MW00377896

PUB. NO. 229
VOL. 2

SIGHT REDUCTION TABLES

FOR

MARINE NAVIGATION

LATITUDES 15°–30°, Inclusive

NATIONAL IMAGERY AND MAPPING AGENCY

INTERPOLATION TABLE

Dec. Inc.	Tens 10′	20′	30′	40′	50′	Decimals ⇓	Units 0′	1′	2′	3′	4′	5′	6′	7′	8′	9′	Double Second Diff.	and Corr.
′	′	′	′	′	′	′	′	′	′	′	′	′	′	′	′	′	′	′
0.0	0.0	0.0	0.0	0.0	0.0	.0	0.0	0.0	0.0	0.0	0.0	0.0	0.0	0.1	0.1	0.1	0.0	0.0
0.1	0.0	0.0	0.0	0.0	0.1	.1	0.0	0.0	0.0	0.0	0.0	0.0	0.1	0.1	0.1	0.1	48.2	
0.2	0.0	0.0	0.1	0.1	0.1	.2	0.0	0.0	0.0	0.0	0.0	0.0	0.1	0.1	0.1	0.1		
0.3	0.0	0.1	0.1	0.2	0.2	.3	0.0	0.0	0.0	0.0	0.0	0.0	0.1	0.1	0.1	0.1		
0.4	0.1	0.1	0.2	0.3	0.3	.4	0.0	0.0	0.0	0.0	0.0	0.0	0.1	0.1	0.1	0.1		
0.5	0.1	0.2	0.3	0.3	0.4	.5	0.0	0.0	0.0	0.0	0.0	0.0	0.1	0.1	0.1	0.1	16.2	0.1
0.6	0.1	0.2	0.3	0.4	0.5	.6	0.0	0.0	0.0	0.0	0.0	0.0	0.1	0.1	0.1	0.1	48.6	
0.7	0.1	0.3	0.4	0.5	0.6	.7	0.0	0.0	0.0	0.0	0.0	0.0	0.1	0.1	0.1	0.1		
0.8	0.2	0.3	0.4	0.6	0.7	.8	0.0	0.0	0.0	0.0	0.0	0.0	0.1	0.1	0.1	0.1		
0.9	0.2	0.3	0.5	0.6	0.8	.9	0.0	0.0	0.0	0.0	0.0	0.0	0.1	0.1	0.1	0.1		
1.0	0.1	0.3	0.5	0.6	0.8	.0	0.0	0.0	0.0	0.1	0.1	0.1	0.1	0.2	0.2	0.2	8.2	0.1
1.1	0.2	0.3	0.5	0.7	0.9	.1	0.0	0.0	0.1	0.1	0.1	0.1	0.2	0.2	0.2	0.2	24.6	0.2
1.2	0.2	0.4	0.6	0.8	1.0	.2	0.0	0.0	0.1	0.1	0.1	0.1	0.2	0.2	0.2	0.2	41.0	
1.3	0.2	0.4	0.6	0.9	1.1	.3	0.0	0.0	0.1	0.1	0.1	0.1	0.2	0.2	0.2	0.2		
1.4	0.2	0.5	0.7	0.9	1.2	.4	0.0	0.0	0.1	0.1	0.1	0.1	0.2	0.2	0.2	0.2		
1.5	0.3	0.5	0.8	1.0	1.3	.5	0.0	0.0	0.1	0.1	0.1	0.1	0.2	0.2	0.2	0.2		
1.6	0.3	0.5	0.8	1.1	1.3	.6	0.0	0.0	0.1	0.1	0.1	0.1	0.2	0.2	0.2	0.2		
1.7	0.3	0.6	0.9	1.2	1.4	.7	0.0	0.0	0.1	0.1	0.1	0.1	0.2	0.2	0.2	0.2		
1.8	0.3	0.6	0.9	1.2	1.5	.8	0.0	0.0	0.1	0.1	0.1	0.1	0.2	0.2	0.2	0.2		
1.9	0.4	0.7	1.0	1.3	1.6	.9	0.0	0.0	0.1	0.1	0.1	0.1	0.2	0.2	0.2	0.2		
2.0	0.3	0.6	1.0	1.3	1.6	.0	0.0	0.0	0.1	0.1	0.2	0.2	0.2	0.3	0.3	0.4	5.0	0.1
2.1	0.3	0.7	1.0	1.4	1.7	.1	0.0	0.0	0.1	0.1	0.2	0.2	0.3	0.3	0.3	0.4	15.0	0.2
2.2	0.3	0.7	1.1	1.4	1.8	.2	0.0	0.0	0.1	0.1	0.2	0.2	0.3	0.3	0.3	0.4	25.0	0.3
2.3	0.4	0.8	1.1	1.5	1.9	.3	0.0	0.1	0.1	0.1	0.2	0.2	0.3	0.3	0.3	0.4	35.1	
2.4	0.4	0.8	1.2	1.6	2.0	.4	0.0	0.1	0.1	0.1	0.2	0.2	0.3	0.3	0.3	0.4		
2.5	0.4	0.8	1.3	1.7	2.1	.5	0.0	0.1	0.1	0.1	0.2	0.2	0.3	0.3	0.4	0.4		
2.6	0.4	0.9	1.3	1.7	2.2	.6	0.0	0.1	0.1	0.1	0.2	0.2	0.3	0.3	0.4	0.4		
2.7	0.5	0.9	1.4	1.8	2.3	.7	0.0	0.1	0.1	0.2	0.2	0.2	0.3	0.3	0.4	0.4		
2.8	0.5	1.0	1.4	1.9	2.4	.8	0.0	0.1	0.1	0.2	0.2	0.2	0.3	0.3	0.4	0.4		
2.9	0.5	1.0	1.5	2.0	2.5	.9	0.0	0.1	0.1	0.2	0.2	0.2	0.3	0.3	0.4	0.4		
3.0	0.5	1.0	1.5	2.0	2.5	.0	0.0	0.1	0.1	0.2	0.2	0.3	0.3	0.4	0.5	0.5	3.6	0.1
3.1	0.5	1.0	1.5	2.0	2.6	.1	0.0	0.1	0.1	0.2	0.2	0.3	0.4	0.4	0.5	0.5	10.9	0.2
3.2	0.5	1.0	1.6	2.1	2.6	.2	0.0	0.1	0.1	0.2	0.2	0.3	0.4	0.4	0.5	0.5	18.2	0.3
3.3	0.5	1.1	1.6	2.2	2.7	.3	0.0	0.1	0.1	0.2	0.3	0.3	0.4	0.4	0.5	0.5	25.5	0.4
3.4	0.6	1.1	1.7	2.3	2.8	.4	0.0	0.1	0.1	0.2	0.3	0.3	0.4	0.4	0.5	0.5	32.8	0.5
3.5	0.6	1.2	1.8	2.3	2.9	.5	0.0	0.1	0.1	0.2	0.3	0.3	0.4	0.4	0.5	0.6	40.1	
3.6	0.6	1.2	1.8	2.4	3.0	.6	0.0	0.1	0.2	0.2	0.3	0.3	0.4	0.4	0.5	0.6		
3.7	0.6	1.3	1.9	2.5	3.1	.7	0.0	0.1	0.2	0.2	0.3	0.3	0.4	0.4	0.5	0.6		
3.8	0.7	1.3	1.9	2.6	3.2	.8	0.0	0.1	0.2	0.2	0.3	0.3	0.4	0.5	0.5	0.6		
3.9	0.7	1.3	2.0	2.6	3.3	.9	0.1	0.1	0.2	0.2	0.3	0.3	0.4	0.5	0.5	0.6		
4.0	0.6	1.3	2.0	2.6	3.3	.0	0.0	0.1	0.1	0.2	0.3	0.4	0.4	0.5	0.6	0.7	2.9	0.1
4.1	0.7	1.3	2.0	2.7	3.4	.1	0.0	0.1	0.2	0.2	0.3	0.4	0.5	0.5	0.6	0.7	8.6	0.2
4.2	0.7	1.4	2.1	2.8	3.5	.2	0.0	0.1	0.2	0.2	0.3	0.4	0.5	0.5	0.6	0.7	14.4	0.3
4.3	0.7	1.4	2.1	2.9	3.6	.3	0.0	0.1	0.2	0.2	0.3	0.4	0.5	0.5	0.6	0.7	20.2	0.4
4.4	0.7	1.5	2.2	2.9	3.7	.4	0.0	0.1	0.2	0.3	0.3	0.4	0.5	0.6	0.6	0.7	25.9	0.5
4.5	0.8	1.5	2.3	3.0	3.8	.5	0.0	0.1	0.2	0.3	0.3	0.4	0.5	0.6	0.6	0.7	31.7	0.6
4.6	0.8	1.5	2.3	3.1	3.8	.6	0.0	0.1	0.2	0.3	0.3	0.4	0.5	0.6	0.6	0.7	37.5	
4.7	0.8	1.6	2.4	3.2	3.9	.7	0.1	0.1	0.2	0.3	0.4	0.4	0.5	0.6	0.7	0.7		
4.8	0.8	1.6	2.4	3.2	4.0	.8	0.1	0.1	0.2	0.3	0.4	0.4	0.5	0.6	0.7	0.7		
4.9	0.9	1.7	2.5	3.3	4.1	.9	0.1	0.1	0.2	0.3	0.4	0.4	0.5	0.6	0.7	0.7		
5.0	0.8	1.6	2.5	3.3	4.1	.0	0.0	0.1	0.2	0.3	0.4	0.5	0.5	0.6	0.7	0.8	2.4	0.1
5.1	0.8	1.7	2.5	3.4	4.2	.1	0.0	0.1	0.2	0.3	0.4	0.5	0.6	0.7	0.7	0.8	7.2	0.2
5.2	0.8	1.7	2.6	3.4	4.3	.2	0.0	0.1	0.2	0.3	0.4	0.5	0.6	0.7	0.8	0.8	12.0	0.3
5.3	0.9	1.8	2.6	3.5	4.4	.3	0.0	0.1	0.2	0.3	0.4	0.5	0.6	0.7	0.8	0.9	16.8	0.4
5.4	0.9	1.8	2.7	3.6	4.5	.4	0.0	0.1	0.2	0.3	0.4	0.5	0.6	0.7	0.8	0.9	21.6	0.5
5.5	0.9	1.8	2.8	3.7	4.6	.5	0.0	0.1	0.2	0.3	0.4	0.5	0.6	0.7	0.8	0.9	26.4	0.6
5.6	0.9	1.9	2.8	3.7	4.7	.6	0.1	0.1	0.2	0.3	0.4	0.5	0.6	0.7	0.8	0.9	31.2	0.7
5.7	1.0	1.9	2.9	3.8	4.8	.7	0.1	0.2	0.2	0.3	0.4	0.5	0.6	0.7	0.8	0.9	36.0	
5.8	1.0	2.0	2.9	3.9	4.9	.8	0.1	0.2	0.3	0.3	0.4	0.5	0.6	0.7	0.8	0.9		
5.9	1.0	2.0	3.0	4.0	5.0	.9	0.1	0.2	0.3	0.4	0.4	0.5	0.6	0.7	0.8	0.9		
6.0	1.0	2.0	3.0	4.0	5.0	.0	0.0	0.1	0.2	0.3	0.4	0.5	0.6	0.8	0.9	1.0	2.1	0.1
6.1	1.0	2.0	3.0	4.0	5.1	.1	0.0	0.1	0.2	0.3	0.4	0.6	0.7	0.8	0.9	1.0	6.2	0.2
6.2	1.0	2.0	3.1	4.1	5.1	.2	0.0	0.1	0.2	0.3	0.5	0.6	0.7	0.8	0.9	1.0	10.4	0.3
6.3	1.0	2.1	3.1	4.2	5.2	.3	0.0	0.1	0.2	0.4	0.5	0.6	0.7	0.8	0.9	1.0	14.5	0.4
6.4	1.1	2.1	3.2	4.3	5.3	.4	0.0	0.2	0.3	0.4	0.5	0.6	0.7	0.8	0.9	1.0	18.6	0.5
6.5	1.1	2.2	3.3	4.3	5.4	.5	0.1	0.2	0.3	0.4	0.5	0.6	0.7	0.8	0.9	1.0	22.8	0.6
6.6	1.1	2.2	3.3	4.4	5.5	.6	0.1	0.2	0.3	0.4	0.5	0.6	0.7	0.8	0.9	1.0	26.9	0.7
6.7	1.1	2.3	3.4	4.5	5.6	.7	0.1	0.2	0.3	0.4	0.5	0.6	0.7	0.8	0.9	1.1	31.1	0.8
6.8	1.2	2.3	3.4	4.6	5.7	.8	0.1	0.2	0.3	0.4	0.5	0.6	0.7	0.8	1.0	1.1	35.2	
6.9	1.2	2.3	3.5	4.6	5.8	.9	0.1	0.2	0.3	0.4	0.5	0.6	0.7	0.9	1.0	1.1		
7.0	1.1	2.3	3.5	4.6	5.8	.0	0.0	0.1	0.2	0.4	0.5	0.6	0.7	0.9	1.0	1.1	1.8	0.1
7.1	1.2	2.3	3.5	4.7	5.9	.1	0.0	0.1	0.3	0.4	0.5	0.6	0.8	0.9	1.0	1.1	5.5	0.2
7.2	1.2	2.4	3.6	4.8	6.0	.2	0.0	0.1	0.3	0.4	0.5	0.6	0.8	0.9	1.0	1.1	9.1	0.3
7.3	1.2	2.4	3.6	4.9	6.1	.3	0.0	0.2	0.3	0.4	0.5	0.7	0.8	0.9	1.0	1.2	12.8	0.4
7.4	1.2	2.5	3.7	4.9	6.2	.4	0.0	0.2	0.3	0.4	0.5	0.7	0.8	0.9	1.0	1.2	16.5	0.5
7.5	1.3	2.5	3.8	5.0	6.3	.5	0.1	0.2	0.3	0.4	0.6	0.7	0.8	0.9	1.1	1.2	20.1	0.6
7.6	1.3	2.5	3.8	5.1	6.3	.6	0.1	0.2	0.3	0.4	0.6	0.7	0.8	0.9	1.1	1.2	23.8	0.7
7.7	1.3	2.6	3.9	5.2	6.4	.7	0.1	0.2	0.3	0.5	0.6	0.7	0.8	1.0	1.1	1.2	27.4	0.8
7.8	1.3	2.6	3.9	5.2	6.5	.8	0.1	0.2	0.3	0.5	0.6	0.7	0.8	1.0	1.1	1.2	31.1	0.9
7.9	1.4	2.7	4.0	5.3	6.6	.9	0.1	0.2	0.4	0.5	0.6	0.7	0.9	1.0	1.1	1.2	34.7	
	10′	20′	30′	40′	50′		0′	1′	2′	3′	4′	5′	6′	7′	8′	9′		

Dec. Inc.	Tens 10′	20′	30′	40′	50′	Decimals ⇓	Units 0′	1′	2′	3′	4′	5′	6′	7′	8′	9′	Double Second Diff.	and Corr.
′	′	′	′	′	′	′	′	′	′	′	′	′	′	′	′	′	′	′
8.0	1.3	2.6	4.0	5.3	6.6	.0	0.0	0.1	0.3	0.4	0.6	0.7	0.8	1.0	1.1	1.3	1.6	0.1
8.1	1.3	2.7	4.0	5.4	6.7	.1	0.0	0.2	0.3	0.4	0.6	0.7	0.9	1.0	1.1	1.3	4.8	0.2
8.2	1.3	2.7	4.1	5.4	6.8	.2	0.0	0.2	0.3	0.5	0.6	0.7	0.9	1.0	1.2	1.3	8.0	0.3
8.3	1.4	2.8	4.1	5.5	6.9	.3	0.0	0.2	0.3	0.5	0.6	0.8	0.9	1.0	1.2	1.3	11.2	0.4
8.4	1.4	2.8	4.2	5.6	7.0	.4	0.1	0.2	0.3	0.5	0.6	0.8	0.9	1.0	1.2	1.3	14.5	0.5
8.5	1.4	2.8	4.3	5.7	7.1	.5	0.1	0.2	0.4	0.5	0.6	0.8	0.9	1.1	1.2	1.3	17.7	0.6
8.6	1.4	2.9	4.3	5.7	7.2	.6	0.1	0.2	0.4	0.5	0.7	0.8	0.9	1.1	1.2	1.4	20.9	0.7
8.7	1.5	2.9	4.4	5.8	7.3	.7	0.1	0.2	0.4	0.5	0.7	0.8	0.9	1.1	1.2	1.4	24.1	0.8
8.8	1.5	3.0	4.4	5.9	7.4	.8	0.1	0.3	0.4	0.5	0.7	0.8	1.0	1.1	1.2	1.4	27.3	0.9
8.9	1.5	3.0	4.5	6.0	7.5	.9	0.1	0.3	0.4	0.6	0.7	0.8	1.0	1.1	1.3	1.4	30.5	1.0
9.0	1.5	3.0	4.5	6.0	7.5	.0	0.0	0.2	0.3	0.5	0.6	0.8	0.9	1.1	1.3	1.4	33.7	1.1
9.1	1.5	3.0	4.5	6.0	7.6	.1	0.0	0.2	0.3	0.5	0.6	0.8	1.0	1.1	1.3	1.4	36.9	
9.2	1.5	3.0	4.6	6.1	7.6	.2	0.0	0.2	0.3	0.5	0.7	0.8	1.0	1.1	1.3	1.5		
9.3	1.5	3.1	4.6	6.2	7.7	.3	0.0	0.2	0.4	0.5	0.7	0.8	1.0	1.2	1.3	1.5		
9.4	1.6	3.1	4.7	6.3	7.8	.4	0.1	0.2	0.4	0.5	0.7	0.9	1.0	1.2	1.3	1.5		
9.5	1.6	3.2	4.8	6.3	7.9	.5	0.1	0.2	0.4	0.6	0.7	0.9	1.0	1.2	1.3	1.5	1.4	0.1
9.6	1.6	3.2	4.8	6.4	8.0	.6	0.1	0.3	0.4	0.6	0.7	0.9	1.0	1.2	1.4	1.5	4.2	0.2
9.7	1.6	3.3	4.9	6.5	8.1	.7	0.1	0.3	0.4	0.6	0.7	0.9	1.1	1.2	1.4	1.5	7.1	0.3
9.8	1.7	3.3	4.9	6.6	8.2	.8	0.1	0.3	0.4	0.6	0.8	0.9	1.1	1.2	1.4	1.6	9.9	0.4
9.9	1.7	3.3	5.0	6.6	8.3	.9	0.1	0.3	0.5	0.6	0.8	0.9	1.1	1.3	1.4	1.6	12.7	0.5
10.0	1.6	3.3	5.0	6.6	8.3	.0	0.0	0.2	0.3	0.5	0.7	0.9	1.0	1.2	1.4	1.6	15.5	0.6
10.1	1.7	3.3	5.0	6.7	8.4	.1	0.0	0.2	0.4	0.5	0.7	0.9	1.1	1.2	1.4	1.6	18.4	0.7
10.2	1.7	3.4	5.1	6.8	8.5	.2	0.0	0.2	0.4	0.6	0.7	0.9	1.1	1.3	1.4	1.6	21.2	0.8
10.3	1.7	3.4	5.1	6.9	8.6	.3	0.1	0.2	0.4	0.6	0.8	0.9	1.1	1.3	1.5	1.6	24.0	0.9
10.4	1.7	3.5	5.2	6.9	8.7	.4	0.1	0.2	0.4	0.6	0.8	0.9	1.1	1.3	1.5	1.6	26.8	1.0
10.5	1.8	3.5	5.3	7.0	8.8	.5	0.1	0.3	0.4	0.6	0.8	1.0	1.1	1.3	1.5	1.7	29.7	1.1
10.6	1.8	3.5	5.3	7.1	8.8	.6	0.1	0.3	0.5	0.6	0.8	1.0	1.2	1.3	1.5	1.7	32.5	1.2
10.7	1.8	3.6	5.4	7.2	8.9	.7	0.1	0.3	0.5	0.6	0.8	1.0	1.2	1.3	1.5	1.7	35.3	
10.8	1.8	3.6	5.4	7.2	9.0	.8	0.1	0.3	0.5	0.7	0.8	1.0	1.2	1.4	1.5	1.7		
10.9	1.9	3.7	5.5	7.3	9.1	.9	0.2	0.3	0.5	0.7	0.9	1.0	1.2	1.4	1.6	1.7		
11.0	1.8	3.6	5.5	7.3	9.1	.0	0.0	0.2	0.4	0.6	0.8	1.0	1.1	1.3	1.5	1.7	1.3	0.1
11.1	1.8	3.7	5.5	7.4	9.2	.1	0.0	0.2	0.4	0.6	0.8	1.0	1.2	1.4	1.6	1.7	3.8	0.2
11.2	1.8	3.7	5.6	7.4	9.3	.2	0.0	0.2	0.4	0.6	0.8	1.0	1.2	1.4	1.6	1.8	6.3	0.3
11.3	1.9	3.8	5.6	7.5	9.4	.3	0.1	0.2	0.4	0.6	0.8	1.0	1.2	1.4	1.6	1.8	8.9	0.4
11.4	1.9	3.8	5.7	7.6	9.5	.4	0.1	0.3	0.5	0.7	0.8	1.0	1.2	1.4	1.6	1.8	11.4	0.5
11.5	1.9	3.8	5.8	7.7	9.6	.5	0.1	0.3	0.5	0.7	0.9	1.1	1.2	1.4	1.6	1.8	14.0	0.6
11.6	1.9	3.9	5.8	7.7	9.7	.6	0.1	0.3	0.5	0.7	0.9	1.1	1.3	1.5	1.6	1.8	16.5	0.7
11.7	2.0	3.9	5.9	7.8	9.8	.7	0.1	0.3	0.5	0.7	0.9	1.1	1.3	1.5	1.7	1.9	19.0	0.8
11.8	2.0	4.0	5.9	7.9	9.9	.8	0.2	0.3	0.5	0.7	0.9	1.1	1.3	1.5	1.7	1.9	21.6	0.9
11.9	2.0	4.0	6.0	8.0	10.0	.9	0.2	0.4	0.6	0.7	0.9	1.1	1.3	1.5	1.7	1.9	24.1	1.0
12.0	2.0	4.0	6.0	8.0	10.0	.0	0.0	0.2	0.4	0.6	0.8	1.0	1.2	1.5	1.7	1.9	26.7	1.1
12.1	2.0	4.0	6.0	8.0	10.1	.1	0.0	0.2	0.4	0.6	0.9	1.1	1.3	1.5	1.7	1.9	29.2	1.2
12.2	2.0	4.0	6.1	8.1	10.1	.2	0.0	0.2	0.5	0.7	0.9	1.1	1.3	1.5	1.7	1.9	31.7	1.3
12.3	2.0	4.1	6.1	8.2	10.2	.3	0.1	0.3	0.5	0.7	0.9	1.1	1.3	1.5	1.7	1.9	34.3	
12.4	2.1	4.1	6.2	8.3	10.3	.4	0.1	0.3	0.5	0.7	0.9	1.1	1.3	1.5	1.7	2.0		
12.5	2.1	4.2	6.3	8.3	10.4	.5	0.1	0.3	0.5	0.7	0.9	1.1	1.4	1.6	1.8	2.0	1.2	0.1
12.6	2.1	4.2	6.3	8.4	10.5	.6	0.1	0.3	0.5	0.7	1.0	1.2	1.4	1.6	1.8	2.0	3.5	0.2
12.7	2.1	4.3	6.4	8.5	10.6	.7	0.1	0.4	0.6	0.8	1.0	1.2	1.4	1.6	1.8	2.0	5.8	0.3
12.8	2.2	4.3	6.4	8.6	10.7	.8	0.2	0.4	0.6	0.8	1.0	1.2	1.4	1.6	1.8	2.0	8.1	0.4
12.9	2.2	4.3	6.5	8.6	10.8	.9	0.2	0.4	0.6	0.8	1.0	1.2	1.4	1.6	1.9	2.1	10.5	0.5
13.0	2.1	4.3	6.5	8.6	10.8	.0	0.0	0.2	0.4	0.7	0.9	1.1	1.3	1.6	1.8	2.0	12.8	0.6
13.1	2.2	4.3	6.5	8.7	10.9	.1	0.0	0.2	0.5	0.7	0.9	1.1	1.4	1.6	1.8	2.0	15.1	0.7
13.2	2.2	4.4	6.6	8.8	11.0	.2	0.0	0.3	0.5	0.7	0.9	1.2	1.4	1.6	1.8	2.1	17.4	0.8
13.3	2.2	4.4	6.6	8.9	11.1	.3	0.1	0.3	0.5	0.7	1.0	1.2	1.4	1.6	1.9	2.1	19.8	0.9
13.4	2.2	4.5	6.7	8.9	11.2	.4	0.1	0.3	0.5	0.8	1.0	1.2	1.4	1.7	1.9	2.1	22.1	1.0
13.5	2.3	4.5	6.8	9.0	11.3	.5	0.1	0.3	0.6	0.8	1.0	1.2	1.5	1.7	1.9	2.1	24.4	1.1
13.6	2.3	4.5	6.8	9.1	11.3	.6	0.1	0.4	0.6	0.8	1.0	1.3	1.5	1.7	1.9	2.2	26.7	1.2
13.7	2.3	4.6	6.9	9.2	11.4	.7	0.2	0.4	0.6	0.8	1.1	1.3	1.5	1.7	2.0	2.2	29.1	1.3
13.8	2.3	4.6	6.9	9.2	11.5	.8	0.2	0.4	0.6	0.9	1.1	1.3	1.5	1.8	2.0	2.2	31.4	1.4
13.9	2.4	4.7	7.0	9.3	11.6	.9	0.2	0.4	0.7	0.9	1.1	1.3	1.6	1.8	2.0	2.2	33.7	1.5
																	36.0	
14.0	2.3	4.6	7.0	9.3	11.6	.0	0.0	0.2	0.5	0.7	1.0	1.2	1.4	1.7	1.9	2.2	1.1	0.1
14.1	2.3	4.7	7.0	9.4	11.7	.1	0.0	0.3	0.5	0.7	1.0	1.2	1.5	1.7	2.0	2.2	3.2	0.2
14.2	2.3	4.7	7.1	9.4	11.8	.2	0.0	0.3	0.5	0.8	1.0	1.3	1.5	1.7	2.0	2.2	5.3	0.3
14.3	2.4	4.8	7.1	9.5	11.9	.3	0.1	0.3	0.6	0.8	1.0	1.3	1.5	1.8	2.0	2.2	7.5	0.4
14.4	2.4	4.8	7.2	9.6	12.0	.4	0.1	0.3	0.6	0.8	1.1	1.3	1.5	1.8	2.0	2.3	9.6	0.5
14.5	2.4	4.8	7.3	9.7	12.1	.5	0.1	0.4	0.6	0.8	1.1	1.3	1.6	1.8	2.1	2.3	11.7	0.6
14.6	2.4	4.9	7.3	9.7	12.2	.6	0.1	0.4	0.6	0.9	1.1	1.4	1.6	1.8	2.1	2.3	13.9	0.7
14.7	2.5	4.9	7.4	9.8	12.3	.7	0.2	0.4	0.7	0.9	1.1	1.4	1.6	1.9	2.1	2.3	16.0	0.8
14.8	2.5	5.0	7.4	9.9	12.4	.8	0.2	0.4	0.7	0.9	1.2	1.4	1.6	1.9	2.1	2.4	18.1	0.9
14.9	2.5	5.0	7.5	10.0	12.5	.9	0.2	0.5	0.7	0.9	1.2	1.4	1.7	1.9	2.2	2.4	20.3	1.0
15.0	2.5	5.0	7.5	10.0	12.5	.0	0.0	0.3	0.5	0.8	1.0	1.3	1.5	1.8	2.1	2.3	22.4	1.1
15.1	2.5	5.0	7.5	10.0	12.6	.1	0.0	0.3	0.5	0.8	1.1	1.3	1.6	1.8	2.1	2.4	24.5	1.2
15.2	2.5	5.0	7.6	10.1	12.6	.2	0.1	0.3	0.6	0.8	1.1	1.3	1.6	1.9	2.1	2.4	26.7	1.3
15.3	2.5	5.1	7.6	10.2	12.7	.3	0.1	0.3	0.6	0.9	1.1	1.4	1.6	1.9	2.1	2.4	28.8	1.4
15.4	2.6	5.1	7.7	10.3	12.8	.4	0.1	0.4	0.6	0.9	1.1	1.4	1.7	1.9	2.2	2.4	30.9	1.5
15.5	2.6	5.2	7.8	10.3	12.9	.5	0.1	0.4	0.6	0.9	1.2	1.4	1.7	1.9	2.2	2.5	33.1	1.6
15.6	2.6	5.2	7.8	10.4	13.0	.6	0.2	0.4	0.7	0.9	1.2	1.4	1.7	2.0	2.2	2.5	35.2	
15.7	2.6	5.3	7.9	10.5	13.1	.7	0.2	0.4	0.7	1.0	1.2	1.5	1.7	2.0	2.2	2.5		
15.8	2.7	5.3	7.9	10.6	13.2	.8	0.2	0.5	0.7	1.0	1.2	1.5	1.8	2.0	2.3	2.5		
15.9	2.7	5.3	8.0	10.6	13.3	.9	0.2	0.5	0.7	1.0	1.3	1.5	1.8	2.0	2.3	2.6		
	10′	20′	30′	40′	50′		0′	1′	2′	3′	4′	5′	6′	7′	8′	9′		

The Double-Second-Difference correction (Corr.) is always to be added to the tabulated altitude.

INTERPOLATION TABLE

Dec. Inc.	Altitude Difference (d)																Double Second Diff. and Corr.
	Tens					Decimals	Units										
	10′	20′	30′	40′	50′	⇓	0′	1′	2′	3′	4′	5′	6′	7′	8′	9′	
16.0	2.6	5.3	8.0	10.6	13.3	.0	0.0	0.3	0.5	0.8	1.1	1.4	1.6	1.9	2.2	2.5	
16.1	2.7	5.3	8.0	10.7	13.4	.1	0.0	0.3	0.6	0.9	1.1	1.4	1.7	2.0	2.2	2.5	
16.2	2.7	5.4	8.1	10.8	13.5	.2	0.1	0.3	0.6	0.9	1.2	1.4	1.7	2.0	2.3	2.5	1.0 0.1
16.3	2.7	5.4	8.1	10.9	13.6	.3	0.1	0.4	0.6	0.9	1.2	1.5	1.7	2.0	2.3	2.6	3.0 0.2
16.4	2.7	5.5	8.2	10.9	13.7	.4	0.1	0.4	0.7	0.9	1.2	1.5	1.8	2.0	2.3	2.6	4.9 0.3 6.9 0.4
16.5	2.8	5.5	8.3	11.0	13.8	.5	0.1	0.4	0.7	1.0	1.2	1.5	1.8	2.1	2.3	2.6	8.9 0.5
16.6	2.8	5.5	8.3	11.1	13.8	.6	0.2	0.4	0.7	1.0	1.3	1.5	1.8	2.1	2.4	2.6	10.8 0.6
16.7	2.8	5.6	8.4	11.2	13.9	.7	0.2	0.5	0.7	1.0	1.3	1.6	1.8	2.1	2.4	2.7	12.8 0.7
16.8	2.8	5.6	8.4	11.2	14.0	.8	0.2	0.5	0.8	1.0	1.3	1.6	1.9	2.1	2.4	2.7	14.8 0.8
16.9	2.9	5.7	8.5	11.3	14.1	.9	0.2	0.5	0.8	1.1	1.3	1.6	1.9	2.2	2.4	2.7	16.7 0.9 18.7 1.0
17.0	2.8	5.6	8.5	11.3	14.1	.0	0.0	0.3	0.6	0.9	1.2	1.5	1.7	2.0	2.3	2.6	20.7 1.1
17.1	2.8	5.7	8.5	11.4	14.2	.1	0.0	0.3	0.6	0.9	1.2	1.5	1.8	2.1	2.4	2.7	22.7 1.2
17.2	2.8	5.7	8.6	11.4	14.3	.2	0.1	0.3	0.6	0.9	1.2	1.5	1.8	2.1	2.4	2.7	24.6 1.3
17.3	2.9	5.8	8.6	11.5	14.4	.3	0.1	0.4	0.7	1.0	1.3	1.5	1.8	2.1	2.4	2.7	26.6 1.4
17.4	2.9	5.8	8.7	11.6	14.5	.4	0.1	0.4	0.7	1.0	1.3	1.6	1.9	2.2	2.4	2.7	28.6 1.5 30.5 1.6
17.5	2.9	5.8	8.8	11.7	14.6	.5	0.1	0.4	0.7	1.0	1.3	1.6	1.9	2.2	2.5	2.8	32.5 1.7
17.6	2.9	5.9	8.8	11.7	14.7	.6	0.2	0.5	0.8	1.0	1.3	1.6	1.9	2.2	2.5	2.8	34.5
17.7	3.0	5.9	8.9	11.8	14.8	.7	0.2	0.5	0.8	1.1	1.4	1.7	2.0	2.2	2.5	2.8	
17.8	3.0	6.0	8.9	11.9	14.9	.8	0.2	0.5	0.8	1.1	1.4	1.7	2.0	2.3	2.6	2.9	
17.9	3.0	6.0	9.0	12.0	15.0	.9	0.3	0.6	0.8	1.1	1.4	1.7	2.0	2.3	2.6	2.9	
18.0	3.0	6.0	9.0	12.0	15.0	.0	0.0	0.3	0.6	0.9	1.2	1.5	1.8	2.2	2.5	2.8	
18.1	3.0	6.0	9.0	12.0	15.1	.1	0.0	0.3	0.6	1.0	1.3	1.6	1.9	2.2	2.5	2.8	0.9
18.2	3.0	6.0	9.1	12.1	15.1	.2	0.1	0.4	0.7	1.0	1.3	1.6	1.9	2.2	2.5	2.8	0.1 2.8
18.3	3.0	6.1	9.1	12.2	15.2	.3	0.1	0.4	0.7	1.0	1.3	1.6	1.9	2.3	2.6	2.9	0.2 4.6
18.4	3.1	6.1	9.2	12.3	15.3	.4	0.1	0.4	0.7	1.0	1.4	1.7	2.0	2.3	2.6	2.9	0.3 6.5 0.4
18.5	3.1	6.2	9.3	12.3	15.4	.5	0.2	0.5	0.8	1.1	1.4	1.7	2.0	2.3	2.6	2.9	8.3 0.5 10.2
18.6	3.1	6.2	9.3	12.4	15.5	.6	0.2	0.5	0.8	1.1	1.4	1.7	2.0	2.3	2.7	3.0	0.6 12.0
18.7	3.1	6.3	9.4	12.5	15.6	.7	0.2	0.5	0.8	1.1	1.4	1.8	2.1	2.4	2.7	3.0	0.7 13.9
18.8	3.2	6.3	9.4	12.6	15.7	.8	0.2	0.6	0.9	1.2	1.5	1.8	2.1	2.4	2.7	3.0	0.8 15.7
18.9	3.2	6.3	9.5	12.6	15.8	.9	0.3	0.6	0.9	1.2	1.5	1.8	2.1	2.4	2.7	3.1	0.9 17.6 1.0
19.0	3.1	6.3	9.5	12.6	15.8	.0	0.0	0.3	0.6	1.0	1.3	1.6	1.9	2.3	2.6	2.9	19.4 1.1 21.3
19.1	3.2	6.3	9.5	12.7	15.9	.1	0.0	0.4	0.7	1.0	1.3	1.7	2.0	2.3	2.6	3.0	1.2 23.1
19.2	3.2	6.4	9.6	12.8	16.0	.2	0.1	0.4	0.7	1.0	1.4	1.7	2.0	2.3	2.7	3.0	1.3 25.0
19.3	3.2	6.4	9.6	12.9	16.1	.3	0.1	0.4	0.7	1.1	1.4	1.7	2.0	2.4	2.7	3.0	1.4 26.8
19.4	3.2	6.5	9.7	12.9	16.2	.4	0.1	0.5	0.8	1.1	1.4	1.8	2.1	2.4	2.7	3.1	1.5 28.7 1.6
19.5	3.3	6.5	9.8	13.0	16.3	.5	0.2	0.5	0.8	1.1	1.5	1.8	2.1	2.4	2.8	3.1	30.5 1.7
19.6	3.3	6.5	9.8	13.1	16.3	.6	0.2	0.5	0.8	1.2	1.5	1.8	2.1	2.5	2.8	3.1	32.3 1.8
19.7	3.3	6.6	9.9	13.2	16.4	.7	0.2	0.6	0.9	1.2	1.5	1.9	2.2	2.5	2.8	3.2	34.2
19.8	3.3	6.6	9.9	13.2	16.5	.8	0.3	0.6	0.9	1.2	1.6	1.9	2.2	2.5	2.9	3.2	
19.9	3.4	6.7	10.0	13.3	16.6	.9	0.3	0.6	0.9	1.3	1.6	1.9	2.2	2.6	2.9	3.2	
20.0	3.3	6.6	10.0	13.3	16.6	.0	0.0	0.3	0.7	1.0	1.4	1.7	2.0	2.4	2.7	3.1	
20.1	3.3	6.7	10.0	13.4	16.7	.1	0.0	0.4	0.7	1.1	1.4	1.7	2.1	2.4	2.8	3.1	0.9
20.2	3.3	6.7	10.1	13.4	16.8	.2	0.1	0.4	0.8	1.1	1.4	1.8	2.1	2.5	2.8	3.1	0.1 2.6
20.3	3.4	6.8	10.1	13.5	16.9	.3	0.1	0.4	0.8	1.1	1.5	1.8	2.2	2.5	2.8	3.2	0.2 4.4
20.4	3.4	6.8	10.2	13.6	17.0	.4	0.1	0.5	0.8	1.2	1.5	1.8	2.2	2.5	2.9	3.2	0.3 6.2 0.4
20.5	3.4	6.8	10.3	13.7	17.1	.5	0.2	0.5	0.9	1.2	1.5	1.9	2.2	2.6	2.9	3.2	7.9 0.5 9.7
20.6	3.4	6.9	10.3	13.7	17.2	.6	0.2	0.5	0.9	1.2	1.6	1.9	2.3	2.6	2.9	3.3	0.6 11.4
20.7	3.5	6.9	10.4	13.8	17.3	.7	0.2	0.6	0.9	1.3	1.6	1.9	2.3	2.6	3.0	3.3	0.7 13.2
20.8	3.5	7.0	10.4	13.9	17.4	.8	0.3	0.6	1.0	1.3	1.6	2.0	2.3	2.7	3.0	3.3	0.8 14.9
20.9	3.5	7.0	10.5	14.0	17.5	.9	0.3	0.6	1.0	1.3	1.7	2.0	2.4	2.7	3.0	3.4	0.9 16.7 1.0
21.0	3.5	7.0	10.5	14.0	17.5	.0	0.0	0.4	0.7	1.1	1.4	1.8	2.1	2.5	2.9	3.2	18.5 1.1 20.2
21.1	3.5	7.0	10.5	14.0	17.6	.1	0.0	0.4	0.8	1.1	1.5	1.8	2.2	2.5	2.9	3.3	1.2 22.0
21.2	3.5	7.0	10.6	14.1	17.6	.2	0.1	0.4	0.8	1.1	1.5	1.9	2.2	2.6	2.9	3.3	1.3 23.7
21.3	3.5	7.1	10.6	14.2	17.7	.3	0.1	0.5	0.8	1.2	1.5	1.9	2.3	2.6	3.0	3.3	1.4 25.5
21.4	3.6	7.1	10.7	14.3	17.8	.4	0.1	0.5	0.9	1.2	1.6	1.9	2.3	2.7	3.0	3.4	1.5 27.3 1.6
21.5	3.6	7.2	10.8	14.3	17.9	.5	0.2	0.5	0.9	1.3	1.6	2.0	2.3	2.7	3.0	3.4	29.0 1.7
21.6	3.6	7.2	10.8	14.4	18.0	.6	0.2	0.6	0.9	1.3	1.6	2.0	2.4	2.7	3.1	3.4	30.8 1.8
21.7	3.6	7.3	10.9	14.5	18.1	.7	0.3	0.6	1.0	1.3	1.7	2.0	2.4	2.8	3.1	3.5	32.5 1.9
21.8	3.7	7.3	10.9	14.6	18.2	.8	0.3	0.6	1.0	1.4	1.7	2.1	2.4	2.8	3.2	3.5	34.3
21.9	3.7	7.3	11.0	14.6	18.3	.9	0.3	0.7	1.0	1.4	1.8	2.1	2.5	2.8	3.2	3.5	
22.0	3.6	7.3	11.0	14.6	18.3	.0	0.0	0.4	0.7	1.1	1.5	1.9	2.2	2.6	3.0	3.4	
22.1	3.7	7.3	11.0	14.7	18.4	.1	0.0	0.4	0.8	1.2	1.5	1.9	2.3	2.7	3.0	3.4	0.8 0.1
22.2	3.7	7.4	11.1	14.8	18.5	.2	0.1	0.4	0.8	1.2	1.6	1.9	2.3	2.7	3.1	3.4	2.5 0.2
22.3	3.7	7.4	11.1	14.9	18.6	.3	0.1	0.5	0.9	1.2	1.6	2.0	2.4	2.7	3.1	3.5	4.2 0.3
22.4	3.7	7.5	11.2	14.9	18.7	.4	0.1	0.5	0.9	1.3	1.6	2.0	2.4	2.8	3.1	3.5	5.9 0.4 7.6
22.5	3.8	7.5	11.3	15.0	18.8	.5	0.2	0.6	0.9	1.3	1.7	2.1	2.4	2.8	3.2	3.6	0.5 9.3 0.6
22.6	3.8	7.5	11.3	15.1	18.8	.6	0.2	0.6	1.0	1.3	1.7	2.1	2.5	2.8	3.2	3.6	11.0 0.7
22.7	3.8	7.6	11.4	15.2	18.9	.7	0.3	0.6	1.0	1.4	1.8	2.1	2.5	2.9	3.3	3.6	12.7 0.8
22.8	3.8	7.6	11.4	15.2	19.0	.8	0.3	0.7	1.0	1.4	1.8	2.2	2.5	2.9	3.3	3.7	14.4 0.9
22.9	3.9	7.7	11.5	15.3	19.1	.9	0.3	0.7	1.1	1.5	1.8	2.2	2.6	3.0	3.3	3.7	16.1 1.0 17.8
23.0	3.8	7.6	11.5	15.3	19.1	.0	0.0	0.4	0.8	1.2	1.6	2.0	2.3	2.7	3.1	3.5	1.1 19.5 1.2
23.1	3.8	7.7	11.5	15.4	19.2	.1	0.0	0.4	0.8	1.2	1.6	2.0	2.4	2.8	3.2	3.6	21.2 1.3
23.2	3.8	7.7	11.6	15.4	19.3	.2	0.1	0.5	0.9	1.3	1.6	2.0	2.4	2.8	3.2	3.6	22.8 1.4
23.3	3.9	7.8	11.6	15.5	19.4	.3	0.1	0.5	0.9	1.3	1.7	2.1	2.5	2.9	3.3	3.6	24.5 1.5
23.4	3.9	7.8	11.7	15.6	19.5	.4	0.2	0.5	0.9	1.3	1.7	2.1	2.5	2.9	3.3	3.7	26.2 1.6 27.9
23.5	3.9	7.8	11.8	15.7	19.6	.5	0.2	0.6	1.0	1.4	1.8	2.2	2.5	2.9	3.3	3.7	1.7 29.6 1.8
23.6	3.9	7.9	11.8	15.7	19.7	.6	0.2	0.6	1.0	1.4	1.8	2.2	2.6	3.0	3.4	3.8	31.3 1.9
23.7	4.0	7.9	11.9	15.8	19.8	.7	0.3	0.7	1.1	1.4	1.8	2.2	2.6	3.0	3.4	3.8	33.0 2.0
23.8	4.0	8.0	11.9	15.9	19.9	.8	0.3	0.7	1.1	1.5	1.9	2.3	2.7	3.1	3.4	3.8	34.7
23.9	4.0	8.0	12.0	16.0	20.0	.9	0.4	0.7	1.1	1.5	1.9	2.3	2.7	3.1	3.5	3.9	
	10′	20′	30′	40′	50′		0′	1′	2′	3′	4′	5′	6′	7′	8′	9′	

Dec. Inc.	Altitude Difference (d)																Double Second Diff. and Corr.
	Tens					Decimals	Units										
	10′	20′	30′	40′	50′	⇓	0′	1′	2′	3′	4′	5′	6′	7′	8′	9′	
24.0	4.0	8.0	12.0	16.0	20.0	.0	0.0	0.4	0.8	1.2	1.6	2.0	2.4	2.9	3.3	3.7	0.8
24.1	4.0	8.0	12.0	16.0	20.1	.1	0.0	0.4	0.9	1.3	1.7	2.1	2.5	2.9	3.3	3.7	0.1 2.5
24.2	4.0	8.0	12.1	16.1	20.1	.2	0.1	0.5	0.9	1.3	1.7	2.1	2.5	2.9	3.3	3.8	0.2 4.1
24.3	4.0	8.1	12.1	16.2	20.2	.3	0.1	0.5	0.9	1.3	1.8	2.2	2.6	3.0	3.4	3.8	0.3 5.8
24.4	4.1	8.1	12.2	16.3	20.3	.4	0.2	0.6	1.0	1.4	1.8	2.2	2.6	3.0	3.4	3.8	0.4 7.4 0.5
24.5	4.1	8.2	12.3	16.3	20.4	.5	0.2	0.6	1.0	1.4	1.8	2.2	2.7	3.1	3.5	3.9	9.1 0.6 10.7
24.6	4.1	8.2	12.3	16.4	20.5	.6	0.2	0.7	1.1	1.5	1.9	2.3	2.7	3.1	3.5	3.9	0.7 12.3
24.7	4.1	8.3	12.4	16.5	20.6	.7	0.3	0.7	1.1	1.5	1.9	2.3	2.7	3.1	3.6	4.0	0.8 14.0
24.8	4.2	8.3	12.4	16.6	20.7	.8	0.3	0.7	1.1	1.6	2.0	2.4	2.8	3.2	3.6	4.0	0.9 15.6
24.9	4.2	8.3	12.5	16.6	20.8	.9	0.4	0.8	1.2	1.6	2.0	2.4	2.8	3.2	3.6	4.0	1.0 17.3 1.1
25.0	4.1	8.3	12.5	16.6	20.8	.0	0.0	0.4	0.8	1.3	1.7	2.1	2.5	3.0	3.4	3.8	18.9 1.2 20.6
25.1	4.2	8.3	12.5	16.7	20.9	.1	0.0	0.5	0.9	1.3	1.7	2.2	2.6	3.0	3.4	3.9	1.3 22.2
25.2	4.2	8.4	12.6	16.8	21.0	.2	0.1	0.5	0.9	1.4	1.8	2.2	2.6	3.1	3.5	3.9	1.4 23.9
25.3	4.2	8.4	12.6	16.9	21.1	.3	0.1	0.6	1.0	1.4	1.8	2.3	2.7	3.1	3.5	4.0	1.5 25.5
25.4	4.2	8.5	12.7	16.9	21.2	.4	0.2	0.6	1.0	1.4	1.9	2.3	2.7	3.1	3.6	4.0	1.6 27.2 1.7
25.5	4.3	8.5	12.8	17.0	21.3	.5	0.2	0.6	1.1	1.5	1.9	2.3	2.8	3.2	3.6	4.0	28.8 1.8
25.6	4.3	8.5	12.8	17.1	21.3	.6	0.3	0.7	1.1	1.5	2.0	2.4	2.8	3.2	3.7	4.1	30.4 1.9
25.7	4.3	8.6	12.9	17.2	21.4	.7	0.3	0.7	1.1	1.6	2.0	2.4	2.8	3.3	3.7	4.1	32.1 2.0
25.8	4.3	8.6	12.9	17.2	21.5	.8	0.3	0.8	1.2	1.6	2.0	2.5	2.9	3.3	3.7	4.2	33.7 2.1
25.9	4.4	8.7	13.0	17.3	21.6	.9	0.4	0.8	1.2	1.7	2.1	2.5	2.9	3.4	3.8	4.2	35.4
26.0	4.3	8.6	13.0	17.3	21.6	.0	0.0	0.4	0.9	1.3	1.8	2.2	2.6	3.1	3.5	4.0	0.8
26.1	4.3	8.7	13.0	17.4	21.7	.1	0.0	0.5	0.9	1.4	1.8	2.3	2.7	3.1	3.6	4.0	0.1 2.4
26.2	4.3	8.7	13.1	17.4	21.8	.2	0.1	0.5	1.0	1.4	1.9	2.3	2.7	3.2	3.6	4.1	0.2 4.0
26.3	4.4	8.8	13.1	17.5	21.9	.3	0.1	0.6	1.0	1.5	1.9	2.3	2.8	3.2	3.7	4.1	0.3 5.7
26.4	4.4	8.8	13.2	17.6	22.0	.4	0.2	0.6	1.1	1.5	1.9	2.4	2.8	3.3	3.7	4.2	0.4 7.3 0.5
26.5	4.4	8.8	13.3	17.7	22.1	.5	0.2	0.7	1.1	1.5	2.0	2.4	2.9	3.3	3.8	4.2	8.9 0.6 10.5
26.6	4.4	8.9	13.3	17.7	22.2	.6	0.3	0.7	1.1	1.6	2.0	2.5	2.9	3.4	3.8	4.2	0.7 12.1
26.7	4.5	8.9	13.4	17.8	22.3	.7	0.3	0.8	1.2	1.6	2.1	2.5	3.0	3.4	3.8	4.3	0.8 13.7
26.8	4.5	9.0	13.4	17.9	22.4	.8	0.4	0.8	1.2	1.7	2.1	2.6	3.0	3.4	3.9	4.3	0.9 15.4
26.9	4.5	9.0	13.5	18.0	22.5	.9	0.4	0.8	1.3	1.7	2.2	2.6	3.0	3.5	3.9	4.4	1.0 17.0 1.1
27.0	4.5	9.0	13.5	18.0	22.5	.0	0.0	0.5	0.9	1.4	1.8	2.3	2.7	3.2	3.7	4.1	18.6 1.2 20.2
27.1	4.5	9.0	13.5	18.0	22.6	.1	0.0	0.5	1.0	1.4	1.9	2.3	2.8	3.3	3.7	4.2	1.3 21.8
27.2	4.5	9.0	13.6	18.1	22.6	.2	0.1	0.5	1.0	1.5	1.9	2.4	2.8	3.3	3.8	4.2	1.4 23.4
27.3	4.5	9.1	13.6	18.2	22.7	.3	0.1	0.6	1.1	1.5	2.0	2.4	2.9	3.3	3.8	4.3	1.5 25.1
27.4	4.6	9.1	13.7	18.3	22.8	.4	0.2	0.6	1.1	1.6	2.0	2.5	2.9	3.4	3.8	4.3	1.6 26.7 1.7
27.5	4.6	9.2	13.8	18.3	22.9	.5	0.2	0.7	1.1	1.6	2.1	2.5	3.0	3.4	3.9	4.4	28.3 1.8
27.6	4.6	9.2	13.8	18.4	23.0	.6	0.3	0.7	1.2	1.6	2.1	2.6	3.0	3.5	3.9	4.4	29.9 1.9
27.7	4.6	9.3	13.9	18.5	23.1	.7	0.3	0.8	1.2	1.7	2.2	2.6	3.1	3.5	4.0	4.4	31.5 2.0
27.8	4.7	9.3	13.9	18.6	23.2	.8	0.4	0.8	1.3	1.7	2.2	2.7	3.1	3.6	4.0	4.5	33.1 2.1
27.9	4.7	9.3	14.0	18.6	23.3	.9	0.4	0.9	1.3	1.8	2.2	2.7	3.2	3.6	4.1	4.5	34.7
28.0	4.6	9.3	14.0	18.6	23.3	.0	0.0	0.5	0.9	1.4	1.9	2.4	2.8	3.3	3.8	4.3	0.8
28.1	4.7	9.3	14.0	18.7	23.4	.1	0.0	0.5	1.0	1.5	1.9	2.4	2.9	3.4	3.8	4.3	0.1 2.4
28.2	4.7	9.4	14.1	18.8	23.5	.2	0.1	0.6	1.0	1.5	2.0	2.5	2.9	3.4	3.9	4.4	0.2 4.0
28.3	4.7	9.4	14.1	18.9	23.6	.3	0.1	0.6	1.1	1.6	2.0	2.5	3.0	3.5	3.9	4.4	0.3 5.6
28.4	4.7	9.5	14.2	18.9	23.7	.4	0.2	0.7	1.1	1.6	2.1	2.6	3.0	3.5	4.0	4.5	0.4 7.2 0.5
28.5	4.8	9.5	14.3	19.0	23.8	.5	0.2	0.7	1.2	1.7	2.1	2.6	3.1	3.6	4.0	4.5	8.8 0.6 10.4
28.6	4.8	9.5	14.3	19.1	23.8	.6	0.3	0.8	1.2	1.7	2.2	2.7	3.1	3.6	4.1	4.6	0.7 12.0
28.7	4.8	9.6	14.4	19.2	23.9	.7	0.3	0.8	1.3	1.8	2.2	2.7	3.2	3.7	4.1	4.6	0.8 13.6
28.8	4.8	9.6	14.4	19.2	24.0	.8	0.4	0.9	1.3	1.8	2.3	2.8	3.2	3.7	4.2	4.7	0.9 15.2
28.9	4.9	9.7	14.5	19.3	24.1	.9	0.4	0.9	1.4	1.9	2.3	2.8	3.3	3.8	4.2	4.7	1.0 16.8 1.1
29.0	4.8	9.6	14.5	19.3	24.1	.0	0.0	0.5	1.0	1.5	2.0	2.5	2.9	3.4	3.9	4.4	18.4 1.2 20.0
29.1	4.8	9.7	14.5	19.4	24.2	.1	0.0	0.5	1.0	1.5	2.0	2.5	3.0	3.5	4.0	4.5	1.3 21.6
29.2	4.8	9.7	14.6	19.4	24.3	.2	0.1	0.6	1.1	1.6	2.1	2.6	3.0	3.5	4.0	4.5	1.4 23.2
29.3	4.9	9.8	14.6	19.5	24.4	.3	0.1	0.6	1.1	1.6	2.1	2.6	3.1	3.6	4.1	4.6	1.5 24.8
29.4	4.9	9.8	14.7	19.6	24.5	.4	0.2	0.7	1.2	1.7	2.2	2.7	3.1	3.6	4.1	4.6	1.6 26.4 1.7
29.5	4.9	9.8	14.8	19.7	24.6	.5	0.2	0.7	1.2	1.7	2.2	2.7	3.2	3.7	4.2	4.7	28.0 1.8
29.6	4.9	9.9	14.8	19.7	24.7	.6	0.3	0.8	1.3	1.8	2.3	2.8	3.2	3.7	4.2	4.7	29.6 1.9
29.7	5.0	9.9	14.9	19.8	24.8	.7	0.3	0.8	1.3	1.8	2.3	2.8	3.3	3.8	4.3	4.8	31.2 2.0
29.8	5.0	10.0	14.9	19.9	24.9	.8	0.4	0.9	1.4	1.9	2.4	2.9	3.3	3.8	4.3	4.8	32.8 2.1
29.9	5.0	10.0	15.0	20.0	25.0	.9	0.4	0.9	1.4	1.9	2.4	2.9	3.4	3.9	4.4	4.9	34.4
30.0	5.0	10.0	15.0	20.0	25.0	.0	0.0	0.5	1.0	1.5	2.0	2.5	3.0	3.6	4.1	4.6	0.8
30.1	5.0	10.0	15.0	20.0	25.1	.1	0.1	0.6	1.1	1.6	2.1	2.6	3.1	3.6	4.1	4.6	0.1 2.4
30.2	5.0	10.0	15.1	20.1	25.1	.2	0.1	0.6	1.1	1.6	2.1	2.6	3.2	3.7	4.2	4.7	0.2 4.0
30.3	5.0	10.1	15.1	20.2	25.2	.3	0.2	0.7	1.2	1.7	2.2	2.7	3.2	3.7	4.2	4.7	0.3 5.6
30.4	5.1	10.1	15.2	20.3	25.3	.4	0.2	0.7	1.2	1.7	2.2	2.7	3.3	3.8	4.3	4.8	0.4 7.2 0.5
30.5	5.1	10.2	15.3	20.3	25.4	.5	0.3	0.8	1.3	1.8	2.3	2.8	3.3	3.8	4.3	4.8	8.8 0.6 10.4
30.6	5.1	10.2	15.3	20.4	25.5	.6	0.3	0.8	1.3	1.8	2.3	2.8	3.4	3.9	4.4	4.9	0.7 12.0
30.7	5.1	10.3	15.4	20.5	25.6	.7	0.4	0.9	1.4	1.9	2.4	2.9	3.4	3.9	4.4	4.9	0.8 13.6
30.8	5.2	10.3	15.4	20.6	25.7	.8	0.4	0.9	1.4	1.9	2.4	2.9	3.5	4.0	4.5	5.0	0.9 15.2
30.9	5.2	10.3	15.5	20.6	25.8	.9	0.5	1.0	1.5	2.0	2.5	3.0	3.5	4.0	4.5	5.0	1.0 16.8 1.1
31.0	5.1	10.3	15.5	20.6	25.8	.0	0.0	0.5	1.0	1.6	2.1	2.6	3.1	3.7	4.2	4.7	18.4 1.2 20.0
31.1	5.2	10.3	15.5	20.7	25.9	.1	0.1	0.6	1.1	1.6	2.2	2.7	3.2	3.7	4.3	4.8	1.3 21.6
31.2	5.2	10.4	15.6	20.8	26.0	.2	0.1	0.6	1.2	1.7	2.2	2.7	3.3	3.8	4.3	4.8	1.4 23.2
31.3	5.2	10.4	15.6	20.9	26.1	.3	0.2	0.7	1.2	1.7	2.3	2.8	3.3	3.8	4.4	4.9	1.5 24.8
31.4	5.2	10.5	15.7	20.9	26.2	.4	0.2	0.7	1.3	1.8	2.3	2.8	3.4	3.9	4.4	4.9	1.6 26.4 1.7
31.5	5.3	10.5	15.8	21.0	26.3	.5	0.3	0.8	1.3	1.8	2.4	2.9	3.4	3.9	4.5	5.0	28.0 1.8
31.6	5.3	10.5	15.8	21.1	26.3	.6	0.3	0.8	1.4	1.9	2.4	2.9	3.5	4.0	4.5	5.0	29.6 1.9
31.7	5.3	10.6	15.9	21.2	26.4	.7	0.4	0.9	1.4	1.9	2.5	3.0	3.5	4.0	4.6	5.1	31.2 2.0
31.8	5.3	10.6	15.9	21.2	26.5	.8	0.4	0.9	1.5	2.0	2.5	3.0	3.6	4.1	4.6	5.1	32.8 2.1
31.9	5.4	10.7	16.0	21.3	26.6	.9	0.5	1.0	1.5	2.0	2.6	3.1	3.6	4.1	4.7	5.2	34.4
	10′	20′	30′	40′	50′		0′	1′	2′	3′	4′	5′	6′	7′	8′	9′	

The Double-Second-Difference correction (Corr.) is always to be added to the tabulated altitude.

INTERPOLATION TABLE

Dec. Inc.	Tens 10′	20′	30′	40′	50′	Decimals ⇓	Units 0′	1′	2′	3′	4′	5′	6′	7′	8′	9′
′	′	′	′	′	′	′	′	′	′	′	′	′	′	′	′	′
28.0	4.6	9.3	14.0	18.6	23.3	.0	0.0	0.5	0.9	1.4	1.9	2.4	2.8	3.3	3.8	4.3
28.1	4.7	9.3	14.0	18.7	23.4	.1	0.0	0.5	1.0	1.5	1.9	2.4	2.9	3.4	3.8	4.3
28.2	4.7	9.4	14.1	18.8	23.5	.2	0.1	0.6	1.0	1.5	2.0	2.5	2.9	3.4	3.9	4.4
28.3	4.7	9.4	14.1	18.9	23.6	.3	0.1	0.6	1.1	1.6	2.0	2.5	3.0	3.5	3.9	4.4
28.4	4.7	9.5	14.2	18.9	23.7	.4	0.2	0.7	1.1	1.6	2.1	2.6	3.0	3.5	4.0	4.5
28.5	4.8	9.5	14.3	19.0	23.8	.5	0.2	0.7	1.2	1.7	2.1	2.6	3.1	3.6	4.0	4.5
28.6	4.8	9.5	14.3	19.1	23.8	.6	0.3	0.8	1.2	1.7	2.2	2.7	3.1	3.6	4.1	4.6
28.7	4.8	9.6	14.4	19.2	23.9	.7	0.3	0.8	1.3	1.8	2.2	2.7	3.2	3.7	4.1	4.6
28.8	4.8	9.6	14.4	19.2	24.0	.8	0.4	0.9	1.3	1.8	2.3	2.8	3.2	3.7	4.2	4.7
28.9	4.9	9.7	14.5	19.3	24.1	.9	0.4	0.9	1.4	1.9	2.3	2.8	3.3	3.8	4.2	4.7
29.0	4.8	9.6	14.5	19.3	24.1	.0	0.0	0.5	1.0	1.5	2.0	2.5	2.9	3.4	3.9	4.4
29.1	4.8	9.7	14.5	19.4	24.2	.1	0.0	0.5	1.0	1.5	2.0	2.5	3.0	3.5	4.0	4.5
29.2	4.8	9.7	14.6	19.4	24.3	.2	0.1	0.6	1.1	1.6	2.1	2.6	3.0	3.5	4.0	4.5
29.3	4.9	9.8	14.6	19.5	24.4	.3	0.1	0.6	1.1	1.6	2.1	2.6	3.1	3.6	4.1	4.6
29.4	4.9	9.8	14.7	19.6	24.5	.4	0.2	0.7	1.2	1.7	2.2	2.7	3.1	3.6	4.1	4.6
29.5	4.9	9.8	14.8	19.7	24.6	.5	0.2	0.7	1.2	1.7	2.2	2.7	3.2	3.7	4.2	4.7
29.6	4.9	9.9	14.8	19.7	24.7	.6	0.3	0.8	1.3	1.8	2.3	2.8	3.2	3.7	4.2	4.7
29.7	5.0	9.9	14.9	19.8	24.8	.7	0.3	0.8	1.3	1.8	2.3	2.8	3.3	3.8	4.3	4.8
29.8	5.0	10.0	14.9	19.9	24.9	.8	0.4	0.9	1.4	1.9	2.4	2.9	3.3	3.8	4.3	4.8
29.9	5.0	10.0	15.0	20.0	25.0	.9	0.4	0.9	1.4	1.9	2.4	2.9	3.4	3.9	4.4	4.9
30.0	5.0	10.0	15.0	20.0	25.0	.0	0.0	0.5	1.0	1.5	2.0	2.5	3.0	3.6	4.1	4.6
30.1	5.0	10.0	15.0	20.0	25.1	.1	0.1	0.6	1.1	1.6	2.1	2.6	3.1	3.6	4.1	4.6
30.2	5.0	10.0	15.1	20.1	25.1	.2	0.1	0.6	1.1	1.6	2.1	2.6	3.2	3.7	4.2	4.7
30.3	5.0	10.1	15.1	20.2	25.2	.3	0.2	0.7	1.2	1.7	2.2	2.7	3.2	3.7	4.2	4.7
30.4	5.1	10.1	15.2	20.3	25.3	.4	0.2	0.7	1.2	1.7	2.2	2.7	3.3	3.8	4.3	4.8
30.5	5.1	10.2	15.3	20.3	25.4	.5	0.3	0.8	1.3	1.8	2.3	2.8	3.3	3.8	4.3	4.8
30.6	5.1	10.2	15.3	20.4	25.5	.6	0.3	0.8	1.3	1.8	2.3	2.8	3.4	3.9	4.4	4.9
30.7	5.1	10.3	15.4	20.5	25.6	.7	0.4	0.9	1.4	1.9	2.4	2.9	3.4	3.9	4.4	4.9
30.8	5.2	10.3	15.4	20.6	25.7	.8	0.4	0.9	1.4	1.9	2.4	2.9	3.5	4.0	4.5	5.0
30.9	5.2	10.3	15.5	20.6	25.8	.9	0.5	1.0	1.5	2.0	2.5	3.0	3.5	4.0	4.5	5.0
31.0	5.1	10.3	15.5	20.6	25.8	.0	0.0	0.5	1.0	1.6	2.1	2.6	3.1	3.7	4.2	4.7
31.1	5.2	10.3	15.5	20.7	25.9	.1	0.1	0.6	1.1	1.6	2.2	2.7	3.2	3.7	4.3	4.8
31.2	5.2	10.4	15.6	20.8	26.0	.2	0.1	0.6	1.2	1.7	2.2	2.7	3.3	3.8	4.3	4.8
31.3	5.2	10.4	15.6	20.9	26.1	.3	0.2	0.7	1.2	1.7	2.3	2.8	3.3	3.8	4.4	4.9
31.4	5.2	10.5	15.7	20.9	26.2	.4	0.2	0.7	1.3	1.8	2.3	2.8	3.4	3.9	4.4	4.9
31.5	5.3	10.5	15.8	21.0	26.3	.5	0.3	0.8	1.3	1.8	2.4	2.9	3.4	3.9	4.5	5.0
31.6	5.3	10.5	15.8	21.1	26.3	.6	0.3	0.8	1.4	1.9	2.4	2.9	3.5	4.0	4.5	5.0
31.7	5.3	10.6	15.9	21.2	26.4	.7	0.4	0.9	1.4	1.9	2.5	3.0	3.5	4.0	4.6	5.1
31.8	5.3	10.6	15.9	21.2	26.5	.8	0.4	0.9	1.5	2.0	2.5	3.0	3.6	4.1	4.6	5.1
31.9	5.4	10.7	16.0	21.3	26.6	.9	0.5	1.0	1.5	2.0	2.6	3.1	3.6	4.1	4.7	5.2
32.0	5.3	10.6	16.0	21.3	26.6	.0	0.0	0.5	1.1	1.6	2.2	2.7	3.2	3.8	4.3	4.9
32.1	5.3	10.7	16.0	21.4	26.7	.1	0.1	0.6	1.1	1.7	2.2	2.8	3.3	3.8	4.4	4.9
32.2	5.3	10.7	16.1	21.4	26.8	.2	0.1	0.6	1.2	1.7	2.3	2.8	3.4	3.9	4.4	5.0
32.3	5.4	10.8	16.1	21.5	26.9	.3	0.2	0.7	1.2	1.8	2.3	2.9	3.4	4.0	4.5	5.0
32.4	5.4	10.8	16.2	21.6	27.0	.4	0.2	0.8	1.3	1.8	2.4	2.9	3.5	4.0	4.5	5.1
32.5	5.4	10.8	16.3	21.7	27.1	.5	0.3	0.8	1.4	1.9	2.4	3.0	3.5	4.1	4.6	5.1
32.6	5.4	10.9	16.3	21.7	27.2	.6	0.3	0.9	1.4	1.9	2.5	3.0	3.6	4.1	4.7	5.2
32.7	5.5	10.9	16.4	21.8	27.3	.7	0.4	0.9	1.5	2.0	2.5	3.1	3.6	4.2	4.7	5.3
32.8	5.5	11.0	16.4	21.9	27.4	.8	0.4	1.0	1.5	2.1	2.6	3.1	3.7	4.2	4.8	5.3
32.9	5.5	11.0	16.5	22.0	27.5	.9	0.5	1.0	1.6	2.1	2.7	3.2	3.7	4.3	4.8	5.4
33.0	5.5	11.0	16.5	22.0	27.5	.0	0.0	0.6	1.1	1.7	2.2	2.8	3.3	3.9	4.5	5.0
33.1	5.5	11.0	16.5	22.0	27.6	.1	0.1	0.6	1.2	1.7	2.3	2.8	3.4	4.0	4.5	5.1
33.2	5.5	11.0	16.6	22.1	27.6	.2	0.1	0.7	1.2	1.8	2.3	2.9	3.5	4.0	4.6	5.1
33.3	5.5	11.1	16.6	22.2	27.7	.3	0.2	0.7	1.3	1.8	2.4	3.0	3.5	4.1	4.6	5.2
33.4	5.6	11.1	16.7	22.3	27.8	.4	0.2	0.8	1.3	1.9	2.5	3.0	3.6	4.1	4.7	5.2
33.5	5.6	11.2	16.8	22.3	27.9	.5	0.3	0.8	1.4	2.0	2.5	3.1	3.6	4.2	4.7	5.3
33.6	5.6	11.2	16.8	22.4	28.0	.6	0.3	0.9	1.5	2.0	2.6	3.1	3.7	4.2	4.8	5.4
33.7	5.6	11.3	16.9	22.5	28.1	.7	0.4	0.9	1.5	2.1	2.6	3.2	3.7	4.3	4.9	5.4
33.8	5.7	11.3	16.9	22.6	28.2	.8	0.4	1.0	1.6	2.1	2.7	3.2	3.8	4.4	4.9	5.5
33.9	5.7	11.3	17.0	22.6	28.3	.9	0.5	1.1	1.6	2.2	2.7	3.3	3.9	4.4	5.0	5.5
34.0	5.6	11.3	17.0	22.6	28.3	.0	0.0	0.6	1.1	1.7	2.3	2.9	3.4	4.0	4.6	5.2
34.1	5.7	11.3	17.0	22.7	28.4	.1	0.1	0.6	1.2	1.8	2.4	2.9	3.5	4.1	4.7	5.2
34.2	5.7	11.4	17.1	22.8	28.5	.2	0.1	0.7	1.3	1.8	2.4	3.0	3.6	4.1	4.7	5.3
34.3	5.7	11.4	17.1	22.9	28.6	.3	0.2	0.7	1.3	1.9	2.5	3.0	3.6	4.2	4.8	5.3
34.4	5.7	11.5	17.2	22.9	28.7	.4	0.2	0.8	1.4	2.0	2.5	3.1	3.7	4.3	4.8	5.4
34.5	5.8	11.5	17.3	23.0	28.8	.5	0.3	0.9	1.4	2.0	2.6	3.2	3.7	4.3	4.9	5.5
34.6	5.8	11.5	17.3	23.1	28.8	.6	0.3	0.9	1.5	2.1	2.6	3.2	3.8	4.4	4.9	5.5
34.7	5.8	11.6	17.4	23.2	28.9	.7	0.4	1.0	1.6	2.1	2.7	3.3	3.9	4.4	5.0	5.6
34.8	5.8	11.6	17.4	23.2	29.0	.8	0.5	1.0	1.6	2.2	2.8	3.3	3.9	4.5	5.1	5.6
34.9	5.9	11.7	17.5	23.3	29.1	.9	0.5	1.1	1.7	2.2	2.8	3.4	4.0	4.5	5.1	5.7
35.0	5.8	11.6	17.5	23.3	29.1	.0	0.0	0.6	1.2	1.8	2.4	3.0	3.5	4.1	4.7	5.3
35.1	5.8	11.7	17.5	23.4	29.2	.1	0.1	0.7	1.2	1.8	2.4	3.0	3.6	4.2	4.8	5.4
35.2	5.8	11.7	17.6	23.4	29.3	.2	0.1	0.7	1.3	1.9	2.5	3.1	3.7	4.3	4.9	5.4
35.3	5.9	11.8	17.6	23.5	29.4	.3	0.2	0.8	1.4	2.0	2.5	3.1	3.7	4.3	4.9	5.5
35.4	5.9	11.8	17.7	23.6	29.5	.4	0.2	0.8	1.4	2.0	2.6	3.2	3.8	4.4	5.0	5.6
35.5	5.9	11.8	17.8	23.7	29.6	.5	0.3	0.9	1.5	2.1	2.7	3.3	3.8	4.4	5.0	5.6
35.6	5.9	11.9	17.8	23.7	29.7	.6	0.4	0.9	1.5	2.1	2.7	3.3	3.9	4.5	5.1	5.7
35.7	6.0	11.9	17.9	23.8	29.8	.7	0.4	1.0	1.6	2.2	2.8	3.4	4.0	4.6	5.1	5.7
35.8	6.0	12.0	17.9	23.9	29.9	.8	0.5	1.1	1.7	2.2	2.8	3.4	4.0	4.6	5.2	5.8
35.9	6.0	12.0	18.0	24.0	30.0	.9	0.5	1.1	1.7	2.3	2.9	3.5	4.1	4.7	5.3	5.9
	10′	20′	30′	40′	50′		0′	1′	2′	3′	4′	5′	6′	7′	8′	9′

Double Second Diff. and Corr. (Dec. Inc. 28.0–29.9 and 30.0–31.9)

Diff. ′	Corr. ′
0.8	
	0.1
2.4	
	0.2
4.0	
	0.3
5.6	
	0.4
7.2	
	0.5
8.8	
	0.6
10.4	
	0.7
12.0	
	0.8
13.6	
	0.9
15.2	
	1.0
16.8	
	1.1
18.4	
	1.2
20.0	
	1.3
21.6	
	1.4
23.2	
	1.5
24.8	
	1.6
26.4	
	1.7
28.0	
	1.8
29.6	
	1.9
31.2	
	2.0
32.8	
	2.1
34.4	

Double Second Diff. and Corr. (Dec. Inc. 32.0–33.9)

Diff. ′	Corr. ′
0.8	
	0.1
2.4	
	0.2
4.0	
	0.3
5.7	
	0.4
7.3	
	0.5
8.9	
	0.6
10.5	
	0.7
12.1	
	0.8
13.7	
	0.9
15.4	
	1.0
17.0	
	1.1
18.6	
	1.2
20.2	
	1.3
21.8	
	1.4
23.4	
	1.5
25.1	
	1.6
26.7	
	1.7
28.3	
	1.8
29.9	
	1.9
31.5	
	2.0
33.1	
	2.1
34.7	

Double Second Diff. and Corr. (Dec. Inc. 34.0–35.9)

Diff. ′	Corr. ′
0.8	
	0.1
2.5	
	0.2
4.1	
	0.3
5.8	
	0.4
7.4	
	0.5
9.1	
	0.6
10.7	
	0.7
12.3	
	0.8
14.0	
	0.9
15.6	
	1.0
17.3	
	1.1
18.9	
	1.2
20.6	
	1.3
22.2	
	1.4
23.9	
	1.5
25.5	
	1.6
27.2	
	1.7
28.8	
	1.8
30.4	
	1.9
32.1	
	2.0
33.7	
	2.1
35.4	

Dec. Inc.	Tens 10′	20′	30′	40′	50′	Decimals ⇓	Units 0′	1′	2′	3′	4′	5′	6′	7′	8′	9′
′	′	′	′	′	′	′	′	′	′	′	′	′	′	′	′	′
36.0	6.0	12.0	18.0	24.0	30.0	.0	0.0	0.6	1.2	1.8	2.4	3.0	3.6	4.3	4.9	5.5
36.1	6.0	12.0	18.0	24.0	30.1	.1	0.1	0.7	1.3	1.9	2.5	3.1	3.7	4.3	4.9	5.5
36.2	6.0	12.0	18.1	24.1	30.1	.2	0.1	0.7	1.3	1.9	2.6	3.2	3.8	4.4	5.0	5.6
36.3	6.0	12.1	18.1	24.2	30.2	.3	0.2	0.8	1.4	2.0	2.6	3.2	3.8	4.4	5.0	5.7
36.4	6.1	12.1	18.2	24.3	30.3	.4	0.2	0.9	1.5	2.1	2.7	3.3	3.9	4.5	5.1	5.7
36.5	6.1	12.2	18.3	24.3	30.4	.5	0.3	0.9	1.5	2.1	2.7	3.3	4.0	4.6	5.2	5.8
36.6	6.1	12.2	18.3	24.4	30.5	.6	0.4	1.0	1.6	2.2	2.8	3.4	4.0	4.6	5.2	5.8
36.7	6.1	12.3	18.4	24.5	30.6	.7	0.4	1.0	1.6	2.3	2.9	3.5	4.1	4.7	5.3	5.9
36.8	6.2	12.3	18.4	24.6	30.7	.8	0.5	1.1	1.7	2.3	2.9	3.5	4.1	4.7	5.4	6.0
36.9	6.2	12.3	18.5	24.6	30.8	.9	0.5	1.2	1.8	2.4	3.0	3.6	4.2	4.8	5.4	6.0
37.0	6.1	12.3	18.5	24.6	30.8	.0	0.0	0.6	1.2	1.9	2.5	3.1	3.7	4.4	5.0	5.6
37.1	6.2	12.3	18.5	24.7	30.9	.1	0.1	0.7	1.3	1.9	2.6	3.2	3.8	4.4	5.1	5.7
37.2	6.2	12.4	18.6	24.8	31.0	.2	0.1	0.7	1.4	2.0	2.6	3.2	3.9	4.5	5.1	5.7
37.3	6.2	12.4	18.6	24.9	31.1	.3	0.2	0.8	1.4	2.1	2.7	3.3	3.9	4.6	5.2	5.8
37.4	6.2	12.5	18.7	24.9	31.2	.4	0.2	0.9	1.5	2.1	2.7	3.4	4.0	4.6	5.2	5.9
37.5	6.3	12.5	18.8	25.0	31.3	.5	0.3	0.9	1.6	2.2	2.8	3.4	4.1	4.7	5.3	5.9
37.6	6.3	12.5	18.8	25.1	31.3	.6	0.4	1.0	1.6	2.2	2.9	3.5	4.1	4.7	5.4	6.0
37.7	6.3	12.6	18.9	25.2	31.4	.7	0.4	1.1	1.7	2.3	2.9	3.6	4.2	4.8	5.4	6.1
37.8	6.3	12.6	18.9	25.2	31.5	.8	0.5	1.1	1.7	2.4	3.0	3.6	4.2	4.9	5.5	6.1
37.9	6.4	12.7	19.0	25.3	31.6	.9	0.6	1.2	1.8	2.4	3.1	3.7	4.3	4.9	5.6	6.2
38.0	6.3	12.6	19.0	25.3	31.6	.0	0.0	0.6	1.3	1.9	2.6	3.2	3.8	4.5	5.1	5.8
38.1	6.3	12.7	19.0	25.4	31.7	.1	0.1	0.7	1.3	2.0	2.6	3.3	3.9	4.6	5.2	5.8
38.2	6.3	12.7	19.1	25.4	31.8	.2	0.1	0.8	1.4	2.1	2.7	3.3	4.0	4.6	5.3	5.9
38.3	6.4	12.8	19.1	25.5	31.9	.3	0.2	0.8	1.5	2.1	2.8	3.4	4.0	4.7	5.3	6.0
38.4	6.4	12.8	19.2	25.6	32.0	.4	0.3	0.9	1.5	2.2	2.8	3.5	4.1	4.7	5.4	6.0
38.5	6.4	12.8	19.3	25.7	32.1	.5	0.3	1.0	1.6	2.2	2.9	3.5	4.2	4.8	5.5	6.1
38.6	6.4	12.9	19.3	25.7	32.2	.6	0.4	1.0	1.7	2.3	3.0	3.6	4.2	4.9	5.5	6.2
38.7	6.5	12.9	19.4	25.8	32.3	.7	0.4	1.1	1.7	2.4	3.0	3.7	4.3	4.9	5.6	6.2
38.8	6.5	13.0	19.4	25.9	32.4	.8	0.5	1.2	1.8	2.4	3.1	3.7	4.4	5.0	5.6	6.3
38.9	6.5	13.0	19.5	26.0	32.5	.9	0.6	1.2	1.9	2.5	3.1	3.8	4.4	5.1	5.7	6.4
39.0	6.5	13.0	19.5	26.0	32.5	.0	0.0	0.7	1.3	2.0	2.6	3.3	3.9	4.6	5.3	5.9
39.1	6.5	13.0	19.5	26.0	32.6	.1	0.1	0.7	1.4	2.0	2.7	3.4	4.0	4.7	5.3	6.0
39.2	6.5	13.0	19.6	26.1	32.6	.2	0.1	0.8	1.4	2.1	2.8	3.4	4.1	4.7	5.4	6.1
39.3	6.5	13.1	19.6	26.2	32.7	.3	0.2	0.9	1.5	2.2	2.8	3.5	4.1	4.8	5.5	6.1
39.4	6.6	13.1	19.7	26.3	32.8	.4	0.3	0.9	1.6	2.2	2.9	3.6	4.2	4.9	5.5	6.2
39.5	6.6	13.2	19.8	26.3	32.9	.5	0.3	1.0	1.6	2.3	3.0	3.6	4.3	4.9	5.6	6.3
39.6	6.6	13.2	19.8	26.4	33.0	.6	0.4	1.1	1.7	2.4	3.0	3.7	4.3	5.0	5.7	6.3
39.7	6.6	13.3	19.9	26.5	33.1	.7	0.5	1.1	1.8	2.4	3.1	3.8	4.4	5.1	5.7	6.4
39.8	6.7	13.3	19.9	26.6	33.2	.8	0.5	1.2	1.8	2.5	3.2	3.8	4.5	5.1	5.8	6.5
39.9	6.7	13.3	20.0	26.6	33.3	.9	0.6	1.3	1.9	2.6	3.2	3.9	4.5	5.2	5.9	6.5
40.0	6.6	13.3	20.0	26.6	33.3	.0	0.0	0.7	1.3	2.0	2.7	3.4	4.0	4.7	5.4	6.1
40.1	6.7	13.3	20.0	26.7	33.4	.1	0.1	0.7	1.4	2.1	2.8	3.4	4.1	4.8	5.5	6.1
40.2	6.7	13.4	20.1	26.8	33.5	.2	0.1	0.8	1.5	2.2	2.8	3.5	4.2	4.9	5.5	6.2
40.3	6.7	13.4	20.1	26.9	33.6	.3	0.2	0.9	1.6	2.2	2.9	3.6	4.3	4.9	5.6	6.3
40.4	6.7	13.5	20.2	26.9	33.7	.4	0.3	0.9	1.6	2.3	3.0	3.6	4.3	5.0	5.7	6.3
40.5	6.8	13.5	20.3	27.0	33.8	.5	0.3	1.0	1.7	2.4	3.0	3.7	4.4	5.1	5.7	6.4
40.6	6.8	13.5	20.3	27.1	33.8	.6	0.4	1.1	1.8	2.4	3.1	3.8	4.5	5.1	5.8	6.5
40.7	6.8	13.6	20.4	27.2	33.9	.7	0.5	1.1	1.8	2.5	3.2	3.8	4.5	5.2	5.9	6.5
40.8	6.8	13.6	20.4	27.2	34.0	.8	0.5	1.2	1.9	2.6	3.2	3.9	4.6	5.3	5.9	6.6
40.9	6.9	13.7	20.5	27.3	34.1	.9	0.6	1.3	2.0	2.6	3.3	4.0	4.7	5.3	6.0	6.7
41.0	6.8	13.6	20.5	27.3	34.1	.0	0.0	0.7	1.4	2.1	2.8	3.5	4.1	4.8	5.5	6.2
41.1	6.8	13.7	20.5	27.4	34.2	.1	0.1	0.8	1.5	2.1	2.8	3.5	4.2	4.9	5.6	6.3
41.2	6.8	13.7	20.6	27.4	34.3	.2	0.1	0.8	1.5	2.2	2.9	3.6	4.3	5.0	5.7	6.4
41.3	6.9	13.8	20.6	27.5	34.4	.3	0.2	0.9	1.6	2.3	3.0	3.7	4.4	5.0	5.7	6.4
41.4	6.9	13.8	20.7	27.6	34.5	.4	0.3	1.0	1.7	2.4	3.0	3.7	4.4	5.1	5.8	6.5
41.5	6.9	13.8	20.8	27.7	34.6	.5	0.3	1.0	1.7	2.4	3.1	3.8	4.5	5.2	5.9	6.6
41.6	6.9	13.9	20.8	27.7	34.7	.6	0.4	1.1	1.8	2.5	3.2	3.9	4.6	5.3	5.9	6.6
41.7	7.0	13.9	20.9	27.8	34.8	.7	0.5	1.2	1.9	2.6	3.3	3.9	4.6	5.3	6.0	6.7
41.8	7.0	14.0	20.9	27.9	34.9	.8	0.6	1.2	1.9	2.6	3.3	4.0	4.7	5.4	6.1	6.8
41.9	7.0	14.0	21.0	28.0	35.0	.9	0.6	1.3	2.0	2.7	3.4	4.1	4.8	5.5	6.2	6.8
42.0	7.0	14.0	21.0	28.0	35.0	.0	0.0	0.7	1.4	2.1	2.8	3.5	4.2	5.0	5.7	6.4
42.1	7.0	14.0	21.0	28.0	35.1	.1	0.1	0.8	1.5	2.2	2.9	3.6	4.3	5.0	5.7	6.4
42.2	7.0	14.0	21.1	28.1	35.1	.2	0.1	0.8	1.6	2.3	3.0	3.7	4.4	5.1	5.8	6.5
42.3	7.0	14.1	21.1	28.2	35.2	.3	0.2	0.9	1.6	2.3	3.0	3.8	4.5	5.2	5.9	6.6
42.4	7.1	14.1	21.2	28.3	35.3	.4	0.3	1.0	1.7	2.4	3.1	3.8	4.5	5.2	5.9	6.7
42.5	7.1	14.2	21.3	28.3	35.4	.5	0.4	1.1	1.8	2.5	3.2	3.9	4.6	5.3	6.0	6.7
42.6	7.1	14.2	21.3	28.4	35.5	.6	0.4	1.1	1.8	2.5	3.3	4.0	4.7	5.4	6.1	6.8
42.7	7.1	14.3	21.4	28.5	35.6	.7	0.5	1.2	1.9	2.6	3.3	4.0	4.7	5.5	6.2	6.9
42.8	7.2	14.3	21.4	28.6	35.7	.8	0.6	1.3	2.0	2.7	3.4	4.1	4.8	5.5	6.2	6.9
42.9	7.2	14.3	21.5	28.6	35.8	.9	0.6	1.3	2.1	2.8	3.5	4.2	4.9	5.6	6.3	7.0
43.0	7.1	14.3	21.5	28.6	35.8	.0	0.0	0.7	1.4	2.2	2.9	3.6	4.3	5.1	5.8	6.5
43.1	7.2	14.3	21.5	28.7	35.9	.1	0.1	0.8	1.5	2.2	3.0	3.7	4.4	5.1	5.9	6.6
43.2	7.2	14.4	21.6	28.8	36.0	.2	0.1	0.9	1.6	2.3	3.0	3.8	4.5	5.2	5.9	6.7
43.3	7.2	14.4	21.6	28.9	36.1	.3	0.2	0.9	1.7	2.4	3.1	3.8	4.6	5.3	6.0	6.7
43.4	7.2	14.5	21.7	28.9	36.2	.4	0.3	1.0	1.7	2.5	3.2	3.9	4.6	5.4	6.1	6.8
43.5	7.3	14.5	21.8	29.0	36.3	.5	0.4	1.1	1.8	2.5	3.3	4.0	4.7	5.4	6.2	6.9
43.6	7.3	14.5	21.8	29.1	36.3	.6	0.4	1.2	1.9	2.6	3.3	4.1	4.8	5.5	6.2	7.0
43.7	7.3	14.6	21.9	29.2	36.4	.7	0.5	1.2	2.0	2.7	3.4	4.1	4.9	5.6	6.3	7.0
43.8	7.3	14.6	21.9	29.2	36.5	.8	0.6	1.3	2.0	2.8	3.5	4.2	4.9	5.7	6.4	7.1
43.9	7.4	14.7	22.0	29.3	36.6	.9	0.7	1.4	2.1	2.8	3.6	4.3	5.0	5.7	6.5	7.2
	10′	20′	30′	40′	50′		0′	1′	2′	3′	4′	5′	6′	7′	8′	9′

Double Second Diff. and Corr. (Dec. Inc. 36.0–37.9)

Diff. ′	Corr. ′
0.8	
	0.1
2.5	
	0.2
4.2	
	0.3
5.9	
	0.4
7.6	
	0.5
9.3	
	0.6
11.0	
	0.7
12.7	
	0.8
14.4	
	0.9
16.1	
	1.0
17.8	
	1.1
19.5	
	1.2
21.2	
	1.3
22.8	
	1.4
24.5	
	1.5
26.2	
	1.6
27.9	
	1.7
29.6	
	1.8
31.3	
	1.9
33.0	
	2.0
34.7	

Double Second Diff. and Corr. (Dec. Inc. 38.0–39.9)

Diff. ′	Corr. ′
0.9	
	0.1
2.6	
	0.2
4.4	
	0.3
6.2	
	0.4
7.9	
	0.5
9.7	
	0.6
11.4	
	0.7
13.2	
	0.8
14.9	
	0.9
16.7	
	1.0
18.5	
	1.1
20.2	
	1.2
22.0	
	1.3
23.7	
	1.4
25.5	
	1.5
27.3	
	1.6
29.0	
	1.7
30.8	
	1.8
32.5	
	1.9
34.3	

Double Second Diff. and Corr. (Dec. Inc. 40.0–41.9)

Diff. ′	Corr. ′
0.9	
	0.1
2.8	
	0.2
4.6	
	0.3
6.5	
	0.4
8.3	
	0.5
10.2	
	0.6
12.0	
	0.7
13.9	
	0.8
15.7	
	0.9
17.6	
	1.0
19.4	
	1.1
21.3	
	1.2
23.1	
	1.3
25.0	
	1.4
26.8	
	1.5
28.7	
	1.6
30.5	
	1.7
32.3	
	1.8
34.2	

Double Second Diff. and Corr. (Dec. Inc. 42.0–43.9)

Diff. ′	Corr. ′
1.0	
	0.1
3.0	
	0.2
4.9	
	0.3
6.9	
	0.4
8.9	
	0.5
10.8	
	0.6
12.8	
	0.7
14.8	
	0.8
16.7	
	0.9
18.7	
	1.0
20.7	
	1.1
22.7	
	1.2
24.6	
	1.3
26.6	
	1.4
28.6	
	1.5
30.5	
	1.6
32.5	
	1.7
34.5	

The Double-Second-Difference correction (Corr.) is always to be added to the tabulated altitude.

INTERPOLATION TABLE

Dec. Inc.	Tens 10′	20′	30′	40′	50′	Decimals	Units 0′	1′	2′	3′	4′	5′	6′	7′	8′	9′
44.0	7.3	14.6	22.0	29.3	36.6	.0	0.0	0.7	1.5	2.2	3.0	3.7	4.4	5.2	5.9	6.7
44.1	7.3	14.7	22.0	29.3	36.7	.1	0.1	0.8	1.6	2.3	3.0	3.8	4.5	5.3	6.0	6.7
44.2	7.3	14.7	22.1	29.4	36.8	.2	0.1	0.9	1.6	2.4	3.1	3.9	4.6	5.3	6.1	6.8
44.3	7.4	14.8	22.1	29.5	36.9	.3	0.2	1.0	1.7	2.4	3.2	3.9	4.7	5.4	6.2	6.9
44.4	7.4	14.8	22.2	29.6	37.0	.4	0.3	1.0	1.8	2.5	3.3	4.0	4.7	5.5	6.2	7.0
44.5	7.4	14.8	22.3	29.7	37.1	.5	0.4	1.1	1.9	2.6	3.3	4.1	4.8	5.6	6.3	7.0
44.6	7.4	14.9	22.3	29.7	37.2	.6	0.4	1.2	1.9	2.7	3.4	4.2	4.9	5.6	6.4	7.1
44.7	7.5	14.9	22.4	29.8	37.3	.7	0.5	1.3	2.0	2.7	3.5	4.2	5.0	5.7	6.5	7.2
44.8	7.5	15.0	22.4	29.9	37.4	.8	0.6	1.3	2.1	2.8	3.6	4.3	5.0	5.8	6.5	7.3
44.9	7.5	15.0	22.5	30.0	37.5	.9	0.7	1.4	2.2	2.9	3.6	4.4	5.1	5.9	6.6	7.3
45.0	7.5	15.0	22.5	30.0	37.5	.0	0.0	0.8	1.5	2.3	3.0	3.8	4.5	5.3	6.1	6.8
45.1	7.5	15.0	22.5	30.0	37.6	.1	0.1	0.8	1.6	2.4	3.1	3.9	4.6	5.4	6.1	6.9
45.2	7.5	15.0	22.6	30.1	37.6	.2	0.2	0.9	1.7	2.4	3.2	3.9	4.7	5.5	6.2	7.0
45.3	7.5	15.1	22.6	30.2	37.7	.3	0.2	1.0	1.7	2.5	3.3	4.0	4.8	5.5	6.3	7.1
45.4	7.6	15.1	22.7	30.3	37.8	.4	0.3	1.1	1.8	2.6	3.3	4.1	4.9	5.6	6.4	7.1
45.5	7.6	15.2	22.8	30.3	37.9	.5	0.4	1.1	1.9	2.7	3.4	4.2	4.9	5.7	6.4	7.2
45.6	7.6	15.2	22.8	30.4	38.0	.6	0.5	1.2	2.0	2.7	3.5	4.2	5.0	5.8	6.5	7.3
45.7	7.6	15.3	22.9	30.5	38.1	.7	0.5	1.3	2.0	2.8	3.6	4.3	5.1	5.8	6.6	7.4
45.8	7.7	15.3	22.9	30.6	38.2	.8	0.6	1.4	2.1	2.9	3.6	4.4	5.2	5.9	6.7	7.4
45.9	7.7	15.3	23.0	30.6	38.3	.9	0.7	1.4	2.2	3.0	3.7	4.5	5.2	6.0	6.7	7.5
46.0	7.6	15.3	23.0	30.6	38.3	.0	0.0	0.8	1.5	2.3	3.1	3.9	4.6	5.4	6.2	7.0
46.1	7.7	15.3	23.0	30.7	38.4	.1	0.1	0.9	1.6	2.4	3.2	4.0	4.7	5.5	6.3	7.1
46.2	7.7	15.4	23.1	30.8	38.5	.2	0.2	0.9	1.7	2.5	3.3	4.0	4.8	5.6	6.4	7.1
46.3	7.7	15.4	23.1	30.9	38.6	.3	0.2	1.0	1.8	2.6	3.3	4.1	4.9	5.7	6.4	7.2
46.4	7.7	15.5	23.2	30.9	38.7	.4	0.3	1.1	1.9	2.6	3.4	4.2	5.0	5.7	6.5	7.3
46.5	7.8	15.5	23.3	31.0	38.8	.5	0.4	1.2	1.9	2.7	3.5	4.3	5.0	5.8	6.6	7.4
46.6	7.8	15.5	23.3	31.1	38.8	.6	0.5	1.2	2.0	2.8	3.6	4.3	5.1	5.9	6.7	7.4
46.7	7.8	15.6	23.4	31.2	38.9	.7	0.5	1.3	2.1	2.9	3.6	4.4	5.2	6.0	6.7	7.5
46.8	7.8	15.6	23.4	31.2	39.0	.8	0.6	1.4	2.2	2.9	3.7	4.5	5.3	6.0	6.8	7.6
46.9	7.9	15.7	23.5	31.3	39.1	.9	0.7	1.5	2.2	3.0	3.8	4.6	5.3	6.1	6.9	7.7
47.0	7.8	15.6	23.5	31.3	39.1	.0	0.0	0.8	1.6	2.4	3.2	4.0	4.7	5.5	6.3	7.1
47.1	7.8	15.7	23.5	31.4	39.2	.1	0.1	0.9	1.7	2.5	3.2	4.0	4.8	5.6	6.4	7.2
47.2	7.8	15.7	23.6	31.4	39.3	.2	0.2	0.9	1.7	2.5	3.3	4.1	4.9	5.7	6.5	7.3
47.3	7.9	15.8	23.6	31.5	39.4	.3	0.2	1.0	1.8	2.6	3.4	4.2	5.0	5.8	6.6	7.4
47.4	7.9	15.8	23.7	31.6	39.5	.4	0.3	1.1	1.9	2.7	3.5	4.3	5.1	5.9	6.6	7.4
47.5	7.9	15.8	23.8	31.7	39.6	.5	0.4	1.2	2.0	2.8	3.6	4.4	5.1	5.9	6.7	7.5
47.6	7.9	15.9	23.8	31.7	39.7	.6	0.5	1.3	2.1	2.8	3.6	4.4	5.2	6.0	6.8	7.6
47.7	8.0	15.9	23.9	31.8	39.8	.7	0.6	1.3	2.1	2.9	3.7	4.5	5.3	6.1	6.9	7.7
47.8	8.0	16.0	23.9	31.9	39.9	.8	0.6	1.4	2.2	3.0	3.8	4.6	5.4	6.2	7.0	7.8
47.9	8.0	16.0	24.0	32.0	40.0	.9	0.7	1.5	2.3	3.1	3.9	4.7	5.5	6.3	7.0	7.8
48.0	8.0	16.0	24.0	32.0	40.0	.0	0.0	0.8	1.6	2.4	3.2	4.0	4.8	5.7	6.5	7.3
48.1	8.0	16.0	24.0	32.0	40.1	.1	0.1	0.9	1.7	2.5	3.3	4.1	4.9	5.7	6.5	7.4
48.2	8.0	16.0	24.1	32.1	40.1	.2	0.2	1.0	1.8	2.6	3.4	4.2	5.0	5.8	6.6	7.4
48.3	8.0	16.1	24.1	32.2	40.2	.3	0.2	1.1	1.9	2.7	3.5	4.3	5.1	5.9	6.7	7.5
48.4	8.1	16.1	24.2	32.3	40.3	.4	0.3	1.1	1.9	2.7	3.6	4.4	5.2	6.0	6.8	7.6
48.5	8.1	16.2	24.3	32.3	40.4	.5	0.4	1.2	2.0	2.8	3.6	4.4	5.3	6.1	6.9	7.7
48.6	8.1	16.2	24.3	32.4	40.5	.6	0.5	1.3	2.1	2.9	3.7	4.5	5.3	6.1	7.0	7.8
48.7	8.1	16.3	24.4	32.5	40.6	.7	0.6	1.4	2.2	3.0	3.8	4.6	5.4	6.2	7.0	7.8
48.8	8.2	16.3	24.4	32.6	40.7	.8	0.6	1.5	2.3	3.1	3.9	4.7	5.5	6.3	7.1	7.9
48.9	8.2	16.3	24.5	32.6	40.8	.9	0.7	1.5	2.3	3.2	4.0	4.8	5.6	6.4	7.2	8.0
49.0	8.1	16.3	24.5	32.6	40.8	.0	0.0	0.8	1.6	2.5	3.3	4.1	4.9	5.8	6.6	7.4
49.1	8.2	16.3	24.5	32.7	40.9	.1	0.1	0.9	1.7	2.6	3.4	4.2	5.0	5.9	6.7	7.5
49.2	8.2	16.4	24.6	32.8	41.0	.2	0.2	1.0	1.8	2.6	3.5	4.3	5.1	5.9	6.8	7.6
49.3	8.2	16.4	24.6	32.9	41.1	.3	0.2	1.1	1.9	2.7	3.5	4.4	5.2	6.0	6.8	7.7
49.4	8.2	16.5	24.7	32.9	41.2	.4	0.3	1.2	2.0	2.8	3.6	4.5	5.3	6.1	6.9	7.8
49.5	8.3	16.5	24.8	33.0	41.3	.5	0.4	1.2	2.1	2.9	3.7	4.5	5.4	6.2	7.0	7.8
49.6	8.3	16.5	24.8	33.1	41.3	.6	0.5	1.3	2.1	3.0	3.8	4.6	5.4	6.3	7.1	7.9
49.7	8.3	16.6	24.9	33.2	41.4	.7	0.6	1.4	2.2	3.1	3.9	4.7	5.5	6.4	7.2	8.0
49.8	8.3	16.6	24.9	33.2	41.5	.8	0.7	1.5	2.3	3.1	4.0	4.8	5.6	6.4	7.3	8.1
49.9	8.4	16.7	25.0	33.3	41.6	.9	0.7	1.6	2.4	3.2	4.0	4.9	5.7	6.5	7.3	8.2
50.0	8.3	16.6	25.0	33.3	41.6	.0	0.0	0.8	1.7	2.5	3.4	4.2	5.0	5.9	6.7	7.6
50.1	8.3	16.7	25.0	33.4	41.7	.1	0.1	0.9	1.8	2.6	3.5	4.3	5.1	6.0	6.8	7.7
50.2	8.3	16.7	25.1	33.4	41.8	.2	0.2	1.0	1.9	2.7	3.5	4.4	5.2	6.1	6.9	7.7
50.3	8.4	16.8	25.1	33.5	41.9	.3	0.3	1.1	1.9	2.8	3.6	4.5	5.3	6.1	7.0	7.8
50.4	8.4	16.8	25.2	33.6	42.0	.4	0.3	1.2	2.0	2.9	3.7	4.5	5.4	6.2	7.1	7.9
50.5	8.4	16.8	25.3	33.7	42.1	.5	0.4	1.3	2.1	2.9	3.8	4.6	5.5	6.3	7.2	8.0
50.6	8.4	16.9	25.3	33.7	42.2	.6	0.5	1.3	2.2	3.0	3.9	4.7	5.6	6.4	7.2	8.1
50.7	8.5	16.9	25.4	33.8	42.3	.7	0.6	1.4	2.3	3.1	4.0	4.8	5.6	6.5	7.3	8.2
50.8	8.5	17.0	25.4	33.9	42.4	.8	0.7	1.5	2.4	3.2	4.0	4.9	5.7	6.6	7.4	8.2
50.9	8.5	17.0	25.5	34.0	42.5	.9	0.8	1.6	2.4	3.3	4.1	5.0	5.8	6.6	7.5	8.3
51.0	8.5	17.0	25.5	34.0	42.5	.0	0.0	0.9	1.7	2.6	3.4	4.3	5.1	6.0	6.9	7.7
51.1	8.5	17.0	25.5	34.0	42.6	.1	0.1	0.9	1.8	2.7	3.5	4.4	5.2	6.1	7.0	7.8
51.2	8.5	17.0	25.6	34.1	42.6	.2	0.2	1.0	1.9	2.7	3.6	4.5	5.3	6.2	7.0	7.9
51.3	8.5	17.1	25.6	34.2	42.7	.3	0.3	1.1	2.0	2.8	3.7	4.5	5.4	6.3	7.1	8.0
51.4	8.6	17.1	25.7	34.3	42.8	.4	0.3	1.2	2.1	2.9	3.8	4.6	5.5	6.4	7.2	8.1
51.5	8.6	17.2	25.8	34.3	42.9	.5	0.4	1.3	2.1	3.0	3.9	4.7	5.6	6.4	7.3	8.2
51.6	8.6	17.2	25.8	34.4	43.0	.6	0.5	1.4	2.2	3.1	3.9	4.8	5.7	6.5	7.4	8.2
51.7	8.6	17.3	25.9	34.5	43.1	.7	0.6	1.5	2.3	3.2	4.0	4.9	5.8	6.6	7.5	8.3
51.8	8.7	17.3	25.9	34.6	43.2	.8	0.7	1.5	2.4	3.3	4.1	5.0	5.8	6.7	7.6	8.4
51.9	8.7	17.3	26.0	34.6	43.3	.9	0.8	1.6	2.5	3.3	4.2	5.1	5.9	6.8	7.6	8.5

Double Second Diff. and Corr.

Dec. Inc.	Double Second Diff. and Corr.
44.0–45.9	1.1, 0.1, 3.2, 0.2, 5.3, 0.3, 7.5, 0.4, 9.6, 0.5, 11.7, 0.6, 13.9, 0.7, 16.0, 0.8, 18.1, 0.9, 20.3, 1.0, 22.4, 1.1, 24.5, 1.2, 26.7, 1.3, 28.8, 1.4, 30.9, 1.5, 33.1, 1.6, 35.2
46.0–47.4	1.2, 0.1, 3.5, 0.2, 5.8, 0.3, 8.1, 0.4, 10.5, 0.5, 12.8, 0.6, 15.1, 0.7, 17.4, 0.8, 19.8, 0.9, 22.1, 1.0, 24.4, 1.1, 26.7, 1.2, 29.1, 1.3, 31.4, 1.4, 33.7, 1.5, 36.0
47.5–48.9	1.3, 0.1, 3.8, 0.2, 6.3, 0.3, 8.9, 0.4, 11.4, 0.5, 14.0, 0.6, 16.5, 0.7, 19.0, 0.8, 21.6, 0.9, 24.1, 1.0, 26.7, 1.1, 29.2, 1.2, 31.7, 1.3, 34.3
49.0–50.4	1.4, 0.1, 4.2, 0.2, 7.1, 0.3, 9.9, 0.4, 12.7, 0.5, 15.5, 0.6, 18.4, 0.7, 21.2, 0.8, 24.0, 0.9, 26.8, 1.0, 29.7, 1.1, 32.5, 1.2, 35.3
50.5–51.9	1.6, 0.1, 4.8, 0.2, 8.0, 0.3, 11.2, 0.4, 14.5, 0.5, 17.7, 0.6, 20.9, 0.7, 24.1, 0.8, 27.3, 0.9, 30.5, 1.0, 33.7, 1.1, 36.9

Dec. Inc.	Tens 10′	20′	30′	40′	50′	Decimals	Units 0′	1′	2′	3′	4′	5′	6′	7′	8′	9′
52.0	8.6	17.3	26.0	34.6	43.3	.0	0.0	0.9	1.7	2.6	3.5	4.4	5.2	6.1	7.0	7.9
52.1	8.7	17.3	26.0	34.7	43.4	.1	0.1	1.0	1.8	2.7	3.6	4.5	5.3	6.2	7.1	8.0
52.2	8.7	17.4	26.1	34.8	43.5	.2	0.2	1.0	1.9	2.8	3.7	4.5	5.4	6.3	7.2	8.0
52.3	8.7	17.4	26.1	34.9	43.6	.3	0.3	1.1	2.0	2.9	3.8	4.6	5.5	6.4	7.3	8.1
52.4	8.7	17.5	26.2	34.9	43.7	.4	0.3	1.2	2.1	3.0	3.8	4.7	5.6	6.5	7.3	8.2
52.5	8.8	17.5	26.3	35.0	43.8	.5	0.4	1.3	2.2	3.1	3.9	4.8	5.7	6.6	7.4	8.3
52.6	8.8	17.5	26.3	35.1	43.8	.6	0.5	1.4	2.3	3.1	4.0	4.9	5.8	6.6	7.5	8.4
52.7	8.8	17.6	26.4	35.2	43.9	.7	0.6	1.5	2.4	3.2	4.1	5.0	5.9	6.7	7.6	8.5
52.8	8.8	17.6	26.4	35.2	44.0	.8	0.7	1.6	2.4	3.3	4.2	5.1	5.9	6.8	7.7	8.6
52.9	8.9	17.7	26.5	35.3	44.1	.9	0.8	1.7	2.5	3.4	4.3	5.2	6.0	6.9	7.8	8.7
53.0	8.8	17.6	26.5	35.3	44.1	.0	0.0	0.9	1.8	2.7	3.6	4.5	5.3	6.2	7.1	8.0
53.1	8.8	17.7	26.5	35.4	44.2	.1	0.1	1.0	1.9	2.8	3.7	4.5	5.4	6.3	7.2	8.1
53.2	8.8	17.7	26.6	35.4	44.3	.2	0.2	1.1	2.0	2.9	3.7	4.6	5.5	6.4	7.3	8.2
53.3	8.9	17.8	26.6	35.5	44.4	.3	0.3	1.2	2.1	2.9	3.8	4.7	5.6	6.5	7.4	8.3
53.4	8.9	17.8	26.7	35.6	44.5	.4	0.4	1.2	2.1	3.0	3.9	4.8	5.7	6.6	7.5	8.4
53.5	8.9	17.8	26.8	35.7	44.6	.5	0.4	1.3	2.2	3.1	4.0	4.9	5.8	6.7	7.6	8.5
53.6	8.9	17.9	26.8	35.7	44.7	.6	0.5	1.4	2.3	3.2	4.1	5.0	5.9	6.8	7.7	8.6
53.7	9.0	17.9	26.9	35.8	44.8	.7	0.6	1.5	2.4	3.3	4.2	5.1	6.0	6.9	7.8	8.6
53.8	9.0	18.0	26.9	35.9	44.9	.8	0.7	1.6	2.5	3.4	4.3	5.2	6.1	7.0	7.8	8.7
53.9	9.0	18.0	27.0	36.0	45.0	.9	0.8	1.7	2.6	3.5	4.4	5.3	6.2	7.0	7.9	8.8
54.0	9.0	18.0	27.0	36.0	45.0	.0	0.0	0.9	1.8	2.7	3.6	4.5	5.4	6.4	7.3	8.2
54.1	9.0	18.0	27.0	36.0	45.1	.1	0.1	1.0	1.9	2.8	3.7	4.6	5.5	6.4	7.4	8.3
54.2	9.0	18.0	27.1	36.1	45.1	.2	0.2	1.1	2.0	2.9	3.8	4.7	5.6	6.5	7.4	8.4
54.3	9.0	18.1	27.1	36.2	45.2	.3	0.3	1.2	2.1	3.0	3.9	4.8	5.7	6.6	7.5	8.4
54.4	9.1	18.1	27.2	36.3	45.3	.4	0.4	1.3	2.2	3.1	4.0	4.9	5.8	6.7	7.6	8.5
54.5	9.1	18.2	27.3	36.3	45.4	.5	0.5	1.4	2.3	3.2	4.1	5.0	5.9	6.8	7.7	8.6
54.6	9.1	18.2	27.3	36.4	45.5	.6	0.5	1.5	2.4	3.3	4.2	5.1	6.0	6.9	7.8	8.7
54.7	9.1	18.3	27.4	36.5	45.6	.7	0.6	1.5	2.5	3.4	4.3	5.2	6.1	7.0	7.9	8.8
54.8	9.2	18.3	27.4	36.6	45.7	.8	0.7	1.6	2.5	3.5	4.4	5.3	6.2	7.1	8.0	8.9
54.9	9.2	18.3	27.5	36.6	45.8	.9	0.8	1.7	2.6	3.5	4.5	5.4	6.3	7.2	8.1	9.0
55.0	9.1	18.3	27.5	36.6	45.8	.0	0.0	0.9	1.8	2.8	3.7	4.6	5.5	6.5	7.4	8.3
55.1	9.2	18.3	27.5	36.7	45.9	.1	0.1	1.0	1.9	2.9	3.8	4.7	5.6	6.6	7.5	8.4
55.2	9.2	18.4	27.6	36.8	46.0	.2	0.2	1.1	2.0	3.0	3.9	4.8	5.7	6.7	7.6	8.5
55.3	9.2	18.4	27.6	36.9	46.1	.3	0.3	1.2	2.1	3.1	4.0	4.9	5.8	6.8	7.7	8.6
55.4	9.2	18.5	27.7	36.9	46.2	.4	0.4	1.3	2.2	3.1	4.1	5.0	5.9	6.8	7.8	8.7
55.5	9.3	18.5	27.8	37.0	46.3	.5	0.5	1.4	2.3	3.2	4.2	5.1	6.0	6.9	7.9	8.8
55.6	9.3	18.5	27.8	37.1	46.3	.6	0.6	1.5	2.4	3.3	4.3	5.2	6.1	7.0	8.0	8.9
55.7	9.3	18.6	27.9	37.2	46.4	.7	0.6	1.6	2.5	3.4	4.3	5.3	6.2	7.1	8.0	9.0
55.8	9.3	18.6	27.9	37.2	46.5	.8	0.7	1.7	2.6	3.5	4.4	5.4	6.3	7.2	8.1	9.1
55.9	9.4	18.7	28.0	37.3	46.6	.9	0.8	1.8	2.7	3.6	4.5	5.5	6.4	7.3	8.2	9.2
56.0	9.3	18.6	28.0	37.3	46.6	.0	0.0	0.9	1.9	2.8	3.8	4.7	5.6	6.6	7.5	8.5
56.1	9.3	18.7	28.0	37.4	46.7	.1	0.1	1.0	2.0	2.9	3.9	4.8	5.7	6.7	7.6	8.6
56.2	9.3	18.7	28.1	37.4	46.8	.2	0.2	1.1	2.1	3.0	4.0	4.9	5.8	6.8	7.7	8.7
56.3	9.4	18.8	28.1	37.5	46.9	.3	0.3	1.2	2.2	3.1	4.0	5.0	5.9	6.9	7.8	8.8
56.4	9.4	18.8	28.2	37.6	47.0	.4	0.4	1.3	2.3	3.2	4.1	5.1	6.0	7.0	7.9	8.9
56.5	9.4	18.8	28.3	37.7	47.1	.5	0.5	1.4	2.4	3.3	4.2	5.2	6.1	7.1	8.0	8.9
56.6	9.4	18.9	28.3	37.7	47.2	.6	0.6	1.5	2.4	3.4	4.3	5.3	6.2	7.2	8.1	9.0
56.7	9.5	18.9	28.4	37.8	47.3	.7	0.7	1.6	2.5	3.5	4.4	5.4	6.3	7.3	8.2	9.1
56.8	9.5	19.0	28.4	37.9	47.4	.8	0.8	1.7	2.6	3.6	4.5	5.5	6.4	7.3	8.3	9.2
56.9	9.5	19.0	28.5	38.0	47.5	.9	0.8	1.8	2.7	3.7	4.6	5.6	6.5	7.4	8.4	9.3
57.0	9.5	19.0	28.5	38.0	47.5	.0	0.0	1.0	1.9	2.9	3.8	4.8	5.7	6.7	7.7	8.6
57.1	9.5	19.0	28.5	38.0	47.6	.1	0.1	1.1	2.0	3.0	3.9	4.9	5.8	6.8	7.8	8.7
57.2	9.5	19.0	28.6	38.1	47.6	.2	0.2	1.1	2.1	3.1	4.0	5.0	5.9	6.9	7.9	8.8
57.3	9.5	19.1	28.6	38.2	47.7	.3	0.3	1.2	2.2	3.2	4.1	5.1	6.0	7.0	8.0	8.9
57.4	9.6	19.1	28.7	38.3	47.8	.4	0.4	1.3	2.3	3.3	4.2	5.2	6.1	7.1	8.0	9.0
57.5	9.6	19.2	28.8	38.3	47.9	.5	0.5	1.4	2.4	3.4	4.3	5.3	6.2	7.2	8.1	9.1
57.6	9.6	19.2	28.8	38.4	48.0	.6	0.6	1.5	2.5	3.4	4.4	5.4	6.3	7.3	8.2	9.2
57.7	9.6	19.3	28.9	38.5	48.1	.7	0.7	1.6	2.6	3.5	4.5	5.5	6.4	7.4	8.3	9.3
57.8	9.7	19.3	28.9	38.6	48.2	.8	0.8	1.7	2.7	3.6	4.6	5.6	6.5	7.5	8.4	9.4
57.9	9.7	19.3	29.0	38.6	48.3	.9	0.9	1.8	2.8	3.7	4.7	5.7	6.6	7.6	8.5	9.5
58.0	9.6	19.3	29.0	38.6	48.3	.0	0.0	1.0	1.9	2.9	3.9	4.9	5.8	6.8	7.8	8.8
58.1	9.7	19.3	29.0	38.7	48.4	.1	0.1	1.1	2.0	3.0	4.0	5.0	5.9	6.9	7.9	8.9
58.2	9.7	19.4	29.1	38.8	48.5	.2	0.2	1.2	2.1	3.1	4.1	5.1	6.0	7.0	8.0	9.0
58.3	9.7	19.4	29.1	38.9	48.6	.3	0.3	1.3	2.2	3.2	4.2	5.2	6.1	7.1	8.1	9.1
58.4	9.7	19.5	29.2	38.9	48.7	.4	0.4	1.4	2.3	3.3	4.3	5.3	6.2	7.2	8.2	9.2
58.5	9.8	19.5	29.3	39.0	48.8	.5	0.5	1.5	2.4	3.4	4.4	5.4	6.3	7.3	8.3	9.3
58.6	9.8	19.5	29.3	39.1	48.8	.6	0.6	1.6	2.5	3.5	4.5	5.5	6.4	7.4	8.4	9.4
58.7	9.8	19.6	29.4	39.2	48.9	.7	0.7	1.7	2.6	3.6	4.6	5.6	6.5	7.5	8.5	9.5
58.8	9.8	19.6	29.4	39.2	49.0	.8	0.8	1.8	2.7	3.7	4.7	5.7	6.6	7.6	8.6	9.6
58.9	9.9	19.7	29.5	39.3	49.1	.9	0.9	1.9	2.8	3.8	4.8	5.8	6.7	7.7	8.7	9.7
59.0	9.8	19.6	29.5	39.3	49.1	.0	0.0	1.0	2.0	3.0	4.0	5.0	5.9	6.9	7.9	8.9
59.1	9.8	19.7	29.5	39.4	49.2	.1	0.1	1.1	2.1	3.1	4.1	5.1	6.0	7.0	8.0	9.0
59.2	9.8	19.7	29.6	39.4	49.3	.2	0.2	1.2	2.2	3.2	4.2	5.2	6.1	7.1	8.1	9.1
59.3	9.9	19.8	29.6	39.5	49.4	.3	0.3	1.3	2.3	3.3	4.3	5.3	6.2	7.2	8.2	9.2
59.4	9.9	19.8	29.7	39.6	49.5	.4	0.4	1.4	2.4	3.4	4.4	5.4	6.3	7.3	8.3	9.3
59.5	9.9	19.8	29.8	39.7	49.6	.5	0.5	1.5	2.5	3.5	4.5	5.5	6.4	7.4	8.4	9.4
59.6	9.9	19.9	29.8	39.7	49.7	.6	0.6	1.6	2.6	3.6	4.6	5.6	6.5	7.5	8.5	9.5
59.7	10.0	19.9	29.9	39.8	49.8	.7	0.7	1.7	2.7	3.7	4.7	5.7	6.6	7.6	8.6	9.6
59.8	10.0	20.0	29.9	39.9	49.9	.8	0.8	1.8	2.8	3.8	4.8	5.8	6.7	7.7	8.7	9.7
59.9	10.0	20.0	30.0	40.0	50.0	.9	0.9	1.9	2.9	3.9	4.9	5.9	6.8	7.8	8.8	9.8

Double Second Diff. and Corr.

Dec. Inc.	Double Second Diff. and Corr.
52.0–52.9	1.8, 0.1, 5.5, 0.2, 9.1, 0.3, 12.8, 0.4, 16.5, 0.5, 20.1, 0.6, 23.8, 0.7, 27.4, 0.8, 31.1, 0.9, 34.7
53.0–53.9	2.1, 0.1, 6.2, 0.2, 10.4, 0.3, 14.5, 0.4, 18.6, 0.5, 22.8, 0.6, 26.9, 0.7, 31.1, 0.8, 35.2
54.0–54.9	2.4, 0.1, 7.2, 0.2, 12.0, 0.3, 16.8, 0.4, 21.6, 0.5, 26.4, 0.6, 31.2, 0.7, 36.0
55.0–55.9	2.9, 0.1, 8.6, 0.2, 14.4, 0.3, 20.2, 0.4, 25.9, 0.5, 31.7, 0.6, 37.5
56.0–56.9	3.6, 0.1, 10.9, 0.2, 18.2, 0.3, 25.5, 0.4, 32.8, 0.5, 40.1
57.0–57.9	5.0, 0.1, 15.0, 0.2, 25.0, 0.3, 35.1
58.0–58.9	8.2, 0.1, 24.6, 0.2, 41.0
59.0–59.4	16.2, 0.1, 48.6
59.5–59.9	0.0, 0.0, 48.2

The Double-Second-Difference correction (Corr.) is always to be added to the tabulated altitude.

PREFACE

This six-volume series of *Sight Reduction Tables for Marine Navigation* is designed to facilitate the practice of celestial navigation at sea by the Marcq Saint Hilaire or intercept method.

The tabular data are the solutions of the navigational triangle of which two sides and the included angle are known and it is necessary to find the values of the third side and adjacent angle.

The tables, intended for use with *The Nautical Almanac*, are designed for precise interpolation of altitude for declination by means of interpolation tables which facilitate linear interpolation and provide additionally for the effect of second differences when required.

The concept, design, development, and preparation of these tables are the results of the collaborative efforts and joint accomplishments of the National Imagery and Mapping Agency, the U.S. Naval Observatory, and Her Majesty's Nautical Almanac Office, Royal Greenwich Observatory. The tabular material in identical format has been published in the United Kingdom by the Hydrographic Department, Ministry of Defence (Navy), as N.P. 401.

This reprint was compiled on a Hewlett Packard K420 server with an HP C180 client workstation, and was composed in its entirety as a digital document.

Users should refer corrections, additions, and comments for improving this product to:

MARINE NAVIGATION DEPARTMENT
ST D 44
NATIONAL IMAGERY AND MAPPING AGENCY
4600 SANGAMORE ROAD
BETHESDA MD 20816-5003

CONTENTS

INTRODUCTION

A. DESCRIPTION OF TABLES

1. Purpose and Scope. The main purpose of these tables is to facilitate the practice of celestial navigation at sea. A secondary purpose is to provide, within the limitations of the tabular precision and interval, a table of the solutions of a spherical triangle of which two sides and the included angle are known and it is necessary to find the values of the third side and adjacent angle.

The tables have been designed primarily for use with the Marcq Saint Hilaire or intercept method of sight reduction, utilizing a position assumed or chosen so that interpolation for latitude and local hour angle is not required.

For entering arguments of integral degrees of latitude, declination, and local hour angle, altitudes and their differences are tabulated to the nearest tenth of a minute, azimuth angles to the nearest tenth of a degree. But the tables are designed for precise interpolation of altitude for declination only by means of interpolation tables which facilitate linear interpolation and provide additionally for the effect of second differences.

The data are applicable to the solutions of sights of all celestial bodies; there are no limiting values of altitude, latitude, hour angle, or declination.

2. Arrangement. The tables are divided into six volumes, each of which includes two eight-degree zones of latitude. An overlap of 1° occurs between volumes. The six volumes cover latitude bands 0° to 15°, 15° to 30°, 30° to 45°, 45° to 60°, 60° to 75°, and 75° to 90°.

Each consecutive opening of the pages of a latitude zone differs from the preceding one by 1° of local hour angle (LHA). As shown in figures 1 and 2, the values of LHA are prominently displayed at the top and bottom of each page; the horizontal argument heading each column is latitude, and the vertical argument is declination.

For each combination of arguments, the tabulations are: the tabular altitude (ht or Tab. Hc), the altitude difference (d) with its sign, and the azimuth angle (Z).

Within each opening, the data on the left-hand page are the altitudes, altitude differences, and azimuth angles of celestial bodies when the latitude of the observer has the same name as the declinations of the bodies. For any LHA tabulated on a left-hand page and any combination of the tabular latitude and declination arguments, the tabular altitude and associated azimuth angle respondents on the left-hand page are those of a body above the celestial horizon of the observer.

The LHA's tabulated on the left-hand pages are limited to the following ranges: 0° increasing to 90° and 360° decreasing to 270°. On any left-hand page there are two tabulated LHA's, one LHA in the range 0° increasing to 90° and the second in the range 360° decreasing to 270°.

On the right-hand page of each opening, the data above the horizontal rules are the tabular altitudes, altitude differences, and azimuth angles of celestial bodies above the celestial horizon when the latitude of the observer has a name contrary to the name of the declinations of the bodies and the LHA's of the bodies are those tabulated at the top of the page. The data below the horizontal rules are the tabular altitudes, altitude differences, and azimuth angles of celestial bodies above the celestial horizon when the latitude of the observer has the same name as the declinations of the bodies and the LHA's of the bodies are those tabulated at the bottom of the page.

The LHA's tabulated at the top of a right-hand page are the same as those tabulated on the left-hand page of the opening. The LHA's tabulated at the bottom of the right-hand page are limited to the range 90° increasing to 270°; one of the two LHA's at the bottom of the page is in the range 90° increasing to 180°; the other LHA is in the range 180° increasing to 270°; the LHA in the range 90° increasing to 180° is the supplement of the LHA at the top of the page in the range 0° increasing to 90°. When the LHA is 90°, the left and right-hand pages are identical.

The horizontal rules, known as the Contrary-Same Line or C-S Line, indicate the degree of declination in which the celestial horizon occurs.

60°, 300° L.H.A.   LATITUDE SAME NAME AS DECLINATION

N. Lat. { L.H.A. greater than 180° .....Zn=Z
{ L.H.A. less than 180°............Zn=360°-Z

Dec.	15° Hc	d	Z	16° Hc	d	Z	17° Hc	d	Z	18° Hc	d	Z	19° Hc	d	Z	20° Hc	d	Z	21° Hc	d	Z	22° Hc	d	Z	Dec.
0	28 52.7	+17.5	98.5	28 43.6	+18.6	99.0	28 33.9	+19.7	99.6	28 23.6	+20.9	100.1	28 12.8	+21.9	100.6	28 01.5	+23.0	101.2	27 49.6	+24.0	101.7	27 37.1	+25.2	102.2	0
1	29 10.2	+16.9	97.4	29 02.2	+18.1	98.0	28 53.6	+19.2	98.5	28 44.5	+20.3	99.0	28 34.7	+21.5	99.6	28 24.5	+22.5	100.1	28 13.6	+23.7	100.7	28 02.3	+24.7	101.2	1
2	29 27.1	+16.4	96.3	29 20.3	+17.5	96.9	29 12.8	+18.7	97.4	29 04.8	+19.8	98.0	28 56.2	+20.9	98.5	28 47.0	+22.0	99.1	28 37.3	+23.1	99.6	28 27.0	+24.2	100.1	2
3	29 43.5	+15.9	95.2	29 37.8	+17.0	95.8	29 31.5	+18.1	96.3	29 24.6	+19.2	96.9	29 17.1	+20.4	97.4	29 09.0	+21.5	98.0	29 00.4	+22.6	98.6	28 51.2	+23.7	99.1	3
4	29 59.4	+15.2	94.1	29 54.8	+16.4	94.7	29 49.6	+17.6	95.2	29 43.8	+18.8	95.8	29 37.5	+19.9	96.4	29 30.5	+21.0	96.9	29 23.0	+22.1	97.5	29 14.9	+23.2	98.0	4
5	30 14.6	+14.7	93.0	30 11.2	+15.9	93.5	30 07.2	+17.0	94.1	30 02.6	+18.2	94.7	29 57.4	+19.3	95.3	29 51.5	+20.5	95.9	29 45.1	+21.6	96.4	29 38.1	+22.7	97.0	5
6	30 29.3	+14.1	91.8	30 27.1	+15.3	92.4	30 24.2	+16.5	93.0	30 20.8	+17.6	93.6	30 16.7	+18.8	94.2	30 12.0	+19.9	94.8	30 06.7	+21.1	95.3	30 00.8	+22.2	95.9	6
7	30 43.4	+13.6	90.7	30 42.4	+14															3	+20.5	94.3	30 23.0	+21.7	94.8	7
8	30 57.0	+12.9	89.6	30 57.1	+14															3	+20.0	93.2	30 44.7	+21.1	93.8	8
9	31 09.9	+12.3	88.4	31 11.2	+13															3	+19.4	92.1	31 05.8	+20.6	92.7	9
10	31 22.2	+11.7	87.3	31 24.7	+12															7	+18.8	91.0	31 26.4	+20.0	91.6	10
11	31 33.9	+11.1	86.1	31 37.6	+12															3	+18.3	89.8	31 46.4	+19.4	90.5	11
12	31 45.0	+10.5	85.0	31 49.9	+11															3	+17.6	88.7	32 05.8	+18.8	89.4	12
13	31 55.5	+9.8	83.8	32 01.6	+11															1	+17.1	87.6	32 24.6	+18.2	88.2	13
14	32 05.3	+9.2	82.7	32 12.7	+10															5	+16.4	86.5	32 42.8	+17.7	87.1	14
15	32 14.5	+8.6	81.5	32 23.1	+9															9	+15.8	85.3	33 00.5	+16.9	86.0	15
16	32 23.1	+7.8	80.3	32 32.8	+9															7	+15.1	84.2	33 17.4	+16.4	84.8	16
17	32 30.9	+7.3	79.2	32 41.9	+8															4	+14.5	83.0	33 33.8	+15.7	83.7	17
18	32 38.2	+6.6	78.0	32 50.4	+7															3	+13.9	81.8	33 49.5	+15.1	82.5	18
19	32 44.8	+5.9	76.8	32 58.1	+7															2	+13.2	80.7	34 04.6	+14.4	81.3	19
20	32 50.7	+5.2	75.6	33 05.2	+6															4	+12.5	79.5	34 19.0	+13.7	80.2	20
21	32 55.9	+4.6	74.4	33 11.7	+5															9	+11.8	78.3	34 32.7	+13.0	79.0	21
22	33 00.5	+3.8	73.2	33 17.4	+5															3	+11.1	77.1	34 45.7	+12.3	77.8	22
23	33 04.3	+3.3	72.0	33 22.5	+4															3	+10.4	75.9	34 58.0	+11.7	76.6	23
24	33 07.6	+2.5	70.9	33 26.9	+3															2	+9.7	74.7	35 09.7	+10.9	75.4	24
25	33 10.1	+1.8	69.7	33 30.6	+3															9	+9.0	73.5	35 20.6	+10.2	74.2	25
26	33 11.9	+1.2	68.5	33 33.6	+2															9	+8.3	72.3	35 30.8	+9.5	73.0	26
27	33 13.1	+0.4	67.3	33 36.0	+1															2	+7.5	71.1	35 40.3	+8.7	71.8	27
28	33 13.5	-0.2	66.1	33 37.6	+0															7	+6.8	69.9	35 49.0	+8.0	70.6	28
29	33 13.3	-0.9	64.9	33 38.5	+0															5	+6.1	68.7	35 57.0	+7.3	69.3	29
30	33 12.4	-1.6	63.7	33 38.7	-0.															5	+5.3	67.4	36 04.3	+6.5	68.1	30
31	33 10.8	-2.2	62.5	33 38.3	-1															4	+4.5	66.2	36 10.8	+5.7	66.9	31
32	33 08.6	-3.0	61.3	33 37.1	-1															4	+3.8	65.0	36 16.5	+5.0	65.6	32
33	33 05.6	-3.6	60.1	33 35.3	-2															3	+3.1	63.7	36 21.5	+4.2	64.4	33
34	33 02.0	-4.3	58.9	33 32.7	-3															3	+2.3	62.5	36 25.7	+3.4	63.2	34
35	32 57.7	-5.0	57.7	33 29.5	-4.															5	+1.5	61.3	36 29.1	+2.7	61.9	35
36	32 52.7	-5.7	56.5	33 25.5	-4.															0	+0.8	60.0	36 31.8	+1.9	60.7	36
37	32 47.0	-6.3	55.4	33 20.9	-5															9	0.0	58.8	36 33.7	+1.1	59.4	37
38	32 40.7	-7.0	54.2	33 15.6	-6															9	-0.7	57.6	36 34.8	+0.3	58.2	38
39	32 33.7	-7.6	53.0	33 09.6	-6															2	-1.6	56.3	36 35.1	-0.4	56.9	39
40	32 26.1	-8.3	51.8	33 03.0	-7.															5	-2.2	55.1	36 34.7	-1.2	55.7	40
41	32 17.8	-9.0	50.6	32 55.6	-8															3	-3.1	53.9	36 33.5	-2.0	54.5	41
42	32 08.8	-9.6	49.5	32 47.6	-8.															3	-3.7	52.6	36 31.5	-2.7	53.2	42
43	31 59.2	-10.2	48.3	32 39.0	-9															5	-4.6	51.4	36 28.8	-3.6	52.0	43
44	31 49.0	-10.8	47.1	32 29.6	-9															)	-5.3	50.2	36 25.2	-4.3	50.7	44
45	31 38.2	-11.5	46.0	32 19.7	-10															7	-6.0	48.9	36 20.9	-5.1	49.5	45
46	31 26.7	-12.1	44.8	32 09.1	-11.															7	-6.8	47.7	36 15.8	-5.8	48.3	46
47	31 14.6	-12.7	43.7	31 57.8	-11.															9	-7.5	46.5	36 10.0	-6.6	47.0	47
48	31 01.9	-13.3	42.6	31 45.9	-12															1	-8.2	45.3	36 03.4	-7.3	45.8	48
49	30 48.6	-13.9	41.4	31 33.4	-13.															2	-9.0	44.1	35 56.1	-8.1	44.6	49
50	30 34.7	-14.5	40.3	31 20.3	-13.7	40.7	32 05.7	-13.0	41.1	32 50.8	-12.2	41.5	33 35.0	-11.4	41.9	34 20.0	-10.5	42.4	35 04.2	-9.7	42.9	35 48.0	-8.8	43.3	50
51	30 20.2	-15.1	39.2	31 06.6	-14.3	39.5	31 52.7	-13.5	39.9	32 38.6	-12.8	40.3	33 24.2	-12.0	40.8	34 09.5	-11.2	41.2	34 54.5	-10.4	41.7	35 39.2	-9.6	42.1	51
52	30 05.1	-15.6	38.0	30 52.3	-14.9	38.4	31 39.2	-14.2	38.8	32 25.8	-13.4	39.2	33 12.2	-12.7	39.6	33 58.3	-11.9	40.0	34 44.1	-11.1	40.5	35 29.6	-10.3	40.9	52
53	29 49.5	-16.2	36.9	30 37.4	-15.5	37.3	31 25.0	-14.8	37.6	32 12.4	-14.1	38.0	32 59.5	-13.3	38.4	33 46.4	-12.6	38.8	34 33.0	-11.8	39.3	35 19.3	-11.0	39.7	53
54	29 33.3	-16.7	35.8	30 21.9	-16.1	36.2	31 10.2	-15.3	36.5	31 58.3	-14.6	36.9	32 46.2	-13.9	37.3	33 33.8	-13.2	37.7	34 21.2	-12.5	38.1	35 08.3	-11.7	38.5	54
55	29 16.6	-17.3	34.7	30 05.8	-16.6	35.0	30 54.9	-16.0	35.4	31 43.7	-15.3	35.7	32 32.3	-14.6	36.1	33 20.6	-13.9	36.5	34 08.7	-13.1	36.9	34 56.6	-12.4	37.3	55
56	28 59.3	-17.8	33.6	29 49.2	-17.2	33.9	30 38.9	-16.5	34.3	31 28.4	-15.9	34.6	32 17.7	-15.2	35.0	33 06.7	-14.5	35.3	33 55.6	-13.8	35.7	34 44.2	-13.1	36.1	56
57	28 41.5	-18.3	32.5	29 32.0	-17.7	32.8	30 22.4	-17.1	33.1	31 12.5	-16.5	33.5	32 02.5	-15.9	33.8	32 52.2	-15.1	34.2	33 41.8	-14.5	34.5	34 31.1	-13.8	34.9	57
58	28 23.2	-18.8	31.4	29 14.3	-18.2	31.7	30 05.3	-17.7	32.0	30 56.0	-17.0	32.3	31 46.6	-16.4	32.7	32 37.1	-15.8	33.0	33 27.3	-15.2	33.4	34 17.3	-14.5	33.7	58
59	28 04.4	-19.4	30.4	28 56.1	-18.8	30.6	29 47.6	-18.2	30.9	30 39.0	-17.6	31.2	31 30.2	-17.0	31.5	32 21.3	-16.4	31.9	33 12.1	-15.7	32.2	34 02.8	-15.1	32.6	59
60	27 45.0	-19.8	29.3	28 37.3	-19.3	29.6	29 29.4	-18.7	29.8	30 21.4	-18.2	30.1	31 13.2	-17.6	30.4	32 04.9	-17.0	30.7	32 56.4	-16.4	31.1	33 47.7	-15.8	31.4	60
61	27 25.2	-20.3	28.2	28 18.0	-19.8	28.5	29 10.7	-19.3	28.7	30 03.2	-18.7	29.0	30 55.6	-18.1	29.3	31 47.9	-17.6	29.6	32 40.0	-17.1	29.9	33 31.9	-16.5	30.2	61
62	27 04.9	-20.8	27.2	27 58.2	-20.3	27.4	28 51.4	-19.7	27.7	29 44.5	-19.2	27.9	30 37.5	-18.8	28.2	31 30.3	-18.2	28.5	32 22.9	-17.6	28.8	33 15.4	-17.0	29.1	62
63	26 44.1	-21.2	26.1	27 37.9	-20.7	26.3	28 31.7	-20.3	26.6	29 25.3	-19.8	26.8	30 18.7	-19.2	27.1	31 12.1	-18.8	27.4	32 05.3	-18.2	27.6	32 58.4	-17.7	27.9	63
64	26 22.9	-21.7	25.1	27 17.2	-21.3	25.3	28 11.4	-20.8	25.5	29 05.5	-20.3	25.8	29 59.5	-19.9	26.0	30 53.3	-19.3	26.3	31 47.1	-18.8	26.5	32 40.7	-18.3	26.8	64
65	26 01.2	-22.2	24.0	26 55.9	-21.7	24.2	27 50.6	-21.3	24.5	28 45.2	-20.8	24.7	29 39.6	-20.3	24.9	30 34.0	-19.9	25.2	31 28.3	-19.4	25.4	32 22.4	-18.9	25.7	65
66	25 39.0	-22.5	23.0	26 34.2	-22.1	23.2	27 29.3	-21.7	23.4	28 24.4	-21.3	23.6	29 19.3	-20.9	23.8	30 14.1	-20.4	24.1	31 08.9	-20.0	24.3	32 03.5	-19.5	24.6	66
67	25 16.5	-23.0	22.0	26 12.1	-22.6	22.2	27 07.6	-22.2	22.3	28 03.1	-21.8	22.5	28 58.4	-21.3	22.8	29 53.7	-20.9	23.0	30 48.9	-20.5	23.2	31 44.0	-20.1	23.4	67
68	24 53.5	-23.4	21.0	25 49.5	-23.1	21.1	26 45.4	-22.7	21.3	27 41.3	-22.3	21.5	28 37.1	-21.9	21.7	29 32.8	-21.5	21.9	30 28.4	-21.1	22.1	31 23.9	-20.6	22.3	68
69	24 30.1	-23.9	19.9	25 26.4	-23.4	20.1	26 22.7	-23.1	20.3	27 19.0	-22.7	20.4	28 15.2	-22.4	20.6	29 11.3	-22.0	20.8	30 07.3	-21.5	21.0	31 03.3	-21.2	21.2	69
70	24 06.2	-24.2	18.9	25 03.0	-23.9	19.1	25 59.6	-23.5	19.2	26 56.3	-23.2	19.4	27 52.8	-22.8	19.6	28 49.3	-22.4	19.8	29 45.8	-22.1	20.0	30 42.1	-21.7	20.2	70
71	23 42.0	-24.6	17.9	24 39.1	-24.3	18.1	25 36.1	-23.9	18.2	26 33.1	-23.7	18.4	27 30.0	-23.3	18.5	28 26.9	-23.0	18.7	29 23.7	-22.7	18.9	30 20.4	-22.3	19.1	71
72	23 17.4	-24.9	16.9	24 14.8	-24.7	17.1	25 12.2	-24.4	17.2	26 09.4	-24.0	17.3	27 06.7	-23.8	17.5	28 03.9	-23.4	17.7	29 01.0	-23.1	17.8	29 58.1	-22.7	18.0	72
73	22 52.5	-25.4	16.0	23 50.1	-25.0	16.1	24 47.8	-24.8	16.2	25 45.4	-24.5	16.3	26 42.9	-24.2	16.5	27 40.5	-23.9	16.6	28 37.9	-23.6	16.8	29 35.4	-23.3	16.9	73
74	22 27.1	-25.6	15.0	23 25.1	-25.4	15.1	24 23.0	-25.2	15.2	25 20.9	-24.9	15.3	26 18.7	-24.6	15.4	27 16.6	-24.4	15.6	28 14.3	-24.0	15.7	29 12.1	-23.8	15.9	74
75	22 01.5	-26.1	14.0	22 59.7	-25.8	14.1	23 57.8	-25.5	14.2	24 56.0	-25.3	14.3	25 54.1	-25.0	14.4	26 52.2	-24.8	14.6	27 50.3	-24.6	14.7	28 48.3	-24.3	14.8	75
76	21 35.4	-26.3	13.0	22 33.9	-26.2	13.1	23 32.3	-25.9	13.2	24 30.7	-25.7	13.3	25 29.1	-25.5	13.4	26 27.4	-25.2	13.5	27 25.7	-24.9	13.7	28 24.0	-24.7	13.8	76
77	21 09.1	-26.7	12.1	22 07.7	-26.5	12.1	23 06.4	-26.3	12.2	24 05.0	-26.1	12.3	25 03.6	-25.8	12.4	26 02.2	-25.6	12.5	27 00.8	-25.5	12.7	27 59.3	-25.2	12.7	77
78	20 42.4	-27.0	11.1	21 41.2	-26.8	11.2	22 40.1	-26.6	11.3	23 38.9	-26.4	11.3	24 37.8	-26.3	11.4	25 36.6	-26.1	11.5	26 35.3	-25.8	11.6	27 34.1	-25.6	11.7	78
79	20 15.4	-27.3	10.1	21 14.4	-27.1	10.2	22 13.3	-27.0	10.3	23 12.5	-26.8	10.3	24 11.5	-26.6	10.4	25 10.5	-26.4	10.5	26 09.5	-26.3	10.5	27 08.5	-26.1	10.7	79
80	19 48.1	-27.7	9.2	20 47.3	-27.5	9.3	21 46.5	-27.3	9.3	22 45.7	-27.2	9.4	23 44.9	-27.0	9.5	24 44.1	-26.9	9.5	25 43.2	-26.6	9.6	26 42.4	-26.5	9.7	80
81	19 20.4	-27.9	8.3	20 19.8	-27.8	8.3	21 19.2	-27.6	8.4	22 18.5	-27.5	8.4	23 17.9	-27.4	8.5	24 17.2	-27.2	8.5	25 16.6	-27.1	8.6	26 15.9	-26.9	8.7	81
82	18 52.5	-28.1	7.3	19 52.0	-28.0	7.4	20 51.6	-27.9	7.4	21 51.0	-27.8	7.5	22 50.5	-27.7	7.5	23 50.0	-27.6	7.6	24 49.5	-27.5	7.6	25 49.0	-27.4	7.7	82
83	18 24.4	-28.5	6.4	19 24.0	-28.4	6.4	20 23.6	-28.2	6.5	21 23.2	-28.1	6.5	22 22.8	-28.0	6.6	23 22.4	-27.9	6.6	24 22.0	-27.8	6.7	25 21.6	-27.7	6.7	83
84	17 55.9	-28.7	5.5	18 55.6	-28.6	5.5	19 55.4	-28.6	5.5	20 55.1	-28.5	5.6	21 54.8	-28.4	5.6	22 54.5	-28.3	5.6	23 54.2	-28.2	5.7	24 53.9	-28.1	5.7	84
85	17 27.2	-29.0	4.5	18 27.1	-28.9	4.6	19 26.8	-28.8	4.6	20 26.6	-28.7	4.6	21 26.4	-28.7	4.7	22 26.2	-28.6	4.7	23 26.0	-28.5	4.7	24 25.8	-28.4	4.8	85
86	16 58.2	-29.2	3.6	17 58.1	-29.2	3.6	18 58.0	-29.1	3.7	19 57.9	-29.1	3.7	20 57.7	-29.0	3.7	21 57.6	-28.9	3.7	22 57.5	-28.9	3.8	23 57.4	-28.9	3.8	86
87	16 29.0	-29.4	2.7	17 28.9	-29.4	2.7	18 28.9	-29.4	2.7	19 28.8	-29.3	2.8	20 28.7	-29.3	2.8	21 28.7	-29.3	2.8	22 28.6	-29.2	2.8	23 28.5	-29.1	2.8	87
88	15 59.6	-29.7	1.8	16 59.5	-29.6	1.8	17 59.5	-29.6	1.8	18 59.5	-29.6	1.8	19 59.4	-29.5	1.8	20 59.4	-29.5	1.9	21 59.4	-29.5	1.9	22 59.4	-29.6	1.9	88
89	15 29.9	-29.9	0.9	16 29.9	-29.9	0.9	17 29.9	-29.9	0.9	18 29.9	-29.9	0.9	19 29.9	-29.9	0.9	20 29.9	-29.9	0.9	21 29.8	-29.8	0.9	22 29.8	-29.8	0.9	89
90	15 00.0	-30.1	0.0	16 00.0	-30.1	0.0	17 00.0	-30.1	0.0	18 00.0	-30.1	0.0	19 00.0	-30.1	0.0	20 00.0	-30.1	0.0	21 00.0	-30.1	0.0	22 00.0	-30.2	0.0	90
	15°			16°			17°			18°			19°			20°			21°			22°			

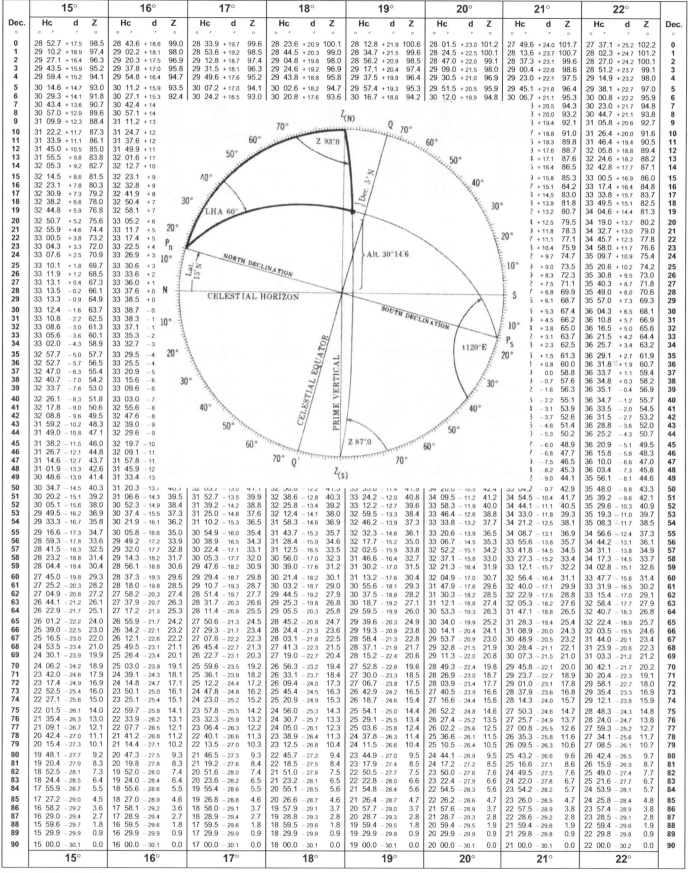

60°, 300° L.H.A.   LATITUDE SAME NAME AS DECLINATION

FIGURE 1

VI

A. DESCRIPTION OF TABLES

LATITUDE CONTRARY NAME TO DECLINATION   L.H.A. 60°, 300°

Dec.	15°			16°			17°			18°			19°			20°			21°			22°			Dec.
	Hc	d	Z	Hc	d	Z	Hc	d	Z	Hc	d	Z	Hc	d	Z	Hc	d	Z	Hc	d	Z	Hc	d	Z	
°	° ′	′	°	° ′	′	°	° ′	′	°	° ′	′	°	° ′	′	°	° ′	′	°	° ′	′	°	° ′	′	°	°
0	28 52.7	−18.0	98.5	28 43.6	−19.1	99.0	28 33.9	−20.2	99.6	28 23.6	−21.3	100.1	28 12.8	−22.4	100.6	28 01.5	−23.5	101.2	27 49.6	−24.6	101.7	27 37.1	−25.5	102.2	0
1	28 34.7	−18.5	99.6	28 24.5	−19.6	100.1	28 13.7	−20.8	100.7	28 02.3	−21.8	101.2	27 50.4	−22.9	101.7	27 38.0	−24.0	102.2	27 25.0	−25.0	102.7	27 11.6	−26.1	103.2	1
2	28 16.2	−19.0	100.7	28 04.9	−20.2	101.2	27 52.9	−21.2	101.7	27 40.5	−22.3	102.2	27 27.5	−23.3	102.7	27 14.0	−24.4	103.2	27 00.0	−25.4	103.7	26 45.5	−26.4	104.2	2
3	27 57.2	−19.5	101.7	27 44.7	−20.6	102.3	27 31.7	−21.7	102.8	27 18.2	−22.7	103.3	27 04.2	−23.8	103.8	26 49.6	−24.8	104.3	26 34.6	−25.9	104.8	26 19.1	−26.9	105.2	3
4	27 37.7	−20.0	102.8	27 24.1	−21.1	103.3	27 10.0	−22.1	103.8	26 55.5	−23.2	104.3	26 40.4	−24.3	104.8	26 24.8	−25.3	105.3	26 08.7	−26.2	105.8	25 52.2	−27.3	106.2	4
5	27 17.7	−20.5	103.9	27 03.0	−21.5	104.4	26 47.9	−22.6	104.9	26 32.3	−23.7	105.3	26 16.1	−24.6	105.8	25 59.5	−25.7	106.3	25 42.5	−26.7	106.8	25 24.9	−27.6	107.2	5
6	26 57.2	−21.0	104.9	26 41.5	−22.0	105.4	26 25.3	−23.1	105.9	26 08.6	−24.1	106.4	25 51.5	−25.1	106.8	25 33.8	−26.0	107.3	25 15.8	−27.1	107.8	24 57.3	−28.1	108.2	6
7	26 36.2	−21.4	106.0	26 19.5	−22.5	106.5	26 02.2	−23.4	106.9	25 44.5	−24.5	107.4	25 26.4	−25.5	107.8	25 07.8	−26.5	108.3	24 48.7	−27.5	108.7	24 29.2	−28.4	109.2	7
8	26 14.8	−21.8	107.0	25 57.0	−22.9															−27.8	109.7	24 00.8	−28.8	110.1	8
9	25 53.0	−22.3	108.1	25 34.1	−23.3															−28.2	110.7	23 32.0	−29.1	111.1	9
10	25 30.7	−22.8	109.1	25 10.8	−23.7															−28.5	111.7	23 02.9	−29.5	112.1	10
11	25 07.9	−23.1	110.1	24 47.1	−24.2															−28.9	112.6	22 33.4	−29.8	113.0	11
12	24 44.8	−23.6	111.1	24 22.9	−24.5															−29.3	113.6	22 03.6	−30.1	113.9	12
13	24 21.2	−24.0	112.1	23 58.4	−24.9															−29.5	114.5	21 33.5	−30.5	114.9	13
14	23 57.2	−24.3	113.1	23 33.5	−25.3															−29.9	115.4	21 03.0	−30.7	115.8	14
15	23 32.9	−24.7	114.1	23 08.2	−25.7															−30.1	116.4	20 32.3	−31.0	116.7	15
16	23 08.2	−25.1	115.1	22 42.5	−26.0															−30.5	117.3	20 01.3	−31.3	117.6	16
17	22 43.1	−25.5	116.1	22 16.5	−26.4															−30.7	118.2	19 30.0	−31.5	118.5	17
18	22 17.6	−25.8	117.1	21 50.1	−26.7															−31.0	119.1	18 58.5	−31.9	119.4	18
19	21 51.8	−26.2	118.1	21 23.4	−27.1															−31.3	120.0	18 26.6	−32.0	120.3	19
20	21 25.6	−26.5	119.0	20 56.3	−27.3															−31.5	120.9	17 54.6	−32.4	121.2	20
21	20 59.1	−26.8	120.0	20 29.0	−27.7															−31.8	121.8	17 22.2	−32.5	122.1	21
22	20 32.3	−27.1	121.0	20 01.3	−28.0															−32.0	122.7	16 49.7	−32.8	123.0	22
23	20 05.2	−27.4	121.9	19 33.3	−28.2															−32.2	123.6	16 16.9	−33.0	123.9	23
24	19 37.8	−27.7	122.9	19 05.1	−28.6															−32.4	124.5	15 43.9	−33.1	124.7	24
25	19 10.1	−28.1	123.8	18 36.5	−28.8															−32.7	125.4	15 10.8	−33.4	125.6	25
26	18 42.0	−28.2	124.7	18 07.7	−29.0															−32.8	126.2	14 37.4	−33.6	126.4	26
27	18 13.8	−28.6	125.7	17 38.7	−29.4															−33.1	127.1	14 03.8	−33.7	127.3	27
28	17 45.2	−28.8	126.6	17 09.3	−29.5															−33.2	128.0	13 30.1	−34.0	128.2	28
29	17 16.4	−29.1	127.5	16 39.8	−29.8															−33.4	128.8	12 56.1	−34.1	129.0	29
30	16 47.3	−29.3	128.4	16 10.0	−30.1															−33.6	129.7	12 22.0	−34.2	129.8	30
31	16 18.0	−29.5	129.3	15 39.9	−30.2															−33.7	130.5	11 47.8	−34.4	130.7	31
32	15 48.5	−29.7	130.2	15 09.7	−30.5															−33.9	131.4	11 13.4	−34.5	131.5	32
33	15 18.8	−30.0	131.1	14 39.2	−30.7															−34.0	132.2	10 38.9	−34.7	132.4	33
34	14 48.8	−30.2	132.0	14 08.5	−30.8															−34.1	133.0	10 04.2	−34.8	133.2	34
35	14 18.6	−30.4	132.9	13 37.7	−31.1															−34.3	133.9	9 29.4	−34.9	134.0	35
36	13 48.2	−30.6	133.8	13 06.6	−31.2															−34.4	134.7	8 54.5	−35.0	134.8	36
37	13 17.6	−30.7	134.7	12 35.4	−31.4															−34.5	135.5	8 19.5	−35.1	135.7	37
38	12 46.9	−30.9	135.6	12 04.0	−31.6															−34.6	136.4	7 44.4	−35.2	136.5	38
39	12 16.0	−31.1	136.5	11 32.4	−31.7															−34.7	137.2	7 09.2	−35.3	137.3	39
40	11 44.9	−31.3	137.3	11 00.7	−31.9															−34.8	138.0	6 33.9	−35.3	138.1	40
41	11 13.6	−31.4	138.2	10 28.8	−32.0															−34.9	138.8	5 58.6	−35.5	138.9	41
42	10 42.2	−31.5	139.1	9 56.8	−32.1															−35.0	139.7	5 23.1	−35.5	139.7	42
43	10 10.7	−31.7	139.9	9 24.7	−32.3															−35.0	140.5	4 47.6	−35.5	140.5	43
44	9 39.0	−31.8	140.8	8 52.4	−32.3															−35.1	141.3	4 12.1	−35.6	141.3	44
45	9 07.2	−32.0	141.7	8 20.1	−32.5															−35.1	142.1	3 36.5	−35.7	142.2	45
46	8 35.2	−32.0	142.5	7 47.6	−32.6															−35.2	142.9	3 00.8	−35.7	143.0	46
47	8 03.2	−32.2	143.4	7 15.0	−32.7															−35.2	143.7	2 25.1	−35.7	143.8	47
48	7 31.0	−32.2	144.2	6 42.3	−32.7															−35.3	144.5	1 49.4	−35.7	144.6	48
49	6 58.8	−32.4	145.1	6 09.6	−32.9															−35.3	145.4	1 13.7	−35.8	145.4	49
50	6 26.4	−32.4	145.9	5 36.7	−32.9															−35.3	146.2	0 37.9	−35.8	146.2	50
51	5 54.0	−32.5	146.8	5 03.8	−33.0	146.8	4 13.6	−33.5	146.9	3 23.3	−33.9	146.9	2 33.0	−34.3	146.9	1 42.7	−34.8	147.0	0 52.4	−35.3	147.0	0 02.1	−35.7	147.0	51
52	5 21.5	−32.6	147.6	4 30.8	−33.0	147.7	3 40.1	−33.5	147.7	2 49.4	−34.0	147.7	1 58.7	−34.5	147.8	1 07.9	−34.9	147.8	0 17.1	−35.3	147.8	0 33.6	+35.8	32.2	52
53	4 48.9	−32.6	148.5	3 57.8	−33.1	148.5	3 06.6	−33.5	148.5	2 15.4	−33.9	148.6	1 24.2	−34.4	148.6	0 33.0	−34.8	148.6				1 09.4	+35.7	31.4	53
54	4 16.3	−32.7	149.3	3 24.7	−33.1	149.3	2 33.1	−33.6	149.4	1 41.5	−34.0	149.4	0 49.8	−34.4	149.4	0 01.8	+34.9	30.6	**C-S Line (Contrary-Same Line)**			1 45.1	+35.7	30.6	54
55	3 43.6	−32.7	150.1	2 51.6	−33.2	150.2	1 59.5	−33.6	150.2	1 07.5	−34.1	150.2	0 15.4	−34.5	150.2	0 36.7	+34.9	29.8				2 20.8	+35.7	29.8	55
56	3 10.9	−32.8	151.0	2 18.4	−33.2	151.0	1 25.9	−33.6	151.0	0 33.4	−34.0	151.0	0 19.1	+34.4	29.0	1 11.6	+34.8	29.0	2 04.0	+35.3	29.0	2 56.5	+35.7	29.0	56
57	2 38.1	−32.8	151.8	1 45.2	−33.2	151.8	0 52.3	−33.6	151.9	0 00.6	+34.0	28.1	0 53.5	+34.4	28.1	1 46.4	+34.8	28.2	2 39.3	+35.2	28.2	3 32.2	+35.6	28.2	57
58	2 05.3	−32.8	152.7	1 12.0	−33.2	152.7	0 18.7	−33.6	152.7	0 34.6	+34.0	27.3	1 27.9	+34.4	27.3	2 21.2	+34.8	27.3	3 14.5	+35.2	27.4	4 07.8	+35.6	27.4	58
59	1 32.5	−32.9	153.5	0 38.8	−33.3	153.5	0 14.9	+33.7	26.5	1 08.6	+34.0	26.5	2 02.3	+34.4	26.5	2 56.0	+34.8	26.5	3 49.7	+35.1	26.6	4 43.4	+35.5	26.6	59
60	0 59.6	−32.9	154.3	0 05.5	−33.2	154.3	0 48.6	+33.6	25.7	1 42.6	+34.0	25.7	2 36.7	+34.4	25.7	3 30.8	+34.7	25.7	4 24.8	+35.1	25.7	5 18.9	+35.4	25.8	60
61	0 26.7	−32.8	155.2	0 27.7	+33.3	24.8	1 22.2	+33.6	24.8	2 16.6	+34.0	24.8	3 11.1	+34.3	24.9	4 05.5	+34.7	24.9	4 59.9	+35.0	24.9	5 54.3	+35.4	25.0	61
62	0 06.1	+32.9	24.0	1 01.0	+33.2	24.0	1 55.8	+33.5	24.0	2 50.6	+33.9	24.0	3 45.4	+34.2	24.0	4 40.2	+34.6	24.1	5 34.9	+35.0	24.1	6 29.7	+35.3	24.2	62
63	0 39.0	+32.9	23.2	1 34.2	+33.2	23.2	2 29.3	+33.6	23.2	3 24.5	+33.9	23.2	4 19.6	+34.3	23.2	5 14.8	+34.5	23.3	6 09.9	+34.9	23.3	7 05.0	+35.2	23.3	63
64	1 11.9	+32.8	22.3	2 07.4	+33.2	22.3	3 02.9	+33.5	22.3	3 58.4	+33.8	22.4	4 53.9	+34.1	22.4	5 49.3	+34.5	22.4	6 44.8	+34.8	22.5	7 40.2	+35.1	22.5	64
65	1 44.7	+32.9	21.5	2 40.6	+33.1	21.5	3 36.4	+33.4	21.5	4 32.2	+33.8	21.5	5 28.0	+34.1	21.6	6 23.8	+34.4	21.6	7 19.6	+34.7	21.7	8 15.3	+35.0	21.7	65
66	2 17.6	+32.8	20.6	3 13.7	+33.1	20.7	4 09.8	+33.4	20.7	5 06.0	+33.7	20.7	6 02.1	+34.0	20.7	6 58.2	+34.3	20.8	7 54.3	+34.6	20.8	8 50.3	+35.0	20.9	66
67	2 50.4	+32.7	19.8	3 46.8	+33.1	19.8	4 43.2	+33.4	19.8	5 39.7	+33.6	19.9	6 36.1	+33.9	19.9	7 32.5	+34.2	20.0	8 28.9	+34.5	20.0	9 25.3	+34.8	20.1	67
68	3 23.1	+32.7	19.0	4 19.9	+33.0	19.0	5 16.6	+33.3	19.0	6 13.3	+33.6	19.0	7 10.0	+33.9	19.1	8 06.7	+34.1	19.1	9 03.4	+34.4	19.2	10 00.1	+34.6	19.2	68
69	3 55.8	+32.7	18.1	4 52.9	+32.9	18.1	5 49.9	+33.2	18.2	6 46.9	+33.4	18.2	7 43.9	+33.7	18.3	8 40.8	+34.0	18.3	9 37.8	+34.3	18.3	10 34.7	+34.6	18.4	69
70	4 28.5	+32.6	17.3	5 25.8	+32.9	17.3	6 23.1	+33.1	17.3	7 20.3	+33.4	17.4	8 17.6	+33.6	17.4	9 14.8	+33.9	17.5	10 12.1	+34.1	17.5	11 09.3	+34.4	17.6	70
71	5 01.1	+32.6	16.4	5 58.7	+32.8	16.5	6 56.2	+33.0	16.5	7 53.7	+33.3	16.5	8 51.2	+33.6	16.6	9 48.7	+33.8	16.6	10 46.2	+34.0	16.7	11 43.7	+34.2	16.7	71
72	5 33.7	+32.4	15.6	6 31.5	+32.7	15.6	7 29.2	+33.0	15.7	8 27.0	+33.2	15.7	9 24.8	+33.4	15.7	10 22.5	+33.6	15.8	11 20.2	+33.9	15.8	12 17.9	+34.1	15.9	72
73	6 06.1	+32.4	14.8	7 04.2	+32.6	14.8	8 02.2	+32.8	14.8	9 00.2	+33.0	14.9	9 58.2	+33.2	14.9	10 56.1	+33.5	14.9	11 54.1	+33.7	15.0	12 52.0	+34.0	15.1	73
74	6 38.5	+32.3	13.9	7 36.8	+32.5	13.9	8 35.0	+32.7	14.0	9 33.2	+33.0	14.0	10 31.4	+33.2	14.1	11 29.6	+33.4	14.1	12 27.8	+33.6	14.2	13 26.0	+33.8	14.2	74
75	7 10.8	+32.3	13.1	8 09.3	+32.4	13.1	9 07.7	+32.6	13.1	10 06.2	+32.8	13.2	11 04.6	+33.0	13.2	12 03.0	+33.2	13.2	13 01.4	+33.4	13.3	13 59.8	+33.6	13.4	75
76	7 43.1	+32.1	12.2	8 41.7	+32.3	12.2	9 40.3	+32.5	12.3	10 39.0	+32.6	12.3	11 37.6	+32.8	12.4	12 36.2	+33.0	12.4	13 34.8	+33.2	12.4	14 33.4	+33.4	12.5	76
77	8 15.2	+32.0	11.4	9 14.0	+32.2	11.4	10 12.8	+32.4	11.4	11 11.6	+32.5	11.5	12 10.4	+32.7	11.5	13 09.2	+32.9	11.5	14 08.0	+33.0	11.6	15 06.8	+33.2	11.6	77
78	8 47.2	+31.9	10.5	9 46.2	+32.0	10.5	10 45.2	+32.2	10.6	11 44.1	+32.4	10.6	12 43.1	+32.5	10.6	13 42.1	+32.7	10.7	14 41.0	+32.9	10.7	15 40.0	+33.0	10.8	78
79	9 19.1	+31.7	9.6	10 18.2	+31.9	9.7	11 17.4	+32.0	9.7	12 16.5	+32.2	9.7	13 15.6	+32.4	9.8	14 14.8	+32.5	9.8	15 13.9	+32.6	9.9	16 13.0	+32.8	9.9	79
80	9 50.8	+31.7	8.8	10 50.1	+31.8	8.8	11 49.4	+31.9	8.8	12 48.7	+32.0	8.9	13 48.0	+32.1	8.9	14 47.3	+32.3	8.9	15 46.5	+32.5	9.0	16 45.8	+32.6	9.0	80
81	10 22.5	+31.5	7.9	11 21.9	+31.6	7.9	12 21.3	+31.7	8.0	13 20.7	+31.9	8.0	14 20.1	+32.0	8.0	15 19.6	+32.0	8.1	16 19.0	+32.2	8.1	17 18.4	+32.3	8.2	81
82	10 54.0	+31.3	7.1	11 53.5	+31.5	7.1	12 53.0	+31.6	7.1	13 52.6	+31.7	7.1	14 52.1	+31.8	7.2	15 51.6	+31.9	7.2	16 51.2	+32.0	7.2	17 50.7	+32.1	7.3	82
83	11 25.3	+31.2	6.2	12 25.0	+31.2	6.2	13 24.6	+31.4	6.2	14 24.3	+31.4	6.3	15 23.9	+31.6	6.3	16 23.5	+31.7	6.3	17 23.2	+31.7	6.3	18 22.8	+31.8	6.4	83
84	11 56.5	+31.0	5.3	12 56.2	+31.2	5.3	13 56.0	+31.2	5.4	14 55.7	+31.3	5.4	15 55.5	+31.3	5.4	16 55.2	+31.4	5.4	17 54.9	+31.5	5.5	18 54.6	+31.6	5.5	84
85	12 27.5	+30.9	4.4	13 27.4	+30.9	4.5	14 27.2	+31.0	4.5	15 27.0	+31.1	4.5	16 26.8	+31.1	4.5	17 26.6	+31.2	4.5	18 26.4	+31.3	4.6	19 26.2	+31.4	4.6	85
86	12 58.4	+30.7	3.6	13 58.3	+30.7	3.6	14 58.2	+30.8	3.6	15 58.1	+30.8	3.6	16 57.9	+30.9	3.6	17 57.8	+31.0	3.6	18 57.7	+31.0	3.7	19 57.6	+31.0	3.7	86
87	13 29.1	+30.5	2.7	14 29.0	+30.6	2.7	15 29.0	+30.5	2.7	16 28.9	+30.6	2.7	17 28.8	+30.7	2.7	18 28.8	+30.6	2.7	19 28.7	+30.7	2.8	20 28.6	+30.8	2.8	87
88	13 59.6	+30.3	1.8	14 59.6	+30.3	1.8	15 59.5	+30.4	1.8	16 59.5	+30.4	1.8	17 59.5	+30.4	1.8	18 59.4	+30.5	1.8	19 59.4	+30.5	1.8	20 59.4	+30.4	1.9	88
89	14 29.9	+30.1	0.9	15 29.9	+30.1	0.9	16 29.9	+30.1	0.9	17 29.9	+30.1	0.9	18 29.9	+30.1	0.9	19 29.9	+30.1	0.9	20 29.9	+30.1	0.9	21 29.8	+30.2	0.9	89
90	15 00.0	+29.9	0.0	16 00.0	+29.9	0.0	17 00.0	+29.9	0.0	18 00.0	+29.9	0.0	19 00.0	+29.9	0.0	20 00.0	+29.9	0.0	21 00.0	+29.8	0.0	22 00.0	+29.8	0.0	90
	15°			16°			17°			18°			19°			20°			21°			22°			

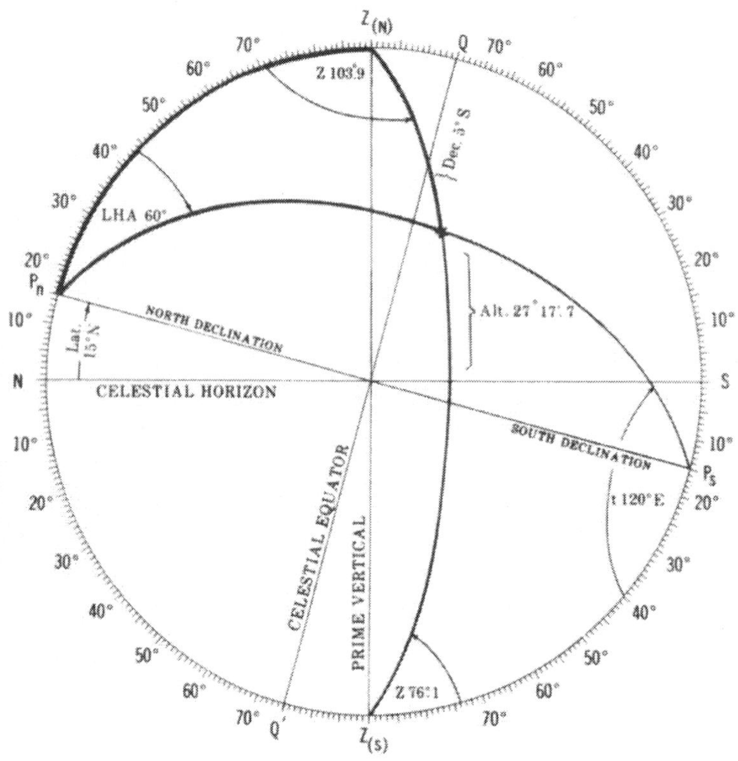

Z(N)
Q
70°
60°
Z 103°.9
50°
Dec. 3° S
40°
30°
LHA 60°
20°
Pn
10°
NORTH DECLINATION
Lat. 15° N
N
CELESTIAL HORIZON
Alt. 27° 17'.7
S
SOUTH DECLINATION
Ps
t 120° E
CELESTIAL EQUATOR
PRIME VERTICAL
Z 76°.1
Q'
Z(S)

S. Lat. { L.H.A. greater than 180° ....Zn=180°–Z
L.H.A. less than 180°...........Zn=180°+Z

LATITUDE SAME NAME AS DECLINATION   L.H.A. 120°, 240°

FIGURE 2

INTRODUCTION

Figures 1 and 2 illustrate four of the eight possible celestial triangles for specific numerical values of latitude and declination and the LHA's tabulated on the left and right-hand pages of an opening of the tables.

The diagram on the plane of the celestial meridian in figure 1 indicates that the celestial body always lies above the celestial horizon when the observer's latitude has the same name as the declination of the body and the values of LHA are those tabulated on the left-hand page of an opening of the tables. The diagram in figure 2 reveals that for the various combinations of arguments on the right-hand page, including whether the name of the observer's latitude is the same as or contrary to the name of the declination, the numerical value of the declination governs whether the body is above or below the celestial horizon. For example, the following arguments are used for entering the tables:

LHA	60°	
Latitude	15° N	(Contrary Name to Declination)
Declination	5° S	

The respondents are:

Tabular altitude,	ht	(Tab. Hc)	27°17.7′
Altitude difference,	d		(−)20.5′
Azimuth angle,	Z		103.9°

As can be verified by an inspection of figures 2 and 4a, the altitude respondent is for a body 27°17.7′ above the celestial horizon. Further inspection of these figures reveals that with the LHA and latitude (Contrary Name) remaining constant, the altitude of the body decreases as the declination increases. Between values of declination 61° and 62° the body crosses the celestial horizon. When the declination reaches 70°, the altitude is 4°28.5′ below the celestial horizon; the tabular azimuth angle is the supplement of the actual azimuth angle of 162.7°.

As an additional example, the following arguments are used for entering the tables:

LHA	240°	(t 120°E)
Latitude	15° S	(Same Name as Declination)
Declination	5° S	

The respondents are:

Tabular altitude,	ht	(Tab. Hc)	27°17.7′
Altitude difference,	d		(−)20.5′
Azimuth angle,	Z		103.9°

However, inspection of the diagram on the plane of the celestial meridian in figures 2 and 4b reveals that the altitude is 27°17.7′ *below* the celestial horizon; the tabular azimuth angle is the *supplement* of the actual azimuth angle of 76.1°. Further inspection of these figures reveals that with the LHA and latitude (Same Name) remaining constant, the altitude of the body increases as the declination increases. Between values of declination of 61° and 62° the body crosses the celestial horizon. When the declination reaches 70°, the altitude is 4°28.5′ above the celestial horizon; the tabular azimuth angle is the actual azimuth angle of 17.3°.

Inspection of figures 1, 2, and 3 reveals that if the left-hand page of an opening of the tables is entered with latitude of contrary name and one of the LHA's tabulated at the bottom of the facing page, the tabular altitudes are negative; the tabular azimuth angles are the supplements of the actual azimuth angles.

A. DESCRIPTION OF TABLES

$Z_{(N)}$, zenith of observer at latitude 15° N.

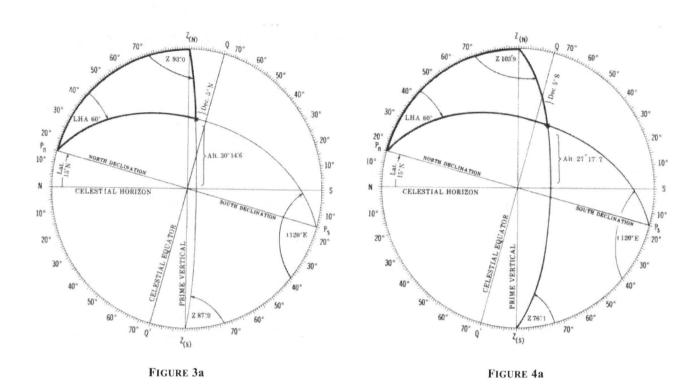

FIGURE 3a   **FIGURE 4a**

$Z_{(S)}$, zenith of observer at latitude 15° S.

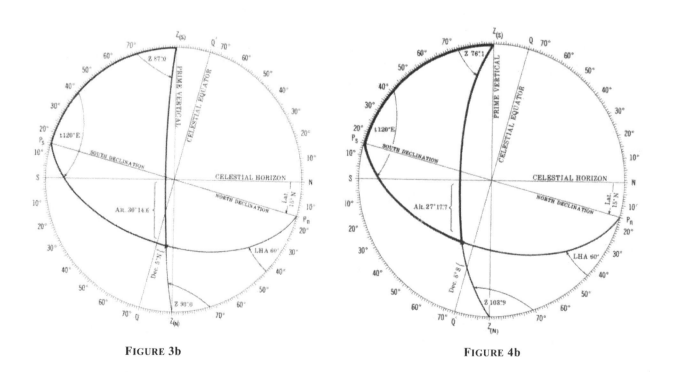

FIGURE 3b   **FIGURE 4b**

B. INTERPOLATION

1. Requirements. In the normal use of the tables with the Marcq Saint Hilaire method, it is only necessary to interpolate the tabular altitude and azimuth angle for the excess of the actual declination of the celestial body over the integral declination argument. When the tabular altitude is less than 60°, the required interpolation can always be effected through the use of the tabulated altitude differences. When the tabular altitude is in excess of 60°, it may be necessary to include the effects of second differences. When the tabular altitude difference is printed in italic type followed by a small dot, the effects of the second differences should be included in the interpolation. Although the effects of second differences may not be required, these effects can always be included in the interpolation whenever it is desired to obtain greater accuracy.

If the sight reduction is from a position such that interpolation for latitude and local hour angle increments is necessary, the required additional interpolation of the altitude can be effected by graphical means.

2. First and Second Differences. The data in the column for latitude 15° (Same Name as Declination) as contained in figure 1 is rearranged in Table I to illustrate the first and second differences.

TABLE I

LHA 60°, Lat. 15° (Same Name as Declination)

Dec.	ht (Tab. Hc)	First Difference	Second Difference
4°	29°59.4′		
		+15.2′	
5°	30°14.6′		-0.5′
		+14.7′	
6°	30°29.3′		-0.6′
		+14.1′	
7°	30°43.4′		

Table I illustrates that the first differences are the differences between successive altitudes in a latitude column; the second differences are the differences between successive first differences.

3. Linear Interpolation. The usual case is that the change of altitude with 60′ increase in declination is nearly linear as illustrated in figure 5. In this case, the required interpolation can be effected by multiplying the altitude difference (a first difference) by the excess of the actual declination over the integral declination argument divided by 60′. This excess of declination in minutes and tenths of minutes of arc is referred to as the declination increment and is abbreviated Dec. Inc.

Using the data of Table I, the computed altitude when the LHA is 60°, the latitude (Same Name) is 15°, and the declination is 5°45.5′ is determined as follows:

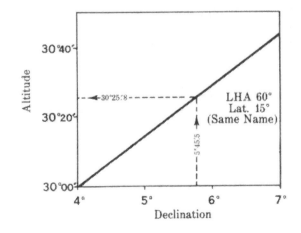

$$\text{Correction} = \text{Altitude difference} \times \frac{\text{Dec. Inc.}}{60'} = (+)14.7' \times \frac{45.5'}{60'} = 11.2'$$

$$\text{Hc} = \text{ht} + \text{correction} = 30°14.6' + 11.2' = 30°25.8'$$

FIGURE 5

x

4. The Interpolation Table.

(a) Design. The main part of the four-page Interpolation Table is basically a multiplication table providing tabulations of:

$$\text{Altitude Difference} \times \frac{\text{Declination Increment}}{60'}$$

The design of the Interpolation Table is such that the desired product must be derived from component parts of the altitude difference. The first part is a multiple of 10′ (10′, 20′, 30′, 40′, or 50′) of the altitude difference; the second part is the remainder in the range 0.0′ to 9.9′. For example, the component parts of altitude difference 14.7′ are 10′ and 4.7′.

In the use of the first part of the altitude difference, the Interpolation Table arguments are Dec. Inc. and the integral multiple of 10′ in the altitude difference, d. The respondent is:

$$\text{Tens} \times \frac{\text{Dec. Inc.}}{60'} \text{ (See figure 6)}$$

In the use of the second part of the altitude difference, the Interpolation Table arguments are the nearest Dec. Inc. ending in 0.5′ and Units and Decimals. The respondent is:

$$\text{Units and Decimals} \times \frac{\text{Dec. Inc.}}{60'}$$

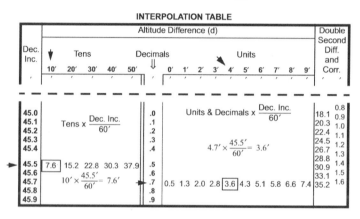

FIGURE 6

In computing the table, the values in the Tens part of the multiplication table were modified by small quantities varying from −0.042′ to +0.033′ before rounding to the tabular precision to compensate for any difference between the actual Dec. Inc. and the nearest Dec. Inc. ending in 0.5′ when using the Units and Decimals part of the table.

(b) Instructions for use of the Interpolation Table.

(i)   Turn to the Interpolation Table on the inside front cover and facing page if the Dec. Inc. is in the range 0.0′ to 31.9′ or on the inside back cover and facing page if the Dec. Inc. is in the range 28.0′ to 59.9′.

(ii)   Enter the Interpolation Table with Dec. Inc. as the vertical argument.

(iii)   On the same horizontal line as the Dec. Inc., extract the altitude correction for the first part of the altitude difference from the appropriate Tens column.

(iv)   From the Units and Decimals subtable immediately to the right, extract the altitude correction for the second part of the altitude difference.

(v)   Add the two parts to form the correction to the tabular altitude for declination increment. The sign of the correction is in accordance with the sign of the altitude difference, d.

(vi)   When the altitude difference, d, is printed in italic type followed by a small dot, enter that compartment of the DSD table opposite the block in which the Dec. Inc. is found with the DSD as the argument to obtain the DSD correction to the altitude. The DSD correction is always plus. (See section B.5)

(c) Example of the Use of Interpolation Table. As an example of the use of the Interpolation Table, the computed altitude and true azimuth are determined for Lat. 15°N, LHA 60°, and Dec. 5°45.5′ N. Data are exhibited in figure 7.

The respondents for the entering arguments (Lat. 15° Same Name as Declination, LHA 60°, and Dec. 5°) are:

tabular altitude,	ht	30°14.6′
altitude difference,	d	(+)14.7′
tabular azimuth angle,	Z	93.0°

Note that Dec. Inc. 45.5′ is the vertical argument for entering the Interpolation Table to extract the correction for tens of minutes of altitude difference, d, and that it also indicates the subtable where the correction for minutes and tenths of minutes (Units and Decimals) of altitude difference, d, is found. Entering the Interpolation Table with Dec. Inc. 45.5′ as the vertical argument, the correction for 10′ of the altitude difference is 7.6′; the correction for 4.7′ of the altitude difference is 3.6′. Adding the two parts, the correction is (+)11.2′, the sign of the correction being in accordance with the sign of the altitude difference, d.

No special table is provided for interpolation of the azimuth angle, and the differences are not tabulated. With latitude and local hour angle constant, the successive azimuth angle differences corresponding to 1° increase in declination are less than 10.0° for altitudes less than 84°, and can easily be found by inspection. If formal interpolation of azimuth angle is desired, the degrees and tenths of degrees of azimuth angle difference are treated as minutes and tenths of minutes in obtaining the required correction from the Units and Decimals subtable to the right of the declination increment. But for most practical applications, interpolation by inspection usually suffices. In this example of formal interpolation, using an azimuth angle difference of −1.2° and a Dec. Inc. of 45.5′, the correction as extracted from the Units and Decimals subtable to the right of the Dec. Inc. is −0.9°. Therefore, the azimuth angle as interpolated for declination increment is 92.1° (93.0° −0.9°). In summary,

tabular altitude	ht	30° 14.6′		tabular azimuth angle	Z	93.0°
correction for 10′ of alt. diff.		(+) 7.6′		correction for Dec. Inc. 45.5′		(−)0.9°
correction for 4.7′ of alt. diff.		(+) 3.6′				
computed altitude	Hc	30° 25.8′		interpolated azimuth angle	Z	N92.1°W
		(See figures 5 and 7)		true azimuth	Zn	267.9°

60°, 300° L.H.A.

LATITUDE SAME NAME

Dec.	15°			16°			17°		
	Hc	d	Z	Hc	d	Z	Hc	d	Z
°	° ′	′	°	° ′	′	°	° ′	′	°
0	28 52.7	+17.5	98.5	28 43.6	+18.6	99.0	28 33.9	+19.7	99.6
1	29 10.2	+16.9	97.4	29 02.2	+18.1	98.0	28 53.6	+19.2	98.5
2	29 27.1	+16.4	96.3	29 20.3	+17.5	96.9	29 12.8	+18.7	97.4
3	29 43.5	+15.9	95.2	29 37.8	+17.0	95.8	29 31.5	+18.1	96.3
4	29 59.4	+15.2	94.1	29 54.8	+16.4	94.7	29 49.6	+17.6	95.2
5	30 14.6	+14.7	93.0	30 11.2	+15.9	93.5	30 07.2	+17.0	94.1
6	30 29.3	+14.1	91.8	30 27.1	+15.3	92.4	30 24.2	+16.5	93.0
7	30 43.4	+13.6	90.7	30 42.4	+14.7	91.3	30 40.7	+15.9	91.9
8	30 57.0	+12.9	89.6	30 57.1	+14.1	90.2	30 56.6	+15.3	90.8
9	31 09.9	+12.3	88.4	31 11.2	+13.5	89.0	31 11.9	+14.7	89.7

Data from Page 122

INTERPOLATION TABLE

Dec. Inc.	Altitude Difference (d)																Double Second Diff. and Corr.	
	Tens					Decimals	Units											
	10′	20′	30′	40′	50′		0′	1′	2′	3′	4′	5′	6′	7′	8′	9′		
45.0	7.5	15.0	22.5	30.0	37.5	.0	0.0	0.8	1.5	2.3	3.0	3.8	4.5	5.3	6.1	6.8	18.1	0.8
45.1	7.5	15.0	22.5	30.0	37.6	.1	0.1	0.8	1.6	2.4	3.1	3.9	4.6	5.4	6.1	6.9	20.3	0.9
45.2	7.5	15.0	22.6	30.1	37.6	.2	0.2	0.9	1.7	2.4	3.2	3.9	4.7	5.5	6.2	7.0	22.4	1.0
45.3	7.5	15.1	22.6	30.2	37.7	.3	0.2	1.0	1.7	2.5	3.3	4.0	4.8	5.5	6.3	7.1	24.5	1.1
45.4	7.6	15.1	22.7	30.3	37.8	.4	0.3	1.1	1.8	2.6	3.3	4.1	4.9	5.6	6.4	7.1	26.7	1.2
																	28.8	1.3
45.5	7.6	15.2	22.8	30.3	37.9	.5	0.4	1.1	1.9	2.7	3.4	4.2	4.9	5.7	6.4	7.2	30.9	1.4
45.6	7.6	15.2	22.8	30.4	38.0	.6	0.5	1.2	2.0	2.7	3.5	4.2	5.0	5.8	6.5	7.3	33.1	1.5
45.7	7.6	15.3	22.9	30.5	38.1	.7	0.5	1.3	2.0	2.8	3.6	4.3	5.1	5.8	6.6	7.4	35.2	1.6
45.8	7.7	15.3	22.9	30.6	38.2	.8	0.6	1.4	2.1	2.9	3.6	4.4	5.2	5.9	6.7	7.4		
45.9	7.7	15.3	23.0	30.6	38.3	.9	0.7	1.4	2.2	3.0	3.7	4.5	5.2	6.0	6.7	7.5		

Data from Interpolation Table

FIGURE 7

5. Interpolation when Second Differences are Required. The accuracy of linear interpolation usually decreases as the altitude increases. At altitudes above 60° it may be necessary to include the effect of second differences in the interpolation. When the altitude difference, d, is printed in italic type followed by a small dot, the second-difference correction may exceed 0.25′, and should normally be applied. The need for a second-difference correction is illustrated by the graph of Table II data in figure 8.

TABLE II

LHA 28°, Lat. 15° (Same Name as Declination)

Dec.	ht (Tab. Hc)	First Difference	Second Difference
15°	62°58.4′		
		+2.8′·	
16°	63°01.2′		−2.0′
		+0.8′·	
17°	63°02.0′		−2.1′
		−1.3′·	
18°	63°00.7′		

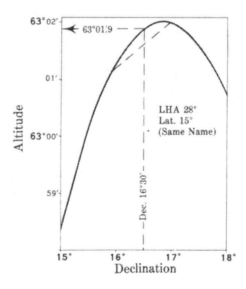

FIGURE 8

Other than graphically, the required correction for the effects of second differences is obtained from the appropriate subtable of the Interpolation Table. However, before the Interpolation Table can be used for this purpose, what is known as the double-second difference (DSD) must be formed.

(a) Forming the Double-Second Difference (DSD)

The double-second difference is the sum of two successive second differences. Although second differences are not tabulated, the DSD can be formed readily by subtracting, algebraically, the tabular altitude difference immediately above the respondent altitude difference from the tabular altitude difference immediately below. The result will always be a negative value.

(b) The Double-Second Difference Correction

As shown in figure 9, that compartment of the DSD table opposite the block in which the Dec. Inc. is found is entered with the DSD to obtain the DSD correction to the altitude. The correction is always plus. Therefore, the sign of the DSD need not be recorded. When the DSD entry corresponds to an exact tabular value, always use the upper of the two possible corrections.

(c)   *Example of the Use of the Double-Second Difference.*

As an example of the use of the double-second difference (DSD) the computed altitude and true azimuth are determined for Lat. 15°N, LHA 28°, and Dec. 16°30.0′N. Data are exhibited in figure 9.

The respondents for the entering arguments (Lat. 15° Same Name as Declination, LHA 28°, and Dec. 16°) are:

tabular altitude,	ht	63°01.2′
altitude difference,	d	(+)0.8′.
azimuth angle,	Z	84.1°

The linear interpolation correction to the tabular altitude for Dec. Inc. 30.0′ is (+)0.4′.

$$Hc = ht + linear\ correction = 63°01.2′ + 0.4′ = 63°01.6′$$

However, by inspection of figure 8, illustrating this solution graphically, the computed altitude should be 63°01.9′. The actual change in altitude with an increase in declination is nonlinear. The altitude value lies on the curve between the points for declination 16° and declination 17° instead of the straight line connecting these points.

The DSD is formed by subtracting, algebraically, the tabular altitude difference immediately above the respondent altitude difference from the tabular altitude difference immediately below. Thus, the DSD is formed by algebraically subtracting (+)2.8′ from (−)1.3′; the result is (−)4.1′.

As shown in figure 9, that compartment of the DSD table opposite the block in which the Dec. Inc. (30.0′) is found is entered with the DSD (4.1′) to obtain the DSD correction to the altitude. The correction is 0.3′. The correction is always plus.

$$Hc = ht + linear\ correction + DSD\ correction$$
$$Hc = 63°01.2′ + 0.4′ + 0.3′ = 63°01.9′$$

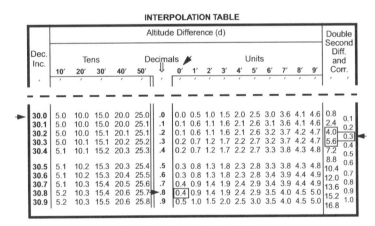

28°, 332° L.H.A.

Data from Page 58

Data from Interpolation Table

FIGURE 9

C. SPECIAL TECHNIQUES

1. Adjustment of Straight Line of Position. The Table of Offsets gives the corrections to the straight line of position (LOP) as drawn on a chart or plotting sheet to provide a closer approximation to the arc of the circle of equal altitude, a small circle of radius equal to the zenith distance. As shown in figure 10, the corrections are offsets of points on the LOP and are drawn at right angles to the LOP in the direction of the observed body. The offset points are joined to obtain the arc of the small circle. Usually the desired approximation to the arc of the small circle can be obtained by drawing a straight line through two offset points. The magnitudes of the offsets are dependent upon altitude and the distance of the offset point from the intercept.

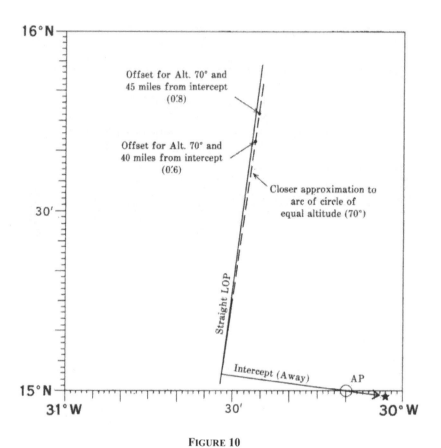

FIGURE 10

TABLE OF OFFSETS

DISTANCE ALONG LINE OF POSITION FROM INTERCEPT

	00′	05′	10′	15′	20′	25′	30′	35′	40′	45′	
ALT.					**OFFSETS**						*ALT.*
0°	0.0′	0.0′	0.0′	0.0′	0.0′	0.0′	0.0′	0.0′	0.0′	0.0′	0°
30	0.0	0.0	0.0	0.0	0.0	0.1	0.1	0.1	0.1	0.2	30
40	0.0	0.0	0.0	0.0	0.1	0.1	0.1	0.2	0.2	0.3	40
50	0.0	0.0	0.0	0.0	0.1	0.1	0.2	0.2	0.3	0.3	50
55	0.0	0.0	0.0	0.0	0.1	0.1	0.2	0.3	0.3	0.4	55
60	0.0	0.0	0.0	0.1	0.1	0.2	0.2	0.3	0.4	0.5	60
62	0.0	0.0	0.0	0.1	0.1	0.2	0.2	0.3	0.4	0.5	62
64	0.0	0.0	0.0	0.1	0.1	0.2	0.3	0.4	0.5	0.6	64
66	0.0	0.0	0.0	0.1	0.1	0.2	0.3	0.4	0.5	0.7	66
68	0.0	0.0	0.0	0.1	0.1	0.2	0.3	0.4	0.6	0.7	68
70	0.0	0.0	0.0	0.1	0.2	0.2	0.4	0.5	0.6	0.8	70
71	0.0	0.0	0.0	0.1	0.2	0.3	0.4	0.5	0.7	0.9	71
72	0.0	0.0	0.0	0.1	0.2	0.3	0.4	0.5	0.7	0.9	72
73	0.0	0.0	0.0	0.1	0.2	0.3	0.4	0.6	0.8	1.0	73
74	0.0	0.0	0.1	0.1	0.2	0.3	0.5	0.6	0.8	1.0	74
75	0.0	0.0	0.1	0.1	0.2	0.3	0.5	0.7	0.9	1.1	75
76	0.0	0.0	0.1	0.1	0.2	0.4	0.5	0.7	0.9	1.2	76
77	0.0	0.0	0.1	0.1	0.3	0.4	0.6	0.8	1.0	1.3	77
78	0.0	0.0	0.1	0.2	0.3	0.4	0.6	0.8	1.1	1.4	78
79	0.0	0.0	0.1	0.2	0.3	0.5	0.7	0.9	1.2	1.5	79
80.0	0.0	0.0	0.1	0.2	0.3	0.5	0.7	1.0	1.3	1.7	80.0
80.5	0.0	0.0	0.1	0.2	0.3	0.5	0.8	1.1	1.4	1.8	80.5
81.0	0.0	0.0	0.1	0.2	0.4	0.6	0.8	1.1	1.5	1.9	81.0
81.5	0.0	0.0	0.1	0.2	0.4	0.6	0.9	1.2	1.6	2.0	81.5
82.0	0.0	0.0	0.1	0.2	0.4	0.6	0.9	1.3	1.7	2.1	82.0
82.5	0.0	0.0	0.1	0.2	0.4	0.7	1.0	1.4	1.8	2.2	82.5
83.0	0.0	0.0	0.1	0.3	0.5	0.7	1.1	1.5	1.9	2.4	83.0
83.5	0.0	0.0	0.1	0.3	0.5	0.8	1.2	1.6	2.0	2.6	83.5
84.0	0.0	0.0	0.1	0.3	0.5	0.9	1.2	1.7	2.2	2.8	84.0
84.5	0.0	0.0	0.2	0.3	0.6	1.0	1.4	1.9	2.4	3.1	84.5
85.0	0.0	0.0	0.2	0.4	0.7	1.0	1.5	2.1	2.7	3.4	85.0
85.5	0.0	0.0	0.2	0.4	0.7	1.2	1.7	2.3	3.0	3.8	85.5
86.0	0.0	0.1	0.2	0.5	0.8	1.3	1.9	2.6	3.4	4.3	86.0
86.5	0.0	0.1	0.2	0.5	1.0	1.5	2.2	2.9	3.8	4.9	86.5
87.0	0.0	0.1	0.3	0.6	1.1	1.7	2.5	3.4	4.5	5.7	87.0
87.5	0.0	0.1	0.3	0.8	1.3	2.1	3.0	4.1	5.4	6.9	87.5
88.0	0.0	0.1	0.4	0.9	1.7	2.7	3.8	5.2	6.9	8.8	88.0
88.5	0.0	0.2	0.6	1.3	2.3	3.5	5.1	7.1	9.4	12.1	88.5
89.0	0.0	0.3	0.8	1.9	3.4	5.5	8.0	11.3	15.3	20.3	89.0

In adjusting the straight LOP to obtain a closer approximation to the arc of the circle of equal altitude, points on the LOP are offset at right angles to the LOP in the direction of the celestial body. The arguments for entering the table are the distance from the intercept to the point on the LOP to be offset and the altitude of the body.

In the use of the table with the graphical method for interpolating altitude for latitude and LHA increments, the offset of the foot of the perpendicular is along the azimuth line in a direction away from the body. The arguments for entering the table are the distance from the DR to the foot of the perpendicular and the altitude of the body.

2. Interpolation for Latitude and Local Hour Angle. The following graphical method can be used to interpolate the altitude for latitude and local hour angle increments. *The basic method should have most frequent application in great-circle solutions.*

In principle the method is the measurement of the difference of the radii of two circles of equal altitude corresponding to the altitudes of a celestial body from two positions at the same instant. One circle passes through the assumed position (AP), and the second circle passes through the dead reckoning position (DR) or other position from which the computed altitude is required.

The measurement, which is the difference in zenith distances as measured from the zenith of the assumed position and the zenith of some nearby position, is effected as follows:

(1) Draw the azimuth line from the assumed position (AP) as shown in figure 11 (the azimuth angle is interpolated for declination increment before conversion to true azimuth).

(2) From the position (DR) for which the computed altitude is required, draw a line perpendicular to the azimuth line or its extension. This line approximates the arc of the circle of equal altitude passing through the DR.

(3) Measure the distance from the foot of the perpendicular to the DR in nautical miles.

(4) Entering the Table of Offsets with the distance of the DR from the foot of the perpendicular and the altitude of the body as interpolated for declination increment, extract the offset.

(5) From the foot of the perpendicular and in a direction away from the celestial body, lay off the offset on the azimuth line or its extension.

(6) As shown in figure 11, a closer approximation to the arc of the circle of equal altitude through the DR is made by drawing a straight line from the offset point to the DR.

(7) The required correction, in units of minutes of latitude, for the latitude and LHA increments is the length along the azimuth line between the AP and the arc of the circle of equal altitude through the DR.

If the arc of the circle of equal altitude through the DR crosses the azimuth line between the AP and the body, the correction is to be added to the altitude interpolated for declination increment; otherwise the correction is to be subtracted. The method will give highly satisfactory results except when plotting on a Mercator chart in high latitudes.

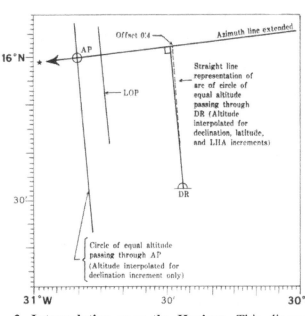

Example:

Computed altitude from AP	Hc	70°05.0′
Observed altitude	Ho	70°00.0′
Intercept	a	5.0 A

Computed altitude from AP	Hc	70°05.0′
Difference of the radii		20.4′
Computed altitude from DR	Hc	69°44.6′

Computed altitude from DR	Hc	69°44.6′
Observed altitude	Ho	70°00.0′
Intercept	a	15.4 T

FIGURE 11

3. Interpolation near the Horizon. This discussion is restricted to the interpolation of altitude for declination within the 1° interval containing the horizon, indicated by the horizontal segments of the C-S Line. Interpolation of altitude in the interval under consideration is accomplished by using the last tabular altitude and altitude difference appearing above the C-S Line. Since the last tabular altitude above the C-S Line indicates the body's altitude above the horizon for LHA at top of page, for the pertinent latitude, and for the last integral declination above the horizontal segment of the C-S Line pertaining to that particular latitude, interpolation resulting in positive altitudes may be carried out for increments of declination of contrary name so long as the interpolated altitude correction does not exceed the last tabular altitude above the C-S Line; for the LHA at bottom of page, positive altitudes will result when interpolating altitude for increments of declination of same name so long as the interpolated altitude correction exceeds the last tabular value above the C-S Line. Interpolation for declinations and increments of declination in excess of the above limits results in negative altitudes.

The tabular azimuth angle pertinent to this one-degree interval of declination is that immediately above or that immediately below the C-S Line, according as the entering arguments are contrary or same name, respectively. The difference in azimuth angle for the interval is determined by taking the value of tabular azimuth angle, on the same side of the C-S Line as the LHA argument, from the supplement of that on the opposite side of the line.

4. Negative Altitudes. This paragraph is restricted to tabular and interpolated altitudes for declinations other than one-degree intervals of declination containing the C-S Line. For all local hour angles at the top of the right-hand page, all tabular or interpolated altitudes on that page for declinations below the C-S Line are negative; also for any local hour angle at the bottom of the right-hand page, all tabular or interpolated altitudes for declinations above the C-S Line are negative; additionally, for these same local hour angles and latitudes changed to Contrary Name, the tabular or interpolated altitudes on the left-hand page are negative. Interpolation of altitudes for declination increments within these areas of negative altitude should, however, be accomplished as if the altitudes were positive, adhering strictly to the sign given to d. Then, after interpolation, regard the results as negative. In all instances involving negative altitudes, except the one-degree interval of declination which includes the C-S Line, the supplement of the pertinent tabular azimuth angle is that to be converted to true azimuth by the rules to be found on each opening of the basic tables.

5. Interpolation near the Zenith. In the region within 4° of the zenith where normal interpolation methods are inadequate, the following method can usually be used to interpolate both altitude and azimuth angle. The Interpolation Table is employed in carrying out the desired interpolation, but the values of altitude and azimuth angle extracted from the basic tables constitute data which require independent differencing; the tabular altitude difference, d, is not used.

To carry out the altitude interpolation, the basic tables are entered with the pertinent LHA and Dec., and with the integral degree of Lat. so chosen that, when increased by the declination increment, it is within 30′ of the known or DR latitude; this practice will prevent long intercepts. For these entering arguments and for a latitude and declination one degree more than the above referenced latitude and declination, respectively, extract the tabular altitudes and azimuth angles. The altitudes and azimuth angles are then differenced and with these differences interpolation of altitude and azimuth angle for the desired declination is made, utilizing the Interpolation Table. The computed altitude is then compared with that observed to determine the intercept, which together with the interpolated azimuth angle converted to true azimuth makes possible the construction of a line of position, which is plotted from the assumed longitude, and from the latitude of the entering argument, augmented by the declination increment.

Example	LHA	Lat.	Dec.	Ho
i	3°18′	24°12′S	21°33.3′S	85°58.2′
ii	356°52′	28°14′S	30°19.7′S	86°33.4′

Example i							*Example ii*					
Lat.	Dec.	Tab. Hc	diff.	Tab. Z	diff.		Lat.	Dec.	Tab. Hc	diff.	Tab. Z	diff
24°	21°	85°55.0′		136.7°			28°	30°	86°42.1′		52.0°	
			(+)0.8′		(+)0.2°					(+)1.2′		(-)0.3°
25°	22°	85°55.8′		136.9°			29°	31°	86°43.3′		51.7°	

Interpolate to Dec.=21°33.3′   Interpolate to Dec.=30°19.7′

Dec. Inc.=33.3′, diff.=(+)0.8′, Z diff.=(+)0.2°   Dec. Inc.=19.7′, diff.=(+)1.2′, Z diff.=(-)0.3°

Tab. Hc	85°55.0′		Tab. Z	136.7°		Tab. Hc	86°42.1′	Tab. Z	52.0°
Correction	(+) 0.4			(+) 0.1		Correction	(+) 0.4		(-) 0.1
Hc	85°55.4′		Z	136.8°		Hc	86°42.5′	Z	51.9°
Ho	85°58.2′					Ho	86°33.4′		
Intercept	2.8 T		Zn	316.8°		Intercept	9.1 A	Zn	128.1°

Plot from Lat. 24°33.3′ S   Plot from Lat. 28°19.7′ S

D. OTHER APPLICATIONS

1. Star Identification. Although no formal star identification tables are included in these volumes, a simple approach to star identification is to scan the pages of the appropriate latitudes and observe the combination of arguments which give the altitude and azimuth angle of the observation. Thus the declination and LHA☆ are determined directly. The star's SHA is found from, SHA☆ = LHA☆−LHAϓ. From these quantities the star can be identified from *The Nautical Almanac*.

Another solution is available through an interchange of arguments using the nearest integral values. The procedure consists of entering the tables with the observer's latitude (Same Name as Declination), with the observed azimuth angle (converted from observed true azimuth as required) as LHA and the observed altitude as declination, and extracting from the tables the altitude and azimuth angle respondents. The extracted altitude becomes the body's declination; the extracted azimuth angle (or its supplement) is the meridian angle of the body. Note that the tables are always entered with latitude of same name as declination. In north latitudes the tables can be entered with true azimuth as LHA.

If the respondents are extracted from above the C-S Line on a right-hand page, the name of the latitude is actually contrary to that of the declination. Otherwise, the declination of the body has the same name as the latitude. If the azimuth angle respondent is extracted from above the C-S Line, the supplement of the tabular value is the meridian angle, t, of the body. If the body is east of the observer's meridian, LHA = 360° − t; if the body is west of the meridian, LHA = t.

EXAMPLES FOR STAR IDENTIFICATION (Selection for illustration only)

Ex.	Lat.	Long.	Obs. Alt.	Obs. Zn	LHAϓ*
1	17° 15′ N	33° 55′ W	54° 36′	20°	189°
2	15 06 N	143 40 W	40 00	96	64
3	15 54 N	168 10 E	19 22	131	288
4	20 38 N	27 27 W	56 56	260	185
5	16 22 N	66 42 E	50 17	235	110
6	18 43 N	165 19 W	47 25	317	351
7	20 55 S	77 33 E	39 32	87	149
8	15 28 S	60 14 E	43 46	22	97
9	19 12 S	34 02 W	45 22	156	274
10	27 43 S	49 17 E	19 35	220	190
11	23 04 S	24 22 W	60 57	276	214
12	15 24 S	127 14 E	31 08	337	305

*LHAϓ from *The Nautical Almanac* for date and GMT of observation.

SOLUTIONS

	Entering Argument					Star Coordinates and Identity				
Ex.	Lat	LHA	Dec.	Page		Dec.	t	LHA☆	SHA☆	Name
1	17°	20°	55°	Left		49°N	17° E	343°	154°	*Alkaid*
2	15	96	40	Right, below C-S Line		5 N	50 E	310	246	*Procyon*
3	16	131	19	Right, above C-S Line		30 S	56 E	304	16	*Fomalhaut*
4	21	260	57	Right, below C-S Line		12 N	33 W	33	208	*Regulus*
5	16	235	50	Right, above C-S Line		8 S	32 W	32	282	*Rigel*
6	19	317	47	Left		45 N	41 W	41	50	*Deneb*
7	21	180−87=93	40	Right, below C-S Line		11 S	51 E	309	160	*Spica*
8	15	180−22=158	44	Right, above C-S Line		28 N	18 E	342	245	*Pollux*
9	19	180−156=24	45	Left		57 S	32 E	328	54	*Peacock*
10	28	220−180=40	20	Left		53 S	93 W	93	263	*Canopus*
11	23	276−180=96	61	Right, below C-S Line		17 S	30 W	30	176	*Gienah*
12	15	337−180=157	31	Right, above C-S Line		39 N	25 W	25	80	*Vega*

SHA☆ = LHA☆−LHAϓ

2. Great-Circle Sailing. The great-circle distance between any two points on the assumed spherical surface of the Earth and the initial great-circle course angle may be found by relating the problems to the solution of the celestial triangle. For by entering the tables with latitude of departure as latitude, latitude of destination as declination, and difference of longitude as LHA, the tabular altitude and azimuth angle may be extracted and converted to distance and course.

The tabular azimuth angle (or its supplement) becomes the initial great-circle course angle, prefixed N or S for the latitude of departure, and suffixed E or W depending upon the destination being east or west of point of departure.

If all entering arguments are integral degrees, the altitude and azimuth angle are obtained directly from the tables without interpolation. If the latitude of destination is nonintegral, interpolation for the additional minutes of latitude is done as in correcting altitude for any declination increment; if either the latitude of departure or difference of longitude, or both, are nonintegral, the additional interpolation is done graphically.

Since the latitude of destination becomes the declination entry, and all declinations appear on every page, the great-circle solution can always be extracted from the volume which covers the latitude of departure.

Great-circle solutions belong in one of the four following cases:

Case I—Latitudes of departure and destination of same name and initial great-circle distance less than 90°.

Enter the tables with latitude of departure as latitude argument (Same Name), latitude of destination as declination argument, and difference of longitude as local hour angle argument. If the respondents as found on a right-hand page do not lie below the C-S Line, Case III is applicable.

Extract the tabular altitude which subtracted from 90° is the desired great-circle distance. The tabular azimuth angle is the initial great-circle course angle.

Case II—Latitudes of departure and destination of contrary name and great-circle distance less than 90°.

Enter the tables with latitude of departure as latitude argument (Contrary Name) and latitude of destination as declination argument, and with the difference of longitude as local hour angle argument. If the respondents do not lie above the C-S Line on the right-hand page, Case IV is applicable.

Extract the tabular altitude which subtracted from 90° is the desired great-circle distance. The tabular azimuth angle is the initial great-circle course angle.

Case III—Latitudes of departure and destination of same name and great-circle distance greater than 90°.

Enter the tables with latitude of departure as latitude argument (Same Name), latitude of destination as declination argument, and difference of longitude as local hour angle argument. If the respondents as found on a right-hand page do not lie above the C-S Line, Case I is applicable.

Extract the tabular altitude which added to 90° gives the desired great-circle distance. The initial great-circle course angle is 180° minus the tabular azimuth angle.

Case IV—Latitudes of departure and destination of contrary name and great-circle distance greater than 90°.

Enter the tables with latitude of departure as latitude argument (Contrary Name), latitude of destination as declination argument and difference of longitude as local hour angle argument. If the respondents as found on a right-hand page do not lie below the C-S Line, Case II is applicable. If the DLo is in excess of 90°, the respondents are found on the facing left-hand page (See section C.4.).

Extract the tabular altitude which added to 90° gives the desired great-circle distance. The initial great-circle course angle is 180° minus the tabular azimuth angle.

The following two great-circle distance and course solutions illustrate Cases I and IV.

Case I

Required.—Distance and initial great-circle course from San Juan (18°28′N, 66°07′W) to Milford Haven (51°43′N, 5°02′W).

Solution.—(l) Case I is assumed to be applicable. Since the latitude of the point of departure, the latitude of the destination, and the difference of longitude (DLo) between the point of departure and destination are not integral degrees, the solution is effected from an adjusted point of departure or assumed position of departure chosen as follows: the latitude of the assumed position (AP) is the integral degrees of latitude nearest to the point of departure; the longitude of the AP is chosen to provide integral degrees of DLo. This AP, which should be within 30′ of the longitude of the point of departure, is at latitude 18°N, longitude 66°02′W. The DLo is 61°.

(2) Enter the tables with 18° as the latitude argument (Same Name), 61° as the LHA argument, and 51° as the declination argument.

(3) From page 124 extract the tabular altitude, altitude difference, and azimuth angle; interpolate altitude and azimuth angle for declination increment. The Dec. Inc. is the minutes that the latitude of the destination is in excess of the integral degrees used as the declination argument.

			ht (Tab. Hc)	d	Z
LHA 61°, Lat. 18° (Same),	Dec.51°		32° 01.6′	(−)11.9′	40.5°
Dec. Inc. 43′, d(−)11.9′	Tens		(−) 7.1		
	Units		(−) 1.4		
Interpolated for Dec. Inc.			31° 53.1′		C N39.6°E
Initial great-circle course from AP					Cn 039.6°
Great-circle distance from AP (90°−31°53.1′)					3486.9 n.mi.

(4) Using the graphical method for interpolating altitude for latitude and LHA increments, the course line is drawn from the AP in the direction of the initial great-circle course from the AP (039.6°). As shown in figure 12, a line is drawn from the point of departure perpendicular to the initial great-circle course line or its extension.

(5) The required correction, in units of minutes of latitude, for the latitude and DLo increments is the length along the course line between the foot of the perpendicular and the AP. The correction as applied to the distance from the AP is −18.4′; the great-circle distance is 3468 nautical miles.

(6) The azimuth angle interpolated for declination, LHA, and latitude increments is 39.8°; the initial great-circle course from the point of departure is 039.8°

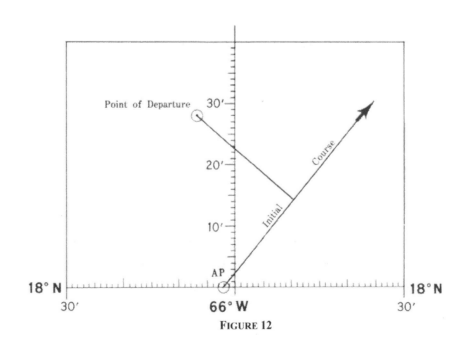

FIGURE 12

Case IV

Required.—Distance and initial great-circle course from Cape Moreton (27°02′S, 153°28′E) to Cape Flattery (48°24′N, 124°44′W).

Solution.—(1) Case IV is assumed to be applicable. Since the latitude of the point of departure, the latitude of the destination, and the difference of longitude (DLo) between the point of departure and destination are not integral degrees, the solution is effected from an adjusted point of departure or assumed position of departure chosen as follows: the latitude of the assumed position (AP) is the integral degrees of latitude nearest to the point of departure; the longitude of the AP is chosen to provide integral degrees of DLo. This AP, which should be within 30′ of the longitude of the point of departure, is at latitude 27°S, longitude 153°16′E. The DLo is 82°.

(2) Enter the tables with 27° as the latitude argument (Contrary Name), 82° as the LHA argument, and 48° as the declination argument.

(3) From page 349 extract the tabular altitude, altitude difference, and azimuth angle; interpolate altitude for Dec. Inc. as if the altitude were positive, adhering strictly to the sign given d. After interpolation regard the results as negative. Subtract tabular azimuth angle from 180°; interpolate for Dec. Inc.

		ht (Tab. Hc)	d	Z
LHA 82°, Lat. 27° (Contrary), Dec.48°		14°44.3′	(+)24.5′	43.2°
Dec. Inc. 24′, d(+)24.5′	Tens	(+) 8.0		180°− Z=136.8°
	Units	(+) 1.8		
Interpolated for Dec. Inc.		(−) 14°54.1′		C S137.2°E
Initial great-circle course from AP				Cn 042.8°
Great-circle distance from AP (90°+14°54.1′)				6294.1 n.mi.

(4) Using the graphical method for interpolating altitude for latitude and LHA increments, the course line is drawn from the AP in the direction of the initial great-circle course from the AP (042.8°). As shown in figure 13 a line is drawn from the point of departure perpendicular to the course line or its extension.

(5) The required additional correction, in units of minutes of latitude, for the latitude and DLo increments is the length along the course line between the foot of the perpendicular and the AP. The correction as applied to the distance from the AP is (−) 5.6′; the great-circle distance is 6288 nautical miles.

(6) The azimuth angle interpolated for declination, LHA, and latitude increments is 137.2°; the initial great-circle course from the point of departure is 042.8°.

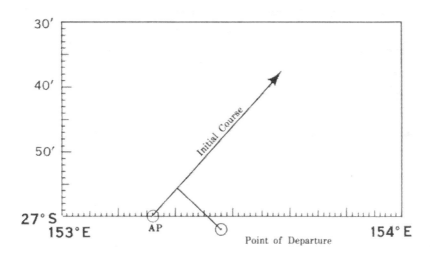

FIGURE 13

3. Points along Great Circle. If the latitude of the point of departure and the initial great-circle course angle are integral degrees, points along the great circle are found by entering the tables with the latitude of departure as the latitude argument (Same Name), the initial great-circle course angle as the LHA argument, and 90° minus distance to a point on the great circle as the declination argument. The latitude of the point on the great circle and the difference of longitude between that point and the point of departure are the tabular altitude and azimuth angle respondents, respectively.

Required.—A number of points at 300-mile intervals along the great circle from latitude 18°N, longitude 66°W when the initial great-circle course angle is N 40° E.

Entering the tables with latitude 18° (Same Name), LHA 40°, and with successive declinations of 85°, 80°, 75°, . . . the latitudes and differences in longitude, from 66°W, are found as tabular altitudes and azimuth angles, respectively.

Distance n. mi, (arc)	300(5°)	600(10°)	900(15°)	1200(20°)
Latitude	21.8°N	25.5°N	29.1°N	32.6°N
DLo	3.5°	7.1°	11.0°	15.1°
Longitude	62.5°W	58.9°W	55.0°W	50.9°W

Note.—If the respondents are abstracted from across the C-S line, the DLo is the supplement of the tabular azimuth angle; the tabular altitudes correspond to latitudes on the side of the equator opposite from the latitude of departure.

4. General Spherical Triangle Solutions. Of the six parts of the spherical astronomical triangle, these tables utilize three as entering arguments and tabulate two as respondents. The only remaining part of the triangle is the parallactic (or position) angle, which is the angle between a body's hour circle and its vertical circle. Values of the parallactic angle, not essential for navigation, have not been included in order to keep the tabulations to a minimum. However, the parallactic angle can be found through the simple interchange of arguments, thus effecting a complete solution. The applicable instructions are as follows:

(a) *When latitude and declination are of same name*, enter the tables with the appropriate local hour angle, with the declination as latitude argument of the same name and the latitude as declination argument, and extract the tabular azimuth angle as the parallactic angle.

(b) *When latitude and declination are of contrary name,* enter the tables with the appropriate local hour angle and with the declination as latitude argument of contrary name and the latitude as declination argument; the tabular azimuth angle is then the supplement of the parallactic angle (i.e., parallactic angle equals 180° minus the azimuth angle). This method generally requires the availability of all volumes of the series.

An approximate value of the parallactic angle, X, accurate enough for most navigational requirements, can be calculated directly from the formula, $\cos X = d/60'$, where d is the difference between successive tabular altitudes for the desired latitude, local hour angle and declination.

Within the limitations of the tabular precision and interval, the tabular data of these tables include the solution of any spherical triangle, given two sides and the included angle. When using the tables for the general solution of the spherical triangle, the use of latitude, declination, and altitude in the tables instead of their corresponding parts of the astronomical triangle must be kept in mind.

In general if any three parts of a spherical triangle are given, these tables can be used to find the remaining parts; this will sometimes mean searching through the volumes to find, for example, a particular altitude in a particular latitude and a given LHA in order to find the corresponding azimuth angle and declination.

5. Compass Error. One of the more frequent applications of sight reduction tables is their use in computing the azimuth of a celestial body for comparison with an observed azimuth in order to determine the error of the compass. In computing the azimuth of a celestial body, for the time and place of observation, it is normally necessary to interpolate the tabular azimuth angle as extracted from the tables for the differences between the table arguments and the actual values of declination, latitude, and local hour angle. The required triple interpolation of the azimuth angle is effected as follows:

(1)   The main tables are entered with the nearest integral values of declination, latitude, and local hour angle; for these arguments, a base azimuth angle is extracted.

(2)   The tables are reentered with the same latitude and LHA arguments but with the declination argument 1° greater or less than the base declination argument depending upon whether the actual declination is greater or less than the base argument. The difference between the respondent azimuth angle and the base azimuth angle establishes the azimuth angle difference (Z Diff.) for the increment of declination.

(3)   The tables are reentered with the base declination and LHA arguments but with the latitude argument 1° greater or less than the base latitude argument depending upon whether the actual (usually DR) latitude is greater or less than the base argument to find the Z Diff. for the increment of latitude.

(4)   The tables are reentered with the base declination and latitude arguments but with the LHA argument 1° greater or less than the base LHA argument depending upon whether the actual LHA is greater or less than the base argument to find the Z Diff. for the increment of LHA.

(5)   The correction to the base azimuth angle for each increment is Z Diff. $\times \dfrac{\text{Inc.}}{60'}$.

Example.—In DR Lat. 23°24.0′N, the azimuth of the Sun is observed as 072.5° pgc. At the time of the observation, the declination of the Sun is 20°13.8′N; the local hour angle of the Sun is 276°41.2′. The error of the gyrocompass is found as follows:

	Actual	Base Arguments	Base Z	Tab* Z	Z Diff.	Increments	Correction (Z Diff×Inc.÷60)
Dec.	20°13.8′N	20°	73.9°	72.9°	-1.0°	13.8′	-0.2°
DR Lat.	23°24.0′N	23° (Same)	73.9°	74.1°	+0.2°	24.0′	+0.1°
LHA	276°41.2′	277°	73.9°	73.5°	-0.4°	18.8′	-0.1°

						Total Corr.	-0.2°

Base Z	73.9°
Corr.	(-) 0.2°
Z	N 73.7°E
Zn	073.7°
Zn pgc	072.5°
Gyro Error	1.2°E

*Respondent for two base arguments and 1° change from third base argument, in vertical order of Dec., DR Lat., and LHA.

E. BACKGROUND

1. Accuracy of Tables. The tabular values as given in these tables have maximum and probable (50%) errors of ±0.05′ and ±0.025′ in altitude and ±0.05° and ±0.025° in azimuth angle.

The maximum error arising from the use of the Interpolation Table for the first-difference correction is ±0.14′, with a probable error of ±0.03′, when used for the interpolation of altitude for declination.

The maximum error arising from the use of the correction for second differences obtained from the Interpolation Table is ±0.12′ with a probable error of ± 0.03′.

When second differences are completely negligible, the maximum error of an interpolated altitude is ±0.19′ with a probable error of ±0.04′; when the second differences are not negligible and the second-difference correction is included in the interpolation, the maximum error of the calculated altitude will be ±0.31′ with a probable error of ±0.05′.

The largest value of the double-second difference when the value of d is not printed in italics is 3.9′, and if the correction for this value is neglected, an error of up to −0.24′ may be introduced into the computed altitude. But such an error is only possible when the altitude is greater than 60° and when the value of Dec. Inc. is close to 30′. The neglect of the second-difference correction when d is not printed in italics will rarely introduce an error as large as −0.2′.

For altitudes less than 86°, i.e., for zenith distances greater than 4°, interpolation of the tabular altitude for declination, utilizing both first and second differences and the Interpolation Table, may be made to within about 0.2′; linear interpolation for azimuth angle can be made to about 0.2°. Closer to the zenith, not only do second differences exceed the limits of the tables but higher differences are also significant.

When the body is in the zenith, its azimuth is indeterminate, that is when LHA is 0° and when latitude and declination are equal and have the Same Name. In these cases Z is tabulated as 90° or as one-half the preceding value. There are 91 of these cases.

When latitude is 90° and declination is 90°, the altitude is 90° for all hour angles. Here the value of Z tabulated is one-half the preceding value. There are 182 of these cases, two of which are included in the previous set. In the above cases the tabulated azimuth angles are the mathematical limits of the azimuth angle when the limit is approached in a specified direction.

In the special cases when the latitude is 90°, i.e., at the poles, all directions from the North Pole are south and from the South Pole are north; the criterion adopted in these cases has been to tabulate the azimuth as equal to 180° minus LHA, i.e., the directions are tabulated as the angular directions from the lower branch of the Greenwich Meridian. There are 90 × 180 of these cases not included in the previous sets.

2. Computation formulas. For latitude (L), declination (d) and local hour angle (LHA), the altitude (Hc) and the azimuth angle (Z) were calculated from the following formulas:

$$\sin Hc = \sin L \sin d + \cos L \cos d \cos LHA$$

$$\tan Z = \frac{\cos d \sin LHA}{\cos L \sin d - \sin L \cos d \cos LHA}$$

All values of altitude within 1°30′ of the zenith were recalculated using a more appropriate formula because determination of these high altitudes from their sines with only nine figures could introduce errors of the order of 0.0005′, which would sometimes affect the rounding off of the altitude to 0.1′. The formula used is equivalent to:

$$\sin^2 \tfrac{1}{2} z = \cos^2 \tfrac{1}{2} LHA \, \sin^2 \tfrac{1}{2} (L-d) + \sin^2 \tfrac{1}{2} LHA \, \cos^2 \tfrac{1}{2} (L+d), \text{ where z is the zenith distance.}$$

F. GLOSSARY

Altitude—the arc of a vertical circle between the horizon and a point or body on the celestial sphere. Altitude as measured by a sextant is called sextant altitude (**hs**). Sextant altitude corrected only for inaccuracies in the reading (instrument, index, and personal errors, as applicable) and inaccuracies in the reference level (principally dip) is called apparent altitude (**ha**). After all corrections are applied, it is called corrected sextant altitude or observed altitude (**Ho**). An altitude taken directly from a table is called a tabular or tabulated altitude (**ht**). Tabular altitude as interpolated for declination, latitude, and LHA increments as required is called computed altitude (**Hc**).

Altitude Difference (d)—the first difference between successive tabulations of altitude in a latitude column of these tables.

Argument—one of the values used for entering a table or diagram.

Assumed (or Chosen) Latitude (aL), Assumed (or Chosen) Longitude (aλ)—geographical coordinates assumed to facilitate sight reduction.

Assumed Position (AP)—a point at which an observer is assumed to be located.

Azimuth (Zn)—the horizontal direction of a celestial body or point from a terrestrial point; the arc of the horizon, or the angle at the zenith, between the north part of the celestial meridian or principal vertical circle and a vertical circle through the body or point, measured from 000° at the north part of the principal vertical circle clockwise through 360°.

Azimuth Angle (Z)—the arc of the horizon, or the angle at the zenith, between the north part or south part of the celestial meridian, according to the elevated pole, and a vertical circle through the body or point, measured from 0° at the north or south reference eastward or westward through 180° according to whether the body is east or west of the local meridian. It is prefixed N or S to agree with the latitude and suffixed E or W to agree with the meridian angle.

Celestial Equator—the primary great circle of the celestial sphere, everywhere 90° from the celestial poles; the intersection of the extended plane of the equator and the celestial sphere. Also called EQUINOCTIAL.

Celestial Horizon—that circle of the celestial sphere formed by the intersection of the celestial sphere and a plane through the center of the Earth and perpendicular to zenith-nadir line.

Celestial Meridian—on the celestial sphere, a great circle through the celestial poles and the zenith. The expression usually refers to the upper branch, that half from pole to pole which passes through the zenith.

Course Angle—course measured from 0° at the reference direction clockwise or counterclockwise through 180°. It is labeled with the reference direction as a prefix and the direction of measurement from the reference direction as a suffix. Thus, course angle S21°E is 21° east of south, or true course 159°.

Course Line—the graphic representation of a ship's course.

Declination (Dec.)—angular distance north or south of the celestial equator; the arc of an hour circle between the celestial equator and a point on the celestial sphere, measured northward or southward from the celestial equator through 90°, and labeled N or S (+ or −) to indicate the direction of measurement.

Declination Increment (Dec. Inc.)—in sight reduction, the excess of the actual declination of a celestial body over the integral declination argument.

Double-Second Difference (DSD)—the sum of successive second differences. Because second differences are not tabulated in these tables, the DSD can be formed most readily by subtracting, algebraically, the first difference immediately above the tabular altitude difference (d) corresponding to the entering arguments from the first difference immediately below. The result will always be a negative value.

Ecliptic—the apparent annual path of the Sun among the stars; the intersection of the plane of the Earth's orbit with the celestial sphere. This is a great circle of the celestial sphere inclined at an angle of about 23°27′ to the celestial equator.

Elevated Pole (Pn or Ps)—the celestial pole above the observer's horizon, agreeing in name with the observer's latitude.

First Difference—the difference between successive tabulations of a quantity.

First Point of Aries (♈)—that point of intersection of the ecliptic and the celestial equator occupied by the Sun as it changes from south to north declination on or about March 21. Also called VERNAL EQUINOX.

Geographical Position (GP)—the point where a line drawn from a celestial body to the Earth's center passes through the Earth's surface.

Great Circle—the intersection of a sphere and a plane through its center.

Great-Circle Course—the direction of the great circle through the point of departure and the destination, expressed as angular distance from a reference direction, usually north, to the direction of the great circle. The angle varies from point to point along the great circle. At the point of departure it is called INITIAL GREAT-CIRCLE COURSE.

Greenwich Hour Angle (GHA)—angular distance west of the Greenwich celestial meridian; the arc of the celestial equator, or the angle at the celestial pole, between the upper branch of the Greenwich celestial meridian and the hour circle of a point on the celestial sphere, measured westward from the Greenwich celestial meridian through 360°.

Hour Circle—on the celestial sphere, a great circle through the celestial poles and a celestial body or the vernal equinox. Hour circles are perpendicular to the celestial equator.

Intercept (a)—the difference in minutes of arc between the computed and observed altitudes (corrected sextant altitudes). It is labeled T (toward) or A (away) as the observed altitude is greater or smaller than the computed altitude; Hc greater than Ho, intercept is away (A); Ho greater than Hc, intercept is toward (T).

Line of Position (LOP)—a line indicating a series of possible positions of a craft, determined by observation or measurement.

Local Hour Angle (LHA)—angular distance west of the local celestial meridian; the arc of the celestial equator, or the angle at the celestial pole, between the upper branch of the local celestial meridian and the hour circle of a celestial body or point on the celestial sphere, measured westward from the local celestial meridian through 360°.

Meridian Angle (t)—angular distance east or west of the local celestial meridian; the arc of the celestial equator, or the angle at the celestial pole, between the upper branch of the local celestial meridian and the hour circle of a celestial body, measured eastward or westward from the local celestial meridian through 180°, and labeled E or W to indicate the direction of measurement.

Nadir (Na)—that point on the celestial sphere 180° from the observer's zenith.

Name—the labels N and S which are attached to latitude and declination are said to be of the same name when they are both N or S and contrary name when one is N and the other is S.

Navigational Triangle—the spherical triangle solved in computing altitude and azimuth and great-circle sailing problems. The celestial triangle is formed on the celestial sphere by the great circles connecting the elevated pole, zenith of the assumed position of the observer, and a celestial body. The terrestrial triangle is formed on the Earth by the great circles connecting the pole and two places on the Earth: the assumed position of the observer and geographical position of the body for celestial observations, and the point of departure and destination for great-circle sailing problems. The term astronomical triangle applies to either the celestial or terrestrial triangle used for solving celestial observations.

Polar Distance (p)—angular distance from a celestial pole; the arc of an hour circle between a celestial pole, usually the elevated pole, and a point on the celestial sphere, measured from the celestial pole through 180°.

Prime Meridian—the meridian of longitude 0°, used as the origin for measurement of longitude.

Prime Vertical—the vertical circle through the east and west points of the horizon.

Principal Vertical Circle—the vertical circle through the north and south points of the horizon, coinciding with the celestial meridian.

Respondent—the value in a table or diagram corresponding to the entering arguments.

Second Difference—the difference between successive first differences.

Sidereal Hour Angle (SHA)—angular distance west of the vernal equinox; the arc of the celestial equator, or the angle at the celestial pole, between the hour circle of the vernal equinox and the hour circle of a point on the celestial sphere, measured westward from the hour circle of the vernal equinox through 360°.

Sight Reduction—the process of deriving from a sight (observation of the altitude, and sometimes also the azimuth, of a celestial body) the information needed for establishing a line of position.

Small Circle—the intersection of a sphere and a plane which does not pass through its center.

Vertical Circle—on the celestial sphere, a great circle through the zenith and nadir. Vertical circles are perpendicular to the horizon.

Zenith (Z)—that point on the celestial sphere vertically overhead.

Zenith Distance (z)—angular distance from the zenith; the arc of a vertical circle between the zenith and a point on the celestial sphere.

G. EXAMPLE SIGHT REDUCTIONS

Example—On September 9, 1974, the 1932 dead reckoning position of a ship is lat. 14°45′ N, long. 30°00′ W. The ship is on course 225°, speed 20 knots. Observations are made from a height of eye of 31 feet using a sextant having an index error of (+) 1.0′ as indicated below. Determine the 1932 fix.

Body	Zone Time	Sextant Altitude	SHA	Declination
Arcturus	19ʰ20ᵐ03ˢ	28°29.5′	146°22.4′	19°18.9′ N
Antares	19ʰ25ᵐ58ˢ	37°57.4′	113°02.0′	26°22.7′ S
Rasalhague	19ʰ32ᵐ01ˢ	72°38.2′	96°34.0′	12°34.9′ N

		ARCTURUS		ANTARES		RASALHAGUE
GMT (Sept. 9) -		21ʰ20ᵐ03ˢ		21ʰ25ᵐ58ˢ		21ʰ32ᵐ01ˢ
GHA ♈ for 21ʰ GMT- - - - - - - - - - - - - - - -		303°31.5′		303°31.5′		303°31.5′
Increments- - - - - - - - - - - - - - - - - - - 20ᵐ03ˢ		5°01.6′	25ᵐ58ˢ	6°30.6′	32ᵐ01ˢ	8°01.6′
SHA -		146°22.4′		113°02.0′		96°34.0′
GHA☆ -		94°55.5′		63°04.1′		48°07.1′
aλ -		29°55.5′W		30°04.1′W		30°07.1′W
LHA☆ -		65°00.0′		33°00.0′		18°00.0′
Dec. -		19°18.9′N		26°22.7′S		12°34.9′N
Dec. Inc. -		18.9′		22.7′		34.9′
aL -		15°00.0′N		15°00.0′N		15°00.0′N
ht (Tab. Hc) -		28°03.0′		37°55.6′		72°14.9′
d and correction - - - - - - - - - - - - - - -(+) 7.3′	(+) 2.3′	(−) 44.9′	(−) 17.0′	(+) 10.6′	(+) 6.6′
Hc -		28°05.3′		37°38.6′		72°21.5′
Ho -		28°21.3′		37°49.8′		72°31.5′
a -		16.0T		11.2T		10.0T
Z and Zn - - - - - - - - - - - - - - - - - - N75.8°W	284.2°	N141.9°W	218.1°	N95.7°W	264.3°

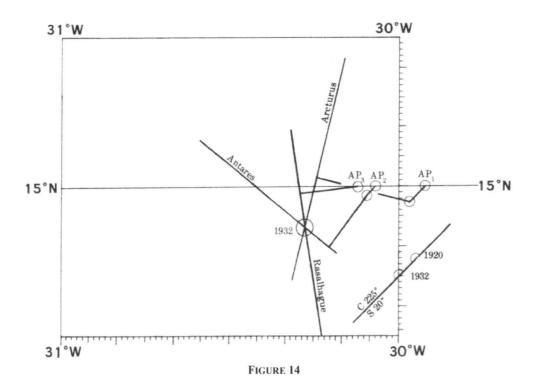

FIGURE 14

Note.——In figure 14 the assumed position of the Arcturus line of position is advanced 4.0 miles for a 12-minute run and the assumed position of the Antares line of position is advanced 2.0 miles for a 6-minute run, both in the direction of the course 225°, to obtain a fix at the time of the Rasalhague sight. Each azimuth angle is interpolated for declination increment. The interpolation of the tabular altitude of the Rasalhague sight includes a DSD correction of (+) 0.4′.

SIGHT REDUCTION TABLES

FOR

MARINE NAVIGATION

LATITUDES 15°–30°, Inclusive

N. Lat. {L.H.A. greater than 180° .....Zn=Z; L.H.A. less than 180°............Zn=360°–Z}

Dec.	15°			16°			17°			18°			19°			20°			21°			22°			Dec.
	Hc	d	Z	Hc	d	Z	Hc	d	Z	Hc	d	Z	Hc	d	Z	Hc	d	Z	Hc	d	Z	Hc	d	Z	
°	° ′	′	°	° ′	′	°	° ′	′	°	° ′	′	°	° ′	′	°	° ′	′	°	° ′	′	°	° ′	′	°	°
0	75 00.0	+60.0	180.0	74 00.0	+60.0	180.0	73 00.0	+60.0	180.0	72 00.0	+60.0	180.0	71 00.0	+60.0	180.0	70 00.0	+60.0	180.0	69 00.0	+60.0	180.0	68 00.0	+60.0	180.0	0
1	76 00.0	+60.0	180.0	75 00.0	+60.0	180.0	74 00.0	+60.0	180.0	73 00.0	+60.0	180.0	72 00.0	+60.0	180.0	71 00.0	+60.0	180.0	70 00.0	+60.0	180.0	69 00.0	+60.0	180.0	1
2	77 00.0	+60.0	180.0	76 00.0	+60.0	180.0	75 00.0	+60.0	180.0	74 00.0	+60.0	180.0	73 00.0	+60.0	180.0	72 00.0	+60.0	180.0	71 00.0	+60.0	180.0	70 00.0	+60.0	180.0	2
3	78 00.0	+60.0	180.0	77 00.0	+60.0	180.0	76 00.0	+60.0	180.0	75 00.0	+60.0	180.0	74 00.0	+60.0	180.0	73 00.0	+60.0	180.0	72 00.0	+60.0	180.0	71 00.0	+60.0	180.0	3
4	79 00.0	+60.0	180.0	78 00.0	+60.0	180.0	77 00.0	+60.0	180.0	76 00.0	+60.0	180.0	75 00.0	+60.0	180.0	74 00.0	+60.0	180.0	73 00.0	+60.0	180.0	72 00.0	+60.0	180.0	4
5	80 00.0	+60.0	180.0	79 00.0	+60.0	180.0	78 00.0	+60.0	180.0	77 00.0	+60.0	180.0	76 00.0	+60.0	180.0	75 00.0	+60.0	180.0	74 00.0	+60.0	180.0	73 00.0	+60.0	180.0	5
6	81 00.0	+60.0	180.0	80 00.0	+60.0	180.0	79 00.0	+60.0	180.0	78 00.0	+60.0	180.0	77 00.0	+60.0	180.0	76 00.0	+60.0	180.0	75 00.0	+60.0	180.0	74 00.0	+60.0	180.0	6
7	82 00.0	+60.0	180.0	81 00.0	+60.0	180.0	80 00.0	+60.0	180.0	79 00.0	+60.0	180.0	78 00.0	+60.0	180.0	77 00.0	+60.0	180.0	76 00.0	+60.0	180.0	75 00.0	+60.0	180.0	7
8	83 00.0	+60.0	180.0	82 00.0	+60.0	180.0	81 00.0	+60.0	180.0	80 00.0	+60.0	180.0	79 00.0	+60.0	180.0	78 00.0	+60.0	180.0	77 00.0	+60.0	180.0	76 00.0	+60.0	180.0	8
9	84 00.0	+60.0	180.0	83 00.0	+60.0	180.0	82 00.0	+60.0	180.0	81 00.0	+60.0	180.0	80 00.0	+60.0	180.0	79 00.0	+60.0	180.0	78 00.0	+60.0	180.0	77 00.0	+60.0	180.0	9
10	85 00.0	+60.0	180.0	84 00.0	+60.0	180.0	83 00.0	+60.0	180.0	82 00.0	+60.0	180.0	81 00.0	+60.0	180.0	80 00.0	+60.0	180.0	79 00.0	+60.0	180.0	78 00.0	+60.0	180.0	10
11	86 00.0	+60.0	180.0	85 00.0	+60.0	180.0	84 00.0	+60.0	180.0	83 00.0	+60.0	180.0	82 00.0	+60.0	180.0	81 00.0	+60.0	180.0	80 00.0	+60.0	180.0	79 00.0	+60.0	180.0	11
12	87 00.0	+60.0	180.0	86 00.0	+60.0	180.0	85 00.0	+60.0	180.0	84 00.0	+60.0	180.0	83 00.0	+60.0	180.0	82 00.0	+60.0	180.0	81 00.0	+60.0	180.0	80 00.0	+60.0	180.0	12
13	88 00.0	+60.0	180.0	87 00.0	+60.0	180.0	86 00.0	+60.0	180.0	85 00.0	+60.0	180.0	84 00.0	+60.0	180.0	83 00.0	+60.0	180.0	82 00.0	+60.0	180.0	81 00.0	+60.0	180.0	13
14	89 00.0	+60.0	180.0	88 00.0	+60.0	180.0	87 00.0	+60.0	180.0	86 00.0	+60.0	180.0	85 00.0	+60.0	180.0	84 00.0	+60.0	180.0	83 00.0	+60.0	180.0	82 00.0	+60.0	180.0	14
15	90 00.0	-60.0	90.0	89 00.0	+60.0	180.0	88 00.0	+60.0	180.0	87 00.0	+60.0	180.0	86 00.0	+60.0	180.0	85 00.0	+60.0	180.0	84 00.0	+60.0	180.0	83 00.0	+60.0	180.0	15
16	89 00.0	-60.0	0.0	90 00.0	-60.0	90.0	89 00.0	+60.0	180.0	88 00.0	+60.0	180.0	87 00.0	+60.0	180.0	86 00.0	+60.0	180.0	85 00.0	+60.0	180.0	84 00.0	+60.0	180.0	16
17	88 00.0	-60.0	0.0	89 00.0	-60.0	0.0	90 00.0	-60.0	90.0	89 00.0	+60.0	180.0	88 00.0	+60.0	180.0	87 00.0	+60.0	180.0	86 00.0	+60.0	180.0	85 00.0	+60.0	180.0	17
18	87 00.0	-60.0	0.0	88 00.0	-60.0	0.0	89 00.0	-60.0	0.0	90 00.0	-60.0	90.0	89 00.0	+60.0	180.0	88 00.0	+60.0	180.0	87 00.0	+60.0	180.0	86 00.0	+60.0	180.0	18
19	86 00.0	-60.0	0.0	87 00.0	-60.0	0.0	88 00.0	-60.0	0.0	89 00.0	-60.0	0.0	90 00.0	-60.0	90.0	89 00.0	+60.0	180.0	88 00.0	+60.0	180.0	87 00.0	+60.0	180.0	19
20	85 00.0	-60.0	0.0	86 00.0	-60.0	0.0	87 00.0	-60.0	0.0	88 00.0	-60.0	0.0	89 00.0	-60.0	0.0	90 00.0	-60.0	90.0	89 00.0	+60.0	180.0	88 00.0	+60.0	180.0	20
21	84 00.0	-60.0	0.0	85 00.0	-60.0	0.0	86 00.0	-60.0	0.0	87 00.0	-60.0	0.0	88 00.0	-60.0	0.0	89 00.0	-60.0	0.0	90 00.0	-60.0	90.0	89 00.0	+60.0	180.0	21
22	83 00.0	-60.0	0.0	84 00.0	-60.0	0.0	85 00.0	-60.0	0.0	86 00.0	-60.0	0.0	87 00.0	-60.0	0.0	88 00.0	-60.0	0.0	89 00.0	-60.0	0.0	90 00.0	-60.0	90.0	22
23	82 00.0	-60.0	0.0	83 00.0	-60.0	0.0	84 00.0	-60.0	0.0	85 00.0	-60.0	0.0	86 00.0	-60.0	0.0	87 00.0	-60.0	0.0	88 00.0	-60.0	0.0	89 00.0	-60.0	0.0	23
24	81 00.0	-60.0	0.0	82 00.0	-60.0	0.0	83 00.0	-60.0	0.0	84 00.0	-60.0	0.0	85 00.0	-60.0	0.0	86 00.0	-60.0	0.0	87 00.0	-60.0	0.0	88 00.0	-60.0	0.0	24
25	80 00.0	-60.0	0.0	81 00.0	-60.0	0.0	82 00.0	-60.0	0.0	83 00.0	-60.0	0.0	84 00.0	-60.0	0.0	85 00.0	-60.0	0.0	86 00.0	-60.0	0.0	87 00.0	-60.0	0.0	25
26	79 00.0	-60.0	0.0	80 00.0	-60.0	0.0	81 00.0	-60.0	0.0	82 00.0	-60.0	0.0	83 00.0	-60.0	0.0	84 00.0	-60.0	0.0	85 00.0	-60.0	0.0	86 00.0	-60.0	0.0	26
27	78 00.0	-60.0	0.0	79 00.0	-60.0	0.0	80 00.0	-60.0	0.0	81 00.0	-60.0	0.0	82 00.0	-60.0	0.0	83 00.0	-60.0	0.0	84 00.0	-60.0	0.0	85 00.0	-60.0	0.0	27
28	77 00.0	-60.0	0.0	78 00.0	-60.0	0.0	79 00.0	-60.0	0.0	80 00.0	-60.0	0.0	81 00.0	-60.0	0.0	82 00.0	-60.0	0.0	83 00.0	-60.0	0.0	84 00.0	-60.0	0.0	28
29	76 00.0	-60.0	0.0	77 00.0	-60.0	0.0	78 00.0	-60.0	0.0	79 00.0	-60.0	0.0	80 00.0	-60.0	0.0	81 00.0	-60.0	0.0	82 00.0	-60.0	0.0	83 00.0	-60.0	0.0	29
30	75 00.0	-60.0	0.0	76 00.0	-60.0	0.0	77 00.0	-60.0	0.0	78 00.0	-60.0	0.0	79 00.0	-60.0	0.0	80 00.0	-60.0	0.0	81 00.0	-60.0	0.0	82 00.0	-60.0	0.0	30
31	74 00.0	-60.0	0.0	75 00.0	-60.0	0.0	76 00.0	-60.0	0.0	77 00.0	-60.0	0.0	78 00.0	-60.0	0.0	79 00.0	-60.0	0.0	80 00.0	-60.0	0.0	81 00.0	-60.0	0.0	31
32	73 00.0	-60.0	0.0	74 00.0	-60.0	0.0	75 00.0	-60.0	0.0	76 00.0	-60.0	0.0	77 00.0	-60.0	0.0	78 00.0	-60.0	0.0	79 00.0	-60.0	0.0	80 00.0	-60.0	0.0	32
33	72 00.0	-60.0	0.0	73 00.0	-60.0	0.0	74 00.0	-60.0	0.0	75 00.0	-60.0	0.0	76 00.0	-60.0	0.0	77 00.0	-60.0	0.0	78 00.0	-60.0	0.0	79 00.0	-60.0	0.0	33
34	71 00.0	-60.0	0.0	72 00.0	-60.0	0.0	73 00.0	-60.0	0.0	74 00.0	-60.0	0.0	75 00.0	-60.0	0.0	76 00.0	-60.0	0.0	77 00.0	-60.0	0.0	78 00.0	-60.0	0.0	34
35	70 00.0	-60.0	0.0	71 00.0	-60.0	0.0	72 00.0	-60.0	0.0	73 00.0	-60.0	0.0	74 00.0	-60.0	0.0	75 00.0	-60.0	0.0	76 00.0	-60.0	0.0	77 00.0	-60.0	0.0	35
36	69 00.0	-60.0	0.0	70 00.0	-60.0	0.0	71 00.0	-60.0	0.0	72 00.0	-60.0	0.0	73 00.0	-60.0	0.0	74 00.0	-60.0	0.0	75 00.0	-60.0	0.0	76 00.0	-60.0	0.0	36
37	68 00.0	-60.0	0.0	69 00.0	-60.0	0.0	70 00.0	-60.0	0.0	71 00.0	-60.0	0.0	72 00.0	-60.0	0.0	73 00.0	-60.0	0.0	74 00.0	-60.0	0.0	75 00.0	-60.0	0.0	37
38	67 00.0	-60.0	0.0	68 00.0	-60.0	0.0	69 00.0	-60.0	0.0	70 00.0	-60.0	0.0	71 00.0	-60.0	0.0	72 00.0	-60.0	0.0	73 00.0	-60.0	0.0	74 00.0	-60.0	0.0	38
39	66 00.0	-60.0	0.0	67 00.0	-60.0	0.0	68 00.0	-60.0	0.0	69 00.0	-60.0	0.0	70 00.0	-60.0	0.0	71 00.0	-60.0	0.0	72 00.0	-60.0	0.0	73 00.0	-60.0	0.0	39
40	65 00.0	-60.0	0.0	66 00.0	-60.0	0.0	67 00.0	-60.0	0.0	68 00.0	-60.0	0.0	69 00.0	-60.0	0.0	70 00.0	-60.0	0.0	71 00.0	-60.0	0.0	72 00.0	-60.0	0.0	40
41	64 00.0	-60.0	0.0	65 00.0	-60.0	0.0	66 00.0	-60.0	0.0	67 00.0	-60.0	0.0	68 00.0	-60.0	0.0	69 00.0	-60.0	0.0	70 00.0	-60.0	0.0	71 00.0	-60.0	0.0	41
42	63 00.0	-60.0	0.0	64 00.0	-60.0	0.0	65 00.0	-60.0	0.0	66 00.0	-60.0	0.0	67 00.0	-60.0	0.0	68 00.0	-60.0	0.0	69 00.0	-60.0	0.0	70 00.0	-60.0	0.0	42
43	62 00.0	-60.0	0.0	63 00.0	-60.0	0.0	64 00.0	-60.0	0.0	65 00.0	-60.0	0.0	66 00.0	-60.0	0.0	67 00.0	-60.0	0.0	68 00.0	-60.0	0.0	69 00.0	-60.0	0.0	43
44	61 00.0	-60.0	0.0	62 00.0	-60.0	0.0	63 00.0	-60.0	0.0	64 00.0	-60.0	0.0	65 00.0	-60.0	0.0	66 00.0	-60.0	0.0	67 00.0	-60.0	0.0	68 00.0	-60.0	0.0	44
45	60 00.0	-60.0	0.0	61 00.0	-60.0	0.0	62 00.0	-60.0	0.0	63 00.0	-60.0	0.0	64 00.0	-60.0	0.0	65 00.0	-60.0	0.0	66 00.0	-60.0	0.0	67 00.0	-60.0	0.0	45
46	59 00.0	-60.0	0.0	60 00.0	-60.0	0.0	61 00.0	-60.0	0.0	62 00.0	-60.0	0.0	63 00.0	-60.0	0.0	64 00.0	-60.0	0.0	65 00.0	-60.0	0.0	66 00.0	-60.0	0.0	46
47	58 00.0	-60.0	0.0	59 00.0	-60.0	0.0	60 00.0	-60.0	0.0	61 00.0	-60.0	0.0	62 00.0	-60.0	0.0	63 00.0	-60.0	0.0	64 00.0	-60.0	0.0	65 00.0	-60.0	0.0	47
48	57 00.0	-60.0	0.0	58 00.0	-60.0	0.0	59 00.0	-60.0	0.0	60 00.0	-60.0	0.0	61 00.0	-60.0	0.0	62 00.0	-60.0	0.0	63 00.0	-60.0	0.0	64 00.0	-60.0	0.0	48
49	56 00.0	-60.0	0.0	57 00.0	-60.0	0.0	58 00.0	-60.0	0.0	59 00.0	-60.0	0.0	60 00.0	-60.0	0.0	61 00.0	-60.0	0.0	62 00.0	-60.0	0.0	63 00.0	-60.0	0.0	49
50	55 00.0	-60.0	0.0	56 00.0	-60.0	0.0	57 00.0	-60.0	0.0	58 00.0	-60.0	0.0	59 00.0	-60.0	0.0	60 00.0	-60.0	0.0	61 00.0	-60.0	0.0	62 00.0	-60.0	0.0	50
51	54 00.0	-60.0	0.0	55 00.0	-60.0	0.0	56 00.0	-60.0	0.0	57 00.0	-60.0	0.0	58 00.0	-60.0	0.0	59 00.0	-60.0	0.0	60 00.0	-60.0	0.0	61 00.0	-60.0	0.0	51
52	53 00.0	-60.0	0.0	54 00.0	-60.0	0.0	55 00.0	-60.0	0.0	56 00.0	-60.0	0.0	57 00.0	-60.0	0.0	58 00.0	-60.0	0.0	59 00.0	-60.0	0.0	60 00.0	-60.0	0.0	52
53	52 00.0	-60.0	0.0	53 00.0	-60.0	0.0	54 00.0	-60.0	0.0	55 00.0	-60.0	0.0	56 00.0	-60.0	0.0	57 00.0	-60.0	0.0	58 00.0	-60.0	0.0	59 00.0	-60.0	0.0	53
54	51 00.0	-60.0	0.0	52 00.0	-60.0	0.0	53 00.0	-60.0	0.0	54 00.0	-60.0	0.0	55 00.0	-60.0	0.0	56 00.0	-60.0	0.0	57 00.0	-60.0	0.0	58 00.0	-60.0	0.0	54
55	50 00.0	-60.0	0.0	51 00.0	-60.0	0.0	52 00.0	-60.0	0.0	53 00.0	-60.0	0.0	54 00.0	-60.0	0.0	55 00.0	-60.0	0.0	56 00.0	-60.0	0.0	57 00.0	-60.0	0.0	55
56	49 00.0	-60.0	0.0	50 00.0	-60.0	0.0	51 00.0	-60.0	0.0	52 00.0	-60.0	0.0	53 00.0	-60.0	0.0	54 00.0	-60.0	0.0	55 00.0	-60.0	0.0	56 00.0	-60.0	0.0	56
57	48 00.0	-60.0	0.0	49 00.0	-60.0	0.0	50 00.0	-60.0	0.0	51 00.0	-60.0	0.0	52 00.0	-60.0	0.0	53 00.0	-60.0	0.0	54 00.0	-60.0	0.0	55 00.0	-60.0	0.0	57
58	47 00.0	-60.0	0.0	48 00.0	-60.0	0.0	49 00.0	-60.0	0.0	50 00.0	-60.0	0.0	51 00.0	-60.0	0.0	52 00.0	-60.0	0.0	53 00.0	-60.0	0.0	54 00.0	-60.0	0.0	58
59	46 00.0	-60.0	0.0	47 00.0	-60.0	0.0	48 00.0	-60.0	0.0	49 00.0	-60.0	0.0	50 00.0	-60.0	0.0	51 00.0	-60.0	0.0	52 00.0	-60.0	0.0	53 00.0	-60.0	0.0	59
60	45 00.0	-60.0	0.0	46 00.0	-60.0	0.0	47 00.0	-60.0	0.0	48 00.0	-60.0	0.0	49 00.0	-60.0	0.0	50 00.0	-60.0	0.0	51 00.0	-60.0	0.0	52 00.0	-60.0	0.0	60
61	44 00.0	-60.0	0.0	45 00.0	-60.0	0.0	46 00.0	-60.0	0.0	47 00.0	-60.0	0.0	48 00.0	-60.0	0.0	49 00.0	-60.0	0.0	50 00.0	-60.0	0.0	51 00.0	-60.0	0.0	61
62	43 00.0	-60.0	0.0	44 00.0	-60.0	0.0	45 00.0	-60.0	0.0	46 00.0	-60.0	0.0	47 00.0	-60.0	0.0	48 00.0	-60.0	0.0	49 00.0	-60.0	0.0	50 00.0	-60.0	0.0	62
63	42 00.0	-60.0	0.0	43 00.0	-60.0	0.0	44 00.0	-60.0	0.0	45 00.0	-60.0	0.0	46 00.0	-60.0	0.0	47 00.0	-60.0	0.0	48 00.0	-60.0	0.0	49 00.0	-60.0	0.0	63
64	41 00.0	-60.0	0.0	42 00.0	-60.0	0.0	43 00.0	-60.0	0.0	44 00.0	-60.0	0.0	45 00.0	-60.0	0.0	46 00.0	-60.0	0.0	47 00.0	-60.0	0.0	48 00.0	-60.0	0.0	64
65	40 00.0	-60.0	0.0	41 00.0	-60.0	0.0	42 00.0	-60.0	0.0	43 00.0	-60.0	0.0	44 00.0	-60.0	0.0	45 00.0	-60.0	0.0	46 00.0	-60.0	0.0	47 00.0	-60.0	0.0	65
66	39 00.0	-60.0	0.0	40 00.0	-60.0	0.0	41 00.0	-60.0	0.0	42 00.0	-60.0	0.0	43 00.0	-60.0	0.0	44 00.0	-60.0	0.0	45 00.0	-60.0	0.0	46 00.0	-60.0	0.0	66
67	38 00.0	-60.0	0.0	39 00.0	-60.0	0.0	40 00.0	-60.0	0.0	41 00.0	-60.0	0.0	42 00.0	-60.0	0.0	43 00.0	-60.0	0.0	44 00.0	-60.0	0.0	45 00.0	-60.0	0.0	67
68	37 00.0	-60.0	0.0	38 00.0	-60.0	0.0	39 00.0	-60.0	0.0	40 00.0	-60.0	0.0	41 00.0	-60.0	0.0	42 00.0	-60.0	0.0	43 00.0	-60.0	0.0	44 00.0	-60.0	0.0	68
69	36 00.0	-60.0	0.0	37 00.0	-60.0	0.0	38 00.0	-60.0	0.0	39 00.0	-60.0	0.0	40 00.0	-60.0	0.0	41 00.0	-60.0	0.0	42 00.0	-60.0	0.0	43 00.0	-60.0	0.0	69
70	35 00.0	-60.0	0.0	36 00.0	-60.0	0.0	37 00.0	-60.0	0.0	38 00.0	-60.0	0.0	39 00.0	-60.0	0.0	40 00.0	-60.0	0.0	41 00.0	-60.0	0.0	42 00.0	-60.0	0.0	70
71	34 00.0	-60.0	0.0	35 00.0	-60.0	0.0	36 00.0	-60.0	0.0	37 00.0	-60.0	0.0	38 00.0	-60.0	0.0	39 00.0	-60.0	0.0	40 00.0	-60.0	0.0	41 00.0	-60.0	0.0	71
72	33 00.0	-60.0	0.0	34 00.0	-60.0	0.0	35 00.0	-60.0	0.0	36 00.0	-60.0	0.0	37 00.0	-60.0	0.0	38 00.0	-60.0	0.0	39 00.0	-60.0	0.0	40 00.0	-60.0	0.0	72
73	32 00.0	-60.0	0.0	33 00.0	-60.0	0.0	34 00.0	-60.0	0.0	35 00.0	-60.0	0.0	36 00.0	-60.0	0.0	37 00.0	-60.0	0.0	38 00.0	-60.0	0.0	39 00.0	-60.0	0.0	73
74	31 00.0	-60.0	0.0	32 00.0	-60.0	0.0	33 00.0	-60.0	0.0	34 00.0	-60.0	0.0	35 00.0	-60.0	0.0	36 00.0	-60.0	0.0	37 00.0	-60.0	0.0	38 00.0	-60.0	0.0	74
75	30 00.0	-60.0	0.0	31 00.0	-60.0	0.0	32 00.0	-60.0	0.0	33 00.0	-60.0	0.0	34 00.0	-60.0	0.0	35 00.0	-60.0	0.0	36 00.0	-60.0	0.0	37 00.0	-60.0	0.0	75
76	29 00.0	-60.0	0.0	30 00.0	-60.0	0.0	31 00.0	-60.0	0.0	32 00.0	-60.0	0.0	33 00.0	-60.0	0.0	34 00.0	-60.0	0.0	35 00.0	-60.0	0.0	36 00.0	-60.0	0.0	76
77	28 00.0	-60.0	0.0	29 00.0	-60.0	0.0	30 00.0	-60.0	0.0	31 00.0	-60.0	0.0	32 00.0	-60.0	0.0	33 00.0	-60.0	0.0	34 00.0	-60.0	0.0	35 00.0	-60.0	0.0	77
78	27 00.0	-60.0	0.0	28 00.0	-60.0	0.0	29 00.0	-60.0	0.0	30 00.0	-60.0	0.0	31 00.0	-60.0	0.0	32 00.0	-60.0	0.0	33 00.0	-60.0	0.0	34 00.0	-60.0	0.0	78
79	26 00.0	-60.0	0.0	27 00.0	-60.0	0.0	28 00.0	-60.0	0.0	29 00.0	-60.0	0.0	30 00.0	-60.0	0.0	31 00.0	-60.0	0.0	32 00.0	-60.0	0.0	33 00.0	-60.0	0.0	79
80	25 00.0	-60.0	0.0	26 00.0	-60.0	0.0	27 00.0	-60.0	0.0	28 00.0	-60.0	0.0	29 00.0	-60.0	0.0	30 00.0	-60.0	0.0	31 00.0	-60.0	0.0	32 00.0	-60.0	0.0	80
81	24 00.0	-60.0	0.0	25 00.0	-60.0	0.0	26 00.0	-60.0	0.0	27 00.0	-60.0	0.0	28 00.0	-60.0	0.0	29 00.0	-60.0	0.0	30 00.0	-60.0	0.0	31 00.0	-60.0	0.0	81
82	23 00.0	-60.0	0.0	24 00.0	-60.0	0.0	25 00.0	-60.0	0.0	26 00.0	-60.0	0.0	27 00.0	-60.0	0.0	28 00.0	-60.0	0.0	29 00.0	-60.0	0.0	30 00.0	-60.0	0.0	82
83	22 00.0	-60.0	0.0	23 00.0	-60.0	0.0	24 00.0	-60.0	0.0	25 00.0	-60.0	0.0	26 00.0	-60.0	0.0	27 00.0	-60.0	0.0	28 00.0	-60.0	0.0	29 00.0	-60.0	0.0	83
84	21 00.0	-60.0	0.0	22 00.0	-60.0	0.0	23 00.0	-60.0	0.0	24 00.0	-60.0	0.0	25 00.0	-60.0	0.0	26 00.0	-60.0	0.0	27 00.0	-60.0	0.0	28 00.0	-60.0	0.0	84
85	20 00.0	-60.0	0.0	21 00.0	-60.0	0.0	22 00.0	-60.0	0.0	23 00.0	-60.0	0.0	24 00.0	-60.0	0.0	25 00.0	-60.0	0.0	26 00.0	-60.0	0.0	27 00.0	-60.0	0.0	85
86	19 00.0	-60.0	0.0	20 00.0	-60.0	0.0	21 00.0	-60.0	0.0	22 00.0	-60.0	0.0	23 00.0	-60.0	0.0	24 00.0	-60.0	0.0	25 00.0	-60.0	0.0	26 00.0	-60.0	0.0	86
87	18 00.0	-60.0	0.0	19 00.0	-60.0	0.0	20 00.0	-60.0	0.0	21 00.0	-60.0	0.0	22 00.0	-60.0	0.0	23 00.0	-60.0	0.0	24 00.0	-60.0	0.0	25 00.0	-60.0	0.0	87
88	17 00.0	-60.0	0.0	18 00.0	-60.0	0.0	19 00.0	-60.0	0.0	20 00.0	-60.0	0.0	21 00.0	-60.0	0.0	22 00.0	-60.0	0.0	23 00.0	-60.0	0.0	24 00.0	-60.0	0.0	88
89	16 00.0	-60.0	0.0	17 00.0	-60.0	0.0	18 00.0	-60.0	0.0	19 00.0	-60.0	0.0	20 00.0	-60.0	0.0	21 00.0	-60.0	0.0	22 00.0	-60.0	0.0	23 00.0	-60.0	0.0	89
90	15 00.0	-60.0	0.0	16 00.0	-60.0	0.0	17 00.0	-60.0	0.0	18 00.0	-60.0	0.0	19 00.0	-60.0	0.0	20 00.0	-60.0	0.0	21 00.0	-60.0	0.0	22 00.0	-60.0	0.0	90
	15°			16°			17°			18°			19°			20°			21°			22°			

0°, 360° L.H.A. LATITUDE SAME NAME AS DECLINATION

LATITUDE **CONTRARY** NAME TO DECLINATION **L.H.A. 0°, 360°**

Dec.	15° Hc	d	Z	16° Hc	d	Z	17° Hc	d	Z	18° Hc	d	Z	19° Hc	d	Z	20° Hc	d	Z	21° Hc	d	Z	22° Hc	d	Z	Dec.
°	° ′	′	°	° ′	′	°	° ′	′	°	° ′	′	°	° ′	′	°	° ′	′	°	° ′	′	°	° ′	′	°	°
0	75 00.0	-60.0	180.0	74 00.0	-60.0	180.0	73 00.0	-60.0	180.0	72 00.0	-60.0	180.0	71 00.0	-60.0	180.0	70 00.0	-60.0	180.0	69 00.0	-60.0	180.0	68 00.0	-60.0	180.0	0
1	74 00.0	-60.0	180.0	73 00.0	-60.0	180.0	72 00.0	-60.0	180.0	71 00.0	-60.0	180.0	70 00.0	-60.0	180.0	69 00.0	-60.0	180.0	68 00.0	-60.0	180.0	67 00.0	-60.0	180.0	1
2	73 00.0	-60.0	180.0	72 00.0	-60.0	180.0	71 00.0	-60.0	180.0	70 00.0	-60.0	180.0	69 00.0	-60.0	180.0	68 00.0	-60.0	180.0	67 00.0	-60.0	180.0	66 00.0	-60.0	180.0	2
3	72 00.0	-60.0	180.0	71 00.0	-60.0	180.0	70 00.0	-60.0	180.0	69 00.0	-60.0	180.0	68 00.0	-60.0	180.0	67 00.0	-60.0	180.0	66 00.0	-60.0	180.0	65 00.0	-60.0	180.0	3
4	71 00.0	-60.0	180.0	70 00.0	-60.0	180.0	69 00.0	-60.0	180.0	68 00.0	-60.0	180.0	67 00.0	-60.0	180.0	66 00.0	-60.0	180.0	65 00.0	-60.0	180.0	64 00.0	-60.0	180.0	4
5	70 00.0	-60.0	180.0	69 00.0	-60.0	180.0	68 00.0	-60.0	180.0	67 00.0	-60.0	180.0	66 00.0	-60.0	180.0	65 00.0	-60.0	180.0	64 00.0	-60.0	180.0	63 00.0	-60.0	180.0	5
6	69 00.0	-60.0	180.0	68 00.0	-60.0	180.0	67 00.0	-60.0	180.0	66 00.0	-60.0	180.0	65 00.0	-60.0	180.0	64 00.0	-60.0	180.0	63 00.0	-60.0	180.0	62 00.0	-60.0	180.0	6
7	68 00.0	-60.0	180.0	67 00.0	-60.0	180.0	66 00.0	-60.0	180.0	65 00.0	-60.0	180.0	64 00.0	-60.0	180.0	63 00.0	-60.0	180.0	62 00.0	-60.0	180.0	61 00.0	-60.0	180.0	7
8	67 00.0	-60.0	180.0	66 00.0	-60.0	180.0	65 00.0	-60.0	180.0	64 00.0	-60.0	180.0	63 00.0	-60.0	180.0	62 00.0	-60.0	180.0	61 00.0	-60.0	180.0	60 00.0	-60.0	180.0	8
9	66 00.0	-60.0	180.0	65 00.0	-60.0	180.0	64 00.0	-60.0	180.0	63 00.0	-60.0	180.0	62 00.0	-60.0	180.0	61 00.0	-60.0	180.0	60 00.0	-60.0	180.0	59 00.0	-60.0	180.0	9
10	65 00.0	-60.0	180.0	64 00.0	-60.0	180.0	63 00.0	-60.0	180.0	62 00.0	-60.0	180.0	61 00.0	-60.0	180.0	60 00.0	-60.0	180.0	59 00.0	-60.0	180.0	58 00.0	-60.0	180.0	10
11	64 00.0	-60.0	180.0	63 00.0	-60.0	180.0	62 00.0	-60.0	180.0	61 00.0	-60.0	180.0	60 00.0	-60.0	180.0	59 00.0	-60.0	180.0	58 00.0	-60.0	180.0	57 00.0	-60.0	180.0	11
12	63 00.0	-60.0	180.0	62 00.0	-60.0	180.0	61 00.0	-60.0	180.0	60 00.0	-60.0	180.0	59 00.0	-60.0	180.0	58 00.0	-60.0	180.0	57 00.0	-60.0	180.0	56 00.0	-60.0	180.0	12
13	62 00.0	-60.0	180.0	61 00.0	-60.0	180.0	60 00.0	-60.0	180.0	59 00.0	-60.0	180.0	58 00.0	-60.0	180.0	57 00.0	-60.0	180.0	56 00.0	-60.0	180.0	55 00.0	-60.0	180.0	13
14	61 00.0	-60.0	180.0	60 00.0	-60.0	180.0	59 00.0	-60.0	180.0	58 00.0	-60.0	180.0	57 00.0	-60.0	180.0	56 00.0	-60.0	180.0	55 00.0	-60.0	180.0	54 00.0	-60.0	180.0	14
15	60 00.0	-60.0	180.0	59 00.0	-60.0	180.0	58 00.0	-60.0	180.0	57 00.0	-60.0	180.0	56 00.0	-60.0	180.0	55 00.0	-60.0	180.0	54 00.0	-60.0	180.0	53 00.0	-60.0	180.0	15
16	59 00.0	-60.0	180.0	58 00.0	-60.0	180.0	57 00.0	-60.0	180.0	56 00.0	-60.0	180.0	55 00.0	-60.0	180.0	54 00.0	-60.0	180.0	53 00.0	-60.0	180.0	52 00.0	-60.0	180.0	16
17	58 00.0	-60.0	180.0	57 00.0	-60.0	180.0	56 00.0	-60.0	180.0	55 00.0	-60.0	180.0	54 00.0	-60.0	180.0	53 00.0	-60.0	180.0	52 00.0	-60.0	180.0	51 00.0	-60.0	180.0	17
18	57 00.0	-60.0	180.0	56 00.0	-60.0	180.0	55 00.0	-60.0	180.0	54 00.0	-60.0	180.0	53 00.0	-60.0	180.0	52 00.0	-60.0	180.0	51 00.0	-60.0	180.0	50 00.0	-60.0	180.0	18
19	56 00.0	-60.0	180.0	55 00.0	-60.0	180.0	54 00.0	-60.0	180.0	53 00.0	-60.0	180.0	52 00.0	-60.0	180.0	51 00.0	-60.0	180.0	50 00.0	-60.0	180.0	49 00.0	-60.0	180.0	19
20	55 00.0	-60.0	180.0	54 00.0	-60.0	180.0	53 00.0	-60.0	180.0	52 00.0	-60.0	180.0	51 00.0	-60.0	180.0	50 00.0	-60.0	180.0	49 00.0	-60.0	180.0	48 00.0	-60.0	180.0	20
21	54 00.0	-60.0	180.0	53 00.0	-60.0	180.0	52 00.0	-60.0	180.0	51 00.0	-60.0	180.0	50 00.0	-60.0	180.0	49 00.0	-60.0	180.0	48 00.0	-60.0	180.0	47 00.0	-60.0	180.0	21
22	53 00.0	-60.0	180.0	52 00.0	-60.0	180.0	51 00.0	-60.0	180.0	50 00.0	-60.0	180.0	49 00.0	-60.0	180.0	48 00.0	-60.0	180.0	47 00.0	-60.0	180.0	46 00.0	-60.0	180.0	22
23	52 00.0	-60.0	180.0	51 00.0	-60.0	180.0	50 00.0	-60.0	180.0	49 00.0	-60.0	180.0	48 00.0	-60.0	180.0	47 00.0	-60.0	180.0	46 00.0	-60.0	180.0	45 00.0	-60.0	180.0	23
24	51 00.0	-60.0	180.0	50 00.0	-60.0	180.0	49 00.0	-60.0	180.0	48 00.0	-60.0	180.0	47 00.0	-60.0	180.0	46 00.0	-60.0	180.0	45 00.0	-60.0	180.0	44 00.0	-60.0	180.0	24
25	50 00.0	-60.0	180.0	49 00.0	-60.0	180.0	48 00.0	-60.0	180.0	47 00.0	-60.0	180.0	46 00.0	-60.0	180.0	45 00.0	-60.0	180.0	44 00.0	-60.0	180.0	43 00.0	-60.0	180.0	25
26	49 00.0	-60.0	180.0	48 00.0	-60.0	180.0	47 00.0	-60.0	180.0	46 00.0	-60.0	180.0	45 00.0	-60.0	180.0	44 00.0	-60.0	180.0	43 00.0	-60.0	180.0	42 00.0	-60.0	180.0	26
27	48 00.0	-60.0	180.0	47 00.0	-60.0	180.0	46 00.0	-60.0	180.0	45 00.0	-60.0	180.0	44 00.0	-60.0	180.0	43 00.0	-60.0	180.0	42 00.0	-60.0	180.0	41 00.0	-60.0	180.0	27
28	47 00.0	-60.0	180.0	46 00.0	-60.0	180.0	45 00.0	-60.0	180.0	44 00.0	-60.0	180.0	43 00.0	-60.0	180.0	42 00.0	-60.0	180.0	41 00.0	-60.0	180.0	40 00.0	-60.0	180.0	28
29	46 00.0	-60.0	180.0	45 00.0	-60.0	180.0	44 00.0	-60.0	180.0	43 00.0	-60.0	180.0	42 00.0	-60.0	180.0	41 00.0	-60.0	180.0	40 00.0	-60.0	180.0	39 00.0	-60.0	180.0	29
30	45 00.0	-60.0	180.0	44 00.0	-60.0	180.0	43 00.0	-60.0	180.0	42 00.0	-60.0	180.0	41 00.0	-60.0	180.0	40 00.0	-60.0	180.0	39 00.0	-60.0	180.0	38 00.0	-60.0	180.0	30
31	44 00.0	-60.0	180.0	43 00.0	-60.0	180.0	42 00.0	-60.0	180.0	41 00.0	-60.0	180.0	40 00.0	-60.0	180.0	39 00.0	-60.0	180.0	38 00.0	-60.0	180.0	37 00.0	-60.0	180.0	31
32	43 00.0	-60.0	180.0	42 00.0	-60.0	180.0	41 00.0	-60.0	180.0	40 00.0	-60.0	180.0	39 00.0	-60.0	180.0	38 00.0	-60.0	180.0	37 00.0	-60.0	180.0	36 00.0	-60.0	180.0	32
33	42 00.0	-60.0	180.0	41 00.0	-60.0	180.0	40 00.0	-60.0	180.0	39 00.0	-60.0	180.0	38 00.0	-60.0	180.0	37 00.0	-60.0	180.0	36 00.0	-60.0	180.0	35 00.0	-60.0	180.0	33
34	41 00.0	-60.0	180.0	40 00.0	-60.0	180.0	39 00.0	-60.0	180.0	38 00.0	-60.0	180.0	37 00.0	-60.0	180.0	36 00.0	-60.0	180.0	35 00.0	-60.0	180.0	34 00.0	-60.0	180.0	34
35	40 00.0	-60.0	180.0	39 00.0	-60.0	180.0	38 00.0	-60.0	180.0	37 00.0	-60.0	180.0	36 00.0	-60.0	180.0	35 00.0	-60.0	180.0	34 00.0	-60.0	180.0	33 00.0	-60.0	180.0	35
36	39 00.0	-60.0	180.0	38 00.0	-60.0	180.0	37 00.0	-60.0	180.0	36 00.0	-60.0	180.0	35 00.0	-60.0	180.0	34 00.0	-60.0	180.0	33 00.0	-60.0	180.0	32 00.0	-60.0	180.0	36
37	38 00.0	-60.0	180.0	37 00.0	-60.0	180.0	36 00.0	-60.0	180.0	35 00.0	-60.0	180.0	34 00.0	-60.0	180.0	33 00.0	-60.0	180.0	32 00.0	-60.0	180.0	31 00.0	-60.0	180.0	37
38	37 00.0	-60.0	180.0	36 00.0	-60.0	180.0	35 00.0	-60.0	180.0	34 00.0	-60.0	180.0	33 00.0	-60.0	180.0	32 00.0	-60.0	180.0	31 00.0	-60.0	180.0	30 00.0	-60.0	180.0	38
39	36 00.0	-60.0	180.0	35 00.0	-60.0	180.0	34 00.0	-60.0	180.0	33 00.0	-60.0	180.0	32 00.0	-60.0	180.0	31 00.0	-60.0	180.0	30 00.0	-60.0	180.0	29 00.0	-60.0	180.0	39
40	35 00.0	-60.0	180.0	34 00.0	-60.0	180.0	33 00.0	-60.0	180.0	32 00.0	-60.0	180.0	31 00.0	-60.0	180.0	30 00.0	-60.0	180.0	29 00.0	-60.0	180.0	28 00.0	-60.0	180.0	40
41	34 00.0	-60.0	180.0	33 00.0	-60.0	180.0	32 00.0	-60.0	180.0	31 00.0	-60.0	180.0	30 00.0	-60.0	180.0	29 00.0	-60.0	180.0	28 00.0	-60.0	180.0	27 00.0	-60.0	180.0	41
42	33 00.0	-60.0	180.0	32 00.0	-60.0	180.0	31 00.0	-60.0	180.0	30 00.0	-60.0	180.0	29 00.0	-60.0	180.0	28 00.0	-60.0	180.0	27 00.0	-60.0	180.0	26 00.0	-60.0	180.0	42
43	32 00.0	-60.0	180.0	31 00.0	-60.0	180.0	30 00.0	-60.0	180.0	29 00.0	-60.0	180.0	28 00.0	-60.0	180.0	27 00.0	-60.0	180.0	26 00.0	-60.0	180.0	25 00.0	-60.0	180.0	43
44	31 00.0	-60.0	180.0	30 00.0	-60.0	180.0	29 00.0	-60.0	180.0	28 00.0	-60.0	180.0	27 00.0	-60.0	180.0	26 00.0	-60.0	180.0	25 00.0	-60.0	180.0	24 00.0	-60.0	180.0	44
45	30 00.0	-60.0	180.0	29 00.0	-60.0	180.0	28 00.0	-60.0	180.0	27 00.0	-60.0	180.0	26 00.0	-60.0	180.0	25 00.0	-60.0	180.0	24 00.0	-60.0	180.0	23 00.0	-60.0	180.0	45
46	29 00.0	-60.0	180.0	28 00.0	-60.0	180.0	27 00.0	-60.0	180.0	26 00.0	-60.0	180.0	25 00.0	-60.0	180.0	24 00.0	-60.0	180.0	23 00.0	-60.0	180.0	22 00.0	-60.0	180.0	46
47	28 00.0	-60.0	180.0	27 00.0	-60.0	180.0	26 00.0	-60.0	180.0	25 00.0	-60.0	180.0	24 00.0	-60.0	180.0	23 00.0	-60.0	180.0	22 00.0	-60.0	180.0	21 00.0	-60.0	180.0	47
48	27 00.0	-60.0	180.0	26 00.0	-60.0	180.0	25 00.0	-60.0	180.0	24 00.0	-60.0	180.0	23 00.0	-60.0	180.0	22 00.0	-60.0	180.0	21 00.0	-60.0	180.0	20 00.0	-60.0	180.0	48
49	26 00.0	-60.0	180.0	25 00.0	-60.0	180.0	24 00.0	-60.0	180.0	23 00.0	-60.0	180.0	22 00.0	-60.0	180.0	21 00.0	-60.0	180.0	20 00.0	-60.0	180.0	19 00.0	-60.0	180.0	49
50	25 00.0	-60.0	180.0	24 00.0	-60.0	180.0	23 00.0	-60.0	180.0	22 00.0	-60.0	180.0	21 00.0	-60.0	180.0	20 00.0	-60.0	180.0	19 00.0	-60.0	180.0	18 00.0	-60.0	180.0	50
51	24 00.0	-60.0	180.0	23 00.0	-60.0	180.0	22 00.0	-60.0	180.0	21 00.0	-60.0	180.0	20 00.0	-60.0	180.0	19 00.0	-60.0	180.0	18 00.0	-60.0	180.0	17 00.0	-60.0	180.0	51
52	23 00.0	-60.0	180.0	22 00.0	-60.0	180.0	21 00.0	-60.0	180.0	20 00.0	-60.0	180.0	19 00.0	-60.0	180.0	18 00.0	-60.0	180.0	17 00.0	-60.0	180.0	16 00.0	-60.0	180.0	52
53	22 00.0	-60.0	180.0	21 00.0	-60.0	180.0	20 00.0	-60.0	180.0	19 00.0	-60.0	180.0	18 00.0	-60.0	180.0	17 00.0	-60.0	180.0	16 00.0	-60.0	180.0	15 00.0	-60.0	180.0	53
54	21 00.0	-60.0	180.0	20 00.0	-60.0	180.0	19 00.0	-60.0	180.0	18 00.0	-60.0	180.0	17 00.0	-60.0	180.0	16 00.0	-60.0	180.0	15 00.0	-60.0	180.0	14 00.0	-60.0	180.0	54
55	20 00.0	-60.0	180.0	19 00.0	-60.0	180.0	18 00.0	-60.0	180.0	17 00.0	-60.0	180.0	16 00.0	-60.0	180.0	15 00.0	-60.0	180.0	14 00.0	-60.0	180.0	13 00.0	-60.0	180.0	55
56	19 00.0	-60.0	180.0	18 00.0	-60.0	180.0	17 00.0	-60.0	180.0	16 00.0	-60.0	180.0	15 00.0	-60.0	180.0	14 00.0	-60.0	180.0	13 00.0	-60.0	180.0	12 00.0	-60.0	180.0	56
57	18 00.0	-60.0	180.0	17 00.0	-60.0	180.0	16 00.0	-60.0	180.0	15 00.0	-60.0	180.0	14 00.0	-60.0	180.0	13 00.0	-60.0	180.0	12 00.0	-60.0	180.0	11 00.0	-60.0	180.0	57
58	17 00.0	-60.0	180.0	16 00.0	-60.0	180.0	15 00.0	-60.0	180.0	14 00.0	-60.0	180.0	13 00.0	-60.0	180.0	12 00.0	-60.0	180.0	11 00.0	-60.0	180.0	10 00.0	-60.0	180.0	58
59	16 00.0	-60.0	180.0	15 00.0	-60.0	180.0	14 00.0	-60.0	180.0	13 00.0	-60.0	180.0	12 00.0	-60.0	180.0	11 00.0	-60.0	180.0	10 00.0	-60.0	180.0	9 00.0	-60.0	180.0	59
60	15 00.0	-60.0	180.0	14 00.0	-60.0	180.0	13 00.0	-60.0	180.0	12 00.0	-60.0	180.0	11 00.0	-60.0	180.0	10 00.0	-60.0	180.0	9 00.0	-60.0	180.0	8 00.0	-60.0	180.0	60
61	14 00.0	-60.0	180.0	13 00.0	-60.0	180.0	12 00.0	-60.0	180.0	11 00.0	-60.0	180.0	10 00.0	-60.0	180.0	9 00.0	-60.0	180.0	8 00.0	-60.0	180.0	7 00.0	-60.0	180.0	61
62	13 00.0	-60.0	180.0	12 00.0	-60.0	180.0	11 00.0	-60.0	180.0	10 00.0	-60.0	180.0	9 00.0	-60.0	180.0	8 00.0	-60.0	180.0	7 00.0	-60.0	180.0	6 00.0	-60.0	180.0	62
63	12 00.0	-60.0	180.0	11 00.0	-60.0	180.0	10 00.0	-60.0	180.0	9 00.0	-60.0	180.0	8 00.0	-60.0	180.0	7 00.0	-60.0	180.0	6 00.0	-60.0	180.0	5 00.0	-60.0	180.0	63
64	11 00.0	-60.0	180.0	10 00.0	-60.0	180.0	9 00.0	-60.0	180.0	8 00.0	-60.0	180.0	7 00.0	-60.0	180.0	6 00.0	-60.0	180.0	5 00.0	-60.0	180.0	4 00.0	-60.0	180.0	64
65	10 00.0	-60.0	180.0	9 00.0	-60.0	180.0	8 00.0	-60.0	180.0	7 00.0	-60.0	180.0	6 00.0	-60.0	180.0	5 00.0	-60.0	180.0	4 00.0	-60.0	180.0	3 00.0	-60.0	180.0	65
66	9 00.0	-60.0	180.0	8 00.0	-60.0	180.0	7 00.0	-60.0	180.0	6 00.0	-60.0	180.0	5 00.0	-60.0	180.0	4 00.0	-60.0	180.0	3 00.0	-60.0	180.0	2 00.0	-60.0	180.0	66
67	8 00.0	-60.0	180.0	7 00.0	-60.0	180.0	6 00.0	-60.0	180.0	5 00.0	-60.0	180.0	4 00.0	-60.0	180.0	3 00.0	-60.0	180.0	2 00.0	-60.0	180.0	1 00.0	-60.0	180.0	67
68	7 00.0	-60.0	180.0	6 00.0	-60.0	180.0	5 00.0	-60.0	180.0	4 00.0	-60.0	180.0	3 00.0	-60.0	180.0	2 00.0	-60.0	180.0	1 00.0	-60.0	180.0	0 00.0	+60.0	0.0	68
69	6 00.0	-60.0	180.0	5 00.0	-60.0	180.0	4 00.0	-60.0	180.0	3 00.0	-60.0	180.0	2 00.0	-60.0	180.0	1 00.0	-60.0	180.0	0 00.0	+60.0	0.0	1 00.0	+60.0	0.0	69
70	5 00.0	-60.0	180.0	4 00.0	-60.0	180.0	3 00.0	-60.0	180.0	2 00.0	-60.0	180.0	1 00.0	-60.0	180.0	0 00.0	+60.0	0.0	1 00.0	+60.0	0.0	2 00.0	+60.0	0.0	70
71	4 00.0	-60.0	180.0	3 00.0	-60.0	180.0	2 00.0	-60.0	180.0	1 00.0	-60.0	180.0	0 00.0	+60.0	0.0	1 00.0	+60.0	0.0	2 00.0	+60.0	0.0	3 00.0	+60.0	0.0	71
72	3 00.0	-60.0	180.0	2 00.0	-60.0	180.0	1 00.0	-60.0	180.0	0 00.0	+60.0	0.0	1 00.0	+60.0	0.0	2 00.0	+60.0	0.0	3 00.0	+60.0	0.0	4 00.0	+60.0	0.0	72
73	2 00.0	-60.0	180.0	1 00.0	-60.0	180.0	0 00.0	+60.0	0.0	1 00.0	+60.0	0.0	2 00.0	+60.0	0.0	3 00.0	+60.0	0.0	4 00.0	+60.0	0.0	5 00.0	+60.0	0.0	73
74	1 00.0	-60.0	180.0	0 00.0	+60.0	0.0	1 00.0	+60.0	0.0	2 00.0	+60.0	0.0	3 00.0	+60.0	0.0	4 00.0	+60.0	0.0	5 00.0	+60.0	0.0	6 00.0	+60.0	0.0	74
75	0 00.0	+60.0	0.0	1 00.0	+60.0	0.0	2 00.0	+60.0	0.0	3 00.0	+60.0	0.0	4 00.0	+60.0	0.0	5 00.0	+60.0	0.0	6 00.0	+60.0	0.0	7 00.0	+60.0	0.0	75
76	1 00.0	+60.0	0.0	2 00.0	+60.0	0.0	3 00.0	+60.0	0.0	4 00.0	+60.0	0.0	5 00.0	+60.0	0.0	6 00.0	+60.0	0.0	7 00.0	+60.0	0.0	8 00.0	+60.0	0.0	76
77	2 00.0	+60.0	0.0	3 00.0	+60.0	0.0	4 00.0	+60.0	0.0	5 00.0	+60.0	0.0	6 00.0	+60.0	0.0	7 00.0	+60.0	0.0	8 00.0	+60.0	0.0	9 00.0	+60.0	0.0	77
78	3 00.0	+60.0	0.0	4 00.0	+60.0	0.0	5 00.0	+60.0	0.0	6 00.0	+60.0	0.0	7 00.0	+60.0	0.0	8 00.0	+60.0	0.0	9 00.0	+60.0	0.0	10 00.0	+60.0	0.0	78
79	4 00.0	+60.0	0.0	5 00.0	+60.0	0.0	6 00.0	+60.0	0.0	7 00.0	+60.0	0.0	8 00.0	+60.0	0.0	9 00.0	+60.0	0.0	10 00.0	+60.0	0.0	11 00.0	+60.0	0.0	79
80	5 00.0	+60.0	0.0	6 00.0	+60.0	0.0	7 00.0	+60.0	0.0	8 00.0	+60.0	0.0	9 00.0	+60.0	0.0	10 00.0	+60.0	0.0	11 00.0	+60.0	0.0	12 00.0	+60.0	0.0	80
81	6 00.0	+60.0	0.0	7 00.0	+60.0	0.0	8 00.0	+60.0	0.0	9 00.0	+60.0	0.0	10 00.0	+60.0	0.0	11 00.0	+60.0	0.0	12 00.0	+60.0	0.0	13 00.0	+60.0	0.0	81
82	7 00.0	+60.0	0.0	8 00.0	+60.0	0.0	9 00.0	+60.0	0.0	10 00.0	+60.0	0.0	11 00.0	+60.0	0.0	12 00.0	+60.0	0.0	13 00.0	+60.0	0.0	14 00.0	+60.0	0.0	82
83	8 00.0	+60.0	0.0	9 00.0	+60.0	0.0	10 00.0	+60.0	0.0	11 00.0	+60.0	0.0	12 00.0	+60.0	0.0	13 00.0	+60.0	0.0	14 00.0	+60.0	0.0	15 00.0	+60.0	0.0	83
84	9 00.0	+60.0	0.0	10 00.0	+60.0	0.0	11 00.0	+60.0	0.0	12 00.0	+60.0	0.0	13 00.0	+60.0	0.0	14 00.0	+60.0	0.0	15 00.0	+60.0	0.0	16 00.0	+60.0	0.0	84
85	10 00.0	+60.0	0.0	11 00.0	+60.0	0.0	12 00.0	+60.0	0.0	13 00.0	+60.0	0.0	14 00.0	+60.0	0.0	15 00.0	+60.0	0.0	16 00.0	+60.0	0.0	17 00.0	+60.0	0.0	85
86	11 00.0	+60.0	0.0	12 00.0	+60.0	0.0	13 00.0	+60.0	0.0	14 00.0	+60.0	0.0	15 00.0	+60.0	0.0	16 00.0	+60.0	0.0	17 00.0	+60.0	0.0	18 00.0	+60.0	0.0	86
87	12 00.0	+60.0	0.0	13 00.0	+60.0	0.0	14 00.0	+60.0	0.0	15 00.0	+60.0	0.0	16 00.0	+60.0	0.0	17 00.0	+60.0	0.0	18 00.0	+60.0	0.0	19 00.0	+60.0	0.0	87
88	13 00.0	+60.0	0.0	14 00.0	+60.0	0.0	15 00.0	+60.0	0.0	16 00.0	+60.0	0.0	17 00.0	+60.0	0.0	18 00.0	+60.0	0.0	19 00.0	+60.0	0.0	20 00.0	+60.0	0.0	88
89	14 00.0	+60.0	0.0	15 00.0	+60.0	0.0	16 00.0	+60.0	0.0	17 00.0	+60.0	0.0	18 00.0	+60.0	0.0	19 00.0	+60.0	0.0	20 00.0	+60.0	0.0	21 00.0	+60.0	0.0	89
90	15 00.0	+60.0	0.0	16 00.0	+60.0	0.0	17 00.0	+60.0	0.0	18 00.0	+60.0	0.0	19 00.0	+60.0	0.0	20 00.0	+60.0	0.0	21 00.0	+60.0	0.0	22 00.0	+60.0	0.0	90
	15°			16°			17°			18°			19°			20°			21°			22°			

S. Lat. { L.H.A. greater than 180° ....Zn=180°−Z
L.H.A. less than 180°...........Zn=180°+Z

LATITUDE **SAME** NAME AS DECLINATION **L.H.A. 180°, 180°**

3

1°, 359° L.H.A. LATITUDE SAME NAME AS DECLINATION

N. Lat. {L.H.A. greater than 180° .....Zn=Z
{L.H.A. less than 180°............Zn=360°−Z

Dec.	15°			16°			17°			18°			19°			20°			21°			22°			Dec.
Dec.	Hc	d	Z	Hc	d	Z	Hc	d	Z	Hc	d	Z	Hc	d	Z	Hc	d	Z	Hc	d	Z	Hc	d	Z	Dec.
°	° ′	′	°	° ′	′	°	° ′	′	°	° ′	′	°	° ′	′	°	° ′	′	°	° ′	′	°	° ′	′	°	°
0	74 58.0	+59.9	176.1	73 58.2	+59.9	176.4	72 58.3	+59.9	176.6	71 58.4	+59.9	176.8	70 58.5	+59.9	176.9	69 58.6	+59.9	177.1	68 58.6	+60.0	177.2	67 58.7	+59.9	177.3	0
1	75 57.9	+59.9	175.9	74 58.1	+59.8	176.1	73 58.2	+59.9	176.4	72 58.3	+59.9	176.6	71 58.4	+59.9	176.8	70 58.5	+59.9	176.9	69 58.6	+59.9	177.1	68 58.6	+60.0	177.2	1
2	76 57.8	+59.8	175.6	75 57.9	+59.9	175.9	74 58.1	+59.8	176.1	73 58.2	+59.9	176.4	72 58.3	+59.9	176.6	71 58.4	+59.9	176.8	70 58.5	+59.9	176.9	69 58.6	+59.9	177.1	2
3	77 57.6	+59.8	175.2	76 57.8	+59.8	175.6	75 57.9	+59.9	175.9	74 58.1	+59.8	176.1	73 58.2	+59.9	176.4	72 58.3	+59.9	176.6	71 58.4	+59.9	176.8	70 58.5	+59.9	176.9	3
4	78 57.4	+59.7	174.8	77 57.6	+59.8	175.2	76 57.8	+59.8	175.6	75 57.9	+59.9	175.9	74 58.1	+59.9	176.2	73 58.2	+59.9	176.4	72 58.3	+59.9	176.6	71 58.4	+59.9	176.8	4
5	79 57.1	+59.7	174.3	78 57.4	+59.7	174.8	77 57.6	+59.8	175.2	76 57.8	+59.8	175.6	75 58.0	+59.8	175.9	74 58.1	+59.9	176.2	73 58.2	+59.9	176.4	72 58.3	+59.9	176.6	5
6	80 56.8	+59.6	173.7	79 57.1	+59.7	174.3	78 57.4	+59.7	174.8	77 57.6	+59.8	175.2	76 57.8	+59.8	175.6	75 58.0	+59.8	175.9	74 58.1	+59.9	176.2	73 58.2	+59.9	176.4	6
7	81 56.4	+59.5	172.9	80 56.8	+59.6	173.7	79 57.1	+59.7	174.3	78 57.4	+59.8	174.8	77 57.6	+59.8	175.2	76 57.8	+59.9	175.6	75 58.0	+59.9	175.9	74 58.1	+59.9	176.2	7
8	82 55.9	+59.4	171.9	81 56.4	+59.5	172.9	80 56.8	+59.7	173.7	79 57.2	+59.7	174.3	78 57.4	+59.8	174.8	77 57.7	+59.8	175.2	76 57.9	+59.8	175.6	75 58.0	+59.9	175.9	8
9	83 55.3	+59.0	170.6	82 55.9	+59.4	171.9	81 56.5	+59.5	172.9	80 56.9	+59.6	173.7	79 57.2	+59.7	174.3	78 57.5	+59.7	174.8	77 57.7	+59.8	175.3	76 57.9	+59.8	175.6	9
10	84 54.3	+58.7	168.8	83 55.3	+59.1	170.7	82 56.0	+59.3	172.0	81 56.5	+59.5	173.0	80 56.9	+59.6	173.7	79 57.2	+59.7	174.3	78 57.5	+59.7	174.9	77 57.7	+59.8	175.3	10
11	85 53.0	+57.8	166.2	84 54.4	+58.6	168.9	83 55.3	+59.1	170.7	82 56.0	+59.4	172.0	81 56.5	+59.5	173.0	80 56.9	+59.7	173.7	79 57.2	+59.8	174.4	78 57.5	+59.8	174.9	11
12	86 50.8	+55.8•	161.9	85 53.0	+57.9	166.2	84 54.4	+58.7	168.9	83 55.4	+59.1	170.7	82 56.0	+59.4	172.0	81 56.6	+59.5	173.0	80 57.0	+59.6	173.8	79 57.3	+59.7	174.4	12
13	87 46.6	+49.9•	154.0	86 50.9	+55.8•	162.0	85 53.1	+57.8	166.3	84 54.5	+58.7	169.0	83 55.4	+59.1	170.8	82 56.1	+59.4	172.1	81 56.6	+59.5	173.0	80 57.0	+59.6	173.8	13
14	88 36.5	+25.5•	135.8	87 46.7	+50.0•	154.1	86 50.9	+56.0•	162.1	85 53.2	+57.8	166.3	84 54.5	+58.7	169.0	83 55.5	+59.1	170.8	82 56.1	+59.4	172.1	81 56.6	+59.6	173.1	14
15	89 02.0	−25.3•	89.9	88 36.7	+25.6•	135.9	87 46.9	+50.0•	154.2	86 51.0	+56.0•	162.1	85 53.2	+57.9	166.4	84 54.6	+58.7	169.0	83 55.5	+59.2	170.8	82 56.2	+59.4	172.1	15
16	88 36.7	−49.8•	43.8	89 02.3	−25.4•	89.9	88 36.9	+25.7•	136.1	87 47.0	+50.1•	154.3	86 51.1	+56.0•	162.2	85 53.3	+57.9	166.5	84 54.7	+58.7	169.1	83 55.6	+59.1	170.9	16
17	87 46.9	−55.9•	25.5	88 36.9	−49.9•	43.7	89 02.6	−25.5•	89.9	88 37.1	+25.8•	136.2	87 47.1	+50.2•	154.4	86 51.2	+56.1•	162.3	85 53.4	+57.9	166.5	84 54.7	+58.8	169.2	17
18	86 51.0	−57.8	17.6	87 47.0	−55.9•	25.4	88 37.1	−50.0•	43.5	89 02.9	−25.6•	89.8	88 37.3	+26.0•	136.4	87 47.3	+50.2•	154.5	86 51.3	+56.1•	162.4	85 53.5	+57.9	166.6	18
19	85 53.2	−58.6	13.3	86 51.1	−57.8	17.5	87 47.1	−55.9•	25.3	88 37.3	−50.0•	43.3	89 03.3	−25.8•	89.8	88 37.5	+26.1•	136.5	87 47.4	+50.4•	154.7	86 51.4	+56.2•	162.5	19
20	84 54.6	−59.1	10.7	85 53.3	−58.6	13.2	86 51.2	−57.8	17.4	87 47.3	−56.0•	25.1	88 37.5	−50.1•	43.1	89 03.6	−25.8•	89.8	88 37.8	+26.2•	136.7	87 47.6	+50.4•	154.8	20
21	83 55.5	−59.3	8.9	84 54.7	−59.1	10.6	85 53.4	−58.7	13.1	86 51.3	−57.8	17.3	87 47.4	−56.0•	25.0	88 37.8	−50.2•	43.0	89 04.0	−26.0•	89.8	88 38.0	+26.4•	136.9	21
22	82 56.2	−59.5	7.6	83 55.6	−59.4	8.8	84 54.7	−59.1	10.5	85 53.5	−58.7	13.1	86 51.4	−57.8	17.2	87 47.6	−56.1•	24.8	88 38.0	−50.3•	42.8	89 04.4	−26.1•	89.8	22
23	81 56.7	−59.6	6.6	82 56.2	−59.5	7.5	83 55.6	−59.3	8.7	84 54.8	−59.1	10.4	85 53.6	−58.7	13.0	86 51.5	−57.9	17.0	87 47.7	−56.0•	24.7	88 38.3	−50.4•	42.5	23
24	80 57.1	−59.7	5.8	81 56.7	−59.6	6.5	82 56.3	−59.5	7.5	83 55.7	−59.4	8.7	84 54.9	−59.2	10.4	85 53.6	−58.7	12.9	86 51.7	−58.0	16.9	87 47.9	−56.1•	24.5	24
25	79 57.4	−59.8	5.2	80 57.1	−59.7	5.8	81 56.8	−59.7	6.5	82 56.3	−59.5	7.4	83 55.7	−59.3	8.6	84 54.9	−59.1	10.3	85 53.7	−58.7	12.8	86 51.8	−58.0	16.8	25
26	78 57.6	−59.8	4.7	79 57.4	−59.7	5.2	80 57.1	−59.7	5.7	81 56.8	−59.6	6.4	82 56.4	−59.6	7.3	83 55.8	−59.4	8.5	84 55.0	−59.1	10.2	85 53.8	−58.7	12.7	26
27	77 57.8	−59.8	4.3	78 57.7	−59.8	4.7	79 57.4	−59.7	5.1	80 57.2	−59.7	5.7	81 56.8	−59.6	6.4	82 56.4	−59.5	7.3	83 55.9	−59.4	8.5	84 55.1	−59.2	10.1	27
28	76 58.0	−59.8	3.9	77 57.9	−59.9	4.2	78 57.7	−59.8	4.6	79 57.5	−59.8	5.1	80 57.2	−59.7	5.6	81 56.9	−59.6	6.3	82 56.5	−59.6	7.2	83 55.9	−59.4	8.4	28
29	75 58.2	−59.9	3.6	76 58.0	−59.8	3.9	77 57.9	−59.8	4.2	78 57.7	−59.8	4.6	79 57.5	−59.7	5.0	80 57.3	−59.7	5.6	81 56.9	−59.6	6.3	82 56.5	−59.5	7.1	29
30	74 58.3	−59.9	3.3	75 58.2	−59.9	3.6	76 58.1	−59.9	3.8	77 57.9	−59.8	4.2	78 57.8	−59.8	4.5	79 57.6	−59.8	5.0	80 57.3	−59.7	5.5	81 57.0	−59.7	6.2	30
31	73 58.4	−59.9	3.1	74 58.3	−59.8	3.3	75 58.2	−59.8	3.5	76 58.1	−59.8	3.8	77 58.0	−59.9	4.1	78 57.8	−59.8	4.5	79 57.6	−59.8	4.9	80 57.3	−59.7	5.5	31
32	72 58.5	−59.9	2.9	73 58.5	−59.9	3.1	74 58.4	−59.9	3.3	75 58.3	−59.9	3.5	76 58.1	−59.8	3.8	77 58.0	−59.8	4.1	78 57.8	−59.8	4.4	79 57.6	−59.7	4.9	32
33	71 58.6	−59.9	2.7	72 58.6	−59.9	2.9	73 58.5	−59.9	3.0	74 58.4	−59.9	3.2	75 58.3	−59.9	3.5	76 58.2	−59.9	3.7	77 58.0	−59.8	4.0	78 57.9	−59.8	4.4	33
34	70 58.7	−59.9	2.5	71 58.7	−60.0	2.7	72 58.6	−59.9	2.8	73 58.5	−59.9	3.0	74 58.4	−59.9	3.2	75 58.3	−59.9	3.4	76 58.2	−59.9	3.7	77 58.1	−59.9	4.0	34
35	69 58.8	−59.9	2.4	70 58.7	−59.9	2.5	71 58.7	−59.9	2.6	72 58.6	−59.9	2.8	73 58.5	−59.9	3.0	74 58.4	−59.8	3.2	75 58.3	−59.8	3.4	76 58.2	−59.8	3.6	35
36	68 58.9	−60.0	2.3	69 58.8	−59.9	2.4	70 58.8	−60.0	2.5	71 58.7	−59.9	2.6	72 58.6	−59.9	2.8	73 58.6	−59.9	2.9	74 58.5	−59.9	3.1	75 58.4	−59.9	3.3	36
37	67 58.9	−59.9	2.1	68 58.9	−60.0	2.2	69 58.8	−59.9	2.3	70 58.8	−59.9	2.5	71 58.7	−59.9	2.6	72 58.7	−60.0	2.7	73 58.6	−59.9	2.9	74 58.5	−59.9	3.1	37
38	66 59.0	−60.0	2.0	67 58.9	−59.9	2.1	68 58.9	−59.9	2.2	69 58.9	−60.0	2.3	70 58.8	−59.9	2.4	71 58.7	−59.9	2.5	72 58.7	−59.9	2.7	73 58.6	−59.9	2.9	38
39	65 59.0	−59.9	1.9	66 59.0	−59.9	2.0	67 59.0	−60.0	2.1	68 58.9	−59.9	2.2	69 58.9	−60.0	2.3	70 58.8	−59.9	2.4	71 58.8	−59.9	2.5	72 58.7	−59.9	2.7	39
40	64 59.1	−60.0	1.8	65 59.1	−60.0	1.9	66 59.0	−59.9	2.0	67 59.0	−60.0	2.0	68 58.9	−59.9	2.1	69 58.9	−59.9	2.2	70 58.9	−60.0	2.4	71 58.8	−59.9	2.5	40
41	63 59.1	−59.9	1.7	64 59.1	−60.0	1.8	65 59.1	−60.0	1.9	66 59.0	−59.9	1.9	67 59.0	−59.9	2.0	68 59.0	−60.0	2.1	69 58.9	−59.9	2.2	70 58.9	−60.0	2.3	41
42	62 59.2	−60.0	1.6	63 59.1	−59.9	1.7	64 59.1	−59.9	1.8	65 59.1	−60.0	1.8	66 59.1	−60.0	1.9	67 59.0	−59.9	2.0	68 59.0	−60.0	2.1	69 58.9	−59.9	2.2	42
43	61 59.2	−60.0	1.6	62 59.2	−60.0	1.6	63 59.2	−60.0	1.7	64 59.1	−59.9	1.7	65 59.1	−59.9	1.8	66 59.1	−60.0	1.9	67 59.0	−59.9	2.0	68 59.0	−59.9	2.0	43
44	60 59.2	−59.9	1.5	61 59.2	−59.9	1.5	62 59.2	−60.0	1.6	63 59.2	−60.0	1.6	64 59.2	−60.0	1.7	65 59.1	−59.9	1.8	66 59.1	−59.9	1.8	67 59.1	−60.0	1.9	44
45	59 59.3	−60.0	1.4	60 59.3	−60.0	1.5	61 59.2	−59.9	1.5	62 59.2	−59.9	1.6	63 59.2	−60.0	1.6	64 59.2	−60.0	1.7	65 59.2	−60.0	1.7	66 59.1	−59.9	1.8	45
46	58 59.3	−60.0	1.3	59 59.3	−60.0	1.4	60 59.3	−60.0	1.4	61 59.3	−60.0	1.5	62 59.2	−59.9	1.5	63 59.2	−59.9	1.6	64 59.2	−60.0	1.6	65 59.2	−60.0	1.7	46
47	57 59.3	−59.9	1.3	58 59.3	−59.9	1.3	59 59.3	−60.0	1.4	60 59.3	−60.0	1.4	61 59.3	−60.0	1.5	62 59.3	−60.0	1.5	63 59.2	−59.9	1.6	64 59.2	−59.9	1.6	47
48	56 59.4	−60.0	1.2	57 59.4	−60.0	1.3	58 59.3	−59.9	1.3	59 59.3	−59.9	1.3	60 59.3	−59.9	1.4	61 59.3	−60.0	1.4	62 59.3	−60.0	1.5	63 59.3	−60.0	1.5	48
49	55 59.4	−60.0	1.2	56 59.4	−60.0	1.2	57 59.4	−60.0	1.2	58 59.4	−60.0	1.3	59 59.4	−60.0	1.3	60 59.3	−59.9	1.4	61 59.3	−59.9	1.4	62 59.3	−60.0	1.4	49
50	54 59.4	−59.9	1.1	55 59.4	−60.0	1.1	56 59.4	−60.0	1.2	57 59.4	−60.0	1.2	58 59.4	−60.0	1.2	59 59.4	−60.0	1.3	60 59.4	−60.0	1.3	61 59.3	−59.9	1.4	50
51	53 59.5	−60.0	1.1	54 59.4	−59.9	1.1	55 59.4	−59.9	1.1	56 59.4	−59.9	1.2	57 59.4	−60.0	1.2	58 59.4	−60.0	1.2	59 59.4	−60.0	1.3	60 59.4	−60.0	1.3	51
52	52 59.5	−60.0	1.0	53 59.5	−60.0	1.0	54 59.5	−60.0	1.1	55 59.5	−60.0	1.1	56 59.4	−59.9	1.1	57 59.4	−59.9	1.2	58 59.4	−60.0	1.2	59 59.4	−60.0	1.2	52
53	51 59.5	−60.0	1.0	52 59.5	−60.0	1.0	53 59.5	−60.0	1.0	54 59.5	−60.0	1.0	55 59.5	−60.0	1.1	56 59.5	−60.0	1.1	57 59.4	−59.9	1.1	58 59.4	−59.9	1.2	53
54	50 59.5	−60.0	0.9	51 59.5	−60.0	1.0	52 59.5	−60.0	1.0	53 59.5	−60.0	1.0	54 59.5	−60.0	1.0	55 59.5	−60.0	1.1	56 59.5	−60.0	1.1	57 59.5	−60.0	1.1	54
55	49 59.5	−59.9	0.9	50 59.5	−59.9	0.9	51 59.5	−59.9	0.9	52 59.5	−60.0	1.0	53 59.5	−60.0	1.0	54 59.5	−60.0	1.0	55 59.5	−60.0	1.0	56 59.5	−60.0	1.1	55
56	48 59.6	−60.0	0.9	49 59.6	−60.0	0.9	50 59.6	−60.0	0.9	51 59.5	−59.9	0.9	52 59.5	−59.9	0.9	53 59.5	−59.9	1.0	54 59.5	−60.0	1.0	55 59.5	−60.0	1.0	56
57	47 59.6	−60.0	0.8	48 59.6	−60.0	0.8	49 59.6	−60.0	0.8	50 59.6	−60.0	0.9	51 59.6	−60.0	0.9	52 59.6	−60.0	0.9	53 59.5	−59.9	0.9	54 59.5	−59.9	0.9	57
58	46 59.6	−60.0	0.8	47 59.6	−60.0	0.8	48 59.6	−60.0	0.8	49 59.6	−60.0	0.8	50 59.6	−60.0	0.8	51 59.6	−60.0	0.9	52 59.6	−60.0	0.9	53 59.6	−60.0	0.9	58
59	45 59.6	−60.0	0.7	46 59.6	−60.0	0.8	47 59.6	−60.0	0.8	48 59.6	−60.0	0.8	49 59.6	−60.0	0.8	50 59.6	−60.0	0.8	51 59.6	−60.0	0.8	52 59.6	−60.0	0.9	59
60	44 59.6	−59.9	0.7	45 59.6	−59.9	0.7	46 59.6	−59.9	0.7	47 59.6	−60.0	0.7	48 59.6	−60.0	0.8	49 59.6	−60.0	0.8	50 59.6	−60.0	0.8	51 59.6	−60.0	0.8	60
61	43 59.7	−60.0	0.7	44 59.7	−60.0	0.7	45 59.7	−60.0	0.7	46 59.6	−59.9	0.7	47 59.6	−59.9	0.7	48 59.6	−59.9	0.7	49 59.6	−59.9	0.8	50 59.6	−60.0	0.8	61
62	42 59.7	−60.0	0.6	43 59.7	−60.0	0.7	44 59.7	−60.0	0.7	45 59.7	−60.0	0.7	46 59.7	−60.0	0.7	47 59.7	−60.0	0.7	48 59.7	−60.0	0.7	49 59.6	−59.9	0.7	62
63	41 59.7	−60.0	0.6	42 59.7	−60.0	0.6	43 59.7	−60.0	0.6	44 59.7	−60.0	0.6	45 59.7	−60.0	0.7	46 59.7	−60.0	0.7	47 59.7	−60.0	0.7	48 59.7	−60.0	0.7	63
64	40 59.7	−60.0	0.6	41 59.7	−60.0	0.6	42 59.7	−60.0	0.6	43 59.7	−60.0	0.6	44 59.7	−60.0	0.6	45 59.7	−60.0	0.6	46 59.7	−60.0	0.6	47 59.7	−60.0	0.7	64
65	39 59.7	−60.0	0.6	40 59.7	−60.0	0.6	41 59.7	−60.0	0.6	42 59.7	−60.0	0.6	43 59.7	−60.0	0.6	44 59.7	−60.0	0.6	45 59.7	−60.0	0.6	46 59.7	−60.0	0.6	65
66	38 59.7	−60.0	0.5	39 59.7	−60.0	0.5	40 59.7	−60.0	0.5	41 59.7	−60.0	0.5	42 59.7	−60.0	0.6	43 59.7	−60.0	0.6	44 59.7	−60.0	0.6	45 59.7	−60.0	0.6	66
67	37 59.7	−59.9	0.5	38 59.7	−59.9	0.5	39 59.7	−59.9	0.5	40 59.7	−59.9	0.5	41 59.7	−59.9	0.5	42 59.7	−59.9	0.5	43 59.7	−60.0	0.5	44 59.7	−60.0	0.6	67
68	36 59.8	−60.0	0.5	37 59.8	−60.0	0.5	38 59.8	−60.0	0.5	39 59.8	−60.0	0.5	40 59.8	−60.0	0.5	41 59.8	−60.0	0.5	42 59.7	−59.9	0.5	43 59.7	−59.9	0.5	68
69	35 59.8	−60.0	0.4	36 59.8	−60.0	0.4	37 59.8	−60.0	0.5	38 59.8	−60.0	0.5	39 59.8	−60.0	0.5	40 59.8	−60.0	0.5	41 59.8	−60.0	0.5	42 59.8	−60.0	0.5	69
70	34 59.8	−60.0	0.4	35 59.8	−60.0	0.4	36 59.8	−60.0	0.4	37 59.8	−60.0	0.4	38 59.8	−60.0	0.4	39 59.8	−60.0	0.4	40 59.8	−60.0	0.5	41 59.8	−60.0	0.5	70
71	33 59.8	−60.0	0.4	34 59.8	−60.0	0.4	35 59.8	−60.0	0.4	36 59.8	−60.0	0.4	37 59.8	−60.0	0.4	38 59.8	−60.0	0.4	39 59.8	−60.0	0.4	40 59.8	−60.0	0.4	71
72	32 59.8	−60.0	0.4	33 59.8	−60.0	0.4	34 59.8	−60.0	0.4	35 59.8	−60.0	0.4	36 59.8	−60.0	0.4	37 59.8	−60.0	0.4	38 59.8	−60.0	0.4	39 59.8	−60.0	0.4	72
73	31 59.8	−60.0	0.3	32 59.8	−60.0	0.3	33 59.8	−60.0	0.4	34 59.8	−60.0	0.4	35 59.8	−60.0	0.4	36 59.8	−60.0	0.4	37 59.8	−60.0	0.4	38 59.8	−60.0	0.4	73
74	30 59.8	−60.0	0.3	31 59.8	−60.0	0.3	32 59.8	−60.0	0.3	33 59.8	−60.0	0.3	34 59.8	−60.0	0.3	35 59.8	−60.0	0.3	36 59.8	−60.0	0.3	37 59.8	−60.0	0.3	74
75	29 59.8	−59.9	0.3	30 59.8	−59.9	0.3	31 59.8	−59.9	0.3	32 59.8	−59.9	0.3	33 59.8	−59.9	0.3	34 59.8	−59.9	0.3	35 59.8	−59.9	0.3	36 59.8	−59.9	0.3	75
76	28 59.9	−60.0	0.3	29 59.9	−60.0	0.3	30 59.9	−60.0	0.3	31 59.9	−60.0	0.3	32 59.9	−60.0	0.3	33 59.9	−60.0	0.3	34 59.9	−60.0	0.3	35 59.9	−60.0	0.3	76
77	27 59.9	−60.0	0.3	28 59.9	−60.0	0.3	29 59.9	−60.0	0.3	30 59.9	−60.0	0.3	31 59.9	−60.0	0.3	32 59.9	−60.0	0.3	33 59.9	−60.0	0.3	34 59.9	−60.0	0.3	77
78	26 59.9	−60.0	0.2	27 59.9	−60.0	0.2	28 59.9	−60.0	0.2	29 59.9	−60.0	0.2	30 59.9	−60.0	0.2	31 59.9	−60.0	0.2	32 59.9	−60.0	0.2	33 59.9	−60.0	0.3	78
79	25 59.9	−60.0	0.2	26 59.9	−60.0	0.2	27 59.9	−60.0	0.2	28 59.9	−60.0	0.2	29 59.9	−60.0	0.2	30 59.9	−60.0	0.2	31 59.9	−60.0	0.2	32 59.9	−60.0	0.2	79
80	24 59.9	−60.0	0.2	25 59.9	−60.0	0.2	26 59.9	−60.0	0.2	27 59.9	−60.0	0.2	28 59.9	−60.0	0.2	29 59.9	−60.0	0.2	30 59.9	−60.0	0.2	31 59.9	−60.0	0.2	80
81	23 59.9	−60.0	0.2	24 59.9	−60.0	0.2	25 59.9	−60.0	0.2	26 59.9	−60.0	0.2	27 59.9	−60.0	0.2	28 59.9	−60.0	0.2	29 59.9	−60.0	0.2	30 59.9	−60.0	0.2	81
82	22 59.9	−60.0	0.2	23 59.9	−60.0	0.2	24 59.9	−60.0	0.2	25 59.9	−60.0	0.2	26 59.9	−60.0	0.2	27 59.9	−60.0	0.2	28 59.9	−60.0	0.2	29 59.9	−60.0	0.2	82
83	21 59.9	−60.0	0.1	22 59.9	−60.0	0.1	23 59.9	−60.0	0.1	24 59.9	−60.0	0.1	25 59.9	−60.0	0.1	26 59.9	−60.0	0.1	27 59.9	−60.0	0.1	28 59.9	−60.0	0.1	83
84	20 59.9	−59.9	0.1	21 59.9	−59.9	0.1	22 59.9	−59.9	0.1	23 59.9	−59.9	0.1	24 59.9	−59.9	0.1	25 59.9	−59.9	0.1	26 59.9	−59.9	0.1	27 59.9	−59.9	0.1	84
85	20 00.0	−60.0	0.1	21 00.0	−60.0	0.1	22 00.0	−60.0	0.1	23 00.0	−60.0	0.1	24 00.0	−60.0	0.1	25 00.0	−60.0	0.1	26 00.0	−60.0	0.1	27 00.0	−60.0	0.1	85
86	19 00.0	−60.0	0.1	20 00.0	−60.0	0.1	21 00.0	−60.0	0.1	22 00.0	−60.0	0.1	23 00.0	−60.0	0.1	24 00.0	−60.0	0.1	25 00.0	−60.0	0.1	26 00.0	−60.0	0.1	86
87	18 00.0	−60.0	0.1	19 00.0	−60.0	0.1	20 00.0	−60.0	0.1	21 00.0	−60.0	0.1	22 00.0	−60.0	0.1	23 00.0	−60.0	0.1	24 00.0	−60.0	0.1	25 00.0	−60.0	0.1	87
88	17 00.0	−60.0	0.0	18 00.0	−60.0	0.0	19 00.0	−60.0	0.0	20 00.0	−60.0	0.0	21 00.0	−60.0	0.0	22 00.0	−60.0	0.0	23 00.0	−60.0	0.0	24 00.0	−60.0	0.0	88
89	16 00.0	−60.0	0.0	17 00.0	−60.0	0.0	18 00.0	−60.0	0.0	19 00.0	−60.0	0.0	20 00.0	−60.0	0.0	21 00.0	−60.0	0.0	22 00.0	−60.0	0.0	23 00.0	−60.0	0.0	89
90	15 00.0	−60.0	0.0	16 00.0	−60.0	0.0	17 00.0	−60.0	0.0	18 00.0	−60.0	0.0	19 00.0	−60.0	0.0	20 00.0	−60.0	0.0	21 00.0	−60.0	0.0	22 00.0	−60.0	0.0	90
	15°			16°			17°			18°			19°			20°			21°			22°			

1°, 359° L.H.A. LATITUDE SAME NAME AS DECLINATION

4

LATITUDE CONTRARY NAME TO DECLINATION L.H.A. 1°, 359°

Dec.	15°			16°			17°			18°			19°			20°			21°			22°			Dec.
	Hc	d	Z	Hc	d	Z	Hc	d	Z	Hc	d	Z	Hc	d	Z	Hc	d	Z	Hc	d	Z	Hc	d	Z	
°	° ′	′	°	° ′	′	°	° ′	′	°	° ′	′	°	° ′	′	°	° ′	′	°	° ′	′	°	° ′	′	°	°
0	74 58.0	-59.8	176.1	73 58.2	-59.9	176.4	72 58.3	-59.9	176.6	71 58.4	-59.9	176.8	70 58.5	-59.9	176.9	69 58.6	-60.0	177.1	68 58.6	-59.9	177.2	67 58.7	-59.9	177.3	0
1	73 58.2	-59.9	176.4	72 58.3	-59.9	176.6	71 58.4	-59.9	176.8	70 58.5	-60.0	176.9	69 58.6	-60.0	177.1	68 58.6	-59.9	177.2	67 58.7	-59.9	177.3	66 58.8	-60.0	177.4	1
2	72 58.3	-59.9	176.6	71 58.4	-59.9	176.8	70 58.5	-60.0	176.9	69 58.5	-59.9	177.1	68 58.6	-59.9	177.2	67 58.7	-60.0	177.3	66 58.8	-60.0	177.4	65 58.8	-59.9	177.5	2
3	71 58.4	-59.9	176.8	70 58.5	-60.0	176.9	69 58.5	-59.9	177.1	68 58.6	-59.9	177.2	67 58.7	-60.0	177.3	66 58.7	-59.9	177.4	65 58.8	-60.0	177.5	64 58.9	-60.0	177.6	3
4	70 58.5	-60.0	176.9	69 58.5	-59.9	177.1	68 58.6	-59.9	177.2	67 58.7	-60.0	177.3	66 58.7	-59.9	177.4	65 58.8	-60.0	177.5	64 58.8	-59.9	177.6	63 58.9	-60.0	177.7	4
5	69 58.5	-59.9	177.1	68 58.6	-59.9	177.2	67 58.7	-60.0	177.3	66 58.7	-59.9	177.5	65 58.8	-60.0	177.6	64 58.8	-59.9	177.6	63 58.9	-60.0	177.7	62 58.9	-59.9	177.8	5
6	68 58.6	-59.9	177.2	67 58.7	-60.0	177.3	66 58.7	-59.9	177.5	65 58.8	-60.0	177.6	64 58.8	-59.9	177.6	63 58.9	-60.0	177.7	62 58.9	-59.9	177.8	61 59.0	-60.0	177.9	6
7	67 58.7	-60.0	177.4	66 58.7	-59.9	177.5	65 58.8	-60.0	177.6	64 58.8	-59.9	177.7	63 58.9	-60.0	177.7	62 58.9	-59.9	177.8	61 59.0	-60.0	177.9	60 59.0	-60.0	178.0	7
8	66 58.7	-59.9	177.5	65 58.8	-60.0	177.6	64 58.8	-59.9	177.7	63 58.9	-60.0	177.7	62 58.9	-59.9	177.8	61 59.0	-60.0	177.9	60 59.0	-60.0	178.0	59 59.0	-59.9	178.0	8
9	65 58.8	-60.0	177.6	64 58.8	-59.9	177.7	63 58.9	-60.0	177.7	62 58.9	-59.9	177.8	61 59.0	-60.0	177.9	60 59.0	-60.0	178.0	59 59.0	-59.9	178.0	58 59.1	-60.0	178.1	9
10	64 58.8	-59.9	177.7	63 58.9	-60.0	177.8	62 58.9	-59.9	177.8	61 59.0	-60.0	177.9	60 59.0	-60.0	178.0	59 59.0	-59.9	178.0	58 59.1	-60.0	178.1	57 59.1	-60.0	178.1	10
11	63 58.9	-60.0	177.7	62 58.9	-59.9	177.8	61 59.0	-60.0	177.9	60 59.0	-60.0	178.0	59 59.0	-59.9	178.0	58 59.1	-60.0	178.1	57 59.1	-60.0	178.1	56 59.1	-59.9	178.2	11
12	62 58.9	-59.9	177.8	61 59.0	-60.0	177.9	60 59.0	-60.0	178.0	59 59.0	-59.9	178.0	58 59.1	-60.0	178.1	57 59.1	-60.0	178.2	56 59.1	-60.0	178.2	55 59.2	-60.0	178.3	12
13	61 59.0	-60.0	177.9	60 59.0	-60.0	178.0	59 59.0	-59.9	178.1	58 59.1	-60.0	178.1	57 59.1	-60.0	178.2	56 59.1	-60.0	178.2	55 59.1	-59.9	178.3	54 59.2	-60.0	178.3	13
14	60 59.0	-60.0	178.0	59 59.0	-59.9	178.1	58 59.1	-60.0	178.1	57 59.1	-60.0	178.2	56 59.1	-60.0	178.2	55 59.1	-59.9	178.3	54 59.2	-60.0	178.3	53 59.2	-60.0	178.3	14
15	59 59.0	-59.9	178.1	58 59.1	-60.0	178.1	57 59.1	-60.0	178.2	56 59.1	-60.0	178.2	55 59.1	-59.9	178.3	54 59.2	-60.0	178.3	53 59.2	-60.0	178.4	52 59.2	-60.0	178.4	15
16	58 59.1	-60.0	178.1	57 59.1	-60.0	178.2	56 59.1	-60.0	178.2	55 59.1	-59.9	178.3	54 59.2	-60.0	178.3	53 59.2	-60.0	178.4	52 59.2	-60.0	178.4	51 59.2	-59.9	178.4	16
17	57 59.1	-60.0	178.2	56 59.1	-60.0	178.2	55 59.1	-59.9	178.3	54 59.2	-60.0	178.3	53 59.2	-60.0	178.4	52 59.2	-60.0	178.4	51 59.2	-59.9	178.4	50 59.3	-60.0	178.5	17
18	56 59.1	-60.0	178.3	55 59.1	-59.9	178.3	54 59.2	-60.0	178.3	53 59.2	-60.0	178.4	52 59.2	-60.0	178.4	51 59.2	-59.9	178.5	50 59.3	-60.0	178.5	49 59.3	-60.0	178.5	18
19	55 59.1	-59.9	178.3	54 59.2	-60.0	178.4	53 59.2	-60.0	178.4	52 59.2	-60.0	178.4	51 59.2	-59.9	178.5	50 59.3	-60.0	178.5	49 59.3	-60.0	178.5	48 59.3	-60.0	178.6	19
20	54 59.2	-60.0	178.4	53 59.2	-60.0	178.4	52 59.2	-60.0	178.4	51 59.2	-59.9	178.5	50 59.3	-60.0	178.5	49 59.3	-60.0	178.5	48 59.3	-60.0	178.6	47 59.3	-60.0	178.6	20
21	53 59.2	-60.0	178.4	52 59.2	-60.0	178.4	51 59.2	-59.9	178.5	50 59.3	-60.0	178.5	49 59.3	-60.0	178.5	48 59.3	-60.0	178.6	47 59.3	-60.0	178.6	46 59.3	-59.9	178.6	21
22	52 59.2	-60.0	178.5	51 59.2	-59.9	178.5	50 59.3	-60.0	178.5	49 59.3	-60.0	178.6	48 59.3	-60.0	178.6	47 59.3	-60.0	178.6	46 59.3	-59.9	178.6	45 59.4	-60.0	178.7	22
23	51 59.2	-59.9	178.5	50 59.3	-60.0	178.5	49 59.3	-60.0	178.6	48 59.3	-60.0	178.6	47 59.3	-60.0	178.6	46 59.3	-59.9	178.7	45 59.4	-60.0	178.7	44 59.4	-60.0	178.7	23
24	50 59.3	-60.0	178.5	49 59.3	-60.0	178.6	48 59.3	-60.0	178.6	47 59.3	-60.0	178.6	46 59.3	-59.9	178.7	45 59.4	-60.0	178.7	44 59.4	-60.0	178.7	43 59.4	-60.0	178.7	24
25	49 59.3	-60.0	178.6	48 59.3	-60.0	178.6	47 59.3	-60.0	178.6	46 59.3	-59.9	178.7	45 59.4	-60.0	178.7	44 59.4	-60.0	178.7	43 59.4	-60.0	178.7	42 59.4	-60.0	178.8	25
26	48 59.3	-60.0	178.6	47 59.3	-60.0	178.7	46 59.3	-59.9	178.7	45 59.4	-60.0	178.7	44 59.4	-60.0	178.7	43 59.4	-60.0	178.8	42 59.4	-60.0	178.8	41 59.4	-60.0	178.8	26
27	47 59.3	-60.0	178.7	46 59.3	-59.9	178.7	45 59.4	-60.0	178.7	44 59.4	-60.0	178.7	43 59.4	-60.0	178.8	42 59.4	-60.0	178.8	41 59.4	-60.0	178.8	40 59.4	-60.0	178.8	27
28	46 59.3	-59.9	178.7	45 59.4	-60.0	178.7	44 59.4	-60.0	178.8	43 59.4	-60.0	178.8	42 59.4	-60.0	178.8	41 59.4	-60.0	178.8	40 59.4	-60.0	178.8	39 59.4	-59.9	178.8	28
29	45 59.4	-60.0	178.7	44 59.4	-60.0	178.8	43 59.4	-60.0	178.8	42 59.4	-60.0	178.8	41 59.4	-60.0	178.8	40 59.4	-60.0	178.8	39 59.4	-59.9	178.9	38 59.5	-60.0	178.9	29
30	44 59.4	-60.0	178.8	43 59.4	-60.0	178.8	42 59.4	-60.0	178.8	41 59.4	-60.0	178.8	40 59.4	-60.0	178.9	39 59.4	-59.9	178.9	38 59.5	-60.0	178.9	37 59.5	-60.0	178.9	30
31	43 59.4	-60.0	178.8	42 59.4	-60.0	178.8	41 59.4	-60.0	178.8	40 59.4	-60.0	178.9	39 59.4	-59.9	178.9	38 59.5	-60.0	178.9	37 59.5	-60.0	178.9	36 59.5	-60.0	178.9	31
32	42 59.4	-60.0	178.8	41 59.4	-60.0	178.9	40 59.4	-59.9	178.9	39 59.4	-59.9	178.9	38 59.5	-60.0	178.9	37 59.5	-60.0	178.9	36 59.5	-60.0	178.9	35 59.5	-60.0	179.0	32
33	41 59.4	-60.0	178.9	40 59.4	-59.9	178.9	39 59.5	-60.0	178.9	38 59.5	-60.0	178.9	37 59.5	-60.0	178.9	36 59.5	-60.0	178.9	35 59.5	-60.0	179.0	34 59.5	-60.0	179.0	33
34	40 59.4	-59.9	178.9	39 59.5	-60.0	178.9	38 59.5	-60.0	178.9	37 59.5	-60.0	178.9	36 59.5	-60.0	179.0	35 59.5	-60.0	179.0	34 59.5	-60.0	179.0	33 59.5	-60.0	179.0	34
35	39 59.5	-60.0	178.9	38 59.5	-60.0	178.9	37 59.5	-60.0	179.0	36 59.5	-60.0	179.0	35 59.5	-60.0	179.0	34 59.5	-60.0	179.0	33 59.5	-60.0	179.0	32 59.5	-60.0	179.0	35
36	38 59.5	-60.0	179.0	37 59.5	-60.0	179.0	36 59.5	-60.0	179.0	35 59.5	-60.0	179.0	34 59.5	-60.0	179.0	33 59.5	-60.0	179.0	32 59.5	-60.0	179.0	31 59.5	-60.0	179.0	36
37	37 59.5	-60.0	179.0	36 59.5	-60.0	179.0	35 59.5	-60.0	179.0	34 59.5	-60.0	179.0	33 59.5	-60.0	179.0	32 59.5	-60.0	179.0	31 59.5	-59.9	179.1	30 59.5	-59.9	179.1	37
38	36 59.5	-60.0	179.0	35 59.5	-60.0	179.0	34 59.5	-60.0	179.0	33 59.5	-60.0	179.0	32 59.5	-60.0	179.1	31 59.5	-59.9	179.1	30 59.6	-60.0	179.1	29 59.6	-60.0	179.1	38
39	35 59.5	-60.0	179.0	34 59.5	-60.0	179.1	33 59.5	-60.0	179.1	32 59.5	-59.9	179.1	31 59.5	-59.9	179.1	30 59.6	-60.0	179.1	29 59.6	-60.0	179.1	28 59.6	-60.0	179.1	39
40	34 59.5	-60.0	179.1	33 59.5	-60.0	179.1	32 59.5	-59.9	179.1	31 59.6	-60.0	179.1	30 59.6	-60.0	179.1	29 59.6	-60.0	179.1	28 59.6	-60.0	179.1	27 59.6	-60.0	179.1	40
41	33 59.5	-59.9	179.1	32 59.5	-59.9	179.1	31 59.6	-60.0	179.1	30 59.6	-60.0	179.1	29 59.6	-60.0	179.1	28 59.6	-60.0	179.1	27 59.6	-60.0	179.1	26 59.6	-60.0	179.2	41
42	32 59.6	-60.0	179.1	31 59.6	-60.0	179.1	30 59.6	-60.0	179.1	29 59.6	-60.0	179.1	28 59.6	-60.0	179.2	27 59.6	-60.0	179.2	26 59.6	-60.0	179.2	25 59.6	-60.0	179.2	42
43	31 59.6	-60.0	179.1	30 59.6	-60.0	179.1	29 59.6	-60.0	179.2	28 59.6	-60.0	179.2	27 59.6	-60.0	179.2	26 59.6	-60.0	179.2	25 59.6	-60.0	179.2	24 59.6	-60.0	179.2	43
44	30 59.6	-60.0	179.2	29 59.6	-60.0	179.2	28 59.6	-60.0	179.2	27 59.6	-60.0	179.2	26 59.6	-60.0	179.2	25 59.6	-60.0	179.2	24 59.6	-60.0	179.2	23 59.6	-60.0	179.2	44
45	29 59.6	-60.0	179.2	28 59.6	-60.0	179.2	27 59.6	-60.0	179.2	26 59.6	-60.0	179.2	25 59.6	-60.0	179.2	24 59.6	-60.0	179.2	23 59.6	-60.0	179.2	22 59.6	-60.0	179.2	45
46	28 59.6	-60.0	179.2	27 59.6	-60.0	179.2	26 59.6	-60.0	179.2	25 59.6	-60.0	179.2	24 59.6	-60.0	179.2	23 59.6	-60.0	179.2	22 59.6	-60.0	179.2	21 59.6	-60.0	179.3	46
47	27 59.6	-60.0	179.2	26 59.6	-60.0	179.2	25 59.6	-60.0	179.2	24 59.6	-60.0	179.2	23 59.6	-60.0	179.3	22 59.6	-60.0	179.3	21 59.6	-60.0	179.3	20 59.6	-59.9	179.3	47
48	26 59.6	-60.0	179.2	25 59.6	-60.0	179.3	24 59.6	-60.0	179.3	23 59.6	-60.0	179.3	22 59.6	-60.0	179.3	21 59.6	-59.9	179.3	20 59.6	-59.9	179.3	19 59.7	-60.0	179.3	48
49	25 59.6	-60.0	179.3	24 59.6	-60.0	179.3	23 59.6	-59.9	179.3	22 59.6	-59.9	179.3	21 59.6	-59.9	179.3	20 59.7	-60.0	179.3	19 59.7	-60.0	179.3	18 59.7	-60.0	179.3	49
50	24 59.6	-59.9	179.3	23 59.6	-59.9	179.3	22 59.7	-60.0	179.3	21 59.7	-60.0	179.3	20 59.7	-60.0	179.3	19 59.7	-60.0	179.3	18 59.7	-60.0	179.3	17 59.7	-60.0	179.3	50
51	23 59.7	-60.0	179.3	22 59.7	-60.0	179.3	21 59.7	-60.0	179.3	20 59.7	-60.0	179.3	19 59.7	-60.0	179.3	18 59.7	-60.0	179.3	17 59.7	-60.0	179.3	16 59.7	-60.0	179.3	51
52	22 59.7	-60.0	179.3	21 59.7	-60.0	179.3	20 59.7	-60.0	179.3	19 59.7	-60.0	179.3	18 59.7	-60.0	179.3	17 59.7	-60.0	179.4	16 59.7	-60.0	179.4	15 59.7	-60.0	179.4	52
53	21 59.7	-60.0	179.4	20 59.7	-60.0	179.4	19 59.7	-60.0	179.4	18 59.7	-60.0	179.4	17 59.7	-60.0	179.4	16 59.7	-60.0	179.4	15 59.7	-60.0	179.4	14 59.7	-60.0	179.4	53
54	20 59.7	-60.0	179.4	19 59.7	-60.0	179.4	18 59.7	-60.0	179.4	17 59.7	-60.0	179.4	16 59.7	-60.0	179.4	15 59.7	-60.0	179.4	14 59.7	-60.0	179.4	13 59.7	-60.0	179.4	54
55	19 59.7	-60.0	179.4	18 59.7	-60.0	179.4	17 59.7	-60.0	179.4	16 59.7	-60.0	179.4	15 59.7	-60.0	179.4	14 59.7	-60.0	179.4	13 59.7	-60.0	179.4	12 59.7	-60.0	179.4	55
56	18 59.7	-60.0	179.4	17 59.7	-60.0	179.4	16 59.7	-60.0	179.4	15 59.7	-60.0	179.4	14 59.7	-60.0	179.4	13 59.7	-60.0	179.4	12 59.7	-60.0	179.4	11 59.7	-60.0	179.4	56
57	17 59.7	-60.0	179.4	16 59.7	-60.0	179.4	15 59.7	-60.0	179.4	14 59.7	-60.0	179.4	13 59.7	-60.0	179.4	12 59.7	-60.0	179.4	11 59.7	-60.0	179.4	10 59.7	-60.0	179.4	57
58	16 59.7	-60.0	179.4	15 59.7	-60.0	179.4	14 59.7	-60.0	179.5	13 59.7	-60.0	179.5	12 59.7	-60.0	179.5	11 59.7	-60.0	179.5	10 59.7	-60.0	179.5	9 59.7	-60.0	179.5	58
59	15 59.7	-60.0	179.5	14 59.7	-60.0	179.5	13 59.7	-60.0	179.5	12 59.7	-60.0	179.5	11 59.7	-60.0	179.5	10 59.7	-59.9	179.5	9 59.7	-59.9	179.5	8 59.7	-59.9	179.5	59
60	14 59.7	-60.0	179.5	13 59.7	-60.0	179.5	12 59.7	-59.9	179.5	11 59.7	-59.9	179.5	10 59.7	-59.9	179.5	9 59.8	-60.0	179.5	8 59.8	-60.0	179.5	7 59.8	-60.0	179.5	60
61	13 59.7	-59.9	179.5	12 59.7	-59.9	179.5	11 59.8	-60.0	179.5	10 59.8	-60.0	179.5	9 59.8	-60.0	179.5	8 59.8	-60.0	179.5	7 59.8	-60.0	179.5	6 59.8	-60.0	179.5	61
62	12 59.8	-60.0	179.5	11 59.8	-60.0	179.5	10 59.8	-60.0	179.5	9 59.8	-60.0	179.5	8 59.8	-60.0	179.5	7 59.8	-60.0	179.5	6 59.8	-60.0	179.5	5 59.8	-60.0	179.5	62
63	11 59.8	-60.0	179.5	10 59.8	-60.0	179.5	9 59.8	-60.0	179.5	8 59.8	-60.0	179.5	7 59.8	-60.0	179.5	6 59.8	-60.0	179.5	5 59.8	-60.0	179.5	4 59.8	-60.0	179.5	63
64	10 59.8	-60.0	179.6	9 59.8	-60.0	179.6	8 59.8	-60.0	179.6	7 59.8	-60.0	179.6	6 59.8	-60.0	179.6	5 59.8	-60.0	179.6	4 59.8	-60.0	179.6	3 59.8	-60.0	179.6	64
65	9 59.8	-60.0	179.6	8 59.8	-60.0	179.6	7 59.8	-60.0	179.6	6 59.8	-60.0	179.6	5 59.8	-60.0	179.6	4 59.8	-60.0	179.6	3 59.8	-60.0	179.6	2 59.8	-60.0	179.6	65
66	8 59.8	-60.0	179.6	7 59.8	-60.0	179.6	6 59.8	-60.0	179.6	5 59.8	-60.0	179.6	4 59.8	-60.0	179.6	3 59.8	-60.0	179.6	2 59.8	-60.0	179.6	1 59.8	-60.0	179.6	66
67	7 59.8	-60.0	179.6	6 59.8	-60.0	179.6	5 59.8	-60.0	179.6	4 59.8	-60.0	179.6	3 59.8	-60.0	179.6	2 59.8	-60.0	179.6	1 59.8	-60.0	179.6	0 59.8	-60.0	179.6	67
68	6 59.8	-60.0	179.6	5 59.8	-60.0	179.6	4 59.8	-60.0	179.6	3 59.8	-60.0	179.6	2 59.8	-60.0	179.6	1 59.8	-60.0	179.6	0 59.8	-60.0	179.6	0 00.2	+60.0	0.4	68
69	5 59.8	-60.0	179.6	4 59.8	-60.0	179.6	3 59.8	-60.0	179.6	2 59.8	-60.0	179.6	1 59.8	-60.0	179.6	0 59.8	-60.0	179.6	0 00.2	+60.0	0.4	1 00.2	+60.0	0.4	69
70	4 59.8	-60.0	179.7	3 59.8	-60.0	179.7	2 59.8	-60.0	179.7	1 59.8	-60.0	179.7	0 59.8	-60.0	179.7	0 00.2	+60.0	0.3	1 00.2	+60.0	0.3	2 00.2	+60.0	0.3	70
71	3 59.8	-60.0	179.7	2 59.8	-60.0	179.7	1 59.8	-60.0	179.7	0 59.8	-60.0	179.7	0 00.2	+60.0	0.3	1 00.2	+60.0	0.3	2 00.2	+60.0	0.3	3 00.2	+60.0	0.3	71
72	2 59.8	-59.9	179.7	1 59.8	-59.9	179.7	0 59.8	-59.9	179.7	0 00.2	+59.9	0.3	1 00.2	+59.9	0.3	2 00.2	+59.9	0.3	3 00.2	+59.9	0.3	4 00.2	+59.9	0.3	72
73	1 59.9	-60.0	179.7	0 59.9	-60.0	179.7	0 00.1	+60.0	0.3	1 00.1	+60.0	0.3	2 00.1	+60.0	0.3	3 00.1	+60.0	0.3	4 00.1	+60.0	0.3	5 00.1	+60.0	0.3	73
74	0 59.9	-60.0	179.7	0 00.1	+60.0	0.3	1 00.1	+60.0	0.3	2 00.1	+60.0	0.3	3 00.1	+60.0	0.3	4 00.1	+60.0	0.3	5 00.1	+60.0	0.3	6 00.1	+60.0	0.3	74
75	0 00.1	+60.0	0.3	1 00.1	+60.0	0.3	2 00.1	+60.0	0.3	3 00.1	+60.0	0.3	4 00.1	+60.0	0.3	5 00.1	+60.0	0.3	6 00.1	+60.0	0.3	7 00.1	+60.0	0.3	75
76	1 00.1	+60.0	0.2	2 00.1	+60.0	0.2	3 00.1	+60.0	0.2	4 00.1	+60.0	0.2	5 00.1	+60.0	0.2	6 00.1	+60.0	0.2	7 00.1	+60.0	0.2	8 00.1	+60.0	0.2	76
77	2 00.1	+60.0	0.2	3 00.1	+60.0	0.2	4 00.1	+60.0	0.2	5 00.1	+60.0	0.2	6 00.1	+60.0	0.2	7 00.1	+60.0	0.2	8 00.1	+60.0	0.2	9 00.1	+60.0	0.2	77
78	3 00.1	+60.0	0.2	4 00.1	+60.0	0.2	5 00.1	+60.0	0.2	6 00.1	+60.0	0.2	7 00.1	+60.0	0.2	8 00.1	+60.0	0.2	9 00.1	+60.0	0.2	10 00.1	+60.0	0.2	78
79	4 00.1	+60.0	0.2	5 00.1	+60.0	0.2	6 00.1	+60.0	0.2	7 00.1	+60.0	0.2	8 00.1	+60.0	0.2	9 00.1	+60.0	0.2	10 00.1	+60.0	0.2	11 00.1	+60.0	0.2	79
80	5 00.1	+60.0	0.2	6 00.1	+60.0	0.2	7 00.1	+60.0	0.2	8 00.1	+60.0	0.2	9 00.1	+60.0	0.2	10 00.1	+60.0	0.2	11 00.1	+60.0	0.2	12 00.1	+60.0	0.2	80
81	6 00.1	+60.0	0.2	7 00.1	+60.0	0.2	8 00.1	+60.0	0.2	9 00.1	+60.0	0.2	10 00.1	+60.0	0.2	11 00.1	+60.0	0.2	12 00.1	+60.0	0.2	13 00.1	+60.0	0.2	81
82	7 00.1	+60.0	0.1	8 00.1	+60.0	0.1	9 00.1	+60.0	0.1	10 00.1	+60.0	0.1	11 00.1	+60.0	0.1	12 00.1	+60.0	0.1	13 00.1	+60.0	0.1	14 00.1	+60.0	0.1	82
83	8 00.1	+60.0	0.1	9 00.1	+60.0	0.1	10 00.1	+60.0	0.1	11 00.1	+60.0	0.1	12 00.1	+60.0	0.1	13 00.1	+60.0	0.1	14 00.1	+60.0	0.1	15 00.1	+60.0	0.1	83
84	9 00.1	+59.9	0.1	10 00.1	+59.9	0.1	11 00.1	+59.9	0.1	12 00.1	+59.9	0.1	13 00.1	+59.9	0.1	14 00.1	+59.9	0.1	15 00.1	+59.9	0.1	16 00.1	+59.9	0.1	84
85	10 00.0	+60.0	0.1	11 00.0	+60.0	0.1	12 00.0	+60.0	0.1	13 00.0	+60.0	0.1	14 00.0	+60.0	0.1	15 00.0	+60.0	0.1	16 00.0	+60.0	0.1	17 00.0	+60.0	0.1	85
86	11 00.0	+60.0	0.1	12 00.0	+60.0	0.1	13 00.0	+60.0	0.1	14 00.0	+60.0	0.1	15 00.0	+60.0	0.1	16 00.0	+60.0	0.1	17 00.0	+60.0	0.1	18 00.0	+60.0	0.1	86
87	12 00.0	+60.0	0.1	13 00.0	+60.0	0.1	14 00.0	+60.0	0.1	15 00.0	+60.0	0.1	16 00.0	+60.0	0.1	17 00.0	+60.0	0.1	18 00.0	+60.0	0.1	19 00.0	+60.0	0.1	87
88	13 00.0	+60.0	0.0	14 00.0	+60.0	0.0	15 00.0	+60.0	0.0	16 00.0	+60.0	0.0	17 00.0	+60.0	0.0	18 00.0	+60.0	0.0	19 00.0	+60.0	0.0	20 00.0	+60.0	0.0	88
89	14 00.0	+60.0	0.0	15 00.0	+60.0	0.0	16 00.0	+60.0	0.0	17 00.0	+60.0	0.0	18 00.0	+60.0	0.0	19 00.0	+60.0	0.0	20 00.0	+60.0	0.0	21 00.0	+60.0	0.0	89
90	15 00.0	+60.0	0.0	16 00.0	+60.0	0.0	17 00.0	+60.0	0.0	18 00.0	+60.0	0.0	19 00.0	+60.0	0.0	20 00.0	+60.0	0.0	21 00.0	+60.0	0.0	22 00.0	+60.0	0.0	90
	15°			16°			17°			18°			19°			20°			21°			22°			

S. Lat. { L.H.A. greater than 180° ....Zn=180°–Z
L.H.A. less than 180°...........Zn=180°+Z

LATITUDE SAME NAME AS DECLINATION L.H.A. 179°, 181°

5

N. Lat. {L.H.A. greater than 180° .....Zn=Z; L.H.A. less than 180°............Zn=360°−Z}

Dec.	15° Hc	15° d	15° Z	16° Hc	16° d	16° Z	17° Hc	17° d	17° Z	18° Hc	18° d	18° Z
°	° ′	′	°	° ′	′	°	° ′	′	°	° ′	′	°
0	74 52.2	+59.5	172.3	73 52.7	+59.6	172.8	72 53.2	+59.6	173.2	71 53.6	+59.6	173.6
1	75 51.7	+59.4	171.8	74 52.3	+59.4	172.3	73 52.8	+59.5	172.8	72 53.2	+59.6	173.2
2	76 51.1	+59.2	171.2	75 51.7	+59.4	171.8	74 52.3	+59.5	172.3	73 52.8	+59.5	172.8
3	77 50.3	+59.2	170.5	76 51.1	+59.3	171.2	75 51.8	+59.4	171.8	74 52.3	+59.5	172.3
4	78 49.5	+59.0	169.7	77 50.4	+59.2	170.5	76 51.2	+59.3	171.2	75 51.8	+59.4	171.8
5	79 48.5	+58.8	168.7	78 49.6	+59.0	169.7	77 50.5	+59.1	170.5	76 51.2	+59.3	171.2
6	80 47.3	+58.5	167.5	79 48.6	+58.8	168.7	78 49.6	+59.1	169.7	77 50.5	+59.2	170.5
7	81 45.8	+58.1	166.0	80 47.4	+58.5	167.5	79 48.7	+58.8	168.7	78 49.7	+59.0	169.7
8	82 43.9	+57.5	164.1	81 45.9	+58.1	166.0	80 47.5	+58.5	167.5	79 48.7	+58.9	168.7
9	83 41.4	+56.6	161.7	82 44.0	+57.5	164.2	81 46.0	+58.1	166.1	80 47.6	+58.5	167.6
10	84 38.0	+55.0	•158.4	83 41.5	+56.6	161.8	82 44.1	+57.6	164.2	81 46.1	+58.2	166.1
11	85 33.0	+52.5	•153.8	84 38.1	+55.2	•158.5	83 41.7	+56.6	161.8	82 44.3	+57.5	164.3
12	86 25.5	+47.3	•146.8	85 33.3	+52.5	•153.9	84 38.3	+55.2	•158.6	83 41.8	+56.7	161.9
13	87 12.8	+36.4	•135.6	86 25.8	+47.4	•146.9	85 33.5	+52.6	•154.0	84 38.5	+55.2	•158.6
14	87 49.2	+14.9	•117.1	87 13.2	+36.5	•135.7	86 26.1	+47.5	•147.0	85 33.7	+52.7	•154.0
15	88 04.1	−14.4	• 89.7	87 49.7	+14.9	•117.2	87 13.6	+36.6	•135.9	86 26.4	+47.6	•147.1
16	87 49.7	−36.1	• 62.3	88 04.6	−14.4	• 89.7	87 50.2	+15.0	•117.3	87 14.0	+36.8	•136.0
17	87 13.6	−47.2	• 43.6	87 50.2	−36.2	• 62.2	88 05.2	−14.4	• 89.7	87 50.8	+15.1	•117.4
18	86 26.4	−52.4	• 32.3	87 14.0	−47.3	• 43.4	87 50.8	−36.4	• 62.0	88 05.9	−14.5	• 89.7
19	85 34.0	−55.1	• 25.3	86 26.7	−52.4	• 32.2	87 14.4	−47.3	• 43.3	87 51.4	−36.5	• 61.9
20	84 38.9	−56.5	20.6	85 34.3	−55.1	• 25.1	86 27.1	−52.6	• 32.0	87 14.9	−47.5	• 43.1
21	83 42.4	−57.5	17.3	84 39.2	−56.6	20.5	85 34.5	−55.1	• 25.0	86 27.4	−52.6	• 31.8
22	82 44.9	−58.1	14.9	83 42.6	−57.5	17.2	84 39.4	−56.6	20.3	85 34.8	−55.1	• 24.8
23	81 46.8	−58.5	13.0	82 45.1	−58.1	14.7	83 42.8	−57.6	17.1	84 39.7	−56.7	20.2
24	80 48.3	−58.8	11.5	81 47.0	−58.5	12.9	82 45.2	−58.1	14.6	83 43.0	−57.6	16.9
25	79 49.5	−59.0	10.3	80 48.5	−58.8	11.4	81 47.1	−58.5	12.8	82 45.4	−58.1	14.5
26	78 50.5	−59.1	9.3	79 49.7	−59.0	10.2	80 48.6	−58.8	11.3	81 47.3	−58.5	12.7
27	77 51.4	−59.3	8.5	78 50.7	−59.2	9.2	79 49.8	−59.0	10.1	80 48.8	−58.8	11.2
28	76 52.1	−59.4	7.8	77 51.5	−59.3	8.4	78 50.8	−59.2	9.2	79 50.0	−59.1	10.1
29	75 52.7	−59.4	7.2	76 52.2	−59.4	7.7	77 51.6	−59.3	8.3	78 50.9	−59.1	9.1
30	74 53.3	−59.6	6.7	75 52.8	−59.4	7.1	76 52.3	−59.4	7.6	77 51.8	−59.4	8.3
31	73 53.7	−59.6	6.2	74 53.4	−59.6	6.6	75 52.9	−59.4	7.0	76 52.4	−59.4	7.6
32	72 54.1	−59.6	5.8	73 53.8	−59.6	6.1	74 53.5	−59.6	6.5	75 53.0	−59.4	7.0
33	71 54.5	−59.6	5.4	72 54.2	−59.6	5.7	73 53.9	−59.6	6.1	74 53.6	−59.6	6.4
34	70 54.9	−59.7	5.1	71 54.6	−59.7	5.3	72 54.3	−59.6	5.6	73 54.0	−59.6	6.0
35	69 55.2	−59.8	4.8	70 54.9	−59.7	5.0	71 54.7	−59.7	5.3	72 54.4	−59.6	5.6
36	68 55.4	−59.7	4.5	69 55.2	−59.7	4.7	70 55.0	−59.7	5.0	71 54.8	−59.7	5.2
37	67 55.7	−59.8	4.3	68 55.5	−59.7	4.4	69 55.3	−59.7	4.7	70 55.1	−59.7	4.9
38	66 55.9	−59.8	4.0	67 55.8	−59.8	4.2	68 55.6	−59.7	4.4	69 55.4	−59.7	4.6
39	65 56.1	−59.8	3.8	66 56.0	−59.8	4.0	67 55.9	−59.8	4.1	68 55.7	−59.8	4.3
40	64 56.3	−59.8	3.6	65 56.2	−59.8	3.8	66 56.1	−59.8	3.9	67 55.9	−59.7	4.1
41	63 56.5	−59.8	3.4	64 56.4	−59.8	3.6	65 56.3	−59.8	3.7	66 56.2	−59.8	3.9
42	62 56.7	−59.8	3.3	63 56.6	−59.8	3.4	64 56.5	−59.8	3.5	65 56.4	−59.8	3.6
43	61 56.9	−59.9	3.1	62 56.8	−59.9	3.2	63 56.7	−59.9	3.3	64 56.6	−59.9	3.5
44	60 57.0	−59.9	3.0	61 56.9	−59.8	3.1	62 56.8	−59.8	3.2	63 56.7	−59.8	3.3
45	59 57.1	−59.8	2.8	60 57.1	−59.9	2.9	61 57.0	−59.9	3.0	62 56.9	−59.8	3.1
46	58 57.3	−59.9	2.7	59 57.2	−59.9	2.8	60 57.1	−59.8	2.9	61 57.1	−59.9	3.0
47	57 57.4	−59.9	2.6	58 57.3	−59.8	2.6	59 57.3	−59.9	2.7	60 57.2	−59.9	2.8
48	56 57.5	−59.9	2.5	57 57.5	−59.9	2.5	58 57.4	−59.9	2.6	59 57.3	−59.8	2.7
49	55 57.6	−59.9	2.3	56 57.6	−59.9	2.4	57 57.5	−59.9	2.5	58 57.5	−59.9	2.5
50	54 57.7	−59.9	2.2	55 57.7	−59.9	2.3	56 57.6	−59.9	2.4	57 57.6	−59.9	2.4
51	53 57.8	−59.9	2.1	54 57.8	−59.9	2.2	55 57.7	−59.8	2.2	56 57.7	−59.9	2.3
52	52 57.9	−59.9	2.0	53 57.9	−59.9	2.1	54 57.9	−59.9	2.1	55 57.8	−59.9	2.2
53	51 58.0	−59.9	2.0	52 58.0	−59.9	2.0	53 58.0	−60.0	2.0	54 57.9	−59.9	2.1
54	50 58.1	−59.9	1.9	51 58.1	−59.9	1.9	52 58.0	−59.9	2.0	53 58.0	−59.9	2.0
55	49 58.2	−59.9	1.8	50 58.2	−60.0	1.8	51 58.1	−59.9	1.9	52 58.1	−59.9	1.9
56	48 58.3	−59.9	1.7	49 58.2	−59.9	1.7	50 58.2	−59.9	1.8	51 58.2	−59.9	1.8
57	47 58.4	−60.0	1.6	48 58.3	−59.9	1.7	49 58.3	−59.9	1.7	50 58.3	−59.9	1.7
58	46 58.4	−59.9	1.6	47 58.4	−59.9	1.6	48 58.4	−59.9	1.6	49 58.4	−60.0	1.6
59	45 58.5	−59.9	1.5	46 58.5	−59.9	1.5	47 58.5	−60.0	1.5	48 58.4	−59.9	1.6
60	44 58.6	−60.0	1.4	45 58.6	−60.0	1.4	46 58.5	−59.9	1.5	47 58.5	−59.9	1.5
61	43 58.6	−59.9	1.3	44 58.6	−60.0	1.4	45 58.6	−59.9	1.4	46 58.6	−59.9	1.4
62	42 58.7	−59.9	1.3	43 58.7	−59.9	1.3	44 58.7	−60.0	1.3	45 58.7	−60.0	1.4
63	41 58.8	−60.0	1.2	42 58.8	−60.0	1.2	43 58.7	−59.9	1.3	44 58.7	−59.9	1.3
64	40 58.8	−59.9	1.2	41 58.8	−59.9	1.2	42 58.8	−59.9	1.2	43 58.8	−60.0	1.2
65	39 58.9	−60.0	1.1	40 58.9	−60.0	1.1	41 58.9	−60.0	1.1	42 58.8	−59.9	1.2
66	38 58.9	−59.9	1.0	39 58.9	−59.9	1.1	40 58.9	−59.9	1.1	41 58.9	−59.9	1.1
67	37 59.0	−59.9	1.0	38 59.0	−60.0	1.0	39 59.0	−60.0	1.0	40 59.0	−60.0	1.0
68	36 59.1	−60.0	0.9	37 59.0	−59.9	1.0	38 59.0	−59.9	1.0	39 59.0	−59.9	1.0
69	35 59.1	−59.9	0.9	36 59.1	−60.0	0.9	37 59.1	−60.0	0.9	38 59.1	−60.0	0.9
70	34 59.2	−60.0	0.8	35 59.1	−59.9	0.8	36 59.1	−59.9	0.9	37 59.1	−59.9	0.9
71	33 59.2	−59.9	0.8	34 59.2	−60.0	0.8	35 59.2	−60.0	0.8	36 59.2	−60.0	0.8
72	32 59.3	−60.0	0.7	33 59.2	−59.9	0.7	34 59.2	−59.9	0.8	35 59.2	−59.9	0.8
73	31 59.3	−60.0	0.7	32 59.3	−60.0	0.7	33 59.3	−60.0	0.7	34 59.3	−60.0	0.7
74	30 59.3	−59.9	0.6	31 59.3	−59.9	0.6	32 59.3	−59.9	0.7	33 59.3	−59.9	0.7
75	29 59.4	−60.0	0.6	30 59.4	−60.0	0.6	31 59.4	−60.0	0.6	32 59.4	−60.0	0.6
76	28 59.4	−59.9	0.6	29 59.4	−59.9	0.6	30 59.4	−60.0	0.6	31 59.4	−59.9	0.6
77	27 59.5	−60.0	0.5	28 59.5	−60.0	0.5	29 59.5	−60.0	0.5	30 59.5	−60.0	0.5
78	26 59.5	−59.9	0.5	27 59.5	−59.9	0.5	28 59.5	−59.9	0.5	29 59.5	−59.9	0.5
79	25 59.6	−60.0	0.4	26 59.6	−60.0	0.4	27 59.6	−60.0	0.4	28 59.6	−60.0	0.4
80	24 59.6	−59.9	0.4	25 59.6	−59.9	0.4	26 59.6	−59.9	0.4	27 59.6	−59.9	0.4
81	23 59.7	−60.0	0.3	24 59.7	−60.0	0.3	25 59.7	−60.0	0.3	26 59.7	−60.0	0.4
82	22 59.7	−60.0	0.3	23 59.7	−60.0	0.3	24 59.7	−60.0	0.3	25 59.7	−60.0	0.3
83	21 59.7	−59.9	0.3	22 59.7	−59.9	0.3	23 59.7	−59.9	0.3	24 59.7	−59.9	0.3
84	20 59.8	−60.0	0.2	21 59.8	−60.0	0.2	22 59.8	−60.0	0.2	23 59.8	−60.0	0.2
85	19 59.8	−59.9	0.2	20 59.8	−59.9	0.2	21 59.8	−59.9	0.2	22 59.8	−59.9	0.2
86	18 59.9	−60.0	0.1	19 59.9	−60.0	0.1	20 59.9	−60.0	0.1	21 59.9	−60.0	0.2
87	17 59.9	−60.0	0.1	18 59.9	−60.0	0.1	19 59.9	−60.0	0.1	20 59.9	−60.0	0.1
88	16 59.9	−59.9	0.1	17 59.9	−59.9	0.1	18 59.9	−59.9	0.1	19 59.9	−59.9	0.1
89	16 00.0	−60.0	0.0	17 00.0	−60.0	0.0	18 00.0	−60.0	0.0	19 00.0	−60.0	0.0
90	15 00.0	−60.0	0.0	16 00.0	−60.0	0.0	17 00.0	−60.0	0.0	18 00.0	−60.0	0.0
	15°			16°			17°			18°		

Dec.	19° Hc	19° d	19° Z	20° Hc	20° d	20° Z	21° Hc	21° d	21° Z	22° Hc	22° d	22° Z
°	° ′	′	°	° ′	′	°	° ′	′	°	° ′	′	°
0	70 53.9	+59.7	173.9	69 54.3	+59.7	174.2	68 54.6	+59.7	174.4	67 54.8	+59.8	174.7
1	71 53.6	+59.7	173.6	70 54.0	+59.7	173.9	69 54.3	+59.7	174.2	68 54.6	+59.7	174.4
2	72 53.3	+59.6	173.2	71 53.7	+59.6	173.6	70 54.0	+59.7	173.9	69 54.3	+59.8	174.2
3	73 52.9	+59.5	172.8	72 53.3	+59.6	173.2	71 53.7	+59.7	173.6	70 54.1	+59.6	173.9
4	74 52.4	+59.5	172.3	73 52.9	+59.6	172.8	72 53.4	+59.6	173.2	71 53.7	+59.7	173.6
5	75 51.9	+59.4	171.8	74 52.5	+59.4	172.3	73 53.0	+59.5	172.8	72 53.4	+59.6	173.2
6	76 51.3	+59.3	171.2	75 51.9	+59.5	171.8	74 52.5	+59.5	172.4	73 53.0	+59.6	172.8
7	77 50.6	+59.2	170.5	76 51.4	+59.3	171.2	75 52.0	+59.4	171.8	74 52.6	+59.5	172.4
8	78 49.8	+59.0	169.7	77 50.7	+59.2	170.6	76 51.4	+59.4	171.3	75 52.1	+59.4	171.9
9	79 48.8	+58.9	168.8	78 49.9	+59.0	169.7	77 50.8	+59.2	170.6	76 51.5	+59.4	171.3
10	80 47.7	+58.5	167.6	79 48.9	+58.9	168.8	78 50.0	+59.0	169.8	77 50.9	+59.2	170.6
11	81 46.2	+58.2	166.2	80 47.8	+58.6	167.6	79 49.0	+58.9	168.8	78 50.1	+59.1	169.8
12	82 44.4	+57.6	164.3	81 46.4	+58.1	166.2	80 47.9	+58.6	167.7	79 49.2	+58.8	168.9
13	83 42.0	+56.7	161.9	82 44.5	+57.7	164.4	81 46.5	+58.2	166.2	80 48.0	+58.6	167.7
14	84 38.7	+55.3	•158.7	83 42.2	+56.7	162.0	82 44.7	+57.7	164.4	81 46.6	+58.3	166.3
15	85 34.0	+52.7	•154.1	84 38.9	+55.4	158.8	83 42.4	+56.8	162.1	82 44.9	+57.7	164.5
16	86 26.7	+47.7	•147.2	85 34.3	+52.8	•154.3	84 39.2	+55.3	158.9	83 42.6	+56.8	162.2
17	87 14.4	+37.0	•136.1	86 27.1	+47.8	•147.4	85 34.5	+52.9	•154.4	84 39.4	+55.4	159.0
18	87 51.4	+15.1	•117.5	87 14.9	+37.1	•136.3	86 27.4	+47.9	•147.5	85 34.8	+53.0	•154.5
19	88 06.5	−14.5	• 89.7	87 52.0	+15.2	•117.6	87 15.3	+37.3	•136.4	86 27.8	+48.0	•147.7
20	87 52.0	−36.7	• 61.7	88 07.2	−14.6	• 89.7	87 52.6	+15.4	•117.7	87 15.8	+37.5	•136.6
21	87 15.3	−47.5	• 42.9	87 52.6	−36.8	• 61.6	88 08.0	−14.7	• 89.6	87 53.3	+15.4	•117.9
22	86 27.8	−52.6	• 31.6	87 15.8	−47.6	• 42.7	87 53.3	−36.9	• 61.4	88 08.7	−14.8	• 89.6
23	85 35.2	−55.3	• 24.7	86 28.2	−52.7	• 31.4	87 16.4	−47.8	• 42.5	87 53.9	−37.0	• 61.2
24	84 39.9	−56.7	20.1	85 35.5	−55.3	• 24.5	86 28.6	−52.8	• 31.3	87 16.9	−47.9	• 42.2
25	83 43.2	−57.6	16.8	84 40.2	−56.7	19.9	85 35.8	−55.3	• 24.3	86 29.0	−52.8	• 31.0
26	82 45.6	−58.1	14.4	83 43.5	−57.7	16.7	84 40.5	−56.8	19.8	85 36.2	−55.4	• 24.1
27	81 47.5	−58.6	12.6	82 45.8	−58.1	14.3	83 43.7	−57.6	16.5	84 40.8	−56.8	19.6
28	80 48.9	−58.8	11.1	81 47.7	−58.6	12.5	82 46.1	−58.2	14.2	83 44.0	−57.7	16.4
29	79 50.1	−59.0	10.0	80 49.1	−58.8	11.0	81 47.9	−58.6	12.4	82 46.3	−58.2	14.0
30	78 51.1	−59.2	9.0	79 50.3	−59.1	9.9	80 49.3	−58.9	10.9	81 48.1	−58.6	12.2
31	77 51.9	−59.3	8.2	78 51.2	−59.2	8.9	79 50.4	−59.0	9.8	80 49.5	−58.9	10.8
32	76 52.6	−59.4	7.5	77 52.0	−59.3	8.1	78 51.4	−59.2	8.8	79 50.6	−59.1	9.7
33	75 53.2	−59.5	6.9	76 52.7	−59.4	7.4	77 52.2	−59.4	8.0	78 51.5	−59.2	8.7
34	74 53.7	−59.6	6.4	75 53.3	−59.5	6.8	76 52.8	−59.4	7.3	77 52.3	−59.3	7.9
35	73 54.1	−59.6	5.9	74 53.8	−59.6	6.3	75 53.4	−59.5	6.7	76 53.0	−59.5	7.2
36	72 54.5	−59.6	5.5	73 54.2	−59.6	5.8	74 53.9	−59.5	6.2	75 53.5	−59.5	6.7
37	71 54.9	−59.7	5.2	72 54.6	−59.6	5.4	73 54.4	−59.7	5.8	74 54.0	−59.5	6.1
38	70 55.2	−59.7	4.8	71 55.0	−59.7	5.1	72 54.7	−59.6	5.4	73 54.5	−59.6	5.7
39	69 55.5	−59.7	4.5	70 55.3	−59.7	4.8	71 55.1	−59.7	5.0	72 54.9	−59.7	5.3
40	68 55.8	−59.8	4.3	69 55.6	−59.7	4.5	70 55.4	−59.7	4.7	71 55.2	−59.7	4.9
41	67 56.0	−59.8	4.0	68 55.9	−59.8	4.2	69 55.7	−59.7	4.4	70 55.5	−59.7	4.6
42	66 56.2	−59.8	3.8	67 56.1	−59.8	4.0	68 56.0	−59.8	4.1	69 55.8	−59.8	4.3
43	65 56.4	−59.8	3.6	66 56.3	−59.8	3.7	67 56.2	−59.8	3.9	68 56.0	−59.7	4.1
44	64 56.6	−59.8	3.4	65 56.5	−59.8	3.5	66 56.4	−59.8	3.7	67 56.3	−59.8	3.8
45	63 56.8	−59.8	3.2	64 56.7	−59.8	3.3	65 56.6	−59.8	3.5	66 56.5	−59.8	3.6
46	62 57.0	−59.9	3.1	63 56.9	−59.9	3.2	64 56.8	−59.8	3.3	65 56.7	−59.8	3.4
47	61 57.1	−59.8	2.9	62 57.0	−59.8	3.0	63 57.0	−59.9	3.1	64 56.9	−59.9	3.2
48	60 57.3	−59.9	2.8	61 57.2	−59.9	2.8	62 57.1	−59.8	2.9	63 57.0	−59.8	3.0
49	59 57.4	−59.9	2.6	60 57.3	−59.8	2.7	61 57.3	−59.9	2.8	62 57.2	−59.9	2.9
50	58 57.5	−59.9	2.5	59 57.5	−59.9	2.6	60 57.4	−59.9	2.6	61 57.3	−59.8	2.7
51	57 57.6	−59.8	2.4	58 57.6	−59.9	2.4	59 57.5	−59.8	2.5	60 57.5	−59.9	2.6
52	56 57.8	−59.9	2.3	57 57.7	−59.9	2.3	58 57.7	−59.9	2.4	59 57.6	−59.9	2.5
53	55 57.9	−59.9	2.2	56 57.8	−59.9	2.2	57 57.8	−59.9	2.3	58 57.7	−59.9	2.3
54	54 58.0	−59.9	2.0	55 57.9	−59.9	2.1	56 57.9	−59.9	2.2	57 57.8	−59.8	2.2
55	53 58.1	−59.9	2.0	54 58.0	−59.9	2.0	55 58.0	−59.9	2.0	56 58.0	−59.9	2.1
56	52 58.2	−60.0	1.9	53 58.1	−59.9	1.9	54 58.1	−59.9	1.9	55 58.1	−59.9	2.0
57	51 58.2	−59.9	1.8	52 58.2	−59.9	1.8	53 58.2	−59.9	1.9	54 58.2	−59.9	1.9
58	50 58.3	−59.9	1.7	51 58.3	−59.9	1.7	52 58.3	−59.9	1.8	53 58.3	−60.0	1.8
59	49 58.4	−59.9	1.6	50 58.4	−59.9	1.6	51 58.4	−60.0	1.7	52 58.3	−59.9	1.7
60	48 58.5	−59.9	1.5	49 58.5	−60.0	1.6	50 58.4	−59.9	1.6	51 58.4	−59.9	1.6
61	47 58.6	−60.0	1.4	48 58.5	−59.9	1.5	49 58.5	−59.9	1.5	50 58.5	−59.9	1.5
62	46 58.6	−59.9	1.4	47 58.6	−59.9	1.4	48 58.6	−59.9	1.4	49 58.6	−59.9	1.5
63	45 58.7	−59.9	1.3	46 58.7	−59.9	1.3	47 58.7	−60.0	1.4	48 58.7	−60.0	1.4
64	44 58.8	−60.0	1.2	45 58.8	−60.0	1.3	46 58.7	−59.9	1.3	47 58.7	−59.9	1.3
65	43 58.8	−59.9	1.2	44 58.8	−59.9	1.2	45 58.8	−59.9	1.2	46 58.8	−59.9	1.2
66	42 58.9	−59.9	1.1	43 58.9	−60.0	1.1	44 58.9	−60.0	1.1	45 58.9	−60.0	1.2
67	41 59.0	−60.0	1.1	42 58.9	−59.9	1.1	43 58.9	−59.9	1.1	44 58.9	−59.9	1.1
68	40 59.0	−59.9	1.0	41 59.0	−59.9	1.0	42 59.0	−59.9	1.0	43 59.0	−60.0	1.0
69	39 59.1	−60.0	0.9	40 59.1	−60.0	0.9	41 59.1	−60.0	1.0	42 59.0	−59.9	1.0
70	38 59.1	−59.9	0.9	39 59.1	−59.9	0.9	40 59.1	−59.9	0.9	41 59.1	−59.9	0.9
71	37 59.2	−60.0	0.8	38 59.2	−60.0	0.8	39 59.2	−60.0	0.8	40 59.2	−60.0	0.9
72	36 59.2	−59.9	0.8	37 59.2	−59.9	0.8	38 59.2	−59.9	0.8	39 59.2	−59.9	0.8
73	35 59.3	−60.0	0.7	36 59.3	−60.0	0.7	37 59.3	−60.0	0.7	38 59.3	−60.0	0.8
74	34 59.3	−59.9	0.7	35 59.3	−59.9	0.7	36 59.3	−59.9	0.7	37 59.3	−59.9	0.7
75	33 59.4	−60.0	0.6	34 59.4	−60.0	0.6	35 59.4	−60.0	0.6	36 59.4	−60.0	0.6
76	32 59.4	−59.9	0.6	33 59.4	−59.9	0.6	34 59.4	−59.9	0.6	35 59.4	−59.9	0.6
77	31 59.5	−60.0	0.5	32 59.5	−60.0	0.5	33 59.5	−60.0	0.5	34 59.5	−60.0	0.5
78	30 59.5	−59.9	0.5	31 59.5	−59.9	0.5	32 59.5	−59.9	0.5	33 59.5	−59.9	0.5
79	29 59.6	−60.0	0.4	30 59.6	−60.0	0.4	31 59.6	−60.0	0.4	32 59.6	−60.0	0.5
80	28 59.6	−60.0	0.4	29 59.6	−60.0	0.4	30 59.6	−60.0	0.4	31 59.6	−60.0	0.4
81	27 59.6	−59.9	0.4	28 59.6	−59.9	0.4	29 59.6	−59.9	0.4	30 59.6	−59.9	0.4
82	26 59.7	−60.0	0.3	27 59.7	−60.0	0.3	28 59.7	−60.0	0.3	29 59.7	−60.0	0.3
83	25 59.7	−59.9	0.3	26 59.7	−59.9	0.3	27 59.7	−59.9	0.3	28 59.7	−59.9	0.3
84	24 59.8	−60.0	0.2	25 59.8	−60.0	0.2	26 59.8	−60.0	0.2	27 59.8	−60.0	0.2
85	23 59.8	−59.9	0.2	24 59.8	−60.0	0.2	25 59.8	−60.0	0.2	26 59.8	−60.0	0.2
86	22 59.9	−60.0	0.2	23 59.8	−59.9	0.2	24 59.8	−59.9	0.2	25 59.8	−59.9	0.2
87	21 59.9	−60.0	0.1	22 59.9	−60.0	0.1	23 59.9	−60.0	0.1	24 59.9	−60.0	0.1
88	20 59.9	−59.9	0.1	21 59.9	−59.9	0.1	22 59.9	−59.9	0.1	23 59.9	−59.9	0.1
89	20 00.0	−60.0	0.0	21 00.0	−60.0	0.0	22 00.0	−60.0	0.0	23 00.0	−60.0	0.0
90	19 00.0	−60.0	0.0	20 00.0	−60.0	0.0	21 00.0	−60.0	0.0	22 00.0	−60.0	0.0
	19°			20°			21°			22°		

2°, 358° L.H.A. LATITUDE SAME NAME AS DECLINATION

LATITUDE **CONTRARY** NAME TO DECLINATION **L.H.A. 2°, 358°**

Dec.	15° Hc	d	Z	16° Hc	d	Z	17° Hc	d	Z	18° Hc	d	Z	Dec.
°	° ′	′	°	° ′	′	°	° ′	′	°	° ′	′	°	°
0	74 52.2	−59.5	172.3	73 52.7	−59.6	172.8	72 53.2	−59.7	173.2	71 53.6	−59.7	173.6	0
1	73 52.7	−59.6	172.8	72 53.1	−59.6	173.2	71 53.5	−59.6	173.6	70 53.9	−59.7	173.9	1
2	72 53.1	−59.6	173.2	71 53.5	−59.7	173.6	70 53.9	−59.7	173.9	69 54.2	−59.7	174.2	2
3	71 53.5	−59.7	173.6	70 53.8	−59.7	173.9	69 54.2	−59.8	174.2	68 54.5	−59.8	174.4	3
4	70 53.8	−59.7	173.9	69 54.1	−59.7	174.2	68 54.4	−59.7	174.4	67 54.7	−59.8	174.7	4
5	69 54.1	−59.7	174.2	68 54.4	−59.7	174.5	67 54.7	−59.8	174.7	66 54.9	−59.8	174.9	5
6	68 54.4	−59.7	174.5	67 54.7	−59.8	174.7	66 54.9	−59.8	174.9	65 55.1	−59.8	175.1	6
7	67 54.7	−59.8	174.7	66 54.9	−59.8	174.9	65 55.1	−59.8	175.1	64 55.3	−59.8	175.3	7
8	66 54.9	−59.8	174.9	65 55.1	−59.8	175.1	64 55.3	−59.8	175.3	63 55.5	−59.8	175.5	8
9	65 55.1	−59.8	175.2	64 55.3	−59.8	175.3	63 55.5	−59.8	175.5	62 55.7	−59.9	175.7	9
10	64 55.3	−59.8	175.3	63 55.5	−59.8	175.5	62 55.7	−59.9	175.7	61 55.8	−59.8	175.8	10
11	63 55.5	−59.9	175.5	62 55.7	−59.9	175.7	61 55.8	−59.8	175.8	60 56.0	−59.9	176.0	11
12	62 55.6	−59.8	175.7	61 55.8	−59.8	175.8	60 56.0	−59.9	176.0	59 56.1	−59.9	176.1	12
13	61 55.8	−59.8	175.9	60 56.0	−59.9	176.0	59 56.1	−59.9	176.1	58 56.2	−59.8	176.2	13
14	60 56.0	−59.9	176.0	59 56.1	−59.9	176.1	58 56.2	−59.8	176.2	57 56.4	−59.9	176.3	14
15	59 56.1	−59.9	176.1	58 56.2	−59.8	176.3	57 56.4	−59.9	176.4	56 56.5	−59.9	176.5	15
16	58 56.2	−59.8	176.3	57 56.4	−59.9	176.4	56 56.5	−59.9	176.5	55 56.6	−59.9	176.6	16
17	57 56.4	−59.9	176.4	56 56.5	−59.9	176.5	55 56.6	−59.9	176.6	54 56.7	−59.9	176.7	17
18	56 56.5	−59.9	176.5	55 56.6	−59.9	176.6	54 56.7	−59.9	176.7	53 56.8	−59.9	176.8	18
19	55 56.6	−59.9	176.6	54 56.7	−59.9	176.7	53 56.8	−59.9	176.8	52 56.9	−59.9	176.9	19
20	54 56.7	−59.9	176.7	53 56.8	−59.9	176.8	52 56.9	−59.9	176.9	51 57.0	−60.0	177.0	20
21	53 56.8	−59.9	176.8	52 56.9	−59.9	176.9	51 57.0	−59.9	177.0	50 57.0	−59.9	177.0	21
22	52 56.9	−59.9	176.9	51 57.0	−59.9	177.0	50 57.1	−60.0	177.1	49 57.1	−59.9	177.1	22
23	51 57.0	−59.9	177.0	50 57.1	−60.0	177.1	49 57.1	−59.9	177.1	48 57.2	−59.9	177.2	23
24	50 57.1	−60.0	177.1	49 57.1	−59.9	177.2	48 57.2	−59.9	177.2	47 57.3	−59.9	177.3	24
25	49 57.1	−59.9	177.2	48 57.2	−59.9	177.2	47 57.3	−59.9	177.3	46 57.4	−60.0	177.3	25
26	48 57.2	−59.9	177.3	47 57.3	−59.9	177.3	46 57.4	−60.0	177.4	45 57.4	−59.9	177.4	26
27	47 57.3	−59.9	177.3	46 57.4	−60.0	177.4	45 57.4	−59.9	177.4	44 57.5	−59.9	177.5	27
28	46 57.4	−59.9	177.4	45 57.4	−59.9	177.5	44 57.5	−59.9	177.5	43 57.6	−60.0	177.5	28
29	45 57.5	−60.0	177.5	44 57.5	−59.9	177.5	43 57.6	−60.0	177.6	42 57.6	−59.9	177.6	29
30	44 57.5	−59.9	177.6	43 57.6	−60.0	177.6	42 57.6	−59.9	177.6	41 57.7	−60.0	177.7	30
31	43 57.6	−59.9	177.6	42 57.6	−59.9	177.7	41 57.7	−59.9	177.7	40 57.7	−59.9	177.7	31
32	42 57.7	−60.0	177.7	41 57.7	−59.9	177.7	40 57.8	−60.0	177.8	39 57.8	−59.9	177.8	32
33	41 57.7	−59.9	177.7	40 57.8	−60.0	177.8	39 57.8	−59.9	177.8	38 57.9	−60.0	177.8	33
34	40 57.8	−60.0	177.8	39 57.8	−59.9	177.8	38 57.9	−60.0	177.9	37 57.9	−59.9	177.9	34
35	39 57.8	−59.9	177.9	38 57.9	−60.0	177.9	37 57.9	−59.9	177.9	36 58.0	−60.0	177.9	35
36	38 57.9	−59.9	177.9	37 57.9	−59.9	177.9	36 58.0	−60.0	178.0	35 58.0	−59.9	178.0	36
37	37 58.0	−60.0	178.0	36 58.0	−60.0	178.0	35 58.0	−59.9	178.0	34 58.1	−60.0	178.1	37
38	36 58.0	−59.9	178.0	35 58.0	−59.9	178.1	34 58.1	−60.0	178.1	33 58.1	−59.9	178.1	38
39	35 58.1	−60.0	178.1	34 58.1	−60.0	178.1	33 58.1	−59.9	178.1	32 58.2	−60.0	178.1	39
40	34 58.1	−59.9	178.1	33 58.1	−59.9	178.2	32 58.2	−60.0	178.2	31 58.2	−60.0	178.2	40
41	33 58.2	−60.0	178.2	32 58.2	−60.0	178.2	31 58.2	−59.9	178.2	30 58.2	−59.9	178.2	41
42	32 58.2	−59.9	178.2	31 58.2	−59.9	178.2	30 58.3	−60.0	178.3	29 58.3	−60.0	178.3	42
43	31 58.3	−60.0	178.3	30 58.3	−60.0	178.3	29 58.3	−59.9	178.3	28 58.3	−59.9	178.3	43
44	30 58.3	−60.0	178.3	29 58.3	−59.9	178.3	28 58.4	−60.0	178.4	27 58.4	−60.0	178.4	44
45	29 58.3	−59.9	178.4	28 58.4	−60.0	178.4	27 58.4	−60.0	178.4	26 58.4	−59.9	178.4	45
46	28 58.4	−60.0	178.4	27 58.4	−59.9	178.4	26 58.4	−59.9	178.4	25 58.5	−60.0	178.5	46
47	27 58.4	−59.9	178.5	26 58.5	−60.0	178.5	25 58.5	−60.0	178.5	24 58.5	−60.0	178.5	47
48	26 58.5	−60.0	178.5	25 58.5	−60.0	178.5	24 58.5	−59.9	178.5	23 58.5	−59.9	178.5	48
49	25 58.5	−59.9	178.5	24 58.5	−59.9	178.6	23 58.6	−60.0	178.6	22 58.6	−60.0	178.6	49
50	24 58.6	−60.0	178.6	23 58.6	−60.0	178.6	22 58.6	−60.0	178.6	21 58.6	−59.9	178.6	50
51	23 58.6	−60.0	178.6	22 58.6	−59.9	178.6	21 58.6	−59.9	178.6	20 58.7	−60.0	178.7	51
52	22 58.6	−59.9	178.7	21 58.7	−60.0	178.7	20 58.7	−60.0	178.7	19 58.7	−60.0	178.7	52
53	21 58.7	−60.0	178.7	20 58.7	−60.0	178.7	19 58.7	−59.9	178.7	18 58.7	−59.9	178.7	53
54	20 58.7	−59.9	178.7	19 58.7	−59.9	178.7	18 58.8	−60.0	178.8	17 58.8	−60.0	178.8	54
55	19 58.8	−60.0	178.8	18 58.8	−60.0	178.8	17 58.8	−60.0	178.8	16 58.8	−60.0	178.8	55
56	18 58.8	−60.0	178.8	17 58.8	−59.9	178.8	16 58.8	−59.9	178.8	15 58.8	−59.9	178.8	56
57	17 58.8	−59.9	178.9	16 58.9	−60.0	178.9	15 58.9	−60.0	178.9	14 58.9	−60.0	178.9	57
58	16 58.9	−60.0	178.9	15 58.9	−60.0	178.9	14 58.9	−60.0	178.9	13 58.9	−60.0	178.9	58
59	15 58.9	−59.9	178.9	14 58.9	−59.9	178.9	13 58.9	−59.9	178.9	12 58.9	−59.9	178.9	59
60	14 59.0	−60.0	179.0	13 59.0	−60.0	179.0	12 59.0	−60.0	179.0	11 59.0	−60.0	179.0	60
61	13 59.0	−60.0	179.0	12 59.0	−60.0	179.0	11 59.0	−60.0	179.0	10 59.0	−59.9	179.0	61
62	12 59.0	−59.9	179.0	11 59.0	−59.9	179.0	10 59.0	−59.9	179.0	9 59.1	−60.0	179.0	62
63	11 59.1	−60.0	179.1	10 59.1	−60.0	179.1	9 59.1	−60.0	179.1	8 59.1	−60.0	179.1	63
64	10 59.1	−60.0	179.1	9 59.1	−60.0	179.1	8 59.1	−60.0	179.1	7 59.1	−59.9	179.1	64
65	9 59.1	−59.9	179.1	8 59.1	−59.9	179.1	7 59.1	−59.9	179.1	6 59.2	−60.0	179.1	65
66	8 59.2	−60.0	179.2	7 59.2	−60.0	179.2	6 59.2	−60.0	179.2	5 59.2	−60.0	179.2	66
67	7 59.2	−60.0	179.2	6 59.2	−60.0	179.2	5 59.2	−60.0	179.2	4 59.2	−59.9	179.2	67
68	6 59.2	−59.9	179.2	5 59.2	−59.9	179.2	4 59.2	−59.9	179.2	3 59.3	−60.0	179.2	68
69	5 59.3	−60.0	179.3	4 59.3	−60.0	179.3	3 59.3	−60.0	179.3	2 59.3	−60.0	179.3	69
70	4 59.3	−60.0	179.3	3 59.3	−60.0	179.3	2 59.3	−60.0	179.3	1 59.3	−59.9	179.3	70
71	3 59.3	−59.9	179.3	2 59.3	−59.9	179.3	1 59.3	−59.9	179.3	0 59.4	−60.0	179.3	71
72	2 59.4	−60.0	179.4	1 59.4	−60.0	179.4	0 59.4	−60.0	179.4	0 00.6	+60.0	0.6	72
73	1 59.4	−60.0	179.4	0 59.4	−60.0	179.4	0 00.6	+60.0	0.6	1 00.6	+59.9	0.6	73
74	0 59.4	−59.9	179.4	0 00.6	+59.9	0.6	1 00.6	+59.9	0.6	2 00.5	+60.0	0.6	74
75	0 00.5	+60.0	0.5	1 00.5	+60.0	0.5	2 00.5	+60.0	0.5	3 00.5	+60.0	0.5	75
76	1 00.5	+60.0	0.5	2 00.5	+60.0	0.5	3 00.5	+60.0	0.5	4 00.5	+59.9	0.5	76
77	2 00.5	+59.9	0.5	3 00.5	+59.9	0.5	4 00.5	+59.9	0.5	5 00.4	+60.0	0.5	77
78	3 00.4	+60.0	0.4	4 00.4	+60.0	0.4	5 00.4	+60.0	0.4	6 00.4	+60.0	0.4	78
79	4 00.4	+60.0	0.4	5 00.4	+60.0	0.4	6 00.4	+60.0	0.4	7 00.4	+59.9	0.4	79
80	5 00.4	+59.9	0.3	6 00.4	+59.9	0.3	7 00.4	+59.9	0.3	8 00.3	+60.0	0.4	80
81	6 00.3	+60.0	0.3	7 00.3	+60.0	0.3	8 00.3	+60.0	0.3	9 00.3	+60.0	0.3	81
82	7 00.3	+59.9	0.3	8 00.3	+59.9	0.3	9 00.3	+59.9	0.3	10 00.3	+59.9	0.3	82
83	8 00.2	+60.0	0.2	9 00.2	+60.0	0.2	10 00.2	+60.0	0.2	11 00.2	+60.0	0.2	83
84	9 00.2	+60.0	0.2	10 00.2	+60.0	0.2	11 00.2	+60.0	0.2	12 00.2	+60.0	0.2	84
85	10 00.2	+59.9	0.2	11 00.2	+59.9	0.2	12 00.2	+59.9	0.2	13 00.2	+59.9	0.2	85
86	11 00.1	+60.0	0.1	12 00.1	+60.0	0.1	13 00.1	+60.0	0.1	14 00.1	+60.0	0.1	86
87	12 00.1	+60.0	0.1	13 00.1	+60.0	0.1	14 00.1	+60.0	0.1	15 00.1	+60.0	0.1	87
88	13 00.1	+59.9	0.1	14 00.1	+59.9	0.1	15 00.1	+59.9	0.1	16 00.1	+59.9	0.1	88
89	14 00.0	+60.0	0.0	15 00.0	+60.0	0.0	16 00.0	+60.0	0.0	17 00.0	+60.0	0.0	89
90	15 00.0	+60.0	0.0	16 00.0	+60.0	0.0	17 00.0	+60.0	0.0	18 00.0	+60.0	0.0	90
	15°			16°			17°			18°			

Dec.	19° Hc	d	Z	20° Hc	d	Z	21° Hc	d	Z	22° Hc	d	Z	Dec.
°	° ′	′	°	° ′	′	°	° ′	′	°	° ′	′	°	°
0	70 53.9	−59.7	173.9	69 54.3	−59.8	174.2	68 54.6	−59.8	174.4	67 54.8	−59.8	174.7	0
1	69 54.2	−59.7	174.2	68 54.5	−59.7	174.4	67 54.8	−59.8	174.7	66 55.0	−59.8	174.9	1
2	68 54.5	−59.8	174.4	67 54.8	−59.8	174.7	66 55.0	−59.8	174.9	65 55.2	−59.8	175.1	2
3	67 54.7	−59.7	174.7	66 55.0	−59.8	174.9	65 55.2	−59.8	175.1	64 55.4	−59.8	175.3	3
4	66 55.0	−59.8	174.9	65 55.2	−59.8	175.1	64 55.4	−59.8	175.3	63 55.6	−59.9	175.5	4
5	65 55.2	−59.9	175.1	64 55.4	−59.9	175.3	63 55.6	−59.9	175.5	62 55.7	−59.8	175.6	5
6	64 55.3	−59.8	175.3	63 55.5	−59.8	175.5	62 55.7	−59.8	175.6	61 55.9	−59.9	175.8	6
7	63 55.5	−59.8	175.5	62 55.7	−59.8	175.6	61 55.9	−59.9	175.8	60 56.0	−59.8	175.9	7
8	62 55.7	−59.9	175.6	61 55.9	−59.9	175.8	60 56.0	−59.9	175.9	59 56.2	−59.9	176.0	8
9	61 55.8	−59.8	175.8	60 56.0	−59.9	175.9	59 56.1	−59.8	176.1	58 56.3	−59.9	176.2	9
10	60 56.0	−59.9	175.9	59 56.1	−59.8	176.1	58 56.3	−59.9	176.2	57 56.4	−59.9	176.3	10
11	59 56.1	−59.9	176.1	58 56.3	−59.9	176.2	57 56.4	−59.9	176.3	56 56.5	−59.9	176.4	11
12	58 56.2	−59.8	176.2	57 56.4	−59.9	176.3	56 56.5	−59.9	176.4	55 56.6	−59.9	176.5	12
13	57 56.4	−59.9	176.3	56 56.5	−59.9	176.4	55 56.6	−59.9	176.5	54 56.7	−59.9	176.6	13
14	56 56.5	−59.9	176.4	55 56.6	−59.9	176.5	54 56.7	−59.9	176.6	53 56.8	−59.9	176.7	14
15	55 56.6	−59.9	176.5	54 56.7	−59.9	176.6	53 56.8	−59.9	176.7	52 56.9	−59.9	176.8	15
16	54 56.7	−59.9	176.7	53 56.8	−59.9	176.7	52 56.9	−59.9	176.8	51 57.0	−59.9	176.9	16
17	53 56.8	−59.9	176.7	52 56.9	−59.9	176.8	51 57.0	−60.0	176.9	50 57.1	−60.0	177.0	17
18	52 56.9	−59.9	176.8	51 57.0	−60.0	176.9	50 57.0	−59.9	177.0	49 57.1	−59.9	177.0	18
19	51 57.0	−60.0	176.9	50 57.0	−59.9	177.0	49 57.1	−59.9	177.1	48 57.2	−59.9	177.1	19
20	50 57.0	−59.9	177.0	49 57.1	−59.9	177.1	48 57.2	−59.9	177.1	47 57.3	−60.0	177.2	20
21	49 57.1	−59.9	177.1	48 57.2	−59.9	177.2	47 57.3	−60.0	177.2	46 57.3	−59.9	177.3	21
22	48 57.2	−59.9	177.2	47 57.3	−60.0	177.2	46 57.3	−59.9	177.3	45 57.4	−59.9	177.3	22
23	47 57.3	−60.0	177.3	46 57.3	−59.9	177.3	45 57.4	−59.9	177.4	44 57.5	−60.0	177.4	23
24	46 57.3	−59.9	177.3	45 57.4	−59.9	177.4	44 57.5	−60.0	177.4	43 57.5	−59.9	177.5	24
25	45 57.4	−59.9	177.4	44 57.5	−60.0	177.4	43 57.5	−59.9	177.5	42 57.6	−59.9	177.5	25
26	44 57.5	−60.0	177.5	43 57.5	−59.9	177.5	42 57.6	−59.9	177.5	41 57.7	−60.0	177.6	26
27	43 57.5	−59.9	177.5	42 57.6	−59.9	177.6	41 57.7	−60.0	177.6	40 57.7	−59.9	177.6	27
28	42 57.6	−59.9	177.6	41 57.7	−60.0	177.6	40 57.7	−59.9	177.7	39 57.8	−60.0	177.7	28
29	41 57.7	−60.0	177.6	40 57.7	−59.9	177.7	39 57.8	−60.0	177.7	38 57.8	−59.9	177.8	29
30	40 57.7	−59.9	177.7	39 57.8	−60.0	177.7	38 57.8	−59.9	177.8	37 57.9	−60.0	177.8	30
31	39 57.8	−60.0	177.8	38 57.8	−59.9	177.8	37 57.9	−60.0	177.8	36 57.9	−59.9	177.9	31
32	38 57.8	−59.9	177.8	37 57.9	−60.0	177.8	36 57.9	−59.9	177.9	35 58.0	−60.0	177.9	32
33	37 57.9	−60.0	177.9	36 57.9	−59.9	177.9	35 58.0	−60.0	177.9	34 58.0	−59.9	178.0	33
34	36 57.9	−59.9	177.9	35 58.0	−60.0	178.0	34 58.0	−59.9	178.0	33 58.1	−60.0	178.0	34
35	35 58.0	−60.0	178.0	34 58.0	−59.9	178.0	33 58.1	−60.0	178.0	32 58.1	−60.0	178.0	35
36	34 58.0	−59.9	178.0	33 58.1	−60.0	178.0	32 58.1	−59.9	178.1	31 58.1	−59.9	178.1	36
37	33 58.1	−60.0	178.1	32 58.1	−59.9	178.1	31 58.2	−60.0	178.1	30 58.2	−60.0	178.1	37
38	32 58.1	−59.9	178.1	31 58.2	−60.0	178.1	30 58.2	−60.0	178.2	29 58.2	−59.9	178.2	38
39	31 58.2	−60.0	178.2	30 58.2	−59.9	178.2	29 58.2	−59.9	178.2	28 58.3	−60.0	178.2	39
40	30 58.2	−59.9	178.2	29 58.3	−60.0	178.2	28 58.3	−60.0	178.2	27 58.3	−59.9	178.3	40
41	29 58.3	−60.0	178.3	28 58.3	−60.0	178.3	27 58.3	−59.9	178.3	26 58.4	−60.0	178.3	41
42	28 58.3	−59.9	178.3	27 58.3	−59.9	178.3	26 58.4	−60.0	178.3	25 58.4	−60.0	178.3	42
43	27 58.4	−60.0	178.3	26 58.4	−60.0	178.4	25 58.4	−60.0	178.4	24 58.4	−59.9	178.4	43
44	26 58.4	−60.0	178.4	25 58.4	−59.9	178.4	24 58.4	−59.9	178.4	23 58.5	−60.0	178.4	44
45	25 58.4	−59.9	178.4	24 58.5	−60.0	178.4	23 58.5	−60.0	178.5	22 58.5	−60.0	178.5	45
46	24 58.5	−60.0	178.5	23 58.5	−60.0	178.5	22 58.5	−59.9	178.5	21 58.5	−59.9	178.5	46
47	23 58.5	−59.9	178.5	22 58.5	−59.9	178.5	21 58.6	−60.0	178.5	20 58.6	−60.0	178.5	47
48	22 58.6	−60.0	178.5	21 58.6	−60.0	178.6	20 58.6	−60.0	178.6	19 58.6	−59.9	178.6	48
49	21 58.6	−60.0	178.6	20 58.6	−59.9	178.6	19 58.6	−59.9	178.6	18 58.7	−60.0	178.6	49
50	20 58.6	−59.9	178.6	19 58.7	−60.0	178.6	18 58.7	−60.0	178.6	17 58.7	−60.0	178.6	50
51	19 58.7	−60.0	178.7	18 58.7	−60.0	178.7	17 58.7	−60.0	178.7	16 58.7	−59.9	178.7	51
52	18 58.7	−60.0	178.7	17 58.7	−59.9	178.7	16 58.7	−59.9	178.7	15 58.8	−60.0	178.7	52
53	17 58.7	−59.9	178.7	16 58.8	−60.0	178.7	15 58.8	−60.0	178.7	14 58.8	−60.0	178.8	53
54	16 58.8	−60.0	178.8	15 58.8	−60.0	178.8	14 58.8	−60.0	178.8	13 58.8	−59.9	178.8	54
55	15 58.8	−59.9	178.8	14 58.8	−59.9	178.8	13 58.8	−59.9	178.8	12 58.9	−60.0	178.8	55
56	14 58.9	−60.0	178.8	13 58.9	−60.0	178.8	12 58.9	−60.0	178.9	11 58.9	−60.0	178.9	56
57	13 58.9	−60.0	178.9	12 58.9	−60.0	178.9	11 58.9	−60.0	178.9	10 58.9	−59.9	178.9	57
58	12 58.9	−59.9	178.9	11 58.9	−59.9	178.9	10 58.9	−59.9	178.9	9 59.0	−60.0	178.9	58
59	11 59.0	−60.0	178.9	10 59.0	−60.0	179.0	9 59.0	−60.0	179.0	8 59.0	−60.0	179.0	59
60	10 59.0	−60.0	179.0	9 59.0	−60.0	179.0	8 59.0	−60.0	179.0	7 59.0	−59.9	179.0	60
61	9 59.0	−59.9	179.0	8 59.0	−59.9	179.0	7 59.0	−59.9	179.0	6 59.1	−60.0	179.0	61
62	8 59.1	−60.0	179.0	7 59.1	−60.0	179.1	6 59.1	−60.0	179.1	5 59.1	−60.0	179.1	62
63	7 59.1	−60.0	179.1	6 59.1	−60.0	179.1	5 59.1	−60.0	179.1	4 59.1	−60.0	179.1	63
64	6 59.1	−59.9	179.1	5 59.1	−59.9	179.1	4 59.1	−59.9	179.1	3 59.1	−59.9	179.1	64
65	5 59.2	−60.0	179.2	4 59.2	−60.0	179.2	3 59.2	−60.0	179.2	2 59.2	−60.0	179.2	65
66	4 59.2	−60.0	179.2	3 59.2	−60.0	179.2	2 59.2	−60.0	179.2	1 59.2	−60.0	179.2	66
67	3 59.2	−59.9	179.2	2 59.2	−59.9	179.2	1 59.2	−59.9	179.2	0 59.2	−59.9	179.2	67
68	2 59.3	−60.0	179.2	1 59.3	−60.0	179.3	0 59.3	−60.0	179.3	0 00.7	+60.0	0.7	68
69	1 59.3	−60.0	179.3	0 59.3	−60.0	179.3	0 00.7	+60.0	0.7	1 00.7	+60.0	0.7	69
70	0 59.3	−59.9	179.3	0 00.7	+59.9	0.7	1 00.7	+59.9	0.7	2 00.7	+59.9	0.7	70
71	0 00.6	+60.0	0.7	1 00.6	+60.0	0.7	2 00.6	+60.0	0.7	3 00.6	+60.0	0.7	71
72	1 00.6	+60.0	0.6	2 00.6	+60.0	0.6	3 00.6	+60.0	0.6	4 00.6	+60.0	0.6	72
73	2 00.6	+59.9	0.6	3 00.6	+59.9	0.6	4 00.6	+59.9	0.6	5 00.6	+59.9	0.6	73
74	3 00.5	+60.0	0.6	4 00.5	+60.0	0.6	5 00.5	+60.0	0.6	6 00.5	+60.0	0.6	74
75	4 00.5	+60.0	0.5	5 00.5	+60.0	0.5	6 00.5	+60.0	0.5	7 00.5	+60.0	0.5	75
76	5 00.5	+59.9	0.5	6 00.5	+59.9	0.5	7 00.5	+59.9	0.5	8 00.5	+59.9	0.5	76
77	6 00.4	+60.0	0.5	7 00.4	+60.0	0.5	8 00.4	+60.0	0.5	9 00.4	+60.0	0.5	77
78	7 00.4	+60.0	0.4	8 00.4	+60.0	0.4	9 00.4	+60.0	0.4	10 00.4	+60.0	0.4	78
79	8 00.4	+59.9	0.4	9 00.4	+59.9	0.4	10 00.4	+59.9	0.4	11 00.4	+59.9	0.4	79
80	9 00.3	+60.0	0.4	10 00.3	+60.0	0.4	11 00.3	+60.0	0.4	12 00.3	+60.0	0.4	80
81	10 00.3	+60.0	0.3	11 00.3	+60.0	0.3	12 00.3	+60.0	0.3	13 00.3	+60.0	0.3	81
82	11 00.3	+59.9	0.3	12 00.3	+59.9	0.3	13 00.3	+59.9	0.3	14 00.3	+59.9	0.3	82
83	12 00.2	+60.0	0.2	13 00.2	+60.0	0.3	14 00.2	+60.0	0.3	15 00.2	+60.0	0.3	83
84	13 00.2	+60.0	0.2	14 00.2	+60.0	0.2	15 00.2	+60.0	0.2	16 00.2	+60.0	0.2	84
85	14 00.2	+59.9	0.2	15 00.2	+59.9	0.2	16 00.2	+59.9	0.2	17 00.2	+59.9	0.2	85
86	15 00.1	+60.0	0.1	16 00.1	+60.0	0.1	17 00.1	+60.0	0.1	18 00.1	+60.0	0.1	86
87	16 00.1	+60.0	0.1	17 00.1	+60.0	0.1	18 00.1	+60.0	0.1	19 00.1	+60.0	0.1	87
88	17 00.1	+59.9	0.1	18 00.1	+59.9	0.1	19 00.1	+59.9	0.1	20 00.1	+59.9	0.1	88
89	18 00.0	+60.0	0.0	19 00.0	+60.0	0.0	20 00.0	+60.0	0.0	21 00.0	+60.0	0.0	89
90	19 00.0	+60.0	0.0	20 00.0	+60.0	0.0	21 00.0	+60.0	0.0	22 00.0	+60.0	0.0	90
	19°			20°			21°			22°			

S. Lat. {L.H.A. greater than 180° ....Zn=180°−Z; L.H.A. less than 180°...........Zn=180°+Z}

LATITUDE **SAME** NAME AS DECLINATION **L.H.A. 178°, 182°**

7

3°, 357° L.H.A. LATITUDE SAME NAME AS DECLINATION

N. Lat. {L.H.A. greater than 180° .....Zn=Z
L.H.A. less than 180°............Zn=360°–Z

	15°			16°			17°			18°			19°			20°			21°			22°			
Dec.	Hc	d	Z	Hc	d	Z	Hc	d	Z	Hc	d	Z	Hc	d	Z	Hc	d	Z	Hc	d	Z	Hc	d	Z	Dec.
°	° ′	′	°	° ′	′	°	° ′	′	°	° ′	′	°	° ′	′	°	° ′	′	°	° ′	′	°	° ′	′	°	°
0	74 42.6	+58.8	168.6	73 43.7	+59.0	169.2	72 44.7	+59.1	169.8	71 45.6	+59.2	170.4	70 46.4	+59.3	170.9	69 47.1	+59.4	171.3	68 47.8	+59.4	171.7	67 48.4	+59.5	172.0	0
1	75 41.4	+58.6	167.8	74 42.7	+58.8	168.6	73 43.8	+59.0	169.2	72 44.8	+59.1	169.8	71 45.7	+59.2	170.4	70 46.5	+59.3	170.9	69 47.2	+59.4	171.3	68 47.9	+59.4	171.7	1
2	76 40.0	+58.5	166.9	75 41.5	+58.6	167.8	74 42.8	+58.8	168.6	73 43.9	+59.0	169.2	72 44.9	+59.1	169.8	71 45.8	+59.2	170.4	70 46.6	+59.3	170.9	69 47.3	+59.4	171.3	2
3	77 38.5	+58.1	165.9	76 40.1	+58.5	166.9	75 41.6	+58.7	167.8	74 42.9	+58.8	168.6	73 44.0	+59.0	169.2	72 45.0	+59.1	169.8	71 45.9	+59.2	170.4	70 46.7	+59.3	170.9	3
4	78 36.6	+57.8	164.7	77 38.6	+58.2	165.9	76 40.3	+58.4	166.9	75 41.7	+58.7	167.8	74 43.0	+58.8	168.6	73 44.1	+59.0	169.3	72 45.1	+59.1	169.9	71 46.0	+59.2	170.4	4
5	79 34.4	+57.4	163.3	78 36.8	+57.8	164.7	77 38.7	+58.2	165.9	76 40.4	+58.5	166.9	75 41.8	+58.7	167.8	74 43.1	+58.9	168.6	73 44.2	+59.1	169.3	72 45.2	+59.2	169.9	5
6	80 31.8	+56.8	161.6	79 34.6	+57.4	163.3	78 36.9	+57.9	164.7	77 38.9	+58.2	165.9	76 40.5	+58.5	166.9	75 42.0	+58.7	167.8	74 43.3	+58.8	168.6	73 44.4	+59.0	169.3	6
7	81 28.6	+55.9	159.5	80 32.0	+56.8	161.6	79 34.8	+57.4	163.3	78 37.1	+57.9	164.7	77 39.0	+58.3	165.9	76 40.7	+58.5	167.0	75 42.1	+58.8	167.9	74 43.4	+58.9	168.6	7
8	82 24.5	+54.8	156.9	81 28.8	+56.0	159.5	80 32.2	+56.8	161.6	79 35.0	+57.4	163.3	78 37.3	+57.9	164.8	77 39.2	+58.3	166.0	76 40.9	+58.5	167.0	75 42.3	+58.7	167.9	8
9	83 19.3	+53.1•	153.6	82 24.8	+54.8	157.0	81 29.0	+56.0	159.6	80 32.4	+56.9	161.7	79 35.2	+57.4	163.4	78 37.5	+57.9	164.8	77 39.4	+58.3	166.0	76 41.0	+58.6	167.0	9
10	84 12.4	+50.4•	149.3	83 19.6	+53.1•	153.7	82 25.0	+54.9	157.0	81 29.3	+56.0	159.6	80 32.6	+56.9	161.7	79 35.4	+57.5	163.4	78 37.7	+57.9	164.8	77 39.6	+58.3	166.0	10
11	85 02.8	+46.2•	143.5	84 12.7	+50.5•	149.4	83 19.9	+53.2•	153.7	82 25.3	+55.0	157.1	81 29.5	+56.1	159.7	80 32.9	+56.9	161.8	79 35.6	+57.6	163.5	78 37.9	+58.0	164.9	11
12	85 49.0	+39.1•	135.4	85 03.2	+46.3•	143.6	84 13.1	+50.6•	149.5	83 20.3	+53.2•	153.8	82 25.6	+55.0	157.1	81 29.8	+56.2	159.7	80 33.2	+56.9	161.8	79 35.9	+57.5	163.5	12
13	86 28.1	+27.6•	124.1	85 49.5	+39.3•	135.5	85 03.7	+46.3•	143.7	84 13.5	+50.7•	149.5	83 20.6	+53.3•	153.9	82 26.0	+55.0	157.2	81 30.1	+56.2	159.8	80 33.4	+57.0	161.9	13
14	86 55.7	+10.4•	108.6	86 28.8	+27.7•	124.2	85 50.0	+39.4•	135.7	85 04.2	+46.4•	143.8	84 13.9	+50.8•	149.6	83 21.0	+53.4•	154.0	82 26.3	+55.1	157.3	81 30.4	+56.3	159.9	14
15	87 06.1	−9.6•	89.6	86 56.5	+10.5•	108.7	86 29.4	+27.9•	124.3	85 50.6	+39.6•	135.8	85 04.7	+46.6•	143.9	84 14.4	+50.8•	149.8	83 21.4	+53.5•	154.1	82 26.7	+55.1	157.4	15
16	86 56.5	−27.1•	70.5	87 07.0	−9.7•	89.6	86 57.3	+10.6•	108.7	86 30.2	+28.0•	124.4	85 51.3	+39.7•	135.9	85 05.2	+46.8•	144.0	84 14.9	+50.9•	149.9	83 21.8	+53.6•	154.2	16
17	86 29.4	−38.8•	54.9	86 57.3	−27.1•	70.4	87 07.9	−9.7•	89.6	86 58.2	+10.6•	108.8	86 31.0	+28.1•	124.6	85 52.0	+39.8•	136.0	85 05.8	+46.9•	144.2	84 15.4	+51.0•	150.0	17
18	85 50.6	−45.9•	43.4	86 30.2	−38.9•	54.7	86 58.2	−27.2•	70.3	87 08.8	−9.7•	89.5	86 59.1	+10.7•	108.9	86 31.8	+28.2•	124.7	85 52.7	+39.9•	136.2	85 06.4	+47.0•	144.3	18
19	85 04.7	−50.3•	35.2	85 51.3	−46.1•	43.2	86 31.0	−39.0•	54.5	86 59.1	−27.3•	70.2	87 09.8	−9.8•	89.5	87 00.0	+10.9•	109.0	86 32.6	+28.4•	124.8	85 53.4	+40.1•	136.3	19
20	84 14.4	−53.0•	29.3	85 05.2	−50.3•	35.0	85 52.0	−46.2•	43.0	86 31.8	−39.1•	54.3	87 00.0	−27.4•	70.0	87 10.9	−9.9•	89.5	87 01.0	+11.0•	109.1	86 33.5	+28.6•	125.0	20
21	83 21.4	−54.7	25.0	84 14.9	−53.1•	29.2	85 05.8	−50.4•	34.9	85 52.7	−46.3•	42.8	86 32.6	−39.2•	54.1	87 01.0	−27.5•	69.9	87 12.0	−9.9•	89.5	87 02.1	+11.0•	109.2	21
22	82 26.7	−55.9	21.7	83 21.8	−54.7	24.8	84 15.4	−53.1•	29.0	85 06.4	−50.5•	34.7	85 53.4	−46.4•	42.6	86 33.5	−39.3•	53.9	87 02.1	−27.6•	69.7	87 13.1	−9.9•	89.4	22
23	81 30.8	−56.8	19.1	82 27.1	−56.0	21.5	83 22.3	−54.8	24.7	84 15.9	−53.1•	28.8	85 07.0	−50.5•	34.5	85 54.2	−46.5•	42.4	86 34.5	−39.5•	53.7	87 03.2	−27.8•	69.6	23
24	80 34.0	−57.3	17.0	81 31.1	−56.7	18.9	82 27.5	−56.0	21.4	83 22.8	−54.9	24.5	84 16.5	−53.3•	28.6	85 07.7	−50.7•	34.3	85 55.0	−46.6•	42.2	86 35.4	−39.6•	53.5	24
25	79 36.7	−57.8	15.3	80 34.4	−57.4	16.8	81 31.5	−56.8	18.8	82 27.9	−56.0	21.2	83 23.2	−54.9	24.3	84 17.0	−53.2•	28.4	85 08.4	−50.8•	34.0	85 55.8	−46.7•	41.9	25
26	78 38.9	−58.1	13.8	79 37.0	−57.8	15.1	80 34.7	−57.4	16.7	81 31.9	−56.8	18.6	82 28.3	−56.0	21.0	83 23.8	−55.0	24.1	84 17.6	−53.3•	28.2	85 09.1	−50.9•	33.8	26
27	77 40.8	−58.5	12.6	78 39.2	−58.2	13.7	79 37.3	−57.8	15.0	80 35.1	−57.5	16.6	81 32.3	−56.9	18.5	82 28.8	−56.1	20.9	83 24.3	−55.0	24.0	84 18.2	−53.4•	28.0	27
28	76 42.3	−58.6	11.6	77 41.0	−58.4	12.5	78 39.5	−58.2	13.6	79 37.6	−57.8	14.9	80 35.4	−57.4	16.4	81 32.7	−56.9	18.3	82 29.3	−56.2	20.7	83 24.8	−55.1	23.8	28
29	75 43.7	−58.8	10.7	76 42.6	−58.7	11.5	77 41.3	−58.5	12.4	78 39.8	−58.2	13.5	79 38.0	−57.9	14.7	80 35.8	−57.5	16.3	81 33.1	−56.9	18.2	82 29.7	−56.2	20.5	29
30	74 44.9	−59.0	9.9	75 43.9	−58.8	10.6	76 42.8	−58.6	11.4	77 41.6	−58.5	12.3	78 40.1	−58.2	13.3	79 38.3	−57.9	14.6	80 36.2	−57.5	16.1	81 33.5	−56.9	18.0	30
31	73 45.9	−59.0	9.2	74 45.1	−58.9	9.8	75 44.2	−58.8	10.5	76 43.1	−58.7	11.3	77 41.9	−58.5	12.2	78 40.4	−58.2	13.2	79 38.7	−58.0	14.5	80 36.6	−57.6	16.0	31
32	72 46.9	−59.2	8.6	73 46.2	−59.1	9.1	74 45.4	−59.0	9.7	75 44.4	−58.8	10.4	76 43.4	−58.7	11.1	77 42.2	−58.5	12.0	78 40.7	−58.2	13.1	79 39.0	−57.9	14.3	32
33	71 47.7	−59.2	8.1	72 47.1	−59.2	8.5	73 46.4	−59.1	9.0	74 45.6	−59.0	9.6	75 44.7	−58.9	10.3	76 43.7	−58.7	11.0	77 42.5	−58.5	11.9	78 41.1	−58.3	12.9	33
34	70 48.5	−59.4	7.6	71 47.9	−59.2	8.0	72 47.3	−59.2	8.4	73 46.6	−59.1	8.9	74 45.8	−59.0	9.5	75 45.0	−58.9	10.2	76 44.0	−58.8	10.9	77 42.8	−58.6	11.8	34
35	69 49.1	−59.3	7.1	70 48.7	−59.4	7.5	71 48.1	−59.2	7.9	72 47.5	−59.2	8.3	73 46.8	−59.1	8.8	74 46.1	−59.0	9.4	75 45.2	−58.8	10.0	76 44.2	−58.7	10.8	35
36	68 49.8	−59.5	6.7	69 49.3	−59.4	7.1	70 48.9	−59.4	7.4	71 48.3	−59.2	7.8	72 47.7	−59.2	8.2	73 47.1	−59.1	8.7	74 46.4	−59.1	9.3	75 45.5	−58.9	9.9	36
37	67 50.3	−59.4	6.4	68 49.9	−59.4	6.6	69 49.5	−59.4	7.0	70 49.1	−59.4	7.3	71 48.5	−59.2	7.7	72 48.0	−59.2	8.1	73 47.3	−59.1	8.6	74 46.6	−59.0	9.2	37
38	66 50.9	−59.6	6.0	67 50.5	−59.5	6.3	68 50.1	−59.4	6.6	69 49.7	−59.4	6.9	70 49.3	−59.4	7.2	71 48.8	−59.3	7.6	72 48.2	−59.2	8.0	73 47.6	−59.1	8.5	38
39	65 51.3	−59.5	5.7	66 51.0	−59.5	5.9	67 50.7	−59.5	6.2	68 50.3	−59.4	6.5	69 49.9	−59.4	6.8	70 49.5	−59.4	7.1	71 49.0	−59.3	7.5	72 48.5	−59.3	7.9	39
40	64 51.8	−59.6	5.4	65 51.5	−59.6	5.6	66 51.2	−59.5	5.9	67 50.9	−59.5	6.1	68 50.5	−59.4	6.4	69 50.1	−59.4	6.7	70 49.7	−59.4	7.0	71 49.2	−59.3	7.4	40
41	63 52.2	−59.6	5.1	64 51.9	−59.6	5.3	65 51.7	−59.6	5.5	66 51.4	−59.6	5.8	67 51.1	−59.5	6.0	68 50.7	−59.5	6.3	69 50.3	−59.4	6.6	70 49.9	−59.4	6.9	41
42	62 52.6	−59.7	4.9	63 52.3	−59.6	5.1	64 52.1	−59.6	5.3	65 51.8	−59.5	5.5	66 51.6	−59.6	5.7	67 51.2	−59.5	5.9	68 50.9	−59.5	6.2	69 50.5	−59.4	6.5	42
43	61 52.9	−59.6	4.7	62 52.7	−59.6	4.8	63 52.5	−59.6	5.0	64 52.3	−59.6	5.2	65 52.0	−59.6	5.4	66 51.7	−59.5	5.6	67 51.4	−59.5	5.8	68 51.1	−59.5	6.1	43
44	60 53.3	−59.7	4.4	61 53.1	−59.7	4.6	62 52.9	−59.7	4.7	63 52.7	−59.7	4.9	64 52.4	−59.6	5.1	65 52.2	−59.6	5.3	66 51.9	−59.5	5.5	67 51.6	−59.5	5.7	44
45	59 53.6	−59.7	4.2	60 53.4	−59.7	4.4	61 53.2	−59.6	4.5	62 53.0	−59.6	4.7	63 52.8	−59.6	4.8	64 52.6	−59.6	5.0	65 52.4	−59.6	5.2	66 52.1	−59.5	5.4	45
46	58 53.9	−59.7	4.0	59 53.7	−59.7	4.2	60 53.6	−59.7	4.3	61 53.4	−59.7	4.4	62 53.2	−59.7	4.6	63 53.0	−59.6	4.7	64 52.8	−59.6	4.9	65 52.6	−59.6	5.1	46
47	57 54.2	−59.8	3.9	58 54.0	−59.7	4.0	59 53.9	−59.7	4.1	60 53.7	−59.7	4.2	61 53.5	−59.6	4.3	62 53.4	−59.7	4.5	63 53.2	−59.7	4.7	64 53.0	−59.7	4.8	47
48	56 54.4	−59.7	3.7	57 54.3	−59.7	3.8	58 54.2	−59.8	3.9	59 54.0	−59.7	4.0	60 53.9	−59.7	4.1	61 53.7	−59.7	4.3	62 53.5	−59.6	4.4	63 53.3	−59.6	4.6	48
49	55 54.7	−59.8	3.5	56 54.6	−59.8	3.6	57 54.4	−59.7	3.7	58 54.3	−59.7	3.8	59 54.2	−59.8	3.9	60 54.0	−59.7	4.0	61 53.9	−59.7	4.2	62 53.7	−59.7	4.3	49
50	54 54.9	−59.8	3.4	55 54.8	−59.8	3.4	56 54.7	−59.8	3.5	57 54.6	−59.8	3.6	58 54.4	−59.7	3.7	59 54.3	−59.7	3.8	60 54.2	−59.7	4.0	61 54.0	−59.7	4.1	50
51	53 55.1	−59.8	3.2	54 55.0	−59.7	3.3	55 54.9	−59.7	3.4	56 54.8	−59.7	3.5	57 54.7	−59.7	3.6	58 54.6	−59.7	3.7	59 54.5	−59.8	3.8	60 54.3	−59.7	3.9	51
52	52 55.3	−59.7	3.1	53 55.3	−59.8	3.1	54 55.2	−59.8	3.2	55 55.1	−59.8	3.3	56 55.0	−59.8	3.4	57 54.9	−59.8	3.5	58 54.7	−59.7	3.6	59 54.6	−59.7	3.7	52
53	51 55.6	−59.8	2.9	52 55.5	−59.8	3.0	53 55.4	−59.8	3.1	54 55.3	−59.8	3.1	55 55.2	−59.8	3.2	56 55.1	−59.7	3.3	57 55.0	−59.7	3.4	58 54.9	−59.7	3.5	53
54	50 55.8	−59.9	2.8	51 55.7	−59.8	2.9	52 55.6	−59.8	2.9	53 55.5	−59.8	3.0	54 55.4	−59.7	3.1	55 55.4	−59.8	3.1	56 55.3	−59.8	3.2	57 55.2	−59.8	3.3	54
55	49 55.9	−59.8	2.7	50 55.9	−59.8	2.7	51 55.8	−59.8	2.8	52 55.7	−59.8	2.9	53 55.7	−59.8	2.9	54 55.6	−59.8	3.0	55 55.5	−59.8	3.1	56 55.4	−59.8	3.2	55
56	48 56.1	−59.8	2.6	49 56.1	−59.9	2.6	50 56.0	−59.8	2.7	51 55.9	−59.8	2.7	52 55.9	−59.8	2.8	53 55.8	−59.8	2.8	54 55.7	−59.8	2.9	55 55.6	−59.7	3.0	56
57	47 56.3	−59.8	2.4	48 56.2	−59.8	2.5	49 56.2	−59.8	2.5	50 56.1	−59.8	2.6	51 56.1	−59.8	2.6	52 56.0	−59.8	2.7	53 55.9	−59.8	2.8	54 55.9	−59.8	2.8	57
58	46 56.5	−59.9	2.3	47 56.4	−59.8	2.4	48 56.4	−59.9	2.4	49 56.3	−59.8	2.5	50 56.3	−59.9	2.5	51 56.2	−59.8	2.6	52 56.1	−59.8	2.6	53 56.1	−59.8	2.7	58
59	45 56.6	−59.8	2.2	46 56.6	−59.9	2.3	47 56.5	−59.8	2.3	48 56.5	−59.8	2.4	49 56.4	−59.8	2.4	50 56.4	−59.8	2.5	51 56.3	−59.8	2.5	52 56.3	−59.8	2.6	59
60	44 56.8	−59.9	2.1	45 56.7	−59.8	2.2	46 56.7	−59.8	2.2	47 56.7	−59.9	2.2	48 56.6	−59.8	2.3	49 56.6	−59.9	2.3	50 56.5	−59.8	2.4	51 56.5	−59.9	2.4	60
61	43 56.9	−59.8	2.0	44 56.9	−59.9	2.1	45 56.9	−59.9	2.1	46 56.8	−59.8	2.1	47 56.8	−59.9	2.2	48 56.7	−59.8	2.2	49 56.7	−59.8	2.3	50 56.6	−59.8	2.3	61
62	42 57.1	−59.9	1.9	43 57.0	−59.8	2.0	44 57.0	−59.8	2.0	45 57.0	−59.9	2.0	46 56.9	−59.8	2.1	47 56.9	−59.8	2.1	48 56.9	−59.9	2.1	49 56.8	−59.8	2.2	62
63	41 57.2	−59.8	1.8	42 57.2	−59.9	1.9	43 57.2	−59.9	1.9	44 57.1	−59.8	1.9	45 57.1	−59.9	2.0	46 57.1	−59.9	2.0	47 57.0	−59.8	2.0	48 57.0	−59.9	2.1	63
64	40 57.4	−59.9	1.7	41 57.3	−59.8	1.8	42 57.3	−59.9	1.8	43 57.3	−59.9	1.8	44 57.2	−59.8	1.9	45 57.2	−59.8	1.9	46 57.2	−59.9	1.9	47 57.1	−59.8	2.0	64
65	39 57.5	−59.9	1.7	40 57.5	−59.9	1.7	41 57.4	−59.8	1.7	42 57.4	−59.9	1.7	43 57.4	−59.9	1.8	44 57.4	−59.9	1.8	45 57.3	−59.8	1.8	46 57.3	−59.9	1.9	65
66	38 57.6	−59.9	1.6	39 57.6	−59.9	1.6	40 57.6	−59.9	1.6	41 57.5	−59.8	1.6	42 57.5	−59.8	1.7	43 57.5	−59.9	1.7	44 57.5	−59.9	1.7	45 57.4	−59.8	1.8	66
67	37 57.7	−59.8	1.5	38 57.7	−59.9	1.5	39 57.7	−59.9	1.5	40 57.7	−59.9	1.6	41 57.7	−59.9	1.6	42 57.6	−59.8	1.6	43 57.6	−59.9	1.6	44 57.6	−59.9	1.7	67
68	36 57.9	−59.9	1.4	37 57.8	−59.8	1.4	38 57.8	−59.8	1.4	39 57.8	−59.9	1.5	40 57.8	−59.9	1.5	41 57.8	−59.9	1.5	42 57.7	−59.8	1.5	43 57.7	−59.8	1.6	68
69	35 58.0	−59.9	1.3	36 58.0	−59.9	1.3	37 58.0	−59.9	1.4	38 57.9	−59.8	1.4	39 57.9	−59.9	1.4	40 57.9	−59.9	1.4	41 57.9	−59.9	1.4	42 57.9	−59.9	1.5	69
70	34 58.1	−59.9	1.3	35 58.1	−59.9	1.3	36 58.1	−59.9	1.3	37 58.1	−59.9	1.3	38 58.0	−59.8	1.3	39 58.0	−59.9	1.3	40 58.0	−59.9	1.4	41 58.0	−59.9	1.4	70
71	33 58.2	−59.9	1.2	34 58.2	−59.9	1.2	35 58.2	−59.9	1.2	36 58.2	−59.9	1.2	37 58.2	−59.9	1.2	38 58.1	−59.8	1.3	39 58.1	−59.8	1.3	40 58.1	−59.9	1.3	71
72	32 58.3	−59.9	1.1	33 58.3	−59.9	1.1	34 58.3	−59.9	1.1	35 58.3	−59.9	1.1	36 58.3	−59.9	1.2	37 58.3	−59.9	1.2	38 58.3	−59.9	1.2	39 58.2	−59.8	1.2	72
73	31 58.4	−59.9	1.0	32 58.4	−59.9	1.0	33 58.4	−59.9	1.1	34 58.4	−59.9	1.1	35 58.4	−59.9	1.1	36 58.4	−59.9	1.1	37 58.4	−59.9	1.1	38 58.4	−59.9	1.1	73
74	30 58.5	−59.9	1.0	31 58.5	−59.9	1.0	32 58.5	−59.9	1.0	33 58.5	−59.9	1.0	34 58.5	−59.9	1.0	35 58.5	−59.9	1.0	36 58.5	−59.9	1.0	37 58.5	−59.9	1.0	74
75	29 58.6	−59.9	0.9	30 58.6	−59.9	0.9	31 58.6	−59.9	0.9	32 58.6	−59.9	0.9	33 58.6	−59.9	0.9	34 58.6	−59.9	0.9	35 58.6	−59.9	1.0	36 58.6	−59.9	1.0	75
76	28 58.7	−59.9	0.8	29 58.7	−59.9	0.8	30 58.7	−59.9	0.8	31 58.7	−59.9	0.9	32 58.7	−59.9	0.9	33 58.7	−59.9	0.9	34 58.7	−59.9	0.9	35 58.7	−59.9	0.9	76
77	27 58.8	−59.9	0.8	28 58.8	−59.9	0.8	29 58.8	−59.9	0.8	30 58.8	−59.9	0.8	31 58.8	−59.9	0.8	32 58.8	−59.9	0.8	33 58.8	−59.9	0.8	34 58.8	−59.9	0.8	77
78	26 58.9	−59.9	0.7	27 58.9	−59.9	0.7	28 58.9	−59.9	0.7	29 58.9	−59.9	0.7	30 58.9	−59.9	0.7	31 58.9	−59.9	0.7	32 58.9	−59.9	0.7	33 58.9	−59.9	0.8	78
79	25 59.0	−59.9	0.6	26 59.0	−59.9	0.6	27 59.0	−59.9	0.6	28 59.0	−59.9	0.7	29 59.0	−59.9	0.7	30 59.0	−59.9	0.7	31 59.0	−59.9	0.7	32 59.0	−59.9	0.7	79
80	24 59.1	−59.9	0.6	25 59.1	−59.9	0.6	26 59.1	−59.9	0.6	27 59.1	−59.9	0.6	28 59.1	−59.9	0.6	29 59.1	−59.9	0.6	30 59.1	−59.9	0.6	31 59.1	−59.9	0.6	80
81	23 59.2	−59.9	0.5	24 59.2	−59.9	0.5	25 59.2	−59.9	0.5	26 59.2	−59.9	0.5	27 59.2	−59.9	0.5	28 59.2	−59.9	0.5	29 59.2	−59.9	0.5	30 59.2	−59.9	0.5	81
82	22 59.3	−59.9	0.5	23 59.3	−59.9	0.5	24 59.3	−59.9	0.5	25 59.3	−59.9	0.5	26 59.3	−59.9	0.5	27 59.3	−59.9	0.5	28 59.3	−59.9	0.5	29 59.3	−59.9	0.5	82
83	21 59.4	−59.9	0.4	22 59.4	−59.9	0.4	23 59.4	−59.9	0.4	24 59.4	−59.9	0.4	25 59.4	−59.9	0.4	26 59.4	−59.9	0.4	27 59.4	−59.9	0.4	28 59.4	−59.9	0.4	83
84	20 59.5	−59.9	0.3	21 59.5	−59.9	0.3	22 59.5	−59.9	0.3	23 59.5	−59.9	0.3	24 59.5	−59.9	0.3	25 59.5	−59.9	0.3	26 59.5	−59.9	0.4	27 59.5	−59.9	0.4	84
85	19 59.6	−59.9	0.3	20 59.6	−59.9	0.3	21 59.6	−59.9	0.3	22 59.6	−59.9	0.3	23 59.6	−59.9	0.3	24 59.6	−59.9	0.3	25 59.6	−59.9	0.3	26 59.6	−59.9	0.3	85
86	18 59.7	−60.0	0.2	19 59.7	−60.0	0.2	20 59.7	−60.0	0.2	21 59.7	−60.0	0.2	22 59.7	−60.0	0.2	23 59.7	−60.0	0.2	24 59.7	−60.0	0.2	25 59.7	−60.0	0.2	86
87	17 59.7	−59.9	0.2	18 59.7	−59.9	0.2	19 59.7	−59.9	0.2	20 59.7	−59.9	0.2	21 59.7	−59.9	0.2	22 59.7	−59.9	0.2	23 59.7	−59.9	0.2	24 59.7	−59.9	0.2	87
88	16 59.8	−59.9	0.1	17 59.8	−59.9	0.1	18 59.8	−59.9	0.1	19 59.8	−59.9	0.1	20 59.8	−59.9	0.1	21 59.8	−59.9	0.1	22 59.8	−59.9	0.1	23 59.8	−59.9	0.1	88
89	15 59.9	−59.9	0.1	16 59.9	−59.9	0.1	17 59.9	−59.9	0.1	18 59.9	−59.9	0.1	19 59.9	−59.9	0.1	20 59.9	−59.9	0.1	21 59.9	−59.9	0.1	22 59.9	−59.9	0.1	89
90	15 00.0	−59.9	0.0	16 00.0	−59.9	0.0	17 00.0	−59.9	0.0	18 00.0	−59.9	0.0	19 00.0	−59.9	0.0	20 00.0	−59.9	0.0	21 00.0	−59.9	0.0	22 00.0	−59.9	0.0	90
	15°			16°			17°			18°			19°			20°			21°			22°			

3°, 357° L.H.A. LATITUDE SAME NAME AS DECLINATION

8

LATITUDE **CONTRARY** NAME TO DECLINATION — L.H.A. 3°, 357°

Dec.	15°			16°			17°			18°			19°			20°			21°			22°			Dec.
	Hc	d	Z	Hc	d	Z	Hc	d	Z	Hc	d	Z	Hc	d	Z	Hc	d	Z	Hc	d	Z	Hc	d	Z	
°	° ′	′	°	° ′	′	°	° ′	′	°	° ′	′	°	° ′	′	°	° ′	′	°	° ′	′	°	° ′	′	°	°
0	74 42.6	-59.0	168.6	73 43.7	-59.1	169.2	72 44.7	-59.2	169.8	71 45.6	-59.3	170.4	70 46.4	-59.4	170.9	69 47.1	-59.4	171.3	68 47.8	-59.5	171.7	67 48.4	-59.5	172.0	0
1	73 43.6	-59.0	169.2	72 44.6	-59.2	169.8	71 45.5	-59.3	170.4	70 46.3	-59.3	170.9	69 47.0	-59.4	171.3	68 47.7	-59.5	171.7	67 48.3	-59.5	172.0	66 48.9	-59.6	172.4	1
2	72 44.6	-59.2	169.8	71 45.4	-59.2	170.4	70 46.2	-59.3	170.9	69 47.0	-59.4	171.3	68 47.6	-59.4	171.7	67 48.2	-59.5	172.0	66 48.8	-59.6	172.4	65 49.3	-59.6	172.7	2
3	71 45.4	-59.3	170.4	70 46.2	-59.3	170.9	69 46.9	-59.4	171.3	68 47.6	-59.5	171.7	67 48.2	-59.5	172.0	66 48.7	-59.5	172.4	65 49.2	-59.5	172.7	64 49.7	-59.6	172.9	3
4	70 46.1	-59.3	170.9	69 46.9	-59.4	171.3	68 47.5	-59.4	171.7	67 48.1	-59.5	172.1	66 48.7	-59.6	172.4	65 49.2	-59.6	172.7	64 49.7	-59.7	172.9	63 50.1	-59.7	173.2	4
5	69 46.8	-59.4	171.3	68 47.5	-59.5	171.7	67 48.1	-59.5	172.1	66 48.6	-59.5	172.4	65 49.1	-59.5	172.7	64 49.6	-59.6	173.0	63 50.0	-59.6	173.2	62 50.4	-59.6	173.4	5
6	68 47.4	-59.4	171.7	67 48.0	-59.5	172.1	66 48.6	-59.6	172.4	65 49.1	-59.6	172.7	64 49.6	-59.7	173.0	63 50.0	-59.7	173.2	62 50.4	-59.7	173.5	61 50.8	-59.7	173.7	6
7	67 48.0	-59.5	172.1	66 48.5	-59.5	172.4	65 49.0	-59.5	172.7	64 49.5	-59.6	173.0	63 49.9	-59.6	173.2	62 50.3	-59.6	173.5	61 50.7	-59.7	173.7	60 51.1	-59.7	173.9	7
8	66 48.5	-59.5	172.4	65 49.0	-59.5	172.7	64 49.5	-59.6	173.0	63 49.9	-59.6	173.3	62 50.3	-59.6	173.5	61 50.7	-59.7	173.7	60 51.0	-59.7	173.9	59 51.4	-59.8	174.1	8
9	65 49.0	-59.6	172.8	64 49.5	-59.6	173.0	63 49.9	-59.6	173.3	62 50.3	-59.7	173.5	61 50.7	-59.7	173.7	60 51.0	-59.7	173.9	59 51.3	-59.7	174.1	58 51.6	-59.7	174.3	9
10	64 49.4	-59.6	173.0	63 49.9	-59.7	173.3	62 50.3	-59.7	173.5	61 50.6	-59.7	173.7	60 51.0	-59.7	173.9	59 51.3	-59.7	174.1	58 51.6	-59.7	174.3	57 51.9	-59.8	174.4	10
11	63 49.8	-59.6	173.3	62 50.2	-59.6	173.5	61 50.6	-59.7	173.7	60 50.9	-59.6	173.9	59 51.3	-59.7	174.1	58 51.6	-59.8	174.3	57 51.9	-59.8	174.5	56 52.1	-59.7	174.6	11
12	62 50.2	-59.6	173.6	61 50.6	-59.7	173.8	60 50.9	-59.7	174.0	59 51.3	-59.8	174.1	58 51.6	-59.8	174.3	57 51.8	-59.7	174.5	56 52.1	-59.8	174.6	55 52.4	-59.8	174.8	12
13	61 50.6	-59.7	173.8	60 50.9	-59.7	174.0	59 51.2	-59.7	174.2	58 51.5	-59.7	174.3	57 51.8	-59.7	174.5	56 52.1	-59.8	174.6	55 52.3	-59.7	174.8	54 52.6	-59.8	174.9	13
14	60 50.9	-59.7	174.0	59 51.2	-59.7	174.2	58 51.5	-59.7	174.4	57 51.8	-59.7	174.5	56 52.1	-59.8	174.7	55 52.3	-59.7	174.8	54 52.6	-59.8	174.9	53 52.8	-59.8	175.1	14
15	59 51.2	-59.7	174.2	58 51.5	-59.7	174.4	57 51.8	-59.7	174.5	56 52.1	-59.8	174.7	55 52.3	-59.8	174.8	54 52.6	-59.8	175.0	53 52.8	-59.8	175.1	52 53.0	-59.8	175.2	15
16	58 51.5	-59.7	174.4	57 51.8	-59.7	174.6	56 52.1	-59.8	174.7	55 52.3	-59.8	174.9	54 52.5	-59.7	175.0	53 52.8	-59.8	175.1	52 53.0	-59.8	175.2	51 53.2	-59.8	175.3	16
17	57 51.8	-59.7	174.6	56 52.1	-59.8	174.7	55 52.3	-59.8	174.9	54 52.5	-59.7	175.0	53 52.8	-59.8	175.1	52 53.0	-59.8	175.2	51 53.2	-59.8	175.3	50 53.4	-59.9	175.4	17
18	56 52.1	-59.8	174.8	55 52.3	-59.8	174.9	54 52.5	-59.7	175.0	53 52.8	-59.8	175.2	52 53.0	-59.8	175.3	51 53.2	-59.8	175.4	50 53.4	-59.9	175.5	49 53.5	-59.8	175.6	18
19	55 52.3	-59.7	174.9	54 52.5	-59.7	175.1	53 52.8	-59.8	175.2	52 53.0	-59.8	175.3	51 53.2	-59.8	175.4	50 53.4	-59.9	175.5	49 53.5	-59.8	175.6	48 53.7	-59.8	175.7	19
20	54 52.6	-59.8	175.1	53 52.8	-59.8	175.2	52 53.0	-59.8	175.3	51 53.2	-59.8	175.4	50 53.4	-59.9	175.5	49 53.5	-59.8	175.6	48 53.7	-59.8	175.7	47 53.9	-59.9	175.8	20
21	53 52.8	-59.8	175.2	52 53.0	-59.8	175.4	51 53.2	-59.8	175.5	50 53.4	-59.9	175.6	49 53.5	-59.8	175.7	48 53.7	-59.8	175.7	47 53.9	-59.9	175.8	46 54.0	-59.8	175.9	21
22	52 53.0	-59.8	175.4	51 53.2	-59.8	175.5	50 53.4	-59.8	175.6	49 53.5	-59.8	175.7	48 53.7	-59.8	175.8	47 53.9	-59.9	175.8	46 54.0	-59.8	175.9	45 54.2	-59.9	176.0	22
23	51 53.2	-59.8	175.5	50 53.4	-59.8	175.6	49 53.6	-59.9	175.7	48 53.7	-59.8	175.8	47 53.9	-59.9	175.9	46 54.0	-59.8	176.0	45 54.2	-59.9	176.0	44 54.3	-59.8	176.1	23
24	50 53.4	-59.8	175.7	49 53.6	-59.8	175.7	48 53.7	-59.8	175.8	47 53.9	-59.8	175.9	46 54.0	-59.8	176.0	45 54.2	-59.9	176.1	44 54.3	-59.8	176.1	43 54.5	-59.9	176.2	24
25	49 53.6	-59.8	175.8	48 53.8	-59.9	175.9	47 53.9	-59.8	175.9	46 54.1	-59.9	176.0	45 54.2	-59.9	176.1	44 54.3	-59.8	176.2	43 54.5	-59.9	176.2	42 54.6	-59.9	176.3	25
26	48 53.8	-59.9	175.9	47 53.9	-59.8	176.0	46 54.1	-59.9	176.1	45 54.2	-59.8	176.1	44 54.3	-59.8	176.2	43 54.5	-59.9	176.3	42 54.6	-59.9	176.3	41 54.7	-59.9	176.4	26
27	47 53.9	-59.8	176.0	46 54.1	-59.9	176.1	45 54.2	-59.8	176.2	44 54.4	-59.9	176.2	43 54.5	-59.9	176.3	42 54.6	-59.9	176.3	41 54.7	-59.8	176.4	40 54.8	-59.8	176.5	27
28	46 54.1	-59.8	176.1	45 54.2	-59.8	176.2	44 54.4	-59.9	176.3	43 54.5	-59.9	176.3	42 54.6	-59.8	176.4	41 54.7	-59.8	176.4	40 54.9	-59.9	176.5	39 55.0	-59.9	176.5	28
29	45 54.3	-59.9	176.2	44 54.4	-59.8	176.3	43 54.5	-59.8	176.4	42 54.6	-59.8	176.4	41 54.8	-59.9	176.5	40 54.9	-59.9	176.5	39 55.0	-59.9	176.6	38 55.1	-59.9	176.6	29
30	44 54.4	-59.8	176.3	43 54.6	-59.9	176.4	42 54.7	-59.9	176.5	41 54.8	-59.9	176.5	40 54.9	-59.9	176.6	39 55.0	-59.9	176.6	38 55.1	-59.9	176.7	37 55.2	-59.9	176.7	30
31	43 54.6	-59.9	176.4	42 54.7	-59.9	176.5	41 54.8	-59.9	176.5	40 54.9	-59.9	176.6	39 55.0	-59.9	176.6	38 55.1	-59.9	176.7	37 55.2	-59.9	176.7	36 55.3	-59.9	176.8	31
32	42 54.7	-59.8	176.5	41 54.8	-59.8	176.6	40 54.9	-59.8	176.6	39 55.0	-59.8	176.7	38 55.1	-59.8	176.7	37 55.2	-59.8	176.8	36 55.3	-59.9	176.8	35 55.4	-59.9	176.9	32
33	41 54.9	-59.9	176.6	40 55.0	-59.9	176.7	39 55.1	-59.9	176.7	38 55.2	-59.9	176.8	37 55.3	-59.9	176.8	36 55.4	-59.9	176.9	35 55.4	-59.8	176.9	34 55.5	-59.9	176.9	33
34	40 55.0	-59.9	176.7	39 55.1	-59.9	176.8	38 55.2	-59.9	176.8	37 55.3	-59.9	176.8	36 55.4	-59.9	176.9	35 55.5	-59.9	176.9	34 55.6	-59.9	177.0	33 55.6	-59.9	177.0	34
35	39 55.1	-59.8	176.8	38 55.2	-59.8	176.8	37 55.3	-59.9	176.9	36 55.4	-59.9	176.9	35 55.5	-59.9	177.0	34 55.6	-59.9	177.0	33 55.7	-59.9	177.0	32 55.7	-59.9	177.1	35
36	38 55.3	-59.9	176.9	37 55.4	-59.8	176.9	36 55.4	-59.8	177.0	35 55.5	-59.9	177.0	34 55.6	-59.9	177.0	33 55.7	-59.9	177.1	32 55.8	-59.9	177.1	31 55.8	-59.9	177.1	36
37	37 55.4	-59.9	177.0	36 55.5	-59.9	177.0	35 55.6	-59.9	177.0	34 55.6	-59.9	177.1	33 55.7	-59.9	177.1	32 55.8	-59.9	177.1	31 55.9	-59.9	177.2	30 55.9	-59.9	177.2	37
38	36 55.5	-59.9	177.0	35 55.6	-59.9	177.1	34 55.7	-59.9	177.1	33 55.7	-59.9	177.2	32 55.8	-59.9	177.2	31 55.9	-59.9	177.2	30 56.0	-59.9	177.2	29 56.0	-59.9	177.3	38
39	35 55.6	-59.9	177.1	34 55.7	-59.9	177.2	33 55.8	-59.9	177.2	32 55.8	-59.8	177.2	31 55.9	-59.9	177.3	30 56.0	-59.9	177.3	29 56.1	-60.0	177.3	28 56.1	-59.9	177.3	39
40	34 55.7	-59.8	177.2	33 55.8	-59.9	177.2	32 55.9	-59.9	177.3	31 56.0	-59.9	177.3	30 56.0	-59.9	177.3	29 56.1	-59.9	177.3	28 56.1	-59.9	177.4	27 56.2	-59.9	177.4	40
41	33 55.9	-59.9	177.3	32 55.9	-59.9	177.3	31 56.0	-59.9	177.3	30 56.1	-59.9	177.4	29 56.1	-59.9	177.4	28 56.2	-59.9	177.4	27 56.2	-59.9	177.4	26 56.3	-59.9	177.5	41
42	32 56.0	-59.9	177.3	31 56.0	-59.9	177.4	30 56.1	-59.9	177.4	29 56.2	-59.9	177.4	28 56.2	-59.9	177.5	27 56.3	-59.9	177.5	26 56.3	-59.9	177.5	25 56.4	-59.9	177.5	42
43	31 56.1	-59.9	177.4	30 56.1	-59.9	177.4	29 56.2	-59.9	177.5	28 56.3	-59.9	177.5	27 56.3	-59.9	177.5	26 56.4	-59.9	177.5	25 56.4	-59.9	177.6	24 56.5	-59.9	177.6	43
44	30 56.2	-59.9	177.5	29 56.2	-59.9	177.5	28 56.3	-59.9	177.5	27 56.4	-60.0	177.6	26 56.4	-59.9	177.6	25 56.5	-60.0	177.6	24 56.5	-59.9	177.6	23 56.6	-60.0	177.6	44
45	29 56.3	-59.9	177.6	28 56.3	-59.9	177.6	27 56.4	-59.9	177.6	26 56.4	-59.9	177.6	25 56.5	-59.9	177.6	24 56.5	-59.9	177.7	23 56.6	-59.9	177.7	22 56.6	-59.9	177.7	45
46	28 56.4	-59.9	177.6	27 56.4	-59.9	177.6	26 56.5	-59.9	177.7	25 56.5	-59.9	177.7	24 56.6	-59.9	177.7	23 56.6	-59.9	177.7	22 56.7	-59.9	177.7	21 56.7	-59.9	177.8	46
47	27 56.5	-59.9	177.7	26 56.5	-59.9	177.7	25 56.6	-59.9	177.7	24 56.6	-59.9	177.7	23 56.7	-59.9	177.8	22 56.7	-59.9	177.8	21 56.8	-60.0	177.8	20 56.8	-59.9	177.8	47
48	26 56.6	-59.9	177.7	25 56.6	-59.9	177.8	24 56.7	-59.9	177.8	23 56.7	-59.9	177.8	22 56.8	-60.0	177.8	21 56.8	-59.9	177.8	20 56.8	-59.9	177.9	19 56.9	-59.9	177.9	48
49	25 56.7	-59.9	177.8	24 56.7	-59.9	177.8	23 56.8	-59.9	177.8	22 56.8	-59.9	177.9	21 56.8	-59.9	177.9	20 56.9	-59.9	177.9	19 56.9	-59.9	177.9	18 57.0	-60.0	177.9	49
50	24 56.8	-59.9	177.9	23 56.8	-59.9	177.9	22 56.9	-60.0	177.9	21 56.9	-59.9	177.9	20 56.9	-59.9	177.9	19 57.0	-59.9	177.9	18 57.0	-59.9	178.0	17 57.0	-59.9	178.0	50
51	23 56.9	-59.9	177.9	22 56.9	-59.9	178.0	21 56.9	-59.9	178.0	20 57.0	-59.9	178.0	19 57.0	-59.9	178.0	18 57.1	-60.0	178.0	17 57.1	-59.9	178.0	16 57.1	-59.9	178.0	51
52	22 57.0	-60.0	178.0	21 57.0	-59.9	178.0	20 57.0	-59.9	178.0	19 57.1	-60.0	178.0	18 57.1	-59.9	178.0	17 57.1	-59.9	178.1	16 57.2	-60.0	178.1	15 57.2	-59.9	178.1	52
53	21 57.0	-59.9	178.1	20 57.1	-59.9	178.1	19 57.1	-59.9	178.1	18 57.1	-59.9	178.1	17 57.2	-59.9	178.1	16 57.2	-59.9	178.1	15 57.2	-59.9	178.1	14 57.3	-59.9	178.1	53
54	20 57.1	-59.9	178.1	19 57.2	-59.9	178.1	18 57.2	-59.9	178.1	17 57.2	-59.9	178.1	16 57.3	-60.0	178.2	15 57.3	-59.9	178.2	14 57.3	-59.9	178.2	13 57.4	-60.0	178.2	54
55	19 57.2	-59.9	178.2	18 57.3	-60.0	178.2	17 57.3	-59.9	178.2	16 57.3	-59.9	178.2	15 57.3	-59.9	178.2	14 57.4	-60.0	178.2	13 57.4	-59.9	178.2	12 57.4	-59.9	178.2	55
56	18 57.3	-59.9	178.2	17 57.3	-59.9	178.2	16 57.4	-60.0	178.2	15 57.4	-59.9	178.3	14 57.4	-59.9	178.3	13 57.4	-59.9	178.3	12 57.5	-59.9	178.3	11 57.5	-59.9	178.3	56
57	17 57.4	-59.9	178.3	16 57.4	-59.9	178.3	15 57.4	-59.9	178.3	14 57.5	-59.9	178.3	13 57.5	-59.9	178.3	12 57.5	-59.9	178.3	11 57.6	-60.0	178.3	10 57.6	-60.0	178.3	57
58	16 57.5	-59.9	178.3	15 57.5	-59.9	178.4	14 57.5	-59.9	178.4	13 57.6	-60.0	178.4	12 57.6	-59.9	178.4	11 57.6	-59.9	178.4	10 57.6	-59.9	178.4	9 57.6	-59.9	178.4	58
59	15 57.6	-60.0	178.4	14 57.6	-59.9	178.4	13 57.6	-59.9	178.4	12 57.6	-59.9	178.4	11 57.7	-60.0	178.4	10 57.7	-59.9	178.4	9 57.7	-59.9	178.4	8 57.7	-59.9	178.4	59
60	14 57.6	-59.9	178.4	13 57.7	-60.0	178.5	12 57.7	-59.9	178.5	11 57.7	-59.9	178.5	10 57.7	-59.9	178.5	9 57.8	-60.0	178.5	8 57.8	-60.0	178.5	7 57.8	-59.9	178.5	60
61	13 57.7	-59.9	178.5	12 57.7	-59.9	178.5	11 57.8	-60.0	178.5	10 57.8	-59.9	178.5	9 57.8	-59.9	178.5	8 57.8	-59.9	178.5	7 57.8	-59.9	178.5	6 57.9	-60.0	178.5	61
62	12 57.8	-59.9	178.6	11 57.8	-59.9	178.6	10 57.8	-59.9	178.6	9 57.9	-60.0	178.6	8 57.9	-59.9	178.6	7 57.9	-59.9	178.6	6 57.9	-59.9	178.6	5 57.9	-59.9	178.6	62
63	11 57.9	-59.9	178.6	10 57.9	-59.9	178.6	9 57.9	-59.9	178.6	8 57.9	-59.9	178.6	7 58.0	-60.0	178.6	6 58.0	-60.0	178.6	5 58.0	-59.9	178.6	4 58.0	-59.9	178.6	63
64	10 58.0	-60.0	178.7	9 58.0	-59.9	178.7	8 58.0	-59.9	178.7	7 58.0	-59.9	178.7	6 58.0	-59.9	178.7	5 58.0	-59.9	178.7	4 58.1	-60.0	178.7	3 58.1	-59.9	178.7	64
65	9 58.0	-59.9	178.7	8 58.1	-60.0	178.7	7 58.1	-59.9	178.7	6 58.1	-59.9	178.7	5 58.1	-59.9	178.7	4 58.1	-59.9	178.7	3 58.1	-59.9	178.7	2 58.2	-60.0	178.7	65
66	8 58.1	-59.9	178.8	7 58.1	-59.9	178.8	6 58.2	-60.0	178.8	5 58.2	-60.0	178.8	4 58.2	-59.9	178.8	3 58.2	-59.9	178.8	2 58.2	-59.9	178.8	1 58.2	-59.9	178.8	66
67	7 58.2	-59.9	178.8	6 58.2	-59.9	178.8	5 58.2	-59.9	178.8	4 58.2	-59.9	178.8	3 58.3	-60.0	178.8	2 58.3	-60.0	178.8	1 58.3	-59.9	178.8	0 58.3	-59.9	178.8	67
68	6 58.3	-59.9	178.9	5 58.3	-59.9	178.9	4 58.3	-59.9	178.9	3 58.3	-59.9	178.9	2 58.3	-59.9	178.9	1 58.3	-59.9	178.9	0 58.4	-60.0	178.9	0 01.6	+60.0	1.1	68
69	5 58.4	-60.0	178.9	4 58.4	-60.0	178.9	3 58.4	-59.9	178.9	2 58.4	-59.9	178.9	1 58.4	-59.9	178.9	0 58.4	-59.9	178.9	0 01.6	+59.9	1.1	1 01.6	+59.9	1.1	69
70	4 58.4	-59.9	179.0	3 58.4	-59.9	179.0	2 58.5	-60.0	179.0	1 58.5	-60.0	179.0	0 58.5	-60.0	179.0	0 01.5	+59.9	1.0	1 01.5	+59.9	1.0	2 01.5	+59.9	1.0	70
71	3 58.5	-59.9	179.0	2 58.5	-59.9	179.0	1 58.5	-59.9	179.0	0 58.5	-59.9	179.0	0 01.5	+59.9	1.0	1 01.4	+60.0	1.0	2 01.4	+60.0	1.0	3 01.4	+60.0	1.0	71
72	2 58.6	-59.9	179.1	1 58.6	-59.9	179.1	0 58.6	-59.9	179.1	0 01.4	+59.9	0.9	1 01.4	+59.9	0.9	2 01.4	+59.9	0.9	3 01.4	+59.9	0.9	4 01.4	+59.9	0.9	72
73	1 58.7	-60.0	179.1	0 58.7	-59.9	179.1	0 01.3	+59.9	0.9	1 01.3	+59.9	0.9	2 01.3	+59.9	0.9	3 01.3	+59.9	0.9	4 01.3	+59.9	0.9	5 01.3	+59.9	0.9	73
74	0 58.7	-59.9	179.2	0 01.2	+60.0	0.8	1 01.2	+60.0	0.8	2 01.2	+60.0	0.8	3 01.2	+60.0	0.8	4 01.2	+60.0	0.8	5 01.2	+59.9	0.8	6 01.2	+59.9	0.8	74
75	0 01.2	+59.9	0.8	1 01.2	+59.9	0.8	2 01.2	+59.9	0.8	3 01.2	+59.9	0.8	4 01.2	+59.9	0.8	5 01.2	+59.9	0.8	6 01.1	+60.0	0.8	7 01.1	+60.0	0.8	75
76	1 01.1	+59.9	0.7	2 01.1	+59.9	0.7	3 01.1	+59.9	0.7	4 01.1	+59.9	0.7	5 01.1	+59.9	0.7	6 01.1	+59.9	0.7	7 01.1	+59.9	0.7	8 01.1	+59.9	0.7	76
77	2 01.0	+59.9	0.7	3 01.0	+59.9	0.7	4 01.0	+59.9	0.7	5 01.0	+59.9	0.7	6 01.0	+59.9	0.7	7 01.0	+59.9	0.7	8 01.0	+59.9	0.7	9 01.0	+59.9	0.7	77
78	3 00.9	+60.0	0.6	4 00.9	+60.0	0.6	5 00.9	+60.0	0.6	6 00.9	+60.0	0.6	7 00.9	+60.0	0.6	8 00.9	+60.0	0.6	9 00.9	+60.0	0.6	10 00.9	+59.9	0.6	78
79	4 00.9	+59.9	0.6	5 00.9	+59.9	0.6	6 00.9	+59.9	0.6	7 00.9	+59.9	0.6	8 00.9	+59.9	0.6	9 00.9	+59.9	0.6	10 00.9	+59.9	0.6	11 00.8	+60.0	0.6	79
80	5 00.8	+59.9	0.5	6 00.8	+59.9	0.5	7 00.8	+59.9	0.5	8 00.8	+59.9	0.5	9 00.8	+59.9	0.5	10 00.8	+59.9	0.5	11 00.8	+59.9	0.5	12 00.8	+59.9	0.5	80
81	6 00.7	+59.9	0.5	7 00.7	+59.9	0.5	8 00.7	+59.9	0.5	9 00.7	+59.9	0.5	10 00.7	+59.9	0.5	11 00.7	+59.9	0.5	12 00.7	+59.9	0.5	13 00.7	+59.9	0.5	81
82	7 00.6	+60.0	0.4	8 00.6	+60.0	0.4	9 00.6	+60.0	0.4	10 00.6	+60.0	0.4	11 00.6	+60.0	0.4	12 00.6	+60.0	0.4	13 00.6	+60.0	0.4	14 00.6	+60.0	0.4	82
83	8 00.6	+59.9	0.4	9 00.6	+59.9	0.4	10 00.6	+59.9	0.4	11 00.6	+59.9	0.4	12 00.6	+59.9	0.4	13 00.6	+59.9	0.4	14 00.6	+59.9	0.4	15 00.6	+59.9	0.4	83
84	9 00.5	+59.9	0.3	10 00.5	+59.9	0.3	11 00.5	+59.9	0.3	12 00.5	+59.9	0.3	13 00.5	+59.9	0.3	14 00.5	+59.9	0.3	15 00.5	+59.9	0.3	16 00.5	+59.9	0.3	84
85	10 00.4	+59.9	0.3	11 00.4	+59.9	0.3	12 00.4	+59.9	0.3	13 00.4	+59.9	0.3	14 00.4	+59.9	0.3	15 00.4	+59.9	0.3	16 00.4	+59.9	0.3	17 00.4	+59.9	0.3	85
86	11 00.3	+59.9	0.2	12 00.3	+59.9	0.2	13 00.3	+59.9	0.2	14 00.3	+59.9	0.2	15 00.3	+59.9	0.2	16 00.3	+59.9	0.2	17 00.3	+59.9	0.2	18 00.3	+59.9	0.2	86
87	12 00.2	+60.0	0.2	13 00.2	+60.0	0.2	14 00.2	+60.0	0.2	15 00.2	+60.0	0.2	16 00.2	+60.0	0.2	17 00.2	+60.0	0.2	18 00.2	+60.0	0.2	19 00.2	+60.0	0.2	87
88	13 00.2	+59.9	0.1	14 00.2	+59.9	0.1	15 00.2	+59.9	0.1	16 00.2	+59.9	0.1	17 00.2	+59.9	0.1	18 00.2	+59.9	0.1	19 00.2	+59.9	0.1	20 00.2	+59.9	0.1	88
89	14 00.1	+59.9	0.1	15 00.1	+59.9	0.1	16 00.1	+59.9	0.1	17 00.1	+59.9	0.1	18 00.1	+59.9	0.1	19 00.1	+59.9	0.1	20 00.1	+59.9	0.1	21 00.1	+59.9	0.1	89
90	15 00.0	+59.9	0.0	16 00.0	+59.9	0.0	17 00.0	+59.9	0.0	18 00.0	+59.9	0.0	19 00.0	+59.9	0.0	20 00.0	+59.9	0.0	21 00.0	+59.9	0.0	22 00.0	+59.9	0.0	90
	15°			16°			17°			18°			19°			20°			21°			22°			

S. Lat. {L.H.A. greater than 180° ....Zn=180°–Z
{L.H.A. less than 180°...........Zn=180°+Z

LATITUDE **SAME** NAME AS DECLINATION — L.H.A. 177°, 183°

4°, 356° L.H.A. LATITUDE SAME NAME AS DECLINATION N. Lat. {L.H.A. greater than 180° .....Zn=Z / L.H.A. less than 180°...........Zn=360°−Z

Dec.	15°			16°			17°			18°			19°			20°			21°			22°			Dec.
	Hc	d	Z	Hc	d	Z	Hc	d	Z	Hc	d	Z	Hc	d	Z	Hc	d	Z	Hc	d	Z	Hc	d	Z	
°	° ′	′	°	° ′	′	°	° ′	′	°	° ′	′	°	° ′	′	°	° ′	′	°	° ′	′	°	° ′	′	°	°
0	74 29.3	+57.9	164.9	73 31.2	+58.2	165.8	72 33.0	+58.4	166.5	71 34.5	+58.6	167.2	70 35.9	+58.8	167.9	69 37.2	+58.9	168.4	68 38.4	+59.0	169.0	67 39.4	+59.1	169.4	0
1	75 27.2	+57.6	163.9	74 29.4	+58.0	164.9	73 31.4	+58.2	165.8	72 33.1	+58.4	166.5	71 34.7	+58.6	167.2	70 36.1	+58.7	167.9	69 37.4	+58.8	168.4	68 38.5	+59.0	169.0	1
2	76 24.8	+57.3	162.7	75 27.4	+57.6	163.9	74 29.6	+58.0	164.9	73 31.5	+58.3	165.8	72 33.3	+58.4	166.6	71 34.8	+58.7	167.3	70 36.2	+58.8	167.9	69 37.5	+58.9	168.4	2
3	77 22.1	+56.9	161.4	76 25.0	+57.3	162.7	75 27.6	+57.6	163.9	74 29.8	+58.0	164.9	73 31.7	+58.3	165.8	72 33.5	+58.4	166.6	71 35.0	+58.7	167.3	70 36.4	+58.8	167.9	3
4	78 19.0	+56.2	159.9	77 22.3	+56.9	161.4	76 25.2	+57.4	162.8	75 27.8	+57.7	163.9	74 30.0	+58.0	164.9	73 31.9	+58.3	165.8	72 33.7	+58.4	166.6	71 35.2	+58.7	167.3	4
5	79 15.2	+55.6	158.1	78 19.2	+56.3	159.9	77 22.6	+56.9	161.5	76 25.5	+57.3	162.8	75 28.0	+57.7	163.9	74 30.2	+58.0	164.9	73 32.1	+58.3	165.8	72 33.9	+58.5	166.6	5
6	80 10.8	+54.6	156.0	79 15.5	+55.6	158.1	78 19.5	+56.3	160.0	77 22.8	+57.0	161.5	76 25.7	+57.4	162.8	75 28.2	+57.8	163.9	74 30.4	+58.1	164.9	73 32.4	+58.3	165.8	6
7	81 05.4	+53.3	153.4	80 11.1	+54.7	156.0	79 15.8	+55.7	158.2	78 19.8	+56.4	160.0	77 23.1	+57.0	161.5	76 26.0	+57.4	162.8	75 28.5	+57.8	164.0	74 30.7	+58.1	165.0	7
8	81 58.7	+51.6•	150.3	81 05.8	+53.3	153.5	80 11.5	+54.7	156.1	79 16.2	+55.6	158.2	78 20.1	+56.4	160.0	77 23.4	+57.0	161.6	76 26.3	+57.5	162.9	75 28.8	+57.8	164.0	8
9	82 50.3	+49.1•	146.5	81 59.1	+51.7•	150.4	81 06.2	+53.4	153.5	80 11.8	+54.8	156.1	79 16.5	+55.7	158.3	78 20.4	+56.5	160.1	77 23.8	+57.0	161.6	76 26.6	+57.5	162.9	9
10	83 39.4	+45.6•	141.6	82 50.8	+49.2•	146.5	81 59.6	+51.7•	150.4	81 06.6	+53.5	153.6	80 12.2	+54.9	156.2	79 16.9	+55.8	158.3	78 20.8	+56.5	160.1	77 24.1	+57.1	161.6	10
11	84 25.0	+40.3•	135.3	83 40.0	+45.6•	141.6	82 51.3	+49.3•	146.6	82 00.1	+51.8•	150.5	81 07.1	+53.5	153.7	80 12.7	+54.8	156.2	79 17.3	+55.8	158.4	78 21.2	+56.5	160.2	11
12	85 05.3	+32.7•	127.2	84 25.6	+40.5•	135.4	83 40.6	+45.8•	141.7	82 51.9	+49.4•	146.7	82 00.6	+51.9•	150.6	81 07.5	+53.7	153.7	80 13.1	+55.0	156.3	79 17.7	+55.9	158.4	12
13	85 38.0	+22.0•	116.8	85 06.1	+32.9•	127.2	84 26.4	+40.6•	135.5	83 41.3	+45.8•	141.8	82 52.5	+49.5•	146.8	82 01.2	+51.9•	150.7	81 08.1	+53.7	153.8	80 13.6	+55.0	156.4	13
14	86 00.0	+8.2•	104.0	85 39.0	+22.1•	116.8	85 07.0	+33.0•	127.3	84 27.1	+40.8•	135.6	83 42.0	+46.0•	141.9	82 53.1	+49.6•	146.9	82 01.8	+52.0•	150.8	81 08.6	+53.8	153.9	14
15	86 08.2	−7.1•	89.5	86 01.1	+8.2•	104.0	85 40.0	+22.2•	116.9	85 07.9	+33.1•	127.5	84 28.0	+40.8•	135.7	83 42.7	+46.1•	142.0	82 53.8	+49.7•	147.0	82 02.4	+52.1•	150.9	15
16	86 01.1	−21.1•	74.9	86 09.3	−7.1•	89.4	86 02.2	+8.3•	104.0	85 41.0	+22.4•	117.0	85 08.8	+33.3•	127.6	84 28.8	+41.1•	135.8	83 43.5	+46.3•	142.2	82 54.5	+49.8•	147.1	16
17	85 40.0	−32.1•	62.0	86 02.2	−21.2•	74.8	86 10.5	−7.1•	89.4	86 03.4	+8.4•	104.1	85 42.1	+22.5•	117.1	85 09.9	+33.4•	127.7	84 29.8	+41.1•	135.9	83 44.3	+46.4•	142.3	17
18	85 07.9	−39.9•	51.4	85 41.0	−32.2•	61.8	86 03.4	−21.3•	74.7	86 11.8	−7.2•	89.4	86 04.6	+8.5•	104.1	85 43.3	+22.7•	117.2	85 10.9	+33.7•	127.8	84 30.7	+41.3•	136.1	18
19	84 28.0	−45.3•	43.2	85 08.8	−40.0•	51.2	85 42.1	−32.2•	61.7	86 04.6	−21.3•	74.6	86 13.1	−7.1•	89.3	86 06.0	+8.5•	104.2	85 44.6	+22.7•	117.3	85 12.0	+33.8•	128.0	19
20	83 42.7	−48.9•	36.8	84 28.8	−45.3•	43.0	85 09.9	−40.1•	51.0	85 43.3	−32.4•	61.5	86 06.0	−21.4•	74.5	86 14.5	−7.2•	89.3	86 07.3	+8.6•	104.2	85 45.8	+23.0•	117.4	20
21	82 53.8	−51.4•	31.8	83 43.5	−49.0•	36.6	84 29.8	−45.5•	42.8	85 10.9	−40.2•	50.8	85 44.6	−32.6•	61.3	86 07.3	−21.5•	74.4	86 15.9	−7.1•	89.3	86 08.8	+8.7•	104.3	21
22	82 02.4	−53.2	27.8	82 54.5	−51.5•	31.6	83 44.3	−49.0•	36.4	84 30.7	−45.5•	42.6	85 12.0	−40.3•	50.6	85 45.8	−32.6•	61.1	86 08.8	−21.6•	74.2	86 17.5	−7.2•	89.3	22
23	81 09.2	−54.5	24.7	82 03.0	−53.2	27.7	82 55.3	−51.6•	31.4	83 45.2	−49.2•	36.2	84 31.7	−45.6•	42.3	85 13.2	−40.4•	50.4	85 47.2	−32.8•	60.9	86 10.3	−21.7•	74.1	23
24	80 14.7	−55.5	22.1	81 09.8	−54.6	24.5	82 03.7	−53.3	27.5	82 56.0	−51.6•	31.2	83 46.1	−49.2•	35.9	84 32.8	−45.8•	42.1	85 14.4	−40.5•	50.2	85 48.6	−32.9•	60.7	24
25	79 19.2	−56.3	19.9	80 15.2	−55.5	21.9	81 10.4	−54.6	24.3	82 04.4	−53.4	27.3	82 56.9	−51.7•	31.0	83 47.0	−49.3•	35.7	84 33.9	−45.9•	41.9	85 15.7	−40.7•	49.9	25
26	78 22.9	−56.8	18.1	79 19.7	−56.3	19.8	80 15.8	−55.6	21.8	81 11.0	−54.6	24.1	82 05.2	−53.5	27.1	82 57.7	−51.8•	30.8	83 48.0	−49.4•	35.5	84 35.0	−46.0•	41.6	26
27	77 26.1	−57.2	16.6	78 23.4	−56.8	18.0	79 20.2	−56.3	19.6	80 16.4	−55.6	21.6	81 11.7	−54.7	24.0	82 05.9	−53.5	26.9	82 58.6	−51.9•	30.5	83 49.0	−49.5•	35.2	27
28	76 28.9	−57.7	15.3	77 26.6	−57.3	16.5	78 23.9	−56.8	17.8	79 20.8	−56.4	19.5	80 17.0	−55.6	21.4	81 12.4	−54.8	23.8	82 06.7	−53.6	26.7	82 59.5	−52.0•	30.3	28
29	75 31.2	−57.9	14.1	76 29.3	−57.6	15.1	77 27.1	−57.4	16.3	78 24.4	−56.9	17.7	79 21.4	−56.4	19.3	80 17.6	−55.7	21.2	81 13.1	−54.8	23.6	82 07.5	−53.6	26.4	29
30	74 33.3	−58.1	13.1	75 31.7	−58.0	14.0	76 29.7	−57.6	15.0	77 27.5	−57.3	16.2	78 25.0	−56.9	17.5	79 21.9	−56.4	19.1	80 18.3	−55.7	21.0	81 13.9	−54.9	23.3	30
31	73 35.2	−58.4	12.2	74 33.7	−58.2	13.0	75 32.1	−58.0	13.8	76 30.2	−57.7	14.8	77 28.1	−57.4	16.0	78 25.5	−56.9	17.3	79 22.6	−56.5	18.9	80 19.0	−55.8	20.8	31
32	72 36.8	−58.5	11.4	73 35.5	−58.3	12.1	74 34.1	−58.2	12.8	75 32.5	−58.0	13.7	76 30.7	−57.7	14.7	77 28.6	−57.4	15.8	78 26.1	−57.0	17.2	79 23.2	−56.5	18.7	32
33	71 38.3	−58.7	10.7	72 37.2	−58.6	11.3	73 35.9	−58.4	12.0	74 34.5	−58.2	12.7	75 33.0	−58.0	13.6	76 31.2	−57.8	14.5	77 29.1	−57.4	15.7	78 26.7	−57.0	17.0	33
34	70 39.6	−58.8	10.1	71 38.6	−58.7	10.6	72 37.5	−58.5	11.2	73 36.3	−58.4	11.8	74 35.0	−58.3	12.6	75 33.4	−58.0	13.4	76 31.7	−57.8	14.4	77 29.7	−57.5	15.5	34
35	69 40.8	−58.9	9.5	70 39.9	−58.8	9.9	71 39.0	−58.7	10.5	72 37.9	−58.6	11.0	73 36.7	−58.4	11.7	74 35.4	−58.2	12.4	75 33.9	−58.0	13.3	76 32.2	−57.8	14.2	35
36	68 41.9	−59.0	8.9	69 41.1	−58.9	9.4	70 40.3	−58.9	9.8	71 39.3	−58.7	10.3	72 38.3	−58.6	10.9	73 37.2	−58.5	11.5	74 35.9	−58.3	12.3	75 34.4	−58.1	13.1	36
37	67 42.9	−59.1	8.4	68 42.2	−59.0	8.8	69 41.4	−58.9	9.2	70 40.6	−58.8	9.7	71 39.7	−58.7	10.2	72 38.7	−58.6	10.8	73 37.6	−58.5	11.4	74 36.3	−58.3	12.1	37
38	66 43.8	−59.2	8.0	67 43.2	−59.1	8.3	68 42.5	−59.0	8.7	69 41.8	−59.0	9.1	70 41.0	−58.9	9.6	71 40.1	−58.7	10.1	72 39.1	−58.6	10.6	73 38.0	−58.4	11.2	38
39	65 44.6	−59.2	7.6	66 44.1	−59.2	7.9	67 43.5	−59.1	8.2	68 42.8	−59.0	8.6	69 42.1	−58.9	9.0	70 41.4	−58.9	9.4	71 40.5	−58.8	9.9	72 39.6	−58.7	10.5	39
40	64 45.4	−59.3	7.2	65 44.9	−59.2	7.5	66 44.4	−59.2	7.8	67 43.8	−59.1	8.1	68 43.2	−59.1	8.5	69 42.5	−59.0	8.9	70 41.7	−58.8	9.3	71 40.9	−58.8	9.8	40
41	63 46.1	−59.3	6.8	64 45.7	−59.3	7.1	65 45.2	−59.2	7.4	66 44.7	−59.2	7.7	67 44.1	−59.1	8.0	68 43.5	−59.0	8.3	69 42.9	−59.0	8.7	70 42.1	−58.9	9.2	41
42	62 46.8	−59.4	6.5	63 46.4	−59.3	6.7	64 46.0	−59.3	7.0	65 45.5	−59.2	7.3	66 45.0	−59.2	7.5	67 44.5	−59.2	7.9	68 43.9	−59.1	8.2	69 43.2	−59.0	8.6	42
43	61 47.4	−59.4	6.2	62 47.1	−59.4	6.4	63 46.7	−59.3	6.6	64 46.3	−59.3	6.9	65 45.8	−59.2	7.1	66 45.3	−59.2	7.4	67 44.8	−59.1	7.7	68 44.2	−59.0	8.1	43
44	60 48.0	−59.4	5.9	61 47.7	−59.4	6.1	62 47.4	−59.4	6.3	63 47.0	−59.4	6.5	64 46.6	−59.3	6.8	65 46.1	−59.2	7.0	66 45.7	−59.2	7.3	67 45.2	−59.2	7.6	44
45	59 48.6	−59.5	5.6	60 48.3	−59.5	5.8	61 48.0	−59.4	6.0	62 47.6	−59.3	6.2	63 47.3	−59.4	6.4	64 46.9	−59.3	6.6	65 46.5	−59.3	6.9	66 46.0	−59.2	7.2	45
46	58 49.1	−59.5	5.4	59 48.8	−59.4	5.5	60 48.6	−59.5	5.7	61 48.3	−59.5	5.9	62 47.9	−59.4	6.1	63 47.6	−59.4	6.3	64 47.2	−59.3	6.5	65 46.8	−59.3	6.8	46
47	57 49.6	−59.5	5.1	58 49.4	−59.5	5.3	59 49.1	−59.5	5.4	60 48.8	−59.4	5.6	61 48.5	−59.4	5.8	62 48.2	−59.4	6.0	63 47.9	−59.4	6.2	64 47.5	−59.3	6.4	47
48	56 50.1	−59.6	4.9	57 49.9	−59.6	5.0	58 49.6	−59.5	5.2	59 49.4	−59.5	5.3	60 49.1	−59.5	5.5	61 48.8	−59.4	5.7	62 48.5	−59.4	5.9	63 48.2	−59.4	6.1	48
49	55 50.5	−59.5	4.7	56 50.3	−59.5	4.8	57 50.1	−59.5	4.9	58 49.9	−59.5	5.1	59 49.6	−59.5	5.2	60 49.4	−59.5	5.4	61 49.1	−59.4	5.6	62 48.8	−59.4	5.7	49
50	54 51.0	−59.6	4.5	55 50.8	−59.6	4.6	56 50.6	−59.6	4.7	57 50.4	−59.6	4.8	58 50.1	−59.5	5.0	59 49.9	−59.5	5.1	60 49.7	−59.5	5.3	61 49.4	−59.5	5.4	50
51	53 51.4	−59.7	4.3	54 51.2	−59.6	4.4	55 51.0	−59.6	4.5	56 50.8	−59.6	4.6	57 50.6	−59.5	4.7	58 50.4	−59.5	4.9	59 50.2	−59.5	5.0	60 49.9	−59.4	5.2	51
52	52 51.7	−59.6	4.1	53 51.6	−59.6	4.2	54 51.4	−59.6	4.3	55 51.2	−59.5	4.4	56 51.1	−59.6	4.5	57 50.9	−59.6	4.6	58 50.7	−59.6	4.8	59 50.5	−59.6	4.9	52
53	51 52.1	−59.6	3.9	52 52.0	−59.7	4.0	53 51.8	−59.6	4.1	54 51.7	−59.7	4.2	55 51.5	−59.6	4.3	56 51.3	−59.6	4.4	57 51.1	−59.5	4.5	58 50.9	−59.5	4.7	53
54	50 52.5	−59.7	3.7	51 52.3	−59.6	3.8	52 52.2	−59.7	3.9	53 52.0	−59.6	4.0	54 51.9	−59.6	4.1	55 51.7	−59.6	4.2	56 51.6	−59.6	4.3	57 51.4	−59.6	4.4	54
55	49 52.8	−59.7	3.6	50 52.7	−59.7	3.6	51 52.5	−59.6	3.7	52 52.4	−59.6	3.8	53 52.3	−59.6	3.9	54 52.1	−59.6	4.0	55 52.0	−59.6	4.1	56 51.8	−59.6	4.2	55
56	48 53.1	−59.7	3.4	49 53.0	−59.7	3.5	50 52.9	−59.7	3.5	51 52.8	−59.7	3.6	52 52.7	−59.7	3.7	53 52.5	−59.6	3.8	54 52.4	−59.6	3.9	55 52.2	−59.6	4.0	56
57	47 53.4	−59.7	3.2	48 53.3	−59.7	3.3	49 53.2	−59.7	3.4	50 53.1	−59.7	3.5	51 53.0	−59.7	3.5	52 52.9	−59.7	3.6	53 52.8	−59.7	3.7	54 52.6	−59.6	3.8	57
58	46 53.7	−59.7	3.1	47 53.6	−59.7	3.2	48 53.5	−59.7	3.2	49 53.4	−59.6	3.3	50 53.3	−59.6	3.4	51 53.2	−59.6	3.4	52 53.1	−59.6	3.5	53 53.0	−59.6	3.6	58
59	45 54.0	−59.7	3.0	46 53.9	−59.7	3.0	47 53.8	−59.7	3.1	48 53.8	−59.7	3.1	49 53.7	−59.7	3.2	50 53.6	−59.7	3.3	51 53.5	−59.7	3.3	52 53.4	−59.7	3.4	59
60	44 54.3	−59.7	2.8	45 54.2	−59.7	2.9	46 54.1	−59.7	2.9	47 54.1	−59.8	3.0	48 54.0	−59.7	3.0	49 53.9	−59.7	3.1	50 53.8	−59.7	3.2	51 53.7	−59.7	3.2	60
61	43 54.6	−59.8	2.7	44 54.5	−59.7	2.7	45 54.4	−59.7	2.8	46 54.3	−59.7	2.8	47 54.3	−59.7	2.9	48 54.2	−59.7	2.9	49 54.1	−59.7	3.0	50 54.0	−59.7	3.1	61
62	42 54.8	−59.7	2.6	43 54.8	−59.8	2.6	44 54.7	−59.8	2.7	45 54.6	−59.7	2.7	46 54.6	−59.8	2.7	47 54.5	−59.7	2.8	48 54.4	−59.7	2.9	49 54.3	−59.7	2.9	62
63	41 55.1	−59.8	2.4	42 55.0	−59.7	2.5	43 54.9	−59.7	2.5	44 54.9	−59.8	2.6	45 54.8	−59.7	2.6	46 54.8	−59.8	2.7	47 54.7	−59.7	2.7	48 54.6	−59.7	2.8	63
64	40 55.3	−59.8	2.3	41 55.3	−59.8	2.4	42 55.2	−59.8	2.4	43 55.1	−59.7	2.4	44 55.1	−59.7	2.5	45 55.0	−59.7	2.5	46 55.0	−59.8	2.6	47 54.9	−59.7	2.6	64
65	39 55.5	−59.7	2.2	40 55.5	−59.8	2.2	41 55.4	−59.7	2.3	42 55.4	−59.8	2.3	43 55.4	−59.8	2.3	44 55.3	−59.7	2.4	45 55.2	−59.7	2.4	46 55.2	−59.7	2.5	65
66	38 55.8	−59.8	2.1	39 55.7	−59.7	2.1	40 55.7	−59.8	2.2	41 55.6	−59.7	2.2	42 55.6	−59.8	2.2	43 55.6	−59.8	2.3	44 55.5	−59.7	2.3	45 55.5	−59.8	2.3	66
67	37 56.0	−59.8	2.0	38 56.0	−59.8	2.0	39 55.9	−59.8	2.0	40 55.9	−59.8	2.1	41 55.8	−59.7	2.1	42 55.8	−59.8	2.1	43 55.8	−59.8	2.2	44 55.7	−59.7	2.2	67
68	36 56.2	−59.8	1.9	37 56.2	−59.8	1.9	38 56.1	−59.7	1.9	39 56.1	−59.8	2.0	40 56.1	−59.8	2.0	41 56.0	−59.7	2.0	42 56.0	−59.8	2.0	43 56.0	−59.8	2.1	68
69	35 56.4	−59.8	1.8	36 56.4	−59.8	1.8	37 56.4	−59.8	1.8	38 56.3	−59.8	1.8	39 56.3	−59.8	1.9	40 56.3	−59.8	1.9	41 56.2	−59.7	1.9	42 56.2	−59.8	2.0	69
70	34 56.6	−59.8	1.7	35 56.6	−59.8	1.7	36 56.6	−59.8	1.7	37 56.5	−59.7	1.7	38 56.5	−59.8	1.8	39 56.5	−59.8	1.8	40 56.5	−59.8	1.8	41 56.4	−59.7	1.8	70
71	33 56.8	−59.8	1.6	34 56.8	−59.8	1.6	35 56.8	−59.8	1.6	36 56.8	−59.8	1.6	37 56.7	−59.8	1.7	38 56.7	−59.8	1.7	39 56.7	−59.8	1.7	40 56.7	−59.8	1.7	71
72	32 57.0	−59.8	1.5	33 57.0	−59.8	1.5	34 57.0	−59.8	1.5	35 57.0	−59.8	1.5	36 56.9	−59.8	1.5	37 56.9	−59.8	1.6	38 56.9	−59.8	1.6	39 56.9	−59.8	1.6	72
73	31 57.2	−59.8	1.4	32 57.2	−59.8	1.4	33 57.2	−59.8	1.4	34 57.2	−59.8	1.4	35 57.1	−59.8	1.4	36 57.1	−59.8	1.5	37 57.1	−59.8	1.5	38 57.1	−59.8	1.5	73
74	30 57.4	−59.8	1.3	31 57.4	−59.8	1.3	32 57.4	−59.8	1.3	33 57.4	−59.9	1.3	34 57.3	−59.8	1.3	35 57.3	−59.8	1.4	36 57.3	−59.8	1.4	37 57.3	−59.8	1.4	74
75	29 57.6	−59.8	1.2	30 57.6	−59.8	1.2	31 57.6	−59.9	1.2	32 57.5	−59.8	1.2	33 57.5	−59.8	1.2	34 57.5	−59.8	1.3	35 57.5	−59.8	1.3	36 57.5	−59.8	1.3	75
76	28 57.8	−59.9	1.1	29 57.8	−59.9	1.1	30 57.7	−59.8	1.1	31 57.7	−59.8	1.1	32 57.7	−59.8	1.2	33 57.7	−59.8	1.2	34 57.7	−59.8	1.2	35 57.7	−59.8	1.2	76
77	27 57.9	−59.8	1.0	28 57.9	−59.8	1.0	29 57.9	−59.8	1.0	30 57.9	−59.8	1.0	31 57.9	−59.8	1.1	32 57.9	−59.8	1.1	33 57.9	−59.8	1.1	34 57.9	−59.8	1.1	77
78	26 58.1	−59.8	0.9	27 58.1	−59.8	0.9	28 58.1	−59.8	0.9	29 58.1	−59.8	0.9	30 58.1	−59.8	1.0	31 58.1	−59.9	1.0	32 58.1	−59.8	1.0	33 58.1	−59.9	1.0	78
79	25 58.3	−59.8	0.8	26 58.3	−59.9	0.9	27 58.3	−59.9	0.9	28 58.3	−59.9	0.9	29 58.3	−59.9	0.9	30 58.2	−59.8	0.9	31 58.2	−59.8	0.9	32 58.2	−59.8	0.9	79
80	24 58.5	−59.9	0.8	25 58.4	−59.8	0.8	26 58.4	−59.8	0.8	27 58.4	−59.8	0.8	28 58.4	−59.8	0.8	29 58.4	−59.8	0.8	30 58.4	−59.8	0.8	31 58.4	−59.8	0.8	80
81	23 58.6	−59.8	0.7	24 58.6	−59.8	0.7	25 58.6	−59.8	0.7	26 58.6	−59.8	0.7	27 58.6	−59.8	0.7	28 58.6	−59.8	0.7	29 58.6	−59.8	0.7	30 58.6	−59.8	0.7	81
82	22 58.8	−59.9	0.6	23 58.8	−59.9	0.6	24 58.8	−59.9	0.6	25 58.8	−59.9	0.6	26 58.8	−59.9	0.6	27 58.8	−59.9	0.6	28 58.8	−59.9	0.6	29 58.8	−59.9	0.6	82
83	21 58.9	−59.8	0.5	22 58.9	−59.8	0.5	23 58.9	−59.8	0.5	24 58.9	−59.8	0.5	25 58.9	−59.8	0.5	26 58.9	−59.8	0.5	27 58.9	−59.8	0.6	28 58.9	−59.8	0.6	83
84	20 59.1	−59.8	0.4	21 59.1	−59.9	0.5	22 59.1	−59.9	0.5	23 59.1	−59.9	0.5	24 59.1	−59.9	0.5	25 59.1	−59.9	0.5	26 59.1	−59.9	0.5	27 59.1	−59.9	0.5	84
85	19 59.3	−59.9	0.4	20 59.2	−59.8	0.4	21 59.2	−59.8	0.4	22 59.2	−59.8	0.4	23 59.2	−59.8	0.4	24 59.2	−59.8	0.4	25 59.2	−59.8	0.4	26 59.2	−59.8	0.4	85
86	18 59.4	−59.8	0.3	19 59.4	−59.8	0.3	20 59.4	−59.8	0.3	21 59.4	−59.8	0.3	22 59.4	−59.8	0.3	23 59.4	−59.8	0.3	24 59.4	−59.8	0.3	25 59.4	−59.8	0.3	86
87	17 59.6	−59.9	0.2	18 59.6	−59.9	0.2	19 59.6	−59.9	0.2	20 59.6	−59.9	0.2	21 59.6	−59.9	0.2	22 59.6	−59.9	0.2	23 59.6	−59.9	0.2	24 59.6	−59.9	0.2	87
88	16 59.7	−59.8	0.1	17 59.7	−59.8	0.1	18 59.7	−59.8	0.1	19 59.7	−59.8	0.1	20 59.7	−59.8	0.1	21 59.7	−59.8	0.2	22 59.7	−59.8	0.2	23 59.7	−59.8	0.2	88
89	15 59.9	−59.9	0.1	16 59.9	−59.9	0.1	17 59.9	−59.9	0.1	18 59.9	−59.9	0.1	19 59.9	−59.9	0.1	20 59.9	−59.9	0.1	21 59.9	−59.9	0.1	22 59.9	−59.9	0.1	89
90	15 00.0	−59.9	0.0	16 00.0	−59.9	0.0	17 00.0	−59.9	0.0	18 00.0	−59.9	0.0	19 00.0	−59.9	0.0	20 00.0	−59.9	0.0	21 00.0	−59.9	0.0	22 00.0	−59.9	0.0	90
	15°			16°			17°			18°			19°			20°			21°			22°			

4°, 356° L.H.A. LATITUDE SAME NAME AS DECLINATION

10

LATITUDE **CONTRARY** NAME TO DECLINATION L.H.A. 4°, 356°

Dec.	15° Hc	15° d	15° Z	16° Hc	16° d	16° Z	17° Hc	17° d	17° Z	18° Hc	18° d	18° Z	Dec.
°	° ′	′	°	° ′	′	°	° ′	′	°	° ′	′	°	°
0	74 29.3	-58.2	164.9	73 31.2	-58.4	165.8	72 33.0	-58.6	166.5	71 34.5	-58.7	167.2	0
1	73 31.1	-58.4	165.8	72 32.8	-58.5	166.6	71 34.4	-58.7	167.3	70 35.8	-58.9	167.9	1
2	72 32.7	-58.5	166.6	71 34.3	-58.7	167.3	70 35.7	-58.9	167.9	69 36.9	-58.9	168.5	2
3	71 34.2	-58.7	167.3	70 35.6	-58.9	167.9	69 36.8	-58.9	168.5	68 38.0	-59.0	169.0	3
4	70 35.5	-58.8	167.9	69 36.7	-58.9	168.5	68 37.9	-59.0	169.0	67 39.0	-59.2	169.5	4
5	69 36.7	-59.0	168.5	68 37.8	-59.0	169.0	67 38.9	-59.1	169.5	66 39.8	-59.2	169.9	5
6	68 37.7	-59.0	169.0	67 38.8	-59.1	169.5	66 39.8	-59.2	169.9	65 40.6	-59.2	170.3	6
7	67 38.7	-59.1	169.5	66 39.7	-59.2	169.9	65 40.6	-59.3	170.3	64 41.4	-59.3	170.7	7
8	66 39.6	-59.1	170.0	65 40.5	-59.2	170.3	64 41.3	-59.2	170.7	63 42.1	-59.3	171.0	8
9	65 40.5	-59.2	170.4	64 41.3	-59.3	170.7	63 42.1	-59.4	171.1	62 42.8	-59.4	171.4	9
10	64 41.3	-59.3	170.8	63 42.0	-59.3	171.1	62 42.7	-59.4	171.4	61 43.4	-59.5	171.7	10
11	63 42.0	-59.3	171.1	62 42.7	-59.4	171.4	61 43.3	-59.4	171.7	60 43.9	-59.4	171.9	11
12	62 42.7	-59.4	171.4	61 43.3	-59.4	171.7	60 43.9	-59.4	172.0	59 44.5	-59.5	172.2	12
13	61 43.3	-59.4	171.8	60 43.9	-59.5	172.0	59 44.5	-59.5	172.2	58 45.0	-59.5	172.5	13
14	60 43.9	-59.5	172.0	59 44.4	-59.4	172.3	58 45.0	-59.5	172.5	57 45.5	-59.6	172.7	14
15	59 44.4	-59.4	172.3	58 45.0	-59.6	172.5	57 45.5	-59.6	172.7	56 45.9	-59.6	172.9	15
16	58 45.0	-59.5	172.6	57 45.4	-59.5	172.8	56 45.9	-59.6	173.0	55 46.3	-59.5	173.2	16
17	57 45.5	-59.6	172.8	56 45.9	-59.6	173.0	55 46.3	-59.5	173.2	54 46.8	-59.7	173.4	17
18	56 45.9	-59.5	173.0	55 46.3	-59.5	173.2	54 46.8	-59.6	173.4	53 47.1	-59.6	173.6	18
19	55 46.4	-59.6	173.3	54 46.8	-59.6	173.4	53 47.2	-59.7	173.6	52 47.5	-59.6	173.7	19
20	54 46.8	-59.6	173.5	53 47.2	-59.7	173.6	52 47.5	-59.6	173.8	51 47.9	-59.7	173.9	20
21	53 47.2	-59.6	173.7	52 47.5	-59.6	173.8	51 47.9	-59.7	174.0	50 48.2	-59.7	174.1	21
22	52 47.6	-59.7	173.9	51 47.9	-59.6	174.0	50 48.2	-59.6	174.1	49 48.5	-59.7	174.2	22
23	51 47.9	-59.6	174.0	50 48.3	-59.7	174.2	49 48.6	-59.7	174.3	48 48.8	-59.7	174.4	23
24	50 48.3	-59.7	174.2	49 48.6	-59.7	174.3	48 48.9	-59.7	174.4	47 49.1	-59.7	174.6	24
25	49 48.6	-59.7	174.4	48 48.9	-59.7	174.5	47 49.2	-59.7	174.6	46 49.4	-59.7	174.7	25
26	48 48.9	-59.7	174.5	47 49.2	-59.7	174.6	46 49.5	-59.8	174.7	45 49.7	-59.7	174.8	26
27	47 49.2	-59.7	174.7	46 49.5	-59.7	174.8	45 49.7	-59.7	174.9	44 50.0	-59.8	175.0	27
28	46 49.5	-59.7	174.8	45 49.8	-59.7	174.9	44 50.0	-59.7	175.0	43 50.2	-59.7	175.1	28
29	45 49.8	-59.7	175.0	44 50.1	-59.8	175.1	43 50.3	-59.8	175.1	42 50.5	-59.8	175.2	29
30	44 50.1	-59.7	175.1	43 50.3	-59.7	175.2	42 50.5	-59.7	175.3	41 50.7	-59.7	175.3	30
31	43 50.4	-59.8	175.2	42 50.6	-59.8	175.3	41 50.8	-59.8	175.4	40 51.0	-59.8	175.5	31
32	42 50.6	-59.7	175.4	41 50.8	-59.7	175.4	40 51.0	-59.8	175.5	39 51.2	-59.8	175.6	32
33	41 50.9	-59.8	175.5	40 51.1	-59.8	175.6	39 51.2	-59.7	175.6	38 51.4	-59.8	175.7	33
34	40 51.1	-59.7	175.6	39 51.3	-59.8	175.7	38 51.5	-59.8	175.7	37 51.6	-59.8	175.8	34
35	39 51.4	-59.8	175.7	38 51.5	-59.8	175.8	37 51.7	-59.8	175.8	36 51.8	-59.8	175.9	35
36	38 51.6	-59.8	175.8	37 51.7	-59.7	175.9	36 51.9	-59.8	176.0	35 52.0	-59.8	176.0	36
37	37 51.8	-59.8	176.0	36 52.0	-59.8	176.0	35 52.1	-59.8	176.1	34 52.2	-59.8	176.1	37
38	36 52.0	-59.8	176.1	35 52.2	-59.8	176.1	34 52.3	-59.8	176.2	33 52.4	-59.8	176.2	38
39	35 52.2	-59.8	176.2	34 52.4	-59.8	176.2	33 52.5	-59.8	176.3	32 52.6	-59.8	176.3	39
40	34 52.4	-59.8	176.3	33 52.6	-59.8	176.3	32 52.7	-59.8	176.4	31 52.8	-59.8	176.4	40
41	33 52.6	-59.8	176.4	32 52.8	-59.8	176.4	31 52.9	-59.8	176.4	30 53.0	-59.8	176.5	41
42	32 52.8	-59.8	176.5	31 53.0	-59.9	176.5	30 53.1	-59.9	176.5	29 53.2	-59.9	176.6	42
43	31 53.0	-59.8	176.6	30 53.1	-59.8	176.6	29 53.2	-59.8	176.6	28 53.3	-59.8	176.7	43
44	30 53.2	-59.8	176.6	29 53.3	-59.8	176.7	28 53.4	-59.8	176.7	27 53.5	-59.8	176.7	44
45	29 53.4	-59.8	176.7	28 53.5	-59.8	176.8	27 53.6	-59.8	176.8	26 53.7	-59.9	176.8	45
46	28 53.6	-59.8	176.8	27 53.7	-59.9	176.9	26 53.8	-59.9	176.9	25 53.8	-59.8	176.9	46
47	27 53.8	-59.9	176.9	26 53.8	-59.8	176.9	25 53.9	-59.8	177.0	24 54.0	-59.8	177.0	47
48	26 53.9	-59.8	177.0	25 54.0	-59.8	177.0	24 54.1	-59.8	177.1	23 54.2	-59.9	177.1	48
49	25 54.1	-59.8	177.1	24 54.2	-59.9	177.1	23 54.3	-59.9	177.1	22 54.3	-59.8	177.2	49
50	24 54.3	-59.9	177.2	23 54.3	-59.8	177.2	22 54.4	-59.8	177.2	21 54.5	-59.9	177.2	50
51	23 54.4	-59.8	177.2	22 54.5	-59.8	177.3	21 54.6	-59.9	177.3	20 54.6	-59.8	177.3	51
52	22 54.6	-59.8	177.3	21 54.7	-59.9	177.3	20 54.7	-59.8	177.4	19 54.8	-59.9	177.4	52
53	21 54.8	-59.9	177.4	20 54.8	-59.8	177.4	19 54.9	-59.9	177.4	18 54.9	-59.8	177.5	53
54	20 54.9	-59.8	177.5	19 55.0	-59.9	177.5	18 55.0	-59.8	177.5	17 55.1	-59.9	177.5	54
55	19 55.1	-59.9	177.6	18 55.1	-59.8	177.6	17 55.2	-59.9	177.6	16 55.2	-59.8	177.6	55
56	18 55.2	-59.8	177.6	17 55.3	-59.9	177.7	16 55.3	-59.8	177.7	15 55.4	-59.9	177.7	56
57	17 55.4	-59.9	177.7	16 55.4	-59.8	177.7	15 55.5	-59.9	177.7	14 55.5	-59.8	177.7	57
58	16 55.5	-59.8	177.8	15 55.6	-59.9	177.8	14 55.6	-59.9	177.8	13 55.7	-59.9	177.8	58
59	15 55.7	-59.9	177.9	14 55.7	-59.8	177.9	13 55.7	-59.8	177.9	12 55.8	-59.9	177.9	59
60	14 55.8	-59.8	177.9	13 55.9	-59.9	177.9	12 55.9	-59.9	177.9	11 55.9	-59.8	178.0	60
61	13 56.0	-59.9	178.0	12 56.0	-59.8	178.0	11 56.0	-59.8	178.0	10 56.1	-59.9	178.0	61
62	12 56.1	-59.9	178.1	11 56.1	-59.8	178.1	10 56.2	-59.9	178.1	9 56.2	-59.9	178.1	62
63	11 56.2	-59.8	178.1	10 56.3	-59.9	178.2	9 56.3	-59.9	178.2	8 56.3	-59.8	178.2	63
64	10 56.4	-59.9	178.2	9 56.4	-59.8	178.2	8 56.4	-59.8	178.2	7 56.5	-59.9	178.2	64
65	9 56.5	-59.8	178.3	8 56.6	-59.9	178.3	7 56.6	-59.9	178.3	6 56.6	-59.9	178.3	65
66	8 56.7	-59.9	178.4	7 56.7	-59.9	178.4	6 56.7	-59.8	178.4	5 56.7	-59.8	178.4	66
67	7 56.8	-59.9	178.4	6 56.8	-59.8	178.4	5 56.9	-59.9	178.4	4 56.9	-59.9	178.4	67
68	6 56.9	-59.8	178.5	5 57.0	-59.9	178.5	4 57.0	-59.9	178.5	3 57.0	-59.9	178.5	68
69	5 57.1	-59.9	178.6	4 57.1	-59.9	178.6	3 57.1	-59.8	178.6	2 57.1	-59.8	178.6	69
70	4 57.2	-59.8	178.6	3 57.2	-59.8	178.6	2 57.3	-59.9	178.6	1 57.3	-59.9	178.6	70
71	3 57.4	-59.8	178.7	2 57.4	-59.8	178.7	1 57.4	-59.9	178.7	0 57.4	-59.9	178.7	71
72	2 57.5	-59.9	178.8	1 57.5	-59.8	178.8	0 57.5	-59.8	178.8	0 02.5	+59.8	1.2	72
73	1 57.6	-59.8	178.8	0 57.6	-59.8	178.8	0 02.3	+59.9	1.2	1 02.3	+59.9	1.2	73
74	0 57.8	-59.9	178.9	0 02.2	+59.9	1.1	1 02.2	+59.9	1.1	2 02.2	+59.9	1.1	74
75	0 02.1	+59.9	1.0	1 02.1	+59.8	1.0	2 02.1	+59.8	1.0	3 02.1	+59.8	1.0	75
76	1 02.0	+59.8	1.0	2 01.9	+59.9	1.0	3 01.9	+59.9	1.0	4 01.9	+59.9	1.0	76
77	2 01.8	+59.9	0.9	3 01.8	+59.9	0.9	4 01.8	+59.9	0.9	5 01.8	+59.9	0.9	77
78	3 01.7	+59.8	0.8	4 01.7	+59.8	0.8	5 01.7	+59.8	0.8	6 01.7	+59.8	0.8	78
79	4 01.5	+59.9	0.8	5 01.5	+59.9	0.8	6 01.5	+59.9	0.8	7 01.5	+59.9	0.8	79
80	5 01.4	+59.9	0.7	6 01.4	+59.9	0.7	7 01.4	+59.9	0.7	8 01.4	+59.9	0.7	80
81	6 01.3	+59.8	0.6	7 01.3	+59.8	0.6	8 01.3	+59.8	0.6	9 01.3	+59.8	0.6	81
82	7 01.1	+59.9	0.6	8 01.1	+59.9	0.6	9 01.1	+59.9	0.6	10 01.1	+59.9	0.6	82
83	8 01.0	+59.9	0.5	9 01.0	+59.9	0.5	10 01.0	+59.9	0.5	11 01.0	+59.9	0.5	83
84	9 00.9	+59.8	0.4	10 00.9	+59.8	0.4	11 00.9	+59.8	0.4	12 00.9	+59.8	0.4	84
85	10 00.7	+59.9	0.4	11 00.7	+59.9	0.4	12 00.7	+59.9	0.4	13 00.7	+59.9	0.4	85
86	11 00.6	+59.8	0.3	12 00.6	+59.8	0.3	13 00.6	+59.8	0.3	14 00.6	+59.8	0.3	86
87	12 00.4	+59.9	0.2	13 00.4	+59.9	0.2	14 00.4	+59.9	0.2	15 00.4	+59.9	0.2	87
88	13 00.3	+59.8	0.1	14 00.3	+59.8	0.1	15 00.3	+59.8	0.1	16 00.3	+59.8	0.1	88
89	14 00.1	+59.9	0.1	15 00.1	+59.9	0.1	16 00.1	+59.9	0.1	17 00.1	+59.9	0.1	89
90	15 00.0	+59.9	0.0	16 00.0	+59.9	0.0	17 00.0	+59.9	0.0	18 00.0	+59.9	0.0	90
	15°			16°			17°			18°			

Dec.	19° Hc	19° d	19° Z	20° Hc	20° d	20° Z	21° Hc	21° d	21° Z	22° Hc	22° d	22° Z	Dec.
°	° ′	′	°	° ′	′	°	° ′	′	°	° ′	′	°	°
0	70 35.9	-58.8	167.9	69 37.2	-59.0	168.4	68 38.4	-59.1	169.0	67 39.4	-59.1	169.4	0
1	69 37.1	-59.0	168.4	68 38.2	-59.0	169.0	67 39.3	-59.2	169.4	66 40.3	-59.3	169.9	1
2	68 38.1	-59.0	169.0	67 39.2	-59.2	169.4	66 40.1	-59.2	169.9	65 41.0	-59.2	170.3	2
3	67 39.1	-59.2	169.4	66 40.0	-59.2	169.9	65 40.9	-59.2	170.3	64 41.8	-59.4	170.6	3
4	66 39.9	-59.2	169.9	65 40.8	-59.2	170.3	64 41.7	-59.4	170.6	63 42.4	-59.4	171.0	4
5	65 40.7	-59.2	170.3	64 41.6	-59.4	170.6	63 42.3	-59.3	171.0	62 43.0	-59.4	171.3	5
6	64 41.5	-59.3	170.7	63 42.2	-59.3	171.0	62 43.0	-59.5	171.3	61 43.6	-59.4	171.6	6
7	63 42.2	-59.4	171.0	62 42.9	-59.4	171.3	61 43.5	-59.4	171.6	60 44.2	-59.5	171.9	7
8	62 42.8	-59.4	171.3	61 43.5	-59.5	171.6	60 44.1	-59.5	171.9	59 44.7	-59.5	172.1	8
9	61 43.4	-59.4	171.6	60 44.0	-59.4	171.9	59 44.6	-59.5	172.1	58 45.2	-59.6	172.4	9
10	60 44.0	-59.5	171.9	59 44.6	-59.5	172.2	58 45.1	-59.5	172.4	57 45.6	-59.6	172.6	10
11	59 44.5	-59.5	172.2	58 45.1	-59.6	172.4	57 45.6	-59.6	172.6	56 46.0	-59.5	172.8	11
12	58 45.0	-59.5	172.4	57 45.5	-59.5	172.7	56 46.0	-59.6	172.8	55 46.5	-59.7	173.0	12
13	57 45.5	-59.6	172.7	56 46.0	-59.6	172.9	55 46.4	-59.6	173.1	54 46.8	-59.6	173.2	13
14	56 45.9	-59.5	172.9	55 46.4	-59.6	173.1	54 46.8	-59.6	173.3	53 47.2	-59.6	173.4	14
15	55 46.4	-59.6	173.1	54 46.8	-59.6	173.3	53 47.2	-59.7	173.5	52 47.6	-59.7	173.6	15
16	54 46.8	-59.6	173.3	53 47.2	-59.7	173.5	52 47.5	-59.6	173.6	51 47.9	-59.7	173.8	16
17	53 47.2	-59.7	173.5	52 47.5	-59.6	173.7	51 47.9	-59.7	173.8	50 48.2	-59.7	173.9	17
18	52 47.5	-59.6	173.7	51 47.9	-59.7	173.8	50 48.2	-59.7	174.0	49 48.5	-59.7	174.1	18
19	51 47.9	-59.7	173.9	50 48.2	-59.7	174.0	49 48.5	-59.7	174.1	48 48.8	-59.7	174.3	19
20	50 48.2	-59.7	174.0	49 48.5	-59.7	174.2	48 48.8	-59.7	174.3	47 49.1	-59.7	174.4	20
21	49 48.5	-59.7	174.2	48 48.8	-59.7	174.3	47 49.1	-59.7	174.4	46 49.4	-59.7	174.5	21
22	48 48.8	-59.7	174.4	47 49.1	-59.7	174.5	46 49.4	-59.7	174.6	45 49.7	-59.8	174.7	22
23	47 49.1	-59.7	174.5	46 49.4	-59.7	174.6	45 49.7	-59.8	174.7	44 49.9	-59.7	174.8	23
24	46 49.4	-59.7	174.7	45 49.7	-59.8	174.8	44 49.9	-59.7	174.8	43 50.2	-59.8	174.9	24
25	45 49.7	-59.7	174.8	44 49.9	-59.7	174.9	43 50.2	-59.8	175.0	42 50.4	-59.8	175.1	25
26	44 50.0	-59.8	174.9	43 50.2	-59.8	175.0	42 50.4	-59.8	175.1	41 50.6	-59.8	175.2	26
27	43 50.2	-59.7	175.1	42 50.4	-59.7	175.1	41 50.6	-59.7	175.2	40 50.8	-59.7	175.3	27
28	42 50.5	-59.8	175.2	41 50.7	-59.8	175.3	40 50.9	-59.8	175.3	39 51.1	-59.8	175.4	28
29	41 50.7	-59.8	175.3	40 50.9	-59.8	175.4	39 51.1	-59.8	175.4	38 51.3	-59.8	175.5	29
30	40 50.9	-59.8	175.4	39 51.1	-59.8	175.5	38 51.3	-59.8	175.6	37 51.5	-59.8	175.6	30
31	39 51.1	-59.7	175.5	38 51.3	-59.8	175.6	37 51.5	-59.8	175.7	36 51.7	-59.8	175.7	31
32	38 51.4	-59.8	175.6	37 51.5	-59.8	175.7	36 51.7	-59.8	175.8	35 51.9	-59.8	175.8	32
33	37 51.6	-59.8	175.8	36 51.7	-59.8	175.8	35 51.9	-59.8	175.9	34 52.1	-59.9	175.9	33
34	36 51.8	-59.8	175.9	35 51.9	-59.8	175.9	34 52.1	-59.8	176.0	33 52.2	-59.8	176.0	34
35	35 52.0	-59.8	176.0	34 52.1	-59.8	176.0	33 52.3	-59.8	176.1	32 52.4	-59.8	176.1	35
36	34 52.2	-59.8	176.1	33 52.3	-59.8	176.1	32 52.5	-59.9	176.1	31 52.6	-59.8	176.2	36
37	33 52.4	-59.8	176.2	32 52.5	-59.8	176.2	31 52.6	-59.8	176.2	30 52.8	-59.9	176.3	37
38	32 52.6	-59.9	176.2	31 52.7	-59.8	176.3	30 52.8	-59.8	176.3	29 52.9	-59.8	176.4	38
39	31 52.7	-59.8	176.3	30 52.9	-59.9	176.4	29 53.0	-59.8	176.4	28 53.1	-59.8	176.5	39
40	30 52.9	-59.8	176.4	29 53.0	-59.8	176.5	28 53.2	-59.9	176.5	27 53.3	-59.9	176.5	40
41	29 53.1	-59.8	176.5	28 53.2	-59.8	176.6	27 53.3	-59.8	176.6	26 53.4	-59.8	176.6	41
42	28 53.3	-59.9	176.6	27 53.4	-59.9	176.6	26 53.5	-59.9	176.7	25 53.6	-59.9	176.7	42
43	27 53.4	-59.8	176.7	26 53.5	-59.8	176.7	25 53.6	-59.8	176.7	24 53.7	-59.8	176.8	43
44	26 53.6	-59.8	176.8	25 53.7	-59.8	176.8	24 53.8	-59.8	176.8	23 53.9	-59.9	176.9	44
45	25 53.8	-59.9	176.9	24 53.9	-59.9	176.9	23 54.0	-59.9	176.9	22 54.0	-59.8	176.9	45
46	24 53.9	-59.8	176.9	23 54.0	-59.8	177.0	22 54.1	-59.8	177.0	21 54.2	-59.9	177.0	46
47	23 54.1	-59.9	177.0	22 54.2	-59.8	177.0	21 54.3	-59.9	177.1	20 54.3	-59.8	177.1	47
48	22 54.2	-59.8	177.1	21 54.3	-59.8	177.1	20 54.4	-59.9	177.1	19 54.5	-59.9	177.2	48
49	21 54.4	-59.9	177.2	20 54.5	-59.9	177.2	19 54.5	-59.8	177.2	18 54.6	-59.8	177.2	49
50	20 54.5	-59.9	177.2	19 54.6	-59.8	177.3	18 54.7	-59.9	177.3	17 54.8	-59.9	177.3	50
51	19 54.7	-59.9	177.3	18 54.8	-59.9	177.3	17 54.8	-59.8	177.4	16 54.9	-59.9	177.4	51
52	18 54.8	-59.8	177.4	17 54.9	-59.9	177.4	16 55.0	-59.9	177.4	15 55.0	-59.8	177.4	52
53	17 55.0	-59.9	177.5	16 55.0	-59.8	177.5	15 55.1	-59.9	177.5	14 55.2	-59.9	177.5	53
54	16 55.1	-59.8	177.5	15 55.2	-59.9	177.6	14 55.2	-59.8	177.6	13 55.3	-59.9	177.6	54
55	15 55.3	-59.9	177.6	14 55.3	-59.8	177.6	13 55.4	-59.9	177.6	12 55.4	-59.8	177.6	55
56	14 55.4	-59.8	177.7	13 55.5	-59.9	177.7	12 55.5	-59.9	177.7	11 55.6	-59.9	177.7	56
57	13 55.6	-59.9	177.8	12 55.6	-59.9	177.8	11 55.6	-59.8	177.8	10 55.7	-59.9	177.8	57
58	12 55.7	-59.9	177.8	11 55.7	-59.8	177.8	10 55.8	-59.9	177.8	9 55.8	-59.8	177.8	58
59	11 55.8	-59.8	177.9	10 55.9	-59.9	177.9	9 55.9	-59.9	177.9	8 56.0	-59.9	177.9	59
60	10 56.0	-59.9	178.0	9 56.0	-59.9	178.0	8 56.0	-59.8	178.0	7 56.1	-59.9	178.0	60
61	9 56.1	-59.9	178.0	8 56.1	-59.8	178.0	7 56.2	-59.9	178.0	6 56.2	-59.9	178.0	61
62	8 56.2	-59.8	178.1	7 56.3	-59.9	178.1	6 56.3	-59.9	178.1	5 56.3	-59.8	178.1	62
63	7 56.4	-59.9	178.2	6 56.4	-59.9	178.2	5 56.4	-59.8	178.2	4 56.5	-59.9	178.2	63
64	6 56.5	-59.9	178.2	5 56.5	-59.8	178.2	4 56.6	-59.9	178.2	3 56.6	-59.9	178.2	64
65	5 56.6	-59.8	178.3	4 56.7	-59.9	178.3	3 56.7	-59.9	178.3	2 56.7	-59.9	178.3	65
66	4 56.8	-59.9	178.4	3 56.8	-59.9	178.4	2 56.8	-59.9	178.4	1 56.8	-59.9	178.4	66
67	3 56.9	-59.9	178.4	2 56.9	-59.8	178.4	1 56.9	-59.8	178.4	0 57.0	-59.9	178.4	67
68	2 57.0	-59.8	178.5	1 57.1	-59.9	178.5	0 57.1	-59.9	178.5	0 02.9	+59.9	1.5	68
69	1 57.2	-59.9	178.6	0 57.2	-59.9	178.6	0 02.8	+59.9	1.4	1 02.8	+59.9	1.4	69
70	0 57.3	-59.9	178.6	0 02.7	+59.9	1.4	1 02.7	+59.8	1.4	2 02.7	+59.8	1.4	70
71	0 02.6	+59.8	1.3	1 02.6	+59.8	1.3	2 02.5	+59.9	1.3	3 02.5	+59.9	1.3	71
72	1 02.4	+59.9	1.2	2 02.4	+59.9	1.2	3 02.4	+59.9	1.2	4 02.4	+59.9	1.2	72
73	2 02.3	+59.9	1.2	3 02.3	+59.9	1.2	4 02.3	+59.9	1.2	5 02.3	+59.9	1.2	73
74	3 02.2	+59.9	1.1	4 02.2	+59.8	1.1	5 02.2	+59.8	1.1	6 02.2	+59.8	1.1	74
75	4 02.1	+59.8	1.0	5 02.0	+59.9	1.0	6 02.0	+59.9	1.0	7 02.0	+59.9	1.0	75
76	5 01.9	+59.9	1.0	6 01.9	+59.9	1.0	7 01.9	+59.9	1.0	8 01.9	+59.9	1.0	76
77	6 01.8	+59.9	0.9	7 01.8	+59.9	0.9	8 01.8	+59.8	0.9	9 01.8	+59.8	0.9	77
78	7 01.7	+59.8	0.8	8 01.7	+59.8	0.8	9 01.6	+59.9	0.8	10 01.6	+59.9	0.8	78
79	8 01.5	+59.9	0.8	9 01.5	+59.9	0.8	10 01.5	+59.9	0.8	11 01.5	+59.9	0.8	79
80	9 01.4	+59.9	0.7	10 01.4	+59.9	0.7	11 01.4	+59.9	0.7	12 01.4	+59.8	0.7	80
81	10 01.3	+59.8	0.6	11 01.3	+59.8	0.6	12 01.3	+59.8	0.6	13 01.2	+59.9	0.6	81
82	11 01.1	+59.8	0.6	12 01.1	+59.9	0.6	13 01.1	+59.9	0.6	14 01.1	+59.9	0.6	82
83	12 01.0	+59.8	0.5	13 01.0	+59.9	0.5	14 01.0	+59.8	0.5	15 01.0	+59.8	0.5	83
84	13 00.8	+59.9	0.4	14 00.8	+59.9	0.4	15 00.8	+59.9	0.4	16 00.8	+59.9	0.4	84
85	14 00.7	+59.8	0.4	15 00.7	+59.9	0.4	16 00.7	+59.9	0.4	17 00.7	+59.9	0.4	85
86	15 00.6	+59.8	0.3	16 00.6	+59.8	0.3	17 00.6	+59.8	0.3	18 00.6	+59.8	0.3	86
87	16 00.4	+59.9	0.2	17 00.4	+59.9	0.2	18 00.4	+59.9	0.2	19 00.4	+59.9	0.2	87
88	17 00.3	+59.8	0.1	18 00.3	+59.8	0.1	19 00.3	+59.8	0.1	20 00.3	+59.8	0.1	88
89	18 00.1	+59.9	0.1	19 00.1	+59.9	0.1	20 00.1	+59.9	0.1	21 00.1	+59.9	0.1	89
90	19 00.0	+59.9	0.0	20 00.0	+59.9	0.0	21 00.0	+59.9	0.0	22 00.0	+59.9	0.0	90
	19°			20°			21°			22°			

S. Lat. {L.H.A. greater than 180° ....Zn=180°–Z
{L.H.A. less than 180°...........Zn=180°+Z

LATITUDE **SAME** NAME AS DECLINATION L.H.A. 176°, 184°

5°, 355° L.H.A.

LATITUDE SAME NAME AS DECLINATION

N. Lat. {L.H.A. greater than 180° .....Zn=Z; L.H.A. less than 180°............Zn=360°−Z}

Dec.	15° Hc	15° d	15° Z	16° Hc	16° d	16° Z	17° Hc	17° d	17° Z	18° Hc	18° d	18° Z
°	° ′	′	°	° ′	′	°	° ′	′	°	° ′	′	°
0	74 12.4	+56.9	161.3	73 15.4	+57.2	162.4	72 18.0	+57.6	163.3	71 20.4	+57.9	164.2
1	75 09.3	+56.4	160.1	74 12.6	+56.9	161.3	73 15.6	+57.3	162.4	72 18.3	+57.6	163.3
2	76 05.7	+55.9	158.7	75 09.5	+56.5	160.1	74 12.9	+56.9	161.3	73 15.9	+57.3	162.4
3	77 01.6	+55.3	157.2	76 06.0	+56.0	158.8	75 09.8	+56.5	160.1	74 13.2	+56.9	161.3
4	77 56.9	+54.5	155.4	77 02.0	+55.3	157.2	76 06.3	+56.0	158.8	75 10.1	+56.6	160.1
5	78 51.4	+53.4	153.3	77 57.3	+54.5	155.4	77 02.3	+55.4	157.2	76 06.7	+56.0	158.8
6	79 44.8	+52.2	150.9	78 51.8	+53.5	153.3	77 57.7	+54.6	155.4	77 02.7	+55.4	157.3
7	80 37.0	+50.5•	148.0	79 45.3	+52.3	150.9	78 52.3	+53.6	153.4	77 58.1	+54.7	155.5
8	81 27.5	+48.2•	144.5	80 37.6	+50.5•	148.0	79 45.9	+52.2	150.9	78 52.8	+53.6	153.4
9	82 15.7	+45.1•	140.3	81 28.1	+48.3•	144.5	80 38.1	+50.7	148.1	79 46.4	+52.4	151.0
10	83 00.8	+41.0•	135.1	82 16.4	+45.2•	140.3	81 28.8	+48.3•	144.6	80 38.8	+50.7	148.1
11	83 41.8	+35.5•	128.8	83 01.6	+41.2•	135.2	82 17.1	+45.4•	140.4	81 29.5	+48.5•	144.7
12	84 17.3	+27.9•	121.1	83 42.8	+35.5•	128.9	83 02.5	+41.3•	135.3	82 18.0	+45.5•	140.5
13	84 45.2	+18.2•	111.8	84 18.3	+28.1•	121.1	83 43.8	+35.7•	129.0	83 03.5	+41.4•	135.4
14	85 03.4	+6.8•	101.0	84 46.4	+18.4•	111.8	84 19.5	+28.2•	121.2	83 44.9	+35.8•	129.1
15	85 10.2	−5.4•	89.4	85 04.8	+6.8•	101.0	84 47.7	+18.5•	111.9	84 20.7	+28.3•	121.3
16	85 04.8	−17.1•	77.6	85 11.6	−5.4•	89.3	85 06.2	+6.9•	101.1	84 49.0	+18.7•	112.0
17	84 47.7	−27.0•	66.7	85 06.2	−17.2•	77.5	85 13.1	−5.4•	89.3	85 07.7	+7.0•	101.1
18	84 20.7	−34.7•	57.3	84 49.0	−27.0•	66.6	85 07.7	−17.2•	77.4	85 14.7	−5.4•	89.2
19	83 46.0	−40.5•	49.4	84 22.0	−34.8•	57.1	84 50.5	−27.1•	66.4	85 09.3	−17.3•	77.3
20	83 05.5	−44.7•	42.9	83 47.2	−40.6•	49.2	84 23.4	−34.9•	56.9	84 52.0	−27.2•	66.3
21	82 20.8	−47.9•	37.7	83 06.6	−44.8•	42.7	83 48.5	−40.7•	49.0	84 24.8	−35.0•	56.7
22	81 32.9	−50.3•	33.4	82 21.8	−48.0•	37.5	83 07.8	−44.9•	42.5	83 49.8	−40.8•	48.8
23	80 42.6	−52.0	29.8	81 33.8	−50.3•	33.1	82 22.9	−48.1•	37.2	83 09.0	−45.0•	42.3
24	79 50.6	−53.3	26.8	80 43.5	−52.0	29.6	81 34.8	−50.4•	32.9	82 24.0	−48.1•	37.0
25	78 57.3	−54.4	24.3	79 51.5	−53.4	26.7	80 44.4	−52.1	29.4	81 35.9	−50.5•	32.7
26	78 02.9	−55.2	22.2	78 58.1	−54.4	24.2	79 52.3	−53.4	26.5	80 45.4	−52.2	29.2
27	77 07.7	−55.8	20.4	78 03.7	−55.3	22.0	78 58.9	−54.5	24.0	79 53.2	−53.5	26.2
28	76 11.9	−56.4	18.8	77 08.4	−55.9	20.2	78 04.4	−55.3	21.9	78 59.7	−54.5	23.8
29	75 15.5	−56.9	17.4	76 12.5	−56.4	18.6	77 09.1	−55.9	20.0	78 05.2	−55.3	21.7
30	74 18.6	−57.1	16.2	75 16.1	−56.8	17.3	76 13.2	−56.4	18.5	77 09.9	−56.0	19.9
31	73 21.5	−57.5	15.1	74 19.3	−57.3	16.0	75 16.8	−56.9	17.1	76 13.9	−56.5	18.3
32	72 24.0	−57.8	14.1	73 22.0	−57.5	15.0	74 19.9	−57.3	15.9	75 17.4	−56.9	16.9
33	71 26.2	−58.0	13.3	72 24.5	−57.7	14.0	73 22.6	−57.5	14.8	74 20.5	−57.2	15.7
34	70 28.2	−58.1	12.5	71 26.8	−58.0	13.1	72 25.1	−57.8	13.8	73 23.3	−57.6	14.6
35	69 30.1	−58.3	11.8	70 28.8	−58.2	12.3	71 27.3	−58.0	13.0	72 25.7	−57.8	13.7
36	68 31.8	−58.5	11.1	69 30.6	−58.3	11.6	70 29.3	−58.2	12.2	71 27.9	−58.0	12.8
37	67 33.3	−58.6	10.5	68 32.3	−58.5	11.0	69 31.1	−58.3	11.5	70 29.9	−58.2	12.0
38	66 34.7	−58.7	9.9	67 33.8	−58.6	10.4	68 32.8	−58.5	10.8	69 31.7	−58.4	11.3
39	65 36.0	−58.7	9.4	66 35.2	−58.7	9.8	67 34.3	−58.6	10.2	68 33.3	−58.5	10.7
40	64 37.3	−58.9	9.0	65 36.5	−58.8	9.3	66 35.7	−58.7	9.7	67 34.8	−58.6	10.1
41	63 38.4	−59.0	8.5	64 37.7	−58.9	8.8	65 37.0	−58.8	9.2	66 36.2	−58.8	9.5
42	62 39.4	−59.0	8.1	63 38.8	−58.9	8.4	64 38.2	−58.9	8.7	65 37.4	−58.8	9.0
43	61 40.4	−59.1	7.7	62 39.9	−59.1	8.0	63 39.3	−59.0	8.3	64 38.6	−58.9	8.6
44	60 41.3	−59.1	7.4	61 40.8	−59.1	7.6	62 40.3	−59.0	7.8	63 39.7	−59.0	8.1
45	59 42.2	−59.2	7.0	60 41.7	−59.1	7.2	61 41.3	−59.1	7.5	62 40.7	−59.0	7.7
46	58 43.0	−59.2	6.7	59 42.6	−59.2	6.9	60 42.2	−59.2	7.1	61 41.7	−59.1	7.3
47	57 43.8	−59.3	6.4	58 43.4	−59.2	6.6	59 43.0	−59.2	6.8	60 42.6	−59.2	7.0
48	56 44.5	−59.3	6.1	57 44.2	−59.3	6.3	58 43.8	−59.2	6.5	59 43.4	−59.2	6.6
49	55 45.2	−59.3	5.8	56 44.9	−59.3	6.0	57 44.6	−59.3	6.2	58 44.2	−59.2	6.3
50	54 45.9	−59.4	5.6	55 45.6	−59.4	5.7	56 45.3	−59.3	5.9	57 45.0	−59.3	6.0
51	53 46.5	−59.4	5.3	54 46.2	−59.3	5.5	55 46.0	−59.4	5.6	56 45.7	−59.4	5.7
52	52 47.1	−59.4	5.1	53 46.9	−59.4	5.2	54 46.6	−59.4	5.3	55 46.3	−59.3	5.5
53	51 47.7	−59.5	4.9	52 47.5	−59.5	5.0	53 47.2	−59.4	5.1	54 47.0	−59.4	5.2
54	50 48.2	−59.5	4.6	51 48.0	−59.4	4.8	52 47.8	−59.4	4.9	53 47.6	−59.4	5.0
55	49 48.7	−59.5	4.4	50 48.6	−59.5	4.5	51 48.4	−59.5	4.6	52 48.2	−59.5	4.7
56	48 49.2	−59.5	4.2	49 49.1	−59.5	4.3	50 48.9	−59.5	4.4	51 48.7	−59.4	4.5
57	47 49.7	−59.5	4.1	48 49.6	−59.5	4.1	49 49.4	−59.5	4.2	50 49.3	−59.5	4.3
58	46 50.2	−59.6	3.9	47 50.1	−59.6	3.9	48 49.9	−59.5	4.0	49 49.8	−59.6	4.1
59	45 50.6	−59.5	3.7	46 50.5	−59.5	3.8	47 50.4	−59.6	3.8	48 50.2	−59.5	3.9
60	44 51.1	−59.6	3.5	45 51.0	−59.6	3.6	46 50.8	−59.5	3.7	47 50.7	−59.5	3.7
61	43 51.5	−59.6	3.4	44 51.4	−59.6	3.4	45 51.3	−59.6	3.5	46 51.2	−59.6	3.5
62	42 51.9	−59.6	3.2	43 51.8	−59.6	3.3	44 51.7	−59.6	3.3	45 51.6	−59.6	3.4
63	41 52.3	−59.6	3.0	42 52.2	−59.6	3.1	43 52.1	−59.6	3.1	44 52.0	−59.6	3.2
64	40 52.7	−59.7	2.9	41 52.6	−59.6	2.9	42 52.5	−59.6	3.0	43 52.4	−59.6	3.0
65	39 53.0	−59.6	2.8	40 53.0	−59.7	2.8	41 52.9	−59.6	2.8	42 52.8	−59.6	2.9
66	38 53.4	−59.7	2.6	39 53.3	−59.6	2.6	40 53.3	−59.7	2.7	41 53.2	−59.6	2.7
67	37 53.7	−59.6	2.5	38 53.7	−59.7	2.5	39 53.6	−59.6	2.5	40 53.6	−59.7	2.6
68	36 54.1	−59.7	2.3	37 54.0	−59.6	2.4	38 54.0	−59.7	2.4	39 53.9	−59.6	2.4
69	35 54.4	−59.7	2.2	36 54.4	−59.7	2.2	37 54.3	−59.7	2.3	38 54.3	−59.7	2.3
70	34 54.7	−59.7	2.1	35 54.7	−59.7	2.1	36 54.6	−59.6	2.1	37 54.6	−59.7	2.2
71	33 55.0	−59.7	2.0	34 55.0	−59.7	2.0	35 55.0	−59.7	2.0	36 54.9	−59.6	2.0
72	32 55.3	−59.7	1.8	33 55.3	−59.7	1.9	34 55.3	−59.7	1.9	35 55.3	−59.7	1.9
73	31 55.6	−59.7	1.7	32 55.6	−59.7	1.7	33 55.6	−59.7	1.8	34 55.6	−59.7	1.8
74	30 55.9	−59.7	1.6	31 55.9	−59.7	1.6	32 55.9	−59.7	1.6	33 55.9	−59.7	1.7
75	29 56.2	−59.7	1.5	30 56.2	−59.7	1.5	31 56.2	−59.7	1.5	32 56.2	−59.7	1.5
76	28 56.5	−59.7	1.4	29 56.5	−59.7	1.4	30 56.5	−59.7	1.4	31 56.5	−59.8	1.4
77	27 56.8	−59.7	1.3	28 56.8	−59.8	1.3	29 56.8	−59.8	1.3	30 56.7	−59.7	1.3
78	26 57.1	−59.8	1.2	27 57.0	−59.7	1.2	28 57.0	−59.7	1.2	29 57.0	−59.7	1.2
79	25 57.3	−59.7	1.1	26 57.3	−59.7	1.1	27 57.3	−59.7	1.1	28 57.3	−59.7	1.1
80	24 57.6	−59.8	1.0	25 57.6	−59.8	1.0	26 57.6	−59.8	1.0	27 57.6	−59.8	1.0
81	23 57.8	−59.7	0.9	24 57.8	−59.7	0.9	25 57.8	−59.8	0.9	26 57.8	−59.7	0.9
82	22 58.1	−59.8	0.8	23 58.1	−59.8	0.8	24 58.1	−59.8	0.8	25 58.1	−59.8	0.8
83	21 58.3	−59.7	0.7	22 58.3	−59.7	0.7	23 58.3	−59.7	0.7	24 58.3	−59.7	0.7
84	20 58.6	−59.8	0.6	21 58.6	−59.8	0.6	22 58.6	−59.8	0.6	23 58.6	−59.8	0.6
85	19 58.8	−59.7	0.5	20 58.8	−59.7	0.5	21 58.8	−59.7	0.5	22 58.8	−59.7	0.5
86	18 59.1	−59.8	0.4	19 59.1	−59.8	0.4	20 59.1	−59.8	0.4	21 59.1	−59.8	0.4
87	17 59.3	−59.8	0.3	18 59.3	−59.8	0.3	19 59.3	−59.8	0.3	20 59.3	−59.8	0.3
88	16 59.5	−59.7	0.2	17 59.5	−59.7	0.2	18 59.5	−59.7	0.2	19 59.5	−59.7	0.2
89	15 59.8	−59.8	0.1	16 59.8	−59.8	0.1	17 59.8	−59.8	0.1	18 59.8	−59.8	0.1
90	15 00.0	−59.8	0.0	16 00.0	−59.8	0.0	17 00.0	−59.8	0.0	18 00.0	−59.8	0.0
	15°			16°			17°			18°		

Dec.	19° Hc	19° d	19° Z	20° Hc	20° d	20° Z	21° Hc	21° d	21° Z	22° Hc	22° d	22° Z
°	° ′	′	°	° ′	′	°	° ′	′	°	° ′	′	°
0	70 22.6	+58.1	165.0	69 24.6	+58.2	165.7	68 26.3	+58.5	166.3	67 28.0	+58.6	166.9
1	71 20.7	+57.8	164.2	70 22.8	+58.1	165.0	69 24.8	+58.3	165.7	68 26.6	+58.4	166.3
2	72 18.5	+57.7	163.3	71 20.9	+57.9	164.2	70 23.1	+58.1	165.0	69 25.0	+58.4	165.7
3	73 16.2	+57.3	162.4	72 18.8	+57.7	163.4	71 21.2	+57.9	164.2	70 23.4	+58.1	165.0
4	74 13.5	+57.0	161.3	73 16.5	+57.3	162.4	72 19.1	+57.7	163.4	71 21.5	+58.0	164.2
5	75 10.5	+56.6	160.2	74 13.8	+57.1	161.4	73 16.8	+57.4	162.4	72 19.5	+57.7	163.4
6	76 07.1	+56.1	158.8	75 10.9	+56.6	160.2	74 14.2	+57.1	161.4	73 17.2	+57.4	162.5
7	77 03.2	+55.4	157.3	76 07.5	+56.1	158.9	75 11.3	+56.6	160.2	74 14.6	+57.1	161.4
8	77 58.6	+54.7	155.5	77 03.6	+55.5	157.3	76 07.9	+56.2	158.9	75 11.7	+56.7	160.3
9	78 53.3	+53.7	153.5	77 59.1	+54.8	155.6	77 04.1	+55.6	157.4	76 08.4	+56.2	158.9
10	79 47.0	+52.5	151.1	78 53.9	+53.8	153.5	77 59.7	+54.8	155.6	77 04.6	+55.7	157.4
11	80 39.5	+50.8•	148.2	79 47.7	+52.5	151.1	78 54.5	+53.8	153.6	78 00.3	+54.8	155.7
12	81 30.3	+48.5•	144.8	80 40.2	+50.9	148.3	79 48.3	+52.7	151.2	78 55.1	+54.0	153.7
13	82 18.8	+45.7•	140.6	81 31.1	+48.7•	144.8	80 41.0	+50.9	148.4	79 49.1	+52.7	151.3
14	83 04.5	+41.5•	135.5	82 19.8	+45.7•	140.7	81 31.9	+48.9•	144.9	80 41.8	+51.1	148.5
15	83 46.0	+36.0•	129.2	83 05.5	+41.7•	135.6	82 20.8	+45.8•	140.8	81 32.9	+48.9•	145.1
16	84 22.0	+28.5•	121.4	83 47.2	+36.2•	129.3	83 06.6	+41.9•	135.7	82 21.8	+46.0•	140.9
17	84 50.5	+18.8•	112.0	84 23.4	+28.6•	121.5	83 48.5	+36.3•	129.4	83 07.8	+42.0•	135.8
18	85 09.3	+7.1•	101.1	84 52.0	+18.9•	112.1	84 24.8	+28.8•	121.6	83 49.8	+36.5•	129.5
19	85 16.4	−5.5•	89.2	85 10.9	+7.2•	101.1	84 53.6	+19.1•	112.2	84 26.3	+29.0•	121.7
20	85 10.9	−17.3•	77.2	85 18.1	−5.4•	89.1	85 12.7	+7.2•	101.2	84 55.3	+19.2•	112.3
21	84 53.6	−27.3•	66.1	85 12.7	−17.4•	77.1	85 19.9	−5.4•	89.1	85 14.5	+7.4•	101.2
22	84 26.3	−35.1•	56.5	84 55.3	−27.4•	65.9	85 14.5	−17.4•	77.0	85 21.9	−5.5•	89.1
23	83 51.2	−40.9•	48.5	84 27.9	−35.2•	56.3	84 57.1	−27.5•	65.7	85 16.4	−17.5•	76.8
24	83 10.3	−45.1•	42.0	83 52.7	−41.0•	48.3	84 29.6	−35.4•	56.1	84 58.9	−27.6•	65.5
25	82 25.2	−48.3•	36.8	83 11.7	−45.3•	41.8	83 54.2	−41.1•	48.1	84 31.3	−35.5•	55.8
26	81 36.9	−50.5	32.5	82 26.4	−48.3•	36.5	83 13.1	−45.4•	41.6	83 55.8	−41.3•	47.8
27	80 46.4	−52.2	29.0	81 38.1	−50.6•	32.3	82 27.7	−48.5•	36.3	83 14.5	−45.5•	41.3
28	79 54.2	−53.6	26.0	80 47.5	−52.4	28.7	81 39.2	−50.7	32.0	82 29.0	−48.6•	36.0
29	79 00.6	−54.6	23.6	79 55.1	−53.6	25.8	80 48.5	−52.4	28.5	81 40.4	−50.8	31.8
30	78 06.0	−55.3	21.5	79 01.5	−54.6	23.4	79 56.1	−53.7	25.6	80 49.6	−52.4	28.3
31	77 10.7	−56.0	19.7	78 06.9	−55.4	21.3	79 02.4	−54.6	23.1	79 57.2	−53.8	25.4
32	76 14.7	−56.6	18.1	77 11.5	−56.1	19.5	78 07.8	−55.5	21.1	79 03.4	−54.7	22.9
33	75 18.1	−56.9	16.7	76 15.4	−56.5	17.9	77 12.3	−56.1	19.3	78 08.7	−55.6	20.8
34	74 21.2	−57.3	15.5	75 18.9	−57.0	16.6	76 16.2	−56.6	17.7	77 13.1	−56.1	19.1
35	73 23.9	−57.6	14.5	74 21.9	−57.3	15.4	75 19.6	−57.0	16.4	76 17.0	−56.6	17.5
36	72 26.3	−57.8	13.5	73 24.6	−57.7	14.3	74 22.6	−57.4	15.2	75 20.4	−57.1	16.2
37	71 28.5	−58.1	12.7	72 26.9	−57.8	13.3	73 25.2	−57.6	14.1	74 23.3	−57.4	15.0
38	70 30.4	−58.2	11.9	71 29.1	−58.1	12.5	72 27.6	−57.9	13.2	73 25.9	−57.7	13.9
39	69 32.2	−58.4	11.2	70 31.0	−58.2	11.7	71 29.7	−58.1	12.3	72 28.2	−57.9	13.0
40	68 33.8	−58.5	10.5	69 32.8	−58.4	11.0	70 31.6	−58.3	11.6	71 30.3	−58.1	12.2
41	67 35.3	−58.6	9.9	68 34.4	−58.6	10.4	69 33.3	−58.4	10.9	70 32.2	−58.3	11.4
42	66 36.7	−58.8	9.4	67 35.8	−58.6	9.8	68 34.9	−58.5	10.2	69 33.9	−58.4	10.7
43	65 37.9	−58.8	8.9	66 37.2	−58.8	9.2	67 36.4	−58.7	9.6	68 35.5	−58.6	10.1
44	64 39.1	−58.9	8.4	65 38.4	−58.8	8.7	66 37.7	−58.8	9.1	67 36.9	−58.7	9.5
45	63 40.2	−59.0	8.0	64 39.6	−59.0	8.3	65 38.9	−58.8	8.6	66 38.2	−58.8	8.9
46	62 41.2	−59.1	7.6	63 40.6	−59.0	7.8	64 40.1	−59.0	8.1	65 39.4	−58.9	8.4
47	61 42.1	−59.1	7.2	62 41.6	−59.0	7.4	63 41.1	−59.0	7.7	64 40.5	−58.9	8.0
48	60 43.0	−59.2	6.8	61 42.6	−59.2	7.1	62 42.1	−59.1	7.3	63 41.6	−59.0	7.6
49	59 43.8	−59.2	6.5	60 43.4	−59.1	6.7	61 43.0	−59.1	6.9	62 42.6	−59.1	7.2
50	58 44.6	−59.2	6.2	59 44.3	−59.3	6.4	60 43.9	−59.2	6.6	61 43.5	−59.2	6.8
51	57 45.4	−59.3	5.9	58 45.0	−59.2	6.1	59 44.7	−59.2	6.2	60 44.3	−59.2	6.4
52	56 46.1	−59.4	5.6	57 45.8	−59.3	5.8	58 45.5	−59.3	5.9	59 45.1	−59.2	6.1
53	55 46.7	−59.3	5.4	56 46.5	−59.4	5.5	57 46.2	−59.3	5.6	58 45.9	−59.3	5.8
54	54 47.4	−59.4	5.1	55 47.1	−59.4	5.2	56 46.9	−59.4	5.4	57 46.6	−59.3	5.5
55	53 48.0	−59.5	4.9	54 47.7	−59.4	5.0	55 47.5	−59.4	5.1	56 47.3	−59.4	5.2
56	52 48.5	−59.4	4.6	53 48.3	−59.4	4.7	54 48.1	−59.4	4.9	55 47.9	−59.4	5.0
57	51 49.1	−59.5	4.4	52 48.9	−59.5	4.5	53 48.7	−59.4	4.6	54 48.5	−59.4	4.7
58	50 49.6	−59.5	4.2	51 49.4	−59.4	4.3	52 49.3	−59.5	4.4	53 49.1	−59.5	4.5
59	49 50.1	−59.5	4.0	50 50.0	−59.5	4.1	51 49.8	−59.5	4.2	52 49.6	−59.4	4.3
60	48 50.6	−59.5	3.8	49 50.5	−59.6	3.9	50 50.3	−59.5	4.0	51 50.2	−59.5	4.0
61	47 51.1	−59.6	3.6	48 50.9	−59.5	3.7	49 50.8	−59.5	3.8	50 50.7	−59.5	3.8
62	46 51.5	−59.6	3.4	47 51.4	−59.6	3.5	48 51.3	−59.6	3.6	49 51.2	−59.6	3.6
63	45 51.9	−59.6	3.3	46 51.8	−59.5	3.3	47 51.7	−59.5	3.4	48 51.6	−59.5	3.4
64	44 52.3	−59.6	3.1	45 52.3	−59.6	3.1	46 52.2	−59.6	3.2	47 52.1	−59.6	3.3
65	43 52.7	−59.6	2.9	44 52.7	−59.6	3.0	45 52.6	−59.6	3.0	46 52.5	−59.6	3.1
66	42 53.1	−59.6	2.8	43 53.1	−59.7	2.8	44 53.0	−59.6	2.9	45 52.9	−59.6	2.9
67	41 53.5	−59.6	2.6	42 53.4	−59.6	2.7	43 53.4	−59.7	2.7	44 53.3	−59.6	2.8
68	40 53.9	−59.7	2.5	41 53.8	−59.6	2.5	42 53.7	−59.6	2.6	43 53.7	−59.6	2.6
69	39 54.2	−59.6	2.3	40 54.2	−59.7	2.4	41 54.1	−59.6	2.4	42 54.1	−59.7	2.4
70	38 54.6	−59.7	2.2	39 54.5	−59.6	2.2	40 54.5	−59.7	2.3	41 54.4	−59.6	2.3
71	37 54.9	−59.7	2.1	38 54.9	−59.7	2.1	39 54.8	−59.7	2.1	40 54.8	−59.7	2.2
72	36 55.2	−59.7	1.9	37 55.2	−59.7	2.0	38 55.1	−59.6	2.0	39 55.1	−59.7	2.0
73	35 55.5	−59.7	1.8	36 55.5	−59.7	1.8	37 55.5	−59.7	1.9	38 55.4	−59.6	1.9
74	34 55.8	−59.7	1.7	35 55.8	−59.7	1.7	36 55.8	−59.7	1.7	37 55.8	−59.7	1.7
75	33 56.1	−59.7	1.6	34 56.1	−59.7	1.6	35 56.1	−59.7	1.6	36 56.1	−59.7	1.6
76	32 56.4	−59.7	1.4	33 56.4	−59.7	1.5	34 56.4	−59.7	1.5	35 56.4	−59.7	1.5
77	31 56.7	−59.7	1.3	32 56.7	−59.7	1.3	33 56.7	−59.7	1.4	34 56.7	−59.7	1.4
78	30 57.0	−59.7	1.2	31 57.0	−59.7	1.2	32 57.0	−59.7	1.2	33 57.0	−59.8	1.3
79	29 57.3	−59.8	1.1	30 57.3	−59.8	1.1	31 57.3	−59.8	1.1	32 57.2	−59.7	1.1
80	28 57.5	−59.7	1.0	29 57.5	−59.7	1.0	30 57.5	−59.7	1.0	31 57.5	−59.7	1.0
81	27 57.8	−59.7	0.9	28 57.8	−59.7	0.9	29 57.8	−59.7	0.9	30 57.8	−59.7	0.9
82	26 58.1	−59.8	0.8	27 58.1	−59.8	0.8	28 58.1	−59.8	0.8	29 58.1	−59.8	0.8
83	25 58.3	−59.7	0.7	26 58.3	−59.7	0.7	27 58.3	−59.7	0.7	28 58.3	−59.7	0.7
84	24 58.6	−59.8	0.6	25 58.6	−59.8	0.6	26 58.6	−59.8	0.6	27 58.6	−59.8	0.6
85	23 58.8	−59.7	0.5	24 58.8	−59.7	0.5	25 58.8	−59.7	0.5	26 58.8	−59.7	0.5
86	22 59.1	−59.8	0.4	23 59.1	−59.8	0.4	24 59.1	−59.8	0.4	25 59.1	−59.8	0.4
87	21 59.3	−59.8	0.3	22 59.3	−59.8	0.3	23 59.3	−59.8	0.3	24 59.3	−59.8	0.3
88	20 59.5	−59.7	0.2	21 59.5	−59.7	0.2	22 59.5	−59.7	0.2	23 59.5	−59.7	0.2
89	19 59.8	−59.8	0.1	20 59.8	−59.8	0.1	21 59.8	−59.8	0.1	22 59.8	−59.8	0.1
90	19 00.0	−59.8	0.0	20 00.0	−59.8	0.0	21 00.0	−59.8	0.0	22 00.0	−59.8	0.0
	19°			20°			21°			22°		

LATITUDE **CONTRARY** NAME TO DECLINATION **L.H.A. 5°, 355°**

Dec.	15°			16°			17°			18°			19°			20°			21°			22°			Dec.
°	Hc ° ′	d ′	Z °	Hc ° ′	d ′	Z °	Hc ° ′	d ′	Z °	Hc ° ′	d ′	Z °	Hc ° ′	d ′	Z °	Hc ° ′	d ′	Z °	Hc ° ′	d ′	Z °	Hc ° ′	d ′	Z °	°
0	74 12.4	-57.2	161.3	73 15.4	-57.6	162.4	72 18.0	-57.8	163.3	71 20.4	-58.0	164.2	70 22.6	-58.3	165.0	69 24.6	-58.5	165.7	68 26.3	-58.5	166.3	67 28.0	-58.7	166.9	0
1	73 15.2	-57.5	162.4	72 17.8	-57.8	163.3	71 20.2	-58.0	164.2	70 22.4	-58.2	165.0	69 24.3	-58.4	165.7	68 26.1	-58.5	166.3	67 27.8	-58.7	166.9	66 29.3	-58.8	167.4	1
2	72 17.7	-57.8	163.4	71 20.0	-58.0	164.2	70 22.2	-58.2	165.0	69 24.2	-58.4	165.7	68 25.9	-58.5	166.3	67 27.6	-58.7	166.9	66 29.1	-58.8	167.4	65 30.5	-58.9	167.9	2
3	71 19.9	-58.0	164.2	70 22.0	-58.2	165.0	69 24.0	-58.4	165.7	68 25.8	-58.5	166.3	67 27.4	-58.6	166.9	66 28.9	-58.8	167.4	65 30.3	-58.9	167.9	64 31.6	-59.0	168.3	3
4	70 21.9	-58.2	165.0	69 23.8	-58.3	165.7	68 25.6	-58.5	166.3	67 27.3	-58.7	166.9	66 28.8	-58.8	167.4	65 30.1	-58.8	167.9	64 31.4	-58.9	168.3	63 32.6	-59.0	168.7	4
5	69 23.7	-58.3	165.7	68 25.5	-58.5	166.3	67 27.1	-58.6	166.9	66 28.6	-58.7	167.4	65 30.0	-58.8	167.9	64 31.3	-59.0	168.4	63 32.5	-59.1	168.8	62 33.6	-59.1	169.1	5
6	68 25.4	-58.5	166.4	67 27.0	-58.6	166.9	66 28.5	-58.7	167.5	65 29.9	-58.9	167.9	64 31.2	-59.0	168.4	63 32.3	-59.0	168.8	62 33.4	-59.0	169.2	61 34.5	-59.2	169.5	6
7	67 26.9	-58.6	167.0	66 28.4	-58.7	167.5	65 29.8	-58.9	168.0	64 31.0	-58.9	168.4	63 32.2	-59.0	168.8	62 33.3	-59.0	169.2	61 34.4	-59.2	169.5	60 35.3	-59.2	169.9	7
8	66 28.3	-58.7	167.5	65 29.7	-58.8	168.0	64 30.9	-58.9	168.4	63 32.1	-59.0	168.8	62 33.2	-59.0	169.2	61 34.3	-59.2	169.6	60 35.2	-59.2	169.9	59 36.1	-59.2	170.2	8
9	65 29.6	-58.8	168.0	64 30.9	-58.9	168.5	63 32.0	-58.9	168.9	62 33.1	-59.0	169.2	61 34.2	-59.2	169.6	60 35.1	-59.2	169.9	59 36.0	-59.2	170.2	58 36.9	-59.3	170.5	9
10	64 30.8	-58.9	168.5	63 32.0	-59.0	168.9	62 33.1	-59.1	169.3	61 34.1	-59.1	169.6	60 35.0	-59.1	169.9	59 35.9	-59.2	170.2	58 36.8	-59.3	170.5	57 37.6	-59.4	170.8	10
11	63 31.9	-58.9	168.9	62 33.0	-59.0	169.3	61 34.0	-59.1	169.6	60 35.0	-59.2	170.0	59 35.9	-59.3	170.3	58 36.7	-59.3	170.5	57 37.5	-59.3	170.8	56 38.2	-59.3	171.1	11
12	62 33.0	-59.0	169.3	61 34.0	-59.1	169.7	60 34.9	-59.1	170.0	59 35.8	-59.2	170.3	58 36.6	-59.2	170.6	57 37.4	-59.3	170.8	56 38.2	-59.4	171.1	55 38.9	-59.4	171.3	12
13	61 34.0	-59.1	169.7	60 34.9	-59.2	170.0	59 35.8	-59.2	170.3	58 36.6	-59.3	170.6	57 37.4	-59.3	170.9	56 38.1	-59.3	171.1	55 38.8	-59.4	171.3	54 39.5	-59.4	171.6	13
14	60 34.9	-59.2	170.1	59 35.7	-59.2	170.4	58 36.6	-59.3	170.7	57 37.3	-59.3	170.9	56 38.1	-59.4	171.2	55 38.8	-59.4	171.4	54 39.4	-59.4	171.6	53 40.1	-59.5	171.8	14
15	59 35.7	-59.2	170.4	58 36.5	-59.2	170.7	57 37.3	-59.3	171.0	56 38.0	-59.3	171.2	55 38.7	-59.3	171.4	54 39.4	-59.4	171.6	53 40.0	-59.4	171.8	52 40.6	-59.5	172.0	15
16	58 36.5	-59.2	170.7	57 37.3	-59.3	171.0	56 38.0	-59.3	171.2	55 38.7	-59.4	171.5	54 39.4	-59.4	171.7	53 40.0	-59.5	171.9	52 40.6	-59.5	172.1	51 41.1	-59.5	172.2	16
17	57 37.3	-59.3	171.0	56 38.0	-59.3	171.3	55 38.7	-59.4	171.5	54 39.3	-59.4	171.7	53 40.0	-59.5	171.9	52 40.5	-59.4	172.1	51 41.1	-59.5	172.3	50 41.6	-59.5	172.4	17
18	56 38.0	-59.3	171.3	55 38.7	-59.3	171.6	54 39.3	-59.3	171.8	53 39.9	-59.4	172.0	52 40.5	-59.4	172.1	51 41.1	-59.5	172.3	50 41.6	-59.5	172.5	49 42.1	-59.5	172.6	18
19	55 38.7	-59.3	171.6	54 39.4	-59.4	171.8	53 40.0	-59.5	172.0	52 40.5	-59.4	172.2	51 41.1	-59.5	172.4	50 41.6	-59.5	172.5	49 42.1	-59.5	172.7	48 42.6	-59.6	172.8	19
20	54 39.4	-59.4	171.9	53 40.0	-59.4	172.1	52 40.5	-59.4	172.2	51 41.1	-59.5	172.4	50 41.6	-59.5	172.6	49 42.1	-59.5	172.7	48 42.6	-59.6	172.9	47 43.0	-59.6	173.0	20
21	53 40.0	-59.4	172.1	52 40.6	-59.5	172.3	51 41.1	-59.5	172.5	50 41.6	-59.5	172.6	49 42.1	-59.5	172.8	48 42.6	-59.6	172.9	47 43.0	-59.6	173.1	46 43.4	-59.5	173.2	21
22	52 40.6	-59.4	172.3	51 41.1	-59.4	172.5	50 41.6	-59.5	172.7	49 42.1	-59.5	172.8	48 42.6	-59.6	173.0	47 43.0	-59.5	173.1	46 43.4	-59.5	173.2	45 43.9	-59.7	173.4	22
23	51 41.2	-59.5	172.6	50 41.7	-59.5	172.7	49 42.1	-59.5	172.9	48 42.6	-59.5	173.0	47 43.0	-59.5	173.2	46 43.5	-59.6	173.3	45 43.9	-59.6	173.4	44 44.2	-59.6	173.5	23
24	50 41.7	-59.5	172.8	49 42.2	-59.5	172.9	48 42.6	-59.5	173.1	47 43.1	-59.6	173.2	46 43.5	-59.6	173.3	45 43.9	-59.6	173.5	44 44.3	-59.7	173.6	43 44.6	-59.6	173.7	24
25	49 42.2	-59.5	173.0	48 42.7	-59.5	173.1	47 43.1	-59.5	173.3	46 43.5	-59.6	173.4	45 43.9	-59.6	173.5	44 44.3	-59.6	173.6	43 44.6	-59.6	173.7	42 45.0	-59.6	173.8	25
26	48 42.7	-59.5	173.2	47 43.2	-59.6	173.3	46 43.6	-59.6	173.4	45 43.9	-59.5	173.6	44 44.3	-59.6	173.7	43 44.7	-59.6	173.8	42 45.0	-59.6	173.9	41 45.4	-59.7	174.0	26
27	47 43.2	-59.5	173.4	46 43.6	-59.5	173.5	45 44.0	-59.6	173.6	44 44.4	-59.6	173.7	43 44.7	-59.6	173.8	42 45.1	-59.7	173.9	41 45.4	-59.7	174.0	40 45.7	-59.7	174.1	27
28	46 43.7	-59.6	173.6	45 44.1	-59.6	173.7	44 44.4	-59.6	173.8	43 44.8	-59.6	173.9	42 45.1	-59.6	174.0	41 45.4	-59.6	174.1	40 45.7	-59.6	174.2	39 46.0	-59.6	174.3	28
29	45 44.1	-59.5	173.7	44 44.5	-59.6	173.8	43 44.8	-59.6	173.9	42 45.2	-59.7	174.0	41 45.5	-59.7	174.1	40 45.8	-59.7	174.2	39 46.1	-59.7	174.3	38 46.4	-59.7	174.4	29
30	44 44.6	-59.6	173.9	43 44.9	-59.6	174.0	42 45.2	-59.6	174.1	41 45.5	-59.6	174.2	40 45.8	-59.6	174.3	39 46.1	-59.6	174.4	38 46.4	-59.7	174.4	37 46.7	-59.7	174.5	30
31	43 45.0	-59.6	174.1	42 45.3	-59.6	174.2	41 45.6	-59.6	174.3	40 45.9	-59.7	174.3	39 46.2	-59.7	174.4	38 46.5	-59.7	174.5	37 46.7	-59.7	174.6	36 47.0	-59.7	174.6	31
32	42 45.4	-59.6	174.2	41 45.7	-59.6	174.3	40 46.0	-59.7	174.4	39 46.2	-59.6	174.5	38 46.5	-59.6	174.6	37 46.8	-59.7	174.6	36 47.0	-59.6	174.7	35 47.3	-59.7	174.8	32
33	41 45.8	-59.7	174.4	40 46.1	-59.7	174.5	39 46.3	-59.6	174.5	38 46.6	-59.7	174.6	37 46.9	-59.7	174.7	36 47.1	-59.7	174.8	35 47.4	-59.7	174.8	34 47.6	-59.7	174.9	33
34	40 46.1	-59.6	174.5	39 46.4	-59.6	174.6	38 46.7	-59.7	174.7	37 46.9	-59.6	174.8	36 47.2	-59.7	174.8	35 47.4	-59.7	174.9	34 47.7	-59.8	175.0	33 47.9	-59.7	175.0	34
35	39 46.5	-59.6	174.7	38 46.8	-59.7	174.7	37 47.0	-59.7	174.8	36 47.3	-59.7	174.9	35 47.5	-59.7	175.0	34 47.7	-59.7	175.0	33 47.9	-59.7	175.1	32 48.2	-59.8	175.1	35
36	38 46.9	-59.7	174.8	37 47.1	-59.7	174.9	36 47.3	-59.6	174.9	35 47.6	-59.7	175.0	34 47.8	-59.7	175.1	33 48.0	-59.7	175.1	32 48.2	-59.7	175.2	31 48.4	-59.7	175.2	36
37	37 47.2	-59.7	174.9	36 47.4	-59.6	175.0	35 47.7	-59.7	175.1	34 47.9	-59.7	175.1	33 48.1	-59.7	175.2	32 48.3	-59.7	175.2	31 48.5	-59.7	175.3	30 48.7	-59.7	175.4	37
38	36 47.5	-59.6	175.1	35 47.8	-59.7	175.1	34 48.0	-59.7	175.2	33 48.2	-59.7	175.3	32 48.4	-59.7	175.3	31 48.6	-59.7	175.4	30 48.8	-59.7	175.4	29 49.0	-59.8	175.5	38
39	35 47.9	-59.7	175.2	34 48.1	-59.7	175.3	33 48.3	-59.7	175.3	32 48.5	-59.7	175.4	31 48.7	-59.7	175.4	30 48.9	-59.8	175.5	29 49.1	-59.8	175.5	28 49.2	-59.7	175.6	39
40	34 48.2	-59.7	175.3	33 48.4	-59.7	175.4	32 48.6	-59.7	175.4	31 48.8	-59.7	175.5	30 49.0	-59.8	175.5	29 49.1	-59.7	175.6	28 49.3	-59.7	175.6	27 49.5	-59.8	175.7	40
41	33 48.5	-59.7	175.5	32 48.7	-59.7	175.5	31 48.9	-59.7	175.6	30 49.1	-59.8	175.6	29 49.2	-59.7	175.7	28 49.4	-59.7	175.7	27 49.6	-59.8	175.7	26 49.7	-59.7	175.8	41
42	32 48.8	-59.7	175.6	31 49.0	-59.7	175.6	30 49.2	-59.8	175.7	29 49.3	-59.7	175.7	28 49.5	-59.7	175.8	27 49.7	-59.8	175.8	26 49.8	-59.7	175.8	25 50.0	-59.8	175.9	42
43	31 49.1	-59.7	175.7	30 49.3	-59.7	175.7	29 49.4	-59.7	175.8	28 49.6	-59.7	175.8	27 49.8	-59.8	175.9	26 49.9	-59.7	175.9	25 50.1	-59.8	175.9	24 50.2	-59.7	176.0	43
44	30 49.4	-59.7	175.8	29 49.6	-59.8	175.9	28 49.7	-59.7	175.9	27 49.9	-59.8	175.9	26 50.0	-59.7	176.0	25 50.2	-59.8	176.0	24 50.3	-59.7	176.0	23 50.5	-59.8	176.1	44
45	29 49.7	-59.7	175.9	28 49.8	-59.7	176.0	27 50.0	-59.7	176.0	26 50.1	-59.7	176.0	25 50.3	-59.8	176.1	24 50.4	-59.7	176.1	23 50.6	-59.8	176.1	22 50.7	-59.8	176.2	45
46	28 50.0	-59.8	176.0	27 50.1	-59.7	176.1	26 50.3	-59.8	176.1	25 50.4	-59.8	176.1	24 50.5	-59.7	176.2	23 50.7	-59.8	176.2	22 50.8	-59.8	176.2	21 50.9	-59.8	176.3	46
47	27 50.2	-59.7	176.1	26 50.4	-59.8	176.2	25 50.5	-59.7	176.2	24 50.6	-59.7	176.2	23 50.8	-59.8	176.3	22 50.9	-59.8	176.3	21 51.0	-59.7	176.3	20 51.1	-59.7	176.4	47
48	26 50.5	-59.7	176.3	25 50.6	-59.8	176.3	24 50.8	-59.8	176.3	23 50.9	-59.8	176.3	22 51.0	-59.7	176.4	21 51.1	-59.7	176.4	20 51.3	-59.8	176.4	19 51.4	-59.8	176.4	48
49	25 50.8	-59.8	176.4	24 50.9	-59.7	176.4	23 51.0	-59.7	176.4	22 51.1	-59.7	176.4	21 51.3	-59.8	176.5	20 51.4	-59.8	176.5	19 51.5	-59.8	176.5	18 51.6	-59.8	176.5	49
50	24 51.0	-59.7	176.5	23 51.2	-59.8	176.5	22 51.3	-59.8	176.5	21 51.4	-59.8	176.5	20 51.5	-59.8	176.6	19 51.6	-59.8	176.6	18 51.7	-59.8	176.6	17 51.8	-59.8	176.6	50
51	23 51.3	-59.8	176.6	22 51.4	-59.7	176.6	21 51.5	-59.7	176.6	20 51.6	-59.7	176.6	19 51.7	-59.8	176.7	18 51.8	-59.8	176.7	17 51.9	-59.8	176.7	16 52.0	-59.8	176.7	51
52	22 51.6	-59.8	176.7	21 51.7	-59.8	176.7	20 51.8	-59.8	176.7	19 51.9	-59.8	176.7	18 51.9	-59.7	176.7	17 52.0	-59.7	176.8	16 52.1	-59.7	176.8	15 52.2	-59.8	176.8	52
53	21 51.8	-59.8	176.8	20 51.9	-59.8	176.8	19 52.0	-59.8	176.8	18 52.1	-59.8	176.8	17 52.2	-59.8	176.8	16 52.3	-59.8	176.9	15 52.4	-59.8	176.9	14 52.4	-59.7	176.9	53
54	20 52.0	-59.7	176.9	19 52.1	-59.7	176.9	18 52.2	-59.7	176.9	17 52.3	-59.8	176.9	16 52.4	-59.8	176.9	15 52.5	-59.8	176.9	14 52.6	-59.8	177.0	13 52.7	-59.8	177.0	54
55	19 52.3	-59.8	177.0	18 52.4	-59.8	177.0	17 52.5	-59.8	177.0	16 52.5	-59.7	177.0	15 52.6	-59.8	177.0	14 52.7	-59.8	177.0	13 52.8	-59.8	177.0	12 52.9	-59.8	177.1	55
56	18 52.5	-59.7	177.0	17 52.6	-59.8	177.1	16 52.7	-59.8	177.1	15 52.8	-59.8	177.1	14 52.8	-59.7	177.1	13 52.9	-59.8	177.1	12 53.0	-59.8	177.1	11 53.1	-59.8	177.1	56
57	17 52.8	-59.8	177.1	16 52.8	-59.7	177.2	15 52.9	-59.8	177.2	14 53.0	-59.8	177.2	13 53.1	-59.8	177.2	12 53.1	-59.8	177.2	11 53.2	-59.8	177.2	10 53.3	-59.8	177.2	57
58	16 53.0	-59.8	177.2	15 53.1	-59.8	177.2	14 53.1	-59.7	177.3	13 53.2	-59.8	177.3	12 53.3	-59.8	177.3	11 53.3	-59.7	177.3	10 53.4	-59.8	177.3	9 53.5	-59.8	177.3	58
59	15 53.2	-59.7	177.3	14 53.3	-59.8	177.3	13 53.4	-59.8	177.3	12 53.4	-59.8	177.4	11 53.5	-59.8	177.4	10 53.6	-59.8	177.4	9 53.6	-59.8	177.4	8 53.7	-59.8	177.4	59
60	14 53.5	-59.8	177.4	13 53.5	-59.8	177.4	12 53.6	-59.8	177.4	11 53.6	-59.7	177.4	10 53.7	-59.8	177.5	9 53.8	-59.8	177.5	8 53.8	-59.8	177.5	7 53.9	-59.8	177.5	60
61	13 53.7	-59.8	177.5	12 53.7	-59.7	177.5	11 53.8	-59.8	177.5	10 53.9	-59.8	177.5	9 53.9	-59.8	177.5	8 54.0	-59.8	177.5	7 54.0	-59.8	177.6	6 54.1	-59.8	177.6	61
62	12 53.9	-59.8	177.6	11 54.0	-59.8	177.6	10 54.0	-59.8	177.6	9 54.1	-59.8	177.6	8 54.1	-59.8	177.6	7 54.2	-59.8	177.6	6 54.2	-59.8	177.6	5 54.3	-59.8	177.6	62
63	11 54.1	-59.7	177.7	10 54.2	-59.8	177.7	9 54.2	-59.8	177.7	8 54.3	-59.8	177.7	7 54.3	-59.8	177.7	6 54.4	-59.8	177.7	5 54.4	-59.8	177.7	4 54.5	-59.8	177.7	63
64	10 54.4	-59.8	177.8	9 54.4	-59.8	177.8	8 54.4	-59.7	177.8	7 54.5	-59.8	177.8	6 54.5	-59.8	177.8	5 54.6	-59.8	177.8	4 54.6	-59.8	177.8	3 54.7	-59.8	177.8	64
65	9 54.6	-59.8	177.9	8 54.6	-59.8	177.9	7 54.7	-59.8	177.9	6 54.7	-59.8	177.9	5 54.7	-59.7	177.9	4 54.8	-59.8	177.9	3 54.8	-59.8	177.9	2 54.9	-59.8	177.9	65
66	8 54.8	-59.8	177.9	7 54.8	-59.8	177.9	6 54.9	-59.8	178.0	5 54.9	-59.8	178.0	4 55.0	-59.8	178.0	3 55.0	-59.8	178.0	2 55.0	-59.8	178.0	1 55.1	-59.8	178.0	66
67	7 55.0	-59.8	178.0	6 55.0	-59.7	178.0	5 55.1	-59.8	178.0	4 55.1	-59.8	178.0	3 55.2	-59.8	178.0	2 55.2	-59.8	178.0	1 55.2	-59.8	178.0	0 55.3	-59.8	178.0	67
68	6 55.2	-59.8	178.1	5 55.3	-59.8	178.1	4 55.3	-59.8	178.1	3 55.3	-59.8	178.1	2 55.4	-59.8	178.1	1 55.4	-59.8	178.1	0 55.4	-59.8	178.1	0 04.5	+59.8	1.9	68
69	5 55.4	-59.7	178.2	4 55.5	-59.8	178.2	3 55.5	-59.8	178.2	2 55.5	-59.8	178.2	1 55.6	-59.8	178.2	0 55.6	-59.8	178.2	0 04.4	+59.8	1.8	1 04.3	+59.9	1.8	69
70	4 55.7	-59.8	178.3	3 55.7	-59.8	178.3	2 55.7	-59.8	178.3	1 55.7	-59.8	178.3	0 55.8	-59.8	178.3	0 04.2	+59.8	1.7	1 04.2	+59.8	1.7	2 04.2	+59.8	1.7	70
71	3 55.9	-59.8	178.4	2 55.9	-59.8	178.4	1 55.9	-59.8	178.4	0 55.9	-59.7	178.4	0 04.0	+59.8	1.6	1 04.0	+59.8	1.6	2 04.0	+59.8	1.6	3 04.0	+59.8	1.6	71
72	2 56.1	-59.8	178.5	1 56.1	-59.8	178.5	0 56.1	-59.8	178.5	0 03.8	+59.8	1.5	1 03.8	+59.8	1.5	2 03.8	+59.8	1.5	3 03.8	+59.8	1.5	4 03.8	+59.8	1.5	72
73	1 56.3	-59.8	178.5	0 56.3	-59.8	178.5	0 03.7	+59.7	1.5	1 03.6	+59.8	1.5	2 03.6	+59.8	1.5	3 03.6	+59.8	1.5	4 03.6	+59.8	1.5	5 03.6	+59.8	1.5	73
74	0 56.5	-59.8	178.6	0 03.5	+59.8	1.4	1 03.4	+59.8	1.4	2 03.4	+59.8	1.4	3 03.4	+59.8	1.4	4 03.4	+59.8	1.4	5 03.4	+59.8	1.4	6 03.4	+59.8	1.4	74
75	0 03.3	+59.8	1.3	1 03.3	+59.7	1.3	2 03.2	+59.8	1.3	3 03.2	+59.8	1.3	4 03.2	+59.8	1.3	5 03.2	+59.8	1.3	6 03.2	+59.8	1.3	7 03.2	+59.8	1.3	75
76	1 03.1	+59.7	1.2	2 03.0	+59.8	1.2	3 03.0	+59.8	1.2	4 03.0	+59.8	1.2	5 03.0	+59.8	1.2	6 03.0	+59.8	1.2	7 03.0	+59.8	1.2	8 03.0	+59.8	1.2	76
77	2 02.8	+59.8	1.1	3 02.8	+59.8	1.1	4 02.8	+59.8	1.1	5 02.8	+59.8	1.1	6 02.8	+59.8	1.1	7 02.8	+59.8	1.1	8 02.8	+59.8	1.1	9 02.8	+59.8	1.1	77
78	3 02.6	+59.8	1.0	4 02.6	+59.8	1.0	5 02.6	+59.8	1.0	6 02.6	+59.8	1.0	7 02.6	+59.8	1.0	8 02.6	+59.8	1.0	9 02.6	+59.8	1.1	10 02.6	+59.8	1.1	78
79	4 02.4	+59.8	1.0	5 02.4	+59.8	1.0	6 02.4	+59.8	1.0	7 02.4	+59.8	1.0	8 02.4	+59.8	1.0	9 02.4	+59.8	1.0	10 02.4	+59.8	1.0	11 02.4	+59.8	1.0	79
80	5 02.2	+59.8	0.9	6 02.2	+59.8	0.9	7 02.2	+59.8	0.9	8 02.2	+59.8	0.9	9 02.2	+59.8	0.9	10 02.2	+59.8	0.9	11 02.2	+59.8	0.9	12 02.2	+59.7	0.9	80
81	6 02.0	+59.8	0.8	7 02.0	+59.8	0.8	8 02.0	+59.8	0.8	9 02.0	+59.8	0.8	10 02.0	+59.8	0.8	11 02.0	+59.7	0.8	12 02.0	+59.7	0.8	13 01.9	+59.8	0.8	81
82	7 01.8	+59.8	0.7	8 01.8	+59.8	0.7	9 01.8	+59.7	0.7	10 01.8	+59.7	0.7	11 01.8	+59.7	0.7	12 01.7	+59.8	0.7	13 01.7	+59.8	0.7	14 01.7	+59.8	0.7	82
83	8 01.6	+59.7	0.6	9 01.6	+59.7	0.6	10 01.5	+59.8	0.6	11 01.5	+59.8	0.6	12 01.5	+59.8	0.6	13 01.5	+59.8	0.6	14 01.5	+59.8	0.6	15 01.5	+59.8	0.6	83
84	9 01.3	+59.8	0.5	10 01.3	+59.8	0.5	11 01.3	+59.8	0.5	12 01.3	+59.8	0.5	13 01.3	+59.8	0.5	14 01.3	+59.8	0.5	15 01.3	+59.8	0.5	16 01.3	+59.8	0.5	84
85	10 01.1	+59.8	0.4	11 01.1	+59.8	0.4	12 01.1	+59.8	0.4	13 01.1	+59.8	0.4	14 01.1	+59.8	0.4	15 01.1	+59.8	0.5	16 01.1	+59.8	0.5	17 01.1	+59.8	0.5	85
86	11 00.9	+59.8	0.4	12 00.9	+59.8	0.4	13 00.9	+59.8	0.4	14 00.9	+59.8	0.4	15 00.9	+59.8	0.4	16 00.9	+59.8	0.4	17 00.9	+59.8	0.4	18 00.9	+59.8	0.4	86
87	12 00.7	+59.8	0.3	13 00.7	+59.8	0.3	14 00.7	+59.8	0.3	15 00.7	+59.8	0.3	16 00.7	+59.8	0.3	17 00.7	+59.8	0.3	18 00.7	+59.8	0.3	19 00.7	+59.8	0.3	87
88	13 00.5	+59.7	0.2	14 00.5	+59.7	0.2	15 00.5	+59.7	0.2	16 00.5	+59.7	0.2	17 00.5	+59.7	0.2	18 00.5	+59.7	0.2	19 00.5	+59.7	0.2	20 00.5	+59.7	0.2	88
89	14 00.2	+59.8	0.1	15 00.2	+59.8	0.1	16 00.2	+59.8	0.1	17 00.2	+59.8	0.1	18 00.2	+59.8	0.1	19 00.2	+59.8	0.1	20 00.2	+59.8	0.1	21 00.2	+59.8	0.1	89
90	15 00.0	+59.8	0.0	16 00.0	+59.8	0.0	17 00.0	+59.8	0.0	18 00.0	+59.8	0.0	19 00.0	+59.8	0.0	20 00.0	+59.8	0.0	21 00.0	+59.8	0.0	22 00.0	+59.8	0.0	90
	15°			16°			17°			18°			19°			20°			21°			22°			

S. Lat. {L.H.A. greater than 180° ....Zn=180°–Z / L.H.A. less than 180°...........Zn=180°+Z

LATITUDE **SAME** NAME AS DECLINATION **L.H.A. 175°, 185°**

13

Dec.	15° Hc	d	Z	16° Hc	d	Z	17° Hc	d	Z	18° Hc	d	Z	Dec.
°	° ′	′	°	° ′	′	°	° ′	′	°	° ′	′	°	°
0	73 52.2	+55.7	157.9	72 56.4	+56.1	159.1	72 00.1	+56.6	160.2	71 03.5	+56.9	161.2	0
1	74 47.9	+55.0	156.5	73 52.5	+55.7	157.9	72 56.7	+56.2	159.1	72 00.4	+56.7	160.2	1
2	75 42.9	+54.4	155.0	74 48.2	+55.1	156.5	73 52.9	+55.7	157.9	72 57.1	+56.2	159.1	2
3	76 37.3	+53.5	153.2	75 43.3	+54.5	155.0	74 48.6	+55.2	156.5	73 53.3	+55.8	157.9	3
4	77 30.8	+52.5	151.2	76 37.8	+53.6	153.2	75 43.8	+54.5	155.0	74 49.1	+55.2	156.5	4
5	78 23.3	+51.2	148.8	77 31.4	+52.5	151.2	76 38.3	+53.6	153.2	75 44.3	+54.5	155.0	5
6	79 14.5	+49.6	146.2	78 23.9	+51.3	148.9	77 31.9	+52.7	151.2	76 38.8	+53.7	153.2	6
7	80 04.1	+47.6•	143.0	79 15.2	+49.7	146.2	78 24.6	+51.3	148.9	77 32.5	+52.8	151.3	7
8	80 51.7	+44.8•	139.3	80 04.9	+47.6•	143.1	79 15.9	+49.8	146.2	78 25.3	+51.4	149.0	8
9	81 36.5	+41.5•	135.0	80 52.5	+45.0•	139.4	80 05.7	+47.7•	143.1	79 16.7	+49.9	146.3	9
10	82 18.0	+37.1•	129.8	81 37.5	+41.6•	135.0	80 53.4	+45.1•	139.4	80 06.6	+47.8•	143.2	10
11	82 55.1	+31.3•	123.7	82 19.1	+37.2•	129.9	81 38.5	+41.7•	135.1	80 54.4	+45.2•	139.5	11
12	83 26.4	+24.3•	116.5	82 56.3	+31.5•	123.7	82 20.2	+37.4•	129.9	81 39.6	+41.9•	135.2	12
13	83 50.7	+15.7•	108.2	83 27.8	+24.4•	116.5	82 57.6	+31.6•	123.8	82 21.5	+37.4•	130.0	13
14	84 06.4	+5.9•	99.0	83 52.2	+15.8•	108.2	83 29.2	+24.6•	116.6	82 58.9	+31.9•	123.9	14
15	84 12.3	-4.3•	89.2	84 08.0	+6.0•	99.0	83 53.8	+15.9•	108.3	83 30.8	+24.6•	116.7	15
16	84 08.0	-14.2•	79.4	84 14.0	-4.3•	89.2	84 09.7	+6.0•	99.0	83 55.4	+16.1•	108.3	16
17	83 53.8	-23.0•	70.1	84 09.7	-14.3•	79.3	84 15.7	-4.2•	89.1	84 11.5	+6.1•	99.0	17
18	83 30.8	-30.4•	61.6	83 55.4	-23.0•	69.9	84 11.5	-14.3•	79.2	84 17.6	-4.2•	89.1	18
19	83 00.4	-36.2•	54.3	83 32.4	-30.4•	61.5	83 57.2	-23.1•	69.8	84 13.4	-14.3•	79.1	19
20	82 24.2	-40.9•	48.0	83 02.0	-36.4•	54.1	83 34.1	-30.5•	61.3	83 59.1	-23.2•	69.6	20
21	81 43.3	-44.4•	42.7	82 25.6	-40.9•	47.8	83 03.6	-36.4•	53.9	83 35.9	-30.6•	61.1	21
22	80 58.9	-47.1•	38.2	81 44.7	-44.5•	42.5	82 27.2	-41.0•	47.6	83 05.3	-36.5•	53.6	22
23	80 11.8	-49.3	34.4	81 00.2	-47.2•	38.0	81 46.2	-44.6•	42.2	82 28.8	-41.1•	47.3	23
24	79 22.5	-51.0	31.2	80 13.0	-49.4	34.2	81 01.6	-47.3•	37.7	81 47.7	-44.7•	42.0	24
25	78 31.5	-52.3	28.4	79 23.6	-51.0	31.0	80 14.3	-49.5	34.0	81 03.0	-47.4•	37.5	25
26	77 39.2	-53.4	26.1	78 32.6	-52.4	28.2	79 24.8	-51.1	30.8	80 15.6	-49.5	33.7	26
27	76 45.8	-54.3	24.0	77 40.2	-53.4	25.9	78 33.7	-52.4	28.0	79 26.1	-51.2	30.5	27
28	75 51.5	-54.9	22.2	76 46.8	-54.3	23.8	77 41.3	-53.5	25.6	78 34.9	-52.5	27.8	28
29	74 56.6	-55.6	20.6	75 52.5	-55.0	22.0	76 47.8	-54.3	23.6	77 42.4	-53.5	25.4	29
30	74 01.0	-56.0	19.2	74 57.5	-55.6	20.4	75 53.5	-55.1	21.8	76 48.9	-54.4	23.4	30
31	73 05.0	-56.5	17.9	74 01.9	-56.1	19.0	74 58.4	-55.6	20.2	75 54.5	-55.1	21.6	31
32	72 08.5	-56.8	16.8	73 05.8	-56.5	17.8	74 02.8	-56.2	18.8	74 59.4	-55.7	20.0	32
33	71 11.7	-57.2	15.8	72 09.3	-56.9	16.6	73 06.6	-56.5	17.6	74 03.7	-56.2	18.6	33
34	70 14.5	-57.3	14.9	71 12.4	-57.1	15.6	72 10.1	-56.9	16.4	73 07.5	-56.5	17.4	34
35	69 17.2	-57.6	14.0	70 15.3	-57.4	14.7	71 13.2	-57.1	15.4	72 11.0	-56.9	16.3	35
36	68 19.6	-57.9	13.2	69 17.9	-57.6	13.8	70 16.1	-57.5	14.5	71 14.1	-57.3	15.2	36
37	67 21.7	-57.9	12.5	68 20.3	-57.9	13.1	69 18.6	-57.6	13.7	70 16.8	-57.4	14.3	37
38	66 23.8	-58.2	11.9	67 22.4	-58.0	12.4	68 21.0	-57.9	12.9	69 19.4	-57.7	13.5	38
39	65 25.6	-58.2	11.3	66 24.4	-58.1	11.7	67 23.1	-58.0	12.2	68 21.7	-57.9	12.7	39
40	64 27.4	-58.4	10.7	65 26.3	-58.3	11.1	66 25.1	-58.2	11.5	67 23.8	-58.0	12.0	40
41	63 29.0	-58.5	10.2	64 28.0	-58.4	10.5	65 26.9	-58.3	10.9	66 25.8	-58.2	11.4	41
42	62 30.5	-58.6	9.7	63 29.6	-58.5	10.0	64 28.6	-58.4	10.4	65 27.6	-58.3	10.8	42
43	61 31.9	-58.7	9.2	62 31.1	-58.6	9.5	63 30.2	-58.5	9.9	64 29.3	-58.4	10.2	43
44	60 33.2	-58.8	8.8	61 32.5	-58.7	9.1	62 31.7	-58.6	9.4	63 30.9	-58.6	9.7	44
45	59 34.4	-58.8	8.4	60 33.8	-58.8	8.6	61 33.1	-58.7	8.9	62 32.3	-58.6	9.2	45
46	58 35.6	-58.9	8.0	59 35.0	-58.8	8.2	60 34.4	-58.8	8.5	61 33.7	-58.7	8.8	46
47	57 36.7	-58.9	7.6	58 36.2	-58.9	7.9	59 35.6	-58.9	8.1	60 35.0	-58.8	8.3	47
48	56 37.8	-59.0	7.3	57 37.3	-59.0	7.5	58 36.7	-58.9	7.7	59 36.2	-58.9	7.9	48
49	55 38.8	-59.1	7.0	56 38.3	-59.0	7.2	57 37.8	-59.0	7.4	58 37.3	-58.9	7.6	49
50	54 39.7	-59.1	6.7	55 39.3	-59.1	6.8	56 38.8	-59.0	7.0	57 38.4	-59.0	7.2	50
51	53 40.6	-59.1	6.4	54 40.2	-59.1	6.5	55 39.8	-59.1	6.7	56 39.4	-59.0	6.9	51
52	52 41.5	-59.2	6.1	53 41.1	-59.1	6.2	54 40.7	-59.1	6.4	55 40.4	-59.1	6.6	52
53	51 42.3	-59.2	5.8	52 42.0	-59.2	6.0	53 41.6	-59.1	6.1	54 41.3	-59.1	6.2	53
54	50 43.1	-59.3	5.6	51 42.8	-59.3	5.7	52 42.5	-59.2	5.8	53 42.2	-59.2	6.0	54
55	49 43.8	-59.3	5.3	50 43.5	-59.2	5.4	51 43.3	-59.3	5.6	52 43.0	-59.2	5.7	55
56	48 44.5	-59.3	5.1	49 44.3	-59.3	5.2	50 44.0	-59.2	5.3	51 43.8	-59.3	5.4	56
57	47 45.2	-59.3	4.9	48 45.0	-59.3	5.0	49 44.8	-59.3	5.1	50 44.5	-59.2	5.2	57
58	46 45.9	-59.4	4.6	47 45.7	-59.3	4.7	48 45.5	-59.3	4.8	49 45.3	-59.3	4.9	58
59	45 46.5	-59.3	4.4	46 46.4	-59.4	4.5	47 46.2	-59.4	4.6	48 46.0	-59.4	4.7	59
60	44 47.2	-59.4	4.2	45 47.0	-59.4	4.3	46 46.8	-59.3	4.4	47 46.6	-59.3	4.5	60
61	43 47.8	-59.5	4.0	44 47.6	-59.4	4.1	45 47.5	-59.4	4.2	46 47.3	-59.4	4.2	61
62	42 48.3	-59.4	3.8	43 48.2	-59.4	3.9	44 48.1	-59.4	4.0	45 47.9	-59.4	4.0	62
63	41 48.9	-59.5	3.7	42 48.8	-59.5	3.7	43 48.7	-59.5	3.8	44 48.5	-59.4	3.8	63
64	40 49.4	-59.4	3.5	41 49.3	-59.4	3.5	42 49.2	-59.4	3.6	43 49.1	-59.4	3.6	64
65	39 50.0	-59.5	3.3	40 49.9	-59.5	3.3	41 49.8	-59.5	3.4	42 49.7	-59.5	3.5	65
66	38 50.5	-59.5	3.1	39 50.4	-59.5	3.2	40 50.3	-59.5	3.2	41 50.2	-59.5	3.3	66
67	37 51.0	-59.5	3.0	38 50.9	-59.5	3.0	39 50.8	-59.5	3.0	40 50.7	-59.4	3.1	67
68	36 51.5	-59.6	2.8	37 51.4	-59.5	2.8	38 51.3	-59.5	2.9	39 51.3	-59.6	2.9	68
69	35 51.9	-59.5	2.6	36 51.9	-59.5	2.7	37 51.8	-59.5	2.7	38 51.7	-59.5	2.8	69
70	34 52.4	-59.5	2.5	35 52.4	-59.6	2.5	36 52.3	-59.5	2.6	37 52.2	-59.5	2.6	70
71	33 52.9	-59.6	2.3	34 52.8	-59.5	2.4	35 52.8	-59.6	2.4	36 52.7	-59.5	2.4	71
72	32 53.3	-59.6	2.2	33 53.3	-59.6	2.2	34 53.2	-59.5	2.3	35 53.2	-59.6	2.3	72
73	31 53.7	-59.5	2.1	32 53.7	-59.6	2.1	33 53.7	-59.6	2.1	34 53.6	-59.6	2.1	73
74	30 54.2	-59.6	1.9	31 54.1	-59.6	1.9	32 54.1	-59.6	2.0	33 54.0	-59.5	2.0	74
75	29 54.6	-59.6	1.8	30 54.5	-59.6	1.8	31 54.5	-59.6	1.8	32 54.5	-59.6	1.8	75
76	28 55.0	-59.6	1.7	29 54.9	-59.6	1.7	30 54.9	-59.6	1.7	31 54.9	-59.6	1.7	76
77	27 55.4	-59.6	1.5	28 55.3	-59.6	1.5	29 55.3	-59.6	1.6	30 55.3	-59.6	1.6	77
78	26 55.8	-59.7	1.4	27 55.7	-59.6	1.4	28 55.7	-59.6	1.4	29 55.7	-59.6	1.4	78
79	25 56.1	-59.6	1.3	26 56.1	-59.6	1.3	27 56.1	-59.6	1.3	28 56.1	-59.6	1.3	79
80	24 56.5	-59.6	1.1	25 56.5	-59.6	1.2	26 56.5	-59.6	1.2	27 56.5	-59.6	1.2	80
81	23 56.9	-59.6	1.0	24 56.9	-59.7	1.0	25 56.9	-59.7	1.0	26 56.9	-59.7	1.1	81
82	22 57.3	-59.7	0.9	23 57.2	-59.6	0.9	24 57.2	-59.6	0.9	25 57.2	-59.6	0.9	82
83	21 57.6	-59.6	0.8	22 57.6	-59.6	0.8	23 57.6	-59.6	0.8	24 57.6	-59.6	0.8	83
84	20 58.0	-59.7	0.7	21 58.0	-59.7	0.7	22 58.0	-59.7	0.7	23 58.0	-59.7	0.7	84
85	19 58.3	-59.6	0.6	20 58.3	-59.6	0.6	21 58.3	-59.6	0.6	22 58.3	-59.6	0.6	85
86	18 58.7	-59.7	0.4	19 58.7	-59.7	0.4	20 58.7	-59.7	0.4	21 58.7	-59.7	0.5	86
87	17 59.0	-59.7	0.3	18 59.0	-59.7	0.3	19 59.0	-59.7	0.3	20 59.0	-59.7	0.3	87
88	16 59.3	-59.6	0.2	17 59.3	-59.6	0.2	18 59.3	-59.6	0.2	19 59.3	-59.6	0.2	88
89	15 59.7	-59.7	0.1	16 59.7	-59.7	0.1	17 59.7	-59.7	0.1	18 59.7	-59.7	0.1	89
90	15 00.0	-59.7	0.0	16 00.0	-59.7	0.0	17 00.0	-59.7	0.0	18 00.0	-59.7	0.0	90
	15°			16°			17°			18°			

Dec.	19° Hc	d	Z	20° Hc	d	Z	21° Hc	d	Z	22° Hc	d	Z	Dec.
°	° ′	′	°	° ′	′	°	° ′	′	°	° ′	′	°	°
0	70 06.5	+57.3	162.1	69 09.3	+57.5	162.9	68 11.8	+57.8	163.7	67 14.1	+58.0	164.3	0
1	71 03.8	+57.0	161.2	70 06.8	+57.4	162.1	69 09.6	+57.6	162.9	68 12.1	+57.9	163.7	1
2	72 00.8	+56.7	160.2	71 04.2	+57.0	161.2	70 07.2	+57.4	162.1	69 10.0	+57.6	162.9	2
3	72 57.5	+56.2	159.1	72 01.2	+56.7	160.2	71 04.6	+57.0	161.2	70 07.6	+57.4	162.1	3
4	73 53.7	+55.9	157.9	72 57.9	+56.3	159.1	72 01.6	+56.8	160.2	71 05.0	+57.1	161.2	4
5	74 49.6	+55.2	156.6	73 54.2	+55.9	157.9	72 58.4	+56.3	159.2	72 02.1	+56.8	160.3	5
6	75 44.8	+54.6	155.0	74 50.1	+55.3	156.6	73 54.7	+56.0	158.0	72 58.9	+56.4	159.2	6
7	76 39.4	+53.8	153.3	75 45.4	+54.7	155.1	74 50.7	+55.3	156.6	73 55.3	+56.0	158.0	7
8	77 33.2	+52.8	151.3	76 40.1	+53.8	153.3	75 46.0	+54.8	155.1	74 51.3	+55.4	156.7	8
9	78 26.0	+51.5	149.0	77 33.9	+52.9	151.3	76 40.8	+53.9	153.4	75 46.7	+54.8	155.2	9
10	79 17.5	+50.0	146.4	78 26.8	+51.6	149.1	77 34.7	+52.9	151.4	76 41.5	+54.0	153.4	10
11	80 07.5	+47.9•	143.3	79 18.4	+50.1	146.4	78 27.6	+51.8	149.1	77 35.5	+53.0	151.5	11
12	80 55.4	+45.4•	139.6	80 08.5	+48.0•	143.3	79 19.4	+50.1	146.5	78 28.5	+51.8	149.2	12
13	81 40.8	+42.0•	135.3	80 56.5	+45.5•	139.7	80 09.5	+48.2•	143.4	79 20.3	+50.3	146.6	13
14	82 22.8	+37.6•	130.1	81 42.0	+42.2•	135.4	80 57.7	+45.6•	139.8	80 10.6	+48.3•	143.5	14
15	83 00.4	+32.0•	124.0	82 24.2	+37.8•	130.2	81 43.3	+42.3•	135.5	80 58.9	+45.8•	139.9	15
16	83 32.4	+24.8•	116.7	83 02.0	+32.1•	124.1	82 25.6	+38.0•	130.3	81 44.7	+42.5•	135.6	16
17	83 57.2	+16.2•	108.4	83 34.1	+25.0•	116.8	83 03.6	+32.3•	124.2	82 27.2	+38.1•	130.4	17
18	84 13.4	+6.2•	99.0	83 59.1	+16.3•	108.4	83 35.9	+25.2•	116.9	83 05.3	+32.5•	124.3	18
19	84 19.6	-4.2•	89.0	84 15.4	+6.3•	99.0	84 01.1	+16.4•	108.5	83 37.8	+25.4•	117.0	19
20	84 15.4	-14.3•	79.0	84 21.7	-4.2•	89.0	84 17.5	+6.4•	99.0	84 03.2	+16.5•	108.6	20
21	84 01.1	-23.3•	69.5	84 17.5	-14.3•	78.9	84 23.9	-4.2•	88.9	84 19.7	+6.5•	99.0	21
22	83 37.8	-30.7•	60.9	84 03.2	-23.4•	69.3	84 19.7	-14.4•	78.8	84 26.2	-4.1•	88.9	22
23	83 07.1	-36.6•	53.4	83 39.8	-30.8•	60.7	84 05.3	-23.4•	69.1	84 22.1	-14.5•	78.6	23
24	82 30.5	-41.3•	47.1	83 09.0	-36.8•	53.2	83 41.9	-31.0•	60.5	84 07.6	-23.6•	68.9	24
25	81 49.2	-44.7•	41.7	82 32.2	-41.3•	46.8	83 10.9	-36.8•	52.9	83 44.0	-31.0•	60.2	25
26	81 04.5	-47.5•	37.3	81 50.9	-44.9•	41.5	82 34.1	-41.5•	46.6	83 13.0	-37.1•	52.7	26
27	80 17.0	-49.6	33.5	81 06.0	-47.6•	37.0	81 52.6	-45.0•	41.2	82 35.9	-41.6•	46.3	27
28	79 27.4	-51.3	30.3	80 18.4	-49.7	33.2	81 07.6	-47.7•	36.7	81 54.3	-45.1•	41.0	28
29	78 36.1	-52.6	27.6	79 28.7	-51.3	30.0	80 19.9	-49.8	33.0	81 09.2	-47.8•	36.5	29
30	77 43.5	-53.6	25.2	78 37.4	-52.7	27.3	79 30.1	-51.4	29.8	80 21.4	-49.9	32.7	30
31	76 49.9	-54.4	23.2	77 44.7	-53.6	25.0	78 38.7	-52.7	27.1	79 31.5	-51.5	29.5	31
32	75 55.5	-55.2	21.4	76 51.1	-54.5	22.9	77 46.0	-53.8	24.7	78 40.0	-52.8	26.8	32
33	75 00.3	-55.7	19.8	75 56.6	-55.2	21.2	76 52.2	-54.5	22.7	77 47.2	-53.8	24.5	33
34	74 04.6	-56.2	18.4	75 01.4	-55.8	19.6	75 57.7	-55.3	20.9	76 53.4	-54.6	22.5	34
35	73 08.4	-56.6	17.2	74 05.6	-56.2	18.2	75 02.4	-55.8	19.4	75 58.8	-55.3	20.7	35
36	72 11.8	-56.9	16.1	73 09.4	-56.7	17.0	74 06.6	-56.3	18.0	75 03.5	-55.9	19.1	36
37	71 14.9	-57.2	15.1	72 12.7	-57.0	15.9	73 10.3	-56.7	16.8	74 07.6	-56.3	17.8	37
38	70 17.7	-57.5	14.1	71 15.7	-57.2	14.9	72 13.6	-57.0	15.7	73 11.3	-56.7	16.5	38
39	69 20.2	-57.7	13.3	70 18.5	-57.5	14.0	71 16.6	-57.3	14.7	72 14.6	-57.1	15.4	39
40	68 22.5	-57.9	12.5	69 21.0	-57.8	13.1	70 19.3	-57.5	13.8	71 17.5	-57.3	14.5	40
41	67 24.6	-58.1	11.9	68 23.2	-57.9	12.4	69 21.8	-57.8	12.9	70 20.2	-57.6	13.6	41
42	66 26.5	-58.2	11.2	67 25.3	-58.1	11.7	68 24.0	-57.9	12.2	69 22.6	-57.8	12.7	42
43	65 28.3	-58.3	10.6	66 27.2	-58.2	11.0	67 26.1	-58.1	11.5	68 24.8	-57.9	12.0	43
44	64 30.0	-58.5	10.1	65 29.0	-58.3	10.4	66 28.0	-58.3	10.9	67 26.9	-58.2	11.3	44
45	63 31.5	-58.5	9.5	64 30.7	-58.5	9.9	65 29.7	-58.3	10.3	66 28.7	-58.2	10.7	45
46	62 33.0	-58.7	9.1	63 32.2	-58.6	9.4	64 31.4	-58.5	9.7	65 30.5	-58.4	10.1	46
47	61 34.3	-58.7	8.6	62 33.6	-58.7	8.9	63 32.9	-58.6	9.2	64 32.1	-58.5	9.5	47
48	60 35.6	-58.8	8.2	61 34.9	-58.7	8.5	62 34.3	-58.7	8.7	63 33.6	-58.7	9.0	48
49	59 36.8	-58.9	7.8	60 36.2	-58.8	8.0	61 35.6	-58.8	8.3	62 34.9	-58.7	8.6	49
50	58 37.9	-58.9	7.4	59 37.4	-58.9	7.6	60 36.8	-58.8	7.9	61 36.2	-58.7	8.1	50
51	57 39.0	-59.0	7.1	58 38.5	-59.0	7.3	59 38.0	-58.9	7.5	60 37.5	-58.9	7.7	51
52	56 40.0	-59.1	6.7	57 39.5	-59.0	6.9	58 39.1	-59.0	7.1	59 38.6	-58.9	7.3	52
53	55 40.9	-59.1	6.4	56 40.5	-59.0	6.6	57 40.1	-59.0	6.8	58 39.7	-59.0	6.9	53
54	54 41.8	-59.1	6.1	55 41.5	-59.1	6.3	56 41.1	-59.1	6.4	57 40.7	-59.0	6.6	54
55	53 42.7	-59.2	5.8	54 42.4	-59.2	6.0	55 42.0	-59.1	6.1	56 41.7	-59.1	6.3	55
56	52 43.5	-59.2	5.5	53 43.2	-59.2	5.7	54 42.9	-59.1	5.8	55 42.6	-59.1	6.0	56
57	51 44.3	-59.3	5.3	52 44.0	-59.2	5.4	53 43.8	-59.2	5.5	54 43.5	-59.2	5.7	57
58	50 45.0	-59.2	5.0	51 44.8	-59.2	5.1	52 44.6	-59.3	5.2	53 44.3	-59.2	5.4	58
59	49 45.8	-59.3	4.8	50 45.6	-59.3	4.9	51 45.3	-59.2	5.0	52 45.1	-59.2	5.1	59
60	48 46.5	-59.4	4.5	49 46.3	-59.3	4.6	50 46.1	-59.3	4.7	51 45.9	-59.3	4.8	60
61	47 47.1	-59.3	4.3	48 47.0	-59.4	4.4	49 46.8	-59.4	4.5	50 46.6	-59.3	4.6	61
62	46 47.8	-59.4	4.1	47 47.6	-59.4	4.2	48 47.4	-59.3	4.3	49 47.3	-59.4	4.4	62
63	45 48.4	-59.4	3.9	46 48.2	-59.3	4.0	47 48.1	-59.4	4.1	48 47.9	-59.3	4.1	63
64	44 49.0	-59.4	3.7	45 48.9	-59.5	3.8	46 48.7	-59.4	3.8	47 48.6	-59.4	3.9	64
65	43 49.6	-59.5	3.5	44 49.4	-59.4	3.6	45 49.3	-59.4	3.6	46 49.2	-59.4	3.7	65
66	42 50.1	-59.5	3.3	43 50.0	-59.4	3.4	44 49.9	-59.4	3.4	45 49.8	-59.4	3.5	66
67	41 50.6	-59.4	3.1	42 50.6	-59.5	3.2	43 50.5	-59.5	3.2	44 50.4	-59.5	3.3	67
68	40 51.2	-59.5	3.0	41 51.1	-59.5	3.0	42 51.0	-59.5	3.1	43 50.9	-59.4	3.1	68
69	39 51.7	-59.5	2.8	40 51.6	-59.5	2.8	41 51.5	-59.5	2.9	42 51.5	-59.5	2.9	69
70	38 52.2	-59.6	2.6	39 52.1	-59.5	2.7	40 52.0	-59.5	2.7	41 52.0	-59.5	2.8	70
71	37 52.6	-59.5	2.5	38 52.6	-59.5	2.5	39 52.5	-59.5	2.5	40 52.5	-59.5	2.6	71
72	36 53.1	-59.5	2.3	37 53.1	-59.6	2.3	38 53.0	-59.5	2.4	39 53.0	-59.6	2.4	72
73	35 53.6	-59.6	2.2	36 53.5	-59.5	2.2	37 53.5	-59.6	2.2	38 53.4	-59.5	2.3	73
74	34 54.0	-59.6	2.0	35 54.0	-59.6	2.0	36 53.9	-59.5	2.1	37 53.9	-59.6	2.1	74
75	33 54.4	-59.5	1.9	34 54.4	-59.6	1.9	35 54.4	-59.6	1.9	36 54.3	-59.5	1.9	75
76	32 54.9	-59.6	1.7	33 54.8	-59.5	1.7	34 54.8	-59.6	1.8	35 54.8	-59.6	1.8	76
77	31 55.3	-59.6	1.6	32 55.3	-59.6	1.6	33 55.2	-59.6	1.6	34 55.2	-59.6	1.6	77
78	30 55.7	-59.6	1.5	31 55.7	-59.6	1.5	32 55.6	-59.6	1.5	33 55.6	-59.6	1.5	78
79	29 56.1	-59.6	1.3	30 56.1	-59.6	1.3	31 56.0	-59.6	1.3	32 56.0	-59.6	1.4	79
80	28 56.5	-59.7	1.2	29 56.5	-59.7	1.2	30 56.4	-59.6	1.2	31 56.4	-59.6	1.2	80
81	27 56.8	-59.6	1.1	28 56.8	-59.6	1.1	29 56.8	-59.6	1.1	30 56.8	-59.6	1.1	81
82	26 57.2	-59.6	0.9	27 57.2	-59.6	0.9	28 57.2	-59.6	1.0	29 57.2	-59.6	1.0	82
83	25 57.6	-59.7	0.8	26 57.6	-59.7	0.8	27 57.6	-59.7	0.8	28 57.6	-59.7	0.8	83
84	24 57.9	-59.6	0.7	25 57.9	-59.6	0.7	26 57.9	-59.6	0.7	27 57.9	-59.6	0.7	84
85	23 58.3	-59.6	0.6	24 58.3	-59.7	0.6	25 58.3	-59.7	0.6	26 58.3	-59.7	0.6	85
86	22 58.7	-59.7	0.5	23 58.6	-59.6	0.5	24 58.6	-59.6	0.5	25 58.6	-59.6	0.5	86
87	21 59.0	-59.7	0.3	22 59.0	-59.7	0.3	23 59.0	-59.7	0.3	24 59.0	-59.7	0.3	87
88	20 59.3	-59.6	0.2	21 59.3	-59.6	0.2	22 59.3	-59.6	0.2	23 59.3	-59.6	0.2	88
89	19 59.7	-59.7	0.1	20 59.7	-59.7	0.1	21 59.7	-59.7	0.1	22 59.7	-59.7	0.1	89
90	19 00.0	-59.7	0.0	20 00.0	-59.7	0.0	21 00.0	-59.7	0.0	22 00.0	-59.7	0.0	90
	19°			20°			21°			22°			

LATITUDE CONTRARY NAME TO DECLINATION L.H.A. 6°, 354°

Dec.	15° Hc	d	Z	16° Hc	d	Z	17° Hc	d	Z	18° Hc	d	Z	19° Hc	d	Z	20° Hc	d	Z	21° Hc	d	Z	22° Hc	d	Z	Dec.
°	° ′	′	°	° ′	′	°	° ′	′	°	° ′	′	°	° ′	′	°	° ′	′	°	° ′	′	°	° ′	′	°	°
0	73 52.2	-56.1	157.9	72 56.4	-56.6	159.1	72 00.1	-56.9	160.2	71 03.5	-57.3	161.2	70 06.5	-57.5	162.1	69 09.3	-57.8	162.9	68 11.8	-58.0	163.7	67 14.1	-58.1	164.3	0
1	72 56.1	-56.5	159.1	71 59.8	-56.9	160.2	71 03.2	-57.3	161.2	70 06.2	-57.5	162.1	69 09.0	-57.8	162.9	68 11.5	-57.9	163.7	67 13.8	-58.1	164.3	66 16.0	-58.3	164.9	1
2	71 59.6	-56.9	160.2	71 02.9	-57.2	161.2	70 05.9	-57.4	162.1	69 08.7	-57.7	162.9	68 11.2	-57.9	163.7	67 13.6	-58.2	164.3	66 15.7	-58.3	165.0	65 17.7	-58.4	165.5	2
3	71 02.7	-57.2	161.3	70 05.7	-57.4	162.1	69 08.5	-57.7	163.0	68 11.0	-57.9	163.7	67 13.3	-58.1	164.4	66 15.4	-58.2	165.0	65 17.4	-58.4	165.5	64 19.3	-58.6	166.1	3
4	70 05.5	-57.4	162.2	69 08.3	-57.7	163.0	68 10.8	-57.9	163.7	67 13.1	-58.1	164.4	66 15.2	-58.2	165.0	65 17.2	-58.4	165.6	64 19.0	-58.5	166.1	63 20.7	-58.6	166.6	4
5	69 08.1	-57.7	163.0	68 10.6	-57.9	163.7	67 12.9	-58.0	164.4	66 15.0	-58.2	165.0	65 17.0	-58.4	165.6	64 18.8	-58.5	166.1	63 20.5	-58.6	166.6	62 22.1	-58.7	167.0	5
6	68 10.4	-57.8	163.8	67 12.7	-58.0	164.4	66 14.9	-58.2	165.0	65 16.8	-58.3	165.6	64 18.6	-58.4	166.1	63 20.3	-58.6	166.6	62 21.9	-58.7	167.0	61 23.4	-58.8	167.5	6
7	67 12.6	-58.0	164.5	66 14.7	-58.2	165.1	65 16.7	-58.4	165.6	64 18.5	-58.5	166.2	63 20.2	-58.6	166.6	62 21.7	-58.7	167.1	61 23.2	-58.8	167.5	60 24.6	-58.9	167.9	7
8	66 14.6	-58.2	165.1	65 16.5	-58.3	165.7	64 18.3	-58.4	166.2	63 20.0	-58.5	166.7	62 21.6	-58.7	167.1	61 23.0	-58.7	167.5	60 24.4	-58.8	167.9	59 25.7	-58.9	168.3	8
9	65 16.4	-58.2	165.7	64 18.2	-58.4	166.2	63 19.9	-58.5	166.7	62 21.5	-58.7	167.1	61 22.9	-58.7	167.6	60 24.3	-58.9	167.9	59 25.6	-58.9	168.3	58 26.8	-59.0	168.6	9
10	64 18.2	-58.5	166.3	63 19.8	-58.5	166.7	62 21.4	-58.7	167.2	61 22.8	-58.7	167.6	60 24.2	-58.9	168.0	59 25.4	-58.9	168.3	58 26.7	-59.0	168.7	57 27.8	-59.1	169.0	10
11	63 19.7	-58.5	166.8	62 21.3	-58.6	167.2	61 22.7	-58.7	167.6	60 24.1	-58.8	168.0	59 25.3	-58.8	168.4	58 26.5	-58.9	168.7	57 27.7	-59.1	169.0	56 28.7	-59.0	169.3	11
12	62 21.2	-58.6	167.3	61 22.7	-58.7	167.7	60 24.0	-58.8	168.1	59 25.3	-58.9	168.4	58 26.5	-59.0	168.7	57 27.6	-59.0	169.0	56 28.6	-59.0	169.3	55 29.7	-59.2	169.6	12
13	61 22.6	-58.7	167.7	60 24.0	-58.8	168.1	59 25.2	-58.9	168.5	58 26.4	-58.9	168.8	57 27.5	-59.0	169.1	56 28.6	-59.1	169.4	55 29.6	-59.2	169.6	54 30.5	-59.2	169.9	13
14	60 23.9	-58.7	168.2	59 25.2	-58.9	168.5	58 26.3	-58.9	168.8	57 27.5	-59.0	169.1	56 28.5	-59.1	169.4	55 29.5	-59.1	169.7	54 30.4	-59.1	169.9	53 31.3	-59.2	170.2	14
15	59 25.2	-58.9	168.6	58 26.3	-58.9	168.9	57 27.4	-59.0	169.2	56 28.5	-59.1	169.5	55 29.4	-59.1	169.7	54 30.4	-59.2	170.0	53 31.3	-59.2	170.2	52 32.1	-59.2	170.4	15
16	58 26.3	-58.9	168.9	57 27.4	-59.0	169.2	56 28.4	-59.0	169.5	55 29.4	-59.1	169.8	54 30.3	-59.1	170.0	53 31.2	-59.2	170.3	52 32.1	-59.3	170.5	51 32.9	-59.3	170.7	16
17	57 27.4	-58.9	169.3	56 28.4	-59.0	169.6	55 29.4	-59.1	169.8	54 30.3	-59.1	170.1	53 31.2	-59.2	170.3	52 32.0	-59.2	170.5	51 32.8	-59.2	170.7	50 33.6	-59.3	170.9	17
18	56 28.5	-59.1	169.6	55 29.4	-59.1	169.9	54 30.3	-59.1	170.1	53 31.2	-59.2	170.4	52 32.0	-59.2	170.6	51 32.8	-59.3	170.8	50 33.6	-59.3	171.0	49 34.3	-59.4	171.2	18
19	55 29.4	-59.0	170.0	54 30.3	-59.1	170.2	53 31.2	-59.2	170.4	52 32.0	-59.2	170.6	51 32.8	-59.3	170.9	50 33.5	-59.3	171.0	49 34.3	-59.4	171.2	48 34.9	-59.3	171.4	19
20	54 30.4	-59.1	170.3	53 31.2	-59.1	170.5	52 32.0	-59.2	170.7	51 32.8	-59.2	170.9	50 33.5	-59.2	171.1	49 34.2	-59.3	171.3	48 34.9	-59.3	171.5	47 35.6	-59.4	171.6	20
21	53 31.3	-59.2	170.6	52 32.1	-59.2	170.8	51 32.8	-59.2	171.0	50 33.6	-59.3	171.2	49 34.3	-59.4	171.3	48 34.9	-59.3	171.5	47 35.6	-59.4	171.7	46 36.2	-59.4	171.8	21
22	52 32.1	-59.2	170.8	51 32.9	-59.3	171.0	50 33.6	-59.3	171.2	49 34.3	-59.3	171.4	48 34.9	-59.3	171.6	47 35.6	-59.4	171.7	46 36.2	-59.4	171.9	45 36.8	-59.5	172.0	22
23	51 32.9	-59.2	171.1	50 33.6	-59.2	171.3	49 34.3	-59.3	171.5	48 35.0	-59.4	171.6	47 35.6	-59.4	171.8	46 36.2	-59.4	171.9	45 36.8	-59.4	172.1	44 37.3	-59.4	172.2	23
24	50 33.7	-59.2	171.4	49 34.4	-59.3	171.5	48 35.0	-59.3	171.7	47 35.6	-59.3	171.9	46 36.2	-59.4	172.0	45 36.8	-59.4	172.2	44 37.4	-59.5	172.3	43 37.9	-59.5	172.4	24
25	49 34.5	-59.3	171.6	48 35.1	-59.3	171.8	47 35.7	-59.3	171.9	46 36.3	-59.4	172.1	45 36.8	-59.4	172.2	44 37.4	-59.4	172.4	43 37.9	-59.4	172.5	42 38.4	-59.5	172.6	25
26	48 35.2	-59.3	171.8	47 35.8	-59.4	172.0	46 36.4	-59.4	172.1	45 36.9	-59.4	172.3	44 37.4	-59.4	172.4	43 38.0	-59.5	172.5	42 38.5	-59.5	172.7	41 38.9	-59.5	172.8	26
27	47 35.9	-59.4	172.1	46 36.4	-59.3	172.2	45 37.0	-59.4	172.3	44 37.5	-59.4	172.5	43 38.0	-59.4	172.6	42 38.5	-59.5	172.7	41 39.0	-59.5	172.8	40 39.4	-59.5	172.9	27
28	46 36.5	-59.3	172.3	45 37.1	-59.4	172.4	44 37.6	-59.4	172.5	43 38.1	-59.5	172.7	42 38.6	-59.5	172.8	41 39.0	-59.5	172.9	40 39.5	-59.5	173.0	39 39.9	-59.5	173.1	28
29	45 37.2	-59.4	172.5	44 37.7	-59.4	172.6	43 38.2	-59.5	172.7	42 38.6	-59.4	172.9	41 39.1	-59.5	173.0	40 39.5	-59.5	173.1	39 40.0	-59.5	173.2	38 40.4	-59.5	173.3	29
30	44 37.8	-59.4	172.7	43 38.3	-59.5	172.8	42 38.7	-59.4	172.9	41 39.2	-59.5	173.0	40 39.6	-59.5	173.1	39 40.0	-59.5	173.2	38 40.5	-59.6	173.3	37 40.9	-59.6	173.4	30
31	43 38.4	-59.4	172.9	42 38.8	-59.4	173.0	41 39.3	-59.5	173.1	40 39.7	-59.5	173.2	39 40.1	-59.5	173.3	38 40.5	-59.5	173.4	37 40.9	-59.5	173.5	36 41.3	-59.6	173.6	31
32	42 39.0	-59.5	173.1	41 39.4	-59.5	173.2	40 39.8	-59.5	173.3	39 40.2	-59.5	173.4	38 40.6	-59.5	173.5	37 41.0	-59.5	173.6	36 41.4	-59.6	173.7	35 41.7	-59.5	173.7	32
33	41 39.5	-59.4	173.3	40 39.9	-59.4	173.4	39 40.3	-59.5	173.5	38 40.7	-59.5	173.6	37 41.1	-59.5	173.6	36 41.5	-59.6	173.7	35 41.8	-59.6	173.8	34 42.2	-59.6	173.9	33
34	40 40.1	-59.5	173.4	39 40.5	-59.5	173.5	38 40.8	-59.5	173.6	37 41.2	-59.5	173.7	36 41.6	-59.6	173.8	35 41.9	-59.6	173.9	34 42.2	-59.5	173.9	33 42.6	-59.6	174.0	34
35	39 40.6	-59.5	173.6	38 41.0	-59.5	173.7	37 41.3	-59.5	173.8	36 41.7	-59.6	173.9	35 42.0	-59.6	173.9	34 42.3	-59.5	174.0	33 42.7	-59.6	174.1	32 43.0	-59.6	174.2	35
36	38 41.1	-59.5	173.8	37 41.5	-59.6	173.9	36 41.8	-59.5	173.9	35 42.1	-59.5	174.0	34 42.4	-59.5	174.1	33 42.8	-59.6	174.2	32 43.1	-59.6	174.2	31 43.4	-59.6	174.3	36
37	37 41.6	-59.5	173.9	36 41.9	-59.5	174.0	35 42.3	-59.6	174.1	34 42.6	-59.6	174.2	33 42.9	-59.6	174.2	32 43.2	-59.6	174.3	31 43.5	-59.6	174.4	30 43.8	-59.7	174.4	37
38	36 42.1	-59.5	174.1	35 42.4	-59.5	174.2	34 42.7	-59.6	174.2	33 43.0	-59.6	174.3	32 43.3	-59.6	174.4	31 43.6	-59.6	174.4	30 43.9	-59.7	174.5	29 44.1	-59.6	174.6	38
39	35 42.6	-59.6	174.3	34 42.9	-59.6	174.3	33 43.1	-59.5	174.4	32 43.4	-59.6	174.5	31 43.7	-59.6	174.5	30 44.0	-59.6	174.6	29 44.2	-59.6	174.6	28 44.5	-59.6	174.7	39
40	34 43.0	-59.5	174.4	33 43.3	-59.6	174.5	32 43.6	-59.6	174.5	31 43.8	-59.5	174.6	30 44.1	-59.6	174.7	29 44.4	-59.7	174.7	28 44.6	-59.6	174.8	27 44.9	-59.7	174.8	40
41	33 43.5	-59.6	174.6	32 43.7	-59.5	174.6	31 44.0	-59.6	174.7	30 44.3	-59.6	174.7	29 44.5	-59.6	174.8	28 44.7	-59.6	174.8	27 45.0	-59.6	174.9	26 45.2	-59.6	174.9	41
42	32 43.9	-59.6	174.7	31 44.2	-59.6	174.8	30 44.4	-59.6	174.8	29 44.7	-59.7	174.9	28 44.9	-59.6	174.9	27 45.1	-59.6	175.0	26 45.4	-59.7	175.0	25 45.6	-59.7	175.1	42
43	31 44.3	-59.5	174.8	30 44.6	-59.6	174.9	29 44.8	-59.6	174.9	28 45.0	-59.6	175.0	27 45.3	-59.7	175.0	26 45.5	-59.6	175.1	25 45.7	-59.6	175.1	24 45.9	-59.6	175.2	43
44	30 44.8	-59.6	175.0	29 45.0	-59.6	175.0	28 45.2	-59.6	175.1	27 45.4	-59.6	175.1	26 45.6	-59.6	175.2	25 45.9	-59.7	175.2	24 46.1	-59.7	175.2	23 46.3	-59.7	175.3	44
45	29 45.2	-59.6	175.1	28 45.4	-59.6	175.2	27 45.6	-59.6	175.2	26 45.8	-59.6	175.3	25 46.0	-59.6	175.3	24 46.2	-59.6	175.3	23 46.4	-59.7	175.4	22 46.6	-59.7	175.4	45
46	28 45.6	-59.6	175.2	27 45.8	-59.6	175.3	26 46.0	-59.7	175.3	25 46.2	-59.7	175.4	24 46.4	-59.7	175.4	23 46.6	-59.7	175.4	22 46.7	-59.6	175.5	21 46.9	-59.6	175.5	46
47	27 46.0	-59.6	175.4	26 46.2	-59.7	175.4	25 46.3	-59.6	175.5	24 46.5	-59.6	175.5	23 46.7	-59.6	175.5	22 46.9	-59.7	175.6	21 47.1	-59.7	175.6	20 47.3	-59.7	175.6	47
48	26 46.4	-59.7	175.5	25 46.5	-59.6	175.5	24 46.7	-59.6	175.6	23 46.9	-59.7	175.6	22 47.1	-59.7	175.6	21 47.2	-59.6	175.7	20 47.4	-59.7	175.7	19 47.6	-59.7	175.7	48
49	25 46.7	-59.6	175.6	24 46.9	-59.6	175.7	23 47.1	-59.7	175.7	22 47.2	-59.6	175.7	21 47.4	-59.7	175.8	20 47.6	-59.7	175.8	19 47.7	-59.6	175.8	18 47.9	-59.7	175.8	49
50	24 47.1	-59.6	175.8	23 47.3	-59.7	175.8	22 47.4	-59.6	175.8	21 47.6	-59.7	175.9	20 47.7	-59.6	175.9	19 47.9	-59.7	175.9	18 48.1	-59.7	175.9	17 48.2	-59.7	176.0	50
51	23 47.5	-59.7	175.9	22 47.6	-59.6	175.9	21 47.8	-59.7	175.9	20 47.9	-59.6	176.0	19 48.1	-59.7	176.0	18 48.2	-59.6	176.0	17 48.4	-59.7	176.0	16 48.5	-59.7	176.1	51
52	22 47.8	-59.6	176.0	21 48.0	-59.7	176.0	20 48.1	-59.6	176.1	19 48.3	-59.7	176.1	18 48.4	-59.7	176.1	17 48.6	-59.7	176.1	16 48.7	-59.7	176.1	15 48.8	-59.7	176.2	52
53	21 48.2	-59.6	176.1	20 48.3	-59.6	176.1	19 48.5	-59.7	176.2	18 48.6	-59.7	176.2	17 48.7	-59.6	176.2	16 48.9	-59.7	176.2	15 49.0	-59.7	176.3	14 49.1	-59.7	176.3	53
54	20 48.6	-59.7	176.2	19 48.7	-59.7	176.3	18 48.8	-59.7	176.3	17 48.9	-59.6	176.3	16 49.1	-59.7	176.3	15 49.2	-59.7	176.3	14 49.3	-59.7	176.4	13 49.4	-59.7	176.4	54
55	19 48.9	-59.7	176.3	18 49.0	-59.6	176.4	17 49.1	-59.6	176.4	16 49.3	-59.7	176.4	15 49.4	-59.7	176.4	14 49.5	-59.7	176.4	13 49.6	-59.7	176.5	12 49.7	-59.7	176.5	55
56	18 49.2	-59.6	176.5	17 49.4	-59.7	176.5	16 49.5	-59.7	176.5	15 49.6	-59.7	176.5	14 49.7	-59.7	176.5	13 49.8	-59.7	176.5	12 49.9	-59.7	176.6	11 50.0	-59.7	176.6	56
57	17 49.6	-59.7	176.6	16 49.7	-59.7	176.6	15 49.8	-59.7	176.6	14 49.9	-59.7	176.6	13 50.0	-59.7	176.6	12 50.1	-59.7	176.7	11 50.2	-59.7	176.7	10 50.3	-59.7	176.7	57
58	16 49.9	-59.6	176.7	15 50.0	-59.6	176.7	14 50.1	-59.7	176.7	13 50.2	-59.7	176.7	12 50.3	-59.7	176.7	11 50.4	-59.7	176.8	10 50.5	-59.7	176.8	9 50.6	-59.7	176.8	58
59	15 50.3	-59.7	176.8	14 50.4	-59.7	176.8	13 50.4	-59.6	176.8	12 50.5	-59.7	176.8	11 50.6	-59.7	176.8	10 50.7	-59.7	176.9	9 50.8	-59.7	176.9	8 50.9	-59.7	176.9	59
60	14 50.6	-59.7	176.9	13 50.7	-59.7	176.9	12 50.8	-59.7	176.9	11 50.8	-59.6	176.9	10 50.9	-59.7	176.9	9 51.0	-59.7	177.0	8 51.1	-59.7	177.0	7 51.2	-59.7	177.0	60
61	13 50.9	-59.7	177.0	12 51.0	-59.7	177.0	11 51.1	-59.7	177.0	10 51.2	-59.7	177.0	9 51.2	-59.7	177.1	8 51.3	-59.7	177.1	7 51.4	-59.7	177.1	6 51.5	-59.7	177.1	61
62	12 51.2	-59.6	177.1	11 51.3	-59.7	177.1	10 51.4	-59.7	177.1	9 51.5	-59.7	177.1	8 51.5	-59.7	177.2	7 51.6	-59.7	177.2	6 51.7	-59.7	177.2	5 51.8	-59.8	177.2	62
63	11 51.6	-59.7	177.2	10 51.6	-59.7	177.2	9 51.7	-59.7	177.2	8 51.8	-59.7	177.2	7 51.8	-59.7	177.3	6 51.9	-59.7	177.3	5 52.0	-59.7	177.3	4 52.0	-59.7	177.3	63
64	10 51.9	-59.7	177.3	9 51.9	-59.6	177.3	8 52.0	-59.7	177.3	7 52.1	-59.7	177.3	6 52.1	-59.7	177.4	5 52.2	-59.7	177.4	4 52.3	-59.7	177.4	3 52.3	-59.7	177.4	64
65	9 52.2	-59.7	177.4	8 52.3	-59.7	177.4	7 52.3	-59.7	177.4	6 52.4	-59.7	177.4	5 52.4	-59.7	177.5	4 52.5	-59.7	177.5	3 52.6	-59.8	177.5	2 52.6	-59.7	177.5	65
66	8 52.5	-59.7	177.5	7 52.6	-59.7	177.5	6 52.6	-59.7	177.5	5 52.7	-59.7	177.6	4 52.7	-59.7	177.6	3 52.8	-59.7	177.6	2 52.8	-59.7	177.6	1 52.9	-59.7	177.6	66
67	7 52.8	-59.7	177.6	6 52.9	-59.7	177.6	5 52.9	-59.7	177.6	4 53.0	-59.7	177.7	3 53.0	-59.7	177.7	2 53.1	-59.7	177.7	1 53.1	-59.7	177.7	0 53.2	-59.7	177.7	67
68	6 53.1	-59.7	177.7	5 53.2	-59.7	177.7	4 53.2	-59.7	177.7	3 53.3	-59.7	177.8	2 53.3	-59.7	177.8	1 53.4	-59.7	177.8	0 53.4	-59.7	177.8	0 06.5	+59.8	2.2	68
69	5 53.4	-59.6	177.8	4 53.5	-59.7	177.8	3 53.5	-59.7	177.8	2 53.6	-59.7	177.9	1 53.6	-59.7	177.9	0 53.7	-59.8	177.9	0 06.3	+59.7	2.1	1 06.3	+59.7	2.1	69
70	4 53.8	-59.7	177.9	3 53.8	-59.7	177.9	2 53.8	-59.7	177.9	1 53.9	-59.7	178.0	0 53.9	-59.7	178.0	0 06.1	+59.7	2.0	1 06.0	+59.7	2.0	2 06.0	+59.7	2.1	70
71	3 54.1	-59.7	178.0	2 54.1	-59.7	178.0	1 54.1	-59.7	178.0	0 54.2	-59.7	178.0	0 05.8	+59.7	2.0	1 05.8	+59.7	2.0	2 05.7	+59.7	2.0	3 05.7	+59.7	2.0	71
72	2 54.4	-59.7	178.1	1 54.4	-59.7	178.1	0 54.4	-59.7	178.1	0 05.5	+59.7	1.9	1 05.5	+59.7	1.9	2 05.5	+59.7	1.9	3 05.4	+59.8	1.9	4 05.4	+59.7	1.9	72
73	1 54.7	-59.7	178.2	0 54.7	-59.7	178.2	0 05.3	+59.7	1.8	1 05.2	+59.7	1.8	2 05.2	+59.7	1.8	3 05.2	+59.7	1.8	4 05.2	+59.7	1.8	5 05.1	+59.7	1.8	73
74	0 55.0	-59.7	178.3	0 05.0	+59.7	1.7	1 05.0	+59.7	1.7	2 04.9	+59.7	1.7	3 04.9	+59.7	1.7	4 04.9	+59.7	1.7	5 04.9	+59.7	1.7	6 04.8	+59.8	1.7	74
75	0 04.7	+59.7	1.6	1 04.7	+59.7	1.6	2 04.7	+59.7	1.6	3 04.6	+59.7	1.6	4 04.6	+59.7	1.6	5 04.6	+59.7	1.6	6 04.6	+59.7	1.6	7 04.6	+59.7	1.6	75
76	1 04.4	+59.7	1.4	2 04.4	+59.7	1.4	3 04.4	+59.7	1.5	4 04.3	+59.7	1.5	5 04.3	+59.7	1.5	6 04.3	+59.7	1.5	7 04.3	+59.7	1.5	8 04.3	+59.7	1.5	76
77	2 04.1	+59.7	1.3	3 04.1	+59.7	1.3	4 04.1	+59.7	1.4	5 04.0	+59.7	1.4	6 04.0	+59.7	1.4	7 04.0	+59.7	1.4	8 04.0	+59.7	1.4	9 04.0	+59.7	1.4	77
78	3 03.8	+59.7	1.2	4 03.8	+59.7	1.2	5 03.8	+59.7	1.3	6 03.7	+59.7	1.3	7 03.7	+59.7	1.3	8 03.7	+59.7	1.3	9 03.7	+59.7	1.3	10 03.7	+59.7	1.3	78
79	4 03.5	+59.7	1.1	5 03.5	+59.7	1.1	6 03.5	+59.7	1.1	7 03.4	+59.7	1.2	8 03.4	+59.7	1.2	9 03.4	+59.7	1.2	10 03.4	+59.7	1.2	11 03.4	+59.7	1.2	79
80	5 03.2	+59.7	1.0	6 03.2	+59.7	1.0	7 03.2	+59.6	1.0	8 03.1	+59.7	1.1	9 03.1	+59.7	1.1	10 03.1	+59.7	1.1	11 03.1	+59.7	1.1	12 03.1	+59.7	1.1	80
81	6 02.9	+59.7	0.9	7 02.9	+59.6	0.9	8 02.8	+59.7	0.9	9 02.8	+59.7	0.9	10 02.8	+59.7	1.0	11 02.8	+59.7	1.0	12 02.8	+59.7	1.0	13 02.8	+59.7	1.0	81
82	7 02.6	+59.6	0.8	8 02.5	+59.7	0.8	9 02.5	+59.7	0.8	10 02.5	+59.7	0.8	11 02.5	+59.7	0.8	12 02.5	+59.7	0.9	13 02.5	+59.7	0.9	14 02.5	+59.7	0.9	82
83	8 02.2	+59.7	0.7	9 02.2	+59.7	0.7	10 02.2	+59.7	0.7	11 02.2	+59.7	0.7	12 02.2	+59.7	0.7	13 02.2	+59.7	0.7	14 02.2	+59.7	0.8	15 02.2	+59.7	0.8	83
84	9 01.9	+59.7	0.6	10 01.9	+59.7	0.6	11 01.9	+59.7	0.6	12 01.9	+59.7	0.6	13 01.9	+59.7	0.6	14 01.9	+59.7	0.6	15 01.9	+59.7	0.6	16 01.9	+59.7	0.7	84
85	10 01.6	+59.7	0.5	11 01.6	+59.7	0.5	12 01.6	+59.7	0.5	13 01.6	+59.7	0.5	14 01.6	+59.7	0.5	15 01.6	+59.7	0.5	16 01.6	+59.7	0.5	17 01.6	+59.7	0.5	85
86	11 01.3	+59.7	0.4	12 01.3	+59.7	0.4	13 01.3	+59.7	0.4	14 01.3	+59.7	0.4	15 01.3	+59.7	0.4	16 01.3	+59.7	0.4	17 01.3	+59.7	0.4	18 01.3	+59.7	0.4	86
87	12 01.0	+59.7	0.3	13 01.0	+59.7	0.3	14 01.0	+59.7	0.3	15 01.0	+59.7	0.3	16 01.0	+59.6	0.3	17 01.0	+59.6	0.3	18 01.0	+59.6	0.3	19 01.0	+59.6	0.3	87
88	13 00.7	+59.6	0.2	14 00.7	+59.6	0.2	15 00.7	+59.6	0.2	16 00.7	+59.7	0.2	17 00.6	+59.7	0.2	18 00.6	+59.7	0.2	19 00.6	+59.7	0.2	20 00.6	+59.7	0.2	88
89	14 00.3	+59.7	0.1	15 00.3	+59.7	0.1	16 00.3	+59.7	0.1	17 00.3	+59.7	0.1	18 00.3	+59.7	0.1	19 00.3	+59.7	0.1	20 00.3	+59.7	0.1	21 00.3	+59.7	0.1	89
90	15 00.0	+59.7	0.0	16 00.0	+59.7	0.0	17 00.0	+59.7	0.0	18 00.0	+59.7	0.0	19 00.0	+59.7	0.0	20 00.0	+59.7	0.0	21 00.0	+59.7	0.0	22 00.0	+59.7	0.0	90
	15°			16°			17°			18°			19°			20°			21°			22°			

S. Lat. {L.H.A. greater than 180° ....Zn=180°−Z; L.H.A. less than 180°............Zn=180°+Z}

LATITUDE SAME NAME AS DECLINATION L.H.A. 174°, 186°

Dec.	15°			16°			17°			18°			19°			20°			21°			22°			Dec.
	Hc	d	Z	Hc	d	Z	Hc	d	Z	Hc	d	Z	Hc	d	Z	Hc	d	Z	Hc	d	Z	Hc	d	Z	
°	° ′	′	°	° ′	′	°	° ′	′	°	° ′	′	°	° ′	′	°	° ′	′	°	° ′	′	°	° ′	′	°	°
0	73 28.9	+54.3	154.6	72 34.3	+55.0	156.0	71 39.3	+55.5	157.2	70 43.7	+56.0	158.3	69 47.8	+56.4	159.3	68 51.5	+56.7	160.3	67 54.9	+57.0	161.1	66 58.0	+57.3	161.9	0
1	74 23.2	+53.5	153.1	73 29.3	+54.3	154.6	72 34.8	+55.0	156.0	71 39.7	+55.6	157.2	70 44.2	+56.0	158.3	69 48.2	+56.5	159.3	68 51.9	+56.8	160.2	67 55.3	+57.1	161.1	1
2	75 16.7	+52.8	151.4	74 23.6	+53.7	153.1	73 29.8	+54.4	154.6	72 35.3	+55.0	156.0	71 40.2	+55.6	157.2	70 44.7	+56.0	158.3	69 48.7	+56.5	159.3	68 52.4	+56.8	160.3	2
3	76 09.5	+51.6	149.4	75 17.3	+52.8	151.4	74 24.2	+53.7	153.1	73 30.3	+54.5	154.6	72 35.8	+55.1	156.0	71 40.7	+55.7	157.2	70 45.2	+56.1	158.3	69 49.2	+56.6	159.3	3
4	77 01.1	+50.5	147.2	76 10.1	+51.7	149.4	75 17.9	+52.8	151.4	74 24.8	+53.7	153.1	73 30.9	+54.5	154.6	72 36.4	+55.2	156.0	71 41.3	+55.7	157.2	70 45.8	+56.1	158.3	4
5	77 51.6	+48.9	144.7	77 01.8	+50.5	147.3	76 10.7	+51.9	149.5	75 18.5	+53.0	151.4	74 25.4	+53.9	153.1	73 31.6	+54.5	154.7	72 37.0	+55.2	156.0	71 41.9	+55.8	157.3	5
6	78 40.5	+47.0•	141.9	77 52.3	+49.0	144.8	77 02.6	+50.6	147.3	76 11.5	+51.9	149.5	75 19.3	+53.0	151.4	74 26.1	+53.9	153.1	73 32.2	+54.7	154.7	72 37.7	+55.3	156.0	6
7	79 27.5	+44.7•	138.6	78 41.3	+47.2•	141.9	77 53.2	+49.1	144.8	77 03.4	+50.7	147.3	76 12.3	+52.0	149.5	75 20.0	+53.1	151.5	74 26.9	+54.0	153.2	73 33.0	+54.7	154.7	7
8	80 12.2	+41.7•	134.8	79 28.5	+44.7•	138.7	78 42.3	+47.2•	142.0	77 54.1	+49.2	144.8	77 04.3	+50.7	147.4	76 13.1	+52.1	149.6	75 20.9	+53.1	151.5	74 27.7	+54.1	153.2	8
9	80 53.9	+38.2•	130.4	80 13.2	+41.9•	134.9	79 29.5	+44.9•	138.7	78 43.3	+47.3•	142.0	77 55.0	+49.3	144.9	77 05.2	+50.9	147.4	76 14.0	+52.2	149.6	75 21.8	+53.2	151.6	9
10	81 32.1	+33.6•	125.4	80 55.1	+38.3•	130.5	80 14.4	+42.0•	134.9	79 30.6	+45.0•	138.8	78 44.3	+47.5•	142.1	77 56.1	+49.4	145.0	77 06.2	+51.0	147.5	76 15.0	+52.3	149.7	10
11	82 05.7	+28.1•	119.6	81 33.4	+33.8•	125.4	80 56.4	+38.4•	130.6	80 15.6	+42.2•	135.0	79 31.8	+45.2•	138.8	78 45.5	+47.6•	142.1	77 57.2	+49.5	145.0	77 07.3	+51.0	147.5	11
12	82 33.8	+21.4•	112.9	82 07.2	+28.2•	119.6	81 34.8	+33.9•	125.5	80 57.8	+38.6•	130.6	80 17.0	+42.3•	135.1	79 33.1	+45.3•	138.9	78 46.7	+47.7•	142.2	77 58.3	+49.7	145.1	12
13	82 55.2	+13.8•	105.5	82 35.4	+21.6•	113.0	82 08.7	+28.4•	119.7	81 36.4	+34.0•	125.6	80 59.3	+38.7•	130.7	80 18.4	+42.4•	135.2	79 34.4	+45.5•	139.0	78 48.0	+47.8•	142.3	13
14	83 09.0	+5.3•	97.5	82 57.0	+13.9•	105.6	82 37.1	+21.8•	113.0	82 10.4	+28.6•	119.7	81 38.0	+34.2•	125.6	81 00.8	+38.9•	130.8	80 19.9	+42.6•	135.2	79 35.8	+45.6•	139.1	14
15	83 14.3	−3.4•	89.1	83 10.9	+5.4•	97.5	82 58.9	+14.0•	105.6	82 39.0	+21.9•	113.1	82 12.2	+28.7•	119.8	81 39.7	+34.4•	125.7	81 02.5	+39.0•	130.9	80 21.4	+42.8•	135.4	15
16	83 10.9	−12.0•	80.6	83 16.3	−3.4•	89.0	83 12.9	+5.5•	97.5	83 00.9	+14.1•	105.6	82 40.9	+22.1•	113.1	82 14.1	+28.9•	119.9	81 41.5	+34.6•	125.8	81 04.2	+39.2•	131.0	16
17	82 58.9	−19.9•	72.5	83 12.9	−12.0•	80.5	83 18.4	−3.4•	89.0	83 15.0	+5.6•	97.5	83 03.0	+14.2•	105.6	82 43.0	+22.2•	113.2	82 16.1	+29.1•	120.0	81 43.4	+34.8•	125.9	17
18	82 39.0	−26.8•	64.9	83 00.9	−20.0•	72.4	83 15.0	−12.0•	80.4	83 20.6	−3.4•	88.9	83 17.2	+5.7•	97.4	83 05.2	+14.4•	105.7	82 45.2	+22.3•	113.2	82 18.2	+29.3•	120.1	18
19	82 12.2	−32.5•	58.2	82 40.9	−26.8•	64.8	83 03.0	−20.0•	72.2	83 17.2	−12.0•	80.3	83 22.9	−3.3•	88.9	83 19.6	+5.8•	97.4	83 07.5	+14.6•	105.7	82 47.5	+22.5•	113.3	19
20	81 39.7	−37.2•	52.2	82 14.1	−32.6•	58.0	82 43.0	−26.9•	64.6	83 05.2	−20.0•	72.1	83 19.6	−12.1•	80.2	83 25.4	−3.3•	88.8	83 22.1	+5.8•	97.4	83 10.0	+14.7•	105.7	20
21	81 02.5	−41.1•	46.9	81 41.5	−37.3•	51.9	82 16.1	−32.7•	57.7	82 45.2	−27.0•	64.4	83 07.5	−20.0•	71.9	83 22.1	−12.1•	80.1	83 27.9	−3.2•	88.7	83 24.7	+5.9•	97.4	21
22	80 21.4	−44.1•	42.4	81 04.2	−41.1•	46.7	81 43.4	−37.4•	51.7	82 18.2	−32.8•	57.5	82 47.5	−27.1•	64.2	83 10.0	−20.1•	71.7	83 24.7	−12.1•	80.0	83 30.6	−3.2•	88.7	22
23	79 37.3	−46.5•	38.5	80 23.1	−44.2•	42.2	81 06.0	−41.2•	46.5	81 45.4	−37.5•	51.5	82 20.4	−32.9•	57.3	82 49.9	−27.2•	64.0	83 12.6	−20.3•	71.6	83 27.4	−12.1•	79.9	23
24	78 50.8	−48.6	35.1	79 38.9	−46.6•	38.3	80 24.8	−44.3•	42.0	81 07.9	−41.3•	46.2	81 47.5	−37.6•	51.2	82 22.7	−33.0•	57.1	82 52.3	−27.2•	63.8	83 15.3	−20.4•	71.4	24
25	78 02.2	−50.1	32.2	78 52.3	−48.6	34.9	79 40.5	−46.7•	38.0	80 26.6	−44.4•	41.7	81 09.9	−41.4•	46.0	81 49.7	−37.7•	51.0	82 25.1	−33.1•	56.8	82 54.9	−27.3•	63.6	25
26	77 12.1	−51.4	29.6	78 03.7	−50.2	32.0	78 53.8	−48.7	34.7	79 42.2	−46.8•	37.8	80 28.5	−44.5•	41.4	81 12.0	−41.6•	45.7	81 52.0	−37.9•	50.7	82 27.6	−33.3•	56.6	26
27	76 20.7	−52.5	27.4	77 13.5	−51.5	29.4	78 05.1	−50.2	31.7	78 55.4	−48.7	34.4	79 44.0	−46.9•	37.5	80 30.4	−44.6•	41.2	81 14.1	−41.7•	45.4	81 54.3	−38.0•	50.5	27
28	75 28.2	−53.5	25.4	76 22.0	−52.6	27.2	77 14.9	−51.6	29.2	78 06.7	−50.4	31.5	78 57.1	−48.9	34.2	79 45.8	−47.0•	37.3	80 32.4	−44.7•	40.9	81 16.3	−41.8•	45.2	28
29	74 34.7	−54.1	23.6	75 29.4	−53.5	25.2	76 23.3	−52.6	26.9	77 16.3	−51.6	28.9	78 08.2	−50.4	31.2	78 58.8	−48.9	33.9	79 47.7	−47.1•	37.0	80 34.5	−44.8•	40.6	29
30	73 40.6	−54.8	22.1	74 35.9	−54.2	23.4	75 30.7	−53.5	25.0	76 24.7	−52.7	26.7	77 17.8	−51.7	28.7	78 09.9	−50.5	31.0	79 00.6	−49.0	33.6	79 49.7	−47.2•	36.7	30
31	72 45.8	−55.3	20.6	73 41.7	−54.8	21.8	74 37.2	−54.3	23.2	75 32.0	−53.6	24.7	76 26.1	−52.7	26.4	77 19.4	−51.8	28.4	78 11.6	−50.6	30.7	79 02.5	−49.2	33.3	31
32	71 50.5	−55.8	19.4	72 46.9	−55.3	20.4	73 42.9	−54.8	21.6	74 38.4	−54.3	23.0	75 33.4	−53.6	24.5	76 27.6	−52.8	26.2	77 21.0	−51.9	28.2	78 13.3	−50.6	30.4	32
33	70 54.7	−56.1	18.2	71 51.6	−55.8	19.2	72 48.1	−55.4	20.2	73 44.1	−54.9	21.4	74 39.8	−54.4	22.7	75 34.8	−53.7	24.2	76 29.1	−52.9	25.9	77 22.7	−52.0	27.9	33
34	69 58.6	−56.5	17.2	70 55.8	−56.2	18.0	71 52.7	−55.9	19.0	72 49.2	−55.4	20.0	73 45.4	−55.0	21.2	74 41.1	−54.4	22.5	75 36.2	−53.7	24.0	76 30.7	−53.0	25.7	34
35	69 02.1	−56.8	16.2	69 59.6	−56.6	17.0	70 56.8	−56.2	17.8	71 53.8	−55.9	18.7	72 50.4	−55.4	19.8	73 46.7	−55.0	20.9	74 42.5	−54.5	22.2	75 37.7	−53.8	23.7	35
36	68 05.3	−57.1	15.3	69 03.0	−56.8	16.0	70 00.6	−56.6	16.8	70 57.9	−56.2	17.6	71 55.0	−56.0	18.5	72 51.7	−55.5	19.5	73 48.0	−55.0	20.7	74 43.9	−54.5	22.0	36
37	67 08.2	−57.3	14.5	68 06.2	−57.1	15.1	69 04.0	−56.8	15.8	70 01.7	−56.6	16.6	70 59.0	−56.3	17.4	71 56.2	−56.0	18.3	72 53.0	−55.6	19.3	73 49.4	−55.1	20.4	37
38	66 10.9	−57.5	13.8	67 09.1	−57.3	14.3	68 07.2	−57.1	14.9	69 05.1	−56.9	15.6	70 02.7	−56.6	16.3	71 00.2	−56.3	17.2	71 57.4	−56.0	18.1	72 54.3	−55.7	19.1	38
39	65 13.4	−57.7	13.1	66 11.8	−57.5	13.6	67 10.1	−57.4	14.1	68 08.2	−57.2	14.7	69 06.1	−56.9	15.4	70 03.9	−56.7	16.1	71 01.4	−56.4	16.9	71 58.6	−56.0	17.8	39
40	64 15.7	−57.8	12.4	65 14.3	−57.7	12.9	66 12.7	−57.5	13.4	67 11.0	−57.3	13.9	68 09.2	−57.2	14.5	69 07.2	−57.0	15.2	70 05.0	−56.7	15.9	71 02.6	−56.5	16.7	40
41	63 17.9	−58.0	11.8	64 16.6	−57.9	12.2	65 15.2	−57.7	12.7	66 13.7	−57.6	13.2	67 12.0	−57.4	13.7	68 10.2	−57.2	14.3	69 08.3	−57.0	15.0	70 06.1	−56.7	15.7	41
42	62 19.9	−58.1	11.2	63 18.7	−57.9	11.6	64 17.5	−57.9	12.1	65 16.1	−57.7	12.5	66 14.6	−57.6	13.0	67 13.0	−57.4	13.5	68 11.3	−57.2	14.1	69 09.4	−57.0	14.7	42
43	61 21.8	−58.2	10.7	62 20.8	−58.2	11.1	63 19.6	−58.0	11.5	64 18.4	−57.9	11.9	65 17.0	−57.7	12.3	66 15.6	−57.6	12.8	67 14.1	−57.5	13.3	68 12.4	−57.3	13.9	43
44	60 23.6	−58.3	10.2	61 22.6	−58.2	10.5	62 21.6	−58.1	10.9	63 20.5	−58.1	11.3	64 19.3	−57.9	11.7	65 18.0	−57.8	12.1	66 16.6	−57.6	12.6	67 15.1	−57.5	13.1	44
45	59 25.3	−58.4	9.8	60 24.4	−58.3	10.0	61 23.5	−58.3	10.4	62 22.4	−58.1	10.7	63 21.4	−58.1	11.1	64 20.2	−57.9	11.5	65 19.0	−57.9	11.9	66 17.6	−57.7	12.4	45
46	58 26.9	−58.5	9.3	59 26.1	−58.5	9.6	60 25.2	−58.3	9.9	61 24.3	−58.3	10.2	62 23.3	−58.2	10.5	63 22.3	−58.1	10.9	64 21.1	−57.9	11.3	65 19.9	−57.8	11.7	46
47	57 28.4	−58.6	8.9	58 27.6	−58.5	9.1	59 26.9	−58.5	9.4	60 26.0	−58.4	9.7	61 25.1	−58.3	10.0	62 24.2	−58.2	10.3	63 23.2	−58.1	10.7	64 22.1	−58.0	11.1	47
48	56 29.8	−58.7	8.5	57 29.1	−58.6	8.7	58 28.4	−58.5	9.0	59 27.6	−58.4	9.2	60 26.8	−58.3	9.5	61 26.0	−58.3	9.8	62 25.1	−58.2	10.1	63 24.1	−58.1	10.5	48
49	55 31.1	−58.7	8.1	56 30.5	−58.6	8.3	57 29.9	−58.6	8.6	58 29.2	−58.6	8.8	59 28.5	−58.5	9.1	60 27.7	−58.4	9.3	61 26.9	−58.4	9.6	62 26.0	−58.2	9.9	49
50	54 32.4	−58.8	7.8	55 31.9	−58.8	8.0	56 31.3	−58.7	8.2	57 30.6	−58.6	8.4	58 30.0	−58.6	8.6	59 29.3	−58.5	8.9	60 28.5	−58.4	9.1	61 27.8	−58.4	9.4	50
51	53 33.6	−58.8	7.4	54 33.1	−58.8	7.6	55 32.6	−58.8	7.8	56 32.0	−58.7	8.0	57 31.4	−58.6	8.2	58 30.8	−58.6	8.4	59 30.1	−58.5	8.7	60 29.4	−58.4	9.0	51
52	52 34.8	−58.9	7.1	53 34.3	−58.8	7.3	54 33.8	−58.8	7.4	55 33.3	−58.7	7.6	56 32.8	−58.7	7.8	57 32.2	−58.7	8.0	58 31.6	−58.6	8.3	59 31.0	−58.6	8.5	52
53	51 35.9	−58.9	6.8	52 35.5	−58.9	6.9	53 35.0	−58.8	7.1	54 34.6	−58.9	7.3	55 34.1	−58.8	7.5	56 33.5	−58.7	7.6	57 33.0	−58.7	7.9	58 32.4	−58.6	8.1	53
54	50 37.0	−59.0	6.5	51 36.6	−59.0	6.6	52 36.2	−58.9	6.8	53 35.7	−58.8	6.9	54 35.3	−58.8	7.1	55 34.8	−58.8	7.3	56 34.3	−58.7	7.5	57 33.8	−58.7	7.7	54
55	49 38.0	−59.0	6.2	50 37.6	−58.9	6.3	51 37.3	−59.0	6.5	52 36.9	−58.9	6.6	53 36.5	−58.9	6.8	54 36.0	−58.8	6.9	55 35.6	−58.8	7.1	56 35.1	−58.7	7.3	55
56	48 39.0	−59.1	5.9	49 38.7	−59.1	6.0	50 38.3	−59.0	6.2	51 38.0	−59.0	6.3	52 37.6	−58.9	6.4	53 37.2	−58.9	6.6	54 36.8	−58.9	6.8	55 36.4	−58.9	6.9	56
57	47 39.9	−59.1	5.7	48 39.6	−59.0	5.8	49 39.3	−59.0	5.9	50 39.0	−59.0	6.0	51 38.7	−59.0	6.1	52 38.3	−58.9	6.3	53 37.9	−58.9	6.4	54 37.5	−58.8	6.6	57
58	46 40.8	−59.1	5.4	47 40.6	−59.1	5.5	48 40.3	−59.1	5.6	49 40.0	−59.1	5.7	50 39.7	−59.0	5.8	51 39.4	−59.0	6.0	52 39.0	−58.9	6.1	53 38.7	−59.0	6.3	58
59	45 41.7	−59.2	5.2	46 41.5	−59.2	5.3	47 41.2	−59.1	5.3	48 40.9	−59.1	5.5	49 40.7	−59.1	5.6	50 40.4	−59.1	5.7	51 40.1	−59.0	5.8	52 39.7	−58.9	5.9	59
60	44 42.5	−59.1	4.9	45 42.3	−59.1	5.0	46 42.1	−59.2	5.1	47 41.8	−59.1	5.2	48 41.6	−59.1	5.3	49 41.3	−59.0	5.4	50 41.1	−59.1	5.5	51 40.8	−59.0	5.6	60
61	43 43.4	−59.3	4.7	44 43.2	−59.2	4.8	45 42.9	−59.1	4.9	46 42.7	−59.1	4.9	47 42.5	−59.1	5.0	48 42.3	−59.1	5.1	49 42.0	−59.1	5.2	50 41.8	−59.1	5.4	61
62	42 44.1	−59.2	4.5	43 44.0	−59.3	4.5	44 43.8	−59.2	4.6	45 43.6	−59.2	4.7	46 43.4	−59.2	4.8	47 43.2	−59.2	4.9	48 42.9	−59.1	5.0	49 42.7	−59.1	5.1	62
63	41 44.9	−59.3	4.3	42 44.7	−59.2	4.3	43 44.6	−59.3	4.4	44 44.4	−59.2	4.5	45 44.2	−59.2	4.5	46 44.0	−59.2	4.6	47 43.8	−59.1	4.7	48 43.6	−59.1	4.8	63
64	40 45.6	−59.2	4.0	41 45.5	−59.3	4.1	42 45.3	−59.2	4.2	43 45.2	−59.3	4.2	44 45.0	−59.2	4.3	45 44.8	−59.2	4.4	46 44.7	−59.2	4.5	47 44.5	−59.2	4.6	64
65	39 46.4	−59.3	3.8	40 46.2	−59.3	3.9	41 46.1	−59.3	4.0	42 45.9	−59.2	4.0	43 45.8	−59.3	4.1	44 45.6	−59.2	4.2	45 45.5	−59.2	4.2	46 45.3	−59.2	4.3	65
66	38 47.1	−59.4	3.6	39 46.9	−59.3	3.7	40 46.8	−59.3	3.8	41 46.7	−59.3	3.8	42 46.5	−59.2	3.9	43 46.4	−59.2	3.9	44 46.3	−59.3	4.0	45 46.1	−59.2	4.1	66
67	37 47.7	−59.3	3.5	38 47.6	−59.3	3.5	39 47.5	−59.3	3.6	40 47.4	−59.3	3.6	41 47.3	−59.3	3.7	42 47.2	−59.3	3.7	43 47.0	−59.2	3.8	44 46.9	−59.3	3.8	67
68	36 48.4	−59.4	3.3	37 48.3	−59.3	3.3	38 48.2	−59.3	3.4	39 48.1	−59.3	3.4	40 48.0	−59.3	3.5	41 47.9	−59.3	3.5	42 47.8	−59.3	3.6	43 47.6	−59.2	3.6	68
69	35 49.0	−59.3	3.1	36 49.0	−59.4	3.1	37 48.9	−59.4	3.2	38 48.8	−59.4	3.2	39 48.7	−59.3	3.3	40 48.6	−59.3	3.3	41 48.5	−59.3	3.4	42 48.4	−59.3	3.4	69
70	34 49.7	−59.4	2.9	35 49.6	−59.4	2.9	36 49.5	−59.4	3.0	37 49.4	−59.3	3.0	38 49.4	−59.4	3.1	39 49.3	−59.4	3.1	40 49.2	−59.4	3.2	41 49.1	−59.3	3.2	70
71	33 50.3	−59.4	2.7	34 50.2	−59.4	2.8	35 50.1	−59.3	2.8	36 50.1	−59.4	2.8	37 50.0	−59.4	2.9	38 49.9	−59.3	2.9	39 49.8	−59.3	3.0	40 49.8	−59.4	3.0	71
72	32 50.9	−59.4	2.6	33 50.8	−59.4	2.6	34 50.8	−59.5	2.6	35 50.7	−59.4	2.7	36 50.6	−59.3	2.7	37 50.6	−59.4	2.7	38 50.5	−59.4	2.8	39 50.4	−59.3	2.8	72
73	31 51.5	−59.5	2.4	32 51.4	−59.4	2.4	33 51.4	−59.4	2.5	34 51.3	−59.4	2.5	35 51.3	−59.4	2.5	36 51.2	−59.4	2.6	37 51.1	−59.3	2.6	38 51.1	−59.4	2.6	73
74	30 52.0	−59.4	2.2	31 52.0	−59.4	2.3	32 52.0	−59.5	2.3	33 51.9	−59.4	2.3	34 51.9	−59.5	2.3	35 51.8	−59.4	2.4	36 51.8	−59.4	2.4	37 51.7	−59.4	2.4	74
75	29 52.6	−59.4	2.1	30 52.6	−59.5	2.1	31 52.5	−59.4	2.1	32 52.5	−59.4	2.2	33 52.4	−59.4	2.2	34 52.4	−59.4	2.2	35 52.4	−59.5	2.2	36 52.3	−59.4	2.3	75
76	28 53.2	−59.5	1.9	29 53.1	−59.4	1.9	30 53.1	−59.5	2.0	31 53.1	−59.5	2.0	32 53.0	−59.4	2.0	33 53.0	−59.5	2.0	34 52.9	−59.4	2.1	35 52.9	−59.4	2.1	76
77	27 53.7	−59.5	1.8	28 53.7	−59.5	1.8	29 53.6	−59.4	1.8	30 53.6	−59.4	1.8	31 53.6	−59.5	1.9	32 53.5	−59.4	1.9	33 53.5	−59.4	1.9	34 53.5	−59.5	1.9	77
78	26 54.2	−59.5	1.6	27 54.2	−59.5	1.6	28 54.2	−59.5	1.7	29 54.2	−59.5	1.7	30 54.1	−59.4	1.7	31 54.1	−59.5	1.7	32 54.1	−59.5	1.7	33 54.0	−59.4	1.7	78
79	25 54.7	−59.4	1.5	26 54.7	−59.5	1.5	27 54.7	−59.5	1.5	28 54.7	−59.5	1.5	29 54.7	−59.5	1.5	30 54.6	−59.4	1.6	31 54.6	−59.4	1.6	32 54.6	−59.5	1.6	79
80	24 55.3	−59.5	1.3	25 55.2	−59.5	1.3	26 55.2	−59.5	1.4	27 55.2	−59.5	1.4	28 55.2	−59.5	1.4	29 55.2	−59.5	1.4	30 55.2	−59.5	1.4	31 55.1	−59.4	1.4	80
81	23 55.8	−59.5	1.2	24 55.7	−59.5	1.2	25 55.7	−59.5	1.2	26 55.7	−59.5	1.2	27 55.7	−59.5	1.2	28 55.7	−59.5	1.2	29 55.7	−59.5	1.3	30 55.7	−59.5	1.3	81
82	22 56.3	−59.6	1.1	23 56.2	−59.5	1.1	24 56.2	−59.5	1.1	25 56.2	−59.5	1.1	26 56.2	−59.5	1.1	27 56.2	−59.5	1.1	28 56.2	−59.5	1.1	29 56.2	−59.5	1.1	82
83	21 56.7	−59.5	0.9	22 56.7	−59.5	0.9	23 56.7	−59.5	0.9	24 56.7	−59.5	0.9	25 56.7	−59.5	0.9	26 56.7	−59.5	1.0	27 56.7	−59.5	1.0	28 56.7	−59.5	1.0	83
84	20 57.2	−59.5	0.8	21 57.2	−59.5	0.8	22 57.2	−59.5	0.8	23 57.2	−59.5	0.8	24 57.2	−59.5	0.8	25 57.2	−59.5	0.8	26 57.2	−59.5	0.8	27 57.2	−59.5	0.8	84
85	19 57.7	−59.5	0.6	20 57.7	−59.5	0.7	21 57.7	−59.5	0.7	22 57.7	−59.5	0.7	23 57.7	−59.5	0.7	24 57.7	−59.5	0.7	25 57.7	−59.5	0.7	26 57.7	−59.5	0.7	85
86	18 58.2	−59.6	0.5	19 58.2	−59.6	0.5	20 58.2	−59.6	0.5	21 58.2	−59.6	0.5	22 58.2	−59.6	0.5	23 58.2	−59.6	0.5	24 58.2	−59.6	0.5	25 58.2	−59.6	0.5	86
87	17 58.6	−59.5	0.4	18 58.6	−59.5	0.4	19 58.6	−59.5	0.4	20 58.6	−59.5	0.4	21 58.6	−59.5	0.4	22 58.6	−59.5	0.4	23 58.6	−59.6	0.4	24 58.6	−59.5	0.4	87
88	16 59.1	−59.5	0.3	17 59.1	−59.5	0.3	18 59.1	−59.5	0.3	19 59.1	−59.5	0.3	20 59.1	−59.6	0.3	21 59.1	−59.6	0.3	22 59.1	−59.6	0.3	23 59.1	−59.6	0.3	88
89	15 59.6	−59.6	0.1	16 59.6	−59.6	0.1	17 59.6	−59.6	0.1	18 59.6	−59.6	0.1	19 59.5	−59.5	0.1	20 59.5	−59.5	0.1	21 59.5	−59.5	0.1	22 59.5	−59.6	0.1	89
90	15 00.0	−59.6	0.0	16 00.0	−59.6	0.0	17 00.0	−59.6	0.0	18 00.0	−59.6	0.0	19 00.0	−59.6	0.0	20 00.0	−59.6	0.0	21 00.0	−59.6	0.0	22 00.0	−59.6	0.0	90
	15°			16°			17°			18°			19°			20°			21°			22°			

LATITUDE **CONTRARY** NAME TO DECLINATION L.H.A. 7°, 353°

Dec.	15°			16°			17°			18°		
	Hc	d	Z	Hc	d	Z	Hc	d	Z	Hc	d	Z
°	° ′	′	°	° ′	′	°	° ′	′	°	° ′	′	°
0	73 28.9	-54.9	154.6	72 34.3	-55.4	156.0	71 39.3	-56.0	157.2	70 43.7	-56.3	158.3
1	72 34.0	-55.5	156.0	71 38.9	-55.9	157.2	70 43.3	-56.3	158.3	69 47.4	-56.7	159.3
2	71 38.5	-55.8	157.2	70 43.0	-56.3	158.4	69 47.0	-56.6	159.4	68 50.7	-57.0	160.3
3	70 42.7	-56.3	158.4	69 46.7	-56.6	159.4	68 50.4	-56.9	160.3	67 53.7	-57.2	161.1
4	69 46.4	-56.5	159.4	68 50.1	-56.9	160.3	67 53.5	-57.2	161.2	66 56.5	-57.4	161.9
5	68 49.9	-56.9	160.4	67 53.2	-57.1	161.2	66 56.3	-57.4	161.9	65 59.1	-57.6	162.6
6	67 53.0	-57.1	161.2	66 56.1	-57.4	162.0	65 58.9	-57.6	162.7	65 01.5	-57.8	163.3
7	66 55.9	-57.3	162.0	65 58.7	-57.5	162.7	65 01.3	-57.7	163.4	64 03.7	-57.9	163.9
8	65 58.6	-57.6	162.8	65 01.2	-57.8	163.4	64 03.6	-57.9	164.0	63 05.8	-58.0	164.5
9	65 01.0	-57.7	163.4	64 03.4	-57.9	164.0	63 05.7	-58.1	164.6	62 07.8	-58.2	165.1
10	64 03.3	-57.8	164.1	63 05.5	-58.0	164.6	62 07.6	-58.1	165.1	61 09.6	-58.3	165.6
11	63 05.5	-58.0	164.7	62 07.5	-58.1	165.2	61 09.5	-58.3	165.6	60 11.3	-58.4	166.1
12	62 07.5	-58.2	165.2	61 09.4	-58.3	165.7	60 11.2	-58.4	166.1	59 12.9	-58.5	166.5
13	61 09.3	-58.2	165.8	60 11.1	-58.3	166.2	59 12.8	-58.5	166.6	58 14.4	-58.6	167.0
14	60 11.1	-58.4	166.2	59 12.8	-58.5	166.6	58 14.3	-58.5	167.0	57 15.8	-58.6	167.4
15	59 12.7	-58.4	166.7	58 14.3	-58.5	167.1	57 15.8	-58.6	167.4	56 17.2	-58.7	167.8
16	58 14.3	-58.5	167.1	57 15.8	-58.6	167.5	56 17.2	-58.7	167.8	55 18.5	-58.8	168.1
17	57 15.8	-58.6	167.6	56 17.2	-58.7	167.9	55 18.5	-58.8	168.2	54 19.7	-58.8	168.5
18	56 17.2	-58.7	167.9	55 18.5	-58.8	168.3	54 19.7	-58.8	168.5	53 20.9	-58.9	168.8
19	55 18.5	-58.7	168.3	54 19.7	-58.8	168.6	53 20.9	-58.9	168.9	52 22.0	-58.9	169.1
20	54 19.8	-58.8	168.7	53 20.9	-58.8	168.9	52 22.0	-58.9	169.2	51 23.1	-59.0	169.4
21	53 21.0	-58.9	169.0	52 22.1	-58.9	169.3	51 23.1	-59.0	169.5	50 24.1	-59.0	169.7
22	52 22.1	-58.9	169.3	51 23.2	-59.0	169.6	50 24.1	-59.0	169.8	49 25.1	-59.1	170.0
23	51 23.2	-58.9	169.6	50 24.2	-59.0	169.9	49 25.1	-59.0	170.1	48 26.0	-59.1	170.3
24	50 24.3	-59.0	169.9	49 25.2	-59.0	170.1	48 26.1	-59.1	170.3	47 26.9	-59.1	170.5
25	49 25.3	-59.0	170.2	48 26.2	-59.1	170.4	47 27.0	-59.1	170.6	46 27.8	-59.2	170.8
26	48 26.3	-59.1	170.5	47 27.1	-59.1	170.7	46 27.9	-59.2	170.8	45 28.6	-59.2	171.0
27	47 27.2	-59.1	170.8	46 28.0	-59.2	170.9	45 28.7	-59.2	171.1	44 29.4	-59.2	171.2
28	46 28.1	-59.1	171.0	45 28.8	-59.1	171.2	44 29.5	-59.2	171.3	43 30.2	-59.2	171.5
29	45 29.0	-59.2	171.3	44 29.7	-59.2	171.4	43 30.3	-59.2	171.5	42 31.0	-59.3	171.7
30	44 29.8	-59.2	171.5	43 30.5	-59.3	171.6	42 31.1	-59.3	171.8	41 31.7	-59.3	171.9
31	43 30.6	-59.2	171.7	42 31.2	-59.2	171.9	41 31.8	-59.2	172.0	40 32.4	-59.3	172.1
32	42 31.4	-59.2	171.9	41 32.0	-59.3	172.1	40 32.6	-59.3	172.2	39 33.1	-59.3	172.3
33	41 32.2	-59.3	172.2	40 32.7	-59.3	172.3	39 33.3	-59.4	172.4	38 33.8	-59.4	172.5
34	40 32.9	-59.3	172.4	39 33.4	-59.3	172.5	38 33.9	-59.3	172.6	37 34.4	-59.3	172.7
35	39 33.6	-59.3	172.6	38 34.1	-59.3	172.7	37 34.6	-59.4	172.8	36 35.1	-59.4	172.9
36	38 34.3	-59.3	172.8	37 34.8	-59.4	172.9	36 35.2	-59.3	172.9	35 35.7	-59.4	173.0
37	37 35.0	-59.4	172.9	36 35.4	-59.3	173.0	35 35.9	-59.4	173.1	34 36.3	-59.4	173.2
38	36 35.6	-59.3	173.1	35 36.1	-59.4	173.2	34 36.5	-59.4	173.3	33 36.9	-59.4	173.4
39	35 36.3	-59.4	173.3	34 36.7	-59.4	173.4	33 37.1	-59.4	173.5	32 37.5	-59.5	173.5
40	34 36.9	-59.4	173.5	33 37.3	-59.4	173.6	32 37.7	-59.5	173.6	31 38.0	-59.4	173.7
41	33 37.5	-59.4	173.7	32 37.9	-59.4	173.7	31 38.2	-59.4	173.8	30 38.6	-59.5	173.9
42	32 38.1	-59.4	173.8	31 38.5	-59.5	173.9	30 38.8	-59.5	174.0	29 39.1	-59.4	174.0
43	31 38.7	-59.4	174.0	30 39.0	-59.4	174.1	29 39.3	-59.4	174.1	28 39.7	-59.5	174.2
44	30 39.3	-59.5	174.2	29 39.6	-59.5	174.2	28 39.9	-59.5	174.3	27 40.2	-59.5	174.3
45	29 39.8	-59.4	174.3	28 40.1	-59.5	174.4	27 40.4	-59.5	174.4	26 40.7	-59.5	174.5
46	28 40.4	-59.5	174.5	27 40.6	-59.4	174.5	26 40.9	-59.5	174.6	25 41.2	-59.5	174.6
47	27 40.9	-59.5	174.6	26 41.2	-59.5	174.7	25 41.4	-59.5	174.7	24 41.7	-59.5	174.8
48	26 41.4	-59.4	174.8	25 41.7	-59.5	174.8	24 41.9	-59.5	174.9	23 42.2	-59.6	174.9
49	25 42.0	-59.5	174.9	24 42.2	-59.5	175.0	23 42.4	-59.5	175.0	22 42.6	-59.5	175.0
50	24 42.5	-59.5	175.1	23 42.7	-59.5	175.1	22 42.9	-59.5	175.1	21 43.1	-59.5	175.2
51	23 43.0	-59.5	175.2	22 43.2	-59.5	175.2	21 43.4	-59.5	175.3	20 43.6	-59.6	175.3
52	22 43.5	-59.6	175.3	21 43.7	-59.6	175.4	20 43.9	-59.6	175.4	19 44.0	-59.5	175.4
53	21 43.9	-59.5	175.5	20 44.1	-59.5	175.5	19 44.3	-59.5	175.5	18 44.5	-59.6	175.6
54	20 44.4	-59.5	175.6	19 44.6	-59.5	175.6	18 44.8	-59.6	175.7	17 44.9	-59.5	175.7
55	19 44.9	-59.5	175.7	18 45.1	-59.6	175.8	17 45.2	-59.5	175.8	16 45.4	-59.6	175.8
56	18 45.4	-59.6	175.9	17 45.5	-59.5	175.9	16 45.7	-59.6	175.9	15 45.8	-59.5	175.9
57	17 45.8	-59.5	176.0	16 46.0	-59.6	176.0	15 46.1	-59.5	176.0	14 46.3	-59.6	176.1
58	16 46.3	-59.6	176.1	15 46.4	-59.5	176.2	14 46.6	-59.6	176.2	13 46.7	-59.6	176.2
59	15 46.7	-59.5	176.3	14 46.9	-59.6	176.3	13 47.0	-59.6	176.3	12 47.1	-59.6	176.3
60	14 47.2	-59.6	176.4	13 47.3	-59.6	176.4	12 47.4	-59.5	176.4	11 47.5	-59.5	176.4
61	13 47.6	-59.5	176.5	12 47.7	-59.5	176.5	11 47.9	-59.6	176.5	10 48.0	-59.6	176.6
62	12 48.1	-59.6	176.6	11 48.2	-59.6	176.6	10 48.3	-59.6	176.7	9 48.4	-59.6	176.7
63	11 48.5	-59.5	176.8	10 48.6	-59.6	176.8	9 48.7	-59.6	176.8	8 48.8	-59.6	176.8
64	10 49.0	-59.6	176.9	9 49.0	-59.5	176.9	8 49.1	-59.6	176.9	7 49.2	-59.6	176.9
65	9 49.4	-59.6	177.0	8 49.5	-59.6	177.0	7 49.5	-59.5	177.0	6 49.6	-59.6	177.0
66	8 49.8	-59.6	177.1	7 49.9	-59.6	177.1	6 50.0	-59.6	177.1	5 50.0	-59.6	177.1
67	7 50.2	-59.5	177.2	6 50.3	-59.6	177.3	5 50.4	-59.6	177.3	4 50.4	-59.6	177.3
68	6 50.7	-59.6	177.4	5 50.7	-59.6	177.4	4 50.8	-59.6	177.4	3 50.8	-59.5	177.4
69	5 51.1	-59.6	177.5	4 51.1	-59.5	177.5	3 51.2	-59.6	177.5	2 51.3	-59.6	177.5
70	4 51.5	-59.6	177.6	3 51.6	-59.6	177.6	2 51.6	-59.6	177.6	1 51.7	-59.6	177.6
71	3 51.9	-59.6	177.7	2 52.0	-59.6	177.7	1 52.0	-59.6	177.7	0 52.1	-59.6	177.7
72	2 52.3	-59.5	177.8	1 52.4	-59.6	177.8	0 52.4	-59.6	177.8	0 07.5	+59.6	2.2
73	1 52.8	-59.6	178.0	0 52.8	-59.6	178.0	0 07.2	+59.6	2.0	1 07.1	+59.6	2.0
74	0 53.2	-59.6	178.1	0 06.8	+59.6	1.9	1 06.8	+59.5	1.9	2 06.7	+59.6	1.9
75	0 06.4	+59.6	1.8	1 06.4	+59.6	1.8	2 06.3	+59.6	1.8	3 06.3	+59.6	1.8
76	1 06.0	+59.6	1.7	2 06.0	+59.5	1.7	3 05.9	+59.6	1.7	4 05.9	+59.6	1.7
77	2 05.6	+59.6	1.6	3 05.5	+59.6	1.6	4 05.5	+59.6	1.6	5 05.5	+59.6	1.6
78	3 05.2	+59.5	1.5	4 05.1	+59.6	1.5	5 05.1	+59.6	1.5	6 05.1	+59.6	1.5
79	4 04.7	+59.6	1.3	5 04.7	+59.6	1.3	6 04.7	+59.6	1.3	7 04.7	+59.6	1.3
80	5 04.3	+59.6	1.2	6 04.3	+59.6	1.2	7 04.3	+59.6	1.2	8 04.3	+59.6	1.2
81	6 03.9	+59.6	1.1	7 03.9	+59.6	1.1	8 03.9	+59.6	1.1	9 03.9	+59.5	1.1
82	7 03.5	+59.5	1.0	8 03.5	+59.5	1.0	9 03.5	+59.5	1.0	10 03.4	+59.6	1.0
83	8 03.0	+59.6	0.9	9 03.0	+59.6	0.9	10 03.0	+59.6	0.9	11 03.0	+59.6	0.9
84	9 02.6	+59.6	0.7	10 02.6	+59.6	0.7	11 02.6	+59.6	0.7	12 02.6	+59.6	0.7
85	10 02.2	+59.6	0.6	11 02.2	+59.6	0.6	12 02.2	+59.6	0.6	13 02.2	+59.6	0.6
86	11 01.8	+59.5	0.5	12 01.8	+59.5	0.5	13 01.8	+59.5	0.5	14 01.8	+59.5	0.5
87	12 01.3	+59.6	0.4	13 01.3	+59.6	0.4	14 01.3	+59.6	0.4	15 01.3	+59.6	0.4
88	13 00.9	+59.5	0.3	14 00.9	+59.5	0.3	15 00.9	+59.5	0.3	16 00.9	+59.5	0.3
89	14 00.4	+59.6	0.1	15 00.4	+59.6	0.1	16 00.4	+59.6	0.1	17 00.4	+59.6	0.1
90	15 00.0	+59.6	0.0	16 00.0	+59.6	0.0	17 00.0	+59.6	0.0	18 00.0	+59.6	0.0
	15°			16°			17°			18°		

Dec.	19°			20°			21°			22°		
	Hc	d	Z	Hc	d	Z	Hc	d	Z	Hc	d	Z
°	° ′	′	°	° ′	′	°	° ′	′	°	° ′	′	°
0	69 47.8	-56.7	159.3	68 51.5	-57.1	160.3	67 54.9	-57.4	161.1	66 58.0	-57.6	161.9
1	68 51.1	-57.0	160.3	67 54.4	-57.2	161.1	66 57.5	-57.5	161.9	66 00.4	-57.7	162.6
2	67 54.1	-57.3	161.1	66 57.2	-57.5	161.9	66 00.0	-57.7	162.6	65 02.7	-57.9	163.2
3	66 56.8	-57.4	161.9	65 59.7	-57.7	162.6	65 02.3	-57.8	163.2	64 04.8	-58.0	163.8
4	65 59.4	-57.6	162.6	65 02.0	-57.8	163.3	64 04.5	-58.0	163.9	63 06.8	-58.2	164.4
5	65 01.8	-57.8	163.3	64 04.2	-58.0	163.9	63 06.5	-58.1	164.4	62 08.6	-58.3	164.9
6	64 04.0	-58.0	163.9	63 06.2	-58.1	164.5	62 08.4	-58.3	165.0	61 10.3	-58.3	165.4
7	63 06.0	-58.1	164.5	62 08.1	-58.2	165.0	61 10.1	-58.4	165.5	60 12.0	-58.5	165.9
8	62 07.9	-58.2	165.0	61 09.9	-58.3	165.5	60 11.7	-58.4	165.9	59 13.5	-58.6	166.4
9	61 09.7	-58.3	165.5	60 11.6	-58.5	166.0	59 13.3	-58.5	166.4	58 14.9	-58.6	166.8
10	60 11.4	-58.4	166.0	59 13.1	-58.5	166.4	58 14.8	-58.7	166.8	57 16.3	-58.7	167.2
11	59 13.0	-58.5	166.5	58 14.6	-58.6	166.9	57 16.1	-58.7	167.2	56 17.6	-58.8	167.6
12	58 14.5	-58.6	166.9	57 16.0	-58.7	167.3	56 17.4	-58.7	167.6	55 18.8	-58.8	167.9
13	57 15.9	-58.7	167.3	56 17.3	-58.7	167.6	55 18.7	-58.8	168.0	54 20.0	-58.9	168.2
14	56 17.2	-58.7	167.7	55 18.6	-58.8	168.0	54 19.9	-58.9	168.3	53 21.1	-59.0	168.6
15	55 18.5	-58.8	168.1	54 19.8	-58.9	168.4	53 21.0	-58.9	168.6	52 22.1	-58.9	168.9
16	54 19.7	-58.8	168.4	53 20.9	-58.9	168.7	52 22.1	-59.0	168.9	51 23.2	-59.1	169.2
17	53 20.9	-58.9	168.7	52 22.0	-58.9	169.0	51 23.1	-59.0	169.2	50 24.1	-59.0	169.5
18	52 22.0	-59.0	169.1	51 23.1	-59.0	169.3	50 24.1	-59.1	169.5	49 25.1	-59.1	169.7
19	51 23.0	-58.9	169.4	50 24.1	-59.1	169.6	49 25.0	-59.1	169.8	48 26.0	-59.2	170.0
20	50 24.1	-59.1	169.6	49 25.0	-59.1	169.9	48 25.9	-59.1	170.1	47 26.8	-59.2	170.3
21	49 25.0	-59.0	169.9	48 25.9	-59.0	170.1	47 26.8	-59.2	170.3	46 27.6	-59.2	170.5
22	48 26.0	-59.2	170.2	47 26.8	-59.1	170.4	46 27.6	-59.2	170.6	45 28.4	-59.2	170.7
23	47 26.8	-59.1	170.5	46 27.7	-59.2	170.6	45 28.4	-59.2	170.8	44 29.2	-59.2	171.0
24	46 27.7	-59.2	170.7	45 28.5	-59.2	170.9	44 29.2	-59.2	171.0	43 30.0	-59.3	171.2
25	45 28.5	-59.2	170.9	44 29.3	-59.3	171.1	43 30.0	-59.3	171.2	42 30.7	-59.3	171.4
26	44 29.3	-59.2	171.2	43 30.0	-59.2	171.3	42 30.7	-59.3	171.5	41 31.4	-59.4	171.6
27	43 30.1	-59.2	171.4	42 30.8	-59.3	171.5	41 31.4	-59.3	171.7	40 32.0	-59.3	171.8
28	42 30.9	-59.3	171.6	41 31.5	-59.3	171.7	40 32.1	-59.3	171.9	39 32.7	-59.4	172.0
29	41 31.6	-59.3	171.8	40 32.2	-59.3	171.9	39 32.8	-59.4	172.1	38 33.3	-59.3	172.2
30	40 32.3	-59.3	172.0	39 32.9	-59.4	172.1	38 33.4	-59.3	172.2	37 34.0	-59.4	172.3
31	39 33.0	-59.4	172.2	38 33.5	-59.3	172.3	37 34.1	-59.4	172.4	36 34.6	-59.4	172.5
32	38 33.6	-59.3	172.4	37 34.2	-59.4	172.5	36 34.7	-59.4	172.6	35 35.2	-59.5	172.7
33	37 34.3	-59.4	172.6	36 34.8	-59.4	172.7	35 35.3	-59.5	172.8	34 35.7	-59.4	172.9
34	36 34.9	-59.4	172.8	35 35.4	-59.4	172.9	34 35.8	-59.4	172.9	33 36.3	-59.5	173.0
35	35 35.5	-59.4	172.9	34 36.0	-59.4	173.0	33 36.4	-59.4	173.1	32 36.8	-59.4	173.2
36	34 36.1	-59.4	173.1	33 36.6	-59.5	173.2	32 37.0	-59.5	173.3	31 37.4	-59.5	173.4
37	33 36.7	-59.4	173.3	32 37.1	-59.4	173.4	31 37.5	-59.5	173.4	30 37.9	-59.5	173.5
38	32 37.3	-59.5	173.5	31 37.7	-59.5	173.5	30 38.0	-59.4	173.6	29 38.4	-59.5	173.7
39	31 37.8	-59.4	173.6	30 38.2	-59.5	173.7	29 38.6	-59.5	173.7	28 38.9	-59.5	173.8
40	30 38.4	-59.5	173.8	29 38.7	-59.4	173.8	28 39.1	-59.5	173.9	27 39.4	-59.5	173.9
41	29 38.9	-59.5	173.9	28 39.3	-59.5	174.0	27 39.6	-59.5	174.0	26 39.9	-59.5	174.1
42	28 39.4	-59.4	174.1	27 39.8	-59.5	174.1	26 40.1	-59.5	174.2	25 40.4	-59.5	174.2
43	27 40.0	-59.5	174.2	26 40.3	-59.5	174.3	25 40.6	-59.5	174.3	24 40.9	-59.6	174.4
44	26 40.5	-59.5	174.4	25 40.8	-59.6	174.4	24 41.0	-59.5	174.5	23 41.3	-59.5	174.5
45	25 41.0	-59.5	174.5	24 41.2	-59.5	174.6	23 41.5	-59.5	174.6	22 41.8	-59.6	174.6
46	24 41.5	-59.6	174.7	23 41.7	-59.5	174.7	22 42.0	-59.6	174.7	21 42.2	-59.5	174.8
47	23 41.9	-59.5	174.8	22 42.2	-59.6	174.8	21 42.4	-59.5	174.9	20 42.7	-59.6	174.9
48	22 42.4	-59.5	174.9	21 42.6	-59.5	175.0	20 42.9	-59.6	175.0	19 43.1	-59.6	175.0
49	21 42.9	-59.6	175.1	20 43.1	-59.6	175.1	19 43.3	-59.6	175.1	18 43.5	-59.5	175.2
50	20 43.3	-59.5	175.2	19 43.5	-59.5	175.2	18 43.7	-59.5	175.3	17 44.0	-59.6	175.3
51	19 43.8	-59.6	175.3	18 44.0	-59.6	175.4	17 44.2	-59.6	175.4	16 44.4	-59.6	175.4
52	18 44.2	-59.5	175.5	17 44.4	-59.5	175.5	16 44.6	-59.6	175.5	15 44.8	-59.6	175.5
53	17 44.7	-59.6	175.6	16 44.9	-59.6	175.6	15 45.0	-59.5	175.6	14 45.2	-59.6	175.7
54	16 45.1	-59.5	175.7	15 45.3	-59.6	175.7	14 45.5	-59.6	175.8	13 45.6	-59.6	175.8
55	15 45.6	-59.6	175.8	14 45.7	-59.6	175.9	13 45.9	-59.6	175.9	12 46.0	-59.6	175.9
56	14 46.0	-59.6	176.0	13 46.1	-59.6	176.0	12 46.3	-59.6	176.0	11 46.4	-59.6	176.0
57	13 46.4	-59.6	176.1	12 46.5	-59.5	176.1	11 46.7	-59.6	176.1	10 46.8	-59.6	176.1
58	12 46.8	-59.6	176.2	11 47.0	-59.6	176.2	10 47.1	-59.6	176.2	9 47.2	-59.6	176.2
59	11 47.2	-59.5	176.3	10 47.4	-59.6	176.3	9 47.5	-59.6	176.3	8 47.6	-59.6	176.4
60	10 47.7	-59.6	176.4	9 47.8	-59.6	176.5	8 47.9	-59.6	176.5	7 48.0	-59.6	176.5
61	9 48.1	-59.6	176.6	8 48.2	-59.6	176.6	7 48.3	-59.6	176.6	6 48.4	-59.6	176.6
62	8 48.5	-59.6	176.7	7 48.6	-59.6	176.7	6 48.7	-59.6	176.7	5 48.8	-59.6	176.7
63	7 48.9	-59.6	176.8	6 49.0	-59.6	176.8	5 49.1	-59.6	176.8	4 49.2	-59.6	176.8
64	6 49.3	-59.6	176.9	5 49.4	-59.6	176.9	4 49.5	-59.6	176.9	3 49.6	-59.7	176.9
65	5 49.7	-59.6	177.0	4 49.8	-59.6	177.0	3 49.9	-59.6	177.0	2 49.9	-59.6	177.0
66	4 50.1	-59.6	177.1	3 50.2	-59.6	177.2	2 50.3	-59.7	177.2	1 50.3	-59.6	177.2
67	3 50.5	-59.6	177.3	2 50.6	-59.6	177.3	1 50.6	-59.6	177.3	0 50.7	-59.6	177.3
68	2 50.9	-59.6	177.4	1 51.0	-59.6	177.4	0 51.0	-59.6	177.4	0 08.9	+59.6	2.6
69	1 51.3	-59.6	177.5	0 51.4	-59.6	177.5	0 08.6	+59.6	2.5	1 08.5	+59.6	2.5
70	0 51.7	-59.6	177.6	0 08.2	+59.6	2.4	1 08.2	+59.6	2.4	2 08.1	+59.6	2.4
71	0 07.9	+59.6	2.3	1 07.8	+59.6	2.3	2 07.8	+59.6	2.3	3 07.7	+59.7	2.3
72	1 07.5	+59.6	2.2	2 07.4	+59.7	2.2	3 07.4	+59.6	2.2	4 07.4	+59.6	2.2
73	2 07.1	+59.6	2.0	3 07.1	+59.6	2.0	4 07.0	+59.6	2.0	5 07.0	+59.6	2.1
74	3 06.7	+59.6	1.9	4 06.7	+59.6	1.9	5 06.6	+59.6	1.9	6 06.6	+59.6	1.9
75	4 06.3	+59.6	1.8	5 06.3	+59.6	1.8	6 06.2	+59.6	1.8	7 06.2	+59.6	1.8
76	5 05.9	+59.6	1.7	6 05.9	+59.6	1.7	7 05.8	+59.6	1.7	8 05.8	+59.6	1.7
77	6 05.5	+59.6	1.6	7 05.5	+59.6	1.6	8 05.4	+59.6	1.6	9 05.4	+59.6	1.6
78	7 05.1	+59.6	1.5	8 05.1	+59.6	1.5	9 05.0	+59.6	1.5	10 05.0	+59.6	1.5
79	8 04.7	+59.6	1.3	9 04.7	+59.5	1.3	10 04.6	+59.6	1.4	11 04.6	+59.6	1.4
80	9 04.3	+59.5	1.2	10 04.2	+59.6	1.2	11 04.2	+59.6	1.2	12 04.2	+59.6	1.2
81	10 03.8	+59.6	1.1	11 03.8	+59.6	1.1	12 03.8	+59.6	1.1	13 03.8	+59.6	1.1
82	11 03.4	+59.6	1.0	12 03.4	+59.6	1.0	13 03.4	+59.6	1.0	14 03.4	+59.6	1.0
83	12 03.0	+59.6	0.9	13 03.0	+59.6	0.9	14 03.0	+59.6	0.9	15 03.0	+59.6	0.9
84	13 02.6	+59.6	0.7	14 02.6	+59.6	0.8	15 02.6	+59.6	0.8	16 02.6	+59.6	0.8
85	14 02.2	+59.5	0.6	15 02.2	+59.5	0.6	16 02.2	+59.5	0.6	17 02.2	+59.5	0.6
86	15 01.7	+59.6	0.5	16 01.7	+59.6	0.5	17 01.7	+59.6	0.5	18 01.7	+59.6	0.5
87	16 01.3	+59.6	0.4	17 01.3	+59.6	0.4	18 01.3	+59.6	0.4	19 01.3	+59.6	0.4
88	17 00.9	+59.5	0.3	18 00.9	+59.5	0.3	19 00.9	+59.5	0.3	20 00.9	+59.5	0.3
89	18 00.4	+59.6	0.1	19 00.4	+59.6	0.1	20 00.4	+59.6	0.1	21 00.4	+59.6	0.1
90	19 00.0	+59.5	0.0	20 00.0	+59.5	0.0	21 00.0	+59.5	0.0	22 00.0	+59.5	0.0
	19°			20°			21°			22°		

S. Lat. {L.H.A. greater than 180° ....Zn=180°−Z; L.H.A. less than 180°...........Zn=180°+Z}

LATITUDE **SAME** NAME AS DECLINATION L.H.A. 173°, 187°

17

Dec.	15°			16°			17°			18°			19°			20°			21°			22°			Dec.
	Hc	d	Z	Hc	d	Z	Hc	d	Z	Hc	d	Z	Hc	d	Z	Hc	d	Z	Hc	d	Z	Hc	d	Z	
°	° ′	′	°	° ′	′	°	° ′	′	°	° ′	′	°	° ′	′	°	° ′	′	°	° ′	′	°	° ′	′	°	°
0	73 02.6	+52.9	151.5	72 09.5	+53.7	153.0	71 15.7	+54.4	154.3	70 21.4	+54.9	155.5	69 26.5	+55.4	156.7	68 31.2	+55.9	157.7	67 35.5	+56.3	158.6	66 39.5	+56.6	159.4	0
1	73 55.5	+52.0	149.8	73 03.2	+52.9	151.5	72 10.1	+53.7	153.0	71 16.3	+54.4	154.3	70 21.9	+55.0	155.5	69 27.1	+55.5	156.6	68 31.8	+55.9	157.7	67 36.1	+56.3	158.6	1
2	74 47.5	+51.0	148.0	73 56.1	+52.1	149.8	73 03.8	+53.0	151.5	72 10.7	+53.8	153.0	71 16.9	+54.5	154.3	70 22.6	+55.0	155.5	69 27.7	+55.5	156.6	68 32.4	+56.0	157.7	2
3	75 38.5	+49.7	145.9	74 48.2	+51.0	148.0	73 56.8	+52.1	149.8	73 04.5	+53.0	151.5	72 11.4	+53.8	153.0	71 17.6	+54.5	154.3	70 23.2	+55.1	155.5	69 28.4	+55.6	156.6	3
4	76 28.2	+48.4	143.6	75 39.2	+49.9	145.9	74 48.9	+51.2	148.0	73 57.5	+52.2	149.8	73 05.2	+53.1	151.5	72 12.1	+53.9	153.0	71 18.3	+54.6	154.3	70 24.0	+55.1	155.6	4
5	77 16.6	+46.6	141.0	76 29.1	+48.4	143.6	75 40.1	+49.9	145.9	74 49.7	+51.3	148.0	73 58.3	+52.4	149.9	73 06.0	+53.2	151.5	72 12.9	+54.0	153.0	71 19.1	+54.7	154.4	5
6	78 03.2	+44.5•	138.0	77 17.5	+46.7	141.0	76 30.0	+48.6	143.6	75 41.0	+50.0	146.0	74 50.7	+51.3	148.0	73 59.2	+52.4	149.9	73 06.9	+53.3	151.5	72 13.8	+54.0	153.0	6
7	78 47.7	+42.0•	134.7	78 04.2	+44.7•	138.1	77 18.6	+46.8	141.0	76 31.0	+48.7	143.7	75 42.0	+50.1	146.0	74 51.6	+51.5	148.1	74 00.2	+52.5	149.9	73 07.8	+53.4	151.6	7
8	79 29.7	+38.9•	130.9	78 48.9	+42.1•	134.7	78 05.4	+44.7•	138.1	77 19.7	+46.9	141.1	76 32.1	+48.8	143.7	75 43.1	+50.2	146.0	74 52.7	+51.5	148.1	74 01.2	+52.6	150.0	8
9	80 08.6	+35.1•	126.6	79 31.0	+39.0•	130.9	78 50.1	+42.3•	134.8	78 06.6	+44.9•	138.1	77 20.9	+47.1	141.1	76 33.3	+48.9	143.8	75 44.2	+50.4	146.1	74 53.8	+51.6	148.2	9
10	80 43.7	+30.7•	121.7	80 10.0	+35.3•	126.6	79 32.4	+39.2•	131.0	78 51.5	+42.4•	134.8	78 08.0	+45.0•	138.2	77 22.2	+47.2	141.2	76 34.6	+49.0	143.8	75 45.4	+50.5	146.1	10
11	81 14.4	+25.4•	116.2	80 45.3	+30.9•	121.7	80 11.6	+35.4•	126.7	79 33.9	+39.3•	131.0	78 53.0	+42.5•	134.9	78 09.4	+45.1•	138.3	77 23.6	+47.3	141.3	76 35.9	+49.1	143.9	11
12	81 39.8	+19.3•	110.1	81 16.2	+25.5•	116.2	80 47.0	+31.0•	121.8	80 13.2	+35.7•	126.7	79 35.5	+39.5•	131.1	78 54.5	+42.7•	135.0	78 10.9	+45.3•	138.3	77 25.0	+47.5	141.3	12
13	81 59.1	+12.4•	103.5	81 41.7	+19.4•	110.1	81 18.0	+25.8•	116.3	80 48.9	+31.1•	121.8	80 15.0	+35.8•	126.8	79 37.2	+39.7•	131.2	78 56.2	+42.8•	135.0	78 12.5	+45.4•	138.4	13
14	82 11.5	+4.9•	96.3	82 01.1	+12.5•	103.5	81 43.8	+19.5•	110.2	81 20.0	+25.9•	116.3	80 50.8	+31.4•	121.9	80 16.9	+36.0•	126.9	79 39.0	+39.9•	131.3	78 57.9	+43.0•	135.1	14
15	82 16.4	-2.8•	89.0	82 13.6	+5.0•	96.3	82 03.3	+12.6•	103.5	81 45.9	+19.7•	110.2	81 22.2	+26.0•	116.4	80 52.9	+31.5•	122.0	80 18.9	+36.1•	127.0	79 40.9	+40.1•	131.4	15
16	82 13.6	-10.3•	81.6	82 18.6	-2.7•	88.9	82 15.9	+5.1•	96.3	82 05.6	+12.7•	103.5	81 48.2	+19.8•	110.2	81 24.4	+26.2•	116.5	80 55.0	+31.7•	122.1	80 21.0	+36.3•	127.1	16
17	82 03.3	-17.4•	74.3	82 15.9	-10.3•	81.4	82 21.0	-2.7•	88.8	82 18.3	+5.2•	96.3	82 08.0	+12.9•	103.5	81 50.6	+20.0•	110.3	81 26.7	+26.4•	116.5	80 57.3	+31.9•	122.2	17
18	81 45.9	-23.7•	67.5	82 05.6	-17.4•	74.2	82 18.3	-10.3•	81.3	82 23.5	-2.6•	88.8	82 20.9	+5.3•	96.2	82 10.6	+13.0•	103.5	81 53.1	+20.2•	110.3	81 29.2	+26.6•	116.6	18
19	81 22.2	-29.3•	61.3	81 48.2	-23.8•	67.4	82 08.0	-17.4•	74.1	82 20.9	-10.3•	81.2	82 26.2	-2.6•	88.7	82 23.6	+5.4•	96.2	82 13.3	+13.2•	103.5	81 55.8	+20.4•	110.4	19
20	80 52.9	-34.0•	55.6	81 24.4	-29.4•	61.1	81 50.6	-23.9•	67.2	82 10.6	-17.5•	73.9	82 23.6	-10.3•	81.1	82 29.0	-2.5•	88.6	82 26.5	+5.4•	96.2	82 16.2	+13.2•	103.5	20
21	80 18.9	-38.0•	50.6	80 55.0	-34.0•	55.4	81 26.7	-29.4•	60.9	81 53.1	-23.9•	67.0	82 13.3	-17.5•	73.8	82 26.5	-10.3•	81.0	82 31.9	-2.5•	88.6	82 29.4	+5.6•	96.2	21
22	79 40.9	-41.1•	46.1	80 21.0	-38.0•	50.3	80 57.3	-34.1•	55.2	81 29.2	-29.5•	60.7	81 55.8	-24.0•	66.8	82 16.2	-17.6•	73.6	82 29.4	-10.3•	80.9	82 35.0	-2.4•	88.5	22
23	78 59.8	-43.9•	42.2	79 43.0	-41.3•	45.9	80 23.2	-38.1•	50.1	80 59.7	-34.2•	54.9	81 31.8	-29.6•	60.4	81 58.6	-24.1•	66.6	82 19.1	-17.6•	73.4	82 32.6	-10.4•	80.8	23
24	78 15.9	-46.0•	38.7	79 01.7	-43.9•	41.9	79 45.1	-41.4•	45.6	80 25.5	-38.2•	49.8	81 02.2	-34.3•	54.7	81 34.5	-29.7•	60.2	82 01.5	-24.1•	66.4	82 22.2	-17.6•	73.3	24
25	77 29.9	-47.9	35.6	78 17.8	-46.2•	38.4	79 03.7	-44.0•	41.7	79 47.3	-41.5•	45.4	80 27.9	-38.3•	49.6	81 04.8	-34.4•	54.4	81 37.4	-29.9•	60.0	82 04.6	-24.3•	66.2	25
26	76 42.0	-49.4	32.9	77 31.6	-47.9	35.4	78 19.7	-46.2•	38.2	79 05.8	-44.1•	41.4	79 49.6	-41.6•	45.1	80 30.4	-38.5•	49.3	81 07.5	-34.6•	54.2	81 40.3	-29.9•	59.7	26
27	75 52.6	-50.7	30.5	76 43.7	-49.5	32.7	77 33.5	-48.0	35.1	78 21.7	-46.3•	37.9	79 08.0	-44.2•	41.1	79 51.9	-41.6•	44.8	80 32.9	-38.5•	49.0	81 10.4	-34.8•	53.9	27
28	75 01.9	-51.7	28.4	75 54.2	-50.7	30.3	76 45.5	-49.6	32.4	77 35.4	-48.1	34.9	78 23.8	-46.4•	37.7	79 10.3	-44.3•	40.8	79 54.4	-41.8•	44.5	80 35.6	-38.6•	48.8	28
29	74 10.2	-52.6	26.5	75 03.5	-51.8	28.2	75 55.9	-50.8	30.1	76 47.3	-49.6	32.2	77 37.4	-48.2	34.6	78 26.0	-46.5•	37.4	79 12.6	-44.4•	40.6	79 57.0	-41.9•	44.2	29
30	73 17.6	-53.4	24.8	74 11.7	-52.7	26.3	75 05.1	-51.8	27.9	75 57.7	-50.9	29.8	76 49.2	-49.7	31.9	77 39.5	-48.3	34.3	78 28.2	-46.6•	37.1	79 15.1	-44.6•	40.3	30
31	72 24.2	-54.1	23.2	73 19.0	-53.4	24.6	74 13.3	-52.8	26.0	75 06.8	-51.9	27.7	75 59.5	-50.9	29.5	76 51.2	-49.8	31.6	77 41.6	-48.4	34.0	78 30.5	-46.7	36.8	31
32	71 30.1	-54.6	21.8	72 25.6	-54.1	23.0	73 20.5	-53.5	24.3	74 14.9	-52.8	25.8	75 08.6	-52.0	27.4	76 01.4	-51.1	29.3	76 53.2	-49.9	31.3	77 43.8	-48.5	33.7	32
33	70 35.5	-55.1	20.6	71 31.5	-54.7	21.6	72 27.0	-54.1	22.8	73 22.1	-53.6	24.1	74 16.6	-52.9	25.5	75 10.3	-52.0	27.1	76 03.3	-51.1	29.0	76 55.3	-50.0	31.1	33
34	69 40.4	-55.5	19.4	70 36.8	-55.1	20.3	71 32.9	-54.7	21.4	72 28.5	-54.2	22.5	73 23.7	-53.6	23.8	74 18.3	-53.0	25.2	75 12.2	-52.1	26.9	76 05.3	-51.2	28.7	34
35	68 44.9	-55.9	18.3	69 41.7	-55.6	19.2	70 38.2	-55.2	20.1	71 34.3	-54.7	21.1	72 30.1	-54.3	22.3	73 25.3	-53.6	23.6	74 20.1	-53.1	25.0	75 14.1	-52.2	26.6	35
36	67 49.0	-56.3	17.3	68 46.1	-55.9	18.1	69 43.0	-55.6	19.0	70 39.6	-55.2	19.9	71 35.8	-54.8	20.9	72 31.7	-54.3	22.0	73 27.0	-53.7	23.3	74 21.9	-53.1	24.7	36
37	66 52.7	-56.5	16.4	67 50.2	-56.3	17.1	68 47.4	-56.0	17.9	69 44.4	-55.7	18.7	70 41.0	-55.2	19.6	71 37.4	-54.9	20.6	72 33.3	-54.4	21.8	73 28.8	-53.8	23.0	37
38	65 56.2	-56.8	15.6	66 53.9	-56.5	16.2	67 51.4	-56.3	16.9	68 48.7	-56.0	17.7	69 45.8	-55.7	18.5	70 42.5	-55.3	19.4	71 38.9	-54.9	20.4	72 35.0	-54.5	21.5	38
39	64 59.4	-56.9	14.8	65 57.4	-56.8	15.4	66 55.1	-56.5	16.0	67 52.7	-56.3	16.7	68 50.1	-56.1	17.4	69 47.2	-55.7	18.2	70 44.0	-55.3	19.1	71 40.5	-54.9	20.1	39
40	64 02.5	-57.2	14.1	65 00.6	-57.0	14.6	65 58.6	-56.9	15.2	66 56.4	-56.6	15.8	67 54.0	-56.3	16.5	68 51.5	-56.1	17.2	69 48.7	-55.8	18.0	70 45.6	-55.5	18.9	40
41	63 05.3	-57.4	13.4	64 03.6	-57.3	13.9	65 01.7	-57.0	14.4	65 59.8	-56.9	15.0	66 57.7	-56.7	15.6	67 55.4	-56.4	16.2	68 52.9	-56.2	16.9	69 50.1	-55.8	17.7	41
42	62 07.9	-57.6	12.8	63 06.3	-57.4	13.2	64 04.7	-57.3	13.7	65 02.9	-57.1	14.2	66 01.0	-56.9	14.7	66 59.0	-56.7	15.3	67 56.7	-56.4	16.0	68 54.3	-56.2	16.7	42
43	61 10.3	-57.7	12.2	62 08.9	-57.5	12.6	63 07.4	-57.4	13.0	64 05.8	-57.2	13.5	65 04.1	-57.1	14.0	66 02.3	-56.9	14.5	67 00.3	-56.7	15.1	67 58.1	-56.4	15.7	43
44	60 12.6	-57.8	11.6	61 11.4	-57.7	12.0	62 10.0	-57.6	12.4	63 08.6	-57.5	12.8	64 07.0	-57.3	13.3	65 05.4	-57.2	13.7	66 03.6	-57.0	14.3	67 01.7	-56.8	14.9	44
45	59 14.8	-57.9	11.1	60 13.7	-57.9	11.4	61 12.4	-57.7	11.8	62 11.1	-57.6	12.2	63 09.7	-57.5	12.6	64 08.2	-57.3	13.0	65 06.6	-57.1	13.5	66 04.9	-57.0	14.0	45
46	58 16.9	-58.1	10.6	59 15.8	-58.0	10.9	60 14.7	-57.9	11.2	61 13.5	-57.7	11.6	62 12.2	-57.6	12.0	63 10.9	-57.5	12.4	64 09.5	-57.4	12.8	65 07.9	-57.2	13.3	46
47	57 18.8	-58.2	10.1	58 17.8	-58.0	10.4	59 16.8	-58.0	10.7	60 15.8	-57.9	11.0	61 14.6	-57.8	11.4	62 13.4	-57.7	11.8	63 12.1	-57.5	12.2	64 10.7	-57.4	12.6	47
48	56 20.6	-58.2	9.7	57 19.8	-58.2	9.9	58 18.8	-58.1	10.2	59 17.9	-58.0	10.5	60 16.8	-57.9	10.8	61 15.7	-57.8	11.2	62 14.6	-57.7	11.5	63 13.3	-57.6	11.9	48
49	55 22.4	-58.3	9.2	56 21.6	-58.3	9.5	57 20.7	-58.1	9.7	58 19.9	-58.2	10.0	59 18.9	-58.0	10.3	60 17.9	-57.9	10.6	61 16.9	-57.9	11.0	62 15.7	-57.7	11.3	49
50	54 24.1	-58.5	8.8	55 23.3	-58.3	9.1	56 22.6	-58.3	9.3	57 21.7	-58.2	9.5	58 20.9	-58.1	9.8	59 20.0	-58.1	10.1	60 19.0	-57.9	10.4	61 18.0	-57.9	10.7	50
51	53 25.6	-58.5	8.5	54 25.0	-58.5	8.7	55 24.3	-58.4	8.9	56 23.5	-58.3	9.1	57 22.8	-58.3	9.4	58 21.9	-58.1	9.6	59 21.1	-58.1	9.9	60 20.1	-57.9	10.2	51
52	52 27.1	-58.5	8.1	53 26.5	-58.5	8.3	54 25.9	-58.4	8.5	55 25.2	-58.4	8.7	56 24.5	-58.3	8.9	57 23.8	-58.3	9.1	58 23.0	-58.2	9.4	59 22.2	-58.1	9.7	52
53	51 28.6	-58.6	7.7	52 28.0	-58.5	7.9	53 27.5	-58.6	8.1	54 26.8	-58.4	8.3	55 26.2	-58.4	8.5	56 25.5	-58.3	8.7	57 24.8	-58.3	8.9	58 24.1	-58.2	9.2	53
54	50 30.0	-58.7	7.4	51 29.5	-58.7	7.5	52 28.9	-58.5	7.7	53 28.4	-58.6	7.9	54 27.8	-58.5	8.1	55 27.2	-58.4	8.3	56 26.5	-58.3	8.5	57 25.9	-58.3	8.7	54
55	49 31.3	-58.7	7.1	50 30.8	-58.6	7.2	51 30.4	-58.7	7.4	52 29.8	-58.5	7.5	53 29.3	-58.5	7.7	54 28.8	-58.5	7.9	55 28.2	-58.5	8.1	56 27.6	-58.4	8.3	55
56	48 32.6	-58.8	6.8	49 32.2	-58.8	6.9	50 31.7	-58.7	7.0	51 31.3	-58.7	7.2	52 30.8	-58.6	7.3	53 30.3	-58.6	7.5	54 29.7	-58.5	7.7	55 29.2	-58.5	7.9	56
57	47 33.8	-58.8	6.4	48 33.4	-58.8	6.6	49 33.0	-58.7	6.7	50 32.6	-58.7	6.9	51 32.2	-58.7	7.0	52 31.7	-58.6	7.2	53 31.2	-58.6	7.3	54 30.7	-58.5	7.5	57
58	46 35.0	-58.9	6.2	47 34.6	-58.8	6.3	48 34.3	-58.8	6.4	49 33.9	-58.8	6.5	50 33.5	-58.7	6.7	51 33.1	-58.7	6.8	52 32.6	-58.6	7.0	53 32.2	-58.6	7.1	58
59	45 36.1	-58.9	5.9	46 35.8	-58.9	6.0	47 35.5	-58.9	6.1	48 35.1	-58.8	6.2	49 34.8	-58.8	6.3	50 34.4	-58.8	6.5	51 34.0	-58.7	6.6	52 33.6	-58.7	6.8	59
60	44 37.2	-58.9	5.6	45 36.9	-58.9	5.7	46 36.6	-58.9	5.8	47 36.3	-58.8	5.9	48 36.0	-58.8	6.0	49 35.6	-58.7	6.2	50 35.3	-58.8	6.3	51 34.9	-58.7	6.4	60
61	43 38.3	-59.0	5.3	44 38.0	-58.9	5.4	45 37.7	-58.9	5.5	46 37.5	-58.9	5.6	47 37.2	-58.9	5.7	48 36.9	-58.9	5.9	49 36.5	-58.8	6.0	50 36.2	-58.8	6.1	61
62	42 39.3	-59.0	5.1	43 39.1	-59.0	5.2	44 38.8	-58.9	5.3	45 38.6	-59.0	5.4	46 38.3	-58.9	5.5	47 38.0	-58.9	5.6	48 37.7	-58.8	5.7	49 37.4	-58.8	5.8	62
63	41 40.3	-59.0	4.9	42 40.1	-59.0	4.9	43 39.9	-59.0	5.0	44 39.6	-58.9	5.1	45 39.4	-59.0	5.2	46 39.1	-58.9	5.3	47 38.9	-58.9	5.4	48 38.6	-58.9	5.5	63
64	40 41.3	-59.1	4.6	41 41.1	-59.1	4.7	42 40.9	-59.1	4.8	43 40.7	-59.0	4.8	44 40.4	-58.9	4.9	45 40.2	-58.9	5.0	46 40.0	-58.9	5.1	47 39.7	-58.9	5.2	64
65	39 42.2	-59.1	4.4	40 42.0	-59.0	4.4	41 41.8	-59.0	4.5	42 41.7	-59.1	4.6	43 41.5	-59.1	4.7	44 41.3	-59.0	4.7	45 41.1	-59.0	4.8	46 40.8	-58.9	4.9	65
66	38 43.1	-59.1	4.2	39 43.0	-59.1	4.2	40 42.8	-59.1	4.3	41 42.6	-59.0	4.3	42 42.4	-59.0	4.4	43 42.3	-59.1	4.5	44 42.1	-59.0	4.6	45 41.9	-59.0	4.6	66
67	37 44.0	-59.1	3.9	38 43.9	-59.2	4.0	39 43.7	-59.1	4.1	40 43.6	-59.1	4.1	41 43.4	-59.1	4.2	42 43.2	-59.0	4.2	43 43.1	-59.1	4.3	44 42.9	-59.0	4.4	67
68	36 44.9	-59.2	3.7	37 44.7	-59.1	3.8	38 44.6	-59.1	3.8	39 44.5	-59.1	3.9	40 44.3	-59.1	3.9	41 44.2	-59.1	4.0	42 44.0	-59.0	4.1	43 43.9	-59.1	4.1	68
69	35 45.7	-59.2	3.5	36 45.6	-59.2	3.6	37 45.5	-59.2	3.6	38 45.4	-59.2	3.7	39 45.2	-59.1	3.7	40 45.1	-59.1	3.8	41 45.0	-59.1	3.8	42 44.8	-59.0	3.9	69
70	34 46.5	-59.2	3.3	35 46.4	-59.2	3.4	36 46.3	-59.2	3.4	37 46.2	-59.2	3.5	38 46.1	-59.2	3.5	39 46.0	-59.2	3.6	40 45.9	-59.2	3.6	41 45.8	-59.2	3.7	70
71	33 47.3	-59.2	3.1	34 47.2	-59.2	3.2	35 47.1	-59.2	3.2	36 47.0	-59.1	3.2	37 46.9	-59.1	3.3	38 46.8	-59.1	3.3	39 46.7	-59.1	3.4	40 46.6	-59.1	3.4	71
72	32 48.1	-59.2	2.9	33 48.0	-59.2	3.0	34 47.9	-59.2	3.0	35 47.9	-59.2	3.0	36 47.8	-59.2	3.1	37 47.7	-59.2	3.1	38 47.6	-59.2	3.2	39 47.5	-59.2	3.2	72
73	31 48.9	-59.3	2.7	32 48.8	-59.2	2.8	33 48.7	-59.2	2.8	34 48.7	-59.3	2.8	35 48.6	-59.2	2.9	36 48.5	-59.2	2.9	37 48.4	-59.2	3.0	38 48.3	-59.1	3.0	73
74	30 49.6	-59.2	2.6	31 49.6	-59.3	2.6	32 49.5	-59.3	2.6	33 49.4	-59.2	2.6	34 49.4	-59.3	2.7	35 49.3	-59.2	2.7	36 49.2	-59.2	2.7	37 49.2	-59.2	2.8	74
75	29 50.4	-59.3	2.4	30 50.3	-59.3	2.4	31 50.2	-59.2	2.4	32 50.2	-59.3	2.5	33 50.1	-59.2	2.5	34 50.1	-59.3	2.5	35 50.0	-59.2	2.5	36 50.0	-59.3	2.6	75
76	28 51.1	-59.3	2.2	29 51.0	-59.3	2.2	30 51.0	-59.3	2.2	31 50.9	-59.2	2.3	32 50.9	-59.3	2.3	33 50.8	-59.2	2.3	34 50.8	-59.3	2.4	35 50.7	-59.2	2.4	76
77	27 51.8	-59.3	2.0	28 51.7	-59.3	2.0	29 51.7	-59.3	2.1	30 51.7	-59.3	2.1	31 51.6	-59.3	2.1	32 51.6	-59.3	2.1	33 51.5	-59.2	2.2	34 51.5	-59.3	2.2	77
78	26 52.5	-59.4	1.9	27 52.4	-59.3	1.9	28 52.4	-59.3	1.9	29 52.4	-59.3	1.9	30 52.3	-59.3	1.9	31 52.3	-59.3	2.0	32 52.3	-59.3	2.0	33 52.2	-59.3	2.0	78
79	25 53.1	-59.3	1.7	26 53.1	-59.3	1.7	27 53.1	-59.3	1.7	28 53.1	-59.4	1.7	29 53.0	-59.3	1.8	30 53.0	-59.3	1.8	31 53.0	-59.3	1.8	32 52.9	-59.2	1.8	79
80	24 53.8	-59.3	1.5	25 53.8	-59.3	1.5	26 53.8	-59.4	1.6	27 53.7	-59.3	1.6	28 53.7	-59.3	1.6	29 53.7	-59.3	1.6	30 53.7	-59.3	1.6	31 53.7	-59.4	1.6	80
81	23 54.5	-59.4	1.4	24 54.5	-59.4	1.4	25 54.4	-59.3	1.4	26 54.4	-59.3	1.4	27 54.4	-59.3	1.4	28 54.4	-59.4	1.4	29 54.4	-59.4	1.4	30 54.3	-59.3	1.5	81
82	22 55.1	-59.3	1.2	23 55.1	-59.4	1.2	24 55.1	-59.4	1.2	25 55.1	-59.4	1.2	26 55.1	-59.4	1.2	27 55.0	-59.3	1.3	28 55.0	-59.3	1.3	29 55.0	-59.3	1.3	82
83	21 55.8	-59.4	1.0	22 55.7	-59.3	1.1	23 55.7	-59.3	1.1	24 55.7	-59.3	1.1	25 55.7	-59.3	1.1	26 55.7	-59.4	1.1	27 55.7	-59.4	1.1	28 55.7	-59.4	1.1	83
84	20 56.4	-59.4	0.9	21 56.4	-59.4	0.9	22 56.4	-59.4	0.9	23 56.4	-59.4	0.9	24 56.4	-59.4	0.9	25 56.3	-59.3	0.9	26 56.3	-59.3	0.9	27 56.3	-59.3	0.9	84
85	19 57.0	-59.4	0.7	20 57.0	-59.4	0.7	21 57.0	-59.4	0.7	22 57.0	-59.4	0.8	23 57.0	-59.4	0.8	24 57.0	-59.4	0.8	25 57.0	-59.4	0.8	26 57.0	-59.4	0.8	85
86	18 57.6	-59.4	0.6	19 57.6	-59.4	0.6	20 57.6	-59.4	0.6	21 57.6	-59.4	0.6	22 57.6	-59.4	0.6	23 57.6	-59.4	0.6	24 57.6	-59.4	0.6	25 57.6	-59.4	0.6	86
87	17 58.2	-59.4	0.4	18 58.2	-59.4	0.4	19 58.2	-59.4	0.4	20 58.2	-59.4	0.4	21 58.2	-59.4	0.5	22 58.2	-59.4	0.5	23 58.2	-59.4	0.5	24 58.2	-59.4	0.5	87
88	16 58.8	-59.4	0.3	17 58.8	-59.4	0.3	18 58.8	-59.4	0.3	19 58.8	-59.4	0.3	20 58.8	-59.4	0.3	21 58.8	-59.4	0.3	22 58.8	-59.4	0.3	23 58.8	-59.4	0.3	88
89	15 59.4	-59.4	0.1	16 59.4	-59.4	0.1	17 59.4	-59.4	0.1	18 59.4	-59.4	0.1	19 59.4	-59.4	0.1	20 59.4	-59.4	0.1	21 59.4	-59.4	0.2	22 59.4	-59.4	0.2	89
90	15 00.0	-59.4	0.0	16 00.0	-59.4	0.0	17 00.0	-59.4	0.0	18 00.0	-59.4	0.0	19 00.0	-59.4	0.0	20 00.0	-59.4	0.0	21 00.0	-59.4	0.0	22 00.0	-59.4	0.0	90
	15°			16°			17°			18°			19°			20°			21°			22°			

LATITUDE CONTRARY NAME TO DECLINATION — L.H.A. 8°, 352°

Dec.	15° Hc	d	Z	16° Hc	d	Z	17° Hc	d	Z	18° Hc	d	Z	Dec.
°	° ′	′	°	° ′	′	°	° ′	′	°	° ′	′	°	°
0	73 02.6	−53.6	151.5	72 09.5	−54.3	153.0	71 15.7	−54.8	154.3	70 21.4	−55.4	155.5	0
1	72 09.0	−54.2	153.0	71 15.2	−54.8	154.3	70 20.9	−55.4	155.6	69 26.0	−55.8	156.7	1
2	71 14.8	−54.8	154.4	70 20.4	−55.3	155.6	69 25.5	−55.7	156.7	68 30.2	−56.1	157.7	2
3	70 20.0	−55.2	155.6	69 25.1	−55.6	156.7	68 29.8	−56.1	157.7	67 34.1	−56.4	158.6	3
4	69 24.8	−55.6	156.7	68 29.5	−56.1	157.7	67 33.7	−56.3	158.7	66 37.7	−56.7	159.5	4
5	68 29.2	−56.0	157.8	67 33.4	−56.3	158.7	66 37.4	−56.7	159.5	65 41.0	−56.9	160.3	5
6	67 33.2	−56.3	158.7	66 37.1	−56.6	159.6	65 40.7	−56.9	160.4	64 44.1	−57.2	161.1	6
7	66 36.9	−56.6	159.6	65 40.5	−56.9	160.4	64 43.8	−57.1	161.1	63 46.9	−57.3	161.8	7
8	65 40.3	−56.9	160.5	64 43.6	−57.1	161.2	63 46.7	−57.3	161.8	62 49.6	−57.5	162.4	8
9	64 43.4	−57.0	161.2	63 46.5	−57.3	161.9	62 49.4	−57.5	162.5	61 52.1	−57.7	163.1	9
10	63 46.4	−57.3	161.9	62 49.2	−57.4	162.5	61 51.9	−57.6	163.1	60 54.4	−57.8	163.6	10
11	62 49.1	−57.4	162.6	61 51.8	−57.6	163.2	60 54.3	−57.8	163.7	59 56.6	−57.9	164.2	11
12	61 51.7	−57.6	163.2	60 54.2	−57.8	163.7	59 56.5	−57.9	164.2	58 58.7	−58.0	164.7	12
13	60 54.1	−57.7	163.8	59 56.4	−57.9	164.3	58 58.6	−58.0	164.7	58 00.7	−58.2	165.2	13
14	59 56.4	−57.9	164.4	58 58.5	−58.0	164.8	58 00.6	−58.1	165.2	57 02.5	−58.2	165.6	14
15	58 58.5	−58.0	164.9	58 00.5	−58.1	165.3	57 02.5	−58.3	165.7	56 04.3	−58.4	166.1	15
16	58 00.5	−58.0	165.4	57 02.4	−58.2	165.8	56 04.2	−58.3	166.1	55 05.9	−58.4	166.5	16
17	57 02.5	−58.2	165.8	56 04.2	−58.3	166.2	55 05.9	−58.4	166.5	54 07.5	−58.5	166.9	17
18	56 04.3	−58.3	166.3	55 05.9	−58.3	166.6	54 07.5	−58.4	166.9	53 09.0	−58.5	167.2	18
19	55 06.0	−58.4	166.7	54 07.6	−58.5	167.0	53 09.1	−58.6	167.3	52 10.5	−58.6	167.6	19
20	54 07.6	−58.4	167.1	53 09.1	−58.5	167.4	52 10.5	−58.6	167.7	51 11.9	−58.7	168.0	20
21	53 09.2	−58.5	167.5	52 10.6	−58.6	167.8	51 11.9	−58.6	168.0	50 13.2	−58.7	168.3	21
22	52 10.7	−58.6	167.9	51 12.0	−58.7	168.1	50 13.3	−58.8	168.4	49 14.5	−58.8	168.6	22
23	51 12.1	−58.6	168.2	50 13.3	−58.7	168.4	49 14.5	−58.7	168.7	48 15.7	−58.8	168.9	23
24	50 13.5	−58.7	168.5	49 14.6	−58.7	168.8	48 15.8	−58.8	169.0	47 16.9	−58.9	169.2	24
25	49 14.8	−58.8	168.9	48 15.9	−58.8	169.1	47 17.0	−58.9	169.3	46 18.0	−58.9	169.5	25
26	48 16.0	−58.7	169.2	47 17.1	−58.8	169.4	46 18.1	−58.9	169.6	45 19.1	−59.0	169.8	26
27	47 17.3	−58.9	169.5	46 18.3	−58.9	169.7	45 19.2	−58.9	169.8	44 20.1	−58.9	170.0	27
28	46 18.4	−58.8	169.8	45 19.4	−59.0	169.9	44 20.3	−59.0	170.1	43 21.2	−59.1	170.3	28
29	45 19.6	−59.0	170.0	44 20.4	−58.9	170.2	43 21.3	−59.0	170.4	42 22.1	−59.0	170.5	29
30	44 20.6	−58.9	170.3	43 21.5	−59.0	170.5	42 22.3	−59.0	170.6	41 23.1	−59.1	170.8	30
31	43 21.7	−59.0	170.6	42 22.5	−59.0	170.7	41 23.3	−59.1	170.9	40 24.0	−59.1	171.0	31
32	42 22.7	−59.0	170.8	41 23.5	−59.1	170.9	40 24.2	−59.1	171.1	39 24.9	−59.1	171.2	32
33	41 23.7	−59.0	171.0	40 24.4	−59.1	171.2	39 25.1	−59.1	171.3	38 25.8	−59.1	171.4	33
34	40 24.7	−59.1	171.3	39 25.3	−59.1	171.4	38 26.0	−59.1	171.5	37 26.7	−59.2	171.6	34
35	39 25.6	−59.1	171.5	38 26.2	−59.1	171.6	37 26.9	−59.2	171.7	36 27.5	−59.2	171.9	35
36	38 26.5	−59.1	171.7	37 27.1	−59.1	171.8	36 27.7	−59.2	172.0	35 28.3	−59.2	172.1	36
37	37 27.4	−59.2	172.0	36 28.0	−59.2	172.1	35 28.5	−59.2	172.2	34 29.1	−59.3	172.3	37
38	36 28.2	−59.1	172.2	35 28.8	−59.2	172.3	34 29.3	−59.2	172.4	33 29.8	−59.2	172.4	38
39	35 29.1	−59.2	172.4	34 29.6	−59.2	172.5	33 30.1	−59.2	172.5	32 30.6	−59.3	172.6	39
40	34 29.9	−59.2	172.6	33 30.4	−59.3	172.7	32 30.9	−59.3	172.7	31 31.3	−59.2	172.8	40
41	33 30.7	−59.3	172.8	32 31.1	−59.2	172.8	31 31.6	−59.3	172.9	30 32.1	−59.3	173.0	41
42	32 31.4	−59.2	173.0	31 31.9	−59.3	173.0	30 32.3	−59.3	173.1	29 32.8	−59.3	173.2	42
43	31 32.2	−59.3	173.1	30 32.6	−59.3	173.2	29 33.0	−59.3	173.3	28 33.5	−59.4	173.3	43
44	30 32.9	−59.2	173.3	29 33.3	−59.2	173.4	28 33.7	−59.3	173.5	27 34.1	−59.3	173.5	44
45	29 33.7	−59.3	173.5	28 34.1	−59.4	173.6	27 34.4	−59.3	173.6	26 34.8	−59.3	173.7	45
46	28 34.4	−59.3	173.7	27 34.7	−59.3	173.7	26 35.1	−59.3	173.8	25 35.5	−59.4	173.8	46
47	27 35.1	−59.3	173.9	26 35.4	−59.3	173.9	25 35.8	−59.4	174.0	24 36.1	−59.4	174.0	47
48	26 35.8	−59.3	174.0	25 36.1	−59.3	174.1	24 36.4	−59.3	174.1	23 36.7	−59.3	174.2	48
49	25 36.5	−59.4	174.2	24 36.8	−59.4	174.2	23 37.1	−59.4	174.3	22 37.4	−59.4	174.3	49
50	24 37.1	−59.3	174.4	23 37.4	−59.4	174.4	22 37.7	−59.4	174.4	21 38.0	−59.4	174.5	50
51	23 37.8	−59.4	174.5	22 38.0	−59.3	174.6	21 38.3	−59.4	174.6	20 38.6	−59.4	174.6	51
52	22 38.4	−59.3	174.7	21 38.7	−59.4	174.7	20 38.9	−59.4	174.7	19 39.2	−59.4	174.8	52
53	21 39.1	−59.4	174.8	20 39.3	−59.4	174.9	19 39.5	−59.4	174.9	18 39.8	−59.4	174.9	53
54	20 39.7	−59.4	175.0	19 39.9	−59.4	175.0	18 40.1	−59.4	175.0	17 40.4	−59.5	175.1	54
55	19 40.3	−59.4	175.1	18 40.5	−59.4	175.2	17 40.7	−59.4	175.2	16 40.9	−59.4	175.2	55
56	18 40.9	−59.4	175.3	17 41.1	−59.4	175.3	16 41.3	−59.4	175.3	15 41.5	−59.4	175.4	56
57	17 41.5	−59.4	175.4	16 41.7	−59.4	175.5	15 41.9	−59.4	175.5	14 42.1	−59.5	175.5	57
58	16 42.1	−59.4	175.6	15 42.3	−59.4	175.6	14 42.5	−59.5	175.6	13 42.6	−59.4	175.6	58
59	15 42.7	−59.4	175.7	14 42.9	−59.5	175.7	13 43.0	−59.4	175.8	12 43.2	−59.5	175.8	59
60	14 43.3	−59.4	175.9	13 43.4	−59.4	175.9	12 43.6	−59.5	175.9	11 43.7	−59.4	175.9	60
61	13 43.9	−59.5	176.0	12 44.0	−59.4	176.0	11 44.2	−59.5	176.0	10 44.3	−59.5	176.1	61
62	12 44.4	−59.4	176.2	11 44.6	−59.5	176.2	10 44.7	−59.4	176.2	9 44.8	−59.4	176.2	62
63	11 45.0	−59.4	176.3	10 45.1	−59.4	176.3	9 45.3	−59.5	176.3	8 45.4	−59.5	176.3	63
64	10 45.6	−59.5	176.4	9 45.7	−59.5	176.5	8 45.8	−59.5	176.5	7 45.9	−59.4	176.5	64
65	9 46.1	−59.4	176.6	8 46.2	−59.5	176.6	7 46.3	−59.4	176.6	6 46.5	−59.5	176.6	65
66	8 46.7	−59.4	176.7	7 46.8	−59.5	176.7	6 46.9	−59.5	176.7	5 47.0	−59.5	176.7	66
67	7 47.3	−59.5	176.9	6 47.3	−59.4	176.9	5 47.4	−59.4	176.9	4 47.5	−59.4	176.9	67
68	6 47.8	−59.4	177.0	5 47.9	−59.5	177.0	4 48.0	−59.5	177.0	3 48.1	−59.5	177.0	68
69	5 48.4	−59.5	177.1	4 48.4	−59.4	177.1	3 48.5	−59.5	177.1	2 48.6	−59.5	177.1	69
70	4 48.9	−59.4	177.3	3 49.0	−59.5	177.3	2 49.0	−59.4	177.3	1 49.1	−59.5	177.3	70
71	3 49.5	−59.5	177.4	2 49.5	−59.4	177.4	1 49.6	−59.5	177.4	0 49.6	−59.4	177.4	71
72	2 50.0	−59.5	177.5	1 50.1	−59.5	177.5	0 50.1	−59.5	177.5	0 09.8	+59.5	2.5	72
73	1 50.5	−59.4	177.7	0 50.6	−59.5	177.7	0 09.4	+59.4	2.3	1 09.3	+59.5	2.3	73
74	0 51.1	−59.5	177.8	0 08.9	+59.4	2.2	1 08.8	+59.5	2.2	2 08.8	+59.4	2.2	74
75	0 08.4	+59.4	2.1	1 08.3	+59.5	2.1	2 08.3	+59.5	2.1	3 08.2	+59.5	2.1	75
76	1 07.8	+59.5	1.9	2 07.8	+59.4	1.9	3 07.8	+59.4	1.9	4 07.7	+59.5	1.9	76
77	2 07.3	+59.4	1.8	3 07.2	+59.5	1.8	4 07.2	+59.5	1.8	5 07.2	+59.5	1.8	77
78	3 06.7	+59.5	1.7	4 06.7	+59.5	1.7	5 06.7	+59.4	1.7	6 06.7	+59.4	1.7	78
79	4 06.2	+59.4	1.5	5 06.2	+59.4	1.5	6 06.1	+59.5	1.5	7 06.1	+59.5	1.5	79
80	5 05.6	+59.5	1.4	6 05.6	+59.5	1.4	7 05.6	+59.5	1.4	8 05.6	+59.4	1.4	80
81	6 05.1	+59.4	1.3	7 05.1	+59.4	1.3	8 05.1	+59.4	1.3	9 05.0	+59.5	1.3	81
82	7 04.5	+59.5	1.1	8 04.5	+59.5	1.1	9 04.5	+59.5	1.1	10 04.5	+59.5	1.1	82
83	8 04.0	+59.4	1.0	9 04.0	+59.4	1.0	10 04.0	+59.4	1.0	11 04.0	+59.4	1.0	83
84	9 03.4	+59.5	0.8	10 03.4	+59.5	0.8	11 03.4	+59.5	0.8	12 03.4	+59.4	0.9	84
85	10 02.9	+59.4	0.7	11 02.9	+59.4	0.7	12 02.9	+59.4	0.7	13 02.8	+59.5	0.7	85
86	11 02.3	+59.4	0.6	12 02.3	+59.4	0.6	13 02.3	+59.4	0.6	14 02.3	+59.4	0.6	86
87	12 01.7	+59.5	0.4	13 01.7	+59.5	0.4	14 01.7	+59.5	0.4	15 01.7	+59.5	0.4	87
88	13 01.2	+59.4	0.3	14 01.2	+59.4	0.3	15 01.2	+59.4	0.3	16 01.2	+59.4	0.3	88
89	14 00.6	+59.4	0.1	15 00.6	+59.4	0.1	16 00.6	+59.4	0.1	17 00.6	+59.4	0.1	89
90	15 00.0	+59.4	0.0	16 00.0	+59.4	0.0	17 00.0	+59.4	0.0	18 00.0	+59.4	0.0	90
	15°			16°			17°			18°			

Dec.	19° Hc	d	Z	20° Hc	d	Z	21° Hc	d	Z	22° Hc	d	Z	Dec.
°	° ′	′	°	° ′	′	°	° ′	′	°	° ′	′	°	°
0	69 26.5	−55.8	156.7	68 31.2	−56.2	157.7	67 35.5	−56.5	158.6	66 39.5	−56.8	159.4	0
1	68 30.7	−56.2	157.7	67 35.0	−56.5	158.6	66 39.0	−56.8	159.4	65 42.7	−57.1	160.2	1
2	67 34.5	−56.4	158.6	66 38.5	−56.8	159.5	65 42.2	−57.1	160.2	64 45.6	−57.3	161.0	2
3	66 38.1	−56.7	159.5	65 41.7	−57.0	160.3	64 45.1	−57.2	161.0	63 48.3	−57.5	161.6	3
4	65 41.4	−57.0	160.3	64 44.7	−57.2	161.0	63 47.9	−57.4	161.7	62 50.8	−57.6	162.3	4
5	64 44.4	−57.2	161.0	63 47.5	−57.4	161.7	62 50.5	−57.6	162.3	61 53.2	−57.8	162.9	5
6	63 47.2	−57.4	161.7	62 50.1	−57.5	162.4	61 52.9	−57.8	162.9	60 55.4	−57.9	163.5	6
7	62 49.8	−57.5	162.4	61 52.6	−57.8	163.0	60 55.1	−57.9	163.5	59 57.5	−58.0	164.0	7
8	61 52.3	−57.7	163.0	60 54.8	−57.8	163.5	59 57.2	−58.0	164.0	58 59.5	−58.2	164.5	8
9	60 54.6	−57.8	163.6	59 57.0	−58.0	164.1	58 59.2	−58.1	164.5	58 01.3	−58.2	165.0	9
10	59 56.8	−58.0	164.1	58 59.0	−58.1	164.6	58 01.1	−58.2	165.0	57 03.1	−58.3	165.4	10
11	58 58.8	−58.0	164.6	58 00.9	−58.2	165.1	57 02.9	−58.3	165.5	56 04.8	−58.4	165.8	11
12	58 00.8	−58.2	165.1	57 02.7	−58.3	165.5	56 04.6	−58.4	165.9	55 06.4	−58.5	166.2	12
13	57 02.6	−58.3	165.6	56 04.4	−58.3	165.9	55 06.2	−58.5	166.3	54 07.9	−58.6	166.6	13
14	56 04.3	−58.3	166.0	55 06.1	−58.5	166.3	54 07.7	−58.5	166.7	53 09.3	−58.6	167.0	14
15	55 06.0	−58.4	166.4	54 07.6	−58.5	166.7	53 09.2	−58.6	167.0	52 10.7	−58.7	167.3	15
16	54 07.6	−58.5	166.8	53 09.1	−58.6	167.1	52 10.6	−58.7	167.4	51 12.0	−58.7	167.7	16
17	53 09.1	−58.6	167.2	52 10.5	−58.6	167.5	51 11.9	−58.7	167.7	50 13.3	−58.8	168.0	17
18	52 10.5	−58.7	167.5	51 11.9	−58.7	167.8	50 13.2	−58.8	168.1	49 14.5	−58.9	168.3	18
19	51 11.8	−58.6	167.9	50 13.2	−58.8	168.1	49 14.4	−58.8	168.4	48 15.6	−58.9	168.6	19
20	50 13.2	−58.8	168.2	49 14.4	−58.8	168.4	48 15.6	−58.9	168.7	47 16.7	−58.9	168.9	20
21	49 14.4	−58.8	168.5	48 15.6	−58.9	168.7	47 16.7	−58.9	169.0	46 17.8	−58.9	169.2	21
22	48 15.6	−58.8	168.8	47 16.7	−58.9	169.0	46 17.8	−58.9	169.2	45 18.9	−59.0	169.4	22
23	47 16.8	−58.9	169.1	46 17.8	−58.9	169.3	45 18.9	−59.0	169.5	44 19.9	−59.1	169.7	23
24	46 17.9	−58.9	169.4	45 18.9	−59.0	169.6	44 19.9	−59.0	169.8	43 20.8	−59.0	169.9	24
25	45 19.0	−59.0	169.7	44 19.9	−59.0	169.8	43 20.9	−59.1	170.0	42 21.8	−59.1	170.2	25
26	44 20.0	−59.0	169.9	43 20.9	−59.0	170.1	42 21.8	−59.1	170.3	41 22.7	−59.2	170.4	26
27	43 21.0	−59.0	170.2	42 21.9	−59.1	170.3	41 22.7	−59.1	170.5	40 23.5	−59.1	170.6	27
28	42 22.0	−59.1	170.4	41 22.8	−59.1	170.6	40 23.6	−59.1	170.7	39 24.4	−59.2	170.8	28
29	41 22.9	−59.0	170.7	40 23.7	−59.1	170.8	39 24.5	−59.2	170.9	38 25.2	−59.2	171.1	29
30	40 23.9	−59.1	170.9	39 24.6	−59.1	171.0	38 25.3	−59.1	171.2	37 26.0	−59.2	171.3	30
31	39 24.8	−59.2	171.1	38 25.5	−59.2	171.2	37 26.2	−59.2	171.4	36 26.8	−59.2	171.5	31
32	38 25.6	−59.1	171.3	37 26.3	−59.2	171.5	36 27.0	−59.3	171.6	35 27.6	−59.3	171.7	32
33	37 26.5	−59.2	171.5	36 27.1	−59.2	171.7	35 27.7	−59.2	171.8	34 28.3	−59.2	171.9	33
34	36 27.3	−59.2	171.8	35 27.9	−59.2	171.9	34 28.5	−59.3	172.0	33 29.1	−59.3	172.0	34
35	35 28.1	−59.2	172.0	34 28.7	−59.3	172.1	33 29.2	−59.2	172.1	32 29.8	−59.3	172.2	35
36	34 28.9	−59.3	172.1	33 29.4	−59.3	172.2	32 30.0	−59.3	172.3	31 30.5	−59.3	172.4	36
37	33 29.6	−59.2	172.3	32 30.1	−59.2	172.4	31 30.7	−59.3	172.5	30 31.2	−59.4	172.6	37
38	32 30.4	−59.3	172.5	31 30.9	−59.3	172.6	30 31.4	−59.4	172.7	29 31.8	−59.3	172.8	38
39	31 31.1	−59.3	172.7	30 31.6	−59.3	172.8	29 32.0	−59.3	172.9	28 32.5	−59.4	172.9	39
40	30 31.8	−59.3	172.9	29 32.3	−59.4	173.0	28 32.7	−59.3	173.0	27 33.1	−59.3	173.1	40
41	29 32.5	−59.3	173.1	28 32.9	−59.3	173.1	27 33.4	−59.4	173.2	26 33.8	−59.4	173.3	41
42	28 33.2	−59.3	173.2	27 33.6	−59.4	173.3	26 34.0	−59.4	173.4	25 34.4	−59.4	173.4	42
43	27 33.9	−59.4	173.4	26 34.2	−59.3	173.5	25 34.6	−59.3	173.5	24 35.0	−59.4	173.6	43
44	26 34.5	−59.3	173.6	25 34.9	−59.4	173.6	24 35.3	−59.4	173.7	23 35.6	−59.4	173.7	44
45	25 35.2	−59.4	173.7	24 35.5	−59.4	173.8	23 35.9	−59.4	173.8	22 36.2	−59.4	173.9	45
46	24 35.8	−59.4	173.9	23 36.1	−59.4	173.9	22 36.5	−59.4	174.0	21 36.8	−59.4	174.0	46
47	23 36.4	−59.4	174.1	22 36.7	−59.4	174.1	21 37.1	−59.5	174.1	20 37.4	−59.5	174.2	47
48	22 37.0	−59.4	174.2	21 37.3	−59.4	174.3	20 37.6	−59.4	174.3	19 37.9	−59.4	174.3	48
49	21 37.6	−59.4	174.4	20 37.9	−59.4	174.4	19 38.2	−59.4	174.4	18 38.5	−59.4	174.5	49
50	20 38.2	−59.4	174.5	19 38.5	−59.4	174.5	18 38.8	−59.4	174.6	17 39.1	−59.5	174.6	50
51	19 38.8	−59.4	174.7	18 39.1	−59.4	174.7	17 39.4	−59.5	174.7	16 39.6	−59.5	174.8	51
52	18 39.4	−59.4	174.8	17 39.7	−59.5	174.8	16 39.9	−59.4	174.9	15 40.1	−59.4	174.9	52
53	17 40.0	−59.4	175.0	16 40.2	−59.4	175.0	15 40.5	−59.5	175.0	14 40.7	−59.5	175.0	53
54	16 40.6	−59.5	175.1	15 40.8	−59.5	175.1	14 41.0	−59.5	175.1	13 41.2	−59.4	175.2	54
55	15 41.1	−59.4	175.2	14 41.3	−59.4	175.3	13 41.5	−59.4	175.3	12 41.8	−59.5	175.3	55
56	14 41.7	−59.4	175.4	13 41.9	−59.5	175.4	12 42.1	−59.5	175.4	11 42.3	−59.5	175.4	56
57	13 42.3	−59.5	175.5	12 42.4	−59.4	175.5	11 42.6	−59.5	175.6	10 42.8	−59.5	175.6	57
58	12 42.8	−59.4	175.7	11 43.0	−59.5	175.7	10 43.1	−59.4	175.7	9 43.3	−59.5	175.7	58
59	11 43.4	−59.5	175.8	10 43.5	−59.5	175.8	9 43.7	−59.5	175.8	8 43.8	−59.5	175.8	59
60	10 43.9	−59.5	175.9	9 44.0	−59.4	176.0	8 44.2	−59.5	176.0	7 44.3	−59.4	176.0	60
61	9 44.4	−59.4	176.1	8 44.6	−59.5	176.1	7 44.7	−59.5	176.1	6 44.9	−59.5	176.1	61
62	8 45.0	−59.5	176.2	7 45.1	−59.5	176.2	6 45.2	−59.5	176.2	5 45.4	−59.5	176.2	62
63	7 45.5	−59.5	176.3	6 45.6	−59.5	176.4	5 45.7	−59.4	176.4	4 45.9	−59.5	176.4	63
64	6 46.0	−59.4	176.5	5 46.1	−59.4	176.5	4 46.3	−59.5	176.5	3 46.4	−59.5	176.5	64
65	5 46.6	−59.5	176.6	4 46.7	−59.5	176.6	3 46.8	−59.5	176.6	2 46.9	−59.5	176.6	65
66	4 47.1	−59.5	176.7	3 47.2	−59.5	176.7	2 47.3	−59.5	176.8	1 47.4	−59.5	176.8	66
67	3 47.6	−59.5	176.9	2 47.7	−59.5	176.9	1 47.8	−59.5	176.9	0 47.9	−59.5	176.9	67
68	2 48.1	−59.4	177.0	1 48.2	−59.5	177.0	0 48.3	−59.5	177.0	0 11.6	+59.5	3.0	68
69	1 48.7	−59.5	177.1	0 48.7	−59.5	177.1	0 11.2	+59.5	2.9	1 11.1	+59.5	2.9	69
70	0 49.2	−59.5	177.3	0 10.8	+59.4	2.7	1 10.7	+59.5	2.7	2 10.6	+59.5	2.7	70
71	0 10.3	+59.5	2.6	1 10.2	+59.5	2.6	2 10.2	+59.5	2.6	3 10.1	+59.5	2.6	71
72	1 09.8	+59.5	2.5	2 09.7	+59.5	2.5	3 09.7	+59.5	2.5	4 09.6	+59.5	2.5	72
73	2 09.3	+59.4	2.3	3 09.2	+59.5	2.3	4 09.2	+59.4	2.3	5 09.1	+59.5	2.3	73
74	3 08.7	+59.5	2.2	4 08.7	+59.5	2.2	5 08.6	+59.5	2.2	6 08.6	+59.5	2.2	74
75	4 08.2	+59.5	2.1	5 08.2	+59.4	2.1	6 08.1	+59.5	2.1	7 08.1	+59.5	2.1	75
76	5 07.7	+59.5	1.9	6 07.6	+59.5	1.9	7 07.6	+59.5	1.9	8 07.6	+59.5	1.9	76
77	6 07.2	+59.4	1.8	7 07.1	+59.5	1.8	8 07.1	+59.5	1.8	9 07.1	+59.5	1.8	77
78	7 06.6	+59.5	1.7	8 06.6	+59.5	1.7	9 06.6	+59.5	1.7	10 06.6	+59.4	1.7	78
79	8 06.1	+59.5	1.5	9 06.1	+59.4	1.5	10 06.1	+59.4	1.5	11 06.0	+59.5	1.6	79
80	9 05.6	+59.4	1.4	10 05.5	+59.5	1.4	11 05.5	+59.5	1.4	12 05.5	+59.5	1.4	80
81	10 05.0	+59.5	1.3	11 05.0	+59.5	1.3	12 05.0	+59.5	1.3	13 05.0	+59.4	1.3	81
82	11 04.5	+59.4	1.1	12 04.5	+59.4	1.1	13 04.5	+59.5	1.1	14 04.4	+59.5	1.1	82
83	12 03.9	+59.5	1.0	13 03.9	+59.5	1.0	14 03.9	+59.5	1.0	15 03.9	+59.5	1.0	83
84	13 03.4	+59.4	0.9	14 03.4	+59.4	0.9	15 03.4	+59.4	0.9	16 03.4	+59.4	0.9	84
85	14 02.8	+59.5	0.7	15 02.8	+59.5	0.7	16 02.8	+59.5	0.7	17 02.8	+59.5	0.7	85
86	15 02.3	+59.4	0.6	16 02.3	+59.4	0.6	17 02.3	+59.4	0.6	18 02.3	+59.4	0.6	86
87	16 01.7	+59.5	0.4	17 01.7	+59.5	0.4	18 01.7	+59.5	0.4	19 01.7	+59.5	0.4	87
88	17 01.2	+59.4	0.3	18 01.2	+59.4	0.3	19 01.2	+59.4	0.3	20 01.2	+59.4	0.3	88
89	18 00.6	+59.4	0.1	19 00.6	+59.4	0.1	20 00.6	+59.4	0.1	21 00.6	+59.4	0.1	89
90	19 00.0	+59.4	0.0	20 00.0	+59.4	0.0	21 00.0	+59.4	0.0	22 00.0	+59.4	0.0	90
	19°			20°			21°			22°			

S. Lat. {L.H.A. greater than 180° ....Zn=180°−Z; L.H.A. less than 180°...........Zn=180°+Z}

LATITUDE SAME NAME AS DECLINATION — L.H.A. 172°, 188°

9°, 351° L.H.A. LATITUDE SAME NAME AS DECLINATION

N. Lat. {L.H.A. greater than 180° .....Zn=Z
L.H.A. less than 180°............Zn=360°-Z}

Dec.	15° Hc	15° d	15° Z	16° Hc	16° d	16° Z	17° Hc	17° d	17° Z	18° Hc	18° d	18° Z
°	° ′	′	°	° ′	′	°	° ′	′	°	° ′	′	°
0	72 33.6	+51.4	148.5	71 42.0	+52.3	150.1	70 49.6	+53.1	151.6	69 56.5	+53.8	152.9
1	73 25.0	+50.4	146.8	72 34.3	+51.5	148.5	71 42.7	+52.4	150.1	70 50.3	+53.2	151.5
2	74 15.4	+49.2	144.8	73 25.8	+50.4	146.8	72 35.1	+51.5	148.5	71 43.5	+52.4	150.1
3	75 04.6	+47.9	142.7	74 16.2	+49.3	144.8	73 26.6	+50.6	146.8	72 35.9	+51.6	148.5
4	75 52.5	+46.2	140.2	75 05.5	+48.0	142.7	74 17.2	+49.4	144.8	73 27.5	+50.7	146.8
5	76 38.7	+44.4•	137.6	75 53.5	+46.4	140.3	75 06.6	+48.0	142.7	74 18.2	+49.5	144.8
6	77 23.1	+42.2•	134.6	76 39.9	+44.5•	137.6	75 54.6	+46.5	140.3	75 07.7	+48.2	142.7
7	78 05.3	+39.4•	131.2	77 24.4	+42.3•	134.6	76 41.1	+44.7•	137.6	75 55.9	+46.6	140.3
8	78 44.7	+36.3•	127.5	78 06.7	+39.6•	131.2	77 25.8	+42.4•	134.6	76 42.5	+44.8•	137.6
9	79 21.0	+32.6•	123.3	78 46.3	+36.4•	127.5	78 08.2	+39.7•	131.3	77 27.3	+42.5•	134.7
10	79 53.6	+28.2•	118.6	79 22.7	+32.8•	123.3	78 47.9	+36.6•	127.5	78 09.8	+39.9•	131.3
11	80 21.8	+23.2•	113.5	79 55.5	+28.3•	118.6	79 24.5	+32.9•	123.3	78 49.7	+36.8•	127.6
12	80 45.0	+17.5•	107.8	80 23.8	+23.4•	113.5	79 57.4	+28.6•	118.7	79 26.5	+33.1•	123.4
13	81 02.5	+11.3•	101.8	80 47.2	+17.6•	107.8	80 26.0	+23.5•	113.5	79 59.6	+28.7•	118.7
14	81 13.8	+4.6•	95.4	81 04.8	+11.4•	101.8	80 49.5	+17.8•	107.8	80 28.3	+23.7•	113.5
15	81 18.4	-2.2•	88.8	81 16.2	+4.8•	95.4	81 07.3	+11.5•	101.7	80 52.0	+17.9•	107.9
16	81 16.2	-8.9•	82.2	81 21.0	-2.2•	88.8	81 18.8	+4.8•	95.3	81 09.9	+11.7•	101.7
17	81 07.3	-15.3•	75.8	81 18.8	-8.9•	82.1	81 23.6	-2.0•	88.7	81 21.6	+4.9•	95.3
18	80 52.0	-21.3•	69.6	81 09.9	-15.3•	75.6	81 21.6	-8.9•	82.0	81 26.5	-2.0•	88.6
19	80 30.7	-26.5•	63.8	80 54.6	-21.3•	69.4	81 12.7	-15.4•	75.5	81 24.5	-8.9•	81.9
20	80 04.2	-31.1•	58.5	80 33.3	-26.6•	63.6	80 57.3	-21.3•	69.2	81 15.6	-15.4•	75.3
21	79 33.1	-35.0•	53.6	80 06.7	-31.1•	58.3	80 36.0	-26.6•	63.4	81 00.2	-21.3•	69.1
22	78 58.1	-38.4•	49.3	79 35.6	-35.1•	53.4	80 09.4	-31.3•	58.0	80 38.9	-26.7•	63.2
23	78 19.7	-41.3•	45.4	79 00.5	-38.5•	49.0	79 38.1	-35.2•	53.2	80 12.2	-31.4•	57.8
24	77 38.4	-43.6•	41.9	78 22.0	-41.3•	45.1	79 02.9	-38.5•	48.8	79 40.8	-35.2•	52.9
25	76 54.8	-45.6	38.8	77 40.7	-43.7•	41.6	78 24.4	-41.4•	44.9	79 05.6	-38.7•	48.5
26	76 09.2	-47.3	36.0	76 57.0	-45.7	38.5	77 43.0	-43.8•	41.4	78 26.9	-41.5•	44.6
27	75 21.9	-48.8	33.5	76 11.3	-47.5	35.7	76 59.2	-45.8	38.2	77 45.4	-43.9•	41.1
28	74 33.1	-50.0	31.2	75 23.8	-48.8	33.2	76 13.4	-47.5	35.5	77 01.5	-45.9	38.0
29	73 43.1	-51.0	29.2	74 35.0	-50.0	31.0	75 25.9	-48.9	33.0	76 15.6	-47.5	35.2
30	72 52.1	-52.0	27.4	73 45.0	-51.1	29.0	74 37.0	-50.1	30.7	75 28.1	-49.0	32.7
31	72 00.1	-52.7	25.7	72 53.9	-52.0	27.1	73 46.9	-51.2	28.7	74 39.1	-50.2	30.4
32	71 07.4	-53.3	24.2	72 01.9	-52.8	25.5	72 55.7	-52.0	26.9	73 48.9	-51.2	28.4
33	70 14.1	-54.0	22.8	71 09.1	-53.4	24.0	72 03.7	-52.8	25.2	72 57.7	-52.1	26.6
34	69 20.1	-54.5	21.6	70 15.7	-54.0	22.6	71 10.9	-53.5	23.7	72 05.6	-52.9	24.9
35	68 25.6	-54.9	20.4	69 21.7	-54.5	21.3	70 17.4	-54.0	22.3	71 12.7	-53.5	23.4
36	67 30.7	-55.3	19.3	68 27.2	-55.0	20.2	69 23.4	-54.6	21.1	70 19.2	-54.1	22.1
37	66 35.4	-55.7	18.3	67 32.2	-55.3	19.1	68 28.8	-55.0	19.9	69 25.1	-54.6	20.8
38	65 39.7	-55.9	17.4	66 36.9	-55.7	18.1	67 33.8	-55.4	18.8	68 30.5	-55.1	19.7
39	64 43.8	-56.3	16.5	65 41.2	-56.0	17.2	66 38.4	-55.7	17.9	67 35.4	-55.4	18.6
40	63 47.5	-56.5	15.7	64 45.2	-56.3	16.3	65 42.7	-56.1	16.9	66 40.0	-55.8	17.6
41	62 51.0	-56.7	15.0	63 48.9	-56.5	15.5	64 46.6	-56.3	16.1	65 44.2	-56.1	16.7
42	61 54.3	-56.9	14.3	62 52.4	-56.8	14.8	63 50.3	-56.5	15.3	64 48.1	-56.3	15.8
43	60 57.4	-57.1	13.6	61 55.6	-56.9	14.1	62 53.8	-56.8	14.5	63 51.8	-56.6	15.1
44	60 00.3	-57.3	13.0	60 58.7	-57.1	13.4	61 57.0	-57.0	13.8	62 55.2	-56.8	14.3
45	59 03.0	-57.4	12.4	60 01.6	-57.3	12.8	61 00.0	-57.1	13.2	61 58.4	-57.0	13.6
46	58 05.6	-57.6	11.9	59 04.3	-57.5	12.2	60 02.9	-57.4	12.6	61 01.4	-57.2	13.0
47	57 08.0	-57.7	11.3	58 06.8	-57.6	11.7	59 05.5	-57.4	12.0	60 04.2	-57.4	12.3
48	56 10.3	-57.8	10.8	57 09.2	-57.7	11.1	58 08.1	-57.6	11.4	59 06.8	-57.5	11.8
49	55 12.5	-57.9	10.4	56 11.5	-57.8	10.6	57 10.5	-57.8	10.9	58 09.3	-57.6	11.2
50	54 14.6	-58.0	9.9	55 13.7	-57.9	10.2	56 12.7	-57.8	10.4	57 11.7	-57.7	10.7
51	53 16.6	-58.1	9.5	54 15.8	-58.1	9.7	55 14.9	-58.0	9.9	56 14.0	-57.9	10.2
52	52 18.5	-58.2	9.1	53 17.7	-58.1	9.3	54 16.9	-58.0	9.5	55 16.1	-58.0	9.7
53	51 20.3	-58.2	8.7	52 19.6	-58.2	8.9	53 18.9	-58.1	9.1	54 18.1	-58.0	9.3
54	50 22.1	-58.4	8.3	51 21.4	-58.2	8.5	52 20.8	-58.2	8.7	53 20.1	-58.2	8.9
55	49 23.7	-58.3	7.9	50 23.2	-58.4	8.1	51 22.6	-58.3	8.3	52 21.9	-58.2	8.4
56	48 25.4	-58.5	7.6	49 24.8	-58.4	7.7	50 24.3	-58.4	7.9	51 23.7	-58.3	8.1
57	47 26.9	-58.5	7.2	48 26.4	-58.5	7.4	49 25.9	-58.4	7.5	50 25.4	-58.4	7.7
58	46 28.4	-58.6	6.9	47 27.9	-58.5	7.0	48 27.5	-58.5	7.2	49 27.0	-58.4	7.3
59	45 29.8	-58.6	6.6	46 29.4	-58.6	6.7	47 29.0	-58.5	6.8	48 28.6	-58.5	7.0
60	44 31.2	-58.6	6.3	45 30.8	-58.6	6.4	46 30.5	-58.6	6.5	47 30.1	-58.6	6.6
61	43 32.6	-58.8	6.0	44 32.2	-58.7	6.1	45 31.9	-58.7	6.2	46 31.5	-58.6	6.3
62	42 33.8	-58.7	5.7	43 33.5	-58.7	5.8	44 33.2	-58.7	5.9	45 32.9	-58.6	6.0
63	41 35.1	-58.8	5.4	42 34.8	-58.7	5.5	43 34.5	-58.7	5.6	44 34.3	-58.7	5.7
64	40 36.3	-58.8	5.2	41 36.1	-58.8	5.3	42 35.8	-58.7	5.3	43 35.6	-58.8	5.4
65	39 37.5	-58.8	4.9	40 37.3	-58.8	5.0	41 37.1	-58.9	5.1	42 36.8	-58.8	5.2
66	38 38.7	-58.9	4.7	39 38.5	-58.9	4.7	40 38.2	-58.8	4.8	41 38.0	-58.8	4.9
67	37 39.8	-58.9	4.4	38 39.6	-58.9	4.5	39 39.4	-58.9	4.6	40 39.2	-58.8	4.6
68	36 40.9	-59.0	4.2	37 40.7	-58.9	4.2	38 40.5	-58.9	4.3	39 40.4	-58.9	4.4
69	35 41.9	-58.9	4.0	36 41.8	-59.0	4.0	37 41.6	-58.9	4.1	38 41.5	-58.9	4.1
70	34 43.0	-59.0	3.7	35 42.8	-58.9	3.8	36 42.7	-59.0	3.8	37 42.6	-59.0	3.9
71	33 44.0	-59.0	3.5	34 43.9	-59.0	3.6	35 43.7	-58.9	3.6	36 43.6	-59.0	3.6
72	32 45.0	-59.1	3.3	33 44.9	-59.1	3.3	34 44.8	-59.1	3.4	35 44.6	-58.9	3.4
73	31 45.9	-59.0	3.1	32 45.8	-59.0	3.1	33 45.7	-59.0	3.2	34 45.7	-59.1	3.2
74	30 46.9	-59.1	2.9	31 46.8	-59.1	2.9	32 46.7	-59.0	2.9	33 46.6	-59.0	3.0
75	29 47.8	-59.1	2.7	30 47.7	-59.1	2.7	31 47.7	-59.1	2.7	32 47.6	-59.1	2.8
76	28 48.7	-59.1	2.5	29 48.6	-59.1	2.5	30 48.6	-59.1	2.5	31 48.5	-59.1	2.6
77	27 49.6	-59.1	2.3	28 49.5	-59.1	2.3	29 49.5	-59.1	2.3	30 49.4	-59.1	2.3
78	26 50.5	-59.2	2.1	27 50.4	-59.1	2.1	28 50.4	-59.1	2.1	29 50.3	-59.1	2.1
79	25 51.3	-59.1	1.9	26 51.3	-59.2	1.9	27 51.3	-59.2	1.9	28 51.2	-59.1	2.0
80	24 52.2	-59.2	1.7	25 52.1	-59.1	1.7	26 52.1	-59.1	1.7	27 52.1	-59.2	1.8
81	23 53.0	-59.2	1.5	24 53.0	-59.2	1.5	25 53.0	-59.2	1.6	26 52.9	-59.1	1.6
82	22 53.8	-59.2	1.4	23 53.8	-59.2	1.4	24 53.8	-59.2	1.4	25 53.8	-59.2	1.4
83	21 54.6	-59.2	1.2	22 54.6	-59.2	1.2	23 54.6	-59.2	1.2	24 54.6	-59.2	1.2
84	20 55.4	-59.2	1.0	21 55.4	-59.2	1.0	22 55.4	-59.2	1.0	23 55.4	-59.2	1.0
85	19 56.2	-59.2	0.8	20 56.2	-59.2	0.8	21 56.2	-59.2	0.8	22 56.2	-59.2	0.8
86	18 57.0	-59.2	0.7	19 57.0	-59.3	0.7	20 57.0	-59.3	0.7	21 57.0	-59.3	0.7
87	17 57.8	-59.3	0.5	18 57.7	-59.2	0.5	19 57.7	-59.2	0.5	20 57.7	-59.2	0.5
88	16 58.5	-59.2	0.3	17 58.5	-59.2	0.3	18 58.5	-59.2	0.3	19 58.5	-59.2	0.3
89	15 59.3	-59.3	0.2	16 59.3	-59.3	0.2	17 59.3	-59.3	0.2	18 59.3	-59.3	0.2
90	15 00.0	-59.3	0.0	16 00.0	-59.3	0.0	17 00.0	-59.3	0.0	18 00.0	-59.3	0.0
	15°			16°			17°			18°		

Dec.	19° Hc	19° d	19° Z	20° Hc	20° d	20° Z	21° Hc	21° d	21° Z	22° Hc	22° d	22° Z	Dec.
°	° ′	′	°	° ′	′	°	° ′	′	°	° ′	′	°	°
0	69 02.9	+54.3	154.1	68 08.6	+55.0	155.2	67 14.0	+55.4	156.2	66 18.9	+55.8	157.1	0
1	69 57.2	+53.9	152.9	69 03.6	+54.4	154.0	68 09.4	+54.9	155.1	67 14.7	+55.4	156.1	1
2	70 51.1	+53.2	151.5	69 58.0	+53.9	152.8	69 04.3	+54.6	154.0	68 10.1	+55.1	155.1	2
3	71 44.3	+52.5	150.1	70 51.9	+53.3	151.5	69 58.9	+53.9	152.8	69 05.2	+54.6	154.0	3
4	72 36.8	+51.7	148.5	71 45.2	+52.6	150.1	70 52.8	+53.4	151.5	69 59.8	+54.0	152.9	4
5	73 28.5	+50.8	146.8	72 37.8	+51.8	148.5	71 46.2	+52.7	150.1	70 53.8	+53.5	151.6	5
6	74 19.3	+49.6	144.9	73 29.6	+50.9	146.8	72 38.9	+51.9	148.6	71 47.3	+52.8	150.1	6
7	75 08.9	+48.3	142.7	74 20.5	+49.7	144.9	73 30.8	+51.0	146.8	72 40.1	+52.0	148.6	7
8	75 57.2	+46.8	140.3	75 10.2	+48.4	142.8	74 21.8	+49.8	144.9	73 32.1	+51.0	146.9	8
9	76 44.0	+44.9•	137.7	75 58.6	+46.9	140.4	75 11.6	+48.6	142.8	74 23.1	+50.0	145.0	9
10	77 28.9	+42.7•	134.7	76 45.5	+45.1•	137.7	76 00.2	+47.0	140.4	75 13.1	+48.7	142.9	10
11	78 11.6	+40.0•	131.4	77 30.6	+42.8•	134.8	76 47.2	+45.2•	137.8	76 01.8	+47.2	140.5	11
12	78 51.6	+37.0•	127.6	78 13.4	+40.3•	131.4	77 32.4	+43.0•	134.8	76 49.0	+45.3•	137.9	12
13	79 28.6	+33.2•	123.4	78 53.7	+37.1•	127.7	78 15.4	+40.4•	131.5	77 34.3	+43.2•	134.9	13
14	80 01.8	+28.9•	118.7	79 30.8	+33.4•	123.5	78 55.8	+37.3•	127.8	78 17.5	+40.6•	131.6	14
15	80 30.7	+23.9•	113.6	80 04.2	+29.1•	118.8	79 33.1	+33.6•	123.6	78 58.1	+37.5•	127.8	15
16	80 54.6	+18.1•	107.9	80 33.3	+24.0•	113.6	80 06.7	+29.3•	118.9	79 35.6	+33.8•	123.6	16
17	81 12.7	+11.8•	101.7	80 57.3	+18.3•	107.9	80 36.0	+24.2•	113.7	80 09.4	+29.5•	118.9	17
18	81 24.5	+5.0•	95.2	81 15.6	+11.9•	101.7	81 00.2	+18.5•	107.9	80 38.9	+24.4•	113.7	18
19	81 29.5	-2.0•	88.5	81 27.5	+5.1•	95.2	81 18.7	+12.0•	101.7	81 03.3	+18.6•	108.0	19
20	81 27.5	-8.8•	81.8	81 32.6	-1.9•	88.5	81 30.7	+5.2•	95.2	81 21.9	+12.2•	101.7	20
21	81 18.7	-15.4•	75.2	81 30.7	-8.8•	81.7	81 35.9	-1.8•	88.4	81 34.1	+5.3•	95.1	21
22	81 03.3	-21.5•	68.9	81 21.9	-15.5•	75.0	81 34.1	-8.9•	81.6	81 39.4	-1.8•	88.3	22
23	80 41.8	-26.7•	63.0	81 06.4	-21.4•	68.7	81 25.2	-15.4•	74.9	81 37.6	-8.8•	81.4	23
24	80 15.1	-31.4•	57.6	80 45.0	-26.9•	62.8	81 09.8	-21.6•	68.5	81 28.8	-15.6•	74.7	24
25	79 43.7	-35.4•	52.7	80 18.1	-31.5•	57.3	80 48.2	-26.9•	62.5	81 13.2	-21.6•	68.3	25
26	79 08.3	-38.8•	48.3	79 46.6	-35.5•	52.4	80 21.3	-31.6•	57.1	80 51.6	-27.0•	62.3	26
27	78 29.5	-41.6•	44.3	79 11.1	-38.9•	48.0	79 49.7	-35.7•	52.1	80 24.6	-31.8•	56.8	27
28	77 47.9	-44.0•	40.8	78 32.2	-41.7•	44.0	79 14.0	-39.0•	47.7	79 52.8	-35.7•	51.8	28
29	77 03.9	-45.9	37.7	77 50.5	-44.1•	40.5	78 35.0	-41.8•	43.7	79 17.1	-39.2•	47.4	29
30	76 18.0	-47.7	34.9	77 06.4	-46.1	37.4	77 53.2	-44.2•	40.2	78 37.9	-41.9•	43.4	30
31	75 30.3	-49.1	32.4	76 20.3	-47.7	34.6	77 09.0	-46.2	37.1	77 56.0	-44.3•	39.9	31
32	74 41.2	-50.2	30.2	75 32.6	-49.2	32.1	76 22.8	-47.8	34.3	77 11.7	-46.3	36.8	32
33	73 51.0	-51.3	28.1	74 43.4	-50.3	29.9	75 35.0	-49.3	31.8	76 25.4	-48.0	34.0	33
34	72 59.7	-52.2	26.3	73 53.1	-51.4	27.9	74 45.7	-50.4	29.6	75 37.4	-49.4	31.5	34
35	72 07.5	-53.0	24.7	73 01.7	-52.3	26.0	73 55.3	-51.5	27.6	74 48.0	-50.5	29.3	35
36	71 14.5	-53.5	23.2	72 09.4	-53.0	24.4	73 03.8	-52.3	25.7	73 57.5	-51.6	27.3	36
37	70 21.0	-54.2	21.8	71 16.4	-53.6	22.9	72 11.5	-53.1	24.1	73 05.9	-52.4	25.5	37
38	69 26.8	-54.7	20.6	70 22.8	-54.2	21.5	71 18.4	-53.7	22.6	72 13.5	-53.1	23.8	38
39	68 32.1	-55.0	19.4	69 28.6	-54.7	20.3	70 24.7	-54.3	21.3	71 20.4	-53.8	22.3	39
40	67 37.1	-55.5	18.3	68 33.9	-55.2	19.1	69 30.4	-54.8	20.0	70 26.6	-54.3	21.0	40
41	66 41.6	-55.8	17.4	67 38.7	-55.5	18.1	68 35.6	-55.1	18.9	69 32.3	-54.9	19.7	41
42	65 45.8	-56.1	16.5	66 43.2	-55.8	17.1	67 40.5	-55.6	17.8	68 37.4	-55.2	18.6	42
43	64 49.7	-56.4	15.6	65 47.4	-56.2	16.2	66 44.9	-55.9	16.8	67 42.2	-55.6	17.6	43
44	63 53.3	-56.7	14.8	64 51.2	-56.4	15.4	65 49.0	-56.2	15.9	66 46.6	-56.0	16.6	44
45	62 56.6	-56.8	14.1	63 54.8	-56.7	14.6	64 52.8	-56.5	15.1	65 50.6	-56.2	15.7	45
46	61 59.8	-57.0	13.4	62 58.1	-56.9	13.8	63 56.3	-56.7	14.3	64 54.4	-56.5	14.8	46
47	61 02.8	-57.3	12.7	62 01.2	-57.0	13.1	62 59.6	-56.9	13.6	63 57.9	-56.8	14.1	47
48	60 05.5	-57.3	12.1	61 04.2	-57.3	12.5	62 02.7	-57.1	12.9	63 01.1	-56.9	13.3	48
49	59 08.2	-57.6	11.5	60 06.9	-57.4	11.9	61 05.6	-57.3	12.3	62 04.2	-57.2	12.7	49
50	58 10.6	-57.6	11.0	59 09.5	-57.5	11.3	60 08.3	-57.4	11.7	61 07.0	-57.3	12.0	50
51	57 13.0	-57.8	10.5	58 12.0	-57.7	10.8	59 10.9	-57.6	11.1	60 09.7	-57.4	11.4	51
52	56 15.2	-57.9	10.0	57 14.3	-57.8	10.3	58 13.3	-57.7	10.5	59 12.3	-57.6	10.8	52
53	55 17.3	-58.0	9.5	56 16.5	-57.9	9.8	57 15.6	-57.8	10.0	58 14.6	-57.7	10.3	53
54	54 19.3	-58.1	9.1	55 18.6	-58.0	9.3	56 17.8	-58.0	9.5	57 16.9	-57.9	9.8	54
55	53 21.2	-58.1	8.6	54 20.6	-58.2	8.9	55 19.8	-58.0	9.1	56 19.0	-57.9	9.3	55
56	52 23.1	-58.3	8.2	53 22.4	-58.1	8.4	54 21.8	-58.1	8.6	55 21.1	-58.1	8.9	56
57	51 24.8	-58.3	7.9	52 24.3	-58.3	8.0	53 23.7	-58.3	8.2	54 23.0	-58.1	8.4	57
58	50 26.5	-58.4	7.5	51 26.0	-58.4	7.6	52 25.4	-58.3	7.8	53 24.9	-58.3	8.0	58
59	49 28.1	-58.4	7.1	50 27.6	-58.4	7.3	51 27.1	-58.3	7.4	52 26.6	-58.3	7.6	59
60	48 29.7	-58.6	6.8	49 29.2	-58.4	6.9	50 28.8	-58.5	7.1	51 28.3	-58.4	7.2	60
61	47 31.1	-58.5	6.4	48 30.8	-58.6	6.6	49 30.3	-58.4	6.7	50 29.9	-58.4	6.8	61
62	46 32.6	-58.7	6.1	47 32.2	-58.6	6.2	48 31.9	-58.6	6.4	49 31.5	-58.5	6.5	62
63	45 33.9	-58.6	5.8	46 33.6	-58.6	5.9	47 33.3	-58.6	6.0	48 33.0	-58.6	6.2	63
64	44 35.3	-58.7	5.5	45 35.0	-58.7	5.6	46 34.7	-58.7	5.7	47 34.4	-58.6	5.8	64
65	43 36.6	-58.8	5.2	44 36.3	-58.7	5.3	45 36.0	-58.7	5.4	46 35.8	-58.7	5.5	65
66	42 37.8	-58.8	5.0	43 37.6	-58.8	5.0	44 37.3	-58.7	5.1	45 37.1	-58.7	5.2	66
67	41 39.0	-58.8	4.7	42 38.8	-58.8	4.8	43 38.6	-58.8	4.8	44 38.4	-58.8	4.9	67
68	40 40.2	-58.9	4.4	41 40.0	-58.8	4.5	42 39.8	-58.8	4.6	43 39.6	-58.8	4.6	68
69	39 41.3	-58.9	4.2	40 41.2	-58.9	4.2	41 41.0	-58.9	4.3	42 40.8	-58.8	4.4	69
70	38 42.4	-58.9	3.9	39 42.3	-58.9	4.0	40 42.1	-58.9	4.0	41 42.0	-58.9	4.1	70
71	37 43.5	-59.0	3.7	38 43.4	-59.0	3.7	39 43.2	-58.9	3.8	40 43.1	-58.9	3.9	71
72	36 44.5	-58.9	3.5	37 44.4	-59.0	3.5	38 44.3	-58.9	3.6	39 44.2	-58.9	3.6	72
73	35 45.6	-59.0	3.2	36 45.5	-59.0	3.3	37 45.4	-59.0	3.3	38 45.3	-59.0	3.4	73
74	34 46.6	-59.1	3.0	35 46.5	-59.1	3.0	36 46.4	-59.0	3.1	37 46.3	-59.0	3.1	74
75	33 47.5	-59.0	2.8	34 47.4	-59.0	2.8	35 47.4	-59.1	2.9	36 47.3	-59.0	2.9	75
76	32 48.5	-59.1	2.6	33 48.4	-59.1	2.6	34 48.3	-59.0	2.6	35 48.3	-59.1	2.7	76
77	31 49.4	-59.1	2.4	32 49.3	-59.0	2.4	33 49.3	-59.1	2.4	34 49.2	-59.0	2.5	77
78	30 50.3	-59.1	2.2	31 50.3	-59.1	2.2	32 50.2	-59.1	2.2	33 50.2	-59.1	2.2	78
79	29 51.2	-59.1	2.0	30 51.2	-59.2	2.0	31 51.1	-59.1	2.0	32 51.1	-59.1	2.0	79
80	28 52.1	-59.2	1.8	29 52.0	-59.1	1.8	30 52.0	-59.1	1.8	31 52.0	-59.2	1.8	80
81	27 52.9	-59.1	1.6	28 52.9	-59.2	1.6	29 52.9	-59.2	1.6	30 52.8	-59.1	1.6	81
82	26 53.8	-59.2	1.4	27 53.7	-59.1	1.4	28 53.7	-59.2	1.4	29 53.7	-59.2	1.4	82
83	25 54.6	-59.2	1.2	26 54.6	-59.2	1.2	27 54.5	-59.1	1.2	28 54.5	-59.1	1.2	83
84	24 55.4	-59.2	1.0	25 55.4	-59.2	1.0	26 55.4	-59.2	1.1	27 55.4	-59.2	1.1	84
85	23 56.2	-59.2	0.9	24 56.2	-59.2	0.9	25 56.2	-59.2	0.9	26 56.2	-59.2	0.9	85
86	22 57.0	-59.3	0.7	23 57.0	-59.3	0.7	24 57.0	-59.3	0.7	25 57.0	-59.3	0.7	86
87	21 57.7	-59.2	0.5	22 57.7	-59.2	0.5	23 57.7	-59.2	0.5	24 57.7	-59.2	0.5	87
88	20 58.5	-59.2	0.3	21 58.5	-59.2	0.3	22 58.5	-59.2	0.3	23 58.5	-59.2	0.3	88
89	19 59.3	-59.3	0.2	20 59.3	-59.3	0.2	21 59.3	-59.3	0.2	22 59.3	-59.3	0.2	89
90	19 00.0	-59.3	0.0	20 00.0	-59.3	0.0	21 00.0	-59.3	0.0	22 00.0	-59.3	0.0	90
	19°			20°			21°			22°			

9°, 351° L.H.A. LATITUDE SAME NAME AS DECLINATION

20

Dec.	15° Hc	d	Z	16° Hc	d	Z	17° Hc	d	Z	18° Hc	d	Z	19° Hc	d	Z	20° Hc	d	Z	21° Hc	d	Z	22° Hc	d	Z	Dec.
°	° ′	′	°	° ′	′	°	° ′	′	°	° ′	′	°	° ′	′	°	° ′	′	°	° ′	′	°	° ′	′	°	°
0	72 33.6	-52.2	148.5	71 42.0	-53.0	150.1	70 49.6	-53.7	151.6	69 56.5	-54.3	152.9	69 02.9	-54.9	154.1	68 08.6	-55.3	155.2	67 14.0	-55.8	156.2	66 18.9	-56.1	157.1	0
1	71 41.4	-52.9	150.1	70 49.0	-53.7	151.6	69 55.9	-54.3	152.9	69 02.2	-54.8	154.1	68 08.0	-55.3	155.2	67 13.3	-55.6	156.2	66 18.2	-56.0	157.1	65 22.8	-56.4	157.9	1
2	70 48.5	-53.6	151.6	69 55.3	-54.2	152.9	69 01.6	-54.7	154.1	68 07.4	-55.2	155.2	67 12.7	-55.6	156.2	66 17.7	-56.0	157.1	65 22.2	-56.3	158.0	64 26.4	-56.6	158.8	2
3	69 54.9	-54.2	152.9	69 01.1	-54.6	154.1	68 06.9	-55.1	155.2	67 12.2	-55.6	156.2	66 17.1	-55.9	157.1	65 21.7	-56.3	158.0	64 25.9	-56.6	158.8	63 29.8	-56.9	159.5	3
4	69 00.7	-54.6	154.2	68 06.5	-55.1	155.3	67 11.8	-55.6	156.3	66 16.6	-55.9	157.2	65 21.2	-56.3	158.0	64 25.4	-56.6	158.8	63 29.3	-56.8	159.5	62 32.9	-57.0	160.2	4
5	68 06.1	-55.1	155.3	67 11.4	-55.5	156.3	66 16.2	-55.8	157.2	65 20.7	-56.2	158.1	64 24.9	-56.5	158.8	63 28.8	-56.7	159.6	62 32.5	-57.0	160.2	61 35.9	-57.2	160.9	5
6	67 11.0	-55.4	156.3	66 15.9	-55.8	157.3	65 20.4	-56.2	158.1	64 24.5	-56.4	158.9	63 28.4	-56.7	159.6	62 32.1	-57.0	160.3	61 35.5	-57.2	160.9	60 38.7	-57.4	161.5	6
7	66 15.6	-55.8	157.3	65 20.1	-56.2	158.2	64 24.2	-56.4	158.9	63 28.1	-56.7	159.7	62 31.7	-56.9	160.3	61 35.1	-57.2	161.0	60 38.3	-57.4	161.5	59 41.3	-57.6	162.1	7
8	65 19.8	-56.1	158.2	64 23.9	-56.3	159.0	63 27.8	-56.6	159.7	62 31.4	-56.9	160.4	61 34.8	-57.1	161.0	60 37.9	-57.3	161.6	59 40.9	-57.5	162.1	58 43.7	-57.6	162.6	8
9	64 23.7	-56.3	159.1	63 27.6	-56.6	159.8	62 31.2	-56.9	160.4	61 34.5	-57.1	161.1	60 37.7	-57.3	161.6	59 40.6	-57.5	162.2	58 43.4	-57.6	162.7	57 46.1	-57.8	163.2	9
10	63 27.4	-56.6	159.8	62 31.0	-56.9	160.5	61 34.3	-57.1	161.1	60 37.4	-57.2	161.7	59 40.4	-57.5	162.2	58 43.1	-57.6	162.7	57 45.8	-57.8	163.2	56 48.3	-57.9	163.7	10
11	62 30.8	-56.8	160.6	61 34.1	-57.0	161.2	60 37.2	-57.2	161.8	59 40.2	-57.4	162.3	58 42.9	-57.6	162.8	57 45.5	-57.7	163.3	56 48.0	-57.9	163.7	55 50.4	-58.1	164.1	11
12	61 34.0	-57.0	161.3	60 37.1	-57.2	161.8	59 40.0	-57.4	162.4	58 42.8	-57.6	162.9	57 45.3	-57.7	163.3	56 47.8	-57.9	163.8	55 50.1	-58.0	164.2	54 52.3	-58.1	164.6	12
13	60 37.0	-57.1	161.9	59 39.9	-57.3	162.4	58 42.6	-57.5	162.9	57 45.2	-57.7	163.4	56 47.6	-57.8	163.8	55 49.9	-57.9	164.3	54 52.1	-58.0	164.6	53 54.2	-58.2	165.0	13
14	59 39.9	-57.4	162.5	58 42.6	-57.5	163.0	57 45.1	-57.7	163.5	56 47.5	-57.8	163.9	55 49.8	-57.9	164.3	54 52.0	-58.1	164.7	53 54.1	-58.2	165.1	52 56.0	-58.2	165.4	14
15	58 42.5	-57.4	163.1	57 45.1	-57.7	163.6	56 47.4	-57.7	164.0	55 49.7	-57.9	164.4	54 51.9	-58.1	164.8	53 53.9	-58.1	165.1	52 55.9	-58.3	165.5	51 57.8	-58.4	165.8	15
16	57 45.1	-57.7	163.6	56 47.4	-57.7	164.1	55 49.7	-57.9	164.5	54 51.8	-58.0	164.9	53 53.8	-58.1	165.2	52 55.8	-58.2	165.6	51 57.6	-58.3	165.9	50 59.4	-58.4	166.2	16
17	56 47.4	-57.7	164.1	55 49.7	-57.9	164.6	54 51.8	-58.0	164.9	53 53.8	-58.1	165.3	52 55.7	-58.2	165.6	51 57.6	-58.4	166.0	50 59.3	-58.4	166.3	50 01.0	-58.5	166.5	17
18	55 49.7	-57.8	164.6	54 51.8	-58.0	165.0	53 53.8	-58.1	165.4	52 55.7	-58.2	165.7	51 57.5	-58.3	166.0	50 59.2	-58.3	166.3	50 00.9	-58.5	166.6	49 02.5	-58.5	166.9	18
19	54 51.9	-58.0	165.1	53 53.8	-58.0	165.5	52 55.7	-58.1	165.8	51 57.5	-58.3	166.1	50 59.2	-58.3	166.4	50 00.9	-58.5	166.7	49 02.4	-58.5	167.0	48 04.0	-58.6	167.2	19
20	53 53.9	-58.0	165.6	52 55.8	-58.2	165.9	51 57.6	-58.3	166.2	50 59.2	-58.3	166.5	50 00.9	-58.5	166.8	49 02.4	-58.5	167.0	48 03.9	-58.5	167.3	47 05.4	-58.7	167.5	20
21	52 55.9	-58.1	166.0	51 57.6	-58.2	166.3	50 59.3	-58.3	166.6	50 00.9	-58.4	166.9	49 02.4	-58.4	167.1	48 03.9	-58.5	167.4	47 05.4	-58.7	167.6	46 06.7	-58.7	167.8	21
22	51 57.8	-58.2	166.4	50 59.4	-58.3	166.7	50 01.0	-58.4	167.0	49 02.5	-58.5	167.2	48 04.0	-58.6	167.5	47 05.4	-58.6	167.7	46 06.7	-58.7	167.9	45 08.0	-58.7	168.1	22
23	50 59.6	-58.3	166.8	50 01.1	-58.4	167.0	49 02.6	-58.4	167.3	48 04.0	-58.5	167.6	47 05.4	-58.6	167.8	46 06.8	-58.7	168.0	45 08.0	-58.7	168.2	44 09.3	-58.8	168.4	23
24	50 01.3	-58.4	167.1	49 02.7	-58.4	167.4	48 04.2	-58.5	167.7	47 05.5	-58.6	167.9	46 06.8	-58.6	168.1	45 08.1	-58.7	168.3	44 09.3	-58.7	168.5	43 10.5	-58.8	168.7	24
25	49 02.9	-58.4	167.5	48 04.3	-58.5	167.7	47 05.7	-58.6	168.0	46 06.9	-58.6	168.2	45 08.2	-58.7	168.4	44 09.4	-58.8	168.6	43 10.6	-58.8	168.8	42 11.7	-58.9	169.0	25
26	48 04.5	-58.5	167.9	47 05.8	-58.5	168.1	46 07.1	-58.6	168.3	45 08.3	-58.7	168.5	44 09.5	-58.7	168.7	43 10.6	-58.7	168.9	42 11.8	-58.9	169.1	41 12.8	-58.9	169.2	26
27	47 06.0	-58.5	168.2	46 07.3	-58.6	168.4	45 08.5	-58.7	168.6	44 09.6	-58.7	168.8	43 10.8	-58.8	169.0	42 11.9	-58.9	169.2	41 12.9	-58.9	169.3	40 13.9	-58.9	169.5	27
28	46 07.5	-58.6	168.5	45 08.7	-58.7	168.7	44 09.8	-58.7	168.9	43 10.9	-58.7	169.1	42 12.0	-58.8	169.3	41 13.0	-58.8	169.4	40 14.0	-58.9	169.6	39 15.0	-58.9	169.7	28
29	45 08.9	-58.6	168.8	44 10.0	-58.7	169.0	43 11.1	-58.7	169.2	42 12.2	-58.8	169.4	41 13.2	-58.9	169.5	40 14.2	-58.9	169.7	39 15.1	-58.9	169.8	38 16.1	-59.0	170.0	29
30	44 10.3	-58.7	169.1	43 11.3	-58.7	169.3	42 12.4	-58.8	169.5	41 13.4	-58.9	169.6	40 14.3	-58.8	169.8	39 15.3	-58.9	169.9	38 16.2	-59.0	170.1	37 17.1	-59.0	170.2	30
31	43 11.6	-58.7	169.4	42 12.6	-58.8	169.6	41 13.6	-58.9	169.7	40 14.5	-58.8	169.9	39 15.5	-58.9	170.0	38 16.4	-59.0	170.2	37 17.2	-59.0	170.3	36 18.1	-59.1	170.4	31
32	42 12.9	-58.8	169.7	41 13.8	-58.8	169.8	40 14.8	-58.9	170.0	39 15.7	-58.9	170.1	38 16.6	-59.0	170.3	37 17.4	-59.0	170.4	36 18.2	-59.0	170.5	35 19.0	-59.0	170.6	32
33	41 14.1	-58.8	170.0	40 15.0	-58.8	170.1	39 15.9	-58.9	170.2	38 16.8	-58.9	170.4	37 17.6	-59.0	170.5	36 18.4	-59.0	170.6	35 19.2	-59.0	170.7	34 20.0	-59.1	170.9	33
34	40 15.3	-58.8	170.2	39 16.2	-58.9	170.4	38 17.0	-58.9	170.5	37 17.9	-59.0	170.6	36 18.6	-58.9	170.7	35 19.4	-59.0	170.9	34 20.2	-59.1	171.0	33 20.9	-59.1	171.1	34
35	39 16.5	-58.8	170.5	38 17.3	-58.9	170.6	37 18.1	-58.9	170.7	36 18.9	-59.0	170.8	35 19.7	-59.1	171.0	34 20.4	-59.1	171.1	33 21.1	-59.1	171.2	32 21.8	-59.1	171.3	35
36	38 17.7	-58.9	170.7	37 18.4	-58.9	170.8	36 19.2	-59.0	171.0	35 19.9	-59.0	171.1	34 20.6	-59.0	171.2	33 21.3	-59.0	171.3	32 22.0	-59.1	171.4	31 22.7	-59.1	171.5	36
37	37 18.8	-59.0	171.0	36 19.5	-59.0	171.1	35 20.2	-59.0	171.2	34 20.9	-59.0	171.3	33 21.6	-59.1	171.4	32 22.3	-59.1	171.5	31 22.9	-59.1	171.6	30 23.6	-59.2	171.7	37
38	36 19.8	-58.9	171.2	35 20.5	-58.9	171.3	34 21.2	-59.0	171.4	33 21.9	-59.1	171.5	32 22.5	-59.1	171.6	31 23.2	-59.1	171.7	30 23.8	-59.2	171.8	29 24.4	-59.2	171.9	38
39	35 20.9	-59.0	171.4	34 21.6	-59.1	171.5	33 22.2	-59.0	171.6	32 22.8	-59.0	171.7	31 23.4	-59.1	171.8	30 24.1	-59.2	171.9	29 24.6	-59.1	172.0	28 25.2	-59.2	172.1	39
40	34 21.9	-59.0	171.7	33 22.5	-59.0	171.7	32 23.2	-59.1	171.8	31 23.8	-59.1	171.9	30 24.3	-59.1	172.0	29 24.9	-59.1	172.1	28 25.5	-59.2	172.2	27 26.0	-59.2	172.2	40
41	33 22.9	-59.0	171.9	32 23.5	-59.0	172.0	31 24.1	-59.1	172.0	30 24.7	-59.1	172.1	29 25.2	-59.1	172.2	28 25.8	-59.2	172.3	27 26.3	-59.2	172.4	26 26.8	-59.2	172.4	41
42	32 23.9	-59.0	172.1	31 24.5	-59.1	172.2	30 25.0	-59.1	172.3	29 25.6	-59.2	172.3	28 26.1	-59.2	172.4	27 26.6	-59.2	172.5	26 27.1	-59.2	172.5	25 27.6	-59.2	172.6	42
43	31 24.9	-59.1	172.3	30 25.4	-59.1	172.4	29 25.9	-59.1	172.5	28 26.4	-59.1	172.5	27 26.9	-59.1	172.6	26 27.4	-59.2	172.7	25 27.9	-59.2	172.7	24 28.4	-59.2	172.8	43
44	30 25.8	-59.1	172.5	29 26.3	-59.1	172.6	28 26.8	-59.1	172.6	27 27.3	-59.2	172.7	26 27.8	-59.2	172.8	25 28.2	-59.2	172.8	24 28.7	-59.2	172.9	23 29.2	-59.3	173.0	44
45	29 26.7	-59.1	172.7	28 27.2	-59.1	172.8	27 27.7	-59.2	172.8	26 28.1	-59.1	172.9	25 28.6	-59.2	173.0	24 29.0	-59.2	173.0	23 29.5	-59.3	173.1	22 29.9	-59.3	173.1	45
46	28 27.6	-59.1	172.9	27 28.1	-59.2	173.0	26 28.5	-59.1	173.0	25 29.0	-59.2	173.1	24 29.4	-59.2	173.1	23 29.8	-59.2	173.2	22 30.2	-59.2	173.2	21 30.6	-59.3	173.3	46
47	27 28.5	-59.1	173.1	26 28.9	-59.1	173.2	25 29.4	-59.2	173.2	24 29.8	-59.2	173.3	23 30.2	-59.2	173.3	22 30.6	-59.3	173.4	21 31.0	-59.3	173.4	20 31.4	-59.3	173.5	47
48	26 29.4	-59.2	173.3	25 29.8	-59.2	173.3	24 30.2	-59.2	173.4	23 30.6	-59.2	173.4	22 31.0	-59.3	173.5	21 31.3	-59.2	173.5	20 31.7	-59.2	173.6	19 32.1	-59.3	173.6	48
49	25 30.2	-59.1	173.5	24 30.6	-59.2	173.5	23 31.0	-59.2	173.6	22 31.4	-59.3	173.6	21 31.7	-59.2	173.7	20 32.1	-59.3	173.7	19 32.5	-59.3	173.7	18 32.8	-59.3	173.8	49
50	24 31.1	-59.2	173.7	23 31.4	-59.2	173.7	22 31.8	-59.2	173.8	21 32.1	-59.2	173.8	20 32.5	-59.3	173.8	19 32.8	-59.2	173.9	18 33.2	-59.3	173.9	17 33.5	-59.3	173.9	50
51	23 31.9	-59.2	173.8	22 32.2	-59.2	173.9	21 32.6	-59.3	173.9	20 32.9	-59.2	174.0	19 33.2	-59.2	174.0	18 33.6	-59.3	174.0	17 33.9	-59.3	174.1	16 34.2	-59.3	174.1	51
52	22 32.7	-59.2	174.0	21 33.0	-59.2	174.1	20 33.3	-59.2	174.1	19 33.7	-59.3	174.1	18 34.0	-59.3	174.2	17 34.3	-59.3	174.2	16 34.6	-59.3	174.2	15 34.9	-59.3	174.3	52
53	21 33.5	-59.2	174.2	20 33.8	-59.2	174.2	19 34.1	-59.2	174.3	18 34.4	-59.2	174.3	17 34.7	-59.3	174.3	16 35.0	-59.3	174.4	15 35.3	-59.3	174.4	14 35.6	-59.4	174.4	53
54	20 34.3	-59.2	174.4	19 34.6	-59.3	174.4	18 34.9	-59.3	174.4	17 35.2	-59.3	174.5	16 35.4	-59.3	174.5	15 35.7	-59.3	174.5	14 36.0	-59.3	174.5	13 36.2	-59.3	174.6	54
55	19 35.1	-59.2	174.5	18 35.3	-59.2	174.6	17 35.6	-59.2	174.6	16 35.9	-59.3	174.6	15 36.1	-59.2	174.7	14 36.4	-59.3	174.7	13 36.7	-59.4	174.7	12 36.9	-59.3	174.7	55
56	18 35.9	-59.3	174.7	17 36.1	-59.2	174.7	16 36.4	-59.3	174.8	15 36.6	-59.3	174.8	14 36.9	-59.3	174.8	13 37.1	-59.3	174.8	12 37.3	-59.3	174.9	11 37.6	-59.4	174.9	56
57	17 36.6	-59.2	174.9	16 36.9	-59.3	174.9	15 37.1	-59.3	174.9	14 37.3	-59.3	174.9	13 37.6	-59.3	175.0	12 37.8	-59.3	175.0	11 38.0	-59.3	175.0	10 38.2	-59.3	175.0	57
58	16 37.4	-59.3	175.0	15 37.6	-59.3	175.1	14 37.8	-59.3	175.1	13 38.0	-59.3	175.1	12 38.3	-59.4	175.1	11 38.5	-59.4	175.1	10 38.7	-59.4	175.2	9 38.9	-59.4	175.2	58
59	15 38.1	-59.2	175.2	14 38.3	-59.2	175.2	13 38.5	-59.3	175.2	12 38.7	-59.3	175.3	11 38.9	-59.3	175.3	10 39.1	-59.3	175.3	9 39.3	-59.3	175.3	8 39.5	-59.3	175.3	59
60	14 38.9	-59.3	175.4	13 39.1	-59.3	175.4	12 39.2	-59.2	175.4	11 39.4	-59.3	175.4	10 39.6	-59.3	175.4	9 39.8	-59.3	175.4	8 40.0	-59.3	175.5	7 40.2	-59.4	175.5	60
61	13 39.6	-59.3	175.5	12 39.8	-59.3	175.5	11 40.0	-59.3	175.6	10 40.1	-59.3	175.6	9 40.3	-59.3	175.6	8 40.5	-59.3	175.6	7 40.7	-59.4	175.6	6 40.8	-59.3	175.6	61
62	12 40.3	-59.3	175.7	11 40.5	-59.3	175.7	10 40.7	-59.3	175.7	9 40.8	-59.3	175.7	8 41.0	-59.3	175.7	7 41.2	-59.4	175.8	6 41.3	-59.3	175.8	5 41.5	-59.4	175.8	62
63	11 41.0	-59.2	175.8	10 41.2	-59.3	175.9	9 41.4	-59.4	175.9	8 41.5	-59.3	175.9	7 41.7	-59.4	175.9	6 41.8	-59.3	175.9	5 42.0	-59.4	175.9	4 42.1	-59.3	175.9	63
64	10 41.8	-59.3	176.0	9 41.9	-59.3	176.0	8 42.0	-59.3	176.0	7 42.2	-59.3	176.0	6 42.3	-59.3	176.0	5 42.5	-59.4	176.0	4 42.6	-59.3	176.1	3 42.8	-59.4	176.1	64
65	9 42.5	-59.3	176.2	8 42.6	-59.3	176.2	7 42.7	-59.3	176.2	6 42.9	-59.4	176.2	5 43.0	-59.3	176.2	4 43.1	-59.3	176.2	3 43.3	-59.4	176.2	2 43.4	-59.4	176.2	65
66	8 43.2	-59.3	176.3	7 43.3	-59.3	176.3	6 43.4	-59.3	176.3	5 43.5	-59.3	176.3	4 43.7	-59.4	176.3	3 43.8	-59.4	176.3	2 43.9	-59.3	176.3	1 44.0	-59.3	176.4	66
67	7 43.9	-59.3	176.5	6 44.0	-59.3	176.5	5 44.1	-59.3	176.5	4 44.2	-59.3	176.5	3 44.3	-59.3	176.5	2 44.4	-59.3	176.5	1 44.6	-59.4	176.5	0 44.7	-59.4	176.5	67
68	6 44.6	-59.3	176.6	5 44.7	-59.3	176.6	4 44.8	-59.3	176.6	3 44.9	-59.3	176.6	2 45.0	-59.3	176.6	1 45.1	-59.4	176.6	0 45.2	-59.4	176.6	0 14.7	+59.4	3.4	68
69	5 45.3	-59.3	176.8	4 45.4	-59.3	176.8	3 45.5	-59.3	176.8	2 45.6	-59.4	176.8	1 45.7	-59.4	176.8	0 45.7	-59.3	176.8	0 14.2	+59.3	3.2	1 14.1	+59.3	3.2	69
70	4 46.0	-59.3	176.9	3 46.1	-59.4	176.9	2 46.1	-59.3	176.9	1 46.2	-59.3	176.9	0 46.3	-59.3	176.9	0 13.6	+59.4	3.1	1 13.5	+59.4	3.1	2 13.4	+59.4	3.1	70
71	3 46.7	-59.3	177.1	2 46.7	-59.3	177.1	1 46.8	-59.3	177.1	0 46.9	-59.3	177.1	0 13.0	+59.4	2.9	1 13.0	+59.3	2.9	2 12.9	+59.3	2.9	3 12.8	+59.4	2.9	71
72	2 47.4	-59.4	177.2	1 47.4	-59.3	177.2	0 47.5	-59.3	177.2	0 12.4	+59.4	2.8	1 12.4	+59.3	2.8	2 12.3	+59.3	2.8	3 12.2	+59.3	2.8	4 12.2	+59.4	2.8	72
73	1 48.0	-59.3	177.4	0 48.1	-59.3	177.4	0 11.8	+59.4	2.6	1 11.8	+59.3	2.6	2 11.7	+59.3	2.6	3 11.6	+59.4	2.6	4 11.6	+59.3	2.6	5 11.5	+59.4	2.6	73
74	0 48.7	-59.3	177.5	0 11.2	+59.3	2.5	1 11.2	+59.3	2.5	2 11.1	+59.3	2.5	3 11.0	+59.4	2.5	4 11.0	+59.3	2.5	5 10.9	+59.4	2.5	6 10.9	+59.3	2.5	74
75	0 10.6	+59.3	2.3	1 10.5	+59.3	2.3	2 10.5	+59.3	2.3	3 10.4	+59.4	2.3	4 10.4	+59.3	2.3	5 10.3	+59.4	2.3	6 10.3	+59.3	2.3	7 10.2	+59.4	2.3	75
76	1 09.9	+59.3	2.2	2 09.8	+59.4	2.2	3 09.8	+59.3	2.2	4 09.8	+59.3	2.2	5 09.7	+59.4	2.2	6 09.7	+59.3	2.2	7 09.6	+59.4	2.2	8 09.6	+59.3	2.2	76
77	2 09.2	+59.3	2.0	3 09.2	+59.3	2.0	4 09.1	+59.3	2.0	5 09.1	+59.3	2.0	6 09.1	+59.3	2.0	7 09.0	+59.4	2.0	8 09.0	+59.3	2.0	9 08.9	+59.4	2.0	77
78	3 08.5	+59.3	1.9	4 08.5	+59.3	1.9	5 08.4	+59.4	1.9	6 08.4	+59.3	1.9	7 08.4	+59.3	1.9	8 08.4	+59.3	1.9	9 08.3	+59.4	1.9	10 08.3	+59.3	1.9	78
79	4 07.8	+59.3	1.7	5 07.8	+59.3	1.7	6 07.8	+59.3	1.7	7 07.7	+59.4	1.7	8 07.7	+59.3	1.7	9 07.7	+59.3	1.7	10 07.7	+59.3	1.7	11 07.6	+59.4	1.7	79
80	5 07.1	+59.3	1.6	6 07.1	+59.3	1.6	7 07.1	+59.3	1.6	8 07.1	+59.3	1.6	9 07.0	+59.4	1.6	10 07.0	+59.3	1.6	11 07.0	+59.3	1.6	12 07.0	+59.3	1.6	80
81	6 06.4	+59.3	1.4	7 06.4	+59.3	1.4	8 06.4	+59.3	1.4	9 06.4	+59.3	1.4	10 06.4	+59.3	1.4	11 06.3	+59.4	1.4	12 06.3	+59.3	1.4	13 06.3	+59.3	1.4	81
82	7 05.7	+59.3	1.3	8 05.7	+59.3	1.3	9 05.7	+59.3	1.3	10 05.7	+59.3	1.3	11 05.7	+59.3	1.3	12 05.7	+59.3	1.3	13 05.6	+59.4	1.3	14 05.6	+59.4	1.3	82
83	8 05.0	+59.3	1.1	9 05.0	+59.3	1.1	10 05.0	+59.3	1.1	11 05.0	+59.3	1.1	12 05.0	+59.3	1.1	13 05.0	+59.3	1.1	14 05.0	+59.3	1.1	15 05.0	+59.3	1.1	83
84	9 04.3	+59.3	0.9	10 04.3	+59.3	1.0	11 04.3	+59.3	1.0	12 04.3	+59.3	1.0	13 04.3	+59.3	1.0	14 04.3	+59.3	1.0	15 04.3	+59.3	1.0	16 04.3	+59.3	1.0	84
85	10 03.6	+59.3	0.8	11 03.6	+59.3	0.8	12 03.6	+59.3	0.8	13 03.6	+59.3	0.8	14 03.6	+59.3	0.8	15 03.6	+59.3	0.8	16 03.6	+59.3	0.8	17 03.6	+59.3	0.8	85
86	11 02.9	+59.3	0.6	12 02.9	+59.3	0.6	13 02.9	+59.3	0.6	14 02.9	+59.3	0.6	15 02.9	+59.3	0.6	16 02.9	+59.3	0.7	17 02.9	+59.3	0.7	18 02.9	+59.3	0.7	86
87	12 02.2	+59.3	0.5	13 02.2	+59.3	0.5	14 02.2	+59.3	0.5	15 02.2	+59.3	0.5	16 02.2	+59.3	0.5	17 02.2	+59.3	0.5	18 02.2	+59.3	0.5	19 02.2	+59.3	0.5	87
88	13 01.5	+59.2	0.3	14 01.5	+59.2	0.3	15 01.5	+59.2	0.3	16 01.5	+59.2	0.3	17 01.5	+59.2	0.3	18 01.5	+59.2	0.3	19 01.5	+59.2	0.3	20 01.5	+59.3	0.3	88
89	14 00.7	+59.3	0.2	15 00.7	+59.3	0.2	16 00.7	+59.3	0.2	17 00.7	+59.3	0.2	18 00.7	+59.3	0.2	19 00.7	+59.2	0.2	20 00.7	+59.3	0.2	21 00.7	+59.3	0.2	89
90	15 00.0	+59.3	0.0	16 00.0	+59.3	0.0	17 00.0	+59.3	0.0	18 00.0	+59.3	0.0	19 00.0	+59.3	0.0	20 00.0	+59.3	0.0	21 00.0	+59.3	0.0	22 00.0	+59.3	0.0	90
	15°			16°			17°			18°			19°			20°			21°			22°			

S. Lat. { L.H.A. greater than 180° ....Zn=180°–Z
{ L.H.A. less than 180°............Zn=180°+Z

10°, 350° L.H.A. LATITUDE SAME NAME AS DECLINATION

N. Lat. {L.H.A. greater than 180° .....Zn=Z; L.H.A. less than 180°............Zn=360°–Z}

Dec.	15° Hc	d	Z	16° Hc	d	Z	17° Hc	d	Z	18° Hc	d	Z
°	° ′	′	°	° ′	′	°	° ′	′	°	° ′	′	°
0	72 02.2	+49.8	145.7	71 12.1	+50.9	147.4	70 21.1	+51.8	148.9	69 29.4	+52.6	150.3
1	72 52.0	+48.8	143.9	72 03.0	+49.9	145.7	71 12.9	+51.0	147.4	70 22.0	+51.8	148.9
2	73 40.8	+47.4	141.9	72 52.9	+48.9	143.9	72 03.9	+50.0	145.7	71 13.8	+51.1	147.4
3	74 28.2	+46.0	139.6	73 41.8	+47.5	141.9	72 53.9	+49.0	143.9	72 04.9	+50.1	145.7
4	75 14.2	+44.3	137.2	74 29.3	+46.1	139.6	73 42.9	+47.7	141.8	72 55.0	+49.1	143.9
5	75 58.5	+42.2•	134.5	75 15.4	+44.4	137.2	74 30.6	+46.2	139.6	73 44.1	+47.8	141.9
6	76 40.7	+39.9•	131.5	75 59.8	+42.4•	134.5	75 16.8	+44.5	137.2	74 31.9	+46.4	139.6
7	77 20.6	+37.2•	128.1	76 42.2	+40.1•	131.5	76 01.3	+42.5•	134.5	75 18.3	+44.6	137.2
8	77 57.8	+34.0•	124.5	77 22.3	+37.3•	128.1	76 43.8	+40.2•	131.5	76 02.9	+42.7•	134.5
9	78 31.8	+30.3•	120.4	77 59.6	+34.1•	124.5	77 24.0	+37.5•	128.2	76 45.6	+40.3•	131.5
10	79 02.1	+26.1•	116.0	78 33.7	+30.5•	120.4	78 01.5	+34.3•	124.5	77 25.9	+37.7•	128.2
11	79 28.2	+21.4•	111.1	79 04.2	+26.3•	116.0	78 35.8	+30.7•	120.4	78 03.6	+34.5•	124.5
12	79 49.6	+16.1•	105.9	79 30.5	+21.5•	111.1	79 06.5	+26.4•	116.0	78 38.1	+30.8•	120.5
13	80 05.7	+10.4•	100.4	79 52.0	+16.2•	105.9	79 32.9	+21.7•	111.1	79 08.9	+26.6•	116.0
14	80 16.1	+4.4•	94.6	80 08.2	+10.6•	100.4	79 54.6	+16.4•	105.9	79 35.5	+21.8•	111.2
15	80 20.5	-1.7•	88.7	80 18.8	+4.5•	94.6	80 11.0	+10.7•	100.3	79 57.3	+16.6•	105.9
16	80 18.8	-7.8•	82.8	80 23.3	-1.6•	88.6	80 21.7	+4.6•	94.5	80 13.9	+10.8•	100.3
17	80 11.0	-13.7•	76.9	80 21.7	-7.8•	82.6	80 26.3	-1.6•	88.5	80 24.7	+4.7•	94.5
18	79 57.3	-19.1•	71.2	80 13.9	-13.6•	76.8	80 24.7	-7.7•	82.5	80 29.4	-1.5•	88.5
19	79 38.2	-24.0•	65.9	80 00.3	-19.1•	71.1	80 17.0	-13.6•	76.6	80 27.9	-7.7•	82.4
20	79 14.2	-28.6•	60.9	79 41.2	-24.2•	65.7	80 03.4	-19.2•	70.9	80 20.2	-13.6•	76.5
21	78 45.6	-32.4•	56.3	79 17.0	-28.5•	60.7	79 44.2	-24.1•	65.5	80 06.6	-19.1•	70.7
22	78 13.2	-35.8•	52.1	78 48.5	-32.5•	56.0	79 20.1	-28.7•	60.5	79 47.5	-24.3•	65.3
23	77 37.4	-38.7•	48.2	78 16.0	-35.9•	51.8	78 51.4	-32.5•	55.8	79 23.2	-28.7•	60.2
24	76 58.7	-41.3•	44.7	77 40.1	-38.8•	48.0	78 18.9	-36.0•	51.6	78 54.5	-32.6•	55.6
25	76 17.4	-43.4•	41.6	77 01.3	-41.4•	44.5	77 42.9	-38.9•	47.7	78 21.9	-36.1•	51.3
26	75 34.0	-45.3	38.8	76 19.9	-43.5	41.3	77 04.0	-41.4•	44.2	77 45.8	-39.0•	47.4
27	74 48.7	-46.8	36.2	75 36.4	-45.3	38.5	76 22.6	-43.6•	41.1	77 06.8	-41.5•	43.9
28	74 01.9	-48.2	33.9	74 51.1	-46.9	35.9	75 39.0	-45.4	38.2	76 25.3	-43.7•	40.8
29	73 13.7	-49.4	31.8	74 04.2	-48.3	33.6	74 53.6	-47.0	35.6	75 41.6	-45.5	37.9
30	72 24.3	-50.4	29.8	73 15.9	-49.4	31.5	74 06.6	-48.4	33.3	74 56.1	-47.0	35.4
31	71 33.9	-51.3	28.1	72 26.5	-50.5	29.6	73 18.2	-49.5	31.2	74 09.1	-48.5	33.0
32	70 42.6	-52.0	26.5	71 36.0	-51.3	27.8	72 28.7	-50.5	29.3	73 20.6	-49.6	30.9
33	69 50.6	-52.8	25.0	70 44.7	-52.1	26.2	71 38.2	-51.4	27.5	72 31.0	-50.6	29.0
34	68 57.8	-53.3	23.6	69 52.6	-52.8	24.7	70 46.8	-52.2	25.9	71 40.4	-51.4	27.2
35	68 04.5	-53.9	22.4	68 59.8	-53.4	23.4	69 54.6	-52.8	24.5	70 49.0	-52.3	25.7
36	67 10.6	-54.3	21.2	68 06.4	-53.9	22.1	69 01.8	-53.5	23.1	69 56.7	-52.9	24.2
37	66 16.3	-54.7	20.2	67 12.5	-54.4	21.0	68 08.3	-53.9	21.9	69 03.8	-53.5	22.8
38	65 21.6	-55.1	19.2	66 18.1	-54.8	19.9	67 14.4	-54.4	20.7	68 10.3	-54.0	21.6
39	64 26.5	-55.5	18.2	65 23.3	-55.1	18.9	66 20.0	-54.8	19.6	67 16.3	-54.4	20.4
40	63 31.0	-55.7	17.4	64 28.2	-55.5	18.0	65 25.2	-55.2	18.6	66 21.9	-54.9	19.4
41	62 35.3	-56.0	16.5	63 32.7	-55.8	17.1	64 30.0	-55.6	17.7	65 27.0	-55.2	18.4
42	61 39.3	-56.3	15.8	62 36.9	-56.0	16.3	63 34.4	-55.8	16.9	64 31.8	-55.6	17.5
43	60 43.0	-56.4	15.0	61 40.9	-56.3	15.5	62 38.6	-56.0	16.0	63 36.2	-55.8	16.6
44	59 46.6	-56.7	14.4	60 44.6	-56.5	14.8	61 42.6	-56.3	15.3	62 40.4	-56.1	15.8
45	58 49.9	-56.9	13.7	59 48.1	-56.7	14.1	60 46.3	-56.6	14.6	61 44.3	-56.4	15.0
46	57 53.0	-57.0	13.1	58 51.4	-56.8	13.5	59 49.7	-56.7	13.9	60 47.9	-56.5	14.3
47	56 56.0	-57.1	12.5	57 54.6	-57.1	12.9	58 53.0	-56.9	13.2	59 51.4	-56.8	13.6
48	55 58.9	-57.4	12.0	56 57.5	-57.2	12.3	57 56.1	-57.1	12.6	58 54.6	-56.9	13.0
49	55 01.5	-57.4	11.5	56 00.3	-57.3	11.8	56 59.0	-57.2	12.1	57 57.7	-57.1	12.4
50	54 04.1	-57.5	11.0	55 03.0	-57.5	11.2	56 01.8	-57.3	11.5	57 00.6	-57.3	11.8
51	53 06.6	-57.7	10.5	54 05.5	-57.5	10.7	55 04.5	-57.5	11.0	56 03.3	-57.4	11.3
52	52 08.9	-57.8	10.0	53 08.0	-57.7	10.3	54 07.0	-57.6	10.5	55 05.9	-57.5	10.8
53	51 11.1	-57.8	9.6	52 10.3	-57.8	9.8	53 09.4	-57.7	10.0	54 08.4	-57.6	10.3
54	50 13.3	-58.0	9.2	51 12.5	-57.9	9.4	52 11.7	-57.8	9.6	53 10.8	-57.7	9.8
55	49 15.3	-58.0	8.8	50 14.6	-58.0	9.0	51 13.9	-57.9	9.2	52 13.1	-57.8	9.4
56	48 17.3	-58.1	8.4	49 16.6	-58.0	8.6	50 16.0	-58.0	8.7	51 15.3	-58.0	8.9
57	47 19.2	-58.2	8.0	48 18.6	-58.1	8.2	49 18.0	-58.1	8.3	50 17.3	-58.0	8.5
58	46 21.0	-58.2	7.7	47 20.5	-58.2	7.8	48 19.9	-58.1	8.0	49 19.3	-58.0	8.1
59	45 22.8	-58.3	7.3	46 22.3	-58.2	7.4	47 21.8	-58.2	7.6	48 21.3	-58.2	7.7
60	44 24.5	-58.3	7.0	45 24.1	-58.4	7.1	46 23.6	-58.3	7.2	47 23.1	-58.2	7.4
61	43 26.2	-58.4	6.7	44 25.7	-58.3	6.8	45 25.3	-58.3	6.9	46 24.9	-58.3	7.0
62	42 27.8	-58.5	6.3	43 27.4	-58.4	6.4	44 27.0	-58.4	6.6	45 26.6	-58.3	6.7
63	41 29.3	-58.5	6.0	42 29.0	-58.5	6.1	43 28.6	-58.4	6.2	44 28.3	-58.4	6.3
64	40 30.8	-58.5	5.7	41 30.5	-58.5	5.8	42 30.2	-58.5	5.9	43 29.9	-58.5	6.0
65	39 32.3	-58.6	5.5	40 32.0	-58.6	5.5	41 31.7	-58.5	5.6	42 31.4	-58.5	5.7
66	38 33.7	-58.6	5.2	39 33.4	-58.6	5.3	40 33.2	-58.6	5.3	41 32.9	-58.5	5.4
67	37 35.1	-58.7	4.9	38 34.8	-58.6	5.0	39 34.6	-58.6	5.1	40 34.4	-58.6	5.1
68	36 36.4	-58.7	4.6	37 36.2	-58.7	4.7	38 36.0	-58.7	4.8	39 35.8	-58.6	4.8
69	35 37.7	-58.7	4.4	36 37.5	-58.7	4.4	37 37.3	-58.6	4.5	38 37.2	-58.7	4.6
70	34 39.0	-58.8	4.1	35 38.8	-58.7	4.2	36 38.7	-58.8	4.2	37 38.5	-58.7	4.3
71	33 40.2	-58.8	3.9	34 40.1	-58.8	3.9	35 39.9	-58.7	4.0	36 39.8	-58.7	4.0
72	32 41.4	-58.8	3.7	33 41.3	-58.8	3.7	34 41.2	-58.8	3.7	35 41.1	-58.8	3.8
73	31 42.6	-58.8	3.4	32 42.5	-58.8	3.5	33 42.4	-58.8	3.5	34 42.3	-58.8	3.5
74	30 43.8	-58.9	3.2	31 43.7	-58.8	3.2	32 43.6	-58.8	3.3	33 43.5	-58.8	3.3
75	29 44.9	-58.8	3.0	30 44.9	-58.9	3.0	31 44.8	-58.9	3.0	32 44.7	-58.9	3.1
76	28 46.1	-58.9	2.7	29 46.0	-58.9	2.8	30 45.9	-58.9	2.8	31 45.8	-58.8	2.8
77	27 47.2	-59.0	2.5	28 47.1	-58.9	2.6	29 47.0	-58.9	2.6	30 47.0	-58.9	2.6
78	26 48.2	-58.9	2.3	27 48.2	-58.9	2.3	28 48.1	-58.9	2.4	29 48.1	-58.9	2.4
79	25 49.3	-59.0	2.1	26 49.3	-59.0	2.1	27 49.2	-58.9	2.1	28 49.2	-59.0	2.2
80	24 50.3	-58.9	1.9	25 50.3	-59.0	1.9	26 50.3	-59.0	1.9	27 50.2	-58.9	2.0
81	23 51.4	-59.0	1.7	24 51.3	-58.9	1.7	25 51.3	-59.0	1.7	26 51.3	-59.0	1.7
82	22 52.4	-59.0	1.5	23 52.4	-59.0	1.5	24 52.3	-59.0	1.5	25 52.3	-59.0	1.5
83	21 53.4	-59.0	1.3	22 53.4	-59.1	1.3	23 53.3	-59.0	1.3	24 53.3	-59.0	1.3
84	20 54.4	-59.1	1.1	21 54.3	-59.0	1.1	22 54.3	-59.0	1.1	23 54.3	-59.0	1.1
85	19 55.3	-59.0	0.9	20 55.3	-59.0	0.9	21 55.3	-59.0	0.9	22 55.3	-59.0	0.9
86	18 56.3	-59.1	0.7	19 56.3	-59.1	0.7	20 56.3	-59.1	0.7	21 56.3	-59.1	0.7
87	17 57.2	-59.0	0.5	18 57.2	-59.0	0.6	19 57.2	-59.0	0.6	20 57.2	-59.0	0.6
88	16 58.2	-59.1	0.4	17 58.2	-59.1	0.4	18 58.2	-59.1	0.4	19 58.2	-59.1	0.4
89	15 59.1	-59.1	0.2	16 59.1	-59.1	0.2	17 59.1	-59.1	0.2	18 59.1	-59.1	0.2
90	15 00.0	-59.1	0.0	16 00.0	-59.1	0.0	17 00.0	-59.1	0.0	18 00.0	-59.1	0.0
	15°			16°			17°			18°		

19° Hc	d	Z	20° Hc	d	Z	21° Hc	d	Z	22° Hc	d	Z	Dec.
° ′	′	°	° ′	′	°	° ′	′	°	° ′	′	°	°
68 36.9	+53.3	151.6	67 43.9	+53.9	152.7	66 50.3	+54.4	153.8	65 56.2	+55.0	154.8	0
69 30.2	+52.7	150.3	68 37.8	+53.3	151.5	67 44.7	+54.0	152.7	66 51.2	+54.5	153.8	1
70 22.9	+52.0	148.9	69 31.1	+52.8	150.3	68 38.7	+53.5	151.5	67 45.7	+54.0	152.7	2
71 14.9	+51.1	147.4	70 23.9	+52.1	148.9	69 32.2	+52.8	150.3	68 39.7	+53.6	151.5	3
72 06.0	+50.3	145.7	71 16.0	+51.2	147.4	70 25.0	+52.2	148.9	69 33.3	+52.9	150.3	4
72 56.3	+49.1	143.9	72 07.2	+50.4	145.7	71 17.2	+51.3	147.4	70 26.2	+52.3	148.9	5
73 45.4	+47.9	141.9	72 57.6	+49.3	143.9	72 08.5	+50.5	145.7	71 18.5	+51.4	147.4	6
74 33.3	+46.5	139.7	73 46.9	+48.0	141.9	72 59.0	+49.4	143.9	72 09.9	+50.6	145.8	7
75 19.8	+44.8	137.2	74 34.9	+46.6	139.7	73 48.4	+48.2	141.9	73 00.5	+49.5	144.0	8
76 04.6	+42.8•	134.5	75 21.5	+45.0	137.3	74 36.6	+46.7	139.7	73 50.0	+48.3	142.0	9
76 47.4	+40.6•	131.6	76 06.5	+42.9•	134.6	75 23.3	+45.1	137.3	74 38.3	+46.9	139.8	10
77 28.0	+37.8•	128.2	76 49.4	+40.7•	131.6	76 08.4	+43.2•	134.6	75 25.2	+45.3	137.4	11
78 05.8	+34.6•	124.6	77 30.1	+38.0•	128.3	76 51.6	+40.8•	131.7	76 10.5	+43.3•	134.7	12
78 40.4	+31.0•	120.5	78 08.1	+34.9•	124.6	77 32.4	+38.2•	128.4	76 53.8	+41.1•	131.7	13
79 11.4	+26.8•	116.0	78 43.0	+31.2•	120.6	78 10.6	+35.0•	124.7	77 34.9	+38.3•	128.4	14
79 38.2	+22.1•	111.2	79 14.2	+27.0•	116.1	78 45.6	+31.4•	120.6	78 13.2	+35.3•	124.8	15
80 00.3	+16.7•	105.9	79 41.2	+22.2•	111.2	79 17.0	+27.2•	116.1	78 48.5	+31.6•	120.7	16
80 17.0	+10.9•	100.3	80 03.4	+16.8•	105.9	79 44.2	+22.4•	111.2	79 20.1	+27.4•	116.2	17
80 27.9	+4.9•	94.4	80 20.2	+11.1•	100.3	80 06.6	+17.1•	105.9	79 47.5	+22.5•	111.3	18
80 32.8	-1.5•	88.4	80 31.3	+5.0•	94.4	80 23.7	+11.2•	100.3	80 10.0	+17.3•	106.0	19
80 31.3	-7.6•	82.3	80 36.3	-1.4•	88.3	80 34.9	+5.0•	94.3	80 27.3	+11.3•	100.3	20
80 23.7	-13.7•	76.3	80 34.9	-7.6•	82.2	80 39.9	-1.3•	88.2	80 38.6	+5.2•	94.3	21
80 10.0	-19.2•	70.5	80 27.3	-13.7•	76.1	80 38.6	-7.6•	82.0	80 43.8	-1.3•	88.1	22
79 50.8	-24.2•	65.1	80 13.6	-19.2•	70.3	80 31.0	-13.6•	76.0	80 42.5	-7.5•	81.9	23
79 26.6	-28.8•	60.0	79 54.4	-24.4•	64.8	80 17.4	-19.3•	70.1	80 35.0	-13.7•	75.8	24
78 57.8	-32.8•	55.3	79 30.0	-28.9•	59.7	79 58.1	-24.5•	64.6	80 21.3	-19.4•	69.9	25
78 25.0	-36.1•	51.0	79 01.1	-32.8•	55.0	79 33.6	-28.9•	59.5	80 01.9	-24.5•	64.4	26
77 48.9	-39.1•	47.1	78 28.3	-36.3•	50.7	79 04.7	-33.0•	54.7	79 37.4	-29.1•	59.2	27
77 09.8	-41.6•	43.6	77 52.0	-39.2•	46.8	78 31.7	-36.4•	50.4	79 08.3	-33.1•	54.5	28
76 28.2	-43.8•	40.5	77 12.8	-41.7•	43.3	77 55.3	-39.3•	46.5	78 35.2	-36.5•	50.1	29
75 44.4	-45.6	37.6	76 31.1	-43.9•	40.2	77 16.0	-41.9•	43.0	77 58.7	-39.5•	46.2	30
74 58.8	-47.2	35.1	75 47.2	-45.7	37.3	76 34.1	-43.9	39.9	77 19.2	-41.9•	42.7	31
74 11.6	-48.5	32.7	75 01.5	-47.2	34.7	75 50.2	-45.8	37.0	76 37.3	-44.1•	39.5	32
73 23.1	-49.7	30.6	74 14.3	-48.6	32.4	75 04.4	-47.4	34.4	75 53.2	-45.9	36.7	33
72 33.4	-50.6	28.7	73 25.7	-49.8	30.3	74 17.0	-48.7	32.1	75 07.3	-47.5	34.1	34
71 42.8	-51.6	27.0	72 35.9	-50.8	28.4	73 28.3	-49.9	30.0	74 19.8	-48.8	31.8	35
70 51.2	-52.3	25.4	71 45.1	-51.6	26.7	72 38.4	-50.8	28.1	73 31.0	-50.0	29.7	36
69 58.9	-53.0	23.9	70 53.5	-52.4	25.1	71 47.6	-51.7	26.4	72 41.0	-50.9	27.8	37
69 05.9	-53.5	22.6	70 01.1	-53.0	23.6	70 55.9	-52.5	24.8	71 50.1	-51.8	26.0	38
68 12.4	-54.1	21.3	69 08.1	-53.6	22.3	70 03.4	-53.1	23.3	70 58.3	-52.5	24.5	39
67 18.3	-54.5	20.2	68 14.5	-54.1	21.0	69 10.3	-53.6	22.0	70 05.8	-53.2	23.0	40
66 23.8	-54.9	19.1	67 20.4	-54.6	19.9	68 16.7	-54.2	20.7	69 12.6	-53.7	21.7	41
65 28.9	-55.3	18.1	66 25.8	-54.9	18.8	67 22.5	-54.6	19.6	68 18.9	-54.3	20.4	42
64 33.6	-55.6	17.2	65 30.9	-55.4	17.8	66 27.9	-55.1	18.5	67 24.6	-54.7	19.3	43
63 38.0	-55.9	16.3	64 35.5	-55.6	16.9	65 32.8	-55.3	17.6	66 29.9	-55.1	18.3	44
62 42.1	-56.1	15.5	63 39.9	-56.0	16.1	64 37.5	-55.7	16.6	65 34.8	-55.4	17.3	45
61 46.0	-56.4	14.8	62 43.9	-56.1	15.3	63 41.8	-56.0	15.8	64 39.4	-55.7	16.4	46
60 49.6	-56.6	14.1	61 47.8	-56.5	14.5	62 45.8	-56.3	15.0	63 43.7	-56.1	15.5	47
59 53.0	-56.8	13.4	60 51.3	-56.6	13.8	61 49.5	-56.4	14.2	62 47.6	-56.2	14.7	48
58 56.2	-56.9	12.8	59 54.7	-56.7	13.1	60 53.1	-56.7	13.5	61 51.4	-56.5	14.0	49
57 59.3	-57.2	12.2	58 57.9	-57.0	12.5	59 56.4	-56.9	12.9	60 54.9	-56.8	13.3	50
57 02.1	-57.2	11.6	58 00.9	-57.2	11.9	58 59.5	-57.0	12.2	59 58.1	-56.9	12.6	51
56 04.9	-57.5	11.0	57 03.7	-57.3	11.3	58 02.5	-57.2	11.7	59 01.2	-57.0	12.0	52
55 07.4	-57.5	10.5	56 06.4	-57.4	10.8	57 05.3	-57.3	11.1	58 04.2	-57.3	11.4	53
54 09.9	-57.6	10.0	55 09.0	-57.6	10.3	56 08.0	-57.5	10.6	57 06.9	-57.3	10.8	54
53 12.3	-57.8	9.6	54 11.4	-57.7	9.8	55 10.5	-57.6	10.0	56 09.6	-57.5	10.3	55
52 14.5	-57.8	9.1	53 13.7	-57.7	9.3	54 12.9	-57.7	9.6	55 12.1	-57.7	9.8	56
51 16.7	-58.0	8.7	52 16.0	-57.9	8.9	53 15.2	-57.8	9.1	54 14.4	-57.7	9.3	57
50 18.7	-58.0	8.3	51 18.1	-58.0	8.5	52 17.4	-57.9	8.7	53 16.7	-57.8	8.9	58
49 20.7	-58.1	7.9	50 20.1	-58.0	8.1	51 19.5	-58.0	8.2	52 18.9	-57.9	8.4	59
48 22.6	-58.2	7.5	49 22.1	-58.2	7.7	50 21.5	-58.0	7.8	51 21.0	-58.1	8.0	60
47 24.4	-58.2	7.1	48 23.9	-58.1	7.3	49 23.5	-58.2	7.4	50 22.9	-58.1	7.6	61
46 26.2	-58.3	6.8	47 25.8	-58.3	6.9	48 25.3	-58.2	7.1	49 24.8	-58.1	7.2	62
45 27.9	-58.4	6.5	46 27.5	-58.3	6.6	47 27.1	-58.3	6.7	48 26.7	-58.3	6.8	63
44 29.5	-58.4	6.1	45 29.2	-58.4	6.2	46 28.8	-58.3	6.3	47 28.4	-58.3	6.5	64
43 31.1	-58.5	5.8	44 30.8	-58.4	5.9	45 30.5	-58.4	6.0	46 30.1	-58.3	6.1	65
42 32.6	-58.5	5.5	43 32.4	-58.5	5.6	44 32.1	-58.5	5.7	45 31.8	-58.5	5.8	66
41 34.1	-58.5	5.2	42 33.9	-58.6	5.3	43 33.6	-58.5	5.4	44 33.3	-58.4	5.5	67
40 35.6	-58.6	4.9	41 35.3	-58.5	5.0	42 35.1	-58.5	5.1	43 34.9	-58.6	5.2	68
39 37.0	-58.7	4.6	40 36.8	-58.7	4.7	41 36.6	-58.6	4.8	42 36.3	-58.5	4.9	69
38 38.3	-58.7	4.4	39 38.1	-58.6	4.4	40 38.0	-58.7	4.5	41 37.8	-58.6	4.6	70
37 39.6	-58.7	4.1	38 39.5	-58.7	4.2	39 39.3	-58.6	4.2	40 39.2	-58.7	4.3	71
36 40.9	-58.7	3.8	37 40.8	-58.7	3.9	38 40.7	-58.8	3.9	39 40.5	-58.7	4.0	72
35 42.2	-58.8	3.6	36 42.1	-58.8	3.6	37 41.9	-58.7	3.7	38 41.8	-58.7	3.7	73
34 43.4	-58.8	3.3	35 43.3	-58.8	3.4	36 43.2	-58.8	3.4	37 43.1	-58.8	3.5	74
33 44.6	-58.8	3.1	34 44.5	-58.8	3.1	35 44.4	-58.8	3.2	36 44.3	-58.8	3.2	75
32 45.8	-58.9	2.9	33 45.7	-58.8	2.9	34 45.6	-58.8	2.9	35 45.5	-58.8	3.0	76
31 46.9	-58.9	2.6	32 46.9	-58.9	2.7	33 46.8	-58.9	2.7	34 46.7	-58.8	2.7	77
30 48.0	-58.9	2.4	31 48.0	-58.9	2.4	32 47.9	-58.9	2.5	33 47.9	-58.9	2.5	78
29 49.1	-58.9	2.2	30 49.1	-58.9	2.2	31 49.0	-58.9	2.2	32 49.0	-58.9	2.3	79
28 50.2	-58.9	2.0	29 50.2	-59.0	2.0	30 50.1	-58.9	2.0	31 50.1	-58.9	2.0	80
27 51.3	-59.0	1.8	28 51.2	-58.9	1.8	29 51.2	-59.0	1.8	30 51.2	-59.0	1.8	81
26 52.3	-59.0	1.6	27 52.3	-59.0	1.6	28 52.2	-58.9	1.6	29 52.2	-58.9	1.6	82
25 53.3	-59.0	1.3	26 53.3	-59.0	1.4	27 53.3	-59.0	1.4	28 53.3	-59.0	1.4	83
24 54.3	-59.0	1.1	25 54.3	-59.0	1.2	26 54.3	-59.0	1.2	27 54.3	-59.0	1.2	84
23 55.3	-59.0	0.9	24 55.3	-59.0	1.0	25 55.3	-59.1	1.0	26 55.3	-59.1	1.0	85
22 56.3	-59.1	0.8	23 56.3	-59.1	0.8	24 56.2	-59.0	0.8	25 56.2	-59.0	0.8	86
21 57.2	-59.0	0.6	22 57.2	-59.0	0.6	23 57.2	-59.0	0.6	24 57.2	-59.0	0.6	87
20 58.2	-59.1	0.4	21 58.2	-59.1	0.4	22 58.2	-59.1	0.4	23 58.2	-59.1	0.4	88
19 59.1	-59.1	0.2	20 59.1	-59.1	0.2	21 59.1	-59.1	0.2	22 59.1	-59.1	0.2	89
19 00.0	-59.1	0.0	20 00.0	-59.1	0.0	21 00.0	-59.1	0.0	22 00.0	-59.1	0.0	90
19°			20°			21°			22°			

10°, 350° L.H.A. LATITUDE SAME NAME AS DECLINATION

LATITUDE CONTRARY NAME TO DECLINATION — L.H.A. 10°, 350°

Dec.	15° Hc	d	Z	16° Hc	d	Z	17° Hc	d	Z	18° Hc	d	Z
°	° ′	′	°	° ′	′	°	° ′	′	°	° ′	′	°
0	72 02.2	-50.8	145.7	71 12.1	-51.7	147.4	70 21.1	-52.5	148.9	69 29.4	-53.2	150.3
1	71 11.4	-51.7	147.4	70 20.4	-52.5	148.9	69 28.6	-53.1	150.3	68 36.2	-53.8	151.6
2	70 19.7	-52.3	149.0	69 27.9	-53.0	150.3	68 35.5	-53.7	151.6	67 42.4	-54.3	152.8
3	69 27.4	-53.1	150.4	68 34.9	-53.7	151.7	67 41.8	-54.2	152.8	66 48.1	-54.6	153.9
4	68 34.3	-53.5	151.7	67 41.2	-54.1	152.9	66 47.6	-54.6	153.9	65 53.5	-55.1	154.9
5	67 40.8	-54.1	152.9	66 47.1	-54.6	154.0	65 53.0	-55.0	155.0	64 58.4	-55.4	155.9
6	66 46.7	-54.5	154.0	65 52.5	-54.9	155.0	64 58.0	-55.4	155.9	64 03.0	-55.7	156.8
7	65 52.2	-54.9	155.1	64 57.6	-55.3	156.0	64 02.6	-55.7	156.8	63 07.3	-56.0	157.6
8	64 57.3	-55.3	156.0	64 02.3	-55.6	156.9	63 06.9	-55.9	157.6	62 11.3	-56.2	158.4
9	64 02.0	-55.6	156.9	63 06.7	-55.9	157.7	62 11.0	-56.2	158.4	61 15.1	-56.5	159.1
10	63 06.4	-55.8	157.8	62 10.8	-56.2	158.5	61 14.8	-56.4	159.2	60 18.6	-56.7	159.8
11	62 10.6	-56.1	158.6	61 14.6	-56.4	159.2	60 18.4	-56.6	159.9	59 21.9	-56.8	160.5
12	61 14.5	-56.4	159.3	60 18.2	-56.6	159.9	59 21.8	-56.9	160.5	58 25.1	-57.0	161.1
13	60 18.1	-56.5	160.0	59 21.6	-56.8	160.6	58 24.9	-57.0	161.2	57 28.1	-57.2	161.7
14	59 21.6	-56.8	160.7	58 24.8	-56.9	161.2	57 27.9	-57.1	161.7	56 30.9	-57.3	162.2
15	58 24.8	-56.9	161.3	57 27.9	-57.1	161.8	56 30.8	-57.3	162.3	55 33.6	-57.5	162.7
16	57 27.9	-57.1	161.9	56 30.8	-57.3	162.4	55 33.5	-57.4	162.8	54 36.1	-57.5	163.3
17	56 30.8	-57.2	162.5	55 33.5	-57.4	162.9	54 36.1	-57.5	163.3	53 38.6	-57.7	163.7
18	55 33.6	-57.4	163.0	54 36.1	-57.5	163.4	53 38.6	-57.7	163.8	52 40.9	-57.8	164.2
19	54 36.2	-57.5	163.5	53 38.6	-57.6	163.9	52 40.9	-57.8	164.3	51 43.1	-57.9	164.6
20	53 38.7	-57.6	164.0	52 41.0	-57.7	164.4	51 43.1	-57.8	164.7	50 45.2	-57.9	165.1
21	52 41.1	-57.7	164.5	51 43.3	-57.9	164.8	50 45.3	-57.9	165.2	49 47.3	-58.1	165.5
22	51 43.4	-57.8	164.9	50 45.4	-57.9	165.3	49 47.4	-58.1	165.6	48 49.2	-58.1	165.8
23	50 45.6	-57.9	165.4	49 47.5	-58.0	165.7	48 49.3	-58.1	165.9	47 51.1	-58.2	166.2
24	49 47.7	-58.0	165.8	48 49.5	-58.1	166.1	47 51.2	-58.1	166.3	46 52.9	-58.2	166.6
25	48 49.7	-58.0	166.2	47 51.4	-58.1	166.4	46 53.1	-58.3	166.7	45 54.7	-58.4	166.9
26	47 51.7	-58.2	166.5	46 53.3	-58.2	166.8	45 54.8	-58.3	167.0	44 56.3	-58.3	167.3
27	46 53.5	-58.2	166.9	45 55.1	-58.3	167.1	44 56.5	-58.3	167.4	43 58.0	-58.5	167.6
28	45 55.3	-58.2	167.3	44 56.8	-58.3	167.5	43 58.2	-58.4	167.7	42 59.5	-58.4	167.9
29	44 57.1	-58.3	167.6	43 58.5	-58.4	167.8	42 59.8	-58.5	168.0	42 01.1	-58.6	168.2
30	43 58.8	-58.4	167.9	43 00.1	-58.5	168.1	42 01.3	-58.5	168.3	41 02.5	-58.5	168.5
31	43 00.4	-58.4	168.3	42 01.6	-58.5	168.4	41 02.8	-58.5	168.6	40 04.0	-58.6	168.8
32	42 02.0	-58.5	168.6	41 03.1	-58.5	168.7	40 04.3	-58.6	168.9	39 05.4	-58.7	169.1
33	41 03.5	-58.5	168.9	40 04.6	-58.6	169.0	39 05.7	-58.7	169.2	38 06.7	-58.7	169.3
34	40 05.0	-58.6	169.2	39 06.0	-58.6	169.3	38 07.0	-58.6	169.5	37 08.0	-58.7	169.6
35	39 06.4	-58.6	169.4	38 07.4	-58.6	169.6	37 08.4	-58.7	169.7	36 09.3	-58.7	169.9
36	38 07.8	-58.6	169.7	37 08.8	-58.7	169.8	36 09.7	-58.8	170.0	35 10.6	-58.8	170.1
37	37 09.2	-58.7	170.0	36 10.1	-58.8	170.1	35 10.9	-58.7	170.2	34 11.8	-58.8	170.3
38	36 10.5	-58.7	170.2	35 11.3	-58.7	170.4	34 12.2	-58.8	170.5	33 13.0	-58.8	170.6
39	35 11.8	-58.8	170.5	34 12.6	-58.8	170.6	33 13.4	-58.8	170.7	32 14.2	-58.9	170.8
40	34 13.0	-58.7	170.7	33 13.8	-58.8	170.8	32 14.6	-58.9	171.0	31 15.3	-58.9	171.0
41	33 14.3	-58.8	171.0	32 15.0	-58.8	171.1	31 15.7	-58.8	171.2	30 16.4	-58.9	171.3
42	32 15.5	-58.8	171.2	31 16.2	-58.9	171.3	30 16.9	-58.9	171.4	29 17.5	-58.9	171.5
43	31 16.7	-58.9	171.5	30 17.3	-58.9	171.5	29 18.0	-58.9	171.6	28 18.6	-58.9	171.7
44	30 17.8	-58.8	171.7	29 18.4	-58.9	171.8	28 19.1	-59.0	171.8	27 19.7	-59.0	171.9
45	29 19.0	-58.9	171.9	28 19.5	-58.9	172.0	27 20.1	-58.9	172.1	26 20.7	-59.0	172.1
46	28 20.1	-59.0	172.1	27 20.6	-58.9	172.2	26 21.2	-59.0	172.3	25 21.7	-59.0	172.3
47	27 21.1	-58.9	172.3	26 21.7	-59.0	172.4	25 22.2	-59.0	172.5	24 22.7	-59.0	172.5
48	26 22.2	-58.9	172.5	25 22.7	-59.0	172.6	24 23.2	-59.0	172.7	23 23.7	-59.0	172.7
49	25 23.3	-59.0	172.8	24 23.7	-58.9	172.8	23 24.2	-59.0	172.9	22 24.7	-59.1	172.9
50	24 24.3	-59.0	173.0	23 24.8	-59.1	173.0	22 25.2	-59.0	173.1	21 25.6	-59.0	173.1
51	23 25.3	-59.0	173.2	22 25.7	-59.0	173.2	21 26.2	-59.1	173.3	20 26.6	-59.1	173.3
52	22 26.3	-59.0	173.4	21 26.7	-59.0	173.4	20 27.1	-59.0	173.4	19 27.5	-59.1	173.5
53	21 27.3	-59.0	173.6	20 27.7	-59.1	173.6	19 28.1	-59.1	173.6	18 28.4	-59.1	173.7
54	20 28.3	-59.0	173.7	19 28.6	-59.0	173.8	18 29.0	-59.1	173.8	17 29.3	-59.1	173.9
55	19 29.3	-59.1	173.9	18 29.6	-59.1	174.0	17 29.9	-59.1	174.0	16 30.2	-59.1	174.0
56	18 30.2	-59.1	174.1	17 30.5	-59.1	174.2	16 30.8	-59.1	174.2	15 31.1	-59.1	174.2
57	17 31.1	-59.0	174.3	16 31.4	-59.0	174.3	15 31.7	-59.1	174.4	14 32.0	-59.1	174.4
58	16 32.1	-59.1	174.5	15 32.4	-59.0	174.5	14 32.6	-59.1	174.5	13 32.9	-59.1	174.6
59	15 33.0	-59.1	174.7	14 33.3	-59.1	174.7	13 33.5	-59.1	174.7	12 33.8	-59.2	174.7
60	14 33.9	-59.1	174.9	13 34.2	-59.2	174.9	12 34.4	-59.1	174.9	11 34.6	-59.1	174.9
61	13 34.8	-59.1	175.0	12 35.0	-59.1	175.1	11 35.3	-59.2	175.1	10 35.5	-59.2	175.1
62	12 35.7	-59.1	175.2	11 35.9	-59.1	175.2	10 36.1	-59.1	175.2	9 36.3	-59.1	175.3
63	11 36.6	-59.1	175.4	10 36.8	-59.1	175.4	9 37.0	-59.2	175.4	8 37.2	-59.2	175.4
64	10 37.5	-59.1	175.6	9 37.7	-59.2	175.6	8 37.8	-59.1	175.6	7 38.0	-59.1	175.6
65	9 38.4	-59.2	175.7	8 38.5	-59.1	175.7	7 38.7	-59.2	175.8	6 38.9	-59.2	175.8
66	8 39.2	-59.1	175.9	7 39.4	-59.2	175.9	6 39.5	-59.1	175.9	5 39.7	-59.2	175.9
67	7 40.1	-59.1	176.1	6 40.2	-59.1	176.1	5 40.4	-59.2	176.1	4 40.5	-59.1	176.1
68	6 41.0	-59.2	176.2	5 41.1	-59.2	176.3	4 41.2	-59.1	176.3	3 41.4	-59.2	176.3
69	5 41.8	-59.1	176.4	4 41.9	-59.1	176.4	3 42.1	-59.2	176.4	2 42.2	-59.2	176.4
70	4 42.7	-59.2	176.6	3 42.8	-59.2	176.6	2 42.9	-59.2	176.6	1 43.0	-59.2	176.6
71	3 43.5	-59.1	176.8	2 43.6	-59.1	176.8	1 43.7	-59.1	176.8	0 43.8	-59.1	176.8
72	2 44.4	-59.2	176.9	1 44.5	-59.2	176.9	0 44.6	-59.2	176.9	0 15.3	+59.2	3.1
73	1 45.2	-59.1	177.1	0 45.3	-59.1	177.1	0 14.6	+59.2	2.9	1 14.5	+59.2	2.9
74	0 46.1	-59.2	177.3	0 13.8	+59.2	2.7	1 13.8	+59.1	2.7	2 13.7	+59.2	2.7
75	0 13.1	+59.1	2.6	1 13.0	+59.2	2.6	2 12.9	+59.2	2.6	3 12.9	+59.1	2.6
76	1 12.2	+59.2	2.4	2 12.2	+59.1	2.4	3 12.1	+59.2	2.4	4 12.0	+59.2	2.4
77	2 11.4	+59.1	2.2	3 11.3	+59.2	2.2	4 11.3	+59.1	2.2	5 11.2	+59.2	2.2
78	3 10.5	+59.2	2.1	4 10.5	+59.1	2.1	5 10.4	+59.2	2.1	6 10.4	+59.2	2.1
79	4 09.7	+59.1	1.9	5 09.6	+59.2	1.9	6 09.6	+59.1	1.9	7 09.6	+59.1	1.9
80	5 08.8	+59.1	1.7	6 08.8	+59.1	1.7	7 08.7	+59.2	1.7	8 08.7	+59.2	1.7
81	6 07.9	+59.2	1.6	7 07.9	+59.2	1.6	8 07.9	+59.1	1.6	9 07.9	+59.1	1.6
82	7 07.1	+59.1	1.4	8 07.1	+59.1	1.4	9 07.0	+59.2	1.4	10 07.0	+59.2	1.4
83	8 06.2	+59.1	1.2	9 06.2	+59.1	1.2	10 06.2	+59.1	1.2	11 06.2	+59.2	1.2
84	9 05.3	+59.2	1.1	10 05.3	+59.2	1.1	11 05.3	+59.2	1.1	12 05.3	+59.1	1.1
85	10 04.5	+59.1	0.9	11 04.5	+59.1	0.9	12 04.5	+59.1	0.9	13 04.4	+59.2	0.9
86	11 03.6	+59.1	0.7	12 03.6	+59.1	0.7	13 03.6	+59.1	0.7	14 03.6	+59.1	0.7
87	12 02.7	+59.1	0.5	13 02.7	+59.1	0.5	14 02.7	+59.1	0.5	15 02.7	+59.1	0.5
88	13 01.8	+59.1	0.4	14 01.8	+59.1	0.4	15 01.8	+59.1	0.4	16 01.8	+59.1	0.4
89	14 00.9	+59.1	0.2	15 00.9	+59.1	0.2	16 00.9	+59.1	0.2	17 00.9	+59.1	0.2
90	15 00.0	+59.1	0.0	16 00.0	+59.1	0.0	17 00.0	+59.1	0.0	18 00.0	+59.1	0.0
	15°			16°			17°			18°		

Dec.	19° Hc	d	Z	20° Hc	d	Z	21° Hc	d	Z	22° Hc	d	Z	Dec.
°	° ′	′	°	° ′	′	°	° ′	′	°	° ′	′	°	°
0	68 36.9	-53.8	151.6	67 43.9	-54.4	152.7	66 50.3	-54.9	153.8	65 56.2	-55.3	154.8	0
1	67 43.1	-54.3	152.7	66 49.5	-54.8	153.8	65 55.4	-55.2	154.8	65 00.9	-55.6	155.7	1
2	66 48.8	-54.8	153.8	65 54.7	-55.2	154.8	65 00.2	-55.6	155.8	64 05.3	-55.9	156.6	2
3	65 54.0	-55.1	154.9	64 59.5	-55.5	155.8	64 04.6	-55.9	156.6	63 09.4	-56.2	157.4	3
4	64 58.9	-55.4	155.8	64 04.0	-55.8	156.7	63 08.7	-56.1	157.5	62 13.2	-56.4	158.2	4
5	64 03.5	-55.8	156.7	63 08.2	-56.1	157.5	62 12.6	-56.4	158.2	61 16.8	-56.7	158.9	5
6	63 07.7	-56.0	157.5	62 12.1	-56.3	158.3	61 16.2	-56.5	158.9	60 20.1	-56.8	159.6	6
7	62 11.7	-56.3	158.3	61 15.8	-56.6	159.0	60 19.7	-56.8	159.6	59 23.3	-57.0	160.2	7
8	61 15.4	-56.5	159.0	60 19.2	-56.7	159.7	59 22.9	-57.0	160.3	58 26.3	-57.2	160.8	8
9	60 18.9	-56.7	159.7	59 22.5	-56.9	160.3	58 25.9	-57.1	160.9	57 29.1	-57.3	161.4	9
10	59 22.2	-56.9	160.4	58 25.6	-57.1	160.9	57 28.8	-57.3	161.5	56 31.8	-57.4	161.9	10
11	58 25.3	-57.1	161.0	57 28.5	-57.3	161.5	56 31.5	-57.4	162.0	55 34.4	-57.6	162.5	11
12	57 28.2	-57.2	161.6	56 31.2	-57.3	162.1	55 34.1	-57.6	162.5	54 36.8	-57.7	162.9	12
13	56 31.0	-57.3	162.1	55 33.9	-57.6	162.6	54 36.5	-57.6	163.0	53 39.1	-57.8	163.4	13
14	55 33.7	-57.5	162.7	54 36.3	-57.6	163.1	53 38.9	-57.8	163.5	52 41.3	-57.9	163.9	14
15	54 36.2	-57.6	163.2	53 38.7	-57.7	163.6	52 41.1	-57.8	163.9	51 43.4	-58.0	164.3	15
16	53 38.6	-57.7	163.6	52 41.0	-57.9	164.0	51 43.3	-58.0	164.4	50 45.4	-58.0	164.7	16
17	52 40.9	-57.8	164.1	51 43.1	-57.9	164.5	50 45.3	-58.0	164.8	49 47.4	-58.2	165.1	17
18	51 43.1	-57.9	164.5	50 45.2	-58.0	164.9	49 47.3	-58.2	165.2	48 49.2	-58.2	165.5	18
19	50 45.2	-58.0	165.0	49 47.2	-58.1	165.3	48 49.1	-58.1	165.6	47 51.0	-58.3	165.8	19
20	49 47.2	-58.1	165.4	48 49.1	-58.1	165.7	47 51.0	-58.3	165.9	46 52.7	-58.3	166.2	20
21	48 49.1	-58.1	165.8	47 51.0	-58.3	166.0	46 52.7	-58.3	166.3	45 54.4	-58.4	166.5	21
22	47 51.0	-58.2	166.1	46 52.7	-58.3	166.4	45 54.4	-58.4	166.6	44 56.0	-58.5	166.9	22
23	46 52.8	-58.3	166.5	45 54.4	-58.3	166.7	44 56.0	-58.4	167.0	43 57.5	-58.5	167.2	23
24	45 54.5	-58.3	166.8	44 56.1	-58.4	167.1	43 57.6	-58.5	167.3	42 59.0	-58.5	167.5	24
25	44 56.2	-58.4	167.2	43 57.7	-58.5	167.4	42 59.1	-58.5	167.6	42 00.5	-58.6	167.8	25
26	43 57.8	-58.5	167.5	42 59.2	-58.5	167.7	42 00.6	-58.6	167.9	41 01.9	-58.7	168.1	26
27	42 59.3	-58.4	167.8	42 00.7	-58.6	168.0	41 02.0	-58.6	168.2	40 03.2	-58.6	168.3	27
28	42 00.9	-58.6	168.1	41 02.1	-58.6	168.3	40 03.4	-58.7	168.4	39 04.6	-58.8	168.6	28
29	41 02.3	-58.6	168.4	40 03.5	-58.6	168.6	39 04.7	-58.7	168.7	38 05.8	-58.7	168.9	29
30	40 03.7	-58.6	168.7	39 04.9	-58.7	168.8	38 06.0	-58.7	169.0	37 07.1	-58.8	169.1	30
31	39 05.1	-58.7	168.9	38 06.2	-58.7	169.1	37 07.3	-58.8	169.2	36 08.3	-58.8	169.4	31
32	38 06.4	-58.6	169.2	37 07.5	-58.8	169.4	36 08.5	-58.8	169.5	35 09.5	-58.8	169.6	32
33	37 07.8	-58.8	169.5	36 08.7	-58.7	169.6	35 09.7	-58.8	169.7	34 10.7	-58.9	169.9	33
34	36 09.0	-58.7	169.7	35 10.0	-58.8	169.9	34 10.9	-58.9	170.0	33 11.8	-58.9	170.1	34
35	35 10.3	-58.8	170.0	34 11.2	-58.9	170.1	33 12.0	-58.8	170.2	32 12.9	-58.9	170.3	35
36	34 11.5	-58.9	170.2	33 12.3	-58.8	170.3	32 13.2	-58.9	170.4	31 14.0	-58.9	170.5	36
37	33 12.6	-58.8	170.5	32 13.5	-58.9	170.6	31 14.3	-59.0	170.7	30 15.1	-59.0	170.8	37
38	32 13.8	-58.9	170.7	31 14.6	-58.9	170.8	30 15.3	-58.9	170.9	29 16.1	-59.0	171.0	38
39	31 14.9	-58.9	170.9	30 15.7	-59.0	171.0	29 16.4	-59.0	171.1	28 17.1	-59.0	171.2	39
40	30 16.0	-58.9	171.1	29 16.7	-58.9	171.2	28 17.4	-58.9	171.3	27 18.1	-59.0	171.4	40
41	29 17.1	-58.9	171.4	28 17.8	-59.0	171.4	27 18.5	-59.0	171.5	26 19.1	-59.0	171.6	41
42	28 18.2	-59.0	171.6	27 18.8	-59.0	171.6	26 19.5	-59.1	171.7	25 20.1	-59.1	171.8	42
43	27 19.2	-59.0	171.8	26 19.8	-59.0	171.9	25 20.4	-59.0	171.9	24 21.0	-59.0	172.0	43
44	26 20.2	-58.9	172.0	25 20.8	-59.0	172.1	24 21.4	-59.0	172.1	23 22.0	-59.1	172.2	44
45	25 21.3	-59.1	172.2	24 21.8	-59.0	172.3	23 22.4	-59.1	172.3	22 22.9	-59.1	172.4	45
46	24 22.2	-59.0	172.4	23 22.8	-59.1	172.4	22 23.3	-59.1	172.5	21 23.8	-59.1	172.6	46
47	23 23.2	-59.0	172.6	22 23.7	-59.0	172.6	21 24.2	-59.1	172.7	20 24.7	-59.1	172.7	47
48	22 24.2	-59.1	172.8	21 24.7	-59.1	172.8	20 25.1	-59.1	172.9	19 25.6	-59.1	172.9	48
49	21 25.1	-59.0	173.0	20 25.6	-59.1	173.0	19 26.0	-59.1	173.1	18 26.5	-59.2	173.1	49
50	20 26.1	-59.1	173.2	19 26.5	-59.1	173.2	18 26.9	-59.1	173.2	17 27.3	-59.1	173.3	50
51	19 27.0	-59.1	173.3	18 27.4	-59.1	173.4	17 27.8	-59.1	173.4	16 28.2	-59.2	173.5	51
52	18 27.9	-59.1	173.5	17 28.3	-59.1	173.6	16 28.7	-59.2	173.6	15 29.0	-59.1	173.6	52
53	17 28.8	-59.1	173.7	16 29.2	-59.2	173.7	15 29.5	-59.1	173.8	14 29.9	-59.2	173.8	53
54	16 29.7	-59.1	173.9	15 30.0	-59.1	173.9	14 30.4	-59.2	173.9	13 30.7	-59.2	174.0	54
55	15 30.6	-59.2	174.1	14 30.9	-59.2	174.1	13 31.2	-59.2	174.1	12 31.5	-59.2	174.1	55
56	14 31.4	-59.1	174.2	13 31.7	-59.1	174.3	12 32.0	-59.1	174.3	11 32.3	-59.1	174.3	56
57	13 32.3	-59.1	174.4	12 32.6	-59.2	174.4	11 32.9	-59.2	174.5	10 33.2	-59.2	174.5	57
58	12 33.2	-59.2	174.6	11 33.4	-59.1	174.6	10 33.7	-59.2	174.6	9 34.0	-59.2	174.6	58
59	11 34.0	-59.1	174.8	10 34.3	-59.2	174.8	9 34.5	-59.2	174.8	8 34.8	-59.2	174.8	59
60	10 34.9	-59.2	174.9	9 35.1	-59.2	174.9	8 35.3	-59.2	175.0	7 35.6	-59.2	175.0	60
61	9 35.7	-59.2	175.1	8 35.9	-59.2	175.1	7 36.1	-59.2	175.1	6 36.4	-59.3	175.1	61
62	8 36.5	-59.1	175.3	7 36.7	-59.1	175.3	6 36.9	-59.2	175.3	5 37.1	-59.2	175.3	62
63	7 37.4	-59.2	175.4	6 37.6	-59.2	175.4	5 37.7	-59.2	175.5	4 37.9	-59.2	175.5	63
64	6 38.2	-59.2	175.6	5 38.4	-59.2	175.6	4 38.5	-59.2	175.6	3 38.7	-59.2	175.6	64
65	5 39.0	-59.2	175.8	4 39.2	-59.2	175.8	3 39.3	-59.2	175.8	2 39.5	-59.2	175.8	65
66	4 39.8	-59.1	175.9	3 40.0	-59.2	175.9	2 40.1	-59.2	175.9	1 40.3	-59.2	175.9	66
67	3 40.7	-59.2	176.1	2 40.8	-59.2	176.1	1 40.9	-59.2	176.1	0 41.1	-59.2	176.1	67
68	2 41.5	-59.2	176.3	1 41.6	-59.2	176.3	0 41.7	-59.2	176.3	0 18.1	+59.3	3.7	68
69	1 42.3	-59.2	176.4	0 42.4	-59.2	176.4	0 17.5	+59.2	3.6	1 17.4	+59.2	3.6	69
70	0 43.1	-59.2	176.6	0 16.8	+59.2	3.4	1 16.7	+59.2	3.4	2 16.6	+59.2	3.4	70
71	0 16.1	+59.2	3.2	1 16.0	+59.2	3.2	2 15.9	+59.2	3.2	3 15.8	+59.2	3.2	71
72	1 15.3	+59.1	3.1	2 15.2	+59.2	3.1	3 15.1	+59.2	3.1	4 15.0	+59.2	3.1	72
73	2 14.4	+59.2	2.9	3 14.4	+59.2	2.9	4 14.3	+59.2	2.9	5 14.2	+59.2	2.9	73
74	3 13.6	+59.2	2.7	4 13.6	+59.2	2.8	5 13.5	+59.2	2.8	6 13.4	+59.2	2.8	74
75	4 12.8	+59.2	2.6	5 12.8	+59.1	2.6	6 12.7	+59.2	2.6	7 12.6	+59.2	2.6	75
76	5 12.0	+59.2	2.4	6 11.9	+59.2	2.4	7 11.9	+59.2	2.4	8 11.8	+59.2	2.4	76
77	6 11.2	+59.1	2.3	7 11.1	+59.2	2.3	8 11.1	+59.2	2.3	9 11.0	+59.2	2.3	77
78	7 10.3	+59.2	2.1	8 10.3	+59.2	2.1	9 10.3	+59.1	2.1	10 10.2	+59.2	2.1	78
79	8 09.5	+59.2	1.9	9 09.5	+59.2	1.9	10 09.4	+59.2	1.9	11 09.4	+59.2	1.9	79
80	9 08.7	+59.1	1.8	10 08.7	+59.1	1.8	11 08.6	+59.2	1.8	12 08.6	+59.2	1.8	80
81	10 07.8	+59.2	1.6	11 07.8	+59.2	1.6	12 07.8	+59.2	1.6	13 07.8	+59.1	1.6	81
82	11 07.0	+59.2	1.4	12 07.0	+59.1	1.4	13 07.0	+59.1	1.4	14 06.9	+59.2	1.4	82
83	12 06.2	+59.1	1.2	13 06.1	+59.2	1.2	14 06.1	+59.2	1.3	15 06.1	+59.2	1.3	83
84	13 05.3	+59.1	1.1	14 05.3	+59.1	1.1	15 05.3	+59.1	1.1	16 05.3	+59.1	1.1	84
85	14 04.4	+59.2	0.9	15 04.4	+59.2	0.9	16 04.4	+59.2	0.9	17 04.4	+59.2	0.9	85
86	15 03.6	+59.1	0.7	16 03.6	+59.1	0.7	17 03.6	+59.1	0.7	18 03.6	+59.1	0.7	86
87	16 02.7	+59.1	0.5	17 02.7	+59.1	0.5	18 02.7	+59.1	0.5	19 02.7	+59.1	0.6	87
88	17 01.8	+59.1	0.4	18 01.8	+59.1	0.4	19 01.8	+59.1	0.4	20 01.8	+59.1	0.4	88
89	18 00.9	+59.1	0.2	19 00.9	+59.1	0.2	20 00.9	+59.1	0.2	21 00.9	+59.1	0.2	89
90	19 00.0	+59.1	0.0	20 00.0	+59.1	0.0	21 00.0	+59.1	0.0	22 00.0	+59.1	0.0	90
	19°			20°			21°			22°			

S. Lat. { L.H.A. greater than 180° ....Zn=180°−Z
{ L.H.A. less than 180°............Zn=180°+Z

LATITUDE SAME NAME AS DECLINATION — L.H.A. 170°, 190°

23

	15°			16°			17°			18°			19°			20°			21°			22°			
Dec.	Hc	d	Z	Hc	d	Z	Hc	d	Z	Hc	d	Z	Hc	d	Z	Hc	d	Z	Hc	d	Z	Hc	d	Z	Dec.
°	° ′	′	°	° ′	′	°	° ′	′	°	° ′	′	°	° ′	′	°	° ′	′	°	° ′	′	°	° ′	′	°	°
0	71 28.4	+48.4	143.1	70 39.9	+49.5	144.8	69 50.4	+50.5	146.4	69 00.0	+51.4	147.8	68 08.9	+52.1	149.2	67 17.0	+52.9	150.4	66 24.6	+53.4	151.5	65 31.6	+54.0	152.6	0
1	72 16.8	+47.1	141.2	71 29.4	+48.4	143.1	70 40.9	+49.6	144.8	69 51.4	+50.6	146.4	69 01.0	+51.5	147.8	68 09.9	+52.2	149.1	67 18.0	+53.0	150.4	66 25.6	+53.6	151.5	1
2	73 03.9	+45.7	139.1	72 17.8	+47.2	141.2	71 30.5	+48.5	143.0	70 42.0	+49.7	144.8	69 52.5	+50.7	146.3	69 02.1	+51.6	147.8	68 11.0	+52.3	149.1	67 19.2	+53.0	150.4	2
3	73 49.6	+44.2	136.8	73 05.0	+45.9	139.1	72 19.0	+47.3	141.1	71 31.7	+48.6	143.0	70 43.2	+49.8	144.8	69 53.7	+50.8	146.3	69 03.3	+51.7	147.8	68 12.2	+52.4	149.1	3
4	74 33.8	+42.3	134.3	73 50.9	+44.3	136.8	73 06.3	+46.0	139.1	72 20.3	+47.5	141.1	71 33.0	+48.7	143.0	70 44.5	+49.9	144.8	69 55.0	+50.9	146.3	69 04.6	+51.8	147.8	4
5	75 16.1	+40.3•	131.6	74 35.2	+42.5	134.3	73 52.3	+44.5	136.8	73 07.8	+46.1	139.1	72 21.7	+47.6	141.1	71 34.4	+48.9	143.0	70 45.9	+50.0	144.8	69 56.4	+51.0	146.3	5
6	75 56.4	+37.8•	128.6	75 17.7	+40.4•	131.6	74 36.8	+42.6•	134.3	73 53.9	+44.5	136.8	73 09.3	+46.3	139.1	72 23.3	+47.7	141.2	71 35.9	+49.0	143.0	70 47.4	+50.1	144.8	6
7	76 34.2	+35.1•	125.4	75 58.1	+37.9•	128.6	75 19.4	+40.5•	131.6	74 38.4	+42.8	134.4	73 55.6	+44.7	136.8	73 11.0	+46.4	139.1	72 24.9	+47.9	141.2	71 37.5	+49.2	143.1	7
8	77 09.3	+31.9•	121.8	76 36.0	+35.3•	125.4	75 59.9	+38.2•	128.7	75 21.2	+40.7•	131.6	74 40.3	+42.9	134.4	73 57.4	+44.8	136.9	73 12.8	+46.5	139.1	72 26.7	+48.0	141.2	8
9	77 41.2	+28.3•	117.9	77 11.3	+32.0•	121.8	76 38.1	+35.4•	125.4	76 01.9	+38.3•	128.7	75 23.2	+40.9•	131.7	74 42.2	+43.1	134.4	73 59.3	+45.0	136.9	73 14.7	+46.7	139.2	9
10	78 09.5	+24.3•	113.7	77 43.3	+28.5•	117.9	77 13.5	+32.2•	121.8	76 40.2	+35.6•	125.4	76 04.1	+38.4•	128.7	75 25.3	+41.0•	131.7	74 44.3	+43.3	134.4	74 01.4	+45.1	136.9	10
11	78 33.8	+19.8•	109.2	78 11.8	+24.5•	113.7	77 45.7	+28.7•	117.9	77 15.8	+32.4•	121.8	76 42.5	+35.8•	125.4	76 06.3	+38.7•	128.7	75 27.6	+41.2•	131.8	74 46.5	+43.5	134.5	11
12	78 53.6	+15.0•	104.3	78 36.3	+20.0•	109.1	78 14.4	+24.6•	113.7	77 48.2	+28.9•	117.9	77 18.3	+32.6•	121.9	76 45.0	+36.0•	125.5	76 08.8	+38.8•	128.8	75 30.0	+41.4•	131.8	12
13	79 08.6	+9.7•	99.2	78 56.3	+15.1•	104.3	78 39.0	+20.2•	109.1	78 17.1	+24.8•	113.7	77 50.9	+29.1•	118.0	77 21.0	+32.8•	121.9	76 47.6	+36.2•	125.5	76 11.4	+39.0•	128.8	13
14	79 18.3	+4.3•	94.0	79 11.4	+9.9•	99.2	78 59.2	+15.2•	104.3	78 41.9	+20.3•	109.1	78 20.0	+25.0•	113.7	77 53.8	+29.2•	118.0	77 23.8	+33.0•	122.0	76 50.4	+36.4•	125.6	14
15	79 22.6	-1.3•	88.6	79 21.3	+4.3•	93.9	79 14.4	+10.0•	99.2	79 02.2	+15.5•	104.3	78 45.0	+20.5•	109.1	78 23.0	+25.2•	113.7	77 56.8	+29.5•	118.0	77 26.8	+33.2•	122.0	15
16	79 21.3	-6.9•	83.2	79 25.6	-1.2•	88.5	79 24.4	+4.5•	93.8	79 17.7	+10.1•	99.1	79 05.5	+15.6•	104.3	78 48.2	+20.7•	109.2	78 26.3	+25.4•	113.8	78 00.0	+29.6•	118.1	16
17	79 14.4	-12.2•	77.8	79 24.4	-6.7•	83.0	79 28.9	-1.1•	88.4	79 27.8	+4.6•	93.8	79 21.1	+10.2•	99.1	79 08.9	+15.8•	104.2	78 51.7	+20.8•	109.2	78 29.6	+25.7•	113.8	17
18	79 02.2	-17.2•	72.6	79 17.7	-12.2•	77.7	79 27.8	-6.7•	82.9	79 32.4	-1.1•	88.3	79 31.3	+4.8•	93.7	79 24.7	+10.4•	99.1	79 12.5	+16.0•	104.2	78 55.3	+21.0•	109.2	18
19	78 45.0	-22.0•	67.6	79 05.5	-17.3•	72.4	79 21.1	-12.2•	77.5	79 31.3	-6.6•	82.8	79 36.1	-1.0•	88.2	79 35.1	+4.8•	93.7	79 28.5	+10.5•	99.0	79 16.3	+16.1•	104.3	19
20	78 23.0	-26.2•	62.9	78 48.2	-21.9•	67.4	79 08.9	-17.2•	72.3	79 24.7	-12.2•	77.4	79 35.1	-6.6•	82.7	79 39.9	-0.9•	88.1	79 39.0	+5.0•	93.6	79 32.4	+10.7•	99.0	20
21	77 56.8	-30.0•	58.5	78 26.3	-26.3•	62.7	78 51.7	-22.1•	67.2	79 12.5	-17.2•	72.1	79 28.5	-12.2•	77.2	79 39.0	-6.6•	82.5	79 44.0	-0.9•	88.0	79 43.1	+5.1•	93.5	21
22	77 26.8	-33.5•	54.5	78 00.0	-30.1•	58.3	78 29.6	-26.3•	62.5	78 55.3	-22.1•	67.0	79 16.3	-17.3•	71.9	79 32.4	-12.1•	77.0	79 43.1	-6.5•	82.4	79 48.2	-0.8•	87.9	22
23	76 53.3	-36.4•	50.7	77 29.9	-33.5•	54.2	78 03.3	-30.1•	58.1	78 33.2	-26.4•	62.3	78 59.0	-22.1•	66.8	79 20.3	-17.3•	71.7	79 36.6	-12.1•	76.9	79 47.4	-6.5•	82.3	23
24	76 16.9	-39.0•	47.3	76 56.4	-36.5•	50.5	77 33.2	-33.6•	54.0	78 06.8	-30.2•	57.8	78 36.9	-26.4•	62.0	79 03.0	-22.2•	66.6	79 24.5	-17.4•	71.5	79 40.9	-12.1•	76.7	24
25	75 37.9	-41.2•	44.2	76 19.9	-39.0•	47.0	76 59.6	-36.5•	50.2	77 36.6	-33.6•	53.7	78 10.5	-30.3•	57.6	78 40.8	-26.5•	61.8	79 07.1	-22.2•	66.4	79 28.8	-17.4•	71.3	25
26	74 56.7	-43.2	41.3	75 40.9	-41.4•	43.9	76 23.1	-39.2•	46.8	77 03.0	-36.7•	49.9	77 40.2	-33.8•	53.4	78 14.3	-30.4•	57.3	78 44.9	-26.6•	61.5	79 11.4	-22.3•	66.1	26
27	74 13.5	-44.9	38.7	74 59.5	-43.3	41.0	75 43.9	-41.4•	43.6	76 26.3	-39.2•	46.5	77 06.4	-36.7•	49.6	77 43.9	-33.8•	53.1	78 18.3	-30.5•	57.0	78 49.1	-26.7•	61.2	27
28	73 28.6	-46.4	36.3	74 16.2	-44.9	38.4	75 02.5	-43.4	40.7	75 47.1	-41.5•	43.3	76 29.7	-39.3•	46.2	77 10.1	-36.9•	49.3	77 47.8	-34.0•	52.8	78 22.4	-30.6•	56.7	28
29	72 42.2	-47.7	34.1	73 31.3	-46.5	36.0	74 19.1	-45.0	38.1	75 05.6	-43.5	40.4	75 50.4	-41.6•	43.0	76 33.2	-39.4•	45.9	77 13.8	-36.9•	49.0	77 51.8	-34.1•	52.5	29
30	71 54.5	-48.9	32.1	72 44.8	-47.8	33.9	73 34.1	-46.6	35.7	74 22.1	-45.1	37.8	75 08.8	-43.6	40.1	75 53.8	-41.7•	42.7	76 36.9	-39.6•	45.5	77 17.7	-37.1•	48.7	30
31	71 05.6	-49.8	30.3	71 57.0	-48.9	31.9	72 47.5	-47.8	33.6	73 37.0	-46.7	35.4	74 25.2	-45.2	37.5	75 12.1	-43.7	39.8	75 57.3	-41.8•	42.4	76 40.6	-39.7•	45.2	31
32	70 15.8	-50.7	28.6	71 08.1	-49.9	30.0	71 59.7	-49.0	31.6	72 50.3	-47.9	33.3	73 40.0	-46.8	35.1	74 28.4	-45.4	37.2	75 15.5	-43.8	39.5	76 00.9	-41.9•	42.0	32
33	69 25.1	-51.5	27.1	70 18.2	-50.7	28.3	71 10.7	-50.0	29.7	72 02.4	-49.1	31.3	72 53.2	-48.0	32.9	73 43.0	-46.8	34.8	74 31.7	-45.5	36.9	75 19.0	-43.9	39.1	33
34	68 33.6	-52.1	25.6	69 27.5	-51.5	26.8	70 20.7	-50.8	28.1	71 13.3	-50.0	29.4	72 05.2	-49.1	31.0	72 56.2	-48.1	32.6	73 46.2	-46.9	34.5	74 35.1	-45.6	36.5	34
35	67 41.5	-52.7	24.3	68 36.0	-52.2	25.4	69 29.9	-51.6	26.5	70 23.3	-50.9	27.8	71 16.1	-50.1	29.1	72 08.1	-49.2	30.6	72 59.3	-48.2	32.3	73 49.5	-47.0	34.1	35
36	66 48.8	-53.3	23.1	67 43.8	-52.8	24.0	68 38.3	-52.2	25.1	69 32.4	-51.6	26.2	70 26.0	-51.0	27.4	71 18.9	-50.2	28.8	72 11.1	-49.3	30.3	73 02.5	-48.3	32.0	36
37	65 55.5	-53.8	21.9	66 51.0	-53.4	22.8	67 46.1	-52.9	23.8	68 40.8	-52.3	24.8	69 35.0	-51.7	25.9	70 28.7	-51.0	27.1	71 21.8	-50.3	28.5	72 14.2	-49.5	30.0	37
38	65 01.7	-54.2	20.9	65 57.6	-53.8	21.7	66 53.2	-53.3	22.5	67 48.5	-52.9	23.5	68 43.3	-52.4	24.5	69 37.7	-51.8	25.6	70 31.5	-51.1	26.8	71 24.7	-50.3	28.1	38
39	64 07.5	-54.5	19.9	65 03.8	-54.2	20.6	65 59.9	-53.9	21.4	66 55.6	-53.5	22.2	67 50.9	-52.9	23.2	68 45.9	-52.5	24.2	69 40.4	-51.9	25.3	70 34.4	-51.2	26.5	39
40	63 13.0	-55.0	18.9	64 09.6	-54.6	19.6	65 06.0	-54.3	20.3	66 02.1	-53.9	21.1	66 58.0	-53.5	21.9	67 53.4	-53.0	22.9	68 48.5	-52.5	23.9	69 43.2	-52.0	24.9	40
41	62 18.0	-55.2	18.0	63 15.0	-55.0	18.7	64 11.7	-54.6	19.3	65 08.2	-54.3	20.0	66 04.5	-54.0	20.8	67 00.4	-53.6	21.6	67 56.0	-53.1	22.5	68 51.2	-52.6	23.5	41
42	61 22.8	-55.5	17.2	62 20.0	-55.2	17.8	63 17.1	-55.0	18.4	64 13.9	-54.7	19.0	65 10.5	-54.4	19.7	66 06.8	-54.0	20.5	67 02.9	-53.6	21.3	67 58.6	-53.2	22.2	42
43	60 27.3	-55.8	16.4	61 24.8	-55.6	17.0	62 22.1	-55.3	17.5	63 19.2	-55.0	18.1	64 16.1	-54.7	18.7	65 12.8	-54.4	19.4	66 09.3	-54.1	20.2	67 05.4	-53.7	21.0	43
44	59 31.5	-56.0	15.7	60 29.2	-55.8	16.2	61 26.8	-55.6	16.7	62 24.2	-55.4	17.2	63 21.4	-55.1	17.8	64 18.4	-54.8	18.5	65 15.2	-54.5	19.1	66 11.7	-54.1	19.9	44
45	58 35.5	-56.2	15.0	59 33.4	-56.0	15.4	60 31.2	-55.9	15.9	61 28.8	-55.6	16.4	62 26.3	-55.4	17.0	63 23.6	-55.2	17.5	64 20.7	-54.9	18.2	65 17.6	-54.6	18.8	45
46	57 39.3	-56.4	14.3	58 37.4	-56.3	14.7	59 35.3	-56.1	15.2	60 33.2	-55.9	15.6	61 30.9	-55.7	16.1	62 28.4	-55.4	16.7	63 25.8	-55.2	17.2	64 23.0	-54.9	17.9	46
47	56 42.9	-56.6	13.7	57 41.1	-56.4	14.1	58 39.2	-56.2	14.5	59 37.3	-56.1	14.9	60 35.2	-55.9	15.4	61 33.0	-55.7	15.9	62 30.6	-55.5	16.4	63 28.1	-55.2	16.9	47
48	55 46.3	-56.8	13.1	56 44.7	-56.7	13.5	57 43.0	-56.5	13.8	58 41.2	-56.4	14.2	59 39.3	-56.2	14.6	60 37.3	-56.0	15.1	61 35.1	-55.7	15.6	62 32.9	-55.6	16.1	48
49	54 49.5	-56.9	12.6	55 48.0	-56.8	12.9	56 46.5	-56.7	13.2	57 44.8	-56.5	13.6	58 43.1	-56.3	14.0	59 41.3	-56.2	14.4	60 39.4	-56.0	14.8	61 37.3	-55.8	15.3	49
50	53 52.6	-57.1	12.0	54 51.2	-56.9	12.3	55 49.8	-56.8	12.6	56 48.3	-56.7	12.9	57 46.8	-56.6	13.3	58 45.1	-56.4	13.7	59 43.4	-56.3	14.1	60 41.5	-56.1	14.5	50
51	52 55.5	-57.2	11.5	53 54.3	-57.1	11.8	54 53.0	-57.0	12.0	55 51.6	-56.8	12.4	56 50.2	-56.7	12.7	57 48.7	-56.6	13.0	58 47.1	-56.4	13.4	59 45.4	-56.2	13.8	51
52	51 58.3	-57.3	11.0	52 57.2	-57.2	11.2	53 56.0	-57.1	11.5	54 54.8	-57.0	11.8	55 53.5	-56.9	12.1	56 52.1	-56.8	12.4	57 50.7	-56.7	12.8	58 49.2	-56.5	13.1	52
53	51 01.0	-57.4	10.5	52 00.0	-57.4	10.7	52 58.9	-57.2	11.0	53 57.8	-57.2	11.3	54 56.6	-57.0	11.5	55 55.3	-56.9	11.8	56 54.0	-56.8	12.1	57 52.7	-56.7	12.5	53
54	50 03.6	-57.5	10.1	51 02.6	-57.4	10.3	52 01.7	-57.4	10.5	53 00.6	-57.2	10.7	53 59.6	-57.2	11.0	54 58.4	-57.0	11.3	55 57.2	-56.9	11.6	56 56.0	-56.8	11.9	54
55	49 06.1	-57.7	9.6	50 05.2	-57.5	9.8	51 04.3	-57.5	10.0	52 03.4	-57.4	10.3	53 02.4	-57.3	10.5	54 01.4	-57.2	10.7	55 00.3	-57.1	11.0	55 59.2	-57.0	11.3	55
56	48 08.4	-57.7	9.2	49 07.7	-57.7	9.4	50 06.8	-57.5	9.6	51 06.0	-57.5	9.8	52 05.1	-57.4	10.0	53 04.2	-57.4	10.2	54 03.2	-57.3	10.5	55 02.2	-57.2	10.7	56
57	47 10.7	-57.8	8.8	48 10.0	-57.7	9.0	49 09.3	-57.7	9.1	50 08.5	-57.6	9.3	51 07.7	-57.5	9.5	52 06.8	-57.4	9.7	53 05.9	-57.3	10.0	54 05.0	-57.3	10.2	57
58	46 12.9	-57.8	8.4	47 12.3	-57.8	8.6	48 11.6	-57.7	8.7	49 10.9	-57.7	8.9	50 10.2	-57.7	9.1	51 09.4	-57.6	9.3	52 08.6	-57.5	9.5	53 07.7	-57.3	9.7	58
59	45 15.1	-58.0	8.0	46 14.5	-57.9	8.2	47 13.9	-57.9	8.3	48 13.2	-57.8	8.5	49 12.5	-57.7	8.7	50 11.8	-57.6	8.8	51 11.1	-57.6	9.0	52 10.4	-57.5	9.2	59
60	44 17.1	-58.0	7.7	45 16.6	-58.0	7.8	46 16.0	-57.9	7.9	47 15.4	-57.8	8.1	48 14.8	-57.8	8.2	49 14.2	-57.7	8.4	50 13.5	-57.6	8.6	51 12.9	-57.7	8.8	60
61	43 19.1	-58.1	7.3	44 18.6	-58.0	7.4	45 18.1	-58.0	7.6	46 17.6	-58.0	7.7	47 17.0	-57.9	7.8	48 16.5	-57.9	8.0	49 15.9	-57.8	8.1	50 15.2	-57.7	8.3	61
62	42 21.0	-58.1	7.0	43 20.6	-58.1	7.1	44 20.1	-58.0	7.2	45 19.6	-58.0	7.3	46 19.1	-57.9	7.5	47 18.6	-57.9	7.6	48 18.1	-57.9	7.7	49 17.5	-57.8	7.9	62
63	41 22.9	-58.2	6.6	42 22.5	-58.1	6.7	43 22.1	-58.1	6.8	44 21.6	-58.0	7.0	45 21.2	-58.0	7.1	46 20.7	-57.9	7.2	47 20.2	-57.9	7.3	48 19.7	-57.8	7.5	63
64	40 24.7	-58.2	6.3	41 24.4	-58.3	6.4	42 24.0	-58.2	6.5	43 23.6	-58.2	6.6	44 23.2	-58.1	6.7	45 22.8	-58.1	6.8	46 22.3	-58.0	7.0	47 21.9	-58.0	7.1	64
65	39 26.5	-58.3	6.0	40 26.1	-58.2	6.1	41 25.8	-58.2	6.2	42 25.4	-58.1	6.3	43 25.1	-58.2	6.4	44 24.7	-58.1	6.5	45 24.3	-58.1	6.6	46 23.9	-58.0	6.7	65
66	38 28.2	-58.3	5.7	39 27.9	-58.3	5.8	40 27.6	-58.3	5.9	41 27.3	-58.3	5.9	42 26.9	-58.2	6.0	43 26.6	-58.2	6.1	44 26.2	-58.1	6.2	45 25.9	-58.1	6.3	66
67	37 29.9	-58.4	5.4	38 29.6	-58.4	5.5	39 29.3	-58.3	5.5	40 29.0	-58.3	5.6	41 28.7	-58.2	5.7	42 28.4	-58.2	5.8	43 28.1	-58.2	5.9	44 27.8	-58.2	6.0	67
68	36 31.5	-58.4	5.1	37 31.2	-58.4	5.2	38 31.0	-58.4	5.2	39 30.7	-58.3	5.3	40 30.5	-58.3	5.4	41 30.2	-58.3	5.5	42 29.9	-58.2	5.6	43 29.6	-58.2	5.7	68
69	35 33.1	-58.5	4.8	36 32.8	-58.4	4.9	37 32.6	-58.4	4.9	38 32.4	-58.4	5.0	39 32.2	-58.4	5.1	40 31.9	-58.3	5.2	41 31.7	-58.3	5.2	42 31.4	-58.3	5.3	69
70	34 34.6	-58.5	4.5	35 34.4	-58.5	4.6	36 34.2	-58.4	4.7	37 34.0	-58.4	4.7	38 33.8	-58.4	4.8	39 33.6	-58.4	4.9	40 33.4	-58.4	4.9	41 33.1	-58.3	5.0	70
71	33 36.1	-58.5	4.3	34 35.9	-58.5	4.3	35 35.8	-58.5	4.4	36 35.6	-58.5	4.4	37 35.4	-58.4	4.5	38 35.2	-58.4	4.6	39 35.0	-58.4	4.6	40 34.8	-58.4	4.7	71
72	32 37.6	-58.6	4.0	33 37.4	-58.5	4.1	34 37.3	-58.6	4.1	35 37.1	-58.5	4.2	36 37.0	-58.5	4.2	37 36.8	-58.5	4.3	38 36.6	-58.4	4.3	39 36.4	-58.4	4.4	72
73	31 39.0	-58.6	3.8	32 38.9	-58.6	3.8	33 38.7	-58.5	3.8	34 38.6	-58.5	3.9	35 38.5	-58.6	3.9	36 38.3	-58.5	4.0	37 38.2	-58.5	4.0	38 38.0	-58.4	4.1	73
74	30 40.4	-58.6	3.5	31 40.3	-58.6	3.5	32 40.2	-58.6	3.6	33 40.1	-58.6	3.6	34 39.9	-58.5	3.7	35 39.8	-58.5	3.7	36 39.7	-58.5	3.8	37 39.6	-58.5	3.8	74
75	29 41.8	-58.7	3.3	30 41.7	-58.6	3.3	31 41.6	-58.6	3.3	32 41.5	-58.6	3.4	33 41.4	-58.6	3.4	34 41.3	-58.6	3.4	35 41.2	-58.6	3.5	36 41.1	-58.6	3.5	75
76	28 43.1	-58.6	3.0	29 43.1	-58.7	3.0	30 43.0	-58.7	3.1	31 42.9	-58.6	3.1	32 42.8	-58.6	3.1	33 42.7	-58.6	3.2	34 42.6	-58.6	3.2	35 42.5	-58.6	3.3	76
77	27 44.5	-58.7	2.8	28 44.4	-58.7	2.8	29 44.3	-58.6	2.8	30 44.3	-58.7	2.9	31 44.2	-58.7	2.9	32 44.1	-58.6	2.9	33 44.0	-58.6	3.0	34 43.9	-58.6	3.0	77
78	26 45.8	-58.7	2.5	27 45.7	-58.7	2.6	28 45.7	-58.7	2.6	29 45.6	-58.7	2.6	30 45.5	-58.6	2.6	31 45.5	-58.7	2.7	32 45.4	-58.7	2.7	33 45.3	-58.6	2.7	78
79	25 47.1	-58.8	2.3	26 47.0	-58.7	2.3	27 47.0	-58.8	2.4	28 46.9	-58.7	2.4	29 46.9	-58.7	2.4	30 46.8	-58.7	2.4	31 46.7	-58.6	2.5	32 46.7	-58.7	2.5	79
80	24 48.3	-58.7	2.1	25 48.3	-58.8	2.1	26 48.2	-58.7	2.1	27 48.2	-58.7	2.1	28 48.2	-58.8	2.2	29 48.1	-58.7	2.2	30 48.1	-58.7	2.2	31 48.0	-58.7	2.2	80
81	23 49.6	-58.8	1.9	24 49.5	-58.7	1.9	25 49.5	-58.8	1.9	26 49.5	-58.8	1.9	27 49.4	-58.7	1.9	28 49.4	-58.7	2.0	29 49.4	-58.8	2.0	30 49.3	-58.7	2.0	81
82	22 50.8	-58.8	1.7	23 50.8	-58.8	1.7	24 50.7	-58.8	1.7	25 50.7	-58.8	1.7	26 50.7	-58.8	1.7	27 50.7	-58.8	1.7	28 50.6	-58.7	1.7	29 50.6	-58.8	1.8	82
83	21 52.0	-58.8	1.4	22 52.0	-58.8	1.4	23 51.9	-58.8	1.5	24 51.9	-58.8	1.5	25 51.9	-58.8	1.5	26 51.9	-58.8	1.5	27 51.9	-58.8	1.5	28 51.8	-58.7	1.5	83
84	20 53.2	-58.9	1.2	21 53.2	-58.9	1.2	22 53.1	-58.8	1.2	23 53.1	-58.8	1.2	24 53.1	-58.8	1.3	25 53.1	-58.8	1.3	26 53.1	-58.8	1.3	27 53.1	-58.8	1.3	84
85	19 54.3	-58.8	1.0	20 54.3	-58.8	1.0	21 54.3	-58.8	1.0	22 54.3	-58.8	1.0	23 54.3	-58.8	1.0	24 54.3	-58.8	1.1	25 54.3	-58.8	1.1	26 54.3	-58.8	1.1	85
86	18 55.5	-58.9	0.8	19 55.5	-58.9	0.8	20 55.5	-58.9	0.8	21 55.5	-58.9	0.8	22 55.5	-58.9	0.8	23 55.5	-58.9	0.8	24 55.5	-58.9	0.8	25 55.5	-58.9	0.8	86
87	17 56.6	-58.8	0.6	18 56.6	-58.8	0.6	19 56.6	-58.8	0.6	20 56.6	-58.8	0.6	21 56.6	-58.8	0.6	22 56.6	-58.8	0.6	23 56.6	-58.8	0.6	24 56.6	-58.8	0.6	87
88	16 57.8	-58.9	0.4	17 57.8	-58.9	0.4	18 57.8	-58.9	0.4	19 57.8	-58.9	0.4	20 57.8	-58.9	0.4	21 57.8	-58.9	0.4	22 57.8	-58.9	0.4	23 57.8	-58.9	0.4	88
89	15 58.9	-58.9	0.2	16 58.9	-58.9	0.2	17 58.9	-58.9	0.2	18 58.9	-58.9	0.2	19 58.9	-58.9	0.2	20 58.9	-58.9	0.2	21 58.9	-58.9	0.2	22 58.9	-58.9	0.2	89
90	15 00.0	-58.9	0.0	16 00.0	-58.9	0.0	17 00.0	-58.9	0.0	18 00.0	-58.9	0.0	19 00.0	-58.9	0.0	20 00.0	-58.9	0.0	21 00.0	-58.9	0.0	22 00.0	-58.9	0.0	90
	15°			16°			17°			18°			19°			20°			21°			22°			

LATITUDE **CONTRARY** NAME TO DECLINATION **L.H.A. 11°, 349°**

Dec.	15°			16°			17°			18°			19°			20°			21°			22°			Dec.
°	Hc ° ′	d ′	Z °	Hc ° ′	d ′	Z °	Hc ° ′	d ′	Z °	Hc ° ′	d ′	Z °	Hc ° ′	d ′	Z °	Hc ° ′	d ′	Z °	Hc ° ′	d ′	Z °	Hc ° ′	d ′	Z °	°
0	71 28.4	-49.3	143.1	70 39.9	-50.4	144.8	69 50.4	-51.3	146.4	69 00.0	-52.1	147.8	68 08.9	-52.8	149.2	67 17.0	-53.4	150.4	66 24.6	-54.0	151.5	65 31.6	-54.5	152.6	0
1	70 39.1	-50.3	144.8	69 49.5	-51.2	146.4	68 59.1	-52.0	147.9	68 07.9	-52.6	149.2	67 16.1	-53.3	150.4	66 23.6	-53.9	151.5	65 30.6	-54.4	152.6	64 37.1	-54.8	153.6	1
2	69 48.8	-51.2	146.5	68 58.3	-51.9	147.9	68 07.1	-52.6	149.2	67 15.3	-53.3	150.4	66 22.8	-53.8	151.6	65 29.7	-54.3	152.6	64 36.2	-54.7	153.6	63 42.3	-55.2	154.5	2
3	68 57.6	-51.8	147.9	68 06.4	-52.5	149.3	67 14.5	-53.2	150.5	66 22.0	-53.7	151.6	65 29.0	-54.3	152.7	64 35.4	-54.7	153.6	63 41.5	-55.1	154.5	62 47.1	-55.5	155.4	3
4	68 05.8	-52.5	149.3	67 13.9	-53.1	150.5	66 21.3	-53.6	151.7	65 28.3	-54.2	152.7	64 34.7	-54.6	153.7	63 40.7	-55.0	154.6	62 46.4	-55.5	155.4	61 51.6	-55.7	156.2	4
5	67 13.3	-53.0	150.6	66 20.8	-53.6	151.7	65 27.7	-54.1	152.8	64 34.1	-54.6	153.7	63 40.1	-55.0	154.6	62 45.7	-55.4	155.5	61 50.9	-55.7	156.2	60 55.9	-56.0	157.0	5
6	66 20.3	-53.5	151.8	65 27.2	-54.1	152.8	64 33.6	-54.5	153.8	63 39.5	-54.9	154.7	62 45.1	-55.3	155.5	61 50.3	-55.6	156.3	60 55.2	-55.9	157.0	59 59.9	-56.3	157.7	6
7	65 26.8	-54.0	152.9	64 33.1	-54.4	153.8	63 39.1	-54.9	154.7	62 44.6	-55.2	155.6	61 49.8	-55.6	156.3	60 54.7	-55.9	157.1	59 59.3	-56.2	157.8	59 03.6	-56.4	158.4	7
8	64 32.8	-54.4	153.9	63 38.7	-54.8	154.8	62 44.2	-55.2	155.6	61 49.4	-55.6	156.4	60 54.2	-55.8	157.1	59 58.8	-56.1	157.8	59 03.1	-56.4	158.4	58 07.2	-56.6	159.0	8
9	63 38.4	-54.8	154.9	62 43.9	-55.2	155.7	61 49.0	-55.5	156.5	60 53.8	-55.8	157.2	59 58.4	-56.1	157.9	59 02.7	-56.4	158.5	58 06.7	-56.5	159.1	57 10.6	-56.8	159.7	9
10	62 43.6	-55.1	155.8	61 48.7	-55.4	156.6	60 53.5	-55.7	157.3	59 58.0	-56.0	157.9	59 02.3	-56.3	158.6	58 06.3	-56.5	159.2	57 10.2	-56.8	159.7	56 13.8	-57.0	160.2	10
11	61 48.5	-55.4	156.6	60 53.3	-55.7	157.4	59 57.8	-56.0	158.0	59 02.0	-56.2	158.7	58 06.0	-56.5	159.2	57 09.8	-56.7	159.8	56 13.4	-56.9	160.3	55 16.8	-57.1	160.8	11
12	60 53.1	-55.6	157.4	59 57.6	-56.0	158.1	59 01.8	-56.2	158.7	58 05.8	-56.5	159.3	57 09.5	-56.7	159.9	56 13.1	-56.9	160.4	55 16.5	-57.1	160.9	54 19.7	-57.2	161.3	12
13	59 57.5	-55.9	158.2	59 01.6	-56.1	158.8	58 05.6	-56.4	159.4	57 09.3	-56.6	160.0	56 12.8	-56.8	160.5	55 16.2	-57.0	161.0	54 19.4	-57.2	161.4	53 22.5	-57.4	161.8	13
14	59 01.6	-56.2	158.9	58 05.5	-56.4	159.5	57 09.2	-56.6	160.0	56 12.7	-56.8	160.6	55 16.0	-57.0	161.0	54 19.2	-57.2	161.5	53 22.2	-57.3	161.9	52 25.1	-57.5	162.3	14
15	58 05.4	-56.3	159.6	57 09.1	-56.6	160.1	56 12.6	-56.8	160.6	55 15.9	-57.0	161.1	54 19.0	-57.1	161.6	53 22.0	-57.3	162.0	52 24.9	-57.4	162.4	51 27.6	-57.5	162.8	15
16	57 09.1	-56.5	160.2	56 12.5	-56.7	160.7	55 15.8	-56.9	161.2	54 18.9	-57.1	161.7	53 21.9	-57.3	162.1	52 24.7	-57.4	162.5	51 27.5	-57.6	162.9	50 30.1	-57.7	163.2	16
17	56 12.6	-56.7	160.8	55 15.8	-56.9	161.3	54 18.9	-57.1	161.8	53 21.8	-57.2	162.2	52 24.6	-57.3	162.6	51 27.3	-57.5	163.0	50 29.9	-57.6	163.3	49 32.4	-57.8	163.7	17
18	55 15.9	-56.9	161.4	54 18.9	-57.0	161.9	53 21.8	-57.2	162.3	52 24.6	-57.3	162.7	51 27.3	-57.5	163.1	50 29.8	-57.6	163.4	49 32.3	-57.8	163.8	48 34.6	-57.8	164.1	18
19	54 19.0	-57.0	162.0	53 21.9	-57.2	162.4	52 24.6	-57.3	162.8	51 27.3	-57.5	163.2	50 29.8	-57.6	163.5	49 32.2	-57.7	163.9	48 34.5	-57.8	164.2	47 36.8	-58.0	164.5	19
20	53 22.0	-57.1	162.5	52 24.7	-57.2	162.9	51 27.3	-57.4	163.3	50 29.8	-57.5	163.6	49 32.2	-57.7	164.0	48 34.5	-57.8	164.3	47 36.7	-57.9	164.6	46 38.8	-58.0	164.9	20
21	52 24.9	-57.3	163.0	51 27.5	-57.4	163.4	50 29.9	-57.5	163.7	49 32.3	-57.7	164.1	48 34.5	-57.7	164.4	47 36.7	-57.9	164.7	46 38.8	-58.0	165.0	45 40.8	-58.1	165.2	21
22	51 27.6	-57.3	163.5	50 30.1	-57.5	163.9	49 32.4	-57.6	164.2	48 34.6	-57.7	164.5	47 36.8	-57.9	164.8	46 38.8	-57.9	165.1	45 40.8	-58.0	165.3	44 42.7	-58.1	165.6	22
23	50 30.3	-57.5	164.0	49 32.6	-57.6	164.3	48 34.8	-57.8	164.6	47 36.9	-57.9	164.9	46 38.9	-57.9	165.2	45 40.9	-58.1	165.4	44 42.8	-58.2	165.7	43 44.6	-58.2	165.9	23
24	49 32.8	-57.6	164.4	48 35.0	-57.7	164.7	47 37.0	-57.8	165.0	46 39.0	-57.9	165.3	45 41.0	-58.0	165.6	44 42.8	-58.1	165.8	43 44.6	-58.1	166.0	42 46.4	-58.3	166.3	24
25	48 35.2	-57.7	164.8	47 37.3	-57.8	165.1	46 39.2	-57.8	165.4	45 41.1	-57.9	165.7	44 43.0	-58.1	165.9	43 44.7	-58.1	166.2	42 46.5	-58.3	166.4	41 48.1	-58.3	166.6	25
26	47 37.5	-57.7	165.3	46 39.5	-57.9	165.5	45 41.4	-58.0	165.8	44 43.2	-58.1	166.0	43 44.9	-58.1	166.3	42 46.6	-58.2	166.5	41 48.2	-58.3	166.7	40 49.8	-58.3	166.9	26
27	46 39.8	-57.8	165.7	45 41.6	-57.9	165.9	44 43.4	-58.0	166.2	43 45.1	-58.1	166.4	42 46.8	-58.2	166.6	41 48.4	-58.3	166.8	40 49.9	-58.3	167.0	39 51.5	-58.5	167.2	27
28	45 42.0	-58.0	166.0	44 43.7	-58.0	166.3	43 45.4	-58.1	166.5	42 47.0	-58.2	166.7	41 48.6	-58.3	166.9	40 50.1	-58.3	167.1	39 51.6	-58.4	167.3	38 53.0	-58.4	167.5	28
29	44 44.0	-57.9	166.4	43 45.7	-58.1	166.6	42 47.3	-58.1	166.9	41 48.8	-58.2	167.1	40 50.3	-58.2	167.3	39 51.8	-58.4	167.4	38 53.2	-58.4	167.6	37 54.6	-58.5	167.8	29
30	43 46.1	-58.1	166.8	42 47.6	-58.1	167.0	41 49.2	-58.2	167.2	40 50.6	-58.3	167.4	39 52.1	-58.4	167.6	38 53.4	-58.4	167.7	37 54.8	-58.5	167.9	36 56.1	-58.5	168.1	30
31	42 48.0	-58.1	167.1	41 49.5	-58.2	167.3	40 51.0	-58.3	167.5	39 52.3	-58.3	167.7	38 53.7	-58.4	167.9	37 55.0	-58.4	168.0	36 56.3	-58.5	168.2	35 57.6	-58.6	168.3	31
32	41 49.9	-58.1	167.5	40 51.3	-58.2	167.6	39 52.7	-58.3	167.8	38 54.0	-58.3	168.0	37 55.3	-58.4	168.2	36 56.6	-58.5	168.3	35 57.8	-58.5	168.5	34 59.0	-58.6	168.6	32
33	40 51.8	-58.3	167.8	39 53.1	-58.3	168.0	38 54.4	-58.4	168.1	37 55.7	-58.5	168.3	36 56.9	-58.5	168.4	35 58.1	-58.5	168.6	34 59.3	-58.6	168.7	34 00.4	-58.6	168.9	33
34	39 53.5	-58.2	168.1	38 54.8	-58.3	168.3	37 56.0	-58.3	168.4	36 57.2	-58.4	168.6	35 58.4	-58.5	168.7	34 59.6	-58.6	168.9	34 00.7	-58.6	169.0	33 01.8	-58.7	169.1	34
35	38 55.3	-58.3	168.4	37 56.5	-58.4	168.6	36 57.7	-58.5	168.7	35 58.8	-58.5	168.9	34 59.9	-58.5	169.0	34 01.0	-58.6	169.1	33 02.1	-58.7	169.3	32 03.1	-58.7	169.4	35
36	37 57.0	-58.4	168.7	36 58.1	-58.4	168.9	35 59.2	-58.5	169.0	35 00.3	-58.5	169.1	34 01.4	-58.6	169.3	33 02.4	-58.6	169.4	32 03.4	-58.7	169.5	31 04.4	-58.7	169.6	36
37	36 58.6	-58.4	169.0	35 59.7	-58.5	169.1	35 00.7	-58.5	169.3	34 01.8	-58.6	169.4	33 02.8	-58.6	169.5	32 03.8	-58.7	169.6	31 04.7	-58.7	169.8	30 05.7	-58.8	169.9	37
38	36 00.2	-58.4	169.3	35 01.2	-58.5	169.4	34 02.2	-58.5	169.5	33 03.2	-58.6	169.7	32 04.2	-58.7	169.8	31 05.1	-58.7	169.9	30 06.0	-58.7	170.0	29 06.9	-58.7	170.1	38
39	35 01.8	-58.5	169.6	34 02.7	-58.5	169.7	33 03.7	-58.6	169.8	32 04.6	-58.6	169.9	31 05.5	-58.6	170.0	30 06.4	-58.7	170.1	29 07.3	-58.7	170.2	28 08.2	-58.8	170.3	39
40	34 03.3	-58.5	169.8	33 04.2	-58.6	170.0	32 05.1	-58.6	170.1	31 06.0	-58.6	170.2	30 06.9	-58.7	170.3	29 07.7	-58.7	170.4	28 08.6	-58.8	170.5	27 09.4	-58.8	170.5	40
41	33 04.8	-58.6	170.1	32 05.6	-58.6	170.2	31 06.5	-58.6	170.3	30 07.4	-58.7	170.4	29 08.2	-58.7	170.5	28 09.0	-58.8	170.6	27 09.8	-58.8	170.7	26 10.6	-58.9	170.8	41
42	32 06.2	-58.6	170.4	31 07.0	-58.6	170.5	30 07.9	-58.7	170.6	29 08.7	-58.7	170.7	28 09.5	-58.8	170.7	27 10.2	-58.7	170.8	26 11.0	-58.8	170.9	25 11.7	-58.8	171.0	42
43	31 07.6	-58.6	170.6	30 08.4	-58.6	170.7	29 09.2	-58.7	170.8	28 10.0	-58.8	170.9	27 10.7	-58.7	171.0	26 11.5	-58.8	171.1	25 12.2	-58.9	171.1	24 12.9	-58.9	171.2	43
44	30 09.0	-58.6	170.9	29 09.8	-58.7	171.0	28 10.5	-58.7	171.0	27 11.2	-58.7	171.1	26 12.0	-58.8	171.2	25 12.7	-58.9	171.3	24 13.3	-58.8	171.3	23 14.0	-58.9	171.4	44
45	29 10.4	-58.7	171.1	28 11.1	-58.7	171.2	27 11.8	-58.7	171.3	26 12.5	-58.8	171.4	25 13.2	-58.8	171.4	24 13.8	-58.8	171.5	23 14.5	-58.9	171.6	22 15.1	-58.9	171.6	45
46	28 11.7	-58.7	171.4	27 12.4	-58.7	171.4	26 13.1	-58.8	171.5	25 13.7	-58.8	171.6	24 14.4	-58.9	171.6	23 15.0	-58.9	171.7	22 15.6	-58.9	171.8	21 16.2	-58.9	171.8	46
47	27 13.0	-58.7	171.6	26 13.7	-58.8	171.7	25 14.3	-58.8	171.7	24 14.9	-58.8	171.8	23 15.5	-58.8	171.9	22 16.1	-58.8	171.9	21 16.7	-58.9	172.0	20 17.3	-58.9	172.0	47
48	26 14.3	-58.7	171.8	25 14.9	-58.7	171.9	24 15.5	-58.8	171.9	23 16.1	-58.8	172.0	22 16.7	-58.9	172.1	21 17.3	-58.9	172.1	20 17.8	-58.9	172.2	19 18.4	-59.0	172.2	48
49	25 15.6	-58.7	172.0	24 16.2	-58.8	172.1	23 16.7	-58.8	172.2	22 17.3	-58.8	172.2	21 17.8	-58.8	172.3	20 18.4	-58.9	172.3	19 18.9	-58.9	172.4	18 19.4	-58.9	172.4	49
50	24 16.9	-58.8	172.3	23 17.4	-58.8	172.3	22 17.9	-58.8	172.4	21 18.5	-58.9	172.4	20 19.0	-58.9	172.5	19 19.5	-58.9	172.5	18 20.0	-58.9	172.6	17 20.5	-59.0	172.6	50
51	23 18.1	-58.8	172.5	22 18.6	-58.8	172.5	21 19.1	-58.8	172.6	20 19.6	-58.9	172.6	19 20.1	-58.9	172.7	18 20.6	-59.0	172.7	17 21.1	-59.0	172.8	16 21.5	-58.9	172.8	51
52	22 19.3	-58.8	172.7	21 19.8	-58.9	172.8	20 20.3	-58.9	172.8	19 20.7	-58.9	172.8	18 21.2	-58.9	172.9	17 21.6	-58.9	172.9	16 22.1	-59.0	173.0	15 22.6	-59.0	173.0	52
53	21 20.5	-58.8	172.9	20 20.9	-58.8	173.0	19 21.4	-58.9	173.0	18 21.8	-58.9	173.1	17 22.3	-58.9	173.1	16 22.7	-58.9	173.2	15 23.1	-58.9	173.2	14 23.6	-59.0	173.2	53
54	20 21.7	-58.9	173.1	19 22.1	-58.9	173.2	18 22.5	-58.9	173.2	17 22.9	-58.9	173.3	16 23.4	-59.0	173.3	15 23.8	-59.0	173.3	14 24.2	-59.0	173.4	13 24.6	-59.0	173.4	54
55	19 22.8	-58.8	173.3	18 23.2	-58.8	173.4	17 23.6	-58.9	173.4	16 24.0	-58.9	173.4	15 24.4	-58.9	173.5	14 24.8	-59.0	173.5	13 25.2	-59.0	173.5	12 25.6	-59.0	173.6	55
56	18 24.0	-58.9	173.5	17 24.4	-58.9	173.6	16 24.7	-58.9	173.6	15 25.1	-58.9	173.6	14 25.5	-59.0	173.7	13 25.8	-58.9	173.7	12 26.2	-59.0	173.7	11 26.6	-59.1	173.8	56
57	17 25.1	-58.9	173.7	16 25.5	-58.9	173.8	15 25.8	-58.9	173.8	14 26.2	-59.0	173.8	13 26.5	-58.9	173.9	12 26.9	-59.0	173.9	11 27.2	-59.0	173.9	10 27.5	-59.0	173.9	57
58	16 26.2	-58.8	173.9	15 26.6	-58.9	174.0	14 26.9	-58.9	174.0	13 27.2	-58.9	174.0	12 27.6	-59.0	174.1	11 27.9	-59.0	174.1	10 28.2	-59.0	174.1	9 28.5	-59.0	174.1	58
59	15 27.4	-58.9	174.1	14 27.7	-59.0	174.2	13 28.0	-59.0	174.2	12 28.3	-59.0	174.2	11 28.6	-59.0	174.2	10 28.9	-59.0	174.3	9 29.2	-59.0	174.3	8 29.5	-59.1	174.3	59
60	14 28.5	-59.0	174.3	13 28.7	-58.9	174.4	12 29.0	-59.0	174.4	11 29.3	-58.9	174.4	10 29.6	-59.0	174.4	9 29.9	-59.0	174.4	8 30.2	-59.1	174.5	7 30.4	-59.0	174.5	60
61	13 29.5	-58.9	174.5	12 29.8	-58.9	174.6	11 30.1	-59.0	174.6	10 30.4	-59.0	174.6	9 30.6	-59.0	174.6	8 30.9	-59.0	174.6	7 31.1	-59.0	174.6	6 31.4	-59.0	174.7	61
62	12 30.6	-58.9	174.7	11 30.9	-59.0	174.8	10 31.1	-58.9	174.8	9 31.4	-59.0	174.8	8 31.6	-59.0	174.8	7 31.9	-59.0	174.8	6 32.1	-59.0	174.8	5 32.4	-59.1	174.8	62
63	11 31.7	-58.9	174.9	10 31.9	-58.9	174.9	9 32.2	-59.0	175.0	8 32.4	-59.0	175.0	7 32.6	-59.0	175.0	6 32.9	-59.1	175.0	5 33.1	-59.0	175.0	4 33.3	-59.0	175.0	63
64	10 32.8	-59.0	175.1	9 33.0	-59.0	175.1	8 33.2	-59.0	175.1	7 33.4	-59.0	175.2	6 33.6	-59.0	175.2	5 33.8	-59.0	175.2	4 34.1	-59.1	175.2	3 34.3	-59.1	175.2	64
65	9 33.8	-58.9	175.3	8 34.0	-58.9	175.3	7 34.2	-58.9	175.3	6 34.4	-59.0	175.3	5 34.6	-59.0	175.4	4 34.8	-59.0	175.4	3 35.0	-59.0	175.4	2 35.2	-59.0	175.4	65
66	8 34.9	-59.0	175.5	7 35.1	-59.0	175.5	6 35.3	-59.0	175.5	5 35.4	-59.0	175.5	4 35.6	-59.0	175.5	3 35.8	-59.0	175.5	2 36.0	-59.1	175.5	1 36.2	-59.1	175.5	66
67	7 35.9	-58.9	175.7	6 36.1	-59.0	175.7	5 36.3	-59.0	175.7	4 36.4	-59.0	175.7	3 36.6	-59.0	175.7	2 36.8	-59.0	175.7	1 36.9	-59.0	175.7	0 37.1	-59.0	175.7	67
68	6 37.0	-59.0	175.9	5 37.1	-58.9	175.9	4 37.3	-59.0	175.9	3 37.4	-59.0	175.9	2 37.6	-59.0	175.9	1 37.8	-59.1	175.9	0 37.9	-59.0	175.9	0 21.9	+59.1	4.1	68
69	5 38.0	-58.9	176.1	4 38.2	-59.0	176.1	3 38.3	-59.0	176.1	2 38.4	-59.0	176.1	1 38.6	-59.0	176.1	0 38.7	-59.0	176.1	0 21.1	+59.1	3.9	1 21.0	+59.0	3.9	69
70	4 39.1	-59.0	176.2	3 39.2	-59.0	176.3	2 39.3	-59.0	176.3	1 39.4	-59.0	176.3	0 39.6	-59.0	176.3	0 20.3	+59.0	3.7	1 20.2	+59.0	3.7	2 20.0	+59.1	3.7	70
71	3 40.1	-59.0	176.4	2 40.2	-59.0	176.4	1 40.3	-59.0	176.4	0 40.4	-59.0	176.4	0 19.4	+59.1	3.6	1 19.3	+59.1	3.6	2 19.2	+59.0	3.6	3 19.1	+59.0	3.6	71
72	2 41.1	-58.9	176.6	1 41.2	-59.0	176.6	0 41.3	-59.0	176.6	0 18.6	+59.0	3.4	1 18.5	+59.0	3.4	2 18.4	+59.0	3.4	3 18.2	+59.1	3.4	4 18.1	+59.1	3.4	72
73	1 42.2	-59.0	176.8	0 42.2	-58.9	176.8	0 17.7	+59.0	3.2	1 17.6	+59.0	3.2	2 17.5	+59.0	3.2	3 17.4	+59.0	3.2	4 17.3	+59.0	3.2	5 17.2	+59.0	3.2	73
74	0 43.2	-59.0	177.0	0 16.7	+59.0	3.0	1 16.7	+58.9	3.0	2 16.6	+59.0	3.0	3 16.5	+59.0	3.0	4 16.4	+59.0	3.0	5 16.3	+59.0	3.0	6 16.2	+59.1	3.0	74
75	0 15.8	+59.0	2.8	1 15.7	+59.0	2.8	2 15.6	+59.0	2.8	3 15.6	+59.0	2.8	4 15.5	+59.0	2.8	5 15.4	+59.0	2.8	6 15.3	+59.1	2.8	7 15.3	+59.0	2.9	75
76	1 14.8	+58.9	2.6	2 14.7	+59.0	2.6	3 14.6	+59.0	2.7	4 14.6	+59.0	2.7	5 14.5	+59.0	2.7	6 14.4	+59.1	2.7	7 14.4	+59.0	2.7	8 14.3	+59.0	2.7	76
77	2 13.7	+59.0	2.5	3 13.7	+59.0	2.5	4 13.6	+59.0	2.5	5 13.6	+59.0	2.5	6 13.5	+59.0	2.5	7 13.5	+59.0	2.5	8 13.4	+59.0	2.5	9 13.3	+59.1	2.5	77
78	3 12.7	+59.0	2.3	4 12.7	+58.9	2.3	5 12.6	+59.0	2.3	6 12.6	+59.0	2.3	7 12.5	+59.0	2.3	8 12.5	+59.0	2.3	9 12.4	+59.0	2.3	10 12.4	+59.0	2.3	78
79	4 11.7	+58.9	2.1	5 11.6	+59.0	2.1	6 11.6	+59.0	2.1	7 11.6	+58.9	2.1	8 11.5	+59.0	2.1	9 11.5	+59.0	2.1	10 11.4	+59.0	2.1	11 11.4	+59.0	2.1	79
80	5 10.6	+59.0	1.9	6 10.6	+59.0	1.9	7 10.6	+58.9	1.9	8 10.5	+59.0	1.9	9 10.5	+59.0	1.9	10 10.5	+59.0	1.9	11 10.4	+59.0	1.9	12 10.4	+59.0	1.9	80
81	6 09.6	+59.0	1.7	7 09.6	+58.9	1.7	8 09.5	+59.0	1.7	9 09.5	+59.0	1.7	10 09.5	+59.0	1.7	11 09.5	+58.9	1.7	12 09.4	+59.0	1.7	13 09.4	+59.0	1.8	81
82	7 08.6	+58.9	1.5	8 08.5	+59.0	1.5	9 08.5	+59.0	1.5	10 08.5	+59.0	1.5	11 08.5	+58.9	1.6	12 08.4	+59.0	1.6	13 08.4	+59.0	1.6	14 08.4	+59.0	1.6	82
83	8 07.5	+59.0	1.3	9 07.5	+58.9	1.3	10 07.5	+58.9	1.4	11 07.5	+58.9	1.4	12 07.4	+59.0	1.4	13 07.4	+59.0	1.4	14 07.4	+59.0	1.4	15 07.4	+59.0	1.4	83
84	9 06.5	+58.9	1.2	10 06.4	+59.0	1.2	11 06.4	+59.0	1.2	12 06.4	+59.0	1.2	13 06.4	+58.9	1.2	14 06.4	+59.0	1.2	15 06.4	+58.9	1.2	16 06.4	+58.9	1.2	84
85	10 05.4	+58.9	1.0	11 05.4	+58.9	1.0	12 05.4	+58.9	1.0	13 05.4	+58.9	1.0	14 05.4	+58.9	1.0	15 05.4	+58.9	1.0	16 05.3	+59.0	1.0	17 05.3	+59.0	1.0	85
86	11 04.3	+59.0	0.8	12 04.3	+59.0	0.8	13 04.3	+59.0	0.8	14 04.3	+59.0	0.8	15 04.3	+58.9	0.8	16 04.3	+58.9	0.8	17 04.3	+58.9	0.8	18 04.3	+58.9	0.8	86
87	12 03.3	+58.9	0.6	13 03.3	+58.9	0.6	14 03.3	+58.9	0.6	15 03.3	+58.9	0.6	16 03.3	+58.9	0.6	17 03.2	+59.0	0.6	18 03.2	+59.0	0.6	19 03.2	+59.0	0.6	87
88	13 02.2	+58.9	0.4	14 02.2	+58.9	0.4	15 02.2	+58.9	0.4	16 02.2	+58.9	0.4	17 02.2	+58.9	0.4	18 02.2	+58.9	0.4	19 02.2	+58.9	0.4	20 02.2	+58.9	0.4	88
89	14 01.1	+58.9	0.2	15 01.1	+58.9	0.2	16 01.1	+58.9	0.2	17 01.1	+58.9	0.2	18 01.1	+58.9	0.2	19 01.1	+58.9	0.2	20 01.1	+58.9	0.2	21 01.1	+58.9	0.2	89
90	15 00.0	+58.9	0.0	16 00.0	+58.9	0.0	17 00.0	+58.9	0.0	18 00.0	+58.9	0.0	19 00.0	+58.9	0.0	20 00.0	+58.9	0.0	21 00.0	+58.9	0.0	22 00.0	+58.9	0.0	90
	15°			16°			17°			18°			19°			20°			21°			22°			

S. Lat. {L.H.A. greater than 180° ....Zn=180°–Z; L.H.A. less than 180°............Zn=180°+Z}

LATITUDE **SAME** NAME AS DECLINATION **L.H.A. 169°, 191°**

25

N. Lat. {L.H.A. greater than 180° .....Zn=Z
{L.H.A. less than 180°............Zn=360°–Z

Dec.	15° Hc	d	Z	16° Hc	d	Z	17° Hc	d	Z	18° Hc	d	Z
°	° ′	′	°	° ′	′	°	° ′	′	°	° ′	′	°
0	70 52.6	+46.8	140.6	70 05.7	+48.0	142.4	69 17.6	+49.2	144.0	68 28.7	+50.1	145.5
1	71 39.4	+45.6	138.7	70 53.7	+47.0	140.6	70 06.8	+48.2	142.3	69 18.8	+49.3	144.0
2	72 25.0	+44.0	136.5	71 40.7	+45.6	138.6	70 55.0	+47.0	140.5	70 08.1	+48.2	142.3
3	73 09.0	+42.4	134.3	72 26.3	+44.2	136.5	71 42.0	+45.8	138.6	70 56.3	+47.2	140.5
4	73 51.4	+40.5•	131.8	73 10.5	+42.5	134.2	72 27.8	+44.3	136.5	71 43.5	+45.9	138.6
5	74 31.9	+38.4•	129.0	73 53.0	+40.7•	131.7	73 12.1	+42.7	134.2	72 29.4	+44.5	136.5
6	75 10.3	+35.9•	126.1	74 33.7	+38.5•	129.0	73 54.8	+40.8•	131.7	73 13.9	+42.8	134.2
7	75 46.2	+33.2•	122.9	75 12.2	+36.1•	126.1	74 35.6	+38.7•	129.0	73 56.7	+41.0	131.7
8	76 19.4	+30.0•	119.5	75 48.3	+33.3•	122.9	75 14.3	+36.3•	126.1	74 37.7	+38.9•	129.0
9	76 49.4	+26.6•	115.7	76 21.6	+30.3•	119.4	75 50.6	+33.5•	122.9	75 16.6	+36.4•	126.1
10	77 16.0	+22.8•	111.7	76 51.9	+26.7•	115.7	76 24.1	+30.4•	119.4	75 53.0	+33.7•	122.9
11	77 38.8	+18.5•	107.5	77 18.6	+22.9•	111.7	76 54.5	+26.9•	115.7	76 26.7	+30.6•	119.5
12	77 57.3	+14.0•	103.0	77 41.5	+18.7•	107.4	77 21.4	+23.1•	111.7	76 57.3	+27.1•	115.7
13	78 11.3	+9.1•	98.3	78 00.2	+14.2•	102.9	77 44.5	+18.9•	107.4	77 24.4	+23.3•	111.7
14	78 20.4	+4.2•	93.4	78 14.4	+9.3•	98.2	78 03.4	+14.3•	102.9	77 47.7	+19.1•	107.4
15	78 24.6	-0.9•	88.4	78 23.7	+4.3•	93.3	78 17.7	+9.5•	98.1	78 06.8	+14.4•	102.9
16	78 23.7	-6.0•	83.5	78 28.0	-0.8•	88.3	78 27.2	+4.4•	93.2	78 21.2	+9.6•	98.1
17	78 17.7	-10.9•	78.5	78 27.2	-6.0•	83.3	78 31.6	-0.8•	88.2	78 30.8	+4.6•	93.2
18	78 06.8	-15.7•	73.7	78 21.2	-10.9•	78.4	78 30.8	-5.8•	83.2	78 35.4	-0.7•	88.1
19	77 51.1	-20.1•	69.1	78 10.3	-15.6•	73.6	78 25.0	-10.9•	78.2	78 34.7	-5.8•	83.1
20	77 31.0	-24.2•	64.7	77 54.7	-20.1•	68.9	78 14.1	-15.6•	73.4	78 28.9	-10.8•	78.1
21	77 06.8	-27.8•	60.5	77 34.6	-24.2•	64.5	77 58.5	-20.2•	68.7	78 18.1	-15.7•	73.2
22	76 39.0	-31.3•	56.6	77 10.4	-27.9•	60.3	77 38.3	-24.2•	64.2	78 02.4	-20.1•	68.5
23	76 07.7	-34.2•	53.0	76 42.5	-31.3•	56.3	77 14.1	-28.0•	60.0	77 42.3	-24.3•	64.0
24	75 33.5	-36.8•	49.6	76 11.2	-34.3•	52.7	76 46.1	-31.3•	56.1	77 18.0	-28.0•	59.8
25	74 56.7	-39.2•	46.5	75 36.9	-36.9•	49.3	76 14.8	-34.3•	52.4	76 50.0	-31.4•	55.8
26	74 17.5	-41.2	43.6	75 00.0	-39.2•	46.2	75 40.5	-37.0•	49.0	76 18.6	-34.4•	52.1
27	73 36.3	-43.0	41.0	74 20.8	-41.3	43.4	75 03.5	-39.3•	45.9	75 44.2	-37.1•	48.8
28	72 53.3	-44.6	38.6	73 39.5	-43.1	40.7	74 24.2	-41.4	43.1	75 07.1	-39.4•	45.6
29	72 08.7	-46.0	36.4	72 56.4	-44.7	38.3	73 42.8	-43.2	40.4	74 27.7	-41.5	42.8
30	71 22.7	-47.3	34.3	72 11.7	-46.1	36.1	72 59.6	-44.7	38.0	73 46.2	-43.2	40.1
31	70 35.4	-48.3	32.4	71 25.6	-47.3	34.0	72 14.9	-46.2	35.8	73 03.0	-44.9	37.7
32	69 47.1	-49.3	30.7	70 38.3	-48.4	32.1	71 28.7	-47.4	33.7	72 18.1	-46.2	35.4
33	68 57.8	-50.1	29.1	69 49.9	-49.3	30.4	70 41.3	-48.4	31.8	71 31.9	-47.5	33.4
34	68 07.7	-50.9	27.6	69 00.6	-50.2	28.8	69 52.9	-49.5	30.1	70 44.4	-48.5	31.5
35	67 16.8	-51.6	26.2	68 10.4	-51.0	27.3	69 03.4	-50.2	28.5	69 55.9	-49.5	29.8
36	66 25.2	-52.2	24.9	67 19.4	-51.6	25.9	68 13.2	-51.1	27.0	69 06.4	-50.4	28.1
37	65 33.0	-52.7	23.7	66 27.8	-52.2	24.6	67 22.1	-51.6	25.6	68 16.0	-51.1	26.6
38	64 40.3	-53.2	22.5	65 35.6	-52.8	23.4	66 30.5	-52.3	24.3	67 24.9	-51.7	25.3
39	63 47.1	-53.7	21.5	64 42.8	-53.3	22.2	65 38.2	-52.9	23.1	66 33.2	-52.4	24.0
40	62 53.4	-54.0	20.5	63 49.5	-53.7	21.2	64 45.3	-53.3	21.9	65 40.8	-52.9	22.8
41	61 59.4	-54.4	19.5	62 55.8	-54.1	20.2	63 52.0	-53.7	20.9	64 47.9	-53.3	21.6
42	61 05.0	-54.8	18.6	62 01.7	-54.4	19.2	62 58.3	-54.2	19.9	63 54.6	-53.8	20.6
43	60 10.2	-55.0	17.8	61 07.3	-54.8	18.4	62 04.1	-54.5	18.9	63 00.8	-54.2	19.6
44	59 15.2	-55.3	17.0	60 12.5	-55.1	17.5	61 09.6	-54.8	18.1	62 06.6	-54.6	18.6
45	58 19.9	-55.6	16.3	59 17.4	-55.3	16.7	60 14.8	-55.1	17.2	61 12.0	-54.8	17.8
46	57 24.3	-55.8	15.6	58 22.1	-55.6	16.0	59 19.7	-55.4	16.4	60 17.2	-55.2	16.9
47	56 28.5	-55.9	14.9	57 26.5	-55.8	15.3	58 24.3	-55.6	15.7	59 22.0	-55.4	16.2
48	55 32.6	-56.2	14.2	56 30.7	-56.1	14.6	57 28.7	-55.9	15.0	58 26.6	-55.7	15.4
49	54 36.4	-56.4	13.6	55 34.6	-56.2	14.0	56 32.8	-56.0	14.3	57 30.9	-55.9	14.7
50	53 40.0	-56.5	13.0	54 38.4	-56.4	13.4	55 36.8	-56.3	13.7	56 35.0	-56.1	14.0
51	52 43.5	-56.7	12.5	53 42.0	-56.5	12.8	54 40.5	-56.4	13.1	55 38.9	-56.3	13.4
52	51 46.8	-56.8	11.9	52 45.5	-56.7	12.2	53 44.1	-56.6	12.5	54 42.6	-56.4	12.8
53	50 50.0	-57.0	11.4	51 48.8	-56.9	11.7	52 47.5	-56.7	11.9	53 46.2	-56.7	12.2
54	49 53.0	-57.0	10.9	50 51.9	-57.0	11.2	51 50.8	-56.9	11.4	52 49.5	-56.7	11.7
55	48 56.0	-57.2	10.5	49 54.9	-57.1	10.7	50 53.9	-57.0	10.9	51 52.8	-56.9	11.1
56	47 58.8	-57.3	10.0	48 57.8	-57.2	10.2	49 56.9	-57.1	10.4	50 55.9	-57.1	10.6
57	47 01.5	-57.4	9.6	48 00.6	-57.3	9.7	48 59.8	-57.3	9.9	49 58.8	-57.1	10.1
58	46 04.1	-57.5	9.1	47 03.3	-57.4	9.3	48 02.5	-57.3	9.5	49 01.7	-57.3	9.7
59	45 06.6	-57.5	8.7	46 05.9	-57.5	8.9	47 05.2	-57.4	9.0	48 04.4	-57.3	9.2
60	44 09.1	-57.7	8.3	45 08.4	-57.6	8.5	46 07.8	-57.6	8.6	47 07.1	-57.5	8.8
61	43 11.4	-57.7	7.9	44 10.8	-57.6	8.1	45 10.2	-57.6	8.2	46 09.6	-57.5	8.4
62	42 13.7	-57.8	7.6	43 13.2	-57.8	7.7	44 12.6	-57.7	7.8	45 12.1	-57.7	8.0
63	41 15.9	-57.8	7.2	42 15.4	-57.8	7.3	43 14.9	-57.7	7.4	44 14.4	-57.7	7.6
64	40 18.1	-57.9	6.9	41 17.6	-57.8	7.0	42 17.2	-57.8	7.1	43 16.7	-57.8	7.2
65	39 20.2	-58.0	6.5	40 19.8	-58.0	6.6	41 19.4	-57.9	6.7	42 18.9	-57.8	6.8
66	38 22.2	-58.0	6.2	39 21.8	-58.0	6.3	40 21.5	-58.0	6.4	41 21.1	-57.9	6.5
67	37 24.2	-58.1	5.9	38 23.8	-58.0	5.9	39 23.5	-58.0	6.0	40 23.2	-58.0	6.1
68	36 26.1	-58.1	5.6	37 25.8	-58.1	5.6	38 25.5	-58.1	5.7	39 25.2	-58.0	5.8
69	35 28.0	-58.2	5.2	36 27.7	-58.1	5.3	37 27.4	-58.1	5.4	38 27.2	-58.1	5.5
70	34 29.8	-58.2	4.9	35 29.6	-58.2	5.0	36 29.3	-58.1	5.1	37 29.1	-58.1	5.1
71	33 31.6	-58.3	4.7	34 31.4	-58.2	4.7	35 31.2	-58.2	4.8	36 31.0	-58.2	4.8
72	32 33.3	-58.3	4.4	33 33.2	-58.3	4.4	34 33.0	-58.3	4.5	35 32.8	-58.2	4.5
73	31 35.0	-58.3	4.1	32 34.9	-58.3	4.1	33 34.7	-58.3	4.2	34 34.6	-58.3	4.2
74	30 36.7	-58.3	3.8	31 36.6	-58.4	3.9	32 36.4	-58.3	3.9	33 36.3	-58.3	3.9
75	29 38.4	-58.4	3.5	30 38.2	-58.3	3.6	31 38.1	-58.3	3.6	32 38.0	-58.3	3.7
76	28 40.0	-58.5	3.3	29 39.9	-58.4	3.3	30 39.8	-58.4	3.4	31 39.7	-58.4	3.4
77	27 41.5	-58.4	3.0	28 41.5	-58.5	3.1	29 41.4	-58.5	3.1	30 41.3	-58.4	3.1
78	26 43.1	-58.5	2.8	27 43.0	-58.4	2.8	28 42.9	-58.4	2.8	29 42.9	-58.5	2.9
79	25 44.6	-58.5	2.5	26 44.6	-58.5	2.5	27 44.5	-58.5	2.6	28 44.4	-58.4	2.6
80	24 46.1	-58.5	2.3	25 46.1	-58.6	2.3	26 46.0	-58.5	2.3	27 46.0	-58.5	2.3
81	23 47.6	-58.6	2.0	24 47.5	-58.5	2.1	25 47.5	-58.5	2.1	26 47.5	-58.6	2.1
82	22 49.0	-58.5	1.8	23 49.0	-58.6	1.8	24 49.0	-58.6	1.8	25 48.9	-58.5	1.8
83	21 50.5	-58.6	1.6	22 50.4	-58.5	1.6	23 50.4	-58.6	1.6	24 50.4	-58.6	1.6
84	20 51.9	-58.6	1.3	21 51.9	-58.6	1.3	22 51.8	-58.6	1.4	23 51.8	-58.6	1.4
85	19 53.3	-58.7	1.1	20 53.3	-58.7	1.1	21 53.2	-58.6	1.1	22 53.2	-58.6	1.1
86	18 54.6	-58.6	0.9	19 54.6	-58.6	0.9	20 54.6	-58.6	0.9	21 54.6	-58.6	0.9
87	17 56.0	-58.6	0.7	18 56.0	-58.6	0.7	19 56.0	-58.7	0.7	20 56.0	-58.7	0.7
88	16 57.4	-58.7	0.4	17 57.4	-58.7	0.4	18 57.3	-58.6	0.4	19 57.3	-58.6	0.4
89	15 58.7	-58.7	0.2	16 58.7	-58.7	0.2	17 58.7	-58.7	0.2	18 58.7	-58.7	0.2
90	15 00.0	-58.7	0.0	16 00.0	-58.7	0.0	17 00.0	-58.7	0.0	18 00.0	-58.7	0.0
	15°			16°			17°			18°		

19° Hc	d	Z	20° Hc	d	Z	21° Hc	d	Z	22° Hc	d	Z	Dec.
° ′	′	°	° ′	′	°	° ′	′	°	° ′	′	°	°
67 38.8	+51.0	146.9	66 48.2	+51.8	148.1	65 56.9	+52.5	149.3	65 05.0	+53.1	150.4	0
68 29.8	+50.3	145.5	67 40.0	+51.1	146.8	66 49.4	+51.9	148.1	65 58.1	+52.6	149.3	1
69 20.1	+49.3	143.9	68 31.1	+50.4	145.4	67 41.3	+51.2	146.8	66 50.7	+52.0	148.1	2
70 09.4	+48.4	142.3	69 21.5	+49.4	143.9	68 32.5	+50.5	145.4	67 42.7	+51.3	146.8	3
70 57.8	+47.3	140.5	70 10.9	+48.6	142.3	69 23.0	+49.6	143.9	68 34.0	+50.6	145.4	4
71 45.1	+46.1	138.6	70 59.5	+47.4	140.5	70 12.6	+48.6	142.3	69 24.6	+49.7	143.9	5
72 31.2	+44.6	136.5	71 46.9	+46.2	138.6	71 01.2	+47.6	140.5	70 14.3	+48.8	142.3	6
73 15.8	+43.0	134.2	72 33.1	+44.8	136.5	71 48.8	+46.4	138.6	71 03.1	+47.8	140.5	7
73 58.8	+41.2•	131.8	73 17.9	+43.1	134.2	72 35.2	+44.9	136.5	71 50.9	+46.5	138.6	8
74 40.0	+39.0•	129.1	74 01.0	+41.4	131.8	73 20.1	+43.3	134.3	72 37.4	+45.1	136.6	9
75 19.0	+36.6•	126.1	74 42.4	+39.2•	129.1	74 03.4	+41.5	131.8	73 22.5	+43.5	134.3	10
75 55.6	+33.9•	122.9	75 21.6	+36.8•	126.1	74 44.9	+39.4•	129.1	74 06.0	+41.6	131.8	11
76 29.5	+30.8•	119.5	75 58.4	+34.1•	123.0	75 24.3	+37.0•	126.2	74 47.6	+39.6•	129.2	12
77 00.3	+27.3•	115.7	76 32.5	+31.0•	119.5	76 01.3	+34.3•	123.0	75 27.2	+37.3•	126.2	13
77 27.6	+23.5•	111.7	77 03.5	+27.5•	115.7	76 35.6	+31.2•	119.5	76 04.5	+34.5•	123.0	14
77 51.1	+19.2•	107.4	77 31.0	+23.7•	111.7	77 06.8	+27.8•	115.8	76 39.0	+31.4•	119.6	15
78 10.3	+14.7•	102.8	77 54.7	+19.4•	107.4	77 34.6	+23.9•	111.7	77 10.4	+27.9•	115.8	16
78 25.0	+9.7•	98.0	78 14.1	+14.8•	102.8	77 58.5	+19.6•	107.4	77 38.3	+24.1•	111.8	17
78 34.7	+4.7•	93.1	78 28.9	+9.9•	98.0	78 18.1	+15.0•	102.8	78 02.4	+19.8•	107.4	18
78 39.4	-0.6•	88.0	78 38.8	+4.8•	93.0	78 33.1	+10.0•	98.0	78 22.2	+15.2•	102.8	19
78 38.8	-5.7•	83.0	78 43.6	-0.5•	87.9	78 43.1	+4.9•	93.0	78 37.4	+10.2•	97.9	20
78 33.1	-10.9•	77.9	78 43.1	-5.7•	82.8	78 48.0	-0.4•	87.8	78 47.6	+5.0•	92.9	21
78 22.2	-15.6•	73.0	78 37.4	-10.8•	77.8	78 47.6	-5.7•	82.7	78 52.6	-0.3•	87.7	22
78 06.6	-20.2•	68.3	78 26.6	-15.7•	72.8	78 41.9	-10.7•	77.6	78 52.3	-5.6•	82.6	23
77 46.4	-24.3•	63.8	78 10.9	-20.2•	68.0	78 31.2	-15.7•	72.6	78 46.7	-10.8•	77.4	24
77 22.1	-28.1•	59.5	77 50.7	-24.4•	63.5	78 15.5	-20.3•	67.8	78 35.9	-15.7•	72.4	25
76 54.0	-31.5•	55.5	77 26.3	-28.1•	59.2	77 55.2	-24.4•	63.2	78 20.2	-20.3•	67.6	26
76 22.5	-34.5•	51.9	76 58.2	-31.6•	55.2	77 30.8	-28.3•	59.0	77 59.9	-24.5•	63.0	27
75 48.0	-37.2•	48.4	76 26.6	-34.6•	51.5	77 02.5	-31.7•	54.9	77 35.4	-28.4•	58.7	28
75 10.8	-39.5•	45.3	75 52.0	-37.3•	48.1	76 30.8	-34.7•	51.2	77 07.0	-31.8•	54.6	29
74 31.3	-41.5	42.4	75 14.7	-39.6•	45.0	75 56.1	-37.4•	47.8	76 35.2	-34.8•	50.9	30
73 49.8	-43.4	39.8	74 35.1	-41.7	42.1	75 18.7	-39.7•	44.7	76 00.4	-37.5•	47.5	31
73 06.4	-44.9	37.4	73 53.4	-43.4	39.5	74 39.0	-41.8	41.8	75 22.9	-39.9•	44.3	32
72 21.5	-46.4	35.1	73 10.0	-45.1	37.0	73 57.2	-43.6	39.1	74 43.0	-41.9	41.4	33
71 35.1	-47.5	33.1	72 24.9	-46.4	34.8	73 13.6	-45.1	36.7	74 01.1	-43.7	38.8	34
70 47.6	-48.6	31.2	71 38.5	-47.6	32.7	72 28.5	-46.5	34.4	73 17.4	-45.3	36.3	35
69 59.0	-49.6	29.4	70 50.9	-48.8	30.8	71 42.0	-47.8	32.4	72 32.1	-46.6	34.1	36
69 09.4	-50.4	27.8	70 02.1	-49.6	29.1	70 54.2	-48.8	30.5	71 45.5	-47.9	32.0	37
68 19.0	-51.2	26.3	69 12.5	-50.5	27.5	70 05.4	-49.8	28.8	70 57.6	-48.9	30.1	38
67 27.8	-51.8	24.9	68 22.0	-51.3	26.0	69 15.6	-50.5	27.1	70 08.7	-49.8	28.4	39
66 36.0	-52.4	23.6	67 30.7	-51.9	24.6	68 25.1	-51.4	25.7	69 18.9	-50.7	26.8	40
65 43.6	-53.0	22.4	66 38.8	-52.4	23.3	67 33.7	-51.9	24.3	68 28.2	-51.4	25.3	41
64 50.6	-53.4	21.3	65 46.4	-53.1	22.1	66 41.8	-52.6	23.0	67 36.8	-52.1	23.9	42
63 57.2	-53.9	20.3	64 53.3	-53.5	21.0	65 49.2	-53.1	21.8	66 44.7	-52.6	22.7	43
63 03.3	-54.2	19.3	63 59.8	-53.9	19.9	64 56.1	-53.5	20.7	65 52.1	-53.2	21.5	44
62 09.1	-54.6	18.3	63 05.9	-54.3	19.0	64 02.6	-54.0	19.6	64 58.9	-53.6	20.3	45
61 14.5	-54.9	17.5	62 11.6	-54.6	18.0	63 08.6	-54.4	18.6	64 05.3	-54.0	19.3	46
60 19.6	-55.2	16.6	61 17.0	-55.0	17.2	62 14.2	-54.7	17.7	63 11.3	-54.5	18.3	47
59 24.4	-55.5	15.9	60 22.0	-55.3	16.3	61 19.5	-55.0	16.9	62 16.8	-54.7	17.4	48
58 28.9	-55.7	15.1	59 26.7	-55.5	15.6	60 24.5	-55.3	16.0	61 22.1	-55.1	16.5	49
57 33.2	-56.0	14.4	58 31.2	-55.7	14.8	59 29.2	-55.6	15.3	60 27.0	-55.4	15.7	50
56 37.2	-56.1	13.8	57 35.5	-56.0	14.1	58 33.6	-55.8	14.5	59 31.6	-55.6	15.0	51
55 41.1	-56.3	13.1	56 39.5	-56.2	13.5	57 37.8	-56.0	13.8	58 36.0	-55.9	14.2	52
54 44.8	-56.5	12.5	55 43.3	-56.4	12.8	56 41.8	-56.3	13.2	57 40.1	-56.0	13.5	53
53 48.3	-56.7	11.9	54 46.9	-56.5	12.2	55 45.5	-56.4	12.5	56 44.1	-56.3	12.9	54
52 51.6	-56.8	11.4	53 50.4	-56.7	11.7	54 49.1	-56.5	11.9	55 47.8	-56.4	12.2	55
51 54.8	-56.9	10.9	52 53.7	-56.8	11.1	53 52.6	-56.8	11.4	54 51.4	-56.7	11.7	56
50 57.9	-57.1	10.4	51 56.9	-57.0	10.6	52 55.8	-56.8	10.8	53 54.7	-56.7	11.1	57
50 00.8	-57.2	9.9	50 59.9	-57.1	10.1	51 59.0	-57.0	10.3	52 58.0	-56.9	10.5	58
49 03.6	-57.3	9.4	50 02.8	-57.2	9.6	51 02.0	-57.2	9.8	52 01.1	-57.1	10.0	59
48 06.3	-57.3	9.0	49 05.6	-57.3	9.1	50 04.8	-57.2	9.3	51 04.0	-57.2	9.5	60
47 09.0	-57.5	8.5	48 08.3	-57.4	8.7	49 07.6	-57.4	8.9	50 06.8	-57.2	9.0	61
46 11.5	-57.6	8.1	47 10.9	-57.6	8.3	48 10.2	-57.4	8.4	49 09.6	-57.4	8.6	62
45 13.9	-57.7	7.7	46 13.3	-57.6	7.8	47 12.8	-57.6	8.0	48 12.2	-57.5	8.1	63
44 16.2	-57.7	7.3	45 15.7	-57.6	7.4	46 15.2	-57.6	7.6	47 14.7	-57.6	7.7	64
43 18.5	-57.8	6.9	44 18.1	-57.8	7.1	45 17.6	-57.7	7.2	46 17.1	-57.6	7.3	65
42 20.7	-57.9	6.6	43 20.3	-57.8	6.7	44 19.9	-57.8	6.8	45 19.5	-57.8	6.9	66
41 22.8	-57.9	6.2	42 22.5	-57.9	6.3	43 22.1	-57.9	6.4	44 21.7	-57.8	6.5	67
40 24.9	-58.0	5.9	41 24.6	-58.0	6.0	42 24.2	-57.9	6.1	43 23.9	-57.9	6.2	68
39 26.9	-58.0	5.5	40 26.6	-58.0	5.6	41 26.3	-58.0	5.7	42 26.0	-57.9	5.8	69
38 28.9	-58.1	5.2	39 28.6	-58.1	5.3	40 28.3	-58.0	5.4	41 28.1	-58.0	5.4	70
37 30.8	-58.2	4.9	38 30.5	-58.1	5.0	39 30.3	-58.1	5.0	40 30.1	-58.1	5.1	71
36 32.6	-58.2	4.6	37 32.4	-58.2	4.6	38 32.2	-58.1	4.7	39 32.0	-58.1	4.8	72
35 34.4	-58.2	4.3	36 34.2	-58.2	4.3	37 34.1	-58.2	4.4	38 33.9	-58.2	4.5	73
34 36.2	-58.3	4.0	35 36.0	-58.3	4.0	36 35.9	-58.3	4.1	37 35.7	-58.2	4.1	74
33 37.9	-58.3	3.7	34 37.7	-58.3	3.7	35 37.6	-58.3	3.8	36 37.5	-58.3	3.8	75
32 39.6	-58.4	3.4	33 39.4	-58.3	3.5	34 39.3	-58.3	3.5	35 39.2	-58.3	3.5	76
31 41.2	-58.4	3.2	32 41.1	-58.4	3.2	33 41.0	-58.4	3.2	34 40.9	-58.3	3.3	77
30 42.8	-58.5	2.9	31 42.7	-58.4	2.9	32 42.6	-58.4	2.9	33 42.6	-58.4	3.0	78
29 44.4	-58.5	2.6	30 44.3	-58.4	2.6	31 44.2	-58.4	2.7	32 44.2	-58.4	2.7	79
28 45.9	-58.5	2.4	29 45.9	-58.5	2.4	30 45.8	-58.5	2.4	31 45.8	-58.5	2.4	80
27 47.4	-58.5	2.1	28 47.4	-58.5	2.1	29 47.3	-58.4	2.1	30 47.3	-58.5	2.2	81
26 48.9	-58.5	1.9	27 48.9	-58.5	1.9	28 48.9	-58.6	1.9	29 48.8	-58.5	1.9	82
25 50.4	-58.6	1.6	26 50.4	-58.6	1.6	27 50.3	-58.5	1.6	28 50.3	-58.5	1.7	83
24 51.8	-58.6	1.4	25 51.8	-58.6	1.4	26 51.8	-58.6	1.4	27 51.8	-58.6	1.4	84
23 53.2	-58.6	1.1	24 53.2	-58.6	1.1	25 53.2	-58.6	1.2	26 53.2	-58.6	1.2	85
22 54.6	-58.6	0.9	23 54.6	-58.6	0.9	24 54.6	-58.6	0.9	25 54.6	-58.6	0.9	86
21 56.0	-58.7	0.7	22 56.0	-58.7	0.7	23 56.0	-58.7	0.7	24 56.0	-58.7	0.7	87
20 57.3	-58.6	0.4	21 57.3	-58.6	0.4	22 57.3	-58.6	0.5	23 57.3	-58.6	0.5	88
19 58.7	-58.7	0.2	20 58.7	-58.7	0.2	21 58.7	-58.7	0.2	22 58.7	-58.7	0.2	89
19 00.0	-58.7	0.0	20 00.0	-58.7	0.0	21 00.0	-58.7	0.0	22 00.0	-58.7	0.0	90
19°			20°			21°			22°			

12°, 348° L.H.A. LATITUDE SAME NAME AS DECLINATION

LATITUDE CONTRARY NAME TO DECLINATION — L.H.A. 12°, 348°

Dec.	15° Hc	15° d	15° Z	16° Hc	16° d	16° Z	17° Hc	17° d	17° Z	18° Hc	18° d	18° Z	19° Hc	19° d	19° Z	20° Hc	20° d	20° Z	21° Hc	21° d	21° Z	22° Hc	22° d	22° Z	Dec.
°	° ′	′	°	° ′	′	°	° ′	′	°	° ′	′	°	° ′	′	°	° ′	′	°	° ′	′	°	° ′	′	°	°
0	70 52.6	−47.9	140.6	70 05.7	−49.1	142.4	69 17.6	−50.0	144.0	68 28.7	−51.0	145.5	67 38.8	−51.7	146.9	66 48.2	−52.4	148.1	65 56.9	−53.0	149.3	65 05.0	−53.6	150.4	0
1	70 04.7	−49.0	142.4	69 16.6	−49.9	144.0	68 27.6	−50.8	145.5	67 37.7	−51.6	146.9	66 47.1	−52.3	148.2	65 55.8	−52.9	149.4	65 03.9	−53.5	150.5	64 11.4	−54.0	151.5	1
2	69 15.7	−49.8	144.1	68 26.7	−50.7	145.6	67 36.8	−51.5	146.9	66 46.1	−52.2	148.2	65 54.8	−52.8	149.4	65 02.9	−53.4	150.5	64 10.4	−53.9	151.5	63 17.4	−54.4	152.5	2
3	68 25.9	−50.7	145.6	67 36.0	−51.5	147.0	66 45.3	−52.1	148.3	65 53.9	−52.7	149.4	65 02.0	−53.4	150.5	64 09.5	−53.9	151.6	63 16.5	−54.3	152.5	62 23.0	−54.7	153.4	3
4	67 35.2	−51.3	147.0	66 44.5	−52.0	148.3	65 53.2	−52.7	149.5	65 01.2	−53.3	150.6	64 08.6	−53.7	151.6	63 15.6	−54.2	152.6	62 22.2	−54.7	153.4	61 28.3	−55.0	154.3	4
5	66 43.9	−52.0	148.4	65 52.5	−52.6	149.6	65 00.5	−53.2	150.6	64 07.9	−53.7	151.7	63 14.9	−54.2	152.6	62 21.4	−54.6	153.5	61 27.5	−55.0	154.3	60 33.3	−55.4	155.1	5
6	65 51.9	−52.5	149.6	64 59.9	−53.1	150.7	64 07.3	−53.6	151.7	63 14.2	−54.1	152.7	62 20.7	−54.5	153.5	61 26.8	−54.9	154.4	60 32.5	−55.2	155.1	59 37.9	−55.6	155.9	6
7	64 59.4	−53.0	150.8	64 06.8	−53.6	151.8	63 13.7	−54.1	152.7	62 20.1	−54.4	153.6	61 26.2	−54.9	154.4	60 31.9	−55.2	155.2	59 37.3	−55.6	155.9	58 42.3	−55.8	156.6	7
8	64 06.4	−53.5	151.9	63 13.2	−54.0	152.8	62 19.6	−54.4	153.7	61 25.7	−54.8	154.5	60 31.3	−55.1	155.3	59 36.7	−55.5	156.0	58 41.7	−55.7	156.7	57 46.5	−56.0	157.3	8
9	63 12.9	−54.0	152.9	62 19.2	−54.3	153.8	61 25.2	−54.7	154.6	60 30.9	−55.1	155.3	59 36.2	−55.4	156.1	58 41.2	−55.7	156.7	57 46.0	−56.0	157.4	56 50.5	−56.3	157.9	9
10	62 18.9	−54.2	153.9	61 24.9	−54.7	154.7	60 30.5	−55.0	155.4	59 35.8	−55.4	156.1	58 40.8	−55.7	156.8	57 45.5	−56.0	157.4	56 50.0	−56.2	158.0	55 54.2	−56.4	158.6	10
11	61 24.7	−54.7	154.8	60 30.2	−55.0	155.5	59 35.5	−55.4	156.2	58 40.4	−55.6	156.9	57 45.1	−55.9	157.5	56 49.5	−56.1	158.1	55 53.8	−56.4	158.7	54 57.8	−56.6	159.2	11
12	60 30.0	−54.9	155.6	59 35.2	−55.2	156.3	58 40.1	−55.5	157.0	57 44.8	−55.8	157.6	56 49.2	−56.1	158.2	55 53.4	−56.3	158.7	54 57.4	−56.6	159.3	54 01.2	−56.8	159.7	12
13	59 35.1	−55.2	156.4	58 40.0	−55.5	157.1	57 44.6	−55.8	157.7	56 49.0	−56.1	158.3	55 53.1	−56.3	158.8	54 57.1	−56.5	159.3	54 00.8	−56.7	159.8	53 04.4	−56.9	160.3	13
14	58 39.9	−55.5	157.2	57 44.5	−55.8	157.8	56 48.8	−56.0	158.4	55 52.9	−56.2	158.9	54 56.8	−56.4	159.4	54 00.6	−56.7	159.9	53 04.1	−56.8	160.4	52 07.5	−57.0	160.8	14
15	57 44.4	−55.7	157.9	56 48.7	−56.0	158.5	55 52.8	−56.2	159.0	54 56.7	−56.4	159.5	54 00.4	−56.7	160.0	53 03.9	−56.8	160.5	52 07.3	−57.0	160.9	51 10.5	−57.2	161.3	15
16	56 48.7	−55.9	158.6	55 52.7	−56.1	159.1	54 56.6	−56.4	159.6	54 00.3	−56.6	160.1	53 03.7	−56.7	160.6	52 07.1	−57.0	161.0	51 10.3	−57.1	161.4	50 13.3	−57.2	161.8	16
17	55 52.8	−56.1	159.2	54 56.6	−56.3	159.7	54 00.2	−56.5	160.2	53 03.7	−56.8	160.7	52 07.0	−56.9	161.1	51 10.1	−57.0	161.5	50 13.2	−57.3	161.9	49 16.1	−57.4	162.3	17
18	54 56.7	−56.3	159.9	54 00.3	−56.6	160.3	53 03.7	−56.7	160.8	52 06.9	−56.8	161.2	51 10.1	−57.1	161.6	50 13.1	−57.2	162.0	49 15.9	−57.3	162.4	48 18.7	−57.5	162.7	18
19	54 00.4	−56.5	160.5	53 03.7	−56.6	160.9	52 07.0	−56.9	161.3	51 10.1	−57.0	161.7	50 13.0	−57.1	162.1	49 15.9	−57.3	162.5	48 18.6	−57.4	162.8	47 21.2	−57.5	163.1	19
20	53 03.9	−56.6	161.0	52 07.1	−56.8	161.4	51 10.1	−56.9	161.8	50 13.1	−57.2	162.2	49 15.9	−57.3	162.6	48 18.6	−57.4	162.9	47 21.2	−57.6	163.2	46 23.7	−57.7	163.5	20
21	52 07.3	−56.8	161.6	51 10.3	−57.0	162.0	50 13.2	−57.1	162.3	49 15.9	−57.2	162.7	48 18.6	−57.4	163.0	47 21.2	−57.5	163.3	46 23.6	−57.6	163.7	45 26.0	−57.7	163.9	21
22	51 10.5	−56.9	162.1	50 13.3	−57.0	162.5	49 16.1	−57.2	162.8	48 18.7	−57.3	163.2	47 21.2	−57.4	163.5	46 23.7	−57.6	163.8	45 26.0	−57.7	164.1	44 28.3	−57.8	164.3	22
23	50 13.6	−57.0	162.6	49 16.3	−57.2	162.9	48 18.9	−57.3	163.3	47 21.4	−57.5	163.6	46 23.8	−57.6	163.9	45 26.1	−57.7	164.2	44 28.3	−57.8	164.4	43 30.5	−57.9	164.7	23
24	49 16.6	−57.2	163.1	48 19.1	−57.3	163.4	47 21.6	−57.4	163.7	46 23.9	−57.5	164.0	45 26.2	−57.6	164.3	44 28.4	−57.7	164.6	43 30.5	−57.8	164.8	42 32.6	−57.9	165.1	24
25	48 19.4	−57.2	163.5	47 21.8	−57.3	163.8	46 24.2	−57.5	164.1	45 26.4	−57.6	164.4	44 28.6	−57.7	164.7	43 30.7	−57.8	164.9	42 32.7	−57.9	165.2	41 34.7	−58.0	165.4	25
26	47 22.2	−57.4	164.0	46 24.5	−57.5	164.3	45 26.7	−57.6	164.6	44 28.8	−57.7	164.8	43 30.9	−57.8	165.1	42 32.9	−57.9	165.3	41 34.8	−58.0	165.5	40 36.7	−58.1	165.7	26
27	46 24.8	−57.4	164.4	45 27.0	−57.6	164.7	44 29.1	−57.7	165.0	43 31.1	−57.8	165.2	42 33.1	−57.9	165.4	41 35.0	−58.0	165.7	40 36.8	−58.0	165.9	39 38.6	−58.1	166.1	27
28	45 27.4	−57.5	164.8	44 29.4	−57.6	165.1	43 31.4	−57.7	165.3	42 33.3	−57.8	165.6	41 35.2	−57.9	165.8	40 37.0	−58.0	166.0	39 38.8	−58.1	166.2	38 40.5	−58.2	166.4	28
29	44 29.9	−57.7	165.2	43 31.8	−57.7	165.5	42 33.7	−57.8	165.7	41 35.5	−57.9	165.9	40 37.3	−58.0	166.1	39 39.0	−58.1	166.3	38 40.7	−58.2	166.5	37 42.3	−58.2	166.7	29
30	43 32.2	−57.6	165.6	42 34.1	−57.8	165.8	41 35.9	−57.9	166.1	40 37.6	−57.9	166.3	39 39.3	−58.0	166.5	38 40.9	−58.1	166.7	37 42.5	−58.1	166.8	36 44.1	−58.3	167.0	30
31	42 34.6	−57.8	166.0	41 36.3	−57.8	166.2	40 38.0	−57.9	166.4	39 39.7	−58.1	166.6	38 41.3	−58.1	166.8	37 42.8	−58.1	167.0	36 44.4	−58.3	167.2	35 45.8	−58.3	167.3	31
32	41 36.8	−57.8	166.4	40 38.5	−58.0	166.6	39 40.1	−58.0	166.8	38 41.6	−58.0	166.9	37 43.2	−58.2	167.1	36 44.7	−58.2	167.3	35 46.1	−58.3	167.4	34 47.5	−58.3	167.6	32
33	40 39.0	−57.9	166.7	39 40.5	−57.9	166.9	38 42.1	−58.1	167.1	37 43.6	−58.1	167.3	36 45.0	−58.2	167.4	35 46.5	−58.3	167.6	34 47.8	−58.3	167.7	33 49.2	−58.4	167.9	33
34	39 41.1	−58.0	167.1	38 42.6	−58.1	167.2	37 44.0	−58.1	167.4	36 45.5	−58.2	167.6	35 46.8	−58.2	167.7	34 48.2	−58.3	167.9	33 49.5	−58.3	168.0	32 50.8	−58.4	168.2	34
35	38 43.1	−58.0	167.4	37 44.5	−58.0	167.6	36 45.9	−58.1	167.7	35 47.3	−58.2	167.9	34 48.6	−58.3	168.0	33 49.9	−58.3	168.2	32 51.2	−58.4	168.3	31 52.4	−58.5	168.4	35
36	37 45.1	−58.0	167.7	36 46.5	−58.2	167.9	35 47.8	−58.2	168.0	34 49.1	−58.3	168.2	33 50.3	−58.3	168.3	32 51.6	−58.4	168.4	31 52.8	−58.5	168.6	30 53.9	−58.4	168.7	36
37	36 47.1	−58.1	168.0	35 48.3	−58.1	168.2	34 49.6	−58.2	168.3	33 50.8	−58.3	168.5	32 52.0	−58.3	168.6	31 53.2	−58.4	168.7	30 54.3	−58.4	168.8	29 55.5	−58.5	169.0	37
38	35 49.0	−58.2	168.3	34 50.2	−58.2	168.5	33 51.4	−58.3	168.6	32 52.5	−58.3	168.8	31 53.7	−58.4	168.9	30 54.8	−58.5	169.0	29 55.9	−58.5	169.1	28 57.0	−58.6	169.2	38
39	34 50.8	−58.2	168.6	33 52.0	−58.3	168.8	32 53.1	−58.3	168.9	31 54.2	−58.4	169.0	30 55.3	−58.4	169.1	29 56.3	−58.4	169.3	28 57.4	−58.5	169.4	27 58.4	−58.6	169.5	39
40	33 52.6	−58.2	168.9	32 53.7	−58.3	169.1	31 54.8	−58.4	169.2	30 55.8	−58.4	169.3	29 56.9	−58.5	169.5	28 57.9	−58.5	169.5	27 58.9	−58.6	169.6	26 59.8	−58.5	169.7	40
41	32 54.4	−58.3	169.2	31 55.4	−58.3	169.3	30 56.4	−58.4	169.5	29 57.4	−58.4	169.6	28 58.4	−58.5	169.7	27 59.4	−58.5	169.8	27 00.3	−58.5	169.9	26 01.3	−58.7	169.9	41
42	31 56.1	−58.3	169.5	30 57.1	−58.4	169.6	29 58.0	−58.4	169.7	28 59.0	−58.5	169.8	27 59.9	−58.5	169.9	27 00.9	−58.6	170.0	26 01.8	−58.6	170.1	25 02.6	−58.6	170.2	42
43	30 57.8	−58.4	169.8	29 58.7	−58.4	169.9	28 59.6	−58.4	170.0	28 00.5	−58.5	170.1	27 01.4	−58.5	170.2	26 02.3	−58.6	170.3	25 03.2	−58.7	170.3	24 04.0	−58.7	170.4	43
44	29 59.4	−58.4	170.1	29 00.3	−58.4	170.2	28 01.2	−58.5	170.2	27 02.0	−58.5	170.3	26 02.9	−58.6	170.4	25 03.7	−58.6	170.5	24 04.5	−58.6	170.6	23 05.3	−58.6	170.6	44
45	29 01.0	−58.4	170.3	28 01.9	−58.5	170.4	27 02.7	−58.5	170.5	26 03.5	−58.5	170.6	25 04.3	−58.5	170.7	24 05.1	−58.6	170.7	23 05.9	−58.7	170.8	22 06.7	−58.7	170.9	45
46	28 02.6	−58.4	170.6	27 03.4	−58.5	170.7	26 04.2	−58.5	170.7	25 05.0	−58.6	170.8	24 05.8	−58.6	170.9	23 06.5	−58.6	171.0	22 07.2	−58.6	171.0	21 08.0	−58.7	171.1	46
47	27 04.2	−58.5	170.8	26 04.9	−58.5	170.9	25 05.7	−58.6	171.0	24 06.4	−58.6	171.1	23 07.2	−58.7	171.1	22 07.9	−58.7	171.2	21 08.6	−58.7	171.3	20 09.3	−58.8	171.3	47
48	26 05.7	−58.5	171.1	25 06.4	−58.5	171.2	24 07.1	−58.5	171.2	23 07.8	−58.6	171.3	22 08.5	−58.6	171.4	21 09.2	−58.7	171.4	20 09.9	−58.7	171.5	19 10.5	−58.7	171.5	48
49	25 07.2	−58.5	171.3	24 07.9	−58.5	171.4	23 08.6	−58.6	171.5	22 09.2	−58.6	171.5	21 09.9	−58.7	171.6	20 10.5	−58.7	171.6	19 11.2	−58.8	171.7	18 11.8	−58.8	171.7	49
50	24 08.7	−58.5	171.6	23 09.4	−58.6	171.6	22 10.0	−58.6	171.7	21 10.6	−58.6	171.8	20 11.2	−58.7	171.8	19 11.8	−58.7	171.9	18 12.4	−58.7	171.9	17 13.0	−58.7	172.0	50
51	23 10.2	−58.6	171.8	22 10.8	−58.6	171.9	21 11.4	−58.7	171.9	20 12.0	−58.7	172.0	19 12.5	−58.6	172.0	18 13.1	−58.7	172.1	17 13.7	−58.8	172.1	16 14.3	−58.8	172.2	51
52	22 11.6	−58.6	172.1	21 12.2	−58.6	172.1	20 12.7	−58.6	172.2	19 13.3	−58.7	172.2	18 13.9	−58.8	172.3	17 14.4	−58.7	172.3	16 14.9	−58.7	172.3	15 15.5	−58.8	172.4	52
53	21 13.0	−58.6	172.3	20 13.6	−58.7	172.3	19 14.1	−58.7	172.4	18 14.6	−58.7	172.4	17 15.1	−58.7	172.5	16 15.7	−58.8	172.5	15 16.2	−58.8	172.5	14 16.7	−58.8	172.6	53
54	20 14.4	−58.6	172.5	19 14.9	−58.6	172.6	18 15.4	−58.6	172.6	17 15.9	−58.7	172.6	16 16.4	−58.7	172.7	15 16.9	−58.8	172.7	14 17.4	−58.8	172.8	13 17.9	−58.8	172.8	54
55	19 15.8	−58.6	172.7	18 16.3	−58.7	172.8	17 16.8	−58.7	172.8	16 17.2	−58.7	172.9	15 17.7	−58.8	172.9	14 18.1	−58.7	172.9	13 18.6	−58.8	173.0	12 19.1	−58.9	173.0	55
56	18 17.2	−58.7	173.0	17 17.6	−58.7	173.0	16 18.1	−58.7	173.0	15 18.5	−58.7	173.1	14 18.9	−58.7	173.1	13 19.4	−58.8	173.1	12 19.8	−58.8	173.2	11 20.2	−58.8	173.2	56
57	17 18.5	−58.6	173.2	16 18.9	−58.6	173.2	15 19.4	−58.8	173.3	14 19.8	−58.8	173.3	13 20.2	−58.8	173.3	12 20.6	−58.8	173.3	11 21.0	−58.8	173.4	10 21.4	−58.8	173.4	57
58	16 19.9	−58.7	173.4	15 20.3	−58.7	173.4	14 20.6	−58.7	173.5	13 21.0	−58.7	173.5	12 21.4	−58.8	173.5	11 21.8	−58.8	173.5	10 22.2	−58.8	173.6	9 22.6	−58.9	173.6	58
59	15 21.2	−58.7	173.6	14 21.6	−58.8	173.7	13 21.9	−58.7	173.7	12 22.3	−58.8	173.7	11 22.6	−58.7	173.7	10 23.0	−58.8	173.8	9 23.4	−58.9	173.8	8 23.7	−58.8	173.8	59
60	14 22.5	−58.7	173.8	13 22.8	−58.7	173.9	12 23.2	−58.8	173.9	11 23.5	−58.8	173.9	10 23.9	−58.8	173.9	9 24.2	−58.8	174.0	8 24.5	−58.8	174.0	7 24.9	−58.9	174.0	60
61	13 23.8	−58.7	174.1	12 24.1	−58.7	174.1	11 24.4	−58.7	174.1	10 24.7	−58.7	174.1	9 25.1	−58.8	174.1	8 25.4	−58.8	174.2	7 25.7	−58.9	174.2	6 26.0	−58.9	174.2	61
62	12 25.1	−58.7	174.3	11 25.4	−58.8	174.3	10 25.7	−58.8	174.3	9 26.0	−58.8	174.3	8 26.3	−58.8	174.3	7 26.6	−58.9	174.4	6 26.8	−58.8	174.4	5 27.1	−58.8	174.4	62
63	11 26.4	−58.8	174.5	10 26.6	−58.7	174.5	9 26.9	−58.8	174.5	8 27.2	−58.8	174.5	7 27.5	−58.9	174.5	6 27.7	−58.8	174.5	5 28.0	−58.9	174.6	4 28.3	−58.9	174.6	63
64	10 27.6	−58.7	174.7	9 27.9	−58.8	174.7	8 28.1	−58.7	174.7	7 28.4	−58.8	174.7	6 28.6	−58.8	174.7	5 28.9	−58.8	174.7	4 29.1	−58.8	174.8	3 29.4	−58.9	174.8	64
65	9 28.9	−58.8	174.9	8 29.1	−58.7	174.9	7 29.4	−58.8	174.9	6 29.6	−58.8	174.9	5 29.8	−58.8	174.9	4 30.1	−58.9	174.9	3 30.3	−58.9	174.9	2 30.5	−58.8	175.0	65
66	8 30.1	−58.7	175.1	7 30.4	−58.8	175.1	6 30.6	−58.8	175.1	5 30.8	−58.8	175.1	4 31.0	−58.8	175.1	3 31.2	−58.8	175.1	2 31.4	−58.8	175.1	1 31.7	−58.9	175.1	66
67	7 31.4	−58.8	175.3	6 31.6	−58.8	175.3	5 31.8	−58.8	175.3	4 32.0	−58.8	175.3	3 32.2	−58.8	175.3	2 32.4	−58.9	175.3	1 32.6	−58.9	175.3	0 32.8	−58.9	175.3	67
68	6 32.6	−58.7	175.5	5 32.8	−58.8	175.5	4 33.0	−58.8	175.5	3 33.2	−58.8	175.5	2 33.4	−58.9	175.5	1 33.5	−58.8	175.5	0 33.7	−58.8	175.5	0 26.1	+58.9	4.5	68
69	5 33.9	−58.8	175.7	4 34.0	−58.8	175.7	3 34.2	−58.8	175.7	2 34.4	−58.8	175.7	1 34.5	−58.8	175.7	0 34.7	−58.8	175.7	0 25.1	+58.9	4.3	1 25.0	+58.8	4.3	69
70	4 35.1	−58.8	175.9	3 35.2	−58.7	175.9	2 35.4	−58.8	175.9	1 35.6	−58.9	175.9	0 35.7	−58.8	175.9	0 24.1	+58.9	4.1	1 24.0	+58.9	4.1	2 23.8	+58.9	4.1	70
71	3 36.3	−58.8	176.1	2 36.5	−58.8	176.1	1 36.6	−58.8	176.1	0 36.7	−58.8	176.1	0 23.1	+58.9	3.9	1 23.0	+58.8	3.9	2 22.9	+58.8	3.9	3 22.7	+58.9	3.9	71
72	2 37.5	−58.7	176.3	1 37.7	−58.8	176.3	0 37.8	−58.8	176.3	0 22.1	+58.8	3.7	1 22.0	+58.9	3.7	2 21.8	+58.9	3.7	3 21.7	+58.9	3.7	4 21.6	+58.9	3.7	72
73	1 38.8	−58.8	176.5	0 38.9	−58.8	176.5	0 21.0	+58.8	3.5	1 20.9	+58.8	3.5	2 20.8	+58.8	3.5	3 20.7	+58.8	3.5	4 20.6	+58.8	3.5	5 20.4	+58.9	3.5	73
74	0 40.0	−58.8	176.7	0 19.9	+58.8	3.3	1 19.8	+58.8	3.3	2 19.7	+58.8	3.3	3 19.6	+58.8	3.3	4 19.5	+58.8	3.3	5 19.4	+58.9	3.3	6 19.3	+58.9	3.3	74
75	0 18.8	+58.8	3.1	1 18.7	+58.8	3.1	2 18.6	+58.8	3.1	3 18.5	+58.8	3.1	4 18.4	+58.9	3.1	5 18.3	+58.9	3.1	6 18.3	+58.8	3.1	7 18.2	+58.8	3.1	75
76	1 17.6	+58.7	2.9	2 17.5	+58.8	2.9	3 17.4	+58.8	2.9	4 17.3	+58.8	2.9	5 17.3	+58.8	2.9	6 17.2	+58.8	2.9	7 17.1	+58.8	2.9	8 17.0	+58.9	2.9	76
77	2 16.3	+58.8	2.7	3 16.3	+58.8	2.7	4 16.2	+58.8	2.7	5 16.1	+58.8	2.7	6 16.1	+58.8	2.7	7 16.0	+58.8	2.7	8 15.9	+58.9	2.7	9 15.9	+58.8	2.7	77
78	3 15.1	+58.8	2.5	4 15.1	+58.7	2.5	5 15.0	+58.8	2.5	6 14.9	+58.8	2.5	7 14.9	+58.8	2.5	8 14.8	+58.8	2.5	9 14.8	+58.8	2.5	10 14.7	+58.8	2.5	78
79	4 13.9	+58.8	2.3	5 13.8	+58.8	2.3	6 13.8	+58.8	2.3	7 13.7	+58.8	2.3	8 13.7	+58.8	2.3	9 13.6	+58.9	2.3	10 13.6	+58.8	2.3	11 13.5	+58.9	2.3	79
80	5 12.7	+58.7	2.1	6 12.6	+58.8	2.1	7 12.6	+58.8	2.1	8 12.5	+58.8	2.1	9 12.5	+58.8	2.1	10 12.5	+58.8	2.1	11 12.4	+58.8	2.1	12 12.4	+58.8	2.1	80
81	6 11.4	+58.8	1.9	7 11.4	+58.8	1.9	8 11.4	+58.7	1.9	9 11.3	+58.8	1.9	10 11.3	+58.8	1.9	11 11.3	+58.7	1.9	12 11.2	+58.8	1.9	13 11.2	+58.8	1.9	81
82	7 10.2	+58.7	1.7	8 10.2	+58.7	1.7	9 10.1	+58.8	1.7	10 10.1	+58.8	1.7	11 10.1	+58.8	1.7	12 10.0	+58.8	1.7	13 10.0	+58.8	1.7	14 10.0	+58.8	1.7	82
83	8 08.9	+58.8	1.5	9 08.9	+58.8	1.5	10 08.9	+58.8	1.5	11 08.9	+58.7	1.5	12 08.9	+58.7	1.5	13 08.8	+58.8	1.5	14 08.8	+58.8	1.5	15 08.8	+58.8	1.5	83
84	9 07.7	+58.7	1.3	10 07.7	+58.7	1.3	11 07.7	+58.7	1.3	12 07.6	+58.8	1.3	13 07.6	+58.8	1.3	14 07.6	+58.8	1.3	15 07.6	+58.8	1.3	16 07.6	+58.7	1.3	84
85	10 06.4	+58.8	1.1	11 06.4	+58.8	1.1	12 06.4	+58.7	1.1	13 06.4	+58.7	1.1	14 06.4	+58.7	1.1	15 06.4	+58.7	1.1	16 06.4	+58.7	1.1	17 06.3	+58.8	1.1	85
86	11 05.2	+58.7	0.8	12 05.2	+58.7	0.8	13 05.1	+58.8	0.9	14 05.1	+58.8	0.9	15 05.1	+58.8	0.9	16 05.1	+58.8	0.9	17 05.1	+58.8	0.9	18 05.1	+58.8	0.9	86
87	12 03.9	+58.7	0.6	13 03.9	+58.7	0.6	14 03.9	+58.7	0.6	15 03.9	+58.7	0.6	16 03.9	+58.7	0.6	17 03.9	+58.7	0.7	18 03.9	+58.7	0.7	19 03.9	+58.7	0.7	87
88	13 02.6	+58.7	0.4	14 02.6	+58.7	0.4	15 02.6	+58.7	0.4	16 02.6	+58.7	0.4	17 02.6	+58.7	0.4	18 02.6	+58.7	0.4	19 02.6	+58.7	0.4	20 02.6	+58.7	0.4	88
89	14 01.3	+58.7	0.2	15 01.3	+58.7	0.2	16 01.3	+58.7	0.2	17 01.3	+58.7	0.2	18 01.3	+58.7	0.2	19 01.3	+58.7	0.2	20 01.3	+58.7	0.2	21 01.3	+58.7	0.2	89
90	15 00.0	+58.7	0.0	16 00.0	+58.7	0.0	17 00.0	+58.7	0.0	18 00.0	+58.7	0.0	19 00.0	+58.7	0.0	20 00.0	+58.7	0.0	21 00.0	+58.7	0.0	22 00.0	+58.7	0.0	90
	15°			16°			17°			18°			19°			20°			21°			22°			

S. Lat. {L.H.A. greater than 180° ....Zn=180°−Z
{L.H.A. less than 180°...........Zn=180°+Z

LATITUDE SAME NAME AS DECLINATION — L.H.A. 168°, 192°

N. Lat. {L.H.A. greater than 180° .....Zn=Z
{L.H.A. less than 180°............Zn=360°-Z

Dec.	15°			16°			17°			18°			19°			20°			21°			22°			Dec.
	Hc	d	Z	Hc	d	Z	Hc	d	Z	Hc	d	Z	Hc	d	Z	Hc	d	Z	Hc	d	Z	Hc	d	Z	
°	° ′	′	°	° ′	′	°	° ′	′	°	° ′	′	°	° ′	′	°	° ′	′	°	° ′	′	°	° ′	′	°	°
0	70 14.9	+45.4	138.3	69 29.5	+46.7	140.1	68 43.0	+47.8	141.7	67 55.4	+48.9	143.2	67 06.9	+49.8	144.7	66 17.5	+50.7	146.0	65 27.4	+51.5	147.2	64 36.7	+52.1	148.4	0
1	71 00.3	+43.9	136.3	70 16.2	+45.4	138.2	69 30.8	+46.8	140.0	68 44.3	+47.9	141.7	67 56.7	+49.0	143.2	67 08.2	+50.0	144.6	66 18.9	+50.8	146.0	65 28.8	+51.6	147.2	1
2	71 44.2	+42.5	134.2	71 01.6	+44.1	136.3	70 17.6	+45.6	138.2	69 32.2	+47.0	140.0	68 45.7	+48.1	141.6	67 58.2	+49.1	143.2	67 09.7	+50.1	144.6	66 20.4	+50.9	145.9	2
3	72 26.7	+40.7	131.9	71 45.7	+42.6	134.1	71 03.2	+44.2	136.2	70 19.2	+45.7	138.2	69 33.8	+47.1	140.0	68 47.3	+48.2	141.6	67 59.8	+49.3	143.2	67 11.3	+50.2	144.6	3
4	73 07.4	+38.8•	129.4	72 28.3	+40.9	131.8	71 47.4	+42.8	134.1	71 04.9	+44.4	136.2	70 20.9	+45.8	138.1	69 35.5	+47.2	139.9	68 49.1	+48.3	141.6	68 01.5	+49.4	143.2	4
5	73 46.2	+36.6•	126.7	73 09.2	+38.9•	129.4	72 30.2	+41.0	131.8	71 49.3	+42.9	134.1	71 06.7	+44.6	136.2	70 22.7	+46.0	138.1	69 37.4	+47.3	139.9	68 50.9	+48.5	141.6	5
6	74 22.8	+34.2•	123.8	73 48.1	+36.8•	126.7	73 11.2	+39.1•	129.3	72 32.2	+41.2	131.8	71 51.3	+43.0	134.1	71 08.7	+44.7	136.2	70 24.7	+46.2	138.1	69 39.4	+47.5	139.9	6
7	74 57.0	+31.4•	120.7	74 24.9	+34.4•	123.8	73 50.3	+37.0•	126.7	73 13.4	+39.2•	129.3	72 34.3	+41.4	131.8	71 53.4	+43.3	134.1	71 10.9	+44.9	136.2	70 26.9	+46.3	138.2	7
8	75 28.4	+28.4•	117.4	74 59.3	+31.6•	120.7	74 27.3	+34.5•	123.8	73 52.6	+37.2•	126.7	73 15.7	+39.5•	129.3	72 36.7	+41.5	131.8	71 55.8	+43.4	134.1	71 13.2	+45.0	136.2	8
9	75 56.8	+25.1•	113.8	75 30.9	+28.6•	117.3	75 01.8	+31.8•	120.7	74 29.8	+34.7•	123.8	73 55.2	+37.3•	126.7	73 18.2	+39.7•	129.3	72 39.2	+41.7	131.8	71 58.2	+43.6	134.1	9
10	76 21.9	+21.3•	110.0	75 59.5	+25.2•	113.8	75 33.6	+28.8•	117.3	75 04.5	+32.0•	120.7	74 32.5	+34.9•	123.8	73 57.9	+37.5•	126.7	73 20.9	+39.8•	129.4	72 41.8	+41.9	131.9	10
11	76 43.2	+17.5•	106.0	76 24.7	+21.6•	110.0	76 02.4	+25.4•	113.8	75 36.5	+29.0•	117.3	75 07.4	+32.2•	120.7	74 35.4	+35.1•	123.8	74 00.7	+37.7•	126.7	73 23.7	+40.1•	129.4	11
12	77 00.7	+13.2•	101.8	76 46.3	+17.6•	105.9	76 27.8	+21.8•	109.9	76 05.5	+25.6•	113.7	75 39.6	+29.2•	117.3	75 10.5	+32.4•	120.7	74 38.4	+35.4•	123.8	74 03.8	+37.9•	126.7	12
13	77 13.9	+8.7•	97.4	77 03.9	+13.3•	101.7	76 49.6	+17.7•	105.9	76 31.1	+21.9•	109.9	76 08.8	+25.8•	113.7	75 42.9	+29.4•	117.3	75 13.8	+32.6•	120.7	74 41.7	+35.5•	123.9	13
14	77 22.6	+4.1•	92.9	77 17.2	+8.9•	97.3	77 07.3	+13.5•	101.7	76 53.0	+18.0•	105.9	76 34.6	+22.1•	109.9	76 12.3	+26.0•	113.7	75 46.4	+29.6•	117.4	75 17.2	+32.9•	120.8	14
15	77 26.7	-0.6•	88.3	77 26.1	+4.2•	92.8	77 20.8	+9.1•	97.3	77 11.0	+13.7•	101.6	76 56.7	+18.2•	105.9	76 38.3	+22.4•	109.9	76 16.0	+26.2•	113.8	75 50.1	+29.8•	117.4	15
16	77 26.1	-5.3•	83.7	77 30.3	-0.4•	88.2	77 29.9	+4.3•	92.7	77 24.7	+9.1•	97.2	77 14.9	+13.8•	101.6	77 00.7	+18.3•	105.8	76 42.2	+22.6•	109.9	76 19.9	+26.5•	113.8	16
17	77 20.8	-9.8•	79.1	77 29.9	-5.2•	83.6	77 34.2	-0.4•	88.1	77 33.8	+4.5•	92.6	77 28.7	+9.4•	97.1	77 19.0	+14.0•	101.5	77 04.8	+18.5•	105.8	76 46.4	+22.7•	109.9	17
18	77 11.0	-14.3•	74.7	77 24.7	-9.8•	79.0	77 33.8	-5.1•	83.4	77 38.3	-0.2•	88.0	77 38.1	+4.6•	92.5	77 33.0	+9.5•	97.1	77 23.3	+14.2•	101.5	77 09.1	+18.8•	105.8	18
19	76 56.7	-18.4•	70.3	77 14.9	-14.2•	74.5	77 28.7	-9.7•	78.8	77 38.1	-5.1•	83.3	77 42.7	-0.2•	87.9	77 42.5	+4.7•	92.5	77 37.5	+9.6•	97.0	77 27.9	+14.3•	101.5	19
20	76 38.3	-22.3•	66.2	77 00.7	-18.5•	70.1	77 19.0	-14.2•	74.3	77 33.0	-9.7•	78.7	77 42.5	-5.0•	83.2	77 47.2	-0.1•	87.8	77 47.1	+4.9•	92.4	77 42.2	+9.8•	97.0	20
21	76 16.0	-25.9•	62.2	76 42.2	-22.3•	65.9	77 04.8	-18.4•	69.9	77 23.3	-14.2•	74.1	77 37.5	-9.6•	78.5	77 47.1	-4.9•	83.0	77 52.0	0.0•	87.7	77 52.0	+5.0•	92.3	21
22	75 50.1	-29.2•	58.5	76 19.9	-26.0•	62.0	76 46.4	-22.4•	65.7	77 09.1	-18.4•	69.7	77 27.9	-14.2•	73.9	77 42.2	-9.6•	78.3	77 52.0	-4.8•	82.9	77 57.0	+0.1•	87.6	22
23	75 20.9	-32.2•	54.9	75 53.9	-29.2•	58.2	76 24.0	-26.0•	61.7	76 50.7	-22.4•	65.5	77 13.7	-18.5•	69.5	77 32.6	-14.2•	73.7	77 47.2	-9.6•	78.2	77 57.1	-4.8•	82.8	23
24	74 48.7	-34.8•	51.7	75 24.7	-32.2•	54.7	75 58.0	-29.3•	57.9	76 28.3	-26.0•	61.5	76 55.2	-22.4•	65.2	77 18.4	-18.4•	69.3	77 37.6	-14.2•	73.5	77 52.3	-9.5•	78.0	24
25	74 13.9	-37.1•	48.6	74 52.5	-34.9•	51.4	75 28.7	-32.2•	54.4	76 02.3	-29.4•	57.7	76 32.8	-26.1•	61.2	77 00.0	-22.5•	65.0	77 23.4	-18.5•	69.0	77 42.8	-14.2•	73.3	25
26	73 36.8	-39.3•	45.8	74 17.6	-37.2•	48.3	74 56.5	-35.0•	51.1	75 32.9	-32.3•	54.1	76 06.7	-29.4•	57.4	76 37.5	-26.2•	60.9	77 04.9	-22.6•	64.7	77 28.6	-18.6•	68.8	26
27	72 57.5	-41.2	43.1	73 40.4	-39.3•	45.5	74 21.5	-37.3•	48.0	75 00.6	-35.0•	50.8	75 37.3	-32.4•	53.8	76 11.3	-29.5•	57.1	76 42.3	-26.2•	60.6	77 10.0	-22.6•	64.5	27
28	72 16.3	-42.8	40.7	73 01.1	-41.3	42.8	73 44.2	-39.4•	45.2	74 25.6	-37.4•	47.7	75 04.9	-35.1•	50.5	75 41.8	-32.5•	53.5	76 16.1	-29.6•	56.8	76 47.4	-26.3•	60.4	28
29	71 33.5	-44.4	38.5	72 19.8	-42.9	40.4	73 04.8	-41.3	42.5	73 48.2	-39.5•	44.9	74 29.8	-37.5•	47.4	75 09.3	-35.2•	50.2	75 46.5	-32.6•	53.2	76 21.1	-29.7•	56.5	29
30	70 49.1	-45.6	36.4	71 36.9	-44.4	38.1	72 23.5	-43.0	40.1	73 08.7	-41.4	42.2	73 52.3	-39.6•	44.5	74 34.1	-37.6•	47.1	75 13.9	-35.3•	49.8	75 51.4	-32.7•	52.9	30
31	70 03.5	-46.8	34.4	70 52.5	-45.7	36.1	71 40.5	-44.5	37.8	72 27.3	-43.1	39.8	73 12.7	-41.5	41.9	73 56.5	-39.7•	44.2	74 38.6	-37.7•	46.7	75 18.7	-35.4•	49.5	31
32	69 16.7	-47.9	32.6	70 06.8	-46.9	34.1	70 56.0	-45.8	35.7	71 44.2	-44.6	37.5	72 31.2	-43.2	39.4	73 16.8	-41.6	41.5	74 00.9	-39.8•	43.8	74 43.3	-37.9•	46.4	32
33	68 28.8	-48.7	31.0	69 19.9	-47.9	32.3	70 10.2	-46.9	33.8	70 59.6	-45.8	35.4	71 48.0	-44.7	37.2	72 35.2	-43.3	39.1	73 21.1	-41.7	41.2	74 05.4	-39.9	43.5	33
34	67 40.1	-49.7	29.4	68 32.0	-48.8	30.6	69 23.3	-48.0	32.0	70 13.8	-47.1	33.5	71 03.3	-45.9	35.1	71 51.9	-44.7	36.8	72 39.4	-43.4	38.7	73 25.5	-41.8	40.8	34
35	66 50.4	-50.3	27.9	67 43.2	-49.7	29.1	68 35.3	-48.9	30.3	69 26.7	-48.1	31.7	70 17.4	-47.1	33.1	71 07.2	-46.1	34.7	71 56.0	-44.9	36.5	72 43.7	-43.5	38.4	35
36	66 00.1	-51.1	26.6	66 53.5	-50.5	27.6	67 46.4	-49.8	28.8	68 38.6	-49.0	30.0	69 30.3	-48.2	31.3	70 21.1	-47.2	32.8	71 11.1	-46.1	34.4	72 00.2	-45.0	36.1	36
37	65 09.0	-51.6	25.3	66 03.0	-51.1	26.3	66 56.6	-50.5	27.3	67 49.6	-49.8	28.4	68 42.1	-49.1	29.6	69 33.9	-48.2	31.0	70 25.0	-47.3	32.4	71 15.2	-46.3	34.0	37
38	64 17.4	-52.2	24.1	65 11.9	-51.7	25.0	66 06.1	-51.2	25.9	66 59.8	-50.5	27.0	67 53.0	-49.9	28.1	68 45.7	-49.2	29.3	69 37.7	-48.4	30.6	70 28.9	-47.4	32.0	38
39	63 25.2	-52.7	23.0	64 20.2	-52.2	23.8	65 14.9	-51.7	24.7	66 09.3	-51.3	25.6	67 03.1	-50.6	26.6	67 56.5	-50.0	27.7	68 49.3	-49.3	28.9	69 41.5	-48.5	30.2	39
40	62 32.5	-53.2	21.9	63 28.0	-52.8	22.7	64 23.2	-52.3	23.5	65 18.0	-51.8	24.4	66 12.5	-51.3	25.3	67 06.5	-50.7	26.3	68 00.0	-50.0	27.4	68 53.0	-49.3	28.6	40
41	61 39.3	-53.5	21.0	62 35.2	-53.1	21.6	63 30.9	-52.8	22.4	64 26.2	-52.4	23.2	65 21.2	-51.9	24.0	66 15.8	-51.4	24.9	67 10.0	-50.8	25.9	68 03.7	-50.2	27.0	41
42	60 45.8	-53.9	20.0	61 42.1	-53.6	20.6	62 38.1	-53.3	21.3	63 33.8	-52.8	22.1	64 29.3	-52.4	22.8	65 24.4	-52.0	23.7	66 19.2	-51.5	24.6	67 13.5	-50.9	25.6	42
43	59 51.9	-54.3	19.1	60 48.5	-54.0	19.7	61 44.8	-53.6	20.3	62 41.0	-53.3	21.0	63 36.9	-53.0	21.7	64 32.4	-52.5	22.5	65 27.7	-52.0	23.3	66 22.6	-51.5	24.2	43
44	58 57.6	-54.5	18.3	59 54.5	-54.3	18.8	60 51.2	-54.0	19.4	61 47.7	-53.7	20.0	62 43.9	-53.3	20.7	63 39.9	-52.9	21.4	64 35.7	-52.6	22.2	65 31.1	-52.2	23.0	44
45	58 03.1	-54.9	17.5	59 00.2	-54.6	18.0	59 57.2	-54.4	18.5	60 54.0	-54.1	19.1	61 50.6	-53.8	19.7	62 47.0	-53.5	20.4	63 43.1	-53.1	21.1	64 38.9	-52.6	21.8	45
46	57 08.2	-55.1	16.7	58 05.6	-54.9	17.2	59 02.8	-54.6	17.7	59 59.9	-54.4	18.2	60 56.8	-54.1	18.8	61 53.5	-53.8	19.4	62 50.0	-53.5	20.0	63 46.3	-53.1	20.7	46
47	56 13.1	-55.3	16.0	57 10.7	-55.1	16.4	58 08.2	-54.9	16.9	59 05.5	-54.7	17.4	60 02.7	-54.4	17.9	60 59.7	-54.1	18.4	61 56.5	-53.8	19.0	62 53.2	-53.6	19.7	47
48	55 17.8	-55.6	15.3	56 15.6	-55.4	15.7	57 13.3	-55.2	16.1	58 10.8	-54.9	16.6	59 08.3	-54.8	17.1	60 05.6	-54.5	17.6	61 02.7	-54.3	18.1	61 59.6	-53.9	18.7	48
49	54 22.2	-55.8	14.7	55 20.2	-55.6	15.0	56 18.1	-55.4	15.4	57 15.9	-55.3	15.8	58 13.5	-55.0	16.3	59 11.1	-54.8	16.7	60 08.4	-54.5	17.2	61 05.7	-54.3	17.8	49
50	53 26.4	-55.9	14.0	54 24.6	-55.8	14.4	55 22.7	-55.7	14.7	56 20.6	-55.4	15.1	57 18.5	-55.3	15.5	58 16.3	-55.1	16.0	59 13.9	-54.9	16.4	60 11.4	-54.7	16.9	50
51	52 30.5	-56.2	13.4	53 28.8	-56.0	13.8	54 27.0	-55.8	14.1	55 25.2	-55.7	14.4	56 23.2	-55.5	14.8	57 21.2	-55.3	15.2	58 19.0	-55.1	15.6	59 16.7	-54.9	16.1	51
52	51 34.3	-56.3	12.9	52 32.8	-56.2	13.2	53 31.2	-56.0	13.5	54 29.5	-55.9	13.8	55 27.7	-55.7	14.1	56 25.9	-55.6	14.5	57 23.9	-55.4	14.9	58 21.8	-55.2	15.3	52
53	50 38.0	-56.4	12.3	51 36.6	-56.3	12.6	52 35.2	-56.2	12.9	53 33.6	-56.0	13.2	54 32.0	-55.9	13.5	55 30.3	-55.8	13.8	56 28.5	-55.6	14.2	57 26.6	-55.4	14.6	53
54	49 41.6	-56.6	11.8	50 40.3	-56.5	12.0	51 39.0	-56.4	12.3	52 37.6	-56.3	12.6	53 36.1	-56.1	12.9	54 34.5	-55.9	13.2	55 32.9	-55.8	13.5	56 31.2	-55.6	13.9	54
55	48 45.0	-56.7	11.3	49 43.8	-56.6	11.5	50 42.6	-56.5	11.8	51 41.3	-56.4	12.0	52 40.0	-56.3	12.3	53 38.6	-56.2	12.6	54 37.1	-56.0	12.9	55 35.6	-55.9	13.2	55
56	47 48.3	-56.8	10.8	48 47.2	-56.7	11.0	49 46.1	-56.6	11.2	50 44.9	-56.5	11.5	51 43.7	-56.4	11.7	52 42.4	-56.3	12.0	53 41.1	-56.2	12.3	54 39.7	-56.1	12.6	56
57	46 51.5	-57.0	10.3	47 50.5	-56.9	10.5	48 49.5	-56.8	10.7	49 48.4	-56.7	10.9	50 47.3	-56.6	11.2	51 46.1	-56.4	11.4	52 44.9	-56.3	11.7	53 43.6	-56.2	12.0	57
58	45 54.5	-57.0	9.9	46 53.6	-56.9	10.0	47 52.7	-56.9	10.2	48 51.7	-56.8	10.4	49 50.7	-56.7	10.7	50 49.7	-56.7	10.9	51 48.6	-56.6	11.1	52 47.4	-56.4	11.4	58
59	44 57.5	-57.2	9.4	45 56.7	-57.1	9.6	46 55.8	-57.0	9.8	47 54.9	-56.9	10.0	48 54.0	-56.8	10.2	49 53.0	-56.7	10.4	50 52.0	-56.6	10.6	51 51.0	-56.6	10.8	59
60	44 00.3	-57.2	9.0	44 59.6	-57.2	9.2	45 58.8	-57.1	9.3	46 58.0	-57.0	9.5	47 57.2	-57.0	9.7	48 56.3	-56.9	9.9	49 55.4	-56.8	10.1	50 54.4	-56.6	10.3	60
61	43 03.1	-57.3	8.6	44 02.4	-57.3	8.7	45 01.7	-57.2	8.9	46 01.0	-57.2	9.0	47 00.2	-57.0	9.2	47 59.4	-57.0	9.4	48 58.6	-56.9	9.6	49 57.8	-56.9	9.8	61
62	42 05.8	-57.4	8.2	43 05.1	-57.3	8.3	44 04.5	-57.3	8.5	45 03.8	-57.2	8.6	46 03.2	-57.2	8.8	47 02.4	-57.1	8.9	48 01.7	-57.0	9.1	49 00.9	-56.9	9.3	62
63	41 08.4	-57.5	7.8	42 07.8	-57.4	7.9	43 07.2	-57.4	8.0	44 06.6	-57.3	8.2	45 06.0	-57.3	8.3	46 05.3	-57.1	8.5	47 04.7	-57.1	8.6	48 04.0	-57.1	8.8	63
64	40 10.9	-57.6	7.4	41 10.4	-57.5	7.5	42 09.8	-57.4	7.6	43 09.3	-57.4	7.8	44 08.7	-57.3	7.9	45 08.2	-57.3	8.0	46 07.6	-57.3	8.2	47 06.9	-57.1	8.3	64
65	39 13.3	-57.6	7.0	40 12.9	-57.6	7.2	41 12.4	-57.6	7.3	42 11.9	-57.5	7.4	43 11.4	-57.4	7.5	44 10.9	-57.4	7.6	45 10.3	-57.3	7.8	46 09.8	-57.3	7.9	65
66	38 15.7	-57.7	6.7	39 15.3	-57.7	6.8	40 14.8	-57.6	6.9	41 14.4	-57.5	7.0	42 14.0	-57.6	7.1	43 13.5	-57.5	7.2	44 13.0	-57.4	7.3	45 12.5	-57.4	7.5	66
67	37 18.0	-57.7	6.3	38 17.6	-57.7	6.4	39 17.2	-57.6	6.5	40 16.9	-57.7	6.6	41 16.4	-57.5	6.7	42 16.0	-57.5	6.8	43 15.6	-57.5	6.9	44 15.1	-57.4	7.0	67
68	36 20.3	-57.9	6.0	37 19.9	-57.7	6.1	38 19.6	-57.8	6.2	39 19.2	-57.7	6.3	40 18.9	-57.7	6.3	41 18.5	-57.6	6.4	42 18.1	-57.6	6.5	43 17.7	-57.5	6.6	68
69	35 22.4	-57.8	5.7	36 22.2	-57.9	5.7	37 21.8	-57.7	5.8	38 21.5	-57.7	5.9	39 21.2	-57.7	6.0	40 20.9	-57.7	6.1	41 20.5	-57.6	6.2	42 20.2	-57.6	6.3	69
70	34 24.6	-57.9	5.4	35 24.3	-57.8	5.4	36 24.1	-57.9	5.5	37 23.8	-57.8	5.6	38 23.5	-57.8	5.6	39 23.2	-57.7	5.7	40 22.9	-57.7	5.8	41 22.6	-57.7	5.9	70
71	33 26.7	-58.0	5.0	34 26.5	-58.0	5.1	35 26.2	-57.9	5.2	36 26.0	-57.9	5.2	37 25.7	-57.8	5.3	38 25.5	-57.8	5.4	39 25.2	-57.8	5.4	40 24.9	-57.7	5.5	71
72	32 28.7	-58.0	4.7	33 28.5	-57.9	4.8	34 28.3	-57.9	4.8	35 28.1	-57.9	4.9	36 27.9	-57.9	5.0	37 27.7	-57.9	5.0	38 27.4	-57.8	5.1	39 27.2	-57.8	5.2	72
73	31 30.7	-58.0	4.4	32 30.6	-58.1	4.5	33 30.4	-58.0	4.5	34 30.2	-58.0	4.6	35 30.0	-58.0	4.6	36 29.8	-57.9	4.7	37 29.6	-57.9	4.8	38 29.4	-57.9	4.8	73
74	30 32.7	-58.1	4.1	31 32.5	-58.0	4.2	32 32.4	-58.1	4.2	33 32.2	-58.0	4.3	34 32.0	-57.9	4.3	35 31.9	-58.0	4.4	36 31.7	-57.9	4.4	37 31.5	-57.9	4.5	74
75	29 34.6	-58.1	3.8	30 34.5	-58.1	3.9	31 34.3	-58.0	3.9	32 34.2	-58.1	4.0	33 34.1	-58.1	4.0	34 33.9	-58.0	4.1	35 33.8	-58.0	4.1	36 33.6	-58.0	4.2	75
76	28 36.5	-58.1	3.6	29 36.4	-58.1	3.6	30 36.3	-58.1	3.6	31 36.1	-58.0	3.7	32 36.0	-58.1	3.7	33 35.9	-58.1	3.7	34 35.8	-58.1	3.8	35 35.6	-58.0	3.8	76
77	27 38.4	-58.2	3.3	28 38.3	-58.2	3.3	29 38.2	-58.2	3.3	30 38.1	-58.2	3.4	31 37.9	-58.1	3.4	32 37.8	-58.1	3.4	33 37.7	-58.1	3.5	34 37.6	-58.0	3.5	77
78	26 40.2	-58.2	3.0	27 40.1	-58.2	3.0	28 40.0	-58.2	3.1	29 39.9	-58.2	3.1	30 39.8	-58.1	3.1	31 39.7	-58.1	3.1	32 39.6	-58.1	3.2	33 39.6	-58.2	3.2	78
79	25 42.0	-58.3	2.7	26 41.9	-58.2	2.8	27 41.8	-58.2	2.8	28 41.7	-58.2	2.8	29 41.7	-58.2	2.8	30 41.6	-58.2	2.9	31 41.5	-58.1	2.9	32 41.4	-58.1	2.9	79
80	24 43.7	-58.3	2.5	25 43.7	-58.3	2.5	26 43.6	-58.3	2.5	27 43.5	-58.2	2.5	28 43.5	-58.2	2.6	29 43.4	-58.2	2.6	30 43.4	-58.2	2.6	31 43.3	-58.2	2.6	80
81	23 45.4	-58.3	2.2	24 45.4	-58.3	2.2	25 45.3	-58.2	2.2	26 45.3	-58.3	2.3	27 45.3	-58.3	2.3	28 45.2	-58.2	2.3	29 45.2	-58.3	2.3	30 45.1	-58.2	2.3	81
82	22 47.1	-58.3	1.9	23 47.1	-58.3	2.0	24 47.1	-58.3	2.0	25 47.0	-58.3	2.0	26 47.0	-58.3	2.0	27 47.0	-58.3	2.0	28 46.9	-58.2	2.0	29 46.9	-58.3	2.1	82
83	21 48.8	-58.3	1.7	22 48.8	-58.3	1.7	23 48.8	-58.4	1.7	24 48.7	-58.3	1.7	25 48.7	-58.3	1.7	26 48.7	-58.3	1.8	27 48.7	-58.3	1.8	28 48.6	-58.3	1.8	83
84	20 50.5	-58.4	1.4	21 50.5	-58.4	1.5	22 50.4	-58.3	1.5	23 50.4	-58.3	1.5	24 50.4	-58.3	1.5	25 50.4	-58.4	1.5	26 50.4	-58.4	1.5	27 50.3	-58.3	1.5	84
85	19 52.1	-58.4	1.2	20 52.1	-58.4	1.2	21 52.1	-58.4	1.2	22 52.1	-58.4	1.2	23 52.1	-58.4	1.2	24 52.0	-58.3	1.2	25 52.0	-58.3	1.2	26 52.0	-58.3	1.3	85
86	18 53.7	-58.4	1.0	19 53.7	-58.4	1.0	20 53.7	-58.4	1.0	21 53.7	-58.4	1.0	22 53.7	-58.4	1.0	23 53.7	-58.4	1.0	24 53.7	-58.4	1.0	25 53.7	-58.4	1.0	86
87	17 55.3	-58.4	0.7	18 55.3	-58.4	0.7	19 55.3	-58.4	0.7	20 55.3	-58.4	0.7	21 55.3	-58.4	0.7	22 55.3	-58.4	0.7	23 55.3	-58.4	0.7	24 55.3	-58.4	0.7	87
88	16 56.9	-58.4	0.5	17 56.9	-58.4	0.5	18 56.9	-58.4	0.5	19 56.9	-58.4	0.5	20 56.9	-58.4	0.5	21 56.9	-58.4	0.5	22 56.9	-58.4	0.5	23 56.9	-58.4	0.5	88
89	15 58.5	-58.5	0.2	16 58.5	-58.5	0.2	17 58.5	-58.5	0.2	18 58.5	-58.5	0.2	19 58.5	-58.5	0.2	20 58.5	-58.5	0.2	21 58.5	-58.5	0.2	22 58.5	-58.5	0.2	89
90	15 00.0	-58.5	0.0	16 00.0	-58.5	0.0	17 00.0	-58.5	0.0	18 00.0	-58.5	0.0	19 00.0	-58.5	0.0	20 00.0	-58.5	0.0	21 00.0	-58.5	0.0	22 00.0	-58.5	0.0	90
	15°			16°			17°			18°			19°			20°			21°			22°			

LATITUDE CONTRARY NAME TO DECLINATION L.H.A. 13°, 347°

Dec.	15° Hc	d	Z	16° Hc	d	Z	17° Hc	d	Z	18° Hc	d	Z
°	° ′	′	°	° ′	′	°	° ′	′	°	° ′	′	°
0	70 14.9	-46.5	138.3	69 29.5	-47.7	140.1	68 43.0	-48.8	141.7	67 55.4	-49.7	143.2
1	69 28.4	-47.6	140.1	68 41.8	-48.7	141.8	67 54.2	-49.6	143.3	67 05.7	-50.5	144.7
2	68 40.8	-48.6	141.8	67 53.1	-49.5	143.3	67 04.6	-50.4	144.7	66 15.2	-51.2	146.1
3	67 52.2	-49.4	143.4	67 03.6	-50.3	144.8	66 14.2	-51.1	146.1	65 24.0	-51.7	147.3
4	67 02.8	-50.2	144.9	66 13.3	-50.9	146.2	65 23.1	-51.6	147.4	64 32.3	-52.3	148.5
5	66 12.6	-50.9	146.3	65 22.4	-51.6	147.5	64 31.5	-52.3	148.6	63 40.0	-52.8	149.7
6	65 21.7	-51.5	147.5	64 30.8	-52.2	148.7	63 39.2	-52.7	149.7	62 47.2	-53.3	150.7
7	64 30.2	-52.1	148.8	63 38.6	-52.6	149.8	62 46.5	-53.2	150.8	61 53.9	-53.6	151.7
8	63 38.1	-52.5	149.9	62 46.0	-53.1	150.9	61 53.3	-53.5	151.8	61 00.3	-54.1	152.6
9	62 45.6	-53.1	151.0	61 52.9	-53.5	151.9	60 59.8	-54.0	152.7	60 06.2	-54.3	153.5
10	61 52.5	-53.4	152.0	60 59.4	-53.9	152.8	60 05.8	-54.3	153.6	59 11.9	-54.7	154.4
11	60 59.1	-53.8	152.9	60 05.5	-54.2	153.7	59 11.5	-54.6	154.5	58 17.2	-54.9	155.2
12	60 05.3	-54.2	153.8	59 11.3	-54.6	154.6	58 16.9	-54.9	155.3	57 22.3	-55.2	155.9
13	59 11.1	-54.5	154.7	58 16.7	-54.8	155.4	57 22.0	-55.1	156.0	56 27.1	-55.5	156.6
14	58 16.6	-54.8	155.5	57 21.9	-55.1	156.1	56 26.9	-55.4	156.7	55 31.6	-55.6	157.3
15	57 21.8	-55.0	156.2	56 26.8	-55.3	156.9	55 31.5	-55.6	157.4	54 36.0	-55.9	158.0
16	56 26.8	-55.3	157.0	55 31.5	-55.6	157.5	54 35.9	-55.8	158.1	53 40.1	-56.0	158.6
17	55 31.5	-55.5	157.7	54 35.9	-55.8	158.2	53 40.1	-56.0	158.7	52 44.1	-56.2	159.2
18	54 36.0	-55.7	158.3	53 40.1	-55.9	158.8	52 44.1	-56.2	159.3	51 47.9	-56.4	159.8
19	53 40.3	-55.9	159.0	52 44.2	-56.2	159.4	51 47.9	-56.3	159.9	50 51.5	-56.5	160.3
20	52 44.4	-56.1	159.6	51 48.0	-56.2	160.0	50 51.6	-56.5	160.4	49 55.0	-56.7	160.8
21	51 48.3	-56.3	160.1	50 51.8	-56.5	160.6	49 55.1	-56.6	161.0	48 58.3	-56.8	161.3
22	50 52.0	-56.4	160.7	49 55.3	-56.6	161.1	48 58.5	-56.8	161.5	48 01.5	-56.9	161.8
23	49 55.6	-56.5	161.2	48 58.7	-56.7	161.6	48 01.7	-56.8	162.0	47 04.6	-57.0	162.3
24	48 59.1	-56.7	161.8	48 02.0	-56.8	162.1	47 04.9	-57.0	162.4	46 07.6	-57.1	162.8
25	48 02.4	-56.8	162.2	47 05.2	-57.0	162.6	46 07.9	-57.1	162.9	45 10.5	-57.2	163.2
26	47 05.6	-56.9	162.7	46 08.2	-57.0	163.0	45 10.8	-57.2	163.3	44 13.3	-57.3	163.6
27	46 08.7	-57.1	163.2	45 11.2	-57.2	163.5	44 13.6	-57.3	163.8	43 16.0	-57.4	164.0
28	45 11.6	-57.1	163.6	44 14.0	-57.2	163.9	43 16.3	-57.3	164.2	42 18.6	-57.5	164.4
29	44 14.5	-57.2	164.1	43 16.8	-57.4	164.3	42 19.0	-57.5	164.6	41 21.1	-57.5	164.8
30	43 17.3	-57.3	164.5	42 19.4	-57.4	164.7	41 21.5	-57.5	165.0	40 23.6	-57.7	165.2
31	42 20.0	-57.4	164.9	41 22.0	-57.5	165.1	40 24.0	-57.6	165.3	39 25.9	-57.7	165.5
32	41 22.6	-57.5	165.3	40 24.5	-57.5	165.5	39 26.4	-57.6	165.7	38 28.2	-57.7	165.9
33	40 25.1	-57.5	165.7	39 27.0	-57.7	165.9	38 28.8	-57.8	166.1	37 30.5	-57.8	166.2
34	39 27.6	-57.6	166.0	38 29.3	-57.7	166.2	37 31.0	-57.7	166.4	36 32.7	-57.9	166.6
35	38 30.0	-57.7	166.4	37 31.6	-57.7	166.6	36 33.3	-57.9	166.7	35 34.8	-57.9	166.9
36	37 32.3	-57.7	166.7	36 33.9	-57.8	166.9	35 35.4	-57.9	167.1	34 36.9	-57.9	167.2
37	36 34.6	-57.8	167.1	35 36.1	-57.9	167.2	34 37.5	-57.9	167.4	33 39.0	-58.0	167.5
38	35 36.8	-57.9	167.4	34 38.2	-57.9	167.6	33 39.6	-58.0	167.7	32 41.0	-58.1	167.8
39	34 38.9	-57.9	167.7	33 40.3	-58.0	167.9	32 41.6	-58.0	168.0	31 42.9	-58.1	168.1
40	33 41.0	-57.9	168.0	32 42.3	-58.0	168.2	31 43.6	-58.1	168.3	30 44.8	-58.1	168.4
41	32 43.1	-58.0	168.4	31 44.3	-58.0	168.5	30 45.5	-58.1	168.6	29 46.7	-58.2	168.7
42	31 45.1	-58.0	168.7	30 46.3	-58.1	168.8	29 47.4	-58.1	168.9	28 48.5	-58.2	169.0
43	30 47.1	-58.1	169.0	29 48.2	-58.1	169.1	28 49.3	-58.2	169.2	27 50.3	-58.2	169.3
44	29 49.0	-58.1	169.3	28 50.1	-58.2	169.4	27 51.1	-58.2	169.5	26 52.1	-58.3	169.5
45	28 50.9	-58.1	169.5	27 51.9	-58.2	169.6	26 52.9	-58.3	169.7	25 53.8	-58.3	169.8
46	27 52.8	-58.2	169.8	26 53.7	-58.2	169.9	25 54.6	-58.3	170.0	24 55.5	-58.3	170.1
47	26 54.6	-58.2	170.1	25 55.5	-58.3	170.2	24 56.3	-58.3	170.3	23 57.2	-58.3	170.3
48	25 56.4	-58.3	170.4	24 57.2	-58.3	170.4	23 58.0	-58.3	170.5	22 58.9	-58.4	170.6
49	24 58.1	-58.2	170.6	23 58.9	-58.3	170.7	22 59.7	-58.3	170.8	22 00.5	-58.4	170.8
50	23 59.9	-58.3	170.9	23 00.6	-58.3	171.0	22 01.4	-58.4	171.0	21 02.1	-58.4	171.1
51	23 01.6	-58.3	171.2	22 02.3	-58.4	171.2	21 03.0	-58.4	171.3	20 03.7	-58.4	171.3
52	22 03.3	-58.4	171.4	21 03.9	-58.3	171.5	20 04.6	-58.4	171.5	19 05.3	-58.5	171.6
53	21 04.9	-58.3	171.7	20 05.6	-58.4	171.7	19 06.2	-58.4	171.8	18 06.8	-58.5	171.8
54	20 06.6	-58.4	171.9	19 07.2	-58.4	172.0	18 07.8	-58.5	172.0	17 08.3	-58.4	172.0
55	19 08.2	-58.4	172.2	18 08.8	-58.5	172.2	17 09.3	-58.5	172.2	16 09.9	-58.5	172.3
56	18 09.8	-58.4	172.4	17 10.3	-58.4	172.4	16 10.8	-58.4	172.5	15 11.4	-58.6	172.5
57	17 11.4	-58.5	172.6	16 11.9	-58.5	172.7	15 12.4	-58.5	172.7	14 12.8	-58.5	172.7
58	16 12.9	-58.4	172.9	15 13.4	-58.5	172.9	14 13.9	-58.6	172.9	13 14.3	-58.5	173.0
59	15 14.5	-58.5	173.1	14 14.9	-58.5	173.1	13 15.3	-58.5	173.2	12 15.8	-58.6	173.2
60	14 16.0	-58.5	173.3	13 16.4	-58.5	173.4	12 16.8	-58.5	173.4	11 17.2	-58.5	173.4
61	13 17.5	-58.5	173.6	12 17.9	-58.5	173.6	11 18.3	-58.6	173.6	10 18.7	-58.6	173.6
62	12 19.0	-58.5	173.8	11 19.4	-58.5	173.8	10 19.7	-58.5	173.8	9 20.1	-58.6	173.9
63	11 20.5	-58.5	174.0	10 20.9	-58.6	174.0	9 21.2	-58.6	174.1	8 21.5	-58.6	174.1
64	10 22.0	-58.5	174.2	9 22.3	-58.5	174.3	8 22.6	-58.5	174.3	7 22.9	-58.6	174.3
65	9 23.5	-58.5	174.5	8 23.8	-58.6	174.5	7 24.1	-58.6	174.5	6 24.3	-58.6	174.5
66	8 25.0	-58.6	174.7	7 25.2	-58.5	174.7	6 25.5	-58.6	174.7	5 25.7	-58.6	174.7
67	7 26.4	-58.5	174.9	6 26.7	-58.6	174.9	5 26.9	-58.6	174.9	4 27.1	-58.6	174.9
68	6 27.9	-58.6	175.1	5 28.1	-58.6	175.1	4 28.3	-58.6	175.2	3 28.5	-58.6	175.2
69	5 29.3	-58.5	175.4	4 29.5	-58.5	175.4	3 29.7	-58.6	175.4	2 29.9	-58.6	175.4
70	4 30.8	-58.6	175.6	3 31.0	-58.6	175.6	2 31.1	-58.5	175.6	1 31.3	-58.6	175.6
71	3 32.2	-58.5	175.8	2 32.4	-58.6	175.8	1 32.6	-58.6	175.8	0 32.7	-58.6	175.8
72	2 33.7	-58.6	176.0	1 33.8	-58.6	176.0	0 34.0	-58.6	176.0	0 25.9	+58.6	4.0
73	1 35.1	-58.6	176.2	0 35.2	-58.5	176.2	0 24.6	+58.6	3.8	1 24.5	+58.6	3.8
74	0 36.5	-58.5	176.4	0 23.3	+58.6	3.6	1 23.2	+58.6	3.6	2 23.1	+58.6	3.6
75	0 22.0	+58.6	3.3	1 21.9	+58.6	3.3	2 21.8	+58.6	3.3	3 21.7	+58.6	3.3
76	1 20.6	+58.6	3.1	2 20.5	+58.6	3.1	3 20.4	+58.6	3.1	4 20.3	+58.6	3.1
77	2 19.2	+58.5	2.9	3 19.1	+58.6	2.9	4 19.0	+58.6	2.9	5 18.9	+58.6	2.9
78	3 17.7	+58.6	2.7	4 17.7	+58.5	2.7	5 17.6	+58.6	2.7	6 17.5	+58.6	2.7
79	4 16.3	+58.5	2.5	5 16.2	+58.6	2.5	6 16.2	+58.5	2.5	7 16.1	+58.6	2.5
80	5 14.8	+58.6	2.2	6 14.8	+58.6	2.3	7 14.7	+58.6	2.3	8 14.7	+58.6	2.3
81	6 13.4	+58.5	2.0	7 13.4	+58.5	2.0	8 13.3	+58.6	2.0	9 13.3	+58.5	2.0
82	7 11.9	+58.6	1.8	8 11.9	+58.6	1.8	9 11.9	+58.5	1.8	10 11.8	+58.6	1.8
83	8 10.5	+58.5	1.6	9 10.5	+58.5	1.6	10 10.4	+58.6	1.6	11 10.4	+58.6	1.6
84	9 09.0	+58.5	1.4	10 09.0	+58.5	1.4	11 09.0	+58.5	1.4	12 09.0	+58.5	1.4
85	10 07.5	+58.5	1.1	11 07.5	+58.5	1.1	12 07.5	+58.5	1.1	13 07.5	+58.5	1.2
86	11 06.0	+58.6	0.9	12 06.0	+58.5	0.9	13 06.0	+58.5	0.9	14 06.0	+58.5	0.9
87	12 04.6	+58.4	0.7	13 04.5	+58.5	0.7	14 04.5	+58.5	0.7	15 04.5	+58.5	0.7
88	13 03.0	+58.5	0.5	14 03.0	+58.5	0.5	15 03.0	+58.5	0.5	16 03.0	+58.5	0.5
89	14 01.5	+58.5	0.2	15 01.5	+58.5	0.2	16 01.5	+58.5	0.2	17 01.5	+58.5	0.2
90	15 00.0	+58.5	0.0	16 00.0	+58.5	0.0	17 00.0	+58.5	0.0	18 00.0	+58.5	0.0
	15°			16°			17°			18°		

Dec.	19° Hc	d	Z	20° Hc	d	Z	21° Hc	d	Z	22° Hc	d	Z	Dec.
°	° ′	′	°	° ′	′	°	° ′	′	°	° ′	′	°	°
0	67 06.9	-50.6	144.7	66 17.5	-51.3	146.0	65 27.4	-52.0	147.2	64 36.7	-52.7	148.4	0
1	66 16.3	-51.3	146.0	65 26.2	-52.0	147.3	64 35.4	-52.6	148.4	63 44.0	-53.1	149.5	1
2	65 25.0	-51.8	147.3	64 34.2	-52.5	148.4	63 42.8	-53.0	149.5	62 50.9	-53.6	150.5	2
3	64 33.2	-52.4	148.5	63 41.7	-52.9	149.5	62 49.8	-53.5	150.5	61 57.3	-54.0	151.5	3
4	63 40.8	-52.9	149.6	62 48.8	-53.4	150.6	61 56.3	-53.9	151.5	61 03.3	-54.3	152.4	4
5	62 47.9	-53.3	150.6	61 55.4	-53.8	151.6	61 02.4	-54.2	152.4	60 09.0	-54.6	153.2	5
6	61 54.6	-53.7	151.6	61 01.6	-54.2	152.5	60 08.2	-54.6	153.3	59 14.4	-54.9	154.1	6
7	61 00.9	-54.1	152.6	60 07.4	-54.5	153.4	59 13.6	-54.9	154.1	58 19.5	-55.2	154.8	7
8	60 06.8	-54.4	153.4	59 12.9	-54.8	154.2	58 18.7	-55.1	154.9	57 24.3	-55.5	155.6	8
9	59 12.4	-54.8	154.3	58 18.1	-55.0	155.0	57 23.6	-55.4	155.6	56 28.8	-55.6	156.3	9
10	58 17.6	-55.0	155.1	57 23.1	-55.3	155.7	56 28.2	-55.6	156.4	55 33.2	-55.9	156.9	10
11	57 22.6	-55.2	155.8	56 27.8	-55.6	156.4	55 32.6	-55.8	157.0	54 37.3	-56.1	157.6	11
12	56 27.4	-55.5	156.5	55 32.2	-55.8	157.1	54 36.8	-56.0	157.7	53 41.2	-56.2	158.2	12
13	55 31.9	-55.7	157.2	54 36.4	-55.9	157.8	53 40.8	-56.2	158.3	52 45.0	-56.4	158.8	13
14	54 36.2	-55.9	157.9	53 40.5	-56.1	158.4	52 44.6	-56.3	158.9	51 48.6	-56.6	159.3	14
15	53 40.3	-56.1	158.5	52 44.4	-56.4	159.0	51 48.3	-56.5	159.4	50 52.0	-56.7	159.9	15
16	52 44.2	-56.3	159.1	51 48.0	-56.4	159.5	50 51.8	-56.7	160.0	49 55.3	-56.8	160.4	16
17	51 47.9	-56.4	159.6	50 51.6	-56.6	160.1	49 55.1	-56.8	160.5	48 58.5	-57.0	160.9	17
18	50 51.5	-56.6	160.2	49 55.0	-56.8	160.6	48 58.3	-56.9	161.0	48 01.5	-57.0	161.3	18
19	49 54.9	-56.7	160.7	48 58.2	-56.8	161.1	48 01.4	-57.0	161.5	47 04.5	-57.2	161.8	19
20	48 58.2	-56.8	161.2	48 01.4	-57.0	161.6	47 04.4	-57.1	161.9	46 07.3	-57.3	162.2	20
21	48 01.4	-56.9	161.7	47 04.4	-57.1	162.0	46 07.3	-57.3	162.4	45 10.0	-57.3	162.7	21
22	47 04.5	-57.1	162.2	46 07.3	-57.2	162.5	45 10.0	-57.3	162.8	44 12.7	-57.5	163.1	22
23	46 07.4	-57.1	162.6	45 10.1	-57.3	162.9	44 12.7	-57.4	163.2	43 15.2	-57.5	163.5	23
24	45 10.3	-57.3	163.1	44 12.8	-57.3	163.3	43 15.3	-57.5	163.6	42 17.7	-57.6	163.9	24
25	44 13.0	-57.3	163.5	43 15.5	-57.5	163.7	42 17.8	-57.6	164.0	41 20.1	-57.7	164.2	25
26	43 15.7	-57.5	163.9	42 18.0	-57.5	164.1	41 20.2	-57.6	164.4	40 22.4	-57.7	164.6	26
27	42 18.2	-57.5	164.3	41 20.5	-57.6	164.5	40 22.6	-57.7	164.7	39 24.7	-57.8	165.0	27
28	41 20.7	-57.5	164.7	40 22.9	-57.7	164.9	39 24.9	-57.8	165.1	38 26.9	-57.9	165.3	28
29	40 23.2	-57.7	165.0	39 25.2	-57.8	165.2	38 27.1	-57.8	165.4	37 29.0	-57.9	165.6	29
30	39 25.5	-57.7	165.4	38 27.4	-57.8	165.6	37 29.3	-57.9	165.8	36 31.1	-58.0	166.0	30
31	38 27.8	-57.8	165.7	37 29.6	-57.8	165.9	36 31.4	-57.9	166.1	35 33.1	-58.0	166.3	31
32	37 30.0	-57.8	166.1	36 31.8	-57.9	166.3	35 33.5	-58.0	166.4	34 35.1	-58.0	166.6	32
33	36 32.2	-57.9	166.4	35 33.9	-58.0	166.6	34 35.5	-58.1	166.8	33 37.1	-58.2	166.9	33
34	35 34.3	-57.9	166.7	34 35.9	-58.0	166.9	33 37.4	-58.0	167.1	32 38.9	-58.1	167.2	34
35	34 36.4	-58.0	167.1	33 37.9	-58.1	167.2	32 39.4	-58.2	167.4	31 40.8	-58.2	167.5	35
36	33 38.4	-58.0	167.4	32 39.8	-58.1	167.5	31 41.2	-58.1	167.7	30 42.6	-58.2	167.8	36
37	32 40.4	-58.1	167.7	31 41.7	-58.1	167.8	30 43.1	-58.2	167.9	29 44.4	-58.3	168.1	37
38	31 42.3	-58.1	168.0	30 43.6	-58.2	168.1	29 44.9	-58.3	168.2	28 46.1	-58.3	168.3	38
39	30 44.2	-58.2	168.3	29 45.4	-58.2	168.4	28 46.6	-58.2	168.5	27 47.8	-58.3	168.6	39
40	29 46.0	-58.2	168.5	28 47.2	-58.2	168.7	27 48.4	-58.3	168.8	26 49.5	-58.4	168.9	40
41	28 47.8	-58.2	168.8	27 49.0	-58.3	168.9	26 50.1	-58.4	169.0	25 51.1	-58.3	169.1	41
42	27 49.6	-58.2	169.1	26 50.7	-58.3	169.2	25 51.7	-58.3	169.3	24 52.8	-58.4	169.4	42
43	26 51.4	-58.3	169.4	25 52.4	-58.4	169.5	24 53.4	-58.4	169.6	23 54.4	-58.5	169.6	43
44	25 53.1	-58.3	169.6	24 54.0	-58.3	169.7	23 55.0	-58.4	169.8	22 55.9	-58.4	169.9	44
45	24 54.8	-58.4	169.9	23 55.7	-58.4	170.0	22 56.6	-58.4	170.1	21 57.5	-58.5	170.1	45
46	23 56.4	-58.3	170.2	22 57.3	-58.4	170.2	21 58.2	-58.5	170.3	20 59.0	-58.5	170.4	46
47	22 58.1	-58.4	170.4	21 58.9	-58.4	170.5	20 59.7	-58.5	170.5	20 00.5	-58.5	170.6	47
48	21 59.7	-58.4	170.7	21 00.5	-58.5	170.7	20 01.2	-58.5	170.8	19 02.0	-58.5	170.8	48
49	21 01.3	-58.5	170.9	20 02.0	-58.5	171.0	19 02.7	-58.5	171.0	18 03.5	-58.6	171.1	49
50	20 02.8	-58.4	171.1	19 03.5	-58.5	171.2	18 04.2	-58.5	171.3	17 04.9	-58.5	171.3	50
51	19 04.4	-58.5	171.4	18 05.0	-58.5	171.4	17 05.7	-58.5	171.5	16 06.4	-58.6	171.5	51
52	18 05.9	-58.5	171.6	17 06.5	-58.5	171.7	16 07.2	-58.6	171.7	15 07.8	-58.6	171.8	52
53	17 07.4	-58.5	171.9	16 08.0	-58.5	171.9	15 08.6	-58.6	171.9	14 09.2	-58.6	172.0	53
54	16 08.9	-58.5	172.1	15 09.5	-58.6	172.1	14 10.0	-58.5	172.2	13 10.6	-58.6	172.2	54
55	15 10.4	-58.5	172.3	14 10.9	-58.5	172.4	13 11.5	-58.6	172.4	12 12.0	-58.6	172.4	55
56	14 11.9	-58.6	172.5	13 12.4	-58.6	172.6	12 12.9	-58.6	172.6	11 13.4	-58.7	172.6	56
57	13 13.3	-58.5	172.8	12 13.8	-58.6	172.8	11 14.3	-58.7	172.8	10 14.7	-58.6	172.8	57
58	12 14.8	-58.6	173.0	11 15.2	-58.6	173.0	10 15.6	-58.6	173.0	9 16.1	-58.7	173.1	58
59	11 16.2	-58.6	173.2	10 16.6	-58.6	173.3	9 17.0	-58.6	173.3	8 17.4	-58.6	173.3	59
60	10 17.6	-58.6	173.4	9 18.0	-58.6	173.5	8 18.4	-58.6	173.5	7 18.8	-58.7	173.5	60
61	9 19.0	-58.6	173.7	8 19.4	-58.6	173.7	7 19.8	-58.7	173.7	6 20.1	-58.6	173.7	61
62	8 20.4	-58.6	173.9	7 20.8	-58.6	173.9	6 21.1	-58.6	173.9	5 21.5	-58.7	173.9	62
63	7 21.8	-58.6	174.1	6 22.2	-58.7	174.1	5 22.5	-58.7	174.1	4 22.8	-58.7	174.1	63
64	6 23.2	-58.6	174.3	5 23.5	-58.6	174.3	4 23.8	-58.6	174.3	3 24.1	-58.7	174.3	64
65	5 24.6	-58.6	174.5	4 24.9	-58.6	174.5	3 25.2	-58.7	174.5	2 25.4	-58.6	174.5	65
66	4 26.0	-58.6	174.7	3 26.3	-58.7	174.7	2 26.5	-58.7	174.7	1 26.8	-58.7	174.7	66
67	3 27.4	-58.6	174.9	2 27.6	-58.6	175.0	1 27.8	-58.6	175.0	0 28.1	-58.7	175.0	67
68	2 28.8	-58.7	175.2	1 29.0	-58.7	175.2	0 29.2	-58.7	175.2	0 30.6	+58.7	4.8	68
69	1 30.1	-58.6	175.4	0 30.3	-58.6	175.4	0 29.5	+58.6	4.6	1 29.3	+58.7	4.6	69
70	0 31.5	-58.6	175.6	0 28.3	+58.7	4.4	1 28.1	+58.7	4.4	2 28.0	+58.6	4.4	70
71	0 27.1	+58.6	4.2	1 27.0	+58.6	4.2	2 26.8	+58.7	4.2	3 26.6	+58.7	4.2	71
72	1 25.7	+58.7	4.0	2 25.6	+58.6	4.0	3 25.5	+58.6	4.0	4 25.3	+58.7	4.0	72
73	2 24.4	+58.6	3.8	3 24.2	+58.7	3.8	4 24.1	+58.7	3.8	5 24.0	+58.6	3.8	73
74	3 23.0	+58.6	3.6	4 22.9	+58.6	3.6	5 22.8	+58.6	3.6	6 22.6	+58.7	3.6	74
75	4 21.6	+58.6	3.3	5 21.5	+58.6	3.4	6 21.4	+58.7	3.4	7 21.3	+58.7	3.4	75
76	5 20.2	+58.6	3.1	6 20.1	+58.7	3.1	7 20.1	+58.6	3.1	8 20.0	+58.6	3.2	76
77	6 18.8	+58.7	2.9	7 18.8	+58.6	2.9	8 18.7	+58.6	2.9	9 18.6	+58.7	2.9	77
78	7 17.5	+58.6	2.7	8 17.4	+58.6	2.7	9 17.3	+58.6	2.7	10 17.3	+58.6	2.7	78
79	8 16.1	+58.6	2.5	9 16.0	+58.6	2.5	10 15.9	+58.7	2.5	11 15.9	+58.6	2.5	79
80	9 14.7	+58.5	2.3	10 14.6	+58.6	2.3	11 14.6	+58.6	2.3	12 14.5	+58.6	2.3	80
81	10 13.2	+58.6	2.0	11 13.2	+58.6	2.1	12 13.2	+58.6	2.1	13 13.1	+58.6	2.1	81
82	11 11.8	+58.6	1.8	12 11.8	+58.6	1.8	13 11.8	+58.5	1.8	14 11.7	+58.6	1.9	82
83	12 10.4	+58.5	1.6	13 10.4	+58.5	1.6	14 10.3	+58.6	1.6	15 10.3	+58.6	1.6	83
84	13 08.9	+58.6	1.4	14 08.9	+58.6	1.4	15 08.9	+58.6	1.4	16 08.9	+58.5	1.4	84
85	14 07.5	+58.5	1.2	15 07.5	+58.5	1.2	16 07.5	+58.5	1.2	17 07.4	+58.6	1.2	85
86	15 06.0	+58.5	0.9	16 06.0	+58.5	0.9	17 06.0	+58.5	0.9	18 06.0	+58.5	0.9	86
87	16 04.5	+58.5	0.7	17 04.5	+58.5	0.7	18 04.5	+58.5	0.7	19 04.5	+58.5	0.7	87
88	17 03.0	+58.5	0.5	18 03.0	+58.5	0.5	19 03.0	+58.5	0.5	20 03.0	+58.5	0.5	88
89	18 01.5	+58.5	0.2	19 01.5	+58.5	0.2	20 01.5	+58.5	0.2	21 01.5	+58.5	0.2	89
90	19 00.0	+58.5	0.0	20 00.0	+58.5	0.0	21 00.0	+58.5	0.0	22 00.0	+58.5	0.0	90
	19°			20°			21°			22°			

S. Lat. {L.H.A. greater than 180° ....Zn=180°–Z
{L.H.A. less than 180°...........Zn=180°+Z

LATITUDE SAME NAME AS DECLINATION L.H.A. 167°, 193°

14°, 346° L.H.A. LATITUDE SAME NAME AS DECLINATION

N. Lat. {L.H.A. greater than 180° .....Zn=Z; L.H.A. less than 180°............Zn=360°-Z

Dec.	15°			16°			17°			18°			19°			20°			21°			22°			Dec.
°	Hc ° ′	d ′	Z °	Hc ° ′	d ′	Z °	Hc ° ′	d ′	Z °	Hc ° ′	d ′	Z °	Hc ° ′	d ′	Z °	Hc ° ′	d ′	Z °	Hc ° ′	d ′	Z °	Hc ° ′	d ′	Z °	°
0	69 35.5	+43.9	136.1	68 51.7	+45.2	137.9	68 06.6	+46.5	139.5	67 20.4	+47.7	141.1	66 33.2	+48.7	142.6	65 45.1	+49.6	143.9	64 56.3	+50.4	145.2	64 06.7	+51.2	146.4	0
1	70 19.4	+42.5	134.1	69 36.9	+44.1	136.0	68 53.1	+45.4	137.8	68 08.1	+46.6	139.5	67 21.9	+47.8	141.1	66 34.7	+48.9	142.5	65 46.7	+49.7	143.9	64 57.9	+50.5	145.1	1
2	71 01.9	+40.9	131.9	70 21.0	+42.6	134.0	69 38.5	+44.2	136.0	68 54.7	+45.6	137.8	68 09.7	+46.8	139.5	67 23.6	+47.9	141.0	66 36.4	+49.0	142.5	65 48.4	+49.9	143.8	2
3	71 42.8	+39.1	129.7	71 03.6	+41.0	131.9	70 22.7	+42.7	134.0	69 40.3	+44.3	135.9	68 56.5	+45.7	137.8	68 11.5	+46.9	139.4	67 25.4	+48.0	141.0	66 38.3	+49.0	142.5	3
4	72 21.9	+37.2•	127.2	71 44.6	+39.3	129.6	71 05.4	+41.3	131.9	70 24.6	+42.9	134.0	69 42.2	+44.5	135.9	68 58.4	+45.9	137.7	68 13.4	+47.1	139.4	67 27.3	+48.2	141.0	4
5	72 59.1	+34.9•	124.6	72 23.9	+37.3•	127.2	71 46.7	+39.4	129.6	71 07.5	+41.4	131.8	70 26.7	+43.0	133.9	69 44.3	+44.6	135.9	69 00.5	+46.0	137.7	68 15.5	+47.3	139.4	5
6	73 34.0	+32.6•	121.7	73 01.2	+35.2•	124.5	72 26.1	+37.5•	127.1	71 48.9	+39.6	129.6	71 09.7	+41.6	131.8	70 28.9	+43.3	133.9	69 46.5	+44.8	135.9	69 02.8	+46.2	137.7	6
7	74 06.6	+29.9•	118.7	73 36.4	+32.8•	121.7	73 03.6	+35.4•	124.5	72 28.5	+37.7•	127.1	71 51.3	+39.8	129.6	71 12.2	+41.7	131.8	70 31.3	+43.5	133.9	69 49.0	+44.9	135.9	7
8	74 36.5	+26.9•	115.5	74 09.2	+30.0•	118.7	73 39.0	+32.9•	121.7	73 06.2	+35.6•	124.5	72 31.1	+37.9•	127.1	71 53.9	+40.0	129.6	71 14.8	+41.9	131.8	70 33.9	+43.6	133.9	8
9	75 03.4	+23.7•	112.1	74 39.2	+27.1•	115.5	74 11.9	+30.3•	118.7	73 41.8	+33.1•	121.7	73 09.0	+35.7•	124.5	72 33.9	+38.1•	127.1	71 56.7	+40.2	129.6	71 17.5	+42.1	131.8	9
10	75 27.1	+20.3•	108.5	75 06.3	+23.9•	112.0	74 42.2	+27.3•	115.4	74 14.9	+30.5•	118.6	73 44.7	+33.4•	121.7	73 12.0	+35.9•	124.5	72 36.9	+38.3•	127.1	71 59.6	+40.4	129.6	10
11	75 47.4	+16.4•	104.7	75 30.2	+20.5•	108.4	75 09.5	+24.1•	112.0	74 45.4	+27.5•	115.4	74 18.1	+30.7•	118.6	73 47.9	+33.6•	121.7	73 15.2	+36.1•	124.5	72 40.0	+38.5•	127.1	11
12	76 03.8	+12.5•	100.7	75 50.7	+16.6•	104.6	75 33.6	+20.6•	108.4	75 12.9	+24.3•	112.0	74 48.8	+27.7•	115.4	74 21.5	+30.9•	118.6	73 51.3	+33.8•	121.7	73 18.5	+36.4•	124.5	12
13	76 16.3	+8.4•	96.6	76 07.3	+12.7•	100.7	75 54.2	+16.8•	104.6	75 37.2	+20.8•	108.4	75 16.5	+24.5•	112.0	74 52.4	+27.9•	115.4	74 25.1	+31.1•	118.7	73 54.9	+34.0•	121.7	13
14	76 24.7	+4.1•	92.4	76 20.0	+8.5•	96.6	76 11.0	+12.9•	100.6	75 58.0	+17.0•	104.5	75 41.0	+21.0•	108.3	75 20.3	+24.7•	112.0	74 56.2	+28.2•	115.4	74 28.9	+31.3•	118.7	14
15	76 28.8	-0.3•	88.2	76 28.5	+4.2•	92.3	76 23.9	+8.6•	96.5	76 15.0	+13.0•	100.5	76 02.0	+17.2•	104.5	75 45.0	+21.2•	108.3	75 24.4	+24.9•	112.0	75 00.2	+28.4•	115.4	15
16	76 28.5	-4.6•	83.9	76 32.7	-0.2•	88.1	76 32.5	+4.4•	92.2	76 28.0	+8.8•	96.4	76 19.2	+13.2•	100.5	76 06.2	+17.4•	104.5	75 49.3	+21.4•	108.3	75 28.6	+25.2•	112.0	16
17	76 23.9	-8.9•	79.7	76 32.5	-4.5•	83.8	76 36.9	-0.1•	87.9	76 36.8	+4.5•	92.1	76 32.4	+9.0•	96.3	76 23.6	+13.4•	100.4	76 10.7	+17.6•	104.4	75 53.8	+21.6•	108.3	17
18	76 15.0	-13.0•	75.5	76 28.0	-8.8•	79.5	76 36.8	-4.4•	83.6	76 41.3	+0.1•	87.8	76 41.4	+4.6•	92.1	76 37.0	+9.1•	96.3	76 28.3	+13.6•	100.4	76 15.4	+17.8•	104.4	18
19	76 02.0	-17.0•	71.4	76 19.2	-13.0•	75.3	76 32.4	-8.8•	79.3	76 41.4	-4.4•	83.5	76 46.0	+0.1•	87.7	76 46.1	+4.8•	92.0	76 41.9	+9.3•	96.2	76 33.2	+13.8•	100.4	19
20	75 45.0	-20.6•	67.5	76 06.2	-16.9•	71.2	76 23.6	-12.9•	75.1	76 37.0	-8.7•	79.2	76 46.1	-4.2•	83.3	76 50.9	+0.3•	87.6	76 51.2	+4.8•	91.9	76 47.0	+9.4•	96.1	20
21	75 24.4	-24.2•	63.7	75 49.3	-20.7•	67.2	76 10.7	-16.9•	71.0	76 28.3	-12.9•	74.9	76 41.9	-8.7•	79.0	76 51.2	-4.2•	83.2	76 56.0	+0.4•	87.5	76 56.4	+5.0•	91.8	21
22	75 00.2	-27.3•	60.1	75 28.6	-24.1•	63.4	75 53.8	-20.7•	67.0	76 15.4	-16.9•	70.8	76 33.2	-12.9•	74.7	76 47.0	-8.6•	78.8	76 56.4	-4.1•	83.1	77 01.4	+0.5•	87.4	22
23	74 32.9	-30.2•	56.7	75 04.5	-27.4•	59.8	75 33.1	-24.2•	63.2	75 58.5	-20.7•	66.8	76 20.3	-16.9•	70.5	76 38.4	-12.9•	74.5	76 52.3	-8.6•	78.7	77 01.9	-4.0•	82.9	23
24	74 02.7	-32.9•	53.5	74 37.1	-30.2•	56.4	75 08.9	-27.3•	59.6	75 37.8	-24.2•	62.9	76 03.4	-20.7•	66.5	76 25.5	-16.9•	70.3	76 43.7	-12.8•	74.3	76 57.9	-8.5•	78.5	24
25	73 29.8	-35.3•	50.5	74 06.9	-33.0•	53.2	74 41.6	-30.4•	56.2	75 13.6	-27.4•	59.3	75 42.7	-24.2•	62.7	76 08.6	-20.8•	66.3	76 30.9	-16.9•	70.1	76 49.4	-12.9•	74.1	25
26	72 54.5	-37.4•	47.7	73 33.9	-35.3•	50.2	74 11.2	-33.0•	52.9	74 46.2	-30.4•	55.9	75 18.5	-27.5•	59.0	75 47.8	-24.3•	62.4	76 14.0	-20.8•	66.0	76 36.5	-17.0•	69.9	26
27	72 17.1	-39.4	45.1	72 58.6	-37.5•	47.4	73 38.2	-35.4•	49.9	74 15.8	-33.1•	52.6	74 51.0	-30.5•	55.6	75 23.5	-27.5•	58.7	75 53.2	-24.4•	62.1	76 19.5	-20.8•	65.8	27
28	71 37.7	-41.0	42.7	72 21.1	-39.4	44.8	73 02.8	-37.5•	47.1	73 42.7	-35.5•	49.6	74 20.5	-33.1•	52.3	74 56.0	-30.6•	55.3	75 28.8	-27.6•	58.4	75 58.7	-24.4•	61.8	28
29	70 56.7	-42.7	40.4	71 41.7	-41.2	42.4	72 25.3	-39.5	44.5	73 07.2	-37.6•	46.8	73 47.4	-35.6•	49.3	74 25.4	-33.2•	52.0	75 01.2	-30.7•	54.9	75 34.3	-27.8•	58.1	29
30	70 14.0	-44.0	38.3	71 00.5	-42.7	40.1	71 45.8	-41.3	42.0	72 29.6	-39.6	44.1	73 11.8	-37.7•	46.4	73 52.2	-35.7•	48.9	74 30.5	-33.3•	51.7	75 06.5	-30.7•	54.6	30
31	69 30.0	-45.3	36.3	70 17.8	-44.1	38.0	71 04.5	-42.8	39.7	71 50.0	-41.3	41.7	72 34.1	-39.7	43.8	73 16.5	-37.8•	46.1	73 57.2	-35.8•	48.6	74 35.8	-33.4•	51.3	31
32	68 44.7	-46.4	34.5	69 33.7	-45.4	36.0	70 21.7	-44.2	37.6	71 08.7	-42.9	39.4	71 54.4	-41.4	41.3	72 38.7	-39.8	43.5	73 21.4	-37.9•	45.8	74 02.4	-35.9•	48.3	32
33	67 58.3	-47.5	32.7	68 48.3	-46.5	34.1	69 37.5	-45.4	35.6	70 25.8	-44.3	37.3	71 13.0	-43.0	39.1	71 58.9	-41.5	41.0	72 43.5	-39.9	43.1	73 26.5	-38.1•	45.4	33
34	67 10.8	-48.3	31.1	68 01.8	-47.4	32.4	68 52.1	-46.6	33.8	69 41.5	-45.5	35.3	70 30.0	-44.4	36.9	71 17.4	-43.1	38.7	72 03.6	-41.6	40.6	72 48.4	-40.0	42.7	34
35	66 22.5	-49.1	29.6	67 14.4	-48.4	30.8	68 05.5	-47.5	32.1	68 56.0	-46.6	33.5	69 45.6	-45.6	34.9	70 34.3	-44.4	36.6	71 22.0	-43.2	38.3	72 08.4	-41.7	40.3	35
36	65 33.4	-49.9	28.2	66 26.0	-49.2	29.3	67 18.0	-48.5	30.5	68 09.4	-47.7	31.7	69 00.0	-46.7	33.1	69 49.9	-45.7	34.6	70 38.8	-44.6	36.2	71 26.7	-43.4	38.0	36
37	64 43.5	-50.5	26.9	65 36.8	-50.0	27.9	66 29.5	-49.2	29.0	67 21.7	-48.5	30.1	68 13.3	-47.7	31.4	69 04.2	-46.9	32.7	69 54.2	-45.8	34.2	70 43.3	-44.6	35.8	37
38	63 53.0	-51.2	25.7	64 46.8	-50.6	26.6	65 40.3	-50.0	27.6	66 33.2	-49.3	28.6	67 25.6	-48.6	29.8	68 17.3	-47.8	31.0	69 08.4	-46.9	32.4	69 58.7	-46.0	33.8	38
39	63 01.8	-51.7	24.5	63 56.2	-51.2	25.3	64 50.3	-50.7	26.2	65 43.9	-50.1	27.2	66 37.0	-49.5	28.3	67 29.5	-48.7	29.4	68 21.5	-47.9	30.6	69 12.7	-47.0	32.0	39
40	62 10.1	-52.1	23.4	63 05.0	-51.7	24.2	63 59.6	-51.2	25.0	64 53.8	-50.7	25.9	65 47.5	-50.1	26.9	66 40.8	-49.5	27.9	67 33.6	-48.8	29.0	68 25.7	-48.0	30.3	40
41	61 18.0	-52.7	22.3	62 13.3	-52.2	23.1	63 08.4	-51.8	23.8	64 03.1	-51.4	24.7	64 57.4	-50.8	25.6	65 51.3	-50.2	26.5	66 44.8	-49.6	27.5	67 37.7	-48.9	28.7	41
42	60 25.3	-53.0	21.4	61 21.1	-52.7	22.0	62 16.6	-52.3	22.7	63 11.7	-51.8	23.5	64 06.6	-51.4	24.3	65 01.1	-50.9	25.2	65 55.2	-50.4	26.1	66 48.8	-49.7	27.2	42
43	59 32.3	-53.5	20.4	60 28.4	-53.1	21.0	61 24.3	-52.8	21.7	62 19.9	-52.4	22.4	63 15.2	-51.9	23.1	64 10.2	-51.5	24.0	65 04.8	-50.9	24.8	65 59.1	-50.4	25.8	43
44	58 38.8	-53.7	19.5	59 35.3	-53.5	20.1	60 31.5	-53.1	20.7	61 27.5	-52.8	21.4	62 23.3	-52.5	22.1	63 18.7	-52.0	22.8	64 13.9	-51.6	23.6	65 08.7	-51.1	24.5	44
45	57 45.1	-54.1	18.7	58 41.8	-53.8	19.2	59 38.4	-53.6	19.8	60 34.7	-53.2	20.4	61 30.8	-52.8	21.0	62 26.7	-52.5	21.7	63 22.3	-52.1	22.4	64 17.6	-51.6	23.2	45
46	56 51.0	-54.4	17.9	57 48.0	-54.2	18.4	58 44.8	-53.8	18.9	59 41.5	-53.6	19.5	60 38.0	-53.3	20.0	61 34.2	-52.9	20.7	62 30.2	-52.5	21.3	63 26.0	-52.2	22.1	46
47	55 56.6	-54.7	17.1	56 53.8	-54.4	17.6	57 51.0	-54.2	18.1	58 47.9	-53.9	18.6	59 44.7	-53.6	19.1	60 41.3	-53.3	19.7	61 37.7	-53.0	20.3	62 33.8	-52.6	21.0	47
48	55 01.9	-54.9	16.4	55 59.4	-54.7	16.8	56 56.8	-54.5	17.3	57 54.0	-54.2	17.7	58 51.1	-54.0	18.2	59 48.0	-53.7	18.8	60 44.7	-53.4	19.3	61 41.2	-53.1	20.0	48
49	54 07.0	-55.1	15.7	55 04.7	-54.9	16.1	56 02.3	-54.7	16.5	56 59.8	-54.6	16.9	57 57.1	-54.3	17.4	58 54.3	-54.1	17.9	59 51.3	-53.8	18.4	60 48.1	-53.5	19.0	49
50	53 11.9	-55.4	15.0	54 09.8	-55.2	15.4	55 07.6	-55.0	15.8	56 05.2	-54.7	16.2	57 02.8	-54.6	16.6	58 00.2	-54.3	17.1	58 57.5	-54.1	17.6	59 54.6	-53.8	18.1	50
51	52 16.5	-55.5	14.4	53 14.6	-55.4	14.7	54 12.6	-55.2	15.1	55 10.5	-55.1	15.5	56 08.2	-54.8	15.9	57 05.9	-54.6	16.3	58 03.4	-54.4	16.7	59 00.8	-54.2	17.2	51
52	51 21.0	-55.8	13.8	52 19.2	-55.6	14.1	53 17.4	-55.5	14.4	54 15.4	-55.2	14.8	55 13.4	-55.1	15.1	56 11.3	-54.9	15.5	57 09.0	-54.7	15.9	58 06.6	-54.4	16.4	52
53	50 25.2	-55.9	13.2	51 23.6	-55.7	13.5	52 21.9	-55.6	13.8	53 20.2	-55.5	14.1	54 18.3	-55.3	14.4	55 16.4	-55.2	14.8	56 14.3	-54.9	15.2	57 12.2	-54.8	15.6	53
54	49 29.3	-56.0	12.6	50 27.9	-56.0	12.9	51 26.3	-55.8	13.2	52 24.7	-55.7	13.5	53 23.0	-55.5	13.8	54 21.2	-55.3	14.1	55 19.4	-55.2	14.5	56 17.4	-55.0	14.8	54
55	48 33.3	-56.2	12.1	49 31.9	-56.1	12.3	50 30.5	-56.0	12.6	51 29.0	-55.8	12.9	52 27.5	-55.7	13.2	53 25.9	-55.6	13.5	54 24.2	-55.4	13.8	55 22.4	-55.2	14.1	55
56	47 37.1	-56.4	11.6	48 35.8	-56.2	11.8	49 34.5	-56.1	12.0	50 33.2	-56.0	12.3	51 31.8	-55.9	12.6	52 30.3	-55.7	12.8	53 28.8	-55.6	13.1	54 27.2	-55.5	13.5	56
57	46 40.7	-56.5	11.1	47 39.6	-56.4	11.3	48 38.4	-56.3	11.5	49 37.2	-56.2	11.7	50 35.9	-56.1	12.0	51 34.6	-56.0	12.2	52 33.2	-55.8	12.5	53 31.7	-55.7	12.8	57
58	45 44.2	-56.5	10.6	46 43.2	-56.5	10.8	47 42.1	-56.4	11.0	48 41.0	-56.3	11.2	49 39.8	-56.2	11.4	50 38.6	-56.1	11.7	51 37.4	-56.0	11.9	52 36.0	-55.8	12.2	58
59	44 47.7	-56.8	10.1	45 46.7	-56.6	10.3	46 45.7	-56.5	10.5	47 44.7	-56.4	10.7	48 43.6	-56.3	10.9	49 42.5	-56.2	11.1	50 41.4	-56.1	11.3	51 40.2	-56.0	11.6	59
60	43 50.9	-56.8	9.7	44 50.1	-56.8	9.8	45 49.2	-56.7	10.0	46 48.3	-56.6	10.2	47 47.3	-56.5	10.4	48 46.3	-56.4	10.6	49 45.3	-56.3	10.8	50 44.2	-56.2	11.0	60
61	42 54.1	-56.9	9.2	43 53.3	-56.8	9.4	44 52.5	-56.7	9.5	45 51.7	-56.7	9.7	46 50.8	-56.6	9.9	47 49.9	-56.5	10.1	48 49.0	-56.5	10.3	49 48.0	-56.3	10.5	61
62	41 57.2	-57.0	8.8	42 56.5	-56.9	8.9	43 55.8	-56.9	9.1	44 55.0	-56.8	9.2	45 54.2	-56.7	9.4	46 53.4	-56.7	9.6	47 52.5	-56.5	9.7	48 51.7	-56.5	9.9	62
63	41 00.2	-57.1	8.4	41 59.6	-57.1	8.5	42 58.9	-57.0	8.6	43 58.2	-56.9	8.8	44 57.5	-56.8	8.9	45 56.7	-56.7	9.1	46 56.0	-56.7	9.3	47 55.2	-56.6	9.4	63
64	40 03.1	-57.2	8.0	41 02.5	-57.1	8.1	42 01.9	-57.0	8.2	43 01.3	-57.0	8.3	44 00.7	-57.0	8.5	45 00.0	-56.9	8.6	45 59.3	-56.8	8.8	46 58.6	-56.7	8.9	64
65	39 05.9	-57.2	7.6	40 05.4	-57.2	7.7	41 04.9	-57.2	7.8	42 04.3	-57.1	7.9	43 03.7	-57.0	8.0	44 03.1	-57.0	8.2	45 02.5	-56.9	8.3	46 01.9	-56.9	8.5	65
66	38 08.7	-57.3	7.2	39 08.2	-57.3	7.3	40 07.7	-57.2	7.4	41 07.2	-57.2	7.5	42 06.7	-57.1	7.6	43 06.1	-57.0	7.7	44 05.6	-57.0	7.9	45 05.0	-56.9	8.0	66
67	37 11.4	-57.4	6.8	38 10.9	-57.3	6.9	39 10.5	-57.3	7.0	40 10.0	-57.2	7.1	41 09.6	-57.2	7.2	42 09.1	-57.2	7.3	43 08.6	-57.1	7.4	44 08.1	-57.1	7.6	67
68	36 14.0	-57.5	6.5	37 13.6	-57.4	6.5	38 13.2	-57.4	6.6	39 12.8	-57.4	6.7	40 12.4	-57.3	6.8	41 11.9	-57.2	6.9	42 11.5	-57.2	7.0	43 11.0	-57.1	7.1	68
69	35 16.5	-57.5	6.1	36 16.2	-57.5	6.2	37 15.8	-57.4	6.3	38 15.4	-57.4	6.3	39 15.1	-57.4	6.4	40 14.7	-57.3	6.5	41 14.3	-57.3	6.6	42 13.9	-57.2	6.7	69
70	34 19.0	-57.6	5.7	35 18.7	-57.6	5.8	36 18.4	-57.5	5.9	37 18.0	-57.4	6.0	38 17.7	-57.4	6.1	39 17.4	-57.4	6.1	40 17.0	-57.3	6.2	41 16.7	-57.3	6.3	70
71	33 21.4	-57.6	5.4	34 21.1	-57.6	5.5	35 20.9	-57.6	5.5	36 20.6	-57.6	5.6	37 20.3	-57.5	5.7	38 20.0	-57.5	5.8	39 19.7	-57.4	5.8	40 19.4	-57.4	5.9	71
72	32 23.8	-57.7	5.1	33 23.5	-57.6	5.1	34 23.3	-57.6	5.2	35 23.0	-57.5	5.3	36 22.8	-57.6	5.3	37 22.5	-57.5	5.4	38 22.3	-57.5	5.5	39 22.0	-57.5	5.5	72
73	31 26.1	-57.7	4.8	32 25.9	-57.7	4.8	33 25.7	-57.7	4.9	34 25.5	-57.7	4.9	35 25.2	-57.6	5.0	36 25.0	-57.6	5.0	37 24.8	-57.6	5.1	38 24.5	-57.5	5.2	73
74	30 28.4	-57.8	4.4	31 28.2	-57.8	4.5	32 28.0	-57.7	4.5	33 27.8	-57.7	4.6	34 27.6	-57.7	4.6	35 27.4	-57.6	4.7	36 27.2	-57.6	4.8	37 27.0	-57.6	4.8	74
75	29 30.6	-57.8	4.1	30 30.4	-57.8	4.2	31 30.3	-57.8	4.2	32 30.1	-57.7	4.3	33 29.9	-57.7	4.3	34 29.8	-57.7	4.4	35 29.6	-57.7	4.4	36 29.4	-57.6	4.5	75
76	28 32.8	-57.9	3.8	29 32.6	-57.8	3.9	30 32.5	-57.8	3.9	31 32.4	-57.8	3.9	32 32.2	-57.8	4.0	33 32.1	-57.8	4.0	34 31.9	-57.7	4.1	35 31.8	-57.7	4.1	76
77	27 34.9	-57.9	3.5	28 34.8	-57.9	3.6	29 34.7	-57.9	3.6	30 34.6	-57.9	3.6	31 34.4	-57.8	3.7	32 34.3	-57.8	3.7	33 34.2	-57.8	3.7	34 34.1	-57.8	3.8	77
78	26 37.0	-57.9	3.2	27 36.9	-57.9	3.3	28 36.8	-57.9	3.3	29 36.7	-57.9	3.3	30 36.6	-57.8	3.4	31 36.5	-57.8	3.4	32 36.4	-57.8	3.4	33 36.3	-57.8	3.5	78
79	25 39.1	-58.0	2.9	26 39.0	-57.9	3.0	27 38.9	-57.9	3.0	28 38.8	-57.9	3.0	29 38.8	-57.9	3.0	30 38.7	-57.9	3.1	31 38.6	-57.9	3.1	32 38.5	-57.9	3.1	79
80	24 41.1	-58.0	2.6	25 41.1	-58.0	2.7	26 41.0	-58.0	2.7	27 40.9	-57.9	2.7	28 40.9	-58.0	2.7	29 40.8	-57.9	2.8	30 40.7	-57.9	2.8	31 40.6	-57.9	2.8	80
81	23 43.1	-58.0	2.4	24 43.1	-58.0	2.4	25 43.0	-58.0	2.4	26 43.0	-58.0	2.4	27 42.9	-58.0	2.5	28 42.9	-58.0	2.5	29 42.8	-58.0	2.5	30 42.7	-57.9	2.5	81
82	22 45.1	-58.1	2.1	23 45.1	-58.1	2.1	24 45.0	-58.0	2.1	25 45.0	-58.0	2.1	26 44.9	-58.0	2.2	27 44.9	-58.0	2.2	28 44.8	-57.9	2.2	29 44.8	-58.0	2.2	82
83	21 47.0	-58.0	1.8	22 47.0	-58.1	1.8	23 47.0	-58.1	1.8	24 47.0	-58.1	1.9	25 46.9	-58.0	1.9	26 46.9	-58.1	1.9	27 46.9	-58.1	1.9	28 46.8	-58.0	1.9	83
84	20 49.0	-58.1	1.6	21 48.9	-58.1	1.6	22 48.9	-58.1	1.6	23 48.9	-58.1	1.6	24 48.9	-58.1	1.6	25 48.8	-58.0	1.6	26 48.8	-58.0	1.6	27 48.8	-58.1	1.6	84
85	19 50.9	-58.2	1.3	20 50.8	-58.1	1.3	21 50.8	-58.1	1.3	22 50.8	-58.1	1.3	23 50.8	-58.1	1.3	24 50.8	-58.1	1.3	25 50.8	-58.1	1.3	26 50.7	-58.0	1.4	85
86	18 52.7	-58.1	1.0	19 52.7	-58.1	1.0	20 52.7	-58.1	1.0	21 52.7	-58.1	1.0	22 52.7	-58.1	1.0	23 52.7	-58.2	1.1	24 52.7	-58.2	1.1	25 52.7	-58.2	1.1	86
87	17 54.6	-58.2	0.8	18 54.6	-58.2	0.8	19 54.6	-58.2	0.8	20 54.6	-58.2	0.8	21 54.6	-58.2	0.8	22 54.5	-58.1	0.8	23 54.5	-58.1	0.8	24 54.5	-58.1	0.8	87
88	16 56.4	-58.2	0.5	17 56.4	-58.2	0.5	18 56.4	-58.2	0.5	19 56.4	-58.2	0.5	20 56.4	-58.2	0.5	21 56.4	-58.2	0.5	22 56.4	-58.2	0.5	23 56.4	-58.2	0.5	88
89	15 58.2	-58.2	0.3	16 58.2	-58.2	0.3	17 58.2	-58.2	0.3	18 58.2	-58.2	0.3	19 58.2	-58.2	0.3	20 58.2	-58.2	0.3	21 58.2	-58.2	0.3	22 58.2	-58.2	0.3	89
90	15 00.0	-58.2	0.0	16 00.0	-58.2	0.0	17 00.0	-58.2	0.0	18 00.0	-58.2	0.0	19 00.0	-58.2	0.0	20 00.0	-58.2	0.0	21 00.0	-58.2	0.0	22 00.0	-58.2	0.0	90
	15°			16°			17°			18°			19°			20°			21°			22°			

14°, 346° L.H.A. LATITUDE SAME NAME AS DECLINATION

30

LATITUDE **CONTRARY** NAME TO DECLINATION **L.H.A. 14°, 346°**

Dec.	15° Hc	d	Z	16° Hc	d	Z	17° Hc	d	Z	18° Hc	d	Z	19° Hc	d	Z	20° Hc	d	Z	21° Hc	d	Z	22° Hc	d	Z	Dec.
°	° ′	′	°	° ′	′	°	° ′	′	°	° ′	′	°	° ′	′	°	° ′	′	°	° ′	′	°	° ′	′	°	°
0	69 35.5	-45.1	136.1	68 51.7	-46.4	137.9	68 06.6	-47.6	139.5	67 20.4	-48.6	141.1	66 33.2	-49.5	142.6	65 45.1	-50.3	143.9	64 56.3	-51.1	145.2	64 06.7	-51.8	146.4	0
1	68 50.4	-46.3	137.9	68 05.3	-47.5	139.6	67 19.0	-48.4	141.2	66 31.8	-49.3	142.6	65 43.7	-50.2	144.0	64 54.8	-50.9	145.2	64 05.2	-51.6	146.4	63 14.9	-52.3	147.5	1
2	68 04.1	-47.3	139.7	67 17.8	-48.3	141.2	66 30.6	-49.3	142.7	65 42.5	-50.1	144.0	64 53.5	-50.8	145.3	64 03.9	-51.6	146.4	63 13.6	-52.2	147.5	62 22.6	-52.7	148.6	2
3	67 16.8	-48.2	141.3	66 29.5	-49.1	142.7	65 41.3	-49.9	144.1	64 52.4	-50.8	145.3	64 02.7	-51.5	146.5	63 12.3	-52.0	147.6	62 21.4	-52.6	148.6	61 29.9	-53.2	149.6	3
4	66 28.6	-49.1	142.8	65 40.4	-49.9	144.1	64 51.4	-50.7	145.4	64 01.6	-51.3	146.6	63 11.2	-51.9	147.7	62 20.3	-52.6	148.7	61 28.8	-53.1	149.6	60 36.7	-53.5	150.5	4
5	65 39.5	-49.7	144.2	64 50.5	-50.6	145.5	64 00.7	-51.2	146.6	63 10.3	-51.9	147.7	62 19.3	-52.5	148.7	61 27.7	-53.0	149.7	60 35.7	-53.5	150.6	59 43.2	-53.9	151.4	5
6	64 49.8	-50.5	145.5	63 59.9	-51.1	146.7	63 09.5	-51.8	147.8	62 18.4	-52.4	148.8	61 26.8	-52.9	149.8	60 34.7	-53.3	150.7	59 42.2	-53.8	151.5	58 49.3	-54.3	152.3	6
7	63 59.3	-51.1	146.8	63 08.8	-51.7	147.9	62 17.7	-52.3	148.9	61 26.0	-52.8	149.9	60 33.9	-53.3	150.8	59 41.4	-53.8	151.6	58 48.4	-54.2	152.4	57 55.0	-54.5	153.1	7
8	63 08.2	-51.6	148.0	62 17.1	-52.2	149.0	61 25.4	-52.7	149.9	60 33.2	-53.2	150.8	59 40.6	-53.6	151.7	58 47.6	-54.1	152.5	57 54.2	-54.4	153.2	57 00.5	-54.8	153.9	8
9	62 16.6	-52.1	149.1	61 24.9	-52.7	150.0	60 32.7	-53.2	150.9	59 40.0	-53.6	151.8	58 47.0	-54.0	152.5	57 53.5	-54.3	153.3	56 59.8	-54.8	154.0	56 05.7	-55.0	154.6	9
10	61 24.5	-52.6	150.1	60 32.2	-53.0	151.0	59 39.5	-53.5	151.9	58 46.4	-53.9	152.6	57 53.0	-54.4	153.4	56 59.2	-54.7	154.1	56 05.0	-54.9	154.7	55 10.7	-55.3	155.3	10
11	60 31.9	-53.0	151.1	59 39.2	-53.5	152.0	58 46.0	-53.9	152.7	57 52.5	-54.3	153.5	56 58.6	-54.6	154.2	56 04.5	-54.9	154.8	55 10.1	-55.3	155.4	54 15.4	-55.5	156.0	11
12	59 38.9	-53.4	152.1	58 45.7	-53.8	152.9	57 52.1	-54.1	153.6	56 58.2	-54.5	154.3	56 04.0	-54.8	154.9	55 09.6	-55.2	155.5	54 14.8	-55.4	156.1	53 19.9	-55.7	156.7	12
13	58 45.5	-53.7	153.0	57 51.9	-54.1	153.7	56 58.0	-54.5	154.4	56 03.7	-54.8	155.0	55 09.2	-55.1	155.6	54 14.4	-55.4	156.2	53 19.4	-55.7	156.8	52 24.2	-55.9	157.3	13
14	57 51.8	-54.1	153.8	56 57.8	-54.4	154.5	56 03.5	-54.7	155.1	55 08.9	-55.0	155.7	54 14.1	-55.3	156.3	53 19.0	-55.6	156.9	52 23.7	-55.8	157.4	51 28.3	-56.1	157.9	14
15	56 57.7	-54.3	154.6	56 03.4	-54.7	155.3	55 08.8	-55.0	155.9	54 13.9	-55.3	156.4	53 18.8	-55.6	157.0	52 23.4	-55.7	157.5	51 27.9	-56.0	158.0	50 32.2	-56.2	158.4	15
16	56 03.4	-54.6	155.4	55 08.7	-54.9	156.0	54 13.8	-55.2	156.6	53 18.6	-55.5	157.1	52 23.2	-55.7	157.6	51 27.7	-56.0	158.1	50 31.9	-56.2	158.5	49 36.0	-56.4	159.0	16
17	55 08.8	-54.9	156.1	54 13.8	-55.2	156.7	53 18.6	-55.5	157.2	52 23.1	-55.6	157.7	51 27.5	-55.9	158.2	50 31.7	-56.1	158.7	49 35.7	-56.3	159.1	48 39.6	-56.5	159.5	17
18	54 13.9	-55.1	156.8	53 18.6	-55.4	157.4	52 23.1	-55.6	157.9	51 27.5	-55.9	158.3	50 31.6	-56.0	158.8	49 35.6	-56.3	159.2	48 39.4	-56.4	159.6	47 43.1	-56.6	160.0	18
19	53 18.8	-55.4	157.5	52 23.2	-55.5	158.0	51 27.5	-55.8	158.5	50 31.6	-56.0	158.9	49 35.6	-56.3	159.3	48 39.3	-56.4	159.7	47 43.0	-56.6	160.1	46 46.5	-56.8	160.5	19
20	52 23.4	-55.5	158.1	51 27.7	-55.8	158.6	50 31.7	-56.0	159.0	49 35.6	-56.2	159.5	48 39.3	-56.3	159.9	47 42.9	-56.5	160.3	46 46.4	-56.7	160.6	45 49.7	-56.8	161.0	20
21	51 27.9	-55.7	158.7	50 31.9	-55.9	159.2	49 35.7	-56.1	159.6	48 39.4	-56.3	160.0	47 43.0	-56.5	160.4	46 46.4	-56.7	160.7	45 49.7	-56.8	161.1	44 52.9	-57.0	161.4	21
22	50 32.2	-55.9	159.3	49 36.0	-56.1	159.8	48 39.6	-56.2	160.1	47 43.1	-56.4	160.5	46 46.5	-56.6	160.9	45 49.7	-56.7	161.2	44 52.9	-56.9	161.5	43 55.9	-57.0	161.9	22
23	49 36.3	-56.0	159.9	48 39.9	-56.2	160.3	47 43.4	-56.5	160.7	46 46.7	-56.6	161.0	45 49.9	-56.8	161.4	44 53.0	-56.9	161.7	43 56.0	-57.1	162.0	42 58.9	-57.2	162.3	23
24	48 40.3	-56.2	160.4	47 43.7	-56.4	160.8	46 46.9	-56.5	161.2	45 50.1	-56.7	161.5	44 53.1	-56.8	161.8	43 56.1	-57.0	162.1	42 58.9	-57.1	162.4	42 01.7	-57.2	162.7	24
25	47 44.1	-56.3	161.0	46 47.3	-56.5	161.3	45 50.4	-56.6	161.7	44 53.4	-56.8	162.0	43 56.3	-56.9	162.3	42 59.1	-57.1	162.6	42 01.8	-57.2	162.8	41 04.5	-57.4	163.1	25
26	46 47.8	-56.5	161.5	45 50.8	-56.6	161.8	44 53.8	-56.8	162.1	43 56.6	-56.9	162.4	42 59.4	-57.1	162.7	42 02.0	-57.1	163.0	41 04.6	-57.3	163.2	40 07.1	-57.4	163.5	26
27	45 51.3	-56.6	162.0	44 54.2	-56.7	162.3	43 57.0	-56.9	162.6	42 59.7	-57.0	162.9	42 02.3	-57.1	163.1	41 04.9	-57.3	163.4	40 07.3	-57.3	163.6	39 09.7	-57.4	163.9	27
28	44 54.7	-56.7	162.4	43 57.5	-56.9	162.7	43 00.1	-56.9	163.0	42 02.7	-57.1	163.3	41 05.2	-57.2	163.5	40 07.6	-57.3	163.8	39 10.0	-57.5	164.0	38 12.3	-57.6	164.2	28
29	43 58.0	-56.8	162.9	43 00.6	-56.9	163.2	42 03.2	-57.1	163.4	41 05.6	-57.2	163.7	40 08.0	-57.3	163.9	39 10.3	-57.4	164.2	38 12.5	-57.5	164.4	37 14.7	-57.6	164.6	29
30	43 01.2	-56.9	163.3	42 03.7	-57.0	163.6	41 06.1	-57.1	163.9	40 08.4	-57.2	164.1	39 10.7	-57.4	164.3	38 12.9	-57.5	164.5	37 15.0	-57.5	164.7	36 17.1	-57.6	164.9	30
31	42 04.3	-57.0	163.8	41 06.7	-57.1	164.0	40 09.0	-57.3	164.3	39 11.2	-57.4	164.5	38 13.3	-57.4	164.7	37 15.4	-57.5	164.9	36 17.5	-57.6	165.1	35 19.5	-57.7	165.3	31
32	41 07.3	-57.1	164.2	40 09.6	-57.2	164.4	39 11.7	-57.3	164.6	38 13.8	-57.4	164.9	37 15.9	-57.5	165.1	36 17.9	-57.6	165.3	35 19.9	-57.7	165.4	34 21.8	-57.8	165.6	32
33	40 10.2	-57.1	164.6	39 12.4	-57.3	164.8	38 14.4	-57.3	165.0	37 16.4	-57.4	165.2	36 18.4	-57.6	165.4	35 20.3	-57.6	165.6	34 22.2	-57.8	165.8	33 24.0	-57.8	165.9	33
34	39 13.1	-57.3	165.0	38 15.1	-57.3	165.2	37 17.1	-57.5	165.4	36 19.0	-57.6	165.6	35 20.8	-57.6	165.8	34 22.7	-57.7	165.9	33 24.4	-57.8	166.1	32 26.2	-57.9	166.3	34
35	38 15.8	-57.3	165.4	37 17.8	-57.5	165.6	36 19.6	-57.5	165.8	35 21.4	-57.6	165.9	34 23.2	-57.7	166.1	33 25.0	-57.8	166.3	32 26.6	-57.8	166.4	31 28.3	-57.9	166.6	35
36	37 18.5	-57.4	165.8	36 20.3	-57.4	165.9	35 22.1	-57.6	166.1	34 23.8	-57.6	166.3	33 25.5	-57.7	166.4	32 27.2	-57.8	166.6	31 28.8	-57.9	166.7	30 30.4	-58.0	166.9	36
37	36 21.1	-57.4	166.1	35 22.9	-57.6	166.3	34 24.5	-57.6	166.5	33 26.2	-57.7	166.6	32 27.8	-57.8	166.8	31 29.4	-57.9	166.9	30 30.9	-57.9	167.0	29 32.4	-57.9	167.2	37
38	35 23.7	-57.5	166.5	34 25.3	-57.6	166.6	33 26.9	-57.6	166.8	32 28.5	-57.8	166.9	31 30.0	-57.8	167.1	30 31.5	-57.9	167.2	29 33.0	-58.0	167.3	28 34.5	-58.1	167.5	38
39	34 26.2	-57.6	166.8	33 27.7	-57.6	167.0	32 29.3	-57.8	167.1	31 30.7	-57.7	167.3	30 32.2	-57.9	167.4	29 33.6	-57.9	167.5	28 35.0	-58.0	167.6	27 36.4	-58.0	167.8	39
40	33 28.6	-57.6	167.2	32 30.1	-57.7	167.3	31 31.5	-57.7	167.4	30 33.0	-57.9	167.6	29 34.3	-57.9	167.7	28 35.7	-58.0	167.8	27 37.0	-58.0	167.9	26 38.4	-58.1	168.0	40
41	32 31.0	-57.7	167.5	31 32.4	-57.8	167.6	30 33.8	-57.9	167.8	29 35.1	-57.9	167.9	28 36.4	-57.9	168.0	27 37.7	-58.0	168.1	26 39.0	-58.1	168.2	25 40.3	-58.2	168.3	41
42	31 33.3	-57.7	167.8	30 34.6	-57.8	167.9	29 35.9	-57.8	168.1	28 37.2	-57.9	168.2	27 38.5	-58.0	168.3	26 39.7	-58.0	168.4	25 40.9	-58.1	168.5	24 42.1	-58.1	168.6	42
43	30 35.6	-57.8	168.1	29 36.8	-57.8	168.3	28 38.1	-57.9	168.4	27 39.3	-58.0	168.5	26 40.5	-58.0	168.6	25 41.7	-58.1	168.7	24 42.8	-58.1	168.8	23 44.0	-58.2	168.9	43
44	29 37.8	-57.8	168.5	28 39.0	-57.9	168.6	27 40.2	-57.9	168.7	26 41.3	-57.9	168.8	25 42.5	-58.1	168.9	24 43.6	-58.1	169.0	23 44.7	-58.1	169.0	22 45.8	-58.2	169.1	44
45	28 40.0	-57.9	168.8	27 41.1	-57.9	168.9	26 42.3	-58.0	169.0	25 43.4	-58.1	169.1	24 44.4	-58.0	169.1	23 45.5	-58.1	169.2	22 46.6	-58.2	169.3	21 47.6	-58.2	169.4	45
46	27 42.1	-57.9	169.1	26 43.2	-57.9	169.2	25 44.3	-58.0	169.2	24 45.3	-58.0	169.3	23 46.4	-58.2	169.4	22 47.4	-58.2	169.5	21 48.4	-58.2	169.6	20 49.4	-58.3	169.6	46
47	26 44.2	-57.9	169.4	25 45.3	-58.0	169.4	24 46.3	-58.1	169.5	23 47.3	-58.1	169.6	22 48.2	-58.1	169.7	21 49.2	-58.2	169.8	20 50.2	-58.3	169.8	19 51.1	-58.3	169.9	47
48	25 46.3	-57.9	169.6	24 47.3	-58.0	169.7	23 48.2	-58.0	169.8	22 49.2	-58.1	169.9	21 50.1	-58.2	170.0	20 51.0	-58.2	170.0	19 51.9	-58.2	170.1	18 52.8	-58.3	170.1	48
49	24 48.4	-58.0	169.9	23 49.3	-58.1	170.0	22 50.2	-58.1	170.1	21 51.1	-58.2	170.2	20 51.9	-58.1	170.2	19 52.8	-58.2	170.3	18 53.7	-58.3	170.3	17 54.5	-58.3	170.4	49
50	23 50.4	-58.1	170.2	22 51.2	-58.0	170.3	21 52.1	-58.1	170.4	20 52.9	-58.1	170.4	19 53.8	-58.2	170.5	18 54.6	-58.3	170.5	17 55.4	-58.3	170.6	16 56.2	-58.3	170.6	50
51	22 52.3	-58.0	170.5	21 53.2	-58.1	170.6	20 54.0	-58.2	170.6	19 54.8	-58.2	170.7	18 55.6	-58.3	170.7	17 56.3	-58.2	170.8	16 57.1	-58.3	170.8	15 57.9	-58.4	170.9	51
52	21 54.3	-58.1	170.8	20 55.1	-58.2	170.8	19 55.8	-58.1	170.9	18 56.6	-58.2	170.9	17 57.3	-58.2	171.0	16 58.1	-58.3	171.0	15 58.8	-58.3	171.1	14 59.5	-58.4	171.1	52
53	20 56.2	-58.1	171.0	19 56.9	-58.1	171.1	18 57.7	-58.2	171.1	17 58.4	-58.3	171.2	16 59.1	-58.3	171.2	15 59.8	-58.3	171.3	15 00.5	-58.4	171.3	14 01.1	-58.3	171.4	53
54	19 58.1	-58.1	171.3	18 58.8	-58.2	171.4	17 59.5	-58.2	171.4	17 00.1	-58.2	171.4	16 00.8	-58.3	171.5	15 01.5	-58.4	171.5	14 02.1	-58.3	171.6	13 02.8	-58.4	171.6	54
55	19 00.0	-58.2	171.6	18 00.6	-58.2	171.6	17 01.3	-58.3	171.7	16 01.9	-58.3	171.7	15 02.5	-58.3	171.7	14 03.1	-58.3	171.8	13 03.8	-58.4	171.8	12 04.4	-58.4	171.8	55
56	18 01.8	-58.1	171.8	17 02.4	-58.2	171.9	16 03.0	-58.2	171.9	15 03.6	-58.2	171.9	14 04.2	-58.3	172.0	13 04.8	-58.3	172.0	12 05.4	-58.4	172.0	11 06.0	-58.5	172.1	56
57	17 03.7	-58.2	172.1	16 04.2	-58.2	172.1	15 04.8	-58.3	172.2	14 05.4	-58.3	172.2	13 05.9	-58.3	172.2	12 06.5	-58.4	172.3	11 07.0	-58.4	172.3	10 07.5	-58.4	172.3	57
58	16 05.5	-58.2	172.3	15 06.0	-58.2	172.4	14 06.5	-58.2	172.4	13 07.1	-58.3	172.4	12 07.6	-58.4	172.5	11 08.1	-58.4	172.5	10 08.6	-58.4	172.5	9 09.1	-58.4	172.5	58
59	15 07.3	-58.3	172.6	14 07.8	-58.3	172.6	13 08.3	-58.3	172.6	12 08.8	-58.4	172.7	11 09.2	-58.3	172.7	10 09.7	-58.4	172.7	9 10.2	-58.4	172.7	8 10.7	-58.5	172.8	59
60	14 09.0	-58.2	172.8	13 09.5	-58.3	172.9	12 10.0	-58.3	172.9	11 10.4	-58.3	172.9	10 10.9	-58.4	172.9	9 11.3	-58.4	173.0	8 11.8	-58.4	173.0	7 12.2	-58.4	173.0	60
61	13 10.8	-58.3	173.1	12 11.2	-58.2	173.1	11 11.7	-58.3	173.1	10 12.1	-58.3	173.2	9 12.5	-58.3	173.2	8 12.9	-58.4	173.2	7 13.4	-58.5	173.2	6 13.8	-58.5	173.2	61
62	12 12.5	-58.2	173.3	11 13.0	-58.3	173.4	10 13.4	-58.4	173.4	9 13.8	-58.4	173.4	8 14.2	-58.4	173.4	7 14.5	-58.4	173.4	6 14.9	-58.4	173.4	5 15.3	-58.4	173.5	62
63	11 14.3	-58.3	173.6	10 14.7	-58.3	173.6	9 15.0	-58.3	173.6	8 15.4	-58.4	173.6	7 15.8	-58.4	173.6	6 16.1	-58.4	173.7	5 16.5	-58.4	173.7	4 16.9	-58.5	173.7	63
64	10 16.0	-58.3	173.8	9 16.4	-58.4	173.8	8 16.7	-58.3	173.8	7 17.0	-58.3	173.9	6 17.4	-58.4	173.9	5 17.7	-58.4	173.9	4 18.1	-58.5	173.9	3 18.4	-58.5	173.9	64
65	9 17.7	-58.3	174.1	8 18.0	-58.3	174.1	7 18.4	-58.4	174.1	6 18.7	-58.4	174.1	5 19.0	-58.4	174.1	4 19.3	-58.4	174.1	3 19.6	-58.4	174.1	2 19.9	-58.4	174.1	65
66	8 19.4	-58.3	174.3	7 19.7	-58.3	174.3	6 20.0	-58.3	174.3	5 20.3	-58.4	174.3	4 20.6	-58.4	174.3	3 20.9	-58.4	174.3	2 21.2	-58.5	174.3	1 21.5	-58.5	174.4	66
67	7 21.1	-58.3	174.5	6 21.4	-58.4	174.5	5 21.7	-58.4	174.6	4 21.9	-58.4	174.6	3 22.2	-58.4	174.6	2 22.5	-58.5	174.6	1 22.7	-58.4	174.6	0 23.0	-58.5	174.6	67
68	6 22.8	-58.3	174.8	5 23.0	-58.3	174.8	4 23.3	-58.4	174.8	3 23.5	-58.3	174.8	2 23.8	-58.4	174.8	1 24.0	-58.4	174.8	0 24.3	-58.5	174.8	0 35.5	+58.4	5.2	68
69	5 24.5	-58.4	175.0	4 24.7	-58.3	175.0	3 24.9	-58.3	175.0	2 25.2	-58.4	175.0	1 25.4	-58.4	175.0	0 25.6	-58.4	175.0	0 34.2	+58.4	5.0	1 33.9	+58.5	5.0	69
70	4 26.1	-58.3	175.2	3 26.4	-58.4	175.2	2 26.6	-58.4	175.2	1 26.8	-58.4	175.3	0 27.0	-58.4	175.3	0 32.8	+58.4	4.7	1 32.6	+58.5	4.7	2 32.4	+58.5	4.8	70
71	3 27.8	-58.3	175.5	2 28.0	-58.3	175.5	1 28.2	-58.4	175.5	0 28.4	-58.4	175.5	0 31.4	+58.4	4.5	1 31.2	+58.5	4.5	2 31.1	+58.4	4.5	3 30.9	+58.4	4.5	71
72	2 29.5	-58.4	175.7	1 29.7	-58.4	175.7	0 29.8	-58.4	175.7	0 30.0	+58.4	4.3	1 29.8	+58.5	4.3	2 29.7	+58.4	4.3	3 29.5	+58.4	4.3	4 29.3	+58.5	4.3	72
73	1 31.1	-58.3	175.9	0 31.3	-58.4	175.9	0 28.6	+58.3	4.1	1 28.4	+58.4	4.1	2 28.3	+58.4	4.1	3 28.1	+58.4	4.1	4 27.9	+58.5	4.1	5 27.8	+58.5	4.1	73
74	0 32.8	-58.3	176.2	0 27.1	+58.3	3.8	1 26.9	+58.4	3.8	2 26.8	+58.4	3.8	3 26.7	+58.4	3.8	4 26.5	+58.4	3.8	5 26.4	+58.4	3.8	6 26.3	+58.4	3.8	74
75	0 25.5	+58.4	3.6	1 25.4	+58.4	3.6	2 25.3	+58.4	3.6	3 25.2	+58.4	3.6	4 25.1	+58.4	3.6	5 24.9	+58.5	3.6	6 24.8	+58.4	3.6	7 24.7	+58.4	3.6	75
76	1 23.9	+58.3	3.4	2 23.8	+58.4	3.4	3 23.7	+58.3	3.4	4 23.6	+58.3	3.4	5 23.5	+58.3	3.4	6 23.4	+58.4	3.4	7 23.2	+58.5	3.4	8 23.1	+58.5	3.4	76
77	2 22.2	+58.3	3.1	3 22.1	+58.4	3.1	4 22.0	+58.4	3.1	5 21.9	+58.4	3.1	6 21.8	+58.4	3.1	7 21.8	+58.4	3.1	8 21.7	+58.4	3.2	9 21.6	+58.4	3.2	77
78	3 20.5	+58.4	2.9	4 20.5	+58.3	2.9	5 20.4	+58.3	2.9	6 20.3	+58.4	2.9	7 20.2	+58.4	2.9	8 20.2	+58.3	2.9	9 20.1	+58.4	2.9	10 20.0	+58.4	2.9	78
79	4 18.9	+58.3	2.7	5 18.8	+58.3	2.7	6 18.7	+58.4	2.7	7 18.7	+58.3	2.7	8 18.6	+58.4	2.7	9 18.5	+58.4	2.7	10 18.5	+58.4	2.7	11 18.4	+58.4	2.7	79
80	5 17.2	+58.3	2.4	6 17.1	+58.4	2.4	7 17.1	+58.3	2.4	8 17.0	+58.4	2.4	9 17.0	+58.3	2.4	10 16.9	+58.4	2.4	11 16.9	+58.4	2.5	12 16.8	+58.4	2.5	80
81	6 15.5	+58.3	2.2	7 15.5	+58.3	2.2	8 15.4	+58.4	2.2	9 15.4	+58.3	2.2	10 15.3	+58.3	2.2	11 15.3	+58.4	2.2	12 15.3	+58.3	2.2	13 15.2	+58.4	2.2	81
82	7 13.8	+58.3	1.9	8 13.8	+58.3	1.9	9 13.8	+58.3	2.0	10 13.7	+58.4	2.0	11 13.7	+58.3	2.0	12 13.7	+58.3	2.0	13 13.6	+58.4	2.0	14 13.6	+58.4	2.0	82
83	8 12.1	+58.3	1.7	9 12.1	+58.3	1.7	10 12.1	+58.3	1.7	11 12.1	+58.3	1.7	12 12.0	+58.4	1.7	13 12.0	+58.3	1.7	14 12.0	+58.3	1.7	15 12.0	+58.3	1.8	83
84	9 10.4	+58.3	1.5	10 10.4	+58.3	1.5	11 10.4	+58.3	1.5	12 10.4	+58.3	1.5	13 10.4	+58.3	1.5	14 10.3	+58.4	1.5	15 10.3	+58.3	1.5	16 10.3	+58.3	1.5	84
85	10 08.7	+58.3	1.2	11 08.7	+58.3	1.2	12 08.7	+58.3	1.2	13 08.7	+58.3	1.2	14 08.7	+58.3	1.2	15 08.7	+58.3	1.3	16 08.6	+58.4	1.3	17 08.6	+58.3	1.3	85
86	11 07.0	+58.3	1.0	12 07.0	+58.3	1.0	13 07.0	+58.3	1.0	14 07.0	+58.3	1.0	15 07.0	+58.3	1.0	16 07.0	+58.3	1.0	17 07.0	+58.2	1.0	18 06.9	+58.3	1.0	86
87	12 05.3	+58.2	0.7	13 05.3	+58.2	0.7	14 05.3	+58.2	0.7	15 05.3	+58.3	0.8	16 05.3	+58.2	0.8	17 05.3	+58.2	0.8	18 05.2	+58.3	0.8	19 05.2	+58.3	0.8	87
88	13 03.5	+58.3	0.5	14 03.5	+58.3	0.5	15 03.5	+58.3	0.5	16 03.5	+58.3	0.5	17 03.5	+58.3	0.5	18 03.5	+58.3	0.5	19 03.5	+58.3	0.5	20 03.5	+58.3	0.5	88
89	14 01.8	+58.2	0.2	15 01.8	+58.2	0.3	16 01.8	+58.2	0.3	17 01.8	+58.2	0.3	18 01.8	+58.2	0.3	19 01.8	+58.2	0.3	20 01.8	+58.2	0.3	21 01.8	+58.2	0.3	89
90	15 00.0	+58.2	0.0	16 00.0	+58.2	0.0	17 00.0	+58.2	0.0	18 00.0	+58.2	0.0	19 00.0	+58.2	0.0	20 00.0	+58.2	0.0	21 00.0	+58.2	0.0	22 00.0	+58.2	0.0	90
	15°			16°			17°			18°			19°			20°			21°			22°			

S. Lat. {L.H.A. greater than 180° ....Zn=180°–Z; L.H.A. less than 180°...........Zn=180°+Z

LATITUDE **SAME** NAME AS DECLINATION **L.H.A. 166°, 194°**

31

15°, 345° L.H.A. LATITUDE SAME NAME AS DECLINATION

N. Lat. {L.H.A. greater than 180° .....Zn=Z; L.H.A. less than 180°............Zn=360°−Z}

Dec.	15° Hc	d	Z	16° Hc	d	Z	17° Hc	d	Z	18° Hc	d	Z	19° Hc	d	Z	20° Hc	d	Z	21° Hc	d	Z	22° Hc	d	Z	Dec.
°	° ′	′	°	° ′	′	°	° ′	′	°	° ′	′	°	° ′	′	°	° ′	′	°	° ′	′	°	° ′	′	°	°
0	68 54.6	+42.4	134.0	68 12.2	+43.9	135.8	67 28.6	+45.2	137.5	66 43.8	+46.4	139.1	65 57.9	+47.6	140.5	65 11.1	+48.6	141.9	64 23.5	+49.4	143.2	63 35.1	+50.2	144.4	0
1	69 37.0	+41.1	132.0	68 56.1	+42.7	133.9	68 13.8	+44.1	135.8	67 30.2	+45.4	137.4	66 45.5	+46.5	139.0	65 59.7	+47.6	140.5	65 12.9	+48.6	141.9	64 25.3	+49.5	143.2	1
2	70 18.1	+39.4	129.9	69 38.8	+41.1	132.0	68 57.9	+42.8	133.9	68 15.6	+44.2	135.7	67 32.0	+45.6	137.4	66 47.3	+46.7	139.0	66 01.5	+47.8	140.5	65 14.8	+48.8	141.8	2
3	70 57.5	+37.6	127.6	70 19.9	+39.6	129.8	69 40.7	+41.3	131.9	68 59.8	+43.0	133.9	68 17.6	+44.4	135.7	67 34.0	+45.7	137.4	66 49.3	+46.9	139.0	66 03.6	+47.9	140.4	3
4	71 35.1	+35.7•	125.2	70 59.5	+37.8	127.6	70 22.0	+39.8	129.8	69 42.8	+41.5	131.9	69 02.0	+43.1	133.8	68 19.7	+44.6	135.6	67 36.2	+45.9	137.3	66 51.5	+47.1	138.9	4
5	72 10.8	+33.5•	122.6	71 37.3	+35.9•	125.1	71 01.8	+38.0	127.5	70 24.3	+39.9	129.8	69 45.1	+41.7	131.8	69 04.3	+43.3	133.8	68 22.1	+44.7	135.6	67 38.6	+46.0	137.3	5
6	72 44.3	+31.0•	119.8	72 13.2	+33.6•	122.6	71 39.8	+36.0•	125.1	71 04.2	+38.2	127.5	70 26.8	+40.1	129.7	69 47.6	+41.9	131.8	69 06.8	+43.5	133.8	68 24.6	+44.9	135.6	6
7	73 15.3	+28.5•	116.9	72 46.8	+31.3•	119.8	72 15.8	+33.8•	122.5	71 42.4	+36.2•	125.1	71 06.9	+38.4	127.5	70 29.5	+40.3	129.7	69 50.3	+42.0	131.8	69 09.5	+43.7	133.8	7
8	73 43.8	+25.6•	113.8	73 18.1	+28.7•	116.9	72 49.6	+31.5•	119.8	72 18.6	+34.1•	122.5	71 45.3	+36.4•	125.1	71 09.8	+38.5	127.5	70 32.3	+40.5	129.7	69 53.2	+42.2	131.8	8
9	74 09.4	+22.5•	110.5	73 46.8	+25.8•	113.8	73 21.1	+28.9•	116.8	72 52.7	+31.7•	119.7	72 21.7	+34.3•	122.5	71 48.3	+36.7•	125.0	71 12.8	+38.8	127.5	70 35.4	+40.7	129.7	9
10	74 31.9	+19.2•	107.1	74 12.6	+22.7•	110.5	73 50.0	+26.0•	113.7	73 24.4	+29.1•	116.8	72 56.0	+31.9•	119.7	72 25.0	+34.4•	122.5	71 51.6	+36.8•	125.0	71 16.1	+39.0	127.5	10
11	74 51.1	+15.7•	103.5	74 35.3	+19.4•	107.1	74 16.0	+22.9•	110.5	73 53.5	+26.2•	113.7	73 27.9	+29.2•	116.8	72 59.4	+32.2•	119.7	72 28.4	+34.8•	122.5	71 55.1	+37.1•	125.1	11
12	75 06.8	+11.9•	99.8	74 54.7	+15.8•	103.5	74 38.9	+19.6•	107.0	74 19.7	+23.1•	110.4	73 57.1	+26.5•	113.7	73 31.6	+29.5•	116.8	73 03.2	+32.3•	119.7	72 32.2	+34.9•	122.5	12
13	75 18.7	+8.1•	96.0	75 10.5	+12.1•	99.7	74 58.5	+16.0•	103.4	74 42.8	+19.8•	107.0	74 23.6	+23.3•	110.4	74 01.1	+26.6•	113.7	73 35.5	+29.7•	116.8	73 07.1	+32.6•	119.7	13
14	75 26.8	+4.0•	92.0	75 22.6	+8.3•	95.9	75 14.5	+12.3•	99.6	75 02.6	+16.2•	103.3	74 46.9	+20.0•	106.9	74 27.7	+23.6•	110.4	74 05.2	+26.9•	113.7	73 39.7	+29.9•	116.8	14
15	75 30.8	+0.1•	88.0	75 30.9	+4.2•	91.9	75 26.8	+8.4•	95.8	75 18.8	+12.5•	99.6	75 06.9	+16.4•	103.3	74 51.3	+20.2•	106.9	74 32.1	+23.8•	110.4	74 09.6	+27.1•	113.7	15
16	75 30.9	-4.1•	84.0	75 35.1	+0.1•	87.9	75 35.2	+4.3•	91.8	75 31.3	+8.5•	95.7	75 23.3	+12.7•	99.5	75 11.5	+16.6•	103.2	74 55.9	+20.4•	106.9	74 36.7	+24.0•	110.3	16
17	75 26.8	-8.0•	80.1	75 35.2	-3.9•	83.9	75 39.5	+0.3•	87.8	75 39.8	+4.5•	91.7	75 36.0	+8.7•	95.6	75 28.1	+12.8•	99.4	75 16.3	+16.8•	103.2	75 00.7	+20.7•	106.8	17
18	75 18.8	-11.9•	76.1	75 31.3	-8.0•	79.9	75 39.8	-3.8•	83.8	75 44.3	+0.4•	87.7	75 44.7	+4.6•	91.6	75 40.9	+8.9•	95.5	75 33.1	+13.0•	99.4	75 21.4	+17.0•	103.2	18
19	75 06.9	-15.6•	72.3	75 23.3	-11.8•	76.0	75 36.0	-7.9•	79.7	75 44.7	-3.8•	83.6	75 49.3	+0.5•	87.5	75 49.8	+4.8•	91.5	75 46.1	+9.1•	95.5	75 38.4	+13.2•	99.3	19
20	74 51.3	-19.2•	68.6	75 11.5	-15.6•	72.1	75 28.1	-11.8•	75.8	75 40.9	-7.8•	79.6	75 49.8	-3.7•	83.5	75 54.6	+0.6•	87.4	75 55.2	+4.9•	91.4	75 51.6	+9.2•	95.4	20
21	74 32.1	-22.5•	65.0	74 55.9	-19.2•	68.3	75 16.3	-15.6•	71.9	75 33.1	-11.7•	75.6	75 46.1	-7.7•	79.4	75 55.2	-3.6•	83.3	76 00.1	+0.7•	87.3	76 00.8	+5.1•	91.3	21
22	74 09.6	-25.6•	61.5	74 36.7	-22.5•	64.7	75 00.7	-19.1•	68.1	75 21.4	-15.6•	71.7	75 38.4	-11.7•	75.4	75 51.6	-7.7•	79.2	76 00.8	-3.5•	83.2	76 05.9	+0.8•	87.2	22
23	73 44.0	-28.4•	58.3	74 14.2	-25.6•	61.3	74 41.6	-22.5•	64.5	75 05.8	-19.1•	67.9	75 26.7	-15.5•	71.4	75 43.9	-11.6•	75.2	75 57.3	-7.6•	79.0	76 06.7	-3.4•	83.0	23
24	73 15.6	-31.1•	55.2	73 48.6	-28.4•	58.0	74 19.1	-25.6•	61.0	74 46.7	-22.5•	64.2	75 11.2	-19.2•	67.6	75 32.3	-15.6•	71.2	75 49.7	-11.6•	75.0	76 03.3	-7.5•	78.9	24
25	72 44.5	-33.4•	52.2	73 20.2	-31.2•	54.9	73 53.5	-28.6•	57.7	74 24.2	-25.7•	60.7	74 52.0	-22.5•	64.0	75 16.7	-19.1•	67.4	75 38.1	-15.5•	71.0	75 55.8	-11.7•	74.8	25
26	72 11.1	-35.7•	49.5	72 49.0	-33.5•	51.9	73 24.9	-31.1•	54.6	73 58.5	-28.6•	57.4	74 29.5	-25.7•	60.5	74 57.6	-22.6•	63.7	75 22.6	-19.2•	67.1	75 44.1	-15.5•	70.8	26
27	71 35.4	-37.6	46.9	72 15.5	-35.7•	49.2	72 53.8	-33.6•	51.6	73 29.9	-31.2•	54.3	74 03.8	-28.7•	57.1	74 35.0	-25.8•	60.2	75 03.4	-22.7•	63.4	75 28.6	-19.2•	66.9	27
28	70 57.8	-39.4	44.5	71 39.8	-37.6	46.6	72 20.2	-35.8•	48.9	72 58.7	-33.6•	51.3	73 35.1	-31.3•	54.0	74 09.2	-28.7•	56.8	74 40.7	-25.8•	59.9	75 09.4	-22.7•	63.1	28
29	70 18.4	-41.0	42.2	71 02.2	-39.5	44.2	71 44.4	-37.7	46.3	72 25.1	-35.9•	48.5	73 03.8	-33.7•	51.0	73 40.5	-31.4•	53.6	74 14.9	-28.8•	56.5	74 46.7	-26.0•	59.6	29
30	69 37.4	-42.5	40.1	70 22.7	-41.1	41.9	71 06.7	-39.5	43.8	71 49.2	-37.8	45.9	72 30.1	-35.9•	48.2	73 09.1	-33.8•	50.7	73 46.1	-31.5•	53.3	74 20.7	-28.8•	56.2	30
31	68 54.9	-43.8	38.1	69 41.6	-42.5	39.7	70 27.2	-41.2	41.5	71 11.4	-39.6	43.5	71 54.2	-37.9	45.6	72 35.3	-36.0•	47.9	73 14.6	-33.9•	50.3	73 51.9	-31.6•	53.0	31
32	68 11.1	-44.9	36.2	68 59.1	-43.9	37.7	69 46.0	-42.6	39.4	70 31.8	-41.3	41.2	71 16.3	-39.8	43.1	71 59.3	-38.0	45.2	72 40.7	-36.1•	47.5	73 20.3	-34.0•	50.0	32
33	67 26.2	-46.1	34.5	68 15.2	-45.0	35.9	69 03.4	-43.9	37.4	69 50.5	-42.7	39.0	70 36.5	-41.3	40.8	71 21.3	-39.8	42.8	72 04.6	-38.1	44.9	72 46.3	-36.3•	47.1	33
34	66 40.1	-47.0	32.8	67 30.2	-46.1	34.1	68 19.5	-45.1	35.5	69 07.8	-44.0	37.0	69 55.2	-42.8	38.7	70 41.5	-41.5	40.5	71 26.5	-39.9	42.4	72 10.0	-38.2	44.5	34
35	65 53.1	-47.8	31.3	66 44.1	-47.1	32.5	67 34.4	-46.2	33.8	68 23.8	-45.2	35.2	69 12.4	-44.1	36.7	70 00.0	-42.8	38.3	70 46.6	-41.6	40.1	71 31.8	-40.0	42.0	35
36	65 05.3	-48.7	29.8	65 57.0	-47.9	30.9	66 48.2	-47.2	32.1	67 38.6	-46.2	33.4	68 28.3	-45.2	34.8	69 17.2	-44.2	36.3	70 05.0	-43.0	37.9	70 51.8	-41.7	39.7	36
37	64 16.6	-49.4	28.4	65 09.1	-48.8	29.5	66 01.0	-48.0	30.6	66 52.4	-47.2	31.8	67 43.1	-46.4	33.0	68 33.0	-45.4	34.4	69 22.0	-44.3	35.9	70 10.1	-43.1	37.5	37
38	63 27.2	-50.1	27.2	64 20.3	-49.4	28.1	65 13.0	-48.8	29.1	66 05.2	-48.1	30.2	66 56.7	-47.3	31.4	67 47.6	-46.5	32.7	68 37.7	-45.5	34.0	69 27.0	-44.4	35.5	38
39	62 37.1	-50.6	25.9	63 30.9	-50.1	26.8	64 24.2	-49.5	27.7	65 17.1	-48.9	28.8	66 09.4	-48.2	29.8	67 01.1	-47.4	31.0	67 52.2	-46.5	32.3	68 42.6	-45.6	33.6	39
40	61 46.5	-51.2	24.8	62 40.8	-50.7	25.6	63 34.7	-50.2	26.5	64 28.2	-49.6	27.4	65 21.2	-48.9	28.4	66 13.7	-48.2	29.5	67 05.7	-47.5	30.6	67 57.0	-46.7	31.9	40
41	60 55.3	-51.7	23.7	61 50.1	-51.3	24.4	62 44.5	-50.8	25.2	63 38.6	-50.3	26.1	64 32.3	-49.7	27.0	65 25.5	-49.1	28.0	66 18.2	-48.4	29.1	67 10.3	-47.6	30.2	41
42	60 03.6	-52.2	22.7	60 58.8	-51.7	23.4	61 53.7	-51.3	24.1	62 48.3	-50.8	24.9	63 42.6	-50.3	25.7	64 36.4	-49.7	26.6	65 29.8	-49.1	27.6	66 22.7	-48.4	28.7	42
43	59 11.4	-52.5	21.7	60 07.1	-52.2	22.3	61 02.4	-51.8	23.0	61 57.5	-51.4	23.7	62 52.3	-50.9	24.5	63 46.7	-50.4	25.4	64 40.7	-49.9	26.3	65 34.3	-49.3	27.2	43
44	58 18.9	-53.0	20.8	59 14.9	-52.7	21.4	60 10.6	-52.2	22.0	61 06.1	-51.8	22.7	62 01.4	-51.5	23.4	62 56.3	-51.0	24.2	63 50.8	-50.5	25.0	64 45.0	-49.9	25.9	44
45	57 25.9	-53.3	19.9	58 22.2	-53.0	20.4	59 18.4	-52.7	21.0	60 14.3	-52.4	21.6	61 09.9	-51.9	22.3	62 05.3	-51.6	23.0	63 00.3	-51.0	23.8	63 55.1	-50.6	24.6	45
46	56 32.6	-53.6	19.0	57 29.2	-53.3	19.5	58 25.7	-53.1	20.1	59 21.9	-52.7	20.7	60 18.0	-52.4	21.3	61 13.7	-52.0	21.9	62 09.3	-51.6	22.6	63 04.5	-51.2	23.4	46
47	55 39.0	-54.0	18.2	56 35.9	-53.7	18.7	57 32.6	-53.4	19.2	58 29.2	-53.1	19.7	59 25.6	-52.8	20.3	60 21.7	-52.4	20.9	61 17.7	-52.1	21.6	62 13.3	-51.7	22.3	47
48	54 45.0	-54.2	17.5	55 42.2	-54.0	17.9	56 39.2	-53.7	18.4	57 36.1	-53.5	18.9	58 32.8	-53.2	19.4	59 29.3	-52.9	19.9	60 25.6	-52.6	20.5	61 21.6	-52.1	21.2	48
49	53 50.8	-54.5	16.7	54 48.2	-54.2	17.1	55 45.5	-54.0	17.6	56 42.6	-53.8	18.0	57 39.6	-53.5	18.5	58 36.4	-53.2	19.0	59 33.0	-52.9	19.6	60 29.5	-52.6	20.2	49
50	52 56.3	-54.7	16.0	53 54.0	-54.6	16.4	54 51.5	-54.3	16.8	55 48.8	-54.0	17.2	56 46.1	-53.9	17.7	57 43.2	-53.6	18.2	58 40.1	-53.3	18.7	59 36.9	-53.1	19.2	50
51	52 01.6	-54.9	15.4	52 59.4	-54.7	15.7	53 57.2	-54.6	16.1	54 54.8	-54.4	16.5	55 52.2	-54.1	16.9	56 49.6	-53.9	17.3	57 46.8	-53.7	17.8	58 43.8	-53.3	18.3	51
52	51 06.7	-55.1	14.7	52 04.7	-55.0	15.0	53 02.6	-54.8	15.4	54 00.4	-54.6	15.7	54 58.1	-54.4	16.1	55 55.7	-54.2	16.5	56 53.1	-53.9	17.0	57 50.5	-53.8	17.4	52
53	50 11.6	-55.4	14.1	51 09.7	-55.1	14.4	52 07.8	-55.0	14.7	53 05.8	-54.8	15.0	54 03.7	-54.7	15.4	55 01.5	-54.5	15.8	55 59.2	-54.3	16.2	56 56.7	-54.0	16.6	53
54	49 16.2	-55.5	13.5	50 14.6	-55.4	13.8	51 12.8	-55.2	14.1	52 11.0	-55.1	14.4	53 09.0	-54.9	14.7	54 07.0	-54.7	15.0	55 04.9	-54.5	15.4	56 02.7	-54.3	15.8	54
55	48 20.7	-55.6	12.9	49 19.2	-55.6	13.2	50 17.6	-55.4	13.4	51 15.9	-55.3	13.7	52 14.1	-55.1	14.0	53 12.3	-54.9	14.4	54 10.4	-54.8	14.7	55 08.4	-54.6	15.1	55
56	47 25.1	-55.9	12.4	48 23.6	-55.7	12.6	49 22.2	-55.6	12.8	50 20.6	-55.4	13.1	51 19.0	-55.3	13.4	52 17.4	-55.2	13.7	53 15.6	-55.0	14.0	54 13.8	-54.8	14.3	56
57	46 29.2	-56.0	11.8	47 27.9	-55.8	12.0	48 26.6	-55.8	12.3	49 25.2	-55.6	12.5	50 23.7	-55.5	12.8	51 22.2	-55.3	13.0	52 20.6	-55.2	13.3	53 19.0	-55.1	13.6	57
58	45 33.2	-56.1	11.3	46 32.1	-56.0	11.5	47 30.8	-55.9	11.7	48 29.6	-55.8	11.9	49 28.2	-55.6	12.2	50 26.9	-55.6	12.4	51 25.4	-55.4	12.7	52 23.9	-55.2	13.0	58
59	44 37.1	-56.2	10.8	45 36.1	-56.2	11.0	46 34.9	-56.0	11.2	47 33.8	-56.0	11.4	48 32.6	-55.9	11.6	49 31.3	-55.7	11.8	50 30.0	-55.6	12.1	51 28.7	-55.5	12.4	59
60	43 40.9	-56.4	10.3	44 39.9	-56.3	10.5	45 38.9	-56.2	10.7	46 37.8	-56.0	10.9	47 36.7	-55.9	11.1	48 35.6	-55.9	11.3	49 34.4	-55.7	11.5	50 33.2	-55.7	11.8	60
61	42 44.5	-56.4	9.8	43 43.6	-56.3	10.0	44 42.7	-56.3	10.2	45 41.8	-56.3	10.3	46 40.8	-56.2	10.5	47 39.7	-56.0	10.7	48 38.7	-56.0	10.9	49 37.5	-55.8	11.2	61
62	41 48.1	-56.6	9.4	42 47.3	-56.6	9.5	43 46.4	-56.4	9.7	44 45.5	-56.3	9.9	45 44.6	-56.2	10.0	46 43.7	-56.2	10.2	47 42.7	-56.0	10.4	48 41.7	-55.9	10.6	62
63	40 51.5	-56.7	8.9	41 50.7	-56.6	9.1	42 50.0	-56.5	9.2	43 49.2	-56.5	9.4	44 48.4	-56.4	9.5	45 47.5	-56.3	9.7	46 46.7	-56.2	9.9	47 45.8	-56.2	10.1	63
64	39 54.8	-56.8	8.5	40 54.1	-56.7	8.6	41 53.5	-56.7	8.8	42 52.7	-56.5	8.9	43 52.0	-56.5	9.1	44 51.2	-56.4	9.2	45 50.5	-56.4	9.4	46 49.6	-56.2	9.5	64
65	38 58.0	-56.8	8.1	39 57.4	-56.8	8.2	40 56.8	-56.7	8.3	41 56.2	-56.7	8.5	42 55.5	-56.6	8.6	43 54.8	-56.5	8.7	44 54.1	-56.4	8.9	45 53.4	-56.4	9.0	65
66	38 01.2	-57.0	7.7	39 00.6	-56.8	7.8	40 00.1	-56.8	7.9	40 59.5	-56.8	8.0	41 58.9	-56.7	8.1	42 58.3	-56.6	8.3	43 57.7	-56.6	8.4	44 57.0	-56.5	8.6	66
67	37 04.2	-57.0	7.3	38 03.8	-57.0	7.4	39 03.3	-57.0	7.5	40 02.7	-56.8	7.6	41 02.2	-56.8	7.7	42 01.7	-56.8	7.8	43 01.1	-56.7	8.0	44 00.5	-56.6	8.1	67
68	36 07.2	-57.1	6.9	37 06.8	-57.1	7.0	38 06.3	-57.0	7.1	39 05.9	-57.0	7.2	40 05.4	-56.9	7.3	41 04.9	-56.8	7.4	42 04.4	-56.8	7.5	43 03.9	-56.7	7.6	68
69	35 10.1	-57.1	6.5	36 09.7	-57.1	6.6	37 09.3	-57.0	6.7	38 08.9	-57.0	6.8	39 08.5	-57.0	6.9	40 08.1	-57.0	7.0	41 07.6	-56.9	7.1	42 07.2	-56.9	7.2	69
70	34 13.0	-57.2	6.1	35 12.6	-57.2	6.2	36 12.3	-57.2	6.3	37 11.9	-57.1	6.4	38 11.5	-57.0	6.5	39 11.1	-57.0	6.6	40 10.7	-56.9	6.7	41 10.3	-56.9	6.8	70
71	33 15.8	-57.3	5.8	34 15.4	-57.2	5.9	35 15.1	-57.2	5.9	36 14.8	-57.2	6.0	37 14.5	-57.2	6.1	38 14.1	-57.1	6.2	39 13.8	-57.1	6.2	40 13.4	-57.0	6.3	71
72	32 18.5	-57.4	5.4	33 18.2	-57.3	5.5	34 17.9	-57.3	5.6	35 17.6	-57.2	5.6	36 17.3	-57.2	5.7	37 17.0	-57.1	5.8	38 16.7	-57.1	5.8	39 16.4	-57.1	5.9	72
73	31 21.1	-57.4	5.1	32 20.9	-57.4	5.1	33 20.6	-57.3	5.2	34 20.4	-57.3	5.3	35 20.1	-57.2	5.3	36 19.9	-57.3	5.4	37 19.6	-57.2	5.5	38 19.3	-57.1	5.5	73
74	30 23.7	-57.4	4.7	31 23.5	-57.4	4.8	32 23.3	-57.4	4.8	33 23.1	-57.4	4.9	34 22.9	-57.4	5.0	35 22.6	-57.3	5.0	36 22.4	-57.3	5.1	37 22.2	-57.3	5.2	74
75	29 26.3	-57.5	4.4	30 26.1	-57.5	4.5	31 25.9	-57.4	4.5	32 25.7	-57.4	4.6	33 25.5	-57.4	4.6	34 25.3	-57.3	4.7	35 25.1	-57.3	4.7	36 24.9	-57.3	4.8	75
76	28 28.8	-57.6	4.1	29 28.6	-57.5	4.1	30 28.5	-57.5	4.2	31 28.3	-57.5	4.2	32 28.1	-57.4	4.3	33 28.0	-57.4	4.3	34 27.8	-57.4	4.4	35 27.6	-57.3	4.4	76
77	27 31.2	-57.6	3.8	28 31.1	-57.6	3.8	29 31.0	-57.6	3.8	30 30.8	-57.5	3.9	31 30.7	-57.5	3.9	32 30.6	-57.5	4.0	33 30.4	-57.4	4.0	34 30.3	-57.5	4.1	77
78	26 33.6	-57.6	3.4	27 33.5	-57.6	3.5	28 33.4	-57.6	3.5	29 33.3	-57.6	3.5	30 33.2	-57.6	3.6	31 33.1	-57.6	3.6	32 33.0	-57.6	3.7	33 32.8	-57.5	3.7	78
79	25 36.0	-57.6	3.1	26 35.9	-57.6	3.2	27 35.8	-57.6	3.2	28 35.7	-57.6	3.2	29 35.6	-57.6	3.3	30 35.5	-57.5	3.3	31 35.4	-57.5	3.3	32 35.3	-57.5	3.4	79
80	24 38.4	-57.8	2.8	25 38.3	-57.7	2.9	26 38.2	-57.7	2.9	27 38.1	-57.6	2.9	28 38.0	-57.6	2.9	29 38.0	-57.7	3.0	30 37.9	-57.6	3.0	31 37.8	-57.6	3.0	80
81	23 40.6	-57.7	2.5	24 40.6	-57.7	2.6	25 40.5	-57.7	2.6	26 40.5	-57.7	2.6	27 40.4	-57.7	2.6	28 40.3	-57.6	2.6	29 40.3	-57.7	2.7	30 40.2	-57.6	2.7	81
82	22 42.9	-57.8	2.2	23 42.9	-57.8	2.3	24 42.8	-57.7	2.3	25 42.8	-57.8	2.3	26 42.7	-57.7	2.3	27 42.7	-57.7	2.3	28 42.6	-57.7	2.4	29 42.6	-57.7	2.4	82
83	21 45.1	-57.8	1.9	22 45.1	-57.8	2.0	23 45.1	-57.8	2.0	24 45.0	-57.7	2.0	25 45.0	-57.8	2.0	26 45.0	-57.8	2.0	27 44.9	-57.7	2.0	28 44.9	-57.7	2.1	83
84	20 47.3	-57.8	1.7	21 47.3	-57.8	1.7	22 47.3	-57.8	1.7	23 47.3	-57.8	1.7	24 47.2	-57.8	1.7	25 47.2	-57.8	1.7	26 47.2	-57.8	1.7	27 47.2	-57.8	1.8	84
85	19 49.5	-57.8	1.4	20 49.5	-57.9	1.4	21 49.5	-57.9	1.4	22 49.5	-57.9	1.4	23 49.4	-57.8	1.4	24 49.4	-57.8	1.4	25 49.4	-57.8	1.4	26 49.4	-57.8	1.4	85
86	18 51.7	-57.9	1.1	19 51.6	-57.8	1.1	20 51.6	-57.8	1.1	21 51.6	-57.8	1.1	22 51.6	-57.8	1.1	23 51.6	-57.9	1.1	24 51.6	-57.9	1.1	25 51.6	-57.9	1.1	86
87	17 53.8	-57.9	0.8	18 53.8	-57.9	0.8	19 53.8	-57.9	0.8	20 53.8	-57.9	0.8	21 53.8	-57.9	0.8	22 53.7	-57.8	0.8	23 53.7	-57.8	0.8	24 53.7	-57.8	0.9	87
88	16 55.9	-58.0	0.5	17 55.9	-58.0	0.5	18 55.9	-58.0	0.5	19 55.9	-58.0	0.6	20 55.9	-58.0	0.6	21 55.9	-58.0	0.6	22 55.9	-58.0	0.6	23 55.9	-58.0	0.6	88
89	15 57.9	-57.9	0.3	16 57.9	-57.9	0.3	17 57.9	-57.9	0.3	18 57.9	-57.9	0.3	19 57.9	-57.9	0.3	20 57.9	-57.9	0.3	21 57.9	-57.9	0.3	22 57.9	-57.9	0.3	89
90	15 00.0	-58.0	0.0	16 00.0	-58.0	0.0	17 00.0	-58.0	0.0	18 00.0	-58.0	0.0	19 00.0	-58.0	0.0	20 00.0	-58.0	0.0	21 00.0	-58.0	0.0	22 00.0	-58.0	0.0	90
	15°			16°			17°			18°			19°			20°			21°			22°			

15°, 345° L.H.A. LATITUDE SAME NAME AS DECLINATION

LATITUDE **CONTRARY** NAME TO DECLINATION — L.H.A. 15°, 345°

Dec.	15°			16°			17°			18°			19°			20°			21°			22°			Dec.
°	Hc ° ′	d ′	Z °	Hc ° ′	d ′	Z °	Hc ° ′	d ′	Z °	Hc ° ′	d ′	Z °	Hc ° ′	d ′	Z °	Hc ° ′	d ′	Z °	Hc ° ′	d ′	Z °	Hc ° ′	d ′	Z °	°
0	68 54.6	-43.8	134.0	68 12.2	-45.1	135.8	67 28.6	-46.3	137.5	66 43.8	-47.4	139.1	65 57.9	-48.3	140.5	65 11.1	-49.2	141.9	64 23.5	-50.1	143.2	63 35.1	-50.9	144.4	0
1	68 10.8	-45.0	135.9	67 27.1	-46.2	137.6	66 42.3	-47.3	139.1	65 56.4	-48.3	140.6	65 09.6	-49.2	142.0	64 21.9	-50.0	143.3	63 33.4	-50.7	144.5	62 44.2	-51.3	145.6	1
2	67 25.8	-46.0	137.6	66 40.9	-47.1	139.2	65 55.0	-48.1	140.7	65 08.1	-49.0	142.0	64 20.4	-49.8	143.3	63 31.9	-50.6	144.5	62 42.7	-51.2	145.7	61 52.9	-51.9	146.7	2
3	66 39.8	-47.1	139.3	65 53.8	-48.0	140.7	65 06.9	-48.9	142.1	64 19.1	-49.7	143.4	63 30.6	-50.5	144.6	62 41.3	-51.1	145.7	61 51.5	-51.8	146.8	61 01.0	-52.4	147.8	3
4	65 52.7	-47.8	140.8	65 05.8	-48.8	142.2	64 18.0	-49.6	143.5	63 29.4	-50.4	144.7	62 40.1	-51.0	145.8	61 50.2	-51.7	146.8	60 59.7	-52.3	147.8	60 08.6	-52.7	148.8	4
5	65 04.9	-48.7	142.3	64 17.0	-49.5	143.5	63 28.4	-50.3	144.7	62 39.0	-50.9	145.9	61 49.1	-51.6	146.9	60 58.5	-52.1	147.9	60 07.4	-52.6	148.8	59 15.9	-53.2	149.7	5
6	64 16.2	-49.4	143.6	63 27.5	-50.2	144.8	62 38.1	-50.8	145.9	61 48.1	-51.5	147.0	60 57.5	-52.1	148.0	60 06.4	-52.6	148.9	59 14.8	-53.1	149.8	58 22.7	-53.5	150.6	6
7	63 26.8	-50.1	144.9	62 37.3	-50.7	146.0	61 47.3	-51.4	147.1	60 56.6	-51.9	148.1	60 05.4	-52.4	149.0	59 13.8	-53.0	149.9	58 21.7	-53.4	150.7	57 29.2	-53.9	151.4	7
8	62 36.7	-50.6	146.1	61 46.6	-51.3	147.2	60 55.9	-51.9	148.2	60 04.7	-52.4	149.1	59 13.0	-52.9	149.9	58 20.8	-53.3	150.8	57 28.3	-53.8	151.5	56 35.3	-54.1	152.3	8
9	61 46.1	-51.2	147.3	60 55.3	-51.8	148.3	60 04.0	-52.3	149.2	59 12.3	-52.8	150.0	58 20.1	-53.3	150.9	57 27.5	-53.7	151.6	56 34.5	-54.1	152.3	55 41.2	-54.5	153.0	9
10	60 54.9	-51.7	148.4	60 03.5	-52.2	149.3	59 11.7	-52.7	150.2	58 19.5	-53.2	151.0	57 26.8	-53.6	151.7	56 33.8	-54.0	152.4	55 40.4	-54.3	153.1	54 46.7	-54.6	153.8	10
11	60 03.2	-52.2	149.4	59 11.3	-52.7	150.3	58 19.0	-53.1	151.1	57 26.3	-53.5	151.8	56 33.2	-53.9	152.6	55 39.8	-54.3	153.2	54 46.1	-54.6	153.9	53 52.1	-55.0	154.5	11
12	59 11.0	-52.6	150.4	58 18.6	-53.0	151.2	57 25.9	-53.5	151.9	56 32.8	-53.9	152.7	55 39.3	-54.2	153.3	54 45.5	-54.5	154.0	53 51.5	-54.9	154.6	52 57.1	-55.1	155.2	12
13	58 18.4	-52.9	151.3	57 25.6	-53.4	152.1	56 32.4	-53.7	152.8	55 38.9	-54.1	153.5	54 45.1	-54.5	154.1	53 51.0	-54.8	154.7	52 56.6	-55.1	155.3	52 02.0	-55.3	155.8	13
14	57 25.5	-53.3	152.2	56 32.2	-53.7	152.9	55 38.7	-54.1	153.6	54 44.8	-54.4	154.2	53 50.6	-54.7	154.8	52 56.2	-55.0	155.4	52 01.5	-55.2	155.9	51 06.7	-55.6	156.4	14
15	56 32.2	-53.7	153.0	55 38.5	-54.0	153.7	54 44.6	-54.3	154.3	53 50.4	-54.7	154.9	52 55.9	-54.9	155.5	52 01.2	-55.2	156.0	51 06.3	-55.5	156.5	50 11.1	-55.7	157.0	15
16	55 38.5	-53.9	153.8	54 44.5	-54.2	154.5	53 50.3	-54.6	155.1	52 55.7	-54.9	155.6	52 01.0	-55.2	156.2	51 06.0	-55.4	156.7	50 10.8	-55.7	157.1	49 15.4	-55.9	157.6	16
17	54 44.6	-54.2	154.6	53 50.3	-54.6	155.2	52 55.7	-54.9	155.8	52 00.8	-55.1	156.3	51 05.8	-55.4	156.8	50 10.6	-55.6	157.3	49 15.1	-55.8	157.7	48 19.5	-56.0	158.1	17
18	53 50.4	-54.5	155.3	52 55.7	-54.7	155.9	52 00.8	-55.0	156.4	51 05.7	-55.3	156.9	50 10.4	-55.5	157.4	49 15.0	-55.8	157.8	48 19.3	-56.0	158.3	47 23.5	-56.2	158.7	18
19	52 55.9	-54.7	156.0	52 01.0	-55.0	156.6	51 05.8	-55.2	157.1	50 10.4	-55.4	157.5	49 14.9	-55.7	158.0	48 19.2	-55.9	158.4	47 23.3	-56.1	158.8	46 27.3	-56.3	159.2	19
20	52 01.2	-54.9	156.7	51 06.0	-55.2	157.2	50 10.6	-55.5	157.7	49 15.0	-55.7	158.1	48 19.2	-55.9	158.5	47 23.3	-56.1	158.9	46 27.2	-56.2	159.3	45 31.0	-56.4	159.7	20
21	51 06.3	-55.2	157.4	50 10.8	-55.4	157.8	49 15.1	-55.6	158.3	48 19.3	-55.8	158.7	47 23.3	-56.0	159.1	46 27.2	-56.2	159.5	45 31.0	-56.4	159.8	44 34.6	-56.6	160.2	21
22	50 11.1	-55.3	158.0	49 15.4	-55.6	158.4	48 19.5	-55.7	158.8	47 23.5	-56.0	159.2	46 27.3	-56.1	159.6	45 31.0	-56.3	160.0	44 34.6	-56.5	160.3	43 38.0	-56.6	160.6	22
23	49 15.8	-55.5	158.6	48 19.8	-55.7	159.0	47 23.8	-56.0	159.4	46 27.5	-56.1	159.8	45 31.2	-56.3	160.1	44 34.7	-56.5	160.5	43 38.1	-56.6	160.8	42 41.4	-56.8	161.1	23
24	48 20.3	-55.7	159.2	47 24.1	-55.8	159.6	46 27.8	-56.0	159.9	45 31.4	-56.2	160.3	44 34.9	-56.4	160.6	43 38.2	-56.5	160.9	42 41.5	-56.7	161.2	41 44.6	-56.9	161.5	24
25	47 24.6	-55.8	159.7	46 28.3	-56.1	160.1	45 31.8	-56.2	160.4	44 35.2	-56.4	160.8	43 38.5	-56.5	161.1	42 41.7	-56.7	161.4	41 44.8	-56.9	161.7	40 47.7	-56.9	161.9	25
26	46 28.8	-56.0	160.3	45 32.2	-56.1	160.6	44 35.6	-56.3	160.9	43 38.8	-56.5	161.2	42 42.0	-56.7	161.5	41 45.0	-56.8	161.8	40 47.9	-56.9	162.1	39 50.8	-57.0	162.4	26
27	45 32.8	-56.1	160.8	44 36.1	-56.3	161.1	43 39.3	-56.5	161.4	42 42.3	-56.5	161.7	41 45.3	-56.7	162.0	40 48.2	-56.8	162.3	39 51.0	-57.0	162.5	38 53.8	-57.2	162.8	27
28	44 36.7	-56.3	161.3	43 39.8	-56.4	161.6	42 42.8	-56.5	161.9	41 45.8	-56.7	162.2	40 48.6	-56.8	162.4	39 51.4	-57.0	162.7	38 54.0	-57.0	162.9	37 56.6	-57.1	163.2	28
29	43 40.4	-56.3	161.8	42 43.4	-56.5	162.1	41 46.3	-56.7	162.3	40 49.1	-56.8	162.6	39 51.8	-56.9	162.8	38 54.4	-57.0	163.1	37 57.0	-57.2	163.3	36 59.5	-57.3	163.5	29
30	42 44.1	-56.5	162.2	41 46.9	-56.6	162.5	40 49.6	-56.7	162.8	39 52.3	-56.9	163.0	38 54.9	-57.0	163.3	37 57.4	-57.1	163.5	36 59.8	-57.2	163.7	36 02.2	-57.3	163.9	30
31	41 47.6	-56.6	162.7	40 50.3	-56.7	162.9	39 52.9	-56.9	163.2	38 55.4	-57.0	163.4	37 57.9	-57.1	163.7	37 00.3	-57.2	163.9	36 02.6	-57.3	164.1	35 04.9	-57.4	164.3	31
32	40 51.0	-56.7	163.1	39 53.6	-56.8	163.4	38 56.0	-56.9	163.6	37 58.4	-57.0	163.8	37 00.8	-57.2	164.0	36 03.1	-57.3	164.2	35 05.3	-57.4	164.4	34 07.5	-57.5	164.6	32
33	39 54.3	-56.7	163.6	38 56.8	-56.9	163.8	37 59.1	-57.0	164.0	37 01.4	-57.1	164.2	36 03.6	-57.2	164.4	35 05.8	-57.3	164.6	34 07.9	-57.4	164.8	33 10.0	-57.5	165.0	33
34	38 57.6	-56.9	164.0	37 59.9	-57.0	164.2	37 02.1	-57.1	164.4	36 04.3	-57.2	164.6	35 06.4	-57.3	164.8	34 08.5	-57.4	165.0	33 10.5	-57.4	165.1	32 12.5	-57.6	165.3	34
35	38 00.7	-56.9	164.4	37 02.9	-57.0	164.6	36 05.0	-57.1	164.8	35 07.1	-57.2	165.0	34 09.1	-57.3	165.2	33 11.1	-57.4	165.3	32 13.1	-57.6	165.5	31 14.9	-57.6	165.6	35
36	37 03.8	-57.0	164.8	36 05.9	-57.2	165.0	35 07.9	-57.2	165.2	34 09.9	-57.4	165.3	33 11.8	-57.4	165.5	32 13.7	-57.5	165.7	31 15.5	-57.6	165.8	30 17.3	-57.6	166.0	36
37	36 06.8	-57.1	165.2	35 08.7	-57.2	165.4	34 10.7	-57.3	165.5	33 12.5	-57.3	165.7	32 14.4	-57.5	165.9	31 16.2	-57.6	166.0	30 17.9	-57.6	166.1	29 19.7	-57.7	166.3	37
38	35 09.7	-57.2	165.6	34 11.5	-57.2	165.7	33 13.4	-57.4	165.9	32 15.2	-57.5	166.0	31 16.9	-57.5	166.2	30 18.6	-57.6	166.3	29 20.3	-57.7	166.5	28 22.0	-57.8	166.6	38
39	34 12.5	-57.2	165.9	33 14.3	-57.3	166.1	32 16.0	-57.4	166.2	31 17.7	-57.4	166.4	30 19.4	-57.6	166.5	29 21.0	-57.6	166.7	28 22.6	-57.7	166.8	27 24.2	-57.8	166.9	39
40	33 15.3	-57.3	166.3	32 17.0	-57.4	166.4	31 18.6	-57.4	166.6	30 20.3	-57.6	166.7	29 21.8	-57.6	166.9	28 23.4	-57.7	167.0	27 24.9	-57.7	167.1	26 26.4	-57.8	167.2	40
41	32 18.0	-57.3	166.6	31 19.6	-57.4	166.8	30 21.2	-57.5	166.9	29 22.7	-57.6	167.0	28 24.2	-57.6	167.2	27 25.7	-57.7	167.3	26 27.2	-57.8	167.4	25 28.6	-57.8	167.5	41
42	31 20.7	-57.4	167.0	30 22.2	-57.5	167.1	29 23.7	-57.6	167.2	28 25.1	-57.6	167.4	27 26.6	-57.7	167.5	26 28.0	-57.8	167.6	25 29.4	-57.8	167.7	24 30.8	-57.9	167.8	42
43	30 23.3	-57.5	167.3	29 24.7	-57.5	167.4	28 26.1	-57.6	167.6	27 27.5	-57.6	167.7	26 28.9	-57.7	167.8	25 30.2	-57.8	167.9	24 31.6	-57.9	168.0	23 32.9	-58.0	168.1	43
44	29 25.8	-57.5	167.7	28 27.2	-57.6	167.8	27 28.5	-57.6	167.9	26 29.9	-57.7	168.0	25 31.2	-57.8	168.1	24 32.4	-57.8	168.2	23 33.7	-57.9	168.3	22 34.9	-57.9	168.4	44
45	28 28.3	-57.5	168.0	27 29.6	-57.6	168.1	26 30.9	-57.7	168.2	25 32.2	-57.8	168.3	24 33.4	-57.8	168.4	23 34.6	-57.9	168.5	22 35.8	-57.9	168.6	21 37.0	-58.0	168.6	45
46	27 30.8	-57.6	168.3	26 32.0	-57.7	168.4	25 33.2	-57.7	168.5	24 34.4	-57.8	168.6	23 35.6	-57.9	168.7	22 36.7	-57.9	168.8	21 37.9	-58.0	168.8	20 39.0	-58.0	168.9	46
47	26 33.2	-57.7	168.6	25 34.3	-57.6	168.7	24 35.5	-57.8	168.8	23 36.6	-57.8	168.9	22 37.7	-57.8	169.0	21 38.8	-57.9	169.1	20 39.9	-57.9	169.1	19 41.0	-58.0	169.2	47
48	25 35.5	-57.6	168.9	24 36.7	-57.8	169.0	23 37.7	-57.7	169.1	22 38.8	-57.8	169.2	21 39.9	-57.9	169.3	20 40.9	-57.9	169.3	19 42.0	-58.0	169.4	18 43.0	-58.1	169.5	48
49	24 37.9	-57.7	169.2	23 38.9	-57.7	169.3	22 40.0	-57.9	169.4	21 41.0	-57.9	169.5	20 42.0	-57.9	169.5	19 43.0	-58.0	169.6	18 44.0	-58.1	169.7	17 44.9	-58.1	169.7	49
50	23 40.2	-57.8	169.5	22 41.2	-57.8	169.6	21 42.1	-57.8	169.7	20 43.1	-57.9	169.8	19 44.1	-58.0	169.8	18 45.0	-58.0	169.9	17 45.9	-58.0	169.9	16 46.8	-58.1	170.0	50
51	22 42.4	-57.7	169.8	21 43.4	-57.8	169.9	20 44.3	-57.9	170.0	19 45.2	-57.9	170.0	18 46.1	-58.0	170.1	17 47.0	-58.0	170.2	16 47.9	-58.1	170.2	15 48.7	-58.1	170.3	51
52	21 44.7	-57.8	170.1	20 45.6	-57.9	170.2	19 46.4	-57.9	170.3	18 47.3	-58.0	170.3	17 48.1	-58.0	170.4	16 49.0	-58.1	170.4	15 49.8	-58.1	170.5	14 50.6	-58.1	170.5	52
53	20 46.9	-57.9	170.4	19 47.7	-57.9	170.5	18 48.5	-57.9	170.5	17 49.3	-57.9	170.6	16 50.1	-58.0	170.6	15 50.9	-58.0	170.7	14 51.7	-58.1	170.7	13 52.5	-58.1	170.8	53
54	19 49.0	-57.8	170.7	18 49.8	-57.9	170.8	17 50.6	-57.9	170.8	16 51.4	-58.0	170.9	15 52.1	-58.0	170.9	14 52.9	-58.1	170.9	13 53.6	-58.1	171.0	12 54.4	-58.2	171.0	54
55	18 51.2	-57.9	171.0	17 51.9	-57.9	171.0	16 52.7	-58.0	171.1	15 53.4	-58.0	171.1	14 54.1	-58.1	171.2	13 54.8	-58.1	171.2	12 55.5	-58.1	171.2	11 56.2	-58.2	171.3	55
56	17 53.3	-57.9	171.3	16 54.0	-58.0	171.3	15 54.7	-58.0	171.3	14 55.4	-58.1	171.4	13 56.0	-58.0	171.4	12 56.7	-58.1	171.5	11 57.4	-58.2	171.5	10 58.0	-58.2	171.5	56
57	16 55.4	-57.9	171.5	15 56.0	-57.9	171.6	14 56.7	-58.0	171.6	13 57.3	-58.0	171.6	12 58.0	-58.1	171.7	11 58.6	-58.1	171.7	10 59.2	-58.1	171.7	9 59.8	-58.2	171.8	57
58	15 57.5	-58.0	171.8	14 58.1	-58.0	171.8	13 58.7	-58.0	171.9	12 59.3	-58.1	171.9	11 59.9	-58.1	171.9	11 00.5	-58.2	172.0	10 01.1	-58.2	172.0	9 01.6	-58.2	172.0	58
59	14 59.5	-57.9	172.1	14 00.1	-58.0	172.1	13 00.7	-58.1	172.1	12 01.2	-58.0	172.2	11 01.8	-58.1	172.2	10 02.3	-58.1	172.2	9 02.9	-58.2	172.2	8 03.4	-58.2	172.3	59
60	14 01.6	-58.0	172.3	13 02.1	-58.0	172.4	12 02.6	-58.0	172.4	11 03.2	-58.1	172.4	10 03.7	-58.2	172.4	9 04.2	-58.2	172.5	8 04.7	-58.2	172.5	7 05.2	-58.2	172.5	60
61	13 03.6	-58.0	172.6	12 04.1	-58.1	172.6	11 04.6	-58.1	172.7	10 05.1	-58.1	172.7	9 05.5	-58.1	172.7	8 06.0	-58.1	172.7	7 06.5	-58.2	172.7	6 07.0	-58.2	172.8	61
62	12 05.6	-58.0	172.9	11 06.0	-58.0	172.9	10 06.5	-58.1	172.9	9 07.0	-58.1	172.9	8 07.4	-58.1	172.9	7 07.9	-58.2	173.0	6 08.3	-58.2	173.0	5 08.8	-58.3	173.0	62
63	11 07.6	-58.1	173.1	10 08.0	-58.1	173.1	9 08.4	-58.1	173.2	8 08.9	-58.2	173.2	7 09.3	-58.2	173.2	6 09.7	-58.2	173.2	5 10.1	-58.2	173.2	4 10.5	-58.2	173.2	63
64	10 09.5	-58.0	173.4	9 09.9	-58.0	173.4	8 10.3	-58.1	173.4	7 10.7	-58.1	173.4	6 11.1	-58.1	173.4	5 11.5	-58.2	173.5	4 11.9	-58.2	173.5	3 12.3	-58.2	173.5	64
65	9 11.5	-58.0	173.6	8 11.9	-58.1	173.7	7 12.2	-58.1	173.7	6 12.6	-58.1	173.7	5 13.0	-58.2	173.7	4 13.3	-58.2	173.7	3 13.7	-58.2	173.7	2 14.1	-58.3	173.7	65
66	8 13.5	-58.1	173.9	7 13.8	-58.1	173.9	6 14.1	-58.1	173.9	5 14.5	-58.2	173.9	4 14.8	-58.2	173.9	3 15.1	-58.2	173.9	2 15.5	-58.2	174.0	1 15.8	-58.2	174.0	66
67	7 15.4	-58.1	174.1	6 15.7	-58.1	174.2	5 16.0	-58.1	174.2	4 16.3	-58.1	174.2	3 16.6	-58.1	174.2	2 16.9	-58.2	174.2	1 17.3	-58.3	174.2	0 17.6	-58.3	174.2	67
68	6 17.3	-58.0	174.4	5 17.6	-58.1	174.4	4 17.9	-58.1	174.4	3 18.2	-58.2	174.4	2 18.5	-58.2	174.4	1 18.7	-58.1	174.4	0 19.0	-58.2	174.4	0 40.7	+58.2	5.6	68
69	5 19.3	-58.1	174.7	4 19.5	-58.1	174.7	3 19.8	-58.2	174.7	2 20.0	-58.1	174.7	1 20.3	-58.2	174.7	0 20.6	-58.2	174.7	0 39.2	+58.2	5.3	1 38.9	+58.3	5.3	69
70	4 21.2	-58.1	174.9	3 21.4	-58.1	174.9	2 21.6	-58.1	174.9	1 21.9	-58.2	174.9	0 22.1	-58.2	174.9	0 37.6	+58.2	5.1	1 37.4	+58.2	5.1	2 37.2	+58.2	5.1	70
71	3 23.1	-58.1	175.2	2 23.3	-58.1	175.2	1 23.5	-58.1	175.2	0 23.7	-58.1	175.2	0 36.1	+58.1	4.8	1 35.8	+58.2	4.8	2 35.6	+58.2	4.8	3 35.4	+58.3	4.8	71
72	2 25.0	-58.1	175.4	1 25.2	-58.1	175.4	0 25.4	-58.2	175.4	0 34.4	+58.2	4.6	1 34.2	+58.2	4.6	2 34.0	+58.2	4.6	3 33.8	+58.3	4.6	4 33.7	+58.2	4.6	72
73	1 26.9	-58.1	175.7	0 27.1	-58.1	175.7	0 32.8	+58.1	4.3	1 32.6	+58.1	4.3	2 32.4	+58.2	4.3	3 32.2	+58.2	4.3	4 32.1	+58.2	4.4	5 31.9	+58.2	4.4	73
74	0 28.8	-58.1	175.9	0 31.0	+58.2	4.1	1 30.9	+58.1	4.1	2 30.7	+58.2	4.1	3 30.6	+58.1	4.1	4 30.4	+58.2	4.1	5 30.3	+58.2	4.1	6 30.1	+58.2	4.1	74
75	0 29.3	+58.1	3.8	1 29.2	+58.1	3.8	2 29.0	+58.1	3.8	3 28.9	+58.1	3.8	4 28.7	+58.2	3.9	5 28.6	+58.2	3.9	6 28.5	+58.2	3.9	7 28.3	+58.2	3.9	75
76	1 27.4	+58.1	3.6	2 27.3	+58.1	3.6	3 27.1	+58.2	3.6	4 27.0	+58.2	3.6	5 26.9	+58.2	3.6	6 26.8	+58.2	3.6	7 26.7	+58.2	3.6	8 26.5	+58.3	3.6	76
77	2 25.5	+58.1	3.3	3 25.4	+58.1	3.3	4 25.3	+58.1	3.3	5 25.2	+58.1	3.4	6 25.1	+58.1	3.4	7 25.0	+58.1	3.4	8 24.9	+58.2	3.4	9 24.8	+58.2	3.4	77
78	3 23.6	+58.0	3.1	4 23.5	+58.1	3.1	5 23.4	+58.1	3.1	6 23.3	+58.2	3.1	7 23.2	+58.2	3.1	8 23.1	+58.2	3.1	9 23.0	+58.2	3.1	10 22.9	+58.2	3.1	78
79	4 21.6	+58.1	2.8	5 21.6	+58.1	2.8	6 21.5	+58.1	2.8	7 21.4	+58.1	2.9	8 21.4	+58.1	2.9	9 21.3	+58.1	2.9	10 21.2	+58.2	2.9	11 21.1	+58.2	2.9	79
80	5 19.7	+58.1	2.6	6 19.7	+58.1	2.6	7 19.6	+58.1	2.6	8 19.5	+58.2	2.6	9 19.5	+58.1	2.6	10 19.4	+58.2	2.6	11 19.4	+58.1	2.6	12 19.3	+58.1	2.6	80
81	6 17.8	+58.1	2.3	7 17.8	+58.0	2.3	8 17.7	+58.1	2.3	9 17.7	+58.1	2.4	10 17.6	+58.1	2.4	11 17.6	+58.2	2.4	12 17.5	+58.1	2.4	13 17.4	+58.2	2.4	81
82	7 15.9	+58.0	2.1	8 15.8	+58.1	2.1	9 15.8	+58.1	2.1	10 15.8	+58.0	2.1	11 15.7	+58.1	2.1	12 15.7	+58.1	2.1	13 15.6	+58.1	2.1	14 15.6	+58.2	2.1	82
83	8 13.9	+58.1	1.8	9 13.9	+58.1	1.8	10 13.9	+58.0	1.8	11 13.8	+58.1	1.8	12 13.8	+58.1	1.8	13 13.8	+58.1	1.9	14 13.7	+58.1	1.9	15 13.7	+58.1	1.9	83
84	9 12.0	+58.0	1.6	10 12.0	+58.0	1.6	11 11.9	+58.1	1.6	12 11.9	+58.1	1.6	13 11.9	+58.1	1.6	14 11.9	+58.0	1.6	15 11.8	+58.1	1.6	16 11.8	+58.1	1.6	84
85	10 10.0	+58.0	1.3	11 10.0	+58.0	1.3	12 10.0	+58.0	1.3	13 10.0	+58.0	1.3	14 10.0	+58.0	1.3	15 09.9	+58.1	1.3	16 09.9	+58.1	1.3	17 09.9	+58.1	1.4	85
86	11 08.0	+58.1	1.1	12 08.0	+58.0	1.1	13 08.0	+58.1	1.1	14 08.0	+58.0	1.1	15 08.0	+58.0	1.1	16 08.0	+58.0	1.1	17 08.0	+58.0	1.1	18 08.0	+58.0	1.1	86
87	12 06.1	+58.0	0.8	13 06.0	+58.1	0.8	14 06.0	+58.0	0.8	15 06.0	+58.0	0.8	16 06.0	+58.0	0.8	17 06.0	+58.0	0.8	18 06.0	+58.0	0.8	19 06.0	+58.0	0.8	87
88	13 04.1	+57.9	0.5	14 04.1	+57.9	0.5	15 04.0	+58.0	0.5	16 04.0	+58.0	0.5	17 04.0	+58.0	0.5	18 04.0	+58.0	0.5	19 04.0	+58.0	0.5	20 04.0	+58.0	0.6	88
89	14 02.0	+58.0	0.3	15 02.0	+58.0	0.3	16 02.0	+58.0	0.3	17 02.0	+58.0	0.3	18 02.0	+58.0	0.3	19 02.0	+58.0	0.3	20 02.0	+58.0	0.3	21 02.0	+58.0	0.3	89
90	15 00.0	+57.9	0.0	16 00.0	+57.9	0.0	17 00.0	+57.9	0.0	18 00.0	+57.9	0.0	19 00.0	+57.9	0.0	20 00.0	+57.9	0.0	21 00.0	+57.9	0.0	22 00.0	+57.9	0.0	90
	15°			16°			17°			18°			19°			20°			21°			22°			

S. Lat. {L.H.A. greater than 180° ....Zn=180°−Z; L.H.A. less than 180°...........Zn=180°+Z}

LATITUDE **SAME** NAME AS DECLINATION — L.H.A. 165°, 195°

Dec.	15° Hc	d	Z	16° Hc	d	Z	17° Hc	d	Z	18° Hc	d	Z	19° Hc	d	Z	20° Hc	d	Z	21° Hc	d	Z	22° Hc	d	Z	Dec.
°	° ′	′	°	° ′	′	°	° ′	′	°	° ′	′	°	° ′	′	°	° ′	′	°	° ′	′	°	° ′	′	°	°
0	68 12.2	+41.1	132.1	67 31.3	+42.6	133.9	66 49.1	+44.0	135.6	66 05.7	+45.2	137.1	65 21.2	+46.3	138.6	64 35.6	+47.5	140.0	63 49.2	+48.4	141.3	63 02.0	+49.2	142.6	0
1	68 53.3	+39.7	130.1	68 13.9	+41.3	132.0	67 33.1	+42.8	133.8	66 50.9	+44.2	135.5	66 07.5	+45.4	137.1	65 23.1	+46.5	138.6	64 37.6	+47.5	140.0	63 51.2	+48.5	141.3	1
2	69 33.0	+38.0	128.0	68 55.2	+39.8	130.0	68 15.9	+41.4	131.9	67 35.1	+42.9	133.7	66 52.9	+44.3	135.4	66 09.6	+45.5	137.0	65 25.1	+46.7	138.5	64 39.7	+47.7	139.9	2
3	70 11.0	+36.2	125.7	69 35.0	+38.2	127.9	68 57.3	+40.0	130.0	68 18.0	+41.6	131.9	67 37.2	+43.2	133.7	66 55.1	+44.5	135.4	66 11.8	+45.8	137.0	65 27.4	+46.9	138.5	3
4	70 47.2	+34.3•	123.3	70 13.2	+36.4	125.7	69 37.3	+38.4	127.8	68 59.6	+40.2	129.9	68 20.4	+41.8	131.8	67 39.6	+43.3	133.7	66 57.6	+44.6	135.4	66 14.3	+45.9	137.0	4
5	71 21.5	+32.0•	120.8	70 49.6	+34.5•	123.3	70 15.7	+36.6	125.6	69 39.8	+38.6	127.8	69 02.2	+40.3	129.9	68 22.9	+42.0	131.8	67 42.2	+43.5	133.6	67 00.2	+44.8	135.3	5
6	71 53.5	+29.8•	118.1	71 24.1	+32.3•	120.7	70 52.3	+34.6•	123.2	70 18.4	+36.8	125.6	69 42.5	+38.8	127.8	69 04.9	+40.6	129.8	68 25.7	+42.2	131.8	67 45.0	+43.7	133.6	6
7	72 23.3	+27.2•	115.3	71 56.4	+29.9•	118.1	71 26.9	+32.5•	120.7	70 55.2	+34.8•	123.2	70 21.3	+37.0	125.5	69 45.5	+38.9	127.7	69 07.9	+40.7	129.8	68 28.7	+42.4	131.8	7
8	72 50.5	+24.4•	112.3	72 26.3	+27.4•	115.2	71 59.4	+30.2•	118.0	71 30.0	+32.7•	120.7	70 58.3	+35.0•	123.2	70 24.4	+37.2	125.5	69 48.6	+39.2	127.7	69 11.1	+40.9	129.8	8
9	73 14.9	+21.5•	109.2	72 53.7	+24.6•	112.2	72 29.6	+27.6•	115.2	72 02.7	+30.4•	118.0	71 33.3	+33.0•	120.6	71 01.6	+35.3•	123.1	70 27.8	+37.4	125.5	69 52.0	+39.4	127.7	9
10	73 36.4	+18.3•	105.9	73 18.3	+21.7•	109.1	72 57.2	+24.8•	112.2	72 33.1	+27.8•	115.1	72 06.3	+30.5•	117.9	71 36.9	+33.1•	120.6	71 05.2	+35.5•	123.1	70 31.4	+37.6	125.5	10
11	73 54.7	+14.9•	102.5	73 40.0	+18.5•	105.8	73 22.0	+21.9•	109.0	73 00.9	+25.1•	112.1	72 36.8	+28.1•	115.1	72 10.0	+30.9•	117.9	71 40.7	+33.4•	120.6	71 09.0	+35.7•	123.1	11
12	74 09.6	+11.5•	99.0	73 58.5	+15.1•	102.4	73 43.9	+18.7•	105.8	73 26.0	+22.0•	109.0	73 04.9	+25.3•	112.1	72 40.9	+28.2•	115.1	72 14.1	+31.0•	117.9	71 44.7	+33.6•	120.6	12
13	74 21.1	+7.7•	95.3	74 13.6	+11.6•	98.9	74 02.6	+15.3•	102.3	73 48.0	+18.9•	105.7	73 30.2	+22.3•	109.0	73 09.1	+25.5•	112.1	72 45.1	+28.5•	115.1	72 18.3	+31.3•	117.9	13
14	74 28.8	+4.1•	91.7	74 25.2	+8.0•	95.2	74 17.9	+11.8•	98.8	74 06.9	+15.6•	102.3	73 52.5	+19.1•	105.6	73 34.6	+22.6•	108.9	73 13.6	+25.8•	112.1	72 49.6	+28.8•	115.1	14
15	74 32.9	+0.3•	87.9	74 33.2	+4.2•	91.5	74 29.7	+8.1•	95.1	74 22.5	+12.0•	98.7	74 11.6	+15.7•	102.2	73 57.2	+19.3•	105.6	73 39.4	+22.7•	108.9	73 18.4	+25.9•	112.1	15
16	74 33.2	-3.5•	84.2	74 37.4	+0.4•	87.8	74 37.8	+4.4•	91.4	74 34.5	+8.3•	95.0	74 27.3	+12.2•	98.6	74 16.5	+15.9•	102.1	74 02.1	+19.6•	105.6	73 44.3	+23.0•	108.9	16
17	74 29.7	-7.2•	80.4	74 37.8	-3.3•	84.0	74 42.2	+0.6•	87.6	74 42.8	+4.5•	91.3	74 39.5	+8.4•	95.0	74 32.4	+12.4•	98.6	74 21.7	+16.1•	102.1	74 07.3	+19.8•	105.5	17
18	74 22.5	-10.9•	76.7	74 34.5	-7.2•	80.2	74 42.8	-3.3•	83.9	74 47.3	+0.6•	87.5	74 47.9	+4.7•	91.2	74 44.8	+8.6•	94.9	74 37.8	+12.6•	98.5	74 27.1	+16.4•	102.0	18
19	74 11.6	-14.4•	73.1	74 27.3	-10.8•	76.5	74 39.5	-7.1•	80.1	74 47.9	-3.1•	83.7	74 52.6	+0.8•	87.4	74 53.4	+4.8•	91.1	74 50.4	+8.8•	94.8	74 43.5	+12.7•	98.4	19
20	73 57.2	-17.8•	69.6	74 16.5	-14.4•	72.9	74 32.4	-10.7•	76.3	74 44.8	-7.0•	79.9	74 53.4	-3.0•	83.5	74 58.2	+1.0•	87.2	74 59.2	+4.9•	91.0	74 56.2	+9.0•	94.7	20
21	73 39.4	-21.0•	66.1	74 02.1	-17.8•	69.3	74 21.7	-14.4•	72.7	74 37.8	-10.7•	76.1	74 50.4	-6.9•	79.7	74 59.2	-3.0•	83.4	75 04.1	+1.1•	87.1	75 05.2	+5.1•	90.9	21
22	73 18.4	-24.0•	62.8	73 44.3	-20.9•	65.9	74 07.3	-17.7•	69.1	74 27.1	-14.3•	72.4	74 43.5	-10.7•	75.9	74 56.2	-6.8•	79.5	75 05.2	-2.9•	83.2	75 10.3	+1.2•	87.0	22
23	72 54.4	-26.8•	59.7	73 23.4	-24.0•	62.6	73 49.6	-21.0•	65.6	74 12.8	-17.7•	68.8	74 32.8	-14.3•	72.2	74 49.4	-10.6•	75.7	75 02.3	-6.7•	79.4	75 11.5	-2.8•	83.1	23
24	72 27.6	-29.4•	56.7	72 59.4	-26.9•	59.4	73 28.6	-24.0•	62.3	73 55.1	-21.0•	65.4	74 18.5	-17.7•	68.6	74 38.8	-14.3•	72.0	74 55.6	-10.6•	75.5	75 08.7	-6.7•	79.2	24
25	71 58.2	-31.7•	53.8	72 32.5	-29.4•	56.4	73 04.6	-26.9•	59.1	73 34.1	-24.1•	62.0	74 00.8	-21.0•	65.1	74 24.5	-17.7•	68.3	74 45.0	-14.2•	71.8	75 02.0	-10.5•	75.3	25
26	71 26.5	-34.0•	51.1	72 03.1	-31.7•	53.5	72 37.7	-29.4•	56.1	73 10.0	-26.8•	58.8	73 39.8	-24.1•	61.7	74 06.8	-21.0•	64.8	74 30.8	-17.8•	68.1	74 51.5	-14.2•	71.5	26
27	70 52.5	-35.9	48.6	71 31.4	-34.0•	50.8	72 08.3	-31.8•	53.2	72 43.2	-29.5•	55.8	73 15.7	-26.9•	58.5	73 45.8	-24.2•	61.4	74 13.0	-21.0•	64.5	74 37.3	-17.8•	67.8	27
28	70 16.6	-37.8	46.1	70 57.4	-36.0	48.2	71 36.5	-34.1•	50.5	72 13.7	-31.9•	52.9	72 48.8	-29.5•	55.5	73 21.6	-26.9•	58.2	73 52.0	-24.2•	61.1	74 19.5	-21.1•	64.3	28
29	69 38.8	-39.4	43.9	70 21.4	-37.8	45.8	71 02.4	-36.0	47.9	71 41.8	-34.1•	50.1	72 19.3	-32.0•	52.5	72 54.7	-29.7•	55.1	73 27.8	-27.1•	57.9	73 58.4	-24.2•	60.8	29
30	68 59.4	-40.9	41.7	69 43.6	-39.5	43.5	70 26.4	-37.9	45.5	71 07.7	-36.2	47.6	71 47.3	-34.2•	49.8	72 25.0	-32.0•	52.2	73 00.7	-29.7•	54.8	73 34.2	-27.2•	57.6	30
31	68 18.5	-42.3	39.7	69 04.1	-41.0	41.4	69 48.5	-39.6	43.2	70 31.5	-37.9	45.1	71 13.1	-36.2	47.2	71 53.0	-34.3•	49.4	72 31.0	-32.1•	51.9	73 07.0	-29.8•	54.4	31
32	67 36.2	-43.5	37.8	68 23.1	-42.3	39.4	69 08.9	-41.0	41.1	69 53.6	-39.6	42.8	70 36.9	-38.1	44.8	71 18.7	-36.3	46.8	71 58.9	-34.4•	49.1	72 37.2	-32.2•	51.5	32
33	66 52.7	-44.6	36.1	67 40.8	-43.6	37.5	68 27.9	-42.4	39.0	69 14.0	-41.2	40.7	69 58.8	-39.7	42.5	70 42.4	-38.1	44.4	71 24.5	-36.4	46.5	72 05.0	-34.5•	48.7	33
34	66 08.1	-45.7	34.4	66 57.2	-44.7	35.7	67 45.5	-43.7	37.1	68 32.8	-42.5	38.7	69 19.1	-41.2	40.3	70 04.3	-39.8	42.1	70 48.1	-38.2	44.0	71 30.5	-36.5	46.1	34
35	65 22.4	-46.6	32.8	66 12.5	-45.8	34.0	67 01.8	-44.8	35.4	67 50.3	-43.7	36.8	68 37.9	-42.6	38.3	69 24.5	-41.4	39.9	70 09.9	-39.9	41.7	70 54.0	-38.4	43.6	35
36	64 35.8	-47.5	31.3	65 26.7	-46.6	32.5	66 17.0	-45.8	33.7	67 06.6	-44.9	35.0	67 55.3	-43.8	36.4	68 43.1	-42.7	37.9	69 30.0	-41.5	39.5	70 15.6	-40.0	41.3	36
37	63 48.3	-48.2	29.9	64 40.1	-47.6	31.0	65 31.2	-46.7	32.1	66 21.7	-45.9	33.3	67 11.5	-45.0	34.6	68 00.4	-43.9	36.0	68 48.5	-42.8	37.5	69 35.6	-41.6	39.1	37
38	63 00.1	-48.9	28.6	63 52.5	-48.3	29.6	64 44.5	-47.6	30.6	65 35.8	-46.8	31.7	66 26.5	-46.0	32.9	67 16.5	-45.0	34.2	68 05.7	-44.0	35.6	68 54.0	-42.9	37.1	38
39	62 11.2	-49.6	27.3	63 04.2	-49.0	28.2	63 56.9	-48.4	29.2	64 49.0	-47.7	30.2	65 40.5	-46.9	31.3	66 31.5	-46.1	32.5	67 21.7	-45.2	33.8	68 11.1	-44.1	35.2	39
40	61 21.6	-50.2	26.1	62 15.2	-49.6	27.0	63 08.5	-49.1	27.9	64 01.3	-48.4	28.8	64 53.6	-47.7	29.8	65 45.4	-47.0	30.9	66 36.5	-46.2	32.1	67 27.0	-45.3	33.4	40
41	60 31.4	-50.7	25.0	61 25.6	-50.2	25.8	62 19.4	-49.7	26.6	63 12.9	-49.2	27.5	64 05.9	-48.6	28.4	64 58.4	-47.9	29.5	65 50.3	-47.1	30.5	66 41.7	-46.3	31.7	41
42	59 40.7	-51.3	23.9	60 35.4	-50.8	24.7	61 29.7	-50.3	25.4	62 23.7	-49.8	26.2	63 17.3	-49.2	27.1	64 10.5	-48.6	28.0	65 03.2	-47.9	29.1	65 55.4	-47.2	30.1	42
43	58 49.4	-51.6	22.9	59 44.6	-51.3	23.6	60 39.4	-50.8	24.3	61 33.9	-50.3	25.0	62 28.1	-49.8	25.9	63 21.9	-49.3	26.7	64 15.3	-48.7	27.7	65 08.2	-48.1	28.6	43
44	57 57.8	-52.1	21.9	58 53.3	-51.7	22.6	59 48.6	-51.4	23.2	60 43.6	-50.9	23.9	61 38.3	-50.5	24.7	62 32.6	-49.9	25.5	63 26.6	-49.4	26.3	64 20.1	-48.8	27.2	44
45	57 05.7	-52.5	21.0	58 01.6	-52.2	21.6	58 57.2	-51.8	22.2	59 52.7	-51.4	22.9	60 47.8	-51.0	23.5	61 42.7	-50.6	24.3	62 37.2	-50.1	25.1	63 31.3	-49.5	25.9	45
46	56 13.2	-52.9	20.1	57 09.4	-52.5	20.7	58 05.4	-52.2	21.2	59 01.3	-51.9	21.8	59 56.8	-51.5	22.5	60 52.1	-51.0	23.2	61 47.1	-50.6	23.9	62 41.8	-50.1	24.7	46
47	55 20.3	-53.2	19.3	56 16.9	-52.9	19.8	57 13.2	-52.6	20.3	58 09.4	-52.3	20.9	59 05.3	-51.9	21.5	60 01.1	-51.6	22.1	60 56.5	-51.1	22.8	61 51.7	-50.7	23.5	47
48	54 27.1	-53.4	18.5	55 24.0	-53.3	19.0	56 20.6	-52.9	19.4	57 17.1	-52.6	20.0	58 13.4	-52.3	20.5	59 09.5	-52.0	21.1	60 05.4	-51.6	21.7	61 01.0	-51.2	22.4	48
49	53 33.7	-53.8	17.7	54 30.7	-53.5	18.1	55 27.7	-53.3	18.6	56 24.5	-53.0	19.1	57 21.1	-52.7	19.6	58 17.5	-52.4	20.1	59 13.8	-52.1	20.7	60 09.8	-51.7	21.3	49
50	52 39.9	-54.1	17.0	53 37.2	-53.8	17.4	54 34.4	-53.6	17.8	55 31.5	-53.4	18.2	56 28.4	-53.1	18.7	57 25.1	-52.8	19.2	58 21.7	-52.5	19.7	59 18.1	-52.2	20.3	50
51	51 45.8	-54.2	16.3	52 43.4	-54.1	16.6	53 40.8	-53.9	17.0	54 38.1	-53.6	17.4	55 35.3	-53.4	17.9	56 32.3	-53.1	18.3	57 29.2	-52.9	18.8	58 25.9	-52.6	19.4	51
52	50 51.6	-54.6	15.6	51 49.3	-54.3	15.9	52 46.9	-54.1	16.3	53 44.5	-53.9	16.7	54 41.9	-53.7	17.1	55 39.2	-53.5	17.5	56 36.3	-53.2	18.0	57 33.3	-52.9	18.4	52
53	49 57.0	-54.7	14.9	50 55.0	-54.6	15.3	51 52.8	-54.4	15.6	52 50.6	-54.2	15.9	53 48.2	-54.0	16.3	54 45.7	-53.7	16.7	55 43.1	-53.5	17.1	56 40.4	-53.3	17.6	53
54	49 02.3	-54.9	14.3	50 00.4	-54.7	14.6	50 58.4	-54.6	14.9	51 56.4	-54.4	15.2	52 54.2	-54.2	15.6	53 52.0	-54.1	15.9	54 49.6	-53.8	16.3	55 47.1	-53.6	16.7	54
55	48 07.4	-55.1	13.7	49 05.7	-55.0	14.0	50 03.8	-54.8	14.3	51 02.0	-54.7	14.6	52 00.0	-54.5	14.9	52 57.9	-54.3	15.2	53 55.8	-54.1	15.6	54 53.5	-53.9	16.0	55
56	47 12.3	-55.3	13.1	48 10.7	-55.2	13.4	49 09.0	-55.0	13.6	50 07.3	-54.9	13.9	51 05.5	-54.7	14.2	52 03.6	-54.5	14.5	53 01.7	-54.4	14.8	53 59.6	-54.1	15.2	56
57	46 17.0	-55.5	12.5	47 15.5	-55.3	12.8	48 14.0	-55.2	13.0	49 12.4	-55.0	13.3	50 10.8	-54.9	13.6	51 09.1	-54.8	13.8	52 07.3	-54.6	14.2	53 05.5	-54.5	14.5	57
58	45 21.5	-55.6	12.0	46 20.2	-55.5	12.2	47 18.8	-55.3	12.4	48 17.4	-55.2	12.7	49 15.9	-55.1	12.9	50 14.3	-54.9	13.2	51 12.7	-54.8	13.5	52 11.0	-54.6	13.8	58
59	44 25.9	-55.7	11.5	45 24.7	-55.6	11.7	46 23.5	-55.6	11.9	47 22.2	-55.4	12.1	48 20.8	-55.3	12.3	49 19.4	-55.2	12.6	50 17.9	-55.0	12.8	51 16.4	-54.9	13.1	59
60	43 30.2	-55.9	11.0	44 29.1	-55.8	11.1	45 27.9	-55.6	11.3	46 26.8	-55.6	11.5	47 25.5	-55.4	11.8	48 24.2	-55.3	12.0	49 22.9	-55.2	12.2	50 21.5	-55.1	12.5	60
61	42 34.3	-56.0	10.5	43 33.3	-55.9	10.6	44 32.3	-55.8	10.8	45 31.2	-55.7	11.0	46 30.1	-55.6	11.2	47 28.9	-55.5	11.4	48 27.7	-55.4	11.6	49 26.4	-55.2	11.9	61
62	41 38.3	-56.1	10.0	42 37.4	-56.0	10.1	43 36.5	-56.0	10.3	44 35.5	-55.9	10.5	45 34.5	-55.8	10.7	46 33.4	-55.7	10.8	47 32.3	-55.5	11.1	48 31.2	-55.5	11.3	62
63	40 42.2	-56.2	9.5	41 41.4	-56.2	9.6	42 40.5	-56.1	9.8	43 39.6	-56.0	10.0	44 38.7	-55.9	10.1	45 37.7	-55.8	10.3	46 36.8	-55.7	10.5	47 35.7	-55.6	10.7	63
64	39 46.0	-56.4	9.0	40 45.2	-56.3	9.2	41 44.4	-56.2	9.3	42 43.6	-56.1	9.5	43 42.8	-56.0	9.6	44 41.9	-55.9	9.8	45 41.1	-55.9	10.0	46 40.1	-55.7	10.1	64
65	38 49.6	-56.4	8.6	39 48.9	-56.3	8.7	40 48.2	-56.3	8.9	41 47.5	-56.2	9.0	42 46.8	-56.2	9.1	43 46.0	-56.1	9.3	44 45.2	-56.0	9.4	45 44.4	-55.9	9.6	65
66	37 53.2	-56.5	8.2	38 52.6	-56.5	8.3	39 51.9	-56.4	8.4	40 51.3	-56.3	8.5	41 50.6	-56.2	8.7	42 49.9	-56.2	8.8	43 49.2	-56.1	8.9	44 48.5	-56.1	9.1	66
67	36 56.7	-56.6	7.7	37 56.1	-56.5	7.8	38 55.5	-56.5	8.0	39 55.0	-56.5	8.1	40 54.4	-56.4	8.2	41 53.7	-56.3	8.3	42 53.1	-56.2	8.5	43 52.4	-56.1	8.6	67
68	36 00.1	-56.7	7.3	36 59.6	-56.7	7.4	37 59.0	-56.5	7.5	38 58.5	-56.5	7.6	39 58.0	-56.5	7.7	40 57.4	-56.4	7.9	41 56.9	-56.4	8.0	42 56.3	-56.3	8.1	68
69	35 03.4	-56.8	6.9	36 02.9	-56.7	7.0	37 02.5	-56.7	7.1	38 02.0	-56.6	7.2	39 01.5	-56.6	7.3	40 01.0	-56.5	7.4	41 00.5	-56.4	7.5	42 00.0	-56.4	7.6	69
70	34 06.6	-56.9	6.5	35 06.2	-56.8	6.6	36 05.8	-56.8	6.7	37 05.4	-56.7	6.8	38 04.9	-56.6	6.9	39 04.5	-56.6	7.0	40 04.1	-56.6	7.1	41 03.6	-56.5	7.2	70
71	33 09.7	-56.9	6.2	34 09.4	-56.9	6.2	35 09.0	-56.8	6.3	36 08.7	-56.8	6.4	37 08.3	-56.8	6.5	38 07.9	-56.7	6.6	39 07.5	-56.7	6.6	40 07.1	-56.6	6.7	71
72	32 12.8	-57.0	5.8	33 12.5	-56.9	5.8	34 12.2	-56.9	5.9	35 11.9	-56.9	6.0	36 11.5	-56.8	6.1	37 11.2	-56.8	6.1	38 10.8	-56.7	6.2	39 10.5	-56.7	6.3	72
73	31 15.8	-57.0	5.4	32 15.6	-57.1	5.5	33 15.3	-57.0	5.5	34 15.0	-56.9	5.6	35 14.7	-56.9	5.7	36 14.4	-56.8	5.7	37 14.1	-56.8	5.8	38 13.8	-56.8	5.9	73
74	30 18.8	-57.1	5.0	31 18.5	-57.0	5.1	32 18.3	-57.0	5.2	33 18.1	-57.0	5.2	34 17.8	-57.0	5.3	35 17.6	-57.0	5.3	36 17.3	-56.9	5.4	37 17.0	-56.8	5.5	74
75	29 21.7	-57.2	4.7	30 21.5	-57.2	4.7	31 21.3	-57.1	4.8	32 21.1	-57.1	4.8	33 20.8	-57.0	4.9	34 20.6	-57.0	5.0	35 20.4	-57.0	5.0	36 20.2	-57.0	5.1	75
76	28 24.5	-57.2	4.3	29 24.3	-57.1	4.4	30 24.2	-57.2	4.4	31 24.0	-57.1	4.5	32 23.8	-57.1	4.5	33 23.6	-57.1	4.6	34 23.4	-57.0	4.6	35 23.2	-57.0	4.7	76
77	27 27.3	-57.3	4.0	28 27.2	-57.3	4.0	29 27.0	-57.2	4.1	30 26.9	-57.2	4.1	31 26.7	-57.2	4.2	32 26.5	-57.1	4.2	33 26.4	-57.1	4.3	34 26.2	-57.1	4.3	77
78	26 30.0	-57.3	3.7	27 29.9	-57.3	3.7	28 29.8	-57.3	3.7	29 29.7	-57.3	3.8	30 29.5	-57.2	3.8	31 29.4	-57.2	3.9	32 29.3	-57.2	3.9	33 29.1	-57.1	3.9	78
79	25 32.7	-57.3	3.3	26 32.6	-57.3	3.4	27 32.5	-57.3	3.4	28 32.4	-57.3	3.4	29 32.3	-57.2	3.5	30 32.2	-57.2	3.5	31 32.1	-57.2	3.5	32 32.0	-57.2	3.6	79
80	24 35.4	-57.4	3.0	25 35.3	-57.4	3.0	26 35.2	-57.3	3.1	27 35.1	-57.3	3.1	28 35.1	-57.4	3.1	29 35.0	-57.3	3.2	30 34.9	-57.3	3.2	31 34.8	-57.3	3.2	80
81	23 38.0	-57.4	2.7	24 37.9	-57.4	2.7	25 37.9	-57.4	2.7	26 37.8	-57.4	2.8	27 37.7	-57.3	2.8	28 37.7	-57.4	2.8	29 37.6	-57.4	2.8	30 37.5	-57.3	2.9	81
82	22 40.6	-57.5	2.4	23 40.5	-57.4	2.4	24 40.5	-57.5	2.4	25 40.4	-57.4	2.4	26 40.4	-57.5	2.5	27 40.3	-57.4	2.5	28 40.2	-57.3	2.5	29 40.2	-57.4	2.5	82
83	21 43.1	-57.5	2.1	22 43.1	-57.5	2.1	23 43.0	-57.4	2.1	24 43.0	-57.5	2.1	25 42.9	-57.4	2.1	26 42.9	-57.4	2.2	27 42.9	-57.5	2.2	28 42.8	-57.4	2.2	83
84	20 45.6	-57.5	1.8	21 45.6	-57.5	1.8	22 45.6	-57.6	1.8	23 45.5	-57.5	1.8	24 45.5	-57.5	1.8	25 45.5	-57.5	1.8	26 45.4	-57.4	1.8	27 45.4	-57.4	1.9	84
85	19 48.1	-57.6	1.5	20 48.1	-57.6	1.5	21 48.0	-57.5	1.5	22 48.0	-57.5	1.5	23 48.0	-57.5	1.5	24 48.0	-57.5	1.5	25 48.0	-57.6	1.5	26 47.9	-57.5	1.5	85
86	18 50.5	-57.6	1.2	19 50.5	-57.6	1.2	20 50.5	-57.6	1.2	21 50.5	-57.6	1.2	22 50.5	-57.6	1.2	23 50.5	-57.6	1.2	24 50.4	-57.5	1.2	25 50.4	-57.5	1.2	86
87	17 52.9	-57.6	0.9	18 52.9	-57.6	0.9	19 52.9	-57.6	0.9	20 52.9	-57.6	0.9	21 52.9	-57.6	0.9	22 52.9	-57.6	0.9	23 52.9	-57.6	0.9	24 52.9	-57.6	0.9	87
88	16 55.3	-57.6	0.6	17 55.3	-57.6	0.6	18 55.3	-57.6	0.6	19 55.3	-57.6	0.6	20 55.3	-57.6	0.6	21 55.3	-57.6	0.6	22 55.3	-57.6	0.6	23 55.3	-57.6	0.6	88
89	15 57.7	-57.7	0.3	16 57.7	-57.7	0.3	17 57.7	-57.7	0.3	18 57.7	-57.7	0.3	19 57.7	-57.7	0.3	20 57.7	-57.7	0.3	21 57.7	-57.7	0.3	22 57.7	-57.7	0.3	89
90	15 00.0	-57.7	0.0	16 00.0	-57.7	0.0	17 00.0	-57.7	0.0	18 00.0	-57.7	0.0	19 00.0	-57.7	0.0	20 00.0	-57.7	0.0	21 00.0	-57.7	0.0	22 00.0	-57.7	0.0	90
	15°			16°			17°			18°			19°			20°			21°			22°			

Dec.	15°			16°			17°			18°			19°			20°			21°			22°			Dec.
°	Hc ° ′	d ′	Z °	Hc ° ′	d ′	Z °	Hc ° ′	d ′	Z °	Hc ° ′	d ′	Z °	Hc ° ′	d ′	Z °	Hc ° ′	d ′	Z °	Hc ° ′	d ′	Z °	Hc ° ′	d ′	Z °	°
0	68 12.2	−42.5	132.1	67 31.3	−43.8	133.9	66 49.1	−45.1	135.6	66 05.7	−46.3	137.1	65 21.2	−47.3	138.6	64 35.6	−48.2	140.0	63 49.2	−49.1	141.3	63 02.0	−49.9	142.6	0
1	67 29.7	−43.7	133.9	66 47.5	−45.0	135.6	66 04.0	−46.1	137.2	65 19.4	−47.1	138.7	64 33.9	−48.1	140.1	63 47.4	−48.9	141.4	63 00.1	−49.7	142.6	62 12.1	−50.5	143.8	1
2	66 46.0	−44.8	135.7	66 02.5	−45.9	137.3	65 17.9	−47.0	138.8	64 32.3	−48.0	140.2	63 45.8	−48.8	141.5	62 58.5	−49.7	142.7	62 10.4	−50.4	143.8	61 21.6	−51.0	144.9	2
3	66 01.2	−45.8	137.4	65 16.6	−46.9	138.8	64 30.9	−47.8	140.2	63 44.3	−48.7	141.5	62 57.0	−49.5	142.8	62 08.8	−50.2	143.9	61 20.0	−50.9	145.0	60 30.6	−51.5	146.0	3
4	65 15.4	−46.7	138.9	64 29.7	−47.7	140.3	63 43.1	−48.6	141.6	62 55.6	−49.3	142.8	62 07.5	−50.1	144.0	61 18.6	−50.8	145.1	60 29.1	−51.4	146.1	59 39.1	−52.0	147.0	4
5	64 28.7	−47.6	140.4	63 42.0	−48.5	141.7	62 54.5	−49.3	142.9	62 06.3	−50.0	144.1	61 17.4	−50.7	145.1	60 27.8	−51.3	146.2	59 37.7	−51.9	147.1	58 47.1	−52.4	148.0	5
6	63 41.1	−48.4	141.8	62 53.5	−49.1	143.0	62 05.2	−49.8	144.2	61 16.3	−50.6	145.2	60 26.7	−51.2	146.2	59 36.5	−51.7	147.2	58 45.8	−52.3	148.1	57 54.7	−52.8	148.9	6
7	62 52.7	−49.0	143.1	62 04.4	−49.8	144.3	61 15.4	−50.5	145.3	60 25.7	−51.1	146.3	59 35.5	−51.7	147.3	58 44.8	−52.2	148.2	57 53.5	−52.6	149.0	57 01.9	−53.2	149.8	7
8	62 03.7	−49.7	144.4	61 14.6	−50.4	145.4	60 24.9	−51.0	146.4	59 34.6	−51.5	147.4	58 43.8	−52.1	148.3	57 52.6	−52.6	149.1	57 00.9	−53.1	149.9	56 08.7	−53.4	150.7	8
9	61 14.0	−50.3	145.5	60 24.2	−50.9	146.5	59 33.9	−51.5	147.5	58 43.1	−52.1	148.4	57 51.7	−52.5	149.2	57 00.0	−53.0	150.0	56 07.8	−53.4	150.8	55 15.3	−53.8	151.5	9
10	60 23.7	−50.8	146.7	59 33.3	−51.3	147.6	58 42.4	−51.9	148.5	57 51.0	−52.4	149.3	56 59.2	−52.8	150.1	56 07.0	−53.3	150.9	55 14.4	−53.7	151.6	54 21.5	−54.1	152.2	10
11	59 32.9	−51.3	147.7	58 42.0	−51.9	148.6	57 50.5	−52.3	149.4	56 58.6	−52.7	150.2	56 06.4	−53.3	151.0	55 13.7	−53.6	151.7	54 20.7	−53.9	152.3	53 27.4	−54.3	153.0	11
12	58 41.6	−51.7	148.7	57 50.1	−52.2	149.6	56 58.2	−52.7	150.4	56 05.9	−53.2	151.1	55 13.1	−53.5	151.8	54 20.1	−53.9	152.5	53 26.8	−54.3	153.1	52 33.1	−54.5	153.7	12
13	57 49.9	−52.2	149.7	56 57.9	−52.6	150.5	56 05.5	−53.1	151.2	55 12.7	−53.4	151.9	54 19.6	−53.8	152.6	53 26.2	−54.1	153.2	52 32.5	−54.5	153.8	51 38.6	−54.8	154.4	13
14	56 57.7	−52.5	150.6	56 05.3	−53.0	151.4	55 12.4	−53.3	152.0	54 19.3	−53.8	152.7	53 25.8	−54.1	153.3	52 32.1	−54.5	153.9	51 38.0	−54.7	154.5	50 43.8	−55.0	155.0	14
15	56 05.2	−52.9	151.5	55 12.3	−53.3	152.2	54 19.1	−53.7	152.8	53 25.5	−54.0	153.5	52 31.7	−54.3	154.0	51 37.6	−54.6	154.6	50 43.3	−54.9	155.1	49 48.8	−55.2	155.6	15
16	55 12.3	−53.2	152.3	54 19.0	−53.6	153.0	53 25.4	−53.9	153.6	52 31.5	−54.2	154.2	51 37.4	−54.6	154.7	50 43.0	−54.9	155.3	49 48.4	−55.1	155.8	48 53.6	−55.4	156.2	16
17	54 19.1	−53.6	153.1	53 25.4	−53.9	153.7	52 31.5	−54.2	154.3	51 37.3	−54.6	154.9	50 42.8	−54.8	155.4	49 48.1	−55.0	155.9	48 53.3	−55.3	156.4	47 58.2	−55.5	156.8	17
18	53 25.5	−53.8	153.9	52 31.5	−54.1	154.5	51 37.3	−54.5	155.0	50 42.7	−54.7	155.5	49 48.0	−55.0	156.0	48 53.1	−55.2	156.5	47 58.0	−55.5	157.0	47 02.7	−55.7	157.4	18
19	52 31.7	−54.1	154.6	51 37.4	−54.4	155.2	50 42.8	−54.7	155.7	49 48.0	−54.9	156.2	48 53.0	−55.1	156.7	47 57.9	−55.5	157.1	47 02.5	−55.6	157.5	46 07.0	−55.9	157.9	19
20	51 37.6	−54.3	155.3	50 43.0	−54.6	155.9	49 48.1	−54.8	156.3	48 53.1	−55.1	156.8	47 57.9	−55.4	157.2	47 02.4	−55.5	157.7	46 06.9	−55.8	158.1	45 11.1	−55.9	158.4	20
21	50 43.3	−54.5	156.0	49 48.4	−54.8	156.5	48 53.3	−55.1	157.0	47 58.0	−55.3	157.4	47 02.5	−55.5	157.8	46 06.9	−55.8	158.2	45 11.1	−55.9	158.6	44 15.2	−56.2	158.9	21
22	49 48.8	−54.8	156.7	48 53.6	−55.0	157.1	47 58.2	−55.2	157.6	47 02.7	−55.5	158.0	46 07.0	−55.7	158.4	45 11.1	−55.8	158.7	44 15.2	−56.1	159.1	43 19.0	−56.2	159.4	22
23	48 54.0	−54.9	157.3	47 58.6	−55.2	157.7	47 03.0	−55.4	158.1	46 07.2	−55.6	158.5	45 11.3	−55.8	158.9	44 15.3	−56.0	159.3	43 19.1	−56.2	159.6	42 22.8	−56.4	159.9	23
24	47 59.1	−55.2	157.9	47 03.4	−55.4	158.3	46 07.6	−55.6	158.7	45 11.6	−55.8	159.1	44 15.5	−56.0	159.4	43 19.3	−56.2	159.8	42 22.9	−56.3	160.1	41 26.4	−56.4	160.4	24
25	47 03.9	−55.3	158.5	46 08.0	−55.5	158.9	45 12.0	−55.7	159.2	44 15.8	−55.9	159.6	43 19.5	−56.0	159.9	42 23.1	−56.2	160.2	41 26.6	−56.4	160.5	40 30.0	−56.6	160.8	25
26	46 08.6	−55.5	159.0	45 12.5	−55.7	159.4	44 16.3	−55.9	159.8	43 19.9	−56.0	160.1	42 23.5	−56.2	160.4	41 26.9	−56.4	160.7	40 30.2	−56.5	161.0	39 33.4	−56.6	161.3	26
27	45 13.1	−55.6	159.6	44 16.8	−55.8	159.9	43 20.4	−56.0	160.3	42 23.9	−56.2	160.6	41 27.3	−56.4	160.9	40 30.5	−56.4	161.2	39 33.7	−56.6	161.4	38 36.8	−56.8	161.7	27
28	44 17.5	−55.7	160.1	43 21.0	−55.9	160.4	42 24.4	−56.1	160.8	41 27.7	−56.2	161.0	40 30.9	−56.4	161.3	39 34.1	−56.6	161.6	38 37.1	−56.7	161.9	37 40.0	−56.8	162.1	28
29	43 21.8	−55.9	160.6	42 25.1	−56.1	160.9	41 28.3	−56.2	161.2	40 31.5	−56.4	161.5	39 34.5	−56.5	161.8	38 37.5	−56.6	162.0	37 40.4	−56.8	162.3	36 43.2	−56.9	162.5	29
30	42 25.9	−56.1	161.1	41 29.0	−56.1	161.4	40 32.1	−56.3	161.7	39 35.1	−56.5	162.0	38 38.0	−56.6	162.2	37 40.9	−56.8	162.4	36 43.6	−56.9	162.7	35 46.3	−57.0	162.9	30
31	41 29.8	−56.1	161.6	40 32.9	−56.3	161.9	39 35.8	−56.4	162.1	38 38.6	−56.5	162.4	37 41.4	−56.7	162.6	36 44.1	−56.8	162.9	35 46.7	−56.9	163.1	34 49.3	−57.0	163.3	31
32	40 33.7	−56.2	162.1	39 36.6	−56.4	162.3	38 39.4	−56.6	162.6	37 42.1	−56.7	162.8	36 44.7	−56.8	163.0	35 47.3	−56.9	163.3	34 49.8	−57.0	163.5	33 52.3	−57.2	163.6	32
33	39 37.5	−56.4	162.5	38 40.2	−56.5	162.8	37 42.8	−56.6	163.0	36 45.4	−56.7	163.2	35 47.9	−56.8	163.4	34 50.4	−57.0	163.6	33 52.8	−57.1	163.8	32 55.1	−57.1	164.0	33
34	38 41.1	−56.5	163.0	37 43.7	−56.6	163.2	36 46.2	−56.7	163.4	35 48.7	−56.8	163.6	34 51.1	−56.9	163.8	33 53.4	−57.0	164.0	32 55.7	−57.1	164.2	31 58.0	−57.3	164.4	34
35	37 44.6	−56.5	163.4	36 47.1	−56.6	163.6	35 49.5	−56.8	163.8	34 51.9	−56.9	164.0	33 54.2	−57.0	164.2	32 56.4	−57.1	164.4	31 58.6	−57.2	164.6	31 00.7	−57.3	164.7	35
36	36 48.1	−56.6	163.8	35 50.5	−56.8	164.0	34 52.7	−56.8	164.2	33 55.0	−57.0	164.4	32 57.2	−57.1	164.6	31 59.3	−57.2	164.8	31 01.4	−57.3	164.9	30 03.4	−57.3	165.1	36
37	35 51.5	−56.7	164.2	34 53.7	−56.8	164.4	33 55.9	−56.9	164.6	32 58.0	−57.0	164.8	32 00.1	−57.1	165.0	31 02.1	−57.2	165.1	30 04.1	−57.3	165.3	29 06.1	−57.4	165.4	37
38	34 54.8	−56.8	164.6	33 56.9	−56.9	164.8	32 59.0	−57.0	165.0	32 01.0	−57.1	165.2	31 03.0	−57.2	165.3	30 04.9	−57.3	165.5	29 06.8	−57.4	165.6	28 08.7	−57.5	165.7	38
39	33 58.0	−56.9	165.0	33 00.0	−57.0	165.2	32 02.0	−57.1	165.4	31 03.9	−57.2	165.5	30 05.8	−57.3	165.7	29 07.6	−57.3	165.8	28 09.4	−57.4	165.9	27 11.2	−57.5	166.1	39
40	33 01.1	−56.9	165.4	32 03.0	−57.0	165.6	31 04.9	−57.1	165.7	30 06.7	−57.2	165.9	29 08.5	−57.3	166.0	28 10.3	−57.4	166.1	27 12.0	−57.4	166.3	26 13.7	−57.5	166.4	40
41	32 04.2	−57.0	165.8	31 06.0	−57.1	165.9	30 07.8	−57.2	166.1	29 09.5	−57.2	166.2	28 11.2	−57.3	166.3	27 12.9	−57.4	166.5	26 14.6	−57.5	166.6	25 16.2	−57.6	166.7	41
42	31 07.2	−57.1	166.2	30 08.9	−57.1	166.3	29 10.6	−57.2	166.4	28 12.3	−57.3	166.6	27 13.9	−57.4	166.7	26 15.5	−57.5	166.8	25 17.1	−57.6	166.9	24 18.6	−57.6	167.0	42
43	30 10.1	−57.1	166.5	29 11.8	−57.2	166.6	28 13.4	−57.3	166.8	27 15.0	−57.4	166.9	26 16.5	−57.4	167.0	25 18.0	−57.5	167.1	24 19.5	−57.5	167.2	23 21.0	−57.6	167.3	43
44	29 13.0	−57.1	166.9	28 14.6	−57.3	167.0	27 16.1	−57.3	167.1	26 17.6	−57.4	167.2	25 19.1	−57.5	167.3	24 20.5	−57.5	167.4	23 22.0	−57.7	167.5	22 23.4	−57.7	167.6	44
45	28 15.9	−57.3	167.2	27 17.3	−57.3	167.3	26 18.8	−57.4	167.4	25 20.2	−57.4	167.5	24 21.6	−57.5	167.6	23 23.0	−57.6	167.7	22 24.3	−57.6	167.8	21 25.7	−57.7	167.9	45
46	27 18.6	−57.2	167.6	26 20.0	−57.3	167.7	25 21.4	−57.4	167.8	24 22.8	−57.5	167.9	23 24.1	−57.5	168.0	22 25.4	−57.6	168.0	21 26.7	−57.7	168.1	20 28.0	−57.8	168.2	46
47	26 21.4	−57.3	167.9	25 22.7	−57.4	168.0	24 24.0	−57.4	168.1	23 25.3	−57.5	168.2	22 26.6	−57.6	168.3	21 27.8	−57.6	168.3	20 29.0	−57.7	168.4	19 30.2	−57.7	168.5	47
48	25 24.1	−57.4	168.2	24 25.3	−57.4	168.3	23 26.6	−57.5	168.4	22 27.8	−57.6	168.5	21 29.0	−57.6	168.6	20 30.2	−57.7	168.6	19 31.3	−57.7	168.7	18 32.5	−57.8	168.8	48
49	24 26.7	−57.4	168.5	23 27.9	−57.5	168.6	22 29.1	−57.6	168.7	21 30.2	−57.6	168.8	20 31.4	−57.7	168.9	19 32.5	−57.7	168.9	18 33.6	−57.8	169.0	17 34.7	−57.8	169.1	49
50	23 29.3	−57.4	168.9	22 30.4	−57.5	168.9	21 31.5	−57.5	169.0	20 32.6	−57.6	169.1	19 33.7	−57.7	169.2	18 34.8	−57.8	169.2	17 35.8	−57.8	169.3	16 36.9	−57.9	169.3	50
51	22 31.9	−57.5	169.2	21 32.9	−57.5	169.3	20 34.0	−57.6	169.3	19 35.0	−57.6	169.4	18 36.0	−57.7	169.5	17 37.0	−57.7	169.5	16 38.0	−57.8	169.6	15 39.0	−57.8	169.6	51
52	21 34.4	−57.5	169.5	20 35.4	−57.6	169.6	19 36.4	−57.6	169.6	18 37.4	−57.7	169.7	17 38.3	−57.7	169.7	16 39.3	−57.8	169.8	15 40.2	−57.8	169.8	14 41.2	−57.9	169.9	52
53	20 36.9	−57.5	169.8	19 37.8	−57.5	169.9	18 38.8	−57.7	169.9	17 39.7	−57.7	170.0	16 40.6	−57.7	170.0	15 41.5	−57.8	170.1	14 42.4	−57.8	170.1	13 43.3	−57.9	170.2	53
54	19 39.4	−57.6	170.1	18 40.3	−57.7	170.2	17 41.1	−57.6	170.2	16 42.0	−57.7	170.3	15 42.9	−57.8	170.3	14 43.7	−57.8	170.4	13 44.6	−57.9	170.4	12 45.4	−57.9	170.4	54
55	18 41.8	−57.6	170.4	17 42.6	−57.6	170.4	16 43.5	−57.7	170.5	15 44.3	−57.8	170.5	14 45.1	−57.8	170.6	13 45.9	−57.8	170.6	12 46.7	−57.9	170.7	11 47.5	−57.9	170.7	55
56	17 44.2	−57.6	170.7	16 45.0	−57.7	170.7	15 45.8	−57.7	170.8	14 46.5	−57.7	170.8	13 47.3	−57.8	170.9	12 48.1	−57.9	170.9	11 48.8	−57.9	170.9	10 49.6	−58.0	171.0	56
57	16 46.6	−57.7	171.0	15 47.3	−57.7	171.0	14 48.1	−57.8	171.1	13 48.8	−57.8	171.1	12 49.5	−57.8	171.1	11 50.2	−57.9	171.2	10 50.9	−57.9	171.2	9 51.6	−57.9	171.2	57
58	15 48.9	−57.6	171.3	14 49.6	−57.7	171.3	13 50.3	−57.7	171.3	12 51.0	−57.8	171.4	11 51.7	−57.9	171.4	10 52.3	−57.8	171.4	9 53.0	−57.9	171.5	8 53.7	−58.0	171.5	58
59	14 51.3	−57.7	171.6	13 51.9	−57.7	171.6	12 52.6	−57.8	171.6	11 53.2	−57.8	171.7	10 53.8	−57.8	171.7	9 54.5	−57.9	171.7	8 55.1	−58.0	171.7	7 55.7	−58.0	171.8	59
60	13 53.6	−57.7	171.8	12 54.2	−57.8	171.9	11 54.8	−57.8	171.9	10 55.4	−57.8	171.9	9 56.0	−57.9	172.0	8 56.6	−57.9	172.0	7 57.1	−57.9	172.0	6 57.7	−58.0	172.0	60
61	12 55.9	−57.8	172.1	11 56.4	−57.7	172.1	10 57.0	−57.8	172.2	9 57.6	−57.9	172.2	8 58.1	−57.9	172.2	7 58.7	−58.0	172.2	6 59.2	−57.9	172.3	5 59.7	−57.9	172.3	61
62	11 58.1	−57.7	172.4	10 58.7	−57.8	172.4	9 59.2	−57.8	172.4	8 59.7	−57.8	172.5	8 00.2	−57.9	172.5	7 00.7	−57.9	172.5	6 01.3	−58.0	172.5	5 01.8	−58.0	172.5	62
63	11 00.4	−57.8	172.7	10 00.9	−57.8	172.7	9 01.4	−57.9	172.7	8 01.9	−57.9	172.7	7 02.3	−57.9	172.8	6 02.8	−57.9	172.8	5 03.3	−58.0	172.8	4 03.8	−58.0	172.8	63
64	10 02.6	−57.7	173.0	9 03.1	−57.8	173.0	8 03.5	−57.8	173.0	7 04.0	−57.9	173.0	6 04.4	−57.9	173.0	5 04.9	−58.0	173.0	4 05.3	−57.9	173.0	3 05.8	−58.0	173.0	64
65	9 04.9	−57.8	173.2	8 05.3	−57.8	173.2	7 05.7	−57.8	173.3	6 06.1	−57.9	173.3	5 06.5	−57.9	173.3	4 06.9	−57.9	173.3	3 07.4	−58.0	173.3	2 07.8	−58.0	173.3	65
66	8 07.1	−57.8	173.5	7 07.5	−57.9	173.5	6 07.9	−57.9	173.5	5 08.2	−57.8	173.5	4 08.6	−57.9	173.5	3 09.0	−58.0	173.6	2 09.4	−58.0	173.6	1 09.8	−58.0	173.6	66
67	7 09.3	−57.8	173.8	6 09.6	−57.8	173.8	5 10.0	−57.9	173.8	4 10.4	−57.9	173.8	3 10.7	−57.9	173.8	2 11.1	−58.0	173.8	1 11.4	−58.0	173.8	0 11.8	−58.1	173.8	67
68	6 11.5	−57.8	174.0	5 11.8	−57.8	174.0	4 12.1	−57.8	174.1	3 12.5	−57.9	174.1	2 12.8	−57.9	174.1	1 13.1	−57.9	174.1	0 13.4	−58.0	174.1	0 46.3	+58.0	5.9	68
69	5 13.7	−57.8	174.3	4 14.0	−57.9	174.3	3 14.3	−57.9	174.3	2 14.6	−57.9	174.3	1 14.9	−58.0	174.3	0 15.2	−58.0	174.3	1 44.6	+57.9	5.7	1 44.3	+58.0	5.7	69
70	4 15.9	−57.9	174.6	3 16.1	−57.8	174.6	2 16.4	−57.9	174.6	1 16.7	−57.9	174.6	0 16.9	−57.9	174.6	0 42.8	+58.0	5.4	1 42.5	+58.0	5.4	2 42.3	+58.0	5.4	70
71	3 18.0	−57.8	174.8	2 18.3	−57.9	174.8	1 18.5	−57.9	174.9	0 18.8	−57.9	174.9	0 41.0	+57.9	5.1	1 40.8	+57.9	5.2	2 40.5	+58.0	5.2	3 40.3	+58.0	5.2	71
72	2 20.2	−57.8	175.1	1 20.4	−57.8	175.1	0 20.6	−57.8	175.1	0 39.1	+57.9	4.9	1 38.9	+57.9	4.9	2 38.7	+57.9	4.9	3 38.5	+58.0	4.9	4 38.3	+58.0	4.9	72
73	1 22.4	−57.9	175.4	0 22.6	−57.9	175.4	0 37.2	+57.9	4.6	1 37.0	+57.9	4.6	2 36.8	+58.0	4.6	3 36.6	+58.0	4.6	4 36.5	+57.9	4.6	5 36.3	+57.9	4.6	73
74	0 24.5	−57.8	175.6	0 35.3	+57.8	4.4	1 35.1	+57.9	4.4	2 34.9	+57.9	4.4	3 34.8	+57.9	4.4	4 34.6	+57.9	4.4	5 34.4	+58.0	4.4	6 34.2	+58.0	4.4	74
75	0 33.3	+57.8	4.1	1 33.1	+57.9	4.1	2 33.0	+57.9	4.1	3 32.8	+57.9	4.1	4 32.7	+57.9	4.1	5 32.5	+58.0	4.1	6 32.4	+57.9	4.1	7 32.2	+58.0	4.1	75
76	1 31.1	+57.9	3.8	2 31.0	+57.8	3.8	3 30.9	+57.8	3.8	4 30.7	+57.9	3.8	5 30.6	+57.9	3.8	6 30.5	+57.9	3.8	7 30.3	+58.0	3.9	8 30.2	+57.9	3.9	76
77	2 29.0	+57.8	3.6	3 28.8	+57.9	3.6	4 28.7	+57.9	3.6	5 28.6	+57.9	3.6	6 28.5	+57.9	3.6	7 28.4	+57.9	3.6	8 28.3	+57.9	3.6	9 28.1	+58.0	3.6	77
78	3 26.8	+57.8	3.3	4 26.7	+57.8	3.3	5 26.6	+57.8	3.3	6 26.5	+57.9	3.3	7 26.4	+57.9	3.3	8 26.3	+57.9	3.3	9 26.2	+57.9	3.3	10 26.1	+57.9	3.3	78
79	4 24.6	+57.8	3.0	5 24.5	+57.9	3.0	6 24.4	+57.9	3.0	7 24.4	+57.8	3.0	8 24.3	+57.8	3.0	9 24.2	+57.9	3.1	10 24.1	+57.9	3.1	11 24.0	+57.9	3.1	79
80	5 22.4	+57.8	2.8	6 22.4	+57.8	2.8	7 22.3	+57.8	2.8	8 22.2	+57.9	2.8	9 22.1	+57.9	2.8	10 22.1	+57.9	2.8	11 22.0	+57.9	2.8	12 21.9	+57.9	2.8	80
81	6 20.2	+57.8	2.5	7 20.2	+57.8	2.5	8 20.1	+57.9	2.5	9 20.1	+57.8	2.5	10 20.0	+57.9	2.5	11 20.0	+57.8	2.5	12 19.9	+57.9	2.5	13 19.8	+57.9	2.5	81
82	7 18.0	+57.8	2.2	8 18.0	+57.8	2.2	9 18.0	+57.8	2.2	10 17.9	+57.8	2.2	11 17.9	+57.8	2.2	12 17.8	+57.9	2.3	13 17.8	+57.8	2.3	14 17.7	+57.9	2.3	82
83	8 15.8	+57.8	1.9	9 15.8	+57.8	2.0	10 15.8	+57.8	2.0	11 15.7	+57.8	2.0	12 15.7	+57.8	2.0	13 15.7	+57.8	2.0	14 15.6	+57.9	2.0	15 15.6	+57.8	2.0	83
84	9 13.6	+57.8	1.7	10 13.6	+57.8	1.7	11 13.6	+57.8	1.7	12 13.5	+57.8	1.7	13 13.5	+57.8	1.7	14 13.5	+57.8	1.7	15 13.5	+57.8	1.7	16 13.4	+57.9	1.7	84
85	10 11.4	+57.7	1.4	11 11.4	+57.7	1.4	12 11.4	+57.7	1.4	13 11.3	+57.8	1.4	14 11.3	+57.8	1.4	15 11.3	+57.8	1.4	16 11.3	+57.8	1.4	17 11.3	+57.8	1.4	85
86	11 09.1	+57.8	1.1	12 09.1	+57.8	1.1	13 09.1	+57.8	1.1	14 09.1	+57.8	1.1	15 09.1	+57.8	1.1	16 09.1	+57.8	1.1	17 09.1	+57.7	1.2	18 09.1	+57.7	1.2	86
87	12 06.9	+57.7	0.8	13 06.9	+57.7	0.8	14 06.9	+57.7	0.9	15 06.9	+57.7	0.9	16 06.9	+57.7	0.9	17 06.9	+57.7	0.9	18 06.8	+57.8	0.9	19 06.8	+57.8	0.9	87
88	13 04.6	+57.7	0.6	14 04.6	+57.7	0.6	15 04.6	+57.7	0.6	16 04.6	+57.7	0.6	17 04.6	+57.7	0.6	18 04.6	+57.7	0.6	19 04.6	+57.7	0.6	20 04.6	+57.7	0.6	88
89	14 02.3	+57.7	0.3	15 02.3	+57.7	0.3	16 02.3	+57.7	0.3	17 02.3	+57.7	0.3	18 02.3	+57.7	0.3	19 02.3	+57.7	0.3	20 02.3	+57.7	0.3	21 02.3	+57.7	0.3	89
90	15 00.0	+57.7	0.0	16 00.0	+57.7	0.0	17 00.0	+57.7	0.0	18 00.0	+57.7	0.0	19 00.0	+57.7	0.0	20 00.0	+57.7	0.0	21 00.0	+57.7	0.0	22 00.0	+57.7	0.0	90
	15°			16°			17°			18°			19°			20°			21°			22°			

S. Lat. {L.H.A. greater than 180° ....Zn=180°−Z
{L.H.A. less than 180°...........Zn=180°+Z

17°, 343° L.H.A. LATITUDE SAME NAME AS DECLINATION N. Lat. {L.H.A. greater than 180° .....Zn=Z / L.H.A. less than 180°............Zn=360°−Z}

Dec.	15°			16°			17°			18°			19°			20°			21°			22°			Dec.
°	Hc ° ′	d ′	Z °	Hc ° ′	d ′	Z °	Hc ° ′	d ′	Z °	Hc ° ′	d ′	Z °	Hc ° ′	d ′	Z °	Hc ° ′	d ′	Z °	Hc ° ′	d ′	Z °	Hc ° ′	d ′	Z °	°
0	67 28.6	+39.8	130.2	66 49.1	+41.4	132.0	66 08.2	+42.8	133.7	65 26.2	+44.1	135.3	64 43.0	+45.2	136.8	63 58.7	+46.4	138.2	63 13.5	+47.4	139.5	62 27.5	+48.2	140.8	0
1	68 08.4	+38.3	128.3	67 30.5	+40.0	130.2	66 51.0	+41.6	132.0	66 10.3	+42.9	133.7	65 28.2	+44.3	135.2	64 45.1	+45.4	136.7	64 00.9	+46.5	138.1	63 15.7	+47.5	139.5	1
2	68 46.7	+36.7	126.2	68 10.5	+38.5	128.2	67 32.6	+40.2	130.1	66 53.2	+41.7	131.9	66 12.5	+43.1	133.6	65 30.5	+44.4	135.2	64 47.4	+45.6	136.7	64 03.2	+46.7	138.1	2
3	69 23.4	+34.9	124.0	68 49.0	+36.8	126.1	68 12.8	+38.6	128.1	67 34.9	+40.4	130.0	66 55.6	+41.9	131.8	66 14.9	+43.3	133.5	65 33.0	+44.6	135.1	64 49.9	+45.8	136.6	3
4	69 58.3	+32.9•	121.6	69 25.8	+35.1	123.9	68 51.4	+37.1	126.0	68 15.3	+38.9	128.1	67 37.5	+40.6	130.0	66 58.2	+42.1	131.8	66 17.6	+43.4	133.5	65 35.7	+44.7	135.1	4
5	70 31.2	+30.9•	119.1	70 00.9	+33.2•	121.5	69 28.5	+35.3	123.8	68 54.2	+37.2	126.0	68 18.1	+39.0	128.0	67 40.3	+40.8	129.9	67 01.0	+42.3	131.8	66 20.4	+43.7	133.5	5
6	71 02.1	+28.5•	116.5	70 34.1	+31.0•	119.1	70 03.8	+33.3•	121.5	69 31.4	+35.5	123.8	68 57.1	+37.5	125.9	68 21.1	+39.2	128.0	67 43.3	+41.0	129.9	67 04.1	+42.5	131.7	6
7	71 30.6	+26.0•	113.8	71 05.1	+28.7•	116.5	70 37.1	+31.3•	119.0	70 06.9	+33.6•	121.4	69 34.6	+35.7	123.7	69 00.3	+37.7	125.9	68 24.3	+39.5	128.0	67 46.6	+41.1	129.9	7
8	71 56.6	+23.4•	110.9	71 33.8	+26.2•	113.7	71 08.4	+28.9•	116.4	70 40.5	+31.4•	119.0	70 10.3	+33.8•	121.4	69 38.0	+35.9	123.7	69 03.8	+37.9	125.9	68 27.7	+39.8	127.9	8
9	72 20.0	+20.5•	107.9	72 00.0	+23.6•	110.8	71 37.3	+26.5•	113.7	71 11.9	+29.2•	116.4	70 44.1	+31.7•	118.9	70 13.9	+34.0•	121.4	69 41.7	+36.1	123.7	69 07.5	+38.1	125.9	9
10	72 40.5	+17.5•	104.8	72 23.6	+20.7•	107.8	72 03.8	+23.8•	110.8	71 41.1	+26.7•	113.6	71 15.8	+29.3•	116.3	70 47.9	+31.9•	118.9	70 17.8	+34.3•	121.3	69 45.6	+36.4	123.7	10
11	72 58.0	+14.3•	101.6	72 44.3	+17.8•	104.7	72 27.6	+20.9•	107.8	72 07.8	+24.0•	110.7	71 45.1	+27.0•	113.6	71 19.8	+29.7•	116.3	70 52.1	+32.1•	118.9	70 22.0	+34.4•	121.3	11
12	73 12.3	+11.0•	98.2	73 02.1	+14.5•	101.5	72 48.5	+17.9•	104.6	72 31.8	+21.1•	107.7	72 12.1	+24.2•	110.7	71 49.5	+27.1•	113.5	71 24.2	+29.9•	116.3	70 56.4	+32.4•	118.9	12
13	73 23.3	+7.6•	94.8	73 16.6	+11.2•	98.1	73 06.4	+14.7•	101.4	72 52.9	+18.2•	104.6	72 36.3	+21.4•	107.7	72 16.6	+24.5•	110.6	71 54.1	+27.3•	113.5	71 28.8	+30.1•	116.2	13
14	73 30.9	+4.1•	91.3	73 27.8	+7.7•	94.7	73 21.1	+11.4•	98.0	73 11.1	+14.9•	101.3	72 57.7	+18.3•	104.5	72 41.1	+21.6•	107.6	72 21.4	+24.7•	110.6	71 58.9	+27.6•	113.5	14
15	73 35.0	+0.5•	87.8	73 35.5	+4.3•	91.2	73 32.5	+8.0•	94.6	73 26.0	+11.6•	97.9	73 16.0	+15.2•	101.2	73 02.7	+18.6•	104.4	72 46.1	+21.9•	107.6	72 26.5	+25.0•	110.6	15
16	73 35.5	−3.0•	84.2	73 39.8	+0.7•	87.6	73 40.5	+4.4•	91.1	73 37.6	+8.1•	94.5	73 31.2	+11.7•	97.8	73 21.3	+15.3•	101.1	73 08.0	+18.8•	104.4	72 51.5	+22.1•	107.5	16
17	73 32.5	−6.5•	80.7	73 40.5	−2.9•	84.1	73 44.9	+0.8•	87.5	73 45.7	+4.6•	90.9	73 42.9	+8.3•	94.4	73 36.6	+12.0•	97.7	73 26.8	+15.5•	101.1	73 13.6	+19.0•	104.3	17
18	73 26.0	−10.0•	77.2	73 37.6	−6.4•	80.5	73 45.7	−2.8•	83.9	73 50.3	+0.9•	87.4	73 51.2	+4.7•	90.8	73 48.6	+8.4•	94.3	73 42.3	+12.2•	97.7	73 32.6	+15.8•	101.0	18
19	73 16.0	−13.3•	73.8	73 31.2	−9.9•	77.0	73 42.9	−6.3•	80.4	73 51.2	−2.6•	83.8	73 55.9	+1.1•	87.2	73 57.0	+4.9•	90.7	73 54.5	+8.7•	94.2	73 48.4	+12.3•	97.6	19
20	73 02.7	−16.6•	70.4	73 21.3	−13.3•	73.6	73 36.6	−9.8•	76.8	73 48.6	−6.3•	80.2	73 57.0	−2.5•	83.6	74 01.9	+1.3•	87.1	74 03.2	+5.0•	90.6	74 00.7	+8.9•	94.1	20
21	72 46.1	−19.6•	67.1	73 08.0	−16.5•	70.2	73 26.8	−13.2•	73.3	73 42.3	−9.7•	76.6	73 54.5	−6.1•	80.0	74 03.2	−2.5•	83.4	74 08.2	+1.4•	86.9	74 09.6	+5.2•	90.5	21
22	72 26.5	−22.5•	64.0	72 51.5	−19.6•	66.9	73 13.6	−16.5•	69.9	73 32.6	−13.2•	73.1	73 48.4	−9.7•	76.4	74 00.7	−6.0•	79.8	74 09.6	−2.4•	83.3	74 14.8	+1.5•	86.8	22
23	72 04.0	−25.2•	60.9	72 31.9	−22.5•	63.7	72 57.1	−19.6•	66.6	73 19.4	−16.4•	69.7	73 38.7	−13.1•	72.9	73 54.7	−9.7•	76.2	74 07.2	−5.9•	79.6	74 16.3	−2.3•	83.1	23
24	71 38.8	−27.8•	58.0	72 09.4	−25.3•	60.7	72 37.5	−22.5•	63.4	73 03.0	−19.6•	66.4	73 25.6	−16.5•	69.4	73 45.0	−13.0•	72.7	74 01.3	−9.6•	76.0	74 14.0	−5.9•	79.4	24
25	71 11.0	−30.1•	55.2	71 44.1	−27.8•	57.7	72 15.0	−25.2•	60.4	72 43.4	−22.5•	63.2	73 09.1	−19.5•	66.1	73 32.0	−16.5•	69.2	73 51.7	−13.1•	72.4	74 08.1	−9.5•	75.8	25
26	70 40.9	−32.3•	52.6	71 16.3	−30.1•	54.9	71 49.8	−27.9•	57.4	72 20.9	−25.3•	60.1	72 49.6	−22.6•	62.9	73 15.5	−19.5•	65.8	73 38.6	−16.4•	68.9	73 58.6	−13.0•	72.2	26
27	70 08.6	−34.4	50.1	70 46.2	−32.4•	52.3	71 21.9	−30.2•	54.6	71 55.6	−27.9•	57.1	72 27.0	−25.3•	59.8	72 56.0	−22.6•	62.6	73 22.2	−19.6•	65.5	73 45.6	−16.4•	68.7	27
28	69 34.2	−36.1	47.7	70 13.8	−34.3	49.7	70 51.7	−32.4•	51.9	71 27.7	−30.2•	54.3	72 01.7	−27.9•	56.8	72 33.4	−25.4•	59.4	73 02.6	−22.6•	62.3	73 29.2	−19.7•	65.3	28
29	68 58.1	−37.9	45.4	69 39.5	−36.2	47.4	70 19.3	−34.4	49.4	70 57.5	−32.5•	51.6	71 33.8	−30.3•	54.0	72 08.0	−27.9•	56.5	72 40.0	−25.4•	59.1	73 09.5	−22.6•	62.0	29
30	68 20.2	−39.3	43.3	69 03.3	−37.9	45.1	69 44.9	−36.3	47.0	70 25.0	−34.4	49.1	71 03.5	−32.5•	51.3	71 40.1	−30.4•	53.6	72 14.6	−28.0•	56.1	72 46.9	−25.5•	58.8	30
31	67 40.9	−40.8	41.3	68 25.4	−39.5	43.0	69 08.6	−37.9	44.7	69 50.6	−36.4	46.7	70 31.0	−34.6	48.7	71 09.7	−32.6•	50.9	71 46.6	−30.5•	53.3	72 21.4	−28.1•	55.8	31
32	67 00.1	−42.1	39.4	67 45.9	−40.8	40.9	68 30.7	−39.5	42.6	69 14.2	−38.0	44.4	69 56.4	−36.4	46.3	70 37.1	−34.7	48.3	71 16.1	−32.7•	50.5	71 53.3	−30.6•	52.9	32
33	66 18.0	−43.3	37.6	67 05.1	−42.2	39.0	67 51.2	−41.0	40.6	68 36.2	−39.6	42.2	69 20.0	−38.2	44.0	70 02.4	−36.5	45.9	70 43.4	−34.7•	48.0	71 22.7	−32.8•	50.2	33
34	65 34.7	−44.3	35.9	66 22.9	−43.3	37.2	67 10.2	−42.2	38.7	67 56.6	−41.0	40.2	68 41.8	−39.6	41.9	69 25.9	−38.2	43.6	70 08.7	−36.7	45.5	70 49.9	−34.8•	47.6	34
35	64 50.4	−45.4	34.3	65 39.6	−44.4	35.5	66 28.0	−43.4	36.9	67 15.6	−42.4	38.3	68 02.2	−41.1	39.8	68 47.7	−39.8	41.5	69 32.0	−38.3	43.2	70 15.1	−36.8	45.1	35
36	64 05.0	−46.2	32.8	64 55.2	−45.4	33.9	65 44.6	−44.5	35.2	66 33.2	−43.4	36.5	67 21.1	−42.4	37.9	68 07.9	−41.2	39.4	68 53.7	−39.9	41.1	69 38.3	−38.4	42.8	36
37	63 18.8	−47.1	31.3	64 09.8	−46.3	32.4	65 00.1	−45.5	33.5	65 49.8	−44.6	34.8	66 38.7	−43.6	36.1	67 26.7	−42.5	37.5	68 13.8	−41.3	39.0	68 59.9	−40.0	40.7	37
38	62 31.7	−47.8	30.0	63 23.5	−47.1	31.0	64 14.6	−46.3	32.0	65 05.2	−45.6	33.2	65 55.1	−44.7	34.4	66 44.2	−43.7	35.7	67 32.5	−42.6	37.1	68 19.9	−41.4	38.6	38
39	61 43.9	−48.5	28.7	62 36.4	−47.9	29.6	63 28.3	−47.2	30.6	64 19.6	−46.4	31.6	65 10.4	−45.6	32.8	66 00.5	−44.7	34.0	66 49.9	−43.8	35.3	67 38.5	−42.7	36.7	39
40	60 55.4	−49.1	27.4	61 48.5	−48.6	28.3	62 41.1	−48.0	29.2	63 33.2	−47.3	30.2	64 24.8	−46.5	31.2	65 15.8	−45.7	32.4	66 06.1	−44.8	33.6	66 55.8	−43.9	34.9	40
41	60 06.3	−49.7	26.3	60 59.9	−49.2	27.1	61 53.1	−48.6	27.9	62 45.9	−48.0	28.8	63 38.3	−47.4	29.8	64 30.1	−46.7	30.8	65 21.3	−45.9	31.9	66 11.9	−45.0	33.1	41
42	59 16.6	−50.3	25.2	60 10.7	−49.8	25.9	61 04.5	−49.3	26.7	61 57.9	−48.7	27.5	62 50.9	−48.1	28.4	63 43.4	−47.4	29.4	64 35.4	−46.7	30.4	65 26.9	−46.0	31.5	42
43	58 26.3	−50.7	24.1	59 20.9	−50.3	24.8	60 15.2	−49.8	25.5	61 09.2	−49.3	26.3	62 02.8	−48.8	27.1	62 56.0	−48.2	28.0	63 48.7	−47.5	29.0	64 40.9	−46.8	30.0	43
44	57 35.6	−51.3	23.1	58 30.6	−50.8	23.7	59 25.4	−50.4	24.4	60 19.9	−50.0	25.1	61 14.0	−49.4	25.9	62 07.8	−48.9	26.7	63 01.2	−48.3	27.6	63 54.1	−47.6	28.6	44
45	56 44.3	−51.6	22.1	57 39.8	−51.3	22.7	58 35.0	−50.9	23.4	59 29.9	−50.4	24.0	60 24.6	−50.0	24.8	61 18.9	−49.5	25.5	62 12.9	−49.0	26.3	63 06.5	−48.4	27.2	45
46	55 52.7	−52.0	21.2	56 48.5	−51.7	21.8	57 44.1	−51.3	22.4	58 39.5	−51.0	23.0	59 34.6	−50.5	23.6	60 29.4	−50.1	24.4	61 23.9	−49.6	25.1	62 18.1	−49.1	25.9	46
47	55 00.7	−52.4	20.3	55 56.8	−52.1	20.9	56 52.8	−51.8	21.4	57 48.5	−51.4	22.0	58 44.1	−51.1	22.6	59 39.3	−50.6	23.2	60 34.3	−50.2	23.9	61 29.0	−49.7	24.7	47
48	54 08.3	−52.8	19.5	55 04.7	−52.4	20.0	56 01.0	−52.1	20.5	56 57.1	−51.8	21.0	57 53.0	−51.4	21.6	58 48.7	−51.1	22.2	59 44.1	−50.6	22.8	60 39.3	−50.3	23.5	48
49	53 15.5	−53.0	18.7	54 12.3	−52.8	19.1	55 08.9	−52.5	19.6	56 05.3	−52.2	20.1	57 01.6	−51.9	20.6	57 57.6	−51.5	21.2	58 53.5	−51.2	21.8	59 49.0	−50.7	22.4	49
50	52 22.5	−53.3	17.9	53 19.5	−53.1	18.3	54 16.4	−52.8	18.8	55 13.1	−52.5	19.2	56 09.7	−52.3	19.7	57 06.1	−52.0	20.2	58 02.3	−51.7	20.8	58 58.3	−51.3	21.4	50
51	51 29.2	−53.6	17.2	52 26.4	−53.4	17.6	53 23.6	−53.2	18.0	54 20.6	−52.9	18.4	55 17.4	−52.6	18.9	56 14.1	−52.3	19.3	57 10.6	−52.0	19.8	58 07.0	−51.7	20.4	51
52	50 35.6	−53.9	16.5	51 33.0	−53.6	16.8	52 30.4	−53.4	17.2	53 27.7	−53.2	17.6	54 24.8	−53.0	18.0	55 21.8	−52.7	18.5	56 18.6	−52.4	18.9	57 15.3	−52.1	19.4	52
53	49 41.7	−54.1	15.8	50 39.4	−53.9	16.1	51 37.0	−53.7	16.5	52 34.5	−53.5	16.8	53 31.8	−53.2	17.2	54 29.1	−53.0	17.6	55 26.2	−52.8	18.1	56 23.2	−52.5	18.5	53
54	48 47.6	−54.3	15.1	49 45.5	−54.2	15.4	50 43.3	−54.0	15.8	51 41.0	−53.8	16.1	52 38.6	−53.6	16.5	53 36.1	−53.4	16.8	54 33.4	−53.1	17.2	55 30.7	−52.9	17.7	54
55	47 53.3	−54.5	14.5	48 51.3	−54.3	14.8	49 49.3	−54.2	15.1	50 47.2	−54.0	15.4	51 45.0	−53.8	15.7	52 42.7	−53.6	16.1	53 40.3	−53.4	16.4	54 37.8	−53.2	16.8	55
56	46 58.8	−54.8	13.9	47 57.0	−54.6	14.1	48 55.1	−54.4	14.4	49 53.2	−54.2	14.7	50 51.2	−54.1	15.0	51 49.1	−53.9	15.3	52 46.9	−53.7	15.7	53 44.6	−53.4	16.0	56
57	46 04.0	−54.8	13.3	47 02.4	−54.7	13.5	48 00.7	−54.6	13.8	48 59.0	−54.5	14.0	49 57.1	−54.3	14.3	50 55.2	−54.1	14.6	51 53.2	−53.9	15.0	52 51.2	−53.8	15.3	57
58	45 09.2	−55.1	12.7	46 07.7	−55.0	12.9	47 06.1	−54.8	13.2	48 04.5	−54.6	13.4	49 02.8	−54.5	13.7	50 01.1	−54.3	14.0	50 59.3	−54.2	14.2	51 57.4	−54.0	14.6	58
59	44 14.1	−55.2	12.1	45 12.7	−55.1	12.3	46 11.3	−55.0	12.6	47 09.9	−54.9	12.8	48 08.3	−54.7	13.0	49 06.8	−54.6	13.3	50 05.1	−54.4	13.6	51 03.4	−54.2	13.9	59
60	43 18.9	−55.4	11.6	44 17.6	−55.2	11.8	45 16.3	−55.1	12.0	46 15.0	−55.0	12.2	47 13.6	−54.9	12.4	48 12.2	−54.8	12.7	49 10.7	−54.6	12.9	50 09.2	−54.5	13.2	60
61	42 23.5	−55.5	11.1	43 22.4	−55.4	11.2	44 21.2	−55.3	11.4	45 20.0	−55.2	11.6	46 18.7	−55.0	11.8	47 17.4	−54.9	12.1	48 16.1	−54.8	12.3	49 14.7	−54.7	12.5	61
62	41 28.0	−55.6	10.6	42 27.0	−55.6	10.7	43 25.9	−55.4	10.9	44 24.8	−55.3	11.1	45 23.7	−55.3	11.3	46 22.5	−55.1	11.5	47 21.3	−55.0	11.7	48 20.0	−54.9	11.9	62
63	40 32.4	−55.8	10.1	41 31.4	−55.7	10.2	42 30.5	−55.6	10.4	43 29.5	−55.5	10.5	44 28.4	−55.4	10.7	45 27.4	−55.3	10.9	46 26.3	−55.2	11.1	47 25.1	−55.0	11.3	63
64	39 36.6	−55.9	9.6	40 35.7	−55.8	9.7	41 34.9	−55.7	9.9	42 34.0	−55.7	10.0	43 33.0	−55.5	10.2	44 32.1	−55.5	10.4	45 31.1	−55.4	10.5	46 30.1	−55.3	10.7	64
65	38 40.7	−56.0	9.1	39 39.9	−55.9	9.2	40 39.2	−55.9	9.4	41 38.3	−55.7	9.5	42 37.5	−55.7	9.7	43 36.6	−55.5	9.8	44 35.7	−55.4	10.0	45 34.8	−55.4	10.2	65
66	37 44.7	−56.1	8.6	38 44.0	−56.0	8.8	39 43.3	−55.9	8.9	40 42.6	−55.9	9.0	41 41.8	−55.8	9.2	42 41.1	−55.8	9.3	43 40.3	−55.7	9.5	44 39.4	−55.5	9.6	66
67	36 48.6	−56.2	8.2	37 48.0	−56.1	8.3	38 47.4	−56.1	8.4	39 46.7	−56.0	8.5	40 46.0	−55.9	8.7	41 45.3	−55.8	8.8	42 44.6	−55.7	8.9	43 43.9	−55.7	9.1	67
68	35 52.4	−56.2	7.8	36 51.9	−56.2	7.9	37 51.3	−56.2	8.0	38 50.7	−56.1	8.1	39 50.1	−56.0	8.2	40 49.5	−56.0	8.3	41 48.9	−55.9	8.5	42 48.2	−55.8	8.6	68
69	34 56.2	−56.4	7.3	35 55.7	−56.4	7.4	36 55.1	−56.2	7.5	37 54.6	−56.2	7.6	38 54.1	−56.2	7.7	39 53.5	−56.0	7.8	40 53.0	−56.1	8.0	41 52.4	−56.0	8.1	69
70	33 59.8	−56.5	6.9	34 59.3	−56.4	7.0	35 58.9	−56.4	7.1	36 58.4	−56.3	7.2	37 57.9	−56.2	7.3	38 57.5	−56.2	7.4	39 56.9	−56.1	7.5	40 56.4	−56.0	7.6	70
71	33 03.3	−56.5	6.5	34 02.9	−56.4	6.6	35 02.5	−56.4	6.7	36 02.1	−56.4	6.8	37 01.7	−56.3	6.8	38 01.3	−56.3	6.9	39 00.8	−56.2	7.0	40 00.4	−56.2	7.1	71
72	32 06.8	−56.6	6.1	33 06.5	−56.6	6.2	34 06.1	−56.5	6.3	35 05.7	−56.4	6.3	36 05.4	−56.5	6.4	37 05.0	−56.4	6.5	38 04.6	−56.3	6.6	39 04.2	−56.3	6.7	72
73	31 10.2	−56.7	5.7	32 09.9	−56.6	5.8	33 09.6	−56.6	5.9	34 09.3	−56.6	5.9	35 08.9	−56.5	6.0	36 08.6	−56.5	6.1	37 08.3	−56.4	6.2	38 07.9	−56.4	6.2	73
74	30 13.5	−56.7	5.4	31 13.3	−56.7	5.4	32 13.0	−56.7	5.5	33 12.7	−56.6	5.5	34 12.4	−56.6	5.6	35 12.1	−56.5	5.7	36 11.9	−56.6	5.7	37 11.5	−56.4	5.8	74
75	29 16.8	−56.8	5.0	30 16.6	−56.8	5.0	31 16.3	−56.7	5.1	32 16.1	−56.7	5.1	33 15.8	−56.6	5.2	34 15.6	−56.6	5.3	35 15.3	−56.5	5.3	36 15.1	−56.6	5.4	75
76	28 20.0	−56.9	4.6	29 19.8	−56.8	4.7	30 19.6	−56.8	4.7	31 19.4	−56.8	4.7	32 19.2	−56.7	4.8	33 19.0	−56.7	4.9	34 18.8	−56.7	4.9	35 18.5	−56.6	5.0	76
77	27 23.1	−56.9	4.2	28 23.0	−56.9	4.3	29 22.8	−56.9	4.3	30 22.6	−56.8	4.4	31 22.5	−56.8	4.4	32 22.3	−56.8	4.5	33 22.1	−56.8	4.5	34 21.9	−56.7	4.6	77
78	26 26.2	−56.9	3.9	27 26.1	−57.0	3.9	28 25.9	−56.9	4.0	29 25.8	−56.9	4.0	30 25.7	−56.9	4.0	31 25.5	−56.8	4.1	32 25.3	−56.8	4.1	33 25.2	−56.8	4.2	78
79	25 29.3	−57.0	3.5	26 29.1	−56.9	3.6	27 29.0	−56.9	3.6	28 28.9	−56.9	3.6	29 28.8	−56.9	3.7	30 28.7	−56.9	3.7	31 28.5	−56.8	3.8	32 28.4	−56.8	3.8	79
80	24 32.3	−57.1	3.2	25 32.2	−57.1	3.2	26 32.1	−57.1	3.3	27 32.0	−57.0	3.3	28 31.9	−57.0	3.3	29 31.8	−57.0	3.3	30 31.7	−57.0	3.4	31 31.6	−57.0	3.4	80
81	23 35.2	−57.1	2.9	24 35.1	−57.1	2.9	25 35.0	−57.0	2.9	26 35.0	−57.1	2.9	27 34.9	−57.0	3.0	28 34.8	−57.0	3.0	29 34.7	−57.0	3.0	30 34.6	−56.9	3.0	81
82	22 38.1	−57.2	2.5	23 38.0	−57.1	2.5	24 38.0	−57.1	2.6	25 37.9	−57.1	2.6	26 37.9	−57.1	2.6	27 37.8	−57.1	2.6	28 37.7	−57.0	2.7	29 37.7	−57.1	2.7	82
83	21 40.9	−57.1	2.2	22 40.9	−57.2	2.2	23 40.9	−57.2	2.2	24 40.8	−57.1	2.2	25 40.8	−57.2	2.3	26 40.7	−57.1	2.3	27 40.7	−57.1	2.3	28 40.6	−57.1	2.3	83
84	20 43.8	−57.2	1.9	21 43.7	−57.2	1.9	22 43.7	−57.2	1.9	23 43.7	−57.2	1.9	24 43.6	−57.1	1.9	25 43.6	−57.2	1.9	26 43.6	−57.2	2.0	27 43.5	−57.1	2.0	84
85	19 46.6	−57.3	1.6	20 46.5	−57.2	1.6	21 46.5	−57.2	1.6	22 46.5	−57.2	1.6	23 46.5	−57.3	1.6	24 46.4	−57.2	1.6	25 46.4	−57.2	1.6	26 46.4	−57.2	1.6	85
86	18 49.3	−57.3	1.2	19 49.3	−57.3	1.2	20 49.3	−57.3	1.3	21 49.3	−57.3	1.3	22 49.2	−57.2	1.3	23 49.2	−57.2	1.3	24 49.2	−57.2	1.3	25 49.2	−57.2	1.3	86
87	17 52.0	−57.3	0.9	18 52.0	−57.3	0.9	19 52.0	−57.3	0.9	20 52.0	−57.3	0.9	21 52.0	−57.3	0.9	22 52.0	−57.3	1.0	23 52.0	−57.3	1.0	24 52.0	−57.3	1.0	87
88	16 54.7	−57.3	0.6	17 54.7	−57.3	0.6	18 54.7	−57.3	0.6	19 54.7	−57.3	0.6	20 54.7	−57.3	0.6	21 54.7	−57.3	0.6	22 54.7	−57.3	0.6	23 54.7	−57.3	0.6	88
89	15 57.4	−57.4	0.3	16 57.4	−57.4	0.3	17 57.4	−57.4	0.3	18 57.4	−57.4	0.3	19 57.4	−57.4	0.3	20 57.4	−57.4	0.3	21 57.4	−57.4	0.3	22 57.4	−57.4	0.3	89
90	15 00.0	−57.4	0.0	16 00.0	−57.4	0.0	17 00.0	−57.4	0.0	18 00.0	−57.4	0.0	19 00.0	−57.4	0.0	20 00.0	−57.4	0.0	21 00.0	−57.4	0.0	22 00.0	−57.4	0.0	90
	15°			16°			17°			18°			19°			20°			21°			22°			

LATITUDE CONTRARY NAME TO DECLINATION   L.H.A. 17°, 343°

Dec.	15°			16°			17°			18°			Dec.
	Hc	d	Z	Hc	d	Z	Hc	d	Z	Hc	d	Z	
°	° ′	′	°	° ′	′	°	° ′	′	°	° ′	′	°	°
0	67 28.6	-41.2	130.2	66 49.1	-42.6	132.0	66 08.2	-43.9	133.7	65 26.2	-45.1	135.3	0
1	66 47.4	-42.5	132.1	66 06.5	-43.8	133.8	65 24.3	-44.9	135.4	64 41.1	-46.1	136.9	1
2	66 04.9	-43.6	133.9	65 22.7	-44.8	135.5	64 39.4	-45.9	137.0	63 55.0	-46.8	138.3	2
3	65 21.3	-44.7	135.6	64 37.9	-45.7	137.0	63 53.5	-46.7	138.4	63 08.2	-47.7	139.7	3
4	64 36.6	-45.6	137.1	63 52.2	-46.7	138.5	63 06.8	-47.6	139.8	62 20.5	-48.4	141.1	4
5	63 51.0	-46.5	138.6	63 05.5	-47.4	139.9	62 19.2	-48.3	141.2	61 32.1	-49.1	142.3	5
6	63 04.5	-47.3	140.0	62 18.1	-48.1	141.3	61 30.9	-48.9	142.4	60 43.0	-49.6	143.5	6
7	62 17.2	-48.0	141.4	61 30.0	-48.8	142.5	60 42.0	-49.5	143.6	59 53.4	-50.2	144.7	7
8	61 29.2	-48.7	142.7	60 41.2	-49.5	143.7	59 52.5	-50.1	144.8	59 03.2	-50.8	145.7	8
9	60 40.5	-49.3	143.9	59 51.7	-49.9	144.9	59 02.4	-50.6	145.9	58 12.4	-51.1	146.8	9
10	59 51.2	-49.9	145.0	59 01.8	-50.6	146.0	58 11.8	-51.1	146.9	57 21.3	-51.7	147.7	10
11	59 01.3	-50.4	146.1	58 11.2	-51.0	147.0	57 20.7	-51.6	147.9	56 29.6	-52.0	148.7	11
12	58 10.9	-50.9	147.2	57 20.2	-51.4	148.0	56 29.1	-51.9	148.8	55 37.6	-52.4	149.6	12
13	57 20.0	-51.4	148.1	56 28.8	-51.8	148.9	55 37.2	-52.3	149.7	54 45.2	-52.7	150.4	13
14	56 28.6	-51.7	149.1	55 37.0	-52.3	149.8	54 44.9	-52.7	150.6	53 52.5	-53.1	151.2	14
15	55 36.9	-52.2	150.0	54 44.7	-52.6	150.7	53 52.2	-53.0	151.4	52 59.4	-53.4	152.0	15
16	54 44.7	-52.5	150.9	53 52.1	-52.9	151.5	52 59.2	-53.2	152.2	52 06.0	-53.6	152.8	16
17	53 52.2	-52.8	151.7	52 59.2	-53.2	152.3	52 06.0	-53.6	152.9	51 12.4	-53.9	153.5	17
18	52 59.4	-53.1	152.5	52 06.0	-53.5	153.1	51 12.4	-53.8	153.7	50 18.5	-54.1	154.2	18
19	52 06.3	-53.5	153.3	51 12.5	-53.7	153.8	50 18.6	-54.1	154.4	49 24.4	-54.4	154.9	19
20	51 12.8	-53.6	154.0	50 18.8	-54.0	154.5	49 24.5	-54.3	155.0	48 30.0	-54.5	155.5	20
21	50 19.2	-54.0	154.7	49 24.8	-54.2	155.2	48 30.2	-54.5	155.7	47 35.5	-54.8	156.1	21
22	49 25.2	-54.1	155.4	48 30.6	-54.5	155.8	47 35.7	-54.7	156.3	46 40.7	-54.9	156.7	22
23	48 31.1	-54.4	156.0	47 36.1	-54.6	156.5	46 41.0	-54.8	156.9	45 45.8	-55.2	157.3	23
24	47 36.7	-54.6	156.7	46 41.5	-54.8	157.1	45 46.2	-55.1	157.5	44 50.6	-55.2	157.9	24
25	46 42.1	-54.8	157.3	45 46.7	-55.0	157.7	44 51.1	-55.2	158.1	43 55.4	-55.4	158.4	25
26	45 47.3	-54.9	157.9	44 51.7	-55.2	158.2	43 55.9	-55.4	158.6	43 00.0	-55.6	158.9	26
27	44 52.4	-55.1	158.4	43 56.5	-55.3	158.8	43 00.5	-55.5	159.1	42 04.4	-55.7	159.5	27
28	43 57.3	-55.3	159.0	43 01.2	-55.5	159.3	42 05.0	-55.6	159.6	41 08.7	-55.8	160.0	28
29	43 02.0	-55.4	159.5	42 05.7	-55.6	159.8	41 09.4	-55.8	160.1	40 12.9	-56.0	160.4	29
30	42 06.6	-55.6	160.0	41 10.1	-55.7	160.3	40 13.6	-55.9	160.6	39 16.9	-56.0	160.9	30
31	41 11.0	-55.6	160.5	40 14.4	-55.8	160.8	39 17.7	-56.0	161.1	38 20.9	-56.2	161.4	31
32	40 15.4	-55.8	161.0	39 18.6	-56.0	161.3	38 21.7	-56.1	161.6	37 24.7	-56.2	161.8	32
33	39 19.6	-55.9	161.5	38 22.6	-56.0	161.8	37 25.6	-56.2	162.0	36 28.5	-56.4	162.2	33
34	38 23.7	-56.1	162.0	37 26.6	-56.2	162.2	36 29.4	-56.3	162.5	35 32.1	-56.4	162.7	34
35	37 27.6	-56.1	162.4	36 30.4	-56.3	162.7	35 33.1	-56.4	162.9	34 35.7	-56.5	163.1	35
36	36 31.5	-56.2	162.9	35 34.1	-56.3	163.1	34 36.7	-56.5	163.3	33 39.2	-56.6	163.5	36
37	35 35.3	-56.3	163.3	34 37.8	-56.5	163.5	33 40.2	-56.5	163.7	32 42.6	-56.7	163.9	37
38	34 39.0	-56.4	163.7	33 41.3	-56.5	163.9	32 43.7	-56.7	164.1	31 45.9	-56.7	164.3	38
39	33 42.6	-56.5	164.1	32 44.8	-56.6	164.3	31 47.0	-56.7	164.5	30 49.2	-56.8	164.7	39
40	32 46.1	-56.5	164.6	31 48.2	-56.6	164.7	30 50.3	-56.7	164.9	29 52.4	-56.9	165.0	40
41	31 49.6	-56.7	164.9	30 51.6	-56.7	165.1	29 53.6	-56.8	165.3	28 55.5	-56.9	165.4	41
42	30 52.9	-56.7	165.3	29 54.9	-56.8	165.5	28 56.8	-56.9	165.6	27 58.6	-57.0	165.8	42
43	29 56.2	-56.7	165.7	28 58.1	-56.9	165.9	27 59.9	-57.0	166.0	27 01.6	-57.0	166.1	43
44	28 59.5	-56.8	166.1	28 01.2	-56.9	166.2	27 02.9	-57.0	166.3	26 04.6	-57.1	166.5	44
45	28 02.7	-56.9	166.5	27 04.3	-56.9	166.6	26 05.9	-57.0	166.7	25 07.5	-57.1	166.8	45
46	27 05.8	-56.9	166.8	26 07.4	-57.1	166.9	25 08.9	-57.1	167.0	24 10.4	-57.1	167.1	46
47	26 08.9	-57.0	167.2	25 10.3	-57.0	167.3	24 11.8	-57.1	167.4	23 13.3	-57.3	167.5	47
48	25 11.9	-57.0	167.5	24 13.3	-57.1	167.6	23 14.7	-57.2	167.7	22 16.0	-57.2	167.8	48
49	24 14.9	-57.1	167.9	23 16.2	-57.2	167.9	22 17.5	-57.2	168.0	21 18.8	-57.3	168.1	49
50	23 17.8	-57.1	168.2	22 19.0	-57.1	168.3	21 20.3	-57.3	168.4	20 21.5	-57.3	168.4	50
51	22 20.7	-57.2	168.5	21 21.9	-57.3	168.6	20 23.0	-57.2	168.7	19 24.2	-57.4	168.8	51
52	21 23.5	-57.2	168.9	20 24.6	-57.2	168.9	19 25.8	-57.4	169.0	18 26.8	-57.3	169.1	52
53	20 26.3	-57.2	169.2	19 27.4	-57.3	169.2	18 28.4	-57.3	169.3	17 29.5	-57.4	169.4	53
54	19 29.1	-57.3	169.5	18 30.1	-57.3	169.6	17 31.1	-57.4	169.6	16 32.1	-57.5	169.7	54
55	18 31.8	-57.3	169.8	17 32.8	-57.4	169.9	16 33.7	-57.4	169.9	15 34.6	-57.4	170.0	55
56	17 34.5	-57.3	170.1	16 35.4	-57.3	170.2	15 36.3	-57.4	170.2	14 37.2	-57.5	170.3	56
57	16 37.2	-57.3	170.4	15 38.1	-57.4	170.5	14 38.9	-57.5	170.5	13 39.7	-57.5	170.6	57
58	15 39.9	-57.4	170.7	14 40.7	-57.5	170.8	13 41.4	-57.4	170.8	12 42.2	-57.5	170.9	58
59	14 42.5	-57.4	171.0	13 43.2	-57.4	171.1	12 44.0	-57.5	171.1	11 44.7	-57.6	171.2	59
60	13 45.1	-57.4	171.3	12 45.8	-57.5	171.4	11 46.5	-57.5	171.4	10 47.1	-57.5	171.4	60
61	12 47.7	-57.5	171.6	11 48.3	-57.5	171.7	10 49.0	-57.6	171.7	9 49.6	-57.6	171.7	61
62	11 50.2	-57.4	171.9	10 50.8	-57.5	172.0	9 51.4	-57.5	172.0	8 52.0	-57.6	172.0	62
63	10 52.8	-57.5	172.2	9 53.3	-57.5	172.3	8 53.9	-57.6	172.3	7 54.4	-57.6	172.3	63
64	9 55.3	-57.5	172.5	8 55.8	-57.5	172.5	7 56.3	-57.5	172.6	6 56.8	-57.6	172.6	64
65	8 57.8	-57.5	172.8	7 58.3	-57.5	172.8	6 58.8	-57.6	172.8	5 59.2	-57.6	172.9	65
66	8 00.3	-57.5	173.1	7 00.8	-57.6	173.1	6 01.2	-57.6	173.1	5 01.6	-57.6	173.1	66
67	7 02.8	-57.5	173.4	6 03.2	-57.5	173.4	5 03.6	-57.6	173.4	4 04.0	-57.6	173.4	67
68	6 05.3	-57.5	173.7	5 05.7	-57.6	173.7	4 06.0	-57.6	173.7	3 06.4	-57.6	173.7	68
69	5 07.8	-57.6	174.0	4 08.1	-57.6	174.0	3 08.4	-57.6	174.0	2 08.8	-57.7	174.0	69
70	4 10.2	-57.5	174.2	3 10.5	-57.6	174.3	2 10.8	-57.6	174.3	1 11.1	-57.6	174.3	70
71	3 12.7	-57.6	174.5	2 12.9	-57.5	174.5	1 13.2	-57.6	174.5	0 13.5	-57.6	174.5	71
72	2 15.1	-57.5	174.8	1 15.4	-57.6	174.8	0 15.6	-57.6	174.8	0 44.1	+57.7	5.2	72
73	1 17.6	-57.6	175.1	0 17.8	-57.6	175.1	0 42.0	+57.6	4.9	1 41.8	+57.6	4.9	73
74	0 20.0	-57.6	175.4	0 39.8	+57.6	4.6	1 39.6	+57.6	4.6	2 39.4	+57.6	4.6	74
75	0 37.6	+57.5	4.3	1 37.4	+57.6	4.3	2 37.2	+57.6	4.3	3 37.0	+57.7	4.3	75
76	1 35.1	+57.6	4.1	2 35.0	+57.5	4.1	3 34.8	+57.6	4.1	4 34.7	+57.6	4.1	76
77	2 32.7	+57.5	3.8	3 32.5	+57.6	3.8	4 32.4	+57.6	3.8	5 32.3	+57.6	3.8	77
78	3 30.2	+57.6	3.5	4 30.1	+57.6	3.5	5 30.0	+57.6	3.5	6 29.9	+57.6	3.5	78
79	4 27.8	+57.5	3.2	5 27.7	+57.5	3.2	6 27.6	+57.5	3.2	7 27.5	+57.6	3.2	79
80	5 25.3	+57.5	2.9	6 25.2	+57.6	2.9	7 25.1	+57.6	2.9	8 25.1	+57.5	2.9	80
81	6 22.8	+57.6	2.6	7 22.8	+57.5	2.6	8 22.7	+57.6	2.6	9 22.6	+57.6	2.7	81
82	7 20.4	+57.5	2.4	8 20.3	+57.5	2.4	9 20.3	+57.5	2.4	10 20.2	+57.5	2.4	82
83	8 17.9	+57.5	2.1	9 17.8	+57.6	2.1	10 17.8	+57.5	2.1	11 17.7	+57.6	2.1	83
84	9 15.4	+57.4	1.8	10 15.3	+57.5	1.8	11 15.3	+57.5	1.8	12 15.3	+57.5	1.8	84
85	10 12.8	+57.5	1.5	11 12.8	+57.5	1.5	12 12.8	+57.5	1.5	13 12.8	+57.5	1.5	85
86	11 10.3	+57.5	1.2	12 10.3	+57.5	1.2	13 10.3	+57.5	1.2	14 10.3	+57.4	1.2	86
87	12 07.8	+57.4	0.9	13 07.8	+57.4	0.9	14 07.8	+57.4	0.9	15 07.7	+57.5	0.9	87
88	13 05.2	+57.4	0.6	14 05.2	+57.4	0.6	15 05.2	+57.4	0.6	16 05.2	+57.4	0.6	88
89	14 02.6	+57.4	0.3	15 02.6	+57.4	0.3	16 02.6	+57.4	0.3	17 02.6	+57.4	0.3	89
90	15 00.0	+57.4	0.0	16 00.0	+57.4	0.0	17 00.0	+57.4	0.0	18 00.0	+57.4	0.0	90
	15°			16°			17°			18°			

Dec.	19°			20°			21°			22°			Dec.
	Hc	d	Z	Hc	d	Z	Hc	d	Z	Hc	d	Z	
°	° ′	′	°	° ′	′	°	° ′	′	°	° ′	′	°	°
0	64 43.0	-46.2	136.8	63 58.7	-47.2	138.2	63 13.5	-48.1	139.5	62 27.5	-49.0	140.8	0
1	63 56.8	-47.0	138.3	63 11.5	-47.9	139.6	62 25.4	-48.8	140.8	61 38.5	-49.6	142.0	1
2	63 09.8	-47.9	139.7	62 23.6	-48.7	140.9	61 36.6	-49.4	142.1	60 48.9	-50.1	143.2	2
3	62 21.9	-48.5	141.0	61 34.9	-49.3	142.2	60 47.2	-50.0	143.3	59 58.8	-50.7	144.3	3
4	61 33.4	-49.2	142.2	60 45.6	-49.9	143.3	59 57.2	-50.6	144.4	59 08.1	-51.2	145.4	4
5	60 44.2	-49.7	143.4	59 55.7	-50.4	144.5	59 06.6	-51.0	145.4	58 16.9	-51.6	146.4	5
6	59 54.5	-50.4	144.6	59 05.3	-51.0	145.5	58 15.6	-51.6	146.4	57 25.3	-52.0	147.3	6
7	59 04.1	-50.8	145.6	58 14.3	-51.4	146.5	57 24.0	-51.9	147.4	56 33.3	-52.5	148.2	7
8	58 13.3	-51.3	146.6	57 22.9	-51.8	147.5	56 32.1	-52.3	148.3	55 40.8	-52.8	149.1	8
9	57 22.0	-51.7	147.6	56 31.1	-52.2	148.4	55 39.8	-52.7	149.2	54 48.0	-53.1	149.9	9
10	56 30.3	-52.1	148.6	55 38.9	-52.6	149.3	54 47.1	-53.0	150.0	53 54.9	-53.4	150.7	10
11	55 38.2	-52.5	149.4	54 46.3	-52.9	150.2	53 54.1	-53.3	150.8	53 01.5	-53.7	151.5	11
12	54 45.7	-52.9	150.3	53 53.4	-53.2	151.0	53 00.8	-53.6	151.6	52 07.8	-53.9	152.2	12
13	53 52.8	-53.1	151.1	53 00.2	-53.6	151.7	52 07.2	-53.9	152.4	51 13.9	-54.2	152.9	13
14	52 59.7	-53.4	151.9	52 06.6	-53.8	152.5	51 13.3	-54.1	153.1	50 19.7	-54.5	153.6	14
15	52 06.3	-53.8	152.6	51 12.8	-54.0	153.2	50 19.2	-54.4	153.7	49 25.2	-54.6	154.3	15
16	51 12.5	-53.9	153.3	50 18.8	-54.3	153.9	49 24.8	-54.6	154.4	48 30.6	-54.9	154.9	16
17	50 18.6	-54.2	154.0	49 24.5	-54.5	154.6	48 30.2	-54.7	155.0	47 35.7	-55.0	155.5	17
18	49 24.4	-54.4	154.7	48 30.0	-54.7	155.2	47 35.5	-55.0	155.7	46 40.7	-55.2	156.1	18
19	48 30.0	-54.7	155.3	47 35.3	-54.9	155.8	46 40.5	-55.1	156.2	45 45.5	-55.4	156.7	19
20	47 35.3	-54.8	156.0	46 40.4	-55.0	156.4	45 45.4	-55.3	156.8	44 50.1	-55.5	157.2	20
21	46 40.5	-55.0	156.6	45 45.4	-55.3	157.0	44 50.1	-55.5	157.4	43 54.6	-55.6	157.7	21
22	45 45.5	-55.2	157.1	44 50.1	-55.4	157.5	43 54.6	-55.6	157.9	42 59.0	-55.8	158.3	22
23	44 50.3	-55.3	157.7	43 54.7	-55.5	158.1	42 59.0	-55.7	158.4	42 03.2	-56.0	158.7	23
24	43 55.0	-55.5	158.2	42 59.2	-55.7	158.6	42 03.3	-55.9	158.9	41 07.2	-56.0	159.2	24
25	42 59.5	-55.6	158.8	42 03.5	-55.8	159.1	41 07.4	-56.0	159.4	40 11.2	-56.1	159.7	25
26	42 03.9	-55.7	159.3	41 07.7	-55.9	159.6	40 11.4	-56.1	159.9	39 15.1	-56.3	160.2	26
27	41 08.2	-55.9	159.8	40 11.8	-56.0	160.1	39 15.3	-56.2	160.3	38 18.8	-56.4	160.6	27
28	40 12.3	-56.0	160.2	39 15.8	-56.2	160.5	38 19.1	-56.3	160.8	37 22.4	-56.4	161.0	28
29	39 16.3	-56.1	160.7	38 19.6	-56.2	161.0	37 22.8	-56.3	161.2	36 26.0	-56.5	161.5	29
30	38 20.2	-56.2	161.2	37 23.4	-56.4	161.4	36 26.5	-56.5	161.7	35 29.5	-56.7	161.9	30
31	37 24.0	-56.3	161.6	36 27.0	-56.4	161.8	35 30.0	-56.6	162.1	34 32.8	-56.7	162.3	31
32	36 27.7	-56.4	162.0	35 30.6	-56.5	162.3	34 33.4	-56.6	162.5	33 36.1	-56.7	162.7	32
33	35 31.3	-56.5	162.5	34 34.1	-56.6	162.7	33 36.8	-56.8	162.9	32 39.4	-56.9	163.1	33
34	34 34.8	-56.5	162.9	33 37.5	-56.7	163.1	32 40.0	-56.8	163.3	31 42.5	-56.9	163.4	34
35	33 38.3	-56.7	163.3	32 40.8	-56.8	163.5	31 43.2	-56.8	163.6	30 45.6	-56.9	163.8	35
36	32 41.6	-56.7	163.7	31 44.0	-56.8	163.9	30 46.4	-56.9	164.0	29 48.7	-57.1	164.2	36
37	31 44.9	-56.7	164.1	30 47.2	-56.9	164.2	29 49.5	-57.0	164.4	28 51.6	-57.0	164.5	37
38	30 48.2	-56.9	164.4	29 50.3	-56.9	164.6	28 52.5	-57.1	164.7	27 54.6	-57.2	164.9	38
39	29 51.3	-56.9	164.8	28 53.4	-57.0	165.0	27 55.4	-57.1	165.1	26 57.4	-57.2	165.2	39
40	28 54.4	-56.9	165.2	27 56.4	-57.1	165.3	26 58.3	-57.1	165.4	26 00.2	-57.2	165.6	40
41	27 57.5	-57.1	165.5	26 59.3	-57.1	165.7	26 01.2	-57.2	165.8	25 03.0	-57.3	165.9	41
42	27 00.4	-57.0	165.9	26 02.2	-57.1	166.0	25 04.0	-57.2	166.1	24 05.7	-57.3	166.2	42
43	26 03.4	-57.1	166.2	25 05.1	-57.2	166.3	24 06.8	-57.3	166.5	23 08.4	-57.3	166.6	43
44	25 06.3	-57.2	166.6	24 07.9	-57.2	166.7	23 09.5	-57.3	166.8	22 11.1	-57.4	166.9	44
45	24 09.1	-57.2	166.9	23 10.7	-57.3	167.0	22 12.2	-57.4	167.1	21 13.7	-57.4	167.2	45
46	23 11.9	-57.2	167.2	22 13.4	-57.3	167.3	21 14.8	-57.3	167.4	20 16.3	-57.5	167.5	46
47	22 14.7	-57.3	167.6	21 16.1	-57.4	167.6	20 17.5	-57.5	167.7	19 18.8	-57.5	167.8	47
48	21 17.4	-57.3	167.9	20 18.7	-57.4	168.0	19 20.0	-57.4	168.0	18 21.3	-57.5	168.1	48
49	20 20.1	-57.4	168.2	19 21.3	-57.4	168.3	18 22.6	-57.5	168.3	17 23.8	-57.5	168.4	49
50	19 22.7	-57.4	168.5	18 23.9	-57.4	168.6	17 25.1	-57.5	168.6	16 26.3	-57.6	168.7	50
51	18 25.3	-57.4	168.8	17 26.5	-57.5	168.9	16 27.6	-57.5	168.9	15 28.7	-57.6	169.0	51
52	17 27.9	-57.4	169.1	16 29.0	-57.5	169.2	15 30.1	-57.6	169.2	14 31.1	-57.6	169.3	52
53	16 30.5	-57.5	169.4	15 31.5	-57.5	169.5	14 32.5	-57.6	169.5	13 33.5	-57.6	169.6	53
54	15 33.0	-57.5	169.7	14 34.0	-57.6	169.8	13 34.9	-57.6	169.8	12 35.9	-57.7	169.9	54
55	14 35.5	-57.5	170.0	13 36.4	-57.5	170.1	12 37.3	-57.6	170.1	11 38.2	-57.6	170.1	55
56	13 38.0	-57.5	170.3	12 38.9	-57.6	170.4	11 39.7	-57.6	170.4	10 40.6	-57.7	170.4	56
57	12 40.5	-57.6	170.6	11 41.3	-57.6	170.6	10 42.1	-57.6	170.7	9 42.9	-57.7	170.7	57
58	11 42.9	-57.5	170.9	10 43.7	-57.6	170.9	9 44.5	-57.7	171.0	8 45.2	-57.7	171.0	58
59	10 45.4	-57.6	171.2	9 46.1	-57.6	171.2	8 46.8	-57.7	171.2	7 47.5	-57.7	171.3	59
60	9 47.8	-57.6	171.5	8 48.5	-57.7	171.5	7 49.1	-57.7	171.5	6 49.8	-57.8	171.5	60
61	8 50.2	-57.6	171.8	7 50.8	-57.6	171.8	6 51.4	-57.7	171.8	5 52.0	-57.7	171.8	61
62	7 52.6	-57.6	172.0	6 53.2	-57.7	172.1	5 53.7	-57.7	172.1	4 54.3	-57.7	172.1	62
63	6 55.0	-57.7	172.3	5 55.5	-57.7	172.3	4 56.0	-57.7	172.3	3 56.6	-57.8	172.4	63
64	5 57.3	-57.6	172.6	4 57.8	-57.6	172.6	3 58.3	-57.7	172.6	2 58.8	-57.7	172.6	64
65	4 59.7	-57.6	172.9	4 00.2	-57.7	172.9	3 00.6	-57.7	172.9	2 01.1	-57.8	172.9	65
66	4 02.1	-57.7	173.2	3 02.5	-57.7	173.2	2 02.9	-57.7	173.2	1 03.3	-57.7	173.2	66
67	3 04.4	-57.7	173.4	2 04.8	-57.7	173.4	1 05.2	-57.7	173.4	0 05.6	-57.8	173.4	67
68	2 06.7	-57.6	173.7	1 07.1	-57.7	173.7	0 07.5	-57.8	173.7	0 52.2	+57.7	6.3	68
69	1 09.1	-57.7	174.0	0 09.4	-57.7	174.0	0 50.3	+57.7	6.0	1 49.9	+57.8	6.0	69
70	0 11.4	-57.6	174.3	0 48.3	+57.7	5.7	1 48.0	+57.7	5.7	2 47.7	+57.7	5.7	70
71	0 46.2	+57.7	5.5	1 46.0	+57.7	5.5	2 45.7	+57.7	5.5	3 45.4	+57.8	5.5	71
72	1 43.9	+57.7	5.2	2 43.7	+57.6	5.2	3 43.4	+57.7	5.2	4 43.2	+57.7	5.2	72
73	2 41.6	+57.6	4.9	3 41.3	+57.7	4.9	4 41.1	+57.7	4.9	5 40.9	+57.7	4.9	73
74	3 39.2	+57.7	4.6	4 39.0	+57.7	4.6	5 38.8	+57.7	4.6	6 38.6	+57.7	4.7	74
75	4 36.9	+57.6	4.4	5 36.7	+57.7	4.4	6 36.5	+57.7	4.4	7 36.3	+57.7	4.4	75
76	5 34.5	+57.6	4.1	6 34.4	+57.6	4.1	7 34.2	+57.7	4.1	8 34.0	+57.7	4.1	76
77	6 32.1	+57.7	3.8	7 32.0	+57.7	3.8	8 31.9	+57.6	3.8	9 31.7	+57.7	3.8	77
78	7 29.8	+57.6	3.5	8 29.7	+57.6	3.5	9 29.5	+57.7	3.5	10 29.4	+57.7	3.5	78
79	8 27.4	+57.6	3.2	9 27.3	+57.6	3.2	10 27.2	+57.6	3.3	11 27.1	+57.6	3.3	79
80	9 25.0	+57.6	2.9	10 24.9	+57.6	3.0	11 24.8	+57.6	3.0	12 24.7	+57.7	3.0	80
81	10 22.6	+57.5	2.7	11 22.5	+57.6	2.7	12 22.4	+57.6	2.7	13 22.4	+57.6	2.7	81
82	11 20.1	+57.6	2.4	12 20.1	+57.6	2.4	13 20.0	+57.6	2.4	14 20.0	+57.6	2.4	82
83	12 17.7	+57.5	2.1	13 17.7	+57.5	2.1	14 17.6	+57.6	2.1	15 17.6	+57.6	2.1	83
84	13 15.2	+57.6	1.8	14 15.2	+57.5	1.8	15 15.2	+57.5	1.8	16 15.2	+57.5	1.8	84
85	14 12.8	+57.5	1.5	15 12.7	+57.5	1.5	16 12.7	+57.5	1.5	17 12.7	+57.5	1.5	85
86	15 10.3	+57.4	1.2	16 10.2	+57.5	1.2	17 10.2	+57.5	1.2	18 10.2	+57.5	1.2	86
87	16 07.7	+57.5	0.9	17 07.7	+57.5	0.9	18 07.7	+57.5	0.9	19 07.7	+57.5	0.9	87
88	17 05.2	+57.4	0.6	18 05.2	+57.4	0.6	19 05.2	+57.4	0.6	20 05.2	+57.4	0.6	88
89	18 02.6	+57.4	0.3	19 02.6	+57.4	0.3	20 02.6	+57.4	0.3	21 02.6	+57.4	0.3	89
90	19 00.0	+57.4	0.0	20 00.0	+57.4	0.0	21 00.0	+57.4	0.0	22 00.0	+57.4	0.0	90
	19°			20°			21°			22°			

S. Lat. {L.H.A. greater than 180° ....Zn=180°–Z
{L.H.A. less than 180°...........Zn=180°+Z

LATITUDE SAME NAME AS DECLINATION   L.H.A. 163°, 197°

18°, 342° L.H.A. LATITUDE SAME NAME AS DECLINATION

N. Lat. {L.H.A. greater than 180° .....Zn=Z
{L.H.A. less than 180°.............Zn=360°-Z

Dec.	15° Hc	15° d	15° Z	16° Hc	16° d	16° Z	17° Hc	17° d	17° Z	18° Hc	18° d	18° Z	Dec.
°	° ′	′	°	° ′	′	°	° ′	′	°	° ′	′	°	°
0	66 43.8	+38.6	128.5	66 05.7	+40.1	130.3	65 26.2	+41.6	132.0	64 45.4	+43.0	133.6	0
1	67 22.4	+37.0	126.6	66 45.8	+38.8	128.5	66 07.8	+40.3	130.2	65 28.4	+41.7	131.9	1
2	67 59.4	+35.5	124.5	67 24.6	+37.3	126.5	66 48.1	+39.0	128.4	66 10.1	+40.6	130.2	2
3	68 34.9	+33.6	122.3	68 01.9	+35.6	124.4	67 27.1	+37.5	126.4	66 50.7	+39.1	128.3	3
4	69 08.5	+31.7	120.0	68 37.5	+33.9	122.2	68 04.6	+35.8	124.3	67 29.8	+37.7	126.3	4
5	69 40.2	+29.7	•117.6	69 11.4	+31.9	•119.9	68 40.4	+34.1	122.2	68 07.5	+36.0	124.3	5
6	70 09.9	+27.4	•115.1	69 43.3	+29.8	•117.5	69 14.5	+32.1	•119.9	68 43.5	+34.3	122.1	6
7	70 37.3	+24.9	•112.4	70 13.1	+27.6	•115.0	69 46.6	+30.1	•117.5	69 17.8	+32.4	•119.8	7
8	71 02.2	+22.4	•109.7	70 40.7	+25.2	•112.3	70 16.7	+27.8	•114.9	69 50.2	+30.3	•117.4	8
9	71 24.6	+19.7	•106.8	71 05.9	+22.6	•109.6	70 44.5	+25.4	•112.3	70 20.5	+28.0	•114.9	9
10	71 44.3	+16.8	•103.8	71 28.5	+19.9	•106.7	71 09.9	+22.8	•109.5	70 48.5	+25.7	•112.2	10
11	72 01.1	+13.8	•100.7	71 48.4	+17.0	•103.7	71 32.7	+20.2	•106.6	71 14.2	+23.1	•109.4	11
12	72 14.9	+10.6	• 97.5	72 05.4	+14.0	•100.6	71 52.9	+17.2	•103.6	71 37.3	+20.3	•106.5	12
13	72 25.5	+7.5	• 94.3	72 19.4	+10.9	• 97.4	72 10.1	+14.2	•100.5	71 57.6	+17.4	•103.5	13
14	72 33.0	+4.1	• 91.0	72 30.3	+7.6	• 94.2	72 24.3	+11.0	• 97.3	72 15.0	+14.4	•100.4	14
15	72 37.1	+0.8	• 87.7	72 37.9	+4.3	• 90.8	72 35.3	+7.8	• 94.0	72 29.4	+11.3	• 97.2	15
16	72 37.9	-2.6	• 84.3	72 42.2	+0.9	• 87.5	72 43.1	+4.5	• 90.7	72 40.7	+7.9	• 93.9	16
17	72 35.3	-5.9	• 81.0	72 43.1	-2.4	• 84.1	72 47.6	+1.0	• 87.3	72 48.6	+4.7	• 90.6	17
18	72 29.4	-9.1	• 77.6	72 40.7	-5.8	• 80.8	72 48.6	-2.3	• 84.0	72 53.3	+1.2	• 87.2	18
19	72 20.3	-12.3	• 74.4	72 34.9	-9.0	• 77.4	72 46.3	-5.6	• 80.6	72 54.5	-2.2	• 83.8	19
20	72 08.0	-15.4	• 71.2	72 25.9	-12.3	• 74.2	72 40.7	-9.0	• 77.2	72 52.3	-5.5	• 80.4	20
21	71 52.6	-18.4	• 68.0	72 13.6	-15.3	• 70.9	72 31.7	-12.2	• 73.9	72 46.8	-8.9	• 77.0	21
22	71 34.2	-21.1	• 65.0	71 58.3	-18.3	• 67.8	72 19.5	-15.3	• 70.7	72 37.9	-12.1	• 73.7	22
23	71 13.1	-23.8	• 62.1	71 40.0	-21.2	• 64.7	72 04.2	-18.2	• 67.5	72 25.8	-15.3	• 70.4	23
24	70 49.3	-26.3	• 59.2	71 18.8	-23.7	• 61.8	71 46.0	-21.1	• 64.5	72 10.5	-18.2	• 67.3	24
25	70 23.0	-28.6	• 56.5	70 55.1	-26.3	• 58.9	71 24.9	-23.8	• 61.5	71 52.3	-21.1	• 64.2	25
26	69 54.4	-30.7	• 53.9	70 28.8	-28.7	• 56.2	71 01.1	-26.3	• 58.6	71 31.2	-23.8	• 61.2	26
27	69 23.7	-32.8	51.5	70 00.1	-30.7	• 53.6	70 34.8	-28.7	• 55.9	71 07.4	-26.4	• 58.3	27
28	68 50.9	-34.6	49.1	69 29.4	-32.8	• 51.1	70 06.1	-30.8	• 53.3	70 41.0	-28.6	• 55.6	28
29	68 16.3	-36.3	46.9	68 56.6	-34.7	48.8	69 35.3	-32.8	• 50.8	70 12.4	-30.9	• 52.9	29
30	67 40.0	-37.9	44.8	68 21.9	-36.4	46.5	69 02.5	-34.8	48.4	69 41.5	-32.9	50.4	30
31	67 02.1	-39.4	42.8	67 45.5	-37.9	44.4	68 27.7	-36.4	46.2	69 08.6	-34.8	48.1	31
32	66 22.7	-40.7	40.8	67 07.6	-39.4	42.4	67 51.3	-38.0	44.0	68 33.8	-36.5	45.8	32
33	65 42.0	-41.9	39.0	66 28.2	-40.8	40.5	67 13.3	-39.5	42.0	67 57.3	-38.1	43.7	33
34	65 00.1	-43.0	37.3	65 47.4	-41.9	38.7	66 33.8	-40.8	40.1	67 19.2	-39.6	41.6	34
35	64 17.1	-44.0	35.7	65 05.5	-43.1	36.9	65 53.0	-42.0	38.3	66 39.6	-40.8	39.7	35
36	63 33.1	-45.0	34.1	64 22.4	-44.1	35.3	65 11.0	-43.2	36.6	65 58.8	-42.2	37.9	36
37	62 48.1	-45.9	32.7	63 38.3	-45.1	33.8	64 27.8	-44.2	34.9	65 16.6	-43.2	36.2	37
38	62 02.2	-46.6	31.3	62 53.2	-45.9	32.3	63 43.6	-45.1	33.4	64 33.4	-44.3	34.5	38
39	61 15.6	-47.4	30.0	62 07.3	-46.7	30.9	62 58.5	-46.0	31.9	63 49.1	-45.2	33.0	39
40	60 28.2	-48.1	28.7	61 20.6	-47.5	29.6	62 12.5	-46.8	30.5	63 03.9	-46.0	31.5	40
41	59 40.1	-48.7	27.5	60 33.1	-48.1	28.3	61 25.7	-47.5	29.2	62 17.9	-46.9	30.1	41
42	58 51.4	-49.3	26.4	59 45.0	-48.8	27.1	60 38.2	-48.2	27.9	61 31.0	-47.6	28.8	42
43	58 02.1	-49.8	25.3	58 56.2	-49.3	26.0	59 50.0	-48.9	26.7	60 43.4	-48.3	27.5	43
44	57 12.3	-50.3	24.2	58 06.9	-49.9	24.9	59 01.1	-49.4	25.6	59 55.1	-48.9	26.3	44
45	56 22.0	-50.8	23.2	57 17.0	-50.4	23.8	58 11.7	-49.9	24.5	59 06.2	-49.5	25.2	45
46	55 31.2	-51.2	22.3	56 26.6	-50.8	22.9	57 21.8	-50.4	23.5	58 16.7	-50.0	24.1	46
47	54 40.0	-51.6	21.4	55 35.8	-51.2	21.9	56 31.4	-50.9	22.5	57 26.7	-50.5	23.1	47
48	53 48.4	-51.9	20.5	54 44.6	-51.7	21.0	55 40.5	-51.3	21.5	56 36.2	-51.0	22.1	48
49	52 56.5	-52.3	19.7	53 52.9	-52.0	20.1	54 49.2	-51.7	20.6	55 45.2	-51.3	21.1	49
50	52 04.2	-52.6	18.9	53 00.9	-52.3	19.3	53 57.5	-52.1	19.7	54 53.9	-51.8	20.2	50
51	51 11.6	-52.9	18.1	52 08.6	-52.7	18.5	53 05.4	-52.4	18.9	54 02.1	-52.1	19.3	51
52	50 18.7	-53.2	17.3	51 15.9	-52.9	17.7	52 13.0	-52.7	18.1	53 10.0	-52.5	18.5	52
53	49 25.5	-53.4	16.6	50 23.0	-53.3	17.0	51 20.3	-53.0	17.3	52 17.5	-52.7	17.7	53
54	48 32.1	-53.7	15.9	49 29.7	-53.4	16.2	50 27.3	-53.3	16.6	51 24.8	-53.1	16.9	54
55	47 38.4	-53.9	15.3	48 36.3	-53.8	15.5	49 34.0	-53.5	15.9	50 31.7	-53.3	16.2	55
56	46 44.5	-54.1	14.6	47 42.5	-53.9	14.9	48 40.5	-53.8	15.2	49 38.4	-53.6	15.5	56
57	45 50.4	-54.3	14.0	46 48.6	-54.2	14.2	47 46.7	-54.0	14.5	48 44.8	-53.9	14.8	57
58	44 56.1	-54.5	13.4	45 54.4	-54.3	13.6	46 52.7	-54.2	13.9	47 50.9	-54.0	14.1	58
59	44 01.6	-54.7	12.8	45 00.1	-54.6	13.0	45 58.5	-54.4	13.2	46 56.9	-54.3	13.5	59
60	43 06.9	-54.8	12.2	44 05.5	-54.7	12.4	45 04.1	-54.6	12.6	46 02.6	-54.4	12.9	60
61	42 12.1	-55.0	11.7	43 10.8	-54.9	11.9	44 09.5	-54.7	12.1	45 08.2	-54.7	12.3	61
62	41 17.1	-55.1	11.1	42 15.9	-55.0	11.3	43 14.8	-55.0	11.5	44 13.5	-54.8	11.7	62
63	40 22.0	-55.3	10.6	41 20.9	-55.2	10.8	42 19.8	-55.0	10.9	43 18.7	-54.9	11.1	63
64	39 26.7	-55.4	10.1	40 25.7	-55.3	10.3	41 24.8	-55.2	10.4	42 23.8	-55.1	10.6	64
65	38 31.3	-55.5	9.6	39 30.4	-55.4	9.7	40 29.6	-55.4	9.9	41 28.7	-55.3	10.0	65
66	37 35.8	-55.7	9.1	38 35.0	-55.6	9.3	39 34.2	-55.5	9.4	40 33.4	-55.4	9.5	66
67	36 40.1	-55.7	8.7	37 39.4	-55.6	8.8	38 38.7	-55.6	8.9	39 38.0	-55.5	9.0	67
68	35 44.4	-55.9	8.2	36 43.8	-55.8	8.3	37 43.1	-55.7	8.4	38 42.5	-55.7	8.5	68
69	34 48.5	-55.9	7.8	35 48.0	-55.9	7.8	36 47.4	-55.8	7.9	37 46.8	-55.7	8.1	69
70	33 52.6	-56.0	7.3	34 52.1	-56.0	7.4	35 51.6	-55.9	7.5	36 51.1	-55.9	7.6	70
71	32 56.6	-56.2	6.9	33 56.1	-56.0	7.0	34 55.7	-56.0	7.0	35 55.2	-55.9	7.1	71
72	32 00.4	-56.2	6.5	33 00.1	-56.2	6.5	33 59.7	-56.1	6.6	34 59.3	-56.1	6.7	72
73	31 04.2	-56.2	6.1	32 03.9	-56.2	6.1	33 03.6	-56.2	6.2	34 03.2	-56.1	6.3	73
74	30 08.0	-56.4	5.7	31 07.7	-56.3	5.7	32 07.4	-56.3	5.8	33 07.1	-56.3	5.8	74
75	29 11.6	-56.4	5.3	30 11.4	-56.4	5.3	31 11.1	-56.3	5.4	32 10.8	-56.3	5.4	75
76	28 15.2	-56.5	4.9	29 15.0	-56.5	4.9	30 14.8	-56.5	5.0	31 14.5	-56.3	5.0	76
77	27 18.7	-56.5	4.5	28 18.5	-56.5	4.5	29 18.3	-56.4	4.6	30 18.2	-56.5	4.6	77
78	26 22.2	-56.6	4.1	27 22.0	-56.5	4.1	28 21.9	-56.6	4.2	29 21.7	-56.5	4.2	78
79	25 25.6	-56.7	3.7	26 25.5	-56.7	3.8	27 25.3	-56.6	3.8	28 25.2	-56.6	3.8	79
80	24 28.9	-56.7	3.4	25 28.8	-56.7	3.4	26 28.7	-56.6	3.4	27 28.6	-56.6	3.5	80
81	23 32.2	-56.7	3.0	24 32.1	-56.7	3.0	25 32.1	-56.8	3.1	26 32.0	-56.7	3.1	81
82	22 35.5	-56.8	2.7	23 35.4	-56.8	2.7	24 35.3	-56.7	2.7	25 35.3	-56.8	2.7	82
83	21 38.7	-56.9	2.3	22 38.6	-56.8	2.3	23 38.6	-56.9	2.4	24 38.5	-56.8	2.4	83
84	20 41.8	-56.9	2.0	21 41.8	-56.9	2.0	22 41.7	-56.8	2.0	23 41.7	-56.8	2.0	84
85	19 44.9	-56.9	1.6	20 44.9	-56.9	1.7	21 44.9	-56.9	1.7	22 44.9	-56.9	1.7	85
86	18 48.0	-56.9	1.3	19 48.0	-56.9	1.3	20 48.0	-57.0	1.3	21 48.0	-57.0	1.3	86
87	17 51.1	-57.0	1.0	18 51.1	-57.0	1.0	19 51.0	-56.9	1.0	20 51.0	-56.9	1.0	87
88	16 54.1	-57.1	0.6	17 54.1	-57.1	0.6	18 54.1	-57.1	0.7	19 54.1	-57.1	0.7	88
89	15 57.0	-57.0	0.3	16 57.0	-57.0	0.3	17 57.0	-57.0	0.3	18 57.0	-57.0	0.3	89
90	15 00.0	-57.1	0.0	16 00.0	-57.1	0.0	17 00.0	-57.1	0.0	18 00.0	-57.1	0.0	90
	15°			16°			17°			18°			

Dec.	19° Hc	19° d	19° Z	20° Hc	20° d	20° Z	21° Hc	21° d	21° Z	22° Hc	22° d	22° Z	Dec.
°	° ′	′	°	° ′	′	°	° ′	′	°	° ′	′	°	°
0	64 03.5	+44.2	135.1	63 20.5	+45.3	136.5	62 36.5	+46.4	137.8	61 51.6	+47.3	139.1	0
1	64 47.7	+43.1	133.5	64 05.8	+44.3	135.0	63 22.9	+45.4	136.4	62 38.9	+46.5	137.7	1
2	65 30.8	+42.0	131.8	64 50.1	+43.3	133.4	64 08.3	+44.5	134.9	63 25.4	+45.7	136.3	2
3	66 12.8	+40.7	130.1	65 33.4	+42.2	131.8	64 52.8	+43.5	133.4	64 11.1	+44.7	134.9	3
4	66 53.5	+39.3	128.2	66 15.6	+40.9	130.0	65 36.3	+42.4	131.7	64 55.8	+43.7	133.3	4
5	67 32.8	+37.9	126.3	66 56.5	+39.6	128.2	66 18.7	+41.1	130.0	65 39.5	+42.5	131.7	5
6	68 10.7	+36.3	124.2	67 36.1	+38.1	126.2	66 59.8	+39.8	128.1	66 22.0	+41.3	129.9	6
7	68 47.0	+34.5	122.1	68 14.2	+36.5	124.2	67 39.6	+38.3	126.2	67 03.3	+40.0	128.1	7
8	69 21.5	+32.6	•119.8	68 50.7	+34.7	122.0	68 17.9	+36.7	124.2	67 43.3	+38.6	126.2	8
9	69 54.1	+30.5	•117.4	69 25.4	+32.8	119.7	68 54.6	+35.0	122.0	68 21.9	+36.9	124.1	9
10	70 24.6	+28.3	•114.8	69 58.2	+30.8	•117.3	69 29.6	+33.0	•119.7	68 58.8	+35.2	122.0	10
11	70 52.9	+25.9	•112.2	70 29.0	+28.5	•114.8	70 02.6	+31.0	•117.3	69 34.0	+33.3	119.7	11
12	71 18.8	+23.3	•109.4	70 57.5	+26.1	•112.1	70 33.6	+28.8	•114.7	70 07.3	+31.3	•117.3	12
13	71 42.1	+20.5	•106.5	71 23.6	+23.6	•109.3	71 02.4	+26.4	•112.1	70 38.6	+29.0	•114.7	13
14	72 02.6	+17.7	•103.4	71 47.2	+20.8	•106.4	71 28.8	+23.8	•109.3	71 07.6	+26.6	•112.0	14
15	72 20.3	+14.6	•100.3	72 08.0	+17.9	•103.4	71 52.6	+21.0	•106.4	71 34.2	+24.1	•109.2	15
16	72 34.9	+11.4	• 97.1	72 25.9	+14.8	•100.2	72 13.6	+18.1	•103.3	71 58.3	+21.2	•106.3	16
17	72 46.3	+8.2	• 93.8	72 40.7	+11.6	• 97.0	72 31.7	+15.1	•100.2	72 19.5	+18.4	•103.3	17
18	72 54.5	+4.8	• 90.4	72 52.3	+8.4	• 93.7	72 46.8	+11.8	• 96.9	72 37.9	+15.3	•100.1	18
19	72 59.3	+1.4	• 87.0	73 00.7	+4.9	• 90.3	72 58.6	+8.5	• 93.6	72 53.2	+12.0	• 96.8	19
20	73 00.7	-2.1	• 83.6	73 05.6	+1.5	• 86.9	73 07.1	+5.2	• 90.2	73 05.2	+8.7	• 93.5	20
21	72 58.6	-5.4	• 80.2	73 07.1	-1.9	• 83.5	73 12.3	+1.6	• 86.8	73 13.9	+5.3	• 90.1	21
22	72 53.2	-8.8	• 76.8	73 05.2	-5.3	• 80.0	73 13.9	-1.8	• 83.3	73 19.2	+1.8	• 86.6	22
23	72 44.4	-12.1	• 73.5	72 59.9	-8.8	• 76.6	73 12.1	-5.2	• 79.8	73 21.0	-1.7	• 83.1	23
24	72 32.3	-15.2	• 70.2	72 51.1	-12.0	• 73.2	73 06.9	-8.7	• 76.4	73 19.3	-5.1	• 79.6	24
25	72 17.1	-18.3	• 67.0	72 39.1	-15.2	• 69.9	72 58.2	-12.0	• 73.0	73 14.2	-8.6	• 76.2	25
26	71 58.8	-21.1	• 63.9	72 23.9	-18.2	• 66.7	72 46.2	-15.1	• 69.7	73 05.6	-12.0	• 72.8	26
27	71 37.7	-23.8	• 60.9	72 05.7	-21.1	• 63.6	72 31.1	-18.3	• 66.4	72 53.6	-15.1	• 69.4	27
28	71 13.9	-26.4	• 58.0	71 44.6	-23.9	• 60.6	72 12.8	-21.1	• 63.3	72 38.5	-18.3	• 66.1	28
29	70 47.5	-28.7	• 55.2	71 20.7	-26.4	• 57.7	71 51.7	-23.9	• 60.2	72 20.2	-21.2	• 63.0	29
30	70 18.8	-30.9	• 52.6	70 54.3	-28.8	• 54.9	71 27.8	-26.5	• 57.3	71 59.0	-23.9	• 59.9	30
31	69 47.9	-33.0	• 50.1	70 25.5	-31.0	• 52.2	71 01.3	-28.9	• 54.5	71 35.1	-26.6	• 57.0	31
32	69 14.9	-34.9	47.7	69 54.5	-33.1	49.7	70 32.4	-31.1	• 51.9	71 08.5	-28.9	• 54.2	32
33	68 40.0	-36.5	45.4	69 21.4	-34.9	47.3	70 01.3	-33.1	49.3	70 39.6	-31.2	• 51.5	33
34	68 03.5	-38.2	43.3	68 46.5	-36.7	45.0	69 28.2	-35.0	46.9	70 08.4	-33.2	• 48.9	34
35	67 25.3	-39.6	41.2	68 09.8	-38.2	42.9	68 53.2	-36.8	44.6	69 35.2	-35.2	46.5	35
36	66 45.7	-41.0	39.3	67 31.6	-39.8	40.8	68 16.4	-38.4	42.5	69 00.0	-36.9	44.2	36
37	66 04.7	-42.2	37.5	66 51.8	-41.0	38.9	67 38.0	-39.8	40.4	68 23.1	-38.4	42.1	37
38	65 22.5	-43.3	35.8	66 10.8	-42.3	37.1	66 58.2	-41.2	38.5	67 44.7	-40.0	40.0	38
39	64 39.2	-44.4	34.1	65 28.5	-43.5	35.3	66 17.0	-42.4	36.7	67 04.7	-41.3	38.1	39
40	63 54.8	-45.3	32.6	64 45.0	-44.4	33.7	65 34.6	-43.5	34.9	66 23.4	-42.5	36.2	40
41	63 09.5	-46.2	31.1	64 00.6	-45.4	32.2	64 51.1	-44.6	33.3	65 40.9	-43.7	34.5	41
42	62 23.3	-46.9	29.7	63 15.2	-46.3	30.7	64 06.5	-45.5	31.7	64 57.2	-44.6	32.9	42
43	61 36.4	-47.7	28.4	62 28.9	-47.0	29.3	63 21.0	-46.3	30.3	64 12.6	-45.6	31.3	43
44	60 48.7	-48.4	27.1	61 41.9	-47.8	28.0	62 34.7	-47.2	28.9	63 27.0	-46.5	29.8	44
45	60 00.3	-49.0	25.9	60 54.1	-48.5	26.7	61 47.5	-47.9	27.5	62 40.5	-47.3	28.4	45
46	59 11.3	-49.5	24.8	60 05.6	-49.0	25.5	60 59.6	-48.5	26.3	61 53.2	-48.0	27.1	46
47	58 21.8	-50.1	23.7	59 16.6	-49.7	24.4	60 11.1	-49.2	25.1	61 05.2	-48.6	25.8	47
48	57 31.7	-50.6	22.7	58 26.9	-50.1	23.3	59 21.9	-49.7	23.9	60 16.6	-49.3	24.6	48
49	56 41.1	-51.0	21.7	57 36.8	-50.7	22.2	58 32.2	-50.3	22.9	59 27.3	-49.8	23.5	49
50	55 50.1	-51.5	20.7	56 46.1	-51.1	21.3	57 41.9	-50.7	21.8	58 37.5	-50.4	22.4	50
51	54 58.6	-51.8	19.8	55 55.0	-51.5	20.3	56 51.2	-51.2	20.8	57 47.1	-50.8	21.4	51
52	54 06.8	-52.2	18.9	55 03.5	-51.9	19.4	56 00.0	-51.6	19.9	56 56.3	-51.3	20.4	52
53	53 14.6	-52.5	18.1	54 11.6	-52.3	18.5	55 08.4	-52.0	19.0	56 05.0	-51.6	19.5	53
54	52 22.1	-52.8	17.3	53 19.3	-52.6	17.7	54 16.4	-52.3	18.1	55 13.4	-52.1	18.6	54
55	51 29.3	-53.2	16.5	52 26.7	-52.9	16.9	53 24.1	-52.7	17.3	54 21.3	-52.4	17.7	55
56	50 36.1	-53.4	15.8	51 33.8	-53.2	16.1	52 31.4	-53.0	16.5	53 28.9	-52.8	16.9	56
57	49 42.7	-53.6	15.1	50 40.6	-53.4	15.4	51 38.4	-53.2	15.7	52 36.1	-53.0	16.1	57
58	48 49.1	-53.9	14.4	49 47.2	-53.7	14.7	50 45.2	-53.6	15.0	51 43.1	-53.4	15.3	58
59	47 55.2	-54.1	13.7	48 53.5	-54.0	14.0	49 51.6	-53.7	14.3	50 49.7	-53.6	14.6	59
60	47 01.1	-54.3	13.1	47 59.5	-54.2	13.3	48 57.9	-54.1	13.6	49 56.1	-53.8	13.9	60
61	46 06.8	-54.5	12.5	47 05.3	-54.3	12.7	48 03.8	-54.2	13.0	49 02.3	-54.1	13.2	61
62	45 12.3	-54.7	11.9	46 11.0	-54.6	12.1	47 09.6	-54.4	12.3	48 08.2	-54.3	12.6	62
63	44 17.6	-54.9	11.3	45 16.4	-54.7	11.5	46 15.2	-54.6	11.7	47 13.9	-54.5	11.9	63
64	43 22.7	-55.0	10.7	44 21.7	-54.9	10.9	45 20.6	-54.8	11.1	46 19.4	-54.7	11.3	64
65	42 27.7	-55.1	10.2	43 26.8	-55.1	10.4	44 25.8	-55.0	10.5	45 24.7	-54.8	10.7	65
66	41 32.6	-55.4	9.7	42 31.7	-55.2	9.8	43 30.8	-55.1	10.0	44 29.9	-55.1	10.1	66
67	40 37.2	-55.4	9.2	41 36.5	-55.4	9.3	42 35.7	-55.3	9.4	43 34.8	-55.1	9.6	67
68	39 41.8	-55.6	8.7	40 41.1	-55.5	8.8	41 40.4	-55.4	8.9	42 39.7	-55.4	9.1	68
69	38 46.2	-55.7	8.2	39 45.6	-55.6	8.3	40 45.0	-55.6	8.4	41 44.3	-55.4	8.5	69
70	37 50.5	-55.7	7.7	38 50.0	-55.7	7.8	39 49.4	-55.6	7.9	40 48.9	-55.6	8.0	70
71	36 54.8	-55.9	7.2	37 54.3	-55.9	7.3	38 53.8	-55.8	7.4	39 53.3	-55.8	7.5	71
72	35 58.9	-56.1	6.8	36 58.4	-55.9	6.9	37 58.0	-55.9	7.0	38 57.5	-55.8	7.1	72
73	35 02.8	-56.0	6.3	36 02.5	-56.1	6.4	37 02.1	-56.0	6.5	38 01.7	-55.9	6.6	73
74	34 06.8	-56.2	5.9	35 06.4	-56.1	6.0	36 06.1	-56.1	6.1	37 05.8	-56.1	6.1	74
75	33 10.6	-56.3	5.5	34 10.3	-56.2	5.5	35 10.0	-56.2	5.6	36 09.7	-56.1	5.7	75
76	32 14.3	-56.3	5.1	33 14.1	-56.3	5.1	34 13.8	-56.2	5.2	35 13.6	-56.3	5.3	76
77	31 18.0	-56.5	4.7	32 17.8	-56.4	4.7	33 17.6	-56.4	4.8	34 17.3	-56.3	4.8	77
78	30 21.5	-56.4	4.3	31 21.4	-56.5	4.3	32 21.2	-56.4	4.4	33 21.0	-56.4	4.4	78
79	29 25.1	-56.6	3.9	30 24.9	-56.5	3.9	31 24.8	-56.5	4.0	32 24.6	-56.5	4.0	79
80	28 28.5	-56.6	3.5	29 28.4	-56.6	3.5	30 28.3	-56.6	3.6	31 28.1	-56.5	3.6	80
81	27 31.9	-56.7	3.1	28 31.8	-56.7	3.2	29 31.7	-56.6	3.2	30 31.6	-56.6	3.2	81
82	26 35.2	-56.7	2.8	27 35.1	-56.7	2.8	28 35.1	-56.7	2.8	29 35.0	-56.7	2.8	82
83	25 38.5	-56.8	2.4	26 38.4	-56.8	2.4	27 38.4	-56.8	2.4	28 38.3	-56.7	2.5	83
84	24 41.7	-56.9	2.0	25 41.6	-56.8	2.1	26 41.6	-56.8	2.1	27 41.6	-56.8	2.1	84
85	23 44.8	-56.8	1.7	24 44.8	-56.9	1.7	25 44.8	-56.9	1.7	26 44.8	-56.9	1.7	85
86	22 48.0	-57.0	1.3	23 47.9	-56.9	1.3	24 47.9	-56.9	1.4	25 47.9	-56.9	1.4	86
87	21 51.0	-56.9	1.0	22 51.0	-56.9	1.0	23 51.0	-57.0	1.0	24 51.0	-57.0	1.0	87
88	20 54.1	-57.1	0.7	21 54.1	-57.1	0.7	22 54.0	-57.0	0.7	23 54.0	-57.0	0.7	88
89	19 57.0	-57.0	0.3	20 57.0	-57.0	0.3	21 57.0	-57.0	0.3	22 57.0	-57.0	0.3	89
90	19 00.0	-57.1	0.0	20 00.0	-57.1	0.0	21 00.0	-57.1	0.0	22 00.0	-57.1	0.0	90
	19°			20°			21°			22°			

18°, 342° L.H.A. LATITUDE SAME NAME AS DECLINATION

38

LATITUDE CONTRARY NAME TO DECLINATION L.H.A. 18°, 342°

Dec.	15°			16°			17°			18°			19°			20°			21°			22°			Dec.
°	Hc ° ′	d ′	Z °	Hc ° ′	d ′	Z °	Hc ° ′	d ′	Z °	Hc ° ′	d ′	Z °	Hc ° ′	d ′	Z °	Hc ° ′	d ′	Z °	Hc ° ′	d ′	Z °	Hc ° ′	d ′	Z °	°
0	66 43.8	−40.0	128.5	66 05.7	−41.5	130.3	65 26.2	−42.8	132.0	64 45.4	−44.0	133.6	64 03.5	−45.1	135.1	63 20.5	−46.1	136.5	62 36.5	−47.1	137.8	61 51.6	−48.0	139.1	0
1	66 03.8	−41.3	130.4	65 24.2	−42.6	132.1	64 43.4	−43.8	133.6	64 01.4	−44.9	135.1	63 18.4	−46.0	136.5	62 34.4	−47.0	137.9	61 49.4	−47.8	139.1	61 03.6	−48.6	140.3	1
2	65 22.5	−42.4	132.2	64 41.6	−43.6	133.7	63 59.6	−44.8	135.2	63 16.5	−45.9	136.6	62 32.4	−46.8	138.0	61 47.4	−47.7	139.2	61 01.6	−48.6	140.4	60 15.0	−49.3	141.5	2
3	64 40.1	−43.5	133.8	63 58.0	−44.7	135.3	63 14.8	−45.7	136.7	62 30.6	−46.6	138.0	61 45.6	−47.6	139.3	60 59.7	−48.4	140.5	60 13.0	−49.1	141.6	59 25.7	−49.9	142.6	3
4	63 56.6	−44.5	135.4	63 13.3	−45.5	136.8	62 29.1	−46.5	138.1	61 44.0	−47.4	139.4	60 58.0	−48.2	140.6	60 11.3	−49.0	141.7	59 23.9	−49.7	142.7	58 35.8	−50.3	143.7	4
5	63 12.1	−45.4	136.9	62 27.8	−46.4	138.3	61 42.6	−47.3	139.5	60 56.6	−48.1	140.7	60 09.8	−48.9	141.8	59 22.3	−49.6	142.8	58 34.2	−50.3	143.8	57 45.5	−50.9	144.8	5
6	62 26.7	−46.3	138.4	61 41.4	−47.1	139.6	60 55.3	−48.0	140.8	60 08.5	−48.8	141.9	59 20.9	−49.4	142.9	58 32.7	−50.1	143.9	57 43.9	−50.7	144.9	56 54.6	−51.3	145.7	6
7	61 40.4	−47.0	139.7	60 54.3	−47.9	140.9	60 07.3	−48.6	142.0	59 19.7	−49.3	143.0	58 31.5	−50.0	144.0	57 42.6	−50.6	145.0	56 53.2	−51.1	145.8	56 03.3	−51.7	146.7	7
8	60 53.4	−47.7	141.0	60 06.4	−48.5	142.1	59 18.7	−49.2	143.2	58 30.4	−49.9	144.1	57 41.5	−50.5	145.1	56 52.0	−51.0	146.0	56 02.1	−51.6	146.8	55 11.6	−52.1	147.6	8
9	60 05.7	−48.4	142.3	59 17.9	−49.1	143.3	58 29.5	−49.7	144.3	57 40.5	−50.3	145.2	56 51.0	−50.9	146.1	56 01.0	−51.5	146.9	55 10.5	−52.0	147.7	54 19.5	−52.4	148.4	9
10	59 17.3	−49.0	143.4	58 28.8	−49.6	144.4	57 39.8	−50.3	145.3	56 50.2	−50.9	146.2	56 00.1	−51.4	147.0	55 09.5	−51.9	147.8	54 18.5	−52.3	148.6	53 27.1	−52.7	149.3	10
11	58 28.3	−49.5	144.5	57 39.2	−50.2	145.5	56 49.5	−50.7	146.3	55 59.3	−51.2	147.2	55 08.7	−51.8	147.9	54 17.6	−52.2	148.7	53 26.2	−52.7	149.4	52 34.4	−53.1	150.1	11
12	57 38.8	−50.1	145.6	56 49.0	−50.6	146.5	55 58.8	−51.2	147.3	55 08.1	−51.7	148.1	54 16.9	−52.1	148.8	53 25.4	−52.6	149.5	52 33.5	−52.9	150.2	51 41.3	−53.3	150.8	12
13	56 48.7	−50.5	146.6	55 58.4	−51.1	147.4	55 07.6	−51.5	148.2	54 16.4	−52.0	149.0	53 24.8	−52.5	149.7	52 32.8	−52.8	150.3	51 40.6	−53.3	151.0	50 48.0	−53.7	151.6	13
14	55 58.2	−50.9	147.6	55 07.3	−51.4	148.4	54 16.1	−52.0	149.1	53 24.4	−52.4	149.8	52 32.3	−52.7	150.5	51 40.0	−53.2	151.1	50 47.3	−53.5	151.7	49 54.3	−53.8	152.3	14
15	55 07.3	−51.4	148.5	54 15.9	−51.9	149.3	53 24.1	−52.3	150.0	52 32.0	−52.7	150.6	51 39.6	−53.1	151.2	50 46.8	−53.4	151.8	49 53.8	−53.8	152.4	49 00.5	−54.1	152.9	15
16	54 15.9	−51.8	149.4	53 24.0	−52.2	150.1	52 31.8	−52.6	150.8	51 39.3	−53.0	151.4	50 46.5	−53.3	152.0	49 53.4	−53.7	152.5	49 00.0	−54.0	153.1	48 06.4	−54.3	153.6	16
17	53 24.1	−52.1	150.3	52 31.8	−52.5	150.9	51 39.2	−52.9	151.6	50 46.3	−53.2	152.1	49 53.2	−53.7	152.7	48 59.7	−53.9	153.2	48 06.0	−54.2	153.7	47 12.1	−54.5	154.2	17
18	52 32.0	−52.4	151.1	51 39.3	−52.8	151.7	50 46.3	−53.1	152.3	49 53.1	−53.6	152.9	48 59.5	−53.8	153.4	48 05.8	−54.2	153.9	47 11.8	−54.4	154.4	46 17.6	−54.7	154.8	18
19	51 39.6	−52.8	151.9	50 46.5	−53.1	152.5	49 53.2	−53.5	153.0	48 59.5	−53.7	153.6	48 05.7	−54.1	154.1	47 11.6	−54.3	154.5	46 17.4	−54.6	155.0	45 22.9	−54.9	155.4	19
20	50 46.8	−53.0	152.7	49 53.4	−53.4	153.2	48 59.7	−53.7	153.7	48 05.8	−54.0	154.2	47 11.6	−54.2	154.7	46 17.3	−54.5	155.2	45 22.8	−54.8	155.6	44 28.0	−55.0	156.0	20
21	49 53.8	−53.3	153.4	49 00.0	−53.6	153.9	48 06.0	−53.9	154.4	47 11.8	−54.2	154.9	46 17.4	−54.5	155.3	45 22.8	−54.8	155.8	44 28.0	−55.0	156.2	43 33.0	−55.2	156.5	21
22	49 00.5	−53.6	154.1	48 06.4	−53.9	154.6	47 12.1	−54.1	155.1	46 17.6	−54.4	155.5	45 22.9	−54.6	155.9	44 28.0	−54.9	156.3	43 33.0	−55.1	156.7	42 37.8	−55.3	157.1	22
23	48 06.9	−53.7	154.8	47 12.5	−54.0	155.2	46 18.0	−54.4	155.7	45 23.2	−54.6	156.1	44 28.3	−54.9	156.5	43 33.1	−55.0	156.9	42 37.9	−55.3	157.3	41 42.5	−55.5	157.6	23
24	47 13.2	−54.1	155.4	46 18.5	−54.3	155.9	45 23.6	−54.5	156.3	44 28.6	−54.7	156.7	43 33.4	−55.0	157.1	42 38.1	−55.2	157.4	41 42.6	−55.4	157.8	40 47.0	−55.6	158.1	24
25	46 19.1	−54.2	156.1	45 24.2	−54.4	156.5	44 29.1	−54.7	156.9	43 33.9	−55.0	157.3	42 38.4	−55.1	157.6	41 42.9	−55.4	158.0	40 47.2	−55.5	158.3	39 51.4	−55.7	158.6	25
26	45 24.9	−54.4	156.7	44 29.8	−54.7	157.1	43 34.4	−54.8	157.5	42 38.9	−55.0	157.8	41 43.3	−55.3	158.2	40 47.5	−55.4	158.5	39 51.7	−55.7	158.8	38 55.7	−55.9	159.1	26
27	44 30.5	−54.5	157.3	43 35.1	−54.8	157.7	42 39.6	−55.1	158.0	41 43.9	−55.3	158.3	40 48.0	−55.4	158.7	39 52.1	−55.6	159.0	38 56.0	−55.8	159.3	37 59.8	−55.9	159.5	27
28	43 36.0	−54.8	157.9	42 40.3	−54.9	158.2	41 44.5	−55.1	158.6	40 48.6	−55.3	158.9	39 52.6	−55.5	159.2	38 56.5	−55.7	159.5	38 00.2	−55.9	159.7	37 03.9	−56.1	160.0	28
29	42 41.2	−54.9	158.4	41 45.4	−55.2	158.8	40 49.4	−55.3	159.1	39 53.3	−55.5	159.4	38 57.1	−55.7	159.7	38 00.8	−55.9	159.9	37 04.3	−55.9	160.2	36 07.8	−56.1	160.4	29
30	41 46.3	−55.1	159.0	40 50.2	−55.2	159.3	39 54.1	−55.5	159.6	38 57.8	−55.6	159.9	38 01.4	−55.8	160.1	37 04.9	−55.9	160.4	36 08.4	−56.1	160.6	35 11.7	−56.2	160.9	30
31	40 51.2	−55.2	159.5	39 55.0	−55.4	159.8	38 58.6	−55.5	160.1	38 02.2	−55.7	160.3	37 05.6	−55.9	160.6	36 09.0	−56.0	160.9	35 12.3	−56.2	161.1	34 15.5	−56.4	161.3	31
32	39 56.0	−55.3	160.0	38 59.6	−55.5	160.3	38 03.1	−55.7	160.6	37 06.5	−55.9	160.8	36 09.7	−55.9	161.1	35 13.0	−56.2	161.3	34 16.1	−56.3	161.5	33 19.1	−56.4	161.7	32
33	39 00.7	−55.4	160.5	38 04.1	−55.6	160.8	37 07.4	−55.8	161.0	36 10.6	−55.9	161.3	35 13.8	−56.1	161.5	34 16.8	−56.2	161.7	33 19.8	−56.3	161.9	32 22.7	−56.4	162.1	33
34	38 05.3	−55.6	161.0	37 08.5	−55.8	161.3	36 11.6	−55.9	161.5	35 14.7	−56.0	161.7	34 17.7	−56.2	161.9	33 20.6	−56.3	162.1	32 23.5	−56.5	162.3	31 26.3	−56.6	162.5	34
35	37 09.7	−55.7	161.5	36 12.7	−55.8	161.7	35 15.7	−55.9	161.9	34 18.7	−56.2	162.2	33 21.5	−56.2	162.4	32 24.3	−56.4	162.6	31 27.0	−56.5	162.7	30 29.7	−56.6	162.9	35
36	36 14.0	−55.8	161.9	35 16.9	−55.9	162.2	34 19.8	−56.1	162.4	33 22.5	−56.2	162.6	32 25.3	−56.4	162.8	31 27.9	−56.4	163.0	30 30.5	−56.5	163.1	29 33.1	−56.7	163.3	36
37	35 18.2	−55.9	162.4	34 21.0	−56.1	162.6	33 23.7	−56.2	162.8	32 26.3	−56.2	163.0	31 28.9	−56.4	163.2	30 31.5	−56.5	163.5	29 34.0	−56.7	163.5	28 36.4	−56.7	163.7	37
38	34 22.3	−56.0	162.8	33 24.9	−56.1	163.0	32 27.5	−56.2	163.2	31 30.1	−56.4	163.4	30 32.5	−56.4	163.6	29 35.0	−56.6	163.7	28 37.3	−56.7	163.9	27 39.7	−56.8	164.0	38
39	33 26.3	−56.0	163.3	32 28.8	−56.2	163.5	31 31.3	−56.3	163.6	30 33.7	−56.4	163.8	29 36.1	−56.6	164.0	28 38.4	−56.7	164.1	27 40.6	−56.7	164.3	26 42.9	−56.9	164.4	39
40	32 30.3	−56.2	163.7	31 32.6	−56.2	163.9	30 35.0	−56.4	164.0	29 37.3	−56.5	164.2	28 39.5	−56.6	164.3	27 41.7	−56.7	164.5	26 43.9	−56.8	164.6	25 46.0	−56.9	164.8	40
41	31 34.1	−56.2	164.1	30 36.4	−56.4	164.3	29 38.6	−56.5	164.4	28 40.8	−56.6	164.6	27 42.9	−56.7	164.7	26 45.0	−56.8	164.9	25 47.1	−56.9	165.0	24 49.1	−57.0	165.1	41
42	30 37.9	−56.4	164.5	29 40.0	−56.4	164.7	28 42.1	−56.5	164.8	27 44.2	−56.6	165.0	26 46.2	−56.7	165.1	25 48.2	−56.8	165.2	24 50.2	−56.9	165.3	23 52.1	−57.0	165.5	42
43	29 41.5	−56.3	164.9	28 43.6	−56.5	165.1	27 45.6	−56.6	165.2	26 47.6	−56.7	165.3	25 49.5	−56.8	165.5	24 51.4	−56.9	165.6	23 53.3	−57.0	165.7	22 55.1	−57.0	165.8	43
44	28 45.2	−56.5	165.3	27 47.1	−56.5	165.4	26 49.0	−56.6	165.6	25 50.9	−56.7	165.7	24 52.7	−56.8	165.8	23 54.5	−56.9	165.9	22 56.3	−57.0	166.0	21 58.1	−57.1	166.1	44
45	27 48.7	−56.5	165.7	26 50.6	−56.6	165.8	25 52.4	−56.7	165.9	24 54.2	−56.8	166.1	23 55.9	−56.9	166.2	22 57.6	−56.9	166.3	21 59.3	−57.0	166.4	21 01.0	−57.1	166.5	45
46	26 52.2	−56.6	166.1	25 54.0	−56.7	166.2	24 55.7	−56.8	166.3	23 57.4	−56.9	166.4	22 59.0	−56.9	166.5	22 00.7	−57.0	166.6	21 02.3	−57.1	166.7	20 03.9	−57.2	166.8	46
47	25 55.6	−56.6	166.4	24 57.3	−56.7	166.6	23 58.9	−56.8	166.7	23 00.5	−56.9	166.8	22 02.1	−57.0	166.9	21 03.7	−57.1	166.9	20 05.2	−57.1	167.0	19 06.7	−57.2	167.1	47
48	24 59.0	−56.7	166.8	24 00.6	−56.8	166.9	23 02.1	−56.8	167.0	22 03.6	−56.9	167.1	21 05.1	−57.0	167.2	20 06.6	−57.0	167.3	19 08.1	−57.2	167.4	18 09.5	−57.2	167.4	48
49	24 02.3	−56.7	167.2	23 03.8	−56.8	167.3	22 05.3	−56.9	167.4	21 06.7	−56.9	167.4	20 08.1	−57.0	167.5	19 09.6	−57.2	167.6	18 10.9	−57.1	167.7	17 12.3	−57.2	167.7	49
50	23 05.6	−56.8	167.5	22 07.0	−56.8	167.6	21 08.4	−56.9	167.7	20 09.8	−57.0	167.8	19 11.1	−57.1	167.9	18 12.4	−57.1	167.9	17 13.8	−57.3	168.0	16 15.1	−57.3	168.1	50
51	22 08.8	−56.8	167.9	21 10.2	−56.9	168.0	20 11.5	−57.0	168.0	19 12.8	−57.1	168.1	18 14.0	−57.1	168.2	17 15.3	−57.2	168.3	16 16.5	−57.2	168.3	15 17.8	−57.3	168.4	51
52	21 12.0	−56.9	168.2	20 13.3	−57.0	168.3	19 14.5	−57.0	168.4	18 15.7	−57.1	168.4	17 16.9	−57.1	168.5	16 18.1	−57.2	168.6	15 19.3	−57.3	168.6	14 20.5	−57.3	168.7	52
53	20 15.1	−56.9	168.6	19 16.3	−56.9	168.6	18 17.5	−57.0	168.7	17 18.6	−57.1	168.8	16 19.8	−57.2	168.8	15 20.9	−57.2	168.9	14 22.0	−57.2	168.9	13 23.2	−57.4	169.0	53
54	19 18.2	−56.9	168.9	18 19.4	−57.0	169.0	17 20.5	−57.1	169.0	16 21.5	−57.1	169.1	15 22.6	−57.2	169.1	14 23.7	−57.3	169.2	13 24.8	−57.4	169.2	12 25.8	−57.4	169.3	54
55	18 21.3	−57.0	169.2	17 22.4	−57.1	169.3	16 23.4	−57.1	169.4	15 24.4	−57.1	169.4	14 25.4	−57.2	169.5	13 26.4	−57.2	169.5	12 27.4	−57.3	169.5	11 28.4	−57.4	169.6	55
56	17 24.3	−57.0	169.6	16 25.3	−57.1	169.6	15 26.3	−57.1	169.7	14 27.3	−57.2	169.7	13 28.2	−57.2	169.8	12 29.2	−57.3	169.8	11 30.1	−57.3	169.8	10 31.0	−57.4	169.9	56
57	16 27.3	−57.0	169.9	15 28.2	−57.0	169.9	14 29.2	−57.2	170.0	13 30.1	−57.2	170.0	12 31.0	−57.3	170.1	11 31.9	−57.3	170.1	10 32.8	−57.4	170.1	9 33.6	−57.4	170.2	57
58	15 30.3	−57.1	170.2	14 31.2	−57.2	170.3	13 32.0	−57.2	170.3	12 32.9	−57.3	170.3	11 33.7	−57.3	170.4	10 34.6	−57.4	170.4	9 35.4	−57.4	170.4	8 36.2	−57.4	170.5	58
59	14 33.2	−57.1	170.5	13 34.0	−57.1	170.6	12 34.8	−57.1	170.6	11 35.6	−57.2	170.6	10 36.4	−57.3	170.7	9 37.2	−57.3	170.7	8 38.0	−57.4	170.7	7 38.8	−57.4	170.8	59
60	13 36.1	−57.1	170.9	12 36.9	−57.2	170.9	11 37.7	−57.3	170.9	10 38.4	−57.3	171.0	9 39.1	−57.3	171.0	8 39.9	−57.4	171.0	7 40.6	−57.4	171.0	6 41.4	−57.5	171.1	60
61	12 39.0	−57.1	171.2	11 39.7	−57.1	171.2	10 40.4	−57.2	171.2	9 41.1	−57.2	171.3	8 41.8	−57.3	171.3	7 42.5	−57.3	171.3	6 43.2	−57.4	171.3	5 43.9	−57.5	171.3	61
62	11 41.9	−57.2	171.5	10 42.6	−57.2	171.5	9 43.2	−57.2	171.5	8 43.9	−57.3	171.6	7 44.5	−57.3	171.6	6 45.2	−57.4	171.6	5 45.8	−57.4	171.6	4 46.4	−57.4	171.6	62
63	10 44.7	−57.1	171.8	9 45.4	−57.3	171.8	8 46.0	−57.3	171.8	7 46.6	−57.3	171.9	6 47.2	−57.4	171.9	5 47.8	−57.4	171.9	4 48.4	−57.5	171.9	3 49.0	−57.5	171.9	63
64	9 47.6	−57.2	172.1	8 48.1	−57.2	172.1	7 48.7	−57.3	172.1	6 49.3	−57.4	172.2	5 49.8	−57.3	172.2	4 50.4	−57.4	172.2	3 50.9	−57.4	172.2	2 51.5	−57.5	172.2	64
65	8 50.4	−57.2	172.4	7 50.9	−57.2	172.4	6 51.4	−57.3	172.4	5 51.9	−57.3	172.5	4 52.5	−57.4	172.5	3 53.0	−57.4	172.5	2 53.5	−57.5	172.5	1 54.0	−57.5	172.5	65
66	7 53.2	−57.2	172.7	6 53.7	−57.3	172.7	5 54.1	−57.3	172.7	4 54.6	−57.3	172.8	3 55.1	−57.4	172.8	2 55.6	−57.4	172.8	1 56.0	−57.4	172.8	0 56.5	−57.5	172.8	66
67	6 56.0	−57.3	173.0	5 56.4	−57.3	173.0	4 56.8	−57.3	173.0	3 57.3	−57.4	173.0	2 57.7	−57.4	173.1	1 58.2	−57.4	173.1	0 58.6	−57.4	173.1	0 01.0	+57.4	6.9	67
68	5 58.7	−57.2	173.3	4 59.1	−57.2	173.3	3 59.5	−57.3	173.3	2 59.9	−57.3	173.3	2 00.3	−57.3	173.3	1 00.8	−57.5	173.4	0 01.2	−57.5	173.4	0 58.4	+57.5	6.6	68
69	5 01.5	−57.3	173.6	4 01.9	−57.3	173.6	3 02.2	−57.3	173.6	2 02.6	−57.4	173.6	1 03.0	−57.4	173.6	0 03.3	−57.4	173.6	0 56.3	+57.4	6.4	1 55.9	+57.5	6.4	69
70	4 04.2	−57.2	173.9	3 04.6	−57.3	173.9	2 04.9	−57.3	173.9	1 05.2	−57.3	173.9	0 05.6	−57.4	173.9	0 54.1	+57.4	6.1	1 53.7	+57.5	6.1	2 53.4	+57.5	6.1	70
71	3 07.0	−57.3	174.2	2 07.3	−57.3	174.2	1 07.6	−57.3	174.2	0 07.9	−57.4	174.2	0 51.8	+57.4	5.8	1 51.5	+57.4	5.8	2 51.2	+57.4	5.8	3 50.9	+57.5	5.8	71
72	2 09.7	−57.2	174.5	1 10.0	−57.3	174.5	0 10.3	−57.3	174.5	0 49.5	+57.3	5.5	1 49.2	+57.4	5.5	2 48.9	+57.4	5.5	3 48.6	+57.4	5.5	4 48.4	+57.5	5.5	72
73	1 12.5	−57.3	174.8	0 12.7	−57.3	174.8	0 47.0	+57.4	5.2	1 46.8	+57.3	5.2	2 46.6	+57.3	5.2	3 46.3	+57.4	5.2	4 46.1	+57.4	5.2	5 45.8	+57.5	5.2	73
74	0 15.2	−57.3	175.1	0 44.6	+57.3	4.9	1 44.4	+57.3	4.9	2 44.1	+57.4	4.9	3 43.9	+57.4	4.9	4 43.7	+57.4	4.9	5 43.5	+57.4	4.9	6 43.3	+57.4	4.9	74
75	0 42.1	+57.2	4.6	1 41.9	+57.3	4.6	2 41.7	+57.3	4.6	3 41.5	+57.3	4.6	4 41.3	+57.4	4.6	5 41.1	+57.4	4.6	6 40.9	+57.4	4.6	7 40.7	+57.4	4.6	75
76	1 39.3	+57.3	4.3	2 39.2	+57.2	4.3	3 39.0	+57.3	4.3	4 38.8	+57.4	4.3	5 38.7	+57.3	4.3	6 38.5	+57.4	4.3	7 38.3	+57.4	4.3	8 38.1	+57.5	4.3	76
77	2 36.6	+57.2	4.0	3 36.4	+57.3	4.0	4 36.3	+57.3	4.0	5 36.2	+57.3	4.0	6 36.0	+57.3	4.0	7 35.9	+57.3	4.0	8 35.7	+57.4	4.0	9 35.6	+57.4	4.0	77
78	3 33.8	+57.3	3.7	4 33.7	+57.3	3.7	5 33.6	+57.3	3.7	6 33.5	+57.3	3.7	7 33.3	+57.4	3.7	8 33.2	+57.4	3.7	9 33.1	+57.4	3.7	10 33.0	+57.4	3.7	78
79	4 31.1	+57.2	3.4	5 31.0	+57.3	3.4	6 30.9	+57.3	3.4	7 30.8	+57.3	3.4	8 30.7	+57.3	3.4	9 30.6	+57.3	3.4	10 30.5	+57.3	3.4	11 30.4	+57.3	3.4	79
80	5 28.3	+57.3	3.1	6 28.3	+57.2	3.1	7 28.2	+57.2	3.1	8 28.1	+57.3	3.1	9 28.0	+57.3	3.1	10 27.9	+57.3	3.1	11 27.8	+57.3	3.1	12 27.7	+57.4	3.2	80
81	6 25.6	+57.2	2.8	7 25.5	+57.2	2.8	8 25.4	+57.3	2.8	9 25.4	+57.2	2.8	10 25.3	+57.3	2.8	11 25.2	+57.3	2.8	12 25.1	+57.4	2.8	13 25.1	+57.3	2.8	81
82	7 22.8	+57.2	2.5	8 22.7	+57.3	2.5	9 22.7	+57.2	2.5	10 22.6	+57.3	2.5	11 22.6	+57.2	2.5	12 22.5	+57.3	2.5	13 22.5	+57.2	2.5	14 22.4	+57.3	2.5	82
83	8 20.0	+57.2	2.2	9 20.0	+57.2	2.2	10 19.9	+57.2	2.2	11 19.9	+57.2	2.2	12 19.8	+57.3	2.2	13 19.8	+57.2	2.2	14 19.7	+57.3	2.2	15 19.7	+57.3	2.2	83
84	9 17.2	+57.2	1.9	10 17.2	+57.2	1.9	11 17.1	+57.2	1.9	12 17.1	+57.2	1.9	13 17.1	+57.2	1.9	14 17.0	+57.3	1.9	15 17.0	+57.3	1.9	16 17.0	+57.2	1.9	84
85	10 14.4	+57.2	1.6	11 14.4	+57.1	1.6	12 14.3	+57.2	1.6	13 14.3	+57.2	1.6	14 14.3	+57.2	1.6	15 14.3	+57.2	1.6	16 14.3	+57.2	1.6	17 14.2	+57.2	1.6	85
86	11 11.6	+57.1	1.3	12 11.5	+57.2	1.3	13 11.5	+57.2	1.3	14 11.5	+57.2	1.3	15 11.5	+57.2	1.3	16 11.5	+57.2	1.3	17 11.5	+57.1	1.3	18 11.4	+57.2	1.3	86
87	12 08.7	+57.1	0.9	13 08.7	+57.1	1.0	14 08.7	+57.1	1.0	15 08.7	+57.1	1.0	16 08.7	+57.1	1.0	17 08.7	+57.1	1.0	18 08.6	+57.2	1.0	19 08.6	+57.2	1.0	87
88	13 05.8	+57.1	0.6	14 05.8	+57.1	0.6	15 05.8	+57.1	0.6	16 05.8	+57.1	0.6	17 05.8	+57.1	0.6	18 05.8	+57.1	0.7	19 05.8	+57.1	0.7	20 05.8	+57.1	0.7	88
89	14 02.9	+57.1	0.3	15 02.9	+57.1	0.3	16 02.9	+57.1	0.3	17 02.9	+57.1	0.3	18 02.9	+57.1	0.3	19 02.9	+57.1	0.3	20 02.9	+57.1	0.3	21 02.9	+57.1	0.3	89
90	15 00.0	+57.0	0.0	16 00.0	+57.0	0.0	17 00.0	+57.0	0.0	18 00.0	+57.0	0.0	19 00.0	+57.0	0.0	20 00.0	+57.0	0.0	21 00.0	+57.0	0.0	22 00.0	+57.0	0.0	90
	15°			16°			17°			18°			19°			20°			21°			22°			

S. Lat. {L.H.A. greater than 180° ....Zn=180°−Z; L.H.A. less than 180°...........Zn=180°+Z}

LATITUDE SAME NAME AS DECLINATION L.H.A. 162°, 198°

Dec.	15°			16°			17°			18°		
Dec.	Hc	d	Z	Hc	d	Z	Hc	d	Z	Hc	d	Z
°	° ′	′	°	° ′	′	°	° ′	′	°	° ′	′	°
0	65 57.9	+37.4	126.9	65 21.2	+38.9	128.7	64 43.0	+40.4	130.3	64 03.5	+41.8	131.9
1	66 35.3	+35.9	125.0	66 00.1	+37.7	126.8	65 23.4	+39.2	128.6	64 45.3	+40.7	130.2
2	67 11.2	+34.3	122.9	66 37.8	+36.0	124.9	66 02.6	+37.8	126.7	65 26.0	+39.4	128.5
3	67 45.5	+32.5	120.8	67 13.8	+34.5	122.9	66 40.4	+36.3	124.8	66 05.4	+38.0	126.7
4	68 18.0	+30.6•	118.6	67 48.3	+32.7	120.7	67 16.7	+34.7	122.8	66 43.4	+36.5	124.7
5	68 48.6	+28.5•	116.2	68 21.0	+30.8	118.5	67 51.4	+32.9	120.6	67 19.9	+34.9	122.7
6	69 17.1	+26.4•	113.7	68 51.8	+28.8•	116.1	68 24.3	+31.1•	118.4	67 54.8	+33.1	120.6
7	69 43.5	+24.0•	111.2	69 20.6	+26.5•	113.7	68 55.4	+28.9•	116.0	68 27.9	+31.3	118.3
8	70 07.5	+21.5•	108.5	69 47.1	+24.3•	111.1	69 24.3	+26.8•	113.6	68 59.2	+29.2•	116.0
9	70 29.0	+18.9•	105.7	70 11.4	+21.7•	108.4	69 51.1	+24.5•	111.0	69 28.4	+27.1•	113.5
10	70 47.9	+16.2•	102.9	70 33.1	+19.2•	105.6	70 15.6	+22.0•	108.3	69 55.5	+24.7•	110.9
11	71 04.1	+13.3•	99.9	70 52.3	+16.4•	102.8	70 37.6	+19.4•	105.5	70 20.2	+22.2•	108.2
12	71 17.4	+10.3•	96.9	71 08.7	+13.5•	99.8	70 57.0	+16.6•	102.7	70 42.4	+19.6•	105.5
13	71 27.7	+7.3•	93.8	71 22.2	+10.5•	96.8	71 13.6	+13.7•	99.7	71 02.0	+16.8•	102.6
14	71 35.0	+4.2•	90.7	71 32.7	+7.5•	93.7	71 27.3	+10.8•	96.7	71 18.8	+14.0•	99.6
15	71 39.2	+1.0•	87.5	71 40.2	+4.3•	90.5	71 38.1	+7.6•	93.6	71 32.8	+10.9•	96.5
16	71 40.2	−2.1•	84.3	71 44.5	+1.2•	87.4	71 45.7	+4.5•	90.4	71 43.7	+7.9•	93.4
17	71 38.1	−5.3•	81.2	71 45.7	−2.0•	84.2	71 50.2	+1.4•	87.2	71 51.6	+4.7•	90.2
18	71 32.8	−8.4•	78.0	71 43.7	−5.1•	81.0	71 51.6	−1.9•	84.0	71 56.3	+1.5•	87.0
19	71 24.4	−11.4•	74.9	71 38.6	−8.3•	77.8	71 49.7	−5.0•	80.8	71 57.8	−1.8•	83.8
20	71 13.0	−14.3•	71.8	71 30.3	−11.3•	74.7	71 44.7	−8.2•	77.6	71 56.0	−4.9•	80.6
21	70 58.7	−17.2•	68.8	71 19.0	−14.3•	71.6	71 36.5	−11.2•	74.4	71 51.1	−8.0•	77.4
22	70 41.5	−19.9•	65.9	71 04.7	−17.1•	68.6	71 25.3	−14.2•	71.3	71 43.1	−11.2•	74.2
23	70 21.6	−22.4•	63.1	70 47.6	−19.8•	65.6	71 11.1	−17.1•	68.3	71 31.9	−14.2•	71.1
24	69 59.2	−24.9•	60.3	70 27.8	−22.4•	62.8	70 54.0	−19.8•	65.4	71 17.7	−17.0•	68.0
25	69 34.3	−27.1•	57.7	70 05.4	−24.9•	60.0	70 34.2	−22.4•	62.5	71 00.7	−19.8•	65.1
26	69 07.2	−29.3•	55.2	69 40.5	−27.2•	57.4	70 11.8	−24.9•	59.7	70 40.9	−22.4•	62.2
27	68 37.9	−31.3	52.8	69 13.3	−29.3•	54.9	69 46.9	−27.1•	57.1	70 18.5	−24.9•	59.4
28	68 06.6	−33.1	50.4	68 44.0	−31.3	52.4	69 19.8	−29.4•	54.5	69 53.6	−27.2•	56.7
29	67 33.5	−34.9	48.2	68 12.7	−33.1	50.1	68 50.4	−31.3	52.1	69 26.4	−29.3•	54.2
30	66 58.6	−36.4	46.1	67 39.6	−34.9	47.9	68 19.1	−33.2	49.7	68 57.1	−31.4•	51.7
31	66 22.2	−37.9	44.1	67 04.7	−36.5	45.8	67 45.9	−35.0	47.5	68 25.7	−33.3	49.4
32	65 44.3	−39.3	42.2	66 28.2	−38.0	43.8	67 10.9	−36.5	45.4	67 52.4	−35.0	47.1
33	65 05.0	−40.5	40.4	65 50.2	−39.3	41.8	66 34.4	−38.1	43.4	67 17.4	−36.6	45.0
34	64 24.5	−41.7	38.7	65 10.9	−40.6	40.0	65 56.3	−39.4	41.5	66 40.8	−38.1	43.0
35	63 42.8	−42.8	37.0	64 30.3	−41.8	38.3	65 16.9	−40.6	39.6	66 02.7	−39.5	41.1
36	63 00.0	−43.8	35.5	63 48.5	−42.8	36.6	64 36.3	−41.9	37.9	65 23.2	−40.8	39.2
37	62 16.2	−44.6	34.0	63 05.7	−43.8	35.1	63 54.4	−42.9	36.2	64 42.4	−41.9	37.5
38	61 31.6	−45.5	32.6	62 21.9	−44.8	33.6	63 11.5	−43.9	34.7	64 00.5	−42.9	35.8
39	60 46.1	−46.3	31.2	61 37.1	−45.5	32.2	62 27.6	−44.8	33.2	63 17.6	−44.0	34.3
40	59 59.8	−47.0	29.9	60 51.6	−46.4	30.8	61 42.8	−45.6	31.8	62 33.6	−44.9	32.8
41	59 12.8	−47.7	28.7	60 05.2	−47.0	29.5	60 57.2	−46.4	30.4	61 48.7	−45.7	31.3
42	58 25.1	−48.3	27.5	59 18.2	−47.8	28.3	60 10.8	−47.2	29.1	61 03.0	−46.5	30.0
43	57 36.8	−48.8	26.4	58 30.4	−48.3	27.1	59 23.6	−47.7	27.9	60 16.5	−47.2	28.7
44	56 48.0	−49.4	25.3	57 42.1	−48.9	26.0	58 35.9	−48.5	26.7	59 29.3	−47.9	27.5
45	55 58.6	−49.8	24.3	56 53.2	−49.5	24.9	57 47.4	−48.9	25.6	58 41.4	−48.5	26.3
46	55 08.8	−50.4	23.3	56 03.7	−49.9	23.9	56 58.5	−49.5	24.5	57 52.9	−49.0	25.2
47	54 18.4	−50.7	22.4	55 13.8	−50.4	22.9	56 09.0	−50.0	23.5	57 03.9	−49.6	24.1
48	53 27.7	−51.1	21.5	54 23.4	−50.8	22.0	55 19.0	−50.5	22.5	56 14.3	−50.1	23.1
49	52 36.6	−51.6	20.6	53 32.6	−51.2	21.1	54 28.5	−50.8	21.6	55 24.2	−50.5	22.1
50	51 45.0	−51.8	19.8	52 41.4	−51.5	20.2	53 37.7	−51.3	20.7	54 33.7	−50.9	21.2
51	50 53.2	−52.2	19.0	51 49.9	−51.9	19.4	52 46.4	−51.6	19.8	53 42.8	−51.3	20.3
52	50 01.0	−52.4	18.2	50 58.0	−52.3	18.6	51 54.8	−52.0	19.0	52 51.5	−51.7	19.4
53	49 08.6	−52.8	17.4	50 05.7	−52.5	17.8	51 02.8	−52.3	18.2	51 59.8	−52.1	18.6
54	48 15.8	−53.0	16.7	49 13.2	−52.8	17.0	50 10.5	−52.5	17.4	51 07.7	−52.3	17.8
55	47 22.8	−53.3	16.0	48 20.4	−53.0	16.3	49 18.0	−52.9	16.6	50 15.4	−52.6	17.0
56	46 29.5	−53.4	15.3	47 27.4	−53.3	15.6	48 25.1	−53.1	15.9	49 22.8	−53.0	16.2
57	45 36.1	−53.8	14.7	46 34.1	−53.6	14.9	47 32.0	−53.4	15.2	48 29.8	−53.1	15.5
58	44 42.3	−53.9	14.0	45 40.5	−53.7	14.3	46 38.6	−53.6	14.6	47 36.7	−53.4	14.8
59	43 48.4	−54.1	13.4	44 46.8	−54.0	13.7	45 45.0	−53.8	13.9	46 43.3	−53.7	14.2
60	42 54.3	−54.2	12.8	43 52.8	−54.1	13.1	44 51.2	−54.0	13.3	45 49.6	−53.8	13.5
61	42 00.1	−54.5	12.3	42 58.7	−54.3	12.5	43 57.2	−54.2	12.7	44 55.8	−54.1	12.9
62	41 05.6	−54.6	11.7	42 04.4	−54.5	11.9	43 03.0	−54.3	12.1	44 01.7	−54.2	12.3
63	40 11.0	−54.7	11.2	41 09.9	−54.7	11.3	42 08.7	−54.6	11.5	43 07.5	−54.5	11.7
64	39 16.3	−54.9	10.6	40 15.2	−54.8	10.8	41 14.1	−54.6	10.9	42 13.0	−54.5	11.1
65	38 21.4	−55.1	10.1	39 20.4	−54.9	10.2	40 19.5	−54.9	10.4	41 18.5	−54.8	10.6
66	37 26.3	−55.1	9.6	38 25.5	−55.1	9.7	39 24.6	−55.0	9.9	40 23.7	−54.9	10.0
67	36 31.2	−55.3	9.1	37 30.4	−55.2	9.2	38 29.6	−55.1	9.4	39 28.8	−55.0	9.5
68	35 35.9	−55.4	8.6	36 35.2	−55.3	8.7	37 34.5	−55.2	8.9	38 33.8	−55.2	9.0
69	34 40.5	−55.5	8.2	35 39.9	−55.4	8.3	36 39.3	−55.4	8.4	37 38.6	−55.3	8.5
70	33 45.0	−55.6	7.7	34 44.5	−55.5	7.8	35 43.9	−55.4	7.9	36 43.3	−55.4	8.0
71	32 49.4	−55.6	7.2	33 49.0	−55.7	7.3	34 48.5	−55.6	7.4	35 47.9	−55.5	7.5
72	31 53.8	−55.8	6.8	32 53.3	−55.7	6.9	33 52.9	−55.7	7.0	34 52.4	−55.6	7.0
73	30 58.0	−55.9	6.4	31 57.6	−55.8	6.4	32 57.2	−55.7	6.5	33 56.8	−55.7	6.6
74	30 02.1	−55.9	5.9	31 01.8	−55.9	6.0	32 01.5	−55.9	6.1	33 01.1	−55.8	6.1
75	29 06.2	−56.0	5.5	30 05.9	−56.0	5.6	31 05.6	−55.9	5.6	32 05.3	−55.9	5.7
76	28 10.2	−56.1	5.1	29 09.9	−56.0	5.2	30 09.7	−56.0	5.2	31 09.4	−56.0	5.3
77	27 14.1	−56.2	4.7	28 13.9	−56.2	4.8	29 13.7	−56.1	4.8	30 13.4	−56.0	4.9
78	26 17.9	−56.2	4.3	27 17.7	−56.1	4.4	28 17.6	−56.2	4.4	29 17.4	−56.1	4.5
79	25 21.7	−56.3	3.9	26 21.6	−56.3	4.0	27 21.4	−56.2	4.0	28 21.3	−56.2	4.0
80	24 25.4	−56.3	3.6	25 25.3	−56.3	3.6	26 25.2	−56.3	3.6	27 25.1	−56.3	3.7
81	23 29.1	−56.4	3.2	24 29.0	−56.4	3.2	25 28.9	−56.4	3.2	26 28.8	−56.3	3.3
82	22 32.7	−56.4	2.8	23 32.6	−56.4	2.8	24 32.5	−56.4	2.9	25 32.5	−56.4	2.9
83	21 36.3	−56.5	2.4	22 36.2	−56.5	2.5	23 36.1	−56.4	2.5	24 36.1	−56.5	2.5
84	20 39.8	−56.6	2.1	21 39.7	−56.5	2.1	22 39.7	−56.5	2.1	23 39.6	−56.4	2.1
85	19 43.2	−56.5	1.7	20 43.2	−56.6	1.7	21 43.2	−56.6	1.8	22 43.2	−56.6	1.8
86	18 46.7	−56.7	1.4	19 46.6	−56.6	1.4	20 46.6	−56.6	1.4	21 46.6	−56.6	1.4
87	17 50.0	−56.6	1.0	18 50.0	−56.6	1.0	19 50.0	−56.6	1.0	20 50.0	−56.6	1.0
88	16 53.4	−56.7	0.7	17 53.4	−56.7	0.7	18 53.4	−56.7	0.7	19 53.4	−56.7	0.7
89	15 56.7	−56.7	0.3	16 56.7	−56.7	0.3	17 56.7	−56.7	0.3	18 56.7	−56.7	0.3
90	15 00.0	−56.7	0.0	16 00.0	−56.7	0.0	17 00.0	−56.7	0.0	18 00.0	−56.7	0.0
	15°			16°			17°			18°		

19°			20°			21°			22°			Dec.
Hc	d	Z	Hc	d	Z	Hc	d	Z	Hc	d	Z	Dec.
° ′	′	°	° ′	′	°	° ′	′	°	° ′	′	°	°
63 22.9	+43.0	133.4	62 41.1	+44.3	134.8	61 58.3	+45.4	136.1	61 14.6	+46.3	137.4	0
64 05.9	+42.1	131.8	63 25.4	+43.2	133.3	62 43.7	+44.4	134.7	62 00.9	+45.5	136.1	1
64 48.0	+40.8	130.2	64 08.6	+42.2	131.7	63 28.1	+43.5	133.2	62 46.4	+44.7	134.7	2
65 28.8	+39.6	128.4	64 50.8	+41.1	130.1	64 11.6	+42.4	131.7	63 31.1	+43.6	133.2	3
66 08.4	+38.2	126.6	65 31.9	+39.8	128.4	64 54.0	+41.2	130.0	64 14.7	+42.7	131.6	4
66 46.6	+36.8	124.7	66 11.7	+38.4	126.5	65 35.2	+40.1	128.3	64 57.4	+41.4	130.0	5
67 23.4	+35.1	122.6	66 50.1	+37.0	124.6	66 15.3	+38.6	126.5	65 38.8	+40.3	128.3	6
67 58.5	+33.4	120.5	67 27.1	+35.3	122.6	66 53.9	+37.2	124.6	66 19.1	+38.9	126.4	7
68 31.9	+31.4	118.3	68 02.4	+33.7	120.4	67 31.1	+35.6	122.5	66 58.0	+37.4	124.5	8
69 03.3	+29.5•	115.9	68 36.1	+31.7•	118.2	68 06.7	+33.8	120.4	67 35.4	+35.8	122.5	9
69 32.8	+27.3•	113.4	69 07.8	+29.7•	115.8	68 40.5	+32.0	118.2	68 11.2	+34.1	120.4	10
70 00.1	+24.9•	110.9	69 37.5	+27.5•	113.4	69 12.5	+30.0•	115.8	68 45.3	+32.2	118.1	11
70 25.0	+22.5•	108.2	70 05.0	+25.2•	110.8	69 42.5	+27.8•	113.3	69 17.5	+30.3•	115.8	12
70 47.5	+19.8•	105.4	70 30.2	+22.7•	108.1	70 10.3	+25.4•	110.7	69 47.8	+28.0•	113.3	13
71 07.3	+17.1•	102.5	70 52.9	+20.1•	105.3	70 35.7	+23.0•	108.0	70 15.8	+25.7•	110.7	14
71 24.4	+14.2•	99.5	71 13.0	+17.3•	102.4	70 58.7	+20.3•	105.2	70 41.5	+23.2•	108.0	15
71 38.6	+11.1•	96.4	71 30.3	+14.4•	99.4	71 19.0	+17.5•	102.3	71 04.7	+20.6•	105.2	16
71 49.7	+8.1•	93.3	71 44.7	+11.3•	96.3	71 36.5	+14.6•	99.3	71 25.3	+17.8•	102.3	17
71 57.8	+4.8•	90.1	71 56.0	+8.3•	93.2	71 51.1	+11.6•	96.2	71 43.1	+14.8•	99.2	18
72 02.6	+1.7•	86.9	72 04.3	+5.0•	90.0	72 02.7	+8.4•	93.1	71 57.9	+11.8•	96.1	19
72 04.3	−1.6•	83.6	72 09.3	+1.8•	86.7	72 11.1	+5.3•	89.8	72 09.7	+8.6•	92.9	20
72 02.7	−4.8•	80.4	72 11.1	−1.4•	83.5	72 16.4	+1.9•	86.6	72 18.3	+5.4•	89.7	21
71 57.9	−8.0•	77.2	72 09.7	−4.7•	80.2	72 18.3	−1.3•	83.3	72 23.7	+2.1•	86.4	22
71 49.9	−11.1•	74.0	72 05.0	−7.9•	76.9	72 17.0	−4.6•	80.0	72 25.8	−1.2•	83.1	23
71 38.8	−14.1•	70.8	71 57.1	−11.0•	73.7	72 12.4	−7.8•	76.7	72 24.6	−4.5•	79.8	24
71 24.7	−17.0•	67.8	71 46.1	−14.1•	70.6	72 04.6	−11.0•	73.5	72 20.1	−7.7•	76.5	25
71 07.7	−19.8•	64.8	71 32.0	−17.0•	67.5	71 53.6	−14.0•	70.3	72 12.4	−11.0•	73.2	26
70 47.9	−22.4•	61.9	71 15.0	−19.8•	64.5	71 39.6	−17.0•	67.2	72 01.4	−14.0•	70.0	27
70 25.5	−24.9•	59.1	70 55.2	−22.4•	61.6	71 22.6	−19.8•	64.2	71 47.4	−16.9•	66.9	28
70 00.6	−27.2•	56.4	70 32.8	−25.0•	58.8	71 02.8	−22.5•	61.2	71 30.5	−19.9•	63.9	29
69 33.4	−29.4•	53.8	70 07.8	−27.2•	56.1	70 40.3	−25.0•	58.4	71 10.6	−22.5•	60.9	30
69 04.0	−31.5	51.4	69 40.6	−29.5•	53.5	70 15.3	−27.3•	55.7	70 48.1	−25.0•	58.1	31
68 32.5	−33.3	49.0	69 11.1	−31.5•	51.0	69 48.0	−29.5•	53.1	70 23.1	−27.4•	55.3	32
67 59.2	−35.1	46.8	68 39.6	−33.5	48.6	69 18.5	−31.6•	50.6	69 55.7	−29.6•	52.7	33
67 24.1	−36.7	44.6	68 06.1	−35.1	46.4	68 46.9	−33.6	48.2	69 26.1	−31.7•	50.2	34
66 47.4	−38.2	42.6	67 31.0	−36.8	44.2	68 13.3	−35.2	46.0	68 54.4	−33.6	47.8	35
66 09.2	−39.6	40.7	66 54.2	−38.3	42.2	67 38.1	−36.9	43.8	68 20.8	−35.4	45.5	36
65 29.6	−40.8	38.8	66 15.9	−39.7	40.2	67 01.2	−38.4	41.8	67 45.4	−37.0	43.4	37
64 48.8	−42.0	37.1	65 36.2	−40.9	38.4	66 22.8	−39.8	39.8	67 08.4	−38.5	41.3	38
64 06.8	−43.1	35.4	64 55.3	−42.1	36.7	65 43.0	−41.0	38.0	66 29.9	−39.9	39.4	39
63 23.7	−44.0	33.8	64 13.2	−43.1	35.0	65 02.0	−42.2	36.2	65 50.0	−41.1	37.5	40
62 39.7	−45.0	32.3	63 30.1	−44.2	33.4	64 19.8	−43.3	34.6	65 08.9	−42.3	35.8	41
61 54.7	−45.8	30.9	62 45.9	−45.1	31.9	63 36.5	−44.2	33.0	64 26.6	−43.4	34.1	42
61 08.9	−46.6	29.6	62 00.8	−45.9	30.5	62 52.3	−45.2	31.5	63 43.2	−44.4	32.5	43
60 22.3	−47.3	28.3	61 14.9	−46.6	29.1	62 07.1	−46.0	30.1	62 58.8	−45.3	31.0	44
59 35.0	−47.9	27.0	60 28.3	−47.4	27.8	61 21.1	−46.8	28.7	62 13.5	−46.1	29.6	45
58 47.1	−48.6	25.9	59 40.9	−48.1	26.6	60 34.3	−47.5	27.4	61 27.4	−46.9	28.2	46
57 58.5	−49.1	24.8	58 52.8	−48.6	25.4	59 46.8	−48.1	26.2	60 40.5	−47.6	27.0	47
57 09.4	−49.7	23.7	58 04.2	−49.2	24.3	58 58.7	−48.7	25.0	59 52.9	−48.2	25.7	48
56 19.7	−50.1	22.7	57 15.0	−49.8	23.3	58 10.0	−49.4	23.9	59 04.7	−48.9	24.6	49
55 29.6	−50.6	21.7	56 25.2	−50.2	22.2	57 20.6	−49.8	22.8	58 15.8	−49.4	23.4	50
54 39.0	−51.0	20.7	55 35.0	−50.7	21.3	56 30.8	−50.3	21.8	57 26.4	−49.9	22.4	51
53 48.0	−51.4	19.8	54 44.3	−51.1	20.3	55 40.5	−50.8	20.8	56 36.5	−50.4	21.4	52
52 56.6	−51.8	19.0	53 53.2	−51.4	19.4	54 49.7	−51.1	19.9	55 46.1	−50.9	20.4	53
52 04.8	−52.1	18.1	53 01.8	−51.9	18.6	53 58.6	−51.6	19.0	54 55.2	−51.2	19.4	54
51 12.7	−52.4	17.3	52 09.9	−52.1	17.7	53 07.0	−51.9	18.1	54 04.0	−51.7	18.6	55
50 20.3	−52.7	16.6	51 17.8	−52.5	16.9	52 15.1	−52.2	17.3	53 12.3	−52.0	17.7	56
49 27.6	−53.0	15.8	50 25.3	−52.8	16.2	51 22.9	−52.6	16.5	52 20.3	−52.3	16.9	57
48 34.6	−53.2	15.1	49 32.5	−53.0	15.4	50 30.3	−52.8	15.7	51 28.0	−52.6	16.1	58
47 41.4	−53.5	14.4	48 39.5	−53.3	14.7	49 37.5	−53.2	15.0	50 35.4	−52.9	15.3	59
46 47.9	−53.7	13.8	47 46.2	−53.6	14.0	48 44.3	−53.3	14.3	49 42.5	−53.2	14.6	60
45 54.2	−53.9	13.1	46 52.6	−53.7	13.4	47 51.0	−53.6	13.6	48 49.3	−53.5	13.9	61
45 00.3	−54.1	12.5	45 58.9	−54.0	12.7	46 57.4	−53.9	12.9	47 55.8	−53.7	13.2	62
44 06.2	−54.3	11.9	45 04.9	−54.2	12.1	46 03.5	−54.0	12.3	47 02.1	−53.9	12.5	63
43 11.9	−54.5	11.3	44 10.7	−54.3	11.5	45 09.5	−54.2	11.7	46 08.2	−54.1	11.9	64
42 17.4	−54.6	10.7	43 16.4	−54.6	10.9	44 15.3	−54.5	11.1	45 14.1	−54.3	11.3	65
41 22.8	−54.8	10.2	42 21.8	−54.7	10.3	43 20.8	−54.6	10.5	44 19.8	−54.5	10.7	66
40 28.0	−55.0	9.6	41 27.1	−54.8	9.8	42 26.2	−54.7	9.9	43 25.3	−54.6	10.1	67
39 33.0	−55.0	9.1	40 32.3	−55.0	9.2	41 31.5	−54.9	9.4	42 30.7	−54.8	9.5	68
38 38.0	−55.2	8.6	39 37.3	−55.1	8.7	40 36.6	−55.1	8.8	41 35.9	−55.0	9.0	69
37 42.8	−55.4	8.1	38 42.2	−55.3	8.2	39 41.5	−55.2	8.3	40 40.9	−55.1	8.4	70
36 47.4	−55.4	7.6	37 46.9	−55.4	7.7	38 46.3	−55.3	7.8	39 45.8	−55.3	7.9	71
35 52.0	−55.6	7.1	36 51.5	−55.5	7.2	37 51.0	−55.4	7.3	38 50.5	−55.3	7.4	72
34 56.4	−55.6	6.7	35 56.0	−55.6	6.8	36 55.6	−55.6	6.8	37 55.2	−55.5	6.9	73
34 00.8	−55.8	6.2	35 00.4	−55.7	6.3	36 00.0	−55.6	6.4	36 59.7	−55.6	6.5	74
33 05.0	−55.8	5.8	34 04.7	−55.8	5.8	35 04.4	−55.8	5.9	36 04.1	−55.7	6.0	75
32 09.2	−56.0	5.3	33 08.9	−55.9	5.4	34 08.6	−55.8	5.5	35 08.4	−55.9	5.5	76
31 13.2	−56.0	4.9	32 13.0	−56.0	5.0	33 12.8	−56.0	5.0	34 12.5	−55.9	5.1	77
30 17.2	−56.1	4.5	31 17.0	−56.0	4.5	32 16.8	−56.0	4.6	33 16.6	−56.0	4.6	78
29 21.1	−56.2	4.1	30 21.0	−56.2	4.1	31 20.8	−56.1	4.2	32 20.6	−56.0	4.2	79
28 24.9	−56.2	3.7	29 24.8	−56.2	3.7	30 24.7	−56.2	3.8	31 24.6	−56.2	3.8	80
27 28.7	−56.3	3.3	28 28.6	−56.3	3.3	29 28.5	−56.3	3.4	30 28.4	−56.2	3.4	81
26 32.4	−56.4	2.9	27 32.3	−56.3	2.9	28 32.2	−56.3	3.0	29 32.2	−56.4	3.0	82
25 36.0	−56.4	2.5	26 36.0	−56.4	2.5	27 35.9	−56.4	2.6	28 35.8	−56.3	2.6	83
24 39.6	−56.5	2.1	25 39.6	−56.5	2.2	26 39.5	−56.4	2.2	27 39.5	−56.5	2.2	84
23 43.1	−56.5	1.8	24 43.1	−56.5	1.8	25 43.1	−56.5	1.8	26 43.0	−56.5	1.8	85
22 46.6	−56.6	1.4	23 46.6	−56.6	1.4	24 46.6	−56.6	1.4	25 46.5	−56.5	1.4	86
21 50.0	−56.6	1.1	22 50.0	−56.6	1.1	23 50.0	−56.6	1.1	24 50.0	−56.6	1.1	87
20 53.4	−56.7	0.7	21 53.4	−56.7	0.7	22 53.4	−56.7	0.7	23 53.4	−56.7	0.7	88
19 56.7	−56.7	0.3	20 56.7	−56.7	0.3	21 56.7	−56.7	0.4	22 56.7	−56.7	0.4	89
19 00.0	−56.7	0.0	20 00.0	−56.8	0.0	21 00.0	−56.8	0.0	22 00.0	−56.8	0.0	90
19°			20°			21°			22°			

LATITUDE **CONTRARY** NAME TO DECLINATION L.H.A. 19°, 341°

Dec.	15° Hc	d	Z	16° Hc	d	Z	17° Hc	d	Z	18° Hc	d	Z	19° Hc	d	Z	20° Hc	d	Z	21° Hc	d	Z	22° Hc	d	Z	Dec.
°	° ′	′	°	° ′	′	°	° ′	′	°	° ′	′	°	° ′	′	°	° ′	′	°	° ′	′	°	° ′	′	°	°
0	65 57.9	-38.8	126.9	65 21.2	-40.3	128.7	64 43.0	-41.7	130.3	64 03.5	-42.9	131.9	63 22.9	-44.1	133.4	62 41.1	-45.2	134.8	61 58.3	-46.1	136.1	61 14.6	-47.1	137.4	0
1	65 19.1	-40.1	128.8	64 40.9	-41.5	130.4	64 01.3	-42.7	132.0	63 20.6	-43.9	133.5	62 38.8	-45.0	134.9	61 55.9	-46.0	136.2	61 12.2	-47.0	137.5	60 27.5	-47.8	138.7	1
2	64 39.0	-41.3	130.5	63 59.4	-42.6	132.1	63 18.6	-43.7	133.6	62 36.7	-44.8	135.0	61 53.8	-45.8	136.3	61 09.9	-46.7	137.6	60 25.2	-47.6	138.8	59 39.7	-48.4	139.9	2
3	63 57.7	-42.4	132.2	63 16.8	-43.5	133.7	62 34.9	-44.7	135.1	61 51.9	-45.7	136.4	61 08.0	-46.6	137.7	60 23.2	-47.5	138.9	59 37.6	-48.2	140.0	58 51.3	-49.0	141.1	3
4	63 15.3	-43.4	133.8	62 33.3	-44.5	135.2	61 50.2	-45.5	136.5	61 06.2	-46.4	137.8	60 21.4	-47.3	139.0	59 35.7	-48.1	140.1	58 49.4	-48.9	141.1	58 02.3	-49.6	142.2	4
5	62 31.9	-44.3	135.3	61 48.8	-45.4	136.6	61 04.7	-46.3	137.9	60 19.8	-47.2	139.1	59 34.1	-48.0	140.2	58 47.6	-48.7	141.2	58 00.5	-49.4	142.3	57 12.7	-50.0	143.2	5
6	61 47.6	-45.2	136.8	61 03.4	-46.1	138.0	60 18.4	-47.0	139.2	59 32.6	-47.8	140.3	58 46.1	-48.6	141.4	57 58.9	-49.3	142.4	57 11.1	-49.9	143.3	56 22.7	-50.5	144.2	6
7	61 02.4	-46.1	138.1	60 17.3	-46.9	139.3	59 31.4	-47.7	140.4	58 44.8	-48.5	141.5	57 57.5	-49.1	142.5	57 09.6	-49.8	143.4	56 21.2	-50.4	144.3	55 32.2	-51.0	145.2	7
8	60 16.3	-46.7	139.4	59 30.4	-47.6	140.6	58 43.7	-48.3	141.6	57 56.3	-49.0	142.6	57 08.4	-49.7	143.5	56 19.8	-50.2	144.4	55 30.8	-50.9	145.3	54 41.2	-51.4	146.1	8
9	59 29.6	-47.4	140.7	58 42.8	-48.2	141.7	57 55.4	-48.9	142.7	57 07.3	-49.5	143.7	56 18.7	-50.1	144.6	55 29.6	-50.8	145.4	54 39.9	-51.2	146.2	53 49.8	-51.7	147.0	9
10	58 42.2	-48.1	141.9	57 54.6	-48.7	142.9	57 06.5	-49.4	143.8	56 17.8	-50.0	144.7	55 28.6	-50.6	145.5	54 38.8	-51.1	146.3	53 48.7	-51.6	147.1	52 58.1	-52.1	147.8	10
11	57 54.1	-48.7	143.0	57 05.9	-49.3	144.0	56 17.1	-49.9	144.8	55 27.8	-50.5	145.7	54 38.0	-51.1	146.5	53 47.7	-51.5	147.2	52 57.1	-52.0	148.0	52 06.0	-52.4	148.7	11
12	57 05.4	-49.2	144.1	56 16.6	-49.8	145.0	55 27.2	-50.4	145.8	54 37.3	-50.9	146.6	53 46.9	-51.4	147.4	52 56.2	-51.9	148.1	52 05.1	-52.3	148.8	51 13.6	-52.7	149.4	12
13	56 16.2	-49.6	145.2	55 26.8	-50.3	146.0	54 36.8	-50.8	146.8	53 46.4	-51.3	147.5	52 55.5	-51.7	148.3	52 04.3	-52.2	148.9	51 12.8	-52.6	149.6	50 20.9	-53.0	150.2	13
14	55 26.6	-50.2	146.2	54 36.5	-50.7	146.9	53 46.0	-51.2	147.7	52 55.1	-51.7	148.4	52 03.8	-52.1	149.1	51 12.1	-52.5	149.7	50 20.2	-52.9	150.3	49 27.9	-53.3	150.9	14
15	54 36.4	-50.6	147.1	53 45.8	-51.1	147.9	52 54.8	-51.6	148.6	52 03.4	-52.0	149.2	51 11.7	-52.4	149.9	50 19.6	-52.8	150.5	49 27.3	-53.2	151.1	48 34.6	-53.5	151.6	15
16	53 45.8	-51.0	148.0	52 54.7	-51.5	148.7	52 03.2	-51.9	149.4	51 11.4	-52.3	150.0	50 19.3	-52.7	150.6	49 26.8	-53.1	151.2	48 34.1	-53.4	151.8	47 41.1	-53.8	152.3	16
17	52 54.8	-51.4	148.9	52 03.2	-51.8	149.6	51 11.3	-52.2	150.2	50 19.1	-52.6	150.8	49 26.6	-53.0	151.4	48 33.7	-53.3	151.9	47 40.7	-53.7	152.5	46 47.3	-53.9	153.0	17
18	52 03.4	-51.7	149.8	51 11.4	-52.1	150.4	50 19.1	-52.5	151.0	49 26.5	-52.9	151.6	48 33.6	-53.3	152.1	47 40.4	-53.6	152.6	46 47.0	-53.9	153.1	45 53.4	-54.2	153.6	18
19	51 11.7	-52.1	150.6	50 19.3	-52.5	151.2	49 26.6	-52.9	151.7	48 33.6	-53.2	152.3	47 40.3	-53.5	152.8	46 46.8	-53.7	153.3	45 53.1	-54.0	153.8	44 59.2	-54.3	154.2	19
20	50 19.6	-52.3	151.4	49 26.8	-52.7	151.9	48 33.7	-53.0	152.5	47 40.4	-53.4	153.0	46 46.8	-53.7	153.5	45 53.1	-54.0	153.9	44 59.1	-54.3	154.4	44 04.9	-54.6	154.8	20
21	49 27.3	-52.7	152.1	48 34.1	-53.0	152.7	47 40.7	-53.4	153.2	46 47.0	-53.6	153.6	45 53.1	-53.9	154.1	44 59.1	-54.2	154.5	44 04.8	-54.5	155.0	43 10.3	-54.7	155.4	21
22	48 34.6	-52.9	152.9	47 41.1	-53.3	153.4	46 47.3	-53.5	153.8	45 53.4	-53.9	154.3	44 59.2	-54.1	154.7	44 04.9	-54.4	155.2	43 10.3	-54.6	155.5	42 15.6	-54.8	155.9	22
23	47 41.7	-53.2	153.6	46 47.8	-53.4	154.0	45 53.8	-53.8	154.5	44 59.5	-54.0	154.9	44 05.1	-54.3	155.3	43 10.5	-54.6	155.7	42 15.7	-54.8	156.1	41 20.8	-55.0	156.5	23
24	46 48.5	-53.4	154.2	45 54.4	-53.7	154.7	45 00.0	-53.9	155.1	44 05.5	-54.2	155.5	43 10.8	-54.5	155.9	42 15.9	-54.7	156.3	41 20.9	-54.9	156.7	40 25.8	-55.2	157.0	24
25	45 55.1	-53.6	154.9	45 00.7	-53.9	155.3	44 06.1	-54.2	155.7	43 11.3	-54.4	156.1	42 16.3	-54.6	156.5	41 21.2	-54.8	156.9	40 26.0	-55.1	157.2	39 30.6	-55.3	157.5	25
26	45 01.5	-53.9	155.5	44 06.8	-54.1	155.9	43 11.9	-54.3	156.3	42 16.9	-54.6	156.7	41 21.7	-54.8	157.1	40 26.4	-55.0	157.4	39 30.9	-55.2	157.7	38 35.3	-55.4	158.0	26
27	44 07.6	-54.0	156.2	43 12.7	-54.3	156.5	42 17.6	-54.6	156.9	41 22.3	-54.7	157.3	40 26.9	-55.0	157.6	39 31.4	-55.2	157.9	38 35.7	-55.3	158.2	37 39.9	-55.5	158.5	27
28	43 13.6	-54.2	156.8	42 18.4	-54.4	157.1	41 23.0	-54.6	157.5	40 27.6	-54.9	157.8	39 31.9	-55.0	158.1	38 36.2	-55.3	158.4	37 40.4	-55.5	158.7	36 44.4	-55.6	159.0	28
29	42 19.4	-54.4	157.3	41 24.0	-54.7	157.7	40 28.4	-54.8	158.0	39 32.7	-55.0	158.3	38 36.9	-55.2	158.6	37 40.9	-55.4	158.9	36 44.9	-55.6	159.2	35 48.8	-55.8	159.4	29
30	41 25.0	-54.5	157.9	40 29.3	-54.7	158.2	39 33.6	-55.0	158.5	38 37.7	-55.2	158.8	37 41.7	-55.4	159.1	36 45.5	-55.5	159.4	35 49.3	-55.6	159.7	34 53.0	-55.8	159.9	30
31	40 30.5	-54.7	158.5	39 34.6	-54.9	158.8	38 38.6	-55.1	159.1	37 42.5	-55.3	159.3	36 46.3	-55.4	159.6	35 50.0	-55.6	159.9	34 53.7	-55.8	160.1	33 57.2	-55.9	160.3	31
32	39 35.8	-54.9	159.0	38 39.7	-55.0	159.3	37 43.5	-55.2	159.6	36 47.2	-55.4	159.8	35 50.9	-55.6	160.1	34 54.4	-55.7	160.3	33 57.9	-55.9	160.6	33 01.3	-56.1	160.8	32
33	38 40.9	-55.0	159.5	37 44.7	-55.2	159.8	36 48.3	-55.3	160.1	35 51.8	-55.5	160.3	34 55.3	-55.6	160.5	33 58.7	-55.8	160.8	33 02.0	-56.0	161.0	32 05.2	-56.1	161.2	33
34	37 45.9	-55.1	160.0	36 49.5	-55.3	160.3	35 53.0	-55.5	160.5	34 56.3	-55.6	160.8	33 59.7	-55.8	161.0	33 02.9	-55.9	161.2	32 06.0	-56.0	161.4	31 09.1	-56.1	161.6	34
35	36 50.8	-55.2	160.5	35 54.2	-55.4	160.8	34 57.5	-55.5	161.0	34 00.7	-55.7	161.2	33 03.9	-55.9	161.4	32 07.0	-56.0	161.6	31 10.0	-56.1	161.8	30 13.0	-56.3	162.0	35
36	35 55.6	-55.4	161.0	34 58.8	-55.5	161.2	34 02.0	-55.7	161.5	33 05.0	-55.8	161.7	32 08.0	-55.9	161.9	31 11.0	-56.1	162.1	30 13.9	-56.2	162.3	29 16.7	-56.3	162.4	36
37	35 00.2	-55.4	161.5	34 03.3	-55.6	161.7	33 06.3	-55.7	161.9	32 09.2	-55.9	162.1	31 12.1	-56.0	162.3	30 14.9	-56.1	162.5	29 17.7	-56.3	162.7	28 20.4	-56.4	162.8	37
38	34 04.8	-55.6	162.0	33 07.7	-55.7	162.2	32 10.6	-55.9	162.4	31 13.3	-55.9	162.5	30 16.1	-56.1	162.7	29 18.8	-56.3	162.9	28 21.4	-56.3	163.1	27 24.0	-56.5	163.2	38
39	33 09.2	-55.6	162.4	32 12.0	-55.8	162.6	31 14.7	-55.9	162.8	30 17.4	-56.1	163.0	29 20.0	-56.2	163.1	28 22.5	-56.2	163.3	27 25.1	-56.4	163.4	26 27.5	-56.5	163.6	39
40	32 13.6	-55.8	162.9	31 16.2	-55.9	163.0	30 18.8	-56.0	163.2	29 21.3	-56.1	163.4	28 23.8	-56.2	163.5	27 26.3	-56.4	163.7	26 28.7	-56.5	163.8	25 31.0	-56.6	164.0	40
41	31 17.8	-55.8	163.3	30 20.3	-55.9	163.5	29 22.8	-56.1	163.6	28 25.2	-56.2	163.8	27 27.6	-56.3	163.9	26 29.9	-56.4	164.1	25 32.2	-56.5	164.2	24 34.4	-56.6	164.3	41
42	30 22.0	-55.9	163.7	29 24.4	-56.1	163.9	28 26.7	-56.1	164.0	27 29.0	-56.2	164.2	26 31.3	-56.4	164.3	25 33.5	-56.5	164.4	24 35.7	-56.6	164.6	23 37.8	-56.7	164.7	42
43	29 26.1	-56.0	164.1	28 28.3	-56.1	164.3	27 30.6	-56.2	164.4	26 32.8	-56.3	164.6	25 34.9	-56.4	164.7	24 37.0	-56.5	164.8	23 39.1	-56.6	164.9	22 41.1	-56.7	165.0	43
44	28 30.1	-56.1	164.5	27 32.2	-56.1	164.7	26 34.4	-56.3	164.8	25 36.4	-56.3	164.9	24 38.5	-56.5	165.1	23 40.5	-56.6	165.2	22 42.5	-56.7	165.3	21 44.4	-56.7	165.4	44
45	27 34.0	-56.1	164.9	26 36.1	-56.3	165.1	25 38.1	-56.4	165.2	24 40.1	-56.5	165.3	23 42.0	-56.5	165.4	22 43.9	-56.6	165.5	21 45.8	-56.7	165.6	20 47.7	-56.9	165.7	45
46	26 37.9	-56.2	165.3	25 39.8	-56.3	165.5	24 41.7	-56.4	165.6	23 43.6	-56.5	165.7	22 45.5	-56.6	165.8	21 47.3	-56.7	165.9	20 49.1	-56.8	166.0	19 50.8	-56.8	166.1	46
47	25 41.7	-56.3	165.7	24 43.5	-56.3	165.9	23 45.3	-56.4	166.0	22 47.1	-56.5	166.1	21 48.9	-56.7	166.2	20 50.6	-56.7	166.3	19 52.3	-56.8	166.3	18 54.0	-56.9	166.4	47
48	24 45.4	-56.3	166.1	23 47.2	-56.4	166.2	22 48.9	-56.5	166.3	21 50.6	-56.6	166.4	20 52.2	-56.6	166.5	19 53.9	-56.8	166.6	18 55.5	-56.8	166.7	17 57.1	-56.9	166.8	48
49	23 49.1	-56.3	166.5	22 50.8	-56.5	166.6	21 52.4	-56.5	166.7	20 54.0	-56.6	166.8	19 55.6	-56.7	166.9	18 57.1	-56.8	166.9	17 58.7	-56.9	167.0	17 00.2	-56.9	167.1	49
50	22 52.8	-56.5	166.9	21 54.3	-56.5	167.0	20 55.9	-56.6	167.1	19 57.4	-56.7	167.1	18 58.9	-56.8	167.2	18 00.3	-56.8	167.3	17 01.8	-56.9	167.4	16 03.3	-57.0	167.4	50
51	21 56.3	-56.4	167.2	20 57.8	-56.5	167.3	19 59.3	-56.7	167.4	19 00.7	-56.7	167.5	18 02.1	-56.8	167.6	17 03.5	-56.8	167.6	16 04.9	-56.9	167.7	15 06.3	-57.0	167.7	51
52	20 59.9	-56.5	167.6	20 01.3	-56.6	167.7	19 02.6	-56.6	167.8	18 04.0	-56.8	167.8	17 05.3	-56.8	167.9	16 06.7	-56.9	168.0	15 08.0	-57.0	168.0	14 09.3	-57.1	168.1	52
53	20 03.4	-56.6	168.0	19 04.7	-56.7	168.0	18 06.0	-56.7	168.1	17 07.2	-56.7	168.2	16 08.5	-56.8	168.2	15 09.8	-57.0	168.3	14 11.0	-57.0	168.3	13 12.2	-57.0	168.4	53
54	19 06.8	-56.6	168.3	18 08.0	-56.6	168.4	17 09.3	-56.8	168.4	16 10.5	-56.9	168.5	15 11.7	-56.9	168.6	14 12.8	-56.9	168.6	13 14.0	-57.0	168.7	12 15.2	-57.1	168.7	54
55	18 10.2	-56.6	168.7	17 11.4	-56.7	168.7	16 12.5	-56.8	168.8	15 13.6	-56.8	168.8	14 14.8	-56.9	168.9	13 15.9	-57.0	168.9	12 17.0	-57.0	169.0	11 18.1	-57.1	169.0	55
56	17 13.6	-56.7	169.0	16 14.7	-56.8	169.1	15 15.7	-56.8	169.1	14 16.8	-56.9	169.2	13 17.9	-57.0	169.2	12 18.9	-57.0	169.3	11 20.0	-57.1	169.3	10 21.0	-57.1	169.3	56
57	16 16.9	-56.7	169.4	15 17.9	-56.8	169.4	14 18.9	-56.8	169.5	13 19.9	-56.9	169.5	12 20.9	-56.9	169.5	11 21.9	-57.0	169.6	10 22.9	-57.1	169.6	9 23.9	-57.1	169.6	57
58	15 20.2	-56.8	169.7	14 21.1	-56.8	169.7	13 22.1	-56.9	169.8	12 23.0	-56.9	169.8	11 24.0	-57.0	169.9	10 24.9	-57.0	169.9	9 25.8	-57.0	169.9	8 26.8	-57.2	170.0	58
59	14 23.4	-56.7	170.0	13 24.3	-56.8	170.1	12 25.2	-56.8	170.1	11 26.1	-56.9	170.1	10 27.0	-57.0	170.2	9 27.9	-57.1	170.2	8 28.8	-57.1	170.2	7 29.6	-57.1	170.3	59
60	13 26.7	-56.8	170.4	12 27.5	-56.8	170.4	11 28.4	-56.9	170.4	10 29.2	-57.0	170.5	9 30.0	-57.0	170.5	8 30.8	-57.0	170.5	7 31.7	-57.2	170.5	6 32.5	-57.2	170.6	60
61	12 29.9	-56.8	170.7	11 30.7	-56.9	170.7	10 31.5	-57.0	170.8	9 32.2	-56.9	170.8	8 33.0	-57.0	170.8	7 33.8	-57.1	170.8	6 34.5	-57.1	170.9	5 35.3	-57.2	170.9	61
62	11 33.1	-56.9	171.0	10 33.8	-56.9	171.0	9 34.5	-56.9	171.1	8 35.3	-57.0	171.1	7 36.0	-57.1	171.1	6 36.7	-57.1	171.1	5 37.4	-57.1	171.2	4 38.1	-57.2	171.2	62
63	10 36.2	-56.8	171.4	9 36.9	-56.9	171.4	8 37.6	-57.0	171.4	7 38.3	-57.0	171.4	6 38.9	-57.0	171.4	5 39.6	-57.1	171.5	4 40.3	-57.2	171.5	3 40.9	-57.2	171.5	63
64	9 39.4	-56.9	171.7	8 40.0	-56.9	171.7	7 40.6	-56.9	171.7	6 41.3	-57.0	171.7	5 41.9	-57.1	171.8	4 42.5	-57.1	171.8	3 43.1	-57.1	171.8	2 43.7	-57.2	171.8	64
65	8 42.5	-56.9	172.0	7 43.1	-56.9	172.0	6 43.7	-57.0	172.0	5 44.3	-57.1	172.1	4 44.8	-57.0	172.1	3 45.4	-57.1	172.1	2 46.0	-57.2	172.1	1 46.5	-57.2	172.1	65
66	7 45.6	-56.9	172.3	6 46.2	-57.0	172.3	5 46.7	-57.0	172.4	4 47.2	-57.0	172.4	3 47.8	-57.1	172.4	2 48.3	-57.1	172.4	1 48.8	-57.1	172.4	0 49.3	-57.2	172.4	66
67	6 48.7	-56.9	172.6	5 49.2	-56.9	172.7	4 49.7	-57.0	172.7	3 50.2	-57.0	172.7	2 50.7	-57.1	172.7	1 51.2	-57.2	172.7	0 51.7	-57.2	172.7	0 07.9	+57.2	7.3	67
68	5 51.8	-56.9	173.0	4 52.3	-57.0	173.0	3 52.7	-57.0	173.0	2 53.2	-57.1	173.0	1 53.6	-57.1	173.0	0 54.0	-57.1	173.0	0 05.5	+57.2	7.0	1 05.1	+57.2	7.0	68
69	4 54.9	-57.0	173.3	3 55.3	-57.0	173.3	2 55.7	-57.0	173.3	1 56.1	-57.0	173.3	0 56.5	-57.1	173.3	0 03.1	+57.1	6.7	1 02.7	+57.1	6.7	2 02.3	+57.2	6.7	69
70	3 57.9	-56.9	173.6	2 58.3	-57.0	173.6	1 58.7	-57.0	173.6	0 59.1	-57.1	173.6	0 00.6	+57.1	6.4	1 00.2	+57.1	6.4	1 59.8	+57.2	6.4	2 59.5	+57.1	6.4	70
71	3 01.0	-57.0	173.9	2 01.3	-57.0	173.9	1 01.7	-57.1	173.9	0 02.0	-57.0	173.9	0 57.7	+57.0	6.1	1 57.3	+57.1	6.1	2 57.0	+57.1	6.1	3 56.6	+57.2	6.1	71
72	2 04.0	-56.9	174.2	1 04.3	-56.9	174.2	0 04.6	-57.0	174.2	0 55.0	+57.1	5.8	1 54.7	+57.1	5.8	2 54.4	+57.1	5.8	3 54.1	+57.2	5.8	4 53.8	+57.2	5.8	72
73	1 07.1	-57.0	174.5	0 07.4	-57.0	174.5	0 52.4	+57.0	5.5	1 52.1	+57.0	5.5	2 51.8	+57.1	5.5	3 51.5	+57.2	5.5	4 51.3	+57.1	5.5	5 51.0	+57.2	5.5	73
74	0 10.1	-56.9	174.9	0 49.6	+57.0	5.1	1 49.4	+57.0	5.2	2 49.1	+57.1	5.2	3 48.9	+57.1	5.2	4 48.7	+57.1	5.2	5 48.4	+57.1	5.2	6 48.2	+57.1	5.2	74
75	0 46.8	+57.0	4.8	1 46.6	+57.0	4.8	2 46.4	+57.0	4.8	3 46.2	+57.0	4.8	4 46.0	+57.0	4.9	5 45.8	+57.0	4.9	6 45.5	+57.2	4.9	7 45.3	+57.2	4.9	75
76	1 43.8	+56.9	4.5	2 43.6	+57.0	4.5	3 43.4	+57.0	4.5	4 43.2	+57.0	4.5	5 43.0	+57.1	4.5	6 42.8	+57.1	4.5	7 42.7	+57.1	4.6	8 42.5	+57.1	4.6	76
77	2 40.7	+57.0	4.2	3 40.6	+56.9	4.2	4 40.4	+57.0	4.2	5 40.2	+57.1	4.2	6 40.1	+57.0	4.2	7 39.9	+57.1	4.2	8 39.8	+57.0	4.2	9 39.6	+57.1	4.3	77
78	3 37.7	+56.9	3.9	4 37.5	+57.0	3.9	5 37.4	+57.0	3.9	6 37.3	+57.0	3.9	7 37.1	+57.0	3.9	8 37.0	+57.0	3.9	9 36.8	+57.1	3.9	10 36.7	+57.1	3.9	78
79	4 34.6	+56.9	3.6	5 34.5	+57.0	3.6	6 34.4	+57.0	3.6	7 34.3	+57.0	3.6	8 34.1	+57.1	3.6	9 34.0	+57.1	3.6	10 33.9	+57.1	3.6	11 33.8	+57.1	3.6	79
80	5 31.5	+57.0	3.3	6 31.5	+56.9	3.3	7 31.4	+56.9	3.3	8 31.3	+56.9	3.3	9 31.2	+57.0	3.3	10 31.1	+57.0	3.3	11 31.0	+57.0	3.3	12 30.9	+57.0	3.3	80
81	6 28.5	+56.9	2.9	7 28.4	+56.9	2.9	8 28.3	+57.0	3.0	9 28.2	+57.0	3.0	10 28.2	+56.9	3.0	11 28.1	+57.0	3.0	12 28.0	+57.0	3.0	13 27.9	+57.0	3.0	81
82	7 25.4	+56.9	2.6	8 25.3	+56.9	2.6	9 25.3	+56.9	2.6	10 25.2	+56.9	2.6	11 25.1	+57.0	2.6	12 25.1	+56.9	2.7	13 25.0	+57.0	2.7	14 24.9	+57.0	2.7	82
83	8 22.3	+56.9	2.3	9 22.2	+56.9	2.3	10 22.2	+56.9	2.3	11 22.1	+56.9	2.3	12 22.1	+56.9	2.3	13 22.0	+57.0	2.3	14 22.0	+56.9	2.3	15 21.9	+57.0	2.4	83
84	9 19.2	+56.8	2.0	10 19.1	+56.9	2.0	11 19.1	+56.9	2.0	12 19.0	+56.9	2.0	13 19.0	+56.9	2.0	14 19.0	+56.9	2.0	15 18.9	+57.0	2.0	16 18.9	+56.9	2.0	84
85	10 16.0	+56.9	1.7	11 16.0	+56.8	1.7	12 16.0	+56.8	1.7	13 15.9	+56.9	1.7	14 15.9	+56.9	1.7	15 15.9	+56.9	1.7	16 15.9	+56.9	1.7	17 15.8	+56.9	1.7	85
86	11 12.9	+56.8	1.3	12 12.8	+56.9	1.3	13 12.8	+56.9	1.3	14 12.8	+56.9	1.3	15 12.8	+56.8	1.3	16 12.8	+56.8	1.4	17 12.8	+56.8	1.4	18 12.7	+56.9	1.4	86
87	12 09.7	+56.8	1.0	13 09.7	+56.8	1.0	14 09.7	+56.8	1.0	15 09.7	+56.8	1.0	16 09.6	+56.9	1.0	17 09.6	+56.9	1.0	18 09.6	+56.9	1.0	19 09.6	+56.9	1.0	87
88	13 06.5	+56.8	0.7	14 06.5	+56.8	0.7	15 06.5	+56.8	0.7	16 06.5	+56.8	0.7	17 06.5	+56.8	0.7	18 06.5	+56.7	0.7	19 06.5	+56.7	0.7	20 06.5	+56.7	0.7	88
89	14 03.3	+56.7	0.3	15 03.3	+56.7	0.3	16 03.3	+56.7	0.3	17 03.3	+56.7	0.3	18 03.3	+56.7	0.3	19 03.2	+56.8	0.3	20 03.2	+56.8	0.3	21 03.2	+56.8	0.3	89
90	15 00.0	+56.7	0.0	16 00.0	+56.7	0.0	17 00.0	+56.7	0.0	18 00.0	+56.7	0.0	19 00.0	+56.7	0.0	20 00.0	+56.7	0.0	21 00.0	+56.7	0.0	22 00.0	+56.7	0.0	90
	15°			16°			17°			18°			19°			20°			21°			22°			

S. Lat. {L.H.A. greater than 180° ....Zn=180°–Z
{L.H.A. less than 180°...........Zn=180°+Z

LATITUDE **SAME** NAME AS DECLINATION L.H.A. 161°, 199°

Dec.	15°			16°			17°			18°		
	Hc	d	Z	Hc	d	Z	Hc	d	Z	Hc	d	Z
°	° ′	′	°	° ′	′	°	° ′	′	°	° ′	′	°
0	65 11.1	+36.3	125.4	64 35.6	+37.9	127.1	63 58.7	+39.4	128.8	63 20.5	+40.8	130.3
1	65 47.4	+34.8	123.5	65 13.5	+36.5	125.3	64 38.1	+38.1	127.0	64 01.3	+39.6	128.7
2	66 22.2	+33.1	121.5	65 50.0	+35.0	123.4	65 16.2	+36.7	125.2	64 40.9	+38.3	126.9
3	66 55.3	+31.4	119.4	66 25.0	+33.4	121.4	65 52.9	+35.2	123.3	65 19.2	+36.9	125.1
4	67 26.7	+29.6	117.2	66 58.4	+31.6	119.3	66 28.1	+33.6	121.3	65 56.1	+35.4	123.2
5	67 56.3	+27.5•	114.9	67 30.0	+29.7	117.1	67 01.7	+31.8	119.2	66 31.5	+33.8	121.2
6	68 23.8	+25.4•	112.5	67 59.7	+27.8•	114.8	67 33.5	+30.0	117.0	67 05.3	+32.1	119.1
7	68 49.2	+23.1•	110.0	68 27.5	+25.6•	112.4	68 03.5	+28.0•	114.7	67 37.4	+30.2	116.9
8	69 12.3	+20.8•	107.4	68 53.1	+23.4•	109.9	68 31.5	+25.9•	112.3	68 07.6	+28.2•	114.6
9	69 33.1	+18.2•	104.8	69 16.5	+21.0•	107.3	68 57.4	+23.6•	109.8	68 35.8	+26.2•	112.2
10	69 51.3	+15.6•	102.0	69 37.5	+18.4•	104.7	69 21.0	+21.2•	107.2	69 02.0	+23.8•	109.7
11	70 06.9	+12.9•	99.2	69 55.9	+15.9•	101.9	69 42.2	+18.7•	104.6	69 25.8	+21.5•	107.1
12	70 19.8	+10.1•	96.3	70 11.8	+13.1•	99.1	70 00.9	+16.1•	101.8	69 47.3	+18.9•	104.5
13	70 29.9	+7.2•	93.4	70 24.9	+10.3•	96.2	70 17.0	+13.3•	99.0	70 06.2	+16.3•	101.7
14	70 37.1	+4.2•	90.4	70 35.2	+7.3•	93.2	70 30.3	+10.5•	96.1	70 22.5	+13.6•	98.9
15	70 41.3	+1.2•	87.4	70 42.5	+4.4•	90.2	70 40.8	+7.5•	93.1	70 36.1	+10.7•	95.9
16	70 42.5	-1.7•	84.4	70 46.9	+1.4•	87.2	70 48.3	+4.6•	90.1	70 46.8	+7.7•	93.0
17	70 40.8	-4.7•	81.3	70 48.3	-1.5•	84.2	70 52.9	+1.6•	87.0	70 54.5	+4.8•	89.9
18	70 36.1	-7.7•	78.3	70 46.8	-4.6•	81.1	70 54.5	-1.4•	84.0	70 59.3	+1.7•	86.9
19	70 28.4	-10.6•	75.4	70 42.2	-7.6•	78.1	70 53.1	-4.5•	80.9	71 01.0	-1.3•	83.8
20	70 17.8	-13.3•	72.4	70 34.6	-10.4•	75.1	70 48.6	-7.4•	77.9	70 59.7	-4.3•	80.7
21	70 04.5	-16.1•	69.5	70 24.2	-13.3•	72.2	70 41.2	-10.4•	74.9	70 55.4	-7.3•	77.7
22	69 48.4	-18.7•	66.7	70 10.9	-16.0•	69.3	70 30.8	-13.2•	71.9	70 48.1	-10.3•	74.7
23	69 29.7	-21.1•	64.0	69 54.9	-18.6•	66.5	70 17.6	-15.9•	69.0	70 37.8	-13.1•	71.7
24	69 08.6	-23.6•	61.4	69 36.3	-21.2•	63.7	70 01.7	-18.6•	66.2	70 24.7	-15.9•	68.7
25	68 45.0	-25.7•	58.8	69 15.1	-23.5•	61.0	69 43.1	-21.1•	63.4	70 08.8	-18.6•	65.9
26	68 19.3	-27.9•	56.3	68 51.6	-25.7•	58.5	69 22.0	-23.5•	60.7	69 50.2	-21.1•	63.1
27	67 51.4	-29.8	53.9	68 25.9	-27.9•	56.0	68 58.5	-25.8•	58.1	69 29.1	-23.5•	60.4
28	67 21.6	-31.8	51.7	67 58.0	-29.9	53.6	68 32.7	-27.9•	55.7	69 05.6	-25.8•	57.8
29	66 49.8	-33.4	49.5	67 28.1	-31.7	51.3	68 04.8	-29.9	53.3	68 39.8	-27.9•	55.3
30	66 16.4	-35.0	47.4	66 56.4	-33.5	49.1	67 34.9	-31.8	51.0	68 11.9	-29.9	52.9
31	65 41.4	-36.5	45.4	66 22.9	-35.1	47.0	67 03.1	-33.5	48.8	67 42.0	-31.8	50.6
32	65 04.9	-38.0	43.5	65 47.8	-36.5	45.0	66 29.6	-35.1	46.7	67 10.2	-33.6	48.4
33	64 26.9	-39.2	41.7	65 11.3	-38.0	43.1	65 54.5	-36.6	44.6	66 36.6	-35.2	46.3
34	63 47.7	-40.4	40.0	64 33.3	-39.3	41.3	65 17.9	-38.1	42.7	66 01.4	-36.7	44.2
35	63 07.3	-41.4	38.3	63 54.0	-40.4	39.6	64 39.8	-39.3	40.9	65 24.7	-38.1	42.3
36	62 25.9	-42.6	36.7	63 13.6	-41.6	37.9	64 00.5	-40.5	39.2	64 46.6	-39.4	40.5
37	61 43.3	-43.4	35.2	62 32.0	-42.6	36.3	63 20.0	-41.6	37.5	64 07.2	-40.6	38.7
38	60 59.9	-44.4	33.8	61 49.4	-43.5	34.8	62 38.4	-42.7	35.9	63 26.6	-41.7	37.1
39	60 15.5	-45.1	32.4	61 05.9	-44.4	33.4	61 55.7	-43.6	34.4	62 44.9	-42.7	35.5
40	59 30.4	-45.9	31.1	60 21.5	-45.2	32.0	61 12.1	-44.4	32.9	62 02.2	-43.7	34.0
41	58 44.5	-46.6	29.8	59 36.3	-46.0	30.7	60 27.7	-45.3	31.6	61 18.5	-44.5	32.5
42	57 57.9	-47.3	28.6	58 50.3	-46.7	29.4	59 42.4	-46.1	30.3	60 34.0	-45.4	31.1
43	57 10.6	-47.9	27.5	58 03.6	-47.3	28.2	58 56.3	-46.7	29.0	59 48.6	-46.1	29.8
44	56 22.7	-48.4	26.4	57 16.3	-47.9	27.1	58 09.6	-47.4	27.8	59 02.5	-46.9	28.6
45	55 34.3	-48.9	25.3	56 28.4	-48.5	26.0	57 22.2	-48.0	26.6	58 15.6	-47.4	27.4
46	54 45.4	-49.5	24.3	55 39.9	-49.0	24.9	56 34.2	-48.6	25.5	57 28.2	-48.1	26.2
47	53 55.9	-49.9	23.3	54 50.9	-49.5	23.9	55 45.6	-49.0	24.5	56 40.1	-48.6	25.1
48	53 06.0	-50.3	22.4	54 01.4	-49.9	22.9	54 56.6	-49.6	23.5	55 51.5	-49.2	24.1
49	52 15.7	-50.7	21.5	53 11.5	-50.4	22.0	54 07.0	-50.0	22.5	55 02.3	-49.6	23.1
50	51 25.0	-51.0	20.6	52 21.1	-50.8	21.1	53 17.0	-50.4	21.6	54 12.7	-50.1	22.1
51	50 34.0	-51.5	19.8	51 30.3	-51.1	20.2	52 26.6	-50.9	20.7	53 22.6	-50.5	21.1
52	49 42.5	-51.7	19.0	50 39.2	-51.5	19.4	51 35.7	-51.2	19.8	52 32.1	-50.9	20.3
53	48 50.8	-52.0	18.2	49 47.7	-51.8	18.6	50 44.5	-51.5	19.0	51 41.2	-51.2	19.4
54	47 58.8	-52.3	17.5	48 55.9	-52.0	17.8	49 53.0	-51.8	18.2	50 50.0	-51.6	18.6
55	47 06.5	-52.6	16.8	48 03.9	-52.4	17.1	49 01.2	-52.2	17.4	49 58.4	-52.0	17.8
56	46 13.9	-52.9	16.1	47 11.5	-52.7	16.3	48 09.0	-52.4	16.7	49 06.4	-52.2	17.0
57	45 21.0	-53.0	15.4	46 18.8	-52.8	15.6	47 16.6	-52.7	15.9	48 14.2	-52.5	16.2
58	44 28.0	-53.3	14.7	45 26.0	-53.2	15.0	46 23.9	-53.0	15.2	47 21.7	-52.7	15.5
59	43 34.7	-53.5	14.1	44 32.8	-53.3	14.3	45 30.9	-53.1	14.6	46 29.0	-53.0	14.8
60	42 41.2	-53.7	13.5	43 39.5	-53.6	13.7	44 37.8	-53.4	13.9	45 36.0	-53.3	14.1
61	41 47.5	-53.9	12.8	42 45.9	-53.7	13.1	43 44.4	-53.6	13.3	44 42.7	-53.4	13.5
62	40 53.6	-54.1	12.3	41 52.2	-53.9	12.5	42 50.8	-53.8	12.7	43 49.3	-53.7	12.9
63	39 59.5	-54.2	11.7	40 58.3	-54.1	11.9	41 57.0	-54.0	12.1	42 55.6	-53.8	12.2
64	39 05.3	-54.3	11.1	40 04.2	-54.3	11.3	41 03.0	-54.2	11.5	42 01.8	-54.0	11.6
65	38 11.0	-54.6	10.6	39 09.9	-54.4	10.7	40 08.8	-54.3	10.9	41 07.8	-54.3	11.1
66	37 16.4	-54.6	10.1	38 15.5	-54.6	10.2	39 14.5	-54.4	10.3	40 13.5	-54.3	10.5
67	36 21.8	-54.8	9.6	37 20.9	-54.7	9.7	38 20.1	-54.6	9.8	39 19.2	-54.5	9.9
68	35 27.0	-54.9	9.0	36 26.2	-54.8	9.2	37 25.5	-54.8	9.3	38 24.7	-54.7	9.4
69	34 32.1	-55.0	8.6	35 31.4	-54.9	8.7	36 30.7	-54.8	8.8	37 30.0	-54.8	8.9
70	33 37.1	-55.2	8.1	34 36.5	-55.1	8.2	35 35.9	-55.0	8.3	36 35.2	-54.9	8.4
71	32 41.9	-55.2	7.6	33 41.4	-55.2	7.7	34 40.9	-55.1	7.8	35 40.3	-55.0	7.9
72	31 46.7	-55.3	7.1	32 46.2	-55.2	7.2	33 45.8	-55.3	7.3	34 45.3	-55.2	7.4
73	30 51.4	-55.4	6.7	31 51.0	-55.4	6.8	32 50.5	-55.3	6.8	33 50.1	-55.2	6.9
74	29 56.0	-55.6	6.2	30 55.6	-55.5	6.3	31 55.2	-55.4	6.4	32 54.9	-55.4	6.4
75	29 00.4	-55.5	5.8	30 00.1	-55.5	5.9	30 59.8	-55.5	5.9	31 59.5	-55.5	6.0
76	28 04.9	-55.7	5.4	29 04.6	-55.6	5.4	30 04.3	-55.6	5.5	31 04.0	-55.5	5.5
77	27 09.2	-55.8	5.0	28 09.0	-55.8	5.0	29 08.7	-55.7	5.1	30 08.5	-55.7	5.1
78	26 13.4	-55.8	4.5	27 13.2	-55.7	4.6	28 13.0	-55.7	4.6	29 12.8	-55.7	4.7
79	25 17.6	-55.9	4.1	26 17.5	-55.9	4.2	27 17.3	-55.8	4.2	28 17.1	-55.8	4.3
80	24 21.7	-55.9	3.7	25 21.6	-55.9	3.8	26 21.5	-55.9	3.8	27 21.3	-55.8	3.8
81	23 25.8	-56.0	3.3	24 25.7	-56.0	3.4	25 25.6	-56.0	3.4	26 25.5	-56.0	3.4
82	22 29.8	-56.1	3.0	23 29.7	-56.0	3.0	24 29.6	-56.0	3.0	25 29.5	-56.0	3.0
83	21 33.7	-56.1	2.6	22 33.7	-56.1	2.6	23 33.6	-56.1	2.6	24 33.5	-56.0	2.6
84	20 37.6	-56.2	2.2	21 37.6	-56.2	2.2	22 37.5	-56.1	2.2	23 37.5	-56.1	2.2
85	19 41.4	-56.2	1.8	20 41.4	-56.2	1.8	21 41.4	-56.2	1.8	22 41.4	-56.2	1.9
86	18 45.2	-56.2	1.4	19 45.2	-56.2	1.5	20 45.2	-56.2	1.5	21 45.2	-56.2	1.5
87	17 49.0	-56.3	1.1	18 49.0	-56.3	1.1	19 49.0	-56.3	1.1	20 49.0	-56.3	1.1
88	16 52.7	-56.3	0.7	17 52.7	-56.3	0.7	18 52.7	-56.3	0.7	19 52.7	-56.3	0.7
89	15 56.4	-56.4	0.4	16 56.4	-56.4	0.4	17 56.4	-56.4	0.4	18 56.4	-56.4	0.4
90	15 00.0	-56.4	0.0	16 00.0	-56.4	0.0	17 00.0	-56.4	0.0	18 00.0	-56.4	0.0
	15°			16°			17°			18°		

19°			20°			21°			22°			Dec.
Hc	d	Z	Hc	d	Z	Hc	d	Z	Hc	d	Z	
° ′	′	°	° ′	′	°	° ′	′	°	° ′	′	°	°
62 41.1	+42.0	131.8	62 00.5	+43.3	133.2	61 18.9	+44.4	134.6	60 36.4	+45.4	135.8	0
63 23.1	+41.0	130.2	62 43.8	+42.2	131.7	62 03.3	+43.5	133.1	61 21.8	+44.5	134.5	1
64 04.1	+39.8	128.6	63 26.0	+41.2	130.2	62 46.8	+42.4	131.6	62 06.3	+43.7	133.1	2
64 43.9	+38.5	126.9	64 07.2	+40.0	128.5	63 29.2	+41.4	130.1	62 50.0	+42.6	131.6	3
65 22.4	+37.1	125.0	64 47.2	+38.7	126.8	64 10.6	+40.2	128.4	63 32.6	+41.6	130.0	4
65 59.5	+35.7	123.1	65 25.9	+37.4	125.0	64 50.8	+39.0	126.7	64 14.2	+40.5	128.4	5
66 35.2	+34.0	121.1	66 03.3	+35.9	123.1	65 29.8	+37.6	124.9	64 54.7	+39.2	126.7	6
67 09.2	+32.4	119.0	66 39.2	+34.3	121.1	66 07.4	+36.1	123.0	65 33.9	+37.8	124.9	7
67 41.6	+30.4	116.8	67 13.5	+32.5	119.0	66 43.5	+34.5	121.0	66 11.7	+36.4	123.0	8
68 12.0	+28.5•	114.5	67 46.0	+30.8	116.8	67 18.0	+32.8	118.9	66 48.1	+34.7	121.0	9
68 40.5	+26.4•	112.1	68 16.8	+28.7•	114.5	67 50.8	+31.0	116.7	67 22.8	+33.1	118.9	10
69 06.9	+24.1•	109.7	68 45.5	+26.6•	112.1	68 21.8	+29.0•	114.4	67 55.9	+31.3	116.7	11
69 31.0	+21.7•	107.1	69 12.1	+24.4•	109.6	68 50.8	+26.9•	112.0	68 27.2	+29.2•	114.4	12
69 52.7	+19.2•	104.4	69 36.5	+21.9•	107.0	69 17.7	+24.6•	109.5	68 56.4	+27.1•	112.0	13
70 11.9	+16.5•	101.6	69 58.4	+19.4•	104.3	69 42.3	+22.2•	106.9	69 23.5	+24.9•	109.5	14
70 28.4	+13.8•	98.7	70 17.8	+16.8•	101.5	70 04.5	+19.7•	104.2	69 48.4	+22.5•	106.8	15
70 42.2	+10.9•	95.8	70 34.6	+14.0•	98.6	70 24.2	+17.0•	101.4	70 10.9	+19.9•	104.1	16
70 53.1	+7.9•	92.8	70 48.6	+11.1•	95.7	70 41.2	+14.2•	98.5	70 30.8	+17.3•	101.3	17
71 01.0	+5.0•	89.8	70 59.7	+8.2•	92.7	70 55.4	+11.4•	95.6	70 48.1	+14.5•	98.4	18
71 06.0	+1.9•	86.7	71 07.9	+5.1•	89.6	71 06.8	+8.3•	92.6	71 02.6	+11.5•	95.5	19
71 07.9	-1.1•	83.6	71 13.0	+2.1•	86.5	71 15.1	+5.3•	89.5	71 14.1	+8.6•	92.4	20
71 06.8	-4.2•	80.5	71 15.1	-1.0•	83.4	71 20.4	+2.3•	86.4	71 22.7	+5.5•	89.3	21
71 02.6	-7.3•	77.5	71 14.1	-4.1•	80.3	71 22.7	-0.9•	83.3	71 28.2	+2.4•	86.2	22
70 55.3	-10.2•	74.4	71 10.0	-7.1•	77.2	71 21.8	-4.0•	80.1	71 30.6	-0.8•	83.1	23
70 45.1	-13.0•	71.4	71 02.9	-10.1•	74.2	71 17.8	-7.0•	77.0	71 29.8	-3.8•	79.9	24
70 32.1	-15.9•	68.5	70 52.8	-13.0•	71.1	71 10.8	-10.0•	73.9	71 26.0	-7.0•	76.8	25
70 16.2	-18.5•	65.6	70 39.8	-15.9•	68.2	71 00.8	-13.0•	70.9	71 19.0	-9.9•	73.7	26
69 57.7	-21.1•	62.8	70 23.9	-18.5•	65.3	70 47.8	-15.8•	67.9	71 09.1	-13.0•	70.6	27
69 36.6	-23.5•	60.1	70 05.4	-21.1•	62.5	70 32.0	-18.5•	65.0	70 56.1	-15.8•	67.6	28
69 13.1	-25.8•	57.5	69 44.3	-23.5•	59.7	70 13.5	-21.1•	62.1	70 40.3	-18.5•	64.7	29
68 47.3	-28.0•	54.9	69 20.8	-25.9•	57.1	69 52.4	-23.6•	59.4	70 21.8	-21.1•	61.8	30
68 19.3	-30.0	52.5	68 54.9	-28.0•	54.6	69 28.8	-25.9•	56.8	70 00.7	-23.7•	59.1	31
67 49.3	-31.9	50.2	68 26.9	-30.0•	52.1	69 02.9	-28.1•	54.2	69 37.0	-25.9•	56.4	32
67 17.4	-33.6	48.0	67 56.9	-32.0	49.8	68 34.8	-30.1	51.8	69 11.1	-28.2•	53.8	33
66 43.8	-35.3	45.9	67 24.9	-33.7	47.6	68 04.7	-32.0	49.4	68 42.9	-30.2	51.4	34
66 08.5	-36.7	43.8	66 51.2	-35.3	45.5	67 32.7	-33.8	47.2	68 12.7	-32.1	49.0	35
65 31.8	-38.2	41.9	66 15.9	-36.9	43.4	66 58.9	-35.5	45.0	67 40.6	-33.9	46.8	36
64 53.6	-39.5	40.1	65 39.0	-38.3	41.5	66 23.4	-36.9	43.0	67 06.7	-35.5	44.6	37
64 14.1	-40.7	38.3	65 00.7	-39.5	39.6	65 46.5	-38.4	41.1	66 31.2	-37.1	42.6	38
63 33.4	-41.8	36.6	64 21.2	-40.8	37.9	65 08.1	-39.7	39.2	65 54.1	-38.4	40.6	39
62 51.6	-42.8	35.1	63 40.4	-41.9	36.2	64 28.4	-40.8	37.4	65 15.7	-39.8	38.8	40
62 08.8	-43.7	33.5	62 58.5	-42.9	34.6	63 47.6	-42.0	35.8	64 35.9	-41.0	37.0	41
61 25.1	-44.7	32.1	62 15.6	-43.9	33.1	63 05.6	-43.1	34.2	63 54.9	-42.1	35.3	42
60 40.4	-45.5	30.7	61 31.7	-44.7	31.6	62 22.5	-43.9	32.6	63 12.8	-43.2	33.7	43
59 54.9	-46.2	29.4	60 47.0	-45.6	30.3	61 38.6	-44.9	31.2	62 29.6	-44.1	32.2	44
59 08.7	-46.9	28.1	60 01.4	-46.3	28.9	60 53.7	-45.6	29.8	61 45.5	-44.9	30.7	45
58 21.8	-47.5	26.9	59 15.1	-47.0	27.7	60 08.1	-46.4	28.5	61 00.6	-45.8	29.4	46
57 34.3	-48.2	25.8	58 28.1	-47.6	26.5	59 21.7	-47.1	27.2	60 14.8	-46.5	28.0	47
56 46.1	-48.7	24.7	57 40.5	-48.3	25.3	58 34.6	-47.8	26.0	59 28.3	-47.2	26.8	48
55 57.4	-49.2	23.6	56 52.2	-48.7	24.2	57 46.8	-48.3	24.9	58 41.1	-47.9	25.6	49
55 08.2	-49.7	22.6	56 03.5	-49.4	23.2	56 58.5	-48.9	23.8	57 53.2	-48.4	24.4	50
54 18.5	-50.2	21.6	55 14.1	-49.8	22.2	56 09.6	-49.4	22.7	57 04.8	-49.0	23.3	51
53 28.3	-50.6	20.7	54 24.3	-50.2	21.2	55 20.2	-49.9	21.7	56 15.8	-49.5	22.3	52
52 37.7	-50.9	19.8	53 34.1	-50.7	20.3	54 30.3	-50.3	20.8	55 26.3	-50.0	21.3	53
51 46.8	-51.4	19.0	52 43.4	-51.0	19.4	53 40.0	-50.8	19.8	54 36.3	-50.4	20.3	54
50 55.4	-51.6	18.1	51 52.4	-51.4	18.5	52 49.2	-51.1	18.9	53 45.9	-50.8	19.4	55
50 03.8	-52.0	17.3	51 01.0	-51.8	17.7	51 58.1	-51.5	18.1	52 55.1	-51.3	18.5	56
49 11.8	-52.3	16.6	50 09.2	-52.0	16.9	51 06.6	-51.8	17.3	52 03.8	-51.5	17.6	57
48 19.5	-52.6	15.8	49 17.2	-52.4	16.1	50 14.8	-52.2	16.5	51 12.3	-51.9	16.8	58
47 26.9	-52.8	15.1	48 24.8	-52.6	15.4	49 22.6	-52.4	15.7	50 20.4	-52.3	16.0	59
46 34.1	-53.0	14.4	47 32.2	-52.9	14.7	48 30.2	-52.7	15.0	49 28.1	-52.5	15.3	60
45 41.1	-53.3	13.7	46 39.3	-53.1	14.0	47 37.5	-53.0	14.2	48 35.6	-52.8	14.5	61
44 47.8	-53.6	13.1	45 46.2	-53.4	13.3	46 44.5	-53.2	13.6	47 42.8	-53.0	13.8	62
43 54.2	-53.7	12.4	44 52.8	-53.6	12.7	45 51.3	-53.4	12.9	46 49.8	-53.3	13.1	63
43 00.5	-53.9	11.8	43 59.2	-53.8	12.0	44 57.9	-53.7	12.2	45 56.5	-53.5	12.5	64
42 06.6	-54.1	11.2	43 05.4	-53.9	11.4	44 04.2	-53.8	11.6	45 03.0	-53.7	11.8	65
41 12.5	-54.2	10.7	42 11.5	-54.2	10.8	43 10.4	-54.0	11.0	44 09.3	-53.9	11.2	66
40 18.3	-54.4	10.1	41 17.3	-54.3	10.2	42 16.4	-54.3	10.4	43 15.4	-54.1	10.6	67
39 23.9	-54.6	9.5	40 23.0	-54.5	9.7	41 22.1	-54.3	9.8	42 21.3	-54.3	10.0	68
38 29.3	-54.7	9.0	39 28.5	-54.6	9.1	40 27.8	-54.6	9.3	41 27.0	-54.5	9.4	69
37 34.6	-54.9	8.5	38 33.9	-54.8	8.6	39 33.2	-54.7	8.7	40 32.5	-54.6	8.9	70
36 39.7	-54.9	8.0	37 39.1	-54.9	8.1	38 38.5	-54.8	8.2	39 37.9	-54.7	8.3	71
35 44.8	-55.1	7.5	36 44.2	-55.0	7.6	37 43.7	-54.9	7.7	38 43.2	-54.9	7.8	72
34 49.7	-55.2	7.0	35 49.2	-55.1	7.1	36 48.8	-55.1	7.2	37 48.3	-55.0	7.3	73
33 54.5	-55.3	6.5	34 54.1	-55.3	6.6	35 53.7	-55.2	6.7	36 53.3	-55.2	6.8	74
32 59.2	-55.4	6.1	33 58.8	-55.3	6.1	34 58.5	-55.3	6.2	35 58.1	-55.2	6.3	75
32 03.8	-55.6	5.6	33 03.5	-55.5	5.7	34 03.2	-55.5	5.7	35 02.9	-55.4	5.8	76
31 08.2	-55.6	5.2	32 08.0	-55.6	5.2	33 07.7	-55.5	5.3	34 07.5	-55.5	5.3	77
30 12.6	-55.6	4.7	31 12.4	-55.6	4.8	32 12.2	-55.6	4.8	33 12.0	-55.6	4.9	78
29 17.0	-55.8	4.3	30 16.8	-55.7	4.3	31 16.6	-55.7	4.4	32 16.4	-55.6	4.4	79
28 21.2	-55.8	3.9	29 21.1	-55.8	3.9	30 20.9	-55.8	3.9	31 20.8	-55.8	4.0	80
27 25.4	-56.0	3.5	28 25.3	-55.9	3.5	29 25.1	-55.8	3.5	30 25.0	-55.8	3.6	81
26 29.4	-55.9	3.0	27 29.4	-56.0	3.1	28 29.3	-56.0	3.1	29 29.2	-55.9	3.1	82
25 33.5	-56.1	2.6	26 33.4	-56.0	2.7	27 33.3	-56.0	2.7	28 33.3	-56.0	2.7	83
24 37.4	-56.1	2.3	25 37.4	-56.1	2.3	26 37.3	-56.0	2.3	27 37.3	-56.1	2.3	84
23 41.3	-56.1	1.9	24 41.3	-56.2	1.9	25 41.3	-56.2	1.9	26 41.2	-56.1	1.9	85
22 45.2	-56.3	1.5	23 45.1	-56.2	1.5	24 45.1	-56.2	1.5	25 45.1	-56.2	1.5	86
21 48.9	-56.2	1.1	22 48.9	-56.2	1.1	23 48.9	-56.2	1.1	24 48.9	-56.2	1.1	87
20 52.7	-56.3	0.7	21 52.7	-56.3	0.7	22 52.7	-56.3	0.7	23 52.7	-56.3	0.7	88
19 56.4	-56.4	0.4	20 56.4	-56.4	0.4	21 56.4	-56.4	0.4	22 56.4	-56.4	0.4	89
19 00.0	-56.4	0.0	20 00.0	-56.4	0.0	21 00.0	-56.4	0.0	22 00.0	-56.4	0.0	90
19°			20°			21°			22°			

LATITUDE **CONTRARY** NAME TO DECLINATION **L.H.A. 20°, 340°**

Dec.	15°			16°			17°			18°			19°			20°			21°			22°			Dec.
	Hc	d	Z	Hc	d	Z	Hc	d	Z	Hc	d	Z	Hc	d	Z	Hc	d	Z	Hc	d	Z	Hc	d	Z	
°	° ′	′	°	° ′	′	°	° ′	′	°	° ′	′	°	° ′	′	°	° ′	′	°	° ′	′	°	° ′	′	°	°
0	65 11.1	−37.6	125.4	64 35.6	−39.1	127.1	63 58.7	−40.5	128.8	63 20.5	−41.8	130.3	62 41.1	−43.1	131.8	62 00.5	−44.1	133.2	61 18.9	−45.2	134.6	60 36.4	−46.2	135.8	0
1	64 33.5	−39.0	127.2	63 56.5	−40.4	128.9	63 18.2	−41.7	130.4	62 38.7	−42.9	131.9	61 58.0	−44.0	133.3	61 16.4	−45.1	134.6	60 33.7	−46.0	135.9	59 50.2	−46.9	137.1	1
2	63 54.5	−40.2	129.0	63 16.1	−41.5	130.5	62 36.5	−42.7	132.0	61 55.8	−43.8	133.4	61 14.0	−44.8	134.7	60 31.3	−45.8	136.0	59 47.7	−46.7	137.2	59 03.3	−47.5	138.3	2
3	63 14.3	−41.3	130.7	62 34.6	−42.5	132.1	61 53.8	−43.6	133.5	61 12.0	−44.7	134.8	60 29.2	−45.7	136.1	59 45.5	−46.5	137.3	59 01.0	−47.4	138.4	58 15.8	−48.2	139.5	3
4	62 33.0	−42.4	132.3	61 52.1	−43.5	133.6	61 10.2	−44.6	135.0	60 27.3	−45.5	136.2	59 43.5	−46.3	137.4	58 59.0	−47.3	138.5	58 13.6	−48.0	139.6	57 27.6	−48.8	140.6	4
5	61 50.6	−43.3	133.8	61 08.6	−44.4	135.1	60 25.6	−45.3	136.3	59 41.8	−46.2	137.5	58 57.2	−47.1	138.7	58 11.7	−47.8	139.7	57 25.6	−48.6	140.7	56 38.8	−49.2	141.7	5
6	61 07.3	−44.2	135.2	60 24.2	−45.1	136.5	59 40.3	−46.1	137.7	58 55.6	−46.9	138.8	58 10.1	−47.7	139.8	57 23.9	−48.5	140.9	56 37.0	−49.1	141.8	55 49.6	−49.8	142.7	6
7	60 23.1	−45.0	136.6	59 39.1	−46.0	137.8	58 54.2	−46.7	138.9	58 08.7	−47.6	140.0	57 22.4	−48.3	141.0	56 35.4	−48.9	141.9	55 47.9	−49.6	142.8	54 59.8	−50.2	143.7	7
8	59 38.1	−45.8	137.9	58 53.1	−46.6	139.0	58 07.5	−47.5	140.1	57 21.1	−48.2	141.1	56 34.1	−48.9	142.1	55 46.5	−49.5	143.0	54 58.3	−50.1	143.8	54 09.6	−50.7	144.7	8
9	58 52.3	−46.5	139.2	58 06.5	−47.3	140.3	57 20.0	−48.0	141.3	56 32.9	−48.7	142.2	55 45.2	−49.3	143.1	54 57.0	−50.0	144.0	54 08.2	−50.5	144.8	53 18.9	−51.0	145.6	9
10	58 05.8	−47.2	140.4	57 19.2	−47.9	141.4	56 32.0	−48.6	142.4	55 44.2	−49.2	143.3	54 55.9	−49.8	144.1	54 07.0	−50.4	144.9	53 17.7	−50.9	145.7	52 27.9	−51.4	146.4	10
11	57 18.6	−47.7	141.6	56 31.3	−48.4	142.5	55 43.4	−49.1	143.4	54 55.0	−49.7	144.3	54 06.1	−50.3	145.1	53 16.6	−50.8	145.8	52 26.8	−51.3	146.6	51 36.5	−51.8	147.3	11
12	56 30.9	−48.4	142.7	55 42.9	−49.0	143.6	54 54.3	−49.5	144.4	54 05.3	−50.1	145.2	53 15.8	−50.7	146.0	52 25.8	−51.1	146.7	51 35.5	−51.7	147.4	50 44.7	−52.0	148.1	12
13	55 42.5	−48.8	143.7	54 53.9	−49.5	144.6	54 04.8	−50.1	145.4	53 15.2	−50.6	146.2	52 25.1	−51.0	146.9	51 34.7	−51.6	147.6	50 43.8	−51.9	148.2	49 52.7	−52.4	148.9	13
14	54 53.7	−49.4	144.8	54 04.4	−49.9	145.6	53 14.7	−50.4	146.3	52 24.6	−50.9	147.0	51 34.1	−51.5	147.7	50 43.1	−51.8	148.4	49 51.9	−52.3	149.0	49 00.3	−52.7	149.6	14
15	54 04.3	−49.8	145.7	53 14.5	−50.3	146.5	52 24.3	−50.9	147.2	51 33.7	−51.4	147.9	50 42.6	−51.7	148.6	49 51.3	−52.2	149.2	48 59.6	−52.6	149.8	48 07.6	−52.9	150.3	15
16	53 14.5	−50.2	146.7	52 24.2	−50.8	147.4	51 33.4	−51.2	148.1	50 42.3	−51.6	148.7	49 50.9	−52.1	149.3	48 59.1	−52.4	149.9	48 07.0	−52.8	150.5	47 14.7	−53.2	151.0	16
17	52 24.3	−50.6	147.6	51 33.4	−51.1	148.3	50 42.2	−51.5	148.9	49 50.7	−52.0	149.5	48 58.8	−52.3	150.1	48 06.7	−52.8	150.7	47 14.2	−53.1	151.2	46 21.5	−53.4	151.7	17
18	51 33.7	−51.1	148.5	50 42.3	−51.4	149.1	49 50.7	−51.9	149.7	48 58.7	−52.2	150.3	48 06.5	−52.6	150.8	47 13.9	−52.9	151.4	46 21.1	−53.3	151.9	45 28.1	−53.6	152.4	18
19	50 42.6	−51.3	149.3	49 50.9	−51.8	149.9	48 58.8	−52.1	150.5	48 06.5	−52.6	151.0	47 13.9	−52.9	151.6	46 21.0	−53.2	152.1	45 27.8	−53.5	152.5	44 34.5	−53.8	153.0	19
20	49 51.3	−51.7	150.1	48 59.1	−52.1	150.7	48 06.7	−52.5	151.2	47 13.9	−52.8	151.8	46 21.0	−53.2	152.3	45 27.8	−53.5	152.7	44 34.3	−53.7	153.2	43 40.7	−54.1	153.6	20
21	48 59.6	−52.0	150.9	48 07.0	−52.3	151.4	47 14.2	−52.7	151.9	46 21.1	−53.0	152.4	45 27.8	−53.3	152.9	44 34.3	−53.6	153.4	43 40.6	−54.0	153.8	42 46.6	−54.2	154.2	21
22	48 07.6	−52.3	151.6	47 14.7	−52.6	152.2	46 21.5	−52.9	152.6	45 28.1	−53.3	153.1	44 34.5	−53.6	153.6	43 40.7	−53.9	154.0	42 46.6	−54.1	154.4	41 52.4	−54.3	154.8	22
23	47 15.3	−52.5	152.4	46 22.1	−52.9	152.9	45 28.6	−53.2	153.3	44 34.8	−53.4	153.8	43 40.9	−53.7	154.2	42 46.8	−54.0	154.6	41 52.5	−54.3	155.0	40 58.1	−54.6	155.4	23
24	46 22.8	−52.8	153.1	45 29.2	−53.1	153.5	44 35.4	−53.4	154.0	43 41.4	−53.7	154.4	42 47.2	−54.0	154.8	41 52.8	−54.2	155.2	40 58.2	−54.4	155.6	40 03.5	−54.6	155.9	24
25	45 30.0	−53.0	153.8	44 36.1	−53.3	154.2	43 42.0	−53.6	154.6	42 47.7	−53.9	155.0	41 53.2	−54.1	155.4	40 58.6	−54.4	155.8	40 03.8	−54.6	156.1	39 08.9	−54.9	156.4	25
26	44 37.0	−53.3	154.4	43 42.8	−53.6	154.8	42 48.4	−53.8	155.2	41 53.8	−54.1	155.6	40 59.1	−54.3	156.0	40 04.2	−54.5	156.3	39 09.2	−54.8	156.6	38 14.0	−54.9	157.0	26
27	43 43.7	−53.5	155.1	42 49.2	−53.7	155.5	41 54.6	−54.0	155.8	40 59.7	−54.2	156.2	40 04.8	−54.5	156.5	39 09.7	−54.7	156.9	38 14.4	−54.8	157.2	37 19.1	−55.1	157.5	27
28	42 50.2	−53.6	155.7	41 55.5	−53.9	156.1	41 00.6	−54.2	156.4	40 05.5	−54.4	156.7	39 10.3	−54.6	157.1	38 15.0	−54.8	157.4	37 19.6	−55.1	157.7	36 24.0	−55.2	158.0	28
29	41 56.6	−53.9	156.3	41 01.6	−54.1	156.6	40 06.4	−54.3	157.0	39 11.1	−54.5	157.3	38 15.7	−54.7	157.6	37 20.2	−55.0	157.9	36 24.5	−55.1	158.2	35 28.8	−55.3	158.4	29
30	41 02.7	−54.0	156.9	40 07.5	−54.3	157.2	39 12.1	−54.5	157.5	38 16.6	−54.7	157.8	37 21.0	−54.9	158.1	36 25.2	−55.0	158.4	35 29.4	−55.2	158.7	34 33.5	−55.5	158.9	30
31	40 08.7	−54.2	157.4	39 13.2	−54.4	157.8	38 17.6	−54.6	158.1	37 21.9	−54.8	158.4	36 26.1	−55.0	158.6	35 30.2	−55.2	158.9	34 34.2	−55.4	159.1	33 38.0	−55.5	159.4	31
32	39 14.5	−54.3	158.0	38 18.8	−54.5	158.3	37 23.0	−54.7	158.6	36 27.1	−54.9	158.9	35 31.1	−55.1	159.1	34 35.0	−55.3	159.4	33 38.8	−55.5	159.6	32 42.5	−55.6	159.8	32
33	38 20.2	−54.5	158.5	37 24.3	−54.7	158.8	36 28.3	−54.9	159.1	35 32.2	−55.1	159.4	34 36.0	−55.2	159.6	33 39.7	−55.4	159.8	32 43.3	−55.5	160.1	31 46.9	−55.7	160.3	33
34	37 25.7	−54.6	159.1	36 29.6	−54.8	159.3	35 33.4	−55.0	159.6	34 37.1	−55.2	159.8	33 40.8	−55.4	160.1	32 44.3	−55.5	160.3	31 47.8	−55.7	160.5	30 51.2	−55.8	160.7	34
35	36 31.1	−54.8	159.6	35 34.8	−55.0	159.9	34 38.4	−55.1	160.1	33 41.9	−55.2	160.3	32 45.4	−55.4	160.5	31 48.8	−55.6	160.7	30 52.1	−55.7	160.9	29 55.4	−55.9	161.1	35
36	35 36.3	−54.9	160.1	34 39.8	−55.0	160.3	33 43.3	−55.2	160.6	32 46.7	−55.4	160.8	31 50.0	−55.6	161.0	30 53.2	−55.7	161.2	29 56.4	−55.8	161.4	28 59.5	−56.0	161.6	36
37	34 41.4	−55.0	160.6	33 44.8	−55.2	160.8	32 48.1	−55.3	161.0	31 51.3	−55.5	161.2	30 54.4	−55.6	161.4	29 57.5	−55.7	161.6	29 00.6	−55.9	161.8	28 03.5	−56.0	162.0	37
38	33 46.4	−55.1	161.1	32 49.6	−55.3	161.3	31 52.8	−55.5	161.5	30 55.8	−55.5	161.7	29 58.8	−55.7	161.9	29 01.8	−55.9	162.0	28 04.7	−56.0	162.2	27 07.5	−56.1	162.4	38
39	32 51.3	−55.2	161.6	31 54.3	−55.3	161.8	30 57.3	−55.5	161.9	30 00.3	−55.7	162.1	29 03.1	−55.8	162.3	28 05.9	−55.9	162.5	27 08.7	−56.0	162.6	26 11.4	−56.1	162.8	39
40	31 56.1	−55.3	162.0	30 59.0	−55.5	162.2	30 01.8	−55.6	162.4	29 04.6	−55.7	162.6	28 07.3	−55.8	162.7	27 10.0	−56.0	162.9	26 12.7	−56.1	163.0	25 15.3	−56.3	163.2	40
41	31 00.8	−55.4	162.5	30 03.5	−55.5	162.6	29 06.2	−55.6	162.8	28 08.9	−55.8	163.0	27 11.5	−55.9	163.1	26 14.0	−56.0	163.3	25 16.6	−56.2	163.4	24 19.0	−56.2	163.5	41
42	30 05.4	−55.5	162.9	29 08.0	−55.6	163.1	28 10.6	−55.8	163.2	27 13.1	−55.9	163.4	26 15.6	−56.0	163.5	25 18.0	−56.1	163.7	24 20.4	−56.2	163.8	23 22.8	−56.4	163.9	42
43	29 09.9	−55.6	163.4	28 12.4	−55.8	163.5	27 14.8	−55.8	163.7	26 17.2	−55.9	163.8	25 19.6	−56.1	163.9	24 21.9	−56.2	164.1	23 24.2	−56.3	164.2	22 26.4	−56.4	164.3	43
44	28 14.3	−55.7	163.8	27 16.6	−55.7	163.9	26 19.0	−55.9	164.1	25 21.3	−56.1	164.2	24 23.5	−56.1	164.3	23 25.7	−56.2	164.4	22 27.9	−56.3	164.6	21 30.0	−56.4	164.7	44
45	27 18.6	−55.7	164.2	26 20.9	−55.9	164.3	25 23.1	−56.0	164.5	24 25.2	−56.0	164.6	23 27.4	−56.2	164.7	22 29.5	−56.3	164.8	21 31.6	−56.4	164.9	20 33.6	−56.5	165.0	45
46	26 22.9	−55.8	164.6	25 25.0	−55.9	164.7	24 27.1	−56.0	164.9	23 29.2	−56.2	165.0	22 31.2	−56.2	165.1	21 33.2	−56.3	165.2	20 35.2	−56.4	165.3	19 37.1	−56.5	165.4	46
47	25 27.1	−55.9	165.0	24 29.1	−56.0	165.1	23 31.1	−56.1	165.3	22 33.0	−56.1	165.4	21 35.0	−56.3	165.5	20 36.9	−56.4	165.6	19 38.8	−56.5	165.7	18 40.6	−56.5	165.7	47
48	24 31.2	−55.9	165.4	23 33.1	−56.0	165.5	22 35.0	−56.1	165.6	21 36.9	−56.3	165.7	20 38.7	−56.3	165.8	19 40.5	−56.4	165.9	18 42.3	−56.5	166.0	17 44.1	−56.6	166.1	48
49	23 35.3	−56.0	165.8	22 37.1	−56.1	165.9	21 38.9	−56.2	166.0	20 40.6	−56.2	166.1	19 42.4	−56.4	166.2	18 44.1	−56.5	166.3	17 45.8	−56.6	166.4	16 47.5	−56.7	166.4	49
50	22 39.3	−56.1	166.2	21 41.0	−56.2	166.3	20 42.7	−56.3	166.4	19 44.4	−56.4	166.5	18 46.0	−56.4	166.6	17 47.6	−56.5	166.7	16 49.2	−56.5	166.7	15 50.8	−56.6	166.8	50
51	21 43.2	−56.1	166.6	20 44.8	−56.1	166.7	19 46.4	−56.2	166.8	18 48.0	−56.3	166.9	17 49.6	−56.5	166.9	16 51.1	−56.5	167.0	15 52.7	−56.7	167.1	14 54.2	−56.7	167.1	51
52	20 47.1	−56.1	167.0	19 48.7	−56.3	167.1	18 50.2	−56.4	167.1	17 51.7	−56.4	167.2	16 53.1	−56.5	167.3	15 54.6	−56.6	167.4	14 56.0	−56.6	167.4	13 57.5	−56.7	167.5	52
53	19 51.0	−56.2	167.4	18 52.4	−56.3	167.4	17 53.8	−56.3	167.5	16 55.3	−56.5	167.6	15 56.6	−56.5	167.6	14 58.0	−56.6	167.7	13 59.4	−56.7	167.8	13 00.8	−56.8	167.8	53
54	18 54.8	−56.3	167.7	17 56.1	−56.3	167.8	16 57.5	−56.4	167.9	15 58.8	−56.5	167.9	15 00.1	−56.5	168.0	14 01.4	−56.6	168.0	13 02.7	−56.7	168.1	12 04.0	−56.7	168.1	54
55	17 58.5	−56.3	168.1	16 59.8	−56.4	168.2	16 01.1	−56.5	168.2	15 02.3	−56.5	168.3	14 03.6	−56.6	168.3	13 04.8	−56.6	168.4	12 06.0	−56.7	168.4	11 07.3	−56.8	168.5	55
56	17 02.2	−56.3	168.5	16 03.4	−56.4	168.5	15 04.6	−56.4	168.6	14 05.8	−56.5	168.6	13 07.0	−56.6	168.7	12 08.2	−56.7	168.7	11 09.3	−56.7	168.8	10 10.5	−56.9	168.8	56
57	16 05.9	−56.3	168.8	15 07.0	−56.4	168.9	14 08.2	−56.5	168.9	13 09.3	−56.6	169.0	12 10.4	−56.6	169.0	11 11.5	−56.7	169.1	10 12.6	−56.8	169.1	9 13.6	−56.8	169.1	57
58	15 09.6	−56.4	169.2	14 10.6	−56.4	169.2	13 11.7	−56.6	169.3	12 12.7	−56.6	169.3	11 13.8	−56.7	169.4	10 14.8	−56.7	169.4	9 15.8	−56.8	169.4	8 16.8	−56.8	169.4	58
59	14 13.2	−56.5	169.5	13 14.2	−56.5	169.6	12 15.1	−56.5	169.6	11 16.1	−56.6	169.7	10 17.1	−56.7	169.7	9 18.1	−56.8	169.7	8 19.0	−56.8	169.7	7 20.0	−56.9	169.8	59
60	13 16.7	−56.4	169.9	12 17.7	−56.5	169.9	11 18.6	−56.6	170.0	10 19.5	−56.6	170.0	9 20.4	−56.7	170.0	8 21.3	−56.7	170.0	7 22.2	−56.8	170.1	6 23.1	−56.8	170.1	60
61	12 20.3	−56.5	170.2	11 21.2	−56.6	170.3	10 22.0	−56.6	170.3	9 22.9	−56.7	170.3	8 23.7	−56.7	170.4	7 24.6	−56.8	170.4	6 25.4	−56.8	170.4	5 26.3	−56.9	170.4	61
62	11 23.8	−56.5	170.6	10 24.6	−56.5	170.6	9 25.4	−56.6	170.6	8 26.2	−56.7	170.7	7 27.0	−56.7	170.7	6 27.8	−56.8	170.7	5 28.6	−56.8	170.7	4 29.4	−56.9	170.7	62
63	10 27.3	−56.5	170.9	9 28.1	−56.6	170.9	8 28.8	−56.6	171.0	7 29.5	−56.6	171.0	6 30.3	−56.8	171.0	5 31.0	−56.8	171.0	4 31.8	−56.9	171.0	3 32.5	−56.9	171.1	63
64	9 30.8	−56.6	171.3	8 31.5	−56.6	171.3	7 32.2	−56.7	171.3	6 32.9	−56.7	171.3	5 33.5	−56.7	171.3	4 34.2	−56.8	171.3	3 34.9	−56.8	171.4	2 35.6	−56.9	171.4	64
65	8 34.2	−56.5	171.6	7 34.9	−56.6	171.6	6 35.5	−56.6	171.6	5 36.2	−56.7	171.6	4 36.8	−56.8	171.7	3 37.4	−56.8	171.7	2 38.1	−56.9	171.7	1 38.7	−56.9	171.7	65
66	7 37.7	−56.6	171.9	6 38.3	−56.7	171.9	5 38.9	−56.7	172.0	4 39.5	−56.8	172.0	3 40.0	−56.7	172.0	2 40.6	−56.8	172.0	1 41.2	−56.8	172.0	0 41.8	−56.9	172.0	66
67	6 41.1	−56.6	172.3	5 41.6	−56.6	172.3	4 42.2	−56.7	172.3	3 42.7	−56.7	172.3	2 43.3	−56.8	172.3	1 43.8	−56.8	172.3	0 44.4	−56.9	172.3	0 15.1	+56.9	7.7	67
68	5 44.5	−56.6	172.6	4 45.0	−56.6	172.6	3 45.5	−56.7	172.6	2 46.0	−56.7	172.6	1 46.5	−56.8	172.6	0 47.0	−56.8	172.6	0 12.5	+56.9	7.4	1 12.0	+56.9	7.4	68
69	4 47.9	−56.6	172.9	3 48.4	−56.7	172.9	2 48.8	−56.7	173.0	1 49.3	−56.8	173.0	0 49.7	−56.7	173.0	0 09.8	+56.8	7.0	1 09.4	+56.8	7.0	2 08.9	+56.9	7.0	69
70	3 51.3	−56.6	173.3	2 51.7	−56.6	173.3	1 52.1	−56.7	173.3	0 52.5	−56.7	173.3	0 07.0	+56.8	6.7	1 06.6	+56.9	6.7	2 06.2	+56.9	6.7	3 05.8	+56.9	6.7	70
71	2 54.7	−56.6	173.6	1 55.1	−56.7	173.6	0 55.4	−56.7	173.6	0 04.2	+56.7	6.4	1 03.8	+56.8	6.4	2 03.5	+56.8	6.4	3 03.1	+56.8	6.4	4 02.7	+56.9	6.4	71
72	1 58.1	−56.7	173.9	0 58.4	−56.7	173.9	0 01.3	+56.7	6.1	1 00.9	+56.8	6.1	2 00.6	+56.8	6.1	3 00.3	+56.8	6.1	3 59.9	+56.9	6.1	4 59.6	+56.9	6.1	72
73	1 01.4	−56.6	174.3	0 01.7	−56.6	174.3	0 58.0	+56.7	5.7	1 57.7	+56.7	5.7	2 57.4	+56.7	5.7	3 57.1	+56.8	5.8	4 56.8	+56.8	5.8	5 56.5	+56.8	5.8	73
74	0 04.8	−56.6	174.6	0 54.9	+56.7	5.4	1 54.7	+56.7	5.4	2 54.4	+56.7	5.4	3 54.1	+56.8	5.4	4 53.9	+56.7	5.4	5 53.6	+56.8	5.4	6 53.3	+56.9	5.4	74
75	0 51.8	+56.7	5.1	1 51.6	+56.6	5.1	2 51.4	+56.6	5.1	3 51.1	+56.7	5.1	4 50.9	+56.7	5.1	5 50.6	+56.8	5.1	6 50.4	+56.8	5.1	7 50.2	+56.8	5.1	75
76	1 48.5	+56.6	4.7	2 48.3	+56.6	4.8	3 48.0	+56.7	4.8	4 47.8	+56.8	4.8	5 47.6	+56.8	4.8	6 47.4	+56.8	4.8	7 47.2	+56.8	4.8	8 47.0	+56.8	4.8	76
77	2 45.1	+56.6	4.4	3 44.9	+56.7	4.4	4 44.7	+56.7	4.4	5 44.6	+56.6	4.4	6 44.4	+56.8	4.4	7 44.2	+56.8	4.5	8 44.0	+56.8	4.5	9 43.8	+56.8	4.5	77
78	3 41.7	+56.6	4.1	4 41.6	+56.6	4.1	5 41.4	+56.7	4.1	6 41.2	+56.7	4.1	7 41.1	+56.7	4.1	8 40.9	+56.8	4.1	9 40.8	+56.7	4.1	10 40.6	+56.8	4.1	78
79	4 38.3	+56.6	3.8	5 38.2	+56.6	3.8	6 38.1	+56.6	3.8	7 37.9	+56.7	3.8	8 37.8	+56.7	3.8	9 37.7	+56.7	3.8	10 37.5	+56.8	3.8	11 37.4	+56.8	3.8	79
80	5 34.9	+56.6	3.4	6 34.8	+56.6	3.4	7 34.7	+56.6	3.4	8 34.6	+56.7	3.4	9 34.5	+56.7	3.5	10 34.4	+56.7	3.5	11 34.3	+56.7	3.5	12 34.2	+56.7	3.5	80
81	6 31.5	+56.6	3.1	7 31.4	+56.6	3.1	8 31.3	+56.7	3.1	9 31.3	+56.6	3.1	10 31.2	+56.6	3.1	11 31.1	+56.6	3.1	12 31.0	+56.7	3.1	13 30.9	+56.7	3.2	81
82	7 28.1	+56.6	2.8	8 28.0	+56.6	2.8	9 28.0	+56.6	2.8	10 27.9	+56.6	2.8	11 27.8	+56.6	2.8	12 27.7	+56.7	2.8	13 27.7	+56.6	2.8	14 27.6	+56.7	2.8	82
83	8 24.7	+56.5	2.4	9 24.6	+56.6	2.4	10 24.6	+56.5	2.4	11 24.5	+56.6	2.4	12 24.4	+56.6	2.4	13 24.4	+56.6	2.5	14 24.3	+56.7	2.5	15 24.3	+56.6	2.5	83
84	9 21.2	+56.5	2.1	10 21.2	+56.5	2.1	11 21.1	+56.5	2.1	12 21.1	+56.5	2.1	13 21.0	+56.6	2.1	14 21.0	+56.6	2.1	15 21.0	+56.6	2.1	16 20.9	+56.6	2.1	84
85	10 17.7	+56.5	1.7	11 17.7	+56.5	1.7	12 17.7	+56.5	1.7	13 17.6	+56.6	1.8	14 17.6	+56.6	1.8	15 17.6	+56.5	1.8	16 17.6	+56.5	1.8	17 17.5	+56.6	1.8	85
86	11 14.2	+56.5	1.4	12 14.2	+56.5	1.4	13 14.2	+56.5	1.4	14 14.2	+56.5	1.4	15 14.2	+56.5	1.4	16 14.1	+56.6	1.4	17 14.1	+56.6	1.4	18 14.1	+56.5	1.4	86
87	12 10.7	+56.5	1.0	13 10.7	+56.5	1.1	14 10.7	+56.5	1.1	15 10.7	+56.5	1.1	16 10.7	+56.5	1.1	17 10.7	+56.5	1.1	18 10.7	+56.4	1.1	19 10.6	+56.5	1.1	87
88	13 07.2	+56.4	0.7	14 07.2	+56.4	0.7	15 07.2	+56.4	0.7	16 07.2	+56.4	0.7	17 07.2	+56.4	0.7	18 07.2	+56.4	0.7	19 07.1	+56.5	0.7	20 07.1	+56.5	0.7	88
89	14 03.6	+56.4	0.4	15 03.6	+56.4	0.4	16 03.6	+56.4	0.4	17 03.6	+56.4	0.4	18 03.6	+56.4	0.4	19 03.6	+56.4	0.4	20 03.6	+56.4	0.4	21 03.6	+56.4	0.4	89
90	15 00.0	+56.4	0.0	16 00.0	+56.4	0.0	17 00.0	+56.4	0.0	18 00.0	+56.4	0.0	19 00.0	+56.4	0.0	20 00.0	+56.4	0.0	21 00.0	+56.4	0.0	22 00.0	+56.4	0.0	90
	15°			16°			17°			18°			19°			20°			21°			22°			

S. Lat. {L.H.A. greater than 180° ....Zn=180°−Z
{L.H.A. less than 180°...........Zn=180°+Z

LATITUDE SAME NAME AS DECLINATION **L.H.A. 160°, 200°**

Dec.	15° Hc	15° d	15° Z	16° Hc	16° d	16° Z	17° Hc	17° d	17° Z	18° Hc	18° d	18° Z	19° Hc	19° d	19° Z	20° Hc	20° d	20° Z	21° Hc	21° d	21° Z	22° Hc	22° d	22° Z	Dec.
°	° ′	′	°	° ′	′	°	° ′	′	°	° ′	′	°	° ′	′	°	° ′	′	°	° ′	′	°	° ′	′	°	°
0	64 23.5	+35.2	124.0	63 49.2	+36.8	125.7	63 13.5	+38.4	127.3	62 36.5	+39.8	128.8	61 58.3	+41.1	130.3	61 18.9	+42.3	131.7	60 38.5	+43.4	133.0	59 57.1	+44.5	134.3	0
1	64 58.7	+33.7	122.1	64 26.0	+35.5	123.9	63 51.9	+37.0	125.6	63 16.3	+38.5	127.2	62 39.4	+39.9	128.7	62 01.2	+41.3	130.2	61 21.9	+42.5	131.6	60 41.6	+43.6	132.9	1
2	65 32.4	+32.1	120.1	65 01.5	+33.9	122.0	64 28.9	+35.6	123.8	63 54.8	+37.3	125.5	63 19.3	+38.8	127.1	62 42.5	+40.1	128.6	62 04.4	+41.5	130.1	61 25.2	+42.7	131.5	2
3	66 04.5	+30.4	118.1	65 35.4	+32.3	120.0	65 04.5	+34.2	121.9	64 32.1	+35.8	123.7	63 58.1	+37.4	125.4	63 22.6	+39.0	127.0	62 45.9	+40.4	128.6	62 07.9	+41.7	130.0	3
4	66 34.9	+28.5	115.9	66 07.7	+30.6	117.9	65 38.7	+32.6	119.9	65 07.9	+34.4	121.8	64 35.5	+36.1	123.6	64 01.6	+37.7	125.3	63 26.3	+39.2	126.9	62 49.6	+40.6	128.5	4
5	67 03.4	+26.6	113.7	66 38.3	+28.8	115.8	66 11.3	+30.8	117.8	65 42.3	+32.8	119.8	65 11.6	+34.7	121.7	64 39.3	+36.4	123.5	64 05.5	+37.9	125.2	63 30.2	+39.4	126.9	5
6	67 30.0	+24.6•	111.4	67 07.1	+26.8•	113.6	66 42.1	+29.0	115.7	66 15.1	+31.1	117.7	65 46.3	+33.0	119.7	65 15.7	+34.8	121.6	64 43.4	+36.6	123.4	64 09.6	+38.2	125.1	6
7	67 54.6	+22.3•	108.9	67 33.9	+24.8•	111.2	67 11.1	+27.1•	113.5	66 46.2	+29.3	115.6	66 19.3	+31.3	117.7	65 50.5	+33.3	119.6	65 20.0	+35.1	121.5	64 47.8	+36.8	123.4	7
8	68 16.9	+20.0•	106.5	67 58.7	+22.6•	108.8	67 38.2	+25.0•	111.1	67 15.5	+27.3•	113.4	66 50.6	+29.6	115.5	66 23.8	+31.6	117.6	65 55.1	+33.5	119.6	65 24.6	+35.4	121.5	8
9	68 36.9	+17.7•	103.9	68 21.3	+20.3•	106.3	68 03.2	+22.8•	108.7	67 42.8	+25.3•	111.0	67 20.2	+27.5•	113.3	66 55.4	+29.8	115.4	66 28.6	+31.9	117.5	66 00.0	+33.8	119.5	9
10	68 54.6	+15.1•	101.3	68 41.6	+17.8•	103.8	68 26.0	+20.6•	106.2	68 08.1	+23.0•	108.6	67 47.7	+25.6•	111.0	67 25.2	+27.8•	113.2	67 00.5	+30.0	115.4	66 33.8	+32.1	117.5	10
11	69 09.7	+12.5•	98.5	68 59.4	+15.4•	101.1	68 46.6	+18.1•	103.7	68 31.1	+20.8•	106.1	68 13.3	+23.3•	108.5	67 53.0	+25.8•	110.9	67 30.5	+28.1	113.1	67 05.9	+30.3	115.3	11
12	69 22.2	+9.8•	95.8	69 14.8	+12.7•	98.4	69 04.7	+15.5•	101.0	68 51.9	+18.4•	103.5	68 36.6	+21.0•	106.0	68 18.8	+23.6•	108.5	67 58.6	+26.1•	110.8	67 36.2	+28.4•	113.1	12
13	69 32.0	+7.1•	93.0	69 27.5	+10.1•	95.6	69 20.2	+13.0•	98.3	69 10.3	+15.8•	100.9	68 57.6	+18.6•	103.4	68 42.4	+21.3•	105.9	68 24.7	+23.8•	108.4	68 04.6	+26.3•	110.7	13
14	69 39.1	+4.3•	90.1	69 37.6	+7.3•	92.8	69 33.2	+10.3•	95.5	69 26.1	+13.2•	98.2	69 16.2	+16.1•	100.8	69 03.7	+18.8•	103.3	68 48.5	+21.6•	105.9	68 30.9	+24.1•	108.3	14
15	69 43.4	+1.5•	87.3	69 44.9	+4.4•	90.0	69 43.5	+7.5•	92.7	69 39.3	+10.5•	95.4	69 32.3	+13.4•	98.0	69 22.5	+16.3•	100.7	69 10.1	+19.1•	103.3	68 55.0	+21.8•	105.8	15
16	69 44.9	−1.4•	84.4	69 49.3	+1.7•	87.1	69 51.0	+4.6•	89.8	69 49.8	+7.7•	92.5	69 45.7	+10.7•	95.2	69 38.8	+13.7•	97.9	69 29.2	+16.5•	100.6	69 16.8	+19.4•	103.2	16
17	69 43.5	−4.2•	81.5	69 51.0	−1.2•	84.2	69 55.6	+1.9•	86.9	69 57.5	+4.8•	89.6	69 56.4	+7.9•	92.4	69 52.5	+10.9•	95.1	69 45.7	+13.9•	97.8	69 36.2	+16.8•	100.5	17
18	69 39.3	−7.0•	78.6	69 49.8	−4.1•	81.3	69 57.5	−1.1•	84.0	70 02.3	+2.0•	86.7	70 04.3	+5.1•	89.5	70 03.4	+8.1•	92.2	69 59.6	+11.2•	95.0	69 53.0	+14.1•	97.7	18
19	69 32.3	−9.8•	75.8	69 45.7	−6.9•	78.4	69 56.4	−3.9•	81.1	70 04.3	−0.9•	83.8	70 09.4	+2.1•	86.5	70 11.5	+5.3•	89.3	70 10.8	+8.3•	92.1	70 07.1	+11.4•	94.9	19
20	69 22.5	−12.4•	72.9	69 38.8	−9.6•	75.5	69 52.5	−6.8•	78.2	70 03.4	−3.8•	80.9	70 11.5	−0.7•	83.6	70 16.8	+2.3•	86.4	70 19.1	+5.4•	89.2	70 18.5	+8.6•	92.0	20
21	69 10.1	−15.1•	70.2	69 29.2	−12.4•	72.7	69 45.7	−9.5•	75.3	69 59.6	−6.6•	77.9	70 10.8	−3.7•	80.6	70 19.1	−0.6•	83.4	70 24.5	+2.6•	86.2	70 27.1	+5.6•	89.0	21
22	68 55.0	−17.5•	67.5	69 16.8	−14.9•	69.9	69 36.2	−12.3•	72.4	69 53.0	−9.4•	75.0	70 07.1	−6.5•	77.7	70 18.5	−3.5•	80.4	70 27.1	−0.5•	83.2	70 32.7	+2.7•	86.0	22
23	68 37.5	−20.0•	64.8	69 01.9	−17.5•	67.2	69 23.9	−14.9•	69.6	69 43.6	−12.2•	72.2	70 00.6	−9.3•	74.8	70 15.0	−6.4•	77.5	70 26.6	−3.4•	80.2	70 35.4	−0.3•	83.0	23
24	68 17.5	−22.3•	62.3	68 44.4	−20.0•	64.5	69 09.0	−17.4•	66.9	69 31.4	−14.8•	69.4	69 51.3	−12.1•	71.9	70 08.6	−9.2•	74.5	70 23.2	−6.3•	77.2	70 35.1	−3.3•	80.0	24
25	67 55.2	−24.4•	59.8	68 24.4	−22.2•	62.0	68 51.6	−19.9•	64.2	69 16.6	−17.4•	66.6	69 39.2	−14.8•	69.1	69 59.4	−12.1•	71.6	70 16.9	−9.1•	74.3	70 31.8	−6.2•	77.0	25
26	67 30.8	−26.6•	57.4	68 02.2	−24.5•	59.5	68 31.7	−22.2•	61.6	68 59.2	−19.9•	63.9	69 24.4	−17.4•	66.3	69 47.3	−14.7•	68.8	70 07.8	−12.0•	71.4	70 25.6	−9.1•	74.0	26
27	67 04.2	−28.5	55.0	67 37.7	−26.5•	57.0	68 09.5	−24.5•	59.1	68 39.3	−22.2•	61.3	69 07.0	−19.8•	63.6	69 32.6	−17.4•	66.0	69 55.8	−14.7•	68.5	70 16.5	−11.9•	71.1	27
28	66 35.7	−30.3	52.8	67 11.2	−28.5	54.7	67 45.0	−26.5•	56.7	68 17.1	−24.5•	58.8	68 47.2	−22.2•	61.0	69 15.2	−19.8•	63.3	69 41.1	−17.3•	65.7	70 04.6	−14.7•	68.2	28
29	66 05.4	−32.1	50.7	66 42.7	−30.3	52.4	67 18.5	−28.5	54.3	67 52.6	−26.5•	56.3	68 25.0	−24.5•	58.4	68 55.4	−22.2•	60.6	69 23.8	−19.9•	63.0	69 49.9	−17.3•	65.4	29
30	65 33.3	−33.6	48.6	66 12.4	−32.1	50.3	66 50.0	−30.4	52.1	67 26.1	−28.6	54.0	68 00.5	−26.6•	56.0	68 33.2	−24.5•	58.1	69 03.9	−22.2•	60.3	69 32.6	−19.9•	62.6	30
31	64 59.7	−35.2	46.6	65 40.3	−33.7	48.2	66 19.6	−32.1	49.9	66 57.5	−30.4	51.7	67 33.9	−28.5	53.6	68 08.7	−26.6•	55.6	68 41.7	−24.5•	57.7	69 12.7	−22.2•	59.9	31
32	64 24.5	−36.6	44.7	65 06.6	−35.2	46.2	65 47.5	−33.7	47.8	66 27.1	−32.1	49.5	67 05.4	−30.5	51.3	67 42.1	−28.7	53.2	68 17.2	−26.7•	55.2	68 50.5	−24.6•	57.3	32
33	63 47.9	−37.8	42.9	64 31.4	−36.6	44.3	65 13.8	−35.3	45.8	65 55.0	−33.8	47.4	66 34.9	−32.2	49.1	67 13.4	−30.5	50.9	67 50.5	−28.7	52.8	68 25.9	−26.7•	54.8	33
34	63 10.1	−39.1	41.2	63 54.8	−38.0	42.5	64 38.5	−36.7	43.9	65 21.2	−35.4	45.4	66 02.7	−33.9	47.0	66 42.9	−32.3	48.7	67 21.8	−30.6	50.5	67 59.2	−28.8•	52.4	34
35	62 31.0	−40.3	39.5	63 16.8	−39.1	40.8	64 01.8	−38.0	42.1	64 45.8	−36.7	43.5	65 28.8	−35.4	45.0	66 10.6	−33.9	46.6	66 51.2	−32.4	48.3	67 30.4	−30.7	50.1	35
36	61 50.7	−41.3	37.9	62 37.7	−40.3	39.1	63 23.8	−39.2	40.3	64 09.1	−38.1	41.7	64 53.4	−36.8	43.1	65 36.7	−35.5	44.6	66 18.8	−34.0	46.2	66 59.7	−32.4	47.9	36
37	61 09.4	−42.2	36.4	61 57.4	−41.4	37.5	62 44.6	−40.3	38.7	63 31.0	−39.2	39.9	64 16.6	−38.1	41.3	65 01.2	−36.9	42.7	65 44.8	−35.5	44.2	66 27.3	−34.1	45.8	37
38	60 27.2	−43.2	34.9	61 16.0	−42.3	36.0	62 04.3	−41.5	37.1	62 51.8	−40.5	38.3	63 38.5	−39.4	39.5	64 24.3	−38.2	40.8	65 09.3	−37.0	42.2	65 53.2	−35.7	43.7	38
39	59 44.0	−44.0	33.5	60 33.7	−43.2	34.5	61 22.8	−42.4	35.6	62 11.3	−41.5	36.7	62 59.1	−40.5	37.8	63 46.1	−39.5	39.1	64 32.3	−38.4	40.4	65 17.5	−37.1	41.8	39
40	59 00.0	−44.9	32.2	59 50.5	−44.1	33.1	60 40.4	−43.3	34.1	61 29.8	−42.4	35.1	62 18.6	−41.6	36.2	63 06.6	−40.6	37.4	63 53.9	−39.5	38.6	64 40.4	−38.5	39.9	40
41	58 15.1	−45.5	30.9	59 06.4	−44.9	31.8	59 57.1	−44.1	32.7	60 47.4	−43.4	33.7	61 37.0	−42.6	34.7	62 26.0	−41.7	35.8	63 14.4	−40.8	36.9	64 01.9	−39.6	38.1	41
42	57 29.6	−46.2	29.7	58 21.5	−45.6	30.5	59 13.0	−45.0	31.4	60 04.0	−44.3	32.3	60 54.4	−43.4	33.2	61 44.3	−42.6	34.2	62 33.6	−41.7	35.3	63 22.3	−40.9	36.5	42
43	56 43.4	−46.9	28.5	57 35.9	−46.3	29.3	58 28.0	−45.7	30.1	59 19.7	−45.0	30.9	60 11.0	−44.4	31.8	61 01.7	−43.6	32.8	61 51.9	−42.8	33.8	62 41.4	−41.9	34.8	43
44	55 56.5	−47.4	27.4	56 49.6	−46.9	28.1	57 42.3	−46.3	28.8	58 34.7	−45.8	29.6	59 26.6	−45.1	30.5	60 18.1	−44.4	31.4	61 09.1	−43.7	32.3	61 59.5	−42.8	33.3	44
45	55 09.1	−48.1	26.3	56 02.7	−47.5	27.0	56 56.0	−47.0	27.7	57 48.9	−46.4	28.4	58 41.5	−45.8	29.2	59 33.7	−45.2	30.0	60 25.4	−44.5	30.9	61 16.7	−43.8	31.8	45
46	54 21.0	−48.5	25.3	55 15.2	−48.1	25.9	56 09.0	−47.6	26.5	57 02.5	−47.1	27.2	57 55.7	−46.5	28.0	58 48.5	−46.0	28.7	59 40.9	−45.3	29.5	60 32.9	−44.7	30.4	46
47	53 32.5	−49.0	24.3	54 27.1	−48.6	24.9	55 21.4	−48.1	25.5	56 15.4	−47.6	26.1	57 09.2	−47.2	26.8	58 02.5	−46.6	27.5	58 55.6	−46.1	28.3	59 48.2	−45.4	29.1	47
48	52 43.5	−49.4	23.3	53 38.5	−49.1	23.9	54 33.3	−48.7	24.4	55 27.8	−48.3	25.0	56 22.0	−47.8	25.7	57 15.9	−47.2	26.3	58 09.5	−46.7	27.0	59 02.8	−46.2	27.8	48
49	51 54.1	−49.9	22.4	52 49.4	−49.5	22.9	53 44.6	−49.1	23.4	54 39.5	−48.7	24.0	55 34.2	−48.3	24.6	56 28.7	−47.9	25.2	57 22.8	−47.3	25.9	58 16.6	−46.8	26.6	49
50	51 04.2	−50.3	21.5	51 59.9	−49.9	22.0	52 55.5	−49.6	22.5	53 50.8	−49.2	23.0	54 45.9	−48.8	23.5	55 40.8	−48.4	24.1	56 35.5	−48.0	24.7	57 29.8	−47.4	25.4	50
51	50 13.9	−50.6	20.6	51 10.0	−50.3	21.1	52 05.9	−50.0	21.5	53 01.6	−49.6	22.0	53 57.1	−49.3	22.5	54 52.4	−48.9	23.1	55 47.5	−48.5	23.7	56 42.4	−48.1	24.3	51
52	49 23.3	−51.0	19.8	50 19.7	−50.7	20.2	51 15.9	−50.4	20.6	52 12.0	−50.1	21.1	53 07.8	−49.7	21.6	54 03.5	−49.3	22.1	54 59.0	−49.0	22.6	55 54.3	−48.6	23.2	52
53	48 32.3	−51.3	19.0	49 29.0	−51.1	19.4	50 25.5	−50.8	19.8	51 21.9	−50.5	20.2	52 18.1	−50.1	20.7	53 14.2	−49.9	21.1	54 10.0	−49.4	21.6	55 05.7	−49.1	22.1	53
54	47 41.0	−51.6	18.2	48 37.9	−51.3	18.6	49 34.7	−51.1	19.0	50 31.4	−50.8	19.3	51 28.0	−50.6	19.8	52 24.3	−50.2	20.2	53 20.6	−49.9	20.7	54 16.6	−49.5	21.1	54
55	46 49.4	−51.9	17.5	47 46.6	−51.7	17.8	48 43.6	−51.4	18.2	49 40.6	−51.2	18.5	50 37.4	−50.9	18.9	51 34.1	−50.6	19.3	52 30.7	−50.4	19.7	53 27.1	−50.0	20.2	55
56	45 57.5	−52.2	16.8	46 54.9	−51.9	17.1	47 52.2	−51.7	17.4	48 49.4	−51.5	17.7	49 46.5	−51.2	18.1	50 43.5	−51.0	18.5	51 40.3	−50.7	18.9	52 37.1	−50.5	19.3	56
57	45 05.3	−52.4	16.0	46 03.0	−52.3	16.3	47 00.5	−52.0	16.6	47 57.9	−51.8	16.9	48 55.3	−51.6	17.3	49 52.5	−51.3	17.6	50 49.6	−51.0	18.0	51 46.6	−50.8	18.4	57
58	44 12.9	−52.6	15.4	45 10.7	−52.4	15.6	46 08.5	−52.3	15.9	47 06.1	−52.0	16.2	48 03.7	−51.9	16.5	49 01.2	−51.7	16.8	49 58.6	−51.4	17.2	50 55.8	−51.1	17.5	58
59	43 20.3	−52.9	14.7	44 18.3	−52.7	14.9	45 16.2	−52.5	15.2	46 14.1	−52.4	15.5	47 11.8	−52.1	15.8	48 09.5	−51.9	16.1	49 07.2	−51.8	16.4	50 04.7	−51.5	16.7	59
60	42 27.4	−53.1	14.1	43 25.6	−53.0	14.3	44 23.7	−52.8	14.5	45 21.7	−52.6	14.8	46 19.7	−52.4	15.0	47 17.6	−52.2	15.3	48 15.4	−52.0	15.6	49 13.2	−51.8	15.9	60
61	41 34.3	−53.3	13.4	42 32.6	−53.1	13.6	43 30.9	−53.0	13.9	44 29.1	−52.8	14.1	45 27.3	−52.7	14.3	46 25.4	−52.5	14.6	47 23.4	−52.3	14.9	48 21.4	−52.1	15.2	61
62	40 41.0	−53.5	12.8	41 39.5	−53.4	13.0	42 37.9	−53.2	13.2	43 36.3	−53.0	13.4	44 34.6	−52.9	13.7	45 32.9	−52.7	13.9	46 31.1	−52.5	14.2	47 29.3	−52.4	14.4	62
63	39 47.5	−53.6	12.2	40 46.1	−53.5	12.4	41 44.7	−53.4	12.6	42 43.3	−53.3	12.8	43 41.7	−53.1	13.0	44 40.2	−53.0	13.2	45 38.6	−52.8	13.5	46 36.9	−52.7	13.7	63
64	38 53.9	−53.8	11.6	39 52.6	−53.7	11.8	40 51.3	−53.5	12.0	41 50.0	−53.4	12.2	42 48.6	−53.3	12.4	43 47.2	−53.2	12.6	44 45.8	−53.1	12.8	45 44.2	−52.8	13.0	64
65	38 00.1	−54.0	11.1	38 58.9	−53.8	11.2	39 57.8	−53.8	11.4	40 56.6	−53.7	11.6	41 55.3	−53.5	11.7	42 54.0	−53.3	11.9	43 52.7	−53.2	12.1	44 51.4	−53.2	12.3	65
66	37 06.1	−54.2	10.5	38 05.1	−54.1	10.7	39 04.0	−53.9	10.8	40 02.9	−53.8	11.0	41 01.8	−53.7	11.1	42 00.7	−53.6	11.3	42 59.5	−53.5	11.5	43 58.2	−53.3	11.7	66
67	36 11.9	−54.2	10.0	37 11.0	−54.1	10.1	38 10.1	−54.1	10.3	39 09.1	−54.0	10.4	40 08.1	−53.9	10.6	41 07.1	−53.8	10.7	42 06.0	−53.6	10.9	43 04.9	−53.5	11.1	67
68	35 17.7	−54.4	9.5	36 16.9	−54.4	9.6	37 16.0	−54.2	9.7	38 15.1	−54.1	9.8	39 14.2	−54.0	10.0	40 13.3	−53.9	10.1	41 12.4	−53.9	10.3	42 11.4	−53.7	10.4	68
69	34 23.3	−54.6	9.0	35 22.5	−54.4	9.1	36 21.8	−54.4	9.2	37 21.0	−54.3	9.3	38 20.2	−54.2	9.4	39 19.4	−54.1	9.6	40 18.5	−54.0	9.7	41 17.7	−53.9	9.8	69
70	33 28.7	−54.6	8.5	34 28.1	−54.6	8.5	35 27.4	−54.5	8.7	36 26.7	−54.4	8.8	37 26.0	−54.3	8.9	38 25.3	−54.3	9.0	39 24.5	−54.1	9.1	40 23.8	−54.1	9.3	70
71	32 34.1	−54.8	8.0	33 33.5	−54.7	8.0	34 32.9	−54.6	8.1	35 32.3	−54.5	8.2	36 31.7	−54.5	8.3	37 31.0	−54.4	8.5	38 30.4	−54.3	8.6	39 29.7	−54.2	8.7	71
72	31 39.3	−54.8	7.5	32 38.8	−54.8	7.6	33 38.3	−54.7	7.6	34 37.8	−54.7	7.7	35 37.2	−54.6	7.8	36 36.6	−54.5	7.9	37 36.1	−54.5	8.0	38 35.5	−54.4	8.1	72
73	30 44.5	−55.0	7.0	31 44.0	−54.9	7.1	32 43.6	−54.9	7.2	33 43.1	−54.8	7.2	34 42.6	−54.7	7.3	35 42.1	−54.7	7.4	36 41.6	−54.6	7.5	37 41.1	−54.5	7.6	73
74	29 49.5	−55.1	6.5	30 49.1	−55.0	6.6	31 48.7	−54.9	6.7	32 48.3	−54.9	6.7	33 47.9	−54.9	6.8	34 47.4	−54.7	6.9	35 47.0	−54.7	7.0	36 46.6	−54.7	7.1	74
75	28 54.4	−55.1	6.1	29 54.1	−55.1	6.1	30 53.8	−55.1	6.2	31 53.4	−55.0	6.3	32 53.0	−54.9	6.3	33 52.7	−54.9	6.4	34 52.3	−54.9	6.5	35 51.9	−54.8	6.6	75
76	27 59.3	−55.3	5.6	28 59.0	−55.2	5.7	29 58.7	−55.2	5.7	30 58.4	−55.1	5.8	31 58.1	−55.1	5.9	32 57.8	−55.0	5.9	33 57.4	−54.9	6.0	34 57.1	−54.9	6.1	76
77	27 04.0	−55.3	5.2	28 03.8	−55.3	5.2	29 03.5	−55.2	5.3	30 03.3	−55.2	5.3	31 03.0	−55.1	5.4	32 02.8	−55.2	5.5	33 02.5	−55.1	5.5	34 02.2	−55.0	5.6	77
78	26 08.7	−55.4	4.8	27 08.5	−55.3	4.8	28 08.3	−55.3	4.8	29 08.1	−55.3	4.9	30 07.9	−55.3	4.9	31 07.6	−55.2	5.0	32 07.4	−55.2	5.0	33 07.2	−55.2	5.1	78
79	25 13.3	−55.4	4.3	26 13.2	−55.5	4.4	27 13.0	−55.4	4.4	28 12.8	−55.4	4.5	29 12.6	−55.3	4.5	30 12.4	−55.3	4.5	31 12.2	−55.2	4.6	32 12.0	−55.2	4.6	79
80	24 17.9	−55.6	3.9	25 17.7	−55.5	3.9	26 17.6	−55.5	4.0	27 17.4	−55.4	4.0	28 17.3	−55.4	4.1	29 17.1	−55.4	4.1	30 17.0	−55.4	4.1	31 16.8	−55.3	4.2	80
81	23 22.3	−55.6	3.5	24 22.2	−55.6	3.5	25 22.1	−55.6	3.6	26 22.0	−55.5	3.6	27 21.9	−55.5	3.6	28 21.7	−55.4	3.7	29 21.6	−55.4	3.7	30 21.5	−55.4	3.7	81
82	22 26.7	−55.6	3.1	23 26.6	−55.6	3.1	24 26.5	−55.6	3.1	25 26.5	−55.6	3.2	26 26.4	−55.6	3.2	27 26.3	−55.6	3.2	28 26.2	−55.6	3.3	29 26.1	−55.5	3.3	82
83	21 31.1	−55.8	2.7	22 31.0	−55.7	2.7	23 30.9	−55.7	2.7	24 30.9	−55.7	2.8	25 30.8	−55.7	2.8	26 30.7	−55.6	2.8	27 30.6	−55.6	2.8	28 30.6	−55.6	2.8	83
84	20 35.3	−55.7	2.3	21 35.3	−55.8	2.3	22 35.2	−55.7	2.3	23 35.2	−55.7	2.3	24 35.1	−55.7	2.4	25 35.1	−55.7	2.4	26 35.0	−55.6	2.4	27 35.0	−55.7	2.4	84
85	19 39.6	−55.9	1.9	20 39.5	−55.8	1.9	21 39.5	−55.8	1.9	22 39.5	−55.8	1.9	23 39.4	−55.7	2.0	24 39.4	−55.8	2.0	25 39.4	−55.8	2.0	26 39.3	−55.7	2.0	85
86	18 43.7	−55.8	1.5	19 43.7	−55.8	1.5	20 43.7	−55.9	1.5	21 43.7	−55.9	1.5	22 43.7	−55.9	1.6	23 43.6	−55.8	1.6	24 43.6	−55.8	1.6	25 43.6	−55.8	1.6	86
87	17 47.9	−55.9	1.1	18 47.9	−56.0	1.1	19 47.8	−55.9	1.1	20 47.8	−55.9	1.1	21 47.8	−55.9	1.2	22 47.8	−55.9	1.2	23 47.8	−55.9	1.2	24 47.8	−55.9	1.2	87
88	16 52.0	−56.0	0.7	17 51.9	−55.9	0.8	18 51.9	−55.9	0.8	19 51.9	−55.9	0.8	20 51.9	−55.9	0.8	21 51.9	−55.9	0.8	22 51.9	−55.9	0.8	23 51.9	−55.9	0.8	88
89	15 56.0	−56.0	0.4	16 56.0	−56.0	0.4	17 56.0	−56.0	0.4	18 56.0	−56.0	0.4	19 56.0	−56.0	0.4	20 56.0	−56.0	0.4	21 56.0	−56.0	0.4	22 56.0	−56.0	0.4	89
90	15 00.0	−56.0	0.0	16 00.0	−56.0	0.0	17 00.0	−56.0	0.0	18 00.0	−56.0	0.0	19 00.0	−56.0	0.0	20 00.0	−56.0	0.0	21 00.0	−56.0	0.0	22 00.0	−56.0	0.0	90
	15°			16°			17°			18°			19°			20°			21°			22°			

LATITUDE CONTRARY NAME TO DECLINATION L.H.A. 21°, 339°

Dec.	15° Hc	d	Z	16° Hc	d	Z	17° Hc	d	Z	18° Hc	d	Z	19° Hc	d	Z	20° Hc	d	Z	21° Hc	d	Z	22° Hc	d	Z	Dec.
°	° ′	′	°	° ′	′	°	° ′	′	°	° ′	′	°	° ′	′	°	° ′	′	°	° ′	′	°	° ′	′	°	°
0	64 23.5	-36.6	124.0	63 49.2	-38.1	125.7	63 13.5	-39.5	127.3	62 36.5	-40.8	128.8	61 58.3	-42.1	130.3	61 18.9	-43.2	131.7	60 38.5	-44.3	133.0	59 57.1	-45.3	134.3	0
1	63 46.9	-37.9	125.8	63 11.1	-39.3	127.4	62 34.0	-40.6	128.9	61 55.7	-41.9	130.4	61 16.2	-43.0	131.8	60 35.7	-44.1	133.1	59 54.2	-45.1	134.4	59 11.8	-46.0	135.6	1
2	63 09.0	-39.2	127.5	62 31.8	-40.5	129.1	61 53.4	-41.7	130.5	61 13.8	-42.8	131.9	60 33.2	-43.9	133.2	59 51.6	-44.9	134.5	59 09.1	-45.8	135.7	58 25.8	-46.7	136.8	2
3	62 29.8	-40.2	129.2	61 51.3	-41.5	130.7	61 11.7	-42.7	132.0	60 31.0	-43.7	133.4	59 49.3	-44.7	134.6	59 06.7	-45.6	135.8	58 23.3	-46.5	136.9	57 39.1	-47.4	138.0	3
4	61 49.6	-41.4	130.8	61 09.8	-42.4	132.2	60 29.0	-43.5	133.5	59 47.3	-44.6	134.7	59 04.6	-45.5	135.9	58 21.1	-46.4	137.1	57 36.8	-47.2	138.1	56 51.7	-47.9	139.2	4
5	61 08.2	-42.2	132.3	60 27.4	-43.4	133.6	59 45.5	-44.4	134.9	59 02.7	-45.3	136.0	58 19.1	-46.2	137.2	57 34.7	-47.0	138.2	56 49.6	-47.8	139.3	56 03.8	-48.5	140.2	5
6	60 26.0	-43.2	133.8	59 44.0	-44.2	135.0	59 01.1	-45.1	136.2	58 17.4	-46.0	137.3	57 32.9	-46.8	138.4	56 47.7	-47.6	139.4	56 01.8	-48.3	140.4	55 15.3	-49.0	141.3	6
7	59 42.8	-44.1	135.1	58 59.8	-45.0	136.3	58 16.0	-45.9	137.4	57 31.4	-46.7	138.5	56 46.1	-47.5	139.5	56 00.1	-48.1	140.5	55 13.5	-48.8	141.4	54 26.3	-49.4	142.3	7
8	58 58.7	-44.8	136.5	58 14.8	-45.7	137.6	57 30.1	-46.5	138.7	56 44.7	-47.3	139.7	55 58.6	-48.0	140.6	55 12.0	-48.7	141.6	54 24.7	-49.4	142.4	53 36.9	-50.0	143.3	8
9	58 13.9	-45.6	137.8	57 29.1	-46.4	138.8	56 43.6	-47.2	139.8	55 57.4	-47.9	140.8	55 10.6	-48.5	141.7	54 23.3	-49.2	142.6	53 35.3	-49.7	143.4	52 46.9	-50.3	144.2	9
10	57 28.3	-46.2	139.0	56 42.7	-47.0	140.0	55 56.4	-47.7	140.9	55 09.5	-48.4	141.8	54 22.1	-49.1	142.7	53 34.1	-49.7	143.5	52 45.6	-50.2	144.3	51 56.6	-50.7	145.1	10
11	56 42.1	-46.9	140.2	55 55.7	-47.6	141.1	55 08.7	-48.3	142.0	54 21.1	-48.9	142.9	53 33.0	-49.5	143.7	52 44.4	-50.0	144.5	51 55.4	-50.6	145.2	51 05.9	-51.1	145.9	11
12	55 55.2	-47.5	141.3	55 08.1	-48.2	142.2	54 20.4	-48.8	143.0	53 32.2	-49.4	143.9	52 43.5	-49.9	144.6	51 54.4	-50.5	145.4	51 04.8	-51.0	146.1	50 14.8	-51.5	146.8	12
13	55 07.7	-48.0	142.4	54 19.9	-48.6	143.2	53 31.6	-49.2	144.0	52 42.8	-49.8	144.8	51 53.6	-50.4	145.5	51 03.9	-50.9	146.2	50 13.8	-51.3	146.9	49 23.3	-51.7	147.6	13
14	54 19.7	-48.6	143.4	53 31.3	-49.2	144.2	52 42.4	-49.7	145.0	51 53.0	-50.2	145.7	51 03.2	-50.7	146.4	50 13.0	-51.1	147.1	49 22.5	-51.6	147.7	48 31.6	-52.1	148.3	14
15	53 31.1	-49.0	144.4	52 42.1	-49.5	145.2	51 52.7	-50.1	145.9	51 02.8	-50.6	146.6	50 12.5	-51.1	147.3	49 21.9	-51.6	147.9	48 30.9	-52.0	148.5	47 39.5	-52.3	149.1	15
16	52 42.1	-49.4	145.4	51 52.6	-50.0	146.1	51 02.6	-50.5	146.8	50 12.2	-51.0	147.4	49 21.4	-51.4	148.1	48 30.3	-51.8	148.7	47 38.9	-52.2	149.2	46 47.2	-52.6	149.8	16
17	51 52.7	-49.9	146.3	51 02.6	-50.4	147.0	50 12.1	-50.9	147.6	49 21.2	-51.3	148.3	48 30.0	-51.7	148.9	47 38.5	-52.1	149.4	46 46.7	-52.5	150.0	45 54.6	-52.8	150.5	17
18	51 02.8	-50.3	147.2	50 12.2	-50.8	147.8	49 21.2	-51.2	148.5	48 29.9	-51.6	149.0	47 38.3	-52.0	149.6	46 46.4	-52.4	150.2	45 54.2	-52.7	150.7	45 01.8	-53.1	151.2	18
19	50 12.5	-50.6	148.0	49 21.4	-51.1	148.7	48 30.0	-51.5	149.2	47 38.3	-51.9	149.8	46 46.3	-52.3	150.3	45 54.0	-52.6	150.9	45 01.5	-53.0	151.4	44 08.7	-53.3	151.8	19
20	49 21.9	-51.0	148.9	48 30.3	-51.4	149.5	47 38.5	-51.8	150.0	46 46.4	-52.2	150.5	45 54.0	-52.5	151.1	45 01.4	-52.9	151.5	44 08.5	-53.2	152.0	43 15.4	-53.5	152.5	20
21	48 30.9	-51.4	149.7	47 38.9	-51.7	150.2	46 46.7	-52.1	150.8	45 54.2	-52.4	151.3	45 01.5	-52.8	151.7	44 08.5	-53.1	152.2	43 15.3	-53.4	152.7	42 21.9	-53.6	153.1	21
22	47 39.5	-51.6	150.4	46 47.2	-52.0	151.0	45 54.6	-52.3	151.5	45 01.8	-52.7	152.0	44 08.7	-53.0	152.4	43 15.4	-53.3	152.9	42 21.9	-53.5	153.3	41 28.3	-53.9	153.7	22
23	46 47.9	-51.9	151.2	45 55.2	-52.2	151.7	45 02.3	-52.6	152.2	44 09.1	-52.9	152.6	43 15.7	-53.2	153.1	42 22.1	-53.5	153.5	41 28.4	-53.8	153.9	40 34.4	-54.0	154.3	23
24	45 56.0	-52.1	151.9	45 03.0	-52.5	152.4	44 09.7	-52.8	152.8	43 16.2	-53.1	153.3	42 22.5	-53.4	153.7	41 28.6	-53.7	154.1	40 34.6	-54.0	154.5	39 40.4	-54.2	154.8	24
25	45 03.9	-52.5	152.6	44 10.5	-52.8	153.1	43 16.9	-53.1	153.5	42 23.1	-53.4	153.9	41 29.1	-53.6	154.3	40 34.9	-53.8	154.7	39 40.6	-54.1	155.0	38 46.2	-54.4	155.4	25
26	44 11.4	-52.6	153.3	43 17.7	-52.9	153.7	42 23.8	-53.2	154.1	41 29.7	-53.5	154.5	40 35.5	-53.8	154.9	39 41.1	-54.1	155.3	38 46.5	-54.3	155.6	37 51.8	-54.5	155.9	26
27	43 18.8	-52.9	154.0	42 24.8	-53.2	154.4	41 30.6	-53.5	154.8	40 36.2	-53.7	155.1	39 41.7	-53.9	155.5	38 47.0	-54.1	155.8	37 52.2	-54.4	156.1	36 57.3	-54.6	156.4	27
28	42 25.9	-53.1	154.6	41 31.6	-53.4	155.0	40 37.1	-53.6	155.4	39 42.5	-53.9	155.7	38 47.8	-54.2	156.0	37 52.9	-54.4	156.4	36 57.8	-54.5	156.7	36 02.7	-54.8	157.0	28
29	41 32.8	-53.3	155.2	40 38.2	-53.5	155.6	39 43.5	-53.8	156.0	38 48.6	-54.0	156.3	37 53.6	-54.2	156.6	36 58.5	-54.5	156.9	36 03.3	-54.7	157.2	35 07.9	-54.9	157.5	29
30	40 39.5	-53.5	155.9	39 44.7	-53.8	156.2	38 49.7	-54.0	156.5	37 54.6	-54.2	156.8	36 59.4	-54.4	157.1	36 04.0	-54.6	157.4	35 08.6	-54.8	157.7	34 13.0	-55.0	158.0	30
31	39 46.0	-53.6	156.4	38 50.9	-53.8	156.8	37 55.7	-54.1	157.1	37 00.4	-54.3	157.4	36 05.0	-54.6	157.7	35 09.4	-54.7	157.9	34 13.8	-55.0	158.2	33 18.0	-55.1	158.4	31
32	38 52.4	-53.9	157.0	37 57.1	-54.1	157.3	37 01.6	-54.2	157.6	36 06.1	-54.5	157.9	35 10.4	-54.6	158.2	34 14.7	-54.9	158.4	33 18.8	-55.0	158.7	32 22.9	-55.2	158.9	32
33	37 58.5	-54.0	157.6	37 03.0	-54.2	157.9	36 07.4	-54.4	158.2	35 11.6	-54.6	158.4	34 15.8	-54.8	158.7	33 19.8	-54.9	158.9	32 23.8	-55.1	159.1	31 27.7	-55.3	159.4	33
34	37 04.5	-54.1	158.1	36 08.8	-54.3	158.4	35 13.0	-54.6	158.7	34 17.0	-54.7	158.9	33 21.0	-54.9	159.2	32 24.9	-55.1	159.4	31 28.7	-55.3	159.6	30 32.4	-55.4	159.8	34
35	36 10.4	-54.3	158.7	35 14.5	-54.5	158.9	34 18.4	-54.6	159.2	33 22.3	-54.8	159.4	32 26.1	-55.0	159.6	31 29.8	-55.2	159.9	30 33.4	-55.3	160.1	29 37.0	-55.5	160.3	35
36	35 16.1	-54.4	159.2	34 20.0	-54.6	159.4	33 23.8	-54.8	159.7	32 27.5	-55.0	159.9	31 31.1	-55.1	160.1	30 34.6	-55.2	160.3	29 38.1	-55.4	160.5	28 41.5	-55.6	160.7	36
37	34 21.7	-54.5	159.7	33 25.4	-54.7	159.9	32 29.0	-54.9	160.2	31 32.5	-55.0	160.4	30 36.0	-55.2	160.6	29 39.4	-55.4	160.8	28 42.7	-55.5	161.0	27 45.9	-55.6	161.1	37
38	33 27.2	-54.6	160.2	32 30.7	-54.8	160.4	31 34.1	-54.9	160.6	30 37.5	-55.1	160.8	29 40.8	-55.3	161.0	28 44.0	-55.4	161.2	27 47.2	-55.6	161.4	26 50.3	-55.7	161.5	38
39	32 32.6	-54.8	160.7	31 35.9	-54.9	160.9	30 39.2	-55.1	161.1	29 42.4	-55.3	161.3	28 45.5	-55.4	161.5	27 48.6	-55.6	161.6	26 51.6	-55.7	161.8	25 54.6	-55.8	162.0	39
40	31 37.8	-54.9	161.2	30 41.0	-55.1	161.4	29 44.1	-55.2	161.6	28 47.1	-55.3	161.7	27 50.1	-55.4	161.9	26 53.0	-55.5	162.1	25 55.9	-55.7	162.2	24 58.8	-55.9	162.4	40
41	30 42.9	-54.9	161.7	29 45.9	-55.1	161.8	28 48.9	-55.3	162.0	27 51.8	-55.4	162.2	26 54.7	-55.6	162.3	25 57.5	-55.7	162.5	25 00.2	-55.8	162.6	24 02.9	-55.9	162.8	41
42	29 48.0	-55.1	162.1	28 50.8	-55.2	162.3	27 53.6	-55.3	162.5	26 56.4	-55.5	162.6	25 59.1	-55.6	162.8	25 01.8	-55.7	162.9	24 04.4	-55.8	163.0	23 07.0	-56.0	163.2	42
43	28 52.9	-55.2	162.6	27 55.6	-55.3	162.7	26 58.3	-55.4	162.9	26 00.9	-55.5	163.0	25 03.5	-55.7	163.2	24 06.1	-55.8	163.3	23 08.6	-56.0	163.4	22 11.0	-56.0	163.6	43
44	27 57.7	-55.2	163.0	27 00.3	-55.4	163.2	26 02.9	-55.5	163.3	25 05.4	-55.7	163.5	24 07.8	-55.7	163.6	23 10.3	-55.9	163.7	22 12.6	-55.9	163.8	21 15.0	-56.1	163.9	44
45	27 02.5	-55.3	163.5	26 04.9	-55.4	163.6	25 07.4	-55.6	163.7	24 09.7	-55.6	163.9	23 12.1	-55.8	164.0	22 14.4	-55.9	164.1	21 16.7	-56.1	164.2	20 18.9	-56.1	164.3	45
46	26 07.2	-55.4	163.9	25 09.5	-55.5	164.0	24 11.8	-55.6	164.2	23 14.1	-55.8	164.3	22 16.3	-55.9	164.4	21 18.5	-56.0	164.5	20 20.6	-56.0	164.6	19 22.8	-56.2	164.7	46
47	25 11.8	-55.5	164.3	24 14.0	-55.6	164.5	23 16.2	-55.7	164.6	22 18.3	-55.8	164.7	21 20.4	-55.9	164.8	20 22.5	-56.0	164.9	19 24.6	-56.2	165.0	18 26.6	-56.2	165.1	47
48	24 16.3	-55.5	164.7	23 18.4	-55.7	164.9	22 20.5	-55.8	165.0	21 22.5	-55.9	165.1	20 24.5	-56.0	165.2	19 26.5	-56.1	165.3	18 28.4	-56.1	165.4	17 30.4	-56.3	165.4	48
49	23 20.8	-55.7	165.2	22 22.7	-55.7	165.3	21 24.7	-55.8	165.4	20 26.6	-55.9	165.5	19 28.5	-56.0	165.6	18 30.4	-56.1	165.6	17 32.3	-56.2	165.7	16 34.1	-56.3	165.8	49
50	22 25.1	-55.6	165.6	21 27.0	-55.7	165.7	20 28.9	-55.9	165.8	19 30.7	-56.0	165.9	18 32.5	-56.0	165.9	17 34.3	-56.1	166.0	16 36.1	-56.3	166.1	15 37.8	-56.3	166.2	50
51	21 29.5	-55.7	166.0	20 31.3	-55.9	166.1	19 33.0	-55.9	166.2	18 34.7	-56.0	166.2	17 36.5	-56.1	166.3	16 38.2	-56.2	166.4	15 39.8	-56.2	166.5	14 41.5	-56.4	166.5	51
52	20 33.8	-55.8	166.4	19 35.4	-55.8	166.5	18 37.1	-56.0	166.5	17 38.7	-56.0	166.6	16 40.4	-56.2	166.7	15 42.0	-56.3	166.8	14 43.6	-56.4	166.8	13 45.1	-56.4	166.9	52
53	19 38.0	-55.8	166.8	18 39.6	-55.9	166.8	17 41.1	-56.0	166.9	16 42.7	-56.1	167.0	15 44.2	-56.2	167.1	14 45.7	-56.2	167.1	13 47.2	-56.3	167.2	12 48.7	-56.4	167.2	53
54	18 42.2	-55.9	167.2	17 43.7	-56.0	167.2	16 45.1	-56.0	167.3	15 46.6	-56.1	167.4	14 48.0	-56.2	167.4	13 49.5	-56.3	167.5	12 50.9	-56.4	167.5	11 52.3	-56.4	167.6	54
55	17 46.3	-55.9	167.5	16 47.7	-56.0	167.6	15 49.1	-56.1	167.7	14 50.5	-56.2	167.7	13 51.8	-56.2	167.8	12 53.2	-56.3	167.8	11 54.5	-56.4	167.9	10 55.9	-56.5	167.9	55
56	16 50.4	-56.0	167.9	15 51.7	-56.0	168.0	14 53.0	-56.1	168.0	13 54.3	-56.2	168.1	12 55.6	-56.3	168.1	11 56.9	-56.4	168.2	10 58.1	-56.4	168.2	9 59.4	-56.5	168.3	56
57	15 54.4	-56.0	168.3	14 55.7	-56.1	168.3	13 56.9	-56.2	168.4	12 58.1	-56.2	168.4	11 59.3	-56.3	168.5	11 00.5	-56.3	168.5	10 01.7	-56.4	168.6	9 02.9	-56.5	168.6	57
58	14 58.4	-56.0	168.7	13 59.6	-56.1	168.7	13 00.7	-56.1	168.8	12 01.9	-56.3	168.8	11 03.0	-56.3	168.8	10 04.2	-56.4	168.9	9 05.3	-56.5	168.9	8 06.4	-56.5	168.9	58
59	14 02.4	-56.1	169.0	13 03.5	-56.2	169.1	12 04.6	-56.3	169.1	11 05.6	-56.2	169.2	10 06.7	-56.3	169.2	9 07.8	-56.5	169.2	8 08.8	-56.5	169.3	7 09.9	-56.6	169.3	59
60	13 06.3	-56.1	169.4	12 07.3	-56.1	169.4	11 08.3	-56.2	169.5	10 09.4	-56.5	169.5	9 10.4	-56.4	169.5	8 11.3	-56.4	169.6	7 12.3	-56.5	169.6	6 13.3	-56.5	169.6	60
61	12 10.2	-56.1	169.8	11 11.2	-56.2	169.8	10 12.1	-56.2	169.8	9 13.1	-56.4	169.9	8 14.0	-56.4	169.9	7 14.9	-56.4	169.9	6 15.8	-56.5	169.9	5 16.8	-56.6	170.0	61
62	11 14.1	-56.2	170.1	10 15.0	-56.2	170.2	9 15.9	-56.3	170.2	8 16.7	-56.3	170.2	7 17.6	-56.4	170.2	6 18.5	-56.5	170.3	5 19.3	-56.5	170.3	4 20.2	-56.6	170.3	62
63	10 17.9	-56.1	170.5	9 18.8	-56.3	170.5	8 19.6	-56.3	170.5	7 20.4	-56.4	170.6	6 21.2	-56.4	170.6	5 22.0	-56.5	170.6	4 22.8	-56.5	170.6	3 23.6	-56.6	170.6	63
64	9 21.8	-56.2	170.8	8 22.5	-56.2	170.9	7 23.3	-56.3	170.9	6 24.0	-56.3	170.9	5 24.8	-56.4	170.9	4 25.5	-56.4	170.9	3 26.3	-56.5	170.9	2 27.0	-56.5	171.0	64
65	8 25.6	-56.2	171.2	7 26.3	-56.3	171.2	6 27.0	-56.3	171.2	5 27.7	-56.4	171.2	4 28.4	-56.5	171.3	3 29.1	-56.5	171.3	2 29.8	-56.6	171.3	1 30.5	-56.6	171.3	65
66	7 29.4	-56.3	171.5	6 30.0	-56.3	171.6	5 30.7	-56.4	171.6	4 31.3	-56.4	171.6	3 31.9	-56.4	171.6	2 32.6	-56.5	171.6	1 33.2	-56.5	171.6	0 33.9	-56.6	171.6	66
67	6 33.1	-56.2	171.9	5 33.7	-56.3	171.9	4 34.3	-56.3	171.9	3 34.9	-56.4	171.9	2 35.5	-56.4	171.9	1 36.1	-56.5	171.9	0 36.7	-56.6	172.0	0 22.7	+56.6	8.0	67
68	5 36.9	-56.3	172.2	4 37.4	-56.3	172.3	3 38.0	-56.4	172.3	2 38.5	-56.4	172.3	1 39.1	-56.5	172.3	0 39.6	-56.5	172.3	0 19.9	+56.5	7.7	1 19.3	+56.6	7.7	68
69	4 40.6	-56.3	172.6	3 41.1	-56.3	172.6	2 41.6	-56.3	172.6	1 42.1	-56.4	172.6	0 42.6	-56.4	172.6	0 16.9	+56.5	7.4	1 16.4	+56.5	7.4	2 15.9	+56.6	7.4	69
70	3 44.3	-56.2	172.9	2 44.8	-56.3	173.0	1 45.3	-56.4	173.0	0 45.7	-56.4	173.0	0 13.8	+56.5	7.0	1 13.4	+56.5	7.0	2 12.9	+56.6	7.0	3 12.5	+56.6	7.1	70
71	2 48.1	-56.3	173.3	1 48.5	-56.3	173.3	0 48.9	-56.4	173.3	0 10.7	+56.4	6.7	1 10.3	+56.4	6.7	2 09.9	+56.5	6.7	3 09.5	+56.5	6.7	4 09.1	+56.5	6.7	71
72	1 51.8	-56.3	173.6	0 52.2	-56.4	173.6	0 07.5	+56.3	6.4	1 07.1	+56.4	6.4	2 06.7	+56.5	6.4	3 06.4	+56.5	6.4	4 06.0	+56.5	6.4	5 05.6	+56.6	6.4	72
73	0 55.5	-56.3	174.0	0 04.2	+56.3	6.0	1 03.8	+56.4	6.0	2 03.5	+56.4	6.0	3 03.2	+56.5	6.0	4 02.9	+56.4	6.0	5 02.5	+56.5	6.0	6 02.2	+56.5	6.0	73
74	0 00.8	+56.3	5.7	1 00.5	+56.3	5.7	2 00.2	+56.4	5.7	2 59.9	+56.4	5.7	3 59.6	+56.4	5.7	4 59.3	+56.5	5.7	5 59.0	+56.5	5.7	6 58.7	+56.6	5.7	74
75	0 57.1	+56.3	5.3	1 56.8	+56.3	5.3	2 56.6	+56.3	5.3	3 56.3	+56.4	5.3	4 56.0	+56.5	5.3	5 55.8	+56.4	5.4	6 55.5	+56.5	5.4	7 55.3	+56.5	5.4	75
76	1 53.4	+56.3	5.0	2 53.1	+56.4	5.0	3 52.9	+56.4	5.0	4 52.7	+56.4	5.0	5 52.5	+56.4	5.0	6 52.2	+56.5	5.0	7 52.0	+56.5	5.0	8 51.8	+56.5	5.0	76
77	2 49.7	+56.2	4.6	3 49.5	+56.3	4.6	4 49.3	+56.3	4.6	5 49.1	+56.3	4.6	6 48.9	+56.4	4.7	7 48.7	+56.4	4.7	8 48.5	+56.4	4.7	9 48.3	+56.4	4.7	77
78	3 45.9	+56.3	4.3	4 45.8	+56.3	4.3	5 45.6	+56.3	4.3	6 45.4	+56.4	4.3	7 45.3	+56.3	4.3	8 45.1	+56.4	4.3	9 44.9	+56.4	4.3	10 44.7	+56.5	4.3	78
79	4 42.2	+56.3	3.9	5 42.1	+56.2	3.9	6 41.9	+56.3	3.9	7 41.8	+56.3	4.0	8 41.6	+56.4	4.0	9 41.5	+56.4	4.0	10 41.3	+56.4	4.0	11 41.2	+56.4	4.0	79
80	5 38.5	+56.2	3.6	6 38.3	+56.3	3.6	7 38.2	+56.3	3.6	8 38.1	+56.3	3.6	9 38.0	+56.3	3.6	10 37.9	+56.3	3.6	11 37.7	+56.4	3.6	12 37.6	+56.4	3.7	80
81	6 34.7	+56.2	3.2	7 34.6	+56.3	3.2	8 34.5	+56.3	3.2	9 34.4	+56.3	3.3	10 34.3	+56.3	3.3	11 34.2	+56.4	3.3	12 34.1	+56.4	3.3	13 34.0	+56.4	3.3	81
82	7 30.9	+56.3	2.9	8 30.9	+56.2	2.9	9 30.8	+56.2	2.9	10 30.7	+56.3	2.9	11 30.6	+56.3	2.9	12 30.6	+56.3	2.9	13 30.5	+56.3	2.9	14 30.4	+56.3	3.0	82
83	8 27.2	+56.2	2.5	9 27.1	+56.2	2.5	10 27.0	+56.3	2.5	11 27.0	+56.2	2.6	12 26.9	+56.3	2.6	13 26.9	+56.2	2.6	14 26.8	+56.3	2.6	15 26.7	+56.3	2.6	83
84	9 23.4	+56.1	2.2	10 23.3	+56.2	2.2	11 23.3	+56.2	2.2	12 23.2	+56.2	2.2	13 23.2	+56.2	2.2	14 23.1	+56.3	2.2	15 23.1	+56.2	2.2	16 23.0	+56.3	2.2	84
85	10 19.5	+56.2	1.8	11 19.5	+56.2	1.8	12 19.5	+56.1	1.8	13 19.4	+56.2	1.8	14 19.4	+56.2	1.8	15 19.4	+56.2	1.9	16 19.3	+56.3	1.9	17 19.3	+56.2	1.9	85
86	11 15.7	+56.1	1.5	12 15.7	+56.1	1.5	13 15.6	+56.2	1.5	14 15.6	+56.2	1.5	15 15.6	+56.2	1.5	16 15.6	+56.1	1.5	17 15.6	+56.1	1.5	18 15.5	+56.2	1.5	86
87	12 11.8	+56.1	1.1	13 11.8	+56.1	1.1	14 11.8	+56.1	1.1	15 11.8	+56.1	1.1	16 11.8	+56.1	1.1	17 11.7	+56.2	1.1	18 11.7	+56.2	1.1	19 11.7	+56.2	1.1	87
88	13 07.9	+56.1	0.7	14 07.9	+56.1	0.7	15 07.9	+56.1	0.7	16 07.9	+56.1	0.7	17 07.9	+56.1	0.7	18 07.9	+56.1	0.8	19 07.9	+56.1	0.8	20 07.9	+56.1	0.8	88
89	14 04.0	+56.0	0.4	15 04.0	+56.0	0.4	16 04.0	+56.0	0.4	17 04.0	+56.0	0.4	18 04.0	+56.0	0.4	19 04.0	+56.0	0.4	20 04.0	+56.0	0.4	21 04.0	+56.0	0.4	89
90	15 00.0	+56.0	0.0	16 00.0	+56.0	0.0	17 00.0	+56.0	0.0	18 00.0	+56.0	0.0	19 00.0	+56.0	0.0	20 00.0	+56.0	0.0	21 00.0	+56.0	0.0	22 00.0	+56.0	0.0	90
	15°			16°			17°			18°			19°			20°			21°			22°			

S. Lat. {L.H.A. greater than 180° ....Zn=180°–Z
{L.H.A. less than 180°...........Zn=180°+Z

LATITUDE SAME NAME AS DECLINATION L.H.A. 159°, 201°

Dec.	15° Hc	d	Z	16° Hc	d	Z	17° Hc	d	Z	18° Hc	d	Z	19° Hc	d	Z	20° Hc	d	Z	21° Hc	d	Z	22° Hc	d	Z	Dec.
°	° ′	′	°	° ′	′	°	° ′	′	°	° ′	′	°	° ′	′	°	° ′	′	°	° ′	′	°	° ′	′	°	°
0	63 35.1	+34.2	122.6	63 02.0	+35.8	124.3	62 27.5	+37.3	125.9	61 51.6	+38.8	127.4	61 14.6	+40.1	128.9	60 36.4	+41.3	130.2	59 57.1	+42.5	131.6	59 16.8	+43.6	132.8	0
1	64 09.3	+32.7	120.8	63 37.8	+34.4	122.5	63 04.8	+36.0	124.2	62 30.4	+37.5	125.8	61 54.7	+38.9	127.3	61 17.7	+40.3	128.8	60 39.6	+41.5	130.1	60 00.4	+42.7	131.5	1
2	64 42.0	+31.1	118.8	64 12.2	+32.9	120.7	63 40.8	+34.7	122.4	63 07.9	+36.3	124.1	62 33.6	+37.8	125.7	61 58.0	+39.2	127.2	61 21.1	+40.5	128.7	60 43.1	+41.7	130.1	2
3	65 13.1	+29.4	116.8	64 45.1	+31.4	118.7	64 15.5	+33.1	120.5	63 44.2	+34.9	122.3	63 11.4	+36.5	124.0	62 37.2	+38.0	125.6	62 01.6	+39.5	127.1	61 24.8	+40.8	128.6	3
4	65 42.5	+27.6	114.7	65 16.5	+29.6	116.7	64 48.6	+31.6	118.6	64 19.1	+33.4	120.4	63 47.9	+35.1	122.2	63 15.2	+36.7	123.9	62 41.1	+38.2	125.5	62 05.6	+39.6	127.0	4
5	66 10.1	+25.8	112.5	65 46.1	+27.9	114.6	65 20.2	+29.9	116.6	64 52.5	+31.8	118.5	64 23.0	+33.7	120.3	63 51.9	+35.4	122.1	63 19.3	+37.0	123.8	62 45.2	+38.5	125.4	5
6	66 35.9	+23.7•	110.3	66 14.0	+26.0	112.4	65 50.1	+28.2	114.5	65 24.3	+30.2	116.5	64 56.7	+32.1	118.4	64 27.3	+33.9	120.2	63 56.3	+35.6	122.0	63 23.7	+37.2	123.7	6
7	66 59.6	+21.6•	108.0	66 40.0	+24.0•	110.2	66 18.3	+26.2•	112.3	65 54.5	+28.4	114.4	65 28.8	+30.4	116.4	65 01.2	+32.3	118.3	64 31.9	+34.2	120.2	64 00.9	+35.9	121.9	7
8	67 21.2	+19.4•	105.5	67 04.0	+21.8•	107.8	66 44.5	+24.2•	110.0	66 22.9	+26.4	112.2	65 59.2	+28.6	114.3	65 33.5	+30.7	116.3	65 06.1	+32.6	118.2	64 36.8	+34.5	120.1	8
9	67 40.6	+17.1•	103.1	67 25.8	+19.6•	105.4	67 08.7	+22.1•	107.7	66 49.3	+24.5•	109.9	66 27.8	+26.8	112.1	66 04.2	+28.9	114.2	65 38.7	+30.9	116.2	65 11.3	+32.8	118.2	9
10	67 57.7	+14.6•	100.5	67 45.4	+17.4•	102.9	67 30.8	+19.9•	105.3	67 13.8	+22.4•	107.6	66 54.6	+24.7•	109.8	66 33.1	+27.0	112.0	66 09.6	+29.2	114.1	65 44.1	+31.3	116.1	10
11	68 12.3	+12.2•	97.9	68 02.8	+14.9•	100.4	67 50.7	+17.6•	102.8	67 36.2	+20.1•	105.2	67 19.3	+22.6•	107.5	67 00.1	+25.0•	109.7	66 38.8	+27.3	111.9	66 15.4	+29.4	114.0	11
12	68 24.5	+9.6•	95.3	68 17.7	+12.4•	97.8	68 08.3	+15.1•	100.3	67 56.3	+17.8•	102.7	67 41.9	+20.4•	105.1	67 25.1	+22.9•	107.4	67 06.1	+25.3•	109.7	66 44.8	+27.6	111.9	12
13	68 34.1	+7.1•	92.6	68 30.1	+9.9•	95.1	68 23.4	+12.7•	97.6	68 14.1	+15.4•	100.1	68 02.3	+18.1•	102.6	67 48.0	+20.7•	105.0	67 31.4	+23.1•	107.3	67 12.4	+25.5•	109.6	13
14	68 41.2	+4.3•	89.9	68 40.0	+7.2•	92.4	68 36.1	+10.1•	95.0	68 29.5	+12.9•	97.5	68 20.4	+15.6•	100.0	68 08.7	+18.3•	102.5	67 54.5	+21.0•	104.9	67 37.9	+23.5•	107.2	14
15	68 45.5	+1.7•	87.1	68 47.2	+4.5•	89.7	68 46.2	+7.4•	92.3	68 42.4	+10.3•	94.8	68 36.0	+13.2•	97.4	68 27.0	+15.9•	99.9	68 15.5	+18.5•	102.4	68 01.4	+21.2•	104.8	15
16	68 47.2	−1.0•	84.4	68 51.7	+1.9•	86.9	68 53.6	+4.7•	89.5	68 52.7	+7.7•	92.1	68 49.2	+10.5•	94.7	68 42.9	+13.4•	97.3	68 34.0	+16.2•	99.8	68 22.6	+18.8•	102.3	16
17	68 46.2	−3.8•	81.6	68 53.6	−0.9•	84.2	68 58.3	+2.1•	86.7	69 00.4	+5.0•	89.3	68 59.7	+7.9•	92.0	68 56.3	+10.8•	94.6	68 50.2	+13.6•	97.1	68 41.4	+16.4•	99.7	17
18	68 42.4	−6.4•	78.8	68 52.7	−3.5•	81.4	69 00.4	−0.7•	84.0	69 05.4	+2.2•	86.6	69 07.6	+5.1•	89.2	69 07.1	+8.1•	91.8	69 03.8	+11.0•	94.4	68 57.8	+13.9•	97.0	18
19	68 36.0	−9.0•	76.1	68 49.2	−6.3•	78.6	68 59.7	−3.4•	81.2	69 07.6	−0.5•	83.8	69 12.7	+2.5•	86.4	69 15.2	+5.3•	89.0	69 14.8	+8.3•	91.7	69 11.7	+11.2•	94.3	19
20	68 27.0	−11.5•	73.4	68 42.9	−8.9•	75.9	68 56.3	−6.1•	78.4	69 07.1	−3.3•	81.0	69 15.2	−0.4•	83.6	69 20.5	+2.6•	86.2	69 23.1	+5.6•	88.8	69 22.9	+8.5•	91.5	20
21	68 15.5	−14.1•	70.8	68 34.0	−11.4•	73.2	68 50.2	−8.8•	75.6	69 03.8	−6.0•	78.2	69 14.8	−3.1•	80.7	69 23.1	−0.2•	83.4	69 28.7	+2.7•	86.0	69 31.4	+5.8•	88.7	21
22	68 01.4	−16.5•	68.1	68 22.6	−14.0•	70.5	68 41.4	−11.3•	72.9	68 57.8	−8.6•	75.4	69 11.7	−5.9•	77.9	69 22.9	−3.0•	80.5	69 31.4	0.0•	83.2	69 37.2	+2.9•	85.8	22
23	67 44.9	−18.9•	65.6	68 08.6	−16.5•	67.9	68 30.1	−14.0•	70.2	68 49.2	−11.3•	72.6	69 05.8	−8.5•	75.1	69 19.9	−5.7•	77.7	69 31.4	−2.8•	80.3	69 40.1	+0.2•	83.0	23
24	67 26.0	−21.1•	63.1	67 52.1	−18.8•	65.3	68 16.1	−16.3•	67.6	68 37.9	−13.8•	69.9	68 57.3	−11.2•	72.4	69 14.2	−8.4•	74.9	69 28.6	−5.6•	77.5	69 40.3	−2.7•	80.1	24
25	67 04.9	−23.2•	60.7	67 33.3	−21.0•	62.8	67 59.8	−18.8•	65.0	68 24.1	−16.4•	67.3	68 46.1	−13.8•	69.6	69 05.8	−11.1•	72.1	69 23.0	−8.4•	74.6	69 37.6	−5.5•	77.2	25
26	66 41.7	−25.3•	58.3	67 12.3	−23.2•	60.3	67 41.0	−21.0•	62.5	68 07.7	−18.7•	64.7	68 32.3	−16.2•	67.0	68 54.7	−13.8•	69.3	69 14.6	−11.0•	71.8	69 32.1	−8.3•	74.4	26
27	66 16.4	−27.2	56.1	66 49.1	−25.2•	58.0	67 20.0	−23.2•	60.0	67 49.0	−21.0•	62.1	68 16.1	−18.7•	64.3	68 40.9	−16.2•	66.7	69 03.6	−13.7•	69.1	69 23.8	−11.0•	71.5	27
28	65 49.2	−29.0	53.9	66 23.9	−27.2	55.7	66 56.8	−25.2•	57.6	67 28.0	−23.1•	59.7	67 57.4	−21.0•	61.8	68 24.7	−18.6•	64.0	68 49.9	−16.2•	66.3	69 12.8	−13.6•	68.8	28
29	65 20.2	−30.7	51.7	65 56.7	−29.0	53.5	66 31.6	−27.2	55.3	67 04.9	−25.3•	57.3	67 36.4	−23.2•	59.3	68 06.1	−21.0•	61.5	68 33.7	−18.6•	63.7	68 59.2	−16.2•	66.0	29
30	64 49.5	−32.3	49.7	65 27.7	−30.8	51.4	66 04.4	−29.0	53.1	66 39.6	−27.2	55.0	67 13.2	−25.2•	56.9	67 45.1	−23.2•	59.0	68 15.1	−21.0•	61.1	68 43.0	−18.6•	63.4	30
31	64 17.2	−33.9	47.7	64 56.9	−32.3	49.3	65 35.4	−30.8	51.0	66 12.4	−29.0	52.7	66 48.0	−27.3	54.6	67 21.9	−25.3•	56.5	67 54.1	−23.2•	58.6	68 24.4	−21.0•	60.8	31
32	63 43.3	−35.2	45.9	64 24.6	−33.9	47.3	65 04.6	−32.4	48.9	65 43.4	−30.8	50.6	66 20.7	−29.1	52.4	66 56.6	−27.3	54.2	67 30.9	−25.3•	56.2	68 03.4	−23.3•	58.2	32
33	63 08.1	−36.6	44.0	63 50.7	−35.3	45.5	64 32.2	−33.9	46.9	65 12.6	−32.5	48.5	65 51.6	−30.8	50.2	66 29.3	−29.1	52.0	67 05.6	−27.4	53.8	67 40.1	−25.3•	55.8	33
34	62 31.5	−37.9	42.3	63 15.4	−36.7	43.6	63 58.3	−35.4	45.1	64 40.1	−34.0	46.5	65 20.8	−32.5	48.1	66 00.2	−30.9	49.8	66 38.2	−29.2	51.6	67 14.8	−27.4•	53.4	34
35	61 53.6	−38.9	40.6	62 38.7	−37.8	41.9	63 22.9	−36.7	43.2	64 06.1	−35.4	44.6	64 48.3	−34.0	46.1	65 29.3	−32.6	47.7	66 09.0	−31.0	49.4	66 47.4	−29.3	51.1	35
36	61 14.7	−40.1	39.0	62 00.9	−39.1	40.2	62 46.2	−37.9	41.5	63 30.7	−36.7	42.8	64 14.3	−35.5	44.2	64 56.7	−34.1	45.7	65 38.0	−32.6	47.3	66 18.1	−31.0	48.9	36
37	60 34.6	−41.1	37.5	61 21.8	−40.1	38.6	62 08.3	−39.1	39.8	62 54.0	−38.0	41.1	63 38.8	−36.8	42.4	64 22.6	−35.5	43.8	65 05.4	−34.2	45.3	65 47.1	−32.8	46.8	37
38	59 53.5	−42.0	36.0	60 41.7	−41.1	37.1	61 29.2	−40.2	38.2	62 16.0	−39.2	39.4	63 02.0	−38.1	40.6	63 47.1	−37.0	41.9	64 31.2	−35.6	43.3	65 14.3	−34.3	44.8	38
39	59 11.5	−42.9	34.6	60 00.6	−42.1	35.6	60 49.0	−41.2	36.7	61 36.8	−40.2	37.8	62 23.9	−39.3	38.9	63 10.1	−38.1	40.2	63 55.6	−37.1	41.5	64 40.0	−35.7	42.9	39
40	58 28.6	−43.7	33.3	59 18.5	−43.0	34.2	60 07.8	−42.1	35.2	60 56.6	−41.3	36.2	61 44.6	−40.3	37.3	62 32.0	−39.4	38.5	63 18.5	−38.2	39.7	64 04.3	−37.1	41.0	40
41	57 44.9	−44.5	32.0	58 35.5	−43.7	32.9	59 25.7	−43.0	33.8	60 15.3	−42.2	34.7	61 04.3	−41.4	35.8	61 52.6	−40.4	36.9	62 40.3	−39.5	38.0	63 27.2	−38.4	39.2	41
42	57 00.4	−45.2	30.7	57 51.8	−44.6	31.6	58 42.7	−43.9	32.4	59 33.1	−43.1	33.3	60 22.9	−42.3	34.3	61 12.2	−41.5	35.3	62 00.8	−40.5	36.4	62 48.8	−39.6	37.5	42
43	56 15.2	−45.8	29.6	57 07.2	−45.2	30.3	57 58.8	−44.6	31.1	58 50.0	−44.0	32.0	59 40.6	−43.2	32.9	60 30.7	−42.4	33.8	61 20.3	−41.6	34.8	62 09.2	−40.6	35.9	43
44	55 29.4	−46.5	28.4	56 22.0	−45.9	29.1	57 14.2	−45.3	29.9	58 06.0	−44.6	30.7	58 57.4	−44.0	31.5	59 48.3	−43.2	32.4	60 38.7	−42.5	33.3	61 28.6	−41.7	34.4	44
45	54 42.9	−47.0	27.3	55 36.1	−46.6	28.0	56 28.9	−46.0	28.7	57 21.4	−45.4	29.4	58 13.4	−44.8	30.2	59 05.1	−44.1	31.0	59 56.2	−43.4	31.9	60 46.9	−42.6	32.9	45
46	53 55.9	−47.6	26.2	54 49.5	−47.1	26.9	55 42.9	−46.6	27.5	56 36.0	−46.1	28.2	57 28.6	−45.4	28.9	58 21.0	−44.9	29.7	59 12.8	−44.2	30.6	60 04.3	−43.5	31.4	46
47	53 08.3	−48.1	25.2	54 02.4	−47.6	25.8	54 56.3	−47.2	26.4	55 49.9	−46.7	27.1	56 43.2	−46.2	27.7	57 36.1	−45.6	28.5	58 28.6	−44.9	29.3	59 20.8	−44.4	30.1	47
48	52 20.2	−48.6	24.2	53 14.8	−48.2	24.8	54 09.1	−47.7	25.3	55 03.2	−47.3	26.0	55 57.0	−46.8	26.6	56 50.5	−46.2	27.3	57 43.7	−45.7	28.0	58 36.4	−45.0	28.8	48
49	51 31.6	−49.0	23.3	52 26.6	−48.7	23.8	53 21.4	−48.3	24.3	54 15.9	−47.8	24.9	55 10.2	−47.3	25.5	56 04.3	−46.9	26.1	56 58.0	−46.4	26.8	57 51.4	−45.8	27.5	49
50	50 42.6	−49.5	22.3	51 37.9	−49.0	22.8	52 33.1	−48.7	23.3	53 28.1	−48.3	23.9	54 22.9	−47.9	24.4	55 17.4	−47.5	25.0	56 11.6	−46.9	25.6	57 05.6	−46.5	26.3	50
51	49 53.1	−49.8	21.5	50 48.9	−49.5	21.9	51 44.4	−49.1	22.4	52 39.8	−48.8	22.9	53 35.0	−48.4	23.4	54 29.9	−47.9	24.0	55 24.7	−47.6	24.5	56 19.1	−47.1	25.2	51
52	49 03.3	−50.2	20.6	49 59.4	−49.9	21.0	50 55.3	−49.6	21.5	51 51.0	−49.2	21.9	52 46.6	−48.9	22.4	53 42.0	−48.5	22.9	54 37.1	−48.1	23.5	55 32.0	−47.6	24.0	52
53	48 13.1	−50.6	19.8	49 09.5	−50.3	20.2	50 05.7	−50.0	20.6	51 01.8	−49.6	21.0	51 57.7	−49.3	21.5	52 53.5	−49.0	21.9	53 49.0	−48.6	22.4	54 44.4	−48.2	23.0	53
54	47 22.5	−50.9	19.0	48 19.2	−50.6	19.3	49 15.7	−50.3	19.7	50 12.2	−50.1	20.1	51 08.4	−49.7	20.5	52 04.5	−49.4	21.0	53 00.4	−49.0	21.5	53 56.2	−48.7	22.0	54
55	46 31.6	−51.1	18.2	47 28.6	−51.0	18.5	48 25.4	−50.7	18.9	49 22.1	−50.4	19.3	50 18.7	−50.1	19.7	51 15.1	−49.8	20.1	52 11.4	−49.5	20.5	53 07.5	−49.2	21.0	55
56	45 40.5	−51.5	17.4	46 37.6	−51.2	17.8	47 34.7	−51.0	18.1	48 31.7	−50.7	18.4	49 28.6	−50.5	18.8	50 25.3	−50.2	19.2	51 21.9	−49.9	19.6	52 18.3	−49.6	20.0	56
57	44 49.0	−51.8	16.7	45 46.4	−51.5	17.0	46 43.7	−51.3	17.3	47 41.0	−51.1	17.6	48 38.1	−50.8	18.0	49 35.1	−50.6	18.3	50 32.0	−50.3	18.7	51 28.7	−50.0	19.1	57
58	43 57.2	−51.9	16.0	44 54.9	−51.8	16.3	45 52.4	−51.6	16.6	46 49.9	−51.4	16.9	47 47.3	−51.2	17.2	48 44.5	−50.9	17.5	49 41.7	−50.7	17.9	50 38.7	−50.3	18.2	58
59	43 05.3	−52.3	15.3	44 03.1	−52.1	15.6	45 00.8	−51.8	15.8	45 58.5	−51.6	16.1	46 56.1	−51.4	16.4	47 53.6	−51.2	16.7	48 51.0	−50.9	17.1	49 48.4	−50.8	17.4	59
60	42 13.0	−52.4	14.6	43 11.0	−52.3	14.9	44 09.0	−52.1	15.1	45 06.9	−52.0	15.4	46 04.7	−51.7	15.7	47 02.4	−51.5	16.0	48 00.1	−51.4	16.3	48 57.6	−51.1	16.6	60
61	41 20.6	−52.7	14.0	42 18.7	−52.5	14.2	43 16.9	−52.4	14.4	44 14.9	−52.1	14.7	45 13.0	−52.0	14.9	46 10.9	−51.8	15.2	47 08.7	−51.6	15.5	48 06.5	−51.4	15.8	61
62	40 27.9	−52.9	13.4	41 26.2	−52.7	13.6	42 24.5	−52.5	13.8	43 22.8	−52.4	14.0	44 21.0	−52.3	14.2	45 19.1	−52.1	14.5	46 17.1	−51.8	14.7	47 15.1	−51.7	15.0	62
63	39 35.0	−53.1	12.7	40 33.5	−52.9	12.9	41 32.0	−52.8	13.1	42 30.4	−52.7	13.3	43 28.7	−52.5	13.6	44 27.0	−52.3	13.8	45 25.3	−52.2	14.0	46 23.4	−51.9	14.3	63
64	38 41.9	−53.2	12.1	39 40.6	−53.2	12.3	40 39.2	−53.0	12.5	41 37.7	−52.8	12.7	42 36.2	−52.7	12.9	43 34.7	−52.6	13.1	44 33.1	−52.4	13.3	45 31.5	−52.3	13.6	64
65	37 48.7	−53.4	11.6	38 47.4	−53.3	11.7	39 46.2	−53.2	11.9	40 44.9	−53.1	12.1	41 43.5	−52.9	12.2	42 42.1	−52.7	12.4	43 40.7	−52.6	12.6	44 39.2	−52.5	12.9	65
66	36 55.3	−53.6	11.0	37 54.1	−53.4	11.1	38 53.0	−53.4	11.3	39 51.8	−53.2	11.4	40 50.6	−53.1	11.6	41 49.4	−53.0	11.8	42 48.1	−52.9	12.0	43 46.7	−52.7	12.2	66
67	36 01.7	−53.8	10.4	37 00.7	−53.7	10.6	37 59.6	−53.5	10.7	38 58.6	−53.4	10.9	39 57.5	−53.3	11.0	40 56.4	−53.2	11.2	41 55.2	−53.0	11.3	42 54.0	−52.9	11.5	67
68	35 07.9	−53.8	9.9	36 07.0	−53.7	10.0	37 06.1	−53.7	10.1	38 05.2	−53.6	10.3	39 04.2	−53.5	10.4	40 03.2	−53.4	10.6	41 02.2	−53.3	10.7	42 01.1	−53.1	10.9	68
69	34 14.1	−54.1	9.3	35 13.3	−54.0	9.5	36 12.4	−53.8	9.6	37 11.6	−53.8	9.7	38 10.7	−53.6	9.8	39 09.8	−53.5	10.0	40 08.9	−53.4	10.1	41 08.0	−53.4	10.3	69
70	33 20.0	−54.1	8.8	34 19.3	−54.0	8.9	35 18.6	−54.0	9.0	36 17.8	−53.9	9.1	37 17.1	−53.8	9.3	38 16.3	−53.7	9.4	39 15.5	−53.7	9.5	40 14.6	−53.5	9.7	70
71	32 25.9	−54.3	8.3	33 25.3	−54.2	8.4	34 24.6	−54.1	8.5	35 23.9	−54.0	8.6	36 23.3	−54.0	8.7	37 22.6	−53.9	8.8	38 21.8	−53.7	8.9	39 21.1	−53.7	9.1	71
72	31 31.6	−54.3	7.8	32 31.1	−54.3	7.9	33 30.5	−54.2	8.0	34 29.9	−54.2	8.1	35 29.3	−54.1	8.2	36 28.7	−54.0	8.3	37 28.1	−54.0	8.4	38 27.4	−53.8	8.5	72
73	30 37.3	−54.5	7.3	31 36.8	−54.5	7.4	32 36.3	−54.4	7.5	33 35.7	−54.3	7.6	34 35.2	−54.2	7.6	35 34.7	−54.2	7.7	36 34.1	−54.1	7.8	37 33.6	−54.1	7.9	73
74	29 42.8	−54.6	6.8	30 42.3	−54.5	6.9	31 41.9	−54.5	7.0	32 41.4	−54.4	7.0	33 41.0	−54.4	7.1	34 40.5	−54.3	7.2	35 40.0	−54.2	7.3	36 39.5	−54.1	7.4	74
75	28 48.2	−54.7	6.4	29 47.8	−54.6	6.4	30 47.4	−54.6	6.5	31 47.0	−54.5	6.5	32 46.6	−54.4	6.6	33 46.2	−54.4	6.7	34 45.8	−54.3	6.8	35 45.4	−54.3	6.9	75
76	27 53.5	−54.8	5.9	28 53.2	−54.8	5.9	29 52.8	−54.7	6.0	30 52.5	−54.6	6.1	31 52.2	−54.6	6.1	32 51.8	−54.5	6.2	33 51.5	−54.5	6.3	34 51.1	−54.4	6.3	76
77	26 58.7	−54.9	5.4	27 58.4	−54.8	5.5	28 58.1	−54.7	5.5	29 57.9	−54.8	5.6	30 57.6	−54.7	5.6	31 57.3	−54.7	5.7	32 57.0	−54.6	5.8	33 56.7	−54.6	5.8	77
78	26 03.8	−54.9	5.0	27 03.6	−54.9	5.0	28 03.4	−54.9	5.1	29 03.1	−54.8	5.1	30 02.9	−54.8	5.2	31 02.6	−54.7	5.2	32 02.4	−54.7	5.3	33 02.1	−54.6	5.3	78
79	25 08.9	−55.1	4.5	26 08.7	−55.0	4.6	27 08.5	−55.0	4.6	28 08.3	−55.0	4.6	29 08.1	−54.9	4.7	30 07.9	−54.9	4.7	31 07.7	−54.9	4.8	32 07.5	−54.8	4.8	79
80	24 13.8	−55.1	4.1	25 13.7	−55.1	4.1	26 13.5	−55.0	4.2	27 13.3	−55.0	4.2	28 13.2	−55.0	4.2	29 13.0	−54.9	4.3	30 12.8	−54.9	4.3	31 12.7	−54.9	4.4	80
81	23 18.7	−55.2	3.7	24 18.6	−55.2	3.7	25 18.5	−55.2	3.7	26 18.3	−55.1	3.7	27 18.2	−55.1	3.8	28 18.1	−55.1	3.8	29 17.9	−55.0	3.9	30 17.8	−55.0	3.9	81
82	22 23.5	−55.2	3.2	23 23.4	−55.2	3.3	24 23.3	−55.2	3.3	25 23.2	−55.1	3.3	26 23.1	−55.1	3.3	27 23.0	−55.1	3.4	28 22.9	−55.1	3.4	29 22.8	−55.1	3.4	82
83	21 28.3	−55.3	2.8	22 28.2	−55.3	2.8	23 28.1	−55.2	2.9	24 28.1	−55.3	2.9	25 28.0	−55.2	2.9	26 27.9	−55.2	2.9	27 27.8	−55.2	2.9	28 27.7	−55.1	3.0	83
84	20 33.0	−55.4	2.4	21 32.9	−55.3	2.4	22 32.9	−55.4	2.4	23 32.8	−55.3	2.4	24 32.8	−55.3	2.5	25 32.7	−55.3	2.5	26 32.6	−55.2	2.5	27 32.6	−55.3	2.5	84
85	19 37.6	−55.4	2.0	20 37.6	−55.4	2.0	21 37.5	−55.4	2.0	22 37.5	−55.4	2.0	23 37.5	−55.4	2.0	24 37.4	−55.3	2.1	25 37.4	−55.4	2.1	26 37.3	−55.3	2.1	85
86	18 42.2	−55.5	1.6	19 42.2	−55.5	1.6	20 42.1	−55.4	1.6	21 42.1	−55.4	1.6	22 42.1	−55.4	1.6	23 42.1	−55.5	1.6	24 42.0	−55.4	1.6	25 42.0	−55.4	1.7	86
87	17 46.7	−55.5	1.2	18 46.7	−55.5	1.2	19 46.7	−55.5	1.2	20 46.7	−55.5	1.2	21 46.7	−55.5	1.2	22 46.6	−55.4	1.2	23 46.6	−55.5	1.2	24 46.6	−55.5	1.2	87
88	16 51.2	−55.6	0.8	17 51.2	−55.6	0.8	18 51.2	−55.6	0.8	19 51.2	−55.6	0.8	20 51.2	−55.6	0.8	21 51.2	−55.6	0.8	22 51.1	−55.5	0.8	23 51.1	−55.5	0.8	88
89	15 55.6	−55.6	0.4	16 55.6	−55.6	0.4	17 55.6	−55.6	0.4	18 55.6	−55.6	0.4	19 55.6	−55.6	0.4	20 55.6	−55.6	0.4	21 55.6	−55.6	0.4	22 55.6	−55.6	0.4	89
90	15 00.0	−55.7	0.0	16 00.0	−55.7	0.0	17 00.0	−55.7	0.0	18 00.0	−55.7	0.0	19 00.0	−55.7	0.0	20 00.0	−55.7	0.0	21 00.0	−55.7	0.0	22 00.0	−55.7	0.0	90
	15°			16°			17°			18°			19°			20°			21°			22°			

LATITUDE **CONTRARY** NAME TO DECLINATION — L.H.A. 22°, 338°

Dec.	15° Hc	d	Z	16° Hc	d	Z	17° Hc	d	Z	18° Hc	d	Z	19° Hc	d	Z	20° Hc	d	Z	21° Hc	d	Z	22° Hc	d	Z	Dec.
°	° ′	′	°	° ′	′	°	° ′	′	°	° ′	′	°	° ′	′	°	° ′	′	°	° ′	′	°	° ′	′	°	°
0	63 35.1	-35.6	122.6	63 02.0	-37.1	124.3	62 27.5	-38.6	125.9	61 51.6	-39.8	127.4	61 14.6	-41.1	128.9	60 36.4	-42.3	130.2	59 57.1	-43.4	131.6	59 16.8	-44.4	132.8	0
1	62 59.5	-36.9	124.4	62 24.9	-38.4	126.0	61 48.9	-39.6	127.5	61 11.8	-40.9	129.0	60 33.5	-42.1	130.4	59 54.1	-43.2	131.7	59 13.7	-44.2	132.9	58 32.4	-45.2	134.1	1
2	62 22.6	-38.1	126.2	61 46.5	-39.4	127.7	61 09.3	-40.7	129.1	60 30.9	-41.9	130.5	59 51.4	-43.0	131.8	59 10.9	-44.0	133.0	58 29.5	-44.9	134.2	57 47.2	-45.8	135.4	2
3	61 44.5	-39.3	127.8	61 07.1	-40.5	129.2	60 28.6	-41.7	130.6	59 49.0	-42.8	131.9	59 08.4	-43.8	133.2	58 26.9	-44.7	134.4	57 44.6	-45.7	135.5	57 01.4	-46.6	136.6	3
4	61 05.2	-40.3	129.4	60 26.6	-41.5	130.8	59 46.9	-42.6	132.1	59 06.2	-43.6	133.3	58 24.6	-44.6	134.5	57 42.2	-45.5	135.6	56 58.9	-46.4	136.7	56 14.8	-47.1	137.7	4
5	60 24.9	-41.3	130.9	59 45.1	-42.4	132.2	59 04.3	-43.4	133.4	58 22.6	-44.4	134.6	57 40.0	-45.3	135.8	56 56.7	-46.2	136.8	56 12.5	-46.9	137.9	55 27.7	-47.7	138.8	5
6	59 43.6	-42.2	132.4	59 02.7	-43.3	133.6	58 20.9	-44.2	134.8	57 38.2	-45.1	135.9	56 54.7	-45.9	137.0	56 10.5	-46.8	138.0	55 25.6	-47.5	139.0	54 40.0	-48.2	139.9	6
7	59 01.4	-43.1	133.7	58 19.4	-44.0	134.9	57 36.7	-45.0	136.0	56 53.1	-45.8	137.1	56 08.8	-46.7	138.1	55 23.7	-47.3	139.1	54 38.1	-48.1	140.0	53 51.8	-48.8	140.9	7
8	58 18.3	-43.9	135.1	57 35.4	-44.8	136.2	56 51.7	-45.7	137.3	56 07.3	-46.5	138.3	55 22.1	-47.2	139.2	54 36.4	-48.0	140.2	53 50.0	-48.6	141.1	53 03.0	-49.2	141.9	8
9	57 34.4	-44.7	136.4	56 50.6	-45.5	137.4	56 06.0	-46.3	138.4	55 20.8	-47.1	139.4	54 34.9	-47.7	140.3	53 48.4	-48.4	141.2	53 01.4	-49.0	142.0	52 13.8	-49.6	142.8	9
10	56 49.7	-45.3	137.6	56 05.1	-46.2	138.6	55 19.7	-46.9	139.6	54 33.7	-47.6	140.5	53 47.2	-48.3	141.4	53 00.0	-48.9	142.2	52 12.4	-49.5	143.0	51 24.2	-50.0	143.7	10
11	56 04.4	-46.0	138.8	55 18.9	-46.7	139.7	54 32.8	-47.4	140.7	53 46.1	-48.1	141.5	52 58.9	-48.8	142.4	52 11.1	-49.3	143.1	51 22.9	-49.9	143.9	50 34.2	-50.4	144.6	11
12	55 18.4	-46.6	139.9	54 32.2	-47.4	140.8	53 45.4	-48.0	141.7	52 58.0	-48.6	142.5	52 10.1	-49.2	143.3	51 21.8	-49.8	144.1	50 33.0	-50.3	144.8	49 43.8	-50.8	145.5	12
13	54 31.8	-47.2	141.0	53 44.8	-47.8	141.9	52 57.4	-48.5	142.7	52 09.4	-49.1	143.5	51 20.9	-49.6	144.2	50 32.0	-50.1	145.0	49 42.7	-50.6	145.6	48 53.0	-51.1	146.3	13
14	53 44.6	-47.7	142.1	52 57.0	-48.4	142.9	52 08.9	-48.9	143.7	51 20.3	-49.5	144.4	50 31.3	-50.0	145.1	49 41.9	-50.5	145.8	48 52.1	-51.0	146.5	48 01.9	-51.5	147.1	14
15	52 56.9	-48.3	143.1	52 08.6	-48.8	143.9	51 20.0	-49.4	144.6	50 30.8	-49.9	145.3	49 41.3	-50.4	146.0	48 51.4	-50.9	146.6	48 01.1	-51.3	147.3	47 10.4	-51.7	147.8	15
16	52 08.6	-48.6	144.1	51 19.8	-49.2	144.8	50 30.6	-49.8	145.5	49 40.9	-50.2	146.2	48 50.9	-50.7	146.8	48 00.5	-51.2	147.4	47 09.8	-51.6	148.0	46 18.7	-52.0	148.6	16
17	51 20.0	-49.2	145.0	50 30.6	-49.6	145.7	49 40.8	-50.1	146.4	48 50.7	-50.7	147.0	48 00.2	-51.1	147.6	47 09.3	-51.5	148.2	46 18.2	-51.9	148.8	45 26.7	-52.2	149.3	17
18	50 30.8	-49.5	145.9	49 40.9	-50.0	146.6	48 50.7	-50.5	147.2	48 00.0	-50.9	147.8	47 09.1	-51.4	148.4	46 17.8	-51.7	149.0	45 26.3	-52.2	149.5	44 34.5	-52.5	150.0	18
19	49 41.3	-49.9	146.8	48 50.9	-50.4	147.4	48 00.2	-50.9	148.0	47 09.1	-51.3	148.6	46 17.7	-51.6	149.2	45 26.1	-52.1	149.7	44 34.1	-52.4	150.2	43 42.0	-52.8	150.7	19
20	48 51.4	-50.3	147.7	48 00.5	-50.7	148.3	47 09.3	-51.1	148.8	46 17.8	-51.5	149.4	45 26.1	-52.0	149.9	44 34.0	-52.3	150.4	43 41.7	-52.6	150.9	42 49.2	-52.9	151.3	20
21	48 01.1	-50.7	148.5	47 09.8	-51.1	149.0	46 18.2	-51.5	149.6	45 26.3	-51.8	150.1	44 34.1	-52.1	150.6	43 41.7	-52.5	151.1	42 49.1	-52.8	151.5	41 56.3	-53.2	152.0	21
22	47 10.4	-50.9	149.3	46 18.7	-51.3	149.8	45 26.7	-51.7	150.3	44 34.5	-52.1	150.8	43 42.0	-52.5	151.3	42 49.2	-52.7	151.7	41 56.3	-53.1	152.2	41 03.1	-53.3	152.6	22
23	46 19.5	-51.3	150.0	45 27.4	-51.7	150.6	44 35.0	-52.0	151.0	43 42.4	-52.3	151.5	42 49.5	-52.6	152.0	41 56.5	-53.0	152.4	41 03.2	-53.2	152.8	40 09.8	-53.6	153.2	23
24	45 28.2	-51.5	150.8	44 35.7	-51.8	151.3	43 43.0	-52.2	151.7	42 50.1	-52.6	152.2	41 56.9	-52.9	152.6	41 03.5	-53.1	153.0	40 10.0	-53.5	153.4	39 16.2	-53.7	153.8	24
25	44 36.7	-51.8	151.5	43 43.9	-52.2	152.0	42 50.8	-52.5	152.4	41 57.5	-52.8	152.8	41 04.0	-53.0	153.2	40 10.4	-53.4	153.6	39 16.5	-53.6	154.0	38 22.5	-53.9	154.3	25
26	43 44.9	-52.0	152.2	42 51.7	-52.4	152.7	41 58.3	-52.7	153.1	41 04.7	-52.9	153.5	40 11.0	-53.3	153.9	39 17.0	-53.5	154.2	38 22.9	-53.8	154.6	37 28.6	-54.0	154.9	26
27	42 52.9	-52.3	152.9	41 59.3	-52.6	153.3	41 05.6	-52.9	153.7	40 11.8	-53.2	154.1	39 17.7	-53.4	154.5	38 23.5	-53.7	154.8	37 29.1	-53.9	155.1	36 34.6	-54.1	155.4	27
28	42 00.6	-52.6	153.6	41 06.7	-52.8	154.0	40 12.7	-53.0	154.3	39 18.6	-53.4	154.7	38 24.3	-53.6	155.0	37 29.8	-53.8	155.4	36 35.2	-54.1	155.7	35 40.5	-54.4	156.0	28
29	41 08.0	-52.7	154.2	40 13.9	-53.0	154.6	39 19.7	-53.3	154.9	38 25.2	-53.5	155.3	37 30.7	-53.8	155.6	36 36.0	-54.0	155.9	35 41.1	-54.2	156.2	34 46.1	-54.4	156.5	29
30	40 15.3	-52.9	154.8	39 20.9	-53.2	155.2	38 26.4	-53.4	155.5	37 31.7	-53.7	155.9	36 36.9	-53.9	156.2	35 42.0	-54.2	156.5	34 46.9	-54.4	156.7	33 51.7	-54.5	157.0	30
31	39 22.4	-53.1	155.5	38 27.7	-53.3	155.8	37 33.0	-53.7	156.1	36 38.0	-53.8	156.4	35 43.0	-54.1	156.7	34 47.8	-54.3	157.0	33 52.5	-54.4	157.2	32 57.2	-54.7	157.5	31
32	38 29.3	-53.3	156.1	37 34.4	-53.6	156.4	36 39.3	-53.7	156.7	35 44.2	-54.0	157.0	34 48.9	-54.2	157.2	33 53.5	-54.4	157.5	32 58.1	-54.6	157.7	32 02.5	-54.8	158.0	32
33	37 36.0	-53.5	156.6	36 40.8	-53.6	156.9	35 45.6	-53.9	157.2	34 50.2	-54.1	157.5	33 54.7	-54.3	157.8	32 59.1	-54.5	158.0	32 03.5	-54.7	158.2	31 07.7	-54.9	158.5	33
34	36 42.5	-53.6	157.2	35 47.2	-53.9	157.5	34 51.7	-54.1	157.8	33 56.1	-54.3	158.0	33 00.4	-54.4	158.3	32 04.6	-54.6	158.5	31 08.8	-54.9	158.7	30 12.8	-55.0	158.9	34
35	35 48.9	-53.8	157.8	34 53.3	-54.0	158.0	33 57.6	-54.2	158.3	33 01.8	-54.3	158.5	32 06.0	-54.6	158.8	31 10.0	-54.8	159.0	30 13.9	-54.9	159.2	29 17.8	-55.1	159.4	35
36	34 55.1	-53.9	158.3	33 59.3	-54.1	158.6	33 03.4	-54.3	158.8	32 07.5	-54.5	159.0	31 11.4	-54.7	159.3	30 15.2	-54.8	159.5	29 19.0	-55.0	159.7	28 22.7	-55.1	159.9	36
37	34 01.2	-54.0	158.8	33 05.2	-54.2	159.1	32 09.1	-54.4	159.3	31 13.0	-54.6	159.5	30 16.7	-54.7	159.7	29 20.4	-54.9	159.9	28 24.0	-55.1	160.1	27 27.6	-55.3	160.3	37
38	33 07.2	-54.2	159.4	32 11.0	-54.4	159.6	31 14.7	-54.5	159.8	30 18.4	-54.7	160.0	29 22.0	-54.9	160.2	28 25.5	-55.1	160.4	27 28.9	-55.2	160.6	26 32.3	-55.3	160.7	38
39	32 13.0	-54.3	159.9	31 16.6	-54.4	160.1	30 20.2	-54.7	160.3	29 23.7	-54.8	160.5	28 27.1	-55.0	160.7	27 30.4	-55.1	160.8	26 33.7	-55.2	161.0	25 37.0	-55.4	161.2	39
40	31 18.7	-54.4	160.4	30 22.2	-54.6	160.6	29 25.5	-54.7	160.8	28 28.9	-54.9	160.9	27 32.1	-55.0	161.1	26 35.3	-55.2	161.3	25 38.5	-55.4	161.4	24 41.6	-55.5	161.6	40
41	30 24.3	-54.5	160.9	29 27.6	-54.7	161.1	28 30.8	-54.8	161.2	27 34.0	-55.0	161.4	26 37.1	-55.2	161.6	25 40.1	-55.2	161.7	24 43.1	-55.4	161.9	23 46.1	-55.6	162.0	41
42	29 29.8	-54.6	161.3	28 32.9	-54.8	161.5	27 36.0	-54.9	161.7	26 39.0	-55.1	161.9	25 41.9	-55.2	162.0	24 44.9	-55.4	162.1	23 47.7	-55.5	162.3	22 50.5	-55.6	162.4	42
43	28 35.2	-54.7	161.8	27 38.1	-54.8	162.0	26 41.1	-55.1	162.1	25 43.9	-55.1	162.3	24 46.7	-55.2	162.4	23 49.5	-55.4	162.6	22 52.2	-55.5	162.7	21 54.9	-55.6	162.8	43
44	27 40.5	-54.9	162.3	26 43.3	-55.0	162.4	25 46.0	-55.0	162.6	24 48.8	-55.3	162.7	23 51.5	-55.4	162.9	22 54.1	-55.5	163.0	21 56.7	-55.6	163.1	20 59.3	-55.7	163.2	44
45	26 45.6	-54.9	162.7	25 48.3	-55.0	162.9	24 51.0	-55.2	163.0	23 53.5	-55.2	163.2	22 56.1	-55.4	163.3	21 58.6	-55.5	163.4	21 01.1	-55.7	163.5	20 03.6	-55.8	163.6	45
46	25 50.7	-54.9	163.2	24 53.3	-55.1	163.3	23 55.8	-55.2	163.5	22 58.3	-55.4	163.6	22 00.7	-55.5	163.7	21 03.1	-55.6	163.8	20 05.4	-55.7	163.9	19 07.8	-55.8	164.0	46
47	24 55.8	-55.1	163.6	23 58.2	-55.2	163.8	23 00.6	-55.3	163.9	22 02.9	-55.4	164.0	21 05.2	-55.5	164.1	20 07.5	-55.7	164.2	19 09.7	-55.7	164.3	18 12.0	-55.9	164.4	47
48	24 00.7	-55.1	164.1	23 03.0	-55.2	164.2	22 05.3	-55.4	164.3	21 07.5	-55.5	164.4	20 09.7	-55.6	164.5	19 11.8	-55.7	164.6	18 14.0	-55.8	164.7	17 16.1	-55.9	164.8	48
49	23 05.6	-55.2	164.5	22 07.8	-55.4	164.6	21 09.9	-55.4	164.7	20 12.0	-55.5	164.8	19 14.1	-55.7	164.9	18 16.1	-55.7	165.0	17 18.2	-55.9	165.1	16 20.2	-56.0	165.2	49
50	22 10.4	-55.3	164.9	21 12.4	-55.3	165.0	20 14.5	-55.5	165.1	19 16.5	-55.6	165.2	18 18.4	-55.7	165.3	17 20.4	-55.8	165.4	16 22.3	-55.9	165.5	15 24.2	-56.0	165.5	50
51	21 15.1	-55.3	165.3	20 17.1	-55.5	165.4	19 19.0	-55.6	165.5	18 20.9	-55.7	165.6	17 22.7	-55.7	165.7	16 24.6	-55.8	165.8	15 26.4	-55.9	165.8	14 28.2	-56.0	165.9	51
52	20 19.8	-55.4	165.8	19 21.6	-55.6	165.9	18 23.4	-55.5	165.9	17 25.2	-55.6	166.0	16 27.0	-55.8	166.1	15 28.8	-55.9	166.2	14 30.5	-56.0	166.2	13 32.2	-56.0	166.3	52
53	19 24.4	-55.4	166.2	18 26.2	-55.6	166.3	17 27.9	-55.7	166.3	16 29.6	-55.8	166.4	15 31.2	-55.8	166.5	14 32.9	-55.9	166.5	13 34.5	-56.0	166.6	12 36.2	-56.1	166.6	53
54	18 29.0	-55.5	166.6	17 30.6	-55.6	166.7	16 32.2	-55.6	166.7	15 33.8	-55.7	166.8	14 35.4	-55.8	166.8	13 37.0	-56.0	166.9	12 38.5	-56.0	167.0	11 40.1	-56.1	167.0	54
55	17 33.5	-55.5	167.0	16 35.0	-55.6	167.0	15 36.6	-55.8	167.1	14 38.1	-55.8	167.2	13 39.6	-55.9	167.2	12 41.0	-55.9	167.3	11 42.5	-56.1	167.3	10 44.0	-56.2	167.4	55
56	16 38.0	-55.6	167.4	15 39.4	-55.7	167.4	14 40.8	-55.7	167.5	13 42.3	-55.9	167.5	12 43.7	-56.0	167.6	11 45.1	-56.0	167.6	10 46.4	-56.0	167.7	9 47.8	-56.1	167.7	56
57	15 42.4	-55.6	167.8	14 43.7	-55.7	167.8	13 45.1	-55.8	167.9	12 46.4	-55.8	167.9	11 47.7	-55.9	168.0	10 49.1	-56.1	168.0	9 50.4	-56.1	168.0	8 51.7	-56.2	168.1	57
58	14 46.8	-55.7	168.2	13 48.0	-55.7	168.2	12 49.3	-55.8	168.3	11 50.6	-55.9	168.3	10 51.8	-56.0	168.3	9 53.0	-56.0	168.4	8 54.3	-56.2	168.4	7 55.5	-56.2	168.4	58
59	13 51.1	-55.7	168.5	12 52.3	-55.8	168.6	11 53.5	-55.8	168.6	10 54.7	-56.0	168.7	9 55.8	-56.0	168.7	8 57.0	-56.1	168.7	7 58.1	-56.1	168.8	6 59.3	-56.2	168.8	59
60	12 55.4	-55.7	168.9	11 56.5	-55.8	169.0	10 57.6	-55.8	169.0	9 58.7	-55.9	169.0	8 59.8	-56.0	169.1	8 00.9	-56.1	169.1	7 02.0	-56.2	169.1	6 03.1	-56.3	169.1	60
61	11 59.7	-55.8	169.3	11 00.7	-55.8	169.3	10 01.8	-55.9	169.4	9 02.8	-56.0	169.4	8 03.8	-56.0	169.4	7 04.8	-56.1	169.5	6 05.8	-56.1	169.5	5 06.8	-56.2	169.5	61
62	11 03.9	-55.8	169.7	10 04.9	-55.9	169.7	9 05.9	-56.0	169.7	8 06.8	-56.0	169.8	7 07.8	-56.1	169.8	6 08.7	-56.1	169.8	5 09.7	-56.2	169.8	4 10.6	-56.2	169.8	62
63	10 08.1	-55.8	170.1	9 09.0	-55.8	170.1	8 09.9	-55.9	170.1	7 10.8	-56.0	170.1	6 11.7	-56.1	170.2	5 12.6	-56.1	170.2	4 13.5	-56.2	170.2	3 14.4	-56.3	170.2	63
64	9 12.3	-55.8	170.4	8 13.2	-55.9	170.4	7 14.0	-56.0	170.5	6 14.8	-56.0	170.5	5 15.6	-56.0	170.5	4 16.5	-56.2	170.5	3 17.3	-56.2	170.5	2 18.1	-56.3	170.5	64
65	8 16.5	-55.9	170.8	7 17.3	-55.9	170.8	6 18.0	-55.9	170.8	5 18.8	-56.0	170.9	4 19.6	-56.1	170.9	3 20.3	-56.1	170.9	2 21.1	-56.2	170.9	1 21.8	-56.2	170.9	65
66	7 20.6	-55.8	171.2	6 21.4	-56.0	171.2	5 22.1	-56.0	171.2	4 22.8	-56.1	171.2	3 23.5	-56.1	171.2	2 24.2	-56.2	171.2	1 24.9	-56.2	171.2	0 25.6	-56.3	171.2	66
67	6 24.8	-55.9	171.5	5 25.4	-55.9	171.5	4 26.1	-56.0	171.6	3 26.7	-56.0	171.6	2 27.4	-56.1	171.6	1 28.0	-56.1	171.6	0 28.7	-56.2	171.6	0 30.7	+56.3	8.4	67
68	5 28.9	-55.9	171.9	4 29.5	-56.0	171.9	3 30.1	-56.0	171.9	2 30.7	-56.1	171.9	1 31.3	-56.1	171.9	0 31.9	-56.2	171.9	0 27.5	+56.3	8.1	1 27.0	+56.2	8.1	68
69	4 33.0	-55.9	172.3	3 33.5	-55.9	172.3	2 34.1	-56.0	172.3	1 34.6	-56.0	172.3	0 35.2	-56.2	172.3	0 24.3	+56.2	7.7	1 23.8	+56.2	7.7	2 23.2	+56.3	7.7	69
70	3 37.1	-56.0	172.6	2 37.6	-56.0	172.6	1 38.1	-56.1	172.6	0 38.6	-56.1	172.6	0 21.0	+56.1	7.4	1 20.5	+56.1	7.4	2 20.0	+56.2	7.4	3 19.5	+56.2	7.4	70
71	2 41.1	-55.9	173.0	1 41.6	-56.0	173.0	0 42.0	-56.0	173.0	0 17.5	+56.1	7.0	1 17.1	+56.1	7.0	2 16.6	+56.2	7.0	3 16.2	+56.2	7.0	4 15.7	+56.3	7.0	71
72	1 45.2	-55.9	173.3	0 45.6	-56.0	173.4	0 14.0	+56.0	6.6	1 13.6	+56.0	6.6	2 13.2	+56.1	6.7	3 12.8	+56.1	6.7	4 12.4	+56.1	6.7	5 12.0	+56.2	6.7	72
73	0 49.3	-56.0	173.7	0 10.4	+55.9	6.3	1 10.0	+56.0	6.3	2 09.6	+56.1	6.3	3 09.3	+56.1	6.3	4 08.9	+56.1	6.3	5 08.5	+56.2	6.3	6 08.2	+56.2	6.3	73
74	0 06.7	+55.9	5.9	1 06.3	+56.0	5.9	2 06.0	+56.0	5.9	3 05.7	+56.0	5.9	4 05.4	+56.0	5.9	5 05.0	+56.0	6.0	6 04.7	+56.2	6.0	7 04.4	+56.2	6.0	74
75	1 02.6	+55.9	5.6	2 02.3	+56.0	5.6	3 02.0	+56.0	5.6	4 01.7	+56.1	5.6	5 01.4	+56.1	5.6	6 01.2	+56.1	5.6	7 00.9	+56.1	5.6	8 00.6	+56.2	5.6	75
76	1 58.5	+55.9	5.2	2 58.3	+55.9	5.2	3 58.0	+56.0	5.2	4 57.8	+56.0	5.2	5 57.5	+56.1	5.2	6 57.3	+56.1	5.2	7 57.0	+56.1	5.3	8 56.8	+56.1	5.3	76
77	2 54.4	+56.0	4.8	3 54.2	+56.0	4.8	4 54.0	+56.0	4.9	5 53.8	+56.0	4.9	6 53.6	+56.0	4.9	7 53.4	+56.0	4.9	8 53.1	+56.2	4.9	9 52.9	+56.2	4.9	77
78	3 50.4	+55.9	4.5	4 50.2	+55.9	4.5	5 50.0	+56.0	4.5	6 49.8	+56.0	4.5	7 49.6	+56.0	4.5	8 49.4	+56.1	4.5	9 49.3	+56.0	4.5	10 49.1	+56.1	4.5	78
79	4 46.3	+55.9	4.1	5 46.1	+55.9	4.1	6 46.0	+55.9	4.1	7 45.8	+56.0	4.1	8 45.6	+56.1	4.1	9 45.5	+56.0	4.2	10 45.3	+56.1	4.2	11 45.2	+56.1	4.2	79
80	5 42.2	+55.9	3.7	6 42.0	+56.0	3.8	7 41.9	+55.9	3.8	8 41.8	+55.9	3.8	9 41.7	+55.9	3.8	10 41.5	+56.0	3.8	11 41.4	+56.0	3.8	12 41.3	+56.0	3.8	80
81	6 38.1	+55.8	3.4	7 38.0	+55.8	3.4	8 37.8	+56.0	3.4	9 37.7	+56.0	3.4	10 37.6	+56.0	3.4	11 37.5	+56.0	3.4	12 37.4	+56.0	3.4	13 37.3	+56.0	3.5	81
82	7 33.9	+55.9	3.0	8 33.8	+55.8	3.0	9 33.8	+55.8	3.0	10 33.7	+55.9	3.0	11 33.6	+55.9	3.1	12 33.5	+56.0	3.1	13 33.4	+56.0	3.1	14 33.3	+56.0	3.1	82
83	8 29.8	+55.8	2.6	9 29.7	+55.9	2.7	10 29.6	+55.9	2.7	11 29.6	+55.9	2.7	12 29.5	+55.8	2.7	13 29.5	+55.9	2.7	14 29.4	+55.9	2.7	15 29.3	+56.0	2.7	83
84	9 25.6	+55.8	2.3	10 25.6	+55.8	2.3	11 25.5	+55.8	2.3	12 25.5	+55.8	2.3	13 25.4	+55.9	2.3	14 25.4	+55.8	2.3	15 25.3	+55.9	2.3	16 25.3	+55.9	2.3	84
85	10 21.4	+55.8	1.9	11 21.4	+55.8	1.9	12 21.3	+55.8	1.9	13 21.3	+55.8	1.9	14 21.3	+55.8	1.9	15 21.2	+55.9	1.9	16 21.2	+55.9	1.9	17 21.2	+55.8	2.0	85
86	11 17.2	+55.7	1.5	12 17.2	+55.7	1.5	13 17.1	+55.8	1.5	14 17.1	+55.8	1.5	15 17.1	+55.8	1.6	16 17.1	+55.8	1.6	17 17.1	+55.8	1.6	18 17.0	+55.9	1.6	86
87	12 12.9	+55.8	1.1	13 12.9	+55.8	1.2	14 12.9	+55.8	1.2	15 12.9	+55.7	1.2	16 12.9	+55.7	1.2	17 12.9	+55.7	1.2	18 12.9	+55.7	1.2	19 12.9	+55.7	1.2	87
88	13 08.7	+55.6	0.8	14 08.7	+55.6	0.8	15 08.7	+55.6	0.8	16 08.6	+55.7	0.8	17 08.6	+55.7	0.8	18 08.6	+55.7	0.8	19 08.6	+55.7	0.8	20 08.6	+55.7	0.8	88
89	14 04.3	+55.7	0.4	15 04.3	+55.7	0.4	16 04.3	+55.7	0.4	17 04.3	+55.7	0.4	18 04.3	+55.7	0.4	19 04.3	+55.7	0.4	20 04.3	+55.7	0.4	21 04.3	+55.7	0.4	89
90	15 00.0	+55.6	0.0	16 00.0	+55.6	0.0	17 00.0	+55.6	0.0	18 00.0	+55.6	0.0	19 00.0	+55.6	0.0	20 00.0	+55.6	0.0	21 00.0	+55.6	0.0	22 00.0	+55.6	0.0	90
	15°			16°			17°			18°			19°			20°			21°			22°			

S. Lat. { L.H.A. greater than 180° ....Zn=180°−Z
{ L.H.A. less than 180°...........Zn=180°+Z

LATITUDE SAME NAME AS DECLINATION — L.H.A. 158°, 202°

23°, 337° L.H.A. LATITUDE SAME NAME AS DECLINATION N. Lat. {L.H.A. greater than 180° .....Zn=Z; L.H.A. less than 180°............Zn=360°–Z}

Dec.	15° Hc	d	Z	16° Hc	d	Z	17° Hc	d	Z	18° Hc	d	Z	19° Hc	d	Z	20° Hc	d	Z	21° Hc	d	Z	22° Hc	d	Z	Dec.
°	° ′	′	°	° ′	′	°	° ′	′	°	° ′	′	°	° ′	′	°	° ′	′	°	° ′	′	°	° ′	′	°	°
0	62 45.9	+33.2	121.4	62 14.0	+34.8	123.0	61 40.6	+36.4	124.6	61 05.9	+37.8	126.1	60 30.0	+39.1	127.5	59 52.9	+40.4	128.9	59 14.7	+41.6	130.2	58 35.5	+42.7	131.4	0
1	63 19.1	+31.8	119.5	62 48.8	+33.5	121.2	62 17.0	+35.0	122.9	61 43.7	+36.6	124.4	61 09.1	+38.0	125.9	60 33.3	+39.4	127.4	59 56.3	+40.6	128.7	59 18.2	+41.8	130.1	1
2	63 50.9	+30.2	117.6	63 22.3	+31.9	119.4	62 52.0	+33.7	121.1	62 20.3	+35.3	122.7	61 47.1	+36.9	124.3	61 12.7	+38.2	125.8	60 36.9	+39.6	127.3	60 00.0	+40.9	128.6	2
3	64 21.1	+28.5	115.6	63 54.2	+30.5	117.5	63 25.7	+32.3	119.3	62 55.6	+33.9	121.0	62 24.0	+35.5	122.6	61 50.9	+37.1	124.2	61 16.5	+38.5	125.7	60 40.9	+39.8	127.2	3
4	64 49.6	+26.8	113.6	64 24.7	+28.8	115.5	63 58.0	+30.6	117.4	63 29.5	+32.5	119.2	62 59.5	+34.2	120.9	62 28.0	+35.8	122.5	61 55.0	+37.4	124.1	61 20.7	+38.8	125.6	4
5	65 16.4	+24.9	111.5	64 53.5	+27.0	113.5	64 28.6	+29.1	115.4	64 02.0	+31.0	117.3	63 33.7	+32.8	119.0	63 03.8	+34.5	120.8	62 32.4	+36.0	122.4	61 59.5	+37.6	124.0	5
6	65 41.3	+23.0•	109.3	65 20.5	+25.2	111.3	64 57.7	+27.3	113.3	64 33.0	+29.3	115.3	64 06.5	+31.2	117.1	63 38.3	+33.0	118.9	63 08.4	+34.7	120.7	62 37.1	+36.3	122.3	6
7	66 04.3	+20.9•	107.0	65 45.7	+23.2•	109.2	65 25.0	+25.4	111.2	65 02.3	+27.5	113.2	64 37.7	+29.5	115.2	64 11.3	+31.4	117.0	63 43.1	+33.3	118.8	63 13.4	+35.0	120.6	7
8	66 25.2	+18.8•	104.7	66 08.9	+21.2•	106.9	65 50.4	+23.5	109.0	65 29.8	+25.7	111.1	65 07.2	+27.8	113.1	64 42.7	+29.9	115.1	64 16.4	+31.8	117.0	63 48.4	+33.5	118.8	8
9	66 44.0	+16.6•	102.3	66 30.1	+19.1•	104.6	66 13.9	+21.5•	106.8	65 55.5	+23.8•	108.9	65 35.0	+26.0	111.0	65 12.6	+28.1	113.0	64 48.2	+30.1	115.0	64 21.9	+32.0	116.9	9
10	67 00.6	+14.3•	99.9	66 49.2	+16.8•	102.2	66 35.4	+19.3•	104.4	66 19.3	+21.7•	106.6	66 01.0	+24.0•	108.8	65 40.7	+26.2	110.9	65 18.3	+28.3	112.9	64 53.9	+30.4	114.9	10
11	67 14.9	+11.9•	97.4	67 06.0	+14.5•	99.7	66 54.7	+17.0•	102.0	66 41.0	+19.6•	104.3	66 25.0	+22.0•	106.5	66 06.9	+24.3	108.7	65 46.6	+26.6	110.8	65 24.3	+28.7	112.8	11
12	67 26.8	+9.4•	94.8	67 20.5	+12.1•	97.2	67 11.7	+14.8•	99.6	67 00.6	+17.3•	101.9	66 47.0	+19.9•	104.2	66 31.2	+22.3•	106.4	66 13.2	+24.5•	108.6	65 53.0	+26.8	110.7	12
13	67 36.2	+7.0•	92.2	67 32.6	+9.7•	94.7	67 26.5	+12.4•	97.1	67 17.9	+15.0•	99.4	67 06.9	+17.6•	101.8	66 53.5	+20.1•	104.1	66 37.7	+22.6•	106.3	66 19.8	+24.8	108.5	13
14	67 43.2	+4.4•	89.6	67 42.3	+7.2•	92.1	67 38.9	+9.9•	94.5	67 32.9	+12.7•	96.9	67 24.5	+15.2•	99.3	67 13.6	+17.8•	101.6	67 00.3	+20.4•	104.0	66 44.6	+22.9•	106.2	14
15	67 47.6	+1.9•	87.0	67 49.5	+4.6•	89.4	67 48.8	+7.4•	91.9	67 45.6	+10.1•	94.3	67 39.7	+12.9•	96.8	67 31.4	+15.6•	99.2	67 20.7	+18.1•	101.5	67 07.5	+20.6•	103.9	15
16	67 49.5	-0.7•	84.3	67 54.1	+2.1•	86.8	67 56.2	+4.9•	89.3	67 55.7	+7.6•	91.7	67 52.6	+10.4•	94.2	67 47.0	+13.1•	96.6	67 38.8	+15.8•	99.0	67 28.1	+18.4•	101.4	16
17	67 48.8	-3.2•	81.7	67 56.2	-0.5•	84.1	68 01.1	+2.2•	86.6	68 03.3	+5.1•	89.1	68 03.0	+7.9•	91.6	68 00.1	+10.6•	94.0	67 54.6	+13.3•	96.5	67 46.5	+16.1•	98.9	17
18	67 45.6	-5.9•	79.0	67 55.7	-3.1•	81.5	68 03.3	-0.3•	83.9	68 08.4	+2.5•	86.4	68 10.9	+5.2•	88.9	68 10.7	+8.1•	91.4	68 07.9	+10.9•	93.9	68 02.6	+13.6•	96.4	18
19	67 39.7	-8.3•	76.4	67 52.6	-5.6•	78.8	68 03.0	-2.9•	81.2	68 10.9	-0.2•	83.7	68 16.1	+2.7•	86.2	68 18.8	+5.5•	88.7	68 18.8	+8.3•	91.2	68 16.2	+11.1•	93.7	19
20	67 31.4	-10.7•	73.8	67 47.0	-8.2•	76.2	68 00.1	-5.5•	78.6	68 10.7	-2.8•	81.0	68 18.8	0.0•	83.5	68 24.3	+2.8•	86.0	68 27.1	+5.7•	88.5	68 27.3	+8.5•	91.1	20
21	67 20.7	-13.2•	71.3	67 38.8	-10.7•	73.6	67 54.6	-8.1•	75.9	68 07.9	-5.3•	78.3	68 18.8	-2.6•	80.8	68 27.1	+0.2•	83.3	68 32.8	+3.0•	85.8	68 35.8	+5.9•	88.4	21
22	67 07.5	-15.6•	68.7	67 28.1	-13.1•	71.0	67 46.5	-10.5•	73.3	68 02.6	-7.9•	75.7	68 16.2	-5.2•	78.1	68 27.3	-2.5•	80.6	68 35.8	+0.4•	83.1	68 41.7	+3.2•	85.6	22
23	66 51.9	-17.8•	66.3	67 15.0	-15.4•	68.5	67 36.0	-13.0•	70.7	67 54.7	-10.5•	73.0	68 11.0	-7.8•	75.4	68 24.8	-5.0•	77.9	68 36.2	-2.3•	80.4	68 44.9	+0.6•	82.9	23
24	66 34.1	-19.9•	63.9	66 59.6	-17.7•	66.0	67 23.0	-15.4•	68.2	67 44.2	-12.9•	70.4	68 03.2	-10.4•	72.8	68 19.8	-7.7•	75.2	68 33.9	-5.0•	77.6	68 45.5	-2.2•	80.1	24
25	66 14.2	-22.1•	61.5	66 41.9	-19.9•	63.5	67 07.6	-17.6•	65.7	67 31.3	-15.3•	67.9	67 52.8	-12.8•	70.1	68 12.1	-10.3•	72.5	68 28.9	-7.6•	74.9	68 43.3	-4.8•	77.4	25
26	65 52.1	-24.0	59.2	66 22.0	-22.0•	61.2	66 50.0	-19.9•	63.2	67 16.0	-17.6•	65.3	67 40.0	-15.2•	67.5	68 01.8	-12.7•	69.8	68 21.3	-10.1•	72.2	68 38.5	-7.5•	74.6	26
27	65 28.1	-26.0	57.0	66 00.0	-24.1	58.9	66 30.1	-22.0•	60.8	66 58.4	-19.8•	62.9	67 24.8	-17.6•	65.0	67 49.1	-15.2•	67.2	68 11.2	-12.7•	69.5	68 31.0	-10.1•	71.9	27
28	65 02.1	-27.7	54.8	65 35.9	-25.9	56.6	66 08.1	-24.0	58.5	66 38.6	-22.0•	60.5	67 07.2	-19.8•	62.5	67 33.9	-17.5•	64.7	67 58.5	-15.2•	66.9	68 20.9	-12.6•	69.2	28
29	64 34.4	-29.4	52.7	65 10.0	-27.7	54.5	65 44.1	-25.9	56.3	66 16.6	-24.0	58.2	66 47.4	-21.9•	60.1	67 16.4	-19.8•	62.2	67 43.3	-17.5•	64.4	68 08.3	-15.1•	66.6	29
30	64 05.0	-31.1	50.7	64 42.3	-29.5	52.4	65 18.2	-27.7	54.1	65 52.6	-25.9	55.9	66 25.5	-24.0•	57.8	66 56.6	-22.0•	59.8	67 25.8	-19.7•	61.8	67 53.2	-17.5•	64.0	30
31	63 33.9	-32.5	48.8	64 12.8	-31.0	50.3	64 50.5	-29.5	52.0	65 26.7	-27.7	53.7	66 01.5	-26.0	55.5	66 34.6	-24.0	57.4	67 06.1	-22.0•	59.4	67 35.7	-19.8•	61.5	31
32	63 01.4	-34.0	46.9	63 41.8	-32.6	48.4	64 21.0	-31.1	50.0	64 59.0	-29.5	51.6	65 35.5	-27.8	53.3	66 10.6	-25.9	55.1	66 44.1	-24.0•	57.0	67 15.9	-22.0•	59.0	32
33	62 27.4	-35.3	45.1	63 09.2	-34.0	46.5	63 49.9	-32.6	48.0	64 29.5	-31.2	49.5	65 07.7	-29.5	51.2	65 44.7	-27.9	52.9	66 20.1	-26.0	54.7	66 53.9	-24.1•	56.6	33
34	61 52.1	-36.6	43.4	62 35.2	-35.4	44.7	63 17.3	-34.1	46.1	63 58.3	-32.6	47.6	64 38.2	-31.2	49.1	65 16.8	-29.5	50.8	65 54.1	-27.9	52.5	66 29.8	-26.0	54.3	34
35	61 15.5	-37.8	41.7	61 59.8	-36.6	43.0	62 43.2	-35.4	44.3	63 25.7	-34.1	45.7	64 07.0	-32.7	47.2	64 47.3	-31.3	48.7	65 26.2	-29.6	50.3	66 03.8	-27.9	52.1	35
36	60 37.7	-38.8	40.1	61 23.2	-37.8	41.3	62 07.8	-36.6	42.5	62 51.6	-35.5	43.9	63 34.3	-34.1	45.3	64 16.0	-32.8	46.7	64 56.6	-31.3	48.3	65 35.9	-29.8	49.9	36
37	59 58.9	-39.9	38.6	60 45.4	-38.9	39.7	61 31.2	-37.9	40.9	62 16.1	-36.7	42.1	63 00.2	-35.6	43.4	63 43.2	-34.2	44.8	64 25.3	-32.9	46.3	65 06.1	-31.3	47.8	37
38	59 19.0	-40.9	37.1	60 06.5	-40.0	38.2	60 53.3	-39.0	39.3	61 39.4	-37.9	40.4	62 24.6	-36.8	41.7	63 09.0	-35.6	43.0	63 52.4	-34.3	44.4	64 34.8	-33.0	45.8	38
39	58 38.1	-41.7	35.7	59 26.5	-40.9	36.7	60 14.3	-40.0	37.7	61 01.5	-39.1	38.8	61 47.8	-38.0	40.0	62 33.4	-36.9	41.2	63 18.1	-35.7	42.5	64 01.8	-34.4	43.9	39
40	57 56.4	-42.6	34.3	58 45.6	-41.8	35.3	59 34.3	-40.9	36.2	60 22.4	-40.1	37.3	61 09.8	-39.1	38.4	61 56.5	-38.1	39.5	62 42.4	-37.0	40.7	63 27.4	-35.8	42.1	40
41	57 13.8	-43.4	33.0	58 03.8	-42.6	33.9	58 53.4	-41.9	34.8	59 42.3	-41.0	35.8	60 30.7	-40.2	36.8	61 18.4	-39.2	37.9	62 05.4	-38.2	39.0	62 51.6	-37.1	40.3	41
42	56 30.4	-44.2	31.7	57 21.2	-43.5	32.6	58 11.5	-42.8	33.4	59 01.3	-42.0	34.3	59 50.5	-41.1	35.3	60 39.2	-40.3	36.3	61 27.2	-39.3	37.4	62 14.5	-38.3	38.6	42
43	55 46.2	-44.8	30.5	56 37.7	-44.2	31.3	57 28.7	-43.5	32.1	58 19.3	-42.8	33.0	59 09.4	-42.0	33.9	59 58.9	-41.2	34.8	60 47.9	-40.4	35.9	61 36.2	-39.4	36.9	43
44	55 01.4	-45.5	29.4	55 53.5	-44.9	30.1	56 45.2	-44.2	30.8	57 36.5	-43.6	31.6	58 27.4	-42.9	32.5	59 17.7	-42.1	33.4	60 07.5	-41.3	34.4	60 56.8	-40.5	35.4	44
45	54 15.9	-46.1	28.2	55 08.6	-45.5	28.9	56 01.0	-45.0	29.6	56 52.9	-44.3	30.4	57 44.5	-43.7	31.2	58 35.6	-43.0	32.0	59 26.2	-42.2	32.9	60 16.3	-41.4	33.9	45
46	53 29.8	-46.6	27.1	54 23.1	-46.2	27.8	55 16.0	-45.6	28.4	56 08.6	-45.1	29.2	57 00.8	-44.5	29.9	57 52.6	-43.8	30.7	58 44.0	-43.1	31.5	59 34.9	-42.4	32.4	46
47	52 43.2	-47.2	26.1	53 36.9	-46.7	26.7	54 30.4	-46.2	27.3	55 23.5	-45.7	28.0	56 16.3	-45.1	28.7	57 08.8	-44.5	29.4	58 00.9	-43.9	30.2	58 52.5	-43.2	31.0	47
48	51 56.0	-47.7	25.1	52 50.2	-47.3	25.6	53 44.2	-46.8	26.2	54 37.8	-46.3	26.9	55 31.2	-45.8	27.5	56 24.3	-45.3	28.2	57 17.0	-44.7	28.9	58 09.3	-44.0	29.7	48
49	51 08.3	-48.2	24.1	52 02.9	-47.7	24.6	52 57.4	-47.4	25.2	53 51.5	-46.8	25.8	54 45.4	-46.4	26.4	55 39.0	-45.8	27.0	56 32.3	-45.3	27.7	57 25.3	-44.8	28.4	49
50	50 20.1	-48.6	23.2	51 15.2	-48.2	23.7	52 10.0	-47.8	24.2	53 04.7	-47.4	24.7	53 59.0	-46.9	25.3	54 53.2	-46.5	25.9	55 47.0	-46.0	26.5	56 40.5	-45.4	27.2	50
51	49 31.5	-49.0	22.3	50 27.0	-48.7	22.7	51 22.2	-48.3	23.2	52 17.3	-47.9	23.7	53 12.1	-47.5	24.2	54 06.7	-47.1	24.8	55 01.0	-46.6	25.4	55 55.1	-46.1	26.0	51
52	48 42.5	-49.4	21.4	49 38.3	-49.1	21.8	50 33.9	-48.7	22.3	51 29.4	-48.4	22.7	52 24.6	-48.0	23.2	53 19.6	-47.6	23.8	54 14.4	-47.1	24.3	55 09.0	-46.7	24.9	52
53	47 53.1	-49.8	20.5	48 49.2	-49.5	20.9	49 45.2	-49.2	21.3	50 41.0	-48.8	21.8	51 36.6	-48.5	22.3	52 32.0	-48.0	22.7	53 27.3	-47.7	23.3	54 22.3	-47.3	23.8	53
54	47 03.3	-50.1	19.7	47 59.7	-49.8	20.1	48 56.0	-49.5	20.5	49 52.2	-49.3	20.9	50 48.1	-48.8	21.3	51 44.0	-48.6	21.8	52 39.6	-48.2	22.2	53 35.0	-47.8	22.8	54
55	46 13.2	-50.4	18.9	47 09.9	-50.2	19.2	48 06.5	-49.9	19.6	49 02.9	-49.6	20.0	49 59.3	-49.4	20.4	50 55.4	-49.0	20.8	51 51.4	-48.6	21.3	52 47.2	-48.3	21.8	55
56	45 22.8	-50.8	18.1	46 19.7	-50.5	18.4	47 16.6	-50.3	18.8	48 13.3	-50.0	19.1	49 09.9	-49.6	19.5	50 06.4	-49.4	19.9	51 02.8	-49.1	20.3	51 58.9	-48.7	20.8	56
57	44 32.0	-51.0	17.4	45 29.2	-50.8	17.7	46 26.3	-50.5	18.0	47 23.3	-50.3	18.3	48 20.3	-50.1	18.7	49 17.0	-49.8	19.0	50 13.7	-49.5	19.4	51 10.2	-49.2	19.8	57
58	43 41.0	-51.4	16.6	44 38.4	-51.1	16.9	45 35.8	-50.9	17.2	46 33.0	-50.6	17.5	47 30.2	-50.4	17.8	48 27.2	-50.1	18.2	49 24.2	-49.9	18.6	50 21.0	-49.6	18.9	58
59	42 49.6	-51.5	15.9	43 47.3	-51.4	16.2	44 44.9	-51.2	16.5	45 42.4	-51.0	16.7	46 39.8	-50.7	17.1	47 37.1	-50.5	17.4	48 34.3	-50.2	17.7	49 31.4	-50.0	18.1	59
60	41 58.1	-51.8	15.2	42 55.9	-51.6	15.5	43 53.7	-51.4	15.7	44 51.4	-51.2	16.0	45 49.1	-51.1	16.3	46 46.6	-50.8	16.6	47 44.1	-50.6	16.9	48 41.4	-50.3	17.2	60
61	41 06.3	-52.1	14.6	42 04.3	-51.9	14.8	43 02.3	-51.7	15.0	44 00.2	-51.5	15.3	44 58.0	-51.3	15.5	45 55.8	-51.1	15.8	46 53.5	-50.9	16.1	47 51.1	-50.7	16.4	61
62	40 14.2	-52.2	13.9	41 12.4	-52.1	14.1	42 10.6	-51.9	14.3	43 08.7	-51.8	14.6	44 06.7	-51.5	14.8	45 04.7	-51.4	15.1	46 02.6	-51.2	15.3	47 00.4	-50.9	15.6	62
63	39 22.0	-52.5	13.3	40 20.3	-52.3	13.5	41 18.7	-52.2	13.7	42 16.9	-52.0	13.9	43 15.2	-51.9	14.1	44 13.3	-51.6	14.3	45 11.4	-51.5	14.6	46 09.5	-51.3	14.8	63
64	38 29.5	-52.7	12.6	39 28.0	-52.5	12.8	40 26.5	-52.4	13.0	41 24.9	-52.2	13.2	42 23.3	-52.0	13.4	43 21.7	-51.9	13.6	44 19.9	-51.7	13.9	45 18.2	-51.6	14.1	64
65	37 36.8	-52.8	12.0	38 35.5	-52.7	12.2	39 34.1	-52.6	12.4	40 32.7	-52.4	12.6	41 31.3	-52.3	12.7	42 29.8	-52.2	12.9	43 28.2	-52.0	13.2	44 26.6	-51.8	13.4	65
66	36 44.0	-53.0	11.4	37 42.8	-52.9	11.6	38 41.5	-52.7	11.7	39 40.3	-52.7	11.9	40 39.0	-52.6	12.1	41 37.6	-52.4	12.3	42 36.2	-52.2	12.5	43 34.8	-52.1	12.7	66
67	35 51.0	-53.2	10.9	36 49.9	-53.1	11.0	37 48.8	-53.0	11.1	38 47.6	-52.8	11.3	39 46.4	-52.7	11.5	40 45.2	-52.6	11.6	41 44.0	-52.5	11.8	42 42.7	-52.3	12.0	67
68	34 57.8	-53.3	10.3	35 56.8	-53.2	10.4	36 55.8	-53.1	10.6	37 54.8	-53.0	10.7	38 53.7	-52.9	10.8	39 52.6	-52.7	11.0	40 51.5	-52.6	11.2	41 50.4	-52.6	11.3	68
69	34 04.5	-53.5	9.7	35 03.6	-53.4	9.8	36 02.7	-53.3	10.0	37 01.8	-53.2	10.1	38 00.8	-53.1	10.2	38 59.9	-53.0	10.4	39 58.9	-52.9	10.5	40 57.8	-52.7	10.7	69
70	33 11.0	-53.6	9.2	34 10.2	-53.5	9.3	35 09.4	-53.4	9.4	36 08.6	-53.4	9.5	37 07.7	-53.2	9.6	38 06.9	-53.2	9.8	39 06.0	-53.0	9.9	40 05.1	-53.0	10.1	70
71	32 17.4	-53.8	8.7	33 16.7	-53.7	8.8	34 16.0	-53.6	8.9	35 15.2	-53.5	9.0	36 14.5	-53.4	9.1	37 13.7	-53.3	9.2	38 13.0	-53.3	9.3	39 12.1	-53.1	9.4	71
72	31 23.6	-53.9	8.1	32 23.0	-53.8	8.2	33 22.4	-53.8	8.3	34 21.7	-53.6	8.4	35 21.1	-53.6	8.5	36 20.4	-53.5	8.6	37 19.7	-53.4	8.7	38 19.0	-53.3	8.9	72
73	30 29.7	-54.0	7.6	31 29.2	-53.9	7.7	32 28.6	-53.8	7.8	33 28.1	-53.8	7.9	34 27.5	-53.7	8.0	35 26.9	-53.6	8.1	36 26.3	-53.5	8.2	37 25.7	-53.5	8.3	73
74	29 35.7	-54.1	7.1	30 35.3	-54.1	7.2	31 34.8	-54.0	7.3	32 34.3	-53.9	7.3	33 33.8	-53.8	7.4	34 33.3	-53.8	7.5	35 32.8	-53.7	7.6	36 32.2	-53.6	7.7	74
75	28 41.6	-54.2	6.6	29 41.2	-54.1	6.7	30 40.8	-54.1	6.8	31 40.4	-54.1	6.8	32 40.0	-54.0	6.9	33 39.5	-53.9	7.0	34 39.1	-53.9	7.1	35 38.6	-53.8	7.1	75
76	27 47.4	-54.3	6.1	28 47.1	-54.3	6.2	29 46.7	-54.2	6.3	30 46.3	-54.1	6.3	31 46.0	-54.1	6.4	32 45.6	-54.0	6.5	33 45.2	-54.0	6.5	34 44.8	-53.9	6.6	76
77	26 53.1	-54.4	5.7	27 52.8	-54.4	5.7	28 52.5	-54.3	5.8	29 52.2	-54.3	5.8	30 51.9	-54.2	5.9	31 51.6	-54.2	5.9	32 51.2	-54.1	6.0	33 50.9	-54.1	6.1	77
78	25 58.7	-54.5	5.2	26 58.4	-54.4	5.2	27 58.2	-54.4	5.3	28 57.9	-54.3	5.3	29 57.7	-54.4	5.4	30 57.4	-54.3	5.4	31 57.1	-54.2	5.5	32 56.8	-54.1	5.6	78
79	25 04.2	-54.6	4.7	26 04.0	-54.6	4.8	27 03.8	-54.5	4.8	28 03.6	-54.5	4.8	29 03.3	-54.4	4.9	30 03.1	-54.4	4.9	31 02.9	-54.4	5.0	32 02.7	-54.3	5.0	79
80	24 09.6	-54.7	4.3	25 09.4	-54.6	4.3	26 09.3	-54.6	4.3	27 09.1	-54.6	4.4	28 08.9	-54.5	4.4	29 08.7	-54.5	4.5	30 08.5	-54.4	4.5	31 08.4	-54.5	4.5	80
81	23 14.9	-54.7	3.8	24 14.8	-54.7	3.8	25 14.7	-54.7	3.9	26 14.5	-54.6	3.9	27 14.4	-54.6	3.9	28 14.2	-54.6	4.0	29 14.1	-54.6	4.0	30 13.9	-54.5	4.1	81
82	22 20.2	-54.8	3.4	23 20.1	-54.8	3.4	24 20.0	-54.8	3.4	25 19.9	-54.8	3.4	26 19.8	-54.8	3.5	27 19.6	-54.6	3.5	28 19.5	-54.6	3.5	29 19.4	-54.6	3.6	82
83	21 25.4	-54.9	2.9	22 25.3	-54.9	3.0	23 25.2	-54.8	3.0	24 25.1	-54.8	3.0	25 25.0	-54.7	3.0	26 25.0	-54.8	3.0	27 24.9	-54.8	3.1	28 24.8	-54.7	3.1	83
84	20 30.5	-55.0	2.5	21 30.4	-54.9	2.5	22 30.4	-54.9	2.5	23 30.3	-54.9	2.6	24 30.3	-54.9	2.6	25 30.2	-54.9	2.6	26 30.1	-54.8	2.6	27 30.1	-54.8	2.6	84
85	19 35.5	-55.0	2.1	20 35.5	-55.0	2.1	21 35.5	-55.0	2.1	22 35.4	-54.9	2.1	23 35.4	-55.0	2.1	24 35.3	-54.9	2.1	25 35.3	-54.9	2.2	26 35.3	-54.9	2.2	85
86	18 40.5	-55.0	1.6	19 40.5	-55.0	1.7	20 40.5	-55.0	1.7	21 40.5	-55.1	1.7	22 40.4	-55.0	1.7	23 40.4	-55.0	1.7	24 40.4	-55.0	1.7	25 40.4	-55.0	1.7	86
87	17 45.5	-55.1	1.2	18 45.5	-55.1	1.2	19 45.5	-55.1	1.2	20 45.4	-55.0	1.3	21 45.4	-55.1	1.3	22 45.4	-55.1	1.3	23 45.4	-55.1	1.3	24 45.4	-55.1	1.3	87
88	16 50.4	-55.2	0.8	17 50.4	-55.2	0.8	18 50.4	-55.2	0.8	19 50.4	-55.2	0.8	20 50.3	-55.1	0.8	21 50.3	-55.1	0.8	22 50.3	-55.1	0.8	23 50.3	-55.1	0.9	88
89	15 55.2	-55.2	0.4	16 55.2	-55.2	0.4	17 55.2	-55.2	0.4	18 55.2	-55.2	0.4	19 55.2	-55.2	0.4	20 55.2	-55.2	0.4	21 55.2	-55.2	0.4	22 55.2	-55.2	0.4	89
90	15 00.0	-55.3	0.0	16 00.0	-55.3	0.0	17 00.0	-55.3	0.0	18 00.0	-55.3	0.0	19 00.0	-55.3	0.0	20 00.0	-55.3	0.0	21 00.0	-55.3	0.0	22 00.0	-55.3	0.0	90
	15°			16°			17°			18°			19°			20°			21°			22°			

23°, 337° L.H.A. LATITUDE SAME NAME AS DECLINATION

LATITUDE **CONTRARY** NAME TO DECLINATION L.H.A. 23°, 337°

Dec.	15° Hc	d	Z	16° Hc	d	Z	17° Hc	d	Z	18° Hc	d	Z	Dec.
°	° ′	′	°	° ′	′	°	° ′	′	°	° ′	′	°	°
0	62 45.9	-34.6	121.4	62 14.0	-36.2	123.0	61 40.6	-37.6	124.6	61 05.9	-38.9	126.1	0
1	62 11.3	-35.9	123.1	61 37.8	-37.3	124.7	61 03.0	-38.7	126.2	60 27.0	-40.0	127.6	1
2	61 35.4	-37.1	124.8	61 00.5	-38.5	126.3	60 24.3	-39.7	127.7	59 47.0	-40.9	129.1	2
3	60 58.3	-38.3	126.5	60 22.0	-39.5	127.9	59 44.6	-40.7	129.3	59 06.1	-41.9	130.5	3
4	60 20.0	-39.3	128.0	59 42.5	-40.6	129.4	59 03.9	-41.7	130.7	58 24.2	-42.7	131.9	4
5	59 40.7	-40.4	129.6	59 01.9	-41.4	130.8	58 22.2	-42.5	132.1	57 41.5	-43.5	133.3	5
6	59 00.3	-41.3	131.0	58 20.5	-42.4	132.2	57 39.7	-43.4	133.4	56 58.0	-44.3	134.5	6
7	58 19.0	-42.1	132.4	57 38.1	-43.1	133.6	56 56.3	-44.0	134.7	56 13.7	-44.9	135.8	7
8	57 36.9	-43.0	133.7	56 55.0	-43.9	134.9	56 12.3	-44.8	135.9	55 28.8	-45.6	136.9	8
9	56 53.9	-43.7	135.0	56 11.1	-44.7	136.1	55 27.5	-45.5	137.1	54 43.2	-46.3	138.1	9
10	56 10.2	-44.5	136.3	55 26.4	-45.2	137.3	54 42.0	-46.1	138.2	53 56.9	-46.8	139.2	10
11	55 25.7	-45.1	137.5	54 41.2	-46.0	138.4	53 55.9	-46.6	139.3	53 10.1	-47.3	140.2	11
12	54 40.6	-45.8	138.6	53 55.2	-46.5	139.5	53 09.3	-47.2	140.4	52 22.8	-47.9	141.2	12
13	53 54.8	-46.3	139.7	53 08.7	-47.0	140.6	52 22.1	-47.7	141.4	51 34.9	-48.3	142.2	13
14	53 08.5	-46.9	140.8	52 21.7	-47.6	141.6	51 34.4	-48.2	142.4	50 46.6	-48.7	143.2	14
15	52 21.6	-47.5	141.8	51 34.1	-48.0	142.6	50 46.2	-48.6	143.4	49 57.9	-49.2	144.1	15
16	51 34.1	-47.9	142.8	50 46.1	-48.5	143.6	49 57.6	-49.1	144.3	49 08.7	-49.6	145.0	16
17	50 46.2	-48.3	143.8	49 57.6	-48.9	144.5	49 08.5	-49.4	145.2	48 19.1	-49.9	145.8	17
18	49 57.9	-48.8	144.7	49 08.7	-49.3	145.4	48 19.1	-49.8	146.0	47 29.2	-50.3	146.6	18
19	49 09.1	-49.2	145.6	48 19.4	-49.7	146.2	47 29.3	-50.2	146.9	46 38.9	-50.6	147.4	19
20	48 19.9	-49.6	146.5	47 29.7	-50.1	147.1	46 39.1	-50.5	147.7	45 48.3	-50.9	148.2	20
21	47 30.3	-50.0	147.3	46 39.6	-50.4	147.9	45 48.6	-50.8	148.4	44 57.4	-51.2	149.0	21
22	46 40.3	-50.2	148.1	45 49.2	-50.7	148.7	44 57.8	-51.1	149.2	44 06.2	-51.5	149.7	22
23	45 50.1	-50.6	148.9	44 58.5	-51.0	149.4	44 06.7	-51.3	149.9	43 14.7	-51.8	150.4	23
24	44 59.5	-50.9	149.7	44 07.5	-51.2	150.2	43 15.4	-51.7	150.7	42 22.9	-51.9	151.1	24
25	44 08.6	-51.2	150.4	43 16.3	-51.6	150.9	42 23.7	-51.8	151.3	41 31.0	-52.2	151.8	25
26	43 17.4	-51.4	151.2	42 24.7	-51.7	151.6	41 31.9	-52.1	152.0	40 38.8	-52.4	152.4	26
27	42 26.0	-51.7	151.9	41 33.0	-52.0	152.3	40 39.8	-52.4	152.7	39 46.4	-52.7	153.1	27
28	41 34.3	-51.9	152.5	40 41.0	-52.3	152.9	39 47.4	-52.5	153.3	38 53.7	-52.8	153.7	28
29	40 42.4	-52.2	153.2	39 48.7	-52.4	153.6	38 54.9	-52.7	153.9	38 00.9	-53.0	154.3	29
30	39 50.2	-52.3	153.9	38 56.3	-52.7	154.2	38 02.2	-52.9	154.6	37 07.9	-53.1	154.9	30
31	38 57.9	-52.6	154.5	38 03.6	-52.8	154.8	37 09.3	-53.1	155.2	36 14.8	-53.4	155.5	31
32	38 05.3	-52.7	155.1	37 10.8	-53.0	155.4	36 16.2	-53.3	155.7	35 21.4	-53.5	156.0	32
33	37 12.6	-52.9	155.7	36 17.8	-53.1	156.0	35 22.9	-53.4	156.3	34 27.9	-53.6	156.6	33
34	36 19.7	-53.1	156.3	35 24.7	-53.4	156.6	34 29.5	-53.5	156.9	33 34.3	-53.8	157.1	34
35	35 26.6	-53.3	156.9	34 31.3	-53.4	157.1	33 36.0	-53.7	157.4	32 40.5	-53.9	157.7	35
36	34 33.3	-53.4	157.4	33 37.9	-53.7	157.7	32 42.3	-53.8	157.9	31 46.6	-54.0	158.2	36
37	33 39.9	-53.5	158.0	32 44.2	-53.7	158.2	31 48.5	-54.0	158.5	30 52.6	-54.1	158.7	37
38	32 46.4	-53.7	158.5	31 50.5	-53.9	158.7	30 54.5	-54.1	159.0	29 58.5	-54.3	159.2	38
39	31 52.7	-53.8	159.0	30 56.6	-54.0	159.3	30 00.4	-54.1	159.5	29 04.2	-54.3	159.7	39
40	30 58.9	-54.0	159.6	30 02.6	-54.1	159.8	29 06.3	-54.3	160.0	28 09.9	-54.5	160.2	40
41	30 04.9	-54.0	160.1	29 08.5	-54.2	160.3	28 12.0	-54.4	160.5	27 15.4	-54.5	160.6	41
42	29 10.9	-54.2	160.6	28 14.3	-54.4	160.8	27 17.6	-54.5	160.9	26 20.9	-54.7	161.1	42
43	28 16.7	-54.2	161.1	27 19.9	-54.4	161.2	26 23.1	-54.6	161.4	25 26.2	-54.7	161.6	43
44	27 22.5	-54.4	161.5	26 25.5	-54.5	161.7	25 28.5	-54.6	161.9	24 31.5	-54.8	162.0	44
45	26 28.1	-54.4	162.0	25 31.0	-54.6	162.2	24 33.9	-54.8	162.3	23 36.7	-54.9	162.5	45
46	25 33.7	-54.6	162.5	24 36.4	-54.7	162.6	23 39.1	-54.8	162.8	22 41.8	-55.0	162.9	46
47	24 39.1	-54.6	163.0	23 41.7	-54.7	163.1	22 44.3	-54.9	163.2	21 46.8	-55.0	163.3	47
48	23 44.5	-54.7	163.4	22 47.0	-54.9	163.5	21 49.4	-54.9	163.6	20 51.8	-55.1	163.8	48
49	22 49.8	-54.8	163.9	21 52.1	-54.9	164.0	20 54.5	-55.1	164.1	19 56.7	-55.1	164.2	49
50	21 55.0	-54.8	164.3	20 57.2	-54.9	164.4	19 59.4	-55.0	164.5	19 01.6	-55.2	164.6	50
51	21 00.2	-54.9	164.7	20 02.3	-55.1	164.8	19 04.4	-55.2	164.9	18 06.4	-55.2	165.0	51
52	20 05.3	-55.0	165.2	19 07.2	-55.0	165.2	18 09.2	-55.2	165.3	17 11.2	-55.3	165.4	52
53	19 10.3	-55.0	165.6	18 12.2	-55.2	165.7	17 14.0	-55.2	165.7	16 15.9	-55.4	165.8	53
54	18 15.3	-55.1	166.0	17 17.0	-55.2	166.1	16 18.8	-55.3	166.2	15 20.5	-55.4	166.2	54
55	17 20.2	-55.2	166.4	16 21.8	-55.2	166.5	15 23.5	-55.3	166.6	14 25.1	-55.4	166.6	55
56	16 25.0	-55.2	166.8	15 26.6	-55.3	166.9	14 28.2	-55.4	167.0	13 29.7	-55.5	167.0	56
57	15 29.8	-55.2	167.2	14 31.3	-55.3	167.3	13 32.8	-55.4	167.4	12 34.2	-55.5	167.4	57
58	14 34.6	-55.2	167.6	13 36.0	-55.4	167.7	12 37.4	-55.5	167.7	11 38.7	-55.5	167.8	58
59	13 39.4	-55.4	168.0	12 40.6	-55.3	168.1	11 41.9	-55.4	168.1	10 43.2	-55.5	168.2	59
60	12 44.0	-55.3	168.4	11 45.3	-55.5	168.5	10 46.5	-55.5	168.5	9 47.7	-55.6	168.6	60
61	11 48.7	-55.4	168.8	10 49.8	-55.4	168.9	9 51.0	-55.6	168.9	8 52.1	-55.6	168.9	61
62	10 53.3	-55.4	169.2	9 54.4	-55.5	169.3	8 55.4	-55.5	169.3	7 56.5	-55.6	169.3	62
63	9 57.9	-55.4	169.6	8 58.9	-55.5	169.7	7 59.9	-55.6	169.7	7 00.8	-55.6	169.7	63
64	9 02.5	-55.5	170.0	8 03.4	-55.5	170.0	7 04.3	-55.6	170.1	6 05.2	-55.7	170.1	64
65	8 07.0	-55.5	170.4	7 07.9	-55.6	170.4	6 08.7	-55.6	170.4	5 09.5	-55.6	170.5	65
66	7 11.5	-55.5	170.8	6 12.3	-55.5	170.8	5 13.1	-55.6	170.8	4 13.9	-55.7	170.8	66
67	6 16.0	-55.5	171.2	5 16.8	-55.6	171.2	4 17.5	-55.7	171.2	3 18.2	-55.7	171.2	67
68	5 20.5	-55.5	171.5	4 21.2	-55.6	171.6	3 21.8	-55.6	171.6	2 22.5	-55.7	171.6	68
69	4 25.0	-55.5	171.9	3 25.6	-55.6	171.9	2 26.2	-55.7	171.9	1 26.8	-55.7	171.9	69
70	3 29.5	-55.6	172.3	2 30.0	-55.6	172.3	1 30.5	-55.6	172.3	0 31.1	-55.7	172.3	70
71	2 33.9	-55.5	172.7	1 34.4	-55.6	172.7	0 34.9	-55.7	172.7	0 24.6	+55.7	7.3	71
72	1 38.4	-55.6	173.1	0 38.8	-55.6	173.1	0 20.8	+55.6	6.9	1 20.3	+55.7	6.9	72
73	0 42.8	-55.6	173.4	0 16.8	+55.6	6.6	1 16.4	+55.7	6.6	2 16.0	+55.7	6.6	73
74	0 12.8	+55.5	6.2	1 12.4	+55.6	6.2	2 12.1	+55.6	6.2	3 11.7	+55.7	6.2	74
75	1 08.3	+55.6	5.8	2 08.0	+55.6	5.8	3 07.7	+55.6	5.8	4 07.4	+55.7	5.8	75
76	2 03.9	+55.5	5.4	3 03.6	+55.6	5.4	4 03.3	+55.7	5.4	5 03.1	+55.6	5.4	76
77	2 59.4	+55.6	5.0	3 59.2	+55.6	5.1	4 59.0	+55.6	5.1	5 58.7	+55.7	5.1	77
78	3 55.0	+55.5	4.7	4 54.8	+55.6	4.7	5 54.6	+55.6	4.7	6 54.4	+55.6	4.7	78
79	4 50.5	+55.5	4.3	5 50.4	+55.5	4.3	6 50.2	+55.6	4.3	7 50.0	+55.6	4.3	79
80	5 46.0	+55.5	3.9	6 45.9	+55.5	3.9	7 45.8	+55.5	3.9	8 45.6	+55.6	3.9	80
81	6 41.5	+55.5	3.5	7 41.4	+55.5	3.5	8 41.3	+55.6	3.5	9 41.2	+55.6	3.6	81
82	7 37.0	+55.5	3.1	8 36.9	+55.5	3.2	9 36.9	+55.5	3.2	10 36.8	+55.5	3.2	82
83	8 32.5	+55.5	2.8	9 32.4	+55.5	2.8	10 32.4	+55.5	2.8	11 32.3	+55.5	2.8	83
84	9 28.0	+55.4	2.4	10 27.9	+55.4	2.4	11 27.9	+55.4	2.4	12 27.8	+55.5	2.4	84
85	10 23.4	+55.4	2.0	11 23.3	+55.4	2.0	12 23.3	+55.4	2.0	13 23.3	+55.4	2.0	85
86	11 18.8	+55.3	1.6	12 18.7	+55.4	1.6	13 18.7	+55.4	1.6	14 18.7	+55.4	1.6	86
87	12 14.1	+55.4	1.2	13 14.1	+55.4	1.2	14 14.1	+55.3	1.2	15 14.1	+55.3	1.2	87
88	13 09.5	+55.2	0.8	14 09.5	+55.2	0.8	15 09.4	+55.3	0.8	16 09.4	+55.3	0.8	88
89	14 04.7	+55.3	0.4	15 04.7	+55.3	0.4	16 04.7	+55.3	0.4	17 04.7	+55.3	0.4	89
90	15 00.0	+55.2	0.0	16 00.0	+55.2	0.0	17 00.0	+55.2	0.0	18 00.0	+55.2	0.0	90
	15°			16°			17°			18°			

Dec.	19° Hc	d	Z	20° Hc	d	Z	21° Hc	d	Z	22° Hc	d	Z	Dec.
°	° ′	′	°	° ′	′	°	° ′	′	°	° ′	′	°	°
0	60 30.0	-40.2	127.5	59 52.9	-41.4	128.9	59 14.7	-42.5	130.2	58 35.5	-43.5	131.4	0
1	59 49.8	-41.1	129.0	59 11.5	-42.2	130.3	58 32.2	-43.3	131.5	57 52.0	-44.3	132.7	1
2	59 08.7	-42.1	130.4	58 29.3	-43.2	131.7	57 48.9	-44.1	132.9	57 07.7	-45.1	134.0	2
3	58 26.6	-42.9	131.8	57 46.1	-43.9	133.0	57 04.8	-44.8	134.1	56 22.6	-45.7	135.2	3
4	57 43.7	-43.7	133.1	57 02.2	-44.6	134.2	56 20.0	-45.5	135.3	55 36.9	-46.3	136.4	4
5	57 00.0	-44.5	134.4	56 17.6	-45.3	135.5	55 34.5	-46.2	136.5	54 50.6	-46.9	137.5	5
6	56 15.5	-45.1	135.6	55 32.3	-46.0	136.6	54 48.3	-46.7	137.6	54 03.7	-47.5	138.5	6
7	55 30.4	-45.8	136.8	54 46.3	-46.6	137.8	54 01.6	-47.3	138.7	53 16.2	-48.0	139.6	7
8	54 44.6	-46.4	137.9	53 59.7	-47.1	138.8	53 14.3	-47.9	139.7	52 28.2	-48.5	140.6	8
9	53 58.2	-47.0	139.0	53 12.6	-47.6	139.9	52 26.4	-48.3	140.7	51 39.7	-48.9	141.5	9
10	53 11.2	-47.5	140.0	52 25.0	-48.2	140.9	51 38.1	-48.7	141.7	50 50.8	-49.3	142.5	10
11	52 23.7	-48.0	141.1	51 36.8	-48.6	141.9	50 49.4	-49.2	142.6	50 01.5	-49.8	143.3	11
12	51 35.7	-48.4	142.0	50 48.2	-49.1	142.8	50 00.2	-49.6	143.5	49 11.7	-50.1	144.2	12
13	50 47.3	-48.9	143.0	49 59.1	-49.4	143.7	49 10.6	-50.0	144.4	48 21.6	-50.5	145.0	13
14	49 58.4	-49.3	143.9	49 09.7	-49.8	144.6	48 20.6	-50.3	145.2	47 31.1	-50.8	145.8	14
15	49 09.1	-49.7	144.8	48 19.9	-50.2	145.4	47 30.3	-50.7	146.0	46 40.3	-51.1	146.6	15
16	48 19.4	-50.1	145.6	47 29.7	-50.6	146.2	46 39.6	-51.0	146.8	45 49.2	-51.4	147.4	16
17	47 29.3	-50.4	146.4	46 39.1	-50.8	147.0	45 48.6	-51.2	147.6	44 57.8	-51.6	148.1	17
18	46 38.9	-50.7	147.2	45 48.3	-51.2	147.8	44 57.4	-51.6	148.3	44 06.2	-52.0	148.8	18
19	45 48.2	-51.1	148.0	44 57.1	-51.4	148.5	44 05.8	-51.8	149.0	43 14.2	-52.2	149.5	19
20	44 57.1	-51.3	148.7	44 05.7	-51.7	149.3	43 14.0	-52.1	149.7	42 22.0	-52.4	150.2	20
21	44 05.8	-51.6	149.5	43 14.0	-52.0	150.0	42 21.9	-52.3	150.4	41 29.6	-52.6	150.9	21
22	43 14.2	-51.8	150.2	42 22.0	-52.1	150.6	41 29.6	-52.5	151.1	40 37.0	-52.8	151.5	22
23	42 22.4	-52.1	150.9	41 29.9	-52.4	151.3	40 37.1	-52.7	151.7	39 44.2	-53.0	152.1	23
24	41 30.3	-52.3	151.5	40 37.5	-52.7	151.9	39 44.4	-52.9	152.3	38 51.2	-53.2	152.7	24
25	40 38.0	-52.5	152.2	39 44.8	-52.8	152.6	38 51.5	-53.1	153.0	37 58.0	-53.4	153.3	25
26	39 45.5	-52.7	152.8	38 52.0	-53.0	153.2	37 58.4	-53.3	153.5	37 04.6	-53.5	153.9	26
27	38 52.8	-52.9	153.4	37 59.0	-53.1	153.8	37 05.1	-53.4	154.1	36 11.1	-53.7	154.4	27
28	37 59.9	-53.1	154.0	37 05.9	-53.4	154.4	36 11.7	-53.6	154.7	35 17.4	-53.9	155.0	28
29	37 06.8	-53.3	154.6	36 12.5	-53.5	154.9	35 18.1	-53.8	155.2	34 23.5	-53.9	155.5	29
30	36 13.5	-53.4	155.2	35 19.0	-53.7	155.5	34 24.3	-53.8	155.8	33 29.6	-54.1	156.1	30
31	35 20.1	-53.6	155.8	34 25.3	-53.8	156.0	33 30.5	-54.1	156.3	32 35.5	-54.3	156.6	31
32	34 26.5	-53.7	156.3	33 31.5	-53.9	156.6	32 36.4	-54.1	156.8	31 41.2	-54.3	157.1	32
33	33 32.8	-53.8	156.8	32 37.6	-54.0	157.1	31 42.3	-54.3	157.3	30 46.9	-54.5	157.6	33
34	32 39.0	-54.0	157.4	31 43.6	-54.2	157.6	30 48.0	-54.4	157.8	29 52.4	-54.6	158.1	34
35	31 45.0	-54.1	157.9	30 49.4	-54.3	158.1	29 53.6	-54.4	158.3	28 57.8	-54.6	158.5	35
36	30 50.9	-54.2	158.4	29 55.1	-54.4	158.6	28 59.2	-54.6	158.8	28 03.2	-54.8	159.0	36
37	29 56.7	-54.3	158.9	29 00.7	-54.5	159.1	28 04.6	-54.7	159.3	27 08.4	-54.8	159.5	37
38	29 02.4	-54.5	159.4	28 06.2	-54.6	159.6	27 09.9	-54.8	159.8	26 13.6	-54.9	159.9	38
39	28 07.9	-54.5	159.9	27 11.6	-54.7	160.0	26 15.1	-54.8	160.2	25 18.7	-55.1	160.4	39
40	27 13.4	-54.6	160.3	26 16.9	-54.8	160.5	25 20.3	-55.0	160.7	24 23.6	-55.0	160.8	40
41	26 18.8	-54.7	160.8	25 22.1	-54.9	161.0	24 25.3	-55.0	161.1	23 28.6	-55.2	161.2	41
42	25 24.1	-54.8	161.2	24 27.2	-54.9	161.4	23 30.3	-55.1	161.5	22 33.4	-55.2	161.7	42
43	24 29.3	-54.9	161.7	23 32.3	-55.0	161.8	22 35.2	-55.1	162.0	21 38.2	-55.3	162.1	43
44	23 34.4	-54.9	162.1	22 37.3	-55.1	162.3	21 40.1	-55.2	162.4	20 42.9	-55.4	162.5	44
45	22 39.5	-55.1	162.6	21 42.2	-55.2	162.7	20 44.9	-55.3	162.8	19 47.5	-55.4	162.9	45
46	21 44.4	-55.0	163.0	20 47.0	-55.2	163.1	19 49.6	-55.3	163.2	18 52.1	-55.4	163.3	46
47	20 49.4	-55.2	163.4	19 51.8	-55.2	163.5	18 54.3	-55.4	163.6	17 56.7	-55.5	163.7	47
48	19 54.2	-55.2	163.9	18 56.6	-55.4	164.0	17 58.9	-55.5	164.0	17 01.2	-55.6	164.1	48
49	18 59.0	-55.3	164.3	18 01.2	-55.3	164.4	17 03.4	-55.4	164.4	16 05.6	-55.6	164.5	49
50	18 03.7	-55.3	164.7	17 05.9	-55.5	164.8	16 08.0	-55.6	164.8	15 10.0	-55.6	164.9	50
51	17 08.4	-55.3	165.1	16 10.4	-55.4	165.2	15 12.4	-55.5	165.2	14 14.4	-55.7	165.3	51
52	16 13.1	-55.4	165.5	15 15.0	-55.5	165.6	14 16.9	-55.6	165.6	13 18.7	-55.7	165.7	52
53	15 17.7	-55.5	165.9	14 19.5	-55.6	166.0	13 21.3	-55.7	166.0	12 23.0	-55.7	166.1	53
54	14 22.2	-55.5	166.3	13 23.9	-55.5	166.3	12 25.6	-55.6	166.4	11 27.3	-55.8	166.4	54
55	13 26.7	-55.5	166.7	12 28.4	-55.7	166.7	11 30.0	-55.8	166.8	10 31.5	-55.8	166.8	55
56	12 31.2	-55.5	167.1	11 32.7	-55.6	167.1	10 34.2	-55.7	167.2	9 35.7	-55.8	167.2	56
57	11 35.7	-55.6	167.5	10 37.1	-55.7	167.5	9 38.5	-55.7	167.5	8 39.9	-55.8	167.6	57
58	10 40.1	-55.6	167.8	9 41.4	-55.7	167.9	8 42.8	-55.8	167.9	7 44.1	-55.9	167.9	58
59	9 44.5	-55.7	168.2	8 45.7	-55.7	168.3	7 47.0	-55.8	168.3	6 48.2	-55.8	168.3	59
60	8 48.8	-55.6	168.6	7 50.0	-55.7	168.6	6 51.2	-55.8	168.7	5 52.4	-55.9	168.7	60
61	7 53.2	-55.7	169.0	6 54.3	-55.8	169.0	5 55.4	-55.8	169.0	4 56.5	-55.9	169.0	61
62	6 57.5	-55.7	169.4	5 58.5	-55.7	169.4	4 59.6	-55.9	169.4	4 00.6	-55.9	169.4	62
63	6 01.8	-55.7	169.7	5 02.8	-55.8	169.7	4 03.7	-55.8	169.8	3 04.7	-55.9	169.8	63
64	5 06.1	-55.7	170.1	4 07.0	-55.8	170.1	3 07.9	-55.9	170.1	2 08.8	-56.0	170.1	64
65	4 10.4	-55.8	170.5	3 11.2	-55.8	170.5	2 12.0	-55.8	170.5	1 12.8	-55.9	170.5	65
66	3 14.6	-55.7	170.8	2 15.4	-55.8	170.8	1 16.2	-55.9	170.9	0 16.9	-55.9	170.9	66
67	2 18.9	-55.8	171.2	1 19.6	-55.8	171.2	0 20.3	-55.9	171.2	0 39.0	+55.9	8.8	67
68	1 23.1	-55.7	171.6	0 23.8	-55.8	171.6	0 35.6	+55.8	8.4	1 34.9	+56.0	8.4	68
69	0 27.4	-55.8	172.0	0 32.0	+55.8	8.0	1 31.4	+55.9	8.1	2 30.9	+55.9	8.1	69
70	0 28.4	+55.7	7.7	1 27.8	+55.8	7.7	2 27.3	+55.9	7.7	3 26.8	+55.9	7.7	70
71	1 24.1	+55.8	7.3	2 23.6	+55.8	7.3	3 23.2	+55.8	7.3	4 22.7	+55.9	7.3	71
72	2 19.9	+55.7	6.9	3 19.4	+55.8	6.9	4 19.0	+55.8	7.0	5 18.6	+55.8	7.0	72
73	3 15.6	+55.8	6.6	4 15.2	+55.8	6.6	5 14.8	+55.9	6.6	6 14.4	+55.8	6.6	73
74	4 11.4	+55.7	6.2	5 11.0	+55.8	6.2	6 10.7	+55.8	6.2	7 10.3	+55.9	6.2	74
75	5 07.1	+55.7	5.8	6 06.8	+55.7	5.8	7 06.5	+55.8	5.8	8 06.2	+55.8	5.9	75
76	6 02.8	+55.7	5.5	7 02.5	+55.8	5.5	8 02.3	+55.7	5.5	9 02.0	+55.8	5.5	76
77	6 58.5	+55.7	5.1	7 58.3	+55.7	5.1	8 58.0	+55.8	5.1	9 57.8	+55.8	5.1	77
78	7 54.2	+55.6	4.7	8 54.0	+55.7	4.7	9 53.8	+55.7	4.7	10 53.6	+55.7	4.7	78
79	8 49.8	+55.7	4.3	9 49.7	+55.6	4.3	10 49.5	+55.7	4.4	11 49.3	+55.7	4.4	79
80	9 45.5	+55.6	3.9	10 45.3	+55.7	4.0	11 45.2	+55.7	4.0	12 45.0	+55.7	4.0	80
81	10 41.1	+55.6	3.6	11 41.0	+55.6	3.6	12 40.9	+55.6	3.6	13 40.7	+55.7	3.6	81
82	11 36.7	+55.5	3.2	12 36.6	+55.6	3.2	13 36.5	+55.6	3.2	14 36.4	+55.6	3.2	82
83	12 32.2	+55.5	2.8	13 32.2	+55.5	2.8	14 32.1	+55.5	2.8	15 32.0	+55.6	2.8	83
84	13 27.7	+55.5	2.4	14 27.7	+55.5	2.4	15 27.6	+55.6	2.4	16 27.6	+55.5	2.4	84
85	14 23.2	+55.5	2.0	15 23.2	+55.4	2.0	16 23.2	+55.4	2.0	17 23.1	+55.5	2.0	85
86	15 18.7	+55.4	1.6	16 18.6	+55.5	1.6	17 18.6	+55.4	1.6	18 18.6	+55.4	1.6	86
87	16 14.1	+55.3	1.2	17 14.1	+55.3	1.2	18 14.0	+55.4	1.2	19 14.0	+55.4	1.2	87
88	17 09.4	+55.3	0.8	18 09.4	+55.3	0.8	19 09.4	+55.3	0.8	20 09.4	+55.3	0.8	88
89	18 04.7	+55.3	0.4	19 04.7	+55.3	0.4	20 04.7	+55.3	0.4	21 04.7	+55.3	0.4	89
90	19 00.0	+55.2	0.0	20 00.0	+55.2	0.0	21 00.0	+55.2	0.0	22 00.0	+55.2	0.0	90
	19°			20°			21°			22°			

S. Lat. {L.H.A. greater than 180° ....Zn=180°−Z; L.H.A. less than 180°..........Zn=180°+Z}

LATITUDE **SAME** NAME AS DECLINATION L.H.A. 157°, 203°

49

Dec.	15° Hc	d	Z	16° Hc	d	Z	17° Hc	d	Z	18° Hc	d	Z	19° Hc	d	Z	20° Hc	d	Z	21° Hc	d	Z	22° Hc	d	Z	Dec.
0	61 56.1	+32.3	120.2	61 25.2	+34.0	121.8	60 53.0	+35.4	123.3	60 19.4	+36.9	124.8	59 44.6	+38.2	126.2	59 08.6	+39.5	127.5	58 31.5	+40.7	128.8	57 53.4	+41.8	130.1	0
1	62 28.4	+30.9	118.4	61 59.2	+32.5	120.0	61 28.4	+34.2	121.6	60 56.3	+35.7	123.2	60 22.8	+37.1	124.6	59 48.1	+38.5	126.0	59 12.2	+39.8	127.4	58 35.2	+41.0	128.7	1
2	62 59.3	+29.3	116.5	62 31.7	+31.1	118.2	62 02.6	+32.8	119.9	61 32.0	+34.4	121.5	60 59.9	+36.0	123.0	60 26.6	+37.3	124.5	59 52.0	+38.7	125.9	59 16.2	+40.0	127.3	2
3	63 28.6	+27.7	114.6	63 02.8	+29.6	116.3	62 35.4	+31.3	118.1	62 06.4	+33.0	119.7	61 35.9	+34.6	121.4	61 03.9	+36.2	122.9	60 30.7	+37.6	124.4	59 56.2	+39.0	125.8	3
4	63 56.3	+26.0	112.6	63 32.4	+27.9	114.4	63 06.7	+29.9	116.2	62 39.4	+31.6	117.9	62 10.5	+33.3	119.6	61 40.1	+34.9	121.2	61 08.3	+36.5	122.8	60 35.2	+37.8	124.3	4
5	64 22.3	+24.2	110.5	64 00.3	+26.3	112.4	63 36.6	+28.2	114.3	63 11.0	+30.1	116.1	62 43.8	+31.9	117.8	62 15.0	+33.6	119.5	61 44.8	+35.1	121.1	61 13.0	+36.7	122.7	5
6	64 46.5	+22.3	108.4	64 26.6	+24.4	110.3	64 04.8	+26.5	112.3	63 41.1	+28.5	114.1	63 15.7	+30.4	116.0	62 48.6	+32.2	117.7	62 19.9	+33.9	119.4	61 49.7	+35.5	121.0	6
7	65 08.8	+20.3	106.2	64 51.0	+22.6	108.2	64 31.3	+24.7	110.2	64 09.6	+26.8	112.0	63 46.1	+28.7	114.0	63 20.8	+30.6	115.9	62 53.8	+32.4	117.6	62 25.2	+34.1	119.3	7
8	65 29.1	+18.2	103.9	65 13.6	+20.6	106.0	64 56.0	+22.8	108.1	64 36.4	+25.0	110.1	64 14.8	+27.1	112.0	63 51.4	+29.1	113.9	63 26.2	+30.9	115.7	62 59.3	+32.7	117.5	8
9	65 47.3	+16.2	101.6	65 34.2	+18.5	103.8	65 18.8	+20.9	105.9	65 01.4	+23.1	107.9	64 41.9	+25.3	110.0	64 20.5	+27.3	111.9	63 57.1	+29.4	113.8	63 32.0	+31.2	115.7	9
10	66 03.5	+13.9	99.2	65 52.7	+16.4	101.4	65 39.7	+18.8	103.6	65 24.5	+21.1	105.7	65 07.2	+23.3	107.8	64 47.8	+25.5	109.8	64 26.5	+27.6	111.8	64 03.2	+29.6	113.7	10
11	66 17.4	+11.6	96.8	66 09.1	+14.1	99.1	65 58.5	+16.6	101.3	65 45.6	+19.1	103.5	65 30.5	+21.4	105.6	65 13.3	+23.7	107.7	64 54.1	+25.8	109.7	64 32.8	+28.0	111.7	11
12	66 29.0	+9.3	94.4	66 23.2	+11.9	96.7	66 15.1	+14.4	98.9	66 04.7	+16.9	101.1	65 51.9	+19.4	103.3	65 37.0	+21.7	105.5	65 19.9	+23.9	107.6	65 00.8	+26.1	109.6	12
13	66 38.3	+6.9	91.9	66 35.1	+9.6	94.2	66 29.5	+12.2	96.5	66 21.6	+14.6	98.8	66 11.3	+17.1	101.0	65 58.7	+19.6	103.2	65 43.8	+22.0	105.4	65 26.9	+24.2	107.5	13
14	66 45.2	+4.6	89.4	66 44.7	+7.1	91.7	66 41.7	+9.8	94.0	66 36.2	+12.4	96.3	66 28.4	+15.0	98.6	66 18.3	+17.4	100.9	66 05.8	+19.9	103.1	65 51.1	+22.3	105.3	14
15	66 49.8	+2.0	86.9	66 51.8	+4.8	89.2	66 51.5	+7.3	91.5	66 48.6	+10.1	93.9	66 43.4	+12.6	96.2	66 35.7	+15.2	98.5	66 25.7	+17.7	100.8	66 13.4	+20.1	103.0	15
16	66 51.8	-0.3	84.3	66 56.6	+2.2	86.6	66 58.8	+5.0	89.0	66 58.7	+7.6	91.4	66 56.0	+10.3	93.7	66 50.9	+12.9	96.0	66 43.4	+15.5	98.3	66 33.5	+18.0	100.6	16
17	66 51.5	-2.9	81.8	66 58.8	-0.1	84.1	67 03.8	+2.5	86.4	67 06.3	+5.1	88.8	67 06.3	+7.8	91.2	67 03.8	+10.5	93.5	66 58.9	+13.1	95.9	66 51.5	+15.8	98.2	17
18	66 48.6	-5.2	79.2	66 58.7	-2.7	81.5	67 06.3	0.0	83.9	67 11.4	+2.7	86.2	67 14.1	+5.4	88.6	67 14.3	+8.1	91.0	67 12.0	+10.8	93.4	67 07.3	+13.4	95.8	18
19	66 43.4	-7.7	76.7	66 56.0	-5.1	79.0	67 06.3	-2.5	81.3	67 14.1	+0.2	83.7	67 19.5	+2.9	86.0	67 22.4	+5.6	88.4	67 22.8	+8.3	90.8	67 20.7	+11.0	93.2	19
20	66 35.7	-10.0	74.2	66 50.9	-7.5	76.4	67 03.8	-4.9	78.7	67 14.3	-2.3	81.1	67 22.4	+0.4	83.4	67 28.0	+3.1	85.8	67 31.1	+5.8	88.3	67 31.7	+8.5	90.7	20
21	66 25.7	-12.3	71.7	66 43.4	-9.9	73.9	66 58.9	-7.4	76.2	67 12.0	-4.7	78.5	67 22.8	-2.1	80.8	67 31.1	+0.6	83.2	67 36.9	+3.3	85.6	67 40.2	+6.0	88.1	21
22	66 13.4	-14.6	69.3	66 33.5	-12.2	71.4	66 51.5	-9.8	73.7	67 07.3	-7.3	75.9	67 20.7	-4.7	78.3	67 31.7	-2.0	80.6	67 40.2	+0.8	83.0	67 46.2	+3.5	85.4	22
23	65 58.8	-16.8	66.9	66 21.3	-14.5	69.0	66 41.7	-12.1	71.2	67 00.0	-9.6	73.4	67 16.0	-7.1	75.7	67 29.7	-4.5	78.0	67 41.0	-1.8	80.4	67 49.7	+1.0	82.8	23
24	65 42.0	-18.9	64.5	66 06.8	-16.7	66.6	66 29.6	-14.4	68.7	66 50.4	-12.0	70.9	67 08.9	-9.5	73.1	67 25.2	-7.0	75.4	67 39.2	-4.4	77.8	67 50.7	-1.7	80.2	24
25	65 23.1	-21.0	62.3	65 50.1	-18.8	64.2	66 15.2	-16.6	66.3	66 38.4	-14.4	68.4	66 59.4	-11.9	70.6	67 18.2	-9.4	72.8	67 34.8	-6.9	75.1	67 49.0	-4.2	77.5	25
26	65 02.1	-22.8	60.0	65 31.3	-20.9	61.9	65 58.6	-18.8	63.9	66 24.0	-16.5	65.9	66 47.5	-14.3	68.1	67 08.8	-11.8	70.3	67 27.9	-9.3	72.5	67 44.8	-6.8	74.9	26
27	64 39.3	-24.8	57.8	65 10.4	-22.9	59.7	65 39.8	-20.8	61.6	66 07.5	-18.8	63.6	66 33.2	-16.5	65.6	66 57.0	-14.2	67.8	67 18.6	-11.8	70.0	67 38.0	-9.2	72.2	27
28	64 14.5	-26.5	55.7	64 47.5	-24.7	57.5	65 19.0	-22.8	59.3	65 48.7	-20.8	61.2	66 16.7	-18.7	63.2	66 42.8	-16.5	65.3	67 06.8	-14.1	67.4	67 28.8	-11.7	69.7	28
29	63 48.0	-28.2	53.7	64 22.8	-26.5	55.4	64 56.2	-24.7	57.1	65 27.9	-22.7	58.9	65 58.0	-20.7	60.9	66 26.3	-18.6	62.9	66 52.7	-16.4	64.9	67 17.1	-14.1	67.1	29
30	63 19.8	-29.8	51.7	63 56.3	-28.2	53.3	64 31.5	-26.5	55.0	65 05.2	-24.7	56.7	65 37.3	-22.8	58.6	66 07.7	-20.8	60.5	66 36.3	-18.6	62.5	67 03.0	-16.4	64.6	30
31	62 50.0	-31.3	49.8	63 28.1	-29.8	51.3	64 05.0	-28.2	52.9	64 40.5	-26.5	54.6	65 14.5	-24.7	56.4	65 46.9	-22.8	58.2	66 17.7	-20.8	60.1	66 46.6	-18.6	62.2	31
32	62 18.7	-32.8	47.9	62 58.3	-31.3	49.4	63 36.8	-29.8	50.9	64 14.0	-28.3	52.5	64 49.8	-26.5	54.2	65 24.1	-24.7	56.0	65 56.9	-22.8	57.8	66 28.0	-20.8	59.8	32
33	61 45.9	-34.0	46.1	62 27.0	-32.8	47.5	63 07.0	-31.4	49.0	63 45.7	-29.8	50.5	64 23.3	-28.3	52.1	64 59.4	-26.5	53.8	65 34.1	-24.7	55.6	66 07.2	-22.8	57.4	33
34	61 11.9	-35.4	44.4	61 54.2	-34.1	45.7	62 35.6	-32.8	47.1	63 15.9	-31.4	48.6	63 55.0	-29.9	50.1	64 32.9	-28.3	51.7	65 09.4	-26.6	53.4	65 44.4	-24.8	55.2	34
35	60 36.5	-36.5	42.8	61 20.1	-35.4	44.0	62 02.8	-34.1	45.3	62 44.5	-32.8	46.7	63 25.1	-31.4	48.1	64 04.6	-30.0	49.7	64 42.8	-28.4	51.3	65 19.6	-26.6	53.0	35
36	60 00.0	-37.7	41.2	60 44.7	-36.5	42.3	61 28.7	-35.5	43.6	62 11.7	-34.2	44.9	62 53.7	-32.9	46.2	63 34.6	-31.4	47.7	64 14.4	-29.9	49.2	64 53.0	-28.4	50.8	36
37	59 22.3	-38.7	39.6	60 08.2	-37.7	40.7	60 53.2	-36.6	41.9	61 37.5	-35.5	43.1	62 20.8	-34.3	44.4	63 03.2	-33.0	45.8	63 44.5	-31.6	47.2	64 24.6	-30.1	48.8	37
38	58 43.6	-39.7	38.1	59 30.5	-38.8	39.1	60 16.6	-37.8	40.3	61 02.0	-36.7	41.4	61 46.5	-35.5	42.7	62 30.2	-34.3	44.0	63 12.9	-33.0	45.3	63 54.5	-31.6	46.8	38
39	58 03.9	-40.6	36.7	58 51.7	-39.8	37.7	59 38.8	-38.8	38.7	60 25.3	-37.8	39.8	61 11.0	-36.8	41.0	61 55.9	-35.7	42.2	62 39.9	-34.5	43.5	63 22.9	-33.1	44.9	39
40	57 23.3	-41.5	35.3	58 11.9	-40.6	36.2	59 00.0	-39.8	37.2	59 47.5	-38.9	38.3	60 34.2	-37.9	39.4	61 20.2	-36.8	40.5	62 05.4	-35.7	41.7	62 49.8	-34.5	43.0	40
41	56 41.8	-42.4	34.0	57 31.3	-41.6	34.9	58 20.2	-40.7	35.8	59 08.6	-39.9	36.8	59 56.3	-38.9	37.8	60 43.4	-38.0	38.9	61 29.7	-36.9	40.0	62 15.3	-35.9	41.3	41
42	55 59.4	-43.0	32.7	56 49.7	-42.4	33.5	57 39.5	-41.7	34.4	58 28.7	-40.8	35.3	59 17.4	-40.0	36.3	60 05.4	-39.1	37.3	60 52.8	-38.1	38.4	61 39.4	-37.0	39.5	42
43	55 16.4	-43.8	31.5	56 07.3	-43.1	32.3	56 57.8	-42.4	33.1	57 47.9	-41.7	33.9	58 37.4	-40.9	34.8	59 26.3	-40.0	35.8	60 14.7	-39.2	36.8	61 02.4	-38.2	37.9	43
44	54 32.6	-44.5	30.3	55 24.2	-43.9	31.0	56 15.4	-43.2	31.8	57 06.2	-42.5	32.6	57 56.5	-41.8	33.5	58 46.3	-41.0	34.4	59 35.5	-40.1	35.3	60 24.2	-39.3	36.3	44
45	53 48.1	-45.1	29.1	54 40.3	-44.5	29.8	55 32.2	-43.9	30.5	56 23.7	-43.3	31.3	57 14.7	-42.6	32.1	58 05.3	-41.9	33.0	58 55.4	-41.1	33.9	59 44.9	-40.3	34.8	45
46	53 03.0	-45.7	28.0	53 55.8	-45.2	28.7	54 48.3	-44.7	29.4	55 40.4	-44.0	30.1	56 32.1	-43.4	30.8	57 23.4	-42.7	31.6	58 14.3	-42.0	32.5	59 04.6	-41.2	33.4	46
47	52 17.3	-46.3	27.0	53 10.6	-45.8	27.6	54 03.6	-45.2	28.2	54 56.4	-44.7	28.9	55 48.7	-44.1	29.6	56 40.7	-43.5	30.3	57 32.3	-42.8	31.1	58 23.4	-42.1	32.0	47
48	51 31.0	-46.8	25.9	52 24.8	-46.3	26.5	53 18.4	-45.8	27.1	54 11.7	-45.4	27.7	55 04.6	-44.8	28.4	55 57.2	-44.2	29.1	56 49.5	-43.6	29.8	57 41.3	-42.9	30.6	48
49	50 44.2	-47.3	24.9	51 38.5	-46.8	25.5	52 32.6	-46.4	26.0	53 26.3	-45.9	26.6	54 19.8	-45.4	27.2	55 13.0	-44.8	27.9	56 05.9	-44.3	28.6	56 58.4	-43.7	29.3	49
50	49 56.9	-47.7	24.0	50 51.7	-47.4	24.5	51 46.2	-47.0	25.0	52 40.4	-46.5	25.5	53 34.4	-46.0	26.1	54 28.2	-45.5	26.7	55 21.6	-45.0	27.4	56 14.7	-44.4	28.1	50
51	49 09.2	-48.2	23.0	50 04.3	-47.8	23.5	50 59.2	-47.4	24.0	51 53.9	-47.0	24.5	52 48.4	-46.5	25.1	53 42.7	-46.1	25.6	54 36.6	-45.6	26.2	55 30.3	-45.1	26.9	51
52	48 21.0	-48.6	22.1	49 16.5	-48.2	22.6	50 11.8	-47.9	23.0	51 06.9	-47.4	23.5	52 01.9	-47.1	24.0	52 56.6	-46.7	24.6	53 51.0	-46.2	25.1	54 45.2	-45.7	25.7	52
53	47 32.4	-49.0	21.3	48 28.3	-48.7	21.7	49 23.9	-48.3	22.1	50 19.5	-48.0	22.5	51 14.8	-47.6	23.0	52 09.8	-47.2	23.5	53 04.8	-46.8	24.0	53 59.5	-46.4	24.6	53
54	46 43.4	-49.3	20.4	47 39.6	-49.0	20.8	48 35.6	-48.7	21.2	49 31.5	-48.4	21.6	50 27.2	-48.1	22.1	51 22.7	-47.7	22.5	52 18.0	-47.3	23.0	53 13.1	-46.8	23.5	54
55	45 54.1	-49.7	19.6	46 50.6	-49.4	19.9	47 46.9	-49.1	20.3	48 43.1	-48.8	20.7	49 39.1	-48.4	21.1	50 35.0	-48.1	21.6	51 30.7	-47.7	22.0	52 26.3	-47.4	22.5	55
56	45 04.4	-50.0	18.8	46 01.2	-49.8	19.1	46 57.8	-49.5	19.5	47 54.3	-49.2	19.8	48 50.7	-48.9	20.2	49 46.9	-48.6	20.6	50 43.0	-48.3	21.1	51 38.9	-47.9	21.5	56
57	44 14.4	-50.3	18.0	45 11.4	-50.1	18.3	46 08.3	-49.8	18.6	47 05.1	-49.6	19.0	48 01.8	-49.3	19.3	48 58.3	-49.0	19.7	49 54.7	-48.6	20.1	50 51.0	-48.4	20.5	57
58	43 24.1	-50.7	17.3	44 21.3	-50.4	17.5	45 18.5	-50.2	17.8	46 15.4	-49.9	18.2	47 12.5	-49.6	18.5	48 09.3	-49.3	18.9	49 06.1	-49.1	19.2	50 02.6	-48.7	19.6	58
59	42 33.4	-50.8	16.5	43 30.9	-50.6	16.8	44 28.3	-50.4	17.1	45 25.6	-50.2	17.4	46 22.9	-50.0	17.7	47 20.0	-49.8	18.0	48 17.0	-49.5	18.3	49 13.9	-49.2	18.7	59
60	41 42.6	-51.2	15.8	42 40.3	-51.0	16.1	43 37.9	-50.8	16.3	44 35.4	-50.5	16.6	45 32.9	-50.3	16.9	46 30.2	-50.0	17.2	47 27.5	-49.8	17.5	48 24.7	-49.6	17.8	60
61	40 51.4	-51.4	15.1	41 49.3	-51.2	15.3	42 47.1	-51.0	15.6	43 44.9	-50.8	15.8	44 42.6	-50.6	16.1	45 40.2	-50.4	16.4	46 37.7	-50.2	16.7	47 35.1	-49.9	17.0	61
62	40 00.0	-51.6	14.4	40 58.1	-51.4	14.6	41 56.1	-51.2	14.9	42 54.1	-51.1	15.1	43 52.0	-50.9	15.4	44 49.8	-50.7	15.6	45 47.5	-50.5	15.9	46 45.2	-50.3	16.2	62
63	39 08.4	-51.8	13.8	40 06.7	-51.7	14.0	41 04.9	-51.6	14.2	42 03.0	-51.3	14.4	43 01.1	-51.2	14.6	43 59.1	-51.0	14.9	44 57.1	-50.8	15.1	45 54.9	-50.6	15.4	63
64	38 16.6	-52.1	13.1	39 15.0	-51.9	13.3	40 13.3	-51.7	13.5	41 11.7	-51.6	13.7	42 09.9	-51.4	13.9	43 08.1	-51.2	14.1	44 06.3	-51.1	14.4	45 04.4	-50.9	14.6	64
65	37 24.5	-52.2	12.5	38 23.1	-52.1	12.7	39 21.6	-52.0	12.8	40 20.1	-51.8	13.0	41 18.5	-51.7	13.2	42 16.9	-51.5	13.4	43 15.2	-51.3	13.7	44 13.5	-51.2	13.9	65
66	36 32.3	-52.5	11.9	37 31.0	-52.3	12.0	38 29.6	-52.1	12.2	39 28.3	-52.1	12.4	40 26.8	-51.8	12.6	41 25.4	-51.8	12.7	42 23.9	-51.6	13.0	43 22.3	-51.4	13.2	66
67	35 39.8	-52.6	11.3	36 38.7	-52.5	11.4	37 37.5	-52.4	11.6	38 36.2	-52.2	11.7	39 35.0	-52.1	11.9	40 33.6	-51.9	12.1	41 32.3	-51.8	12.3	42 30.9	-51.7	12.5	67
68	34 47.2	-52.7	10.7	35 46.2	-52.7	10.8	36 45.1	-52.5	11.0	37 44.0	-52.4	11.1	38 42.9	-52.3	11.3	39 41.7	-52.2	11.4	40 40.5	-52.1	11.6	41 39.2	-51.9	11.8	68
69	33 54.5	-53.0	10.1	34 53.5	-52.8	10.2	35 52.6	-52.8	10.4	36 51.6	-52.6	10.5	37 50.6	-52.5	10.6	38 49.5	-52.4	10.8	39 48.4	-52.2	10.9	40 47.3	-52.1	11.1	69
70	33 01.5	-53.0	9.6	34 00.7	-53.0	9.7	34 59.8	-52.8	9.8	35 59.0	-52.8	9.9	36 58.1	-52.7	10.0	37 57.1	-52.6	10.2	38 56.2	-52.5	10.3	39 55.2	-52.4	10.5	70
71	32 08.5	-53.3	9.0	33 07.7	-53.1	9.1	34 07.0	-53.1	9.2	35 06.2	-53.0	9.3	36 05.4	-52.9	9.4	37 04.5	-52.7	9.6	38 03.7	-52.7	9.7	39 02.8	-52.5	9.9	71
72	31 15.2	-53.3	8.5	32 14.6	-53.3	8.5	33 13.9	-53.2	8.6	34 13.2	-53.1	8.7	35 12.5	-53.0	8.8	36 11.8	-52.9	9.0	37 11.0	-52.8	9.1	38 10.3	-52.8	9.2	72
73	30 21.9	-53.5	7.9	31 21.3	-53.4	8.0	32 20.7	-53.3	8.1	33 20.1	-53.2	8.2	34 19.5	-53.2	8.3	35 18.9	-53.1	8.4	36 18.2	-53.0	8.5	37 17.5	-52.9	8.6	73
74	29 28.4	-53.6	7.4	30 27.9	-53.5	7.5	31 27.4	-53.5	7.6	32 26.9	-53.4	7.6	33 26.3	-53.3	7.7	34 25.8	-53.3	7.8	35 25.2	-53.2	7.9	36 24.6	-53.1	8.0	74
75	28 34.8	-53.7	6.9	29 34.4	-53.7	7.0	30 33.9	-53.6	7.0	31 33.5	-53.6	7.1	32 33.0	-53.5	7.2	33 32.5	-53.4	7.3	34 32.0	-53.3	7.3	35 31.5	-53.2	7.4	75
76	27 41.1	-53.8	6.4	28 40.7	-53.8	6.5	29 40.3	-53.7	6.5	30 39.9	-53.6	6.6	31 39.5	-53.5	6.6	32 39.1	-53.5	6.7	33 38.7	-53.4	6.8	34 38.3	-53.4	6.9	76
77	26 47.3	-54.0	5.9	27 46.9	-53.8	5.9	28 46.6	-53.8	6.0	29 46.3	-53.8	6.1	30 46.0	-53.8	6.1	31 45.6	-53.7	6.2	32 45.3	-53.6	6.2	33 44.9	-53.6	6.3	77
78	25 53.3	-54.0	5.4	26 53.1	-54.0	5.4	27 52.8	-53.9	5.5	28 52.5	-53.9	5.5	29 52.2	-53.9	5.6	30 51.9	-53.7	5.7	31 51.7	-53.8	5.7	32 51.3	-53.6	5.8	78
79	24 59.2	-54.1	4.9	25 59.1	-54.1	5.0	26 58.9	-54.1	5.0	27 58.6	-54.0	5.0	28 58.3	-53.9	5.1	29 58.2	-53.9	5.1	30 57.9	-53.8	5.2	31 57.7	-53.8	5.2	79
80	24 05.2	-54.2	4.4	25 05.0	-54.2	4.5	26 04.8	-54.2	4.5	27 04.6	-54.1	4.5	28 04.5	-54.1	4.6	29 04.3	-54.1	4.6	30 04.1	-54.0	4.7	31 03.9	-54.0	4.7	80
81	23 11.0	-54.3	4.0	24 10.8	-54.2	4.0	25 10.7	-54.2	4.1	26 10.6	-54.2	4.1	27 10.4	-54.2	4.1	28 10.2	-54.1	4.1	29 10.1	-54.1	4.2	30 09.9	-54.0	4.2	81
82	22 16.7	-54.3	3.5	23 16.6	-54.3	3.5	24 16.5	-54.3	3.6	25 16.4	-54.3	3.6	26 16.2	-54.2	3.6	27 16.1	-54.2	3.6	28 16.0	-54.2	3.7	29 15.9	-54.2	3.7	82
83	21 22.3	-54.4	3.1	22 22.3	-54.4	3.1	23 22.2	-54.4	3.1	24 22.1	-54.4	3.1	25 22.0	-54.3	3.1	26 21.9	-54.3	3.2	27 21.8	-54.3	3.2	28 21.7	-54.3	3.2	83
84	20 27.9	-54.5	2.6	21 27.9	-54.5	2.6	22 27.8	-54.5	2.7	23 27.7	-54.5	2.7	24 27.7	-54.5	2.7	25 27.6	-54.4	2.7	26 27.5	-54.4	2.7	27 27.5	-54.4	2.7	84
85	19 33.4	-54.6	2.2	20 33.4	-54.6	2.2	21 33.3	-54.5	2.2	22 33.3	-54.5	2.2	23 33.2	-54.5	2.2	24 33.2	-54.5	2.2	25 33.1	-54.4	2.3	26 33.1	-54.5	2.3	85
86	18 38.8	-54.6	1.7	19 38.8	-54.6	1.7	20 38.8	-54.6	1.7	21 38.8	-54.6	1.7	22 38.7	-54.6	1.8	23 38.7	-54.6	1.8	24 38.7	-54.6	1.8	25 38.6	-54.5	1.8	86
87	17 44.2	-54.7	1.3	18 44.2	-54.7	1.3	19 44.2	-54.7	1.3	20 44.2	-54.7	1.3	21 44.1	-54.7	1.3	22 44.1	-54.7	1.3	23 44.1	-54.6	1.3	24 44.1	-54.6	1.3	87
88	16 49.5	-54.7	0.8	17 49.5	-54.7	0.8	18 49.5	-54.8	0.9	19 49.5	-54.7	0.9	20 49.5	-54.7	0.9	21 49.5	-54.7	0.9	22 49.5	-54.7	0.9	23 49.5	-54.7	0.9	88
89	15 54.8	-54.8	0.4	16 54.8	-54.8	0.4	17 54.8	-54.8	0.4	18 54.8	-54.8	0.4	19 54.8	-54.8	0.4	20 54.8	-54.8	0.4	21 54.8	-54.8	0.4	22 54.8	-54.8	0.4	89
90	15 00.0	-54.8	0.0	16 00.0	-54.8	0.0	17 00.0	-54.8	0.0	18 00.0	-54.8	0.0	19 00.0	-54.8	0.0	20 00.0	-54.8	0.0	21 00.0	-54.8	0.0	22 00.0	-54.8	0.0	90

24°, 336° L.H.A.　　LATITUDE **SAME** NAME AS DECLINATION

LATITUDE **CONTRARY** NAME TO DECLINATION **L.H.A. 24°, 336°**

Dec.	15° Hc	15° d	15° Z	16° Hc	16° d	16° Z	17° Hc	17° d	17° Z	18° Hc	18° d	18° Z	19° Hc	19° d	19° Z	20° Hc	20° d	20° Z	21° Hc	21° d	21° Z	22° Hc	22° d	22° Z	Dec.
°	° ′	′	°	° ′	′	°	° ′	′	°	° ′	′	°	° ′	′	°	° ′	′	°	° ′	′	°	° ′	′	°	°
0	61 56.1	-33.7	120.2	61 25.2	-35.2	121.8	60 53.0	-36.7	123.3	60 19.4	-38.0	124.8	59 44.6	-39.3	126.2	59 08.6	-40.5	127.5	58 31.5	-41.6	128.8	57 53.4	-42.7	130.1	0
1	61 22.4	-34.9	121.9	60 50.0	-36.4	123.4	60 16.3	-37.7	124.9	59 41.4	-39.0	126.3	59 05.3	-40.3	127.7	58 28.1	-41.4	129.0	57 49.9	-42.5	130.2	57 10.7	-43.5	131.4	1
2	60 47.5	-36.2	123.6	60 13.6	-37.5	125.1	59 38.6	-38.9	126.5	59 02.4	-40.1	127.8	58 25.0	-41.1	129.1	57 46.7	-42.2	130.3	57 07.4	-43.3	131.5	56 27.2	-44.2	132.6	2
3	60 11.3	-37.3	125.2	59 36.1	-38.6	126.6	58 59.7	-39.8	128.0	58 22.3	-40.9	129.2	57 43.9	-42.1	130.5	57 04.5	-43.1	131.6	56 24.1	-44.0	132.8	55 43.0	-44.9	133.9	3
4	59 34.0	-38.4	126.8	58 57.5	-39.6	128.1	58 19.9	-40.7	129.4	57 41.4	-41.9	130.6	57 01.8	-42.8	131.8	56 21.4	-43.8	132.9	55 40.1	-44.7	134.0	54 58.1	-45.6	135.0	4
5	58 55.6	-39.4	128.3	58 17.9	-40.6	129.6	57 39.2	-41.7	130.8	56 59.5	-42.6	131.9	56 19.0	-43.6	133.1	55 37.6	-44.5	134.1	54 55.4	-45.3	135.2	54 12.5	-46.1	136.1	5
6	58 16.2	-40.4	129.7	57 37.3	-41.4	130.9	56 57.5	-42.4	132.1	56 16.9	-43.4	133.2	55 35.4	-44.3	134.3	54 53.1	-45.2	135.3	54 10.1	-46.0	136.3	53 26.4	-46.8	137.2	6
7	57 35.8	-41.2	131.1	56 55.9	-42.3	132.3	56 15.1	-43.2	133.4	55 33.5	-44.2	134.5	54 51.1	-45.0	135.5	54 07.9	-45.7	136.4	53 24.1	-46.5	137.4	52 39.6	-47.2	138.3	7
8	56 54.6	-42.1	132.5	56 13.6	-43.0	133.6	55 31.9	-44.0	134.6	54 49.3	-44.7	135.6	54 06.1	-45.6	136.6	53 22.2	-46.4	137.5	52 37.6	-47.1	138.4	51 52.4	-47.8	139.3	8
9	56 12.5	-42.9	133.8	55 30.6	-43.8	134.8	54 47.9	-44.6	135.8	54 04.6	-45.5	136.8	53 20.5	-46.2	137.7	52 35.8	-46.9	138.6	51 50.5	-47.6	139.4	51 04.6	-48.2	140.3	9
10	55 29.6	-43.5	135.0	54 46.8	-44.4	136.0	54 03.3	-45.2	137.0	53 19.1	-46.0	137.9	52 34.3	-46.7	138.8	51 48.9	-47.4	139.6	51 02.9	-48.0	140.4	50 16.4	-48.6	141.2	10
11	54 46.1	-44.3	136.2	54 02.4	-45.1	137.2	53 18.1	-45.9	138.1	52 33.1	-46.5	139.0	51 47.6	-47.3	139.8	51 01.5	-47.9	140.6	50 14.9	-48.5	141.4	49 27.8	-49.1	142.1	11
12	54 01.8	-44.9	137.4	53 17.3	-45.7	138.3	52 32.2	-46.4	139.1	51 46.6	-47.1	140.0	51 00.3	-47.7	140.8	50 13.6	-48.3	141.5	49 26.4	-48.9	142.3	48 38.7	-49.5	143.0	12
13	53 16.9	-45.6	138.5	52 31.6	-46.2	139.4	51 45.8	-46.9	140.2	50 59.5	-47.6	141.0	50 12.6	-48.2	141.7	49 25.3	-48.8	142.5	48 37.5	-49.3	143.2	47 49.2	-49.8	143.8	13
14	52 31.3	-46.0	139.6	51 45.4	-46.8	140.4	50 58.9	-47.4	141.2	50 11.9	-48.0	141.9	49 24.4	-48.6	142.7	48 36.5	-49.1	143.4	47 48.2	-49.7	144.0	46 59.4	-50.1	144.6	14
15	51 45.3	-46.7	140.6	50 58.6	-47.4	141.4	50 11.5	-47.9	142.1	49 23.9	-48.5	142.9	48 35.8	-49.0	143.6	47 47.4	-49.6	144.2	46 58.5	-50.0	144.8	46 09.3	-50.5	145.4	15
16	50 58.6	-47.1	141.6	50 11.3	-47.7	142.4	49 23.6	-48.3	143.1	48 35.4	-48.8	143.8	47 46.8	-49.4	144.4	46 57.8	-49.8	145.0	46 08.5	-50.4	145.6	45 18.8	-50.8	146.2	16
17	50 11.5	-47.6	142.6	49 23.6	-48.2	143.3	48 35.3	-48.7	144.0	47 46.6	-49.3	144.6	46 57.4	-49.7	145.3	46 08.0	-50.3	145.9	45 18.1	-50.6	146.4	44 28.0	-51.1	147.0	17
18	49 23.9	-48.1	143.5	48 35.4	-48.6	144.2	47 46.6	-49.2	144.9	46 57.3	-49.6	145.5	46 07.7	-50.1	146.1	45 17.7	-50.5	146.6	44 27.5	-51.0	147.2	43 36.9	-51.4	147.7	18
19	48 35.8	-48.4	144.4	47 46.8	-49.0	145.1	46 57.4	-49.4	145.7	46 07.7	-50.0	146.3	45 17.6	-50.4	146.9	44 27.2	-50.8	147.4	43 36.5	-51.2	147.9	42 45.5	-51.6	148.4	19
20	47 47.4	-48.9	145.3	46 57.8	-49.3	145.9	46 08.0	-49.9	146.5	45 17.7	-50.2	147.1	44 27.2	-50.7	147.6	43 36.4	-51.1	148.1	42 45.3	-51.5	148.6	41 53.9	-51.8	149.1	20
21	46 58.5	-49.2	146.2	46 08.5	-49.7	146.8	45 18.1	-50.1	147.3	44 27.5	-50.6	147.9	43 36.5	-51.0	148.4	42 45.3	-51.4	148.9	41 53.8	-51.7	149.3	41 02.1	-52.1	149.8	21
22	46 09.3	-49.6	147.0	45 18.8	-50.1	147.6	44 28.0	-50.5	148.1	43 36.9	-50.9	148.6	42 45.5	-51.2	149.1	41 53.9	-51.6	149.6	41 02.1	-52.0	150.0	40 10.0	-52.3	150.4	22
23	45 19.7	-50.0	147.8	44 28.7	-50.3	148.3	43 37.5	-50.7	148.9	42 46.0	-51.1	149.3	41 54.3	-51.5	149.8	41 02.3	-51.8	150.2	40 10.1	-52.1	150.7	39 17.7	-52.5	151.1	23
24	44 29.7	-50.2	148.6	43 38.4	-50.6	149.1	42 46.8	-51.0	149.6	41 54.9	-51.4	150.0	41 02.8	-51.7	150.5	40 10.5	-52.1	150.9	39 18.0	-52.4	151.3	38 25.2	-52.7	151.7	24
25	43 39.5	-50.5	149.4	42 47.8	-50.9	149.8	41 55.8	-51.3	150.3	41 03.5	-51.6	150.7	40 11.1	-52.0	151.1	39 18.4	-52.2	151.5	38 25.6	-52.6	151.9	37 32.5	-52.8	152.3	25
26	42 49.0	-50.8	150.1	41 56.9	-51.2	150.6	41 04.5	-51.5	151.0	40 11.9	-51.8	151.4	39 19.1	-52.1	151.8	38 26.2	-52.5	152.2	37 33.0	-52.8	152.5	36 39.7	-53.1	152.9	26
27	41 58.2	-51.1	150.8	41 05.7	-51.4	151.3	40 13.0	-51.8	151.7	39 20.1	-52.1	152.1	38 27.0	-52.4	152.4	37 33.7	-52.7	152.8	36 40.2	-52.9	153.1	35 46.6	-53.2	153.5	27
28	41 07.1	-51.3	151.5	40 14.3	-51.7	151.9	39 21.2	-51.9	152.3	38 28.0	-52.3	152.7	37 34.6	-52.6	153.1	36 41.0	-52.8	153.4	35 47.3	-53.1	153.7	34 53.4	-53.3	154.0	28
29	40 15.8	-51.6	152.2	39 22.6	-51.8	152.6	38 29.3	-52.2	153.0	37 35.7	-52.4	153.3	36 42.0	-52.7	153.7	35 48.2	-53.0	154.0	34 54.2	-53.3	154.3	34 00.1	-53.5	154.6	29
30	39 24.2	-51.7	152.9	38 30.8	-52.1	153.2	37 37.1	-52.4	153.6	36 43.3	-52.7	153.9	35 49.3	-52.9	154.3	34 55.2	-53.2	154.6	34 00.9	-53.4	154.9	33 06.6	-53.7	155.1	30
31	38 32.5	-52.0	153.5	37 38.7	-52.3	153.9	36 44.7	-52.5	154.2	35 50.6	-52.8	154.5	34 56.4	-53.1	154.8	34 02.0	-53.3	155.1	33 07.5	-53.5	155.4	32 12.9	-53.7	155.7	31
32	37 40.5	-52.2	154.2	36 46.4	-52.4	154.5	35 52.2	-52.7	154.8	34 57.8	-52.9	155.1	34 03.3	-53.2	155.4	33 08.7	-53.4	155.7	32 14.0	-53.7	155.9	31 19.2	-53.9	156.2	32
33	36 48.3	-52.4	154.8	35 54.0	-52.7	155.1	34 59.5	-52.9	155.4	34 04.9	-53.2	155.7	33 10.1	-53.3	156.0	32 15.3	-53.6	156.2	31 20.3	-53.8	156.5	30 25.3	-54.1	156.7	33
34	35 55.9	-52.5	155.4	35 01.3	-52.8	155.7	34 06.6	-53.1	156.0	33 11.7	-53.3	156.2	32 16.8	-53.5	156.5	31 21.7	-53.7	156.7	30 26.5	-53.9	157.0	29 31.2	-54.1	157.2	34
35	35 03.4	-52.7	156.0	34 08.5	-52.9	156.3	33 13.5	-53.2	156.5	32 18.4	-53.4	156.8	31 23.3	-53.7	157.0	30 28.0	-53.9	157.3	29 32.6	-54.1	157.5	28 37.1	-54.2	157.7	35
36	34 10.7	-52.9	156.6	33 15.6	-53.2	156.8	32 20.3	-53.3	157.1	31 25.0	-53.5	157.3	30 29.6	-53.7	157.6	29 34.1	-53.9	157.8	28 38.5	-54.1	158.0	27 42.9	-54.4	158.2	36
37	33 17.8	-53.1	157.1	32 22.4	-53.2	157.4	31 27.0	-53.5	157.6	30 31.5	-53.7	157.8	29 35.9	-53.9	158.1	28 40.2	-54.1	158.3	27 44.4	-54.2	158.5	26 48.5	-54.4	158.7	37
38	32 24.7	-53.1	157.7	31 29.2	-53.4	157.9	30 33.5	-53.5	158.1	29 37.8	-53.8	158.4	28 42.0	-54.0	158.6	27 46.1	-54.2	158.8	26 50.2	-54.4	158.9	25 54.1	-54.5	159.1	38
39	31 31.6	-53.3	158.2	30 35.8	-53.5	158.5	29 40.0	-53.8	158.7	28 44.0	-53.9	158.9	27 48.0	-54.1	159.1	26 51.9	-54.2	159.2	25 55.8	-54.4	159.4	24 59.6	-54.6	159.6	39
40	30 38.3	-53.5	158.8	29 42.3	-53.7	159.0	28 46.2	-53.8	159.2	27 50.1	-54.0	159.4	26 53.9	-54.1	159.6	25 57.7	-54.4	159.7	25 01.4	-54.5	159.9	24 05.0	-54.7	160.0	40
41	29 44.8	-53.6	159.3	28 48.6	-53.7	159.5	27 52.4	-53.9	159.7	26 56.1	-54.1	159.9	25 59.8	-54.3	160.0	25 03.3	-54.4	160.2	24 06.9	-54.6	160.3	23 10.3	-54.7	160.5	41
42	28 51.2	-53.6	159.8	27 54.9	-53.9	160.0	26 58.5	-54.1	160.2	26 02.0	-54.2	160.3	25 05.5	-54.4	160.5	24 08.9	-54.5	160.7	23 12.3	-54.7	160.8	22 15.6	-54.9	160.9	42
43	27 57.6	-53.8	160.3	27 01.0	-53.9	160.5	26 04.4	-54.1	160.7	25 07.8	-54.3	160.8	24 11.1	-54.4	161.0	23 14.4	-54.6	161.1	22 17.6	-54.8	161.2	21 20.7	-54.9	161.4	43
44	27 03.8	-53.9	160.8	26 07.1	-54.1	161.0	25 10.3	-54.2	161.1	24 13.5	-54.4	161.3	23 16.7	-54.6	161.4	22 19.8	-54.7	161.6	21 22.8	-54.8	161.7	20 25.8	-54.9	161.8	44
45	26 09.9	-54.0	161.3	25 13.0	-54.1	161.5	24 16.1	-54.3	161.6	23 19.1	-54.4	161.7	22 22.1	-54.6	161.9	21 25.1	-54.8	162.0	20 28.0	-54.9	162.1	19 30.9	-55.0	162.2	45
46	25 15.9	-54.1	161.8	24 18.9	-54.3	161.9	23 21.8	-54.4	162.1	22 24.7	-54.5	162.2	21 27.5	-54.6	162.3	20 30.3	-54.8	162.4	19 33.1	-54.9	162.6	18 35.9	-55.1	162.7	46
47	24 21.8	-54.2	162.3	23 24.6	-54.3	162.4	22 27.4	-54.5	162.5	21 30.2	-54.7	162.7	20 32.9	-54.8	162.8	19 35.5	-54.8	162.9	18 38.2	-55.0	163.0	17 40.8	-55.1	163.1	47
48	23 27.6	-54.2	162.7	22 30.3	-54.4	162.9	21 32.9	-54.5	163.0	20 35.5	-54.6	163.1	19 38.1	-54.8	163.2	18 40.7	-55.0	163.3	17 43.2	-55.1	163.4	16 45.7	-55.2	163.5	48
49	22 33.4	-54.4	163.2	21 35.9	-54.5	163.3	20 38.4	-54.6	163.4	19 40.9	-54.8	163.5	18 43.3	-54.8	163.6	17 45.7	-54.9	163.7	16 48.1	-55.1	163.8	15 50.5	-55.2	163.9	49
50	21 39.0	-54.4	163.7	20 41.4	-54.5	163.8	19 43.8	-54.7	163.9	18 46.1	-54.7	164.0	17 48.5	-55.0	164.1	16 50.8	-55.1	164.1	15 53.0	-55.1	164.2	14 55.3	-55.3	164.3	50
51	20 44.6	-54.5	164.1	19 46.9	-54.6	164.2	18 49.1	-54.7	164.3	17 51.4	-54.9	164.4	16 53.5	-54.9	164.5	15 55.7	-55.1	164.6	14 57.9	-55.2	164.6	14 00.0	-55.3	164.7	51
52	19 50.1	-54.5	164.6	18 52.3	-54.7	164.7	17 54.4	-54.8	164.7	16 56.5	-54.9	164.8	15 58.6	-55.0	164.9	15 00.6	-55.1	165.0	14 02.7	-55.2	165.0	13 04.7	-55.3	165.1	52
53	18 55.6	-54.6	165.0	17 57.6	-54.7	165.1	16 59.6	-54.8	165.2	16 01.6	-54.9	165.2	15 03.6	-55.1	165.3	14 05.5	-55.1	165.4	13 07.5	-55.3	165.4	12 09.4	-55.4	165.5	53
54	18 01.0	-54.7	165.4	17 02.9	-54.8	165.5	16 04.8	-54.9	165.6	15 06.7	-55.0	165.7	14 08.5	-55.1	165.7	13 10.4	-55.2	165.8	12 12.2	-55.3	165.8	11 14.0	-55.4	165.9	54
55	17 06.3	-54.7	165.9	16 08.1	-54.8	165.9	15 09.9	-54.9	166.0	14 11.7	-55.1	166.1	13 13.4	-55.1	166.1	12 15.2	-55.3	166.2	11 16.9	-55.4	166.2	10 18.6	-55.4	166.3	55
56	16 11.6	-54.8	166.3	15 13.3	-54.9	166.4	14 15.0	-55.0	166.4	13 16.6	-55.1	166.5	12 18.3	-55.2	166.5	11 19.9	-55.3	166.6	10 21.5	-55.3	166.6	9 23.2	-55.5	166.7	56
57	15 16.8	-54.8	166.7	14 18.4	-54.9	166.8	13 20.0	-55.0	166.8	12 21.5	-55.0	166.9	11 23.1	-55.2	166.9	10 24.6	-55.3	167.0	9 26.2	-55.4	167.0	8 27.7	-55.5	167.1	57
58	14 22.0	-54.9	167.1	13 23.5	-55.0	167.2	12 25.0	-55.1	167.2	11 26.4	-55.1	167.3	10 27.9	-55.2	167.3	9 29.3	-55.3	167.4	8 30.8	-55.4	167.4	7 32.2	-55.5	167.4	58
59	13 27.1	-54.9	167.6	12 28.5	-55.0	167.6	11 29.9	-55.1	167.7	10 31.3	-55.2	167.7	9 32.7	-55.3	167.7	8 34.0	-55.3	167.8	7 35.4	-55.5	167.8	6 36.7	-55.5	167.8	59
60	12 32.2	-54.9	168.0	11 33.5	-55.0	168.0	10 34.8	-55.1	168.1	9 36.1	-55.2	168.1	8 37.4	-55.3	168.1	7 38.7	-55.4	168.2	6 39.9	-55.4	168.2	5 41.2	-55.5	168.2	60
61	11 37.3	-55.0	168.4	10 38.5	-55.1	168.4	9 39.7	-55.1	168.5	8 40.9	-55.2	168.5	7 42.1	-55.3	168.5	6 43.3	-55.4	168.5	5 44.5	-55.5	168.6	4 45.7	-55.6	168.6	61
62	10 42.3	-55.0	168.8	9 43.4	-55.1	168.8	8 44.6	-55.2	168.9	7 45.7	-55.3	168.9	6 46.8	-55.3	168.9	5 47.9	-55.4	168.9	4 49.0	-55.4	169.0	3 50.1	-55.5	169.0	62
63	9 47.3	-55.1	169.2	8 48.3	-55.1	169.2	7 49.4	-55.2	169.3	6 50.4	-55.2	169.3	5 51.5	-55.4	169.3	4 52.5	-55.4	169.3	3 53.6	-55.5	169.3	2 54.6	-55.6	169.3	63
64	8 52.2	-55.0	169.6	7 53.2	-55.1	169.6	6 54.2	-55.2	169.7	5 55.2	-55.3	169.7	4 56.1	-55.3	169.7	3 57.1	-55.4	169.7	2 58.1	-55.5	169.7	1 59.0	-55.5	169.7	64
65	7 57.2	-55.1	170.0	6 58.1	-55.2	170.0	5 59.0	-55.3	170.0	4 59.9	-55.3	170.1	4 00.8	-55.4	170.1	3 01.7	-55.5	170.1	2 02.6	-55.5	170.1	1 03.5	-55.6	170.1	65
66	7 02.1	-55.1	170.4	6 02.9	-55.2	170.4	5 03.7	-55.2	170.4	4 04.6	-55.3	170.5	3 05.4	-55.4	170.5	2 06.2	-55.4	170.5	1 07.1	-55.5	170.5	0 07.9	-55.6	170.5	66
67	6 07.0	-55.2	170.8	5 07.7	-55.2	170.8	4 08.5	-55.3	170.8	3 09.3	-55.3	170.8	2 10.0	-55.3	170.8	1 10.8	-55.4	170.9	0 11.6	-55.5	170.9	0 47.7	+55.5	9.1	67
68	5 11.8	-55.1	171.2	4 12.5	-55.2	171.2	3 13.2	-55.2	171.2	2 14.0	-55.4	171.2	1 14.7	-55.4	171.2	0 15.4	-55.5	171.2	0 43.9	+55.5	8.8	1 43.2	+55.6	8.8	68
69	4 16.7	-55.2	171.6	3 17.3	-55.2	171.6	2 18.0	-55.3	171.6	1 18.6	-55.3	171.6	0 19.3	-55.4	171.6	0 40.1	+55.4	8.4	1 39.4	+55.5	8.4	2 38.8	+55.6	8.4	69
70	3 21.5	-55.1	172.0	2 22.1	-55.2	172.0	1 22.7	-55.3	172.0	0 23.3	-55.3	172.0	0 36.1	+55.4	8.0	1 35.5	+55.5	8.0	2 34.9	+55.5	8.0	3 34.4	+55.5	8.0	70
71	2 26.4	-55.2	172.4	1 26.9	-55.2	172.4	0 27.4	-55.2	172.4	0 32.0	+55.4	7.6	1 31.5	+55.4	7.6	2 31.0	+55.4	7.6	3 30.4	+55.5	7.6	4 29.9	+55.5	7.6	71
72	1 31.2	-55.2	172.8	0 31.7	-55.2	172.8	0 27.8	+55.3	7.2	1 27.4	+55.3	7.2	2 26.9	+55.4	7.2	3 26.4	+55.4	7.2	4 25.9	+55.5	7.2	5 25.4	+55.6	7.3	72
73	0 36.0	-55.1	173.2	0 23.5	+55.3	6.8	1 23.1	+55.3	6.8	2 22.7	+55.3	6.8	3 22.3	+55.3	6.8	4 21.8	+55.4	6.8	5 21.4	+55.5	6.9	6 21.0	+55.5	6.9	73
74	0 19.1	+55.2	6.4	1 18.8	+55.2	6.4	2 18.4	+55.2	6.4	3 18.0	+55.3	6.4	4 17.6	+55.4	6.5	5 17.2	+55.4	6.5	6 16.9	+55.4	6.5	7 16.5	+55.5	6.5	74
75	1 14.3	+55.2	6.0	2 14.0	+55.2	6.0	3 13.6	+55.3	6.1	4 13.3	+55.3	6.1	5 13.0	+55.3	6.1	6 12.6	+55.4	6.1	7 12.3	+55.4	6.1	8 12.0	+55.4	6.1	75
76	2 09.5	+55.1	5.7	3 09.2	+55.2	5.7	4 08.9	+55.2	5.7	5 08.6	+55.3	5.7	6 08.3	+55.3	5.7	7 08.0	+55.4	5.7	8 07.7	+55.4	5.7	9 07.4	+55.5	5.7	76
77	3 04.6	+55.2	5.3	4 04.4	+55.2	5.3	5 04.1	+55.3	5.3	6 03.9	+55.2	5.3	7 03.6	+55.3	5.3	8 03.4	+55.3	5.3	9 03.1	+55.4	5.3	10 02.9	+55.4	5.3	77
78	3 59.8	+55.1	4.9	4 59.6	+55.2	4.9	5 59.4	+55.2	4.9	6 59.1	+55.3	4.9	7 58.9	+55.3	4.9	8 58.7	+55.3	4.9	9 58.5	+55.3	4.9	10 58.3	+55.3	4.9	78
79	4 54.9	+55.2	4.5	5 54.8	+55.1	4.5	6 54.6	+55.2	4.5	7 54.4	+55.2	4.5	8 54.2	+55.3	4.5	9 54.0	+55.3	4.5	10 53.8	+55.4	4.5	11 53.6	+55.4	4.5	79
80	5 50.1	+55.1	4.1	6 49.9	+55.2	4.1	7 49.8	+55.1	4.1	8 49.6	+55.2	4.1	9 49.5	+55.2	4.1	10 49.3	+55.3	4.1	11 49.2	+55.2	4.1	12 49.0	+55.3	4.2	80
81	6 45.2	+55.1	3.7	7 45.1	+55.1	3.7	8 44.9	+55.2	3.7	9 44.8	+55.2	3.7	10 44.7	+55.2	3.7	11 44.6	+55.2	3.7	12 44.4	+55.3	3.7	13 44.3	+55.3	3.8	81
82	7 40.3	+55.1	3.3	8 40.2	+55.1	3.3	9 40.1	+55.1	3.3	10 40.0	+55.1	3.3	11 39.9	+55.2	3.3	12 39.8	+55.2	3.3	13 39.7	+55.2	3.3	14 39.6	+55.2	3.4	82
83	8 35.4	+55.0	2.9	9 35.3	+55.0	2.9	10 35.2	+55.1	2.9	11 35.1	+55.1	2.9	12 35.1	+55.1	2.9	13 35.0	+55.1	2.9	14 34.9	+55.2	2.9	15 34.8	+55.2	2.9	83
84	9 30.4	+55.0	2.5	10 30.3	+55.1	2.5	11 30.3	+55.0	2.5	12 30.2	+55.1	2.5	13 30.2	+55.1	2.5	14 30.1	+55.1	2.5	15 30.1	+55.1	2.5	16 30.0	+55.1	2.5	84
85	10 25.4	+55.0	2.1	11 25.4	+55.0	2.1	12 25.3	+55.1	2.1	13 25.3	+55.0	2.1	14 25.3	+55.0	2.1	15 25.2	+55.1	2.1	16 25.2	+55.1	2.1	17 25.1	+55.1	2.1	85
86	11 20.4	+55.0	1.7	12 20.4	+55.0	1.7	13 20.4	+54.9	1.7	14 20.3	+55.0	1.7	15 20.3	+55.0	1.7	16 20.3	+55.0	1.7	17 20.3	+55.0	1.7	18 20.2	+55.1	1.7	86
87	12 15.4	+54.9	1.2	13 15.4	+54.9	1.3	14 15.3	+55.0	1.3	15 15.3	+55.0	1.3	16 15.3	+55.0	1.3	17 15.3	+55.0	1.3	18 15.3	+54.9	1.3	19 15.3	+54.9	1.3	87
88	13 10.3	+54.9	0.8	14 10.3	+54.9	0.8	15 10.3	+54.9	0.8	16 10.3	+54.9	0.8	17 10.3	+54.9	0.9	18 10.3	+54.9	0.9	19 10.2	+55.0	0.9	20 10.2	+55.0	0.9	88
89	14 05.2	+54.8	0.4	15 05.2	+54.8	0.4	16 05.2	+54.8	0.4	17 05.2	+54.8	0.4	18 05.2	+54.8	0.4	19 05.2	+54.8	0.4	20 05.2	+54.8	0.4	21 05.2	+54.8	0.4	89
90	15 00.0	+54.8	0.0	16 00.0	+54.8	0.0	17 00.0	+54.8	0.0	18 00.0	+54.8	0.0	19 00.0	+54.8	0.0	20 00.0	+54.8	0.0	21 00.0	+54.8	0.0	22 00.0	+54.8	0.0	90
	15°			16°			17°			18°			19°			20°			21°			22°			

S. Lat. {L.H.A. greater than 180° ....Zn=180°−Z
{L.H.A. less than 180°...........Zn=180°+Z

LATITUDE **SAME** NAME AS DECLINATION **L.H.A. 156°, 204°**

51

25°, 335° L.H.A. LATITUDE SAME NAME AS DECLINATION

N. Lat. {L.H.A. greater than 180° .....Zn=Z
{L.H.A. less than 180°............Zn=360°–Z

Dec.	15° Hc	d	Z	16° Hc	d	Z	17° Hc	d	Z	18° Hc	d	Z
°	° ′	′	°	° ′	′	°	° ′	′	°	° ′	′	°
0	61 05.7	+31.5	119.0	60 35.9	+33.0	120.6	60 04.7	+34.5	122.1	59 32.2	+36.0	123.5
1	61 37.2	+30.0	117.3	61 08.9	+31.7	118.9	60 39.2	+33.3	120.4	60 08.2	+34.8	121.9
2	62 07.2	+28.5	115.4	61 40.6	+30.3	117.1	61 12.5	+32.0	118.7	60 43.0	+33.5	120.3
3	62 35.7	+26.9	113.5	62 10.9	+28.8	115.3	61 44.5	+30.5	116.9	61 16.5	+32.2	118.6
4	63 02.6	+25.2	111.6	62 39.7	+27.1	113.4	62 15.0	+29.0	115.1	61 48.7	+30.8	116.8
5	63 27.8	+23.5	109.5	63 06.8	+25.5	111.4	62 44.0	+27.5	113.2	62 19.5	+29.3	115.0
6	63 51.3	+21.7	107.5	63 32.3	+23.8	109.4	63 11.5	+25.8	111.3	62 48.8	+27.8	113.1
7	64 13.0	+19.7	105.3	63 56.1	+21.9	107.3	63 37.3	+24.0	109.2	63 16.6	+26.0	111.1
8	64 32.7	+17.8•	103.2	64 18.0	+20.1	105.2	64 01.3	+22.2	107.2	63 42.6	+24.4	109.1
9	64 50.5	+15.7•	100.9	64 38.1	+18.0•	103.0	64 23.5	+20.3	105.0	64 07.0	+22.4	107.0
10	65 06.2	+13.6•	98.6	64 56.1	+16.0•	100.8	64 43.8	+18.3•	102.8	64 29.4	+20.6	104.9
11	65 19.8	+11.4•	96.3	65 12.1	+13.8•	98.5	65 02.1	+16.3•	100.6	64 50.0	+18.6•	102.7
12	65 31.2	+9.2•	94.0	65 25.9	+11.7•	96.1	65 18.4	+14.1•	98.3	65 08.6	+16.5•	100.4
13	65 40.4	+6.9•	91.6	65 37.6	+9.4•	93.8	65 32.5	+11.9•	96.0	65 25.1	+14.4•	98.1
14	65 47.3	+4.6•	89.2	65 47.0	+7.2•	91.4	65 44.4	+9.7•	93.6	65 39.5	+12.2•	95.8
15	65 51.9	+2.3•	86.7	65 54.2	+4.8•	88.9	65 54.1	+7.4•	91.2	65 51.7	+9.9•	93.4
16	65 54.2	−0.1•	84.3	65 59.0	+2.5•	86.5	66 01.5	+5.0•	88.7	66 01.6	+7.6•	91.0
17	65 54.1	−2.4•	81.8	66 01.5	+0.1•	84.0	66 06.5	+2.7•	86.3	66 09.2	+5.3•	88.5
18	65 51.7	−4.7•	79.4	66 01.6	−2.2•	81.6	66 09.2	+0.4•	83.8	66 14.5	+2.9•	86.1
19	65 47.0	−7.1•	76.9	65 59.4	−4.6•	79.1	66 09.6	−2.1•	81.3	66 17.4	+0.6•	83.6
20	65 39.9	−9.3•	74.5	65 54.8	−6.9•	76.7	66 07.5	−4.4•	78.9	66 18.0	−1.9•	81.1
21	65 30.6	−11.5•	72.1	65 47.9	−9.1•	74.3	66 03.1	−6.7•	76.4	66 16.1	−4.2•	78.6
22	65 19.1	−13.8•	69.8	65 38.8	−11.4•	71.8	65 56.4	−9.0•	74.0	66 11.9	−6.6•	76.2
23	65 05.3	−15.8•	67.5	65 27.4	−13.6•	69.5	65 47.4	−11.3•	71.6	66 05.3	−8.9•	73.7
24	64 49.5	−17.9•	65.2	65 13.8	−15.8•	67.1	65 36.1	−13.5•	69.2	65 56.4	−11.2•	71.3
25	64 31.6	−19.9	62.9	64 58.0	−17.8•	64.8	65 22.6	−15.7•	66.8	65 45.2	−13.4•	68.9
26	64 11.7	−21.7	60.8	64 40.2	−19.8	62.6	65 06.9	−17.7•	64.5	65 31.8	−15.6•	66.5
27	63 50.0	−23.6	58.6	64 20.4	−21.7	60.4	64 49.2	−19.7•	62.3	65 16.2	−17.6•	64.2
28	63 26.4	−25.4	56.6	63 58.7	−23.6	58.3	64 29.5	−21.7	60.1	64 58.6	−19.7•	61.9
29	63 01.0	−27.0	54.6	63 35.1	−25.3	56.2	64 07.8	−23.6	57.9	64 38.9	−21.7	59.7
30	62 34.0	−28.6	52.6	63 09.8	−27.0	54.2	63 44.2	−25.3	55.8	64 17.2	−23.5	57.5
31	62 05.4	−30.1	50.7	62 42.8	−28.6	52.2	63 18.9	−26.9	53.8	63 53.7	−25.3	55.4
32	61 35.3	−31.5	48.9	62 14.2	−30.1	50.3	62 52.0	−28.6	51.8	63 28.4	−27.0	53.4
33	61 03.8	−32.9	47.1	61 44.1	−31.5	48.5	62 23.4	−30.1	49.9	63 01.4	−28.6	51.4
34	60 30.9	−34.1	45.4	61 12.6	−32.9	46.7	61 53.3	−31.6	48.0	62 32.8	−30.1	49.5
35	59 56.8	−35.3	43.7	60 39.7	−34.2	45.0	61 21.7	−32.9	46.2	62 02.7	−31.6	47.6
36	59 21.5	−36.5	42.1	60 05.5	−35.3	43.3	60 48.8	−34.2	44.5	61 31.1	−33.0	45.8
37	58 45.0	−37.6	40.6	59 30.2	−36.6	41.7	60 14.6	−35.5	42.8	60 58.1	−34.2	44.1
38	58 07.4	−38.5	39.1	58 53.6	−37.5	40.1	59 39.1	−36.5	41.2	60 23.9	−35.5	42.4
39	57 28.9	−39.5	37.7	58 16.1	−38.7	38.6	59 02.6	−37.7	39.7	59 48.4	−36.6	40.8
40	56 49.4	−40.4	36.3	57 37.4	−39.5	37.2	58 24.9	−38.6	38.2	59 11.8	−37.7	39.2
41	56 09.0	−41.3	34.9	56 57.9	−40.5	35.8	57 46.3	−39.6	36.7	58 34.1	−38.8	37.7
42	55 27.7	−42.0	33.6	56 17.4	−41.2	34.5	57 06.7	−40.6	35.3	57 55.3	−39.7	36.3
43	54 45.7	−42.8	32.4	55 36.2	−42.1	33.2	56 26.1	−41.3	34.0	57 15.6	−40.5	34.9
44	54 02.9	−43.4	31.2	54 54.1	−42.9	31.9	55 44.8	−42.2	32.7	56 35.1	−41.5	33.5
45	53 19.5	−44.1	30.0	54 11.2	−43.5	30.7	55 02.6	−42.9	31.4	55 53.6	−42.2	32.2
46	52 35.4	−44.8	28.9	53 27.7	−44.2	29.5	54 19.7	−43.6	30.2	55 11.4	−43.0	30.9
47	51 50.6	−45.3	27.8	52 43.5	−44.8	28.4	53 36.1	−44.2	29.1	54 28.4	−43.7	29.7
48	51 05.3	−45.9	26.8	51 58.7	−45.3	27.3	52 51.9	−44.9	27.9	53 44.7	−44.3	28.6
49	50 19.4	−46.4	25.7	51 13.4	−46.0	26.3	52 07.0	−45.4	26.8	53 00.4	−44.9	27.4
50	49 33.0	−46.8	24.8	50 27.4	−46.4	25.3	51 21.6	−46.0	25.8	52 15.5	−45.6	26.3
51	48 46.2	−47.4	23.8	49 41.0	−47.0	24.3	50 35.6	−46.6	24.8	51 29.9	−46.1	25.3
52	47 58.8	−47.7	22.9	48 54.0	−47.4	23.3	49 49.0	−47.0	23.8	50 43.8	−46.6	24.3
53	47 11.1	−48.2	22.0	48 06.6	−47.8	22.4	49 02.0	−47.4	22.8	49 57.2	−47.1	23.3
54	46 22.9	−48.6	21.1	47 18.8	−48.2	21.5	48 14.6	−47.9	21.9	49 10.1	−47.5	22.3
55	45 34.3	−48.9	20.3	46 30.6	−48.7	20.6	47 26.7	−48.4	21.0	48 22.6	−48.0	21.4
56	44 45.4	−49.2	19.4	45 41.9	−48.9	19.8	46 38.3	−48.6	20.1	47 34.6	−48.4	20.5
57	43 56.2	−49.6	18.6	44 53.0	−49.4	19.0	45 49.7	−49.1	19.3	46 46.2	−48.7	19.6
58	43 06.6	−49.9	17.9	44 03.6	−49.6	18.2	45 00.6	−49.4	18.5	45 57.5	−49.2	18.8
59	42 16.7	−50.2	17.1	43 14.0	−50.0	17.4	44 11.2	−49.7	17.7	45 08.3	−49.5	18.0
60	41 26.5	−50.5	16.4	42 24.0	−50.2	16.6	43 21.5	−50.0	16.9	44 18.8	−49.8	17.2
61	40 36.0	−50.7	15.7	41 33.8	−50.5	15.9	42 31.5	−50.4	16.1	43 29.0	−50.1	16.4
62	39 45.3	−50.9	15.0	40 43.3	−50.8	15.2	41 41.1	−50.6	15.4	42 38.9	−50.3	15.6
63	38 54.4	−51.2	14.3	39 52.5	−51.0	14.5	40 50.5	−50.8	14.7	41 48.6	−50.7	14.9
64	38 03.2	−51.5	13.6	39 01.5	−51.3	13.8	39 59.7	−51.1	14.0	40 57.9	−50.9	14.2
65	37 11.7	−51.6	13.0	38 10.2	−51.5	13.1	39 08.6	−51.3	13.3	40 07.0	−51.2	13.5
66	36 20.1	−51.8	12.3	37 18.7	−51.7	12.5	38 17.3	−51.6	12.7	39 15.8	−51.4	12.8
67	35 28.3	−52.0	11.7	36 27.0	−51.8	11.8	37 25.7	−51.7	12.0	38 24.4	−51.6	12.2
68	34 36.3	−52.2	11.1	35 35.2	−52.1	11.2	36 34.0	−52.0	11.4	37 32.8	−51.8	11.5
69	33 44.1	−52.4	10.5	34 43.1	−52.3	10.6	35 42.0	−52.1	10.7	36 41.0	−52.0	10.9
70	32 51.7	−52.5	9.9	33 50.8	−52.4	10.0	34 49.9	−52.3	10.1	35 49.0	−52.2	10.3
71	31 59.2	−52.6	9.3	32 58.4	−52.5	9.4	33 57.6	−52.5	9.5	34 56.8	−52.4	9.7
72	31 06.6	−52.9	8.8	32 05.9	−52.8	8.9	33 05.1	−52.6	9.0	34 04.4	−52.6	9.1
73	30 13.7	−52.9	8.2	31 13.1	−52.8	8.3	32 12.5	−52.8	8.4	33 11.8	−52.7	8.5
74	29 20.8	−53.1	7.7	30 20.3	−53.0	7.8	31 19.7	−52.9	7.8	32 19.1	−52.8	7.9
75	28 27.7	−53.2	7.1	29 27.3	−53.2	7.2	30 26.8	−53.1	7.3	31 26.3	−53.0	7.4
76	27 34.5	−53.3	6.6	28 34.1	−53.2	6.7	29 33.7	−53.2	6.8	30 33.3	−53.1	6.8
77	26 41.2	−53.4	6.1	27 40.9	−53.4	6.2	28 40.5	−53.3	6.2	29 40.2	−53.3	6.3
78	25 47.8	−53.5	5.6	26 47.5	−53.5	5.6	27 47.2	−53.4	5.7	28 46.9	−53.4	5.8
79	24 54.3	−53.7	5.1	25 54.0	−53.6	5.1	26 53.8	−53.6	5.2	27 53.5	−53.5	5.2
80	24 00.6	−53.7	4.6	25 00.4	−53.7	4.6	26 00.2	−53.6	4.7	27 00.0	−53.6	4.7
81	23 06.9	−53.8	4.1	24 06.7	−53.7	4.2	25 06.6	−53.7	4.2	26 06.4	−53.7	4.2
82	22 13.1	−53.9	3.6	23 13.0	−53.9	3.7	24 12.9	−53.9	3.7	25 12.7	−53.8	3.7
83	21 19.2	−54.0	3.2	22 19.1	−53.9	3.2	23 19.0	−53.9	3.2	24 18.9	−53.9	3.2
84	20 25.2	−54.0	2.7	21 25.2	−54.1	2.7	22 25.1	−54.0	2.7	23 25.0	−54.0	2.8
85	19 31.2	−54.1	2.2	20 31.1	−54.1	2.3	21 31.1	−54.1	2.3	22 31.0	−54.0	2.3
86	18 37.1	−54.2	1.8	19 37.0	−54.1	1.8	20 37.0	−54.1	1.8	21 37.0	−54.2	1.8
87	17 42.9	−54.2	1.3	18 42.9	−54.3	1.3	19 42.9	−54.3	1.3	20 42.8	−54.2	1.4
88	16 48.7	−54.3	0.9	17 48.6	−54.2	0.9	18 48.6	−54.3	0.9	19 48.6	−54.3	0.9
89	15 54.4	−54.4	0.4	16 54.4	−54.4	0.4	17 54.3	−54.3	0.4	18 54.3	−54.3	0.4
90	15 00.0	−54.4	0.0	16 00.0	−54.4	0.0	17 00.0	−54.4	0.0	18 00.0	−54.4	0.0
	15°			16°			17°			18°		

19° Hc	d	Z	20° Hc	d	Z	21° Hc	d	Z	22° Hc	d	Z	Dec.
° ′	′	°	° ′	′	°	° ′	′	°	° ′	′	°	°
58 58.4	+37.4	124.9	58 23.5	+38.7	126.3	57 47.5	+39.8	127.5	57 10.4	+41.0	128.8	0
59 35.8	+36.2	123.4	59 02.2	+37.6	124.8	58 27.3	+39.0	126.1	57 51.4	+40.1	127.4	1
60 12.0	+35.1	121.8	59 39.8	+36.5	123.3	59 06.3	+37.8	124.7	58 31.5	+39.2	126.0	2
60 47.1	+33.8	120.2	60 16.3	+35.3	121.7	59 44.1	+36.8	123.1	59 10.7	+38.1	124.5	3
61 20.9	+32.5	118.4	60 51.6	+34.1	120.0	60 20.9	+35.6	121.6	59 48.8	+37.1	123.0	4
61 53.4	+31.1	116.7	61 25.7	+32.8	118.3	60 56.5	+34.4	119.9	60 25.9	+35.9	121.4	5
62 24.5	+29.6	114.8	61 58.5	+31.3	116.6	61 30.9	+33.0	118.2	61 01.8	+34.6	119.8	6
62 54.1	+28.0	113.0	62 29.8	+29.9	114.7	62 03.9	+31.6	116.4	61 36.4	+33.3	118.1	7
63 22.1	+26.3	111.0	62 59.7	+28.3	112.8	62 35.5	+30.2	114.6	62 09.7	+31.9	116.3	8
63 48.4	+24.6	109.0	63 28.0	+26.6	110.9	63 05.7	+28.6	112.7	62 41.6	+30.5	114.5	9
64 13.0	+22.8	106.9	63 54.6	+24.9	108.8	63 34.3	+26.9	110.8	63 12.1	+28.9	112.6	10
64 35.8	+20.8	104.8	64 19.5	+23.0	106.8	64 01.2	+25.2	108.7	63 41.0	+27.2	110.7	11
64 56.6	+18.9•	102.6	64 42.5	+21.2	104.6	64 26.4	+23.3	106.6	64 08.2	+25.5	108.6	12
65 15.5	+16.8•	100.3	65 03.7	+19.1•	102.4	64 49.7	+21.5	104.5	64 33.7	+23.6	106.5	13
65 32.3	+14.7•	98.0	65 22.8	+17.1•	100.2	65 11.2	+19.4•	102.3	64 57.3	+21.8	104.4	14
65 47.0	+12.4•	95.6	65 39.9	+14.9•	97.8	65 30.6	+17.3•	100.0	65 19.1	+19.7•	102.2	15
65 59.4	+10.2•	93.2	65 54.8	+12.7•	95.5	65 47.9	+15.2•	97.7	65 38.8	+17.6•	99.9	16
66 09.6	+7.8•	90.8	66 07.5	+10.5•	93.1	66 03.1	+13.0•	95.3	65 56.4	+15.5•	97.6	17
66 17.4	+5.5•	88.4	66 18.0	+8.1•	90.6	66 16.1	+10.7•	92.9	66 11.9	+13.2•	95.2	18
66 22.9	+3.2•	85.9	66 26.1	+5.7•	88.2	66 26.8	+8.3•	90.5	66 25.1	+10.9•	92.7	19
66 26.1	+0.7•	83.4	66 31.8	+3.3•	85.7	66 35.1	+6.0•	88.0	66 36.0	+8.6•	90.3	20
66 26.8	−1.7•	80.9	66 35.1	+0.9•	83.2	66 41.1	+3.5•	85.5	66 44.6	+6.2•	87.8	21
66 25.1	−4.1•	78.4	66 36.0	−1.5•	80.6	66 44.6	+1.1•	82.9	66 50.8	+3.7•	85.3	22
66 21.0	−6.4•	75.9	66 34.5	−3.9•	78.1	66 45.7	−1.3•	80.4	66 54.5	+1.3•	82.7	23
66 14.6	−8.8•	73.4	66 30.6	−6.3•	75.6	66 44.4	−3.8•	77.9	66 55.8	−1.1•	80.2	24
66 05.8	−11.0•	71.0	66 24.3	−8.6•	73.1	66 40.6	−6.1•	75.3	66 54.7	−3.6•	77.6	25
65 54.8	−13.4•	68.5	66 15.7	−11.0•	70.7	66 34.5	−8.6•	72.8	66 51.1	−6.1•	75.1	26
65 41.4	−15.5•	66.2	66 04.7	−13.2•	68.2	66 25.9	−10.9•	70.4	66 45.0	−8.4•	72.5	27
65 25.9	−17.6•	63.8	65 51.5	−15.5•	65.8	66 15.0	−13.1•	67.9	66 36.6	−10.8•	70.0	28
65 08.3	−19.6•	61.5	65 36.0	−17.6•	63.5	66 01.9	−15.4•	65.5	66 25.8	−13.1•	67.6	29
64 48.7	−21.7	59.3	65 18.4	−19.6•	61.2	65 46.5	−17.6•	63.1	66 12.7	−15.4•	65.1	30
64 27.0	−23.5	57.1	64 58.8	−21.6	58.9	65 28.9	−19.6•	60.8	65 57.3	−17.5•	62.8	31
64 03.5	−25.3	55.0	64 37.2	−23.5	56.7	65 09.3	−21.6	58.5	65 39.8	−19.6•	60.4	32
63 38.2	−27.0	53.0	64 13.7	−25.3	54.6	64 47.7	−23.5	56.3	65 20.2	−21.7	58.1	33
63 11.2	−28.6	51.0	63 48.4	−27.1	52.5	64 24.2	−25.4	54.2	64 58.5	−23.5	55.9	34
62 42.6	−30.2	49.0	63 21.3	−28.6	50.5	63 58.8	−27.0	52.1	64 35.0	−25.4	53.8	35
62 12.4	−31.6	47.2	62 52.7	−30.3	48.6	63 31.8	−28.8	50.1	64 09.6	−27.1	51.7	36
61 40.8	−33.0	45.4	62 22.4	−31.7	46.7	63 03.0	−30.3	48.1	63 42.5	−28.8	49.6	37
61 07.8	−34.4	43.6	61 50.7	−33.1	44.9	62 32.7	−31.7	46.2	63 13.7	−30.4	47.7	38
60 33.4	−35.5	41.9	61 17.6	−34.3	43.1	62 01.0	−33.2	44.4	62 43.3	−31.8	45.8	39
59 57.9	−36.7	40.3	60 43.3	−35.7	41.5	61 27.8	−34.5	42.7	62 11.5	−33.3	43.9	40
59 21.2	−37.8	38.7	60 07.6	−36.7	39.8	60 53.3	−35.7	41.0	61 38.2	−34.5	42.2	41
58 43.4	−38.8	37.2	59 30.9	−37.9	38.2	60 17.6	−36.8	39.3	61 03.7	−35.8	40.5	42
58 04.6	−39.8	35.8	58 53.0	−38.9	36.7	59 40.8	−38.0	37.8	60 27.9	−37.0	38.8	43
57 24.8	−40.6	34.4	58 14.1	−39.9	35.3	59 02.8	−39.0	36.2	59 50.9	−38.1	37.2	44
56 44.2	−41.6	33.0	57 34.2	−40.7	33.9	58 23.8	−40.0	34.8	59 12.8	−39.1	35.7	45
56 02.6	−42.3	31.7	56 53.5	−41.6	32.5	57 43.8	−40.8	33.4	58 33.7	−40.1	34.3	46
55 20.3	−43.0	30.5	56 11.9	−42.4	31.2	57 03.0	−41.8	32.0	57 53.6	−41.0	32.8	47
54 37.3	−43.8	29.2	55 29.5	−43.2	29.9	56 21.2	−42.5	30.7	57 12.6	−41.8	31.5	48
53 53.5	−44.4	28.1	54 46.3	−43.9	28.7	55 38.7	−43.2	29.4	56 30.8	−42.6	30.2	49
53 09.1	−45.1	26.9	54 02.4	−44.5	27.6	54 55.5	−44.0	28.2	55 48.2	−43.4	28.9	50
52 24.0	−45.6	25.8	53 17.9	−45.1	26.4	54 11.5	−44.6	27.0	55 04.8	−44.1	27.7	51
51 38.4	−46.2	24.8	52 32.8	−45.8	25.3	53 26.9	−45.3	25.9	54 20.7	−44.7	26.5	52
50 52.2	−46.6	23.8	51 47.0	−46.2	24.3	52 41.6	−45.8	24.8	53 36.0	−45.4	25.4	53
50 05.6	−47.2	22.8	51 00.8	−46.8	23.3	51 55.8	−46.4	23.8	52 50.6	−45.9	24.3	54
49 18.4	−47.7	21.8	50 14.0	−47.3	22.3	51 09.4	−46.9	22.7	52 04.7	−46.5	23.2	55
48 30.7	−48.0	20.9	49 26.7	−47.7	21.3	50 22.5	−47.4	21.8	51 18.2	−47.0	22.2	56
47 42.7	−48.5	20.0	48 39.0	−48.2	20.4	49 35.1	−47.8	20.8	50 31.2	−47.5	21.2	57
46 54.2	−48.9	19.1	47 50.8	−48.5	19.5	48 47.3	−48.2	19.9	49 43.7	−48.0	20.3	58
46 05.3	−49.2	18.3	47 02.3	−49.0	18.6	47 59.1	−48.7	19.0	48 55.7	−48.3	19.3	59
45 16.1	−49.5	17.5	46 13.3	−49.3	17.8	47 10.4	−48.8	18.1	48 07.4	−48.8	18.5	60
44 26.6	−49.9	16.7	45 24.0	−49.6	17.0	46 21.3	−49.4	17.3	47 18.6	−49.2	17.6	61
43 36.7	−50.2	15.9	44 34.4	−50.0	16.2	45 31.9	−49.7	16.5	46 29.4	−49.5	16.7	62
42 46.5	−50.5	15.2	43 44.4	−50.3	15.4	44 42.2	−50.1	15.7	45 39.9	−49.8	15.9	63
41 56.0	−50.7	14.4	42 54.1	−50.5	14.6	43 52.1	−50.3	14.9	44 50.1	−50.2	15.1	64
41 05.3	−51.0	13.7	42 03.6	−50.9	13.9	43 01.8	−50.7	14.1	43 59.9	−50.4	14.4	65
40 14.3	−51.3	13.0	41 12.7	−51.1	13.2	42 11.1	−50.9	13.4	43 09.5	−50.8	13.6	66
39 23.0	−51.4	12.3	40 21.6	−51.3	12.5	41 20.2	−51.2	12.7	42 18.7	−51.0	12.9	67
38 31.6	−51.7	11.7	39 30.3	−51.5	11.8	40 29.0	−51.4	12.0	41 27.7	−51.3	12.2	68
37 39.9	−51.9	11.0	38 38.8	−51.8	11.2	39 37.6	−51.6	11.3	40 36.4	−51.5	11.5	69
36 48.0	−52.1	10.4	37 47.0	−52.0	10.5	38 46.0	−51.9	10.7	39 44.9	−51.7	10.8	70
35 55.9	−52.3	9.8	36 55.0	−52.2	9.9	37 54.1	−52.1	10.0	38 53.2	−52.0	10.2	71
35 03.6	−52.4	9.2	36 02.8	−52.3	9.3	37 02.0	−52.2	9.4	38 01.2	−52.1	9.5	72
34 11.2	−52.6	8.6	35 10.5	−52.5	8.7	36 09.8	−52.4	8.8	37 09.1	−52.4	8.9	73
33 18.6	−52.8	8.0	34 18.0	−52.7	8.1	35 17.4	−52.7	8.2	36 16.7	−52.5	8.3	74
32 25.8	−52.9	7.4	33 25.3	−52.9	7.5	34 24.7	−52.7	7.6	35 24.2	−52.7	7.7	75
31 32.9	−53.1	6.9	32 32.4	−53.0	7.0	33 32.0	−53.0	7.0	34 31.5	−52.8	7.1	76
30 39.8	−53.2	6.3	31 39.4	−53.1	6.4	32 39.0	−53.0	6.5	33 38.7	−53.1	6.6	77
29 46.6	−53.3	5.8	30 46.3	−53.3	5.9	31 46.0	−53.2	5.9	32 45.6	−53.1	6.0	78
28 53.3	−53.5	5.3	29 53.0	−53.4	5.3	30 52.8	−53.4	5.4	31 52.5	−53.3	5.4	79
27 59.8	−53.5	4.8	28 59.6	−53.5	4.8	29 59.4	−53.5	4.9	30 59.2	−53.4	4.9	80
27 06.3	−53.7	4.3	28 06.1	−53.6	4.3	29 05.9	−53.6	4.3	30 05.8	−53.6	4.4	81
26 12.6	−53.8	3.8	27 12.5	−53.8	3.8	28 12.3	−53.7	3.8	29 12.2	−53.7	3.9	82
25 18.8	−53.8	3.3	26 18.7	−53.8	3.3	27 18.6	−53.8	3.3	28 18.5	−53.8	3.4	83
24 25.0	−54.0	2.8	25 24.9	−53.9	2.8	26 24.8	−53.9	2.8	27 24.7	−53.8	2.9	84
23 31.0	−54.0	2.3	24 31.0	−54.1	2.3	25 30.9	−54.0	2.3	26 30.9	−54.0	2.4	85
22 37.0	−54.1	1.8	23 36.9	−54.1	1.8	24 36.9	−54.1	1.9	25 36.9	−54.1	1.9	86
21 42.8	−54.2	1.4	22 42.8	−54.2	1.4	23 42.8	−54.2	1.4	24 42.8	−54.2	1.4	87
20 48.6	−54.3	0.9	21 48.6	−54.3	0.9	22 48.6	−54.3	0.9	23 48.6	−54.3	0.9	88
19 54.3	−54.3	0.4	20 54.3	−54.3	0.5	21 54.3	−54.3	0.5	22 54.3	−54.3	0.5	89
19 00.0	−54.4	0.0	20 00.0	−54.4	0.0	21 00.0	−54.4	0.0	22 00.0	−54.4	0.0	90
19°			20°			21°			22°			

25°, 335° L.H.A. LATITUDE SAME NAME AS DECLINATION

52

LATITUDE **CONTRARY** NAME TO DECLINATION L.H.A. 25°, 335°

Dec.	15° Hc	d	Z	16° Hc	d	Z	17° Hc	d	Z	18° Hc	d	Z	19° Hc	d	Z	20° Hc	d	Z	21° Hc	d	Z	22° Hc	d	Z	Dec.
°	° ′	′	°	° ′	′	°	° ′	′	°	° ′	′	°	° ′	′	°	° ′	′	°	° ′	′	°	° ′	′	°	°
0	61 05.7	-32.8	119.0	60 35.9	-34.3	120.6	60 04.7	-35.8	122.1	59 32.2	-37.1	123.5	58 58.4	-38.4	124.9	58 23.5	-39.6	126.3	57 47.5	-40.8	127.5	57 10.4	-41.9	128.8	0
1	60 32.9	-34.0	120.7	60 01.6	-35.5	122.2	59 28.9	-36.8	123.7	58 55.1	-38.2	125.1	58 20.0	-39.4	126.4	57 43.9	-40.6	127.7	57 06.7	-41.7	128.9	56 28.5	-42.7	130.1	1
2	59 58.9	-35.3	122.4	59 26.1	-36.7	123.8	58 52.1	-38.0	125.2	58 16.9	-39.2	126.5	57 40.6	-40.3	127.8	57 03.3	-41.4	129.0	56 25.0	-42.4	130.2	55 45.8	-43.4	131.3	2
3	59 23.6	-36.4	124.0	58 49.4	-37.7	125.4	58 14.1	-38.9	126.7	57 37.7	-40.1	128.0	57 00.3	-41.2	129.2	56 21.9	-42.2	130.4	55 42.6	-43.2	131.5	55 02.4	-44.1	132.6	3
4	58 47.2	-37.5	125.6	58 11.7	-38.7	126.9	57 35.2	-39.9	128.1	56 57.6	-40.9	129.4	56 19.1	-42.0	130.5	55 39.7	-43.0	131.6	54 59.4	-43.9	132.7	54 18.3	-44.8	133.7	4
5	58 09.7	-38.5	127.1	57 33.0	-39.7	128.3	56 55.3	-40.7	129.5	56 16.7	-41.8	130.7	55 37.1	-42.8	131.8	54 56.7	-43.7	132.9	54 15.5	-44.6	133.9	53 33.5	-45.4	134.9	5
6	57 31.2	-39.5	128.5	56 53.3	-40.5	129.7	56 14.6	-41.6	130.9	55 34.9	-42.6	132.0	54 54.3	-43.5	133.0	54 13.0	-44.4	134.0	53 30.9	-45.2	135.0	52 48.1	-45.9	136.0	6
7	56 51.7	-40.3	129.9	56 12.8	-41.4	131.0	55 33.0	-42.4	132.1	54 52.3	-43.3	133.2	54 10.8	-44.1	134.2	53 28.6	-45.0	135.2	52 45.7	-45.8	136.1	52 02.2	-46.6	137.0	7
8	56 11.4	-41.2	131.2	55 31.4	-42.2	132.3	54 50.6	-43.1	133.4	54 09.0	-44.0	134.4	53 26.7	-44.8	135.4	52 43.6	-45.5	136.3	51 59.9	-46.3	137.2	51 15.6	-47.0	138.0	8
9	55 30.2	-42.0	132.5	54 49.2	-42.9	133.6	54 07.5	-43.8	134.6	53 25.0	-44.6	135.5	52 41.9	-45.4	136.5	51 58.1	-46.2	137.4	51 13.6	-46.8	138.2	50 28.6	-47.5	139.0	9
10	54 48.2	-42.7	133.8	54 06.3	-43.6	134.8	53 23.7	-44.4	135.7	52 40.4	-45.2	136.7	51 56.5	-46.0	137.5	51 11.9	-46.7	138.4	50 26.8	-47.4	139.2	49 41.1	-48.0	140.0	10
11	54 05.5	-43.4	135.0	53 22.7	-44.2	135.9	52 39.3	-45.1	136.9	51 55.2	-45.8	137.7	51 10.5	-46.5	138.6	50 25.2	-47.1	139.4	49 39.4	-47.8	140.1	48 53.1	-48.4	140.9	11
12	53 22.1	-44.1	136.1	52 38.5	-44.9	137.1	51 54.2	-45.6	137.9	51 09.4	-46.3	138.8	50 24.0	-47.0	139.6	49 38.1	-47.6	140.3	48 51.6	-48.2	141.1	48 04.7	-48.8	141.8	12
13	52 38.0	-44.7	137.3	51 53.6	-45.4	138.1	51 08.6	-46.1	139.0	50 23.1	-46.8	139.8	49 37.0	-47.4	140.5	48 50.5	-48.1	141.3	48 03.4	-48.6	142.0	47 15.9	-49.1	142.6	13
14	51 53.3	-45.3	138.4	51 08.2	-46.0	139.2	50 22.5	-46.7	140.0	49 36.3	-47.3	140.7	48 49.6	-47.9	141.5	48 02.4	-48.5	142.2	47 14.8	-49.0	142.8	46 26.8	-49.6	143.5	14
15	51 08.0	-45.8	139.4	50 22.2	-46.5	140.2	49 35.8	-47.1	141.0	48 49.0	-47.8	141.7	48 01.7	-48.4	142.4	47 13.9	-48.8	143.0	46 25.8	-49.4	143.7	45 37.2	-49.8	144.3	15
16	50 22.2	-46.4	140.4	49 35.7	-47.0	141.2	48 48.7	-47.6	141.9	48 01.2	-48.1	142.6	47 13.3	-48.7	143.3	46 25.1	-49.3	143.9	45 36.4	-49.7	144.5	44 47.4	-50.2	145.1	16
17	49 35.8	-46.8	141.4	48 48.7	-47.5	142.1	48 01.1	-48.0	142.8	47 13.1	-48.6	143.5	46 24.6	-49.0	144.1	45 35.8	-49.5	144.7	44 46.7	-50.0	145.3	43 57.2	-50.5	145.8	17
18	49 49.0	-47.3	142.4	48 01.2	-47.9	143.1	47 13.1	-48.5	143.7	46 24.5	-48.9	144.3	45 35.6	-49.5	144.9	44 46.3	-49.9	145.5	43 56.7	-50.4	146.1	43 06.7	-50.7	146.6	18
19	48 01.7	-47.8	143.3	47 13.3	-48.2	144.0	46 24.6	-48.8	144.6	45 35.6	-49.3	145.2	44 46.1	-49.7	145.7	43 56.4	-50.2	146.3	43 06.3	-50.6	146.8	42 16.0	-51.1	147.3	19
20	47 13.9	-48.1	144.2	46 25.1	-48.7	144.8	45 35.8	-49.1	145.4	44 46.3	-49.6	146.0	43 56.4	-50.1	146.5	43 06.2	-50.5	147.0	42 15.7	-50.9	147.5	41 24.9	-51.3	148.0	20
21	46 25.8	-48.6	145.1	45 36.4	-49.0	145.7	44 46.7	-49.5	146.2	43 56.7	-50.0	146.8	43 06.3	-50.3	147.3	42 15.7	-50.8	147.8	41 24.8	-51.2	148.3	40 33.6	-51.5	148.7	21
22	45 37.2	-48.9	145.9	44 47.4	-49.4	146.5	43 57.2	-49.8	147.0	43 06.7	-50.2	147.5	42 16.0	-50.7	148.0	41 24.9	-51.0	148.5	40 33.6	-51.3	149.0	39 42.1	-51.7	149.4	22
23	44 48.3	-49.2	146.7	43 58.0	-49.7	147.3	43 07.4	-50.1	147.8	42 16.5	-50.5	148.3	41 25.3	-50.9	148.7	40 33.9	-51.3	149.2	39 42.3	-51.7	149.6	38 50.4	-52.0	150.0	23
24	43 59.1	-49.6	147.5	43 08.3	-50.0	148.1	42 17.3	-50.4	148.5	41 26.0	-50.8	149.0	40 34.4	-51.1	149.5	39 42.6	-51.5	149.9	38 50.6	-51.8	150.3	37 58.4	-52.1	150.7	24
25	43 09.5	-49.8	148.3	42 18.3	-50.2	148.8	41 26.9	-50.7	149.3	40 35.2	-51.0	149.7	39 43.3	-51.4	150.1	38 51.1	-51.7	150.5	37 58.8	-52.1	150.9	37 06.3	-52.4	151.3	25
26	42 19.7	-50.2	149.1	41 28.1	-50.6	149.5	40 36.2	-50.9	150.0	39 44.2	-51.3	150.4	38 51.9	-51.6	150.8	37 59.4	-51.9	151.2	37 06.7	-52.2	151.6	36 13.9	-52.5	151.9	26
27	41 29.5	-50.5	149.8	40 37.5	-50.8	150.3	39 45.3	-51.2	150.7	38 52.9	-51.5	151.1	38 00.3	-51.8	151.5	37 07.5	-52.1	151.8	36 14.5	-52.4	152.2	35 21.4	-52.7	152.5	27
28	40 39.0	-50.7	150.5	39 46.7	-51.1	151.0	38 54.1	-51.3	151.3	38 01.4	-51.7	151.7	37 08.5	-52.0	152.1	36 15.4	-52.4	152.4	35 22.1	-52.6	152.8	34 28.7	-52.9	153.1	28
29	39 48.3	-50.9	151.2	38 55.6	-51.2	151.6	38 02.8	-51.6	152.0	37 09.7	-51.9	152.4	36 16.5	-52.3	152.7	35 23.0	-52.4	153.0	34 29.5	-52.8	153.4	33 35.8	-53.0	153.7	29
30	38 57.4	-51.2	151.9	38 04.4	-51.5	152.3	37 11.2	-51.8	152.7	36 17.8	-52.1	153.0	35 24.2	-52.3	153.3	34 30.6	-52.7	153.6	33 36.7	-52.9	153.9	32 42.8	-53.2	154.2	30
31	38 06.2	-51.4	152.6	37 12.9	-51.7	152.9	36 19.4	-52.0	153.3	35 25.7	-52.3	153.6	34 31.9	-52.6	153.9	33 37.9	-52.8	154.2	32 43.8	-53.0	154.5	31 49.6	-53.3	154.8	31
32	37 14.8	-51.6	153.2	36 21.2	-51.9	153.6	35 27.4	-52.2	153.9	34 33.4	-52.5	154.2	33 39.3	-52.7	154.5	32 45.1	-53.0	154.8	31 50.8	-53.2	155.0	30 56.3	-53.4	155.3	32
33	36 23.2	-51.8	153.9	35 29.3	-52.1	154.2	34 35.2	-52.4	154.5	33 40.9	-52.6	154.8	32 46.6	-52.9	155.1	31 52.1	-53.1	155.3	30 57.6	-53.4	155.6	30 02.9	-53.6	155.8	33
34	35 31.4	-52.0	154.5	34 37.2	-52.3	154.8	33 42.8	-52.5	155.1	32 48.3	-52.7	155.4	31 53.7	-53.0	155.6	30 59.0	-53.2	155.9	30 04.2	-53.4	156.1	29 09.3	-53.7	156.3	34
35	34 39.4	-52.2	155.1	33 44.9	-52.4	155.4	32 50.3	-52.7	155.7	31 55.6	-53.0	155.9	31 00.7	-53.1	156.2	30 05.8	-53.4	156.4	29 10.8	-53.6	156.6	28 15.6	-53.8	156.9	35
36	33 47.2	-52.3	155.7	32 52.5	-52.6	156.0	31 57.6	-52.8	156.2	31 02.6	-53.0	156.5	30 07.6	-53.3	156.7	29 12.4	-53.5	156.9	28 17.2	-53.7	157.2	27 21.8	-53.9	157.4	36
37	32 54.9	-52.5	156.3	31 59.9	-52.8	156.5	31 04.8	-53.0	156.8	30 09.6	-53.2	157.0	29 14.3	-53.4	157.2	28 18.9	-53.6	157.5	27 23.5	-53.8	157.7	26 27.9	-54.0	157.9	37
38	32 02.4	-52.7	156.9	31 07.1	-52.9	157.1	30 11.8	-53.1	157.3	29 16.4	-53.3	157.6	28 20.9	-53.5	157.8	27 25.3	-53.7	158.0	26 29.7	-53.9	158.2	25 33.9	-54.0	158.3	38
39	31 09.7	-52.8	157.4	30 14.2	-53.0	157.7	29 18.7	-53.2	157.9	28 23.1	-53.4	158.1	27 27.4	-53.6	158.3	26 31.6	-53.8	158.5	25 35.8	-54.0	158.6	24 39.9	-54.2	158.8	39
40	30 16.9	-52.9	158.0	29 21.2	-53.1	158.2	28 25.5	-53.4	158.4	27 29.7	-53.6	158.6	26 33.8	-53.8	158.8	25 37.8	-53.9	159.0	24 41.8	-54.1	159.1	23 45.7	-54.3	159.3	40
41	29 24.0	-53.1	158.5	28 28.1	-53.3	158.7	27 32.1	-53.4	158.9	26 36.1	-53.6	159.1	25 40.0	-53.8	159.3	24 43.9	-54.0	159.4	23 47.7	-54.2	159.6	22 51.4	-54.3	159.7	41
42	28 30.9	-53.2	159.1	27 34.8	-53.4	159.2	26 38.7	-53.6	159.4	25 42.5	-53.8	159.6	24 46.2	-53.9	159.8	23 49.9	-54.1	159.9	22 53.5	-54.3	160.1	21 57.1	-54.5	160.2	42
43	27 37.7	-53.3	159.6	26 41.4	-53.5	159.8	25 45.1	-53.7	159.9	24 48.7	-53.8	160.1	23 52.3	-54.0	160.2	22 55.8	-54.2	160.4	21 59.2	-54.3	160.5	21 02.6	-54.4	160.7	43
44	26 44.4	-53.4	160.1	25 47.9	-53.6	160.3	24 51.4	-53.7	160.4	23 54.9	-54.0	160.6	22 58.3	-54.1	160.7	22 01.6	-54.2	160.9	21 04.9	-54.4	161.0	20 08.2	-54.6	161.1	44
45	25 51.0	-53.6	160.6	24 54.3	-53.7	160.8	23 57.7	-53.9	160.9	23 00.9	-54.0	161.1	22 04.2	-54.2	161.2	21 07.4	-54.4	161.3	20 10.5	-54.5	161.4	19 13.6	-54.6	161.5	45
46	24 57.4	-53.6	161.1	24 00.6	-53.7	161.3	23 03.8	-53.9	161.4	22 06.9	-54.1	161.5	21 10.0	-54.3	161.7	20 13.0	-54.4	161.8	19 16.0	-54.5	161.9	18 19.0	-54.7	162.0	46
47	24 03.8	-53.7	161.6	23 06.9	-53.9	161.7	22 09.9	-54.1	161.9	21 12.8	-54.2	162.0	20 15.7	-54.3	162.1	19 18.6	-54.4	162.2	18 21.5	-54.6	162.3	17 24.3	-54.7	162.4	47
48	23 10.1	-53.8	162.1	22 13.0	-54.0	162.2	21 15.8	-54.1	162.3	20 18.6	-54.2	162.5	19 21.4	-54.4	162.6	18 24.2	-54.6	162.7	17 26.9	-54.7	162.8	16 29.6	-54.8	162.8	48
49	22 16.3	-53.9	162.6	21 19.0	-54.0	162.7	20 21.7	-54.1	162.8	19 24.4	-54.3	162.9	18 27.0	-54.4	163.0	17 29.6	-54.5	163.1	16 32.2	-54.7	163.2	15 34.8	-54.9	163.3	49
50	21 22.4	-54.0	163.0	20 25.0	-54.1	163.2	19 27.6	-54.3	163.3	18 30.1	-54.4	163.4	17 32.6	-54.5	163.4	16 35.1	-54.7	163.5	15 37.5	-54.7	163.6	14 39.9	-54.8	163.7	50
51	20 28.4	-54.0	163.5	19 30.9	-54.2	163.6	18 33.3	-54.3	163.7	17 35.7	-54.4	163.8	16 38.1	-54.6	163.9	15 40.4	-54.6	164.0	14 42.8	-54.8	164.0	13 45.1	-55.0	164.1	51
52	19 34.4	-54.1	164.0	18 36.7	-54.2	164.1	17 39.0	-54.4	164.2	16 41.3	-54.5	164.2	15 43.5	-54.6	164.3	14 45.8	-54.8	164.4	13 48.0	-54.9	164.5	12 50.1	-54.9	164.5	52
53	18 40.3	-54.2	164.4	17 42.5	-54.3	164.5	16 44.6	-54.4	164.6	15 46.8	-54.5	164.7	14 48.9	-54.6	164.7	13 51.0	-54.8	164.8	12 53.1	-54.9	164.9	11 55.2	-55.0	164.9	53
54	17 46.1	-54.2	164.9	16 48.2	-54.4	165.0	15 50.2	-54.4	165.0	14 52.3	-54.6	165.1	13 54.3	-54.7	165.2	12 56.2	-54.8	165.2	11 58.2	-54.9	165.3	11 00.2	-55.0	165.3	54
55	16 51.9	-54.3	165.3	15 53.8	-54.4	165.4	14 55.8	-54.6	165.5	13 57.7	-54.7	165.5	12 59.6	-54.8	165.6	12 01.4	-54.8	165.7	11 03.3	-55.0	165.7	10 05.2	-55.1	165.7	55
56	15 57.6	-54.4	165.8	14 59.4	-54.4	165.8	14 01.2	-54.5	165.9	13 03.0	-54.6	166.0	12 04.8	-54.8	166.0	11 06.6	-54.9	166.1	10 08.3	-54.9	166.1	9 10.1	-55.1	166.1	56
57	15 03.2	-54.4	166.2	14 05.0	-54.6	166.3	13 06.7	-54.6	166.3	12 08.4	-54.8	166.4	11 10.0	-54.8	166.4	10 11.7	-54.9	166.5	9 13.4	-55.0	166.5	8 15.0	-55.1	166.6	57
58	14 08.8	-54.4	166.6	13 10.4	-54.5	166.7	12 12.1	-54.7	166.8	11 13.6	-54.7	166.8	10 15.2	-54.8	166.8	9 16.8	-55.0	166.9	8 18.4	-55.1	166.9	7 19.9	-55.1	167.0	58
59	13 14.4	-54.5	167.1	12 15.9	-54.6	167.1	11 17.4	-54.7	167.2	10 18.9	-54.8	167.2	9 20.4	-54.9	167.3	8 21.8	-54.9	167.3	7 23.3	-55.0	167.3	6 24.8	-55.2	167.3	59
60	12 19.9	-54.5	167.5	11 21.3	-54.6	167.6	10 22.7	-54.7	167.6	9 24.1	-54.8	167.6	8 25.5	-54.9	167.7	7 26.9	-55.0	167.7	6 28.3	-55.1	167.7	5 29.6	-55.1	167.7	60
61	11 25.4	-54.6	167.9	10 26.7	-54.7	168.0	9 28.0	-54.7	168.0	8 29.3	-54.8	168.0	7 30.6	-54.9	168.1	6 31.9	-55.0	168.1	5 33.2	-55.1	168.1	4 34.5	-55.2	168.1	61
62	10 30.8	-54.6	168.4	9 32.0	-54.7	168.4	8 33.3	-54.8	168.4	7 34.5	-54.9	168.5	6 35.7	-55.0	168.5	5 36.9	-55.0	168.5	4 38.1	-55.1	168.5	3 39.3	-55.2	168.5	62
63	9 36.2	-54.6	168.8	8 37.3	-54.7	168.8	7 38.5	-54.8	168.8	6 39.6	-54.9	168.9	5 40.7	-54.9	168.9	4 41.9	-55.1	168.9	3 43.0	-55.1	168.9	2 44.1	-55.2	168.9	63
64	8 41.6	-54.7	169.2	7 42.6	-54.7	169.2	6 43.7	-54.8	169.2	5 44.7	-54.9	169.3	4 45.8	-55.0	169.3	3 46.8	-55.0	169.3	2 47.9	-55.2	169.3	1 48.9	-55.2	169.3	64
65	7 46.9	-54.7	169.6	6 47.9	-54.8	169.6	5 48.9	-54.9	169.7	4 49.8	-54.9	169.7	3 50.8	-55.0	169.7	2 51.8	-55.1	169.7	1 52.7	-55.1	169.7	0 53.7	-55.2	169.7	65
66	6 52.2	-54.7	170.0	5 53.1	-54.7	170.0	4 54.0	-54.8	170.1	3 54.9	-54.9	170.1	2 55.8	-55.0	170.1	1 56.7	-55.0	170.1	0 57.6	-55.1	170.1	0 01.5	+55.2	9.9	66
67	5 57.5	-54.7	170.4	4 58.4	-54.8	170.5	3 59.2	-54.9	170.5	3 00.0	-54.9	170.5	2 00.8	-55.0	170.5	1 01.7	-55.1	170.5	0 02.5	-55.1	170.5	0 56.7	+55.2	9.5	67
68	5 02.8	-54.7	170.9	4 03.6	-54.8	170.9	3 04.3	-54.8	170.9	2 05.1	-55.0	170.9	1 05.8	-55.0	170.9	0 06.6	-55.1	170.9	0 52.6	+55.2	9.1	1 51.9	+55.2	9.1	68
69	4 08.1	-54.8	171.3	3 08.8	-54.9	171.3	2 09.5	-54.9	171.3	1 10.1	-54.9	171.3	0 10.8	-55.0	171.3	0 48.5	+55.0	8.7	1 47.8	+55.1	8.7	2 47.1	+55.2	8.7	69
70	3 13.3	-54.7	171.7	2 13.9	-54.8	171.7	1 14.6	-54.9	171.7	0 15.2	-54.9	171.7	0 44.2	+55.0	8.3	1 43.5	+55.1	8.3	2 42.9	+55.1	8.3	3 42.3	+55.1	8.3	70
71	2 18.6	-54.8	172.1	1 19.1	-54.8	172.1	0 19.7	-54.9	172.1	0 39.7	+55.0	7.9	1 39.2	+55.0	7.9	2 38.6	+55.0	7.9	3 38.0	+55.1	7.9	4 37.4	+55.2	7.9	71
72	1 23.8	-54.8	172.5	0 24.3	-54.8	172.5	0 35.2	+54.9	7.5	1 34.7	+54.9	7.5	2 34.2	+54.9	7.5	3 33.6	+55.1	7.5	4 33.1	+55.1	7.5	5 32.6	+55.2	7.5	72
73	0 29.0	-54.8	172.9	0 30.5	+54.8	7.1	1 30.1	+54.8	7.1	2 29.6	+54.9	7.1	3 29.1	+55.0	7.1	4 28.7	+55.0	7.1	5 28.2	+55.1	7.1	6 27.8	+55.1	7.1	73
74	0 25.8	+54.7	6.7	1 25.3	+54.9	6.7	2 24.9	+54.9	6.7	3 24.5	+54.9	6.7	4 24.1	+55.0	6.7	5 23.7	+55.0	6.7	6 23.3	+55.1	6.7	7 22.9	+55.1	6.7	74
75	1 20.5	+54.8	6.3	2 20.2	+54.8	6.3	3 19.8	+54.9	6.3	4 19.4	+54.9	6.3	5 19.1	+54.9	6.3	6 18.7	+55.0	6.3	7 18.4	+55.1	6.3	8 18.0	+55.1	6.3	75
76	2 15.3	+54.8	5.9	3 15.0	+54.8	5.9	4 14.7	+54.8	5.9	5 14.3	+54.9	5.9	6 14.0	+55.0	5.9	7 13.7	+55.0	5.9	8 13.4	+55.0	5.9	9 13.1	+55.0	5.9	76
77	3 10.1	+54.7	5.5	4 09.8	+54.8	5.5	5 09.5	+54.8	5.5	6 09.2	+54.9	5.5	7 09.0	+54.9	5.5	8 08.7	+54.9	5.5	9 08.4	+55.0	5.5	10 08.1	+55.1	5.5	77
78	4 04.8	+54.7	5.1	5 04.6	+54.8	5.1	6 04.3	+54.9	5.1	7 04.1	+54.9	5.1	8 03.9	+54.9	5.1	9 03.6	+55.0	5.1	10 03.4	+55.0	5.1	11 03.2	+54.9	5.1	78
79	4 59.5	+54.8	4.6	5 59.4	+54.7	4.7	6 59.2	+54.7	4.7	7 59.0	+54.8	4.7	8 58.8	+54.8	4.7	9 58.6	+54.8	4.7	10 58.4	+54.9	4.7	11 58.1	+55.0	4.7	79
80	5 54.3	+54.7	4.2	6 54.1	+54.7	4.2	7 53.9	+54.8	4.2	8 53.8	+54.8	4.3	9 53.6	+54.8	4.3	10 53.4	+54.9	4.3	11 53.3	+54.9	4.3	12 53.1	+54.9	4.3	80
81	6 49.0	+54.7	3.8	7 48.8	+54.8	3.8	8 48.7	+54.7	3.8	9 48.6	+54.7	3.8	10 48.4	+54.8	3.9	11 48.3	+54.8	3.9	12 48.2	+54.8	3.9	13 48.0	+54.9	3.9	81
82	7 43.7	+54.6	3.4	8 43.6	+54.6	3.4	9 43.4	+54.8	3.4	10 43.3	+54.8	3.4	11 43.2	+54.8	3.4	12 43.1	+54.8	3.5	13 43.0	+54.8	3.5	14 42.9	+54.8	3.5	82
83	8 38.3	+54.7	3.0	9 38.2	+54.7	3.0	10 38.2	+54.6	3.0	11 38.1	+54.7	3.0	12 38.0	+54.7	3.0	13 37.9	+54.7	3.0	14 37.8	+54.8	3.1	15 37.7	+54.8	3.1	83
84	9 33.0	+54.6	2.6	10 32.9	+54.6	2.6	11 32.8	+54.7	2.6	12 32.8	+54.6	2.6	13 32.7	+54.7	2.6	14 32.6	+54.7	2.6	15 32.6	+54.7	2.6	16 32.5	+54.8	2.6	84
85	10 27.6	+54.5	2.1	11 27.5	+54.6	2.2	12 27.5	+54.6	2.2	13 27.4	+54.6	2.2	14 27.4	+54.6	2.2	15 27.3	+54.7	2.2	16 27.3	+54.7	2.2	17 27.3	+54.6	2.2	85
86	11 22.1	+54.6	1.7	12 22.1	+54.5	1.7	13 22.1	+54.5	1.7	14 22.0	+54.6	1.7	15 22.0	+54.6	1.8	16 22.0	+54.6	1.8	17 22.0	+54.6	1.8	18 21.9	+54.6	1.8	86
87	12 16.7	+54.4	1.3	13 16.6	+54.5	1.3	14 16.6	+54.5	1.3	15 16.6	+54.5	1.3	16 16.6	+54.5	1.3	17 16.6	+54.5	1.3	18 16.6	+54.5	1.3	19 16.5	+54.6	1.3	87
88	13 11.1	+54.5	0.9	14 11.1	+54.5	0.9	15 11.1	+54.5	0.9	16 11.1	+54.5	0.9	17 11.1	+54.5	0.9	18 11.1	+54.5	0.9	19 11.1	+54.5	0.9	20 11.1	+54.5	0.9	88
89	14 05.6	+54.4	0.4	15 05.6	+54.4	0.4	16 05.6	+54.4	0.4	17 05.6	+54.4	0.4	18 05.6	+54.4	0.4	19 05.6	+54.4	0.4	20 05.6	+54.4	0.5	21 05.6	+54.4	0.5	89
90	15 00.0	+54.4	0.0	16 00.0	+54.4	0.0	17 00.0	+54.3	0.0	18 00.0	+54.3	0.0	19 00.0	+54.3	0.0	20 00.0	+54.3	0.0	21 00.0	+54.3	0.0	22 00.0	+54.3	0.0	90
	15°			16°			17°			18°			19°			20°			21°			22°			

S. Lat. { L.H.A. greater than 180° ....Zn=180°–Z
L.H.A. less than 180°...........Zn=180°+Z

LATITUDE **SAME** NAME AS DECLINATION L.H.A. 155°, 205°

53

N. Lat. {L.H.A. greater than 180° .....Zn=Z; L.H.A. less than 180°............Zn=360°-Z}

Dec.	15°			16°			17°			18°			19°			20°			21°			22°			Dec.
	Hc	d	Z	Hc	d	Z	Hc	d	Z	Hc	d	Z	Hc	d	Z	Hc	d	Z	Hc	d	Z	Hc	d	Z	
°	° ′	′	°	° ′	′	°	° ′	′	°	° ′	′	°	° ′	′	°	° ′	′	°	° ′	′	°	° ′	′	°	°
0	60 14.8	+30.6	118.0	59 46.0	+32.2	119.5	59 15.8	+33.7	120.9	58 44.3	+35.1	122.4	58 11.6	+36.5	123.7	57 37.7	+37.8	125.0	57 02.7	+39.1	126.3	56 26.6	+40.3	127.5	0
1	60 45.4	+29.2	116.2	60 18.2	+30.8	117.8	59 49.5	+32.5	119.3	59 19.4	+34.0	120.8	58 48.1	+35.4	122.2	58 15.5	+36.8	123.6	57 41.8	+38.0	124.9	57 06.9	+39.3	126.2	1
2	61 14.6	+27.7	114.4	60 49.0	+29.5	116.0	60 22.0	+31.1	117.6	59 53.4	+32.8	119.2	59 23.5	+34.3	120.6	58 52.3	+35.7	122.1	58 19.8	+37.1	123.4	57 46.2	+38.3	124.8	2
3	61 42.3	+26.2	112.5	61 18.5	+28.0	114.2	60 53.1	+29.7	115.9	60 26.2	+31.4	117.5	59 57.8	+33.0	119.0	59 28.0	+34.5	120.5	58 56.9	+36.0	121.9	58 24.5	+37.4	123.3	3
4	62 08.5	+24.6	110.6	61 46.5	+26.5	112.4	61 22.8	+28.3	114.1	60 57.6	+30.0	115.7	60 30.8	+31.7	117.3	60 02.5	+33.3	118.9	59 32.9	+34.8	120.4	59 01.9	+36.2	121.8	4
5	62 33.1	+22.8	108.7	62 13.0	+24.8	110.5	61 51.1	+26.8	112.2	61 27.6	+28.6	113.9	61 02.5	+30.3	115.6	60 35.8	+32.0	117.2	60 07.7	+33.5	118.7	59 38.1	+35.1	120.2	5
6	62 55.9	+21.1	106.7	62 37.8	+23.1	108.5	62 17.9	+25.1	110.3	61 56.2	+27.0	112.1	61 32.8	+28.8	113.8	61 07.8	+30.6	115.5	60 41.2	+32.3	117.1	60 13.2	+33.9	118.6	6
7	63 17.0	+19.2	104.6	63 00.9	+21.4	106.5	62 43.0	+23.4	108.3	62 23.2	+25.4	110.2	62 01.6	+27.3	111.9	61 38.4	+29.1	113.7	61 13.5	+30.9	115.3	60 47.1	+32.5	116.9	7
8	63 36.2	+17.3	102.5	63 22.3	+19.5	104.4	63 06.4	+21.6	106.3	62 48.6	+23.7	108.2	62 28.9	+25.7	110.0	62 07.5	+27.6	111.8	61 44.4	+29.4	113.5	61 19.6	+31.3	115.2	8
9	63 53.5	+15.4•	100.3	63 41.8	+17.6	102.3	63 28.0	+19.8	104.2	63 12.3	+21.9	106.2	62 54.6	+24.0	108.1	62 35.1	+26.0	109.9	62 13.8	+27.9	111.7	61 50.8	+29.7	113.4	9
10	64 08.9	+13.3•	98.1	63 59.4	+15.6•	100.1	63 47.8	+17.9	102.1	63 34.2	+20.1	104.1	63 18.6	+22.2	106.0	63 01.1	+24.3	107.9	62 41.7	+26.3	109.8	62 20.5	+28.2	111.6	10
11	64 22.2	+11.2•	95.8	64 15.0	+13.6•	97.9	64 05.7	+15.9•	99.9	63 54.3	+18.1	102.0	63 40.8	+20.4	103.9	63 25.4	+22.5	105.9	63 08.0	+24.6	107.8	62 48.7	+26.6	109.6	11
12	64 33.4	+9.1•	93.6	64 28.6	+11.4•	95.7	64 21.6	+13.8•	97.7	64 12.4	+16.2•	99.8	64 01.2	+18.4	101.8	63 47.9	+20.6	103.8	63 32.6	+22.8	105.8	63 15.3	+24.9	107.7	12
13	64 42.5	+6.8•	91.3	64 40.0	+9.4•	93.4	64 35.4	+11.7•	95.5	64 28.6	+14.1•	97.6	64 19.6	+16.5•	99.6	64 08.5	+18.8	101.7	63 55.4	+21.0	103.7	63 40.2	+23.1	105.6	13
14	64 49.3	+4.7•	88.9	64 49.4	+7.1•	91.1	64 47.1	+9.6•	93.2	64 42.7	+12.0•	95.3	64 36.1	+14.4•	97.4	64 27.3	+16.7•	99.5	64 16.4	+19.0•	101.5	64 03.3	+21.3	103.5	14
15	64 54.0	+2.5•	86.6	64 56.5	+4.9•	88.7	64 56.7	+7.4•	90.9	64 54.7	+9.9•	93.0	64 50.5	+12.2•	95.1	64 44.0	+14.7•	97.2	64 35.4	+17.0•	99.3	64 24.6	+19.3•	101.4	15
16	64 56.5	+0.2•	84.2	65 01.4	+2.7•	86.4	65 04.1	+5.2•	88.5	65 04.6	+7.6•	90.7	65 02.7	+10.1•	92.8	64 58.7	+12.5•	94.9	64 52.4	+14.9•	97.1	64 43.9	+17.3•	99.2	16
17	64 56.7	-2.0•	81.9	65 04.1	+0.5•	84.0	65 09.3	+2.9•	86.1	65 12.2	+5.4•	88.3	65 12.8	+7.9•	90.5	65 11.2	+10.4•	92.6	65 07.3	+12.9•	94.8	65 01.2	+15.3•	96.9	17
18	64 54.7	-4.2•	79.5	65 04.6	-1.9•	81.6	65 12.2	+0.6•	83.8	65 17.6	+3.1•	85.9	65 20.7	+5.7•	88.1	65 21.6	+8.1•	90.3	65 20.2	+10.6•	92.5	65 16.5	+13.0•	94.6	18
19	64 50.5	-6.5•	77.2	65 02.7	-4.0•	79.2	65 12.8	-1.6•	81.4	65 20.7	+0.9•	83.5	65 26.4	+3.3•	85.7	65 29.7	+5.9•	87.9	65 30.8	+8.4•	90.1	65 29.5	+10.9•	92.3	19
20	64 44.0	-8.6•	74.8	64 58.7	-6.3•	76.9	65 11.2	-3.9•	79.0	65 21.6	-1.4•	81.1	65 29.7	+1.1•	83.3	65 35.6	+3.6•	85.5	65 39.2	+6.0•	87.7	65 40.4	+8.6•	89.9	20
21	64 35.4	-10.8•	72.5	64 52.4	-8.5•	74.5	65 07.3	-6.1•	76.6	65 20.2	-3.7•	78.7	65 30.8	-1.3•	80.9	65 39.2	+1.2•	83.1	65 45.2	+3.8•	85.3	65 49.0	+6.4•	87.5	21
22	64 24.6	-12.9•	70.2	64 43.9	-10.6•	72.2	65 01.2	-8.3•	74.3	65 16.5	-6.0•	76.3	65 29.5	-3.5•	78.5	65 40.4	-1.0•	80.6	65 49.0	+1.5•	82.8	65 55.4	+4.0•	85.1	22
23	64 11.7	-14.9•	68.0	64 33.3	-12.8•	69.9	64 52.9	-10.5•	71.9	65 10.5	-8.2•	74.0	65 26.0	-5.8•	76.1	65 39.4	-3.4•	78.2	65 50.5	-0.9•	80.4	65 59.4	+1.6•	82.6	23
24	63 56.8	-16.9•	65.8	64 20.5	-14.8•	67.6	64 42.4	-12.7•	69.6	65 02.3	-10.4•	71.6	65 20.2	-8.1•	73.7	65 36.0	-5.7•	75.8	65 49.6	-3.2•	78.0	66 01.0	-0.7•	80.1	24
25	63 39.9	-18.9	63.6	64 05.7	-16.8•	65.4	64 29.7	-14.7•	67.3	64 51.9	-12.5•	69.3	65 12.1	-10.2•	71.3	65 30.3	-7.9•	73.4	65 46.4	-5.5•	75.5	66 00.3	-3.0•	77.7	25
26	63 21.0	-20.7	61.5	63 48.9	-18.8	63.2	64 15.0	-16.7•	65.1	64 39.4	-14.7•	67.0	65 01.9	-12.5•	69.0	65 22.4	-10.1•	71.0	65 40.9	-7.8•	73.1	65 57.3	-5.4•	75.2	26
27	63 00.3	-22.5	59.4	63 30.1	-20.7	61.1	63 58.3	-18.7	62.9	64 24.7	-16.6•	64.7	64 49.4	-14.5•	66.7	65 12.3	-12.4•	68.6	65 33.1	-10.0•	70.7	65 51.9	-7.7•	72.8	27
28	62 37.8	-24.2	57.3	63 09.4	-22.4	59.0	63 39.6	-20.6	60.7	64 08.1	-18.7	62.5	64 34.9	-16.6•	64.4	64 59.9	-14.5•	66.3	65 23.1	-12.3•	68.3	65 44.2	-9.9•	70.4	28
29	62 13.6	-25.9	55.4	62 47.0	-24.2	57.0	63 19.0	-22.4	58.6	63 49.4	-20.5	60.4	64 18.3	-18.6	62.2	64 45.4	-16.5•	64.0	65 10.8	-14.4•	66.0	65 34.3	-12.2•	68.0	29
30	61 47.7	-27.4	53.4	62 22.8	-25.8	55.0	62 56.6	-24.2	56.6	63 28.9	-22.4	58.2	63 59.7	-20.5	60.0	64 28.9	-18.6	61.8	64 56.4	-16.5•	63.7	65 22.1	-14.4•	65.6	30
31	61 20.3	-28.9	51.6	61 57.0	-27.4	53.0	62 32.4	-25.8	54.6	63 06.5	-24.1	56.2	63 39.2	-22.4	57.9	64 10.3	-20.4	59.6	64 39.9	-18.5•	61.4	65 07.7	-16.4•	63.3	31
32	60 51.4	-30.4	49.8	61 29.6	-28.9	51.2	62 06.6	-27.4	52.6	62 42.4	-25.8	54.2	63 16.8	-24.1	55.8	63 49.9	-22.4	57.5	64 21.4	-20.5	59.2	64 51.3	-18.6•	61.0	32
33	60 21.0	-31.6	48.0	61 00.7	-30.4	49.3	61 39.2	-28.9	50.7	62 16.6	-27.4	52.2	62 52.7	-25.8	53.8	63 27.5	-24.1	55.4	64 00.9	-22.4	57.0	64 32.7	-20.4	58.8	33
34	59 49.4	-33.0	46.3	60 30.3	-31.7	47.6	61 10.3	-30.4	48.9	61 49.2	-29.0	50.3	62 26.9	-27.4	51.8	63 03.4	-25.9	53.3	63 38.5	-24.1	54.9	64 12.3	-22.4	56.6	34
35	59 16.4	-34.2	44.7	59 58.6	-32.9	45.9	60 39.9	-31.7	47.1	61 20.2	-30.3	48.5	61 59.5	-29.0	49.9	62 37.5	-27.4	51.3	63 14.4	-25.9	52.9	63 49.9	-24.2	54.5	35
36	58 42.2	-35.3	43.1	59 25.7	-34.2	44.2	60 08.2	-33.0	45.4	60 49.9	-31.8	46.7	61 30.5	-30.4	48.0	62 10.1	-29.0	49.4	62 48.5	-27.5	50.9	63 25.7	-25.9	52.5	36
37	58 06.9	-36.4	41.5	58 51.5	-35.4	42.6	59 35.2	-34.2	43.8	60 18.1	-33.0	45.0	61 00.1	-31.8	46.2	61 41.1	-30.5	47.6	62 21.0	-29.0	49.0	62 59.8	-27.5	50.5	37
38	57 30.5	-37.4	40.0	58 16.1	-36.4	41.1	59 01.0	-35.4	42.1	59 45.1	-34.3	43.3	60 28.3	-33.1	44.5	61 10.6	-31.8	45.8	61 52.0	-30.5	47.1	62 32.3	-29.1	48.5	38
39	56 53.1	-38.4	38.6	57 39.7	-37.5	39.6	58 25.6	-36.5	40.6	59 10.8	-35.5	41.7	59 55.2	-34.3	42.8	60 38.8	-33.2	44.0	61 21.5	-32.0	45.3	62 03.2	-30.6	46.6	39
40	56 14.7	-39.3	37.2	57 02.2	-38.4	38.1	57 49.1	-37.5	39.1	58 35.3	-36.5	40.1	59 20.9	-35.6	41.2	60 05.6	-34.4	42.3	60 49.5	-33.2	43.5	61 32.6	-32.0	44.8	40
41	55 35.4	-40.2	35.8	56 23.8	-39.4	36.7	57 11.6	-38.5	37.6	57 58.8	-37.6	38.6	58 45.3	-36.6	39.6	59 31.2	-35.6	40.7	60 16.3	-34.5	41.8	61 00.6	-33.4	43.0	41
42	54 55.2	-40.9	34.5	55 44.4	-40.2	35.4	56 33.1	-39.4	36.2	57 21.2	-38.5	37.1	58 08.7	-37.6	38.1	58 55.6	-36.7	39.1	59 41.8	-35.7	40.2	60 27.2	-34.6	41.3	42
43	54 14.3	-41.7	33.3	55 04.2	-41.0	34.1	55 53.7	-40.3	34.9	56 42.7	-39.5	35.7	57 31.1	-38.6	36.7	58 18.9	-37.7	37.6	59 06.1	-36.8	38.6	59 52.6	-35.7	39.7	43
44	53 32.6	-42.5	32.1	54 23.2	-41.8	32.8	55 13.4	-41.1	33.6	56 03.2	-40.4	34.4	56 52.5	-39.6	35.2	57 41.2	-38.7	36.2	58 29.3	-37.8	37.1	59 16.9	-36.9	38.1	44
45	52 50.1	-43.1	30.9	53 41.4	-42.5	31.6	54 32.3	-41.8	32.3	55 22.8	-41.1	33.1	56 12.9	-40.4	33.9	57 02.5	-39.7	34.7	57 51.5	-38.8	35.6	58 40.0	-38.0	36.6	45
46	52 07.0	-43.8	29.7	52 58.9	-43.2	30.4	53 50.5	-42.6	31.1	54 41.7	-41.9	31.8	55 32.5	-41.3	32.6	56 22.8	-40.5	33.4	57 12.7	-39.8	34.2	58 02.0	-38.9	35.1	46
47	51 23.2	-44.4	28.6	52 15.7	-43.8	29.2	53 07.9	-43.2	29.9	53 59.8	-42.7	30.6	54 51.2	-42.0	31.3	55 42.3	-41.3	32.0	56 32.9	-40.6	32.8	57 23.1	-39.9	33.7	47
48	50 38.8	-44.9	27.6	51 31.9	-44.4	28.1	52 24.7	-43.9	28.7	53 17.1	-43.3	29.4	54 09.2	-42.7	30.1	55 01.0	-42.2	30.8	55 52.3	-41.4	31.5	56 43.2	-40.7	32.3	48
49	49 53.9	-45.5	26.5	50 47.5	-45.0	27.1	51 40.8	-44.5	27.6	52 33.8	-44.0	28.2	53 26.5	-43.5	28.9	54 18.8	-42.8	29.5	55 10.9	-42.3	30.2	56 02.5	-41.6	31.0	49
50	49 08.4	-46.0	25.5	50 02.5	-45.6	26.0	50 56.3	-45.1	26.6	51 49.8	-44.6	27.1	52 43.0	-44.0	27.7	53 36.0	-43.5	28.3	54 28.6	-42.9	29.0	55 20.9	-42.3	29.7	50
51	48 22.4	-46.4	24.5	49 16.9	-46.0	25.0	50 11.2	-45.6	25.5	51 05.2	-45.2	26.1	51 59.0	-44.7	26.6	52 52.5	-44.2	27.2	53 45.7	-43.6	27.8	54 38.6	-43.1	28.5	51
52	47 36.0	-46.9	23.6	48 30.9	-46.6	24.0	49 25.6	-46.2	24.5	50 20.0	-45.7	25.0	51 14.3	-45.3	25.5	52 08.3	-44.8	26.1	53 02.1	-44.3	26.7	53 55.5	-43.7	27.3	52
53	46 49.1	-47.4	22.7	47 44.3	-46.9	23.1	48 39.4	-46.6	23.5	49 34.3	-46.2	24.0	50 29.0	-45.7	24.5	51 23.5	-45.3	25.0	52 17.8	-44.9	25.6	53 11.8	-44.4	26.1	53
54	46 01.7	-47.7	21.8	46 57.4	-47.5	22.2	47 52.8	-47.0	22.6	48 48.1	-46.6	23.0	49 43.3	-46.3	23.5	50 38.2	-45.9	24.0	51 32.9	-45.4	24.5	52 27.4	-45.0	25.0	54
55	45 14.0	-48.2	20.9	46 09.9	-47.8	21.3	47 05.8	-47.5	21.7	48 01.5	-47.2	22.1	48 57.0	-46.8	22.5	49 52.3	-46.4	23.0	50 47.5	-46.0	23.4	51 42.4	-45.6	23.9	55
56	44 25.8	-48.5	20.1	45 22.1	-48.2	20.4	46 18.3	-47.9	20.8	47 14.3	-47.6	21.2	48 10.2	-47.2	21.6	49 05.9	-46.9	22.0	50 01.5	-46.5	22.4	50 56.8	-46.1	22.9	56
57	43 37.3	-48.8	19.3	44 33.9	-48.5	19.6	45 30.4	-48.3	19.9	46 26.7	-47.9	20.3	47 23.0	-47.7	20.6	48 19.0	-47.3	21.0	49 15.0	-47.0	21.5	50 10.7	-46.6	21.9	57
58	42 48.5	-49.1	18.5	43 45.4	-48.9	18.8	44 42.1	-48.6	19.1	45 38.8	-48.4	19.4	46 35.3	-48.0	19.8	47 31.7	-47.7	20.1	48 28.0	-47.4	20.5	49 24.1	-47.1	20.9	58
59	41 59.4	-49.5	17.7	42 56.5	-49.2	18.0	43 53.5	-49.0	18.3	44 50.4	-48.7	18.6	45 47.3	-48.5	18.9	46 44.0	-48.2	19.2	47 40.6	-47.9	19.6	48 37.0	-47.5	20.0	59
60	41 09.9	-49.8	16.9	42 07.3	-49.6	17.2	43 04.5	-49.3	17.5	44 01.7	-49.0	17.7	44 58.8	-48.8	18.1	45 55.8	-48.5	18.4	46 52.7	-48.3	18.7	47 49.5	-48.0	19.1	60
61	40 20.1	-50.0	16.2	41 17.7	-49.8	16.4	42 15.2	-49.6	16.7	43 12.7	-49.4	17.0	44 10.0	-49.1	17.2	45 07.3	-48.9	17.5	46 04.4	-48.6	17.8	47 01.5	-48.4	18.2	61
62	39 30.1	-50.3	15.5	40 27.9	-50.1	15.7	41 25.6	-49.8	15.9	42 23.3	-49.7	16.2	43 20.9	-49.5	16.4	44 18.4	-49.2	16.7	45 15.8	-49.0	17.0	46 13.1	-48.7	17.3	62
63	38 39.8	-50.5	14.8	39 37.8	-50.3	15.0	40 35.8	-50.2	15.2	41 33.6	-49.9	15.4	42 31.4	-49.7	15.7	43 29.2	-49.6	15.9	44 26.8	-49.3	16.2	45 24.4	-49.1	16.5	63
64	37 49.3	-50.8	14.1	38 47.5	-50.6	14.3	39 45.6	-50.4	14.5	40 43.7	-50.3	14.7	41 41.7	-50.1	14.9	42 39.6	-49.8	15.1	43 37.5	-49.7	15.4	44 35.3	-49.4	15.7	64
65	36 58.5	-51.0	13.4	37 56.9	-50.9	13.6	38 55.2	-50.7	13.8	39 53.4	-50.5	14.0	40 51.6	-50.3	14.2	41 49.8	-50.2	14.4	42 47.8	-49.9	14.6	43 45.9	-49.8	14.9	65
66	36 07.5	-51.2	12.8	37 06.0	-51.0	12.9	38 04.5	-50.9	13.1	39 02.9	-50.7	13.3	40 01.3	-50.6	13.5	40 59.6	-50.4	13.7	41 57.9	-50.2	13.9	42 56.1	-50.0	14.1	66
67	35 16.3	-51.4	12.1	36 15.0	-51.3	12.3	37 13.6	-51.1	12.4	38 12.2	-51.0	12.6	39 10.7	-50.8	12.8	40 09.2	-50.7	13.0	41 07.7	-50.5	13.1	42 06.1	-50.4	13.3	67
68	34 24.9	-51.5	11.5	35 23.7	-51.4	11.6	36 22.5	-51.3	11.8	37 21.2	-51.2	11.9	38 19.9	-51.1	12.1	39 18.5	-50.9	12.3	40 17.2	-50.8	12.4	41 15.7	-50.6	12.6	68
69	33 33.4	-51.8	10.9	34 32.3	-51.7	11.0	35 31.2	-51.6	11.1	36 30.0	-51.4	11.3	37 28.8	-51.2	11.4	38 27.6	-51.1	11.6	39 26.4	-51.0	11.7	40 25.1	-50.8	11.9	69
70	32 41.6	-51.9	10.3	33 40.6	-51.8	10.4	34 39.6	-51.7	10.5	35 38.6	-51.6	10.6	36 37.6	-51.5	10.8	37 36.5	-51.4	10.9	38 35.4	-51.2	11.1	39 34.3	-51.1	11.2	70
71	31 49.7	-52.1	9.7	32 48.8	-52.0	9.8	33 47.9	-51.9	9.9	34 47.0	-51.8	10.0	35 46.1	-51.7	10.1	36 45.1	-51.5	10.3	37 44.2	-51.5	10.4	38 43.2	-51.4	10.5	71
72	30 57.6	-52.3	9.1	31 56.8	-52.2	9.2	32 56.0	-52.0	9.3	33 55.2	-51.9	9.4	34 54.4	-51.9	9.5	35 53.6	-51.8	9.6	36 52.7	-51.6	9.8	37 51.8	-51.5	9.9	72
73	30 05.3	-52.4	8.5	31 04.6	-52.3	8.6	32 04.0	-52.3	8.7	33 03.3	-52.2	8.8	34 02.5	-52.0	8.9	35 01.8	-51.9	9.0	36 01.1	-51.9	9.1	37 00.3	-51.7	9.2	73
74	29 12.9	-52.5	8.0	30 12.3	-52.4	8.0	31 11.7	-52.3	8.1	32 11.1	-52.3	8.2	33 10.5	-52.2	8.3	34 09.9	-52.1	8.4	35 09.2	-52.0	8.5	36 08.6	-52.0	8.6	74
75	28 20.4	-52.7	7.4	29 19.9	-52.6	7.5	30 19.4	-52.6	7.6	31 18.8	-52.4	7.6	32 18.3	-52.4	7.7	33 17.8	-52.3	7.8	34 17.2	-52.2	7.9	35 16.6	-52.1	8.0	75
76	27 27.7	-52.8	6.9	28 27.3	-52.7	6.9	29 26.8	-52.6	7.0	30 26.4	-52.6	7.1	31 25.9	-52.5	7.1	32 25.5	-52.5	7.2	33 25.0	-52.4	7.3	34 24.5	-52.3	7.4	76
77	26 34.9	-52.9	6.3	27 34.6	-52.9	6.4	28 34.2	-52.8	6.4	29 33.8	-52.7	6.5	30 33.4	-52.7	6.6	31 33.0	-52.6	6.6	32 32.6	-52.5	6.7	33 32.2	-52.5	6.8	77
78	25 42.0	-53.0	5.8	26 41.7	-52.9	5.9	27 41.4	-52.9	5.9	28 41.1	-52.9	6.0	29 40.7	-52.7	6.0	30 40.4	-52.7	6.1	31 40.1	-52.7	6.1	32 39.7	-52.6	6.2	78
79	24 49.0	-53.1	5.3	25 48.8	-53.1	5.3	26 48.5	-53.0	5.4	27 48.2	-53.0	5.4	28 48.0	-53.0	5.5	29 47.7	-52.9	5.5	30 47.4	-52.8	5.6	31 47.1	-52.8	5.6	79
80	23 55.9	-53.2	4.8	24 55.7	-53.2	4.8	25 55.5	-53.2	4.9	26 55.2	-53.0	4.9	27 55.0	-53.0	4.9	28 54.8	-53.0	5.0	29 54.6	-53.0	5.0	30 54.3	-52.9	5.1	80
81	23 02.7	-53.4	4.3	24 02.5	-53.3	4.3	25 02.3	-53.2	4.3	26 02.2	-53.3	4.4	27 02.0	-53.2	4.4	28 01.8	-53.1	4.5	29 01.6	-53.1	4.5	30 01.4	-53.0	4.5	81
82	22 09.3	-53.4	3.8	23 09.2	-53.4	3.8	24 09.1	-53.4	3.8	25 08.9	-53.3	3.9	26 08.8	-53.3	3.9	27 08.7	-53.3	3.9	28 08.5	-53.2	4.0	29 08.4	-53.2	4.0	82
83	21 15.9	-53.4	3.3	22 15.8	-53.4	3.3	23 15.7	-53.4	3.3	24 15.6	-53.4	3.4	25 15.5	-53.3	3.4	26 15.4	-53.3	3.4	27 15.3	-53.3	3.4	28 15.2	-53.3	3.5	83
84	20 22.5	-53.6	2.8	21 22.4	-53.6	2.8	22 22.3	-53.5	2.8	23 22.2	-53.5	2.9	24 22.2	-53.5	2.9	25 22.1	-53.5	2.9	26 22.0	-53.4	2.9	27 21.9	-53.4	3.0	84
85	19 28.9	-53.7	2.3	20 28.8	-53.6	2.3	21 28.8	-53.6	2.4	22 28.7	-53.6	2.4	23 28.7	-53.6	2.4	24 28.6	-53.5	2.4	25 28.6	-53.6	2.4	26 28.5	-53.5	2.4	85
86	18 35.2	-53.7	1.8	19 35.2	-53.7	1.9	20 35.2	-53.7	1.9	21 35.1	-53.6	1.9	22 35.1	-53.6	1.9	23 35.1	-53.7	1.9	24 35.0	-53.6	1.9	25 35.0	-53.6	1.9	86
87	17 41.5	-53.8	1.4	18 41.5	-53.8	1.4	19 41.5	-53.8	1.4	20 41.5	-53.8	1.4	21 41.5	-53.8	1.4	22 41.4	-53.7	1.4	23 41.4	-53.7	1.4	24 41.4	-53.7	1.4	87
88	16 47.7	-53.8	0.9	17 47.7	-53.8	0.9	18 47.7	-53.8	0.9	19 47.7	-53.8	0.9	20 47.7	-53.8	0.9	21 47.7	-53.8	0.9	22 47.7	-53.8	1.0	23 47.7	-53.8	1.0	88
89	15 53.9	-53.9	0.5	16 53.9	-53.9	0.5	17 53.9	-53.9	0.5	18 53.9	-53.9	0.5	19 53.9	-53.9	0.5	20 53.9	-53.9	0.5	21 53.9	-53.9	0.5	22 53.9	-53.9	0.5	89
90	15 00.0	-54.0	0.0	16 00.0	-54.0	0.0	17 00.0	-54.0	0.0	18 00.0	-54.0	0.0	19 00.0	-54.0	0.0	20 00.0	-54.0	0.0	21 00.0	-54.0	0.0	22 00.0	-54.0	0.0	90
	15°			16°			17°			18°			19°			20°			21°			22°			

LATITUDE CONTRARY NAME TO DECLINATION — L.H.A. 26°, 334°

Dec. °	15° Hc ° ′	15° d ′	15° Z °	16° Hc ° ′	16° d ′	16° Z °	17° Hc ° ′	17° d ′	17° Z °	18° Hc ° ′	18° d ′	18° Z °
0	60 14.8	-32.0	118.0	59 46.0	-33.5	119.5	59 15.8	-34.9	120.9	58 44.3	-36.3	122.4
1	59 42.8	-33.2	119.6	59 12.5	-34.7	121.1	58 40.9	-36.1	122.5	58 08.0	-37.3	123.9
2	59 09.6	-34.4	121.3	58 37.8	-35.7	122.7	58 04.8	-37.0	124.0	57 30.7	-38.3	125.3
3	58 35.2	-35.5	122.9	58 02.1	-36.9	124.2	57 27.8	-38.1	125.5	56 52.4	-39.3	126.8
4	57 59.7	-36.6	124.4	57 25.2	-37.8	125.7	56 49.7	-39.0	126.9	56 13.1	-40.1	128.1
5	57 23.1	-37.6	125.9	56 47.4	-38.8	127.1	56 10.7	-39.9	128.3	55 33.0	-41.0	129.5
6	56 45.5	-38.6	127.3	56 08.6	-39.7	128.5	55 30.8	-40.8	129.6	54 52.0	-41.7	130.7
7	56 06.9	-39.5	128.7	55 28.9	-40.5	129.8	54 50.0	-41.5	130.9	54 10.3	-42.5	132.0
8	55 27.4	-40.3	130.0	54 48.4	-41.4	131.1	54 08.5	-42.3	132.2	53 27.8	-43.2	133.2
9	54 47.1	-41.1	131.3	54 07.0	-42.0	132.4	53 26.2	-43.0	133.4	52 44.6	-43.8	134.3
10	54 06.0	-41.9	132.6	53 25.0	-42.8	133.6	52 43.2	-43.6	134.5	52 00.8	-44.4	135.5
11	53 24.1	-42.6	133.8	52 42.2	-43.4	134.8	51 59.6	-44.2	135.7	51 16.4	-45.0	136.5
12	52 41.5	-43.3	135.0	51 58.8	-44.1	135.9	51 15.4	-44.9	136.8	50 31.4	-45.6	137.6
13	51 58.2	-43.9	136.1	51 14.7	-44.7	137.0	50 30.5	-45.4	137.8	49 45.8	-46.1	138.6
14	51 14.3	-44.4	137.2	50 30.0	-45.2	138.0	49 45.1	-45.9	138.8	48 59.7	-46.6	139.6
15	50 29.9	-45.1	138.3	49 44.8	-45.7	139.1	48 59.2	-46.4	139.8	48 13.1	-47.0	140.5
16	49 44.8	-45.6	139.3	48 59.1	-46.3	140.1	48 12.8	-46.8	140.8	47 26.1	-47.4	141.5
17	48 59.2	-46.1	140.3	48 12.8	-46.7	141.0	47 26.0	-47.3	141.7	46 38.7	-47.9	142.4
18	48 13.1	-46.5	141.3	47 26.1	-47.1	141.9	46 38.7	-47.8	142.6	45 50.8	-48.3	143.2
19	47 26.6	-47.0	142.2	46 39.0	-47.6	142.9	45 50.9	-48.1	143.5	45 02.5	-48.6	144.1
20	46 39.6	-47.4	143.1	45 51.4	-48.0	143.7	45 02.8	-48.4	144.3	44 13.9	-49.0	144.9
21	45 52.2	-47.9	144.0	45 03.4	-48.3	144.6	44 14.4	-48.9	145.2	43 24.9	-49.3	145.7
22	45 04.3	-48.2	144.9	44 15.1	-48.7	145.4	43 25.5	-49.1	146.0	42 35.6	-49.6	146.5
23	44 16.1	-48.5	145.7	43 26.4	-49.0	146.2	42 36.4	-49.5	146.8	41 46.0	-49.8	147.2
24	43 27.6	-48.9	146.5	42 37.4	-49.4	147.0	41 46.9	-49.8	147.5	40 56.2	-50.2	148.0
25	42 38.7	-49.3	147.3	41 48.0	-49.6	147.8	40 57.1	-50.0	148.3	40 06.0	-50.5	148.7
26	41 49.4	-49.5	148.1	40 58.4	-49.9	148.5	40 07.1	-50.3	149.0	39 15.5	-50.6	149.4
27	40 59.9	-49.8	148.8	40 08.5	-50.2	149.3	39 16.8	-50.6	149.7	38 24.9	-51.0	150.1
28	40 10.1	-50.1	149.6	39 18.3	-50.5	150.0	38 26.2	-50.8	150.4	37 33.9	-51.1	150.8
29	39 20.0	-50.3	150.3	38 27.8	-50.7	150.7	37 35.4	-51.0	151.1	36 42.8	-51.3	151.4
30	38 29.7	-50.6	151.0	37 37.1	-50.9	151.4	36 44.4	-51.3	151.7	35 51.5	-51.6	152.1
31	37 39.1	-50.8	151.7	36 46.2	-51.1	152.0	35 53.1	-51.4	152.4	34 59.9	-51.7	152.7
32	36 48.3	-51.0	152.3	35 55.1	-51.4	152.7	35 01.7	-51.6	153.0	34 08.2	-52.0	153.3
33	35 57.3	-51.3	153.0	35 03.7	-51.5	153.3	34 10.1	-51.9	153.6	33 16.2	-52.0	153.9
34	35 06.0	-51.4	153.6	34 12.2	-51.7	153.9	33 18.2	-51.9	154.2	32 24.2	-52.3	154.5
35	34 14.6	-51.6	154.3	33 20.5	-51.9	154.5	32 26.3	-52.2	154.8	31 31.9	-52.4	155.1
36	33 23.0	-51.8	154.9	32 28.6	-52.1	155.1	31 34.1	-52.3	155.4	30 39.5	-52.6	155.7
37	32 31.2	-52.0	155.5	31 36.5	-52.2	155.7	30 41.8	-52.5	156.0	29 46.9	-52.7	156.2
38	31 39.2	-52.1	156.1	30 44.3	-52.3	156.3	29 49.3	-52.6	156.5	28 54.2	-52.8	156.8
39	30 47.1	-52.3	156.6	29 52.0	-52.6	156.9	28 56.7	-52.7	157.1	28 01.4	-52.9	157.3
40	29 54.8	-52.4	157.2	28 59.4	-52.6	157.4	28 04.0	-52.9	157.6	27 08.5	-53.1	157.8
41	29 02.4	-52.6	157.8	28 06.8	-52.8	158.0	27 11.1	-52.9	158.2	26 15.4	-53.2	158.4
42	28 09.8	-52.7	158.3	27 14.0	-52.9	158.5	26 18.2	-53.1	158.7	25 22.2	-53.3	158.9
43	27 17.1	-52.8	158.9	26 21.1	-53.0	159.0	25 25.1	-53.2	159.2	24 28.9	-53.3	159.4
44	26 24.3	-52.9	159.4	25 28.1	-53.1	159.6	24 31.9	-53.3	159.7	23 35.6	-53.5	159.9
45	25 31.4	-53.1	159.9	24 35.0	-53.2	160.1	23 38.6	-53.4	160.2	22 42.1	-53.6	160.4
46	24 38.3	-53.1	160.4	23 41.8	-53.3	160.6	22 45.2	-53.5	160.7	21 48.5	-53.6	160.9
47	23 45.2	-53.2	160.9	22 48.5	-53.4	161.1	21 51.7	-53.6	161.2	20 54.9	-53.8	161.3
48	22 52.0	-53.4	161.4	21 55.1	-53.5	161.6	20 58.1	-53.6	161.7	20 01.1	-53.8	161.8
49	21 58.6	-53.4	161.9	21 01.6	-53.6	162.1	20 04.5	-53.8	162.2	19 07.3	-53.8	162.3
50	21 05.2	-53.5	162.4	20 08.0	-53.7	162.5	19 10.7	-53.8	162.6	18 13.5	-54.0	162.7
51	20 11.7	-53.6	162.9	19 14.3	-53.7	163.0	18 16.9	-53.8	163.1	17 19.5	-54.0	163.2
52	19 18.1	-53.6	163.4	18 20.6	-53.8	163.5	17 23.1	-54.0	163.6	16 25.5	-54.1	163.7
53	18 24.5	-53.8	163.9	17 26.8	-53.9	163.9	16 29.1	-54.0	164.0	15 31.4	-54.1	164.1
54	17 30.7	-53.8	164.3	16 32.9	-53.9	164.4	15 35.1	-54.0	164.5	14 37.3	-54.1	164.6
55	16 36.9	-53.8	164.8	15 39.0	-54.0	164.9	14 41.1	-54.1	164.9	13 43.2	-54.3	165.0
56	15 43.1	-53.9	165.2	14 45.0	-54.0	165.3	13 47.0	-54.1	165.4	12 48.9	-54.2	165.4
57	14 49.2	-54.0	165.7	13 51.0	-54.1	165.8	12 52.9	-54.2	165.8	11 54.7	-54.3	165.9
58	13 55.2	-54.0	166.2	12 56.9	-54.1	166.2	11 58.7	-54.3	166.3	11 00.4	-54.4	166.3
59	13 01.2	-54.1	166.6	12 02.8	-54.1	166.7	11 04.4	-54.2	166.7	10 06.0	-54.3	166.7
60	12 07.1	-54.1	167.0	11 08.7	-54.2	167.1	10 10.2	-54.3	167.1	9 11.7	-54.4	167.2
61	11 13.0	-54.1	167.5	10 14.5	-54.3	167.5	9 15.9	-54.4	167.6	8 17.3	-54.5	167.6
62	10 18.9	-54.2	167.9	9 20.2	-54.3	168.0	8 21.5	-54.3	168.0	7 22.8	-54.4	168.0
63	9 24.7	-54.2	168.4	8 25.9	-54.3	168.4	7 27.2	-54.4	168.4	6 28.4	-54.5	168.4
64	8 30.5	-54.2	168.8	7 31.6	-54.3	168.8	6 32.8	-54.4	168.8	5 33.9	-54.5	168.9
65	7 36.3	-54.3	169.2	6 37.3	-54.3	169.3	5 38.4	-54.4	169.3	4 39.4	-54.5	169.3
66	6 42.0	-54.3	169.7	5 43.0	-54.4	169.7	4 44.0	-54.5	169.7	3 44.9	-54.5	169.7
67	5 47.7	-54.3	170.1	4 48.6	-54.4	170.1	3 49.5	-54.4	170.1	2 50.4	-54.5	170.1
68	4 53.4	-54.3	170.5	3 54.2	-54.4	170.5	2 55.1	-54.5	170.5	1 55.9	-54.6	170.5
69	3 59.1	-54.3	170.9	2 59.8	-54.4	170.9	2 00.6	-54.5	171.0	1 01.3	-54.5	171.0
70	3 04.8	-54.4	171.4	2 05.4	-54.4	171.4	1 06.1	-54.4	171.4	0 06.8	-54.5	171.4
71	2 10.4	-54.3	171.8	1 11.0	-54.4	171.8	0 11.7	-54.5	171.8	0 47.7	+54.6	8.2
72	1 16.1	-54.4	172.2	0 16.6	-54.4	172.2	0 42.8	+54.5	7.8	1 42.3	+54.5	7.8
73	0 21.7	-54.3	172.6	0 37.8	+54.4	7.4	1 37.3	+54.5	7.4	2 36.8	+54.5	7.4
74	0 32.6	+54.4	6.9	1 32.2	+54.4	6.9	2 31.8	+54.4	6.9	3 31.3	+54.5	7.0
75	1 27.0	+54.3	6.5	2 26.6	+54.4	6.5	3 26.2	+54.5	6.5	4 25.8	+54.5	6.5
76	2 21.3	+54.4	6.1	3 21.0	+54.4	6.1	4 20.7	+54.4	6.1	5 20.3	+54.5	6.1
77	3 15.7	+54.3	5.7	4 15.4	+54.4	5.7	5 15.1	+54.4	5.7	6 14.8	+54.5	5.7
78	4 10.0	+54.3	5.2	5 09.8	+54.3	5.3	6 09.5	+54.4	5.3	7 09.3	+54.4	5.3
79	5 04.3	+54.3	4.8	6 04.1	+54.4	4.8	7 03.9	+54.4	4.8	8 03.7	+54.4	4.8
80	5 58.6	+54.3	4.4	6 58.5	+54.3	4.4	7 58.3	+54.3	4.4	8 58.1	+54.4	4.4
81	6 52.9	+54.3	4.0	7 52.8	+54.2	4.0	8 52.6	+54.3	4.0	9 52.5	+54.3	4.0
82	7 47.2	+54.2	3.5	8 47.0	+54.3	3.5	9 46.9	+54.3	3.5	10 46.8	+54.3	3.6
83	8 41.4	+54.2	3.1	9 41.3	+54.2	3.1	10 41.2	+54.3	3.1	11 41.1	+54.3	3.1
84	9 35.6	+54.2	2.7	10 35.5	+54.2	2.7	11 35.5	+54.2	2.7	12 35.4	+54.2	2.7
85	10 29.8	+54.1	2.2	11 29.7	+54.2	2.2	12 29.7	+54.1	2.2	13 29.6	+54.2	2.3
86	11 23.9	+54.1	1.8	12 23.9	+54.1	1.8	13 23.8	+54.2	1.8	14 23.8	+54.1	1.8
87	12 18.0	+54.0	1.3	13 18.0	+54.0	1.4	14 18.0	+54.0	1.4	15 17.9	+54.1	1.4
88	13 12.0	+54.0	0.9	14 12.0	+54.0	0.9	15 12.0	+54.0	0.9	16 12.0	+54.0	0.9
89	14 06.0	+54.0	0.5	15 06.0	+54.0	0.5	16 06.0	+54.0	0.5	17 06.0	+54.0	0.5
90	15 00.0	+53.9	0.0	16 00.0	+53.9	0.0	17 00.0	+53.9	0.0	18 00.0	+53.9	0.0
	15°			16°			17°			18°		

Dec. °	19° Hc ° ′	19° d ′	19° Z °	20° Hc ° ′	20° d ′	20° Z °	21° Hc ° ′	21° d ′	21° Z °	22° Hc ° ′	22° d ′	22° Z °
0	58 11.6	-37.6	123.7	57 37.7	-38.8	125.0	57 02.7	-40.0	126.3	56 26.6	-41.0	127.5
1	57 34.0	-38.6	125.2	56 58.9	-39.8	126.5	56 22.7	-40.8	127.7	55 45.6	-41.9	128.8
2	56 55.4	-39.5	126.6	56 19.1	-40.5	127.8	55 41.9	-41.7	129.0	55 03.7	-42.7	130.1
3	56 15.9	-40.3	128.0	55 38.6	-41.5	129.1	55 00.2	-42.4	130.2	54 21.0	-43.3	131.3
4	55 35.6	-41.2	129.3	54 57.1	-42.1	130.4	54 17.8	-43.1	131.5	53 37.7	-44.0	132.5
5	54 54.4	-42.0	130.6	54 15.0	-42.9	131.6	53 34.7	-43.8	132.6	52 53.7	-44.7	133.6
6	54 12.4	-42.6	131.8	53 32.1	-43.6	132.8	52 50.9	-44.4	133.8	52 09.0	-45.2	134.7
7	53 29.8	-43.4	133.0	52 48.5	-44.3	134.0	52 06.5	-45.1	134.9	51 23.8	-45.8	135.8
8	52 46.4	-44.0	134.1	52 04.2	-44.8	135.1	51 21.4	-45.6	136.0	50 38.0	-46.3	136.8
9	52 02.4	-44.7	135.3	51 19.4	-45.4	136.1	50 35.8	-46.1	137.0	49 51.7	-46.8	137.8
10	51 17.7	-45.2	136.3	50 34.0	-45.9	137.2	49 49.7	-46.6	138.0	49 04.9	-47.3	138.8
11	50 32.5	-45.7	137.4	49 48.1	-46.5	138.2	49 03.1	-47.1	139.0	48 17.6	-47.7	139.7
12	49 46.8	-46.3	138.4	49 01.6	-46.9	139.2	48 16.0	-47.5	139.9	47 29.9	-48.2	140.6
13	49 00.5	-46.7	139.4	48 14.7	-47.3	140.1	47 28.5	-48.0	140.8	46 41.7	-48.5	141.5
14	48 13.8	-47.2	140.3	47 27.4	-47.8	141.0	46 40.5	-48.3	141.7	45 53.2	-48.9	142.3
15	47 26.6	-47.6	141.2	46 39.6	-48.2	141.9	45 52.2	-48.8	142.5	45 04.3	-49.2	143.2
16	46 39.0	-48.1	142.1	45 51.4	-48.6	142.8	45 03.4	-49.0	143.4	44 15.1	-49.6	144.0
17	45 50.9	-48.4	143.0	45 02.8	-48.9	143.6	44 14.4	-49.5	144.2	43 25.5	-49.9	144.7
18	45 02.5	-48.7	143.8	44 13.9	-49.3	144.4	43 24.9	-49.7	145.0	42 35.6	-50.1	145.5
19	44 13.8	-49.2	144.7	43 24.6	-49.5	145.2	42 35.2	-50.0	145.7	41 45.5	-50.5	146.2
20	43 24.6	-49.4	145.5	42 35.1	-49.9	146.0	41 45.2	-50.3	146.5	40 55.0	-50.7	147.0
21	42 35.2	-49.7	146.2	41 45.2	-50.2	146.7	40 54.9	-50.6	147.2	40 04.3	-50.9	147.7
22	41 45.5	-50.0	147.0	40 55.0	-50.4	147.5	40 04.3	-50.8	147.9	39 13.4	-51.2	148.4
23	40 55.5	-50.3	147.7	40 04.6	-50.7	148.2	39 13.5	-51.1	148.6	38 22.2	-51.5	149.0
24	40 05.2	-50.6	148.4	39 13.9	-50.9	148.9	38 22.4	-51.2	149.3	37 30.7	-51.6	149.7
25	39 14.6	-50.8	149.1	38 23.0	-51.2	149.5	37 31.2	-51.6	149.9	36 39.1	-51.8	150.3
26	38 23.8	-51.0	149.8	37 31.8	-51.4	150.2	36 39.6	-51.7	150.6	35 47.3	-52.0	150.9
27	37 32.8	-51.3	150.5	36 40.4	-51.5	150.9	35 47.9	-51.9	151.2	34 55.3	-52.2	151.6
28	36 41.5	-51.5	151.1	35 48.9	-51.8	151.5	34 56.0	-52.0	151.8	34 03.1	-52.4	152.1
29	35 50.0	-51.6	151.8	34 57.1	-52.0	152.1	34 04.0	-52.3	152.4	33 10.7	-52.5	152.7
30	34 58.4	-51.9	152.4	34 05.1	-52.1	152.7	33 11.7	-52.4	153.0	32 18.2	-52.7	153.3
31	34 06.5	-52.0	153.0	33 13.0	-52.3	153.3	32 19.3	-52.6	153.6	31 25.5	-52.8	153.9
32	33 14.5	-52.2	153.6	32 20.7	-52.5	153.9	31 26.7	-52.7	154.2	30 32.7	-53.0	154.4
33	32 22.3	-52.4	154.2	31 28.2	-52.6	154.5	30 34.0	-52.8	154.7	29 39.7	-53.1	155.0
34	31 29.9	-52.5	154.8	30 35.6	-52.8	155.0	29 41.2	-53.0	155.3	28 46.6	-53.2	155.5
35	30 37.4	-52.6	155.3	29 42.8	-52.8	155.6	28 48.2	-53.1	155.8	27 53.4	-53.3	156.0
36	29 44.8	-52.8	155.9	28 50.0	-53.1	156.1	27 55.1	-53.3	156.3	27 00.1	-53.5	156.5
37	28 52.0	-52.9	156.4	27 56.9	-53.1	156.7	27 01.8	-53.3	156.9	26 06.6	-53.5	157.1
38	27 59.1	-53.1	157.0	27 03.8	-53.2	157.2	26 08.5	-53.5	157.4	25 13.1	-53.7	157.6
39	27 06.0	-53.1	157.5	26 10.6	-53.4	157.7	25 15.0	-53.5	157.9	24 19.4	-53.7	158.0
40	26 12.9	-53.3	158.0	25 17.2	-53.5	158.2	24 21.5	-53.7	158.4	23 25.7	-53.9	158.5
41	25 19.6	-53.4	158.5	24 23.7	-53.5	158.7	23 27.8	-53.7	158.9	22 31.8	-53.9	159.0
42	24 26.2	-53.4	159.0	23 30.2	-53.7	159.2	22 34.1	-53.9	159.3	21 37.9	-54.0	159.5
43	23 32.8	-53.6	159.5	22 36.5	-53.7	159.7	21 40.2	-53.9	159.8	20 43.9	-54.1	160.0
44	22 39.2	-53.6	160.0	21 42.8	-53.8	160.2	20 46.3	-54.0	160.3	19 49.8	-54.1	160.4
45	21 45.6	-53.8	160.5	20 49.0	-53.9	160.6	19 52.3	-54.0	160.8	18 55.7	-54.2	160.9
46	20 51.8	-53.8	161.0	19 55.1	-54.0	161.1	18 58.3	-54.1	161.2	18 01.5	-54.3	161.3
47	19 58.0	-53.9	161.5	19 01.1	-54.0	161.6	18 04.2	-54.2	161.7	17 07.2	-54.3	161.8
48	19 04.1	-53.9	161.9	18 07.1	-54.1	162.0	17 10.0	-54.3	162.1	16 12.9	-54.4	162.2
49	18 10.2	-54.1	162.4	17 13.0	-54.2	162.5	16 15.7	-54.3	162.6	15 18.5	-54.5	162.7
50	17 16.1	-54.0	162.8	16 18.8	-54.2	162.9	15 21.4	-54.3	163.0	14 24.0	-54.4	163.1
51	16 22.1	-54.2	163.3	15 24.6	-54.3	163.4	14 27.1	-54.4	163.4	13 29.6	-54.6	163.5
52	15 27.9	-54.2	163.7	14 30.3	-54.3	163.8	13 32.7	-54.5	163.9	12 35.0	-54.5	163.9
53	14 33.7	-54.2	164.2	13 36.0	-54.4	164.3	12 38.2	-54.5	164.3	11 40.5	-54.7	164.4
54	13 39.5	-54.3	164.6	12 41.6	-54.4	164.7	11 43.7	-54.5	164.7	10 45.8	-54.6	164.8
55	12 45.2	-54.3	165.1	11 47.2	-54.4	165.1	10 49.2	-54.5	165.2	9 51.2	-54.7	165.2
56	11 50.9	-54.4	165.5	10 52.8	-54.5	165.5	9 54.7	-54.6	165.6	8 56.5	-54.7	165.6
57	10 56.5	-54.4	165.9	9 58.3	-54.5	166.0	9 00.1	-54.7	166.0	8 01.8	-54.7	166.0
58	10 02.1	-54.5	166.4	9 03.8	-54.6	166.4	8 05.4	-54.6	166.4	7 07.1	-54.7	166.5
59	9 07.6	-54.4	166.8	8 09.2	-54.6	166.8	7 10.8	-54.7	166.8	6 12.4	-54.8	166.9
60	8 13.2	-54.5	167.2	7 14.6	-54.5	167.2	6 16.1	-54.7	167.3	5 17.6	-54.8	167.3
61	7 18.7	-54.6	167.6	6 20.1	-54.7	167.7	5 21.4	-54.7	167.7	4 22.8	-54.8	167.7
62	6 24.1	-54.5	168.0	5 25.4	-54.6	168.1	4 26.7	-54.7	168.1	3 28.0	-54.8	168.1
63	5 29.6	-54.6	168.5	4 30.8	-54.6	168.5	3 32.0	-54.7	168.5	2 33.2	-54.8	168.5
64	4 35.0	-54.5	168.9	3 36.2	-54.7	168.9	2 37.3	-54.8	168.9	1 38.4	-54.8	168.9
65	3 40.5	-54.6	169.3	2 41.5	-54.7	169.3	1 42.5	-54.7	169.3	0 43.6	-54.8	169.3
66	2 45.9	-54.6	169.7	1 46.8	-54.6	169.7	0 47.8	-54.7	169.7	0 11.2	+54.9	10.3
67	1 51.3	-54.6	170.1	0 52.2	-54.7	170.1	0 06.9	+54.8	9.9	1 06.1	+54.8	9.9
68	0 56.7	-54.6	170.5	0 02.5	+54.7	9.5	1 01.7	+54.7	9.5	2 00.9	+54.8	9.5
69	0 02.1	-54.6	171.0	0 57.2	+54.6	9.0	1 56.4	+54.8	9.0	2 55.7	+54.8	9.1
70	0 52.5	+54.6	8.6	1 51.8	+54.7	8.6	2 51.2	+54.7	8.6	3 50.5	+54.8	8.6
71	1 47.1	+54.6	8.2	2 46.5	+54.7	8.2	3 45.9	+54.7	8.2	4 45.3	+54.7	8.2
72	2 41.7	+54.6	7.8	3 41.2	+54.6	7.8	4 40.6	+54.7	7.8	5 40.0	+54.8	7.8
73	3 36.3	+54.6	7.4	4 35.8	+54.6	7.4	5 35.3	+54.7	7.4	6 34.8	+54.7	7.4
74	4 30.9	+54.5	7.0	5 30.4	+54.6	7.0	6 30.0	+54.6	7.0	7 29.5	+54.8	7.0
75	5 25.4	+54.6	6.5	6 25.0	+54.6	6.6	7 24.6	+54.7	6.6	8 24.3	+54.6	6.6
76	6 20.0	+54.5	6.1	7 19.6	+54.6	6.1	8 19.3	+54.6	6.2	9 18.9	+54.7	6.2
77	7 14.5	+54.5	5.7	8 14.2	+54.5	5.7	9 13.9	+54.6	5.7	10 13.6	+54.6	5.8
78	8 09.0	+54.5	5.3	9 08.7	+54.6	5.3	10 08.5	+54.5	5.3	11 08.2	+54.6	5.3
79	9 03.5	+54.4	4.9	10 03.3	+54.4	4.9	11 03.0	+54.6	4.9	12 02.8	+54.6	4.9
80	9 57.9	+54.4	4.4	10 57.7	+54.5	4.4	11 57.6	+54.4	4.5	12 57.4	+54.5	4.5
81	10 52.3	+54.4	4.0	11 52.2	+54.4	4.0	12 52.0	+54.5	4.0	13 51.9	+54.4	4.1
82	11 46.7	+54.3	3.6	12 46.6	+54.3	3.6	13 46.5	+54.4	3.6	14 46.3	+54.5	3.6
83	12 41.0	+54.3	3.1	13 40.9	+54.4	3.2	14 40.9	+54.3	3.2	15 40.8	+54.3	3.2
84	13 35.3	+54.3	2.7	14 35.3	+54.2	2.7	15 35.2	+54.3	2.7	16 35.1	+54.3	2.7
85	14 29.6	+54.2	2.3	15 29.5	+54.2	2.3	16 29.5	+54.2	2.3	17 29.4	+54.3	2.3
86	15 23.8	+54.1	1.8	16 23.7	+54.2	1.8	17 23.7	+54.2	1.8	18 23.7	+54.2	1.8
87	16 17.9	+54.1	1.4	17 17.9	+54.1	1.4	18 17.9	+54.1	1.4	19 17.9	+54.1	1.4
88	17 12.0	+54.0	0.9	18 12.0	+54.0	0.9	19 12.0	+54.0	0.9	20 12.0	+54.0	0.9
89	18 06.0	+54.0	0.5	19 06.0	+54.0	0.5	20 06.0	+54.0	0.5	21 06.0	+54.0	0.5
90	19 00.0	+53.9	0.0	20 00.0	+53.9	0.0	21 00.0	+53.9	0.0	22 00.0	+53.9	0.0
	19°			20°			21°			22°		

S. Lat. {L.H.A. greater than 180° ....Zn=180°–Z
{L.H.A. less than 180°...........Zn=180°+Z

LATITUDE SAME NAME AS DECLINATION — L.H.A. 154°, 206°

27°, 333° L.H.A. LATITUDE SAME NAME AS DECLINATION

N. Lat. {L.H.A. greater than 180° .....Zn=Z; L.H.A. less than 180°............Zn=360°–Z}

Dec.	15° Hc	d	Z	16° Hc	d	Z	17° Hc	d	Z	18° Hc	d	Z	19° Hc	d	Z	20° Hc	d	Z	21° Hc	d	Z	22° Hc	d	Z	Dec.
°	° ′	′	°	° ′	′	°	° ′	′	°	° ′	′	°	° ′	′	°	° ′	′	°	° ′	′	°	° ′	′	°	°
0	59 23.4	+29.8	116.9	58 55.5	+31.4	118.4	58 26.3	+32.9	119.8	57 55.8	+34.3	121.2	57 24.1	+35.7	122.6	56 51.2	+37.0	123.9	56 17.2	+38.3	125.1	55 42.2	+39.4	126.3	0
1	59 53.2	+28.4	115.2	59 26.9	+30.1	116.7	58 59.2	+31.7	118.2	58 30.1	+33.2	119.7	57 59.8	+34.6	121.1	57 28.2	+36.0	122.4	56 55.5	+37.3	123.7	56 21.6	+38.6	125.0	1
2	60 21.6	+27.0	113.4	59 57.0	+28.7	115.0	59 30.9	+30.4	116.6	59 03.3	+32.0	118.1	58 34.4	+33.5	119.5	58 04.2	+34.9	120.9	57 32.8	+36.3	122.3	57 00.2	+37.5	123.6	2
3	60 48.6	+25.5	111.6	60 25.7	+27.3	113.3	60 01.3	+29.0	114.9	59 35.3	+30.6	116.4	59 07.9	+32.2	117.9	58 39.1	+33.8	119.4	58 09.1	+35.1	120.8	57 37.7	+36.6	122.1	3
4	61 14.1	+23.9	109.8	60 53.0	+25.8	111.5	60 30.3	+27.5	113.1	60 05.9	+29.3	114.7	59 40.1	+31.0	116.3	59 12.9	+32.5	117.8	58 44.2	+34.1	119.2	58 14.3	+35.5	120.6	4
5	61 38.0	+22.3	107.8	61 18.8	+24.2	109.6	60 57.8	+26.1	111.3	60 35.2	+27.9	112.9	60 11.1	+29.6	114.5	59 45.4	+31.2	116.1	59 18.3	+32.8	117.6	58 49.8	+34.3	119.1	5
6	62 00.3	+20.5	105.9	61 43.0	+22.5	107.7	61 23.9	+24.5	109.4	61 03.1	+26.4	111.1	60 40.7	+28.1	112.8	60 16.6	+29.9	114.4	59 51.1	+31.5	116.0	59 24.1	+33.1	117.5	6
7	62 20.8	+18.8	103.9	62 05.5	+20.8	105.7	61 48.4	+22.8	107.5	61 29.5	+24.7	109.3	61 08.8	+26.7	111.0	60 46.5	+28.5	112.6	60 22.6	+30.2	114.3	59 57.2	+31.9	115.8	7
8	62 39.6	+16.9	101.8	62 26.3	+19.1	103.7	62 11.2	+21.1	105.5	61 54.2	+23.1	107.3	61 35.5	+25.0	109.1	61 15.0	+26.9	110.8	60 52.8	+28.8	112.5	60 29.1	+30.5	114.1	8
9	62 56.5	+15.0	99.7	62 45.4	+17.1	101.6	62 32.3	+19.3	103.5	62 17.3	+21.5	105.4	62 00.5	+23.5	107.2	61 41.9	+25.4	109.0	61 21.6	+27.2	110.7	60 59.6	+29.0	112.4	9
10	63 11.5	+13.0•	97.6	63 02.5	+15.3	99.5	62 51.6	+17.5	101.4	62 38.8	+19.6	103.3	62 24.0	+21.7	105.2	62 07.3	+23.7	107.0	61 48.8	+25.7	108.8	61 28.6	+27.6	110.6	10
11	63 24.5	+11.0•	95.4	63 17.8	+13.3•	97.4	63 09.1	+15.6	99.3	62 58.4	+17.7	101.3	62 45.7	+19.9	103.2	62 31.0	+22.0	105.1	62 14.5	+24.1	106.9	61 56.2	+26.0	108.7	11
12	63 35.5	+9.0•	93.2	63 31.1	+11.3•	95.2	63 24.7	+13.6•	97.2	63 16.1	+15.9	99.2	63 05.6	+18.0	101.1	62 53.0	+20.3	103.0	62 38.6	+22.3	104.9	62 22.2	+24.3	106.8	12
13	63 44.5	+6.9•	91.0	63 42.4	+9.3•	93.0	63 38.3	+11.5•	95.0	63 32.0	+13.9•	97.0	63 23.6	+16.2	99.0	63 13.3	+18.3	100.9	63 00.9	+20.5	102.9	62 46.5	+22.7	104.8	13
14	63 51.4	+4.8•	88.7	63 51.7	+7.1•	90.7	63 49.8	+9.6•	92.8	63 45.9	+11.8•	94.8	63 39.8	+14.1•	96.8	63 31.6	+16.4	98.8	63 21.4	+18.6	100.8	63 09.2	+20.8	102.7	14
15	63 56.2	+2.6•	86.4	63 58.8	+5.1•	88.5	63 59.4	+7.4•	90.5	63 57.7	+9.8•	92.6	63 53.9	+12.2•	94.6	63 48.0	+14.5•	96.7	63 40.0	+16.8	98.7	63 30.0	+18.9	100.6	15
16	63 58.8	+0.6•	84.2	64 03.9	+2.9•	86.2	64 06.8	+5.2•	88.3	64 07.5	+7.7•	90.3	64 06.1	+10.0•	92.4	64 02.5	+12.4•	94.4	63 56.8	+14.7•	96.5	63 48.9	+17.1	98.5	16
17	63 59.4	-1.7•	81.9	64 06.8	+0.7•	83.9	64 12.0	+3.2•	86.0	64 15.2	+5.5•	88.1	64 16.1	+7.9•	90.1	64 14.9	+10.3•	92.2	64 11.5	+12.7•	94.3	64 06.0	+15.0•	96.3	17
18	63 57.7	-3.8•	79.6	64 07.5	-1.4•	81.6	64 15.2	+0.9•	83.7	64 20.7	+3.3•	85.8	64 24.0	+5.8•	87.8	64 25.2	+8.2•	89.9	64 24.2	+10.6•	92.0	64 21.0	+12.9•	94.1	18
19	63 53.9	-5.9•	77.3	64 06.1	-3.6•	79.3	64 16.1	-1.2•	81.4	64 24.0	+1.2•	83.4	64 29.8	+3.6•	85.5	64 33.4	+6.0•	87.6	64 34.8	+8.4•	89.7	64 33.9	+10.9•	91.8	19
20	63 48.0	-8.0•	75.1	64 02.5	-5.7•	77.1	64 14.9	-3.4•	79.1	64 25.2	-1.0•	81.1	64 33.4	+1.4•	83.2	64 39.4	+3.8•	85.3	64 43.2	+6.2•	87.4	64 44.8	+8.7•	89.5	20
21	63 40.0	-10.0•	72.8	63 56.8	-7.9•	74.8	64 11.5	-5.5•	76.8	64 24.2	-3.2•	78.8	64 34.8	-0.9•	80.9	64 43.2	+1.6•	83.0	64 49.4	+4.1•	85.1	64 53.5	+6.4•	87.2	21
22	63 30.0	-12.1•	70.6	63 48.9	-9.9•	72.5	64 06.0	-7.7•	74.5	64 21.0	-5.4•	76.5	64 33.9	-3.0•	78.6	64 44.8	-0.6•	80.6	64 53.5	+1.8•	82.7	64 59.9	+4.3•	84.9	22
23	63 17.9	-14.1	68.4	63 39.0	-11.9•	70.3	63 58.3	-9.8•	72.2	64 15.6	-7.5•	74.2	64 30.9	-5.2•	76.2	64 44.2	-2.9•	78.3	64 55.3	-0.5•	80.4	65 04.2	+2.0•	82.5	23
24	63 03.8	-16.0	66.3	63 27.1	-14.0•	68.1	63 48.5	-11.8•	70.0	64 08.1	-9.6•	71.9	64 25.7	-7.3•	73.9	64 41.3	-5.0•	75.9	64 54.8	-2.6•	78.0	65 06.2	-0.2•	80.1	24
25	62 47.8	-17.9	64.2	63 13.1	-15.9	65.9	63 36.7	-13.8•	67.8	63 58.5	-11.7•	69.7	64 18.4	-9.5•	71.6	64 36.3	-7.2•	73.6	64 52.2	-4.9•	75.7	65 06.0	-2.5•	77.7	25
26	62 29.9	-19.7	62.1	62 57.2	-17.8	63.8	63 22.9	-15.8	65.6	63 46.8	-13.8•	67.4	64 08.9	-11.6•	69.4	64 29.1	-9.4•	71.3	64 47.3	-7.1•	73.3	65 03.5	-4.8•	75.4	26
27	62 10.2	-21.4	60.1	62 39.4	-19.6	61.7	63 07.1	-17.7	63.5	63 33.0	-15.7	65.3	63 57.3	-13.7•	67.1	64 19.7	-11.5•	69.0	64 40.2	-9.3•	71.0	64 58.7	-6.9•	73.0	27
28	61 48.8	-23.1	58.1	62 19.8	-21.4	59.7	62 49.4	-19.6	61.4	63 17.3	-17.6	63.1	63 43.6	-15.6	64.9	64 08.2	-13.6•	66.8	64 30.9	-11.4•	68.7	64 51.8	-9.2•	70.7	28
29	61 25.7	-24.8	56.1	61 58.4	-23.0	57.7	62 29.8	-21.3	59.3	62 59.7	-19.5	61.0	63 28.0	-17.6	62.7	63 54.6	-15.5	64.5	64 19.5	-13.4•	66.4	64 42.6	-11.3•	68.4	29
30	61 00.9	-26.3	54.2	61 35.4	-24.7	55.7	62 08.5	-23.1	57.3	62 40.2	-21.3	58.9	63 10.4	-19.4	60.6	63 39.1	-17.5•	62.4	64 06.1	-15.5•	64.2	64 31.3	-13.4•	66.1	30
31	60 34.6	-27.7	52.4	61 10.7	-26.3	53.8	61 45.4	-24.6	55.3	62 18.9	-23.0	56.9	62 51.0	-21.3	58.5	63 21.6	-19.5	60.2	63 50.6	-17.5	62.0	64 17.9	-15.4•	63.8	31
32	60 06.9	-29.2	50.6	60 44.4	-27.8	52.0	61 20.8	-26.3	53.4	61 55.9	-24.7	54.9	62 29.7	-23.0	56.5	63 02.1	-21.2	58.1	63 33.1	-19.4	59.8	64 02.5	-17.5•	61.6	32
33	59 37.7	-30.5	48.9	60 16.6	-29.1	50.2	60 54.5	-27.7	51.5	61 31.2	-26.2	53.0	62 06.7	-24.6	54.5	62 40.9	-23.0	56.1	63 13.7	-21.2	57.7	63 45.0	-19.4	59.4	33
34	59 07.2	-31.8	47.2	59 47.5	-30.6	48.4	60 26.8	-29.2	49.7	61 05.0	-27.7	51.1	61 42.1	-26.3	52.6	62 17.9	-24.6	54.1	62 52.5	-23.0	55.6	63 25.6	-21.2	57.3	34
35	58 35.4	-33.1	45.5	59 16.9	-31.8	46.7	59 57.6	-30.5	48.0	60 37.3	-29.2	49.3	61 15.8	-27.7	50.7	61 53.3	-26.3	52.1	62 29.5	-24.7	53.6	63 04.4	-23.0	55.2	35
36	58 02.3	-34.1	43.9	58 45.1	-33.0	45.1	59 27.1	-31.9	46.3	60 08.1	-30.6	47.5	60 48.1	-29.3	48.8	61 27.0	-27.8	50.2	62 04.8	-26.3	51.7	62 41.4	-24.7	53.2	36
37	57 28.2	-35.3	42.4	58 12.1	-34.2	43.5	58 55.2	-33.0	44.6	59 37.5	-31.9	45.8	60 18.8	-30.6	47.1	60 59.2	-29.3	48.4	61 38.5	-27.8	49.8	62 16.7	-26.3	51.2	37
38	56 52.9	-36.3	40.9	57 37.9	-35.3	41.9	58 22.2	-34.3	43.0	59 05.6	-33.1	44.1	59 48.2	-31.9	45.3	60 29.9	-30.6	46.6	61 10.7	-29.3	47.9	61 50.4	-27.9	49.3	38
39	56 16.6	-37.3	39.5	57 02.6	-36.3	40.4	57 47.9	-35.3	41.5	58 32.5	-34.3	42.5	59 16.3	-33.1	43.7	59 59.3	-32.0	44.9	60 41.4	-30.7	46.1	61 22.5	-29.4	47.4	39
40	55 39.3	-38.2	38.1	56 26.3	-37.3	39.0	57 12.6	-36.4	40.0	57 58.2	-35.3	41.0	58 43.2	-34.4	42.1	59 27.3	-33.2	43.2	60 10.7	-32.1	44.4	60 53.1	-30.8	45.6	40
41	55 01.1	-39.1	36.7	55 49.0	-38.3	37.6	56 36.2	-37.4	38.5	57 22.9	-36.5	39.5	58 08.8	-35.4	40.5	58 54.1	-34.4	41.6	59 38.6	-33.3	42.7	60 22.3	-32.1	43.9	41
42	54 22.0	-39.9	35.4	55 10.7	-39.1	36.2	55 58.8	-38.3	37.1	56 46.4	-37.4	38.0	57 33.4	-36.5	39.0	58 19.7	-35.5	40.0	59 05.3	-34.5	41.1	59 50.2	-33.4	42.2	42
43	53 42.1	-40.7	34.1	54 31.6	-40.0	34.9	55 20.5	-39.1	35.7	56 09.0	-38.4	36.6	56 56.9	-37.5	37.5	57 44.2	-36.6	38.5	58 30.8	-35.6	39.5	59 16.8	-34.6	40.5	43
44	53 01.4	-41.4	32.9	53 51.6	-40.7	33.6	54 41.4	-40.1	34.4	55 30.6	-39.2	35.2	56 19.4	-38.5	36.1	57 07.6	-37.6	37.0	57 55.2	-36.7	37.9	58 42.2	-35.7	39.0	44
45	52 20.0	-42.1	31.7	53 10.9	-41.5	32.4	54 01.3	-40.8	33.1	54 51.4	-40.1	33.9	55 40.9	-39.3	34.7	56 30.0	-38.5	35.6	57 18.5	-37.7	36.5	58 06.5	-36.8	37.4	45
46	51 37.9	-42.8	30.5	52 29.4	-42.2	31.2	53 20.5	-41.5	31.9	54 11.3	-40.9	32.6	55 01.6	-40.2	33.4	55 51.5	-39.5	34.2	56 40.8	-38.6	35.0	57 29.7	-37.8	35.9	46
47	50 55.1	-43.4	29.4	51 47.2	-42.8	30.0	52 39.0	-42.3	30.7	53 30.4	-41.6	31.4	54 21.4	-40.9	32.1	55 12.0	-40.2	32.9	56 02.2	-39.5	33.7	56 51.9	-38.7	34.5	47
48	50 11.7	-44.0	28.3	51 04.4	-43.5	28.9	51 56.7	-42.9	29.5	52 48.8	-42.4	30.2	53 40.5	-41.8	30.9	54 31.8	-41.1	31.6	55 22.7	-40.4	32.3	56 13.2	-39.7	33.1	48
49	49 27.7	-44.6	27.3	50 20.9	-44.1	27.8	51 13.8	-43.5	28.4	52 06.4	-43.0	29.0	52 58.7	-42.4	29.6	53 50.7	-41.8	30.3	54 42.3	-41.2	31.0	55 33.5	-40.5	31.8	49
50	48 43.1	-45.1	26.3	49 36.8	-44.6	26.8	50 30.3	-44.2	27.3	51 23.4	-43.6	27.9	52 16.3	-43.1	28.5	53 08.9	-42.5	29.1	54 01.1	-41.9	29.8	54 53.0	-41.2	30.5	50
51	47 58.0	-45.5	25.3	48 52.2	-45.2	25.7	49 46.1	-44.7	26.3	50 39.8	-44.2	26.8	51 33.2	-43.7	27.4	52 26.4	-43.2	27.9	53 19.2	-42.6	28.6	54 11.8	-42.1	29.2	51
52	47 12.5	-46.1	24.3	48 07.0	-45.6	24.8	49 01.4	-45.2	25.2	49 55.6	-44.8	25.7	50 49.5	-44.3	26.3	51 43.2	-43.8	26.8	52 36.6	-43.3	27.4	53 29.7	-42.7	28.0	52
53	46 26.4	-46.5	23.4	47 21.4	-46.1	23.8	48 16.2	-45.7	24.2	49 10.8	-45.3	24.7	50 05.2	-44.9	25.2	50 59.4	-44.4	25.7	51 53.3	-43.9	26.3	52 47.0	-43.4	26.9	53
54	45 39.9	-46.9	22.4	46 35.3	-46.6	22.8	47 30.5	-46.2	23.3	48 25.5	-45.8	23.7	49 20.3	-45.4	24.2	50 15.0	-45.0	24.7	51 09.4	-44.5	25.2	52 03.6	-44.1	25.7	54
55	44 53.0	-47.4	21.6	45 48.7	-47.0	21.9	46 44.3	-46.7	22.3	47 39.7	-46.3	22.7	48 34.9	-45.9	23.2	49 30.0	-45.5	23.6	50 24.9	-45.1	24.1	51 19.5	-44.6	24.6	55
56	44 05.6	-47.7	20.7	45 01.7	-47.4	21.1	45 57.6	-47.0	21.4	46 53.4	-46.7	21.8	47 49.0	-46.3	22.2	48 44.5	-46.0	22.6	49 39.8	-45.6	23.1	50 34.9	-45.2	23.6	56
57	43 17.9	-48.0	19.9	44 14.3	-47.8	20.2	45 10.6	-47.5	20.5	46 06.7	-47.2	20.9	47 02.7	-46.8	21.3	47 58.5	-46.5	21.7	48 54.2	-46.1	22.1	49 49.7	-45.7	22.5	57
58	42 29.9	-48.4	19.0	43 26.5	-48.1	19.4	44 23.1	-47.8	19.7	45 19.5	-47.5	20.0	46 15.9	-47.3	20.4	47 12.0	-46.9	20.7	48 08.1	-46.6	21.1	49 04.0	-46.3	21.5	58
59	41 41.5	-48.7	18.2	42 38.4	-48.5	18.5	43 35.3	-48.3	18.8	44 32.0	-47.9	19.1	45 28.6	-47.6	19.5	46 25.1	-47.3	19.8	47 21.5	-47.0	20.2	48 17.7	-46.7	20.6	59
60	40 52.8	-49.1	17.5	41 49.9	-48.7	17.7	42 47.0	-48.5	18.0	43 44.1	-48.3	18.3	44 41.0	-48.0	18.6	45 37.8	-47.8	18.9	46 34.5	-47.5	19.3	47 31.0	-47.1	19.6	60
61	40 03.7	-49.3	16.7	41 01.2	-49.1	17.0	41 58.5	-48.9	17.2	42 55.8	-48.6	17.5	43 53.0	-48.4	17.8	44 50.0	-48.1	18.1	45 47.0	-47.8	18.4	46 43.9	-47.6	18.7	61
62	39 14.4	-49.6	16.0	40 12.1	-49.4	16.2	41 09.6	-49.1	16.4	42 07.2	-49.0	16.7	43 04.6	-48.7	17.0	44 01.9	-48.4	17.2	44 59.2	-48.2	17.5	45 56.3	-47.9	17.8	62
63	38 24.8	-49.8	15.3	39 22.7	-49.7	15.5	40 20.5	-49.5	15.7	41 18.2	-49.2	15.9	42 15.9	-49.1	16.2	43 13.5	-48.9	16.4	44 11.0	-48.6	16.7	45 08.4	-48.3	17.0	63
64	37 35.0	-50.1	14.5	38 33.0	-49.9	14.7	39 31.0	-49.7	15.0	40 29.0	-49.6	15.2	41 26.8	-49.3	15.4	42 24.6	-49.1	15.6	43 22.4	-48.9	15.9	44 20.1	-48.7	16.2	64
65	36 44.9	-50.4	13.9	37 43.1	-50.2	14.0	38 41.3	-50.0	14.2	39 39.4	-49.8	14.4	40 37.5	-49.6	14.6	41 35.5	-49.4	14.9	42 33.5	-49.2	15.1	43 31.4	-49.0	15.3	65
66	35 54.5	-50.5	13.2	36 52.9	-50.4	13.3	37 51.3	-50.2	13.5	38 49.6	-50.1	13.7	39 47.9	-49.9	13.9	40 46.1	-49.7	14.1	41 44.3	-49.6	14.3	42 42.4	-49.4	14.6	66
67	35 04.0	-50.8	12.5	36 02.5	-50.6	12.7	37 01.1	-50.5	12.8	37 59.5	-50.3	13.0	38 58.0	-50.2	13.2	39 56.4	-50.0	13.4	40 54.7	-49.8	13.6	41 53.0	-49.6	13.8	67
68	34 13.2	-50.9	11.9	35 11.9	-50.8	12.0	36 10.6	-50.7	12.2	37 09.2	-50.5	12.3	38 07.8	-50.4	12.5	39 06.4	-50.3	12.7	40 04.9	-50.1	12.8	41 03.4	-49.9	13.0	68
69	33 22.3	-51.2	11.2	34 21.1	-51.0	11.4	35 19.9	-50.9	11.5	36 18.7	-50.8	11.6	37 17.4	-50.6	11.8	38 16.1	-50.4	12.0	39 14.8	-50.3	12.1	40 13.5	-50.2	12.3	69
70	32 31.1	-51.3	10.6	33 30.1	-51.3	10.7	34 29.0	-51.1	10.9	35 27.9	-51.0	11.0	36 26.8	-50.9	11.1	37 25.7	-50.8	11.3	38 24.5	-50.6	11.4	39 23.3	-50.5	11.6	70
71	31 39.8	-51.5	10.0	32 38.8	-51.4	10.1	33 37.9	-51.3	10.2	34 36.9	-51.1	10.3	35 35.9	-51.0	10.5	36 34.9	-50.9	10.6	37 33.9	-50.8	10.7	38 32.8	-50.7	10.9	71
72	30 48.3	-51.7	9.4	31 47.4	-51.5	9.5	32 46.6	-51.5	9.6	33 45.8	-51.4	9.7	34 44.9	-51.3	9.8	35 44.0	-51.2	10.0	36 43.1	-51.1	10.1	37 42.1	-50.9	10.2	72
73	29 56.6	-51.8	8.8	30 55.9	-51.8	8.9	31 55.1	-51.6	9.0	32 54.4	-51.6	9.1	33 53.6	-51.4	9.2	34 52.8	-51.3	9.3	35 52.0	-51.2	9.4	36 51.2	-51.1	9.5	73
74	29 04.8	-52.0	8.2	30 04.1	-51.9	8.3	31 03.5	-51.8	8.4	32 02.8	-51.7	8.5	33 02.2	-51.6	8.6	34 01.5	-51.5	8.7	35 00.8	-51.4	8.8	36 00.1	-51.3	8.9	74
75	28 12.8	-52.1	7.7	29 12.2	-52.0	7.7	30 11.7	-52.0	7.8	31 11.1	-51.8	7.9	32 10.6	-51.8	8.0	33 10.0	-51.7	8.1	34 09.4	-51.7	8.2	35 08.8	-51.6	8.3	75
76	27 20.7	-52.3	7.1	28 20.2	-52.2	7.2	29 19.7	-52.1	7.2	30 19.3	-52.1	7.3	31 18.8	-52.0	7.4	32 18.3	-51.9	7.5	33 17.7	-51.8	7.6	34 17.2	-51.7	7.6	76
77	26 28.4	-52.3	6.6	27 28.0	-52.3	6.6	28 27.6	-52.2	6.7	29 27.2	-52.2	6.7	30 26.8	-52.1	6.8	31 26.4	-52.1	6.9	32 25.9	-51.9	6.9	33 25.5	-51.9	7.0	77
78	25 36.1	-52.5	6.0	26 35.7	-52.4	6.1	27 35.4	-52.4	6.1	28 35.0	-52.3	6.2	29 34.7	-52.3	6.2	30 34.3	-52.2	6.3	31 34.0	-52.2	6.4	32 33.6	-52.1	6.4	78
79	24 43.6	-52.6	5.5	25 43.3	-52.6	5.5	26 43.0	-52.5	5.6	27 42.7	-52.4	5.6	28 42.4	-52.3	5.7	29 42.1	-52.3	5.7	30 41.8	-52.2	5.8	31 41.5	-52.2	5.8	79
80	23 51.0	-52.7	4.9	24 50.7	-52.6	5.0	25 50.5	-52.6	5.0	26 50.3	-52.6	5.1	27 50.1	-52.6	5.1	28 49.8	-52.5	5.2	29 49.6	-52.5	5.2	30 49.3	-52.4	5.3	80
81	22 58.3	-52.8	4.4	23 58.1	-52.8	4.5	24 57.9	-52.7	4.5	25 57.7	-52.7	4.5	26 57.5	-52.6	4.6	27 57.3	-52.6	4.6	28 57.1	-52.5	4.7	29 56.9	-52.5	4.7	81
82	22 05.5	-52.9	3.9	23 05.3	-52.8	3.9	24 05.2	-52.9	4.0	25 05.0	-52.8	4.0	26 04.9	-52.8	4.0	27 04.7	-52.7	4.1	28 04.6	-52.7	4.1	29 04.4	-52.6	4.1	82
83	21 12.6	-53.0	3.4	22 12.5	-53.0	3.4	23 12.3	-52.9	3.5	24 12.2	-52.9	3.5	25 12.1	-52.8	3.5	26 12.0	-52.8	3.5	27 11.9	-52.8	3.6	28 11.8	-52.8	3.6	83
84	20 19.6	-53.1	2.9	21 19.5	-53.1	2.9	22 19.4	-53.0	2.9	23 19.3	-53.0	3.0	24 19.3	-53.0	3.0	25 19.2	-53.0	3.0	26 19.1	-52.9	3.0	27 19.0	-52.9	3.1	84
85	19 26.5	-53.2	2.4	20 26.4	-53.1	2.4	21 26.4	-53.1	2.4	22 26.3	-53.1	2.5	23 26.3	-53.1	2.5	24 26.2	-53.0	2.5	25 26.2	-53.1	2.5	26 26.1	-53.0	2.5	85
86	18 33.3	-53.2	1.9	19 33.3	-53.2	1.9	20 33.3	-53.2	1.9	21 33.2	-53.2	2.0	22 33.2	-53.2	2.0	23 33.2	-53.2	2.0	24 33.1	-53.1	2.0	25 33.1	-53.1	2.0	86
87	17 40.1	-53.3	1.4	18 40.1	-53.3	1.4	19 40.1	-53.3	1.4	20 40.0	-53.2	1.5	21 40.0	-53.2	1.5	22 40.0	-53.2	1.5	23 40.0	-53.3	1.5	24 40.0	-53.3	1.5	87
88	16 46.8	-53.4	0.9	17 46.8	-53.4	1.0	18 46.8	-53.4	1.0	19 46.8	-53.4	1.0	20 46.8	-53.4	1.0	21 46.8	-53.4	1.0	22 46.7	-53.3	1.0	23 46.7	-53.3	1.0	88
89	15 53.4	-53.4	0.5	16 53.4	-53.4	0.5	17 53.4	-53.4	0.5	18 53.4	-53.4	0.5	19 53.4	-53.4	0.5	20 53.4	-53.4	0.5	21 53.4	-53.4	0.5	22 53.4	-53.4	0.5	89
90	15 00.0	-53.5	0.0	16 00.0	-53.5	0.0	17 00.0	-53.5	0.0	18 00.0	-53.5	0.0	19 00.0	-53.5	0.0	20 00.0	-53.5	0.0	21 00.0	-53.5	0.0	22 00.0	-53.5	0.0	90
	15°			16°			17°			18°			19°			20°			21°			22°			

27°, 333° L.H.A. LATITUDE SAME NAME AS DECLINATION

56

LATITUDE CONTRARY NAME TO DECLINATION L.H.A. 27°, 333°

Dec.	15°			16°			17°			18°		
	Hc	d	Z	Hc	d	Z	Hc	d	Z	Hc	d	Z
°	° ′	′	°	° ′	′	°	° ′	′	°	° ′	′	°
0	59 23.4	-31.2	116.9	58 55.5	-32.7	118.4	58 26.3	-34.1	119.8	57 55.8	-35.5	121.2
1	58 52.2	-32.4	118.6	58 22.8	-33.8	120.0	57 52.2	-35.2	121.4	57 20.3	-36.5	122.7
2	58 19.8	-33.6	120.2	57 49.0	-34.9	121.6	57 17.0	-36.3	122.9	56 43.8	-37.5	124.2
3	57 46.2	-34.7	121.8	57 14.1	-36.0	123.1	56 40.7	-37.2	124.4	56 06.3	-38.4	125.6
4	57 11.5	-35.7	123.3	56 38.1	-37.1	124.6	56 03.5	-38.2	125.8	55 27.9	-39.3	127.0
5	56 35.8	-36.8	124.8	56 01.0	-37.9	126.0	55 25.3	-39.1	127.2	54 48.6	-40.2	128.3
6	55 59.0	-37.7	126.2	55 23.1	-38.9	127.4	54 46.2	-39.9	128.5	54 08.4	-40.9	129.6
7	55 21.3	-38.6	127.6	54 44.2	-39.7	128.7	54 06.3	-40.7	129.8	53 27.5	-41.7	130.8
8	54 42.7	-39.5	128.9	54 04.5	-40.4	130.0	53 25.6	-41.5	131.0	52 45.8	-42.4	132.0
9	54 03.2	-40.3	130.2	53 24.1	-41.3	131.2	52 44.1	-42.2	132.2	52 03.4	-43.0	133.2
10	53 22.9	-41.0	131.4	52 42.8	-42.0	132.4	52 01.9	-42.8	133.4	51 20.4	-43.7	134.3
11	52 41.9	-41.8	132.7	52 00.8	-42.6	133.6	51 19.1	-43.5	134.5	50 36.7	-44.2	135.4
12	52 00.1	-42.5	133.8	51 18.2	-43.3	134.7	50 35.6	-44.0	135.6	49 52.5	-44.9	136.4
13	51 17.6	-43.0	135.0	50 34.9	-43.9	135.8	49 51.6	-44.7	136.7	49 07.6	-45.3	137.5
14	50 34.6	-43.7	136.1	49 51.0	-44.4	136.9	49 06.9	-45.1	137.7	48 22.3	-45.8	138.5
15	49 50.9	-44.3	137.2	49 06.6	-45.0	137.9	48 21.8	-45.7	138.7	47 36.5	-46.4	139.4
16	49 06.6	-44.8	138.2	48 21.6	-45.5	138.9	47 36.1	-46.1	139.7	46 50.1	-46.7	140.4
17	48 21.8	-45.3	139.2	47 36.1	-46.0	139.9	46 50.0	-46.6	140.6	46 03.4	-47.2	141.3
18	47 36.5	-45.9	140.2	46 50.1	-46.4	140.9	46 03.4	-47.0	141.5	45 16.2	-47.6	142.2
19	46 50.6	-46.2	141.1	46 03.7	-46.8	141.8	45 16.4	-47.5	142.4	44 28.6	-47.9	143.0
20	46 04.4	-46.7	142.1	45 16.9	-47.3	142.7	44 28.9	-47.8	143.3	43 40.7	-48.3	143.9
21	45 17.7	-47.2	143.0	44 29.6	-47.7	143.5	43 41.1	-48.1	144.1	42 52.4	-48.7	144.7
22	44 30.5	-47.5	143.8	43 41.9	-48.0	144.4	42 53.0	-48.5	144.9	42 03.7	-49.0	145.5
23	43 43.0	-47.8	144.7	42 53.9	-48.3	145.2	42 04.5	-48.8	145.7	41 14.7	-49.2	146.2
24	42 55.2	-48.3	145.5	42 05.6	-48.7	146.0	41 15.7	-49.2	146.5	40 25.5	-49.6	147.0
25	42 06.9	-48.5	146.3	41 16.9	-49.0	146.8	40 26.5	-49.4	147.3	39 35.9	-49.8	147.7
26	41 18.4	-48.9	147.1	40 27.9	-49.3	147.6	39 37.1	-49.7	148.0	38 46.1	-50.1	148.4
27	40 29.5	-49.2	147.9	39 38.6	-49.6	148.3	38 47.4	-50.0	148.7	37 56.0	-50.3	149.1
28	39 40.3	-49.4	148.6	38 49.0	-49.8	149.0	37 57.4	-50.2	149.4	37 05.7	-50.6	149.8
29	38 50.9	-49.7	149.3	37 59.2	-50.1	149.7	37 07.2	-50.4	150.1	36 15.1	-50.8	150.5
30	38 01.2	-50.0	150.1	37 09.1	-50.3	150.4	36 16.8	-50.7	150.8	35 24.3	-51.0	151.2
31	37 11.2	-50.2	150.8	36 18.8	-50.6	151.1	35 26.1	-50.8	151.5	34 33.3	-51.2	151.8
32	36 21.0	-50.4	151.4	35 28.2	-50.8	151.8	34 35.3	-51.1	152.1	33 42.1	-51.3	152.4
33	35 30.6	-50.7	152.1	34 37.4	-50.9	152.4	33 44.2	-51.3	152.8	32 50.8	-51.6	153.1
34	34 39.9	-50.9	152.8	33 46.5	-51.2	153.1	32 52.9	-51.4	153.4	31 59.2	-51.7	153.7
35	33 49.0	-51.0	153.4	32 55.3	-51.3	153.7	32 01.5	-51.7	154.0	31 07.5	-51.9	154.3
36	32 58.0	-51.3	154.0	32 04.0	-51.5	154.3	31 09.8	-51.7	154.6	30 15.6	-52.0	154.8
37	32 06.7	-51.4	154.7	31 12.5	-51.7	154.9	30 18.1	-52.0	155.2	29 23.6	-52.2	155.4
38	31 15.3	-51.6	155.3	30 20.8	-51.9	155.5	29 26.1	-52.1	155.7	28 31.4	-52.4	156.0
39	30 23.7	-51.7	155.9	29 28.9	-52.0	156.1	28 34.0	-52.2	156.3	27 39.0	-52.4	156.5
40	29 32.0	-51.9	156.4	28 36.9	-52.1	156.7	27 41.8	-52.3	156.9	26 46.6	-52.6	157.1
41	28 40.1	-52.0	157.0	27 44.8	-52.2	157.2	26 49.5	-52.5	157.4	25 54.0	-52.7	157.6
42	27 48.1	-52.2	157.6	26 52.6	-52.4	157.8	25 57.0	-52.6	158.0	25 01.3	-52.8	158.1
43	26 55.9	-52.3	158.1	26 00.2	-52.6	158.3	25 04.4	-52.7	158.5	24 08.5	-52.9	158.7
44	26 03.6	-52.4	158.7	25 07.6	-52.6	158.9	24 11.7	-52.9	159.0	23 15.6	-53.0	159.2
45	25 11.2	-52.6	159.2	24 15.0	-52.7	159.4	23 18.8	-52.9	159.5	22 22.6	-53.1	159.7
46	24 18.6	-52.6	159.8	23 22.3	-52.8	159.9	22 25.9	-53.0	160.1	21 29.5	-53.2	160.2
47	23 26.0	-52.8	160.3	22 29.5	-53.0	160.4	21 32.9	-53.1	160.6	20 36.3	-53.3	160.7
48	22 33.2	-52.8	160.8	21 36.5	-53.0	160.9	20 39.8	-53.2	161.1	19 43.0	-53.3	161.2
49	21 40.4	-53.0	161.3	20 43.5	-53.1	161.4	19 46.6	-53.3	161.5	18 49.7	-53.5	161.7
50	20 47.4	-53.0	161.8	19 50.4	-53.2	161.9	18 53.3	-53.3	162.0	17 56.2	-53.5	162.1
51	19 54.4	-53.1	162.3	18 57.2	-53.3	162.4	18 00.0	-53.4	162.5	17 02.7	-53.5	162.6
52	19 01.3	-53.2	162.8	18 03.9	-53.3	162.9	17 06.6	-53.5	163.0	16 09.2	-53.7	163.1
53	18 08.1	-53.3	163.3	17 10.6	-53.4	163.4	16 13.1	-53.6	163.5	15 15.5	-53.6	163.5
54	17 14.8	-53.3	163.8	16 17.2	-53.5	163.9	15 19.5	-53.6	163.9	14 21.9	-53.8	164.0
55	16 21.5	-53.4	164.3	15 23.7	-53.5	164.3	14 25.9	-53.6	164.4	13 28.1	-53.8	164.5
56	15 28.1	-53.5	164.7	14 30.2	-53.6	164.8	13 32.3	-53.7	164.9	12 34.3	-53.8	164.9
57	14 34.6	-53.5	165.2	13 36.6	-53.6	165.3	12 38.6	-53.8	165.3	11 40.5	-53.9	165.4
58	13 41.1	-53.6	165.7	12 43.0	-53.7	165.7	11 44.8	-53.8	165.8	10 46.6	-53.9	165.8
59	12 47.5	-53.6	166.1	11 49.3	-53.8	166.2	10 51.0	-53.8	166.2	9 52.7	-53.9	166.3
60	11 53.9	-53.6	166.6	10 55.5	-53.7	166.6	9 57.2	-53.9	166.7	8 58.8	-54.0	166.7
61	11 00.3	-53.7	167.0	10 01.8	-53.8	167.1	9 03.3	-53.9	167.1	8 04.8	-54.0	167.2
62	10 06.6	-53.8	167.5	9 08.0	-53.9	167.5	8 09.4	-54.0	167.6	7 10.8	-54.0	167.6
63	9 12.8	-53.8	167.9	8 14.1	-53.8	168.0	7 15.4	-53.9	168.0	6 16.8	-54.1	168.0
64	8 19.0	-53.8	168.4	7 20.3	-53.9	168.4	6 21.5	-54.0	168.4	5 22.7	-54.1	168.5
65	7 25.2	-53.8	168.8	6 26.4	-53.9	168.9	5 27.5	-54.0	168.9	4 28.6	-54.1	168.9
66	6 31.4	-53.8	169.3	5 32.5	-54.0	169.3	4 33.5	-54.0	169.3	3 34.5	-54.1	169.3
67	5 37.6	-53.9	169.7	4 38.5	-53.9	169.7	3 39.5	-54.0	169.8	2 40.4	-54.1	169.8
68	4 43.7	-53.9	170.2	3 44.6	-54.0	170.2	2 45.5	-54.1	170.2	1 46.3	-54.1	170.2
69	3 49.8	-53.9	170.6	2 50.6	-54.0	170.6	1 51.4	-54.0	170.6	0 52.2	-54.1	170.6
70	2 55.9	-53.9	171.1	1 56.6	-53.9	171.1	0 57.4	-54.1	171.1	0 01.9	+54.1	8.9
71	2 02.0	-53.9	171.5	1 02.7	-54.0	171.5	0 03.3	-54.0	171.5	0 56.0	+54.1	8.5
72	1 08.1	-53.9	171.9	0 08.7	-54.0	171.9	0 50.7	+54.1	8.1	1 50.1	+54.1	8.1
73	0 14.2	-54.0	172.4	0 45.3	+54.0	7.6	1 44.8	+54.0	7.6	2 44.2	+54.1	7.6
74	0 39.8	+53.9	7.2	1 39.3	+54.0	7.2	2 38.8	+54.1	7.2	3 38.3	+54.1	7.2
75	1 33.7	+53.9	6.8	2 33.3	+53.9	6.8	3 32.9	+54.0	6.8	4 32.4	+54.1	6.8
76	2 27.6	+53.9	6.3	3 27.2	+54.0	6.3	4 26.9	+54.0	6.3	5 26.5	+54.1	6.3
77	3 21.5	+53.9	5.9	4 21.2	+53.9	5.9	5 20.9	+54.0	5.9	6 20.6	+54.0	5.9
78	4 15.4	+53.9	5.4	5 15.1	+54.0	5.4	6 14.9	+53.9	5.4	7 14.6	+54.0	5.5
79	5 09.3	+53.8	5.0	6 09.1	+53.9	5.0	7 08.8	+54.0	5.0	8 08.6	+54.0	5.0
80	6 03.1	+53.9	4.5	7 03.0	+53.8	4.6	8 02.8	+53.9	4.6	9 02.6	+53.9	4.6
81	6 57.0	+53.8	4.1	7 56.8	+53.9	4.1	8 56.7	+53.9	4.1	9 56.5	+53.9	4.1
82	7 50.8	+53.8	3.7	8 50.7	+53.8	3.7	9 50.6	+53.8	3.7	10 50.4	+53.9	3.7
83	8 44.6	+53.7	3.2	9 44.5	+53.8	3.2	10 44.4	+53.8	3.2	11 44.3	+53.8	3.2
84	9 38.3	+53.8	2.8	10 38.3	+53.7	2.8	11 38.2	+53.8	2.8	12 38.1	+53.8	2.8
85	10 32.1	+53.6	2.3	11 32.0	+53.7	2.3	12 32.0	+53.7	2.3	13 31.9	+53.7	2.3
86	11 25.7	+53.7	1.9	12 25.7	+53.7	1.9	13 25.7	+53.6	1.9	14 25.6	+53.7	1.9
87	12 19.4	+53.6	1.4	13 19.4	+53.6	1.4	14 19.3	+53.7	1.4	15 19.3	+53.6	1.4
88	13 13.0	+53.5	0.9	14 13.0	+53.5	0.9	15 13.0	+53.5	0.9	16 12.9	+53.6	0.9
89	14 06.5	+53.5	0.5	15 06.5	+53.5	0.5	16 06.5	+53.5	0.5	17 06.5	+53.5	0.5
90	15 00.0	+53.4	0.0	16 00.0	+53.4	0.0	17 00.0	+53.4	0.0	18 00.0	+53.4	0.0
	15°			16°			17°			18°		

19°			20°			21°			22°			Dec.
Hc	d	Z	Hc	d	Z	Hc	d	Z	Hc	d	Z	
° ′	′	°	° ′	′	°	° ′	′	°	° ′	′	°	°
57 24.1	-36.8	122.6	56 51.2	-38.0	123.9	56 17.2	-39.2	125.1	55 42.2	-40.3	126.3	0
56 47.3	-37.7	124.0	56 13.2	-38.9	125.3	55 38.0	-40.0	126.5	55 01.9	-41.2	127.6	1
56 09.6	-38.7	125.4	55 34.3	-39.9	126.6	54 58.0	-40.9	127.8	54 20.7	-41.8	128.9	2
55 30.9	-39.6	126.8	54 54.4	-40.6	127.9	54 17.1	-41.6	129.0	53 38.9	-42.6	130.1	3
54 51.3	-40.4	128.1	54 13.8	-41.4	129.2	53 35.5	-42.4	130.3	52 56.3	-43.3	131.3	4
54 10.9	-41.1	129.4	53 32.4	-42.1	130.4	52 53.1	-43.0	131.5	52 13.0	-43.9	132.4	5
53 29.8	-41.9	130.6	52 50.3	-42.8	131.6	52 10.1	-43.7	132.6	51 29.1	-44.5	133.5	6
52 47.9	-42.6	131.8	52 07.5	-43.5	132.8	51 26.4	-44.3	133.7	50 44.6	-45.1	134.6	7
52 05.3	-43.3	133.0	51 24.0	-44.1	133.9	50 42.1	-44.9	134.8	49 59.5	-45.6	135.6	8
51 22.0	-43.9	134.1	50 39.9	-44.6	135.0	49 57.2	-45.4	135.8	49 13.9	-46.1	136.6	9
50 38.1	-44.4	135.2	49 55.3	-45.2	136.0	49 11.8	-45.9	136.8	48 27.8	-46.6	137.6	10
49 53.7	-45.0	136.2	49 10.1	-45.7	137.0	48 25.9	-46.4	137.8	47 41.2	-47.1	138.5	11
49 08.7	-45.5	137.2	48 24.4	-46.3	138.0	47 39.5	-46.9	138.8	46 54.1	-47.4	139.5	12
48 23.2	-46.1	138.2	47 38.1	-46.6	139.0	46 52.6	-47.2	139.7	46 06.7	-47.9	140.4	13
47 37.1	-46.5	139.2	46 51.5	-47.1	139.9	46 05.4	-47.7	140.6	45 18.8	-48.3	141.2	14
46 50.6	-46.9	140.1	46 04.4	-47.5	140.8	45 17.7	-48.1	141.4	44 30.5	-48.6	142.1	15
46 03.7	-47.3	141.0	45 16.9	-48.0	141.7	44 29.6	-48.5	142.3	43 41.9	-48.9	142.9	16
45 16.4	-47.8	141.9	44 28.9	-48.2	142.5	43 41.1	-48.7	143.1	42 53.0	-49.3	143.7	17
44 28.6	-48.1	142.8	43 40.7	-48.6	143.3	42 52.4	-49.1	143.9	42 03.7	-49.6	144.4	18
43 40.5	-48.4	143.6	42 52.1	-49.0	144.1	42 03.3	-49.5	144.7	41 14.1	-49.8	145.2	19
42 52.1	-48.8	144.4	42 03.1	-49.3	144.9	41 13.8	-49.7	145.4	40 24.3	-50.2	145.9	20
42 03.3	-49.2	145.2	41 13.8	-49.5	145.7	40 24.1	-50.0	146.2	39 34.1	-50.3	146.6	21
41 14.1	-49.4	146.0	40 24.3	-49.9	146.4	39 34.1	-50.2	146.9	38 43.8	-50.7	147.3	22
40 24.7	-49.7	146.7	39 34.4	-50.1	147.2	38 43.9	-50.5	147.6	37 53.1	-50.8	148.0	23
39 35.0	-49.9	147.4	38 44.3	-50.3	147.9	37 53.4	-50.7	148.3	37 02.3	-51.1	148.7	24
38 45.1	-50.2	148.2	37 54.0	-50.6	148.6	37 02.7	-51.0	149.0	36 11.2	-51.3	149.4	25
37 54.9	-50.5	148.9	37 03.4	-50.8	149.2	36 11.7	-51.1	149.6	35 19.9	-51.5	150.0	26
37 04.4	-50.7	149.5	36 12.6	-51.1	149.9	35 20.6	-51.4	150.3	34 28.4	-51.7	150.6	27
36 13.7	-50.9	150.2	35 21.5	-51.2	150.6	34 29.2	-51.5	150.9	33 36.7	-51.9	151.2	28
35 22.8	-51.1	150.9	34 30.3	-51.4	151.2	33 37.7	-51.8	151.5	32 44.8	-52.0	151.8	29
34 31.7	-51.3	151.5	33 38.9	-51.6	151.8	32 45.9	-51.9	152.1	31 52.8	-52.2	152.4	30
33 40.4	-51.5	152.1	32 47.3	-51.8	152.4	31 54.0	-52.1	152.7	31 00.6	-52.3	153.0	31
32 48.9	-51.7	152.7	31 55.5	-52.0	153.0	31 01.9	-52.2	153.3	30 08.3	-52.5	153.6	32
31 57.2	-51.8	153.3	31 03.5	-52.1	153.6	30 09.7	-52.3	153.9	29 15.8	-52.6	154.1	33
31 05.4	-52.0	153.9	30 11.4	-52.2	154.2	29 17.4	-52.6	154.4	28 23.2	-52.8	154.7	34
30 13.4	-52.2	154.5	29 19.2	-52.4	154.8	28 24.8	-52.6	155.0	27 30.4	-52.8	155.2	35
29 21.2	-52.3	155.1	28 26.8	-52.6	155.3	27 32.2	-52.8	155.5	26 37.6	-53.0	155.7	36
28 28.9	-52.5	155.6	27 34.2	-52.6	155.9	26 39.4	-52.8	156.1	25 44.6	-53.1	156.3	37
27 36.5	-52.5	156.2	26 41.6	-52.8	156.4	25 46.6	-53.0	156.6	24 51.5	-53.2	156.8	38
26 44.0	-52.7	156.7	25 48.8	-52.9	156.9	24 53.6	-53.1	157.1	23 58.3	-53.3	157.3	39
25 51.3	-52.8	157.3	24 55.9	-53.0	157.4	24 00.5	-53.2	157.6	23 05.0	-53.4	157.8	40
24 58.5	-52.9	157.8	24 02.9	-53.1	158.0	23 07.3	-53.3	158.1	22 11.6	-53.5	158.3	41
24 05.6	-53.0	158.3	23 09.8	-53.2	158.5	22 14.0	-53.4	158.6	21 18.1	-53.6	158.8	42
23 12.6	-53.1	158.8	22 16.6	-53.3	159.0	21 20.6	-53.5	159.1	20 24.5	-53.6	159.3	43
22 19.5	-53.2	159.3	21 23.3	-53.3	159.5	20 27.1	-53.5	159.6	19 30.9	-53.8	159.7	44
21 26.3	-53.3	159.8	20 30.0	-53.5	160.0	19 33.6	-53.7	160.1	18 37.1	-53.8	160.2	45
20 33.0	-53.3	160.3	19 36.5	-53.5	160.4	18 39.9	-53.7	160.6	17 43.3	-53.8	160.7	46
19 39.7	-53.5	160.8	18 43.0	-53.6	160.9	17 46.2	-53.7	161.0	16 49.5	-53.9	161.1	47
18 46.2	-53.5	161.3	17 49.4	-53.7	161.4	16 52.5	-53.8	161.5	15 55.6	-54.0	161.6	48
17 52.7	-53.6	161.8	16 55.7	-53.7	161.9	15 58.7	-53.9	162.0	15 01.6	-54.0	162.0	49
16 59.1	-53.6	162.2	16 02.0	-53.8	162.3	15 04.8	-54.0	162.4	14 07.6	-54.1	162.5	50
16 05.5	-53.7	162.7	15 08.2	-53.9	162.8	14 10.8	-53.9	162.9	13 13.5	-54.1	162.9	51
15 11.8	-53.8	163.2	14 14.3	-53.9	163.2	13 16.9	-54.1	163.3	12 19.4	-54.2	163.4	52
14 18.0	-53.8	163.6	13 20.4	-53.9	163.7	12 22.8	-54.1	163.8	11 25.2	-54.2	163.8	53
13 24.2	-53.9	164.1	12 26.5	-54.0	164.1	11 28.7	-54.1	164.2	10 31.0	-54.2	164.3	54
12 30.3	-53.9	164.5	11 32.5	-54.1	164.6	10 34.6	-54.1	164.6	9 36.8	-54.3	164.7	55
11 36.4	-54.0	165.0	10 38.4	-54.0	165.0	9 40.5	-54.2	165.1	8 42.5	-54.3	165.1	56
10 42.4	-53.9	165.4	9 44.4	-54.1	165.5	8 46.3	-54.2	165.5	7 48.2	-54.3	165.5	57
9 48.5	-54.1	165.9	8 50.3	-54.2	165.9	7 52.1	-54.3	165.9	6 53.9	-54.4	166.0	58
8 54.4	-54.0	166.3	7 56.1	-54.1	166.3	6 57.8	-54.2	166.4	5 59.5	-54.4	166.4	59
8 00.4	-54.1	166.7	7 02.0	-54.2	166.8	6 03.6	-54.3	166.8	5 05.1	-54.3	166.8	60
7 06.3	-54.1	167.2	6 07.8	-54.2	167.2	5 09.3	-54.3	167.2	4 10.8	-54.4	167.3	61
6 12.2	-54.1	167.6	5 13.6	-54.2	167.6	4 15.0	-54.4	167.7	3 16.4	-54.5	167.7	62
5 18.1	-54.2	168.1	4 19.4	-54.3	168.1	3 20.6	-54.3	168.1	2 21.9	-54.4	168.1	63
4 23.9	-54.2	168.5	3 25.1	-54.2	168.5	2 26.3	-54.3	168.5	1 27.5	-54.4	168.5	64
3 29.7	-54.1	168.9	2 30.9	-54.3	168.9	1 32.0	-54.4	168.9	0 33.1	-54.4	168.9	65
2 35.6	-54.2	169.3	1 36.6	-54.3	169.4	0 37.6	-54.3	169.4	0 21.3	+54.5	10.6	66
1 41.4	-54.2	169.8	0 42.3	-54.2	169.8	0 16.7	+54.3	10.2	1 15.8	+54.4	10.2	67
0 47.2	-54.2	170.2	0 11.9	+54.3	9.8	1 11.0	+54.4	9.8	2 10.2	+54.4	9.8	68
0 07.0	+54.2	9.4	1 06.2	+54.2	9.4	2 05.4	+54.3	9.4	3 04.6	+54.4	9.4	69
1 01.2	+54.2	8.9	2 00.4	+54.3	8.9	2 59.7	+54.3	8.9	3 59.0	+54.4	9.0	70
1 55.4	+54.1	8.5	2 54.7	+54.2	8.5	3 54.0	+54.4	8.5	4 53.4	+54.4	8.5	71
2 49.5	+54.2	8.1	3 48.9	+54.3	8.1	4 48.4	+54.2	8.1	5 47.8	+54.3	8.1	72
3 43.7	+54.2	7.6	4 43.2	+54.2	7.7	5 42.6	+54.3	7.7	6 42.1	+54.3	7.7	73
4 37.9	+54.1	7.2	5 37.4	+54.2	7.2	6 36.9	+54.3	7.2	7 36.4	+54.3	7.3	74
5 32.0	+54.1	6.8	6 31.6	+54.2	6.8	7 31.2	+54.2	6.8	8 30.7	+54.3	6.8	75
6 26.1	+54.1	6.3	7 25.8	+54.1	6.4	8 25.4	+54.2	6.4	9 25.0	+54.3	6.4	76
7 20.2	+54.1	5.9	8 19.9	+54.1	5.9	9 19.6	+54.2	5.9	10 19.3	+54.2	6.0	77
8 14.3	+54.1	5.5	9 14.0	+54.1	5.5	10 13.8	+54.1	5.5	11 13.5	+54.2	5.5	78
9 08.4	+54.0	5.0	10 08.1	+54.1	5.0	11 07.9	+54.1	5.1	12 07.7	+54.1	5.1	79
10 02.4	+54.0	4.6	11 02.2	+54.0	4.6	12 02.0	+54.0	4.6	13 01.8	+54.1	4.6	80
10 56.4	+53.9	4.1	11 56.2	+54.0	4.2	12 56.0	+54.0	4.2	13 55.9	+54.0	4.2	81
11 50.3	+53.9	3.7	12 50.2	+53.9	3.7	13 50.0	+54.0	3.7	14 49.9	+54.0	3.7	82
12 44.2	+53.9	3.3	13 44.1	+53.9	3.3	14 44.0	+53.9	3.3	15 43.9	+53.9	3.3	83
13 38.1	+53.8	2.8	14 38.0	+53.8	2.8	15 37.9	+53.9	2.8	16 37.8	+53.9	2.8	84
14 31.9	+53.7	2.3	15 31.8	+53.8	2.4	16 31.8	+53.7	2.4	17 31.7	+53.8	2.4	85
15 25.6	+53.7	1.9	16 25.6	+53.7	1.9	17 25.5	+53.8	1.9	18 25.5	+53.7	1.9	86
16 19.3	+53.6	1.4	17 19.3	+53.6	1.4	18 19.3	+53.6	1.4	19 19.2	+53.7	1.4	87
17 12.9	+53.6	1.0	18 12.9	+53.6	1.0	19 12.9	+53.6	1.0	20 12.9	+53.6	1.0	88
18 06.5	+53.5	0.5	19 06.5	+53.5	0.5	20 06.5	+53.5	0.5	21 06.5	+53.5	0.5	89
19 00.0	+53.4	0.0	20 00.0	+53.4	0.0	21 00.0	+53.4	0.0	22 00.0	+53.4	0.0	90
19°			20°			21°			22°			

S. Lat. { L.H.A. greater than 180° ....Zn=180°–Z
L.H.A. less than 180°...........Zn=180°+Z

LATITUDE SAME NAME AS DECLINATION L.H.A. 153°, 207°

57

28°, 332° L.H.A. LATITUDE SAME NAME AS DECLINATION

N. Lat. {L.H.A. greater than 180° .....Zn=Z; L.H.A. less than 180°............Zn=360°–Z}

Dec.	15°			16°			17°			18°			19°			20°			21°			22°			Dec.
°	Hc ° ′	d ′	Z °	Hc ° ′	d ′	Z °	Hc ° ′	d ′	Z °	Hc ° ′	d ′	Z °	Hc ° ′	d ′	Z °	Hc ° ′	d ′	Z °	Hc ° ′	d ′	Z °	Hc ° ′	d ′	Z °	°
0	58 31.5	+29.0	116.0	58 04.5	+30.7	117.4	57 36.3	+32.1	118.8	57 06.7	+33.6	120.2	56 36.0	+34.9	121.5	56 04.1	+36.2	122.8	55 31.1	+37.5	124.0	54 57.0	+38.7	125.2	0
1	59 00.5	+27.8	114.3	58 35.2	+29.3	115.8	58 08.4	+30.9	117.2	57 40.3	+32.4	118.6	57 10.9	+33.9	120.0	56 40.3	+35.3	121.3	56 08.6	+36.5	122.6	55 35.7	+37.8	123.8	1
2	59 28.3	+26.3	112.5	59 04.5	+28.1	114.1	58 39.3	+29.7	115.6	58 12.7	+31.3	117.0	57 44.8	+32.7	118.5	57 15.6	+34.1	119.8	56 45.1	+35.6	121.2	56 13.5	+36.8	122.4	2
3	59 54.6	+24.8	110.8	59 32.6	+26.6	112.3	59 09.0	+28.3	113.9	58 44.0	+29.9	115.4	58 17.5	+31.5	116.9	57 49.7	+33.0	118.3	57 20.7	+34.4	119.7	56 50.3	+35.9	121.0	3
4	60 19.4	+23.3	108.9	59 59.2	+25.1	110.6	59 37.3	+26.9	112.2	59 13.9	+28.6	113.7	58 49.0	+30.3	115.2	58 22.7	+31.9	116.7	57 55.1	+33.3	118.1	57 26.2	+34.7	119.5	4
5	60 42.7	+21.7	107.1	60 24.3	+23.6	108.7	60 04.2	+25.4	110.4	59 42.5	+27.2	112.0	59 19.3	+28.9	113.6	58 54.6	+30.5	115.1	58 28.4	+32.1	116.6	58 00.9	+33.6	118.0	5
6	61 04.4	+20.1	105.1	60 47.9	+22.0	106.9	60 29.6	+23.9	108.6	60 09.7	+25.7	110.2	59 48.2	+27.5	111.8	59 25.1	+29.2	113.4	59 00.5	+30.9	114.9	58 34.5	+32.4	116.4	6
7	61 24.5	+18.3	103.2	61 09.9	+20.3	104.9	60 53.5	+22.3	106.7	60 35.4	+24.2	108.4	60 15.7	+26.0	110.1	59 54.3	+27.8	111.7	59 31.4	+29.5	113.3	59 06.9	+31.2	114.8	7
8	61 42.8	+16.5	101.2	61 30.2	+18.6	103.0	61 15.8	+20.6	104.8	60 59.6	+22.6	106.5	60 41.7	+24.5	108.2	60 22.1	+26.4	109.9	60 00.9	+28.1	111.5	59 38.1	+29.8	113.1	8
9	61 59.3	+14.7	99.1	61 48.8	+16.8	101.0	61 36.4	+18.9	102.8	61 22.2	+20.9	104.6	61 06.2	+22.9	106.3	60 48.5	+24.8	108.1	60 29.0	+26.7	109.7	60 07.9	+28.5	111.4	9
10	62 14.0	+12.8	97.1	62 05.6	+15.0	98.9	61 55.3	+17.1	100.8	61 43.1	+19.2	102.6	61 29.1	+21.3	104.4	61 13.3	+23.2	106.2	60 55.7	+25.1	107.9	60 36.4	+27.0	109.6	10
11	62 26.8	+10.9	95.0	62 20.6	+13.1	96.9	62 12.4	+15.3	98.8	62 02.3	+17.5	100.6	61 50.4	+19.5	102.5	61 36.5	+21.5	104.3	61 20.8	+23.5	106.0	61 03.4	+25.4	107.8	11
12	62 37.7	+8.9•	92.8	62 33.7	+11.1	94.8	62 27.7	+13.4	96.7	62 19.8	+15.5	98.6	62 09.9	+17.7	100.4	61 58.0	+19.8	102.3	61 44.3	+21.9	104.1	61 28.8	+23.8	105.9	12
13	62 46.6	+6.9•	90.7	62 44.8	+9.2	92.6	62 41.1	+11.4	94.6	62 35.3	+13.7	96.5	62 27.6	+15.8	98.4	62 17.8	+18.1	100.3	62 06.2	+20.1	102.1	61 52.6	+22.2	104.0	13
14	62 53.5	+4.9•	88.5	62 54.0	+7.2•	90.5	62 52.5	+9.5•	92.4	62 49.0	+11.7•	94.4	62 43.4	+14.0	96.3	62 35.9	+16.1	98.2	62 26.3	+18.3	100.1	62 14.8	+20.5	102.0	14
15	62 58.4	+2.8•	86.3	63 01.2	+5.1•	88.3	63 02.0	+7.4•	90.2	63 00.7	+9.7•	92.2	62 57.4	+12.0•	94.2	62 52.0	+14.3	96.1	62 44.6	+16.5	98.0	62 35.3	+18.6	99.9	15
16	63 01.2	+0.8•	84.1	63 06.3	+3.1•	86.1	63 09.4	+5.4•	88.0	63 10.4	+7.7•	90.0	63 09.4	+10.0•	92.0	63 06.3	+12.2•	94.0	63 01.1	+14.5	95.9	62 53.9	+16.7	97.9	16
17	63 02.0	–1.3•	81.9	63 09.4	+1.0•	83.9	63 14.8	+3.3•	85.8	63 18.1	+5.7•	87.8	63 19.4	+7.9•	89.8	63 18.5	+10.3•	91.8	63 15.6	+12.6•	93.8	63 10.6	+14.9	95.8	17
18	63 00.7	–3.3•	79.7	63 10.4	–1.0•	81.6	63 18.1	+1.3•	83.6	63 23.8	+3.5•	85.6	63 27.3	+5.9•	87.6	63 28.8	+8.2•	89.6	63 28.2	+10.5•	91.6	63 25.5	+12.8•	93.6	18
19	62 57.4	–5.4•	77.5	63 09.4	–3.1•	79.4	63 19.4	–0.9•	81.4	63 27.3	+1.5•	83.4	63 33.2	+3.8•	85.4	63 37.0	+6.2•	87.4	63 38.7	+8.5•	89.4	63 38.3	+10.9•	91.4	19
20	62 52.0	–7.4	75.3	63 06.3	–5.2•	77.2	63 18.5	–2.9•	79.2	63 28.8	–0.6•	81.1	63 37.0	+1.7•	83.1	63 43.2	+4.0•	85.1	63 47.2	+6.4•	87.1	63 49.2	+8.7•	89.2	20
21	62 44.6	–9.3•	73.1	63 01.1	–7.2•	75.0	63 15.6	–5.0•	76.9	63 28.2	–2.7•	78.9	63 38.7	–0.4•	80.9	63 47.2	+2.0•	82.9	63 53.6	+4.3•	84.9	63 57.9	+6.7•	86.9	21
22	62 35.3	–11.4	71.0	62 53.9	–9.2•	72.8	63 10.6	–7.0•	74.7	63 25.5	–4.8•	76.7	63 38.3	–2.5•	78.6	63 49.2	–0.3•	80.6	63 57.9	+2.1•	82.6	64 04.6	+4.5•	84.7	22
23	62 23.9	–13.2	68.9	62 44.7	–11.2	70.7	63 03.6	–9.0•	72.5	63 20.7	–6.9•	74.4	63 35.8	–4.6•	76.4	63 48.9	–2.3•	78.3	64 00.0	0.0•	80.3	64 09.1	+2.3•	82.4	23
24	62 10.7	–15.2	66.8	62 33.5	–13.1	68.5	62 54.6	–11.1•	70.4	63 13.8	–8.9•	72.2	63 31.2	–6.7•	74.1	63 46.6	–4.4•	76.1	64 00.0	–2.1•	78.1	64 11.4	+0.2•	80.1	24
25	61 55.5	–16.9	64.7	62 20.4	–15.0	66.4	62 43.5	–13.0	68.2	63 04.9	–10.9•	70.0	63 24.5	–8.8•	71.9	63 42.2	–6.6•	73.8	63 57.9	–4.3•	75.8	64 11.6	–2.0•	77.8	25
26	61 38.6	–18.7	62.7	62 05.4	–16.9	64.3	62 30.5	–14.9	66.1	62 54.0	–12.9	67.9	63 15.7	–10.8	69.7	63 35.6	–8.6•	71.6	63 53.6	–6.4•	73.5	64 09.6	–4.1•	75.5	26
27	61 19.9	–20.5	60.7	61 48.5	–18.6	62.3	62 15.6	–16.7	64.0	62 41.1	–14.8	65.7	63 04.9	–12.7•	67.5	63 27.0	–10.7•	69.4	63 47.2	–8.5•	71.3	64 05.5	–6.3•	73.2	27
28	60 59.4	–22.0	58.7	61 29.9	–20.4	60.3	61 58.9	–18.6	61.9	62 26.3	–16.7	63.6	62 52.2	–14.8	65.4	63 16.3	–12.7	67.2	63 38.7	–10.6•	69.0	63 59.2	–8.3•	70.9	28
29	60 37.4	–23.7	56.8	61 09.5	–22.0	58.3	61 40.3	–20.3	59.9	62 09.6	–18.4	61.6	62 37.4	–16.5	63.2	63 03.6	–14.6	65.0	63 28.1	–12.5•	66.8	63 50.9	–10.5•	68.7	29
30	60 13.7	–25.2	55.0	60 47.5	–23.6	56.4	61 20.0	–21.9	57.9	61 51.2	–20.3	59.5	62 20.9	–18.5	61.2	62 49.0	–16.5	62.9	63 15.6	–14.6•	64.6	63 40.4	–12.5•	66.5	30
31	59 48.5	–26.7	53.1	60 23.9	–25.2	54.6	60 58.1	–23.6	56.0	61 30.9	–21.9	57.5	62 02.4	–20.1	59.1	62 32.5	–18.4	60.8	63 01.0	–16.5	62.5	63 27.9	–14.5	64.3	31
32	59 21.8	–28.0	51.4	59 58.7	–26.6	52.7	60 34.5	–25.1	54.1	61 09.0	–23.5	55.6	61 42.3	–21.9	57.1	62 14.1	–20.1	58.7	62 44.5	–18.3	60.4	63 13.4	–16.4	62.1	32
33	58 53.8	–29.4	49.7	59 32.1	–28.0	50.9	60 09.4	–26.7	52.3	60 45.5	–25.1	53.7	61 20.4	–23.6	55.2	61 54.0	–21.9	56.7	62 26.2	–20.1	58.3	62 57.0	–18.3	60.0	33
34	58 24.4	–30.7	48.0	59 04.1	–29.4	49.2	59 42.7	–28.0	50.5	60 20.4	–26.7	51.9	60 56.8	–25.1	53.3	61 32.1	–23.5	54.7	62 06.1	–21.9	56.3	62 38.7	–20.1	57.9	34
35	57 53.7	–31.9	46.4	58 34.7	–30.7	47.5	59 14.7	–29.4	48.8	59 53.7	–28.0	50.1	60 31.7	–26.6	51.4	61 08.6	–25.2	52.8	61 44.2	–23.5	54.3	62 18.6	–21.9	55.8	35
36	57 21.8	–33.0	44.8	58 04.0	–31.9	45.9	58 45.3	–30.7	47.1	59 25.7	–29.4	48.3	60 05.1	–28.1	49.6	60 43.4	–26.6	51.0	61 20.7	–25.2	52.4	61 56.7	–23.6	53.9	36
37	56 48.8	–34.2	43.2	57 32.1	–33.1	44.3	58 14.6	–31.9	45.4	58 56.3	–30.7	46.6	59 37.0	–29.4	47.8	60 16.8	–28.1	49.1	60 55.5	–26.6	50.5	61 33.1	–25.1	51.9	37
38	56 14.6	–35.2	41.7	56 59.0	–34.1	42.8	57 42.7	–33.1	43.8	58 25.6	–32.0	45.0	59 07.6	–30.7	46.1	59 48.7	–29.5	47.4	60 28.9	–28.2	48.7	61 08.0	–26.8	50.0	38
39	55 39.4	–36.1	40.3	56 24.9	–35.2	41.3	57 09.6	–34.2	42.3	57 53.6	–33.1	43.4	58 36.9	–32.0	44.5	59 19.2	–30.7	45.6	60 00.7	–29.5	46.9	60 41.2	–28.1	48.2	39
40	55 03.3	–37.2	38.9	55 49.7	–36.3	39.8	56 35.4	–35.2	40.8	57 20.5	–34.2	41.8	58 04.9	–33.2	42.9	58 48.5	–32.1	44.0	59 31.2	–30.9	45.2	60 13.1	–29.6	46.4	40
41	54 26.1	–38.0	37.5	55 13.4	–37.1	38.4	56 00.2	–36.3	39.3	56 46.3	–35.3	40.3	57 31.7	–34.3	41.3	58 16.4	–33.2	42.4	59 00.3	–32.1	43.5	59 43.5	–31.0	44.7	41
42	53 48.1	–38.8	36.2	54 36.3	–38.1	37.0	55 23.9	–37.2	37.9	56 11.0	–36.4	38.8	56 57.4	–35.4	39.8	57 43.2	–34.4	40.8	58 28.2	–33.3	41.8	59 12.5	–32.2	43.0	42
43	53 09.3	–39.7	34.9	53 58.2	–38.9	35.7	54 46.7	–38.1	36.5	55 34.6	–37.2	37.4	56 22.0	–36.4	38.3	57 08.8	–35.5	39.3	57 54.9	–34.4	40.3	58 40.3	–33.4	41.3	43
44	52 29.6	–40.4	33.7	53 19.3	–39.7	34.4	54 08.6	–39.0	35.2	54 57.4	–38.2	36.0	55 45.6	–37.3	36.9	56 33.3	–36.4	37.8	57 20.5	–35.6	38.7	58 06.9	–34.5	39.7	44
45	51 49.2	–41.1	32.5	52 39.6	–40.4	33.2	53 29.6	–39.7	33.9	54 19.2	–39.0	34.7	55 08.3	–38.2	35.5	55 56.9	–37.4	36.4	56 44.9	–36.5	37.3	57 32.4	–35.7	38.2	45
46	51 08.1	–41.8	31.3	51 59.2	–41.2	32.0	52 49.9	–40.5	32.7	53 40.2	–39.8	33.4	54 30.1	–39.1	34.2	55 19.5	–38.4	35.0	56 08.4	–37.5	35.8	56 56.7	–36.6	36.7	46
47	50 26.3	–42.5	30.2	51 18.0	–41.9	30.8	52 09.4	–41.3	31.5	53 00.4	–40.6	32.1	53 51.0	–40.0	32.9	54 41.1	–39.2	33.6	55 30.9	–38.5	34.4	56 20.1	–37.6	35.3	47
48	49 43.8	–43.0	29.1	50 36.1	–42.5	29.7	51 28.1	–41.9	30.3	52 19.8	–41.4	30.9	53 11.0	–40.6	31.6	54 01.9	–40.0	32.3	54 52.4	–39.3	33.1	55 42.5	–38.6	33.9	48
49	49 00.8	–43.6	28.0	49 53.6	–43.1	28.6	50 46.2	–42.6	29.1	51 38.4	–42.0	29.8	52 30.4	–41.5	30.4	53 21.9	–40.8	31.1	54 13.1	–40.1	31.8	55 03.9	–39.4	32.5	49
50	48 17.2	–44.2	27.0	49 10.5	–43.7	27.5	50 03.6	–43.2	28.0	50 56.4	–42.6	28.6	51 48.9	–42.1	29.2	52 41.1	–41.5	29.9	53 33.0	–40.9	30.5	54 24.5	–40.2	31.2	50
51	47 33.0	–44.7	26.0	48 26.8	–44.2	26.4	49 20.4	–43.7	27.0	50 13.8	–43.3	27.5	51 06.8	–42.7	28.1	51 59.6	–42.2	28.7	52 52.1	–41.6	29.3	53 44.3	–41.0	30.0	51
52	46 48.3	–45.2	25.0	47 42.6	–44.8	25.4	48 36.7	–44.4	25.9	49 30.5	–43.9	26.4	50 24.1	–43.4	27.0	51 17.4	–42.8	27.5	52 10.5	–42.3	28.1	53 03.3	–41.8	28.7	52
53	46 03.1	–45.6	24.0	46 57.8	–45.2	24.5	47 52.3	–44.8	24.9	48 46.6	–44.3	25.4	49 40.7	–43.9	25.9	50 34.6	–43.5	26.4	51 28.2	–43.0	27.0	52 21.5	–42.4	27.6	53
54	45 17.5	–46.1	23.1	46 12.6	–45.7	23.5	47 07.5	–45.3	23.9	48 02.3	–45.0	24.4	48 56.8	–44.5	24.8	49 51.1	–44.0	25.3	50 45.2	–43.5	25.9	51 39.1	–43.1	26.4	54
55	44 31.4	–46.5	22.2	45 26.9	–46.2	22.6	46 22.2	–45.8	23.0	47 17.3	–45.4	23.4	48 12.3	–45.0	23.8	49 07.1	–44.6	24.3	50 01.7	–44.2	24.8	50 56.0	–43.6	25.3	55
56	43 44.9	–46.9	21.3	44 40.7	–46.6	21.7	45 36.4	–46.2	22.0	46 31.9	–45.9	22.4	47 27.3	–45.5	22.8	48 22.5	–45.1	23.3	49 17.5	–44.7	23.7	50 12.4	–44.3	24.2	56
57	42 58.0	–47.3	20.5	43 54.1	–46.9	20.8	44 50.2	–46.7	21.1	45 46.0	–46.3	21.5	46 41.8	–46.0	21.9	47 37.4	–45.6	22.3	48 32.8	–45.2	22.7	49 28.1	–44.8	23.2	57
58	42 10.7	–47.6	19.6	43 07.2	–47.4	19.9	44 03.5	–47.0	20.3	44 59.7	–46.7	20.6	45 55.8	–46.4	21.0	46 51.8	–46.1	21.3	47 47.6	–45.7	21.7	48 43.3	–45.4	22.2	58
59	41 23.1	–48.0	18.8	42 19.8	–47.7	19.1	43 16.5	–47.5	19.4	44 13.0	–47.1	19.7	45 09.4	–46.8	20.1	46 05.7	–46.5	20.4	47 01.9	–46.2	20.8	47 57.9	–45.8	21.2	59
60	40 35.1	–48.3	18.0	41 32.1	–48.0	18.3	42 29.0	–47.7	18.6	43 25.9	–47.5	18.9	44 22.6	–47.2	19.2	45 19.2	–46.9	19.5	46 15.7	–46.6	19.8	47 12.1	–46.3	20.2	60
61	39 46.8	–48.6	17.2	40 44.1	–48.4	17.5	41 41.3	–48.1	17.7	42 38.4	–47.9	18.0	43 35.4	–47.6	18.3	44 32.3	–47.3	18.6	45 29.1	–47.0	18.9	46 25.8	–46.8	19.3	61
62	38 58.2	–48.9	16.5	39 55.7	–48.6	16.7	40 53.2	–48.5	16.9	41 50.5	–48.2	17.2	42 47.8	–48.0	17.5	43 45.0	–47.7	17.8	44 42.1	–47.5	18.1	45 39.0	–47.1	18.4	62
63	38 09.3	–49.1	15.7	39 07.1	–49.0	15.9	40 04.7	–48.7	16.2	41 02.3	–48.5	16.4	41 59.8	–48.3	16.7	42 57.3	–48.1	16.9	43 54.6	–47.8	17.2	44 51.9	–47.5	17.5	63
64	37 20.2	–49.4	15.0	38 18.1	–49.2	15.2	39 16.0	–49.0	15.4	40 13.8	–48.8	15.6	41 11.5	–48.6	15.9	42 09.2	–48.4	16.1	43 06.8	–48.1	16.4	44 04.4	–48.0	16.6	64
65	36 30.8	–49.7	14.3	37 28.9	–49.5	14.5	38 27.0	–49.3	14.7	39 25.0	–49.1	14.9	40 22.9	–48.9	15.1	41 20.8	–48.7	15.3	42 18.7	–48.5	15.6	43 16.4	–48.2	15.8	65
66	35 41.1	–49.9	13.6	36 39.4	–49.7	13.8	37 37.7	–49.6	14.0	38 35.9	–49.4	14.1	39 34.0	–49.2	14.3	40 32.1	–49.0	14.6	41 30.2	–48.8	14.8	42 28.2	–48.6	15.0	66
67	34 51.2	–50.1	12.9	35 49.7	–50.0	13.1	36 48.1	–49.8	13.2	37 46.5	–49.6	13.4	38 44.8	–49.4	13.6	39 43.1	–49.3	13.8	40 41.4	–49.1	14.0	41 39.6	–49.0	14.2	67
68	34 01.1	–50.3	12.3	34 59.7	–50.2	12.4	35 58.3	–50.0	12.6	36 56.9	–49.9	12.7	37 55.4	–49.8	12.9	38 53.8	–49.5	13.1	39 52.3	–49.4	13.2	40 50.6	–49.2	13.4	68
69	33 10.8	–50.5	11.6	34 09.5	–50.4	11.7	35 08.3	–50.3	11.9	36 07.0	–50.1	12.0	37 05.6	–49.9	12.2	38 04.3	–49.8	12.3	39 02.9	–49.7	12.5	40 01.4	–49.5	12.7	69
70	32 20.3	–50.8	11.0	33 19.1	–50.5	11.1	34 18.0	–50.5	11.2	35 16.9	–50.4	11.3	36 15.7	–50.2	11.5	37 14.5	–50.1	11.6	38 13.2	–49.9	11.8	39 11.9	–49.8	12.0	70
71	31 29.5	–50.9	10.3	32 28.6	–50.8	10.4	33 27.5	–50.6	10.6	34 26.5	–50.5	10.7	35 25.5	–50.5	10.8	36 24.4	–50.3	10.9	37 23.3	–50.2	11.1	38 22.1	–50.0	11.2	71
72	30 38.6	–51.0	9.7	31 37.8	–51.0	9.8	32 36.9	–50.9	9.9	33 36.0	–50.8	10.0	34 35.0	–50.6	10.1	35 34.1	–50.5	10.3	36 33.1	–50.4	10.4	37 32.1	–50.3	10.5	72
73	29 47.6	–51.3	9.1	30 46.8	–51.1	9.2	31 46.0	–51.0	9.3	32 45.2	–50.9	9.4	33 44.4	–50.8	9.5	34 43.6	–50.8	9.6	35 42.7	–50.6	9.7	36 41.8	–50.5	9.9	73
74	28 56.3	–51.4	8.5	29 55.7	–51.3	8.6	30 55.0	–51.2	8.7	31 54.3	–51.1	8.8	32 53.6	–51.1	8.9	33 52.8	–50.9	9.0	34 52.1	–50.8	9.1	35 51.3	–50.7	9.2	74
75	28 04.9	–51.5	7.9	29 04.4	–51.5	8.0	30 03.8	–51.4	8.1	31 03.2	–51.3	8.2	32 02.5	–51.2	8.2	33 01.9	–51.1	8.3	34 01.3	–51.0	8.4	35 00.6	–50.9	8.5	75
76	27 13.4	–51.7	7.3	28 12.9	–51.6	7.4	29 12.4	–51.5	7.5	30 11.9	–51.5	7.6	31 11.3	–51.3	7.6	32 10.8	–51.3	7.7	33 10.3	–51.2	7.8	34 09.7	–51.1	7.9	76
77	26 21.7	–51.8	6.8	27 21.3	–51.8	6.8	28 20.9	–51.7	6.9	29 20.4	–51.6	7.0	30 20.0	–51.6	7.0	31 19.5	–51.4	7.1	32 19.1	–51.4	7.2	33 18.6	–51.3	7.3	77
78	25 29.9	–51.9	6.2	26 29.5	–51.8	6.3	27 29.2	–51.8	6.3	28 28.8	–51.7	6.4	29 28.4	–51.7	6.4	30 28.1	–51.7	6.5	31 27.7	–51.6	6.6	32 27.3	–51.5	6.6	78
79	24 38.0	–52.1	5.7	25 37.7	–52.0	5.7	26 37.4	–52.0	5.8	27 37.1	–51.9	5.8	28 36.7	–51.8	5.9	29 36.4	–51.7	5.9	30 36.1	–51.7	6.0	31 35.8	–51.7	6.0	79
80	23 45.9	–52.2	5.1	24 45.7	–52.2	5.2	25 45.4	–52.1	5.2	26 45.2	–52.1	5.2	27 44.9	–52.0	5.3	28 44.7	–52.0	5.3	29 44.4	–51.9	5.4	30 44.1	–51.8	5.4	80
81	22 53.7	–52.3	4.6	23 53.5	–52.2	4.6	24 53.3	–52.2	4.6	25 53.1	–52.1	4.7	26 52.9	–52.1	4.7	27 52.7	–52.0	4.8	28 52.5	–52.0	4.8	29 52.3	–52.0	4.9	81
82	22 01.4	–52.3	4.0	23 01.3	–52.4	4.1	24 01.1	–52.3	4.1	25 01.0	–52.3	4.1	26 00.8	–52.2	4.2	27 00.7	–52.2	4.2	28 00.5	–52.1	4.2	29 00.3	–52.1	4.3	82
83	21 09.1	–52.5	3.5	22 08.9	–52.4	3.5	23 08.8	–52.4	3.6	24 08.7	–52.4	3.6	25 08.6	–52.4	3.6	26 08.5	–52.3	3.7	27 08.4	–52.3	3.7	28 08.2	–52.2	3.7	83
84	20 16.6	–52.6	3.0	21 16.5	–52.5	3.0	22 16.4	–52.5	3.0	23 16.3	–52.5	3.1	24 16.2	–52.4	3.1	25 16.2	–52.5	3.1	26 16.1	–52.4	3.1	27 16.0	–52.4	3.2	84
85	19 24.0	–52.6	2.5	20 24.0	–52.7	2.5	21 23.9	–52.6	2.5	22 23.8	–52.5	2.5	23 23.8	–52.6	2.6	24 23.7	–52.5	2.6	25 23.7	–52.6	2.6	26 23.6	–52.5	2.6	85
86	18 31.4	–52.8	2.0	19 31.3	–52.7	2.0	20 31.3	–52.7	2.0	21 31.3	–52.7	2.0	22 31.2	–52.6	2.0	23 31.2	–52.7	2.0	24 31.1	–52.6	2.1	25 31.1	–52.6	2.1	86
87	17 38.6	–52.8	1.5	18 38.6	–52.8	1.5	19 38.6	–52.8	1.5	20 38.6	–52.8	1.5	21 38.6	–52.8	1.5	22 38.5	–52.7	1.5	23 38.5	–52.7	1.5	24 38.5	–52.7	1.5	87
88	16 45.8	–52.9	1.0	17 45.8	–52.9	1.0	18 45.8	–52.9	1.0	19 45.8	–52.8	1.0	20 45.8	–52.9	1.0	21 45.8	–52.9	1.0	22 45.8	–52.9	1.0	23 45.8	–52.9	1.0	88
89	15 52.9	–52.9	0.5	16 52.9	–52.9	0.5	17 52.9	–52.9	0.5	18 52.9	–52.9	0.5	19 52.9	–52.9	0.5	20 52.9	–52.9	0.5	21 52.9	–52.9	0.5	22 52.9	–52.9	0.5	89
90	15 00.0	–53.0	0.0	16 00.0	–53.0	0.0	17 00.0	–53.0	0.0	18 00.0	–53.0	0.0	19 00.0	–53.0	0.0	20 00.0	–53.0	0.0	21 00.0	–53.0	0.0	22 00.0	–53.0	0.0	90
	15°			16°			17°			18°			19°			20°			21°			22°			

28°, 332° L.H.A. LATITUDE SAME NAME AS DECLINATION

58

LATITUDE CONTRARY NAME TO DECLINATION — L.H.A. 28°, 332°

Dec.	15° Hc	d	Z	16° Hc	d	Z	17° Hc	d	Z	18° Hc	d	Z
°	° ′	′	°	° ′	′	°	° ′	′	°	° ′	′	°
0	58 31.5	-30.4	116.0	58 04.5	-31.9	117.4	57 36.3	-33.4	118.8	57 06.7	-34.7	120.2
1	58 01.1	-31.6	117.6	57 32.6	-33.0	119.0	57 02.9	-34.4	120.3	56 32.0	-35.7	121.7
2	57 29.5	-32.8	119.2	56 59.6	-34.1	120.5	56 28.5	-35.4	121.8	55 56.3	-36.7	123.1
3	56 56.7	-33.9	120.7	56 25.5	-35.2	122.0	55 53.1	-36.5	123.3	55 19.6	-37.6	124.5
4	56 22.8	-34.9	122.2	55 50.3	-36.2	123.5	55 16.6	-37.4	124.7	54 42.0	-38.6	125.9
5	55 47.9	-36.0	123.7	55 14.1	-37.2	124.9	54 39.2	-38.2	126.1	54 03.4	-39.3	127.2
6	55 11.9	-36.9	125.1	54 36.9	-38.0	126.3	54 01.0	-39.2	127.4	53 24.1	-40.2	128.5
7	54 35.0	-37.8	126.5	53 58.9	-38.9	127.6	53 21.8	-39.9	128.7	52 43.9	-40.9	129.7
8	53 57.2	-38.6	127.8	53 20.0	-39.7	128.9	52 41.9	-40.7	129.9	52 03.0	-41.6	130.9
9	53 18.6	-39.5	129.1	52 40.3	-40.4	130.1	52 01.2	-41.3	131.1	51 21.4	-42.2	132.1
10	52 39.1	-40.2	130.3	51 59.9	-41.2	131.3	51 19.9	-42.1	132.3	50 39.2	-43.0	133.2
11	51 58.9	-41.0	131.6	51 18.7	-41.9	132.5	50 37.8	-42.7	133.4	49 56.2	-43.5	134.3
12	51 17.9	-41.6	132.7	50 36.8	-42.5	133.6	49 55.1	-43.3	134.5	49 12.7	-44.0	135.3
13	50 36.3	-42.3	133.9	49 54.3	-43.1	134.7	49 11.8	-43.9	135.6	48 28.7	-44.7	136.4
14	49 54.0	-43.0	135.0	49 11.2	-43.7	135.8	48 27.9	-44.4	136.6	47 44.0	-45.1	137.4
15	49 11.0	-43.5	136.1	48 27.5	-44.2	136.9	47 43.5	-44.9	137.6	46 58.9	-45.6	138.3
16	48 27.5	-44.0	137.1	47 43.3	-44.7	137.9	46 58.6	-45.5	138.6	46 13.3	-46.0	139.3
17	47 43.5	-44.6	138.1	46 58.6	-45.3	138.9	46 13.1	-45.8	139.5	45 27.3	-46.5	140.2
18	46 58.9	-45.0	139.1	46 13.3	-45.7	139.8	45 27.3	-46.3	140.5	44 40.8	-46.9	141.1
19	46 13.9	-45.6	140.1	45 27.6	-46.1	140.7	44 41.0	-46.8	141.4	43 53.9	-47.3	142.0
20	45 28.3	-46.0	141.0	44 41.5	-46.6	141.6	43 54.2	-47.1	142.2	43 06.6	-47.7	142.8
21	44 42.3	-46.4	141.9	43 54.9	-47.0	142.5	43 07.1	-47.5	143.1	42 18.9	-47.9	143.6
22	43 55.9	-46.8	142.8	43 07.9	-47.3	143.4	42 19.6	-47.8	143.9	41 31.0	-48.4	144.5
23	43 09.1	-47.2	143.7	42 20.6	-47.7	144.2	41 31.8	-48.2	144.7	40 42.6	-48.6	145.2
24	42 21.9	-47.5	144.5	41 32.9	-48.0	145.0	40 43.6	-48.5	145.5	39 54.0	-49.0	146.0
25	41 34.4	-47.9	145.3	40 44.9	-48.4	145.8	39 55.1	-48.8	146.3	39 05.0	-49.2	146.8
26	40 46.5	-48.2	146.1	39 56.5	-48.6	146.6	39 06.3	-49.1	147.1	38 15.8	-49.5	147.5
27	39 58.3	-48.5	146.9	39 07.9	-49.0	147.4	38 17.2	-49.3	147.8	37 26.3	-49.7	148.2
28	39 09.8	-48.9	147.7	38 18.9	-49.2	148.1	37 27.9	-49.6	148.5	36 36.6	-50.0	148.9
29	38 20.9	-49.0	148.4	37 29.7	-49.5	148.8	36 38.3	-49.9	149.2	35 46.6	-50.2	149.6
30	37 31.9	-49.4	149.2	36 40.2	-49.7	149.5	35 48.4	-50.1	149.9	34 56.4	-50.4	150.3
31	36 42.5	-49.6	149.9	35 50.5	-49.9	150.2	34 58.3	-50.3	150.6	34 06.0	-50.6	150.9
32	35 52.9	-49.8	150.6	35 00.6	-50.2	150.9	34 08.0	-50.5	151.2	33 15.4	-50.9	151.6
33	35 03.1	-50.1	151.3	34 10.4	-50.4	151.6	33 17.5	-50.7	151.9	32 24.5	-51.0	152.2
34	34 13.0	-50.3	151.9	33 20.0	-50.6	152.2	32 26.8	-50.9	152.5	31 33.5	-51.2	152.8
35	33 22.7	-50.5	152.6	32 29.4	-50.8	152.9	31 35.9	-51.1	153.2	30 42.3	-51.3	153.4
36	32 32.2	-50.6	153.2	31 38.6	-51.0	153.5	30 44.8	-51.2	153.8	29 51.0	-51.6	154.0
37	31 41.6	-50.9	153.9	30 47.6	-51.1	154.1	29 53.6	-51.4	154.4	28 59.4	-51.6	154.6
38	30 50.7	-51.0	154.5	29 56.5	-51.3	154.7	29 02.2	-51.6	155.0	28 07.8	-51.8	155.2
39	29 59.7	-51.2	155.1	29 05.2	-51.5	155.3	28 10.6	-51.7	155.6	27 16.0	-52.0	155.8
40	29 08.5	-51.4	155.7	28 13.7	-51.6	155.9	27 18.9	-51.8	156.1	26 24.0	-52.1	156.3
41	28 17.1	-51.5	156.3	27 22.1	-51.7	156.5	26 27.1	-52.0	156.7	25 31.9	-52.2	156.9
42	27 25.6	-51.6	156.9	26 30.4	-51.9	157.1	25 35.1	-52.1	157.2	24 39.7	-52.3	157.4
43	26 34.0	-51.8	157.4	25 38.5	-52.0	157.6	24 43.0	-52.2	157.8	23 47.4	-52.4	158.0
44	25 42.2	-51.9	158.0	24 46.5	-52.1	158.2	23 50.8	-52.3	158.3	22 55.0	-52.5	158.5
45	24 50.3	-52.1	158.5	23 54.4	-52.2	158.7	22 58.5	-52.5	158.9	22 02.5	-52.7	159.0
46	23 58.2	-52.1	159.1	23 02.2	-52.4	159.2	22 06.0	-52.5	159.4	21 09.8	-52.7	159.5
47	23 06.1	-52.3	159.6	22 09.8	-52.4	159.8	21 13.5	-52.6	159.9	20 17.1	-52.8	160.0
48	22 13.8	-52.3	160.2	21 17.4	-52.6	160.3	20 20.9	-52.8	160.4	19 24.3	-52.9	160.5
49	21 21.5	-52.5	160.7	20 24.8	-52.6	160.8	19 28.1	-52.8	160.9	18 31.4	-52.9	161.0
50	20 29.0	-52.5	161.2	19 32.2	-52.7	161.3	18 35.3	-52.8	161.4	17 38.5	-53.1	161.5
51	19 36.5	-52.7	161.7	18 39.5	-52.8	161.8	17 42.5	-53.0	161.9	16 45.4	-53.1	162.0
52	18 43.8	-52.7	162.2	17 46.7	-52.9	162.3	16 49.5	-53.0	162.4	15 52.3	-53.2	162.5
53	17 51.1	-52.8	162.7	16 53.8	-52.9	162.8	15 56.5	-53.1	162.9	14 59.1	-53.2	163.0
54	16 58.3	-52.8	163.2	16 00.9	-53.0	163.3	15 03.4	-53.2	163.4	14 05.9	-53.3	163.5
55	16 05.5	-52.9	163.7	15 07.9	-53.1	163.8	14 10.2	-53.2	163.9	13 12.6	-53.3	163.9
56	15 12.6	-53.0	164.2	14 14.8	-53.1	164.3	13 17.0	-53.2	164.4	12 19.3	-53.4	164.4
57	14 19.6	-53.1	164.7	13 21.7	-53.2	164.8	12 23.8	-53.3	164.8	11 25.9	-53.5	164.9
58	13 26.5	-53.1	165.2	12 28.5	-53.2	165.2	11 30.5	-53.4	165.3	10 32.4	-53.4	165.3
59	12 33.4	-53.2	165.7	11 35.3	-53.3	165.7	10 37.1	-53.4	165.8	9 39.0	-53.6	165.8
60	11 40.2	-53.2	166.1	10 42.0	-53.3	166.2	9 43.7	-53.4	166.2	8 45.4	-53.5	166.3
61	10 47.0	-53.2	166.6	9 48.7	-53.4	166.6	8 50.3	-53.5	166.7	7 51.9	-53.6	166.7
62	9 53.8	-53.3	167.1	8 55.3	-53.4	167.1	7 56.8	-53.5	167.1	6 58.3	-53.6	167.2
63	9 00.5	-53.3	167.5	8 01.9	-53.4	167.6	7 03.3	-53.5	167.6	6 04.7	-53.6	167.6
64	8 07.2	-53.4	168.0	7 08.5	-53.4	168.0	6 09.8	-53.5	168.1	5 11.1	-53.6	168.1
65	7 13.8	-53.3	168.5	6 15.1	-53.5	168.5	5 16.3	-53.6	168.5	4 17.5	-53.7	168.5
66	6 20.5	-53.4	168.9	5 21.6	-53.5	168.9	4 22.7	-53.6	169.0	3 23.8	-53.7	169.0
67	5 27.1	-53.5	169.4	4 28.1	-53.5	169.4	3 29.1	-53.6	169.4	2 30.1	-53.6	169.4
68	4 33.6	-53.4	169.8	3 34.6	-53.5	169.9	2 35.5	-53.6	169.9	1 36.5	-53.7	169.9
69	3 40.2	-53.5	170.3	2 41.1	-53.6	170.3	1 41.9	-53.6	170.3	0 42.8	-53.7	170.3
70	2 46.7	-53.4	170.7	1 47.5	-53.5	170.8	0 48.3	-53.6	170.8	0 10.9	+53.7	9.2
71	1 53.3	-53.5	171.2	0 54.0	-53.6	171.2	0 05.3	+53.6	8.8	1 04.6	+53.7	8.8
72	0 59.8	-53.5	171.7	0 00.4	-53.5	171.7	0 58.9	+53.6	8.3	1 58.3	+53.6	8.3
73	0 06.3	-53.4	172.1	0 53.1	+53.5	7.9	1 52.5	+53.6	7.9	2 52.0	+53.6	7.9
74	0 47.1	+53.5	7.4	1 46.6	+53.6	7.4	2 46.1	+53.6	7.4	3 45.6	+53.7	7.5
75	1 40.6	+53.5	7.0	2 40.2	+53.5	7.0	3 39.7	+53.6	7.0	4 39.3	+53.6	7.0
76	2 34.1	+53.4	6.5	3 33.7	+53.5	6.5	4 33.3	+53.6	6.5	5 32.9	+53.6	6.6
77	3 27.5	+53.5	6.1	4 27.2	+53.5	6.1	5 26.9	+53.5	6.1	6 26.5	+53.6	6.1
78	4 21.0	+53.4	5.6	5 20.7	+53.5	5.6	6 20.4	+53.5	5.6	7 20.1	+53.6	5.6
79	5 14.4	+53.4	5.2	6 14.2	+53.4	5.2	7 13.9	+53.5	5.2	8 13.7	+53.5	5.2
80	6 07.8	+53.4	4.7	7 07.6	+53.4	4.7	8 07.4	+53.5	4.7	9 07.2	+53.5	4.7
81	7 01.2	+53.4	4.2	8 01.0	+53.4	4.3	9 00.9	+53.4	4.3	10 00.7	+53.5	4.3
82	7 54.6	+53.3	3.8	8 54.4	+53.4	3.8	9 54.3	+53.4	3.8	10 54.2	+53.4	3.8
83	8 47.9	+53.3	3.3	9 47.8	+53.3	3.3	10 47.7	+53.3	3.3	11 47.6	+53.3	3.4
84	9 41.2	+53.2	2.9	10 41.1	+53.3	2.9	11 41.0	+53.3	2.9	12 40.9	+53.4	2.9
85	10 34.4	+53.2	2.4	11 34.4	+53.2	2.4	12 34.3	+53.3	2.4	13 34.3	+53.2	2.4
86	11 27.6	+53.2	1.9	12 27.6	+53.2	1.9	13 27.6	+53.2	1.9	14 27.5	+53.3	1.9
87	12 20.8	+53.1	1.4	13 20.8	+53.1	1.4	14 20.8	+53.1	1.5	15 20.8	+53.1	1.5
88	13 13.9	+53.1	1.0	14 13.9	+53.1	1.0	15 13.9	+53.1	1.0	16 13.9	+53.1	1.0
89	14 07.0	+53.0	0.5	15 07.0	+53.0	0.5	16 07.0	+53.0	0.5	17 07.0	+53.0	0.5
90	15 00.0	+52.9	0.0	16 00.0	+52.9	0.0	17 00.0	+52.9	0.0	18 00.0	+52.9	0.0
	15°			16°			17°			18°		

19° Hc	d	Z	20° Hc	d	Z	21° Hc	d	Z	22° Hc	d	Z	Dec.
° ′	′	°	° ′	′	°	° ′	′	°	° ′	′	°	°
56 36.0	-36.0	121.5	56 04.1	-37.3	122.8	55 31.1	-38.5	124.0	54 57.0	-39.5	125.2	0
56 00.0	-37.0	122.9	55 26.8	-38.1	124.1	54 52.6	-39.2	125.3	54 17.5	-40.4	126.5	1
55 23.0	-37.9	124.3	54 48.7	-39.1	125.5	54 13.4	-40.2	126.6	53 37.1	-41.1	127.7	2
54 45.1	-38.8	125.7	54 09.6	-39.8	126.8	53 33.2	-40.8	127.9	52 56.0	-41.9	128.9	3
54 06.3	-39.6	127.0	53 29.8	-40.6	128.1	52 52.4	-41.7	129.1	52 14.1	-42.5	130.1	4
53 26.7	-40.4	128.3	52 49.2	-41.4	129.3	52 10.7	-42.3	130.3	51 31.6	-43.2	131.3	5
52 46.3	-41.1	129.5	52 07.8	-42.1	130.5	51 28.4	-42.9	131.4	50 48.4	-43.8	132.4	6
52 05.2	-41.8	130.7	51 25.7	-42.7	131.6	50 45.5	-43.6	132.6	50 04.6	-44.4	133.4	7
51 23.4	-42.5	131.8	50 43.0	-43.3	132.8	50 01.9	-44.1	133.6	49 20.1	-44.9	134.5	8
50 40.9	-43.1	133.0	49 59.7	-44.0	133.8	49 17.8	-44.7	134.7	48 35.3	-45.4	135.5	9
49 57.8	-43.8	134.1	49 15.7	-44.5	134.9	48 33.1	-45.2	135.7	47 49.9	-46.0	136.5	10
49 14.0	-44.2	135.1	48 31.2	-45.0	135.9	47 47.9	-45.7	136.7	47 03.9	-46.3	137.4	11
48 29.8	-44.8	136.1	47 46.2	-45.5	136.9	47 02.2	-46.2	137.6	46 17.6	-46.8	138.3	12
47 45.0	-45.4	137.1	47 00.7	-46.0	137.9	46 16.0	-46.6	138.6	45 30.8	-47.3	139.2	13
46 59.6	-45.7	138.1	46 14.7	-46.4	138.8	45 29.4	-47.1	139.5	44 43.5	-47.6	140.1	14
46 13.9	-46.3	139.0	45 28.3	-46.8	139.7	44 42.3	-47.4	140.4	43 55.9	-48.0	141.0	15
45 27.6	-46.6	140.0	44 41.5	-47.3	140.6	43 54.9	-47.8	141.2	43 07.9	-48.3	141.8	16
44 41.0	-47.1	140.8	43 54.2	-47.6	141.5	43 07.1	-48.2	142.0	42 19.6	-48.6	142.6	17
43 53.9	-47.5	141.7	43 06.6	-48.0	142.3	42 18.9	-48.4	142.9	41 31.0	-49.0	143.4	18
43 06.4	-47.8	142.6	42 18.6	-48.3	143.1	41 30.5	-48.8	143.6	40 42.0	-49.3	144.2	19
42 18.6	-48.1	143.4	41 30.3	-48.6	143.9	40 41.7	-49.2	144.4	39 52.7	-49.5	144.9	20
41 30.5	-48.5	144.2	40 41.7	-49.0	144.7	39 52.5	-49.3	145.2	39 03.2	-49.8	145.6	21
40 42.0	-48.8	145.0	39 52.7	-49.2	145.4	39 03.2	-49.7	145.9	38 13.3	-50.0	146.4	22
39 53.2	-49.1	145.7	39 03.5	-49.5	146.2	38 13.5	-49.9	146.6	37 23.3	-50.4	147.1	23
39 04.1	-49.4	146.5	38 14.0	-49.8	146.9	37 23.6	-50.2	147.3	36 32.9	-50.5	147.7	24
38 14.7	-49.6	147.2	37 24.2	-50.0	147.6	36 33.4	-50.4	148.0	35 42.4	-50.7	148.4	25
37 25.1	-49.9	147.9	36 34.2	-50.3	148.3	35 43.0	-50.6	148.7	34 51.7	-51.0	149.1	26
36 35.2	-50.1	148.6	35 43.9	-50.5	149.0	34 52.4	-50.8	149.3	34 00.7	-51.2	149.7	27
35 45.1	-50.3	149.3	34 53.4	-50.6	149.6	34 01.6	-51.0	150.0	33 09.5	-51.3	150.3	28
34 54.8	-50.6	150.0	34 02.8	-50.9	150.3	33 10.6	-51.3	150.6	32 18.2	-51.5	150.9	29
34 04.2	-50.7	150.6	33 11.9	-51.1	150.9	32 19.3	-51.3	151.2	31 26.7	-51.7	151.5	30
33 13.5	-51.0	151.2	32 20.8	-51.3	151.6	31 28.0	-51.6	151.8	30 35.0	-51.9	152.1	31
32 22.5	-51.1	151.9	31 29.5	-51.4	152.2	30 36.4	-51.7	152.4	29 43.1	-52.0	152.7	32
31 31.4	-51.3	152.5	30 38.1	-51.6	152.8	29 44.7	-51.9	153.0	28 51.1	-52.1	153.3	33
30 40.1	-51.5	153.1	29 46.5	-51.7	153.4	28 52.8	-52.0	153.6	27 59.0	-52.3	153.8	34
29 48.6	-51.6	153.7	28 54.8	-51.9	153.9	28 00.8	-52.1	154.2	27 06.7	-52.4	154.4	35
28 57.0	-51.8	154.3	28 02.9	-52.1	154.5	27 08.7	-52.3	154.7	26 14.3	-52.5	154.9	36
28 05.2	-51.9	154.9	27 10.8	-52.1	155.1	26 16.4	-52.4	155.3	25 21.8	-52.6	155.5	37
27 13.3	-52.1	155.4	26 18.7	-52.3	155.6	25 24.0	-52.6	155.8	24 29.2	-52.8	156.0	38
26 21.2	-52.2	156.0	25 26.4	-52.4	156.2	24 31.4	-52.6	156.4	23 36.4	-52.8	156.5	39
25 29.0	-52.3	156.5	24 34.0	-52.6	156.7	23 38.8	-52.7	156.9	22 43.6	-53.0	157.1	40
24 36.7	-52.4	157.1	23 41.4	-52.6	157.2	22 46.1	-52.9	157.4	21 50.6	-53.0	157.6	41
23 44.3	-52.5	157.6	22 48.8	-52.7	157.8	21 53.2	-52.9	157.9	20 57.6	-53.1	158.1	42
22 51.8	-52.6	158.1	21 56.1	-52.9	158.3	21 00.3	-53.0	158.4	20 04.5	-53.2	158.6	43
21 59.2	-52.8	158.6	21 03.2	-52.9	158.8	20 07.3	-53.1	158.9	19 11.3	-53.3	159.0	44
21 06.4	-52.8	159.2	20 10.3	-53.0	159.3	19 14.2	-53.2	159.4	18 18.0	-53.4	159.5	45
20 13.6	-52.9	159.7	19 17.3	-53.1	159.8	18 21.0	-53.3	159.9	17 24.6	-53.4	160.0	46
19 20.7	-53.0	160.2	18 24.2	-53.1	160.3	17 27.7	-53.3	160.4	16 31.2	-53.5	160.5	47
18 27.7	-53.0	160.7	17 31.1	-53.2	160.8	16 34.4	-53.4	160.9	15 37.7	-53.5	161.0	48
17 34.7	-53.2	161.2	16 37.9	-53.3	161.2	15 41.0	-53.4	161.3	14 44.2	-53.6	161.4	49
16 41.5	-53.2	161.6	15 44.6	-53.4	161.7	14 47.6	-53.5	161.8	13 50.6	-53.7	161.9	50
15 48.3	-53.2	162.1	14 51.2	-53.4	162.2	13 54.1	-53.6	162.3	12 56.9	-53.7	162.4	51
14 55.1	-53.4	162.6	13 57.8	-53.5	162.7	13 00.5	-53.6	162.7	12 03.2	-53.8	162.8	52
14 01.7	-53.3	163.1	13 04.3	-53.5	163.1	12 06.9	-53.7	163.2	11 09.4	-53.7	163.3	53
13 08.4	-53.5	163.5	12 10.8	-53.6	163.6	11 13.2	-53.7	163.7	10 15.7	-53.9	163.7	54
12 14.9	-53.4	164.0	11 17.2	-53.6	164.1	10 19.5	-53.7	164.1	9 21.8	-53.8	164.2	55
11 21.5	-53.6	164.5	10 23.6	-53.6	164.5	9 25.8	-53.8	164.6	8 28.0	-53.9	164.6	56
10 27.9	-53.5	164.9	9 30.0	-53.7	165.0	8 32.0	-53.8	165.0	7 34.1	-53.9	165.1	57
9 34.4	-53.6	165.4	8 36.3	-53.7	165.4	7 38.2	-53.8	165.5	6 40.2	-54.0	165.5	58
8 40.8	-53.6	165.8	7 42.6	-53.7	165.9	6 44.4	-53.8	165.9	5 46.2	-54.0	165.9	59
7 47.2	-53.7	166.3	6 48.9	-53.8	166.3	5 50.6	-53.9	166.4	4 52.2	-53.9	166.4	60
6 53.5	-53.7	166.7	5 55.1	-53.8	166.8	4 56.7	-53.9	166.8	3 58.3	-54.0	166.8	61
5 59.8	-53.7	167.2	5 01.3	-53.8	167.2	4 02.8	-53.9	167.2	3 04.3	-54.0	167.2	62
5 06.1	-53.7	167.6	4 07.5	-53.8	167.7	3 08.9	-53.9	167.7	2 10.3	-54.0	167.7	63
4 12.4	-53.7	168.1	3 13.7	-53.8	168.1	2 15.0	-54.0	168.1	1 16.3	-54.1	168.1	64
3 18.7	-53.8	168.5	2 19.9	-53.9	168.5	1 21.0	-53.9	168.6	0 22.2	-54.0	168.6	65
2 24.9	-53.7	169.0	1 26.0	-53.8	169.0	0 27.1	-53.9	169.0	0 31.8	+54.0	11.0	66
1 31.2	-53.8	169.4	0 32.2	-53.9	169.4	0 26.8	+53.9	10.6	1 25.8	+54.0	10.6	67
0 37.4	-53.8	169.9	0 21.7	+53.8	10.1	1 20.7	+54.0	10.1	2 19.8	+54.0	10.1	68
0 16.4	+53.7	9.7	1 15.5	+53.9	9.7	2 14.7	+53.9	9.7	3 13.8	+54.0	9.7	69
1 10.1	+53.8	9.2	2 09.4	+53.8	9.2	3 08.6	+53.9	9.3	4 07.8	+54.0	9.3	70
2 03.9	+53.7	8.8	3 03.2	+53.8	8.8	4 02.5	+53.9	8.8	5 01.8	+53.9	8.8	71
2 57.6	+53.8	8.4	3 57.0	+53.8	8.4	4 56.4	+53.8	8.4	5 55.7	+54.0	8.4	72
3 51.4	+53.7	7.9	4 50.8	+53.8	7.9	5 50.2	+53.9	7.9	6 49.7	+53.9	7.9	73
4 45.1	+53.7	7.5	5 44.6	+53.8	7.5	6 44.1	+53.8	7.5	7 43.6	+53.9	7.5	74
5 38.8	+53.7	7.0	6 38.4	+53.7	7.0	7 37.9	+53.8	7.0	8 37.5	+53.8	7.1	75
6 32.5	+53.7	6.6	7 32.1	+53.7	6.6	8 31.7	+53.8	6.6	9 31.3	+53.9	6.6	76
7 26.2	+53.6	6.1	8 25.8	+53.7	6.1	9 25.5	+53.7	6.1	10 25.2	+53.7	6.2	77
8 19.8	+53.6	5.7	9 19.5	+53.7	5.7	10 19.2	+53.7	5.7	11 18.9	+53.8	5.7	78
9 13.4	+53.6	5.2	10 13.2	+53.6	5.2	11 12.9	+53.7	5.2	12 12.7	+53.7	5.3	79
10 07.0	+53.5	4.8	11 06.8	+53.6	4.8	12 06.6	+53.6	4.8	13 06.4	+53.6	4.8	80
11 00.5	+53.5	4.3	12 00.4	+53.5	4.3	13 00.2	+53.6	4.3	14 00.0	+53.6	4.3	81
11 54.0	+53.5	3.8	12 53.9	+53.5	3.8	13 53.8	+53.5	3.9	14 53.6	+53.6	3.9	82
12 47.5	+53.4	3.4	13 47.4	+53.4	3.4	14 47.3	+53.4	3.4	15 47.2	+53.4	3.4	83
13 40.9	+53.3	2.9	14 40.8	+53.4	2.9	15 40.7	+53.4	2.9	16 40.6	+53.5	2.9	84
14 34.2	+53.3	2.4	15 34.2	+53.3	2.4	16 34.1	+53.3	2.4	17 34.1	+53.3	2.5	85
15 27.5	+53.2	1.9	16 27.5	+53.2	2.0	17 27.4	+53.3	2.0	18 27.4	+53.3	2.0	86
16 20.7	+53.2	1.5	17 20.7	+53.2	1.5	18 20.7	+53.2	1.5	19 20.7	+53.2	1.5	87
17 13.9	+53.1	1.0	18 13.9	+53.1	1.0	19 13.9	+53.1	1.0	20 13.9	+53.1	1.0	88
18 07.0	+53.0	0.5	19 07.0	+53.0	0.5	20 07.0	+53.0	0.5	21 07.0	+53.0	0.5	89
19 00.0	+52.9	0.0	20 00.0	+52.9	0.0	21 00.0	+52.9	0.0	22 00.0	+52.9	0.0	90
19°			20°			21°			22°			

S. Lat. {L.H.A. greater than 180° ....Zn=180°–Z; L.H.A. less than 180°...........Zn=180°+Z

LATITUDE SAME NAME AS DECLINATION — L.H.A. 152°, 208°

Dec.	15°			16°			17°			18°		
	Hc	d	Z	Hc	d	Z	Hc	d	Z	Hc	d	Z
°	° ′	′	°	° ′	′	°	° ′	′	°	° ′	′	°
0	57 39.1	+28.4	115.0	57 13.1	+29.9	116.4	56 45.7	+31.5	117.8	56 17.1	+32.9	119.1
1	58 07.5	+27.1	113.4	57 43.0	+28.7	114.8	57 17.2	+30.2	116.2	56 50.0	+31.7	117.6
2	58 34.6	+25.7	111.7	58 11.7	+27.3	113.2	57 47.4	+28.9	114.6	57 21.7	+30.5	116.1
3	59 00.3	+24.2	109.9	58 39.0	+26.0	111.5	58 16.3	+27.7	113.0	57 52.2	+29.3	114.4
4	59 24.5	+22.7	108.1	59 05.0	+24.5	109.7	58 44.0	+26.3	111.3	58 21.5	+27.9	112.8
5	59 47.2	+21.2	106.3	59 29.5	+23.1	107.9	59 10.3	+24.8	109.5	58 49.4	+26.6	111.1
6	60 08.4	+19.6	104.4	59 52.6	+21.5	106.1	59 35.1	+23.3	107.8	59 16.0	+25.2	109.4
7	60 28.0	+17.8	102.5	60 14.1	+19.8	104.2	59 58.4	+21.8	105.9	59 41.2	+23.6	107.6
8	60 45.8	+16.2	100.6	60 33.9	+18.2	102.3	60 20.2	+20.2	104.0	60 04.8	+22.1	105.7
9	61 02.0	+14.4	98.6	60 52.1	+16.5	100.4	60 40.4	+18.5	102.1	60 26.9	+20.5	103.9
10	61 16.4	+12.6	96.6	61 08.6	+14.7	98.4	60 58.9	+16.8	100.2	60 47.4	+18.8	101.9
11	61 29.0	+10.8	94.6	61 23.3	+12.9	96.4	61 15.7	+15.0	98.2	61 06.2	+17.1	100.0
12	61 39.8	+8.8	92.5	61 36.2	+11.0	94.3	61 30.7	+13.2	96.2	61 23.3	+15.3	98.0
13	61 48.6	+6.9	90.4	61 47.2	+9.1	92.3	61 43.9	+11.3	94.1	61 38.6	+13.5	96.0
14	61 55.5	+5.0	88.3	61 56.3	+7.2	90.2	61 55.2	+9.4	92.0	61 52.1	+11.6	93.9
15	62 00.5	+3.0	86.2	62 03.5	+5.3	88.1	62 04.6	+7.5	89.9	62 03.7	+9.7	91.8
16	62 03.5	+1.1	84.0	62 08.8	+3.3•	85.9	62 12.1	+5.5•	87.8	62 13.4	+7.7	89.7
17	62 04.6	-0.9•	81.9	62 12.1	+1.3•	83.8	62 17.6	+3.5•	85.7	62 21.1	+5.8	87.6
18	62 03.7	-2.9•	79.8	62 13.4	-0.7•	81.6	62 21.1	+1.5	83.5	62 26.9	+3.8•	85.4
19	62 00.8	-4.9	77.6	62 12.7	-2.7•	79.5	62 22.6	-0.4•	81.4	62 30.7	+1.7•	83.3
20	61 55.9	-6.8	75.5	62 10.0	-4.7	77.4	62 22.2	-2.5•	79.2	62 32.4	-0.2•	81.1
21	61 49.1	-8.7	73.4	62 05.3	-6.6	75.2	62 19.7	-4.4•	77.1	62 32.2	-2.3•	78.9
22	61 40.4	-10.6	71.3	61 58.7	-8.5	73.1	62 15.3	-6.5	74.9	62 29.9	-4.2•	76.8
23	61 29.8	-12.5	69.3	61 50.2	-10.5	71.0	62 08.8	-8.3	72.8	62 25.7	-6.3•	74.6
24	61 17.3	-14.3	67.2	61 39.7	-12.3	68.9	62 00.5	-10.3	70.7	62 19.4	-8.2	72.5
25	61 03.0	-16.0	65.2	61 27.4	-14.1	66.9	61 50.2	-12.2	68.6	62 11.2	-10.1	70.3
26	60 47.0	-17.8	63.2	61 13.3	-16.0	64.8	61 38.0	-14.1	66.5	62 01.1	-12.1	68.2
27	60 29.2	-19.5	61.3	60 57.3	-17.7	62.8	61 23.9	-15.8	64.5	61 49.0	-13.9	66.2
28	60 09.7	-21.0	59.4	60 39.6	-19.3	60.9	61 08.1	-17.6	62.5	61 35.1	-15.8	64.1
29	59 48.7	-22.7	57.5	60 20.3	-21.0	59.0	60 50.5	-19.3	60.5	61 19.3	-17.5	62.1
30	59 26.0	-24.1	55.7	59 59.3	-22.6	57.1	60 31.2	-20.9	58.6	61 01.8	-19.2	60.1
31	59 01.9	-25.6	53.9	59 36.7	-24.1	55.2	60 10.3	-22.5	56.7	60 42.6	-20.9	58.2
32	58 36.3	-26.9	52.1	59 12.6	-25.5	53.4	59 47.8	-24.1	54.8	60 21.7	-22.4	56.2
33	58 09.4	-28.3	50.4	58 47.1	-27.0	51.7	59 23.7	-25.5	53.0	59 59.3	-24.0	54.4
34	57 41.1	-29.6	48.8	58 20.1	-28.2	50.0	58 58.2	-26.9	51.2	59 35.3	-25.5	52.6
35	57 11.5	-30.8	47.1	57 51.9	-29.6	48.3	58 31.3	-28.3	49.5	59 09.8	-27.0	50.8
36	56 40.7	-31.9	45.6	57 22.3	-30.8	46.7	58 03.0	-29.5	47.8	58 42.8	-28.2	49.0
37	56 08.8	-33.1	44.0	56 51.5	-31.9	45.1	57 33.5	-30.8	46.2	58 14.6	-29.6	47.4
38	55 35.7	-34.1	42.5	56 19.6	-33.1	43.6	57 02.7	-32.0	44.6	57 45.0	-30.8	45.7
39	55 01.6	-35.0	41.1	55 46.5	-34.1	42.1	56 30.7	-33.1	43.1	57 14.2	-32.0	44.1
40	54 26.6	-36.1	39.7	55 12.4	-35.1	40.6	55 57.6	-34.1	41.6	56 42.2	-33.1	42.6
41	53 50.5	-36.9	38.3	54 37.3	-36.1	39.2	55 23.5	-35.2	40.1	56 09.1	-34.2	41.1
42	53 13.6	-37.8	37.0	54 01.2	-36.9	37.8	54 48.3	-36.1	38.7	55 34.9	-35.2	39.6
43	52 35.8	-38.6	35.7	53 24.3	-37.9	36.5	54 12.2	-37.0	37.3	54 59.7	-36.2	38.2
44	51 57.2	-39.4	34.5	52 46.4	-38.6	35.2	53 35.2	-37.9	36.0	54 23.5	-37.1	36.8
45	51 17.8	-40.1	33.2	52 07.8	-39.5	33.9	52 57.3	-38.7	34.7	53 46.4	-37.9	35.5
46	50 37.7	-40.9	32.1	51 28.3	-40.2	32.7	52 18.6	-39.5	33.4	53 08.5	-38.8	34.2
47	49 56.8	-41.4	30.9	50 48.1	-40.8	31.5	51 39.1	-40.2	32.2	52 29.7	-39.6	32.9
48	49 15.4	-42.1	29.8	50 07.3	-41.6	30.4	50 58.9	-41.0	31.0	51 50.1	-40.3	31.7
49	48 33.3	-42.7	28.7	49 25.7	-42.1	29.3	50 17.9	-41.6	29.9	51 09.8	-41.0	30.5
50	47 50.6	-43.3	27.7	48 43.6	-42.8	28.2	49 36.3	-42.2	28.7	50 28.8	-41.7	29.3
51	47 07.3	-43.8	26.6	48 00.8	-43.3	27.1	48 54.1	-42.8	27.7	49 47.1	-42.3	28.2
52	46 23.5	-44.3	25.6	47 17.5	-43.9	26.1	48 11.3	-43.4	26.6	49 04.8	-42.9	27.1
53	45 39.2	-44.8	24.7	46 33.6	-44.3	25.1	47 27.9	-44.0	25.6	48 21.9	-43.5	26.0
54	44 54.4	-45.2	23.7	45 49.3	-44.9	24.1	46 43.9	-44.4	24.6	47 38.4	-44.0	25.0
55	44 09.2	-45.7	22.8	45 04.4	-45.3	23.2	45 59.5	-44.9	23.6	46 54.4	-44.5	24.0
56	43 23.5	-46.1	21.9	44 19.1	-45.7	22.3	45 14.6	-45.4	22.6	46 09.9	-45.0	23.0
57	42 37.4	-46.4	21.0	43 33.4	-46.2	21.4	44 29.2	-45.8	21.7	45 24.9	-45.5	22.1
58	41 51.0	-46.9	20.2	42 47.2	-46.5	20.5	43 43.4	-46.3	20.8	44 39.4	-45.9	21.2
59	41 04.1	-47.2	19.3	42 00.7	-46.9	19.6	42 57.1	-46.6	19.9	43 53.5	-46.3	20.3
60	40 16.9	-47.5	18.5	41 13.8	-47.3	18.8	42 10.5	-47.0	19.1	43 07.2	-46.7	19.4
61	39 29.4	-47.8	17.7	40 26.5	-47.6	18.0	41 23.5	-47.3	18.3	42 20.5	-47.1	18.5
62	38 41.6	-48.2	17.0	39 38.9	-47.9	17.2	40 36.2	-47.7	17.4	41 33.4	-47.4	17.7
63	37 53.4	-48.4	16.2	38 51.0	-48.2	16.4	39 48.5	-48.0	16.6	40 46.0	-47.8	16.9
64	37 05.0	-48.7	15.5	38 02.8	-48.5	15.7	39 00.5	-48.3	15.9	39 58.2	-48.1	16.1
65	36 16.3	-49.0	14.7	37 14.3	-48.8	14.9	38 12.2	-48.6	15.1	39 10.1	-48.4	15.3
66	35 27.3	-49.2	14.0	36 25.5	-49.1	14.2	37 23.6	-48.8	14.4	38 21.7	-48.6	14.6
67	34 38.1	-49.5	13.3	35 36.4	-49.2	13.5	36 34.8	-49.1	13.6	37 33.1	-49.0	13.8
68	33 48.6	-49.6	12.6	34 47.2	-49.6	12.8	35 45.7	-49.4	12.9	36 44.1	-49.2	13.1
69	32 59.0	-49.9	12.0	33 57.6	-49.7	12.1	34 56.3	-49.6	12.2	35 54.9	-49.4	12.4
70	32 09.1	-50.1	11.3	33 07.9	-50.0	11.4	34 06.7	-49.8	11.6	35 05.5	-49.7	11.7
71	31 19.0	-50.3	10.6	32 17.9	-50.1	10.8	33 16.9	-50.1	10.9	34 15.8	-49.9	11.0
72	30 28.7	-50.5	10.0	31 27.8	-50.4	10.1	32 26.8	-50.2	10.2	33 25.9	-50.1	10.3
73	29 38.2	-50.6	9.4	30 37.4	-50.5	9.5	31 36.6	-50.4	9.6	32 35.8	-50.4	9.7
74	28 47.6	-50.8	8.8	29 46.9	-50.7	8.9	30 46.2	-50.6	8.9	31 45.4	-50.5	9.0
75	27 56.8	-50.9	8.2	28 56.2	-50.9	8.2	29 55.6	-50.8	8.3	30 54.9	-50.6	8.4
76	27 05.9	-51.1	7.6	28 05.3	-51.0	7.6	29 04.8	-50.9	7.7	30 04.3	-50.9	7.8
77	26 14.8	-51.3	7.0	27 14.3	-51.2	7.0	28 13.9	-51.1	7.1	29 13.4	-51.0	7.2
78	25 23.5	-51.3	6.4	26 23.1	-51.3	6.5	27 22.8	-51.3	6.5	28 22.4	-51.2	6.6
79	24 32.2	-51.6	5.8	25 31.8	-51.4	5.9	26 31.5	-51.4	5.9	27 31.2	-51.3	6.0
80	23 40.6	-51.6	5.3	24 40.4	-51.6	5.3	25 40.1	-51.5	5.4	26 39.9	-51.5	5.4
81	22 49.0	-51.7	4.7	23 48.8	-51.7	4.8	24 48.6	-51.6	4.8	25 48.4	-51.6	4.8
82	21 57.3	-51.9	4.2	22 57.1	-51.8	4.2	23 57.0	-51.8	4.2	24 56.8	-51.7	4.3
83	21 05.4	-51.9	3.6	22 05.3	-51.9	3.7	23 05.2	-51.9	3.7	24 05.1	-51.9	3.7
84	20 13.5	-52.0	3.1	21 13.4	-52.0	3.1	22 13.3	-52.0	3.1	23 13.2	-51.9	3.2
85	19 21.5	-52.2	2.6	20 21.4	-52.1	2.6	21 21.3	-52.0	2.6	22 21.3	-52.1	2.6
86	18 29.3	-52.2	2.0	19 29.3	-52.2	2.1	20 29.3	-52.2	2.1	21 29.2	-52.2	2.1
87	17 37.1	-52.3	1.5	18 37.1	-52.3	1.5	19 37.1	-52.3	1.5	20 37.0	-52.2	1.6
88	16 44.8	-52.4	1.0	17 44.8	-52.4	1.0	18 44.8	-52.4	1.0	19 44.8	-52.4	1.0
89	15 52.4	-52.4	0.5	16 52.4	-52.4	0.5	17 52.4	-52.4	0.5	18 52.4	-52.4	0.5
90	15 00.0	-52.5	0.0	16 00.0	-52.5	0.0	17 00.0	-52.5	0.0	18 00.0	-52.5	0.0
	15°			16°			17°			18°		

Dec.	19°			20°			21°			22°			Dec.
	Hc	d	Z	Hc	d	Z	Hc	d	Z	Hc	d	Z	
°	° ′	′	°	° ′	′	°	° ′	′	°	° ′	′	°	°
0	55 47.3	+34.2	120.4	55 16.4	+35.5	121.7	54 44.3	+36.8	122.9	54 11.2	+38.0	124.1	0
1	56 21.5	+33.2	119.0	55 51.9	+34.5	120.3	55 21.1	+35.8	121.5	54 49.2	+37.1	122.7	1
2	56 54.7	+32.0	117.4	56 26.4	+33.5	118.8	55 56.9	+34.8	120.1	55 26.3	+36.1	121.3	2
3	57 26.7	+30.8	115.9	56 59.9	+32.3	117.3	56 31.7	+33.8	118.6	56 02.4	+35.1	119.9	3
4	57 57.5	+29.6	114.3	57 32.2	+31.1	115.7	57 05.5	+32.6	117.1	56 37.5	+34.1	118.5	4
5	58 27.1	+28.3	112.6	58 03.3	+29.9	114.1	57 38.1	+31.4	115.5	57 11.6	+32.9	117.0	5
6	58 55.4	+26.8	110.9	58 33.2	+28.5	112.5	58 09.5	+30.2	113.9	57 44.5	+31.7	115.4	6
7	59 22.2	+25.5	109.2	59 01.7	+27.3	110.8	58 39.7	+28.9	112.3	58 16.2	+30.6	113.8	7
8	59 47.7	+24.0	107.4	59 29.0	+25.7	109.0	59 08.6	+27.6	110.6	58 46.8	+29.2	112.1	8
9	60 11.7	+22.4	105.6	59 54.7	+24.3	107.2	59 36.2	+26.1	108.9	59 16.0	+27.8	110.5	9
10	60 34.1	+20.8	103.7	60 19.0	+22.8	105.4	60 02.3	+24.6	107.1	59 43.8	+26.5	108.7	10
11	60 54.9	+19.1	101.8	60 41.8	+21.1	103.5	60 26.9	+23.0	105.2	60 10.3	+24.9	106.9	11
12	61 14.0	+17.4	99.8	61 02.9	+19.4	101.6	60 49.9	+21.4	103.3	60 35.2	+23.4	105.1	12
13	61 31.4	+15.6	97.8	61 22.3	+17.7	99.6	61 11.3	+19.8	101.4	60 58.6	+21.7	103.2	13
14	61 47.0	+13.8	95.8	61 40.0	+15.9	97.6	61 31.1	+18.0	99.4	61 20.3	+20.1	101.3	14
15	62 00.8	+11.9	93.7	61 55.9	+14.1	95.6	61 49.1	+16.2	97.4	61 40.4	+18.3	99.3	15
16	62 12.7	+9.9	91.6	62 10.0	+12.2	93.5	62 05.3	+14.4	95.4	61 58.7	+16.6	97.3	16
17	62 22.6	+8.1	89.5	62 22.2	+10.2	91.4	62 19.7	+12.5	93.3	62 15.3	+14.6	95.2	17
18	62 30.7	+6.0•	87.3	62 32.4	+8.3	89.3	62 32.2	+10.5	91.2	62 29.9	+12.8	93.1	18
19	62 36.7	+4.0•	85.2	62 40.7	+6.3•	87.1	62 42.7	+8.6•	89.1	62 42.7	+10.8	91.0	19
20	62 40.7	+2.0•	83.0	62 47.0	+4.3•	84.9	62 51.3	+6.5•	86.9	62 53.5	+8.9•	88.8	20
21	62 42.7	0.0•	80.8	62 51.3	+2.2•	82.8	62 57.8	+4.6•	84.7	63 02.4	+6.8•	86.7	21
22	62 42.7	-2.0•	78.7	62 53.5	+0.2•	80.6	63 02.4	+2.4•	82.5	63 09.2	+4.7•	84.5	22
23	62 40.7	-4.1•	76.5	62 53.7	-1.8•	78.4	63 04.8	+0.4•	80.3	63 13.9	+2.7•	82.3	23
24	62 36.6	-6.1	74.3	62 51.9	-3.9•	76.2	63 05.2	-1.6•	78.1	63 16.6	+0.6•	80.0	24
25	62 30.5	-8.0•	72.1	62 48.0	-5.9•	74.0	63 03.6	-3.7•	75.9	63 17.2	-1.4•	77.8	25
26	62 22.5	-10.1	70.0	62 42.1	-7.9•	71.8	62 59.9	-5.8•	73.7	63 15.8	-3.6•	75.6	26
27	62 12.4	-11.9	67.9	62 34.2	-9.9•	69.7	62 54.1	-7.8	71.5	63 12.2	-5.6•	73.4	27
28	62 00.5	-13.8	65.8	62 24.3	-11.9	67.5	62 46.3	-9.7•	69.3	63 06.6	-7.6•	71.2	28
29	61 46.7	-15.7	63.7	62 12.4	-13.7	65.4	62 36.6	-11.8	67.2	62 59.0	-9.7•	69.0	29
30	61 31.0	-17.4	61.7	61 58.7	-15.5	63.3	62 24.8	-13.6	65.0	62 49.3	-11.6	66.8	30
31	61 13.6	-19.2	59.7	61 43.2	-17.4	61.3	62 11.2	-15.5	63.0	62 37.7	-13.6	64.7	31
32	60 54.4	-20.8	57.7	61 25.8	-19.1	59.3	61 55.7	-17.3	60.9	62 24.1	-15.4	62.6	32
33	60 33.6	-22.4	55.8	61 06.7	-20.8	57.3	61 38.4	-19.1	58.9	62 08.7	-17.3	60.5	33
34	60 11.2	-24.0	53.9	60 45.9	-22.5	55.4	61 19.3	-20.8	56.9	61 51.4	-19.0	58.4	34
35	59 47.2	-25.5	52.1	60 23.4	-24.0	53.5	60 58.5	-22.4	54.9	61 32.4	-20.8	56.4	35
36	59 21.7	-27.0	50.3	59 59.4	-25.5	51.6	60 36.1	-24.0	53.0	61 11.6	-22.5	54.5	36
37	58 54.7	-28.2	48.6	59 33.9	-26.9	49.8	60 12.1	-25.5	51.2	60 49.1	-24.0	52.6	37
38	58 26.5	-29.6	46.9	59 07.0	-28.3	48.1	59 46.6	-27.0	49.4	60 25.1	-25.5	50.7	38
39	57 56.9	-30.9	45.2	58 38.7	-29.7	46.4	59 19.6	-28.4	47.6	59 59.6	-27.1	48.9	39
40	57 26.0	-32.0	43.6	58 09.0	-30.9	44.7	58 51.2	-29.7	45.9	59 32.5	-28.4	47.1	40
41	56 54.0	-33.2	42.1	57 38.1	-32.1	43.1	58 21.5	-30.9	44.2	59 04.1	-29.7	45.4	41
42	56 20.8	-34.2	40.6	57 06.0	-33.2	41.6	57 50.6	-32.2	42.6	58 34.4	-31.1	43.7	42
43	55 46.6	-35.3	39.1	56 32.8	-34.3	40.0	57 18.4	-33.3	41.0	58 03.3	-32.2	42.1	43
44	55 11.3	-36.3	37.7	55 58.5	-35.3	38.6	56 45.1	-34.4	39.5	57 31.1	-33.4	40.5	44
45	54 35.0	-37.1	36.3	55 23.2	-36.4	37.1	56 10.7	-35.4	38.0	56 57.7	-34.5	39.0	45
46	53 57.9	-38.1	34.9	54 46.8	-37.2	35.7	55 35.3	-36.4	36.6	56 23.2	-35.5	37.5	46
47	53 19.8	-38.8	33.6	54 09.6	-38.1	34.4	54 58.9	-37.4	35.2	55 47.7	-36.6	36.0	47
48	52 41.0	-39.7	32.4	53 31.5	-39.0	33.1	54 21.5	-38.2	33.8	55 11.1	-37.4	34.6	48
49	52 01.3	-40.4	31.1	52 52.5	-39.7	31.8	53 43.3	-39.0	32.5	54 33.7	-38.3	33.3	49
50	51 20.9	-41.1	29.9	52 12.8	-40.5	30.6	53 04.3	-39.9	31.2	53 55.4	-39.2	32.0	50
51	50 39.8	-41.7	28.8	51 32.3	-41.2	29.4	52 24.4	-40.6	30.0	53 16.2	-40.0	30.7	51
52	49 58.1	-42.4	27.6	50 51.1	-41.9	28.2	51 43.8	-41.3	28.8	52 36.2	-40.7	29.4	52
53	49 15.7	-43.0	26.6	50 09.2	-42.5	27.1	51 02.5	-42.0	27.6	51 55.5	-41.4	28.2	53
54	48 32.7	-43.6	25.5	49 26.7	-43.1	26.0	50 20.5	-42.6	26.5	51 14.1	-42.1	27.1	54
55	47 49.1	-44.1	24.5	48 43.6	-43.7	24.9	49 37.9	-43.2	25.4	50 32.0	-42.7	25.9	55
56	47 05.0	-44.6	23.5	47 59.9	-44.2	23.9	48 54.7	-43.8	24.4	49 49.3	-43.4	24.8	56
57	46 20.4	-45.1	22.5	47 15.7	-44.7	22.9	48 10.9	-44.3	23.3	49 05.9	-43.9	23.8	57
58	45 35.3	-45.6	21.5	46 31.0	-45.2	21.9	47 26.6	-44.8	22.3	48 22.0	-44.4	22.7	58
59	44 49.7	-46.0	20.6	45 45.8	-45.7	21.0	46 41.8	-45.4	21.3	47 37.6	-45.0	21.7	59
60	44 03.7	-46.4	19.7	45 00.1	-46.1	20.0	45 56.4	-45.7	20.4	46 52.6	-45.4	20.8	60
61	43 17.3	-46.8	18.8	44 14.0	-46.5	19.1	45 10.7	-46.3	19.5	46 07.2	-45.9	19.8	61
62	42 30.5	-47.2	18.0	43 27.5	-46.9	18.3	44 24.4	-46.6	18.6	45 21.3	-46.4	18.9	62
63	41 43.3	-47.5	17.2	42 40.6	-47.3	17.4	43 37.8	-47.0	17.7	44 34.9	-46.7	18.0	63
64	40 55.8	-47.9	16.3	41 53.3	-47.6	16.6	42 50.8	-47.4	16.9	43 48.2	-47.1	17.1	64
65	40 07.9	-48.1	15.5	41 05.7	-47.9	15.8	42 03.4	-47.7	16.0	43 01.1	-47.5	16.3	65
66	39 19.8	-48.5	14.8	40 17.8	-48.3	15.0	41 15.7	-48.1	15.2	42 13.6	-47.9	15.4	66
67	38 31.3	-48.8	14.0	39 29.5	-48.6	14.2	40 27.6	-48.4	14.4	41 25.7	-48.2	14.6	67
68	37 42.5	-49.0	13.3	38 40.9	-48.9	13.5	39 39.2	-48.6	13.6	40 37.5	-48.5	13.8	68
69	36 53.5	-49.3	12.5	37 52.0	-49.1	12.7	38 50.6	-49.0	12.9	39 49.0	-48.8	13.1	69
70	36 04.2	-49.5	11.8	37 02.9	-49.4	12.0	38 01.6	-49.3	12.2	39 00.2	-49.1	12.3	70
71	35 14.7	-49.8	11.1	36 13.5	-49.6	11.3	37 12.3	-49.5	11.4	38 11.1	-49.3	11.6	71
72	34 24.9	-50.0	10.5	35 23.9	-49.9	10.6	36 22.8	-49.7	10.7	37 21.8	-49.6	10.9	72
73	33 34.9	-50.2	9.8	34 34.0	-50.1	9.9	35 33.1	-50.0	10.0	36 32.2	-49.9	10.2	73
74	32 44.7	-50.4	9.1	33 43.9	-50.3	9.2	34 43.1	-50.2	9.4	35 42.3	-50.1	9.5	74
75	31 54.3	-50.6	8.5	32 53.6	-50.5	8.6	33 52.9	-50.4	8.7	34 52.2	-50.3	8.8	75
76	31 03.7	-50.8	7.9	32 03.1	-50.7	8.0	33 02.5	-50.6	8.0	34 01.9	-50.5	8.1	76
77	30 12.9	-50.9	7.3	31 12.4	-50.8	7.3	32 11.9	-50.7	7.4	33 11.4	-50.7	7.5	77
78	29 22.0	-51.1	6.6	30 21.6	-51.1	6.7	31 21.2	-51.0	6.8	32 20.7	-50.9	6.9	78
79	28 30.9	-51.3	6.0	29 30.5	-51.2	6.1	30 30.2	-51.2	6.2	31 29.8	-51.0	6.2	79
80	27 39.6	-51.4	5.5	28 39.3	-51.3	5.5	29 39.0	-51.3	5.6	30 38.8	-51.3	5.6	80
81	26 48.2	-51.6	4.9	27 48.0	-51.5	4.9	28 47.7	-51.4	5.0	29 47.5	-51.4	5.0	81
82	25 56.6	-51.6	4.3	26 56.5	-51.7	4.3	27 56.3	-51.6	4.4	28 56.1	-51.5	4.4	82
83	25 05.0	-51.9	3.7	26 04.8	-51.7	3.8	27 04.7	-51.7	3.8	28 04.6	-51.7	3.8	83
84	24 13.1	-51.9	3.2	25 13.1	-51.9	3.2	26 13.0	-51.9	3.2	27 12.9	-51.9	3.3	84
85	23 21.2	-52.0	2.6	24 21.2	-52.1	2.7	25 21.1	-52.0	2.7	26 21.0	-51.9	2.7	85
86	22 29.2	-52.2	2.1	23 29.1	-52.1	2.1	24 29.1	-52.1	2.1	25 29.1	-52.1	2.1	86
87	21 37.0	-52.2	1.6	22 37.0	-52.2	1.6	23 37.0	-52.2	1.6	24 37.0	-52.3	1.6	87
88	20 44.8	-52.4	1.0	21 44.8	-52.4	1.0	22 44.8	-52.4	1.1	23 44.7	-52.3	1.1	88
89	19 52.4	-52.4	0.5	20 52.4	-52.4	0.5	21 52.4	-52.4	0.5	22 52.4	-52.4	0.5	89
90	19 00.0	-52.5	0.0	20 00.0	-52.5	0.0	21 00.0	-52.5	0.0	22 00.0	-52.5	0.0	90
	19°			20°			21°			22°			

29°, 331° L.H.A. LATITUDE SAME NAME AS DECLINATION

LATITUDE CONTRARY NAME TO DECLINATION L.H.A. 29°, 331°

Dec.	15° Hc	d	Z	16° Hc	d	Z	17° Hc	d	Z	18° Hc	d	Z
°	° ′	′	°	° ′	′	°	° ′	′	°	° ′	′	°
0	57 39.1	-29.6	115.0	57 13.1	-31.1	116.4	56 45.7	-32.5	117.8	56 17.1	-33.9	119.1
1	57 09.5	-30.9	116.6	56 42.0	-32.3	118.0	56 13.2	-33.7	119.3	55 43.2	-35.0	120.6
2	56 38.6	-32.0	118.2	56 09.7	-33.4	119.5	55 39.5	-34.7	120.8	55 08.2	-35.9	122.0
3	56 06.6	-33.1	119.7	55 36.3	-34.4	121.0	55 04.8	-35.7	122.2	54 32.3	-36.9	123.4
4	55 33.5	-34.1	121.2	55 01.9	-35.4	122.5	54 29.1	-36.6	123.6	53 55.4	-37.7	124.8
5	54 59.4	-35.2	122.7	54 26.5	-36.4	123.9	53 52.5	-37.5	125.0	53 17.7	-38.6	126.1
6	54 24.2	-36.1	124.1	53 50.1	-37.2	125.2	53 15.0	-38.3	126.3	52 39.1	-39.4	127.4
7	53 48.1	-37.0	125.4	53 12.9	-38.1	126.5	52 36.7	-39.1	127.6	51 59.7	-40.2	128.6
8	53 11.1	-37.9	126.8	52 34.8	-38.9	127.8	51 57.6	-39.9	128.8	51 19.5	-40.8	129.8
9	52 33.2	-38.6	128.0	51 55.9	-39.7	129.1	51 17.7	-40.7	130.0	50 38.7	-41.5	131.0
10	51 54.6	-39.5	129.3	51 16.2	-40.4	130.3	50 37.0	-41.3	131.2	49 57.2	-42.2	132.1
11	51 15.1	-40.1	130.5	50 35.8	-41.1	131.4	49 55.7	-41.9	132.3	49 15.0	-42.8	133.2
12	50 35.0	-40.9	131.7	49 54.7	-41.7	132.6	49 13.8	-42.5	133.4	48 32.2	-43.3	134.3
13	49 54.1	-41.5	132.8	49 13.0	-42.3	133.7	48 31.3	-43.2	134.5	47 48.9	-43.9	135.3
14	49 12.6	-42.1	133.9	48 30.7	-43.0	134.8	47 48.1	-43.7	135.5	47 05.0	-44.4	136.3
15	48 30.5	-42.8	135.0	47 47.7	-43.5	135.8	47 04.4	-44.2	136.6	46 20.6	-44.9	137.3
16	47 47.7	-43.3	136.1	47 04.2	-44.0	136.8	46 20.2	-44.7	137.5	45 35.7	-45.4	138.2
17	47 04.4	-43.8	137.1	46 20.2	-44.5	137.8	45 35.5	-45.2	138.5	44 50.3	-45.8	139.2
18	46 20.6	-44.3	138.1	45 35.7	-45.0	138.8	44 50.3	-45.6	139.4	44 04.5	-46.2	140.1
19	45 36.3	-44.8	139.1	44 50.7	-45.4	139.7	44 04.7	-46.0	140.4	43 18.3	-46.6	141.0
20	44 51.5	-45.3	140.0	44 05.3	-45.9	140.6	43 18.7	-46.4	141.2	42 31.7	-47.0	141.8
21	44 06.2	-45.7	140.9	43 19.4	-46.3	141.5	42 32.3	-46.9	142.1	41 44.7	-47.3	142.7
22	43 20.5	-46.1	141.8	42 33.1	-46.6	142.4	41 45.4	-47.2	142.9	40 57.4	-47.7	143.5
23	42 34.4	-46.5	142.7	41 46.5	-47.0	143.2	40 58.2	-47.5	143.8	40 09.7	-48.0	144.3
24	41 47.9	-46.9	143.6	40 59.5	-47.4	144.1	40 10.7	-47.8	144.6	39 21.7	-48.3	145.1
25	41 01.0	-47.2	144.4	40 12.1	-47.7	144.9	39 22.9	-48.2	145.4	38 33.4	-48.6	145.8
26	40 13.8	-47.5	145.2	39 24.4	-48.0	145.7	38 34.7	-48.4	146.1	37 44.8	-48.9	146.6
27	39 26.3	-47.9	146.0	38 36.4	-48.3	146.4	37 46.3	-48.8	146.9	36 55.9	-49.2	147.3
28	38 38.4	-48.2	146.8	37 48.1	-48.6	147.2	36 57.5	-49.0	147.6	36 06.7	-49.3	148.0
29	37 50.2	-48.4	147.5	36 59.5	-48.9	147.9	36 08.5	-49.2	148.3	35 17.4	-49.7	148.7
30	37 01.8	-48.8	148.3	36 10.6	-49.1	148.7	35 19.3	-49.5	149.0	34 27.7	-49.8	149.4
31	36 13.0	-49.0	149.0	35 21.5	-49.4	149.4	34 29.8	-49.7	149.7	33 37.9	-50.1	150.1
32	35 24.0	-49.2	149.7	34 32.1	-49.5	150.1	33 40.1	-50.0	150.4	32 47.8	-50.3	150.7
33	34 34.8	-49.4	150.4	33 42.6	-49.8	150.7	32 50.1	-50.1	151.1	31 57.5	-50.4	151.4
34	33 45.4	-49.7	151.1	32 52.8	-50.1	151.4	32 00.0	-50.3	151.7	31 07.1	-50.7	152.0
35	32 55.7	-49.9	151.8	32 02.7	-50.2	152.1	31 09.7	-50.6	152.3	30 16.4	-50.8	152.6
36	32 05.8	-50.1	152.4	31 12.5	-50.4	152.7	30 19.1	-50.7	153.0	29 25.6	-51.0	153.2
37	31 15.7	-50.3	153.1	30 22.1	-50.6	153.3	29 28.4	-50.8	153.6	28 34.6	-51.1	153.8
38	30 25.4	-50.5	153.7	29 31.5	-50.7	154.0	28 37.6	-51.1	154.2	27 43.5	-51.3	154.4
39	29 34.9	-50.6	154.3	28 40.8	-50.9	154.6	27 46.5	-51.1	154.8	26 52.2	-51.4	155.0
40	28 44.3	-50.8	154.9	27 49.9	-51.1	155.2	26 55.4	-51.4	155.4	26 00.8	-51.6	155.6
41	27 53.5	-51.0	155.5	26 58.8	-51.2	155.8	26 04.0	-51.4	156.0	25 09.2	-51.7	156.2
42	27 02.5	-51.1	156.1	26 07.6	-51.4	156.3	25 12.6	-51.6	156.5	24 17.5	-51.8	156.7
43	26 11.4	-51.3	156.7	25 16.2	-51.5	156.9	24 21.0	-51.7	157.1	23 25.7	-51.9	157.3
44	25 20.1	-51.3	157.3	24 24.7	-51.6	157.5	23 29.3	-51.8	157.7	22 33.8	-52.1	157.8
45	24 28.8	-51.6	157.9	23 33.1	-51.7	158.0	22 37.5	-52.0	158.2	21 41.7	-52.1	158.3
46	23 37.2	-51.6	158.4	22 41.4	-51.8	158.6	21 45.5	-52.0	158.7	20 49.6	-52.3	158.9
47	22 45.6	-51.7	159.0	21 49.6	-52.0	159.1	20 53.5	-52.2	159.3	19 57.3	-52.3	159.4
48	21 53.9	-51.9	159.5	20 57.6	-52.0	159.7	20 01.3	-52.2	159.8	19 05.0	-52.4	159.9
49	21 02.0	-51.9	160.1	20 05.6	-52.1	160.2	19 09.1	-52.3	160.3	18 12.6	-52.5	160.4
50	20 10.1	-52.1	160.6	19 13.5	-52.3	160.7	18 16.8	-52.4	160.8	17 20.1	-52.6	160.9
51	19 18.0	-52.1	161.1	18 21.2	-52.3	161.2	17 24.4	-52.5	161.4	16 27.5	-52.6	161.4
52	18 25.9	-52.2	161.7	17 28.9	-52.4	161.8	16 31.9	-52.5	161.9	15 34.9	-52.7	161.9
53	17 33.7	-52.3	162.2	16 36.5	-52.4	162.3	15 39.4	-52.7	162.4	14 42.2	-52.8	162.4
54	16 41.4	-52.4	162.7	15 44.1	-52.6	162.8	14 46.7	-52.6	162.9	13 49.4	-52.8	162.9
55	15 49.0	-52.5	163.2	14 51.5	-52.6	163.3	13 54.1	-52.8	163.4	12 56.6	-52.9	163.4
56	14 56.5	-52.5	163.7	13 58.9	-52.6	163.8	13 01.3	-52.8	163.8	12 03.7	-53.0	163.9
57	14 04.0	-52.6	164.2	13 06.3	-52.7	164.3	12 08.5	-52.8	164.3	11 10.7	-52.9	164.4
58	13 11.4	-52.6	164.7	12 13.6	-52.8	164.8	11 15.7	-52.9	164.8	10 17.8	-53.1	164.9
59	12 18.8	-52.7	165.2	11 20.8	-52.8	165.2	10 22.8	-53.0	165.3	9 24.7	-53.0	165.3
60	11 26.1	-52.7	165.7	10 28.0	-52.9	165.7	9 29.8	-52.9	165.8	8 31.7	-53.1	165.8
61	10 33.4	-52.8	166.2	9 35.1	-52.9	166.2	8 36.9	-53.1	166.2	7 38.6	-53.2	166.3
62	9 40.6	-52.8	166.7	8 42.2	-52.9	166.7	7 43.8	-53.0	166.7	6 45.4	-53.1	166.8
63	8 47.8	-52.8	167.1	7 49.3	-53.0	167.2	6 50.8	-53.1	167.2	5 52.3	-53.2	167.2
64	7 55.0	-52.9	167.6	6 56.3	-52.9	167.6	5 57.7	-53.1	167.7	4 59.1	-53.2	167.7
65	7 02.1	-52.9	168.1	6 03.4	-53.1	168.1	5 04.6	-53.1	168.1	4 05.9	-53.2	168.1
66	6 09.2	-53.0	168.6	5 10.3	-53.0	168.6	4 11.5	-53.1	168.6	3 12.7	-53.2	168.6
67	5 16.2	-53.0	169.0	4 17.3	-53.0	169.0	3 18.4	-53.1	169.1	2 19.5	-53.2	169.1
68	4 23.2	-52.9	169.5	3 24.3	-53.1	169.5	2 25.3	-53.2	169.5	1 26.3	-53.3	169.5
69	3 30.3	-53.0	170.0	2 31.2	-53.1	170.0	1 32.1	-53.2	170.0	0 33.0	-53.2	170.0
70	2 37.3	-53.0	170.4	1 38.1	-53.1	170.5	0 38.9	-53.1	170.5	0 20.2	+53.3	9.5
71	1 44.3	-53.0	170.9	0 45.0	-53.1	170.9	0 14.2	+53.2	9.1	1 13.5	+53.2	9.1
72	0 51.3	-53.1	171.4	0 08.1	+53.0	8.6	1 07.4	+53.1	8.6	2 06.7	+53.2	8.6
73	0 01.8	+53.0	8.1	1 01.1	+53.1	8.2	2 00.5	+53.2	8.2	2 59.9	+53.2	8.2
74	0 54.8	+53.0	7.7	1 54.2	+53.1	7.7	2 53.7	+53.1	7.7	3 53.1	+53.2	7.7
75	1 47.8	+53.0	7.2	2 47.3	+53.1	7.2	3 46.8	+53.1	7.2	4 46.3	+53.2	7.2
76	2 40.8	+53.0	6.7	3 40.4	+53.0	6.7	4 39.9	+53.1	6.8	5 39.5	+53.2	6.8
77	3 33.8	+52.9	6.3	4 33.4	+53.0	6.3	5 33.0	+53.1	6.3	6 32.7	+53.1	6.3
78	4 26.7	+53.0	5.8	5 26.4	+53.0	5.8	6 26.1	+53.1	5.8	7 25.8	+53.1	5.8
79	5 19.7	+52.9	5.3	6 19.4	+53.0	5.3	7 19.2	+53.0	5.4	8 18.9	+53.1	5.4
80	6 12.6	+53.0	4.9	7 12.4	+53.0	4.9	8 12.2	+53.0	4.9	9 12.0	+53.0	4.9
81	7 05.6	+52.8	4.4	8 05.4	+52.9	4.4	9 05.2	+53.0	4.4	10 05.0	+53.0	4.4
82	7 58.4	+52.9	3.9	8 58.3	+52.9	3.9	9 58.2	+52.9	3.9	10 58.0	+53.0	3.9
83	8 51.3	+52.8	3.4	9 51.2	+52.8	3.4	10 51.1	+52.8	3.4	11 51.0	+52.9	3.5
84	9 44.1	+52.8	2.9	10 44.0	+52.8	3.0	11 43.9	+52.9	3.0	12 43.9	+52.8	3.0
85	10 36.9	+52.7	2.5	11 36.8	+52.8	2.5	12 36.8	+52.7	2.5	13 36.7	+52.8	2.5
86	11 29.6	+52.7	2.0	12 29.6	+52.7	2.0	13 29.5	+52.8	2.0	14 29.5	+52.7	2.0
87	12 22.3	+52.6	1.5	13 22.3	+52.6	1.5	14 22.3	+52.6	1.5	15 22.2	+52.7	1.5
88	13 14.9	+52.6	1.0	14 14.9	+52.6	1.0	15 14.9	+52.6	1.0	16 14.9	+52.6	1.0
89	14 07.5	+52.5	0.5	15 07.5	+52.5	0.5	16 07.5	+52.5	0.5	17 07.5	+52.5	0.5
90	15 00.0	+52.4	0.0	16 00.0	+52.4	0.0	17 00.0	+52.4	0.0	18 00.0	+52.4	0.0
	15°			16°			17°			18°		

Dec.	19° Hc	d	Z	20° Hc	d	Z	21° Hc	d	Z	22° Hc	d	Z
°	° ′	′	°	° ′	′	°	° ′	′	°	° ′	′	°
0	55 47.3	-35.2	120.4	55 16.4	-36.5	121.7	54 44.3	-37.7	122.9	54 11.2	-38.8	124.1
1	55 12.1	-36.2	121.9	54 39.9	-37.4	123.1	54 06.6	-38.5	124.2	53 32.4	-39.6	125.3
2	54 35.9	-37.2	123.2	54 02.5	-38.3	124.4	53 28.1	-39.4	125.5	52 52.8	-40.5	126.6
3	53 58.7	-38.0	124.6	53 24.2	-39.1	125.7	52 48.7	-40.1	126.8	52 12.3	-41.1	127.8
4	53 20.7	-38.8	125.9	52 45.1	-39.9	127.0	52 08.6	-40.9	128.0	51 31.2	-41.8	129.0
5	52 41.9	-39.7	127.2	52 05.2	-40.6	128.2	51 27.7	-41.6	129.2	50 49.4	-42.5	130.1
6	52 02.2	-40.4	128.4	51 24.6	-41.4	129.4	50 46.1	-42.2	130.3	50 06.9	-43.1	131.2
7	51 21.8	-41.0	129.6	50 43.2	-42.0	130.5	50 03.9	-42.9	131.4	49 23.8	-43.7	132.3
8	50 40.8	-41.8	130.7	50 01.2	-42.6	131.7	49 21.0	-43.4	132.5	48 40.1	-44.2	133.4
9	49 59.0	-42.4	131.9	49 18.6	-43.2	132.7	48 37.6	-44.0	133.6	47 55.9	-44.7	134.4
10	49 16.6	-43.0	133.0	48 35.4	-43.8	133.8	47 53.6	-44.6	134.6	47 11.2	-45.3	135.4
11	48 33.6	-43.5	134.0	47 51.6	-44.3	134.8	47 09.0	-45.0	135.6	46 25.9	-45.7	136.3
12	47 50.1	-44.1	135.1	47 07.3	-44.8	135.8	46 24.0	-45.5	136.6	45 40.2	-46.2	137.3
13	47 06.0	-44.6	136.1	46 22.5	-45.3	136.8	45 38.5	-45.9	137.5	44 54.0	-46.5	138.2
14	46 21.4	-45.1	137.0	45 37.2	-45.7	137.7	44 52.6	-46.4	138.4	44 07.5	-47.0	139.1
15	45 36.3	-45.6	138.0	44 51.5	-46.2	138.7	44 06.2	-46.8	139.3	43 20.5	-47.4	139.9
16	44 50.7	-46.0	138.9	44 05.3	-46.6	139.5	43 19.4	-47.1	140.2	42 33.1	-47.7	140.8
17	44 04.7	-46.4	139.8	43 18.7	-47.0	140.4	42 32.3	-47.6	141.0	41 45.4	-48.0	141.6
18	43 18.3	-46.8	140.7	42 31.7	-47.3	141.3	41 44.7	-47.8	141.8	40 57.4	-48.4	142.4
19	42 31.5	-47.1	141.5	41 44.4	-47.7	142.1	40 56.9	-48.2	142.6	40 09.0	-48.7	143.2
20	41 44.4	-47.5	142.4	40 56.7	-48.0	142.9	40 08.7	-48.5	143.4	39 20.3	-48.9	143.9
21	40 56.9	-47.9	143.2	40 08.7	-48.4	143.7	39 20.2	-48.8	144.2	38 31.4	-49.3	144.7
22	40 09.0	-48.2	144.0	39 20.3	-48.6	144.5	38 31.4	-49.1	144.9	37 42.1	-49.5	145.4
23	39 20.8	-48.4	144.8	38 31.7	-48.9	145.2	37 42.3	-49.4	145.7	36 52.6	-49.7	146.1
24	38 32.4	-48.8	145.5	37 42.8	-49.2	146.0	36 52.9	-49.6	146.4	36 02.9	-50.0	146.8
25	37 43.6	-49.0	146.3	36 53.6	-49.4	146.7	36 03.3	-49.8	147.1	35 12.9	-50.2	147.5
26	36 54.6	-49.3	147.0	36 04.2	-49.7	147.4	35 13.5	-50.0	147.8	34 22.7	-50.5	148.1
27	36 05.3	-49.5	147.7	35 14.5	-49.9	148.1	34 23.5	-50.3	148.4	33 32.2	-50.6	148.8
28	35 15.8	-49.8	148.4	34 24.6	-50.2	148.7	33 33.2	-50.5	149.1	32 41.6	-50.8	149.4
29	34 26.0	-50.0	149.1	33 34.4	-50.3	149.4	32 42.7	-50.7	149.7	31 50.8	-51.0	150.1
30	33 36.0	-50.2	149.7	32 44.1	-50.5	150.1	31 52.0	-50.8	150.4	30 59.8	-51.2	150.7
31	32 45.8	-50.4	150.4	31 53.6	-50.8	150.7	31 01.2	-51.1	151.0	30 08.6	-51.3	151.3
32	31 55.4	-50.6	151.0	31 02.8	-50.9	151.3	30 10.1	-51.2	151.6	29 17.3	-51.5	151.9
33	31 04.8	-50.8	151.7	30 11.9	-51.0	151.9	29 18.9	-51.3	152.2	28 25.8	-51.7	152.5
34	30 14.0	-50.9	152.3	29 20.9	-51.3	152.5	28 27.6	-51.5	152.8	27 34.1	-51.7	153.0
35	29 23.1	-51.1	152.9	28 29.6	-51.4	153.1	27 36.1	-51.7	153.4	26 42.4	-52.0	153.6
36	28 32.0	-51.3	153.5	27 38.2	-51.5	153.7	26 44.4	-51.8	153.9	25 50.4	-52.0	154.2
37	27 40.7	-51.4	154.1	26 46.7	-51.6	154.3	25 52.6	-51.9	154.5	24 58.4	-52.2	154.7
38	26 49.3	-51.5	154.7	25 55.1	-51.8	154.9	25 00.7	-52.1	155.1	24 06.2	-52.2	155.3
39	25 57.8	-51.7	155.2	25 03.3	-52.0	155.4	24 08.6	-52.1	155.6	23 14.0	-52.4	155.8
40	25 06.1	-51.8	155.8	24 11.3	-52.0	156.0	23 16.5	-52.3	156.2	22 21.6	-52.5	156.3
41	24 14.3	-51.9	156.3	23 19.3	-52.2	156.5	22 24.2	-52.3	156.7	21 29.1	-52.6	156.8
42	23 22.4	-52.1	156.9	22 27.1	-52.2	157.1	21 31.9	-52.5	157.2	20 36.5	-52.7	157.4
43	22 30.3	-52.1	157.4	21 34.9	-52.4	157.6	20 39.4	-52.6	157.7	19 43.8	-52.7	157.9
44	21 38.2	-52.3	158.0	20 42.5	-52.4	158.1	19 46.8	-52.6	158.2	18 51.1	-52.9	158.4
45	20 45.9	-52.3	158.5	19 50.1	-52.6	158.6	18 54.2	-52.7	158.8	17 58.2	-52.9	158.9
46	19 53.6	-52.4	159.0	18 57.5	-52.6	159.1	18 01.5	-52.9	159.3	17 05.3	-53.0	159.4
47	19 01.2	-52.6	159.5	18 04.9	-52.7	159.6	17 08.6	-52.8	159.8	16 12.3	-53.0	159.9
48	18 08.6	-52.6	160.0	17 12.2	-52.7	160.1	16 15.8	-53.0	160.2	15 19.3	-53.1	160.3
49	17 16.0	-52.6	160.5	16 19.5	-52.9	160.6	15 22.8	-53.0	160.7	14 26.2	-53.2	160.8
50	16 23.4	-52.8	161.0	15 26.6	-52.9	161.1	14 29.8	-53.1	161.2	13 33.0	-53.2	161.3
51	15 30.6	-52.8	161.5	14 33.7	-53.0	161.6	13 36.7	-53.1	161.7	12 39.8	-53.3	161.8
52	14 37.8	-52.8	162.0	13 40.7	-53.0	162.1	12 43.6	-53.2	162.2	11 46.5	-53.3	162.2
53	13 45.0	-53.0	162.5	12 47.7	-53.1	162.6	11 50.4	-53.2	162.7	10 53.2	-53.4	162.7
54	12 52.0	-53.0	163.0	11 54.6	-53.1	163.1	10 57.2	-53.2	163.1	9 59.8	-53.4	163.2
55	11 59.0	-53.0	163.5	11 01.5	-53.2	163.5	10 04.0	-53.3	163.6	9 06.4	-53.4	163.6
56	11 06.0	-53.1	164.0	10 08.3	-53.2	164.0	9 10.7	-53.4	164.1	8 13.0	-53.5	164.1
57	10 12.9	-53.1	164.4	9 15.1	-53.2	164.5	8 17.3	-53.4	164.5	7 19.5	-53.5	164.6
58	9 19.8	-53.1	164.9	8 21.9	-53.3	164.9	7 23.9	-53.4	165.0	6 26.0	-53.5	165.0
59	8 26.7	-53.2	165.4	7 28.6	-53.3	165.4	6 30.5	-53.4	165.4	5 32.5	-53.6	165.5
60	7 33.5	-53.2	165.8	6 35.3	-53.3	165.9	5 37.1	-53.4	165.9	4 38.9	-53.5	165.9
61	6 40.3	-53.3	166.3	5 42.0	-53.4	166.3	4 43.7	-53.5	166.4	3 45.4	-53.6	166.4
62	5 47.0	-53.2	166.8	4 48.6	-53.3	166.8	3 50.2	-53.5	166.8	2 51.8	-53.6	166.8
63	4 53.8	-53.3	167.2	3 55.3	-53.4	167.3	2 56.7	-53.5	167.3	1 58.2	-53.6	167.3
64	4 00.5	-53.3	167.7	3 01.9	-53.4	167.7	2 03.2	-53.5	167.7	1 04.6	-53.6	167.7
65	3 07.2	-53.3	168.2	2 08.5	-53.4	168.2	1 09.7	-53.5	168.2	0 11.0	-53.6	168.2
66	2 13.9	-53.3	168.6	1 15.1	-53.4	168.6	0 16.2	-53.5	168.6	0 42.6	+53.6	11.4
67	1 20.6	-53.4	169.1	0 21.7	-53.5	169.1	0 37.3	+53.5	10.9	1 36.2	+53.6	10.9
68	0 27.2	-53.3	169.5	0 31.8	+53.4	10.5	1 30.8	+53.4	10.5	2 29.8	+53.5	10.5
69	0 26.1	+53.3	10.0	1 25.2	+53.4	10.0	2 24.2	+53.5	10.0	3 23.3	+53.6	10.0
70	1 19.4	+53.3	9.5	2 18.6	+53.4	9.6	3 17.7	+53.5	9.6	4 16.9	+53.5	9.6
71	2 12.7	+53.3	9.1	3 12.0	+53.3	9.1	4 11.2	+53.5	9.1	5 10.4	+53.6	9.1
72	3 06.0	+53.3	8.6	4 05.3	+53.4	8.6	5 04.7	+53.4	8.7	6 04.0	+53.5	8.7
73	3 59.3	+53.3	8.2	4 58.7	+53.4	8.2	5 58.1	+53.4	8.2	6 57.5	+53.5	8.2
74	4 52.6	+53.3	7.7	5 52.1	+53.3	7.7	6 51.5	+53.4	7.7	7 51.0	+53.4	7.8
75	5 45.9	+53.2	7.2	6 45.4	+53.3	7.3	7 44.9	+53.4	7.3	8 44.4	+53.4	7.3
76	6 39.1	+53.2	6.8	7 38.7	+53.3	6.8	8 38.3	+53.3	6.8	9 37.8	+53.4	6.8
77	7 32.3	+53.2	6.3	8 32.0	+53.2	6.3	9 31.6	+53.3	6.3	10 31.2	+53.4	6.4
78	8 25.5	+53.2	5.8	9 25.2	+53.2	5.9	10 24.9	+53.2	5.9	11 24.6	+53.3	5.9
79	9 18.7	+53.1	5.4	10 18.4	+53.2	5.4	11 18.1	+53.2	5.4	12 17.9	+53.2	5.4
80	10 11.8	+53.0	4.9	11 11.6	+53.1	4.9	12 11.3	+53.2	4.9	13 11.1	+53.2	5.0
81	11 04.8	+53.1	4.4	12 04.7	+53.0	4.4	13 04.5	+53.1	4.5	14 04.3	+53.1	4.5
82	11 57.9	+53.0	4.0	12 57.7	+53.0	4.0	13 57.6	+53.0	4.0	14 57.4	+53.1	4.0
83	12 50.9	+52.9	3.5	13 50.7	+53.0	3.5	14 50.6	+53.0	3.5	15 50.5	+53.0	3.5
84	13 43.8	+52.9	3.0	14 43.7	+52.9	3.0	15 43.6	+52.9	3.0	16 43.5	+53.0	3.0
85	14 36.7	+52.8	2.5	15 36.6	+52.8	2.5	16 36.5	+52.9	2.5	17 36.5	+52.9	2.5
86	15 29.5	+52.7	2.0	16 29.4	+52.8	2.0	17 29.4	+52.8	2.0	18 29.4	+52.7	2.0
87	16 22.2	+52.7	1.5	17 22.2	+52.7	1.5	18 22.2	+52.7	1.5	19 22.1	+52.8	1.5
88	17 14.9	+52.6	1.0	18 14.9	+52.6	1.0	19 14.9	+52.6	1.0	20 14.9	+52.6	1.0
89	18 07.5	+52.5	0.5	19 07.5	+52.5	0.5	20 07.5	+52.5	0.5	21 07.5	+52.5	0.5
90	19 00.0	+52.4	0.0	20 00.0	+52.4	0.0	21 00.0	+52.4	0.0	22 00.0	+52.4	0.0
	19°			20°			21°			22°		

S. Lat. {L.H.A. greater than 180° ....Zn=180°–Z
{L.H.A. less than 180°............Zn=180°+Z

LATITUDE SAME NAME AS DECLINATION L.H.A. 151°, 209°

61

Dec.	15°			16°			17°			18°			19°			20°			21°			22°			Dec.
	Hc	d	Z	Hc	d	Z	Hc	d	Z	Hc	d	Z	Hc	d	Z	Hc	d	Z	Hc	d	Z	Hc	d	Z	
°	° ′	′	°	° ′	′	°	° ′	′	°	° ′	′	°	° ′	′	°	° ′	′	°	° ′	′	°	° ′	′	°	°
0	56 46.4	+27.8	114.1	56 21.2	+29.3	115.5	55 54.8	+30.7	116.9	55 27.0	+32.2	118.2	54 58.1	+33.6	119.4	54 28.1	+34.8	120.6	53 57.0	+36.1	121.8	53 24.8	+37.3	123.0	0
1	57 14.2	+26.4	112.5	56 50.5	+28.0	113.9	56 25.5	+29.5	115.3	55 59.2	+31.0	116.7	55 31.7	+32.4	118.0	55 02.9	+33.9	119.2	54 33.1	+35.1	120.5	54 02.1	+36.4	121.7	1
2	57 40.6	+25.0	110.8	57 18.5	+26.7	112.3	56 55.0	+28.4	113.7	56 30.2	+29.9	115.1	56 04.1	+31.4	116.5	55 36.8	+32.7	117.8	55 08.2	+34.1	119.1	54 38.5	+35.4	120.3	2
3	58 05.6	+23.7	109.1	57 45.2	+25.4	110.6	57 23.4	+27.0	112.1	57 00.1	+28.6	113.5	56 35.5	+30.1	114.9	56 09.5	+31.7	116.3	55 42.3	+33.1	117.6	55 13.9	+34.5	118.9	3
4	58 29.3	+22.2	107.4	58 10.6	+24.0	108.9	57 50.4	+25.7	110.4	57 28.7	+27.3	111.9	57 05.6	+29.0	113.3	56 41.2	+30.4	114.7	56 15.4	+32.0	116.1	55 48.4	+33.3	117.4	4
5	58 51.5	+20.7	105.6	58 34.6	+22.5	107.2	58 16.1	+24.2	108.7	57 56.0	+26.0	110.2	57 34.6	+27.6	111.7	57 11.6	+29.3	113.2	56 47.4	+30.8	114.6	56 21.7	+32.3	115.9	5
6	59 12.2	+19.1	103.8	58 57.1	+21.0	105.4	58 40.3	+22.9	107.0	58 22.0	+24.6	108.5	58 02.2	+26.3	110.1	57 40.9	+28.0	111.5	57 18.2	+29.5	113.0	56 54.0	+31.2	114.4	6
7	59 31.3	+17.5	101.9	59 18.1	+19.4	103.6	59 03.2	+21.3	105.2	58 46.6	+23.2	106.8	58 28.5	+25.0	108.4	58 08.9	+26.6	109.9	57 47.7	+28.3	111.4	57 25.2	+29.9	112.8	7
8	59 48.8	+15.9	100.0	59 37.5	+17.8	101.7	59 24.5	+19.7	103.4	59 09.8	+21.6	105.0	58 53.5	+23.4	106.6	58 35.5	+25.3	108.2	58 16.0	+27.0	109.7	57 55.1	+28.6	111.2	8
9	60 04.7	+14.1	98.1	59 55.3	+16.2	99.8	59 44.2	+18.2	101.5	59 31.4	+20.1	103.2	59 16.9	+22.0	104.8	59 00.8	+23.8	106.4	58 43.0	+25.6	108.0	58 23.7	+27.3	109.6	9
10	60 18.8	+12.4	96.1	60 11.5	+14.5	97.9	60 02.4	+16.5	99.6	59 51.5	+18.5	101.3	59 38.9	+20.4	103.0	59 24.6	+22.2	104.6	59 08.6	+24.1	106.3	58 51.0	+25.9	107.8	10
11	60 31.2	+10.7	94.2	60 26.0	+12.7	95.9	60 18.9	+14.7	97.7	60 10.0	+16.7	99.4	59 59.3	+18.8	101.1	59 46.8	+20.8	102.8	59 32.7	+22.6	104.5	59 16.9	+24.5	106.1	11
12	60 41.9	+8.8	92.2	60 38.7	+10.9	93.9	60 33.6	+13.0	95.7	60 26.7	+15.1	97.5	60 18.1	+17.1	99.2	60 07.6	+19.1	100.9	59 55.3	+21.1	102.6	59 41.4	+22.9	104.3	12
13	60 50.7	+6.9	90.1	60 49.6	+9.1	91.9	60 46.6	+11.2	93.7	60 41.8	+13.3	95.5	60 35.2	+15.3	97.3	60 26.7	+17.4	99.0	60 16.4	+19.4	100.7	60 04.3	+21.4	102.4	13
14	60 57.6	+5.1	88.1	60 58.7	+7.2	89.9	60 57.8	+9.4	91.7	60 55.1	+11.5	93.5	60 50.5	+13.7	95.3	60 44.1	+15.7	97.1	60 35.8	+17.7	98.8	60 25.7	+19.7	100.6	14
15	61 02.7	+3.2	86.0	61 05.9	+5.4	87.8	61 07.2	+7.5	89.7	61 06.6	+9.7	91.5	61 04.2	+11.8	93.3	60 59.8	+13.9	95.1	60 53.5	+16.1	96.9	60 45.4	+18.1	98.6	15
16	61 05.9	+1.3	84.0	61 11.3	+3.4	85.8	61 14.7	+5.7	87.6	61 16.3	+7.8	89.4	61 16.0	+9.9	91.2	61 13.7	+12.1	93.1	61 09.6	+14.2	94.9	61 03.5	+16.3	96.7	16
17	61 07.2	-0.6	81.9	61 14.7	+1.6	83.7	61 20.4	+3.7	85.5	61 24.1	+5.9	87.3	61 25.9	+8.1	89.2	61 25.8	+10.3	91.0	61 23.8	+12.4	92.9	61 19.8	+14.6	94.7	17
18	61 06.6	-2.4	79.8	61 16.3	-0.3	81.6	61 24.1	+1.8	83.4	61 30.0	+4.0	85.3	61 34.0	+6.2	87.1	61 36.1	+8.3	89.0	61 36.2	+10.5	90.8	61 34.4	+12.7	92.7	18
19	61 04.2	-4.4	77.8	61 16.0	-2.3	79.5	61 25.9	-0.1	81.3	61 34.0	+2.1	83.2	61 40.2	+4.2	85.0	61 44.4	+6.5	86.9	61 46.7	+8.7	88.7	61 47.1	+10.8	90.6	19
20	60 59.8	-6.3	75.7	61 13.7	-4.1	77.5	61 25.8	-2.0	79.3	61 36.1	+0.1	81.1	61 44.4	+2.3	82.9	61 50.9	+4.5•	84.8	61 55.4	+6.7•	86.6	61 57.9	+8.9	88.5	20
21	60 53.5	-8.1	73.7	61 09.6	-6.1	75.4	61 23.8	-4.0	77.2	61 36.2	-1.8	79.0	61 46.7	+0.4	80.8	61 55.4	+2.5	82.6	62 02.1	+4.7	84.5	62 06.8	+7.0	86.4	21
22	60 45.4	-9.9	71.6	61 03.5	-7.9	73.3	61 19.8	-5.8	75.1	61 34.4	-3.8	76.9	61 47.1	-1.6	78.7	61 57.9	+0.6	80.5	62 06.8	+2.8	82.4	62 13.8	+5.0•	84.3	22
23	60 35.5	-11.7	69.6	60 55.6	-9.7	71.3	61 14.0	-7.7	73.0	61 30.6	-5.6	74.8	61 45.5	-3.5	76.6	61 58.5	-1.4	78.4	62 09.6	+0.8•	80.2	62 18.8	+3.0	82.1	23
24	60 23.8	-13.5	67.6	60 45.9	-11.6	69.3	61 06.3	-9.6	71.0	61 25.0	-7.6	72.7	61 42.0	-5.5	74.5	61 57.1	-3.3	76.3	62 10.4	-1.2	78.1	62 21.8	+1.1•	80.0	24
25	60 10.3	-15.2	65.7	60 34.3	-13.3	67.3	60 56.7	-11.4	68.9	61 17.4	-9.4	70.6	61 36.5	-7.4	72.4	61 53.8	-5.3•	74.1	62 09.2	-3.1	76.0	62 22.9	-1.0•	77.8	25
26	59 55.1	-16.9	63.7	60 21.0	-15.1	65.3	60 45.3	-13.2	66.9	61 08.0	-11.3	68.6	61 29.1	-9.3	70.3	61 48.5	-7.3	72.0	62 06.1	-5.1•	73.8	62 21.9	-3.0•	75.7	26
27	59 38.2	-18.5	61.8	60 05.9	-16.8	63.3	60 32.1	-15.0	64.9	60 56.7	-13.0	66.5	61 19.8	-11.1	68.2	61 41.2	-9.1	69.9	62 01.0	-7.1	71.7	62 18.9	-5.0	73.5	27
28	59 19.7	-20.1	59.9	59 49.1	-18.4	61.4	60 17.1	-16.6	63.0	60 43.7	-14.9	64.5	61 08.7	-13.0	66.2	61 32.1	-11.0	67.9	61 53.9	-9.0	69.6	62 13.9	-6.9	71.4	28
29	58 59.6	-21.6	58.1	59 30.7	-20.0	59.5	60 00.5	-18.4	61.0	60 28.8	-16.6	62.6	60 55.7	-14.7	64.2	61 21.1	-12.9	65.8	61 44.9	-10.9	67.5	62 07.0	-8.9	69.2	29
30	58 38.0	-23.1	56.3	59 10.7	-21.6	57.7	59 42.1	-19.9	59.1	60 12.2	-18.2	60.6	60 41.0	-16.5	62.2	61 08.2	-14.6	63.8	61 34.0	-12.8	65.4	61 58.1	-10.8	67.1	30
31	58 14.9	-24.5	54.5	58 49.1	-23.0	55.9	59 22.2	-21.5	57.3	59 54.0	-19.9	58.7	60 24.5	-18.2	60.2	60 53.6	-16.4	61.8	61 21.2	-14.5	63.4	61 47.3	-12.6	65.0	31
32	57 50.4	-25.9	52.8	58 26.1	-24.5	54.1	59 00.7	-23.0	55.4	59 34.1	-21.4	56.8	60 06.3	-19.8	58.3	60 37.2	-18.1	59.8	61 06.7	-16.4	61.4	61 34.7	-14.5	63.0	32
33	57 24.5	-27.3	51.1	58 01.6	-25.8	52.4	58 37.7	-24.4	53.7	59 12.7	-22.9	55.0	59 46.5	-21.4	56.4	60 19.1	-19.8	57.9	60 50.3	-18.1	59.4	61 20.2	-16.3	61.0	33
34	56 57.2	-28.4	49.5	57 35.8	-27.2	50.7	58 13.3	-25.9	51.9	58 49.8	-24.5	53.2	59 25.1	-22.9	54.6	59 59.3	-21.4	56.0	60 32.2	-19.7	57.4	61 03.9	-18.1	59.0	34
35	56 28.8	-29.7	47.9	57 08.6	-28.5	49.0	57 47.4	-27.1	50.2	58 25.3	-25.8	51.5	59 02.2	-24.4	52.8	59 37.9	-22.9	54.1	60 12.5	-21.3	55.5	60 45.8	-19.7	57.0	35
36	55 59.1	-30.9	46.3	56 40.1	-29.7	47.4	57 20.3	-28.5	48.5	57 59.5	-27.2	49.7	58 37.8	-25.8	51.0	59 15.0	-24.4	52.3	59 51.2	-22.9	53.7	60 26.1	-21.3	55.1	36
37	55 28.2	-31.9	44.8	56 10.4	-30.8	45.8	56 51.8	-29.7	46.9	57 32.3	-28.4	48.1	58 12.0	-27.2	49.3	58 50.6	-25.8	50.5	59 28.3	-24.5	51.8	60 04.8	-22.9	53.2	37
38	54 56.3	-33.0	43.3	55 39.6	-32.0	44.3	56 22.1	-30.8	45.3	57 03.9	-29.7	46.4	57 44.8	-28.5	47.6	58 24.8	-27.2	48.8	59 03.8	-25.8	50.0	59 41.9	-24.5	51.3	38
39	54 23.3	-34.1	41.9	55 07.6	-33.0	42.8	55 51.3	-32.0	43.8	56 34.2	-30.9	44.9	57 16.3	-29.7	45.9	57 57.6	-28.5	47.1	58 38.0	-27.2	48.3	59 17.4	-25.8	49.5	39
40	53 49.2	-34.9	40.5	54 34.6	-34.0	41.4	55 19.3	-33.0	42.3	56 03.3	-32.0	43.3	56 46.6	-30.9	44.4	57 29.1	-29.8	45.4	58 10.8	-28.6	46.6	58 51.6	-27.3	47.8	40
41	53 14.3	-35.9	39.1	54 00.6	-35.0	40.0	54 46.3	-34.1	40.9	55 31.3	-33.1	41.8	56 15.7	-32.1	42.8	56 59.3	-30.9	43.8	57 42.2	-29.8	44.9	58 24.3	-28.6	46.1	41
42	52 38.4	-36.8	37.8	53 25.6	-36.0	38.6	54 12.2	-35.0	39.4	54 58.2	-34.1	40.3	55 43.6	-33.1	41.3	56 28.4	-32.1	42.3	57 12.4	-31.0	43.3	57 55.7	-29.9	44.4	42
43	52 01.6	-37.5	36.5	52 49.6	-36.7	37.2	53 37.2	-36.0	38.1	54 24.1	-35.1	38.9	55 10.5	-34.2	39.8	55 56.3	-33.2	40.8	56 41.4	-32.2	41.7	57 25.8	-31.1	42.8	43
44	51 24.1	-38.4	35.2	52 12.9	-37.7	35.9	53 01.2	-36.8	36.7	53 49.0	-36.0	37.5	54 36.3	-35.1	38.4	55 23.1	-34.3	39.3	56 09.2	-33.3	40.2	56 54.7	-32.3	41.2	44
45	50 45.7	-39.1	34.0	51 35.2	-38.4	34.7	52 24.4	-37.7	35.4	53 13.0	-36.9	36.2	54 01.2	-36.1	37.0	54 48.8	-35.2	37.8	55 35.9	-34.3	38.7	56 22.4	-33.3	39.7	45
46	50 06.6	-39.9	32.8	50 56.8	-39.1	33.5	51 46.7	-38.5	34.2	52 36.1	-37.7	34.9	53 25.1	-37.0	35.6	54 13.6	-36.1	36.5	55 01.6	-35.3	37.3	55 49.1	-34.4	38.2	46
47	49 26.7	-40.5	31.6	50 17.7	-39.9	32.3	51 08.2	-39.2	32.9	51 58.4	-38.6	33.6	52 48.1	-37.8	34.3	53 37.5	-37.1	35.1	54 26.3	-36.2	35.9	55 14.7	-35.4	36.7	47
48	48 46.2	-41.1	30.5	49 37.8	-40.6	31.1	50 29.0	-39.9	31.7	51 19.8	-39.2	32.4	52 10.3	-38.6	33.1	53 00.4	-37.9	33.8	53 50.1	-37.2	34.5	54 39.3	-36.4	35.3	48
49	48 05.1	-41.7	29.4	48 57.2	-41.2	30.0	49 49.1	-40.7	30.6	50 40.6	-40.1	31.2	51 31.7	-39.4	31.8	52 22.5	-38.7	32.5	53 12.9	-38.0	33.2	54 02.9	-37.3	34.0	49
50	47 23.4	-42.4	28.3	48 16.0	-41.8	28.9	49 08.4	-41.2	29.4	50 00.5	-40.7	30.0	50 52.3	-40.1	30.6	51 43.8	-39.5	31.3	52 34.9	-38.8	31.9	53 25.6	-38.1	32.6	50
51	46 41.0	-42.9	27.3	47 34.2	-42.4	27.8	48 27.2	-41.9	28.3	49 19.8	-41.3	28.9	50 12.2	-40.7	29.4	51 04.3	-40.2	30.1	51 56.1	-39.6	30.7	52 47.5	-38.9	31.4	51
52	45 58.1	-43.4	26.3	46 51.8	-42.9	26.8	47 45.3	-42.5	27.2	48 38.5	-42.0	27.8	49 31.5	-41.5	28.3	50 24.1	-40.8	28.9	51 16.5	-40.3	29.5	52 08.6	-39.7	30.1	52
53	45 14.7	-43.9	25.3	46 08.9	-43.5	25.7	47 02.8	-43.0	26.2	47 56.5	-42.5	26.7	48 50.0	-42.0	27.2	49 43.3	-41.6	27.7	50 36.2	-41.0	28.3	51 28.9	-40.4	28.9	53
54	44 30.8	-44.3	24.3	45 25.4	-44.0	24.8	46 19.8	-43.5	25.2	47 14.0	-43.1	25.6	48 08.0	-42.7	26.1	49 01.7	-42.1	26.6	49 55.2	-41.6	27.2	50 48.5	-41.1	27.7	54
55	43 46.5	-44.9	23.4	44 41.4	-44.4	23.8	45 36.3	-44.1	24.2	46 30.9	-43.6	24.6	47 25.3	-43.2	25.1	48 19.6	-42.8	25.6	49 13.6	-42.3	26.0	50 07.4	-41.8	26.6	55
56	43 01.6	-45.2	22.5	43 57.0	-44.9	22.9	44 52.2	-44.5	23.2	45 47.3	-44.2	23.6	46 42.1	-43.7	24.1	47 36.8	-43.3	24.5	48 31.3	-42.8	25.0	49 25.6	-42.4	25.5	56
57	42 16.4	-45.7	21.6	43 12.1	-45.3	21.9	44 07.7	-45.0	22.3	45 03.1	-44.6	22.7	45 58.4	-44.2	23.1	46 53.5	-43.8	23.5	47 48.5	-43.4	23.9	48 43.2	-43.0	24.4	57
58	41 30.7	-46.0	20.7	42 26.8	-45.7	21.0	43 22.7	-45.4	21.4	44 18.5	-45.0	21.7	45 14.2	-44.7	22.1	46 09.7	-44.3	22.5	47 05.1	-44.0	22.9	48 00.2	-43.5	23.3	58
59	40 44.7	-46.4	19.9	41 41.1	-46.2	20.2	42 37.3	-45.8	20.5	43 33.5	-45.5	20.8	44 29.5	-45.2	21.2	45 25.4	-44.8	21.5	46 21.1	-44.4	21.9	47 16.7	-44.1	22.3	59
60	39 58.3	-46.8	19.0	40 54.9	-46.4	19.3	41 51.5	-46.2	19.6	42 48.0	-45.9	19.9	43 44.3	-45.6	20.2	44 40.6	-45.3	20.6	45 36.7	-45.0	20.9	46 32.6	-44.5	21.3	60
61	39 11.5	-47.1	18.2	40 08.5	-46.9	18.5	41 05.3	-46.5	18.8	42 02.1	-46.3	19.0	42 58.7	-45.9	19.3	43 55.3	-45.7	19.7	44 51.7	-45.3	20.0	45 48.1	-45.1	20.3	61
62	38 24.4	-47.4	17.4	39 21.6	-47.1	17.7	40 18.8	-47.0	17.9	41 15.8	-46.6	18.2	42 12.8	-46.4	18.5	43 09.6	-46.1	18.8	44 06.4	-45.8	19.1	45 03.0	-45.5	19.4	62
63	37 37.0	-47.7	16.7	38 34.5	-47.5	16.9	39 31.8	-47.2	17.1	40 29.2	-47.0	17.4	41 26.4	-46.8	17.6	42 23.5	-46.5	17.9	43 20.6	-46.2	18.2	44 17.5	-45.9	18.5	63
64	36 49.3	-48.0	15.9	37 47.0	-47.8	16.1	38 44.6	-47.6	16.3	39 42.2	-47.4	16.6	40 39.6	-47.1	16.8	41 37.0	-46.8	17.0	42 34.4	-46.6	17.3	43 31.6	-46.3	17.6	64
65	36 01.3	-48.2	15.1	36 59.2	-48.0	15.3	37 57.0	-47.8	15.5	38 54.8	-47.6	15.8	39 52.5	-47.4	16.0	40 50.2	-47.2	16.2	41 47.8	-47.0	16.5	42 45.3	-46.8	16.7	65
66	35 13.1	-48.6	14.4	36 11.2	-48.4	14.6	37 09.2	-48.2	14.8	38 07.2	-48.0	15.0	39 05.1	-47.7	15.2	40 03.0	-47.5	15.4	41 00.8	-47.3	15.6	41 58.5	-47.0	15.9	66
67	34 24.5	-48.7	13.7	35 22.8	-48.6	13.9	36 21.0	-48.4	14.0	37 19.2	-48.2	14.2	38 17.4	-48.1	14.4	39 15.5	-47.9	14.6	40 13.5	-47.7	14.8	41 11.5	-47.5	15.0	67
68	33 35.8	-49.0	13.0	34 34.2	-48.8	13.1	35 32.6	-48.6	13.3	36 31.0	-48.5	13.5	37 29.3	-48.3	13.7	38 27.6	-48.1	13.8	39 25.8	-47.9	14.0	40 24.0	-47.7	14.2	68
69	32 46.8	-49.2	12.3	33 45.4	-49.1	12.4	34 44.0	-49.0	12.6	35 42.5	-48.8	12.7	36 41.0	-48.6	12.9	37 39.5	-48.5	13.1	38 37.9	-48.3	13.3	39 36.3	-48.1	13.4	69
70	31 57.6	-49.5	11.6	32 56.3	-49.3	11.8	33 55.0	-49.1	11.9	34 53.7	-49.0	12.0	35 52.4	-48.9	12.2	36 51.0	-48.7	12.3	37 49.6	-48.5	12.5	38 48.2	-48.4	12.7	70
71	31 08.1	-49.6	11.0	32 07.0	-49.5	11.1	33 05.9	-49.4	11.2	34 04.7	-49.2	11.3	35 03.5	-49.1	11.5	36 02.3	-48.9	11.6	37 01.1	-48.8	11.8	37 59.8	-48.7	11.9	71
72	30 18.5	-49.8	10.3	31 17.5	-49.7	10.4	32 16.5	-49.6	10.5	33 15.5	-49.5	10.6	34 14.4	-49.3	10.8	35 13.3	-49.2	10.9	36 12.3	-49.1	11.0	37 11.1	-48.9	11.2	72
73	29 28.7	-50.1	9.7	30 27.8	-49.9	9.8	31 26.9	-49.8	9.9	32 26.0	-49.7	10.0	33 25.1	-49.6	10.1	34 24.2	-49.5	10.2	35 23.2	-49.3	10.3	36 22.2	-49.2	10.5	73
74	28 38.6	-50.1	9.0	29 37.9	-50.1	9.1	30 37.1	-50.0	9.2	31 36.3	-49.8	9.3	32 35.5	-49.7	9.4	33 34.7	-49.6	9.5	34 33.9	-49.5	9.6	35 33.0	-49.4	9.8	74
75	27 48.5	-50.4	8.4	28 47.8	-50.2	8.5	29 47.1	-50.1	8.6	30 46.5	-50.1	8.7	31 45.8	-50.0	8.8	32 45.1	-49.9	8.9	33 44.4	-49.8	9.0	34 43.6	-49.6	9.1	75
76	26 58.1	-50.5	7.8	27 57.6	-50.5	7.9	28 57.0	-50.3	7.9	29 56.4	-50.2	8.0	30 55.8	-50.1	8.1	31 55.2	-50.1	8.2	32 54.6	-50.0	8.3	33 54.0	-49.9	8.4	76
77	26 07.6	-50.6	7.2	27 07.1	-50.5	7.3	28 06.7	-50.5	7.3	29 06.2	-50.5	7.4	30 05.7	-50.4	7.5	31 05.1	-50.2	7.5	32 04.6	-50.2	7.6	33 04.1	-50.1	7.7	77
78	25 17.0	-50.8	6.6	26 16.6	-50.8	6.7	27 16.2	-50.7	6.7	28 15.7	-50.5	6.8	29 15.3	-50.5	6.8	30 14.9	-50.5	6.9	31 14.4	-50.3	7.0	32 14.0	-50.3	7.1	78
79	24 26.2	-51.0	6.0	25 25.8	-50.8	6.1	26 25.5	-50.8	6.1	27 25.2	-50.8	6.2	28 24.8	-50.7	6.2	29 24.4	-50.6	6.3	30 24.1	-50.6	6.4	31 23.7	-50.5	6.4	79
80	23 35.2	-51.0	5.4	24 35.0	-51.0	5.5	25 34.7	-51.0	5.5	26 34.4	-50.9	5.6	27 34.1	-50.8	5.6	28 33.8	-50.7	5.7	29 33.5	-50.7	5.7	30 33.2	-50.6	5.8	80
81	22 44.2	-51.2	4.9	23 44.0	-51.2	4.9	24 43.7	-51.0	4.9	25 43.5	-51.0	5.0	26 43.3	-51.0	5.0	27 43.1	-51.0	5.1	28 42.8	-50.9	5.1	29 42.6	-50.8	5.2	81
82	21 53.0	-51.3	4.3	22 52.8	-51.2	4.3	23 52.7	-51.2	4.4	24 52.5	-51.2	4.4	25 52.3	-51.1	4.4	26 52.1	-51.0	4.5	27 51.9	-51.0	4.5	28 51.8	-51.0	4.6	82
83	21 01.7	-51.4	3.7	22 01.6	-51.4	3.8	23 01.5	-51.4	3.8	24 01.3	-51.3	3.8	25 01.2	-51.3	3.9	26 01.1	-51.3	3.9	27 00.9	-51.2	3.9	28 00.8	-51.2	4.0	83
84	20 10.3	-51.5	3.2	21 10.2	-51.4	3.2	22 10.1	-51.4	3.2	23 10.0	-51.4	3.3	24 09.9	-51.3	3.3	25 09.8	-51.3	3.3	26 09.7	-51.3	3.3	27 09.6	-51.2	3.4	84
85	19 18.8	-51.6	2.6	20 18.8	-51.6	2.7	21 18.7	-51.6	2.7	22 18.6	-51.5	2.7	23 18.6	-51.5	2.7	24 18.5	-51.5	2.7	25 18.4	-51.4	2.8	26 18.4	-51.5	2.8	85
86	18 27.2	-51.7	2.1	19 27.2	-51.7	2.1	20 27.1	-51.6	2.1	21 27.1	-51.6	2.1	22 27.1	-51.6	2.2	23 27.0	-51.6	2.2	24 27.0	-51.6	2.2	25 26.9	-51.5	2.2	86
87	17 35.5	-51.7	1.6	18 35.5	-51.7	1.6	19 35.5	-51.7	1.6	20 35.5	-51.8	1.6	21 35.5	-51.8	1.6	22 35.4	-51.7	1.6	23 35.4	-51.7	1.6	24 35.4	-51.7	1.6	87
88	16 43.8	-51.9	1.0	17 43.8	-51.9	1.0	18 43.8	-51.9	1.1	19 43.7	-51.8	1.1	20 43.7	-51.8	1.1	21 43.7	-51.8	1.1	22 43.7	-51.8	1.1	23 43.7	-51.8	1.1	88
89	15 51.9	-51.9	0.5	16 51.9	-51.9	0.5	17 51.9	-51.9	0.5	18 51.9	-51.9	0.5	19 51.9	-51.9	0.5	20 51.9	-51.9	0.5	21 51.9	-51.9	0.5	22 51.9	-51.9	0.5	89
90	15 00.0	-52.0	0.0	16 00.0	-52.0	0.0	17 00.0	-52.0	0.0	18 00.0	-52.0	0.0	19 00.0	-52.0	0.0	20 00.0	-52.0	0.0	21 00.0	-52.0	0.0	22 00.0	-52.0	0.0	90
	15°			16°			17°			18°			19°			20°			21°			22°			

LATITUDE **CONTRARY** NAME TO DECLINATION **L.H.A. 30°, 330°**

Dec.	15° Hc	d	Z	16° Hc	d	Z	17° Hc	d	Z	18° Hc	d	Z	19° Hc	d	Z	20° Hc	d	Z	21° Hc	d	Z	22° Hc	d	Z	Dec.
°	° ′	′	°	° ′	′	°	° ′	′	°	° ′	′	°	° ′	′	°	° ′	′	°	° ′	′	°	° ′	′	°	°
0	56 46.4	-28.9	114.1	56 21.2	-30.4	115.5	55 54.8	-31.9	116.9	55 27.0	-33.2	118.2	54 58.1	-34.5	119.4	54 28.1	-35.8	120.6	53 57.0	-37.0	121.8	53 24.8	-38.1	123.0	0
1	56 17.5	-30.2	115.7	55 50.8	-31.6	117.1	55 22.9	-32.9	118.4	54 53.8	-34.2	119.6	54 23.6	-35.5	120.8	53 52.3	-36.7	122.0	53 20.0	-37.8	123.2	52 46.7	-38.9	124.3	1
2	55 47.3	-31.2	117.3	55 19.2	-32.6	118.6	54 50.0	-34.0	119.8	54 19.6	-35.2	121.0	53 48.1	-36.4	122.2	53 15.6	-37.5	123.3	52 42.2	-38.7	124.4	52 07.8	-39.7	125.5	2
3	55 16.1	-32.4	118.8	54 46.6	-33.7	120.0	54 16.0	-34.9	121.2	53 44.4	-36.2	122.4	53 11.7	-37.3	123.5	52 38.1	-38.4	124.6	52 03.5	-39.4	125.7	51 28.1	-40.5	126.7	3
4	54 43.7	-33.4	120.3	54 12.9	-34.6	121.5	53 41.1	-35.9	122.6	53 08.2	-37.0	123.8	52 34.4	-38.1	124.8	51 59.7	-39.2	125.9	51 24.1	-40.2	126.9	50 47.6	-41.1	127.9	4
5	54 10.3	-34.4	121.7	53 38.3	-35.6	122.8	53 05.2	-36.7	124.0	52 31.2	-37.8	125.1	51 56.3	-38.9	126.1	51 20.5	-39.9	127.1	50 43.9	-40.8	128.1	50 06.5	-41.8	129.0	5
6	53 35.9	-35.3	123.1	53 02.7	-36.5	124.2	52 28.5	-37.6	125.3	51 53.4	-38.6	126.3	51 17.4	-39.6	127.3	50 40.6	-40.6	128.3	50 03.1	-41.6	129.2	49 24.7	-42.4	130.2	6
7	53 00.6	-36.2	124.4	52 26.2	-37.3	125.5	51 50.9	-38.4	126.5	51 14.8	-39.4	127.6	50 37.8	-40.4	128.5	50 00.0	-41.2	129.5	49 21.5	-42.1	130.4	48 42.3	-43.0	131.2	7
8	52 24.4	-37.1	125.7	51 48.9	-38.2	126.8	51 12.5	-39.1	127.8	50 35.4	-40.1	128.7	49 57.4	-41.0	129.7	49 18.8	-41.9	130.6	48 39.4	-42.8	131.4	47 59.3	-43.5	132.3	8
9	51 47.3	-37.9	127.0	51 10.7	-38.9	128.0	50 33.4	-39.9	129.0	49 55.3	-40.8	129.9	49 16.4	-41.7	130.8	48 36.9	-42.6	131.7	47 56.6	-43.3	132.5	47 15.8	-44.1	133.3	9
10	51 09.4	-38.7	128.3	50 31.8	-39.6	129.2	49 53.5	-40.5	130.2	49 14.5	-41.5	131.0	48 34.7	-42.2	131.9	47 54.3	-43.0	132.7	47 13.3	-43.8	133.5	46 31.7	-44.6	134.3	10
11	50 30.7	-39.3	129.5	49 52.2	-40.3	130.4	49 13.0	-41.2	131.3	48 33.0	-42.0	132.1	47 52.5	-42.9	133.0	47 11.3	-43.6	133.8	46 29.5	-44.4	134.5	45 47.1	-45.0	135.3	11
12	49 51.4	-40.1	130.7	49 11.9	-41.0	131.5	48 31.8	-41.8	132.4	47 51.0	-42.6	133.2	47 09.6	-43.4	134.0	46 27.7	-44.2	134.8	45 45.1	-44.8	135.5	45 02.1	-45.5	136.2	12
13	49 11.3	-40.8	131.8	48 30.9	-41.6	132.7	47 50.0	-42.4	133.5	47 08.4	-43.2	134.3	46 26.2	-43.9	135.0	45 43.5	-44.6	135.7	45 00.3	-45.3	136.4	44 16.6	-46.0	137.1	13
14	48 30.5	-41.4	132.9	47 49.3	-42.1	133.7	47 07.6	-43.0	134.5	46 25.2	-43.7	135.3	45 42.3	-44.4	136.0	44 58.9	-45.1	136.7	44 15.0	-45.7	137.4	43 30.6	-46.3	138.0	14
15	47 49.1	-41.9	134.0	47 07.2	-42.8	134.8	46 24.6	-43.5	135.5	45 41.5	-44.2	136.3	44 57.9	-44.9	137.0	44 13.8	-45.5	137.6	43 29.3	-46.2	138.3	42 44.3	-46.7	138.9	15
16	47 07.2	-42.6	135.1	46 24.4	-43.3	135.8	45 41.1	-44.0	136.5	44 57.3	-44.6	137.2	44 13.0	-45.3	137.9	43 28.3	-45.9	138.5	42 43.1	-46.5	139.1	41 57.6	-47.1	139.7	16
17	46 24.6	-43.1	136.1	45 41.1	-43.8	136.8	44 57.1	-44.4	137.5	44 12.7	-45.2	138.2	43 27.7	-45.7	138.8	42 42.4	-46.3	139.4	41 56.6	-46.9	140.0	41 10.5	-47.5	140.6	17
18	45 41.5	-43.6	137.1	44 57.3	-44.3	137.8	44 12.7	-45.0	138.4	43 27.5	-45.5	139.1	42 42.0	-46.1	139.7	41 56.1	-46.7	140.3	41 09.7	-47.2	140.8	40 23.0	-47.7	141.4	18
19	44 57.9	-44.1	138.1	44 13.0	-44.7	138.7	43 27.7	-45.3	139.4	42 42.0	-45.9	140.0	41 55.9	-46.5	140.5	41 09.4	-47.1	141.1	40 22.5	-47.6	141.6	39 35.3	-48.1	142.2	19
20	44 13.8	-44.5	139.0	43 28.3	-45.2	139.7	42 42.4	-45.8	140.3	41 56.1	-46.4	140.8	41 09.4	-46.9	141.4	40 22.3	-47.4	141.9	39 34.9	-47.9	142.4	38 47.2	-48.4	142.9	20
21	43 29.3	-45.0	140.0	42 43.1	-45.5	140.6	41 56.6	-46.1	141.1	41 09.7	-46.7	141.7	40 22.5	-47.2	142.2	39 34.9	-47.7	142.7	38 47.0	-48.2	143.2	37 58.8	-48.7	143.7	21
22	42 44.3	-45.4	140.9	41 57.6	-46.0	141.4	41 10.5	-46.5	142.0	40 23.0	-47.0	142.5	39 35.3	-47.6	143.0	38 47.2	-48.0	143.5	37 58.8	-48.5	144.0	37 10.1	-48.9	144.4	22
23	41 58.9	-45.8	141.7	41 11.6	-46.4	142.3	40 24.0	-46.9	142.8	39 36.0	-47.4	143.3	38 47.7	-47.8	143.8	37 59.2	-48.4	144.3	37 10.3	-48.8	144.7	36 21.2	-49.2	145.1	23
24	41 13.1	-46.2	142.6	40 25.2	-46.7	143.1	39 37.1	-47.2	143.6	38 48.6	-47.7	144.1	37 59.9	-48.2	144.6	37 10.8	-48.6	145.0	36 21.5	-49.0	145.4	35 32.0	-49.4	145.9	24
25	40 26.9	-46.6	143.5	39 38.5	-47.0	144.0	38 49.9	-47.6	144.4	38 00.9	-48.0	144.9	37 11.7	-48.4	145.3	36 22.2	-48.8	145.8	35 32.5	-49.2	146.2	34 42.6	-49.7	146.5	25
26	39 40.3	-46.8	144.3	38 51.5	-47.4	144.8	38 02.3	-47.8	145.2	37 12.9	-48.2	145.6	36 23.3	-48.7	146.1	35 33.4	-49.1	146.5	34 43.3	-49.5	146.9	33 52.9	-49.9	147.2	26
27	38 53.5	-47.3	145.1	38 04.1	-47.6	145.5	37 14.5	-48.1	146.0	36 24.7	-48.6	146.4	35 34.6	-49.0	146.8	34 44.3	-49.4	147.2	33 53.8	-49.8	147.5	33 03.0	-50.1	147.9	27
28	38 06.2	-47.5	145.9	37 16.5	-48.0	146.3	36 26.4	-48.4	146.7	35 36.1	-48.8	147.1	34 45.6	-49.1	147.5	33 54.9	-49.5	147.9	33 04.0	-49.9	148.2	32 12.9	-50.2	148.5	28
29	37 18.7	-47.8	146.6	36 28.5	-48.3	147.1	35 38.0	-48.6	147.4	34 47.3	-49.0	147.8	33 56.5	-49.5	148.2	33 05.4	-49.8	148.5	32 14.1	-50.1	148.9	31 22.7	-50.5	149.2	29
30	36 30.9	-48.1	147.4	35 40.2	-48.5	147.8	34 49.4	-48.9	148.2	33 58.3	-49.3	148.5	33 07.0	-49.6	148.9	32 15.6	-50.0	149.2	31 24.0	-50.4	149.5	30 32.2	-50.7	149.8	30
31	35 42.8	-48.4	148.1	34 51.7	-48.7	148.5	34 00.5	-49.1	148.9	33 09.0	-49.5	149.2	32 17.4	-49.8	149.5	31 25.6	-50.2	149.9	30 33.6	-50.5	150.2	29 41.5	-50.8	150.4	31
32	34 54.4	-48.6	148.9	34 03.0	-49.0	149.2	33 11.4	-49.4	149.6	32 19.5	-49.7	149.9	31 27.6	-50.1	150.2	30 35.4	-50.3	150.5	29 43.1	-50.6	150.8	28 50.7	-51.0	151.0	32
33	34 05.8	-48.8	149.6	33 14.0	-49.2	149.9	32 22.0	-49.6	150.2	31 29.8	-49.9	150.5	30 37.5	-50.2	150.8	29 45.1	-50.6	151.1	28 52.5	-50.9	151.4	27 59.7	-51.1	151.6	33
34	33 17.0	-49.1	150.3	32 24.8	-49.4	150.6	31 32.4	-49.7	150.9	30 39.9	-50.1	151.2	29 47.3	-50.4	151.5	28 54.5	-50.7	151.7	28 01.6	-51.0	152.0	27 08.6	-51.3	152.2	34
35	32 27.9	-49.3	151.0	31 35.4	-49.7	151.3	30 42.7	-50.0	151.6	29 49.8	-50.2	151.8	28 56.9	-50.6	152.1	28 03.8	-50.9	152.3	27 10.6	-51.1	152.6	26 17.3	-51.4	152.8	35
36	31 38.6	-49.5	151.6	30 45.7	-49.8	151.9	29 52.7	-50.1	152.2	28 59.6	-50.5	152.5	28 06.3	-50.7	152.7	27 12.9	-51.0	152.9	26 19.5	-51.3	153.2	25 25.9	-51.6	153.4	36
37	30 49.1	-49.7	152.3	29 55.9	-50.0	152.6	29 02.6	-50.3	152.8	28 09.1	-50.6	153.1	27 15.6	-50.9	153.3	26 21.9	-51.1	153.5	25 28.2	-51.5	153.7	24 34.3	-51.7	154.0	37
38	29 59.4	-49.9	152.9	29 05.9	-50.2	153.2	28 12.3	-50.5	153.4	27 18.5	-50.7	153.7	26 24.7	-51.0	153.9	25 30.8	-51.3	154.1	24 36.7	-51.5	154.3	23 42.6	-51.8	154.5	38
39	29 09.5	-50.1	153.6	28 15.7	-50.4	153.8	27 21.8	-50.7	154.1	26 27.8	-50.9	154.3	25 33.7	-51.2	154.5	24 39.5	-51.4	154.7	23 45.2	-51.7	154.9	22 50.8	-51.9	155.1	39
40	28 19.4	-50.3	154.2	27 25.3	-50.5	154.4	26 31.1	-50.8	154.7	25 36.9	-51.1	154.9	24 42.5	-51.3	155.1	23 48.1	-51.6	155.3	22 53.5	-51.8	155.4	21 58.9	-52.0	155.6	40
41	27 29.1	-50.4	154.8	26 34.8	-50.7	155.0	25 40.3	-50.9	155.2	24 45.8	-51.2	155.4	23 51.2	-51.4	155.6	22 56.5	-51.7	155.8	22 01.7	-51.9	156.0	21 06.9	-52.1	156.1	41
42	26 38.7	-50.5	155.4	25 44.1	-50.8	155.6	24 49.4	-51.0	155.8	23 54.6	-51.3	156.0	22 59.8	-51.6	156.2	22 04.8	-51.7	156.4	21 09.8	-51.9	156.5	20 14.8	-52.2	156.7	42
43	25 48.2	-50.7	156.0	24 53.3	-51.0	156.2	23 58.4	-51.2	156.4	23 03.3	-51.4	156.6	22 08.2	-51.6	156.7	21 13.1	-51.9	156.9	20 17.9	-52.1	157.1	19 22.6	-52.3	157.2	43
44	24 57.5	-50.9	156.6	24 02.3	-51.0	156.8	23 07.2	-51.4	157.0	22 11.9	-51.5	157.1	21 16.6	-51.8	157.3	20 21.2	-52.0	157.4	19 25.8	-52.2	157.6	18 30.3	-52.4	157.7	44
45	24 06.6	-51.0	157.2	23 11.3	-51.2	157.4	22 15.8	-51.4	157.5	21 20.4	-51.7	157.7	20 24.8	-51.8	157.8	19 29.2	-52.0	158.0	18 33.6	-52.3	158.1	17 37.9	-52.5	158.2	45
46	23 15.6	-51.1	157.8	22 20.1	-51.4	157.9	21 24.4	-51.5	158.1	20 28.7	-51.7	158.2	19 33.0	-52.0	158.4	18 37.2	-52.2	158.5	17 41.3	-52.3	158.6	16 45.4	-52.5	158.7	46
47	22 24.5	-51.2	158.4	21 28.7	-51.4	158.5	20 32.9	-51.7	158.6	19 37.0	-51.9	158.8	18 41.0	-52.0	158.9	17 45.0	-52.2	159.0	16 49.0	-52.4	159.1	15 52.9	-52.6	159.2	47
48	21 33.3	-51.3	158.9	20 37.3	-51.5	159.1	19 41.2	-51.7	159.2	18 45.1	-51.9	159.3	17 49.0	-52.1	159.4	16 52.8	-52.3	159.5	15 56.6	-52.5	159.6	15 00.3	-52.7	159.7	48
49	20 42.0	-51.5	159.5	19 45.8	-51.7	159.6	18 49.5	-51.8	159.7	17 53.2	-52.0	159.8	16 56.9	-52.2	159.9	16 00.5	-52.4	160.0	15 04.1	-52.6	160.1	14 07.6	-52.7	160.2	49
50	19 50.5	-51.5	160.0	18 54.1	-51.7	160.1	17 57.7	-51.9	160.3	17 01.2	-52.1	160.4	16 04.7	-52.3	160.5	15 08.1	-52.4	160.6	14 11.5	-52.6	160.6	13 14.9	-52.8	160.7	50
51	18 59.0	-51.6	160.6	18 02.4	-51.8	160.7	17 05.8	-52.0	160.8	16 09.1	-52.2	160.9	15 12.4	-52.3	161.0	14 15.7	-52.5	161.1	13 18.9	-52.7	161.1	12 22.1	-52.8	161.2	51
52	18 07.4	-51.7	161.1	17 10.6	-51.9	161.2	16 13.8	-52.1	161.3	15 16.9	-52.2	161.4	14 20.1	-52.4	161.5	13 23.2	-52.6	161.6	12 26.2	-52.7	161.6	11 29.3	-52.9	161.7	52
53	17 15.7	-51.8	161.6	16 18.7	-52.0	161.7	15 21.7	-52.1	161.8	14 24.7	-52.3	161.9	13 27.7	-52.5	162.0	12 30.6	-52.6	162.0	11 33.5	-52.8	162.1	10 36.4	-52.9	162.2	53
54	16 23.9	-51.9	162.2	15 26.7	-52.0	162.2	14 29.6	-52.2	162.3	13 32.4	-52.4	162.4	12 35.2	-52.5	162.5	11 38.0	-52.7	162.5	10 40.7	-52.8	162.6	9 43.5	-53.0	162.7	54
55	15 32.0	-52.0	162.7	14 34.7	-52.1	162.8	13 37.4	-52.3	162.8	12 40.0	-52.4	162.9	11 42.7	-52.6	163.0	10 45.3	-52.7	163.0	9 47.9	-52.9	163.1	8 50.5	-53.0	163.1	55
56	14 40.0	-52.0	163.2	13 42.6	-52.2	163.3	12 45.1	-52.3	163.3	11 47.6	-52.5	163.4	10 50.1	-52.6	163.5	9 52.6	-52.8	163.5	8 55.0	-52.9	163.6	7 57.5	-53.0	163.6	56
57	13 48.0	-52.1	163.7	12 50.4	-52.2	163.8	11 52.8	-52.4	163.8	10 55.1	-52.5	163.9	9 57.5	-52.7	163.9	8 59.8	-52.8	164.0	8 02.1	-52.9	164.0	7 04.5	-53.1	164.1	57
58	12 55.9	-52.1	164.2	11 58.2	-52.3	164.3	11 00.4	-52.4	164.3	10 02.6	-52.5	164.4	9 04.8	-52.7	164.4	8 07.0	-52.8	164.5	7 09.2	-52.9	164.5	6 11.4	-53.1	164.5	58
59	12 03.8	-52.2	164.7	11 05.9	-52.3	164.8	10 08.0	-52.5	164.8	9 10.1	-52.6	164.9	8 12.1	-52.7	164.9	7 14.2	-52.9	165.0	6 16.3	-53.0	165.0	5 18.3	-53.1	165.0	59
60	11 11.6	-52.3	165.2	10 13.6	-52.4	165.3	9 15.5	-52.5	165.3	8 17.5	-52.7	165.4	7 19.4	-52.8	165.4	6 21.3	-52.8	165.4	5 23.3	-53.0	165.5	4 25.2	-53.1	165.5	60
61	10 19.3	-52.3	165.7	9 21.2	-52.4	165.8	8 23.0	-52.5	165.8	7 24.8	-52.6	165.9	6 26.6	-52.7	165.9	5 28.5	-52.9	165.9	4 30.3	-53.1	165.9	3 32.1	-53.2	165.9	61
62	9 27.0	-52.3	166.2	8 28.8	-52.5	166.3	7 30.5	-52.6	166.3	6 32.2	-52.7	166.3	5 33.9	-52.8	166.4	4 35.6	-53.0	166.4	3 37.2	-53.0	166.4	2 38.9	-53.1	166.4	62
63	8 34.7	-52.4	166.7	7 36.3	-52.5	166.8	6 37.9	-52.6	166.8	5 39.5	-52.7	166.8	4 41.1	-52.8	166.8	3 42.6	-52.9	166.9	2 44.2	-53.1	166.9	1 45.8	-53.2	166.9	63
64	7 42.3	-52.4	167.2	6 43.8	-52.5	167.2	5 45.3	-52.6	167.3	4 46.8	-52.8	167.3	3 48.2	-52.8	167.3	2 49.7	-53.0	167.3	1 51.1	-53.0	167.3	0 52.6	-53.2	167.3	64
65	6 49.9	-52.4	167.7	5 51.3	-52.6	167.7	4 52.7	-52.7	167.8	3 54.0	-52.7	167.8	2 55.4	-52.9	167.8	1 56.7	-52.9	167.8	0 58.1	-53.1	167.8	0 00.6	+53.1	12.2	65
66	5 57.5	-52.5	168.2	4 58.7	-52.5	168.2	4 00.0	-52.7	168.2	3 01.3	-52.8	168.2	2 02.5	-52.8	168.3	1 03.8	-53.0	168.3	0 05.0	-53.0	168.3	0 53.7	+53.2	11.7	66
67	5 05.0	-52.5	168.7	4 06.2	-52.6	168.7	3 07.3	-52.6	168.7	2 08.5	-52.8	168.7	1 09.7	-52.9	168.7	0 10.8	-53.0	168.7	0 48.0	+53.1	11.3	1 46.9	+53.1	11.3	67
68	4 12.5	-52.5	169.2	3 13.6	-52.6	169.2	2 14.7	-52.7	169.2	1 15.7	-52.8	169.2	0 16.8	-52.9	169.2	0 42.2	+52.9	10.8	1 41.1	+53.0	10.8	2 40.0	+53.2	10.8	68
69	3 20.0	-52.5	169.7	2 21.0	-52.6	169.7	1 22.0	-52.7	169.7	0 22.9	-52.7	169.7	0 36.1	+52.9	10.3	1 35.1	+53.0	10.3	2 34.1	+53.1	10.3	3 33.2	+53.1	10.3	69
70	2 27.5	-52.5	170.1	1 28.4	-52.6	170.2	0 29.3	-52.7	170.2	0 29.8	+52.8	9.8	1 29.0	+52.8	9.8	2 28.1	+52.9	9.9	3 27.2	+53.0	9.9	4 26.3	+53.1	9.9	70
71	1 35.0	-52.6	170.6	0 35.8	-52.6	170.6	0 23.4	+52.7	9.4	1 22.6	+52.8	9.4	2 21.8	+52.9	9.4	3 21.0	+52.9	9.4	4 20.2	+53.0	9.4	5 19.4	+53.1	9.4	71
72	0 42.4	-52.5	171.1	0 16.8	+52.6	8.9	1 16.1	+52.7	8.9	2 15.4	+52.8	8.9	3 14.7	+52.8	8.9	4 13.9	+53.0	8.9	5 13.2	+53.0	8.9	6 12.5	+53.1	8.9	72
73	0 10.1	+52.5	8.4	1 09.4	+52.7	8.4	2 08.8	+52.7	8.4	3 08.2	+52.7	8.4	4 07.5	+52.8	8.4	5 06.9	+52.9	8.4	6 06.2	+53.0	8.5	7 05.6	+53.0	8.5	73
74	1 02.6	+52.6	7.9	2 02.1	+52.6	7.9	3 01.5	+52.7	7.9	4 00.9	+52.7	7.9	5 00.3	+52.8	8.0	5 59.8	+52.8	8.0	6 59.2	+52.9	8.0	7 58.6	+53.0	8.0	74
75	1 55.2	+52.5	7.4	2 54.7	+52.5	7.4	3 54.2	+52.6	7.5	4 53.6	+52.8	7.5	5 53.1	+52.8	7.5	6 52.6	+52.9	7.5	7 52.1	+52.9	7.5	8 51.6	+53.0	7.5	75
76	2 47.7	+52.5	7.0	3 47.2	+52.6	7.0	4 46.8	+52.7	7.0	5 46.4	+52.7	7.0	6 45.9	+52.8	7.0	7 45.5	+52.8	7.0	8 45.0	+52.9	7.0	9 44.6	+52.9	7.0	76
77	3 40.2	+52.5	6.5	4 39.8	+52.6	6.5	5 39.4	+52.6	6.5	6 39.1	+52.6	6.5	7 38.7	+52.7	6.5	8 38.3	+52.7	6.5	9 37.9	+52.8	6.6	10 37.5	+52.9	6.6	77
78	4 32.7	+52.5	6.0	5 32.4	+52.5	6.0	6 32.0	+52.6	6.0	7 31.7	+52.6	6.0	8 31.4	+52.7	6.0	9 31.0	+52.8	6.1	10 30.7	+52.8	6.1	11 30.4	+52.8	6.1	78
79	5 25.2	+52.4	5.5	6 24.9	+52.5	5.5	7 24.6	+52.6	5.5	8 24.3	+52.6	5.5	9 24.1	+52.6	5.5	10 23.8	+52.7	5.6	11 23.5	+52.7	5.6	12 23.2	+52.8	5.6	79
80	6 17.6	+52.5	5.0	7 17.4	+52.5	5.0	8 17.2	+52.5	5.0	9 16.9	+52.6	5.0	10 16.7	+52.6	5.1	11 16.5	+52.6	5.1	12 16.2	+52.7	5.1	13 16.0	+52.7	5.1	80
81	7 10.1	+52.4	4.5	8 09.9	+52.4	4.5	9 09.7	+52.5	4.5	10 09.5	+52.5	4.6	11 09.3	+52.6	4.6	12 09.1	+52.6	4.6	13 08.9	+52.6	4.6	14 08.7	+52.7	4.6	81
82	8 02.5	+52.3	4.0	9 02.3	+52.4	4.0	10 02.2	+52.4	4.1	11 02.0	+52.5	4.1	12 01.9	+52.5	4.1	13 01.7	+52.5	4.1	14 01.5	+52.6	4.1	15 01.4	+52.6	4.1	82
83	8 54.8	+52.3	3.5	9 54.7	+52.4	3.5	10 54.6	+52.4	3.6	11 54.5	+52.4	3.6	12 54.4	+52.4	3.6	13 54.2	+52.5	3.6	14 54.1	+52.5	3.6	15 54.0	+52.5	3.6	83
84	9 47.1	+52.3	3.0	10 47.1	+52.3	3.0	11 47.0	+52.3	3.1	12 46.9	+52.3	3.1	13 46.8	+52.4	3.1	14 46.7	+52.4	3.1	15 46.6	+52.4	3.1	16 46.5	+52.5	3.1	84
85	10 39.4	+52.2	2.5	11 39.4	+52.2	2.6	12 39.3	+52.3	2.6	13 39.2	+52.3	2.6	14 39.2	+52.3	2.6	15 39.1	+52.3	2.6	16 39.0	+52.4	2.6	17 39.0	+52.4	2.6	85
86	11 31.6	+52.2	2.0	12 31.6	+52.2	2.0	13 31.6	+52.2	2.1	14 31.5	+52.3	2.1	15 31.5	+52.2	2.1	16 31.4	+52.3	2.1	17 31.4	+52.3	2.1	18 31.4	+52.3	2.1	86
87	12 23.8	+52.1	1.5	13 23.8	+52.1	1.5	14 23.8	+52.1	1.5	15 23.8	+52.1	1.6	16 23.7	+52.2	1.6	17 23.7	+52.2	1.6	18 23.7	+52.2	1.6	19 23.7	+52.2	1.6	87
88	13 15.9	+52.1	1.0	14 15.9	+52.1	1.0	15 15.9	+52.1	1.0	16 15.9	+52.1	1.0	17 15.9	+52.1	1.0	18 15.9	+52.1	1.1	19 15.9	+52.1	1.1	20 15.9	+52.1	1.1	88
89	14 08.0	+52.0	0.5	15 08.0	+52.0	0.5	16 08.0	+52.0	0.5	17 08.0	+52.0	0.5	18 08.0	+52.0	0.5	19 08.0	+52.0	0.5	20 08.0	+52.0	0.5	21 08.0	+52.0	0.5	89
90	15 00.0	+51.9	0.0	16 00.0	+51.9	0.0	17 00.0	+51.9	0.0	18 00.0	+51.9	0.0	19 00.0	+51.9	0.0	20 00.0	+51.9	0.0	21 00.0	+51.9	0.0	22 00.0	+51.9	0.0	90
	15°			16°			17°			18°			19°			20°			21°			22°			

S. Lat. {L.H.A. greater than 180° ....Zn=180°−Z
{L.H.A. less than 180°...........Zn=180°+Z

LATITUDE **SAME** NAME AS DECLINATION **L.H.A. 150°, 210°**

63

Dec.	15°			16°			17°			18°			19°			20°			21°			22°			Dec.
	Hc	d	Z	Hc	d	Z	Hc	d	Z	Hc	d	Z	Hc	d	Z	Hc	d	Z	Hc	d	Z	Hc	d	Z	
°	° ′	′	°	° ′	′	°	° ′	′	°	° ′	′	°	° ′	′	°	° ′	′	°	° ′	′	°	° ′	′	°	°
0	55 53.4	+27.1	113.3	55 29.0	+28.6	114.6	55 03.4	+30.0	115.9	54 36.5	+31.5	117.2	54 08.5	+32.8	118.5	53 39.4	+34.1	119.6	53 09.2	+35.3	120.8	52 37.9	+36.6	121.9	0
1	56 20.5	+25.8	111.7	55 57.6	+27.4	113.1	55 33.4	+28.9	114.4	55 08.0	+30.4	115.7	54 41.3	+31.8	117.0	54 13.5	+33.2	118.3	53 44.5	+34.5	119.5	53 14.5	+35.7	120.6	1
2	56 46.3	+24.5	110.1	56 25.0	+26.1	111.5	56 02.3	+27.7	112.9	55 38.4	+29.2	114.2	55 13.1	+30.7	115.5	54 46.7	+32.1	116.8	54 19.0	+33.5	118.1	53 50.2	+34.8	119.3	2
3	57 10.8	+23.1	108.4	56 51.1	+24.8	109.8	56 30.0	+26.5	111.3	56 07.6	+28.0	112.7	55 43.8	+29.6	114.0	55 18.8	+31.0	115.3	54 52.5	+32.4	116.6	54 25.0	+33.8	117.9	3
4	57 33.9	+21.7	106.7	57 15.9	+23.5	108.2	56 56.5	+25.1	109.6	56 35.6	+26.8	111.1	56 13.4	+28.3	112.5	55 49.8	+29.8	113.8	55 24.9	+31.3	115.2	54 58.8	+32.7	116.5	4
5	57 55.6	+20.2	104.9	57 39.4	+22.0	106.5	57 21.6	+23.8	108.0	57 02.4	+25.4	109.4	56 41.7	+27.1	110.9	56 19.6	+28.7	112.3	55 56.2	+30.2	113.6	55 31.5	+31.7	115.0	5
6	58 15.8	+18.7	103.2	58 01.4	+20.5	104.7	57 45.4	+22.3	106.2	57 27.8	+24.1	107.8	57 08.8	+25.8	109.2	56 48.3	+27.4	110.7	56 26.4	+29.0	112.1	56 03.2	+30.5	113.5	6
7	58 34.5	+17.2	101.3	58 21.9	+19.1	102.9	58 07.7	+20.9	104.5	57 51.9	+22.7	106.0	57 34.6	+24.4	107.6	57 15.7	+26.1	109.0	56 55.4	+27.8	110.5	56 33.7	+29.3	111.9	7
8	58 51.7	+15.6	99.5	58 41.0	+17.5	101.1	58 28.6	+19.4	102.7	58 14.6	+21.2	104.3	57 59.0	+23.0	105.8	57 41.8	+24.8	107.4	57 23.2	+26.4	108.9	57 03.0	+28.1	110.3	8
9	59 07.3	+13.9	97.6	58 58.5	+15.8	99.3	58 48.0	+17.8	100.9	58 35.8	+19.7	102.5	58 22.0	+21.5	104.1	58 06.6	+23.3	105.7	57 49.6	+25.1	107.2	57 31.1	+26.8	108.7	9
10	59 21.2	+12.2	95.7	59 14.3	+14.3	97.4	59 05.8	+16.2	99.0	58 55.5	+18.1	100.7	58 43.5	+20.0	102.3	58 29.9	+21.9	103.9	58 14.7	+23.7	105.5	57 57.9	+25.5	107.0	10
11	59 33.4	+10.5	93.8	59 28.6	+12.5	95.5	59 22.0	+14.5	97.2	59 13.6	+16.5	98.8	59 03.5	+18.5	100.5	58 51.8	+20.4	102.1	58 38.4	+22.2	103.7	58 23.4	+24.0	105.3	11
12	59 43.9	+8.8	91.8	59 41.1	+10.8	93.5	59 36.5	+12.9	95.3	59 30.1	+14.9	96.9	59 22.0	+16.8	98.6	59 12.2	+18.7	100.3	59 00.6	+20.7	101.9	58 47.4	+22.5	103.5	12
13	59 52.7	+7.0	89.9	59 51.9	+9.1	91.6	59 49.4	+11.1	93.3	59 45.0	+13.2	95.0	59 38.8	+15.2	96.7	59 30.9	+17.2	98.4	59 21.3	+19.1	100.1	59 09.9	+21.1	101.7	13
14	59 59.7	+5.2	87.9	60 01.0	+7.3	89.6	60 00.5	+9.3	91.4	59 58.2	+11.4	93.1	59 54.0	+13.5	94.8	59 48.1	+15.5	96.5	59 40.4	+17.5	98.2	59 31.0	+19.4	99.9	14
15	60 04.9	+3.4	85.9	60 08.3	+5.5	87.6	60 09.8	+7.6	89.4	60 09.6	+9.6	91.1	60 07.5	+11.7	92.9	60 03.6	+13.8	94.6	59 57.9	+15.8	96.3	59 50.4	+17.8	98.0	15
16	60 08.3	+1.5	83.9	60 13.8	+3.6	85.6	60 17.4	+5.8	87.4	60 19.2	+7.9	89.1	60 19.2	+10.0	90.9	60 17.4	+12.0	92.6	60 13.7	+14.1	94.4	60 08.2	+16.2	96.1	16
17	60 09.8	-0.2	81.9	60 17.4	+1.8	83.6	60 23.2	+3.9	85.4	60 27.1	+6.1	87.1	60 29.2	+8.2	88.9	60 29.4	+10.3	90.7	60 27.8	+12.4	92.4	60 24.4	+14.4	94.2	17
18	60 09.6	-2.1	79.9	60 19.2	0.0	81.6	60 27.1	+2.1	83.3	60 33.2	+4.2	85.1	60 37.4	+6.3	86.9	60 39.7	+8.4	88.6	60 40.2	+10.5	90.4	60 38.8	+12.7	92.2	18
19	60 07.5	-3.9	77.9	60 19.2	-1.8	79.6	60 29.2	+0.2	81.3	60 37.4	+2.3	83.1	60 43.7	+4.4	84.8	60 48.1	+6.6	86.6	60 50.7	+8.8	88.4	60 51.5	+10.8	90.2	19
20	60 03.6	-5.7	75.9	60 17.4	-3.7	77.6	60 29.4	-1.6	79.3	60 39.7	+0.5	81.0	60 48.1	+2.6	82.8	60 54.7	+4.8	84.6	60 59.5	+6.8	86.4	61 02.3	+9.0	88.2	20
21	59 57.9	-7.5	73.9	60 13.7	-5.5	75.5	60 27.8	-3.4	77.3	60 40.2	-1.4	79.0	60 50.7	+0.8	80.7	60 59.5	+2.8	82.5	61 06.3	+5.0	84.3	61 11.3	+7.2	86.1	21
22	59 50.4	-9.3	71.9	60 08.2	-7.3	73.5	60 24.4	-5.3	75.2	60 38.8	-3.2	77.0	60 51.5	-1.2	78.7	61 02.3	+1.0	80.5	61 11.3	+3.1	82.3	61 18.5	+5.2	84.1	22
23	59 41.1	-11.0	69.9	60 00.9	-9.0	71.6	60 19.1	-7.1	73.2	60 35.6	-5.1	74.9	60 50.3	-3.0	76.6	61 03.3	-1.0	78.4	61 14.4	+1.2	80.2	61 23.7	+3.4	82.0	23
24	59 30.1	-12.7	68.0	59 51.9	-10.9	69.6	60 12.0	-8.9	71.2	60 30.5	-6.9	72.9	60 47.3	-4.9	74.6	61 02.3	-2.8	76.3	61 15.6	-0.7	78.1	61 27.1	+1.4	79.9	24
25	59 17.4	-14.3	66.1	59 41.0	-12.5	67.6	60 03.1	-10.7	69.2	60 23.6	-8.8	70.9	60 42.4	-6.8	72.6	60 59.5	-4.7	74.3	61 14.9	-2.6	76.0	61 28.5	-0.5	77.8	25
26	59 03.1	-16.1	64.2	59 28.5	-14.3	65.7	59 52.4	-12.4	67.3	60 14.8	-10.5	68.9	60 35.6	-8.5	70.5	60 54.8	-6.6	72.2	61 12.3	-4.6	74.0	61 28.0	-2.5	75.7	26
27	58 47.0	-17.6	62.3	59 14.2	-15.9	63.8	59 40.0	-14.1	65.3	60 04.3	-12.3	66.9	60 27.1	-10.4	68.5	60 48.2	-8.4	70.2	61 07.7	-6.4	71.9	61 25.5	-4.3	73.6	27
28	58 29.4	-19.1	60.5	58 58.3	-17.4	61.9	59 25.9	-15.8	63.4	59 52.0	-13.9	64.9	60 16.7	-12.1	66.5	60 39.8	-10.2	68.2	61 01.3	-8.2	69.8	61 21.2	-6.3	71.5	28
29	58 10.3	-20.7	58.7	58 40.9	-19.1	60.1	59 10.1	-17.4	61.5	59 38.1	-15.7	63.0	60 04.6	-13.9	64.6	60 29.6	-12.0	66.1	60 53.1	-10.1	67.8	61 14.9	-8.1	69.5	29
30	57 49.6	-22.1	56.9	58 21.8	-20.6	58.2	58 52.7	-18.9	59.7	59 22.4	-17.3	61.1	59 50.7	-15.6	62.6	60 17.6	-13.8	64.2	60 43.0	-11.9	65.8	61 06.8	-10.0	67.4	30
31	57 27.5	-23.5	55.2	58 01.2	-22.0	56.5	58 33.8	-20.5	57.8	59 05.1	-18.9	59.2	59 35.1	-17.2	60.7	60 03.8	-15.5	62.2	60 31.1	-13.7	63.8	60 56.8	-11.8	65.4	31
32	57 04.0	-24.9	53.5	57 39.2	-23.5	54.7	58 13.3	-22.0	56.0	58 46.2	-20.4	57.4	59 17.9	-18.8	58.8	59 48.3	-17.1	60.3	60 17.4	-15.4	61.8	60 45.0	-13.6	63.4	32
33	56 39.1	-26.1	51.8	57 15.7	-24.8	53.0	57 51.3	-23.4	54.3	58 25.8	-21.9	55.6	58 59.1	-20.4	57.0	59 31.2	-18.8	58.4	60 02.0	-17.1	59.9	60 31.4	-15.3	61.4	33
34	56 13.0	-27.5	50.2	56 50.9	-26.1	51.3	57 27.9	-24.8	52.6	58 03.9	-23.4	53.8	58 38.7	-21.9	55.1	59 12.4	-20.3	56.5	59 44.9	-18.7	57.9	60 16.1	-17.0	59.4	34
35	55 45.5	-28.6	48.6	56 24.8	-27.4	49.7	57 03.1	-26.1	50.9	57 40.5	-24.7	52.1	58 16.8	-23.3	53.4	58 52.1	-21.9	54.7	59 26.2	-20.3	56.1	59 59.1	-18.7	57.5	35
36	55 16.9	-29.8	47.0	55 57.4	-28.6	48.1	56 37.0	-27.3	49.2	57 15.8	-26.1	50.4	57 53.5	-24.7	51.6	58 30.2	-23.3	52.9	59 05.9	-21.9	54.2	59 40.4	-20.3	55.6	36
37	54 47.1	-30.9	45.5	55 28.8	-29.8	46.5	56 09.7	-28.6	47.6	56 49.7	-27.4	48.7	57 28.8	-26.1	49.9	58 06.9	-24.7	51.1	58 44.0	-23.3	52.4	59 20.1	-21.9	53.8	37
38	54 16.2	-31.9	44.0	54 59.0	-30.8	45.0	55 41.1	-29.8	46.0	56 22.3	-28.6	47.1	57 02.7	-27.4	48.3	57 42.2	-26.1	49.4	58 20.7	-24.7	50.7	58 58.2	-23.3	51.9	38
39	53 44.3	-32.9	42.6	54 28.2	-32.0	43.5	55 11.3	-30.9	44.5	55 53.7	-29.8	45.5	56 35.3	-28.6	46.6	57 16.1	-27.4	47.8	57 56.0	-26.1	48.9	58 34.9	-24.8	50.2	39
40	53 11.4	-34.0	41.2	53 56.2	-33.0	42.1	54 40.4	-32.0	43.0	55 23.9	-30.9	44.0	56 06.7	-29.8	45.0	56 48.7	-28.7	46.1	57 29.9	-27.5	47.2	58 10.1	-26.1	48.4	40
41	52 37.4	-34.8	39.8	53 23.2	-33.9	40.7	54 08.4	-32.9	41.6	54 53.0	-32.0	42.5	55 36.9	-31.0	43.5	56 20.0	-29.8	44.5	57 02.4	-28.7	45.6	57 44.0	-27.5	46.7	41
42	52 02.6	-35.7	38.5	52 49.3	-34.8	39.3	53 35.5	-34.0	40.2	54 21.0	-33.0	41.0	55 05.9	-32.0	42.0	55 50.2	-31.0	43.0	56 33.7	-29.9	44.0	57 16.5	-28.7	45.1	42
43	51 26.9	-36.6	37.2	52 14.5	-35.8	38.0	53 01.5	-34.9	38.8	53 48.0	-34.0	39.6	54 33.9	-33.1	40.5	55 19.2	-32.1	41.5	56 03.8	-31.0	42.4	56 47.8	-30.0	43.5	43
44	50 50.3	-37.3	35.9	51 38.7	-36.6	36.7	52 26.6	-35.8	37.4	53 14.0	-35.0	38.2	54 00.8	-34.0	39.1	54 47.1	-33.1	40.0	55 32.8	-32.2	40.9	56 17.8	-31.1	41.9	44
45	50 13.0	-38.1	34.7	51 02.1	-37.4	35.4	51 50.8	-36.6	36.1	52 39.0	-35.8	36.9	53 26.8	-35.0	37.7	54 14.0	-34.2	38.5	55 00.6	-33.2	39.4	55 46.7	-32.3	40.4	45
46	49 34.9	-38.8	33.5	50 24.7	-38.1	34.2	51 14.2	-37.5	34.8	52 03.2	-36.7	35.6	52 51.8	-35.9	36.3	53 39.8	-35.0	37.1	54 27.4	-34.2	38.0	55 14.4	-33.3	38.9	46
47	48 56.1	-39.6	32.3	49 46.6	-38.9	33.0	50 36.7	-38.2	33.6	51 26.5	-37.5	34.3	52 15.9	-36.8	35.0	53 04.8	-36.0	35.8	53 53.2	-35.2	36.6	54 41.1	-34.3	37.4	47
48	48 16.5	-40.2	31.2	49 07.7	-39.6	31.8	49 58.5	-38.9	32.4	50 49.0	-38.3	33.1	51 39.1	-37.6	33.7	52 28.8	-36.9	34.5	53 18.0	-36.0	35.2	54 06.8	-35.3	36.0	48
49	47 36.3	-40.8	30.1	48 28.1	-40.2	30.6	49 19.6	-39.6	31.2	50 10.7	-39.0	31.8	51 01.5	-38.3	32.5	51 51.9	-37.6	33.2	52 42.0	-37.0	33.9	53 31.5	-36.1	34.6	49
50	46 55.5	-41.4	29.0	47 47.9	-40.9	29.5	48 40.0	-40.3	30.1	49 31.7	-39.7	30.7	50 23.2	-39.1	31.3	51 14.3	-38.5	31.9	52 05.0	-37.8	32.6	52 55.4	-37.1	33.3	50
51	46 14.1	-41.9	27.9	47 07.0	-41.4	28.4	47 59.7	-41.0	29.0	48 52.0	-40.4	29.5	49 44.1	-39.8	30.1	50 35.8	-39.2	30.7	51 27.2	-38.5	31.3	52 18.3	-37.9	32.0	51
52	45 32.2	-42.5	26.9	46 25.6	-42.1	27.4	47 18.7	-41.5	27.9	48 11.6	-41.0	28.4	49 04.3	-40.5	28.9	49 56.6	-39.9	29.5	50 48.7	-39.3	30.1	51 40.4	-38.6	30.8	52
53	44 49.7	-43.0	25.9	45 43.5	-42.5	26.4	46 37.2	-42.1	26.8	47 30.6	-41.6	27.3	48 23.8	-41.1	27.8	49 16.7	-40.5	28.4	50 09.4	-40.0	28.9	51 01.8	-39.5	29.5	53
54	44 06.7	-43.5	24.9	45 01.0	-43.1	25.4	45 55.1	-42.6	25.8	46 49.0	-42.2	26.3	47 42.7	-41.7	26.7	48 36.2	-41.2	27.2	49 29.4	-40.7	27.8	50 22.3	-40.1	28.3	54
55	43 23.2	-44.0	24.0	44 17.9	-43.6	24.4	45 12.5	-43.2	24.8	46 06.8	-42.7	25.2	47 01.0	-42.3	25.7	47 55.0	-41.8	26.2	48 48.7	-41.3	26.7	49 42.2	-40.8	27.2	55
56	42 39.2	-44.4	23.1	43 34.3	-44.0	23.4	44 29.3	-43.6	23.8	45 24.1	-43.2	24.2	46 18.7	-42.8	24.6	47 13.2	-42.4	25.1	48 07.4	-41.9	25.6	49 01.4	-41.4	26.1	56
57	41 54.8	-44.8	22.1	42 50.3	-44.5	22.5	43 45.7	-44.2	22.9	44 40.9	-43.8	23.2	45 35.9	-43.3	23.6	46 30.8	-42.9	24.1	47 25.5	-42.5	24.5	48 20.0	-42.0	25.0	57
58	41 10.0	-45.3	21.3	42 05.8	-44.9	21.6	43 01.5	-44.5	21.9	43 57.1	-44.2	22.3	44 52.6	-43.8	22.7	45 47.9	-43.5	23.0	46 43.0	-43.0	23.5	47 38.0	-42.7	23.9	58
59	40 24.7	-45.6	20.4	41 20.9	-45.3	20.7	42 17.0	-45.0	21.0	43 12.9	-44.6	21.3	44 08.8	-44.3	21.7	45 04.4	-43.9	22.1	46 00.0	-43.6	22.4	46 55.3	-43.1	22.9	59
60	39 39.1	-45.9	19.5	40 35.6	-45.7	19.8	41 32.0	-45.4	20.1	42 28.3	-45.1	20.4	43 24.5	-44.8	20.8	44 20.5	-44.4	21.1	45 16.4	-44.0	21.5	46 12.2	-43.7	21.8	60
61	38 53.2	-46.4	18.7	39 49.9	-46.0	19.0	40 46.6	-45.7	19.3	41 43.2	-45.4	19.5	42 39.7	-45.2	19.8	43 36.1	-44.9	20.2	44 32.4	-44.6	20.5	45 28.5	-44.2	20.9	61
62	38 06.8	-46.6	17.9	39 03.9	-46.4	18.1	40 00.9	-46.2	18.4	40 57.8	-45.9	18.7	41 54.5	-45.5	19.0	42 51.2	-45.2	19.3	43 47.8	-44.9	19.6	44 44.3	-44.6	19.9	62
63	37 20.2	-47.0	17.1	38 17.5	-46.7	17.3	39 14.7	-46.4	17.6	40 11.9	-46.2	17.8	41 09.0	-46.0	18.1	42 06.0	-45.7	18.4	43 02.9	-45.4	18.7	43 59.7	-45.1	19.0	63
64	36 33.2	-47.2	16.3	37 30.8	-47.0	16.5	38 28.3	-46.8	16.8	39 25.7	-46.6	17.0	40 23.0	-46.3	17.2	41 20.3	-46.1	17.5	42 17.5	-45.8	17.8	43 14.6	-45.6	18.1	64
65	35 46.0	-47.6	15.6	36 43.8	-47.4	15.8	37 41.5	-47.1	16.0	38 39.1	-46.9	16.2	39 36.7	-46.7	16.4	40 34.2	-46.4	16.7	41 31.7	-46.2	16.9	42 29.0	-45.9	17.2	65
66	34 58.4	-47.8	14.8	35 56.4	-47.6	15.0	36 54.4	-47.5	15.2	37 52.2	-47.2	15.4	38 50.0	-46.9	15.6	39 47.8	-46.8	15.8	40 45.5	-46.5	16.1	41 43.1	-46.3	16.3	66
67	34 10.6	-48.0	14.1	35 08.8	-47.9	14.2	36 06.9	-47.7	14.4	37 05.0	-47.5	14.6	38 03.1	-47.3	14.8	39 01.0	-47.1	15.0	39 59.0	-46.9	15.2	40 56.8	-46.6	15.5	67
68	33 22.6	-48.3	13.4	34 20.9	-48.1	13.5	35 19.2	-47.9	13.7	36 17.5	-47.8	13.8	37 15.8	-47.7	14.0	38 13.9	-47.4	14.2	39 12.1	-47.2	14.4	40 10.2	-47.1	14.6	68
69	32 34.3	-48.6	12.7	33 32.8	-48.4	12.8	34 31.3	-48.3	12.9	35 29.7	-48.0	13.1	36 28.1	-47.8	13.3	37 26.5	-47.7	13.4	38 24.9	-47.6	13.6	39 23.1	-47.3	13.8	69
70	31 45.7	-48.8	12.0	32 44.4	-48.6	12.1	33 43.0	-48.4	12.2	34 41.7	-48.3	12.4	35 40.3	-48.2	12.5	36 38.8	-48.0	12.7	37 37.3	-47.8	12.9	38 35.8	-47.6	13.0	70
71	30 56.9	-48.9	11.3	31 55.8	-48.9	11.4	32 54.6	-48.7	11.5	33 53.4	-48.6	11.7	34 52.1	-48.4	11.8	35 50.8	-48.2	11.9	36 49.5	-48.1	12.1	37 48.2	-48.0	12.3	71
72	30 08.0	-49.2	10.6	31 06.9	-49.0	10.7	32 05.9	-49.0	10.8	33 04.8	-48.8	10.9	34 03.7	-48.7	11.1	35 02.6	-48.6	11.2	36 01.4	-48.4	11.3	37 00.2	-48.2	11.5	72
73	29 18.8	-49.4	9.9	30 17.9	-49.3	10.0	31 16.9	-49.1	10.1	32 16.0	-49.0	10.3	33 15.0	-48.9	10.4	34 14.0	-48.7	10.5	35 13.0	-48.6	10.6	36 12.0	-48.5	10.8	73
74	28 29.4	-49.5	9.3	29 28.6	-49.4	9.4	30 27.8	-49.3	9.5	31 27.0	-49.2	9.6	32 26.1	-49.1	9.7	33 25.3	-49.0	9.8	34 24.4	-48.9	9.9	35 23.5	-48.8	10.0	74
75	27 39.9	-49.8	8.7	28 39.2	-49.7	8.7	29 38.5	-49.6	8.8	30 37.8	-49.5	8.9	31 37.0	-49.3	9.0	32 36.3	-49.2	9.1	33 35.5	-49.1	9.2	34 34.7	-49.0	9.3	75
76	26 50.1	-49.9	8.0	27 49.5	-49.8	8.1	28 48.9	-49.7	8.2	29 48.3	-49.6	8.3	30 47.7	-49.5	8.3	31 47.1	-49.5	8.4	32 46.4	-49.3	8.5	33 45.7	-49.2	8.6	76
77	26 00.2	-50.0	7.4	26 59.7	-49.9	7.5	27 59.2	-49.9	7.5	28 58.7	-49.8	7.6	29 58.2	-49.7	7.7	30 57.6	-49.6	7.8	31 57.1	-49.6	7.8	32 56.5	-49.4	7.9	77
78	25 10.2	-50.2	6.8	26 09.8	-50.1	6.9	27 09.3	-50.0	6.9	28 08.9	-50.0	7.0	29 08.5	-49.9	7.0	30 08.0	-49.8	7.1	31 07.5	-49.7	7.2	32 07.1	-49.7	7.3	78
79	24 20.0	-50.3	6.2	25 19.7	-50.3	6.2	26 19.3	-50.2	6.3	27 18.9	-50.1	6.4	28 18.6	-50.1	6.4	29 18.2	-50.0	6.5	30 17.8	-49.9	6.5	31 17.4	-49.9	6.6	79
80	23 29.7	-50.5	5.6	24 29.4	-50.4	5.6	25 29.1	-50.4	5.7	26 28.8	-50.3	5.7	27 28.5	-50.2	5.8	28 28.2	-50.2	5.8	29 27.9	-50.1	5.9	30 27.5	-50.0	6.0	80
81	22 39.2	-50.6	5.0	23 39.0	-50.6	5.0	24 38.7	-50.5	5.1	25 38.5	-50.4	5.1	26 38.3	-50.4	5.2	27 38.0	-50.3	5.2	28 37.8	-50.3	5.3	29 37.5	-50.2	5.3	81
82	21 48.6	-50.7	4.4	22 48.4	-50.7	4.5	23 48.2	-50.6	4.5	24 48.1	-50.6	4.5	25 47.9	-50.6	4.6	26 47.7	-50.5	4.6	27 47.5	-50.5	4.6	28 47.3	-50.4	4.7	82
83	20 57.9	-50.8	3.9	21 57.7	-50.7	3.9	22 57.6	-50.7	3.9	23 57.5	-50.8	3.9	24 57.3	-50.7	4.0	25 57.2	-50.7	4.0	26 57.0	-50.6	4.0	27 56.9	-50.6	4.1	83
84	20 07.1	-51.0	3.3	21 07.0	-51.0	3.3	22 06.9	-50.9	3.3	23 06.7	-50.8	3.4	24 06.6	-50.8	3.4	25 06.5	-50.7	3.4	26 06.4	-50.7	3.4	27 06.3	-50.7	3.5	84
85	19 16.1	-51.0	2.7	20 16.0	-51.0	2.7	21 16.0	-51.0	2.8	22 15.9	-51.0	2.8	23 15.8	-50.9	2.8	24 15.8	-51.0	2.8	25 15.7	-50.9	2.8	26 15.6	-50.8	2.9	85
86	18 25.1	-51.2	2.2	19 25.0	-51.1	2.2	20 25.0	-51.1	2.2	21 24.9	-51.0	2.2	22 24.9	-51.1	2.2	23 24.8	-51.0	2.2	24 24.8	-51.0	2.3	25 24.8	-51.0	2.3	86
87	17 33.9	-51.2	1.6	18 33.9	-51.2	1.6	19 33.9	-51.2	1.6	20 33.9	-51.2	1.6	21 33.8	-51.1	1.7	22 33.8	-51.2	1.7	23 33.8	-51.2	1.7	24 33.8	-51.2	1.7	87
88	16 42.7	-51.3	1.1	17 42.7	-51.3	1.1	18 42.7	-51.3	1.1	19 42.7	-51.3	1.1	20 42.7	-51.3	1.1	21 42.6	-51.2	1.1	22 42.6	-51.2	1.1	23 42.6	-51.2	1.1	88
89	15 51.4	-51.4	0.5	16 51.4	-51.4	0.5	17 51.4	-51.4	0.5	18 51.4	-51.4	0.5	19 51.4	-51.4	0.5	20 51.4	-51.4	0.6	21 51.4	-51.4	0.6	22 51.4	-51.4	0.6	89
90	15 00.0	-51.5	0.0	16 00.0	-51.5	0.0	17 00.0	-51.5	0.0	18 00.0	-51.5	0.0	19 00.0	-51.5	0.0	20 00.0	-51.5	0.0	21 00.0	-51.5	0.0	22 00.0	-51.5	0.0	90
	15°			16°			17°			18°			19°			20°			21°			22°			

LATITUDE CONTRARY NAME TO DECLINATION L.H.A. 31°, 329°

Dec.	15°			16°			17°			18°			19°			20°			21°			22°			Dec.
	Hc	d	Z	Hc	d	Z	Hc	d	Z	Hc	d	Z	Hc	d	Z	Hc	d	Z	Hc	d	Z	Hc	d	Z	
°	° ′	′	°	° ′	′	°	° ′	′	°	° ′	′	°	° ′	′	°	° ′	′	°	° ′	′	°	° ′	′	°	°
0	55 53.4	−28.3	113.3	55 29.0	−29.8	114.6	55 03.4	−31.2	115.9	54 36.5	−32.5	117.2	54 08.5	−33.8	118.5	53 39.4	−35.1	119.6	53 09.2	−36.3	120.8	52 37.9	−37.4	121.9	0
1	55 25.1	−29.5	114.9	54 59.2	−30.8	116.2	54 32.2	−32.2	117.4	54 04.0	−33.6	118.7	53 34.7	−34.8	119.9	53 04.3	−36.0	121.0	52 32.9	−37.2	122.1	52 00.5	−38.3	123.2	1
2	54 55.6	−30.5	116.4	54 28.4	−32.0	117.7	54 00.0	−33.3	118.9	53 30.4	−34.5	120.1	52 59.9	−35.7	121.2	52 28.3	−36.9	122.3	51 55.7	−38.0	123.4	51 22.2	−39.0	124.5	2
3	54 25.1	−31.7	117.9	53 56.4	−32.9	119.1	53 26.7	−34.2	120.3	52 55.9	−35.4	121.4	52 24.2	−36.6	122.5	51 51.4	−37.7	123.6	51 17.7	−38.7	124.7	50 43.2	−39.8	125.7	3
4	53 53.4	−32.7	119.3	53 23.5	−33.9	120.5	52 52.5	−35.1	121.7	52 20.5	−36.3	122.8	51 47.6	−37.4	123.8	51 13.7	−38.4	124.9	50 39.0	−39.5	125.9	50 03.4	−40.4	126.8	4
5	53 20.7	−33.6	120.7	52 49.6	−34.9	121.9	52 17.4	−36.0	123.0	51 44.2	−37.1	124.1	51 10.2	−38.2	125.1	50 35.3	−39.2	126.1	49 59.5	−40.1	127.1	49 23.0	−41.1	128.0	5
6	52 47.1	−34.6	122.1	52 14.7	−35.7	123.2	51 41.4	−36.9	124.3	51 07.1	−37.9	125.3	50 32.0	−38.9	126.3	49 56.1	−39.9	127.3	49 19.4	−40.9	128.2	48 41.9	−41.7	129.1	6
7	52 12.5	−35.5	123.5	51 39.0	−36.6	124.5	51 04.5	−37.6	125.5	50 29.2	−38.7	126.5	49 53.1	−39.7	127.5	49 16.2	−40.6	128.4	48 38.5	−41.4	129.3	48 00.2	−42.4	130.2	7
8	51 37.0	−36.3	124.8	51 02.4	−37.4	125.8	50 26.9	−38.4	126.8	49 50.5	−39.3	127.7	49 13.4	−40.3	128.7	48 35.6	−41.2	129.5	47 57.1	−42.1	130.4	47 17.8	−42.8	131.2	8
9	51 00.7	−37.1	126.0	50 25.0	−38.1	127.0	49 48.5	−39.2	128.0	49 11.2	−40.1	128.9	48 33.1	−40.9	129.8	47 54.4	−41.8	130.6	47 15.0	−42.6	131.5	46 35.0	−43.5	132.3	9
10	50 23.6	−37.9	127.3	49 46.9	−38.9	128.2	49 09.3	−39.8	129.1	48 31.1	−40.7	130.0	47 52.2	−41.6	130.9	47 12.6	−42.4	131.7	46 32.4	−43.2	132.5	45 51.5	−43.9	133.3	10
11	49 45.7	−38.6	128.5	49 08.0	−39.6	129.4	48 29.5	−40.4	130.3	47 50.4	−41.3	131.1	47 10.6	−42.1	131.9	46 30.2	−42.9	132.7	45 49.2	−43.7	133.5	45 07.6	−44.4	134.2	11
12	49 07.1	−39.4	129.7	48 28.4	−40.2	130.5	47 49.1	−41.1	131.4	47 09.1	−41.9	132.2	46 28.5	−42.7	133.0	45 47.3	−43.5	133.7	45 05.5	−44.2	134.5	44 23.2	−44.9	135.2	12
13	48 27.7	−40.0	130.8	47 48.2	−40.9	131.7	47 08.0	−41.7	132.5	46 27.2	−42.5	133.2	45 45.8	−43.2	134.0	45 03.8	−43.9	134.7	44 21.3	−44.6	135.4	43 38.3	−45.2	136.1	13
14	47 47.7	−40.6	131.9	47 07.3	−41.4	132.7	46 26.3	−42.2	133.5	45 44.7	−43.0	134.3	45 02.6	−43.8	135.0	44 19.9	−44.4	135.7	43 36.7	−45.1	136.4	42 53.1	−45.8	137.0	14
15	47 07.1	−41.2	133.0	46 25.9	−42.1	133.8	45 44.1	−42.8	134.5	45 01.7	−43.5	135.3	44 18.8	−44.2	136.0	43 35.5	−44.9	136.6	42 51.6	−45.5	137.3	42 07.3	−46.1	137.9	15
16	46 25.9	−41.8	134.1	45 43.8	−42.5	134.8	45 01.3	−43.3	135.5	44 18.2	−44.0	136.2	43 34.6	−44.6	136.9	42 50.6	−45.3	137.5	42 06.1	−45.9	138.1	41 21.2	−46.4	138.7	16
17	45 44.1	−42.4	135.1	45 01.3	−43.1	135.8	44 18.0	−43.8	136.5	43 34.2	−44.4	137.2	42 50.0	−45.1	137.8	42 05.3	−45.7	138.4	41 20.2	−46.2	139.0	40 34.8	−46.9	139.6	17
18	45 01.7	−42.9	136.1	44 18.2	−43.6	136.8	43 34.2	−44.2	137.5	42 49.8	−44.9	138.1	42 04.9	−45.5	138.7	41 19.6	−46.0	139.3	40 34.0	−46.7	139.8	39 47.9	−47.1	140.4	18
19	44 18.8	−43.3	137.1	43 34.6	−44.0	137.8	42 50.0	−44.7	138.4	42 04.9	−45.3	139.0	41 19.4	−45.8	139.6	40 33.6	−46.4	140.1	39 47.3	−46.9	140.7	39 00.8	−47.5	141.2	19
20	43 35.5	−43.9	138.1	42 50.6	−44.5	138.7	42 05.3	−45.1	139.3	41 19.6	−45.6	139.9	40 33.6	−46.3	140.4	39 47.2	−46.8	141.0	39 00.4	−47.3	141.5	38 13.3	−47.8	142.0	20
21	42 51.6	−44.3	139.0	42 06.1	−44.9	139.6	41 20.2	−45.4	140.2	40 34.0	−46.1	140.7	39 47.3	−46.5	141.3	39 00.4	−47.1	141.8	38 13.1	−47.6	142.3	37 25.5	−48.1	142.7	21
22	42 07.3	−44.7	139.9	41 21.2	−45.3	140.5	40 34.8	−45.9	141.0	39 47.9	−46.4	141.6	39 00.8	−47.0	142.1	38 13.3	−47.4	142.6	37 25.5	−47.9	143.0	36 37.4	−48.4	143.5	22
23	41 22.6	−45.1	140.8	40 35.9	−45.6	141.4	39 48.9	−46.2	141.9	39 01.5	−46.7	142.4	38 13.8	−47.2	142.9	37 25.9	−47.8	143.3	36 37.6	−48.2	143.8	35 49.0	−48.6	144.2	23
24	40 37.5	−45.5	141.7	39 50.3	−46.1	142.2	39 02.7	−46.6	142.7	38 14.8	−47.1	143.2	37 26.6	−47.5	143.7	36 38.1	−48.0	144.1	35 49.4	−48.4	144.5	35 00.4	−48.9	144.9	24
25	39 52.0	−45.9	142.5	39 04.2	−46.4	143.0	38 16.1	−46.9	143.5	37 27.7	−47.3	144.0	36 39.1	−47.9	144.4	35 50.1	−48.2	144.8	35 01.0	−48.7	145.3	34 11.5	−49.1	145.6	25
26	39 06.1	−46.2	143.4	38 17.8	−46.7	143.9	37 29.2	−47.2	144.3	36 40.4	−47.7	144.7	35 51.2	−48.0	145.2	35 01.9	−48.5	145.6	34 12.3	−49.0	146.0	33 22.4	−49.3	146.3	26
27	38 19.9	−46.5	144.2	37 31.1	−47.0	144.6	36 42.0	−47.4	145.1	35 52.7	−47.9	145.5	35 03.2	−48.4	145.9	34 13.4	−48.8	146.3	33 23.3	−49.1	146.7	32 33.1	−49.5	147.0	27
28	37 33.4	−46.9	145.0	36 44.1	−47.3	145.4	35 54.6	−47.8	145.8	35 04.8	−48.2	146.2	34 14.8	−48.6	146.6	33 24.6	−49.0	147.0	32 34.2	−49.4	147.3	31 43.6	−49.8	147.7	28
29	36 46.5	−47.2	145.8	35 56.8	−47.7	146.2	35 06.8	−48.0	146.6	34 16.6	−48.5	147.0	33 26.2	−48.9	147.3	32 35.6	−49.2	147.7	31 44.8	−49.6	148.0	30 53.8	−49.9	148.3	29
30	35 59.3	−47.4	146.5	35 09.1	−47.8	146.9	34 18.8	−48.3	147.3	33 28.1	−48.6	147.7	32 37.3	−49.0	148.0	31 46.4	−49.5	148.4	30 55.2	−49.8	148.7	30 03.9	−50.2	149.0	30
31	35 11.9	−47.8	147.3	34 21.3	−48.2	147.7	33 30.5	−48.6	148.0	32 39.5	−48.9	148.4	31 48.3	−49.3	148.7	30 56.9	−49.6	149.0	30 05.4	−50.0	149.3	29 13.7	−50.3	149.6	31
32	34 24.1	−48.0	148.0	33 33.1	−48.4	148.4	32 41.9	−48.7	148.7	31 50.6	−49.2	149.1	30 59.0	−49.5	149.4	30 07.3	−49.8	149.7	29 15.4	−50.1	150.0	28 23.4	−50.5	150.2	32
33	33 36.1	−48.2	148.8	32 44.7	−48.6	149.1	31 53.2	−49.0	149.4	31 01.4	−49.3	149.7	30 09.5	−49.6	150.0	29 17.5	−50.0	150.3	28 25.3	−50.3	150.6	27 32.9	−50.6	150.8	33
34	32 47.9	−48.5	149.5	31 56.1	−48.8	149.8	31 04.2	−49.2	150.1	30 12.1	−49.5	150.4	29 19.9	−49.9	150.7	28 27.5	−50.2	150.9	27 35.0	−50.5	151.2	26 42.3	−50.8	151.4	34
35	31 59.4	−48.7	150.2	31 07.3	−49.1	150.5	30 15.0	−49.4	150.8	29 22.6	−49.8	151.0	28 30.0	−50.0	151.3	27 37.3	−50.3	151.6	26 44.5	−50.7	151.8	25 51.5	−50.9	152.0	35
36	31 10.7	−48.9	150.9	30 18.2	−49.2	151.1	29 25.6	−49.6	151.4	28 32.8	−49.8	151.7	27 40.0	−50.2	151.9	26 47.0	−50.5	152.2	25 53.8	−50.7	152.4	25 00.6	−51.0	152.6	36
37	30 21.8	−49.1	151.5	29 29.0	−49.5	151.8	28 36.0	−49.7	152.1	27 43.0	−50.1	152.3	26 49.8	−50.4	152.6	25 56.5	−50.7	152.8	25 03.1	−51.0	153.0	24 09.6	−51.2	153.2	37
38	29 32.7	−49.4	152.2	28 39.5	−49.6	152.5	27 46.3	−50.0	152.7	26 52.9	−50.2	152.9	25 59.4	−50.5	153.2	25 05.8	−50.8	153.4	24 12.1	−51.0	153.6	23 18.4	−51.3	153.8	38
39	28 43.3	−49.5	152.8	27 49.9	−49.8	153.1	26 56.3	−50.1	153.3	26 02.7	−50.4	153.5	25 08.9	−50.6	153.8	24 15.0	−50.9	154.0	23 21.1	−51.2	154.2	22 27.1	−51.5	154.3	39
40	27 53.8	−49.6	153.5	27 00.1	−50.0	153.7	26 06.2	−50.2	153.9	25 12.3	−50.5	154.1	24 18.3	−50.8	154.3	23 24.1	−51.0	154.5	22 29.9	−51.3	154.7	21 35.6	−51.5	154.9	40
41	27 04.2	−49.9	154.1	26 10.1	−50.1	154.3	25 16.0	−50.4	154.5	24 21.8	−50.7	154.7	23 27.5	−50.9	154.9	22 33.1	−51.2	155.1	21 38.6	−51.4	155.3	20 44.1	−51.7	155.4	41
42	26 14.3	−50.0	154.7	25 20.0	−50.3	154.9	24 25.6	−50.5	155.1	23 31.1	−50.8	155.3	22 36.6	−51.1	155.5	21 41.9	−51.2	155.7	20 47.2	−51.5	155.8	19 52.4	−51.7	156.0	42
43	25 24.3	−50.1	155.4	24 29.7	−50.4	155.5	23 35.1	−50.7	155.7	22 40.3	−50.9	155.9	21 45.5	−51.1	156.1	20 50.7	−51.4	156.2	19 55.7	−51.6	156.4	19 00.7	−51.8	156.5	43
44	24 34.2	−50.3	156.0	23 39.3	−50.5	156.1	22 44.4	−50.8	156.3	21 49.4	−51.0	156.5	20 54.4	−51.3	156.6	19 59.3	−51.5	156.8	19 04.1	−51.7	156.9	18 08.9	−51.9	157.1	44
45	23 43.9	−50.5	156.6	22 48.8	−50.7	156.7	21 53.6	−50.9	156.9	20 58.4	−51.1	157.0	20 03.1	−51.3	157.2	19 07.8	−51.6	157.3	18 12.4	−51.8	157.5	17 17.0	−52.0	157.6	45
46	22 53.4	−50.5	157.1	21 58.1	−50.8	157.3	21 02.7	−51.0	157.5	20 07.3	−51.3	157.6	19 11.8	−51.5	157.7	18 16.2	−51.6	157.9	17 20.6	−51.9	158.0	16 25.0	−52.1	158.1	46
47	22 02.9	−50.7	157.7	21 07.3	−50.9	157.9	20 11.7	−51.1	158.0	19 16.0	−51.3	158.2	18 20.3	−51.5	158.3	17 24.6	−51.8	158.4	16 28.7	−51.9	158.5	15 32.9	−52.2	158.6	47
48	21 12.2	−50.8	158.3	20 16.4	−51.0	158.4	19 20.6	−51.3	158.6	18 24.7	−51.4	158.7	17 28.8	−51.7	158.8	16 32.8	−51.8	158.9	15 36.8	−52.0	159.0	14 40.7	−52.2	159.1	48
49	20 21.4	−50.9	158.9	19 25.4	−51.1	159.0	18 29.3	−51.3	159.1	17 33.3	−51.6	159.2	16 37.1	−51.7	159.4	15 41.0	−51.9	159.5	14 44.8	−52.1	159.5	13 48.5	−52.2	159.6	49
50	19 30.5	−51.0	159.4	18 34.3	−51.2	159.6	17 38.0	−51.4	159.7	16 41.7	−51.6	159.8	15 45.4	−51.8	159.9	14 49.1	−52.0	160.0	13 52.7	−52.2	160.1	12 56.3	−52.4	160.1	50
51	18 39.5	−51.2	160.0	17 43.1	−51.3	160.1	16 46.6	−51.5	160.2	15 50.1	−51.6	160.3	14 53.6	−51.8	160.4	13 57.1	−52.0	160.5	13 00.5	−52.2	160.6	12 03.9	−52.4	160.6	51
52	17 48.3	−51.2	160.5	16 51.8	−51.4	160.7	15 55.1	−51.5	160.7	14 58.5	−51.8	160.8	14 01.8	−52.0	160.9	13 05.1	−52.1	161.0	12 08.3	−52.3	161.1	11 11.5	−52.4	161.1	52
53	16 57.1	−51.2	161.1	16 00.4	−51.5	161.2	15 03.6	−51.7	161.3	14 06.7	−51.8	161.4	13 09.8	−51.9	161.4	12 13.0	−52.2	161.5	11 16.0	−52.3	161.6	10 19.1	−52.5	161.6	53
54	16 05.9	−51.4	161.6	15 08.9	−51.5	161.7	14 11.9	−51.7	161.8	13 14.9	−51.9	161.9	12 17.9	−52.1	162.0	11 20.8	−52.2	162.0	10 23.7	−52.3	162.1	9 26.6	−52.5	162.1	54
55	15 14.5	−51.5	162.2	14 17.4	−51.7	162.3	13 20.2	−51.8	162.3	12 23.0	−51.9	162.4	11 25.8	−52.1	162.5	10 28.6	−52.3	162.5	9 31.4	−52.4	162.6	8 34.1	−52.5	162.6	55
56	14 23.0	−51.5	162.7	13 25.7	−51.6	162.8	12 28.4	−51.8	162.8	11 31.1	−52.0	162.9	10 33.7	−52.1	163.0	9 36.3	−52.3	163.0	8 39.0	−52.5	163.1	7 41.6	−52.6	163.1	56
57	13 31.5	−51.6	163.2	12 34.1	−51.8	163.3	11 36.6	−51.9	163.4	10 39.1	−52.1	163.4	9 41.6	−52.2	163.5	8 44.0	−52.3	163.5	7 46.5	−52.5	163.6	6 49.0	−52.7	163.6	57
58	12 39.9	−51.6	163.8	11 42.3	−51.8	163.8	10 44.7	−51.9	163.9	9 47.0	−52.0	163.9	8 49.4	−52.2	164.0	7 51.7	−52.4	164.0	6 54.0	−52.5	164.0	5 56.3	−52.6	164.1	58
59	11 48.3	−51.7	164.3	10 50.5	−51.8	164.3	9 52.8	−52.0	164.4	8 55.0	−52.2	164.4	7 57.2	−52.3	164.5	6 59.3	−52.4	164.5	6 01.5	−52.5	164.5	5 03.7	−52.7	164.6	59
60	10 56.6	−51.8	164.8	9 58.7	−51.9	164.8	9 00.8	−52.1	164.9	8 02.8	−52.1	164.9	7 04.9	−52.3	165.0	6 06.9	−52.4	165.0	5 09.0	−52.6	165.0	4 11.0	−52.7	165.0	60
61	10 04.8	−51.8	165.3	9 06.8	−51.9	165.4	8 08.7	−52.0	165.4	7 10.7	−52.2	165.4	6 12.6	−52.3	165.5	5 14.5	−52.4	165.5	4 16.4	−52.5	165.5	3 18.3	−52.6	165.5	61
62	9 13.0	−51.8	165.8	8 14.9	−52.0	165.9	7 16.7	−52.1	165.9	6 18.5	−52.2	165.9	5 20.3	−52.4	165.9	4 22.1	−52.5	166.0	3 23.9	−52.6	166.0	2 25.7	−52.8	166.0	62
63	8 21.2	−51.9	166.3	7 22.9	−52.0	166.4	6 24.6	−52.1	166.4	5 26.3	−52.3	166.4	4 27.9	−52.3	166.4	3 29.6	−52.5	166.5	2 31.3	−52.6	166.5	1 32.9	−52.7	166.5	63
64	7 29.3	−51.9	166.8	6 30.9	−52.0	166.9	5 32.5	−52.2	166.9	4 34.0	−52.2	166.9	3 35.6	−52.4	166.9	2 37.1	−52.5	166.9	1 38.7	−52.6	166.9	0 40.2	−52.7	167.0	64
65	6 37.4	−51.9	167.3	5 38.9	−52.1	167.4	4 40.3	−52.2	167.4	3 41.8	−52.3	167.4	2 43.2	−52.4	167.4	1 44.6	−52.5	167.4	0 46.1	−52.6	167.4	0 12.5	+52.7	12.6	65
66	5 45.5	−52.0	167.8	4 46.8	−52.1	167.9	3 48.1	−52.2	167.9	2 49.5	−52.3	167.9	1 50.8	−52.4	167.9	0 52.1	−52.5	167.9	0 06.5	+52.6	12.1	1 05.2	+52.7	12.1	66
67	4 53.5	−52.0	168.3	3 54.7	−52.1	168.4	2 55.9	−52.2	168.4	1 57.2	−52.3	168.4	0 58.4	−52.4	168.4	0 00.4	+52.5	11.6	0 59.1	+52.6	11.6	1 57.9	+52.7	11.6	67
68	4 01.5	−52.0	168.8	3 02.6	−52.1	168.9	2 03.7	−52.2	168.9	1 04.9	−52.3	168.9	0 06.0	−52.4	168.9	0 52.9	+52.5	11.1	1 51.7	+52.6	11.1	2 50.6	+52.7	11.1	68
69	3 09.5	−52.1	169.3	2 10.5	−52.1	169.4	1 11.5	−52.2	169.4	0 12.6	−52.3	169.4	0 46.4	+52.4	10.6	1 45.4	+52.5	10.6	2 44.3	+52.6	10.6	3 43.3	+52.7	10.7	69
70	2 17.4	−52.0	169.8	1 18.4	−52.2	169.9	0 19.3	−52.2	169.9	0 39.7	+52.4	10.1	1 38.8	+52.4	10.2	2 37.9	+52.4	10.2	3 36.9	+52.6	10.2	4 36.0	+52.6	10.2	70
71	1 25.4	−52.0	170.3	0 26.2	−52.1	170.3	0 32.9	+52.2	9.7	1 32.1	+52.3	9.7	2 31.2	+52.4	9.7	3 30.3	+52.5	9.7	4 29.5	+52.5	9.7	5 28.6	+52.7	9.7	71
72	0 33.4	−52.1	170.8	0 25.9	+52.1	9.2	1 25.1	+52.2	9.2	2 24.4	+52.2	9.2	3 23.6	+52.4	9.2	4 22.8	+52.5	9.2	5 22.0	+52.6	9.2	6 21.3	+52.6	9.2	72
73	0 18.7	+52.0	8.7	1 18.0	+52.1	8.7	2 17.3	+52.2	8.7	3 16.6	+52.3	8.7	4 16.0	+52.3	8.7	5 15.3	+52.4	8.7	6 14.6	+52.5	8.7	7 13.9	+52.6	8.7	73
74	1 10.7	+52.1	8.2	2 10.1	+52.1	8.2	3 09.5	+52.2	8.2	4 08.9	+52.3	8.2	5 08.3	+52.3	8.2	6 07.7	+52.4	8.2	7 07.1	+52.4	8.2	8 06.5	+52.5	8.2	74
75	2 02.8	+52.0	7.7	3 02.2	+52.1	7.7	4 01.7	+52.2	7.7	5 01.2	+52.2	7.7	6 00.6	+52.3	7.7	7 00.1	+52.4	7.7	7 59.5	+52.5	7.7	8 59.0	+52.5	7.8	75
76	2 54.8	+52.0	7.2	3 54.3	+52.1	7.2	4 53.9	+52.1	7.2	5 53.4	+52.2	7.2	6 52.9	+52.3	7.2	7 52.5	+52.3	7.2	8 52.0	+52.4	7.2	9 51.5	+52.5	7.3	76
77	3 46.8	+52.0	6.7	4 46.4	+52.1	6.7	5 46.0	+52.1	6.7	6 45.6	+52.2	6.7	7 45.2	+52.2	6.7	8 44.8	+52.3	6.7	9 44.4	+52.3	6.8	10 44.0	+52.4	6.8	77
78	4 38.8	+52.0	6.2	5 38.5	+52.0	6.2	6 38.1	+52.1	6.2	7 37.8	+52.1	6.2	8 37.4	+52.2	6.2	9 37.1	+52.2	6.2	10 36.7	+52.3	6.3	11 36.4	+52.3	6.3	78
79	5 30.8	+52.0	5.7	6 30.5	+52.0	5.7	7 30.2	+52.1	5.7	8 29.9	+52.1	5.7	9 29.6	+52.2	5.7	10 29.3	+52.2	5.7	11 29.0	+52.3	5.8	12 28.7	+52.3	5.8	79
80	6 22.8	+51.9	5.2	7 22.5	+52.0	5.2	8 22.3	+52.0	5.2	9 22.0	+52.1	5.2	10 21.8	+52.1	5.2	11 21.5	+52.2	5.2	12 21.3	+52.2	5.3	13 21.0	+52.3	5.3	80
81	7 14.7	+51.9	4.7	8 14.5	+51.9	4.7	9 14.3	+52.0	4.7	10 14.1	+52.0	4.7	11 13.9	+52.1	4.7	12 13.7	+52.1	4.7	13 13.5	+52.1	4.7	14 13.3	+52.2	4.8	81
82	8 06.6	+51.8	4.2	9 06.4	+51.9	4.2	10 06.3	+51.9	4.2	11 06.1	+52.0	4.2	12 06.0	+52.0	4.2	13 05.8	+52.0	4.2	14 05.6	+52.1	4.2	15 05.5	+52.1	4.3	82
83	8 58.4	+51.9	3.6	9 58.3	+51.9	3.7	10 58.2	+51.9	3.7	11 58.1	+51.9	3.7	12 58.0	+51.9	3.7	13 57.8	+52.0	3.7	14 57.7	+52.0	3.7	15 57.6	+52.0	3.7	83
84	9 50.3	+51.7	3.1	10 50.2	+51.8	3.1	11 50.1	+51.8	3.2	12 50.0	+51.8	3.2	13 49.9	+51.9	3.2	14 49.8	+51.9	3.2	15 49.7	+51.9	3.2	16 49.6	+52.0	3.2	84
85	10 42.0	+51.7	2.6	11 42.0	+51.7	2.6	12 41.9	+51.8	2.6	13 41.8	+51.8	2.6	14 41.8	+51.8	2.7	15 41.7	+51.8	2.7	16 41.6	+51.9	2.7	17 41.6	+51.8	2.7	85
86	11 33.7	+51.7	2.1	12 33.7	+51.7	2.1	13 33.7	+51.7	2.1	14 33.6	+51.7	2.1	15 33.6	+51.7	2.1	16 33.5	+51.8	2.1	17 33.5	+51.8	2.2	18 33.4	+51.8	2.2	86
87	12 25.4	+51.6	1.6	13 25.4	+51.6	1.6	14 25.4	+51.6	1.6	15 25.3	+51.7	1.6	16 25.3	+51.7	1.6	17 25.3	+51.6	1.6	18 25.3	+51.6	1.6	19 25.2	+51.7	1.6	87
88	13 17.0	+51.5	1.1	14 17.0	+51.5	1.1	15 17.0	+51.5	1.1	16 17.0	+51.5	1.1	17 17.0	+51.5	1.1	18 16.9	+51.6	1.1	19 16.9	+51.6	1.1	20 16.9	+51.6	1.1	88
89	14 08.5	+51.5	0.5	15 08.5	+51.5	0.5	16 08.5	+51.5	0.5	17 08.5	+51.5	0.5	18 08.5	+51.5	0.5	19 08.5	+51.5	0.5	20 08.5	+51.5	0.5	21 08.5	+51.5	0.6	89
90	15 00.0	+51.4	0.0	16 00.0	+51.4	0.0	17 00.0	+51.4	0.0	18 00.0	+51.4	0.0	19 00.0	+51.4	0.0	20 00.0	+51.4	0.0	21 00.0	+51.4	0.0	22 00.0	+51.4	0.0	90
	15°			16°			17°			18°			19°			20°			21°			22°			

S. Lat. {L.H.A. greater than 180° ....Zn=180°−Z
{L.H.A. less than 180°...........Zn=180°+Z

LATITUDE SAME NAME AS DECLINATION L.H.A. 149°, 211°

32°, 328° L.H.A. LATITUDE SAME NAME AS DECLINATION

N. Lat. {L.H.A. greater than 180°.....Zn=Z; L.H.A. less than 180°............Zn=360°–Z}

Dec.	15° Hc	15° d	15° Z	16° Hc	16° d	16° Z	17° Hc	17° d	17° Z	18° Hc	18° d	18° Z	19° Hc	19° d	19° Z	20° Hc	20° d	20° Z	21° Hc	21° d	21° Z	22° Hc	22° d	22° Z	Dec.
°	° ′	′	°	° ′	′	°	° ′	′	°	° ′	′	°	° ′	′	°	° ′	′	°	° ′	′	°	° ′	′	°	°
0	55 00.0	+26.5	112.5	54 36.4	+28.0	113.8	54 11.6	+29.4	115.1	53 45.6	+30.8	116.3	53 18.4	+32.2	117.5	52 50.1	+33.5	118.7	52 20.8	+34.7	119.8	51 50.4	+36.0	120.9	0
1	55 26.5	+25.2	110.9	55 04.4	+26.8	112.3	54 41.0	+28.3	113.6	54 16.4	+29.8	114.9	53 50.6	+31.1	116.1	53 23.6	+32.5	117.3	52 55.5	+33.9	118.5	52 26.4	+35.1	119.6	1
2	55 51.7	+23.9	109.3	55 31.2	+25.5	110.7	55 09.3	+27.1	112.0	54 46.2	+28.6	113.4	54 21.7	+30.1	114.6	53 56.1	+31.5	115.9	53 29.4	+32.8	117.1	53 01.5	+34.1	118.3	2
3	56 15.6	+22.7	107.7	55 56.7	+24.3	109.1	55 36.4	+25.9	110.5	55 14.8	+27.4	111.8	54 51.8	+29.0	113.1	54 27.6	+30.4	114.4	54 02.2	+31.8	115.7	53 35.6	+33.2	116.9	3
4	56 38.3	+21.2	106.0	56 21.0	+22.9	107.4	56 02.3	+24.6	108.9	55 42.2	+26.2	110.3	55 20.8	+27.7	111.6	54 58.0	+29.3	112.9	54 34.0	+30.7	114.2	54 08.8	+32.1	115.5	4
5	56 59.5	+19.8	104.3	56 43.9	+21.6	105.8	56 26.9	+23.3	107.2	56 08.4	+25.0	108.7	55 48.5	+26.6	110.0	55 27.3	+28.1	111.4	55 04.7	+29.7	112.8	54 40.9	+31.1	114.1	5
6	57 19.3	+18.4	102.6	57 05.5	+20.2	104.1	56 50.2	+21.9	105.5	56 33.4	+23.6	107.0	56 15.1	+25.3	108.4	55 55.4	+26.9	109.8	55 34.4	+28.4	111.2	55 12.0	+29.9	112.6	6
7	57 37.7	+16.8	100.8	57 25.7	+18.6	102.3	57 12.1	+20.5	103.8	56 57.0	+22.2	105.3	56 40.4	+23.9	106.8	56 22.3	+25.6	108.2	56 02.8	+27.2	109.7	55 41.9	+28.8	111.0	7
8	57 54.5	+15.3	99.0	57 44.3	+17.2	100.5	57 32.6	+19.0	102.1	57 19.2	+20.8	103.6	57 04.3	+22.6	105.1	56 47.9	+24.3	106.6	56 30.0	+26.0	108.1	56 10.7	+27.6	109.5	8
9	58 09.8	+13.7	97.2	58 01.5	+15.6	98.7	57 51.6	+17.5	100.3	57 40.0	+19.4	101.9	57 26.9	+21.1	103.4	57 12.2	+22.9	104.9	56 56.0	+24.6	106.4	56 38.3	+26.3	107.9	9
10	58 23.5	+12.1	95.3	58 17.1	+14.0	96.9	58 09.1	+15.9	98.5	57 59.4	+17.8	100.1	57 48.0	+19.7	101.7	57 35.1	+21.5	103.2	57 20.6	+23.3	104.7	57 04.6	+25.0	106.2	10
11	58 35.6	+10.4	93.4	58 31.1	+12.4	95.1	58 25.0	+14.3	96.7	58 17.2	+16.3	98.3	58 07.7	+18.2	99.9	57 56.6	+20.0	101.5	57 43.9	+21.8	103.0	57 29.6	+23.6	104.5	11
12	58 46.0	+8.7	91.5	58 43.5	+10.8	93.2	58 39.3	+12.8	94.8	58 33.5	+14.6	96.4	58 25.9	+16.6	98.1	58 16.6	+18.5	99.7	58 05.7	+20.4	101.3	57 53.2	+22.2	102.8	12
13	58 54.7	+7.1	89.6	58 54.3	+9.0	91.3	58 52.1	+11.0	92.9	58 48.1	+13.1	94.6	58 42.5	+15.0	96.2	58 35.1	+17.0	97.9	58 26.1	+18.8	99.5	58 15.4	+20.7	101.1	13
14	59 01.8	+5.3	87.7	59 03.3	+7.4	89.4	59 03.1	+9.4	91.0	59 01.2	+11.3	92.7	58 57.5	+13.3	94.4	58 52.1	+15.3	96.0	58 44.9	+17.3	97.6	58 36.1	+19.2	99.3	14
15	59 07.1	+3.6	85.8	59 10.7	+5.6	87.4	59 12.5	+7.6	89.1	59 12.5	+9.7	90.8	59 10.8	+11.7	92.5	59 07.4	+13.7	94.1	59 02.2	+15.7	95.8	58 55.3	+17.6	97.4	15
16	59 10.7	+1.8	83.8	59 16.3	+3.8	85.5	59 20.1	+5.9	87.2	59 22.2	+7.9	88.8	59 22.5	+10.0	90.5	59 21.1	+12.0	92.2	59 17.9	+14.0	93.9	59 12.9	+16.0	95.6	16
17	59 12.5	0.0	81.9	59 20.1	+2.1	83.5	59 26.0	+4.1	85.2	59 30.1	+6.2	86.9	59 32.5	+8.2	88.6	59 33.1	+10.2	90.3	59 31.9	+12.3	92.0	59 28.9	+14.3	93.7	17
18	59 12.5	-1.7	79.9	59 22.2	+0.3	81.6	59 30.1	+2.4	83.2	59 36.3	+4.4	84.9	59 40.7	+6.5	86.6	59 43.3	+8.6	88.3	59 44.2	+10.5	90.1	59 43.2	+12.6	91.8	18
19	59 10.8	-3.4	78.0	59 22.5	-1.4	79.6	59 32.5	+0.6	81.3	59 40.7	+2.6	83.0	59 47.2	+4.7	84.7	59 51.9	+6.7	86.4	59 54.7	+8.9	88.1	59 55.8	+10.9	89.8	19
20	59 07.4	-5.2	76.0	59 21.1	-3.2	77.6	59 33.1	-1.2	79.3	59 43.3	+0.9	81.0	59 51.9	+2.8	82.7	59 58.6	+5.0	84.4	60 03.6	+7.0	86.1	60 06.7	+9.1	87.9	20
21	59 02.2	-6.9	74.1	59 17.9	-5.0	75.7	59 31.9	-3.0	77.3	59 44.2	-1.0	79.0	59 54.7	+1.1	80.7	60 03.6	+3.1	82.4	60 10.6	+5.2	84.1	60 15.8	+7.3	85.9	21
22	58 55.3	-8.6	72.1	59 12.9	-6.7	73.7	59 28.9	-4.8	75.4	59 43.2	-2.7	77.0	59 55.8	-0.7	78.7	60 06.7	+1.3	80.4	60 15.8	+3.4	82.1	60 23.1	+5.5	83.9	22
23	58 46.7	-10.4	70.2	59 06.2	-8.4	71.8	59 24.1	-6.5	73.4	59 40.5	-4.6	75.0	59 55.1	-2.5	76.7	60 08.0	-0.5	78.4	60 19.2	+1.6	80.1	60 28.6	+3.7	81.9	23
24	58 36.3	-11.9	68.3	58 57.8	-10.2	69.9	59 17.6	-8.2	71.4	59 35.9	-6.3	73.1	59 52.6	-4.4	74.7	60 07.5	-2.3	76.4	60 20.8	-0.3	78.1	60 32.3	+1.8	79.8	24
25	58 24.4	-13.6	66.5	58 47.6	-11.8	68.0	59 09.4	-10.0	69.5	59 29.6	-8.1	71.1	59 48.2	-6.1	72.7	60 05.2	-4.1	74.4	60 20.5	-2.1	76.1	60 34.1	0.0	77.8	25
26	58 10.8	-15.2	64.6	58 35.8	-13.4	66.1	58 59.4	-11.6	67.6	59 21.5	-9.7	69.2	59 42.1	-7.9	70.7	60 01.1	-5.9	72.4	60 18.4	-3.9	74.1	60 34.1	-2.0	75.8	26
27	57 55.6	-16.7	62.8	58 22.4	-15.0	64.2	58 47.8	-13.3	65.7	59 11.8	-11.5	67.2	59 34.2	-9.6	68.8	59 55.2	-7.8	70.4	60 14.5	-5.8	72.0	60 32.1	-3.7	73.7	27
28	57 38.9	-18.3	61.0	58 07.4	-16.7	62.4	58 34.5	-14.9	63.8	59 00.3	-13.2	65.3	59 24.6	-11.3	66.8	59 47.4	-9.4	68.4	60 08.7	-7.5	70.0	60 28.4	-5.6	71.7	28
29	57 20.6	-19.7	59.2	57 50.7	-18.1	60.6	58 19.6	-16.5	62.0	58 47.1	-14.8	63.4	59 13.3	-13.1	64.9	59 38.0	-11.2	66.5	60 01.2	-9.4	68.0	60 22.8	-7.4	69.7	29
30	57 00.9	-21.1	57.5	57 32.6	-19.6	58.8	58 03.1	-18.0	60.1	58 32.3	-16.4	61.6	59 00.2	-14.6	63.0	59 26.8	-13.0	64.5	59 51.8	-11.1	66.1	60 15.4	-9.2	67.7	30
31	56 39.8	-22.5	55.7	57 13.0	-21.1	57.0	57 45.1	-19.6	58.3	58 15.9	-17.9	59.7	58 45.6	-16.3	61.1	59 13.8	-14.5	62.6	59 40.7	-12.8	64.1	60 06.2	-11.0	65.7	31
32	56 17.3	-23.9	54.1	56 51.9	-22.4	55.3	57 25.5	-20.9	56.6	57 58.0	-19.4	57.9	58 29.3	-17.9	59.3	58 59.3	-16.2	60.7	59 27.9	-14.5	62.2	59 55.2	-12.7	63.7	32
33	55 53.4	-25.2	52.4	56 29.5	-23.8	53.6	57 04.6	-22.4	54.9	57 38.6	-21.0	56.1	58 11.4	-19.4	57.5	58 43.1	-17.8	58.9	59 13.4	-16.1	60.3	59 42.5	-14.4	61.8	33
34	55 28.2	-26.3	50.8	56 05.7	-25.1	52.0	56 42.2	-23.8	53.2	57 17.6	-22.3	54.4	57 52.0	-20.8	55.7	58 25.3	-19.4	57.0	58 57.3	-17.7	58.4	59 28.1	-16.1	59.9	34
35	55 01.9	-27.6	49.2	55 40.6	-26.3	50.3	56 18.4	-25.0	51.5	56 55.3	-23.7	52.7	57 31.2	-22.3	53.9	58 05.9	-20.8	55.2	58 39.6	-19.3	56.6	59 12.0	-17.7	58.0	35
36	54 34.3	-28.8	47.7	55 14.3	-27.6	48.8	55 53.4	-26.3	49.9	56 31.6	-25.0	51.0	57 08.9	-23.7	52.2	57 45.1	-22.3	53.5	58 20.3	-20.8	54.8	58 54.3	-19.2	56.1	36
37	54 05.5	-29.8	46.2	54 46.7	-28.7	47.2	55 27.1	-27.6	48.3	56 06.6	-26.3	49.4	56 45.2	-25.0	50.5	57 22.8	-23.6	51.7	57 59.5	-22.3	53.0	58 35.1	-20.8	54.3	37
38	53 35.7	-30.9	44.7	54 18.0	-29.8	45.7	54 59.5	-28.7	46.7	55 40.3	-27.6	47.8	56 20.2	-26.3	48.9	56 59.2	-25.1	50.0	57 37.2	-23.6	51.2	58 14.3	-22.3	52.5	38
39	53 04.8	-31.9	43.3	53 48.2	-30.9	44.2	54 30.8	-29.8	45.2	55 12.7	-28.7	46.2	55 53.9	-27.6	47.3	56 34.1	-26.3	48.4	57 13.6	-25.1	49.5	57 52.0	-23.7	50.7	39
40	52 32.9	-32.8	41.9	53 17.3	-31.9	42.8	54 01.0	-30.9	43.7	54 44.0	-29.8	44.7	55 26.3	-28.7	45.7	56 07.8	-27.5	46.8	56 48.5	-26.3	47.9	57 28.3	-25.0	49.0	40
41	52 00.1	-33.8	40.5	52 45.4	-32.9	41.4	53 30.1	-31.9	42.3	54 14.2	-30.9	43.2	54 57.6	-29.9	44.2	55 40.3	-28.8	45.2	56 22.2	-27.6	46.2	57 03.3	-26.4	47.3	41
42	51 26.3	-34.7	39.2	52 12.5	-33.8	40.0	52 58.2	-32.9	40.8	53 43.3	-32.0	41.7	54 27.7	-30.9	42.7	55 11.5	-29.9	43.6	55 54.6	-28.8	44.6	56 36.9	-27.6	45.7	42
43	50 51.6	-35.5	37.9	51 38.7	-34.7	38.6	52 25.3	-33.8	39.5	53 11.3	-32.9	40.3	53 56.8	-32.0	41.2	54 41.6	-31.0	42.1	55 25.8	-29.9	43.1	56 09.3	-28.9	44.1	43
44	50 16.1	-36.4	36.6	51 04.0	-35.6	37.3	51 51.5	-34.8	38.1	52 38.4	-33.9	38.9	53 24.8	-33.0	39.8	54 10.6	-32.0	40.6	54 55.9	-31.1	41.6	55 40.4	-30.0	42.5	44
45	49 39.7	-37.1	35.4	50 28.4	-36.3	36.1	51 16.7	-35.6	36.8	52 04.5	-34.8	37.6	52 51.8	-33.9	38.4	53 38.6	-33.1	39.2	54 24.8	-32.1	40.1	55 10.4	-31.1	41.0	45
46	49 02.6	-37.8	34.2	49 52.1	-37.2	34.8	50 41.1	-36.4	35.5	51 29.7	-35.6	36.2	52 17.9	-34.9	37.0	53 05.5	-34.0	37.8	53 52.7	-33.1	38.6	54 39.3	-32.2	39.5	46
47	48 24.8	-38.6	33.0	49 14.9	-37.9	33.6	50 04.7	-37.2	34.3	50 54.1	-36.5	35.0	51 43.0	-35.7	35.7	52 31.5	-34.9	36.4	53 19.6	-34.1	37.2	54 07.1	-33.3	38.1	47
48	47 46.2	-39.2	31.8	48 37.0	-38.6	32.4	49 27.5	-37.9	33.1	50 17.6	-37.3	33.7	51 07.3	-36.5	34.4	51 56.6	-35.8	35.1	52 45.5	-35.0	35.9	53 33.8	-34.1	36.7	48
49	47 07.0	-39.8	30.7	47 58.4	-39.2	31.3	48 49.6	-38.7	31.9	49 40.3	-38.0	32.5	50 30.8	-37.4	33.1	51 20.8	-36.6	33.8	52 10.5	-35.9	34.5	52 59.7	-35.2	35.3	49
50	46 27.2	-40.5	29.6	47 19.2	-39.9	30.2	48 10.9	-39.3	30.7	49 02.3	-38.7	31.3	49 53.4	-38.0	31.9	50 44.2	-37.4	32.6	51 34.6	-36.8	33.2	52 24.5	-35.9	33.9	50
51	45 46.7	-41.0	28.6	46 39.3	-40.5	29.1	47 31.6	-40.0	29.6	48 23.6	-39.4	30.1	49 15.4	-38.9	30.7	50 06.8	-38.2	31.3	50 57.8	-37.5	32.0	51 48.6	-36.9	32.6	51
52	45 05.7	-41.6	27.5	45 58.8	-41.1	28.0	46 51.6	-40.6	28.5	47 44.2	-40.0	29.0	48 36.5	-39.4	29.6	49 28.6	-38.9	30.1	50 20.3	-38.3	30.7	51 11.7	-37.6	31.4	52
53	44 24.1	-42.1	26.5	45 17.7	-41.7	27.0	46 11.0	-41.1	27.4	47 04.2	-40.7	27.9	47 57.1	-40.2	28.4	48 49.7	-39.6	29.0	49 42.0	-39.0	29.5	50 34.1	-38.4	30.1	53
54	43 42.0	-42.7	25.5	44 36.0	-42.2	25.9	45 29.9	-41.8	26.4	46 23.5	-41.2	26.8	47 16.9	-40.7	27.3	48 10.1	-40.2	27.8	49 03.0	-39.7	28.4	49 55.7	-39.1	28.9	54
55	42 59.3	-43.1	24.6	43 53.8	-42.7	24.9	44 48.1	-42.2	25.4	45 42.3	-41.9	25.8	46 36.2	-41.4	26.3	47 29.9	-40.9	26.7	48 23.3	-40.3	27.2	49 16.6	-39.9	27.8	55
56	42 16.2	-43.5	23.6	43 11.1	-43.1	24.0	44 05.9	-42.8	24.4	45 00.4	-42.3	24.8	45 54.8	-41.9	25.2	46 49.0	-41.4	25.7	47 43.0	-41.0	26.1	48 36.7	-40.4	26.6	56
57	41 32.7	-44.0	22.7	42 28.0	-43.6	23.0	43 23.1	-43.2	23.4	44 18.1	-42.8	23.8	45 12.9	-42.4	24.2	46 07.6	-42.0	24.6	47 02.0	-41.5	25.1	47 56.3	-41.1	25.5	57
58	40 48.7	-44.4	21.8	41 44.4	-44.1	22.1	42 39.9	-43.7	22.5	43 35.3	-43.4	22.8	44 30.5	-43.0	23.2	45 25.6	-42.6	23.6	46 20.5	-42.2	24.0	47 15.2	-41.7	24.4	58
59	40 04.3	-44.8	20.9	41 00.3	-44.5	21.2	41 56.2	-44.2	21.5	42 51.9	-43.8	21.9	43 47.5	-43.4	22.2	44 43.0	-43.0	22.6	45 38.3	-42.6	23.0	46 33.5	-42.3	23.4	59
60	39 19.5	-45.2	20.0	40 15.8	-44.8	20.3	41 12.0	-44.5	20.6	42 08.1	-44.2	20.9	43 04.1	-43.9	21.3	44 00.0	-43.6	21.6	44 55.7	-43.2	22.0	45 51.2	-42.8	22.4	60
61	38 34.3	-45.5	19.2	39 31.0	-45.3	19.5	40 27.5	-45.0	19.7	41 23.9	-44.6	20.0	42 20.2	-44.3	20.3	43 16.4	-44.0	20.7	44 12.5	-43.7	21.0	45 08.4	-43.3	21.4	61
62	37 48.8	-45.9	18.4	38 45.7	-45.6	18.6	39 42.5	-45.3	18.9	40 39.3	-45.1	19.1	41 35.9	-44.8	19.4	42 32.4	-44.4	19.7	43 28.8	-44.1	20.1	44 25.1	-43.7	20.4	62
63	37 02.9	-46.2	17.5	38 00.1	-45.9	17.8	38 57.2	-45.7	18.0	39 54.2	-45.4	18.3	40 51.1	-45.1	18.5	41 48.0	-44.9	18.8	42 44.7	-44.5	19.1	43 41.4	-44.3	19.4	63
64	36 16.7	-46.5	16.7	37 14.2	-46.3	17.0	38 11.5	-46.0	17.2	39 08.8	-45.8	17.4	40 06.0	-45.5	17.7	41 03.1	-45.2	17.9	42 00.2	-45.0	18.2	42 57.1	-44.7	18.5	64
65	35 30.2	-46.8	16.0	36 27.9	-46.6	16.2	37 25.5	-46.4	16.4	38 23.0	-46.1	16.6	39 20.5	-45.9	16.8	40 17.9	-45.7	17.1	41 15.2	-45.4	17.3	42 12.4	-45.1	17.6	65
66	34 43.4	-47.1	15.2	35 41.3	-46.9	15.4	36 39.1	-46.6	15.6	37 36.9	-46.5	15.8	38 34.6	-46.2	16.0	39 32.2	-46.0	16.2	40 29.8	-45.7	16.5	41 27.3	-45.5	16.7	66
67	33 56.3	-47.3	14.5	34 54.4	-47.1	14.6	35 52.5	-47.0	14.8	36 50.4	-46.7	15.0	37 48.4	-46.6	15.2	38 46.2	-46.3	15.4	39 44.1	-46.1	15.6	40 41.8	-45.9	15.8	67
68	33 09.0	-47.6	13.7	34 07.3	-47.5	13.9	35 05.5	-47.2	14.0	36 03.7	-47.1	14.2	37 01.8	-46.8	14.4	37 59.9	-46.7	14.6	38 58.0	-46.5	14.8	39 55.9	-46.2	15.0	68
69	32 21.4	-47.9	13.0	33 19.8	-47.6	13.1	34 18.3	-47.6	13.3	35 16.6	-47.3	13.5	36 15.0	-47.2	13.6	37 13.2	-46.9	13.8	38 11.5	-46.8	14.0	39 09.7	-46.6	14.2	69
70	31 33.5	-48.0	12.3	32 32.2	-48.0	12.4	33 30.7	-47.7	12.6	34 29.3	-47.6	12.7	35 27.8	-47.4	12.9	36 26.3	-47.3	13.0	37 24.7	-47.1	13.2	38 23.1	-46.9	13.4	70
71	30 45.5	-48.3	11.6	31 44.2	-48.1	11.7	32 43.0	-48.1	11.8	33 41.7	-47.9	12.0	34 40.4	-47.8	12.1	35 39.0	-47.5	12.3	36 37.6	-47.4	12.4	37 36.2	-47.2	12.6	71
72	29 57.2	-48.6	10.9	30 56.1	-48.4	11.0	31 54.9	-48.2	11.1	32 53.8	-48.1	11.2	33 52.6	-47.9	11.4	34 51.5	-47.9	11.5	35 50.2	-47.6	11.7	36 49.0	-47.5	11.8	72
73	29 08.6	-48.7	10.2	30 07.7	-48.6	10.3	31 06.7	-48.5	10.4	32 05.7	-48.3	10.5	33 04.7	-48.2	10.7	34 03.6	-48.0	10.8	35 02.6	-48.0	10.9	36 01.5	-47.8	11.0	73
74	28 19.9	-48.9	9.6	29 19.1	-48.8	9.6	30 18.2	-48.6	9.7	31 17.4	-48.6	9.8	32 16.5	-48.5	9.9	33 15.6	-48.4	10.1	34 14.6	-48.2	10.2	35 13.7	-48.1	10.3	74
75	27 31.0	-49.1	8.9	28 30.3	-49.0	9.0	29 29.6	-48.9	9.1	30 28.8	-48.8	9.2	31 28.0	-48.6	9.3	32 27.2	-48.5	9.4	33 26.4	-48.4	9.5	34 25.6	-48.3	9.6	75
76	26 41.9	-49.2	8.3	27 41.3	-49.2	8.3	28 40.7	-49.1	8.4	29 40.0	-49.0	8.5	30 39.4	-48.9	8.6	31 38.7	-48.8	8.7	32 38.0	-48.7	8.8	33 37.3	-48.6	8.9	76
77	25 52.7	-49.5	7.6	26 52.1	-49.3	7.7	27 51.6	-49.3	7.7	28 51.0	-49.1	7.8	29 50.5	-49.1	7.9	30 49.9	-49.0	8.0	31 49.3	-48.9	8.1	32 48.7	-48.8	8.2	77
78	25 03.2	-49.5	7.0	26 02.8	-49.5	7.0	27 02.3	-49.4	7.1	28 01.9	-49.4	7.2	29 01.4	-49.3	7.2	30 00.9	-49.2	7.3	31 00.4	-49.1	7.4	31 59.9	-49.0	7.5	78
79	24 13.7	-49.8	6.4	25 13.3	-49.7	6.4	26 12.9	-49.6	6.5	27 12.5	-49.5	6.5	28 12.1	-49.4	6.6	29 11.7	-49.3	6.7	30 11.3	-49.3	6.7	31 10.9	-49.2	6.8	79
80	23 23.9	-49.8	5.8	24 23.6	-49.8	5.8	25 23.3	-49.7	5.8	26 23.0	-49.7	5.9	27 22.7	-49.6	5.9	28 22.4	-49.6	6.0	29 22.0	-49.5	6.1	30 21.7	-49.4	6.1	80
81	22 34.1	-50.0	5.2	23 33.8	-49.9	5.2	24 33.6	-49.9	5.2	25 33.3	-49.8	5.3	26 33.1	-49.8	5.3	27 32.8	-49.7	5.4	28 32.5	-49.6	5.4	29 32.3	-49.6	5.5	81
82	21 44.1	-50.2	4.6	22 43.9	-50.1	4.6	23 43.7	-50.1	4.6	24 43.5	-50.0	4.7	25 43.3	-50.0	4.7	26 43.1	-49.9	4.7	27 42.9	-49.9	4.8	28 42.7	-49.8	4.8	82
83	20 53.9	-50.2	4.0	21 53.8	-50.2	4.0	22 53.6	-50.1	4.0	23 53.5	-50.1	4.1	24 53.3	-50.0	4.1	25 53.2	-50.1	4.1	26 53.0	-50.0	4.2	27 52.9	-50.0	4.2	83
84	20 03.7	-50.4	3.4	21 03.6	-50.4	3.4	22 03.5	-50.3	3.4	23 03.4	-50.3	3.5	24 03.3	-50.3	3.5	25 03.1	-50.2	3.5	26 03.0	-50.1	3.5	27 02.9	-50.1	3.6	84
85	19 13.3	-50.5	2.8	20 13.2	-50.4	2.8	21 13.2	-50.4	2.8	22 13.1	-50.4	2.9	23 13.0	-50.3	2.9	24 12.9	-50.3	2.9	25 12.9	-50.3	2.9	26 12.8	-50.3	3.0	85
86	18 22.8	-50.5	2.2	19 22.8	-50.6	2.2	20 22.8	-50.6	2.3	21 22.7	-50.5	2.3	22 22.7	-50.5	2.3	23 22.6	-50.5	2.3	24 22.6	-50.5	2.3	25 22.5	-50.4	2.3	86
87	17 32.3	-50.7	1.7	18 32.2	-50.6	1.7	19 32.2	-50.6	1.7	20 32.2	-50.6	1.7	21 32.2	-50.6	1.7	22 32.1	-50.6	1.7	23 32.1	-50.6	1.7	24 32.1	-50.6	1.7	87
88	16 41.6	-50.8	1.1	17 41.6	-50.8	1.1	18 41.6	-50.8	1.1	19 41.6	-50.8	1.1	20 41.6	-50.8	1.1	21 41.5	-50.7	1.1	22 41.5	-50.7	1.1	23 41.5	-50.7	1.2	88
89	15 50.8	-50.8	0.6	16 50.8	-50.8	0.6	17 50.8	-50.8	0.6	18 50.8	-50.8	0.6	19 50.8	-50.8	0.6	20 50.8	-50.8	0.6	21 50.8	-50.8	0.6	22 50.8	-50.8	0.6	89
90	15 00.0	-50.9	0.0	16 00.0	-50.9	0.0	17 00.0	-50.9	0.0	18 00.0	-50.9	0.0	19 00.0	-50.9	0.0	20 00.0	-50.9	0.0	21 00.0	-50.9	0.0	22 00.0	-50.9	0.0	90
	15°			16°			17°			18°			19°			20°			21°			22°			

32°, 328° L.H.A. LATITUDE SAME NAME AS DECLINATION

66

LATITUDE **CONTRARY** NAME TO DECLINATION L.H.A. 32°, 328°

Dec.	15° Hc	d	Z	16° Hc	d	Z	17° Hc	d	Z	18° Hc	d	Z	19° Hc	d	Z	20° Hc	d	Z	21° Hc	d	Z	22° Hc	d	Z	Dec.
°	° ′	′	°	° ′	′	°	° ′	′	°	° ′	′	°	° ′	′	°	° ′	′	°	° ′	′	°	° ′	′	°	°
0	55 00.0	-27.7	112.5	54 36.4	-29.1	113.8	54 11.6	-30.5	115.1	53 45.6	-31.9	116.3	53 18.4	-33.2	117.5	52 50.1	-34.4	118.7	52 20.8	-35.6	119.8	51 50.4	-36.7	120.9	0
1	54 32.3	-28.8	114.0	54 07.3	-30.2	115.3	53 41.1	-31.6	116.5	53 13.7	-32.9	117.7	52 45.2	-34.1	118.9	52 15.7	-35.3	120.0	51 45.2	-36.5	121.1	51 13.7	-37.6	122.2	1
2	54 03.5	-29.9	115.5	53 37.1	-31.3	116.8	53 09.5	-32.6	118.0	52 40.8	-33.8	119.1	52 11.1	-35.0	120.3	51 40.4	-36.2	121.4	51 08.7	-37.3	122.4	50 36.1	-38.4	123.4	2
3	53 33.6	-30.9	117.0	53 05.8	-32.2	118.2	52 36.9	-33.5	119.4	52 07.0	-34.7	120.5	51 36.1	-35.9	121.6	51 04.2	-37.0	122.6	50 31.4	-38.1	123.7	49 57.7	-39.1	124.7	3
4	53 02.7	-32.0	118.4	52 33.6	-33.3	119.6	52 03.4	-34.4	120.7	51 32.3	-35.6	121.8	51 00.2	-36.7	122.9	50 27.2	-37.8	123.9	49 53.3	-38.8	124.9	49 18.6	-39.8	125.8	4
5	52 30.7	-32.9	119.8	52 00.3	-34.1	121.0	51 29.0	-35.3	122.0	50 56.7	-36.4	123.1	50 23.5	-37.5	124.1	49 49.4	-38.5	125.1	49 14.5	-39.5	126.0	48 38.8	-40.4	127.0	5
6	51 57.8	-33.9	121.2	51 26.2	-35.0	122.3	50 53.7	-36.1	123.3	50 20.3	-37.2	124.3	49 46.0	-38.2	125.3	49 10.9	-39.2	126.3	48 35.0	-40.1	127.2	47 58.4	-41.1	128.1	6
7	51 23.9	-34.7	122.5	50 51.2	-35.9	123.6	50 17.6	-37.0	124.6	49 43.1	-38.0	125.6	49 07.8	-39.0	126.5	48 31.7	-39.9	127.4	47 54.9	-40.8	128.3	47 17.3	-41.6	129.2	7
8	50 49.2	-35.6	123.8	50 15.3	-36.6	124.8	49 40.6	-37.7	125.8	49 05.1	-38.7	126.8	48 28.8	-39.6	127.7	47 51.8	-40.5	128.5	47 14.1	-41.4	129.4	46 35.7	-42.3	130.2	8
9	50 13.6	-36.4	125.1	49 38.7	-37.5	126.1	49 02.9	-38.4	127.0	48 26.4	-39.3	127.9	47 49.2	-40.2	128.8	47 11.3	-41.1	129.6	46 32.7	-42.0	130.4	45 53.4	-42.7	131.2	9
10	49 37.2	-37.2	126.3	49 01.2	-38.1	127.3	48 24.5	-39.1	128.2	47 47.1	-40.0	129.0	47 09.0	-40.9	129.9	46 30.2	-41.7	130.7	45 50.7	-42.5	131.5	45 10.7	-43.3	132.2	10
11	49 00.0	-37.9	127.5	48 23.1	-38.8	128.4	47 45.4	-39.7	129.3	47 07.1	-40.6	130.1	46 28.1	-41.5	131.0	45 48.5	-42.3	131.7	45 08.2	-43.0	132.5	44 27.4	-43.8	133.2	11
12	48 22.1	-38.5	128.7	47 44.3	-39.5	129.6	47 05.7	-40.4	130.4	46 26.5	-41.2	131.2	45 46.6	-42.0	132.0	45 06.2	-42.8	132.7	44 25.2	-43.5	133.5	43 43.6	-44.2	134.2	12
13	47 43.6	-39.3	129.9	47 04.8	-40.2	130.7	46 25.3	-40.9	131.5	45 45.3	-41.8	132.3	45 04.6	-42.5	133.0	44 23.4	-43.3	133.7	43 41.7	-44.0	134.4	42 59.4	-44.6	135.1	13
14	47 04.3	-39.9	131.0	46 24.6	-40.7	131.8	45 44.4	-41.6	132.5	45 03.5	-42.3	133.3	44 22.1	-43.1	134.0	43 40.1	-43.7	134.7	42 57.7	-44.4	135.4	42 14.8	-45.1	136.0	14
15	46 24.4	-40.5	132.1	45 43.9	-41.3	132.8	45 02.8	-42.1	133.6	44 21.2	-42.8	134.3	43 39.0	-43.5	135.0	42 56.4	-44.2	135.6	42 13.3	-44.9	136.3	41 29.7	-45.5	136.9	15
16	45 43.9	-41.1	133.1	45 02.6	-41.9	133.9	44 20.7	-42.5	134.6	43 38.4	-43.3	135.3	42 55.5	-44.0	135.9	42 12.2	-44.6	136.6	41 28.4	-45.3	137.2	40 44.2	-45.9	137.8	16
17	45 02.8	-41.6	134.2	44 20.7	-42.3	134.9	43 38.2	-43.1	135.6	42 55.1	-43.8	136.2	42 11.5	-44.4	136.8	41 27.6	-45.1	137.5	40 43.1	-45.6	138.0	39 58.3	-46.2	138.6	17
18	44 21.2	-42.2	135.2	43 38.4	-42.9	135.9	42 55.1	-43.6	136.5	42 11.3	-44.2	137.1	41 27.1	-44.8	137.7	40 42.5	-45.3	138.3	39 57.5	-46.0	138.9	39 12.1	-46.6	139.4	18
19	43 39.0	-42.6	136.2	42 55.5	-43.3	136.8	42 11.5	-43.9	137.4	41 27.1	-44.6	138.0	40 42.3	-45.2	138.6	39 57.1	-45.8	139.2	39 11.5	-46.4	139.7	38 25.5	-46.9	140.2	19
20	42 56.4	-43.1	137.1	42 12.2	-43.8	137.8	41 27.6	-44.5	138.4	40 42.5	-45.0	138.9	39 57.1	-45.6	139.5	39 11.3	-46.2	140.0	38 25.1	-46.7	140.5	37 38.6	-47.2	141.0	20
21	42 13.3	-43.6	138.1	41 28.4	-44.2	138.7	40 43.1	-44.8	139.3	39 57.5	-45.4	139.8	39 11.5	-46.0	140.3	38 25.1	-46.5	140.8	37 38.4	-47.0	141.3	36 51.4	-47.5	141.8	21
22	41 29.7	-44.0	139.0	40 44.2	-44.6	139.6	39 58.3	-45.2	140.1	39 12.1	-45.8	140.7	38 25.5	-46.3	141.2	37 38.6	-46.8	141.6	36 51.4	-47.3	142.1	36 03.9	-47.7	142.6	22
23	40 45.7	-44.5	139.9	39 59.6	-45.0	140.5	39 13.1	-45.5	141.0	38 26.3	-46.1	141.5	37 39.2	-46.6	142.0	36 51.8	-47.1	142.4	36 04.1	-47.6	142.9	35 16.2	-48.1	143.3	23
24	40 01.2	-44.8	140.8	39 14.6	-45.4	141.3	38 27.6	-45.9	141.8	37 40.2	-46.4	142.3	36 52.6	-46.9	142.8	36 04.7	-47.4	143.2	35 16.5	-47.8	143.6	34 28.1	-48.3	144.0	24
25	39 16.4	-45.2	141.7	38 29.2	-45.7	142.2	37 41.7	-46.3	142.6	36 53.8	-46.7	143.1	36 05.7	-47.2	143.5	35 17.3	-47.7	144.0	34 28.7	-48.1	144.4	33 39.8	-48.6	144.8	25
26	38 31.2	-45.5	142.5	37 43.5	-46.1	143.0	36 55.4	-46.6	143.4	36 07.1	-47.1	143.9	35 18.5	-47.5	144.3	34 29.6	-47.9	144.7	33 40.6	-48.4	145.1	32 51.2	-48.7	145.5	26
27	37 45.7	-45.9	143.3	36 57.4	-46.4	143.8	36 08.8	-46.8	144.2	35 20.0	-47.3	144.6	34 31.0	-47.8	145.0	33 41.7	-48.2	145.4	32 52.2	-48.6	145.8	32 02.5	-49.0	146.2	27
28	36 59.8	-46.3	144.1	36 11.0	-46.7	144.6	35 22.0	-47.2	145.0	34 32.7	-47.6	145.4	33 43.2	-48.0	145.8	32 53.5	-48.4	146.1	32 03.6	-48.8	146.5	31 13.5	-49.2	146.8	28
29	36 13.5	-46.5	144.9	35 24.3	-47.0	145.3	34 34.8	-47.4	145.7	33 45.1	-47.8	146.1	32 55.2	-48.2	146.5	32 05.1	-48.7	146.8	31 14.8	-49.1	147.2	30 24.3	-49.5	147.5	29
30	35 27.0	-46.8	145.7	34 37.3	-47.2	146.1	33 47.4	-47.7	146.5	32 57.3	-48.1	146.8	32 07.0	-48.5	147.2	31 16.4	-48.8	147.5	30 25.7	-49.2	147.8	29 34.8	-49.6	148.1	30
31	34 40.2	-47.1	146.5	33 50.1	-47.6	146.8	32 59.7	-47.9	147.2	32 09.2	-48.3	147.6	31 18.5	-48.7	147.9	30 27.6	-49.1	148.2	29 36.5	-49.5	148.5	28 45.2	-49.7	148.8	31
32	33 53.1	-47.4	147.2	33 02.5	-47.7	147.6	32 11.8	-48.2	147.9	31 20.9	-48.6	148.3	30 29.8	-49.0	148.6	29 38.5	-49.3	148.9	28 47.0	-49.6	149.2	27 55.5	-50.0	149.4	32
33	33 05.7	-47.6	148.0	32 14.8	-48.0	148.3	31 23.6	-48.4	148.6	30 32.3	-48.7	148.9	29 40.8	-49.1	149.2	28 49.2	-49.4	149.5	27 57.4	-49.8	149.8	27 05.5	-50.1	150.1	33
34	32 18.1	-47.9	148.7	31 26.8	-48.3	149.0	30 35.2	-48.6	149.3	29 43.6	-49.0	149.6	28 51.7	-49.3	149.9	27 59.8	-49.7	150.2	27 07.6	-49.9	150.4	26 15.4	-50.3	150.7	34
35	31 30.2	-48.1	149.4	30 38.5	-48.4	149.7	29 46.6	-48.8	150.0	28 54.6	-49.2	150.3	28 02.4	-49.5	150.5	27 10.1	-49.8	150.8	26 17.7	-50.1	151.0	25 25.1	-50.4	151.3	35
36	30 42.1	-48.3	150.1	29 50.1	-48.7	150.4	28 57.8	-49.0	150.7	28 05.4	-49.3	150.9	27 12.9	-49.6	151.2	26 20.3	-49.9	151.4	25 27.6	-50.3	151.7	24 34.7	-50.5	151.9	36
37	29 53.8	-48.5	150.8	29 01.4	-48.9	151.1	28 08.8	-49.2	151.3	27 16.1	-49.5	151.6	26 23.3	-49.8	151.8	25 30.4	-50.2	152.0	24 37.3	-50.4	152.3	23 44.2	-50.7	152.5	37
38	29 05.3	-48.7	151.5	28 12.5	-49.0	151.7	27 19.6	-49.3	152.0	26 26.6	-49.7	152.2	25 33.5	-50.0	152.4	24 40.2	-50.2	152.6	23 46.9	-50.5	152.8	22 53.5	-50.9	153.0	38
39	28 16.6	-49.0	152.1	27 23.5	-49.3	152.4	26 30.3	-49.6	152.6	25 36.9	-49.8	152.8	24 43.5	-50.1	153.0	23 50.0	-50.4	153.2	22 56.4	-50.7	153.4	22 02.6	-50.9	153.6	39
40	27 27.6	-49.1	152.8	26 34.2	-49.4	153.0	25 40.7	-49.7	153.2	24 47.1	-50.0	153.4	23 53.4	-50.3	153.6	22 59.6	-50.6	153.8	22 05.7	-50.8	154.0	21 11.7	-51.0	154.2	40
41	26 38.5	-49.2	153.4	25 44.8	-49.5	153.6	24 51.0	-49.8	153.8	23 57.1	-50.1	154.0	23 03.1	-50.4	154.2	22 09.0	-50.6	154.4	21 14.9	-50.9	154.6	20 20.7	-51.2	154.8	41
42	25 49.3	-49.5	154.1	24 55.3	-49.7	154.3	24 01.2	-50.0	154.5	23 07.0	-50.3	154.6	22 12.7	-50.5	154.8	21 18.4	-50.8	155.0	20 24.0	-51.0	155.2	19 29.5	-51.2	155.3	42
43	24 59.8	-49.6	154.7	24 05.6	-49.9	154.9	23 11.2	-50.1	155.1	22 16.7	-50.3	155.2	21 22.2	-50.6	155.4	20 27.6	-50.8	155.6	19 33.0	-51.1	155.7	18 38.3	-51.4	155.9	43
44	24 10.2	-49.7	155.3	23 15.7	-50.0	155.5	22 21.1	-50.3	155.7	21 26.4	-50.5	155.8	20 31.6	-50.8	156.0	19 36.8	-51.0	156.1	18 41.9	-51.3	156.3	17 46.9	-51.4	156.4	44
45	23 20.5	-49.9	155.9	22 25.7	-50.1	156.1	21 30.8	-50.4	156.2	20 35.9	-50.7	156.4	19 40.8	-50.8	156.5	18 45.8	-51.1	156.7	17 50.6	-51.3	156.8	16 55.5	-51.6	156.9	45
46	22 30.6	-50.0	156.5	21 35.6	-50.3	156.7	20 40.4	-50.5	156.8	19 45.2	-50.7	157.0	18 50.0	-51.0	157.1	17 54.7	-51.2	157.2	16 59.3	-51.4	157.4	16 03.9	-51.6	157.5	46
47	21 40.6	-50.1	157.1	20 45.3	-50.4	157.3	19 49.9	-50.6	157.4	18 54.5	-50.8	157.5	17 59.0	-51.0	157.7	17 03.5	-51.2	157.8	16 07.9	-51.4	157.9	15 12.3	-51.6	158.0	47
48	20 50.5	-50.3	157.7	19 54.9	-50.5	157.8	18 59.3	-50.7	158.0	18 03.7	-50.9	158.1	17 08.0	-51.1	158.2	16 12.3	-51.4	158.3	15 16.5	-51.6	158.4	14 20.7	-51.8	158.5	48
49	20 00.2	-50.4	158.3	19 04.4	-50.5	158.4	18 08.6	-50.8	158.5	17 12.8	-51.0	158.7	16 16.9	-51.3	158.8	15 20.9	-51.4	158.9	14 24.9	-51.6	159.0	13 28.9	-51.8	159.1	49
50	19 09.8	-50.4	158.9	18 13.9	-50.7	159.0	17 17.8	-50.9	159.1	16 21.8	-51.1	159.2	15 25.6	-51.3	159.3	14 29.5	-51.5	159.4	13 33.3	-51.7	159.5	12 37.1	-51.9	159.6	50
51	18 19.4	-50.6	159.4	17 23.2	-50.8	159.5	16 26.9	-51.0	159.7	15 30.7	-51.2	159.8	14 34.3	-51.3	159.8	13 38.0	-51.6	159.9	12 41.6	-51.7	160.0	11 45.2	-51.9	160.1	51
52	17 28.8	-50.7	160.0	16 32.4	-50.9	160.1	15 35.9	-51.0	160.2	14 39.5	-51.3	160.3	13 43.0	-51.5	160.4	12 46.4	-51.6	160.5	11 49.9	-51.8	160.5	10 53.3	-52.0	160.6	52
53	16 38.1	-50.8	160.6	15 41.5	-50.9	160.7	14 44.9	-51.2	160.7	13 48.2	-51.3	160.8	12 51.5	-51.5	160.9	11 54.8	-51.6	161.0	10 58.1	-51.9	161.0	10 01.3	-52.0	161.1	53
54	15 47.3	-50.8	161.1	14 50.6	-51.1	161.2	13 53.7	-51.2	161.3	12 56.9	-51.4	161.4	12 00.0	-51.5	161.4	11 03.2	-51.8	161.5	10 06.2	-51.9	161.6	9 09.3	-52.0	161.6	54
55	14 56.5	-50.9	161.7	13 59.5	-51.1	161.7	13 02.5	-51.2	161.8	12 05.5	-51.4	161.9	11 08.5	-51.6	162.0	10 11.4	-51.8	162.0	9 14.3	-51.9	162.1	8 17.3	-52.1	162.1	55
56	14 05.6	-51.0	162.2	13 08.4	-51.1	162.3	12 11.3	-51.4	162.4	11 14.1	-51.5	162.4	10 16.9	-51.7	162.5	9 19.6	-51.8	162.5	8 22.4	-52.0	162.6	7 25.2	-52.2	162.6	56
57	13 14.6	-51.1	162.8	12 17.3	-51.3	162.8	11 19.9	-51.4	162.9	10 22.6	-51.6	162.9	9 25.2	-51.7	163.0	8 27.8	-51.8	163.0	7 30.4	-52.0	163.1	6 33.0	-52.1	163.1	57
58	12 23.5	-51.1	163.3	11 26.0	-51.3	163.4	10 28.5	-51.4	163.4	9 31.0	-51.6	163.5	8 33.5	-51.7	163.5	7 36.0	-51.9	163.5	6 38.4	-52.0	163.6	5 40.9	-52.2	163.6	58
59	11 32.4	-51.2	163.8	10 34.7	-51.3	163.9	9 37.1	-51.5	163.9	8 39.4	-51.6	164.0	7 41.8	-51.8	164.0	6 44.1	-52.0	164.0	5 46.4	-52.1	164.1	4 48.7	-52.2	164.1	59
60	10 41.2	-51.3	164.4	9 43.4	-51.4	164.4	8 45.6	-51.5	164.4	7 47.8	-51.7	164.5	6 50.0	-51.8	164.5	5 52.1	-51.9	164.6	4 54.3	-52.1	164.6	3 56.5	-52.3	164.6	60
61	9 49.9	-51.3	164.9	8 52.0	-51.4	164.9	7 54.1	-51.6	165.0	6 56.1	-51.7	165.0	5 58.2	-51.9	165.0	5 00.2	-52.0	165.1	4 02.2	-52.1	165.1	3 04.2	-52.2	165.1	61
62	8 58.6	-51.3	165.4	8 00.6	-51.5	165.4	7 02.5	-51.6	165.5	6 04.4	-51.7	165.5	5 06.3	-51.9	165.5	4 08.2	-52.0	165.6	3 10.1	-52.1	165.6	2 12.0	-52.3	165.6	62
63	8 07.3	-51.4	165.9	7 09.1	-51.5	166.0	6 10.9	-51.6	166.0	5 12.7	-51.8	166.0	4 14.4	-51.8	166.0	3 16.2	-52.0	166.1	2 18.0	-52.2	166.1	1 19.7	-52.2	166.1	63
64	7 15.9	-51.4	166.5	6 17.6	-51.5	166.5	5 19.3	-51.7	166.5	4 20.9	-51.8	166.5	3 22.6	-51.9	166.5	2 24.2	-52.0	166.6	1 25.8	-52.1	166.6	0 27.5	-52.3	166.6	64
65	6 24.5	-51.4	167.0	5 26.1	-51.6	167.0	4 27.6	-51.7	167.0	3 29.1	-51.8	167.0	2 30.7	-52.0	167.0	1 32.2	-52.0	167.1	0 33.7	-52.1	167.1	0 24.8	+52.2	12.9	65
66	5 33.1	-51.5	167.5	4 34.5	-51.6	167.5	3 35.9	-51.7	167.5	2 37.3	-51.8	167.5	1 38.7	-51.9	167.5	0 40.2	-52.1	167.6	0 18.4	+52.2	12.4	1 17.0	+52.3	12.5	66
67	4 41.6	-51.5	168.0	3 42.9	-51.6	168.0	2 44.2	-51.7	168.0	1 45.5	-51.8	168.0	0 46.8	-51.9	168.0	0 11.9	+52.0	11.9	1 10.6	+52.1	12.0	2 09.3	+52.2	12.0	67
68	3 50.1	-51.5	168.5	2 51.3	-51.6	168.5	1 52.5	-51.7	168.5	0 53.7	-51.8	168.5	0 05.1	+51.9	11.4	1 03.9	+52.0	11.5	2 02.7	+52.1	11.5	3 01.5	+52.2	11.5	68
69	2 58.6	-51.5	169.0	1 59.7	-51.6	169.0	1 00.8	-51.7	169.1	0 01.9	-51.8	169.1	0 57.0	+51.9	10.9	1 55.9	+52.1	11.0	2 54.8	+52.2	11.0	3 53.7	+52.3	11.0	69
70	2 07.1	-51.6	169.6	1 08.1	-51.7	169.6	0 09.1	-51.8	169.6	0 49.9	+51.9	10.4	1 48.9	+52.0	10.4	2 48.0	+52.0	10.5	3 47.0	+52.1	10.5	4 46.0	+52.1	10.5	70
71	1 15.5	-51.5	170.1	0 16.4	-51.6	170.1	0 42.7	+51.7	9.9	1 41.8	+51.8	9.9	2 40.9	+51.9	9.9	3 40.0	+51.9	10.0	4 39.1	+52.0	10.0	5 38.1	+52.2	10.0	71
72	0 24.0	-51.5	170.6	0 35.2	+51.6	9.4	1 34.4	+51.7	9.4	2 33.6	+51.8	9.4	3 32.8	+51.8	9.4	4 31.9	+52.0	9.5	5 31.1	+52.1	9.5	6 30.3	+52.1	9.5	72
73	0 27.5	+51.6	8.9	1 26.8	+51.6	8.9	2 26.1	+51.7	8.9	3 25.4	+51.8	8.9	4 24.6	+51.9	8.9	5 23.9	+52.0	9.0	6 23.2	+52.0	9.0	7 22.4	+52.1	9.0	73
74	1 19.1	+51.5	8.4	2 18.4	+51.7	8.4	3 17.8	+51.7	8.4	4 17.2	+51.7	8.4	5 16.5	+51.8	8.4	6 15.9	+51.9	8.4	7 15.2	+52.0	8.5	8 14.5	+52.1	8.5	74
75	2 10.6	+51.5	7.9	3 10.1	+51.6	7.9	4 09.5	+51.7	7.9	5 08.9	+51.8	7.9	6 08.3	+51.9	7.9	7 07.8	+51.8	7.9	8 07.2	+51.9	8.0	9 06.6	+52.0	8.0	75
76	3 02.1	+51.6	7.4	4 01.7	+51.5	7.4	5 01.2	+51.6	7.4	6 00.7	+51.7	7.4	7 00.2	+51.7	7.4	7 59.6	+51.9	7.4	8 59.1	+52.0	7.5	9 58.6	+52.0	7.5	76
77	3 53.7	+51.5	6.9	4 53.2	+51.6	6.9	5 52.8	+51.6	6.9	6 52.4	+51.6	6.9	7 51.9	+51.8	6.9	8 51.5	+51.8	6.9	9 51.1	+51.8	6.9	10 50.6	+51.9	7.0	77
78	4 45.2	+51.4	6.3	5 44.8	+51.5	6.4	6 44.4	+51.6	6.4	7 44.0	+51.7	6.4	8 43.7	+51.7	6.4	9 43.3	+51.8	6.4	10 42.9	+51.8	6.4	11 42.5	+51.9	6.5	78
79	5 36.6	+51.5	5.8	6 36.3	+51.5	5.8	7 36.0	+51.5	5.9	8 35.7	+51.6	5.9	9 35.4	+51.6	5.9	10 35.1	+51.7	5.9	11 34.7	+51.8	5.9	12 34.4	+51.8	5.9	79
80	6 28.1	+51.4	5.3	7 27.8	+51.5	5.3	8 27.5	+51.5	5.3	9 27.3	+51.5	5.4	10 27.0	+51.6	5.4	11 26.8	+51.6	5.4	12 26.5	+51.7	5.4	13 26.2	+51.8	5.4	80
81	7 19.5	+51.3	4.8	8 19.3	+51.4	4.8	9 19.0	+51.5	4.8	10 18.8	+51.5	4.8	11 18.6	+51.6	4.8	12 18.4	+51.6	4.9	13 18.2	+51.6	4.9	14 18.0	+51.7	4.9	81
82	8 10.8	+51.4	4.3	9 10.7	+51.3	4.3	10 10.5	+51.4	4.3	11 10.3	+51.5	4.3	12 10.2	+51.5	4.3	13 10.0	+51.5	4.3	14 09.8	+51.6	4.4	15 09.7	+51.6	4.4	82
83	9 02.2	+51.3	3.7	10 02.0	+51.4	3.8	11 01.9	+51.4	3.8	12 01.8	+51.4	3.8	13 01.7	+51.4	3.8	14 01.5	+51.5	3.8	15 01.4	+51.5	3.8	16 01.3	+51.5	3.9	83
84	9 53.5	+51.2	3.2	10 53.4	+51.2	3.2	11 53.3	+51.3	3.2	12 53.2	+51.3	3.3	13 53.1	+51.3	3.3	14 53.0	+51.4	3.3	15 52.9	+51.4	3.3	16 52.8	+51.4	3.3	84
85	10 44.7	+51.2	2.7	11 44.6	+51.3	2.7	12 44.6	+51.2	2.7	13 44.5	+51.3	2.7	14 44.4	+51.3	2.7	15 44.4	+51.3	2.8	16 44.3	+51.3	2.8	17 44.2	+51.4	2.8	85
86	11 35.9	+51.1	2.2	12 35.9	+51.1	2.2	13 35.8	+51.2	2.2	14 35.8	+51.1	2.2	15 35.7	+51.2	2.2	16 35.7	+51.2	2.2	17 35.6	+51.3	2.2	18 35.6	+51.2	2.2	86
87	12 27.0	+51.1	1.6	13 27.0	+51.1	1.6	14 27.0	+51.1	1.6	15 26.9	+51.2	1.6	16 26.9	+51.1	1.7	17 26.9	+51.1	1.7	18 26.9	+51.1	1.7	19 26.8	+51.2	1.7	87
88	13 18.1	+51.0	1.1	14 18.1	+51.0	1.1	15 18.1	+51.0	1.1	16 18.1	+51.0	1.1	17 18.0	+51.1	1.1	18 18.0	+51.1	1.1	19 18.0	+51.1	1.1	20 18.0	+51.1	1.1	88
89	14 09.1	+50.9	0.5	15 09.1	+50.9	0.5	16 09.1	+50.9	0.6	17 09.1	+50.9	0.6	18 09.1	+50.9	0.6	19 09.1	+50.9	0.6	20 09.1	+50.9	0.6	21 09.1	+50.9	0.6	89
90	15 00.0	+50.8	0.0	16 00.0	+50.8	0.0	17 00.0	+50.8	0.0	18 00.0	+50.8	0.0	19 00.0	+50.8	0.0	20 00.0	+50.8	0.0	21 00.0	+50.8	0.0	22 00.0	+50.8	0.0	90
	15°			16°			17°			18°			19°			20°			21°			22°			

S. Lat. {L.H.A. greater than 180° ....Zn=180°–Z
{L.H.A. less than 180°...........Zn=180°+Z

LATITUDE **SAME** NAME AS DECLINATION L.H.A. 148°, 212°

67

33°, 327° L.H.A. LATITUDE SAME NAME AS DECLINATION N. Lat. {L.H.A. greater than 180° .....Zn=Z; L.H.A. less than 180°.............Zn=360°−Z}

	15°			16°			17°			18°			19°			20°			21°			22°			
Dec.	Hc	d	Z	Hc	d	Z	Hc	d	Z	Hc	d	Z	Hc	d	Z	Hc	d	Z	Hc	d	Z	Hc	d	Z	Dec.
°	° ′	′	°	° ′	′	°	° ′	′	°	° ′	′	°	° ′	′	°	° ′	′	°	° ′	′	°	° ′	′	°	°
0	54 06.3	+25.9	111.7	53 43.5	+27.4	113.0	53 19.4	+28.9	114.2	52 54.2	+30.2	115.4	52 27.9	+31.6	116.6	52 00.5	+32.8	117.8	51 32.0	+34.1	118.9	51 02.5	+35.3	120.0	0
1	54 32.2	+24.7	110.2	54 10.9	+26.2	111.5	53 48.3	+27.7	112.8	53 24.4	+29.2	114.0	52 59.5	+30.5	115.2	52 33.3	+31.9	116.4	52 06.1	+33.2	117.6	51 37.8	+34.5	118.7	1
2	54 56.9	+23.4	108.6	54 37.1	+25.0	109.9	54 16.0	+26.5	111.3	53 53.6	+28.1	112.5	53 30.0	+29.5	113.8	53 05.2	+30.9	115.0	52 39.3	+32.2	116.2	52 12.3	+33.5	117.4	2
3	55 20.3	+22.2	107.0	55 02.1	+23.8	108.4	54 42.5	+25.4	109.7	54 21.7	+26.8	111.0	53 59.5	+28.4	112.3	53 36.1	+29.8	113.6	53 11.5	+31.3	114.8	52 45.8	+32.6	116.0	3
4	55 42.5	+20.8	105.4	55 25.9	+22.4	106.8	55 07.9	+24.1	108.1	54 48.5	+25.7	109.5	54 27.9	+27.2	110.8	54 05.9	+28.8	112.1	53 42.8	+30.1	113.4	53 18.4	+31.5	114.6	4
5	56 03.3	+19.4	103.7	55 48.3	+21.2	105.1	55 32.0	+22.8	106.5	55 14.2	+24.5	107.9	54 55.1	+26.1	109.3	54 34.7	+27.5	110.6	54 12.9	+29.1	111.9	53 49.9	+30.5	113.2	5
6	56 22.7	+18.0	102.0	56 09.5	+19.7	103.4	55 54.8	+21.5	104.9	55 38.7	+23.1	106.3	55 21.2	+24.7	107.7	55 02.2	+26.4	109.1	54 42.0	+27.9	110.4	54 20.4	+29.5	111.7	6
7	56 40.7	+16.5	100.2	56 29.2	+18.4	101.7	56 16.3	+20.1	103.2	56 01.8	+21.9	104.7	55 45.9	+23.6	106.1	55 28.6	+25.2	107.5	55 09.9	+26.8	108.8	54 49.9	+28.3	110.2	7
8	56 57.2	+15.1	98.5	56 47.6	+16.9	100.0	56 36.4	+18.7	101.5	56 23.7	+20.4	103.0	56 09.5	+22.1	104.4	55 53.8	+23.8	105.9	55 36.7	+25.5	107.3	55 18.2	+27.0	108.7	8
9	57 12.3	+13.5	96.7	57 04.5	+15.3	98.2	56 55.1	+17.2	99.8	56 44.1	+19.0	101.3	56 31.6	+20.8	102.8	56 17.6	+22.5	104.2	56 02.2	+24.2	105.7	55 45.2	+25.9	107.1	9
10	57 25.8	+11.9	94.9	57 19.8	+13.9	96.5	57 12.3	+15.7	98.0	57 03.1	+17.6	99.5	56 52.4	+19.4	101.0	56 40.1	+21.2	102.5	56 26.4	+22.8	104.0	56 11.1	+24.6	105.5	10
11	57 37.7	+10.4	93.1	57 33.7	+12.2	94.7	57 28.0	+14.2	96.2	57 20.7	+16.0	97.8	57 11.8	+17.9	99.3	57 01.3	+19.7	100.8	56 49.2	+21.5	102.3	56 35.7	+23.2	103.8	11
12	57 48.1	+8.7	91.2	57 45.9	+10.7	92.8	57 42.2	+12.6	94.4	57 36.7	+14.5	96.0	57 29.7	+16.4	97.5	57 21.0	+18.2	99.1	57 10.7	+20.1	100.6	56 58.9	+21.8	102.1	12
13	57 56.8	+7.1	89.4	57 56.6	+9.0	91.0	57 54.8	+10.9	92.6	57 51.2	+13.0	94.2	57 46.1	+14.8	95.7	57 39.2	+16.8	97.3	57 30.8	+18.6	98.9	57 20.7	+20.4	100.4	13
14	58 03.9	+5.4	87.5	58 05.6	+7.4	89.1	58 05.7	+9.4	90.7	58 04.2	+11.3	92.3	58 00.9	+13.2	93.9	57 56.0	+15.1	95.5	57 49.4	+17.0	97.1	57 41.1	+19.0	98.7	14
15	58 09.3	+3.7	85.6	58 13.0	+5.8	87.2	58 15.1	+7.7	88.8	58 15.5	+9.6	90.5	58 14.1	+11.7	92.1	58 11.1	+13.6	93.7	58 06.4	+15.6	95.3	58 00.1	+17.4	96.9	15
16	58 13.0	+2.1	83.7	58 18.8	+4.0	85.3	58 22.8	+6.0	87.0	58 25.1	+8.1	88.6	58 25.8	+10.0	90.2	58 24.7	+12.0	91.8	58 22.0	+13.9	93.5	58 17.5	+15.8	95.1	16
17	58 15.1	+0.4	81.8	58 22.8	+2.3	83.4	58 28.8	+4.4	85.1	58 33.2	+6.3	86.7	58 35.8	+8.3	88.3	58 36.7	+10.3	90.0	58 35.9	+12.3	91.6	58 33.3	+14.3	93.2	17
18	58 15.5	−1.4	79.9	58 25.1	+0.7	81.5	58 33.2	+2.6	83.1	58 39.5	+4.6	84.8	58 44.1	+6.6	86.4	58 47.0	+8.6	88.1	58 48.2	+10.6	89.7	58 47.6	+12.6	91.4	18
19	58 14.1	−3.0	78.0	58 25.8	−1.1	79.6	58 35.8	+0.9	81.2	58 44.1	+2.9	82.9	58 50.7	+4.9	84.5	58 55.6	+6.9	86.1	58 58.8	+8.9	87.8	59 00.2	+10.9	89.5	19
20	58 11.1	−4.7	76.1	58 24.7	−2.7	77.7	58 36.7	−0.8	79.3	58 47.0	+1.2	80.9	58 55.6	+3.2	82.6	59 02.5	+5.2	84.2	59 07.7	+7.2	85.9	59 11.1	+9.2	87.6	20
21	58 06.4	−6.3	74.2	58 22.0	−4.5	75.8	58 35.9	−2.6	77.4	58 48.2	−0.6	79.0	58 58.8	+1.4	80.6	59 07.7	+3.4	82.3	59 14.9	+5.4	83.9	59 20.3	+7.5	85.6	21
22	58 00.1	−8.0	72.4	58 17.5	−6.1	73.9	58 33.3	−4.2	75.5	58 47.6	−2.3	77.1	59 00.2	−0.3	78.7	59 11.1	+1.7	80.3	59 20.3	+3.8	82.0	59 27.8	+5.8	83.7	22
23	57 52.1	−9.7	70.5	58 11.4	−7.8	72.0	58 29.1	−5.9	73.6	58 45.3	−4.0	75.1	58 59.9	−2.1	76.7	59 12.8	−0.1	78.4	59 24.1	+1.9	80.0	59 33.6	+3.9	81.7	23
24	57 42.4	−11.2	68.6	58 03.6	−9.5	70.1	58 23.2	−7.6	71.7	58 41.3	−5.7	73.2	58 57.8	−3.8	74.8	59 12.7	−1.8	76.4	59 26.0	+0.2	78.1	59 37.5	+2.2	79.7	24
25	57 31.2	−12.8	66.8	57 54.1	−11.1	68.3	58 15.6	−9.3	69.8	58 35.6	−7.4	71.3	58 54.0	−5.5	72.9	59 10.9	−3.6	74.5	59 26.2	−1.6	76.1	59 39.7	+0.4	77.8	25
26	57 18.4	−14.4	65.0	57 43.0	−12.6	66.4	58 06.3	−10.9	67.9	58 28.2	−9.1	69.4	58 48.5	−7.2	70.9	59 07.3	−5.3	72.5	59 24.6	−3.4	74.1	59 40.1	−1.4	75.8	26
27	57 04.0	−15.9	63.2	57 30.4	−14.2	64.6	57 55.4	−12.5	66.0	58 19.1	−10.7	67.5	58 41.3	−8.9	69.0	59 02.0	−7.0	70.6	59 21.2	−5.2	72.2	59 38.7	−3.1	73.8	27
28	56 48.1	−17.4	61.4	57 16.2	−15.8	62.8	57 42.9	−14.1	64.2	58 08.4	−12.4	65.6	58 32.4	−10.6	67.1	58 55.0	−8.8	68.7	59 16.0	−6.8	70.2	59 35.6	−5.0	71.8	28
29	56 30.7	−18.8	59.7	57 00.4	−17.2	61.0	57 28.8	−15.6	62.4	57 56.0	−13.9	63.8	58 21.8	−12.2	65.3	58 46.2	−10.4	66.7	59 09.2	−8.6	68.3	59 30.6	−6.7	69.9	29
30	56 11.9	−20.2	58.0	56 43.2	−18.7	59.3	57 13.2	−17.1	60.6	57 42.1	−15.5	62.0	58 09.6	−13.8	63.4	58 35.8	−12.1	64.9	59 00.6	−10.3	66.4	59 23.9	−8.5	67.9	30
31	55 51.7	−21.5	56.3	56 24.5	−20.1	57.5	56 56.1	−18.6	58.8	57 26.6	−17.1	60.2	57 55.8	−15.4	61.6	58 23.7	−13.7	63.0	58 50.3	−12.0	64.4	59 15.4	−10.1	66.0	31
32	55 30.2	−22.9	54.6	56 04.4	−21.5	55.8	56 37.5	−20.0	57.1	57 09.5	−18.5	58.4	57 40.4	−17.0	59.7	58 10.0	−15.3	61.1	58 38.3	−13.6	62.6	59 05.3	−11.9	64.0	32
33	55 07.3	−24.2	53.0	55 42.9	−22.8	54.2	56 17.5	−21.4	55.4	56 51.0	−19.9	56.6	57 23.4	−18.4	58.0	57 54.7	−16.9	59.3	58 24.7	−15.2	60.7	58 53.4	−13.5	62.1	33
34	54 43.1	−25.3	51.4	55 20.1	−24.1	52.5	55 56.1	−22.8	53.7	56 31.1	−21.4	54.9	57 05.0	−19.9	56.2	57 37.8	−18.3	57.5	58 09.5	−16.8	58.9	58 39.9	−15.2	60.3	34
35	54 17.8	−26.6	49.9	54 56.0	−25.3	50.9	55 33.3	−24.0	52.1	56 09.7	−22.6	53.2	56 45.1	−21.2	54.5	57 19.5	−19.9	55.7	57 52.7	−18.3	57.0	58 24.7	−16.7	58.4	35
36	53 51.2	−27.7	48.3	54 30.7	−26.5	49.4	55 09.3	−25.3	50.5	55 47.1	−24.0	51.6	56 23.9	−22.7	52.8	56 59.6	−21.2	54.0	57 34.4	−19.8	55.3	58 08.0	−18.3	56.6	36
37	53 23.5	−28.8	46.8	54 04.2	−27.7	47.8	54 44.0	−26.5	48.9	55 23.1	−25.3	50.0	56 01.2	−24.0	51.1	56 38.4	−22.6	52.3	57 14.6	−21.2	53.5	57 49.7	−19.7	54.8	37
38	52 54.7	−29.8	45.4	53 36.5	−28.8	46.3	54 17.5	−27.6	47.3	54 57.8	−26.5	48.4	55 37.2	−25.2	49.5	56 15.8	−24.0	50.6	56 53.4	−22.6	51.8	57 30.0	−21.2	53.0	38
39	52 24.9	−30.9	43.9	53 07.7	−29.8	44.9	53 49.9	−28.8	45.8	54 31.3	−27.6	46.8	55 12.0	−26.5	47.9	55 51.8	−25.2	49.0	56 30.8	−24.0	50.1	57 08.8	−22.6	51.3	39
40	51 54.0	−31.8	42.5	52 37.9	−30.9	43.4	53 21.1	−29.8	44.3	54 03.7	−28.8	45.3	54 45.5	−27.6	46.3	55 26.6	−26.5	47.4	56 06.8	−25.3	48.4	56 46.2	−24.0	49.6	40
41	51 22.2	−32.8	41.2	52 07.0	−31.8	42.0	52 51.3	−30.9	42.9	53 34.9	−29.8	43.8	54 17.9	−28.8	44.8	55 00.1	−27.7	45.8	55 41.5	−26.5	46.8	56 22.2	−25.3	47.9	41
42	50 49.4	−33.7	39.8	51 35.2	−32.8	40.6	52 20.4	−31.8	41.5	53 05.1	−30.9	42.4	53 49.1	−29.9	43.3	54 32.4	−28.8	44.2	55 15.0	−27.7	45.2	55 56.9	−26.6	46.3	42
43	50 15.7	−34.5	38.5	51 02.4	−33.7	39.3	51 48.6	−32.8	40.1	52 34.2	−31.9	40.9	53 19.2	−30.9	41.8	54 03.6	−29.9	42.7	54 47.3	−28.8	43.7	55 30.3	−27.7	44.7	43
44	49 41.2	−35.3	37.3	50 28.7	−34.5	38.0	51 15.8	−33.7	38.8	52 02.3	−32.8	39.6	52 48.3	−31.9	40.4	53 33.7	−31.0	41.3	54 18.5	−30.0	42.2	55 02.6	−28.9	43.1	44
45	49 05.9	−36.1	36.0	49 54.2	−35.3	36.7	50 42.1	−34.6	37.4	51 29.5	−33.8	38.2	52 16.4	−32.9	39.0	53 02.7	−32.0	39.8	53 48.5	−31.0	40.7	54 33.7	−30.1	41.6	45
46	48 29.8	−36.9	34.8	49 18.9	−36.2	35.5	50 07.5	−35.4	36.2	50 55.7	−34.6	36.9	51 43.5	−33.8	37.6	52 30.7	−32.9	38.4	53 17.5	−32.1	39.3	54 03.6	−31.1	40.1	46
47	47 52.9	−37.5	33.6	48 42.7	−36.9	34.3	49 32.1	−36.2	34.9	50 21.1	−35.4	35.6	51 09.7	−34.7	36.3	51 57.8	−33.9	37.1	52 45.4	−33.0	37.9	53 32.5	−32.2	38.7	47
48	47 15.4	−38.3	32.5	48 05.8	−37.6	33.1	48 55.9	−36.9	33.7	49 45.7	−36.3	34.3	50 35.0	−35.5	35.0	51 23.9	−34.7	35.7	52 12.4	−33.9	36.5	53 00.4	−33.1	37.3	48
49	46 37.1	−38.9	31.3	47 28.2	−38.3	31.9	48 19.0	−37.7	32.5	49 09.4	−37.0	33.1	49 59.5	−36.3	33.8	50 49.2	−35.6	34.4	51 38.5	−34.9	35.2	52 27.3	−34.1	35.9	49
50	45 58.2	−39.5	30.2	46 49.9	−38.9	30.8	47 41.3	−38.3	31.3	48 32.4	−37.7	31.9	49 23.2	−37.1	32.5	50 13.6	−36.4	33.2	51 03.6	−35.7	33.8	51 53.2	−34.9	34.6	50
51	45 18.7	−40.1	29.2	46 11.0	−39.6	29.7	47 03.0	−39.0	30.2	47 54.7	−38.4	30.8	48 46.1	−37.8	31.3	49 37.2	−37.2	31.9	50 27.9	−36.5	32.6	51 18.3	−35.8	33.2	51
52	44 38.6	−40.7	28.1	45 31.4	−40.1	28.6	46 24.0	−39.7	29.1	47 16.3	−39.1	29.6	48 08.3	−38.5	30.2	49 00.0	−37.9	30.7	49 51.4	−37.2	31.3	50 42.5	−36.6	32.0	52
53	43 57.9	−41.2	27.1	44 51.3	−40.8	27.5	45 44.3	−40.2	28.0	46 37.2	−39.7	28.5	47 29.8	−39.2	29.0	48 22.1	−38.6	29.6	49 14.2	−38.0	30.1	50 05.9	−37.4	30.7	53
54	43 16.7	−41.7	26.1	44 10.5	−41.3	26.5	45 04.1	−40.8	27.0	45 57.5	−40.3	27.4	46 50.6	−39.8	27.9	47 43.5	−39.2	28.4	48 36.2	−38.7	29.0	49 28.5	−38.1	29.5	54
55	42 35.0	−42.2	25.1	43 29.2	−41.7	25.5	44 23.3	−41.3	25.9	45 17.2	−40.9	26.4	46 10.8	−40.4	26.8	47 04.3	−39.9	27.3	47 57.5	−39.4	27.8	48 50.4	−38.8	28.3	55
56	41 52.8	−42.7	24.1	42 47.5	−42.3	24.5	43 42.0	−41.9	24.9	44 36.3	−41.4	25.3	45 30.4	−41.0	25.8	46 24.4	−40.6	26.2	47 18.1	−40.0	26.7	48 11.6	−39.5	27.2	56
57	41 10.1	−43.1	23.2	42 05.2	−42.8	23.6	43 00.1	−42.4	23.9	43 54.9	−42.0	24.3	44 49.4	−41.5	24.7	45 43.8	−41.0	25.1	46 38.1	−40.7	25.6	47 32.1	−40.2	26.1	57
58	40 27.0	−43.6	22.3	41 22.4	−43.2	22.6	42 17.7	−42.8	23.0	43 12.9	−42.5	23.3	44 07.9	−42.0	23.7	45 02.8	−41.7	24.1	45 57.4	−41.2	24.5	46 51.9	−40.7	25.0	58
59	39 43.4	−44.0	21.4	40 39.2	−43.6	21.7	41 34.9	−43.3	22.0	42 30.4	−42.9	22.4	43 25.9	−42.6	22.7	44 21.1	−42.1	23.1	45 16.2	−41.7	23.5	46 11.2	−41.4	23.9	59
60	38 59.4	−44.3	20.5	39 55.6	−44.1	20.8	40 51.6	−43.7	21.1	41 47.5	−43.4	21.4	42 43.3	−43.0	21.8	43 39.0	−42.7	22.1	44 34.5	−42.3	22.5	45 29.8	−41.8	22.9	60
61	38 15.1	−44.8	19.6	39 11.5	−44.4	19.9	40 07.9	−44.1	20.2	41 04.1	−43.8	20.5	42 00.3	−43.5	20.8	42 56.3	−43.1	21.1	43 52.2	−42.8	21.5	44 48.0	−42.4	21.8	61
62	37 30.3	−45.0	18.8	38 27.1	−44.8	19.1	39 23.8	−44.6	19.3	40 20.3	−44.2	19.6	41 16.8	−43.9	19.9	42 13.2	−43.6	20.2	43 09.4	−43.2	20.5	44 05.6	−43.0	20.9	62
63	36 45.3	−45.5	18.0	37 42.3	−45.2	18.2	38 39.2	−44.8	18.5	39 36.1	−44.6	18.7	40 32.9	−44.3	19.0	41 29.6	−44.0	19.3	42 26.2	−43.7	19.6	43 22.6	−43.3	19.9	63
64	35 59.8	−45.7	17.2	36 57.1	−45.5	17.4	37 54.4	−45.3	17.6	38 51.5	−45.0	17.9	39 48.6	−44.7	18.1	40 45.6	−44.5	18.4	41 42.5	−44.2	18.7	42 39.3	−43.9	18.9	64
65	35 14.1	−46.1	16.4	36 11.6	−45.8	16.6	37 09.1	−45.6	16.8	38 06.5	−45.3	17.0	39 03.9	−45.1	17.2	40 01.1	−44.8	17.5	40 58.3	−44.5	17.7	41 55.4	−44.3	18.0	65
66	34 28.0	−46.3	15.6	35 25.8	−46.1	15.8	36 23.5	−45.9	16.0	37 21.2	−45.7	16.2	38 18.8	−45.5	16.4	39 16.3	−45.2	16.6	40 13.8	−45.0	16.9	41 11.1	−44.7	17.1	66
67	33 41.7	−46.6	14.8	34 39.7	−46.4	15.0	35 37.6	−46.2	15.2	36 35.5	−46.0	15.4	37 33.3	−45.8	15.6	38 31.1	−45.6	15.8	39 28.8	−45.3	16.0	40 26.4	−45.0	16.2	67
68	32 55.1	−46.9	14.1	33 53.3	−46.7	14.2	34 51.4	−46.5	14.4	35 49.5	−46.3	14.6	36 47.5	−46.1	14.8	37 45.5	−45.9	15.0	38 43.5	−45.7	15.2	39 41.4	−45.5	15.4	68
69	32 08.2	−47.1	13.3	33 06.6	−47.0	13.5	34 04.9	−46.8	13.6	35 03.2	−46.6	13.8	36 01.4	−46.4	14.0	36 59.6	−46.2	14.1	37 57.8	−46.0	14.3	38 55.9	−45.8	14.5	69
70	31 21.1	−47.4	12.6	32 19.6	−47.2	12.7	33 18.1	−47.1	12.9	34 16.6	−46.9	13.0	35 15.0	−46.7	13.2	36 13.4	−46.5	13.4	37 11.8	−46.4	13.5	38 10.1	−46.2	13.7	70
71	30 33.7	−47.6	11.9	31 32.4	−47.5	12.0	32 31.0	−47.3	12.1	33 29.7	−47.2	12.3	34 28.3	−47.0	12.4	35 26.9	−46.8	12.6	36 25.4	−46.6	12.7	37 23.9	−46.4	12.9	71
72	29 46.1	−47.9	11.2	30 44.9	−47.7	11.3	31 43.7	−47.5	11.4	32 42.5	−47.4	11.5	33 41.3	−47.2	11.7	34 40.1	−47.2	11.8	35 38.8	−47.0	12.0	36 37.5	−46.8	12.1	72
73	28 58.2	−48.0	10.5	29 57.2	−47.9	10.6	30 56.2	−47.8	10.7	31 55.1	−47.6	10.8	32 54.1	−47.6	10.9	33 52.9	−47.3	11.1	34 51.8	−47.2	11.2	35 50.7	−47.1	11.3	73
74	28 10.2	−48.3	9.8	29 09.3	−48.1	9.9	30 08.4	−48.0	10.0	31 07.5	−47.9	10.1	32 06.5	−47.7	10.2	33 05.6	−47.7	10.3	34 04.6	−47.5	10.4	35 03.6	−47.4	10.6	74
75	27 21.9	−48.4	9.1	28 21.2	−48.4	9.2	29 20.4	−48.2	9.3	30 19.6	−48.1	9.4	31 18.8	−48.0	9.5	32 17.9	−47.8	9.6	33 17.1	−47.8	9.7	34 16.2	−47.6	9.8	75
76	26 33.5	−48.6	8.5	27 32.8	−48.5	8.5	28 32.2	−48.4	8.6	29 31.5	−48.3	8.7	30 30.8	−48.2	8.8	31 30.1	−48.1	8.9	32 29.3	−47.9	9.0	33 28.6	−47.9	9.1	76
77	25 44.9	−48.8	7.8	26 44.3	−48.7	7.9	27 43.8	−48.7	8.0	28 43.2	−48.5	8.0	29 42.6	−48.4	8.1	30 42.0	−48.3	8.2	31 41.4	−48.3	8.3	32 40.7	−48.1	8.4	77
78	24 56.1	−48.9	7.2	25 55.6	−48.8	7.2	26 55.1	−48.7	7.3	27 54.7	−48.7	7.4	28 54.2	−48.7	7.4	29 53.7	−48.6	7.5	30 53.1	−48.4	7.6	31 52.6	−48.3	7.7	78
79	24 07.2	−49.2	6.5	25 06.8	−49.1	6.6	26 06.4	−49.0	6.6	27 06.0	−48.9	6.7	28 05.5	−48.8	6.8	29 05.1	−48.7	6.8	30 04.7	−48.7	6.9	31 04.3	−48.6	7.0	79
80	23 18.0	−49.2	5.9	24 17.7	−49.2	6.0	25 17.4	−49.1	6.0	26 17.1	−49.1	6.1	27 16.7	−49.0	6.1	28 16.4	−48.9	6.2	29 16.0	−48.8	6.2	30 15.7	−48.8	6.3	80
81	22 28.8	−49.4	5.3	23 28.5	−49.3	5.3	24 28.3	−49.3	5.4	25 28.0	−49.2	5.4	26 27.7	−49.1	5.5	27 27.5	−49.1	5.5	28 27.2	−49.1	5.6	29 26.9	−49.0	5.6	81
82	21 39.4	−49.5	4.7	22 39.2	−49.5	4.7	23 39.0	−49.4	4.7	24 38.8	−49.4	4.8	25 38.6	−49.4	4.8	26 38.4	−49.3	4.9	27 38.1	−49.2	4.9	28 37.9	−49.1	5.0	82
83	20 49.9	−49.7	4.1	21 49.7	−49.6	4.1	22 49.6	−49.6	4.1	23 49.4	−49.5	4.2	24 49.2	−49.4	4.2	25 49.1	−49.5	4.2	26 48.9	−49.4	4.3	27 48.8	−49.4	4.3	83
84	20 00.2	−49.8	3.5	21 00.1	−49.7	3.5	22 00.0	−49.7	3.5	22 59.9	−49.7	3.5	23 59.8	−49.7	3.6	24 59.6	−49.6	3.6	25 59.5	−49.5	3.6	26 59.4	−49.5	3.7	84
85	19 10.4	−49.8	2.9	20 10.4	−49.9	2.9	21 10.3	−49.8	2.9	22 10.2	−49.8	2.9	23 10.1	−49.7	3.0	24 10.0	−49.7	3.0	25 10.0	−49.7	3.0	26 09.9	−49.7	3.0	85
86	18 20.6	−50.0	2.3	19 20.5	−50.0	2.3	20 20.5	−50.0	2.3	21 20.4	−49.9	2.3	22 20.4	−49.9	2.4	23 20.3	−49.9	2.4	24 20.3	−49.9	2.4	25 20.2	−49.8	2.4	86
87	17 30.6	−50.1	1.7	18 30.5	−50.0	1.7	19 30.5	−50.1	1.7	20 30.5	−50.1	1.7	21 30.5	−50.1	1.8	22 30.4	−50.0	1.8	23 30.4	−50.0	1.8	24 30.4	−50.0	1.8	87
88	16 40.5	−50.2	1.1	17 40.5	−50.2	1.1	18 40.4	−50.1	1.1	19 40.4	−50.1	1.2	20 40.4	−50.1	1.2	21 40.4	−50.1	1.2	22 40.4	−50.1	1.2	23 40.4	−50.1	1.2	88
89	15 50.3	−50.3	0.6	16 50.3	−50.3	0.6	17 50.3	−50.3	0.6	18 50.3	−50.3	0.6	19 50.3	−50.3	0.6	20 50.3	−50.3	0.6	21 50.3	−50.3	0.6	22 50.3	−50.3	0.6	89
90	15 00.0	−50.4	0.0	16 00.0	−50.4	0.0	17 00.0	−50.4	0.0	18 00.0	−50.4	0.0	19 00.0	−50.4	0.0	20 00.0	−50.4	0.0	21 00.0	−50.4	0.0	22 00.0	−50.4	0.0	90
	15°			16°			17°			18°			19°			20°			21°			22°			

33°, 327° L.H.A. LATITUDE SAME NAME AS DECLINATION

68

	15°			16°			17°			18°			19°			20°			21°			22°			
Dec.	Hc	d	Z	Hc	d	Z	Hc	d	Z	Hc	d	Z	Hc	d	Z	Hc	d	Z	Hc	d	Z	Hc	d	Z	Dec.
°	° ′	′	°	° ′	′	°	° ′	′	°	° ′	′	°	° ′	′	°	° ′	′	°	° ′	′	°	° ′	′	°	°
0	54 06.3	-27.1	111.7	53 43.5	-28.5	113.0	53 19.4	-29.9	114.2	52 54.2	-31.2	115.4	52 27.9	-32.6	116.6	52 00.5	-33.8	117.8	51 32.0	-35.0	118.9	51 02.5	-36.2	120.0	0
1	53 39.2	-28.1	113.2	53 15.0	-29.6	114.5	52 49.5	-30.9	115.7	52 23.0	-32.2	116.9	51 55.3	-33.4	118.0	51 26.7	-34.7	119.1	50 57.0	-35.9	120.2	50 26.3	-36.9	121.2	1
2	53 11.1	-29.3	114.7	52 45.4	-30.6	115.9	52 18.6	-31.9	117.1	51 50.8	-33.2	118.2	51 21.9	-34.4	119.3	50 52.0	-35.5	120.4	50 21.1	-36.6	121.5	49 49.4	-37.7	122.5	2
3	52 41.8	-30.3	116.2	52 14.8	-31.6	117.3	51 46.7	-32.8	118.5	51 17.6	-34.1	119.6	50 47.5	-35.2	120.6	50 16.5	-36.4	121.7	49 44.5	-37.4	122.7	49 11.7	-38.5	123.7	3
4	52 11.5	-31.3	117.6	51 43.2	-32.6	118.7	51 13.9	-33.8	119.8	50 43.5	-34.9	120.9	50 12.3	-36.0	121.9	49 40.1	-37.1	122.9	49 07.1	-38.2	123.9	48 33.2	-39.1	124.8	4
5	51 40.2	-32.2	119.0	51 10.6	-33.4	120.1	50 40.1	-34.6	121.1	50 08.6	-35.7	122.2	49 36.3	-36.9	123.2	49 03.0	-37.8	124.1	48 28.9	-38.8	125.1	47 54.1	-39.8	126.0	5
6	51 08.0	-33.2	120.3	50 37.2	-34.3	121.4	50 05.5	-35.5	122.4	49 32.9	-36.5	123.4	48 59.4	-37.5	124.4	48 25.2	-38.6	125.3	47 50.1	-39.5	126.2	47 14.3	-40.4	127.1	6
7	50 34.8	-34.0	121.6	50 02.9	-35.2	122.7	49 30.0	-36.2	123.7	48 56.4	-37.3	124.6	48 21.9	-38.3	125.5	47 46.6	-39.2	126.4	47 10.6	-40.1	127.3	46 33.9	-41.0	128.2	7
8	50 00.8	-34.9	122.9	49 27.7	-35.9	123.9	48 53.8	-37.0	124.9	48 19.1	-38.0	125.8	47 43.6	-38.9	126.7	47 07.4	-39.8	127.6	46 30.5	-40.7	128.4	45 52.9	-41.6	129.2	8
9	49 25.9	-35.7	124.2	48 51.8	-36.7	125.1	48 16.8	-37.7	126.1	47 41.1	-38.6	127.0	47 04.7	-39.6	127.8	46 27.6	-40.5	128.7	45 49.8	-41.4	129.5	45 11.3	-42.1	130.2	9
10	48 50.2	-36.4	125.4	48 15.1	-37.5	126.3	47 39.1	-38.4	127.2	47 02.5	-39.3	128.1	46 25.1	-40.2	128.9	45 47.1	-41.0	129.7	45 08.4	-41.8	130.5	44 29.2	-42.7	131.3	10
11	48 13.8	-37.2	126.6	47 37.6	-38.1	127.5	47 00.7	-39.0	128.4	46 23.2	-40.0	129.2	45 44.9	-40.7	130.0	45 06.1	-41.6	130.8	44 26.6	-42.4	131.5	43 46.5	-43.1	132.2	11
12	47 36.6	-37.8	127.8	46 59.5	-38.8	128.6	46 21.7	-39.7	129.5	45 43.2	-40.5	130.3	45 04.2	-41.4	131.0	44 24.5	-42.2	131.8	43 44.2	-42.9	132.5	43 03.4	-43.6	133.2	12
13	46 58.8	-38.6	128.9	46 20.7	-39.4	129.8	45 42.0	-40.2	130.5	45 02.7	-41.1	131.3	44 22.8	-41.8	132.1	43 42.3	-42.6	132.8	43 01.3	-43.3	133.5	42 19.8	-44.0	134.1	13
14	46 20.2	-39.1	130.1	45 41.3	-40.0	130.8	45 01.8	-40.9	131.6	44 21.6	-41.6	132.3	43 41.0	-42.4	133.1	42 59.7	-43.1	133.7	42 18.0	-43.8	134.4	41 35.8	-44.5	135.0	14
15	45 41.1	-39.8	131.1	45 01.3	-40.6	131.9	44 20.9	-41.3	132.6	43 40.0	-42.1	133.3	42 58.6	-42.9	134.0	42 16.6	-43.5	134.7	41 34.2	-44.2	135.3	40 51.3	-44.9	135.9	15
16	45 01.3	-40.4	132.2	44 20.7	-41.1	132.9	43 39.6	-41.9	133.6	42 57.9	-42.6	134.3	42 15.7	-43.3	135.0	41 33.1	-44.0	135.6	40 50.0	-44.7	136.2	40 06.4	-45.2	136.8	16
17	44 20.9	-40.9	133.3	43 39.6	-41.7	134.0	42 57.7	-42.4	134.6	42 15.3	-43.1	135.3	41 32.4	-43.8	135.9	40 49.1	-44.4	136.5	40 05.3	-45.0	137.1	39 21.2	-45.6	137.7	17
18	43 40.0	-41.4	134.3	42 57.9	-42.2	134.9	42 15.3	-42.9	135.6	41 32.2	-43.6	136.2	40 48.6	-44.1	136.8	40 04.7	-44.8	137.4	39 20.3	-45.4	138.0	38 35.6	-46.0	138.5	18
19	42 58.6	-42.0	135.3	42 15.7	-42.6	135.9	41 32.4	-43.3	136.5	40 48.6	-43.9	137.1	40 04.5	-44.6	137.7	39 19.9	-45.2	138.3	38 34.9	-45.7	138.8	37 49.6	-46.3	139.3	19
20	42 16.6	-42.4	136.2	41 33.1	-43.1	136.9	40 49.1	-43.8	137.4	40 04.7	-44.4	138.0	39 19.9	-45.0	138.6	38 34.7	-45.5	139.1	37 49.2	-46.1	139.6	37 03.3	-46.6	140.1	20
21	41 34.2	-42.9	137.2	40 50.0	-43.6	137.8	40 05.3	-44.1	138.3	39 20.3	-44.7	138.9	38 34.9	-45.3	139.4	37 49.2	-45.9	139.9	37 03.1	-46.4	140.4	36 16.7	-46.9	140.9	21
22	40 51.3	-43.3	138.1	40 06.4	-43.9	138.7	39 21.2	-44.5	139.2	38 35.6	-45.1	139.8	37 49.6	-45.7	140.3	37 03.3	-46.2	140.7	36 16.7	-46.7	141.2	35 29.8	-47.2	141.7	22
23	40 08.0	-43.8	139.0	39 22.5	-44.3	139.6	38 36.7	-45.0	140.1	37 50.5	-45.5	140.6	37 03.9	-45.9	141.1	36 17.1	-46.5	141.5	35 30.0	-47.0	142.0	34 42.6	-47.5	142.4	23
24	39 24.2	-44.1	139.9	38 38.2	-44.7	140.4	37 51.7	-45.2	140.9	37 05.0	-45.8	141.4	36 18.0	-46.4	141.9	35 30.6	-46.8	142.3	34 43.0	-47.3	142.7	33 55.1	-47.7	143.2	24
25	38 40.1	-44.5	140.8	37 53.5	-45.1	141.3	37 06.5	-45.6	141.8	36 19.2	-46.1	142.2	35 31.6	-46.6	142.7	34 43.8	-47.1	143.1	33 55.7	-47.5	143.5	33 07.4	-48.0	143.9	25
26	37 55.6	-44.9	141.6	37 08.4	-45.4	142.1	36 20.9	-45.9	142.6	35 33.1	-46.4	143.0	34 45.0	-46.9	143.4	33 56.7	-47.3	143.8	33 08.2	-47.8	144.2	32 19.4	-48.3	144.6	26
27	37 10.7	-45.2	142.5	36 23.0	-45.8	142.9	35 35.0	-46.3	143.4	34 46.7	-46.7	143.8	33 58.1	-47.1	144.2	33 09.4	-47.6	144.6	32 20.4	-48.1	144.9	31 31.1	-48.4	145.3	27
28	36 25.5	-45.6	143.3	35 37.2	-46.0	143.7	34 48.7	-46.5	144.1	34 00.0	-47.0	144.5	33 11.0	-47.5	144.9	32 21.8	-47.9	145.3	31 32.3	-48.2	145.7	30 42.7	-48.7	146.0	28
29	35 39.9	-45.9	144.1	34 51.2	-46.4	144.5	34 02.2	-46.8	144.9	33 13.0	-47.3	145.3	32 23.5	-47.6	145.7	31 33.9	-48.1	146.0	30 44.1	-48.5	146.3	29 54.0	-48.8	146.7	29
30	34 54.0	-46.2	144.9	34 04.8	-46.6	145.3	33 15.4	-47.1	145.7	32 25.7	-47.5	146.0	31 35.9	-47.9	146.4	30 45.8	-48.3	146.7	29 55.6	-48.7	147.0	29 05.2	-49.1	147.3	30
31	34 07.8	-46.4	145.7	33 18.2	-46.9	146.0	32 28.3	-47.3	146.4	31 38.2	-47.7	146.7	30 48.0	-48.2	147.1	29 57.5	-48.5	147.4	29 06.9	-48.9	147.7	28 16.1	-49.3	148.0	31
32	33 21.4	-46.8	146.4	32 31.3	-47.2	146.8	31 41.0	-47.6	147.1	30 50.5	-48.0	147.5	29 59.8	-48.3	147.8	29 09.0	-48.7	148.1	28 18.0	-49.1	148.4	27 26.8	-49.4	148.6	32
33	32 34.6	-47.0	147.2	31 44.1	-47.4	147.5	30 53.4	-47.8	147.8	30 02.5	-48.1	148.2	29 11.5	-48.6	148.5	28 20.3	-48.9	148.7	27 28.9	-49.2	149.0	26 37.4	-49.6	149.3	33
34	31 47.6	-47.2	147.9	30 56.7	-47.6	148.2	30 05.6	-48.0	148.5	29 14.4	-48.4	148.8	28 22.9	-48.7	149.1	27 31.4	-49.1	149.4	26 39.7	-49.5	149.7	25 47.8	-49.7	149.9	34
35	31 00.4	-47.5	148.6	30 09.1	-47.9	148.9	29 17.6	-48.2	149.2	28 26.0	-48.6	149.5	27 34.2	-48.9	149.8	26 42.3	-49.3	150.0	25 50.2	-49.5	150.3	24 58.1	-49.9	150.5	35
36	30 12.9	-47.7	149.3	29 21.2	-48.1	149.6	28 29.4	-48.4	149.9	27 37.4	-48.8	150.2	26 45.3	-49.1	150.4	25 53.0	-49.4	150.7	25 00.7	-49.8	150.9	24 08.2	-50.1	151.1	36
37	29 25.2	-47.9	150.0	28 33.1	-48.2	150.3	27 41.0	-48.7	150.6	26 48.6	-48.9	150.8	25 56.2	-49.3	151.1	25 03.6	-49.6	151.3	24 10.9	-49.9	151.5	23 18.1	-50.2	151.7	37
38	28 37.3	-48.2	150.7	27 44.9	-48.5	151.0	26 52.3	-48.8	151.2	25 59.7	-49.1	151.5	25 06.9	-49.4	151.7	24 14.0	-49.7	151.9	23 21.0	-50.0	152.1	22 27.9	-50.3	152.3	38
39	27 49.1	-48.3	151.4	26 56.4	-48.7	151.7	26 03.5	-48.9	151.9	25 10.6	-49.3	152.1	24 17.5	-49.6	152.3	23 24.3	-49.9	152.5	22 31.0	-50.2	152.7	21 37.6	-50.4	152.9	39
40	27 00.8	-48.5	152.1	26 07.7	-48.8	152.3	25 14.6	-49.2	152.5	24 21.3	-49.5	152.7	23 27.9	-49.7	152.9	22 34.4	-50.0	153.1	21 40.8	-50.2	153.3	20 47.2	-50.6	153.5	40
41	26 12.3	-48.7	152.7	25 18.9	-49.0	153.0	24 25.4	-49.3	153.2	23 31.8	-49.5	153.4	22 38.2	-49.9	153.6	21 44.4	-50.1	153.7	20 50.6	-50.4	153.9	19 56.6	-50.6	154.1	41
42	25 23.6	-48.8	153.4	24 29.9	-49.1	153.6	23 36.1	-49.4	153.8	22 42.3	-49.8	154.0	21 48.3	-50.0	154.2	20 54.3	-50.3	154.3	20 00.2	-50.6	154.5	19 06.0	-50.8	154.6	42
43	24 34.8	-49.1	154.0	23 40.8	-49.3	154.2	22 46.7	-49.6	154.4	21 52.5	-49.8	154.6	20 58.3	-50.1	154.7	20 04.0	-50.4	154.9	19 09.6	-50.6	155.1	18 15.2	-50.9	155.2	43
44	23 45.7	-49.1	154.7	22 51.5	-49.5	154.8	21 57.1	-49.7	155.0	21 02.7	-50.0	155.2	20 08.2	-50.2	155.3	19 13.6	-50.4	155.5	18 19.0	-50.7	155.6	17 24.3	-50.9	155.8	44
45	22 56.6	-49.4	155.3	22 02.0	-49.6	155.5	21 07.4	-49.8	155.6	20 12.7	-50.1	155.8	19 18.0	-50.4	155.9	18 23.2	-50.6	156.1	17 28.3	-50.8	156.2	16 33.4	-51.1	156.3	45
46	22 07.2	-49.4	155.9	21 12.4	-49.7	156.1	20 17.6	-50.0	156.2	19 22.6	-50.2	156.4	18 27.6	-50.4	156.5	17 32.6	-50.7	156.6	16 37.5	-50.9	156.7	15 42.3	-51.1	156.9	46
47	21 17.8	-49.6	156.5	20 22.7	-49.8	156.7	19 27.6	-50.1	156.8	18 32.4	-50.3	156.9	17 37.2	-50.5	157.1	16 41.9	-50.7	157.2	15 46.6	-51.0	157.3	14 51.2	-51.2	157.4	47
48	20 28.2	-49.7	157.1	19 32.9	-49.9	157.2	18 37.5	-50.1	157.4	17 42.1	-50.4	157.5	16 46.7	-50.7	157.6	15 51.2	-50.9	157.7	14 55.6	-51.0	157.8	14 00.0	-51.2	157.9	48
49	19 38.5	-49.8	157.7	18 43.0	-50.1	157.8	17 47.4	-50.3	158.0	16 51.7	-50.5	158.1	15 56.0	-50.7	158.2	15 00.3	-50.9	158.3	14 04.6	-51.2	158.4	13 08.8	-51.4	158.5	49
50	18 48.7	-50.0	158.3	17 52.9	-50.2	158.4	16 57.1	-50.4	158.5	16 01.2	-50.6	158.6	15 05.3	-50.8	158.7	14 09.4	-51.0	158.8	13 13.4	-51.2	158.9	12 17.4	-51.4	159.0	50
51	17 58.7	-50.0	158.9	17 02.7	-50.2	159.0	16 06.7	-50.4	159.1	15 10.6	-50.6	159.2	14 14.5	-50.8	159.3	13 18.4	-51.1	159.4	12 22.2	-51.2	159.5	11 26.0	-51.4	159.5	51
52	17 08.7	-50.1	159.5	16 12.5	-50.3	159.6	15 16.3	-50.6	159.7	14 20.0	-50.8	159.8	13 23.7	-51.0	159.8	12 27.3	-51.1	159.9	11 31.0	-51.3	160.0	10 34.6	-51.5	160.1	52
53	16 18.6	-50.3	160.0	15 22.2	-50.5	160.1	14 25.7	-50.6	160.2	13 29.2	-50.8	160.3	12 32.7	-51.0	160.4	11 36.2	-51.2	160.5	10 39.7	-51.4	160.5	9 43.1	-51.6	160.6	53
54	15 28.3	-50.3	160.6	14 31.7	-50.5	160.7	13 35.1	-50.7	160.8	12 38.4	-50.9	160.8	11 41.7	-51.0	160.9	10 45.0	-51.2	161.0	9 48.3	-51.4	161.0	8 51.5	-51.6	161.1	54
55	14 38.0	-50.4	161.2	13 41.2	-50.6	161.2	12 44.4	-50.8	161.3	11 47.5	-50.9	161.4	10 50.7	-51.1	161.5	9 53.8	-51.3	161.5	8 56.9	-51.5	161.6	7 59.9	-51.6	161.6	55
56	13 47.6	-50.4	161.7	12 50.6	-50.6	161.8	11 53.6	-50.8	161.9	10 56.6	-51.0	161.9	9 59.6	-51.2	162.0	9 02.5	-51.4	162.0	8 05.4	-51.5	162.1	7 08.3	-51.7	162.1	56
57	12 57.2	-50.6	162.3	12 00.0	-50.7	162.3	11 02.8	-50.9	162.4	10 05.6	-51.0	162.5	9 08.4	-51.2	162.5	8 11.1	-51.3	162.6	7 13.9	-51.5	162.6	6 16.6	-51.7	162.6	57
58	12 06.6	-50.6	162.8	11 09.3	-50.8	162.9	10 11.9	-50.9	162.9	9 14.6	-51.1	163.0	8 17.2	-51.3	163.0	7 19.8	-51.4	163.1	6 22.4	-51.6	163.1	5 24.9	-51.7	163.1	58
59	11 16.0	-50.7	163.4	10 18.5	-50.8	163.4	9 21.0	-51.0	163.5	8 23.5	-51.2	163.5	7 25.9	-51.3	163.6	6 28.4	-51.5	163.6	5 30.8	-51.6	163.6	4 33.2	-51.7	163.7	59
60	10 25.3	-50.7	163.9	9 27.7	-50.9	164.0	8 30.0	-51.0	164.0	7 32.3	-51.2	164.1	6 34.6	-51.3	164.1	5 36.9	-51.5	164.1	4 39.2	-51.6	164.1	3 41.5	-51.8	164.2	60
61	9 34.6	-50.8	164.5	8 36.8	-50.9	164.5	7 39.0	-51.1	164.5	6 41.1	-51.2	164.6	5 43.3	-51.4	164.6	4 45.4	-51.4	164.6	3 47.6	-51.6	164.7	2 49.7	-51.7	164.7	61
62	8 43.8	-50.8	165.0	7 45.9	-51.0	165.0	6 47.9	-51.1	165.1	5 49.9	-51.2	165.1	4 51.9	-51.3	165.1	3 54.0	-51.6	165.2	2 56.0	-51.7	165.2	1 58.0	-51.8	165.2	62
63	7 53.0	-50.8	165.5	6 54.9	-51.0	165.6	5 56.8	-51.1	165.6	4 58.7	-51.3	165.6	4 00.6	-51.4	165.6	3 02.4	-51.5	165.7	2 04.3	-51.7	165.7	1 06.2	-51.8	165.7	63
64	7 02.2	-50.9	166.1	6 03.9	-51.0	166.1	5 05.7	-51.2	166.1	4 07.4	-51.3	166.2	3 09.2	-51.4	166.2	2 10.9	-51.5	166.2	1 12.6	-51.6	166.2	0 14.4	-51.8	166.2	64
65	6 11.3	-50.9	166.6	5 12.9	-51.0	166.6	4 14.5	-51.1	166.7	3 16.1	-51.3	166.7	2 17.8	-51.5	166.7	1 19.4	-51.6	166.7	0 21.0	-51.7	166.7	0 37.4	+51.8	13.3	65
66	5 20.4	-51.0	167.1	4 21.9	-51.1	167.2	3 23.4	-51.2	167.2	2 24.8	-51.3	167.2	1 26.3	-51.4	167.2	0 27.8	-51.5	167.2	0 30.7	+51.6	12.8	1 29.2	+51.8	12.8	66
67	4 29.4	-51.0	167.7	3 30.8	-51.1	167.7	2 32.2	-51.2	167.7	1 33.5	-51.3	167.7	0 34.9	-51.4	167.7	0 23.7	+51.6	12.3	1 22.3	+51.7	12.3	2 21.0	+51.8	12.3	67
68	3 38.4	-51.0	168.2	2 39.7	-51.1	168.2	1 41.0	-51.3	168.2	0 42.2	-51.3	168.2	0 16.5	+51.5	11.8	1 15.3	+51.5	11.8	2 14.0	+51.6	11.8	3 12.7	+51.8	11.8	68
69	2 47.4	-51.0	168.7	1 48.6	-51.1	168.7	0 49.7	-51.2	168.7	0 09.1	+51.3	11.3	1 08.0	+51.4	11.3	2 06.8	+51.5	11.3	3 05.6	+51.7	11.3	4 04.5	+51.7	11.3	69
70	1 56.4	-51.0	169.3	0 57.5	-51.2	169.3	0 01.5	+51.2	10.7	1 00.4	+51.3	10.7	1 59.4	+51.4	10.7	2 58.3	+51.5	10.8	3 57.3	+51.6	10.8	4 56.2	+51.7	10.8	70
71	1 05.4	-51.0	169.8	0 06.3	-51.1	169.8	0 52.7	+51.2	10.2	1 51.7	+51.4	10.2	2 50.8	+51.4	10.2	3 49.8	+51.5	10.2	4 48.9	+51.6	10.3	5 47.9	+51.7	10.3	71
72	0 14.4	-51.1	170.3	0 44.8	+51.1	9.7	1 43.9	+51.2	9.7	2 43.1	+51.3	9.7	3 42.2	+51.4	9.7	4 41.3	+51.5	9.7	5 40.5	+51.5	9.7	6 39.6	+51.7	9.8	72
73	0 36.7	+51.0	9.2	1 35.9	+51.1	9.2	2 35.1	+51.2	9.2	3 34.4	+51.2	9.2	4 33.6	+51.3	9.2	5 32.8	+51.5	9.2	6 32.0	+51.6	9.2	7 31.3	+51.6	9.2	73
74	1 27.7	+51.0	8.6	2 27.0	+51.1	8.6	3 26.3	+51.2	8.6	4 25.6	+51.3	8.7	5 24.9	+51.4	8.7	6 24.3	+51.4	8.7	7 23.6	+51.5	8.7	8 22.9	+51.5	8.7	74
75	2 18.7	+51.0	8.1	3 18.1	+51.1	8.1	4 17.5	+51.1	8.1	5 16.9	+51.2	8.1	6 16.3	+51.3	8.2	7 15.7	+51.4	8.2	8 15.1	+51.4	8.2	9 14.4	+51.6	8.2	75
76	3 09.7	+51.0	7.6	4 09.2	+51.0	7.6	5 08.6	+51.2	7.6	6 08.1	+51.2	7.6	7 07.6	+51.3	7.6	8 07.1	+51.3	7.6	9 06.5	+51.4	7.7	10 06.0	+51.5	7.7	76
77	4 00.7	+50.9	7.1	5 00.2	+51.1	7.1	5 59.8	+51.1	7.1	6 59.3	+51.2	7.1	7 58.9	+51.2	7.1	8 58.4	+51.3	7.1	9 57.9	+51.4	7.1	10 57.5	+51.4	7.2	77
78	4 51.6	+51.0	6.5	5 51.3	+51.0	6.5	6 50.9	+51.0	6.5	7 50.5	+51.1	6.6	8 50.1	+51.2	6.6	9 49.7	+51.2	6.6	10 49.3	+51.3	6.6	11 48.9	+51.4	6.6	78
79	5 42.6	+50.9	6.0	6 42.3	+50.9	6.0	7 41.9	+51.1	6.0	8 41.6	+51.1	6.0	9 41.3	+51.1	6.1	10 40.9	+51.2	6.1	11 40.6	+51.2	6.1	12 40.3	+51.3	6.1	79
80	6 33.5	+50.9	5.5	7 33.2	+51.0	5.5	8 33.0	+50.9	5.5	9 32.7	+51.0	5.5	10 32.4	+51.1	5.5	11 32.1	+51.2	5.5	12 31.8	+51.2	5.6	13 31.6	+51.2	5.6	80
81	7 24.4	+50.8	4.9	8 24.2	+50.8	4.9	9 23.9	+51.0	5.0	10 23.7	+51.0	5.0	11 23.5	+51.0	5.0	12 23.3	+51.0	5.0	13 23.0	+51.1	5.0	14 22.8	+51.2	5.0	81
82	8 15.2	+50.8	4.4	9 15.0	+50.9	4.4	10 14.9	+50.8	4.4	11 14.7	+50.9	4.4	12 14.5	+51.0	4.4	13 14.3	+51.0	4.5	14 14.1	+51.1	4.5	15 14.0	+51.0	4.5	82
83	9 06.0	+50.8	3.9	10 05.9	+50.8	3.9	11 05.7	+50.9	3.9	12 05.6	+50.9	3.9	13 05.5	+50.9	3.9	14 05.3	+51.0	3.9	15 05.2	+51.0	3.9	16 05.0	+51.1	4.0	83
84	9 56.8	+50.7	3.3	10 56.7	+50.7	3.3	11 56.6	+50.7	3.3	12 56.5	+50.8	3.3	13 56.4	+50.8	3.4	14 56.3	+50.8	3.4	15 56.2	+50.8	3.4	16 56.1	+50.9	3.4	84
85	10 47.5	+50.6	2.8	11 47.4	+50.7	2.8	12 47.3	+50.7	2.8	13 47.3	+50.7	2.8	14 47.2	+50.7	2.8	15 47.1	+50.8	2.8	16 47.0	+50.8	2.8	17 47.0	+50.8	2.9	85
86	11 38.1	+50.6	2.2	12 38.1	+50.6	2.2	13 38.0	+50.6	2.2	14 38.0	+50.6	2.3	15 37.9	+50.7	2.3	16 37.9	+50.7	2.3	17 37.8	+50.7	2.3	18 37.8	+50.7	2.3	86
87	12 28.7	+50.5	1.7	13 28.7	+50.5	1.7	14 28.6	+50.6	1.7	15 28.6	+50.6	1.7	16 28.6	+50.6	1.7	17 28.6	+50.5	1.7	18 28.5	+50.6	1.7	19 28.5	+50.6	1.7	87
88	13 19.2	+50.4	1.1	14 19.2	+50.4	1.1	15 19.2	+50.4	1.1	16 19.2	+50.4	1.1	17 19.2	+50.4	1.1	18 19.1	+50.5	1.1	19 19.1	+50.5	1.2	20 19.1	+50.5	1.2	88
89	14 09.6	+50.4	0.6	15 09.6	+50.4	0.6	16 09.6	+50.4	0.6	17 09.6	+50.4	0.6	18 09.6	+50.4	0.6	19 09.6	+50.4	0.6	20 09.6	+50.4	0.6	21 09.6	+50.4	0.6	89
90	15 00.0	+50.3	0.0	16 00.0	+50.3	0.0	17 00.0	+50.3	0.0	18 00.0	+50.3	0.0	19 00.0	+50.3	0.0	20 00.0	+50.3	0.0	21 00.0	+50.3	0.0	22 00.0	+50.3	0.0	90
	15°			16°			17°			18°			19°			20°			21°			22°			

S. Lat. {L.H.A. greater than 180° ....Zn=180°−Z; L.H.A. less than 180°...........Zn=180°+Z

34°, 326° L.H.A. LATITUDE SAME NAME AS DECLINATION

N. Lat. {L.H.A. greater than 180° .....Zn=Z; L.H.A. less than 180°............Zn=360°-Z}

Dec.	15° Hc	d	Z	16° Hc	d	Z	17° Hc	d	Z	18° Hc	d	Z	19° Hc	d	Z	20° Hc	d	Z	21° Hc	d	Z	22° Hc	d	Z	Dec.
°	° ′	′	°	° ′	′	°	° ′	′	°	° ′	′	°	° ′	′	°	° ′	′	°	° ′	′	°	° ′	′	°	°
0	53 12.3	+25.4	111.0	52 50.2	+26.9	112.2	52 26.9	+28.3	113.4	52 02.5	+29.7	114.6	51 37.0	+31.0	115.8	51 10.4	+32.2	116.9	50 42.7	+33.5	118.0	50 14.1	+34.7	119.0	0
1	53 37.7	+24.2	109.5	53 17.1	+25.6	110.7	52 55.2	+27.2	112.0	52 32.2	+28.5	113.2	52 08.0	+29.9	114.4	51 42.6	+31.3	115.5	51 16.2	+32.6	116.7	50 48.8	+33.9	117.8	1
2	54 01.9	+22.9	107.9	53 42.7	+24.6	109.2	53 22.4	+26.0	110.5	53 00.7	+27.5	111.7	52 37.9	+29.0	113.0	52 13.9	+30.4	114.2	51 48.8	+31.7	115.3	51 22.7	+32.9	116.4	2
3	54 24.8	+21.7	106.3	54 07.3	+23.2	107.7	53 48.4	+24.8	109.0	53 28.2	+26.4	110.3	53 06.9	+27.8	111.5	52 44.3	+29.2	112.7	52 20.5	+30.7	113.9	51 55.6	+32.0	115.1	3
4	54 46.5	+20.4	104.7	54 30.5	+22.1	106.1	54 13.2	+23.7	107.4	53 54.6	+25.2	108.7	53 34.7	+26.7	110.0	53 13.5	+28.2	111.3	52 51.2	+29.6	112.5	52 27.6	+31.0	113.7	4
5	55 06.9	+19.0	103.1	54 52.6	+20.7	104.5	54 36.9	+22.4	105.8	54 19.8	+24.0	107.2	54 01.4	+25.6	108.5	53 41.7	+27.1	109.8	53 20.8	+28.6	111.1	52 58.6	+30.0	112.3	5
6	55 25.9	+17.7	101.4	55 13.3	+19.4	102.8	54 59.3	+21.1	104.2	54 43.8	+22.8	105.6	54 27.0	+24.3	107.0	54 08.8	+25.9	108.3	53 49.4	+27.4	109.6	53 28.6	+28.9	110.9	6
7	55 43.6	+16.3	99.7	55 32.7	+18.0	101.2	55 20.4	+19.7	102.6	55 06.6	+21.4	104.0	54 51.3	+23.1	105.4	54 34.7	+24.7	106.7	54 16.8	+26.3	108.1	53 57.5	+27.8	109.4	7
8	55 59.9	+14.8	98.0	55 50.7	+16.6	99.5	55 40.1	+18.4	100.9	55 28.0	+20.1	102.4	55 14.4	+21.8	103.8	54 59.4	+23.5	105.2	54 43.1	+25.0	106.5	54 25.3	+26.7	107.9	8
9	56 14.7	+13.3	96.3	56 07.3	+15.2	97.8	55 58.5	+16.9	99.2	55 48.1	+18.7	100.7	55 36.2	+20.5	102.1	55 22.9	+22.1	103.5	55 08.1	+23.8	104.9	54 52.0	+25.4	106.3	9
10	56 28.0	+11.8	94.5	56 22.5	+13.7	96.0	56 15.4	+15.5	97.5	56 06.8	+17.3	99.0	55 56.7	+19.0	100.5	55 45.0	+20.8	101.9	55 31.9	+22.5	103.3	55 17.4	+24.2	104.7	10
11	56 39.8	+10.3	92.7	56 36.2	+12.1	94.3	56 30.9	+14.0	95.8	56 24.1	+15.9	97.3	56 15.7	+17.7	98.8	56 05.8	+19.5	100.2	55 54.4	+21.2	101.7	55 41.6	+22.8	103.1	11
12	56 50.1	+8.7	90.9	56 48.3	+10.6	92.5	56 44.9	+12.5	94.0	56 40.0	+14.3	95.5	56 33.4	+16.2	97.0	56 25.3	+18.0	98.5	56 15.6	+19.8	100.0	56 04.4	+21.6	101.5	12
13	56 58.8	+7.2	89.1	56 58.9	+9.1	90.7	56 57.4	+11.0	92.2	56 54.3	+12.8	93.7	56 49.6	+14.7	95.3	56 43.3	+16.5	96.8	56 35.4	+18.4	98.3	56 26.0	+20.1	99.8	13
14	57 06.0	+5.5	87.3	57 08.0	+7.4	88.9	57 08.4	+9.3	90.4	57 07.1	+11.3	92.0	57 04.3	+13.1	93.5	56 59.8	+15.1	95.0	56 53.8	+16.8	96.6	56 46.1	+18.7	98.1	14
15	57 11.5	+3.9	85.5	57 15.4	+5.9	87.0	57 17.7	+7.8	88.6	57 18.4	+9.7	90.1	57 17.4	+11.7	91.7	57 14.9	+13.5	93.3	57 10.6	+15.4	94.8	57 04.8	+17.3	96.3	15
16	57 15.4	+2.3	83.6	57 21.3	+4.2	85.2	57 25.5	+6.2	86.7	57 28.1	+8.1	88.3	57 29.1	+10.0	89.9	57 28.4	+11.9	91.4	57 26.0	+13.9	93.0	57 22.1	+15.7	94.6	16
17	57 17.7	+0.7	81.8	57 25.5	+2.6	83.3	57 31.7	+4.5	84.9	57 36.2	+6.5	86.5	57 39.1	+8.4	88.0	57 40.3	+10.3	89.6	57 39.9	+12.2	91.2	57 37.8	+14.2	92.8	17
18	57 18.4	-1.0	79.9	57 28.1	+1.0	81.5	57 36.2	+2.9	83.0	57 42.7	+4.8	84.6	57 47.5	+6.7	86.2	57 50.6	+8.8	87.8	57 52.1	+10.7	89.4	57 52.0	+12.6	91.0	18
19	57 17.4	-2.5	78.1	57 29.1	-0.7	79.6	57 39.1	+1.2	81.2	57 47.5	+3.1	82.7	57 54.2	+5.2	84.3	57 59.4	+7.0	85.9	58 02.8	+9.0	87.5	58 04.6	+11.0	89.1	19
20	57 14.9	-4.3	76.2	57 28.4	-2.4	77.8	57 40.3	-0.4	79.3	57 50.6	+1.5	80.9	57 59.4	+3.4	82.4	58 06.4	+5.4	84.0	58 11.8	+7.4	85.6	58 15.6	+9.3	87.2	20
21	57 10.6	-5.8	74.4	57 26.0	-3.9	75.9	57 39.9	-2.1	77.4	57 52.1	-0.1	79.0	58 02.8	+1.8	80.6	58 11.8	+3.8	82.1	58 19.2	+5.7	83.7	58 24.9	+7.7	85.4	21
22	57 04.8	-7.4	72.6	57 22.1	-5.6	74.0	57 37.8	-3.7	75.6	57 52.0	-1.9	77.1	58 04.6	+0.1	78.7	58 15.6	+2.0	80.2	58 24.9	+4.0	81.8	58 32.6	+5.9	83.5	22
23	56 57.4	-9.0	70.7	57 16.5	-7.2	72.2	57 34.1	-5.4	73.7	57 50.1	-3.4	75.2	58 04.7	-1.6	76.8	58 17.6	+0.3	78.3	58 28.9	+2.3	79.9	58 38.5	+4.3	81.6	23
24	56 48.4	-10.6	68.9	57 09.3	-8.8	70.4	57 28.7	-7.0	71.8	57 46.7	-5.2	73.3	58 03.1	-3.3	74.9	58 17.9	-1.3	76.4	58 31.2	+0.6	78.0	58 42.8	+2.6	79.6	24
25	56 37.8	-12.0	67.1	57 00.5	-10.4	68.5	57 21.7	-8.6	70.0	57 41.5	-6.8	71.5	57 59.8	-4.9	73.0	58 16.6	-3.1	74.5	58 31.8	-1.1	76.1	58 45.4	+0.8	77.7	25
26	56 25.8	-13.6	65.4	56 50.1	-11.9	66.7	57 13.1	-10.2	68.2	57 34.7	-8.4	69.6	57 54.9	-6.6	71.1	58 13.5	-4.7	72.6	58 30.7	-2.9	74.2	58 46.2	-0.9	75.8	26
27	56 12.2	-15.1	63.6	56 38.2	-13.4	65.0	57 02.9	-11.7	66.4	57 26.3	-10.0	67.8	57 48.3	-8.2	69.3	58 08.8	-6.4	70.8	58 27.8	-4.5	72.3	58 45.3	-2.6	73.9	27
28	55 57.1	-16.5	61.9	56 24.8	-15.0	63.2	56 51.2	-13.3	64.6	57 16.3	-11.6	66.0	57 40.1	-9.9	67.4	58 02.4	-8.0	68.9	58 23.3	-6.2	70.4	58 42.7	-4.3	71.9	28
29	55 40.6	-18.0	60.2	56 09.8	-16.3	61.4	56 37.9	-14.8	62.8	57 04.7	-13.1	64.1	57 30.2	-11.4	65.6	57 54.4	-9.7	67.0	58 17.1	-7.9	68.5	58 38.4	-6.1	70.0	29
30	55 22.6	-19.2	58.5	55 53.5	-17.8	59.7	56 23.1	-16.2	61.0	56 51.6	-14.7	62.4	57 18.8	-13.0	63.7	57 44.7	-11.3	65.1	58 09.2	-9.5	66.6	58 32.3	-7.7	68.1	30
31	55 03.4	-20.7	56.8	55 35.7	-19.2	58.0	56 06.9	-17.7	59.3	56 36.9	-16.1	60.6	57 05.8	-14.5	61.9	57 33.4	-12.9	63.3	57 59.7	-11.2	64.7	58 24.6	-9.4	66.2	31
32	54 42.7	-21.9	55.2	55 16.5	-20.5	56.4	55 49.2	-19.1	57.6	56 20.8	-17.6	58.8	56 51.3	-16.1	60.1	57 20.5	-14.4	61.5	57 48.5	-12.7	62.9	58 15.2	-11.1	64.3	32
33	54 20.8	-23.2	53.6	54 56.0	-21.9	54.7	55 30.1	-20.4	55.9	56 03.2	-19.0	57.1	56 35.2	-17.5	58.4	57 06.1	-15.9	59.7	57 35.8	-14.4	61.1	58 04.1	-12.6	62.5	33
34	53 57.6	-24.3	52.0	54 34.1	-23.1	53.1	55 09.7	-21.8	54.2	55 44.2	-20.3	55.4	56 17.7	-18.9	56.7	56 50.2	-17.4	57.9	57 21.4	-15.8	59.3	57 51.5	-14.2	60.6	34
35	53 33.3	-25.6	50.5	54 11.0	-24.3	51.5	54 47.9	-23.0	52.6	55 23.9	-21.7	53.8	55 58.8	-20.3	55.0	56 32.8	-18.9	56.2	57 05.6	-17.4	57.5	57 37.3	-15.8	58.8	35
36	53 07.7	-26.7	48.9	53 46.7	-25.5	50.0	54 24.9	-24.3	51.0	55 02.2	-23.0	52.1	55 38.5	-21.6	53.3	56 13.9	-20.3	54.5	56 48.2	-18.8	55.7	57 21.5	-17.3	57.0	36
37	52 41.0	-27.8	47.4	53 21.2	-26.6	48.4	54 00.6	-25.5	49.5	54 39.2	-24.2	50.5	55 16.9	-23.0	51.6	55 53.6	-21.6	52.8	56 29.4	-20.2	54.0	57 04.2	-18.8	55.2	37
38	52 13.2	-28.8	46.0	52 54.6	-27.8	46.9	53 35.1	-26.6	47.9	54 15.0	-25.5	49.0	54 53.9	-24.2	50.0	55 32.0	-22.9	51.1	56 09.2	-21.6	52.3	56 45.4	-20.2	53.5	38
39	51 44.4	-29.8	44.6	52 26.8	-28.8	45.5	53 08.5	-27.7	46.4	53 49.5	-26.6	47.4	54 29.7	-25.4	48.4	55 09.1	-24.2	49.5	55 47.6	-22.9	50.6	56 25.2	-21.6	51.8	39
40	51 14.6	-30.8	43.2	51 58.0	-29.8	44.0	52 40.8	-28.8	45.0	53 22.9	-27.7	45.9	54 04.3	-26.6	46.9	54 44.9	-25.4	47.9	55 24.7	-24.2	49.0	56 03.6	-22.9	50.1	40
41	50 43.8	-31.8	41.8	51 28.2	-30.8	42.6	52 12.0	-29.8	43.5	52 55.2	-28.8	44.4	53 37.7	-27.7	45.4	54 19.5	-26.6	46.4	55 00.5	-25.4	47.4	55 40.7	-24.2	48.5	41
42	50 12.0	-32.6	40.5	50 57.4	-31.8	41.3	51 42.2	-30.8	42.1	52 26.4	-29.8	43.0	53 10.0	-28.9	43.9	53 52.9	-27.8	44.8	54 35.1	-26.7	45.8	55 16.5	-25.5	46.8	42
43	49 39.4	-33.5	39.2	50 25.6	-32.6	39.9	51 11.4	-31.8	40.7	51 56.6	-30.9	41.6	52 41.1	-29.8	42.4	53 25.1	-28.8	43.3	54 08.4	-27.8	44.3	54 51.0	-26.7	45.3	43
44	49 05.9	-34.3	37.9	49 53.0	-33.5	38.6	50 39.6	-32.7	39.4	51 25.7	-31.8	40.2	52 11.3	-30.9	41.0	52 56.3	-29.9	41.9	53 40.6	-28.9	42.8	54 24.3	-27.8	43.7	44
45	48 31.6	-35.1	36.7	49 19.5	-34.4	37.3	50 06.9	-33.5	38.1	50 53.9	-32.7	38.8	51 40.4	-31.8	39.6	52 26.4	-30.9	40.4	53 11.7	-29.9	41.3	53 56.5	-29.0	42.2	45
46	47 56.5	-35.9	35.4	48 45.1	-35.1	36.1	49 33.4	-34.4	36.8	50 21.2	-33.6	37.5	51 08.6	-32.8	38.3	51 55.5	-31.9	39.0	52 41.8	-31.0	39.9	53 27.5	-30.0	40.7	46
47	47 20.6	-36.6	34.3	48 10.0	-35.9	34.9	48 59.0	-35.1	35.5	49 47.6	-34.4	36.2	50 35.8	-33.6	36.9	51 23.6	-32.8	37.7	52 10.8	-31.9	38.5	52 57.5	-31.0	39.3	47
48	46 44.0	-37.3	33.1	47 34.1	-36.6	33.7	48 23.9	-36.0	34.3	49 13.2	-35.2	35.0	50 02.2	-34.5	35.6	50 50.8	-33.8	36.3	51 38.9	-32.9	37.1	52 26.5	-32.1	37.9	48
49	46 06.7	-37.9	32.0	46 57.5	-37.3	32.5	47 47.9	-36.7	33.1	48 38.0	-36.0	33.7	49 27.7	-35.3	34.4	50 17.0	-34.5	35.0	51 06.0	-33.8	35.7	51 54.4	-33.0	36.5	49
50	45 28.8	-38.6	30.8	46 20.2	-38.0	31.4	47 11.2	-37.3	31.9	48 02.0	-36.7	32.5	48 52.4	-36.0	33.1	49 42.5	-35.4	33.8	50 32.2	-34.7	34.4	51 21.4	-33.8	35.1	50
51	44 50.2	-39.1	29.8	45 42.2	-38.6	30.3	46 33.9	-38.1	30.8	47 25.3	-37.5	31.3	48 16.4	-36.9	31.9	49 07.1	-36.1	32.5	49 57.5	-35.4	33.2	50 47.6	-34.8	33.8	51
52	44 11.1	-39.8	28.7	45 03.6	-39.3	29.2	45 55.8	-38.7	29.7	46 47.8	-38.1	30.2	47 39.5	-37.5	30.7	48 31.0	-36.9	31.3	49 22.1	-36.3	31.9	50 12.8	-35.6	32.5	52
53	43 31.3	-40.3	27.7	44 24.3	-39.8	28.1	45 17.1	-39.2	28.6	46 09.7	-38.7	29.1	47 02.0	-38.2	29.6	47 54.1	-37.7	30.1	48 45.8	-37.0	30.7	49 37.2	-36.3	31.3	53
54	42 51.0	-40.8	26.6	43 44.5	-40.3	27.1	44 37.9	-39.9	27.5	45 31.0	-39.4	28.0	46 23.8	-38.8	28.5	47 16.4	-38.2	29.0	48 08.8	-37.7	29.5	49 00.9	-37.1	30.1	54
55	42 10.2	-41.4	25.6	43 04.2	-40.9	26.0	43 58.0	-40.5	26.5	44 51.6	-40.0	26.9	45 45.0	-39.5	27.4	46 38.2	-39.0	27.8	47 31.1	-38.4	28.4	48 23.8	-37.9	28.9	55
56	41 28.8	-41.8	24.7	42 23.3	-41.4	25.0	43 17.5	-40.9	25.4	44 11.6	-40.5	25.9	45 05.5	-40.0	26.3	45 59.2	-39.5	26.7	46 52.7	-39.1	27.2	47 45.9	-38.5	27.7	56
57	40 47.0	-42.3	23.7	41 41.9	-41.9	24.1	42 36.6	-41.5	24.4	43 31.1	-41.0	24.8	44 25.5	-40.6	25.2	45 19.7	-40.2	25.7	46 13.6	-39.6	26.1	47 07.4	-39.2	26.6	57
58	40 04.7	-42.7	22.8	41 00.0	-42.3	23.1	41 55.1	-42.0	23.5	42 50.1	-41.6	23.8	43 44.9	-41.2	24.2	44 39.5	-40.7	24.6	45 34.0	-40.3	25.0	46 28.2	-39.8	25.5	58
59	39 22.0	-43.1	21.9	40 17.7	-42.8	22.2	41 13.1	-42.4	22.5	42 08.5	-42.0	22.9	43 03.7	-41.6	23.2	43 58.8	-41.3	23.6	44 53.7	-40.8	24.0	45 48.4	-40.4	24.4	59
60	38 38.9	-43.5	21.0	39 34.9	-43.2	21.3	40 30.7	-42.8	21.6	41 26.5	-42.6	21.9	42 22.1	-42.2	22.2	43 17.5	-41.7	22.6	44 12.9	-41.4	23.0	45 08.0	-40.9	23.3	60
61	37 55.4	-44.0	20.1	38 51.7	-43.6	20.4	39 47.9	-43.3	20.7	40 43.9	-42.9	21.0	41 39.9	-42.6	21.3	42 35.8	-42.3	21.6	43 31.5	-41.9	22.0	44 27.1	-41.6	22.3	61
62	37 11.4	-44.2	19.2	38 08.1	-44.0	19.5	39 04.6	-43.7	19.8	40 01.0	-43.4	20.0	40 57.3	-43.1	20.3	41 53.5	-42.7	20.7	42 49.6	-42.4	21.0	43 45.5	-42.0	21.3	62
63	36 27.2	-44.7	18.4	37 24.1	-44.4	18.6	38 20.9	-44.1	18.9	39 17.6	-43.8	19.1	40 14.2	-43.5	19.4	41 10.8	-43.2	19.7	42 07.2	-42.9	20.0	43 03.5	-42.5	20.3	63
64	35 42.5	-44.9	17.6	36 39.7	-44.7	17.8	37 36.8	-44.5	18.0	38 33.8	-44.2	18.3	39 30.7	-43.9	18.5	40 27.6	-43.6	18.8	41 24.3	-43.3	19.1	42 21.0	-43.0	19.4	64
65	34 57.6	-45.3	16.8	35 55.0	-45.1	17.0	36 52.3	-44.7	17.2	37 49.6	-44.5	17.4	38 46.8	-44.2	17.6	39 44.0	-44.0	17.9	40 41.0	-43.7	18.2	41 38.0	-43.4	18.4	65
66	34 12.3	-45.6	16.0	35 09.9	-45.3	16.2	36 07.6	-45.2	16.4	37 05.1	-44.9	16.6	38 02.6	-44.7	16.8	39 00.0	-44.4	17.0	39 57.3	-44.1	17.3	40 54.6	-43.9	17.5	66
67	33 26.7	-45.9	15.2	34 24.6	-45.7	15.4	35 22.4	-45.4	15.5	36 20.2	-45.2	15.7	37 17.9	-45.0	15.9	38 15.6	-44.8	16.2	39 13.2	-44.5	16.4	40 10.7	-44.3	16.6	67
68	32 40.8	-46.1	14.4	33 38.9	-45.9	14.6	34 37.0	-45.8	14.7	35 35.0	-45.6	14.9	36 32.9	-45.3	15.1	37 30.8	-45.1	15.3	38 28.7	-44.9	15.5	39 26.4	-44.6	15.7	68
69	31 54.7	-46.4	13.7	32 53.0	-46.3	13.8	33 51.2	-46.0	14.0	34 49.4	-45.8	14.1	35 47.6	-45.7	14.3	36 45.7	-45.5	14.5	37 43.8	-45.3	14.7	38 41.8	-45.1	14.9	69
70	31 08.3	-46.7	12.9	32 06.7	-46.5	13.0	33 05.2	-46.4	13.2	34 03.6	-46.2	13.3	35 01.9	-45.9	13.5	36 00.2	-45.7	13.7	36 58.5	-45.6	13.9	37 56.7	-45.3	14.0	70
71	30 21.6	-46.9	12.2	31 20.2	-46.7	12.3	32 18.8	-46.6	12.4	33 17.4	-46.4	12.6	34 16.0	-46.3	12.7	35 14.5	-46.1	12.9	36 12.9	-45.9	13.0	37 11.4	-45.8	13.2	71
72	29 34.7	-47.2	11.5	30 33.5	-47.0	11.6	31 32.2	-46.8	11.7	32 31.0	-46.7	11.8	33 29.7	-46.5	12.0	34 28.4	-46.4	12.1	35 27.0	-46.2	12.2	36 25.6	-46.0	12.4	72
73	28 47.5	-47.3	10.8	29 46.5	-47.2	10.9	30 45.4	-47.1	11.0	31 44.3	-47.0	11.1	32 43.2	-46.8	11.2	33 42.0	-46.7	11.3	34 40.8	-46.5	11.5	35 39.6	-46.3	11.6	73
74	28 00.2	-47.6	10.1	28 59.3	-47.5	10.1	29 58.3	-47.3	10.2	30 57.3	-47.1	10.4	31 56.4	-47.1	10.5	32 55.3	-46.9	10.6	33 54.3	-46.8	10.7	34 53.3	-46.7	10.8	74
75	27 12.6	-47.7	9.4	28 11.8	-47.6	9.5	29 11.0	-47.5	9.5	30 10.2	-47.5	9.6	31 09.3	-47.3	9.7	32 08.4	-47.1	9.8	33 07.5	-47.0	10.0	34 06.6	-46.9	10.1	75
76	26 24.9	-48.0	8.7	27 24.2	-47.9	8.8	28 23.5	-47.8	8.8	29 22.7	-47.6	8.9	30 22.0	-47.5	9.0	31 21.3	-47.5	9.1	32 20.5	-47.3	9.2	33 19.7	-47.2	9.3	76
77	25 36.9	-48.1	8.0	26 36.3	-48.0	8.1	27 35.7	-47.9	8.2	28 35.1	-47.8	8.2	29 34.5	-47.8	8.3	30 33.8	-47.6	8.4	31 33.2	-47.6	8.5	32 32.5	-47.4	8.6	77
78	24 48.8	-48.3	7.4	25 48.3	-48.2	7.4	26 47.8	-48.2	7.5	27 47.3	-48.1	7.6	28 46.7	-47.9	7.6	29 46.2	-47.9	7.7	30 45.6	-47.7	7.8	31 45.1	-47.7	7.9	78
79	24 00.5	-48.5	6.7	25 00.1	-48.4	6.8	25 59.6	-48.3	6.8	26 59.2	-48.2	6.9	27 58.8	-48.2	6.9	28 58.3	-48.0	7.0	29 57.9	-48.0	7.1	30 57.4	-47.9	7.1	79
80	23 12.0	-48.6	6.1	24 11.7	-48.6	6.1	25 11.3	-48.5	6.2	26 11.0	-48.4	6.2	27 10.6	-48.3	6.3	28 10.3	-48.3	6.3	29 09.9	-48.2	6.4	30 09.5	-48.1	6.4	80
81	22 23.4	-48.8	5.4	23 23.1	-48.7	5.5	24 22.8	-48.6	5.5	25 22.6	-48.6	5.6	26 22.3	-48.6	5.6	27 22.0	-48.5	5.7	28 21.7	-48.4	5.7	29 21.4	-48.3	5.8	81
82	21 34.6	-48.9	4.8	22 34.4	-48.9	4.8	23 34.2	-48.8	4.9	24 34.0	-48.8	4.9	25 33.7	-48.7	4.9	26 33.5	-48.6	5.0	27 33.3	-48.6	5.0	28 33.1	-48.6	5.1	82
83	20 45.7	-49.0	4.2	21 45.5	-49.0	4.2	22 45.4	-49.0	4.2	23 45.2	-48.9	4.3	24 45.0	-48.8	4.3	25 44.9	-48.8	4.3	26 44.7	-48.8	4.4	27 44.5	-48.7	4.4	83
84	19 56.7	-49.2	3.6	20 56.5	-49.1	3.6	21 56.4	-49.1	3.6	22 56.3	-49.1	3.6	23 56.2	-49.0	3.7	24 56.1	-49.0	3.7	25 55.9	-48.9	3.7	26 55.8	-48.9	3.8	84
85	19 07.5	-49.3	3.0	20 07.4	-49.2	3.0	21 07.3	-49.2	3.0	22 07.2	-49.2	3.0	23 07.2	-49.2	3.0	24 07.1	-49.2	3.1	25 07.0	-49.1	3.1	26 06.9	-49.1	3.1	85
86	18 18.2	-49.4	2.4	19 18.2	-49.4	2.4	20 18.1	-49.4	2.4	21 18.0	-49.3	2.4	22 18.0	-49.3	2.4	23 17.9	-49.2	2.4	24 17.9	-49.3	2.5	25 17.8	-49.2	2.5	86
87	17 28.8	-49.5	1.8	18 28.8	-49.5	1.8	19 28.7	-49.4	1.8	20 28.7	-49.4	1.8	21 28.7	-49.4	1.8	22 28.7	-49.5	1.8	23 28.6	-49.4	1.8	24 28.6	-49.4	1.8	87
88	16 39.3	-49.6	1.2	17 39.3	-49.6	1.2	18 39.3	-49.6	1.2	19 39.3	-49.6	1.2	20 39.3	-49.6	1.2	21 39.2	-49.5	1.2	22 39.2	-49.5	1.2	23 39.2	-49.5	1.2	88
89	15 49.7	-49.7	0.6	16 49.7	-49.7	0.6	17 49.7	-49.7	0.6	18 49.7	-49.7	0.6	19 49.7	-49.7	0.6	20 49.7	-49.7	0.6	21 49.7	-49.7	0.6	22 49.7	-49.7	0.6	89
90	15 00.0	-49.8	0.0	16 00.0	-49.8	0.0	17 00.0	-49.8	0.0	18 00.0	-49.8	0.0	19 00.0	-49.8	0.0	20 00.0	-49.8	0.0	21 00.0	-49.8	0.0	22 00.0	-49.8	0.0	90
	15°			16°			17°			18°			19°			20°			21°			22°			

34°, 326° L.H.A. LATITUDE SAME NAME AS DECLINATION

LATITUDE **CONTRARY** NAME TO DECLINATION **L.H.A. 34°, 326°**

Dec.	15° Hc	d	Z	16° Hc	d	Z	17° Hc	d	Z	18° Hc	d	Z	Dec.
°	° ′	′	°	° ′	′	°	° ′	′	°	° ′	′	°	°
0	53 12.3	−26.5	111.0	52 50.2	−27.9	112.2	52 26.9	−29.3	113.4	52 02.5	−30.6	114.6	0
1	52 45.8	−27.5	112.5	52 22.3	−29.0	113.7	51 57.6	−30.3	114.9	51 31.9	−31.6	116.0	1
2	52 18.3	−28.7	113.9	51 53.3	−29.9	115.1	51 27.3	−31.2	116.3	51 00.3	−32.5	117.4	2
3	51 49.6	−29.7	115.4	51 23.4	−31.0	116.5	50 56.1	−32.2	117.6	50 27.8	−33.5	118.7	3
4	51 19.9	−30.6	116.8	50 52.4	−31.9	117.9	50 23.9	−33.1	118.9	49 54.3	−34.2	120.0	4
5	50 49.3	−31.6	118.1	50 20.5	−32.8	119.2	49 50.8	−34.0	120.2	49 20.1	−35.1	121.3	5
6	50 17.7	−32.5	119.5	49 47.7	−33.6	120.5	49 16.8	−34.8	121.5	48 45.0	−35.8	122.5	6
7	49 45.2	−33.3	120.8	49 14.1	−34.5	121.8	48 42.0	−35.5	122.8	48 09.2	−36.6	123.7	7
8	49 11.9	−34.2	122.1	48 39.6	−35.2	123.0	48 06.5	−36.3	124.0	47 32.6	−37.3	124.9	8
9	48 37.7	−35.0	123.3	48 04.4	−36.1	124.3	47 30.2	−37.0	125.2	46 55.3	−38.0	126.0	9
10	48 02.7	−35.7	124.5	47 28.3	−36.7	125.4	46 53.2	−37.7	126.3	46 17.3	−38.6	127.2	10
11	47 27.0	−36.4	125.7	46 51.6	−37.4	126.6	46 15.5	−38.4	127.4	45 38.7	−39.3	128.3	11
12	46 50.6	−37.2	126.9	46 14.2	−38.1	127.7	45 37.1	−39.0	128.6	44 59.4	−39.8	129.3	12
13	46 13.4	−37.8	128.0	45 36.1	−38.7	128.9	44 58.1	−39.5	129.6	44 19.6	−40.4	130.4	13
14	45 35.6	−38.5	129.2	44 57.4	−39.3	129.9	44 18.6	−40.2	130.7	43 39.2	−41.0	131.4	14
15	44 57.1	−39.0	130.2	44 18.1	−39.9	131.0	43 38.4	−40.7	131.7	42 58.2	−41.5	132.4	15
16	44 18.1	−39.7	131.3	43 38.2	−40.5	132.0	42 57.7	−41.2	132.7	42 16.7	−41.9	133.4	16
17	43 38.4	−40.2	132.4	42 57.7	−41.0	133.1	42 16.5	−41.7	133.7	41 34.8	−42.4	134.4	17
18	42 58.2	−40.7	133.4	42 16.7	−41.4	134.0	41 34.8	−42.2	134.7	40 52.4	−42.9	135.3	18
19	42 17.5	−41.3	134.4	41 35.3	−42.0	135.0	40 52.6	−42.6	135.6	40 09.5	−43.3	136.2	19
20	41 36.2	−41.7	135.4	40 53.3	−42.4	136.0	40 10.0	−43.1	136.6	39 26.2	−43.7	137.1	20
21	40 54.5	−42.2	136.3	40 10.9	−42.9	136.9	39 26.9	−43.5	137.5	38 42.5	−44.1	138.0	21
22	40 12.3	−42.6	137.2	39 28.0	−43.2	137.8	38 43.4	−43.9	138.4	37 58.4	−44.5	138.9	22
23	39 29.7	−43.1	138.2	38 44.8	−43.7	138.7	37 59.5	−44.2	139.2	37 13.9	−44.8	139.7	23
24	38 46.6	−43.5	139.1	38 01.1	−44.1	139.6	37 15.3	−44.7	140.1	36 29.1	−45.2	140.6	24
25	38 03.1	−43.8	139.9	37 17.0	−44.4	140.4	36 30.6	−44.9	140.9	35 43.9	−45.5	141.4	25
26	37 19.3	−44.2	140.8	36 32.6	−44.7	141.3	35 45.7	−45.3	141.7	34 58.4	−45.8	142.2	26
27	36 35.1	−44.6	141.6	35 47.9	−45.1	142.1	35 00.4	−45.6	142.5	34 12.6	−46.1	143.0	27
28	35 50.5	−44.9	142.5	35 02.8	−45.4	142.9	34 14.8	−45.9	143.3	33 26.5	−46.3	143.7	28
29	35 05.6	−45.2	143.3	34 17.4	−45.8	143.7	33 28.9	−46.2	144.1	32 40.2	−46.7	144.5	29
30	34 20.4	−45.6	144.1	33 31.6	−46.0	144.5	32 42.7	−46.5	144.9	31 53.5	−46.9	145.2	30
31	33 34.8	−45.8	144.9	32 45.6	−46.2	145.3	31 56.2	−46.7	145.6	31 06.6	−47.1	146.0	31
32	32 49.0	−46.1	145.6	31 59.4	−46.6	146.0	31 09.5	−46.9	146.3	30 19.5	−47.4	146.7	32
33	32 02.9	−46.4	146.4	31 12.8	−46.8	146.7	30 22.6	−47.2	147.1	29 32.1	−47.6	147.4	33
34	31 16.5	−46.6	147.2	30 26.0	−47.0	147.5	29 35.4	−47.5	147.8	28 44.5	−47.8	148.1	34
35	30 29.9	−46.9	147.9	29 39.0	−47.3	148.2	28 47.9	−47.6	148.5	27 56.7	−48.0	148.8	35
36	29 43.0	−47.1	148.6	28 51.7	−47.4	148.9	28 00.3	−47.8	149.2	27 08.7	−48.2	149.4	36
37	28 55.9	−47.3	149.3	28 04.3	−47.7	149.6	27 12.5	−48.1	149.9	26 20.5	−48.4	150.1	37
38	28 08.6	−47.5	150.0	27 16.6	−47.9	150.3	26 24.4	−48.2	150.5	25 32.1	−48.5	150.8	38
39	27 21.1	−47.7	150.7	26 28.7	−48.1	151.0	25 36.2	−48.4	151.2	24 43.6	−48.8	151.4	39
40	26 33.4	−48.0	151.4	25 40.6	−48.2	151.6	24 47.8	−48.6	151.8	23 54.8	−48.8	152.1	40
41	25 45.4	−48.1	152.1	24 52.4	−48.4	152.3	23 59.2	−48.7	152.5	23 06.0	−49.1	152.7	41
42	24 57.3	−48.2	152.7	24 04.0	−48.6	152.9	23 10.5	−48.9	153.1	22 16.9	−49.1	153.3	42
43	24 09.1	−48.5	153.4	23 15.4	−48.7	153.6	22 21.6	−49.0	153.8	21 27.8	−49.3	153.9	43
44	23 20.6	−48.6	154.0	22 26.7	−48.9	154.2	21 32.6	−49.2	154.4	20 38.5	−49.5	154.5	44
45	22 32.0	−48.7	154.7	21 37.8	−49.0	154.8	20 43.4	−49.3	155.0	19 49.0	−49.5	155.1	45
46	21 43.3	−48.9	155.3	20 48.8	−49.2	155.4	19 54.1	−49.4	155.6	18 59.5	−49.7	155.7	46
47	20 54.4	−49.0	155.9	19 59.6	−49.3	156.1	19 04.7	−49.5	156.2	18 09.8	−49.8	156.3	47
48	20 05.4	−49.2	156.5	19 10.3	−49.4	156.7	18 15.2	−49.6	156.8	17 20.0	−49.8	156.9	48
49	19 16.2	−49.2	157.1	18 20.9	−49.5	157.3	17 25.6	−49.8	157.4	16 30.2	−50.0	157.5	49
50	18 27.0	−49.4	157.7	17 31.4	−49.6	157.9	16 35.8	−49.8	158.0	15 40.2	−50.1	158.1	50
51	17 37.6	−49.5	158.3	16 41.8	−49.7	158.4	15 46.0	−49.9	158.6	14 50.1	−50.1	158.7	51
52	16 48.1	−49.6	158.9	15 52.1	−49.8	159.0	14 56.1	−50.1	159.1	14 00.0	−50.2	159.2	52
53	15 58.5	−49.7	159.5	15 02.3	−49.9	159.6	14 06.0	−50.0	159.7	13 09.8	−50.3	159.8	53
54	15 08.8	−49.7	160.1	14 12.4	−50.0	160.2	13 16.0	−50.2	160.3	12 19.5	−50.4	160.3	54
55	14 19.1	−49.9	160.7	13 22.4	−50.0	160.8	12 25.8	−50.3	160.8	11 29.1	−50.4	160.9	55
56	13 29.2	−49.9	161.2	12 32.4	−50.1	161.3	11 35.5	−50.3	161.4	10 38.7	−50.5	161.4	56
57	12 39.3	−50.0	161.8	11 42.3	−50.2	161.9	10 45.2	−50.3	161.9	9 48.2	−50.5	162.0	57
58	11 49.3	−50.1	162.4	10 52.1	−50.3	162.4	9 54.9	−50.4	162.5	8 57.7	−50.6	162.5	58
59	10 59.2	−50.1	162.9	10 01.8	−50.2	163.0	9 04.5	−50.5	163.0	8 07.1	−50.7	163.1	59
60	10 09.1	−50.2	163.5	9 11.6	−50.4	163.5	8 14.0	−50.5	163.6	7 16.4	−50.6	163.6	60
61	9 18.9	−50.2	164.1	8 21.2	−50.4	164.1	7 23.5	−50.6	164.1	6 25.8	−50.7	164.2	61
62	8 28.7	−50.3	164.6	7 30.8	−50.4	164.6	6 32.9	−50.5	164.7	5 35.1	−50.8	164.7	62
63	7 38.4	−50.4	165.2	6 40.4	−50.5	165.2	5 42.4	−50.7	165.2	4 44.3	−50.7	165.2	63
64	6 48.0	−50.3	165.7	5 49.9	−50.5	165.7	4 51.7	−50.6	165.8	3 53.6	−50.8	165.8	64
65	5 57.7	−50.4	166.3	4 59.4	−50.5	166.3	4 01.1	−50.7	166.3	3 02.8	−50.8	166.3	65
66	5 07.3	−50.4	166.8	4 08.9	−50.6	166.8	3 10.4	−50.6	166.8	2 12.0	−50.8	166.8	66
67	4 16.9	−50.5	167.3	3 18.3	−50.5	167.4	2 19.8	−50.7	167.4	1 21.2	−50.8	167.4	67
68	3 26.4	−50.4	167.9	2 27.8	−50.6	167.9	1 29.1	−50.7	167.9	0 30.4	−50.8	167.9	68
69	2 36.0	−50.5	168.4	1 37.2	−50.6	168.4	0 38.4	−50.7	168.4	0 20.4	+50.8	11.6	69
70	1 45.5	−50.5	169.0	0 46.6	−50.6	169.0	0 12.3	+50.7	11.0	1 11.2	+50.8	11.0	70
71	0 55.0	−50.5	169.5	0 04.0	+50.6	10.5	1 03.0	+50.7	10.5	2 02.0	+50.8	10.5	71
72	0 04.5	−50.5	170.0	0 54.6	+50.6	10.0	1 53.7	+50.7	10.0	2 52.8	+50.8	10.0	72
73	0 46.0	+50.5	9.4	1 45.2	+50.6	9.4	2 44.4	+50.7	9.4	3 43.6	+50.7	9.4	73
74	1 36.5	+50.5	8.9	2 35.8	+50.5	8.9	3 35.1	+50.6	8.9	4 34.3	+50.8	8.9	74
75	2 27.0	+50.4	8.3	3 26.3	+50.6	8.3	4 25.7	+50.6	8.3	5 25.1	+50.7	8.4	75
76	3 17.4	+50.5	7.8	4 16.9	+50.5	7.8	5 16.3	+50.6	7.8	6 15.8	+50.7	7.8	76
77	4 07.9	+50.4	7.2	5 07.4	+50.5	7.3	6 06.9	+50.6	7.3	7 06.5	+50.6	7.3	77
78	4 58.3	+50.4	6.7	5 57.9	+50.5	6.7	6 57.5	+50.5	6.7	7 57.1	+50.6	6.7	78
79	5 48.7	+50.4	6.2	6 48.4	+50.4	6.2	7 48.0	+50.5	6.2	8 47.7	+50.5	6.2	79
80	6 39.1	+50.3	5.6	7 38.8	+50.4	5.6	8 38.5	+50.5	5.6	9 38.2	+50.5	5.7	80
81	7 29.4	+50.3	5.1	8 29.2	+50.3	5.1	9 29.0	+50.3	5.1	10 28.7	+50.5	5.1	81
82	8 19.7	+50.3	4.5	9 19.5	+50.3	4.5	10 19.3	+50.4	4.5	11 19.2	+50.3	4.6	82
83	9 10.0	+50.2	4.0	10 09.8	+50.3	4.0	11 09.7	+50.3	4.0	12 09.5	+50.3	4.0	83
84	10 00.2	+50.1	3.4	11 00.1	+50.1	3.4	12 00.0	+50.2	3.4	12 59.8	+50.3	3.4	84
85	10 50.3	+50.1	2.8	11 50.2	+50.1	2.9	12 50.2	+50.1	2.9	13 50.1	+50.1	2.9	85
86	11 40.4	+50.0	2.3	12 40.3	+50.1	2.3	13 40.3	+50.0	2.3	14 40.2	+50.1	2.3	86
87	12 30.4	+49.9	1.7	13 30.4	+49.9	1.7	14 30.3	+50.0	1.7	15 30.3	+50.0	1.7	87
88	13 20.3	+49.9	1.1	14 20.3	+49.9	1.2	15 20.3	+49.9	1.2	16 20.3	+49.9	1.2	88
89	14 10.2	+49.8	0.6	15 10.2	+49.8	0.6	16 10.2	+49.8	0.6	17 10.2	+49.8	0.6	89
90	15 00.0	+49.7	0.0	16 00.0	+49.7	0.0	17 00.0	+49.7	0.0	18 00.0	+49.7	0.0	90
	15°			16°			17°			18°			

Dec.	19° Hc	d	Z	20° Hc	d	Z	21° Hc	d	Z	22° Hc	d	Z	Dec.
°	° ′	′	°	° ′	′	°	° ′	′	°	° ′	′	°	°
0	51 37.0	−32.0	115.8	51 10.4	−33.2	116.9	50 42.7	−34.4	118.0	50 14.1	−35.6	119.0	0
1	51 05.0	−32.8	117.1	50 37.2	−34.1	118.2	50 08.3	−35.2	119.3	49 38.5	−36.3	120.3	1
2	50 32.2	−33.7	118.4	50 03.1	−34.9	119.5	49 33.1	−36.0	120.5	49 02.2	−37.1	121.5	2
3	49 58.5	−34.6	119.7	49 28.2	−35.7	120.8	48 57.1	−36.8	121.7	48 25.1	−37.8	122.7	3
4	49 23.9	−35.4	121.0	48 52.5	−36.4	122.0	48 20.3	−37.5	122.9	47 47.3	−38.5	123.9	4
5	48 48.5	−36.1	122.2	48 16.1	−37.2	123.2	47 42.8	−38.2	124.1	47 08.8	−39.2	125.0	5
6	48 12.4	−36.9	123.4	47 38.9	−37.9	124.4	47 04.6	−38.8	125.3	46 29.6	−39.7	126.1	6
7	47 35.5	−37.6	124.6	47 01.0	−38.6	125.5	46 25.8	−39.5	126.4	45 49.9	−40.4	127.2	7
8	46 57.9	−38.3	125.8	46 22.4	−39.2	126.6	45 46.3	−40.1	127.4	45 09.5	−41.0	128.3	8
9	46 19.6	−38.9	126.9	45 43.2	−39.8	127.7	45 06.2	−40.7	128.5	44 28.5	−41.5	129.3	9
10	45 40.7	−39.5	128.0	45 03.4	−40.3	128.8	44 25.5	−41.2	129.5	43 47.0	−42.0	130.3	10
11	45 01.2	−40.1	129.1	44 23.1	−41.0	129.8	43 44.3	−41.7	130.6	43 05.0	−42.5	131.3	11
12	44 21.1	−40.7	130.1	43 42.1	−41.5	130.8	43 02.6	−42.2	131.5	42 22.5	−42.9	132.2	12
13	43 40.4	−41.2	131.1	43 00.6	−41.9	131.8	42 20.4	−42.7	132.5	41 39.6	−43.5	133.2	13
14	42 59.2	−41.7	132.1	42 18.7	−42.5	132.8	41 37.7	−43.2	133.5	40 56.1	−43.8	134.1	14
15	42 17.5	−42.2	133.1	41 36.2	−42.9	133.8	40 54.5	−43.6	134.4	40 12.3	−44.3	135.0	15
16	41 35.3	−42.7	134.1	40 53.3	−43.3	134.7	40 10.9	−44.0	135.3	39 28.0	−44.6	135.9	16
17	40 52.6	−43.1	135.0	40 10.0	−43.8	135.6	39 26.9	−44.4	136.2	38 43.4	−45.0	136.7	17
18	40 09.5	−43.5	135.9	39 26.2	−44.2	136.5	38 42.5	−44.8	137.0	37 58.4	−45.4	137.6	18
19	39 26.0	−44.0	136.8	38 42.0	−44.5	137.4	37 57.7	−45.1	137.9	37 13.0	−45.7	138.4	19
20	38 42.0	−44.3	137.7	37 57.5	−44.9	138.2	37 12.6	−45.5	138.7	36 27.3	−46.0	139.2	20
21	37 57.7	−44.7	138.5	37 12.6	−45.3	139.0	36 27.1	−45.8	139.5	35 41.3	−46.4	140.0	21
22	37 13.0	−45.0	139.4	36 27.3	−45.6	139.9	35 41.3	−46.1	140.3	34 54.9	−46.6	140.8	22
23	36 28.0	−45.4	140.2	35 41.7	−45.9	140.7	34 55.2	−46.5	141.1	34 08.3	−46.9	141.5	23
24	35 42.6	−45.7	141.0	34 55.8	−46.2	141.5	34 08.7	−46.7	141.9	33 21.4	−47.2	142.3	24
25	34 56.9	−46.0	141.8	34 09.6	−46.5	142.2	33 22.0	−46.9	142.6	32 34.2	−47.4	143.0	25
26	34 10.9	−46.3	142.6	33 23.1	−46.8	143.0	32 35.1	−47.2	143.4	31 46.8	−47.7	143.8	26
27	33 24.6	−46.6	143.4	32 36.3	−47.0	143.7	31 47.9	−47.5	144.1	30 59.1	−47.9	144.5	27
28	32 38.0	−46.8	144.1	31 49.3	−47.2	144.5	31 00.4	−47.7	144.8	30 11.2	−48.1	145.2	28
29	31 51.2	−47.1	144.8	31 02.1	−47.6	145.2	30 12.7	−47.9	145.5	29 23.1	−48.3	145.9	29
30	31 04.1	−47.3	145.6	30 14.5	−47.7	145.9	29 24.8	−48.2	146.2	28 34.8	−48.5	146.5	30
31	30 16.8	−47.5	146.3	29 26.8	−47.9	146.6	28 36.6	−48.3	146.9	27 46.3	−48.7	147.2	31
32	29 29.3	−47.8	147.0	28 38.9	−48.2	147.3	27 48.3	−48.5	147.6	26 57.6	−48.9	147.9	32
33	28 41.5	−48.0	147.7	27 50.7	−48.4	148.0	26 59.8	−48.8	148.2	26 08.7	−49.1	148.5	33
34	27 53.5	−48.2	148.4	27 02.3	−48.5	148.6	26 11.0	−48.8	148.9	25 19.6	−49.2	149.1	34
35	27 05.3	−48.3	149.0	26 13.8	−48.7	149.3	25 22.2	−49.1	149.5	24 30.4	−49.4	149.8	35
36	26 17.0	−48.6	149.7	25 25.1	−48.9	149.9	24 33.1	−49.2	150.2	23 41.0	−49.5	150.4	36
37	25 28.4	−48.7	150.4	24 36.2	−49.0	150.6	23 43.9	−49.4	150.8	22 51.5	−49.7	151.0	37
38	24 39.7	−48.9	151.0	23 47.2	−49.2	151.2	22 54.5	−49.5	151.4	22 01.8	−49.8	151.6	38
39	23 50.8	−49.0	151.6	22 58.0	−49.4	151.8	22 05.0	−49.6	152.0	21 12.0	−49.9	152.2	39
40	23 01.8	−49.2	152.3	22 08.6	−49.4	152.5	21 15.4	−49.8	152.6	20 22.1	−50.1	152.8	40
41	22 12.6	−49.3	152.9	21 19.2	−49.7	153.1	20 25.6	−49.9	153.2	19 32.0	−50.1	153.4	41
42	21 23.3	−49.5	153.5	20 29.5	−49.7	153.7	19 35.7	−50.0	153.8	18 41.9	−50.3	154.0	42
43	20 33.8	−49.6	154.1	19 39.8	−49.8	154.3	18 45.7	−50.1	154.4	17 51.6	−50.4	154.6	43
44	19 44.2	−49.7	154.7	18 50.0	−50.0	154.8	17 55.6	−50.2	155.0	17 01.2	−50.4	155.1	44
45	18 54.5	−49.8	155.3	18 00.0	−50.1	155.4	17 05.4	−50.3	155.6	16 10.8	−50.6	155.7	45
46	18 04.7	−49.9	155.9	17 09.9	−50.1	156.0	16 15.1	−50.4	156.1	15 20.2	−50.6	156.2	46
47	17 14.8	−50.0	156.5	16 19.8	−50.3	156.6	15 24.7	−50.5	156.7	14 29.6	−50.7	156.8	47
48	16 24.8	−50.1	157.0	15 29.5	−50.3	157.2	14 34.2	−50.5	157.3	13 38.9	−50.8	157.4	48
49	15 34.7	−50.2	157.6	14 39.2	−50.4	157.7	13 43.7	−50.7	157.8	12 48.1	−50.9	157.9	49
50	14 44.5	−50.3	158.2	13 48.8	−50.5	158.3	12 53.0	−50.7	158.4	11 57.2	−50.9	158.4	50
51	13 54.2	−50.3	158.7	12 58.3	−50.6	158.8	12 02.3	−50.7	158.9	11 06.3	−50.9	159.0	51
52	13 03.9	−50.5	159.3	12 07.7	−50.6	159.4	11 11.6	−50.9	159.5	10 15.4	−51.1	159.5	52
53	12 13.4	−50.5	159.9	11 17.1	−50.7	159.9	10 20.7	−50.9	160.0	9 24.3	−51.0	160.1	53
54	11 22.9	−50.5	160.4	10 26.4	−50.7	160.5	9 29.8	−50.9	160.5	8 33.3	−51.1	160.6	54
55	10 32.4	−50.6	161.0	9 35.7	−50.8	161.0	8 38.9	−51.0	161.1	7 42.2	−51.2	161.1	55
56	9 41.8	−50.7	161.5	8 44.9	−50.9	161.6	7 47.9	−51.0	161.6	6 51.0	−51.2	161.6	56
57	8 51.1	−50.7	162.0	7 54.0	−50.8	162.1	6 56.9	−51.0	162.1	5 59.8	−51.2	162.2	57
58	8 00.4	−50.7	162.6	7 03.2	−51.0	162.6	6 05.9	−51.1	162.7	5 08.6	−51.2	162.7	58
59	7 09.7	−50.8	163.1	6 12.2	−50.9	163.2	5 14.8	−51.1	163.2	4 17.4	−51.3	163.2	59
60	6 18.9	−50.9	163.7	5 21.3	−51.0	163.7	4 23.7	−51.1	163.7	3 26.1	−51.3	163.7	60
61	5 28.0	−50.8	164.2	4 30.3	−51.0	164.2	3 32.6	−51.2	164.2	2 34.8	−51.3	164.3	61
62	4 37.2	−50.9	164.7	3 39.3	−51.0	164.7	2 41.4	−51.1	164.8	1 43.5	−51.3	164.8	62
63	3 46.3	−50.9	165.3	2 48.3	−51.0	165.3	1 50.3	−51.2	165.3	0 52.2	−51.3	165.3	63
64	2 55.4	−50.9	165.8	1 57.3	−51.1	165.8	0 59.1	−51.2	165.8	0 00.9	−51.3	165.8	64
65	2 04.5	−50.9	166.3	1 06.2	−51.0	166.3	0 07.9	−51.2	166.3	0 50.4	+51.3	13.7	65
66	1 13.6	−50.9	166.9	0 15.2	−51.1	166.9	0 43.3	+51.1	13.1	1 41.7	+51.3	13.2	66
67	0 22.7	−51.0	167.4	0 35.9	+51.0	12.6	1 34.4	+51.2	12.6	2 33.0	+51.3	12.6	67
68	0 28.3	+50.9	12.1	1 26.9	+51.1	12.1	2 25.6	+51.1	12.1	3 24.3	+51.2	12.1	68
69	1 19.2	+50.9	11.6	2 18.0	+51.0	11.6	3 16.7	+51.2	11.6	4 15.5	+51.3	11.6	69
70	2 10.1	+50.9	11.0	3 09.0	+51.0	11.0	4 07.9	+51.1	11.1	5 06.8	+51.2	11.1	70
71	3 01.0	+50.9	10.5	4 00.0	+51.0	10.5	4 59.0	+51.1	10.5	5 58.0	+51.2	10.5	71
72	3 51.9	+50.9	10.0	4 51.0	+51.0	10.0	5 50.1	+51.0	10.0	6 49.2	+51.1	10.0	72
73	4 42.8	+50.8	9.4	5 42.0	+50.9	9.5	6 41.1	+51.1	9.5	7 40.3	+51.1	9.5	73
74	5 33.6	+50.8	8.9	6 32.9	+50.9	8.9	7 32.2	+50.9	8.9	8 31.4	+51.1	9.0	74
75	6 24.4	+50.8	8.4	7 23.8	+50.9	8.4	8 23.1	+51.0	8.4	9 22.5	+51.0	8.4	75
76	7 15.2	+50.8	7.8	8 14.7	+50.8	7.9	9 14.1	+50.9	7.9	10 13.5	+51.0	7.9	76
77	8 06.0	+50.7	7.3	9 05.5	+50.8	7.3	10 05.0	+50.8	7.3	11 04.5	+50.9	7.4	77
78	8 56.7	+50.6	6.7	9 56.3	+50.7	6.8	10 55.8	+50.8	6.8	11 55.4	+50.9	6.8	78
79	9 47.3	+50.6	6.2	10 47.0	+50.6	6.2	11 46.6	+50.7	6.3	12 46.3	+50.7	6.3	79
80	10 37.9	+50.6	5.7	11 37.6	+50.6	5.7	12 37.3	+50.7	5.7	13 37.0	+50.8	5.7	80
81	11 28.5	+50.5	5.1	12 28.2	+50.6	5.1	13 28.0	+50.6	5.2	14 27.8	+50.6	5.2	81
82	12 19.0	+50.4	4.6	13 18.8	+50.4	4.6	14 18.6	+50.5	4.6	15 18.4	+50.5	4.6	82
83	13 09.4	+50.3	4.0	14 09.2	+50.4	4.0	15 09.1	+50.4	4.0	16 08.9	+50.5	4.1	83
84	13 59.7	+50.3	3.5	14 59.6	+50.3	3.5	15 59.5	+50.4	3.5	16 59.4	+50.4	3.5	84
85	14 50.0	+50.2	2.9	15 49.9	+50.2	2.9	16 49.9	+50.2	2.9	17 49.8	+50.2	2.9	85
86	15 40.2	+50.1	2.3	16 40.1	+50.2	2.3	17 40.1	+50.1	2.3	18 40.0	+50.2	2.4	86
87	16 30.3	+50.0	1.7	17 30.3	+50.0	1.8	18 30.2	+50.1	1.8	19 30.2	+50.1	1.8	87
88	17 20.3	+49.9	1.2	18 20.3	+49.9	1.2	19 20.3	+49.9	1.2	20 20.3	+49.9	1.2	88
89	18 10.2	+49.8	0.6	19 10.2	+49.8	0.6	20 10.2	+49.8	0.6	21 10.2	+49.8	0.6	89
90	19 00.0	+49.7	0.0	20 00.0	+49.7	0.0	21 00.0	+49.7	0.0	22 00.0	+49.7	0.0	90
	19°			20°			21°			22°			

S. Lat. {L.H.A. greater than 180° ....Zn=180°−Z
{L.H.A. less than 180°...........Zn=180°+Z

LATITUDE **SAME** NAME AS DECLINATION **L.H.A. 146°, 214°**

71

35°, 325° L.H.A. LATITUDE SAME NAME AS DECLINATION N. Lat. {L.H.A. greater than 180° .....Zn=Z; L.H.A. less than 180°............Zn=360°−Z

Dec.	15° Hc	d	Z	16° Hc	d	Z	17° Hc	d	Z	18° Hc	d	Z	19° Hc	d	Z	20° Hc	d	Z	21° Hc	d	Z	22° Hc	d	Z	Dec.
°	° ′	′	°	° ′	′	°	° ′	′	°	° ′	′	°	° ′	′	°	° ′	′	°	° ′	′	°	° ′	′	°	°
0	52 18.1	+24.8	110.3	51 56.7	+26.3	111.5	51 34.1	+27.8	112.7	51 10.5	+29.0	113.8	50 45.7	+30.4	114.9	50 19.9	+31.7	116.0	49 53.1	+32.9	117.1	49 25.2	+34.2	118.1	0
1	52 42.9	+23.7	108.8	52 23.0	+25.2	110.0	52 01.9	+26.6	111.2	51 39.5	+28.1	112.4	51 16.1	+29.4	113.6	50 51.6	+30.7	114.7	50 26.0	+32.0	115.8	49 59.4	+33.3	116.9	1
2	53 06.6	+22.5	107.3	52 48.2	+24.0	108.5	52 28.5	+25.5	109.8	52 07.6	+27.0	111.0	51 45.5	+28.4	112.2	51 22.3	+29.8	113.3	50 58.0	+31.1	114.5	50 32.7	+32.3	115.6	2
3	53 29.1	+21.3	105.7	53 12.2	+22.8	107.0	52 54.0	+24.4	108.3	52 34.6	+25.9	109.5	52 13.9	+27.4	110.7	51 52.1	+28.8	111.9	51 29.1	+30.2	113.1	51 05.0	+31.5	114.2	3
4	53 50.4	+20.0	104.1	53 35.0	+21.7	105.5	53 18.4	+23.2	106.7	53 00.5	+24.7	108.0	52 41.3	+26.2	109.3	52 20.9	+27.7	110.5	51 59.3	+29.1	111.7	51 36.5	+30.5	112.9	4
5	54 10.4	+18.7	102.5	53 56.7	+20.3	103.9	53 41.6	+22.0	105.2	53 25.2	+23.6	106.5	53 07.5	+25.1	107.8	52 48.6	+26.6	109.0	52 28.4	+28.1	110.3	52 07.0	+29.5	111.5	5
6	54 29.1	+17.3	100.9	54 17.0	+19.1	102.3	54 03.6	+20.7	103.6	53 48.8	+22.3	105.0	53 32.6	+24.0	106.3	53 15.2	+25.4	107.6	52 56.5	+26.9	108.8	52 36.5	+28.4	110.1	6
7	54 46.4	+16.0	99.2	54 36.1	+17.7	100.6	54 24.3	+19.4	102.0	54 11.1	+21.1	103.4	53 56.6	+22.7	104.7	53 40.6	+24.3	106.0	53 23.4	+25.9	107.3	53 04.9	+27.4	108.6	7
8	55 02.4	+14.7	97.6	54 53.8	+16.4	99.0	54 43.7	+18.1	100.4	54 32.2	+19.8	101.8	54 19.3	+21.4	103.1	54 04.9	+23.1	104.5	53 49.3	+24.6	105.8	53 32.3	+26.2	107.1	8
9	55 17.1	+13.1	95.9	55 10.2	+14.9	97.3	55 01.8	+16.7	98.7	54 52.0	+18.4	100.1	54 40.7	+20.1	101.5	54 28.0	+21.8	102.9	54 13.9	+23.5	104.3	53 58.5	+25.0	105.6	9
10	55 30.2	+11.7	94.2	55 25.1	+13.5	95.6	55 18.5	+15.3	97.0	55 10.4	+17.1	98.5	55 00.8	+18.8	99.9	54 49.8	+20.5	101.3	54 37.4	+22.1	102.7	54 23.5	+23.8	104.0	10
11	55 41.9	+10.3	92.4	55 38.6	+12.1	93.9	55 33.8	+13.9	95.3	55 27.5	+15.6	96.8	55 19.6	+17.5	98.2	55 10.3	+19.2	99.6	54 59.5	+20.9	101.1	54 47.3	+22.6	102.4	11
12	55 52.2	+8.7	90.7	55 50.7	+10.6	92.1	55 47.7	+12.4	93.6	55 43.1	+14.3	95.1	55 37.1	+16.0	96.5	55 29.5	+17.8	98.0	55 20.4	+19.5	99.4	55 09.9	+21.2	100.8	12
13	56 00.9	+7.2	88.9	56 01.3	+9.0	90.4	56 00.1	+10.9	91.9	55 57.4	+12.7	93.3	55 53.1	+14.5	94.8	55 47.3	+16.3	96.3	55 39.9	+18.2	97.7	55 31.1	+19.9	99.2	13
14	56 08.1	+5.6	87.1	56 10.3	+7.5	88.6	56 11.0	+9.4	90.1	56 10.1	+11.2	91.6	56 07.6	+13.1	93.1	56 03.6	+15.0	94.6	55 58.1	+16.7	96.0	55 51.0	+18.5	97.5	14
15	56 13.7	+4.1	85.3	56 17.8	+6.0	86.8	56 20.4	+7.8	88.3	56 21.3	+9.8	89.8	56 20.7	+11.6	91.3	56 18.6	+13.4	92.8	56 14.8	+15.3	94.3	56 09.5	+17.1	95.8	15
16	56 17.8	+2.6	83.5	56 23.8	+4.4	85.0	56 28.2	+6.3	86.5	56 31.1	+8.1	88.0	56 32.3	+10.1	89.6	56 32.0	+11.9	91.1	56 30.1	+13.8	92.6	56 26.6	+15.6	94.1	16
17	56 20.4	+0.9	81.7	56 28.2	+2.9	83.2	56 34.5	+4.7	84.7	56 39.2	+6.6	86.2	56 42.4	+8.5	87.8	56 43.9	+10.4	89.3	56 43.9	+12.2	90.8	56 42.2	+14.1	92.3	17
18	56 21.3	−0.6	79.9	56 31.1	+1.2	81.4	56 39.2	+3.2	82.9	56 45.8	+5.1	84.4	56 50.9	+6.9	86.0	56 54.3	+8.8	87.5	56 56.1	+10.7	89.0	56 56.3	+12.6	90.6	18
19	56 20.7	−2.1	78.1	56 32.3	−0.3	79.6	56 42.4	+1.5	81.1	56 50.9	+3.4	82.6	56 57.8	+5.3	84.1	57 03.1	+7.3	85.7	57 06.8	+9.2	87.2	57 08.9	+11.1	88.8	19
20	56 18.6	−3.8	76.3	56 32.0	−1.9	77.8	56 43.9	0.0	79.3	56 54.3	+1.8	80.8	57 03.1	+3.7	82.3	57 10.4	+5.6	83.8	57 16.0	+7.5	85.4	57 20.0	+9.5	86.9	20
21	56 14.8	−5.3	74.5	56 30.1	−3.5	76.0	56 43.9	−1.7	77.5	56 56.1	+0.2	79.0	57 06.8	+2.1	80.5	57 16.0	+4.0	82.0	57 23.5	+6.0	83.6	57 29.5	+7.8	85.1	21
22	56 09.5	−6.8	72.7	56 26.6	−5.1	74.2	56 42.2	−3.2	75.6	56 56.3	−1.3	77.1	57 08.9	+0.5	78.6	57 20.0	+2.4	80.2	57 29.5	+4.2	81.7	57 37.3	+6.2	83.3	22
23	56 02.7	−8.4	71.0	56 21.5	−6.6	72.4	56 39.0	−4.8	73.8	56 55.0	−3.0	75.3	57 09.4	−1.1	76.8	57 22.4	+0.7	78.3	57 33.7	+2.7	79.8	57 43.5	+4.6	81.4	23
24	55 54.3	−9.9	69.2	56 14.9	−8.2	70.6	56 34.2	−6.4	72.0	56 52.0	−4.6	73.5	57 08.3	−2.8	74.9	57 23.1	−0.9	76.5	57 36.4	+1.0	78.0	57 48.1	+2.9	79.5	24
25	55 44.4	−11.4	67.4	56 06.7	−9.6	68.8	56 27.8	−8.0	70.2	56 47.4	−6.2	71.6	57 05.5	−4.3	73.1	57 22.2	−2.5	74.6	57 37.4	−0.6	76.1	57 51.0	+1.3	77.7	25
26	55 33.0	−12.8	65.7	55 57.1	−11.2	67.0	56 19.8	−9.5	68.4	56 41.2	−7.8	69.8	57 01.2	−6.0	71.3	57 19.7	−4.1	72.7	57 36.8	−2.3	74.2	57 52.3	−0.4	75.8	26
27	55 20.2	−14.3	64.0	55 45.9	−12.7	65.3	56 10.3	−11.0	66.6	56 33.4	−9.3	68.0	56 55.2	−7.5	69.4	57 15.6	−5.8	70.9	57 34.5	−4.0	72.4	57 51.9	−2.1	73.9	27
28	55 05.9	−15.7	62.3	55 33.2	−14.1	63.6	55 59.3	−12.5	64.9	56 24.1	−10.8	66.2	56 47.7	−9.2	67.6	57 09.8	−7.4	69.1	57 30.5	−5.6	70.5	57 49.8	−3.8	72.0	28
29	54 50.2	−17.1	60.6	55 19.1	−15.5	61.8	55 46.8	−14.0	63.1	56 13.3	−12.3	64.5	56 38.5	−10.6	65.8	57 02.4	−8.9	67.2	57 24.9	−7.1	68.7	57 46.0	−5.3	70.1	29
30	54 33.1	−18.4	58.9	55 03.6	−17.0	60.1	55 32.8	−15.4	61.4	56 01.0	−13.9	62.7	56 27.9	−12.2	64.0	56 53.5	−10.6	65.4	57 17.8	−8.8	66.8	57 40.7	−7.1	68.3	30
31	54 14.7	−19.7	57.3	54 46.6	−18.3	58.5	55 17.4	−16.8	59.7	55 47.1	−15.2	61.0	56 15.7	−13.7	62.3	56 42.9	−12.0	63.6	57 09.0	−10.4	65.0	57 33.6	−8.6	66.4	31
32	53 55.0	−21.0	55.7	54 28.3	−19.6	56.8	55 00.6	−18.1	58.0	55 31.9	−16.7	59.3	56 02.0	−15.2	60.5	56 30.9	−13.6	61.8	56 58.6	−11.9	63.2	57 25.0	−10.3	64.6	32
33	53 34.0	−22.2	54.1	54 08.7	−20.8	55.2	54 42.5	−19.5	56.4	55 15.2	−18.1	57.6	55 46.8	−16.6	58.8	56 17.3	−15.0	60.1	56 46.7	−13.5	61.4	57 14.7	−11.8	62.8	33
34	53 11.8	−23.4	52.5	53 47.9	−22.2	53.6	54 23.0	−20.8	54.7	54 57.1	−19.4	55.9	55 30.2	−17.9	57.1	56 02.3	−16.5	58.3	56 33.2	−15.0	59.6	57 02.9	−13.3	61.0	34
35	52 48.4	−24.6	51.0	53 25.7	−23.3	52.1	54 02.2	−22.1	53.1	54 37.7	−20.7	54.3	55 12.3	−19.4	55.4	55 45.8	−17.9	56.6	56 18.2	−16.4	57.9	56 49.6	−14.9	59.2	35
36	52 23.8	−25.7	49.5	53 02.4	−24.5	50.5	53 40.1	−23.3	51.6	54 17.0	−22.0	52.6	54 52.9	−20.7	53.8	55 27.9	−19.3	54.9	56 01.8	−17.8	56.1	56 34.7	−16.3	57.4	36
37	51 58.1	−26.8	48.0	52 37.9	−25.7	49.0	53 16.8	−24.4	50.0	53 55.0	−23.3	51.1	54 32.2	−21.9	52.1	55 08.6	−20.6	53.3	55 44.0	−19.3	54.4	56 18.4	−17.8	55.7	37
38	51 31.3	−27.8	46.6	52 12.2	−26.7	47.5	52 52.4	−25.6	48.5	53 31.7	−24.4	49.5	54 10.3	−23.2	50.5	54 48.0	−21.9	51.6	55 24.7	−20.5	52.8	56 00.6	−19.2	53.9	38
39	51 03.5	−28.8	45.2	51 45.5	−27.8	46.1	52 26.8	−26.7	47.0	53 07.3	−25.6	48.0	53 47.1	−24.4	49.0	54 26.1	−23.2	50.0	55 04.2	−21.9	51.1	55 41.4	−20.6	52.3	39
40	50 34.7	−29.8	43.8	51 17.7	−28.8	44.6	52 00.1	−27.8	45.5	52 41.7	−26.7	46.5	53 22.7	−25.6	47.4	54 02.9	−24.4	48.5	54 42.3	−23.2	49.5	55 20.8	−21.9	50.6	40
41	50 04.9	−30.7	42.4	50 48.9	−29.8	43.2	51 32.3	−28.8	44.1	52 15.0	−27.7	45.0	52 57.1	−26.7	45.9	53 38.5	−25.6	46.9	54 19.1	−24.4	47.9	54 58.9	−23.2	49.0	41
42	49 34.2	−31.7	41.1	50 19.1	−30.7	41.9	51 03.5	−29.8	42.7	51 47.3	−28.8	43.6	52 30.4	−27.7	44.5	53 12.9	−26.7	45.4	53 54.7	−25.6	46.4	54 35.7	−24.4	47.4	42
43	49 02.5	−32.5	39.8	49 48.4	−31.7	40.5	50 33.7	−30.7	41.3	51 18.5	−29.8	42.1	52 02.7	−28.9	43.0	52 46.2	−27.8	43.9	53 29.1	−26.7	44.8	54 11.3	−25.6	45.8	43
44	48 30.0	−33.3	38.5	49 16.7	−32.5	39.2	50 03.0	−31.7	40.0	50 48.7	−30.8	40.8	51 33.8	−29.8	41.6	52 18.4	−28.8	42.4	53 02.4	−27.8	43.3	53 45.7	−26.8	44.3	44
45	47 56.7	−34.1	37.3	48 44.2	−33.3	37.9	49 31.3	−32.5	38.7	50 17.9	−31.6	39.4	51 04.0	−30.8	40.2	51 49.6	−29.9	41.0	52 34.6	−28.9	41.9	53 18.9	−27.9	42.8	45
46	47 22.6	−34.9	36.0	48 10.9	−34.1	36.7	48 58.8	−33.4	37.4	49 46.3	−32.6	38.1	50 33.2	−31.7	38.8	51 19.7	−30.8	39.6	52 05.7	−30.0	40.4	52 51.0	−28.9	41.3	46
47	46 47.7	−35.6	34.8	47 36.8	−34.9	35.5	48 25.4	−34.1	36.1	49 13.7	−33.4	36.8	50 01.5	−32.6	37.5	50 48.9	−31.8	38.3	51 35.7	−30.8	39.0	52 22.1	−30.0	39.8	47
48	46 12.1	−36.3	33.7	47 01.9	−35.7	34.3	47 51.3	−35.0	34.9	48 40.3	−34.2	35.5	49 28.9	−33.4	36.2	50 17.1	−32.7	36.9	51 04.9	−31.9	37.7	51 52.1	−31.0	38.4	48
49	45 35.8	−37.0	32.5	46 26.2	−36.3	33.1	47 16.3	−35.7	33.7	48 06.1	−35.0	34.3	48 55.5	−34.3	34.9	49 44.4	−33.5	35.6	50 33.0	−32.7	36.3	51 21.1	−31.9	37.1	49
50	44 58.8	−37.6	31.4	45 49.9	−37.0	31.9	46 40.6	−36.3	32.5	47 31.1	−35.8	33.1	48 21.2	−35.1	33.7	49 10.9	−34.3	34.3	50 00.3	−33.6	35.0	50 49.2	−32.8	35.7	50
51	44 21.2	−38.2	30.3	45 12.9	−37.7	30.8	46 04.3	−37.1	31.4	46 55.3	−36.4	31.9	47 46.1	−35.8	32.5	48 36.6	−35.2	33.1	49 26.7	−34.5	33.7	50 16.4	−33.7	34.4	51
52	43 43.0	−38.8	29.2	44 35.2	−38.3	29.7	45 27.2	−37.7	30.2	46 18.9	−37.2	30.7	47 10.3	−36.5	31.3	48 01.4	−35.9	31.9	48 52.2	−35.2	32.5	49 42.7	−34.6	33.1	52
53	43 04.2	−39.4	28.2	43 56.9	−38.9	28.6	44 49.5	−38.4	29.1	45 41.7	−37.7	29.6	46 33.8	−37.2	30.1	47 25.5	−36.6	30.7	48 17.0	−36.0	31.2	49 08.1	−35.3	31.8	53
54	42 24.8	−40.0	27.2	43 18.0	−39.4	27.6	44 11.1	−38.9	28.0	45 04.0	−38.5	28.5	45 56.6	−37.9	29.0	46 48.9	−37.3	29.5	47 41.0	−36.7	30.1	48 32.8	−36.1	30.6	54
55	41 44.8	−40.4	26.2	42 38.6	−40.0	26.6	43 32.2	−39.5	27.0	44 25.5	−39.0	27.4	45 18.7	−38.5	27.9	46 11.6	−38.0	28.4	47 04.3	−37.5	28.9	47 56.7	−36.9	29.4	55
56	41 04.4	−40.9	25.2	41 58.6	−40.5	25.6	42 52.7	−40.1	26.0	43 46.5	−39.6	26.4	44 40.2	−39.1	26.8	45 33.6	−38.6	27.3	46 26.8	−38.1	27.7	47 19.8	−37.5	28.2	56
57	40 23.5	−41.4	24.2	41 18.1	−41.0	24.6	42 12.6	−40.6	24.9	43 06.9	−40.1	25.3	44 01.1	−39.7	25.7	44 55.0	−39.2	26.2	45 48.7	−38.7	26.6	46 42.3	−38.2	27.1	57
58	39 42.1	−41.9	23.3	40 37.1	−41.4	23.6	41 32.0	−41.0	24.0	42 26.8	−40.7	24.3	43 21.4	−40.3	24.7	44 15.8	−39.8	25.1	45 10.0	−39.3	25.5	46 04.1	−38.9	26.0	58
59	39 00.2	−42.3	22.3	39 55.7	−42.0	22.7	40 51.0	−41.6	23.0	41 46.1	−41.1	23.3	42 41.1	−40.7	23.7	43 36.0	−40.3	24.1	44 30.7	−39.9	24.5	45 25.2	−39.4	24.9	59
60	38 17.9	−42.7	21.4	39 13.7	−42.3	21.7	40 09.4	−42.0	22.0	41 05.0	−41.7	22.4	42 00.4	−41.3	22.7	42 55.7	−40.9	23.1	43 50.8	−40.5	23.4	44 45.8	−40.1	23.8	60
61	37 35.2	−43.1	20.5	38 31.4	−42.8	20.8	39 27.4	−42.4	21.1	40 23.3	−42.1	21.4	41 19.1	−41.7	21.7	42 14.8	−41.4	22.1	43 10.3	−41.0	22.4	44 05.7	−40.6	22.8	61
62	36 52.1	−43.4	19.7	37 48.6	−43.2	19.9	38 45.0	−42.9	20.2	39 41.2	−42.5	20.5	40 37.4	−42.2	20.8	41 33.4	−41.9	21.1	42 29.3	−41.5	21.4	43 25.1	−41.1	21.8	62
63	36 08.7	−43.9	18.8	37 05.4	−43.5	19.1	38 02.1	−43.3	19.3	38 58.7	−43.0	19.6	39 55.2	−42.7	19.8	40 51.5	−42.3	20.1	41 47.8	−42.0	20.4	42 44.0	−41.6	20.8	63
64	35 24.8	−44.1	18.0	36 21.9	−43.9	18.2	37 18.8	−43.6	18.4	38 15.7	−43.3	18.7	39 12.5	−43.0	18.9	40 09.2	−42.7	19.2	41 05.8	−42.4	19.5	42 02.4	−42.2	19.8	64
65	34 40.7	−44.5	17.1	35 38.0	−44.3	17.4	36 35.2	−44.0	17.6	37 32.4	−43.8	17.8	38 29.5	−43.5	18.0	39 26.5	−43.2	18.3	40 23.4	−42.9	18.6	41 20.2	−42.6	18.8	65
66	33 56.2	−44.8	16.3	34 53.7	−44.6	16.5	35 51.2	−44.3	16.7	36 48.6	−44.1	16.9	37 46.0	−43.8	17.2	38 43.3	−43.6	17.4	39 40.5	−43.3	17.6	40 37.6	−43.0	17.9	66
67	33 11.4	−45.2	15.5	34 09.1	−44.9	15.7	35 06.9	−44.7	15.9	36 04.5	−44.4	16.1	37 02.2	−44.2	16.3	37 59.7	−43.9	16.5	38 57.2	−43.7	16.7	39 54.6	−43.4	17.0	67
68	32 26.2	−45.4	14.7	33 24.2	−45.2	14.9	34 22.2	−45.0	15.1	35 20.1	−44.8	15.3	36 18.0	−44.6	15.5	37 15.8	−44.4	15.7	38 13.5	−44.1	15.9	39 11.2	−43.9	16.1	68
69	31 40.8	−45.6	14.0	32 39.0	−45.4	14.1	33 37.2	−45.3	14.3	34 35.3	−45.1	14.5	35 33.4	−44.9	14.6	36 31.4	−44.6	14.8	37 29.4	−44.4	15.0	38 27.3	−44.2	15.2	69
70	30 55.2	−46.0	13.2	31 53.6	−45.8	13.4	32 51.9	−45.6	13.5	33 50.2	−45.4	13.7	34 48.5	−45.2	13.8	35 46.8	−45.1	14.0	36 45.0	−44.9	14.2	37 43.1	−44.6	14.4	70
71	30 09.2	−46.2	12.5	31 07.8	−46.0	12.6	32 06.3	−45.8	12.7	33 04.8	−45.6	12.9	34 03.3	−45.5	13.0	35 01.7	−45.3	13.2	36 00.1	−45.1	13.3	36 58.5	−44.9	13.5	71
72	29 23.0	−46.4	11.7	30 21.8	−46.3	11.9	31 20.5	−46.1	12.0	32 19.2	−46.0	12.1	33 17.8	−45.8	12.2	34 16.4	−45.6	12.4	35 15.0	−45.4	12.5	36 13.6	−45.3	12.7	72
73	28 36.6	−46.7	11.0	29 35.5	−46.5	11.1	30 34.4	−46.4	11.2	31 33.2	−46.2	11.3	32 32.0	−46.1	11.5	33 30.8	−45.9	11.6	34 29.6	−45.8	11.7	35 28.3	−45.6	11.9	73
74	27 49.9	−46.8	10.3	28 49.0	−46.8	10.4	29 48.0	−46.6	10.5	30 47.0	−46.5	10.6	31 45.9	−46.3	10.7	32 44.9	−46.2	10.8	33 43.8	−46.1	11.0	34 42.7	−45.9	11.1	74
75	27 03.1	−47.1	9.6	28 02.2	−46.9	9.7	29 01.4	−46.9	9.8	30 00.5	−46.7	9.9	30 59.6	−46.6	10.0	31 58.7	−46.5	10.1	32 57.7	−46.3	10.2	33 56.8	−46.2	10.3	75
76	26 16.0	−47.3	8.9	27 15.3	−47.2	9.0	28 14.5	−47.0	9.1	29 13.8	−47.0	9.1	30 13.0	−46.8	9.2	31 12.2	−46.7	9.3	32 11.4	−46.6	9.4	33 10.6	−46.5	9.5	76
77	25 28.7	−47.4	8.2	26 28.1	−47.4	8.3	27 27.5	−47.3	8.4	28 26.8	−47.1	8.4	29 26.2	−47.1	8.5	30 25.5	−47.0	8.6	31 24.8	−46.8	8.7	32 24.1	−46.7	8.8	77
78	24 41.3	−47.7	7.5	25 40.7	−47.5	7.6	26 40.2	−47.5	7.7	27 39.7	−47.4	7.7	28 39.1	−47.3	7.8	29 38.5	−47.1	7.9	30 38.0	−47.1	8.0	31 37.4	−47.0	8.1	78
79	23 53.6	−47.8	6.9	24 53.2	−47.8	6.9	25 52.7	−47.6	7.0	26 52.3	−47.6	7.0	27 51.8	−47.5	7.1	28 51.4	−47.4	7.2	29 50.9	−47.3	7.2	30 50.4	−47.2	7.3	79
80	23 05.8	−48.0	6.2	24 05.4	−47.9	6.3	25 05.1	−47.8	6.3	26 04.7	−47.7	6.4	27 04.3	−47.6	6.4	28 04.0	−47.6	6.5	29 03.6	−47.6	6.5	30 03.2	−47.5	6.6	80
81	22 17.8	−48.1	5.6	23 17.5	−48.0	5.6	24 17.3	−48.1	5.6	25 17.0	−48.0	5.7	26 16.7	−47.9	5.7	27 16.4	−47.9	5.8	28 16.0	−47.7	5.8	29 15.7	−47.6	5.9	81
82	21 29.7	−48.3	4.9	22 29.5	−48.2	5.0	23 29.2	−48.1	5.0	24 29.0	−48.1	5.0	25 28.8	−48.1	5.1	26 28.5	−47.9	5.1	27 28.3	−47.9	5.2	28 28.1	−47.9	5.2	82
83	20 41.4	−48.4	4.3	21 41.3	−48.4	4.3	22 41.1	−48.3	4.3	23 40.9	−48.3	4.4	24 40.7	−48.2	4.4	25 40.6	−48.2	4.4	26 40.4	−48.2	4.5	27 40.2	−48.1	4.5	83
84	19 53.0	−48.5	3.7	20 52.9	−48.5	3.7	21 52.8	−48.5	3.7	22 52.6	−48.4	3.7	23 52.5	−48.4	3.8	24 52.4	−48.4	3.8	25 52.2	−48.3	3.8	26 52.1	−48.3	3.9	84
85	19 04.5	−48.7	3.0	20 04.4	−48.7	3.1	21 04.3	−48.6	3.1	22 04.2	−48.6	3.1	23 04.1	−48.5	3.1	24 04.0	−48.5	3.1	25 03.9	−48.4	3.2	26 03.8	−48.4	3.2	85
86	18 15.8	−48.8	2.4	19 15.7	−48.7	2.4	20 15.7	−48.8	2.4	21 15.6	−48.7	2.5	22 15.6	−48.7	2.5	23 15.5	−48.6	2.5	24 15.5	−48.7	2.5	25 15.4	−48.6	2.5	86
87	17 27.0	−48.9	1.8	18 27.0	−48.9	1.8	19 26.9	−48.8	1.8	20 26.9	−48.8	1.8	21 26.9	−48.8	1.8	22 26.9	−48.9	1.9	23 26.8	−48.8	1.9	24 26.8	−48.8	1.9	87
88	16 38.1	−49.0	1.2	17 38.1	−49.0	1.2	18 38.1	−49.0	1.2	19 38.1	−49.0	1.2	20 38.1	−49.0	1.2	21 38.0	−48.9	1.2	22 38.0	−48.9	1.2	23 38.0	−48.9	1.3	88
89	15 49.1	−49.1	0.6	16 49.1	−49.1	0.6	17 49.1	−49.1	0.6	18 49.1	−49.1	0.6	19 49.1	−49.1	0.6	20 49.1	−49.1	0.6	21 49.1	−49.1	0.6	22 49.1	−49.1	0.6	89
90	15 00.0	−49.2	0.0	16 00.0	−49.2	0.0	17 00.0	−49.2	0.0	18 00.0	−49.2	0.0	19 00.0	−49.2	0.0	20 00.0	−49.2	0.0	21 00.0	−49.2	0.0	22 00.0	−49.2	0.0	90
	15°			16°			17°			18°			19°			20°			21°			22°			

35°, 325° L.H.A. LATITUDE SAME NAME AS DECLINATION

72

LATITUDE CONTRARY NAME TO DECLINATION L.H.A. 35°, 325°

Dec.	15° Hc	d	Z	16° Hc	d	Z	17° Hc	d	Z	18° Hc	d	Z	19° Hc	d	Z	20° Hc	d	Z	21° Hc	d	Z	22° Hc	d	Z	Dec.
°	° ′	′	°	° ′	′	°	° ′	′	°	° ′	′	°	° ′	′	°	° ′	′	°	° ′	′	°	° ′	′	°	°
0	52 18.1	-26.0	110.3	51 56.7	-27.4	111.5	51 34.1	-28.7	112.7	51 10.5	-30.1	113.8	50 45.7	-31.3	114.9	50 19.9	-32.6	116.0	49 53.1	-33.8	117.1	49 25.2	-34.9	118.1	0
1	51 52.1	-27.0	111.8	51 29.3	-28.3	112.9	51 05.4	-29.7	114.1	50 40.4	-31.0	115.2	50 14.4	-32.3	116.3	49 47.3	-33.5	117.3	49 19.3	-34.7	118.4	48 50.3	-35.8	119.4	1
2	51 25.1	-28.0	113.2	51 01.0	-29.4	114.3	50 35.7	-30.7	115.4	50 09.4	-31.9	116.5	49 42.1	-33.1	117.6	49 13.8	-34.2	118.6	48 44.6	-35.4	119.6	48 14.5	-36.4	120.6	2
3	50 57.1	-29.1	114.6	50 31.6	-30.4	115.7	50 05.0	-31.6	116.8	49 37.5	-32.8	117.8	49 09.0	-34.0	118.9	48 39.6	-35.1	119.9	48 09.2	-36.1	120.8	47 38.1	-37.2	121.8	3
4	50 28.0	-30.0	116.0	50 01.2	-31.2	117.1	49 33.4	-32.4	118.1	49 04.7	-33.6	119.1	48 35.0	-34.7	120.1	48 04.5	-35.8	121.1	47 33.1	-36.9	122.0	47 00.9	-37.9	122.9	4
5	49 58.0	-30.9	117.3	49 30.0	-32.2	118.4	49 01.0	-33.3	119.4	48 31.1	-34.5	120.4	48 00.3	-35.5	121.3	47 28.7	-36.6	122.3	46 56.2	-37.6	123.2	46 23.0	-38.6	124.1	5
6	49 27.1	-31.9	118.7	48 57.8	-33.0	119.7	48 27.7	-34.1	120.7	47 56.6	-35.2	121.6	47 24.8	-36.3	122.5	46 52.1	-37.3	123.5	46 18.6	-38.2	124.3	45 44.4	-39.1	125.2	6
7	48 55.2	-32.6	120.0	48 24.8	-33.8	120.9	47 53.6	-34.9	121.9	47 21.4	-35.9	122.8	46 48.5	-36.9	123.7	46 14.8	-37.9	124.6	45 40.4	-38.8	125.4	45 05.3	-39.8	126.3	7
8	48 22.6	-33.5	121.2	47 51.0	-34.6	122.2	47 18.7	-35.7	123.1	46 45.5	-36.6	124.0	46 11.6	-37.6	124.9	45 36.9	-38.5	125.7	45 01.6	-39.5	126.5	44 25.5	-40.3	127.3	8
9	47 49.1	-34.3	122.5	47 16.4	-35.3	123.4	46 43.0	-36.3	124.3	46 08.9	-37.4	125.1	45 34.0	-38.3	126.0	44 58.4	-39.2	126.8	44 22.1	-40.0	127.6	43 45.2	-40.9	128.3	9
10	47 14.8	-35.1	123.7	46 41.1	-36.1	124.6	46 06.7	-37.0	125.4	45 31.5	-37.9	126.3	44 55.7	-38.9	127.1	44 19.2	-39.7	127.9	43 42.1	-40.6	128.6	43 04.3	-41.4	129.4	10
11	46 39.7	-35.7	124.9	46 05.0	-36.7	125.7	45 29.7	-37.7	126.6	44 53.6	-38.6	127.4	44 16.8	-39.4	128.1	43 39.5	-40.3	128.9	43 01.5	-41.1	129.6	42 22.9	-41.9	130.3	11
12	46 04.0	-36.5	126.0	45 28.3	-37.4	126.9	44 52.0	-38.3	127.7	44 15.0	-39.2	128.4	43 37.4	-40.0	129.2	42 59.2	-40.9	129.9	42 20.4	-41.6	130.6	41 41.0	-42.3	131.3	12
13	45 27.5	-37.1	127.2	44 50.9	-38.0	128.0	44 13.7	-38.9	128.7	43 35.8	-39.7	129.5	42 57.4	-40.6	130.2	42 18.3	-41.3	130.9	41 38.8	-42.1	131.6	40 58.7	-42.8	132.2	13
14	44 50.4	-37.8	128.3	44 12.9	-38.7	129.1	43 34.8	-39.5	129.8	42 56.1	-40.3	130.5	42 16.8	-41.1	131.2	41 37.0	-41.8	131.9	40 56.7	-42.6	132.5	40 15.9	-43.3	133.2	14
15	44 12.6	-38.4	129.4	43 34.2	-39.2	130.1	42 55.3	-40.0	130.8	42 15.8	-40.8	131.5	41 35.7	-41.5	132.2	40 55.2	-42.3	132.8	40 14.1	-42.9	133.5	39 32.6	-43.6	134.1	15
16	43 34.2	-38.9	130.4	42 55.0	-39.7	131.2	42 15.3	-40.6	131.8	41 35.0	-41.3	132.5	40 54.2	-42.0	133.2	40 12.9	-42.7	133.8	39 31.2	-43.4	134.4	38 49.0	-44.1	135.0	16
17	42 55.3	-39.5	131.5	42 15.3	-40.3	132.2	41 34.7	-41.0	132.8	40 53.7	-41.8	133.5	40 12.2	-42.5	134.1	39 30.2	-43.2	134.7	38 47.8	-43.8	135.3	38 04.9	-44.4	135.8	17
18	42 15.8	-40.1	132.5	41 35.0	-40.8	133.2	40 53.7	-41.5	133.8	40 11.9	-42.2	134.4	39 29.7	-42.9	135.0	38 47.0	-43.5	135.6	38 04.0	-44.2	136.1	37 20.5	-44.8	136.7	18
19	41 35.7	-40.5	133.5	40 54.2	-41.3	134.1	40 12.2	-42.0	134.8	39 29.7	-42.7	135.3	38 46.8	-43.3	135.9	38 03.5	-43.9	136.5	37 19.8	-44.5	137.0	36 35.7	-45.1	137.5	19
20	40 55.2	-41.1	134.5	40 12.9	-41.7	135.1	39 30.2	-42.4	135.7	38 47.0	-43.0	136.3	38 03.5	-43.7	136.8	37 19.6	-44.3	137.3	36 35.3	-44.9	137.8	35 50.6	-45.4	138.3	20
21	40 14.1	-41.5	135.5	39 31.2	-42.2	136.0	38 47.8	-42.9	136.6	38 04.0	-43.5	137.1	37 19.8	-44.1	137.7	36 35.3	-44.7	138.2	35 50.4	-45.2	138.7	35 05.2	-45.8	139.1	21
22	39 32.6	-41.9	136.4	38 49.0	-42.6	137.0	38 04.9	-43.2	137.5	37 20.5	-43.8	138.0	36 35.7	-44.4	138.5	35 50.6	-45.0	139.0	35 05.2	-45.5	139.5	34 19.4	-46.0	139.9	22
23	38 50.7	-42.4	137.3	38 06.4	-43.0	137.9	37 21.7	-43.6	138.4	36 36.7	-44.2	138.9	35 51.3	-44.7	139.4	35 05.6	-45.3	139.8	34 19.7	-45.9	140.3	33 33.4	-46.4	140.7	23
24	38 08.3	-42.8	138.2	37 23.4	-43.4	138.7	36 38.1	-44.0	139.2	35 52.5	-44.5	139.7	35 06.6	-45.1	140.2	34 20.3	-45.6	140.6	33 33.8	-46.1	141.0	32 47.0	-46.6	141.4	24
25	37 25.5	-43.2	139.1	36 40.0	-43.8	139.6	35 54.1	-44.3	140.1	35 08.0	-44.9	140.5	34 21.5	-45.4	141.0	33 34.7	-45.9	141.4	32 47.7	-46.4	141.8	32 00.4	-46.8	142.2	25
26	36 42.3	-43.5	140.0	35 56.2	-44.1	140.5	35 09.8	-44.6	140.9	34 23.1	-45.2	141.3	33 36.1	-45.7	141.8	32 48.8	-46.1	142.2	32 01.3	-46.6	142.6	31 13.6	-47.1	142.9	26
27	35 58.8	-43.9	140.8	35 12.1	-44.4	141.3	34 25.2	-45.0	141.7	33 37.9	-45.5	142.1	32 50.4	-45.9	142.5	32 02.7	-46.5	142.9	31 14.7	-46.9	143.3	30 26.5	-47.4	143.6	27
28	35 14.9	-44.3	141.7	34 27.7	-44.8	142.1	33 40.2	-45.3	142.5	32 52.4	-45.7	142.9	32 04.5	-46.3	143.3	31 16.2	-46.7	143.7	30 27.8	-47.1	144.0	29 39.1	-47.5	144.4	28
29	34 30.6	-44.5	142.5	33 42.9	-45.1	142.9	32 54.9	-45.6	143.3	32 06.7	-46.1	143.7	31 18.2	-46.5	144.0	30 29.5	-46.9	144.4	29 40.7	-47.4	144.7	28 51.6	-47.8	145.1	29
30	33 46.1	-44.9	143.3	32 57.8	-45.4	143.7	32 09.3	-45.8	144.1	31 20.6	-46.2	144.4	30 31.7	-46.7	144.8	29 42.6	-47.1	145.1	28 53.3	-47.6	145.4	28 03.8	-48.0	145.7	30
31	33 01.2	-45.2	144.1	32 12.4	-45.6	144.5	31 23.5	-46.1	144.8	30 34.4	-46.6	145.2	29 45.0	-47.0	145.5	28 55.5	-47.4	145.8	28 05.7	-47.8	146.1	27 15.8	-48.2	146.4	31
32	32 16.0	-45.5	144.9	31 26.8	-45.9	145.2	30 37.4	-46.4	145.6	29 47.8	-46.8	145.9	28 58.0	-47.2	146.2	28 08.1	-47.6	146.5	27 17.9	-47.9	146.8	26 27.6	-48.3	147.1	32
33	31 30.5	-45.7	145.7	30 40.9	-46.2	146.0	29 51.0	-46.5	146.3	29 01.0	-47.0	146.6	28 10.8	-47.4	146.9	27 20.5	-47.8	147.2	26 30.0	-48.2	147.5	25 39.3	-48.5	147.7	33
34	30 44.8	-46.0	146.4	29 54.7	-46.4	146.7	29 04.5	-46.9	147.0	28 14.0	-47.2	147.3	27 23.4	-47.6	147.6	26 32.7	-48.0	147.9	25 41.8	-48.4	148.1	24 50.8	-48.7	148.4	34
35	29 58.8	-46.3	147.2	29 08.3	-46.7	147.5	28 17.6	-47.0	147.8	27 26.8	-47.4	148.0	26 35.8	-47.8	148.3	25 44.7	-48.2	148.6	24 53.4	-48.5	148.8	24 02.1	-48.9	149.0	35
36	29 12.5	-46.4	147.9	28 21.6	-46.8	148.2	27 30.6	-47.3	148.5	26 39.4	-47.6	148.7	25 48.0	-48.0	149.0	24 56.5	-48.3	149.2	24 04.9	-48.6	149.5	23 13.2	-49.0	149.7	36
37	28 26.1	-46.7	148.6	27 34.8	-47.1	148.9	26 43.3	-47.4	149.1	25 51.8	-47.9	149.4	25 00.0	-48.1	149.6	24 08.2	-48.5	149.9	23 16.3	-48.9	150.1	22 24.2	-49.2	150.3	37
38	27 39.4	-47.0	149.3	26 47.7	-47.3	149.6	25 55.9	-47.7	149.8	25 03.9	-47.9	150.1	24 11.9	-48.3	150.3	23 19.7	-48.6	150.5	22 27.4	-48.9	150.7	21 35.0	-49.2	150.9	38
39	26 52.4	-47.1	150.0	26 00.4	-47.5	150.3	25 08.2	-47.8	150.5	24 16.0	-48.2	150.7	23 23.6	-48.5	150.9	22 31.1	-48.8	151.1	21 38.5	-49.2	151.3	20 45.8	-49.5	151.5	39
40	26 05.3	-47.3	150.7	25 12.9	-47.6	150.9	24 20.4	-48.0	151.2	23 27.8	-48.3	151.4	22 35.1	-48.7	151.6	21 42.3	-49.0	151.8	20 49.3	-49.2	152.0	19 56.3	-49.5	152.1	40
41	25 18.0	-47.5	151.4	24 25.3	-47.9	151.6	23 32.4	-48.1	151.8	22 39.5	-48.5	152.0	21 46.4	-48.7	152.2	20 53.3	-49.1	152.4	20 00.1	-49.4	152.6	19 06.8	-49.6	152.7	41
42	24 30.5	-47.7	152.1	23 37.4	-48.0	152.3	22 44.3	-48.3	152.5	21 51.0	-48.6	152.7	20 57.7	-48.9	152.8	20 04.2	-49.2	153.0	19 10.7	-49.4	153.2	18 17.2	-49.8	153.3	42
43	23 42.8	-47.8	152.7	22 49.4	-48.1	152.9	21 56.0	-48.5	153.1	21 02.4	-48.8	153.3	20 08.8	-49.1	153.5	19 15.0	-49.3	153.6	18 21.3	-49.6	153.8	17 27.4	-49.9	153.9	43
44	22 55.0	-48.1	153.4	22 01.3	-48.3	153.6	21 07.5	-48.6	153.7	20 13.6	-48.8	153.9	19 19.7	-49.1	154.1	18 25.7	-49.4	154.2	17 31.7	-49.7	154.4	16 37.5	-49.9	154.5	44
45	22 06.9	-48.1	154.0	21 13.0	-48.5	154.2	20 18.9	-48.7	154.4	19 24.8	-49.0	154.5	18 30.6	-49.3	154.7	17 36.3	-49.5	154.8	16 42.0	-49.8	154.9	15 47.6	-50.1	155.1	45
46	21 18.8	-48.3	154.7	20 24.5	-48.6	154.8	19 30.2	-48.9	155.0	18 35.8	-49.2	155.1	17 41.3	-49.4	155.3	16 46.8	-49.7	155.4	15 52.2	-49.9	155.5	14 57.5	-50.1	155.6	46
47	20 30.5	-48.5	155.3	19 35.9	-48.7	155.5	18 41.3	-49.0	155.6	17 46.6	-49.2	155.7	16 51.9	-49.5	155.9	15 57.1	-49.7	156.0	15 02.3	-50.0	156.1	14 07.4	-50.2	156.2	47
48	19 42.0	-48.5	155.9	18 47.2	-48.8	156.1	17 52.3	-49.1	156.2	16 57.4	-49.3	156.3	16 02.4	-49.6	156.5	15 07.4	-49.8	156.6	14 12.3	-50.0	156.7	13 17.2	-50.3	156.8	48
49	18 53.5	-48.7	156.6	17 58.4	-49.0	156.7	17 03.2	-49.1	156.8	16 08.1	-49.5	156.9	15 12.8	-49.6	157.0	14 17.6	-49.9	157.2	13 22.3	-50.2	157.2	12 26.9	-50.3	157.3	49
50	18 04.8	-48.9	157.2	17 09.4	-49.0	157.3	16 14.1	-49.3	157.4	15 18.6	-49.5	157.5	14 23.2	-49.8	157.6	13 27.7	-50.0	157.7	12 32.1	-50.2	157.8	11 36.6	-50.5	157.9	50
51	17 15.9	-48.9	157.8	16 20.4	-49.2	157.9	15 24.8	-49.4	158.0	14 29.1	-49.6	158.1	13 33.4	-49.8	158.2	12 37.7	-50.1	158.3	11 41.9	-50.2	158.4	10 46.1	-50.4	158.4	51
52	16 27.0	-49.0	158.4	15 31.2	-49.2	158.5	14 35.4	-49.5	158.6	13 39.5	-49.7	158.7	12 43.6	-49.9	158.8	11 47.6	-50.1	158.9	10 51.7	-50.4	158.9	9 55.7	-50.6	159.0	52
53	15 38.0	-49.1	159.0	14 42.0	-49.4	159.1	13 45.9	-49.6	159.2	12 49.8	-49.8	159.3	11 53.7	-50.0	159.3	10 57.5	-50.2	159.4	10 01.3	-50.4	159.5	9 05.1	-50.6	159.5	53
54	14 48.9	-49.2	159.6	13 52.6	-49.4	159.7	12 56.3	-49.6	159.8	12 00.0	-49.8	159.8	11 03.7	-50.0	159.9	10 07.3	-50.2	160.0	9 10.9	-50.4	160.0	8 14.5	-50.6	160.1	54
55	13 59.7	-49.3	160.2	13 03.2	-49.5	160.3	12 06.7	-49.7	160.3	11 10.2	-49.9	160.4	10 13.7	-50.1	160.5	9 17.1	-50.3	160.5	8 20.5	-50.5	160.6	7 23.9	-50.6	160.6	55
56	13 10.4	-49.4	160.8	12 13.7	-49.6	160.8	11 17.0	-49.8	160.9	10 20.3	-50.0	161.0	9 23.6	-50.2	161.0	8 26.8	-50.3	161.1	7 30.0	-50.5	161.1	6 33.3	-50.7	161.2	56
57	12 21.0	-49.5	161.3	11 24.1	-49.6	161.4	10 27.2	-49.8	161.5	9 30.3	-50.0	161.5	8 33.4	-50.2	161.6	7 36.5	-50.4	161.6	6 39.5	-50.5	161.7	5 42.6	-50.8	161.7	57
58	11 31.5	-49.5	161.9	10 34.5	-49.7	162.0	9 37.4	-49.9	162.0	8 40.3	-50.0	162.1	7 43.2	-50.2	162.1	6 46.1	-50.4	162.2	5 49.0	-50.6	162.2	4 51.8	-50.7	162.2	58
59	10 42.0	-49.6	162.5	9 44.8	-49.8	162.6	8 47.5	-49.9	162.6	7 50.3	-50.1	162.7	6 53.0	-50.3	162.7	5 55.7	-50.4	162.7	4 58.4	-50.6	162.8	4 01.1	-50.8	162.8	59
60	9 52.4	-49.6	163.1	8 55.0	-49.8	163.1	7 57.6	-50.0	163.2	7 00.2	-50.2	163.2	6 02.7	-50.3	163.2	5 05.3	-50.5	163.3	4 07.8	-50.6	163.3	3 10.3	-50.8	163.3	60
61	9 02.8	-49.7	163.6	8 05.2	-49.9	163.7	7 07.6	-50.0	163.7	6 10.0	-50.2	163.8	5 12.4	-50.3	163.8	4 14.8	-50.5	163.8	3 17.2	-50.7	163.8	2 19.5	-50.8	163.8	61
62	8 13.1	-49.8	164.2	7 15.3	-49.9	164.2	6 17.6	-50.1	164.3	5 19.8	-50.2	164.3	4 22.1	-50.4	164.3	3 24.3	-50.5	164.4	2 26.5	-50.6	164.4	1 28.7	-50.8	164.4	62
63	7 23.3	-49.7	164.8	6 25.4	-49.9	164.8	5 27.5	-50.0	164.8	4 29.6	-50.2	164.9	3 31.7	-50.4	164.9	2 33.8	-50.5	164.9	1 35.9	-50.7	164.9	0 37.9	-50.8	164.9	63
64	6 33.6	-49.9	165.3	5 35.5	-50.0	165.4	4 37.5	-50.2	165.4	3 39.4	-50.3	165.4	2 41.3	-50.4	165.4	1 43.3	-50.6	165.4	0 45.2	-50.7	165.4	0 12.9	+50.8	14.6	64
65	5 43.7	-49.8	165.9	4 45.5	-50.0	165.9	3 47.3	-50.1	165.9	2 49.1	-50.2	166.0	1 50.9	-50.4	166.0	0 52.7	-50.5	166.0	0 05.5	+50.7	14.0	1 03.7	+50.8	14.0	65
66	4 53.9	-49.9	166.5	3 55.5	-50.0	166.5	2 57.2	-50.1	166.5	1 58.9	-50.3	166.5	1 00.5	-50.4	166.5	0 02.2	-50.6	166.5	0 56.2	+50.6	13.5	1 54.5	+50.8	13.5	66
67	4 04.0	-49.9	167.0	3 05.5	-50.0	167.0	2 07.1	-50.2	167.0	1 08.6	-50.3	167.0	0 10.1	-50.4	167.0	0 48.4	+50.5	13.0	1 46.8	+50.7	13.0	2 45.3	+50.8	13.0	67
68	3 14.1	-49.9	167.6	2 15.5	-50.0	167.6	1 16.9	-50.2	167.6	0 18.3	-50.3	167.6	0 40.3	+50.4	12.4	1 38.9	+50.5	12.4	2 37.5	+50.6	12.4	3 36.1	+50.7	12.4	68
69	2 24.2	-50.0	168.1	1 25.5	-50.1	168.1	0 26.7	-50.1	168.1	0 32.0	+50.3	11.9	1 30.7	+50.4	11.9	2 29.4	+50.5	11.9	3 28.1	+50.7	11.9	4 26.8	+50.8	11.9	69
70	1 34.2	-49.9	168.7	0 35.4	-50.1	168.7	0 23.4	+50.2	11.3	1 22.3	+50.2	11.3	2 21.1	+50.4	11.3	3 19.9	+50.5	11.3	4 18.8	+50.6	11.3	5 17.6	+50.7	11.4	70
71	0 44.3	-50.0	169.2	0 14.7	+50.0	10.8	1 13.6	+50.2	10.8	2 12.5	+50.3	10.8	3 11.5	+50.3	10.8	4 10.4	+50.5	10.8	5 09.4	+50.5	10.8	6 08.3	+50.7	10.8	71
72	0 05.7	+49.9	10.2	1 04.7	+50.1	10.2	2 03.8	+50.1	10.2	3 02.8	+50.2	10.2	4 01.8	+50.4	10.2	5 00.9	+50.4	10.2	5 59.9	+50.6	10.3	6 59.0	+50.6	10.3	72
73	0 55.6	+49.9	9.7	1 54.8	+50.0	9.7	2 53.9	+50.1	9.7	3 53.0	+50.3	9.7	4 52.2	+50.3	9.7	5 51.3	+50.5	9.7	6 50.5	+50.5	9.7	7 49.6	+50.6	9.7	73
74	1 45.5	+50.0	9.1	2 44.8	+50.0	9.1	3 44.0	+50.1	9.1	4 43.3	+50.2	9.1	5 42.5	+50.3	9.1	6 41.8	+50.3	9.2	7 41.0	+50.4	9.2	8 40.2	+50.6	9.2	74
75	2 35.5	+49.9	8.5	3 34.8	+50.0	8.6	4 34.1	+50.1	8.6	5 33.5	+50.1	8.6	6 32.8	+50.3	8.6	7 32.1	+50.4	8.6	8 31.4	+50.5	8.6	9 30.8	+50.5	8.7	75
76	3 25.4	+49.9	8.0	4 24.8	+50.0	8.0	5 24.2	+50.1	8.0	6 23.6	+50.2	8.0	7 23.1	+50.2	8.0	8 22.5	+50.3	8.1	9 21.9	+50.3	8.1	10 21.3	+50.4	8.1	76
77	4 15.3	+49.9	7.4	5 14.8	+49.9	7.4	6 14.3	+50.0	7.5	7 13.8	+50.1	7.5	8 13.3	+50.1	7.5	9 12.8	+50.2	7.5	10 12.2	+50.4	7.5	11 11.7	+50.4	7.6	77
78	5 05.2	+49.8	6.9	6 04.7	+50.0	6.9	7 04.3	+50.0	6.9	8 03.9	+50.0	6.9	9 03.4	+50.2	6.9	10 03.0	+50.2	7.0	11 02.6	+50.2	7.0	12 02.1	+50.3	7.0	78
79	5 55.0	+49.8	6.3	6 54.7	+49.8	6.3	7 54.3	+49.9	6.3	8 53.9	+50.0	6.4	9 53.6	+50.0	6.4	10 53.2	+50.1	6.4	11 52.8	+50.2	6.4	12 52.4	+50.3	6.4	79
80	6 44.8	+49.8	5.8	7 44.5	+49.9	5.8	8 44.2	+49.9	5.8	9 43.9	+50.0	5.8	10 43.6	+50.0	5.8	11 43.3	+50.1	5.8	12 43.0	+50.1	5.9	13 42.7	+50.1	5.9	80
81	7 34.6	+49.7	5.2	8 34.4	+49.7	5.2	9 34.1	+49.8	5.2	10 33.9	+49.8	5.2	11 33.6	+49.9	5.3	12 33.4	+49.9	5.3	13 33.1	+50.0	5.3	14 32.8	+50.1	5.3	81
82	8 24.3	+49.7	4.6	9 24.1	+49.8	4.6	10 23.9	+49.8	4.7	11 23.7	+49.9	4.7	12 23.5	+49.9	4.7	13 23.3	+50.0	4.7	14 23.1	+50.0	4.7	15 22.9	+50.0	4.7	82
83	9 14.0	+49.7	4.1	10 13.9	+49.6	4.1	11 13.7	+49.7	4.1	12 13.6	+49.7	4.1	13 13.4	+49.8	4.1	14 13.3	+49.8	4.1	15 13.1	+49.9	4.2	16 12.9	+50.0	4.2	83
84	10 03.7	+49.5	3.5	11 03.5	+49.6	3.5	12 03.4	+49.7	3.5	13 03.3	+49.7	3.5	14 03.2	+49.7	3.5	15 03.1	+49.7	3.6	16 03.0	+49.7	3.6	17 02.9	+49.8	3.6	84
85	10 53.2	+49.5	2.9	11 53.1	+49.6	2.9	12 53.1	+49.5	2.9	13 53.0	+49.6	3.0	14 52.9	+49.6	3.0	15 52.8	+49.7	3.0	16 52.7	+49.7	3.0	17 52.7	+49.7	3.0	85
86	11 42.7	+49.5	2.3	12 42.7	+49.4	2.4	13 42.6	+49.5	2.4	14 42.6	+49.5	2.4	15 42.5	+49.5	2.4	16 42.5	+49.5	2.4	17 42.4	+49.6	2.4	18 42.4	+49.6	2.4	86
87	12 32.2	+49.3	1.8	13 32.1	+49.4	1.8	14 32.1	+49.4	1.8	15 32.1	+49.4	1.8	16 32.0	+49.5	1.8	17 32.0	+49.5	1.8	18 32.0	+49.4	1.8	19 32.0	+49.5	1.8	87
88	13 21.5	+49.3	1.2	14 21.5	+49.3	1.2	15 21.5	+49.3	1.2	16 21.5	+49.3	1.2	17 21.5	+49.3	1.2	18 21.5	+49.3	1.2	19 21.4	+49.4	1.2	20 21.4	+49.4	1.2	88
89	14 10.8	+49.2	0.6	15 10.8	+49.2	0.6	16 10.8	+49.2	0.6	17 10.8	+49.2	0.6	18 10.8	+49.2	0.6	19 10.8	+49.2	0.6	20 10.8	+49.2	0.6	21 10.8	+49.2	0.6	89
90	15 00.0	+49.1	0.0	16 00.0	+49.1	0.0	17 00.0	+49.1	0.0	18 00.0	+49.1	0.0	19 00.0	+49.1	0.0	20 00.0	+49.1	0.0	21 00.0	+49.1	0.0	22 00.0	+49.1	0.0	90
	15°			16°			17°			18°			19°			20°			21°			22°			

S. Lat. {L.H.A. greater than 180° ....Zn=180°–Z; L.H.A. less than 180°...........Zn=180°+Z

LATITUDE SAME NAME AS DECLINATION L.H.A. 145°, 215°

73

36°, 324° L.H.A. LATITUDE SAME NAME AS DECLINATION N. Lat. {L.H.A. greater than 180° .....Zn=Z; L.H.A. less than 180°............Zn=360°−Z}

Dec.	15° Hc	d	Z	16° Hc	d	Z	17° Hc	d	Z	18° Hc	d	Z	19° Hc	d	Z	20° Hc	d	Z	21° Hc	d	Z	22° Hc	d	Z	Dec.
°	° ′	′	°	° ′	′	°	° ′	′	°	° ′	′	°	° ′	′	°	° ′	′	°	° ′	′	°	° ′	′	°	°
0	51 23.6	+24.4	109.6	51 02.9	+25.8	110.8	50 41.1	+27.1	111.9	50 18.1	+28.6	113.0	49 54.1	+29.9	114.1	49 29.1	+31.1	115.2	49 03.0	+32.4	116.3	48 36.0	+33.6	117.3	0
1	51 48.0	+23.2	108.1	51 28.7	+24.7	109.3	51 08.2	+26.2	110.5	50 46.7	+27.5	111.7	50 24.0	+28.9	112.8	50 00.2	+30.2	113.9	49 35.4	+31.5	115.0	49 09.6	+32.7	116.0	1
2	52 11.2	+22.0	106.6	51 53.4	+23.6	107.9	51 34.4	+25.0	109.1	51 14.2	+26.5	110.2	50 52.9	+27.9	111.4	50 30.4	+29.3	112.5	50 06.9	+30.6	113.6	49 42.3	+31.9	114.7	2
3	52 33.2	+20.9	105.1	52 17.0	+22.4	106.4	51 59.4	+24.0	107.6	51 40.7	+25.4	108.8	51 20.8	+26.8	110.0	50 59.7	+28.2	111.2	50 37.5	+29.6	112.3	50 14.2	+30.9	113.4	3
4	52 54.1	+19.6	103.6	52 39.4	+21.2	104.8	52 23.4	+22.8	106.1	52 06.1	+24.3	107.3	51 47.6	+25.8	108.6	51 27.9	+27.3	109.7	51 07.1	+28.6	110.9	50 45.1	+30.0	112.1	4
5	53 13.7	+18.4	102.0	53 00.6	+20.0	103.3	52 46.2	+21.5	104.6	52 30.4	+23.2	105.8	52 13.4	+24.7	107.1	51 55.2	+26.1	108.3	51 35.7	+27.6	109.5	51 15.1	+29.0	110.7	5
6	53 32.1	+17.1	100.4	53 20.6	+18.8	101.7	53 07.7	+20.4	103.0	52 53.6	+21.9	104.3	52 38.1	+23.5	105.6	52 21.3	+25.1	106.8	52 03.3	+26.5	108.1	51 44.1	+28.0	109.3	6
7	53 49.2	+15.8	98.8	53 39.4	+17.4	100.1	53 28.1	+19.1	101.5	53 15.5	+20.8	102.8	53 01.6	+22.3	104.1	52 46.4	+23.9	105.3	52 29.8	+25.5	106.6	52 12.1	+26.9	107.8	7
8	54 05.0	+14.4	97.1	53 56.8	+16.1	98.5	53 47.2	+17.8	99.9	53 36.3	+19.4	101.2	53 23.9	+21.1	102.5	53 10.3	+22.7	103.8	52 55.3	+24.2	105.1	52 39.0	+25.8	106.4	8
9	54 19.4	+13.0	95.5	54 12.9	+14.8	96.9	54 05.0	+16.5	98.2	53 55.7	+18.2	99.6	53 45.0	+19.9	100.9	53 33.0	+21.5	102.3	53 19.5	+23.1	103.6	53 04.8	+24.6	104.9	9
10	54 32.4	+11.6	93.8	54 27.7	+13.4	95.2	54 21.5	+15.2	96.6	54 13.9	+16.9	98.0	54 04.9	+18.6	99.3	53 54.5	+20.2	100.7	53 42.6	+21.9	102.0	53 29.4	+23.5	103.4	10
11	54 44.0	+10.2	92.1	54 41.1	+12.0	93.5	54 36.7	+13.7	94.9	54 30.8	+15.5	96.3	54 23.5	+17.2	97.7	54 14.7	+18.9	99.1	54 04.5	+20.6	100.5	53 52.9	+22.3	101.8	11
12	54 54.2	+8.7	90.4	54 53.1	+10.5	91.8	54 50.4	+12.3	93.2	54 46.3	+14.1	94.7	54 40.7	+15.8	96.1	54 33.6	+17.6	97.5	54 25.1	+19.3	98.8	54 15.2	+20.9	100.2	12
13	55 02.9	+7.3	88.7	55 03.6	+9.1	90.1	55 02.7	+10.9	91.5	55 00.4	+12.7	93.0	54 56.5	+14.5	94.4	54 51.2	+16.2	95.8	54 44.4	+18.0	97.2	54 36.1	+19.7	98.6	13
14	55 10.2	+5.8	86.9	55 12.7	+7.6	88.4	55 13.6	+9.4	89.8	55 13.1	+11.2	91.3	55 11.0	+13.0	92.7	55 07.4	+14.8	94.1	55 02.4	+16.5	95.6	54 55.8	+18.3	97.0	14
15	55 16.0	+4.3	85.2	55 20.3	+6.1	86.6	55 23.0	+8.0	88.1	55 24.3	+9.7	89.5	55 24.0	+11.6	91.0	55 22.2	+13.4	92.4	55 18.9	+15.2	93.9	55 14.1	+17.0	95.3	15
16	55 20.3	+2.7	83.4	55 26.4	+4.6	84.9	55 31.0	+6.4	86.3	55 34.0	+8.3	87.8	55 35.6	+10.1	89.2	55 35.6	+11.9	90.7	55 34.1	+13.8	92.2	55 31.1	+15.5	93.6	16
17	55 23.0	+1.3	81.7	55 31.0	+3.0	83.1	55 37.4	+4.9	84.6	55 42.3	+6.8	86.0	55 45.7	+8.6	87.5	55 47.5	+10.5	89.0	55 47.9	+12.2	90.4	55 46.6	+14.1	91.9	17
18	55 24.3	−0.3	79.9	55 34.0	+1.6	81.4	55 42.3	+3.4	82.8	55 49.1	+5.2	84.3	55 54.3	+7.1	85.7	55 58.0	+8.9	87.2	56 00.1	+10.8	88.7	56 00.7	+12.6	90.2	18
19	55 24.0	−1.8	78.2	55 35.6	0.0	79.6	55 45.7	+1.8	81.0	55 54.3	+3.7	82.5	56 01.4	+5.5	84.0	56 06.9	+7.4	85.4	56 10.9	+9.3	86.9	56 13.3	+11.1	88.4	19
20	55 22.2	−3.3	76.4	55 35.6	−1.5	77.8	55 47.5	+0.4	79.3	55 58.0	+2.1	80.7	56 06.9	+4.0	82.2	56 14.3	+5.9	83.7	56 20.2	+7.7	85.2	56 24.4	+9.6	86.7	20
21	55 18.9	−4.8	74.6	55 34.1	−3.0	76.1	55 47.9	−1.3	77.5	56 00.1	+0.6	78.9	56 10.9	+2.4	80.4	56 20.2	+4.2	81.9	56 27.9	+6.1	83.4	56 34.0	+8.1	84.9	21
22	55 14.1	−6.3	72.9	55 31.1	−4.6	74.3	55 46.6	−2.7	75.7	56 00.7	−0.9	77.1	56 13.3	+0.9	78.6	56 24.4	+2.8	80.1	56 34.0	+4.6	81.6	56 42.1	+6.4	83.1	22
23	55 07.8	−7.7	71.2	55 26.5	−6.0	72.5	55 43.9	−4.3	73.9	55 59.8	−2.6	75.3	56 14.2	−0.7	76.8	56 27.2	+1.1	78.3	56 38.6	+3.0	79.7	56 48.5	+4.9	81.2	23
24	55 00.1	−9.3	69.4	55 20.5	−7.6	70.8	55 39.6	−5.9	72.2	55 57.2	−4.0	73.6	56 13.5	−2.3	75.0	56 28.3	−0.4	76.4	56 41.6	+1.4	77.9	56 53.4	+3.3	79.4	24
25	54 50.8	−10.7	67.7	55 12.9	−9.0	69.0	55 33.7	−7.3	70.4	55 53.2	−5.6	71.8	56 11.2	−3.8	73.2	56 27.9	−2.0	74.6	56 43.0	−0.2	76.1	56 56.7	+1.6	77.6	25
26	54 40.1	−12.1	66.0	55 03.9	−10.5	67.3	55 26.4	−8.8	68.6	55 47.6	−7.1	70.0	56 07.4	−5.3	71.4	56 25.9	−3.6	72.8	56 42.8	−1.7	74.3	56 58.3	+0.1	75.8	26
27	54 28.0	−13.5	64.3	54 53.4	−11.9	65.6	55 17.6	−10.3	66.9	55 40.5	−8.6	68.2	56 02.1	−7.0	69.6	56 22.3	−5.2	71.0	56 41.1	−3.4	72.5	56 58.4	−1.5	73.9	27
28	54 14.5	−14.9	62.6	54 41.5	−13.3	63.9	55 07.3	−11.8	65.2	55 31.9	−10.1	66.5	55 55.1	−8.4	67.8	56 17.1	−6.7	69.2	56 37.7	−5.0	70.6	56 56.9	−3.2	72.1	28
29	53 59.6	−16.2	61.0	54 28.2	−14.8	62.2	54 55.5	−13.1	63.5	55 21.8	−11.6	64.8	55 46.7	−9.9	66.1	56 10.4	−8.3	67.4	56 32.7	−6.5	68.8	56 53.7	−4.8	70.3	29
30	53 43.4	−17.6	59.4	54 13.4	−16.1	60.5	54 42.4	−14.6	61.8	55 10.2	−13.0	63.0	55 36.8	−11.4	64.3	56 02.1	−9.7	65.7	56 26.2	−8.1	67.0	56 48.9	−6.3	68.4	30
31	53 25.8	−18.8	57.7	53 57.3	−17.4	58.9	54 27.8	−15.9	60.1	54 57.2	−14.5	61.3	55 25.4	−12.9	62.6	55 52.4	−11.3	63.9	56 18.1	−9.6	65.2	56 42.6	−7.9	66.6	31
32	53 07.0	−20.1	56.2	53 39.9	−18.7	57.3	54 11.9	−17.3	58.4	54 42.7	−15.8	59.6	55 12.5	−14.3	60.9	55 41.1	−12.7	62.2	56 08.5	−11.1	63.5	56 34.7	−9.5	64.8	32
33	52 46.9	−21.3	54.6	53 21.2	−19.9	55.7	53 54.6	−18.6	56.8	54 26.9	−17.2	58.0	54 58.2	−15.7	59.2	55 28.4	−14.2	60.4	55 57.4	−12.6	61.7	56 25.2	−11.0	63.0	33
34	52 25.6	−22.4	53.0	53 01.3	−21.2	54.1	53 36.0	−19.9	55.2	54 09.7	−18.5	56.3	54 42.5	−17.1	57.5	55 14.2	−15.6	58.7	55 44.8	−14.1	60.0	56 14.2	−12.5	61.3	34
35	52 03.2	−23.6	51.5	52 40.1	−22.4	52.6	53 16.1	−21.1	53.6	53 51.2	−19.7	54.7	54 25.4	−18.4	55.9	54 58.6	−17.0	57.0	55 30.7	−15.5	58.2	56 01.7	−14.0	59.5	35
36	51 39.6	−24.8	50.0	52 17.7	−23.5	51.0	52 55.0	−22.3	52.1	53 31.5	−21.1	53.1	54 07.0	−19.7	54.2	54 41.6	−18.3	55.4	55 15.2	−16.9	56.5	55 47.7	−15.4	57.8	36
37	51 14.8	−25.8	48.6	51 54.2	−24.7	49.5	52 32.7	−23.5	50.5	53 10.4	−22.2	51.6	53 47.3	−21.0	52.6	54 23.3	−19.7	53.7	54 58.3	−18.3	54.9	55 32.3	−16.8	56.1	37
38	50 49.0	−26.8	47.1	51 29.5	−25.7	48.1	52 09.2	−24.6	49.0	52 48.2	−23.4	50.0	53 26.3	−22.2	51.0	54 03.6	−20.9	52.1	54 40.0	−19.6	53.2	55 15.5	−18.3	54.4	38
39	50 22.2	−27.8	45.7	51 03.8	−26.8	46.6	51 44.6	−25.7	47.5	52 24.8	−24.6	48.5	53 04.1	−23.4	49.5	53 42.7	−22.2	50.5	54 20.4	−20.9	51.6	54 57.2	−19.5	52.7	39
40	49 54.4	−28.8	44.4	50 37.0	−27.8	45.2	51 18.9	−26.8	46.1	52 00.2	−25.7	47.0	52 40.7	−24.5	48.0	53 20.5	−23.4	49.0	53 59.5	−22.1	50.0	54 37.7	−20.9	51.1	40
41	49 25.6	−29.8	43.0	50 09.2	−28.8	43.8	50 52.1	−27.7	44.7	51 34.5	−26.7	45.5	52 16.2	−25.7	46.5	52 57.1	−24.5	47.4	53 37.4	−23.4	48.4	54 16.8	−22.2	49.4	41
42	48 55.8	−30.6	41.7	49 40.4	−29.7	42.5	50 24.4	−28.8	43.3	51 07.8	−27.8	44.1	51 50.5	−26.7	45.0	52 32.6	−25.7	45.9	53 14.0	−24.5	46.9	53 54.6	−23.3	47.9	42
43	48 25.2	−31.5	40.4	49 10.7	−30.7	41.1	49 55.6	−29.7	41.9	50 40.0	−28.8	42.7	51 23.8	−27.8	43.5	52 06.9	−26.7	44.4	52 49.5	−25.7	45.3	53 31.3	−24.6	46.3	43
44	47 53.7	−32.3	39.1	48 40.0	−31.5	39.8	49 25.9	−30.6	40.6	50 11.2	−29.7	41.3	50 56.0	−28.8	42.1	51 40.2	−27.8	43.0	52 23.8	−26.8	43.9	53 06.7	−25.7	44.8	44
45	47 21.4	−33.1	37.8	48 08.5	−32.3	38.5	48 55.3	−31.6	39.2	49 41.5	−30.7	40.0	50 27.2	−29.8	40.8	51 12.4	−28.8	41.6	51 57.0	−27.9	42.4	52 41.0	−26.9	43.3	45
46	46 48.3	−33.9	36.6	47 36.2	−33.1	37.3	48 23.7	−32.3	37.9	49 10.8	−31.5	38.7	49 57.4	−30.6	39.4	50 43.6	−29.8	40.2	51 29.1	−28.8	41.0	52 14.1	−27.9	41.8	46
47	46 14.4	−34.7	35.4	47 03.1	−33.9	36.0	47 51.4	−33.2	36.7	48 39.3	−32.4	37.4	49 26.8	−31.6	38.1	50 13.8	−30.8	38.8	51 00.3	−29.9	39.6	51 46.2	−28.9	40.4	47
48	45 39.7	−35.3	34.2	46 29.2	−34.7	34.8	47 18.2	−33.9	35.5	48 06.9	−33.2	36.1	48 55.2	−32.5	36.8	49 43.0	−31.6	37.5	50 30.4	−30.8	38.2	51 17.3	−29.9	39.0	48
49	45 04.4	−36.0	33.1	45 54.5	−35.4	33.7	46 44.3	−34.7	34.2	47 33.7	−34.0	34.9	48 22.7	−33.2	35.5	49 11.4	−32.5	36.2	49 59.6	−31.7	36.9	50 47.4	−30.9	37.6	49
50	44 28.4	−36.7	32.0	45 19.1	−36.0	32.5	46 09.6	−35.4	33.1	46 59.7	−34.7	33.6	47 49.5	−34.1	34.2	48 38.9	−33.3	34.9	49 27.9	−32.6	35.5	50 16.5	−31.8	36.2	50
51	43 51.7	−37.3	30.9	44 43.1	−36.7	31.4	45 34.2	−36.1	31.9	46 25.0	−35.5	32.4	47 15.4	−34.8	33.0	48 05.6	−34.2	33.6	48 55.3	−33.4	34.3	49 44.7	−32.6	34.9	51
52	43 14.4	−37.9	29.8	44 06.4	−37.4	30.3	44 58.1	−36.8	30.8	45 49.5	−36.2	31.3	46 40.6	−35.5	31.8	47 31.4	−34.9	32.4	48 21.9	−34.2	33.0	49 12.1	−33.6	33.6	52
53	42 36.5	−38.4	28.7	43 29.0	−37.9	29.2	44 21.3	−37.4	29.7	45 13.3	−36.8	30.1	46 05.1	−36.3	30.7	46 56.5	−35.6	31.2	47 47.7	−35.0	31.8	48 38.5	−34.3	32.4	53
54	41 58.1	−39.0	27.7	42 51.1	−38.5	28.1	43 43.9	−38.0	28.6	44 36.5	−37.5	29.0	45 28.8	−36.9	29.5	46 20.9	−36.3	30.0	47 12.7	−35.7	30.6	48 04.2	−35.1	31.1	54
55	41 19.1	−39.6	26.7	42 12.6	−39.1	27.1	43 05.9	−38.6	27.5	43 59.0	−38.1	27.9	44 51.9	−37.5	28.4	45 44.6	−37.0	28.9	46 37.0	−36.5	29.4	47 29.1	−35.8	29.9	55
56	40 39.5	−40.0	25.7	41 33.5	−39.6	26.1	42 27.3	−39.1	26.5	43 20.9	−38.6	26.9	44 14.4	−38.2	27.3	45 07.6	−37.7	27.8	46 00.5	−37.1	28.2	46 53.3	−36.6	28.7	56
57	39 59.5	−40.5	24.7	40 53.9	−40.1	25.1	41 48.2	−39.7	25.4	42 42.3	−39.2	25.8	43 36.2	−38.8	26.2	44 29.9	−38.3	26.7	45 23.4	−37.7	27.1	46 16.7	−37.2	27.6	57
58	39 19.0	−41.0	23.7	40 13.8	−40.6	24.1	41 08.5	−40.2	24.4	42 03.1	−39.8	24.8	42 57.4	−39.3	25.2	43 51.6	−38.8	25.6	44 45.7	−38.4	26.0	45 39.5	−37.9	26.5	58
59	38 38.0	−41.5	22.8	39 33.2	−41.0	23.1	40 28.3	−40.6	23.5	41 23.3	−40.3	23.8	42 18.1	−39.8	24.2	43 12.8	−39.4	24.5	44 07.3	−39.0	24.9	45 01.6	−38.5	25.4	59
60	37 56.5	−41.8	21.9	38 52.2	−41.5	22.2	39 47.7	−41.2	22.5	40 43.0	−40.7	22.8	41 38.3	−40.4	23.2	42 33.4	−40.0	23.5	43 28.3	−39.5	23.9	44 23.1	−39.1	24.3	60
61	37 14.7	−42.3	21.0	38 10.7	−42.0	21.3	39 06.5	−41.6	21.5	40 02.3	−41.3	21.9	40 57.9	−40.9	22.2	41 53.4	−40.5	22.5	42 48.8	−40.1	22.9	43 44.0	−39.7	23.2	61
62	36 32.4	−42.6	20.1	37 28.7	−42.3	20.3	38 24.9	−42.0	20.6	39 21.0	−41.6	20.9	40 17.0	−41.3	21.2	41 12.9	−41.0	21.5	42 08.7	−40.6	21.8	43 04.3	−40.2	22.2	62
63	35 49.8	−43.0	19.2	36 46.4	−42.7	19.5	37 42.9	−42.4	19.7	38 39.4	−42.1	20.0	39 35.7	−41.8	20.3	40 31.9	−41.4	20.6	41 28.1	−41.1	20.9	42 24.1	−40.8	21.2	63
64	35 06.8	−43.4	18.4	36 03.7	−43.1	18.6	37 00.5	−42.8	18.8	37 57.3	−42.6	19.1	38 53.9	−42.2	19.3	39 50.5	−41.9	19.6	40 47.0	−41.6	19.9	41 43.3	−41.2	20.2	64
65	34 23.4	−43.7	17.5	35 20.6	−43.5	17.7	36 17.7	−43.2	18.0	37 14.7	−42.9	18.2	38 11.7	−42.6	18.4	39 08.6	−42.3	18.7	40 05.4	−42.0	18.9	41 02.1	−41.7	19.2	65
66	33 39.7	−44.0	16.7	34 37.1	−43.8	16.9	35 34.5	−43.5	17.1	36 31.8	−43.2	17.3	37 29.1	−43.0	17.5	38 26.3	−42.8	17.8	39 23.4	−42.5	18.0	40 20.4	−42.2	18.3	66
67	32 55.7	−44.4	15.9	33 53.3	−44.1	16.1	34 51.0	−43.9	16.3	35 48.6	−43.7	16.5	36 46.1	−43.4	16.7	37 43.5	−43.1	16.9	38 40.9	−42.9	17.1	39 38.2	−42.6	17.4	67
68	32 11.3	−44.6	15.1	33 09.2	−44.4	15.2	34 07.1	−44.2	15.4	35 04.9	−44.0	15.6	36 02.7	−43.8	15.8	37 00.4	−43.5	16.0	37 58.0	−43.3	16.2	38 55.6	−43.0	16.4	68
69	31 26.7	−44.9	14.3	32 24.8	−44.7	14.4	33 22.9	−44.5	14.6	34 20.9	−44.3	14.8	35 18.9	−44.1	15.0	36 16.9	−43.9	15.1	37 14.7	−43.6	15.3	38 12.6	−43.4	15.5	69
70	30 41.8	−45.2	13.5	31 40.1	−45.0	13.7	32 38.4	−44.9	13.8	33 36.6	−44.6	14.0	34 34.8	−44.4	14.1	35 33.0	−44.3	14.3	36 31.1	−44.0	14.5	37 29.2	−43.8	14.7	70
71	29 56.6	−45.5	12.8	30 55.1	−45.3	12.9	31 53.5	−45.1	13.0	32 52.0	−45.0	13.2	33 50.4	−44.8	13.3	34 48.7	−44.5	13.5	35 47.1	−44.4	13.6	36 45.4	−44.2	13.8	71
72	29 11.1	−45.7	12.0	30 09.8	−45.6	12.1	31 08.4	−45.4	12.3	32 07.0	−45.2	12.4	33 05.6	−45.0	12.5	34 04.2	−44.9	12.7	35 02.7	−44.7	12.8	36 01.2	−44.5	13.0	72
73	28 25.4	−45.9	11.3	29 24.2	−45.8	11.4	30 23.0	−45.6	11.5	31 21.8	−45.5	11.6	32 20.6	−45.3	11.7	33 19.3	−45.1	11.9	34 18.0	−45.0	12.0	35 16.7	−44.8	12.2	73
74	27 39.5	−46.2	10.5	28 38.4	−46.0	10.6	29 37.4	−45.9	10.7	30 36.3	−45.7	10.9	31 35.3	−45.6	11.0	32 34.2	−45.5	11.1	33 33.0	−45.3	11.2	34 31.9	−45.2	11.3	74
75	26 53.3	−46.4	9.8	27 52.4	−46.2	9.9	28 51.5	−46.1	10.0	29 50.6	−46.0	10.1	30 49.7	−45.9	10.2	31 48.7	−45.7	10.3	32 47.7	−45.6	10.4	33 46.7	−45.4	10.5	75
76	26 06.9	−46.6	9.1	27 06.2	−46.5	9.2	28 05.4	−46.4	9.3	29 04.6	−46.2	9.4	30 03.8	−46.1	9.5	31 03.0	−46.0	9.6	32 02.1	−45.8	9.7	33 01.3	−45.8	9.8	76
77	25 20.3	−46.7	8.4	26 19.7	−46.7	8.5	27 19.0	−46.5	8.6	28 18.4	−46.5	8.6	29 17.7	−46.4	8.7	30 17.0	−46.3	8.8	31 16.3	−46.2	8.9	32 15.5	−46.0	9.0	77
78	24 33.6	−47.0	7.7	25 33.0	−46.9	7.8	26 32.5	−46.8	7.9	27 31.9	−46.7	7.9	28 31.3	−46.6	8.0	29 30.7	−46.5	8.1	30 30.1	−46.4	8.2	31 29.5	−46.3	8.2	78
79	23 46.6	−47.1	7.0	24 46.1	−47.0	7.1	25 45.7	−47.0	7.2	26 45.2	−46.9	7.2	27 44.7	−46.8	7.3	28 44.2	−46.7	7.3	29 43.7	−46.6	7.4	30 43.2	−46.5	7.5	79
80	22 59.5	−47.4	6.4	23 59.1	−47.3	6.4	24 58.7	−47.2	6.5	25 58.3	−47.1	6.5	26 57.9	−47.0	6.6	27 57.5	−46.9	6.6	28 57.1	−46.8	6.7	29 56.7	−46.8	6.8	80
81	22 12.1	−47.4	5.7	23 11.8	−47.4	5.7	24 11.5	−47.3	5.8	25 11.2	−47.2	5.8	26 10.9	−47.2	5.9	27 10.6	−47.1	5.9	28 10.3	−47.1	6.0	29 09.9	−46.9	6.0	81
82	21 24.7	−47.7	5.0	22 24.4	−47.5	5.1	23 24.2	−47.5	5.1	24 24.0	−47.5	5.2	25 23.7	−47.4	5.2	26 23.5	−47.4	5.2	27 23.2	−47.3	5.3	28 23.0	−47.3	5.3	82
83	20 37.0	−47.7	4.4	21 36.9	−47.8	4.4	22 36.7	−47.7	4.5	23 36.5	−47.6	4.5	24 36.3	−47.6	4.5	25 36.1	−47.5	4.6	26 35.9	−47.4	4.6	27 35.7	−47.4	4.6	83
84	19 49.3	−47.9	3.7	20 49.1	−47.8	3.8	21 49.0	−47.8	3.8	22 48.9	−47.8	3.8	23 48.7	−47.7	3.9	24 48.6	−47.7	3.9	25 48.5	−47.7	3.9	26 48.3	−47.6	3.9	84
85	19 01.4	−48.1	3.1	20 01.3	−48.0	3.1	21 01.2	−48.0	3.1	22 01.1	−48.0	3.2	23 01.0	−47.9	3.2	24 00.9	−47.9	3.2	25 00.8	−47.8	3.2	26 00.7	−47.8	3.3	85
86	18 13.3	−48.1	2.5	19 13.3	−48.2	2.5	20 13.2	−48.1	2.5	21 13.1	−48.0	2.5	22 13.1	−48.1	2.5	23 13.0	−48.0	2.6	24 13.0	−48.0	2.6	25 12.9	−48.0	2.6	86
87	17 25.2	−48.3	1.8	18 25.1	−48.2	1.9	19 25.1	−48.2	1.9	20 25.1	−48.3	1.9	21 25.0	−48.2	1.9	22 25.0	−48.2	1.9	23 25.0	−48.2	1.9	24 24.9	−48.1	1.9	87
88	16 36.9	−48.4	1.2	17 36.9	−48.4	1.2	18 36.9	−48.4	1.2	19 36.8	−48.3	1.2	20 36.8	−48.3	1.3	21 36.8	−48.3	1.3	22 36.8	−48.3	1.3	23 36.8	−48.3	1.3	88
89	15 48.5	−48.5	0.6	16 48.5	−48.5	0.6	17 48.5	−48.5	0.6	18 48.5	−48.5	0.6	19 48.5	−48.5	0.6	20 48.5	−48.5	0.6	21 48.5	−48.5	0.6	22 48.5	−48.5	0.6	89
90	15 00.0	−48.6	0.0	16 00.0	−48.6	0.0	17 00.0	−48.6	0.0	18 00.0	−48.6	0.0	19 00.0	−48.6	0.0	20 00.0	−48.6	0.0	21 00.0	−48.6	0.0	22 00.0	−48.6	0.0	90
	15°			16°			17°			18°			19°			20°			21°			22°			

36°, 324° L.H.A. LATITUDE SAME NAME AS DECLINATION

74

LATITUDE CONTRARY NAME TO DECLINATION L.H.A. 36°, 324°

Dec.	15° Hc	15° d	15° Z	16° Hc	16° d	16° Z	17° Hc	17° d	17° Z	18° Hc	18° d	18° Z	19° Hc	19° d	19° Z	20° Hc	20° d	20° Z	21° Hc	21° d	21° Z	22° Hc	22° d	22° Z	Dec.
°	° ′	′	°	° ′	′	°	° ′	′	°	° ′	′	°	° ′	′	°	° ′	′	°	° ′	′	°	° ′	′	°	°
0	51 23.6	−25.4	109.6	51 02.9	−26.8	110.8	50 41.1	−28.2	111.9	50 18.1	−29.5	113.0	49 54.1	−30.8	114.1	49 29.1	−32.1	115.2	49 03.0	−33.2	116.3	48 36.0	−34.4	117.3	0
1	50 58.2	−26.5	111.1	50 36.1	−27.9	112.2	50 12.9	−29.2	113.3	49 48.6	−30.4	114.4	49 23.3	−31.7	115.5	48 57.0	−32.8	116.5	48 29.8	−34.1	117.5	48 01.6	−35.2	118.5	1
2	50 31.7	−27.5	112.5	50 08.2	−28.8	113.6	49 43.7	−30.1	114.7	49 18.2	−31.4	115.7	48 51.6	−32.5	116.8	48 24.2	−33.7	117.8	47 55.7	−34.8	118.8	47 26.4	−35.9	119.7	2
3	50 04.2	−28.4	113.9	49 39.4	−29.7	114.9	49 13.6	−31.0	116.0	48 46.8	−32.1	117.0	48 19.1	−33.3	118.0	47 50.5	−34.5	119.0	47 20.9	−35.5	120.0	46 50.5	−36.6	120.9	3
4	49 35.8	−29.5	115.2	49 09.7	−30.7	116.3	48 42.6	−31.8	117.3	48 14.7	−33.1	118.3	47 45.8	−34.2	119.3	47 16.0	−35.2	120.2	46 45.4	−36.3	121.1	46 13.9	−37.3	122.0	4
5	49 06.3	−30.3	116.6	48 39.0	−31.5	117.6	48 10.8	−32.7	118.6	47 41.6	−33.8	119.5	47 11.6	−34.9	120.5	46 40.8	−36.0	121.4	46 09.1	−37.0	122.3	45 36.6	−37.9	123.2	5
6	48 36.0	−31.2	117.9	48 07.5	−32.3	118.9	47 38.1	−33.5	119.8	47 07.8	−34.5	120.8	46 36.7	−35.6	121.7	46 04.8	−36.6	122.6	45 32.1	−37.6	123.4	44 58.7	−38.5	124.3	6
7	48 04.8	−32.0	119.2	47 35.2	−33.2	120.1	47 04.6	−34.2	121.1	46 33.3	−35.3	122.0	46 01.1	−36.3	122.8	45 28.2	−37.3	123.7	44 54.5	−38.2	124.5	44 20.2	−39.2	125.3	7
8	47 32.8	−32.9	120.4	47 02.0	−34.0	121.4	46 30.4	−35.0	122.3	45 58.0	−36.1	123.1	45 24.8	−37.0	124.0	44 50.9	−37.9	124.8	44 16.3	−38.9	125.6	43 41.0	−39.7	126.4	8
9	46 59.9	−33.6	121.7	46 28.0	−34.6	122.6	45 55.4	−35.7	123.4	45 21.9	−36.6	124.3	44 47.8	−37.6	125.1	44 13.0	−38.6	125.9	43 37.4	−39.4	126.7	43 01.3	−40.3	127.4	9
10	46 26.3	−34.4	122.9	45 53.4	−35.4	123.7	45 19.7	−36.4	124.6	44 45.3	−37.3	125.4	44 10.2	−38.3	126.2	43 34.4	−39.1	127.0	42 58.0	−39.9	127.7	42 21.0	−40.8	128.4	10
11	45 51.9	−35.1	124.0	45 18.0	−36.1	124.9	44 43.3	−37.0	125.7	44 08.0	−38.0	126.5	43 31.9	−38.8	127.3	42 55.3	−39.7	128.0	42 18.1	−40.5	128.7	41 40.2	−41.2	129.4	11
12	45 16.8	−35.7	125.2	44 41.9	−36.7	126.0	44 06.3	−37.7	126.8	43 30.0	−38.5	127.6	42 53.1	−39.3	128.3	42 15.6	−40.2	129.0	41 37.6	−41.0	129.7	40 59.0	−41.8	130.4	12
13	44 41.1	−36.5	126.3	44 05.2	−37.4	127.1	43 28.6	−38.2	127.9	42 51.5	−39.1	128.6	42 13.8	−40.0	129.3	41 35.4	−40.7	130.0	40 56.6	−41.5	130.7	40 17.2	−42.2	131.3	13
14	44 04.6	−37.1	127.5	43 27.8	−37.9	128.2	42 50.4	−38.8	128.9	42 12.4	−39.6	129.7	41 33.8	−40.4	130.3	40 54.7	−41.2	131.0	40 15.1	−41.9	131.6	39 35.0	−42.6	132.3	14
15	43 27.5	−37.6	128.5	42 49.9	−38.6	129.3	42 11.6	−39.4	130.0	41 32.8	−40.2	130.7	40 53.4	−40.9	131.3	40 13.5	−41.6	132.0	39 33.2	−42.4	132.6	38 52.4	−43.1	133.2	15
16	42 49.9	−38.3	129.6	42 11.3	−39.1	130.3	41 32.2	−39.8	131.0	40 52.6	−40.6	131.6	40 12.5	−41.4	132.3	39 31.9	−42.1	132.9	38 50.8	−42.8	133.5	38 09.3	−43.4	134.1	16
17	42 11.6	−38.8	130.7	41 32.2	−39.6	131.3	40 52.4	−40.4	132.0	40 12.0	−41.1	132.6	39 31.1	−41.8	133.2	38 49.8	−42.5	133.8	38 08.0	−43.1	134.4	37 25.9	−43.9	134.9	17
18	41 32.8	−39.4	131.7	40 52.6	−40.1	132.3	40 12.0	−40.9	133.0	39 30.9	−41.6	133.6	38 49.3	−42.3	134.2	38 07.3	−42.9	134.7	37 24.9	−43.6	135.3	36 42.0	−44.1	135.8	18
19	40 53.4	−39.9	132.7	40 12.5	−40.6	133.3	39 31.1	−41.3	133.9	38 49.3	−42.0	134.5	38 07.0	−42.6	135.1	37 24.4	−43.4	135.6	36 41.3	−43.9	136.1	35 57.9	−44.6	136.6	19
20	40 13.5	−40.3	133.7	39 31.9	−41.1	134.3	38 49.8	−41.8	134.8	38 07.3	−42.4	135.4	37 24.4	−43.1	135.9	36 41.0	−43.6	136.5	35 57.4	−44.3	137.0	35 13.3	−44.8	137.5	20
21	39 33.2	−40.8	134.6	38 50.8	−41.5	135.2	38 08.0	−42.1	135.8	37 24.9	−42.9	136.3	36 41.3	−43.4	136.8	35 57.4	−44.1	137.3	35 13.1	−44.6	137.8	34 28.5	−45.2	138.3	21
22	38 52.4	−41.3	135.6	38 09.3	−41.9	136.1	37 25.9	−42.6	136.7	36 42.0	−43.2	137.2	35 57.9	−43.8	137.7	35 13.3	−44.3	138.2	34 28.5	−45.0	138.6	33 43.3	−45.5	139.1	22
23	38 11.1	−41.7	136.5	37 27.4	−42.4	137.0	36 43.3	−43.0	137.5	35 58.8	−43.5	138.0	35 14.1	−44.2	138.5	34 29.0	−44.7	139.0	33 43.5	−45.2	139.4	32 57.8	−45.7	139.8	23
24	37 29.4	−42.1	137.4	36 45.0	−42.7	137.9	36 00.3	−43.3	138.4	35 15.3	−43.9	138.9	34 29.9	−44.4	139.3	33 44.3	−45.1	139.8	32 58.3	−45.5	140.2	32 12.1	−46.1	140.6	24
25	36 47.3	−42.5	138.3	36 02.3	−43.1	138.8	35 17.0	−43.7	139.3	34 31.4	−44.3	139.7	33 45.5	−44.8	140.2	32 59.2	−45.3	140.6	32 12.8	−45.8	141.0	31 26.0	−46.3	141.4	25
26	36 04.8	−42.9	139.2	35 19.2	−43.5	139.6	34 33.3	−44.0	140.1	33 47.1	−44.5	140.5	33 00.7	−45.1	140.9	32 13.9	−45.5	141.4	31 27.0	−46.1	141.7	30 39.7	−46.5	142.1	26
27	35 21.9	−43.3	140.0	34 35.7	−43.8	140.5	33 49.3	−44.3	140.9	33 02.6	−44.9	141.3	32 15.6	−45.4	141.7	31 28.4	−45.9	142.1	30 40.9	−46.3	142.5	29 53.2	−46.8	142.8	27
28	34 38.6	−43.6	140.9	33 51.9	−44.1	141.3	33 05.0	−44.7	141.7	32 17.7	−45.1	142.1	31 30.2	−45.6	142.5	30 42.5	−46.1	142.9	29 54.6	−46.6	143.2	29 06.4	−47.0	143.6	28
29	33 55.0	−43.9	141.7	33 07.8	−44.4	142.1	32 20.3	−44.9	142.5	31 32.6	−45.5	142.9	30 44.6	−45.9	143.3	29 56.4	−46.3	143.6	29 08.0	−46.8	143.9	28 19.4	−47.2	144.3	29
30	33 11.1	−44.2	142.5	32 23.4	−44.8	142.9	31 35.4	−45.3	143.3	30 47.1	−45.6	143.7	29 58.7	−46.1	144.0	29 10.1	−46.6	144.3	28 21.2	−47.0	144.7	27 32.2	−47.5	145.0	30
31	32 26.9	−44.6	143.3	31 38.6	−45.0	143.7	30 50.1	−45.4	144.1	30 01.5	−46.0	144.4	29 12.6	−46.4	144.7	28 23.5	−46.8	145.1	27 34.2	−47.2	145.4	26 44.7	−47.6	145.7	31
32	31 42.3	−44.8	144.1	30 53.6	−45.3	144.5	30 04.7	−45.8	144.8	29 15.5	−46.2	145.2	28 26.2	−46.6	145.5	27 36.7	−47.1	145.8	26 47.0	−47.5	146.1	25 57.1	−47.8	146.3	32
33	30 57.5	−45.1	144.9	30 08.3	−45.5	145.2	29 18.9	−46.0	145.6	28 29.3	−46.4	145.9	27 39.6	−46.9	146.2	26 49.6	−47.2	146.5	25 59.5	−47.6	146.7	25 09.3	−48.0	147.0	33
34	30 12.4	−45.4	145.7	29 22.8	−45.8	146.0	28 32.9	−46.2	146.3	27 42.9	−46.6	146.6	26 52.7	−47.0	146.9	26 02.4	−47.4	147.2	25 11.9	−47.8	147.4	24 21.3	−48.2	147.7	34
35	29 27.0	−45.6	146.4	28 37.0	−46.1	146.7	27 46.7	−46.4	147.0	26 56.3	−46.9	147.3	26 05.7	−47.2	147.6	25 15.0	−47.6	147.8	24 24.1	−47.9	148.1	23 33.1	−48.3	148.3	35
36	28 41.4	−45.8	147.2	27 50.9	−46.2	147.5	27 00.3	−46.7	147.7	26 09.4	−47.0	148.0	25 18.5	−47.4	148.3	24 27.4	−47.8	148.5	23 36.2	−48.2	148.7	22 44.8	−48.5	149.0	36
37	27 55.6	−46.1	147.9	27 04.7	−46.5	148.2	26 13.6	−46.9	148.4	25 22.4	−47.2	148.7	24 31.1	−47.6	148.9	23 39.6	−47.9	149.2	22 48.0	−48.3	149.4	21 56.3	−48.6	149.6	37
38	27 09.5	−46.3	148.6	26 18.2	−46.7	148.9	25 26.7	−47.0	149.1	24 35.2	−47.4	149.4	23 43.5	−47.8	149.6	22 51.7	−48.1	149.8	21 59.7	−48.4	150.0	21 07.7	−48.7	150.2	38
39	26 23.2	−46.5	149.3	25 31.5	−46.9	149.6	24 39.7	−47.2	149.8	23 47.8	−47.6	150.1	22 55.7	−47.9	150.3	22 03.6	−48.3	150.5	21 11.3	−48.6	150.7	20 19.0	−48.9	150.9	39
40	25 36.7	−46.7	150.0	24 44.6	−47.0	150.3	23 52.5	−47.5	150.5	23 00.2	−47.8	150.7	22 07.8	−48.1	150.9	21 15.3	−48.4	151.1	20 22.7	−48.7	151.3	19 30.1	−49.1	151.5	40
41	24 50.0	−46.9	150.7	23 57.6	−47.3	151.0	23 05.0	−47.5	151.2	22 12.4	−47.9	151.4	21 19.7	−48.2	151.6	20 26.9	−48.5	151.7	19 34.0	−48.8	151.9	18 41.0	−49.1	152.1	41
42	24 03.1	−47.1	151.4	23 10.3	−47.4	151.6	22 17.5	−47.8	151.8	21 24.5	−48.0	152.0	20 31.5	−48.4	152.2	19 38.4	−48.7	152.4	18 45.2	−49.0	152.5	17 51.9	−49.2	152.7	42
43	23 16.0	−47.3	152.1	22 22.9	−47.6	152.3	21 29.7	−47.9	152.5	20 36.5	−48.2	152.7	19 43.1	−48.5	152.8	18 49.7	−48.8	153.0	17 56.2	−49.0	153.1	17 02.7	−49.4	153.3	43
44	22 28.7	−47.4	152.8	21 35.3	−47.7	153.0	20 41.8	−48.0	153.1	19 48.3	−48.3	153.3	18 54.6	−48.6	153.5	18 00.9	−48.9	153.6	17 07.2	−49.2	153.7	16 13.3	−49.4	153.9	44
45	21 41.3	−47.6	153.4	20 47.6	−47.9	153.6	19 53.8	−48.2	153.8	19 00.0	−48.5	153.9	18 06.0	−48.7	154.1	17 12.0	−49.0	154.2	16 18.0	−49.3	154.3	15 23.9	−49.6	154.5	45
46	20 53.7	−47.7	154.1	19 59.7	−48.0	154.2	19 05.6	−48.3	154.4	18 11.5	−48.6	154.5	17 17.3	−48.9	154.7	16 23.0	−49.1	154.8	15 28.7	−49.4	154.9	14 34.3	−49.6	155.0	46
47	20 06.0	−47.9	154.7	19 11.7	−48.1	154.9	18 17.3	−48.4	155.0	17 22.9	−48.7	155.2	16 28.4	−48.9	155.3	15 33.9	−49.2	155.4	14 39.3	−49.4	155.5	13 44.7	−49.7	155.6	47
48	19 18.1	−48.0	155.4	18 23.6	−48.3	155.5	17 28.9	−48.5	155.6	16 34.2	−48.7	155.8	15 39.5	−49.0	155.9	14 44.7	−49.3	156.0	13 49.9	−49.6	156.1	12 55.0	−49.8	156.2	48
49	18 30.1	−48.1	156.0	17 35.3	−48.4	156.1	16 40.4	−48.6	156.3	15 45.5	−48.9	156.4	14 50.5	−49.2	156.5	13 55.4	−49.4	156.6	13 00.3	−49.6	156.7	12 05.2	−49.8	156.8	49
50	17 42.0	−48.2	156.6	16 46.9	−48.5	156.8	15 51.8	−48.8	156.9	14 56.6	−49.0	157.0	14 01.3	−49.2	157.1	13 06.0	−49.4	157.2	12 10.7	−49.7	157.3	11 15.4	−50.0	157.3	50
51	16 53.8	−48.4	157.3	15 58.4	−48.6	157.4	15 03.0	−48.8	157.5	14 07.6	−49.1	157.6	13 12.1	−49.3	157.7	12 16.6	−49.5	157.8	11 21.0	−49.7	157.8	10 25.4	−49.9	157.9	51
52	16 05.4	−48.4	157.9	15 09.8	−48.7	158.0	14 14.2	−48.9	158.1	13 18.5	−49.1	158.2	12 22.8	−49.4	158.3	11 27.1	−49.6	158.3	10 31.3	−49.8	158.4	9 35.5	−50.1	158.5	52
53	15 17.0	−48.6	158.5	14 21.1	−48.7	158.6	13 25.3	−49.0	158.7	12 29.4	−49.3	158.8	11 33.4	−49.4	158.8	10 37.5	−49.7	158.9	9 41.5	−49.9	159.0	8 45.4	−50.0	159.0	53
54	14 28.4	−48.6	159.1	13 32.4	−48.9	159.2	12 36.3	−49.1	159.3	11 40.1	−49.3	159.3	10 44.0	−49.5	159.4	9 47.8	−49.7	159.5	8 51.6	−49.9	159.5	7 55.4	−50.2	159.6	54
55	13 39.8	−48.8	159.7	12 43.5	−49.0	159.8	11 47.2	−49.2	159.9	10 50.8	−49.3	159.9	9 54.5	−49.6	160.0	8 58.1	−49.8	160.0	8 01.7	−50.0	160.1	7 05.2	−50.1	160.1	55
56	12 51.0	−48.8	160.3	11 54.5	−49.0	160.4	10 58.0	−49.2	160.4	10 01.5	−49.5	160.5	9 04.9	−49.6	160.6	8 08.3	−49.8	160.6	7 11.7	−50.0	160.7	6 15.1	−50.2	160.7	56
57	12 02.2	−48.9	160.9	11 05.5	−49.1	161.0	10 08.8	−49.3	161.0	9 12.0	−49.4	161.1	8 15.3	−49.7	161.1	7 18.5	−49.9	161.2	6 21.7	−50.0	161.2	5 24.9	−50.2	161.2	57
58	11 13.3	−48.9	161.5	10 16.4	−49.1	161.5	9 19.5	−49.3	161.6	8 22.6	−49.6	161.6	7 25.6	−49.7	161.7	6 28.6	−49.9	161.7	5 31.7	−50.1	161.8	4 34.7	−50.3	161.8	58
59	10 24.4	−49.1	162.1	9 27.3	−49.2	162.1	8 30.2	−49.4	162.2	7 33.0	−49.5	162.2	6 35.9	−49.8	162.3	5 38.7	−49.9	162.3	4 41.6	−50.1	162.3	3 44.4	−50.3	162.3	59
60	9 35.3	−49.0	162.7	8 38.1	−49.3	162.7	7 40.8	−49.5	162.7	6 43.5	−49.6	162.8	5 46.1	−49.7	162.8	4 48.8	−49.9	162.8	3 51.5	−50.1	162.9	2 54.1	−50.2	162.9	60
61	8 46.3	−49.2	163.2	7 48.8	−49.3	163.3	6 51.3	−49.4	163.3	5 53.9	−49.7	163.4	4 56.4	−49.8	163.4	3 58.9	−50.0	163.4	3 01.4	−50.2	163.4	2 03.9	−50.3	163.4	61
62	7 57.1	−49.2	163.8	6 59.5	−49.4	163.9	6 01.9	−49.6	163.9	5 04.2	−49.7	163.9	4 06.6	−49.9	163.9	3 08.9	−50.0	164.0	2 11.2	−50.1	164.0	1 13.6	−50.3	164.0	62
63	7 07.9	−49.2	164.4	6 10.1	−49.3	164.4	5 12.3	−49.5	164.5	4 14.5	−49.7	164.5	3 16.7	−49.8	164.5	2 18.9	−50.0	164.5	1 21.1	−50.2	164.5	0 23.3	−50.4	164.5	63
64	6 18.7	−49.3	165.0	5 20.8	−49.5	165.0	4 22.8	−49.6	165.0	3 24.8	−49.7	165.0	2 26.9	−49.9	165.1	1 28.9	−50.0	165.1	0 30.9	−50.1	165.1	0 27.1	+50.3	14.9	64
65	5 29.4	−49.3	165.5	4 31.3	−49.4	165.6	3 33.2	−49.6	165.6	2 35.1	−49.7	165.6	1 37.0	−49.9	165.6	0 38.9	−50.0	165.6	0 19.2	+50.2	14.4	1 17.4	+50.3	14.4	65
66	4 40.1	−49.3	166.1	3 41.9	−49.5	166.1	2 43.6	−49.6	166.2	1 45.4	−49.8	166.2	0 47.1	−49.9	166.2	0 11.1	+50.0	13.8	1 09.4	+50.1	13.8	2 07.7	+50.2	13.8	66
67	3 50.8	−49.3	166.7	2 52.4	−49.5	166.7	1 54.0	−49.6	166.7	0 55.6	−49.7	166.7	0 02.8	+49.8	13.3	1 01.1	+50.1	13.3	1 59.5	+50.2	13.3	2 57.9	+50.2	13.3	67
68	3 01.5	−49.4	167.3	2 02.9	−49.4	167.3	1 04.4	−49.6	167.3	0 05.9	−49.8	167.3	0 52.6	+49.9	12.7	1 51.2	+50.0	12.7	2 49.7	+50.1	12.7	3 48.2	+50.3	12.7	68
69	2 12.1	−49.4	167.8	1 13.5	−49.5	167.8	0 14.8	−49.6	167.8	0 43.9	+49.7	12.2	1 42.5	+49.9	12.2	2 41.2	+49.9	12.2	3 39.8	+50.1	12.2	4 38.5	+50.2	12.2	69
70	1 22.7	−49.4	168.4	0 24.0	−49.6	168.4	0 34.8	+49.6	11.6	1 33.6	+49.7	11.6	2 32.4	+49.8	11.6	3 31.1	+50.0	11.6	4 29.9	+50.1	11.6	5 28.7	+50.2	11.7	70
71	0 33.3	−49.4	169.0	0 25.6	+49.5	11.0	1 24.4	+49.7	11.0	2 23.3	+49.8	11.0	3 22.2	+49.9	11.1	4 21.1	+49.9	11.1	5 20.0	+50.0	11.1	6 18.9	+50.1	11.1	71
72	0 16.1	+49.3	10.5	1 15.1	+49.5	10.5	2 14.1	+49.6	10.5	3 13.1	+49.7	10.5	4 12.1	+49.8	10.5	5 11.0	+50.0	10.5	6 10.0	+50.1	10.5	7 09.0	+50.1	10.5	72
73	1 05.4	+49.4	9.9	2 04.6	+49.4	9.9	3 03.7	+49.5	9.9	4 02.8	+49.6	9.9	5 01.9	+49.7	9.9	6 01.0	+49.8	10.0	7 00.1	+49.9	10.0	7 59.1	+50.1	10.0	73
74	1 54.8	+49.4	9.3	2 54.0	+49.5	9.3	3 53.2	+49.6	9.3	4 52.4	+49.7	9.4	5 51.6	+49.8	9.4	6 50.8	+49.9	9.4	7 50.0	+50.0	9.4	8 49.2	+50.0	9.4	74
75	2 44.2	+49.4	8.8	3 43.5	+49.4	8.8	4 42.8	+49.5	8.8	5 42.1	+49.6	8.8	6 41.4	+49.7	8.8	7 40.7	+49.8	8.8	8 40.0	+49.8	8.9	9 39.2	+50.0	8.9	75
76	3 33.6	+49.3	8.2	4 32.9	+49.5	8.2	5 32.3	+49.5	8.2	6 31.7	+49.6	8.2	7 31.1	+49.7	8.2	8 30.5	+49.7	8.3	9 29.8	+49.9	8.3	10 29.2	+49.9	8.3	76
77	4 22.9	+49.3	7.6	5 22.4	+49.3	7.6	6 21.8	+49.5	7.6	7 21.3	+49.5	7.7	8 20.8	+49.6	7.7	9 20.2	+49.7	7.7	10 19.7	+49.7	7.7	11 19.1	+49.9	7.7	77
78	5 12.2	+49.3	7.0	6 11.7	+49.4	7.1	7 11.3	+49.4	7.1	8 10.8	+49.5	7.1	9 10.4	+49.5	7.1	10 09.9	+49.6	7.1	11 09.4	+49.7	7.2	12 09.0	+49.8	7.2	78
79	6 01.5	+49.2	6.5	7 01.1	+49.3	6.5	8 00.7	+49.4	6.5	9 00.3	+49.5	6.5	9 59.9	+49.5	6.5	10 59.5	+49.6	6.6	11 59.1	+49.7	6.6	12 58.8	+49.7	6.6	79
80	6 50.7	+49.2	5.9	7 50.4	+49.3	5.9	8 50.1	+49.3	5.9	9 49.8	+49.3	5.9	10 49.4	+49.5	6.0	11 49.1	+49.5	6.0	12 48.8	+49.5	6.0	13 48.5	+49.6	6.0	80
81	7 39.9	+49.2	5.3	8 39.7	+49.2	5.3	9 39.4	+49.3	5.4	10 39.1	+49.4	5.4	11 38.9	+49.3	5.4	12 38.6	+49.4	5.4	13 38.3	+49.5	5.4	14 38.1	+49.5	5.5	81
82	8 29.1	+49.1	4.7	9 28.9	+49.1	4.8	10 28.7	+49.2	4.8	11 28.5	+49.2	4.8	12 28.2	+49.3	4.8	13 28.0	+49.4	4.8	14 27.8	+49.4	4.8	15 27.6	+49.4	4.9	82
83	9 18.2	+49.0	4.2	10 18.0	+49.1	4.2	11 17.9	+49.1	4.2	12 17.7	+49.2	4.2	13 17.5	+49.3	4.2	14 17.4	+49.2	4.2	15 17.2	+49.3	4.3	16 17.0	+49.4	4.3	83
84	10 07.2	+49.0	3.6	11 07.1	+49.0	3.6	12 07.0	+49.0	3.6	13 06.9	+49.1	3.6	14 06.8	+49.1	3.6	15 06.6	+49.2	3.6	16 06.5	+49.2	3.7	17 06.4	+49.2	3.7	84
85	10 56.2	+48.9	3.0	11 56.1	+49.0	3.0	12 56.0	+49.0	3.0	13 56.0	+49.0	3.0	14 55.9	+49.0	3.0	15 55.8	+49.1	3.1	16 55.7	+49.1	3.1	17 55.6	+49.1	3.1	85
86	11 45.1	+48.9	2.4	12 45.1	+48.8	2.4	13 45.0	+48.9	2.4	14 45.0	+48.9	2.4	15 44.9	+48.9	2.4	16 44.9	+48.9	2.5	17 44.8	+49.0	2.5	18 44.7	+49.1	2.5	86
87	12 34.0	+48.7	1.8	13 33.9	+48.8	1.8	14 33.9	+48.8	1.8	15 33.9	+48.8	1.8	16 33.8	+48.9	1.8	17 33.8	+48.9	1.8	18 33.8	+48.8	1.9	19 33.8	+48.8	1.9	87
88	13 22.7	+48.7	1.2	14 22.7	+48.7	1.2	15 22.7	+48.7	1.2	16 22.7	+48.7	1.2	17 22.7	+48.7	1.2	18 22.7	+48.7	1.2	19 22.6	+48.8	1.2	20 22.6	+48.8	1.3	88
89	14 11.4	+48.6	0.6	15 11.4	+48.6	0.6	16 11.4	+48.6	0.6	17 11.4	+48.6	0.6	18 11.4	+48.6	0.6	19 11.4	+48.6	0.6	20 11.4	+48.6	0.6	21 11.4	+48.6	0.6	89
90	15 00.0	+48.5	0.0	16 00.0	+48.5	0.0	17 00.0	+48.5	0.0	18 00.0	+48.5	0.0	19 00.0	+48.5	0.0	20 00.0	+48.5	0.0	21 00.0	+48.5	0.0	22 00.0	+48.5	0.0	90
	15°			16°			17°			18°			19°			20°			21°			22°			

S. Lat. { L.H.A. greater than 180° ....Zn=180°−Z
L.H.A. less than 180°...........Zn=180°+Z

LATITUDE SAME NAME AS DECLINATION L.H.A. 144°, 216°

37°, 323° L.H.A. LATITUDE SAME NAME AS DECLINATION N. Lat. {L.H.A. greater than 180° .....Zn=Z; L.H.A. less than 180°............Zn=360°−Z

Dec.	15° Hc	d	Z	16° Hc	d	Z	17° Hc	d	Z	18° Hc	d	Z
°	° ′	′	°	° ′	′	°	° ′	′	°	° ′	′	°
0	50 28.9	+23.9	109.0	50 08.9	+25.2	110.1	49 47.7	+26.7	111.2	49 25.5	+28.0	112.3
1	50 52.8	+22.8	107.5	50 34.1	+24.3	108.7	50 14.4	+25.6	109.8	49 53.5	+27.0	110.9
2	51 15.6	+21.6	106.0	50 58.4	+23.1	107.2	50 40.0	+24.6	108.4	50 20.5	+26.1	109.5
3	51 37.2	+20.5	104.5	51 21.5	+22.0	105.8	51 04.6	+23.6	106.9	50 46.6	+24.9	108.1
4	51 57.7	+19.3	103.0	51 43.5	+20.9	104.3	51 28.2	+22.3	105.5	51 11.5	+23.9	106.7
5	52 17.0	+18.1	101.5	52 04.4	+19.7	102.7	51 50.5	+21.3	104.0	51 35.4	+22.8	105.2
6	52 35.1	+16.8	99.9	52 24.1	+18.4	101.2	52 11.8	+20.0	102.5	51 58.2	+21.6	103.7
7	52 51.9	+15.5	98.3	52 42.5	+17.2	99.6	52 31.8	+18.9	100.9	52 19.8	+20.4	102.2
8	53 07.4	+14.3	96.7	52 59.7	+15.9	98.0	52 50.7	+17.5	99.4	52 40.2	+19.2	100.6
9	53 21.7	+12.9	95.1	53 15.6	+14.6	96.4	53 08.2	+16.3	97.8	52 59.4	+18.0	99.1
10	53 34.6	+11.5	93.5	53 30.2	+13.3	94.8	53 24.5	+15.0	96.2	53 17.4	+16.6	97.5
11	53 46.1	+10.2	91.8	53 43.5	+11.9	93.2	53 39.5	+13.6	94.5	53 34.0	+15.4	95.9
12	53 56.3	+8.7	90.1	53 55.4	+10.5	91.5	53 53.1	+12.3	92.9	53 49.4	+14.0	94.2
13	54 05.0	+7.3	88.4	54 05.9	+9.1	89.8	54 05.4	+10.8	91.2	54 03.4	+12.6	92.6
14	54 12.3	+5.9	86.8	54 15.0	+7.7	88.1	54 16.2	+9.5	89.5	54 16.0	+11.2	90.9
15	54 18.2	+4.5	85.1	54 22.7	+6.2	86.4	54 25.7	+8.0	87.8	54 27.2	+9.8	89.2
16	54 22.7	+3.0	83.3	54 28.9	+4.8	84.7	54 33.7	+6.6	86.1	54 37.0	+8.4	87.5
17	54 25.7	+1.5	81.6	54 33.7	+3.3	83.0	54 40.3	+5.1	84.4	54 45.4	+6.9	85.8
18	54 27.2	+0.1	79.9	54 37.0	+1.9	81.3	54 45.4	+3.6	82.7	54 52.3	+5.4	84.1
19	54 27.3	-1.4	78.2	54 38.9	+0.3	79.6	54 49.0	+2.2	81.0	54 57.7	+4.0	82.4
20	54 25.9	-2.9	76.5	54 39.2	-1.1	77.8	54 51.2	+0.6	79.2	55 01.7	+2.4	80.6
21	54 23.0	-4.3	74.7	54 38.1	-2.5	76.1	54 51.8	-0.8	77.5	55 04.1	+1.0	78.9
22	54 18.7	-5.7	73.0	54 35.6	-4.1	74.4	54 51.0	-2.3	75.7	55 05.1	-0.6	77.1
23	54 13.0	-7.2	71.3	54 31.5	-5.5	72.7	54 48.7	-3.8	74.0	55 04.5	-2.0	75.4
24	54 05.8	-8.7	69.6	54 26.0	-7.0	70.9	54 44.9	-5.2	72.3	55 02.5	-3.5	73.6
25	53 57.1	-10.0	68.0	54 19.0	-8.4	69.2	54 39.7	-6.8	70.6	54 59.0	-5.1	71.9
26	53 47.1	-11.4	66.3	54 10.6	-9.8	67.5	54 32.9	-8.1	68.8	54 53.9	-6.5	70.2
27	53 35.7	-12.8	64.6	54 00.8	-11.2	65.9	54 24.8	-9.6	67.1	54 47.4	-7.9	68.4
28	53 22.9	-14.1	63.0	53 49.6	-12.5	64.2	54 15.2	-11.1	65.4	54 39.5	-9.4	66.7
29	53 08.8	-15.4	61.4	53 37.1	-14.0	62.5	54 04.1	-12.4	63.8	54 30.1	-10.8	65.0
30	52 53.4	-16.7	59.7	53 23.1	-15.2	60.9	53 51.7	-13.7	62.1	54 19.3	-12.3	63.3
31	52 36.7	-18.0	58.2	53 07.9	-16.6	59.3	53 38.0	-15.1	60.5	54 07.0	-13.6	61.7
32	52 18.7	-19.1	56.6	52 51.3	-17.8	57.7	53 22.9	-16.5	58.8	53 53.4	-15.0	60.0
33	51 59.6	-20.4	55.1	52 33.5	-19.1	56.1	53 06.4	-17.7	57.2	53 38.4	-16.3	58.4
34	51 39.2	-21.6	53.5	52 14.4	-20.3	54.6	52 48.7	-18.9	55.6	53 22.1	-17.6	56.7
35	51 17.6	-22.6	52.0	51 54.1	-21.4	53.0	52 29.8	-20.2	54.1	53 04.5	-18.8	55.1
36	50 55.0	-23.8	50.6	51 32.7	-22.6	51.5	52 09.6	-21.3	52.5	52 45.7	-20.1	53.6
37	50 31.2	-24.8	49.1	51 10.1	-23.7	50.0	51 48.3	-22.6	51.0	52 25.6	-21.3	52.0
38	50 06.4	-25.9	47.7	50 46.4	-24.7	48.6	51 25.7	-23.6	49.5	52 04.3	-22.4	50.5
39	49 40.5	-26.8	46.3	50 21.7	-25.9	47.1	51 02.1	-24.7	48.1	51 41.9	-23.6	49.0
40	49 13.7	-27.9	44.9	49 55.8	-26.8	45.7	50 37.4	-25.8	46.6	51 18.3	-24.7	47.5
41	48 45.8	-28.7	43.6	49 29.0	-27.8	44.4	50 11.6	-26.8	45.2	50 53.6	-25.8	46.1
42	48 17.1	-29.7	42.2	49 01.2	-28.7	43.0	49 44.8	-27.7	43.8	50 27.8	-26.7	44.6
43	47 47.4	-30.5	40.9	48 32.5	-29.6	41.7	49 17.1	-28.7	42.4	50 01.1	-27.8	43.2
44	47 16.9	-31.3	39.7	48 02.9	-30.5	40.4	48 48.4	-29.7	41.1	49 33.3	-28.7	41.9
45	46 45.6	-32.1	38.4	47 32.4	-31.3	39.1	48 18.7	-30.5	39.8	49 04.6	-29.6	40.5
46	46 13.5	-33.0	37.2	47 01.1	-32.2	37.8	47 48.2	-31.3	38.5	48 35.0	-30.5	39.2
47	45 40.5	-33.6	36.0	46 28.9	-32.9	36.6	47 16.9	-32.2	37.2	48 04.5	-31.4	37.9
48	45 06.9	-34.4	34.8	45 56.0	-33.7	35.4	46 44.7	-32.9	36.0	47 33.1	-32.2	36.6
49	44 32.5	-35.0	33.6	45 22.3	-34.4	34.2	46 11.8	-33.7	34.8	47 00.9	-33.0	35.4
50	43 57.5	-35.7	32.5	44 47.9	-35.1	33.0	45 38.1	-34.5	33.6	46 27.9	-33.8	34.2
51	43 21.8	-36.4	31.4	44 12.8	-35.7	31.9	45 03.6	-35.1	32.4	45 54.1	-34.5	33.0
52	42 45.4	-36.9	30.3	43 37.1	-36.4	30.8	44 28.5	-35.8	31.3	45 19.6	-35.2	31.8
53	42 08.5	-37.6	29.2	43 00.7	-37.0	29.7	43 52.7	-36.4	30.2	44 44.4	-35.8	30.7
54	41 30.9	-38.1	28.2	42 23.7	-37.6	28.6	43 16.3	-37.1	29.1	44 08.6	-36.5	29.5
55	40 52.8	-38.6	27.2	41 46.1	-38.1	27.6	42 39.2	-37.7	28.0	43 32.1	-37.2	28.4
56	40 14.2	-39.2	26.2	41 08.0	-38.7	26.5	42 01.5	-38.2	26.9	42 54.9	-37.7	27.4
57	39 35.0	-39.6	25.2	40 29.3	-39.2	25.5	41 23.3	-38.7	25.9	42 17.2	-38.3	26.3
58	38 55.4	-40.1	24.2	39 50.1	-39.7	24.5	40 44.6	-39.3	24.9	41 38.9	-38.8	25.3
59	38 15.3	-40.6	23.2	39 10.4	-40.2	23.6	40 05.3	-39.8	23.9	41 00.1	-39.4	24.2
60	37 34.7	-41.0	22.3	38 30.2	-40.6	22.6	39 25.5	-40.2	22.9	40 20.7	-39.9	23.3
61	36 53.7	-41.4	21.4	37 49.6	-41.1	21.7	38 45.3	-40.8	22.0	39 40.8	-40.3	22.3
62	36 12.3	-41.8	20.5	37 08.5	-41.5	20.8	38 04.5	-41.1	21.0	39 00.5	-40.8	21.3
63	35 30.5	-42.2	19.6	36 27.0	-41.9	19.9	37 23.4	-41.6	20.1	38 19.7	-41.3	20.4
64	34 48.3	-42.5	18.7	35 45.1	-42.2	19.0	36 41.8	-42.0	19.2	37 38.4	-41.6	19.5
65	34 05.8	-42.9	17.9	35 02.9	-42.7	18.1	35 59.8	-42.3	18.3	36 56.8	-42.1	18.6
66	33 22.9	-43.3	17.0	34 20.2	-43.0	17.2	35 17.5	-42.7	17.5	36 14.7	-42.5	17.7
67	32 39.6	-43.5	16.2	33 37.2	-43.3	16.4	34 34.8	-43.1	16.6	35 32.2	-42.8	16.8
68	31 56.1	-43.9	15.4	32 53.9	-43.6	15.6	33 51.7	-43.4	15.8	34 49.4	-43.2	15.9
69	31 12.2	-44.1	14.6	32 10.3	-44.0	14.8	33 08.3	-43.8	14.9	34 06.2	-43.5	15.1
70	30 28.1	-44.5	13.8	31 26.3	-44.2	14.0	32 24.5	-44.0	14.1	33 22.7	-43.9	14.3
71	29 43.6	-44.7	13.0	30 42.1	-44.6	13.2	31 40.5	-44.4	13.3	32 38.8	-44.1	13.5
72	28 58.9	-44.9	12.3	29 57.5	-44.8	12.4	30 56.1	-44.6	12.5	31 54.7	-44.5	12.7
73	28 14.0	-45.3	11.5	29 12.7	-45.0	11.6	30 11.5	-44.9	11.7	31 10.2	-44.7	11.9
74	27 28.7	-45.4	10.8	28 27.7	-45.3	10.9	29 26.6	-45.2	11.0	30 25.5	-45.0	11.1
75	26 43.3	-45.7	10.0	27 42.4	-45.6	10.1	28 41.4	-45.4	10.2	29 40.5	-45.3	10.3
76	25 57.6	-45.8	9.3	26 56.8	-45.7	9.4	27 56.0	-45.6	9.5	28 55.2	-45.5	9.6
77	25 11.8	-46.1	8.6	26 11.1	-46.0	8.7	27 10.4	-45.9	8.8	28 09.7	-45.8	8.8
78	24 25.7	-46.3	7.9	25 25.1	-46.2	8.0	26 24.5	-46.1	8.0	27 23.9	-45.9	8.1
79	23 39.4	-46.4	7.2	24 38.9	-46.3	7.3	25 38.4	-46.2	7.3	26 38.0	-46.2	7.4
80	22 53.0	-46.7	6.5	23 52.6	-46.6	6.6	24 52.2	-46.5	6.6	25 51.8	-46.4	6.7
81	22 06.3	-46.8	5.8	23 06.0	-46.7	5.9	24 05.7	-46.7	5.9	25 05.4	-46.6	6.0
82	21 19.5	-46.9	5.2	22 19.3	-46.9	5.2	23 19.0	-46.8	5.2	24 18.8	-46.8	5.3
83	20 32.6	-47.2	4.5	21 32.4	-47.1	4.5	22 32.2	-47.0	4.6	23 32.0	-47.0	4.6
84	19 45.4	-47.2	3.8	20 45.3	-47.2	3.9	21 45.2	-47.2	3.9	22 45.0	-47.1	3.9
85	18 58.2	-47.4	3.2	19 58.1	-47.4	3.2	20 58.0	-47.3	3.2	21 57.9	-47.3	3.2
86	18 10.8	-47.5	2.5	19 10.7	-47.5	2.5	20 10.7	-47.5	2.6	21 10.6	-47.4	2.6
87	17 23.3	-47.7	1.9	18 23.2	-47.6	1.9	19 23.2	-47.6	1.9	20 23.2	-47.6	1.9
88	16 35.6	-47.7	1.3	17 35.6	-47.7	1.3	18 35.6	-47.7	1.3	19 35.6	-47.7	1.3
89	15 47.9	-47.9	0.6	16 47.9	-47.9	0.6	17 47.9	-47.9	0.6	18 47.9	-47.9	0.6
90	15 00.0	-48.0	0.0	16 00.0	-48.0	0.0	17 00.0	-48.0	0.0	18 00.0	-48.0	0.0

Dec.	19° Hc	d	Z	20° Hc	d	Z	21° Hc	d	Z	22° Hc	d	Z
°	° ′	′	°	° ′	′	°	° ′	′	°	° ′	′	°
0	49 02.2	+29.3	113.4	48 37.9	+30.6	114.4	48 12.6	+31.8	115.4	47 46.3	+33.1	116.4
1	49 31.5	+28.4	112.0	49 08.5	+29.7	113.1	48 44.4	+31.0	114.2	48 19.4	+32.2	115.2
2	49 59.9	+27.4	110.7	49 38.2	+28.8	111.8	49 15.4	+30.1	112.9	48 51.6	+31.4	113.9
3	50 27.3	+26.4	109.3	50 07.0	+27.7	110.4	49 45.5	+29.1	111.5	49 23.0	+30.4	112.6
4	50 53.7	+25.4	107.9	50 34.7	+26.8	109.0	50 14.6	+28.2	110.2	49 53.4	+29.5	111.3
5	51 19.1	+24.2	106.4	51 01.5	+25.8	107.6	50 42.8	+27.2	108.8	50 22.9	+28.6	109.9
6	51 43.3	+23.2	104.9	51 27.3	+24.6	106.2	51 10.0	+26.1	107.4	50 51.5	+27.5	108.5
7	52 06.5	+22.0	103.4	51 51.9	+23.5	104.7	51 36.1	+25.0	105.9	51 19.0	+26.5	107.1
8	52 28.5	+20.8	101.9	52 15.4	+22.4	103.2	52 01.1	+23.9	104.4	51 45.5	+25.4	105.7
9	52 49.3	+19.6	100.4	52 37.8	+21.2	101.7	52 25.0	+22.8	102.9	52 10.9	+24.4	104.2
10	53 08.9	+18.3	98.8	52 59.0	+20.0	100.1	52 47.8	+21.6	101.4	52 35.3	+23.1	102.7
11	53 27.2	+17.0	97.2	53 19.0	+18.7	98.6	53 09.4	+20.3	99.9	52 58.4	+22.0	101.2
12	53 44.2	+15.7	95.6	53 37.7	+17.4	97.0	53 29.7	+19.1	98.3	53 20.4	+20.7	99.6
13	53 59.9	+14.4	94.0	53 55.1	+16.1	95.3	53 48.8	+17.8	96.7	53 41.1	+19.5	98.1
14	54 14.3	+13.0	92.3	54 11.2	+14.7	93.7	54 06.6	+16.4	95.1	54 00.6	+18.1	96.4
15	54 27.3	+11.6	90.6	54 25.9	+13.3	92.0	54 23.0	+15.1	93.4	54 18.7	+16.9	94.8
16	54 38.9	+10.1	88.9	54 39.2	+12.0	90.4	54 38.1	+13.7	91.8	54 35.6	+15.4	93.2
17	54 49.0	+8.7	87.2	54 51.2	+10.5	88.7	54 51.8	+12.3	90.1	54 51.0	+14.1	91.5
18	54 57.7	+7.3	85.5	55 01.7	+9.0	86.9	55 04.1	+10.9	88.4	55 05.1	+12.6	89.8
19	55 05.0	+5.7	83.8	55 10.7	+7.6	85.2	55 15.0	+9.4	86.6	55 17.7	+11.2	88.1
20	55 10.7	+4.3	82.0	55 18.3	+6.1	83.5	55 24.4	+7.8	84.9	55 28.9	+9.7	86.4
21	55 15.0	+2.7	80.3	55 24.4	+4.5	81.7	55 32.2	+6.4	83.2	55 38.6	+8.3	84.6
22	55 17.7	+1.3	78.5	55 28.9	+3.1	80.0	55 38.6	+4.9	81.4	55 46.9	+6.7	82.9
23	55 19.0	-0.3	76.8	55 32.0	+1.5	78.2	55 43.5	+3.3	79.6	55 53.6	+5.1	81.1
24	55 18.7	-1.8	75.0	55 33.5	0.0	76.4	55 46.8	+1.9	77.9	55 58.7	+3.7	79.3
25	55 16.9	-3.3	73.3	55 33.5	-1.5	74.7	55 48.7	+0.2	76.1	56 02.4	+2.0	77.5
26	55 13.6	-4.8	71.5	55 32.0	-3.1	72.9	55 48.9	-1.3	74.3	56 04.4	+0.6	75.7
27	55 08.8	-6.2	69.8	55 28.9	-4.5	71.1	55 47.6	-2.8	72.5	56 05.0	-1.1	73.9
28	55 02.6	-7.8	68.0	55 24.4	-6.1	69.4	55 44.8	-4.3	70.7	56 03.9	-2.6	72.1
29	54 54.8	-9.2	66.3	55 18.3	-7.6	67.6	55 40.5	-5.9	69.0	56 01.3	-4.1	70.4
30	54 45.6	-10.7	64.6	55 10.7	-9.0	65.9	55 34.6	-7.4	67.2	55 57.2	-5.7	68.6
31	54 34.9	-12.0	62.9	55 01.7	-10.5	64.2	55 27.2	-8.8	65.5	55 51.5	-7.2	66.8
32	54 22.9	-13.5	61.2	54 51.2	-11.9	62.4	55 18.4	-10.4	63.7	55 44.3	-8.7	65.0
33	54 09.4	-14.9	59.5	54 39.3	-13.4	60.7	55 08.0	-11.8	62.0	55 35.6	-10.2	63.3
34	53 54.5	-16.1	57.9	54 25.9	-14.7	59.1	54 56.2	-13.2	60.3	55 25.4	-11.7	61.5
35	53 38.4	-17.5	56.3	54 11.2	-16.1	57.4	54 43.0	-14.6	58.6	55 13.7	-13.1	59.8
36	53 20.9	-18.8	54.6	53 55.1	-17.4	55.8	54 28.4	-16.0	56.9	55 00.6	-14.5	58.1
37	53 02.1	-20.0	53.1	53 37.7	-18.7	54.1	54 12.4	-17.4	55.3	54 46.1	-16.0	56.4
38	52 42.1	-21.3	51.5	53 19.0	-20.0	52.5	53 55.0	-18.6	53.6	54 30.1	-17.2	54.8
39	52 20.8	-22.4	50.0	52 59.0	-21.2	51.0	53 36.4	-19.9	52.0	54 12.9	-18.6	53.1
40	51 58.4	-23.5	48.5	52 37.8	-22.3	49.4	53 16.5	-21.2	50.4	53 54.3	-19.9	51.5
41	51 34.9	-24.7	47.0	52 15.5	-23.6	47.9	52 55.3	-22.3	48.9	53 34.4	-21.2	49.9
42	51 10.2	-25.7	45.5	51 51.9	-24.6	46.4	52 33.0	-23.6	47.3	53 13.2	-22.3	48.3
43	50 44.5	-26.8	44.1	51 27.3	-25.7	44.9	52 09.4	-24.6	45.8	52 50.9	-23.6	46.8
44	50 17.7	-27.7	42.7	51 01.6	-26.8	43.5	51 44.8	-25.8	44.4	52 27.3	-24.6	45.3
45	49 50.0	-28.8	41.3	50 34.8	-27.8	42.1	51 19.0	-26.8	42.9	52 02.7	-25.8	43.8
46	49 21.2	-29.6	39.9	50 07.0	-28.8	40.7	50 52.2	-27.8	41.5	51 36.9	-26.9	42.3
47	48 51.6	-30.6	38.6	49 38.2	-29.7	39.3	50 24.4	-28.8	40.1	51 10.0	-27.9	40.9
48	48 21.0	-31.4	37.3	49 08.5	-30.6	38.0	49 55.6	-29.8	38.7	50 42.1	-28.8	39.5
49	47 49.6	-32.3	36.0	48 37.9	-31.5	36.7	49 25.8	-30.7	37.4	50 13.3	-29.9	38.1
50	47 17.3	-33.0	34.8	48 06.4	-32.3	35.4	48 55.1	-31.5	36.1	49 43.4	-30.7	36.8
51	46 44.3	-33.8	33.5	47 34.1	-33.1	34.1	48 23.6	-32.4	34.8	49 12.7	-31.7	35.4
52	46 10.5	-34.6	32.3	47 01.0	-33.9	32.9	47 51.2	-33.2	33.5	48 41.0	-32.4	34.1
53	45 35.9	-35.2	31.2	46 27.1	-34.6	31.7	47 18.0	-34.0	32.3	48 08.6	-33.4	32.9
54	45 00.7	-36.0	30.0	45 52.5	-35.4	30.5	46 44.0	-34.7	31.1	47 35.2	-34.0	31.6
55	44 24.7	-36.6	28.9	45 17.1	-36.0	29.4	46 09.3	-35.5	29.9	47 01.2	-34.9	30.4
56	43 48.1	-37.2	27.8	44 41.1	-36.7	28.3	45 33.8	-36.1	28.7	46 26.3	-35.6	29.2
57	43 10.9	-37.8	26.7	44 04.4	-37.3	27.1	44 57.7	-36.8	27.6	45 50.7	-36.2	28.1
58	42 33.1	-38.4	25.7	43 27.1	-37.9	26.1	44 20.9	-37.4	26.5	45 14.5	-36.9	26.9
59	41 54.7	-38.9	24.6	42 49.2	-38.5	25.0	43 43.5	-38.1	25.4	44 37.6	-37.6	25.8
60	41 15.8	-39.5	23.6	42 10.7	-39.1	24.0	43 05.4	-38.6	24.3	44 00.0	-38.2	24.7
61	40 36.3	-40.0	22.6	41 31.6	-39.6	22.9	42 26.8	-39.2	23.3	43 21.8	-38.7	23.7
62	39 56.3	-40.4	21.6	40 52.0	-40.0	21.9	41 47.6	-39.7	22.3	42 43.1	-39.3	22.6
63	39 15.9	-40.9	20.7	40 12.0	-40.6	21.0	41 07.9	-40.2	21.3	42 03.8	-39.9	21.6
64	38 35.0	-41.4	19.7	39 31.4	-41.0	20.0	40 27.7	-40.7	20.3	41 23.9	-40.3	20.6
65	37 53.6	-41.8	18.8	38 50.4	-41.5	19.1	39 47.0	-41.1	19.3	40 43.6	-40.8	19.6
66	37 11.8	-42.2	17.9	38 08.9	-41.9	18.1	39 05.9	-41.6	18.4	40 02.8	-41.4	18.6
67	36 29.6	-42.5	17.0	37 27.0	-42.3	17.2	38 24.3	-42.1	17.5	39 21.4	-41.7	17.7
68	35 47.1	-43.0	16.1	36 44.7	-42.7	16.3	37 42.2	-42.4	16.6	38 39.7	-42.2	16.8
69	35 04.1	-43.3	15.3	36 02.0	-43.1	15.5	36 59.8	-42.9	15.7	37 57.5	-42.6	15.9
70	34 20.8	-43.6	14.4	35 18.9	-43.4	14.6	36 16.9	-43.2	14.8	37 14.9	-43.0	15.0
71	33 37.2	-44.0	13.6	34 35.5	-43.8	13.8	35 33.7	-43.5	13.9	36 31.9	-43.3	14.1
72	32 53.2	-44.3	12.8	33 51.7	-44.1	12.9	34 50.2	-44.0	13.1	35 48.6	-43.7	13.3
73	32 08.9	-44.5	12.0	33 07.6	-44.4	12.1	34 06.2	-44.2	12.3	35 04.9	-44.1	12.4
74	31 24.4	-44.9	11.2	32 23.2	-44.7	11.3	33 22.0	-44.5	11.5	34 20.8	-44.4	11.6
75	30 39.5	-45.1	10.4	31 38.5	-45.0	10.5	32 37.5	-44.9	10.7	33 36.4	-44.7	10.8
76	29 54.4	-45.4	9.7	30 53.5	-45.3	9.8	31 52.6	-45.1	9.9	32 51.7	-45.0	10.0
77	29 09.0	-45.7	8.9	30 08.2	-45.5	9.0	31 07.5	-45.4	9.1	32 06.7	-45.3	9.2
78	28 23.3	-45.8	8.2	29 22.7	-45.8	8.3	30 22.1	-45.7	8.3	31 21.4	-45.5	8.4
79	27 37.5	-46.1	7.4	28 36.9	-46.0	7.5	29 36.4	-45.9	7.6	30 35.9	-45.8	7.7
80	26 51.4	-46.4	6.7	27 50.9	-46.2	6.8	28 50.5	-46.1	6.9	29 50.1	-46.1	6.9
81	26 05.0	-46.5	6.0	27 04.7	-46.4	6.1	28 04.4	-46.4	6.1	29 04.0	-46.3	6.2
82	25 18.5	-46.7	5.3	26 18.3	-46.7	5.4	27 18.0	-46.6	5.4	28 17.7	-46.5	5.5
83	24 31.8	-46.9	4.6	25 31.6	-46.9	4.7	26 31.4	-46.8	4.7	27 31.2	-46.7	4.7
84	23 44.9	-47.1	3.9	24 44.7	-47.0	4.0	25 44.6	-47.0	4.0	26 44.5	-47.0	4.0
85	22 57.8	-47.3	3.3	23 57.7	-47.2	3.3	24 57.6	-47.2	3.3	25 57.5	-47.1	3.3
86	22 10.5	-47.4	2.6	23 10.5	-47.4	2.6	24 10.4	-47.3	2.6	25 10.4	-47.4	2.7
87	21 23.1	-47.5	1.9	22 23.1	-47.5	2.0	23 23.1	-47.6	2.0	24 23.0	-47.5	2.0
88	20 35.6	-47.7	1.3	21 35.6	-47.8	1.3	22 35.5	-47.7	1.3	23 35.5	-47.7	1.3
89	19 47.9	-47.9	0.6	20 47.8	-47.8	0.6	21 47.8	-47.8	0.6	22 47.8	-47.8	0.7
90	19 00.0	-48.0	0.0	20 00.0	-48.0	0.0	21 00.0	-48.0	0.0	22 00.0	-48.0	0.0

37°, 323° L.H.A. LATITUDE SAME NAME AS DECLINATION

76

LATITUDE **CONTRARY** NAME TO DECLINATION — **L.H.A. 37°, 323°**

Dec.	15°			16°			17°			18°			19°			20°			21°			22°			Dec.
	Hc	d	Z	Hc	d	Z	Hc	d	Z	Hc	d	Z	Hc	d	Z	Hc	d	Z	Hc	d	Z	Hc	d	Z	
°	° ′	′	°	° ′	′	°	° ′	′	°	° ′	′	°	° ′	′	°	° ′	′	°	° ′	′	°	° ′	′	°	°
0	50 28.9	−24.9	109.0	50 08.9	−26.4	110.1	49 47.7	−27.7	111.2	49 25.5	−29.0	112.3	49 02.2	−30.3	113.4	48 37.9	−31.5	114.4	48 12.6	−32.7	115.4	47 46.3	−33.8	116.4	0
1	50 04.0	−26.0	110.4	49 42.5	−27.3	111.5	49 20.0	−28.6	112.6	48 56.5	−29.9	113.6	48 31.9	−31.1	114.7	48 06.4	−32.3	115.7	47 39.9	−33.5	116.7	47 12.5	−34.6	117.7	1
2	49 38.0	−26.9	111.8	49 15.2	−28.2	112.9	48 51.4	−29.5	113.9	48 26.6	−30.8	115.0	48 00.8	−32.0	116.0	47 34.1	−33.1	116.9	47 06.4	−34.2	117.9	46 37.9	−35.3	118.9	2
3	49 11.1	−27.9	113.2	48 47.0	−29.2	114.2	48 21.9	−30.4	115.2	47 55.8	−31.6	116.2	47 28.8	−32.7	117.2	47 01.0	−33.9	118.2	46 32.2	−35.0	119.1	46 02.6	−36.0	120.0	3
4	48 43.2	−28.9	114.5	48 17.8	−30.1	115.5	47 51.5	−31.3	116.5	47 24.2	−32.4	117.5	46 56.1	−33.6	118.5	46 27.1	−34.7	119.4	45 57.2	−35.7	120.3	45 26.6	−36.8	121.2	4
5	48 14.3	−29.7	115.8	47 47.7	−30.9	116.8	47 20.2	−32.1	117.8	46 51.8	−33.2	118.7	46 22.5	−34.3	119.7	45 52.4	−35.3	120.6	45 21.5	−36.3	121.4	44 49.8	−37.3	122.3	5
6	47 44.6	−30.6	117.1	47 16.8	−31.7	118.1	46 48.1	−32.8	119.0	46 18.6	−34.0	119.9	45 48.2	−35.0	120.8	45 17.1	−36.1	121.7	44 45.2	−37.1	122.6	44 12.5	−38.0	123.4	6
7	47 14.0	−31.4	118.4	46 45.1	−32.6	119.3	46 15.3	−33.7	120.2	45 44.6	−34.7	121.1	45 13.2	−35.7	122.0	44 41.0	−36.6	122.8	44 08.1	−37.6	123.7	43 34.5	−38.5	124.5	7
8	46 42.6	−32.2	119.6	46 12.5	−33.3	120.6	45 41.6	−34.3	121.4	45 09.9	−35.3	122.3	44 37.5	−36.4	123.1	44 04.4	−37.4	124.0	43 30.5	−38.2	124.7	42 56.0	−39.2	125.5	8
9	46 10.4	−33.0	120.9	45 39.2	−34.0	121.7	45 07.3	−35.1	122.6	44 34.6	−36.1	123.4	44 01.1	−37.0	124.3	43 27.0	−37.9	125.0	42 52.3	−38.8	125.8	42 16.8	−39.6	126.5	9
10	45 37.4	−33.7	122.1	45 05.2	−34.8	122.9	44 32.2	−35.7	123.8	43 58.5	−36.7	124.6	43 24.1	−37.6	125.3	42 49.1	−38.5	126.1	42 13.5	−39.4	126.8	41 37.2	−40.2	127.6	10
11	45 03.7	−34.4	123.2	44 30.4	−35.4	124.1	43 56.5	−36.4	124.9	43 21.8	−37.3	125.7	42 46.5	−38.1	126.4	42 10.6	−39.0	127.1	41 34.1	−39.9	127.9	40 57.0	−40.7	128.5	11
12	44 29.3	−35.2	124.4	43 55.0	−36.1	125.2	43 20.1	−37.0	126.0	42 44.5	−37.9	126.7	42 08.4	−38.8	127.5	41 31.6	−39.6	128.2	40 54.2	−40.4	128.8	40 16.3	−41.1	129.5	12
13	43 54.1	−35.7	125.5	43 18.9	−36.7	126.3	42 43.1	−37.6	127.0	42 06.6	−38.4	127.8	41 29.6	−39.3	128.5	40 52.0	−40.1	129.2	40 13.8	−40.8	129.8	39 35.2	−41.7	130.5	13
14	43 18.4	−36.4	126.6	42 42.2	−37.3	127.4	42 05.5	−38.1	128.1	41 28.2	−39.0	128.8	40 50.3	−39.8	129.5	40 11.9	−40.6	130.1	39 33.0	−41.3	130.8	38 53.5	−42.0	131.4	14
15	42 42.0	−37.1	127.7	42 04.9	−37.8	128.4	41 27.4	−38.7	129.1	40 49.2	−39.5	129.8	40 10.5	−40.3	130.5	39 31.3	−41.0	131.1	38 51.7	−41.8	131.7	38 11.5	−42.5	132.3	15
16	42 04.9	−37.5	128.8	41 27.1	−38.4	129.5	40 48.7	−39.3	130.2	40 09.7	−40.0	130.8	39 30.2	−40.7	131.4	38 50.3	−41.5	132.0	38 09.9	−42.2	132.6	37 29.0	−42.8	133.2	16
17	41 27.4	−38.2	129.8	40 48.7	−39.0	130.5	40 09.4	−39.7	131.1	39 29.7	−40.5	131.8	38 49.5	−41.2	132.4	38 08.8	−41.9	133.0	37 27.7	−42.6	133.5	36 46.2	−43.2	134.1	17
18	40 49.2	−38.7	130.9	40 09.7	−39.5	131.5	39 29.7	−40.2	132.1	38 49.2	−40.9	132.7	38 08.3	−41.6	133.3	37 26.9	−42.3	133.9	36 45.1	−42.9	134.4	36 03.0	−43.6	134.9	18
19	40 10.5	−39.2	131.9	39 30.2	−39.9	132.5	38 49.5	−40.7	133.1	38 08.3	−41.4	133.7	37 26.7	−42.1	134.2	36 44.6	−42.7	134.8	36 02.2	−43.4	135.3	35 19.4	−44.0	135.8	19
20	39 31.3	−39.6	132.9	38 50.3	−40.4	133.4	38 08.8	−41.1	134.0	37 26.9	−41.8	134.6	36 44.6	−42.4	135.1	36 01.9	−43.1	135.6	35 18.8	−43.6	136.1	34 35.4	−44.3	136.6	20
21	38 51.7	−40.2	133.8	38 09.9	−40.9	134.4	37 27.7	−41.5	134.9	36 45.1	−42.1	135.5	36 02.2	−42.8	136.0	35 18.8	−43.4	136.5	34 35.2	−44.1	137.0	33 51.1	−44.6	137.4	21
22	38 11.5	−40.6	134.8	37 29.0	−41.2	135.3	36 46.2	−41.9	135.8	36 03.0	−42.6	136.4	35 19.4	−43.2	136.9	34 35.4	−43.8	137.3	33 51.1	−44.3	137.8	33 06.5	−44.9	138.2	22
23	37 30.9	−41.0	135.7	36 47.8	−41.7	136.2	36 04.3	−42.4	136.7	35 20.4	−42.9	137.2	34 36.2	−43.5	137.7	33 51.6	−44.1	138.2	33 06.8	−44.7	138.6	32 21.6	−45.1	139.0	23
24	36 49.9	−41.5	136.6	36 06.1	−42.1	137.1	35 21.9	−42.7	137.6	34 37.5	−43.3	138.1	33 52.7	−43.9	138.5	33 07.5	−44.4	139.0	32 22.1	−44.9	139.4	31 36.5	−45.5	139.8	24
25	36 08.4	−41.8	137.5	35 24.0	−42.5	138.0	34 39.2	−43.0	138.5	33 54.2	−43.6	138.9	33 08.8	−44.2	139.4	32 23.1	−44.7	139.8	31 37.2	−45.2	140.2	30 51.0	−45.7	140.6	25
26	35 26.6	−42.3	138.4	34 41.5	−42.8	138.9	33 56.2	−43.4	139.3	33 10.6	−44.0	139.7	32 24.6	−44.4	140.2	31 38.4	−45.0	140.6	30 52.0	−45.5	140.9	30 05.3	−46.0	141.3	26
27	34 44.3	−42.5	139.3	33 58.7	−43.1	139.7	33 12.8	−43.7	140.1	32 26.6	−44.2	140.6	31 40.2	−44.8	140.9	30 53.4	−45.2	141.3	30 06.5	−45.8	141.7	29 19.3	−46.2	142.0	27
28	34 01.8	−43.0	140.1	33 15.6	−43.5	140.5	32 29.1	−44.0	141.0	31 42.4	−44.6	141.3	30 55.4	−45.0	141.7	30 08.2	−45.5	142.1	29 20.7	−46.0	142.4	28 33.1	−46.5	142.8	28
29	33 18.8	−43.2	141.0	32 32.1	−43.8	141.4	31 45.1	−44.3	141.8	30 57.8	−44.8	142.1	30 10.4	−45.3	142.5	29 22.7	−45.8	142.8	28 34.7	−46.2	143.2	27 46.6	−46.7	143.5	29
30	32 35.6	−43.6	141.8	31 48.3	−44.1	142.2	31 00.8	−44.6	142.5	30 13.0	−45.1	142.9	29 25.1	−45.6	143.2	28 36.9	−46.0	143.6	27 48.5	−46.4	143.9	26 59.9	−46.8	144.2	30
31	31 52.0	−43.9	142.6	31 04.2	−44.4	143.0	30 16.2	−44.9	143.3	29 27.9	−45.3	143.7	28 39.5	−45.8	144.0	27 50.9	−46.3	144.3	27 02.1	−46.7	144.6	26 13.1	−47.1	144.9	31
32	31 08.1	−44.2	143.4	30 19.8	−44.7	143.8	29 31.3	−45.1	144.1	28 42.6	−45.6	144.4	27 53.7	−46.0	144.7	27 04.6	−46.4	145.0	26 15.4	−46.9	145.3	25 26.0	−47.3	145.6	32
33	30 23.9	−44.5	144.2	29 35.1	−44.9	144.5	28 46.2	−45.4	144.8	27 57.0	−45.8	145.2	27 07.7	−46.2	145.5	26 18.2	−46.7	145.7	25 28.5	−47.0	146.0	24 38.7	−47.5	146.3	33
34	29 39.4	−44.7	145.0	28 50.2	−45.2	145.3	28 00.8	−45.6	145.6	27 11.2	−46.0	145.9	26 21.5	−46.5	146.2	25 31.5	−46.8	146.4	24 41.5	−47.3	146.7	23 51.2	−47.6	146.9	34
35	28 54.7	−45.0	145.7	28 05.0	−45.4	146.0	27 15.2	−45.9	146.3	26 25.2	−46.3	146.6	25 35.0	−46.6	146.9	24 44.7	−47.1	147.1	23 54.2	−47.4	147.4	23 03.6	−47.8	147.6	35
36	28 09.7	−45.2	146.5	27 19.6	−45.6	146.8	26 29.3	−46.0	147.0	25 38.9	−46.4	147.3	24 48.4	−46.9	147.6	23 57.6	−47.2	147.8	23 06.8	−47.6	148.0	22 15.8	−47.9	148.3	36
37	27 24.5	−45.5	147.2	26 34.0	−45.9	147.5	25 43.3	−46.3	147.8	24 52.5	−46.7	148.0	24 01.5	−47.0	148.2	23 10.4	−47.4	148.5	22 19.2	−47.7	148.7	21 27.9	−48.1	148.9	37
38	26 39.0	−45.7	148.0	25 48.1	−46.1	148.2	24 57.0	−46.4	148.5	24 05.8	−46.8	148.7	23 14.5	−47.2	148.9	22 23.0	−47.5	149.1	21 31.5	−47.9	149.4	20 39.8	−48.2	149.5	38
39	25 53.3	−45.9	148.7	25 02.0	−46.3	148.9	24 10.6	−46.7	149.2	23 19.0	−47.0	149.4	22 27.3	−47.4	149.6	21 35.5	−47.7	149.8	20 43.6	−48.1	150.0	19 51.6	−48.4	150.2	39
40	25 07.4	−46.1	149.4	24 15.7	−46.4	149.6	23 23.9	−46.8	149.8	22 32.0	−47.2	150.1	21 39.9	−47.5	150.3	20 47.8	−47.9	150.5	19 55.5	−48.1	150.6	19 03.2	−48.5	150.8	40
41	24 21.3	−46.3	150.1	23 29.3	−46.7	150.3	22 37.1	−47.0	150.5	21 44.8	−47.3	150.7	20 52.4	−47.6	150.9	19 59.9	−47.9	151.1	19 07.4	−48.3	151.3	18 14.7	−48.6	151.4	41
42	23 35.0	−46.4	150.8	22 42.6	−46.8	151.0	21 50.1	−47.2	151.2	20 57.5	−47.5	151.4	20 04.8	−47.8	151.6	19 12.0	−48.2	151.7	18 19.1	−48.5	151.9	17 26.1	−48.7	152.0	42
43	22 48.6	−46.7	151.5	21 55.8	−47.0	151.7	21 02.9	−47.3	151.9	20 10.0	−47.6	152.0	19 17.0	−48.0	152.2	18 23.8	−48.2	152.4	17 30.6	−48.5	152.5	16 37.4	−48.8	152.7	43
44	22 01.9	−46.8	152.2	21 08.8	−47.1	152.3	20 15.6	−47.4	152.5	19 22.4	−47.8	152.7	18 29.0	−48.0	152.8	17 35.6	−48.4	153.0	16 42.1	−48.6	153.1	15 48.6	−49.0	153.3	44
45	21 15.1	−47.0	152.8	20 21.7	−47.3	153.0	19 28.2	−47.6	153.2	18 34.6	−47.9	153.3	17 41.0	−48.2	153.5	16 47.2	−48.4	153.6	15 53.5	−48.8	153.7	14 59.6	−49.0	153.9	45
46	20 28.1	−47.1	153.5	19 34.4	−47.4	153.7	18 40.6	−47.7	153.8	17 46.7	−48.0	154.0	16 52.8	−48.3	154.1	15 58.8	−48.6	154.2	15 04.7	−48.8	154.3	14 10.6	−49.1	154.5	46
47	19 41.0	−47.3	154.2	18 47.0	−47.6	154.3	17 52.9	−47.9	154.5	16 58.7	−48.1	154.6	16 04.5	−48.4	154.7	15 10.2	−48.7	154.8	14 15.9	−49.0	154.9	13 21.5	−49.2	155.0	47
48	18 53.7	−47.4	154.8	17 59.4	−47.7	155.0	17 05.0	−47.9	155.1	16 10.6	−48.3	155.2	15 16.1	−48.5	155.3	14 21.5	−48.7	155.4	13 26.9	−49.0	155.5	12 32.3	−49.3	155.6	48
49	18 06.3	−47.5	155.5	17 11.7	−47.8	155.6	16 17.1	−48.1	155.7	15 22.3	−48.3	155.8	14 27.6	−48.6	155.9	13 32.8	−48.9	156.0	12 37.9	−49.1	156.1	11 43.0	−49.3	156.2	49
50	17 18.8	−47.7	156.1	16 23.9	−47.9	156.2	15 29.0	−48.2	156.3	14 34.0	−48.4	156.4	13 39.0	−48.7	156.5	12 43.9	−48.9	156.6	11 48.8	−49.1	156.7	10 53.7	−49.4	156.8	50
51	16 31.1	−47.7	156.7	15 36.0	−48.0	156.8	14 40.8	−48.3	157.0	13 45.6	−48.5	157.1	12 50.3	−48.8	157.1	11 55.0	−49.0	157.2	10 59.7	−49.3	157.3	10 04.3	−49.5	157.4	51
52	15 43.4	−47.9	157.4	14 48.0	−48.2	157.5	13 52.5	−48.3	157.6	12 57.1	−48.7	157.7	12 01.5	−48.8	157.7	11 06.0	−49.1	157.8	10 10.4	−49.3	157.9	9 14.8	−49.5	158.0	52
53	14 55.5	−48.0	158.0	13 59.8	−48.2	158.1	13 04.2	−48.5	158.2	12 08.4	−48.6	158.3	11 12.7	−48.9	158.3	10 16.9	−49.1	158.4	9 21.1	−49.3	158.5	8 25.3	−49.6	158.5	53
54	14 07.5	−48.1	158.6	13 11.6	−48.3	158.7	12 15.7	−48.5	158.8	11 19.8	−48.8	158.9	10 23.8	−49.0	158.9	9 27.8	−49.2	159.0	8 31.8	−49.4	159.0	7 35.7	−49.6	159.1	54
55	13 19.4	−48.1	159.2	12 23.3	−48.4	159.3	11 27.2	−48.6	159.4	10 31.0	−48.8	159.4	9 34.8	−49.0	159.5	8 38.6	−49.2	159.6	7 42.4	−49.5	159.6	6 46.1	−49.6	159.7	55
56	12 31.3	−48.3	159.8	11 34.9	−48.4	159.9	10 38.6	−48.7	160.0	9 42.2	−48.9	160.0	8 45.8	−49.1	160.1	7 49.4	−49.3	160.1	6 52.9	−49.5	160.2	5 56.5	−49.7	160.2	56
57	11 43.0	−48.3	160.4	10 46.5	−48.5	160.5	9 49.9	−48.7	160.6	8 53.3	−48.9	160.6	7 56.7	−49.1	160.7	7 00.1	−49.3	160.7	6 03.4	−49.5	160.8	5 06.8	−49.7	160.8	57
58	10 54.7	−48.4	161.0	9 58.0	−48.6	161.1	9 01.2	−48.8	161.2	8 04.4	−49.0	161.2	7 07.6	−49.2	161.3	6 10.8	−49.4	161.3	5 13.9	−49.5	161.3	4 17.1	−49.8	161.3	58
59	10 06.3	−48.4	161.6	9 09.4	−48.7	161.7	8 12.4	−48.8	161.7	7 15.4	−49.0	161.8	6 18.4	−49.2	161.8	5 21.4	−49.4	161.9	4 24.4	−49.6	161.9	3 27.3	−49.7	161.9	59
60	9 17.9	−48.5	162.2	8 20.7	−48.7	162.3	7 23.6	−48.9	162.3	6 26.4	−49.1	162.4	5 29.2	−49.3	162.4	4 32.0	−49.4	162.4	3 34.8	−49.6	162.5	2 37.6	−49.8	162.5	60
61	8 29.4	−48.6	162.8	7 32.0	−48.7	162.9	6 34.7	−49.0	162.9	5 37.3	−49.1	163.0	4 39.9	−49.2	163.0	3 42.6	−49.5	163.0	2 45.2	−49.6	163.0	1 47.8	−49.8	163.0	61
62	7 40.8	−48.6	163.4	6 43.3	−48.8	163.5	5 45.7	−48.9	163.5	4 48.2	−49.1	163.5	3 50.7	−49.3	163.6	2 53.1	−49.4	163.6	1 55.6	−49.7	163.6	0 58.0	−49.8	163.6	62
63	6 52.2	−48.7	164.0	5 54.5	−48.8	164.1	4 56.8	−49.0	164.1	3 59.1	−49.2	164.1	3 01.4	−49.3	164.1	2 03.7	−49.5	164.1	1 05.9	−49.6	164.1	0 08.2	−49.8	164.1	63
64	6 03.5	−48.7	164.6	5 05.7	−48.9	164.6	4 07.8	−49.0	164.7	3 09.9	−49.1	164.7	2 12.1	−49.4	164.7	1 14.2	−49.5	164.7	0 16.3	−49.6	164.7	0 41.6	+49.7	15.3	64
65	5 14.8	−48.7	165.2	4 16.8	−48.9	165.2	3 18.8	−49.1	165.2	2 20.8	−49.2	165.3	1 22.7	−49.3	165.3	0 24.7	−49.5	165.3	0 33.3	+49.6	14.7	1 31.3	+49.8	14.7	65
66	4 26.1	−48.8	165.8	3 27.9	−48.9	165.8	2 29.7	−49.0	165.8	1 31.6	−49.2	165.8	0 33.4	−49.3	165.8	0 24.8	+49.5	14.2	1 22.9	+49.7	14.2	2 21.1	+49.8	14.2	66
67	3 37.3	−48.8	166.4	2 39.0	−48.9	166.4	1 40.7	−49.1	166.4	0 42.4	−49.2	166.4	0 15.9	+49.4	13.6	1 14.3	+49.4	13.6	2 12.6	+49.6	13.6	3 10.9	+49.7	13.6	67
68	2 48.5	−48.8	167.0	1 50.1	−48.9	167.0	0 51.6	−49.0	167.0	0 06.8	+49.2	13.0	1 05.3	+49.3	13.0	2 03.7	+49.5	13.0	3 02.2	+49.6	13.0	4 00.6	+49.8	13.1	68
69	1 59.7	−48.8	167.5	1 01.2	−49.0	167.5	0 02.6	−49.1	167.5	0 56.0	+49.2	12.5	1 54.6	+49.3	12.5	2 53.2	+49.4	12.5	3 51.8	+49.5	12.5	4 50.4	+49.6	12.5	69
70	1 10.9	−48.8	168.1	0 12.2	−48.9	168.1	0 46.5	+49.1	11.9	1 45.2	+49.2	11.9	2 43.9	+49.3	11.9	3 42.6	+49.5	11.9	4 41.3	+49.6	11.9	5 40.0	+49.7	11.9	70
71	0 22.1	−48.8	168.7	0 36.7	+49.0	11.3	1 35.6	+49.0	11.3	2 34.4	+49.2	11.3	3 33.2	+49.3	11.3	4 32.1	+49.4	11.3	5 30.9	+49.5	11.4	6 29.7	+49.6	11.4	71
72	0 26.7	+48.8	10.7	1 25.7	+48.9	10.7	2 24.6	+49.1	10.7	3 23.6	+49.1	10.7	4 22.5	+49.3	10.7	5 21.5	+49.3	10.8	6 20.4	+49.5	10.8	7 19.3	+49.6	10.8	72
73	1 15.5	+48.8	10.1	2 14.6	+48.9	10.1	3 13.7	+49.0	10.2	4 12.7	+49.1	10.2	5 11.8	+49.2	10.2	6 10.8	+49.4	10.2	7 09.9	+49.4	10.2	8 08.9	+49.6	10.2	73
74	2 04.3	+48.8	9.6	3 03.5	+48.9	9.6	4 02.7	+49.0	9.6	5 01.8	+49.1	9.6	6 01.0	+49.2	9.6	7 00.2	+49.2	9.6	7 59.3	+49.4	9.6	8 58.5	+49.4	9.7	74
75	2 53.1	+48.8	9.0	3 52.4	+48.9	9.0	4 51.7	+48.9	9.0	5 50.9	+49.1	9.0	6 50.2	+49.1	9.0	7 49.4	+49.3	9.0	8 48.7	+49.3	9.1	9 47.9	+49.5	9.1	75
76	3 41.9	+48.8	8.4	4 41.3	+48.8	8.4	5 40.6	+49.0	8.4	6 40.0	+49.0	8.4	7 39.3	+49.1	8.4	8 38.7	+49.2	8.5	9 38.0	+49.3	8.5	10 37.4	+49.3	8.5	76
77	4 30.7	+48.7	7.8	5 30.1	+48.8	7.8	6 29.6	+48.8	7.8	7 29.0	+49.0	7.8	8 28.4	+49.1	7.9	9 27.9	+49.1	7.9	10 27.3	+49.2	7.9	11 26.7	+49.3	7.9	77
78	5 19.4	+48.7	7.2	6 18.9	+48.8	7.2	7 18.4	+48.9	7.2	8 18.0	+48.9	7.3	9 17.5	+49.0	7.3	10 17.0	+49.1	7.3	11 16.5	+49.1	7.3	12 16.0	+49.2	7.4	78
79	6 08.1	+48.6	6.6	7 07.7	+48.7	6.6	8 07.3	+48.8	6.7	9 06.9	+48.8	6.7	10 06.5	+48.9	6.7	11 06.1	+49.0	6.7	12 05.6	+49.1	6.7	13 05.2	+49.2	6.8	79
80	6 56.7	+48.7	6.0	7 56.4	+48.7	6.1	8 56.1	+48.7	6.1	9 55.7	+48.8	6.1	10 55.4	+48.9	6.1	11 55.1	+48.9	6.1	12 54.7	+49.0	6.2	13 54.4	+49.0	6.2	80
81	7 45.4	+48.5	5.5	8 45.1	+48.6	5.5	9 44.8	+48.7	5.5	10 44.5	+48.8	5.5	11 44.3	+48.8	5.5	12 44.0	+48.8	5.5	13 43.7	+48.9	5.6	14 43.4	+49.0	5.6	81
82	8 33.9	+48.5	4.9	9 33.7	+48.6	4.9	10 33.5	+48.6	4.9	11 33.3	+48.6	4.9	12 33.1	+48.7	4.9	13 32.8	+48.8	4.9	14 32.6	+48.8	5.0	15 32.4	+48.8	5.0	82
83	9 22.4	+48.5	4.3	10 22.3	+48.5	4.3	11 22.1	+48.5	4.3	12 21.9	+48.6	4.3	13 21.8	+48.6	4.3	14 21.6	+48.7	4.3	15 21.4	+48.7	4.4	16 21.2	+48.8	4.4	83
84	10 10.9	+48.4	3.7	11 10.8	+48.4	3.7	12 10.6	+48.5	3.7	13 10.5	+48.5	3.7	14 10.4	+48.5	3.7	15 10.3	+48.5	3.7	16 10.1	+48.6	3.8	17 10.0	+48.7	3.8	84
85	10 59.3	+48.3	3.1	11 59.2	+48.3	3.1	12 59.1	+48.4	3.1	13 59.0	+48.4	3.1	14 58.9	+48.5	3.1	15 58.8	+48.5	3.1	16 58.7	+48.5	3.1	17 58.7	+48.5	3.2	85
86	11 47.6	+48.2	2.5	12 47.5	+48.3	2.5	13 47.5	+48.3	2.5	14 47.4	+48.3	2.5	15 47.4	+48.3	2.5	16 47.3	+48.4	2.5	17 47.2	+48.4	2.5	18 47.2	+48.4	2.5	86
87	12 35.8	+48.2	1.8	13 35.8	+48.2	1.9	14 35.8	+48.1	1.9	15 35.7	+48.2	1.9	16 35.7	+48.2	1.9	17 35.7	+48.2	1.9	18 35.6	+48.3	1.9	19 35.6	+48.3	1.9	87
88	13 24.0	+48.0	1.2	14 24.0	+48.0	1.2	15 23.9	+48.1	1.2	16 23.9	+48.1	1.3	17 23.9	+48.1	1.3	18 23.9	+48.1	1.3	19 23.9	+48.1	1.3	20 23.9	+48.1	1.3	88
89	14 12.0	+48.0	0.6	15 12.0	+48.0	0.6	16 12.0	+48.0	0.6	17 12.0	+48.0	0.6	18 12.0	+48.0	0.6	19 12.0	+48.0	0.6	20 12.0	+48.0	0.6	21 12.0	+48.0	0.6	89
90	15 00.0	+47.9	0.0	16 00.0	+47.9	0.0	17 00.0	+47.9	0.0	18 00.0	+47.9	0.0	19 00.0	+47.9	0.0	20 00.0	+47.8	0.0	21 00.0	+47.8	0.0	22 00.0	+47.8	0.0	90
	15°			16°			17°			18°			19°			20°			21°			22°			

S. Lat. {L.H.A. greater than 180° ....Zn=180°−Z; L.H.A. less than 180°...........Zn=180°+Z}

LATITUDE **SAME** NAME AS DECLINATION — **L.H.A. 143°, 217°**

77

38°, 322° L.H.A. LATITUDE SAME NAME AS DECLINATION N. Lat. {L.H.A. greater than 180° .....Zn=Z; L.H.A. less than 180°............Zn=360°–Z}

Dec.	15° Hc	d	Z	16° Hc	d	Z	17° Hc	d	Z	18° Hc	d	Z	19° Hc	d	Z	20° Hc	d	Z	21° Hc	d	Z	22° Hc	d	Z	Dec.
°	° ′	′	°	° ′	′	°	° ′	′	°	° ′	′	°	° ′	′	°	° ′	′	°	° ′	′	°	° ′	′	°	°
0	49 34.0	+23.4	108.3	49 14.6	+24.8	109.4	48 54.1	+26.2	110.5	48 32.5	+27.6	111.6	48 10.0	+28.8	112.6	47 46.4	+30.1	113.6	47 21.8	+31.4	114.6	46 56.4	+32.5	115.6	0
1	49 57.4	+22.4	106.9	49 39.4	+23.8	108.0	49 20.3	+25.2	109.1	49 00.1	+26.5	110.2	48 38.8	+27.9	111.3	48 16.5	+29.2	112.3	47 53.2	+30.4	113.4	47 28.9	+31.7	114.4	1
2	50 19.8	+21.2	105.5	50 03.2	+22.7	106.6	49 45.5	+24.2	107.7	49 26.6	+25.6	108.9	49 06.7	+27.0	110.0	48 45.7	+28.3	111.0	48 23.6	+29.6	112.1	48 00.6	+30.8	113.1	2
3	50 41.0	+20.2	104.0	50 25.9	+21.7	105.2	50 09.7	+23.1	106.3	49 52.2	+24.6	107.5	49 33.7	+25.9	108.6	49 14.0	+27.3	109.7	48 53.2	+28.7	110.8	48 31.4	+30.0	111.8	3
4	51 01.2	+18.9	102.5	50 47.6	+20.5	103.7	50 32.8	+22.0	104.9	50 16.8	+23.5	106.0	49 59.6	+25.0	107.2	49 41.3	+26.4	108.3	49 21.9	+27.8	109.4	49 01.4	+29.1	110.5	4
5	51 20.1	+17.8	101.0	51 08.1	+19.4	102.2	50 54.8	+20.9	103.4	50 40.3	+22.4	104.6	50 24.6	+23.9	105.8	50 07.7	+25.3	106.9	49 49.7	+26.7	108.1	49 30.5	+28.1	109.2	5
6	51 37.9	+16.6	99.4	51 27.5	+18.1	100.7	51 15.7	+19.7	101.9	51 02.7	+21.3	103.1	50 48.5	+22.8	104.3	50 33.0	+24.3	105.5	50 16.4	+25.7	106.7	49 58.6	+27.2	107.8	6
7	51 54.5	+15.4	97.9	51 45.6	+17.0	99.2	51 35.4	+18.6	100.4	51 24.0	+20.1	101.6	51 11.3	+21.6	102.9	50 57.3	+23.2	104.1	50 42.1	+24.7	105.2	50 25.8	+26.1	106.4	7
8	52 09.9	+14.0	96.3	52 02.6	+15.7	97.6	51 54.0	+17.3	98.9	51 44.1	+19.0	100.1	51 32.9	+20.5	101.4	51 20.5	+22.0	102.6	51 06.8	+23.6	103.8	50 51.9	+25.0	105.0	8
9	52 23.9	+12.8	94.7	52 18.3	+14.5	96.0	52 11.3	+16.1	97.3	52 03.1	+17.7	98.6	51 53.4	+19.4	99.8	51 42.5	+21.0	101.1	51 30.4	+22.4	102.3	51 16.9	+24.0	103.5	9
10	52 36.7	+11.5	93.1	52 32.8	+13.1	94.4	52 27.4	+14.9	95.7	52 20.8	+16.5	97.0	52 12.8	+18.1	98.3	52 03.5	+19.7	99.6	51 52.8	+21.3	100.8	51 40.9	+22.9	102.1	10
11	52 48.2	+10.1	91.5	52 45.9	+11.8	92.8	52 42.3	+13.5	94.1	52 37.3	+15.2	95.4	52 30.9	+16.9	96.7	52 23.2	+18.5	98.0	52 14.1	+20.1	99.3	52 03.8	+21.7	100.6	11
12	52 58.3	+8.8	89.9	52 57.7	+10.5	91.2	52 55.8	+12.2	92.5	52 52.5	+13.9	93.8	52 47.8	+15.5	95.2	52 41.7	+17.2	96.5	52 34.2	+18.9	97.8	52 25.5	+20.5	99.1	12
13	53 07.1	+7.4	88.2	53 08.2	+9.2	89.6	53 08.0	+10.9	90.9	53 06.4	+12.5	92.2	53 03.3	+14.3	93.6	52 58.9	+16.0	94.9	52 53.1	+17.7	96.2	52 46.0	+19.2	97.5	13
14	53 14.5	+6.0	86.6	53 17.4	+7.7	87.9	53 18.9	+9.5	89.3	53 18.9	+11.3	90.6	53 17.6	+13.0	91.9	53 14.9	+14.6	93.3	53 10.8	+16.3	94.6	53 05.2	+18.1	95.9	14
15	53 20.5	+4.6	84.9	53 25.1	+6.4	86.2	53 28.4	+8.1	87.6	53 30.2	+9.8	88.9	53 30.6	+11.6	90.3	53 29.5	+13.4	91.6	53 27.1	+15.0	93.0	53 23.3	+16.7	94.3	15
16	53 25.1	+3.3	83.2	53 31.5	+5.0	84.6	53 36.5	+6.7	85.9	53 40.0	+8.5	87.3	53 42.2	+10.2	88.6	53 42.9	+11.9	90.0	53 42.1	+13.7	91.4	53 40.0	+15.4	92.7	16
17	53 28.4	+1.8	81.6	53 36.5	+3.5	82.9	53 43.2	+5.3	84.3	53 48.5	+7.0	85.6	53 52.4	+8.8	87.0	53 54.8	+10.6	88.3	53 55.8	+12.3	89.7	53 55.4	+14.1	91.1	17
18	53 30.2	+0.4	79.9	53 40.0	+2.2	81.2	53 48.5	+3.9	82.6	53 55.5	+5.7	83.9	54 01.2	+7.4	85.3	54 05.4	+9.1	86.7	54 08.1	+11.0	88.1	54 09.5	+12.6	89.4	18
19	53 30.6	−1.1	78.2	53 42.2	+0.7	79.5	53 52.4	+2.4	80.9	54 01.2	+4.2	82.2	54 08.6	+5.9	83.6	54 14.5	+7.8	85.0	54 19.1	+9.5	86.4	54 22.1	+11.3	87.8	19
20	53 29.5	−2.4	76.5	53 42.9	−0.8	77.8	53 54.8	+1.0	79.2	54 05.4	+2.7	80.5	54 14.5	+4.6	81.9	54 22.3	+6.3	83.3	54 28.6	+8.0	84.7	54 33.4	+9.9	86.1	20
21	53 27.1	−3.8	74.8	53 42.1	−2.1	76.2	53 55.8	−0.4	77.5	54 08.1	+1.4	78.8	54 19.1	+3.0	80.2	54 28.6	+4.8	81.6	54 36.6	+6.7	83.0	54 43.3	+8.4	84.4	21
22	53 23.3	−5.3	73.2	53 40.0	−3.6	74.5	53 55.4	−1.9	75.8	54 09.5	−0.2	77.1	54 22.1	+1.6	78.5	54 33.4	+3.4	79.9	54 43.3	+5.1	81.2	54 51.7	+6.9	82.7	22
23	53 18.0	−6.6	71.5	53 36.4	−4.9	72.8	53 53.5	−3.3	74.1	54 09.3	−1.6	75.4	54 23.7	+0.2	76.8	54 36.8	+1.9	78.1	54 48.4	+3.7	79.5	54 58.6	+5.5	80.9	23
24	53 11.4	−8.0	69.8	53 31.5	−6.4	71.1	53 50.2	−4.7	72.4	54 07.7	−3.0	73.7	54 23.9	−1.3	75.0	54 38.7	+0.4	76.4	54 52.1	+2.2	77.8	55 04.1	+3.9	79.2	24
25	53 03.4	−9.4	68.2	53 25.1	−7.8	69.4	53 45.5	−6.1	70.7	54 04.7	−4.5	72.0	54 22.6	−2.8	73.3	54 39.1	−1.0	74.7	54 54.3	+0.7	76.0	55 08.0	+2.5	77.4	25
26	52 54.0	−10.7	66.5	53 17.3	−9.1	67.8	53 39.4	−7.5	69.0	54 00.2	−5.9	70.3	54 19.8	−4.2	71.6	54 38.1	−2.5	73.0	54 55.0	−0.8	74.3	55 10.5	+1.0	75.7	26
27	52 43.3	−12.1	64.9	53 08.2	−10.6	66.1	53 31.9	−9.0	67.4	53 54.3	−7.3	68.6	54 15.6	−5.7	69.9	54 35.6	−4.0	71.2	54 54.2	−2.3	72.6	55 11.5	−0.5	73.9	27
28	52 31.2	−13.3	63.3	52 57.6	−11.8	64.5	53 22.9	−10.3	65.7	53 47.0	−8.7	66.9	54 09.9	−7.1	68.2	54 31.6	−5.5	69.5	54 51.9	−3.7	70.8	55 11.0	−2.1	72.2	28
29	52 17.9	−14.6	61.7	52 45.8	−13.2	62.9	53 12.6	−11.6	64.0	53 38.3	−10.1	65.3	54 02.8	−8.5	66.5	54 26.1	−6.9	67.8	54 48.2	−5.3	69.1	55 08.9	−3.5	70.4	29
30	52 03.3	−15.9	60.1	52 32.6	−14.4	61.2	53 01.0	−13.0	62.4	53 28.2	−11.5	63.6	53 54.3	−9.9	64.8	54 19.2	−8.3	66.1	54 42.9	−6.7	67.4	55 05.4	−5.1	68.7	30
31	51 47.4	−17.1	58.6	52 18.2	−15.8	59.7	52 48.0	−14.3	60.8	53 16.7	−12.8	62.0	53 44.4	−11.3	63.2	54 10.9	−9.8	64.4	54 36.2	−8.1	65.7	55 00.3	−6.5	67.0	31
32	51 30.3	−18.4	57.0	52 02.4	−16.9	58.1	52 33.7	−15.6	59.2	53 03.9	−14.1	60.3	53 33.1	−12.7	61.5	54 01.1	−11.1	62.7	54 28.1	−9.6	63.9	54 53.8	−8.0	65.2	32
33	51 11.9	−19.5	55.5	51 45.5	−18.2	56.5	52 18.1	−16.8	57.6	52 49.8	−15.5	58.7	53 20.4	−14.0	59.9	53 50.0	−12.5	61.0	54 18.5	−11.0	62.3	54 45.8	−9.4	63.5	33
34	50 52.4	−20.6	54.0	51 27.3	−19.4	55.0	52 01.3	−18.1	56.0	52 34.3	−16.7	57.1	53 06.4	−15.3	58.2	53 37.5	−13.9	59.4	54 07.5	−12.4	60.6	54 36.4	−10.8	61.8	34
35	50 31.8	−21.7	52.5	51 07.9	−20.5	53.5	51 43.2	−19.3	54.5	52 17.6	−18.0	55.5	52 51.1	−16.6	56.6	53 23.6	−15.2	57.7	53 55.1	−13.8	58.9	54 25.6	−12.3	60.1	35
36	50 10.1	−22.9	51.0	50 47.4	−21.7	52.0	51 23.9	−20.4	53.0	51 59.6	−19.1	54.0	52 34.5	−17.9	55.0	53 08.4	−16.5	56.1	53 41.3	−15.1	57.3	54 13.3	−13.7	58.4	36
37	49 47.2	−23.9	49.6	50 25.7	−22.7	50.5	51 03.5	−21.6	51.5	51 40.5	−20.4	52.5	52 16.6	−19.1	53.5	52 51.9	−17.8	54.5	53 26.2	−16.4	55.6	53 59.6	−15.0	56.8	37
38	49 23.3	−24.9	48.2	50 03.0	−23.8	49.1	50 41.9	−22.6	50.0	51 20.1	−21.5	50.9	51 57.5	−20.2	51.9	52 34.1	−19.0	53.0	53 09.8	−17.7	54.0	53 44.6	−16.3	55.1	38
39	48 58.4	−25.8	46.8	49 39.2	−24.8	47.6	50 19.3	−23.8	48.5	50 58.6	−22.6	49.5	51 37.3	−21.5	50.4	52 15.1	−20.2	51.4	52 52.1	−18.9	52.4	53 28.3	−17.7	53.5	39
40	48 32.6	−26.9	45.4	49 14.4	−25.9	46.2	49 55.5	−24.8	47.1	50 36.0	−23.7	48.0	51 15.8	−22.5	48.9	51 54.9	−21.4	49.9	52 33.2	−20.2	50.9	53 10.6	−18.9	51.9	40
41	48 05.7	−27.8	44.1	48 48.5	−26.8	44.9	49 30.7	−25.8	45.7	50 12.3	−24.7	46.5	50 53.3	−23.7	47.4	51 33.5	−22.6	48.4	52 13.0	−21.4	49.3	52 51.7	−20.2	50.3	41
42	47 37.9	−28.6	42.8	48 21.7	−27.7	43.5	49 04.9	−26.7	44.3	49 47.6	−25.8	45.1	50 29.6	−24.7	46.0	51 10.9	−23.6	46.9	51 51.6	−22.5	47.8	52 31.5	−21.3	48.8	42
43	47 09.3	−29.6	41.5	47 54.0	−28.7	42.2	48 38.2	−27.7	42.9	49 21.8	−26.7	43.7	50 04.9	−25.8	44.6	50 47.3	−24.7	45.4	51 29.1	−23.7	46.3	52 10.2	−22.5	47.2	43
44	46 39.7	−30.3	40.2	47 25.3	−29.5	40.9	48 10.5	−28.7	41.6	48 55.1	−27.8	42.4	49 39.1	−26.7	43.2	50 22.6	−25.8	44.0	51 05.4	−24.7	44.8	51 47.7	−23.7	45.7	44
45	46 09.4	−31.2	38.9	46 55.8	−30.3	39.6	47 41.8	−29.5	40.3	48 27.3	−28.6	41.0	49 12.4	−27.8	41.8	49 56.8	−26.8	42.6	50 40.7	−25.8	43.4	51 24.0	−24.8	44.3	45
46	45 38.2	−31.9	37.7	46 25.5	−31.2	38.3	47 12.3	−30.3	39.0	47 58.7	−29.5	39.7	48 44.6	−28.6	40.4	49 30.0	−27.7	41.2	50 14.9	−26.8	42.0	50 59.2	−25.8	42.8	46
47	45 06.3	−32.7	36.5	45 54.3	−31.9	37.1	46 42.0	−31.2	37.8	47 29.2	−30.4	38.4	48 16.0	−29.6	39.1	49 02.3	−28.7	39.8	49 48.1	−27.8	40.6	50 33.4	−26.8	41.4	47
48	44 33.6	−33.4	35.3	45 22.4	−32.7	35.9	46 10.8	−32.0	36.5	46 58.8	−31.2	37.1	47 46.4	−30.4	37.8	48 33.6	−29.6	38.5	49 20.3	−28.7	39.2	50 06.6	−27.9	40.0	48
49	44 00.2	−34.1	34.2	44 49.7	−33.4	34.7	45 38.8	−32.7	35.3	46 27.6	−32.0	35.9	47 16.0	−31.2	36.5	48 04.0	−30.4	37.2	48 51.6	−29.6	37.9	49 38.7	−28.7	38.6	49
50	43 26.1	−34.8	33.0	44 16.3	−34.2	33.6	45 06.1	−33.5	34.1	45 55.6	−32.8	34.7	46 44.8	−32.1	35.3	47 33.6	−31.3	35.9	48 22.0	−30.6	36.6	49 10.0	−29.8	37.2	50
51	42 51.3	−35.4	31.9	43 42.1	−34.8	32.4	44 32.6	−34.1	32.9	45 22.8	−33.5	33.5	46 12.7	−32.8	34.0	47 02.3	−32.1	34.6	47 51.4	−31.3	35.3	48 40.2	−30.6	35.9	51
52	42 15.9	−36.0	30.8	43 07.3	−35.4	31.3	43 58.5	−34.9	31.8	44 49.3	−34.2	32.3	45 39.9	−33.6	32.8	46 30.2	−32.9	33.4	47 20.1	−32.2	34.0	48 09.6	−31.4	34.6	52
53	41 39.9	−36.6	29.7	42 31.9	−36.0	30.2	43 23.6	−35.4	30.7	44 15.1	−34.9	31.1	45 06.3	−34.2	31.7	45 57.3	−33.7	32.2	46 47.9	−33.0	32.8	47 38.2	−32.3	33.4	53
54	41 03.3	−37.2	28.7	41 55.9	−36.7	29.1	42 48.2	−36.1	29.6	43 40.2	−35.5	30.0	44 32.1	−35.0	30.5	45 23.6	−34.3	31.0	46 14.9	−33.7	31.6	47 05.9	−33.1	32.1	54
55	40 26.1	−37.7	27.6	41 19.2	−37.2	28.0	42 12.1	−36.8	28.5	43 04.7	−36.2	28.9	43 57.1	−35.6	29.4	44 49.3	−35.1	29.9	45 41.2	−34.5	30.4	46 32.8	−33.9	30.9	55
56	39 48.4	−38.2	26.6	40 42.0	−37.8	27.0	41 35.3	−37.2	27.4	42 28.5	−36.8	27.8	43 21.5	−36.3	28.3	44 14.2	−35.7	28.7	45 06.7	−35.2	29.2	45 58.9	−34.6	29.7	56
57	39 10.2	−38.8	25.6	40 04.2	−38.3	26.0	40 58.1	−37.9	26.4	41 51.7	−37.3	26.8	42 45.2	−36.9	27.2	43 38.5	−36.4	27.6	44 31.5	−35.8	28.1	45 24.4	−35.3	28.5	57
58	38 31.4	−39.2	24.6	39 25.9	−38.8	25.0	40 20.2	−38.4	25.3	41 14.4	−38.0	25.7	42 08.3	−37.4	26.1	43 02.1	−37.0	26.5	43 55.7	−36.5	26.9	44 49.1	−36.0	27.4	58
59	37 52.2	−39.7	23.7	38 47.1	−39.3	24.0	39 41.8	−38.8	24.3	40 36.4	−38.4	24.7	41 30.9	−38.0	25.1	42 25.1	−37.5	25.4	43 19.2	−37.1	25.8	44 13.1	−36.6	26.3	59
60	37 12.5	−40.1	22.7	38 07.8	−39.7	23.0	39 03.0	−39.4	23.4	39 58.0	−39.0	23.7	40 52.9	−38.6	24.0	41 47.6	−38.1	24.4	42 42.1	−37.6	24.8	43 36.5	−37.2	25.2	60
61	36 32.4	−40.5	21.8	37 28.1	−40.2	22.1	38 23.6	−39.8	22.4	39 19.0	−39.4	22.7	40 14.3	−39.1	23.0	41 09.5	−38.7	23.4	42 04.5	−38.3	23.7	42 59.3	−37.8	24.1	61
62	35 51.9	−41.0	20.9	36 47.9	−40.7	21.2	37 43.8	−40.3	21.4	38 39.6	−40.0	21.7	39 35.2	−39.5	22.0	40 30.8	−39.2	22.3	41 26.2	−38.8	22.7	42 21.5	−38.4	23.0	62
63	35 10.9	−41.4	20.0	36 07.2	−41.0	20.2	37 03.5	−40.7	20.5	37 59.6	−40.4	20.8	38 55.7	−40.1	21.1	39 51.6	−39.7	21.4	40 47.4	−39.3	21.7	41 43.1	−38.9	22.0	63
64	34 29.5	−41.7	19.1	35 26.2	−41.4	19.3	36 22.8	−41.2	19.6	37 19.2	−40.8	19.8	38 15.6	−40.5	20.1	39 11.9	−40.1	20.4	40 08.1	−39.8	20.7	41 04.2	−39.4	21.0	64
65	33 47.8	−42.1	18.2	34 44.8	−41.9	18.5	35 41.6	−41.5	18.7	36 38.4	−41.2	18.9	37 35.1	−40.9	19.2	38 31.8	−40.6	19.4	39 28.3	−40.3	19.7	40 24.8	−40.0	20.0	65
66	33 05.7	−42.4	17.4	34 02.9	−42.1	17.6	35 00.1	−41.9	17.8	35 57.2	−41.6	18.0	36 54.2	−41.3	18.2	37 51.2	−41.1	18.5	38 48.0	−40.7	18.7	39 44.8	−40.4	19.0	66
67	32 23.3	−42.8	16.6	33 20.8	−42.5	16.7	34 18.2	−42.3	16.9	35 15.6	−42.0	17.1	36 12.9	−41.8	17.3	37 10.1	−41.4	17.6	38 07.3	−41.2	17.8	39 04.4	−40.9	18.1	67
68	31 40.5	−43.0	15.7	32 38.3	−42.9	15.9	33 35.9	−42.6	16.1	34 33.6	−42.4	16.3	35 31.1	−42.1	16.5	36 28.7	−41.9	16.7	37 26.1	−41.6	16.9	38 23.5	−41.4	17.1	68
69	30 57.5	−43.4	14.9	31 55.4	−43.1	15.1	32 53.3	−42.9	15.2	33 51.2	−42.7	15.4	34 49.0	−42.5	15.6	35 46.8	−42.3	15.8	36 44.5	−42.0	16.0	37 42.1	−41.7	16.2	69
70	30 14.1	−43.7	14.1	31 12.3	−43.5	14.3	32 10.4	−43.3	14.4	33 08.5	−43.1	14.6	34 06.5	−42.8	14.7	35 04.5	−42.6	14.9	36 02.5	−42.4	15.1	37 00.4	−42.2	15.3	70
71	29 30.4	−43.9	13.3	30 28.8	−43.8	13.4	31 27.1	−43.6	13.6	32 25.4	−43.4	13.7	33 23.7	−43.2	13.9	34 21.9	−43.0	14.1	35 20.1	−42.8	14.2	36 18.2	−42.5	14.4	71
72	28 46.5	−44.2	12.5	29 45.0	−44.0	12.7	30 43.5	−43.8	12.8	31 42.0	−43.6	12.9	32 40.5	−43.5	13.1	33 38.9	−43.3	13.2	34 37.3	−43.1	13.4	35 35.7	−42.9	13.5	72
73	28 02.3	−44.5	11.8	29 01.0	−44.3	11.9	29 59.7	−44.2	12.0	30 58.4	−44.0	12.1	31 57.0	−43.8	12.2	32 55.6	−43.6	12.4	33 54.2	−43.4	12.5	34 52.8	−43.3	12.7	73
74	27 17.8	−44.7	11.0	28 16.7	−44.6	11.1	29 15.5	−44.4	11.2	30 14.4	−44.3	11.3	31 13.2	−44.1	11.4	32 12.0	−43.9	11.6	33 10.8	−43.8	11.7	34 09.5	−43.6	11.8	74
75	26 33.1	−44.9	10.3	27 32.1	−44.8	10.4	28 31.1	−44.6	10.4	29 30.1	−44.5	10.5	30 29.1	−44.4	10.7	31 28.1	−44.3	10.8	32 27.0	−44.1	10.9	33 25.9	−43.9	11.0	75
76	25 48.2	−45.2	9.5	26 47.3	−45.0	9.6	27 46.5	−44.9	9.7	28 45.6	−44.8	9.8	29 44.7	−44.6	9.9	30 43.8	−44.5	10.0	31 42.9	−44.4	10.1	32 42.0	−44.3	10.2	76
77	25 03.0	−45.4	8.8	26 02.3	−45.3	8.9	27 01.6	−45.2	8.9	28 00.8	−45.0	9.0	29 00.1	−44.9	9.1	29 59.3	−44.8	9.2	30 58.5	−44.6	9.3	31 57.7	−44.5	9.4	77
78	24 17.6	−45.5	8.1	25 17.0	−45.4	8.1	26 16.4	−45.3	8.2	27 15.8	−45.3	8.3	28 15.2	−45.2	8.4	29 14.5	−45.0	8.4	30 13.9	−45.0	8.5	31 13.2	−44.8	8.6	78
79	23 32.1	−45.8	7.4	24 31.6	−45.7	7.4	25 31.1	−45.6	7.5	26 30.5	−45.4	7.5	27 30.0	−45.4	7.6	28 29.5	−45.3	7.7	29 28.9	−45.1	7.8	30 28.4	−45.1	7.8	79
80	22 46.3	−45.9	6.7	23 45.9	−45.9	6.7	24 45.5	−45.8	6.8	25 45.1	−45.7	6.8	26 44.6	−45.6	6.9	27 44.2	−45.5	6.9	28 43.8	−45.5	7.0	29 43.3	−45.3	7.1	80
81	22 00.4	−46.2	6.0	23 00.0	−46.0	6.0	23 59.7	−46.0	6.1	24 59.4	−45.9	6.1	25 59.0	−45.8	6.2	26 58.7	−45.8	6.2	27 58.3	−45.7	6.3	28 58.0	−45.6	6.3	81
82	21 14.2	−46.2	5.3	22 14.0	−46.2	5.3	23 13.7	−46.1	5.4	24 13.5	−46.1	5.4	25 13.2	−46.0	5.4	26 12.9	−45.9	5.5	27 12.6	−45.8	5.5	28 12.4	−45.9	5.6	82
83	20 28.0	−46.5	4.6	21 27.8	−46.4	4.6	22 27.6	−46.4	4.7	23 27.4	−46.3	4.7	24 27.2	−46.3	4.7	25 27.0	−46.2	4.8	26 26.8	−46.2	4.8	27 26.5	−46.0	4.8	83
84	19 41.5	−46.6	3.9	20 41.4	−46.6	3.9	21 41.2	−46.5	4.0	22 41.1	−46.5	4.0	23 40.9	−46.4	4.0	24 40.8	−46.4	4.1	25 40.6	−46.3	4.1	26 40.5	−46.3	4.1	84
85	18 54.9	−46.7	3.3	19 54.8	−46.7	3.3	20 54.7	−46.6	3.3	21 54.6	−46.6	3.3	22 54.5	−46.6	3.3	23 54.4	−46.5	3.4	24 54.3	−46.5	3.4	25 54.2	−46.5	3.4	85
86	18 08.2	−46.9	2.6	19 08.1	−46.8	2.6	20 08.1	−46.8	2.6	21 08.0	−46.8	2.6	22 07.9	−46.7	2.7	23 07.9	−46.7	2.7	24 07.8	−46.7	2.7	25 07.7	−46.6	2.7	86
87	17 21.3	−47.0	1.9	18 21.3	−47.0	1.9	19 21.3	−47.0	2.0	20 21.2	−46.9	2.0	21 21.2	−46.9	2.0	22 21.2	−46.9	2.0	23 21.1	−46.9	2.0	24 21.1	−46.9	2.0	87
88	16 34.3	−47.1	1.3	17 34.3	−47.1	1.3	18 34.3	−47.1	1.3	19 34.3	−47.1	1.3	20 34.3	−47.1	1.3	21 34.3	−47.1	1.3	22 34.2	−47.0	1.3	23 34.2	−47.0	1.3	88
89	15 47.2	−47.2	0.6	16 47.2	−47.2	0.6	17 47.2	−47.2	0.6	18 47.2	−47.2	0.7	19 47.2	−47.2	0.7	20 47.2	−47.2	0.7	21 47.2	−47.2	0.7	22 47.2	−47.2	0.7	89
90	15 00.0	−47.3	0.0	16 00.0	−47.3	0.0	17 00.0	−47.3	0.0	18 00.0	−47.3	0.0	19 00.0	−47.3	0.0	20 00.0	−47.4	0.0	21 00.0	−47.4	0.0	22 00.0	−47.4	0.0	90
	15°			16°			17°			18°			19°			20°			21°			22°			

38°, 322° L.H.A. LATITUDE SAME NAME AS DECLINATION

78

LATITUDE **CONTRARY** NAME TO DECLINATION L.H.A. 38°, 322°

Dec.	15° Hc	d	Z	16° Hc	d	Z	17° Hc	d	Z	18° Hc	d	Z	Dec.
°	° ′	′	°	° ′	′	°	° ′	′	°	° ′	′	°	°
0	49 34.0	-24.5	108.3	49 14.6	-25.8	109.4	48 54.1	-27.2	110.5	48 32.5	-28.4	111.6	0
1	49 09.5	-25.4	109.7	48 48.8	-26.8	110.8	48 26.9	-28.1	111.9	48 04.1	-29.4	112.9	1
2	48 44.1	-26.4	111.1	48 22.0	-27.8	112.2	47 58.8	-29.0	113.2	47 34.7	-30.2	114.2	2
3	48 17.7	-27.4	112.5	47 54.2	-28.6	113.5	47 29.8	-29.8	114.5	47 04.5	-31.1	115.5	3
4	47 50.3	-28.3	113.8	47 25.6	-29.5	114.8	47 00.0	-30.7	115.8	46 33.4	-31.8	116.7	4
5	47 22.0	-29.1	115.1	46 56.1	-30.3	116.1	46 29.3	-31.5	117.0	46 01.6	-32.7	118.0	5
6	46 52.9	-30.0	116.4	46 25.8	-31.2	117.3	45 57.8	-32.3	118.3	45 28.9	-33.3	119.2	6
7	46 22.9	-30.8	117.7	45 54.6	-31.9	118.6	45 25.5	-33.0	119.5	44 55.6	-34.1	120.3	7
8	45 52.1	-31.7	118.9	45 22.7	-32.7	119.8	44 52.5	-33.8	120.6	44 21.5	-34.8	121.5	8
9	45 20.4	-32.3	120.1	44 50.0	-33.5	121.0	44 18.7	-34.4	121.8	43 46.7	-35.4	122.6	9
10	44 48.1	-33.1	121.3	44 16.5	-34.1	122.1	43 44.3	-35.1	122.9	43 11.3	-36.1	123.7	10
11	44 15.0	-33.8	122.5	43 42.4	-34.8	123.3	43 09.2	-35.8	124.1	42 35.2	-36.6	124.8	11
12	43 41.2	-34.5	123.6	43 07.6	-35.4	124.4	42 33.4	-36.3	125.2	41 58.6	-37.3	125.9	12
13	43 06.7	-35.1	124.7	42 32.2	-36.0	125.5	41 57.1	-37.0	126.2	41 21.3	-37.8	126.9	13
14	42 31.6	-35.7	125.8	41 56.2	-36.7	126.6	41 20.1	-37.5	127.3	40 43.5	-38.4	128.0	14
15	41 55.9	-36.4	126.9	41 19.5	-37.2	127.6	40 42.6	-38.1	128.3	40 05.1	-38.9	129.0	15
16	41 19.5	-36.9	128.0	40 42.3	-37.8	128.7	40 04.5	-38.5	129.3	39 26.2	-39.3	130.0	16
17	40 42.6	-37.5	129.0	40 04.5	-38.3	129.7	39 26.0	-39.1	130.3	38 46.9	-39.9	131.0	17
18	40 05.1	-38.0	130.1	39 26.2	-38.8	130.7	38 46.9	-39.6	131.3	38 07.0	-40.3	131.9	18
19	39 27.1	-38.5	131.1	38 47.4	-39.2	131.7	38 07.3	-40.0	132.3	37 26.7	-40.7	132.8	19
20	38 48.6	-39.0	132.1	38 08.2	-39.8	132.6	37 27.3	-40.5	133.2	36 46.0	-41.2	133.8	20
21	38 09.6	-39.5	133.0	37 28.4	-40.2	133.6	36 46.8	-40.9	134.1	36 04.8	-41.5	134.7	21
22	37 30.1	-40.0	134.0	36 48.2	-40.6	134.5	36 05.9	-41.3	135.1	35 23.3	-42.0	135.6	22
23	36 50.1	-40.3	134.9	36 07.6	-41.1	135.4	35 24.6	-41.6	135.9	34 41.3	-42.3	136.4	23
24	36 09.8	-40.8	135.8	35 26.5	-41.4	136.3	34 43.0	-42.1	136.8	33 59.0	-42.6	137.3	24
25	35 29.0	-41.2	136.7	34 45.1	-41.8	137.2	34 00.9	-42.4	137.7	33 16.4	-43.0	138.1	25
26	34 47.8	-41.6	137.6	34 03.3	-42.2	138.1	33 18.5	-42.8	138.5	32 33.4	-43.3	139.0	26
27	34 06.2	-41.9	138.5	33 21.1	-42.5	139.0	32 35.7	-43.0	139.4	31 50.1	-43.7	139.8	27
28	33 24.3	-42.3	139.4	32 38.6	-42.8	139.8	31 52.7	-43.4	140.2	31 06.4	-43.9	140.6	28
29	32 42.0	-42.6	140.2	31 55.8	-43.2	140.6	31 09.3	-43.7	141.0	30 22.5	-44.2	141.4	29
30	31 59.4	-42.9	141.0	31 12.6	-43.4	141.4	30 25.6	-44.0	141.8	29 38.3	-44.5	142.2	30
31	31 16.5	-43.3	141.9	30 29.2	-43.8	142.2	29 41.6	-44.2	142.6	28 53.8	-44.7	142.9	31
32	30 33.2	-43.5	142.7	29 45.4	-44.0	143.0	28 57.4	-44.6	143.4	28 09.1	-45.0	143.7	32
33	29 49.7	-43.8	143.5	29 01.4	-44.3	143.8	28 12.8	-44.7	144.1	27 24.1	-45.2	144.4	33
34	29 05.9	-44.1	144.3	28 17.1	-44.6	144.6	27 28.1	-45.0	144.9	26 38.9	-45.4	145.2	34
35	28 21.8	-44.4	145.0	27 32.5	-44.8	145.3	26 43.1	-45.3	145.6	25 53.5	-45.7	145.9	35
36	27 37.4	-44.6	145.8	26 47.7	-45.0	146.1	25 57.8	-45.4	146.4	25 07.8	-45.9	146.6	36
37	26 52.8	-44.8	146.5	26 02.7	-45.3	146.8	25 12.4	-45.7	147.1	24 21.9	-46.0	147.3	37
38	26 08.0	-45.1	147.3	25 17.4	-45.4	147.5	24 26.7	-45.8	147.8	23 35.9	-46.3	148.0	38
39	25 22.9	-45.3	148.0	24 32.0	-45.7	148.3	23 40.9	-46.1	148.5	22 49.6	-46.4	148.7	39
40	24 37.6	-45.4	148.7	23 46.3	-45.9	149.0	22 54.8	-46.2	149.2	22 03.2	-46.6	149.4	40
41	23 52.2	-45.7	149.5	23 00.4	-46.0	149.7	22 08.6	-46.4	149.9	21 16.6	-46.7	150.1	41
42	23 06.5	-45.9	150.2	22 14.4	-46.2	150.4	21 22.2	-46.6	150.6	20 29.9	-46.9	150.8	42
43	22 20.6	-46.0	150.9	21 28.2	-46.4	151.1	20 35.6	-46.7	151.2	19 43.0	-47.1	151.4	43
44	21 34.6	-46.2	151.6	20 41.8	-46.6	151.7	19 48.9	-46.9	151.9	18 55.9	-47.2	152.1	44
45	20 48.4	-46.4	152.2	19 55.2	-46.7	152.4	19 02.0	-47.0	152.6	18 08.7	-47.3	152.7	45
46	20 02.0	-46.5	152.9	19 08.5	-46.8	153.1	18 15.0	-47.1	153.2	17 21.4	-47.4	153.4	46
47	19 15.5	-46.7	153.6	18 21.7	-47.0	153.7	17 27.9	-47.3	153.9	16 34.0	-47.6	154.0	47
48	18 28.8	-46.8	154.3	17 34.7	-47.1	154.4	16 40.6	-47.4	154.5	15 46.4	-47.7	154.7	48
49	17 42.0	-46.9	154.9	16 47.6	-47.2	155.0	15 53.2	-47.5	155.2	14 58.7	-47.7	155.3	49
50	16 55.1	-47.1	155.6	16 00.4	-47.3	155.7	15 05.7	-47.6	155.8	14 11.0	-47.9	155.9	50
51	16 08.0	-47.2	156.2	15 13.1	-47.5	156.3	14 18.1	-47.7	156.4	13 23.1	-48.0	156.5	51
52	15 20.8	-47.3	156.9	14 25.6	-47.5	157.0	13 30.4	-47.8	157.1	12 35.1	-48.0	157.1	52
53	14 33.5	-47.4	157.5	13 38.1	-47.7	157.6	12 42.6	-47.9	157.7	11 47.1	-48.1	157.8	53
54	13 46.1	-47.4	158.1	12 50.4	-47.7	158.2	11 54.7	-47.9	158.3	10 59.0	-48.2	158.4	54
55	12 58.7	-47.6	158.8	12 02.7	-47.8	158.8	11 06.8	-48.1	158.9	10 10.8	-48.3	159.0	55
56	12 11.1	-47.7	159.4	11 14.9	-47.9	159.5	10 18.7	-48.1	159.5	9 22.5	-48.3	159.6	56
57	11 23.4	-47.7	160.0	10 27.0	-47.9	160.1	9 30.6	-48.1	160.1	8 34.2	-48.4	160.2	57
58	10 35.7	-47.8	160.6	9 39.1	-48.0	160.7	8 42.5	-48.3	160.7	7 45.8	-48.4	160.8	58
59	9 47.9	-47.9	161.2	8 51.1	-48.1	161.3	7 54.2	-48.2	161.3	6 57.4	-48.5	161.4	59
60	9 00.0	-47.9	161.8	8 03.0	-48.1	161.9	7 06.0	-48.4	161.9	6 08.9	-48.5	162.0	60
61	8 12.1	-48.0	162.4	7 14.9	-48.2	162.5	6 17.6	-48.3	162.5	5 20.4	-48.5	162.6	61
62	7 24.1	-48.1	163.1	6 26.7	-48.2	163.1	5 29.3	-48.4	163.1	4 31.9	-48.6	163.1	62
63	6 36.0	-48.0	163.7	5 38.5	-48.3	163.7	4 40.9	-48.5	163.7	3 43.3	-48.6	163.7	63
64	5 48.0	-48.2	164.3	4 50.2	-48.3	164.3	3 52.4	-48.4	164.3	2 54.7	-48.6	164.3	64
65	4 59.8	-48.1	164.9	4 01.9	-48.3	164.9	3 04.0	-48.5	164.9	2 06.1	-48.7	164.9	65
66	4 11.7	-48.2	165.5	3 13.6	-48.3	165.5	2 15.5	-48.5	165.5	1 17.4	-48.6	165.5	66
67	3 23.5	-48.2	166.1	2 25.3	-48.4	166.1	1 27.0	-48.5	166.1	0 28.8	-48.6	166.1	67
68	2 35.3	-48.2	166.7	1 36.9	-48.3	166.7	0 38.5	-48.4	166.7	0 19.8	+48.7	13.3	68
69	1 47.1	-48.2	167.2	0 48.6	-48.4	167.3	0 09.9	+48.5	12.7	1 08.5	+48.6	12.7	69
70	0 58.9	-48.3	167.8	0 00.2	-48.4	167.8	0 58.4	+48.5	12.2	1 57.1	+48.6	12.2	70
71	0 10.6	-48.2	168.4	0 48.2	+48.3	11.6	1 46.9	+48.5	11.6	2 45.7	+48.6	11.6	71
72	0 37.6	+48.2	11.0	1 36.5	+48.4	11.0	2 35.4	+48.5	11.0	3 34.3	+48.6	11.0	72
73	1 25.8	+48.3	10.4	2 24.9	+48.3	10.4	3 23.9	+48.4	10.4	4 22.9	+48.5	10.4	73
74	2 14.1	+48.2	9.8	3 13.2	+48.3	9.8	4 12.3	+48.4	9.8	5 11.4	+48.6	9.8	74
75	3 02.3	+48.2	9.2	4 01.5	+48.3	9.2	5 00.7	+48.4	9.2	6 00.0	+48.4	9.2	75
76	3 50.5	+48.1	8.6	4 49.8	+48.2	8.6	5 49.1	+48.4	8.6	6 48.4	+48.5	8.6	76
77	4 38.6	+48.2	8.0	5 38.0	+48.3	8.0	6 37.5	+48.3	8.0	7 36.9	+48.4	8.0	77
78	5 26.8	+48.1	7.4	6 26.3	+48.1	7.4	7 25.8	+48.2	7.4	8 25.3	+48.3	7.4	78
79	6 14.9	+48.0	6.8	7 14.4	+48.2	6.8	8 14.0	+48.2	6.8	9 13.6	+48.3	6.8	79
80	7 02.9	+48.0	6.2	8 02.6	+48.0	6.2	9 02.2	+48.2	6.2	10 01.9	+48.2	6.2	80
81	7 50.9	+48.0	5.6	8 50.6	+48.1	5.6	9 50.4	+48.0	5.6	10 50.1	+48.1	5.6	81
82	8 38.9	+47.9	5.0	9 38.7	+47.9	5.0	10 38.4	+48.0	5.0	11 38.2	+48.1	5.0	82
83	9 26.8	+47.8	4.4	10 26.6	+47.9	4.4	11 26.4	+48.0	4.4	12 26.3	+47.9	4.4	83
84	10 14.6	+47.8	3.7	11 14.5	+47.8	3.8	12 14.4	+47.8	3.8	13 14.2	+47.9	3.8	84
85	11 02.4	+47.7	3.1	12 02.3	+47.7	3.1	13 02.2	+47.8	3.2	14 02.1	+47.8	3.2	85
86	11 50.1	+47.6	2.5	12 50.0	+47.7	2.5	13 50.0	+47.6	2.5	14 49.9	+47.7	2.5	86
87	12 37.7	+47.5	1.9	13 37.7	+47.5	1.9	14 37.6	+47.6	1.9	15 37.6	+47.6	1.9	87
88	13 25.2	+47.5	1.3	14 25.2	+47.5	1.3	15 25.2	+47.5	1.3	16 25.2	+47.5	1.3	88
89	14 12.7	+47.3	0.6	15 12.7	+47.3	0.6	16 12.7	+47.3	0.6	17 12.7	+47.3	0.6	89
90	15 00.0	+47.2	0.0	16 00.0	+47.2	0.0	17 00.0	+47.2	0.0	18 00.0	+47.2	0.0	90
	15°			16°			17°			18°			

Dec.	19° Hc	d	Z	20° Hc	d	Z	21° Hc	d	Z	22° Hc	d	Z	Dec.
°	° ′	′	°	° ′	′	°	° ′	′	°	° ′	′	°	°
0	48 10.0	-29.8	112.6	47 46.4	-31.0	113.6	47 21.8	-32.1	114.6	46 56.4	-33.3	115.6	0
1	47 40.2	-30.6	113.9	47 15.4	-31.8	114.9	46 49.7	-32.9	115.9	46 23.1	-34.1	116.8	1
2	47 09.6	-31.4	115.2	46 43.6	-32.5	116.2	46 16.8	-33.7	117.1	45 49.0	-34.8	118.0	2
3	46 38.2	-32.2	116.4	46 11.1	-33.4	117.4	45 43.1	-34.5	118.3	45 14.2	-35.5	119.2	3
4	46 06.0	-33.0	117.7	45 37.7	-34.0	118.6	45 08.6	-35.1	119.5	44 38.7	-36.1	120.3	4
5	45 33.0	-33.7	118.9	45 03.7	-34.8	119.7	44 33.5	-35.8	120.6	44 02.6	-36.8	121.4	5
6	44 59.3	-34.4	120.0	44 28.9	-35.4	120.9	43 57.7	-36.4	121.7	43 25.8	-37.4	122.5	6
7	44 24.9	-35.1	121.2	43 53.5	-36.1	122.0	43 21.3	-37.1	122.8	42 48.4	-38.0	123.6	7
8	43 49.8	-35.8	122.3	43 17.4	-36.8	123.1	42 44.2	-37.6	123.9	42 10.4	-38.5	124.6	8
9	43 14.0	-36.4	123.4	42 40.6	-37.3	124.2	42 06.6	-38.2	124.9	41 31.9	-39.1	125.7	9
10	42 37.6	-37.0	124.5	42 03.3	-37.9	125.3	41 28.4	-38.8	126.0	40 52.8	-39.6	126.7	10
11	42 00.6	-37.5	125.6	41 25.4	-38.4	126.3	40 49.6	-39.3	127.0	40 13.2	-40.1	127.7	11
12	41 23.1	-38.2	126.6	40 47.0	-39.0	127.3	40 10.3	-39.8	128.0	39 33.1	-40.5	128.6	12
13	40 44.9	-38.6	127.6	40 08.0	-39.5	128.3	39 30.5	-40.2	129.0	38 52.6	-41.1	129.6	13
14	40 06.3	-39.2	128.6	39 28.5	-39.9	129.3	38 50.3	-40.7	129.9	38 11.5	-41.4	130.5	14
15	39 27.1	-39.7	129.6	38 48.6	-40.4	130.3	38 09.6	-41.2	130.9	37 30.1	-41.9	131.4	15
16	38 47.4	-40.1	130.6	38 08.2	-40.9	131.2	37 28.4	-41.6	131.8	36 48.2	-42.3	132.3	16
17	38 07.3	-40.6	131.5	37 27.3	-41.3	132.1	36 46.8	-42.0	132.7	36 05.9	-42.6	133.2	17
18	37 26.7	-41.0	132.5	36 46.0	-41.7	133.0	36 04.8	-42.3	133.6	35 23.3	-43.0	134.1	18
19	36 45.7	-41.4	133.4	36 04.3	-42.1	133.9	35 22.5	-42.8	134.4	34 40.3	-43.4	134.9	19
20	36 04.3	-41.8	134.3	35 22.2	-42.5	134.8	34 39.7	-43.1	135.3	33 56.9	-43.7	135.8	20
21	35 22.5	-42.2	135.2	34 39.7	-42.8	135.7	33 56.6	-43.4	136.1	33 13.2	-44.0	136.6	21
22	34 40.3	-42.6	136.0	33 56.9	-43.2	136.5	33 13.2	-43.8	137.0	32 29.2	-44.3	137.4	22
23	33 57.7	-42.9	136.9	33 13.7	-43.5	137.4	32 29.4	-44.0	137.8	31 44.9	-44.7	138.2	23
24	33 14.8	-43.3	137.7	32 30.2	-43.8	138.2	31 45.4	-44.4	138.6	31 00.2	-44.9	139.0	24
25	32 31.5	-43.5	138.6	31 46.4	-44.1	139.0	31 01.0	-44.6	139.4	30 15.3	-45.1	139.8	25
26	31 48.0	-43.9	139.4	31 02.3	-44.4	139.8	30 16.4	-44.9	140.2	29 30.2	-45.4	140.5	26
27	31 04.1	-44.1	140.2	30 17.9	-44.7	140.6	29 31.5	-45.2	140.9	28 44.8	-45.7	141.3	27
28	30 20.0	-44.5	141.0	29 33.2	-44.9	141.3	28 46.3	-45.4	141.7	27 59.1	-45.9	142.0	28
29	29 35.5	-44.7	141.7	28 48.3	-45.2	142.1	28 00.9	-45.7	142.4	27 13.2	-46.1	142.7	29
30	28 50.8	-44.9	142.5	28 03.1	-45.4	142.8	27 15.2	-45.9	143.1	26 27.1	-46.3	143.5	30
31	28 05.9	-45.2	143.3	27 17.7	-45.7	143.6	26 29.3	-46.1	143.9	25 40.8	-46.6	144.2	31
32	27 20.7	-45.5	144.0	26 32.0	-45.8	144.3	25 43.2	-46.3	144.6	24 54.2	-46.7	144.9	32
33	26 35.2	-45.6	144.7	25 46.2	-46.1	145.0	24 56.9	-46.5	145.3	24 07.5	-46.9	145.5	33
34	25 49.6	-45.9	145.5	25 00.1	-46.3	145.7	24 10.4	-46.7	146.0	23 20.6	-47.1	146.2	34
35	25 03.7	-46.1	146.2	24 13.8	-46.5	146.4	23 23.7	-46.8	146.7	22 33.5	-47.2	146.9	35
36	24 17.6	-46.2	146.9	23 27.3	-46.6	147.1	22 36.9	-47.1	147.3	21 46.3	-47.4	147.6	36
37	23 31.4	-46.5	147.6	22 40.7	-46.9	147.8	21 49.8	-47.2	148.0	20 58.9	-47.6	148.2	37
38	22 44.9	-46.6	148.3	21 53.8	-47.0	148.5	21 02.6	-47.3	148.7	20 11.3	-47.7	148.9	38
39	21 58.3	-46.8	148.9	21 06.8	-47.1	149.1	20 15.3	-47.5	149.3	19 23.6	-47.8	149.5	39
40	21 11.5	-46.9	149.6	20 19.7	-47.3	149.8	19 27.8	-47.6	150.0	18 35.8	-48.0	150.2	40
41	20 24.6	-47.1	150.3	19 32.4	-47.4	150.5	18 40.2	-47.8	150.6	17 47.8	-48.0	150.8	41
42	19 37.5	-47.3	150.9	18 45.0	-47.6	151.1	17 52.4	-47.9	151.3	16 59.8	-48.2	151.4	42
43	18 50.2	-47.3	151.6	17 57.4	-47.7	151.7	17 04.5	-48.0	151.9	16 11.6	-48.3	152.0	43
44	18 02.9	-47.5	152.2	17 09.7	-47.8	152.4	16 16.5	-48.1	152.5	15 23.3	-48.4	152.7	44
45	17 15.4	-47.7	152.9	16 21.9	-47.9	153.0	15 28.4	-48.2	153.1	14 34.9	-48.5	153.3	45
46	16 27.7	-47.7	153.5	15 34.0	-48.0	153.6	14 40.2	-48.3	153.8	13 46.4	-48.6	153.9	46
47	15 40.0	-47.9	154.1	14 46.0	-48.2	154.3	13 51.9	-48.4	154.4	12 57.8	-48.7	154.5	47
48	14 52.1	-47.9	154.8	13 57.8	-48.2	154.9	13 03.5	-48.5	155.0	12 09.1	-48.7	155.1	48
49	14 04.2	-48.0	155.4	13 09.6	-48.3	155.5	12 15.0	-48.6	155.6	11 20.4	-48.9	155.7	49
50	13 16.2	-48.2	156.0	12 21.3	-48.4	156.1	11 26.4	-48.6	156.2	10 31.5	-48.8	156.3	50
51	12 28.0	-48.2	156.6	11 32.9	-48.4	156.7	10 37.8	-48.7	156.8	9 42.7	-49.0	156.9	51
52	11 39.8	-48.3	157.2	10 44.5	-48.6	157.3	9 49.1	-48.8	157.4	8 53.7	-49.0	157.4	52
53	10 51.5	-48.3	157.8	9 55.9	-48.5	157.9	9 00.3	-48.8	158.0	8 04.7	-49.0	158.0	53
54	10 03.2	-48.5	158.4	9 07.4	-48.7	158.5	8 11.5	-48.9	158.6	7 15.7	-49.1	158.6	54
55	9 14.7	-48.4	159.0	8 18.7	-48.7	159.1	7 22.6	-48.9	159.1	6 26.6	-49.2	159.2	55
56	8 26.3	-48.6	159.6	7 30.0	-48.7	159.7	6 33.7	-48.9	159.7	5 37.4	-49.1	159.8	56
57	7 37.7	-48.6	160.2	6 41.3	-48.8	160.3	5 44.8	-49.0	160.3	4 48.3	-49.2	160.3	57
58	6 49.1	-48.6	160.8	5 52.5	-48.9	160.9	4 55.8	-49.0	160.9	3 59.1	-49.2	160.9	58
59	6 00.5	-48.7	161.4	5 03.6	-48.8	161.4	4 06.8	-49.1	161.5	3 09.9	-49.3	161.5	59
60	5 11.8	-48.6	162.0	4 14.8	-48.9	162.0	3 17.7	-49.1	162.0	2 20.6	-49.2	162.1	60
61	4 23.2	-48.6	162.6	3 25.9	-48.9	162.6	2 28.6	-49.0	162.6	1 31.4	-49.3	162.6	61
62	3 34.4	-48.7	163.2	2 37.0	-48.9	163.2	1 39.6	-49.1	163.2	0 42.1	-49.2	163.2	62
63	2 45.7	-48.8	163.7	1 48.1	-49.0	163.8	0 50.5	-49.1	163.8	0 07.1	+49.3	16.2	63
64	1 56.9	-48.8	164.3	0 59.1	-48.9	164.3	0 01.4	-49.1	164.3	0 56.4	+49.3	15.7	64
65	1 08.1	-48.7	164.9	0 10.2	-48.9	164.9	0 47.7	+49.1	15.1	1 45.7	+49.2	15.1	65
66	0 19.4	-48.8	165.5	0 38.7	+49.0	14.5	1 36.8	+49.1	14.5	2 34.9	+49.2	14.5	66
67	0 29.4	+48.8	13.9	1 27.7	+48.9	13.9	2 25.9	+49.1	13.9	3 24.1	+49.3	13.9	67
68	1 18.2	+48.8	13.3	2 16.6	+48.9	13.3	3 15.0	+49.0	13.4	4 13.4	+49.1	13.4	68
69	2 07.0	+48.8	12.8	3 05.5	+48.9	12.8	4 04.0	+49.0	12.8	5 02.5	+49.2	12.8	69
70	2 55.8	+48.7	12.2	3 54.4	+48.9	12.2	4 53.0	+49.0	12.2	5 51.7	+49.1	12.2	70
71	3 44.5	+48.7	11.6	4 43.3	+48.8	11.6	5 42.0	+49.0	11.6	6 40.8	+49.1	11.6	71
72	4 33.2	+48.7	11.0	5 32.1	+48.8	11.0	6 31.0	+48.9	11.0	7 29.9	+49.0	11.1	72
73	5 21.9	+48.7	10.4	6 20.9	+48.8	10.4	7 19.9	+48.9	10.5	8 18.9	+49.0	10.5	73
74	6 10.6	+48.6	9.8	7 09.7	+48.7	9.8	8 08.8	+48.8	9.9	9 07.9	+48.9	9.9	74
75	6 59.2	+48.6	9.2	7 58.4	+48.7	9.3	8 57.6	+48.8	9.3	9 56.8	+48.9	9.3	75
76	7 47.8	+48.5	8.6	8 47.1	+48.6	8.7	9 46.4	+48.7	8.7	10 45.7	+48.8	8.7	76
77	8 36.3	+48.5	8.1	9 35.7	+48.5	8.1	10 35.1	+48.6	8.1	11 34.5	+48.7	8.1	77
78	9 24.8	+48.4	7.5	10 24.2	+48.5	7.5	11 23.7	+48.6	7.5	12 23.2	+48.7	7.5	78
79	10 13.2	+48.3	6.9	11 12.7	+48.5	6.9	12 12.3	+48.5	6.9	13 11.9	+48.5	6.9	79
80	11 01.5	+48.3	6.3	12 01.2	+48.3	6.3	13 00.8	+48.4	6.3	14 00.4	+48.5	6.3	80
81	11 49.8	+48.2	5.6	12 49.5	+48.2	5.7	13 49.2	+48.3	5.7	14 48.9	+48.4	5.7	81
82	12 38.0	+48.1	5.0	13 37.7	+48.2	5.1	14 37.5	+48.2	5.1	15 37.3	+48.2	5.1	82
83	13 26.1	+48.0	4.4	14 25.9	+48.1	4.4	15 25.7	+48.1	4.5	16 25.5	+48.2	4.5	83
84	14 14.1	+47.9	3.8	15 14.0	+47.9	3.8	16 13.8	+48.0	3.8	17 13.7	+48.1	3.9	84
85	15 02.0	+47.9	3.2	16 01.9	+47.9	3.2	17 01.8	+47.9	3.2	18 01.8	+47.9	3.2	85
86	15 49.9	+47.7	2.6	16 49.8	+47.7	2.6	17 49.7	+47.8	2.6	18 49.7	+47.8	2.6	86
87	16 37.6	+47.6	1.9	17 37.5	+47.7	1.9	18 37.5	+47.6	1.9	19 37.5	+47.6	2.0	87
88	17 25.2	+47.4	1.3	18 25.2	+47.4	1.3	19 25.1	+47.5	1.3	20 25.1	+47.5	1.3	88
89	18 12.7	+47.3	0.6	19 12.6	+47.4	0.7	20 12.6	+47.4	0.7	21 12.6	+47.4	0.7	89
90	19 00.0	+47.2	0.0	20 00.0	+47.2	0.0	21 00.0	+47.2	0.0	22 00.0	+47.2	0.0	90
	19°			20°			21°			22°			

S. Lat. { L.H.A. greater than 180° ....Zn=180°–Z
L.H.A. less than 180°...........Zn=180°+Z

LATITUDE **SAME** NAME AS DECLINATION L.H.A. 142°, 218°

39°, 321° L.H.A. LATITUDE SAME NAME AS DECLINATION N. Lat. {L.H.A. greater than 180° .....Zn=Z; L.H.A. less than 180°............Zn=360°−Z}

Dec.	15° Hc	d	Z	16° Hc	d	Z	17° Hc	d	Z	18° Hc	d	Z	19° Hc	d	Z	20° Hc	d	Z	21° Hc	d	Z	22° Hc	d	Z	Dec.
°	° ′	′	°	° ′	′	°	° ′	′	°	° ′	′	°	° ′	′	°	° ′	′	°	° ′	′	°	° ′	′	°	°
0	48 38.9	+23.0	107.7	48 20.1	+24.4	108.8	48 00.2	+25.8	109.9	47 39.3	+27.1	110.9	47 17.4	+28.4	111.9	46 54.6	+29.6	112.9	46 30.8	+30.8	113.9	46 06.0	+32.1	114.8	0
1	49 01.9	+21.9	106.3	48 44.5	+23.3	107.4	48 26.0	+24.7	108.5	48 06.4	+26.1	109.6	47 45.8	+27.5	110.6	47 24.2	+28.7	111.6	47 01.6	+30.0	112.6	46 38.1	+31.2	113.6	1
2	49 23.8	+20.9	104.9	49 07.8	+22.4	106.0	48 50.7	+23.8	107.1	48 32.5	+25.2	108.2	48 13.3	+26.5	109.3	47 52.9	+27.9	110.3	47 31.6	+29.1	111.3	47 09.3	+30.4	112.4	2
3	49 44.7	+19.8	103.5	49 30.2	+21.3	104.6	49 14.5	+22.7	105.7	48 57.7	+24.2	106.8	48 39.8	+25.5	107.9	48 20.8	+26.9	109.0	48 00.7	+28.3	110.0	47 39.7	+29.5	111.1	3
4	50 04.5	+18.7	102.0	49 51.5	+20.2	103.1	49 37.2	+21.7	104.3	49 21.9	+23.1	105.4	49 05.3	+24.6	106.5	48 47.7	+25.9	107.6	48 29.0	+27.3	108.7	48 09.2	+28.6	109.8	4
5	50 23.2	+17.5	100.5	50 11.7	+19.0	101.7	49 58.9	+20.6	102.8	49 45.0	+22.1	104.0	49 29.9	+23.5	105.1	49 13.6	+25.0	106.3	48 56.3	+26.3	107.4	48 37.8	+27.7	108.5	5
6	50 40.7	+16.4	99.0	50 30.7	+18.0	100.2	50 19.5	+19.5	101.4	50 07.1	+20.9	102.6	49 53.4	+22.5	103.7	49 38.6	+23.9	104.9	49 22.6	+25.4	106.0	49 05.5	+26.8	107.1	6
7	50 57.1	+15.1	97.5	50 48.7	+16.7	98.7	50 39.0	+18.3	99.9	50 28.0	+19.9	101.1	50 15.9	+21.4	102.3	50 02.5	+22.9	103.4	49 48.0	+24.3	104.6	49 32.3	+25.8	105.7	7
8	51 12.2	+14.0	95.9	51 05.4	+15.5	97.2	50 57.3	+17.1	98.4	50 47.9	+18.7	99.6	50 37.3	+20.2	100.8	50 25.4	+21.8	102.0	50 12.3	+23.3	103.2	49 58.1	+24.7	104.3	8
9	51 26.2	+12.6	94.4	51 20.9	+14.3	95.6	51 14.4	+15.9	96.9	51 06.6	+17.5	98.1	50 57.5	+19.1	99.3	50 47.2	+20.6	100.5	50 35.6	+22.2	101.7	50 22.8	+23.7	102.9	9
10	51 38.8	+11.4	92.8	51 35.2	+13.1	94.1	51 30.3	+14.7	95.3	51 24.1	+16.3	96.6	51 16.6	+17.9	97.8	51 07.8	+19.5	99.0	50 57.8	+21.0	100.3	50 46.5	+22.5	101.5	10
11	51 50.2	+10.1	91.2	51 48.3	+11.8	92.5	51 45.0	+13.5	93.8	51 40.4	+15.1	95.0	51 34.5	+16.7	96.3	51 27.3	+18.3	97.5	51 18.8	+19.9	98.8	51 09.0	+21.5	100.0	11
12	52 00.3	+8.9	89.6	52 00.1	+10.5	90.9	51 58.5	+12.1	92.2	51 55.5	+13.8	93.5	51 51.2	+15.5	94.7	51 45.6	+17.1	96.0	51 38.7	+18.7	97.3	51 30.5	+20.3	98.5	12
13	52 09.2	+7.4	88.0	52 10.6	+9.1	89.3	52 10.6	+10.9	90.6	52 09.3	+12.6	91.9	52 06.7	+14.2	93.2	52 02.7	+15.9	94.4	51 57.4	+17.5	95.7	51 50.8	+19.1	97.0	13
14	52 16.6	+6.2	86.4	52 19.7	+7.9	87.7	52 21.5	+9.5	89.0	52 21.9	+11.2	90.3	52 20.9	+12.9	91.6	52 18.6	+14.6	92.9	52 14.9	+16.3	94.2	52 09.9	+17.9	95.4	14
15	52 22.8	+4.8	84.8	52 27.6	+6.5	86.1	52 31.0	+8.2	87.4	52 33.1	+9.9	88.7	52 33.8	+11.6	90.0	52 33.2	+13.3	91.3	52 31.2	+14.9	92.6	52 27.8	+16.6	93.9	15
16	52 27.6	+3.4	83.1	52 34.1	+5.1	84.4	52 39.2	+6.9	85.7	52 43.0	+8.6	87.0	52 45.4	+10.3	88.4	52 46.5	+12.0	89.7	52 46.1	+13.7	91.0	52 44.4	+15.4	92.3	16
17	52 31.0	+2.1	81.5	52 39.2	+3.8	82.8	52 46.1	+5.5	84.1	52 51.6	+7.2	85.4	52 55.7	+8.9	86.7	52 58.5	+10.6	88.0	52 59.8	+12.4	89.4	52 59.8	+14.0	90.7	17
18	52 33.1	+0.7	79.8	52 43.0	+2.4	81.1	52 51.6	+4.1	82.4	52 58.8	+5.8	83.8	53 04.6	+7.6	85.1	53 09.1	+9.3	86.4	53 12.2	+11.0	87.7	53 13.8	+12.8	89.1	18
19	52 33.8	-0.6	78.2	52 45.4	+1.1	79.5	52 55.7	+2.8	80.8	53 04.6	+4.5	82.1	53 12.2	+6.2	83.4	53 18.4	+7.9	84.8	53 23.2	+9.6	86.1	53 26.6	+11.3	87.4	19
20	52 33.2	-2.0	76.6	52 46.5	-0.4	77.8	52 58.5	+1.3	79.1	53 09.1	+3.1	80.4	53 18.4	+4.8	81.8	53 26.3	+6.5	83.1	53 32.8	+8.3	84.4	53 37.9	+10.0	85.8	20
21	52 31.2	-3.4	74.9	52 46.1	-1.7	76.2	52 59.8	0.0	77.5	53 12.2	+1.6	78.8	53 23.2	+3.4	80.1	53 32.8	+5.1	81.4	53 41.1	+6.8	82.8	53 47.9	+8.6	84.1	21
22	52 27.8	-4.8	73.3	52 44.4	-3.1	74.5	52 59.8	-1.4	75.8	53 13.8	+0.3	77.1	53 26.6	+1.9	78.4	53 37.9	+3.7	79.7	53 47.9	+5.4	81.1	53 56.5	+7.2	82.4	22
23	52 23.0	-6.0	71.6	52 41.3	-4.4	72.9	52 58.4	-2.9	74.1	53 14.1	-1.1	75.4	53 28.5	+0.6	76.7	53 41.6	+2.3	78.1	53 53.3	+4.1	79.4	54 03.7	+5.7	80.8	23
24	52 17.0	-7.5	70.0	52 36.9	-5.9	71.2	52 55.5	-4.1	72.5	53 13.0	-2.6	73.8	53 29.1	-0.9	75.1	53 43.9	+0.8	76.4	53 57.4	+2.5	77.7	54 09.4	+4.4	79.1	24
25	52 09.5	-8.7	68.4	52 31.0	-7.1	69.6	52 51.4	-5.6	70.8	53 10.4	-3.9	72.1	53 28.2	-2.2	73.4	53 44.7	-0.5	74.7	53 59.9	+1.2	76.0	54 13.8	+2.8	77.4	25
26	52 00.8	-10.1	66.8	52 23.9	-8.5	68.0	52 45.8	-6.9	69.2	53 06.5	-5.3	70.4	53 26.0	-3.7	71.7	53 44.2	-2.0	73.0	54 01.1	-0.3	74.3	54 16.6	+1.4	75.6	26
27	51 50.7	-11.3	65.2	52 15.4	-9.9	66.4	52 38.9	-8.3	67.5	53 01.2	-6.7	68.8	53 22.3	-5.1	70.0	53 42.2	-3.5	71.3	54 00.8	-1.8	72.6	54 18.0	0.0	73.9	27
28	51 39.4	-12.6	63.6	52 05.5	-11.1	64.7	52 30.6	-9.6	65.9	52 54.5	-8.1	67.1	53 17.2	-6.4	68.4	53 38.7	-4.8	69.6	53 59.0	-3.2	70.9	54 18.0	-1.5	72.2	28
29	51 26.8	-13.9	62.0	51 54.4	-12.4	63.1	52 21.0	-11.0	64.3	52 46.4	-9.4	65.5	53 10.8	-7.9	66.7	53 33.9	-6.3	67.9	53 55.8	-4.6	69.2	54 16.5	-3.0	70.5	29
30	51 12.9	-15.1	60.5	51 42.0	-13.7	61.6	52 10.0	-12.2	62.7	52 37.0	-10.7	63.9	53 02.9	-9.2	65.0	53 27.6	-7.6	66.3	53 51.2	-6.0	67.5	54 13.5	-4.4	68.8	30
31	50 57.8	-16.3	58.9	51 28.3	-14.9	60.0	51 57.8	-13.5	61.1	52 26.3	-12.1	62.2	52 53.7	-10.6	63.4	53 20.0	-9.0	64.6	53 45.2	-7.5	65.8	54 09.1	-5.8	67.1	31
32	50 41.5	-17.4	57.4	51 13.4	-16.1	58.4	51 44.3	-14.7	59.5	52 14.2	-13.3	60.6	52 43.1	-11.8	61.8	53 11.0	-10.4	62.9	53 37.7	-8.8	64.2	54 03.3	-7.3	65.4	32
33	50 24.1	-18.7	55.9	50 57.3	-17.4	56.9	51 29.6	-16.0	58.0	52 00.9	-14.6	59.0	52 31.3	-13.2	60.2	53 00.6	-11.7	61.3	53 28.9	-10.3	62.5	53 56.0	-8.7	63.7	33
34	50 05.4	-19.7	54.4	50 39.9	-18.5	55.4	51 13.6	-17.2	56.4	51 46.3	-15.9	57.5	52 18.1	-14.5	58.6	52 48.9	-13.1	59.7	53 18.6	-11.5	60.8	53 47.3	-10.0	62.0	34
35	49 45.7	-20.9	52.9	50 21.4	-19.6	53.9	50 56.4	-18.4	54.9	51 30.4	-17.0	55.9	52 03.6	-15.7	57.0	52 35.8	-14.3	58.1	53 07.1	-13.0	59.2	53 37.3	-11.5	60.4	35
36	49 24.8	-21.9	51.5	50 01.8	-20.7	52.4	50 38.0	-19.5	53.4	51 13.4	-18.3	54.4	51 47.9	-17.0	55.4	52 21.5	-15.6	56.5	52 54.1	-14.2	57.6	53 25.8	-12.8	58.7	36
37	49 02.9	-22.9	50.1	49 41.1	-21.8	51.0	50 18.5	-20.6	51.9	50 55.1	-19.4	52.9	51 30.9	-18.1	53.9	52 05.9	-16.9	54.9	52 39.9	-15.5	56.0	53 13.0	-14.1	57.1	37
38	48 40.0	-24.0	48.7	49 19.3	-22.9	49.5	49 57.9	-21.8	50.4	50 35.7	-20.6	51.4	51 12.8	-19.4	52.3	51 49.0	-18.1	53.3	52 24.4	-16.8	54.4	52 58.9	-15.5	55.5	38
39	48 16.0	-24.9	47.3	48 56.4	-23.9	48.1	49 36.1	-22.8	49.0	50 15.1	-21.6	49.9	50 53.4	-20.5	50.8	51 30.9	-19.3	51.8	52 07.6	-18.0	52.8	52 43.4	-16.7	53.9	39
40	47 51.1	-25.9	45.9	48 32.5	-24.8	46.7	49 13.3	-23.8	47.6	49 53.5	-22.8	48.4	50 32.9	-21.6	49.3	51 11.6	-20.4	50.3	51 49.6	-19.2	51.3	52 26.7	-17.9	52.3	40
41	47 25.2	-26.8	44.6	48 07.7	-25.9	45.4	48 49.5	-24.8	46.2	49 30.7	-23.7	47.0	50 11.3	-22.7	47.9	50 51.2	-21.6	48.8	51 30.4	-20.4	49.7	52 08.8	-19.2	50.7	41
42	46 58.4	-27.7	43.3	47 41.8	-26.7	44.0	48 24.7	-25.8	44.8	49 07.0	-24.8	45.6	49 48.6	-23.7	46.4	50 29.6	-22.6	47.3	51 10.0	-21.6	48.2	51 49.6	-20.4	49.2	42
43	46 30.7	-28.5	42.0	47 15.1	-27.7	42.7	47 58.9	-26.7	43.4	48 42.2	-25.8	44.2	49 24.9	-24.8	45.0	50 07.0	-23.7	45.9	50 48.4	-22.6	46.7	51 29.2	-21.5	47.7	43
44	46 02.2	-29.4	40.7	46 47.4	-28.5	41.4	47 32.2	-27.7	42.1	48 16.4	-26.7	42.9	49 00.1	-25.7	43.6	49 43.3	-24.8	44.4	50 25.8	-23.7	45.3	51 07.7	-22.7	46.2	44
45	45 32.8	-30.2	39.4	46 18.9	-29.4	40.1	47 04.5	-28.5	40.8	47 49.7	-27.6	41.5	48 34.4	-26.7	42.3	49 18.5	-25.8	43.0	50 02.1	-24.8	43.9	50 45.0	-23.7	44.7	45
46	45 02.6	-31.0	38.2	45 49.5	-30.2	38.9	46 36.0	-29.4	39.5	47 22.1	-28.6	40.2	48 07.7	-27.7	40.9	48 52.7	-26.7	41.7	49 37.3	-25.8	42.4	50 21.3	-24.8	43.2	46
47	44 31.6	-31.7	37.0	45 19.3	-31.0	37.6	46 06.6	-30.1	38.2	46 53.5	-29.3	38.9	47 40.0	-28.5	39.6	48 26.0	-27.7	40.3	49 11.5	-26.7	41.1	49 56.5	-25.8	41.8	47
48	43 59.9	-32.5	35.8	44 48.3	-31.7	36.4	45 36.5	-31.0	37.0	46 24.2	-30.2	37.6	47 11.5	-29.4	38.3	47 58.3	-28.5	39.0	48 44.8	-27.8	39.7	49 30.7	-26.8	40.4	48
49	43 27.4	-33.1	34.7	44 16.6	-32.4	35.2	45 05.5	-31.8	35.8	45 54.0	-31.1	36.4	46 42.1	-30.3	37.0	47 29.8	-29.5	37.7	48 17.0	-28.6	38.3	49 03.9	-27.8	39.1	49
50	42 54.3	-33.8	33.5	43 44.2	-33.2	34.0	44 33.7	-32.5	34.6	45 22.9	-31.7	35.2	46 11.8	-31.0	35.8	47 00.3	-30.3	36.4	47 48.4	-29.5	37.0	48 36.1	-28.7	37.7	50
51	42 20.5	-34.5	32.4	43 11.0	-33.8	32.9	44 01.2	-33.1	33.4	44 51.2	-32.6	34.0	45 40.8	-31.9	34.5	46 30.0	-31.1	35.1	47 18.9	-30.4	35.7	48 07.4	-29.6	36.4	51
52	41 46.0	-35.0	31.3	42 37.2	-34.5	31.8	43 28.1	-33.9	32.3	44 18.6	-33.2	32.8	45 08.9	-32.5	33.3	45 58.9	-31.9	33.9	46 48.5	-31.1	34.5	47 37.8	-30.4	35.1	52
53	41 11.0	-35.7	30.2	42 02.7	-35.1	30.7	42 54.2	-34.5	31.1	43 45.4	-33.9	31.6	44 36.4	-33.3	32.1	45 27.0	-32.6	32.7	46 17.4	-32.0	33.2	47 07.4	-31.3	33.8	53
54	40 35.3	-36.2	29.2	41 27.6	-35.7	29.6	42 19.7	-35.2	30.0	43 11.5	-34.6	30.5	44 03.1	-34.0	31.0	44 54.4	-33.4	31.5	45 45.4	-32.8	32.0	46 36.1	-32.1	32.6	54
55	39 59.1	-36.8	28.1	40 51.9	-36.3	28.5	41 44.5	-35.8	28.9	42 36.9	-35.2	29.4	43 29.1	-34.7	29.8	44 21.0	-34.1	30.3	45 12.6	-33.4	30.8	46 04.0	-32.8	31.3	55
56	39 22.3	-37.4	27.1	40 15.6	-36.9	27.5	41 08.7	-36.3	27.9	42 01.7	-35.9	28.3	42 54.4	-35.3	28.7	43 46.9	-34.7	29.2	44 39.2	-34.2	29.6	45 31.2	-33.6	30.1	56
57	38 44.9	-37.8	26.1	39 38.7	-37.4	26.4	40 32.4	-36.9	26.8	41 25.8	-36.4	27.2	42 19.1	-35.9	27.6	43 12.2	-35.4	28.0	44 05.0	-34.9	28.5	44 57.6	-34.3	29.0	57
58	38 07.1	-38.4	25.1	39 01.3	-37.9	25.4	39 55.5	-37.5	25.8	40 49.4	-37.0	26.1	41 43.2	-36.5	26.5	42 36.8	-36.1	26.9	43 30.1	-35.5	27.4	44 23.3	-35.0	27.8	58
59	37 28.7	-38.8	24.1	38 23.4	-38.3	24.4	39 18.0	-38.0	24.8	40 12.4	-37.5	25.1	41 06.7	-37.1	25.5	42 00.7	-36.6	25.9	42 54.6	-36.1	26.3	43 48.3	-35.6	26.7	59
60	36 49.9	-39.2	23.1	37 45.1	-38.9	23.5	38 40.0	-38.4	23.8	39 34.9	-38.1	24.1	40 29.6	-37.7	24.4	41 24.1	-37.2	24.8	42 18.5	-36.7	25.2	43 12.7	-36.3	25.6	60
61	36 10.7	-39.7	22.2	37 06.2	-39.3	22.5	38 01.6	-39.0	22.8	38 56.8	-38.5	23.1	39 51.9	-38.1	23.4	40 46.9	-37.7	23.8	41 41.8	-37.4	24.1	42 36.4	-36.8	24.5	61
62	35 31.0	-40.1	21.3	36 26.9	-39.8	21.5	37 22.6	-39.4	21.8	38 18.3	-39.1	22.1	39 13.8	-38.7	22.4	40 09.2	-38.3	22.7	41 04.4	-37.8	23.1	41 59.6	-37.5	23.4	62
63	34 50.9	-40.5	20.4	35 47.1	-40.2	20.6	36 43.2	-39.8	20.9	37 39.2	-39.5	21.2	38 35.1	-39.1	21.4	39 30.9	-38.8	21.7	40 26.6	-38.4	22.0	41 22.1	-38.0	22.4	63
64	34 10.4	-40.9	19.5	35 06.9	-40.6	19.7	36 03.4	-40.3	20.0	36 59.7	-39.9	20.2	37 56.0	-39.6	20.5	38 52.1	-39.2	20.8	39 48.2	-38.9	21.0	40 44.1	-38.5	21.4	64
65	33 29.5	-41.3	18.6	34 26.3	-40.9	18.8	35 23.1	-40.7	19.0	36 19.8	-40.4	19.3	37 16.4	-40.1	19.5	38 12.9	-39.8	19.8	39 09.3	-39.4	20.1	40 05.6	-39.1	20.3	65
66	32 48.2	-41.6	17.7	33 45.4	-41.4	17.9	34 42.4	-41.1	18.1	35 39.4	-40.8	18.4	36 36.3	-40.5	18.6	37 33.1	-40.2	18.8	38 29.9	-39.9	19.1	39 26.5	-39.5	19.4	66
67	32 06.6	-41.9	16.9	33 04.0	-41.7	17.1	34 01.3	-41.4	17.3	34 58.6	-41.2	17.5	35 55.8	-40.9	17.7	36 52.9	-40.6	17.9	37 50.0	-40.3	18.1	38 47.0	-40.0	18.4	67
68	31 24.7	-42.3	16.0	32 22.3	-42.0	16.2	33 19.9	-41.8	16.4	34 17.4	-41.5	16.6	35 14.9	-41.3	16.8	36 12.3	-41.0	17.0	37 09.7	-40.8	17.2	38 07.0	-40.5	17.4	68
69	30 42.4	-42.6	15.2	31 40.3	-42.4	15.4	32 38.1	-42.1	15.5	33 35.9	-41.9	15.7	34 33.6	-41.6	15.9	35 31.3	-41.4	16.1	36 28.9	-41.1	16.3	37 26.5	-40.9	16.5	69
70	29 59.8	-42.9	14.4	30 57.9	-42.7	14.5	31 56.0	-42.5	14.7	32 54.0	-42.3	14.9	33 52.0	-42.1	15.0	34 49.9	-41.8	15.2	35 47.8	-41.6	15.4	36 45.6	-41.3	15.6	70
71	29 16.9	-43.1	13.6	30 15.2	-42.9	13.7	31 13.5	-42.8	13.9	32 11.7	-42.5	14.0	33 09.9	-42.3	14.2	34 08.1	-42.2	14.3	35 06.2	-41.9	14.5	36 04.3	-41.8	14.7	71
72	28 33.8	-43.5	12.8	29 32.3	-43.3	12.9	30 30.7	-43.1	13.0	31 29.2	-42.9	13.2	32 27.6	-42.7	13.3	33 25.9	-42.5	13.5	34 24.3	-42.3	13.6	35 22.5	-42.1	13.8	72
73	27 50.3	-43.7	12.0	28 49.0	-43.5	12.1	29 47.6	-43.3	12.2	30 46.3	-43.2	12.4	31 44.9	-43.1	12.5	32 43.4	-42.8	12.6	33 42.0	-42.7	12.8	34 40.4	-42.4	12.9	73
74	27 06.6	-43.9	11.2	28 05.5	-43.8	11.3	29 04.3	-43.7	11.4	30 03.1	-43.5	11.6	31 01.8	-43.3	11.7	32 00.6	-43.2	11.8	32 59.3	-43.0	11.9	33 58.0	-42.8	12.1	74
75	26 22.7	-44.2	10.5	27 21.7	-44.1	10.6	28 20.6	-43.9	10.7	29 19.6	-43.8	10.8	30 18.5	-43.6	10.9	31 17.4	-43.4	11.0	32 16.3	-43.3	11.1	33 15.2	-43.2	11.2	75
76	25 38.5	-44.5	9.7	26 37.6	-44.3	9.8	27 36.7	-44.1	9.9	28 35.8	-44.0	10.0	29 34.9	-43.9	10.1	30 34.0	-43.8	10.2	31 33.0	-43.6	10.3	32 32.0	-43.4	10.4	76
77	24 54.0	-44.6	9.0	25 53.3	-44.5	9.1	26 52.6	-44.5	9.1	27 51.8	-44.3	9.2	28 51.0	-44.2	9.3	29 50.2	-44.0	9.4	30 49.4	-43.9	9.5	31 48.6	-43.8	9.6	77
78	24 09.4	-44.8	8.2	25 08.8	-44.8	8.3	26 08.1	-44.6	8.4	27 07.5	-44.5	8.5	28 06.8	-44.4	8.5	29 06.2	-44.3	8.6	30 05.5	-44.2	8.7	31 04.8	-44.1	8.8	78
79	23 24.6	-45.1	7.5	24 24.0	-44.9	7.6	25 23.5	-44.8	7.6	26 23.0	-44.8	7.7	27 22.4	-44.6	7.8	28 21.9	-44.6	7.8	29 21.3	-44.4	7.9	30 20.7	-44.3	8.0	79
80	22 39.5	-45.2	6.8	23 39.1	-45.2	6.9	24 38.7	-45.1	6.9	25 38.2	-45.0	7.0	26 37.8	-44.9	7.0	27 37.3	-44.8	7.1	28 36.9	-44.8	7.2	29 36.4	-44.6	7.2	80
81	21 54.3	-45.4	6.1	22 53.9	-45.3	6.1	23 53.6	-45.3	6.2	24 53.2	-45.2	6.2	25 52.9	-45.1	6.3	26 52.5	-45.0	6.3	27 52.1	-44.9	6.4	28 51.8	-44.9	6.5	81
82	21 08.9	-45.6	5.4	22 08.6	-45.5	5.4	23 08.3	-45.4	5.5	24 08.0	-45.3	5.5	25 07.8	-45.4	5.6	26 07.5	-45.3	5.6	27 07.2	-45.2	5.6	28 06.9	-45.1	5.7	82
83	20 23.3	-45.8	4.7	21 23.1	-45.7	4.7	22 22.9	-45.7	4.8	23 22.7	-45.6	4.8	24 22.4	-45.5	4.8	25 22.2	-45.4	4.9	26 22.0	-45.4	4.9	27 21.8	-45.4	5.0	83
84	19 37.5	-45.9	4.0	20 37.4	-45.9	4.0	21 37.2	-45.8	4.1	22 37.1	-45.8	4.1	23 36.9	-45.7	4.1	24 36.8	-45.7	4.1	25 36.6	-45.6	4.2	26 36.4	-45.5	4.2	84
85	18 51.6	-46.0	3.3	19 51.5	-46.0	3.3	20 51.4	-46.0	3.4	21 51.3	-45.9	3.4	22 51.2	-45.9	3.4	23 51.1	-45.9	3.4	24 51.0	-45.8	3.5	25 50.9	-45.8	3.5	85
86	18 05.6	-46.2	2.6	19 05.5	-46.2	2.7	20 05.4	-46.1	2.7	21 05.4	-46.2	2.7	22 05.3	-46.1	2.7	23 05.2	-46.0	2.7	24 05.2	-46.1	2.8	25 05.1	-46.0	2.8	86
87	17 19.4	-46.4	2.0	18 19.3	-46.3	2.0	19 19.3	-46.3	2.0	20 19.2	-46.2	2.0	21 19.2	-46.2	2.0	22 19.2	-46.3	2.0	23 19.1	-46.2	2.1	24 19.1	-46.2	2.1	87
88	16 33.0	-46.4	1.3	17 33.0	-46.4	1.3	18 33.0	-46.4	1.3	19 33.0	-46.4	1.3	20 33.0	-46.4	1.3	21 32.9	-46.3	1.4	22 32.9	-46.4	1.4	23 32.9	-46.4	1.4	88
89	15 46.6	-46.6	0.7	16 46.6	-46.6	0.7	17 46.6	-46.6	0.7	18 46.6	-46.6	0.7	19 46.6	-46.6	0.7	20 46.6	-46.6	0.7	21 46.5	-46.5	0.7	22 46.5	-46.5	0.7	89
90	15 00.0	-46.7	0.0	16 00.0	-46.7	0.0	17 00.0	-46.7	0.0	18 00.0	-46.7	0.0	19 00.0	-46.7	0.0	20 00.0	-46.7	0.0	21 00.0	-46.7	0.0	22 00.0	-46.7	0.0	90
	15°			16°			17°			18°			19°			20°			21°			22°			

39°, 321° L.H.A. LATITUDE SAME NAME AS DECLINATION

80

LATITUDE CONTRARY NAME TO DECLINATION — L.H.A. 39°, 321°

Dec.	15° Hc	d	Z	16° Hc	d	Z	17° Hc	d	Z	18° Hc	d	Z	19° Hc	d	Z	20° Hc	d	Z	21° Hc	d	Z	22° Hc	d	Z	Dec.
°	° ′	′	°	° ′	′	°	° ′	′	°	° ′	′	°	° ′	′	°	° ′	′	°	° ′	′	°	° ′	′	°	°
0	48 38.9	-24.0	107.7	48 20.1	-25.4	108.8	48 00.2	-26.7	109.9	47 39.3	-27.9	110.9	47 17.4	-29.2	111.9	46 54.6	-30.5	112.9	46 30.8	-31.7	113.9	46 06.0	-32.8	114.8	0
1	48 14.9	-25.0	109.1	47 54.7	-26.3	110.2	47 33.5	-27.6	111.2	47 11.4	-28.9	112.2	46 48.2	-30.1	113.2	46 24.1	-31.2	114.2	45 59.1	-32.4	115.1	45 33.2	-33.5	116.0	1
2	47 49.9	-25.9	110.5	47 28.4	-27.2	111.5	47 05.9	-28.4	112.5	46 42.5	-29.7	113.5	46 18.1	-30.8	114.4	45 52.9	-32.1	115.4	45 26.7	-33.2	116.3	44 59.7	-34.3	117.2	2
3	47 24.0	-26.9	111.8	47 01.2	-28.1	112.8	46 37.5	-29.4	113.8	46 12.8	-30.5	114.7	45 47.3	-31.7	115.7	45 20.8	-32.8	116.6	44 53.5	-33.8	117.5	44 25.4	-34.9	118.4	3
4	46 57.1	-27.7	113.1	46 33.1	-29.0	114.1	46 08.1	-30.1	115.0	45 42.3	-31.3	116.0	45 15.6	-32.4	116.9	44 48.0	-33.5	117.8	44 19.7	-34.6	118.6	43 50.5	-35.6	119.5	4
5	46 29.4	-28.6	114.4	46 04.1	-29.8	115.4	45 38.0	-30.9	116.3	45 11.0	-32.1	117.2	44 43.2	-33.2	118.1	44 14.5	-34.2	118.9	43 45.1	-35.2	119.8	43 14.9	-36.2	120.6	5
6	46 00.8	-29.4	115.7	45 34.3	-30.5	116.6	45 07.1	-31.8	117.5	44 38.9	-32.8	118.4	44 10.0	-33.8	119.2	43 40.3	-34.9	120.1	43 09.9	-35.9	120.9	42 38.7	-36.8	121.7	6
7	45 31.4	-30.3	116.9	45 03.8	-31.4	117.8	44 35.3	-32.4	118.7	44 06.1	-33.5	119.6	43 36.2	-34.6	120.4	43 05.4	-35.5	121.2	42 34.0	-36.5	122.0	42 01.9	-37.5	122.8	7
8	45 01.1	-31.0	118.2	44 32.4	-32.1	119.0	44 02.9	-33.2	119.9	43 32.6	-34.1	120.7	43 01.6	-35.1	121.5	42 29.9	-36.1	122.3	41 57.5	-37.1	123.1	41 24.4	-37.9	123.8	8
9	44 30.1	-31.7	119.4	44 00.3	-32.8	120.2	43 29.7	-33.8	121.0	42 58.5	-34.9	121.8	42 26.5	-35.8	122.6	41 53.8	-36.8	123.4	41 20.4	-37.6	124.1	40 46.5	-38.5	124.8	9
10	43 58.4	-32.5	120.6	43 27.5	-33.5	121.4	42 55.9	-34.5	122.2	42 23.6	-35.4	122.9	41 50.7	-36.4	123.7	41 17.0	-37.3	124.4	40 42.8	-38.2	125.2	40 08.0	-39.1	125.8	10
11	43 25.9	-33.2	121.7	42 54.0	-34.2	122.5	42 21.4	-35.1	123.3	41 48.2	-36.1	124.0	41 14.3	-37.0	124.8	40 39.7	-37.8	125.5	40 04.6	-38.7	126.2	39 28.9	-39.5	126.8	11
12	42 52.7	-33.8	122.9	42 19.8	-34.8	123.6	41 46.3	-35.8	124.4	41 12.1	-36.7	125.1	40 37.3	-37.5	125.8	40 01.9	-38.4	126.5	39 25.9	-39.2	127.2	38 49.4	-40.0	127.8	12
13	42 18.9	-34.5	124.0	41 45.0	-35.4	124.7	41 10.5	-36.3	125.4	40 35.4	-37.2	126.1	39 59.8	-38.1	126.8	39 23.5	-38.9	127.5	38 46.7	-39.6	128.1	38 09.4	-40.4	128.8	13
14	41 44.4	-35.1	125.1	41 09.6	-36.0	125.8	40 34.2	-36.9	126.5	39 58.2	-37.7	127.2	39 21.7	-38.5	127.8	38 44.6	-39.3	128.5	38 07.1	-40.2	129.1	37 29.0	-40.9	129.7	14
15	41 09.3	-35.7	126.2	40 33.6	-36.6	126.9	39 57.3	-37.4	127.5	39 20.5	-38.2	128.2	38 43.2	-39.1	128.8	38 05.3	-39.8	129.4	37 26.9	-40.5	130.0	36 48.1	-41.3	130.6	15
16	40 33.6	-36.3	127.2	39 57.0	-37.1	127.9	39 19.9	-37.9	128.5	38 42.3	-38.8	129.2	38 04.1	-39.5	129.8	37 25.5	-40.3	130.4	36 46.4	-41.0	131.0	36 06.8	-41.7	131.5	16
17	39 57.3	-36.8	128.3	39 19.9	-37.6	128.9	38 42.0	-38.5	129.5	38 03.5	-39.2	130.2	37 24.6	-40.0	130.7	36 45.2	-40.7	131.3	36 05.4	-41.4	131.9	35 25.1	-42.0	132.4	17
18	39 20.5	-37.3	129.3	38 42.3	-38.2	129.9	38 03.5	-38.9	130.5	37 24.3	-39.7	131.1	36 44.6	-40.4	131.7	36 04.5	-41.1	132.2	35 24.0	-41.8	132.8	34 43.1	-42.5	133.3	18
19	38 43.2	-37.9	130.3	38 04.1	-38.6	130.9	37 24.6	-39.4	131.5	36 44.6	-40.1	132.0	36 04.2	-40.8	132.6	35 23.4	-41.5	133.1	34 42.2	-42.2	133.6	34 00.6	-42.8	134.1	19
20	38 05.3	-38.4	131.3	37 25.5	-39.1	131.9	36 45.2	-39.8	132.4	36 04.5	-40.5	133.0	35 23.4	-41.2	133.5	34 41.9	-41.9	134.0	34 00.0	-42.5	134.5	33 17.8	-43.1	135.0	20
21	37 26.9	-38.8	132.3	36 46.4	-39.6	132.8	36 05.4	-40.3	133.4	35 24.0	-40.9	133.9	34 42.2	-41.6	134.4	34 00.0	-42.2	134.9	33 17.5	-42.8	135.3	32 34.7	-43.5	135.8	21
22	36 48.1	-39.3	133.2	36 06.8	-40.0	133.8	35 25.1	-40.6	134.3	34 43.1	-41.4	134.8	34 00.6	-41.9	135.3	33 17.8	-42.6	135.7	32 34.7	-43.2	136.2	31 51.2	-43.7	136.6	22
23	36 08.8	-39.7	134.2	35 26.8	-40.3	134.7	34 44.5	-41.1	135.2	34 01.7	-41.6	135.7	33 18.7	-42.3	136.1	32 35.2	-42.9	136.6	31 51.5	-43.5	137.0	31 07.5	-44.1	137.4	23
24	35 29.1	-40.1	135.1	34 46.5	-40.8	135.6	34 03.4	-41.4	136.1	33 20.1	-42.1	136.5	32 36.4	-42.7	137.0	31 52.3	-43.2	137.4	31 08.0	-43.7	137.8	30 23.4	-44.3	138.2	24
25	34 49.0	-40.5	136.0	34 05.7	-41.2	136.5	33 22.0	-41.8	136.9	32 38.0	-42.4	137.4	31 53.7	-42.9	137.8	31 09.1	-43.5	138.2	30 24.3	-44.1	138.6	29 39.1	-44.6	139.0	25
26	34 08.5	-40.9	136.9	33 24.5	-41.5	137.3	32 40.2	-42.1	137.8	31 55.6	-42.7	138.2	31 10.8	-43.3	138.6	30 25.6	-43.8	139.0	29 40.2	-44.3	139.4	28 54.5	-44.8	139.7	26
27	33 27.6	-41.3	137.8	32 43.0	-41.9	138.2	31 58.1	-42.4	138.6	31 12.9	-43.0	139.0	30 27.5	-43.6	139.4	29 41.8	-44.1	139.8	28 55.9	-44.6	140.2	28 09.7	-45.1	140.5	27
28	32 46.3	-41.6	138.6	32 01.1	-42.2	139.1	31 15.7	-42.8	139.5	30 29.9	-43.3	139.8	29 43.9	-43.8	140.2	28 57.7	-44.3	140.6	28 11.3	-44.9	140.9	27 24.6	-45.4	141.2	28
29	32 04.7	-42.0	139.5	31 18.9	-42.5	139.9	30 32.9	-43.1	140.3	29 46.6	-43.6	140.6	29 00.1	-44.1	141.0	28 13.4	-44.6	141.3	27 26.4	-45.1	141.7	26 39.2	-45.5	142.0	29
30	31 22.7	-42.3	140.3	30 36.4	-42.8	140.7	29 49.8	-43.3	141.1	29 03.0	-43.8	141.4	28 16.0	-44.4	141.8	27 28.8	-44.9	142.1	26 41.3	-45.3	142.4	25 53.7	-45.8	142.7	30
31	30 40.4	-42.6	141.2	29 53.6	-43.2	141.5	29 06.5	-43.7	141.9	28 19.2	-44.2	142.2	27 31.6	-44.6	142.5	26 43.9	-45.1	142.8	25 56.0	-45.5	143.1	25 07.9	-46.0	143.4	31
32	29 57.8	-42.9	142.0	29 10.4	-43.4	142.3	28 22.8	-43.9	142.7	27 35.0	-44.3	143.0	26 47.0	-44.8	143.3	25 58.8	-45.3	143.6	25 10.5	-45.8	143.9	24 21.9	-46.1	144.1	32
33	29 14.9	-43.2	142.8	28 27.0	-43.6	143.1	27 38.9	-44.1	143.4	26 50.7	-44.7	143.7	26 02.2	-45.1	144.0	25 13.5	-45.5	144.3	24 24.7	-45.9	144.6	23 35.8	-46.4	144.8	33
34	28 31.7	-43.4	143.6	27 43.4	-44.0	143.9	26 54.8	-44.4	144.2	26 06.0	-44.8	144.5	25 17.1	-45.3	144.8	24 28.0	-45.7	145.0	23 38.8	-46.1	145.3	22 49.4	-46.5	145.5	34
35	27 48.3	-43.7	144.4	26 59.4	-44.2	144.7	26 10.4	-44.6	144.9	25 21.2	-45.1	145.2	24 31.8	-45.4	145.5	23 42.3	-45.9	145.7	22 52.7	-46.3	146.0	22 02.9	-46.7	146.2	35
36	27 04.6	-44.0	145.1	26 15.2	-44.4	145.4	25 25.8	-44.9	145.7	24 36.1	-45.2	145.9	23 46.4	-45.7	146.2	22 56.4	-46.1	146.4	22 06.4	-46.5	146.7	21 16.2	-46.9	146.9	36
37	26 20.6	-44.2	145.9	25 30.8	-44.6	146.2	24 40.9	-45.0	146.4	23 50.9	-45.5	146.7	23 00.7	-45.9	146.9	22 10.3	-46.2	147.1	21 19.9	-46.7	147.3	20 29.3	-47.0	147.6	37
38	25 36.4	-44.4	146.6	24 46.2	-44.8	146.9	23 55.9	-45.3	147.1	23 05.4	-45.7	147.4	22 14.8	-46.0	147.6	21 24.1	-46.4	147.8	20 33.2	-46.8	148.0	19 42.3	-47.2	148.2	38
39	24 52.0	-44.7	147.4	24 01.4	-45.1	147.6	23 10.6	-45.4	147.9	22 19.7	-45.8	148.1	21 28.8	-46.3	148.3	20 37.7	-46.6	148.5	19 46.4	-46.9	148.7	18 55.1	-47.3	148.9	39
40	24 07.3	-44.9	148.1	23 16.3	-45.3	148.3	22 25.2	-45.7	148.6	21 33.9	-46.0	148.8	20 42.5	-46.3	149.0	19 51.1	-46.8	149.2	18 59.5	-47.1	149.3	18 07.8	-47.4	149.5	40
41	23 22.4	-45.0	148.8	22 31.0	-45.4	149.1	21 39.5	-45.8	149.3	20 47.9	-46.2	149.5	19 56.2	-46.6	149.7	19 04.3	-46.8	149.8	18 12.4	-47.2	150.0	17 20.4	-47.5	150.2	41
42	22 37.4	-45.3	149.6	21 45.6	-45.6	149.8	20 53.7	-46.0	150.0	20 01.7	-46.3	150.1	19 09.6	-46.6	150.3	18 17.5	-47.0	150.5	17 25.2	-47.3	150.6	16 32.9	-47.7	150.8	42
43	21 52.1	-45.4	150.3	21 00.0	-45.8	150.5	20 07.7	-46.1	150.6	19 15.4	-46.5	150.8	18 23.0	-46.8	151.0	17 30.5	-47.2	151.1	16 37.9	-47.5	151.3	15 45.2	-47.8	151.4	43
44	21 06.7	-45.6	151.0	20 14.2	-45.9	151.2	19 21.6	-46.3	151.3	18 28.9	-46.6	151.5	17 36.2	-47.0	151.6	16 43.3	-47.2	151.8	15 50.4	-47.5	151.9	14 57.4	-47.8	152.1	44
45	20 21.1	-45.7	151.7	19 28.3	-46.1	151.8	18 35.3	-46.4	152.0	17 42.3	-46.7	152.2	16 49.2	-47.0	152.3	15 56.1	-47.4	152.4	15 02.9	-47.7	152.6	14 09.6	-48.0	152.7	45
46	19 35.4	-46.0	152.4	18 42.2	-46.3	152.5	17 48.9	-46.5	152.7	16 55.6	-46.9	152.8	16 02.2	-47.2	152.9	15 08.7	-47.5	153.1	14 15.2	-47.8	153.2	13 21.6	-48.0	153.3	46
47	18 49.4	-46.0	153.0	17 55.9	-46.3	153.2	17 02.4	-46.7	153.3	16 08.7	-47.0	153.5	15 15.0	-47.3	153.6	14 21.2	-47.5	153.7	13 27.4	-47.8	153.8	12 33.6	-48.2	153.9	47
48	18 03.4	-46.2	153.7	17 09.6	-46.5	153.9	16 15.7	-46.8	154.0	15 21.7	-47.1	154.1	14 27.7	-47.4	154.2	13 33.7	-47.7	154.3	12 39.6	-48.0	154.4	11 45.4	-48.2	154.5	48
49	17 17.2	-46.4	154.4	16 23.1	-46.7	154.5	15 28.9	-47.0	154.6	14 34.6	-47.2	154.7	13 40.3	-47.4	154.9	12 46.0	-47.8	155.0	11 51.6	-48.0	155.0	10 57.2	-48.3	155.1	49
50	16 30.8	-46.4	155.0	15 36.4	-46.7	155.2	14 41.9	-47.0	155.3	13 47.4	-47.3	155.4	12 52.9	-47.6	155.5	11 58.2	-47.8	155.6	11 03.6	-48.1	155.7	10 08.9	-48.3	155.7	50
51	15 44.4	-46.6	155.7	14 49.7	-46.9	155.8	13 54.9	-47.1	155.9	13 00.1	-47.4	156.0	12 05.3	-47.7	156.1	11 10.4	-47.9	156.2	10 15.5	-48.2	156.3	9 20.6	-48.5	156.3	51
52	14 57.8	-46.7	156.4	14 02.8	-46.9	156.5	13 07.8	-47.2	156.6	12 12.7	-47.4	156.6	11 17.6	-47.7	156.7	10 22.5	-48.0	156.8	9 27.3	-48.2	156.9	8 32.1	-48.4	156.9	52
53	14 11.1	-46.8	157.0	13 15.9	-47.1	157.1	12 20.6	-47.3	157.2	11 25.3	-47.6	157.3	10 29.9	-47.8	157.3	9 34.5	-48.0	157.4	8 39.1	-48.3	157.5	7 43.7	-48.5	157.5	53
54	13 24.3	-46.9	157.6	12 28.8	-47.1	157.7	11 33.3	-47.4	157.8	10 37.7	-47.6	157.9	9 42.1	-47.9	158.0	8 46.5	-48.1	158.0	7 50.8	-48.3	158.1	6 55.2	-48.6	158.1	54
55	12 37.4	-46.9	158.3	11 41.7	-47.2	158.4	10 45.9	-47.5	158.4	9 50.1	-47.7	158.5	8 54.2	-47.9	158.6	7 58.4	-48.2	158.6	7 02.5	-48.4	158.7	6 06.6	-48.6	158.7	55
56	11 50.5	-47.1	158.9	10 54.5	-47.3	159.0	9 58.4	-47.5	159.1	9 02.4	-47.8	159.1	8 06.3	-48.0	159.2	7 10.2	-48.2	159.2	6 14.1	-48.4	159.3	5 18.0	-48.6	159.3	56
57	11 03.4	-47.2	159.6	10 07.2	-47.4	159.6	9 10.9	-47.6	159.7	8 14.6	-47.8	159.7	7 18.3	-48.0	159.8	6 22.0	-48.2	159.8	5 25.7	-48.5	159.9	4 29.4	-48.7	159.9	57
58	10 16.2	-47.2	160.2	9 19.8	-47.4	160.2	8 23.3	-47.6	160.3	7 26.8	-47.8	160.3	6 30.3	-48.1	160.4	5 33.8	-48.3	160.4	4 37.2	-48.4	160.5	3 40.7	-48.7	160.5	58
59	9 29.0	-47.3	160.8	8 32.4	-47.5	160.9	7 35.7	-47.7	160.9	6 39.0	-48.0	161.0	5 42.2	-48.1	161.0	4 45.5	-48.3	161.0	3 48.8	-48.6	161.0	2 52.0	-48.7	161.1	59
60	8 41.7	-47.3	161.4	7 44.9	-47.6	161.5	6 48.0	-47.8	161.5	5 51.0	-47.9	161.6	4 54.1	-48.1	161.6	3 57.2	-48.3	161.6	3 00.2	-48.5	161.6	2 03.3	-48.7	161.6	60
61	7 54.4	-47.4	162.1	6 57.3	-47.6	162.1	6 00.2	-47.8	162.1	5 03.1	-48.0	162.2	4 06.0	-48.2	162.2	3 08.9	-48.4	162.2	2 11.7	-48.5	162.2	1 14.6	-48.7	162.2	61
62	7 07.0	-47.4	162.7	6 09.7	-47.6	162.7	5 12.4	-47.8	162.7	4 15.1	-48.0	162.8	3 17.8	-48.2	162.8	2 20.5	-48.4	162.8	1 23.2	-48.6	162.8	0 25.9	-48.8	162.8	62
63	6 19.6	-47.5	163.3	5 22.1	-47.7	163.3	4 24.6	-47.8	163.3	3 27.1	-48.0	163.4	2 29.6	-48.2	163.4	1 32.1	-48.3	163.4	0 34.6	-48.5	163.4	0 22.9	+48.7	16.6	63
64	5 32.1	-47.6	163.9	4 34.4	-47.7	163.9	3 36.8	-47.9	164.0	2 39.1	-48.1	164.0	1 41.4	-48.2	164.0	0 43.8	-48.4	164.0	0 13.9	+48.6	16.0	1 11.6	+48.7	16.0	64
65	4 44.5	-47.5	164.5	3 46.7	-47.7	164.5	2 48.9	-47.9	164.6	1 51.0	-48.0	164.6	0 53.2	-48.2	164.6	0 04.6	+48.4	15.4	1 02.5	+48.5	15.4	2 00.3	+48.7	15.4	65
66	3 57.0	-47.6	165.1	2 59.0	-47.8	165.1	2 01.0	-47.9	165.2	1 03.0	-48.1	165.2	0 05.0	-48.2	165.2	0 53.0	+48.4	14.8	1 51.0	+48.5	14.8	2 49.0	+48.7	14.8	66
67	3 09.4	-47.6	165.7	2 11.2	-47.7	165.8	1 13.1	-47.9	165.8	0 14.9	-48.0	165.8	0 43.2	+48.2	14.2	1 41.4	+48.4	14.2	2 39.5	+48.6	14.3	3 37.7	+48.7	14.3	67
68	2 21.8	-47.6	166.4	1 23.5	-47.8	166.4	0 25.2	-47.9	166.4	0 33.1	+48.1	13.6	1 31.4	+48.3	13.6	2 29.8	+48.3	13.6	3 28.1	+48.5	13.7	4 26.4	+48.6	13.7	68
69	1 34.2	-47.7	167.0	0 35.7	-47.8	167.0	0 22.7	+48.0	13.0	1 21.2	+48.1	13.0	2 19.7	+48.1	13.0	3 18.1	+48.3	13.1	4 16.6	+48.4	13.1	5 15.0	+48.6	13.1	69
70	0 46.5	-47.6	167.6	0 12.1	+47.7	12.4	1 10.7	+47.9	12.4	2 09.3	+48.0	12.4	3 07.8	+48.2	12.4	4 06.4	+48.3	12.5	5 05.0	+48.5	12.5	6 03.6	+48.6	12.5	70
71	0 01.1	+47.7	11.8	0 59.8	+47.8	11.8	1 58.6	+47.9	11.8	2 57.3	+48.0	11.8	3 56.0	+48.2	11.9	4 54.7	+48.3	11.9	5 53.5	+48.4	11.9	6 52.2	+48.5	11.9	71
72	0 48.8	+47.6	11.2	1 47.6	+47.8	11.2	2 46.5	+47.8	11.2	3 45.3	+48.0	11.2	4 44.2	+48.1	11.3	5 43.0	+48.2	11.3	6 41.9	+48.3	11.3	7 40.7	+48.5	11.3	72
73	1 36.4	+47.6	10.6	2 35.4	+47.7	10.6	3 34.3	+47.9	10.6	4 33.3	+48.0	10.6	5 32.3	+48.1	10.7	6 31.2	+48.2	10.7	7 30.2	+48.3	10.7	8 29.2	+48.4	10.7	73
74	2 24.0	+47.6	10.0	3 23.1	+47.7	10.0	4 22.2	+47.8	10.0	5 21.3	+47.9	10.0	6 20.4	+48.0	10.1	7 19.4	+48.2	10.1	8 18.5	+48.3	10.1	9 17.6	+48.3	10.1	74
75	3 11.6	+47.6	9.4	4 10.8	+47.7	9.4	5 10.0	+47.8	9.4	6 09.2	+47.9	9.4	7 08.4	+48.0	9.4	8 07.6	+48.1	9.5	9 06.8	+48.2	9.5	10 05.9	+48.3	9.5	75
76	3 59.2	+47.6	8.8	4 58.5	+47.7	8.8	5 57.8	+47.8	8.8	6 57.1	+47.8	8.8	7 56.4	+47.9	8.8	8 55.7	+48.0	8.9	9 55.0	+48.1	8.9	10 54.2	+48.2	8.9	76
77	4 46.8	+47.5	8.2	5 46.2	+47.6	8.2	6 45.6	+47.7	8.2	7 44.9	+47.8	8.2	8 44.3	+47.9	8.2	9 43.7	+48.0	8.3	10 43.1	+48.0	8.3	11 42.4	+48.2	8.3	77
78	5 34.3	+47.5	7.6	6 33.8	+47.5	7.6	7 33.3	+47.6	7.6	8 32.7	+47.8	7.6	9 32.2	+47.8	7.6	10 31.7	+47.9	7.6	11 31.1	+48.0	7.7	12 30.6	+48.1	7.7	78
79	6 21.8	+47.4	6.9	7 21.3	+47.6	7.0	8 20.9	+47.6	7.0	9 20.5	+47.6	7.0	10 20.0	+47.8	7.0	11 19.6	+47.8	7.0	12 19.1	+47.9	7.1	13 18.7	+47.9	7.1	79
80	7 09.2	+47.4	6.3	8 08.9	+47.4	6.3	9 08.5	+47.5	6.4	10 08.1	+47.6	6.4	11 07.8	+47.6	6.4	12 07.4	+47.7	6.4	13 07.0	+47.8	6.4	14 06.6	+47.9	6.5	80
81	7 56.6	+47.4	5.7	8 56.3	+47.4	5.7	9 56.0	+47.5	5.7	10 55.7	+47.6	5.8	11 55.4	+47.6	5.8	12 55.1	+47.7	5.8	13 54.8	+47.7	5.8	14 54.5	+47.8	5.8	81
82	8 44.0	+47.3	5.1	9 43.7	+47.4	5.1	10 43.5	+47.4	5.1	11 43.3	+47.4	5.1	12 43.0	+47.5	5.2	13 42.8	+47.5	5.2	14 42.5	+47.6	5.2	15 42.3	+47.6	5.2	82
83	9 31.3	+47.2	4.5	10 31.1	+47.2	4.5	11 30.9	+47.3	4.5	12 30.7	+47.4	4.5	13 30.5	+47.4	4.5	14 30.3	+47.5	4.5	15 30.1	+47.5	4.6	16 29.9	+47.6	4.6	83
84	10 18.5	+47.1	3.8	11 18.3	+47.2	3.8	12 18.2	+47.2	3.9	13 18.1	+47.2	3.9	14 17.9	+47.3	3.9	15 17.8	+47.3	3.9	16 17.6	+47.4	3.9	17 17.5	+47.4	4.0	84
85	11 05.6	+47.1	3.2	12 05.5	+47.1	3.2	13 05.4	+47.1	3.2	14 05.3	+47.2	3.2	15 05.2	+47.2	3.3	16 05.1	+47.3	3.3	17 05.0	+47.3	3.3	18 04.9	+47.3	3.3	85
86	11 52.7	+46.9	2.6	12 52.6	+47.0	2.6	13 52.5	+47.1	2.6	14 52.5	+47.0	2.6	15 52.4	+47.1	2.6	16 52.4	+47.1	2.6	17 52.3	+47.1	2.6	18 52.2	+47.2	2.7	86
87	12 39.6	+46.9	1.9	13 39.6	+46.9	1.9	14 39.6	+46.9	2.0	15 39.5	+47.0	2.0	16 39.5	+47.0	2.0	17 39.5	+47.0	2.0	18 39.4	+47.0	2.0	19 39.4	+47.0	2.0	87
88	13 26.5	+46.8	1.3	14 26.5	+46.8	1.3	15 26.5	+46.8	1.3	16 26.5	+46.8	1.3	17 26.5	+46.8	1.3	18 26.5	+46.8	1.3	19 26.4	+46.9	1.3	20 26.4	+46.9	1.3	88
89	14 13.3	+46.7	0.6	15 13.3	+46.7	0.7	16 13.3	+46.7	0.7	17 13.3	+46.7	0.7	18 13.3	+46.7	0.7	19 13.3	+46.7	0.7	20 13.3	+46.7	0.7	21 13.3	+46.7	0.7	89
90	15 00.0	+46.6	0.0	16 00.0	+46.6	0.0	17 00.0	+46.6	0.0	18 00.0	+46.6	0.0	19 00.0	+46.6	0.0	20 00.0	+46.6	0.0	21 00.0	+46.5	0.0	22 00.0	+46.5	0.0	90
	15°			16°			17°			18°			19°			20°			21°			22°			

S. Lat. { L.H.A. greater than 180° ....Zn=180°–Z
L.H.A. less than 180°............Zn=180°+Z

LATITUDE SAME NAME AS DECLINATION — L.H.A. 141°, 219°

40°, 320° L.H.A. LATITUDE **SAME** NAME AS DECLINATION N. Lat. {L.H.A. greater than 180° .....Zn=Z; L.H.A. less than 180°............Zn=360°–Z

Dec.	15° Hc	d	Z	16° Hc	d	Z	17° Hc	d	Z	18° Hc	d	Z
°	° ′	′	°	° ′	′	°	° ′	′	°	° ′	′	°
0	47 43.6	+22.6	107.1	47 25.4	+23.9	108.2	47 06.1	+25.4	109.2	46 45.9	+26.6	110.2
1	48 06.2	+21.6	105.8	47 49.3	+23.0	106.8	47 31.5	+24.3	107.9	47 12.5	+25.7	108.9
2	48 27.8	+20.5	104.4	48 12.3	+22.0	105.4	47 55.8	+23.4	106.5	47 38.2	+24.8	107.6
3	48 48.3	+19.5	102.9	48 34.3	+21.0	104.0	48 19.2	+22.4	105.1	48 03.0	+23.8	106.2
4	49 07.8	+18.4	101.5	48 55.3	+19.8	102.6	48 41.6	+21.3	103.7	48 26.8	+22.7	104.8
5	49 26.2	+17.3	100.0	49 15.1	+18.8	101.2	49 02.9	+20.3	102.3	48 49.5	+21.8	103.4
6	49 43.5	+16.1	98.6	49 33.9	+17.7	99.7	49 23.2	+19.2	100.9	49 11.3	+20.7	102.0
7	49 59.6	+15.0	97.1	49 51.6	+16.5	98.2	49 42.4	+18.1	99.4	49 32.0	+19.6	100.6
8	50 14.6	+13.8	95.6	50 08.1	+15.4	96.7	50 00.5	+16.9	97.9	49 51.6	+18.5	99.1
9	50 28.4	+12.5	94.0	50 23.5	+14.2	95.2	50 17.4	+15.8	96.4	50 10.1	+17.3	97.6
10	50 40.9	+11.4	92.5	50 37.7	+13.0	93.7	50 33.2	+14.6	94.9	50 27.4	+16.2	96.1
11	50 52.3	+10.1	90.9	50 50.7	+11.7	92.2	50 47.8	+13.3	93.4	50 43.6	+14.9	94.6
12	51 02.4	+8.8	89.4	51 02.4	+10.5	90.6	51 01.1	+12.1	91.8	50 58.5	+13.8	93.1
13	51 11.2	+7.6	87.8	51 12.9	+9.2	89.0	51 13.2	+10.9	90.3	51 12.3	+12.5	91.5
14	51 18.8	+6.3	86.2	51 22.1	+8.0	87.5	51 24.1	+9.6	88.7	51 24.8	+11.3	90.0
15	51 25.1	+5.0	84.6	51 30.1	+6.6	85.9	51 33.7	+8.3	87.1	51 36.1	+9.9	88.4
16	51 30.1	+3.6	83.0	51 36.7	+5.3	84.3	51 42.0	+7.0	85.5	51 46.0	+8.7	86.8
17	51 33.7	+2.4	81.4	51 42.0	+4.0	82.7	51 49.0	+5.7	83.9	51 54.7	+7.4	85.2
18	51 36.1	+1.0	79.8	51 46.0	+2.7	81.1	51 54.7	+4.4	82.3	52 02.1	+6.0	83.6
19	51 37.1	−0.3	78.2	51 48.7	+1.4	79.4	51 59.1	+3.0	80.7	52 08.1	+4.7	82.0
20	51 36.8	−1.6	76.6	51 50.1	0.0	77.8	52 02.1	+1.7	79.1	52 12.8	+3.4	80.3
21	51 35.2	−2.9	75.0	51 50.1	−1.3	76.2	52 03.8	+0.3	77.4	52 16.2	+2.0	78.7
22	51 32.3	−4.3	73.4	51 48.8	−2.6	74.6	52 04.1	−0.9	75.8	52 18.2	+0.7	77.1
23	51 28.0	−5.5	71.8	51 46.2	−4.0	73.0	52 03.2	−2.4	74.2	52 18.9	−0.7	75.4
24	51 22.5	−6.9	70.2	51 42.2	−5.2	71.4	52 00.8	−3.7	72.6	52 18.2	−2.1	73.8
25	51 15.6	−8.1	68.6	51 37.0	−6.6	69.8	51 57.1	−5.0	70.9	52 16.1	−3.4	72.2
26	51 07.5	−9.4	67.0	51 30.4	−7.9	68.2	51 52.1	−6.3	69.3	52 12.7	−4.7	70.5
27	50 58.1	−10.7	65.4	51 22.5	−9.2	66.6	51 45.8	−7.6	67.7	52 08.0	−6.1	68.9
28	50 47.4	−11.9	63.9	51 13.3	−10.4	65.0	51 38.2	−9.0	66.1	52 01.9	−7.4	67.3
29	50 35.5	−13.1	62.3	51 02.9	−11.7	63.4	51 29.2	−10.2	64.5	51 54.5	−8.7	65.7
30	50 22.4	−14.3	60.8	50 51.2	−12.9	61.9	51 19.0	−11.5	63.0	51 45.8	−10.1	64.1
31	50 08.1	−15.5	59.3	50 38.3	−14.1	60.3	51 07.5	−12.7	61.4	51 35.7	−11.3	62.5
32	49 52.6	−16.6	57.8	50 24.2	−15.4	58.8	50 54.8	−14.0	59.8	51 24.4	−12.5	60.9
33	49 36.0	−17.8	56.3	50 08.8	−16.4	57.3	50 40.8	−15.1	58.3	51 11.9	−13.8	59.3
34	49 18.2	−18.9	54.8	49 52.4	−17.7	55.8	50 25.7	−16.4	56.8	50 58.1	−15.0	57.8
35	48 59.3	−19.9	53.4	49 34.7	−18.7	54.3	50 09.3	−17.5	55.3	50 43.1	−16.2	56.3
36	48 39.4	−21.1	51.9	49 16.0	−19.9	52.8	49 51.8	−18.6	53.8	50 26.9	−17.4	54.8
37	48 18.3	−22.0	50.5	48 56.1	−20.9	51.4	49 33.2	−19.7	52.3	50 09.5	−18.5	53.3
38	47 56.3	−23.0	49.1	48 35.2	−21.9	50.0	49 13.5	−20.8	50.9	49 51.0	−19.6	51.8
39	47 33.3	−24.0	47.7	48 13.3	−22.9	48.6	48 52.7	−21.9	49.4	49 31.4	−20.8	50.3
40	47 09.3	−24.9	46.4	47 50.4	−24.0	47.2	48 30.8	−22.8	48.0	49 10.6	−21.7	48.8
41	46 44.4	−25.9	45.1	47 26.4	−24.8	45.8	48 08.0	−23.9	46.6	48 48.9	−22.9	47.5
42	46 18.5	−26.7	43.8	47 01.6	−25.8	44.5	47 44.1	−24.8	45.3	48 26.0	−23.8	46.1
43	45 51.8	−27.6	42.5	46 35.8	−26.7	43.2	47 19.3	−25.8	43.9	48 02.2	−24.8	44.7
44	45 24.2	−28.5	41.2	46 09.1	−27.6	41.9	46 53.5	−26.6	42.6	47 37.4	−25.7	43.3
45	44 55.7	−29.2	39.9	45 41.5	−28.4	40.6	46 26.9	−27.6	41.3	47 11.7	−26.6	42.0
46	44 26.5	−30.0	38.7	45 13.1	−29.2	39.3	45 59.3	−28.4	40.0	46 45.1	−27.6	40.7
47	43 56.5	−30.7	37.5	44 43.9	−30.0	38.1	45 30.9	−29.2	38.7	46 17.5	−28.4	39.4
48	43 25.8	−31.5	36.3	44 13.9	−30.7	36.9	45 01.7	−30.0	37.5	45 49.1	−29.2	38.1
49	42 54.3	−32.2	35.1	43 43.2	−31.5	35.7	44 31.7	−30.7	36.3	45 19.9	−30.0	36.9
50	42 22.1	−32.9	34.0	43 11.7	−32.2	34.5	44 01.0	−31.6	35.1	44 49.9	−30.8	35.6
51	41 49.2	−33.5	32.9	42 39.5	−32.9	33.4	43 29.4	−32.2	33.9	44 19.1	−31.5	34.4
52	41 15.7	−34.1	31.8	42 06.6	−33.5	32.2	42 57.2	−32.9	32.7	43 47.6	−32.3	33.2
53	40 41.6	−34.7	30.7	41 33.1	−34.2	31.1	42 24.3	−33.5	31.6	43 15.3	−33.0	32.1
54	40 06.9	−35.4	29.6	40 58.9	−34.8	30.0	41 50.8	−34.3	30.5	42 42.3	−33.6	30.9
55	39 31.5	−35.8	28.6	40 24.1	−35.3	29.0	41 16.5	−34.8	29.4	42 08.7	−34.3	29.8
56	38 55.7	−36.4	27.5	39 48.8	−35.9	27.9	40 41.7	−35.4	28.3	41 34.4	−34.8	28.7
57	38 19.3	−37.0	26.5	39 12.9	−36.5	26.9	40 06.3	−36.0	27.2	40 59.6	−35.5	27.6
58	37 42.3	−37.4	25.5	38 36.4	−37.0	25.8	39 30.3	−36.5	26.2	40 24.1	−36.1	26.6
59	37 04.9	−37.9	24.5	37 59.4	−37.5	24.8	38 53.8	−37.1	25.2	39 48.0	−36.6	25.5
60	36 27.0	−38.4	23.6	37 21.9	−38.0	23.9	38 16.7	−37.5	24.2	39 11.4	−37.2	24.5
61	35 48.6	−38.8	22.6	36 43.9	−38.4	22.9	37 39.2	−38.1	23.2	38 34.2	−37.6	23.5
62	35 09.8	−39.3	21.7	36 05.5	−38.9	21.9	37 01.1	−38.5	22.2	37 56.6	−38.2	22.5
63	34 30.5	−39.6	20.7	35 26.6	−39.3	21.0	36 22.6	−39.0	21.3	37 18.4	−38.6	21.5
64	33 50.9	−40.1	19.8	34 47.3	−39.7	20.1	35 43.6	−39.4	20.3	36 39.8	−39.0	20.6
65	33 10.8	−40.4	18.9	34 07.6	−40.2	19.2	35 04.2	−39.8	19.4	36 00.8	−39.5	19.6
66	32 30.4	−40.8	18.1	33 27.4	−40.5	18.3	34 24.4	−40.2	18.5	35 21.3	−40.0	18.7
67	31 49.6	−41.1	17.2	32 46.9	−40.8	17.4	33 44.2	−40.6	17.6	34 41.3	−40.3	17.8
68	31 08.5	−41.4	16.3	32 06.1	−41.2	16.5	33 03.6	−41.0	16.7	34 01.0	−40.7	16.9
69	30 27.1	−41.8	15.5	31 24.9	−41.6	15.7	32 22.6	−41.3	15.8	33 20.3	−41.1	16.0
70	29 45.3	−42.1	14.7	30 43.3	−41.9	14.8	31 41.3	−41.7	15.0	32 39.2	−41.4	15.1
71	29 03.2	−42.4	13.9	30 01.4	−42.2	14.0	30 59.6	−42.0	14.1	31 57.8	−41.8	14.3
72	28 20.8	−42.7	13.0	29 19.2	−42.4	13.2	30 17.6	−42.3	13.3	31 16.0	−42.1	13.4
73	27 38.1	−42.9	12.2	28 36.8	−42.8	12.4	29 35.4	−42.6	12.5	30 33.9	−42.4	12.6
74	26 55.2	−43.2	11.5	27 54.0	−43.0	11.6	28 52.8	−42.9	11.7	29 51.5	−42.7	11.8
75	26 12.0	−43.4	10.7	27 11.0	−43.3	10.8	28 09.9	−43.1	10.9	29 08.8	−43.0	11.0
76	25 28.6	−43.7	9.9	26 27.7	−43.6	10.0	27 26.8	−43.4	10.1	28 25.8	−43.2	10.2
77	24 44.9	−43.9	9.2	25 44.1	−43.7	9.2	26 43.4	−43.7	9.3	27 42.6	−43.6	9.4
78	24 01.0	−44.1	8.4	25 00.4	−44.0	8.5	25 59.7	−43.9	8.6	26 59.0	−43.8	8.6
79	23 16.9	−44.3	7.7	24 16.4	−44.3	7.7	25 15.8	−44.1	7.8	26 15.2	−44.0	7.9
80	22 32.6	−44.5	6.9	23 32.1	−44.4	7.0	24 31.7	−44.4	7.0	25 31.2	−44.2	7.1
81	21 48.1	−44.7	6.2	22 47.7	−44.6	6.3	23 47.3	−44.5	6.3	24 47.0	−44.5	6.4
82	21 03.4	−44.9	5.5	22 03.1	−44.8	5.5	23 02.8	−44.7	5.6	24 02.5	−44.7	5.6
83	20 18.5	−45.1	4.8	21 18.3	−45.0	4.8	22 18.1	−45.0	4.9	23 17.8	−44.8	4.9
84	19 33.4	−45.2	4.1	20 33.3	−45.2	4.1	21 33.1	−45.1	4.1	22 33.0	−45.1	4.2
85	18 48.2	−45.4	3.4	19 48.1	−45.3	3.4	20 48.0	−45.3	3.4	21 47.9	−45.3	3.5
86	18 02.8	−45.5	2.7	19 02.8	−45.5	2.7	20 02.7	−45.4	2.7	21 02.6	−45.4	2.8
87	17 17.3	−45.6	2.0	18 17.3	−45.6	2.0	19 17.3	−45.6	2.0	20 17.2	−45.6	2.1
88	16 31.7	−45.8	1.3	17 31.7	−45.8	1.3	18 31.7	−45.8	1.4	19 31.6	−45.7	1.4
89	15 45.9	−45.9	0.7	16 45.9	−45.9	0.7	17 45.9	−45.9	0.7	18 45.9	−45.9	0.7
90	15 00.0	−46.0	0.0	16 00.0	−46.0	0.0	17 00.0	−46.0	0.0	18 00.0	−46.0	0.0

Dec.	19° Hc	d	Z	20° Hc	d	Z	21° Hc	d	Z	22° Hc	d	Z
°	° ′	′	°	° ′	′	°	° ′	′	°	° ′	′	°
0	46 24.7	+27.9	111.2	46 02.5	+29.2	112.2	45 39.4	+30.4	113.1	45 15.4	+31.5	114.1
1	46 52.6	+27.0	109.9	46 31.7	+28.3	110.9	46 09.8	+29.5	111.9	45 46.9	+30.8	112.8
2	47 19.6	+26.1	108.6	47 00.0	+27.4	109.6	46 39.3	+28.7	110.6	46 17.7	+29.9	111.6
3	47 45.7	+25.2	107.3	47 27.4	+26.5	108.3	47 08.0	+27.8	109.3	46 47.6	+29.1	110.3
4	48 10.9	+24.1	105.9	47 53.9	+25.5	107.0	47 35.8	+26.9	108.0	47 16.7	+28.3	109.1
5	48 35.0	+23.2	104.5	48 19.4	+24.6	105.6	48 02.7	+26.0	106.7	47 45.0	+27.3	107.8
6	48 58.2	+22.2	103.1	48 44.0	+23.6	104.2	48 28.7	+25.0	105.3	48 12.3	+26.4	106.4
7	49 20.4	+21.1	101.7	49 07.6	+22.6	102.8	48 53.7	+24.0	104.0	48 38.7	+25.4	105.1
8	49 41.5	+20.0	100.3	49 30.2	+21.5	101.4	49 17.7	+23.0	102.6	49 04.1	+24.4	103.7
9	50 01.5	+18.9	98.8	49 51.7	+20.4	100.0	49 40.7	+21.9	101.1	49 28.5	+23.4	102.3
10	50 20.4	+17.7	97.3	50 12.1	+19.3	98.5	50 02.6	+20.8	99.7	49 51.9	+22.3	100.9
11	50 38.1	+16.6	95.8	50 31.4	+18.1	97.0	50 23.4	+19.7	98.2	50 14.2	+21.2	99.4
12	50 54.7	+15.3	94.3	50 49.5	+17.0	95.5	50 43.1	+18.6	96.8	50 35.4	+20.1	98.0
13	51 10.0	+14.2	92.8	51 06.5	+15.8	94.0	51 01.7	+17.3	95.2	50 55.5	+19.0	96.5
14	51 24.2	+12.9	91.2	51 22.3	+14.5	92.5	51 19.0	+16.2	93.7	51 14.5	+17.8	95.0
15	51 37.1	+11.6	89.6	51 36.8	+13.3	90.9	51 35.2	+14.9	92.2	51 32.3	+16.5	93.4
16	51 48.7	+10.4	88.1	51 50.1	+12.0	89.3	51 50.1	+13.7	90.6	51 48.8	+15.3	91.9
17	51 59.1	+9.0	86.5	52 02.1	+10.7	87.7	52 03.8	+12.4	89.0	52 04.1	+14.1	90.3
18	52 08.1	+7.8	84.9	52 12.8	+9.5	86.1	52 16.2	+11.1	87.4	52 18.2	+12.8	88.7
19	52 15.9	+6.4	83.2	52 22.3	+8.0	84.5	52 27.3	+9.8	85.8	52 31.0	+11.5	87.1
20	52 22.3	+5.0	81.6	52 30.3	+6.8	82.9	52 37.1	+8.4	84.2	52 42.5	+10.1	85.5
21	52 27.3	+3.7	80.0	52 37.1	+5.4	81.3	52 45.5	+7.1	82.6	52 52.6	+8.8	83.9
22	52 31.0	+2.3	78.3	52 42.5	+4.0	79.6	52 52.6	+5.7	80.9	53 01.4	+7.4	82.2
23	52 33.3	+1.0	76.7	52 46.5	+2.6	78.0	52 58.3	+4.3	79.3	53 08.8	+6.0	80.6
24	52 34.3	−0.4	75.1	52 49.1	+1.3	76.3	53 02.6	+3.0	77.6	53 14.8	+4.7	78.9
25	52 33.9	−1.8	73.4	52 50.4	−0.2	74.7	53 05.6	+1.5	76.0	53 19.5	+3.2	77.3
26	52 32.1	−3.1	71.8	52 50.2	−1.5	73.0	53 07.1	+0.2	74.3	53 22.7	+1.9	75.6
27	52 29.0	−4.5	70.1	52 48.7	−2.8	71.4	53 07.3	−1.2	72.6	53 24.6	+0.4	73.9
28	52 24.5	−5.9	68.5	52 45.9	−4.3	69.7	53 06.1	−2.7	71.0	53 25.0	−1.0	72.2
29	52 18.6	−7.2	66.9	52 41.6	−5.6	68.1	53 03.4	−4.0	69.3	53 24.0	−2.3	70.6
30	52 11.4	−8.5	65.2	52 36.0	−7.0	66.4	52 59.4	−5.4	67.6	53 21.7	−3.8	68.9
31	52 02.9	−9.8	63.6	52 29.0	−8.3	64.8	52 54.0	−6.7	66.0	53 17.9	−5.2	67.2
32	51 53.1	−11.1	62.0	52 20.7	−9.6	63.2	52 47.3	−8.2	64.3	53 12.7	−6.6	65.5
33	51 42.0	−12.4	60.4	52 11.1	−11.0	61.6	52 39.1	−9.4	62.7	53 06.1	−7.9	63.9
34	51 29.6	−13.6	58.9	52 00.1	−12.2	60.0	52 29.7	−10.8	61.1	52 58.2	−9.3	62.2
35	51 16.0	−14.9	57.3	51 47.9	−13.5	58.4	52 18.9	−12.1	59.5	52 48.9	−10.7	60.6
36	51 01.1	−16.1	55.8	51 34.4	−14.8	56.8	52 06.8	−13.4	57.9	52 38.2	−12.0	59.0
37	50 45.0	−17.3	54.2	51 19.6	−15.9	55.2	51 53.4	−14.6	56.3	52 26.2	−13.2	57.4
38	50 27.7	−18.4	52.7	51 03.7	−17.2	53.7	51 38.8	−15.9	54.7	52 13.0	−14.6	55.8
39	50 09.3	−19.6	51.2	50 46.5	−18.4	52.2	51 22.9	−17.1	53.2	51 58.4	−15.8	54.2
40	49 49.7	−20.6	49.8	50 28.1	−19.4	50.7	51 05.8	−18.3	51.6	51 42.6	−17.0	52.6
41	49 29.1	−21.7	48.3	50 08.7	−20.6	49.2	50 47.5	−19.4	50.1	51 25.6	−18.2	51.1
42	49 07.4	−22.8	46.9	49 48.1	−21.7	47.7	50 28.1	−20.6	48.6	51 07.4	−19.4	49.6
43	48 44.6	−23.8	45.5	49 26.4	−22.8	46.3	50 07.5	−21.7	47.2	50 48.0	−20.6	48.1
44	48 20.8	−24.8	44.1	49 03.6	−23.7	44.9	49 45.8	−22.7	45.7	50 27.4	−21.6	46.6
45	47 56.0	−25.7	42.7	48 39.9	−24.8	43.5	49 23.1	−23.8	44.3	50 05.8	−22.8	45.1
46	47 30.3	−26.6	41.4	48 15.1	−25.7	42.1	48 59.3	−24.7	42.9	49 43.0	−23.8	43.7
47	47 03.7	−27.6	40.1	47 49.4	−26.7	40.8	48 34.6	−25.8	41.5	49 19.2	−24.8	42.3
48	46 36.1	−28.4	38.8	47 22.7	−27.6	39.4	48 08.8	−26.7	40.1	48 54.4	−25.8	40.9
49	46 07.7	−29.2	37.5	46 55.1	−28.4	38.1	47 42.1	−27.6	38.8	48 28.6	−26.7	39.5
50	45 38.5	−30.1	36.2	46 26.7	−29.3	36.8	47 14.5	−28.5	37.5	48 01.9	−27.7	38.2
51	45 08.4	−30.8	35.0	45 57.4	−30.1	35.6	46 46.0	−29.3	36.2	47 34.2	−28.5	36.8
52	44 37.6	−31.6	33.8	45 27.3	−30.9	34.3	46 16.7	−30.2	34.9	47 05.7	−29.5	35.5
53	44 06.0	−32.3	32.6	44 56.4	−31.7	33.1	45 46.5	−31.0	33.7	46 36.2	−30.2	34.3
54	43 33.7	−33.1	31.4	44 24.7	−32.4	31.9	45 15.5	−31.7	32.5	46 06.0	−31.1	33.0
55	43 00.6	−33.6	30.3	43 52.3	−33.1	30.8	44 43.8	−32.5	31.3	45 34.9	−31.8	31.8
56	42 27.0	−34.4	29.2	43 19.2	−33.7	29.6	44 11.3	−33.2	30.1	45 03.1	−32.6	30.6
57	41 52.6	−35.0	28.0	42 45.5	−34.5	28.5	43 38.1	−33.9	28.9	44 30.5	−33.3	29.4
58	41 17.6	−35.5	27.0	42 11.0	−35.0	27.4	43 04.2	−34.5	27.8	43 57.2	−34.0	28.2
59	40 42.1	−36.2	25.9	41 36.0	−35.7	26.3	42 29.7	−35.2	26.7	43 23.2	−34.7	27.1
60	40 05.9	−36.7	24.8	41 00.3	−36.3	25.2	41 54.5	−35.8	25.6	42 48.5	−35.3	26.0
61	39 29.2	−37.2	23.8	40 24.0	−36.8	24.2	41 18.7	−36.4	24.5	42 13.2	−35.9	24.9
62	38 52.0	−37.8	22.8	39 47.2	−37.3	23.1	40 42.3	−36.9	23.5	41 37.3	−36.5	23.8
63	38 14.2	−38.2	21.8	39 09.9	−37.9	22.1	40 05.4	−37.5	22.4	41 00.8	−37.1	22.8
64	37 36.0	−38.8	20.8	38 32.0	−38.4	21.1	39 27.9	−38.0	21.4	40 23.7	−37.6	21.7
65	36 57.2	−39.2	19.9	37 53.6	−38.8	20.1	38 49.9	−38.5	20.4	39 46.1	−38.2	20.7
66	36 18.0	−39.6	18.9	37 14.8	−39.3	19.2	38 11.4	−39.0	19.4	39 07.9	−38.6	19.7
67	35 38.4	−40.0	18.0	36 35.5	−39.8	18.2	37 32.4	−39.4	18.5	38 29.3	−39.2	18.7
68	34 58.4	−40.5	17.1	35 55.7	−40.2	17.3	36 53.0	−39.9	17.5	37 50.1	−39.6	17.8
69	34 17.9	−40.8	16.2	35 15.5	−40.5	16.4	36 13.1	−40.3	16.6	37 10.5	−40.0	16.8
70	33 37.1	−41.2	15.3	34 35.0	−41.0	15.5	35 32.8	−40.8	15.7	36 30.5	−40.5	15.9
71	32 55.9	−41.5	14.4	33 54.0	−41.3	14.6	34 52.0	−41.1	14.8	35 50.0	−40.8	15.0
72	32 14.4	−41.9	13.6	33 12.7	−41.7	13.7	34 10.9	−41.5	13.9	35 09.2	−41.3	14.1
73	31 32.5	−42.3	12.7	32 31.0	−42.1	12.9	33 29.4	−41.8	13.0	34 27.9	−41.7	13.2
74	30 50.2	−42.5	11.9	31 48.9	−42.3	12.0	32 47.6	−42.2	12.2	33 46.2	−42.0	12.3
75	30 07.7	−42.8	11.1	31 06.6	−42.7	11.2	32 05.4	−42.5	11.3	33 04.2	−42.3	11.5
76	29 24.9	−43.2	10.3	30 23.9	−43.0	10.4	31 22.9	−42.8	10.5	32 21.9	−42.7	10.6
77	28 41.7	−43.4	9.5	29 40.9	−43.3	9.6	30 40.1	−43.2	9.7	31 39.2	−43.0	9.8
78	27 58.3	−43.6	8.7	28 57.6	−43.5	8.8	29 56.9	−43.4	8.9	30 56.2	−43.3	9.0
79	27 14.7	−43.9	7.9	28 14.1	−43.8	8.0	29 13.5	−43.7	8.1	30 12.9	−43.6	8.2
80	26 30.8	−44.2	7.2	27 30.3	−44.1	7.2	28 29.8	−44.0	7.3	29 29.3	−43.8	7.4
81	25 46.6	−44.4	6.4	26 46.2	−44.3	6.5	27 45.8	−44.2	6.5	28 45.5	−44.2	6.6
82	25 02.2	−44.6	5.7	26 01.9	−44.5	5.7	27 01.6	−44.4	5.8	28 01.3	−44.4	5.8
83	24 17.6	−44.8	4.9	25 17.4	−44.8	5.0	26 17.2	−44.7	5.0	27 16.9	−44.6	5.1
84	23 32.8	−45.0	4.2	24 32.6	−44.9	4.2	25 32.5	−44.9	4.3	26 32.3	−44.9	4.3
85	22 47.8	−45.2	3.5	23 47.7	−45.2	3.5	24 47.6	−45.2	3.5	25 47.4	−45.0	3.6
86	22 02.6	−45.4	2.8	23 02.5	−45.4	2.8	24 02.4	−45.3	2.8	25 02.4	−45.3	2.8
87	21 17.2	−45.6	2.1	22 17.1	−45.5	2.1	23 17.1	−45.5	2.1	24 17.1	−45.5	2.1
88	20 31.6	−45.7	1.4	21 31.6	−45.7	1.4	22 31.6	−45.7	1.4	23 31.6	−45.7	1.4
89	19 45.9	−45.9	0.7	20 45.9	−45.9	0.7	21 45.9	−45.9	0.7	22 45.9	−45.9	0.7
90	19 00.0	−46.0	0.0	20 00.0	−46.0	0.0	21 00.0	−46.0	0.0	22 00.0	−46.0	0.0

15° 16° 17° 18° 19° 20° 21° 22°

40°, 320° L.H.A. LATITUDE **SAME** NAME AS DECLINATION

LATITUDE **CONTRARY** NAME TO DECLINATION — L.H.A. 40°, 320°

Dec.	15° Hc	d	Z	16° Hc	d	Z	17° Hc	d	Z	18° Hc	d	Z	19° Hc	d	Z	20° Hc	d	Z	21° Hc	d	Z	22° Hc	d	Z	Dec.
°	° ′	′	°	° ′	′	°	° ′	′	°	° ′	′	°	° ′	′	°	° ′	′	°	° ′	′	°	° ′	′	°	°
0	47 43.6	−23.6	107.1	47 25.4	−24.9	108.2	47 06.1	−26.2	109.2	46 45.9	−27.5	110.2	46 24.7	−28.8	111.2	46 02.5	−30.0	112.2	45 39.4	−31.2	113.1	45 15.4	−32.3	114.1	0
1	47 20.0	−24.5	108.5	47 00.5	−25.9	109.5	46 39.9	−27.1	110.5	46 18.4	−28.4	111.5	45 55.9	−29.5	112.5	45 32.5	−30.7	113.4	45 08.2	−31.9	114.3	44 43.1	−33.1	115.2	1
2	46 55.5	−25.5	109.8	46 34.6	−26.7	110.8	46 12.8	−28.0	111.8	45 50.0	−29.2	112.8	45 26.4	−30.4	113.7	45 01.8	−31.6	114.6	44 36.3	−32.6	115.5	44 10.0	−33.7	116.4	2
3	46 30.0	−26.3	111.2	46 07.9	−27.6	112.1	45 44.8	−28.8	113.1	45 20.8	−30.0	114.0	44 56.0	−31.2	114.9	44 30.2	−32.2	115.8	44 03.7	−33.4	116.7	43 36.3	−34.4	117.6	3
4	46 03.7	−27.2	112.5	45 40.3	−28.4	113.4	45 16.0	−29.6	114.3	44 50.8	−30.7	115.3	44 24.8	−31.9	116.1	43 58.0	−33.0	117.0	43 30.3	−34.0	117.9	43 01.9	−35.1	118.7	4
5	45 36.5	−28.1	113.7	45 11.9	−29.3	114.7	44 46.4	−30.4	115.6	44 20.1	−31.5	116.5	43 52.9	−32.6	117.3	43 25.0	−33.7	118.2	42 56.3	−34.7	119.0	42 26.8	−35.6	119.8	5
6	45 08.4	−28.9	115.0	44 42.6	−30.0	115.9	44 16.0	−31.2	116.8	43 48.6	−32.3	117.6	43 20.3	−33.3	118.5	42 51.3	−34.3	119.3	42 21.6	−35.3	120.1	41 51.2	−36.3	120.9	6
7	44 39.5	−29.6	116.2	44 12.6	−30.8	117.1	43 44.8	−31.8	118.0	43 16.3	−32.9	118.8	42 47.0	−33.9	119.6	42 17.0	−35.0	120.4	41 46.3	−35.9	121.2	41 14.9	−36.9	121.9	7
8	44 09.9	−30.5	117.5	43 41.8	−31.5	118.3	43 13.0	−32.6	119.1	42 43.4	−33.6	120.0	42 13.1	−34.6	120.7	41 42.0	−35.5	121.5	41 10.4	−36.6	122.3	40 38.0	−37.4	123.0	8
9	43 39.4	−31.1	118.7	43 10.3	−32.2	119.5	42 40.4	−33.3	120.3	42 09.8	−34.3	121.1	41 38.5	−35.3	121.8	41 06.5	−36.2	122.6	40 33.8	−37.0	123.3	40 00.6	−38.0	124.0	9
10	43 08.3	−31.9	119.8	42 38.1	−32.9	120.6	42 07.1	−33.9	121.4	41 35.5	−34.8	122.2	41 03.2	−35.8	122.9	40 30.3	−36.7	123.6	39 56.8	−37.6	124.3	39 22.6	−38.4	125.0	10
11	42 36.4	−32.6	121.0	42 05.2	−33.6	121.8	41 33.2	−34.5	122.5	41 00.7	−35.5	123.3	40 27.4	−36.3	124.0	39 53.6	−37.3	124.7	39 19.2	−38.1	125.4	38 44.2	−39.0	126.0	11
12	42 03.8	−33.2	122.1	41 31.6	−34.2	122.9	40 58.7	−35.1	123.6	40 25.2	−36.1	124.3	39 51.1	−37.0	125.0	39 16.3	−37.8	125.7	38 41.1	−38.7	126.3	38 05.2	−39.4	127.0	12
13	41 30.6	−33.8	123.2	40 57.4	−34.8	124.0	40 23.6	−35.7	124.7	39 49.1	−36.6	125.4	39 14.1	−37.4	126.0	38 38.5	−38.2	126.7	38 02.4	−39.1	127.3	37 25.8	−39.9	127.9	13
14	40 56.8	−34.5	124.3	40 22.6	−35.4	125.0	39 47.9	−36.3	125.7	39 12.5	−37.1	126.4	38 36.7	−38.0	127.0	38 00.3	−38.8	127.7	37 23.3	−39.5	128.3	36 45.9	−40.3	128.9	14
15	40 22.3	−35.1	125.4	39 47.2	−35.9	126.1	39 11.6	−36.8	126.8	38 35.4	−37.6	127.4	37 58.7	−38.4	128.0	37 21.5	−39.2	128.6	36 43.8	−40.0	129.2	36 05.6	−40.7	129.8	15
16	39 47.2	−35.6	126.5	39 11.3	−36.5	127.1	38 34.8	−37.3	127.8	37 57.8	−38.2	128.4	37 20.3	−39.0	129.0	36 42.3	−39.7	129.6	36 03.8	−40.4	130.1	35 24.9	−41.1	130.7	16
17	39 11.6	−36.2	127.5	38 34.8	−37.0	128.2	37 57.5	−37.9	128.8	37 19.6	−38.6	129.4	36 41.3	−39.3	130.0	36 02.6	−40.1	130.5	35 23.4	−40.8	131.1	34 43.8	−41.5	131.6	17
18	38 35.4	−36.7	128.5	37 57.8	−37.5	129.2	37 19.6	−38.3	129.8	36 41.0	−39.0	130.3	36 02.0	−39.8	130.9	35 22.5	−40.5	131.4	34 42.6	−41.2	132.0	34 02.3	−41.9	132.5	18
19	37 58.7	−37.2	129.6	37 20.3	−38.0	130.1	36 41.3	−38.7	130.7	36 02.0	−39.5	131.3	35 22.2	−40.2	131.8	34 42.0	−40.9	132.3	34 01.4	−41.6	132.8	33 20.4	−42.2	133.3	19
20	37 21.5	−37.7	130.5	36 42.3	−38.5	131.1	36 02.6	−39.2	131.7	35 22.5	−39.9	132.2	34 42.0	−40.6	132.7	34 01.1	−41.3	133.2	33 19.8	−41.9	133.7	32 38.2	−42.6	134.2	20
21	36 43.8	−38.2	131.5	36 03.8	−38.9	132.1	35 23.4	−39.6	132.6	34 42.6	−40.3	133.1	34 01.4	−41.0	133.6	33 19.8	−41.6	134.1	32 37.9	−42.3	134.6	31 55.6	−42.8	135.0	21
22	36 05.6	−38.6	132.5	35 24.9	−39.3	133.0	34 43.8	−40.0	133.5	34 02.3	−40.7	134.0	33 20.4	−41.3	134.5	32 38.2	−42.0	134.9	31 55.6	−42.6	135.4	31 12.8	−43.2	135.8	22
23	35 27.0	−39.1	133.4	34 45.6	−39.8	133.9	34 03.8	−40.5	134.4	33 21.6	−41.1	134.9	32 39.1	−41.7	135.4	31 56.2	−42.3	135.8	31 13.0	−42.9	136.2	30 29.6	−43.5	136.6	23
24	34 47.9	−39.4	134.3	34 05.8	−40.1	134.8	33 23.3	−40.8	135.3	32 40.5	−41.4	135.8	31 57.4	−42.1	136.2	31 13.9	−42.6	136.6	30 30.1	−43.2	137.0	29 46.1	−43.8	137.4	24
25	34 08.5	−39.9	135.3	33 25.7	−40.5	135.7	32 42.5	−41.1	136.2	31 59.1	−41.8	136.6	31 15.3	−42.3	137.0	30 31.3	−43.0	137.4	29 46.9	−43.5	137.8	29 02.3	−44.0	138.2	25
26	33 28.6	−40.3	136.2	32 45.2	−40.9	136.6	32 01.4	−41.5	137.0	31 17.3	−42.1	137.5	30 33.0	−42.7	137.9	29 48.3	−43.2	138.3	29 03.4	−43.7	138.6	28 18.3	−44.3	139.0	26
27	32 48.3	−40.6	137.0	32 04.3	−41.3	137.5	31 19.9	−41.8	137.9	30 35.2	−42.3	138.3	29 50.3	−42.9	138.7	29 05.1	−43.5	139.1	28 19.7	−44.0	139.4	27 34.0	−44.5	139.8	27
28	32 07.7	−41.0	137.9	31 23.0	−41.5	138.3	30 38.1	−42.2	138.7	29 52.9	−42.7	139.1	29 07.4	−43.3	139.5	28 21.6	−43.7	139.8	27 35.7	−44.3	140.2	26 49.5	−44.8	140.5	28
29	31 26.7	−41.3	138.8	30 41.5	−41.9	139.2	29 55.9	−42.4	139.6	29 10.2	−43.0	139.9	28 24.1	−43.5	140.3	27 37.9	−44.1	140.6	26 51.4	−44.5	140.9	26 04.7	−45.0	141.3	29
30	30 45.4	−41.6	139.6	29 59.6	−42.2	140.0	29 13.5	−42.7	140.4	28 27.2	−43.3	140.7	27 40.6	−43.7	141.1	26 53.8	−44.2	141.4	26 06.9	−44.8	141.7	25 19.7	−45.2	142.0	30
31	30 03.8	−42.0	140.5	29 17.4	−42.5	140.8	28 30.8	−43.0	141.2	27 43.9	−43.5	141.5	26 56.9	−44.1	141.8	26 09.6	−44.5	142.1	25 22.1	−44.9	142.4	24 34.5	−45.4	142.7	31
32	29 21.8	−42.2	141.3	28 34.9	−42.8	141.6	27 47.8	−43.3	142.0	27 00.4	−43.8	142.3	26 12.8	−44.2	142.6	25 25.1	−44.7	142.9	24 37.2	−45.2	143.2	23 49.1	−45.7	143.4	32
33	28 39.6	−42.6	142.1	27 52.1	−43.0	142.4	27 04.5	−43.6	142.7	26 16.6	−44.0	143.0	25 28.6	−44.5	143.3	24 40.4	−45.0	143.6	23 52.0	−45.4	143.9	23 03.4	−45.8	144.1	33
34	27 57.0	−42.8	142.9	27 09.1	−43.3	143.2	26 20.9	−43.7	143.5	25 32.6	−44.2	143.8	24 44.1	−44.7	144.1	23 55.4	−45.1	144.3	23 06.6	−45.6	144.6	22 17.6	−45.9	144.8	34
35	27 14.2	−43.1	143.7	26 25.8	−43.6	144.0	25 37.2	−44.1	144.3	24 48.4	−44.5	144.5	23 59.4	−44.9	144.8	23 10.3	−45.3	145.1	22 21.0	−45.7	145.3	21 31.7	−46.2	145.5	35
36	26 31.1	−43.3	144.5	25 42.2	−43.8	144.8	24 53.1	−44.2	145.0	24 03.9	−44.7	145.3	23 14.5	−45.1	145.5	22 25.0	−45.5	145.8	21 35.3	−45.9	146.0	20 45.5	−46.3	146.2	36
37	25 47.8	−43.6	145.2	24 58.4	−44.0	145.5	24 08.9	−44.4	145.8	23 19.2	−44.8	146.0	22 29.4	−45.3	146.2	21 39.5	−45.7	146.5	20 49.4	−46.1	146.7	19 59.2	−46.5	146.9	37
38	25 04.2	−43.8	146.0	24 14.4	−44.2	146.3	23 24.5	−44.7	146.5	22 34.4	−45.1	146.7	21 44.1	−45.4	147.0	20 53.8	−45.9	147.2	20 03.3	−46.2	147.4	19 12.7	−46.6	147.6	38
39	24 20.4	−44.0	146.8	23 30.2	−44.4	147.0	22 39.8	−44.8	147.2	21 49.3	−45.2	147.4	20 58.7	−45.7	147.7	20 07.9	−46.0	147.9	19 17.1	−46.4	148.0	18 26.1	−46.7	148.2	39
40	23 36.4	−44.2	147.5	22 45.8	−44.7	147.7	21 55.0	−45.1	147.9	21 04.1	−45.5	148.2	20 13.0	−45.8	148.3	19 21.9	−46.2	148.5	18 30.7	−46.5	148.7	17 39.4	−46.9	148.9	40
41	22 52.2	−44.4	148.2	22 01.1	−44.8	148.4	21 09.9	−45.2	148.7	20 18.6	−45.5	148.8	19 27.2	−45.9	149.0	18 35.7	−46.3	149.2	17 44.2	−46.7	149.4	16 52.5	−47.0	149.5	41
42	22 07.8	−44.7	149.0	21 16.3	−45.0	149.2	20 24.7	−45.3	149.4	19 33.1	−45.8	149.5	18 41.3	−46.1	149.7	17 49.4	−46.4	149.9	16 57.5	−46.8	150.0	16 05.5	−47.1	150.2	42
43	21 23.1	−44.8	149.7	20 31.3	−45.2	149.9	19 39.4	−45.6	150.1	18 47.3	−45.9	150.2	17 55.2	−46.2	150.4	17 03.0	−46.6	150.5	16 10.7	−46.9	150.7	15 18.4	−47.3	150.8	43
44	20 38.3	−44.9	150.4	19 46.1	−45.3	150.6	18 53.8	−45.7	150.7	18 01.4	−46.0	150.9	17 09.0	−46.4	151.1	16 16.4	−46.7	151.2	15 23.8	−47.0	151.3	14 31.1	−47.3	151.5	44
45	19 53.4	−45.2	151.1	19 00.8	−45.5	151.3	18 08.1	−45.8	151.4	17 15.4	−46.1	151.6	16 22.6	−46.5	151.7	15 29.7	−46.8	151.9	14 36.8	−47.1	152.0	13 43.8	−47.4	152.1	45
46	19 08.2	−45.3	151.8	18 15.3	−45.6	152.0	17 22.3	−46.0	152.1	16 29.3	−46.3	152.2	15 36.1	−46.6	152.4	14 42.9	−46.9	152.5	13 49.7	−47.2	152.6	12 56.4	−47.6	152.7	46
47	18 22.9	−45.4	152.5	17 29.7	−45.8	152.6	16 36.3	−46.0	152.8	15 43.0	−46.4	152.9	14 49.5	−46.7	153.0	13 56.0	−47.0	153.1	13 02.5	−47.4	153.3	12 08.8	−47.6	153.4	47
48	17 37.5	−45.6	153.2	16 43.9	−45.9	153.3	15 50.3	−46.3	153.4	14 56.6	−46.6	153.6	14 02.8	−46.8	153.7	13 09.0	−47.1	153.8	12 15.1	−47.4	153.9	11 21.2	−47.6	154.0	48
49	16 51.9	−45.7	153.9	15 58.0	−46.0	154.0	15 04.0	−46.3	154.1	14 10.0	−46.6	154.2	13 16.0	−46.9	154.3	12 21.9	−47.2	154.4	11 27.7	−47.4	154.5	10 33.6	−47.8	154.6	49
50	16 06.2	−45.9	154.5	15 12.0	−46.2	154.6	14 17.7	−46.4	154.8	13 23.4	−46.7	154.9	12 29.1	−47.0	155.0	11 34.7	−47.3	155.1	10 40.3	−47.6	155.1	9 45.8	−47.8	155.2	50
51	15 20.3	−46.0	155.2	14 25.8	−46.2	155.3	13 31.3	−46.6	155.4	12 36.7	−46.8	155.5	11 42.1	−47.1	155.6	10 47.4	−47.3	155.7	9 52.7	−47.6	155.8	8 58.0	−47.9	155.8	51
52	14 34.3	−46.0	155.9	13 39.6	−46.4	156.0	12 44.7	−46.6	156.1	11 49.9	−46.9	156.2	10 55.0	−47.2	156.2	10 00.1	−47.5	156.3	9 05.1	−47.7	156.4	8 10.1	−47.9	156.4	52
53	13 48.3	−46.2	156.5	12 53.2	−46.5	156.6	11 58.1	−46.7	156.7	11 03.0	−47.0	156.8	10 07.8	−47.2	156.9	9 12.6	−47.4	156.9	8 17.4	−47.7	157.0	7 22.2	−48.0	157.0	53
54	13 02.1	−46.3	157.2	12 06.7	−46.5	157.3	11 11.4	−46.8	157.3	10 16.0	−47.0	157.4	9 20.6	−47.3	157.5	8 25.2	−47.6	157.5	7 29.7	−47.8	157.6	6 34.2	−48.0	157.6	54
55	12 15.8	−46.4	157.8	11 20.2	−46.6	157.9	10 24.6	−46.9	158.0	9 29.0	−47.2	158.1	8 33.3	−47.4	158.1	7 37.6	−47.6	158.2	6 41.9	−47.8	158.2	5 46.2	−48.1	158.2	55
56	11 29.4	−46.5	158.5	10 33.6	−46.7	158.6	9 37.7	−46.9	158.6	8 41.8	−47.1	158.7	7 45.9	−47.4	158.7	6 50.0	−47.6	158.8	5 54.1	−47.9	158.8	4 58.1	−48.1	158.9	56
57	10 42.9	−46.5	159.1	9 46.9	−46.8	159.2	8 50.8	−47.0	159.2	7 54.7	−47.3	159.3	6 58.5	−47.4	159.3	6 02.4	−47.7	159.4	5 06.2	−47.9	159.4	4 10.0	−48.1	159.5	57
58	9 56.4	−46.6	159.8	9 00.1	−46.8	159.8	8 03.8	−47.1	159.9	7 07.4	−47.3	159.9	6 11.1	−47.5	160.0	5 14.7	−47.7	160.0	4 18.3	−47.9	160.0	3 21.9	−48.1	160.0	58
59	9 09.8	−46.7	160.4	8 13.3	−46.9	160.5	7 16.7	−47.1	160.5	6 20.1	−47.3	160.5	5 23.6	−47.6	160.6	4 27.0	−47.8	160.6	3 30.4	−48.0	160.6	2 33.8	−48.2	160.6	59
60	8 23.1	−46.7	161.0	7 26.4	−47.0	161.1	6 29.6	−47.2	161.1	5 32.8	−47.4	161.2	4 36.0	−47.6	161.2	3 39.2	−47.8	161.2	2 42.4	−48.0	161.2	1 45.6	−48.2	161.2	60
61	7 36.4	−46.8	161.7	6 39.4	−47.0	161.7	5 42.4	−47.2	161.7	4 45.4	−47.4	161.8	3 48.4	−47.5	161.8	2 51.4	−47.7	161.8	1 54.4	−47.9	161.8	0 57.4	−48.1	161.8	61
62	6 49.6	−46.9	162.3	5 52.4	−47.0	162.3	4 55.2	−47.2	162.4	3 58.0	−47.4	162.4	3 00.9	−47.7	162.4	2 03.7	−47.9	162.4	1 06.5	−48.0	162.4	0 09.3	−48.2	162.4	62
63	6 02.7	−46.9	162.9	5 05.4	−47.1	163.0	4 08.0	−47.3	163.0	3 10.6	−47.4	163.0	2 13.2	−47.6	163.0	1 15.8	−47.8	163.0	0 18.5	−48.0	163.0	0 38.9	+48.2	17.0	63
64	5 15.8	−46.9	163.6	4 18.3	−47.1	163.6	3 20.7	−47.3	163.6	2 23.2	−47.5	163.6	1 25.6	−47.6	163.6	0 28.0	−47.8	163.6	0 29.5	+48.0	16.4	1 27.1	+48.2	16.4	64
65	4 28.9	−46.9	164.2	3 31.2	−47.2	164.2	2 33.4	−47.3	164.2	1 35.7	−47.5	164.2	0 38.0	−47.7	164.2	0 19.8	+47.8	15.8	1 17.5	+48.0	15.8	2 15.3	+48.1	15.8	65
66	3 42.0	−47.0	164.8	2 44.0	−47.1	164.8	1 46.1	−47.3	164.8	0 48.2	−47.5	164.8	0 09.7	+47.6	15.2	1 07.6	+47.8	15.2	2 05.5	+48.0	15.2	3 03.4	+48.2	15.2	66
67	2 55.0	−47.0	165.4	1 56.9	−47.2	165.4	0 58.8	−47.3	165.5	0 00.7	−47.4	165.5	0 57.3	+47.7	14.5	1 55.4	+47.8	14.6	2 53.5	+47.9	14.6	3 51.6	+48.1	14.6	67
68	2 08.0	−47.1	166.1	1 09.7	−47.1	166.1	0 11.5	−47.3	166.1	0 46.7	+47.5	13.9	1 45.0	+47.6	13.9	2 43.2	+47.8	13.9	3 41.4	+48.0	14.0	4 39.7	+48.0	14.0	68
69	1 20.9	−47.0	166.7	0 22.6	−47.2	166.7	0 35.8	+47.4	13.3	1 34.2	+47.5	13.3	2 32.6	+47.6	13.3	3 31.0	+47.7	13.3	4 29.4	+47.9	13.4	5 27.7	+48.1	13.4	69
70	0 33.9	−47.0	167.3	0 24.6	+47.2	12.7	1 23.2	+47.3	12.7	2 21.7	+47.4	12.7	3 20.2	+47.6	12.7	4 18.7	+47.8	12.7	5 17.3	+47.8	12.8	6 15.8	+48.0	12.8	70
71	0 13.1	+47.1	12.1	1 11.8	+47.2	12.1	2 10.5	+47.3	12.1	3 09.1	+47.5	12.1	4 07.8	+47.6	12.1	5 06.5	+47.6	12.1	6 05.1	+47.8	12.1	7 03.8	+47.9	12.2	71
72	1 00.2	+47.0	11.5	1 59.0	+47.1	11.5	2 57.8	+47.2	11.5	3 56.6	+47.4	11.5	4 55.4	+47.5	11.5	5 54.1	+47.7	11.5	6 52.9	+47.8	11.5	7 51.7	+47.9	11.6	72
73	1 47.2	+47.0	10.8	2 46.1	+47.1	10.8	3 45.0	+47.3	10.9	4 44.0	+47.3	10.9	5 42.9	+47.5	10.9	6 41.8	+47.6	10.9	7 40.7	+47.7	10.9	8 39.6	+47.9	11.0	73
74	2 34.2	+47.0	10.2	3 33.2	+47.1	10.2	4 32.3	+47.2	10.2	5 31.3	+47.4	10.3	6 30.4	+47.4	10.3	7 29.4	+47.6	10.3	8 28.4	+47.7	10.3	9 27.5	+47.7	10.3	74
75	3 21.2	+47.0	9.6	4 20.3	+47.1	9.6	5 19.5	+47.2	9.6	6 18.7	+47.2	9.6	7 17.8	+47.4	9.7	8 17.0	+47.5	9.7	9 16.1	+47.6	9.7	10 15.2	+47.7	9.7	75
76	4 08.2	+46.9	9.0	5 07.4	+47.1	9.0	6 06.7	+47.1	9.0	7 05.9	+47.3	9.0	8 05.2	+47.3	9.0	9 04.5	+47.4	9.1	10 03.7	+47.5	9.1	11 02.9	+47.7	9.1	76
77	4 55.1	+46.9	8.3	5 54.5	+47.0	8.4	6 53.8	+47.1	8.4	7 53.2	+47.2	8.4	8 52.5	+47.3	8.4	9 51.9	+47.4	8.4	10 51.2	+47.5	8.5	11 50.6	+47.5	8.5	77
78	5 42.0	+46.9	7.7	6 41.5	+46.9	7.7	7 40.9	+47.0	7.8	8 40.4	+47.1	7.8	9 39.8	+47.2	7.8	10 39.3	+47.2	7.8	11 38.7	+47.4	7.8	12 38.1	+47.5	7.9	78
79	6 28.9	+46.8	7.1	7 28.4	+46.9	7.1	8 27.9	+47.0	7.1	9 27.5	+47.0	7.1	10 27.0	+47.1	7.2	11 26.5	+47.3	7.2	12 26.1	+47.3	7.2	13 25.6	+47.4	7.2	79
80	7 15.7	+46.8	6.5	8 15.3	+46.8	6.5	9 14.9	+46.9	6.5	10 14.5	+47.0	6.5	11 14.1	+47.1	6.5	12 13.8	+47.1	6.6	13 13.4	+47.2	6.6	14 13.0	+47.2	6.6	80
81	8 02.5	+46.7	5.8	9 02.1	+46.8	5.8	10 01.8	+46.9	5.9	11 01.5	+46.9	5.9	12 01.2	+47.0	5.9	13 00.9	+47.0	5.9	14 00.6	+47.1	5.9	15 00.2	+47.2	6.0	81
82	8 49.2	+46.6	5.2	9 48.9	+46.7	5.2	10 48.7	+46.7	5.2	11 48.4	+46.8	5.2	12 48.2	+46.8	5.3	13 47.9	+46.9	5.3	14 47.7	+46.9	5.3	15 47.4	+47.0	5.3	82
83	9 35.8	+46.6	4.6	10 35.6	+46.6	4.6	11 35.4	+46.7	4.6	12 35.2	+46.8	4.6	13 35.0	+46.8	4.6	14 34.8	+46.9	4.6	15 34.6	+46.9	4.7	16 34.4	+47.0	4.7	83
84	10 22.4	+46.5	3.9	11 22.2	+46.6	3.9	12 22.1	+46.6	3.9	13 22.0	+46.6	4.0	14 21.8	+46.7	4.0	15 21.7	+46.7	4.0	16 21.5	+46.8	4.0	17 21.4	+46.8	4.0	84
85	11 08.9	+46.4	3.3	12 08.8	+46.4	3.3	13 08.7	+46.5	3.3	14 08.6	+46.5	3.3	15 08.5	+46.5	3.3	16 08.4	+46.6	3.3	17 08.3	+46.6	3.4	18 08.2	+46.6	3.4	85
86	11 55.3	+46.3	2.6	12 55.2	+46.4	2.6	13 55.2	+46.3	2.6	14 55.1	+46.4	2.7	15 55.0	+46.5	2.7	16 55.0	+46.4	2.7	17 54.9	+46.5	2.7	18 54.8	+46.6	2.7	86
87	12 41.6	+46.3	2.0	13 41.6	+46.2	2.0	14 41.5	+46.3	2.0	15 41.5	+46.3	2.0	16 41.5	+46.3	2.0	17 41.4	+46.4	2.0	18 41.4	+46.4	2.0	19 41.4	+46.3	2.0	87
88	13 27.9	+46.1	1.3	14 27.8	+46.2	1.3	15 27.8	+46.2	1.3	16 27.8	+46.2	1.3	17 27.8	+46.2	1.3	18 27.8	+46.2	1.4	19 27.8	+46.2	1.4	20 27.7	+46.3	1.4	88
89	14 14.0	+46.0	0.7	15 14.0	+46.0	0.7	16 14.0	+46.0	0.7	17 14.0	+46.0	0.7	18 14.0	+46.0	0.7	19 14.0	+46.0	0.7	20 14.0	+46.0	0.7	21 14.0	+46.0	0.7	89
90	15 00.0	+45.9	0.0	16 00.0	+45.9	0.0	17 00.0	+45.9	0.0	18 00.0	+45.9	0.0	19 00.0	+45.9	0.0	20 00.0	+45.9	0.0	21 00.0	+45.9	0.0	22 00.0	+45.9	0.0	90
	15°			16°			17°			18°			19°			20°			21°			22°			

S. Lat. {L.H.A. greater than 180° ....Zn=180°−Z; L.H.A. less than 180°...........Zn=180°+Z

LATITUDE **SAME** NAME AS DECLINATION — L.H.A. 140°, 220°

41°, 319° L.H.A. LATITUDE **SAME** NAME AS DECLINATION N. Lat. {L.H.A. greater than 180° .....Zn=Z; L.H.A. less than 180°............Zn=360°–Z

Dec.	15° Hc	d	Z	16° Hc	d	Z	17° Hc	d	Z	18° Hc	d	Z	19° Hc	d	Z	20° Hc	d	Z	21° Hc	d	Z	22° Hc	d	Z	Dec.
°	° ′	′	°	° ′	′	°	° ′	′	°	° ′	′	°	° ′	′	°	° ′	′	°	° ′	′	°	° ′	′	°	°
0	46 48.1	+22.2	106.6	46 30.5	+23.6	107.6	46 11.9	+24.9	108.6	45 52.2	+26.2	109.6	45 31.7	+27.4	110.5	45 10.2	+28.7	111.5	44 47.7	+30.0	112.4	44 24.4	+31.1	113.3	0
1	47 10.3	+21.3	105.2	46 54.1	+22.6	106.3	46 36.8	+23.9	107.3	46 18.4	+25.3	108.3	45 59.1	+26.6	109.3	45 38.9	+27.8	110.2	45 17.7	+29.1	111.2	44 55.5	+30.3	112.1	1
2	47 31.6	+20.2	103.8	47 16.7	+21.6	104.9	47 00.7	+23.0	105.9	46 43.7	+24.4	107.0	46 25.7	+25.7	108.0	46 06.7	+27.0	109.0	45 46.8	+28.2	109.9	45 25.8	+29.6	110.9	2
3	47 51.8	+19.1	102.4	47 38.3	+20.6	103.5	47 23.7	+22.1	104.6	47 08.1	+23.4	105.6	46 51.4	+24.8	106.6	46 33.7	+26.2	107.7	46 15.0	+27.5	108.7	45 55.4	+28.6	109.6	3
4	48 10.9	+18.2	101.0	47 58.9	+19.6	102.1	47 45.8	+21.0	103.2	47 31.5	+22.5	104.3	47 16.2	+23.9	105.3	46 59.9	+25.2	106.3	46 42.5	+26.5	107.4	46 24.0	+27.9	108.4	4
5	48 29.1	+17.0	99.6	48 18.5	+18.5	100.7	48 06.8	+20.0	101.8	47 54.0	+21.4	102.9	47 40.1	+22.8	104.0	47 25.1	+24.2	105.0	47 09.0	+25.6	106.1	46 51.9	+26.9	107.1	5
6	48 46.1	+16.0	98.1	48 37.0	+17.5	99.3	48 26.8	+19.0	100.4	48 15.4	+20.4	101.5	48 02.9	+21.9	102.6	47 49.3	+23.3	103.7	47 34.6	+24.7	104.7	47 18.8	+26.1	105.8	6
7	49 02.1	+14.8	96.7	48 54.5	+16.3	97.8	48 45.8	+17.8	98.9	48 35.8	+19.4	100.1	48 24.8	+20.8	101.2	48 12.6	+22.3	102.3	47 59.3	+23.7	103.4	47 44.9	+25.1	104.4	7
8	49 16.9	+13.6	95.2	49 10.8	+15.3	96.3	49 03.6	+16.8	97.5	48 55.2	+18.3	98.6	48 45.6	+19.8	99.8	48 34.9	+21.2	100.9	48 23.0	+22.7	102.0	48 10.0	+24.1	103.1	8
9	49 30.5	+12.5	93.7	49 26.1	+14.0	94.9	49 20.4	+15.6	96.0	49 13.5	+17.1	97.2	49 05.4	+18.7	98.3	48 56.1	+20.2	99.5	48 45.7	+21.6	100.6	48 34.1	+23.1	101.7	9
10	49 43.0	+11.3	92.2	49 40.1	+12.9	93.4	49 36.0	+14.5	94.5	49 30.6	+16.1	95.7	49 24.1	+17.6	96.9	49 16.3	+19.1	98.0	49 07.3	+20.6	99.2	48 57.2	+22.1	100.3	10
11	49 54.3	+10.1	90.7	49 53.0	+11.7	91.8	49 50.5	+13.3	93.0	49 46.7	+14.9	94.2	49 41.7	+16.4	95.4	49 35.4	+18.0	96.6	49 27.9	+19.6	97.7	49 19.3	+21.0	98.9	11
12	50 04.4	+8.9	89.1	50 04.7	+10.5	90.3	50 03.8	+12.1	91.5	50 01.6	+13.7	92.7	49 58.1	+15.3	93.9	49 53.4	+16.8	95.1	49 47.5	+18.4	96.3	49 40.3	+19.9	97.4	12
13	50 13.3	+7.7	87.6	50 15.2	+9.3	88.8	50 15.9	+10.9	90.0	50 15.3	+12.5	91.2	50 13.4	+14.1	92.4	50 10.2	+15.7	93.6	50 05.9	+17.2	94.8	50 00.2	+18.8	96.0	13
14	50 21.0	+6.4	86.0	50 24.5	+8.0	87.2	50 26.8	+9.6	88.4	50 27.8	+11.2	89.7	50 27.5	+12.9	90.9	50 25.9	+14.5	92.1	50 23.1	+16.1	93.3	50 19.0	+17.7	94.5	14
15	50 27.4	+5.1	84.5	50 32.5	+6.8	85.7	50 36.4	+8.4	86.9	50 39.0	+10.1	88.1	50 40.4	+11.6	89.3	50 40.4	+13.3	90.6	50 39.2	+14.9	91.8	50 36.7	+16.5	93.0	15
16	50 32.5	+3.9	82.9	50 39.3	+5.5	84.1	50 44.8	+7.2	85.3	50 49.1	+8.8	86.6	50 52.0	+10.5	87.8	50 53.7	+12.1	89.0	50 54.1	+13.7	90.2	50 53.2	+15.3	91.5	16
17	50 36.4	+2.6	81.3	50 44.8	+4.3	82.5	50 52.0	+5.9	83.8	50 57.9	+7.5	85.0	51 02.5	+9.1	86.2	51 05.8	+10.8	87.5	51 07.8	+12.4	88.7	51 08.5	+14.1	89.9	17
18	50 39.0	+1.4	79.8	50 49.1	+2.9	81.0	50 57.9	+4.6	82.2	51 05.4	+6.2	83.4	51 11.6	+7.9	84.6	51 16.6	+9.5	85.9	51 20.2	+11.2	87.1	51 22.6	+12.8	88.4	18
19	50 40.4	0.0	78.2	50 52.0	+1.7	79.4	51 02.5	+3.3	80.6	51 11.6	+5.0	81.8	51 19.5	+6.6	83.1	51 26.1	+8.3	84.3	51 31.4	+10.0	85.6	51 35.4	+11.6	86.8	19
20	50 40.4	-1.2	76.6	50 53.7	+0.4	77.8	51 05.8	+2.0	79.0	51 16.6	+3.6	80.2	51 26.1	+5.3	81.5	51 34.4	+7.0	82.7	51 41.4	+8.6	84.0	51 47.0	+10.3	85.2	20
21	50 39.2	-2.5	75.0	50 54.1	-0.9	76.2	51 07.8	+0.7	77.4	51 20.2	+2.4	78.6	51 31.4	+4.0	79.9	51 41.4	+5.6	81.1	51 50.0	+7.3	82.4	51 57.3	+9.0	83.6	21
22	50 36.7	-3.7	73.5	50 53.2	-2.2	74.6	51 08.5	-0.6	75.8	51 22.6	+1.0	77.0	51 35.4	+2.7	78.3	51 47.0	+4.3	79.5	51 57.3	+6.0	80.8	52 06.3	+7.6	82.0	22
23	50 33.0	-5.1	71.9	50 51.0	-3.4	73.0	51 07.9	-1.8	74.2	51 23.6	-0.2	75.4	51 38.1	+1.4	76.7	51 51.3	+3.0	77.9	52 03.3	+4.6	79.1	52 13.9	+6.4	80.4	23
24	50 27.9	-6.3	70.3	50 47.6	-4.8	71.5	51 06.1	-3.2	72.6	51 23.4	-1.6	73.8	51 39.5	0.0	75.0	51 54.3	+1.7	76.3	52 07.9	+3.3	77.5	52 20.3	+4.9	78.8	24
25	50 21.6	-7.5	68.8	50 42.8	-6.0	69.9	51 02.9	-4.5	71.0	51 21.8	-2.9	72.2	51 39.5	-1.3	73.4	51 56.0	+0.3	74.7	52 11.2	+2.0	75.9	52 25.2	+3.7	77.2	25
26	50 14.1	-8.8	67.2	50 36.8	-7.3	68.3	50 58.4	-5.7	69.5	51 18.9	-4.2	70.6	51 38.2	-2.6	71.8	51 56.3	-1.0	73.0	52 13.2	+0.6	74.3	52 28.9	+2.2	75.5	26
27	50 05.3	-10.0	65.7	50 29.5	-8.5	66.8	50 52.7	-7.1	67.9	51 14.7	-5.5	69.0	51 35.6	-3.9	70.2	51 55.3	-2.3	71.4	52 13.8	-0.7	72.6	52 31.1	+0.9	73.9	27
28	49 55.3	-11.2	64.1	50 21.0	-9.7	65.2	50 45.6	-8.2	66.3	51 09.2	-6.8	67.4	51 31.7	-5.3	68.6	51 53.0	-3.7	69.8	52 13.1	-2.1	71.0	52 32.0	-0.4	72.2	28
29	49 44.1	-12.4	62.6	50 11.3	-11.0	63.7	50 37.4	-9.6	64.7	51 02.4	-8.0	65.9	51 26.4	-6.5	67.0	51 49.3	-5.0	68.2	52 11.0	-3.4	69.4	52 31.6	-1.9	70.6	29
30	49 31.7	-13.5	61.1	50 00.3	-12.2	62.1	50 27.8	-10.7	63.2	50 54.4	-9.3	64.3	51 19.9	-7.8	65.4	51 44.3	-6.3	66.6	52 07.6	-4.8	67.7	52 29.7	-3.1	68.9	30
31	49 18.2	-14.7	59.6	49 48.1	-13.4	60.6	50 17.1	-12.0	61.7	50 45.1	-10.6	62.7	51 12.1	-9.2	63.8	51 38.0	-7.6	65.0	52 02.8	-6.1	66.1	52 26.6	-4.6	67.3	31
32	49 03.5	-15.8	58.1	49 34.7	-14.5	59.1	50 05.1	-13.2	60.1	50 34.5	-11.8	61.2	51 02.9	-10.3	62.3	51 30.4	-8.9	63.4	51 56.7	-7.4	64.5	52 22.0	-5.9	65.7	32
33	48 47.7	-17.0	56.6	49 20.2	-15.6	57.6	49 51.9	-14.3	58.6	50 22.7	-13.0	59.6	50 52.6	-11.6	60.7	51 21.5	-10.2	61.8	51 49.3	-8.7	62.9	52 16.1	-7.2	64.0	33
34	48 30.7	-18.0	55.2	49 04.6	-16.8	56.1	49 37.6	-15.5	57.1	50 09.7	-14.2	58.1	50 41.0	-12.9	59.1	51 11.3	-11.5	60.2	51 40.6	-10.0	61.3	52 08.9	-8.6	62.4	34
35	48 12.7	-19.1	53.8	48 47.8	-17.9	54.7	49 22.1	-16.7	55.6	49 55.5	-15.3	56.6	50 28.1	-14.0	57.6	50 59.8	-12.7	58.6	51 30.6	-11.3	59.7	52 00.3	-9.8	60.8	35
36	47 53.6	-20.1	52.3	48 29.9	-19.0	53.2	49 05.4	-17.7	54.1	49 40.2	-16.5	55.1	50 14.1	-15.2	56.1	50 47.1	-13.9	57.1	51 19.3	-12.6	58.1	51 50.5	-11.2	59.2	36
37	47 33.5	-21.1	50.9	48 10.9	-20.0	51.8	48 47.7	-18.8	52.7	49 23.7	-17.7	53.6	49 58.9	-16.4	54.6	50 33.2	-15.1	55.6	51 06.7	-13.8	56.6	51 39.3	-12.4	57.6	37
38	47 12.4	-22.2	49.6	47 50.9	-21.0	50.4	48 28.9	-19.9	51.3	49 06.0	-18.7	52.1	49 42.5	-17.5	53.1	50 18.1	-16.3	54.0	50 52.9	-15.0	55.0	51 26.9	-13.7	56.1	38
39	46 50.2	-23.0	48.2	47 29.9	-22.0	49.0	48 09.0	-21.0	49.8	48 47.3	-19.8	50.7	49 25.0	-18.7	51.6	50 01.8	-17.4	52.5	50 37.9	-16.2	53.5	51 13.2	-14.9	54.5	39
40	46 27.2	-24.0	46.8	47 07.9	-23.0	47.6	47 48.0	-21.9	48.4	48 27.5	-20.8	49.3	49 06.3	-19.7	50.1	49 44.4	-18.5	51.0	50 21.7	-17.3	52.0	50 58.3	-16.1	52.9	40
41	46 03.2	-24.9	45.5	46 44.9	-23.9	46.3	47 26.1	-22.9	47.1	48 06.7	-21.9	47.9	48 46.6	-20.8	48.7	49 25.9	-19.7	49.6	50 04.4	-18.5	50.5	50 42.2	-17.3	51.4	41
42	45 38.3	-25.8	44.2	46 21.0	-24.8	44.9	47 03.2	-23.9	45.7	47 44.8	-22.8	46.5	48 25.8	-21.8	47.3	49 06.2	-20.7	48.1	49 45.9	-19.6	49.0	50 24.9	-18.4	49.9	42
43	45 12.5	-26.7	42.9	45 56.2	-25.8	43.6	46 39.3	-24.8	44.4	47 22.0	-23.9	45.1	48 04.0	-22.8	45.9	48 45.5	-21.8	46.7	49 26.3	-20.7	47.6	50 06.5	-19.6	48.4	43
44	44 45.8	-27.4	41.7	45 30.4	-26.6	42.3	46 14.5	-25.7	43.0	46 58.1	-24.7	43.8	47 41.2	-23.8	44.5	48 23.7	-22.8	45.3	49 05.6	-21.8	46.1	49 46.9	-20.7	47.0	44
45	44 18.4	-28.3	40.4	45 03.8	-27.4	41.1	45 48.8	-26.5	41.7	46 33.4	-25.7	42.4	47 17.4	-24.7	43.2	48 00.9	-23.8	43.9	48 43.8	-22.7	44.7	49 26.2	-21.7	45.5	45
46	43 50.1	-29.1	39.2	44 36.4	-28.3	39.8	45 22.3	-27.4	40.4	46 07.7	-26.6	41.1	46 52.7	-25.7	41.8	47 37.1	-24.7	42.5	48 21.1	-23.8	43.3	49 04.5	-22.8	44.1	46
47	43 21.0	-29.8	38.0	44 08.1	-29.0	38.6	44 54.9	-28.3	39.2	45 41.1	-27.4	39.8	46 27.0	-26.6	40.5	47 12.4	-25.7	41.2	47 57.3	-24.8	41.9	48 41.7	-23.8	42.7	47
48	42 51.2	-30.5	36.8	43 39.1	-29.8	37.4	44 26.6	-29.0	37.9	45 13.7	-28.2	38.6	46 00.4	-27.4	39.2	46 46.7	-26.5	39.9	47 32.5	-25.6	40.6	48 17.9	-24.8	41.3	48
49	42 20.7	-31.2	35.6	43 09.3	-30.5	36.2	43 57.6	-29.8	36.7	44 45.5	-29.0	37.3	45 33.0	-28.2	37.9	46 20.2	-27.5	38.6	47 06.9	-26.7	39.2	47 53.1	-25.7	39.9	49
50	41 49.5	-31.9	34.5	42 38.8	-31.2	35.0	43 27.8	-30.5	35.5	44 16.5	-29.9	36.1	45 04.8	-29.1	36.7	45 52.7	-28.3	37.3	46 40.2	-27.4	37.9	47 27.4	-26.7	38.6	50
51	41 17.6	-32.6	33.3	42 07.6	-31.9	33.8	42 57.3	-31.3	34.3	43 46.6	-30.5	34.9	44 35.7	-29.8	35.4	45 24.4	-29.1	36.0	46 12.8	-28.4	36.6	47 00.7	-27.5	37.3	51
52	40 45.0	-33.2	32.2	41 35.7	-32.6	32.7	42 26.0	-31.9	33.2	43 16.1	-31.3	33.7	44 05.9	-30.7	34.2	44 55.3	-29.9	34.8	45 44.4	-29.2	35.4	46 33.2	-28.5	36.0	52
53	40 11.8	-33.8	31.1	41 03.1	-33.2	31.6	41 54.1	-32.6	32.0	42 44.8	-32.0	32.5	43 35.2	-31.3	33.0	44 25.4	-30.7	33.6	45 15.2	-29.9	34.1	46 04.7	-29.2	34.7	53
54	39 38.0	-34.3	30.0	40 29.9	-33.9	30.5	41 21.5	-33.3	30.9	42 12.8	-32.6	31.4	43 03.9	-32.0	31.9	43 54.7	-31.4	32.4	44 45.3	-30.8	32.9	45 35.5	-30.1	33.4	54
55	39 03.7	-35.0	29.0	39 56.0	-34.4	29.4	40 48.2	-33.9	29.8	41 40.2	-33.4	30.2	42 31.9	-32.8	30.7	43 23.3	-32.1	31.2	44 14.5	-31.5	31.7	45 05.4	-30.8	32.2	55
56	38 28.7	-35.5	27.9	39 21.6	-35.0	28.3	40 14.3	-34.4	28.7	41 06.8	-33.9	29.1	41 59.1	-33.3	29.6	42 51.2	-32.8	30.0	43 43.0	-32.2	30.5	44 34.6	-31.6	31.0	56
57	37 53.2	-36.0	26.9	38 46.6	-35.5	27.3	39 39.9	-35.1	27.7	40 32.9	-34.5	28.0	41 25.8	-34.1	28.5	42 18.4	-33.5	28.9	43 10.8	-32.9	29.3	44 03.0	-32.3	29.8	57
58	37 17.2	-36.5	25.9	38 11.1	-36.1	26.3	39 04.8	-35.6	26.6	39 58.4	-35.2	27.0	40 51.7	-34.6	27.4	41 44.9	-34.1	27.8	42 37.9	-33.6	28.2	43 30.7	-33.0	28.6	58
59	36 40.7	-37.1	24.9	37 35.0	-36.6	25.2	38 29.2	-36.1	25.6	39 23.2	-35.6	25.9	40 17.1	-35.2	26.3	41 10.8	-34.7	26.7	42 04.3	-34.2	27.1	42 57.7	-33.7	27.5	59
60	36 03.6	-37.4	23.9	36 58.4	-37.1	24.2	37 53.1	-36.7	24.6	38 47.6	-36.3	24.9	39 41.9	-35.8	25.2	40 36.1	-35.3	25.6	41 30.1	-34.8	26.0	42 24.0	-34.4	26.4	60
61	35 26.2	-38.0	23.0	36 21.3	-37.5	23.3	37 16.4	-37.2	23.6	38 11.3	-36.7	23.9	39 06.1	-36.3	24.2	40 00.8	-35.9	24.5	40 55.3	-35.4	24.9	41 49.6	-34.9	25.3	61
62	34 48.2	-38.4	22.0	35 43.8	-38.0	22.3	36 39.2	-37.6	22.6	37 34.6	-37.3	22.9	38 29.8	-36.8	23.2	39 24.9	-36.4	23.5	40 19.9	-36.0	23.8	41 14.7	-35.6	24.2	62
63	34 09.8	-38.7	21.1	35 05.8	-38.5	21.3	36 01.6	-38.1	21.6	36 57.3	-37.7	21.9	37 53.0	-37.4	22.2	38 48.5	-37.0	22.5	39 43.9	-36.6	22.8	40 39.1	-36.1	23.1	63
64	33 31.1	-39.2	20.2	34 27.3	-38.8	20.4	35 23.5	-38.5	20.7	36 19.6	-38.2	20.9	37 15.6	-37.8	21.2	38 11.5	-37.5	21.5	39 07.3	-37.1	21.8	40 03.0	-36.7	22.1	64
65	32 51.9	-39.6	19.3	33 48.5	-39.3	19.5	34 45.0	-39.0	19.7	35 41.4	-38.6	20.0	36 37.8	-38.3	20.2	37 34.0	-37.9	20.5	38 30.2	-37.6	20.8	39 26.3	-37.3	21.0	65
66	32 12.3	-39.9	18.4	33 09.2	-39.6	18.6	34 06.0	-39.3	18.8	35 02.8	-39.0	19.0	35 59.5	-38.8	19.3	36 56.1	-38.4	19.5	37 52.6	-38.1	19.8	38 49.0	-37.7	20.0	66
67	31 32.4	-40.3	17.5	32 29.6	-40.1	17.7	33 26.7	-39.8	17.9	34 23.8	-39.5	18.1	35 20.7	-39.1	18.3	36 17.7	-38.9	18.5	37 14.5	-38.5	18.8	38 11.3	-38.3	19.0	67
68	30 52.1	-40.7	16.6	31 49.5	-40.4	16.8	32 46.9	-40.1	17.0	33 44.3	-39.9	17.2	34 41.6	-39.6	17.4	35 38.8	-39.3	17.6	36 36.0	-39.1	17.8	37 33.0	-38.7	18.1	68
69	30 11.4	-40.9	15.8	31 09.1	-40.7	15.9	32 06.8	-40.5	16.1	33 04.4	-40.2	16.3	34 02.0	-40.0	16.5	34 59.5	-39.7	16.7	35 56.9	-39.4	16.9	36 54.3	-39.1	17.1	69
70	29 30.5	-41.3	14.9	30 28.4	-41.0	15.1	31 26.3	-40.8	15.2	32 24.2	-40.6	15.4	33 22.0	-40.4	15.6	34 19.8	-40.1	15.8	35 17.5	-39.9	16.0	36 15.2	-39.7	16.2	70
71	28 49.2	-41.6	14.1	29 47.4	-41.4	14.2	30 45.5	-41.2	14.4	31 43.6	-41.0	14.5	32 41.6	-40.7	14.7	33 39.7	-40.5	14.9	34 37.6	-40.2	15.0	35 35.5	-40.0	15.2	71
72	28 07.6	-41.9	13.3	29 06.0	-41.7	13.4	30 04.3	-41.5	13.5	31 02.6	-41.2	13.7	32 00.9	-41.1	13.8	32 59.2	-40.9	14.0	33 57.4	-40.7	14.1	34 55.5	-40.4	14.3	72
73	27 25.7	-42.1	12.5	28 24.3	-42.0	12.6	29 22.8	-41.7	12.7	30 21.4	-41.6	12.8	31 19.8	-41.4	13.0	32 18.3	-41.2	13.1	33 16.7	-41.0	13.3	34 15.1	-40.8	13.4	73
74	26 43.6	-42.4	11.7	27 42.3	-42.2	11.8	28 41.1	-42.1	11.9	29 39.8	-42.0	12.0	30 38.4	-41.7	12.1	31 37.1	-41.6	12.3	32 35.7	-41.4	12.4	33 34.3	-41.2	12.5	74
75	26 01.2	-42.7	10.9	27 00.1	-42.5	11.0	27 59.0	-42.4	11.1	28 57.8	-42.2	11.2	29 56.7	-42.1	11.3	30 55.5	-41.9	11.4	31 54.3	-41.7	11.5	32 53.1	-41.6	11.7	75
76	25 18.5	-42.9	10.1	26 17.6	-42.8	10.2	27 16.6	-42.6	10.3	28 15.6	-42.5	10.4	29 14.6	-42.3	10.5	30 13.6	-42.2	10.6	31 12.6	-42.0	10.7	32 11.5	-41.8	10.8	76
77	24 35.6	-43.1	9.3	25 34.8	-43.0	9.4	26 34.0	-42.9	9.5	27 33.1	-42.7	9.6	28 32.3	-42.6	9.7	29 31.4	-42.4	9.8	30 30.6	-42.4	9.9	31 29.7	-42.2	10.0	77
78	23 52.5	-43.4	8.6	24 51.8	-43.3	8.6	25 51.1	-43.2	8.7	26 50.4	-43.0	8.8	27 49.7	-42.9	8.9	28 49.0	-42.8	9.0	29 48.2	-42.6	9.0	30 47.5	-42.6	9.1	78
79	23 09.1	-43.6	7.8	24 08.5	-43.5	7.9	25 07.9	-43.3	7.9	26 07.4	-43.3	8.0	27 06.8	-43.2	8.1	28 06.2	-43.1	8.2	29 05.6	-43.0	8.2	30 04.9	-42.8	8.3	79
80	22 25.5	-43.8	7.1	23 25.0	-43.6	7.1	24 24.6	-43.6	7.2	25 24.1	-43.5	7.2	26 23.6	-43.4	7.3	27 23.1	-43.3	7.4	28 22.6	-43.2	7.4	29 22.1	-43.1	7.5	80
81	21 41.7	-44.0	6.3	22 41.4	-43.9	6.4	23 41.0	-43.8	6.4	24 40.6	-43.7	6.5	25 40.2	-43.6	6.5	26 39.8	-43.5	6.6	27 39.4	-43.5	6.7	28 39.0	-43.4	6.7	81
82	20 57.7	-44.1	5.6	21 57.5	-44.1	5.6	22 57.2	-44.1	5.7	23 56.9	-44.0	5.7	24 56.6	-43.9	5.8	25 56.3	-43.8	5.8	26 55.9	-43.7	5.9	27 55.6	-43.6	5.9	82
83	20 13.6	-44.3	4.9	21 13.4	-44.3	4.9	22 13.1	-44.2	5.0	23 12.9	-44.1	5.0	24 12.7	-44.1	5.0	25 12.5	-44.1	5.1	26 12.2	-43.9	5.1	27 12.0	-43.9	5.2	83
84	19 29.3	-44.6	4.2	20 29.1	-44.5	4.2	21 28.9	-44.4	4.2	22 28.8	-44.4	4.3	23 28.6	-44.3	4.3	24 28.4	-44.2	4.3	25 28.3	-44.2	4.4	26 28.1	-44.2	4.4	84
85	18 44.7	-44.6	3.5	19 44.6	-44.6	3.5	20 44.5	-44.6	3.5	21 44.4	-44.5	3.5	22 44.3	-44.5	3.6	23 44.2	-44.5	3.6	24 44.1	-44.4	3.6	25 43.9	-44.3	3.6	85
86	18 00.1	-44.8	2.8	19 00.0	-44.8	2.8	19 59.9	-44.7	2.8	20 59.9	-44.7	2.8	21 59.8	-44.7	2.8	22 59.7	-44.6	2.8	23 59.7	-44.7	2.9	24 59.6	-44.6	2.9	86
87	17 15.3	-45.0	2.1	18 15.2	-44.9	2.1	19 15.2	-44.9	2.1	20 15.2	-44.9	2.1	21 15.1	-44.9	2.1	22 15.1	-44.9	2.1	23 15.0	-44.8	2.1	24 15.0	-44.8	2.2	87
88	16 30.3	-45.1	1.4	17 30.3	-45.1	1.4	18 30.3	-45.1	1.4	19 30.3	-45.1	1.4	20 30.2	-45.0	1.4	21 30.2	-45.0	1.4	22 30.2	-45.0	1.4	23 30.2	-45.0	1.4	88
89	15 45.2	-45.2	0.7	16 45.2	-45.2	0.7	17 45.2	-45.2	0.7	18 45.2	-45.2	0.7	19 45.2	-45.2	0.7	20 45.2	-45.2	0.7	21 45.2	-45.2	0.7	22 45.2	-45.2	0.7	89
90	15 00.0	-45.3	0.0	16 00.0	-45.3	0.0	17 00.0	-45.4	0.0	18 00.0	-45.4	0.0	19 00.0	-45.4	0.0	20 00.0	-45.4	0.0	21 00.0	-45.4	0.0	22 00.0	-45.4	0.0	90
	15°			16°			17°			18°			19°			20°			21°			22°			

41°, 319° L.H.A. LATITUDE **SAME** NAME AS DECLINATION

84

LATITUDE CONTRARY NAME TO DECLINATION — L.H.A. 41°, 319°

Dec.	15°			16°			17°			18°			19°			20°			21°			22°			Dec.
	Hc	d	Z	Hc	d	Z	Hc	d	Z	Hc	d	Z	Hc	d	Z	Hc	d	Z	Hc	d	Z	Hc	d	Z	
°	° ′	′	°	° ′	′	°	° ′	′	°	° ′	′	°	° ′	′	°	° ′	′	°	° ′	′	°	° ′	′	°	°
0	46 48.1	−23.1	106.6	46 30.5	−24.5	107.6	46 11.9	−25.8	108.6	45 52.2	−27.0	109.6	45 31.7	−28.3	110.5	45 10.2	−29.5	111.5	44 47.7	−30.6	112.4	44 24.4	−31.8	113.3	0
1	46 25.0	−24.1	107.9	46 06.0	−25.4	108.9	45 46.1	−26.7	109.9	45 25.2	−27.9	110.8	45 03.4	−29.1	111.8	44 40.7	−30.3	112.7	44 17.1	−31.5	113.6	43 52.6	−32.5	114.5	1
2	46 00.9	−25.0	109.2	45 40.6	−26.2	110.2	45 19.4	−27.5	111.2	44 57.3	−28.7	112.1	44 34.3	−29.9	113.0	44 10.4	−31.1	113.9	43 45.6	−32.1	114.8	43 20.1	−33.3	115.7	2
3	45 35.9	−25.9	110.6	45 14.4	−27.2	111.5	44 51.9	−28.3	112.4	44 28.6	−29.5	113.3	44 04.4	−30.7	114.2	43 39.3	−31.7	115.1	43 13.5	−32.9	116.0	42 46.8	−33.9	116.8	3
4	45 10.0	−26.7	111.8	44 47.2	−27.9	112.8	44 23.6	−29.1	113.7	43 59.1	−30.3	114.6	43 33.7	−31.3	115.4	43 07.6	−32.5	116.3	42 40.6	−33.5	117.1	42 12.9	−34.5	117.9	4
5	44 43.3	−27.6	113.1	44 19.3	−28.7	114.0	43 54.5	−29.9	114.9	43 28.8	−31.0	115.7	43 02.4	−32.1	116.6	42 35.1	−33.1	117.4	42 07.1	−34.1	118.2	41 38.4	−35.2	119.0	5
6	44 15.7	−28.3	114.3	43 50.6	−29.5	115.2	43 24.6	−30.6	116.1	42 57.8	−31.7	116.9	42 30.3	−32.8	117.7	42 02.0	−33.8	118.5	41 33.0	−34.8	119.3	41 03.2	−35.7	120.1	6
7	43 47.4	−29.1	115.6	43 21.1	−30.2	116.4	42 54.0	−31.3	117.3	42 26.1	−32.3	118.1	41 57.5	−33.4	118.9	41 28.2	−34.4	119.7	40 58.2	−35.4	120.4	40 27.5	−36.4	121.2	7
8	43 18.3	−29.9	116.8	42 50.9	−31.0	117.6	42 22.7	−32.0	118.4	41 53.8	−33.1	119.2	41 24.1	−34.0	120.0	40 53.8	−35.0	120.7	40 22.8	−36.0	121.5	39 51.1	−36.8	122.2	8
9	42 48.4	−30.6	118.0	42 19.9	−31.6	118.8	41 50.7	−32.7	119.6	41 20.7	−33.7	120.3	40 50.1	−34.7	121.1	40 18.8	−35.6	121.8	39 46.8	−36.5	122.5	39 14.3	−37.4	123.2	9
10	42 17.8	−31.3	119.1	41 48.3	−32.4	119.9	41 18.0	−33.3	120.7	40 47.0	−34.3	121.4	40 15.4	−35.2	122.2	39 43.2	−36.2	122.9	39 10.3	−37.0	123.6	38 36.9	−38.0	124.2	10
11	41 46.5	−31.9	120.3	41 15.9	−32.9	121.0	40 44.7	−34.0	121.8	40 12.7	−34.9	122.5	39 40.2	−35.8	123.2	39 07.0	−36.7	123.9	38 33.3	−37.6	124.6	37 58.9	−38.4	125.2	11
12	41 14.6	−32.6	121.4	40 43.0	−33.6	122.2	40 10.7	−34.5	122.9	39 37.8	−35.4	123.6	39 04.4	−36.4	124.2	38 30.3	−37.2	124.9	37 55.7	−38.0	125.6	37 20.5	−38.8	126.2	12
13	40 42.0	−33.3	122.5	40 09.4	−34.2	123.2	39 36.2	−35.1	123.9	39 02.4	−36.0	124.6	38 28.0	−36.8	125.3	37 53.1	−37.7	125.9	37 17.7	−38.6	126.5	36 41.7	−39.3	127.1	13
14	40 08.7	−33.8	123.6	39 35.2	−34.8	124.3	39 01.1	−35.7	125.0	38 26.4	−36.5	125.6	37 51.2	−37.4	126.3	37 15.4	−38.2	126.9	36 39.1	−38.9	127.5	36 02.4	−39.8	128.1	14
15	39 34.9	−34.5	124.7	39 00.4	−35.3	125.4	38 25.4	−36.2	126.0	37 49.9	−37.1	126.6	37 13.8	−37.9	127.3	36 37.2	−38.6	127.9	36 00.2	−39.5	128.4	35 22.6	−40.1	129.0	15
16	39 00.4	−35.0	125.8	38 25.1	−35.9	126.4	37 49.2	−36.7	127.0	37 12.8	−37.5	127.6	36 35.9	−38.3	128.2	35 58.6	−39.1	128.8	35 20.7	−39.8	129.4	34 42.5	−40.6	129.9	16
17	38 25.4	−35.5	126.8	37 49.2	−36.4	127.4	37 12.5	−37.2	128.0	36 35.3	−38.0	128.6	35 57.6	−38.7	129.2	35 19.5	−39.5	129.7	34 40.9	−40.2	130.3	34 01.9	−40.9	130.8	17
18	37 49.9	−36.1	127.8	37 12.8	−36.9	128.4	36 35.3	−37.7	129.0	35 57.3	−38.4	129.6	35 18.9	−39.2	130.1	34 40.0	−39.9	130.7	34 00.7	−40.6	131.2	33 21.0	−41.3	131.7	18
19	37 13.8	−36.6	128.8	36 35.9	−37.3	129.4	35 57.6	−38.1	130.0	35 18.9	−38.9	130.5	34 39.7	−39.6	131.0	34 00.1	−40.4	131.6	33 20.1	−41.0	132.1	32 39.7	−41.7	132.5	19
20	36 37.2	−37.0	129.8	35 58.6	−37.9	130.4	35 19.5	−38.6	130.9	34 40.0	−39.3	131.4	34 00.1	−40.0	132.0	33 19.7	−40.6	132.5	32 39.1	−41.4	132.9	31 58.0	−42.0	133.4	20
21	36 00.2	−37.6	130.8	35 20.7	−38.2	131.3	34 40.9	−39.0	131.9	34 00.7	−39.7	132.4	33 20.1	−40.4	132.9	32 39.1	−41.1	133.3	31 57.7	−41.7	133.8	31 16.0	−42.3	134.2	21
22	35 22.6	−37.9	131.8	34 42.5	−38.7	132.3	34 01.9	−39.4	132.8	33 21.0	−40.1	133.3	32 39.7	−40.8	133.7	31 58.0	−41.4	134.2	31 16.0	−42.0	134.6	30 33.7	−42.6	135.1	22
23	34 44.7	−38.5	132.7	34 03.8	−39.1	133.2	33 22.5	−39.8	133.7	32 40.9	−40.5	134.2	31 58.9	−41.1	134.6	31 16.6	−41.7	135.0	30 34.0	−42.3	135.5	29 51.1	−42.9	135.9	23
24	34 06.2	−38.8	133.6	33 24.7	−39.5	134.1	32 42.7	−40.1	134.6	32 00.4	−40.8	135.0	31 17.8	−41.4	135.5	30 34.9	−42.0	135.9	29 51.7	−42.6	136.3	29 08.2	−43.2	136.7	24
25	33 27.4	−39.2	134.5	32 45.2	−39.9	135.0	32 02.6	−40.6	135.5	31 19.6	−41.1	135.9	30 36.4	−41.7	136.3	29 52.9	−42.4	136.7	29 09.1	−42.9	137.1	28 25.0	−43.5	137.5	25
26	32 48.2	−39.6	135.5	32 05.3	−40.3	135.9	31 22.0	−40.8	136.3	30 38.5	−41.5	136.7	29 54.7	−42.1	137.1	29 10.5	−42.6	137.5	28 26.2	−43.2	137.9	27 41.5	−43.7	138.2	26
27	32 08.6	−40.0	136.3	31 25.0	−40.6	136.8	30 41.2	−41.2	137.2	29 57.0	−41.8	137.6	29 12.6	−42.4	138.0	28 27.9	−42.9	138.3	27 43.0	−43.5	138.7	26 57.8	−44.0	139.0	27
28	31 28.6	−40.3	137.2	30 44.4	−40.9	137.6	30 00.0	−41.5	138.0	29 15.2	−42.1	138.4	28 30.2	−42.6	138.8	27 45.0	−43.2	139.1	26 59.5	−43.7	139.5	26 13.8	−44.2	139.8	28
29	30 48.3	−40.7	138.1	30 03.5	−41.3	138.5	29 18.5	−41.9	138.9	28 33.1	−42.3	139.2	27 47.6	−42.9	139.6	27 01.8	−43.4	139.9	26 15.8	−43.9	140.2	25 29.6	−44.4	140.5	29
30	30 07.6	−41.0	138.9	29 22.2	−41.5	139.3	28 36.6	−42.1	139.7	27 50.8	−42.7	140.0	27 04.7	−43.2	140.3	26 18.4	−43.7	140.7	25 31.9	−44.2	141.0	24 45.2	−44.7	141.3	30
31	29 26.6	−41.3	139.8	28 40.7	−41.9	140.1	27 54.5	−42.4	140.5	27 08.1	−42.9	140.8	26 21.5	−43.4	141.1	25 34.7	−43.9	141.4	24 47.7	−44.4	141.7	24 00.5	−44.9	142.0	31
32	28 45.3	−41.6	140.6	27 58.8	−42.1	140.9	27 12.1	−42.6	141.3	26 25.2	−43.2	141.6	25 38.1	−43.7	141.9	24 50.8	−44.1	142.2	24 03.3	−44.6	142.5	23 15.6	−45.0	142.7	32
33	28 03.7	−41.9	141.4	27 16.7	−42.4	141.8	26 29.5	−43.0	142.1	25 42.0	−43.4	142.4	24 54.4	−43.8	142.7	24 06.7	−44.4	142.9	23 18.7	−44.8	143.2	22 30.6	−45.3	143.4	33
34	27 21.8	−42.2	142.2	26 34.3	−42.7	142.5	25 46.5	−43.1	142.8	24 58.6	−43.6	143.1	24 10.6	−44.1	143.4	23 22.3	−44.6	143.7	22 33.9	−45.0	143.9	21 45.3	−45.4	144.2	34
35	26 39.6	−42.4	143.0	25 51.6	−42.9	143.3	25 03.4	−43.4	143.6	24 15.0	−43.9	143.9	23 26.5	−44.4	144.1	22 37.7	−44.7	144.4	21 48.9	−45.2	144.6	20 59.9	−45.6	144.9	35
36	25 57.2	−42.7	143.8	25 08.7	−43.2	144.1	24 20.0	−43.6	144.4	23 31.1	−44.0	144.6	22 42.1	−44.5	144.9	21 53.0	−44.9	145.1	21 03.7	−45.3	145.3	20 14.3	−45.8	145.5	36
37	25 14.5	−42.9	144.6	24 25.5	−43.4	144.9	23 36.4	−43.9	145.1	22 47.1	−44.3	145.4	21 57.6	−44.7	145.6	21 08.1	−45.2	145.8	20 18.4	−45.6	146.0	19 28.5	−45.9	146.2	37
38	24 31.6	−43.2	145.4	23 42.1	−43.6	145.6	22 52.5	−44.0	145.9	22 02.8	−44.5	146.1	21 12.9	−44.8	146.3	20 22.9	−45.2	146.5	19 32.8	−45.6	146.7	18 42.6	−46.0	146.9	38
39	23 48.4	−43.4	146.1	22 58.5	−43.8	146.4	22 08.5	−44.2	146.6	21 18.3	−44.6	146.8	20 28.1	−45.1	147.0	19 37.7	−45.5	147.2	18 47.2	−45.9	147.4	17 56.6	−46.2	147.6	39
40	23 05.0	−43.6	146.9	22 14.7	−44.0	147.1	21 24.3	−44.5	147.3	20 33.7	−44.8	147.5	19 43.0	−45.2	147.7	18 52.2	−45.6	147.9	18 01.3	−45.9	148.1	17 10.4	−46.4	148.3	40
41	22 21.4	−43.8	147.6	21 30.7	−44.2	147.8	20 39.8	−44.6	148.1	19 48.9	−45.0	148.2	18 57.8	−45.4	148.4	18 06.6	−45.7	148.6	17 15.4	−46.1	148.8	16 24.0	−46.4	148.9	41
42	21 37.6	−44.0	148.4	20 46.5	−44.4	148.6	19 55.2	−44.7	148.8	19 03.9	−45.2	148.9	18 12.4	−45.5	149.1	17 20.9	−45.9	149.3	16 29.3	−46.3	149.4	15 37.6	−46.6	149.6	42
43	20 53.6	−44.1	149.1	20 02.1	−44.6	149.3	19 10.5	−45.0	149.5	18 18.7	−45.3	149.6	17 26.9	−45.6	149.8	16 35.0	−46.0	150.0	15 43.0	−46.3	150.1	14 51.0	−46.7	150.2	43
44	20 09.5	−44.4	149.8	19 17.5	−44.7	150.0	18 25.5	−45.0	150.2	17 33.4	−45.4	150.3	16 41.3	−45.8	150.5	15 49.0	−46.1	150.6	14 56.7	−46.5	150.8	14 04.3	−46.8	150.9	44
45	19 25.1	−44.5	150.5	18 32.8	−44.9	150.7	17 40.5	−45.3	150.9	16 48.0	−45.6	151.0	15 55.5	−45.9	151.2	15 02.9	−46.2	151.3	14 10.2	−46.5	151.4	13 17.5	−46.9	151.5	45
46	18 40.6	−44.7	151.2	17 47.9	−45.0	151.4	16 55.2	−45.3	151.6	16 02.4	−45.7	151.7	15 09.6	−46.1	151.8	14 16.7	−46.4	151.9	13 23.7	−46.7	152.1	12 30.6	−46.9	152.2	46
47	17 55.9	−44.8	151.9	17 02.9	−45.1	152.1	16 09.9	−45.5	152.2	15 16.7	−45.8	152.4	14 23.5	−46.1	152.5	13 30.3	−46.4	152.6	12 37.0	−46.7	152.7	11 43.7	−47.1	152.8	47
48	17 11.1	−45.0	152.6	16 17.8	−45.3	152.8	15 24.4	−45.7	152.9	14 30.9	−45.9	153.0	13 37.4	−46.2	153.1	12 43.9	−46.6	153.3	11 50.3	−46.9	153.4	10 56.6	−47.1	153.4	48
49	16 26.1	−45.1	153.3	15 32.5	−45.5	153.5	14 38.7	−45.7	153.6	13 45.0	−46.0	153.7	12 51.2	−46.4	153.8	11 57.3	−46.6	153.9	11 03.4	−46.9	154.0	10 09.5	−47.2	154.1	49
50	15 41.0	−45.2	154.0	14 47.0	−45.5	154.1	13 53.0	−45.8	154.3	12 59.0	−46.2	154.4	12 04.8	−46.4	154.5	11 10.7	−46.7	154.5	10 16.5	−47.0	154.6	9 22.3	−47.3	154.7	50
51	14 55.8	−45.4	154.7	14 01.5	−45.7	154.8	13 07.2	−46.0	154.9	12 12.8	−46.2	155.0	11 18.4	−46.5	155.1	10 24.0	−46.8	155.2	9 29.5	−47.1	155.3	8 35.0	−47.3	155.3	51
52	14 10.4	−45.4	155.4	13 15.8	−45.7	155.5	12 21.2	−46.0	155.6	11 26.6	−46.3	155.7	10 31.9	−46.6	155.7	9 37.2	−46.9	155.8	8 42.4	−47.1	155.9	7 47.7	−47.4	155.9	52
53	13 25.0	−45.6	156.1	12 30.1	−45.9	156.1	11 35.2	−46.1	156.2	10 40.3	−46.4	156.3	9 45.3	−46.6	156.4	8 50.3	−46.9	156.4	7 55.3	−47.2	156.5	7 00.3	−47.5	156.6	53
54	12 39.4	−45.7	156.7	11 44.2	−45.9	156.8	10 49.1	−46.2	156.9	9 53.9	−46.5	157.0	8 58.7	−46.8	157.0	8 03.4	−47.0	157.1	7 08.1	−47.2	157.1	6 12.8	−47.4	157.2	54
55	11 53.7	−45.8	157.4	10 58.3	−46.0	157.5	10 02.9	−46.3	157.5	9 07.4	−46.5	157.6	8 11.9	−46.8	157.7	7 16.4	−47.0	157.7	6 20.9	−47.3	157.8	5 25.4	−47.6	157.8	55
56	11 07.9	−45.8	158.0	10 12.3	−46.1	158.1	9 16.6	−46.4	158.2	8 20.9	−46.6	158.2	7 25.1	−46.8	158.3	6 29.4	−47.1	158.3	5 33.6	−47.3	158.4	4 37.8	−47.5	158.4	56
57	10 22.1	−45.9	158.7	9 26.2	−46.2	158.8	8 30.2	−46.4	158.8	7 34.3	−46.7	158.9	6 38.3	−46.9	158.9	5 42.3	−47.1	159.0	4 46.3	−47.3	159.0	3 50.3	−47.6	159.0	57
58	9 36.2	−46.0	159.4	8 40.0	−46.2	159.4	7 43.8	−46.4	159.5	6 47.6	−46.7	159.5	5 51.4	−46.9	159.5	4 55.2	−47.1	159.6	3 59.0	−47.4	159.6	3 02.7	−47.6	159.6	58
59	8 50.2	−46.1	160.0	7 53.8	−46.3	160.1	6 57.4	−46.6	160.1	6 00.9	−46.7	160.1	5 04.5	−47.0	160.2	4 08.1	−47.2	160.2	3 11.6	−47.4	160.2	2 15.1	−47.6	160.2	59
60	8 04.1	−46.1	160.7	7 07.5	−46.4	160.7	6 10.8	−46.5	160.7	5 14.2	−46.8	160.8	4 17.5	−47.0	160.8	3 20.9	−47.2	160.8	2 24.2	−47.4	160.8	1 27.5	−47.6	160.8	60
61	7 18.0	−46.2	161.3	6 21.1	−46.4	161.3	5 24.3	−46.6	161.4	4 27.4	−46.8	161.4	3 30.5	−47.0	161.4	2 33.7	−47.2	161.4	1 36.8	−47.4	161.4	0 39.9	−47.6	161.5	61
62	6 31.8	−46.3	161.9	5 34.7	−46.4	162.0	4 37.7	−46.7	162.0	3 40.6	−46.8	162.0	2 43.5	−47.0	162.0	1 46.5	−47.3	162.1	0 49.4	−47.5	162.1	0 07.7	+47.6	17.9	62
63	5 45.5	−46.2	162.6	4 48.3	−46.5	162.6	3 51.0	−46.6	162.6	2 53.8	−46.9	162.6	1 56.5	−47.1	162.7	0 59.2	−47.2	162.7	0 01.9	−47.4	162.7	0 55.3	+47.6	17.3	63
64	4 59.3	−46.3	163.2	4 01.8	−46.5	163.2	3 04.4	−46.7	163.3	2 06.9	−46.9	163.3	1 09.4	−47.0	163.3	0 12.0	−47.3	163.3	0 45.5	+47.4	16.7	1 42.9	+47.7	16.7	64
65	4 13.0	−46.4	163.9	3 15.3	−46.5	163.9	2 17.7	−46.7	163.9	1 20.0	−46.8	163.9	0 22.4	−47.1	163.9	0 35.3	+47.2	16.1	1 32.9	+47.4	16.1	2 30.6	+47.5	16.1	65
66	3 26.6	−46.4	164.5	2 28.8	−46.5	164.5	1 31.0	−46.7	164.5	0 33.2	−46.9	164.5	0 24.7	+47.0	15.5	1 22.5	+47.2	15.5	2 20.3	+47.4	15.5	3 18.1	+47.6	15.5	66
67	2 40.2	−46.3	165.1	1 42.3	−46.6	165.1	0 44.3	−46.8	165.1	0 13.7	+46.9	14.9	1 11.7	+47.1	14.9	2 09.7	+47.2	14.9	3 07.7	+47.4	14.9	4 05.7	+47.5	14.9	67
68	1 53.9	−46.4	165.8	0 55.7	−46.6	165.8	0 02.5	+46.7	14.2	1 00.6	+46.9	14.2	1 58.8	+47.0	14.2	2 56.9	+47.2	14.2	3 55.1	+47.3	14.3	4 53.2	+47.5	14.3	68
69	1 07.5	−46.5	166.4	0 09.1	−46.5	166.4	0 49.2	+46.7	13.6	1 47.5	+46.9	13.6	2 45.8	+47.0	13.6	3 44.1	+47.2	13.6	4 42.4	+47.4	13.6	5 40.7	+47.5	13.7	69
70	0 21.0	−46.4	167.0	0 37.4	+46.6	13.0	1 35.9	+46.7	13.0	2 34.4	+46.8	13.0	3 32.8	+47.0	13.0	4 31.3	+47.1	13.0	5 29.8	+47.2	13.0	6 28.2	+47.4	13.1	70
71	0 25.4	+46.4	12.3	1 24.0	+46.5	12.3	2 22.6	+46.7	12.3	3 21.2	+46.8	12.4	4 19.8	+47.0	12.4	5 18.4	+47.1	12.4	6 17.0	+47.3	12.4	7 15.6	+47.4	12.4	71
72	1 11.8	+46.4	11.7	2 10.5	+46.6	11.7	3 09.3	+46.7	11.7	4 08.0	+46.8	11.7	5 06.8	+46.9	11.7	6 05.5	+47.1	11.8	7 04.3	+47.1	11.8	8 03.0	+47.3	11.8	72
73	1 58.2	+46.4	11.1	2 57.1	+46.5	11.1	3 56.0	+46.6	11.1	4 54.8	+46.8	11.1	5 53.7	+46.9	11.1	6 52.6	+47.0	11.1	7 51.4	+47.2	11.2	8 50.3	+47.3	11.2	73
74	2 44.6	+46.3	10.4	3 43.6	+46.5	10.4	4 42.6	+46.6	10.5	5 41.6	+46.7	10.5	6 40.6	+46.8	10.5	7 39.6	+46.9	10.5	8 38.6	+47.0	10.5	9 37.6	+47.1	10.6	74
75	3 30.9	+46.4	9.8	4 30.1	+46.4	9.8	5 29.2	+46.6	9.8	6 28.3	+46.7	9.8	7 27.4	+46.8	9.9	8 26.5	+46.9	9.9	9 25.6	+47.0	9.9	10 24.7	+47.2	9.9	75
76	4 17.3	+46.3	9.2	5 16.5	+46.4	9.2	6 15.8	+46.5	9.2	7 15.0	+46.6	9.2	8 14.2	+46.7	9.2	9 13.4	+46.9	9.3	10 12.6	+47.0	9.3	11 11.9	+47.0	9.3	76
77	5 03.6	+46.3	8.5	6 02.9	+46.4	8.5	7 02.3	+46.4	8.6	8 01.6	+46.6	8.6	9 00.9	+46.7	8.6	10 00.3	+46.7	8.6	10 59.6	+46.8	8.6	11 58.9	+46.9	8.7	77
78	5 49.9	+46.2	7.9	6 49.3	+46.3	7.9	7 48.7	+46.4	7.9	8 48.2	+46.5	7.9	9 47.6	+46.6	8.0	10 47.0	+46.7	8.0	11 46.4	+46.8	8.0	12 45.8	+46.9	8.0	78
79	6 36.1	+46.2	7.2	7 35.6	+46.3	7.3	8 35.1	+46.4	7.3	9 34.7	+46.4	7.3	10 34.2	+46.5	7.3	11 33.7	+46.6	7.3	12 33.2	+46.7	7.4	13 32.7	+46.7	7.4	79
80	7 22.3	+46.1	6.6	8 21.9	+46.2	6.6	9 21.5	+46.3	6.6	10 21.1	+46.3	6.7	11 20.7	+46.4	6.7	12 20.3	+46.5	6.7	13 19.9	+46.5	6.7	14 19.4	+46.7	6.8	80
81	8 08.4	+46.1	6.0	9 08.1	+46.1	6.0	10 07.8	+46.1	6.0	11 07.4	+46.3	6.0	12 07.1	+46.3	6.0	13 06.8	+46.4	6.0	14 06.4	+46.5	6.1	15 06.1	+46.5	6.1	81
82	8 54.5	+46.0	5.3	9 54.2	+46.1	5.3	10 53.9	+46.2	5.3	11 53.7	+46.2	5.4	12 53.4	+46.3	5.4	13 53.2	+46.3	5.4	14 52.9	+46.3	5.4	15 52.6	+46.4	5.4	82
83	9 40.5	+45.9	4.7	10 40.3	+45.9	4.7	11 40.1	+46.0	4.7	12 39.9	+46.0	4.7	13 39.7	+46.1	4.7	14 39.5	+46.1	4.7	15 39.2	+46.3	4.8	16 39.0	+46.3	4.8	83
84	10 26.4	+45.8	4.0	11 26.2	+45.9	4.0	12 26.1	+45.9	4.0	13 25.9	+46.0	4.0	14 25.8	+46.0	4.1	15 25.6	+46.1	4.1	16 25.5	+46.1	4.1	17 25.3	+46.2	4.1	84
85	11 12.2	+45.8	3.3	12 12.1	+45.8	3.4	13 12.0	+45.8	3.4	14 11.9	+45.9	3.4	15 11.8	+45.9	3.4	16 11.7	+45.9	3.4	17 11.6	+46.0	3.4	18 11.5	+46.0	3.5	85
86	11 58.0	+45.6	2.7	12 57.9	+45.7	2.7	13 57.8	+45.8	2.7	14 57.8	+45.7	2.7	15 57.7	+45.8	2.7	16 57.6	+45.9	2.7	17 57.6	+45.8	2.8	18 57.5	+45.9	2.8	86
87	12 43.6	+45.6	2.0	13 43.6	+45.6	2.0	14 43.6	+45.6	2.0	15 43.5	+45.7	2.0	16 43.5	+45.6	2.1	17 43.5	+45.6	2.1	18 43.4	+45.7	2.1	19 43.4	+45.7	2.1	87
88	13 29.2	+45.5	1.3	14 29.2	+45.5	1.4	15 29.2	+45.4	1.4	16 29.2	+45.4	1.4	17 29.1	+45.5	1.4	18 29.1	+45.5	1.4	19 29.1	+45.5	1.4	20 29.1	+45.5	1.4	88
89	14 14.7	+45.3	0.7	15 14.7	+45.3	0.7	16 14.6	+45.4	0.7	17 14.6	+45.4	0.7	18 14.6	+45.4	0.7	19 14.6	+45.4	0.7	20 14.6	+45.4	0.7	21 14.6	+45.4	0.7	89
90	15 00.0	+45.2	0.0	16 00.0	+45.2	0.0	17 00.0	+45.2	0.0	18 00.0	+45.2	0.0	19 00.0	+45.2	0.0	20 00.0	+45.2	0.0	21 00.0	+45.2	0.0	22 00.0	+45.2	0.0	90
	15°			16°			17°			18°			19°			20°			21°			22°			

S. Lat. {L.H.A. greater than 180° ....Zn=180°−Z
{L.H.A. less than 180°...........Zn=180°+Z

LATITUDE SAME NAME AS DECLINATION — L.H.A. 139°, 221°

42°, 318° L.H.A. LATITUDE SAME NAME AS DECLINATION

N. Lat. {L.H.A. greater than 180° .....Zn=Z; L.H.A. less than 180°............Zn=360°−Z}

Dec. °	15° Hc ° ′	d ′	Z °	16° Hc ° ′	d ′	Z °	17° Hc ° ′	d ′	Z °	18° Hc ° ′	d ′	Z °
0	45 52.5	+21.8	106.0	45 35.4	+23.2	107.0	45 17.4	+24.5	108.0	44 58.4	+25.8	108.9
1	46 14.3	+20.9	104.7	45 58.6	+22.3	105.7	45 41.9	+23.6	106.7	45 24.2	+24.9	107.7
2	46 35.2	+19.9	103.3	46 20.9	+21.3	104.4	46 05.5	+22.6	105.4	45 49.1	+24.0	106.4
3	46 55.1	+18.9	102.0	46 42.2	+20.3	103.0	46 28.1	+21.7	104.0	46 13.1	+23.1	105.0
4	47 14.0	+17.9	100.6	47 02.5	+19.3	101.6	46 49.8	+20.8	102.7	46 36.2	+22.1	103.7
5	47 31.9	+16.8	99.2	47 21.8	+18.3	100.2	47 10.6	+19.7	101.3	46 58.3	+21.2	102.3
6	47 48.7	+15.8	97.7	47 40.1	+17.2	98.8	47 30.3	+18.7	99.9	47 19.5	+20.1	101.0
7	48 04.5	+14.6	96.3	47 57.3	+16.2	97.4	47 49.0	+17.7	98.5	47 39.6	+19.1	99.6
8	48 19.1	+13.6	94.8	48 13.5	+15.1	96.0	48 06.7	+16.6	97.1	47 58.7	+18.1	98.2
9	48 32.7	+12.4	93.4	48 28.6	+13.9	94.5	48 23.3	+15.5	95.6	48 16.8	+17.0	96.7
10	48 45.1	+11.3	91.9	48 42.5	+12.9	93.0	48 38.8	+14.4	94.2	48 33.8	+16.0	95.3
11	48 56.4	+10.1	90.4	48 55.4	+11.7	91.5	48 53.2	+13.2	92.7	48 49.8	+14.7	93.8
12	49 06.5	+8.9	88.9	49 07.1	+10.5	90.0	49 06.4	+12.1	91.2	49 04.5	+13.7	92.4
13	49 15.4	+7.8	87.4	49 17.6	+9.3	88.5	49 18.5	+10.9	89.7	49 18.2	+12.5	90.9
14	49 23.2	+6.5	85.9	49 26.9	+8.1	87.0	49 29.4	+9.7	88.2	49 30.7	+11.3	89.4
15	49 29.7	+5.3	84.3	49 35.0	+7.0	85.5	49 39.1	+8.6	86.7	49 42.0	+10.1	87.8
16	49 35.0	+4.1	82.8	49 42.0	+5.7	84.0	49 47.7	+7.3	85.1	49 52.1	+8.9	86.3
17	49 39.1	+2.9	81.3	49 47.7	+4.4	82.4	49 55.0	+6.0	83.6	50 01.0	+7.7	84.8
18	49 42.0	+1.6	79.7	49 52.1	+3.3	80.9	50 01.0	+4.9	82.0	50 08.7	+6.5	83.2
19	49 43.6	+0.5	78.2	49 55.4	+2.0	79.3	50 05.9	+3.6	80.5	50 15.2	+5.2	81.7
20	49 44.1	−0.9	76.6	49 57.4	+0.7	77.8	50 09.5	+2.3	78.9	50 20.4	+3.9	80.1
21	49 43.2	−2.0	75.1	49 58.1	−0.5	76.2	50 11.8	+1.1	77.4	50 24.3	+2.7	78.6
22	49 41.2	−3.3	73.5	49 57.6	−1.7	74.7	50 12.9	−0.2	75.8	50 27.0	+1.4	77.0
23	49 37.9	−4.6	72.0	49 55.9	−3.0	73.1	50 12.7	−1.4	74.3	50 28.4	+0.2	75.4
24	49 33.3	−5.7	70.4	49 52.9	−4.3	71.6	50 11.3	−2.7	72.7	50 28.6	−1.2	73.8
25	49 27.6	−7.0	68.9	49 48.6	−5.4	70.0	50 08.6	−3.9	71.1	50 27.4	−2.4	72.3
26	49 20.6	−8.1	67.4	49 43.2	−6.7	68.5	50 04.7	−5.2	69.6	50 25.0	−3.6	70.7
27	49 12.5	−9.4	65.9	49 36.5	−7.9	66.9	49 59.5	−6.4	68.0	50 21.4	−4.9	69.1
28	49 03.1	−10.5	64.4	49 28.6	−9.1	65.4	49 53.1	−7.7	66.5	50 16.5	−6.2	67.6
29	48 52.6	−11.7	62.9	49 19.5	−10.3	63.9	49 45.4	−8.8	64.9	50 10.3	−7.4	66.0
30	48 40.9	−12.8	61.4	49 09.2	−11.4	62.4	49 36.6	−10.1	63.4	50 02.9	−8.6	64.5
31	48 28.1	−13.9	59.9	48 57.8	−12.6	60.9	49 26.5	−11.2	61.9	49 54.3	−9.8	62.9
32	48 14.2	−15.0	58.4	48 45.2	−13.8	59.4	49 15.3	−12.4	60.4	49 44.5	−11.1	61.4
33	47 59.2	−16.2	57.0	48 31.4	−14.8	57.9	49 02.9	−13.6	58.9	49 33.4	−12.2	59.9
34	47 43.0	−17.2	55.5	48 16.6	−16.0	56.5	48 49.3	−14.7	57.4	49 21.2	−13.4	58.4
35	47 25.8	−18.2	54.1	48 00.6	−17.0	55.0	48 34.6	−15.8	55.9	49 07.8	−14.5	56.9
36	47 07.6	−19.2	52.7	47 43.6	−18.1	53.6	48 18.8	−16.9	54.5	48 53.3	−15.7	55.4
37	46 48.4	−20.3	51.3	47 25.5	−19.1	52.2	48 01.9	−17.9	53.0	48 37.6	−16.7	54.0
38	46 28.1	−21.2	50.0	47 06.4	−20.1	50.8	47 44.0	−19.0	51.6	48 20.9	−17.9	52.5
39	46 06.9	−22.2	48.6	46 46.3	−21.1	49.4	47 25.0	−20.0	50.2	48 03.0	−18.9	51.1
40	45 44.7	−23.0	47.3	46 25.2	−22.1	48.0	47 05.0	−21.0	48.8	47 44.1	−19.9	49.7
41	45 21.7	−24.0	45.9	46 03.1	−23.0	46.7	46 44.0	−22.0	47.5	47 24.2	−20.9	48.3
42	44 57.7	−24.9	44.6	45 40.1	−23.9	45.4	46 22.0	−22.9	46.1	47 03.3	−21.9	46.9
43	44 32.8	−25.7	43.4	45 16.2	−24.8	44.1	45 59.1	−23.9	44.8	46 41.4	−22.9	45.5
44	44 07.1	−26.5	42.1	44 51.4	−25.6	42.8	45 35.2	−24.7	43.5	46 18.5	−23.8	44.2
45	43 40.6	−27.3	40.9	44 25.8	−26.5	41.5	45 10.5	−25.6	42.2	45 54.7	−24.7	42.8
46	43 13.3	−28.1	39.6	43 59.3	−27.3	40.2	44 44.9	−26.5	40.9	45 30.0	−25.6	41.5
47	42 45.2	−28.9	38.4	43 32.0	−28.1	39.0	44 18.4	−27.2	39.6	45 04.4	−26.4	40.3
48	42 16.3	−29.5	37.2	43 03.9	−28.8	37.8	43 51.2	−28.1	38.4	44 38.0	−27.3	39.0
49	41 46.8	−30.3	36.1	42 35.1	−29.5	36.6	43 23.1	−28.8	37.2	44 10.7	−28.0	37.7
50	41 16.5	−31.0	34.9	42 05.6	−30.3	35.4	42 54.3	−29.6	36.0	43 42.7	−28.9	36.5
51	40 45.5	−31.6	33.8	41 35.3	−31.0	34.3	42 24.7	−30.3	34.8	43 13.8	−29.5	35.3
52	40 13.9	−32.2	32.7	41 04.3	−31.6	33.1	41 54.4	−30.9	33.6	42 44.3	−30.4	34.1
53	39 41.7	−32.9	31.6	40 32.7	−32.3	32.0	41 23.5	−31.7	32.5	42 13.9	−31.0	32.9
54	39 08.8	−33.4	30.5	40 00.4	−32.9	30.9	40 51.8	−32.3	31.3	41 42.9	−31.7	31.8
55	38 35.4	−34.0	29.4	39 27.5	−33.4	29.8	40 19.5	−32.9	30.2	41 11.2	−32.3	30.7
56	38 01.4	−34.6	28.4	38 54.1	−34.1	28.7	39 46.6	−33.6	29.1	40 38.9	−33.0	29.5
57	37 26.8	−35.1	27.3	38 20.0	−34.6	27.7	39 13.0	−34.1	28.1	40 05.9	−33.6	28.5
58	36 51.7	−35.6	26.3	37 45.4	−35.2	26.6	38 38.9	−34.7	27.0	39 32.3	−34.2	27.4
59	36 16.1	−36.2	25.3	37 10.2	−35.6	25.6	38 04.2	−35.2	26.0	38 58.1	−34.7	26.3
60	35 39.9	−36.5	24.3	36 34.6	−36.2	24.6	37 29.0	−35.7	24.9	38 23.4	−35.3	25.3
61	35 03.4	−37.1	23.3	35 58.4	−36.7	23.6	36 53.3	−36.3	23.9	37 48.1	−35.9	24.2
62	34 26.3	−37.5	22.4	35 21.7	−37.1	22.7	36 17.0	−36.7	22.9	37 12.2	−36.3	23.2
63	33 48.8	−37.9	21.4	34 44.6	−37.5	21.7	35 40.3	−37.2	22.0	36 35.9	−36.8	22.2
64	33 10.9	−38.3	20.5	34 07.1	−38.0	20.8	35 03.1	−37.6	21.0	35 59.1	−37.3	21.3
65	32 32.6	−38.7	19.6	33 29.1	−38.4	19.8	34 25.5	−38.1	20.0	35 21.8	−37.7	20.3
66	31 53.9	−39.1	18.7	32 50.7	−38.8	18.9	33 47.4	−38.5	19.1	34 44.1	−38.2	19.3
67	31 14.8	−39.5	17.8	32 11.9	−39.2	18.0	33 08.9	−38.9	18.2	34 05.9	−38.6	18.4
68	30 35.3	−39.8	16.9	31 32.7	−39.5	17.1	32 30.0	−39.3	17.3	33 27.3	−39.0	17.5
69	29 55.5	−40.1	16.1	30 53.2	−39.9	16.2	31 50.7	−39.6	16.4	32 48.3	−39.4	16.6
70	29 15.4	−40.5	15.2	30 13.3	−40.3	15.4	31 11.1	−40.0	15.5	32 08.9	−39.8	15.7
71	28 34.9	−40.7	14.4	29 33.0	−40.5	14.5	30 31.1	−40.3	14.6	31 29.1	−40.1	14.8
72	27 54.2	−41.1	13.5	28 52.5	−40.9	13.7	29 50.8	−40.7	13.8	30 49.0	−40.4	13.9
73	27 13.1	−41.4	12.7	28 11.6	−41.2	12.8	29 10.1	−41.0	12.9	30 08.6	−40.8	13.1
74	26 31.7	−41.6	11.9	27 30.4	−41.4	12.0	28 29.1	−41.3	12.1	29 27.8	−41.1	12.2
75	25 50.1	−41.9	11.1	26 49.0	−41.7	11.2	27 47.8	−41.5	11.3	28 46.7	−41.4	11.4
76	25 08.2	−42.1	10.3	26 07.3	−42.0	10.4	27 06.3	−41.9	10.5	28 05.3	−41.7	10.6
77	24 26.1	−42.4	9.5	25 25.3	−42.3	9.6	26 24.4	−42.1	9.7	27 23.6	−42.0	9.8
78	23 43.7	−42.6	8.7	24 43.0	−42.5	8.8	25 42.3	−42.4	8.9	26 41.6	−42.3	9.0
79	23 01.1	−42.8	8.0	24 00.5	−42.7	8.0	24 59.9	−42.6	8.1	25 59.3	−42.5	8.2
80	22 18.3	−43.0	7.2	23 17.8	−42.9	7.3	24 17.3	−42.8	7.3	25 16.8	−42.7	7.4
81	21 35.3	−43.3	6.5	22 34.9	−43.2	6.5	23 34.5	−43.1	6.6	24 34.1	−43.0	6.6
82	20 52.0	−43.4	5.7	21 51.7	−43.3	5.8	22 51.4	−43.3	5.8	23 51.1	−43.2	5.8
83	20 08.6	−43.6	5.0	21 08.4	−43.6	5.0	22 08.1	−43.4	5.1	23 07.9	−43.4	5.1
84	19 25.0	−43.8	4.3	20 24.8	−43.7	4.3	21 24.7	−43.7	4.3	22 24.5	−43.6	4.3
85	18 41.2	−43.9	3.5	19 41.1	−43.9	3.6	20 41.0	−43.9	3.6	21 40.9	−43.8	3.6
86	17 57.3	−44.1	2.8	18 57.2	−44.1	2.8	19 57.1	−44.0	2.8	20 57.0	−44.0	2.9
87	17 13.2	−44.3	2.1	18 13.1	−44.2	2.1	19 13.1	−44.2	2.1	20 13.0	−44.1	2.1
88	16 28.9	−44.4	1.4	17 28.9	−44.4	1.4	18 28.9	−44.4	1.4	19 28.9	−44.4	1.4
89	15 44.5	−44.5	0.7	16 44.5	−44.5	0.7	17 44.5	−44.5	0.7	18 44.5	−44.5	0.7
90	15 00.0	−44.7	0.0	16 00.0	−44.7	0.0	17 00.0	−44.7	0.0	18 00.0	−44.7	0.0

Dec. °	19° Hc ° ′	d ′	Z °	20° Hc ° ′	d ′	Z °	21° Hc ° ′	d ′	Z °	22° Hc ° ′	d ′	Z °
0	44 38.4	+27.1	109.9	44 17.6	+28.3	110.8	43 55.8	+29.5	111.7	43 33.2	+30.7	112.6
1	45 05.5	+26.2	108.6	44 45.9	+27.4	109.6	44 25.3	+28.7	110.5	44 03.9	+29.8	111.4
2	45 31.7	+25.3	107.3	45 13.3	+26.6	108.3	44 54.0	+27.9	109.3	44 33.7	+29.2	110.2
3	45 57.0	+24.4	106.0	45 39.9	+25.8	107.0	45 21.9	+27.0	108.0	45 02.9	+28.2	109.0
4	46 21.4	+23.5	104.7	46 05.7	+24.8	105.7	45 48.9	+26.2	106.7	45 31.1	+27.5	107.7
5	46 44.9	+22.6	103.4	46 30.5	+24.0	104.4	46 15.1	+25.3	105.4	45 58.6	+26.6	106.4
6	47 07.5	+21.6	102.0	46 54.5	+22.9	103.1	46 40.4	+24.3	104.1	46 25.2	+25.7	105.1
7	47 29.1	+20.6	100.7	47 17.4	+22.0	101.7	47 04.7	+23.4	102.8	46 50.9	+24.8	103.8
8	47 49.7	+19.5	99.3	47 39.4	+21.1	100.3	47 28.1	+22.5	101.4	47 15.7	+23.8	102.5
9	48 09.2	+18.5	97.8	48 00.5	+19.9	98.9	47 50.6	+21.4	100.0	47 39.5	+22.9	101.1
10	48 27.7	+17.5	96.4	48 20.4	+19.0	97.5	48 12.0	+20.4	98.6	48 02.4	+21.9	99.7
11	48 45.2	+16.3	95.0	48 39.4	+17.8	96.1	48 32.4	+19.4	97.2	48 24.3	+20.8	98.3
12	49 01.5	+15.2	93.5	48 57.2	+16.8	94.7	48 51.8	+18.2	95.8	48 45.1	+19.8	96.9
13	49 16.7	+14.0	92.0	49 14.0	+15.6	93.2	49 10.0	+17.2	94.3	49 04.9	+18.7	95.5
14	49 30.7	+12.9	90.5	49 29.6	+14.5	91.7	49 27.2	+16.0	92.9	49 23.6	+17.6	94.0
15	49 43.6	+11.8	89.0	49 44.1	+13.3	90.2	49 43.2	+14.9	91.4	49 41.2	+16.4	92.6
16	49 55.4	+10.5	87.5	49 57.4	+12.1	88.7	49 58.1	+13.7	89.9	49 57.6	+15.3	91.1
17	50 05.9	+9.3	86.0	50 09.5	+10.9	87.2	50 11.8	+12.5	88.4	50 12.9	+14.1	89.6
18	50 15.2	+8.0	84.4	50 20.4	+9.6	85.6	50 24.3	+11.3	86.8	50 27.0	+12.9	88.0
19	50 23.2	+6.8	82.9	50 30.0	+8.5	84.1	50 35.6	+10.1	85.3	50 39.9	+11.7	86.5
20	50 30.0	+5.6	81.3	50 38.5	+7.2	82.5	50 45.7	+8.8	83.7	50 51.6	+10.4	85.0
21	50 35.6	+4.3	79.7	50 45.7	+5.9	81.0	50 54.5	+7.5	82.2	51 02.0	+9.2	83.4
22	50 39.9	+3.0	78.2	50 51.6	+4.6	79.4	51 02.0	+6.3	80.6	51 11.2	+7.9	81.8
23	50 42.9	+1.8	76.6	50 56.2	+3.4	77.8	51 08.3	+5.0	79.0	51 19.1	+6.6	80.2
24	50 44.7	+0.4	75.0	50 59.6	+2.0	76.2	51 13.3	+3.6	77.4	51 25.7	+5.3	78.6
25	50 45.1	−0.8	73.4	51 01.6	+0.8	74.6	51 16.9	+2.4	75.8	51 31.0	+4.0	77.0
26	50 44.3	−2.1	71.9	51 02.4	−0.5	73.0	51 19.3	+1.1	74.2	51 35.0	+2.7	75.4
27	50 42.2	−3.4	70.3	51 01.9	−1.8	71.4	51 20.4	−0.3	72.6	51 37.7	+1.4	73.8
28	50 38.8	−4.6	68.7	51 00.1	−3.2	69.9	51 20.1	−1.5	71.0	51 39.1	0.0	72.2
29	50 34.2	−5.9	67.1	50 56.9	−4.4	68.3	51 18.6	−2.9	69.4	51 39.1	−1.3	70.6
30	50 28.3	−7.2	65.6	50 52.5	−5.6	66.7	51 15.7	−4.1	67.8	51 37.8	−2.6	69.0
31	50 21.1	−8.4	64.0	50 46.9	−7.0	65.1	51 11.6	−5.5	66.2	51 35.2	−3.9	67.4
32	50 12.7	−9.6	62.5	50 39.9	−8.2	63.5	51 06.1	−6.7	64.6	51 31.3	−5.2	65.8
33	50 03.1	−10.9	60.9	50 31.7	−9.4	62.0	50 59.4	−8.0	63.1	51 26.1	−6.6	64.2
34	49 52.2	−12.0	59.4	50 22.3	−10.7	60.4	50 51.4	−9.3	61.5	51 19.5	−7.8	62.6
35	49 40.2	−13.3	57.9	50 11.6	−11.9	58.9	50 42.1	−10.5	59.9	51 11.7	−9.1	61.0
36	49 26.9	−14.4	56.4	49 59.7	−13.1	57.4	50 31.6	−11.7	58.4	51 02.6	−10.3	59.4
37	49 12.5	−15.5	54.9	49 46.6	−14.2	55.8	50 19.9	−12.9	56.8	50 52.3	−11.6	57.9
38	48 57.0	−16.6	53.4	49 32.4	−15.4	54.3	50 07.0	−14.2	55.3	50 40.7	−12.9	56.3
39	48 40.4	−17.7	52.0	49 17.0	−16.5	52.9	49 52.8	−15.3	53.8	50 27.8	−14.0	54.8
40	48 22.7	−18.8	50.5	49 00.5	−17.7	51.4	49 37.5	−16.4	52.3	50 13.8	−15.2	53.3
41	48 03.9	−19.9	49.1	48 42.8	−18.7	49.9	49 21.1	−17.6	50.8	49 58.6	−16.4	51.7
42	47 44.0	−20.9	47.7	48 24.1	−19.8	48.5	49 03.5	−18.7	49.4	49 42.2	−17.5	50.3
43	47 23.1	−21.8	46.3	48 04.3	−20.8	47.1	48 44.8	−19.7	47.9	49 24.7	−18.6	48.8
44	47 01.3	−22.8	44.9	47 43.5	−21.8	45.7	48 25.1	−20.8	46.5	49 06.1	−19.7	47.3
45	46 38.5	−23.8	43.6	47 21.7	−22.8	44.3	48 04.3	−21.8	45.1	48 46.4	−20.8	45.9
46	46 14.7	−24.7	42.2	46 58.9	−23.8	42.9	47 42.5	−22.8	43.7	48 25.6	−21.8	44.5
47	45 50.0	−25.6	40.9	46 35.1	−24.7	41.6	47 19.7	−23.7	42.3	48 03.8	−22.8	43.1
48	45 24.4	−26.4	39.6	46 10.4	−25.6	40.3	46 56.0	−24.7	41.0	47 41.0	−23.8	41.7
49	44 58.0	−27.3	38.3	45 44.8	−26.4	39.0	46 31.3	−25.6	39.6	47 17.2	−24.7	40.3
50	44 30.7	−28.1	37.1	45 18.4	−27.3	37.7	46 05.7	−26.5	38.3	46 52.5	−25.6	39.0
51	44 02.6	−28.8	35.9	44 51.1	−28.1	36.4	45 39.2	−27.4	37.0	46 26.9	−26.6	37.7
52	43 33.8	−29.7	34.6	44 23.0	−28.9	35.2	45 11.8	−28.1	35.8	46 00.3	−27.4	36.4
53	43 04.1	−30.3	33.5	43 54.1	−29.7	34.0	44 43.7	−29.0	34.5	45 32.9	−28.2	35.1
54	42 33.8	−31.1	32.3	43 24.4	−30.4	32.8	44 14.7	−29.8	33.3	45 04.7	−29.1	33.8
55	42 02.7	−31.7	31.1	42 54.0	−31.2	31.6	43 44.9	−30.5	32.1	44 35.6	−29.8	32.6
56	41 31.0	−32.5	30.0	42 22.8	−31.8	30.4	43 14.4	−31.2	30.9	44 05.8	−30.6	31.4
57	40 58.5	−33.0	28.9	41 51.0	−32.5	29.3	42 43.2	−31.9	29.7	43 35.2	−31.4	30.2
58	40 25.5	−33.7	27.8	41 18.5	−33.2	28.2	42 11.3	−32.6	28.6	43 03.8	−32.0	29.0
59	39 51.8	−34.3	26.7	40 45.3	−33.7	27.1	41 38.7	−33.3	27.5	42 31.8	−32.7	27.9
60	39 17.5	−34.8	25.6	40 11.6	−34.4	26.0	41 05.4	−33.9	26.4	41 59.1	−33.4	26.7
61	38 42.7	−35.4	24.6	39 37.2	−34.9	24.9	40 31.5	−34.4	25.3	41 25.7	−34.0	25.6
62	38 07.3	−35.9	23.5	39 02.3	−35.5	23.9	39 57.1	−35.1	24.2	40 51.7	−34.6	24.5
63	37 31.4	−36.4	22.5	38 26.8	−36.1	22.8	39 22.0	−35.6	23.1	40 17.1	−35.2	23.5
64	36 55.0	−37.0	21.5	37 50.7	−36.5	21.8	38 46.4	−36.2	22.1	39 41.9	−35.8	22.4
65	36 18.0	−37.4	20.5	37 14.2	−37.1	20.8	38 10.2	−36.7	21.1	39 06.1	−36.3	21.4
66	35 40.6	−37.8	19.6	36 37.1	−37.5	19.8	37 33.5	−37.2	20.1	38 29.8	−36.8	20.3
67	35 02.8	−38.3	18.6	35 59.6	−38.0	18.9	36 56.3	−37.6	19.1	37 53.0	−37.3	19.3
68	34 24.5	−38.7	17.7	35 21.6	−38.4	17.9	36 18.7	−38.2	18.1	37 15.7	−37.9	18.4
69	33 45.8	−39.2	16.8	34 43.2	−38.9	17.0	35 40.5	−38.5	17.2	36 37.8	−38.3	17.4
70	33 06.6	−39.5	15.9	34 04.3	−39.2	16.0	35 02.0	−39.0	16.2	35 59.5	−38.7	16.4
71	32 27.1	−39.9	15.0	33 25.1	−39.7	15.1	34 23.0	−39.4	15.3	35 20.8	−39.2	15.5
72	31 47.2	−40.2	14.1	32 45.4	−40.0	14.2	33 43.6	−39.9	14.4	34 41.6	−39.5	14.6
73	31 07.0	−40.6	13.2	32 05.4	−40.4	13.4	33 03.7	−40.1	13.5	34 02.1	−40.0	13.7
74	30 26.4	−40.9	12.4	31 25.0	−40.7	12.5	32 23.6	−40.6	12.6	33 22.1	−40.4	12.8
75	29 45.5	−41.3	11.5	30 44.3	−41.1	11.6	31 43.0	−40.9	11.7	32 41.7	−40.7	11.9
76	29 04.2	−41.5	10.7	30 03.2	−41.4	10.8	31 02.1	−41.2	10.9	32 01.0	−41.0	11.0
77	28 22.7	−41.9	9.9	29 21.8	−41.7	9.9	30 20.9	−41.6	10.0	31 20.0	−41.5	10.1
78	27 40.8	−42.1	9.0	28 40.1	−42.0	9.1	29 39.3	−41.8	9.2	30 38.5	−41.7	9.3
79	26 58.7	−42.4	8.2	27 58.1	−42.3	8.3	28 57.5	−42.2	8.4	29 56.8	−42.0	8.5
80	26 16.3	−42.6	7.4	27 15.8	−42.5	7.5	28 15.3	−42.4	7.6	29 14.8	−42.4	7.7
81	25 33.7	−42.9	6.7	26 33.3	−42.8	6.7	27 32.9	−42.7	6.8	28 32.4	−42.6	6.8
82	24 50.8	−43.1	5.9	25 50.5	−43.1	5.9	26 50.2	−43.0	6.0	27 49.8	−42.9	6.0
83	24 07.7	−43.4	5.1	25 07.4	−43.3	5.2	26 07.2	−43.2	5.2	27 06.9	−43.1	5.3
84	23 24.3	−43.6	4.4	24 24.1	−43.5	4.4	25 24.0	−43.5	4.4	26 23.8	−43.4	4.5
85	22 40.7	−43.7	3.6	23 40.6	−43.7	3.7	24 40.5	−43.7	3.7	25 40.4	−43.7	3.7
86	21 57.0	−44.0	2.9	22 56.9	−43.9	2.9	23 56.8	−43.9	2.9	24 56.7	−43.8	3.0
87	21 13.0	−44.2	2.2	22 13.0	−44.2	2.2	23 12.9	−44.1	2.2	24 12.9	−44.1	2.2
88	20 28.8	−44.3	1.4	21 28.8	−44.3	1.4	22 28.8	−44.3	1.4	23 28.8	−44.3	1.5
89	19 44.5	−44.5	0.7	20 44.5	−44.5	0.7	21 44.5	−44.5	0.7	22 44.5	−44.5	0.7
90	19 00.0	−44.7	0.0	20 00.0	−44.7	0.0	21 00.0	−44.7	0.0	22 00.0	−44.7	0.0

15° 16° 17° 18° 19° 20° 21° 22°

42°, 318° L.H.A. LATITUDE SAME NAME AS DECLINATION

LATITUDE CONTRARY NAME TO DECLINATION — L.H.A. 42°, 318°

Dec.	15° Hc	d	Z	16° Hc	d	Z	17° Hc	d	Z	18° Hc	d	Z
°	° '	'	°	° '	'	°	° '	'	°	° '	'	°
0	45 52.5	−22.8	106.0	45 35.4	−24.1	107.0	45 17.4	−25.4	108.0	44 58.4	−26.7	108.9
1	45 29.7	−23.6	107.4	45 11.3	−24.9	108.3	44 52.0	−26.2	109.3	44 31.7	−27.4	110.2
2	45 06.1	−24.6	108.7	44 46.4	−25.8	109.6	44 25.8	−27.0	110.5	44 04.3	−28.2	111.4
3	44 41.5	−25.4	110.0	44 20.6	−26.7	110.9	43 58.8	−27.9	111.8	43 36.1	−29.1	112.7
4	44 16.1	−26.2	111.2	43 53.9	−27.4	112.1	43 30.9	−28.6	113.0	43 07.0	−29.7	113.9
5	43 49.9	−27.1	112.5	43 26.5	−28.2	113.4	43 02.3	−29.4	114.2	42 37.3	−30.5	115.1
6	43 22.8	−27.8	113.7	42 58.3	−29.0	114.6	42 32.9	−30.1	115.4	42 06.8	−31.2	116.2
7	42 55.0	−28.6	114.9	42 29.3	−29.7	115.8	42 02.8	−30.8	116.6	41 35.6	−31.8	117.4
8	42 26.4	−29.3	116.1	41 59.6	−30.4	116.9	41 32.0	−31.4	117.7	41 03.8	−32.5	118.5
9	41 57.1	−30.1	117.3	41 29.2	−31.1	118.1	41 00.6	−32.1	118.9	40 31.3	−33.2	119.6
10	41 27.0	−30.7	118.5	40 58.1	−31.8	119.2	40 28.5	−32.8	120.0	39 58.1	−33.7	120.7
11	40 56.3	−31.4	119.6	40 26.3	−32.4	120.3	39 55.7	−33.4	121.1	39 24.4	−34.3	121.8
12	40 24.9	−32.0	120.7	39 53.9	−33.0	121.4	39 22.3	−33.9	122.1	38 50.1	−34.9	122.8
13	39 52.9	−32.7	121.8	39 20.9	−33.6	122.5	38 48.4	−34.5	123.2	38 15.2	−35.4	123.9
14	39 20.2	−33.2	122.9	38 47.3	−34.1	123.6	38 13.9	−35.1	124.3	37 39.8	−35.9	124.9
15	38 47.0	−33.8	124.0	38 13.2	−34.8	124.6	37 38.8	−35.6	125.3	37 03.9	−36.5	125.9
16	38 13.2	−34.4	125.0	37 38.4	−35.2	125.7	37 03.2	−36.1	126.3	36 27.4	−36.9	126.9
17	37 38.8	−34.9	126.1	37 03.2	−35.8	126.7	36 27.1	−36.6	127.3	35 50.5	−37.4	127.9
18	37 03.9	−35.5	127.1	36 27.4	−36.3	127.7	35 50.5	−37.1	128.3	35 13.1	−37.9	128.8
19	36 28.4	−35.9	128.1	35 51.1	−36.7	128.7	35 13.4	−37.5	129.2	34 35.2	−38.2	129.8
20	35 52.5	−36.5	129.1	35 14.4	−37.2	129.7	34 35.9	−38.0	130.2	33 57.0	−38.7	130.7
21	35 16.0	−36.8	130.1	34 37.2	−37.7	130.6	33 57.9	−38.3	131.1	33 18.3	−39.1	131.6
22	34 39.2	−37.4	131.0	33 59.5	−38.0	131.6	33 19.6	−38.8	132.1	32 39.2	−39.5	132.5
23	34 01.8	−37.8	132.0	33 21.5	−38.5	132.5	32 40.8	−39.2	133.0	31 59.7	−39.8	133.4
24	33 24.0	−38.1	132.9	32 43.0	−38.9	133.4	32 01.6	−39.5	133.9	31 19.9	−40.2	134.3
25	32 45.9	−38.6	133.8	32 04.1	−39.2	134.3	31 22.1	−39.9	134.7	30 39.7	−40.6	135.2
26	32 07.3	−39.0	134.8	31 24.9	−39.6	135.2	30 42.2	−40.3	135.6	29 59.1	−40.8	136.0
27	31 28.3	−39.3	135.7	30 45.3	−40.0	136.1	30 01.9	−40.6	136.5	29 18.3	−41.2	136.9
28	30 49.0	−39.7	136.5	30 05.3	−40.3	136.9	29 21.3	−40.9	137.3	28 37.1	−41.5	137.7
29	30 09.3	−40.0	137.4	29 25.0	−40.6	137.8	28 40.4	−41.2	138.2	27 55.6	−41.8	138.5
30	29 29.3	−40.4	138.3	28 44.4	−40.9	138.6	27 59.2	−41.5	139.0	27 13.8	−42.0	139.3
31	28 48.9	−40.6	139.1	28 03.5	−41.3	139.5	27 17.7	−41.7	139.8	26 31.8	−42.3	140.1
32	28 08.3	−41.0	139.9	27 22.2	−41.5	140.3	26 36.0	−42.1	140.6	25 49.5	−42.6	140.9
33	27 27.3	−41.2	140.8	26 40.7	−41.8	141.1	25 53.9	−42.3	141.4	25 06.9	−42.8	141.7
34	26 46.1	−41.6	141.6	25 58.9	−42.0	141.9	25 11.6	−42.5	142.2	24 24.1	−43.0	142.5
35	26 04.5	−41.8	142.4	25 16.9	−42.3	142.7	24 29.1	−42.8	143.0	23 41.1	−43.2	143.2
36	25 22.7	−42.0	143.2	24 34.6	−42.5	143.5	23 46.3	−43.0	143.7	22 57.9	−43.5	144.0
37	24 40.7	−42.3	144.0	23 52.1	−42.8	144.2	23 03.3	−43.2	144.5	22 14.4	−43.7	144.7
38	23 58.4	−42.5	144.8	23 09.3	−43.0	145.0	22 20.1	−43.4	145.2	21 30.7	−43.8	145.5
39	23 15.9	−42.8	145.5	22 26.3	−43.2	145.8	21 36.7	−43.7	146.0	20 46.9	−44.1	146.2
40	22 33.1	−43.0	146.3	21 43.1	−43.4	146.5	20 53.0	−43.8	146.7	20 02.8	−44.2	146.9
41	21 50.1	−43.1	147.0	20 59.7	−43.5	147.3	20 09.2	−44.0	147.5	19 18.6	−44.4	147.6
42	21 07.0	−43.4	147.8	20 16.2	−43.8	148.0	19 25.2	−44.1	148.2	18 34.2	−44.6	148.4
43	20 23.6	−43.5	148.5	19 32.4	−43.9	148.7	18 41.1	−44.4	148.9	17 49.6	−44.6	149.1
44	19 40.1	−43.7	149.3	18 48.5	−44.1	149.4	17 56.7	−44.4	149.6	17 05.0	−44.9	149.8
45	18 56.4	−43.9	150.0	18 04.4	−44.3	150.2	17 12.3	−44.6	150.3	16 20.1	−45.0	150.5
46	18 12.5	−44.1	150.7	17 20.1	−44.4	150.9	16 27.7	−44.8	151.0	15 35.1	−45.1	151.1
47	17 28.4	−44.2	151.4	16 35.7	−44.6	151.6	15 42.9	−44.9	151.7	14 50.0	−45.2	151.8
48	16 44.2	−44.3	152.1	15 51.1	−44.6	152.3	14 58.0	−45.0	152.4	14 04.8	−45.3	152.5
49	15 59.9	−44.5	152.8	15 06.5	−44.8	153.0	14 13.0	−45.1	153.1	13 19.5	−45.5	153.2
50	15 15.4	−44.6	153.5	14 21.7	−45.0	153.6	13 27.9	−45.3	153.8	12 34.0	−45.5	153.9
51	14 30.8	−44.7	154.2	13 36.7	−45.0	154.3	12 42.6	−45.3	154.4	11 48.5	−45.6	154.5
52	13 46.1	−44.9	154.9	12 51.7	−45.1	155.0	11 57.3	−45.4	155.1	11 02.9	−45.8	155.2
53	13 01.2	−44.9	155.6	12 06.6	−45.3	155.7	11 11.9	−45.6	155.8	10 17.1	−45.8	155.8
54	12 16.3	−45.1	156.3	11 21.3	−45.3	156.3	10 26.3	−45.6	156.4	9 31.3	−45.8	156.5
55	11 31.2	−45.1	156.9	10 36.0	−45.4	157.0	9 40.7	−45.6	157.1	8 45.5	−46.0	157.1
56	10 46.1	−45.3	157.6	9 50.6	−45.5	157.7	8 55.1	−45.8	157.7	7 59.5	−46.0	157.8
57	10 00.8	−45.3	158.3	9 05.1	−45.6	158.3	8 09.3	−45.8	158.4	7 13.5	−46.0	158.4
58	9 15.5	−45.3	158.9	8 19.5	−45.6	159.0	7 23.5	−45.9	159.0	6 27.5	−46.1	159.1
59	8 30.2	−45.5	159.6	7 33.9	−45.7	159.7	6 37.6	−45.9	159.7	5 41.4	−46.2	159.7
60	7 44.7	−45.5	160.3	6 48.2	−45.7	160.3	5 51.7	−45.9	160.3	4 55.2	−46.2	160.4
61	6 59.2	−45.6	160.9	6 02.5	−45.8	161.0	5 05.8	−46.0	161.0	4 09.0	−46.2	161.0
62	6 13.6	−45.6	161.6	5 16.7	−45.8	161.6	4 19.8	−46.1	161.6	3 22.8	−46.2	161.7
63	5 28.0	−45.6	162.2	4 30.9	−45.9	162.3	3 33.7	−46.0	162.3	2 36.6	−46.3	162.3
64	4 42.4	−45.7	162.9	3 45.0	−45.9	162.9	2 47.7	−46.1	162.9	1 50.3	−46.2	162.9
65	3 56.7	−45.7	163.5	2 59.1	−45.9	163.6	2 01.6	−46.1	163.6	1 04.1	−46.3	163.6
66	3 11.0	−45.8	164.2	2 13.2	−45.9	164.2	1 15.5	−46.1	164.2	0 17.8	−46.3	164.2
67	2 25.2	−45.7	164.8	1 27.3	−45.9	164.8	0 29.4	−46.1	164.8	0 28.5	+46.3	15.2
68	1 39.5	−45.8	165.5	0 41.4	−46.0	165.5	0 16.7	+46.1	14.5	1 14.8	+46.3	14.5
69	0 53.7	−45.8	166.1	0 04.6	+45.9	13.9	1 02.8	+46.1	13.9	2 01.1	+46.2	13.9
70	0 07.9	−45.8	166.8	0 50.5	+45.9	13.2	1 48.9	+46.1	13.2	2 47.3	+46.2	13.2
71	0 37.9	+45.8	12.6	1 36.4	+46.0	12.6	2 35.0	+46.1	12.6	3 33.5	+46.3	12.6
72	1 23.7	+45.7	11.9	2 22.4	+45.9	11.9	3 21.1	+46.0	12.0	4 19.8	+46.1	12.0
73	2 09.4	+45.8	11.3	3 08.3	+45.8	11.3	4 07.1	+46.0	11.3	5 05.9	+46.2	11.3
74	2 55.2	+45.7	10.6	3 54.1	+45.9	10.7	4 53.1	+46.0	10.7	5 52.1	+46.1	10.7
75	3 40.9	+45.7	10.0	4 40.0	+45.8	10.0	5 39.1	+45.9	10.0	6 38.2	+46.0	10.0
76	4 26.6	+45.7	9.3	5 25.8	+45.8	9.4	6 25.0	+45.9	9.4	7 24.2	+46.0	9.4
77	5 12.3	+45.6	8.7	6 11.6	+45.7	8.7	7 10.9	+45.8	8.7	8 10.2	+45.9	8.7
78	5 57.9	+45.6	8.0	6 57.3	+45.7	8.1	7 56.7	+45.8	8.1	8 56.1	+45.9	8.1
79	6 43.5	+45.5	7.4	7 43.0	+45.6	7.4	8 42.5	+45.7	7.4	9 42.0	+45.8	7.4
80	7 29.0	+45.5	6.7	8 28.6	+45.5	6.7	9 28.2	+45.6	6.8	10 27.8	+45.7	6.8
81	8 14.5	+45.4	6.1	9 14.1	+45.5	6.1	10 13.8	+45.5	6.1	11 13.5	+45.6	6.1
82	8 59.9	+45.3	5.4	9 59.6	+45.4	5.4	10 59.3	+45.5	5.4	11 59.1	+45.5	5.5
83	9 45.2	+45.3	4.7	10 45.0	+45.3	4.8	11 44.8	+45.4	4.8	12 44.6	+45.4	4.8
84	10 30.5	+45.1	4.1	11 30.3	+45.2	4.1	12 30.2	+45.2	4.1	13 30.0	+45.3	4.1
85	11 15.6	+45.1	3.4	12 15.5	+45.1	3.4	13 15.4	+45.2	3.4	14 15.3	+45.2	3.4
86	12 00.7	+45.0	2.7	13 00.6	+45.1	2.7	14 00.6	+45.0	2.8	15 00.5	+45.1	2.8
87	12 45.7	+44.9	2.1	13 45.7	+44.9	2.1	14 45.6	+44.9	2.1	15 45.6	+44.9	2.1
88	13 30.6	+44.7	1.4	14 30.6	+44.7	1.4	15 30.5	+44.8	1.4	16 30.5	+44.8	1.4
89	14 15.3	+44.7	0.7	15 15.3	+44.7	0.7	16 15.3	+44.7	0.7	17 15.3	+44.7	0.7
90	15 00.0	+44.5	0.0	16 00.0	+44.5	0.0	17 00.0	+44.5	0.0	18 00.0	+44.5	0.0
	15°			16°			17°			18°		

Dec.	19° Hc	d	Z	20° Hc	d	Z	21° Hc	d	Z	22° Hc	d	Z
°	° '	'	°	° '	'	°	° '	'	°	° '	'	°
0	44 38.4	−27.8	109.9	44 17.6	−29.1	110.8	43 55.8	−30.2	111.7	43 33.2	−31.4	112.6
1	44 10.6	−28.7	111.1	43 48.5	−29.8	112.0	43 25.6	−31.0	112.9	43 01.8	−32.0	113.8
2	43 41.9	−29.4	112.3	43 18.7	−30.6	113.2	42 54.6	−31.6	114.1	42 29.8	−32.8	114.9
3	43 12.5	−30.1	113.5	42 48.1	−31.2	114.4	42 23.0	−32.4	115.2	41 57.0	−33.4	116.0
4	42 42.4	−30.9	114.7	42 16.9	−32.0	115.6	41 50.6	−33.0	116.4	41 23.6	−34.1	117.2
5	42 11.5	−31.6	115.9	41 44.9	−32.6	116.7	41 17.6	−33.7	117.5	40 49.5	−34.6	118.2
6	41 39.9	−32.2	117.0	41 12.3	−33.3	117.8	40 43.9	−34.2	118.6	40 14.9	−35.2	119.3
7	41 07.7	−32.9	118.2	40 39.0	−33.9	118.9	40 09.7	−34.9	119.7	39 39.7	−35.8	120.4
8	40 34.8	−33.5	119.3	40 05.1	−34.4	120.0	39 34.8	−35.4	120.7	39 03.9	−36.4	121.4
9	40 01.3	−34.1	120.3	39 30.7	−35.1	121.1	38 59.4	−36.0	121.8	38 27.5	−36.9	122.4
10	39 27.2	−34.7	121.4	38 55.6	−35.6	122.1	38 23.4	−36.5	122.8	37 50.6	−37.3	123.4
11	38 52.5	−35.2	122.5	38 20.0	−36.1	123.1	37 46.9	−37.0	123.8	37 13.3	−37.9	124.4
12	38 17.3	−35.8	123.5	37 43.9	−36.7	124.2	37 09.9	−37.5	124.8	36 35.4	−38.3	125.4
13	37 41.5	−36.3	124.5	37 07.2	−37.1	125.1	36 32.4	−37.9	125.8	35 57.1	−38.8	126.4
14	37 05.2	−36.8	125.5	36 30.1	−37.6	126.1	35 54.5	−38.5	126.7	35 18.3	−39.1	127.3
15	36 28.4	−37.3	126.5	35 52.5	−38.1	127.1	35 16.0	−38.8	127.7	34 39.2	−39.7	128.2
16	35 51.1	−37.7	127.5	35 14.4	−38.5	128.0	34 37.2	−39.3	128.6	33 59.5	−39.9	129.1
17	35 13.4	−38.2	128.4	34 35.9	−38.9	129.0	33 57.9	−39.6	129.5	33 19.6	−40.4	130.0
18	34 35.2	−38.6	129.4	33 57.0	−39.4	129.9	33 18.3	−40.1	130.4	32 39.2	−40.8	130.9
19	33 56.6	−39.0	130.3	33 17.6	−39.7	130.8	32 38.2	−40.4	131.3	31 58.4	−41.1	131.8
20	33 17.6	−39.4	131.2	32 37.9	−40.1	131.7	31 57.8	−40.8	132.2	31 17.3	−41.4	132.6
21	32 38.2	−39.8	132.1	31 57.8	−40.5	132.6	31 17.0	−41.1	133.0	30 35.9	−41.7	133.5
22	31 58.4	−40.1	133.0	31 17.3	−40.8	133.4	30 35.9	−41.4	133.9	29 54.2	−42.1	134.3
23	31 18.3	−40.5	133.9	30 36.5	−41.1	134.3	29 54.5	−41.8	134.7	29 12.1	−42.3	135.1
24	30 37.8	−40.8	134.7	29 55.4	−41.4	135.1	29 12.7	−42.0	135.5	28 29.8	−42.7	135.9
25	29 57.0	−41.2	135.6	29 14.0	−41.8	136.0	28 30.7	−42.4	136.4	27 47.1	−42.9	136.7
26	29 15.8	−41.5	136.4	28 32.2	−42.0	136.8	27 48.3	−42.6	137.2	27 04.2	−43.2	137.5
27	28 34.3	−41.7	137.2	27 50.2	−42.4	137.6	27 05.7	−42.9	138.0	26 21.0	−43.4	138.3
28	27 52.6	−42.1	138.1	27 07.8	−42.6	138.4	26 22.8	−43.1	138.7	25 37.6	−43.6	139.1
29	27 10.5	−42.3	138.9	26 25.2	−42.8	139.2	25 39.7	−43.4	139.5	24 54.0	−43.9	139.8
30	26 28.2	−42.6	139.7	25 42.4	−43.1	140.0	24 56.3	−43.6	140.3	24 10.1	−44.1	140.6
31	25 45.6	−42.8	140.4	24 59.3	−43.3	140.7	24 12.7	−43.8	141.0	23 26.0	−44.3	141.3
32	25 02.8	−43.0	141.2	24 16.0	−43.6	141.5	23 28.9	−44.0	141.8	22 41.7	−44.5	142.0
33	24 19.8	−43.3	142.0	23 32.4	−43.8	142.3	22 44.9	−44.3	142.5	21 57.2	−44.7	142.8
34	23 36.5	−43.5	142.7	22 48.6	−43.9	143.0	22 00.6	−44.4	143.2	21 12.5	−44.9	143.5
35	22 53.0	−43.8	143.5	22 04.7	−44.2	143.7	21 16.2	−44.6	144.0	20 27.6	−45.0	144.2
36	22 09.2	−43.9	144.2	21 20.5	−44.4	144.5	20 31.6	−44.8	144.7	19 42.6	−45.2	144.9
37	21 25.3	−44.1	145.0	20 36.1	−44.5	145.2	19 46.8	−44.9	145.4	18 57.4	−45.4	145.6
38	20 41.2	−44.3	145.7	19 51.6	−44.7	145.9	19 01.9	−45.2	146.1	18 12.0	−45.5	146.3
39	19 56.9	−44.4	146.4	19 06.9	−44.9	146.6	18 16.7	−45.2	146.8	17 26.5	−45.7	147.0
40	19 12.5	−44.7	147.1	18 22.0	−45.0	147.3	17 31.5	−45.4	147.5	16 40.8	−45.7	147.6
41	18 27.8	−44.7	147.8	17 37.0	−45.2	148.0	16 46.1	−45.6	148.2	15 55.1	−45.9	148.3
42	17 43.1	−45.0	148.5	16 51.8	−45.3	148.7	16 00.5	−45.6	148.8	15 09.2	−46.1	149.0
43	16 58.1	−45.0	149.2	16 06.5	−45.4	149.4	15 14.9	−45.8	149.5	14 23.1	−46.1	149.7
44	16 13.1	−45.2	149.9	15 21.1	−45.5	150.1	14 29.1	−45.9	150.2	13 37.0	−46.2	150.3
45	15 27.9	−45.4	150.6	14 35.6	−45.7	150.7	13 43.2	−46.0	150.9	12 50.8	−46.4	151.0
46	14 42.5	−45.4	151.3	13 49.9	−45.8	151.4	12 57.2	−46.1	151.5	12 04.4	−46.4	151.6
47	13 57.1	−45.5	152.0	13 04.1	−45.8	152.1	12 11.1	−46.2	152.2	11 18.0	−46.5	152.3
48	13 11.6	−45.7	152.6	12 18.3	−46.0	152.7	11 24.9	−46.3	152.8	10 31.5	−46.6	152.9
49	12 25.9	−45.8	153.3	11 32.3	−46.1	153.4	10 38.6	−46.3	153.5	9 44.9	−46.6	153.5
50	11 40.1	−45.8	153.9	10 46.2	−46.1	154.0	9 52.3	−46.5	154.1	8 58.3	−46.8	154.2
51	10 54.3	−45.9	154.6	10 00.1	−46.2	154.7	9 05.8	−46.5	154.8	8 11.5	−46.7	154.8
52	10 08.4	−46.0	155.3	9 13.9	−46.3	155.3	8 19.3	−46.5	155.4	7 24.8	−46.9	155.5
53	9 22.4	−46.1	155.9	8 27.6	−46.4	156.0	7 32.8	−46.6	156.0	6 37.9	−46.8	156.1
54	8 36.3	−46.1	156.6	7 41.2	−46.4	156.6	6 46.2	−46.7	156.7	5 51.1	−47.0	156.7
55	7 50.2	−46.2	157.2	6 54.8	−46.4	157.3	5 59.5	−46.7	157.3	5 04.1	−46.9	157.3
56	7 04.0	−46.3	157.8	6 08.4	−46.5	157.9	5 12.8	−46.8	157.9	4 17.2	−47.0	158.0
57	6 17.7	−46.3	158.5	5 21.9	−46.6	158.5	4 26.0	−46.7	158.6	3 30.2	−47.0	158.6
58	5 31.4	−46.3	159.1	4 35.3	−46.5	159.2	3 39.3	−46.8	159.2	2 43.2	−47.1	159.2
59	4 45.1	−46.4	159.8	3 48.8	−46.6	159.8	2 52.5	−46.9	159.8	1 56.1	−47.0	159.8
60	3 58.7	−46.4	160.4	3 02.2	−46.7	160.4	2 05.6	−46.8	160.4	1 09.1	−47.1	160.4
61	3 12.3	−46.4	161.0	2 15.5	−46.6	161.1	1 18.8	−46.9	161.1	0 22.0	−47.0	161.1
62	2 25.9	−46.5	161.7	1 28.9	−46.6	161.7	0 31.9	−46.8	161.7	0 25.0	+47.1	18.3
63	1 39.4	−46.4	162.3	0 42.3	−46.7	162.3	0 14.9	+46.9	17.7	1 12.1	+47.0	17.7
64	0 53.0	−46.5	162.9	0 04.4	+46.7	17.1	1 01.8	+46.8	17.1	1 59.1	+47.0	17.1
65	0 06.5	−46.5	163.6	0 51.1	+46.6	16.4	1 48.6	+46.8	16.4	2 46.1	+47.1	16.4
66	0 40.0	+46.4	15.8	1 37.7	+46.6	15.8	2 35.4	+46.8	15.8	3 33.2	+46.9	15.8
67	1 26.4	+46.5	15.2	2 24.3	+46.7	15.2	3 22.2	+46.8	15.2	4 20.1	+47.0	15.2
68	2 12.9	+46.4	14.5	3 11.0	+46.5	14.5	4 09.0	+46.8	14.6	5 07.1	+46.9	14.6
69	2 59.3	+46.4	13.9	3 57.5	+46.6	13.9	4 55.8	+46.7	13.9	5 54.0	+46.9	13.9
70	3 45.7	+46.4	13.3	4 44.1	+46.5	13.3	5 42.5	+46.7	13.3	6 40.9	+46.8	13.3
71	4 32.1	+46.3	12.6	5 30.6	+46.5	12.6	6 29.2	+46.6	12.7	7 27.7	+46.8	12.7
72	5 18.4	+46.4	12.0	6 17.1	+46.5	12.0	7 15.8	+46.6	12.0	8 14.5	+46.7	12.1
73	6 04.8	+46.2	11.3	7 03.6	+46.4	11.4	8 02.4	+46.5	11.4	9 01.2	+46.7	11.4
74	6 51.0	+46.2	10.7	7 50.0	+46.3	10.7	8 48.9	+46.5	10.8	9 47.9	+46.5	10.8
75	7 37.2	+46.2	10.1	8 36.3	+46.3	10.1	9 35.4	+46.4	10.1	10 34.4	+46.5	10.1
76	8 23.4	+46.1	9.4	9 22.6	+46.2	9.4	10 21.8	+46.3	9.5	11 20.9	+46.5	9.5
77	9 09.5	+46.0	8.8	10 08.8	+46.1	8.8	11 08.1	+46.2	8.8	12 07.4	+46.3	8.9
78	9 55.5	+46.0	8.1	10 54.9	+46.1	8.1	11 54.3	+46.1	8.2	12 53.7	+46.2	8.2
79	10 41.5	+45.8	7.5	11 41.0	+45.9	7.5	12 40.4	+46.1	7.5	13 39.9	+46.1	7.6
80	11 27.3	+45.8	6.8	12 26.9	+45.9	6.8	13 26.5	+45.9	6.9	14 26.0	+46.1	6.9
81	12 13.1	+45.7	6.1	13 12.8	+45.7	6.2	14 12.4	+45.8	6.2	15 12.1	+45.9	6.2
82	12 58.8	+45.6	5.5	13 58.5	+45.7	5.5	14 58.2	+45.7	5.5	15 58.0	+45.7	5.6
83	13 44.4	+45.4	4.8	14 44.2	+45.5	4.8	15 43.9	+45.6	4.9	16 43.7	+45.7	4.9
84	14 29.8	+45.4	4.1	15 29.7	+45.4	4.2	16 29.5	+45.5	4.2	17 29.4	+45.5	4.2
85	15 15.2	+45.2	3.5	16 15.1	+45.3	3.5	17 15.0	+45.3	3.5	18 14.9	+45.3	3.5
86	16 00.4	+45.1	2.8	17 00.4	+45.1	2.8	18 00.3	+45.2	2.8	19 00.2	+45.2	2.8
87	16 45.5	+45.0	2.1	17 45.5	+45.0	2.1	18 45.5	+45.0	2.1	19 45.4	+45.1	2.1
88	17 30.5	+44.8	1.4	18 30.5	+44.8	1.4	19 30.5	+44.8	1.4	20 30.5	+44.8	1.4
89	18 15.3	+44.7	0.7	19 15.3	+44.7	0.7	20 15.3	+44.7	0.7	21 15.3	+44.7	0.7
90	19 00.0	+44.5	0.0	20 00.0	+44.5	0.0	21 00.0	+44.5	0.0	22 00.0	+44.5	0.0
	19°			20°			21°			22°		

S. Lat. { L.H.A. greater than 180° ....Zn=180°−Z ; L.H.A. less than 180°............Zn=180°+Z }

LATITUDE SAME NAME AS DECLINATION — L.H.A. 138°, 222°

43°, 317° L.H.A. LATITUDE **SAME** NAME AS DECLINATION N. Lat. {L.H.A. greater than 180° .....Zn=Z
L.H.A. less than 180°............Zn=360°-Z

Dec.	15° Hc	d	Z	16° Hc	d	Z	17° Hc	d	Z	18° Hc	d	Z	19° Hc	d	Z	20° Hc	d	Z	21° Hc	d	Z	22° Hc	d	Z	Dec.
°	° ′	′	°	° ′	′	°	° ′	′	°	° ′	′	°	° ′	′	°	° ′	′	°	° ′	′	°	° ′	′	°	°
0	44 56.7	+21.5	105.5	44 40.2	+22.8	106.5	44 22.7	+24.1	107.4	44 04.3	+25.4	108.3	43 45.0	+26.6	109.2	43 24.8	+27.8	110.1	43 03.7	+29.0	111.0	42 41.7	+30.2	111.9	0
1	45 18.2	+20.6	104.2	45 03.0	+21.9	105.2	44 46.8	+23.3	106.1	44 29.7	+24.5	107.1	44 11.6	+25.8	108.0	43 52.6	+27.1	108.9	43 32.7	+28.3	109.8	43 11.9	+29.5	110.7	1
2	45 38.8	+19.6	102.8	45 24.9	+21.0	103.8	45 10.1	+22.3	104.8	44 54.2	+23.7	105.8	44 37.4	+25.0	106.7	44 19.7	+26.2	107.7	44 01.0	+27.5	108.6	43 41.4	+28.7	109.5	2
3	45 58.4	+18.6	101.5	45 45.9	+20.0	102.5	45 32.4	+21.4	103.5	45 17.9	+22.8	104.5	45 02.4	+24.1	105.5	44 45.9	+25.4	106.4	44 28.5	+26.7	107.4	44 10.1	+28.0	108.3	3
4	46 17.0	+17.6	100.1	46 05.9	+19.1	101.1	45 53.8	+20.5	102.2	45 40.7	+21.8	103.2	45 26.5	+23.2	104.2	45 11.3	+24.5	105.1	44 55.2	+25.8	106.1	44 38.1	+27.1	107.0	4
5	46 34.6	+16.7	98.7	46 25.0	+18.1	99.8	46 14.3	+19.5	100.8	46 02.5	+20.9	101.8	45 49.7	+22.3	102.8	45 35.8	+23.7	103.8	45 21.0	+25.0	104.8	45 05.2	+26.2	105.8	5
6	46 51.3	+15.5	97.3	46 43.1	+17.0	98.4	46 33.8	+18.5	99.4	46 23.4	+19.9	100.5	46 12.0	+21.3	101.5	45 59.5	+22.7	102.5	45 46.0	+24.0	103.5	45 31.4	+25.4	104.5	6
7	47 06.8	+14.6	95.9	47 00.1	+16.0	97.0	46 52.3	+17.4	98.0	46 43.3	+18.9	99.1	46 33.3	+20.3	100.1	46 22.2	+21.7	101.2	46 10.0	+23.2	102.2	45 56.8	+24.5	103.2	7
8	47 21.4	+13.4	94.5	47 16.1	+15.0	95.6	47 09.7	+16.5	96.6	47 02.2	+17.9	97.7	46 53.6	+19.4	98.8	46 43.9	+20.8	99.8	46 33.2	+22.2	100.9	46 21.3	+23.6	101.9	8
9	47 34.8	+12.4	93.0	47 31.1	+13.8	94.1	47 26.2	+15.3	95.2	47 20.1	+16.9	96.3	47 13.0	+18.3	97.4	47 04.7	+19.8	98.4	46 55.4	+21.2	99.5	46 44.9	+22.6	100.6	9
10	47 47.2	+11.2	91.6	47 44.9	+12.8	92.7	47 41.5	+14.3	93.8	47 37.0	+15.8	94.9	47 31.3	+17.3	96.0	47 24.5	+18.8	97.1	47 16.6	+20.2	98.1	47 07.5	+21.7	99.2	10
11	47 58.4	+10.2	90.1	47 57.7	+11.7	91.2	47 55.8	+13.2	92.3	47 52.8	+14.7	93.5	47 48.6	+16.2	94.6	47 43.3	+17.7	95.7	47 36.8	+19.2	96.7	47 29.2	+20.7	97.8	11
12	48 08.6	+8.9	88.7	48 09.4	+10.5	89.8	48 09.0	+12.1	90.9	48 07.5	+13.6	92.0	48 04.8	+15.2	93.1	48 01.0	+16.7	94.2	47 56.0	+18.2	95.3	47 49.9	+19.6	96.4	12
13	48 17.5	+7.9	87.2	48 19.9	+9.4	88.3	48 21.1	+11.0	89.4	48 21.1	+12.5	90.5	48 20.0	+14.0	91.7	48 17.7	+15.5	92.8	48 14.2	+17.0	93.9	48 09.5	+18.6	95.0	13
14	48 25.4	+6.6	85.7	48 29.3	+8.2	86.8	48 32.1	+9.8	87.9	48 33.6	+11.4	89.1	48 34.0	+12.9	90.2	48 33.2	+14.5	91.3	48 31.2	+16.0	92.5	48 28.1	+17.5	93.6	14
15	48 32.0	+5.5	84.2	48 37.5	+7.1	85.3	48 41.9	+8.6	86.4	48 45.0	+10.2	87.6	48 46.9	+11.8	88.7	48 47.7	+13.3	89.9	48 47.2	+14.9	91.0	48 45.6	+16.4	92.1	15
16	48 37.5	+4.4	82.7	48 44.6	+5.9	83.8	48 50.5	+7.4	84.9	48 55.2	+9.0	86.1	48 58.7	+10.6	87.2	49 01.0	+12.2	88.4	49 02.1	+13.7	89.5	49 02.0	+15.3	90.7	16
17	48 41.9	+3.1	81.2	48 50.5	+4.7	82.3	48 57.9	+6.3	83.4	49 04.2	+7.9	84.6	49 09.3	+9.4	85.7	49 13.2	+11.0	86.9	49 15.8	+12.6	88.0	49 17.3	+14.1	89.2	17
18	48 45.0	+1.9	79.6	48 55.2	+3.5	80.8	49 04.2	+5.1	81.9	49 12.1	+6.6	83.1	49 18.7	+8.2	84.2	49 24.2	+9.8	85.4	49 28.4	+11.4	86.5	49 31.4	+13.0	87.7	18
19	48 46.9	+0.8	78.1	48 58.7	+2.3	79.3	49 09.3	+3.9	80.4	49 18.7	+5.5	81.5	49 26.9	+7.1	82.7	49 34.0	+8.6	83.9	49 39.8	+10.2	85.0	49 44.4	+11.8	86.2	19
20	48 47.7	-0.5	76.6	49 01.0	+1.1	77.7	49 13.2	+2.6	78.9	49 24.2	+4.2	80.0	49 34.0	+5.8	81.2	49 42.6	+7.4	82.3	49 50.0	+9.0	83.5	49 56.2	+10.6	84.7	20
21	48 47.2	-1.6	75.1	49 02.1	-0.1	76.2	49 15.8	+1.5	77.3	49 28.4	+3.0	78.5	49 39.8	+4.6	79.6	49 50.0	+6.2	80.8	49 59.0	+7.8	82.0	50 06.8	+9.3	83.1	21
22	48 45.6	-2.9	73.6	49 02.0	-1.3	74.7	49 17.3	+0.2	75.8	49 31.4	+1.8	76.9	49 44.4	+3.3	78.1	49 56.2	+4.9	79.2	50 06.8	+6.5	80.4	50 16.1	+8.2	81.6	22
23	48 42.7	-4.0	72.1	49 00.7	-2.6	73.2	49 17.5	-1.0	74.3	49 33.2	+0.5	75.4	49 47.7	+2.2	76.5	50 01.1	+3.7	77.7	50 13.3	+5.3	78.9	50 24.3	+6.9	80.1	23
24	48 38.7	-5.2	70.6	48 58.1	-3.7	71.6	49 16.5	-2.2	72.7	49 33.7	-0.6	73.9	49 49.9	+0.8	75.0	50 04.8	+2.5	76.1	50 18.6	+4.0	77.3	50 31.2	+5.6	78.5	24
25	48 33.5	-6.4	69.0	48 54.4	-4.9	70.1	49 14.3	-3.4	71.2	49 33.1	-1.9	72.3	49 50.7	-0.3	73.4	50 07.3	+1.2	74.6	50 22.6	+2.8	75.7	50 36.8	+4.4	76.9	25
26	48 27.1	-7.5	67.5	48 49.5	-6.1	68.6	49 10.9	-4.6	69.7	49 31.2	-3.1	70.8	49 50.4	-1.6	71.9	50 08.5	-0.1	73.0	50 25.4	+1.5	74.2	50 41.2	+3.1	75.4	26
27	48 19.6	-8.8	66.1	48 43.4	-7.3	67.1	49 06.3	-5.9	68.2	49 28.1	-4.4	69.2	49 48.8	-2.9	70.3	50 08.4	-1.3	71.5	50 26.9	+0.3	72.6	50 44.3	+1.8	73.8	27
28	48 10.8	-9.8	64.6	48 36.1	-8.4	65.6	49 00.4	-7.0	66.6	49 23.7	-5.5	67.7	49 45.9	-4.0	68.8	50 07.1	-2.5	69.9	50 27.2	-1.1	71.0	50 46.1	+0.5	72.2	28
29	48 01.0	-11.0	63.1	48 27.7	-9.6	64.1	48 53.4	-8.2	65.1	49 18.2	-6.8	66.2	49 41.9	-5.3	67.2	50 04.6	-3.9	68.3	50 26.1	-2.2	69.5	50 46.6	-0.7	70.6	29
30	47 50.0	-12.1	61.6	48 18.1	-10.8	62.6	48 45.2	-9.3	63.6	49 11.4	-8.0	64.7	49 36.6	-6.5	65.7	50 00.7	-5.0	66.8	50 23.9	-3.6	67.9	50 45.9	-2.0	69.0	30
31	47 37.9	-13.2	60.2	48 07.3	-11.8	61.1	48 35.9	-10.6	62.1	49 03.4	-9.1	63.1	49 30.1	-7.8	64.2	49 55.7	-6.3	65.2	50 20.3	-4.8	66.3	50 43.9	-3.4	67.5	31
32	47 24.7	-14.2	58.7	47 55.5	-13.0	59.7	48 25.3	-11.6	60.6	48 54.3	-10.3	61.6	49 22.3	-8.9	62.7	49 49.4	-7.5	63.7	50 15.5	-6.1	64.8	50 40.5	-4.5	65.9	32
33	47 10.5	-15.4	57.3	47 42.5	-14.1	58.2	48 13.7	-12.8	59.2	48 44.0	-11.5	60.1	49 13.4	-10.1	61.1	49 41.9	-8.7	62.2	50 09.4	-7.3	63.2	50 36.0	-5.9	64.3	33
34	46 55.1	-16.3	55.9	47 28.4	-15.1	56.8	48 00.9	-13.9	57.7	48 32.5	-12.6	58.6	49 03.3	-11.3	59.6	49 33.2	-9.9	60.6	50 02.1	-8.5	61.7	50 30.1	-7.1	62.7	34
35	46 38.8	-17.4	54.5	47 13.3	-16.2	55.3	47 47.0	-15.0	56.2	48 19.9	-13.7	57.2	48 52.0	-12.4	58.1	49 23.3	-11.1	59.1	49 53.6	-9.7	60.1	50 23.0	-8.3	61.2	35
36	46 21.4	-18.4	53.1	46 57.1	-17.3	53.9	47 32.0	-16.0	54.8	48 06.2	-14.8	55.7	48 39.6	-13.5	56.6	49 12.2	-12.3	57.6	49 43.9	-11.0	58.6	50 14.7	-9.6	59.6	36
37	46 03.0	-19.4	51.7	46 39.8	-18.2	52.5	47 16.0	-17.1	53.4	47 51.4	-15.9	54.3	48 26.1	-14.7	55.2	48 59.9	-13.4	56.1	49 32.9	-12.1	57.1	50 05.1	-10.8	58.1	37
38	45 43.6	-20.3	50.3	46 21.6	-19.2	51.1	46 58.9	-18.1	52.0	47 35.5	-17.0	52.8	48 11.4	-15.8	53.7	48 46.5	-14.5	54.6	49 20.8	-13.3	55.6	49 54.3	-12.0	56.6	38
39	45 23.3	-21.3	49.0	46 02.4	-20.3	49.8	46 40.8	-19.1	50.6	47 18.5	-18.0	51.4	47 55.6	-16.8	52.3	48 32.0	-15.7	53.2	49 07.5	-14.4	54.1	49 42.3	-13.1	55.0	39
40	45 02.0	-22.1	47.7	45 42.1	-21.1	48.4	46 21.7	-20.1	49.2	47 00.5	-19.0	50.0	47 38.8	-17.9	50.8	48 16.3	-16.7	51.7	48 53.1	-15.5	52.6	49 29.2	-14.4	53.5	40
41	44 39.9	-23.1	46.4	45 21.0	-22.1	47.1	46 01.6	-21.1	47.8	46 41.5	-20.0	48.6	47 20.9	-19.0	49.4	47 59.6	-17.9	50.3	48 37.6	-16.7	51.1	49 14.8	-15.4	52.0	41
42	44 16.8	-23.9	45.1	44 58.9	-23.0	45.8	45 40.5	-22.0	46.5	46 21.5	-21.0	47.3	47 01.9	-19.9	48.0	47 41.7	-18.8	48.9	48 20.9	-17.7	49.7	48 59.4	-16.6	50.6	42
43	43 52.9	-24.8	43.8	44 35.9	-23.8	44.5	45 18.5	-22.9	45.2	46 00.5	-21.9	45.9	46 42.0	-20.9	46.7	47 22.9	-19.9	47.4	48 03.2	-18.8	48.3	48 42.8	-17.7	49.1	43
44	43 28.1	-25.6	42.5	44 12.1	-24.7	43.2	44 55.6	-23.8	43.9	45 38.6	-22.8	44.6	46 21.1	-21.9	45.3	47 03.0	-20.9	46.1	47 44.4	-19.9	46.8	48 25.1	-18.8	47.7	44
45	43 02.5	-26.3	41.3	43 47.4	-25.5	41.9	44 31.8	-24.6	42.6	45 15.8	-23.8	43.2	45 59.2	-22.8	44.0	46 42.1	-21.8	44.7	47 24.5	-20.8	45.4	48 06.3	-19.8	46.2	45
46	42 36.2	-27.2	40.1	43 21.9	-26.4	40.7	44 07.2	-25.5	41.3	44 52.0	-24.6	41.9	45 36.4	-23.7	42.6	46 20.3	-22.8	43.3	47 03.7	-21.8	44.1	47 46.5	-20.8	44.8	46
47	42 09.0	-27.9	38.9	42 55.5	-27.1	39.4	43 41.7	-26.3	40.0	44 27.4	-25.5	40.7	45 12.7	-24.6	41.3	45 57.5	-23.7	42.0	46 41.9	-22.8	42.7	47 25.7	-21.8	43.4	47
48	41 41.1	-28.6	37.7	42 28.4	-27.8	38.2	43 15.4	-27.1	38.8	44 01.9	-26.3	39.4	44 48.1	-25.5	40.0	45 33.8	-24.6	40.7	46 19.1	-23.7	41.4	47 03.9	-22.8	42.1	48
49	41 12.5	-29.3	36.5	42 00.6	-28.7	37.0	42 48.3	-27.9	37.6	43 35.6	-27.0	38.2	44 22.6	-26.3	38.8	45 09.2	-25.4	39.4	45 55.4	-24.6	40.0	46 41.1	-23.7	40.7	49
50	40 43.2	-30.1	35.3	41 31.9	-29.3	35.8	42 20.4	-28.6	36.4	43 08.6	-27.9	36.9	43 56.3	-27.1	37.5	44 43.8	-26.4	38.1	45 30.8	-25.5	38.7	46 17.4	-24.7	39.4	50
51	40 13.1	-30.6	34.2	41 02.6	-30.0	34.7	41 51.8	-29.3	35.2	42 40.7	-28.6	35.7	43 29.2	-27.8	36.3	44 17.4	-27.1	36.8	45 05.3	-26.4	37.4	45 52.7	-25.5	38.1	51
52	39 42.5	-31.3	33.1	40 32.6	-30.6	33.5	41 22.5	-30.0	34.0	42 12.1	-29.4	34.5	43 01.4	-28.7	35.1	43 50.3	-27.9	35.6	44 38.9	-27.2	36.2	45 27.2	-26.4	36.8	52
53	39 11.2	-31.9	32.0	40 02.0	-31.4	32.4	40 52.5	-30.7	32.9	41 42.7	-30.0	33.4	42 32.7	-29.4	33.9	43 22.4	-28.7	34.4	44 11.7	-27.9	34.9	45 00.8	-27.3	35.5	53
54	38 39.3	-32.6	30.9	39 30.6	-31.9	31.3	40 21.8	-31.4	31.7	41 12.7	-30.7	32.2	42 03.3	-30.1	32.7	42 53.7	-29.5	33.2	43 43.8	-28.8	33.7	44 33.5	-28.0	34.2	54
55	38 06.7	-33.1	29.8	38 58.7	-32.5	30.2	39 50.4	-31.9	30.6	40 42.0	-31.4	31.1	41 33.2	-30.8	31.5	42 24.2	-30.1	32.0	43 15.0	-29.5	32.5	44 05.5	-28.9	33.0	55
56	37 33.6	-33.6	28.8	38 26.2	-33.2	29.1	39 18.5	-32.6	29.5	40 10.6	-32.1	29.9	41 02.4	-31.4	30.4	41 54.1	-30.9	30.8	42 45.5	-30.3	31.3	43 36.6	-29.6	31.8	56
57	37 00.0	-34.2	27.7	37 53.0	-33.7	28.1	38 45.9	-33.2	28.4	39 38.5	-32.6	28.8	40 31.0	-32.1	29.2	41 23.2	-31.5	29.7	42 15.2	-30.9	30.1	43 07.0	-30.3	30.6	57
58	36 25.8	-34.7	26.7	37 19.3	-34.2	27.0	38 12.7	-33.7	27.4	39 05.9	-33.2	27.8	39 58.9	-32.7	28.1	40 51.7	-32.2	28.5	41 44.3	-31.6	29.0	42 36.7	-31.1	29.4	58
59	35 51.1	-35.2	25.7	36 45.1	-34.7	26.0	37 39.0	-34.3	26.3	38 32.7	-33.9	26.7	39 26.2	-33.3	27.1	40 19.5	-32.8	27.4	41 12.7	-32.3	27.8	42 05.6	-31.7	28.3	59
60	35 15.9	-35.7	24.7	36 10.4	-35.3	25.0	37 04.7	-34.8	25.3	37 58.8	-34.3	25.6	38 52.9	-33.9	26.0	39 46.7	-33.4	26.3	40 40.4	-32.9	26.7	41 33.9	-32.4	27.1	60
61	34 40.2	-36.1	23.7	35 35.1	-35.7	24.0	36 29.9	-35.4	24.3	37 24.5	-34.9	24.6	38 19.0	-34.5	24.9	39 13.3	-34.0	25.3	40 07.5	-33.5	25.6	41 01.5	-33.0	26.0	61
62	34 04.1	-36.6	22.7	34 59.4	-36.3	23.0	35 54.5	-35.8	23.3	36 49.6	-35.4	23.6	37 44.5	-35.0	23.9	38 39.3	-34.6	24.2	39 34.0	-34.2	24.5	40 28.5	-33.7	24.9	62
63	33 27.5	-37.1	21.8	34 23.1	-36.6	22.0	35 18.7	-36.3	22.3	36 14.2	-35.9	22.6	37 09.5	-35.5	22.9	38 04.7	-35.1	23.2	38 59.8	-34.7	23.5	39 54.8	-34.3	23.8	63
64	32 50.4	-37.4	20.8	33 46.5	-37.1	21.1	34 42.4	-36.7	21.3	35 38.3	-36.4	21.6	36 34.0	-36.0	21.9	37 29.6	-35.6	22.1	38 25.1	-35.2	22.4	39 20.5	-34.8	22.7	64
65	32 13.0	-37.8	19.9	33 09.4	-37.6	20.1	34 05.7	-37.2	20.4	35 01.9	-36.9	20.6	35 58.0	-36.5	20.9	36 54.0	-36.1	21.1	37 49.9	-35.8	21.4	38 45.7	-35.4	21.7	65
66	31 35.2	-38.3	19.0	32 31.8	-37.9	19.2	33 28.5	-37.6	19.4	34 25.0	-37.3	19.6	35 21.5	-37.0	19.9	36 17.9	-36.7	20.1	37 14.1	-36.2	20.4	38 10.3	-35.9	20.7	66
67	30 56.9	-38.6	18.1	31 53.9	-38.3	18.3	32 50.9	-38.1	18.5	33 47.7	-37.7	18.7	34 44.5	-37.4	18.9	35 41.2	-37.1	19.2	36 37.9	-36.8	19.4	37 34.4	-36.4	19.6	67
68	30 18.3	-38.9	17.2	31 15.6	-38.7	17.4	32 12.8	-38.4	17.6	33 10.0	-38.1	17.8	34 07.1	-37.8	18.0	35 04.1	-37.5	18.2	36 01.1	-37.2	18.4	36 58.0	-36.9	18.6	68
69	29 39.4	-39.3	16.3	30 36.9	-39.0	16.5	31 34.4	-38.8	16.7	32 31.9	-38.6	16.9	33 29.3	-38.3	17.0	34 26.6	-38.0	17.2	35 23.9	-37.7	17.4	36 21.1	-37.4	17.7	69
70	29 00.1	-39.7	15.5	29 57.9	-39.4	15.6	30 55.6	-39.1	15.8	31 53.3	-38.9	15.9	32 51.0	-38.6	16.1	33 48.6	-38.4	16.3	34 46.2	-38.1	16.5	35 43.7	-37.9	16.7	70
71	28 20.4	-39.9	14.6	29 18.5	-39.8	14.8	30 16.5	-39.5	14.9	31 14.4	-39.2	15.1	32 12.4	-39.1	15.2	33 10.2	-38.8	15.4	34 08.1	-38.6	15.6	35 05.8	-38.3	15.7	71
72	27 40.5	-40.3	13.8	28 38.7	-40.0	13.9	29 37.0	-39.9	14.0	30 35.2	-39.7	14.2	31 33.3	-39.4	14.3	32 31.4	-39.1	14.5	33 29.5	-38.9	14.6	34 27.5	-38.7	14.8	72
73	27 00.2	-40.5	12.9	27 58.7	-40.4	13.0	28 57.1	-40.1	13.2	29 55.5	-39.9	13.3	30 53.9	-39.7	13.4	31 52.3	-39.6	13.6	32 50.6	-39.4	13.7	33 48.8	-39.1	13.9	73
74	26 19.7	-40.8	12.1	27 18.3	-40.6	12.2	28 17.0	-40.5	12.3	29 15.6	-40.3	12.4	30 14.2	-40.1	12.6	31 12.7	-39.9	12.7	32 11.2	-39.7	12.8	33 09.7	-39.5	13.0	74
75	25 38.9	-41.1	11.3	26 37.7	-40.9	11.4	27 36.5	-40.8	11.5	28 35.3	-40.6	11.6	29 34.1	-40.5	11.7	30 32.8	-40.3	11.8	31 31.5	-40.1	12.0	32 30.2	-39.9	12.1	75
76	24 57.8	-41.4	10.5	25 56.8	-41.2	10.6	26 55.7	-41.0	10.7	27 54.7	-40.9	10.8	28 53.6	-40.7	10.9	29 52.5	-40.5	11.0	30 51.4	-40.4	11.1	31 50.3	-40.2	11.2	76
77	24 16.4	-41.6	9.7	25 15.6	-41.5	9.8	26 14.7	-41.3	9.8	27 13.8	-41.2	9.9	28 12.9	-41.0	10.0	29 12.0	-40.9	10.1	30 11.0	-40.7	10.2	31 10.1	-40.6	10.3	77
78	23 34.8	-41.8	8.9	24 34.1	-41.7	9.0	25 33.4	-41.6	9.0	26 32.6	-41.4	9.1	27 31.9	-41.4	9.2	28 31.1	-41.2	9.3	29 30.3	-41.1	9.4	30 29.5	-41.0	9.5	78
79	22 53.0	-42.1	8.1	23 52.4	-41.9	8.2	24 51.8	-41.9	8.2	25 51.2	-41.8	8.3	26 50.5	-41.6	8.4	27 49.9	-41.5	8.5	28 49.2	-41.3	8.5	29 48.5	-41.2	8.6	79
80	22 10.9	-42.2	7.3	23 10.5	-42.2	7.4	24 09.9	-42.0	7.5	25 09.4	-41.9	7.5	26 08.9	-41.9	7.6	27 08.4	-41.8	7.6	28 07.9	-41.7	7.7	29 07.3	-41.5	7.8	80
81	21 28.7	-42.5	6.6	22 28.3	-42.4	6.6	23 27.9	-42.3	6.7	24 27.5	-42.3	6.7	25 27.0	-42.1	6.8	26 26.6	-42.0	6.8	27 26.2	-41.9	6.9	28 25.8	-41.9	7.0	81
82	20 46.2	-42.7	5.8	21 45.9	-42.6	5.9	22 45.6	-42.6	5.9	23 45.2	-42.4	6.0	24 44.9	-42.3	6.0	25 44.6	-42.3	6.0	26 44.3	-42.3	6.1	27 43.9	-42.1	6.2	82
83	20 03.5	-42.8	5.1	21 03.3	-42.8	5.1	22 03.0	-42.7	5.1	23 02.8	-42.7	5.2	24 02.6	-42.6	5.2	25 02.3	-42.5	5.3	26 02.0	-42.4	5.3	27 01.8	-42.4	5.4	83
84	19 20.7	-43.1	4.3	20 20.5	-43.0	4.4	21 20.3	-42.9	4.4	22 20.1	-42.8	4.4	23 20.0	-42.9	4.5	24 19.8	-42.8	4.5	25 19.6	-42.7	4.5	26 19.4	-42.7	4.6	84
85	18 37.6	-43.2	3.6	19 37.5	-43.2	3.6	20 37.4	-43.2	3.6	21 37.3	-43.1	3.7	22 37.1	-43.0	3.7	23 37.0	-43.0	3.7	24 36.9	-43.0	3.7	25 36.7	-42.9	3.8	85
86	17 54.4	-43.4	2.9	18 54.3	-43.3	2.9	19 54.2	-43.3	2.9	20 54.2	-43.3	2.9	21 54.1	-43.2	2.9	22 54.0	-43.2	3.0	23 53.9	-43.1	3.0	24 53.8	-43.1	3.0	86
87	17 11.0	-43.5	2.1	18 11.0	-43.5	2.2	19 10.9	-43.4	2.2	20 10.9	-43.5	2.2	21 10.9	-43.5	2.2	22 10.8	-43.4	2.2	23 10.8	-43.4	2.2	24 10.7	-43.3	2.2	87
88	16 27.5	-43.7	1.4	17 27.5	-43.7	1.4	18 27.5	-43.7	1.4	19 27.4	-43.6	1.4	20 27.4	-43.6	1.5	21 27.4	-43.6	1.5	22 27.4	-43.6	1.5	23 27.4	-43.6	1.5	88
89	15 43.8	-43.8	0.7	16 43.8	-43.8	0.7	17 43.8	-43.8	0.7	18 43.8	-43.8	0.7	19 43.8	-43.8	0.7	20 43.8	-43.8	0.7	21 43.8	-43.8	0.7	22 43.8	-43.8	0.7	89
90	15 00.0	-43.9	0.0	16 00.0	-43.9	0.0	17 00.0	-44.0	0.0	18 00.0	-44.0	0.0	19 00.0	-44.0	0.0	20 00.0	-44.0	0.0	21 00.0	-44.0	0.0	22 00.0	-44.0	0.0	90
	15°			16°			17°			18°			19°			20°			21°			22°			

43°, 317° L.H.A. LATITUDE **SAME** NAME AS DECLINATION

LATITUDE **CONTRARY** NAME TO DECLINATION — L.H.A. 43°, 317°

Dec.	15° Hc	d	Z	16° Hc	d	Z	17° Hc	d	Z	18° Hc	d	Z
°	° ′	′	°	° ′	′	°	° ′	′	°	° ′	′	°
0	44 56.7	-22.4	105.5	44 40.2	-23.7	106.5	44 22.7	-24.9	107.4	44 04.3	-26.2	108.3
1	44 34.3	-23.2	106.8	44 16.5	-24.5	107.8	43 57.8	-25.8	108.7	43 38.1	-27.0	109.6
2	44 11.1	-24.2	108.1	43 52.0	-25.4	109.0	43 32.0	-26.6	109.9	43 11.1	-27.8	110.8
3	43 46.9	-24.9	109.4	43 26.6	-26.2	110.3	43 05.4	-27.4	111.2	42 43.3	-28.6	112.0
4	43 22.0	-25.8	110.6	43 00.4	-27.0	111.5	42 38.0	-28.2	112.4	42 14.7	-29.3	113.2
5	42 56.2	-26.6	111.9	42 33.4	-27.7	112.7	42 09.8	-28.8	113.6	41 45.4	-29.9	114.4
6	42 29.6	-27.3	113.1	42 05.7	-28.5	113.9	41 41.0	-29.6	114.7	41 15.5	-30.7	115.5
7	42 02.3	-28.1	114.3	41 37.2	-29.2	115.1	41 11.4	-30.3	115.9	40 44.8	-31.3	116.7
8	41 34.2	-28.8	115.5	41 08.0	-29.9	116.3	40 41.1	-30.9	117.0	40 13.5	-32.0	117.8
9	41 05.4	-29.5	116.7	40 38.1	-30.5	117.4	40 10.2	-31.6	118.2	39 41.5	-32.6	118.9
10	40 35.9	-30.1	117.8	40 07.6	-31.2	118.6	39 38.6	-32.2	119.3	39 08.9	-33.2	120.0
11	40 05.8	-30.9	118.9	39 36.4	-31.8	119.7	39 06.4	-32.8	120.4	38 35.7	-33.7	121.1
12	39 34.9	-31.4	120.1	39 04.6	-32.5	120.8	38 33.6	-33.4	121.4	38 02.0	-34.4	122.1
13	39 03.5	-32.1	121.2	38 32.1	-33.0	121.8	38 00.2	-34.0	122.5	37 27.6	-34.8	123.2
14	38 31.4	-32.6	122.2	37 59.1	-33.6	122.9	37 26.2	-34.5	123.5	36 52.8	-35.4	124.2
15	37 58.8	-33.3	123.3	37 25.5	-34.1	124.0	36 51.7	-35.0	124.6	36 17.4	-35.8	125.2
16	37 25.5	-33.8	124.4	36 51.4	-34.7	125.0	36 16.7	-35.5	125.6	35 41.6	-36.4	126.2
17	36 51.7	-34.3	125.4	36 16.7	-35.1	126.0	35 41.2	-36.0	126.6	35 05.2	-36.8	127.2
18	36 17.4	-34.8	126.4	35 41.6	-35.7	127.0	35 05.2	-36.5	127.6	34 28.4	-37.2	128.1
19	35 42.6	-35.3	127.4	35 05.9	-36.1	128.0	34 28.7	-36.9	128.5	33 51.2	-37.7	129.1
20	35 07.3	-35.8	128.4	34 29.8	-36.6	129.0	33 51.8	-37.3	129.5	33 13.5	-38.1	130.0
21	34 31.5	-36.3	129.4	33 53.2	-37.0	129.9	33 14.5	-37.8	130.4	32 35.4	-38.5	130.9
22	33 55.2	-36.7	130.4	33 16.2	-37.5	130.9	32 36.7	-38.2	131.3	31 56.9	-38.9	131.8
23	33 18.5	-37.1	131.3	32 38.7	-37.8	131.8	31 58.5	-38.5	132.3	31 18.0	-39.2	132.7
24	32 41.4	-37.6	132.2	32 00.9	-38.3	132.7	31 20.0	-38.9	133.2	30 38.8	-39.6	133.6
25	32 03.8	-37.9	133.2	31 22.6	-38.6	133.6	30 41.1	-39.3	134.1	29 59.2	-39.9	134.5
26	31 25.9	-38.3	134.1	30 44.0	-39.0	134.5	30 01.8	-39.7	134.9	29 19.3	-40.3	135.3
27	30 47.6	-38.7	135.0	30 05.0	-39.3	135.4	29 22.1	-39.9	135.8	28 39.0	-40.6	136.2
28	30 08.9	-39.1	135.9	29 25.7	-39.7	136.3	28 42.2	-40.3	136.6	27 58.4	-40.8	137.0
29	29 29.8	-39.3	136.7	28 46.0	-40.0	137.1	28 01.9	-40.6	137.5	27 17.6	-41.2	137.8
30	28 50.5	-39.8	137.6	28 06.0	-40.3	138.0	27 21.3	-40.8	138.3	26 36.4	-41.4	138.7
31	28 10.7	-40.0	138.5	27 25.7	-40.6	138.8	26 40.5	-41.2	139.1	25 55.0	-41.7	139.5
32	27 30.7	-40.3	139.3	26 45.1	-40.9	139.6	25 59.3	-41.4	140.0	25 13.3	-42.0	140.3
33	26 50.4	-40.6	140.1	26 04.2	-41.1	140.4	25 17.9	-41.7	140.8	24 31.3	-42.2	141.0
34	26 09.8	-40.9	141.0	25 23.1	-41.4	141.3	24 36.2	-41.9	141.5	23 49.1	-42.4	141.8
35	25 28.9	-41.1	141.8	24 41.7	-41.7	142.1	23 54.3	-42.2	142.3	23 06.7	-42.7	142.6
36	24 47.8	-41.5	142.6	24 00.0	-41.9	142.8	23 12.1	-42.4	143.1	22 24.0	-42.8	143.4
37	24 06.3	-41.6	143.4	23 18.1	-42.1	143.6	22 29.7	-42.6	143.9	21 41.2	-43.1	144.1
38	23 24.7	-41.9	144.2	22 36.0	-42.4	144.4	21 47.1	-42.8	144.6	20 58.1	-43.2	144.9
39	22 42.8	-42.1	144.9	21 53.6	-42.5	145.2	21 04.3	-43.0	145.4	20 14.9	-43.5	145.6
40	22 00.7	-42.3	145.7	21 11.1	-42.8	145.9	20 21.3	-43.2	146.1	19 31.4	-43.6	146.3
41	21 18.4	-42.6	146.5	20 28.3	-43.0	146.7	19 38.1	-43.4	146.9	18 47.8	-43.8	147.1
42	20 35.8	-42.7	147.2	19 45.3	-43.1	147.4	18 54.7	-43.5	147.6	18 04.0	-43.9	147.8
43	19 53.1	-42.9	148.0	19 02.2	-43.3	148.2	18 11.2	-43.7	148.3	17 20.1	-44.1	148.5
44	19 10.2	-43.1	148.7	18 18.9	-43.5	148.9	17 27.5	-43.9	149.1	16 36.0	-44.3	149.2
45	18 27.1	-43.2	149.4	17 35.4	-43.6	149.6	16 43.6	-44.0	149.8	15 51.7	-44.3	149.9
46	17 43.9	-43.4	150.2	16 51.8	-43.8	150.3	15 59.6	-44.1	150.5	15 07.4	-44.5	150.6
47	17 00.5	-43.6	150.9	16 08.0	-43.9	151.0	15 15.5	-44.3	151.2	14 22.9	-44.7	151.3
48	16 16.9	-43.7	151.6	15 24.1	-44.1	151.7	14 31.2	-44.4	151.9	13 38.2	-44.7	152.0
49	15 33.2	-43.9	152.3	14 40.0	-44.2	152.5	13 46.8	-44.5	152.6	12 53.5	-44.8	152.7
50	14 49.3	-43.9	153.0	13 55.8	-44.3	153.1	13 02.3	-44.7	153.3	12 08.7	-45.0	153.4
51	14 05.4	-44.1	153.7	13 11.5	-44.4	153.8	12 17.6	-44.7	153.9	11 23.7	-45.0	154.0
52	13 21.3	-44.3	154.4	12 27.1	-44.5	154.5	11 32.9	-44.8	154.6	10 38.7	-45.1	154.7
53	12 37.0	-44.3	155.1	11 42.6	-44.6	155.2	10 48.1	-44.9	155.3	9 53.6	-45.2	155.4
54	11 52.7	-44.4	155.8	10 58.0	-44.7	155.9	10 03.2	-45.0	156.0	9 08.4	-45.3	156.0
55	11 08.3	-44.5	156.5	10 13.3	-44.8	156.6	9 18.2	-45.1	156.6	8 23.1	-45.3	156.7
56	10 23.8	-44.6	157.2	9 28.5	-44.9	157.3	8 33.1	-45.1	157.3	7 37.8	-45.4	157.4
57	9 39.2	-44.7	157.9	8 43.6	-44.9	157.9	7 48.0	-45.2	158.0	6 52.4	-45.5	158.0
58	8 54.5	-44.7	158.5	7 58.7	-45.0	158.6	7 02.8	-45.2	158.6	6 06.9	-45.5	158.7
59	8 09.8	-44.8	159.2	7 13.7	-45.1	159.3	6 17.6	-45.4	159.3	5 21.4	-45.5	159.3
60	7 25.0	-44.9	159.9	6 28.6	-45.1	159.9	5 32.2	-45.3	160.0	4 35.9	-45.6	160.0
61	6 40.1	-44.9	160.6	5 43.5	-45.2	160.6	4 46.9	-45.4	160.6	3 50.3	-45.6	160.6
62	5 55.2	-45.0	161.2	4 58.3	-45.2	161.3	4 01.5	-45.4	161.3	3 04.7	-45.6	161.3
63	5 10.2	-45.0	161.9	4 13.1	-45.2	161.9	3 16.1	-45.4	161.9	2 19.1	-45.7	161.9
64	4 25.2	-45.1	162.6	3 27.9	-45.2	162.6	2 30.7	-45.5	162.6	1 33.4	-45.6	162.6
65	3 40.1	-45.1	163.2	2 42.7	-45.3	163.2	1 45.2	-45.5	163.2	0 47.8	-45.7	163.2
66	2 55.0	-45.1	163.9	1 57.4	-45.3	163.9	0 59.7	-45.4	163.9	0 02.1	-45.7	163.9
67	2 09.9	-45.1	164.5	1 12.1	-45.3	164.5	0 14.3	-45.5	164.5	0 43.6	+45.6	15.5
68	1 24.8	-45.1	165.2	0 26.8	-45.3	165.2	0 31.2	+45.5	14.8	1 29.2	+45.7	14.8
69	0 39.7	-45.2	165.9	0 18.5	+45.3	14.1	1 16.7	+45.5	14.2	2 14.9	+45.6	14.2
70	0 05.5	+45.1	13.5	1 03.8	+45.3	13.5	2 02.2	+45.4	13.5	3 00.5	+45.6	13.5
71	0 50.6	+45.2	12.8	1 49.1	+45.3	12.8	2 47.6	+45.5	12.8	3 46.1	+45.6	12.9
72	1 35.8	+45.1	12.2	2 34.4	+45.3	12.2	3 33.1	+45.4	12.2	4 31.7	+45.5	12.2
73	2 20.9	+45.1	11.5	3 19.7	+45.2	11.5	4 18.5	+45.3	11.5	5 17.2	+45.6	11.6
74	3 06.0	+45.1	10.9	4 04.9	+45.2	10.9	5 03.8	+45.4	10.9	6 02.8	+45.4	10.9
75	3 51.1	+45.0	10.2	4 50.1	+45.2	10.2	5 49.2	+45.2	10.2	6 48.2	+45.4	10.2
76	4 36.1	+45.0	9.5	5 35.3	+45.1	9.5	6 34.4	+45.3	9.6	7 33.6	+45.4	9.6
77	5 21.1	+45.0	8.9	6 20.4	+45.1	8.9	7 19.7	+45.1	8.9	8 19.0	+45.2	8.9
78	6 06.1	+44.9	8.2	7 05.5	+45.0	8.2	8 04.8	+45.2	8.2	9 04.2	+45.2	8.3
79	6 51.0	+44.9	7.5	7 50.5	+44.9	7.5	8 50.0	+45.0	7.6	9 49.4	+45.2	7.6
80	7 35.9	+44.8	6.9	8 35.4	+44.9	6.9	9 35.0	+45.0	6.9	10 34.6	+45.0	6.9
81	8 20.7	+44.7	6.2	9 20.3	+44.8	6.2	10 20.0	+44.8	6.2	11 19.6	+45.0	6.2
82	9 05.4	+44.7	5.5	10 05.1	+44.7	5.5	11 04.8	+44.8	5.6	12 04.6	+44.8	5.6
83	9 50.1	+44.5	4.8	10 49.8	+44.7	4.9	11 49.6	+44.7	4.9	12 49.4	+44.7	4.9
84	10 34.6	+44.5	4.2	11 34.5	+44.5	4.2	12 34.3	+44.6	4.2	13 34.1	+44.7	4.2
85	11 19.1	+44.4	3.5	12 19.0	+44.4	3.5	13 18.9	+44.5	3.5	14 18.8	+44.5	3.5
86	12 03.5	+44.3	2.8	13 03.4	+44.4	2.8	14 03.4	+44.3	2.8	15 03.3	+44.4	2.8
87	12 47.8	+44.2	2.1	13 47.8	+44.2	2.1	14 47.7	+44.3	2.1	15 47.7	+44.2	2.1
88	13 32.0	+44.1	1.4	14 32.0	+44.1	1.4	15 32.0	+44.0	1.4	16 31.9	+44.1	1.4
89	14 16.1	+43.9	0.7	15 16.1	+43.9	0.7	16 16.0	+44.0	0.7	17 16.0	+44.0	0.7
90	15 00.0	+43.8	0.0	16 00.0	+43.8	0.0	17 00.0	+43.8	0.0	18 00.0	+43.8	0.0
	15°			16°			17°			18°		

19° Hc	d	Z	20° Hc	d	Z	21° Hc	d	Z	22° Hc	d	Z	Dec.
° ′	′	°	° ′	′	°	° ′	′	°	° ′	′	°	°
43 45.0	-27.5	109.2	43 24.8	-28.7	110.1	43 03.7	-29.8	111.0	42 41.7	-30.9	111.9	0
43 17.5	-28.2	110.5	42 56.1	-29.4	111.3	42 33.9	-30.5	112.2	42 10.8	-31.6	113.0	1
42 49.3	-28.9	111.7	42 26.7	-30.1	112.5	42 03.4	-31.3	113.4	41 39.2	-32.3	114.2	2
42 20.4	-29.7	112.9	41 56.6	-30.7	113.7	41 32.1	-31.8	114.5	41 06.9	-33.0	115.3	3
41 50.7	-30.4	114.0	41 25.9	-31.5	114.8	41 00.3	-32.6	115.6	40 33.9	-33.5	116.4	4
41 20.3	-31.1	115.2	40 54.4	-32.2	116.0	40 27.7	-33.1	116.8	40 00.4	-34.2	117.5	5
40 49.2	-31.7	116.3	40 22.2	-32.7	117.1	39 54.6	-33.8	117.8	39 26.2	-34.7	118.6	6
40 17.5	-32.4	117.4	39 49.5	-33.4	118.2	39 20.8	-34.3	118.9	38 51.5	-35.3	119.6	7
39 45.1	-32.9	118.5	39 16.1	-33.9	119.3	38 46.5	-34.9	120.0	38 16.2	-35.8	120.7	8
39 12.2	-33.6	119.6	38 42.2	-34.5	120.3	38 11.6	-35.5	121.0	37 40.4	-36.4	121.7	9
38 38.6	-34.1	120.7	38 07.7	-35.1	121.4	37 36.1	-35.9	122.0	37 04.0	-36.8	122.7	10
38 04.5	-34.7	121.7	37 32.6	-35.6	122.4	37 00.2	-36.5	123.0	36 27.2	-37.3	123.7	11
37 29.8	-35.2	122.8	36 57.0	-36.1	123.4	36 23.7	-36.9	124.0	35 49.9	-37.8	124.6	12
36 54.6	-35.8	123.8	36 20.9	-36.6	124.4	35 46.8	-37.5	125.0	35 12.1	-38.2	125.6	13
36 18.8	-36.2	124.8	35 44.3	-37.0	125.4	35 09.3	-37.8	126.0	34 33.9	-38.7	126.5	14
35 42.6	-36.7	125.8	35 07.3	-37.5	126.4	34 31.5	-38.3	126.9	33 55.2	-39.0	127.5	15
35 05.9	-37.2	126.7	34 29.8	-38.0	127.3	33 53.2	-38.7	127.8	33 16.2	-39.5	128.4	16
34 28.7	-37.5	127.7	33 51.8	-38.3	128.2	33 14.5	-39.1	128.8	32 36.7	-39.8	129.3	17
33 51.2	-38.1	128.6	33 13.5	-38.8	129.2	32 35.4	-39.5	129.7	31 56.9	-40.2	130.1	18
33 13.1	-38.4	129.6	32 34.7	-39.1	130.1	31 55.9	-39.9	130.6	31 16.7	-40.5	131.0	19
32 34.7	-38.8	130.5	31 55.6	-39.6	131.0	31 16.0	-40.2	131.4	30 36.2	-40.9	131.9	20
31 55.9	-39.2	131.4	31 16.0	-39.8	131.9	30 35.8	-40.5	132.3	29 55.3	-41.2	132.7	21
31 16.7	-39.6	132.3	30 36.2	-40.3	132.7	29 55.3	-40.9	133.1	29 14.1	-41.5	133.6	22
30 37.1	-39.9	133.2	29 55.9	-40.5	133.6	29 14.4	-41.2	134.0	28 32.6	-41.8	134.4	23
29 57.2	-40.2	134.0	29 15.4	-40.9	134.4	28 33.2	-41.4	134.8	27 50.8	-42.1	135.2	24
29 17.0	-40.6	134.9	28 34.5	-41.2	135.3	27 51.8	-41.8	135.6	27 08.7	-42.3	136.0	25
28 36.4	-40.8	135.7	27 53.3	-41.4	136.1	27 10.0	-42.1	136.5	26 26.4	-42.6	136.8	26
27 55.6	-41.2	136.5	27 11.9	-41.8	136.9	26 27.9	-42.3	137.2	25 43.8	-42.9	137.6	27
27 14.4	-41.4	137.4	26 30.1	-42.0	137.7	25 45.6	-42.5	138.0	25 00.9	-43.1	138.4	28
26 33.0	-41.8	138.2	25 48.1	-42.2	138.5	25 03.1	-42.8	138.8	24 17.8	-43.3	139.1	29
25 51.2	-41.9	139.0	25 05.9	-42.5	139.3	24 20.3	-43.1	139.6	23 34.5	-43.5	139.9	30
25 09.3	-42.3	139.8	24 23.4	-42.8	140.1	23 37.2	-43.2	140.4	22 51.0	-43.8	140.6	31
24 27.0	-42.4	140.6	23 40.6	-43.0	140.8	22 54.0	-43.5	141.1	22 07.2	-43.9	141.4	32
23 44.6	-42.7	141.3	22 57.6	-43.2	141.6	22 10.5	-43.6	141.9	21 23.3	-44.2	142.1	33
23 01.9	-42.9	142.1	22 14.4	-43.3	142.3	21 26.9	-43.9	142.6	20 39.1	-44.3	142.8	34
22 19.0	-43.2	142.9	21 31.1	-43.6	143.1	20 43.0	-44.0	143.3	19 54.8	-44.5	143.5	35
21 35.8	-43.3	143.6	20 47.5	-43.8	143.8	19 59.0	-44.3	144.0	19 10.3	-44.6	144.3	36
20 52.5	-43.5	144.3	20 03.7	-44.0	144.6	19 14.7	-44.3	144.8	18 25.7	-44.8	145.0	37
20 09.0	-43.7	145.1	19 19.7	-44.1	145.3	18 30.4	-44.6	145.5	17 40.9	-45.0	145.7	38
19 25.3	-43.9	145.8	18 35.6	-44.3	146.0	17 45.8	-44.7	146.2	16 55.9	-45.1	146.4	39
18 41.4	-44.0	146.5	17 51.3	-44.4	146.7	17 01.1	-44.8	146.9	16 10.8	-45.2	147.0	40
17 57.4	-44.2	147.2	17 06.9	-44.6	147.4	16 16.3	-45.0	147.6	15 25.6	-45.4	147.7	41
17 13.2	-44.3	148.0	16 22.3	-44.7	148.1	15 31.3	-45.1	148.3	14 40.2	-45.4	148.4	42
16 28.9	-44.5	148.7	15 37.6	-44.9	148.8	14 46.2	-45.2	148.9	13 54.8	-45.6	149.1	43
15 44.4	-44.6	149.4	14 52.7	-44.9	149.5	14 01.0	-45.3	149.6	13 09.2	-45.7	149.7	44
14 59.8	-44.7	150.0	14 07.8	-45.1	150.2	13 15.7	-45.5	150.3	12 23.5	-45.7	150.4	45
14 15.1	-44.9	150.7	13 22.7	-45.2	150.9	12 30.2	-45.5	151.0	11 37.8	-45.9	151.1	46
13 30.2	-45.0	151.4	12 37.5	-45.3	151.5	11 44.7	-45.6	151.6	10 51.9	-46.0	151.7	47
12 45.2	-45.0	152.1	11 52.2	-45.4	152.2	10 59.1	-45.7	152.3	10 05.9	-46.0	152.4	48
12 00.2	-45.2	152.8	11 06.8	-45.5	152.9	10 13.4	-45.8	153.0	9 19.9	-46.1	153.0	49
11 15.0	-45.2	153.5	10 21.3	-45.5	153.5	9 27.6	-45.9	153.6	8 33.8	-46.1	153.7	50
10 29.8	-45.4	154.1	9 35.8	-45.6	154.2	8 41.7	-45.9	154.3	7 47.7	-46.3	154.3	51
9 44.4	-45.4	154.8	8 50.1	-45.7	154.9	7 55.8	-46.0	154.9	7 01.4	-46.2	155.0	52
8 59.0	-45.5	155.4	8 04.4	-45.7	155.5	7 09.8	-46.0	155.6	6 15.2	-46.3	155.6	53
8 13.5	-45.5	156.1	7 18.7	-45.9	156.2	6 23.8	-46.1	156.2	5 28.9	-46.4	156.3	54
7 28.0	-45.6	156.8	6 32.8	-45.8	156.8	5 37.7	-46.2	156.9	4 42.5	-46.4	156.9	55
6 42.4	-45.7	157.4	5 47.0	-46.0	157.5	4 51.5	-46.1	157.5	3 56.1	-46.4	157.5	56
5 56.7	-45.7	158.1	5 01.0	-45.9	158.1	4 05.4	-46.2	158.1	3 09.7	-46.5	158.2	57
5 11.0	-45.7	158.7	4 15.1	-46.0	158.8	3 19.2	-46.3	158.8	2 23.2	-46.4	158.8	58
4 25.3	-45.8	159.4	3 29.1	-46.0	159.4	2 32.9	-46.2	159.4	1 36.8	-46.5	159.4	59
3 39.5	-45.8	160.0	2 43.1	-46.0	160.0	1 46.7	-46.3	160.1	0 50.3	-46.5	160.1	60
2 53.7	-45.8	160.7	1 57.1	-46.1	160.7	1 00.4	-46.2	160.7	0 03.8	-46.5	160.7	61
2 07.9	-45.9	161.3	1 11.0	-46.0	161.3	0 14.2	-46.3	161.3	0 42.7	+46.4	18.7	62
1 22.0	-45.8	162.0	0 25.0	-46.1	162.0	0 32.1	+46.2	18.0	1 29.1	+46.5	18.0	63
0 36.2	-45.9	162.6	0 21.1	+46.1	17.4	1 18.3	+46.3	17.4	2 15.6	+46.5	17.4	64
0 09.7	+45.9	16.8	1 07.2	+46.0	16.8	2 04.6	+46.2	16.8	3 02.1	+46.4	16.8	65
0 55.6	+45.8	16.1	1 53.2	+46.0	16.1	2 50.8	+46.3	16.1	3 48.5	+46.4	16.1	66
1 41.4	+45.8	15.5	2 39.2	+46.0	15.5	3 37.1	+46.1	15.5	4 34.9	+46.3	15.5	67
2 27.2	+45.9	14.8	3 25.2	+46.0	14.8	4 23.2	+46.2	14.8	5 21.2	+46.4	14.9	68
3 13.1	+45.8	14.2	4 11.2	+46.0	14.2	5 09.4	+46.1	14.2	6 07.6	+46.2	14.2	69
3 58.9	+45.7	13.5	4 57.2	+45.9	13.5	5 55.5	+46.1	13.6	6 53.8	+46.3	13.6	70
4 44.6	+45.7	12.9	5 43.1	+45.9	12.9	6 41.6	+46.0	12.9	7 40.1	+46.1	12.9	71
5 30.3	+45.7	12.2	6 29.0	+45.8	12.2	7 27.6	+46.0	12.3	8 26.2	+46.1	12.3	72
6 16.0	+45.7	11.6	7 14.8	+45.8	11.6	8 13.6	+45.9	11.6	9 12.3	+46.1	11.7	73
7 01.7	+45.5	10.9	8 00.6	+45.7	10.9	8 59.5	+45.8	11.0	9 58.4	+45.9	11.0	74
7 47.2	+45.6	10.3	8 46.3	+45.6	10.3	9 45.3	+45.8	10.3	10 44.3	+45.9	10.4	75
8 32.8	+45.4	9.6	9 31.9	+45.6	9.6	10 31.1	+45.7	9.7	11 30.2	+45.8	9.7	76
9 18.2	+45.4	8.9	10 17.5	+45.5	9.0	11 16.8	+45.5	9.0	12 16.0	+45.7	9.0	77
10 03.6	+45.3	8.3	11 03.0	+45.4	8.3	12 02.3	+45.5	8.3	13 01.7	+45.6	8.4	78
10 48.9	+45.2	7.6	11 48.4	+45.3	7.6	12 47.8	+45.4	7.7	13 47.3	+45.5	7.7	79
11 34.1	+45.1	6.9	12 33.7	+45.2	7.0	13 33.2	+45.3	7.0	14 32.8	+45.4	7.0	80
12 19.2	+45.1	6.3	13 18.9	+45.1	6.3	14 18.5	+45.2	6.3	15 18.2	+45.2	6.4	81
13 04.3	+44.9	5.6	14 04.0	+45.0	5.6	15 03.7	+45.0	5.6	16 03.4	+45.1	5.7	82
13 49.2	+44.8	4.9	14 49.0	+44.8	4.9	15 48.7	+45.0	5.0	16 48.5	+45.0	5.0	83
14 34.0	+44.7	4.2	15 33.8	+44.8	4.2	16 33.7	+44.7	4.3	17 33.5	+44.8	4.3	84
15 18.7	+44.5	3.5	16 18.6	+44.5	3.6	17 18.4	+44.7	3.6	18 18.3	+44.7	3.6	85
16 03.2	+44.4	2.8	17 03.1	+44.4	2.9	18 03.1	+44.5	2.9	19 03.0	+44.5	2.9	86
16 47.6	+44.3	2.1	17 47.6	+44.3	2.1	18 47.6	+44.3	2.2	19 47.5	+44.4	2.2	87
17 31.9	+44.1	1.4	18 31.9	+44.1	1.4	19 31.9	+44.1	1.4	20 31.9	+44.1	1.5	88
18 16.0	+44.0	0.7	19 16.0	+44.0	0.7	20 16.0	+44.0	0.7	21 16.0	+44.0	0.7	89
19 00.0	+43.8	0.0	20 00.0	+43.8	0.0	21 00.0	+43.8	0.0	22 00.0	+43.8	0.0	90
19°			20°			21°			22°			

S. Lat. {L.H.A. greater than 180° ....Zn=180°–Z; L.H.A. less than 180°...........Zn=180°+Z}

LATITUDE **SAME** NAME AS DECLINATION — L.H.A. 137°, 223°

44°, 316° L.H.A. LATITUDE SAME NAME AS DECLINATION

N. Lat. {L.H.A. greater than 180° .....Zn=Z
L.H.A. less than 180°............Zn=360°–Z}

Dec.	15° Hc	d	Z	16° Hc	d	Z	17° Hc	d	Z	18° Hc	d	Z	19° Hc	d	Z	20° Hc	d	Z	21° Hc	d	Z	22° Hc	d	Z	Dec.
°	° ′	′	°	° ′	′	°	° ′	′	°	° ′	′	°	° ′	′	°	° ′	′	°	° ′	′	°	° ′	′	°	°
0	44 00.8	+21.2	105.0	43 44.8	+22.5	105.9	43 27.9	+23.7	106.8	43 10.0	+25.1	107.7	42 51.3	+26.3	108.6	42 31.7	+27.5	109.5	42 11.3	+28.6	110.4	41 50.0	+29.8	111.2	0
1	44 22.0	+20.2	103.7	44 07.3	+21.6	104.6	43 51.6	+22.9	105.6	43 35.1	+24.1	106.5	43 17.6	+25.4	107.4	42 59.2	+26.7	108.3	42 39.9	+27.9	109.2	42 19.8	+29.1	110.0	1
2	44 42.2	+19.3	102.4	44 28.9	+20.6	103.3	44 14.5	+22.0	104.3	43 59.2	+23.4	105.2	43 43.0	+24.6	106.2	43 25.9	+25.9	107.1	43 07.8	+27.1	108.0	42 48.9	+28.3	108.8	2
3	45 01.5	+18.4	101.0	44 49.5	+19.8	102.0	44 36.5	+21.2	103.0	44 22.6	+22.4	103.9	44 07.6	+23.8	104.9	43 51.8	+25.0	105.8	43 34.9	+26.4	106.7	43 17.2	+27.6	107.6	3
4	45 19.9	+17.4	99.7	45 09.3	+18.8	100.7	44 57.7	+20.2	101.7	44 45.0	+21.6	102.6	44 31.4	+22.9	103.6	44 16.8	+24.2	104.6	44 01.3	+25.5	105.5	43 44.8	+26.8	106.4	4
5	45 37.3	+16.5	98.3	45 28.1	+17.9	99.3	45 17.9	+19.2	100.3	45 06.6	+20.6	101.3	44 54.3	+22.0	102.3	44 41.0	+23.4	103.3	44 26.8	+24.6	104.2	44 11.6	+25.9	105.2	5
6	45 53.8	+15.4	96.9	45 46.0	+16.8	98.0	45 37.1	+18.3	99.0	45 27.2	+19.7	100.0	45 16.3	+21.1	101.0	45 04.4	+22.4	102.0	44 51.4	+23.8	102.9	44 37.5	+25.1	103.9	6
7	46 09.2	+14.4	95.6	46 02.8	+15.9	96.6	45 55.4	+17.3	97.6	45 46.9	+18.8	98.6	45 37.4	+20.1	99.6	45 26.8	+21.5	100.7	45 15.2	+22.9	101.6	45 02.6	+24.2	102.6	7
8	46 23.6	+13.3	94.2	46 18.7	+14.8	95.2	46 12.7	+16.3	96.2	46 05.7	+17.7	97.3	45 57.5	+19.2	98.3	45 48.3	+20.6	99.3	45 38.1	+22.0	100.3	45 26.8	+23.4	101.3	8
9	46 36.9	+12.3	92.7	46 33.5	+13.8	93.8	46 29.0	+15.3	94.8	46 23.4	+16.7	95.9	46 16.7	+18.2	96.9	46 08.9	+19.6	98.0	46 00.1	+21.0	99.0	45 50.2	+22.4	100.0	9
10	46 49.2	+11.3	91.3	46 47.3	+12.7	92.4	46 44.3	+14.2	93.4	46 40.1	+15.7	94.5	46 34.9	+17.1	95.5	46 28.5	+18.7	96.6	46 21.1	+20.0	97.6	46 12.6	+21.4	98.7	10
11	47 00.5	+10.1	89.9	47 00.0	+11.7	90.9	46 58.5	+13.2	92.0	46 55.8	+14.7	93.1	46 52.0	+16.2	94.2	46 47.2	+17.6	95.2	46 41.1	+19.1	96.3	46 34.0	+20.5	97.3	11
12	47 10.6	+9.1	88.4	47 11.7	+10.6	89.5	47 11.7	+12.0	90.6	47 10.5	+13.6	91.7	47 08.2	+15.1	92.7	47 04.8	+16.5	93.8	47 00.2	+18.1	94.9	46 54.5	+19.5	95.9	12
13	47 19.7	+7.9	87.0	47 22.3	+9.4	88.1	47 23.7	+11.0	89.1	47 24.1	+12.5	90.2	47 23.3	+14.0	91.3	47 21.3	+15.5	92.4	47 18.3	+17.0	93.5	47 14.0	+18.5	94.6	13
14	47 27.6	+6.8	85.5	47 31.7	+8.4	86.6	47 34.7	+9.9	87.7	47 36.6	+11.4	88.8	47 37.3	+12.9	89.9	47 36.8	+14.5	91.0	47 35.3	+15.9	92.1	47 32.5	+17.5	93.2	14
15	47 34.4	+5.7	84.0	47 40.1	+7.2	85.1	47 44.6	+8.7	86.2	47 48.0	+10.3	87.3	47 50.2	+11.8	88.4	47 51.3	+13.3	89.5	47 51.2	+14.9	90.6	47 50.0	+16.3	91.7	15
16	47 40.1	+4.5	82.6	47 47.3	+6.0	83.6	47 53.3	+7.7	84.7	47 58.3	+9.1	85.8	48 02.0	+10.7	87.0	48 04.6	+12.3	88.1	48 06.1	+13.7	89.2	48 06.3	+15.3	90.3	16
17	47 44.6	+3.4	81.1	47 53.3	+5.0	82.2	48 01.0	+6.4	83.3	48 07.4	+8.0	84.4	48 12.7	+9.6	85.5	48 16.9	+11.1	86.6	48 19.8	+12.7	87.7	48 21.6	+14.2	88.8	17
18	47 48.0	+2.2	79.6	47 58.3	+3.7	80.7	48 07.4	+5.3	81.8	48 15.4	+6.9	82.9	48 22.3	+8.4	84.0	48 28.0	+9.9	85.1	48 32.5	+11.5	86.2	48 35.8	+13.1	87.4	18
19	47 50.2	+1.1	78.1	48 02.0	+2.6	79.2	48 12.7	+4.2	80.3	48 22.3	+5.7	81.4	48 30.7	+7.2	82.5	48 37.9	+8.8	83.6	48 44.0	+10.4	84.8	48 48.9	+11.9	85.9	19
20	47 51.3	-0.1	76.6	48 04.6	+1.5	77.7	48 16.9	+2.9	78.8	48 28.0	+4.5	79.9	48 37.9	+6.1	81.0	48 46.7	+7.7	82.1	48 54.4	+9.1	83.3	49 00.8	+10.7	84.4	20
21	47 51.2	-1.2	75.1	48 06.1	+0.2	76.2	48 19.8	+1.8	77.3	48 32.5	+3.3	78.4	48 44.0	+4.9	79.5	48 54.4	+6.4	80.6	49 03.5	+8.0	81.8	49 11.5	+9.6	82.9	21
22	47 50.0	-2.4	73.6	48 06.3	-0.8	74.7	48 21.6	+0.7	75.8	48 35.8	+2.2	76.9	48 48.9	+3.7	78.0	49 00.8	+5.2	79.1	49 11.5	+6.9	80.2	49 21.1	+8.4	81.4	22
23	47 47.6	-3.6	72.1	48 05.5	-2.1	73.2	48 22.3	-0.6	74.3	48 38.0	+0.9	75.4	48 52.6	+2.5	76.5	49 06.0	+4.1	77.6	49 18.4	+5.6	78.7	49 29.5	+7.2	79.9	23
24	47 44.0	-4.7	70.7	48 03.4	-3.2	71.7	48 21.7	-1.7	72.8	48 38.9	-0.2	73.9	48 55.1	+1.3	75.0	49 10.1	+2.8	76.1	49 24.0	+4.4	77.2	49 36.7	+5.9	78.3	24
25	47 39.3	-5.8	69.2	48 00.2	-4.4	70.2	48 20.0	-2.9	71.3	48 38.7	-1.4	72.3	48 56.4	+0.1	73.4	49 12.9	+1.6	74.5	49 28.4	+3.1	75.7	49 42.6	+4.8	76.8	25
26	47 33.5	-7.0	67.7	47 55.8	-5.5	68.7	48 17.1	-4.1	69.8	48 37.3	-2.6	70.8	48 56.5	-1.1	71.9	49 14.5	+0.5	73.0	49 31.5	+2.0	74.1	49 47.4	+3.5	75.3	26
27	47 26.5	-8.0	66.2	47 50.3	-6.7	67.2	48 13.0	-5.3	68.3	48 34.7	-3.8	69.3	48 55.4	-2.4	70.4	49 15.0	-0.8	71.5	49 33.5	+0.7	72.6	49 50.9	+2.2	73.7	27
28	47 18.5	-9.2	64.8	47 43.6	-7.8	65.8	48 07.7	-6.4	66.8	48 30.9	-5.0	67.8	48 53.0	-3.5	68.9	49 14.2	-2.1	69.9	49 34.2	-0.5	71.0	49 53.1	+1.0	72.2	28
29	47 09.3	-10.3	63.3	47 35.8	-9.0	64.3	48 01.3	-7.5	65.3	48 25.9	-6.1	66.3	48 49.5	-4.7	67.3	49 12.1	-3.2	68.4	49 33.7	-1.8	69.5	49 54.1	-0.2	70.6	29
30	46 59.0	-11.4	61.9	47 26.8	-10.0	62.8	47 53.8	-8.7	63.8	48 19.8	-7.3	64.8	48 44.8	-5.8	65.8	49 08.9	-4.4	66.9	49 31.9	-2.9	68.0	49 53.9	-1.4	69.1	30
31	46 47.6	-12.5	60.4	47 16.8	-11.2	61.4	47 45.1	-9.8	62.3	48 12.5	-8.5	63.3	48 39.0	-7.1	64.3	49 04.5	-5.7	65.4	49 29.0	-4.2	66.4	49 52.5	-2.7	67.5	31
32	46 35.1	-13.5	59.0	47 05.6	-12.2	59.9	47 35.3	-11.0	60.9	48 04.0	-9.5	61.8	48 31.9	-8.2	62.8	48 58.8	-6.8	63.8	49 24.8	-5.4	64.9	49 49.8	-4.0	66.0	32
33	46 21.6	-14.5	57.6	46 53.4	-13.3	58.5	47 24.3	-12.0	59.4	47 54.5	-10.8	60.4	48 23.7	-9.4	61.3	48 52.0	-8.0	62.3	49 19.4	-6.6	63.4	49 45.8	-5.2	64.4	33
34	46 07.1	-15.6	56.2	46 40.1	-14.4	57.1	47 12.3	-13.1	58.0	47 43.7	-11.8	58.9	48 14.3	-10.5	59.8	48 44.0	-9.2	60.8	49 12.8	-7.8	61.8	49 40.6	-6.4	62.9	34
35	45 51.5	-16.6	54.8	46 25.7	-15.3	55.6	46 59.2	-14.1	56.5	47 31.9	-12.9	57.4	48 03.8	-11.6	58.4	48 34.8	-10.3	59.3	49 05.0	-9.0	60.3	49 34.2	-7.6	61.3	35
36	45 34.9	-17.5	53.4	46 10.4	-16.4	54.2	46 45.1	-15.3	55.1	47 19.0	-14.0	56.0	47 52.2	-12.8	56.9	48 24.5	-11.5	57.8	48 56.0	-10.1	58.8	49 26.6	-8.8	59.8	36
37	45 17.4	-18.5	52.1	45 54.0	-17.4	52.9	46 29.8	-16.2	53.7	47 05.0	-15.1	54.6	47 39.4	-13.8	55.5	48 13.0	-12.6	56.4	48 45.9	-11.4	57.3	49 17.8	-10.0	58.3	37
38	44 58.9	-19.5	50.7	45 36.6	-18.4	51.5	46 13.6	-17.3	52.3	46 49.9	-16.1	53.1	47 25.6	-15.0	54.0	48 00.4	-13.7	54.9	48 34.5	-12.4	55.8	49 07.8	-11.1	56.8	38
39	44 39.4	-20.3	49.4	45 18.2	-19.3	50.1	45 56.3	-18.2	50.9	46 33.8	-17.1	51.7	47 10.6	-15.9	52.6	47 46.7	-14.8	53.5	48 22.1	-13.6	54.4	48 56.7	-12.4	55.3	39
40	44 19.1	-21.3	48.1	44 58.9	-20.3	48.8	45 38.1	-19.2	49.6	46 16.7	-18.1	50.3	46 54.7	-17.0	51.2	47 31.9	-15.8	52.0	48 08.5	-14.7	52.9	48 44.3	-13.4	53.8	40
41	43 57.8	-22.2	46.7	44 38.6	-21.1	47.5	45 18.9	-20.1	48.2	45 58.6	-19.1	49.0	46 37.7	-18.1	49.8	47 16.1	-16.9	50.6	47 53.8	-15.7	51.4	48 30.9	-14.6	52.3	41
42	43 35.6	-23.0	45.5	44 17.5	-22.1	46.2	44 58.8	-21.1	46.9	45 39.5	-20.1	47.6	46 19.6	-19.0	48.4	46 59.2	-18.0	49.2	47 38.1	-16.9	50.0	48 16.3	-15.7	50.9	42
43	43 12.6	-23.8	44.2	43 55.4	-22.9	44.9	44 37.7	-22.0	45.5	45 19.4	-21.0	46.3	46 00.6	-20.0	47.0	46 41.2	-18.9	47.8	47 21.2	-17.8	48.6	48 00.6	-16.7	49.4	43
44	42 48.8	-24.7	42.9	43 32.5	-23.8	43.6	44 15.7	-22.8	44.2	44 58.4	-21.9	44.9	45 40.6	-20.9	45.7	46 22.3	-19.9	46.4	47 03.4	-18.9	47.2	47 43.9	-17.9	48.0	44
45	42 24.1	-25.4	41.7	43 08.7	-24.6	42.3	43 52.9	-23.7	43.0	44 36.5	-22.8	43.6	45 19.7	-21.8	44.3	46 02.4	-20.9	45.0	46 44.5	-19.9	45.8	47 26.0	-18.8	46.6	45
46	41 58.7	-26.2	40.5	42 44.1	-25.4	41.1	43 29.2	-24.6	41.7	44 13.7	-23.6	42.3	44 57.9	-22.8	43.0	45 41.5	-21.8	43.7	46 24.6	-20.8	44.4	47 07.2	-19.9	45.2	46
47	41 32.5	-27.0	39.3	42 18.7	-26.1	39.8	43 04.6	-25.3	40.4	43 50.1	-24.5	41.1	44 35.1	-23.6	41.7	45 19.7	-22.8	42.4	46 03.8	-21.9	43.1	46 47.3	-20.8	43.8	47
48	41 05.5	-27.7	38.1	41 52.6	-26.9	38.6	42 39.3	-26.2	39.2	43 25.6	-25.4	39.8	44 11.5	-24.5	40.4	44 56.9	-23.6	41.1	45 41.9	-22.7	41.7	46 26.5	-21.8	42.4	48
49	40 37.8	-28.3	36.9	41 25.7	-27.7	37.4	42 13.1	-26.9	38.0	43 00.2	-26.1	38.5	43 47.0	-25.3	39.1	44 33.3	-24.5	39.8	45 19.2	-23.6	40.4	46 04.7	-22.8	41.1	49
50	40 09.5	-29.1	35.7	40 58.0	-28.4	36.3	41 46.2	-27.6	36.8	42 34.1	-26.9	37.3	43 21.7	-26.2	37.9	44 08.8	-25.3	38.5	44 55.6	-24.5	39.1	45 41.9	-23.6	39.7	50
51	39 40.4	-29.7	34.6	40 29.6	-29.0	35.1	41 18.6	-28.4	35.6	42 07.2	-27.6	36.1	42 55.5	-26.9	36.7	43 43.5	-26.2	37.2	44 31.1	-25.4	37.8	45 18.3	-24.6	38.4	51
52	39 10.7	-30.4	33.5	40 00.6	-29.7	33.9	40 50.2	-29.0	34.4	41 39.6	-28.4	34.9	42 28.6	-27.7	35.4	43 17.3	-26.9	36.0	44 05.7	-26.2	36.5	44 53.7	-25.4	37.1	52
53	38 40.3	-31.0	32.4	39 30.9	-30.4	32.8	40 21.2	-29.8	33.3	41 11.2	-29.1	33.7	42 00.9	-28.4	34.2	42 50.4	-27.7	34.8	43 39.5	-27.0	35.3	44 28.3	-26.2	35.9	53
54	38 09.3	-31.5	31.3	39 00.5	-31.0	31.7	39 51.4	-30.4	32.1	40 42.1	-29.8	32.6	41 32.5	-29.1	33.1	42 22.7	-28.5	33.6	43 12.5	-27.7	34.1	44 02.1	-27.1	34.6	54
55	37 37.8	-32.2	30.2	38 29.5	-31.6	30.6	39 21.0	-31.0	31.0	40 12.3	-30.4	31.4	41 03.4	-29.8	31.9	41 54.2	-29.2	32.4	42 44.8	-28.6	32.9	43 35.0	-27.8	33.4	55
56	37 05.6	-32.7	29.1	37 57.9	-32.2	29.5	38 50.0	-31.6	29.9	39 41.9	-31.1	30.3	40 33.6	-30.5	30.8	41 25.0	-29.8	31.2	42 16.2	-29.2	31.7	43 07.2	-28.6	32.2	56
57	36 32.9	-33.3	28.1	37 25.7	-32.7	28.5	38 18.4	-32.3	28.8	39 10.8	-31.6	29.2	40 01.3	-31.1	29.6	40 55.2	-30.6	30.0	41 47.0	-30.0	30.5	42 38.6	-29.4	31.0	57
58	35 59.6	-33.8	27.1	36 53.0	-33.3	27.4	37 46.1	-32.8	27.8	38 39.2	-32.3	28.1	39 32.0	-31.8	28.5	40 24.6	-31.2	28.9	41 17.0	-30.6	29.3	42 09.2	-30.1	29.8	58
59	35 25.8	-34.3	26.0	36 19.7	-33.9	26.4	37 13.3	-33.3	26.7	38 06.9	-32.9	27.0	39 00.2	-32.4	27.4	39 53.4	-31.9	27.8	40 46.4	-31.3	28.2	41 39.1	-30.7	28.6	59
60	34 51.5	-34.7	25.0	35 45.8	-34.3	25.3	36 40.0	-33.9	25.7	37 34.0	-33.4	26.0	38 27.8	-32.9	26.3	39 21.5	-32.4	26.7	40 15.1	-32.0	27.1	41 08.4	-31.4	27.5	60
61	34 16.8	-35.3	24.1	35 11.5	-34.8	24.3	36 06.1	-34.4	24.6	37 00.6	-34.0	24.9	37 54.9	-33.5	25.3	38 49.1	-33.1	25.6	39 43.1	-32.6	26.0	40 37.0	-32.1	26.3	61
62	33 41.5	-35.7	23.1	34 36.7	-35.4	23.3	35 31.7	-34.9	23.6	36 26.6	-34.5	23.9	37 21.4	-34.1	24.2	38 16.0	-33.6	24.5	39 10.5	-33.1	24.9	40 04.9	-32.7	25.2	62
63	33 05.8	-36.1	22.1	34 01.3	-35.7	22.4	34 56.8	-35.4	22.6	35 52.1	-35.0	22.9	36 47.3	-34.6	23.2	37 42.4	-34.2	23.5	38 37.4	-33.8	23.8	39 32.2	-33.3	24.1	63
64	32 29.7	-36.6	21.2	33 25.6	-36.2	21.4	34 21.4	-35.9	21.6	35 17.1	-35.5	21.9	36 12.7	-35.1	22.2	37 08.2	-34.7	22.5	38 03.6	-34.3	22.8	38 58.9	-33.9	23.1	64
65	31 53.1	-37.0	20.2	32 49.4	-36.7	20.4	33 45.5	-36.3	20.7	34 41.6	-35.9	20.9	35 37.6	-35.6	21.2	36 33.5	-35.2	21.4	37 29.3	-34.8	21.7	38 25.0	-34.4	22.0	65
66	31 16.1	-37.3	19.3	32 12.7	-37.0	19.5	33 09.2	-36.7	19.7	34 05.7	-36.4	19.9	35 02.0	-36.0	20.2	35 58.3	-35.7	20.4	36 54.5	-35.4	20.7	37 50.6	-35.0	21.0	66
67	30 38.8	-37.8	18.4	31 35.7	-37.5	18.6	32 32.5	-37.1	18.8	33 29.3	-36.8	19.0	34 26.0	-36.5	19.2	35 22.6	-36.2	19.4	36 19.1	-35.8	19.7	37 15.6	-35.5	19.9	67
68	30 01.0	-38.1	17.5	30 58.2	-37.8	17.7	31 55.4	-37.6	17.9	32 52.5	-37.3	18.0	33 49.5	-37.0	18.3	34 46.4	-36.6	18.5	35 43.3	-36.3	18.7	36 40.1	-36.0	18.9	68
69	29 22.9	-38.4	16.6	30 20.4	-38.2	16.8	31 17.8	-37.9	16.9	32 15.2	-37.7	17.1	33 12.5	-37.4	17.3	34 09.8	-37.1	17.5	35 07.0	-36.8	17.7	36 04.1	-36.5	17.9	69
70	28 44.5	-38.8	15.7	29 42.2	-38.5	15.9	30 39.9	-38.3	16.0	31 37.5	-38.0	16.2	32 35.1	-37.7	16.4	33 32.7	-37.5	16.6	34 30.2	-37.3	16.8	35 27.6	-37.0	17.0	70
71	28 05.7	-39.1	14.9	29 03.7	-38.9	15.0	30 01.6	-38.7	15.1	30 59.5	-38.4	15.3	31 57.4	-38.2	15.5	32 55.2	-38.0	15.6	33 52.9	-37.7	15.8	34 50.6	-37.4	16.0	71
72	27 26.6	-39.4	14.0	28 24.8	-39.2	14.1	29 22.9	-38.9	14.3	30 21.1	-38.8	14.4	31 19.2	-38.6	14.6	32 17.2	-38.3	14.7	33 15.2	-38.0	14.9	34 13.2	-37.8	15.0	72
73	26 47.2	-39.8	13.2	27 45.6	-39.6	13.3	28 44.0	-39.4	13.4	29 42.3	-39.1	13.5	30 40.6	-38.9	13.7	31 38.9	-38.7	13.8	32 37.2	-38.5	14.0	33 35.4	-38.3	14.1	73
74	26 07.4	-40.0	12.3	27 06.0	-39.8	12.4	28 04.6	-39.6	12.5	29 03.2	-39.5	12.7	30 01.7	-39.3	12.8	31 00.2	-39.1	12.9	31 58.7	-38.9	13.0	32 57.1	-38.6	13.2	74
75	25 27.4	-40.3	11.5	26 26.2	-40.1	11.6	27 25.0	-40.0	11.7	28 23.7	-39.7	11.8	29 22.4	-39.6	11.9	30 21.1	-39.4	12.0	31 19.8	-39.2	12.2	32 18.5	-39.1	12.3	75
76	24 47.1	-40.5	10.7	25 46.1	-40.4	10.8	26 45.0	-40.2	10.8	27 44.0	-40.1	10.9	28 42.8	-39.9	11.0	29 41.7	-39.7	11.2	30 40.6	-39.6	11.3	31 39.4	-39.4	11.4	76
77	24 06.6	-40.8	9.9	25 05.7	-40.7	9.9	26 04.8	-40.5	10.0	27 03.9	-40.4	10.1	28 02.9	-40.2	10.2	29 02.0	-40.1	10.3	30 01.0	-39.9	10.4	31 00.0	-39.8	10.5	77
78	23 25.8	-41.1	9.1	24 25.0	-40.9	9.1	25 24.3	-40.8	9.2	26 23.5	-40.7	9.3	27 22.7	-40.5	9.4	28 21.9	-40.4	9.4	29 21.1	-40.3	9.5	30 20.2	-40.1	9.6	78
79	22 44.7	-41.2	8.3	23 44.1	-41.1	8.3	24 43.5	-41.1	8.4	25 42.8	-40.9	8.5	26 42.2	-40.8	8.5	27 41.5	-40.7	8.6	28 40.8	-40.5	8.7	29 40.1	-40.4	8.8	79
80	22 03.5	-41.5	7.5	23 03.0	-41.4	7.5	24 02.4	-41.3	7.6	25 01.9	-41.2	7.7	26 01.4	-41.1	7.7	27 00.8	-41.0	7.8	28 00.3	-40.9	7.9	28 59.7	-40.8	7.9	80
81	21 22.0	-41.7	6.7	22 21.6	-41.7	6.7	23 21.1	-41.5	6.8	24 20.7	-41.4	6.9	25 20.3	-41.4	6.9	26 19.8	-41.2	7.0	27 19.4	-41.2	7.0	28 18.9	-41.0	7.1	81
82	20 40.3	-42.0	5.9	21 39.9	-41.8	6.0	22 39.6	-41.7	6.0	23 39.3	-41.7	6.1	24 38.9	-41.6	6.1	25 38.6	-41.5	6.2	26 38.2	-41.4	6.2	27 37.9	-41.3	6.3	82
83	19 58.3	-42.1	5.2	20 58.1	-42.0	5.2	21 57.9	-42.0	5.2	22 57.6	-41.9	5.3	23 57.3	-41.8	5.3	24 57.1	-41.8	5.4	25 56.8	-41.7	5.4	26 56.6	-41.7	5.4	83
84	19 16.2	-42.3	4.4	20 16.1	-42.3	4.4	21 15.9	-42.2	4.5	22 15.7	-42.1	4.5	23 15.5	-42.1	4.5	24 15.3	-42.0	4.6	25 15.1	-41.9	4.6	26 14.9	-41.9	4.6	84
85	18 33.9	-42.4	3.7	19 33.8	-42.4	3.7	20 33.7	-42.4	3.7	21 33.6	-42.4	3.7	22 33.4	-42.2	3.8	23 33.3	-42.2	3.8	24 33.2	-42.2	3.8	25 33.0	-42.1	3.8	85
86	17 51.5	-42.7	2.9	18 51.4	-42.6	2.9	19 51.3	-42.6	3.0	20 51.2	-42.5	3.0	21 51.2	-42.5	3.0	22 51.1	-42.5	3.0	23 51.0	-42.4	3.0	24 50.9	-42.4	3.1	86
87	17 08.8	-42.8	2.2	18 08.8	-42.8	2.2	19 08.7	-42.7	2.2	20 08.7	-42.7	2.2	21 08.7	-42.7	2.2	22 08.6	-42.7	2.2	23 08.6	-42.7	2.3	24 08.5	-42.6	2.3	87
88	16 26.0	-42.9	1.4	17 26.0	-42.9	1.5	18 26.0	-42.9	1.5	19 26.0	-42.9	1.5	20 26.0	-42.9	1.5	21 25.9	-42.8	1.5	22 25.9	-42.8	1.5	23 25.9	-42.8	1.5	88
89	15 43.1	-43.1	0.7	16 43.1	-43.1	0.7	17 43.1	-43.1	0.7	18 43.1	-43.1	0.7	19 43.1	-43.1	0.7	20 43.1	-43.1	0.7	21 43.1	-43.1	0.7	22 43.1	-43.1	0.8	89
90	15 00.0	-43.2	0.0	16 00.0	-43.2	0.0	17 00.0	-43.2	0.0	18 00.0	-43.2	0.0	19 00.0	-43.2	0.0	20 00.0	-43.3	0.0	21 00.0	-43.3	0.0	22 00.0	-43.3	0.0	90
	15°			16°			17°			18°			19°			20°			21°			22°			

44°, 316° L.H.A. LATITUDE SAME NAME AS DECLINATION

LATITUDE **CONTRARY** NAME TO DECLINATION — L.H.A. 44°, 316°

Dec.	15° Hc	d	Z	16° Hc	d	Z	17° Hc	d	Z	18° Hc	d	Z	19° Hc	d	Z	20° Hc	d	Z	21° Hc	d	Z	22° Hc	d	Z	Dec.
°	° ′	′	°	° ′	′	°	° ′	′	°	° ′	′	°	° ′	′	°	° ′	′	°	° ′	′	°	° ′	′	°	°
0	44 00.8	−22.0	105.0	43 44.8	−23.3	105.9	43 27.9	−24.6	106.8	43 10.0	−25.8	107.7	42 51.3	−27.0	108.6	42 31.7	−28.2	109.5	42 11.3	−29.4	110.4	41 50.0	−30.5	111.2	0
1	43 38.8	−22.9	106.3	43 21.5	−24.2	107.2	43 03.3	−25.4	108.1	42 44.2	−26.6	109.0	42 24.3	−27.8	109.8	42 03.5	−29.0	110.7	41 41.9	−30.1	111.5	41 19.5	−31.2	112.4	1
2	43 15.9	−23.7	107.6	42 57.3	−24.9	108.5	42 37.9	−26.2	109.3	42 17.6	−27.3	110.2	41 56.5	−28.5	111.0	41 34.5	−29.6	111.9	41 11.8	−30.8	112.7	40 48.3	−31.9	113.5	2
3	42 52.2	−24.6	108.8	42 32.4	−25.8	109.7	42 11.7	−26.9	110.6	41 50.3	−28.1	111.4	41 28.0	−29.3	112.2	41 04.9	−30.4	113.0	40 41.0	−31.4	113.8	40 16.4	−32.4	114.6	3
4	42 27.6	−25.3	110.1	42 06.6	−26.5	110.9	41 44.8	−27.7	111.8	41 22.2	−28.9	112.6	40 58.7	−29.9	113.4	40 34.5	−31.0	114.2	40 09.6	−32.0	114.9	39 44.0	−33.1	115.7	4
5	42 02.3	−26.1	111.3	41 40.1	−27.3	112.1	41 17.1	−28.4	112.9	40 53.3	−29.5	113.7	40 28.8	−30.6	114.5	40 03.5	−31.6	115.3	39 37.6	−32.7	116.0	39 10.9	−33.7	116.8	5
6	41 36.2	−26.9	112.5	41 12.8	−27.9	113.3	40 48.7	−29.1	114.1	40 23.8	−30.1	114.9	39 58.2	−31.2	115.7	39 31.9	−32.3	116.4	39 04.9	−33.3	117.1	38 37.2	−34.3	117.8	6
7	41 09.3	−27.5	113.7	40 44.9	−28.7	114.5	40 19.6	−29.7	115.3	39 53.7	−30.9	116.0	39 27.0	−31.9	116.8	38 59.6	−32.8	117.5	38 31.6	−33.8	118.2	38 02.9	−34.8	118.9	7
8	40 41.8	−28.3	114.9	40 16.2	−29.4	115.6	39 49.9	−30.5	116.4	39 22.8	−31.4	117.1	38 55.1	−32.4	117.9	38 26.8	−33.5	118.6	37 57.8	−34.4	119.2	37 28.1	−35.3	119.9	8
9	40 13.5	−29.0	116.0	39 46.8	−30.0	116.8	39 19.4	−31.0	117.5	38 51.4	−32.1	118.2	38 22.7	−33.1	118.9	37 53.3	−34.0	119.6	37 23.4	−34.9	120.3	36 52.8	−35.8	120.9	9
10	39 44.5	−29.6	117.2	39 16.8	−30.7	117.9	38 48.4	−31.7	118.6	38 19.3	−32.6	119.3	37 49.6	−33.6	120.0	37 19.3	−34.5	120.7	36 48.5	−35.5	121.3	36 17.0	−36.3	121.9	10
11	39 14.9	−30.3	118.3	38 46.1	−31.3	119.0	38 16.7	−32.3	119.7	37 46.7	−33.3	120.4	37 16.0	−34.1	121.0	36 44.8	−35.1	121.7	36 13.0	−35.9	122.3	35 40.7	−36.8	122.9	11
12	38 44.6	−30.9	119.4	38 14.8	−31.8	120.1	37 44.4	−32.8	120.8	37 13.4	−33.7	121.4	36 41.9	−34.7	122.1	36 09.7	−35.5	122.7	35 37.1	−36.4	123.3	35 03.9	−37.3	123.9	12
13	38 13.7	−31.5	120.5	37 43.0	−32.5	121.2	37 11.6	−33.4	121.8	36 39.7	−34.3	122.5	36 07.2	−35.2	123.1	35 34.2	−36.0	123.7	35 00.7	−36.9	124.3	34 26.6	−37.7	124.8	13
14	37 42.2	−32.1	121.6	37 10.5	−33.0	122.2	36 38.2	−33.9	122.9	36 05.4	−34.8	123.5	35 32.0	−35.6	124.1	34 58.2	−36.5	124.7	34 23.8	−37.3	125.2	33 48.9	−38.1	125.8	14
15	37 10.1	−32.6	122.6	36 37.5	−33.6	123.3	36 04.3	−34.4	123.9	35 30.6	−35.3	124.5	34 56.4	−36.2	125.1	34 21.7	−37.0	125.6	33 46.5	−37.8	126.2	33 10.8	−38.5	126.7	15
16	36 37.5	−33.2	123.7	36 03.9	−34.0	124.3	35 29.9	−35.0	124.9	34 55.3	−35.8	125.5	34 20.2	−36.6	126.0	33 44.7	−37.4	126.6	33 08.7	−38.1	127.1	32 32.3	−38.9	127.6	16
17	36 04.3	−33.7	124.7	35 29.9	−34.6	125.3	34 54.9	−35.4	125.9	34 19.5	−36.2	126.4	33 43.6	−37.0	127.0	33 07.3	−37.8	127.5	32 30.6	−38.6	128.0	31 53.4	−39.3	128.5	17
18	35 30.6	−34.2	125.7	34 55.3	−35.1	126.3	34 19.5	−35.9	126.9	33 43.3	−36.7	127.4	33 06.6	−37.4	127.9	32 29.5	−38.2	128.4	31 52.0	−38.9	128.9	31 14.1	−39.6	129.4	18
19	34 56.4	−34.7	126.8	34 20.2	−35.5	127.3	33 43.6	−36.3	127.8	33 06.6	−37.1	128.4	32 29.2	−37.9	128.9	31 51.3	−38.5	129.4	31 13.1	−39.3	129.8	30 34.5	−40.0	130.3	19
20	34 21.7	−35.2	127.7	33 44.7	−36.0	128.3	33 07.3	−36.7	128.8	32 29.5	−37.5	129.3	31 51.3	−38.2	129.8	31 12.8	−39.0	130.2	30 33.8	−39.6	130.7	29 54.5	−40.3	131.1	20
21	33 46.5	−35.7	128.7	33 08.7	−36.4	129.2	32 30.6	−37.2	129.7	31 52.0	−37.9	130.2	31 13.1	−38.6	130.7	30 33.8	−39.3	131.1	29 54.2	−40.0	131.6	29 14.2	−40.7	132.0	21
22	33 10.8	−36.0	129.7	32 32.3	−36.8	130.2	31 53.4	−37.6	130.7	31 14.1	−38.2	131.1	30 34.5	−39.0	131.6	29 54.5	−39.6	132.0	29 14.2	−40.3	132.4	28 33.5	−40.9	132.8	22
23	32 34.8	−36.6	130.6	31 55.5	−37.3	131.1	31 15.8	−37.9	131.6	30 35.9	−38.7	132.0	29 55.5	−39.3	132.5	29 14.9	−40.0	132.9	28 33.9	−40.6	133.3	27 52.6	−41.2	133.7	23
24	31 58.2	−36.9	131.6	31 18.2	−37.6	132.0	30 37.9	−38.3	132.5	29 57.2	−39.0	132.9	29 16.2	−39.6	133.3	28 34.9	−40.3	133.7	27 53.3	−40.9	134.1	27 11.4	−41.6	134.5	24
25	31 21.3	−37.3	132.5	30 40.6	−38.0	132.9	29 59.6	−38.7	133.4	29 18.2	−39.3	133.8	28 36.6	−40.0	134.2	27 54.6	−40.6	134.6	27 12.4	−41.2	134.9	26 29.8	−41.8	135.3	25
26	30 44.0	−37.7	133.4	30 02.6	−38.3	133.8	29 20.9	−39.0	134.3	28 38.9	−39.7	134.6	27 56.6	−40.3	135.0	27 14.0	−40.9	135.4	26 31.2	−41.5	135.8	25 48.0	−42.0	136.1	26
27	30 06.3	−38.0	134.3	29 24.3	−38.7	134.7	28 41.9	−39.3	135.1	27 59.2	−39.9	135.5	27 16.3	−40.6	135.9	26 33.1	−41.1	136.2	25 49.7	−41.8	136.6	25 06.0	−42.3	136.9	27
28	29 28.3	−38.4	135.2	28 45.6	−39.1	135.6	28 02.6	−39.7	136.0	27 19.3	−40.3	136.3	26 35.7	−40.8	136.7	25 52.0	−41.5	137.0	25 07.9	−42.0	137.4	24 23.7	−42.5	137.7	28
29	28 49.9	−38.8	136.1	28 06.5	−39.3	136.5	27 22.9	−40.0	136.8	26 39.0	−40.5	137.2	25 54.9	−41.1	137.5	25 10.5	−41.7	137.8	24 25.9	−42.2	138.1	23 41.2	−42.8	138.4	29
30	28 11.1	−39.0	137.0	27 27.2	−39.7	137.3	26 42.9	−40.2	137.7	25 58.5	−40.9	138.0	25 13.8	−41.4	138.3	24 28.8	−41.9	138.6	23 43.7	−42.4	138.9	22 58.4	−43.0	139.2	30
31	27 32.1	−39.4	137.8	26 47.5	−40.0	138.2	26 02.7	−40.6	138.5	25 17.6	−41.1	138.8	24 32.4	−41.7	139.1	23 46.9	−42.2	139.4	23 01.3	−42.7	139.7	22 15.4	−43.2	140.0	31
32	26 52.7	−39.7	138.7	26 07.5	−40.2	139.0	25 22.1	−40.8	139.3	24 36.5	−41.3	139.6	23 50.7	−41.8	139.9	23 04.7	−42.3	140.2	22 18.6	−42.9	140.4	21 32.2	−43.4	140.7	32
33	26 13.0	−40.0	139.5	25 27.3	−40.5	139.8	24 41.3	−41.0	140.1	23 55.2	−41.6	140.4	23 08.9	−42.1	140.7	22 22.4	−42.6	140.9	21 35.7	−43.1	141.2	20 48.8	−43.5	141.4	33
34	25 33.0	−40.2	140.3	24 46.8	−40.8	140.6	24 00.3	−41.3	140.9	23 13.6	−41.8	141.2	22 26.8	−42.4	141.5	21 39.8	−42.9	141.7	20 52.6	−43.3	141.9	20 05.3	−43.8	142.2	34
35	24 52.8	−40.5	141.2	24 06.0	−41.1	141.4	23 19.0	−41.6	141.7	22 31.8	−42.1	142.0	21 44.4	−42.5	142.2	20 56.9	−43.0	142.5	20 09.3	−43.5	142.7	19 21.5	−43.9	142.9	35
36	24 12.3	−40.8	142.0	23 24.9	−41.2	142.2	22 37.4	−41.7	142.5	21 49.7	−42.2	142.7	21 01.9	−42.7	143.0	20 13.9	−43.2	143.2	19 25.8	−43.6	143.4	18 37.6	−44.1	143.6	36
37	23 31.5	−41.0	142.8	22 43.7	−41.5	143.0	21 55.7	−42.0	143.3	21 07.5	−42.5	143.5	20 19.2	−42.9	143.7	19 30.7	−43.3	143.9	18 42.2	−43.8	144.1	17 53.5	−44.3	144.3	37
38	22 50.5	−41.2	143.6	22 02.2	−41.8	143.8	21 13.7	−42.2	144.0	20 25.0	−42.6	144.3	19 36.3	−43.1	144.5	18 47.4	−43.6	144.7	17 58.4	−44.0	144.9	17 09.2	−44.5	145.0	38
39	22 09.3	−41.5	144.3	21 20.4	−41.9	144.6	20 31.5	−42.4	144.8	19 42.4	−42.9	145.0	18 53.2	−43.3	145.2	18 03.8	−43.7	145.4	17 14.4	−44.1	145.6	16 24.8	−44.5	145.8	39
40	21 27.8	−41.7	145.1	20 38.5	−42.1	145.3	19 49.1	−42.6	145.6	18 59.5	−43.0	145.8	18 09.9	−43.4	145.9	17 20.1	−43.8	146.1	16 30.3	−44.3	146.3	15 40.3	−44.6	146.4	40
41	20 46.1	−41.9	145.9	19 56.4	−42.4	146.1	19 06.5	−42.7	146.3	18 16.5	−43.1	146.5	17 26.5	−43.6	146.7	16 36.3	−44.0	146.8	15 46.0	−44.4	147.0	14 55.7	−44.8	147.1	41
42	20 04.2	−42.1	146.7	19 14.0	−42.5	146.9	18 23.8	−43.0	147.0	17 33.4	−43.4	147.2	16 42.9	−43.8	147.4	15 52.3	−44.2	147.5	15 01.6	−44.5	147.7	14 10.9	−44.9	147.8	42
43	19 22.1	−42.2	147.4	18 31.5	−42.6	147.6	17 40.8	−43.1	147.8	16 50.0	−43.5	147.9	15 59.1	−43.9	148.1	15 08.1	−44.2	148.2	14 17.1	−44.7	148.4	13 26.0	−45.1	148.5	43
44	18 39.9	−42.5	148.2	17 48.9	−42.9	148.3	16 57.7	−43.2	148.5	16 06.5	−43.6	148.7	15 15.2	−44.0	148.8	14 23.9	−44.4	148.9	13 32.4	−44.7	149.1	12 40.9	−45.1	149.2	44
45	17 57.4	−42.6	148.9	17 06.0	−43.0	149.1	16 14.5	−43.4	149.2	15 22.9	−43.8	149.4	14 31.2	−44.1	149.5	13 39.5	−44.5	149.6	12 47.7	−44.9	149.8	11 55.8	−45.2	149.9	45
46	17 14.8	−42.8	149.7	16 23.0	−43.2	149.8	15 31.1	−43.5	149.9	14 39.1	−43.9	150.1	13 47.1	−44.3	150.2	12 55.0	−44.6	150.3	12 02.8	−44.9	150.4	11 10.6	−45.3	150.5	46
47	16 32.0	−42.9	150.4	15 39.8	−43.3	150.5	14 47.6	−43.7	150.7	13 55.2	−44.0	150.8	13 02.8	−44.3	150.9	12 10.4	−44.7	151.0	11 17.9	−45.1	151.1	10 25.3	−45.4	151.2	47
48	15 49.1	−43.1	151.1	14 56.5	−43.4	151.2	14 03.9	−43.8	151.4	13 11.2	−44.1	151.5	12 18.5	−44.5	151.6	11 25.7	−44.8	151.7	10 32.8	−45.1	151.8	9 39.9	−45.4	151.9	48
49	15 06.0	−43.2	151.8	14 13.1	−43.5	152.0	13 20.1	−43.9	152.1	12 27.1	−44.2	152.2	11 34.0	−44.6	152.3	10 40.9	−44.9	152.4	9 47.7	−45.2	152.5	8 54.5	−45.6	152.5	49
50	14 22.8	−43.3	152.6	13 29.6	−43.7	152.7	12 36.2	−44.0	152.8	11 42.9	−44.4	152.9	10 49.4	−44.6	153.0	9 56.0	−45.0	153.0	9 02.5	−45.3	153.1	8 08.9	−45.6	153.2	50
51	13 39.5	−43.5	153.3	12 45.9	−43.8	153.4	11 52.2	−44.1	153.5	10 58.5	−44.4	153.6	10 04.8	−44.8	153.6	9 11.0	−45.0	153.7	8 17.2	−45.4	153.8	7 23.3	−45.6	153.8	51
52	12 56.0	−43.5	154.0	12 02.1	−43.9	154.1	11 08.1	−44.2	154.2	10 14.1	−44.5	154.2	9 20.0	−44.8	154.3	8 26.0	−45.2	154.4	7 31.8	−45.4	154.4	6 37.7	−45.7	154.5	52
53	12 12.5	−43.7	154.7	11 18.2	−44.0	154.8	10 23.9	−44.3	154.8	9 29.6	−44.6	154.9	8 35.2	−44.9	155.0	7 40.8	−45.1	155.0	6 46.4	−45.4	155.1	5 52.0	−45.8	155.1	53
54	11 28.8	−43.8	155.4	10 34.2	−44.1	155.5	9 39.6	−44.3	155.5	8 45.0	−44.7	155.6	7 50.3	−44.9	155.7	6 55.7	−45.3	155.7	6 01.0	−45.5	155.8	5 06.2	−45.7	155.8	54
55	10 45.0	−43.9	156.1	9 50.1	−44.1	156.1	8 55.3	−44.5	156.2	8 00.3	−44.7	156.3	7 05.4	−45.0	156.3	6 10.4	−45.2	156.4	5 15.5	−45.6	156.4	4 20.5	−45.9	156.4	55
56	10 01.1	−43.9	156.8	9 06.0	−44.3	156.8	8 10.8	−44.5	156.9	7 15.6	−44.8	156.9	6 20.4	−45.1	157.0	5 25.2	−45.4	157.0	4 29.9	−45.6	157.1	3 34.6	−45.8	157.1	56
57	9 17.2	−44.1	157.5	8 21.7	−44.3	157.5	7 26.3	−44.6	157.6	6 30.8	−44.8	157.6	5 35.3	−45.1	157.7	4 39.8	−45.3	157.7	3 44.3	−45.6	157.7	2 48.8	−45.9	157.7	57
58	8 33.1	−44.1	158.1	7 37.4	−44.3	158.2	6 41.7	−44.6	158.2	5 46.0	−44.9	158.3	4 50.2	−45.1	158.3	3 54.5	−45.4	158.3	2 58.7	−45.6	158.4	2 02.9	−45.9	158.4	58
59	7 49.0	−44.1	158.8	6 53.1	−44.5	158.9	5 57.1	−44.7	158.9	5 01.1	−44.9	159.0	4 05.1	−45.2	159.0	3 09.1	−45.4	159.0	2 13.1	−45.7	159.0	1 17.0	−45.8	159.0	59
60	7 04.9	−44.3	159.5	6 08.6	−44.4	159.6	5 12.4	−44.7	159.6	4 16.2	−45.0	159.6	3 19.9	−45.2	159.6	2 23.7	−45.5	159.7	1 27.4	−45.7	159.7	0 31.2	−45.9	159.7	60
61	6 20.6	−44.3	160.2	5 24.2	−44.6	160.2	4 27.7	−44.8	160.3	3 31.2	−45.0	160.3	2 34.7	−45.2	160.3	1 38.2	−45.4	160.3	0 41.7	−45.6	160.3	0 14.7	+45.9	19.7	61
62	5 36.3	−44.3	160.9	4 39.6	−44.5	160.9	3 42.9	−44.7	160.9	2 46.2	−45.0	160.9	1 49.5	−45.2	161.0	0 52.8	−45.5	161.0	0 03.9	+45.7	19.0	1 00.6	+45.9	19.0	62
63	4 52.0	−44.4	161.5	3 55.1	−44.6	161.6	2 58.2	−44.9	161.6	2 01.2	−45.0	161.6	1 04.3	−45.3	161.6	0 07.3	−45.4	161.6	0 49.6	+45.7	18.4	1 46.5	+45.9	18.4	63
64	4 07.6	−44.4	162.2	3 10.5	−44.6	162.2	2 13.3	−44.8	162.3	1 16.2	−45.0	162.3	0 19.0	−45.2	162.3	0 38.1	+45.5	17.7	1 35.3	+45.6	17.7	2 32.4	+45.9	17.7	64
65	3 23.2	−44.4	162.9	2 25.9	−44.7	162.9	1 28.5	−44.8	162.9	0 31.2	−45.1	162.9	0 26.2	+45.2	17.1	1 23.6	+45.4	17.1	2 20.9	+45.6	17.1	3 18.3	+45.8	17.1	65
66	2 38.8	−44.5	163.6	1 41.2	−44.6	163.6	0 43.7	−44.9	163.6	0 13.9	+45.0	16.4	1 11.4	+45.3	16.4	2 09.0	+45.4	16.4	3 06.5	+45.7	16.4	4 04.1	+45.8	16.5	66
67	1 54.3	−44.5	164.2	0 56.6	−44.7	164.2	0 01.2	+44.8	15.7	0 58.9	+45.1	15.8	1 56.7	+45.2	15.8	2 54.4	+45.4	15.8	3 52.2	+45.5	15.8	4 49.9	+45.7	15.8	67
68	1 09.8	−44.4	164.9	0 11.9	−44.7	164.9	0 46.0	+44.9	15.1	1 44.0	+45.0	15.1	2 41.9	+45.2	15.1	3 39.8	+45.4	15.1	4 37.7	+45.6	15.1	5 35.6	+45.8	15.2	68
69	0 25.4	−44.5	165.6	0 32.8	+44.6	14.4	1 30.9	+44.8	14.4	2 29.0	+45.0	14.4	3 27.1	+45.1	14.4	4 25.2	+45.3	14.5	5 23.3	+45.5	14.5	6 21.4	+45.6	14.5	69
70	0 19.1	+44.5	13.7	1 17.4	+44.7	13.7	2 15.7	+44.8	13.8	3 14.0	+44.9	13.8	4 12.2	+45.2	13.8	5 10.5	+45.3	13.8	6 08.8	+45.4	13.8	7 07.0	+45.7	13.9	70
71	1 03.6	+44.5	13.1	2 02.1	+44.6	13.1	3 00.5	+44.8	13.1	3 58.9	+45.0	13.1	4 57.4	+45.1	13.1	5 55.8	+45.3	13.1	6 54.2	+45.4	13.2	7 52.7	+45.5	13.2	71
72	1 48.1	+44.5	12.4	2 46.7	+44.6	12.4	3 45.3	+44.7	12.4	4 43.9	+44.9	12.4	5 42.5	+45.0	12.5	6 41.1	+45.1	12.5	7 39.6	+45.4	12.5	8 38.2	+45.5	12.5	72
73	2 32.6	+44.4	11.7	3 31.3	+44.6	11.7	4 30.0	+44.8	11.8	5 28.8	+44.8	11.8	6 27.5	+45.0	11.8	7 26.2	+45.2	11.8	8 25.0	+45.2	11.8	9 23.7	+45.4	11.9	73
74	3 17.0	+44.4	11.1	4 15.9	+44.5	11.1	5 14.8	+44.6	11.1	6 13.6	+44.8	11.1	7 12.5	+45.0	11.1	8 11.4	+45.1	11.2	9 10.2	+45.2	11.2	10 09.1	+45.3	11.2	74
75	4 01.4	+44.4	10.4	5 00.4	+44.5	10.4	5 59.4	+44.7	10.4	6 58.4	+44.8	10.4	7 57.5	+44.8	10.5	8 56.5	+44.9	10.5	9 55.4	+45.2	10.5	10 54.4	+45.3	10.6	75
76	4 45.8	+44.3	9.7	5 44.9	+44.5	9.7	6 44.1	+44.5	9.7	7 43.2	+44.7	9.8	8 42.3	+44.8	9.8	9 41.4	+45.0	9.8	10 40.6	+45.0	9.8	11 39.7	+45.1	9.9	76
77	5 30.1	+44.3	9.0	6 29.4	+44.4	9.0	7 28.6	+44.5	9.1	8 27.9	+44.6	9.1	9 27.1	+44.8	9.1	10 26.4	+44.8	9.1	11 25.6	+44.9	9.2	12 24.8	+45.1	9.2	77
78	6 14.4	+44.3	8.4	7 13.8	+44.3	8.4	8 13.1	+44.5	8.4	9 12.5	+44.5	8.4	10 11.9	+44.6	8.4	11 11.2	+44.7	8.5	12 10.5	+44.9	8.5	13 09.9	+44.9	8.5	78
79	6 58.7	+44.1	7.7	7 58.1	+44.3	7.7	8 57.6	+44.4	7.7	9 57.0	+44.5	7.7	10 56.5	+44.5	7.8	11 55.9	+44.7	7.8	12 55.4	+44.7	7.8	13 54.8	+44.9	7.8	79
80	7 42.9	+44.1	7.0	8 42.4	+44.2	7.0	9 42.0	+44.2	7.0	10 41.5	+44.4	7.1	11 41.0	+44.5	7.1	12 40.6	+44.5	7.1	13 40.1	+44.6	7.1	14 39.7	+44.7	7.2	80
81	8 27.0	+44.0	6.3	9 26.6	+44.1	6.3	10 26.2	+44.2	6.3	11 25.9	+44.2	6.4	12 25.5	+44.3	6.4	13 25.1	+44.4	6.4	14 24.7	+44.5	6.4	15 24.4	+44.5	6.5	81
82	9 11.0	+44.0	5.6	10 10.7	+44.1	5.6	11 10.4	+44.1	5.7	12 10.1	+44.2	5.7	13 09.8	+44.3	5.7	14 09.5	+44.4	5.7	15 09.2	+44.4	5.7	16 08.9	+44.5	5.8	82
83	9 55.0	+43.9	4.9	10 54.8	+43.9	4.9	11 54.5	+44.0	5.0	12 54.3	+44.1	5.0	13 54.1	+44.1	5.0	14 53.9	+44.1	5.0	15 53.6	+44.3	5.0	16 53.4	+44.3	5.1	83
84	10 38.9	+43.8	4.2	11 38.7	+43.8	4.3	12 38.5	+43.9	4.3	13 38.4	+43.9	4.3	14 38.2	+44.0	4.3	15 38.0	+44.1	4.3	16 37.9	+44.1	4.3	17 37.7	+44.1	4.4	84
85	11 22.7	+43.7	3.5	12 22.5	+43.8	3.6	13 22.4	+43.8	3.6	14 22.3	+43.8	3.6	15 22.2	+43.9	3.6	16 22.1	+43.9	3.6	17 22.0	+43.9	3.6	18 21.8	+44.0	3.7	85
86	12 06.4	+43.5	2.8	13 06.3	+43.6	2.9	14 06.2	+43.7	2.9	15 06.1	+43.7	2.9	16 06.1	+43.7	2.9	17 06.0	+43.7	2.9	18 05.9	+43.8	2.9	19 05.8	+43.8	2.9	86
87	12 49.9	+43.5	2.1	13 49.9	+43.5	2.1	14 49.9	+43.5	2.2	15 49.8	+43.6	2.2	16 49.8	+43.6	2.2	17 49.7	+43.6	2.2	18 49.7	+43.6	2.2	19 49.6	+43.7	2.2	87
88	13 33.4	+43.4	1.4	14 33.4	+43.4	1.4	15 33.4	+43.4	1.4	16 33.4	+43.4	1.4	17 33.3	+43.5	1.5	18 33.3	+43.4	1.5	19 33.3	+43.4	1.5	20 33.3	+43.4	1.5	88
89	14 16.8	+43.2	0.7	15 16.8	+43.2	0.7	16 16.8	+43.2	0.7	17 16.8	+43.2	0.7	18 16.8	+43.2	0.7	19 16.7	+43.3	0.7	20 16.7	+43.3	0.7	21 16.7	+43.3	0.7	89
90	15 00.0	+43.1	0.0	16 00.0	+43.1	0.0	17 00.0	+43.1	0.0	18 00.0	+43.1	0.0	19 00.0	+43.1	0.0	20 00.0	+43.1	0.0	21 00.0	+43.1	0.0	22 00.0	+43.1	0.0	90
	15°			16°			17°			18°			19°			20°			21°			22°			

S. Lat. {L.H.A. greater than 180° ....Zn=180°−Z; L.H.A. less than 180°...........Zn=180°+Z

LATITUDE **SAME** NAME AS DECLINATION — L.H.A. 136°, 224°

91

45°, 315° L.H.A. LATITUDE SAME NAME AS DECLINATION N. Lat. {L.H.A. greater than 180° .....Zn=Z; L.H.A. less than 180°............Zn=360°–Z

Dec.	15° Hc	d	Z	16° Hc	d	Z	17° Hc	d	Z	18° Hc	d	Z	19° Hc	d	Z	20° Hc	d	Z	21° Hc	d	Z	22° Hc	d	Z	Dec.
°	° ′	′	°	° ′	′	°	° ′	′	°	° ′	′	°	° ′	′	°	° ′	′	°	° ′	′	°	° ′	′	°	°
0	43 04.8	+20.8	104.5	42 49.3	+22.1	105.4	42 32.9	+23.4	106.3	42 15.6	+24.7	107.2	41 57.5	+25.8	108.0	41 38.5	+27.1	108.9	41 18.6	+28.3	109.7	40 58.0	+29.4	110.5	0
1	43 25.6	+20.0	103.2	43 11.4	+21.3	104.1	42 56.3	+22.6	105.0	42 40.3	+23.8	105.9	42 23.3	+25.2	106.8	42 05.6	+26.3	107.7	41 46.9	+27.5	108.5	41 27.4	+28.7	109.4	1
2	43 45.6	+19.0	101.9	43 32.7	+20.4	102.9	43 18.9	+21.7	103.8	43 04.1	+23.0	104.7	42 48.5	+24.2	105.6	42 31.9	+25.5	106.5	42 14.4	+26.8	107.3	41 56.1	+28.0	108.2	2
3	44 04.6	+18.1	100.6	43 53.1	+19.5	101.6	43 40.6	+20.8	102.5	43 27.1	+22.2	103.4	43 12.7	+23.5	104.3	42 57.4	+24.8	105.2	42 41.2	+26.0	106.1	42 24.1	+27.2	107.0	3
4	44 22.7	+17.3	99.3	44 12.6	+18.6	100.2	44 01.4	+20.0	101.2	43 49.3	+21.3	102.1	43 36.2	+22.6	103.1	43 22.2	+23.9	104.0	43 07.2	+25.2	104.9	42 51.3	+26.5	105.8	4
5	44 40.0	+16.2	97.9	44 31.2	+17.6	98.9	44 21.4	+19.0	99.9	44 10.6	+20.4	100.8	43 58.8	+21.8	101.8	43 46.1	+23.1	102.7	43 32.4	+24.4	103.7	43 17.8	+25.6	104.6	5
6	44 56.2	+15.3	96.6	44 48.8	+16.7	97.6	44 40.4	+18.1	98.5	44 31.0	+19.5	99.5	44 20.6	+20.8	100.5	44 09.2	+22.2	101.4	43 56.8	+23.5	102.4	43 43.4	+24.9	103.3	6
7	45 11.5	+14.3	95.2	45 05.5	+15.7	96.2	44 58.5	+17.2	97.2	44 50.5	+18.5	98.2	44 41.4	+20.0	99.2	44 31.4	+21.3	100.1	44 20.3	+22.7	101.1	44 08.3	+23.9	102.1	7
8	45 25.8	+13.2	93.8	45 21.2	+14.8	94.8	45 15.7	+16.1	95.8	45 09.0	+17.6	96.8	45 01.4	+19.0	97.8	44 52.7	+20.4	98.8	44 43.0	+21.7	99.8	44 32.2	+23.1	100.8	8
9	45 39.0	+12.3	92.4	45 36.0	+13.7	93.5	45 31.8	+15.2	94.5	45 26.6	+16.6	95.5	45 20.4	+18.0	96.5	45 13.1	+19.4	97.5	45 04.7	+20.8	98.5	44 55.3	+22.3	99.5	9
10	45 51.3	+11.2	91.0	45 49.7	+12.7	92.1	45 47.0	+14.2	93.1	45 43.2	+15.6	94.1	45 38.4	+17.1	95.1	45 32.5	+18.5	96.1	45 25.5	+19.9	97.2	45 17.6	+21.2	98.2	10
11	46 02.5	+10.2	89.6	46 02.4	+11.6	90.7	46 01.2	+13.1	91.7	45 58.8	+14.6	92.7	45 55.5	+16.0	93.8	45 51.0	+17.5	94.8	45 45.4	+19.0	95.8	45 38.8	+20.4	96.8	11
12	46 12.7	+9.1	88.2	46 14.0	+10.6	89.2	46 14.3	+12.1	90.3	46 13.4	+13.6	91.3	46 11.5	+15.1	92.4	46 08.5	+16.5	93.4	46 04.4	+17.9	94.4	45 59.2	+19.4	95.5	12
13	46 21.8	+8.0	86.8	46 24.6	+9.6	87.8	46 26.4	+11.0	88.9	46 27.0	+12.5	89.9	46 26.6	+14.0	91.0	46 25.0	+15.5	92.0	46 22.3	+17.0	93.1	46 18.6	+18.4	94.1	13
14	46 29.8	+7.0	85.3	46 34.2	+8.4	86.4	46 37.4	+10.0	87.4	46 39.5	+11.5	88.5	46 40.6	+12.9	89.6	46 40.5	+14.4	90.6	46 39.3	+15.9	91.7	46 37.0	+17.4	92.7	14
15	46 36.8	+5.8	83.9	46 42.6	+7.4	84.9	46 47.4	+8.8	86.0	46 51.0	+10.4	87.1	46 53.5	+11.9	88.1	46 54.9	+13.4	89.2	46 55.2	+14.9	90.3	46 54.4	+16.3	91.3	15
16	46 42.6	+4.8	82.4	46 50.0	+6.2	83.5	46 56.2	+7.8	84.5	47 01.4	+9.2	85.6	47 05.4	+10.8	86.7	47 08.3	+12.3	87.8	47 10.1	+13.8	88.8	47 10.7	+15.3	89.9	16
17	46 47.4	+3.6	81.0	46 56.2	+5.2	82.0	47 04.0	+6.6	83.1	47 10.6	+8.2	84.2	47 16.2	+9.7	85.2	47 20.6	+11.2	86.3	47 23.9	+12.7	87.4	47 26.0	+14.3	88.5	17
18	46 51.0	+2.5	79.5	47 01.4	+4.0	80.6	47 10.6	+5.6	81.6	47 18.8	+7.1	82.7	47 25.9	+8.6	83.8	47 31.8	+10.1	84.9	47 36.6	+11.6	86.0	47 40.3	+13.1	87.1	18
19	46 53.5	+1.4	78.1	47 05.4	+2.9	79.1	47 16.2	+4.4	80.2	47 25.9	+5.9	81.2	47 34.5	+7.4	82.3	47 41.9	+9.0	83.4	47 48.2	+10.5	84.5	47 53.4	+12.0	85.6	19
20	46 54.9	+0.3	76.6	47 08.3	+1.8	77.6	47 20.6	+3.3	78.7	47 31.8	+4.8	79.8	47 41.9	+6.3	80.8	47 50.9	+7.8	81.9	47 58.7	+9.4	83.0	48 05.4	+11.0	84.1	20
21	46 55.2	-0.8	75.1	47 10.1	+0.6	76.2	47 23.9	+2.1	77.2	47 36.6	+3.7	78.3	47 48.2	+5.2	79.4	47 58.7	+6.7	80.5	48 08.1	+8.3	81.6	48 16.4	+9.7	82.7	21
22	46 54.4	-2.0	73.7	47 10.7	-0.5	74.7	47 26.0	+1.0	75.7	47 40.3	+2.5	76.8	47 53.4	+4.0	77.9	48 05.4	+5.6	79.0	48 16.4	+7.0	80.1	48 26.1	+8.6	81.2	22
23	46 52.4	-3.1	72.2	47 10.2	-1.6	73.2	47 27.0	-0.1	74.3	47 42.8	+1.3	75.3	47 57.4	+2.9	76.4	48 11.0	+4.4	77.5	48 23.4	+5.9	78.6	48 34.7	+7.5	79.7	23
24	46 49.3	-4.1	70.7	47 08.6	-2.7	71.8	47 26.9	-1.3	72.8	47 44.1	+0.2	73.8	48 00.3	+1.7	74.9	48 15.4	+3.2	76.0	48 29.3	+4.8	77.1	48 42.2	+6.3	78.2	24
25	46 45.2	-5.3	69.3	47 05.9	-3.9	70.3	47 25.6	-2.4	71.3	47 44.3	-0.9	72.4	48 02.0	+0.5	73.4	48 18.6	+2.0	74.5	48 34.1	+3.6	75.6	48 48.5	+5.1	76.7	25
26	46 39.9	-6.4	67.8	47 02.0	-5.0	68.8	47 23.2	-3.5	69.8	47 43.4	-2.1	70.9	48 02.5	-0.6	71.9	48 20.6	+0.9	73.0	48 37.7	+2.3	74.1	48 53.6	+3.9	75.2	26
27	46 33.5	-7.5	66.4	46 57.0	-6.0	67.4	47 19.7	-4.7	68.4	47 41.3	-3.3	69.4	48 01.9	-1.8	70.4	48 21.5	-0.3	71.5	48 40.0	+1.2	72.5	48 57.5	+2.7	73.6	27
28	46 26.0	-8.6	64.9	46 51.0	-7.2	65.9	47 15.0	-5.8	66.9	47 38.0	-4.3	67.9	48 00.1	-2.9	68.9	48 21.2	-1.5	70.0	48 41.2	0.0	71.0	49 00.2	+1.5	72.1	28
29	46 17.4	-9.6	63.5	46 43.8	-8.3	64.5	47 09.2	-6.9	65.4	47 33.7	-5.6	66.4	47 57.2	-4.1	67.4	48 19.7	-2.7	68.5	48 41.2	-1.2	69.5	49 01.7	+0.3	70.6	29
30	46 07.8	-10.7	62.1	46 35.5	-9.4	63.0	47 02.3	-8.1	64.0	47 28.1	-6.6	64.9	47 53.1	-5.3	65.9	48 17.0	-3.8	67.0	48 40.0	-2.4	68.0	49 02.0	-0.9	69.1	30
31	45 57.1	-11.7	60.7	46 26.1	-10.4	61.6	46 54.2	-9.1	62.5	47 21.5	-7.8	63.5	47 47.8	-6.4	64.5	48 13.2	-5.0	65.5	48 37.6	-3.5	66.5	49 01.1	-2.2	67.5	31
32	45 45.4	-12.8	59.3	46 15.7	-11.5	60.2	46 45.1	-10.2	61.1	47 13.7	-8.9	62.0	47 41.4	-7.5	63.0	48 08.2	-6.2	64.0	48 34.1	-4.8	65.0	48 58.9	-3.3	66.0	32
33	45 32.6	-13.8	57.9	46 04.2	-12.6	58.7	46 34.9	-11.3	59.6	47 04.8	-10.0	60.6	47 33.9	-8.7	61.5	48 02.0	-7.3	62.5	48 29.3	-5.9	63.5	48 55.6	-4.5	64.5	33
34	45 18.8	-14.7	56.5	45 51.6	-13.6	57.3	46 23.6	-12.3	58.2	46 54.8	-11.0	59.1	47 25.2	-9.8	60.0	47 54.7	-8.4	61.0	48 23.4	-7.1	62.0	48 51.1	-5.7	63.0	34
35	45 04.1	-15.8	55.1	45 38.0	-14.5	55.9	46 11.3	-13.4	56.8	46 43.8	-12.2	57.7	47 15.4	-10.8	58.6	47 46.3	-9.6	59.5	48 16.3	-8.3	60.5	48 45.4	-6.9	61.5	35
36	44 48.3	-16.7	53.7	45 23.5	-15.6	54.5	45 57.9	-14.4	55.4	46 31.6	-13.2	56.2	47 04.6	-12.0	57.1	47 36.7	-10.7	58.1	48 08.0	-9.3	59.0	48 38.5	-8.0	60.0	36
37	44 31.6	-17.7	52.4	45 07.9	-16.6	53.2	45 43.5	-15.4	54.0	46 18.4	-14.2	54.8	46 52.6	-13.0	55.7	47 26.0	-11.8	56.6	47 58.7	-10.6	57.5	48 30.5	-9.3	58.5	37
38	44 13.9	-18.6	51.0	44 51.3	-17.5	51.8	45 28.1	-16.4	52.6	46 04.2	-15.3	53.4	46 39.6	-14.1	54.3	47 14.2	-12.8	55.2	47 48.1	-11.6	56.1	48 21.2	-10.3	57.0	38
39	43 55.3	-19.5	49.7	44 33.8	-18.4	50.5	45 11.7	-17.4	51.2	45 48.9	-16.2	52.0	46 25.5	-15.1	52.9	47 01.4	-14.0	53.7	47 36.5	-12.7	54.6	48 10.9	-11.5	55.5	39
40	43 35.8	-20.4	48.4	44 15.4	-19.4	49.1	44 54.3	-18.3	49.9	45 32.7	-17.3	50.7	46 10.4	-16.1	51.5	46 47.4	-15.0	52.3	47 23.8	-13.8	53.1	47 59.4	-12.6	54.0	40
41	43 15.4	-21.2	47.1	43 56.0	-20.3	47.8	44 36.0	-19.2	48.5	45 15.4	-18.2	49.3	45 54.3	-17.2	50.1	46 32.4	-16.0	50.9	47 10.0	-14.9	51.7	47 46.8	-13.7	52.6	41
42	42 54.2	-22.1	45.8	43 35.7	-21.1	46.5	44 16.8	-20.2	47.2	44 57.2	-19.1	47.9	45 37.1	-18.1	48.7	46 16.4	-17.0	49.5	46 55.1	-16.0	50.3	47 33.1	-14.8	51.1	42
43	42 32.1	-22.9	44.6	43 14.6	-22.0	45.2	43 56.6	-21.1	45.9	44 38.1	-20.1	46.6	45 19.0	-19.0	47.3	45 59.4	-18.0	48.1	46 39.1	-16.9	48.9	47 18.3	-15.9	49.7	43
44	42 09.2	-23.8	43.3	42 52.6	-22.9	44.0	43 35.5	-21.9	44.6	44 18.0	-21.0	45.3	45 00.0	-20.0	46.0	45 41.4	-19.0	46.7	46 22.2	-18.0	47.5	47 02.4	-16.9	48.3	44
45	41 45.4	-24.5	42.1	42 29.7	-23.6	42.7	43 13.6	-22.8	43.3	43 57.0	-21.8	44.0	44 40.0	-21.0	44.7	45 22.4	-20.0	45.4	46 04.2	-18.9	46.1	46 45.5	-17.9	46.9	45
46	41 20.9	-25.3	40.9	42 06.1	-24.5	41.5	42 50.8	-23.5	42.1	43 35.2	-22.7	42.7	44 19.0	-21.8	43.4	45 02.4	-20.9	44.0	45 45.3	-19.9	44.7	46 27.6	-18.9	45.5	46
47	40 55.6	-26.0	39.7	41 41.6	-25.2	40.2	42 27.3	-24.4	40.8	43 12.5	-23.6	41.4	43 57.2	-22.7	42.1	44 41.5	-21.7	42.7	45 25.4	-20.9	43.4	46 08.7	-19.9	44.1	47
48	40 29.6	-26.7	38.5	41 16.4	-26.0	39.0	42 02.9	-25.2	39.6	42 48.9	-24.4	40.2	43 34.5	-23.5	40.8	44 19.8	-22.7	41.4	45 04.5	-21.7	42.1	45 48.8	-20.8	42.8	48
49	40 02.9	-27.5	37.3	40 50.4	-26.7	37.8	41 37.7	-26.0	38.4	42 24.5	-25.1	38.9	43 11.0	-24.3	39.5	43 57.1	-23.5	40.1	44 42.8	-22.7	40.8	45 28.0	-21.8	41.4	49
50	39 35.4	-28.1	36.1	40 23.7	-27.4	36.6	41 11.7	-26.7	37.2	41 59.4	-26.0	37.7	42 46.7	-25.2	38.3	43 33.6	-24.4	38.8	44 20.1	-23.5	39.5	45 06.2	-22.6	40.1	50
51	39 07.3	-28.8	35.0	39 56.3	-28.1	35.5	40 45.0	-27.4	36.0	41 33.4	-26.6	36.5	42 21.5	-25.9	37.0	43 09.2	-25.1	37.6	43 56.6	-24.4	38.2	44 43.6	-23.6	38.8	51
52	38 38.5	-29.4	33.9	39 28.2	-28.7	34.3	40 17.6	-28.1	34.8	41 06.8	-27.5	35.3	41 55.6	-26.7	35.8	42 44.1	-26.0	36.3	43 32.2	-25.2	36.9	44 20.0	-24.4	37.5	52
53	38 09.1	-30.0	32.8	38 59.5	-29.5	33.2	39 49.5	-28.8	33.6	40 39.3	-28.1	34.1	41 28.9	-27.5	34.6	42 18.1	-26.7	35.1	43 07.0	-26.0	35.7	43 55.6	-25.3	36.2	53
54	37 39.1	-30.7	31.7	38 30.0	-30.0	32.1	39 20.7	-29.4	32.5	40 11.2	-28.8	33.0	41 01.4	-28.1	33.4	41 51.4	-27.5	33.9	42 41.0	-26.8	34.4	43 30.3	-26.0	35.0	54
55	37 08.4	-31.2	30.6	38 00.0	-30.7	31.0	38 51.3	-30.1	31.4	39 42.4	-29.5	31.8	40 33.3	-28.9	32.3	41 23.9	-28.2	32.7	42 14.2	-27.5	33.2	43 04.3	-26.9	33.7	55
56	36 37.2	-31.8	29.5	37 29.3	-31.2	29.9	38 21.2	-30.6	30.3	39 12.9	-30.1	30.7	40 04.4	-29.5	31.1	40 55.7	-28.9	31.6	41 46.7	-28.3	32.0	42 37.4	-27.6	32.5	56
57	36 05.4	-32.3	28.5	36 58.1	-31.8	28.8	37 50.6	-31.3	29.2	38 42.8	-30.7	29.6	39 34.9	-30.2	30.0	40 26.8	-29.6	30.4	41 18.4	-29.0	30.8	42 09.8	-28.4	31.3	57
58	35 33.1	-32.9	27.4	36 26.3	-32.4	27.8	37 19.3	-31.9	28.1	38 12.1	-31.3	28.5	39 04.7	-30.8	28.9	39 57.2	-30.3	29.3	40 49.4	-29.6	29.7	41 41.4	-29.0	30.1	58
59	35 00.2	-33.4	26.4	35 53.9	-32.9	26.7	36 47.4	-32.4	27.0	37 40.8	-32.0	27.4	38 33.9	-31.4	27.8	39 26.9	-30.8	28.1	40 19.8	-30.4	28.5	41 12.4	-29.8	29.0	59
60	34 26.8	-33.8	25.4	35 21.0	-33.4	25.7	36 15.0	-33.0	26.0	37 08.8	-32.5	26.3	38 02.5	-32.0	26.7	38 56.1	-31.5	27.0	39 49.4	-31.0	27.4	40 42.6	-30.5	27.8	60
61	33 53.0	-34.4	24.4	34 47.6	-34.0	24.7	35 42.0	-33.5	25.0	36 36.3	-33.0	25.3	37 30.5	-32.5	25.6	38 24.6	-32.1	25.9	39 18.4	-31.6	26.3	40 12.1	-31.1	26.7	61
62	33 18.6	-34.8	23.4	34 13.6	-34.4	23.7	35 08.5	-33.9	24.0	36 03.3	-33.5	24.2	36 58.0	-33.2	24.5	37 52.5	-32.7	24.9	38 46.8	-32.2	25.2	39 41.0	-31.7	25.6	62
63	32 43.8	-35.2	22.4	33 39.2	-34.8	22.7	34 34.6	-34.5	22.9	35 29.8	-34.1	23.2	36 24.8	-33.6	23.5	37 19.8	-33.2	23.8	38 14.6	-32.8	24.1	39 09.3	-32.3	24.5	63
64	32 08.6	-35.7	21.5	33 04.4	-35.3	21.7	34 00.1	-35.0	22.0	34 55.7	-34.6	22.2	35 51.2	-34.2	22.5	36 46.6	-33.8	22.8	37 41.8	-33.3	23.1	38 37.0	-33.0	23.4	64
65	31 32.9	-36.1	20.5	32 29.1	-35.8	20.7	33 25.1	-35.4	21.0	34 21.1	-35.0	21.2	35 17.0	-34.7	21.5	36 12.8	-34.3	21.7	37 08.5	-33.9	22.0	38 04.0	-33.5	22.3	65
66	30 56.8	-36.4	19.6	31 53.3	-36.1	19.8	32 49.7	-35.8	20.0	33 46.1	-35.5	20.2	34 42.3	-35.1	20.5	35 38.5	-34.8	20.7	36 34.6	-34.5	21.0	37 30.5	-34.0	21.3	66
67	30 20.4	-36.9	18.7	31 17.2	-36.6	18.9	32 13.9	-36.2	19.1	33 10.6	-36.0	19.3	34 07.2	-35.6	19.5	35 03.7	-35.3	19.7	36 00.1	-34.9	20.0	36 56.5	-34.6	20.2	67
68	29 43.5	-37.3	17.8	30 40.6	-37.0	17.9	31 37.7	-36.7	18.1	32 34.6	-36.3	18.3	33 31.6	-36.1	18.5	34 28.4	-35.7	18.7	35 25.2	-35.4	19.0	36 21.9	-35.1	19.2	68
69	29 06.2	-37.5	16.9	30 03.6	-37.3	17.0	31 01.0	-37.1	17.2	31 58.3	-36.8	17.4	32 55.5	-36.5	17.6	33 52.7	-36.2	17.8	34 49.8	-35.9	18.0	35 46.8	-35.6	18.2	69
70	28 28.7	-38.0	16.0	29 26.3	-37.7	16.1	30 23.9	-37.4	16.3	31 21.5	-37.2	16.5	32 19.0	-36.9	16.6	33 16.5	-36.6	16.8	34 13.9	-36.4	17.0	35 11.2	-36.0	17.2	70
71	27 50.7	-38.3	15.1	28 48.6	-38.0	15.2	29 46.5	-37.8	15.4	30 44.3	-37.5	15.5	31 42.1	-37.3	15.7	32 39.9	-37.1	15.9	33 37.5	-36.7	16.0	34 35.2	-36.5	16.2	71
72	27 12.4	-38.5	14.2	28 10.6	-38.4	14.4	29 08.7	-38.1	14.5	30 06.8	-37.9	14.6	31 04.8	-37.7	14.8	32 02.8	-37.4	14.9	33 00.8	-37.3	15.1	33 58.7	-37.0	15.3	72
73	26 33.9	-38.9	13.4	27 32.2	-38.7	13.5	28 30.6	-38.5	13.6	29 28.9	-38.3	13.7	30 27.1	-38.0	13.9	31 25.4	-37.9	14.0	32 23.5	-37.6	14.2	33 21.7	-37.4	14.3	73
74	25 55.0	-39.2	12.5	26 53.5	-39.0	12.6	27 52.1	-38.8	12.7	28 50.6	-38.6	12.9	29 49.1	-38.5	13.0	30 47.5	-38.2	13.1	31 45.9	-38.0	13.3	32 44.3	-37.8	13.4	74
75	25 15.8	-39.5	11.7	26 14.5	-39.3	11.8	27 13.3	-39.2	11.9	28 12.0	-39.0	12.0	29 10.6	-38.7	12.1	30 09.3	-38.6	12.2	31 07.9	-38.4	12.3	32 06.5	-38.2	12.5	75
76	24 36.3	-39.7	10.8	25 35.2	-39.5	10.9	26 34.1	-39.4	11.0	27 33.0	-39.2	11.1	28 31.9	-39.1	11.2	29 30.7	-38.9	11.3	30 29.5	-38.7	11.5	31 28.3	-38.5	11.6	76
77	23 56.6	-40.0	10.0	24 55.7	-39.9	10.1	25 54.7	-39.7	10.2	26 53.8	-39.6	10.3	27 52.8	-39.4	10.4	28 51.8	-39.2	10.5	29 50.8	-39.1	10.6	30 49.8	-38.9	10.7	77
78	23 16.6	-40.3	9.2	24 15.8	-40.1	9.3	25 15.0	-40.0	9.4	26 14.2	-39.8	9.4	27 13.4	-39.7	9.5	28 12.6	-39.6	9.6	29 11.7	-39.4	9.7	30 10.9	-39.3	9.8	78
79	22 36.3	-40.4	8.4	23 35.7	-40.4	8.5	24 35.0	-40.2	8.5	25 34.4	-40.2	8.6	26 33.7	-40.0	8.7	27 33.0	-39.9	8.8	28 32.3	-39.8	8.8	29 31.6	-39.6	8.9	79
80	21 55.9	-40.7	7.6	22 55.3	-40.6	7.7	23 54.8	-40.5	7.7	24 54.2	-40.3	7.8	25 53.7	-40.3	7.8	26 53.1	-40.1	7.9	27 52.5	-40.0	8.0	28 52.0	-40.0	8.1	80
81	21 15.2	-41.0	6.8	22 14.7	-40.8	6.9	23 14.3	-40.8	6.9	24 13.9	-40.7	7.0	25 13.4	-40.5	7.0	26 13.0	-40.5	7.1	27 12.5	-40.4	7.1	28 12.0	-40.2	7.2	81
82	20 34.2	-41.1	6.0	21 33.9	-41.1	6.1	22 33.5	-40.9	6.1	23 33.2	-40.9	6.2	24 32.9	-40.9	6.2	25 32.5	-40.7	6.3	26 32.1	-40.6	6.3	27 31.8	-40.6	6.4	82
83	19 53.1	-41.4	5.3	20 52.8	-41.2	5.3	21 52.6	-41.2	5.3	22 52.3	-41.1	5.4	23 52.0	-41.0	5.4	24 51.8	-41.0	5.5	25 51.5	-40.9	5.5	26 51.2	-40.8	5.5	83
84	19 11.7	-41.5	4.5	20 11.6	-41.5	4.5	21 11.4	-41.4	4.5	22 11.2	-41.4	4.6	23 11.0	-41.3	4.6	24 10.8	-41.2	4.6	25 10.6	-41.2	4.7	26 10.4	-41.1	4.7	84
85	18 30.2	-41.7	3.7	19 30.1	-41.7	3.7	20 30.0	-41.7	3.8	21 29.8	-41.5	3.8	22 29.7	-41.5	3.8	23 29.6	-41.5	3.9	24 29.4	-41.4	3.9	25 29.3	-41.4	3.9	85
86	17 48.5	-41.9	3.0	18 48.4	-41.8	3.0	19 48.3	-41.8	3.0	20 48.3	-41.8	3.0	21 48.2	-41.8	3.0	22 48.1	-41.7	3.1	23 48.0	-41.7	3.1	24 47.9	-41.6	3.1	86
87	17 06.6	-42.0	2.2	18 06.6	-42.1	2.2	19 06.5	-42.0	2.2	20 06.5	-42.0	2.3	21 06.4	-41.9	2.3	22 06.4	-41.9	2.3	23 06.3	-41.9	2.3	24 06.3	-41.9	2.3	87
88	16 24.6	-42.2	1.5	17 24.5	-42.2	1.5	18 24.5	-42.2	1.5	19 24.5	-42.2	1.5	20 24.5	-42.2	1.5	21 24.5	-42.2	1.5	22 24.4	-42.1	1.5	23 24.4	-42.1	1.5	88
89	15 42.4	-42.4	0.7	16 42.3	-42.3	0.7	17 42.3	-42.3	0.7	18 42.3	-42.2	0.7	19 42.3	-42.3	0.8	20 42.3	-42.3	0.8	21 42.3	-42.3	0.8	22 42.3	-42.3	0.8	89
90	15 00.0	-42.5	0.0	16 00.0	-42.5	0.0	17 00.0	-42.5	0.0	18 00.0	-42.5	0.0	19 00.0	-42.5	0.0	20 00.0	-42.5	0.0	21 00.0	-42.5	0.0	22 00.0	-42.5	0.0	90
	15°			16°			17°			18°			19°			20°			21°			22°			

45°, 315° L.H.A. LATITUDE SAME NAME AS DECLINATION

92

LATITUDE **CONTRARY** NAME TO DECLINATION — L.H.A. 45°, 315°

Dec.	15° Hc	d	Z	16° Hc	d	Z	17° Hc	d	Z	18° Hc	d	Z	19° Hc	d	Z	20° Hc	d	Z	21° Hc	d	Z	22° Hc	d	Z	Dec.
°	° ′	′	°	° ′	′	°	° ′	′	°	° ′	′	°	° ′	′	°	° ′	′	°	° ′	′	°	° ′	′	°	°
0	43 04.8	-21.7	104.5	42 49.3	-23.0	105.4	42 32.9	-24.2	106.3	42 15.6	-25.4	107.2	41 57.5	-26.7	108.0	41 38.5	-27.9	108.9	41 18.6	-28.9	109.7	40 58.0	-30.1	110.5	0
1	42 43.1	-22.5	105.8	42 26.3	-23.8	106.7	42 08.7	-25.0	107.5	41 50.2	-26.2	108.4	41 30.8	-27.4	109.2	41 10.6	-28.5	110.1	40 49.7	-29.7	110.9	40 27.9	-30.8	111.7	1
2	42 20.6	-23.4	107.0	42 02.5	-24.5	107.9	41 43.7	-25.8	108.8	41 24.0	-27.0	109.6	41 03.4	-28.1	110.4	40 42.1	-29.2	111.2	40 20.0	-30.3	112.0	39 57.1	-31.4	112.8	2
3	41 57.2	-24.1	108.3	41 38.0	-25.4	109.1	41 17.9	-26.5	110.0	40 57.0	-27.6	110.8	40 35.3	-28.8	111.6	40 12.9	-29.9	112.4	39 49.7	-31.0	113.1	39 25.7	-32.0	113.9	3
4	41 33.1	-24.9	109.5	41 12.6	-26.0	110.3	40 51.4	-27.2	111.2	40 29.4	-28.4	112.0	40 06.5	-29.4	112.7	39 43.0	-30.6	113.5	39 18.7	-31.6	114.3	38 53.7	-32.7	115.0	4
5	41 08.2	-25.7	110.7	40 46.6	-26.8	111.5	40 24.2	-28.0	112.3	40 01.0	-29.1	113.1	39 37.1	-30.2	113.9	39 12.4	-31.2	114.6	38 47.1	-32.2	115.4	38 21.0	-33.2	116.1	5
6	40 42.5	-26.3	111.9	40 19.8	-27.6	112.7	39 56.2	-28.6	113.5	39 31.9	-29.7	114.2	39 06.9	-30.7	115.0	38 41.2	-31.7	115.7	38 14.9	-32.8	116.4	37 47.8	-33.7	117.1	6
7	40 16.2	-27.1	113.1	39 52.2	-28.2	113.9	39 27.6	-29.3	114.6	39 02.2	-30.3	115.4	38 36.2	-31.4	116.1	38 09.5	-32.4	116.8	37 42.1	-33.4	117.5	37 14.1	-34.3	118.2	7
8	39 49.1	-27.8	114.3	39 24.0	-28.8	115.0	38 58.3	-29.9	115.8	38 31.9	-31.0	116.5	38 04.8	-31.9	117.2	37 37.1	-33.0	117.9	37 08.7	-33.9	118.5	36 39.8	-34.9	119.2	8
9	39 21.3	-28.5	115.4	38 55.2	-29.5	116.1	38 28.4	-30.6	116.9	38 00.9	-31.5	117.6	37 32.9	-32.6	118.3	37 04.1	-33.4	118.9	36 34.8	-34.4	119.6	36 04.9	-35.3	120.2	9
10	38 52.8	-29.1	116.6	38 25.7	-30.2	117.3	37 57.8	-31.1	118.0	37 29.4	-32.1	118.6	37 00.3	-33.1	119.3	36 30.7	-34.1	120.0	36 00.4	-34.9	120.6	35 29.6	-35.8	121.2	10
11	38 23.7	-29.7	117.7	37 55.5	-30.7	118.4	37 26.7	-31.7	119.0	36 57.3	-32.7	119.7	36 27.2	-33.6	120.3	35 56.6	-34.5	121.0	35 25.5	-35.4	121.6	34 53.8	-36.3	122.2	11
12	37 54.0	-30.4	118.8	37 24.8	-31.4	119.4	36 55.0	-32.3	120.1	36 24.6	-33.2	120.7	35 53.6	-34.1	121.4	35 22.1	-35.0	122.0	34 50.1	-35.9	122.6	34 17.5	-36.7	123.2	12
13	37 23.6	-30.9	119.9	36 53.4	-31.9	120.5	36 22.7	-32.9	121.2	35 51.4	-33.8	121.8	35 19.5	-34.7	122.4	34 47.1	-35.5	123.0	34 14.2	-36.4	123.6	33 40.8	-37.2	124.1	13
14	36 52.7	-31.5	120.9	36 21.5	-32.4	121.6	35 49.8	-33.3	122.2	35 17.6	-34.2	122.8	34 44.8	-35.1	123.4	34 11.6	-36.0	124.0	33 37.8	-36.8	124.5	33 03.6	-37.6	125.1	14
15	36 21.2	-32.1	122.0	35 49.1	-33.0	122.6	35 16.5	-33.9	123.2	34 43.4	-34.8	123.8	34 09.7	-35.5	124.4	33 35.6	-36.4	124.9	33 01.0	-37.2	125.5	32 26.0	-38.0	126.0	15
16	35 49.1	-32.6	123.0	35 16.1	-33.5	123.6	34 42.6	-34.3	124.2	34 08.6	-35.2	124.8	33 34.2	-36.1	125.3	32 59.2	-36.8	125.9	32 23.8	-37.6	126.4	31 48.0	-38.3	126.9	16
17	35 16.5	-33.1	124.1	34 42.6	-34.0	124.7	34 08.3	-34.9	125.2	33 33.4	-35.6	125.8	32 58.1	-36.4	126.3	32 22.4	-37.2	126.8	31 46.2	-38.0	127.3	31 09.7	-38.8	127.8	17
18	34 43.4	-33.7	125.1	34 08.6	-34.4	125.7	33 33.4	-35.3	126.2	32 57.8	-36.1	126.7	32 21.7	-36.9	127.2	31 45.2	-37.7	127.7	31 08.2	-38.3	128.2	30 30.9	-39.1	128.7	18
19	34 09.7	-34.1	126.1	33 34.2	-35.0	126.6	32 58.1	-35.7	127.2	32 21.7	-36.5	127.7	31 44.8	-37.3	128.2	31 07.5	-38.0	128.6	30 29.9	-38.8	129.1	29 51.8	-39.4	129.6	19
20	33 35.6	-34.6	127.1	32 59.2	-35.4	127.6	32 22.4	-36.2	128.1	31 45.2	-37.0	128.6	31 07.5	-37.6	129.1	30 29.5	-38.4	129.5	29 51.1	-39.1	130.0	29 12.4	-39.8	130.4	20
21	33 01.0	-35.0	128.1	32 23.8	-35.8	128.6	31 46.2	-36.5	129.1	31 08.2	-37.3	129.5	30 29.9	-38.1	130.0	29 51.1	-38.7	130.4	29 12.0	-39.4	130.9	28 32.6	-40.1	131.3	21
22	32 26.0	-35.4	129.0	31 48.0	-36.2	129.5	31 09.7	-37.0	130.0	30 30.9	-37.7	130.4	29 51.8	-38.4	130.9	29 12.4	-39.1	131.3	28 32.6	-39.7	131.7	27 52.5	-40.4	132.1	22
23	31 50.6	-35.9	130.0	31 11.8	-36.6	130.5	30 32.7	-37.3	130.9	29 53.2	-38.0	131.3	29 13.4	-38.7	131.8	28 33.3	-39.4	132.2	27 52.9	-40.1	132.6	27 12.1	-40.7	133.0	23
24	31 14.7	-36.3	130.9	30 35.2	-37.0	131.4	29 55.4	-37.8	131.8	29 15.2	-38.4	132.2	28 34.7	-39.1	132.6	27 53.9	-39.7	133.0	27 12.8	-40.3	133.4	26 31.4	-40.9	133.8	24
25	30 38.4	-36.7	131.9	29 58.2	-37.4	132.3	29 17.6	-38.0	132.7	28 36.8	-38.7	133.1	27 55.6	-39.3	133.5	27 14.2	-40.0	133.9	26 32.5	-40.7	134.2	25 50.5	-41.3	134.6	25
26	30 01.7	-37.1	132.8	29 20.8	-37.7	133.2	28 39.6	-38.4	133.6	27 58.1	-39.1	134.0	27 16.3	-39.7	134.4	26 34.2	-40.3	134.7	25 51.8	-40.9	135.1	25 09.2	-41.5	135.4	26
27	29 24.6	-37.4	133.7	28 43.1	-38.1	134.1	28 01.2	-38.8	134.5	27 19.0	-39.4	134.8	26 36.6	-40.0	135.2	25 53.9	-40.6	135.5	25 10.9	-41.2	135.9	24 27.7	-41.7	136.2	27
28	28 47.2	-37.7	134.6	28 05.0	-38.4	135.0	27 22.4	-39.0	135.3	26 39.6	-39.6	135.7	25 56.6	-40.3	136.0	25 13.3	-40.9	136.4	24 29.7	-41.4	136.7	23 46.0	-42.0	137.0	28
29	28 09.5	-38.2	135.5	27 26.6	-38.8	135.8	26 43.4	-39.4	136.2	26 00.0	-40.0	136.5	25 16.3	-40.5	136.9	24 32.4	-41.1	137.2	23 48.3	-41.6	137.5	23 04.0	-42.2	137.8	29
30	27 31.3	-38.4	136.3	26 47.8	-39.0	136.7	26 04.0	-39.6	137.0	25 20.0	-40.2	137.3	24 35.8	-40.8	137.7	23 51.3	-41.3	138.0	23 06.7	-41.9	138.3	22 21.8	-42.4	138.5	30
31	26 52.9	-38.7	137.2	26 08.8	-39.4	137.5	25 24.4	-39.9	137.9	24 39.8	-40.5	138.2	23 55.0	-41.0	138.5	23 10.0	-41.6	138.8	22 24.8	-42.1	139.0	21 39.4	-42.7	139.3	31
32	26 14.2	-39.1	138.0	25 29.4	-39.6	138.4	24 44.5	-40.2	138.7	23 59.3	-40.7	139.0	23 14.0	-41.3	139.3	22 28.4	-41.8	139.5	21 42.7	-42.4	139.8	20 56.7	-42.8	140.1	32
33	25 35.1	-39.3	138.9	24 49.8	-39.9	139.2	24 04.3	-40.4	139.5	23 18.6	-41.0	139.8	22 32.7	-41.5	140.1	21 46.6	-42.0	140.3	21 00.3	-42.5	140.6	20 13.9	-43.0	140.8	33
34	24 55.8	-39.6	139.7	24 09.9	-40.1	140.0	23 23.9	-40.7	140.3	22 37.6	-41.2	140.6	21 51.2	-41.8	140.8	21 04.6	-42.3	141.1	20 17.8	-42.7	141.3	19 30.9	-43.2	141.5	34
35	24 16.2	-39.9	140.6	23 29.8	-40.4	140.8	22 43.2	-41.0	141.1	21 56.4	-41.4	141.4	21 09.4	-41.9	141.6	20 22.3	-42.4	141.8	19 35.1	-42.9	142.1	18 47.7	-43.4	142.3	35
36	23 36.3	-40.1	141.4	22 49.4	-40.7	141.6	22 02.2	-41.1	141.9	21 15.0	-41.7	142.1	20 27.5	-42.1	142.4	19 39.9	-42.6	142.6	18 52.2	-43.1	142.8	18 04.3	-43.5	143.0	36
37	22 56.2	-40.4	142.2	22 08.7	-40.8	142.4	21 21.1	-41.4	142.7	20 33.3	-41.8	142.9	19 45.4	-42.3	143.1	18 57.3	-42.8	143.3	18 09.1	-43.2	143.5	17 20.8	-43.7	143.7	37
38	22 15.8	-40.6	143.0	21 27.9	-41.1	143.2	20 39.7	-41.5	143.5	19 51.5	-42.1	143.7	19 03.1	-42.5	143.9	18 14.5	-42.9	144.1	17 25.9	-43.4	144.3	16 37.1	-43.8	144.4	38
39	21 35.2	-40.8	143.8	20 46.8	-41.3	144.0	19 58.2	-41.8	144.2	19 09.4	-42.2	144.4	18 20.6	-42.7	144.6	17 31.6	-43.1	144.8	16 42.5	-43.6	145.0	15 53.3	-44.0	145.2	39
40	20 54.4	-41.0	144.6	20 05.5	-41.5	144.8	19 16.4	-42.0	145.0	18 27.2	-42.4	145.2	17 37.9	-42.9	145.4	16 48.5	-43.3	145.5	15 58.9	-43.6	145.7	15 09.3	-44.1	145.9	40
41	20 13.4	-41.3	145.3	19 24.0	-41.7	145.5	18 34.4	-42.1	145.7	17 44.8	-42.6	145.9	16 55.0	-42.9	146.1	16 05.2	-43.4	146.3	15 15.3	-43.9	146.4	14 25.2	-44.2	146.6	41
42	19 32.1	-41.4	146.1	18 42.3	-41.9	146.3	17 52.3	-42.3	146.5	17 02.2	-42.7	146.7	16 12.1	-43.2	146.8	15 21.8	-43.6	147.0	14 31.4	-43.9	147.1	13 41.0	-44.3	147.3	42
43	18 50.7	-41.6	146.9	18 00.4	-42.1	147.1	17 10.0	-42.5	147.2	16 19.5	-42.9	147.4	15 28.9	-43.3	147.5	14 38.2	-43.6	147.7	13 47.5	-44.1	147.8	12 56.7	-44.5	148.0	43
44	18 09.1	-41.8	147.6	17 18.3	-42.2	147.8	16 27.5	-42.6	148.0	15 36.6	-43.0	148.1	14 45.6	-43.4	148.3	13 54.6	-43.8	148.4	13 03.4	-44.1	148.5	12 12.2	-44.5	148.6	44
45	17 27.3	-42.0	148.4	16 36.1	-42.3	148.6	15 44.9	-42.8	148.7	14 53.6	-43.2	148.8	14 02.2	-43.5	149.0	13 10.8	-43.9	149.1	12 19.3	-44.3	149.2	11 27.7	-44.7	149.3	45
46	16 45.3	-42.1	149.1	15 53.8	-42.6	149.3	15 02.1	-42.9	149.4	14 10.4	-43.2	149.6	13 18.7	-43.7	149.7	12 26.9	-44.1	149.8	11 35.0	-44.4	149.9	10 43.0	-44.7	150.0	46
47	16 03.2	-42.3	149.9	15 11.2	-42.6	150.0	14 19.2	-43.0	150.2	13 27.2	-43.4	150.3	12 35.0	-43.7	150.4	11 42.8	-44.1	150.5	10 50.6	-44.5	150.6	9 58.3	-44.8	150.7	47
48	15 20.9	-42.4	150.6	14 28.6	-42.8	150.7	13 36.2	-43.2	150.9	12 43.8	-43.6	151.0	11 51.3	-43.9	151.1	10 58.7	-44.2	151.2	10 06.1	-44.5	151.3	9 13.5	-44.9	151.4	48
49	14 38.5	-42.6	151.3	13 45.8	-42.9	151.5	12 53.0	-43.2	151.6	12 00.2	-43.6	151.7	11 07.4	-44.0	151.8	10 14.5	-44.3	151.9	9 21.6	-44.7	152.0	8 28.6	-45.0	152.0	49
50	13 55.9	-42.7	152.1	13 02.9	-43.1	152.2	12 09.8	-43.4	152.3	11 16.6	-43.7	152.4	10 23.4	-44.0	152.5	9 30.2	-44.4	152.6	8 36.9	-44.7	152.6	7 43.6	-45.0	152.7	50
51	13 13.2	-42.8	152.8	12 19.8	-43.1	152.9	11 26.4	-43.5	153.0	10 32.9	-43.8	153.1	9 39.4	-44.2	153.2	8 45.8	-44.4	153.2	7 52.2	-44.7	153.3	6 58.6	-45.1	153.4	51
52	12 30.4	-42.9	153.5	11 36.7	-43.3	153.6	10 42.9	-43.6	153.7	9 49.1	-43.9	153.8	8 55.2	-44.2	153.9	8 01.4	-44.5	153.9	7 07.5	-44.9	154.0	6 13.5	-45.1	154.0	52
53	11 47.5	-43.1	154.2	10 53.4	-43.3	154.3	9 59.3	-43.6	154.4	9 05.2	-44.0	154.5	8 11.0	-44.2	154.5	7 16.9	-44.6	154.6	6 22.6	-44.8	154.6	5 28.4	-45.2	154.7	53
54	11 04.4	-43.1	154.9	10 10.1	-43.5	155.0	9 15.7	-43.8	155.1	8 21.2	-44.0	155.2	7 26.8	-44.4	155.2	6 32.3	-44.7	155.3	5 37.8	-45.0	155.3	4 43.2	-45.2	155.4	54
55	10 21.3	-43.2	155.7	9 26.6	-43.5	155.7	8 31.9	-43.8	155.8	7 37.2	-44.1	155.8	6 42.4	-44.4	155.9	5 47.6	-44.6	155.9	4 52.8	-44.9	156.0	3 58.0	-45.2	156.0	55
56	9 38.1	-43.3	156.4	8 43.1	-43.6	156.4	7 48.1	-43.9	156.5	6 53.1	-44.2	156.5	5 58.0	-44.4	156.6	5 03.0	-44.8	156.6	4 07.9	-45.0	156.6	3 12.8	-45.3	156.7	56
57	8 54.8	-43.4	157.1	7 59.5	-43.7	157.1	7 04.2	-43.9	157.2	6 08.9	-44.2	157.2	5 13.6	-44.5	157.2	4 18.2	-44.7	157.3	3 22.9	-45.0	157.3	2 27.5	-45.2	157.3	57
58	8 11.4	-43.5	157.8	7 15.8	-43.7	157.8	6 20.3	-44.0	157.9	5 24.7	-44.3	157.9	4 29.1	-44.5	157.9	3 33.5	-44.8	157.9	2 37.9	-45.1	158.0	1 42.3	-45.3	158.0	58
59	7 27.9	-43.5	158.5	6 32.1	-43.8	158.5	5 36.3	-44.1	158.5	4 40.4	-44.3	158.6	3 44.6	-44.6	158.6	2 48.7	-44.8	158.6	1 52.8	-45.0	158.6	0 57.0	-45.3	158.6	59
60	6 44.4	-43.6	159.1	5 48.3	-43.8	159.2	4 52.2	-44.1	159.2	3 56.1	-44.3	159.2	3 00.0	-44.6	159.3	2 03.9	-44.8	159.3	1 07.8	-45.1	159.3	0 11.7	-45.4	159.3	60
61	6 00.8	-43.6	159.8	5 04.5	-43.9	159.9	4 08.1	-44.1	159.9	3 11.8	-44.3	159.9	2 15.4	-44.6	159.9	1 19.1	-44.9	159.9	0 22.7	-45.1	160.0	0 33.7	+45.3	20.0	61
62	5 17.2	-43.7	160.5	4 20.6	-43.9	160.6	3 24.0	-44.1	160.6	2 27.4	-44.3	160.6	1 30.8	-44.6	160.6	0 34.2	-44.8	160.6	0 22.4	+45.0	19.4	1 19.0	+45.2	19.4	62
63	4 33.5	-43.7	161.2	3 36.7	-44.0	161.2	2 39.9	-44.2	161.3	1 43.1	-44.4	161.3	0 46.2	-44.6	161.3	0 10.6	+44.8	18.7	1 07.4	+45.1	18.7	2 04.2	+45.3	18.7	63
64	3 49.8	-43.8	161.9	2 52.7	-43.9	161.9	1 55.7	-44.2	161.9	0 58.7	-44.4	161.9	0 01.6	-44.6	161.9	0 55.4	+44.9	18.1	1 52.5	+45.0	18.1	2 49.5	+45.3	18.1	64
65	3 06.0	-43.8	162.6	2 08.8	-44.0	162.6	1 11.5	-44.2	162.6	0 14.3	-44.5	162.6	0 43.0	+44.6	17.4	1 40.3	+44.8	17.4	2 37.5	+45.0	17.4	3 34.8	+45.2	17.4	65
66	2 22.2	-43.8	163.3	1 24.8	-44.0	163.3	0 27.3	-44.2	163.3	0 30.2	+44.4	16.7	1 27.6	+44.6	16.7	2 25.1	+44.8	16.7	3 22.5	+45.0	16.7	4 20.0	+45.2	16.8	66
67	1 38.4	-43.8	164.0	0 40.8	-44.0	164.0	0 16.9	+44.2	16.0	1 14.6	+44.3	16.0	2 12.2	+44.6	16.1	3 09.9	+44.7	16.1	4 07.5	+45.0	16.1	5 05.2	+45.1	16.1	67
68	0 54.6	-43.8	164.6	0 03.2	+44.0	15.4	1 01.1	+44.2	15.4	1 58.9	+44.4	15.4	2 56.8	+44.6	15.4	3 54.6	+44.8	15.4	4 52.5	+44.9	15.4	5 50.3	+45.1	15.4	68
69	0 10.8	-43.8	165.3	0 47.2	+44.0	14.7	1 45.3	+44.2	14.7	2 43.3	+44.4	14.7	3 41.4	+44.5	14.7	4 39.4	+44.7	14.7	5 37.4	+44.9	14.8	6 35.4	+45.1	14.8	69
70	0 33.0	+43.8	14.0	1 31.2	+44.0	14.0	2 29.5	+44.1	14.0	3 27.7	+44.3	14.0	4 25.9	+44.5	14.0	5 24.1	+44.6	14.1	6 22.3	+44.8	14.1	7 20.5	+45.0	14.1	70
71	1 16.8	+43.9	13.3	2 15.2	+44.0	13.3	3 13.6	+44.1	13.3	4 12.0	+44.3	13.3	5 10.4	+44.4	13.4	6 08.7	+44.7	13.4	7 07.1	+44.8	13.4	8 05.5	+44.9	13.4	71
72	2 00.7	+43.7	12.6	2 59.2	+43.9	12.6	3 57.7	+44.1	12.7	4 56.3	+44.2	12.7	5 54.8	+44.4	12.7	6 53.4	+44.5	12.7	7 51.9	+44.7	12.7	8 50.4	+44.9	12.8	72
73	2 44.4	+43.8	11.9	3 43.1	+44.0	12.0	4 41.8	+44.1	12.0	5 40.5	+44.2	12.0	6 39.2	+44.4	12.0	7 37.9	+44.5	12.0	8 36.6	+44.6	12.1	9 35.3	+44.7	12.1	73
74	3 28.2	+43.7	11.3	4 27.1	+43.8	11.3	5 25.9	+44.0	11.3	6 24.7	+44.2	11.3	7 23.6	+44.2	11.3	8 22.4	+44.4	11.4	9 21.2	+44.6	11.4	10 20.0	+44.7	11.4	74
75	4 11.9	+43.8	10.6	5 10.9	+43.9	10.6	6 09.9	+44.0	10.6	7 08.9	+44.1	10.6	8 07.8	+44.3	10.7	9 06.8	+44.4	10.7	10 05.8	+44.4	10.7	11 04.7	+44.6	10.7	75
76	4 55.7	+43.6	9.9	5 54.8	+43.7	9.9	6 53.9	+43.9	9.9	7 53.0	+44.0	9.9	8 52.1	+44.1	10.0	9 51.2	+44.2	10.0	10 50.2	+44.4	10.0	11 49.3	+44.5	10.1	76
77	5 39.3	+43.6	9.2	6 38.5	+43.8	9.2	7 37.8	+43.8	9.2	8 37.0	+43.9	9.3	9 36.2	+44.1	9.3	10 35.4	+44.2	9.3	11 34.6	+44.3	9.3	12 33.8	+44.4	9.4	77
78	6 22.9	+43.6	8.5	7 22.3	+43.6	8.5	8 21.6	+43.8	8.5	9 20.9	+43.9	8.6	10 20.3	+43.9	8.6	11 19.6	+44.1	8.6	12 18.9	+44.2	8.7	13 18.2	+44.3	8.7	78
79	7 06.5	+43.5	7.8	8 05.9	+43.6	7.8	9 05.4	+43.6	7.9	10 04.8	+43.8	7.9	11 04.2	+43.9	7.9	12 03.7	+43.9	7.9	13 03.1	+44.0	8.0	14 02.5	+44.2	8.0	79
80	7 50.0	+43.4	7.1	8 49.5	+43.5	7.1	9 49.0	+43.6	7.2	10 48.6	+43.7	7.2	11 48.1	+43.8	7.2	12 47.6	+43.9	7.2	13 47.1	+44.0	7.3	14 46.7	+44.0	7.3	80
81	8 33.4	+43.3	6.4	9 33.0	+43.4	6.4	10 32.6	+43.5	6.5	11 32.3	+43.5	6.5	12 31.9	+43.6	6.5	13 31.5	+43.7	6.5	14 31.1	+43.8	6.6	15 30.7	+43.9	6.6	81
82	9 16.7	+43.3	5.7	10 16.4	+43.4	5.7	11 16.1	+43.4	5.8	12 15.8	+43.5	5.8	13 15.5	+43.6	5.8	14 15.2	+43.6	5.8	15 14.9	+43.7	5.9	16 14.6	+43.8	5.9	82
83	10 00.0	+43.2	5.0	10 59.8	+43.3	5.0	11 59.5	+43.3	5.1	12 59.3	+43.4	5.1	13 59.1	+43.4	5.1	14 58.8	+43.5	5.1	15 58.6	+43.5	5.1	16 58.4	+43.6	5.2	83
84	10 43.2	+43.1	4.3	11 43.0	+43.2	4.3	12 42.8	+43.2	4.3	13 42.7	+43.2	4.4	14 42.5	+43.3	4.4	15 42.3	+43.4	4.4	16 42.1	+43.4	4.4	17 42.0	+43.4	4.4	84
85	11 26.3	+43.0	3.6	12 26.2	+43.0	3.6	13 26.0	+43.1	3.6	14 25.9	+43.1	3.6	15 25.8	+43.1	3.7	16 25.7	+43.2	3.7	17 25.5	+43.3	3.7	18 25.4	+43.3	3.7	85
86	12 09.3	+42.8	2.9	13 09.2	+42.9	2.9	14 09.1	+42.9	2.9	15 09.0	+43.0	2.9	16 08.9	+43.0	2.9	17 08.9	+43.0	3.0	18 08.8	+43.1	3.0	19 08.7	+43.1	3.0	86
87	12 52.1	+42.8	2.2	13 52.1	+42.8	2.2	14 52.0	+42.8	2.2	15 52.0	+42.8	2.2	16 51.9	+42.9	2.2	17 51.9	+42.9	2.2	18 51.9	+42.9	2.2	19 51.8	+42.9	2.3	87
88	13 34.9	+42.6	1.5	14 34.9	+42.6	1.5	15 34.8	+42.7	1.5	16 34.8	+42.7	1.5	17 34.8	+42.7	1.5	18 34.8	+42.7	1.5	19 34.8	+42.7	1.5	20 34.7	+42.8	1.5	88
89	14 17.5	+42.5	0.7	15 17.5	+42.5	0.7	16 17.5	+42.5	0.7	17 17.5	+42.5	0.7	18 17.5	+42.5	0.7	19 17.5	+42.5	0.7	20 17.5	+42.5	0.8	21 17.5	+42.5	0.8	89
90	15 00.0	+42.4	0.0	16 00.0	+42.3	0.0	17 00.0	+42.3	0.0	18 00.0	+42.3	0.0	19 00.0	+42.3	0.0	20 00.0	+42.3	0.0	21 00.0	+42.3	0.0	22 00.0	+42.3	0.0	90
	15°			16°			17°			18°			19°			20°			21°			22°			

S. Lat. {L.H.A. greater than 180° ....Zn=180°−Z; L.H.A. less than 180°...........Zn=180°+Z}

LATITUDE **SAME** NAME AS DECLINATION — L.H.A. 135°, 225°

46°, 314° L.H.A. LATITUDE **SAME** NAME AS DECLINATION N. Lat. {L.H.A. greater than 180° .....Zn=Z; L.H.A. less than 180°............Zn=360°−Z

Dec.	15°			16°			17°			18°			Dec.
	Hc	d	Z	Hc	d	Z	Hc	d	Z	Hc	d	Z	
°	° ′	′	°	° ′	′	°	° ′	′	°	° ′	′	°	°
0	42 08.6	+20.5	104.0	41 53.6	+21.8	104.9	41 37.7	+23.1	105.8	41 21.0	+24.3	106.6	0
1	42 29.1	+19.7	102.8	42 15.4	+21.0	103.7	42 00.8	+22.3	104.5	41 45.3	+23.5	105.4	1
2	42 48.8	+18.8	101.5	42 36.4	+20.1	102.4	42 23.1	+21.4	103.3	42 08.8	+22.8	104.2	2
3	43 07.6	+17.9	100.2	42 56.5	+19.3	101.1	42 44.5	+20.6	102.0	42 31.6	+21.9	102.9	3
4	43 25.5	+17.0	98.9	43 15.8	+18.4	99.8	43 05.1	+19.7	100.7	42 53.5	+21.0	101.6	4
5	43 42.5	+16.1	97.5	43 34.2	+17.4	98.5	43 24.8	+18.8	99.4	43 14.5	+20.2	100.4	5
6	43 58.6	+15.1	96.2	43 51.6	+16.6	97.2	43 43.6	+18.0	98.1	43 34.7	+19.3	99.1	6
7	44 13.7	+14.2	94.9	44 08.2	+15.5	95.8	44 01.6	+17.0	96.8	43 54.0	+18.3	97.7	7
8	44 27.9	+13.2	93.5	44 23.7	+14.7	94.5	44 18.6	+16.0	95.5	44 12.3	+17.5	96.4	8
9	44 41.1	+12.3	92.1	44 38.4	+13.6	93.1	44 34.6	+15.1	94.1	44 29.8	+16.5	95.1	9
10	44 53.4	+11.2	90.8	44 52.0	+12.7	91.7	44 49.7	+14.1	92.7	44 46.3	+15.5	93.7	10
11	45 04.6	+10.2	89.4	45 04.7	+11.7	90.4	45 03.8	+13.1	91.4	45 01.8	+14.6	92.4	11
12	45 14.8	+9.1	88.0	45 16.4	+10.6	89.0	45 16.9	+12.1	90.0	45 16.4	+13.6	91.0	12
13	45 23.9	+8.2	86.6	45 27.0	+9.6	87.6	45 29.0	+11.1	88.6	45 30.0	+12.5	89.6	13
14	45 32.1	+7.0	85.1	45 36.6	+8.6	86.2	45 40.1	+10.0	87.2	45 42.5	+11.5	88.2	14
15	45 39.1	+6.1	83.7	45 45.2	+7.5	84.8	45 50.1	+9.0	85.8	45 54.0	+10.5	86.8	15
16	45 45.2	+4.9	82.3	45 52.7	+6.4	83.3	45 59.1	+7.9	84.4	46 04.5	+9.4	85.4	16
17	45 50.1	+3.9	80.9	45 59.1	+5.4	81.9	46 07.0	+6.9	82.9	46 13.9	+8.3	84.0	17
18	45 54.0	+2.8	79.4	46 04.5	+4.3	80.5	46 13.9	+5.8	81.5	46 22.2	+7.3	82.5	18
19	45 56.8	+1.7	78.0	46 08.8	+3.2	79.0	46 19.7	+4.6	80.1	46 29.5	+6.2	81.1	19
20	45 58.5	+0.7	76.6	46 12.0	+2.1	77.6	46 24.3	+3.6	78.6	46 35.7	+5.0	79.6	20
21	45 59.2	−0.5	75.1	46 14.1	+1.0	76.1	46 27.9	+2.5	77.2	46 40.7	+4.0	78.2	21
22	45 58.7	−1.5	73.7	46 15.1	−0.1	74.7	46 30.4	+1.4	75.7	46 44.7	+2.9	76.7	22
23	45 57.2	−2.6	72.3	46 15.0	−1.2	73.2	46 31.8	+0.3	74.3	46 47.6	+1.7	75.3	23
24	45 54.6	−3.7	70.8	46 13.8	−2.2	71.8	46 32.1	−0.8	72.8	46 49.3	+0.7	73.8	24
25	45 50.9	−4.7	69.4	46 11.6	−3.4	70.4	46 31.3	−2.0	71.3	46 50.0	−0.5	72.4	25
26	45 46.2	−5.9	68.0	46 08.2	−4.4	68.9	46 29.3	−3.0	69.9	46 49.5	−1.6	70.9	26
27	45 40.3	−6.8	66.5	46 03.8	−5.5	67.5	46 26.3	−4.1	68.4	46 47.9	−2.7	69.4	27
28	45 33.5	−8.0	65.1	45 58.3	−6.6	66.0	46 22.2	−5.2	67.0	46 45.2	−3.9	68.0	28
29	45 25.5	−9.0	63.7	45 51.7	−7.7	64.6	46 17.0	−6.3	65.6	46 41.3	−4.9	66.5	29
30	45 16.5	−10.0	62.3	45 44.0	−8.7	63.2	46 10.7	−7.4	64.1	46 36.4	−6.0	65.1	30
31	45 06.5	−11.0	60.9	45 35.3	−9.7	61.8	46 03.3	−8.5	62.7	46 30.4	−7.1	63.6	31
32	44 55.5	−12.0	59.5	45 25.6	−10.8	60.4	45 54.8	−9.5	61.3	46 23.3	−8.2	62.2	32
33	44 43.5	−13.0	58.1	45 14.8	−11.8	59.0	45 45.3	−10.5	59.8	46 15.1	−9.3	60.7	33
34	44 30.5	−14.0	56.7	45 03.0	−12.8	57.6	45 34.8	−11.6	58.4	46 05.8	−10.3	59.3	34
35	44 16.5	−15.0	55.4	44 50.2	−13.8	56.2	45 23.2	−12.6	57.0	45 55.5	−11.4	57.9	35
36	44 01.5	−15.9	54.0	44 36.4	−14.8	54.8	45 10.6	−13.6	55.6	45 44.1	−12.4	56.5	36
37	43 45.6	−16.8	52.7	44 21.6	−15.7	53.5	44 57.0	−14.6	54.3	45 31.7	−13.4	55.1	37
38	43 28.8	−17.8	51.4	44 05.9	−16.7	52.1	44 42.4	−15.5	52.9	45 18.3	−14.4	53.7	38
39	43 11.0	−18.6	50.1	43 49.2	−17.6	50.8	44 26.9	−16.6	51.5	45 03.9	−15.5	52.3	39
40	42 52.4	−19.5	48.8	43 31.6	−18.5	49.5	44 10.3	−17.4	50.2	44 48.4	−16.3	51.0	40
41	42 32.9	−20.4	47.5	43 13.1	−19.3	48.2	43 52.9	−18.4	48.9	44 32.1	−17.4	49.6	41
42	42 12.5	−21.2	46.2	42 53.8	−20.3	46.9	43 34.5	−19.2	47.6	44 14.7	−18.2	48.3	42
43	41 51.3	−22.0	44.9	42 33.5	−21.1	45.6	43 15.3	−20.2	46.2	43 56.5	−19.2	46.9	43
44	41 29.3	−22.9	43.7	42 12.4	−21.9	44.3	42 55.1	−21.0	45.0	43 37.3	−20.0	45.6	44
45	41 06.4	−23.5	42.5	41 50.5	−22.7	43.1	42 34.1	−21.8	43.7	43 17.3	−21.0	44.3	45
46	40 42.9	−24.4	41.2	41 27.8	−23.5	41.8	42 12.3	−22.7	42.4	42 56.3	−21.7	43.0	46
47	40 18.5	−25.1	40.0	41 04.3	−24.3	40.6	41 49.6	−23.4	41.2	42 34.6	−22.6	41.8	47
48	39 53.4	−25.8	38.9	40 40.0	−25.1	39.4	41 26.2	−24.3	39.9	42 12.0	−23.5	40.5	48
49	39 27.6	−26.5	37.7	40 14.9	−25.7	38.2	41 01.9	−25.0	38.7	41 48.5	−24.2	39.3	49
50	39 01.1	−27.2	36.5	39 49.2	−26.5	37.0	40 36.9	−25.7	37.5	41 24.3	−24.9	38.1	50
51	38 33.9	−27.8	35.4	39 22.7	−27.2	35.8	40 11.2	−26.5	36.3	40 59.4	−25.8	36.9	51
52	38 06.1	−28.5	34.2	38 55.5	−27.8	34.7	39 44.7	−27.1	35.2	40 33.6	−26.4	35.7	52
53	37 37.6	−29.1	33.1	38 27.7	−28.5	33.6	39 17.6	−27.8	34.0	40 07.2	−27.2	34.5	53
54	37 08.5	−29.7	32.0	37 59.2	−29.1	32.4	38 49.8	−28.5	32.9	39 40.0	−27.8	33.3	54
55	36 38.8	−30.3	30.9	37 30.1	−29.7	31.3	38 21.3	−29.1	31.7	39 12.2	−28.5	32.2	55
56	36 08.5	−30.9	29.9	37 00.4	−30.3	30.2	37 52.2	−29.8	30.6	38 43.7	−29.2	31.0	56
57	35 37.6	−31.4	28.8	36 30.1	−30.9	29.2	37 22.4	−30.3	29.5	38 14.5	−29.8	29.9	57
58	35 06.2	−31.9	27.8	35 59.2	−31.4	28.1	36 52.1	−30.9	28.5	37 44.7	−30.3	28.8	58
59	34 34.3	−32.5	26.7	35 27.8	−32.0	27.1	36 21.2	−31.5	27.4	37 14.4	−31.0	27.7	59
60	34 01.8	−32.9	25.7	34 55.8	−32.5	26.0	35 49.7	−32.0	26.3	36 43.4	−31.6	26.7	60
61	33 28.9	−33.4	24.7	34 23.3	−33.0	25.0	35 17.7	−32.6	25.3	36 11.8	−32.1	25.6	61
62	32 55.5	−33.9	23.7	33 50.3	−33.4	24.0	34 45.1	−33.1	24.3	35 39.7	−32.6	24.6	62
63	32 21.6	−34.4	22.7	33 16.9	−34.0	23.0	34 12.0	−33.5	23.3	35 07.1	−33.1	23.5	63
64	31 47.2	−34.7	21.8	32 42.9	−34.4	22.0	33 38.5	−34.0	22.3	34 34.0	−33.7	22.5	64
65	31 12.5	−35.2	20.8	32 08.5	−34.8	21.0	33 04.5	−34.5	21.3	34 00.3	−34.1	21.5	65
66	30 37.3	−35.6	19.9	31 33.7	−35.3	20.1	32 30.0	−35.0	20.3	33 26.2	−34.6	20.5	66
67	30 01.7	−36.0	18.9	30 58.4	−35.7	19.1	31 55.0	−35.3	19.3	32 51.6	−35.0	19.5	67
68	29 25.7	−36.4	18.0	30 22.7	−36.1	18.2	31 19.7	−35.8	18.4	32 16.6	−35.5	18.6	68
69	28 49.3	−36.7	17.1	29 46.6	−36.4	17.3	30 43.9	−36.2	17.5	31 41.1	−35.9	17.6	69
70	28 12.6	−37.1	16.2	29 10.2	−36.8	16.4	30 07.7	−36.5	16.5	31 05.2	−36.3	16.7	70
71	27 35.5	−37.4	15.3	28 33.4	−37.2	15.5	29 31.2	−37.0	15.6	30 28.9	−36.6	15.8	71
72	26 58.1	−37.7	14.4	27 56.2	−37.5	14.6	28 54.2	−37.2	14.7	29 52.3	−37.1	14.9	72
73	26 20.4	−38.1	13.6	27 18.7	−37.9	13.7	28 17.0	−37.7	13.8	29 15.2	−37.4	13.9	73
74	25 42.3	−38.3	12.7	26 40.8	−38.1	12.8	27 39.3	−37.9	12.9	28 37.8	−37.8	13.1	74
75	25 04.0	−38.7	11.9	26 02.7	−38.5	12.0	27 01.4	−38.3	12.1	28 00.0	−38.1	12.2	75
76	24 25.3	−38.9	11.0	25 24.2	−38.7	11.1	26 23.1	−38.6	11.2	27 21.9	−38.4	11.3	76
77	23 46.4	−39.2	10.2	24 45.5	−39.1	10.3	25 44.5	−38.9	10.3	26 43.5	−38.7	10.4	77
78	23 07.2	−39.4	9.4	24 06.4	−39.3	9.4	25 05.6	−39.1	9.5	26 04.8	−39.0	9.6	78
79	22 27.8	−39.7	8.5	23 27.1	−39.5	8.6	24 26.5	−39.5	8.7	25 25.8	−39.3	8.7	79
80	21 48.1	−39.9	7.7	22 47.6	−39.8	7.8	23 47.0	−39.7	7.8	24 46.5	−39.6	7.9	80
81	21 08.2	−40.1	6.9	22 07.8	−40.1	7.0	23 07.3	−39.9	7.0	24 06.9	−39.9	7.1	81
82	20 28.1	−40.4	6.1	21 27.7	−40.2	6.2	22 27.4	−40.2	6.2	23 27.0	−40.1	6.3	82
83	19 47.7	−40.5	5.3	20 47.5	−40.5	5.4	21 47.2	−40.4	5.4	22 46.9	−40.3	5.5	83
84	19 07.2	−40.8	4.6	20 07.0	−40.7	4.6	21 06.8	−40.7	4.6	22 06.6	−40.6	4.7	84
85	18 26.4	−40.9	3.8	19 26.3	−40.9	3.8	20 26.1	−40.8	3.8	21 26.0	−40.8	3.9	85
86	17 45.5	−41.2	3.0	18 45.4	−41.1	3.0	19 45.3	−41.0	3.1	20 45.2	−41.0	3.1	86
87	17 04.3	−41.2	2.3	18 04.3	−41.3	2.3	19 04.3	−41.3	2.3	20 04.2	−41.2	2.3	87
88	16 23.1	−41.5	1.5	17 23.0	−41.4	1.5	18 23.0	−41.4	1.5	19 23.0	−41.4	1.5	88
89	15 41.6	−41.6	0.7	16 41.6	−41.6	0.8	17 41.6	−41.6	0.8	18 41.6	−41.6	0.8	89
90	15 00.0	−41.8	0.0	16 00.0	−41.8	0.0	17 00.0	−41.8	0.0	18 00.0	−41.8	0.0	90
	15°			16°			17°			18°			

Dec.	19°			20°			21°			22°			Dec.
	Hc	d	Z	Hc	d	Z	Hc	d	Z	Hc	d	Z	
°	° ′	′	°	° ′	′	°	° ′	′	°	° ′	′	°	°
0	41 03.4	+25.6	107.5	40 45.0	+26.8	108.3	40 25.8	+27.9	109.1	40 05.8	+29.0	109.9	0
1	41 29.0	+24.7	106.2	41 11.8	+25.9	107.1	40 53.7	+27.2	107.9	40 34.8	+28.4	108.7	1
2	41 53.7	+24.0	105.0	41 37.7	+25.3	105.9	41 20.9	+26.4	106.7	41 03.2	+27.6	107.6	2
3	42 17.7	+23.2	103.8	42 03.0	+24.4	104.7	41 47.3	+25.7	105.5	41 30.8	+26.9	106.4	3
4	42 40.9	+22.3	102.5	42 27.4	+23.6	103.4	42 13.0	+24.9	104.3	41 57.7	+26.2	105.2	4
5	43 03.2	+21.5	101.3	42 51.0	+22.9	102.2	42 37.9	+24.1	103.1	42 23.9	+25.3	104.0	5
6	43 24.7	+20.7	100.0	43 13.9	+21.9	100.9	43 02.0	+23.3	101.8	42 49.2	+24.6	102.8	6
7	43 45.4	+19.7	98.7	43 35.8	+21.1	99.6	43 25.3	+22.4	100.6	43 13.8	+23.7	101.5	7
8	44 05.1	+18.9	97.4	43 56.9	+20.2	98.3	43 47.7	+21.6	99.3	43 37.5	+22.9	100.2	8
9	44 24.0	+17.9	96.1	44 17.1	+19.3	97.0	44 09.3	+20.6	98.0	44 00.4	+22.0	99.0	9
10	44 41.9	+16.9	94.7	44 36.4	+18.4	95.7	44 29.9	+19.8	96.7	44 22.4	+21.2	97.7	10
11	44 58.8	+16.0	93.4	44 54.8	+17.4	94.4	44 49.7	+18.8	95.4	44 43.6	+20.2	96.3	11
12	45 14.8	+15.0	92.0	45 12.2	+16.4	93.0	45 08.5	+17.9	94.0	45 03.8	+19.3	95.0	12
13	45 29.8	+14.0	90.6	45 28.6	+15.5	91.6	45 26.4	+16.9	92.7	45 23.1	+18.3	93.7	13
14	45 43.8	+13.0	89.2	45 44.1	+14.4	90.3	45 43.3	+15.9	91.3	45 41.4	+17.3	92.3	14
15	45 56.8	+12.0	87.8	45 58.5	+13.5	88.9	45 59.2	+14.9	89.9	45 58.7	+16.4	90.9	15
16	46 08.8	+10.9	86.4	46 12.0	+12.3	87.5	46 14.1	+13.8	88.5	46 15.1	+15.3	89.6	16
17	46 19.7	+9.8	85.0	46 24.3	+11.4	86.0	46 27.9	+12.8	87.1	46 30.4	+14.3	88.1	17
18	46 29.5	+8.7	83.6	46 35.7	+10.2	84.6	46 40.7	+11.7	85.7	46 44.7	+13.2	86.7	18
19	46 38.2	+7.7	82.1	46 45.9	+9.2	83.2	46 52.5	+10.6	84.2	46 57.9	+12.2	85.3	19
20	46 45.9	+6.6	80.7	46 55.1	+8.0	81.7	47 03.1	+9.6	82.8	47 10.1	+11.1	83.9	20
21	46 52.5	+5.4	79.2	47 03.1	+7.0	80.3	47 12.7	+8.5	81.4	47 21.2	+10.0	82.4	21
22	46 57.9	+4.4	77.8	47 10.1	+5.9	78.8	47 21.2	+7.3	79.9	47 31.2	+8.8	81.0	22
23	47 02.3	+3.2	76.3	47 16.0	+4.7	77.4	47 28.5	+6.3	78.4	47 40.0	+7.8	79.5	23
24	47 05.5	+2.1	74.8	47 20.7	+3.6	75.9	47 34.8	+5.1	77.0	47 47.8	+6.6	78.0	24
25	47 07.6	+1.0	73.4	47 24.3	+2.4	74.4	47 39.9	+3.9	75.5	47 54.4	+5.4	76.5	25
26	47 08.6	−0.1	71.9	47 26.7	+1.3	72.9	47 43.8	+2.8	74.0	47 59.8	+4.3	75.1	26
27	47 08.5	−1.3	70.4	47 28.0	+0.2	71.5	47 46.6	+1.6	72.5	48 04.1	+3.1	73.6	27
28	47 07.2	−2.4	69.0	47 28.2	−1.0	70.0	47 48.2	+0.5	71.0	48 07.2	+2.0	72.1	28
29	47 04.8	−3.6	67.5	47 27.2	−2.1	68.5	47 48.7	−0.6	69.5	48 09.2	+0.8	70.6	29
30	47 01.2	−4.6	66.0	47 25.1	−3.2	67.0	47 48.1	−1.8	68.0	48 10.0	−0.4	69.1	30
31	46 56.6	−5.8	64.6	47 21.9	−4.4	65.6	47 46.3	−3.0	66.6	48 09.6	−1.5	67.6	31
32	46 50.8	−6.8	63.1	47 17.5	−5.5	64.1	47 43.3	−4.1	65.1	48 08.1	−2.7	66.1	32
33	46 44.0	−8.0	61.7	47 12.0	−6.6	62.6	47 39.2	−5.3	63.6	48 05.4	−3.9	64.6	33
34	46 36.0	−9.0	60.2	47 05.4	−7.7	61.2	47 33.9	−6.4	62.1	48 01.5	−5.0	63.1	34
35	46 27.0	−10.1	58.8	46 57.7	−8.9	59.7	47 27.5	−7.5	60.6	47 56.5	−6.2	61.6	35
36	46 16.9	−11.2	57.4	46 48.8	−9.9	58.3	47 20.0	−8.6	59.2	47 50.3	−7.3	60.1	36
37	46 05.7	−12.2	55.9	46 38.9	−11.0	56.8	47 11.4	−9.8	57.7	47 43.0	−8.5	58.6	37
38	45 53.5	−13.3	54.5	46 27.9	−12.1	55.4	47 01.6	−10.8	56.3	47 34.5	−9.5	57.2	38
39	45 40.2	−14.3	53.1	46 15.8	−13.1	54.0	46 50.8	−11.9	54.8	47 25.0	−10.7	55.7	39
40	45 25.9	−15.2	51.7	46 02.7	−14.1	52.6	46 38.9	−13.0	53.4	47 14.3	−11.8	54.3	40
41	45 10.7	−16.3	50.4	45 48.6	−15.1	51.2	46 25.9	−14.0	52.0	47 02.5	−12.8	52.8	41
42	44 54.4	−17.2	49.0	45 33.5	−16.2	49.8	46 11.9	−15.0	50.6	46 49.7	−13.9	51.4	42
43	44 37.2	−18.2	47.7	45 17.3	−17.1	48.4	45 56.9	−16.1	49.2	46 35.8	−15.0	50.0	43
44	44 19.0	−19.0	46.3	45 00.2	−18.1	47.0	45 40.8	−17.0	47.8	46 20.8	−16.0	48.6	44
45	44 00.0	−20.0	45.0	44 42.1	−19.0	45.7	45 23.8	−18.1	46.4	46 04.8	−16.9	47.2	45
46	43 40.0	−20.9	43.7	44 23.1	−19.9	44.4	45 05.7	−18.9	45.1	45 47.9	−18.0	45.8	46
47	43 19.1	−21.7	42.4	44 03.2	−20.9	43.0	44 46.8	−19.9	43.7	45 29.9	−18.9	44.4	47
48	42 57.4	−22.6	41.1	43 42.3	−21.7	41.7	44 26.9	−20.8	42.4	45 11.0	−19.9	43.1	48
49	42 34.8	−23.4	39.9	43 20.6	−22.5	40.5	44 06.1	−21.7	41.1	44 51.1	−20.8	41.7	49
50	42 11.4	−24.2	38.6	42 58.1	−23.4	39.2	43 44.4	−22.6	39.8	44 30.3	−21.7	40.4	50
51	41 47.2	−25.0	37.4	42 34.7	−24.2	37.9	43 21.8	−23.4	38.5	44 08.6	−22.6	39.1	51
52	41 22.2	−25.7	36.2	42 10.5	−25.0	36.7	42 58.4	−24.2	37.2	43 46.0	−23.4	37.8	52
53	40 56.5	−26.5	35.0	41 45.5	−25.7	35.5	42 34.2	−25.0	36.0	43 22.6	−24.3	36.6	53
54	40 30.0	−27.2	33.8	41 19.8	−26.5	34.3	42 09.2	−25.8	34.8	42 58.3	−25.1	35.3	54
55	40 02.8	−27.8	32.6	40 53.3	−27.3	33.1	41 43.4	−26.6	33.6	42 33.2	−25.8	34.1	55
56	39 35.0	−28.6	31.5	40 26.0	−27.9	31.9	41 16.8	−27.3	32.4	42 07.4	−26.6	32.8	56
57	39 06.4	−29.2	30.3	39 58.1	−28.6	30.7	40 49.5	−28.0	31.2	41 40.8	−27.4	31.6	57
58	38 37.2	−29.8	29.2	39 29.5	−29.3	29.6	40 21.5	−28.6	30.0	41 13.4	−28.1	30.5	58
59	38 07.4	−30.5	28.1	39 00.2	−29.9	28.5	39 52.9	−29.4	28.9	40 45.3	−28.8	29.3	59
60	37 36.9	−31.0	27.0	38 30.3	−30.5	27.4	39 23.5	−30.0	27.7	40 16.5	−29.5	28.1	60
61	37 05.9	−31.7	25.9	37 59.8	−31.2	26.3	38 53.5	−30.7	26.6	39 47.0	−30.1	27.0	61
62	36 34.2	−32.1	24.9	37 28.6	−31.7	25.2	38 22.8	−31.2	25.5	39 16.9	−30.8	25.9	62
63	36 02.1	−32.8	23.8	36 56.9	−32.3	24.1	37 51.6	−31.9	24.4	38 46.1	−31.3	24.8	63
64	35 29.3	−33.2	22.8	36 24.6	−32.8	23.1	37 19.7	−32.4	23.4	38 14.8	−32.0	23.7	64
65	34 56.1	−33.7	21.8	35 51.8	−33.4	22.0	36 47.3	−32.9	22.3	37 42.8	−32.6	22.6	65
66	34 22.4	−34.3	20.8	35 18.4	−33.9	21.0	36 14.4	−33.5	21.3	37 10.2	−33.1	21.5	66
67	33 48.1	−34.7	19.8	34 44.5	−34.3	20.0	35 40.9	−34.0	20.2	36 37.1	−33.6	20.5	67
68	33 13.4	−35.1	18.8	34 10.2	−34.9	19.0	35 06.9	−34.5	19.2	36 03.5	−34.2	19.5	68
69	32 38.3	−35.6	17.8	33 35.3	−35.2	18.0	34 32.4	−35.0	18.2	35 29.3	−34.6	18.5	69
70	32 02.7	−36.0	16.9	33 00.1	−35.8	17.1	33 57.4	−35.5	17.3	34 54.7	−35.2	17.5	70
71	31 26.7	−36.5	15.9	32 24.3	−36.1	16.1	33 21.9	−35.8	16.3	34 19.5	−35.6	16.5	71
72	30 50.2	−36.8	15.0	31 48.2	−36.6	15.2	32 46.1	−36.4	15.3	33 43.9	−36.1	15.5	72
73	30 13.4	−37.2	14.1	31 11.6	−37.0	14.2	32 09.7	−36.7	14.4	33 07.8	−36.5	14.5	73
74	29 36.2	−37.5	13.2	30 34.6	−37.3	13.3	31 33.0	−37.1	13.5	32 31.3	−36.9	13.6	74
75	28 58.7	−37.9	12.3	29 57.3	−37.7	12.4	30 55.9	−37.6	12.5	31 54.4	−37.3	12.7	75
76	28 20.8	−38.3	11.4	29 19.6	−38.1	11.5	30 18.3	−37.8	11.6	31 17.1	−37.7	11.7	76
77	27 42.5	−38.6	10.5	28 41.5	−38.4	10.6	29 40.5	−38.2	10.7	30 39.4	−38.1	10.8	77
78	27 03.9	−38.8	9.7	28 03.1	−38.8	9.8	29 02.2	−38.6	9.8	30 01.3	−38.4	9.9	78
79	26 25.1	−39.2	8.8	27 24.3	−39.0	8.9	28 23.6	−38.9	9.0	29 22.9	−38.8	9.1	79
80	25 45.9	−39.5	8.0	26 45.3	−39.4	8.0	27 44.7	−39.2	8.1	28 44.1	−39.1	8.2	80
81	25 06.4	−39.7	7.1	26 05.9	−39.6	7.2	27 05.5	−39.6	7.3	28 05.0	−39.5	7.3	81
82	24 26.7	−40.0	6.3	25 26.3	−39.9	6.4	26 25.9	−39.8	6.4	27 25.5	−39.7	6.5	82
83	23 46.7	−40.3	5.5	24 46.4	−40.2	5.5	25 46.1	−40.1	5.6	26 45.8	−40.0	5.6	83
84	23 06.4	−40.5	4.7	24 06.2	−40.5	4.7	25 06.0	−40.4	4.8	26 05.8	−40.4	4.8	84
85	22 25.9	−40.8	3.9	23 25.7	−40.7	3.9	24 25.6	−40.6	3.9	25 25.4	−40.5	4.0	85
86	21 45.1	−40.9	3.1	22 45.0	−40.9	3.1	23 45.0	−40.9	3.1	24 44.9	−40.9	3.2	86
87	21 04.2	−41.2	2.3	22 04.1	−41.1	2.3	23 04.1	−41.2	2.3	24 04.0	−41.1	2.4	87
88	20 23.0	−41.4	1.5	21 23.0	−41.4	1.5	22 22.9	−41.3	1.6	23 22.9	−41.3	1.6	88
89	19 41.6	−41.6	0.8	20 41.6	−41.6	0.8	21 41.6	−41.6	0.8	22 41.6	−41.6	0.8	89
90	19 00.0	−41.8	0.0	20 00.0	−41.8	0.0	21 00.0	−41.8	0.0	22 00.0	−41.8	0.0	90
	19°			20°			21°			22°			

LATITUDE CONTRARY NAME TO DECLINATION — L.H.A. 46°, 314°

Dec.	15° Hc	d	Z	16° Hc	d	Z	17° Hc	d	Z	18° Hc	d	Z	19° Hc	d	Z	20° Hc	d	Z	21° Hc	d	Z	22° Hc	d	Z	Dec.
°	° ′	′	°	° ′	′	°	° ′	′	°	° ′	′	°	° ′	′	°	° ′	′	°	° ′	′	°	° ′	′	°	°
0	42 08.6	-21.4	104.0	41 53.6	-22.6	104.9	41 37.7	-23.8	105.8	41 21.0	-25.1	106.6	41 03.4	-26.2	107.5	40 45.0	-27.4	108.3	40 25.8	-28.6	109.1	40 05.8	-29.7	109.9	0
1	41 47.2	-22.1	105.3	41 31.0	-23.4	106.1	41 13.9	-24.6	107.0	40 55.9	-25.8	107.8	40 37.2	-27.0	108.6	40 17.6	-28.2	109.4	39 57.2	-29.3	110.2	39 36.1	-30.4	111.0	1
2	41 25.1	-23.0	106.5	41 07.6	-24.2	107.4	40 49.3	-25.4	108.2	40 30.1	-26.5	109.0	40 10.2	-27.7	109.8	39 49.4	-28.8	110.6	39 27.9	-29.9	111.4	39 05.7	-31.0	112.1	2
3	41 02.1	-23.7	107.8	40 43.4	-24.9	108.6	40 23.9	-26.1	109.4	40 03.6	-27.3	110.2	39 42.5	-28.4	111.0	39 20.6	-29.5	111.7	38 58.0	-30.5	112.5	38 34.7	-31.6	113.2	3
4	40 38.4	-24.5	109.0	40 18.5	-25.7	109.8	39 57.8	-26.8	110.6	39 36.3	-27.9	111.3	39 14.1	-29.0	112.1	38 51.1	-30.1	112.9	38 27.5	-31.2	113.6	38 03.1	-32.2	114.3	4
5	40 13.9	-25.2	110.2	39 52.8	-26.4	111.0	39 31.0	-27.5	111.7	39 08.4	-28.6	112.5	38 45.1	-29.7	113.2	38 21.0	-30.7	114.0	37 56.3	-31.7	114.7	37 30.9	-32.7	115.4	5
6	39 48.7	-26.0	111.4	39 26.4	-27.0	112.1	39 03.5	-28.2	112.9	38 39.8	-29.3	113.6	38 15.4	-30.3	114.3	37 50.3	-31.3	115.1	37 24.6	-32.4	115.8	36 58.2	-33.3	116.4	6
7	39 22.7	-26.6	112.5	38 59.4	-27.8	113.3	38 35.3	-28.8	114.0	38 10.5	-29.8	114.7	37 45.1	-30.9	115.4	37 19.0	-31.9	116.1	36 52.2	-32.8	116.8	36 24.9	-33.9	117.5	7
8	38 56.1	-27.3	113.7	38 31.6	-28.3	114.4	38 06.5	-29.4	115.1	37 40.7	-30.5	115.8	37 14.2	-31.5	116.5	36 47.1	-32.5	117.2	36 19.4	-33.4	117.9	35 51.0	-34.3	118.5	8
9	38 28.8	-28.0	114.8	38 03.3	-29.1	115.5	37 37.1	-30.1	116.2	37 10.2	-31.0	116.9	36 42.7	-32.0	117.6	36 14.6	-33.0	118.2	35 46.0	-34.0	118.9	35 16.7	-34.9	119.5	9
10	38 00.8	-28.6	116.0	37 34.2	-29.6	116.6	37 07.0	-30.6	117.3	36 39.2	-31.7	118.0	36 10.7	-32.6	118.6	35 41.6	-33.5	119.3	35 12.0	-34.4	119.9	34 41.8	-35.3	120.5	10
11	37 32.2	-29.2	117.1	37 04.6	-30.2	117.7	36 36.4	-31.2	118.4	36 07.5	-32.1	119.0	35 38.1	-33.1	119.7	35 08.1	-34.0	120.3	34 37.6	-34.9	120.9	34 06.5	-35.8	121.5	11
12	37 03.0	-29.8	118.2	36 34.4	-30.8	118.8	36 05.2	-31.8	119.5	35 35.4	-32.7	120.1	35 05.0	-33.6	120.7	34 34.1	-34.5	121.3	34 02.7	-35.4	121.9	33 30.7	-36.2	122.4	12
13	36 33.2	-30.4	119.2	36 03.6	-31.4	119.9	35 33.4	-32.3	120.5	35 02.7	-33.2	121.1	34 31.4	-34.1	121.7	33 59.6	-35.0	122.3	33 27.3	-35.8	122.9	32 54.5	-36.6	123.4	13
14	36 02.8	-31.0	120.3	35 32.2	-31.9	120.9	35 01.1	-32.8	121.5	34 29.5	-33.7	122.1	33 57.3	-34.6	122.7	33 24.6	-35.4	123.3	32 51.5	-36.3	123.8	32 17.9	-37.1	124.3	14
15	35 31.8	-31.5	121.4	35 00.3	-32.4	122.0	34 28.3	-33.3	122.6	33 55.8	-34.2	123.1	33 22.7	-35.0	123.7	32 49.2	-35.9	124.2	32 15.2	-36.7	124.8	31 40.8	-37.5	125.3	15
16	35 00.3	-32.0	122.4	34 27.9	-32.9	123.0	33 55.0	-33.8	123.6	33 21.6	-34.7	124.1	32 47.7	-35.5	124.7	32 13.3	-36.3	125.2	31 38.5	-37.0	125.7	31 03.3	-37.8	126.2	16
17	34 28.3	-32.5	123.4	33 55.0	-33.4	124.0	33 21.2	-34.3	124.6	32 46.9	-35.1	125.1	32 12.2	-35.9	125.6	31 37.0	-36.6	126.1	31 01.5	-37.5	126.6	30 25.5	-38.2	127.1	17
18	33 55.8	-33.1	124.5	33 21.6	-33.9	125.0	32 46.9	-34.7	125.5	32 11.8	-35.5	126.1	31 36.3	-36.3	126.6	31 00.4	-37.1	127.0	30 24.0	-37.8	127.5	29 47.3	-38.6	128.0	18
19	33 22.7	-33.5	125.5	32 47.7	-34.4	126.0	32 12.2	-35.2	126.5	31 36.3	-35.9	127.0	31 00.0	-36.7	127.5	30 23.3	-37.5	128.0	29 46.2	-38.2	128.4	29 08.7	-38.9	128.9	19
20	32 49.2	-34.0	126.5	32 13.3	-34.8	127.0	31 37.0	-35.5	127.5	31 00.4	-36.4	127.9	30 23.3	-37.1	128.4	29 45.8	-37.8	128.9	29 08.0	-38.6	129.3	28 29.8	-39.2	129.7	20
21	32 15.2	-34.4	127.4	31 38.5	-35.2	127.9	31 01.5	-36.0	128.4	30 24.0	-36.7	128.9	29 46.2	-37.5	129.3	29 08.0	-38.2	129.8	28 29.4	-38.8	130.2	27 50.6	-39.6	130.6	21
22	31 40.8	-34.9	128.4	31 03.3	-35.6	128.9	30 25.5	-36.4	129.3	29 47.3	-37.1	129.8	29 08.7	-37.8	130.2	28 29.8	-38.5	130.6	27 50.6	-39.2	131.0	27 11.0	-39.8	131.4	22
23	31 05.9	-35.2	129.3	30 27.7	-36.0	129.8	29 49.1	-36.7	130.3	29 10.2	-37.5	130.7	28 30.9	-38.2	131.1	27 51.3	-38.8	131.5	27 11.4	-39.5	131.9	26 31.2	-40.2	132.3	23
24	30 30.7	-35.7	130.3	29 51.7	-36.4	130.7	29 12.4	-37.1	131.2	28 32.7	-37.8	131.6	27 52.7	-38.4	132.0	27 12.5	-39.2	132.4	26 31.9	-39.8	132.7	25 51.0	-40.4	133.1	24
25	29 55.0	-36.1	131.2	29 15.3	-36.8	131.6	28 35.3	-37.5	132.1	27 54.9	-38.1	132.5	27 14.3	-38.8	132.8	26 33.3	-39.4	133.2	25 52.1	-40.1	133.6	25 10.6	-40.7	133.9	25
26	29 18.9	-36.4	132.1	28 38.5	-37.1	132.6	27 57.8	-37.8	132.9	27 16.8	-38.5	133.3	26 35.5	-39.1	133.7	25 53.9	-39.8	134.1	25 12.0	-40.3	134.4	24 29.9	-40.9	134.7	26
27	28 42.5	-36.8	133.0	28 01.4	-37.5	133.4	27 20.0	-38.1	133.8	26 38.3	-38.8	134.2	25 56.4	-39.4	134.5	25 14.1	-40.0	134.9	24 31.7	-40.6	135.2	23 49.0	-41.2	135.5	27
28	28 05.7	-37.1	133.9	27 23.9	-37.8	134.3	26 41.9	-38.5	134.7	25 59.5	-39.0	135.0	25 17.0	-39.7	135.4	24 34.1	-40.2	135.7	23 51.1	-40.9	136.0	23 07.8	-41.4	136.3	28
29	27 28.6	-37.5	134.8	26 46.1	-38.1	135.2	26 03.4	-38.7	135.5	25 20.5	-39.4	135.9	24 37.3	-40.0	136.2	23 53.9	-40.6	136.5	23 10.2	-41.1	136.8	22 26.4	-41.7	137.1	29
30	26 51.1	-37.8	135.7	26 08.0	-38.4	136.1	25 24.7	-39.0	136.4	24 41.1	-39.6	136.7	23 57.3	-40.2	137.0	23 13.3	-40.7	137.3	22 29.1	-41.3	137.6	21 44.7	-41.8	137.9	30
31	26 13.3	-38.1	136.6	25 29.6	-38.7	136.9	24 45.7	-39.3	137.2	24 01.5	-39.9	137.5	23 17.1	-40.4	137.8	22 32.6	-41.0	138.1	21 47.8	-41.5	138.4	21 02.9	-42.1	138.6	31
32	25 35.2	-38.4	137.4	24 50.9	-39.0	137.8	24 06.4	-39.6	138.1	23 21.6	-40.1	138.4	22 36.7	-40.7	138.6	21 51.6	-41.2	138.9	21 06.3	-41.8	139.2	20 20.8	-42.3	139.4	32
33	24 56.8	-38.7	138.3	24 11.9	-39.3	138.6	23 26.8	-39.8	138.9	22 41.5	-40.3	139.2	21 56.0	-40.9	139.4	21 10.4	-41.5	139.7	20 24.5	-41.9	139.9	19 38.5	-42.4	140.2	33
34	24 18.1	-38.9	139.1	23 32.6	-39.5	139.4	22 47.0	-40.1	139.7	22 01.1	-40.6	140.0	21 15.1	-41.1	140.2	20 28.9	-41.6	140.5	19 42.6	-42.2	140.7	18 56.1	-42.7	140.9	34
35	23 39.2	-39.3	140.0	22 53.1	-39.8	140.2	22 06.9	-40.3	140.5	21 20.5	-40.8	140.8	20 34.0	-41.4	141.0	19 47.3	-41.9	141.2	19 00.4	-42.3	141.4	18 13.4	-42.8	141.7	35
36	22 59.9	-39.5	140.8	22 13.3	-40.0	141.0	21 26.6	-40.5	141.3	20 39.7	-41.0	141.5	19 52.6	-41.5	141.8	19 05.4	-42.0	142.0	18 18.1	-42.5	142.2	17 30.6	-42.9	142.4	36
37	22 20.4	-39.7	141.6	21 33.3	-40.2	141.9	20 46.1	-40.8	142.1	19 58.7	-41.3	142.3	19 11.1	-41.7	142.5	18 23.4	-42.2	142.7	17 35.6	-42.7	142.9	16 47.7	-43.2	143.1	37
38	21 40.7	-39.9	142.4	20 53.1	-40.5	142.6	20 05.3	-40.9	142.9	19 17.4	-41.4	143.1	18 29.4	-41.9	143.3	17 41.2	-42.3	143.5	16 52.9	-42.8	143.7	16 04.5	-43.2	143.8	38
39	21 00.8	-40.2	143.2	20 12.6	-40.6	143.4	19 24.4	-41.2	143.7	18 36.0	-41.6	143.9	17 47.5	-42.1	144.0	16 58.9	-42.6	144.2	16 10.1	-42.9	144.4	15 21.3	-43.4	144.6	39
40	20 20.6	-40.4	144.0	19 32.0	-40.9	144.2	18 43.2	-41.3	144.4	17 54.4	-41.8	144.6	17 05.4	-42.2	144.8	16 16.3	-42.6	145.0	15 27.2	-43.2	145.1	14 37.9	-43.6	145.3	40
41	19 40.2	-40.6	144.8	18 51.1	-41.0	145.0	18 01.9	-41.5	145.2	17 12.6	-42.0	145.4	16 23.2	-42.4	145.5	15 33.7	-42.9	145.7	14 44.0	-43.2	145.9	13 54.3	-43.6	146.0	41
42	18 59.6	-40.8	145.6	18 10.1	-41.3	145.8	17 20.4	-41.7	145.9	16 30.6	-42.1	146.1	15 40.8	-42.6	146.3	14 50.8	-42.9	146.4	14 00.8	-43.4	146.6	13 10.7	-43.8	146.7	42
43	18 18.8	-41.0	146.3	17 28.8	-41.4	146.5	16 38.7	-41.8	146.7	15 48.5	-42.2	146.9	14 58.2	-42.6	147.0	14 07.9	-43.1	147.1	13 17.4	-43.4	147.3	12 26.9	-43.9	147.4	43
44	17 37.8	-41.1	147.1	16 47.4	-41.6	147.3	15 56.9	-42.0	147.4	15 06.3	-42.4	147.6	14 15.6	-42.8	147.7	13 24.8	-43.2	147.9	12 34.0	-43.6	148.0	11 43.0	-43.9	148.1	44
45	16 56.7	-41.3	147.9	16 05.8	-41.7	148.0	15 14.9	-42.2	148.2	14 23.9	-42.6	148.3	13 32.8	-43.0	148.5	12 41.6	-43.3	148.6	11 50.4	-43.7	148.7	10 59.1	-44.1	148.8	45
46	16 15.4	-41.5	148.6	15 24.1	-41.9	148.8	14 32.7	-42.2	148.9	13 41.3	-42.7	149.0	12 49.8	-43.0	149.2	11 58.3	-43.5	149.3	11 06.7	-43.8	149.4	10 15.0	-44.2	149.5	46
47	15 33.9	-41.7	149.4	14 42.2	-42.0	149.5	13 50.5	-42.4	149.7	12 58.6	-42.7	149.8	12 06.8	-43.2	149.9	11 14.8	-43.5	150.0	10 22.9	-43.9	150.1	9 30.8	-44.2	150.2	47
48	14 52.2	-41.7	150.1	14 00.2	-42.2	150.3	13 08.1	-42.6	150.4	12 15.9	-42.9	150.5	11 23.6	-43.2	150.6	10 31.3	-43.6	150.7	9 39.0	-44.0	150.8	8 46.6	-44.3	150.9	48
49	14 10.5	-41.9	150.9	13 18.0	-42.3	151.0	12 25.5	-42.6	151.1	11 33.0	-43.0	151.2	10 40.4	-43.4	151.3	9 47.7	-43.7	151.4	8 55.0	-44.0	151.5	8 02.3	-44.4	151.5	49
50	13 28.6	-42.1	151.6	12 35.7	-42.4	151.7	11 42.9	-42.8	151.8	10 50.0	-43.1	151.9	9 57.0	-43.4	152.0	9 04.0	-43.8	152.1	8 11.0	-44.1	152.2	7 17.9	-44.4	152.2	50
51	12 46.5	-42.1	152.3	11 53.3	-42.5	152.4	11 00.1	-42.8	152.5	10 06.9	-43.2	152.6	9 13.6	-43.6	152.7	8 20.2	-43.8	152.8	7 26.9	-44.2	152.8	6 33.5	-44.5	152.9	51
52	12 04.4	-42.3	153.1	11 10.8	-42.6	153.2	10 17.3	-43.0	153.2	9 23.7	-43.3	153.3	8 30.0	-43.5	153.4	7 36.4	-43.9	153.5	6 42.7	-44.2	153.5	5 49.0	-44.6	153.6	52
53	11 22.1	-42.4	153.8	10 28.2	-42.7	153.9	9 34.3	-43.0	154.0	8 40.4	-43.3	154.0	7 46.5	-43.7	154.1	6 52.5	-44.0	154.1	5 58.5	-44.3	154.2	5 04.4	-44.6	154.2	53
54	10 39.7	-42.5	154.5	9 45.5	-42.8	154.6	8 51.3	-43.1	154.7	7 57.1	-43.5	154.7	7 02.8	-43.7	154.8	6 08.5	-44.0	154.8	5 14.2	-44.3	154.9	4 19.8	-44.6	154.9	54
55	9 57.2	-42.6	155.2	9 02.7	-42.9	155.3	8 08.2	-43.2	155.4	7 13.6	-43.4	155.4	6 19.1	-43.8	155.5	5 24.5	-44.1	155.5	4 29.9	-44.4	155.6	3 35.2	-44.6	155.6	55
56	9 14.6	-42.6	155.9	8 19.8	-42.9	156.0	7 25.0	-43.2	156.1	6 30.2	-43.6	156.1	5 35.3	-43.8	156.2	4 40.4	-44.1	156.2	3 45.5	-44.4	156.2	2 50.6	-44.7	156.3	56
57	8 32.0	-42.7	156.7	7 36.9	-43.0	156.7	6 41.8	-43.3	156.8	5 46.6	-43.6	156.8	4 51.5	-43.9	156.8	3 56.3	-44.2	156.9	3 01.1	-44.4	156.9	2 05.9	-44.7	156.9	57
58	7 49.3	-42.8	157.4	6 53.9	-43.1	157.4	5 58.5	-43.4	157.5	5 03.0	-43.6	157.5	4 07.6	-43.9	157.5	3 12.1	-44.1	157.6	2 16.7	-44.5	157.6	1 21.2	-44.7	157.6	58
59	7 06.5	-42.9	158.1	6 10.8	-43.2	158.1	5 15.1	-43.4	158.2	4 19.4	-43.7	158.2	3 23.7	-43.9	158.2	2 28.0	-44.2	158.2	1 32.2	-44.4	158.2	0 36.5	-44.7	158.3	59
60	6 23.6	-42.9	158.8	5 27.6	-43.1	158.8	4 31.7	-43.4	158.9	3 35.7	-43.7	158.9	2 39.8	-44.0	158.9	1 43.8	-44.2	158.9	0 47.8	-44.5	158.9	0 08.2	+44.7	21.1	60
61	5 40.7	-43.0	159.5	4 44.5	-43.3	159.5	3 48.3	-43.5	159.5	2 52.0	-43.7	159.6	1 55.8	-44.0	159.6	0 59.6	-44.2	159.6	0 03.3	-44.4	159.6	0 52.9	+44.7	20.4	61
62	4 57.7	-43.0	160.2	4 01.2	-43.2	160.2	3 04.8	-43.5	160.2	2 08.3	-43.7	160.2	1 11.8	-43.9	160.3	0 15.4	-44.3	160.3	0 41.1	+44.5	19.7	1 37.6	+44.7	19.7	62
63	4 14.7	-43.1	160.9	3 18.0	-43.3	160.9	2 21.3	-43.6	160.9	1 24.6	-43.8	160.9	0 27.9	-44.0	160.9	0 28.9	+44.2	19.1	1 25.6	+44.4	19.1	2 22.3	+44.6	19.1	63
64	3 31.6	-43.1	161.6	2 34.7	-43.3	161.6	1 37.7	-43.5	161.6	0 40.8	-43.7	161.6	0 16.1	+44.0	18.4	1 13.1	+44.2	18.4	2 10.0	+44.4	18.4	3 06.9	+44.7	18.4	64
65	2 48.5	-43.1	162.3	1 51.4	-43.4	162.3	0 54.2	-43.5	162.3	0 02.9	+43.8	17.7	1 00.1	+44.0	17.7	1 57.3	+44.2	17.7	2 54.4	+44.4	17.7	3 51.6	+44.6	17.7	65
66	2 05.4	-43.1	163.0	1 08.0	-43.3	163.0	0 10.7	-43.6	163.0	0 46.7	+43.8	17.0	1 44.1	+43.9	17.0	2 41.5	+44.1	17.0	3 38.8	+44.4	17.0	4 36.2	+44.5	17.1	66
67	1 22.3	-43.2	163.7	0 24.7	-43.3	163.7	0 32.9	+43.5	16.3	1 30.5	+43.7	16.3	2 28.0	+44.0	16.3	3 25.6	+44.1	16.4	4 23.2	+44.3	16.4	5 20.7	+44.6	16.4	67
68	0 39.1	-43.1	164.4	0 18.6	+43.4	15.6	1 16.4	+43.6	15.6	2 14.2	+43.7	15.6	3 12.0	+43.9	15.7	4 09.7	+44.1	15.7	5 07.5	+44.3	15.7	6 05.3	+44.4	15.7	68
69	0 04.0	+43.2	14.9	1 02.0	+43.3	14.9	2 00.0	+43.5	14.9	2 57.9	+43.7	15.0	3 55.9	+43.9	15.0	4 53.8	+44.1	15.0	5 51.8	+44.2	15.0	6 49.7	+44.5	15.0	69
70	0 47.2	+43.1	14.2	1 45.3	+43.3	14.2	2 43.5	+43.5	14.3	3 41.6	+43.7	14.3	4 39.8	+43.8	14.3	5 37.9	+44.0	14.3	6 36.0	+44.2	14.3	7 34.2	+44.3	14.4	70
71	1 30.3	+43.1	13.5	2 28.6	+43.3	13.6	3 27.0	+43.4	13.6	4 25.3	+43.6	13.6	5 23.6	+43.8	13.6	6 21.9	+44.0	13.6	7 20.2	+44.1	13.7	8 18.5	+44.3	13.7	71
72	2 13.4	+43.1	12.9	3 11.9	+43.3	12.9	4 10.4	+43.4	12.9	5 08.9	+43.6	12.9	6 07.4	+43.7	12.9	7 05.9	+43.9	12.9	8 04.3	+44.1	13.0	9 02.8	+44.2	13.0	72
73	2 56.5	+43.1	12.2	3 55.2	+43.2	12.2	4 53.8	+43.4	12.2	5 52.5	+43.5	12.2	6 51.1	+43.7	12.2	7 49.8	+43.8	12.3	8 48.4	+44.0	12.3	9 47.0	+44.1	12.3	73
74	3 39.6	+43.1	11.5	4 38.4	+43.2	11.5	5 37.2	+43.4	11.5	6 36.0	+43.5	11.5	7 34.8	+43.6	11.5	8 33.6	+43.8	11.6	9 32.4	+43.9	11.6	10 31.1	+44.1	11.6	74
75	4 22.7	+43.0	10.8	5 21.6	+43.2	10.8	6 20.6	+43.2	10.8	7 19.5	+43.4	10.8	8 18.4	+43.6	10.8	9 17.4	+43.6	10.9	10 16.3	+43.8	10.9	11 15.2	+43.9	10.9	75
76	5 05.7	+43.0	10.1	6 04.8	+43.1	10.1	7 03.8	+43.3	10.1	8 02.9	+43.3	10.1	9 02.0	+43.4	10.1	10 01.0	+43.6	10.2	11 00.1	+43.7	10.2	11 59.1	+43.9	10.2	76
77	5 48.7	+42.9	9.4	6 47.9	+43.0	9.4	7 47.1	+43.1	9.4	8 46.2	+43.3	9.4	9 45.4	+43.4	9.5	10 44.6	+43.5	9.5	11 43.8	+43.6	9.5	12 43.0	+43.7	9.5	77
78	6 31.6	+42.8	8.7	7 30.9	+42.9	8.7	8 30.2	+43.1	8.7	9 29.5	+43.2	8.7	10 28.8	+43.3	8.7	11 28.1	+43.4	8.8	12 27.4	+43.5	8.8	13 26.7	+43.6	8.8	78
79	7 14.4	+42.8	8.0	8 13.8	+42.9	8.0	9 13.3	+43.0	8.0	10 12.7	+43.1	8.0	11 12.1	+43.2	8.0	12 11.5	+43.3	8.1	13 10.9	+43.4	8.1	14 10.3	+43.5	8.1	79
80	7 57.2	+42.7	7.2	8 56.7	+42.8	7.3	9 56.3	+42.8	7.3	10 55.8	+43.0	7.3	11 55.3	+43.1	7.3	12 54.8	+43.2	7.4	13 54.3	+43.2	7.4	14 53.8	+43.3	7.4	80
81	8 39.9	+42.7	6.5	9 39.5	+42.8	6.6	10 39.1	+42.9	6.6	11 38.8	+42.8	6.6	12 38.4	+42.9	6.6	13 38.0	+43.0	6.6	14 37.5	+43.2	6.7	15 37.1	+43.3	6.7	81
82	9 22.6	+42.5	5.8	10 22.3	+42.6	5.8	11 22.0	+42.6	5.9	12 21.6	+42.8	5.9	13 21.3	+42.9	5.9	14 21.0	+42.9	5.9	15 20.7	+43.0	6.0	16 20.4	+43.0	6.0	82
83	10 05.1	+42.5	5.1	11 04.9	+42.5	5.1	12 04.6	+42.6	5.1	13 04.4	+42.7	5.2	14 04.2	+42.7	5.2	15 03.9	+42.8	5.2	16 03.7	+42.8	5.2	17 03.4	+42.9	5.3	83
84	10 47.6	+42.3	4.4	11 47.4	+42.4	4.4	12 47.2	+42.5	4.4	13 47.1	+42.5	4.4	14 46.9	+42.6	4.5	15 46.7	+42.6	4.5	16 46.5	+42.7	4.5	17 46.3	+42.8	4.5	84
85	11 29.9	+42.3	3.7	12 29.8	+42.3	3.7	13 29.7	+42.3	3.7	14 29.6	+42.4	3.7	15 29.5	+42.4	3.7	16 29.3	+42.5	3.7	17 29.2	+42.5	3.8	18 29.1	+42.5	3.8	85
86	12 12.2	+42.1	2.9	13 12.1	+42.2	3.0	14 12.0	+42.3	3.0	15 12.0	+42.2	3.0	16 11.9	+42.3	3.0	17 11.8	+42.3	3.0	18 11.7	+42.4	3.0	19 11.6	+42.4	3.0	86
87	12 54.3	+42.1	2.2	13 54.3	+42.0	2.2	14 54.3	+42.0	2.2	15 54.2	+42.1	2.2	16 54.2	+42.1	2.3	17 54.1	+42.2	2.3	18 54.1	+42.1	2.3	19 54.0	+42.2	2.3	87
88	13 36.4	+41.8	1.5	14 36.3	+41.9	1.5	15 36.3	+41.9	1.5	16 36.3	+41.9	1.5	17 36.3	+41.9	1.5	18 36.3	+41.9	1.5	19 36.2	+42.0	1.5	20 36.2	+42.0	1.5	88
89	14 18.2	+41.8	0.7	15 18.2	+41.8	0.7	16 18.2	+41.8	0.7	17 18.2	+41.8	0.8	18 18.2	+41.8	0.8	19 18.2	+41.8	0.8	20 18.2	+41.8	0.8	21 18.2	+41.8	0.8	89
90	15 00.0	+41.6	0.0	16 00.0	+41.6	0.0	17 00.0	+41.6	0.0	18 00.0	+41.6	0.0	19 00.0	+41.6	0.0	20 00.0	+41.6	0.0	21 00.0	+41.6	0.0	22 00.0	+41.6	0.0	90
	15°			16°			17°			18°			19°			20°			21°			22°			

S. Lat. { L.H.A. greater than 180° ....Zn=180°−Z
L.H.A. less than 180°...........Zn=180°+Z

LATITUDE SAME NAME AS DECLINATION — L.H.A. 134°, 226°

47°, 313° L.H.A. LATITUDE SAME NAME AS DECLINATION N. Lat. {L.H.A. greater than 180° .....Zn=Z / L.H.A. less than 180°............Zn=360°-Z}

Dec.	15° Hc	d	Z	16° Hc	d	Z	17° Hc	d	Z	18° Hc	d	Z	Dec.
°	° ′	′	°	° ′	′	°	° ′	′	°	° ′	′	°	°
0	41 12.3	+20.3	103.6	40 57.8	+21.5	104.4	40 42.5	+22.7	105.3	40 26.3	+23.9	106.1	0
1	41 32.6	+19.4	102.3	41 19.3	+20.7	103.2	41 05.2	+22.0	104.0	40 50.2	+23.3	104.9	1
2	41 52.0	+18.5	101.0	41 40.0	+19.9	101.9	41 27.2	+21.1	102.8	41 13.5	+22.4	103.6	2
3	42 10.5	+17.7	99.8	41 59.9	+19.0	100.7	41 48.3	+20.4	101.5	41 35.9	+21.6	102.4	3
4	42 28.2	+16.8	98.5	42 18.9	+18.2	99.4	42 08.7	+19.5	100.3	41 57.5	+20.8	101.2	4
5	42 45.0	+16.0	97.2	42 37.1	+17.3	98.1	42 28.2	+18.6	99.0	42 18.3	+20.0	99.9	5
6	43 01.0	+15.0	95.9	42 54.4	+16.4	96.8	42 46.8	+17.8	97.7	42 38.3	+19.1	98.6	6
7	43 16.0	+14.1	94.5	43 10.8	+15.4	95.5	43 04.6	+16.8	96.4	42 57.4	+18.2	97.3	7
8	43 30.1	+13.1	93.2	43 26.2	+14.6	94.1	43 21.4	+16.0	95.1	43 15.6	+17.3	96.0	8
9	43 43.2	+12.2	91.8	43 40.8	+13.6	92.8	43 37.4	+15.0	93.7	43 32.9	+16.4	94.7	9
10	43 55.4	+11.2	90.5	43 54.4	+12.6	91.4	43 52.4	+14.0	92.4	43 49.3	+15.5	93.4	10
11	44 06.6	+10.3	89.1	44 07.0	+11.7	90.1	44 06.4	+13.1	91.1	44 04.8	+14.5	92.0	11
12	44 16.9	+9.2	87.7	44 18.7	+10.7	88.7	44 19.5	+12.2	89.7	44 19.3	+13.6	90.7	12
13	44 26.1	+8.2	86.4	44 29.4	+9.7	87.3	44 31.7	+11.1	88.3	44 32.9	+12.6	89.3	13
14	44 34.3	+7.2	85.0	44 39.1	+8.6	86.0	44 42.8	+10.1	86.9	44 45.5	+11.5	87.9	14
15	44 41.5	+6.2	83.6	44 47.7	+7.7	84.6	44 52.9	+9.1	85.6	44 57.0	+10.6	86.6	15
16	44 47.7	+5.2	82.2	44 55.4	+6.6	83.2	45 02.0	+8.1	84.2	45 07.6	+9.5	85.2	16
17	44 52.9	+4.1	80.8	45 02.0	+5.6	81.8	45 10.1	+7.0	82.8	45 17.1	+8.6	83.8	17
18	44 57.0	+3.1	79.4	45 07.6	+4.5	80.4	45 17.1	+6.1	81.3	45 25.7	+7.4	82.3	18
19	45 00.1	+2.1	78.0	45 12.1	+3.5	78.9	45 23.2	+4.9	79.9	45 33.1	+6.4	80.9	19
20	45 02.2	+1.0	76.5	45 15.6	+2.5	77.5	45 28.1	+3.9	78.5	45 39.5	+5.4	79.5	20
21	45 03.2	-0.1	75.1	45 18.1	+1.4	76.1	45 32.0	+2.8	77.1	45 44.9	+4.3	78.1	21
22	45 03.1	-1.1	73.7	45 19.5	+0.3	74.7	45 34.8	+1.8	75.7	45 49.2	+3.2	76.7	22
23	45 02.0	-2.1	72.3	45 19.8	-0.8	73.3	45 36.6	+0.7	74.2	45 52.4	+2.1	75.2	23
24	44 59.9	-3.2	70.9	45 19.0	-1.8	71.8	45 37.3	-0.4	72.8	45 54.5	+1.1	73.8	24
25	44 56.7	-4.3	69.5	45 17.2	-2.8	70.4	45 36.9	-1.5	71.4	45 55.6	-0.1	72.3	25
26	44 52.4	-5.2	68.1	45 14.4	-3.9	69.0	45 35.4	-2.5	69.9	45 55.5	-1.1	70.9	26
27	44 47.2	-6.3	66.7	45 10.5	-5.0	67.6	45 32.9	-3.6	68.5	45 54.4	-2.2	69.5	27
28	44 40.9	-7.4	65.3	45 05.5	-6.0	66.2	45 29.3	-4.6	67.1	45 52.2	-3.2	68.0	28
29	44 33.5	-8.3	63.9	44 59.5	-7.0	64.8	45 24.7	-5.7	65.7	45 49.0	-4.4	66.6	29
30	44 25.2	-9.3	62.5	44 52.5	-8.0	63.4	45 19.0	-6.7	64.3	45 44.6	-5.4	65.2	30
31	44 15.9	-10.4	61.1	44 44.5	-9.1	62.0	45 12.3	-7.8	62.8	45 39.2	-6.4	63.7	31
32	44 05.5	-11.3	59.7	44 35.4	-10.1	60.6	45 04.5	-8.8	61.4	45 32.8	-7.6	62.3	32
33	43 54.2	-12.3	58.4	44 25.3	-11.1	59.2	44 55.7	-9.9	60.0	45 25.2	-8.5	60.9	33
34	43 41.9	-13.2	57.0	44 14.2	-12.0	57.8	44 45.8	-10.8	58.6	45 16.7	-9.6	59.5	34
35	43 28.7	-14.2	55.6	44 02.2	-13.0	56.4	44 35.0	-11.8	57.3	45 07.1	-10.6	58.1	35
36	43 14.5	-15.1	54.3	43 49.2	-14.0	55.1	44 23.2	-12.8	55.9	44 56.5	-11.7	56.7	36
37	42 59.4	-16.0	53.0	43 35.2	-14.9	53.7	44 10.4	-13.8	54.5	44 44.8	-12.6	55.3	37
38	42 43.4	-16.9	51.7	43 20.3	-15.8	52.4	43 56.6	-14.8	53.2	44 32.2	-13.6	54.0	38
39	42 26.5	-17.8	50.4	43 04.5	-16.8	51.1	43 41.8	-15.6	51.8	44 18.6	-14.6	52.6	39
40	42 08.7	-18.7	49.1	42 47.7	-17.6	49.8	43 26.2	-16.6	50.5	44 04.0	-15.5	51.2	40
41	41 50.0	-19.5	47.8	42 30.1	-18.5	48.5	43 09.6	-17.5	49.2	43 48.5	-16.4	49.9	41
42	41 30.5	-20.3	46.5	42 11.6	-19.4	47.2	42 52.1	-18.4	47.9	43 32.1	-17.4	48.6	42
43	41 10.2	-21.1	45.3	41 52.2	-20.2	45.9	42 33.7	-19.2	46.6	43 14.7	-18.3	47.2	43
44	40 49.1	-21.9	44.0	41 32.0	-21.0	44.7	42 14.5	-20.1	45.3	42 56.4	-19.1	45.9	44
45	40 27.2	-22.7	42.8	41 11.0	-21.8	43.4	41 54.4	-21.0	44.0	42 37.3	-20.0	44.7	45
46	40 04.5	-23.4	41.6	40 49.2	-22.6	42.2	41 33.4	-21.7	42.8	42 17.3	-20.9	43.4	46
47	39 41.1	-24.2	40.4	40 26.6	-23.4	40.9	41 11.7	-22.5	41.5	41 56.4	-21.6	42.1	47
48	39 16.9	-24.9	39.2	40 03.2	-24.1	39.7	40 49.2	-23.3	40.3	41 34.8	-22.5	40.9	48
49	38 52.0	-25.5	38.0	39 39.1	-24.8	38.5	40 25.9	-24.1	39.1	41 12.3	-23.3	39.6	49
50	38 26.5	-26.3	36.9	39 14.3	-25.5	37.4	40 01.8	-24.8	37.9	40 49.0	-24.0	38.4	50
51	38 00.2	-26.9	35.7	38 48.8	-26.2	36.2	39 37.0	-25.5	36.7	40 25.0	-24.8	37.2	51
52	37 33.3	-27.5	34.6	38 22.6	-26.9	35.1	39 11.5	-26.2	35.5	40 00.2	-25.5	36.0	52
53	37 05.8	-28.2	33.5	37 55.7	-27.5	33.9	38 45.3	-26.8	34.4	39 34.7	-26.2	34.8	53
54	36 37.6	-28.8	32.4	37 28.2	-28.2	32.8	38 18.5	-27.6	33.2	39 08.5	-26.8	33.7	54
55	36 08.8	-29.3	31.3	37 00.0	-28.8	31.7	37 50.9	-28.1	32.1	38 41.7	-27.6	32.5	55
56	35 39.5	-29.9	30.2	36 31.2	-29.3	30.6	37 22.8	-28.8	31.0	38 14.1	-28.2	31.4	56
57	35 09.6	-30.5	29.2	36 01.9	-30.0	29.5	36 54.0	-29.4	29.9	37 45.9	-28.8	30.3	57
58	34 39.1	-31.0	28.1	35 31.9	-30.5	28.4	36 24.6	-30.0	28.8	37 17.1	-29.4	29.2	58
59	34 08.1	-31.6	27.1	35 01.4	-31.0	27.4	35 54.6	-30.5	27.7	36 47.7	-30.1	28.1	59
60	33 36.5	-32.0	26.0	34 30.4	-31.6	26.3	35 24.1	-31.1	26.7	36 17.6	-30.6	27.0	60
61	33 04.5	-32.5	25.0	33 58.8	-32.0	25.3	34 53.0	-31.6	25.6	35 47.0	-31.1	25.9	61
62	32 32.0	-33.0	24.0	33 26.8	-32.6	24.3	34 21.4	-32.2	24.6	35 15.9	-31.7	24.9	62
63	31 59.0	-33.4	23.0	32 54.2	-33.0	23.3	33 49.2	-32.6	23.6	34 44.2	-32.2	23.8	63
64	31 25.6	-33.9	22.1	32 21.2	-33.5	22.3	33 16.6	-33.1	22.5	34 12.0	-32.7	22.8	64
65	30 51.7	-34.3	21.1	31 47.7	-34.0	21.3	32 43.5	-33.6	21.6	33 39.3	-33.2	21.8	65
66	30 17.4	-34.7	20.2	31 13.7	-34.3	20.4	32 09.9	-34.0	20.6	33 06.1	-33.7	20.8	66
67	29 42.7	-35.1	19.2	30 39.4	-34.8	19.4	31 35.9	-34.4	19.6	32 32.4	-34.1	19.8	67
68	29 07.6	-35.5	18.3	30 04.6	-35.2	18.5	31 01.5	-34.9	18.6	31 58.3	-34.6	18.8	68
69	28 32.1	-35.8	17.4	29 29.4	-35.6	17.5	30 26.6	-35.3	17.7	31 23.7	-35.0	17.9	69
70	27 56.3	-36.2	16.4	28 53.8	-35.9	16.6	29 51.3	-35.7	16.8	30 48.7	-35.4	16.9	70
71	27 20.1	-36.6	15.5	28 17.9	-36.3	15.7	29 15.6	-36.0	15.8	30 13.3	-35.8	16.0	71
72	26 43.5	-36.8	14.7	27 41.6	-36.7	14.8	28 39.6	-36.4	14.9	29 37.5	-36.2	15.1	72
73	26 06.7	-37.2	13.8	27 04.9	-37.0	13.9	28 03.2	-36.8	14.0	29 01.3	-36.5	14.2	73
74	25 29.5	-37.5	12.9	26 27.9	-37.3	13.0	27 26.4	-37.1	13.1	28 24.8	-36.9	13.2	74
75	24 52.0	-37.8	12.0	25 50.6	-37.6	12.1	26 49.3	-37.4	12.2	27 47.9	-37.2	12.4	75
76	24 14.2	-38.1	11.2	25 13.0	-37.9	11.3	26 11.9	-37.8	11.4	27 10.7	-37.6	11.5	76
77	23 36.1	-38.4	10.3	24 35.1	-38.2	10.4	25 34.1	-38.0	10.5	26 33.1	-37.9	10.6	77
78	22 57.7	-38.6	9.5	23 56.9	-38.5	9.6	24 56.1	-38.4	9.7	25 55.2	-38.2	9.7	78
79	22 19.1	-38.8	8.7	23 18.4	-38.7	8.7	24 17.7	-38.6	8.8	25 17.0	-38.5	8.9	79
80	21 40.3	-39.1	7.9	22 39.7	-39.0	7.9	23 39.1	-38.8	8.0	24 38.5	-38.7	8.0	80
81	21 01.2	-39.4	7.0	22 00.7	-39.2	7.1	23 00.3	-39.2	7.1	23 59.8	-39.1	7.2	81
82	20 21.8	-39.5	6.2	21 21.5	-39.5	6.3	22 21.1	-39.4	6.3	23 20.7	-39.2	6.4	82
83	19 42.3	-39.8	5.4	20 42.0	-39.7	5.5	21 41.7	-39.6	5.5	22 41.5	-39.6	5.5	83
84	19 02.5	-39.9	4.6	20 02.3	-39.9	4.7	21 02.1	-39.8	4.7	22 01.9	-39.8	4.7	84
85	18 22.6	-40.2	3.9	19 22.4	-40.1	3.9	20 22.3	-40.1	3.9	21 22.1	-40.0	3.9	85
86	17 42.4	-40.4	3.1	18 42.3	-40.3	3.1	19 42.2	-40.2	3.1	20 42.1	-40.2	3.1	86
87	17 02.0	-40.5	2.3	18 02.0	-40.5	2.3	19 02.0	-40.5	2.3	20 01.9	-40.4	2.3	87
88	16 21.5	-40.7	1.5	17 21.5	-40.7	1.5	18 21.5	-40.7	1.5	19 21.5	-40.7	1.6	88
89	15 40.8	-40.8	0.8	16 40.8	-40.8	0.8	17 40.8	-40.8	0.8	18 40.8	-40.8	0.8	89
90	15 00.0	-41.0	0.0	16 00.0	-41.0	0.0	17 00.0	-41.0	0.0	18 00.0	-41.0	0.0	90
	15°			16°			17°			18°			

Dec.	19° Hc	d	Z	20° Hc	d	Z	21° Hc	d	Z	22° Hc	d	Z	Dec.
°	° ′	′	°	° ′	′	°	° ′	′	°	° ′	′	°	°
0	40 09.2	+25.2	106.9	39 51.4	+26.4	107.7	39 32.8	+27.5	108.5	39 13.4	+28.7	109.3	0
1	40 34.4	+24.5	105.7	40 17.8	+25.6	106.5	40 00.3	+26.9	107.3	39 42.1	+28.0	108.1	1
2	40 58.9	+23.7	104.5	40 43.4	+25.0	105.3	40 27.2	+26.1	106.2	40 10.1	+27.3	107.0	2
3	41 22.6	+22.9	103.3	41 08.4	+24.1	104.1	40 53.3	+25.4	105.0	40 37.4	+26.6	105.8	3
4	41 45.5	+22.1	102.0	41 32.5	+23.4	102.9	41 18.7	+24.6	103.8	41 04.0	+25.8	104.6	4
5	42 07.6	+21.2	100.8	41 55.9	+22.5	101.7	41 43.3	+23.8	102.5	41 29.8	+25.1	103.4	5
6	42 28.8	+20.5	99.5	42 18.4	+21.8	100.4	42 07.1	+23.1	101.3	41 54.9	+24.3	102.2	6
7	42 49.3	+19.5	98.2	42 40.2	+20.9	99.2	42 30.2	+22.2	100.1	42 19.2	+23.5	101.0	7
8	43 08.8	+18.7	97.0	43 01.1	+20.0	97.9	42 52.4	+21.4	98.8	42 42.7	+22.7	99.7	8
9	43 27.5	+17.8	95.6	43 21.1	+19.2	96.6	43 13.8	+20.5	97.5	43 05.4	+21.9	98.4	9
10	43 45.3	+16.9	94.3	43 40.3	+18.2	95.3	43 34.3	+19.6	96.2	43 27.3	+21.0	97.2	10
11	44 02.2	+15.9	93.0	43 58.5	+17.4	94.0	43 53.9	+18.7	94.9	43 48.3	+20.1	95.9	11
12	44 18.1	+15.0	91.6	44 15.9	+16.4	92.6	44 12.6	+17.8	93.6	44 08.4	+19.1	94.6	12
13	44 33.1	+14.0	90.3	44 32.3	+15.4	91.3	44 30.4	+16.9	92.3	44 27.5	+18.3	93.2	13
14	44 47.1	+13.0	88.9	44 47.7	+14.5	89.9	44 47.3	+15.9	90.9	44 45.8	+17.3	91.9	14
15	45 00.1	+12.0	87.5	45 02.2	+13.4	88.5	45 03.2	+14.9	89.5	45 03.1	+16.4	90.6	15
16	45 12.1	+11.1	86.2	45 15.6	+12.5	87.2	45 18.1	+13.9	88.2	45 19.5	+15.3	89.2	16
17	45 23.2	+9.9	84.8	45 28.1	+11.4	85.8	45 32.0	+12.9	86.8	45 34.8	+14.4	87.8	17
18	45 33.1	+9.0	83.4	45 39.5	+10.4	84.4	45 44.9	+11.9	85.4	45 49.2	+13.3	86.4	18
19	45 42.1	+7.8	81.9	45 49.9	+9.4	83.0	45 56.8	+10.8	84.0	46 02.5	+12.3	85.0	19
20	45 49.9	+6.9	80.5	45 59.3	+8.3	81.5	46 07.6	+9.8	82.6	46 14.8	+11.3	83.6	20
21	45 56.8	+5.7	79.1	46 07.6	+7.2	80.1	46 17.4	+8.7	81.1	46 26.1	+10.1	82.2	21
22	46 02.5	+4.7	77.7	46 14.8	+6.2	78.7	46 26.1	+7.6	79.7	46 36.2	+9.1	80.7	22
23	46 07.2	+3.6	76.2	46 21.0	+5.0	77.2	46 33.7	+6.5	78.3	46 45.3	+8.1	79.3	23
24	46 10.8	+2.5	74.8	46 26.0	+4.0	75.8	46 40.2	+5.4	76.8	46 53.4	+6.9	77.9	24
25	46 13.3	+1.4	73.3	46 30.0	+2.8	74.3	46 45.6	+4.4	75.4	47 00.3	+5.8	76.4	25
26	46 14.7	+0.3	71.9	46 32.8	+1.8	72.9	46 50.0	+3.2	73.9	47 06.1	+4.7	74.9	26
27	46 15.0	-0.8	70.4	46 34.6	+0.6	71.4	46 53.2	+2.1	72.5	47 10.8	+3.5	73.5	27
28	46 14.2	-1.9	69.0	46 35.2	-0.4	70.0	46 55.3	+1.0	71.0	47 14.3	+2.5	72.0	28
29	46 12.3	-2.9	67.6	46 34.8	-1.6	68.5	46 56.3	-0.2	69.5	47 16.8	+1.2	70.5	29
30	46 09.4	-4.1	66.1	46 33.2	-2.6	67.1	46 56.1	-1.2	68.1	47 18.0	+0.2	69.1	30
31	46 05.3	-5.1	64.7	46 30.6	-3.8	65.6	46 54.9	-2.4	66.6	47 18.2	-1.0	67.6	31
32	46 00.2	-6.2	63.2	46 26.8	-4.9	64.2	46 52.5	-3.5	65.1	47 17.2	-2.1	66.1	32
33	45 54.0	-7.3	61.8	46 21.9	-5.9	62.7	46 49.0	-4.6	63.7	47 15.1	-3.2	64.6	33
34	45 46.7	-8.3	60.4	46 16.0	-7.1	61.3	46 44.4	-5.7	62.2	47 11.9	-4.4	63.2	34
35	45 38.4	-9.4	59.0	46 08.9	-8.1	59.9	46 38.7	-6.8	60.8	47 07.5	-5.4	61.7	35
36	45 29.0	-10.4	57.6	46 00.8	-9.1	58.4	46 31.9	-7.9	59.3	47 02.1	-6.6	60.2	36
37	45 18.6	-11.4	56.2	45 51.7	-10.3	57.0	46 24.0	-9.0	57.9	46 55.5	-7.7	58.8	37
38	45 07.2	-12.5	54.8	45 41.4	-11.2	55.6	46 15.0	-10.1	56.5	46 47.8	-8.8	57.3	38
39	44 54.7	-13.4	53.4	45 30.2	-12.3	54.2	46 04.9	-11.1	55.0	46 39.0	-9.9	55.9	39
40	44 41.3	-14.4	52.0	45 17.9	-13.3	52.8	45 53.8	-12.1	53.6	46 29.1	-11.0	54.5	40
41	44 26.9	-15.4	50.6	45 04.6	-14.3	51.4	45 41.7	-13.1	52.2	46 18.1	-12.0	53.0	41
42	44 11.5	-16.3	49.3	44 50.3	-15.2	50.0	45 28.6	-14.2	50.8	46 06.1	-13.0	51.6	42
43	43 55.2	-17.3	47.9	44 35.1	-16.3	48.7	45 14.4	-15.2	49.4	45 53.1	-14.1	50.2	43
44	43 37.9	-18.2	46.6	44 18.8	-17.1	47.3	44 59.2	-16.1	48.1	45 39.0	-15.0	48.8	44
45	43 19.7	-19.0	45.3	44 01.7	-18.1	46.0	44 43.1	-17.1	46.7	45 24.0	-16.1	47.4	45
46	43 00.7	-20.0	44.0	43 43.6	-19.0	44.7	44 26.0	-18.0	45.4	45 07.9	-17.0	46.1	46
47	42 40.7	-20.8	42.7	43 24.6	-19.9	43.4	44 08.0	-19.0	44.0	44 50.9	-18.0	44.7	47
48	42 19.9	-21.6	41.5	43 04.7	-20.8	42.1	43 49.0	-19.8	42.7	44 32.9	-19.0	43.4	48
49	41 58.3	-22.4	40.2	42 43.9	-21.6	40.8	43 29.2	-20.8	41.4	44 13.9	-19.8	42.0	49
50	41 35.9	-23.3	38.9	42 22.3	-22.4	39.5	43 08.4	-21.6	40.1	43 54.1	-20.7	40.7	50
51	41 12.6	-24.0	37.7	41 59.9	-23.2	38.3	42 46.8	-22.4	38.8	43 33.4	-21.6	39.4	51
52	40 48.6	-24.8	36.5	41 36.7	-24.0	37.0	42 24.4	-23.2	37.6	43 11.8	-22.5	38.1	52
53	40 23.8	-25.5	35.3	41 12.7	-24.8	35.8	42 01.2	-24.1	36.3	42 49.3	-23.3	36.9	53
54	39 58.3	-26.2	34.1	40 47.9	-25.6	34.6	41 37.1	-24.8	35.1	42 26.0	-24.0	35.6	54
55	39 32.1	-26.9	33.0	40 22.3	-26.2	33.4	41 12.3	-25.6	33.9	42 02.0	-24.9	34.4	55
56	39 05.2	-27.6	31.8	39 56.1	-27.0	32.2	40 46.7	-26.3	32.7	41 37.1	-25.7	33.2	56
57	38 37.6	-28.2	30.7	39 29.1	-27.6	31.1	40 20.4	-27.0	31.5	41 11.4	-26.3	32.0	57
58	38 09.4	-28.9	29.5	39 01.5	-28.3	29.9	39 53.4	-27.7	30.3	40 45.1	-27.2	30.8	58
59	37 40.5	-29.5	28.4	38 33.2	-29.0	28.8	39 25.7	-28.4	29.2	40 17.9	-27.8	29.6	59
60	37 11.0	-30.1	27.3	38 04.2	-29.5	27.7	38 57.3	-29.1	28.0	39 50.1	-28.5	28.4	60
61	36 40.9	-30.7	26.2	37 34.7	-30.2	26.6	38 28.2	-29.6	26.9	39 21.6	-29.1	27.3	61
62	36 10.2	-31.2	25.2	37 04.5	-30.8	25.5	37 58.6	-30.3	25.8	38 52.5	-29.8	26.2	62
63	35 39.0	-31.8	24.1	36 33.7	-31.3	24.4	37 28.3	-30.9	24.7	38 22.7	-30.4	25.1	63
64	35 07.2	-32.3	23.1	36 02.4	-31.9	23.4	36 57.4	-31.5	23.7	37 52.3	-31.0	24.0	64
65	34 34.9	-32.8	22.0	35 30.5	-32.4	22.3	36 25.9	-32.0	22.6	37 21.3	-31.6	22.9	65
66	34 02.1	-33.3	21.0	34 58.1	-33.0	21.3	35 53.9	-32.5	21.5	36 49.7	-32.2	21.8	66
67	33 28.8	-33.8	20.0	34 25.1	-33.4	20.3	35 21.4	-33.1	20.5	36 17.5	-32.7	20.8	67
68	32 55.0	-34.2	19.0	33 51.7	-33.9	19.3	34 48.3	-33.6	19.5	35 44.8	-33.2	19.7	68
69	32 20.8	-34.7	18.1	33 17.8	-34.4	18.3	34 14.7	-34.0	18.5	35 11.6	-33.7	18.7	69
70	31 46.1	-35.1	17.1	32 43.4	-34.8	17.3	33 40.7	-34.6	17.5	34 37.9	-34.3	17.7	70
71	31 11.0	-35.6	16.2	32 08.6	-35.3	16.3	33 06.1	-35.0	16.5	34 03.6	-34.7	16.7	71
72	30 35.4	-35.9	15.2	31 33.3	-35.7	15.4	32 31.1	-35.4	15.5	33 28.9	-35.1	15.7	72
73	29 59.5	-36.3	14.3	30 57.6	-36.1	14.4	31 55.7	-35.8	14.6	32 53.8	-35.6	14.8	73
74	29 23.2	-36.7	13.4	30 21.5	-36.4	13.5	31 19.9	-36.3	13.7	32 18.2	-36.1	13.8	74
75	28 46.5	-37.0	12.5	29 45.1	-36.9	12.6	30 43.6	-36.6	12.7	31 42.1	-36.4	12.9	75
76	28 09.5	-37.4	11.6	29 08.2	-37.2	11.7	30 07.0	-37.1	11.8	31 05.7	-36.8	11.9	76
77	27 32.1	-37.8	10.7	28 31.0	-37.5	10.8	29 29.9	-37.3	10.9	30 28.9	-37.3	11.0	77
78	26 54.3	-38.0	9.8	27 53.5	-37.9	9.9	28 52.6	-37.8	10.0	29 51.6	-37.6	10.1	78
79	26 16.3	-38.3	9.0	27 15.6	-38.3	9.0	28 14.8	-38.1	9.1	29 14.0	-37.9	9.2	79
80	25 38.0	-38.7	8.1	26 37.3	-38.5	8.2	27 36.7	-38.4	8.2	28 36.1	-38.3	8.3	80
81	24 59.3	-38.9	7.3	25 58.8	-38.8	7.3	26 58.3	-38.7	7.4	27 57.8	-38.6	7.4	81
82	24 20.4	-39.2	6.4	25 20.0	-39.1	6.5	26 19.6	-39.0	6.5	27 19.2	-38.9	6.6	82
83	23 41.2	-39.5	5.6	24 40.9	-39.4	5.6	25 40.6	-39.3	5.7	26 40.3	-39.2	5.7	83
84	23 01.7	-39.7	4.8	24 01.5	-39.6	4.8	25 01.3	-39.6	4.8	26 01.1	-39.5	4.9	84
85	22 22.0	-40.0	4.0	23 21.9	-40.0	4.0	24 21.7	-39.8	4.0	25 21.6	-39.8	4.0	85
86	21 42.0	-40.1	3.1	22 41.9	-40.1	3.2	23 41.9	-40.2	3.2	24 41.8	-40.1	3.2	86
87	21 01.9	-40.5	2.4	22 01.8	-40.4	2.4	23 01.7	-40.3	2.4	24 01.7	-40.3	2.4	87
88	20 21.4	-40.6	1.6	21 21.4	-40.6	1.6	22 21.4	-40.6	1.6	23 21.4	-40.6	1.6	88
89	19 40.8	-40.8	0.8	20 40.8	-40.8	0.8	21 40.8	-40.8	0.8	22 40.8	-40.8	0.8	89
90	19 00.0	-41.0	0.0	20 00.0	-41.0	0.0	21 00.0	-41.0	0.0	22 00.0	-41.0	0.0	90
	19°			20°			21°			22°			

47°, 313° L.H.A. LATITUDE SAME NAME AS DECLINATION

96

LATITUDE CONTRARY NAME TO DECLINATION L.H.A. 47°, 313°

Dec.	15°			16°			17°			18°		
	Hc	d	Z	Hc	d	Z	Hc	d	Z	Hc	d	Z
°	° ′	′	°	° ′	′	°	° ′	′	°	° ′	′	°
0	41 12.3	-21.0	103.6	40 57.8	-22.3	104.4	40 42.5	-23.6	105.3	40 26.3	-24.8	106.1
1	40 51.3	-21.9	104.8	40 35.5	-23.0	105.6	40 18.9	-24.2	106.5	40 01.5	-25.4	107.3
2	40 29.4	-22.6	106.0	40 12.5	-23.9	106.9	39 54.7	-25.0	107.7	39 36.1	-26.2	108.4
3	40 06.8	-23.3	107.3	39 48.6	-24.5	108.1	39 29.7	-25.7	108.8	39 09.9	-26.8	109.6
4	39 43.5	-24.1	108.5	39 24.1	-25.2	109.2	39 04.0	-26.4	110.0	38 43.1	-27.6	110.8
5	39 19.4	-24.8	109.6	38 58.9	-26.0	110.4	38 37.6	-27.1	111.2	38 15.5	-28.1	111.9
6	38 54.6	-25.5	110.8	38 32.9	-26.6	111.6	38 10.5	-27.7	112.3	37 47.4	-28.8	113.0
7	38 29.1	-26.2	112.0	38 06.3	-27.3	112.7	37 42.8	-28.4	113.4	37 18.6	-29.4	114.1
8	38 02.9	-26.8	113.1	37 39.0	-27.9	113.8	37 14.4	-28.9	114.5	36 49.2	-30.0	115.2
9	37 36.1	-27.5	114.3	37 11.1	-28.5	114.9	36 45.5	-29.6	115.6	36 19.2	-30.6	116.3
10	37 08.6	-28.1	115.4	36 42.6	-29.2	116.0	36 15.9	-30.1	116.7	35 48.6	-31.1	117.4
11	36 40.5	-28.7	116.5	36 13.4	-29.7	117.1	35 45.8	-30.7	117.8	35 17.5	-31.7	118.4
12	36 11.8	-29.3	117.6	35 43.7	-30.3	118.2	35 15.1	-31.3	118.8	34 45.8	-32.1	119.4
13	35 42.5	-29.9	118.6	35 13.4	-30.8	119.3	34 43.8	-31.8	119.9	34 13.7	-32.7	120.5
14	35 12.6	-30.4	119.7	34 42.6	-31.4	120.3	34 12.0	-32.2	120.9	33 41.0	-33.2	121.5
15	34 42.2	-31.0	120.8	34 11.2	-31.8	121.4	33 39.8	-32.8	121.9	33 07.8	-33.7	122.5
16	34 11.2	-31.4	121.8	33 39.4	-32.4	122.4	33 07.0	-33.3	122.9	32 34.1	-34.1	123.5
17	33 39.8	-32.0	122.8	33 07.0	-32.9	123.4	32 33.7	-33.7	123.9	32 00.0	-34.5	124.4
18	33 07.8	-32.5	123.8	32 34.1	-33.3	124.4	32 00.0	-34.1	124.9	31 25.5	-35.0	125.4
19	32 35.3	-32.9	124.8	32 00.8	-33.7	125.4	31 25.9	-34.6	125.9	30 50.5	-35.3	126.4
20	32 02.4	-33.4	125.8	31 27.1	-34.2	126.3	30 51.3	-35.0	126.8	30 15.2	-35.8	127.3
21	31 29.0	-33.8	126.8	30 52.9	-34.7	127.3	30 16.3	-35.4	127.8	29 39.4	-36.2	128.2
22	30 55.2	-34.3	127.8	30 18.2	-35.0	128.2	29 40.9	-35.8	128.7	29 03.2	-36.5	129.1
23	30 20.9	-34.6	128.7	29 43.2	-35.4	129.2	29 05.1	-36.1	129.6	28 26.7	-36.9	130.0
24	29 46.3	-35.1	129.7	29 07.8	-35.8	130.1	28 29.0	-36.6	130.5	27 49.8	-37.2	130.9
25	29 11.2	-35.4	130.6	28 32.0	-36.2	131.0	27 52.4	-36.8	131.4	27 12.6	-37.6	131.8
26	28 35.8	-35.9	131.5	27 55.8	-36.5	131.9	27 15.6	-37.2	132.3	26 35.0	-37.8	132.7
27	27 59.9	-36.1	132.4	27 19.3	-36.8	132.8	26 38.4	-37.5	133.2	25 57.2	-38.2	133.6
28	27 23.8	-36.5	133.3	26 42.5	-37.2	133.7	26 00.9	-37.9	134.1	25 19.0	-38.5	134.4
29	26 47.3	-36.9	134.2	26 05.3	-37.5	134.6	25 23.0	-38.1	134.9	24 40.5	-38.7	135.3
30	26 10.4	-37.1	135.1	25 27.8	-37.8	135.5	24 44.9	-38.4	135.8	24 01.8	-39.0	136.1
31	25 33.3	-37.5	136.0	24 50.0	-38.1	136.3	24 06.5	-38.7	136.6	23 22.8	-39.3	136.9
32	24 55.8	-37.8	136.8	24 11.9	-38.4	137.2	23 27.8	-39.0	137.5	22 43.5	-39.5	137.7
33	24 18.0	-38.0	137.7	23 33.5	-38.6	138.0	22 48.8	-39.2	138.3	22 04.0	-39.8	138.6
34	23 40.0	-38.4	138.5	22 54.9	-38.9	138.8	22 09.6	-39.4	139.1	21 24.2	-40.0	139.4
35	23 01.6	-38.5	139.4	22 16.0	-39.1	139.7	21 30.2	-39.7	139.9	20 44.2	-40.2	140.2
36	22 23.1	-38.9	140.2	21 36.9	-39.4	140.5	20 50.5	-39.9	140.7	20 04.0	-40.4	141.0
37	21 44.2	-39.1	141.0	20 57.5	-39.6	141.3	20 10.6	-40.1	141.5	19 23.6	-40.7	141.7
38	21 05.1	-39.3	141.9	20 17.9	-39.8	142.1	19 30.5	-40.3	142.3	18 42.9	-40.8	142.5
39	20 25.8	-39.5	142.7	19 38.1	-40.1	142.9	18 50.2	-40.6	143.1	18 02.1	-41.0	143.3
40	19 46.3	-39.7	143.5	18 58.0	-40.2	143.7	18 09.6	-40.7	143.9	17 21.1	-41.2	144.1
41	19 06.6	-40.0	144.3	18 17.8	-40.4	144.5	17 28.9	-40.9	144.6	16 39.9	-41.3	144.8
42	18 26.6	-40.1	145.0	17 37.4	-40.6	145.2	16 48.0	-41.0	145.4	15 58.6	-41.5	145.6
43	17 46.5	-40.4	145.8	16 56.8	-40.8	146.0	16 07.0	-41.2	146.2	15 17.1	-41.6	146.3
44	17 06.1	-40.5	146.6	16 16.0	-40.9	146.8	15 25.8	-41.4	146.9	14 35.5	-41.8	147.1
45	16 25.6	-40.6	147.4	15 35.1	-41.1	147.5	14 44.4	-41.5	147.7	13 53.7	-41.9	147.8
46	15 45.0	-40.9	148.1	14 54.0	-41.3	148.3	14 02.9	-41.6	148.4	13 11.8	-42.1	148.5
47	15 04.1	-40.9	148.9	14 12.7	-41.3	149.0	13 21.3	-41.8	149.2	12 29.7	-42.2	149.3
48	14 23.2	-41.2	149.7	13 31.4	-41.6	149.8	12 39.5	-41.9	149.9	11 47.5	-42.2	150.0
49	13 42.0	-41.2	150.4	12 49.8	-41.6	150.5	11 57.6	-42.0	150.6	11 05.3	-42.4	150.7
50	13 00.8	-41.4	151.2	12 08.2	-41.7	151.3	11 15.6	-42.1	151.4	10 22.9	-42.5	151.4
51	12 19.4	-41.5	151.9	11 26.5	-41.9	152.0	10 33.5	-42.2	152.1	9 40.4	-42.5	152.2
52	11 37.9	-41.6	152.6	10 44.6	-42.0	152.7	9 51.3	-42.4	152.8	8 57.9	-42.7	152.9
53	10 56.3	-41.7	153.4	10 02.6	-42.0	153.4	9 08.9	-42.3	153.5	8 15.2	-42.7	153.6
54	10 14.6	-41.8	154.1	9 20.6	-42.2	154.2	8 26.6	-42.5	154.2	7 32.5	-42.8	154.3
55	9 32.8	-42.0	154.8	8 38.4	-42.2	154.9	7 44.1	-42.5	155.0	6 49.7	-42.8	155.0
56	8 50.8	-41.9	155.6	7 56.2	-42.3	155.6	7 01.6	-42.6	155.7	6 06.9	-42.9	155.7
57	8 08.9	-42.1	156.3	7 13.9	-42.4	156.3	6 19.0	-42.7	156.4	5 24.0	-43.0	156.4
58	7 26.8	-42.2	157.0	6 31.5	-42.4	157.0	5 36.3	-42.7	157.1	4 41.0	-43.0	157.1
59	6 44.6	-42.2	157.7	5 49.1	-42.5	157.8	4 53.6	-42.8	157.8	3 58.0	-43.0	157.8
60	6 02.4	-42.2	158.4	5 06.6	-42.5	158.5	4 10.8	-42.8	158.5	3 15.0	-43.1	158.5
61	5 20.2	-42.3	159.1	4 24.1	-42.5	159.2	3 28.0	-42.8	159.2	2 31.9	-43.0	159.2
62	4 37.9	-42.4	159.9	3 41.6	-42.6	159.9	2 45.2	-42.8	159.9	1 48.9	-43.1	159.9
63	3 55.5	-42.3	160.6	2 59.0	-42.7	160.6	2 02.4	-42.9	160.6	1 05.8	-43.1	160.6
64	3 13.2	-42.5	161.3	2 16.3	-42.6	161.3	1 19.5	-42.9	161.3	0 22.7	-43.1	161.3
65	2 30.7	-42.4	162.0	1 33.7	-42.7	162.0	0 36.6	-42.9	162.0	0 20.4	+43.1	18.0
66	1 48.3	-42.5	162.7	0 51.0	-42.6	162.7	0 06.3	+42.8	17.3	1 03.5	+43.1	17.3
67	1 05.8	-42.4	163.4	0 08.4	-42.7	163.4	0 49.1	+42.9	16.6	1 46.6	+43.1	16.6
68	0 23.4	-42.5	164.1	0 34.3	+42.7	15.9	1 32.0	+42.9	15.9	2 29.7	+43.1	15.9
69	0 19.1	+42.4	15.2	1 17.0	+42.6	15.2	2 14.9	+42.8	15.2	3 12.8	+43.0	15.2
70	1 01.5	+42.5	14.5	1 59.6	+42.7	14.5	2 57.7	+42.8	14.5	3 55.8	+43.0	14.5
71	1 44.0	+42.4	13.8	2 42.3	+42.6	13.8	3 40.5	+42.8	13.8	4 38.8	+43.0	13.8
72	2 26.4	+42.5	13.1	3 24.9	+42.6	13.1	4 23.3	+42.8	13.1	5 21.8	+42.9	13.1
73	3 08.9	+42.3	12.4	4 07.5	+42.5	12.4	5 06.1	+42.7	12.4	6 04.7	+42.8	12.4
74	3 51.2	+42.4	11.7	4 50.0	+42.5	11.7	5 48.8	+42.6	11.7	6 47.5	+42.8	11.7
75	4 33.6	+42.3	10.9	5 32.5	+42.4	11.0	6 31.4	+42.6	11.0	7 30.3	+42.7	11.0
76	5 15.9	+42.3	10.2	6 14.9	+42.4	10.3	7 14.0	+42.5	10.3	8 13.0	+42.7	10.3
77	5 58.2	+42.2	9.5	6 57.3	+42.4	9.5	7 56.5	+42.4	9.6	8 55.7	+42.5	9.6
78	6 40.4	+42.1	8.8	7 39.7	+42.2	8.8	8 38.9	+42.4	8.8	9 38.2	+42.5	8.9
79	7 22.5	+42.1	8.1	8 21.9	+42.2	8.1	9 21.3	+42.3	8.1	10 20.7	+42.4	8.2
80	8 04.6	+42.0	7.4	9 04.1	+42.1	7.4	10 03.6	+42.2	7.4	11 03.1	+42.3	7.4
81	8 46.6	+41.9	6.6	9 46.2	+42.0	6.7	10 45.8	+42.1	6.7	11 45.4	+42.1	6.7
82	9 28.5	+41.8	5.9	10 28.2	+41.9	5.9	11 27.9	+41.9	6.0	12 27.5	+42.1	6.0
83	10 10.3	+41.8	5.2	11 10.1	+41.8	5.2	12 09.8	+41.9	5.2	13 09.6	+41.9	5.3
84	10 52.1	+41.6	4.5	11 51.9	+41.7	4.5	12 51.7	+41.7	4.5	13 51.5	+41.8	4.5
85	11 33.7	+41.5	3.7	12 33.6	+41.5	3.7	13 33.4	+41.6	3.8	14 33.3	+41.7	3.8
86	12 15.2	+41.4	3.0	13 15.1	+41.5	3.0	14 15.0	+41.5	3.0	15 15.0	+41.5	3.0
87	12 56.6	+41.3	2.3	13 56.6	+41.2	2.3	14 56.5	+41.3	2.3	15 56.5	+41.3	2.3
88	13 37.9	+41.1	1.5	14 37.8	+41.2	1.5	15 37.8	+41.2	1.5	16 37.8	+41.2	1.5
89	14 19.0	+41.0	0.8	15 19.0	+41.0	0.8	16 19.0	+41.0	0.8	17 19.0	+41.0	0.8
90	15 00.0	+40.8	0.0	16 00.0	+40.8	0.0	17 00.0	+40.8	0.0	18 00.0	+40.8	0.0
	15°			16°			17°			18°		

Dec.	19°			20°			21°			22°		
	Hc	d	Z	Hc	d	Z	Hc	d	Z	Hc	d	Z
°	° ′	′	°	° ′	′	°	° ′	′	°	° ′	′	°
0	40 09.2	-25.9	106.9	39 51.4	-27.1	107.7	39 32.8	-28.2	108.5	39 13.4	-29.4	109.3
1	39 43.3	-26.6	108.1	39 24.3	-27.7	108.8	39 04.6	-28.9	109.6	38 44.0	-29.9	110.4
2	39 16.7	-27.3	109.2	38 56.6	-28.5	110.0	38 35.7	-29.5	110.7	38 14.1	-30.6	111.5
3	38 49.4	-28.0	110.4	38 28.1	-29.0	111.1	38 06.2	-30.2	111.9	37 43.5	-31.2	112.6
4	38 21.4	-28.6	111.5	37 59.1	-29.7	112.2	37 36.0	-30.7	113.0	37 12.3	-31.8	113.7
5	37 52.8	-29.2	112.6	37 29.4	-30.3	113.3	37 05.3	-31.3	114.0	36 40.5	-32.3	114.7
6	37 23.6	-29.9	113.7	36 59.1	-30.9	114.4	36 34.0	-31.9	115.1	36 08.2	-32.8	115.8
7	36 53.7	-30.4	114.8	36 28.2	-31.4	115.5	36 02.1	-32.4	116.1	35 35.4	-33.4	116.8
8	36 23.3	-31.0	115.9	35 56.8	-32.0	116.5	35 29.7	-33.0	117.2	35 02.0	-33.9	117.8
9	35 52.3	-31.5	116.9	35 24.8	-32.5	117.6	34 56.7	-33.4	118.2	34 28.1	-34.4	118.8
10	35 20.8	-32.1	118.0	34 52.3	-33.0	118.6	34 23.3	-33.9	119.2	33 53.7	-34.8	119.8
11	34 48.7	-32.6	119.0	34 19.3	-33.5	119.6	33 49.4	-34.5	120.2	33 18.9	-35.3	120.8
12	34 16.1	-33.1	120.0	33 45.8	-34.0	120.6	33 14.9	-34.8	121.2	32 43.6	-35.7	121.7
13	33 43.0	-33.6	121.1	33 11.8	-34.5	121.6	32 40.1	-35.3	122.2	32 07.9	-36.2	122.7
14	33 09.4	-34.1	122.0	32 37.3	-34.9	122.6	32 04.8	-35.8	123.1	31 31.7	-36.5	123.6
15	32 35.3	-34.5	123.0	32 02.4	-35.3	123.6	31 29.0	-36.1	124.1	30 55.2	-37.0	124.6
16	32 00.8	-34.9	124.0	31 27.1	-35.8	124.5	30 52.9	-36.6	125.0	30 18.2	-37.3	125.5
17	31 25.9	-35.4	124.9	30 51.3	-36.1	125.4	30 16.3	-36.9	125.9	29 40.9	-37.7	126.4
18	30 50.5	-35.7	125.9	30 15.2	-36.6	126.4	29 39.4	-37.3	126.8	29 03.2	-38.0	127.3
19	30 14.8	-36.2	126.8	29 38.6	-36.9	127.3	29 02.1	-37.7	127.7	28 25.2	-38.4	128.2
20	29 38.6	-36.5	127.7	29 01.7	-37.3	128.2	28 24.4	-38.0	128.6	27 46.8	-38.7	129.0
21	29 02.1	-36.9	128.7	28 24.4	-37.6	129.1	27 46.4	-38.3	129.5	27 08.1	-39.0	129.9
22	28 25.2	-37.3	129.6	27 46.8	-37.9	130.0	27 08.1	-38.6	130.4	26 29.1	-39.3	130.7
23	27 47.9	-37.5	130.4	27 08.9	-38.3	130.8	26 29.5	-39.0	131.2	25 49.8	-39.6	131.6
24	27 10.4	-38.0	131.3	26 30.6	-38.6	131.7	25 50.5	-39.2	132.1	25 10.2	-39.9	132.4
25	26 32.4	-38.2	132.2	25 52.0	-38.9	132.6	25 11.3	-39.5	132.9	24 30.3	-40.1	133.2
26	25 54.2	-38.5	133.1	25 13.1	-39.1	133.4	24 31.8	-39.8	133.7	23 50.2	-40.4	134.1
27	25 15.7	-38.8	133.9	24 34.0	-39.5	134.2	23 52.0	-40.0	134.6	23 09.8	-40.7	134.9
28	24 36.9	-39.1	134.7	23 54.5	-39.7	135.1	23 12.0	-40.3	135.4	22 29.1	-40.8	135.7
29	23 57.8	-39.4	135.6	23 14.8	-39.9	135.9	22 31.7	-40.6	136.2	21 48.3	-41.1	136.5
30	23 18.4	-39.6	136.4	22 34.9	-40.2	136.7	21 51.1	-40.7	137.0	21 07.2	-41.3	137.2
31	22 38.8	-39.8	137.2	21 54.7	-40.4	137.5	21 10.4	-41.0	137.8	20 25.9	-41.5	138.0
32	21 59.0	-40.1	138.0	21 14.3	-40.7	138.3	20 29.4	-41.2	138.5	19 44.4	-41.7	138.8
33	21 18.9	-40.3	138.8	20 33.6	-40.8	139.1	19 48.2	-41.3	139.3	19 02.7	-41.9	139.5
34	20 38.6	-40.6	139.6	19 52.8	-41.1	139.9	19 06.9	-41.6	140.1	18 20.8	-42.1	140.3
35	19 58.0	-40.7	140.4	19 11.7	-41.2	140.6	18 25.3	-41.8	140.8	17 38.7	-42.3	141.0
36	19 17.3	-40.9	141.2	18 30.5	-41.4	141.4	17 43.5	-41.9	141.6	16 56.4	-42.4	141.8
37	18 36.4	-41.1	142.0	17 49.1	-41.7	142.2	17 01.6	-42.1	142.3	16 14.0	-42.5	142.5
38	17 55.3	-41.4	142.7	17 07.4	-41.7	142.9	16 19.5	-42.2	143.1	15 31.5	-42.7	143.3
39	17 13.9	-41.4	143.5	16 25.7	-42.0	143.7	15 37.3	-42.4	143.8	14 48.8	-42.8	144.0
40	16 32.5	-41.7	144.2	15 43.7	-42.0	144.4	14 54.9	-42.5	144.6	14 06.0	-43.0	144.7
41	15 50.8	-41.7	145.0	15 01.7	-42.3	145.1	14 12.4	-42.7	145.3	13 23.0	-43.1	145.4
42	15 09.1	-42.0	145.7	14 19.4	-42.3	145.9	13 29.7	-42.8	146.0	12 39.9	-43.2	146.1
43	14 27.1	-42.0	146.5	13 37.1	-42.5	146.6	12 46.9	-42.9	146.7	11 56.7	-43.3	146.9
44	13 45.1	-42.2	147.2	12 54.6	-42.6	147.3	12 04.0	-43.0	147.5	11 13.4	-43.4	147.6
45	13 02.9	-42.4	147.9	12 12.0	-42.7	148.1	11 21.0	-43.1	148.2	10 30.0	-43.5	148.3
46	12 20.5	-42.4	148.7	11 29.3	-42.9	148.8	10 37.9	-43.2	148.9	9 46.5	-43.5	149.0
47	11 38.1	-42.5	149.4	10 46.4	-42.9	149.5	9 54.7	-43.3	149.6	9 03.0	-43.7	149.7
48	10 55.6	-42.7	150.1	10 03.5	-43.0	150.2	9 11.4	-43.3	150.3	8 19.3	-43.7	150.4
49	10 12.9	-42.7	150.8	9 20.5	-43.1	150.9	8 28.1	-43.5	151.0	7 35.6	-43.8	151.0
50	9 30.2	-42.9	151.5	8 37.4	-43.2	151.6	7 44.6	-43.5	151.7	6 51.8	-43.9	151.7
51	8 47.3	-42.9	152.2	7 54.2	-43.2	152.3	7 01.1	-43.6	152.4	6 07.9	-43.9	152.4
52	8 04.4	-42.9	152.9	7 11.0	-43.3	153.0	6 17.5	-43.6	153.1	5 24.0	-43.9	153.1
53	7 21.5	-43.1	153.7	6 27.7	-43.4	153.7	5 33.9	-43.7	153.8	4 40.1	-44.0	153.8
54	6 38.4	-43.1	154.4	5 44.3	-43.4	154.4	4 50.2	-43.7	154.4	3 56.1	-44.1	154.5
55	5 55.3	-43.1	155.1	5 00.9	-43.4	155.1	4 06.5	-43.8	155.1	3 12.0	-44.0	155.2
56	5 12.2	-43.2	155.8	4 17.5	-43.5	155.8	3 22.7	-43.8	155.8	2 28.0	-44.1	155.8
57	4 29.0	-43.3	156.5	3 34.0	-43.6	156.5	2 38.9	-43.8	156.5	1 43.9	-44.1	156.5
58	3 45.7	-43.2	157.1	2 50.4	-43.5	157.2	1 55.1	-43.8	157.2	0 59.8	-44.1	157.2
59	3 02.5	-43.3	157.8	2 06.9	-43.6	157.9	1 11.3	-43.8	157.9	0 15.7	-44.1	157.9
60	2 19.2	-43.4	158.5	1 23.3	-43.6	158.5	0 27.5	-43.9	158.6	0 28.4	+44.1	21.5
61	1 35.8	-43.3	159.2	0 39.7	-43.5	159.2	0 16.4	+43.8	20.8	1 12.5	+44.0	20.8
62	0 52.5	-43.3	159.9	0 03.8	+43.6	20.1	1 00.2	+43.8	20.1	1 56.5	+44.1	20.1
63	0 09.2	-43.4	160.6	0 47.4	+43.6	19.4	1 44.0	+43.8	19.4	2 40.6	+44.1	19.4
64	0 34.2	+43.3	18.7	1 31.0	+43.6	18.7	2 27.8	+43.8	18.7	3 24.7	+44.0	18.7
65	1 17.5	+43.3	18.0	2 14.6	+43.5	18.0	3 11.6	+43.8	18.0	4 08.7	+43.9	18.1
66	2 00.8	+43.3	17.3	2 58.1	+43.5	17.3	3 55.4	+43.7	17.3	4 52.6	+44.0	17.4
67	2 44.1	+43.3	16.6	3 41.6	+43.5	16.6	4 39.1	+43.7	16.7	5 36.6	+43.9	16.7
68	3 27.4	+43.3	15.9	4 25.1	+43.5	15.9	5 22.8	+43.6	16.0	6 20.5	+43.8	16.0
69	4 10.7	+43.2	15.2	5 08.6	+43.4	15.3	6 06.4	+43.6	15.3	7 04.3	+43.8	15.3
70	4 53.9	+43.2	14.5	5 52.0	+43.3	14.6	6 50.0	+43.6	14.6	7 48.1	+43.7	14.6
71	5 37.1	+43.1	13.8	6 35.3	+43.3	13.9	7 33.6	+43.4	13.9	8 31.8	+43.6	13.9
72	6 20.2	+43.1	13.1	7 18.6	+43.2	13.2	8 17.0	+43.4	13.2	9 15.4	+43.6	13.2
73	7 03.3	+43.0	12.4	8 01.8	+43.2	12.5	9 00.4	+43.3	12.5	9 59.0	+43.5	12.5
74	7 46.3	+42.9	11.7	8 45.0	+43.1	11.8	9 43.7	+43.3	11.8	10 42.5	+43.3	11.8
75	8 29.2	+42.9	11.0	9 28.1	+43.0	11.1	10 27.0	+43.1	11.1	11 25.8	+43.3	11.1
76	9 12.1	+42.7	10.3	10 11.1	+42.9	10.4	11 10.1	+43.0	10.4	12 09.1	+43.2	10.4
77	9 54.8	+42.7	9.6	10 54.0	+42.8	9.6	11 53.1	+43.0	9.7	12 52.3	+43.0	9.7
78	10 37.5	+42.6	8.9	11 36.8	+42.7	8.9	12 36.1	+42.8	9.0	13 35.3	+42.9	9.0
79	11 20.1	+42.5	8.2	12 19.5	+42.6	8.2	13 18.9	+42.7	8.2	14 18.2	+42.8	8.3
80	12 02.6	+42.4	7.5	13 02.1	+42.4	7.5	14 01.6	+42.5	7.5	15 01.0	+42.7	7.6
81	12 45.0	+42.2	6.7	13 44.5	+42.4	6.8	14 44.1	+42.4	6.8	15 43.7	+42.5	6.8
82	13 27.2	+42.1	6.0	14 26.9	+42.2	6.0	15 26.5	+42.3	6.1	16 26.2	+42.4	6.1
83	14 09.3	+42.0	5.3	15 09.1	+42.0	5.3	16 08.8	+42.1	5.3	17 08.6	+42.2	5.4
84	14 51.3	+41.9	4.5	15 51.1	+41.9	4.6	16 50.9	+42.0	4.6	17 50.8	+42.0	4.6
85	15 33.2	+41.7	3.8	16 33.0	+41.8	3.8	17 32.9	+41.8	3.8	18 32.8	+41.8	3.9
86	16 14.9	+41.5	3.0	17 14.8	+41.6	3.1	18 14.7	+41.6	3.1	19 14.6	+41.7	3.1
87	16 56.4	+41.4	2.3	17 56.4	+41.4	2.3	18 56.3	+41.4	2.3	19 56.3	+41.4	2.3
88	17 37.8	+41.2	1.5	18 37.8	+41.2	1.5	19 37.7	+41.3	1.6	20 37.7	+41.3	1.6
89	18 19.0	+41.0	0.8	19 19.0	+41.0	0.8	20 19.0	+41.0	0.8	21 19.0	+41.0	0.8
90	19 00.0	+40.8	0.0	20 00.0	+40.8	0.0	21 00.0	+40.8	0.0	22 00.0	+40.8	0.0
	19°			20°			21°			22°		

S. Lat. {L.H.A. greater than 180° ....Zn=180°–Z
{L.H.A. less than 180°...........Zn=180°+Z

LATITUDE SAME NAME AS DECLINATION L.H.A. 133°, 227°

48°, 312° L.H.A. LATITUDE SAME NAME AS DECLINATION

N. Lat. {L.H.A. greater than 180° .....Zn=Z
{L.H.A. less than 180°............Zn=360°-Z

Dec.	15°			16°			17°			18°			19°			20°			21°			22°			Dec.
	Hc	d	Z	Hc	d	Z	Hc	d	Z	Hc	d	Z	Hc	d	Z	Hc	d	Z	Hc	d	Z	Hc	d	Z	
°	° ′	′	°	° ′	′	°	° ′	′	°	° ′	′	°	° ′	′	°	° ′	′	°	° ′	′	°	° ′	′	°	°
0	40 15.9	+20.0	103.1	40 01.9	+21.2	103.9	39 47.0	+22.5	104.7	39 31.3	+23.7	105.5	39 14.9	+24.8	106.3	38 57.6	+26.0	107.1	38 39.6	+27.2	107.9	38 20.8	+28.3	108.6	0
1	40 35.9	+19.1	101.9	40 23.1	+20.4	102.7	40 09.5	+21.7	103.5	39 55.0	+22.9	104.4	39 39.7	+24.2	105.2	39 23.6	+25.4	106.0	39 06.8	+26.5	106.7	38 49.1	+27.7	107.5	1
2	40 55.0	+18.4	100.6	40 43.5	+19.7	101.5	40 31.2	+20.9	102.3	40 17.9	+22.2	103.1	40 03.9	+23.4	104.0	39 49.0	+24.6	104.8	39 33.3	+25.8	105.6	39 16.8	+27.0	106.4	2
3	41 13.4	+17.5	99.4	41 03.2	+18.8	100.2	40 52.1	+20.1	101.1	40 40.1	+21.4	101.9	40 27.3	+22.6	102.8	40 13.6	+23.9	103.6	39 59.1	+25.1	104.4	39 43.8	+26.3	105.2	3
4	41 30.9	+16.6	98.1	41 22.0	+18.0	99.0	41 12.2	+19.3	99.8	41 01.5	+20.6	100.7	40 49.9	+21.9	101.5	40 37.5	+23.1	102.4	40 24.2	+24.4	103.2	40 10.1	+25.5	104.0	4
5	41 47.5	+15.8	96.8	41 40.0	+17.1	97.7	41 31.5	+18.4	98.6	41 22.1	+19.7	99.4	41 11.8	+21.0	100.3	41 00.6	+22.4	101.2	40 48.6	+23.6	102.0	40 35.6	+24.9	102.9	5
6	42 03.3	+14.9	95.5	41 57.1	+16.2	96.4	41 49.9	+17.6	97.3	41 41.8	+19.0	98.2	41 32.8	+20.3	99.1	41 23.0	+21.5	99.9	41 12.2	+22.8	100.8	41 00.5	+24.1	101.6	6
7	42 18.2	+14.0	94.2	42 13.3	+15.4	95.1	42 07.5	+16.7	96.0	42 00.8	+18.0	96.9	41 53.1	+19.4	97.8	41 44.5	+20.7	98.7	41 35.0	+22.0	99.6	41 24.6	+23.3	100.4	7
8	42 32.2	+13.1	92.9	42 28.7	+14.5	93.8	42 24.2	+15.9	94.7	42 18.8	+17.3	95.6	42 12.5	+18.6	96.5	42 05.2	+19.9	97.4	41 57.0	+21.2	98.3	41 47.9	+22.5	99.2	8
9	42 45.3	+12.1	91.6	42 43.2	+13.5	92.5	42 40.1	+14.9	93.4	42 36.1	+16.3	94.3	42 31.1	+17.6	95.2	42 25.1	+19.0	96.1	42 18.2	+20.4	97.1	42 10.4	+21.7	98.0	9
10	42 57.4	+11.3	90.2	42 56.7	+12.7	91.2	42 55.0	+14.1	92.1	42 52.4	+15.4	93.0	42 48.7	+16.8	93.9	42 44.1	+18.2	94.9	42 38.6	+19.5	95.8	42 32.1	+20.8	96.7	10
11	43 08.7	+10.2	88.9	43 09.4	+11.6	89.8	43 09.1	+13.1	90.8	43 07.8	+14.5	91.7	43 05.5	+15.9	92.6	43 02.3	+17.3	93.6	42 58.1	+18.6	94.5	42 52.9	+20.0	95.4	11
12	43 18.9	+9.4	87.5	43 21.0	+10.8	88.5	43 22.2	+12.1	89.4	43 22.3	+13.5	90.4	43 21.4	+15.0	91.3	43 19.6	+16.3	92.2	43 16.7	+17.7	93.2	43 12.9	+19.1	94.1	12
13	43 28.3	+8.3	86.2	43 31.8	+9.7	87.1	43 34.3	+11.2	88.1	43 35.8	+12.6	89.0	43 36.4	+14.0	90.0	43 35.9	+15.4	90.9	43 34.4	+16.9	91.9	43 32.0	+18.2	92.8	13
14	43 36.6	+7.4	84.8	43 41.5	+8.8	85.7	43 45.5	+10.2	86.7	43 48.4	+11.7	87.7	43 50.4	+13.1	88.6	43 51.3	+14.5	89.6	43 51.3	+15.9	90.5	43 50.2	+17.3	91.5	14
15	43 44.0	+6.3	83.4	43 50.3	+7.8	84.4	43 55.7	+9.2	85.3	44 00.1	+10.7	86.3	44 03.5	+12.1	87.3	44 05.8	+13.5	88.2	44 07.2	+14.9	89.2	44 07.5	+16.3	90.2	15
16	43 50.3	+5.4	82.0	43 58.1	+6.8	83.0	44 04.9	+8.3	84.0	44 10.8	+9.6	84.9	44 15.6	+11.1	85.9	44 19.3	+12.6	86.9	44 22.1	+14.0	87.8	44 23.8	+15.4	88.8	16
17	43 55.7	+4.4	80.7	44 04.9	+5.9	81.6	44 13.2	+7.2	82.6	44 20.4	+8.7	83.6	44 26.7	+10.1	84.5	44 31.9	+11.5	85.5	44 36.1	+13.0	86.5	44 39.2	+14.5	87.5	17
18	44 00.1	+3.4	79.3	44 10.8	+4.8	80.2	44 20.4	+6.3	81.2	44 29.1	+7.7	82.2	44 36.8	+9.1	83.1	44 43.4	+10.6	84.1	44 49.1	+12.0	85.1	44 53.7	+13.4	86.1	18
19	44 03.5	+2.3	77.9	44 15.6	+3.7	78.8	44 26.7	+5.2	79.8	44 36.8	+6.6	80.8	44 45.9	+8.1	81.8	44 54.0	+9.5	82.7	45 01.1	+11.0	83.7	45 07.1	+12.4	84.7	19
20	44 05.8	+1.4	76.5	44 19.3	+2.8	77.4	44 31.9	+4.2	78.4	44 43.4	+5.7	79.4	44 54.0	+7.1	80.4	45 03.5	+8.6	81.3	45 12.1	+9.9	82.3	45 19.5	+11.5	83.3	20
21	44 07.2	+0.3	75.1	44 22.1	+1.7	76.1	44 36.1	+3.1	77.0	44 49.1	+4.6	78.0	45 01.1	+6.0	79.0	45 12.1	+7.4	79.9	45 22.0	+9.0	80.9	45 31.0	+10.4	81.9	21
22	44 07.5	-0.7	73.7	44 23.8	+0.8	74.7	44 39.2	+2.2	75.6	44 53.7	+3.5	76.6	45 07.1	+5.0	77.5	45 19.5	+6.5	78.5	45 31.0	+7.9	79.5	45 41.4	+9.3	80.5	22
23	44 06.8	-1.7	72.3	44 24.6	-0.4	73.3	44 41.4	+1.1	74.2	44 57.2	+2.5	75.2	45 12.1	+3.9	76.1	45 26.0	+5.4	77.1	45 38.9	+6.8	78.1	45 50.7	+8.3	79.1	23
24	44 05.1	-2.7	70.9	44 24.2	-1.3	71.9	44 42.5	0.0	72.8	44 59.7	+1.5	73.7	45 16.0	+2.9	74.7	45 31.4	+4.3	75.7	45 45.7	+5.8	76.7	45 59.0	+7.2	77.7	24
25	44 02.4	-3.7	69.5	44 22.9	-2.4	70.5	44 42.5	-1.0	71.4	45 01.2	+0.4	72.3	45 18.9	+1.9	73.3	45 35.7	+3.3	74.3	45 51.5	+4.7	75.3	46 06.2	+6.2	76.3	25
26	43 58.7	-4.8	68.2	44 20.5	-3.3	69.1	44 41.5	-2.0	70.0	45 01.6	-0.6	70.9	45 20.8	+0.7	71.9	45 39.0	+2.1	72.8	45 56.2	+3.6	73.8	46 12.4	+5.0	74.8	26
27	43 53.9	-5.7	66.8	44 17.2	-4.4	67.7	44 39.5	-3.0	68.6	45 01.0	-1.7	69.5	45 21.5	-0.2	70.4	45 41.1	+1.2	71.4	45 59.8	+2.5	72.4	46 17.4	+4.0	73.4	27
28	43 48.2	-6.7	65.4	44 12.8	-5.4	66.3	44 36.5	-4.1	67.2	44 59.3	-2.7	68.1	45 21.3	-1.4	69.0	45 42.3	0.0	70.0	46 02.3	+1.5	71.0	46 21.4	+2.9	71.9	28
29	43 41.5	-7.7	64.0	44 07.4	-6.5	64.9	44 32.4	-5.1	65.8	44 56.6	-3.8	66.7	45 19.9	-2.4	67.6	45 42.3	-1.0	68.5	46 03.8	+0.4	69.5	46 24.3	+1.8	70.5	29
30	43 33.8	-8.7	62.6	44 00.9	-7.4	63.5	44 27.3	-6.1	64.4	44 52.8	-4.8	65.3	45 17.5	-3.5	66.2	45 41.3	-2.1	67.1	46 04.2	-0.8	68.1	46 26.1	+0.7	69.0	30
31	43 25.1	-9.7	61.3	43 53.5	-8.4	62.1	44 21.2	-7.1	63.0	44 48.0	-5.8	63.9	45 14.0	-4.5	64.8	45 39.2	-3.2	65.7	46 03.4	-1.8	66.6	46 26.8	-0.4	67.6	31
32	43 15.4	-10.6	59.9	43 45.1	-9.4	60.7	44 14.1	-8.2	61.6	44 42.2	-6.9	62.5	45 09.5	-5.5	63.3	45 36.0	-4.2	64.3	46 01.6	-2.8	65.2	46 26.4	-1.5	66.1	32
33	43 04.8	-11.5	58.6	43 35.7	-10.3	59.4	44 05.9	-9.1	60.2	44 35.3	-7.8	61.1	45 04.0	-6.6	61.9	45 31.8	-5.3	62.8	45 58.8	-4.0	63.7	46 24.9	-2.7	64.7	33
34	42 53.3	-12.5	57.2	43 25.4	-11.3	58.0	43 56.8	-10.1	58.8	44 27.5	-8.9	59.7	44 57.4	-7.6	60.5	45 26.5	-6.4	61.4	45 54.8	-5.1	62.3	46 22.2	-3.7	63.2	34
35	42 40.8	-13.4	55.9	43 14.1	-12.3	56.7	43 46.7	-11.1	57.5	44 18.6	-9.9	58.3	44 49.8	-8.7	59.1	45 20.1	-7.3	60.0	45 49.7	-6.1	60.9	46 18.5	-4.8	61.8	35
36	42 27.4	-14.4	54.6	43 01.8	-13.2	55.3	43 35.6	-12.0	56.1	44 08.7	-10.9	56.9	44 41.1	-9.7	57.7	45 12.8	-8.5	58.6	45 43.6	-7.1	59.5	46 13.7	-5.9	60.4	36
37	42 13.0	-15.2	53.3	42 48.6	-14.1	54.0	43 23.6	-13.0	54.8	43 57.8	-11.8	55.5	44 31.4	-10.6	56.4	45 04.3	-9.4	57.2	45 36.5	-8.2	58.0	46 07.8	-6.9	58.9	37
38	41 57.8	-16.1	52.0	42 34.5	-15.0	52.7	43 10.6	-13.9	53.4	43 46.0	-12.8	54.2	44 20.8	-11.7	55.0	44 54.9	-10.5	55.8	45 28.3	-9.3	56.6	46 00.9	-8.0	57.5	38
39	41 41.7	-16.9	50.7	42 19.5	-15.9	51.4	42 56.7	-14.9	52.1	43 33.2	-13.7	52.8	44 09.1	-12.6	53.6	44 44.4	-11.5	54.4	45 19.0	-10.3	55.2	45 52.9	-9.1	56.1	39
40	41 24.8	-17.8	49.4	42 03.6	-16.8	50.1	42 41.8	-15.7	50.8	43 19.5	-14.7	51.5	43 56.5	-13.6	52.2	44 32.9	-12.4	53.0	45 08.7	-11.3	53.8	45 43.8	-10.2	54.6	40
41	41 07.0	-18.6	48.1	41 46.8	-17.6	48.8	42 26.1	-16.7	49.5	43 04.8	-15.6	50.2	43 42.9	-14.5	50.9	44 20.5	-13.5	51.6	44 57.4	-12.3	52.4	45 33.6	-11.1	53.2	41
42	40 48.4	-19.5	46.9	41 29.2	-18.5	47.5	42 09.4	-17.5	48.2	42 49.2	-16.5	48.8	43 28.4	-15.5	49.6	44 07.0	-14.4	50.3	44 45.1	-13.3	51.0	45 22.5	-12.2	51.8	42
43	40 28.9	-20.2	45.6	41 10.7	-19.3	46.2	41 51.9	-18.3	46.9	42 32.7	-17.4	47.5	43 12.9	-16.3	48.2	43 52.6	-15.3	48.9	44 31.8	-14.3	49.7	45 10.3	-13.2	50.4	43
44	40 08.7	-21.0	44.4	40 51.4	-20.2	45.0	41 33.6	-19.2	45.6	42 15.3	-18.2	46.2	42 56.6	-17.3	46.9	43 37.3	-16.3	47.6	44 17.5	-15.3	48.3	44 57.1	-14.2	49.1	44
45	39 47.7	-21.8	43.2	40 31.2	-20.9	43.7	41 14.4	-20.0	44.3	41 57.1	-19.1	45.0	42 39.3	-18.2	45.6	43 21.0	-17.2	46.3	44 02.2	-16.2	47.0	44 42.9	-15.2	47.7	45
46	39 25.9	-22.5	41.9	40 10.3	-21.6	42.5	40 54.4	-20.9	43.1	41 38.0	-20.0	43.7	42 21.1	-19.0	44.3	43 03.8	-18.0	45.0	43 46.0	-17.1	45.6	44 27.7	-16.1	46.3	46
47	39 03.4	-23.3	40.7	39 48.7	-22.5	41.3	40 33.5	-21.6	41.8	41 18.0	-20.7	42.4	42 02.1	-19.8	43.0	42 45.8	-19.0	43.7	43 28.9	-18.0	44.3	44 11.6	-17.0	45.0	47
48	38 40.1	-23.9	39.6	39 26.2	-23.2	40.1	40 11.9	-22.3	40.6	40 57.3	-21.5	41.2	41 42.3	-20.7	41.8	42 26.8	-19.8	42.4	43 10.9	-18.9	43.0	43 54.6	-18.0	43.6	48
49	38 16.2	-24.7	38.4	39 03.0	-23.8	38.9	39 49.6	-23.1	39.4	40 35.8	-22.4	39.9	41 21.6	-21.5	40.5	42 07.0	-20.7	41.1	42 52.0	-19.8	41.7	43 36.6	-18.9	42.3	49
50	37 51.5	-25.3	37.2	38 39.2	-24.6	37.7	39 26.5	-23.9	38.2	40 13.4	-23.0	38.7	41 00.1	-22.3	39.3	41 46.3	-21.4	39.8	42 32.2	-20.6	40.4	43 17.7	-19.8	41.0	50
51	37 26.2	-26.0	36.1	38 14.6	-25.3	36.5	39 02.6	-24.5	37.0	39 50.4	-23.8	37.5	40 37.8	-23.1	38.0	41 24.9	-22.3	38.6	42 11.6	-21.5	39.1	42 57.9	-20.6	39.7	51
52	37 00.2	-26.6	35.0	37 49.3	-25.9	35.4	38 38.1	-25.3	35.9	39 26.6	-24.6	36.3	40 14.7	-23.8	36.8	41 02.6	-23.1	37.3	41 50.1	-22.2	37.9	42 37.3	-21.5	38.4	52
53	36 33.6	-27.2	33.8	37 23.4	-26.6	34.3	38 12.8	-25.9	34.7	39 02.0	-25.2	35.2	39 50.9	-24.5	35.6	40 39.5	-23.8	36.1	41 27.9	-23.1	36.6	42 15.8	-22.3	37.2	53
54	36 06.4	-27.8	32.7	36 56.8	-27.2	33.1	37 46.9	-26.6	33.6	38 36.8	-26.0	34.0	39 26.4	-25.3	34.4	40 15.7	-24.5	34.9	41 04.8	-23.9	35.4	41 53.5	-23.1	35.9	54
55	35 38.6	-28.4	31.6	36 29.6	-27.9	32.0	37 20.3	-27.2	32.4	38 10.8	-26.5	32.8	39 01.1	-25.9	33.3	39 51.2	-25.3	33.7	40 40.9	-24.6	34.2	41 30.4	-23.9	34.7	55
56	35 10.2	-29.0	30.6	36 01.7	-28.4	30.9	36 53.1	-27.8	31.3	37 44.3	-27.3	31.7	38 35.2	-26.6	32.1	39 25.9	-26.0	32.5	40 16.3	-25.3	33.0	41 06.5	-24.6	33.5	56
57	34 41.2	-29.6	29.5	35 33.3	-29.0	29.8	36 25.3	-28.5	30.2	37 17.0	-27.8	30.6	38 08.6	-27.3	31.0	38 59.9	-26.7	31.4	39 51.0	-26.0	31.8	40 41.9	-25.4	32.3	57
58	34 11.6	-30.0	28.4	35 04.3	-29.5	28.8	35 56.8	-29.0	29.1	36 49.2	-28.5	29.5	37 41.3	-27.9	29.8	38 33.2	-27.3	30.2	39 25.0	-26.8	30.6	40 16.5	-26.2	31.1	58
59	33 41.6	-30.6	27.4	34 34.8	-30.2	27.7	35 27.8	-29.6	28.0	36 20.7	-29.1	28.4	37 13.4	-28.6	28.7	38 05.9	-28.0	29.1	38 58.2	-27.4	29.5	39 50.3	-26.8	29.9	59
60	33 11.0	-31.1	26.4	34 04.6	-30.6	26.7	34 58.2	-30.1	27.0	35 51.6	-29.6	27.3	36 44.8	-29.1	27.6	37 37.9	-28.6	28.0	38 30.8	-28.1	28.4	39 23.5	-27.5	28.7	60
61	32 39.9	-31.6	25.3	33 34.0	-31.1	25.6	34 28.1	-30.7	25.9	35 22.0	-30.3	26.2	36 15.7	-29.7	26.5	37 09.3	-29.2	26.9	38 02.7	-28.7	27.2	38 56.0	-28.2	27.6	61
62	32 08.3	-32.1	24.3	33 02.9	-31.7	24.6	33 57.4	-31.2	24.9	34 51.7	-30.7	25.2	35 46.0	-30.3	25.5	36 40.1	-29.8	25.8	37 34.0	-29.3	26.1	38 27.8	-28.8	26.5	62
63	31 36.2	-32.5	23.3	32 31.2	-32.1	23.6	33 26.2	-31.7	23.8	34 21.0	-31.3	24.1	35 15.7	-30.8	24.4	36 10.3	-30.4	24.7	37 04.7	-29.9	25.0	37 59.0	-29.4	25.3	63
64	31 03.7	-33.0	22.4	31 59.1	-32.5	22.6	32 54.5	-32.2	22.8	33 49.7	-31.7	23.1	34 44.9	-31.4	23.4	35 39.9	-30.9	23.6	36 34.8	-30.5	23.9	37 29.6	-30.1	24.2	64
65	30 30.7	-33.4	21.4	31 26.6	-33.1	21.6	32 22.3	-32.7	21.8	33 18.0	-32.3	22.1	34 13.5	-31.9	22.3	35 09.0	-31.5	22.6	36 04.3	-31.1	22.9	36 59.5	-30.6	23.2	65
66	29 57.3	-33.8	20.4	30 53.5	-33.4	20.6	31 49.6	-33.1	20.8	32 45.7	-32.8	21.1	33 41.6	-32.4	21.3	34 37.5	-32.0	21.6	35 33.2	-31.6	21.8	36 28.9	-31.2	22.1	66
67	29 23.5	-34.2	19.5	30 20.1	-33.9	19.7	31 16.5	-33.5	19.9	32 12.9	-33.2	20.1	33 09.2	-32.8	20.3	34 05.5	-32.5	20.5	35 01.6	-32.1	20.8	35 57.7	-31.8	21.0	67
68	28 49.3	-34.6	18.5	29 46.2	-34.3	18.7	30 43.0	-34.0	18.9	31 39.7	-33.6	19.1	32 36.4	-33.3	19.3	33 33.0	-33.0	19.5	34 29.5	-32.6	19.7	35 25.9	-32.3	20.0	68
69	28 14.7	-34.9	17.6	29 11.9	-34.7	17.8	30 09.0	-34.4	17.9	31 06.1	-34.1	18.1	32 03.1	-33.8	18.3	33 00.0	-33.5	18.5	33 56.9	-33.2	18.7	34 53.6	-32.8	18.9	69
70	27 39.8	-35.4	16.7	28 37.2	-35.0	16.8	29 34.6	-34.7	17.0	30 32.0	-34.5	17.2	31 29.3	-34.2	17.3	32 26.5	-33.9	17.5	33 23.7	-33.6	17.7	34 20.8	-33.3	17.9	70
71	27 04.4	-35.6	15.8	28 02.2	-35.5	15.9	28 59.9	-35.2	16.1	29 57.5	-34.9	16.2	30 55.1	-34.7	16.4	31 52.6	-34.3	16.6	32 50.1	-34.1	16.7	33 47.5	-33.8	16.9	71
72	26 28.8	-36.0	14.9	27 26.7	-35.7	15.0	28 24.7	-35.5	15.1	29 22.6	-35.3	15.3	30 20.4	-35.0	15.4	31 18.3	-34.8	15.6	32 16.0	-34.5	15.8	33 13.7	-34.2	15.9	72
73	25 52.8	-36.4	14.0	26 51.0	-36.1	14.1	27 49.2	-35.9	14.2	28 47.3	-35.7	14.4	29 45.4	-35.4	14.5	30 43.5	-35.2	14.6	31 41.5	-34.9	14.8	32 39.5	-34.7	15.0	73
74	25 16.4	-36.6	13.1	26 14.9	-36.5	13.2	27 13.3	-36.3	13.3	28 11.6	-36.0	13.4	29 10.0	-35.8	13.6	30 08.3	-35.6	13.7	31 06.6	-35.4	13.8	32 04.8	-35.1	14.0	74
75	24 39.8	-37.0	12.2	25 38.4	-36.7	12.3	26 37.0	-36.5	12.4	27 35.6	-36.4	12.5	28 34.2	-36.2	12.7	29 32.7	-36.0	12.8	30 31.2	-35.8	12.9	31 29.7	-35.6	13.0	75
76	24 02.8	-37.2	11.4	25 01.7	-37.1	11.4	26 00.5	-36.9	11.5	26 59.2	-36.7	11.6	27 58.0	-36.5	11.7	28 56.7	-36.3	11.9	29 55.4	-36.1	12.0	30 54.1	-35.9	12.1	76
77	23 25.6	-37.5	10.5	24 24.6	-37.4	10.6	25 23.6	-37.2	10.7	26 22.5	-37.0	10.8	27 21.5	-36.9	10.8	28 20.4	-36.7	10.9	29 19.3	-36.5	11.1	30 18.2	-36.4	11.2	77
78	22 48.1	-37.8	9.6	23 47.2	-37.6	9.7	24 46.4	-37.5	9.8	25 45.5	-37.3	9.9	26 44.6	-37.2	10.0	27 43.7	-37.1	10.1	28 42.8	-36.9	10.1	29 41.8	-36.7	10.2	78
79	22 10.3	-38.0	8.8	23 09.6	-37.9	8.9	24 08.9	-37.8	8.9	25 08.2	-37.7	9.0	26 07.4	-37.5	9.1	27 06.6	-37.3	9.2	28 05.9	-37.3	9.3	29 05.1	-37.1	9.3	79
80	21 32.3	-38.3	8.0	22 31.7	-38.2	8.0	23 31.1	-38.0	8.1	24 30.5	-37.9	8.2	25 29.9	-37.8	8.2	26 29.3	-37.7	8.3	27 28.6	-37.5	8.4	28 28.0	-37.4	8.4	80
81	20 54.0	-38.5	7.1	21 53.5	-38.4	7.2	22 53.1	-38.3	7.2	23 52.6	-38.2	7.3	24 52.1	-38.1	7.4	25 51.6	-38.0	7.4	26 51.1	-37.9	7.5	27 50.6	-37.8	7.6	81
82	20 15.5	-38.7	6.3	21 15.1	-38.6	6.4	22 14.8	-38.6	6.4	23 14.4	-38.5	6.5	24 14.0	-38.4	6.5	25 13.6	-38.3	6.6	26 13.2	-38.2	6.6	27 12.8	-38.1	6.7	82
83	19 36.8	-39.0	5.5	20 36.5	-38.9	5.6	21 36.2	-38.8	5.6	22 35.9	-38.7	5.6	23 35.6	-38.6	5.7	24 35.3	-38.6	5.7	25 35.0	-38.5	5.8	26 34.7	-38.4	5.8	83
84	18 57.8	-39.2	4.7	19 57.6	-39.1	4.7	20 57.4	-39.1	4.8	21 57.2	-39.0	4.8	22 57.0	-38.9	4.8	23 56.7	-38.8	4.9	24 56.5	-38.7	4.9	25 56.3	-38.7	5.0	84
85	18 18.6	-39.3	3.9	19 18.5	-39.3	3.9	20 18.3	-39.2	4.0	21 18.2	-39.2	4.0	22 18.1	-39.2	4.0	23 17.9	-39.1	4.0	24 17.8	-39.1	4.1	25 17.6	-39.0	4.1	85
86	17 39.3	-39.6	3.1	18 39.2	-39.5	3.1	19 39.1	-39.5	3.2	20 39.0	-39.4	3.2	21 38.9	-39.4	3.2	22 38.8	-39.3	3.2	23 38.7	-39.3	3.2	24 38.6	-39.3	3.3	86
87	16 59.7	-39.7	2.3	17 59.7	-39.7	2.3	18 59.6	-39.7	2.4	19 59.6	-39.7	2.4	20 59.5	-39.6	2.4	21 59.5	-39.6	2.4	22 59.4	-39.6	2.4	23 59.3	-39.5	2.4	87
88	16 20.0	-39.9	1.5	17 20.0	-39.9	1.6	18 19.9	-39.8	1.6	19 19.9	-39.8	1.6	20 19.9	-39.9	1.6	21 19.9	-39.9	1.6	22 19.8	-39.8	1.6	23 19.8	-39.8	1.6	88
89	15 40.1	-40.1	0.8	16 40.1	-40.1	0.8	17 40.1	-40.1	0.8	18 40.1	-40.1	0.8	19 40.0	-40.0	0.8	20 40.0	-40.0	0.8	21 40.0	-40.0	0.8	22 40.0	-40.0	0.8	89
90	15 00.0	-40.2	0.0	16 00.0	-40.2	0.0	17 00.0	-40.2	0.0	18 00.0	-40.2	0.0	19 00.0	-40.2	0.0	20 00.0	-40.3	0.0	21 00.0	-40.3	0.0	22 00.0	-40.3	0.0	90
	15°			16°			17°			18°			19°			20°			21°			22°			

48°, 312° L.H.A. LATITUDE SAME NAME AS DECLINATION

98

LATITUDE **CONTRARY** NAME TO DECLINATION **L.H.A. 48°, 312°**

Dec.	15° Hc	d	Z	16° Hc	d	Z	17° Hc	d	Z	18° Hc	d	Z	19° Hc	d	Z	20° Hc	d	Z	21° Hc	d	Z	22° Hc	d	Z	Dec.
°	° ′	′	°	° ′	′	°	° ′	′	°	° ′	′	°	° ′	′	°	° ′	′	°	° ′	′	°	° ′	′	°	°
0	40 15.9	-20.7	103.1	40 01.9	-22.0	103.9	39 47.0	-23.2	104.7	39 31.3	-24.3	105.5	39 14.9	-25.6	106.3	38 57.6	-26.7	107.1	38 39.6	-27.9	107.9	38 20.8	-29.0	108.6	0
1	39 55.2	-21.5	104.3	39 39.9	-22.7	105.2	39 23.8	-23.9	105.9	39 07.0	-25.1	106.7	38 49.3	-26.3	107.5	38 30.9	-27.4	108.3	38 11.7	-28.5	109.0	37 51.8	-29.6	109.8	1
2	39 33.7	-22.3	105.6	39 17.2	-23.5	106.3	38 59.9	-24.6	107.1	38 41.9	-25.8	107.9	38 23.0	-26.9	108.7	38 03.5	-28.1	109.4	37 43.2	-29.1	110.1	37 22.2	-30.2	110.9	2
3	39 11.4	-23.0	106.8	38 53.7	-24.1	107.5	38 35.3	-25.4	108.3	38 16.1	-26.5	109.1	37 56.1	-27.6	109.8	37 35.4	-28.6	110.5	37 14.1	-29.8	111.2	36 52.0	-30.8	111.9	3
4	38 48.4	-23.7	107.9	38 29.6	-24.9	108.7	38 09.9	-25.9	109.5	37 49.6	-27.1	110.2	37 28.5	-28.2	110.9	37 06.8	-29.3	111.6	36 44.3	-30.3	112.3	36 21.2	-31.3	113.0	4
5	38 24.7	-24.4	109.1	38 04.7	-25.5	109.9	37 44.0	-26.7	110.6	37 22.5	-27.8	111.3	37 00.3	-28.8	112.0	36 37.5	-29.9	112.7	36 14.0	-30.9	113.4	35 49.9	-31.9	114.1	5
6	38 00.3	-25.1	110.3	37 39.2	-26.2	111.0	37 17.3	-27.3	111.7	36 54.7	-28.3	112.4	36 31.5	-29.4	113.1	36 07.6	-30.4	113.8	35 43.1	-31.4	114.5	35 18.0	-32.4	115.1	6
7	37 35.2	-25.7	111.4	37 13.0	-26.9	112.1	36 50.0	-27.9	112.8	36 26.4	-29.0	113.5	36 02.1	-30.0	114.2	35 37.2	-31.0	114.9	35 11.7	-32.0	115.5	34 45.6	-33.0	116.1	7
8	37 09.5	-26.4	112.6	36 46.1	-27.4	113.3	36 22.1	-28.5	113.9	35 57.4	-29.5	114.6	35 32.1	-30.5	115.3	35 06.2	-31.5	115.9	34 39.7	-32.5	116.5	34 12.6	-33.4	117.1	8
9	36 43.1	-27.0	113.7	36 18.7	-28.1	114.4	35 53.6	-29.1	115.0	35 27.9	-30.1	115.7	35 01.6	-31.1	116.3	34 34.7	-32.0	116.9	34 07.2	-33.0	117.5	33 39.2	-33.9	118.1	9
10	36 16.1	-27.6	114.8	35 50.6	-28.6	115.5	35 24.5	-29.6	116.1	34 57.8	-30.6	116.7	34 30.5	-31.6	117.4	34 02.7	-32.6	118.0	33 34.2	-33.4	118.6	33 05.3	-34.4	119.1	10
11	35 48.5	-28.2	115.9	35 22.0	-29.3	116.5	34 54.9	-30.3	117.2	34 27.2	-31.2	117.8	33 58.9	-32.1	118.4	33 30.1	-33.0	119.0	33 00.8	-33.9	119.5	32 30.9	-34.8	120.1	11
12	35 20.3	-28.8	117.0	34 52.7	-29.7	117.6	34 24.6	-30.7	118.2	33 56.0	-31.7	118.8	33 26.8	-32.6	119.4	32 57.1	-33.5	120.0	32 26.9	-34.4	120.5	31 56.1	-35.2	121.1	12
13	34 51.5	-29.4	118.1	34 23.0	-30.3	118.7	33 53.9	-31.2	119.3	33 24.3	-32.2	119.8	32 54.2	-33.1	120.4	32 23.6	-34.0	121.0	31 52.5	-34.8	121.5	31 20.9	-35.7	122.0	13
14	34 22.1	-29.9	119.1	33 52.7	-30.9	119.7	33 22.7	-31.8	120.3	32 52.1	-32.6	120.9	32 21.1	-33.5	121.4	31 49.6	-34.4	121.9	31 17.7	-35.3	122.5	30 45.2	-36.0	123.0	14
15	33 52.2	-30.4	120.2	33 21.8	-31.3	120.7	32 50.9	-32.2	121.3	32 19.5	-33.1	121.8	31 47.6	-34.0	122.4	31 15.2	-34.8	122.9	30 42.4	-35.6	123.4	30 09.2	-36.5	123.9	15
16	33 21.8	-30.9	121.2	32 50.5	-31.8	121.8	32 18.7	-32.7	122.3	31 46.4	-33.6	122.8	31 13.6	-34.4	123.3	30 40.4	-35.2	123.8	30 06.8	-36.0	124.3	29 32.7	-36.8	124.8	16
17	32 50.9	-31.4	122.2	32 18.7	-32.3	122.8	31 46.0	-33.2	123.3	31 12.8	-34.0	123.8	30 39.2	-34.8	124.3	30 05.2	-35.6	124.8	29 30.8	-36.5	125.3	28 55.9	-37.1	125.7	17
18	32 19.5	-31.9	123.2	31 46.4	-32.8	123.8	31 12.8	-33.6	124.3	30 38.8	-34.4	124.8	30 04.4	-35.2	125.2	29 29.6	-36.0	125.7	28 54.3	-36.7	126.2	28 18.8	-37.6	126.6	18
19	31 47.6	-32.4	124.2	31 13.6	-33.2	124.7	30 39.2	-34.0	125.2	30 04.4	-34.8	125.7	29 29.2	-35.6	126.2	28 53.6	-36.4	126.6	28 17.6	-37.1	127.1	27 41.2	-37.8	127.5	19
20	31 15.2	-32.8	125.2	30 40.4	-33.6	125.7	30 05.2	-34.4	126.2	29 29.6	-35.3	126.7	28 53.6	-36.0	127.1	28 17.2	-36.7	127.5	27 40.5	-37.5	128.0	27 03.4	-38.2	128.4	20
21	30 42.4	-33.2	126.2	30 06.8	-34.1	126.7	29 30.8	-34.9	127.1	28 54.3	-35.5	127.6	28 17.6	-36.4	128.0	27 40.5	-37.1	128.4	27 03.0	-37.8	128.8	26 25.2	-38.5	129.2	21
22	30 09.2	-33.7	127.2	29 32.7	-34.4	127.6	28 55.9	-35.2	128.1	28 18.8	-36.0	128.5	27 41.2	-36.6	128.9	27 03.4	-37.4	129.3	26 25.2	-38.1	129.7	25 46.7	-38.7	130.1	22
23	29 35.5	-34.0	128.1	28 58.3	-34.8	128.6	28 20.7	-35.6	129.0	27 42.8	-36.3	129.4	27 04.6	-37.1	129.8	26 26.0	-37.7	130.2	25 47.1	-38.4	130.6	25 08.0	-39.1	130.9	23
24	29 01.5	-34.5	129.1	28 23.5	-35.2	129.5	27 45.1	-35.9	129.9	27 06.5	-36.6	130.3	26 27.5	-37.3	130.7	25 48.3	-38.0	131.1	25 08.7	-38.7	131.4	24 28.9	-39.3	131.8	24
25	28 27.0	-34.8	130.0	27 48.3	-35.6	130.4	27 09.2	-36.3	130.8	26 29.9	-37.0	131.2	25 50.2	-37.6	131.6	25 10.3	-38.3	131.9	24 30.0	-38.9	132.3	23 49.6	-39.6	132.6	25
26	27 52.2	-35.2	130.9	27 12.7	-35.9	131.3	26 32.9	-36.6	131.7	25 52.9	-37.3	132.1	25 12.6	-38.0	132.4	24 32.0	-38.6	132.8	23 51.1	-39.2	133.1	23 10.0	-39.9	133.4	26
27	27 17.0	-35.6	131.8	26 36.8	-36.2	132.2	25 56.3	-36.9	132.6	25 15.6	-37.6	132.9	24 34.6	-38.2	133.3	23 53.4	-38.9	133.6	23 11.9	-39.5	133.9	22 30.1	-40.1	134.2	27
28	26 41.4	-35.9	132.7	26 00.6	-36.6	133.1	25 19.4	-37.2	133.5	24 38.0	-37.8	133.8	23 56.4	-38.5	134.1	23 14.5	-39.1	134.4	22 32.4	-39.7	134.7	21 50.0	-40.3	135.0	28
29	26 05.5	-36.2	133.6	25 24.0	-36.9	134.0	24 42.2	-37.5	134.3	24 00.2	-38.2	134.6	23 17.9	-38.8	135.0	22 35.4	-39.4	135.3	21 52.7	-40.0	135.5	21 09.7	-40.5	135.8	29
30	25 29.3	-36.5	134.5	24 47.1	-37.2	134.9	24 04.7	-37.8	135.2	23 22.0	-38.4	135.5	22 39.1	-39.0	135.8	21 56.0	-39.6	136.1	21 12.7	-40.2	136.3	20 29.2	-40.8	136.6	30
31	24 52.8	-36.9	135.4	24 09.9	-37.4	135.7	23 26.9	-38.1	136.0	22 43.6	-38.7	136.3	22 00.1	-39.3	136.6	21 16.4	-39.9	136.9	20 32.5	-40.4	137.1	19 48.4	-40.9	137.4	31
32	24 15.9	-37.1	136.3	23 32.5	-37.8	136.6	22 48.8	-38.4	136.9	22 04.9	-38.9	137.1	21 20.8	-39.5	137.4	20 36.5	-40.0	137.7	19 52.1	-40.6	137.9	19 07.5	-41.2	138.2	32
33	23 38.8	-37.4	137.1	22 54.7	-38.0	137.4	22 10.4	-38.5	137.7	21 26.0	-39.2	138.0	20 41.3	-39.7	138.2	19 56.5	-40.3	138.5	19 11.5	-40.8	138.7	18 26.3	-41.3	138.9	33
34	23 01.4	-37.7	138.0	22 16.7	-38.2	138.3	21 31.9	-38.9	138.5	20 46.8	-39.4	138.8	20 01.6	-39.9	139.0	19 16.2	-40.5	139.3	18 30.7	-41.0	139.5	17 45.0	-41.5	139.7	34
35	22 23.7	-37.9	138.8	21 38.5	-38.6	139.1	20 53.0	-39.0	139.3	20 07.4	-39.6	139.6	19 21.7	-40.2	139.8	18 35.7	-40.6	140.0	17 49.7	-41.2	140.2	17 03.5	-41.7	140.4	35
36	21 45.8	-38.2	139.7	20 59.9	-38.7	139.9	20 14.0	-39.3	140.2	19 27.8	-39.8	140.4	18 41.5	-40.3	140.6	17 55.1	-40.9	140.8	17 08.5	-41.3	141.0	16 21.8	-41.8	141.2	36
37	21 07.6	-38.5	140.5	20 21.2	-39.0	140.7	19 34.7	-39.5	141.0	18 48.0	-40.0	141.2	18 01.2	-40.5	141.4	17 14.2	-41.0	141.6	16 27.2	-41.5	141.8	15 40.0	-42.0	141.9	37
38	20 29.1	-38.6	141.3	19 42.2	-39.2	141.5	18 55.2	-39.7	141.8	18 08.0	-40.2	142.0	17 20.7	-40.7	142.2	16 33.2	-41.2	142.3	15 45.7	-41.7	142.5	14 58.0	-42.1	142.7	38
39	19 50.5	-38.9	142.1	19 03.0	-39.4	142.3	18 15.5	-39.9	142.5	17 27.8	-40.4	142.7	16 40.0	-40.9	142.9	15 52.0	-41.3	143.1	15 04.0	-41.8	143.3	14 15.9	-42.3	143.4	39
40	19 11.6	-39.1	142.9	18 23.6	-39.5	143.1	17 35.6	-40.1	143.3	16 47.4	-40.6	143.5	15 59.1	-41.0	143.7	15 10.7	-41.5	143.9	14 22.2	-41.9	144.0	13 33.6	-42.4	144.2	40
41	18 32.5	-39.3	143.7	17 44.1	-39.8	143.9	16 55.5	-40.3	144.1	16 06.8	-40.7	144.3	15 18.1	-41.2	144.4	14 29.2	-41.6	144.6	13 40.3	-42.1	144.7	12 51.2	-42.5	144.9	41
42	17 53.2	-39.5	144.5	17 04.3	-40.0	144.7	16 15.2	-40.4	144.9	15 26.1	-40.9	145.0	14 36.9	-41.3	145.2	13 47.6	-41.8	145.3	12 58.2	-42.2	145.5	12 08.7	-42.6	145.6	42
43	17 13.7	-39.7	145.3	16 24.3	-40.1	145.5	15 34.8	-40.6	145.7	14 45.2	-41.0	145.8	13 55.6	-41.5	145.9	13 05.8	-41.9	146.1	12 16.0	-42.3	146.2	11 26.1	-42.7	146.3	43
44	16 34.0	-39.8	146.1	15 44.2	-40.3	146.3	14 54.2	-40.7	146.4	14 04.2	-41.1	146.6	13 14.1	-41.6	146.7	12 23.9	-42.0	146.8	11 33.7	-42.4	146.9	10 43.4	-42.8	147.0	44
45	15 54.2	-40.0	146.9	15 03.9	-40.5	147.0	14 13.5	-40.9	147.2	13 23.1	-41.3	147.3	12 32.5	-41.7	147.4	11 41.9	-42.1	147.5	10 51.3	-42.5	147.7	10 00.6	-43.0	147.8	45
46	15 14.2	-40.2	147.7	14 23.4	-40.5	147.8	13 32.6	-41.0	147.9	12 41.8	-41.5	148.1	11 50.8	-41.8	148.2	10 59.8	-42.2	148.3	10 08.8	-42.7	148.4	9 17.6	-43.0	148.5	46
47	14 34.0	-40.3	148.4	13 42.9	-40.8	148.6	12 51.6	-41.1	148.7	12 00.3	-41.5	148.8	11 09.0	-41.9	148.9	10 17.6	-42.3	149.0	9 26.1	-42.6	149.1	8 34.6	-43.0	149.2	47
48	13 53.7	-40.5	149.2	13 02.1	-40.8	149.3	12 10.5	-41.3	149.4	11 18.8	-41.6	149.5	10 27.1	-42.1	149.6	9 35.3	-42.4	149.7	8 43.5	-42.8	149.8	7 51.6	-43.2	149.9	48
49	13 13.2	-40.6	149.9	12 21.3	-41.0	150.1	11 29.2	-41.3	150.2	10 37.2	-41.8	150.3	9 45.0	-42.1	150.4	8 52.9	-42.5	150.4	8 00.7	-42.9	150.5	7 08.4	-43.2	150.6	49
50	12 32.6	-40.7	150.7	11 40.3	-41.1	150.8	10 47.9	-41.5	150.9	9 55.4	-41.8	151.0	9 02.9	-42.2	151.1	8 10.4	-42.6	151.1	7 17.8	-42.9	151.2	6 25.2	-43.2	151.3	50
51	11 51.9	-40.8	151.5	10 59.2	-41.2	151.5	10 06.4	-41.6	151.6	9 13.6	-41.9	151.7	8 20.7	-42.3	151.8	7 27.8	-42.6	151.9	6 34.9	-43.0	151.9	5 42.0	-43.3	152.0	51
52	11 11.1	-41.0	152.2	10 18.0	-41.3	152.3	9 24.8	-41.6	152.4	8 31.7	-42.0	152.4	7 38.4	-42.3	152.5	6 45.2	-42.7	152.6	5 51.9	-43.0	152.6	4 58.7	-43.4	152.7	52
53	10 30.1	-41.0	152.9	9 36.7	-41.4	153.0	8 43.2	-41.8	153.1	7 49.7	-42.1	153.2	6 56.1	-42.4	153.2	6 02.5	-42.7	153.3	5 08.9	-43.0	153.3	4 15.3	-43.4	153.4	53
54	9 49.1	-41.2	153.7	8 55.3	-41.5	153.8	8 01.4	-41.8	153.8	7 07.6	-42.2	153.9	6 13.7	-42.5	153.9	5 19.8	-42.8	154.0	4 25.9	-43.2	154.0	3 31.9	-43.4	154.0	54
55	9 07.9	-41.2	154.4	8 13.8	-41.6	154.5	7 19.6	-41.9	154.5	6 25.4	-42.2	154.6	5 31.2	-42.5	154.6	4 37.0	-42.8	154.7	3 42.7	-43.1	154.7	2 48.5	-43.5	154.7	55
56	8 26.7	-41.3	155.2	7 32.2	-41.6	155.2	6 37.7	-41.9	155.3	5 43.2	-42.2	155.3	4 48.7	-42.6	155.4	3 54.2	-42.9	155.4	2 59.6	-43.2	155.4	2 05.0	-43.4	155.4	56
57	7 45.4	-41.4	155.9	6 50.6	-41.7	155.9	5 55.8	-42.0	156.0	5 01.0	-42.3	156.0	4 06.1	-42.6	156.1	3 11.3	-42.9	156.1	2 16.4	-43.2	156.1	1 21.6	-43.5	156.1	57
58	7 04.0	-41.5	156.6	6 08.9	-41.8	156.7	5 13.8	-42.1	156.7	4 18.7	-42.4	156.7	3 23.5	-42.6	156.8	2 28.4	-42.9	156.8	1 33.2	-43.2	156.8	0 38.1	-43.5	156.8	58
59	6 22.5	-41.5	157.3	5 27.1	-41.8	157.4	4 31.7	-42.1	157.4	3 36.3	-42.4	157.4	2 40.9	-42.7	157.5	1 45.5	-43.0	157.5	0 50.0	-43.2	157.5	0 05.4	+43.5	22.5	59
60	5 41.0	-41.6	158.1	4 45.3	-41.9	158.1	3 49.6	-42.1	158.1	2 53.9	-42.4	158.2	1 58.2	-42.6	158.2	1 02.5	-42.9	158.2	0 06.8	-43.2	158.2	0 48.9	+43.4	21.8	60
61	4 59.4	-41.6	158.8	4 03.4	-41.8	158.8	3 07.5	-42.2	158.8	2 11.5	-42.4	158.9	1 15.6	-42.7	158.9	0 19.6	-43.0	158.9	0 36.4	+43.2	21.1	1 32.3	+43.5	21.1	61
62	4 17.8	-41.7	159.5	3 21.6	-42.0	159.5	2 25.3	-42.2	159.6	1 29.1	-42.4	159.6	0 32.9	-42.7	159.6	0 23.4	+42.9	20.4	1 19.6	+43.2	20.4	2 15.8	+43.4	20.4	62
63	3 36.1	-41.7	160.2	2 39.6	-41.9	160.3	1 43.1	-42.2	160.3	0 46.7	-42.5	160.3	0 09.8	+42.7	19.7	1 06.3	+42.9	19.7	2 02.8	+43.2	19.7	2 59.2	+43.5	19.7	63
64	2 54.4	-41.7	161.0	1 57.7	-42.0	161.0	1 00.9	-42.2	161.0	0 04.2	-42.4	161.0	0 52.5	+42.7	19.0	1 49.2	+42.9	19.0	2 45.9	+43.2	19.0	3 42.7	+43.3	19.1	64
65	2 12.7	-41.8	161.7	1 15.7	-42.0	161.7	0 18.7	-42.2	161.7	0 38.2	+42.5	18.3	1 35.2	+42.7	18.3	2 32.1	+42.9	18.3	3 29.1	+43.1	18.3	4 26.0	+43.4	18.4	65
66	1 30.9	-41.7	162.4	0 33.7	-42.0	162.4	0 23.5	+42.2	17.6	1 20.7	+42.4	17.6	2 17.9	+42.6	17.6	3 15.0	+42.9	17.6	4 12.2	+43.1	17.6	5 09.4	+43.3	17.7	66
67	0 49.2	-41.8	163.1	0 08.3	+41.9	16.9	1 05.7	+42.2	16.9	2 03.1	+42.4	16.9	3 00.5	+42.6	16.9	3 57.9	+42.8	16.9	4 55.3	+43.0	16.9	5 52.7	+43.2	17.0	67
68	0 07.4	-41.8	163.8	0 50.2	+42.0	16.2	1 47.9	+42.2	16.2	2 45.5	+42.4	16.2	3 43.1	+42.6	16.2	4 40.7	+42.8	16.2	5 38.3	+43.0	16.2	6 35.9	+43.2	16.3	68
69	0 34.4	+41.8	15.4	1 32.2	+42.0	15.5	2 30.1	+42.1	15.5	3 27.9	+42.3	15.5	4 25.7	+42.6	15.5	5 23.5	+42.8	15.5	6 21.3	+43.0	15.5	7 19.1	+43.2	15.6	69
70	1 16.2	+41.7	14.7	2 14.2	+41.9	14.7	3 12.2	+42.1	14.7	4 10.2	+42.3	14.8	5 08.3	+42.4	14.8	6 06.3	+42.6	14.8	7 04.3	+42.8	14.8	8 02.3	+43.0	14.9	70
71	1 57.9	+41.8	14.0	2 56.1	+41.9	14.0	3 54.3	+42.1	14.0	4 52.5	+42.3	14.1	5 50.7	+42.5	14.1	6 48.9	+42.7	14.1	7 47.1	+42.8	14.1	8 45.3	+43.0	14.2	71
72	2 39.7	+41.7	13.3	3 38.0	+41.9	13.3	4 36.4	+42.1	13.3	5 34.8	+42.2	13.3	6 33.2	+42.4	13.4	7 31.6	+42.5	13.4	8 29.9	+42.8	13.4	9 28.3	+42.9	13.5	72
73	3 21.4	+41.6	12.6	4 19.9	+41.9	12.6	5 18.5	+42.0	12.6	6 17.0	+42.2	12.6	7 15.6	+42.3	12.7	8 14.1	+42.5	12.7	9 12.7	+42.6	12.7	10 11.2	+42.8	12.8	73
74	4 03.0	+41.7	11.9	5 01.8	+41.8	11.9	6 00.5	+41.9	11.9	6 59.2	+42.1	11.9	7 57.9	+42.2	11.9	8 56.6	+42.4	12.0	9 55.3	+42.5	12.0	10 54.0	+42.7	12.0	74
75	4 44.7	+41.6	11.1	5 43.6	+41.7	11.1	6 42.4	+41.9	11.2	7 41.3	+42.0	11.2	8 40.1	+42.2	11.2	9 39.0	+42.3	11.3	10 37.8	+42.5	11.3	11 36.7	+42.6	11.3	75
76	5 26.3	+41.5	10.4	6 25.3	+41.7	10.4	7 24.3	+41.8	10.4	8 23.3	+41.9	10.5	9 22.3	+42.1	10.5	10 21.3	+42.2	10.5	11 20.3	+42.3	10.6	12 19.3	+42.4	10.6	76
77	6 07.8	+41.5	9.7	7 07.0	+41.6	9.7	8 06.1	+41.7	9.7	9 05.2	+41.9	9.7	10 04.4	+42.0	9.8	11 03.5	+42.1	9.8	12 02.6	+42.3	9.8	13 01.7	+42.4	9.9	77
78	6 49.3	+41.4	9.0	7 48.6	+41.5	9.0	8 47.8	+41.7	9.0	9 47.1	+41.8	9.0	10 46.4	+41.8	9.0	11 45.6	+42.0	9.1	12 44.9	+42.1	9.1	13 44.1	+42.2	9.2	78
79	7 30.7	+41.4	8.2	8 30.1	+41.5	8.2	9 29.5	+41.6	8.3	10 28.9	+41.6	8.3	11 28.2	+41.8	8.3	12 27.6	+41.9	8.3	13 27.0	+42.0	8.4	14 26.3	+42.1	8.4	79
80	8 12.1	+41.3	7.5	9 11.6	+41.3	7.5	10 11.1	+41.4	7.5	11 10.5	+41.6	7.6	12 10.0	+41.7	7.6	13 09.5	+41.7	7.6	14 09.0	+41.8	7.6	15 08.4	+42.0	7.7	80
81	8 53.4	+41.1	6.8	9 52.9	+41.3	6.8	10 52.5	+41.4	6.8	11 52.1	+41.4	6.8	12 51.7	+41.5	6.8	13 51.2	+41.7	6.9	14 50.8	+41.7	6.9	15 50.4	+41.8	6.9	81
82	9 34.5	+41.1	6.0	10 34.2	+41.2	6.0	11 33.9	+41.2	6.1	12 33.5	+41.4	6.1	13 33.2	+41.4	6.1	14 32.9	+41.4	6.1	15 32.5	+41.6	6.2	16 32.2	+41.6	6.2	82
83	10 15.6	+41.0	5.3	11 15.4	+41.0	5.3	12 15.1	+41.1	5.3	13 14.9	+41.1	5.3	14 14.6	+41.2	5.4	15 14.3	+41.4	5.4	16 14.1	+41.4	5.4	17 13.8	+41.5	5.4	83
84	10 56.6	+40.9	4.5	11 56.4	+41.0	4.6	12 56.2	+41.0	4.6	13 56.0	+41.1	4.6	14 55.8	+41.2	4.6	15 55.7	+41.1	4.6	16 55.5	+41.2	4.7	17 55.3	+41.2	4.7	84
85	11 37.5	+40.8	3.8	12 37.4	+40.8	3.8	13 37.2	+40.9	3.8	14 37.1	+40.9	3.8	15 37.0	+40.9	3.9	16 36.8	+41.0	3.9	17 36.7	+41.0	3.9	18 36.5	+41.1	3.9	85
86	12 18.3	+40.6	3.0	13 18.2	+40.6	3.1	14 18.1	+40.7	3.1	15 18.0	+40.8	3.1	16 17.9	+40.8	3.1	17 17.8	+40.9	3.1	18 17.7	+40.9	3.1	19 17.6	+40.9	3.1	86
87	12 58.9	+40.5	2.3	13 58.8	+40.6	2.3	14 58.8	+40.6	2.3	15 58.8	+40.5	2.3	16 58.7	+40.6	2.3	17 58.7	+40.6	2.3	18 58.6	+40.7	2.4	19 58.5	+40.8	2.4	87
88	13 39.4	+40.4	1.5	14 39.4	+40.4	1.5	15 39.4	+40.4	1.5	16 39.3	+40.5	1.6	17 39.3	+40.5	1.6	18 39.3	+40.4	1.6	19 39.3	+40.4	1.6	20 39.3	+40.4	1.6	88
89	14 19.8	+40.2	0.8	15 19.8	+40.2	0.8	16 19.8	+40.2	0.8	17 19.8	+40.2	0.8	18 19.8	+40.2	0.8	19 19.7	+40.3	0.8	20 19.7	+40.3	0.8	21 19.7	+40.3	0.8	89
90	15 00.0	+40.1	0.0	16 00.0	+40.1	0.0	17 00.0	+40.1	0.0	18 00.0	+40.1	0.0	19 00.0	+40.0	0.0	20 00.0	+40.0	0.0	21 00.0	+40.0	0.0	22 00.0	+40.0	0.0	90
	15°			16°			17°			18°			19°			20°			21°			22°			

S. Lat. {L.H.A. greater than 180° ....Zn=180°−Z; L.H.A. less than 180°...........Zn=180°+Z}

LATITUDE **SAME** NAME AS DECLINATION **L.H.A. 132°, 228°**

99

49°, 311° L.H.A. LATITUDE SAME NAME AS DECLINATION

N. Lat. {L.H.A. greater than 180° .....Zn=Z; L.H.A. less than 180°............Zn=360°−Z}

Dec.	15° Hc	d	Z	16° Hc	d	Z	17° Hc	d	Z	18° Hc	d	Z
°	° ′	′	°	° ′	′	°	° ′	′	°	° ′	′	°
0	39 19.4	+19.7	102.7	39 05.9	+20.9	103.5	38 51.5	+22.1	104.3	38 36.3	+23.4	105.0
1	39 39.1	+18.9	101.5	39 26.8	+20.2	102.3	39 13.6	+21.5	103.1	38 59.7	+22.6	103.9
2	39 58.0	+18.2	100.2	39 47.0	+19.4	101.0	39 35.1	+20.6	101.9	39 22.3	+21.9	102.7
3	40 16.2	+17.3	99.0	40 06.4	+18.6	99.8	39 55.7	+19.9	100.6	39 44.2	+21.2	101.5
4	40 33.5	+16.5	97.7	40 25.0	+17.8	98.6	40 15.6	+19.1	99.4	40 05.4	+20.4	100.2
5	40 50.0	+15.6	96.4	40 42.8	+16.9	97.3	40 34.7	+18.3	98.2	40 25.8	+19.5	99.0
6	41 05.6	+14.8	95.2	40 59.7	+16.2	96.0	40 53.0	+17.4	96.9	40 45.3	+18.8	97.8
7	41 20.4	+13.9	93.9	41 15.9	+15.2	94.8	41 10.4	+16.6	95.6	41 04.1	+17.9	96.5
8	41 34.3	+13.0	92.6	41 31.1	+14.4	93.5	41 27.0	+15.8	94.4	41 22.0	+17.1	95.2
9	41 47.3	+12.2	91.3	41 45.5	+13.6	92.2	41 42.8	+14.9	93.1	41 39.1	+16.3	93.9
10	41 59.5	+11.2	90.0	41 59.1	+12.6	90.9	41 57.7	+14.0	91.8	41 55.4	+15.3	92.7
11	42 10.7	+10.3	88.6	42 11.7	+11.7	89.5	42 11.7	+13.1	90.4	42 10.7	+14.5	91.4
12	42 21.0	+9.4	87.3	42 23.4	+10.8	88.2	42 24.8	+12.2	89.1	42 25.2	+13.6	90.0
13	42 30.4	+8.5	86.0	42 34.2	+9.8	86.9	42 37.0	+11.2	87.8	42 38.8	+12.6	88.7
14	42 38.9	+7.5	84.6	42 44.0	+8.9	85.5	42 48.2	+10.3	86.5	42 51.4	+11.7	87.4
15	42 46.4	+6.5	83.3	42 52.9	+8.0	84.2	42 58.5	+9.4	85.1	43 03.1	+10.8	86.1
16	42 52.9	+5.6	81.9	43 00.9	+7.0	82.8	43 07.9	+8.4	83.8	43 13.9	+9.8	84.7
17	42 58.5	+4.6	80.6	43 07.9	+6.0	81.5	43 16.3	+7.4	82.4	43 23.7	+8.9	83.3
18	43 03.1	+3.7	79.2	43 13.9	+5.1	80.1	43 23.7	+6.5	81.0	43 32.6	+7.9	82.0
19	43 06.8	+2.7	77.8	43 19.0	+4.0	78.7	43 30.2	+5.5	79.7	43 40.5	+6.9	80.6
20	43 09.5	+1.6	76.5	43 23.0	+3.1	77.4	43 35.7	+4.5	78.3	43 47.4	+5.9	79.2
21	43 11.1	+0.8	75.1	43 26.1	+2.1	76.0	43 40.2	+3.5	76.9	43 53.3	+4.9	77.9
22	43 11.9	−0.3	73.7	43 28.2	+1.1	74.6	43 43.7	+2.5	75.5	43 58.2	+3.9	76.5
23	43 11.6	−1.3	72.3	43 29.3	+0.1	73.2	43 46.2	+1.5	74.2	44 02.1	+2.9	75.1
24	43 10.3	−2.2	71.0	43 29.4	−0.9	71.9	43 47.7	+0.4	72.8	44 05.0	+1.8	73.7
25	43 08.1	−3.3	69.6	43 28.5	−1.8	70.5	43 48.1	−0.5	71.4	44 06.8	+0.9	72.3
26	43 04.8	−4.2	68.2	43 26.7	−2.9	69.1	43 47.6	−1.5	70.0	44 07.7	−0.2	70.9
27	43 00.6	−5.1	66.9	43 23.8	−3.9	67.7	43 46.1	−2.5	68.6	44 07.5	−1.1	69.5
28	42 55.5	−6.2	65.5	43 19.9	−4.8	66.4	43 43.6	−3.5	67.2	44 06.4	−2.2	68.1
29	42 49.3	−7.0	64.2	43 15.1	−5.8	65.0	43 40.1	−4.6	65.9	44 04.2	−3.2	66.7
30	42 42.3	−8.1	62.8	43 09.3	−6.8	63.6	43 35.5	−5.5	64.5	44 01.0	−4.2	65.3
31	42 34.2	−9.0	61.5	43 02.5	−7.7	62.3	43 30.0	−6.5	63.1	43 56.8	−5.2	64.0
32	42 25.2	−9.9	60.1	42 54.8	−8.7	60.9	43 23.5	−7.4	61.7	43 51.6	−6.2	62.6
33	42 15.3	−10.8	58.8	42 46.1	−9.7	59.6	43 16.1	−8.5	60.4	43 45.4	−7.2	61.2
34	42 04.5	−11.8	57.5	42 36.4	−10.6	58.2	43 07.6	−9.3	59.0	43 38.2	−8.2	59.8
35	41 52.7	−12.6	56.1	42 25.8	−11.5	56.9	42 58.3	−10.4	57.7	43 30.0	−9.2	58.5
36	41 40.1	−13.6	54.8	42 14.3	−12.4	55.6	42 47.9	−11.3	56.3	43 20.8	−10.1	57.1
37	41 26.5	−14.4	53.5	42 01.9	−13.3	54.2	42 36.6	−12.2	55.0	43 10.7	−11.0	55.7
38	41 12.1	−15.3	52.2	41 48.6	−14.3	52.9	42 24.4	−13.1	53.7	42 59.7	−12.0	54.4
39	40 56.8	−16.1	50.9	41 34.3	−15.0	51.6	42 11.3	−14.0	52.3	42 47.7	−13.0	53.1
40	40 40.7	−17.0	49.7	41 19.3	−16.0	50.3	41 57.3	−14.9	51.0	42 34.7	−13.8	51.7
41	40 23.7	−17.7	48.4	41 03.3	−16.8	49.1	41 42.4	−15.8	49.7	42 20.9	−14.8	50.4
42	40 06.0	−18.6	47.2	40 46.5	−17.6	47.8	41 26.6	−16.6	48.4	42 06.1	−15.6	49.1
43	39 47.4	−19.4	45.9	40 28.9	−18.4	46.5	41 10.0	−17.5	47.2	41 50.5	−16.5	47.8
44	39 28.0	−20.1	44.7	40 10.5	−19.2	45.3	40 52.5	−18.3	45.9	41 34.0	−17.3	46.5
45	39 07.9	−20.9	43.5	39 51.3	−20.0	44.0	40 34.2	−19.1	44.6	41 16.7	−18.2	45.2
46	38 47.0	−21.6	42.3	39 31.3	−20.8	42.8	40 15.1	−19.9	43.4	40 58.5	−19.1	44.0
47	38 25.4	−22.3	41.1	39 10.5	−21.5	41.6	39 55.2	−20.7	42.2	40 39.4	−19.8	42.7
48	38 03.1	−23.0	39.9	38 49.0	−22.3	40.4	39 34.5	−21.5	40.9	40 19.6	−20.6	41.5
49	37 40.1	−23.8	38.7	38 26.7	−22.9	39.2	39 13.0	−22.1	39.7	39 59.0	−21.4	40.3
50	37 16.3	−24.3	37.6	38 03.8	−23.7	38.0	38 50.9	−23.0	38.5	39 37.6	−22.1	39.0
51	36 52.0	−25.1	36.4	37 40.1	−24.3	36.9	38 27.9	−23.6	37.3	39 15.5	−22.9	37.8
52	36 26.9	−25.7	35.3	37 15.8	−25.0	35.7	38 04.3	−24.3	36.2	38 52.6	−23.6	36.6
53	36 01.2	−26.3	34.2	36 50.8	−25.7	34.6	37 40.0	−24.9	35.0	38 29.0	−24.3	35.5
54	35 34.9	−26.9	33.1	36 25.1	−26.3	33.5	37 15.1	−25.7	33.9	38 04.7	−24.9	34.3
55	35 08.0	−27.4	32.0	35 58.8	−26.8	32.3	36 49.4	−26.2	32.7	37 39.8	−25.7	33.2
56	34 40.6	−28.1	30.9	35 32.0	−27.5	31.2	36 23.2	−26.9	31.6	37 14.1	−26.2	32.0
57	34 12.5	−28.6	29.8	35 04.5	−28.1	30.1	35 56.3	−27.5	30.5	36 47.9	−27.0	30.9
58	33 43.9	−29.1	28.7	34 36.4	−28.6	29.1	35 28.8	−28.1	29.4	36 20.9	−27.5	29.8
59	33 14.8	−29.7	27.7	34 07.8	−29.2	28.0	35 00.7	−28.7	28.3	35 53.4	−28.1	28.7
60	32 45.1	−30.2	26.7	33 38.6	−29.7	27.0	34 32.0	−29.2	27.3	35 25.3	−28.7	27.6
61	32 14.9	−30.6	25.6	33 08.9	−30.2	25.9	34 02.8	−29.7	26.2	34 56.6	−29.2	26.5
62	31 44.3	−31.2	24.6	32 38.7	−30.7	24.9	33 33.1	−30.2	25.2	34 27.4	−29.8	25.4
63	31 13.1	−31.6	23.6	32 08.0	−31.1	23.9	33 02.9	−30.8	24.1	33 57.6	−30.4	24.4
64	30 41.5	−32.0	22.6	31 36.9	−31.7	22.9	32 32.1	−31.3	23.1	33 27.2	−30.8	23.4
65	30 09.5	−32.5	21.6	31 05.2	−32.1	21.9	32 00.8	−31.7	22.1	32 56.4	−31.4	22.3
66	29 37.0	−32.9	20.7	30 33.1	−32.6	20.9	31 29.1	−32.2	21.1	32 25.0	−31.8	21.3
67	29 04.1	−33.3	19.7	30 00.5	−32.9	19.9	30 56.9	−32.6	20.1	31 53.2	−32.3	20.3
68	28 30.8	−33.7	18.8	29 27.6	−33.4	18.9	30 24.3	−33.1	19.1	31 20.9	−32.7	19.3
69	27 57.1	−34.1	17.8	28 54.2	−33.8	18.0	29 51.2	−33.4	18.2	30 48.2	−33.2	18.4
70	27 23.0	−34.4	16.9	28 20.4	−34.1	17.1	29 17.8	−33.9	17.2	30 15.0	−33.6	17.4
71	26 48.6	−34.8	16.0	27 46.3	−34.6	16.1	28 43.9	−34.3	16.3	29 41.4	−34.0	16.4
72	26 13.8	−35.1	15.1	27 11.7	−34.9	15.2	28 09.6	−34.6	15.3	29 07.4	−34.3	15.5
73	25 38.7	−35.5	14.2	26 36.8	−35.2	14.3	27 35.0	−35.0	14.4	28 33.1	−34.8	14.5
74	25 03.2	−35.8	13.3	26 01.6	−35.6	13.4	27 00.0	−35.4	13.5	27 58.3	−35.2	13.6
75	24 27.4	−36.0	12.4	25 26.0	−35.9	12.5	26 24.6	−35.7	12.6	27 23.1	−35.5	12.7
76	23 51.4	−36.4	11.5	24 50.1	−36.2	11.6	25 48.9	−36.0	11.7	26 47.6	−35.8	11.8
77	23 15.0	−36.7	10.6	24 13.9	−36.5	10.7	25 12.9	−36.4	10.8	26 11.8	−36.2	10.9
78	22 38.3	−36.9	9.8	23 37.4	−36.7	9.9	24 36.5	−36.6	9.9	25 35.6	−36.4	10.0
79	22 01.4	−37.2	8.9	23 00.7	−37.1	9.0	23 59.9	−36.9	9.1	24 59.2	−36.8	9.1
80	21 24.2	−37.5	8.1	22 23.6	−37.3	8.1	23 23.0	−37.2	8.2	24 22.4	−37.1	8.3
81	20 46.7	−37.6	7.3	21 46.3	−37.6	7.3	22 45.8	−37.5	7.4	23 45.3	−37.4	7.4
82	20 09.1	−38.0	6.4	21 08.7	−37.8	6.5	22 08.3	−37.7	6.5	23 07.9	−37.6	6.6
83	19 31.1	−38.1	5.6	20 30.9	−38.1	5.6	21 30.6	−38.0	5.7	22 30.3	−37.9	5.7
84	18 53.0	−38.4	4.8	19 52.8	−38.3	4.8	20 52.6	−38.2	4.8	21 52.4	−38.2	4.9
85	18 14.6	−38.5	4.0	19 14.5	−38.5	4.0	20 14.4	−38.5	4.0	21 14.2	−38.4	4.0
86	17 36.1	−38.8	3.2	18 36.0	−38.7	3.2	19 35.9	−38.7	3.2	20 35.8	−38.6	3.2
87	16 57.3	−38.9	2.4	17 57.3	−38.9	2.4	18 57.2	−38.8	2.4	19 57.2	−38.9	2.4
88	16 18.4	−39.1	1.6	17 18.4	−39.1	1.6	18 18.4	−39.1	1.6	19 18.3	−39.0	1.6
89	15 39.3	−39.3	0.8	16 39.3	−39.3	0.8	17 39.3	−39.3	0.8	18 39.3	−39.3	0.8
90	15 00.0	−39.4	0.0	16 00.0	−39.4	0.0	17 00.0	−39.5	0.0	18 00.0	−39.5	0.0
	15°			16°			17°			18°		

19° Hc	d	Z	20° Hc	d	Z	21° Hc	d	Z	22° Hc	d	Z	Dec.
° ′	′	°	° ′	′	°	° ′	′	°	° ′	′	°	°
38 20.4	+24.5	105.8	38 03.6	+25.8	106.6	37 46.2	+26.8	107.3	37 27.9	+28.0	108.0	0
38 44.9	+23.9	104.6	38 29.4	+25.0	105.4	38 13.0	+26.2	106.2	37 55.9	+27.4	106.9	1
39 08.8	+23.1	103.5	38 54.4	+24.3	104.2	38 39.2	+25.6	105.0	38 23.3	+26.7	105.8	2
39 31.9	+22.4	102.3	39 18.7	+23.7	103.1	39 04.8	+24.8	103.9	38 50.0	+26.0	104.6	3
39 54.3	+21.6	101.1	39 42.4	+22.9	101.9	39 29.6	+24.1	102.7	39 16.0	+25.3	103.5	4
40 15.9	+20.9	99.8	40 05.3	+22.1	100.7	39 53.7	+23.4	101.5	39 41.3	+24.6	102.3	5
40 36.8	+20.1	98.6	40 27.4	+21.3	99.5	40 17.1	+22.6	100.3	40 05.9	+23.9	101.1	6
40 56.9	+19.2	97.4	40 48.7	+20.6	98.2	40 39.7	+21.8	99.1	40 29.8	+23.1	99.9	7
41 16.1	+18.4	96.1	41 09.3	+19.7	97.0	41 01.5	+21.1	97.8	40 52.9	+22.3	98.7	8
41 34.5	+17.6	94.8	41 29.0	+18.9	95.7	41 22.6	+20.2	96.6	41 15.2	+21.6	97.5	9
41 52.1	+16.7	93.6	41 47.9	+18.1	94.4	41 42.8	+19.4	95.3	41 36.8	+20.7	96.2	10
42 08.8	+15.9	92.3	42 06.0	+17.2	93.2	42 02.2	+18.6	94.1	41 57.5	+19.9	95.0	11
42 24.7	+14.9	91.0	42 23.2	+16.3	91.9	42 20.8	+17.7	92.8	42 17.4	+19.0	93.7	12
42 39.6	+14.1	89.6	42 39.5	+15.5	90.6	42 38.5	+16.8	91.5	42 36.4	+18.2	92.4	13
42 53.7	+13.1	88.3	42 55.0	+14.5	89.2	42 55.3	+15.8	90.2	42 54.6	+17.3	91.1	14
43 06.8	+12.2	87.0	43 09.5	+13.5	87.9	43 11.1	+15.0	88.9	43 11.9	+16.3	89.8	15
43 19.0	+11.2	85.6	43 23.0	+12.7	86.6	43 26.1	+14.1	87.5	43 28.2	+15.5	88.5	16
43 30.2	+10.3	84.3	43 35.7	+11.7	85.2	43 40.2	+13.1	86.2	43 43.7	+14.5	87.1	17
43 40.5	+9.3	82.9	43 47.4	+10.7	83.9	43 53.3	+12.1	84.8	43 58.2	+13.5	85.8	18
43 49.8	+8.3	81.6	43 58.1	+9.7	82.5	44 05.4	+11.2	83.5	44 11.7	+12.6	84.4	19
43 58.1	+7.3	80.2	44 07.8	+8.8	81.1	44 16.6	+10.1	82.1	44 24.3	+11.6	83.1	20
44 05.4	+6.3	78.8	44 16.6	+7.7	79.8	44 26.7	+9.2	80.7	44 35.9	+10.6	81.7	21
44 11.7	+5.3	77.4	44 24.3	+6.7	78.4	44 35.9	+8.2	79.3	44 46.5	+9.6	80.3	22
44 17.0	+4.3	76.0	44 31.0	+5.7	77.0	44 44.1	+7.1	77.9	44 56.1	+8.6	78.9	23
44 21.3	+3.3	74.6	44 36.7	+4.7	75.6	44 51.2	+6.1	76.5	45 04.7	+7.5	77.5	24
44 24.6	+2.3	73.2	44 41.4	+3.7	74.2	44 57.3	+5.1	75.1	45 12.2	+6.5	76.1	25
44 26.9	+1.2	71.8	44 45.1	+2.6	72.8	45 02.4	+4.0	73.7	45 18.7	+5.4	74.7	26
44 28.1	+0.2	70.4	44 47.7	+1.6	71.4	45 06.4	+3.0	72.3	45 24.1	+4.4	73.3	27
44 28.3	−0.9	69.0	44 49.3	+0.5	70.0	45 09.4	+1.9	70.9	45 28.5	+3.4	71.9	28
44 27.4	−1.8	67.6	44 49.8	−0.5	68.6	45 11.3	+0.9	69.5	45 31.9	+2.2	70.4	29
44 25.6	−2.9	66.2	44 49.3	−1.5	67.1	45 12.2	−0.2	68.1	45 34.1	+1.3	69.0	30
44 22.7	−3.9	64.8	44 47.8	−2.6	65.7	45 12.0	−1.2	66.6	45 35.4	+0.1	67.6	31
44 18.8	−4.9	63.4	44 45.2	−3.6	64.3	45 10.8	−2.3	65.2	45 35.5	−0.9	66.2	32
44 13.9	−5.9	62.1	44 41.6	−4.6	62.9	45 08.5	−3.3	63.8	45 34.6	−2.0	64.7	33
44 08.0	−7.0	60.7	44 37.0	−5.7	61.5	45 05.2	−4.4	62.4	45 32.6	−3.1	63.3	34
44 01.0	−7.9	59.3	44 31.3	−6.7	60.1	45 00.8	−5.4	61.0	45 29.5	−4.1	61.9	35
43 53.1	−8.9	57.9	44 24.6	−7.7	58.7	44 55.4	−6.5	59.6	45 25.4	−5.2	60.4	36
43 44.2	−9.9	56.5	44 16.9	−8.7	57.3	44 48.9	−7.5	58.2	45 20.2	−6.3	59.0	37
43 34.3	−10.9	55.2	44 08.2	−9.7	56.0	44 41.4	−8.5	56.8	45 13.9	−7.2	57.6	38
43 23.4	−11.8	53.8	43 58.5	−10.7	54.6	44 32.9	−9.5	55.4	45 06.7	−8.3	56.2	39
43 11.6	−12.8	52.5	43 47.8	−11.6	53.2	44 23.4	−10.5	54.0	44 58.4	−9.4	54.8	40
42 58.8	−13.7	51.1	43 36.2	−12.6	51.9	44 12.9	−11.5	52.6	44 49.0	−10.3	53.4	41
42 45.1	−14.6	49.8	43 23.6	−13.6	50.5	44 01.4	−12.4	51.3	44 38.7	−11.4	52.0	42
42 30.5	−15.5	48.5	43 10.0	−14.4	49.2	43 49.0	−13.4	49.9	44 27.3	−12.3	50.6	43
42 15.0	−16.3	47.2	42 55.6	−15.4	47.9	43 35.6	−14.4	48.6	44 15.0	−13.3	49.3	44
41 58.7	−17.3	45.9	42 40.2	−16.3	46.5	43 21.2	−15.3	47.2	44 01.7	−14.3	47.9	45
41 41.4	−18.1	44.6	42 23.9	−17.2	45.2	43 05.9	−16.2	45.9	43 47.4	−15.2	46.6	46
41 23.3	−18.9	43.3	42 06.7	−18.0	43.9	42 49.7	−17.1	44.6	43 32.2	−16.1	45.2	47
41 04.4	−19.8	42.1	41 48.7	−18.9	42.7	42 32.6	−18.0	43.3	43 16.1	−17.1	43.9	48
40 44.6	−20.5	40.8	41 29.8	−19.7	41.4	42 14.6	−18.8	42.0	42 59.0	−17.9	42.6	49
40 24.1	−21.4	39.6	41 10.1	−20.5	40.1	41 55.8	−19.7	40.7	42 41.1	−18.8	41.3	50
40 02.7	−22.1	38.3	40 49.6	−21.3	38.9	41 36.1	−20.5	39.4	42 22.3	−19.7	40.0	51
39 40.6	−22.8	37.1	40 28.3	−22.1	37.6	41 15.6	−21.3	38.2	42 02.6	−20.5	38.7	52
39 17.8	−23.6	35.9	40 06.2	−22.9	36.4	40 54.3	−22.1	36.9	41 42.1	−21.3	37.5	53
38 54.2	−24.3	34.8	39 43.3	−23.6	35.2	40 32.2	−22.9	35.7	41 20.8	−22.2	36.2	54
38 29.9	−25.0	33.6	39 19.7	−24.3	34.0	40 09.3	−23.6	34.5	40 58.6	−22.9	35.0	55
38 04.9	−25.7	32.4	38 55.4	−25.0	32.9	39 45.7	−24.3	33.3	40 35.7	−23.7	33.8	56
37 39.2	−26.3	31.3	38 30.4	−25.7	31.7	39 21.4	−25.1	32.1	40 12.0	−24.4	32.6	57
37 12.9	−26.9	30.1	38 04.7	−26.4	30.5	38 56.3	−25.8	30.9	39 47.6	−25.1	31.4	58
36 46.0	−27.6	29.0	37 38.3	−27.0	29.4	38 30.5	−26.4	29.8	39 22.5	−25.9	30.2	59
36 18.4	−28.2	27.9	37 11.3	−27.6	28.3	38 04.1	−27.1	28.6	38 56.6	−26.5	29.0	60
35 50.2	−28.7	26.8	36 43.7	−28.3	27.2	37 37.0	−27.7	27.5	38 30.1	−27.2	27.9	61
35 21.5	−29.4	25.8	36 15.4	−28.8	26.1	37 09.3	−28.4	26.4	38 02.9	−27.8	26.7	62
34 52.1	−29.8	24.7	35 46.6	−29.4	25.0	36 40.9	−28.9	25.3	37 35.1	−28.5	25.6	63
34 22.3	−30.5	23.6	35 17.2	−30.0	23.9	36 12.0	−29.6	24.2	37 06.6	−29.1	24.5	64
33 51.8	−30.9	22.6	34 47.2	−30.6	22.9	35 42.4	−30.1	23.1	36 37.5	−29.6	23.4	65
33 20.9	−31.4	21.6	34 16.6	−31.0	21.8	35 12.3	−30.6	22.1	36 07.9	−30.3	22.3	66
32 49.5	−32.0	20.5	33 45.6	−31.6	20.8	34 41.7	−31.2	21.0	35 37.6	−30.8	21.3	67
32 17.5	−32.4	19.5	33 14.0	−32.0	19.8	34 10.5	−31.7	20.0	35 06.8	−31.3	20.2	68
31 45.1	−32.8	18.5	32 42.0	−32.6	18.7	33 38.8	−32.2	19.0	34 35.5	−31.9	19.2	69
31 12.3	−33.3	17.6	32 09.4	−33.0	17.8	33 06.6	−32.7	17.9	34 03.6	−32.4	18.2	70
30 39.0	−33.8	16.6	31 36.4	−33.4	16.8	32 33.9	−33.2	17.0	33 31.2	−32.8	17.1	71
30 05.2	−34.1	15.6	31 03.0	−33.9	15.8	32 00.7	−33.6	16.0	32 58.4	−33.4	16.1	72
29 31.1	−34.5	14.7	30 29.1	−34.3	14.8	31 27.1	−34.0	15.0	32 25.0	−33.7	15.2	73
28 56.6	−34.9	13.8	29 54.8	−34.7	13.9	30 53.1	−34.5	14.0	31 51.3	−34.3	14.2	74
28 21.7	−35.3	12.8	29 20.1	−35.0	12.9	30 18.6	−34.9	13.1	31 17.0	−34.6	13.2	75
27 46.4	−35.7	11.9	28 45.1	−35.5	12.0	29 43.7	−35.2	12.1	30 42.4	−35.1	12.3	76
27 10.7	−36.0	11.0	28 09.6	−35.8	11.1	29 08.5	−35.7	11.2	30 07.3	−35.5	11.3	77
26 34.7	−36.3	10.1	27 33.8	−36.2	10.2	28 32.8	−36.0	10.3	29 31.8	−35.8	10.4	78
25 58.4	−36.7	9.2	26 57.6	−36.5	9.3	27 56.8	−36.4	9.4	28 56.0	−36.2	9.5	79
25 21.7	−36.9	8.3	26 21.1	−36.8	8.4	27 20.4	−36.7	8.5	28 19.8	−36.6	8.6	80
24 44.8	−37.3	7.5	25 44.3	−37.2	7.5	26 43.7	−37.0	7.6	27 43.2	−36.9	7.7	81
24 07.5	−37.5	6.6	25 07.1	−37.4	6.7	26 06.7	−37.4	6.7	27 06.3	−37.3	6.8	82
23 30.0	−37.9	5.8	24 29.7	−37.8	5.8	25 29.3	−37.6	5.8	26 29.0	−37.5	5.9	83
22 52.1	−38.0	4.9	23 51.9	−38.0	4.9	24 51.7	−38.0	5.0	25 51.5	−37.9	5.0	84
22 14.1	−38.4	4.1	23 13.9	−38.3	4.1	24 13.7	−38.2	4.1	25 13.6	−38.2	4.2	85
21 35.7	−38.6	3.2	22 35.6	−38.5	3.3	23 35.5	−38.5	3.3	24 35.4	−38.4	3.3	86
20 57.1	−38.8	2.4	21 57.1	−38.8	2.4	22 57.0	−38.7	2.5	23 57.0	−38.8	2.5	87
20 18.3	−39.0	1.6	21 18.3	−39.0	1.6	22 18.3	−39.1	1.6	23 18.2	−39.0	1.6	88
19 39.3	−39.3	0.8	20 39.3	−39.3	0.8	21 39.2	−39.2	0.8	22 39.2	−39.2	0.8	89
19 00.0	−39.5	0.0	20 00.0	−39.5	0.0	21 00.0	−39.5	0.0	22 00.0	−39.5	0.0	90
19°			20°			21°			22°			

49°, 311° L.H.A. LATITUDE SAME NAME AS DECLINATION

Dec.	15° Hc	15° d	15° Z	16° Hc	16° d	16° Z	17° Hc	17° d	17° Z	18° Hc	18° d	18° Z	19° Hc	19° d	19° Z	20° Hc	20° d	20° Z	21° Hc	21° d	21° Z	22° Hc	22° d	22° Z	Dec.
°	° ′	′	°	° ′	′	°	° ′	′	°	° ′	′	°	° ′	′	°	° ′	′	°	° ′	′	°	° ′	′	°	°
0	39 19.4	−20.4	102.7	39 05.9	−21.7	103.5	38 51.5	−22.9	104.3	38 36.3	−24.1	105.0	38 20.4	−25.3	105.8	38 03.6	−26.4	106.6	37 46.2	−27.6	107.3	37 27.9	−28.6	108.0	0
1	38 59.0	−21.2	103.9	38 44.2	−22.4	104.7	38 28.6	−23.6	105.4	38 12.2	−24.7	106.2	37 55.1	−25.9	107.0	37 37.2	−27.0	107.7	37 18.6	−28.1	108.4	36 59.3	−29.2	109.1	1
2	38 37.8	−21.9	105.1	38 21.8	−23.1	105.9	38 05.0	−24.3	106.6	37 47.5	−25.5	107.4	37 29.2	−26.6	108.1	37 10.2	−27.7	108.8	36 50.5	−28.8	109.5	36 30.1	−29.8	110.2	2
3	38 15.9	−22.7	106.3	37 58.7	−23.8	107.0	37 40.7	−24.9	107.8	37 22.0	−26.1	108.5	37 02.6	−27.2	109.2	36 42.5	−28.2	109.9	36 21.7	−29.3	110.6	36 00.3	−30.4	111.3	3
4	37 53.2	−23.3	107.5	37 34.9	−24.5	108.2	37 15.8	−25.7	108.9	36 55.9	−26.7	109.6	36 35.4	−27.8	110.3	36 14.3	−28.9	111.0	35 52.4	−29.9	111.7	35 29.9	−31.0	112.4	4
5	37 29.9	−24.0	108.6	37 10.4	−25.2	109.3	36 50.1	−26.2	110.1	36 29.2	−27.3	110.8	36 07.6	−28.4	111.4	35 45.4	−29.5	112.1	35 22.5	−30.5	112.8	34 58.9	−31.4	113.4	5
6	37 05.9	−24.7	109.8	36 45.2	−25.8	110.5	36 23.9	−26.9	111.2	36 01.9	−27.9	111.9	35 39.2	−29.0	112.5	35 15.9	−30.0	113.2	34 52.0	−31.0	113.8	34 27.5	−32.0	114.5	6
7	36 41.2	−25.3	110.9	36 19.4	−26.4	111.6	35 57.0	−27.5	112.3	35 34.0	−28.6	112.9	35 10.2	−29.5	113.6	34 45.9	−30.5	114.2	34 21.0	−31.5	114.9	33 55.5	−32.5	115.5	7
8	36 15.9	−26.0	112.0	35 53.0	−27.0	112.7	35 29.5	−28.0	113.4	35 05.4	−29.1	114.0	34 40.7	−30.1	114.7	34 15.4	−31.1	115.3	33 49.5	−32.1	115.9	33 23.0	−33.0	116.5	8
9	35 49.9	−26.5	113.2	35 26.0	−27.6	113.8	35 01.5	−28.6	114.5	34 36.3	−29.6	115.1	34 10.6	−30.6	115.7	33 44.3	−31.6	116.3	33 17.4	−32.5	116.9	32 50.0	−33.4	117.5	9
10	35 23.4	−27.2	114.3	34 58.4	−28.2	114.9	34 32.9	−29.2	115.5	34 06.7	−30.2	116.1	33 40.0	−31.1	116.7	33 12.7	−32.1	117.3	32 44.9	−33.0	117.9	32 16.6	−33.9	118.5	10
11	34 56.2	−27.7	115.4	34 30.2	−28.7	116.0	34 03.7	−29.7	116.6	33 36.5	−30.6	117.2	33 08.9	−31.7	117.8	32 40.6	−32.5	118.3	32 11.9	−33.5	118.9	31 42.7	−34.4	119.4	11
12	34 28.5	−28.3	116.4	34 01.5	−29.3	117.0	33 34.0	−30.3	117.6	33 05.9	−31.2	118.2	32 37.2	−32.1	118.8	32 08.1	−33.0	119.3	31 38.4	−33.9	119.9	31 08.3	−34.7	120.4	12
13	34 00.2	−28.8	117.5	33 32.2	−29.8	118.1	33 03.7	−30.7	118.7	32 34.7	−31.7	119.2	32 05.1	−32.6	119.8	31 35.1	−33.5	120.3	31 04.5	−34.3	120.8	30 33.6	−35.2	121.4	13
14	33 31.4	−29.4	118.6	33 02.4	−30.3	119.1	32 33.0	−31.3	119.7	32 03.0	−32.2	120.2	31 32.5	−33.0	120.8	31 01.6	−33.9	121.3	30 30.2	−34.7	121.8	29 58.4	−35.6	122.3	14
15	33 02.0	−29.9	119.6	32 32.1	−30.8	120.2	32 01.7	−31.7	120.7	31 30.8	−32.5	121.2	30 59.5	−33.5	121.7	30 27.7	−34.3	122.2	29 55.5	−35.2	122.7	29 22.8	−35.9	123.2	15
16	32 32.1	−30.4	120.6	32 01.3	−31.3	121.2	31 30.0	−32.2	121.7	30 58.3	−33.1	122.2	30 26.0	−33.8	122.7	29 53.4	−34.7	123.2	29 20.3	−35.5	123.7	28 46.9	−36.3	124.1	16
17	32 01.7	−30.9	121.6	31 30.0	−31.7	122.2	30 57.8	−32.6	122.7	30 25.2	−33.5	123.2	29 52.2	−34.3	123.7	29 18.7	−35.1	124.1	28 44.8	−35.9	124.6	28 10.6	−36.7	125.0	17
18	31 30.8	−31.3	122.7	30 58.3	−32.3	123.2	30 25.2	−33.0	123.7	29 51.7	−33.8	124.1	29 17.9	−34.7	124.6	28 43.6	−35.5	125.1	28 08.9	−36.2	125.5	27 33.9	−37.0	125.9	18
19	30 59.5	−31.8	123.7	30 26.0	−32.6	124.1	29 52.2	−33.5	124.6	29 17.9	−34.3	125.1	28 43.2	−35.1	125.5	28 08.1	−35.8	126.0	27 32.7	−36.6	126.4	26 56.9	−37.3	126.8	19
20	30 27.7	−32.2	124.6	29 53.4	−33.1	125.1	29 18.7	−33.9	125.6	28 43.6	−34.7	126.0	28 08.1	−35.4	126.5	27 32.3	−36.2	126.9	26 56.1	−36.9	127.3	26 19.6	−37.7	127.7	20
21	29 55.5	−32.7	125.6	29 20.3	−33.4	126.1	28 44.8	−34.2	126.5	28 08.9	−35.0	127.0	27 32.7	−35.8	127.4	26 56.1	−36.5	127.8	26 19.2	−37.3	128.2	25 41.9	−37.9	128.6	21
22	29 22.8	−33.1	126.6	28 46.9	−33.9	127.0	28 10.6	−34.7	127.5	27 33.9	−35.4	127.9	26 56.9	−36.1	128.3	26 19.6	−36.9	128.7	25 41.9	−37.5	129.1	25 04.0	−38.3	129.4	22
23	28 49.7	−33.4	127.5	28 13.0	−34.2	128.0	27 35.9	−35.0	128.4	26 58.5	−35.7	128.8	26 20.8	−36.5	129.2	25 42.7	−37.1	129.6	25 04.4	−37.9	129.9	24 25.7	−38.5	130.3	23
24	28 16.3	−33.9	128.5	27 38.8	−34.6	128.9	27 00.9	−35.3	129.3	26 22.8	−36.1	129.7	25 44.3	−36.8	130.1	25 05.6	−37.5	130.4	24 26.5	−38.1	130.8	23 47.2	−38.8	131.1	24
25	27 42.4	−34.2	129.4	27 04.2	−35.0	129.8	26 25.6	−35.7	130.2	25 46.7	−36.4	130.6	25 07.5	−37.0	130.9	24 28.1	−37.8	131.3	23 48.4	−38.4	131.6	23 08.4	−39.1	131.9	25
26	27 08.2	−34.6	130.3	26 29.2	−35.3	130.7	25 49.9	−36.0	131.1	25 10.3	−36.7	131.5	24 30.5	−37.4	131.8	23 50.3	−38.0	132.1	23 10.0	−38.7	132.5	22 29.3	−39.3	132.8	26
27	26 33.6	−34.9	131.3	25 53.9	−35.7	131.6	25 13.9	−36.3	132.0	24 33.6	−37.0	132.3	23 53.1	−37.7	132.7	23 12.3	−38.3	133.0	22 31.3	−38.9	133.3	21 50.0	−39.5	133.6	27
28	25 58.7	−35.3	132.2	25 18.2	−35.9	132.5	24 37.6	−36.7	132.9	23 56.6	−37.3	133.2	23 15.4	−37.9	133.5	22 34.0	−38.5	133.8	21 52.4	−39.2	134.1	21 10.5	−39.8	134.4	28
29	25 23.4	−35.6	133.1	24 42.3	−36.3	133.4	24 00.9	−36.9	133.7	23 19.3	−37.5	134.0	22 37.5	−38.2	134.3	21 55.5	−38.8	134.6	21 13.2	−39.4	134.9	20 30.7	−40.0	135.2	29
30	24 47.8	−35.9	133.9	24 06.0	−36.5	134.3	23 24.0	−37.2	134.6	22 41.8	−37.8	134.9	21 59.3	−38.4	135.2	21 16.7	−39.1	135.5	20 33.8	−39.6	135.7	19 50.7	−40.2	136.0	30
31	24 11.9	−36.2	134.8	23 29.5	−36.9	135.1	22 46.8	−37.5	135.4	22 04.0	−38.1	135.7	21 20.9	−38.7	136.0	20 37.6	−39.2	136.3	19 54.2	−39.9	136.5	19 10.5	−40.4	136.8	31
32	23 35.7	−36.5	135.7	22 52.6	−37.1	136.0	22 09.3	−37.7	136.3	21 25.9	−38.3	136.6	20 42.2	−38.9	136.8	19 58.4	−39.5	137.1	19 14.3	−40.0	137.3	18 30.1	−40.5	137.6	32
33	22 59.2	−36.8	136.6	22 15.5	−37.4	136.8	21 31.6	−38.0	137.1	20 47.6	−38.6	137.4	20 03.3	−39.1	137.6	19 18.9	−39.7	137.9	18 34.3	−40.2	138.1	17 49.6	−40.8	138.3	33
34	22 22.4	−37.1	137.4	21 38.1	−37.6	137.7	20 53.6	−38.2	138.0	20 09.0	−38.8	138.2	19 24.2	−39.4	138.4	18 39.2	−39.9	138.7	17 54.1	−40.5	138.9	17 08.8	−41.0	139.1	34
35	21 45.3	−37.3	138.3	21 00.5	−37.9	138.5	20 15.4	−38.4	138.8	19 30.2	−39.0	139.0	18 44.8	−39.5	139.2	17 59.3	−40.1	139.5	17 13.6	−40.5	139.7	16 27.8	−41.1	139.9	35
36	21 08.0	−37.5	139.1	20 22.6	−38.1	139.4	19 37.0	−38.7	139.6	18 51.2	−39.2	139.8	18 05.3	−39.7	140.0	17 19.2	−40.2	140.2	16 33.1	−40.8	140.4	15 46.7	−41.2	140.6	36
37	20 30.5	−37.8	139.9	19 44.5	−38.4	140.2	18 58.3	−38.9	140.4	18 12.0	−39.4	140.6	17 25.6	−40.0	140.8	16 39.0	−40.4	141.0	15 52.3	−40.9	141.2	15 05.5	−41.4	141.4	37
38	19 52.7	−38.0	140.8	19 06.1	−38.5	141.0	18 19.4	−39.0	141.2	17 32.6	−39.6	141.4	16 45.6	−40.0	141.6	15 58.6	−40.6	141.8	15 11.4	−41.1	142.0	14 24.1	−41.6	142.1	38
39	19 14.7	−38.3	141.6	18 27.6	−38.8	141.8	17 40.4	−39.3	142.0	16 53.0	−39.7	142.2	16 05.6	−40.3	142.4	15 18.0	−40.8	142.5	14 30.3	−41.2	142.7	13 42.5	−41.7	142.9	39
40	18 36.4	−38.4	142.4	17 48.8	−38.9	142.6	17 01.1	−39.4	142.8	16 13.3	−40.0	143.0	15 25.3	−40.4	143.1	14 37.2	−40.9	143.3	13 49.1	−41.4	143.5	13 00.8	−41.8	143.6	40
41	17 58.0	−38.6	143.2	17 09.9	−39.2	143.4	16 21.7	−39.7	143.6	15 33.3	−40.1	143.8	14 44.9	−40.6	143.9	13 56.3	−41.0	144.1	13 07.7	−41.5	144.2	12 19.0	−41.9	144.3	41
42	17 19.4	−38.9	144.0	16 30.7	−39.3	144.2	15 42.0	−39.8	144.4	14 53.2	−40.2	144.5	14 04.3	−40.7	144.7	13 15.3	−41.2	144.8	12 26.2	−41.6	144.9	11 37.1	−42.1	145.1	42
43	16 40.5	−39.0	144.8	15 51.4	−39.5	145.0	15 02.2	−39.9	145.1	14 13.0	−40.4	145.3	13 23.6	−40.8	145.4	12 34.1	−41.2	145.6	11 44.6	−41.7	145.7	10 55.0	−42.1	145.8	43
44	16 01.5	−39.2	145.6	15 11.9	−39.6	145.8	14 22.3	−40.1	145.9	13 32.6	−40.6	146.1	12 42.8	−41.0	146.2	11 52.9	−41.4	146.3	11 02.9	−41.8	146.4	10 12.9	−42.2	146.5	44
45	15 22.3	−39.3	146.4	14 32.3	−39.8	146.5	13 42.2	−40.2	146.7	12 52.0	−40.6	146.8	12 01.8	−41.1	146.9	11 11.5	−41.5	147.0	10 21.1	−41.9	147.1	9 30.7	−42.4	147.2	45
46	14 43.0	−39.5	147.2	13 52.5	−39.9	147.3	13 02.0	−40.4	147.4	12 11.4	−40.8	147.6	11 20.7	−41.2	147.7	10 30.0	−41.6	147.8	9 39.2	−42.0	147.9	8 48.3	−42.4	148.0	46
47	14 03.5	−39.7	148.0	13 12.6	−40.1	148.1	12 21.6	−40.5	148.2	11 30.6	−40.9	148.3	10 39.5	−41.3	148.4	9 48.4	−41.8	148.5	8 57.2	−42.1	148.6	8 05.9	−42.5	148.7	47
48	13 23.8	−39.8	148.7	12 32.5	−40.2	148.8	11 41.1	−40.6	149.0	10 49.7	−41.0	149.1	9 58.2	−41.4	149.2	9 06.6	−41.7	149.2	8 15.1	−42.2	149.3	7 23.4	−42.5	149.4	48
49	12 44.0	−39.9	149.5	11 52.3	−40.4	149.6	11 00.5	−40.7	149.7	10 08.7	−41.1	149.8	9 16.8	−41.5	149.9	8 24.9	−41.9	150.0	7 32.9	−42.2	150.0	6 40.9	−42.6	150.1	49
50	12 04.1	−40.1	150.3	11 11.9	−40.4	150.4	10 19.8	−40.8	150.5	9 27.6	−41.2	150.5	8 35.3	−41.6	150.6	7 43.0	−41.9	150.7	6 50.7	−42.3	150.8	5 58.3	−42.7	150.8	50
51	11 24.0	−40.2	151.0	10 31.5	−40.5	151.1	9 39.0	−41.0	151.2	8 46.4	−41.3	151.3	7 53.7	−41.6	151.3	7 01.1	−42.1	151.4	6 08.4	−42.4	151.5	5 15.6	−42.7	151.5	51
52	10 43.8	−40.2	151.8	9 51.0	−40.7	151.9	8 58.0	−41.0	151.9	8 05.1	−41.4	152.0	7 12.1	−41.7	152.1	6 19.0	−42.0	152.1	5 26.0	−42.4	152.2	4 32.9	−42.7	152.2	52
53	10 03.6	−40.4	152.5	9 10.3	−40.7	152.6	8 17.0	−41.1	152.7	7 23.7	−41.4	152.7	6 30.4	−41.8	152.8	5 37.0	−42.1	152.8	4 43.6	−42.5	152.9	3 50.2	−42.8	152.9	53
54	9 23.2	−40.5	153.3	8 29.6	−40.8	153.4	7 35.9	−41.1	153.4	6 42.3	−41.5	153.5	5 48.6	−41.9	153.5	4 54.9	−42.2	153.6	4 01.1	−42.5	153.6	3 07.4	−42.8	153.6	54
55	8 42.7	−40.6	154.0	7 48.8	−40.9	154.1	6 54.8	−41.3	154.1	6 00.8	−41.6	154.2	5 06.7	−41.8	154.2	4 12.7	−42.2	154.3	3 18.6	−42.5	154.3	2 24.6	−42.9	154.3	55
56	8 02.1	−40.6	154.8	7 07.9	−41.0	154.8	6 13.5	−41.2	154.9	5 19.2	−41.6	154.9	4 24.9	−42.0	155.0	3 30.5	−42.2	155.0	2 36.1	−42.5	155.0	1 41.7	−42.8	155.0	56
57	7 21.5	−40.7	155.5	6 26.9	−41.0	155.6	5 32.3	−41.4	155.6	4 37.6	−41.6	155.6	3 42.9	−41.9	155.7	2 48.3	−42.3	155.7	1 53.6	−42.6	155.7	0 58.9	−42.9	155.7	57
58	6 40.8	−40.8	156.3	5 45.9	−41.1	156.3	4 50.9	−41.4	156.3	3 56.0	−41.7	156.4	3 01.0	−42.0	156.4	2 06.0	−42.3	156.4	1 11.0	−42.6	156.4	0 16.0	−42.8	156.4	58
59	6 00.0	−40.8	157.0	5 04.8	−41.2	157.0	4 09.5	−41.4	157.1	3 14.3	−41.8	157.1	2 19.0	−42.0	157.1	1 23.7	−42.3	157.1	0 28.4	−42.5	157.1	0 26.8	+42.9	22.9	59
60	5 19.2	−40.9	157.7	4 23.6	−41.1	157.8	3 28.1	−41.5	157.8	2 32.5	−41.7	157.8	1 37.0	−42.0	157.8	0 41.4	−42.3	157.8	0 14.1	+42.6	22.2	1 09.7	+42.9	22.2	60
61	4 38.3	−41.0	158.5	3 42.5	−41.3	158.5	2 46.6	−41.5	158.5	1 50.8	−41.8	158.5	0 55.0	−42.1	158.5	0 00.9	+42.3	21.5	0 56.7	+42.6	21.5	1 52.6	+42.8	21.5	61
62	3 57.3	−40.9	159.2	3 01.2	−41.2	159.2	2 05.1	−41.5	159.2	1 09.0	−41.7	159.2	0 12.9	−42.0	159.2	0 43.2	+42.3	20.8	1 39.3	+42.5	20.8	2 35.4	+42.8	20.8	62
63	3 16.4	−41.1	159.9	2 20.0	−41.3	159.9	1 23.6	−41.5	160.0	0 27.3	−41.8	160.0	0 29.1	+42.0	20.0	1 25.5	+42.3	20.0	2 21.8	+42.6	20.1	3 18.2	+42.8	20.1	63
64	2 35.3	−41.0	160.7	1 38.7	−41.3	160.7	0 42.1	−41.5	160.7	0 14.5	+41.8	19.3	1 11.1	+42.1	19.3	2 07.8	+42.2	19.3	3 04.4	+42.5	19.3	4 01.0	+42.7	19.4	64
65	1 54.3	−41.0	161.4	0 57.4	−41.2	161.4	0 00.6	−41.5	161.4	0 56.3	+41.8	18.6	1 53.2	+42.0	18.6	2 50.0	+42.2	18.6	3 46.9	+42.4	18.6	4 43.7	+42.7	18.7	65
66	1 13.3	−41.1	162.1	0 16.2	−41.3	162.1	0 40.9	+41.6	17.9	1 38.1	+41.7	17.9	2 35.2	+41.9	17.9	3 32.2	+42.2	17.9	4 29.3	+42.5	17.9	5 26.4	+42.7	18.0	66
67	0 32.2	−41.1	162.8	0 25.1	+41.3	17.2	1 22.5	+41.5	17.2	2 19.8	+41.7	17.2	3 17.1	+42.0	17.2	4 14.4	+42.2	17.2	5 11.8	+42.3	17.2	6 09.1	+42.6	17.3	67
68	0 08.9	+41.0	16.4	1 06.4	+41.3	16.4	2 04.0	+41.5	16.4	3 01.5	+41.7	16.4	3 59.1	+41.9	16.5	4 56.6	+42.1	16.5	5 54.1	+42.4	16.5	6 51.7	+42.5	16.5	68
69	0 49.9	+41.1	15.7	1 47.7	+41.3	15.7	2 45.5	+41.4	15.7	3 43.2	+41.7	15.7	4 41.0	+41.8	15.7	5 38.7	+42.1	15.8	6 36.5	+42.2	15.8	7 34.2	+42.5	15.8	69
70	1 31.0	+41.1	15.0	2 29.0	+41.2	15.0	3 26.9	+41.5	15.0	4 24.9	+41.6	15.0	5 22.8	+41.9	15.0	6 20.8	+42.0	15.1	7 18.7	+42.2	15.1	8 16.7	+42.3	15.1	70
71	2 12.1	+41.0	14.2	3 10.2	+41.2	14.2	4 08.4	+41.4	14.3	5 06.5	+41.6	14.3	6 04.7	+41.7	14.3	7 02.8	+41.9	14.3	8 00.9	+42.1	14.4	8 59.0	+42.3	14.4	71
72	2 53.1	+41.0	13.5	3 51.4	+41.2	13.5	4 49.8	+41.3	13.5	5 48.1	+41.5	13.6	6 46.4	+41.7	13.6	7 44.7	+41.9	13.6	8 43.0	+42.1	13.6	9 41.3	+42.3	13.7	72
73	3 34.1	+40.9	12.8	4 32.6	+41.1	12.8	5 31.1	+41.3	12.8	6 29.6	+41.5	12.8	7 28.1	+41.6	12.9	8 26.6	+41.8	12.9	9 25.1	+41.9	12.9	10 23.6	+42.1	13.0	73
74	4 15.0	+41.0	12.0	5 13.7	+41.1	12.1	6 12.4	+41.2	12.1	7 11.1	+41.3	12.1	8 09.7	+41.6	12.1	9 08.4	+41.7	12.2	10 07.0	+41.9	12.2	11 05.7	+42.0	12.2	74
75	4 56.0	+40.8	11.3	5 54.8	+41.0	11.3	6 53.6	+41.2	11.3	7 52.4	+41.4	11.4	8 51.3	+41.4	11.4	9 50.1	+41.6	11.4	10 48.9	+41.7	11.5	11 47.7	+41.9	11.5	75
76	5 36.8	+40.8	10.6	6 35.8	+41.0	10.6	7 34.8	+41.1	10.6	8 33.8	+41.2	10.6	9 32.7	+41.4	10.7	10 31.7	+41.5	10.7	11 30.6	+41.7	10.7	12 29.6	+41.8	10.8	76
77	6 17.6	+40.8	9.8	7 16.8	+40.8	9.9	8 15.9	+41.0	9.9	9 15.0	+41.1	9.9	10 14.1	+41.3	9.9	11 13.2	+41.4	10.0	12 12.3	+41.5	10.0	13 11.4	+41.6	10.0	77
78	6 58.4	+40.7	9.1	7 57.6	+40.9	9.1	8 56.9	+40.9	9.1	9 56.1	+41.1	9.2	10 55.4	+41.1	9.2	11 54.6	+41.3	9.2	12 53.8	+41.4	9.3	13 53.0	+41.5	9.3	78
79	7 39.1	+40.6	8.4	8 38.5	+40.7	8.4	9 37.8	+40.8	8.4	10 37.2	+40.9	8.4	11 36.5	+41.1	8.5	12 35.9	+41.1	8.5	13 35.2	+41.3	8.5	14 34.5	+41.4	8.6	79
80	8 19.7	+40.5	7.6	9 19.2	+40.6	7.6	10 18.6	+40.8	7.7	11 18.1	+40.8	7.7	12 17.6	+40.9	7.7	13 17.0	+41.0	7.7	14 16.5	+41.1	7.8	15 15.9	+41.2	7.8	80
81	9 00.2	+40.5	6.9	9 59.8	+40.5	6.9	10 59.4	+40.6	6.9	11 58.9	+40.7	6.9	12 58.5	+40.8	7.0	13 58.0	+40.9	7.0	14 57.6	+41.0	7.0	15 57.1	+41.1	7.1	81
82	9 40.7	+40.3	6.1	10 40.3	+40.4	6.1	11 40.0	+40.5	6.2	12 39.6	+40.6	6.2	13 39.3	+40.6	6.2	14 38.9	+40.8	6.2	15 38.6	+40.8	6.3	16 38.2	+40.9	6.3	82
83	10 21.0	+40.2	5.4	11 20.7	+40.3	5.4	12 20.5	+40.3	5.4	13 20.2	+40.4	5.4	14 19.9	+40.5	5.4	15 19.7	+40.5	5.5	16 19.4	+40.6	5.5	17 19.1	+40.7	5.5	83
84	11 01.2	+40.2	4.6	12 01.0	+40.2	4.6	13 00.8	+40.3	4.6	14 00.6	+40.3	4.7	15 00.4	+40.4	4.7	16 00.2	+40.5	4.7	17 00.0	+40.5	4.7	17 59.8	+40.6	4.8	84
85	11 41.4	+40.0	3.9	12 41.2	+40.1	3.9	13 41.1	+40.1	3.9	14 40.9	+40.2	3.9	15 40.8	+40.2	3.9	16 40.7	+40.2	3.9	17 40.5	+40.3	4.0	18 40.4	+40.3	4.0	85
86	12 21.4	+39.8	3.1	13 21.3	+39.9	3.1	14 21.2	+39.9	3.1	15 21.1	+40.0	3.1	16 21.0	+40.0	3.1	17 20.9	+40.1	3.2	18 20.8	+40.1	3.2	19 20.7	+40.2	3.2	86
87	13 01.2	+39.8	2.3	14 01.2	+39.7	2.3	15 01.1	+39.8	2.3	16 01.1	+39.8	2.4	17 01.0	+39.9	2.4	18 01.0	+39.9	2.4	19 00.9	+39.9	2.4	20 00.9	+39.9	2.4	87
88	13 41.0	+39.6	1.6	14 40.9	+39.7	1.6	15 40.9	+39.6	1.6	16 40.9	+39.6	1.6	17 40.9	+39.6	1.6	18 40.9	+39.6	1.6	19 40.8	+39.7	1.6	20 40.8	+39.7	1.6	88
89	14 20.6	+39.4	0.8	15 20.6	+39.4	0.8	16 20.5	+39.5	0.8	17 20.5	+39.5	0.8	18 20.5	+39.5	0.8	19 20.5	+39.5	0.8	20 20.5	+39.5	0.8	21 20.5	+39.5	0.8	89
90	15 00.0	+39.3	0.0	16 00.0	+39.3	0.0	17 00.0	+39.3	0.0	18 00.0	+39.3	0.0	19 00.0	+39.3	0.0	20 00.0	+39.3	0.0	21 00.0	+39.2	0.0	22 00.0	+39.2	0.0	90
	15°			16°			17°			18°			19°			20°			21°			22°			

S. Lat. {L.H.A. greater than 180° ....Zn=180°−Z; L.H.A. less than 180°...........Zn=180°+Z

50°, 310° L.H.A. **LATITUDE SAME NAME AS DECLINATION** N. Lat. {L.H.A. greater than 180° .....Zn=Z; L.H.A. less than 180°............Zn=360°−Z}

Dec.	15° Hc	d	Z	16° Hc	d	Z	17° Hc	d	Z	18° Hc	d	Z	19° Hc	d	Z	20° Hc	d	Z	21° Hc	d	Z	22° Hc	d	Z	Dec.
°	° ′	′	°	° ′	′	°	° ′	′	°	° ′	′	°	° ′	′	°	° ′	′	°	° ′	′	°	° ′	′	°	°
0	38 22.8	+19.5	102.3	38 09.7	+20.7	103.0	37 55.8	+21.9	103.8	37 41.1	+23.1	104.5	37 25.7	+24.3	105.3	37 09.5	+25.4	106.0	36 52.6	+26.6	106.7	36 35.0	+27.6	107.4	0
1	38 42.3	+18.7	101.0	38 30.4	+19.9	101.8	38 17.7	+21.2	102.6	38 04.2	+22.4	103.4	37 50.0	+23.5	104.1	37 34.9	+24.8	104.9	37 19.2	+25.9	105.6	37 02.6	+27.1	106.3	1
2	39 01.0	+17.9	99.8	38 50.3	+19.2	100.6	38 38.9	+20.4	101.4	38 26.6	+21.7	102.2	38 13.5	+22.9	103.0	37 59.7	+24.1	103.7	37 45.1	+25.2	104.5	37 29.7	+26.4	105.2	2
3	39 18.9	+17.1	98.6	39 09.5	+18.4	99.4	38 59.3	+19.7	100.2	38 48.3	+20.9	101.0	38 36.4	+22.2	101.8	38 23.8	+23.3	102.6	38 10.3	+24.6	103.3	37 56.1	+25.8	104.1	3
4	39 36.0	+16.3	97.4	39 27.9	+17.6	98.2	39 19.0	+18.9	99.0	39 09.2	+20.2	99.8	38 58.6	+21.4	100.6	38 47.1	+22.7	101.4	38 34.9	+23.9	102.2	38 21.9	+25.0	102.9	4
5	39 52.3	+15.6	96.1	39 45.5	+16.9	96.9	39 37.9	+18.1	97.8	39 29.4	+19.4	98.6	39 20.0	+20.7	99.4	39 09.8	+21.9	100.2	38 58.8	+23.1	101.0	38 46.9	+24.4	101.8	5
6	40 07.9	+14.7	94.8	40 02.4	+16.0	95.7	39 56.0	+17.3	96.5	39 48.8	+18.6	97.3	39 40.7	+19.9	98.2	39 31.7	+21.2	99.0	39 21.9	+22.5	99.8	39 11.3	+23.7	100.6	6
7	40 22.6	+13.8	93.6	40 18.4	+15.2	94.4	40 13.3	+16.5	95.3	40 07.4	+17.8	96.1	40 00.6	+19.1	96.9	39 52.9	+20.4	97.8	39 44.4	+21.6	98.6	39 35.0	+22.9	99.4	7
8	40 36.4	+13.0	92.3	40 33.6	+14.3	93.1	40 29.8	+15.7	94.0	40 25.2	+17.0	94.8	40 19.7	+18.3	95.7	40 13.3	+19.6	96.5	40 06.0	+20.9	97.4	39 57.9	+22.2	98.2	8
9	40 49.4	+12.1	91.0	40 47.9	+13.5	91.9	40 45.5	+14.8	92.7	40 42.2	+16.2	93.6	40 38.0	+17.5	94.4	40 32.9	+18.8	95.3	40 26.9	+20.1	96.1	40 20.1	+21.4	97.0	9
10	41 01.5	+11.3	89.7	41 01.4	+12.6	90.6	41 00.3	+14.0	91.4	40 58.4	+15.3	92.3	40 55.5	+16.7	93.2	40 51.7	+18.0	94.0	40 47.0	+19.3	94.9	40 41.5	+20.6	95.8	10
11	41 12.8	+10.4	88.4	41 14.0	+11.7	89.3	41 14.3	+13.1	90.2	41 13.7	+14.4	91.0	41 12.2	+15.8	91.9	41 09.7	+17.1	92.8	41 06.3	+18.5	93.7	41 02.1	+19.8	94.5	11
12	41 23.2	+9.4	87.1	41 25.7	+10.9	88.0	41 27.4	+12.2	88.9	41 28.1	+13.6	89.7	41 28.0	+14.9	90.6	41 26.8	+16.3	91.5	41 24.8	+17.7	92.4	41 21.9	+18.9	93.3	12
13	41 32.6	+8.6	85.8	41 36.6	+9.9	86.7	41 39.6	+11.4	87.5	41 41.7	+12.7	88.4	41 42.9	+14.1	89.3	41 43.1	+15.5	90.2	41 42.5	+16.7	91.1	41 40.8	+18.2	92.0	13
14	41 41.2	+7.6	84.4	41 46.5	+9.1	85.3	41 51.0	+10.4	86.2	41 54.4	+11.8	87.1	41 57.0	+13.1	88.0	41 58.6	+14.5	88.9	41 59.2	+15.9	89.8	41 59.0	+17.2	90.7	14
15	41 48.8	+6.8	83.1	41 55.6	+8.1	84.0	42 01.4	+9.5	84.9	42 06.2	+10.9	85.8	42 10.1	+12.3	86.7	42 13.1	+13.7	87.6	42 15.1	+15.1	88.5	42 16.2	+16.4	89.4	15
16	41 55.6	+5.8	81.8	42 03.7	+7.2	82.7	42 10.9	+8.5	83.6	42 17.1	+10.0	84.5	42 22.4	+11.4	85.4	42 26.8	+12.7	86.3	42 30.2	+14.1	87.2	42 32.6	+15.5	88.1	16
17	42 01.4	+4.8	80.4	42 10.9	+6.2	81.3	42 19.4	+7.7	82.2	42 27.1	+9.0	83.1	42 33.8	+10.4	84.1	42 39.5	+11.8	85.0	42 44.3	+13.2	85.9	42 48.1	+14.6	86.8	17
18	42 06.2	+3.9	79.1	42 17.1	+5.3	80.0	42 27.1	+6.7	80.9	42 36.1	+8.1	81.8	42 44.2	+9.5	82.7	42 51.3	+10.9	83.6	42 57.5	+12.3	84.6	43 02.7	+13.7	85.5	18
19	42 10.1	+3.0	77.8	42 22.4	+4.4	78.6	42 33.8	+5.7	79.5	42 44.2	+7.1	80.5	42 53.7	+8.5	81.4	43 02.2	+9.9	82.3	43 09.8	+11.3	83.2	43 16.4	+12.7	84.2	19
20	42 13.1	+2.0	76.4	42 26.8	+3.4	77.3	42 39.5	+4.8	78.2	42 51.3	+6.2	79.1	43 02.2	+7.6	80.0	43 12.1	+9.0	80.9	43 21.1	+10.4	81.9	43 29.1	+11.8	82.8	20
21	42 15.1	+1.1	75.1	42 30.2	+2.4	75.9	42 44.3	+3.8	76.8	42 57.5	+5.2	77.7	43 09.8	+6.6	78.7	43 21.1	+8.0	79.6	43 31.5	+9.4	80.5	43 40.9	+10.8	81.5	21
22	42 16.2	+0.1	73.7	42 32.6	+1.5	74.6	42 48.1	+2.9	75.5	43 02.7	+4.2	76.4	43 16.4	+5.6	77.3	43 29.1	+7.0	78.2	43 40.9	+8.4	79.1	43 51.7	+9.8	80.1	22
23	42 16.3	−0.8	72.4	42 34.1	+0.5	73.2	42 51.0	+1.8	74.1	43 06.9	+3.3	75.0	43 22.0	+4.6	75.9	43 36.1	+6.1	76.8	43 49.3	+7.4	77.8	44 01.5	+8.9	78.7	23
24	42 15.5	−1.8	71.0	42 34.6	−0.4	71.9	42 52.8	+1.0	72.8	43 10.2	+2.3	73.6	43 26.6	+3.7	74.6	43 42.2	+5.0	75.5	43 56.7	+6.5	76.4	44 10.4	+7.8	77.3	24
25	42 13.7	−2.7	69.7	42 34.2	−1.4	70.5	42 53.8	−0.1	71.4	43 12.5	+1.3	72.3	43 30.3	+2.7	73.2	43 47.2	+4.0	74.1	44 03.2	+5.4	75.0	44 18.2	+6.9	76.0	25
26	42 11.0	−3.7	68.3	42 32.8	−2.4	69.2	42 53.7	−1.0	70.0	43 13.8	+0.3	70.9	43 33.0	+1.6	71.8	43 51.2	+3.1	72.7	44 08.6	+4.4	73.6	44 25.1	+5.8	74.6	26
27	42 07.3	−4.6	67.0	42 30.4	−3.3	67.8	42 52.7	−2.0	68.7	43 14.1	−0.7	69.5	43 34.6	+0.7	70.4	43 54.3	+2.0	71.3	44 13.0	+3.5	72.2	44 30.9	+4.8	73.2	27
28	42 02.7	−5.5	65.6	42 27.1	−4.3	66.4	42 50.7	−3.0	67.3	43 13.4	−1.7	68.2	43 35.3	−0.3	69.0	43 56.3	+1.1	69.9	44 16.5	+2.4	70.8	44 35.7	+3.8	71.8	28
29	41 57.2	−6.5	64.3	42 22.8	−5.2	65.1	42 47.7	−4.0	65.9	43 11.7	−2.6	66.8	43 35.0	−1.3	67.7	43 57.4	0.0	68.5	44 18.9	+1.3	69.5	44 39.5	+2.7	70.4	29
30	41 50.7	−7.4	62.9	42 17.6	−6.2	63.7	42 43.7	−4.9	64.6	43 09.1	−3.6	65.4	43 33.7	−2.4	66.3	43 57.4	−1.0	67.2	44 20.2	+0.4	68.1	44 42.2	+1.7	69.0	30
31	41 43.3	−8.4	61.6	42 11.4	−7.1	62.4	42 38.8	−5.8	63.2	43 05.5	−4.6	64.0	43 31.3	−3.3	64.9	43 56.4	−2.0	65.8	44 20.6	−0.7	66.7	44 43.9	+0.7	67.6	31
32	41 34.9	−9.2	60.3	42 04.3	−8.0	61.1	42 33.0	−6.8	61.9	43 00.9	−5.6	62.7	43 28.0	−4.3	63.5	43 54.4	−3.0	64.4	44 19.9	−1.7	65.3	44 44.6	−0.4	66.2	32
33	41 25.7	−10.1	59.0	41 56.3	−9.0	59.7	42 26.2	−7.8	60.5	42 55.3	−6.5	61.3	43 23.7	−5.2	62.1	43 51.4	−4.0	63.0	44 18.2	−2.7	63.9	44 44.2	−1.4	64.7	33
34	41 15.6	−11.1	57.7	41 47.3	−9.8	58.4	42 18.4	−8.7	59.2	42 48.8	−7.5	60.0	43 18.5	−6.3	60.8	43 47.4	−5.0	61.6	44 15.5	−3.7	62.5	44 42.8	−2.4	63.3	34
35	41 04.5	−11.9	56.3	41 37.5	−10.8	57.1	42 09.7	−9.6	57.8	42 41.3	−8.4	58.6	43 12.2	−7.2	59.4	43 42.4	−6.0	60.2	44 11.8	−4.8	61.1	44 40.4	−3.5	61.9	35
36	40 52.6	−12.8	55.0	41 26.7	−11.7	55.8	42 00.1	−10.5	56.5	42 32.9	−9.4	57.3	43 05.0	−8.2	58.1	43 36.4	−7.0	58.9	44 07.0	−5.7	59.7	44 36.9	−4.5	60.5	36
37	40 39.8	−13.6	53.8	41 15.0	−12.5	54.5	41 49.6	−11.5	55.2	42 23.5	−10.3	55.9	42 56.8	−9.1	56.7	43 29.4	−8.0	57.5	44 01.3	−6.8	58.3	44 32.4	−5.5	59.1	37
38	40 26.2	−14.5	52.5	41 02.5	−13.4	53.2	41 38.1	−12.3	53.9	42 13.2	−11.2	54.6	42 47.7	−10.1	55.3	43 21.4	−8.9	56.1	43 54.5	−7.7	56.9	44 26.9	−6.5	57.7	38
39	40 11.7	−15.3	51.2	40 49.1	−14.3	51.9	41 25.8	−13.2	52.6	42 02.0	−12.1	53.3	42 37.6	−11.1	54.0	43 12.5	−9.9	54.8	43 46.8	−8.7	55.5	44 20.4	−7.6	56.3	39
40	39 56.4	−16.1	49.9	40 34.8	−15.1	50.6	41 12.6	−14.1	51.3	41 49.9	−13.1	52.0	42 26.5	−11.9	52.7	43 02.6	−10.8	53.4	43 38.1	−9.7	54.2	44 12.8	−8.5	55.0	40
41	39 40.3	−16.9	48.7	40 19.7	−16.0	49.3	40 58.5	−14.9	50.0	41 36.8	−13.9	50.7	42 14.6	−12.9	51.3	42 51.8	−11.8	52.1	43 28.4	−10.7	52.8	44 04.3	−9.5	53.6	41
42	39 23.4	−17.7	47.4	40 03.7	−16.7	48.1	40 43.6	−15.8	48.7	41 22.9	−14.8	49.4	42 01.7	−13.7	50.0	42 40.0	−12.7	50.7	43 17.7	−11.6	51.5	43 54.8	−10.6	52.2	42
43	39 05.7	−18.5	46.2	39 47.0	−17.6	46.8	40 27.8	−16.6	47.4	41 08.1	−15.6	48.1	41 48.0	−14.6	48.7	42 27.3	−13.6	49.4	43 06.1	−12.6	50.1	43 44.2	−11.4	50.8	43
44	38 47.2	−19.3	45.0	39 29.4	−18.3	45.6	40 11.2	−17.4	46.2	40 52.5	−16.5	46.8	41 33.4	−15.6	47.4	42 13.7	−14.5	48.1	42 53.5	−13.5	48.8	43 32.8	−12.5	49.5	44
45	38 27.9	−20.0	43.8	39 11.1	−19.2	44.3	39 53.8	−18.3	44.9	40 36.0	−17.3	45.5	41 17.8	−16.3	46.1	41 59.2	−15.4	46.8	42 40.0	−14.4	47.4	43 20.3	−13.4	48.1	45
46	38 07.9	−20.7	42.6	38 51.9	−19.8	43.1	39 35.5	−19.0	43.7	40 18.7	−18.1	44.3	41 01.5	−17.2	44.9	41 43.8	−16.3	45.5	42 25.6	−15.3	46.1	43 06.9	−14.3	46.8	46
47	37 47.2	−21.4	41.4	38 32.1	−20.6	41.9	39 16.5	−19.7	42.4	40 00.6	−18.9	43.0	40 44.3	−18.0	43.6	41 27.5	−17.1	44.2	42 10.3	−16.2	44.8	42 52.6	−15.2	45.5	47
48	37 25.8	−22.1	40.2	38 11.5	−21.4	40.7	38 56.8	−20.6	41.2	39 41.7	−19.7	41.8	40 26.3	−18.9	42.3	41 10.4	−17.9	42.9	41 54.1	−17.0	43.5	42 37.4	−16.1	44.2	48
49	37 03.7	−22.8	39.0	37 50.1	−22.0	39.5	38 36.2	−21.2	40.0	39 22.0	−20.4	40.5	40 07.4	−19.6	41.1	40 52.5	−18.8	41.7	41 37.1	−17.9	42.2	42 21.3	−17.0	42.8	49
50	36 40.9	−23.5	37.9	37 28.1	−22.7	38.3	38 15.0	−22.0	38.8	39 01.6	−21.2	39.3	39 47.8	−20.4	39.9	40 33.7	−19.6	40.4	41 19.2	−18.8	41.0	42 04.3	−17.9	41.6	50
51	36 17.4	−24.1	36.7	37 05.4	−23.4	37.2	37 53.0	−22.7	37.6	38 40.4	−22.0	38.1	39 27.4	−21.2	38.6	40 14.1	−20.4	39.2	41 00.4	−19.5	39.7	41 46.4	−18.7	40.3	51
52	35 53.3	−24.7	35.6	36 42.0	−24.1	36.0	37 30.3	−23.3	36.5	38 18.4	−22.6	36.9	39 06.2	−21.9	37.4	39 53.7	−21.1	37.9	40 40.9	−20.4	38.5	41 27.7	−19.6	39.0	52
53	35 28.6	−25.4	34.5	36 17.9	−24.7	34.9	37 07.0	−24.1	35.3	37 55.8	−23.3	35.8	38 44.3	−22.6	36.2	39 32.6	−21.9	36.7	40 20.5	−21.1	37.2	41 08.1	−20.3	37.7	53
54	35 03.2	−26.0	33.4	35 53.2	−25.3	33.8	36 42.9	−24.6	34.2	37 32.5	−24.1	34.6	38 21.7	−23.3	35.0	39 10.7	−22.6	35.5	39 59.4	−21.9	36.0	40 47.8	−21.2	36.5	54
55	34 37.2	−26.5	32.3	35 27.9	−26.0	32.6	36 18.3	−25.4	33.0	37 08.4	−24.6	33.4	37 58.4	−24.0	33.9	38 48.1	−23.4	34.3	39 37.5	−22.7	34.8	40 26.6	−21.9	35.3	55
56	34 10.7	−27.1	31.2	35 01.9	−26.5	31.5	35 52.9	−25.9	31.9	36 43.8	−25.4	32.3	37 34.4	−24.7	32.7	38 24.7	−24.0	33.1	39 14.8	−23.3	33.6	40 04.7	−22.7	34.0	56
57	33 43.6	−27.7	30.1	34 35.4	−27.1	30.5	35 27.0	−26.5	30.8	36 18.4	−25.9	31.2	37 09.7	−25.4	31.6	38 00.7	−24.8	32.0	38 51.5	−24.1	32.4	39 42.0	−23.4	32.8	57
58	33 15.9	−28.2	29.0	34 08.3	−27.7	29.4	35 00.5	−27.2	29.7	35 52.5	−26.6	30.1	36 44.3	−26.0	30.4	37 35.9	−25.3	30.8	38 27.4	−24.8	31.2	39 18.6	−24.2	31.6	58
59	32 47.7	−28.7	28.0	33 40.6	−28.2	28.3	34 33.3	−27.7	28.6	35 25.9	−27.1	29.0	36 18.3	−26.6	29.3	37 10.6	−26.1	29.7	38 02.6	−25.5	30.1	38 54.4	−24.9	30.5	59
60	32 19.0	−29.3	27.0	33 12.4	−28.8	27.2	34 05.6	−28.2	27.5	34 58.8	−27.8	27.9	35 51.7	−27.2	28.2	36 44.5	−26.7	28.6	37 37.1	−26.1	28.9	38 29.5	−25.5	29.3	60
61	31 49.7	−29.7	25.9	32 43.6	−29.3	26.2	33 37.4	−28.8	26.5	34 31.0	−28.3	26.8	35 24.5	−27.8	27.1	36 17.8	−27.3	27.4	37 11.0	−26.8	27.8	38 04.0	−26.2	28.1	61
62	31 20.0	−30.2	24.9	32 14.3	−29.7	25.2	33 08.6	−29.3	25.4	34 02.7	−28.8	25.7	34 56.7	−28.4	26.0	35 50.5	−27.8	26.3	36 44.2	−27.3	26.7	37 37.8	−26.9	27.0	62
63	30 49.8	−30.7	23.9	31 44.6	−30.3	24.1	32 39.3	−29.8	24.4	33 33.9	−29.4	24.7	34 28.3	−28.9	25.0	35 22.7	−28.5	25.2	36 16.9	−28.0	25.6	37 10.9	−27.5	25.9	63
64	30 19.1	−31.1	22.9	31 14.3	−30.7	23.1	32 09.5	−30.4	23.4	33 04.5	−29.9	23.6	33 59.4	−29.5	23.9	34 54.2	−29.0	24.2	35 48.9	−28.6	24.5	36 43.4	−28.1	24.8	64
65	29 48.0	−31.6	21.9	30 43.6	−31.2	22.1	31 39.1	−30.8	22.4	32 34.6	−30.4	22.6	33 29.9	−30.0	22.8	34 25.2	−29.6	23.1	35 20.3	−29.2	23.4	36 15.3	−28.7	23.7	65
66	29 16.4	−32.0	20.9	30 12.4	−31.6	21.1	31 08.3	−31.2	21.3	32 04.2	−30.9	21.6	32 59.9	−30.5	21.8	33 55.6	−30.1	22.1	34 51.1	−29.6	22.3	35 46.6	−29.3	22.6	66
67	28 44.4	−32.4	20.0	29 40.8	−32.1	20.2	30 37.1	−31.7	20.4	31 33.3	−31.4	20.6	32 29.4	−31.0	20.8	33 25.5	−30.6	21.0	34 21.5	−30.3	21.3	35 17.3	−29.8	21.5	67
68	28 12.0	−32.7	19.0	29 08.7	−32.4	19.2	30 05.4	−32.2	19.4	31 01.9	−31.8	19.6	31 58.4	−31.4	19.8	32 54.9	−31.1	20.0	33 51.2	−30.7	20.2	34 47.5	−30.4	20.5	68
69	27 39.3	−33.2	18.1	28 36.3	−32.9	18.2	29 33.2	−32.5	18.4	30 30.1	−32.2	18.6	31 27.0	−32.0	18.8	32 23.8	−31.6	19.0	33 20.5	−31.3	19.2	34 17.1	−30.9	19.4	69
70	27 06.1	−33.6	17.1	28 03.4	−33.3	17.3	29 00.7	−33.0	17.4	29 57.9	−32.7	17.6	30 55.0	−32.3	17.8	31 52.2	−32.1	18.0	32 49.2	−31.8	18.2	33 46.2	−31.5	18.4	70
71	26 32.5	−33.9	16.2	27 30.1	−33.6	16.3	28 27.7	−33.4	16.5	29 25.2	−33.1	16.6	30 22.7	−32.8	16.8	31 20.1	−32.5	17.0	32 17.4	−32.2	17.2	33 14.7	−31.9	17.4	71
72	25 58.6	−34.2	15.3	26 56.5	−34.0	15.4	27 54.3	−33.7	15.5	28 52.1	−33.5	15.7	29 49.9	−33.3	15.8	30 47.6	−33.0	16.0	31 45.2	−32.7	16.2	32 42.8	−32.4	16.3	72
73	25 24.4	−34.6	14.4	26 22.5	−34.3	14.5	27 20.6	−34.1	14.6	28 18.6	−33.8	14.7	29 16.6	−33.6	14.9	30 14.6	−33.4	15.0	31 12.5	−33.1	15.2	32 10.4	−32.8	15.3	73
74	24 49.8	−34.9	13.5	25 48.2	−34.7	13.6	26 46.5	−34.5	13.7	27 44.8	−34.3	13.8	28 43.0	−34.0	13.9	29 41.2	−33.8	14.1	30 39.4	−33.6	14.2	31 37.6	−33.4	14.4	74
75	24 14.9	−35.2	12.6	25 13.5	−35.0	12.7	26 12.0	−34.8	12.8	27 10.5	−34.6	12.9	28 09.0	−34.4	13.0	29 07.4	−34.2	13.1	30 05.8	−33.9	13.2	31 04.2	−33.7	13.4	75
76	23 39.7	−35.5	11.7	24 38.5	−35.4	11.8	25 37.2	−35.2	11.9	26 35.9	−35.0	12.0	27 34.6	−34.8	12.1	28 33.2	−34.5	12.2	29 31.9	−34.4	12.3	30 30.5	−34.2	12.4	76
77	23 04.2	−35.8	10.8	24 03.1	−35.6	10.9	25 02.0	−35.4	11.0	26 00.9	−35.3	11.1	26 59.8	−35.1	11.2	27 58.7	−35.0	11.3	28 57.5	−34.8	11.4	29 56.3	−34.6	11.5	77
78	22 28.4	−36.1	9.9	23 27.5	−35.9	10.0	24 26.6	−35.8	10.1	25 25.6	−35.6	10.2	26 24.7	−35.5	10.2	27 23.7	−35.3	10.3	28 22.7	−35.1	10.4	29 21.7	−34.9	10.5	78
79	21 52.3	−36.3	9.1	22 51.6	−36.2	9.1	23 50.8	−36.1	9.2	24 50.0	−35.9	9.3	25 49.2	−35.8	9.3	26 48.4	−35.6	9.4	27 47.6	−35.5	9.5	28 46.8	−35.4	9.6	79
80	21 16.0	−36.6	8.2	22 15.4	−36.5	8.3	23 14.7	−36.3	8.3	24 14.1	−36.2	8.4	25 13.4	−36.1	8.5	26 12.8	−36.0	8.5	27 12.1	−35.8	8.6	28 11.4	−35.7	8.7	80
81	20 39.4	−36.9	7.4	21 38.9	−36.8	7.4	22 38.4	−36.7	7.5	23 37.9	−36.6	7.5	24 37.3	−36.4	7.6	25 36.8	−36.3	7.6	26 36.3	−36.2	7.7	27 35.7	−36.0	7.8	81
82	20 02.5	−37.1	6.5	21 02.1	−37.0	6.6	22 01.7	−36.9	6.6	23 01.3	−36.8	6.7	24 00.9	−36.7	6.7	25 00.5	−36.6	6.8	26 00.1	−36.5	6.8	26 59.7	−36.4	6.9	82
83	19 25.4	−37.3	5.7	20 25.1	−37.2	5.7	21 24.8	−37.1	5.8	22 24.5	−37.0	5.8	23 24.2	−37.0	5.8	24 23.9	−36.9	5.9	25 23.6	−36.8	5.9	26 23.3	−36.7	6.0	83
84	18 48.1	−37.5	4.9	19 47.9	−37.4	4.9	20 47.7	−37.4	4.9	21 47.5	−37.4	4.9	22 47.2	−37.2	5.0	23 47.0	−37.2	5.0	24 46.8	−37.1	5.1	25 46.6	−37.1	5.1	84
85	18 10.6	−37.7	4.0	19 10.5	−37.7	4.1	20 10.3	−37.6	4.1	21 10.1	−37.5	4.1	22 10.0	−37.5	4.1	23 09.8	−37.4	4.2	24 09.7	−37.4	4.2	25 09.5	−37.3	4.2	85
86	17 32.9	−38.0	3.2	18 32.8	−37.9	3.2	19 32.7	−37.9	3.3	20 32.6	−37.8	3.3	21 32.5	−37.8	3.3	22 32.4	−37.7	3.3	23 32.3	−37.7	3.3	24 32.2	−37.7	3.4	86
87	16 54.9	−38.1	2.4	17 54.9	−38.1	2.4	18 54.8	−38.1	2.4	19 54.8	−38.1	2.4	20 54.7	−38.0	2.5	21 54.7	−38.0	2.5	22 54.6	−38.0	2.5	23 54.5	−37.9	2.5	87
88	16 16.8	−38.3	1.6	17 16.8	−38.3	1.6	18 16.7	−38.2	1.6	19 16.7	−38.2	1.6	20 16.7	−38.2	1.6	21 16.7	−38.2	1.6	22 16.6	−38.2	1.7	23 16.6	−38.2	1.7	88
89	15 38.5	−38.5	0.8	16 38.5	−38.5	0.8	17 38.5	−38.5	0.8	18 38.5	−38.5	0.8	19 38.5	−38.5	0.8	20 38.5	−38.5	0.8	21 38.4	−38.4	0.8	22 38.4	−38.4	0.8	89
90	15 00.0	−38.6	0.0	16 00.0	−38.7	0.0	17 00.0	−38.7	0.0	18 00.0	−38.7	0.0	19 00.0	−38.7	0.0	20 00.0	−38.7	0.0	21 00.0	−38.7	0.0	22 00.0	−38.7	0.0	90
	15°			16°			17°			18°			19°			20°			21°			22°			

50°, 310° L.H.A. **LATITUDE SAME NAME AS DECLINATION**

102

LATITUDE **CONTRARY** NAME TO DECLINATION **L.H.A. 50°, 310°**

Dec.	15°			16°			17°			18°			19°			20°			21°			22°			Dec.
	Hc	d	Z	Hc	d	Z	Hc	d	Z	Hc	d	Z	Hc	d	Z	Hc	d	Z	Hc	d	Z	Hc	d	Z	
°	° ′	′	°	° ′	′	°	° ′	′	°	° ′	′	°	° ′	′	°	° ′	′	°	° ′	′	°	° ′	′	°	°
0	38 22.8	-20.1	102.3	38 09.7	-21.4	103.0	37 55.8	-22.6	103.8	37 41.1	-23.7	104.5	37 25.7	-24.9	105.3	37 09.5	-26.1	106.0	36 52.6	-27.2	106.7	36 35.0	-28.3	107.4	0
1	38 02.7	-20.9	103.5	37 48.3	-22.1	104.2	37 33.2	-23.3	105.0	37 17.4	-24.5	105.7	37 00.8	-25.6	106.4	36 43.4	-26.7	107.1	36 25.4	-27.8	107.8	36 06.7	-28.9	108.5	1
2	37 41.8	-21.6	104.6	37 26.2	-22.8	105.4	37 09.9	-23.9	106.1	36 52.9	-25.1	106.8	36 35.2	-26.2	107.6	36 16.7	-27.3	108.3	35 57.6	-28.4	108.9	35 37.8	-29.5	109.6	2
3	37 20.2	-22.3	105.8	37 03.4	-23.4	106.5	36 46.0	-24.6	107.3	36 27.8	-25.7	108.0	36 09.0	-26.9	108.7	35 49.4	-27.9	109.4	35 29.2	-29.0	110.0	35 08.3	-30.0	110.7	3
4	36 57.9	-23.0	107.0	36 40.0	-24.1	107.7	36 21.4	-25.2	108.4	36 02.1	-26.3	109.1	35 42.1	-27.4	109.8	35 21.5	-28.5	110.4	35 00.2	-29.5	111.1	34 38.3	-30.5	111.8	4
5	36 34.9	-23.6	108.1	36 15.9	-24.8	108.8	35 56.2	-25.9	109.5	35 35.8	-27.0	110.2	35 14.7	-28.0	110.9	34 53.0	-29.0	111.5	34 30.7	-30.1	112.2	34 07.8	-31.1	112.8	5
6	36 11.3	-24.3	109.3	35 51.1	-25.4	110.0	35 30.3	-26.5	110.6	35 08.8	-27.5	111.3	34 46.7	-28.6	111.9	34 24.0	-29.6	112.6	34 00.6	-30.6	113.2	33 36.7	-31.6	113.8	6
7	35 47.0	-24.9	110.4	35 25.7	-26.0	111.1	35 03.8	-27.0	111.7	34 41.3	-28.1	112.4	34 18.1	-29.1	113.0	33 54.4	-30.1	113.6	33 30.0	-31.1	114.2	33 05.1	-32.1	114.8	7
8	35 22.1	-25.6	111.5	34 59.7	-26.6	112.2	34 36.8	-27.7	112.8	34 13.2	-28.7	113.5	33 49.0	-29.6	114.1	33 24.3	-30.7	114.7	32 58.9	-31.6	115.3	32 33.0	-32.5	115.8	8
9	34 56.5	-26.1	112.6	34 33.1	-27.1	113.3	34 09.1	-28.1	113.9	33 44.5	-29.1	114.5	33 19.4	-30.2	115.1	32 53.6	-31.1	115.7	32 27.3	-32.0	116.3	32 00.5	-33.0	116.8	9
10	34 30.4	-26.7	113.7	34 06.0	-27.7	114.3	33 41.0	-28.8	115.0	33 15.4	-29.8	115.6	32 49.2	-30.7	116.1	32 22.5	-31.6	116.7	31 55.3	-32.6	117.3	31 27.5	-33.4	117.8	10
11	34 03.7	-27.2	114.8	33 38.3	-28.3	115.4	33 12.2	-29.2	116.0	32 45.6	-30.2	116.6	32 18.5	-31.1	117.2	31 50.9	-32.1	117.7	31 22.7	-33.0	118.3	30 54.1	-33.9	118.8	11
12	33 36.5	-27.8	115.9	33 10.0	-28.8	116.5	32 43.0	-29.8	117.1	32 15.4	-30.7	117.6	31 47.4	-31.7	118.2	31 18.8	-32.6	118.7	30 49.7	-33.4	119.2	30 20.2	-34.3	119.8	12
13	33 08.7	-28.4	116.9	32 41.2	-29.3	117.5	32 13.2	-30.2	118.1	31 44.7	-31.2	118.6	31 15.7	-32.1	119.2	30 46.2	-32.9	119.7	30 16.3	-33.9	120.2	29 45.9	-34.7	120.7	13
14	32 40.3	-28.8	118.0	32 11.9	-29.8	118.6	31 43.0	-30.8	119.1	31 13.5	-31.6	119.6	30 43.6	-32.5	120.2	30 13.3	-33.4	120.7	29 42.4	-34.2	121.2	29 11.2	-35.1	121.6	14
15	32 11.5	-29.4	119.0	31 42.1	-30.3	119.6	31 12.2	-31.2	120.1	30 41.9	-32.1	120.6	30 11.1	-33.0	121.1	29 39.9	-33.8	121.6	29 08.2	-34.6	122.1	28 36.1	-35.4	122.6	15
16	31 42.1	-29.9	120.1	31 11.8	-30.8	120.6	30 41.0	-31.6	121.1	30 09.8	-32.5	121.6	29 38.1	-33.3	122.1	29 06.1	-34.2	122.6	28 33.6	-35.1	123.0	28 00.7	-35.9	123.5	16
17	31 12.2	-30.3	121.1	30 41.0	-31.2	121.6	30 09.4	-32.1	122.1	29 37.3	-33.0	122.6	29 04.8	-33.8	123.0	28 31.9	-34.6	123.5	27 58.5	-35.3	124.0	27 24.8	-36.1	124.4	17
18	30 41.9	-30.8	122.1	30 09.8	-31.7	122.6	29 37.3	-32.5	123.1	29 04.3	-33.3	123.5	28 31.0	-34.2	124.0	27 57.3	-35.0	124.4	27 23.2	-35.8	124.9	26 48.7	-36.5	125.3	18
19	30 11.1	-31.2	123.1	29 38.1	-32.0	123.6	29 04.8	-32.9	124.0	28 31.0	-33.7	124.5	27 56.8	-34.5	124.9	27 22.3	-35.3	125.4	26 47.4	-36.1	125.8	26 12.2	-36.8	126.2	19
20	29 39.9	-31.7	124.1	29 06.1	-32.5	124.5	28 31.9	-33.4	125.0	27 57.3	-34.1	125.4	27 22.3	-34.9	125.8	26 47.0	-35.7	126.3	26 11.3	-36.4	126.7	25 35.4	-37.2	127.0	20
21	29 08.2	-32.1	125.0	28 33.6	-32.9	125.5	27 58.5	-33.7	125.9	27 23.2	-34.5	126.3	26 47.4	-35.2	126.8	26 11.3	-35.9	127.2	25 34.9	-36.7	127.5	24 58.2	-37.4	127.9	21
22	28 36.1	-32.5	126.0	28 00.7	-33.3	126.4	27 24.8	-34.0	126.9	26 48.7	-34.9	127.3	26 12.2	-35.6	127.7	25 35.4	-36.3	128.0	24 58.2	-37.0	128.4	24 20.8	-37.7	128.8	22
23	28 03.6	-32.9	127.0	27 27.4	-33.7	127.4	26 50.8	-34.5	127.8	26 13.8	-35.1	128.2	25 36.6	-35.9	128.6	24 59.1	-36.7	128.9	24 21.2	-37.3	129.3	23 43.1	-38.0	129.6	23
24	27 30.7	-33.2	127.9	26 53.7	-34.0	128.3	26 16.3	-34.7	128.7	25 38.7	-35.5	129.1	25 00.7	-36.2	129.4	24 22.4	-36.9	129.8	23 43.9	-37.6	130.1	23 05.1	-38.3	130.5	24
25	26 57.5	-33.7	128.8	26 19.7	-34.4	129.2	25 41.6	-35.1	129.6	25 03.2	-35.8	130.0	24 24.5	-36.5	130.3	23 45.5	-37.2	130.7	23 06.3	-37.9	131.0	22 26.8	-38.5	131.3	25
26	26 23.8	-34.0	129.8	25 45.3	-34.7	130.1	25 06.5	-35.5	130.5	24 27.4	-36.2	130.9	23 48.0	-36.8	131.2	23 08.3	-37.4	131.5	22 28.4	-38.1	131.8	21 48.3	-38.8	132.1	26
27	25 49.8	-34.3	130.7	25 10.6	-35.1	131.0	24 31.0	-35.7	131.4	23 51.2	-36.4	131.7	23 11.2	-37.1	132.1	22 30.9	-37.8	132.4	21 50.3	-38.4	132.7	21 09.5	-39.0	133.0	27
28	25 15.5	-34.7	131.6	24 35.5	-35.3	131.9	23 55.3	-36.0	132.3	23 14.8	-36.7	132.6	22 34.1	-37.4	132.9	21 53.1	-38.0	133.2	21 11.9	-38.6	133.5	20 30.5	-39.2	133.8	28
29	24 40.8	-34.9	132.5	24 00.2	-35.7	132.8	23 19.3	-36.4	133.1	22 38.1	-37.0	133.5	21 56.7	-37.6	133.8	21 15.1	-38.2	134.0	20 33.3	-38.8	134.3	19 51.3	-39.4	134.6	29
30	24 05.9	-35.3	133.4	23 24.5	-35.9	133.7	22 42.9	-36.5	134.0	22 01.1	-37.2	134.3	21 19.1	-37.8	134.6	20 36.9	-38.5	134.9	19 54.5	-39.1	135.1	19 11.9	-39.7	135.4	30
31	23 30.6	-35.6	134.3	22 48.6	-36.3	134.6	22 06.4	-36.9	134.9	21 23.9	-37.5	135.2	20 41.3	-38.1	135.4	19 58.4	-38.6	135.7	19 15.4	-39.2	135.9	18 32.2	-39.8	136.2	31
32	22 55.0	-35.9	135.1	22 12.3	-36.5	135.4	21 29.5	-37.1	135.7	20 46.4	-37.7	136.0	20 03.2	-38.3	136.2	19 19.8	-38.9	136.5	18 36.2	-39.5	136.7	17 52.4	-40.0	137.0	32
33	22 19.1	-36.1	136.0	21 35.8	-36.7	136.3	20 52.4	-37.4	136.6	20 08.7	-37.9	136.8	19 24.9	-38.6	137.1	18 40.9	-39.1	137.3	17 56.7	-39.7	137.5	17 12.4	-40.3	137.7	33
34	21 43.0	-36.4	136.9	20 59.1	-37.0	137.1	20 15.0	-37.6	137.4	19 30.8	-38.2	137.6	18 46.3	-38.7	137.9	18 01.8	-39.3	138.1	17 17.0	-39.8	138.3	16 32.1	-40.3	138.5	34
35	21 06.6	-36.7	137.7	20 22.1	-37.3	138.0	19 37.4	-37.8	138.2	18 52.6	-38.4	138.5	18 07.6	-39.0	138.7	17 22.5	-39.5	138.9	16 37.2	-40.0	139.1	15 51.8	-40.6	139.3	35
36	20 29.9	-36.9	138.6	19 44.8	-37.5	138.8	18 59.6	-38.1	139.0	18 14.2	-38.6	139.3	17 28.6	-39.1	139.5	16 43.0	-39.7	139.7	15 57.2	-40.2	139.9	15 11.2	-40.7	140.0	36
37	19 53.0	-37.2	139.4	19 07.3	-37.7	139.6	18 21.5	-38.2	139.9	17 35.6	-38.8	140.1	16 49.5	-39.3	140.3	16 03.3	-39.8	140.5	15 17.0	-40.4	140.6	14 30.5	-40.8	140.8	37
38	19 15.8	-37.3	140.2	18 29.6	-37.9	140.5	17 43.3	-38.5	140.7	16 56.8	-39.0	140.9	16 10.2	-39.5	141.1	15 23.5	-40.0	141.2	14 36.6	-40.5	141.4	13 49.7	-41.0	141.6	38
39	18 38.5	-37.6	141.1	17 51.7	-38.1	141.3	17 04.8	-38.6	141.5	16 17.8	-39.1	141.7	15 30.7	-39.6	141.8	14 43.5	-40.2	142.0	13 56.1	-40.6	142.2	13 08.7	-41.1	142.3	39
40	18 00.9	-37.8	141.9	17 13.6	-38.3	142.1	16 26.2	-38.8	142.3	15 38.7	-39.3	142.5	14 51.1	-39.8	142.6	14 03.3	-40.3	142.8	13 15.5	-40.8	142.9	12 27.6	-41.2	143.1	40
41	17 23.1	-38.0	142.7	16 35.3	-38.5	142.9	15 47.4	-39.0	143.1	14 59.4	-39.5	143.2	14 11.3	-40.0	143.4	13 23.0	-40.4	143.5	12 34.7	-40.8	143.7	11 46.4	-41.2	143.8	41
42	16 45.1	-38.2	143.5	15 56.8	-38.7	143.7	15 08.4	-39.2	143.9	14 19.9	-39.6	144.0	13 31.3	-40.1	144.2	12 42.6	-40.5	144.3	11 53.9	-41.1	144.4	11 05.0	-41.4	144.5	42
43	16 06.9	-38.3	144.3	15 18.1	-38.8	144.5	14 29.2	-39.3	144.6	13 40.3	-39.8	144.8	12 51.2	-40.2	144.9	12 02.1	-40.7	145.1	11 12.8	-41.1	145.2	10 23.6	-41.6	145.3	43
44	15 28.6	-38.6	145.1	14 39.3	-39.0	145.3	13 49.9	-39.4	145.4	13 00.5	-39.9	145.6	12 11.0	-40.4	145.7	11 21.4	-40.8	145.8	10 31.7	-41.2	145.9	9 42.0	-41.6	146.0	44
45	14 50.0	-38.6	145.9	14 00.3	-39.1	146.1	13 10.5	-39.6	146.2	12 20.6	-40.0	146.3	11 30.6	-40.4	146.4	10 40.6	-40.9	146.5	9 50.5	-41.3	146.6	9 00.4	-41.8	146.7	45
46	14 11.4	-38.9	146.7	13 21.2	-39.3	146.8	12 30.9	-39.7	147.0	11 40.6	-40.2	147.1	10 50.2	-40.6	147.2	9 59.7	-41.0	147.3	9 09.2	-41.4	147.4	8 18.6	-41.8	147.5	46
47	13 32.5	-39.0	147.5	12 41.9	-39.5	147.6	11 51.2	-39.9	147.7	11 00.4	-40.3	147.8	10 09.6	-40.7	147.9	9 18.7	-41.1	148.0	8 27.8	-41.5	148.1	7 36.8	-41.9	148.2	47
48	12 53.5	-39.1	148.3	12 02.4	-39.5	148.4	11 11.3	-39.9	148.5	10 20.1	-40.3	148.6	9 28.9	-40.8	148.7	8 37.6	-41.2	148.8	7 46.3	-41.6	148.8	6 54.9	-41.9	148.9	48
49	12 14.4	-39.3	149.1	11 22.9	-39.7	149.2	10 31.4	-40.1	149.3	9 39.8	-40.5	149.3	8 48.1	-40.8	149.4	7 56.4	-41.2	149.5	7 04.7	-41.6	149.6	6 13.0	-42.0	149.6	49
50	11 35.1	-39.3	149.8	10 43.2	-39.7	149.9	9 51.3	-40.2	150.0	8 59.3	-40.6	150.1	8 07.3	-41.0	150.2	7 15.2	-41.3	150.2	6 23.1	-41.7	150.3	5 31.0	-42.1	150.4	50
51	10 55.8	-39.5	150.6	10 03.5	-39.9	150.7	9 11.1	-40.2	150.8	8 18.7	-40.6	150.8	7 26.3	-41.0	150.9	6 33.9	-41.4	151.0	5 41.4	-41.7	151.0	4 48.9	-42.1	151.1	51
52	10 16.3	-39.6	151.4	9 23.6	-40.0	151.4	8 30.9	-40.4	151.5	7 38.1	-40.7	151.6	6 45.3	-41.1	151.6	5 52.5	-41.4	151.7	4 59.7	-41.8	151.7	4 06.8	-42.1	151.8	52
53	9 36.7	-39.8	152.1	8 43.6	-40.1	152.2	7 50.5	-40.4	152.3	6 57.4	-40.8	152.3	6 04.2	-41.1	152.4	5 11.1	-41.5	152.4	4 17.9	-41.9	152.5	3 24.7	-42.2	152.5	53
54	8 56.9	-39.7	152.9	8 03.5	-40.1	153.0	7 10.1	-40.5	153.0	6 16.6	-40.8	153.1	5 23.1	-41.2	153.1	4 29.6	-41.6	153.1	3 36.0	-41.8	153.2	2 42.5	-42.2	153.2	54
55	8 17.2	-39.9	153.6	7 23.4	-40.2	153.7	6 29.6	-40.6	153.8	5 35.8	-41.0	153.8	4 41.9	-41.2	153.8	3 48.0	-41.5	153.9	2 54.2	-41.9	153.9	2 00.3	-42.2	153.9	55
56	7 37.3	-40.0	154.4	6 43.2	-40.3	154.4	5 49.0	-40.6	154.5	4 54.8	-40.9	154.5	4 00.7	-41.3	154.6	3 06.5	-41.6	154.6	2 12.3	-41.9	154.6	1 18.1	-42.3	154.6	56
57	6 57.3	-40.0	155.1	6 02.9	-40.4	155.2	5 08.4	-40.7	155.2	4 13.9	-41.0	155.3	3 19.4	-41.3	155.3	2 24.9	-41.6	155.3	1 30.4	-42.0	155.3	0 35.8	-42.2	155.3	57
58	6 17.3	-40.1	155.9	5 22.5	-40.4	155.9	4 27.7	-40.7	156.0	3 32.9	-41.0	156.0	2 38.1	-41.3	156.0	1 43.3	-41.7	156.0	0 48.4	-41.9	156.0	0 06.4	+42.2	24.0	58
59	5 37.2	-40.2	156.6	4 42.1	-40.5	156.7	3 47.0	-40.8	156.7	2 51.9	-41.1	156.7	1 56.8	-41.4	156.7	1 01.6	-41.6	156.8	0 06.5	-41.9	156.8	0 48.6	+42.3	23.2	59
60	4 57.0	-40.2	157.4	4 01.6	-40.4	157.4	3 06.2	-40.7	157.4	2 10.8	-41.0	157.5	1 15.4	-41.4	157.5	0 20.0	-41.7	157.5	0 35.4	+42.0	22.5	1 30.9	+42.2	22.5	60
61	4 16.8	-40.2	158.1	3 21.2	-40.6	158.2	2 25.5	-40.9	158.2	1 29.8	-41.1	158.2	0 34.0	-41.3	158.2	0 21.7	+41.6	21.8	1 17.4	+41.9	21.8	2 13.1	+42.2	21.8	61
62	3 36.6	-40.3	158.9	2 40.6	-40.5	158.9	1 44.6	-40.8	158.9	0 48.7	-41.1	158.9	0 07.3	+41.4	21.1	1 03.3	+41.6	21.1	1 59.3	+41.9	21.1	2 55.3	+42.1	21.1	62
63	2 56.3	-40.3	159.6	2 00.1	-40.6	159.6	1 03.8	-40.8	159.6	0 07.6	-41.1	159.6	0 48.7	+41.3	20.4	1 44.9	+41.7	20.4	2 41.2	+41.9	20.4	3 37.4	+42.2	20.4	63
64	2 16.0	-40.3	160.4	1 19.5	-40.6	160.4	0 23.0	-40.9	160.4	0 33.5	+41.1	19.6	1 30.0	+41.4	19.6	2 26.6	+41.6	19.6	3 23.1	+41.8	19.7	4 19.6	+42.1	19.7	64
65	1 35.7	-40.4	161.1	0 38.9	-40.6	161.1	0 17.9	+40.8	18.9	1 14.6	+41.1	18.9	2 11.4	+41.3	18.9	3 08.2	+41.5	18.9	4 04.9	+41.8	18.9	5 01.7	+42.0	19.0	65
66	0 55.3	-40.3	161.8	0 01.7	+40.6	18.2	0 58.7	+40.8	18.2	1 55.7	+41.1	18.2	2 52.7	+41.3	18.2	3 49.7	+41.5	18.2	4 46.7	+41.8	18.2	5 43.7	+42.0	18.2	66
67	0 15.0	-40.4	162.6	0 42.3	+40.6	17.4	1 39.5	+40.8	17.4	2 36.8	+41.0	17.4	3 34.0	+41.3	17.5	4 31.2	+41.5	17.5	5 28.5	+41.7	17.5	6 25.7	+41.9	17.5	67
68	0 25.4	+40.3	16.7	1 22.9	+40.5	16.7	2 20.3	+40.8	16.7	3 17.8	+41.0	16.7	4 15.3	+41.2	16.7	5 12.7	+41.5	16.7	6 10.2	+41.6	16.8	7 07.6	+41.9	16.8	68
69	1 05.7	+40.4	15.9	2 03.4	+40.6	15.9	3 01.1	+40.8	16.0	3 58.8	+41.0	16.0	4 56.5	+41.2	16.0	5 54.2	+41.3	16.0	6 51.8	+41.6	16.1	7 49.5	+41.8	16.1	69
70	1 46.1	+40.3	15.2	2 44.0	+40.5	15.2	3 41.9	+40.7	15.2	4 39.8	+40.9	15.2	5 37.7	+41.1	15.3	6 35.5	+41.4	15.3	7 33.4	+41.5	15.3	8 31.3	+41.7	15.4	70
71	2 26.4	+40.3	14.5	3 24.5	+40.5	14.5	4 22.6	+40.7	14.5	5 20.7	+40.9	14.5	6 18.8	+41.0	14.5	7 16.9	+41.2	14.6	8 14.9	+41.5	14.6	9 13.0	+41.6	14.6	71
72	3 06.7	+40.3	13.7	4 05.0	+40.5	13.7	5 03.3	+40.6	13.7	6 01.6	+40.8	13.8	6 59.8	+41.0	13.8	7 58.1	+41.2	13.8	8 56.4	+41.3	13.9	9 54.6	+41.5	13.9	72
73	3 47.0	+40.2	13.0	4 45.5	+40.4	13.0	5 43.9	+40.6	13.0	6 42.4	+40.7	13.0	7 40.8	+40.9	13.1	8 39.3	+41.1	13.1	9 37.7	+41.3	13.1	10 36.1	+41.5	13.2	73
74	4 27.2	+40.2	12.2	5 25.9	+40.3	12.2	6 24.5	+40.5	12.3	7 23.1	+40.7	12.3	8 21.7	+40.9	12.3	9 20.4	+40.9	12.4	10 19.0	+41.1	12.4	11 17.6	+41.3	12.4	74
75	5 07.4	+40.1	11.5	6 06.2	+40.3	11.5	7 05.0	+40.4	11.5	8 03.8	+40.6	11.6	9 02.6	+40.7	11.6	10 01.3	+40.9	11.6	11 00.1	+41.1	11.7	11 58.9	+41.2	11.7	75
76	5 47.5	+40.1	10.7	6 46.5	+40.2	10.8	7 45.4	+40.4	10.8	8 44.4	+40.5	10.8	9 43.3	+40.7	10.8	10 42.2	+40.8	10.9	11 41.2	+40.9	10.9	12 40.1	+41.0	10.9	76
77	6 27.6	+40.0	10.0	7 26.7	+40.2	10.0	8 25.8	+40.3	10.0	9 24.9	+40.4	10.1	10 24.0	+40.5	10.1	11 23.0	+40.7	10.1	12 22.1	+40.8	10.2	13 21.1	+41.0	10.2	77
78	7 07.6	+40.0	9.2	8 06.9	+40.0	9.3	9 06.1	+40.2	9.3	10 05.3	+40.3	9.3	11 04.5	+40.4	9.3	12 03.7	+40.5	9.4	13 02.9	+40.7	9.4	14 02.1	+40.8	9.4	78
79	7 47.6	+39.8	8.5	8 46.9	+40.0	8.5	9 46.3	+40.0	8.5	10 45.6	+40.2	8.6	11 44.9	+40.3	8.6	12 44.2	+40.5	8.6	13 43.6	+40.5	8.7	14 42.9	+40.6	8.7	79
80	8 27.4	+39.8	7.7	9 26.9	+39.9	7.8	10 26.3	+40.0	7.8	11 25.8	+40.1	7.8	12 25.2	+40.2	7.8	13 24.7	+40.3	7.9	14 24.1	+40.4	7.9	15 23.5	+40.5	7.9	80
81	9 07.2	+39.7	7.0	10 06.8	+39.7	7.0	11 06.3	+39.9	7.0	12 05.9	+39.9	7.0	13 05.4	+40.1	7.1	14 05.0	+40.1	7.1	15 04.5	+40.2	7.1	16 04.0	+40.4	7.2	81
82	9 46.9	+39.6	6.2	10 46.5	+39.7	6.2	11 46.2	+39.7	6.3	12 45.8	+39.8	6.3	13 45.5	+39.9	6.3	14 45.1	+40.0	6.3	15 44.7	+40.1	6.4	16 44.4	+40.1	6.4	82
83	10 26.5	+39.4	5.4	11 26.2	+39.5	5.5	12 25.9	+39.6	5.5	13 25.6	+39.7	5.5	14 25.4	+39.7	5.5	15 25.1	+39.8	5.6	16 24.8	+39.9	5.6	17 24.5	+40.0	5.6	83
84	11 05.9	+39.4	4.7	12 05.7	+39.4	4.7	13 05.5	+39.5	4.7	14 05.3	+39.6	4.7	15 05.1	+39.6	4.8	16 04.9	+39.7	4.8	17 04.7	+39.7	4.8	18 04.5	+39.8	4.8	84
85	11 45.3	+39.2	3.9	12 45.1	+39.3	3.9	13 45.0	+39.3	3.9	14 44.9	+39.3	4.0	15 44.7	+39.4	4.0	16 44.6	+39.4	4.0	17 44.4	+39.5	4.0	18 44.3	+39.6	4.0	85
86	12 24.5	+39.1	3.1	13 24.4	+39.1	3.1	14 24.3	+39.2	3.2	15 24.2	+39.2	3.2	16 24.1	+39.3	3.2	17 24.0	+39.3	3.2	18 23.9	+39.4	3.2	19 23.9	+39.3	3.2	86
87	13 03.6	+38.9	2.4	14 03.5	+39.0	2.4	15 03.5	+39.0	2.4	16 03.4	+39.1	2.4	17 03.4	+39.1	2.4	18 03.3	+39.1	2.4	19 03.3	+39.1	2.4	20 03.2	+39.2	2.4	87
88	13 42.5	+38.9	1.6	14 42.5	+38.8	1.6	15 42.5	+38.8	1.6	16 42.5	+38.8	1.6	17 42.5	+38.8	1.6	18 42.4	+38.9	1.6	19 42.4	+38.9	1.6	20 42.4	+38.9	1.6	88
89	14 21.4	+38.6	0.8	15 21.3	+38.7	0.8	16 21.3	+38.7	0.8	17 21.3	+38.7	0.8	18 21.3	+38.7	0.8	19 21.3	+38.7	0.8	20 21.3	+38.7	0.8	21 21.3	+38.7	0.8	89
90	15 00.0	+38.5	0.0	16 00.0	+38.5	0.0	17 00.0	+38.5	0.0	18 00.0	+38.5	0.0	19 00.0	+38.5	0.0	20 00.0	+38.5	0.0	21 00.0	+38.4	0.0	22 00.0	+38.4	0.0	90
	15°			16°			17°			18°			19°			20°			21°			22°			

S. Lat. {L.H.A. greater than 180° ....Zn=180°–Z
{L.H.A. less than 180°............Zn=180°+Z **LATITUDE SAME NAME AS DECLINATION** **L.H.A. 130°, 230°**

103

51°, 309° L.H.A. LATITUDE **SAME** NAME AS DECLINATION N. Lat. {L.H.A. greater than 180° .....Zn=Z; L.H.A. less than 180°............Zn=360°−Z}

Dec.	15°			16°			17°			18°			Dec.
	Hc	d	Z	Hc	d	Z	Hc	d	Z	Hc	d	Z	
°	° ′	′	°	° ′	′	°	° ′	′	°	° ′	′	°	°
0	37 26.2	+19.2	101.8	37 13.5	+20.4	102.6	37 00.0	+21.7	103.3	36 45.8	+22.8	104.0	0
1	37 45.4	+18.4	100.6	37 33.9	+19.7	101.4	37 21.7	+20.9	102.1	37 08.6	+22.2	102.9	1
2	38 03.8	+17.8	99.4	37 53.6	+19.0	100.2	37 42.6	+20.2	101.0	37 30.8	+21.4	101.7	2
3	38 21.6	+16.9	98.2	38 12.6	+18.2	99.0	38 02.8	+19.5	99.8	37 52.2	+20.7	100.5	3
4	38 38.5	+16.2	97.0	38 30.8	+17.5	97.8	38 22.3	+18.7	98.6	38 12.9	+20.0	99.4	4
5	38 54.7	+15.4	95.8	38 48.3	+16.7	96.6	38 41.0	+18.0	97.4	38 32.9	+19.2	98.1	5
6	39 10.1	+14.6	94.5	39 05.0	+15.9	95.3	38 59.0	+17.2	96.1	38 52.1	+18.5	96.9	6
7	39 24.7	+13.8	93.3	39 20.9	+15.1	94.1	39 16.2	+16.4	94.9	39 10.6	+17.7	95.7	7
8	39 38.5	+13.0	92.0	39 36.0	+14.3	92.8	39 32.6	+15.6	93.7	39 28.3	+16.9	94.5	8
9	39 51.5	+12.1	90.7	39 50.3	+13.4	91.6	39 48.2	+14.8	92.4	39 45.2	+16.1	93.2	9
10	40 03.6	+11.3	89.5	40 03.7	+12.6	90.3	40 03.0	+13.9	91.1	40 01.3	+15.3	92.0	10
11	40 14.9	+10.4	88.2	40 16.3	+11.8	89.0	40 16.9	+13.1	89.9	40 16.6	+14.5	90.7	11
12	40 25.3	+9.5	86.9	40 28.1	+10.9	87.7	40 30.0	+12.3	88.6	40 31.1	+13.6	89.4	12
13	40 34.8	+8.7	85.6	40 39.0	+10.1	86.4	40 42.3	+11.4	87.3	40 44.7	+12.7	88.2	13
14	40 43.5	+7.8	84.3	40 49.1	+9.1	85.1	40 53.7	+10.5	86.0	40 57.4	+11.9	86.9	14
15	40 51.3	+6.9	83.0	40 58.2	+8.3	83.8	41 04.2	+9.7	84.7	41 09.3	+11.0	85.6	15
16	40 58.2	+6.0	81.6	41 06.5	+7.4	82.5	41 13.9	+8.7	83.4	41 20.3	+10.1	84.3	16
17	41 04.2	+5.1	80.3	41 13.9	+6.4	81.2	41 22.6	+7.8	82.1	41 30.4	+9.2	82.9	17
18	41 09.3	+4.2	79.0	41 20.3	+5.6	79.9	41 30.4	+7.0	80.7	41 39.6	+8.3	81.6	18
19	41 13.5	+3.3	77.7	41 25.9	+4.6	78.5	41 37.4	+6.0	79.4	41 47.9	+7.4	80.3	19
20	41 16.8	+2.4	76.4	41 30.5	+3.7	77.2	41 43.4	+5.0	78.1	41 55.3	+6.4	79.0	20
21	41 19.2	+1.4	75.0	41 34.2	+2.8	75.9	41 48.4	+4.2	76.7	42 01.7	+5.6	77.6	21
22	41 20.6	+0.5	73.7	41 37.0	+1.9	74.5	41 52.6	+3.2	75.4	42 07.3	+4.5	76.3	22
23	41 21.1	−0.4	72.4	41 38.9	+0.9	73.2	41 55.8	+2.3	74.1	42 11.8	+3.6	74.9	23
24	41 20.7	−1.3	71.0	41 39.8	0.0	71.9	41 58.1	+1.3	72.7	42 15.4	+2.7	73.6	24
25	41 19.4	−2.3	69.7	41 39.8	−0.9	70.5	41 59.4	+0.4	71.4	42 18.1	+1.7	72.2	25
26	41 17.1	−3.1	68.4	41 38.9	−1.9	69.2	41 59.8	−0.6	70.0	42 19.8	+0.8	70.9	26
27	41 14.0	−4.1	67.0	41 37.0	−2.8	67.9	41 59.2	−1.5	68.7	42 20.6	−0.2	69.5	27
28	41 09.9	−5.0	65.7	41 34.2	−3.7	66.5	41 57.7	−2.4	67.3	42 20.4	−1.1	68.2	28
29	41 04.9	−5.9	64.4	41 30.5	−4.7	65.2	41 55.3	−3.4	66.0	42 19.3	−2.1	66.8	29
30	40 59.0	−6.8	63.1	41 25.8	−5.5	63.9	41 51.9	−4.3	64.7	42 17.2	−3.0	65.5	30
31	40 52.2	−7.6	61.8	41 20.3	−6.5	62.5	41 47.6	−5.2	63.3	42 14.2	−4.0	64.1	31
32	40 44.6	−8.6	60.4	41 13.8	−7.4	61.2	41 42.4	−6.2	62.0	42 10.2	−5.0	62.8	32
33	40 36.0	−9.5	59.1	41 06.4	−8.2	59.9	41 36.2	−7.1	60.6	42 05.2	−5.8	61.4	33
34	40 26.5	−10.3	57.8	40 58.2	−9.2	58.6	41 29.1	−8.0	59.3	41 59.4	−6.8	60.1	34
35	40 16.2	−11.1	56.5	40 49.0	−10.1	57.3	41 21.1	−8.9	58.0	41 52.6	−7.8	58.8	35
36	40 05.1	−12.1	55.3	40 38.9	−10.9	56.0	41 12.2	−9.8	56.7	41 44.8	−8.6	57.4	36
37	39 53.0	−12.8	54.0	40 28.0	−11.8	54.7	41 02.4	−10.7	55.4	41 36.2	−9.6	56.1	37
38	39 40.2	−13.7	52.7	40 16.2	−12.6	53.4	40 51.7	−11.5	54.1	41 26.6	−10.4	54.8	38
39	39 26.5	−14.5	51.4	40 03.6	−13.5	52.1	40 40.2	−12.4	52.8	41 16.2	−11.3	53.5	39
40	39 12.0	−15.3	50.2	39 50.1	−14.3	50.8	40 27.8	−13.3	51.5	41 04.9	−12.3	52.2	40
41	38 56.7	−16.1	48.9	39 35.8	−15.1	49.6	40 14.5	−14.1	50.2	40 52.6	−13.0	50.9	41
42	38 40.6	−16.9	47.7	39 20.7	−15.9	48.3	40 00.4	−14.9	48.9	40 39.6	−14.0	49.6	42
43	38 23.7	−17.6	46.5	39 04.8	−16.7	47.1	39 45.5	−15.8	47.7	40 25.6	−14.8	48.3	43
44	38 06.1	−18.4	45.3	38 48.1	−17.4	45.8	39 29.7	−16.5	46.4	40 10.8	−15.6	47.0	44
45	37 47.7	−19.1	44.1	38 30.7	−18.3	44.6	39 13.2	−17.4	45.2	39 55.2	−16.4	45.8	45
46	37 28.6	−19.8	42.9	38 12.4	−19.0	43.4	38 55.8	−18.1	43.9	39 38.8	−17.2	44.5	46
47	37 08.8	−20.5	41.7	37 53.4	−19.7	42.2	38 37.7	−18.9	42.7	39 21.6	−18.0	43.3	47
48	36 48.3	−21.2	40.5	37 33.7	−20.4	41.0	38 18.8	−19.6	41.5	39 03.6	−18.8	42.0	48
49	36 27.1	−21.9	39.3	37 13.3	−21.1	39.8	37 59.2	−20.3	40.3	38 44.8	−19.5	40.8	49
50	36 05.2	−22.6	38.2	36 52.2	−21.8	38.6	37 38.9	−21.0	39.1	38 25.3	−20.3	39.6	50
51	35 42.6	−23.2	37.0	36 30.4	−22.5	37.5	37 17.9	−21.8	37.9	38 05.0	−21.0	38.4	51
52	35 19.4	−23.8	35.9	36 07.9	−23.1	36.3	36 56.1	−22.4	36.8	37 44.0	−21.7	37.2	52
53	34 55.6	−24.4	34.8	35 44.8	−23.8	35.2	36 33.7	−23.1	35.6	37 22.3	−22.4	36.1	53
54	34 31.2	−25.0	33.7	35 21.0	−24.4	34.1	36 10.6	−23.7	34.5	36 59.9	−23.0	34.9	54
55	34 06.2	−25.7	32.6	34 56.6	−25.0	32.9	35 46.9	−24.4	33.3	36 36.9	−23.8	33.7	55
56	33 40.5	−26.1	31.5	34 31.6	−25.6	31.8	35 22.5	−25.0	32.2	36 13.1	−24.3	32.6	56
57	33 14.4	−26.8	30.4	34 06.0	−26.2	30.7	34 57.5	−25.6	31.1	35 48.8	−25.0	31.5	57
58	32 47.6	−27.2	29.3	33 39.8	−26.7	29.7	34 31.9	−26.2	30.0	35 23.8	−25.6	30.3	58
59	32 20.4	−27.8	28.3	33 13.1	−27.3	28.6	34 05.7	−26.7	28.9	34 58.2	−26.2	29.2	59
60	31 52.6	−28.3	27.2	32 45.8	−27.8	27.5	33 39.0	−27.3	27.8	34 32.0	−26.8	28.1	60
61	31 24.3	−28.8	26.2	32 18.0	−28.3	26.5	33 11.7	−27.9	26.8	34 05.2	−27.4	27.1	61
62	30 55.5	−29.3	25.2	31 49.7	−28.8	25.4	32 43.8	−28.3	25.7	33 37.8	−27.9	26.0	62
63	30 26.2	−29.8	24.2	31 20.9	−29.3	24.4	32 15.5	−28.9	24.7	33 09.9	−28.4	24.9	63
64	29 56.4	−30.2	23.2	30 51.6	−29.8	23.4	31 46.6	−29.4	23.6	32 41.5	−29.0	23.9	64
65	29 26.2	−30.6	22.2	30 21.8	−30.3	22.4	31 17.2	−29.9	22.6	32 12.5	−29.4	22.8	65
66	28 55.6	−31.1	21.2	29 51.5	−30.7	21.4	30 47.3	−30.3	21.6	31 43.1	−30.0	21.8	66
67	28 24.5	−31.4	20.2	29 20.8	−31.1	20.4	30 17.0	−30.8	20.6	31 13.1	−30.4	20.8	67
68	27 53.1	−31.9	19.2	28 49.7	−31.6	19.4	29 46.2	−31.2	19.6	30 42.7	−30.8	19.8	68
69	27 21.2	−32.3	18.3	28 18.1	−31.9	18.4	29 15.0	−31.6	18.6	30 11.9	−31.4	18.8	69
70	26 48.9	−32.6	17.3	27 46.2	−32.4	17.5	28 43.4	−32.1	17.6	29 40.5	−31.7	17.8	70
71	26 16.3	−33.0	16.4	27 13.8	−32.7	16.5	28 11.3	−32.4	16.7	29 08.8	−32.2	16.8	71
72	25 43.3	−33.4	15.5	26 41.1	−33.1	15.6	27 38.9	−32.9	15.7	28 36.6	−32.6	15.9	72
73	25 09.9	−33.7	14.5	26 08.0	−33.5	14.7	27 06.0	−33.2	14.8	28 04.0	−32.9	14.9	73
74	24 36.2	−34.0	13.6	25 34.5	−33.8	13.7	26 32.8	−33.6	13.9	27 31.1	−33.4	14.0	74
75	24 02.2	−34.3	12.7	25 00.7	−34.1	12.8	25 59.2	−33.9	12.9	26 57.7	−33.7	13.0	75
76	23 27.9	−34.6	11.8	24 26.6	−34.4	11.9	25 25.3	−34.2	12.0	26 24.0	−34.1	12.1	76
77	22 53.3	−35.0	10.9	23 52.2	−34.8	11.0	24 51.1	−34.6	11.1	25 49.9	−34.4	11.2	77
78	22 18.3	−35.2	10.1	23 17.4	−35.0	10.1	24 16.5	−34.9	10.2	25 15.5	−34.7	10.3	78
79	21 43.1	−35.5	9.2	22 42.4	−35.4	9.3	23 41.6	−35.2	9.3	24 40.8	−35.1	9.4	79
80	21 07.6	−35.7	8.3	22 07.0	−35.6	8.4	23 06.4	−35.5	8.4	24 05.7	−35.4	8.5	80
81	20 31.9	−36.0	7.5	21 31.4	−35.9	7.5	22 30.9	−35.8	7.6	23 30.3	−35.6	7.6	81
82	19 55.9	−36.2	6.6	20 55.5	−36.1	6.6	21 55.1	−36.0	6.7	22 54.7	−36.0	6.7	82
83	19 19.7	−36.5	5.8	20 19.4	−36.4	5.8	21 19.1	−36.4	5.8	22 18.7	−36.2	5.9	83
84	18 43.2	−36.7	4.9	19 43.0	−36.7	5.0	20 42.7	−36.5	5.0	21 42.5	−36.5	5.0	84
85	18 06.5	−36.9	4.1	19 06.3	−36.8	4.1	20 06.2	−36.8	4.1	21 06.0	−36.7	4.2	85
86	17 29.6	−37.1	3.3	18 29.5	−37.1	3.3	19 29.4	−37.0	3.3	20 29.3	−37.0	3.3	86
87	16 52.5	−37.3	2.4	17 52.4	−37.3	2.4	18 52.4	−37.3	2.5	19 52.3	−37.2	2.5	87
88	16 15.2	−37.5	1.6	17 15.1	−37.4	1.6	18 15.1	−37.4	1.6	19 15.1	−37.4	1.6	88
89	15 37.7	−37.7	0.8	16 37.7	−37.7	0.8	17 37.7	−37.7	0.8	18 37.7	−37.7	0.8	89
90	15 00.0	−37.8	0.0	16 00.0	−37.8	0.0	17 00.0	−37.9	0.0	18 00.0	−37.9	0.0	90
	15°			16°			17°			18°			

Dec.	19°			20°			21°			22°			Dec.
	Hc	d	Z	Hc	d	Z	Hc	d	Z	Hc	d	Z	
°	° ′	′	°	° ′	′	°	° ′	′	°	° ′	′	°	°
0	36 30.9	+24.0	104.8	36 15.2	+25.2	105.5	35 58.9	+26.2	106.2	35 41.8	+27.4	106.9	0
1	36 54.9	+23.3	103.6	36 40.4	+24.5	104.4	36 25.1	+25.7	105.1	36 09.2	+26.8	105.8	1
2	37 18.2	+22.6	102.5	37 04.9	+23.8	103.2	36 50.8	+25.0	103.9	36 36.0	+26.1	104.7	2
3	37 40.8	+22.0	101.3	37 28.7	+23.1	102.1	37 15.8	+24.3	102.8	37 02.1	+25.5	103.5	3
4	38 02.8	+21.2	100.1	37 51.8	+22.5	100.9	37 40.1	+23.6	101.7	37 27.6	+24.8	102.4	4
5	38 24.0	+20.5	98.9	38 14.3	+21.7	99.7	38 03.7	+23.0	100.5	37 52.4	+24.2	101.3	5
6	38 44.5	+19.7	97.7	38 36.0	+21.0	98.5	38 26.7	+22.2	99.3	38 16.6	+23.4	100.1	6
7	39 04.2	+19.0	96.5	38 57.0	+20.3	97.3	38 48.9	+21.5	98.1	38 40.0	+22.8	98.9	7
8	39 23.2	+18.2	95.3	39 17.3	+19.4	96.1	39 10.4	+20.8	96.9	39 02.8	+22.0	97.7	8
9	39 41.4	+17.4	94.1	39 36.7	+18.8	94.9	39 31.2	+20.0	95.7	39 24.8	+21.3	96.5	9
10	39 58.8	+16.6	92.8	39 55.5	+17.9	93.6	39 51.2	+19.2	94.5	39 46.1	+20.5	95.3	10
11	40 15.4	+15.8	91.6	40 13.4	+17.1	92.4	40 10.4	+18.4	93.2	40 06.6	+19.7	94.1	11
12	40 31.2	+15.0	90.3	40 30.5	+16.3	91.1	40 28.8	+17.6	92.0	40 26.3	+18.9	92.8	12
13	40 46.2	+14.1	89.0	40 46.8	+15.4	89.9	40 46.4	+16.8	90.7	40 45.2	+18.1	91.6	13
14	41 00.3	+13.2	87.7	41 02.2	+14.6	88.6	41 03.2	+16.0	89.5	41 03.3	+17.3	90.3	14
15	41 13.5	+12.4	86.4	41 16.8	+13.7	87.3	41 19.2	+15.0	88.2	41 20.6	+16.4	89.1	15
16	41 25.9	+11.5	85.1	41 30.5	+12.9	86.0	41 34.2	+14.2	86.9	41 37.0	+15.6	87.8	16
17	41 37.4	+10.5	83.8	41 43.4	+11.9	84.7	41 48.4	+13.3	85.6	41 52.6	+14.7	86.5	17
18	41 47.9	+9.7	82.5	41 55.3	+11.0	83.4	42 01.7	+12.5	84.3	42 07.3	+13.7	85.2	18
19	41 57.6	+8.7	81.2	42 06.3	+10.2	82.1	42 14.2	+11.5	83.0	42 21.0	+12.9	83.9	19
20	42 06.3	+7.9	79.8	42 16.5	+9.2	80.7	42 25.7	+10.5	81.6	42 33.9	+12.0	82.5	20
21	42 14.2	+6.8	78.5	42 25.7	+8.2	79.4	42 36.2	+9.7	80.3	42 45.9	+11.0	81.2	21
22	42 21.0	+6.0	77.2	42 33.9	+7.3	78.1	42 45.9	+8.7	79.0	42 56.9	+10.1	79.9	22
23	42 27.0	+5.0	75.8	42 41.2	+6.4	76.7	42 54.6	+7.7	77.6	43 07.0	+9.1	78.5	23
24	42 32.0	+4.0	74.5	42 47.6	+5.4	75.4	43 02.3	+6.8	76.3	43 16.1	+8.2	77.2	24
25	42 36.0	+3.1	73.1	42 53.0	+4.4	74.0	43 09.1	+5.8	74.9	43 24.3	+7.1	75.8	25
26	42 39.1	+2.1	71.7	42 57.4	+3.5	72.6	43 14.9	+4.8	73.5	43 31.4	+6.2	74.4	26
27	42 41.2	+1.1	70.4	43 00.9	+2.5	71.3	43 19.7	+3.9	72.2	43 37.6	+5.3	73.1	27
28	42 42.3	+0.2	69.0	43 03.4	+1.5	69.9	43 23.6	+2.8	70.8	43 42.9	+4.2	71.7	28
29	42 42.5	−0.8	67.7	43 04.9	+0.5	68.5	43 26.4	+1.9	69.4	43 47.1	+3.2	70.3	29
30	42 41.7	−1.7	66.3	43 05.4	−0.4	67.2	43 28.3	+0.9	68.0	43 50.3	+2.2	68.9	30
31	42 40.0	−2.8	64.9	43 05.0	−1.5	65.8	43 29.2	−0.2	66.7	43 52.5	+1.2	67.5	31
32	42 37.2	−3.6	63.6	43 03.5	−2.4	64.4	43 29.0	−1.1	65.3	43 53.7	+0.2	66.1	32
33	42 33.6	−4.7	62.2	43 01.1	−3.3	63.1	43 27.9	−2.1	63.9	43 53.9	−0.8	64.8	33
34	42 28.9	−5.6	60.9	42 57.8	−4.4	61.7	43 25.8	−3.1	62.5	43 53.1	−1.8	63.4	34
35	42 23.3	−6.5	59.5	42 53.4	−5.3	60.3	43 22.7	−4.0	61.1	43 51.3	−2.8	62.0	35
36	42 16.8	−7.5	58.2	42 48.1	−6.3	59.0	43 18.7	−5.1	59.8	43 48.5	−3.8	60.6	36
37	42 09.3	−8.4	56.8	42 41.8	−7.2	57.6	43 13.6	−6.0	58.4	43 44.7	−4.8	59.2	37
38	42 00.9	−9.3	55.5	42 34.6	−8.2	56.3	43 07.6	−7.0	57.0	43 39.9	−5.8	57.8	38
39	41 51.6	−10.2	54.2	42 26.4	−9.1	54.9	43 00.6	−8.0	55.7	43 34.1	−6.8	56.5	39
40	41 41.4	−11.2	52.9	42 17.3	−10.1	53.6	42 52.6	−8.9	54.3	43 27.3	−7.8	55.1	40
41	41 30.2	−12.0	51.6	42 07.2	−10.9	52.3	42 43.7	−9.9	53.0	43 19.5	−8.7	53.7	41
42	41 18.2	−12.9	50.2	41 56.3	−11.9	50.9	42 33.8	−10.8	51.6	43 10.8	−9.7	52.4	42
43	41 05.3	−13.8	48.9	41 44.4	−12.7	49.6	42 23.0	−11.7	50.3	43 01.1	−10.7	51.0	43
44	40 51.5	−14.6	47.7	41 31.7	−13.7	48.3	42 11.3	−12.6	49.0	42 50.4	−11.6	49.7	44
45	40 36.9	−15.5	46.4	41 18.0	−14.5	47.0	41 58.7	−13.5	47.7	42 38.8	−12.5	48.3	45
46	40 21.4	−16.3	45.1	41 03.5	−15.4	45.7	41 45.2	−14.5	46.4	42 26.3	−13.4	47.0	46
47	40 05.1	−17.1	43.8	40 48.1	−16.0	44.4	41 30.7	−15.2	45.1	42 12.9	−14.3	45.7	47
48	39 48.0	−18.0	42.6	40 31.9	−17.0	43.2	41 15.5	−16.2	43.8	41 58.6	−15.2	44.4	48
49	39 30.0	−18.7	41.4	40 14.9	−17.9	41.9	40 59.3	−16.9	42.5	41 43.4	−16.1	43.1	49
50	39 11.3	−19.4	40.1	39 57.0	−18.6	40.7	40 42.4	−17.8	41.3	41 27.3	−16.9	41.8	50
51	38 51.9	−20.2	38.9	39 38.4	−19.4	39.4	40 24.6	−18.7	40.0	41 10.4	−17.8	40.5	51
52	38 31.7	−21.0	37.7	39 19.0	−20.2	38.2	40 05.9	−19.4	38.7	40 52.6	−18.6	39.3	52
53	38 10.7	−21.7	36.5	38 58.8	−21.0	37.0	39 46.5	−20.1	37.5	40 34.0	−19.4	38.0	53
54	37 49.0	−22.4	35.3	38 37.8	−21.6	35.8	39 26.4	−21.0	36.3	40 14.6	−20.2	36.8	54
55	37 26.6	−23.0	34.2	38 16.2	−22.4	34.6	39 05.4	−21.7	35.1	39 54.4	−21.0	35.5	55
56	37 03.6	−23.8	33.0	37 53.8	−23.1	33.4	38 43.7	−22.4	33.9	39 33.4	−21.7	34.3	56
57	36 39.8	−24.3	31.8	37 30.7	−23.8	32.2	38 21.3	−23.1	32.7	39 11.7	−22.4	33.1	57
58	36 15.5	−25.1	30.7	37 06.9	−24.4	31.1	37 58.2	−23.8	31.5	38 49.3	−23.2	31.9	58
59	35 50.4	−25.6	29.6	36 42.5	−25.1	30.0	37 34.4	−24.5	30.3	38 26.1	−23.9	30.7	59
60	35 24.8	−26.3	28.5	36 17.4	−25.7	28.8	37 09.9	−25.1	29.2	38 02.2	−24.6	29.6	60
61	34 58.5	−26.8	27.4	35 51.7	−26.3	27.7	36 44.8	−25.8	28.0	37 37.6	−25.2	28.4	61
62	34 31.7	−27.4	26.3	35 25.4	−26.9	26.6	36 19.0	−26.4	26.9	37 12.4	−25.9	27.3	62
63	34 04.3	−28.0	25.2	34 58.5	−27.5	25.5	35 52.6	−27.0	25.8	36 46.5	−26.5	26.1	63
64	33 36.3	−28.5	24.1	34 31.0	−28.1	24.4	35 25.6	−27.6	24.7	36 20.0	−27.1	25.0	64
65	33 07.8	−29.1	23.1	34 02.9	−28.6	23.4	34 58.0	−28.2	23.6	35 52.9	−27.8	23.9	65
66	32 38.7	−29.5	22.0	33 34.3	−29.1	22.3	34 29.8	−28.8	22.6	35 25.1	−28.3	22.8	66
67	32 09.2	−30.1	21.0	33 05.2	−29.7	21.2	34 01.0	−29.2	21.5	34 56.8	−28.9	21.7	67
68	31 39.1	−30.5	20.0	32 35.5	−30.2	20.2	33 31.8	−29.9	20.4	34 27.9	−29.4	20.7	68
69	31 08.6	−31.0	19.0	32 05.3	−30.6	19.2	33 01.9	−30.3	19.4	33 58.5	−30.0	19.6	69
70	30 37.6	−31.4	18.0	31 34.7	−31.2	18.2	32 31.6	−30.8	18.4	33 28.5	−30.4	18.6	70
71	30 06.2	−31.9	17.0	31 03.5	−31.6	17.2	32 00.8	−31.3	17.4	32 58.1	−31.0	17.6	71
72	29 34.3	−32.3	16.0	30 31.9	−32.0	16.2	31 29.5	−31.7	16.4	32 27.1	−31.5	16.5	72
73	29 02.0	−32.7	15.1	29 59.9	−32.5	15.2	30 57.8	−32.2	15.4	31 55.6	−31.9	15.5	73
74	28 29.3	−33.2	14.1	29 27.4	−32.8	14.2	30 25.6	−32.7	14.4	31 23.7	−32.4	14.5	74
75	27 56.1	−33.5	13.2	28 54.6	−33.3	13.3	29 52.9	−33.0	13.4	30 51.3	−32.9	13.6	75
76	27 22.6	−33.8	12.2	28 21.3	−33.7	12.3	29 19.9	−33.5	12.5	30 18.4	−33.2	12.6	76
77	26 48.8	−34.3	11.3	27 47.6	−34.1	11.4	28 46.4	−33.9	11.5	29 45.2	−33.7	11.6	77
78	26 14.5	−34.5	10.4	27 13.5	−34.4	10.5	28 12.5	−34.2	10.6	29 11.5	−34.1	10.7	78
79	25 40.0	−35.0	9.5	26 39.1	−34.7	9.6	27 38.3	−34.6	9.6	28 37.4	−34.4	9.7	79
80	25 05.0	−35.2	8.6	26 04.4	−35.1	8.6	27 03.7	−35.0	8.7	28 03.0	−34.8	8.8	80
81	24 29.8	−35.5	7.7	25 29.3	−35.5	7.7	26 28.7	−35.3	7.8	27 28.2	−35.2	7.9	81
82	23 54.3	−35.9	6.8	24 53.8	−35.7	6.8	25 53.4	−35.6	6.9	26 53.0	−35.6	7.0	82
83	23 18.4	−36.1	5.9	24 18.1	−36.0	6.0	25 17.8	−36.0	6.0	26 17.4	−35.8	6.1	83
84	22 42.3	−36.4	5.1	23 42.1	−36.4	5.1	24 41.8	−36.3	5.1	25 41.6	−36.2	5.2	84
85	22 05.9	−36.7	4.2	23 05.7	−36.6	4.2	24 05.5	−36.5	4.3	25 05.4	−36.5	4.3	85
86	21 29.2	−36.9	3.3	22 29.1	−36.9	3.4	23 29.0	−36.8	3.4	24 28.9	−36.8	3.4	86
87	20 52.3	−37.2	2.5	21 52.2	−37.2	2.5	22 52.1	−37.1	2.5	23 52.1	−37.1	2.5	87
88	20 15.1	−37.5	1.7	21 15.0	−37.4	1.7	22 15.0	−37.4	1.7	23 15.0	−37.4	1.7	88
89	19 37.6	−37.6	0.8	20 37.6	−37.6	0.8	21 37.6	−37.6	0.8	22 37.6	−37.6	0.8	89
90	19 00.0	−37.9	0.0	20 00.0	−37.9	0.0	21 00.0	−37.9	0.0	22 00.0	−37.9	0.0	90
	19°			20°			21°			22°			

51°, 309° L.H.A. LATITUDE **SAME** NAME AS DECLINATION

104

LATITUDE **CONTRARY** NAME TO DECLINATION L.H.A. 51°, 309°

Dec.	15° Hc	d	Z	16° Hc	d	Z	17° Hc	d	Z	18° Hc	d	Z	19° Hc	d	Z	20° Hc	d	Z	21° Hc	d	Z	22° Hc	d	Z	Dec.
°	° ′	′	°	° ′	′	°	° ′	′	°	° ′	′	°	° ′	′	°	° ′	′	°	° ′	′	°	° ′	′	°	°
0	37 26.2	-19.9	101.8	37 13.5	-21.1	102.6	37 00.0	-22.3	103.3	36 45.8	-23.4	104.0	36 30.9	-24.6	104.8	36 15.2	-25.7	105.5	35 58.9	-26.9	106.2	35 41.8	-28.0	106.9	0
1	37 06.3	-20.7	103.0	36 52.4	-21.8	103.8	36 37.7	-22.9	104.5	36 22.4	-24.2	105.2	36 06.3	-25.3	105.9	35 49.5	-26.4	106.6	35 32.0	-27.5	107.3	35 13.8	-28.5	108.0	1
2	36 45.6	-21.3	104.2	36 30.6	-22.5	104.9	36 14.8	-23.7	105.6	35 58.2	-24.7	106.3	35 41.0	-25.9	107.0	35 23.1	-27.0	107.7	35 04.5	-28.0	108.4	34 45.3	-29.1	109.0	2
3	36 24.3	-21.9	105.4	36 08.1	-23.1	106.1	35 51.1	-24.2	106.8	35 33.5	-25.4	107.5	35 15.1	-26.4	108.1	34 56.1	-27.5	108.8	34 36.5	-28.6	109.5	34 16.2	-29.7	110.1	3
4	36 02.4	-22.7	106.5	35 45.0	-23.8	107.2	35 26.9	-24.9	107.9	35 08.1	-26.0	108.6	34 48.7	-27.1	109.2	34 28.6	-28.1	109.9	34 07.9	-29.2	110.5	33 46.5	-30.1	111.1	4
5	35 39.7	-23.2	107.7	35 21.2	-24.4	108.3	35 02.0	-25.5	109.0	34 42.1	-26.5	109.7	34 21.6	-27.6	110.3	34 00.5	-28.7	110.9	33 38.7	-29.7	111.6	33 16.4	-30.7	112.2	5
6	35 16.5	-23.9	108.8	34 56.8	-25.0	109.5	34 36.5	-26.1	110.1	34 15.6	-27.2	110.7	33 54.0	-28.2	111.4	33 31.8	-29.2	112.0	33 09.0	-30.2	112.6	32 45.7	-31.2	113.2	6
7	34 52.6	-24.5	109.9	34 31.8	-25.6	110.6	34 10.4	-26.6	111.2	33 48.4	-27.7	111.8	33 25.8	-28.7	112.4	33 02.6	-29.7	113.0	32 38.8	-30.6	113.6	32 14.5	-31.7	114.2	7
8	34 28.1	-25.1	111.0	34 06.2	-26.1	111.7	33 43.8	-27.2	112.3	33 20.7	-28.2	112.9	32 57.1	-29.2	113.5	32 32.9	-30.2	114.1	32 08.2	-31.2	114.7	31 42.8	-32.1	115.2	8
9	34 03.0	-25.7	112.1	33 40.1	-26.8	112.7	33 16.6	-27.8	113.3	32 52.5	-28.7	113.9	32 27.9	-29.8	114.5	32 02.7	-30.7	115.1	31 37.0	-31.7	115.7	31 10.7	-32.5	116.2	9
10	33 37.3	-26.3	113.2	33 13.3	-27.2	113.8	32 48.8	-28.3	114.4	32 23.8	-29.3	115.0	31 58.1	-30.2	115.6	31 32.0	-31.2	116.1	31 05.3	-32.1	116.7	30 38.2	-33.0	117.2	10
11	33 11.0	-26.8	114.3	32 46.1	-27.8	114.9	32 20.5	-28.7	115.5	31 54.5	-29.8	116.0	31 27.9	-30.7	116.6	31 00.8	-31.6	117.1	30 33.2	-32.5	117.6	30 05.2	-33.5	118.2	11
12	32 44.2	-27.3	115.4	32 18.3	-28.4	115.9	31 51.8	-29.3	116.5	31 24.7	-30.2	117.0	30 57.2	-31.2	117.6	30 29.2	-32.1	118.1	30 00.7	-33.0	118.6	29 31.7	-33.8	119.1	12
13	32 16.9	-27.9	116.4	31 49.9	-28.8	117.0	31 22.5	-29.8	117.5	30 54.5	-30.7	118.0	30 26.0	-31.6	118.6	29 57.1	-32.5	119.1	29 27.7	-33.3	119.6	28 57.9	-34.2	120.1	13
14	31 49.0	-28.4	117.5	31 21.1	-29.3	118.0	30 52.7	-30.3	118.5	30 23.8	-31.2	119.0	29 54.4	-32.0	119.6	29 24.6	-32.9	120.0	28 54.4	-33.8	120.5	28 23.7	-34.6	121.0	14
15	31 20.6	-28.8	118.5	30 51.8	-29.8	119.0	30 22.4	-30.7	119.5	29 52.6	-31.5	120.0	29 22.4	-32.5	120.5	28 51.7	-33.3	121.0	28 20.6	-34.2	121.5	27 49.1	-35.0	121.9	15
16	30 51.8	-29.4	119.5	30 22.0	-30.3	120.0	29 51.7	-31.1	120.5	29 21.1	-32.1	121.0	28 49.9	-32.8	121.5	28 18.4	-33.7	122.0	27 46.4	-34.5	122.4	27 14.1	-35.3	122.8	16
17	30 22.4	-29.8	120.5	29 51.7	-30.6	121.0	29 20.6	-31.6	121.5	28 49.0	-32.4	122.0	28 17.1	-33.3	122.4	27 44.7	-34.1	122.9	27 11.9	-34.9	123.3	26 38.8	-35.7	123.7	17
18	29 52.6	-30.2	121.5	29 21.1	-31.2	122.0	28 49.0	-31.9	122.5	28 16.6	-32.8	122.9	27 43.8	-33.6	123.4	27 10.6	-34.4	123.8	26 37.0	-35.2	124.2	26 03.1	-36.0	124.6	18
19	29 22.4	-30.7	122.5	28 49.9	-31.5	123.0	28 17.1	-32.4	123.4	27 43.8	-33.2	123.9	27 10.2	-34.0	124.3	26 36.2	-34.8	124.7	26 01.8	-35.6	125.1	25 27.1	-36.3	125.5	19
20	28 51.7	-31.1	123.5	28 18.4	-32.0	124.0	27 44.7	-32.8	124.4	27 10.6	-33.6	124.8	26 36.2	-34.4	125.2	26 01.4	-35.2	125.6	25 26.2	-35.9	126.0	24 50.8	-36.7	126.4	20
21	28 20.6	-31.5	124.5	27 46.4	-32.3	124.9	27 11.9	-33.1	125.3	26 37.0	-33.9	125.8	26 01.8	-34.7	126.2	25 26.2	-35.4	126.5	24 50.3	-36.2	126.9	24 14.1	-36.9	127.3	21
22	27 49.1	-32.0	125.4	27 14.1	-32.7	125.9	26 38.8	-33.6	126.3	26 03.1	-34.3	126.7	25 27.1	-35.0	127.1	24 50.8	-35.8	127.4	24 14.1	-36.4	127.8	23 37.2	-37.2	128.1	22
23	27 17.1	-32.3	126.4	26 41.4	-33.1	126.8	26 05.2	-33.8	127.2	25 28.8	-34.6	127.6	24 52.1	-35.4	128.0	24 15.0	-36.1	128.3	23 37.7	-36.8	128.7	23 00.0	-37.4	129.0	23
24	26 44.8	-32.7	127.3	26 08.3	-33.5	127.7	25 31.4	-34.2	128.1	24 54.2	-34.9	128.5	24 16.7	-35.7	128.8	23 38.9	-36.3	129.2	23 00.9	-37.1	129.5	22 22.6	-37.8	129.8	24
25	26 12.1	-33.0	128.3	25 34.8	-33.8	128.7	24 57.2	-34.5	129.0	24 19.3	-35.3	129.4	23 41.0	-35.9	129.7	23 02.6	-36.7	130.1	22 23.8	-37.3	130.4	21 44.8	-38.0	130.7	25
26	25 39.1	-33.4	129.2	25 01.0	-34.1	129.6	24 22.7	-34.9	129.9	23 44.0	-35.5	130.3	23 05.1	-36.2	130.6	22 25.9	-36.9	130.9	21 46.5	-37.6	131.2	21 06.8	-38.2	131.5	26
27	25 05.7	-33.7	130.1	24 26.9	-34.5	130.5	23 47.8	-35.1	130.8	23 08.5	-35.9	131.1	22 28.9	-36.6	131.5	21 49.0	-37.2	131.8	21 08.9	-37.8	132.1	20 28.6	-38.4	132.3	27
28	24 32.0	-34.1	131.0	23 52.4	-34.7	131.4	23 12.7	-35.5	131.7	22 32.6	-36.1	132.0	21 52.3	-36.7	132.3	21 11.8	-37.4	132.6	20 31.1	-38.1	132.9	19 50.2	-38.7	133.2	28
29	23 57.9	-34.4	131.9	23 17.7	-35.1	132.3	22 37.2	-35.7	132.6	21 56.5	-36.4	132.9	21 15.6	-37.1	133.2	20 34.4	-37.7	133.4	19 53.0	-38.2	133.7	19 11.5	-38.9	134.0	29
30	23 23.5	-34.6	132.8	22 42.6	-35.3	133.1	22 01.5	-36.0	133.4	21 20.1	-36.6	133.7	20 38.5	-37.2	134.0	19 56.7	-37.9	134.3	19 14.8	-38.5	134.5	18 32.6	-39.1	134.8	30
31	22 48.9	-35.0	133.7	22 07.3	-35.6	134.0	21 25.5	-36.3	134.3	20 43.5	-36.9	134.6	20 01.3	-37.5	134.8	19 18.8	-38.1	135.1	18 36.3	-38.7	135.3	17 53.5	-39.3	135.6	31
32	22 13.9	-35.2	134.6	21 31.7	-35.9	134.9	20 49.2	-36.5	135.2	20 06.6	-37.1	135.4	19 23.8	-37.8	135.7	18 40.7	-38.3	135.9	17 57.6	-38.9	136.1	17 14.2	-39.5	136.4	32
33	21 38.7	-35.6	135.5	20 55.8	-36.2	135.7	20 12.7	-36.7	136.0	19 29.5	-37.4	136.3	18 46.0	-37.9	136.5	18 02.4	-38.5	136.7	17 18.7	-39.1	136.9	16 34.7	-39.6	137.2	33
34	21 03.1	-35.7	136.3	20 19.6	-36.3	136.6	19 36.0	-37.0	136.9	18 52.1	-37.6	137.1	18 08.1	-38.2	137.3	17 23.9	-38.7	137.5	16 39.6	-39.3	137.7	15 55.1	-39.8	137.9	34
35	20 27.4	-36.1	137.2	19 43.3	-36.7	137.4	18 59.0	-37.2	137.7	18 14.5	-37.8	137.9	17 29.9	-38.3	138.1	16 45.2	-38.9	138.3	16 00.3	-39.5	138.5	15 15.3	-40.0	138.7	35
36	19 51.3	-36.2	138.1	19 06.6	-36.8	138.3	18 21.8	-37.5	138.5	17 36.7	-37.9	138.7	16 51.6	-38.6	138.9	16 06.3	-39.1	139.1	15 20.8	-39.6	139.3	14 35.3	-40.1	139.5	36
37	19 15.1	-36.5	138.9	18 29.8	-37.1	139.1	17 44.3	-37.6	139.3	16 58.8	-38.2	139.5	16 13.0	-38.7	139.7	15 27.2	-39.2	139.9	14 41.2	-39.7	140.1	13 55.2	-40.3	140.3	37
38	18 38.6	-36.7	139.7	17 52.7	-37.3	139.9	17 06.7	-37.8	140.2	16 20.6	-38.4	140.3	15 34.3	-38.8	140.5	14 48.0	-39.4	140.7	14 01.5	-39.9	140.9	13 14.9	-40.4	141.0	38
39	18 01.9	-37.0	140.6	17 15.4	-37.4	140.8	16 28.9	-38.0	141.0	15 42.2	-38.5	141.1	14 55.5	-39.1	141.3	14 08.6	-39.6	141.5	13 21.6	-40.1	141.6	12 34.5	-40.5	141.8	39
40	17 24.9	-37.1	141.4	16 38.0	-37.7	141.6	15 50.9	-38.2	141.8	15 03.7	-38.7	141.9	14 16.4	-39.2	142.1	13 29.0	-39.7	142.3	12 41.5	-40.1	142.4	11 54.0	-40.7	142.5	40
41	16 47.8	-37.4	142.2	16 00.3	-37.8	142.4	15 12.7	-38.3	142.6	14 25.0	-38.8	142.7	13 37.2	-39.3	142.9	12 49.3	-39.8	143.0	12 01.4	-40.3	143.2	11 13.3	-40.8	143.3	41
42	16 10.4	-37.5	143.0	15 22.5	-38.1	143.2	14 34.4	-38.6	143.4	13 46.2	-39.0	143.5	12 57.9	-39.5	143.7	12 09.5	-39.9	143.8	11 21.1	-40.5	143.9	10 32.5	-40.8	144.0	42
43	15 32.9	-37.7	143.8	14 44.4	-38.2	144.0	13 55.8	-38.6	144.2	13 07.2	-39.2	144.3	12 18.4	-39.6	144.4	11 29.6	-40.1	144.5	10 40.6	-40.5	144.7	9 51.7	-41.0	144.8	43
44	14 55.2	-37.8	144.7	14 06.2	-38.3	144.8	13 17.2	-38.8	144.9	12 28.0	-39.3	145.1	11 38.8	-39.7	145.2	10 49.5	-40.2	145.3	10 00.1	-40.6	145.4	9 10.7	-41.1	145.5	44
45	14 17.4	-38.1	145.5	13 27.9	-38.5	145.6	12 38.4	-39.0	145.7	11 48.7	-39.3	145.8	10 59.1	-39.9	146.0	10 09.3	-40.3	146.1	9 19.5	-40.7	146.2	8 29.6	-41.1	146.2	45
46	13 39.3	-38.1	146.3	12 49.4	-38.6	146.4	11 59.4	-39.1	146.5	11 09.4	-39.6	146.6	10 19.2	-39.9	146.7	9 29.0	-40.3	146.8	8 38.8	-40.8	146.9	7 48.5	-41.2	147.0	46
47	13 01.2	-38.3	147.0	12 10.8	-38.8	147.2	11 20.3	-39.2	147.3	10 29.8	-39.6	147.4	9 39.3	-40.1	147.5	8 48.7	-40.5	147.6	7 58.0	-40.9	147.6	7 07.3	-41.3	147.7	47
48	12 22.9	-38.5	147.8	11 32.0	-38.9	147.9	10 41.1	-39.3	148.0	9 50.2	-39.7	148.1	8 59.2	-40.1	148.2	8 08.2	-40.6	148.3	7 17.1	-40.9	148.4	6 26.0	-41.3	148.4	48
49	11 44.4	-38.6	148.6	10 53.1	-39.0	148.7	10 01.8	-39.4	148.8	9 10.5	-39.8	148.9	8 19.1	-40.2	149.0	7 27.6	-40.6	149.1	6 36.2	-41.0	149.1	5 44.7	-41.4	149.2	49
50	11 05.8	-38.7	149.4	10 14.1	-39.1	149.5	9 22.4	-39.5	149.6	8 30.7	-39.9	149.7	7 38.9	-40.3	149.7	6 47.0	-40.7	149.8	5 55.2	-41.1	149.9	5 03.3	-41.5	149.9	50
51	10 27.1	-38.8	150.2	9 35.0	-39.2	150.3	8 42.9	-39.6	150.3	7 50.8	-40.0	150.4	6 58.6	-40.4	150.5	6 06.3	-40.7	150.5	5 14.1	-41.1	150.6	4 21.8	-41.5	150.6	51
52	9 48.3	-38.9	151.0	8 55.8	-39.3	151.0	8 03.3	-39.7	151.1	7 10.8	-40.1	151.2	6 18.2	-40.4	151.2	5 25.6	-40.8	151.3	4 33.0	-41.2	151.3	3 40.3	-41.5	151.4	52
53	9 09.4	-39.0	151.7	8 16.5	-39.4	151.8	7 23.6	-39.7	151.9	6 30.7	-40.1	151.9	5 37.8	-40.5	152.0	4 44.8	-40.9	152.0	3 51.8	-41.2	152.0	2 58.8	-41.6	152.1	53
54	8 30.4	-39.2	152.5	7 37.1	-39.4	152.6	6 43.9	-39.9	152.6	5 50.6	-40.2	152.7	4 57.3	-40.6	152.7	4 03.9	-40.9	152.7	3 10.6	-41.3	152.8	2 17.2	-41.6	152.8	54
55	7 51.2	-39.1	153.3	6 57.7	-39.6	153.3	6 04.0	-39.9	153.4	5 10.4	-40.3	153.4	4 16.7	-40.6	153.4	3 23.0	-40.9	153.5	2 29.3	-41.2	153.5	1 35.6	-41.5	153.5	55
56	7 12.1	-39.3	154.0	6 18.1	-39.6	154.1	5 24.1	-39.9	154.1	4 30.1	-40.2	154.2	3 36.1	-40.6	154.2	2 42.1	-40.9	154.2	1 48.1	-41.3	154.2	0 54.1	-41.6	154.2	56
57	6 32.8	-39.3	154.8	5 38.5	-39.7	154.8	4 44.2	-40.0	154.9	3 49.9	-40.4	154.9	2 55.5	-40.6	154.9	2 01.2	-41.0	154.9	1 06.8	-41.3	155.0	0 12.5	-41.6	155.0	57
58	5 53.5	-39.4	155.5	4 58.8	-39.7	155.6	4 04.2	-40.1	155.6	3 09.5	-40.3	155.6	2 14.9	-40.7	155.7	1 20.2	-41.0	155.7	0 25.5	-41.3	155.7	0 29.1	+41.6	24.3	58
59	5 14.1	-39.5	156.3	4 19.1	-39.8	156.3	3 24.1	-40.0	156.4	2 29.2	-40.4	156.4	1 34.2	-40.7	156.4	0 39.2	-41.0	156.4	0 15.8	+41.3	23.6	1 10.7	+41.6	23.6	59
60	4 34.6	-39.5	157.1	3 39.3	-39.8	157.1	2 44.1	-40.1	157.1	1 48.8	-40.4	157.1	0 53.5	-40.7	157.1	0 01.8	+41.0	22.9	0 57.1	+41.2	22.9	1 52.3	+41.6	22.9	60
61	3 55.1	-39.5	157.8	2 59.5	-39.8	157.8	2 04.0	-40.1	157.9	1 08.4	-40.4	157.9	0 12.8	-40.7	157.9	0 42.8	+40.9	22.1	1 38.3	+41.3	22.1	2 33.9	+41.5	22.2	61
62	3 15.6	-39.6	158.6	2 19.7	-39.8	158.6	1 23.9	-40.2	158.6	0 28.0	-40.4	158.6	0 27.9	+40.7	21.4	1 23.7	+41.0	21.4	2 19.6	+41.2	21.4	3 15.4	+41.6	21.4	62
63	2 36.0	-39.6	159.3	1 39.9	-39.9	159.3	0 43.7	-40.1	159.3	0 12.4	+40.4	20.7	1 08.6	+40.6	20.7	2 04.7	+41.0	20.7	3 00.8	+41.2	20.7	3 57.0	+41.4	20.7	63
64	1 56.4	-39.6	160.1	1 00.0	-39.9	160.1	0 03.6	-40.2	160.1	0 52.8	+40.4	19.9	1 49.2	+40.7	19.9	2 45.7	+40.9	19.9	3 42.0	+41.2	20.0	4 38.4	+41.5	20.0	64
65	1 16.8	-39.7	160.8	0 20.1	-39.9	160.8	0 36.6	+40.1	19.2	1 33.2	+40.4	19.2	2 29.9	+40.6	19.2	3 26.6	+40.9	19.2	4 23.2	+41.2	19.2	5 19.9	+41.4	19.3	65
66	0 37.1	-39.6	161.6	0 19.8	+39.9	18.4	1 16.7	+40.1	18.4	2 13.6	+40.4	18.4	3 10.5	+40.7	18.5	4 07.5	+40.8	18.5	5 04.4	+41.0	18.5	6 01.3	+41.3	18.5	66
67	0 02.5	+39.6	17.7	0 59.7	+39.8	17.7	1 56.8	+40.1	17.7	2 54.0	+40.3	17.7	3 51.2	+40.5	17.7	4 48.3	+40.8	17.7	5 45.4	+41.1	17.8	6 42.6	+41.2	17.8	67
68	0 42.1	+39.7	16.9	1 39.5	+39.9	16.9	2 36.9	+40.1	16.9	3 34.3	+40.3	17.0	4 31.7	+40.5	17.0	5 29.1	+40.7	17.0	6 26.5	+40.9	17.0	7 23.8	+41.2	17.1	68
69	1 21.8	+39.6	16.2	2 19.4	+39.8	16.2	3 17.0	+40.1	16.2	4 14.6	+40.3	16.2	5 12.2	+40.5	16.2	6 09.8	+40.7	16.3	7 07.4	+40.9	16.3	8 05.0	+41.1	16.3	69
70	2 01.4	+39.6	15.4	2 59.2	+39.8	15.4	3 57.1	+40.0	15.5	4 54.9	+40.2	15.5	5 52.7	+40.4	15.5	6 50.5	+40.6	15.5	7 48.3	+40.9	15.6	8 46.1	+41.1	15.6	70
71	2 41.0	+39.6	14.7	3 39.0	+39.8	14.7	4 37.1	+39.9	14.7	5 35.1	+40.2	14.7	6 33.1	+40.4	14.8	7 31.1	+40.6	14.8	8 29.2	+40.7	14.8	9 27.2	+40.9	14.9	71
72	3 20.6	+39.5	13.9	4 18.8	+39.7	13.9	5 17.0	+39.9	14.0	6 15.3	+40.0	14.0	7 13.5	+40.2	14.0	8 11.7	+40.4	14.0	9 09.9	+40.6	14.1	10 08.1	+40.8	14.1	72
73	4 00.1	+39.5	13.2	4 58.5	+39.7	13.2	5 56.9	+39.9	13.2	6 55.3	+40.1	13.2	7 53.7	+40.2	13.3	8 52.1	+40.4	13.3	9 50.5	+40.6	13.3	10 48.9	+40.7	13.4	73
74	4 39.6	+39.4	12.4	5 38.2	+39.6	12.4	6 36.8	+39.8	12.5	7 35.4	+39.9	12.5	8 33.9	+40.1	12.5	9 32.5	+40.3	12.5	10 31.1	+40.4	12.6	11 29.6	+40.6	12.6	74
75	5 19.0	+39.4	11.7	6 17.8	+39.5	11.7	7 16.6	+39.7	11.7	8 15.3	+39.9	11.7	9 14.0	+40.1	11.8	10 12.8	+40.2	11.8	11 11.5	+40.3	11.8	12 10.2	+40.5	11.9	75
76	5 58.4	+39.4	10.9	6 57.3	+39.5	10.9	7 56.3	+39.6	10.9	8 55.2	+39.7	11.0	9 54.1	+39.9	11.0	10 53.0	+40.0	11.0	11 51.8	+40.2	11.1	12 50.7	+40.4	11.1	76
77	6 37.8	+39.2	10.1	7 36.8	+39.4	10.2	8 35.9	+39.5	10.2	9 34.9	+39.7	10.2	10 34.0	+39.8	10.2	11 33.0	+39.9	10.3	12 32.0	+40.1	10.3	13 31.1	+40.2	10.4	77
78	7 17.0	+39.2	9.4	8 16.2	+39.3	9.4	9 15.4	+39.4	9.4	10 14.6	+39.5	9.5	11 13.8	+39.7	9.5	12 12.9	+39.9	9.5	13 12.1	+40.0	9.6	14 11.3	+40.1	9.6	78
79	7 56.2	+39.1	8.6	8 55.5	+39.2	8.6	9 54.8	+39.4	8.7	10 54.1	+39.5	8.7	11 53.5	+39.5	8.7	12 52.8	+39.6	8.7	13 52.1	+39.8	8.8	14 51.4	+39.9	8.8	79
80	8 35.3	+39.0	7.8	9 34.7	+39.1	7.9	10 34.2	+39.2	7.9	11 33.6	+39.3	7.9	12 33.0	+39.4	7.9	13 32.4	+39.6	8.0	14 31.9	+39.6	8.0	15 31.3	+39.7	8.1	80
81	9 14.3	+38.9	7.1	10 13.8	+39.0	7.1	11 13.4	+39.1	7.1	12 12.9	+39.2	7.1	13 12.4	+39.3	7.2	14 12.0	+39.4	7.2	15 11.5	+39.5	7.2	16 11.0	+39.6	7.3	81
82	9 53.2	+38.8	6.3	10 52.8	+38.9	6.3	11 52.5	+38.9	6.3	12 52.1	+39.1	6.4	13 51.7	+39.2	6.4	14 51.4	+39.2	6.4	15 51.0	+39.3	6.5	16 50.6	+39.4	6.5	82
83	10 32.0	+38.7	5.5	11 31.7	+38.8	5.5	12 31.4	+38.9	5.6	13 31.2	+38.9	5.6	14 30.9	+39.0	5.6	15 30.6	+39.0	5.6	16 30.3	+39.1	5.7	17 30.0	+39.2	5.7	83
84	11 10.7	+38.6	4.7	12 10.5	+38.6	4.8	13 10.3	+38.7	4.8	14 10.1	+38.7	4.8	15 09.9	+38.8	4.8	16 09.6	+38.9	4.9	17 09.4	+39.0	4.9	18 09.2	+39.0	4.9	84
85	11 49.3	+38.4	4.0	12 49.1	+38.5	4.0	13 49.0	+38.5	4.0	14 48.8	+38.6	4.0	15 48.7	+38.6	4.0	16 48.5	+38.7	4.1	17 48.4	+38.7	4.1	18 48.2	+38.8	4.1	85
86	12 27.7	+38.3	3.2	13 27.6	+38.3	3.2	14 27.5	+38.4	3.2	15 27.4	+38.4	3.2	16 27.3	+38.5	3.2	17 27.2	+38.5	3.3	18 27.1	+38.6	3.3	19 27.0	+38.6	3.3	86
87	13 06.0	+38.2	2.4	14 05.9	+38.2	2.4	15 05.9	+38.2	2.4	16 05.8	+38.3	2.4	17 05.8	+38.3	2.4	18 05.7	+38.3	2.5	19 05.7	+38.3	2.5	20 05.6	+38.4	2.5	87
88	13 44.2	+38.0	1.6	14 44.1	+38.1	1.6	15 44.1	+38.0	1.6	16 44.1	+38.0	1.6	17 44.1	+38.0	1.6	18 44.0	+38.1	1.6	19 44.0	+38.1	1.7	20 44.0	+38.1	1.7	88
89	14 22.2	+37.8	0.8	15 22.2	+37.8	0.8	16 22.1	+37.9	0.8	17 22.1	+37.9	0.8	18 22.1	+37.9	0.8	19 22.1	+37.9	0.8	20 22.1	+37.9	0.8	21 22.1	+37.9	0.8	89
90	15 00.0	+37.7	0.0	16 00.0	+37.7	0.0	17 00.0	+37.7	0.0	18 00.0	+37.7	0.0	19 00.0	+37.6	0.0	20 00.0	+37.6	0.0	21 00.0	+37.6	0.0	22 00.0	+37.6	0.0	90
	15°			16°			17°			18°			19°			20°			21°			22°			

S. Lat. {L.H.A. greater than 180° ....Zn=180°–Z; L.H.A. less than 180°...........Zn=180°+Z}

LATITUDE **SAME** NAME AS DECLINATION L.H.A. 129°, 231°

105

52°, 308° L.H.A. LATITUDE SAME NAME AS DECLINATION

N. Lat. {L.H.A. greater than 180° .....Zn=Z; L.H.A. less than 180°............Zn=360°−Z}

Dec.	15° Hc	d	Z	16° Hc	d	Z	17° Hc	d	Z	18° Hc	d	Z	19° Hc	d	Z	20° Hc	d	Z	21° Hc	d	Z	22° Hc	d	Z	Dec.
°	° ′	′	°	° ′	′	°	° ′	′	°	° ′	′	°	° ′	′	°	° ′	′	°	° ′	′	°	° ′	′	°	°
0	36 29.4	+19.0	101.4	36 17.1	+20.2	102.2	36 04.1	+21.4	102.9	35 50.4	+22.6	103.6	35 36.0	+23.7	104.3	35 20.8	+24.9	105.0	35 05.0	+26.0	105.6	34 48.5	+27.1	106.3	0
1	36 48.4	+18.2	100.2	36 37.3	+19.5	101.0	36 25.5	+20.7	101.7	36 13.0	+21.9	102.4	35 59.7	+23.1	103.1	35 45.7	+24.2	103.8	35 31.0	+25.4	104.5	35 15.6	+26.5	105.2	1
2	37 06.6	+17.6	99.1	36 56.8	+18.8	99.8	36 46.2	+20.0	100.5	36 34.9	+21.2	101.3	36 22.8	+22.4	102.0	36 09.9	+23.6	102.7	35 56.4	+24.7	103.4	35 42.1	+25.8	104.1	2
3	37 24.2	+16.8	97.9	37 15.6	+18.0	98.6	37 06.2	+19.3	99.4	36 56.1	+20.5	100.1	36 45.2	+21.7	100.8	36 33.5	+22.9	101.6	36 21.1	+24.1	102.3	36 07.9	+25.3	103.0	3
4	37 41.0	+16.0	96.6	37 33.6	+17.3	97.4	37 25.5	+18.6	98.2	37 16.6	+19.8	98.9	37 06.9	+21.0	99.7	36 56.4	+22.3	100.4	36 45.2	+23.4	101.2	36 33.2	+24.6	101.9	4
5	37 57.0	+15.3	95.4	37 50.9	+16.6	96.2	37 44.1	+17.8	97.0	37 36.4	+19.1	97.7	37 27.9	+20.3	98.5	37 18.7	+21.5	99.3	37 08.6	+22.8	100.0	36 57.8	+24.0	100.7	5
6	38 12.3	+14.5	94.2	38 07.5	+15.8	95.0	38 01.9	+17.1	95.8	37 55.5	+18.3	96.5	37 48.2	+19.6	97.3	37 40.2	+20.8	98.1	37 31.4	+22.1	98.8	37 21.8	+23.3	99.6	6
7	38 26.8	+13.8	93.0	38 23.3	+15.0	93.8	38 19.0	+16.3	94.5	38 13.8	+17.6	95.3	38 07.8	+18.9	96.1	38 01.0	+20.2	96.9	37 53.5	+21.3	97.7	37 45.1	+22.5	98.4	7
8	38 40.6	+12.9	91.7	38 38.3	+14.3	92.5	38 35.3	+15.5	93.3	38 31.4	+16.9	94.1	38 26.7	+18.1	94.9	38 21.2	+19.4	95.7	38 14.8	+20.6	96.5	38 07.6	+21.9	97.3	8
9	38 53.5	+12.1	90.5	38 52.6	+13.4	91.3	38 50.8	+14.8	92.1	38 48.3	+16.0	92.9	38 44.8	+17.4	93.7	38 40.6	+18.6	94.5	38 35.4	+19.9	95.3	38 29.5	+21.2	96.1	9
10	39 05.6	+11.3	89.2	39 06.0	+12.7	90.0	39 05.6	+14.0	90.8	39 04.3	+15.3	91.6	39 02.2	+16.5	92.5	38 59.2	+17.8	93.3	38 55.3	+19.2	94.1	38 50.7	+20.4	94.9	10
11	39 16.9	+10.5	87.9	39 18.7	+11.8	88.8	39 19.6	+13.1	89.6	39 19.6	+14.4	90.4	39 18.7	+15.8	91.2	39 17.0	+17.1	92.0	39 14.5	+18.4	92.8	39 11.1	+19.6	93.7	11
12	39 27.4	+9.7	86.7	39 30.5	+11.0	87.5	39 32.7	+12.3	88.3	39 34.0	+13.7	89.1	39 34.5	+15.0	90.0	39 34.1	+16.3	90.8	39 32.9	+17.5	91.6	39 30.7	+18.9	92.4	12
13	39 37.1	+8.8	85.4	39 41.5	+10.1	86.2	39 45.0	+11.5	87.0	39 47.7	+12.8	87.9	39 49.5	+14.1	88.7	39 50.4	+15.4	89.5	39 50.4	+16.8	90.4	39 49.6	+18.1	91.2	13
14	39 45.9	+7.9	84.1	39 51.6	+9.3	84.9	39 56.5	+10.6	85.8	40 00.5	+11.9	86.6	40 03.6	+13.3	87.4	40 05.8	+14.7	88.3	40 07.2	+16.0	89.1	40 07.7	+17.3	90.0	14
15	39 53.8	+7.1	82.8	40 00.9	+8.4	83.6	40 07.1	+9.8	84.5	40 12.4	+11.2	85.3	40 16.9	+12.5	86.2	40 20.5	+13.8	87.0	40 23.2	+15.1	87.9	40 25.0	+16.4	88.7	15
16	40 00.9	+6.2	81.5	40 09.3	+7.6	82.3	40 16.9	+8.9	83.2	40 23.6	+10.2	84.0	40 29.4	+11.6	84.9	40 34.3	+12.9	85.7	40 38.3	+14.3	86.6	40 41.4	+15.7	87.4	16
17	40 07.1	+5.3	80.2	40 16.9	+6.7	81.0	40 25.8	+8.0	81.9	40 33.8	+9.4	82.7	40 41.0	+10.7	83.6	40 47.2	+12.1	84.4	40 52.6	+13.4	85.3	40 57.1	+14.7	86.2	17
18	40 12.4	+4.5	78.9	40 23.6	+5.8	79.7	40 33.8	+7.2	80.6	40 43.2	+8.5	81.4	40 51.7	+9.9	82.3	40 59.3	+11.2	83.1	41 06.0	+12.6	84.0	41 11.8	+13.9	84.9	18
19	40 16.9	+3.6	77.6	40 29.4	+4.9	78.4	40 41.0	+6.2	79.3	40 51.7	+7.6	80.1	41 01.6	+8.9	81.0	41 10.5	+10.3	81.8	41 18.6	+11.7	82.7	41 25.7	+13.1	83.6	19
20	40 20.5	+2.7	76.3	40 34.3	+4.0	77.1	40 47.2	+5.4	78.0	40 59.3	+6.7	78.8	41 10.5	+8.1	79.7	41 20.8	+9.5	80.5	41 30.3	+10.7	81.4	41 38.8	+12.1	82.3	20
21	40 23.2	+1.8	75.0	40 38.3	+3.1	75.8	40 52.6	+4.5	76.6	41 06.0	+5.8	77.5	41 18.6	+7.1	78.3	41 30.3	+8.5	79.2	41 41.0	+9.9	80.1	41 50.9	+11.3	81.0	21
22	40 25.0	+0.9	73.7	40 41.4	+2.3	74.5	40 57.1	+3.5	75.3	41 11.8	+4.9	76.2	41 25.7	+6.3	77.0	41 38.8	+7.6	77.9	41 50.9	+9.0	78.8	42 02.2	+10.3	79.6	22
23	40 25.9	0.0	72.4	40 43.7	+1.3	73.2	41 00.6	+2.7	74.0	41 16.7	+4.0	74.8	41 32.0	+5.3	75.7	41 46.4	+6.7	76.6	41 59.9	+8.0	77.4	42 12.5	+9.4	78.3	23
24	40 25.9	−0.9	71.0	40 45.0	+0.4	71.9	41 03.3	+1.7	72.7	41 20.7	+3.1	73.5	41 37.3	+4.4	74.4	41 53.1	+5.7	75.2	42 07.9	+7.1	76.1	42 21.9	+8.4	77.0	24
25	40 25.0	−1.7	69.7	40 45.4	−0.5	70.5	41 05.0	+0.8	71.4	41 23.8	+2.1	72.2	41 41.7	+3.5	73.0	41 58.8	+4.8	73.9	42 15.0	+6.2	74.8	42 30.3	+7.6	75.6	25
26	40 23.3	−2.7	68.4	40 44.9	−1.3	69.2	41 05.8	0.0	70.0	41 25.9	+1.3	70.9	41 45.2	+2.5	71.7	42 03.6	+3.9	72.5	42 21.2	+5.2	73.4	42 37.9	+6.5	74.3	26
27	40 20.6	−3.5	67.1	40 43.6	−2.3	67.9	41 05.8	−1.0	68.7	41 27.2	+0.3	69.5	41 47.7	+1.7	70.4	42 07.5	+2.9	71.2	42 26.4	+4.3	72.1	42 44.4	+5.7	72.9	27
28	40 17.1	−4.5	65.8	40 41.3	−3.2	66.6	41 04.8	−1.9	67.4	41 27.5	−0.7	68.2	41 49.4	+0.6	69.0	42 10.4	+2.0	69.9	42 30.7	+3.3	70.7	42 50.1	+4.6	71.6	28
29	40 12.6	−5.3	64.5	40 38.1	−4.1	65.3	41 02.9	−2.9	66.0	41 26.8	−1.5	66.8	41 50.0	−0.2	67.7	42 12.4	+1.1	68.5	42 34.0	+2.3	69.4	42 54.7	+3.7	70.2	29
30	40 07.3	−6.1	63.2	40 34.0	−4.9	63.9	41 00.0	−3.7	64.7	41 25.3	−2.5	65.5	41 49.8	−1.2	66.3	42 13.5	0.0	67.2	42 36.3	+1.4	68.0	42 58.4	+2.7	68.9	30
31	40 01.2	−7.1	61.9	40 29.1	−5.9	62.6	40 56.3	−4.6	63.4	41 22.8	−3.4	64.2	41 48.6	−2.2	65.0	42 13.5	−0.8	65.8	42 37.7	+0.5	66.6	43 01.1	+1.7	67.5	31
32	39 54.1	−7.9	60.6	40 23.2	−6.7	61.3	40 51.7	−5.6	62.1	41 19.4	−4.3	62.9	41 46.4	−3.0	63.6	42 12.7	−1.8	64.5	42 38.2	−0.6	65.3	43 02.8	+0.8	66.1	32
33	39 46.2	−8.8	59.3	40 16.5	−7.6	60.0	40 46.1	−6.4	60.8	41 15.1	−5.2	61.5	41 43.4	−4.1	62.3	42 10.9	−2.8	63.1	42 37.6	−1.5	63.9	43 03.6	−0.2	64.8	33
34	39 37.4	−9.6	58.0	40 08.9	−8.5	58.7	40 39.7	−7.3	59.5	41 09.9	−6.1	60.2	41 39.3	−4.9	61.0	42 08.1	−3.7	61.8	42 36.1	−2.4	62.6	43 03.4	−1.2	63.4	34
35	39 27.8	−10.4	56.7	40 00.4	−9.3	57.4	40 32.4	−8.2	58.1	41 03.8	−7.1	58.9	41 34.4	−5.8	59.6	42 04.4	−4.6	60.4	42 33.7	−3.5	61.2	43 02.2	−2.2	62.0	35
36	39 17.4	−11.3	55.5	39 51.1	−10.2	56.1	40 24.2	−9.0	56.8	40 56.7	−7.9	57.6	41 28.6	−6.8	58.3	41 59.8	−5.6	59.1	42 30.2	−4.3	59.9	43 00.0	−3.1	60.7	36
37	39 06.1	−12.1	54.2	39 40.9	−11.0	54.9	40 15.2	−10.0	55.5	40 48.8	−8.8	56.3	41 21.8	−7.7	57.0	41 54.2	−6.5	57.7	42 25.9	−5.4	58.5	42 56.9	−4.2	59.3	37
38	38 54.0	−12.9	52.9	39 29.9	−11.9	53.6	40 05.2	−10.8	54.3	40 40.0	−9.7	54.9	41 14.1	−8.5	55.7	41 47.7	−7.5	56.4	42 20.5	−6.2	57.2	42 52.7	−5.0	57.9	38
39	38 41.1	−13.7	51.7	39 18.0	−12.6	52.3	39 54.4	−11.6	53.0	40 30.3	−10.6	53.7	41 05.6	−9.5	54.3	41 40.2	−8.3	55.1	42 14.3	−7.2	55.8	42 47.7	−6.1	56.6	39
40	38 27.4	−14.5	50.4	39 05.4	−13.5	51.1	39 42.8	−12.5	51.7	40 19.7	−11.4	52.4	40 56.1	−10.4	53.0	41 31.9	−9.3	53.7	42 07.1	−8.2	54.5	42 41.6	−7.0	55.2	40
41	38 12.9	−15.3	49.2	38 51.9	−14.3	49.8	39 30.3	−13.2	50.4	40 08.3	−12.3	51.1	40 45.7	−11.2	51.7	41 22.6	−10.1	52.4	41 58.9	−9.1	53.1	42 34.6	−8.0	53.9	41
42	37 57.6	−16.0	48.0	38 37.6	−15.1	48.6	39 17.1	−14.1	49.2	39 56.0	−13.1	49.8	40 34.5	−12.1	50.4	41 12.5	−11.1	51.1	41 49.8	−9.9	51.8	42 26.6	−8.8	52.5	42
43	37 41.6	−16.8	46.7	38 22.5	−15.8	47.3	39 03.0	−14.9	47.9	39 42.9	−13.9	48.5	40 22.4	−12.9	49.2	41 01.4	−11.9	49.8	41 39.9	−10.9	50.5	42 17.8	−9.9	51.2	43
44	37 24.8	−17.5	45.5	38 06.7	−16.6	46.1	38 48.1	−15.7	46.7	39 29.0	−14.7	47.3	40 09.5	−13.8	47.9	40 49.5	−12.8	48.5	41 29.0	−11.8	49.2	42 07.9	−10.7	49.9	44
45	37 07.3	−18.2	44.3	37 50.1	−17.4	44.9	38 32.4	−16.5	45.4	39 14.3	−15.6	46.0	39 55.7	−14.6	46.6	40 36.7	−13.6	47.2	41 17.2	−12.7	47.9	41 57.2	−11.6	48.5	45
46	36 49.1	−18.9	43.1	37 32.7	−18.1	43.7	38 15.9	−17.2	44.2	38 58.7	−16.3	44.8	39 41.1	−15.4	45.3	40 23.1	−14.5	45.9	41 04.5	−13.5	46.6	41 45.6	−12.6	47.2	46
47	36 30.2	−19.7	42.0	37 14.6	−18.8	42.5	37 58.7	−18.0	43.0	38 42.4	−17.1	43.5	39 25.7	−16.2	44.1	40 08.6	−15.3	44.7	40 51.0	−14.4	45.3	41 33.0	−13.4	45.9	47
48	36 10.5	−20.3	40.8	36 55.8	−19.5	41.3	37 40.7	−18.7	41.8	38 25.3	−17.9	42.3	39 09.5	−17.0	42.8	39 53.3	−16.2	43.4	40 36.6	−15.2	44.0	41 19.6	−14.3	44.6	48
49	35 50.2	−21.0	39.6	36 36.3	−20.2	40.1	37 22.0	−19.4	40.6	38 07.4	−18.6	41.1	38 52.5	−17.8	41.6	39 37.1	−16.9	42.2	40 21.4	−16.0	42.7	41 05.3	−15.2	43.3	49
50	35 29.2	−21.6	38.5	36 16.1	−20.9	38.9	37 02.6	−20.1	39.4	37 48.8	−19.3	39.9	38 34.7	−18.6	40.4	39 20.2	−17.7	40.9	40 05.4	−16.9	41.5	40 50.1	−16.0	42.0	50
51	35 07.6	−22.3	37.3	35 55.2	−21.6	37.8	36 42.5	−20.8	38.2	37 29.5	−20.1	38.7	38 16.1	−19.2	39.2	39 02.5	−18.5	39.7	39 48.5	−17.7	40.2	40 34.1	−16.8	40.8	51
52	34 45.3	−22.9	36.2	35 33.6	−22.2	36.6	36 21.7	−21.5	37.0	37 09.4	−20.8	37.5	37 56.9	−20.1	38.0	38 44.0	−19.2	38.5	39 30.8	−18.4	39.0	40 17.3	−17.7	39.5	52
53	34 22.4	−23.5	35.1	35 11.4	−22.8	35.5	36 00.2	−22.2	35.9	36 48.6	−21.4	36.3	37 36.8	−20.7	36.8	38 24.8	−20.0	37.2	39 12.4	−19.3	37.7	39 59.6	−18.4	38.2	53
54	33 58.9	−24.1	34.0	34 48.6	−23.5	34.3	35 38.0	−22.8	34.7	36 27.2	−22.1	35.2	37 16.1	−21.4	35.6	38 04.8	−20.7	36.0	38 53.1	−19.9	36.5	39 41.2	−19.2	37.0	54
55	33 34.8	−24.6	32.9	34 25.1	−24.0	33.2	35 15.2	−23.4	33.6	36 05.1	−22.8	34.0	36 54.7	−22.1	34.4	37 44.1	−21.5	34.9	38 33.2	−20.8	35.3	39 22.0	−20.0	35.8	55
56	33 10.2	−25.3	31.8	34 01.1	−24.7	32.1	34 51.8	−24.1	32.5	35 42.3	−23.4	32.9	36 32.6	−22.8	33.3	37 22.6	−22.1	33.7	38 12.4	−21.4	34.1	39 02.0	−20.8	34.6	56
57	32 44.9	−25.8	30.7	33 36.4	−25.2	31.0	34 27.7	−24.6	31.4	35 18.9	−24.1	31.7	36 09.8	−23.4	32.1	37 00.5	−22.8	32.5	37 51.0	−22.2	32.9	38 41.2	−21.4	33.4	57
58	32 19.1	−26.3	29.6	33 11.2	−25.8	29.9	34 03.1	−25.2	30.3	34 54.8	−24.6	30.6	35 46.4	−24.1	31.0	36 37.7	−23.4	31.4	37 28.8	−22.8	31.8	38 19.8	−22.2	32.2	58
59	31 52.8	−26.9	28.6	32 45.4	−26.3	28.9	33 37.9	−25.8	29.2	34 30.2	−25.3	29.5	35 22.3	−24.7	29.8	36 14.3	−24.2	30.2	37 06.0	−23.5	30.6	37 57.6	−22.9	31.0	59
60	31 25.9	−27.4	27.5	32 19.1	−26.9	27.8	33 12.1	−26.4	28.1	34 04.9	−25.8	28.4	34 57.6	−25.3	28.7	35 50.1	−24.7	29.1	36 42.5	−24.2	29.4	37 34.7	−23.6	29.8	60
61	30 58.5	−27.8	26.5	31 52.2	−27.4	26.7	32 45.7	−26.9	27.0	33 39.1	−26.4	27.3	34 32.3	−25.8	27.6	35 25.4	−25.3	28.0	36 18.3	−24.8	28.3	37 11.1	−24.3	28.7	61
62	30 30.7	−28.4	25.4	31 24.8	−27.9	25.7	32 18.8	−27.4	26.0	33 12.7	−26.9	26.2	34 06.5	−26.5	26.5	35 00.1	−26.0	26.8	35 53.5	−25.4	27.2	36 46.8	−24.9	27.5	62
63	30 02.3	−28.8	24.4	30 56.9	−28.4	24.7	31 51.4	−27.9	24.9	32 45.8	−27.5	25.2	33 40.0	−27.0	25.5	34 34.1	−26.5	25.8	35 28.1	−26.1	26.1	36 21.9	−25.5	26.4	63
64	29 33.5	−29.2	23.4	30 28.5	−28.8	23.6	31 23.5	−28.5	23.9	32 18.3	−28.0	24.1	33 13.0	−27.6	24.4	34 07.6	−27.1	24.7	35 02.0	−26.6	25.0	35 56.4	−26.2	25.3	64
65	29 04.3	−29.7	22.4	29 59.7	−29.3	22.6	30 55.0	−28.9	22.8	31 50.3	−28.5	23.1	32 45.4	−28.1	23.3	33 40.5	−27.7	23.6	34 35.4	−27.2	23.9	35 30.2	−26.8	24.1	65
66	28 34.6	−30.2	21.4	29 30.4	−29.8	21.6	30 26.1	−29.4	21.8	31 21.8	−29.0	22.0	32 17.3	−28.6	22.3	33 12.8	−28.2	22.5	34 08.2	−27.8	22.8	35 03.4	−27.3	23.1	66
67	28 04.4	−30.5	20.4	29 00.6	−30.2	20.6	29 56.7	−29.8	20.8	30 52.8	−29.5	21.0	31 48.7	−29.1	21.2	32 44.6	−28.7	21.5	33 40.4	−28.3	21.7	34 36.1	−27.9	22.0	67
68	27 33.9	−31.0	19.5	28 30.4	−30.6	19.6	29 26.9	−30.3	19.8	30 23.3	−29.9	20.0	31 19.6	−29.5	20.2	32 15.9	−29.2	20.4	33 12.1	−28.9	20.7	34 08.2	−28.5	20.9	68
69	27 02.9	−31.3	18.5	27 59.8	−31.1	18.7	28 56.6	−30.7	18.8	29 53.4	−30.4	19.0	30 50.1	−30.1	19.2	31 46.7	−29.7	19.4	32 43.2	−29.3	19.6	33 39.7	−29.0	19.8	69
70	26 31.6	−31.8	17.5	27 28.7	−31.4	17.7	28 25.9	−31.1	17.8	29 23.0	−30.9	18.0	30 20.0	−30.5	18.2	31 17.0	−30.2	18.4	32 13.9	−29.9	18.6	33 10.7	−29.5	18.8	70
71	25 59.8	−32.1	16.6	26 57.3	−31.8	16.7	27 54.8	−31.6	16.9	28 52.1	−31.2	17.0	29 49.5	−31.0	17.2	30 46.8	−30.7	17.4	31 44.0	−30.3	17.6	32 41.2	−30.0	17.7	71
72	25 27.7	−32.4	15.6	26 25.5	−32.2	15.8	27 23.2	−31.9	15.9	28 20.9	−31.7	16.1	29 18.5	−31.3	16.2	30 16.1	−31.1	16.4	31 13.7	−30.9	16.5	32 11.2	−30.6	16.7	72
73	24 55.3	−32.8	14.7	25 53.3	−32.5	14.8	26 51.3	−32.3	15.0	27 49.2	−32.0	15.1	28 47.2	−31.8	15.2	29 45.0	−31.5	15.4	30 42.8	−31.2	15.5	31 40.6	−31.0	15.7	73
74	24 22.5	−33.1	13.8	25 20.8	−32.9	13.9	26 19.0	−32.7	14.0	27 17.2	−32.4	14.1	28 15.4	−32.2	14.3	29 13.5	−32.0	14.4	30 11.6	−31.7	14.6	31 09.6	−31.4	14.7	74
75	23 49.4	−33.4	12.9	24 47.9	−33.3	13.0	25 46.3	−33.0	13.1	26 44.8	−32.9	13.2	27 43.2	−32.6	13.3	28 41.5	−32.3	13.4	29 39.9	−32.2	13.6	30 38.2	−31.9	13.7	75
76	23 16.0	−33.8	12.0	24 14.6	−33.5	12.1	25 13.3	−33.4	12.2	26 11.9	−33.1	12.3	27 10.6	−33.0	12.4	28 09.2	−32.8	12.5	29 07.7	−32.5	12.6	30 06.3	−32.4	12.7	76
77	22 42.2	−34.0	11.1	23 41.1	−33.9	11.1	24 39.9	−33.7	11.2	25 38.8	−33.5	11.3	26 37.6	−33.3	11.4	27 36.4	−33.2	11.5	28 35.2	−33.0	11.6	29 33.9	−32.7	11.8	77
78	22 08.2	−34.4	10.2	23 07.2	−34.2	10.3	24 06.2	−34.0	10.3	25 05.3	−33.9	10.4	26 04.3	−33.7	10.5	27 03.2	−33.5	10.6	28 02.2	−33.3	10.7	29 01.2	−33.2	10.8	78
79	21 33.8	−34.6	9.3	22 33.0	−34.4	9.4	23 32.2	−34.3	9.4	24 31.4	−34.2	9.5	25 30.6	−34.1	9.6	26 29.7	−33.9	9.7	27 28.9	−33.8	9.8	28 28.0	−33.6	9.8	79
80	20 59.2	−34.9	8.4	21 58.6	−34.8	8.5	22 57.9	−34.6	8.5	23 57.2	−34.5	8.6	24 56.5	−34.3	8.7	25 55.8	−34.2	8.8	26 55.1	−34.0	8.8	27 54.4	−33.9	8.9	80
81	20 24.3	−35.1	7.6	21 23.8	−35.0	7.6	22 23.3	−34.9	7.7	23 22.7	−34.8	7.7	24 22.2	−34.7	7.8	25 21.6	−34.5	7.8	26 21.1	−34.5	7.9	27 20.5	−34.3	8.0	81
82	19 49.2	−35.4	6.7	20 48.8	−35.3	6.7	21 48.4	−35.2	6.8	22 47.9	−35.0	6.8	23 47.5	−35.0	6.9	24 47.1	−34.9	6.9	25 46.6	−34.7	7.0	26 46.2	−34.7	7.1	82
83	19 13.8	−35.6	5.8	20 13.5	−35.5	5.9	21 13.2	−35.5	5.9	22 12.9	−35.4	6.0	23 12.5	−35.2	6.0	24 12.2	−35.2	6.0	25 11.9	−35.1	6.1	26 11.5	−35.0	6.1	83
84	18 38.2	−35.9	5.0	19 38.0	−35.8	5.0	20 37.7	−35.7	5.0	21 37.5	−35.6	5.1	22 37.3	−35.6	5.1	23 37.0	−35.5	5.2	24 36.8	−35.4	5.2	25 36.5	−35.3	5.2	84
85	18 02.3	−36.0	4.1	19 02.2	−36.0	4.2	20 02.0	−35.9	4.2	21 01.9	−35.9	4.2	22 01.7	−35.8	4.2	23 01.5	−35.7	4.3	24 01.4	−35.7	4.3	25 01.2	−35.7	4.3	85
86	17 26.3	−36.3	3.3	18 26.2	−36.3	3.3	19 26.1	−36.2	3.3	20 26.0	−36.2	3.4	21 25.9	−36.1	3.4	22 25.8	−36.1	3.4	23 25.7	−36.1	3.4	24 25.5	−35.9	3.5	86
87	16 50.0	−36.5	2.5	17 49.9	−36.4	2.5	18 49.9	−36.4	2.5	19 49.8	−36.4	2.5	20 49.8	−36.4	2.5	21 49.7	−36.3	2.5	22 49.6	−36.2	2.6	23 49.6	−36.3	2.6	87
88	16 13.5	−36.6	1.6	17 13.5	−36.7	1.6	18 13.5	−36.7	1.7	19 13.4	−36.6	1.7	20 13.4	−36.6	1.7	21 13.4	−36.6	1.7	22 13.4	−36.6	1.7	23 13.3	−36.5	1.7	88
89	15 36.9	−36.9	0.8	16 36.8	−36.8	0.8	17 36.8	−36.8	0.8	18 36.8	−36.8	0.8	19 36.8	−36.8	0.8	20 36.8	−36.8	0.8	21 36.8	−36.8	0.8	22 36.8	−36.8	0.9	89
90	15 00.0	−37.0	0.0	16 00.0	−37.0	0.0	17 00.0	−37.0	0.0	18 00.0	−37.0	0.0	19 00.0	−37.0	0.0	20 00.0	−37.1	0.0	21 00.0	−37.1	0.0	22 00.0	−37.1	0.0	90
	15°			16°			17°			18°			19°			20°			21°			22°			

52°, 308° L.H.A. LATITUDE SAME NAME AS DECLINATION

106

LATITUDE CONTRARY NAME TO DECLINATION — L.H.A. 52°, 308°

Dec. °	15° Hc ° ′	d ′	Z °	16° Hc ° ′	d ′	Z °	17° Hc ° ′	d ′	Z °	18° Hc ° ′	d ′	Z °
0	36 29.4	-19.7	101.4	36 17.1	-20.8	102.2	36 04.1	-22.0	102.9	35 50.4	-23.2	103.6
1	36 09.7	-20.3	102.6	35 56.3	-21.5	103.3	35 42.1	-22.7	104.0	35 27.2	-23.8	104.7
2	35 49.4	-21.0	103.8	35 34.8	-22.2	104.5	35 19.4	-23.3	105.2	35 03.4	-24.4	105.8
3	35 28.4	-21.7	104.9	35 12.6	-22.8	105.6	34 56.1	-23.9	106.3	34 39.0	-25.1	106.9
4	35 06.7	-22.3	106.1	34 49.8	-23.4	106.7	34 32.2	-24.5	107.4	34 13.9	-25.6	108.0
5	34 44.4	-22.9	107.2	34 26.4	-24.1	107.9	34 07.7	-25.2	108.5	33 48.3	-26.2	109.1
6	34 21.5	-23.5	108.3	34 02.3	-24.6	109.0	33 42.5	-25.7	109.6	33 22.1	-26.7	110.2
7	33 58.0	-24.1	109.4	33 37.7	-25.2	110.1	33 16.8	-26.2	110.7	32 55.4	-27.3	111.3
8	33 33.9	-24.7	110.5	33 12.5	-25.7	111.1	32 50.6	-26.8	111.8	32 28.1	-27.9	112.3
9	33 09.2	-25.3	111.6	32 46.8	-26.3	112.2	32 23.8	-27.3	112.8	32 00.2	-28.3	113.4
10	32 43.9	-25.8	112.7	32 20.5	-26.9	113.3	31 56.5	-27.9	113.9	31 31.9	-28.8	114.4
11	32 18.1	-26.4	113.8	31 53.6	-27.3	114.3	31 28.6	-28.3	114.9	31 03.1	-29.3	115.5
12	31 51.7	-26.9	114.8	31 26.3	-27.9	115.4	31 00.3	-28.9	115.9	30 33.8	-29.8	116.5
13	31 24.8	-27.3	115.9	30 58.4	-28.4	116.4	30 31.4	-29.3	117.0	30 04.0	-30.2	117.5
14	30 57.5	-27.9	116.9	30 30.0	-28.8	117.5	30 02.1	-29.7	118.0	29 33.8	-30.7	118.5
15	30 29.6	-28.4	118.0	30 01.2	-29.3	118.5	29 32.4	-30.2	119.0	29 03.1	-31.1	119.5
16	30 01.2	-28.8	119.0	29 31.9	-29.7	119.5	29 02.2	-30.7	120.0	28 32.0	-31.5	120.4
17	29 32.4	-29.3	120.0	29 02.2	-30.2	120.5	28 31.5	-31.0	120.9	28 00.5	-31.9	121.4
18	29 03.1	-29.7	121.0	28 32.0	-30.6	121.5	28 00.5	-31.5	121.9	27 28.6	-32.3	122.4
19	28 33.4	-30.2	122.0	28 01.4	-31.0	122.4	27 29.0	-31.8	122.9	26 56.3	-32.7	123.3
20	28 03.2	-30.5	123.0	27 30.4	-31.4	123.4	26 57.2	-32.3	123.8	26 23.6	-33.1	124.2
21	27 32.7	-31.0	123.9	26 59.0	-31.8	124.4	26 24.9	-32.6	124.8	25 50.5	-33.4	125.2
22	27 01.7	-31.4	124.9	26 27.2	-32.2	125.3	25 52.3	-32.9	125.7	25 17.1	-33.7	126.1
23	26 30.3	-31.7	125.8	25 55.0	-32.5	126.2	25 19.4	-33.3	126.6	24 43.4	-34.1	127.0
24	25 58.6	-32.1	126.8	25 22.5	-32.9	127.2	24 46.1	-33.7	127.6	24 09.3	-34.3	127.9
25	25 26.5	-32.5	127.7	24 49.6	-33.2	128.1	24 12.4	-33.9	128.5	23 35.0	-34.7	128.8
26	24 54.0	-32.8	128.7	24 16.4	-33.6	129.0	23 38.5	-34.3	129.4	23 00.3	-35.0	129.7
27	24 21.2	-33.1	129.6	23 42.8	-33.8	129.9	23 04.2	-34.6	130.3	22 25.3	-35.3	130.6
28	23 48.1	-33.5	130.5	23 09.0	-34.2	130.8	22 29.6	-34.8	131.1	21 50.0	-35.5	131.4
29	23 14.6	-33.7	131.4	22 34.8	-34.4	131.7	21 54.8	-35.2	132.0	21 14.5	-35.8	132.3
30	22 40.9	-34.1	132.3	22 00.4	-34.8	132.6	21 19.6	-35.4	132.9	20 38.7	-36.1	133.2
31	22 06.8	-34.3	133.2	21 25.6	-35.0	133.5	20 44.2	-35.6	133.8	20 02.6	-36.3	134.0
32	21 32.5	-34.7	134.1	20 50.6	-35.3	134.4	20 08.6	-35.9	134.6	19 26.3	-36.5	134.9
33	20 57.8	-34.9	134.9	20 15.3	-35.5	135.2	19 32.7	-36.2	135.5	18 49.8	-36.7	135.7
34	20 22.9	-35.1	135.8	19 39.8	-35.7	136.1	18 56.5	-36.3	136.3	18 13.1	-37.0	136.5
35	19 47.8	-35.4	136.7	19 04.1	-36.0	136.9	18 20.2	-36.6	137.2	17 36.1	-37.2	137.4
36	19 12.4	-35.6	137.5	18 28.1	-36.3	137.8	17 43.6	-36.8	138.0	16 58.9	-37.4	138.2
37	18 36.8	-35.9	138.4	17 51.8	-36.4	138.6	17 06.8	-37.0	138.8	16 21.5	-37.5	139.0
38	18 00.9	-36.1	139.2	17 15.4	-36.6	139.4	16 29.8	-37.2	139.6	15 44.0	-37.8	139.8
39	17 24.8	-36.2	140.1	16 38.8	-36.9	140.3	15 52.6	-37.4	140.5	15 06.2	-37.9	140.6
40	16 48.6	-36.5	140.9	16 01.9	-37.0	141.1	15 15.2	-37.6	141.3	14 28.3	-38.0	141.4
41	16 12.1	-36.7	141.7	15 24.9	-37.2	141.9	14 37.6	-37.7	142.1	13 50.3	-38.1	142.2
42	15 35.4	-36.9	142.6	14 47.7	-37.4	142.7	13 59.9	-37.9	142.9	13 12.0	-38.3	143.0
43	14 58.5	-37.0	143.4	14 10.3	-37.5	143.5	13 22.0	-38.0	143.7	12 33.7	-38.5	143.8
44	14 21.5	-37.2	144.2	13 32.8	-37.7	144.3	12 44.0	-38.1	144.5	11 55.2	-38.7	144.6
45	13 44.3	-37.3	145.0	12 55.1	-37.8	145.1	12 05.9	-38.3	145.3	11 16.5	-38.7	145.4
46	13 07.0	-37.5	145.8	12 17.3	-38.0	145.9	11 27.6	-38.5	146.0	10 37.8	-38.9	146.2
47	12 29.5	-37.7	146.6	11 39.3	-38.1	146.7	10 49.1	-38.5	146.8	9 58.9	-39.0	146.9
48	11 51.8	-37.8	147.4	11 01.2	-38.2	147.5	10 10.6	-38.7	147.6	9 19.9	-39.1	147.7
49	11 14.0	-37.9	148.2	10 23.0	-38.3	148.3	9 31.9	-38.7	148.4	8 40.8	-39.1	148.5
50	10 36.1	-38.0	149.0	9 44.7	-38.5	149.1	8 53.2	-38.9	149.2	8 01.7	-39.3	149.2
51	9 58.1	-38.1	149.8	9 06.2	-38.5	149.9	8 14.3	-38.9	149.9	7 22.4	-39.3	150.0
52	9 20.0	-38.3	150.6	8 27.7	-38.6	150.6	7 35.4	-39.0	150.7	6 43.1	-39.4	150.8
53	8 41.7	-38.3	151.3	7 49.1	-38.7	151.4	6 56.4	-39.1	151.5	6 03.7	-39.5	151.5
54	8 03.4	-38.4	152.1	7 10.4	-38.8	152.2	6 17.3	-39.2	152.2	5 24.2	-39.5	152.3
55	7 25.0	-38.5	152.9	6 31.6	-38.9	152.9	5 38.1	-39.2	153.0	4 44.7	-39.6	153.0
56	6 46.5	-38.6	153.7	5 52.7	-38.9	153.7	4 58.9	-39.2	153.7	4 05.1	-39.6	153.8
57	6 07.9	-38.6	154.4	5 13.8	-39.0	154.5	4 19.7	-39.4	154.5	3 25.5	-39.7	154.5
58	5 29.3	-38.7	155.2	4 34.8	-39.0	155.2	3 40.3	-39.3	155.3	2 45.8	-39.6	155.3
59	4 50.6	-38.7	156.0	3 55.8	-39.1	156.0	3 01.0	-39.4	156.0	2 06.2	-39.7	156.0
60	4 11.9	-38.8	156.7	3 16.7	-39.1	156.8	2 21.6	-39.4	156.8	1 26.5	-39.8	156.8
61	3 33.1	-38.9	157.5	2 37.6	-39.1	157.5	1 42.2	-39.4	157.5	0 46.7	-39.7	157.5
62	2 54.2	-38.8	158.3	1 58.5	-39.1	158.3	1 02.8	-39.5	158.3	0 07.0	-39.7	158.3
63	2 15.4	-38.9	159.0	1 19.4	-39.2	159.0	0 23.3	-39.4	159.0	0 32.7	+39.7	21.0
64	1 36.5	-38.9	159.8	0 40.2	-39.2	159.8	0 16.1	+39.4	20.2	1 12.4	+39.7	20.2
65	0 57.6	-38.9	160.5	0 01.0	-39.1	160.5	0 55.5	+39.5	19.5	1 52.1	+39.7	19.5
66	0 18.7	-38.9	161.3	0 38.1	+39.2	18.7	1 35.0	+39.4	18.7	2 31.8	+39.7	18.7
67	0 20.2	+38.9	17.9	1 17.3	+39.2	17.9	2 14.4	+39.4	17.9	3 11.5	+39.6	18.0
68	0 59.1	+38.9	17.2	1 56.5	+39.1	17.2	2 53.8	+39.3	17.2	3 51.1	+39.6	17.2
69	1 38.0	+38.9	16.4	2 35.6	+39.1	16.4	3 33.1	+39.4	16.4	4 30.7	+39.5	16.5
70	2 16.9	+38.9	15.6	3 14.7	+39.1	15.7	4 12.5	+39.2	15.7	5 10.2	+39.5	15.7
71	2 55.8	+38.8	14.9	3 53.8	+39.0	14.9	4 51.7	+39.3	14.9	5 49.7	+39.4	14.9
72	3 34.6	+38.8	14.1	4 32.8	+39.0	14.1	5 31.0	+39.1	14.2	6 29.1	+39.4	14.2
73	4 13.4	+38.7	13.4	5 11.8	+38.9	13.4	6 10.1	+39.1	13.4	7 08.5	+39.3	13.4
74	4 52.1	+38.7	12.6	5 50.7	+38.8	12.6	6 49.2	+39.1	12.6	7 47.8	+39.2	12.7
75	5 30.8	+38.7	11.8	6 29.5	+38.8	11.8	7 28.3	+38.9	11.9	8 27.0	+39.1	11.9
76	6 09.5	+38.5	11.1	7 08.3	+38.8	11.1	8 07.2	+38.9	11.1	9 06.1	+39.0	11.1
77	6 48.0	+38.5	10.3	7 47.1	+38.6	10.3	8 46.1	+38.8	10.3	9 45.1	+38.9	10.4
78	7 26.5	+38.4	9.5	8 25.7	+38.5	9.5	9 24.9	+38.6	9.6	10 24.0	+38.8	9.6
79	8 04.9	+38.4	8.7	9 04.2	+38.5	8.8	10 03.5	+38.6	8.8	11 02.8	+38.7	8.8
80	8 43.3	+38.2	8.0	9 42.7	+38.3	8.0	10 42.1	+38.4	8.0	11 41.5	+38.6	8.0
81	9 21.5	+38.1	7.2	10 21.0	+38.2	7.2	11 20.5	+38.4	7.2	12 20.1	+38.4	7.2
82	9 59.6	+38.0	6.4	10 59.2	+38.1	6.4	11 58.9	+38.1	6.4	12 58.5	+38.3	6.5
83	10 37.6	+37.9	5.6	11 37.3	+38.0	5.6	12 37.0	+38.1	5.6	13 36.8	+38.1	5.7
84	11 15.5	+37.8	4.8	12 15.3	+37.8	4.8	13 15.1	+37.9	4.9	14 14.9	+37.9	4.9
85	11 53.3	+37.6	4.0	12 53.1	+37.7	4.0	13 53.0	+37.7	4.1	14 52.8	+37.8	4.1
86	12 30.9	+37.5	3.2	13 30.8	+37.6	3.2	14 30.7	+37.6	3.3	15 30.6	+37.7	3.3
87	13 08.4	+37.4	2.4	14 08.4	+37.4	2.4	15 08.3	+37.4	2.4	16 08.3	+37.4	2.5
88	13 45.8	+37.2	1.6	14 45.8	+37.2	1.6	15 45.7	+37.3	1.6	16 45.7	+37.3	1.6
89	14 23.0	+37.0	0.8	15 23.0	+37.0	0.8	16 23.0	+37.0	0.8	17 23.0	+37.0	0.8
90	15 00.0	+36.9	0.0	16 00.0	+36.8	0.0	17 00.0	+36.8	0.0	18 00.0	+36.8	0.0
	15°			16°			17°			18°		

19° Hc ° ′	d ′	Z °	20° Hc ° ′	d ′	Z °	21° Hc ° ′	d ′	Z °	22° Hc ° ′	d ′	Z °	Dec. °
35 36.0	-24.4	104.3	35 20.8	-25.4	105.0	35 05.0	-26.6	105.6	34 48.5	-27.7	106.3	0
35 11.6	-24.9	105.4	34 55.4	-26.1	106.1	34 38.4	-27.1	106.7	34 20.8	-28.2	107.4	1
34 46.7	-25.6	106.5	34 29.3	-26.6	107.2	34 11.3	-27.7	107.8	33 52.6	-28.8	108.5	2
34 21.1	-26.1	107.6	34 02.7	-27.2	108.2	33 43.6	-28.3	108.9	33 23.8	-29.2	109.5	3
33 55.0	-26.7	108.7	33 35.5	-27.8	109.3	33 15.3	-28.8	109.9	32 54.6	-29.9	110.6	4
33 28.3	-27.2	109.8	33 07.7	-28.3	110.4	32 46.5	-29.3	111.0	32 24.7	-30.3	111.6	5
33 01.1	-27.8	110.8	32 39.4	-28.8	111.4	32 17.2	-29.8	112.0	31 54.4	-30.7	112.6	6
32 33.3	-28.3	111.9	32 10.6	-29.3	112.5	31 47.4	-30.3	113.0	31 23.7	-31.3	113.6	7
32 05.0	-28.9	112.9	31 41.3	-29.8	113.5	31 17.1	-30.7	114.1	30 52.4	-31.7	114.6	8
31 36.1	-29.3	114.0	31 11.5	-30.3	114.5	30 46.4	-31.3	115.1	30 20.7	-32.2	115.6	9
31 06.8	-29.8	115.0	30 41.2	-30.7	115.5	30 15.1	-31.6	116.1	29 48.5	-32.5	116.6	10
30 37.0	-30.2	116.0	30 10.5	-31.2	116.5	29 43.5	-32.1	117.0	29 16.0	-33.0	117.5	11
30 06.8	-30.7	117.0	29 39.3	-31.6	117.5	29 11.4	-32.5	118.0	28 43.0	-33.4	118.5	12
29 36.1	-31.2	118.0	29 07.7	-32.0	118.5	28 38.9	-32.9	119.0	28 09.6	-33.8	119.4	13
29 04.9	-31.5	119.0	28 35.7	-32.5	119.4	28 06.0	-33.3	119.9	27 35.8	-34.1	120.4	14
28 33.4	-32.0	119.9	28 03.2	-32.8	120.4	27 32.7	-33.7	120.9	27 01.7	-34.5	121.3	15
28 01.4	-32.4	120.9	27 30.4	-33.2	121.3	26 59.0	-34.1	121.8	26 27.2	-34.9	122.2	16
27 29.0	-32.7	121.8	26 57.2	-33.6	122.3	26 24.9	-34.4	122.7	25 52.3	-35.2	123.1	17
26 56.3	-33.2	122.8	26 23.6	-34.0	123.2	25 50.5	-34.7	123.6	25 17.1	-35.5	124.0	18
26 23.1	-33.5	123.7	25 49.6	-34.2	124.1	25 15.8	-35.0	124.5	24 41.6	-35.8	124.9	19
25 49.6	-33.8	124.6	25 15.4	-34.6	125.0	24 40.8	-35.4	125.4	24 05.8	-36.1	125.8	20
25 15.8	-34.2	125.6	24 40.8	-35.0	125.9	24 05.4	-35.7	126.3	23 29.7	-36.4	126.7	21
24 41.6	-34.5	126.5	24 05.8	-35.2	126.8	23 29.7	-36.0	127.2	22 53.3	-36.7	127.5	22
24 07.1	-34.8	127.4	23 30.6	-35.6	127.7	22 53.7	-36.2	128.1	22 16.6	-36.9	128.4	23
23 32.3	-35.1	128.3	22 55.0	-35.8	128.6	22 17.5	-36.5	128.9	21 39.7	-37.2	129.2	24
22 57.2	-35.4	129.1	22 19.2	-36.1	129.5	21 41.0	-36.8	129.8	21 02.5	-37.5	130.1	25
22 21.8	-35.7	130.0	21 43.1	-36.3	130.3	21 04.2	-37.1	130.6	20 25.0	-37.6	130.9	26
21 46.1	-35.9	130.9	21 06.8	-36.7	131.2	20 27.1	-37.2	131.5	19 47.3	-37.9	131.7	27
21 10.2	-36.2	131.7	20 30.1	-36.8	132.0	19 49.9	-37.5	132.3	19 09.4	-38.2	132.6	28
20 34.0	-36.5	132.6	19 53.3	-37.1	132.9	19 12.4	-37.8	133.1	18 31.2	-38.3	133.4	29
19 57.5	-36.7	133.4	19 16.2	-37.3	133.7	18 34.6	-37.9	133.9	17 52.9	-38.5	134.2	30
19 20.8	-36.9	134.3	18 38.9	-37.6	134.5	17 56.7	-38.2	134.8	17 14.4	-38.8	135.0	31
18 43.9	-37.1	135.1	18 01.3	-37.7	135.4	17 18.5	-38.3	135.6	16 35.6	-38.9	135.8	32
18 06.8	-37.4	135.9	17 23.6	-38.0	136.2	16 40.2	-38.5	136.4	15 56.7	-39.1	136.6	33
17 29.4	-37.5	136.8	16 45.6	-38.1	137.0	16 01.7	-38.7	137.2	15 17.6	-39.2	137.4	34
16 51.9	-37.8	137.6	16 07.5	-38.3	137.8	15 23.0	-38.9	138.0	14 38.4	-39.5	138.2	35
16 14.1	-37.9	138.4	15 29.2	-38.5	138.6	14 44.1	-39.0	138.8	13 58.9	-39.5	138.9	36
15 36.2	-38.1	139.2	14 50.7	-38.7	139.4	14 05.1	-39.2	139.5	13 19.4	-39.7	139.7	37
14 58.1	-38.3	140.0	14 12.0	-38.8	140.2	13 25.9	-39.3	140.3	12 39.7	-39.8	140.5	38
14 19.8	-38.4	140.8	13 33.2	-38.9	141.0	12 46.6	-39.5	141.1	11 59.9	-40.0	141.2	39
13 41.4	-38.6	141.6	12 54.3	-39.1	141.7	12 07.1	-39.5	141.9	11 19.9	-40.1	142.0	40
13 02.8	-38.7	142.4	12 15.2	-39.2	142.5	11 27.6	-39.7	142.6	10 39.8	-40.1	142.8	41
12 24.1	-38.9	143.2	11 36.0	-39.3	143.3	10 47.9	-39.9	143.4	9 59.7	-40.3	143.5	42
11 45.2	-39.0	143.9	10 56.7	-39.5	144.1	10 08.0	-39.9	144.2	9 19.4	-40.4	144.3	43
11 06.2	-39.1	144.7	10 17.2	-39.6	144.8	9 28.1	-40.0	144.9	8 39.0	-40.5	145.0	44
10 27.1	-39.2	145.5	9 37.6	-39.6	145.6	8 48.1	-40.1	145.7	7 58.5	-40.5	145.8	45
9 47.9	-39.3	146.3	8 58.0	-39.8	146.3	8 08.0	-40.2	146.4	7 18.0	-40.6	146.5	46
9 08.6	-39.4	147.0	8 18.2	-39.8	147.1	7 27.8	-40.2	147.2	6 37.4	-40.7	147.2	47
8 29.2	-39.5	147.8	7 38.4	-39.9	147.9	6 47.6	-40.4	147.9	5 56.7	-40.7	148.0	48
7 49.7	-39.6	148.5	6 58.5	-40.0	148.6	6 07.2	-40.4	148.7	5 16.0	-40.8	148.7	49
7 10.1	-39.7	149.3	6 18.5	-40.1	149.4	5 26.8	-40.4	149.4	4 35.2	-40.9	149.5	50
6 30.4	-39.7	150.1	5 38.4	-40.1	150.1	4 46.4	-40.5	150.2	3 54.3	-40.8	150.2	51
5 50.7	-39.8	150.8	4 58.3	-40.2	150.9	4 05.9	-40.5	150.9	3 13.5	-40.9	150.9	52
5 10.9	-39.8	151.6	4 18.1	-40.2	151.6	3 25.4	-40.6	151.6	2 32.6	-41.0	151.7	53
4 31.1	-39.9	152.3	3 37.9	-40.2	152.3	2 44.8	-40.6	152.4	1 51.6	-40.9	152.4	54
3 51.2	-39.9	153.1	2 57.7	-40.3	153.1	2 04.2	-40.6	153.1	1 10.7	-41.0	153.1	55
3 11.3	-40.0	153.8	2 17.4	-40.3	153.8	1 23.6	-40.7	153.8	0 29.7	-41.0	153.9	56
2 31.3	-40.0	154.6	1 37.1	-40.3	154.6	0 42.9	-40.6	154.6	0 11.3	+40.9	25.4	57
1 51.3	-40.0	155.3	0 56.8	-40.3	155.3	0 02.3	-40.6	155.3	0 52.2	+41.0	24.7	58
1 11.3	-40.0	156.0	0 16.5	-40.3	156.1	0 38.3	+40.7	23.9	1 33.2	+40.9	24.0	59
0 31.3	-40.0	156.8	0 23.8	+40.4	23.2	1 19.0	+40.6	23.2	2 14.1	+40.9	23.2	60
0 08.7	+40.0	22.5	1 04.2	+40.3	22.5	1 59.6	+40.6	22.5	2 55.0	+40.9	22.5	61
0 48.7	+40.0	21.7	1 44.5	+40.3	21.7	2 40.2	+40.6	21.7	3 35.9	+40.9	21.8	62
1 28.7	+40.0	21.0	2 24.8	+40.2	21.0	3 20.8	+40.5	21.0	4 16.8	+40.8	21.0	63
2 08.7	+40.0	20.2	3 05.0	+40.3	20.2	4 01.3	+40.5	20.3	4 57.6	+40.8	20.3	64
2 48.7	+39.9	19.5	3 45.3	+40.2	19.5	4 41.8	+40.5	19.5	5 38.4	+40.7	19.6	65
3 28.6	+39.9	18.7	4 25.5	+40.1	18.8	5 22.3	+40.4	18.8	6 19.1	+40.6	18.8	66
4 08.5	+39.9	18.0	5 05.6	+40.1	18.0	6 02.7	+40.3	18.0	6 59.7	+40.6	18.1	67
4 48.4	+39.8	17.2	5 45.7	+40.1	17.3	6 43.0	+40.3	17.3	7 40.3	+40.5	17.3	68
5 28.2	+39.8	16.5	6 25.8	+39.9	16.5	7 23.3	+40.2	16.5	8 20.8	+40.4	16.6	69
6 08.0	+39.7	15.7	7 05.7	+39.9	15.8	8 03.5	+40.1	15.8	9 01.2	+40.3	15.8	70
6 47.7	+39.6	15.0	7 45.6	+39.9	15.0	8 43.6	+40.0	15.0	9 41.5	+40.3	15.1	71
7 27.3	+39.6	14.2	8 25.5	+39.7	14.3	9 23.6	+39.9	14.3	10 21.8	+40.1	14.3	72
8 06.9	+39.4	13.5	9 05.2	+39.6	13.5	10 03.5	+39.9	13.5	11 01.9	+40.0	13.6	73
8 46.3	+39.4	12.7	9 44.8	+39.6	12.7	10 43.4	+39.7	12.8	11 41.9	+39.9	12.8	74
9 25.7	+39.3	11.9	10 24.4	+39.4	12.0	11 23.1	+39.6	12.0	12 21.8	+39.7	12.1	75
10 05.0	+39.1	11.2	11 03.8	+39.3	11.2	12 02.7	+39.4	11.2	13 01.5	+39.6	11.3	76
10 44.1	+39.1	10.4	11 43.1	+39.2	10.4	12 42.1	+39.4	10.5	13 41.1	+39.5	10.5	77
11 23.2	+38.9	9.6	12 22.3	+39.1	9.7	13 21.5	+39.2	9.7	14 20.6	+39.3	9.7	78
12 02.1	+38.8	8.8	13 01.4	+38.9	8.9	14 00.7	+39.0	8.9	14 59.9	+39.2	9.0	79
12 40.9	+38.7	8.1	13 40.3	+38.8	8.1	14 39.7	+38.9	8.1	15 39.1	+39.0	8.2	80
13 19.6	+38.5	7.3	14 19.1	+38.6	7.3	15 18.6	+38.7	7.3	16 18.1	+38.8	7.4	81
13 58.1	+38.4	6.5	14 57.7	+38.5	6.5	15 57.3	+38.6	6.5	16 56.9	+38.7	6.6	82
14 36.5	+38.2	5.7	15 36.2	+38.2	5.7	16 35.9	+38.3	5.8	17 35.6	+38.4	5.8	83
15 14.7	+38.0	4.9	16 14.4	+38.1	4.9	17 14.2	+38.2	4.9	18 14.0	+38.2	5.0	84
15 52.7	+37.8	4.1	16 52.5	+37.9	4.1	17 52.4	+37.9	4.1	18 52.2	+38.0	4.2	85
16 30.5	+37.7	3.3	17 30.4	+37.8	3.3	18 30.3	+37.8	3.3	19 30.2	+37.8	3.3	86
17 08.2	+37.5	2.5	18 08.2	+37.5	2.5	19 08.1	+37.5	2.5	20 08.0	+37.6	2.5	87
17 45.7	+37.2	1.7	18 45.7	+37.2	1.7	19 45.6	+37.3	1.7	20 45.6	+37.3	1.7	88
18 22.9	+37.1	0.8	19 22.9	+37.1	0.8	20 22.9	+37.1	0.8	21 22.9	+37.1	0.8	89
19 00.0	+36.8	0.0	20 00.0	+36.8	0.0	21 00.0	+36.8	0.0	22 00.0	+36.8	0.0	90
19°			20°			21°			22°			

S. Lat. {L.H.A. greater than 180° ....Zn=180°−Z; L.H.A. less than 180°...........Zn=180°+Z

LATITUDE SAME NAME AS DECLINATION — L.H.A. 128°, 232°

53°, 307° L.H.A. LATITUDE SAME NAME AS DECLINATION N. Lat. {L.H.A. greater than 180° .....Zn=Z; L.H.A. less than 180°............Zn=360°-Z}

Dec.	15°			16°			17°			18°			19°			20°			21°			22°			Dec.
	Hc	d	Z	Hc	d	Z	Hc	d	Z	Hc	d	Z	Hc	d	Z	Hc	d	Z	Hc	d	Z	Hc	d	Z	
°	° ′	′	°	° ′	′	°	° ′	′	°	° ′	′	°	° ′	′	°	° ′	′	°	° ′	′	°	° ′	′	°	°
0	35 32.6	+18.7	101.0	35 20.7	+20.0	101.7	35 08.2	+21.1	102.4	34 54.9	+22.3	103.1	34 40.9	+23.5	103.8	34 26.3	+24.6	104.5	34 11.0	+25.7	105.1	33 55.0	+26.8	105.8	0
1	35 51.3	+18.1	99.9	35 40.7	+19.2	100.6	35 29.3	+20.5	101.3	35 17.2	+21.6	102.0	35 04.4	+22.8	102.7	34 50.9	+24.0	103.3	34 36.7	+25.1	104.0	34 21.8	+26.3	104.7	1
2	36 09.4	+17.3	98.7	35 59.9	+18.6	99.4	35 49.8	+19.8	100.1	35 38.8	+21.0	100.8	35 27.2	+22.2	101.5	35 14.9	+23.3	102.2	35 01.8	+24.5	102.9	34 48.1	+25.6	103.6	2
3	36 26.7	+16.7	97.5	36 18.5	+17.9	98.2	36 09.6	+19.1	99.0	35 59.8	+20.4	99.7	35 49.4	+21.5	100.4	35 38.2	+22.7	101.1	35 26.3	+23.9	101.8	35 13.7	+25.0	102.5	3
4	36 43.4	+15.9	96.3	36 36.4	+17.2	97.0	36 28.7	+18.4	97.8	36 20.2	+19.6	98.5	36 10.9	+20.9	99.2	36 00.9	+22.1	100.0	35 50.2	+23.2	100.7	35 38.7	+24.4	101.4	4
5	36 59.3	+15.2	95.1	36 53.6	+16.4	95.8	36 47.1	+17.7	96.6	36 39.8	+19.0	97.3	36 31.8	+20.1	98.1	36 23.0	+21.4	98.8	36 13.4	+22.6	99.5	36 03.1	+23.8	100.2	5
6	37 14.5	+14.4	93.9	37 10.0	+15.8	94.6	37 04.8	+17.0	95.4	36 58.8	+18.2	96.1	36 51.9	+19.5	96.9	36 44.4	+20.7	97.6	36 36.0	+21.9	98.4	36 26.9	+23.1	99.1	6
7	37 28.9	+13.7	92.7	37 25.8	+14.9	93.4	37 21.8	+16.2	94.2	37 17.0	+17.5	95.0	37 11.4	+18.8	95.7	37 05.1	+19.9	96.5	36 57.9	+21.2	97.2	36 50.0	+22.4	98.0	7
8	37 42.6	+12.9	91.4	37 40.7	+14.2	92.2	37 38.0	+15.5	93.0	37 34.5	+16.8	93.7	37 30.2	+18.0	94.5	37 25.0	+19.3	95.3	37 19.1	+20.6	96.0	37 12.4	+21.8	96.8	8
9	37 55.5	+12.2	90.2	37 54.9	+13.5	91.0	37 53.5	+14.7	91.8	37 51.3	+16.0	92.5	37 48.2	+17.3	93.3	37 44.3	+18.6	94.1	37 39.7	+19.8	94.9	37 34.2	+21.0	95.6	9
10	38 07.7	+11.3	89.0	38 08.4	+12.6	89.7	38 08.2	+14.0	90.5	38 07.3	+15.2	91.3	38 05.5	+16.5	92.1	38 02.9	+17.8	92.9	37 59.5	+19.0	93.7	37 55.2	+20.3	94.4	10
11	38 19.0	+10.6	87.7	38 21.0	+11.9	88.5	38 22.2	+13.1	89.3	38 22.5	+14.5	90.1	38 22.0	+15.8	90.9	38 20.7	+17.0	91.7	38 18.5	+18.4	92.5	38 15.5	+19.6	93.2	11
12	38 29.6	+9.7	86.4	38 32.9	+11.0	87.2	38 35.3	+12.4	88.0	38 37.0	+13.6	88.8	38 37.8	+15.0	89.6	38 37.7	+16.3	90.4	38 36.9	+17.5	91.2	38 35.1	+18.9	92.0	12
13	38 39.3	+8.9	85.2	38 43.9	+10.3	86.0	38 47.7	+11.6	86.8	38 50.6	+12.9	87.6	38 52.8	+14.1	88.4	38 54.0	+15.5	89.2	38 54.4	+16.8	90.0	38 54.0	+18.1	90.8	13
14	38 48.2	+8.1	83.9	38 54.2	+9.4	84.7	38 59.3	+10.7	85.5	39 03.5	+12.1	86.3	39 06.9	+13.4	87.1	39 09.5	+14.7	88.0	39 11.2	+16.0	88.8	39 12.1	+17.3	89.6	14
15	38 56.3	+7.3	82.6	39 03.6	+8.6	83.5	39 10.0	+9.9	84.3	39 15.6	+11.2	85.1	39 20.3	+12.6	85.9	39 24.2	+13.9	86.7	39 27.2	+15.2	87.5	39 29.4	+16.5	88.4	15
16	39 03.6	+6.4	81.4	39 12.2	+7.7	82.2	39 19.9	+9.1	83.0	39 26.8	+10.4	83.8	39 32.9	+11.7	84.6	39 38.1	+13.0	85.4	39 42.4	+14.4	86.3	39 45.9	+15.7	87.1	16
17	39 10.0	+5.6	80.1	39 19.9	+6.9	80.9	39 29.0	+8.2	81.7	39 37.2	+9.6	82.5	39 44.6	+10.9	83.3	39 51.1	+12.2	84.2	39 56.8	+13.5	85.0	40 01.6	+14.8	85.8	17
18	39 15.6	+4.7	78.8	39 26.8	+6.1	79.6	39 37.2	+7.4	80.4	39 46.8	+8.7	81.2	39 55.5	+10.0	82.1	40 03.3	+11.4	82.9	40 10.3	+12.7	83.7	40 16.4	+14.1	84.6	18
19	39 20.3	+3.9	77.5	39 32.9	+5.2	78.3	39 44.6	+6.5	79.1	39 55.5	+7.8	80.0	40 05.5	+9.2	80.8	40 14.7	+10.5	81.6	40 23.0	+11.9	82.5	40 30.5	+13.2	83.3	19
20	39 24.2	+3.0	76.2	39 38.1	+4.3	77.0	39 51.1	+5.7	77.8	40 03.3	+7.0	78.7	40 14.7	+8.3	79.5	40 25.2	+9.7	80.3	40 34.9	+11.0	81.2	40 43.7	+12.3	82.0	20
21	39 27.2	+2.2	74.9	39 42.4	+3.5	75.7	39 56.8	+4.8	76.5	40 10.3	+6.1	77.4	40 23.0	+7.5	78.2	40 34.9	+8.8	79.0	40 45.9	+10.1	79.9	40 56.0	+11.4	80.7	21
22	39 29.4	+1.3	73.6	39 45.9	+2.6	74.4	40 01.6	+3.9	75.2	40 16.4	+5.3	76.1	40 30.5	+6.5	76.9	40 43.7	+7.9	77.7	40 56.0	+9.2	78.6	41 07.4	+10.6	79.4	22
23	39 30.7	+0.4	72.3	39 48.5	+1.7	73.1	40 05.5	+3.0	73.9	40 21.7	+4.3	74.8	40 37.0	+5.7	75.6	40 51.6	+7.0	76.4	41 05.2	+8.4	77.3	41 18.0	+9.7	78.1	23
24	39 31.1	-0.4	71.0	39 50.2	+0.8	71.8	40 08.5	+2.2	72.6	40 26.0	+3.5	73.4	40 42.7	+4.8	74.3	40 58.6	+6.1	75.1	41 13.6	+7.4	75.9	41 27.7	+8.8	76.8	24
25	39 30.7	-1.3	69.7	39 51.0	0.0	70.5	40 10.7	+1.2	71.3	40 29.5	+2.5	72.1	40 47.5	+3.9	72.9	41 04.7	+5.2	73.8	41 21.0	+6.5	74.6	41 36.5	+7.8	75.5	25
26	39 29.4	-2.2	68.5	39 51.0	-0.9	69.2	40 11.9	+0.4	70.0	40 32.0	+1.7	70.8	40 51.4	+2.9	71.6	41 09.9	+4.2	72.5	41 27.5	+5.6	73.3	41 44.3	+7.0	74.1	26
27	39 27.2	-3.0	67.2	39 50.1	-1.7	67.9	40 12.3	-0.5	68.7	40 33.7	+0.8	69.5	40 54.3	+2.1	70.3	41 14.1	+3.4	71.1	41 33.1	+4.7	72.0	41 51.3	+6.0	72.8	27
28	39 24.2	-3.9	65.9	39 48.4	-2.7	66.6	40 11.8	-1.4	67.4	40 34.5	-0.1	68.2	40 56.4	+1.2	69.0	41 17.5	+2.5	69.8	41 37.8	+3.8	70.6	41 57.3	+5.1	71.5	28
29	39 20.3	-4.7	64.6	39 45.7	-3.5	65.3	40 10.4	-2.3	66.1	40 34.4	-1.1	66.9	40 57.6	+0.2	67.7	41 20.0	+1.5	68.5	41 41.6	+2.8	69.3	42 02.4	+4.1	70.1	29
30	39 15.6	-5.6	63.3	39 42.2	-4.4	64.0	40 08.1	-3.1	64.8	40 33.3	-1.9	65.5	40 57.8	-0.7	66.3	41 21.5	+0.6	67.1	41 44.4	+1.9	68.0	42 06.5	+3.2	68.8	30
31	39 10.0	-6.4	62.0	39 37.8	-5.2	62.7	40 05.0	-4.0	63.5	40 31.4	-2.8	64.2	40 57.1	-1.5	65.0	41 22.1	-0.3	65.8	41 46.3	+1.0	66.6	42 09.7	+2.3	67.4	31
32	39 03.6	-7.3	60.7	39 32.6	-6.1	61.4	40 01.0	-4.9	62.2	40 28.6	-3.7	62.9	40 55.6	-2.5	63.7	41 21.8	-1.2	64.5	41 47.3	0.0	65.3	42 12.0	+1.3	66.1	32
33	38 56.3	-8.1	59.4	39 26.5	-6.9	60.1	39 56.1	-5.8	60.9	40 24.9	-4.6	61.6	40 53.1	-3.4	62.4	41 20.6	-2.2	63.1	41 47.3	-0.9	63.9	42 13.3	+0.3	64.7	33
34	38 48.2	-8.9	58.2	39 19.6	-7.8	58.9	39 50.3	-6.7	59.6	40 20.3	-5.4	60.3	40 49.7	-4.3	61.0	41 18.4	-3.0	61.8	41 46.4	-1.8	62.6	42 13.6	-0.6	63.4	34
35	38 39.3	-9.7	56.9	39 11.8	-8.6	57.6	39 43.6	-7.5	58.3	40 14.9	-6.4	59.0	40 45.4	-5.1	59.7	41 15.4	-4.0	60.5	41 44.6	-2.8	61.3	42 13.0	-1.5	62.0	35
36	38 29.6	-10.6	55.6	39 03.2	-9.5	56.3	39 36.1	-8.3	57.0	40 08.5	-7.2	57.7	40 40.3	-6.1	58.4	41 11.4	-4.9	59.2	41 41.8	-3.7	59.9	42 11.5	-2.5	60.7	36
37	38 19.0	-11.3	54.4	38 53.7	-10.3	55.0	39 27.8	-9.2	55.7	40 01.3	-8.1	56.4	40 34.2	-7.0	57.1	41 06.5	-5.8	57.8	41 38.1	-4.6	58.6	42 09.0	-3.4	59.4	37
38	38 07.7	-12.1	53.1	38 43.4	-11.1	53.8	39 18.6	-10.0	54.4	39 53.2	-8.9	55.1	40 27.2	-7.8	55.8	41 00.7	-6.7	56.5	41 33.5	-5.6	57.2	42 05.6	-4.4	58.0	38
39	37 55.6	-13.0	51.9	38 32.3	-11.9	52.5	39 08.6	-10.9	53.2	39 44.3	-9.8	53.8	40 19.4	-8.7	54.5	40 54.0	-7.6	55.2	41 27.9	-6.5	55.9	42 01.2	-5.3	56.7	39
40	37 42.6	-13.6	50.7	38 20.4	-12.7	51.3	38 57.7	-11.6	51.9	39 34.5	-10.6	52.5	40 10.7	-9.6	53.2	40 46.4	-8.5	53.9	41 21.4	-7.3	54.6	41 55.9	-6.3	55.3	40
41	37 29.0	-14.5	49.4	38 07.7	-13.4	50.0	38 46.1	-12.5	50.6	39 23.9	-11.5	51.3	40 01.1	-10.4	51.9	40 37.9	-9.4	52.6	41 14.1	-8.3	53.3	41 49.6	-7.1	54.0	41
42	37 14.5	-15.2	48.2	37 54.3	-14.3	48.8	38 33.6	-13.3	49.4	39 12.4	-12.3	50.0	39 50.7	-11.2	50.6	40 28.5	-10.2	51.3	41 05.8	-9.2	52.0	41 42.5	-8.1	52.7	42
43	36 59.3	-15.9	47.0	37 40.0	-15.0	47.6	38 20.3	-14.1	48.1	39 00.1	-13.1	48.7	39 39.5	-12.2	49.3	40 18.3	-11.1	50.0	40 56.6	-10.1	50.6	41 34.4	-9.0	51.3	43
44	36 43.4	-16.7	45.8	37 25.0	-15.7	46.3	38 06.2	-14.8	46.9	38 47.0	-13.9	47.5	39 27.3	-12.9	48.1	40 07.2	-11.9	48.7	40 46.5	-10.9	49.3	41 25.4	-9.9	50.0	44
45	36 26.7	-17.3	44.6	37 09.3	-16.5	45.1	37 51.4	-15.6	45.7	38 33.1	-14.6	46.2	39 14.4	-13.7	46.8	39 55.3	-12.8	47.4	40 35.6	-11.8	48.0	41 15.5	-10.8	48.7	45
46	36 09.4	-18.1	43.4	36 52.8	-17.2	43.9	37 35.8	-16.3	44.4	38 18.5	-15.5	45.0	39 00.7	-14.6	45.6	39 42.5	-13.6	46.1	40 23.8	-12.6	46.8	41 04.7	-11.7	47.4	46
47	35 51.3	-18.7	42.2	36 35.6	-17.9	42.7	37 19.5	-17.1	43.2	38 03.0	-16.2	43.8	38 46.1	-15.3	44.3	39 28.9	-14.5	44.9	40 11.2	-13.5	45.5	40 53.0	-12.5	46.1	47
48	35 32.6	-19.4	41.1	36 17.7	-18.7	41.5	37 02.4	-17.8	42.0	37 46.8	-17.0	42.5	38 30.8	-16.1	43.1	39 14.4	-15.2	43.6	39 57.7	-14.4	44.2	40 40.5	-13.4	44.8	48
49	35 13.2	-20.1	39.9	35 59.0	-19.3	40.4	36 44.6	-18.5	40.8	37 29.8	-17.7	41.3	38 14.7	-16.9	41.8	38 59.2	-16.0	42.4	39 43.3	-15.1	42.9	40 27.1	-14.3	43.5	49
50	34 53.1	-20.7	38.7	35 39.7	-19.9	39.2	36 26.1	-19.2	39.6	37 12.1	-18.4	40.1	37 57.8	-17.6	40.6	38 43.2	-16.8	41.1	39 28.2	-16.0	41.7	40 12.8	-15.1	42.2	50
51	34 32.4	-21.4	37.6	35 19.8	-20.7	38.0	36 06.9	-19.9	38.5	36 53.7	-19.1	38.9	37 40.2	-18.3	39.4	38 26.4	-17.6	39.9	39 12.2	-16.7	40.4	39 57.7	-15.9	41.0	51
52	34 11.0	-22.0	36.5	34 59.1	-21.3	36.9	35 47.0	-20.6	37.3	36 34.6	-19.9	37.8	37 21.9	-19.1	38.2	38 08.8	-18.3	38.7	38 55.5	-17.5	39.2	39 41.8	-16.7	39.7	52
53	33 49.0	-22.6	35.3	34 37.8	-21.9	35.7	35 26.4	-21.2	36.2	36 14.7	-20.5	36.6	37 02.8	-19.8	37.0	37 50.5	-19.0	37.5	38 38.0	-18.3	38.0	39 25.1	-17.5	38.5	53
54	33 26.4	-23.1	34.2	34 15.9	-22.5	34.6	35 05.2	-21.9	35.0	35 54.2	-21.2	35.4	36 43.0	-20.5	35.8	37 31.5	-19.8	36.3	38 19.7	-19.0	36.8	39 07.6	-18.2	37.2	54
55	33 03.3	-23.8	33.1	33 53.4	-23.1	33.5	34 43.3	-22.4	33.9	35 33.0	-21.8	34.3	36 22.5	-21.1	34.7	37 11.7	-20.4	35.1	38 00.7	-19.8	35.5	38 49.4	-19.1	36.0	55
56	32 39.5	-24.3	32.0	33 30.3	-23.7	32.4	34 20.9	-23.1	32.7	35 11.2	-22.4	33.1	36 01.4	-21.9	33.5	36 51.3	-21.2	33.9	37 40.9	-20.5	34.4	38 30.3	-19.8	34.8	56
57	32 15.2	-24.8	31.0	33 06.6	-24.3	31.3	33 57.8	-23.7	31.6	34 48.8	-23.1	32.0	35 39.5	-22.4	32.4	36 30.1	-21.8	32.8	37 20.4	-21.1	33.2	38 10.5	-20.5	33.6	57
58	31 50.4	-25.4	29.9	32 42.3	-24.8	30.2	33 34.1	-24.3	30.5	34 25.7	-23.7	30.9	35 17.1	-23.1	31.2	36 08.3	-22.5	31.6	36 59.3	-21.9	32.0	37 50.0	-21.2	32.4	58
59	31 25.0	-26.0	28.8	32 17.5	-25.4	29.1	33 09.8	-24.9	29.4	34 02.0	-24.3	29.8	34 54.0	-23.8	30.1	35 45.8	-23.2	30.5	36 37.4	-22.5	30.8	37 28.8	-21.9	31.2	59
60	30 59.0	-26.4	27.8	31 52.1	-26.0	28.0	32 44.9	-25.4	28.3	33 37.7	-24.9	28.7	34 30.2	-24.3	29.0	35 22.6	-23.7	29.3	36 14.9	-23.2	29.7	37 06.9	-22.6	30.1	60
61	30 32.6	-26.9	26.7	31 26.1	-26.4	27.0	32 19.5	-25.9	27.3	33 12.8	-25.4	27.6	34 05.9	-24.9	27.9	34 58.9	-24.4	28.2	35 51.7	-23.9	28.5	36 44.3	-23.3	28.9	61
62	30 05.7	-27.4	25.7	30 59.7	-26.9	25.9	31 53.6	-26.5	26.2	32 47.4	-26.0	26.5	33 41.0	-25.5	26.8	34 34.5	-25.0	27.1	35 27.8	-24.4	27.4	36 21.0	-23.9	27.7	62
63	29 38.3	-27.9	24.7	30 32.8	-27.5	24.9	31 27.1	-27.0	25.2	32 21.4	-26.5	25.4	33 15.5	-26.0	25.7	34 09.5	-25.6	26.0	35 03.4	-25.1	26.3	35 57.1	-24.6	26.6	63
64	29 10.4	-28.3	23.6	30 05.3	-27.9	23.9	31 00.1	-27.4	24.1	31 54.9	-27.1	24.4	32 49.5	-26.6	24.6	33 43.9	-26.1	24.9	34 38.3	-25.7	25.2	35 32.5	-25.1	25.5	64
65	28 42.1	-28.8	22.6	29 37.4	-28.4	22.8	30 32.7	-28.0	23.1	31 27.8	-27.5	23.3	32 22.9	-27.2	23.6	33 17.8	-26.7	23.8	34 12.6	-26.2	24.1	35 07.4	-25.8	24.4	65
66	28 13.3	-29.2	21.6	29 09.0	-28.8	21.8	30 04.7	-28.5	22.0	31 00.3	-28.1	22.3	31 55.7	-27.6	22.5	32 51.1	-27.2	22.7	33 46.4	-26.8	23.0	34 41.6	-26.4	23.3	66
67	27 44.1	-29.6	20.6	28 40.2	-29.3	20.8	29 36.2	-28.9	21.0	30 32.2	-28.5	21.2	31 28.1	-28.2	21.5	32 23.9	-27.8	21.7	33 19.6	-27.4	21.9	34 15.2	-26.9	22.2	67
68	27 14.5	-30.1	19.7	28 10.9	-29.7	19.8	29 07.3	-29.3	20.0	30 03.7	-29.0	20.2	30 59.9	-28.6	20.4	31 56.1	-28.2	20.6	32 52.2	-27.9	20.9	33 48.3	-27.5	21.1	68
69	26 44.4	-30.4	18.7	27 41.2	-30.1	18.9	28 38.0	-29.8	19.0	29 34.7	-29.5	19.2	30 31.3	-29.1	19.4	31 27.9	-28.8	19.6	32 24.3	-28.4	19.8	33 20.8	-28.1	20.0	69
70	26 14.0	-30.8	17.7	27 11.1	-30.5	17.9	28 08.2	-30.2	18.0	29 05.2	-29.9	18.2	30 02.2	-29.6	18.4	30 59.1	-29.2	18.6	31 55.9	-28.9	18.8	32 52.7	-28.6	19.0	70
71	25 43.2	-31.2	16.8	26 40.6	-30.9	16.9	27 38.0	-30.6	17.1	28 35.3	-30.3	17.2	29 32.6	-30.0	17.4	30 29.9	-29.8	17.6	31 27.0	-29.4	17.7	32 24.1	-29.0	17.9	71
72	25 12.0	-31.5	15.8	26 09.7	-31.2	16.0	27 07.4	-31.0	16.1	28 05.0	-30.7	16.2	29 02.6	-30.4	16.4	30 00.1	-30.1	16.6	30 57.6	-29.8	16.7	31 55.1	-29.6	16.9	72
73	24 40.5	-31.9	14.9	25 38.5	-31.7	15.0	26 36.4	-31.4	15.1	27 34.3	-31.1	15.3	28 32.2	-30.9	15.4	29 30.0	-30.6	15.6	30 27.8	-30.4	15.7	31 25.5	-30.1	15.9	73
74	24 08.6	-32.2	14.0	25 06.8	-32.0	14.1	26 05.0	-31.7	14.2	27 03.2	-31.6	14.3	28 01.3	-31.3	14.4	28 59.4	-31.1	14.6	29 57.4	-30.8	14.7	30 55.4	-30.5	14.9	74
75	23 36.4	-32.5	13.0	24 34.8	-32.3	13.1	25 33.3	-32.2	13.2	26 31.6	-31.9	13.4	27 30.0	-31.7	13.5	28 28.3	-31.4	13.6	29 26.6	-31.2	13.7	30 24.9	-31.0	13.9	75
76	23 03.9	-32.9	12.1	24 02.5	-32.7	12.2	25 01.1	-32.4	12.3	25 59.7	-32.2	12.4	26 58.3	-32.0	12.5	27 56.9	-31.9	12.6	28 55.4	-31.6	12.8	29 53.9	-31.4	12.9	76
77	22 31.0	-33.2	11.2	23 29.8	-32.9	11.3	24 28.7	-32.8	11.4	25 27.5	-32.6	11.5	26 26.3	-32.5	11.6	27 25.0	-32.2	11.7	28 23.8	-32.1	11.8	29 22.5	-31.8	11.9	77
78	21 57.8	-33.4	10.3	22 56.9	-33.3	10.4	23 55.9	-33.2	10.5	24 54.9	-33.0	10.5	25 53.8	-32.7	10.6	26 52.8	-32.6	10.7	27 51.7	-32.4	10.8	28 50.7	-32.3	10.9	78
79	21 24.4	-33.7	9.4	22 23.6	-33.6	9.5	23 22.7	-33.4	9.6	24 21.9	-33.3	9.6	25 21.1	-33.2	9.7	26 20.2	-33.0	9.8	27 19.3	-32.8	9.9	28 18.4	-32.6	10.0	79
80	20 50.7	-34.0	8.5	21 50.0	-33.9	8.6	22 49.3	-33.7	8.7	23 48.6	-33.6	8.7	24 47.9	-33.4	8.8	25 47.2	-33.3	8.9	26 46.5	-33.2	8.9	27 45.8	-33.1	9.0	80
81	20 16.7	-34.3	7.7	21 16.1	-34.1	7.7	22 15.6	-34.1	7.8	23 15.0	-33.9	7.8	24 14.5	-33.8	7.9	25 13.9	-33.7	7.9	26 13.3	-33.5	8.0	27 12.7	-33.4	8.1	81
82	19 42.4	-34.5	6.8	20 42.0	-34.4	6.8	21 41.5	-34.3	6.9	22 41.1	-34.2	6.9	23 40.7	-34.1	7.0	24 40.2	-34.0	7.0	25 39.8	-33.9	7.1	26 39.3	-33.8	7.1	82
83	19 07.9	-34.8	5.9	20 07.6	-34.7	5.9	21 07.2	-34.6	6.0	22 06.9	-34.5	6.0	23 06.6	-34.4	6.1	24 06.2	-34.3	6.1	25 05.9	-34.2	6.2	26 05.5	-34.1	6.2	83
84	18 33.1	-35.0	5.1	19 32.9	-34.9	5.1	20 32.6	-34.8	5.1	21 32.4	-34.8	5.1	22 32.2	-34.7	5.2	23 31.9	-34.6	5.2	24 31.7	-34.6	5.3	25 31.4	-34.5	5.3	84
85	17 58.1	-35.2	4.2	18 58.0	-35.2	4.2	19 57.8	-35.1	4.2	20 57.6	-35.0	4.3	21 57.5	-35.0	4.3	22 57.3	-34.9	4.3	23 57.1	-34.8	4.4	24 56.9	-34.7	4.4	85
86	17 22.9	-35.4	3.3	18 22.8	-35.4	3.4	19 22.7	-35.3	3.4	20 22.6	-35.3	3.4	21 22.5	-35.3	3.4	22 22.4	-35.2	3.5	23 22.3	-35.2	3.5	24 22.2	-35.1	3.5	86
87	16 47.5	-35.7	2.5	17 47.4	-35.6	2.5	18 47.4	-35.6	2.5	19 47.3	-35.5	2.5	20 47.2	-35.5	2.6	21 47.2	-35.5	2.6	22 47.1	-35.4	2.6	23 47.1	-35.4	2.6	87
88	16 11.8	-35.8	1.7	17 11.8	-35.8	1.7	18 11.8	-35.8	1.7	19 11.8	-35.8	1.7	20 11.7	-35.7	1.7	21 11.7	-35.7	1.7	22 11.7	-35.7	1.7	23 11.7	-35.7	1.7	88
89	15 36.0	-36.0	0.8	16 36.0	-36.0	0.8	17 36.0	-36.0	0.8	18 36.0	-36.0	0.8	19 36.0	-36.0	0.8	20 36.0	-36.0	0.9	21 36.0	-36.0	0.9	22 36.0	-36.0	0.9	89
90	15 00.0	-36.2	0.0	16 00.0	-36.2	0.0	17 00.0	-36.2	0.0	18 00.0	-36.2	0.0	19 00.0	-36.2	0.0	20 00.0	-36.2	0.0	21 00.0	-36.2	0.0	22 00.0	-36.2	0.0	90
	15°			16°			17°			18°			19°			20°			21°			22°			

53°, 307° L.H.A. LATITUDE SAME NAME AS DECLINATION

108

Dec.	15° Hc	d	Z	16° Hc	d	Z	17° Hc	d	Z	18° Hc	d	Z	Dec.
°	° ′	′	°	° ′	′	°	° ′	′	°	° ′	′	°	°
0	35 32.6	-19.5	101.0	35 20.7	-20.6	101.7	35 08.2	-21.8	102.4	34 54.9	-22.9	103.1	0
1	35 13.1	-20.0	102.2	35 00.1	-21.2	102.9	34 46.4	-22.4	103.6	34 32.0	-23.6	104.2	1
2	34 53.1	-20.8	103.3	34 38.9	-21.9	104.0	34 24.0	-23.0	104.7	34 08.4	-24.1	105.3	2
3	34 32.3	-21.3	104.5	34 17.0	-22.5	105.2	34 01.0	-23.6	105.8	33 44.3	-24.7	106.5	3
4	34 11.0	-22.0	105.6	33 54.5	-23.1	106.3	33 37.4	-24.2	106.9	33 19.6	-25.3	107.5	4
5	33 49.0	-22.6	106.7	33 31.4	-23.7	107.4	33 13.2	-24.8	108.0	32 54.3	-25.8	108.6	5
6	33 26.4	-23.1	107.9	33 07.7	-24.2	108.5	32 48.4	-25.3	109.1	32 28.5	-26.4	109.7	6
7	33 03.3	-23.8	109.0	32 43.5	-24.9	109.6	32 23.1	-25.9	110.2	32 02.1	-26.9	110.8	7
8	32 39.5	-24.3	110.1	32 18.6	-25.3	110.6	31 57.2	-26.4	111.2	31 35.2	-27.4	111.8	8
9	32 15.2	-24.9	111.1	31 53.3	-25.9	111.7	31 30.8	-26.9	112.3	31 07.8	-28.0	112.9	9
10	31 50.3	-25.4	112.2	31 27.4	-26.4	112.8	31 03.9	-27.4	113.3	30 39.8	-28.4	113.9	10
11	31 24.9	-25.9	113.3	31 01.0	-27.0	113.8	30 36.5	-27.9	114.4	30 11.4	-28.8	114.9	11
12	30 59.0	-26.4	114.3	30 34.0	-27.4	114.9	30 08.6	-28.4	115.4	29 42.6	-29.4	115.9	12
13	30 32.6	-26.9	115.4	30 06.6	-27.9	115.9	29 40.2	-28.9	116.4	29 13.2	-29.7	116.9	13
14	30 05.7	-27.4	116.4	29 38.7	-28.3	116.9	29 11.3	-29.2	117.4	28 43.5	-30.2	117.9	14
15	29 38.3	-27.9	117.4	29 10.4	-28.8	117.9	28 42.1	-29.8	118.4	28 13.3	-30.6	118.9	15
16	29 10.4	-28.3	118.5	28 41.6	-29.3	118.9	28 12.3	-30.1	119.4	27 42.7	-31.1	119.9	16
17	28 42.1	-28.8	119.5	28 12.3	-29.6	119.9	27 42.2	-30.6	120.4	27 11.6	-31.4	120.8	17
18	28 13.3	-29.2	120.5	27 42.7	-30.1	120.9	27 11.6	-30.9	121.4	26 40.2	-31.8	121.8	18
19	27 44.1	-29.7	121.4	27 12.6	-30.5	121.9	26 40.7	-31.4	122.3	26 08.4	-32.1	122.7	19
20	27 14.4	-30.0	122.4	26 42.1	-30.9	122.9	26 09.3	-31.7	123.3	25 36.3	-32.6	123.7	20
21	26 44.4	-30.4	123.4	26 11.2	-31.2	123.8	25 37.6	-32.0	124.2	25 03.7	-32.8	124.6	21
22	26 14.0	-30.8	124.4	25 40.0	-31.7	124.8	25 05.6	-32.4	125.1	24 30.9	-33.2	125.5	22
23	25 43.2	-31.2	125.3	25 08.3	-31.9	125.7	24 33.2	-32.8	126.1	23 57.7	-33.5	126.4	23
24	25 12.0	-31.5	126.3	24 36.4	-32.4	126.6	24 00.4	-33.1	127.0	23 24.2	-33.9	127.3	24
25	24 40.5	-31.9	127.2	24 04.0	-32.6	127.6	23 27.3	-33.4	127.9	22 50.3	-34.1	128.2	25
26	24 08.6	-32.2	128.1	23 31.4	-33.0	128.5	22 53.9	-33.7	128.8	22 16.2	-34.4	129.1	26
27	23 36.4	-32.6	129.1	22 58.4	-33.2	129.4	22 20.2	-34.0	129.7	21 41.8	-34.7	130.0	27
28	23 03.8	-32.8	130.0	22 25.2	-33.6	130.3	21 46.2	-34.2	130.6	21 07.1	-35.0	130.9	28
29	22 31.0	-33.2	130.9	21 51.6	-33.9	131.2	21 12.0	-34.6	131.5	20 32.1	-35.2	131.8	29
30	21 57.8	-33.4	131.8	21 17.7	-34.1	132.1	20 37.4	-34.8	132.4	19 56.9	-35.5	132.6	30
31	21 24.4	-33.8	132.7	20 43.6	-34.4	133.0	20 02.6	-35.1	133.2	19 21.4	-35.7	133.5	31
32	20 50.6	-34.0	133.6	20 09.2	-34.7	133.8	19 27.5	-35.3	134.1	18 45.7	-35.9	134.3	32
33	20 16.6	-34.2	134.4	19 34.5	-34.9	134.7	18 52.2	-35.5	134.9	18 09.8	-36.2	135.2	33
34	19 42.4	-34.5	135.3	18 59.6	-35.1	135.6	18 16.7	-35.8	135.8	17 33.6	-36.4	136.0	34
35	19 07.9	-34.8	136.2	18 24.5	-35.4	136.4	17 40.9	-35.9	136.6	16 57.2	-36.5	136.8	35
36	18 33.1	-35.0	137.0	17 49.1	-35.6	137.3	17 05.0	-36.2	137.5	16 20.7	-36.8	137.7	36
37	17 58.1	-35.2	137.9	17 13.5	-35.8	138.1	16 28.8	-36.4	138.3	15 43.9	-36.9	138.5	37
38	17 22.9	-35.4	138.7	16 37.7	-36.0	138.9	15 52.4	-36.6	139.1	15 07.0	-37.2	139.3	38
39	16 47.5	-35.7	139.6	16 01.7	-36.2	139.8	15 15.8	-36.7	140.0	14 29.8	-37.2	140.1	39
40	16 11.8	-35.8	140.4	15 25.5	-36.4	140.6	14 39.1	-36.9	140.8	13 52.6	-37.5	140.9	40
41	15 36.0	-36.0	141.3	14 49.1	-36.5	141.4	14 02.2	-37.1	141.6	13 15.1	-37.6	141.7	41
42	15 00.0	-36.2	142.1	14 12.6	-36.7	142.2	13 25.1	-37.2	142.4	12 37.5	-37.7	142.5	42
43	14 23.8	-36.4	142.9	13 35.9	-36.9	143.1	12 47.9	-37.4	143.2	11 59.8	-37.9	143.3	43
44	13 47.4	-36.5	143.7	12 59.0	-37.0	143.9	12 10.5	-37.5	144.0	11 21.9	-38.0	144.1	44
45	13 10.9	-36.7	144.5	12 22.0	-37.2	144.7	11 33.0	-37.7	144.8	10 43.9	-38.1	144.9	45
46	12 34.2	-36.8	145.4	11 44.8	-37.3	145.5	10 55.3	-37.7	145.6	10 05.8	-38.2	145.7	46
47	11 57.4	-37.0	146.2	11 07.5	-37.4	146.3	10 17.6	-37.9	146.4	9 27.6	-38.4	146.5	47
48	11 20.4	-37.1	147.0	10 30.1	-37.6	147.1	9 39.7	-38.0	147.2	8 49.2	-38.4	147.3	48
49	10 43.3	-37.2	147.8	9 52.5	-37.6	147.9	9 01.7	-38.1	148.0	8 10.8	-38.5	148.0	49
50	10 06.1	-37.3	148.6	9 14.9	-37.8	148.7	8 23.6	-38.2	148.7	7 32.3	-38.6	148.8	50
51	9 28.8	-37.5	149.4	8 37.1	-37.9	149.4	7 45.4	-38.3	149.5	6 53.7	-38.7	149.6	51
52	8 51.3	-37.5	150.2	7 59.2	-37.9	150.2	7 07.1	-38.3	150.3	6 15.0	-38.7	150.4	52
53	8 13.8	-37.7	150.9	7 21.3	-38.0	151.0	6 28.8	-38.4	151.1	5 36.3	-38.8	151.1	53
54	7 36.1	-37.7	151.7	6 43.3	-38.1	151.8	5 50.4	-38.5	151.8	4 57.5	-38.9	151.9	54
55	6 58.4	-37.8	152.5	6 05.2	-38.2	152.6	5 11.9	-38.5	152.6	4 18.6	-38.9	152.7	55
56	6 20.6	-37.8	153.3	5 27.0	-38.2	153.3	4 33.4	-38.6	153.4	3 39.7	-38.9	153.4	56
57	5 42.8	-38.0	154.1	4 48.8	-38.3	154.1	3 54.8	-38.6	154.2	3 00.8	-39.0	154.2	57
58	5 04.8	-38.0	154.9	4 10.5	-38.3	154.9	3 16.2	-38.7	154.9	2 21.8	-39.0	154.9	58
59	4 26.8	-38.0	155.6	3 32.2	-38.4	155.7	2 37.5	-38.7	155.7	1 42.8	-39.0	155.7	59
60	3 48.8	-38.1	156.4	2 53.8	-38.4	156.4	1 58.8	-38.7	156.4	1 03.8	-39.0	156.5	60
61	3 10.7	-38.1	157.2	2 15.4	-38.4	157.2	1 20.1	-38.7	157.2	0 24.8	-39.0	157.2	61
62	2 32.6	-38.1	158.0	1 37.0	-38.4	158.0	0 41.4	-38.7	158.0	0 14.2	+39.1	22.0	62
63	1 54.5	-38.2	158.7	0 58.6	-38.5	158.7	0 02.7	-38.8	158.7	0 53.3	+39.0	21.3	63
64	1 16.3	-38.1	159.5	0 20.1	-38.4	159.5	0 36.1	+38.7	20.5	1 32.3	+39.0	20.5	64
65	0 38.2	-38.2	160.3	0 18.3	+38.5	19.7	1 14.8	+38.7	19.7	2 11.3	+38.9	19.7	65
66	0 00.0	-38.2	161.0	0 56.8	+38.4	19.0	1 53.5	+38.7	19.0	2 50.2	+39.0	19.0	66
67	0 38.2	+38.2	18.2	1 35.2	+38.4	18.2	2 32.2	+38.7	18.2	3 29.2	+38.9	18.2	67
68	1 16.4	+38.1	17.4	2 13.6	+38.4	17.4	3 10.9	+38.6	17.4	4 08.1	+38.9	17.5	68
69	1 54.5	+38.2	16.6	2 52.0	+38.4	16.7	3 49.5	+38.6	16.7	4 47.0	+38.8	16.7	69
70	2 32.7	+38.1	15.9	3 30.4	+38.3	15.9	4 28.1	+38.5	15.9	5 25.8	+38.7	15.9	70
71	3 10.8	+38.0	15.1	4 08.7	+38.3	15.1	5 06.6	+38.5	15.1	6 04.5	+38.7	15.2	71
72	3 48.8	+38.1	14.3	4 47.0	+38.2	14.3	5 45.1	+38.4	14.4	6 43.2	+38.6	14.4	72
73	4 26.9	+38.0	13.5	5 25.2	+38.2	13.6	6 23.5	+38.4	13.6	7 21.8	+38.6	13.6	73
74	5 04.9	+37.9	12.8	6 03.4	+38.1	12.8	7 01.9	+38.3	12.8	8 00.4	+38.4	12.8	74
75	5 42.8	+37.8	12.0	6 41.5	+38.0	12.0	7 40.2	+38.1	12.0	8 38.8	+38.4	12.1	75
76	6 20.6	+37.8	11.2	7 19.5	+37.9	11.2	8 18.3	+38.2	11.3	9 17.2	+38.2	11.3	76
77	6 58.4	+37.8	10.4	7 57.4	+37.9	10.5	8 56.5	+38.0	10.5	9 55.4	+38.2	10.5	77
78	7 36.2	+37.6	9.6	8 35.3	+37.8	9.7	9 34.5	+37.9	9.7	10 33.6	+38.0	9.7	78
79	8 13.8	+37.5	8.9	9 13.1	+37.6	8.9	10 12.4	+37.7	8.9	11 11.6	+37.9	8.9	79
80	8 51.3	+37.5	8.1	9 50.7	+37.6	8.1	10 50.1	+37.7	8.1	11 49.5	+37.8	8.1	80
81	9 28.8	+37.3	7.3	10 28.3	+37.4	7.3	11 27.8	+37.5	7.3	12 27.3	+37.6	7.4	81
82	10 06.1	+37.2	6.5	11 05.7	+37.3	6.5	12 05.3	+37.4	6.5	13 04.9	+37.5	6.6	82
83	10 43.3	+37.1	5.7	11 43.0	+37.2	5.7	12 42.7	+37.3	5.7	13 42.4	+37.4	5.7	83
84	11 20.4	+37.0	4.9	12 20.2	+37.0	4.9	13 20.0	+37.1	4.9	14 19.8	+37.1	4.9	84
85	11 57.4	+36.8	4.1	12 57.2	+36.9	4.1	13 57.1	+36.9	4.1	14 56.9	+37.0	4.1	85
86	12 34.2	+36.7	3.3	13 34.1	+36.8	3.3	14 34.0	+36.8	3.3	15 33.9	+36.8	3.3	86
87	13 10.9	+36.5	2.5	14 10.9	+36.5	2.5	15 10.8	+36.6	2.5	16 10.7	+36.7	2.5	87
88	13 47.4	+36.4	1.6	14 47.4	+36.4	1.7	15 47.4	+36.4	1.7	16 47.4	+36.4	1.7	88
89	14 23.8	+36.2	0.8	15 23.8	+36.2	0.8	16 23.8	+36.2	0.8	17 23.8	+36.2	0.8	89
90	15 00.0	+36.0	0.0	16 00.0	+36.0	0.0	17 00.0	+36.0	0.0	18 00.0	+36.0	0.0	90
	15°			16°			17°			18°			

Dec.	19° Hc	d	Z	20° Hc	d	Z	21° Hc	d	Z	22° Hc	d	Z	Dec.
°	° ′	′	°	° ′	′	°	° ′	′	°	° ′	′	°	°
0	34 40.9	-24.0	103.8	34 26.3	-25.2	104.5	34 11.0	-26.3	105.1	33 55.0	-27.3	105.8	0
1	34 16.9	-24.7	104.9	34 01.1	-25.7	105.6	33 44.7	-26.8	106.2	33 27.7	-27.9	106.8	1
2	33 52.2	-25.2	106.0	33 35.4	-26.3	106.6	33 17.9	-27.4	107.3	32 59.8	-28.5	107.9	2
3	33 27.0	-25.8	107.1	33 09.1	-26.9	107.7	32 50.5	-27.9	108.3	32 31.3	-28.9	108.9	3
4	33 01.2	-26.4	108.2	32 42.2	-27.4	108.8	32 22.6	-28.5	109.4	32 02.4	-29.5	110.0	4
5	32 34.8	-26.9	109.2	32 14.8	-27.9	109.8	31 54.1	-28.9	110.4	31 32.9	-29.9	111.0	5
6	32 07.9	-27.4	110.3	31 46.9	-28.5	110.9	31 25.2	-29.4	111.5	31 03.0	-30.4	112.0	6
7	31 40.5	-27.9	111.3	31 18.4	-28.9	111.9	30 55.8	-29.9	112.5	30 32.6	-30.9	113.0	7
8	31 12.6	-28.4	112.4	30 49.5	-29.4	112.9	30 25.9	-30.4	113.5	30 01.7	-31.3	114.0	8
9	30 44.2	-28.9	113.4	30 20.1	-29.9	113.9	29 55.5	-30.8	114.5	29 30.4	-31.7	115.0	9
10	30 15.3	-29.4	114.4	29 50.2	-30.3	114.9	29 24.7	-31.3	115.5	28 58.7	-32.2	116.0	10
11	29 45.9	-29.8	115.4	29 19.9	-30.7	115.9	28 53.4	-31.6	116.4	28 26.5	-32.6	116.9	11
12	29 16.1	-30.2	116.4	28 49.2	-31.2	116.9	28 21.8	-32.1	117.4	27 53.9	-32.9	117.9	12
13	28 45.9	-30.7	117.4	28 18.0	-31.6	117.9	27 49.7	-32.4	118.4	27 21.0	-33.3	118.8	13
14	28 15.2	-31.1	118.4	27 46.4	-32.0	118.9	27 17.3	-32.9	119.3	26 47.7	-33.7	119.8	14
15	27 44.1	-31.5	119.4	27 14.4	-32.3	119.8	26 44.4	-33.2	120.3	26 14.0	-34.0	120.7	15
16	27 12.6	-31.9	120.3	26 42.1	-32.8	120.8	26 11.2	-33.6	121.2	25 40.0	-34.4	121.6	16
17	26 40.7	-32.3	121.3	26 09.3	-33.0	121.7	25 37.6	-33.9	122.1	25 05.6	-34.7	122.5	17
18	26 08.4	-32.6	122.2	25 36.3	-33.5	122.6	25 03.7	-34.2	123.0	24 30.9	-35.1	123.4	18
19	25 35.8	-33.0	123.1	25 02.8	-33.8	123.5	24 29.5	-34.6	123.9	23 55.8	-35.3	124.3	19
20	25 02.8	-33.3	124.1	24 29.0	-34.1	124.4	23 54.9	-34.8	124.8	23 20.5	-35.6	125.2	20
21	24 29.5	-33.7	125.0	23 54.9	-34.4	125.4	23 20.1	-35.2	125.7	22 44.9	-35.9	126.1	21
22	23 55.8	-33.9	125.9	23 20.5	-34.7	126.2	22 44.9	-35.5	126.6	22 09.0	-36.2	126.9	22
23	23 21.9	-34.3	126.8	22 45.8	-35.0	127.1	22 09.4	-35.7	127.5	21 32.8	-36.4	127.8	23
24	22 47.6	-34.6	127.7	22 10.8	-35.3	128.0	21 33.7	-36.0	128.3	20 56.4	-36.7	128.6	24
25	22 13.0	-34.8	128.6	21 35.5	-35.5	128.9	20 57.7	-36.2	129.2	20 19.7	-36.9	129.5	25
26	21 38.2	-35.1	129.4	21 00.0	-35.9	129.7	20 21.5	-36.5	130.0	19 42.8	-37.2	130.3	26
27	21 03.1	-35.4	130.3	20 24.1	-36.0	130.6	19 45.0	-36.8	130.9	19 05.6	-37.4	131.1	27
28	20 27.7	-35.7	131.2	19 48.1	-36.3	131.5	19 08.2	-36.9	131.7	18 28.2	-37.6	132.0	28
29	19 52.0	-35.8	132.0	19 11.8	-36.6	132.3	18 31.3	-37.2	132.6	17 50.6	-37.8	132.8	29
30	19 16.2	-36.2	132.9	18 35.2	-36.7	133.1	17 54.1	-37.4	133.4	17 12.8	-38.0	133.6	30
31	18 40.0	-36.3	133.7	17 58.5	-37.0	134.0	17 16.7	-37.6	134.2	16 34.8	-38.2	134.4	31
32	18 03.7	-36.6	134.6	17 21.5	-37.2	134.8	16 39.1	-37.7	135.0	15 56.6	-38.3	135.2	32
33	17 27.1	-36.7	135.4	16 44.3	-37.3	135.6	16 01.4	-38.0	135.8	15 18.3	-38.6	136.0	33
34	16 50.4	-37.0	136.2	16 07.0	-37.6	136.4	15 23.4	-38.1	136.6	14 39.7	-38.7	136.8	34
35	16 13.4	-37.2	137.1	15 29.4	-37.7	137.2	14 45.3	-38.3	137.4	14 01.0	-38.8	137.6	35
36	15 36.2	-37.3	137.9	14 51.7	-37.9	138.1	14 07.0	-38.4	138.2	13 22.2	-39.0	138.4	36
37	14 58.9	-37.5	138.7	14 13.8	-38.1	138.9	13 28.6	-38.6	139.0	12 43.2	-39.1	139.2	37
38	14 21.4	-37.7	139.5	13 35.7	-38.2	139.6	12 50.0	-38.8	139.8	12 04.1	-39.3	139.9	38
39	13 43.7	-37.8	140.3	12 57.5	-38.3	140.4	12 11.2	-38.8	140.6	11 24.8	-39.3	140.7	39
40	13 05.9	-37.9	141.1	12 19.2	-38.5	141.2	11 32.4	-39.0	141.4	10 45.5	-39.5	141.5	40
41	12 28.0	-38.2	141.9	11 40.7	-38.6	142.0	10 53.4	-39.1	142.1	10 06.0	-39.6	142.2	41
42	11 49.8	-38.2	142.7	11 02.1	-38.7	142.8	10 14.3	-39.2	142.9	9 26.4	-39.7	143.0	42
43	11 11.6	-38.3	143.5	10 23.4	-38.9	143.6	9 35.1	-39.4	143.7	8 46.7	-39.8	143.8	43
44	10 33.3	-38.5	144.2	9 44.5	-38.9	144.3	8 55.7	-39.4	144.4	8 06.9	-39.9	144.5	44
45	9 54.8	-38.6	145.0	9 05.6	-39.1	145.1	8 16.3	-39.5	145.2	7 27.0	-39.9	145.3	45
46	9 16.2	-38.7	145.8	8 26.5	-39.1	145.9	7 36.8	-39.5	146.0	6 47.1	-40.0	146.0	46
47	8 37.5	-38.8	146.6	7 47.4	-39.2	146.7	6 57.3	-39.7	146.7	6 07.1	-40.1	146.8	47
48	7 58.7	-38.8	147.3	7 08.2	-39.3	147.4	6 17.6	-39.7	147.5	5 27.0	-40.1	147.5	48
49	7 19.9	-39.0	148.1	6 28.9	-39.3	148.2	5 37.9	-39.7	148.2	4 46.9	-40.2	148.3	49
50	6 40.9	-39.0	148.9	5 49.6	-39.5	148.9	4 58.2	-39.9	149.0	4 06.7	-40.2	149.0	50
51	6 01.9	-39.0	149.6	5 10.1	-39.4	149.7	4 18.3	-39.8	149.7	3 26.5	-40.3	149.8	51
52	5 22.9	-39.2	150.4	4 30.7	-39.5	150.4	3 38.5	-39.9	150.5	2 46.2	-40.2	150.5	52
53	4 43.7	-39.2	151.2	3 51.2	-39.6	151.2	2 58.6	-40.0	151.2	2 06.0	-40.3	151.3	53
54	4 04.5	-39.2	151.9	3 11.6	-39.6	152.0	2 18.6	-39.9	152.0	1 25.7	-40.3	152.0	54
55	3 25.3	-39.2	152.7	2 32.0	-39.6	152.7	1 38.7	-40.0	152.7	0 45.4	-40.4	152.7	55
56	2 46.1	-39.3	153.4	1 52.4	-39.6	153.5	0 58.7	-40.0	153.5	0 05.0	-40.3	153.5	56
57	2 06.8	-39.3	154.2	1 12.8	-39.7	154.2	0 18.7	-40.0	154.2	0 35.3	+40.3	25.8	57
58	1 27.5	-39.4	155.0	0 33.1	-39.6	155.0	0 21.3	+39.9	25.0	1 15.6	+40.3	25.0	58
59	0 48.1	-39.3	155.7	0 06.5	+39.7	24.3	1 01.2	+40.0	24.3	1 55.9	+40.3	24.3	59
60	0 08.8	-39.3	156.5	0 46.2	+39.6	23.5	1 41.2	+40.0	23.5	2 36.2	+40.3	23.6	60
61	0 30.5	+39.4	22.8	1 25.8	+39.7	22.8	2 21.2	+39.9	22.8	3 16.5	+40.2	22.8	61
62	1 09.9	+39.3	22.0	2 05.5	+39.6	22.0	3 01.1	+39.9	22.1	3 56.7	+40.2	22.1	62
63	1 49.2	+39.3	21.3	2 45.1	+39.6	21.3	3 41.0	+39.8	21.3	4 36.9	+40.1	21.3	63
64	2 28.5	+39.2	20.5	3 24.7	+39.5	20.5	4 20.8	+39.9	20.6	5 17.0	+40.1	20.6	64
65	3 07.7	+39.3	19.8	4 04.2	+39.5	19.8	5 00.7	+39.7	19.8	5 57.1	+40.0	19.8	65
66	3 47.0	+39.2	19.0	4 43.7	+39.5	19.0	5 40.4	+39.7	19.1	6 37.1	+40.0	19.1	66
67	4 26.2	+39.1	18.2	5 23.2	+39.4	18.3	6 20.1	+39.7	18.3	7 17.1	+39.9	18.3	67
68	5 05.3	+39.1	17.5	6 02.6	+39.3	17.5	6 59.8	+39.5	17.5	7 57.0	+39.8	17.6	68
69	5 44.4	+39.1	16.7	6 41.9	+39.3	16.7	7 39.3	+39.5	16.8	8 36.8	+39.7	16.8	69
70	6 23.5	+38.9	16.0	7 21.2	+39.1	16.0	8 18.8	+39.4	16.0	9 16.5	+39.6	16.1	70
71	7 02.4	+38.9	15.2	8 00.3	+39.1	15.2	8 58.2	+39.3	15.3	9 56.1	+39.5	15.3	71
72	7 41.3	+38.8	14.4	8 39.4	+39.1	14.5	9 37.5	+39.2	14.5	10 35.6	+39.4	14.5	72
73	8 20.1	+38.8	13.7	9 18.5	+38.9	13.7	10 16.7	+39.1	13.7	11 15.0	+39.3	13.8	73
74	8 58.9	+38.6	12.9	9 57.4	+38.8	12.9	10 55.8	+39.0	13.0	11 54.3	+39.2	13.0	74
75	9 37.5	+38.5	12.1	10 36.2	+38.7	12.1	11 34.8	+38.9	12.2	12 33.5	+39.0	12.2	75
76	10 16.0	+38.4	11.3	11 14.9	+38.5	11.4	12 13.7	+38.7	11.4	13 12.5	+38.9	11.4	76
77	10 54.4	+38.3	10.5	11 53.4	+38.5	10.6	12 52.4	+38.6	10.6	13 51.4	+38.7	10.7	77
78	11 32.7	+38.2	9.8	12 31.9	+38.3	9.8	13 31.0	+38.4	9.8	14 30.1	+38.6	9.9	78
79	12 10.9	+38.0	9.0	13 10.2	+38.1	9.0	14 09.4	+38.3	9.0	15 08.7	+38.4	9.1	79
80	12 48.9	+37.9	8.2	13 48.3	+38.0	8.2	14 47.7	+38.1	8.2	15 47.1	+38.2	8.3	80
81	13 26.8	+37.8	7.4	14 26.3	+37.9	7.4	15 25.8	+38.0	7.4	16 25.3	+38.0	7.5	81
82	14 04.6	+37.5	6.6	15 04.2	+37.6	6.6	16 03.8	+37.7	6.6	17 03.3	+37.9	6.7	82
83	14 42.1	+37.4	5.8	15 41.8	+37.5	5.8	16 41.5	+37.6	5.8	17 41.2	+37.7	5.9	83
84	15 19.5	+37.3	5.0	16 19.3	+37.3	5.0	17 19.1	+37.4	5.0	18 18.9	+37.4	5.0	84
85	15 56.8	+37.0	4.2	16 56.6	+37.1	4.2	17 56.5	+37.1	4.2	18 56.3	+37.2	4.2	85
86	16 33.8	+36.9	3.3	17 33.7	+36.9	3.3	18 33.6	+37.0	3.4	19 33.5	+37.0	3.4	86
87	17 10.7	+36.6	2.5	18 10.6	+36.7	2.5	19 10.6	+36.7	2.5	20 10.5	+36.8	2.6	87
88	17 47.3	+36.5	1.7	18 47.3	+36.5	1.7	19 47.3	+36.5	1.7	20 47.3	+36.5	1.7	88
89	18 23.8	+36.2	0.8	19 23.8	+36.2	0.8	20 23.8	+36.2	0.9	21 23.8	+36.2	0.9	89
90	19 00.0	+36.0	0.0	20 00.0	+36.0	0.0	21 00.0	+36.0	0.0	22 00.0	+36.0	0.0	90
	19°			20°			21°			22°			

S. Lat. {L.H.A. greater than 180° ....Zn=180°–Z
{L.H.A. less than 180°............Zn=180°+Z

LATITUDE **SAME** NAME AS DECLINATION   L.H.A. 127°, 233°

LATITUDE SAME NAME AS DECLINATION

N. Lat. { L.H.A. greater than 180° .....Zn=Z
{ L.H.A. less than 180°............Zn=360°−Z

Dec.	15° Hc	d	Z	16° Hc	d	Z	17° Hc	d	Z	18° Hc	d	Z	19° Hc	d	Z	20° Hc	d	Z	21° Hc	d	Z	22° Hc	d	Z	Dec.
0	34 35.6	+18.6	100.6	34 24.2	+19.7	101.3	34 12.1	+20.9	102.0	33 59.3	+22.0	102.7	33 45.8	+23.2	103.3	33 31.7	+24.3	104.0	33 16.9	+25.4	104.6	33 01.4	+26.6	105.2	0
1	34 54.2	+17.8	99.5	34 43.9	+19.1	100.2	34 33.0	+20.2	100.9	34 21.3	+21.5	101.5	34 09.0	+22.6	102.2	33 56.0	+23.7	102.9	33 42.3	+24.9	103.5	33 28.0	+25.9	104.2	1
2	35 12.0	+17.2	98.3	35 03.0	+18.4	99.0	34 53.2	+19.6	99.7	34 42.8	+20.8	100.4	34 31.6	+22.0	101.1	34 19.7	+23.1	101.7	34 07.2	+24.2	102.4	33 53.9	+25.4	103.1	2
3	35 29.2	+16.6	97.2	35 21.4	+17.7	97.9	35 12.8	+19.0	98.6	35 03.6	+20.1	99.3	34 53.6	+21.3	99.9	34 42.8	+22.5	100.6	34 31.4	+23.7	101.3	34 19.3	+24.8	102.0	3
4	35 45.8	+15.8	96.0	35 39.1	+17.1	96.7	35 31.8	+18.3	97.4	35 23.7	+19.5	98.1	35 14.9	+20.7	98.8	35 05.3	+21.9	99.5	34 55.1	+23.0	100.2	34 44.1	+24.2	100.9	4
5	36 01.6	+15.1	94.8	35 56.2	+16.3	95.5	35 50.1	+17.5	96.2	35 43.2	+18.8	96.9	35 35.6	+20.0	97.6	35 27.2	+21.2	98.4	35 18.1	+22.4	99.1	35 08.3	+23.6	99.8	5
6	36 16.7	+14.3	93.6	36 12.5	+15.7	94.3	36 07.6	+16.9	95.0	36 02.0	+18.1	95.8	35 55.6	+19.3	96.5	35 48.4	+20.6	97.2	35 40.5	+21.8	97.9	35 31.9	+23.0	98.6	6
7	36 31.0	+13.7	92.4	36 28.2	+14.9	93.1	36 24.5	+16.2	93.8	36 20.1	+17.4	94.6	36 14.9	+18.7	95.3	36 09.0	+19.9	96.0	36 02.3	+21.1	96.8	35 54.9	+22.3	97.5	7
8	36 44.7	+12.9	91.2	36 43.1	+14.2	91.9	36 40.7	+15.4	92.7	36 37.5	+16.7	93.4	36 33.6	+17.9	94.1	36 28.9	+19.2	94.9	36 23.4	+20.4	95.6	36 17.2	+21.6	96.3	8
9	36 57.6	+12.1	89.9	36 57.3	+13.4	90.7	36 56.1	+14.7	91.4	36 54.2	+16.0	92.2	36 51.5	+17.3	92.9	36 48.1	+18.5	93.7	36 43.8	+19.7	94.4	36 38.8	+20.9	95.2	9
10	37 09.7	+11.4	88.7	37 10.7	+12.7	89.5	37 10.8	+14.0	90.2	37 10.2	+15.2	91.0	37 08.8	+16.5	91.7	37 06.6	+17.7	92.5	37 03.5	+19.1	93.3	36 59.7	+20.3	94.0	10
11	37 21.1	+10.6	87.5	37 23.4	+11.9	88.2	37 24.8	+13.2	89.0	37 25.4	+14.5	89.8	37 25.3	+15.7	90.5	37 24.3	+17.1	91.3	37 22.6	+18.2	92.1	37 20.0	+19.5	92.8	11
12	37 31.7	+9.9	86.2	37 35.3	+11.1	87.0	37 38.0	+12.4	87.8	37 39.9	+13.7	88.5	37 41.0	+15.0	89.3	37 41.4	+16.2	90.1	37 40.8	+17.6	90.9	37 39.5	+18.9	91.6	12
13	37 41.6	+9.0	85.0	37 46.4	+10.3	85.8	37 50.4	+11.7	86.5	37 53.6	+13.0	87.3	37 56.0	+14.3	88.1	37 57.6	+15.6	88.9	37 58.4	+16.8	89.7	37 58.4	+18.0	90.4	13
14	37 50.6	+8.3	83.7	37 56.7	+9.6	84.5	38 02.1	+10.8	85.3	38 06.6	+12.1	86.1	38 10.3	+13.4	86.9	38 13.2	+14.7	87.6	38 15.2	+16.1	88.4	38 16.4	+17.4	89.2	14
15	37 58.9	+7.4	82.5	38 06.3	+8.7	83.3	38 12.9	+10.1	84.0	38 18.7	+11.4	84.8	38 23.7	+12.7	85.6	38 27.9	+14.0	86.4	38 31.3	+15.2	87.2	38 33.8	+16.5	88.0	15
16	38 06.3	+6.6	81.2	38 15.0	+8.0	82.0	38 23.0	+9.2	82.8	38 30.1	+10.6	83.6	38 36.4	+11.9	84.4	38 41.9	+13.1	85.2	38 46.5	+14.5	86.0	38 50.3	+15.8	86.8	16
17	38 12.9	+5.8	80.0	38 23.0	+7.1	80.7	38 32.2	+8.5	81.5	38 40.7	+9.7	82.3	38 48.3	+11.0	83.1	38 55.0	+12.4	83.9	39 01.0	+13.7	84.7	39 06.1	+15.0	85.5	17
18	38 18.7	+5.0	78.7	38 30.1	+6.3	79.5	38 40.7	+7.6	80.3	38 50.4	+8.9	81.1	38 59.3	+10.3	81.9	39 07.4	+11.6	82.7	39 14.7	+12.8	83.5	39 21.1	+14.1	84.3	18
19	38 23.7	+4.2	77.4	38 36.4	+5.5	78.2	38 48.3	+6.7	79.0	38 59.3	+8.1	79.8	39 09.6	+9.4	80.6	39 19.0	+10.7	81.4	39 27.5	+12.1	82.2	39 35.2	+13.4	83.0	19
20	38 27.9	+3.4	76.2	38 41.9	+4.6	76.9	38 55.0	+6.0	77.7	39 07.4	+7.3	78.5	39 19.0	+8.5	79.3	39 29.7	+9.9	80.1	39 39.6	+11.2	80.9	39 48.6	+12.5	81.8	20
21	38 31.3	+2.5	74.9	38 46.5	+3.8	75.6	39 01.0	+5.1	76.4	39 14.7	+6.4	77.2	39 27.5	+7.7	78.0	39 39.6	+9.0	78.8	39 50.8	+10.3	79.7	40 01.1	+11.7	80.5	21
22	38 33.8	+1.6	73.6	38 50.3	+3.0	74.4	39 06.1	+4.2	75.1	39 21.1	+5.5	75.9	39 35.2	+6.9	76.7	39 48.6	+8.2	77.5	40 01.1	+9.5	78.4	40 12.8	+10.9	79.2	22
23	38 35.4	+0.9	72.3	38 53.3	+2.1	73.1	39 10.3	+3.5	73.9	39 26.6	+4.7	74.7	39 42.1	+6.0	75.4	39 56.8	+7.3	76.3	40 10.6	+8.6	77.1	40 23.6	+10.0	77.9	23
24	38 36.3	0.0	71.0	38 55.4	+1.3	71.8	39 13.8	+2.5	72.6	39 31.3	+3.8	73.4	39 48.1	+5.2	74.2	40 04.1	+6.4	75.0	40 19.2	+7.8	75.8	40 33.6	+9.0	76.6	24
25	38 36.3	−0.8	69.8	38 56.7	+0.4	70.5	39 16.3	+1.7	71.3	39 35.2	+2.9	72.1	39 53.3	+4.2	72.9	40 10.5	+5.6	73.7	40 27.0	+6.9	74.5	40 42.6	+8.2	75.3	25
26	38 35.5	−1.7	68.5	38 57.1	−0.4	69.2	39 18.0	+0.8	70.0	39 38.1	+2.2	70.8	39 57.5	+3.4	71.6	40 16.1	+4.7	72.4	40 33.9	+6.0	73.2	40 50.8	+7.4	74.0	26
27	38 33.8	−2.5	67.2	38 56.7	−1.3	67.9	39 18.8	0.0	68.7	39 40.3	+1.2	69.5	40 00.9	+2.5	70.3	40 20.8	+3.8	71.1	40 39.9	+5.1	71.9	40 58.2	+6.4	72.7	27
28	38 31.3	−3.3	65.9	38 55.4	−2.1	66.7	39 18.8	−0.8	67.4	39 41.5	+0.4	68.2	40 03.4	+1.7	68.9	40 24.6	+2.9	69.7	40 45.0	+4.2	70.5	41 04.6	+5.5	71.4	28
29	38 28.0	−4.2	64.6	38 53.3	−3.0	65.4	39 18.0	−1.8	66.1	39 41.9	−0.5	66.9	40 05.1	+0.7	67.6	40 27.5	+2.0	68.4	40 49.2	+3.3	69.2	41 10.1	+4.6	70.0	29
30	38 23.8	−5.0	63.4	38 50.3	−3.7	64.1	39 16.2	−2.6	64.8	39 41.4	−1.4	65.6	40 05.8	−0.1	66.3	40 29.5	+1.2	67.1	40 52.5	+2.4	67.9	41 14.7	+3.7	68.7	30
31	38 18.8	−5.8	62.1	38 46.6	−4.7	62.8	39 13.6	−3.4	63.5	39 40.0	−2.2	64.3	40 05.7	−1.0	65.0	40 30.7	+0.2	65.8	40 54.9	+1.5	66.6	41 18.4	+2.7	67.4	31
32	38 13.0	−6.6	60.8	38 41.9	−5.4	61.5	39 10.2	−4.3	62.2	39 37.8	−3.1	63.0	40 04.7	−1.9	63.7	40 30.9	−0.6	64.5	40 56.4	+0.6	65.3	41 21.1	+1.9	66.1	32
33	38 06.4	−7.4	59.6	38 36.5	−6.3	60.3	39 05.9	−5.1	61.0	39 34.7	−4.0	61.7	40 02.8	−2.7	62.4	40 30.3	−1.6	63.2	40 57.0	−0.3	63.9	41 23.0	+0.9	64.7	33
34	37 59.0	−8.3	58.3	38 30.2	−7.1	59.0	39 00.8	−6.0	59.7	39 30.7	−4.8	60.4	40 00.1	−3.7	61.1	40 28.7	−2.4	61.9	40 56.7	−1.3	62.6	41 23.9	0.0	63.4	34
35	37 50.7	−9.0	57.1	38 23.1	−8.0	57.7	38 54.8	−6.8	58.4	39 25.9	−5.6	59.1	39 56.4	−4.5	59.8	40 26.3	−3.4	60.5	40 55.4	−2.1	61.3	41 23.9	−0.9	62.1	35
36	37 41.7	−9.8	55.8	38 15.1	−8.7	56.5	38 48.0	−7.6	57.1	39 20.3	−6.6	57.8	39 51.9	−5.4	58.5	40 22.9	−4.2	59.2	40 53.3	−3.0	60.0	41 23.0	−1.9	60.7	36
37	37 31.9	−10.6	54.6	38 06.4	−9.6	55.2	38 40.4	−8.5	55.9	39 13.7	−7.3	56.5	39 46.5	−6.2	57.2	40 18.7	−5.1	57.9	40 50.3	−4.0	58.6	41 21.1	−2.7	59.4	37
38	37 21.3	−11.4	53.3	37 56.8	−10.3	53.9	38 31.9	−9.3	54.6	39 06.4	−8.2	55.2	39 40.3	−7.1	55.9	40 13.6	−6.0	56.6	40 46.3	−4.8	57.3	41 18.4	−3.7	58.1	38
39	37 09.9	−12.1	52.1	37 46.5	−11.1	52.7	38 22.6	−10.1	53.3	38 58.2	−9.1	54.0	39 33.2	−8.0	54.6	40 07.6	−6.8	55.3	40 41.5	−5.8	56.0	41 14.7	−4.6	56.7	39
40	36 57.8	−12.9	50.9	37 35.4	−11.9	51.5	38 12.5	−10.9	52.1	38 49.1	−9.8	52.7	39 25.2	−8.8	53.3	40 00.8	−7.7	54.0	40 35.7	−6.6	54.7	41 10.1	−5.5	55.4	40
41	36 44.9	−13.7	49.6	37 23.5	−12.7	50.2	38 01.6	−11.6	50.8	38 39.3	−10.7	51.4	39 16.4	−9.6	52.1	39 53.1	−8.6	52.7	40 29.1	−7.5	53.4	41 04.6	−6.4	54.1	41
42	36 31.2	−14.3	48.4	37 10.8	−13.4	49.0	37 50.0	−12.5	49.6	38 28.6	−11.4	50.2	39 06.8	−10.4	50.8	39 44.5	−9.4	51.4	40 21.6	−8.4	52.1	40 58.2	−7.3	52.8	42
43	36 16.9	−15.1	47.2	36 57.4	−14.2	47.8	37 37.5	−13.2	48.3	38 17.2	−12.3	48.9	38 56.4	−11.3	49.5	39 35.1	−10.3	50.2	40 13.2	−9.2	50.8	40 50.9	−8.2	51.5	43
44	36 01.8	−15.8	46.0	36 43.2	−14.9	46.6	37 24.3	−14.0	47.1	38 04.9	−13.0	47.7	38 45.1	−12.1	48.3	39 24.8	−11.1	48.9	40 04.0	−10.1	49.5	40 42.7	−9.1	50.2	44
45	35 46.0	−16.5	44.8	36 28.3	−15.6	45.3	37 10.3	−14.7	45.9	37 51.9	−13.9	46.4	38 33.0	−12.9	47.0	39 13.7	−12.0	47.6	39 53.9	−11.0	48.2	40 33.6	−9.9	48.8	45
46	35 29.5	−17.2	43.6	36 12.7	−16.3	44.1	36 55.6	−15.5	44.7	37 38.0	−14.5	45.2	38 20.1	−13.7	45.8	39 01.7	−12.7	46.3	39 42.9	−11.7	46.9	40 23.7	−10.8	47.6	46
47	35 12.3	−17.9	42.5	35 56.4	−17.1	43.0	36 40.1	−16.2	43.5	37 23.5	−15.4	44.0	38 06.4	−14.4	44.5	38 49.0	−13.5	45.1	39 31.2	−12.7	45.7	40 12.9	−11.7	46.3	47
48	34 54.4	−18.5	41.3	35 39.3	−17.7	41.8	36 23.9	−16.9	42.3	37 08.1	−16.1	42.8	37 52.0	−15.2	43.3	38 35.5	−14.4	43.8	39 18.5	−13.4	44.4	40 01.2	−12.5	45.0	48
49	34 35.9	−19.2	40.1	35 21.6	−18.4	40.6	36 07.0	−17.6	41.1	36 52.0	−16.7	41.6	37 36.8	−16.0	42.1	38 21.1	−15.1	42.6	39 05.1	−14.2	43.1	39 48.7	−13.4	43.7	49
50	34 16.7	−19.8	39.0	35 03.2	−19.1	39.4	35 49.4	−18.3	39.9	36 35.3	−17.6	40.4	37 20.8	−16.7	40.9	38 06.0	−15.9	41.4	38 50.9	−15.1	41.9	39 35.3	−14.1	42.4	50
51	33 56.9	−20.5	37.9	34 44.1	−19.7	38.3	35 31.1	−19.0	38.7	36 17.7	−18.2	39.2	37 04.1	−17.4	39.6	37 50.1	−16.6	40.1	38 35.8	−15.8	40.6	39 21.2	−15.0	41.2	51
52	33 36.4	−21.0	36.7	34 24.4	−20.4	37.1	35 12.1	−19.6	37.6	35 59.5	−18.9	38.0	36 46.7	−18.2	38.5	37 33.5	−17.4	38.9	38 20.0	−16.6	39.4	39 06.2	−15.8	39.9	52
53	33 15.4	−21.7	35.6	34 04.0	−20.9	36.0	34 52.5	−20.3	36.4	35 40.6	−19.5	36.8	36 28.5	−18.8	37.3	37 16.1	−18.1	37.7	38 03.4	−17.3	38.2	38 50.4	−16.5	38.7	53
54	32 53.7	−22.2	34.5	33 43.1	−21.6	34.9	34 32.2	−20.9	35.3	35 21.1	−20.3	35.7	36 09.7	−19.6	36.1	36 58.0	−18.8	36.5	37 46.1	−18.1	37.0	38 33.9	−17.3	37.5	54
55	32 31.5	−22.8	33.4	33 21.5	−22.2	33.7	34 11.3	−21.6	34.1	35 00.8	−20.9	34.5	35 50.1	−20.3	34.9	36 39.2	−19.5	35.3	37 28.0	−18.9	35.8	38 16.6	−18.1	36.2	55
56	32 08.7	−23.4	32.3	32 59.3	−22.8	32.6	33 49.7	−22.1	33.0	34 39.9	−21.5	33.4	35 29.9	−20.8	33.8	36 19.7	−20.2	34.2	37 09.2	−19.5	34.6	37 58.5	−18.8	35.0	56
57	31 45.3	−23.9	31.2	32 36.5	−23.3	31.5	33 27.6	−22.8	31.9	34 18.4	−22.1	32.3	35 09.1	−21.5	32.6	35 59.5	−20.9	33.0	36 49.7	−20.2	33.4	37 39.7	−19.6	33.8	57
58	31 21.4	−24.5	30.1	32 13.2	−23.9	30.4	33 04.8	−23.3	30.8	33 56.3	−22.8	31.1	34 47.6	−22.1	31.5	35 38.6	−21.5	31.8	36 29.5	−20.9	32.2	37 20.1	−20.2	32.6	58
59	30 56.9	−25.0	29.1	31 49.3	−24.5	29.4	32 41.5	−23.9	29.7	33 33.5	−23.3	30.0	34 25.4	−22.8	30.3	35 17.1	−22.2	30.7	36 08.6	−21.6	31.1	36 59.9	−21.0	31.4	59
60	30 31.9	−25.5	28.0	31 24.8	−24.9	28.3	32 17.6	−24.5	28.6	33 10.2	−23.9	28.9	34 02.6	−23.3	29.2	34 54.9	−22.8	29.6	35 47.0	−22.2	29.9	36 38.9	−21.6	30.3	60
61	30 06.4	−25.9	27.0	30 59.9	−25.5	27.2	31 53.1	−24.9	27.5	32 46.3	−24.5	27.8	33 39.3	−24.0	28.1	34 32.1	−23.4	28.4	35 24.8	−22.9	28.8	36 17.3	−22.3	29.1	61
62	29 40.5	−26.5	25.9	30 34.4	−26.0	26.2	31 28.2	−25.6	26.4	32 21.8	−25.0	26.7	33 15.3	−24.5	27.0	34 08.7	−24.0	27.3	35 01.9	−23.4	27.6	35 55.0	−22.9	28.0	62
63	29 14.0	−26.9	24.9	30 08.4	−26.5	25.1	31 02.6	−26.0	25.4	31 56.8	−25.6	25.6	32 50.8	−25.1	25.9	33 44.7	−24.6	26.2	34 38.5	−24.1	26.5	35 32.1	−23.6	26.8	63
64	28 47.1	−27.4	23.9	29 41.9	−27.0	24.1	30 36.6	−26.5	24.3	31 31.2	−26.1	24.6	32 25.7	−25.6	24.8	33 20.1	−25.2	25.1	34 14.4	−24.7	25.4	35 08.5	−24.2	25.7	64
65	28 19.7	−27.9	22.9	29 14.9	−27.4	23.1	30 10.1	−27.1	23.3	31 05.1	−26.5	23.5	32 00.1	−26.2	23.8	32 54.9	−25.7	24.0	33 49.7	−25.3	24.3	34 44.3	−24.8	24.6	65
66	27 51.8	−28.2	21.9	28 47.5	−27.9	22.1	29 43.0	−27.5	22.3	30 38.5	−27.1	22.5	31 33.9	−26.7	22.7	32 29.2	−26.3	23.0	33 24.4	−25.8	23.2	34 19.5	−25.4	23.5	66
67	27 23.6	−28.7	20.9	28 19.6	−28.3	21.0	29 15.5	−27.9	21.2	30 11.4	−27.5	21.5	31 07.2	−27.2	21.7	32 02.9	−26.7	21.9	32 58.6	−26.4	22.1	33 54.1	−26.0	22.4	67
68	26 54.9	−29.1	19.9	27 51.3	−28.8	20.0	28 47.6	−28.4	20.2	29 43.9	−28.1	20.4	30 40.0	−27.6	20.6	31 36.2	−27.3	20.8	32 32.2	−26.9	21.1	33 28.1	−26.5	21.3	68
69	26 25.8	−29.5	18.9	27 22.5	−29.2	19.1	28 19.2	−28.9	19.2	29 15.8	−28.5	19.4	30 12.4	−28.2	19.6	31 08.9	−27.9	19.8	32 05.3	−27.5	20.0	33 01.6	−27.1	20.2	69
70	25 56.3	−29.9	17.9	26 53.3	−29.5	18.1	27 50.3	−29.2	18.2	28 47.3	−28.9	18.4	29 44.2	−28.6	18.6	30 41.0	−28.2	18.8	31 37.8	−27.9	19.0	32 34.5	−27.6	19.2	70
71	25 26.4	−30.3	17.0	26 23.8	−30.0	17.1	27 21.1	−29.7	17.3	28 18.4	−29.4	17.5	29 15.6	−29.1	17.6	30 12.8	−28.8	17.7	31 09.9	−28.5	17.9	32 06.9	−28.1	18.1	71
72	24 56.1	−30.6	16.0	25 53.8	−30.4	16.1	26 51.4	−30.1	16.3	27 49.0	−29.8	16.4	28 46.5	−29.6	16.6	29 44.0	−29.2	16.7	30 41.4	−28.9	16.9	31 38.8	−28.6	17.1	72
73	24 25.5	−30.9	15.1	25 23.4	−30.7	15.2	26 21.3	−30.4	15.3	27 19.2	−30.2	15.5	28 17.0	−29.9	15.6	29 14.8	−29.7	15.8	30 12.5	−29.4	15.9	31 10.2	−29.1	16.0	73
74	23 54.6	−31.4	14.1	24 52.7	−31.0	14.2	25 50.9	−30.9	14.3	26 49.0	−30.6	14.5	27 47.1	−30.4	14.6	28 45.1	−30.1	14.7	29 43.1	−29.8	14.9	30 41.1	−29.6	15.0	74
75	23 23.2	−31.6	13.2	24 21.7	−31.5	13.3	25 20.0	−31.2	13.4	26 18.4	−31.0	13.5	27 16.7	−30.7	13.6	28 15.0	−30.5	13.8	29 13.3	−30.3	13.9	30 11.5	−30.0	14.0	75
76	22 51.6	−31.9	12.3	23 50.2	−31.7	12.4	24 48.8	−31.5	12.5	25 47.4	−31.3	12.6	26 46.0	−31.2	12.7	27 44.5	−30.9	12.8	28 43.0	−30.7	13.0	29 41.5	−30.5	13.0	76
77	22 19.7	−32.3	11.3	23 18.5	−32.1	11.4	24 17.3	−31.9	11.5	25 16.1	−31.7	11.6	26 14.8	−31.4	11.7	27 13.6	−31.4	11.8	28 12.3	−31.1	11.9	29 11.0	−30.9	12.0	77
78	21 47.4	−32.6	10.4	22 46.4	−32.4	10.5	23 45.4	−32.2	10.6	24 44.4	−32.1	10.7	25 43.3	−31.9	10.8	26 42.2	−31.7	10.9	27 41.2	−31.6	10.9	28 40.1	−31.4	11.1	78
79	21 14.8	−32.9	9.5	22 14.0	−32.7	9.6	23 13.2	−32.6	9.7	24 12.3	−32.4	9.7	25 11.4	−32.2	9.8	26 10.5	−32.0	9.9	27 09.6	−31.9	10.0	28 08.7	−31.7	10.1	79
80	20 42.0	−33.1	8.6	21 41.3	−33.0	8.7	22 40.6	−32.8	8.8	23 39.9	−32.7	8.8	24 39.2	−32.6	8.9	25 38.5	−32.4	9.0	26 37.7	−32.2	9.0	27 37.0	−32.1	9.1	80
81	20 08.9	−33.4	7.7	21 08.3	−33.2	7.8	22 07.8	−33.2	7.9	23 07.2	−33.0	7.9	24 06.6	−32.9	8.0	25 06.1	−32.8	8.0	26 05.5	−32.7	8.1	27 04.9	−32.6	8.2	81
82	19 35.5	−33.6	6.9	20 35.1	−33.6	6.9	21 34.6	−33.4	7.0	22 34.2	−33.3	7.1	23 33.7	−33.2	7.1	24 33.3	−33.1	7.1	25 32.8	−33.0	7.2	26 32.3	−32.8	7.2	82
83	19 01.9	−33.9	6.0	20 01.5	−33.8	6.0	21 01.2	−33.7	6.1	22 00.9	−33.6	6.1	23 00.5	−33.5	6.1	24 00.2	−33.5	6.2	24 59.8	−33.3	6.2	25 59.5	−33.3	6.3	83
84	18 28.0	−34.1	5.1	19 27.7	−34.0	5.1	20 27.5	−34.0	5.2	21 27.3	−33.9	5.2	22 27.0	−33.8	5.3	23 26.7	−33.7	5.3	24 26.5	−33.7	5.3	25 26.2	−33.5	5.4	84
85	17 53.9	−34.4	4.2	18 53.7	−34.3	4.3	19 53.5	−34.2	4.3	20 53.4	−34.2	4.3	21 53.2	−34.1	4.4	22 53.0	−34.0	4.4	23 52.8	−33.9	4.4	24 52.7	−34.0	4.5	85
86	17 19.5	−34.6	3.4	18 19.4	−34.5	3.4	19 19.3	−34.5	3.4	20 19.2	−34.4	3.5	21 19.1	−34.4	3.5	22 19.0	−34.4	3.5	23 18.9	−34.3	3.5	24 18.7	−34.2	3.6	86
87	16 44.9	−34.7	2.5	17 44.9	−34.8	2.6	18 44.8	−34.7	2.6	19 44.8	−34.7	2.6	20 44.7	−34.7	2.6	21 44.6	−34.6	2.6	22 44.6	−34.6	2.7	23 44.5	−34.5	2.7	87
88	16 10.2	−35.0	1.7	17 10.1	−34.9	1.7	18 10.1	−34.9	1.7	19 10.1	−34.9	1.7	20 10.0	−34.9	1.7	21 10.0	−34.9	1.7	22 10.0	−34.9	1.7	23 10.0	−34.9	1.8	88
89	15 35.2	−35.2	0.8	16 35.2	−35.2	0.8	17 35.2	−35.2	0.8	18 35.2	−35.2	0.9	19 35.1	−35.1	0.9	20 35.1	−35.1	0.9	21 35.1	−35.1	0.9	22 35.1	−35.1	0.9	89
90	15 00.0	−35.4	0.0	16 00.0	−35.4	0.0	17 00.0	−35.4	0.0	18 00.0	−35.4	0.0	19 00.0	−35.4	0.0	20 00.0	−35.4	0.0	21 00.0	−35.4	0.0	22 00.0	−35.4	0.0	90
	15°			16°			17°			18°			19°			20°			21°			22°			

LATITUDE **CONTRARY** NAME TO DECLINATION **L.H.A. 54°, 306°**

	15°			16°			17°			18°			19°			20°			21°			22°			
Dec.	Hc	d	Z	Hc	d	Z	Hc	d	Z	Hc	d	Z	Hc	d	Z	Hc	d	Z	Hc	d	Z	Hc	d	Z	Dec.
°	° ′	′	°	° ′	′	°	° ′	′	°	° ′	′	°	° ′	′	°	° ′	′	°	° ′	′	°	° ′	′	°	°
0	34 35.6	-19.2	100.6	34 24.2	-20.4	101.3	34 12.1	-21.5	102.0	33 59.3	-22.7	102.7	33 45.8	-23.8	103.3	33 31.7	-25.0	104.0	33 16.9	-26.0	104.6	33 01.4	-27.1	105.2	0
1	34 16.4	-19.8	101.8	34 03.8	-20.9	102.5	33 50.6	-22.2	103.1	33 36.6	-23.2	103.8	33 22.0	-24.4	104.4	33 06.7	-25.4	105.0	32 50.9	-26.6	105.7	32 34.3	-27.6	106.3	1
2	33 56.6	-20.4	102.9	33 42.9	-21.6	103.6	33 28.4	-22.7	104.2	33 13.4	-23.9	104.9	32 57.6	-24.9	105.5	32 41.3	-26.0	106.1	32 24.3	-27.1	106.7	32 06.7	-28.1	107.3	2
3	33 36.2	-21.1	104.1	33 21.3	-22.2	104.7	33 05.7	-23.3	105.3	32 49.5	-24.4	106.0	32 32.7	-25.5	106.6	32 15.3	-26.6	107.2	31 57.2	-27.6	107.8	31 38.6	-28.6	108.4	3
4	33 15.1	-21.7	105.2	32 59.1	-22.8	105.8	32 42.4	-23.9	106.4	32 25.1	-24.9	107.1	32 07.2	-26.0	107.7	31 48.7	-27.0	108.2	31 29.6	-28.1	108.8	31 10.0	-29.1	109.4	4
5	32 53.4	-22.2	106.3	32 36.3	-23.4	106.9	32 18.5	-24.4	107.5	32 00.2	-25.5	108.1	31 41.2	-26.6	108.7	31 21.7	-27.6	109.3	31 01.5	-28.5	109.9	30 40.9	-29.6	110.4	5
6	32 31.2	-22.8	107.4	32 12.9	-23.9	108.0	31 54.1	-25.0	108.6	31 34.7	-26.1	109.2	31 14.6	-27.0	109.8	30 54.1	-28.1	110.3	30 33.0	-29.1	110.9	30 11.3	-30.0	111.4	6
7	32 08.4	-23.4	108.5	31 49.0	-24.4	109.1	31 29.1	-25.5	109.7	31 08.6	-26.5	110.2	30 47.6	-27.5	110.8	30 26.0	-28.5	111.4	30 03.9	-29.5	111.9	29 41.3	-30.5	112.4	7
8	31 45.0	-23.9	109.6	31 24.6	-25.0	110.2	31 03.6	-26.0	110.7	30 42.1	-27.0	111.3	30 20.1	-28.1	111.8	29 57.5	-29.0	112.4	29 34.4	-30.0	112.9	29 10.8	-31.0	113.4	8
9	31 21.1	-24.5	110.7	30 59.6	-25.5	111.2	30 37.6	-26.5	111.8	30 15.1	-27.5	112.3	29 52.0	-28.5	112.9	29 28.5	-29.5	113.4	29 04.4	-30.4	113.9	28 39.8	-31.3	114.4	9
10	30 56.6	-25.0	111.7	30 34.1	-26.0	112.3	30 11.1	-27.0	112.8	29 47.6	-28.0	113.4	29 23.5	-28.9	113.9	28 59.0	-29.9	114.4	28 34.0	-30.8	114.9	28 08.5	-31.7	115.4	10
11	30 31.6	-25.5	112.8	30 08.1	-26.5	113.3	29 44.1	-27.5	113.9	29 19.6	-28.5	114.4	28 54.6	-29.4	114.9	28 29.1	-30.3	115.4	28 03.2	-31.3	115.9	27 36.8	-32.2	116.3	11
12	30 06.1	-26.0	113.8	29 41.6	-27.0	114.4	29 16.6	-27.9	114.9	28 51.1	-28.9	115.4	28 25.2	-29.8	115.9	27 58.8	-30.8	116.4	27 31.9	-31.6	116.8	27 04.6	-32.5	117.3	12
13	29 40.1	-26.5	114.9	29 14.6	-27.4	115.4	28 48.7	-28.4	115.9	28 22.2	-29.3	116.4	27 55.4	-30.3	116.9	27 28.0	-31.1	117.3	27 00.3	-32.0	117.8	26 32.1	-32.9	118.2	13
14	29 13.6	-26.9	115.9	28 47.2	-27.9	116.4	28 20.3	-28.8	116.9	27 52.9	-29.7	117.4	27 25.1	-30.6	117.8	26 56.9	-31.5	118.3	26 28.3	-32.4	118.7	25 59.2	-33.2	119.2	14
15	28 46.7	-27.4	116.9	28 19.3	-28.3	117.4	27 51.5	-29.3	117.9	27 23.2	-30.2	118.3	26 54.5	-31.0	118.8	26 25.4	-31.9	119.2	25 55.9	-32.8	119.7	25 26.0	-33.6	120.1	15
16	28 19.3	-27.8	117.9	27 51.0	-28.8	118.4	27 22.2	-29.6	118.9	26 53.0	-30.5	119.3	26 23.5	-31.5	119.8	25 53.5	-32.3	120.2	25 23.1	-33.1	120.6	24 52.4	-33.9	121.0	16
17	27 51.5	-28.3	118.9	27 22.2	-29.2	119.4	26 52.6	-30.1	119.8	26 22.5	-30.9	120.3	25 52.0	-31.7	120.7	25 21.2	-32.6	121.1	24 50.0	-33.4	121.5	24 18.5	-34.2	121.9	17
18	27 23.2	-28.7	119.9	26 53.0	-29.5	120.4	26 22.5	-30.5	120.8	25 51.6	-31.3	121.2	25 20.3	-32.2	121.6	24 48.6	-32.9	122.0	24 16.6	-33.7	122.4	23 44.3	-34.6	122.8	18
19	26 54.5	-29.1	120.9	26 23.5	-30.0	121.4	25 52.0	-30.8	121.8	25 20.3	-31.7	122.2	24 48.1	-32.4	122.6	24 15.7	-33.3	123.0	23 42.9	-34.1	123.3	23 09.7	-34.8	123.7	19
20	26 25.4	-29.5	121.9	25 53.5	-30.4	122.3	25 21.2	-31.2	122.7	24 48.6	-32.0	123.1	24 15.7	-32.8	123.5	23 42.4	-33.6	123.9	23 08.8	-34.4	124.2	22 34.9	-35.1	124.6	20
21	25 55.9	-29.9	122.9	25 23.1	-30.7	123.3	24 50.0	-31.5	123.7	24 16.6	-32.3	124.0	23 42.9	-33.2	124.4	23 08.8	-33.9	124.8	22 34.4	-34.6	125.1	21 59.8	-35.5	125.5	21
22	25 26.0	-30.3	123.8	24 52.4	-31.1	124.2	24 18.5	-31.9	124.6	23 44.3	-32.7	125.0	23 09.7	-33.4	125.3	22 34.9	-34.2	125.7	21 59.8	-35.0	126.0	21 24.3	-35.6	126.3	22
23	24 55.7	-30.6	124.8	24 21.3	-31.4	125.2	23 46.6	-32.2	125.5	23 11.6	-33.0	125.9	22 36.3	-33.8	126.2	22 00.7	-34.5	126.6	21 24.8	-35.2	126.9	20 48.7	-36.0	127.2	23
24	24 25.1	-31.0	125.7	23 49.9	-31.7	126.1	23 14.4	-32.5	126.5	22 38.6	-33.3	126.8	22 02.5	-34.0	127.1	21 26.2	-34.8	127.4	20 49.6	-35.5	127.7	20 12.7	-36.1	128.0	24
25	23 54.1	-31.3	126.7	23 18.2	-32.1	127.0	22 41.9	-32.8	127.4	22 05.3	-33.6	127.7	21 28.5	-34.3	128.0	20 51.4	-35.0	128.3	20 14.1	-35.7	128.6	19 36.6	-36.4	128.9	25
26	23 22.8	-31.6	127.6	22 46.1	-32.4	127.9	22 09.1	-33.2	128.3	21 31.8	-33.9	128.6	20 54.2	-34.6	128.9	20 16.4	-35.3	129.2	19 38.4	-36.0	129.5	19 00.2	-36.7	129.7	26
27	22 51.2	-32.0	128.5	22 13.7	-32.7	128.9	21 35.9	-33.4	129.2	20 57.9	-34.1	129.5	20 19.6	-34.8	129.8	19 41.1	-35.5	130.0	19 02.4	-36.2	130.3	18 23.5	-36.8	130.6	27
28	22 19.2	-32.2	129.5	21 41.0	-33.0	129.8	21 02.5	-33.7	130.1	20 23.8	-34.4	130.4	19 44.8	-35.1	130.6	19 05.6	-35.7	130.9	18 26.2	-36.4	131.2	17 46.7	-37.1	131.4	28
29	21 47.0	-32.6	130.4	21 08.0	-33.3	130.7	20 28.8	-34.0	130.9	19 49.4	-34.7	131.2	19 09.7	-35.3	131.5	18 29.9	-36.0	131.7	17 49.8	-36.6	132.0	17 09.6	-37.3	132.2	29
30	21 14.4	-32.8	131.3	20 34.7	-33.5	131.5	19 54.8	-34.2	131.8	19 14.7	-34.9	132.1	18 34.4	-35.5	132.3	17 53.9	-36.2	132.6	17 13.2	-36.8	132.8	16 32.3	-37.4	133.0	30
31	20 41.6	-33.1	132.2	20 01.2	-33.8	132.4	19 20.6	-34.5	132.7	18 39.8	-35.1	132.9	17 58.9	-35.8	133.2	17 17.7	-36.4	133.4	16 36.4	-37.0	133.6	15 54.9	-37.7	133.9	31
32	20 08.5	-33.4	133.0	19 27.4	-34.0	133.3	18 46.1	-34.7	133.6	18 04.7	-35.3	133.8	17 23.1	-36.0	134.0	16 41.3	-36.6	134.3	15 59.4	-37.3	134.5	15 17.2	-37.8	134.7	32
33	19 35.1	-33.7	133.9	18 53.4	-34.3	134.2	18 11.4	-34.9	134.4	17 29.4	-35.6	134.7	16 47.1	-36.2	134.9	16 04.7	-36.8	135.1	15 22.1	-37.3	135.3	14 39.4	-37.9	135.5	33
34	19 01.4	-33.9	134.8	18 19.1	-34.6	135.0	17 36.5	-35.1	135.3	16 53.8	-35.8	135.5	16 10.9	-36.3	135.7	15 27.9	-37.0	135.9	14 44.8	-37.6	136.1	14 01.5	-38.2	136.3	34
35	18 27.5	-34.1	135.7	17 44.5	-34.7	135.9	17 01.4	-35.4	136.1	16 18.0	-35.9	136.3	15 34.6	-36.6	136.5	14 50.9	-37.1	136.7	14 07.2	-37.7	136.9	13 23.3	-38.2	137.1	35
36	17 53.4	-34.3	136.5	17 09.8	-35.0	136.8	16 26.0	-35.6	137.0	15 42.1	-36.2	137.2	14 58.0	-36.7	137.4	14 13.8	-37.3	137.5	13 29.5	-37.9	137.7	12 45.1	-38.5	137.9	36
37	17 19.1	-34.6	137.4	16 34.8	-35.2	137.6	15 50.4	-35.7	137.8	15 05.9	-36.3	138.0	14 21.3	-36.9	138.2	13 36.5	-37.5	138.3	12 51.6	-38.0	138.5	12 06.6	-38.5	138.6	37
38	16 44.5	-34.8	138.3	15 59.6	-35.3	138.5	15 14.7	-36.0	138.6	14 29.6	-36.5	138.8	13 44.4	-37.1	139.0	12 59.0	-37.6	139.1	12 13.6	-38.1	139.3	11 28.1	-38.7	139.4	38
39	16 09.7	-35.0	139.1	15 24.3	-35.6	139.3	14 38.7	-36.1	139.5	13 53.1	-36.7	139.6	13 07.3	-37.2	139.8	12 21.4	-37.7	139.9	11 35.5	-38.3	140.1	10 49.4	-38.8	140.2	39
40	15 34.7	-35.2	140.0	14 48.7	-35.7	140.1	14 02.6	-36.3	140.3	13 16.4	-36.8	140.4	12 30.1	-37.4	140.6	11 43.7	-37.9	140.7	10 57.2	-38.4	140.9	10 10.6	-38.9	141.0	40
41	14 59.5	-35.3	140.8	14 13.0	-35.9	141.0	13 26.3	-36.4	141.1	12 39.6	-37.0	141.3	11 52.7	-37.4	141.4	11 05.8	-38.0	141.5	10 18.8	-38.5	141.6	9 31.7	-39.0	141.7	41
42	14 24.2	-35.6	141.6	13 37.1	-36.1	141.8	12 49.9	-36.6	141.9	12 02.6	-37.1	142.1	11 15.3	-37.7	142.2	10 27.8	-38.1	142.3	9 40.3	-38.6	142.4	8 52.7	-39.1	142.5	42
43	13 48.6	-35.7	142.5	13 01.0	-36.2	142.6	12 13.3	-36.7	142.7	11 25.5	-37.2	142.9	10 37.6	-37.7	143.0	9 49.7	-38.2	143.1	9 01.7	-38.7	143.2	8 13.6	-39.2	143.3	43
44	13 12.9	-35.8	143.3	12 24.8	-36.4	143.4	11 36.6	-36.9	143.6	10 48.3	-37.4	143.7	9 59.9	-37.8	143.8	9 11.5	-38.3	143.9	8 23.0	-38.8	144.0	7 34.4	-39.2	144.0	44
45	12 37.1	-36.0	144.1	11 48.4	-36.5	144.2	10 59.7	-37.0	144.4	10 10.9	-37.4	144.5	9 22.1	-38.0	144.6	8 33.2	-38.5	144.7	7 44.2	-38.9	144.7	6 55.2	-39.4	144.8	45
46	12 01.1	-36.2	144.9	11 11.9	-36.6	145.0	10 22.7	-37.1	145.2	9 33.5	-37.6	145.3	8 44.1	-38.0	145.3	7 54.7	-38.5	145.4	7 05.3	-38.9	145.5	6 15.8	-39.4	145.6	46
47	11 24.9	-36.3	145.7	10 35.3	-36.8	145.9	9 45.6	-37.2	146.0	8 55.9	-37.7	146.0	8 06.1	-38.2	146.1	7 16.2	-38.5	146.2	6 26.4	-39.1	146.3	5 36.4	-39.4	146.3	47
48	10 48.6	-36.4	146.6	9 58.5	-36.8	146.7	9 08.4	-37.3	146.7	8 18.2	-37.8	146.8	7 27.9	-38.2	146.9	6 37.7	-38.7	147.0	5 47.3	-39.1	147.0	4 57.0	-39.5	147.1	48
49	10 12.2	-36.5	147.4	9 21.7	-37.0	147.5	8 31.1	-37.5	147.5	7 40.4	-37.8	147.6	6 49.7	-38.3	147.7	5 59.0	-38.7	147.7	5 08.2	-39.1	147.8	4 17.5	-39.6	147.8	49
50	9 35.7	-36.7	148.2	8 44.7	-37.1	148.3	7 53.6	-37.5	148.3	7 02.6	-38.0	148.4	6 11.4	-38.3	148.5	5 20.3	-38.8	148.5	4 29.1	-39.2	148.6	3 37.9	-39.6	148.6	50
51	8 59.0	-36.7	149.0	8 07.6	-37.2	149.0	7 16.1	-37.6	149.1	6 24.6	-38.0	149.2	5 33.1	-38.4	149.2	4 41.5	-38.8	149.3	3 49.9	-39.2	149.3	2 58.3	-39.6	149.3	51
52	8 22.3	-36.8	149.8	7 30.4	-37.2	149.8	6 38.5	-37.6	149.9	5 46.6	-38.1	150.0	4 54.7	-38.5	150.0	4 02.7	-38.9	150.0	3 10.7	-39.3	150.1	2 18.7	-39.7	150.1	52
53	7 45.5	-37.0	150.6	6 53.2	-37.4	150.6	6 00.9	-37.8	150.7	5 08.5	-38.1	150.7	4 16.2	-38.5	150.8	3 23.8	-38.9	150.8	2 31.4	-39.2	150.8	1 39.0	-39.6	150.9	53
54	7 08.5	-37.0	151.4	6 15.8	-37.4	151.4	5 23.1	-37.7	151.5	4 30.4	-38.2	151.5	3 37.7	-38.6	151.5	2 44.9	-38.9	151.6	1 52.2	-39.4	151.6	0 59.4	-39.7	151.6	54
55	6 31.5	-37.1	152.2	5 38.4	-37.4	152.2	4 45.4	-37.9	152.2	3 52.2	-38.2	152.3	2 59.1	-38.6	152.3	2 06.0	-39.0	152.3	1 12.8	-39.3	152.3	0 19.7	-39.7	152.4	55
56	5 54.4	-37.1	152.9	5 01.0	-37.5	153.0	4 07.5	-37.9	153.0	3 14.0	-38.2	153.1	2 20.5	-38.6	153.1	1 27.0	-38.9	153.1	0 33.5	-39.3	153.1	0 20.0	+39.7	26.9	56
57	5 17.3	-37.2	153.7	4 23.5	-37.6	153.8	3 29.6	-37.9	153.8	2 35.8	-38.3	153.8	1 41.9	-38.6	153.8	0 48.1	-39.0	153.9	0 05.8	+39.3	26.1	0 59.7	+39.6	26.1	57
58	4 40.1	-37.3	154.5	3 45.9	-37.6	154.6	2 51.7	-38.0	154.6	1 57.5	-38.3	154.6	1 03.3	-38.6	154.6	0 09.1	-39.0	154.6	0 45.1	+39.3	25.4	1 39.3	+39.7	25.4	58
59	4 02.8	-37.3	155.3	3 08.3	-37.7	155.3	2 13.7	-37.9	155.4	1 19.2	-38.3	155.4	0 24.7	-38.7	155.4	0 29.9	+39.0	24.6	1 24.4	+39.3	24.6	2 19.0	+39.6	24.6	59
60	3 25.5	-37.4	156.1	2 30.6	-37.7	156.1	1 35.8	-38.0	156.1	0 40.9	-38.3	156.1	0 14.0	+38.6	23.9	1 08.9	+38.9	23.9	2 03.7	+39.3	23.9	2 58.6	+39.6	23.9	60
61	2 48.1	-37.4	156.9	1 52.9	-37.7	156.9	0 57.8	-38.1	156.9	0 02.6	-38.4	156.9	0 52.6	+38.7	23.1	1 47.8	+39.0	23.1	2 43.0	+39.3	23.1	3 38.2	+39.5	23.1	61
62	2 10.7	-37.4	157.7	1 15.2	-37.7	157.7	0 19.7	-38.0	157.7	0 35.8	+38.3	22.3	1 31.3	+38.6	22.3	2 26.8	+38.9	22.3	3 22.3	+39.2	22.4	4 17.7	+39.6	22.4	62
63	1 33.3	-37.4	158.4	0 37.5	-37.7	158.5	0 18.3	+38.0	21.5	1 14.1	+38.3	21.6	2 09.9	+38.6	21.6	3 05.7	+38.9	21.6	4 01.5	+39.1	21.6	4 57.3	+39.4	21.6	63
64	0 55.9	-37.4	159.2	0 00.2	+37.7	20.8	0 56.3	+38.0	20.8	1 52.4	+38.3	20.8	2 48.5	+38.5	20.8	3 44.6	+38.8	20.8	4 40.6	+39.2	20.8	5 36.7	+39.4	20.9	64
65	0 18.5	-37.5	160.0	0 37.9	+37.7	20.0	1 34.3	+38.0	20.0	2 30.7	+38.2	20.0	3 27.0	+38.6	20.0	4 23.4	+38.8	20.1	5 19.8	+39.0	20.1	6 16.1	+39.3	20.1	65
66	0 19.0	+37.4	19.2	1 15.6	+37.7	19.2	2 12.3	+37.9	19.2	3 08.9	+38.2	19.2	4 05.6	+38.5	19.3	5 02.2	+38.7	19.3	5 58.8	+39.0	19.3	6 55.4	+39.3	19.4	66
67	0 56.4	+37.4	18.4	1 53.3	+37.7	18.4	2 50.2	+38.0	18.5	3 47.1	+38.2	18.5	4 44.1	+38.4	18.5	5 40.9	+38.7	18.5	6 37.8	+39.0	18.6	7 34.7	+39.2	18.6	67
68	1 33.8	+37.4	17.6	2 31.0	+37.6	17.7	3 28.2	+37.9	17.7	4 25.3	+38.2	17.7	5 22.5	+38.4	17.7	6 19.6	+38.6	17.8	7 16.8	+38.8	17.8	8 13.9	+39.1	17.8	68
69	2 11.2	+37.4	16.9	3 08.6	+37.7	16.9	4 06.1	+37.8	16.9	5 03.5	+38.0	16.9	6 00.9	+38.3	16.9	6 58.2	+38.6	17.0	7 55.6	+38.8	17.0	8 53.0	+39.0	17.1	69
70	2 48.6	+37.4	16.1	3 46.3	+37.5	16.1	4 43.9	+37.8	16.1	5 41.5	+38.1	16.1	6 39.2	+38.2	16.2	7 36.8	+38.4	16.2	8 34.4	+38.7	16.2	9 32.0	+38.9	16.3	70
71	3 26.0	+37.3	15.3	4 23.8	+37.6	15.3	5 21.7	+37.7	15.3	6 19.6	+37.9	15.4	7 17.4	+38.2	15.4	8 15.2	+38.4	15.4	9 13.1	+38.6	15.5	10 10.9	+38.8	15.5	71
72	4 03.3	+37.2	14.5	5 01.4	+37.4	14.5	5 59.4	+37.7	14.6	6 57.5	+37.9	14.6	7 55.6	+38.0	14.6	8 53.6	+38.3	14.7	9 51.7	+38.4	14.7	10 49.7	+38.7	14.7	72
73	4 40.5	+37.2	13.7	5 38.8	+37.4	13.8	6 37.1	+37.6	13.8	7 35.4	+37.8	13.8	8 33.6	+38.0	13.8	9 31.9	+38.1	13.9	10 30.1	+38.4	13.9	11 28.4	+38.5	14.0	73
74	5 17.7	+37.2	12.9	6 16.2	+37.4	13.0	7 14.7	+37.5	13.0	8 13.2	+37.6	13.0	9 11.6	+37.9	13.1	10 10.0	+38.1	13.1	11 08.5	+38.2	13.1	12 06.9	+38.4	13.2	74
75	5 54.9	+37.1	12.2	6 53.6	+37.2	12.2	7 52.2	+37.4	12.2	8 50.8	+37.6	12.2	9 49.5	+37.7	12.3	10 48.1	+37.9	12.3	11 46.7	+38.1	12.4	12 45.3	+38.3	12.4	75
76	6 32.0	+37.0	11.4	7 30.8	+37.2	11.4	8 29.6	+37.4	11.4	9 28.4	+37.5	11.4	10 27.2	+37.7	11.5	11 26.0	+37.8	11.5	12 24.8	+38.0	11.6	13 23.6	+38.1	11.6	76
77	7 09.0	+36.9	10.6	8 08.0	+37.1	10.6	9 07.0	+37.2	10.6	10 05.9	+37.4	10.7	11 04.9	+37.5	10.7	12 03.8	+37.8	10.7	13 02.8	+37.8	10.8	14 01.7	+38.0	10.8	77
78	7 45.9	+36.9	9.8	8 45.1	+36.9	9.8	9 44.2	+37.1	9.8	10 43.3	+37.3	9.9	11 42.4	+37.4	9.9	12 41.5	+37.5	9.9	13 40.6	+37.7	10.0	14 39.7	+37.8	10.0	78
79	8 22.8	+36.7	9.0	9 22.0	+36.9	9.0	10 21.3	+37.0	9.0	11 20.6	+37.1	9.1	12 19.8	+37.3	9.1	13 19.0	+37.4	9.1	14 18.3	+37.5	9.2	15 17.5	+37.6	9.2	79
80	8 59.5	+36.7	8.2	9 58.9	+36.8	8.2	10 58.3	+36.9	8.2	11 57.7	+37.0	8.3	12 57.1	+37.1	8.3	13 56.4	+37.2	8.3	14 55.8	+37.3	8.4	15 55.1	+37.5	8.4	80
81	9 36.2	+36.5	7.4	10 35.7	+36.6	7.4	11 35.2	+36.7	7.4	12 34.7	+36.8	7.5	13 34.2	+36.9	7.5	14 33.6	+37.1	7.5	15 33.1	+37.2	7.5	16 32.6	+37.3	7.6	81
82	10 12.7	+36.4	6.6	11 12.3	+36.5	6.6	12 11.9	+36.6	6.6	13 11.5	+36.7	6.6	14 11.1	+36.8	6.7	15 10.7	+36.9	6.7	16 10.3	+36.9	6.7	17 09.9	+37.0	6.8	82
83	10 49.1	+36.3	5.8	11 48.8	+36.4	5.8	12 48.5	+36.4	5.8	13 48.2	+36.5	5.8	14 47.9	+36.6	5.9	15 47.6	+36.7	5.9	16 47.2	+36.8	5.9	17 46.9	+36.9	5.9	83
84	11 25.4	+36.1	4.9	12 25.2	+36.2	5.0	13 24.9	+36.3	5.0	14 24.7	+36.4	5.0	15 24.5	+36.4	5.0	16 24.3	+36.4	5.1	17 24.0	+36.6	5.1	18 23.8	+36.6	5.1	84
85	12 01.5	+36.1	4.1	13 01.4	+36.1	4.2	14 01.2	+36.1	4.2	15 01.1	+36.1	4.2	16 00.9	+36.2	4.2	17 00.7	+36.3	4.2	18 00.6	+36.3	4.3	19 00.4	+36.4	4.3	85
86	12 37.6	+35.8	3.3	13 37.5	+35.9	3.3	14 37.3	+36.0	3.3	15 37.2	+36.0	3.4	16 37.1	+36.1	3.4	17 37.0	+36.1	3.4	18 36.9	+36.2	3.4	19 36.8	+36.2	3.4	86
87	13 13.4	+35.7	2.5	14 13.4	+35.7	2.5	15 13.3	+35.8	2.5	16 13.2	+35.8	2.5	17 13.2	+35.8	2.5	18 13.1	+35.9	2.6	19 13.1	+35.9	2.6	20 13.0	+35.9	2.6	87
88	13 49.1	+35.5	1.7	14 49.1	+35.5	1.7	15 49.1	+35.5	1.7	16 49.0	+35.6	1.7	17 49.0	+35.6	1.7	18 49.0	+35.6	1.7	19 49.0	+35.6	1.7	20 48.9	+35.7	1.7	88
89	14 24.6	+35.4	0.8	15 24.6	+35.4	0.8	16 24.6	+35.4	0.8	17 24.6	+35.4	0.8	18 24.6	+35.4	0.9	19 24.6	+35.4	0.9	20 24.6	+35.4	0.9	21 24.6	+35.4	0.9	89
90	15 00.0	+35.2	0.0	16 00.0	+35.2	0.0	17 00.0	+35.2	0.0	18 00.0	+35.2	0.0	19 00.0	+35.1	0.0	20 00.0	+35.1	0.0	21 00.0	+35.1	0.0	22 00.0	+35.1	0.0	90
	15°			16°			17°			18°			19°			20°			21°			22°			

S. Lat. { L.H.A. greater than 180° ....Zn=180°–Z
L.H.A. less than 180°...........Zn=180°+Z

LATITUDE **SAME** NAME AS DECLINATION **L.H.A. 126°, 234°**

111

55°, 305° L.H.A. LATITUDE SAME NAME AS DECLINATION

N. Lat. {L.H.A. greater than 180° .....Zn=Z
{L.H.A. less than 180°............Zn=360°-Z

Dec.	15° Hc	d	Z	16° Hc	d	Z	17° Hc	d	Z	18° Hc	d	Z
°	° ′	′	°	° ′	′	°	° ′	′	°	° ′	′	°
0	33 38.6	+18.4	100.3	33 27.6	+19.5	100.9	33 15.9	+20.7	101.6	33 03.5	+21.9	102.2
1	33 57.0	+17.7	99.1	33 47.1	+18.9	99.8	33 36.6	+20.0	100.4	33 25.4	+21.2	101.1
2	34 14.7	+17.0	98.0	34 06.0	+18.3	98.6	33 56.6	+19.5	99.3	33 46.6	+20.6	100.0
3	34 31.7	+16.4	96.8	34 24.3	+17.5	97.5	34 16.1	+18.8	98.2	34 07.2	+20.0	98.8
4	34 48.1	+15.7	95.6	34 41.8	+17.0	96.3	34 34.9	+18.1	97.0	34 27.2	+19.3	97.7
5	35 03.8	+15.0	94.5	34 58.8	+16.2	95.2	34 53.0	+17.5	95.9	34 46.5	+18.7	96.5
6	35 18.8	+14.3	93.3	35 15.0	+15.6	94.0	35 10.5	+16.8	94.7	35 05.2	+18.0	95.4
7	35 33.1	+13.6	92.1	35 30.6	+14.8	92.8	35 27.3	+16.1	93.5	35 23.2	+17.4	94.2
8	35 46.7	+12.9	90.9	35 45.4	+14.2	91.6	35 43.4	+15.4	92.3	35 40.6	+16.6	93.0
9	35 59.6	+12.2	89.7	35 59.6	+13.4	90.4	35 58.8	+14.7	91.1	35 57.2	+16.0	91.9
10	36 11.8	+11.4	88.5	36 13.0	+12.7	89.2	36 13.5	+13.9	89.9	36 13.2	+15.2	90.7
11	36 23.2	+10.7	87.3	36 25.7	+12.0	88.0	36 27.4	+13.3	88.7	36 28.4	+14.5	89.5
12	36 33.9	+9.9	86.0	36 37.7	+11.2	86.8	36 40.7	+12.5	87.5	36 42.9	+13.7	88.3
13	36 43.8	+9.2	84.8	36 48.9	+10.4	85.5	36 53.2	+11.7	86.3	36 56.6	+13.1	87.0
14	36 53.0	+8.4	83.6	36 59.3	+9.7	84.3	37 04.9	+11.0	85.1	37 09.7	+12.2	85.8
15	37 01.4	+7.6	82.3	37 09.0	+8.9	83.1	37 15.9	+10.2	83.8	37 21.9	+11.5	84.6
16	37 09.0	+6.9	81.1	37 17.9	+8.2	81.8	37 26.1	+9.4	82.6	37 33.4	+10.7	83.4
17	37 15.9	+6.0	79.8	37 26.1	+7.3	80.6	37 35.5	+8.6	81.3	37 44.1	+9.9	82.1
18	37 21.9	+5.3	78.6	37 33.4	+6.6	79.3	37 44.1	+7.9	80.1	37 54.0	+9.2	80.9
19	37 27.2	+4.4	77.3	37 40.0	+5.7	78.1	37 52.0	+7.0	78.8	38 03.2	+8.3	79.6
20	37 31.6	+3.7	76.1	37 45.7	+4.9	76.8	37 59.0	+6.2	77.6	38 11.5	+7.5	78.3
21	37 35.3	+2.9	74.8	37 50.6	+4.2	75.6	38 05.2	+5.4	76.3	38 19.0	+6.7	77.1
22	37 38.2	+2.0	73.6	37 54.8	+3.3	74.3	38 10.6	+4.6	75.1	38 25.7	+5.9	75.8
23	37 40.2	+1.3	72.3	37 58.1	+2.5	73.0	38 15.2	+3.8	73.8	38 31.6	+5.1	74.5
24	37 41.5	+0.4	71.0	38 00.6	+1.7	71.8	38 19.0	+3.0	72.5	38 36.7	+4.2	73.3
25	37 41.9	-0.4	69.8	38 02.3	+0.9	70.5	38 22.0	+2.1	71.2	38 40.9	+3.4	72.0
26	37 41.5	-1.1	68.5	38 03.2	0.0	69.2	38 24.1	+1.3	70.0	38 44.3	+2.5	70.7
27	37 40.4	-2.0	67.2	38 03.2	-0.7	68.0	38 25.4	+0.4	68.7	38 46.8	+1.7	69.4
28	37 38.4	-2.8	66.0	38 02.5	-1.6	66.7	38 25.8	-0.3	67.4	38 48.5	+0.9	68.2
29	37 35.6	-3.6	64.7	38 00.9	-2.4	65.4	38 25.5	-1.2	66.1	38 49.4	0.0	66.9
30	37 32.0	-4.4	63.5	37 58.5	-3.3	64.1	38 24.3	-2.0	64.9	38 49.4	-0.8	65.6
31	37 27.6	-5.2	62.2	37 55.2	-4.0	62.9	38 22.3	-2.9	63.6	38 48.6	-1.6	64.3
32	37 22.4	-6.0	60.9	37 51.2	-4.8	61.6	38 19.4	-3.7	62.3	38 47.0	-2.5	63.0
33	37 16.4	-6.8	59.7	37 46.4	-5.7	60.4	38 15.7	-4.5	61.0	38 44.5	-3.4	61.7
34	37 09.6	-7.6	58.4	37 40.7	-6.4	59.1	38 11.2	-5.3	59.8	38 41.1	-4.2	60.5
35	37 02.0	-8.3	57.2	37 34.3	-7.3	57.8	38 05.9	-6.1	58.5	38 36.9	-5.0	59.2
36	36 53.7	-9.1	56.0	37 27.0	-8.0	56.6	37 59.8	-7.0	57.2	38 31.9	-5.8	57.9
37	36 44.6	-9.9	54.7	37 19.0	-8.8	55.3	37 52.8	-7.7	56.0	38 26.1	-6.6	56.6
38	36 34.7	-10.6	53.5	37 10.2	-9.6	54.1	37 45.1	-8.6	54.7	38 19.5	-7.5	55.4
39	36 24.1	-11.4	52.3	37 00.6	-10.4	52.9	37 36.5	-9.3	53.5	38 12.0	-8.3	54.1
40	36 12.7	-12.1	51.1	36 50.2	-11.1	51.6	37 27.2	-10.1	52.2	38 03.7	-9.1	52.8
41	36 00.6	-12.8	49.8	36 39.1	-11.9	50.4	37 17.1	-10.9	51.0	37 54.6	-9.8	51.6
42	35 47.8	-13.6	48.6	36 27.2	-12.6	49.2	37 06.2	-11.6	49.8	37 44.8	-10.7	50.3
43	35 34.2	-14.2	47.4	36 14.6	-13.3	48.0	36 54.6	-12.4	48.5	37 34.1	-11.5	49.1
44	35 20.0	-15.0	46.2	36 01.3	-14.1	46.8	36 42.2	-13.2	47.3	37 22.6	-12.2	47.9
45	35 05.0	-15.6	45.1	35 47.2	-14.8	45.6	36 29.0	-13.9	46.1	37 10.4	-12.9	46.6
46	34 49.4	-16.3	43.9	35 32.4	-15.4	44.4	36 15.1	-14.6	44.9	36 57.5	-13.7	45.4
47	34 33.1	-17.0	42.7	35 17.0	-16.2	43.2	36 00.5	-15.3	43.7	36 43.8	-14.5	44.2
48	34 16.1	-17.7	41.5	35 00.8	-16.8	42.0	35 45.2	-16.0	42.5	36 29.3	-15.2	43.0
49	33 58.4	-18.3	40.4	34 44.0	-17.5	40.8	35 29.2	-16.7	41.3	36 14.1	-15.9	41.8
50	33 40.1	-18.9	39.2	34 26.5	-18.2	39.7	35 12.5	-17.4	40.1	35 58.2	-16.6	40.6
51	33 21.2	-19.5	38.1	34 08.3	-18.8	38.5	34 55.1	-18.1	39.0	35 41.6	-17.3	39.4
52	33 01.7	-20.2	37.0	33 49.5	-19.5	37.4	34 37.0	-18.7	37.8	35 24.3	-18.0	38.2
53	32 41.5	-20.7	35.9	33 30.0	-20.0	36.2	34 18.3	-19.3	36.6	35 06.3	-18.6	37.1
54	32 20.8	-21.3	34.7	33 10.0	-20.7	35.1	33 59.0	-20.0	35.5	34 47.7	-19.3	35.9
55	31 59.5	-21.9	33.6	32 49.3	-21.2	34.0	33 39.0	-20.6	34.4	34 28.4	-20.0	34.7
56	31 37.6	-22.4	32.5	32 28.1	-21.9	32.9	33 18.4	-21.2	33.2	34 08.4	-20.5	33.6
57	31 15.2	-23.0	31.5	32 06.2	-22.4	31.8	32 57.2	-21.8	32.1	33 47.9	-21.2	32.5
58	30 52.2	-23.6	30.4	31 43.8	-22.9	30.7	32 35.4	-22.4	31.0	33 26.7	-21.8	31.3
59	30 28.6	-24.0	29.3	31 20.9	-23.5	29.6	32 13.0	-23.0	29.9	33 04.9	-22.4	30.2
60	30 04.6	-24.5	28.2	30 57.4	-24.0	28.5	31 50.0	-23.5	28.8	32 42.5	-22.9	29.1
61	29 40.1	-25.1	27.2	30 33.4	-24.6	27.5	31 26.5	-24.0	27.7	32 19.6	-23.6	28.0
62	29 15.0	-25.5	26.2	30 08.8	-25.0	26.4	31 02.5	-24.6	26.7	31 56.0	-24.0	26.9
63	28 49.5	-26.0	25.1	29 43.8	-25.6	25.4	30 37.9	-25.0	25.6	31 32.0	-24.6	25.9
64	28 23.5	-26.4	24.1	29 18.2	-26.0	24.3	30 12.9	-25.6	24.6	31 07.4	-25.2	24.8
65	27 57.1	-26.9	23.1	28 52.2	-26.5	23.3	29 47.3	-26.1	23.5	30 42.2	-25.6	23.7
66	27 30.2	-27.4	22.1	28 25.7	-26.9	22.3	29 21.2	-26.5	22.5	30 16.6	-26.1	22.7
67	27 02.8	-27.7	21.1	27 58.8	-27.4	21.2	28 54.7	-27.0	21.4	29 50.5	-26.7	21.7
68	26 35.1	-28.2	20.1	27 31.4	-27.8	20.2	28 27.7	-27.5	20.4	29 23.8	-27.0	20.6
69	26 06.9	-28.6	19.1	27 03.6	-28.3	19.2	28 00.2	-27.9	19.4	28 56.8	-27.6	19.6
70	25 38.3	-28.9	18.1	26 35.3	-28.6	18.3	27 32.3	-28.3	18.4	28 29.2	-28.0	18.6
71	25 09.4	-29.3	17.1	26 06.7	-29.0	17.3	27 04.0	-28.8	17.4	28 01.2	-28.4	17.6
72	24 40.1	-29.7	16.2	25 37.7	-29.4	16.3	26 35.2	-29.1	16.4	27 32.8	-28.9	16.6
73	24 10.4	-30.1	15.2	25 08.3	-29.8	15.3	26 06.1	-29.5	15.5	27 03.9	-29.3	15.6
74	23 40.3	-30.3	14.3	24 38.5	-30.2	14.4	25 36.6	-29.9	14.5	26 34.6	-29.6	14.6
75	23 10.0	-30.8	13.3	24 08.3	-30.5	13.4	25 06.7	-30.3	13.5	26 05.0	-30.1	13.7
76	22 39.2	-31.0	12.4	23 37.8	-30.8	12.5	24 36.4	-30.6	12.6	25 34.9	-30.4	12.7
77	22 08.2	-31.4	11.5	23 07.0	-31.2	11.6	24 05.8	-31.0	11.6	25 04.5	-30.8	11.7
78	21 36.8	-31.6	10.6	22 35.8	-31.5	10.6	23 34.8	-31.3	10.7	24 33.7	-31.1	10.8
79	21 05.2	-31.9	9.6	22 04.3	-31.7	9.7	23 03.5	-31.7	9.8	24 02.6	-31.5	9.9
80	20 33.3	-32.3	8.7	21 32.6	-32.1	8.8	22 31.8	-31.9	8.9	23 31.1	-31.8	8.9
81	20 01.0	-32.5	7.8	21 00.5	-32.4	7.9	21 59.9	-32.3	7.9	22 59.3	-32.1	8.0
82	19 28.5	-32.7	6.9	20 28.1	-32.6	7.0	21 27.6	-32.5	7.0	22 27.2	-32.4	7.1
83	18 55.8	-33.0	6.1	19 55.5	-33.0	6.1	20 55.1	-32.8	6.1	21 54.8	-32.8	6.2
84	18 22.8	-33.3	5.2	19 22.5	-33.1	5.2	20 22.3	-33.1	5.2	21 22.0	-33.0	5.3
85	17 49.5	-33.4	4.3	18 49.4	-33.4	4.3	19 49.2	-33.4	4.4	20 49.0	-33.3	4.4
86	17 16.1	-33.7	3.4	18 16.0	-33.7	3.4	19 15.8	-33.6	3.5	20 15.7	-33.5	3.5
87	16 42.4	-34.0	2.6	17 42.3	-33.9	2.6	18 42.2	-33.8	2.6	19 42.2	-33.7	2.6
88	16 08.4	-34.1	1.7	17 08.4	-34.1	1.7	18 08.4	-34.1	1.7	19 08.4	-34.1	1.7
89	15 34.3	-34.3	0.9	16 34.3	-34.3	0.9	17 34.3	-34.3	0.9	18 34.3	-34.3	0.9
90	15 00.0	-34.5	0.0	16 00.0	-34.5	0.0	17 00.0	-34.5	0.0	18 00.0	-34.5	0.0
	15°			16°			17°			18°		

19° Hc	d	Z	20° Hc	d	Z	21° Hc	d	Z	22° Hc	d	Z	Dec.
° ′	′	°	° ′	′	°	° ′	′	°	° ′	′	°	°
32 50.5	+23.0	102.8	32 36.9	+24.1	103.5	32 22.6	+25.2	104.1	32 07.7	+26.2	104.7	0
33 13.5	+22.4	101.7	33 01.0	+23.5	102.4	32 47.8	+24.6	103.0	32 33.9	+25.8	103.6	1
33 35.9	+21.7	100.6	33 24.5	+22.9	101.3	33 12.4	+24.1	101.9	32 59.7	+25.2	102.6	2
33 57.6	+21.2	99.5	33 47.4	+22.3	100.2	33 36.5	+23.4	100.8	33 24.9	+24.6	101.5	3
34 18.8	+20.5	98.4	34 09.7	+21.7	99.0	33 59.9	+22.9	99.7	33 49.5	+24.0	100.4	4
34 39.3	+19.9	97.2	34 31.4	+21.1	97.9	34 22.8	+22.2	98.6	34 13.5	+23.4	99.3	5
34 59.2	+19.2	96.1	34 52.5	+20.4	96.8	34 45.0	+21.7	97.5	34 36.9	+22.8	98.2	6
35 18.4	+18.6	94.9	35 12.9	+19.8	95.6	35 06.7	+20.9	96.3	34 59.7	+22.1	97.0	7
35 37.0	+17.9	93.8	35 32.7	+19.1	94.5	35 27.6	+20.4	95.2	35 21.8	+21.6	95.9	8
35 54.9	+17.2	92.6	35 51.8	+18.4	93.3	35 48.0	+19.6	94.0	35 43.4	+20.8	94.7	9
36 12.1	+16.5	91.4	36 10.2	+17.8	92.1	36 07.6	+19.0	92.9	36 04.2	+20.2	93.6	10
36 28.6	+15.7	90.2	36 28.0	+17.0	90.9	36 26.6	+18.2	91.7	36 24.4	+19.5	92.4	11
36 44.3	+15.1	89.0	36 45.0	+16.3	89.8	36 44.8	+17.6	90.5	36 43.9	+18.8	91.2	12
36 59.4	+14.2	87.8	37 01.3	+15.5	88.5	37 02.4	+16.8	89.3	37 02.7	+18.1	90.1	13
37 13.6	+13.6	86.6	37 16.8	+14.8	87.3	37 19.2	+16.1	88.1	37 20.8	+17.4	88.9	14
37 27.2	+12.8	85.4	37 31.6	+14.1	86.1	37 35.3	+15.3	86.9	37 38.2	+16.6	87.7	15
37 40.0	+12.0	84.1	37 45.7	+13.3	84.9	37 50.6	+14.6	85.7	37 54.8	+15.8	86.4	16
37 52.0	+11.2	82.9	37 59.0	+12.5	83.7	38 05.2	+13.8	84.4	38 10.6	+15.1	85.2	17
38 03.2	+10.4	81.6	38 11.5	+11.7	82.4	38 19.0	+13.0	83.2	38 25.7	+14.3	84.0	18
38 13.6	+9.6	80.4	38 23.2	+10.9	81.2	38 32.0	+12.3	81.9	38 40.0	+13.6	82.7	19
38 23.2	+8.8	79.1	38 34.1	+10.2	79.9	38 44.3	+11.4	80.7	38 53.6	+12.7	81.5	20
38 32.0	+8.0	77.9	38 44.3	+9.3	78.6	38 55.7	+10.6	79.4	39 06.3	+11.9	80.2	21
38 40.0	+7.2	76.6	38 53.6	+8.4	77.4	39 06.3	+9.7	78.2	39 18.2	+11.0	79.0	22
38 47.2	+6.3	75.3	39 02.0	+7.7	76.1	39 16.0	+9.0	76.9	39 29.2	+10.3	77.7	23
38 53.5	+5.6	74.0	39 09.7	+6.7	74.8	39 25.0	+8.0	75.6	39 39.5	+9.4	76.4	24
38 59.1	+4.6	72.8	39 16.4	+6.0	73.5	39 33.0	+7.3	74.3	39 48.9	+8.5	75.1	25
39 03.7	+3.8	71.5	39 22.4	+5.1	72.3	39 40.3	+6.4	73.0	39 57.4	+7.7	73.8	26
39 07.5	+3.0	70.2	39 27.5	+4.2	71.0	39 46.7	+5.5	71.7	40 05.1	+6.8	72.5	27
39 10.5	+2.1	68.9	39 31.7	+3.4	69.7	39 52.2	+4.6	70.5	40 11.9	+5.9	71.2	28
39 12.6	+1.3	67.6	39 35.1	+2.5	68.4	39 56.8	+3.8	69.2	40 17.8	+5.0	69.9	29
39 13.9	+0.4	66.3	39 37.6	+1.7	67.1	40 00.6	+2.9	67.9	40 22.8	+4.2	68.6	30
39 14.3	-0.5	65.0	39 39.3	+0.7	65.8	40 03.5	+2.0	66.5	40 27.0	+3.3	67.3	31
39 13.8	-1.3	63.7	39 40.0	-0.1	64.5	40 05.5	+1.2	65.2	40 30.3	+2.4	66.0	32
39 12.5	-2.1	62.5	39 39.9	-0.9	63.2	40 06.7	+0.2	63.9	40 32.7	+1.5	64.7	33
39 10.4	-3.0	61.2	39 39.0	-1.8	61.9	40 06.9	-0.6	62.6	40 34.2	+0.6	63.4	34
39 07.4	-3.9	59.9	39 37.2	-2.7	60.6	40 06.3	-1.5	61.3	40 34.8	-0.3	62.1	35
39 03.5	-4.7	58.6	39 34.5	-3.6	59.3	40 04.8	-2.4	60.0	40 34.5	-1.2	60.7	36
38 58.8	-5.5	57.3	39 30.9	-4.4	58.0	40 02.4	-3.3	58.7	40 33.3	-2.1	59.4	37
38 53.3	-6.4	56.0	39 26.5	-5.3	56.7	39 59.1	-4.1	57.4	40 31.2	-3.0	58.1	38
38 46.9	-7.2	54.7	39 21.2	-6.1	55.4	39 55.0	-5.0	56.1	40 28.2	-3.9	56.8	39
38 39.7	-8.0	53.5	39 15.1	-6.9	54.1	39 50.0	-5.9	54.8	40 24.3	-4.8	55.5	40
38 31.7	-8.9	52.2	39 08.2	-7.8	52.8	39 44.1	-6.7	53.5	40 19.5	-5.6	54.2	41
38 22.8	-9.7	50.9	39 00.4	-8.7	51.6	39 37.4	-7.6	52.2	40 13.9	-6.6	52.9	42
38 13.1	-10.4	49.7	38 51.7	-9.4	50.3	39 29.8	-8.4	50.9	40 07.3	-7.4	51.6	43
38 02.7	-11.3	48.4	38 42.3	-10.3	49.0	39 21.4	-9.3	49.6	39 59.9	-8.2	50.3	44
37 51.4	-12.0	47.2	38 32.0	-11.1	47.8	39 12.1	-10.1	48.4	39 51.7	-9.1	49.0	45
37 39.4	-12.8	46.0	38 20.9	-11.9	46.5	39 02.0	-11.0	47.1	39 42.6	-10.0	47.7	46
37 26.6	-13.6	44.7	38 09.0	-12.7	45.3	38 51.0	-11.7	45.8	39 32.6	-10.8	46.4	47
37 13.0	-14.3	43.5	37 56.3	-13.4	44.0	38 39.3	-12.6	44.6	39 21.8	-11.6	45.1	48
36 58.7	-15.1	42.3	37 42.9	-14.2	42.8	38 26.7	-13.3	43.3	39 10.2	-12.5	43.9	49
36 43.6	-15.8	41.1	37 28.7	-15.0	41.6	38 13.4	-14.1	42.1	38 57.7	-13.2	42.6	50
36 27.8	-16.5	39.9	37 13.7	-15.7	40.3	37 59.3	-14.9	40.8	38 44.5	-14.1	41.4	51
36 11.3	-17.2	38.7	36 58.0	-16.5	39.1	37 44.4	-15.7	39.6	38 30.4	-14.8	40.1	52
35 54.1	-17.9	37.5	36 41.5	-17.1	37.9	37 28.7	-16.4	38.4	38 15.6	-15.6	38.9	53
35 36.2	-18.6	36.3	36 24.4	-17.9	36.7	37 12.3	-17.1	37.2	38 00.0	-16.4	37.7	54
35 17.6	-19.3	35.1	36 06.5	-18.6	35.6	36 55.2	-17.9	36.0	37 43.6	-17.1	36.4	55
34 58.3	-19.9	34.0	35 47.9	-19.2	34.4	36 37.3	-18.5	34.8	37 26.5	-17.9	35.2	56
34 38.4	-20.6	32.8	35 28.7	-19.9	33.2	36 18.8	-19.3	33.6	37 08.6	-18.5	34.0	57
34 17.8	-21.1	31.7	35 08.8	-20.6	32.1	35 59.5	-19.9	32.4	36 50.1	-19.3	32.8	58
33 56.7	-21.8	30.6	34 48.2	-21.2	30.9	35 39.6	-20.6	31.3	36 30.8	-20.0	31.7	59
33 34.9	-22.4	29.4	34 27.0	-21.8	29.8	35 19.0	-21.2	30.1	36 10.8	-20.6	30.5	60
33 12.5	-23.0	28.3	34 05.2	-22.5	28.7	34 57.8	-21.9	29.0	35 50.2	-21.4	29.3	61
32 49.5	-23.6	27.2	33 42.7	-23.0	27.5	34 35.9	-22.5	27.9	35 28.8	-21.9	28.2	62
32 25.9	-24.1	26.1	33 19.7	-23.6	26.4	34 13.4	-23.2	26.7	35 06.9	-22.6	27.0	63
32 01.8	-24.7	25.1	32 56.1	-24.2	25.3	33 50.2	-23.7	25.6	34 44.3	-23.2	25.9	64
31 37.1	-25.2	24.0	32 31.9	-24.8	24.2	33 26.5	-24.3	24.5	34 21.1	-23.9	24.8	65
31 11.9	-25.7	22.9	32 07.1	-25.3	23.2	33 02.2	-24.8	23.4	33 57.2	-24.4	23.7	66
30 46.2	-26.2	21.9	31 41.8	-25.8	22.1	32 37.4	-25.4	22.3	33 32.8	-25.0	22.6	67
30 20.0	-26.8	20.8	31 16.0	-26.3	21.0	32 12.0	-26.0	21.3	33 07.8	-25.5	21.5	68
29 53.2	-27.2	19.8	30 49.7	-26.9	20.0	31 46.0	-26.5	20.2	32 42.3	-26.1	20.4	69
29 26.0	-27.6	18.8	30 22.8	-27.3	19.0	31 19.5	-27.0	19.1	32 16.2	-26.7	19.4	70
28 58.4	-28.2	17.7	29 55.5	-27.8	17.9	30 52.5	-27.4	18.1	31 49.5	-27.1	18.3	71
28 30.2	-28.5	16.7	29 27.7	-28.3	16.9	30 25.1	-28.0	17.1	31 22.4	-27.7	17.2	72
28 01.7	-29.0	15.7	28 59.4	-28.7	15.9	29 57.1	-28.4	16.0	30 54.7	-28.1	16.2	73
27 32.7	-29.4	14.8	28 30.7	-29.2	14.9	29 28.7	-28.9	15.0	30 26.6	-28.6	15.2	74
27 03.3	-29.8	13.8	28 01.5	-29.5	13.9	28 59.8	-29.4	14.0	29 58.0	-29.1	14.2	75
26 33.5	-30.2	12.8	27 32.0	-30.0	12.9	28 30.4	-29.7	13.0	29 28.9	-29.6	13.2	76
26 03.3	-30.6	11.8	27 02.0	-30.4	11.9	28 00.7	-30.2	12.0	28 59.3	-30.0	12.2	77
25 32.7	-31.0	10.9	26 31.6	-30.8	11.0	27 30.5	-30.6	11.1	28 29.3	-30.4	11.2	78
25 01.7	-31.3	9.9	26 00.8	-31.2	10.0	26 59.9	-31.0	10.1	27 58.9	-30.8	10.2	79
24 30.4	-31.7	9.0	25 29.6	-31.5	9.1	26 28.9	-31.4	9.1	27 28.1	-31.2	9.2	80
23 58.7	-32.0	8.1	24 58.1	-31.8	8.1	25 57.5	-31.7	8.2	26 56.9	-31.6	8.3	81
23 26.7	-32.3	7.1	24 26.3	-32.2	7.2	25 25.8	-32.1	7.3	26 25.3	-32.0	7.3	82
22 54.4	-32.6	6.2	23 54.1	-32.6	6.3	24 53.7	-32.4	6.3	25 53.3	-32.3	6.4	83
22 21.8	-33.0	5.3	23 21.5	-32.8	5.4	24 21.3	-32.8	5.4	25 21.0	-32.7	5.4	84
21 48.8	-33.2	4.4	22 48.7	-33.2	4.4	23 48.5	-33.1	4.5	24 48.3	-33.0	4.5	85
21 15.6	-33.5	3.5	22 15.5	-33.5	3.5	23 15.4	-33.4	3.6	24 15.3	-33.4	3.6	86
20 42.1	-33.8	2.6	21 42.0	-33.7	2.6	22 42.0	-33.7	2.7	23 41.9	-33.7	2.7	87
20 08.3	-34.0	1.7	21 08.3	-34.0	1.8	22 08.3	-34.0	1.8	23 08.2	-33.9	1.8	88
19 34.3	-34.3	0.9	20 34.3	-34.3	0.9	21 34.3	-34.3	0.9	22 34.3	-34.3	0.9	89
19 00.0	-34.5	0.0	20 00.0	-34.5	0.0	21 00.0	-34.5	0.0	22 00.0	-34.6	0.0	90
19°			20°			21°			22°			

55°, 305° L.H.A. LATITUDE SAME NAME AS DECLINATION

112

LATITUDE **CONTRARY** NAME TO DECLINATION **L.H.A. 55°, 305°**

Dec.	15° Hc	d	Z	16° Hc	d	Z	17° Hc	d	Z	18° Hc	d	Z	Dec.
°	° ′	′	°	° ′	′	°	° ′	′	°	° ′	′	°	°
0	33 38.6	−18.9	100.3	33 27.6	−20.1	100.9	33 15.9	−21.3	101.6	33 03.5	−22.4	102.2	0
1	33 19.7	−19.6	101.4	33 07.5	−20.8	102.1	32 54.6	−21.8	102.7	32 41.1	−23.0	103.3	1
2	33 00.1	−20.2	102.5	32 46.7	−21.3	103.2	32 32.8	−22.5	103.8	32 18.1	−23.5	104.4	2
3	32 39.9	−20.8	103.7	32 25.4	−21.9	104.3	32 10.3	−23.0	104.9	31 54.6	−24.1	105.5	3
4	32 19.1	−21.3	104.8	32 03.5	−22.5	105.4	31 47.3	−23.6	106.0	31 30.5	−24.7	106.6	4
5	31 57.8	−22.0	105.9	31 41.0	−23.0	106.5	31 23.7	−24.1	107.1	31 05.8	−25.1	107.6	5
6	31 35.8	−22.5	107.0	31 18.0	−23.5	107.6	30 59.6	−24.6	108.1	30 40.7	−25.7	108.7	6
7	31 13.3	−23.0	108.1	30 54.5	−24.1	108.6	30 35.0	−25.1	109.2	30 15.0	−26.2	109.7	7
8	30 50.3	−23.6	109.1	30 30.4	−24.6	109.7	30 09.9	−25.7	110.2	29 48.8	−26.6	110.8	8
9	30 26.7	−24.0	110.2	30 05.8	−25.2	110.7	29 44.2	−26.1	111.3	29 22.2	−27.1	111.8	9
10	30 02.7	−24.6	111.3	29 40.6	−25.6	111.8	29 18.1	−26.6	112.3	28 55.1	−27.6	112.8	10
11	29 38.1	−25.1	112.3	29 15.0	−26.0	112.8	28 51.5	−27.0	113.3	28 27.5	−28.0	113.8	11
12	29 13.0	−25.6	113.4	28 49.0	−26.6	113.9	28 24.5	−27.6	114.4	27 59.5	−28.5	114.9	12
13	28 47.4	−26.0	114.4	28 22.4	−27.0	114.9	27 56.9	−27.9	115.4	27 31.0	−28.9	115.8	13
14	28 21.4	−26.5	115.4	27 55.4	−27.4	115.9	27 29.0	−28.4	116.4	27 02.1	−29.3	116.8	14
15	27 54.9	−26.9	116.4	27 28.0	−27.9	116.9	27 00.6	−28.8	117.4	26 32.8	−29.6	117.8	15
16	27 28.0	−27.4	117.4	27 00.1	−28.3	117.9	26 31.8	−29.1	118.3	26 03.2	−30.1	118.8	16
17	27 00.6	−27.8	118.4	26 31.8	−28.6	118.9	26 02.7	−29.6	119.3	25 33.1	−30.5	119.7	17
18	26 32.8	−28.2	119.4	26 03.2	−29.1	119.9	25 33.1	−30.0	120.3	25 02.6	−30.8	120.7	18
19	26 04.6	−28.6	120.4	25 34.1	−29.5	120.8	25 03.1	−30.3	121.2	24 31.8	−31.1	121.6	19
20	25 36.0	−28.9	121.4	25 04.6	−29.8	121.8	24 32.8	−30.7	122.2	24 00.7	−31.5	122.6	20
21	25 07.1	−29.4	122.4	24 34.8	−30.2	122.8	24 02.1	−31.0	123.1	23 29.2	−31.8	123.5	21
22	24 37.7	−29.7	123.3	24 04.6	−30.6	123.7	23 31.1	−31.3	124.1	22 57.4	−32.2	124.4	22
23	24 08.0	−30.1	124.3	23 34.0	−30.8	124.6	22 59.8	−31.7	125.0	22 25.2	−32.4	125.3	23
24	23 37.9	−30.4	125.2	23 03.2	−31.2	125.6	22 28.1	−32.0	125.9	21 52.8	−32.8	126.3	24
25	23 07.5	−30.7	126.2	22 32.0	−31.6	126.5	21 56.1	−32.3	126.8	21 20.0	−33.0	127.2	25
26	22 36.8	−31.1	127.1	22 00.4	−31.8	127.4	21 23.8	−32.5	127.7	20 47.0	−33.3	128.0	26
27	22 05.7	−31.4	128.0	21 28.6	−32.1	128.3	20 51.3	−32.9	128.6	20 13.7	−33.6	128.9	27
28	21 34.3	−31.6	128.9	20 56.5	−32.4	129.2	20 18.4	−33.1	129.5	19 40.1	−33.8	129.8	28
29	21 02.7	−32.0	129.9	20 24.1	−32.7	130.1	19 45.3	−33.4	130.4	19 06.3	−34.1	130.7	29
30	20 30.7	−32.2	130.8	19 51.4	−32.9	131.0	19 11.9	−33.6	131.3	18 32.2	−34.3	131.6	30
31	19 58.5	−32.6	131.7	19 18.5	−33.2	131.9	18 38.3	−33.9	132.2	17 57.9	−34.6	132.4	31
32	19 25.9	−32.7	132.6	18 45.3	−33.5	132.8	18 04.4	−34.1	133.1	17 23.3	−34.7	133.3	32
33	18 53.2	−33.1	133.4	18 11.8	−33.7	133.7	17 30.3	−34.3	133.9	16 48.6	−35.0	134.1	33
34	18 20.1	−33.2	134.3	17 38.1	−33.9	134.6	16 56.0	−34.6	134.8	16 13.6	−35.2	135.0	34
35	17 46.9	−33.5	135.2	17 04.2	−34.1	135.4	16 21.4	−34.7	135.6	15 38.4	−35.3	135.8	35
36	17 13.4	−33.7	136.1	16 30.1	−34.3	136.3	15 46.7	−35.0	136.5	15 03.1	−35.6	136.7	36
37	16 39.7	−34.0	136.9	15 55.8	−34.6	137.1	15 11.7	−35.1	137.3	14 27.5	−35.7	137.5	37
38	16 05.7	−34.1	137.8	15 21.2	−34.7	138.0	14 36.6	−35.3	138.2	13 51.8	−35.9	138.3	38
39	15 31.6	−34.3	138.6	14 46.5	−34.9	138.8	14 01.3	−35.5	139.0	13 15.9	−36.0	139.2	39
40	14 57.3	−34.6	139.5	14 11.6	−35.1	139.7	13 25.8	−35.7	139.8	12 39.9	−36.2	140.0	40
41	14 22.7	−34.7	140.3	13 36.5	−35.3	140.5	12 50.1	−35.8	140.6	12 03.7	−36.3	140.8	41
42	13 48.0	−34.8	141.2	13 01.2	−35.4	141.3	12 14.3	−35.9	141.5	11 27.4	−36.5	141.6	42
43	13 13.2	−35.1	142.0	12 25.8	−35.5	142.2	11 38.4	−36.1	142.3	10 50.9	−36.6	142.4	43
44	12 38.1	−35.2	142.9	11 50.3	−35.7	143.0	11 02.3	−36.2	143.1	10 14.3	−36.7	143.2	44
45	12 02.9	−35.3	143.7	11 14.6	−35.9	143.8	10 26.1	−36.3	143.9	9 37.6	−36.8	144.0	45
46	11 27.6	−35.5	144.5	10 38.7	−35.9	144.6	9 49.8	−36.5	144.7	9 00.8	−37.0	144.8	46
47	10 52.1	−35.6	145.3	10 02.8	−36.1	145.4	9 13.3	−36.5	145.5	8 23.8	−37.0	145.6	47
48	10 16.5	−35.7	146.1	9 26.7	−36.2	146.2	8 36.8	−36.7	146.3	7 46.8	−37.1	146.4	48
49	9 40.8	−35.8	147.0	8 50.5	−36.3	147.1	8 00.1	−36.7	147.1	7 09.7	−37.2	147.2	49
50	9 05.0	−36.0	147.8	8 14.2	−36.4	147.9	7 23.4	−36.9	147.9	6 32.5	−37.3	148.0	50
51	8 29.0	−36.0	148.6	7 37.8	−36.5	148.7	6 46.5	−36.9	148.7	5 55.2	−37.3	148.8	51
52	7 53.0	−36.2	149.4	7 01.3	−36.6	149.5	6 09.6	−37.0	149.5	5 17.9	−37.4	149.6	52
53	7 16.8	−36.2	150.2	6 24.7	−36.6	150.3	5 32.6	−37.0	150.3	4 40.5	−37.5	150.4	53
54	6 40.6	−36.3	151.0	5 48.1	−36.7	151.1	4 55.6	−37.1	151.1	4 03.0	−37.5	151.1	54
55	6 04.3	−36.4	151.8	5 11.4	−36.8	151.9	4 18.5	−37.2	151.9	3 25.5	−37.5	151.9	55
56	5 27.9	−36.4	152.6	4 34.6	−36.8	152.6	3 41.3	−37.2	152.7	2 48.0	−37.5	152.7	56
57	4 51.5	−36.5	153.4	3 57.8	−36.8	153.4	3 04.1	−37.2	153.5	2 10.5	−37.6	153.5	57
58	4 15.0	−36.6	154.2	3 21.0	−36.9	154.2	2 26.9	−37.2	154.2	1 32.9	−37.6	154.3	58
59	3 38.4	−36.6	155.0	2 44.1	−37.0	155.0	1 49.7	−37.3	155.0	0 55.3	−37.6	155.0	59
60	3 01.8	−36.6	155.8	2 07.1	−36.9	155.8	1 12.4	−37.3	155.8	0 17.7	−37.7	155.8	60
61	2 25.2	−36.6	156.6	1 30.2	−37.0	156.6	0 35.1	−37.3	156.6	0 20.0	+37.6	23.4	61
62	1 48.6	−36.7	157.4	0 53.2	−37.0	157.4	0 02.2	+37.3	22.6	0 57.6	+37.6	22.6	62
63	1 11.9	−36.7	158.2	0 16.2	−37.0	158.2	0 39.5	+37.3	21.8	1 35.2	+37.6	21.8	63
64	0 35.2	−36.7	159.0	0 20.8	+37.0	21.0	1 16.8	+37.2	21.0	2 12.8	+37.5	21.1	64
65	0 01.5	+36.7	20.3	0 57.8	+36.9	20.3	1 54.0	+37.3	20.3	2 50.3	+37.6	20.3	65
66	0 38.2	+36.6	19.5	1 34.7	+37.0	19.5	2 31.3	+37.2	19.5	3 27.9	+37.4	19.5	66
67	1 14.8	+36.7	18.7	2 11.7	+36.9	18.7	3 08.5	+37.2	18.7	4 05.3	+37.5	18.7	67
68	1 51.5	+36.6	17.9	2 48.6	+36.9	17.9	3 45.7	+37.1	17.9	4 42.8	+37.4	17.9	68
69	2 28.1	+36.7	17.1	3 25.5	+36.9	17.1	4 22.8	+37.1	17.1	5 20.2	+37.3	17.1	69
70	3 04.8	+36.5	16.3	4 02.4	+36.8	16.3	4 59.9	+37.1	16.3	5 57.5	+37.3	16.4	70
71	3 41.3	+36.6	15.5	4 39.2	+36.7	15.5	5 37.0	+36.9	15.5	6 34.8	+37.2	15.6	71
72	4 17.9	+36.5	14.7	5 15.9	+36.7	14.7	6 13.9	+36.9	14.8	7 12.0	+37.1	14.8	72
73	4 54.4	+36.4	13.9	5 52.6	+36.6	13.9	6 50.8	+36.9	14.0	7 49.1	+37.0	14.0	73
74	5 30.8	+36.4	13.1	6 29.2	+36.6	13.1	7 27.7	+36.7	13.2	8 26.1	+36.9	13.2	74
75	6 07.2	+36.3	12.3	7 05.8	+36.5	12.3	8 04.4	+36.7	12.4	9 03.0	+36.8	12.4	75
76	6 43.5	+36.2	11.5	7 42.3	+36.4	11.5	8 41.1	+36.5	11.6	9 39.8	+36.7	11.6	76
77	7 19.7	+36.1	10.7	8 18.7	+36.2	10.7	9 17.6	+36.4	10.8	10 16.5	+36.6	10.8	77
78	7 55.8	+36.1	9.9	8 54.9	+36.2	9.9	9 54.0	+36.4	10.0	10 53.1	+36.5	10.0	78
79	8 31.9	+35.9	9.1	9 31.1	+36.1	9.1	10 30.4	+36.2	9.1	11 29.6	+36.3	9.2	79
80	9 07.8	+35.9	8.3	10 07.2	+35.9	8.3	11 06.6	+36.0	8.3	12 05.9	+36.2	8.4	80
81	9 43.7	+35.7	7.5	10 43.1	+35.9	7.5	11 42.6	+36.0	7.5	12 42.1	+36.0	7.5	81
82	10 19.4	+35.6	6.7	11 19.0	+35.7	6.7	12 18.6	+35.7	6.7	13 18.1	+35.9	6.7	82
83	10 55.0	+35.4	5.8	11 54.7	+35.5	5.9	12 54.3	+35.7	5.9	13 54.0	+35.7	5.9	83
84	11 30.4	+35.3	5.0	12 30.2	+35.4	5.0	13 30.0	+35.4	5.1	14 29.7	+35.6	5.1	84
85	12 05.7	+35.2	4.2	13 05.6	+35.2	4.2	14 05.4	+35.3	4.2	15 05.3	+35.3	4.2	85
86	12 40.9	+35.0	3.4	13 40.8	+35.1	3.4	14 40.7	+35.1	3.4	15 40.6	+35.2	3.4	86
87	13 15.9	+34.9	2.5	14 15.9	+34.9	2.5	15 15.8	+35.0	2.5	16 15.8	+34.9	2.6	87
88	13 50.8	+34.7	1.7	14 50.8	+34.7	1.7	15 50.8	+34.7	1.7	16 50.7	+34.8	1.7	88
89	14 25.5	+34.5	0.8	15 25.5	+34.5	0.8	16 25.5	+34.5	0.9	17 25.5	+34.5	0.9	89
90	15 00.0	+34.3	0.0	16 00.0	+34.3	0.0	17 00.0	+34.3	0.0	18 00.0	+34.3	0.0	90
	15°			16°			17°			18°			

Dec.	19° Hc	d	Z	20° Hc	d	Z	21° Hc	d	Z	22° Hc	d	Z	Dec.
°	° ′	′	°	° ′	′	°	° ′	′	°	° ′	′	°	°
0	32 50.5	−23.5	102.8	32 36.9	−24.7	103.5	32 22.6	−25.7	104.1	32 07.7	−26.8	104.7	0
1	32 27.0	−24.1	103.9	32 12.2	−25.2	104.5	31 56.9	−26.3	105.2	31 40.9	−27.3	105.8	1
2	32 02.9	−24.6	105.0	31 47.0	−25.7	105.6	31 30.6	−26.8	106.2	31 13.6	−27.9	106.8	2
3	31 38.3	−25.2	106.1	31 21.3	−26.2	106.7	31 03.8	−27.3	107.3	30 45.7	−28.3	107.8	3
4	31 13.1	−25.7	107.2	30 55.1	−26.7	107.7	30 36.5	−27.7	108.3	30 17.4	−28.8	108.9	4
5	30 47.4	−26.2	108.2	30 28.4	−27.3	108.8	30 08.8	−28.3	109.3	29 48.6	−29.2	109.9	5
6	30 21.2	−26.7	109.3	30 01.1	−27.7	109.8	29 40.5	−28.7	110.3	29 19.4	−29.7	110.9	6
7	29 54.5	−27.2	110.3	29 33.4	−28.2	110.8	29 11.8	−29.1	111.3	28 49.7	−30.1	111.9	7
8	29 27.3	−27.7	111.3	29 05.2	−28.6	111.8	28 42.7	−29.6	112.3	28 19.6	−30.5	112.8	8
9	28 59.6	−28.1	112.3	28 36.6	−29.1	112.8	28 13.1	−30.0	113.3	27 49.1	−31.0	113.8	9
10	28 31.5	−28.5	113.3	28 07.5	−29.5	113.8	27 43.1	−30.5	114.3	27 18.1	−31.3	114.8	10
11	28 03.0	−29.0	114.3	27 38.0	−29.9	114.8	27 12.6	−30.8	115.3	26 46.8	−31.7	115.7	11
12	27 34.0	−29.4	115.3	27 08.1	−30.3	115.8	26 41.8	−31.2	116.3	26 15.1	−32.1	116.7	12
13	27 04.6	−29.8	116.3	26 37.8	−30.7	116.8	26 10.6	−31.6	117.2	25 43.0	−32.5	117.6	13
14	26 34.8	−30.2	117.3	26 07.1	−31.1	117.7	25 39.0	−31.9	118.2	25 10.5	−32.8	118.6	14
15	26 04.6	−30.5	118.2	25 36.0	−31.4	118.7	25 07.1	−32.3	119.1	24 37.7	−33.1	119.5	15
16	25 34.1	−31.0	119.2	25 04.6	−31.8	119.6	24 34.8	−32.7	120.0	24 04.6	−33.5	120.4	16
17	25 03.1	−31.3	120.2	24 32.8	−32.1	120.5	24 02.1	−32.9	120.9	23 31.1	−33.7	121.3	17
18	24 31.8	−31.6	121.1	24 00.7	−32.5	121.5	23 29.2	−33.3	121.9	22 57.4	−34.1	122.2	18
19	24 00.2	−32.0	122.0	23 28.2	−32.8	122.4	22 55.9	−33.6	122.8	22 23.3	−34.4	123.1	19
20	23 28.2	−32.3	122.9	22 55.4	−33.1	123.3	22 22.3	−33.9	123.7	21 48.9	−34.6	124.0	20
21	22 55.9	−32.6	123.9	22 22.3	−33.4	124.2	21 48.4	−34.1	124.5	21 14.3	−34.9	124.9	21
22	22 23.3	−32.9	124.8	21 48.9	−33.7	125.1	21 14.3	−34.5	125.4	20 39.4	−35.2	125.7	22
23	21 50.4	−33.3	125.7	21 15.2	−33.9	126.0	20 39.8	−34.7	126.3	20 04.2	−35.4	126.6	23
24	21 17.1	−33.4	126.6	20 41.3	−34.3	126.9	20 05.1	−34.9	127.2	19 28.8	−35.7	127.5	24
25	20 43.7	−33.8	127.5	20 07.0	−34.5	127.8	19 30.2	−35.2	128.0	18 53.1	−35.9	128.3	25
26	20 09.9	−34.0	128.3	19 32.5	−34.7	128.6	18 55.0	−35.5	128.9	18 17.2	−36.1	129.2	26
27	19 35.9	−34.3	129.2	18 57.8	−35.0	129.5	18 19.5	−35.6	129.7	17 41.1	−36.3	130.0	27
28	19 01.6	−34.5	130.1	18 22.8	−35.2	130.3	17 43.9	−35.9	130.6	17 04.8	−36.6	130.8	28
29	18 27.1	−34.8	131.0	17 47.6	−35.4	131.2	17 08.0	−36.1	131.4	16 28.2	−36.7	131.7	29
30	17 52.3	−35.0	131.8	17 12.2	−35.6	132.0	16 31.9	−36.2	132.3	15 51.5	−36.9	132.5	30
31	17 17.3	−35.2	132.7	16 36.6	−35.9	132.9	15 55.7	−36.5	133.1	15 14.6	−37.1	133.3	31
32	16 42.1	−35.4	133.5	16 00.7	−36.0	133.7	15 19.2	−36.7	133.9	14 37.5	−37.3	134.1	32
33	16 06.7	−35.6	134.3	15 24.7	−36.2	134.6	14 42.5	−36.8	134.7	14 00.2	−37.4	134.9	33
34	15 31.1	−35.8	135.2	14 48.5	−36.4	135.4	14 05.7	−37.0	135.6	13 22.8	−37.5	135.7	34
35	14 55.3	−35.9	136.0	14 12.1	−36.6	136.2	13 28.7	−37.1	136.4	12 45.3	−37.8	136.5	35
36	14 19.4	−36.2	136.8	13 35.5	−36.7	137.0	12 51.6	−37.3	137.2	12 07.5	−37.8	137.3	36
37	13 43.2	−36.3	137.7	12 58.8	−36.8	137.8	12 14.3	−37.4	138.0	11 29.7	−38.0	138.1	37
38	13 06.9	−36.4	138.5	12 22.0	−37.0	138.6	11 36.9	−37.6	138.8	10 51.7	−38.1	138.9	38
39	12 30.5	−36.6	139.3	11 45.0	−37.2	139.4	10 59.3	−37.6	139.6	10 13.6	−38.2	139.7	39
40	11 53.9	−36.7	140.1	11 07.8	−37.3	140.2	10 21.7	−37.8	140.4	9 35.4	−38.3	140.5	40
41	11 17.2	−36.9	140.9	10 30.5	−37.3	141.0	9 43.9	−37.9	141.2	8 57.1	−38.4	141.3	41
42	10 40.3	−37.0	141.7	9 53.2	−37.5	141.8	9 06.0	−38.1	141.9	8 18.7	−38.5	142.0	42
43	10 03.3	−37.1	142.5	9 15.7	−37.6	142.6	8 27.9	−38.1	142.7	7 40.2	−38.6	142.8	43
44	9 26.2	−37.2	143.3	8 38.1	−37.7	143.4	7 49.8	−38.1	143.5	7 01.6	−38.7	143.6	44
45	8 49.0	−37.3	144.1	8 00.4	−37.8	144.2	7 11.7	−38.3	144.3	6 22.9	−38.7	144.3	45
46	8 11.7	−37.4	144.9	7 22.6	−37.9	145.0	6 33.4	−38.3	145.1	5 44.2	−38.8	145.1	46
47	7 34.3	−37.5	145.7	6 44.7	−37.9	145.8	5 55.1	−38.4	145.8	5 05.4	−38.8	145.9	47
48	6 56.8	−37.6	146.5	6 06.8	−38.1	146.5	5 16.7	−38.5	146.6	4 26.6	−38.9	146.6	48
49	6 19.2	−37.6	147.3	5 28.7	−38.0	147.3	4 38.2	−38.5	147.4	3 47.7	−39.0	147.4	49
50	5 41.6	−37.7	148.1	4 50.7	−38.2	148.1	3 59.7	−38.5	148.1	3 08.7	−38.9	148.2	50
51	5 03.9	−37.8	148.8	4 12.5	−38.1	148.9	3 21.2	−38.6	148.9	2 29.8	−39.0	148.9	51
52	4 26.1	−37.8	149.6	3 34.4	−38.2	149.6	2 42.6	−38.6	149.7	1 50.8	−39.0	149.7	52
53	3 48.3	−37.8	150.4	2 56.2	−38.3	150.4	2 04.0	−38.7	150.4	1 11.8	−39.0	150.5	53
54	3 10.5	−37.9	151.2	2 17.9	−38.3	151.2	1 25.3	−38.6	151.2	0 32.8	−39.1	151.2	54
55	2 32.6	−37.9	151.9	1 39.6	−38.2	152.0	0 46.7	−38.7	152.0	0 06.3	+39.0	28.0	55
56	1 54.7	−37.9	152.7	1 01.4	−38.3	152.7	0 08.0	−38.6	152.7	0 45.3	+39.0	27.3	56
57	1 16.8	−38.0	153.5	0 23.1	−38.3	153.5	0 30.6	+38.7	26.5	1 24.3	+39.0	26.5	57
58	0 38.8	−37.9	154.3	0 15.2	+38.3	25.7	1 09.3	+38.6	25.7	2 03.3	+39.0	25.7	58
59	0 00.9	−38.0	155.0	0 53.5	+38.3	25.0	1 47.9	+38.6	25.0	2 42.3	+39.0	25.0	59
60	0 37.1	+37.9	24.2	1 31.8	+38.3	24.2	2 26.5	+38.6	24.2	3 21.3	+38.9	24.2	60
61	1 15.0	+38.0	23.4	2 10.1	+38.2	23.4	3 05.1	+38.6	23.4	4 00.2	+38.9	23.5	61
62	1 53.0	+37.9	22.6	2 48.3	+38.3	22.6	3 43.7	+38.5	22.7	4 39.1	+38.8	22.7	62
63	2 30.9	+37.9	21.9	3 26.6	+38.1	21.9	4 22.2	+38.5	21.9	5 17.9	+38.8	21.9	63
64	3 08.8	+37.8	21.1	4 04.7	+38.2	21.1	5 00.7	+38.4	21.1	5 56.7	+38.7	21.2	64
65	3 46.6	+37.8	20.3	4 42.9	+38.1	20.3	5 39.1	+38.4	20.4	6 35.4	+38.6	20.4	65
66	4 24.4	+37.8	19.5	5 21.0	+38.0	19.6	6 17.5	+38.3	19.6	7 14.0	+38.6	19.6	66
67	5 02.2	+37.7	18.7	5 59.0	+37.9	18.8	6 55.8	+38.2	18.8	7 52.6	+38.4	18.9	67
68	5 39.9	+37.6	18.0	6 36.9	+37.9	18.0	7 34.0	+38.1	18.0	8 31.0	+38.4	18.1	68
69	6 17.5	+37.6	17.2	7 14.8	+37.8	17.2	8 12.1	+38.1	17.3	9 09.4	+38.3	17.3	69
70	6 55.1	+37.5	16.4	7 52.6	+37.7	16.4	8 50.2	+37.9	16.5	9 47.7	+38.2	16.5	70
71	7 32.6	+37.4	15.6	8 30.3	+37.7	15.6	9 28.1	+37.9	15.7	10 25.9	+38.0	15.7	71
72	8 10.0	+37.3	14.8	9 08.0	+37.5	14.9	10 06.0	+37.7	14.9	11 03.9	+38.0	14.9	72
73	8 47.3	+37.2	14.0	9 45.5	+37.4	14.1	10 43.7	+37.6	14.1	11 41.9	+37.8	14.2	73
74	9 24.5	+37.1	13.2	10 22.9	+37.3	13.3	11 21.3	+37.5	13.3	12 19.7	+37.6	13.4	74
75	10 01.6	+37.0	12.4	11 00.2	+37.2	12.5	11 58.8	+37.3	12.5	12 57.3	+37.6	12.6	75
76	10 38.6	+36.9	11.6	11 37.4	+37.0	11.7	12 36.1	+37.2	11.7	13 34.9	+37.3	11.8	76
77	11 15.5	+36.7	10.8	12 14.4	+36.9	10.9	13 13.3	+37.1	10.9	14 12.2	+37.2	11.0	77
78	11 52.2	+36.6	10.0	12 51.3	+36.7	10.1	13 50.4	+36.9	10.1	14 49.4	+37.1	10.1	78
79	12 28.8	+36.5	9.2	13 28.0	+36.6	9.2	14 27.3	+36.7	9.3	15 26.5	+36.8	9.3	79
80	13 05.3	+36.3	8.4	14 04.6	+36.5	8.4	15 04.0	+36.5	8.5	16 03.3	+36.7	8.5	80
81	13 41.6	+36.1	7.6	14 41.1	+36.2	7.6	15 40.5	+36.4	7.6	16 40.0	+36.5	7.7	81
82	14 17.7	+36.0	6.8	15 17.3	+36.1	6.8	16 16.9	+36.2	6.8	17 16.5	+36.2	6.9	82
83	14 53.7	+35.8	5.9	15 53.4	+35.9	6.0	16 53.1	+35.9	6.0	17 52.7	+36.1	6.0	83
84	15 29.5	+35.6	5.1	16 29.3	+35.6	5.1	17 29.0	+35.8	5.2	18 28.8	+35.8	5.2	84
85	16 05.1	+35.4	4.3	17 04.9	+35.5	4.3	18 04.8	+35.5	4.3	19 04.6	+35.6	4.3	85
86	16 40.5	+35.2	3.4	17 40.4	+35.2	3.4	18 40.3	+35.3	3.5	19 40.2	+35.3	3.5	86
87	17 15.7	+35.0	2.6	18 15.6	+35.1	2.6	19 15.6	+35.0	2.6	20 15.5	+35.1	2.6	87
88	17 50.7	+34.8	1.7	18 50.7	+34.8	1.7	19 50.6	+34.8	1.7	20 50.6	+34.8	1.8	88
89	18 25.5	+34.5	0.9	19 25.5	+34.5	0.9	20 25.5	+34.5	0.9	21 25.4	+34.6	0.9	89
90	19 00.0	+34.3	0.0	20 00.0	+34.3	0.0	21 00.0	+34.3	0.0	22 00.0	+34.3	0.0	90
	19°			20°			21°			22°			

S. Lat. { L.H.A. greater than 180° ....Zn=180°−Z
L.H.A. less than 180°...........Zn=180°+Z

LATITUDE **SAME** NAME AS DECLINATION **L.H.A. 125°, 235°**

113

56°, 304° L.H.A. LATITUDE SAME NAME AS DECLINATION

N. Lat. {L.H.A. greater than 180° .....Zn=Z
{L.H.A. less than 180°............Zn=360°–Z

Dec.	15° Hc	d	Z	16° Hc	d	Z	17° Hc	d	Z	18° Hc	d	Z	19° Hc	d	Z	20° Hc	d	Z	21° Hc	d	Z	22° Hc	d	Z	Dec.
°	° ′	′	°	° ′	′	°	° ′	′	°	° ′	′	°	° ′	′	°	° ′	′	°	° ′	′	°	° ′	′	°	°
0	32 41.6	+18.1	99.9	32 30.9	+19.4	100.5	32 19.7	+20.4	101.2	32 07.7	+21.6	101.8	31 55.2	+22.7	102.4	31 42.0	+23.8	103.0	31 28.2	+24.9	103.6	31 13.8	+26.0	104.2	0
1	32 59.7	+17.6	98.8	32 50.3	+18.7	99.4	32 40.1	+19.9	100.0	32 29.3	+21.1	100.7	32 17.9	+22.2	101.3	32 05.8	+23.3	101.9	31 53.1	+24.4	102.5	31 39.8	+25.5	103.1	1
2	33 17.3	+16.9	97.6	33 09.0	+18.0	98.3	33 00.0	+19.3	98.9	32 50.4	+20.4	99.6	32 40.1	+21.6	100.2	32 29.1	+22.8	100.8	32 17.5	+23.9	101.4	32 05.3	+25.0	102.1	2
3	33 34.2	+16.2	96.5	33 27.0	+17.5	97.1	33 19.3	+18.6	97.8	33 10.8	+19.8	98.4	33 01.7	+20.9	99.1	32 51.9	+22.1	99.7	32 41.4	+23.3	100.4	32 30.3	+24.4	101.0	3
4	33 50.4	+15.6	95.3	33 44.5	+16.8	96.0	33 37.9	+18.0	96.6	33 30.6	+19.2	97.3	33 22.6	+20.4	98.0	33 14.0	+21.5	98.6	33 04.7	+22.7	99.3	32 54.7	+23.8	99.9	4
5	34 06.0	+14.9	94.2	34 01.3	+16.2	94.8	33 55.9	+17.4	95.5	33 49.8	+18.6	96.2	33 43.0	+19.8	96.8	33 35.5	+21.0	97.5	33 27.4	+22.1	98.1	33 18.5	+23.3	98.8	5
6	34 20.9	+14.3	93.0	34 17.5	+15.5	93.7	34 13.3	+16.7	94.3	34 08.4	+17.9	95.0	34 02.8	+19.1	95.7	33 56.5	+20.3	96.4	33 49.5	+21.5	97.0	33 41.8	+22.6	97.7	6
7	34 35.2	+13.6	91.8	34 33.0	+14.8	92.5	34 30.0	+16.0	93.2	34 26.3	+17.3	93.9	34 21.9	+18.5	94.5	34 16.8	+19.7	95.2	34 11.0	+20.8	95.9	34 04.4	+22.1	96.6	7
8	34 48.8	+12.9	90.6	34 47.8	+14.1	91.3	34 46.0	+15.4	92.0	34 43.6	+16.6	92.7	34 40.4	+17.8	93.4	34 36.5	+19.0	94.1	34 31.8	+20.3	94.8	34 26.5	+21.4	95.5	8
9	35 01.7	+12.2	89.4	35 01.9	+13.5	90.1	35 01.4	+14.7	90.8	35 00.2	+15.9	91.5	34 58.2	+17.2	92.2	34 55.5	+18.4	92.9	34 52.1	+19.6	93.6	34 47.9	+20.8	94.3	9
10	35 13.9	+11.4	88.2	35 15.4	+12.7	88.9	35 16.1	+14.0	89.6	35 16.1	+15.2	90.4	35 15.4	+16.4	91.1	35 13.9	+17.7	91.8	35 11.7	+18.9	92.5	35 08.7	+20.1	93.2	10
11	35 25.3	+10.8	87.0	35 28.1	+12.0	87.7	35 30.1	+13.3	88.5	35 31.3	+14.6	89.2	35 31.8	+15.8	89.9	35 31.6	+17.0	90.6	35 30.6	+18.2	91.3	35 28.8	+19.5	92.0	11
12	35 36.1	+10.0	85.8	35 40.1	+11.3	86.5	35 43.4	+12.5	87.3	35 45.9	+13.8	88.0	35 47.6	+15.1	88.7	35 48.6	+16.3	89.4	35 48.8	+17.6	90.1	35 48.3	+18.8	90.9	12
13	35 46.1	+9.3	84.6	35 51.4	+10.6	85.3	35 55.9	+11.8	86.0	35 59.7	+13.1	86.8	36 02.7	+14.3	87.5	36 04.9	+15.6	88.2	36 06.4	+16.8	89.0	36 07.1	+18.1	89.7	13
14	35 55.4	+8.6	83.4	36 02.0	+9.8	84.1	36 07.7	+11.1	84.8	36 12.8	+12.3	85.6	36 17.0	+13.6	86.3	36 20.5	+14.9	87.0	36 23.2	+16.2	87.8	36 25.2	+17.4	88.5	14
15	36 04.0	+7.8	82.2	36 11.8	+9.1	82.9	36 18.8	+10.4	83.6	36 25.1	+11.6	84.3	36 30.6	+12.9	85.1	36 35.4	+14.2	85.8	36 39.4	+15.4	86.6	36 42.6	+16.7	87.3	15
16	36 11.8	+7.0	80.9	36 20.9	+8.3	81.7	36 29.2	+9.6	82.4	36 36.7	+10.9	83.1	36 43.5	+12.2	83.9	36 49.6	+13.4	84.6	36 54.8	+14.7	85.4	36 59.3	+15.9	86.1	16
17	36 18.8	+6.3	79.7	36 29.2	+7.5	80.4	36 38.8	+8.8	81.2	36 47.6	+10.1	81.9	36 55.7	+11.4	82.6	37 03.0	+12.6	83.4	37 09.5	+13.9	84.1	37 15.2	+15.2	84.9	17
18	36 25.1	+5.5	78.5	36 36.7	+6.8	79.2	36 47.6	+8.1	79.9	36 57.7	+9.4	80.7	37 07.1	+10.6	81.4	37 15.6	+11.9	82.2	37 23.4	+13.2	82.9	37 30.4	+14.5	83.7	18
19	36 30.6	+4.8	77.2	36 43.5	+6.1	78.0	36 55.7	+7.3	78.7	37 07.1	+8.5	79.4	37 17.7	+9.8	80.2	37 27.5	+11.2	80.9	37 36.6	+12.4	81.7	37 44.9	+13.7	82.5	19
20	36 35.4	+4.0	76.0	36 49.6	+5.2	76.7	37 03.0	+6.5	77.4	37 15.6	+7.8	78.2	37 27.5	+9.1	78.9	37 38.7	+10.3	79.7	37 49.0	+11.6	80.5	37 58.6	+12.9	81.2	20
21	36 39.4	+3.2	74.7	36 54.8	+4.5	75.5	37 09.5	+5.7	76.2	37 23.4	+7.0	76.9	37 36.6	+8.3	77.7	37 49.0	+9.6	78.4	38 00.6	+10.9	79.2	38 11.5	+12.1	80.0	21
22	36 42.6	+2.4	73.5	36 59.3	+3.6	74.2	37 15.2	+5.0	75.0	37 30.4	+6.2	75.7	37 44.9	+7.4	76.4	37 58.6	+8.7	77.2	38 11.5	+10.0	78.0	38 23.6	+11.3	78.7	22
23	36 45.0	+1.7	72.3	37 02.9	+2.9	73.0	37 20.2	+4.1	73.7	37 36.6	+5.4	74.4	37 52.3	+6.7	75.2	38 07.3	+8.0	75.9	38 21.5	+9.2	76.7	38 34.9	+10.5	77.5	23
24	36 46.7	+0.8	71.0	37 05.8	+2.1	71.7	37 24.3	+3.3	72.4	37 42.0	+4.6	73.2	37 59.0	+5.9	73.9	38 15.3	+7.1	74.7	38 30.7	+8.4	75.4	38 45.4	+9.7	76.2	24
25	36 47.5	+0.1	69.8	37 07.9	+1.3	70.5	37 27.6	+2.6	71.2	37 46.6	+3.8	71.9	38 04.9	+5.0	72.7	38 22.4	+6.3	73.4	38 39.1	+7.6	74.2	38 55.1	+8.9	75.0	25
26	36 47.6	-0.7	68.5	37 09.2	+0.6	69.2	37 30.2	+1.7	69.9	37 50.4	+3.0	70.7	38 09.9	+4.3	71.4	38 28.7	+5.5	72.1	38 46.7	+6.8	72.9	39 04.0	+8.0	73.7	26
27	36 46.9	-1.5	67.3	37 09.8	-0.3	68.0	37 31.9	+1.0	68.7	37 53.4	+2.2	69.4	38 14.2	+3.4	70.1	38 34.2	+4.7	70.9	38 53.5	+5.9	71.6	39 12.0	+7.2	72.4	27
28	36 45.4	-2.2	66.0	37 09.5	-1.1	66.7	37 32.9	+0.1	67.4	37 55.6	+1.3	68.1	38 17.6	+2.6	68.9	38 38.9	+3.8	69.6	38 59.4	+5.1	70.4	39 19.2	+6.4	71.1	28
29	36 43.2	-3.1	64.8	37 08.4	-1.9	65.4	37 33.0	-0.7	66.1	37 56.9	+0.6	66.9	38 20.2	+1.7	67.6	38 42.7	+3.0	68.3	39 04.5	+4.2	69.1	39 25.6	+5.5	69.8	29
30	36 40.1	-3.8	63.5	37 06.5	-2.6	64.2	37 32.3	-1.4	64.9	37 57.5	-0.3	65.6	38 21.9	+1.0	66.3	38 45.7	+2.1	67.0	39 08.7	+3.4	67.8	39 31.1	+4.6	68.5	30
31	36 36.3	-4.6	62.3	37 03.9	-3.5	62.9	37 30.9	-2.3	63.6	37 57.2	-1.1	64.3	38 22.9	+0.1	65.0	38 47.8	+1.4	65.8	39 12.1	+2.6	66.5	39 35.7	+3.8	67.3	31
32	36 31.7	-5.4	61.0	37 00.4	-4.2	61.7	37 28.6	-3.1	62.4	37 56.1	-1.9	63.1	38 23.0	-0.8	63.8	38 49.2	+0.4	64.5	39 14.7	+1.7	65.2	39 39.5	+2.9	66.0	32
33	36 26.3	-6.1	59.8	36 56.2	-5.0	60.4	37 25.5	-3.9	61.1	37 54.2	-2.7	61.8	38 22.2	-1.5	62.5	38 49.6	-0.3	63.2	39 16.4	+0.8	63.9	39 42.4	+2.0	64.7	33
34	36 20.2	-6.9	58.6	36 51.2	-5.8	59.2	37 21.6	-4.6	59.8	37 51.5	-3.6	60.5	38 20.7	-2.4	61.2	38 49.3	-1.3	61.9	39 17.2	0.0	62.6	39 44.4	+1.2	63.4	34
35	36 13.3	-7.7	57.3	36 45.4	-6.6	58.0	37 17.0	-5.5	58.6	37 47.9	-4.3	59.3	38 18.3	-3.2	59.9	38 48.0	-2.0	60.6	39 17.2	-0.9	61.3	39 45.6	+0.3	62.1	35
36	36 05.6	-8.4	56.1	36 38.8	-7.3	56.7	37 11.5	-6.3	57.3	37 43.6	-5.2	58.0	38 15.1	-4.0	58.7	38 46.0	-2.9	59.3	39 16.3	-1.8	60.0	39 45.9	-0.6	60.8	36
37	35 57.2	-9.1	54.9	36 31.5	-8.1	55.5	37 05.2	-7.0	56.1	37 38.4	-5.9	56.7	38 11.1	-4.9	57.4	38 43.1	-3.7	58.1	39 14.5	-2.6	58.7	39 45.3	-1.4	59.5	37
38	35 48.1	-9.9	53.7	36 23.4	-8.9	54.2	36 58.2	-7.8	54.9	37 32.5	-6.8	55.5	38 06.2	-5.7	56.1	38 39.4	-4.6	56.8	39 11.9	-3.4	57.5	39 43.9	-2.3	58.2	38
39	35 38.2	-10.6	52.4	36 14.5	-9.6	53.0	36 50.4	-8.6	53.6	37 25.7	-7.5	54.2	38 00.5	-6.4	54.9	38 34.8	-5.4	55.5	39 08.5	-4.3	56.2	39 41.6	-3.2	56.9	39
40	35 27.6	-11.3	51.2	36 04.9	-10.3	51.8	36 41.8	-9.3	52.4	37 18.2	-8.3	53.0	37 54.1	-7.3	53.6	38 29.4	-6.2	54.2	39 04.2	-5.1	54.9	39 38.4	-4.0	55.6	40
41	35 16.3	-12.1	50.0	35 54.6	-11.1	50.6	36 32.5	-10.1	51.1	37 09.9	-9.1	51.7	37 46.8	-8.1	52.3	38 23.2	-7.1	53.0	38 59.1	-6.0	53.6	39 34.4	-4.9	54.3	41
42	35 04.2	-12.7	48.8	35 43.5	-11.8	49.4	36 22.4	-10.9	49.9	37 00.8	-9.9	50.5	37 38.7	-8.9	51.1	38 16.1	-7.8	51.7	38 53.1	-6.8	52.3	39 29.5	-5.8	53.0	42
43	34 51.5	-13.5	47.6	35 31.7	-12.5	48.2	36 11.5	-11.6	48.7	36 50.9	-10.6	49.3	37 29.8	-9.6	49.8	38 08.3	-8.7	50.4	38 46.3	-7.7	51.0	39 23.7	-6.6	51.7	43
44	34 38.0	-14.1	46.5	35 19.2	-13.2	47.0	35 59.9	-12.3	47.5	36 40.3	-11.4	48.0	37 20.2	-10.4	48.6	37 59.6	-9.4	49.2	38 38.6	-8.4	49.8	39 17.1	-7.4	50.4	44
45	34 23.9	-14.8	45.3	35 06.0	-14.0	45.8	35 47.6	-13.0	46.3	36 28.9	-12.1	46.8	37 09.8	-11.2	47.4	37 50.2	-10.3	47.9	38 30.2	-9.3	48.5	39 09.7	-8.3	49.1	45
46	34 09.1	-15.4	44.1	34 52.0	-14.6	44.6	35 34.6	-13.8	45.1	36 16.8	-12.9	45.6	36 58.6	-12.0	46.1	37 39.9	-11.0	46.7	38 20.9	-10.1	47.3	39 01.4	-9.1	47.8	46
47	33 53.7	-16.2	42.9	34 37.4	-15.3	43.4	35 20.8	-14.4	43.9	36 03.9	-13.6	44.4	36 46.6	-12.7	44.9	37 28.9	-11.8	45.4	38 10.8	-10.9	46.0	38 52.3	-10.0	46.6	47
48	33 37.5	-16.7	41.8	34 22.1	-15.9	42.2	35 06.4	-15.2	42.7	35 50.3	-14.3	43.2	36 33.9	-13.5	43.7	37 17.1	-12.6	44.2	37 59.9	-11.7	44.7	38 42.3	-10.7	45.3	48
49	33 20.8	-17.4	40.6	34 06.2	-16.7	41.1	34 51.2	-15.8	41.5	35 36.0	-15.0	42.0	36 20.4	-14.1	42.5	37 04.5	-13.3	43.0	37 48.2	-12.4	43.5	38 31.6	-11.6	44.0	49
50	33 03.4	-18.0	39.5	33 49.5	-17.2	39.9	34 35.4	-16.5	40.3	35 21.0	-15.7	40.8	36 06.3	-14.9	41.3	36 51.2	-14.1	41.8	37 35.8	-13.2	42.3	38 20.0	-12.4	42.8	50
51	32 45.4	-18.7	38.3	33 32.3	-17.9	38.8	34 18.9	-17.1	39.2	35 05.3	-16.4	39.6	35 51.4	-15.6	40.1	36 37.1	-14.8	40.5	37 22.6	-14.0	41.0	38 07.6	-13.1	41.5	51
52	32 26.7	-19.2	37.2	33 14.4	-18.5	37.6	34 01.8	-17.8	38.0	34 48.9	-17.0	38.4	35 35.8	-16.3	38.9	36 22.3	-15.5	39.3	37 08.6	-14.8	39.8	37 54.5	-13.9	40.3	52
53	32 07.5	-19.8	36.1	32 55.9	-19.2	36.5	33 44.0	-18.5	36.9	34 31.9	-17.8	37.3	35 19.5	-17.0	37.7	36 06.8	-16.2	38.1	36 53.8	-15.4	38.6	37 40.6	-14.7	39.1	53
54	31 47.7	-20.4	35.0	32 36.7	-19.7	35.3	33 25.5	-19.0	35.7	34 14.1	-18.3	36.1	35 02.5	-17.7	36.5	35 50.6	-17.0	37.0	36 38.4	-16.2	37.4	37 25.9	-15.4	37.9	54
55	31 27.3	-21.0	33.9	32 17.0	-20.3	34.2	33 06.5	-19.7	34.6	33 55.8	-19.0	35.0	34 44.8	-18.3	35.4	35 33.6	-17.6	35.8	36 22.2	-16.9	36.2	37 10.5	-16.2	36.6	55
56	31 06.3	-21.5	32.8	31 56.7	-20.9	33.1	32 46.8	-20.2	33.5	33 36.8	-19.7	33.8	34 26.5	-19.0	34.2	35 16.0	-18.3	34.6	36 05.3	-17.6	35.0	36 54.3	-16.9	35.4	56
57	30 44.8	-22.0	31.7	31 35.8	-21.5	32.0	32 26.6	-20.9	32.3	33 17.1	-20.2	32.7	34 07.5	-19.6	33.1	34 57.7	-18.9	33.4	35 47.7	-18.3	33.8	36 37.4	-17.6	34.2	57
58	30 22.8	-22.6	30.6	31 14.3	-22.0	30.9	32 05.7	-21.4	31.2	32 56.9	-20.8	31.6	33 47.9	-20.2	31.9	34 38.8	-19.6	32.3	35 29.4	-19.0	32.7	36 19.8	-18.3	33.0	58
59	30 00.2	-23.1	29.5	30 52.3	-22.6	29.8	31 44.3	-22.0	30.1	32 36.1	-21.4	30.5	33 27.7	-20.8	30.8	34 19.2	-20.3	31.1	35 10.4	-19.6	31.5	36 01.5	-19.0	31.9	59
60	29 37.1	-23.6	28.5	30 29.7	-23.0	28.8	31 22.3	-22.6	29.0	32 14.7	-22.0	29.3	33 06.9	-21.5	29.7	33 58.9	-20.8	30.0	34 50.8	-20.3	30.3	35 42.5	-19.7	30.7	60
61	29 13.5	-24.1	27.4	30 06.7	-23.6	27.7	30 59.7	-23.1	28.0	31 52.7	-22.6	28.2	32 45.4	-22.0	28.6	33 38.1	-21.5	28.9	34 30.5	-20.9	29.2	35 22.8	-20.3	29.5	61
62	28 49.4	-24.6	26.4	29 43.1	-24.1	26.6	30 36.6	-23.6	26.9	31 30.1	-23.1	27.2	32 23.4	-22.6	27.4	33 16.6	-22.1	27.7	34 09.6	-21.5	28.1	35 02.5	-21.0	28.4	62
63	28 24.8	-25.1	25.3	29 19.0	-24.6	25.6	30 13.0	-24.1	25.8	31 07.0	-23.7	26.1	32 00.8	-23.1	26.4	32 54.5	-22.6	26.6	33 48.1	-22.2	26.9	34 41.5	-21.6	27.2	63
64	27 59.7	-25.5	24.3	28 54.4	-25.1	24.5	29 48.9	-24.6	24.8	30 43.3	-24.1	25.0	31 37.7	-23.7	25.3	32 31.9	-23.3	25.5	33 25.9	-22.7	25.8	34 19.9	-22.3	26.1	64
65	27 34.2	-25.9	23.3	28 29.3	-25.5	23.5	29 24.3	-25.1	23.7	30 19.2	-24.7	23.9	31 14.0	-24.3	24.2	32 08.6	-23.7	24.4	33 03.2	-23.3	24.7	33 57.6	-22.8	25.0	65
66	27 08.3	-26.4	22.3	28 03.8	-26.0	22.5	28 59.2	-25.6	22.7	29 54.5	-25.2	22.9	30 49.7	-24.7	23.1	31 44.9	-24.4	23.4	32 39.9	-23.9	23.6	33 34.8	-23.4	23.9	66
67	26 41.9	-26.8	21.3	27 37.8	-26.5	21.4	28 33.6	-26.1	21.6	29 29.3	-25.6	21.8	30 25.0	-25.3	22.1	31 20.5	-24.8	22.3	32 16.0	-24.4	22.5	33 11.4	-24.0	22.8	67
68	26 15.1	-27.2	20.3	27 11.3	-26.8	20.4	28 07.5	-26.5	20.6	29 03.7	-26.2	20.8	29 59.7	-25.8	21.0	30 55.7	-25.4	21.2	31 51.6	-25.0	21.4	32 47.4	-24.6	21.7	68
69	25 47.9	-27.7	19.3	26 44.5	-27.3	19.4	27 41.0	-26.9	19.6	28 37.5	-26.6	19.8	29 33.9	-26.2	20.0	30 30.3	-25.9	20.2	31 26.6	-25.5	20.4	32 22.8	-25.1	20.6	69
70	25 20.2	-28.0	18.3	26 17.2	-27.7	18.4	27 14.1	-27.4	18.6	28 10.9	-27.0	18.8	29 07.7	-26.7	18.9	30 04.4	-26.3	19.1	31 01.1	-26.0	19.3	31 57.7	-25.7	19.5	70
71	24 52.2	-28.4	17.3	25 49.5	-28.1	17.4	26 46.7	-27.8	17.6	27 43.9	-27.5	17.8	28 41.0	-27.2	17.9	29 38.1	-26.9	18.1	30 35.1	-26.6	18.3	31 32.0	-26.2	18.5	71
72	24 23.8	-28.7	16.3	25 21.4	-28.5	16.5	26 18.9	-28.2	16.6	27 16.4	-27.9	16.8	28 13.8	-27.6	16.9	29 11.2	-27.3	17.1	30 08.5	-27.0	17.2	31 05.8	-26.7	17.4	72
73	23 55.1	-29.1	15.4	24 52.9	-28.8	15.5	25 50.7	-28.6	15.6	26 48.5	-28.3	15.8	27 46.2	-28.0	15.9	28 43.9	-27.8	16.0	29 41.5	-27.4	16.2	30 39.1	-27.2	16.4	73
74	23 26.0	-29.5	14.4	24 24.1	-29.2	14.5	25 22.1	-28.9	14.6	26 20.2	-28.8	14.8	27 18.2	-28.5	14.9	28 16.1	-28.2	15.0	29 14.1	-28.0	15.2	30 11.9	-27.6	15.3	74
75	22 56.5	-29.8	13.5	23 54.9	-29.6	13.6	24 53.2	-29.4	13.7	25 51.4	-29.1	13.8	26 49.7	-28.9	13.9	27 47.9	-28.6	14.0	28 46.1	-28.4	14.2	29 44.3	-28.2	14.3	75
76	22 26.7	-30.1	12.5	23 25.3	-29.9	12.6	24 23.8	-29.7	12.7	25 22.3	-29.5	12.8	26 20.8	-29.2	12.9	27 19.3	-29.1	13.0	28 17.7	-28.8	13.2	29 16.1	-28.6	13.3	76
77	21 56.6	-30.4	11.6	22 55.4	-30.3	11.7	23 54.1	-30.0	11.8	24 52.8	-29.8	11.9	25 51.6	-29.7	12.0	26 50.2	-29.4	12.1	27 48.9	-29.2	12.2	28 47.5	-29.0	12.3	77
78	21 26.2	-30.8	10.7	22 25.1	-30.5	10.7	23 24.1	-30.4	10.8	24 23.0	-30.2	10.9	25 21.9	-30.0	11.0	26 20.8	-29.9	11.1	27 19.7	-29.7	11.2	28 18.5	-29.5	11.3	78
79	20 55.4	-31.0	9.8	21 54.6	-30.9	9.8	22 53.7	-30.7	9.9	23 52.8	-30.6	10.0	24 51.9	-30.4	10.0	25 50.9	-30.2	10.1	26 50.0	-30.1	10.2	27 49.0	-29.8	10.3	79
80	20 24.4	-31.3	8.8	21 23.7	-31.2	8.9	22 23.0	-31.1	9.0	23 22.2	-30.9	9.0	24 21.5	-30.8	9.1	25 20.7	-30.6	9.2	26 19.9	-30.4	9.2	27 19.2	-30.3	9.3	80
81	19 53.1	-31.6	7.9	20 52.5	-31.5	8.0	21 51.9	-31.3	8.0	22 51.3	-31.2	8.1	23 50.7	-31.1	8.2	24 50.1	-30.9	8.2	25 49.5	-30.8	8.3	26 48.9	-30.7	8.4	81
82	19 21.5	-31.9	7.0	20 21.0	-31.7	7.1	21 20.6	-31.7	7.1	22 20.1	-31.5	7.2	23 19.6	-31.4	7.2	24 19.2	-31.3	7.3	25 18.7	-31.2	7.3	26 18.2	-31.1	7.4	82
83	18 49.6	-32.1	6.1	19 49.3	-32.0	6.2	20 48.9	-31.9	6.2	21 48.6	-31.8	6.2	22 48.2	-31.7	6.3	23 47.9	-31.7	6.3	24 47.5	-31.5	6.4	25 47.1	-31.4	6.4	83
84	18 17.5	-32.3	5.2	19 17.3	-32.3	5.3	20 17.0	-32.2	5.3	21 16.8	-32.2	5.3	22 16.5	-32.0	5.4	23 16.2	-31.9	5.4	24 16.0	-31.9	5.5	25 15.7	-31.8	5.5	84
85	17 45.2	-32.6	4.4	18 45.0	-32.5	4.4	19 44.8	-32.5	4.4	20 44.6	-32.4	4.4	21 44.5	-32.4	4.5	22 44.3	-32.3	4.5	23 44.1	-32.2	4.5	24 43.9	-32.1	4.6	85
86	17 12.6	-32.9	3.5	18 12.5	-32.8	3.5	19 12.3	-32.7	3.5	20 12.2	-32.6	3.5	21 12.1	-32.6	3.6	22 12.0	-32.6	3.6	23 11.9	-32.5	3.6	24 11.8	-32.5	3.6	86
87	16 39.7	-33.0	2.6	17 39.7	-33.0	2.6	18 39.6	-32.9	2.6	19 39.6	-33.0	2.6	20 39.5	-32.9	2.7	21 39.4	-32.8	2.7	22 39.4	-32.9	2.7	23 39.3	-32.8	2.7	87
88	16 06.7	-33.2	1.7	17 06.7	-33.3	1.7	18 06.7	-33.3	1.7	19 06.6	-33.2	1.8	20 06.6	-33.2	1.8	21 06.6	-33.2	1.8	22 06.5	-33.1	1.8	23 06.5	-33.1	1.8	88
89	15 33.5	-33.5	0.9	16 33.4	-33.4	0.9	17 33.4	-33.4	0.9	18 33.4	-33.4	0.9	19 33.4	-33.4	0.9	20 33.4	-33.4	0.9	21 33.4	-33.4	0.9	22 33.4	-33.4	0.9	89
90	15 00.0	-33.6	0.0	16 00.0	-33.7	0.0	17 00.0	-33.7	0.0	18 00.0	-33.7	0.0	19 00.0	-33.7	0.0	20 00.0	-33.7	0.0	21 00.0	-33.7	0.0	22 00.0	-33.7	0.0	90
	15°			16°			17°			18°			19°			20°			21°			22°			

56°, 304° L.H.A. LATITUDE SAME NAME AS DECLINATION

114

LATITUDE **CONTRARY** NAME TO DECLINATION **L.H.A. 56°, 304°**

Dec.	15° Hc	d	Z	16° Hc	d	Z	17° Hc	d	Z	18° Hc	d	Z	19° Hc	d	Z	20° Hc	d	Z	21° Hc	d	Z	22° Hc	d	Z	Dec.
°	° ′	′	°	° ′	′	°	° ′	′	°	° ′	′	°	° ′	′	°	° ′	′	°	° ′	′	°	° ′	′	°	°
0	32 41.6	-18.8	99.9	32 30.9	-19.9	100.5	32 19.7	-21.1	101.2	32 07.7	-22.1	101.8	31 55.2	-23.3	102.4	31 42.0	-24.4	103.0	31 28.2	-25.5	103.6	31 13.8	-26.5	104.2	0
1	32 22.8	-19.3	101.0	32 11.0	-20.5	101.6	31 58.6	-21.6	102.3	31 45.6	-22.8	102.9	31 31.9	-23.9	103.5	31 17.6	-24.9	104.1	31 02.7	-26.0	104.6	30 47.3	-27.1	105.2	1
2	32 03.5	-20.0	102.1	31 50.5	-21.0	102.8	31 37.0	-22.2	103.4	31 22.8	-23.3	104.0	31 08.0	-24.3	104.5	30 52.7	-25.4	105.1	30 36.7	-26.4	105.7	30 20.2	-27.5	106.3	2
3	31 43.5	-20.5	103.3	31 29.5	-21.7	103.9	31 14.8	-22.7	104.4	30 59.5	-23.8	105.0	30 43.7	-24.9	105.6	30 27.3	-26.0	106.2	30 10.3	-27.0	106.7	29 52.7	-28.0	107.3	3
4	31 23.0	-21.0	104.4	31 07.8	-22.1	104.9	30 52.1	-23.3	105.5	30 35.7	-24.3	106.1	30 18.8	-25.4	106.7	30 01.3	-26.4	107.2	29 43.3	-27.5	107.8	29 24.7	-28.5	108.3	4
5	31 02.0	-21.7	105.5	30 45.7	-22.7	106.0	30 28.8	-23.8	106.6	30 11.4	-24.8	107.2	29 53.4	-25.9	107.7	29 34.9	-26.9	108.3	29 15.8	-27.9	108.8	28 56.2	-28.9	109.3	5
6	30 40.3	-22.1	106.5	30 23.0	-23.3	107.1	30 05.0	-24.3	107.7	29 46.6	-25.4	108.2	29 27.5	-26.3	108.8	29 08.0	-27.4	109.3	28 47.9	-28.3	109.8	28 27.3	-29.3	110.3	6
7	30 18.2	-22.7	107.6	29 59.7	-23.7	108.2	29 40.7	-24.7	108.7	29 21.2	-25.8	109.3	29 01.2	-26.8	109.8	28 40.6	-27.8	110.3	28 19.6	-28.8	110.8	27 58.0	-29.8	111.3	7
8	29 55.5	-23.2	108.7	29 36.0	-24.3	109.2	29 16.0	-25.3	109.8	28 55.4	-26.3	110.3	28 34.4	-27.3	110.8	28 12.8	-28.3	111.3	27 50.8	-29.3	111.8	27 28.2	-30.1	112.3	8
9	29 32.3	-23.7	109.8	29 11.7	-24.7	110.3	28 50.7	-25.8	110.8	28 29.1	-26.7	111.3	28 07.1	-27.7	111.8	27 44.5	-28.6	112.3	27 21.5	-29.6	112.8	26 58.1	-30.6	113.3	9
10	29 08.6	-24.2	110.8	28 47.0	-25.2	111.3	28 24.9	-26.2	111.8	28 02.4	-27.2	112.3	27 39.4	-28.2	112.8	27 15.9	-29.1	113.3	26 51.9	-30.0	113.8	26 27.5	-30.9	114.2	10
11	28 44.4	-24.7	111.9	28 21.8	-25.7	112.4	27 58.7	-26.6	112.9	27 35.2	-27.6	113.3	27 11.2	-28.6	113.8	26 46.8	-29.5	114.3	26 21.9	-30.4	114.7	25 56.6	-31.4	115.2	11
12	28 19.7	-25.1	112.9	27 56.1	-26.1	113.4	27 32.1	-27.1	113.9	27 07.6	-28.1	114.3	26 42.6	-28.9	114.8	26 17.3	-29.9	115.2	25 51.5	-30.8	115.7	25 25.2	-31.6	116.1	12
13	27 54.6	-25.6	113.9	27 30.0	-26.6	114.4	27 05.0	-27.5	114.9	26 39.5	-28.4	115.3	26 13.7	-29.4	115.8	25 47.4	-30.3	116.2	25 20.7	-31.2	116.6	24 53.6	-32.1	117.1	13
14	27 29.0	-26.1	114.9	27 03.4	-27.0	115.4	26 37.5	-28.0	115.9	26 11.1	-28.9	116.3	25 44.3	-29.8	116.7	25 17.1	-30.6	117.2	24 49.5	-31.5	117.6	24 21.5	-32.3	118.0	14
15	27 02.9	-26.5	116.0	26 36.4	-27.4	116.4	26 09.5	-28.3	116.9	25 42.2	-29.2	117.3	25 14.5	-30.1	117.7	24 46.5	-31.0	118.1	24 18.0	-31.9	118.5	23 49.2	-32.7	118.9	15
16	26 36.4	-26.9	117.0	26 09.0	-27.8	117.4	25 41.2	-28.7	117.8	25 13.0	-29.6	118.3	24 44.4	-30.5	118.7	24 15.5	-31.4	119.1	23 46.1	-32.1	119.5	23 16.5	-33.0	119.8	16
17	26 09.5	-27.3	118.0	25 41.2	-28.2	118.4	25 12.5	-29.1	118.8	24 43.4	-30.0	119.2	24 13.9	-30.8	119.6	23 44.1	-31.7	120.0	23 14.0	-32.5	120.4	22 43.5	-33.4	120.7	17
18	25 42.2	-27.7	118.9	25 13.0	-28.6	119.4	24 43.4	-29.5	119.8	24 13.4	-30.3	120.2	23 43.1	-31.2	120.5	23 12.4	-31.9	120.9	22 41.5	-32.9	121.3	22 10.1	-33.6	121.6	18
19	25 14.5	-28.0	119.9	24 44.4	-28.9	120.3	24 13.9	-29.8	120.7	23 43.1	-30.7	121.1	23 11.9	-31.4	121.5	22 40.5	-32.4	121.8	22 08.6	-33.1	122.2	21 36.5	-33.9	122.5	19
20	24 46.5	-28.5	120.9	24 15.5	-29.4	121.3	23 44.1	-30.1	121.7	23 12.4	-30.9	122.0	22 40.5	-31.9	122.4	22 08.1	-32.6	122.8	21 35.5	-33.4	123.1	21 02.6	-34.1	123.4	20
21	24 18.0	-28.8	121.9	23 46.1	-29.6	122.3	23 14.0	-30.5	122.6	22 41.5	-31.4	123.0	22 08.6	-32.1	123.3	21 35.5	-32.9	123.7	21 02.1	-33.6	124.0	20 28.5	-34.5	124.3	21
22	23 49.2	-29.2	122.8	23 16.5	-30.1	123.2	22 43.5	-30.9	123.6	22 10.1	-31.6	123.9	21 36.5	-32.4	124.2	21 02.6	-33.1	124.6	20 28.5	-34.0	124.9	19 54.0	-34.6	125.2	22
23	23 20.0	-29.6	123.8	22 46.4	-30.3	124.1	22 12.6	-31.1	124.5	21 38.5	-31.9	124.8	21 04.1	-32.7	125.1	20 29.5	-33.5	125.4	19 54.5	-34.2	125.7	19 19.4	-35.0	126.0	23
24	22 50.4	-29.8	124.7	22 16.1	-30.7	125.1	21 41.5	-31.5	125.4	21 06.6	-32.2	125.7	20 31.4	-32.9	126.0	19 56.0	-33.7	126.3	19 20.3	-34.4	126.6	18 44.4	-35.1	126.9	24
25	22 20.6	-30.2	125.7	21 45.4	-30.9	126.0	21 10.0	-31.7	126.3	20 34.4	-32.5	126.6	19 58.5	-33.3	126.9	19 22.3	-34.0	127.2	18 45.9	-34.7	127.5	18 09.3	-35.4	127.7	25
26	21 50.4	-30.5	126.6	21 14.5	-31.3	126.9	20 38.3	-32.0	127.2	20 01.9	-32.8	127.5	19 25.2	-33.5	127.8	18 48.3	-34.2	128.1	18 11.2	-34.9	128.3	17 33.9	-35.6	128.6	26
27	21 19.9	-30.8	127.5	20 43.2	-31.5	127.8	20 06.3	-32.3	128.1	19 29.1	-33.0	128.4	18 51.7	-33.7	128.7	18 14.1	-34.4	128.9	17 36.3	-35.1	129.2	16 58.3	-35.8	129.4	27
28	20 49.1	-31.1	128.5	20 11.7	-31.9	128.7	19 34.0	-32.6	129.0	18 56.1	-33.3	129.3	18 18.0	-34.0	129.6	17 39.7	-34.7	129.8	17 01.2	-35.4	130.0	16 22.5	-36.0	130.3	28
29	20 18.0	-31.4	129.4	19 39.8	-32.1	129.6	19 01.4	-32.8	129.9	18 22.8	-33.5	130.2	17 44.0	-34.2	130.4	17 05.0	-34.8	130.7	16 25.8	-35.5	130.9	15 46.5	-36.2	131.1	29
30	19 46.6	-31.6	130.3	19 07.7	-32.3	130.5	18 28.6	-33.0	130.8	17 49.3	-33.7	131.0	17 09.8	-34.4	131.3	16 30.2	-35.1	131.5	15 50.3	-35.7	131.7	15 10.3	-36.4	131.9	30
31	19 15.0	-31.9	131.2	18 35.4	-32.6	131.4	17 55.6	-33.3	131.7	17 15.6	-34.0	131.9	16 35.4	-34.6	132.1	15 55.1	-35.3	132.4	15 14.6	-35.9	132.6	14 33.9	-36.5	132.8	31
32	18 43.1	-32.2	132.1	18 02.8	-32.9	132.3	17 22.3	-33.5	132.6	16 41.6	-34.1	132.8	16 00.8	-34.8	133.0	15 19.8	-35.5	133.2	14 38.7	-36.1	133.4	13 57.4	-36.7	133.6	32
33	18 10.9	-32.4	133.0	17 29.9	-33.0	133.2	16 48.8	-33.7	133.4	16 07.5	-34.4	133.6	15 26.0	-35.0	133.8	14 44.3	-35.6	134.0	14 02.6	-36.3	134.2	13 20.7	-36.9	134.4	33
34	17 38.5	-32.6	133.8	16 56.9	-33.3	134.1	16 15.1	-34.0	134.3	15 33.1	-34.6	134.5	14 51.0	-35.2	134.7	14 08.7	-35.8	134.9	13 26.3	-36.4	135.0	12 43.8	-37.0	135.2	34
35	17 05.9	-32.9	134.7	16 23.6	-33.5	134.9	15 41.1	-34.1	135.1	14 58.5	-34.8	135.3	14 15.8	-35.4	135.5	13 32.9	-36.0	135.7	12 49.9	-36.6	135.9	12 06.8	-37.2	136.0	35
36	16 33.0	-33.1	135.6	15 50.1	-33.8	135.8	15 07.0	-34.4	136.0	14 23.7	-34.9	136.2	13 40.4	-35.5	136.3	12 56.9	-36.1	136.5	12 13.3	-36.7	136.7	11 29.6	-37.2	136.8	36
37	15 59.9	-33.3	136.5	15 16.3	-33.9	136.7	14 32.6	-34.5	136.8	13 48.8	-35.1	137.0	13 04.9	-35.7	137.2	12 20.8	-36.3	137.3	11 36.6	-36.8	137.5	10 52.4	-37.4	137.6	37
38	15 26.6	-33.5	137.3	14 42.4	-34.1	137.5	13 58.1	-34.7	137.7	13 13.7	-35.3	137.8	12 29.2	-35.9	138.0	11 44.5	-36.4	138.1	10 59.8	-37.0	138.3	10 15.0	-37.6	138.4	38
39	14 53.1	-33.7	138.2	14 08.3	-34.2	138.4	13 23.4	-34.8	138.5	12 38.4	-35.4	138.7	11 53.3	-36.0	138.8	11 08.1	-36.5	139.0	10 22.8	-37.1	139.1	9 37.4	-37.6	139.2	39
40	14 19.4	-33.8	139.0	13 34.1	-34.5	139.2	12 48.6	-35.0	139.4	12 03.0	-35.6	139.5	11 17.3	-36.1	139.6	10 31.6	-36.7	139.8	9 45.7	-37.2	139.9	8 59.8	-37.7	140.0	40
41	13 45.6	-34.1	139.9	12 59.6	-34.6	140.0	12 13.6	-35.2	140.2	11 27.4	-35.7	140.3	10 41.2	-36.2	140.5	9 54.9	-36.8	140.6	9 08.5	-37.3	140.7	8 22.1	-37.8	140.8	41
42	13 11.5	-34.2	140.7	12 25.0	-34.7	140.9	11 38.4	-35.3	141.0	10 51.7	-35.8	141.1	10 05.0	-36.4	141.3	9 18.1	-36.8	141.4	8 31.2	-37.4	141.5	7 44.3	-37.9	141.6	42
43	12 37.3	-34.3	141.6	11 50.3	-34.9	141.7	11 03.1	-35.4	141.8	10 15.9	-36.0	142.0	9 28.6	-36.5	142.1	8 41.3	-37.0	142.2	7 53.8	-37.4	142.3	7 06.4	-38.0	142.3	43
44	12 03.0	-34.6	142.4	11 15.4	-35.1	142.6	10 27.7	-35.6	142.7	9 39.9	-36.0	142.8	8 52.1	-36.5	142.9	8 04.3	-37.1	143.0	7 16.4	-37.6	143.0	6 28.4	-38.1	143.1	44
45	11 28.4	-34.6	143.3	10 40.3	-35.1	143.4	9 52.1	-35.6	143.5	9 03.9	-36.2	143.6	8 15.6	-36.7	143.7	7 27.2	-37.2	143.8	6 38.8	-37.7	143.8	5 50.3	-38.1	143.9	45
46	10 53.8	-34.8	144.1	10 05.2	-35.3	144.2	9 16.5	-35.8	144.3	8 27.7	-36.3	144.4	7 38.9	-36.8	144.5	6 50.0	-37.2	144.5	6 01.1	-37.7	144.6	5 12.2	-38.2	144.7	46
47	10 19.0	-34.9	144.9	9 29.9	-35.4	145.0	8 40.7	-35.9	145.1	7 51.4	-36.3	145.2	7 02.1	-36.8	145.3	6 12.8	-37.3	145.3	5 23.4	-37.7	145.4	4 34.0	-38.2	145.4	47
48	9 44.1	-35.1	145.7	8 54.5	-35.6	145.8	8 04.8	-36.0	145.9	7 15.1	-36.5	146.0	6 25.3	-36.9	146.1	5 35.5	-37.4	146.1	4 45.7	-37.9	146.2	3 55.8	-38.3	146.2	48
49	9 09.0	-35.1	146.6	8 18.9	-35.6	146.7	7 28.8	-36.1	146.7	6 38.6	-36.5	146.8	5 48.4	-37.0	146.9	4 58.1	-37.4	146.9	4 07.8	-37.8	147.0	3 17.5	-38.3	147.0	49
50	8 33.9	-35.3	147.4	7 43.3	-35.7	147.5	6 52.7	-36.1	147.5	6 02.1	-36.6	147.6	5 11.4	-37.0	147.7	4 20.7	-37.5	147.7	3 30.0	-37.9	147.7	2 39.2	-38.3	147.8	50
51	7 58.6	-35.3	148.2	7 07.6	-35.8	148.3	6 16.6	-36.3	148.3	5 25.5	-36.7	148.4	4 34.4	-37.1	148.4	3 43.2	-37.5	148.5	2 52.1	-38.0	148.5	2 00.9	-38.3	148.5	51
52	7 23.3	-35.4	149.0	6 31.8	-35.8	149.1	5 40.3	-36.3	149.1	4 48.8	-36.7	149.2	3 57.3	-37.2	149.2	3 05.7	-37.5	149.3	2 14.1	-37.9	149.3	1 22.6	-38.4	149.3	52
53	6 47.9	-35.6	149.8	5 56.0	-36.0	149.9	5 04.0	-36.3	149.9	4 12.1	-36.8	150.0	3 20.1	-37.1	150.0	2 28.2	-37.6	150.0	1 36.2	-38.0	150.1	0 44.2	-38.4	150.1	53
54	6 12.3	-35.6	150.6	5 20.0	-36.0	150.7	4 27.7	-36.4	150.7	3 35.3	-36.8	150.8	2 43.0	-37.2	150.8	1 50.6	-37.6	150.8	0 58.2	-38.0	150.8	0 05.8	-38.4	150.8	54
55	5 36.7	-35.6	151.5	4 44.0	-36.0	151.5	3 51.3	-36.5	151.5	2 58.5	-36.8	151.6	2 05.8	-37.3	151.6	1 13.0	-37.6	151.6	0 20.2	-38.0	151.6	0 32.6	+38.3	28.4	55
56	5 01.1	-35.7	152.3	4 08.0	-36.1	152.3	3 14.8	-36.4	152.3	2 21.7	-36.9	152.4	1 28.5	-37.2	152.4	0 35.4	-37.6	152.4	0 17.8	+38.0	27.6	1 10.9	+38.4	27.6	56
57	4 25.4	-35.8	153.1	3 31.9	-36.2	153.1	2 38.4	-36.6	153.1	1 44.8	-36.9	153.1	0 51.3	-37.3	153.2	0 02.2	+37.7	26.8	0 55.8	+38.0	26.8	1 49.3	+38.3	26.9	57
58	3 49.6	-35.8	153.9	2 55.7	-36.2	153.9	2 01.8	-36.5	153.9	1 07.9	-36.9	153.9	0 14.0	-37.2	153.9	0 39.9	+37.6	26.1	1 33.8	+37.9	26.1	2 27.6	+38.4	26.1	58
59	3 13.8	-35.9	154.7	2 19.5	-36.2	154.7	1 25.3	-36.6	154.7	0 31.0	-36.9	154.7	0 23.2	+37.3	25.3	1 17.5	+37.6	25.3	2 11.7	+38.0	25.3	3 06.0	+38.2	25.3	59
60	2 37.9	-35.8	155.5	1 43.3	-36.2	155.5	0 48.7	-36.5	155.5	0 05.9	+36.9	24.5	1 00.5	+37.2	24.5	1 55.1	+37.5	24.5	2 49.7	+37.9	24.5	3 44.2	+38.3	24.5	60
61	2 02.1	-36.0	156.3	1 07.1	-36.2	156.3	0 12.2	-36.6	156.3	0 42.8	+36.9	23.7	1 37.7	+37.2	23.7	2 32.6	+37.6	23.7	3 27.6	+37.8	23.7	4 22.5	+38.2	23.8	61
62	1 26.1	-35.9	157.1	0 30.9	-36.3	157.1	0 24.4	+36.6	22.9	1 19.7	+36.8	22.9	2 14.9	+37.2	22.9	3 10.2	+37.5	22.9	4 05.4	+37.9	23.0	5 00.7	+38.1	23.0	62
63	0 50.2	-35.9	157.9	0 05.4	+36.2	22.1	1 01.0	+36.5	22.1	1 56.5	+36.9	22.1	2 52.1	+37.2	22.1	3 47.7	+37.5	22.2	4 43.3	+37.7	22.2	5 38.8	+38.1	22.2	63
64	0 14.3	-35.9	158.7	0 41.6	+36.2	21.3	1 37.5	+36.5	21.3	2 33.4	+36.8	21.3	3 29.3	+37.1	21.4	4 25.2	+37.4	21.4	5 21.0	+37.7	21.4	6 16.9	+38.0	21.4	64
65	0 21.6	+36.0	20.5	1 17.8	+36.3	20.5	2 14.0	+36.5	20.5	3 10.2	+36.8	20.5	4 06.4	+37.1	20.6	5 02.6	+37.3	20.6	5 58.7	+37.7	20.6	6 54.9	+37.9	20.7	65
66	0 57.6	+35.9	19.7	1 54.1	+36.2	19.7	2 50.5	+36.5	19.7	3 47.0	+36.8	19.8	4 43.5	+37.0	19.8	5 39.9	+37.3	19.8	6 36.4	+37.6	19.8	7 32.8	+37.9	19.9	66
67	1 33.5	+35.9	18.9	2 30.3	+36.1	18.9	3 27.0	+36.5	18.9	4 23.8	+36.7	19.0	5 20.5	+37.0	19.0	6 17.2	+37.3	19.0	7 14.0	+37.4	19.1	8 10.7	+37.7	19.1	67
68	2 09.4	+35.9	18.1	3 06.4	+36.2	18.1	4 03.5	+36.3	18.1	5 00.5	+36.6	18.2	5 57.5	+36.9	18.2	6 54.5	+37.1	18.2	7 51.4	+37.5	18.3	8 48.4	+37.7	18.3	68
69	2 45.3	+35.8	17.3	3 42.6	+36.1	17.3	4 39.8	+36.4	17.3	5 37.1	+36.6	17.4	6 34.4	+36.8	17.4	7 31.6	+37.1	17.4	8 28.9	+37.3	17.5	9 26.1	+37.5	17.5	69
70	3 21.1	+35.8	16.5	4 18.7	+36.0	16.5	5 16.2	+36.2	16.5	6 13.7	+36.5	16.6	7 11.2	+36.7	16.6	8 08.7	+37.0	16.6	9 06.2	+37.2	16.7	10 03.6	+37.5	16.7	70
71	3 56.9	+35.8	15.7	4 54.7	+36.0	15.7	5 52.4	+36.2	15.7	6 50.2	+36.4	15.8	7 47.9	+36.7	15.8	8 45.7	+36.8	15.8	9 43.4	+37.1	15.9	10 41.1	+37.3	15.9	71
72	4 32.7	+35.7	14.9	5 30.7	+35.9	14.9	6 28.6	+36.2	14.9	7 26.6	+36.4	15.0	8 24.6	+36.5	15.0	9 22.5	+36.8	15.0	10 20.5	+36.9	15.1	11 18.4	+37.2	15.1	72
73	5 08.4	+35.6	14.1	6 06.6	+35.8	14.1	7 04.8	+36.0	14.1	8 03.0	+36.2	14.2	9 01.1	+36.5	14.2	9 59.3	+36.6	14.2	10 57.4	+36.9	14.3	11 55.6	+37.0	14.3	73
74	5 44.0	+35.6	13.3	6 42.4	+35.8	13.3	7 40.8	+36.0	13.3	8 39.2	+36.1	13.4	9 37.6	+36.3	13.4	10 35.9	+36.6	13.4	11 34.3	+36.7	13.5	12 32.6	+36.9	13.5	74
75	6 19.6	+35.5	12.5	7 18.2	+35.7	12.5	8 16.8	+35.8	12.5	9 15.3	+36.1	12.6	10 13.9	+36.2	12.6	11 12.5	+36.4	12.6	12 11.0	+36.6	12.7	13 09.5	+36.8	12.7	75
76	6 55.1	+35.4	11.7	7 53.9	+35.6	11.7	8 52.6	+35.8	11.7	9 51.4	+35.9	11.7	10 50.1	+36.1	11.8	11 48.9	+36.2	11.8	12 47.6	+36.4	11.9	13 46.3	+36.6	11.9	76
77	7 30.5	+35.4	10.8	8 29.5	+35.4	10.9	9 28.4	+35.6	10.9	10 27.3	+35.8	10.9	11 26.2	+36.0	11.0	12 25.1	+36.1	11.0	13 24.0	+36.3	11.1	14 22.9	+36.4	11.1	77
78	8 05.9	+35.2	10.0	9 04.9	+35.4	10.1	10 04.0	+35.5	10.1	11 03.1	+35.7	10.1	12 02.2	+35.8	10.2	13 01.2	+36.0	10.2	14 00.3	+36.1	10.2	14 59.3	+36.3	10.3	78
79	8 41.1	+35.1	9.2	9 40.3	+35.3	9.2	10 39.5	+35.4	9.3	11 38.8	+35.5	9.3	12 38.0	+35.6	9.3	13 37.2	+35.8	9.4	14 36.4	+35.9	9.4	15 35.6	+36.0	9.5	79
80	9 16.2	+35.0	8.4	10 15.6	+35.1	8.4	11 14.9	+35.3	8.4	12 14.3	+35.4	8.5	13 13.6	+35.5	8.5	14 13.0	+35.6	8.5	15 12.3	+35.7	8.6	16 11.6	+35.9	8.6	80
81	9 51.2	+34.9	7.6	10 50.7	+35.0	7.6	11 50.2	+35.1	7.6	12 49.7	+35.2	7.6	13 49.1	+35.3	7.7	14 48.6	+35.4	7.7	15 48.0	+35.6	7.7	16 47.5	+35.6	7.8	81
82	10 26.1	+34.8	6.7	11 25.7	+34.9	6.8	12 25.3	+34.9	6.8	13 24.9	+35.0	6.8	14 24.4	+35.2	6.8	15 24.0	+35.3	6.9	16 23.6	+35.3	6.9	17 23.1	+35.5	6.9	82
83	11 00.9	+34.6	5.9	12 00.6	+34.7	5.9	13 00.2	+34.8	6.0	13 59.9	+34.9	6.0	14 59.6	+35.0	6.0	15 59.3	+35.0	6.0	16 58.9	+35.2	6.1	17 58.6	+35.2	6.1	83
84	11 35.5	+34.5	5.1	12 35.3	+34.5	5.1	13 35.0	+34.7	5.1	14 34.8	+34.7	5.1	15 34.6	+34.7	5.2	16 34.3	+34.9	5.2	17 34.1	+34.9	5.2	18 33.8	+35.0	5.2	84
85	12 10.0	+34.3	4.2	13 09.8	+34.4	4.3	14 09.7	+34.4	4.3	15 09.5	+34.5	4.3	16 09.3	+34.6	4.3	17 09.2	+34.6	4.3	18 09.0	+34.7	4.4	19 08.8	+34.8	4.4	85
86	12 44.3	+34.2	3.4	13 44.2	+34.3	3.4	14 44.1	+34.3	3.4	15 44.0	+34.3	3.4	16 43.9	+34.4	3.5	17 43.8	+34.4	3.5	18 43.7	+34.4	3.5	19 43.6	+34.5	3.5	86
87	13 18.5	+34.0	2.6	14 18.5	+34.0	2.6	15 18.4	+34.1	2.6	16 18.3	+34.1	2.6	17 18.3	+34.1	2.6	18 18.2	+34.2	2.6	19 18.1	+34.3	2.6	20 18.1	+34.2	2.7	87
88	13 52.5	+33.9	1.7	14 52.5	+33.8	1.7	15 52.5	+33.8	1.7	16 52.4	+33.9	1.7	17 52.4	+33.9	1.7	18 52.4	+33.9	1.8	19 52.4	+33.9	1.8	20 52.3	+34.0	1.8	88
89	14 26.4	+33.6	0.9	15 26.3	+33.7	0.9	16 26.3	+33.7	0.9	17 26.3	+33.7	0.9	18 26.3	+33.7	0.9	19 26.3	+33.7	0.9	20 26.3	+33.7	0.9	21 26.3	+33.7	0.9	89
90	15 00.0	+33.5	0.0	16 00.0	+33.4	0.0	17 00.0	+33.4	0.0	18 00.0	+33.4	0.0	19 00.0	+33.4	0.0	20 00.0	+33.4	0.0	21 00.0	+33.4	0.0	22 00.0	+33.4	0.0	90
	15°			16°			17°			18°			19°			20°			21°			22°			

S. Lat. { L.H.A. greater than 180° ....Zn=180°−Z
L.H.A. less than 180°...........Zn=180°+Z

LATITUDE **SAME** NAME AS DECLINATION **L.H.A. 124°, 236°**

115

57°, 303° L.H.A. LATITUDE SAME NAME AS DECLINATION

N. Lat. {L.H.A. greater than 180° .....Zn=Z; L.H.A. less than 180°............Zn=360°−Z}

Dec.	15°			16°			17°			18°			19°			20°			21°			22°			Dec.
	Hc	d	Z	Hc	d	Z	Hc	d	Z	Hc	d	Z	Hc	d	Z	Hc	d	Z	Hc	d	Z	Hc	d	Z	
°	° ′	′	°	° ′	′	°	° ′	′	°	° ′	′	°	° ′	′	°	° ′	′	°	° ′	′	°	° ′	′	°	°
0	31 44.5	+17.9	99.5	31 34.2	+19.1	100.1	31 23.3	+20.3	100.8	31 11.8	+21.4	101.3	30 59.7	+22.5	101.9	30 47.0	+23.6	102.5	30 33.7	+24.7	103.1	30 19.8	+25.8	103.7	0
1	32 02.4	+17.4	98.4	31 53.3	+18.6	99.0	31 43.6	+19.7	99.6	31 33.2	+20.9	100.3	31 22.2	+22.0	100.9	31 10.6	+23.1	101.5	30 58.4	+24.2	102.0	30 45.6	+25.3	102.6	1
2	32 19.8	+16.7	97.3	32 11.9	+17.9	97.9	32 03.3	+19.1	98.5	31 54.1	+20.2	99.2	31 44.2	+21.4	99.8	31 33.7	+22.5	100.4	31 22.6	+23.6	101.0	31 10.9	+24.7	101.6	2
3	32 36.5	+16.2	96.1	32 29.8	+17.3	96.8	32 22.4	+18.5	97.4	32 14.3	+19.7	98.0	32 05.6	+20.8	98.7	31 56.2	+22.0	99.3	31 46.2	+23.2	99.9	31 35.6	+24.2	100.5	3
4	32 52.7	+15.5	95.0	32 47.1	+16.7	95.6	32 40.9	+17.9	96.3	32 34.0	+19.1	96.9	32 26.4	+20.3	97.6	32 18.2	+21.4	98.2	32 09.4	+22.5	98.8	31 59.8	+23.7	99.4	4
5	33 08.2	+14.9	93.9	33 03.8	+16.1	94.5	32 58.8	+17.3	95.1	32 53.1	+18.4	95.8	32 46.7	+19.6	96.4	32 39.6	+20.8	97.1	32 31.9	+22.0	97.7	32 23.5	+23.1	98.3	5
6	33 23.1	+14.2	92.7	33 19.9	+15.4	93.3	33 16.1	+16.6	94.0	33 11.5	+17.9	94.7	33 06.3	+19.0	95.3	33 00.4	+20.2	96.0	32 53.9	+21.3	96.6	32 46.6	+22.6	97.2	6
7	33 37.3	+13.5	91.5	33 35.3	+14.8	92.2	33 32.7	+16.0	92.9	33 29.4	+17.2	93.5	33 25.3	+18.4	94.2	33 20.6	+19.6	94.8	33 15.2	+20.8	95.5	33 09.2	+21.9	96.1	7
8	33 50.8	+12.9	90.4	33 50.1	+14.1	91.0	33 48.7	+15.3	91.7	33 46.6	+16.5	92.4	33 43.7	+17.8	93.0	33 40.2	+19.0	93.7	33 36.0	+20.2	94.4	33 31.1	+21.3	95.0	8
9	34 03.7	+12.2	89.2	34 04.2	+13.5	89.9	34 04.0	+14.7	90.5	34 03.1	+15.9	91.2	34 01.5	+17.1	91.9	33 59.2	+18.3	92.6	33 56.2	+19.5	93.2	33 52.4	+20.7	93.9	9
10	34 15.9	+11.6	88.0	34 17.7	+12.8	88.7	34 18.7	+14.0	89.4	34 19.0	+15.3	90.0	34 18.6	+16.5	90.7	34 17.5	+17.7	91.4	34 15.7	+18.9	92.1	34 13.1	+20.1	92.8	10
11	34 27.5	+10.8	86.8	34 30.5	+12.0	87.5	34 32.7	+13.3	88.2	34 34.3	+14.5	88.9	34 35.1	+15.8	89.6	34 35.2	+17.0	90.2	34 34.6	+18.2	90.9	34 33.2	+19.5	91.6	11
12	34 38.3	+10.1	85.6	34 42.5	+11.4	86.3	34 46.0	+12.7	87.0	34 48.8	+13.9	87.7	34 50.9	+15.1	88.4	34 52.2	+16.4	89.1	34 52.8	+17.6	89.8	34 52.7	+18.8	90.5	12
13	34 48.4	+9.5	84.4	34 53.9	+10.7	85.1	34 58.7	+11.9	85.8	35 02.7	+13.2	86.5	35 06.0	+14.4	87.2	35 08.6	+15.6	87.9	35 10.4	+16.9	88.6	35 11.5	+18.1	89.3	13
14	34 57.9	+8.7	83.2	35 04.6	+10.0	83.9	35 10.6	+11.2	84.6	35 15.9	+12.4	85.3	35 20.4	+13.7	86.0	35 24.2	+15.0	86.7	35 27.3	+16.2	87.4	35 29.6	+17.4	88.1	14
15	35 06.6	+8.0	82.0	35 14.6	+9.2	82.7	35 21.8	+10.5	83.4	35 28.3	+11.8	84.1	35 34.1	+13.0	84.8	35 39.2	+14.2	85.5	35 43.5	+15.5	86.2	35 47.0	+16.8	87.0	15
16	35 14.6	+7.2	80.8	35 23.8	+8.5	81.5	35 32.3	+9.8	82.2	35 40.1	+11.0	82.9	35 47.1	+12.3	83.6	35 53.4	+13.6	84.3	35 59.0	+14.8	85.1	36 03.8	+16.0	85.8	16
17	35 21.8	+6.5	79.6	35 32.3	+7.8	80.3	35 42.1	+9.0	81.0	35 51.1	+10.3	81.7	35 59.4	+11.6	82.4	36 07.0	+12.8	83.1	36 13.8	+14.1	83.9	36 19.8	+15.3	84.6	17
18	35 28.3	+5.8	78.4	35 40.1	+7.0	79.1	35 51.1	+8.3	79.8	36 01.4	+9.6	80.5	36 11.0	+10.8	81.2	36 19.8	+12.1	81.9	36 27.9	+13.3	82.7	36 35.1	+14.6	83.4	18
19	35 34.1	+5.1	77.1	35 47.1	+6.3	77.8	35 59.4	+7.6	78.5	36 11.0	+8.8	79.3	36 21.8	+10.1	80.0	36 31.9	+11.3	80.7	36 41.2	+12.6	81.4	36 49.7	+13.9	82.2	19
20	35 39.2	+4.3	75.9	35 53.4	+5.6	76.6	36 07.0	+6.8	77.3	36 19.8	+8.1	78.0	36 31.9	+9.3	78.7	36 43.2	+10.6	79.5	36 53.8	+11.8	80.2	37 03.6	+13.1	81.0	20
21	35 43.5	+3.5	74.7	35 59.0	+4.8	75.4	36 13.8	+6.0	76.1	36 27.9	+7.2	76.8	36 41.2	+8.5	77.5	36 53.8	+9.8	78.3	37 05.6	+11.1	79.0	37 16.7	+12.3	79.7	21
22	35 47.0	+2.8	73.4	36 03.8	+4.0	74.1	36 19.8	+5.3	74.8	36 35.1	+6.6	75.6	36 49.7	+7.8	76.3	37 03.6	+9.0	77.0	37 16.7	+10.3	77.8	37 29.0	+11.6	78.5	22
23	35 49.8	+2.1	72.2	36 07.8	+3.3	72.9	36 25.1	+4.5	73.6	36 41.7	+5.7	74.3	36 57.5	+7.0	75.0	37 12.6	+8.3	75.8	37 27.0	+9.5	76.5	37 40.6	+10.8	77.3	23
24	35 51.9	+1.3	71.0	36 11.1	+2.5	71.7	36 29.6	+3.7	72.4	36 47.4	+5.0	73.1	37 04.5	+6.2	73.8	37 20.9	+7.5	74.5	37 36.5	+8.8	75.3	37 51.4	+10.0	76.0	24
25	35 53.2	+0.5	69.7	36 13.6	+1.7	70.4	36 33.3	+3.0	71.1	36 52.4	+4.2	71.8	37 10.7	+5.5	72.6	37 28.4	+6.7	73.3	37 45.3	+7.9	74.0	38 01.4	+9.2	74.8	25
26	35 53.7	-0.2	68.5	36 15.3	+1.0	69.2	36 36.3	+2.2	69.9	36 56.6	+3.4	70.6	37 16.2	+4.6	71.3	37 35.1	+5.8	72.0	37 53.2	+7.1	72.8	38 10.6	+8.4	73.5	26
27	35 53.5	-1.0	67.3	36 16.3	+0.2	68.0	36 38.5	+1.4	68.6	37 00.0	+2.6	69.3	37 20.8	+3.9	70.0	37 40.9	+5.1	70.8	38 00.3	+6.4	71.5	38 19.0	+7.6	72.3	27
28	35 52.5	-1.8	66.0	36 16.5	-0.6	66.7	36 39.9	+0.6	67.4	37 02.6	+1.9	68.1	37 24.7	+3.0	68.8	37 46.0	+4.3	69.5	38 06.7	+5.5	70.2	38 26.6	+6.8	71.0	28
29	35 50.7	-2.5	64.8	36 15.9	-1.3	65.5	36 40.5	-0.1	66.1	37 04.5	+1.0	66.8	37 27.7	+2.3	67.5	37 50.3	+3.5	68.2	38 12.2	+4.7	69.0	38 33.4	+5.9	69.7	29
30	35 48.2	-3.2	63.6	36 14.6	-2.1	64.2	36 40.4	-0.9	64.9	37 05.5	+0.3	65.6	37 30.0	+1.4	66.3	37 53.8	+2.6	67.0	38 16.9	+3.9	67.7	38 39.3	+5.1	68.4	30
31	35 45.0	-4.0	62.3	36 12.5	-2.9	63.0	36 39.5	-1.8	63.7	37 05.8	-0.6	64.3	37 31.4	+0.7	65.0	37 56.4	+1.9	65.7	38 20.8	+3.0	66.4	38 44.4	+4.3	67.2	31
32	35 41.0	-4.8	61.1	36 09.6	-3.6	61.8	36 37.7	-2.4	62.4	37 05.2	-1.3	63.1	37 32.1	-0.2	63.8	37 58.3	+1.0	64.5	38 23.8	+2.3	65.2	38 48.7	+3.4	65.9	32
33	35 36.2	-5.5	59.9	36 06.0	-4.4	60.5	36 35.3	-3.3	61.2	37 03.9	-2.1	61.8	37 31.9	-0.9	62.5	37 59.3	+0.2	63.2	38 26.1	+1.3	63.9	38 52.1	+2.6	64.6	33
34	35 30.7	-6.2	58.7	36 01.6	-5.1	59.3	36 32.0	-4.0	59.9	37 01.8	-2.9	60.6	37 31.0	-1.8	61.2	37 59.5	-0.6	61.9	38 27.4	+0.6	62.6	38 54.7	+1.8	63.3	34
35	35 24.5	-7.0	57.4	35 56.5	-5.9	58.1	36 28.0	-4.8	58.7	36 58.9	-3.7	59.3	37 29.2	-2.6	60.0	37 58.9	-1.4	60.6	38 28.0	-0.3	61.3	38 56.5	+0.9	62.0	35
36	35 17.5	-7.7	56.2	35 50.6	-6.7	56.8	36 23.2	-5.6	57.4	36 55.2	-4.5	58.1	37 26.6	-3.4	58.7	37 57.5	-2.3	59.4	38 27.7	-1.1	60.1	38 57.4	0.0	60.8	36
37	35 09.8	-8.4	55.0	35 43.9	-7.3	55.6	36 17.6	-6.3	56.2	36 50.7	-5.3	56.8	37 23.2	-4.1	57.5	37 55.2	-3.0	58.1	38 26.6	-1.9	58.8	38 57.4	-0.8	59.5	37
38	35 01.4	-9.2	53.8	35 36.6	-8.2	54.4	36 11.3	-7.1	55.0	36 45.4	-6.0	55.6	37 19.1	-5.0	56.2	37 52.2	-3.9	56.8	38 24.7	-2.8	57.5	38 56.6	-1.6	58.2	38
39	34 52.2	-9.8	52.6	35 28.4	-8.8	53.2	36 04.2	-7.9	53.7	36 39.4	-6.8	54.3	37 14.1	-5.7	54.9	37 48.3	-4.7	55.6	38 21.9	-3.5	56.2	38 55.0	-2.5	56.9	39
40	34 42.4	-10.6	51.4	35 19.6	-9.6	51.9	35 56.3	-8.6	52.5	36 32.6	-7.6	53.1	37 08.4	-6.6	53.7	37 43.6	-5.4	54.3	38 18.4	-4.5	55.0	38 52.5	-3.3	55.6	40
41	34 31.8	-11.3	50.2	35 10.0	-10.3	50.7	35 47.7	-9.3	51.3	36 25.0	-8.3	51.9	37 01.8	-7.3	52.5	37 38.2	-6.3	53.1	38 13.9	-5.2	53.7	38 49.2	-4.2	54.3	41
42	34 20.5	-11.9	49.0	34 59.7	-11.0	49.5	35 38.4	-10.0	50.1	36 16.7	-9.1	50.6	36 54.5	-8.1	51.2	37 31.9	-7.1	51.8	38 08.7	-6.0	52.4	38 45.0	-4.9	53.1	42
43	34 08.6	-12.6	47.8	34 48.7	-11.7	48.3	35 28.4	-10.8	48.9	36 07.6	-9.8	49.4	36 46.4	-8.8	50.0	37 24.8	-7.9	50.6	38 02.7	-6.9	51.2	38 40.1	-5.9	51.8	43
44	33 56.0	-13.3	46.6	34 37.0	-12.4	47.1	35 17.6	-11.5	47.7	35 57.8	-10.6	48.2	36 37.6	-9.6	48.7	37 16.9	-8.6	49.3	37 55.8	-7.6	49.9	38 34.2	-6.6	50.5	44
45	33 42.7	-14.0	45.5	34 24.6	-13.1	46.0	35 06.1	-12.2	46.5	35 47.2	-11.3	47.0	36 28.0	-10.4	47.5	37 08.3	-9.4	48.1	37 48.2	-8.5	48.6	38 27.6	-7.5	49.2	45
46	33 28.7	-14.6	44.3	34 11.5	-13.8	44.8	34 53.9	-12.9	45.3	35 35.9	-12.0	45.8	36 17.6	-11.1	46.3	36 58.9	-10.2	46.8	37 39.7	-9.2	47.4	38 20.1	-8.3	48.0	46
47	33 14.1	-15.3	43.1	33 57.7	-14.4	43.6	34 41.0	-13.6	44.1	35 23.9	-12.7	44.6	36 06.5	-11.9	45.1	36 48.7	-11.0	45.6	37 30.5	-10.1	46.1	38 11.8	-9.1	46.7	47
48	32 58.8	-15.8	42.0	33 43.3	-15.1	42.4	34 27.4	-14.3	42.9	35 11.2	-13.4	43.4	35 54.6	-12.5	43.9	36 37.7	-11.7	44.4	37 20.4	-10.8	44.9	38 02.7	-9.9	45.4	48
49	32 43.0	-16.6	40.8	33 28.2	-15.7	41.3	34 13.1	-14.9	41.7	34 57.8	-14.2	42.2	35 42.1	-13.3	42.7	36 26.0	-12.4	43.1	37 09.6	-11.6	43.7	37 52.8	-10.7	44.2	49
50	32 26.4	-17.1	39.7	33 12.5	-16.4	40.1	33 58.2	-15.6	40.5	34 43.6	-14.8	41.0	35 28.8	-14.0	41.5	36 13.6	-13.2	41.9	36 58.0	-12.3	42.4	37 42.1	-11.4	42.9	50
51	32 09.3	-17.7	38.6	32 56.1	-17.0	39.0	33 42.6	-16.2	39.4	34 28.8	-15.4	39.8	35 14.8	-14.7	40.3	36 00.4	-13.9	40.7	36 45.7	-13.1	41.2	37 30.7	-12.3	41.7	51
52	31 51.6	-18.3	37.4	32 39.1	-17.6	37.8	33 26.4	-16.9	38.2	34 13.4	-16.2	38.6	35 00.1	-15.4	39.1	35 46.5	-14.6	39.5	36 32.6	-13.8	40.0	37 18.4	-13.0	40.5	52
53	31 33.3	-19.0	36.3	32 21.5	-18.2	36.7	33 09.5	-17.5	37.1	33 57.2	-16.8	37.5	34 44.7	-16.1	37.9	35 31.9	-15.3	38.3	36 18.8	-14.5	38.8	37 05.4	-13.7	39.3	53
54	31 14.3	-19.4	35.2	32 03.3	-18.8	35.6	32 52.0	-18.2	35.9	33 40.4	-17.4	36.3	34 28.6	-16.7	36.7	35 16.6	-16.0	37.1	36 04.3	-15.3	37.6	36 51.7	-14.5	38.0	54
55	30 54.9	-20.1	34.1	31 44.5	-19.4	34.4	32 33.8	-18.7	34.8	33 23.0	-18.1	35.2	34 11.9	-17.4	35.6	35 00.6	-16.7	36.0	35 49.0	-15.9	36.4	36 37.2	-15.2	36.8	55
56	30 34.8	-20.5	33.0	31 25.1	-20.0	33.3	32 15.1	-19.3	33.7	33 04.9	-18.7	34.0	33 54.5	-18.0	34.4	34 43.9	-17.3	34.8	35 33.1	-16.7	35.2	36 22.0	-16.0	35.6	56
57	30 14.3	-21.2	31.9	31 05.1	-20.5	32.2	31 55.8	-19.9	32.6	32 46.2	-19.3	32.9	33 36.5	-18.6	33.3	34 26.6	-18.0	33.6	35 16.4	-17.3	34.0	36 06.0	-16.6	34.4	57
58	29 53.1	-21.6	30.8	30 44.6	-21.1	31.1	31 35.9	-20.5	31.5	32 26.9	-19.8	31.8	33 17.9	-19.3	32.1	34 08.6	-18.7	32.5	34 59.1	-18.0	32.9	35 49.4	-17.4	33.2	58
59	29 31.5	-22.2	29.8	30 23.5	-21.6	30.1	31 15.4	-21.1	30.4	32 07.1	-20.5	30.7	32 58.6	-19.9	31.0	33 49.9	-19.2	31.3	34 41.1	-18.7	31.7	35 32.0	-18.0	32.1	59
60	29 09.3	-22.6	28.7	30 01.9	-22.1	29.0	30 54.3	-21.6	29.3	31 46.6	-21.0	29.6	32 38.7	-20.5	29.9	33 30.7	-19.9	30.2	34 22.4	-19.3	30.5	35 14.0	-18.7	30.9	60
61	28 46.7	-23.2	27.6	29 39.8	-22.7	27.9	30 32.7	-22.1	28.2	31 25.6	-21.6	28.5	32 18.2	-21.0	28.8	33 10.8	-20.5	29.1	34 03.1	-19.9	29.4	34 55.3	-19.3	29.7	61
62	28 23.5	-23.6	26.6	29 17.1	-23.1	26.8	30 10.6	-22.6	27.1	31 04.0	-22.2	27.4	31 57.2	-21.7	27.6	32 50.3	-21.1	27.9	33 43.2	-20.6	28.3	34 36.0	-20.1	28.6	62
63	27 59.9	-24.1	25.5	28 54.0	-23.7	25.8	29 48.0	-23.2	26.0	30 41.8	-22.7	26.3	31 35.5	-22.1	26.6	32 29.2	-21.7	26.8	33 22.6	-21.1	27.1	34 15.9	-20.6	27.4	63
64	27 35.8	-24.6	24.5	28 30.3	-24.1	24.7	29 24.8	-23.7	25.0	30 19.1	-23.2	25.2	31 13.4	-22.8	25.5	32 07.5	-22.3	25.7	33 01.5	-21.8	26.0	33 55.3	-21.2	26.3	64
65	27 11.2	-25.0	23.5	28 06.2	-24.6	23.7	29 01.1	-24.1	23.9	29 55.9	-23.7	24.1	30 50.6	-23.2	24.4	31 45.2	-22.8	24.6	32 39.7	-22.3	24.9	33 34.1	-21.9	25.2	65
66	26 46.2	-25.4	22.5	27 41.6	-25.0	22.7	28 37.0	-24.7	22.9	29 32.2	-24.2	23.1	30 27.4	-23.8	23.3	31 22.4	-23.3	23.5	32 17.4	-22.9	23.8	33 12.2	-22.4	24.1	66
67	26 20.8	-25.9	21.4	27 16.6	-25.5	21.6	28 12.3	-25.1	21.8	29 08.0	-24.7	22.0	30 03.6	-24.3	22.2	30 59.1	-23.9	22.5	31 54.5	-23.5	22.7	32 49.8	-23.1	23.0	67
68	25 54.9	-26.2	20.4	26 51.1	-25.9	20.6	27 47.2	-25.5	20.8	28 43.3	-25.2	21.0	29 39.3	-24.8	21.2	30 35.2	-24.4	21.4	31 31.0	-24.0	21.6	32 26.7	-23.6	21.9	68
69	25 28.7	-26.7	19.4	26 25.2	-26.3	19.6	27 21.7	-26.0	19.8	28 18.1	-25.6	20.0	29 14.5	-25.3	20.1	30 10.8	-24.9	20.3	31 07.0	-24.5	20.6	32 03.1	-24.1	20.8	69
70	25 02.0	-27.1	18.5	25 58.9	-26.8	18.6	26 55.7	-26.4	18.8	27 52.5	-26.1	18.9	28 49.2	-25.7	19.1	29 45.9	-25.4	19.3	30 42.5	-25.1	19.5	31 39.0	-24.7	19.7	70
71	24 34.9	-27.4	17.5	25 32.1	-27.1	17.6	26 29.3	-26.9	17.8	27 26.4	-26.5	17.9	28 23.5	-26.2	18.1	29 20.5	-25.9	18.3	30 17.4	-25.5	18.4	31 14.3	-25.2	18.6	71
72	24 07.5	-27.9	16.5	25 05.0	-27.6	16.6	26 02.4	-27.2	16.8	26 59.9	-27.0	16.9	27 57.3	-26.7	17.1	28 54.6	-26.4	17.2	29 51.9	-26.1	17.4	30 49.1	-25.7	17.6	72
73	23 39.6	-28.1	15.5	24 37.4	-27.9	15.6	25 35.2	-27.6	15.8	26 32.9	-27.4	15.9	27 30.6	-27.1	16.0	28 28.2	-26.8	16.2	29 25.8	-26.5	16.4	30 23.4	-26.2	16.5	73
74	23 11.5	-28.6	14.6	24 09.5	-28.3	14.7	25 07.6	-28.1	14.8	26 05.5	-27.7	14.9	27 03.5	-27.5	15.0	28 01.4	-27.2	15.2	28 59.3	-27.0	15.3	29 57.2	-26.7	15.5	74
75	22 42.9	-28.8	13.6	23 41.2	-28.6	13.7	24 39.5	-28.4	13.8	25 37.8	-28.2	13.9	26 36.0	-27.9	14.0	27 34.2	-27.7	14.2	28 32.3	-27.4	14.3	29 30.5	-27.2	14.4	75
76	22 14.1	-29.2	12.7	23 12.6	-29.0	12.8	24 11.1	-28.7	12.9	25 09.6	-28.5	13.0	26 08.1	-28.4	13.1	27 06.5	-28.1	13.2	28 04.9	-27.9	13.3	29 03.3	-27.7	13.4	76
77	21 44.9	-29.5	11.7	22 43.6	-29.3	11.8	23 42.4	-29.2	11.9	24 41.1	-29.0	12.0	25 39.7	-28.7	12.1	26 38.4	-28.5	12.2	27 37.0	-28.3	12.3	28 35.6	-28.0	12.4	77
78	21 15.4	-29.8	10.8	22 14.3	-29.6	10.9	23 13.2	-29.4	10.9	24 12.1	-29.2	11.0	25 11.0	-29.1	11.1	26 09.9	-28.9	11.2	27 08.7	-28.7	11.3	28 07.6	-28.6	11.4	78
79	20 45.6	-30.1	9.9	21 44.7	-30.0	9.9	22 43.8	-29.8	10.0	23 42.9	-29.7	10.1	24 41.9	-29.4	10.1	25 41.0	-29.3	10.2	26 40.0	-29.1	10.3	27 39.0	-28.9	10.4	79
80	20 15.5	-30.5	8.9	21 14.7	-30.2	9.0	22 14.0	-30.1	9.1	23 13.2	-29.9	9.1	24 12.5	-29.9	9.2	25 11.7	-29.7	9.3	26 10.9	-29.5	9.3	27 10.1	-29.4	9.4	80
81	19 45.0	-30.6	8.0	20 44.5	-30.6	8.1	21 43.9	-30.5	8.1	22 43.3	-30.3	8.2	23 42.6	-30.1	8.2	24 42.0	-30.0	8.3	25 41.4	-29.9	8.4	26 40.7	-29.7	8.4	81
82	19 14.4	-31.0	7.1	20 13.9	-30.8	7.1	21 13.4	-30.7	7.2	22 13.0	-30.7	7.2	23 12.5	-30.5	7.3	24 12.0	-30.4	7.4	25 11.5	-30.3	7.4	26 11.0	-30.2	7.5	82
83	18 43.4	-31.2	6.2	19 43.1	-31.2	6.2	20 42.7	-31.0	6.3	21 42.3	-30.9	6.3	22 42.0	-30.8	6.4	23 41.6	-30.7	6.4	24 41.2	-30.6	6.5	25 40.8	-30.5	6.5	83
84	18 12.2	-31.5	5.3	19 11.9	-31.3	5.3	20 11.7	-31.3	5.4	21 11.4	-31.2	5.4	22 11.2	-31.2	5.4	23 10.9	-31.1	5.5	24 10.6	-31.0	5.5	25 10.3	-30.8	5.6	84
85	17 40.7	-31.7	4.4	18 40.6	-31.7	4.4	19 40.4	-31.6	4.5	20 40.2	-31.5	4.5	21 40.0	-31.4	4.5	22 39.8	-31.3	4.5	23 39.6	-31.3	4.6	24 39.5	-31.3	4.6	85
86	17 09.0	-31.9	3.5	18 08.9	-31.9	3.5	19 08.8	-31.8	3.6	20 08.7	-31.8	3.6	21 08.6	-31.7	3.6	22 08.5	-31.7	3.6	23 08.3	-31.6	3.6	24 08.2	-31.6	3.7	86
87	16 37.1	-32.1	2.6	17 37.0	-32.1	2.6	18 37.0	-32.1	2.7	19 36.9	-32.0	2.7	20 36.9	-32.1	2.7	21 36.8	-32.0	2.7	22 36.7	-31.9	2.7	23 36.6	-31.9	2.7	87
88	16 05.0	-32.4	1.7	17 04.9	-32.3	1.8	18 04.9	-32.3	1.8	19 04.9	-32.3	1.8	20 04.8	-32.3	1.8	21 04.8	-32.3	1.8	22 04.8	-32.3	1.8	23 04.7	-32.2	1.8	88
89	15 32.6	-32.6	0.9	16 32.6	-32.6	0.9	17 32.6	-32.6	0.9	18 32.6	-32.6	0.9	19 32.5	-32.5	0.9	20 32.5	-32.5	0.9	21 32.5	-32.5	0.9	22 32.5	-32.5	0.9	89
90	15 00.0	-32.8	0.0	16 00.0	-32.8	0.0	17 00.0	-32.8	0.0	18 00.0	-32.8	0.0	19 00.0	-32.8	0.0	20 00.0	-32.8	0.0	21 00.0	-32.8	0.0	22 00.0	-32.8	0.0	90
	15°			16°			17°			18°			19°			20°			21°			22°			

57°, 303° L.H.A. LATITUDE SAME NAME AS DECLINATION

LATITUDE **CONTRARY** NAME TO DECLINATION **L.H.A. 57°, 303°**

Dec.	15° Hc	d	Z	16° Hc	d	Z	17° Hc	d	Z	18° Hc	d	Z	19° Hc	d	Z	20° Hc	d	Z	21° Hc	d	Z	22° Hc	d	Z	Dec.
°	° ′	′	°	° ′	′	°	° ′	′	°	° ′	′	°	° ′	′	°	° ′	′	°	° ′	′	°	° ′	′	°	°
0	31 44.5	−18.6	99.5	31 34.2	−19.7	100.1	31 23.3	−20.8	100.8	31 11.8	−21.9	101.3	30 59.7	−23.0	101.9	30 47.0	−24.1	102.5	30 33.7	−25.2	103.1	30 19.8	−26.3	103.7	0
1	31 25.9	−19.1	100.7	31 14.5	−20.3	101.3	31 02.5	−21.4	101.8	30 49.9	−22.5	102.4	30 36.7	−23.6	103.0	30 22.9	−24.7	103.6	30 08.5	−25.8	104.2	29 53.5	−26.8	104.7	1
2	31 06.8	−19.7	101.8	30 54.2	−20.8	102.4	30 41.1	−21.9	102.9	30 27.4	−23.0	103.5	30 13.1	−24.1	104.1	29 58.2	−25.2	104.6	29 42.7	−26.2	105.2	29 26.7	−27.2	105.7	2
3	30 47.1	−20.3	102.9	30 33.4	−21.3	103.4	30 19.2	−22.5	104.0	30 04.4	−23.6	104.6	29 49.0	−24.6	105.1	29 33.0	−25.6	105.7	29 16.5	−26.6	106.2	28 59.5	−27.7	106.8	3
4	30 26.8	−20.8	104.0	30 12.1	−21.9	104.5	29 56.7	−22.9	105.1	29 40.8	−24.0	105.6	29 24.4	−25.1	106.2	29 07.4	−26.1	106.7	28 49.9	−27.2	107.3	28 31.8	−28.1	107.8	4
5	30 06.0	−21.3	105.0	29 50.2	−22.4	105.6	29 33.8	−23.5	106.2	29 16.8	−24.5	106.7	28 59.3	−25.6	107.2	28 41.3	−26.6	107.8	28 22.7	−27.6	108.3	28 03.7	−28.6	108.8	5
6	29 44.7	−21.8	106.1	29 27.8	−22.9	106.7	29 10.3	−24.0	107.2	28 52.3	−25.0	107.7	28 33.7	−26.0	108.3	28 14.7	−27.0	108.8	27 55.1	−28.0	109.3	27 35.1	−29.0	109.8	6
7	29 22.9	−22.4	107.2	29 04.9	−23.4	107.7	28 46.3	−24.4	108.3	28 27.3	−25.5	108.8	28 07.7	−26.5	109.3	27 47.7	−27.5	109.8	27 27.1	−28.4	110.3	27 06.1	−29.4	110.8	7
8	29 00.5	−22.8	108.3	28 41.5	−23.9	108.8	28 21.9	−24.9	109.3	28 01.8	−25.9	109.8	27 41.2	−26.9	110.3	27 20.2	−27.9	110.8	26 58.7	−28.9	111.3	26 36.7	−29.8	111.7	8
9	28 37.7	−23.4	109.3	28 17.6	−24.4	109.8	27 57.0	−25.4	110.3	27 35.9	−26.4	110.8	27 14.3	−27.3	111.3	26 52.3	−28.3	111.8	26 29.8	−29.3	112.2	26 06.9	−30.2	112.7	9
10	28 14.3	−23.8	110.4	27 53.2	−24.8	110.9	27 31.6	−25.8	111.4	27 09.5	−26.8	111.8	26 47.0	−27.8	112.3	26 24.0	−28.7	112.8	26 00.5	−29.6	113.2	25 36.7	−30.6	113.7	10
11	27 50.5	−24.3	111.4	27 28.4	−25.3	111.9	27 05.8	−26.3	112.4	26 42.7	−27.2	112.8	26 19.2	−28.2	113.3	25 55.3	−29.2	113.7	25 30.9	−30.0	114.2	25 06.1	−30.9	114.6	11
12	27 26.2	−24.7	112.4	27 03.1	−25.7	112.9	26 39.5	−26.7	113.4	26 15.5	−27.6	113.8	25 51.0	−28.5	114.3	25 26.1	−29.4	114.7	25 00.9	−30.4	115.1	24 35.2	−31.3	115.6	12
13	27 01.5	−25.2	113.5	26 37.4	−26.2	113.9	26 12.8	−27.1	114.4	25 47.9	−28.1	114.8	25 22.5	−29.0	115.3	24 56.7	−29.9	115.7	24 30.5	−30.8	116.1	24 03.9	−31.6	116.5	13
14	26 36.3	−25.6	114.5	26 11.2	−26.5	114.9	25 45.7	−27.5	115.4	25 19.8	−28.4	115.8	24 53.5	−29.3	116.2	24 26.8	−30.2	116.6	23 59.7	−31.1	117.0	23 32.3	−32.0	117.4	14
15	26 10.7	−26.0	115.5	25 44.7	−27.0	115.9	25 18.2	−27.8	116.4	24 51.4	−28.8	116.8	24 24.2	−29.7	117.2	23 56.6	−30.6	117.6	23 28.6	−31.4	118.0	23 00.3	−32.2	118.3	15
16	25 44.7	−26.5	116.5	25 17.7	−27.3	116.9	24 50.4	−28.3	117.3	24 22.6	−29.1	117.7	23 54.5	−30.0	118.1	23 26.0	−30.8	118.5	22 57.2	−31.7	118.9	22 28.1	−32.6	119.3	16
17	25 18.2	−26.8	117.5	24 50.4	−27.8	117.9	24 22.1	−28.6	118.3	23 53.5	−29.5	118.7	23 24.5	−30.4	119.1	22 55.2	−31.3	119.5	22 25.5	−32.1	119.8	21 55.5	−32.9	120.2	17
18	24 51.4	−27.2	118.5	24 22.6	−28.1	118.9	23 53.5	−29.0	119.3	23 24.0	−29.9	119.6	22 54.1	−30.7	120.0	22 23.9	−31.5	120.4	21 53.4	−32.3	120.7	21 22.6	−33.1	121.1	18
19	24 24.2	−27.6	119.5	23 54.5	−28.5	119.8	23 24.5	−29.3	120.2	22 54.1	−30.2	120.6	22 23.4	−31.0	120.9	21 52.4	−31.8	121.3	21 21.1	−32.6	121.6	20 49.5	−33.5	122.0	19
20	23 56.6	−28.0	120.4	23 26.0	−28.8	120.8	22 55.2	−29.7	121.2	22 23.9	−30.5	121.5	21 52.4	−31.3	121.9	21 20.6	−32.1	122.2	20 48.5	−33.0	122.5	20 16.0	−33.6	122.8	20
21	23 28.6	−28.3	121.4	22 57.2	−29.1	121.8	22 25.5	−30.0	122.1	21 53.4	−30.8	122.5	21 21.1	−31.6	122.8	20 48.5	−32.5	123.1	20 15.5	−33.1	123.4	19 42.4	−34.0	123.7	21
22	23 00.3	−28.6	122.4	22 28.1	−29.5	122.7	21 55.5	−30.3	123.0	21 22.6	−31.1	123.4	20 49.5	−31.9	123.7	20 16.0	−32.6	124.0	19 42.4	−33.5	124.3	19 08.4	−34.2	124.6	22
23	22 31.7	−29.0	123.3	21 58.6	−29.8	123.6	21 25.2	−30.6	124.0	20 51.5	−31.4	124.3	20 17.6	−32.2	124.6	19 43.4	−33.0	124.9	19 08.9	−33.7	125.2	18 34.2	−34.4	125.5	23
24	22 02.7	−29.3	124.2	21 28.8	−30.2	124.6	20 54.6	−30.9	124.9	20 20.1	−31.7	125.2	19 45.4	−32.5	125.5	19 10.4	−33.2	125.8	18 35.2	−33.9	126.1	17 59.8	−34.7	126.3	24
25	21 33.4	−29.7	125.2	20 58.6	−30.4	125.5	20 23.7	−31.2	125.8	19 48.4	−31.9	126.1	19 12.9	−32.7	126.4	18 37.2	−33.4	126.7	18 01.3	−34.2	126.9	17 25.1	−34.9	127.2	25
26	21 03.7	−29.9	126.1	20 28.2	−30.7	126.4	19 52.5	−31.5	126.7	19 16.5	−32.2	127.0	18 40.2	−32.9	127.3	18 03.8	−33.7	127.5	17 27.1	−34.4	127.8	16 50.2	−35.0	128.0	26
27	20 33.8	−30.2	127.0	19 57.5	−31.0	127.3	19 21.0	−31.7	127.6	18 44.3	−32.5	127.9	18 07.3	−33.2	128.2	17 30.1	−33.9	128.4	16 52.7	−34.6	128.7	16 15.2	−35.3	128.9	27
28	20 03.6	−30.6	128.0	19 26.5	−31.2	128.3	18 49.3	−32.0	128.5	18 11.8	−32.7	128.8	17 34.1	−33.4	129.0	16 56.2	−34.1	129.3	16 18.1	−34.8	129.5	15 39.9	−35.5	129.7	28
29	19 33.0	−30.7	128.9	18 55.3	−31.5	129.2	18 17.3	−32.3	129.4	17 39.1	−33.0	129.7	17 00.7	−33.7	129.9	16 22.1	−34.3	130.1	15 43.3	−35.0	130.4	15 04.4	−35.7	130.6	29
30	19 02.3	−31.1	129.8	18 23.8	−31.8	130.1	17 45.0	−32.4	130.3	17 06.1	−33.1	130.5	16 27.0	−33.8	130.8	15 47.8	−34.6	131.0	15 08.3	−35.2	131.2	14 28.7	−35.8	131.4	30
31	18 31.2	−31.3	130.7	17 52.0	−32.0	130.9	17 12.6	−32.7	131.2	16 33.0	−33.4	131.4	15 53.2	−34.1	131.6	15 13.2	−34.7	131.8	14 33.1	−35.3	132.0	13 52.9	−36.0	132.2	31
32	17 59.9	−31.6	131.6	17 20.0	−32.3	131.8	16 39.9	−33.0	132.1	15 59.6	−33.6	132.3	15 19.1	−34.2	132.5	14 38.5	−34.9	132.7	13 57.8	−35.5	132.9	13 16.9	−36.2	133.0	32
33	17 28.3	−31.8	132.5	16 47.7	−32.4	132.7	16 06.9	−33.1	132.9	15 26.0	−33.8	133.1	14 44.9	−34.4	133.3	14 03.6	−35.0	133.5	13 22.3	−35.7	133.7	12 40.7	−36.3	133.9	33
34	16 56.5	−32.0	133.4	16 15.3	−32.7	133.6	15 33.8	−33.3	133.8	14 52.2	−34.0	134.0	14 10.5	−34.7	134.2	13 28.6	−35.3	134.4	12 46.6	−35.9	134.5	12 04.4	−36.4	134.7	34
35	16 24.5	−32.2	134.3	15 42.6	−32.9	134.5	15 00.5	−33.6	134.7	14 18.2	−34.1	134.8	13 35.8	−34.7	135.0	12 53.3	−35.4	135.2	12 10.7	−36.0	135.3	11 28.0	−36.6	135.5	35
36	15 52.3	−32.5	135.1	15 09.7	−33.1	135.3	14 26.9	−33.7	135.5	13 44.1	−34.4	135.7	13 01.1	−35.0	135.9	12 17.9	−35.5	136.0	11 34.7	−36.1	136.2	10 51.4	−36.7	136.3	36
37	15 19.8	−32.6	136.0	14 36.6	−33.3	136.2	13 53.2	−33.9	136.4	13 09.7	−34.5	136.5	12 26.1	−35.1	136.7	11 42.4	−35.7	136.8	10 58.6	−36.3	137.0	10 14.7	−36.9	137.1	37
38	14 47.2	−32.9	136.9	14 03.3	−33.4	137.1	13 19.3	−34.0	137.2	12 35.2	−34.6	137.4	11 51.0	−35.2	137.5	11 06.7	−35.8	137.7	10 22.3	−36.3	137.8	9 37.8	−36.9	137.9	38
39	14 14.3	−33.0	137.7	13 29.9	−33.7	137.9	12 45.3	−34.3	138.1	12 00.6	−34.8	138.2	11 15.8	−35.4	138.4	10 30.9	−35.9	138.5	9 46.0	−36.5	138.6	9 00.9	−37.0	138.7	39
40	13 41.3	−33.2	138.6	12 56.2	−33.8	138.8	12 11.0	−34.3	138.9	11 25.8	−35.0	139.0	10 40.4	−35.5	139.2	9 55.0	−36.1	139.3	9 09.5	−36.6	139.4	8 23.9	−37.2	139.5	40
41	13 08.1	−33.4	139.5	12 22.4	−33.9	139.6	11 36.7	−34.5	139.7	10 50.8	−35.0	139.9	10 04.9	−35.6	140.0	9 18.9	−36.1	140.1	8 32.9	−36.7	140.2	7 46.7	−37.2	140.3	41
42	12 34.7	−33.6	140.3	11 48.5	−34.1	140.5	11 02.2	−34.7	140.6	10 15.8	−35.2	140.7	9 29.3	−35.7	140.8	8 42.8	−36.3	140.9	7 56.2	−36.8	141.0	7 09.5	−37.3	141.1	42
43	12 01.1	−33.7	141.2	11 14.4	−34.3	141.3	10 27.5	−34.8	141.4	9 40.6	−35.3	141.5	8 53.6	−35.9	141.6	8 06.5	−36.4	141.7	7 19.4	−36.9	141.8	6 32.2	−37.4	141.9	43
44	11 27.4	−33.8	142.0	10 40.1	−34.4	142.1	9 52.7	−34.9	142.2	9 05.3	−35.5	142.3	8 17.7	−35.9	142.4	7 30.1	−36.4	142.5	6 42.5	−36.9	142.6	5 54.8	−37.4	142.7	44
45	10 53.6	−34.0	142.8	10 05.7	−34.5	143.0	9 17.8	−35.0	143.1	8 29.8	−35.5	143.2	7 41.8	−36.0	143.2	6 53.7	−36.5	143.3	6 05.6	−37.1	143.4	5 17.4	−37.5	143.4	45
46	10 19.6	−34.1	143.7	9 31.2	−34.6	143.8	8 42.8	−35.1	143.9	7 54.3	−35.6	144.0	7 05.8	−36.2	144.0	6 17.2	−36.6	144.1	5 28.5	−37.0	144.2	4 39.9	−37.6	144.2	46
47	9 45.5	−34.2	144.5	8 56.6	−34.7	144.6	8 07.7	−35.2	144.7	7 18.7	−35.7	144.8	6 29.6	−36.1	144.9	5 40.6	−36.7	144.9	4 51.5	−37.2	145.0	4 02.3	−37.6	145.0	47
48	9 11.3	−34.4	145.4	8 21.9	−34.8	145.4	7 32.5	−35.3	145.5	6 43.0	−35.8	145.6	5 53.5	−36.3	145.7	5 03.9	−36.7	145.7	4 14.3	−37.2	145.8	3 24.7	−37.6	145.8	48
49	8 36.9	−34.4	146.2	7 47.1	−35.0	146.3	6 57.2	−35.4	146.3	6 07.2	−35.9	146.4	5 17.2	−36.3	146.5	4 27.2	−36.8	146.5	3 37.1	−37.2	146.5	2 47.1	−37.7	146.6	49
50	8 02.5	−34.6	147.0	7 12.1	−35.0	147.1	6 21.8	−35.5	147.2	5 31.3	−35.9	147.2	4 40.9	−36.4	147.3	3 50.4	−36.8	147.3	2 59.9	−37.3	147.3	2 09.4	−37.7	147.4	50
51	7 27.9	−34.6	147.8	6 37.1	−35.1	147.9	5 46.3	−35.6	148.0	4 55.4	−36.0	148.0	4 04.5	−36.4	148.1	3 13.6	−36.9	148.1	2 22.6	−37.2	148.1	1 31.7	−37.7	148.1	51
52	6 53.3	−34.7	148.7	6 02.0	−35.1	148.7	5 10.7	−35.6	148.8	4 19.4	−36.0	148.8	3 28.1	−36.5	148.8	2 36.7	−36.9	148.9	1 45.4	−37.3	148.9	0 54.0	−37.7	148.9	52
53	6 18.6	−34.8	149.5	5 26.9	−35.3	149.5	4 35.1	−35.6	149.6	3 43.4	−36.1	149.6	2 51.6	−36.5	149.6	1 59.8	−36.9	149.7	1 08.1	−37.4	149.7	0 16.3	−37.8	149.7	53
54	5 43.8	−34.9	150.3	4 51.6	−35.2	150.3	3 59.5	−35.7	150.4	3 07.3	−36.1	150.4	2 15.1	−36.5	150.4	1 22.9	−36.9	150.5	0 30.7	−37.3	150.5	0 21.5	+37.7	29.5	54
55	5 08.9	−34.9	151.1	4 16.4	−35.4	151.2	3 23.8	−35.8	151.2	2 31.2	−36.1	151.2	1 38.6	−36.5	151.2	0 46.0	−36.9	151.2	0 06.6	+37.3	28.8	0 59.2	+37.7	28.8	55
56	4 34.0	−35.0	151.9	3 41.0	−35.4	152.0	2 48.0	−35.7	152.0	1 55.1	−36.2	152.0	1 02.1	−36.6	152.0	0 09.1	−36.9	152.0	0 43.9	+37.3	28.0	1 36.9	+37.7	28.0	56
57	3 59.0	−35.1	152.7	3 05.6	−35.4	152.8	2 12.3	−35.8	152.8	1 18.9	−36.2	152.8	0 25.5	−36.5	152.8	0 27.8	+37.0	27.2	1 21.2	+37.3	27.2	2 14.6	+37.7	27.2	57
58	3 23.9	−35.0	153.6	2 30.2	−35.4	153.6	1 36.5	−35.9	153.6	0 42.7	−36.2	153.6	0 11.0	+36.6	26.4	1 04.8	+36.9	26.4	1 58.5	+37.3	26.4	2 52.3	+37.6	26.4	58
59	2 48.9	−35.1	154.4	1 54.8	−35.5	154.4	1 00.6	−35.8	154.4	0 06.5	−36.2	154.4	0 47.6	+36.5	25.6	1 41.7	+36.9	25.6	2 35.8	+37.2	25.6	3 29.9	+37.6	25.6	59
60	2 13.8	−35.2	155.2	1 19.3	−35.5	155.2	0 24.8	−35.8	155.2	0 29.7	+36.1	24.8	1 24.1	+36.5	24.8	2 18.6	+36.9	24.8	3 13.0	+37.3	24.8	4 07.5	+37.5	24.9	60
61	1 38.6	−35.1	156.0	0 43.8	−35.5	156.0	0 11.0	+35.9	24.0	1 05.8	+36.2	24.0	2 00.6	+36.6	24.0	2 55.5	+36.8	24.0	3 50.3	+37.1	24.0	4 45.0	+37.5	24.1	61
62	1 03.5	−35.2	156.8	0 08.3	−35.5	156.8	0 46.9	+35.8	23.2	1 42.0	+36.2	23.2	2 37.2	+36.4	23.2	3 32.3	+36.8	23.2	4 27.4	+37.1	23.3	5 22.5	+37.5	23.3	62
63	0 28.3	−35.2	157.6	0 27.2	+35.5	22.4	1 22.7	+35.8	22.4	2 18.2	+36.1	22.4	3 13.6	+36.5	22.4	4 09.1	+36.7	22.4	5 04.5	+37.1	22.5	6 00.0	+37.3	22.5	63
64	0 06.9	+35.2	21.6	1 02.7	+35.5	21.6	1 58.5	+35.8	21.6	2 54.3	+36.1	21.6	3 50.1	+36.4	21.6	4 45.8	+36.7	21.6	5 41.6	+37.0	21.7	6 37.3	+37.3	21.7	64
65	0 42.1	+35.1	20.8	1 38.2	+35.4	20.8	2 34.3	+35.7	20.8	3 30.4	+36.0	20.8	4 26.5	+36.3	20.8	5 22.5	+36.7	20.9	6 18.6	+36.9	20.9	7 14.6	+37.3	20.9	65
66	1 17.2	+35.2	20.0	2 13.6	+35.5	20.0	3 10.0	+35.8	20.0	4 06.4	+36.0	20.0	5 02.8	+36.3	20.0	5 59.2	+36.5	20.1	6 55.5	+36.9	20.1	7 51.9	+37.1	20.1	66
67	1 52.4	+35.1	19.1	2 49.1	+35.4	19.2	3 45.8	+35.6	19.2	4 42.4	+36.0	19.2	5 39.1	+36.2	19.2	6 35.7	+36.5	19.3	7 32.4	+36.7	19.3	8 29.0	+37.0	19.3	67
68	2 27.5	+35.1	18.3	3 24.5	+35.3	18.3	4 21.4	+35.6	18.4	5 18.4	+35.8	18.4	6 15.3	+36.1	18.4	7 12.2	+36.4	18.5	8 09.1	+36.7	18.5	9 06.0	+36.9	18.6	68
69	3 02.6	+35.1	17.5	3 59.8	+35.4	17.5	4 57.0	+35.6	17.6	5 54.2	+35.9	17.6	6 51.4	+36.1	17.6	7 48.6	+36.3	17.7	8 45.8	+36.5	17.7	9 42.9	+36.8	17.8	69
70	3 37.7	+35.0	16.7	4 35.2	+35.2	16.7	5 32.6	+35.5	16.7	6 30.1	+35.7	16.8	7 27.5	+36.0	16.8	8 24.9	+36.2	16.9	9 22.3	+36.5	16.9	10 19.7	+36.7	17.0	70
71	4 12.7	+35.0	15.9	5 10.4	+35.2	15.9	6 08.1	+35.4	15.9	7 05.8	+35.6	16.0	8 03.5	+35.9	16.0	9 01.1	+36.2	16.0	9 58.8	+36.3	16.1	10 56.4	+36.6	16.1	71
72	4 47.7	+34.9	15.1	5 45.6	+35.1	15.1	6 43.5	+35.4	15.1	7 41.4	+35.6	15.2	8 39.4	+35.7	15.2	9 37.3	+35.9	15.2	10 35.1	+36.2	15.3	11 33.0	+36.4	15.3	72
73	5 22.6	+34.8	14.3	6 20.7	+35.1	14.3	7 18.9	+35.2	14.3	8 17.0	+35.5	14.3	9 15.1	+35.7	14.4	10 13.2	+35.9	14.4	11 11.3	+36.1	14.5	12 09.4	+36.3	14.5	73
74	5 57.4	+34.8	13.4	6 55.8	+35.0	13.5	7 54.1	+35.2	13.5	8 52.5	+35.3	13.5	9 50.8	+35.6	13.6	10 49.1	+35.8	13.6	11 47.4	+36.0	13.7	12 45.7	+36.2	13.7	74
75	6 32.2	+34.7	12.6	7 30.8	+34.8	12.6	8 29.3	+35.1	12.7	9 27.8	+35.3	12.7	10 26.4	+35.4	12.8	11 24.9	+35.6	12.8	12 23.4	+35.8	12.8	13 21.9	+35.9	12.9	75
76	7 06.9	+34.6	11.8	8 05.6	+34.8	11.8	9 04.4	+34.9	11.9	10 03.1	+35.1	11.9	11 01.8	+35.3	11.9	12 00.5	+35.4	12.0	12 59.2	+35.6	12.0	13 57.8	+35.9	12.1	76
77	7 41.5	+34.5	11.0	8 40.4	+34.7	11.0	9 39.3	+34.8	11.0	10 38.2	+35.0	11.1	11 37.1	+35.1	11.1	12 35.9	+35.3	11.1	13 34.8	+35.5	11.2	14 33.7	+35.6	11.2	77
78	8 16.0	+34.4	10.1	9 15.1	+34.5	10.2	10 14.1	+34.7	10.2	11 13.2	+34.8	10.2	12 12.2	+35.0	10.3	13 11.2	+35.2	10.3	14 10.3	+35.3	10.4	15 09.3	+35.4	10.4	78
79	8 50.4	+34.3	9.3	9 49.6	+34.5	9.3	10 48.8	+34.6	9.4	11 48.0	+34.7	9.4	12 47.2	+34.9	9.4	13 46.4	+35.0	9.5	14 45.6	+35.1	9.5	15 44.7	+35.3	9.6	79
80	9 24.7	+34.2	8.5	10 24.1	+34.3	8.5	11 23.4	+34.4	8.5	12 22.7	+34.6	8.6	13 22.1	+34.6	8.6	14 21.4	+34.8	8.6	15 20.7	+34.9	8.7	16 20.0	+35.1	8.7	80
81	9 58.9	+34.1	7.7	10 58.4	+34.1	7.7	11 57.8	+34.3	7.7	12 57.3	+34.4	7.7	13 56.7	+34.5	7.8	14 56.2	+34.6	7.8	15 55.6	+34.8	7.8	16 55.1	+34.8	7.9	81
82	10 33.0	+33.9	6.8	11 32.5	+34.1	6.8	12 32.1	+34.1	6.9	13 31.7	+34.2	6.9	14 31.2	+34.4	6.9	15 30.8	+34.4	7.0	16 30.4	+34.5	7.0	17 29.9	+34.6	7.0	82
83	11 06.9	+33.8	6.0	12 06.6	+33.8	6.0	13 06.2	+34.0	6.0	14 05.9	+34.0	6.0	15 05.6	+34.1	6.1	16 05.2	+34.2	6.1	17 04.9	+34.3	6.1	18 04.5	+34.4	6.2	83
84	11 40.7	+33.6	5.1	12 40.4	+33.7	5.2	13 40.2	+33.8	5.2	14 39.9	+33.9	5.2	15 39.7	+33.9	5.2	16 39.4	+34.1	5.3	17 39.2	+34.1	5.3	18 38.9	+34.2	5.3	84
85	12 14.3	+33.5	4.3	13 14.1	+33.6	4.3	14 14.0	+33.6	4.3	15 13.8	+33.7	4.3	16 13.6	+33.8	4.4	17 13.5	+33.7	4.4	18 13.3	+33.8	4.4	19 13.1	+33.9	4.4	85
86	12 47.8	+33.3	3.4	13 47.7	+33.4	3.5	14 47.6	+33.4	3.5	15 47.5	+33.4	3.5	16 47.4	+33.5	3.5	17 47.2	+33.6	3.5	18 47.1	+33.6	3.5	19 47.0	+33.7	3.6	86
87	13 21.1	+33.2	2.6	14 21.1	+33.1	2.6	15 21.0	+33.2	2.6	16 20.9	+33.3	2.6	17 20.9	+33.2	2.6	18 20.8	+33.3	2.7	19 20.7	+33.4	2.7	20 20.7	+33.4	2.7	87
88	13 54.3	+32.9	1.7	14 54.2	+33.0	1.7	15 54.2	+33.0	1.7	16 54.2	+33.0	1.8	17 54.1	+33.1	1.8	18 54.1	+33.1	1.8	19 54.1	+33.1	1.8	20 54.1	+33.1	1.8	88
89	14 27.2	+32.8	0.9	15 27.2	+32.8	0.9	16 27.2	+32.8	0.9	17 27.2	+32.8	0.9	18 27.2	+32.8	0.9	19 27.2	+32.8	0.9	20 27.2	+32.8	0.9	21 27.2	+32.8	0.9	89
90	15 00.0	+32.6	0.0	16 00.0	+32.6	0.0	17 00.0	+32.6	0.0	18 00.0	+32.6	0.0	19 00.0	+32.5	0.0	20 00.0	+32.5	0.0	21 00.0	+32.5	0.0	22 00.0	+32.5	0.0	90
	15°			16°			17°			18°			19°			20°			21°			22°			

S. Lat. { L.H.A. greater than 180° ....Zn=180°−Z; L.H.A. less than 180°...........Zn=180°+Z

LATITUDE **SAME** NAME AS DECLINATION **L.H.A. 123°, 237°**

117

Dec.	15° Hc	15° d	15° Z	16° Hc	16° d	16° Z	17° Hc	17° d	17° Z	18° Hc	18° d	18° Z	19° Hc	19° d	19° Z	20° Hc	20° d	20° Z	21° Hc	21° d	21° Z	22° Hc	22° d	22° Z	Dec.
°	° ′	′	°	° ′	′	°	° ′	′	°	° ′	′	°	° ′	′	°	° ′	′	°	° ′	′	°	° ′	′	°	°
0	30 47.3	+17.8	99.2	30 37.4	+18.9	99.8	30 26.9	+20.1	100.4	30 15.8	+21.2	100.9	30 04.2	+22.3	101.5	29 51.9	+23.4	102.1	29 39.1	+24.5	102.6	29 25.7	+25.6	103.2	0
1	31 05.1	+17.2	98.1	30 56.3	+18.4	98.7	30 47.0	+19.5	99.3	30 37.0	+20.7	99.8	30 26.5	+21.8	100.4	30 15.3	+22.9	101.0	30 03.6	+24.0	101.6	29 51.3	+25.0	102.1	1
2	31 22.3	+16.6	97.0	31 14.7	+17.8	97.6	31 06.5	+19.0	98.2	30 57.7	+20.1	98.8	30 48.3	+21.2	99.3	30 38.2	+22.4	99.9	30 27.6	+23.4	100.5	30 16.3	+24.6	101.1	2
3	31 38.9	+16.0	95.8	31 32.5	+17.2	96.4	31 25.5	+18.3	97.0	31 17.8	+19.5	97.7	31 09.5	+20.7	98.3	31 00.6	+21.8	98.8	30 51.0	+23.0	99.4	30 40.9	+24.0	100.0	3
4	31 54.9	+15.5	94.7	31 49.7	+16.6	95.3	31 43.8	+17.8	95.9	31 37.3	+19.0	96.5	31 30.2	+20.1	97.2	31 22.4	+21.2	97.8	31 14.0	+22.4	98.4	31 04.9	+23.5	99.0	4
5	32 10.4	+14.8	93.6	32 06.3	+16.0	94.2	32 01.6	+17.2	94.8	31 56.3	+18.3	95.4	31 50.3	+19.5	96.0	31 43.6	+20.7	96.7	31 36.4	+21.8	97.3	31 28.4	+23.0	97.9	5
6	32 25.2	+14.1	92.4	32 22.3	+15.4	93.0	32 18.8	+16.6	93.7	32 14.6	+17.8	94.3	32 09.8	+18.9	94.9	32 04.3	+20.1	95.6	31 58.2	+21.2	96.2	31 51.4	+22.4	96.8	6
7	32 39.3	+13.6	91.3	32 37.7	+14.7	91.9	32 35.4	+15.9	92.5	32 32.4	+17.1	93.2	32 28.7	+18.4	93.8	32 24.4	+19.5	94.4	32 19.4	+20.7	95.1	32 13.8	+21.9	95.7	7
8	32 52.9	+12.9	90.1	32 52.4	+14.2	90.7	32 51.3	+15.4	91.4	32 49.5	+16.6	92.0	32 47.1	+17.7	92.7	32 43.9	+19.0	93.3	32 40.1	+20.1	94.0	32 35.7	+21.2	94.6	8
9	33 05.8	+12.2	88.9	33 06.6	+13.4	89.6	33 06.7	+14.6	90.2	33 06.1	+15.9	90.9	33 04.8	+17.1	91.5	33 02.9	+18.2	92.2	33 00.2	+19.5	92.8	32 56.9	+20.7	93.5	9
10	33 18.0	+11.6	87.8	33 20.0	+12.8	88.4	33 21.3	+14.1	89.1	33 22.0	+15.2	89.7	33 21.9	+16.5	90.4	33 21.1	+17.7	91.1	33 19.7	+18.9	91.7	33 17.6	+20.0	92.4	10
11	33 29.6	+10.9	86.6	33 32.8	+12.2	87.2	33 35.4	+13.4	87.9	33 37.2	+14.6	88.6	33 38.4	+15.8	89.2	33 38.8	+17.0	89.9	33 38.6	+18.2	90.6	33 37.6	+19.4	91.2	11
12	33 40.5	+10.3	85.4	33 45.0	+11.5	86.1	33 48.8	+12.7	86.7	33 51.8	+14.0	87.4	33 54.2	+15.1	88.1	33 55.8	+16.4	88.8	33 56.8	+17.6	89.4	33 57.0	+18.8	90.1	12
13	33 50.8	+9.5	84.2	33 56.5	+10.8	84.9	34 01.5	+12.0	85.6	34 05.8	+13.2	86.2	34 09.3	+14.5	86.9	34 12.2	+15.7	87.6	34 14.4	+16.9	88.3	34 15.8	+18.2	88.9	13
14	34 00.3	+8.9	83.0	34 07.3	+10.1	83.7	34 13.5	+11.3	84.4	34 19.0	+12.6	85.1	34 23.8	+13.9	85.7	34 27.9	+15.1	86.4	34 31.3	+16.3	87.1	34 34.0	+17.5	87.8	14
15	34 09.2	+8.2	81.8	34 17.4	+9.4	82.5	34 24.8	+10.7	83.2	34 31.6	+11.9	83.9	34 37.7	+13.1	84.6	34 43.0	+14.3	85.2	34 47.6	+15.6	85.9	34 51.5	+16.8	86.6	15
16	34 17.4	+7.4	80.6	34 26.8	+8.7	81.3	34 35.5	+9.9	82.0	34 43.5	+11.2	82.7	34 50.8	+12.4	83.4	34 57.3	+13.7	84.1	35 03.2	+14.9	84.8	35 08.3	+16.2	85.5	16
17	34 24.8	+6.8	79.4	34 35.5	+8.0	80.1	34 45.4	+9.3	80.8	34 54.7	+10.5	81.5	35 03.2	+11.7	82.2	35 11.0	+13.0	82.9	35 18.1	+14.2	83.6	35 24.5	+15.4	84.3	17
18	34 31.6	+6.1	78.2	34 43.5	+7.3	78.9	34 54.7	+8.5	79.6	35 05.2	+9.7	80.3	35 14.9	+11.1	81.0	35 24.0	+12.3	81.7	35 32.3	+13.5	82.4	35 39.9	+14.7	83.1	18
19	34 37.7	+5.3	77.0	34 50.8	+6.5	77.7	35 03.2	+7.8	78.4	35 14.9	+9.1	79.1	35 26.0	+10.3	79.8	35 36.3	+11.5	80.5	35 45.8	+12.8	81.2	35 54.6	+14.1	81.9	19
20	34 43.0	+4.6	75.8	34 57.3	+5.9	76.5	35 11.0	+7.1	77.2	35 24.0	+8.3	77.9	35 36.3	+9.5	78.6	35 47.8	+10.8	79.3	35 58.6	+12.1	80.0	36 08.7	+13.3	80.7	20
21	34 47.6	+3.9	74.6	35 03.2	+5.1	75.3	35 18.1	+6.4	76.0	35 32.3	+7.6	76.6	35 45.8	+8.8	77.3	35 58.6	+10.1	78.1	36 10.7	+11.3	78.8	36 22.0	+12.5	79.5	21
22	34 51.5	+3.1	73.4	35 08.3	+4.4	74.1	35 24.5	+5.6	74.7	35 39.9	+6.8	75.4	35 54.6	+8.1	76.1	36 08.7	+9.3	76.8	36 22.0	+10.6	77.5	36 34.5	+11.9	78.3	22
23	34 54.6	+2.5	72.2	35 12.7	+3.6	72.8	35 30.1	+4.8	73.5	35 46.7	+6.1	74.2	36 02.7	+7.4	74.9	36 18.0	+8.6	75.6	36 32.6	+9.8	76.3	36 46.4	+11.0	77.0	23
24	34 57.1	+1.7	70.9	35 16.3	+3.0	71.6	35 34.9	+4.2	72.3	35 52.8	+5.4	73.0	36 10.1	+6.5	73.7	36 26.6	+7.8	74.4	36 42.4	+9.0	75.1	36 57.4	+10.4	75.8	24
25	34 58.8	+1.0	69.7	35 19.3	+2.1	70.4	35 39.1	+3.3	71.1	35 58.2	+4.6	71.7	36 16.6	+5.9	72.4	36 34.4	+7.0	73.1	36 51.4	+8.3	73.9	37 07.8	+9.5	74.6	25
26	34 59.8	+0.2	68.5	35 21.4	+1.4	69.2	35 42.4	+2.7	69.8	36 02.8	+3.8	70.5	36 22.5	+5.0	71.2	36 41.4	+6.3	71.9	36 59.7	+7.5	72.6	37 17.3	+8.7	73.3	26
27	35 00.0	−0.5	67.3	35 22.8	+0.7	67.9	35 45.1	+1.8	68.6	36 06.6	+3.1	69.3	36 27.5	+4.3	70.0	36 47.7	+5.5	70.7	37 07.2	+6.8	71.4	37 26.0	+8.0	72.1	27
28	34 59.5	−1.2	66.1	35 23.5	0.0	66.7	35 46.9	+1.2	67.4	36 09.7	+2.3	68.0	36 31.8	+3.5	68.7	36 53.2	+4.8	69.4	37 14.0	+5.9	70.1	37 34.0	+7.2	70.9	28
29	34 58.3	−2.0	64.8	35 23.5	−0.8	65.5	35 48.1	+0.3	66.1	36 12.0	+1.6	66.8	36 35.3	+2.8	67.5	36 58.0	+3.9	68.2	37 19.9	+5.2	68.9	37 41.2	+6.4	69.6	29
30	34 56.3	−2.7	63.6	35 22.7	−1.6	64.3	35 48.4	−0.4	64.9	36 13.6	+0.7	65.6	36 38.1	+1.9	66.2	37 01.9	+3.2	66.9	37 25.1	+4.3	67.6	37 47.6	+5.6	68.3	30
31	34 53.6	−3.4	62.4	35 21.1	−2.3	63.0	35 48.0	−1.1	63.7	36 14.3	0.0	64.3	36 40.0	+1.2	65.0	37 05.1	+2.3	65.7	37 29.4	+3.6	66.4	37 53.2	+4.7	67.1	31
32	34 50.2	−4.2	61.2	35 18.8	−3.0	61.8	35 46.9	−1.9	62.4	36 14.3	−0.7	63.1	36 41.2	+0.4	63.7	37 07.4	+1.6	64.4	37 33.0	+2.8	65.1	37 57.9	+4.0	65.8	32
33	34 46.0	−4.8	60.0	35 15.8	−3.8	60.6	35 45.0	−2.7	61.2	36 13.6	−1.5	61.8	36 41.6	−0.4	62.5	37 09.0	+0.8	63.2	37 35.8	+1.9	63.9	38 01.9	+3.1	64.5	33
34	34 41.2	−5.6	58.8	35 12.0	−4.5	59.4	35 42.3	−3.4	60.0	36 12.1	−2.3	60.6	36 41.2	−1.1	61.3	37 09.8	0.0	61.9	37 37.7	+1.2	62.6	38 05.0	+2.3	63.3	34
35	34 35.6	−6.3	57.6	35 07.5	−5.2	58.1	35 38.9	−4.1	58.7	36 09.8	−3.1	59.4	36 40.1	−2.0	60.0	37 09.8	−0.8	60.7	37 38.9	+0.3	61.3	38 07.3	+1.5	62.0	35
36	34 29.3	−7.0	56.3	35 02.3	−6.0	56.9	35 34.8	−4.9	57.5	36 06.7	−3.8	58.1	36 38.1	−2.7	58.8	37 09.0	−1.6	59.4	37 39.2	−0.5	60.1	38 08.8	+0.7	60.7	36
37	34 22.3	−7.7	55.1	34 56.3	−6.7	55.7	35 29.9	−5.7	56.3	36 02.9	−4.6	56.9	36 35.4	−3.5	57.5	37 07.4	−2.4	58.1	37 38.7	−1.2	58.8	38 09.5	−0.1	59.5	37
38	34 14.6	−8.5	53.9	34 49.6	−7.4	54.5	35 24.2	−6.3	55.1	35 58.3	−5.3	55.7	36 31.9	−4.2	56.3	37 05.0	−3.2	56.9	37 37.5	−2.1	57.5	38 09.4	−1.0	58.2	38
39	34 06.1	−9.1	52.7	34 42.2	−8.1	53.3	35 17.9	−7.1	53.9	35 53.0	−6.1	54.4	36 27.7	−5.1	55.0	37 01.8	−4.0	55.6	37 35.4	−2.9	56.3	38 08.4	−1.8	56.9	39
40	33 57.0	−9.8	51.6	34 34.1	−8.8	52.1	35 10.8	−7.9	52.6	35 46.9	−6.8	53.2	36 22.6	−5.8	53.8	36 57.8	−4.7	54.4	37 32.5	−3.7	55.0	38 06.6	−2.6	55.7	40
41	33 47.2	−10.5	50.4	34 25.3	−9.5	50.9	35 02.9	−8.5	51.4	35 40.1	−7.6	52.0	36 16.8	−6.5	52.6	36 53.1	−5.6	53.1	37 28.8	−4.5	53.8	38 04.0	−3.4	54.4	41
42	33 36.7	−11.1	49.2	34 15.8	−10.3	49.7	34 54.4	−9.3	50.2	35 32.5	−8.3	50.8	36 10.3	−7.3	51.3	36 47.5	−6.3	51.9	37 24.3	−5.3	52.5	38 00.6	−4.3	53.1	42
43	33 25.6	−11.8	48.0	34 05.5	−10.9	48.5	34 45.1	−10.0	49.0	35 24.2	−9.0	49.5	36 03.0	−8.1	50.1	36 41.2	−7.1	50.7	37 19.0	−6.1	51.2	37 56.3	−5.0	51.9	43
44	33 13.8	−12.5	46.8	33 54.6	−11.5	47.3	34 35.1	−10.7	47.8	35 15.2	−9.7	48.3	35 54.9	−8.8	48.9	36 34.1	−7.8	49.4	37 12.9	−6.8	50.0	37 51.3	−5.9	50.6	44
45	33 01.3	−13.1	45.7	33 43.1	−12.3	46.1	34 24.4	−11.3	46.6	35 05.5	−10.5	47.1	35 46.1	−9.6	47.7	36 26.3	−8.6	48.2	37 06.1	−7.7	48.8	37 45.4	−6.7	49.3	45
46	32 48.2	−13.8	44.5	33 30.8	−12.9	45.0	34 13.1	−12.1	45.4	34 55.0	−11.2	45.9	35 36.5	−10.2	46.4	36 17.7	−9.4	47.0	36 58.4	−8.4	47.5	37 38.7	−7.4	48.1	46
47	32 34.4	−14.4	43.3	33 17.9	−13.6	43.8	34 01.0	−12.7	44.2	34 43.8	−11.8	44.7	35 26.3	−11.0	45.2	36 08.3	−10.1	45.7	36 50.0	−9.2	46.3	37 31.3	−8.3	46.8	47
48	32 20.0	−15.0	42.2	33 04.3	−14.2	42.6	33 48.3	−13.4	43.1	34 32.0	−12.6	43.5	35 15.3	−11.7	44.0	35 58.2	−10.8	44.5	36 40.8	−9.9	45.0	37 23.0	−9.0	45.6	48
49	32 05.0	−15.7	41.0	32 50.1	−14.9	41.5	33 34.9	−14.1	41.9	34 19.4	−13.3	42.4	35 03.6	−12.4	42.8	35 47.4	−11.6	43.3	36 30.9	−10.7	43.8	37 14.0	−9.8	44.3	49
50	31 49.3	−16.2	39.9	32 35.2	−15.5	40.3	33 20.8	−14.7	40.7	34 06.1	−13.9	41.2	34 51.2	−13.2	41.6	35 35.8	−12.2	42.1	36 20.2	−11.4	42.6	37 04.2	−10.6	43.1	50
51	31 33.1	−16.8	38.8	32 19.7	−16.1	39.2	33 06.1	−15.3	39.6	33 52.2	−14.5	40.0	34 38.0	−13.7	40.4	35 23.6	−13.0	40.9	36 08.8	−12.2	41.4	36 53.6	−11.3	41.9	51
52	31 16.3	−17.5	37.7	32 03.6	−16.7	38.0	32 50.8	−16.0	38.4	33 37.7	−15.3	38.8	34 24.3	−14.5	39.3	35 10.6	−13.7	39.7	35 56.6	−12.9	40.2	36 42.3	−12.1	40.6	52
53	30 58.8	−18.0	36.5	31 46.9	−17.3	36.9	32 34.8	−16.6	37.3	33 22.4	−15.9	37.7	34 09.8	−15.2	38.1	34 56.9	−14.4	38.5	35 43.7	−13.6	39.0	36 30.2	−12.8	39.4	53
54	30 40.8	−18.5	35.4	31 29.6	−17.9	35.8	32 18.2	−17.2	36.1	33 06.5	−16.5	36.5	33 54.6	−15.8	36.9	34 42.5	−15.1	37.3	35 30.1	−14.4	37.8	36 17.4	−13.6	38.2	54
55	30 22.3	−19.1	34.3	31 11.7	−18.4	34.7	32 01.0	−17.8	35.0	32 50.0	−17.1	35.4	33 38.8	−16.4	35.8	34 27.4	−15.7	36.2	35 15.7	−15.0	36.6	36 03.8	−14.3	37.0	55
56	30 03.2	−19.7	33.2	30 53.3	−19.0	33.5	31 43.2	−18.4	33.9	32 32.9	−17.7	34.2	33 22.4	−17.1	34.6	34 11.7	−16.4	35.0	35 00.7	−15.7	35.4	35 49.5	−15.0	35.8	56
57	29 43.5	−20.2	32.1	30 34.3	−19.6	32.4	31 24.8	−19.0	32.8	32 15.2	−18.4	33.1	33 05.3	−17.7	33.5	33 55.3	−17.1	33.8	34 45.0	−16.4	34.2	35 34.5	−15.7	34.6	57
58	29 23.3	−20.7	31.0	30 14.7	−20.2	31.3	31 05.8	−19.5	31.7	31 56.8	−18.9	32.0	32 47.6	−18.3	32.3	33 38.2	−17.7	32.7	34 28.6	−17.0	33.0	35 18.8	−16.4	33.4	58
59	29 02.6	−21.2	30.0	29 54.5	−20.6	30.3	30 46.3	−20.1	30.6	31 37.9	−19.5	30.9	32 29.3	−18.9	31.2	33 20.5	−18.3	31.5	34 11.6	−17.7	31.9	35 02.4	−17.0	32.2	59
60	28 41.4	−21.7	28.9	29 33.9	−21.2	29.2	30 26.2	−20.6	29.5	31 18.4	−20.1	29.8	32 10.4	−19.5	30.1	33 02.2	−18.9	30.4	33 53.9	−18.4	30.7	34 45.4	−17.8	31.1	60
61	28 19.7	−22.2	27.8	29 12.7	−21.7	28.1	30 05.6	−21.2	28.4	30 58.3	−20.7	28.7	31 50.9	−20.1	28.9	32 43.3	−19.6	29.3	33 35.5	−18.9	29.6	34 27.6	−18.3	29.9	61
62	27 57.5	−22.7	26.8	28 51.0	−22.2	27.0	29 44.4	−21.7	27.3	30 37.6	−21.1	27.6	31 30.8	−20.7	27.8	32 23.7	−20.1	28.1	33 16.6	−19.6	28.4	34 09.3	−19.1	28.8	62
63	27 34.8	−23.1	25.7	28 28.8	−22.7	26.0	29 22.7	−22.2	26.2	30 16.5	−21.8	26.5	31 10.1	−21.2	26.7	32 03.6	−20.7	27.0	32 57.0	−20.2	27.3	33 50.2	−19.6	27.6	63
64	27 11.7	−23.6	24.7	28 06.1	−23.1	24.9	29 00.5	−22.7	25.2	29 54.7	−22.2	25.4	30 48.9	−21.8	25.6	31 42.9	−21.3	25.9	32 36.8	−20.8	26.2	33 30.6	−20.3	26.5	64
65	26 48.1	−24.1	23.7	27 43.0	−23.7	23.9	28 37.8	−23.2	24.1	29 32.5	−22.7	24.3	30 27.1	−22.3	24.6	31 21.6	−21.8	24.8	32 16.0	−21.3	25.1	33 10.3	−20.8	25.4	65
66	26 24.0	−24.5	22.6	27 19.3	−24.0	22.8	28 14.6	−23.7	23.1	29 09.8	−23.3	23.3	30 04.8	−22.8	23.5	30 59.8	−22.4	23.7	31 54.7	−21.9	24.0	32 49.5	−21.5	24.2	66
67	25 59.5	−24.9	21.6	26 55.3	−24.6	21.8	27 50.9	−24.1	22.0	28 46.5	−23.7	22.2	29 42.0	−23.3	22.4	30 37.4	−22.9	22.6	31 32.8	−22.5	22.9	32 28.0	−22.1	23.1	67
68	25 34.6	−25.3	20.6	26 30.7	−24.9	20.8	27 26.8	−24.6	21.0	28 22.8	−24.2	21.2	29 18.7	−23.8	21.4	30 14.5	−23.4	21.6	31 10.3	−23.0	21.8	32 05.9	−22.6	22.0	68
69	25 09.3	−25.7	19.6	26 05.8	−25.4	19.8	27 02.2	−25.0	20.0	27 58.6	−24.7	20.1	28 54.9	−24.3	20.3	29 51.1	−23.9	20.5	30 47.3	−23.6	20.7	31 43.3	−23.1	20.9	69
70	24 43.6	−26.2	18.6	25 40.4	−25.8	18.8	26 37.2	−25.5	18.9	27 33.9	−25.1	19.1	28 30.6	−24.8	19.3	29 27.2	−24.5	19.5	30 23.7	−24.1	19.6	31 20.2	−23.7	19.9	70
71	24 17.4	−26.5	17.6	25 14.6	−26.2	17.8	26 11.7	−25.9	17.9	27 08.8	−25.6	18.1	28 05.8	−25.3	18.2	29 02.7	−24.9	18.4	29 59.6	−24.5	18.6	30 56.5	−24.3	18.8	71
72	23 50.9	−26.8	16.7	24 48.4	−26.6	16.8	25 45.8	−26.3	16.9	26 43.2	−26.0	17.1	27 40.5	−25.7	17.2	28 37.8	−25.4	17.4	29 35.1	−25.1	17.5	30 32.2	−24.7	17.7	72
73	23 24.1	−27.3	15.7	24 21.8	−27.0	15.8	25 19.5	−26.7	15.9	26 17.2	−26.4	16.1	27 14.8	−26.1	16.2	28 12.4	−25.8	16.3	29 10.0	−25.5	16.5	30 07.5	−25.2	16.7	73
74	22 56.8	−27.6	14.7	23 54.8	−27.3	14.8	24 52.8	−27.0	14.9	25 50.8	−26.8	15.1	26 48.7	−26.5	15.2	27 46.6	−26.3	15.3	28 44.5	−26.1	15.5	29 42.3	−25.8	15.6	74
75	22 29.2	−27.9	13.7	23 27.5	−27.7	13.8	24 25.8	−27.5	13.9	25 24.0	−27.2	14.1	26 22.2	−27.0	14.2	27 20.3	−26.7	14.3	28 18.4	−26.4	14.4	29 16.5	−26.2	14.6	75
76	22 01.3	−28.2	12.8	22 59.8	−28.0	12.9	23 58.3	−27.8	13.0	24 56.8	−27.6	13.1	25 55.2	−27.4	13.2	26 53.6	−27.2	13.3	27 52.0	−26.9	13.4	28 50.3	−26.7	13.5	76
77	21 33.1	−28.6	11.8	22 31.8	−28.4	11.9	23 30.5	−28.2	12.0	24 29.2	−28.0	12.1	25 27.8	−27.8	12.2	26 26.4	−27.5	12.3	27 25.1	−27.4	12.4	28 23.6	−27.1	12.5	77
78	21 04.5	−28.9	10.9	22 03.4	−28.7	11.0	23 02.3	−28.5	11.0	24 01.2	−28.4	11.1	25 00.0	−28.1	11.2	25 58.9	−28.0	11.3	26 57.7	−27.8	11.4	27 56.5	−27.6	11.5	78
79	20 35.6	−29.2	10.0	21 34.7	−29.0	10.0	22 33.8	−28.9	10.1	23 32.8	−28.7	10.2	24 31.9	−28.5	10.2	25 30.9	−28.3	10.3	26 29.9	−28.1	10.4	27 28.9	−28.0	10.5	79
80	20 06.4	−29.5	9.0	21 05.7	−29.4	9.1	22 04.9	−29.2	9.1	23 04.1	−29.0	9.2	24 03.4	−28.9	9.3	25 02.6	−28.8	9.4	26 01.8	−28.6	9.4	27 00.9	−28.4	9.5	80
81	19 36.9	−29.7	8.1	20 36.3	−29.6	8.1	21 35.7	−29.5	8.2	22 35.1	−29.4	8.3	23 34.5	−29.3	8.3	24 33.8	−29.1	8.4	25 33.2	−29.0	8.5	26 32.5	−28.8	8.5	81
82	19 07.2	−30.1	7.2	20 06.7	−29.9	7.2	21 06.2	−29.8	7.3	22 05.7	−29.7	7.3	23 05.2	−29.5	7.4	24 04.7	−29.4	7.4	25 04.2	−29.3	7.5	26 03.7	−29.2	7.5	82
83	18 37.1	−30.3	6.3	19 36.8	−30.2	6.3	20 36.4	−30.1	6.3	21 36.0	−30.0	6.4	22 35.7	−29.9	6.4	23 35.3	−29.8	6.5	24 34.9	−29.7	6.5	25 34.5	−29.6	6.6	83
84	18 06.8	−30.5	5.4	19 06.6	−30.5	5.4	20 06.3	−30.4	5.4	21 06.0	−30.3	5.5	22 05.8	−30.3	5.5	23 05.5	−30.2	5.5	24 05.2	−30.1	5.6	25 04.9	−29.9	5.6	84
85	17 36.3	−30.8	4.4	18 36.1	−30.7	4.5	19 35.9	−30.7	4.5	20 35.7	−30.6	4.5	21 35.5	−30.5	4.6	22 35.3	−30.4	4.6	23 35.1	−30.3	4.6	24 35.0	−30.4	4.7	85
86	17 05.5	−31.1	3.5	18 05.4	−31.0	3.6	19 05.2	−30.9	3.6	20 05.1	−30.9	3.6	21 05.0	−30.8	3.6	22 04.9	−30.8	3.7	23 04.8	−30.8	3.7	24 04.6	−30.6	3.7	86
87	16 34.4	−31.2	2.7	17 34.4	−31.3	2.7	18 34.3	−31.2	2.7	19 34.2	−31.1	2.7	20 34.2	−31.1	2.7	21 34.1	−31.1	2.7	22 34.0	−31.0	2.8	23 34.0	−31.0	2.8	87
88	16 03.2	−31.5	1.8	17 03.1	−31.4	1.8	18 03.1	−31.4	1.8	19 03.1	−31.4	1.8	20 03.1	−31.4	1.8	21 03.0	−31.3	1.8	22 03.0	−31.4	1.8	23 03.0	−31.4	1.8	88
89	15 31.7	−31.7	0.9	16 31.7	−31.7	0.9	17 31.7	−31.7	0.9	18 31.7	−31.7	0.9	19 31.7	−31.7	0.9	20 31.7	−31.7	0.9	21 31.6	−31.6	0.9	22 31.6	−31.6	0.9	89
90	15 00.0	−31.9	0.0	16 00.0	−31.9	0.0	17 00.0	−31.9	0.0	18 00.0	−31.9	0.0	19 00.0	−31.9	0.0	20 00.0	−31.9	0.0	21 00.0	−31.9	0.0	22 00.0	−31.9	0.0	90
	15°			16°			17°			18°			19°			20°			21°			22°			

Dec.	15° Hc	d	Z	16° Hc	d	Z	17° Hc	d	Z	18° Hc	d	Z
°	° ′	′	°	° ′	′	°	° ′	′	°	° ′	′	°
0	30 47.3	-18.4	99.2	30 37.4	-19.5	99.8	30 26.9	-20.6	100.4	30 15.8	-21.7	100.9
1	30 28.9	-18.9	100.3	30 17.9	-20.0	100.9	30 06.3	-21.2	101.4	29 54.1	-22.3	102.0
2	30 10.0	-19.5	101.4	29 57.9	-20.6	102.0	29 45.1	-21.6	102.5	29 31.8	-22.7	103.1
3	29 50.5	-20.0	102.5	29 37.3	-21.1	103.0	29 23.5	-22.2	103.6	29 09.1	-23.3	104.1
4	29 30.5	-20.5	103.6	29 16.2	-21.6	104.1	29 01.3	-22.7	104.7	28 45.8	-23.7	105.2
5	29 10.0	-21.0	104.6	28 54.6	-22.1	105.2	28 38.6	-23.2	105.7	28 22.1	-24.2	106.2
6	28 49.0	-21.6	105.7	28 32.5	-22.6	106.2	28 15.4	-23.6	106.8	27 57.9	-24.7	107.3
7	28 27.4	-22.0	106.8	28 09.9	-23.1	107.3	27 51.8	-24.1	107.8	27 33.2	-25.2	108.3
8	28 05.4	-22.5	107.8	27 46.8	-23.6	108.3	27 27.7	-24.6	108.8	27 08.0	-25.5	109.3
9	27 42.9	-23.0	108.9	27 23.2	-24.0	109.4	27 03.1	-25.0	109.9	26 42.5	-26.1	110.3
10	27 19.9	-23.4	109.9	26 59.2	-24.4	110.4	26 38.1	-25.5	110.9	26 16.4	-26.4	111.3
11	26 56.5	-23.9	111.0	26 34.8	-24.9	111.4	26 12.6	-25.9	111.9	25 50.0	-26.8	112.3
12	26 32.6	-24.4	112.0	26 09.9	-25.3	112.4	25 46.7	-26.2	112.9	25 23.2	-27.2	113.3
13	26 08.2	-24.7	113.0	25 44.6	-25.8	113.5	25 20.5	-26.7	113.9	24 56.0	-27.7	114.3
14	25 43.5	-25.2	114.0	25 18.8	-26.1	114.5	24 53.8	-27.1	114.9	24 28.3	-27.9	115.3
15	25 18.3	-25.6	115.0	24 52.7	-26.5	115.5	24 26.7	-27.4	115.9	24 00.4	-28.4	116.3
16	24 52.7	-26.0	116.0	24 26.2	-26.9	116.4	23 59.3	-27.8	116.8	23 32.0	-28.7	117.2
17	24 26.7	-26.3	117.0	23 59.3	-27.3	117.4	23 31.5	-28.2	117.8	23 03.3	-29.1	118.2
18	24 00.4	-26.8	118.0	23 32.0	-27.6	118.4	23 03.3	-28.5	118.8	22 34.2	-29.3	119.1
19	23 33.6	-27.1	119.0	23 04.4	-28.0	119.4	22 34.8	-28.9	119.7	22 04.9	-29.7	120.1
20	23 06.5	-27.5	120.0	22 36.4	-28.3	120.3	22 05.9	-29.1	120.7	21 35.2	-30.0	121.0
21	22 39.0	-27.8	120.9	22 08.1	-28.7	121.3	21 36.8	-29.5	121.6	21 05.2	-30.4	121.9
22	22 11.2	-28.1	121.9	21 39.4	-29.0	122.2	21 07.3	-29.8	122.5	20 34.8	-30.6	122.9
23	21 43.1	-28.5	122.8	21 10.4	-29.3	123.2	20 37.5	-30.1	123.5	20 04.2	-30.9	123.8
24	21 14.6	-28.7	123.8	20 41.1	-29.5	124.1	20 07.4	-30.4	124.4	19 33.3	-31.1	124.7
25	20 45.9	-29.1	124.7	20 11.6	-29.9	125.0	19 37.0	-30.7	125.3	19 02.2	-31.4	125.6
26	20 16.8	-29.4	125.7	19 41.7	-30.2	125.9	19 06.3	-30.9	126.2	18 30.8	-31.7	126.5
27	19 47.4	-29.7	126.6	19 11.5	-30.4	126.9	18 35.4	-31.2	127.1	17 59.1	-31.9	127.4
28	19 17.7	-29.9	127.5	18 41.1	-30.7	127.8	18 04.2	-31.4	128.0	17 27.2	-32.2	128.3
29	18 47.8	-30.2	128.4	18 10.4	-30.9	128.7	17 32.8	-31.7	128.9	16 55.0	-32.4	129.2
30	18 17.6	-30.5	129.3	17 39.5	-31.2	129.6	17 01.1	-31.9	129.8	16 22.6	-32.6	130.0
31	17 47.1	-30.7	130.2	17 08.3	-31.5	130.5	16 29.2	-32.1	130.7	15 50.0	-32.8	130.9
32	17 16.4	-31.0	131.1	16 36.8	-31.6	131.4	15 57.1	-32.3	131.6	15 17.2	-33.0	131.8
33	16 45.4	-31.1	132.0	16 05.2	-31.9	132.3	15 24.8	-32.6	132.5	14 44.2	-33.2	132.7
34	16 14.3	-31.4	132.9	15 33.3	-32.1	133.1	14 52.2	-32.7	133.3	14 11.0	-33.4	133.5
35	15 42.9	-31.7	133.8	15 01.2	-32.2	134.0	14 19.5	-32.9	134.2	13 37.6	-33.6	134.4
36	15 11.2	-31.8	134.7	14 29.0	-32.5	134.9	13 46.6	-33.1	135.1	13 04.0	-33.7	135.2
37	14 39.4	-32.0	135.6	13 56.5	-32.6	135.7	13 13.5	-33.3	135.9	12 30.3	-33.9	136.1
38	14 07.4	-32.2	136.4	13 23.9	-32.9	136.6	12 40.2	-33.4	136.8	11 56.4	-34.0	136.9
39	13 35.2	-32.4	137.3	12 51.0	-33.0	137.5	12 06.8	-33.6	137.6	11 22.4	-34.2	137.8
40	13 02.8	-32.6	138.2	12 18.0	-33.1	138.3	11 33.2	-33.8	138.5	10 48.2	-34.3	138.6
41	12 30.2	-32.7	139.0	11 44.9	-33.3	139.2	10 59.4	-33.8	139.3	10 13.9	-34.4	139.4
42	11 57.5	-32.9	139.9	11 11.6	-33.5	140.0	10 25.6	-34.1	140.1	9 39.5	-34.6	140.3
43	11 24.6	-33.0	140.7	10 38.1	-33.5	140.9	9 51.5	-34.1	141.0	9 04.9	-34.7	141.1
44	10 51.6	-33.2	141.6	10 04.6	-33.8	141.7	9 17.4	-34.2	141.8	8 30.2	-34.8	141.9
45	10 18.4	-33.3	142.4	9 30.8	-33.8	142.6	8 43.2	-34.4	142.7	7 55.4	-34.8	142.7
46	9 45.1	-33.4	143.3	8 57.0	-33.9	143.4	8 08.8	-34.4	143.5	7 20.6	-35.0	143.6
47	9 11.7	-33.5	144.1	8 23.1	-34.1	144.2	7 34.4	-34.6	144.3	6 45.6	-35.0	144.4
48	8 38.2	-33.7	145.0	7 49.0	-34.1	145.1	6 59.8	-34.6	145.1	6 10.6	-35.1	145.2
49	8 04.5	-33.7	145.8	7 14.9	-34.3	145.9	6 25.2	-34.7	146.0	5 35.5	-35.2	146.0
50	7 30.8	-33.9	146.6	6 40.6	-34.3	146.7	5 50.5	-34.8	146.8	5 00.3	-35.3	146.8
51	6 56.9	-33.9	147.5	6 06.3	-34.4	147.5	5 15.7	-34.9	147.6	4 25.0	-35.3	147.6
52	6 23.0	-34.0	148.3	5 31.9	-34.4	148.4	4 40.8	-34.9	148.4	3 49.7	-35.3	148.4
53	5 49.0	-34.1	149.1	4 57.5	-34.5	149.2	4 05.9	-34.9	149.2	3 14.4	-35.4	149.3
54	5 14.9	-34.1	150.0	4 23.0	-34.6	150.0	3 31.0	-35.0	150.0	2 39.0	-35.4	150.1
55	4 40.8	-34.2	150.8	3 48.4	-34.6	150.8	2 56.0	-35.0	150.9	2 03.6	-35.5	150.9
56	4 06.6	-34.3	151.6	3 13.8	-34.7	151.6	2 21.0	-35.1	151.7	1 28.1	-35.4	151.7
57	3 32.3	-34.3	152.4	2 39.1	-34.7	152.5	1 45.9	-35.1	152.5	0 52.7	-35.5	152.5
58	2 58.0	-34.3	153.3	2 04.4	-34.7	153.3	1 10.8	-35.1	153.3	0 17.2	-35.5	153.3
59	2 23.7	-34.4	154.1	1 29.7	-34.7	154.1	0 35.7	-35.1	154.1	0 18.3	+35.4	25.9
60	1 49.3	-34.4	154.9	0 55.0	-34.8	154.9	0 00.6	-35.1	154.9	0 53.7	+35.5	25.1
61	1 14.9	-34.4	155.7	0 20.2	-34.7	155.7	0 34.5	+35.1	24.3	1 29.2	+35.4	24.3
62	0 40.5	-34.4	156.5	0 14.5	+34.8	23.5	1 09.6	+35.1	23.5	2 04.6	+35.4	23.5
63	0 06.1	-34.4	157.4	0 49.3	+34.7	22.6	1 44.7	+35.0	22.7	2 40.0	+35.4	22.7
64	0 28.3	+34.4	21.8	1 24.0	+34.7	21.8	2 19.7	+35.1	21.8	3 15.4	+35.3	21.9
65	1 02.7	+34.4	21.0	1 58.7	+34.7	21.0	2 54.8	+34.9	21.0	3 50.7	+35.3	21.1
66	1 37.1	+34.4	20.2	2 33.4	+34.7	20.2	3 29.7	+35.0	20.2	4 26.0	+35.3	20.2
67	2 11.5	+34.4	19.4	3 08.1	+34.6	19.4	4 04.7	+34.9	19.4	5 01.3	+35.2	19.4
68	2 45.9	+34.3	18.5	3 42.7	+34.6	18.6	4 39.6	+34.9	18.6	5 36.5	+35.1	18.6
69	3 20.2	+34.2	17.7	4 17.3	+34.5	17.7	5 14.5	+34.7	17.8	6 11.6	+35.0	17.8
70	3 54.4	+34.3	16.9	4 51.8	+34.5	16.9	5 49.2	+34.8	17.0	6 46.6	+35.0	17.0
71	4 28.7	+34.1	16.1	5 26.3	+34.4	16.1	6 24.0	+34.6	16.1	7 21.6	+34.9	16.2
72	5 02.8	+34.1	15.3	6 00.7	+34.3	15.3	6 58.6	+34.5	15.3	7 56.5	+34.7	15.3
73	5 36.9	+34.1	14.4	6 35.0	+34.3	14.5	7 33.1	+34.5	14.5	8 31.2	+34.7	14.5
74	6 11.0	+33.9	13.6	7 09.3	+34.2	13.6	8 07.6	+34.4	13.7	9 05.9	+34.6	13.7
75	6 44.9	+33.9	12.8	7 43.5	+34.0	12.8	8 42.0	+34.2	12.8	9 40.5	+34.4	12.9
76	7 18.8	+33.8	11.9	8 17.5	+34.0	12.0	9 16.2	+34.1	12.0	10 14.9	+34.3	12.0
77	7 52.6	+33.7	11.1	8 51.5	+33.8	11.1	9 50.3	+34.1	11.2	10 49.2	+34.2	11.2
78	8 26.3	+33.6	10.3	9 25.3	+33.8	10.3	10 24.4	+33.8	10.3	11 23.4	+34.0	10.4
79	8 59.9	+33.4	9.4	9 59.1	+33.6	9.5	10 58.2	+33.8	9.5	11 57.4	+33.9	9.5
80	9 33.3	+33.4	8.6	10 32.7	+33.4	8.6	11 32.0	+33.6	8.6	12 31.3	+33.7	8.7
81	10 06.7	+33.2	7.7	11 06.1	+33.4	7.8	12 05.6	+33.4	7.8	13 05.0	+33.6	7.8
82	10 39.9	+33.1	6.9	11 39.5	+33.1	6.9	12 39.0	+33.3	6.9	13 38.6	+33.4	7.0
83	11 13.0	+32.9	6.0	12 12.6	+33.0	6.1	13 12.3	+33.1	6.1	14 12.0	+33.1	6.1
84	11 45.9	+32.8	5.2	12 45.6	+32.9	5.2	13 45.4	+32.9	5.2	14 45.1	+33.1	5.3
85	12 18.7	+32.6	4.3	13 18.5	+32.7	4.4	14 18.3	+32.8	4.4	15 18.2	+32.8	4.4
86	12 51.3	+32.4	3.5	13 51.2	+32.5	3.5	14 51.1	+32.5	3.5	15 51.0	+32.6	3.5
87	13 23.7	+32.3	2.6	14 23.7	+32.3	2.6	15 23.6	+32.4	2.6	16 23.6	+32.3	2.7
88	13 56.0	+32.1	1.7	14 56.0	+32.1	1.8	15 56.0	+32.1	1.8	16 55.9	+32.2	1.8
89	14 28.1	+31.9	0.9	15 28.1	+31.9	0.9	16 28.1	+31.9	0.9	17 28.1	+31.9	0.9
90	15 00.0	+31.7	0.0	16 00.0	+31.7	0.0	17 00.0	+31.7	0.0	18 00.0	+31.7	0.0
	15°			16°			17°			18°		

19° Hc	d	Z	20° Hc	d	Z	21° Hc	d	Z	22° Hc	d	Z	Dec.
° ′	′	°	° ′	′	°	° ′	′	°	° ′	′	°	°
30 04.2	-22.9	101.5	29 51.9	-23.9	102.1	29 39.1	-25.0	102.6	29 25.7	-26.1	103.2	0
29 41.3	-23.3	102.6	29 28.0	-24.4	103.1	29 14.1	-25.5	103.7	28 59.6	-26.5	104.2	1
29 18.0	-23.8	103.6	29 03.6	-24.9	104.2	28 48.6	-25.9	104.7	28 33.1	-26.9	105.2	2
28 54.2	-24.4	104.7	28 38.7	-25.4	105.2	28 22.7	-26.4	105.7	28 06.2	-27.5	106.2	3
28 29.8	-24.8	105.7	28 13.3	-25.8	106.2	27 56.3	-26.9	106.7	27 38.7	-27.8	107.3	4
28 05.0	-25.2	106.8	27 47.5	-26.3	107.3	27 29.4	-27.2	107.8	27 10.9	-28.3	108.2	5
27 39.8	-25.7	107.8	27 21.2	-26.7	108.3	27 02.2	-27.7	108.8	26 42.6	-28.6	109.2	6
27 14.1	-26.2	108.8	26 54.5	-27.1	109.3	26 34.5	-28.1	109.8	26 14.0	-29.1	110.2	7
26 47.9	-26.5	109.8	26 27.4	-27.6	110.3	26 06.4	-28.6	110.7	25 44.9	-29.5	111.2	8
26 21.4	-27.0	110.8	25 59.8	-27.9	111.3	25 37.8	-28.8	111.7	25 15.4	-29.8	112.2	9
25 54.4	-27.4	111.8	25 31.9	-28.4	112.2	25 09.0	-29.3	112.7	24 45.6	-30.2	113.1	10
25 27.0	-27.8	112.8	25 03.5	-28.7	113.2	24 39.7	-29.7	113.6	24 15.4	-30.5	114.1	11
24 59.2	-28.2	113.8	24 34.8	-29.1	114.2	24 10.0	-30.0	114.6	23 44.9	-30.9	115.0	12
24 31.0	-28.5	114.7	24 05.7	-29.4	115.2	23 40.0	-30.3	115.6	23 14.0	-31.2	115.9	13
24 02.5	-28.9	115.7	23 36.3	-29.8	116.1	23 09.7	-30.7	116.5	22 42.8	-31.6	116.9	14
23 33.6	-29.2	116.7	23 06.5	-30.1	117.0	22 39.0	-30.9	117.4	22 11.2	-31.8	117.8	15
23 04.4	-29.6	117.6	22 36.4	-30.5	118.0	22 08.1	-31.3	118.4	21 39.4	-32.1	118.7	16
22 34.8	-29.9	118.6	22 05.9	-30.7	118.9	21 36.8	-31.6	119.3	21 07.3	-32.5	119.6	17
22 04.9	-30.3	119.5	21 35.2	-31.1	119.8	21 05.2	-31.9	120.2	20 34.8	-32.7	120.5	18
21 34.6	-30.5	120.4	21 04.1	-31.4	120.8	20 33.3	-32.2	121.1	20 02.1	-32.9	121.4	19
21 04.1	-30.8	121.4	20 32.7	-31.6	121.7	20 01.1	-32.5	122.0	19 29.2	-33.3	122.3	20
20 33.3	-31.2	122.3	20 01.1	-31.9	122.6	19 28.6	-32.7	122.9	18 55.9	-33.4	123.2	21
20 02.1	-31.4	123.2	19 29.2	-32.2	123.5	18 55.9	-32.9	123.8	18 22.5	-33.7	124.1	22
19 30.7	-31.6	124.1	18 57.0	-32.5	124.4	18 23.0	-33.2	124.7	17 48.8	-34.0	124.9	23
18 59.1	-32.0	125.0	18 24.5	-32.6	125.3	17 49.8	-33.4	125.5	17 14.8	-34.2	125.8	24
18 27.1	-32.1	125.9	17 51.9	-33.0	126.1	17 16.4	-33.7	126.4	16 40.6	-34.3	126.6	25
17 55.0	-32.5	126.8	17 18.9	-33.1	127.0	16 42.7	-33.9	127.3	16 06.3	-34.6	127.5	26
17 22.5	-32.6	127.7	16 45.8	-33.4	127.9	16 08.8	-34.0	128.1	15 31.7	-34.8	128.3	27
16 49.9	-32.9	128.5	16 12.4	-33.6	128.8	15 34.8	-34.3	129.0	14 56.9	-34.9	129.2	28
16 17.0	-33.1	129.4	15 38.8	-33.8	129.6	15 00.5	-34.5	129.8	14 22.0	-35.2	130.0	29
15 43.9	-33.3	130.3	15 05.0	-33.9	130.5	14 26.0	-34.6	130.7	13 46.8	-35.3	130.9	30
15 10.6	-33.5	131.1	14 31.1	-34.2	131.3	13 51.4	-34.8	131.5	13 11.5	-35.4	131.7	31
14 37.1	-33.6	132.0	13 56.9	-34.3	132.2	13 16.6	-35.0	132.4	12 36.1	-35.6	132.5	32
14 03.5	-33.9	132.8	13 22.6	-34.5	133.0	12 41.6	-35.2	133.2	12 00.5	-35.8	133.4	33
13 29.6	-34.0	133.7	12 48.1	-34.7	133.9	12 06.4	-35.2	134.0	11 24.7	-35.9	134.2	34
12 55.6	-34.2	134.5	12 13.4	-34.8	134.7	11 31.2	-35.4	134.8	10 48.8	-36.0	135.0	35
12 21.4	-34.4	135.4	11 38.6	-34.9	135.5	10 55.8	-35.6	135.7	10 12.8	-36.2	135.8	36
11 47.0	-34.4	136.2	11 03.7	-35.1	136.4	10 20.2	-35.7	136.5	9 36.6	-36.2	136.6	37
11 12.6	-34.7	137.1	10 28.6	-35.2	137.2	9 44.5	-35.8	137.3	9 00.4	-36.4	137.4	38
10 37.9	-34.7	137.9	9 53.4	-35.4	138.0	9 08.7	-35.9	138.1	8 24.0	-36.4	138.2	39
10 03.2	-34.9	138.7	9 18.0	-35.4	138.8	8 32.8	-36.0	138.9	7 47.6	-36.6	139.0	40
9 28.3	-35.0	139.5	8 42.6	-35.6	139.6	7 56.8	-36.1	139.7	7 11.0	-36.6	139.8	41
8 53.3	-35.1	140.4	8 07.0	-35.6	140.5	7 20.7	-36.1	140.5	6 34.4	-36.7	140.6	42
8 18.2	-35.2	141.2	7 31.4	-35.7	141.3	6 44.6	-36.3	141.4	5 57.7	-36.8	141.4	43
7 43.0	-35.3	142.0	6 55.7	-35.9	142.1	6 08.3	-36.3	142.2	5 20.9	-36.8	142.2	44
7 07.7	-35.4	142.8	6 19.8	-35.8	142.9	5 32.0	-36.4	143.0	4 44.1	-36.9	143.0	45
6 32.3	-35.5	143.6	5 44.0	-36.0	143.7	4 55.6	-36.5	143.8	4 07.2	-37.0	143.8	46
5 56.8	-35.5	144.4	5 08.0	-36.0	144.5	4 19.1	-36.5	144.5	3 30.2	-36.9	144.6	47
5 21.3	-35.6	145.3	4 32.0	-36.1	145.3	3 42.6	-36.5	145.3	2 53.3	-37.0	145.4	48
4 45.7	-35.7	146.1	3 55.9	-36.1	146.1	3 06.1	-36.6	146.1	2 16.3	-37.1	146.2	49
4 10.0	-35.7	146.9	3 19.8	-36.2	146.9	2 29.5	-36.6	146.9	1 39.2	-37.0	147.0	50
3 34.3	-35.7	147.7	2 43.6	-36.2	147.7	1 52.9	-36.6	147.7	1 02.2	-37.1	147.8	51
2 58.6	-35.8	148.5	2 07.4	-36.2	148.5	1 16.3	-36.7	148.5	0 25.1	-37.1	148.5	52
2 22.8	-35.8	149.3	1 31.2	-36.2	149.3	0 39.6	-36.6	149.3	0 12.0	+37.0	30.7	53
1 47.0	-35.8	150.1	0 55.0	-36.3	150.1	0 03.0	-36.7	150.1	0 49.0	+37.1	29.9	54
1 11.2	-35.9	150.9	0 18.7	-36.2	150.9	0 33.7	+36.6	29.1	1 26.1	+37.0	29.1	55
0 35.3	-35.8	151.7	0 17.5	+36.2	28.3	1 10.3	+36.7	28.3	2 03.1	+37.1	28.3	56
0 00.5	+35.9	27.5	0 53.7	+36.3	27.5	1 47.0	+36.6	27.5	2 40.2	+37.0	27.5	57
0 36.4	+35.8	26.7	1 30.0	+36.2	26.7	2 23.6	+36.6	26.7	3 17.2	+36.9	26.8	58
1 12.2	+35.9	25.9	2 06.2	+36.2	25.9	3 00.2	+36.5	25.9	3 54.1	+36.9	26.0	59
1 48.1	+35.8	25.1	2 42.4	+36.1	25.1	3 36.7	+36.5	25.1	4 31.0	+36.9	25.2	60
2 23.9	+35.7	24.3	3 18.5	+36.2	24.3	4 13.2	+36.5	24.3	5 07.9	+36.8	24.4	61
2 59.6	+35.8	23.5	3 54.7	+36.0	23.5	4 49.7	+36.4	23.6	5 44.7	+36.7	23.6	62
3 35.4	+35.7	22.7	4 30.7	+36.1	22.7	5 26.1	+36.3	22.8	6 21.4	+36.7	22.8	63
4 11.1	+35.6	21.9	5 06.8	+35.9	21.9	6 02.4	+36.3	22.0	6 58.1	+36.5	22.0	64
4 46.7	+35.6	21.1	5 42.7	+35.9	21.1	6 38.7	+36.2	21.2	7 34.6	+36.5	21.2	65
5 22.3	+35.6	20.3	6 18.6	+35.8	20.3	7 14.9	+36.1	20.3	8 11.1	+36.4	20.4	66
5 57.9	+35.4	19.5	6 54.4	+35.8	19.5	7 51.0	+36.0	19.5	8 47.5	+36.3	19.6	67
6 33.3	+35.4	18.6	7 30.2	+35.6	18.7	8 27.0	+35.9	18.7	9 23.8	+36.2	18.8	68
7 08.7	+35.3	17.8	8 05.8	+35.6	17.9	9 02.9	+35.8	17.9	10 00.0	+36.1	18.0	69
7 44.0	+35.2	17.0	8 41.4	+35.4	17.1	9 38.7	+35.7	17.1	10 36.1	+35.9	17.2	70
8 19.2	+35.1	16.2	9 16.8	+35.4	16.2	10 14.4	+35.6	16.3	11 12.0	+35.8	16.3	71
8 54.3	+35.0	15.4	9 52.2	+35.2	15.4	10 50.0	+35.4	15.5	11 47.8	+35.7	15.5	72
9 29.3	+34.9	14.6	10 27.4	+35.1	14.6	11 25.4	+35.3	14.7	12 23.5	+35.5	14.7	73
10 04.2	+34.7	13.7	11 02.5	+34.9	13.8	12 00.7	+35.2	13.8	12 59.0	+35.4	13.9	74
10 38.9	+34.7	12.9	11 37.4	+34.8	12.9	12 35.9	+35.0	13.0	13 34.4	+35.1	13.0	75
11 13.6	+34.5	12.1	12 12.2	+34.7	12.1	13 10.9	+34.8	12.2	14 09.5	+35.1	12.2	76
11 48.1	+34.3	11.2	12 46.9	+34.5	11.3	13 45.7	+34.7	11.3	14 44.6	+34.8	11.4	77
12 22.4	+34.2	10.4	13 21.4	+34.3	10.4	14 20.4	+34.5	10.5	15 19.4	+34.7	10.5	78
12 56.6	+34.0	9.6	13 55.7	+34.2	9.6	14 54.9	+34.3	9.6	15 54.1	+34.4	9.7	79
13 30.6	+33.9	8.7	14 29.9	+34.0	8.7	15 29.2	+34.1	8.8	16 28.5	+34.2	8.8	80
14 04.5	+33.6	7.9	15 03.9	+33.8	7.9	16 03.3	+33.9	7.9	17 02.7	+34.1	8.0	81
14 38.1	+33.5	7.0	15 37.7	+33.6	7.0	16 37.2	+33.7	7.1	17 36.8	+33.8	7.1	82
15 11.6	+33.3	6.1	16 11.3	+33.3	6.2	17 10.9	+33.5	6.2	18 10.6	+33.5	6.2	83
15 44.9	+33.1	5.3	16 44.6	+33.2	5.3	17 44.4	+33.2	5.3	18 44.1	+33.3	5.4	84
16 18.0	+32.8	4.4	17 17.8	+32.9	4.4	18 17.6	+33.0	4.5	19 17.4	+33.1	4.5	85
16 50.8	+32.7	3.5	17 50.7	+32.7	3.6	18 50.6	+32.8	3.6	19 50.5	+32.8	3.6	86
17 23.5	+32.4	2.7	18 23.4	+32.5	2.7	19 23.4	+32.4	2.7	20 23.3	+32.5	2.7	87
17 55.9	+32.2	1.8	18 55.9	+32.2	1.8	19 55.8	+32.3	1.8	20 55.8	+32.3	1.8	88
18 28.1	+31.9	0.9	19 28.1	+31.9	0.9	20 28.1	+31.9	0.9	21 28.1	+31.9	0.9	89
19 00.0	+31.7	0.0	20 00.0	+31.7	0.0	21 00.0	+31.6	0.0	22 00.0	+31.6	0.0	90
19°			20°			21°			22°			

S. Lat. {L.H.A. greater than 180° ....Zn=180°–Z
{L.H.A. less than 180°...........Zn=180°+Z

59°, 301° L.H.A. LATITUDE SAME NAME AS DECLINATION

N. Lat. {L.H.A. greater than 180° .....Zn=Z; L.H.A. less than 180°............Zn=360°−Z}

Dec.	15°			16°			17°			18°			19°			20°			21°			22°			Dec.
	Hc	d	Z	Hc	d	Z	Hc	d	Z	Hc	d	Z	Hc	d	Z	Hc	d	Z	Hc	d	Z	Hc	d	Z	
°	° ′	′	°	° ′	′	°	° ′	′	°	° ′	′	°	° ′	′	°	° ′	′	°	° ′	′	°	° ′	′	°	°
0	29 50.0	+17.7	98.8	29 40.5	+18.8	99.4	29 30.4	+19.9	100.0	29 19.8	+21.0	100.5	29 08.5	+22.1	101.1	28 56.7	+23.2	101.6	28 44.4	+24.3	102.2	28 31.5	+25.3	102.7	0
1	30 07.7	+17.0	97.7	29 59.3	+18.2	98.3	29 50.3	+19.4	98.9	29 40.8	+20.5	99.4	29 30.6	+21.6	100.0	29 19.9	+22.7	100.6	29 08.7	+23.7	101.1	28 56.8	+24.9	101.7	1
2	30 24.7	+16.5	96.6	30 17.5	+17.7	97.2	30 09.7	+18.8	97.8	30 01.3	+19.9	98.4	29 52.2	+21.1	98.9	29 42.6	+22.2	99.5	29 32.4	+23.3	100.1	29 21.7	+24.4	100.6	2
3	30 41.2	+16.0	95.5	30 35.2	+17.1	96.1	30 28.5	+18.2	96.7	30 21.2	+19.4	97.3	30 13.3	+20.5	97.8	30 04.8	+21.7	98.4	29 55.7	+22.8	99.0	29 46.1	+23.8	99.6	3
4	30 57.2	+15.3	94.4	30 52.3	+16.5	95.0	30 46.7	+17.7	95.6	30 40.6	+18.8	96.2	30 33.8	+20.0	96.8	30 26.5	+21.1	97.3	30 18.5	+22.3	97.9	30 09.9	+23.4	98.5	4
5	31 12.5	+14.8	93.3	31 08.8	+15.9	93.9	31 04.4	+17.1	94.5	30 59.4	+18.3	95.1	30 53.8	+19.5	95.7	30 47.6	+20.6	96.3	30 40.8	+21.7	96.8	30 33.3	+22.8	97.4	5
6	31 27.3	+14.1	92.1	31 24.7	+15.3	92.7	31 21.5	+16.5	93.3	31 17.7	+17.7	94.0	31 13.3	+18.8	94.6	31 08.2	+20.0	95.2	31 02.5	+21.1	95.8	30 56.1	+22.3	96.4	6
7	31 41.4	+13.5	91.0	31 40.0	+14.8	91.6	31 38.0	+16.0	92.2	31 35.4	+17.1	92.8	31 32.1	+18.3	93.4	31 28.2	+19.4	94.1	31 23.6	+20.6	94.7	31 18.4	+21.8	95.3	7
8	31 54.9	+12.9	89.8	31 54.8	+14.1	90.5	31 54.0	+15.3	91.1	31 52.5	+16.5	91.7	31 50.4	+17.7	92.3	31 47.6	+18.9	92.9	31 44.2	+20.1	93.6	31 40.2	+21.2	94.2	8
9	32 07.8	+12.3	88.7	32 08.9	+13.5	89.3	32 09.3	+14.7	89.9	32 09.0	+15.9	90.6	32 08.1	+17.1	91.2	32 06.5	+18.3	91.8	32 04.3	+19.4	92.5	32 01.4	+20.6	93.1	9
10	32 20.1	+11.7	87.5	32 22.4	+12.8	88.2	32 24.0	+14.0	88.8	32 24.9	+15.3	89.4	32 25.2	+16.4	90.1	32 24.8	+17.6	90.7	32 23.7	+18.9	91.3	32 22.0	+20.0	92.0	10
11	32 31.8	+11.0	86.4	32 35.2	+12.3	87.0	32 38.0	+13.5	87.6	32 40.2	+14.6	88.3	32 41.6	+15.9	88.9	32 42.4	+17.1	89.6	32 42.6	+18.2	90.2	32 42.0	+19.4	90.8	11
12	32 42.8	+10.3	85.2	32 47.5	+11.5	85.8	32 51.5	+12.8	86.5	32 54.8	+14.0	87.1	32 57.5	+15.2	87.8	32 59.5	+16.4	88.4	33 00.8	+17.6	89.1	33 01.4	+18.8	89.7	12
13	32 53.1	+9.7	84.0	32 59.0	+10.9	84.7	33 04.3	+12.1	85.3	33 08.8	+13.4	86.0	33 12.7	+14.6	86.6	33 15.9	+15.8	87.3	33 18.4	+17.0	87.9	33 20.2	+18.2	88.6	13
14	33 02.8	+9.0	82.8	33 09.9	+10.3	83.5	33 16.4	+11.5	84.1	33 22.2	+12.7	84.8	33 27.3	+13.9	85.5	33 31.7	+15.1	86.1	33 35.4	+16.3	86.8	33 38.4	+17.6	87.4	14
15	33 11.8	+8.4	81.7	33 20.2	+9.6	82.3	33 27.9	+10.8	83.0	33 34.9	+12.0	83.6	33 41.2	+13.2	84.3	33 46.8	+14.5	85.0	33 51.7	+15.7	85.6	33 56.0	+16.9	86.3	15
16	33 20.2	+7.7	80.5	33 29.8	+8.9	81.1	33 38.7	+10.1	81.8	33 46.9	+11.4	82.5	33 54.4	+12.6	83.1	34 01.3	+13.8	83.8	34 07.4	+15.1	84.5	34 12.9	+16.2	85.1	16
17	33 27.9	+7.0	79.3	33 38.7	+8.2	79.9	33 48.8	+9.5	80.6	33 58.3	+10.6	81.3	34 07.0	+11.9	81.9	34 15.1	+13.1	82.6	34 22.5	+14.3	83.3	34 29.1	+15.6	84.0	17
18	33 34.9	+6.3	78.1	33 46.9	+7.5	78.8	33 58.3	+8.7	79.4	34 08.9	+10.0	80.1	34 18.9	+11.2	80.8	34 28.2	+12.5	81.4	34 36.8	+13.7	82.1	34 44.7	+14.9	82.8	18
19	33 41.2	+5.6	76.9	33 54.4	+6.9	77.6	34 07.0	+8.1	78.2	34 18.9	+9.3	78.9	34 30.1	+10.6	79.6	34 40.7	+11.7	80.2	34 50.5	+13.0	80.9	34 59.6	+14.2	81.6	19
20	33 46.8	+4.9	75.7	34 01.3	+6.1	76.4	34 15.1	+7.4	77.0	34 28.2	+8.6	77.7	34 40.7	+9.8	78.4	34 52.4	+11.1	79.0	35 03.5	+12.2	79.7	35 13.8	+13.5	80.4	20
21	33 51.7	+4.3	74.5	34 07.4	+5.5	75.2	34 22.5	+6.6	75.8	34 36.8	+7.9	76.5	34 50.5	+9.1	77.2	35 03.5	+10.3	77.8	35 15.7	+11.6	78.5	35 27.3	+12.8	79.2	21
22	33 56.0	+3.5	73.3	34 12.9	+4.7	74.0	34 29.1	+6.0	74.6	34 44.7	+7.2	75.3	34 59.6	+8.4	76.0	35 13.8	+9.6	76.6	35 27.3	+10.8	77.3	35 40.1	+12.1	78.0	22
23	33 59.5	+2.8	72.1	34 17.6	+4.0	72.8	34 35.1	+5.2	73.4	34 51.9	+6.4	74.1	35 08.0	+7.6	74.8	35 23.4	+8.9	75.4	35 38.1	+10.2	76.1	35 52.2	+11.3	76.8	23
24	34 02.3	+2.1	70.9	34 21.6	+3.3	71.5	34 40.3	+4.5	72.2	34 58.3	+5.7	72.9	35 15.6	+7.0	73.5	35 32.3	+8.2	74.2	35 48.3	+9.4	74.9	36 03.5	+10.6	75.6	24
25	34 04.4	+1.4	69.7	34 24.9	+2.6	70.3	34 44.8	+3.8	71.0	35 04.0	+5.0	71.6	35 22.6	+6.2	72.3	35 40.5	+7.4	73.0	35 57.7	+8.6	73.7	36 14.1	+9.9	74.4	25
26	34 05.8	+0.7	68.5	34 27.5	+1.9	69.1	34 48.6	+3.0	69.8	35 09.0	+4.3	70.4	35 28.8	+5.4	71.1	35 47.9	+6.6	71.8	36 06.3	+7.9	72.5	36 24.0	+9.1	73.2	26
27	34 06.5	0.0	67.3	34 29.4	+1.2	67.9	34 51.6	+2.4	68.6	35 13.3	+3.5	69.2	35 34.2	+4.8	69.9	35 54.5	+6.0	70.6	36 14.2	+7.1	71.2	36 33.1	+8.4	71.9	27
28	34 06.5	−0.7	66.1	34 30.6	+0.4	66.7	34 54.0	+1.6	67.3	35 16.8	+2.8	68.0	35 39.0	+3.9	68.6	36 00.5	+5.1	69.3	36 21.3	+6.4	70.0	36 41.5	+7.6	70.7	28
29	34 05.8	−1.4	64.9	34 31.0	−0.3	65.5	34 55.6	+0.9	66.1	35 19.6	+2.0	66.8	35 42.9	+3.2	67.4	36 05.6	+4.4	68.1	36 27.7	+5.6	68.8	36 49.1	+6.8	69.5	29
30	34 04.4	−2.2	63.7	34 30.7	−1.0	64.3	34 56.5	+0.1	64.9	35 21.6	+1.3	65.5	35 46.1	+2.5	66.2	36 10.0	+3.7	66.9	36 33.3	+4.8	67.5	36 55.9	+6.0	68.2	30
31	34 02.2	−2.8	62.5	34 29.7	−1.7	63.1	34 56.6	−0.6	63.7	35 22.9	+0.6	64.3	35 48.6	+1.7	65.0	36 13.7	+2.9	65.6	36 38.1	+4.1	66.3	37 01.9	+5.3	67.0	31
32	33 59.4	−3.5	61.2	34 28.0	−2.5	61.8	34 56.0	−1.3	62.5	35 23.5	−0.2	63.1	35 50.3	+1.0	63.7	36 16.6	+2.1	64.4	36 42.2	+3.3	65.1	37 07.2	+4.5	65.7	32
33	33 55.9	−4.3	60.0	34 25.5	−3.1	60.6	34 54.7	−2.1	61.2	35 23.3	−1.0	61.9	35 51.3	+0.2	62.5	36 18.7	+1.3	63.1	36 45.5	+2.5	63.8	37 11.7	+3.6	64.5	33
34	33 51.6	−4.9	58.8	34 22.4	−3.9	59.4	34 52.6	−2.7	60.0	35 22.3	−1.6	60.6	35 51.5	−0.6	61.3	36 20.0	+0.6	61.9	36 48.0	+1.7	62.6	37 15.3	+2.9	63.2	34
35	33 46.7	−5.7	57.6	34 18.5	−4.6	58.2	34 49.9	−3.5	58.8	35 20.7	−2.5	59.4	35 50.9	−1.3	60.0	36 20.6	−0.2	60.7	36 49.7	+1.0	61.3	37 18.2	+2.1	62.0	35
36	33 41.0	−6.3	56.4	34 13.9	−5.3	57.0	34 46.4	−4.3	57.6	35 18.2	−3.1	58.2	35 49.6	−2.1	58.8	36 20.4	−0.9	59.4	36 50.7	+0.1	60.1	37 20.3	+1.3	60.7	36
37	33 34.7	−7.0	55.3	34 08.6	−5.9	55.8	34 42.1	−4.9	56.4	35 15.1	−3.9	57.0	35 47.5	−2.8	57.6	36 19.5	−1.8	58.2	36 50.8	−0.6	58.8	37 21.6	+0.5	59.5	37
38	33 27.7	−7.7	54.1	34 02.7	−6.7	54.6	34 37.2	−5.7	55.2	35 11.2	−4.6	55.7	35 44.7	−3.6	56.3	36 17.7	−2.5	56.9	36 50.2	−1.4	57.6	37 22.1	−0.3	58.2	38
39	33 20.0	−8.4	52.9	33 56.0	−7.4	53.4	34 31.5	−6.4	54.0	35 06.6	−5.4	54.5	35 41.1	−4.3	55.1	36 15.2	−3.2	55.7	36 48.8	−2.2	56.3	37 21.8	−1.1	56.9	39
40	33 11.6	−9.1	51.7	33 48.6	−8.1	52.2	34 25.1	−7.1	52.7	35 01.2	−6.1	53.3	35 36.8	−5.0	53.9	36 12.0	−4.1	54.5	36 46.6	−3.0	55.1	37 20.7	−1.9	55.7	40
41	33 02.5	−9.7	50.5	33 40.5	−8.8	51.0	34 18.0	−7.8	51.5	34 55.1	−6.8	52.1	35 31.8	−5.9	52.6	36 07.9	−4.8	53.2	36 43.6	−3.8	53.8	37 18.8	−2.7	54.4	41
42	32 52.8	−10.3	49.3	33 31.7	−9.4	49.8	34 10.2	−8.5	50.3	34 48.3	−7.5	50.9	35 25.9	−6.5	51.4	36 03.1	−5.5	52.0	36 39.8	−4.5	52.6	37 16.1	−3.5	53.2	42
43	32 42.5	−11.1	48.2	33 22.3	−10.1	48.6	34 01.7	−9.1	49.2	34 40.8	−8.3	49.7	35 19.4	−7.3	50.2	35 57.6	−6.3	50.8	36 35.3	−5.3	51.3	37 12.6	−4.3	51.9	43
44	32 31.4	−11.6	47.0	33 12.2	−10.8	47.5	33 52.6	−9.9	48.0	34 32.5	−8.9	48.5	35 12.1	−8.0	49.0	35 51.3	−7.1	49.5	36 30.0	−6.1	50.1	37 08.3	−5.1	50.7	44
45	32 19.8	−12.3	45.8	33 01.4	−11.4	46.3	33 42.7	−10.6	46.8	34 23.6	−9.6	47.3	35 04.1	−8.7	47.8	35 44.2	−7.8	48.3	36 23.9	−6.8	48.9	37 03.2	−5.9	49.4	45
46	32 07.5	−12.9	44.7	32 50.0	−12.1	45.1	33 32.1	−11.2	45.6	34 14.0	−10.4	46.1	34 55.4	−9.5	46.6	35 36.4	−8.5	47.1	36 17.1	−7.6	47.6	36 57.3	−6.6	48.2	46
47	31 54.6	−13.6	43.5	32 37.9	−12.7	44.0	33 20.9	−11.9	44.4	34 03.6	−11.0	44.9	34 45.9	−10.1	45.4	35 27.9	−9.2	45.9	36 09.5	−8.3	46.4	36 50.7	−7.4	46.9	47
48	31 41.0	−14.2	42.4	32 25.2	−13.4	42.8	33 09.0	−12.5	43.2	33 52.6	−11.7	43.7	34 35.8	−10.8	44.2	35 18.7	−10.0	44.7	36 01.2	−9.1	45.2	36 43.3	−8.2	45.7	48
49	31 26.8	−14.7	41.2	32 11.8	−14.0	41.6	32 56.5	−13.2	42.1	33 40.9	−12.4	42.5	34 25.0	−11.6	43.0	35 08.7	−10.7	43.5	35 52.1	−9.9	43.9	36 35.1	−9.0	44.5	49
50	31 12.1	−15.4	40.1	31 57.8	−14.6	40.5	32 43.3	−13.8	40.9	33 28.5	−13.0	41.3	34 13.4	−12.2	41.8	34 58.0	−11.4	42.2	35 42.2	−10.5	42.7	36 26.1	−9.7	43.2	50
51	30 56.7	−15.9	39.0	31 43.2	−15.2	39.4	32 29.5	−14.5	39.8	33 15.5	−13.7	40.2	34 01.2	−12.9	40.6	34 46.6	−12.1	41.1	35 31.7	−11.3	41.5	36 16.4	−10.4	42.0	51
52	30 40.8	−16.5	37.9	31 28.0	−15.8	38.2	32 15.0	−15.0	38.6	33 01.8	−14.3	39.0	33 48.3	−13.6	39.4	34 34.5	−12.8	39.9	35 20.4	−12.0	40.3	36 06.0	−11.2	40.8	52
53	30 24.3	−17.1	36.7	31 12.2	−16.4	37.1	32 00.0	−15.7	37.5	32 47.5	−15.0	37.9	33 34.7	−14.2	38.3	34 21.7	−13.5	38.7	35 08.4	−12.7	39.1	35 54.8	−11.9	39.6	53
54	30 07.2	−17.7	35.6	30 55.8	−16.9	36.0	31 44.3	−16.3	36.3	32 32.5	−15.6	36.7	33 20.5	−14.9	37.1	34 08.2	−14.1	37.5	34 55.7	−13.4	37.9	35 42.9	−12.6	38.4	54
55	29 49.5	−18.2	34.5	30 38.9	−17.6	34.9	31 28.0	−16.9	35.2	32 16.9	−16.2	35.6	33 05.6	−15.5	35.9	33 54.1	−14.8	36.3	34 42.3	−14.1	36.7	35 30.3	−13.4	37.2	55
56	29 31.3	−18.7	33.4	30 21.3	−18.1	33.7	31 11.1	−17.4	34.1	32 00.7	−16.8	34.4	32 50.1	−16.1	34.8	33 39.3	−15.5	35.2	34 28.2	−14.8	35.5	35 16.9	−14.0	36.0	56
57	29 12.6	−19.2	32.3	30 03.2	−18.6	32.6	30 53.7	−18.1	33.0	31 43.9	−17.4	33.3	32 34.0	−16.8	33.6	33 23.8	−16.1	34.0	34 13.4	−15.4	34.4	35 02.9	−14.8	34.8	57
58	28 53.4	−19.8	31.3	29 44.6	−19.2	31.5	30 35.6	−18.6	31.8	31 26.5	−18.0	32.2	32 17.2	−17.4	32.5	33 07.7	−16.7	32.8	33 58.0	−16.1	33.2	34 48.1	−15.4	33.6	58
59	28 33.6	−20.3	30.2	29 25.4	−19.7	30.5	30 17.0	−19.1	30.7	31 08.5	−18.5	31.1	31 59.8	−17.9	31.4	32 51.0	−17.4	31.7	33 41.9	−16.7	32.0	34 32.7	−16.1	32.4	59
60	28 13.3	−20.8	29.1	29 05.7	−20.3	29.4	29 57.9	−19.7	29.7	30 50.0	−19.2	29.9	31 41.9	−18.6	30.2	32 33.6	−17.9	30.6	33 25.2	−17.4	30.9	34 16.6	−16.8	31.2	60
61	27 52.5	−21.2	28.0	28 45.4	−20.7	28.3	29 38.2	−20.2	28.6	30 30.8	−19.6	28.8	31 23.3	−19.1	29.1	32 15.7	−18.6	29.4	33 07.8	−18.0	29.8	33 59.8	−17.4	30.1	61
62	27 31.3	−21.7	27.0	28 24.7	−21.2	27.2	29 18.0	−20.7	27.5	30 11.2	−20.3	27.7	31 04.2	−19.7	28.0	31 57.1	−19.2	28.3	32 49.8	−18.6	28.6	33 42.4	−18.0	28.9	62
63	27 09.6	−22.2	25.9	28 03.5	−21.8	26.2	28 57.3	−21.3	26.4	29 50.9	−20.7	26.7	30 44.5	−20.3	26.9	31 37.9	−19.7	27.2	32 31.2	−19.2	27.5	33 24.4	−18.7	27.8	63
64	26 47.4	−22.7	24.9	27 41.7	−22.2	25.1	28 36.0	−21.7	25.3	29 30.2	−21.3	25.6	30 24.2	−20.7	25.8	31 18.2	−20.3	26.1	32 12.0	−19.8	26.4	33 05.7	−19.3	26.6	64
65	26 24.7	−23.1	23.9	27 19.5	−22.6	24.1	28 14.3	−22.3	24.3	29 08.9	−21.8	24.5	30 03.5	−21.4	24.7	30 57.9	−20.9	25.0	31 52.2	−20.4	25.2	32 46.4	−19.9	25.5	65
66	26 01.6	−23.5	22.8	26 56.9	−23.2	23.0	27 52.0	−22.7	23.2	28 47.1	−22.2	23.4	29 42.1	−21.8	23.7	30 37.0	−21.4	23.9	31 31.8	−20.9	24.1	32 26.5	−20.4	24.4	66
67	25 38.1	−24.0	21.8	26 33.7	−23.5	22.0	27 29.3	−23.1	22.2	28 24.9	−22.8	22.4	29 20.3	−22.4	22.6	30 15.6	−21.9	22.8	31 10.9	−21.5	23.0	32 06.1	−21.1	23.3	67
68	25 14.1	−24.4	20.8	26 10.2	−24.0	21.0	27 06.2	−23.7	21.1	28 02.1	−23.2	21.3	28 57.9	−22.8	21.5	29 53.7	−22.4	21.7	30 49.4	−22.0	22.0	31 45.0	−21.6	22.2	68
69	24 49.7	−24.7	19.8	25 46.2	−24.4	19.9	26 42.5	−24.0	20.1	27 38.9	−23.7	20.3	28 35.1	−23.3	20.5	29 31.3	−23.0	20.7	30 27.4	−22.6	20.9	31 23.4	−22.2	21.1	69
70	24 25.0	−25.2	18.8	25 21.8	−24.9	18.9	26 18.5	−24.5	19.1	27 15.2	−24.2	19.3	28 11.8	−23.8	19.4	29 08.3	−23.4	19.6	30 04.8	−23.1	19.8	31 01.2	−22.7	20.0	70
71	23 59.8	−25.5	17.8	24 56.9	−25.2	17.9	25 54.0	−24.9	18.1	26 51.0	−24.6	18.2	27 48.0	−24.3	18.4	28 44.9	−24.0	18.6	29 41.7	−23.6	18.7	30 38.5	−23.2	18.9	71
72	23 34.3	−26.0	16.8	24 31.7	−25.7	16.9	25 29.1	−25.4	17.1	26 26.4	−25.0	17.2	27 23.7	−24.7	17.4	28 20.9	−24.4	17.5	29 18.1	−24.1	17.7	30 15.3	−23.8	17.9	72
73	23 08.3	−26.3	15.8	24 06.0	−26.0	15.9	25 03.7	−25.7	16.1	26 01.4	−25.5	16.2	26 59.0	−25.2	16.3	27 56.5	−24.9	16.5	28 54.0	−24.5	16.6	29 51.5	−24.3	16.8	73
74	22 42.0	−26.6	14.8	23 40.0	−26.3	14.9	24 38.0	−26.1	15.1	25 35.9	−25.9	15.2	26 33.8	−25.6	15.3	27 31.6	−25.3	15.5	28 29.5	−25.1	15.6	29 27.2	−24.7	15.7	74
75	22 15.4	−27.0	13.9	23 13.7	−26.8	14.0	24 11.9	−26.5	14.1	25 10.0	−26.2	14.2	26 08.2	−26.0	14.3	27 06.3	−25.7	14.4	28 04.4	−25.5	14.6	29 02.5	−25.3	14.7	75
76	21 48.4	−27.3	12.9	22 46.9	−27.1	13.0	23 45.4	−26.9	13.1	24 43.8	−26.7	13.2	25 42.2	−26.4	13.3	26 40.6	−26.2	13.4	27 38.9	−25.9	13.5	28 37.2	−25.7	13.7	76
77	21 21.1	−27.6	11.9	22 19.8	−27.4	12.0	23 18.5	−27.3	12.1	24 17.1	−27.0	12.2	25 15.8	−26.9	12.3	26 14.4	−26.6	12.4	27 13.0	−26.4	12.5	28 11.5	−26.1	12.6	77
78	20 53.5	−28.0	11.0	21 52.4	−27.8	11.1	22 51.2	−27.5	11.2	23 50.1	−27.4	11.2	24 48.9	−27.2	11.3	25 47.8	−27.0	11.4	26 46.6	−26.8	11.5	27 45.4	−26.7	11.6	78
79	20 25.5	−28.2	10.1	21 24.6	−28.1	10.1	22 23.7	−28.0	10.2	23 22.7	−27.7	10.3	24 21.7	−27.5	10.3	25 20.8	−27.4	10.4	26 19.8	−27.3	10.5	27 18.7	−27.0	10.6	79
80	19 57.3	−28.6	9.1	20 56.5	−28.4	9.2	21 55.7	−28.2	9.2	22 55.0	−28.1	9.3	23 54.2	−28.0	9.4	24 53.4	−27.8	9.4	25 52.5	−27.6	9.5	26 51.7	−27.5	9.6	80
81	19 28.7	−28.8	8.2	20 28.1	−28.7	8.2	21 27.5	−28.6	8.3	22 26.9	−28.5	8.3	23 26.2	−28.3	8.4	24 25.6	−28.2	8.5	25 24.9	−28.0	8.5	26 24.2	−27.8	8.6	81
82	18 59.9	−29.1	7.2	19 59.4	−29.0	7.3	20 58.9	−28.9	7.3	21 58.4	−28.7	7.4	22 57.9	−28.6	7.4	23 57.4	−28.5	7.5	24 56.9	−28.4	7.6	25 56.4	−28.3	7.6	82
83	18 30.8	−29.4	6.3	19 30.4	−29.3	6.4	20 30.0	−29.1	6.4	21 29.7	−29.1	6.4	22 29.3	−29.0	6.5	23 28.9	−28.9	6.5	24 28.5	−28.8	6.6	25 28.1	−28.7	6.6	83
84	18 01.4	−29.6	5.4	19 01.1	−29.5	5.4	20 00.9	−29.5	5.5	21 00.6	−29.4	5.5	22 00.3	−29.3	5.5	23 00.0	−29.2	5.6	23 59.7	−29.1	5.6	24 59.4	−29.0	5.7	84
85	17 31.8	−29.9	4.5	18 31.6	−29.8	4.5	19 31.4	−29.8	4.5	20 31.2	−29.7	4.6	21 31.0	−29.6	4.6	22 30.8	−29.5	4.6	23 30.6	−29.5	4.7	24 30.4	−29.4	4.7	85
86	17 01.9	−30.2	3.6	18 01.8	−30.1	3.6	19 01.6	−30.0	3.6	20 01.5	−30.0	3.6	21 01.4	−29.9	3.7	22 01.3	−29.9	3.7	23 01.1	−29.8	3.7	24 01.0	−29.7	3.8	86
87	16 31.7	−30.3	2.7	17 31.7	−30.3	2.7	18 31.6	−30.3	2.7	19 31.5	−30.2	2.7	20 31.5	−30.2	2.7	21 31.4	−30.2	2.8	22 31.3	−30.1	2.8	23 31.3	−30.1	2.8	87
88	16 01.4	−30.6	1.8	17 01.4	−30.6	1.8	18 01.3	−30.5	1.8	19 01.3	−30.5	1.8	20 01.3	−30.5	1.8	21 01.2	−30.4	1.8	22 01.2	−30.4	1.8	23 01.2	−30.5	1.9	88
89	15 30.8	−30.8	0.9	16 30.8	−30.8	0.9	17 30.8	−30.8	0.9	18 30.8	−30.8	0.9	19 30.8	−30.8	0.9	20 30.8	−30.8	0.9	21 30.8	−30.8	0.9	22 30.7	−30.7	0.9	89
90	15 00.0	−31.0	0.0	16 00.0	−31.0	0.0	17 00.0	−31.0	0.0	18 00.0	−31.0	0.0	19 00.0	−31.0	0.0	20 00.0	−31.0	0.0	21 00.0	−31.0	0.0	22 00.0	−31.1	0.0	90
	15°			16°			17°			18°			19°			20°			21°			22°			

59°, 301° L.H.A. LATITUDE SAME NAME AS DECLINATION

120

LATITUDE **CONTRARY** NAME TO DECLINATION L.H.A. 59°, 301°

Dec.	15°			16°			17°			18°			19°			20°			21°			22°			Dec.
	Hc	d	Z	Hc	d	Z	Hc	d	Z	Hc	d	Z	Hc	d	Z	Hc	d	Z	Hc	d	Z	Hc	d	Z	
°	° ′	′	°	° ′	′	°	° ′	′	°	° ′	′	°	° ′	′	°	° ′	′	°	° ′	′	°	° ′	′	°	°
0	29 50.0	−18.1	98.8	29 40.5	−19.3	99.4	29 30.4	−20.4	100.0	29 19.8	−21.6	100.5	29 08.5	−22.6	101.1	28 56.7	−23.7	101.6	28 44.4	−24.8	102.2	28 31.5	−25.8	102.7	0
1	29 31.9	−18.7	99.9	29 21.2	−19.8	100.5	29 10.0	−20.9	101.0	28 58.2	−22.0	101.6	28 45.9	−23.1	102.1	28 33.0	−24.1	102.7	28 19.6	−25.2	103.2	28 05.7	−26.3	103.7	1
2	29 13.2	−19.3	101.0	29 01.4	−20.3	101.6	28 49.1	−21.5	102.1	28 36.2	−22.5	102.6	28 22.8	−23.6	103.2	28 08.9	−24.7	103.7	27 54.4	−25.7	104.2	27 39.4	−26.7	104.7	2
3	28 53.9	−19.7	102.1	28 41.1	−20.9	102.6	28 27.6	−21.9	103.2	28 13.7	−23.0	103.7	27 59.2	−24.0	104.2	27 44.2	−25.1	104.7	27 28.7	−26.1	105.2	27 12.7	−27.2	105.7	3
4	28 34.2	−20.3	103.2	28 20.2	−21.3	103.7	28 05.7	−22.4	104.2	27 50.7	−23.5	104.7	27 35.2	−24.5	105.3	27 19.1	−25.5	105.8	27 02.6	−26.6	106.3	26 45.5	−27.5	106.7	4
5	28 13.9	−20.8	104.3	27 58.9	−21.9	104.8	27 43.3	−22.9	105.3	27 27.2	−23.9	105.8	27 10.7	−25.0	106.3	26 53.6	−26.0	106.8	26 36.0	−26.9	107.3	26 18.0	−28.0	107.7	5
6	27 53.1	−21.2	105.3	27 37.0	−22.3	105.8	27 20.4	−23.3	106.3	27 03.3	−24.4	106.8	26 45.7	−25.4	107.3	26 27.6	−26.4	107.8	26 09.1	−27.4	108.3	25 50.0	−28.3	108.7	6
7	27 31.9	−21.7	106.4	27 14.7	−22.7	106.9	26 57.1	−23.8	107.4	26 38.9	−24.8	107.8	26 20.3	−25.8	108.3	26 01.2	−26.8	108.8	25 41.7	−27.8	109.2	25 21.7	−28.8	109.7	7
8	27 10.2	−22.2	107.4	26 52.0	−23.3	107.9	26 33.3	−24.3	108.4	26 14.1	−25.2	108.9	25 54.5	−26.2	109.3	25 34.4	−27.2	109.8	25 13.9	−28.2	110.2	24 52.9	−29.1	110.7	8
9	26 48.0	−22.6	108.5	26 28.7	−23.6	108.9	26 09.0	−24.6	109.4	25 48.9	−25.7	109.9	25 28.3	−26.7	110.3	25 07.2	−27.6	110.8	24 45.7	−28.5	111.2	24 23.8	−29.5	111.6	9
10	26 25.4	−23.1	109.5	26 05.1	−24.1	110.0	25 44.4	−25.1	110.4	25 23.2	−26.0	110.9	25 01.6	−27.0	111.3	24 39.6	−28.0	111.7	24 17.2	−28.9	112.2	23 54.3	−29.8	112.6	10
11	26 02.3	−23.6	110.5	25 41.0	−24.5	111.0	25 19.3	−25.5	111.4	24 57.2	−26.5	111.9	24 34.6	−27.4	112.3	24 11.6	−28.3	112.7	23 48.3	−29.3	113.1	23 24.5	−30.2	113.5	11
12	25 38.7	−23.9	111.6	25 16.5	−24.9	112.0	24 53.8	−25.9	112.4	24 30.7	−26.8	112.9	24 07.2	−27.8	113.3	23 43.3	−28.7	113.7	23 19.0	−29.6	114.1	22 54.3	−30.5	114.5	12
13	25 14.8	−24.4	112.6	24 51.6	−25.4	113.0	24 27.9	−26.3	113.4	24 03.9	−27.3	113.8	23 39.4	−28.1	114.2	23 14.6	−29.0	114.6	22 49.4	−29.9	115.0	22 23.8	−30.8	115.4	13
14	24 50.4	−24.7	113.6	24 26.2	−25.7	114.0	24 01.6	−26.6	114.4	23 36.6	−27.5	114.8	23 11.3	−28.5	115.2	22 45.6	−29.4	115.6	22 19.5	−30.3	116.0	21 53.0	−31.1	116.3	14
15	24 25.7	−25.2	114.6	24 00.5	−26.1	115.0	23 35.0	−27.0	115.4	23 09.1	−27.9	115.8	22 42.8	−28.8	116.2	22 16.2	−29.7	116.5	21 49.2	−30.6	116.9	21 21.9	−31.4	117.2	15
16	24 00.5	−25.5	115.6	23 34.4	−26.4	116.0	23 08.0	−27.4	116.4	22 41.2	−28.3	116.7	22 14.0	−29.2	117.1	21 46.5	−30.0	117.5	21 18.6	−30.8	117.8	20 50.5	−31.7	118.2	16
17	23 35.0	−25.9	116.6	23 08.0	−26.8	117.0	22 40.6	−27.7	117.3	22 12.9	−28.6	117.7	21 44.8	−29.4	118.1	21 16.5	−30.4	118.4	20 47.8	−31.2	118.7	20 18.8	−32.0	119.1	17
18	23 09.1	−26.3	117.5	22 41.2	−27.2	117.9	22 12.9	−28.1	118.3	21 44.3	−28.9	118.6	21 15.4	−29.8	119.0	20 46.1	−30.6	119.3	20 16.6	−31.4	119.6	19 46.8	−32.3	120.0	18
19	22 42.8	−26.6	118.5	22 14.0	−27.5	118.9	21 44.8	−28.3	119.2	21 15.4	−29.3	119.6	20 45.6	−30.1	119.9	20 15.5	−30.9	120.2	19 45.2	−31.8	120.6	19 14.5	−32.5	120.9	19
20	22 16.2	−27.0	119.5	21 46.5	−27.9	119.8	21 16.5	−28.7	120.2	20 46.1	−29.5	120.5	20 15.5	−30.3	120.8	19 44.6	−31.2	121.2	19 13.4	−31.9	121.5	18 42.0	−32.8	121.7	20
21	21 49.2	−27.3	120.5	21 18.6	−28.1	120.8	20 47.8	−29.0	121.1	20 16.6	−29.8	121.4	19 45.2	−30.7	121.8	19 13.4	−31.4	122.1	18 41.5	−32.3	122.4	18 09.2	−33.0	122.6	21
22	21 21.9	−27.6	121.4	20 50.5	−28.5	121.7	20 18.8	−29.3	122.1	19 46.8	−30.1	122.4	19 14.5	−30.9	122.7	18 42.0	−31.7	123.0	18 09.2	−32.4	123.2	17 36.2	−33.2	123.5	22
23	20 54.3	−28.0	122.4	20 22.0	−28.8	122.7	19 49.5	−29.6	123.0	19 16.7	−30.4	123.3	18 43.6	−31.2	123.6	18 10.3	−31.9	123.9	17 36.8	−32.7	124.1	17 03.0	−33.5	124.4	23
24	20 26.3	−28.2	123.3	19 53.2	−29.0	123.6	19 19.9	−29.9	123.9	18 46.3	−30.7	124.2	18 12.4	−31.4	124.5	17 38.4	−32.2	124.7	17 04.1	−33.0	125.0	16 29.5	−33.6	125.2	24
25	19 58.1	−28.6	124.3	19 24.2	−29.4	124.5	18 50.0	−30.1	124.8	18 15.6	−30.9	125.1	17 41.0	−31.6	125.4	17 06.2	−32.4	125.6	16 31.1	−33.1	125.9	15 55.9	−33.9	126.1	25
26	19 29.5	−28.8	125.2	18 54.8	−29.6	125.5	18 19.9	−30.4	125.7	17 44.7	−31.1	126.0	17 09.4	−31.9	126.3	16 33.8	−32.7	126.5	15 58.0	−33.4	126.7	15 22.0	−34.1	127.0	26
27	19 00.7	−29.1	126.1	18 25.2	−29.8	126.4	17 49.5	−30.6	126.7	17 13.6	−31.4	126.9	16 37.5	−32.2	127.1	16 01.1	−32.8	127.4	15 24.6	−33.5	127.6	14 47.9	−34.3	127.8	27
28	18 31.6	−29.4	127.0	17 55.4	−30.2	127.3	17 18.9	−30.9	127.6	16 42.2	−31.6	127.8	16 05.3	−32.3	128.0	15 28.3	−33.1	128.3	14 51.1	−33.8	128.5	14 13.6	−34.4	128.7	28
29	18 02.2	−29.6	128.0	17 25.2	−30.4	128.2	16 48.0	−31.1	128.5	16 10.6	−31.8	128.7	15 33.0	−32.5	128.9	14 55.2	−33.2	129.1	14 17.3	−33.9	129.3	13 39.2	−34.6	129.5	29
30	17 32.6	−29.9	128.9	16 54.8	−30.6	129.1	16 16.9	−31.3	129.3	15 38.8	−32.1	129.6	15 00.5	−32.8	129.8	14 22.0	−33.4	130.0	13 43.4	−34.1	130.2	13 04.6	−34.8	130.4	30
31	17 02.7	−30.1	129.8	16 24.2	−30.8	130.0	15 45.6	−31.6	130.2	15 06.7	−32.2	130.4	14 27.7	−32.9	130.6	13 48.6	−33.6	130.8	13 09.3	−34.3	131.0	12 29.8	−34.9	131.2	31
32	16 32.6	−30.4	130.7	15 53.4	−31.1	130.9	15 14.0	−31.7	131.1	14 34.5	−32.4	131.3	13 54.8	−33.1	131.5	13 15.0	−33.8	131.7	12 35.0	−34.4	131.9	11 54.9	−35.1	132.0	32
33	16 02.2	−30.5	131.6	15 22.3	−31.2	131.8	14 42.3	−32.0	132.0	14 02.1	−32.7	132.2	13 21.7	−33.3	132.4	12 41.2	−33.9	132.5	12 00.6	−34.6	132.7	11 19.8	−35.2	132.8	33
34	15 31.7	−30.8	132.5	14 51.1	−31.5	132.7	14 10.3	−32.1	132.9	13 29.4	−32.8	133.0	12 48.4	−33.4	133.2	12 07.3	−34.1	133.4	11 26.0	−34.7	133.5	10 44.6	−35.3	133.7	34
35	15 00.9	−31.0	133.4	14 19.6	−31.7	133.6	13 38.2	−32.3	133.7	12 56.6	−32.9	133.9	12 15.0	−33.6	134.1	11 33.2	−34.2	134.2	10 51.3	−34.9	134.4	10 09.3	−35.5	134.5	35
36	14 29.9	−31.2	134.3	13 47.9	−31.8	134.4	13 05.9	−32.5	134.6	12 23.7	−33.1	134.8	11 41.4	−33.8	134.9	10 59.0	−34.4	135.1	10 16.4	−34.9	135.2	9 33.8	−35.5	135.3	36
37	13 58.7	−31.4	135.1	13 16.1	−32.0	135.3	12 33.4	−32.7	135.5	11 50.6	−33.3	135.6	11 07.6	−33.9	135.8	10 24.6	−34.5	135.9	9 41.5	−35.1	136.0	8 58.3	−35.7	136.1	37
38	13 27.3	−31.6	136.0	12 44.1	−32.2	136.2	12 00.7	−32.8	136.3	11 17.3	−33.4	136.5	10 33.7	−34.0	136.6	9 50.1	−34.6	136.7	9 06.4	−35.2	136.8	8 22.6	−35.8	136.9	38
39	12 55.7	−31.7	136.9	12 11.9	−32.4	137.0	11 27.9	−32.9	137.2	10 43.9	−33.6	137.3	9 59.7	−34.1	137.4	9 15.5	−34.7	137.6	8 31.2	−35.3	137.7	7 46.8	−35.9	137.8	39
40	12 24.0	−31.9	137.8	11 39.5	−32.5	137.9	10 55.0	−33.1	138.0	10 10.3	−33.7	138.2	9 25.6	−34.3	138.3	8 40.8	−34.9	138.4	7 55.9	−35.4	138.5	7 10.9	−35.9	138.6	40
41	11 52.1	−32.1	138.6	11 07.0	−32.6	138.8	10 21.9	−33.3	138.9	9 36.6	−33.8	139.0	8 51.3	−34.4	139.1	8 05.9	−34.9	139.2	7 20.5	−35.5	139.3	6 35.0	−36.1	139.4	41
42	11 20.0	−32.2	139.5	10 34.4	−32.8	139.6	9 48.6	−33.3	139.7	9 02.8	−33.9	139.8	8 16.9	−34.4	139.9	7 31.0	−35.0	140.0	6 45.0	−35.6	140.1	5 58.9	−36.1	140.2	42
43	10 47.8	−32.3	140.3	10 01.6	−32.9	140.5	9 15.3	−33.5	140.6	8 28.9	−34.0	140.7	7 42.5	−34.6	140.8	6 56.0	−35.1	140.8	6 09.4	−35.6	140.9	5 22.8	−36.2	141.0	43
44	10 15.5	−32.5	141.2	9 28.7	−33.1	141.3	8 41.8	−33.6	141.4	7 54.9	−34.2	141.5	7 07.9	−34.7	141.6	6 20.8	−35.1	141.7	5 33.8	−35.7	141.7	4 46.6	−36.2	141.8	44
45	9 43.0	−32.7	142.1	8 55.6	−33.1	142.2	8 08.2	−33.7	142.2	7 20.7	−34.2	142.3	6 33.2	−34.7	142.4	5 45.7	−35.3	142.5	4 58.1	−35.8	142.5	4 10.4	−36.2	142.6	45
46	9 10.3	−32.7	142.9	8 22.5	−33.3	143.0	7 34.5	−33.8	143.1	6 46.5	−34.3	143.2	5 58.5	−34.8	143.2	5 10.4	−35.3	143.3	4 22.3	−35.8	143.3	3 34.2	−36.4	143.4	46
47	8 37.6	−32.8	143.8	7 49.2	−33.4	143.8	7 00.7	−33.8	143.9	6 12.2	−34.4	144.0	5 23.7	−34.9	144.0	4 35.1	−35.4	144.1	3 46.5	−35.9	144.1	2 57.8	−36.3	144.2	47
48	8 04.8	−33.0	144.6	7 15.8	−33.4	144.7	6 26.9	−34.0	144.7	5 37.8	−34.4	144.8	4 48.8	−34.9	144.9	3 59.7	−35.4	144.9	3 10.6	−35.9	144.9	2 21.5	−36.4	145.0	48
49	7 31.8	−33.0	145.4	6 42.4	−33.6	145.5	5 52.9	−34.0	145.6	5 03.4	−34.5	145.6	4 13.9	−35.0	145.7	3 24.3	−35.5	145.7	2 34.7	−35.9	145.7	1 45.1	−36.4	145.8	49
50	6 58.8	−33.2	146.3	6 08.8	−33.6	146.3	5 18.9	−34.1	146.4	4 28.9	−34.6	146.4	3 38.9	−35.1	146.5	2 48.8	−35.5	146.5	1 58.8	−36.0	146.5	1 08.7	−36.4	146.6	50
51	6 25.6	−33.2	147.1	5 35.2	−33.7	147.2	4 44.8	−34.2	147.2	3 54.3	−34.6	147.3	3 03.8	−35.0	147.3	2 13.3	−35.5	147.3	1 22.8	−35.9	147.3	0 32.3	−36.4	147.4	51
52	5 52.4	−33.3	148.0	5 01.5	−33.7	148.0	4 10.6	−34.2	148.1	3 19.7	−34.6	148.1	2 28.8	−35.1	148.1	1 37.8	−35.5	148.1	0 46.9	−36.0	148.1	0 04.1	+36.4	31.9	52
53	5 19.1	−33.3	148.8	4 27.8	−33.8	148.8	3 36.4	−34.2	148.9	2 45.1	−34.7	148.9	1 53.7	−35.1	148.9	1 02.3	−35.6	148.9	0 10.9	−36.0	148.9	0 40.5	+36.4	31.1	53
54	4 45.8	−33.5	149.6	3 54.0	−33.9	149.7	3 02.2	−34.3	149.7	2 10.4	−34.7	149.7	1 18.6	−35.2	149.7	0 26.7	−35.5	149.7	0 25.1	+36.0	30.3	1 16.9	+36.4	30.3	54
55	4 12.3	−33.4	150.5	3 20.1	−33.9	150.5	2 27.9	−34.3	150.5	1 35.7	−34.8	150.5	0 43.4	−35.1	150.5	0 08.8	+35.6	29.4	1 01.1	+35.9	29.5	1 53.3	+36.4	29.5	55
56	3 38.9	−33.6	151.3	2 46.2	−33.9	151.3	1 53.6	−34.4	151.3	1 00.9	−34.7	151.4	0 08.3	−35.2	151.4	0 44.4	+35.5	28.6	1 37.0	+36.0	28.7	2 29.7	+36.3	28.7	56
57	3 05.3	−33.5	152.1	2 12.3	−34.0	152.1	1 19.2	−34.3	152.2	0 26.2	−34.8	152.2	0 26.9	+35.1	27.8	1 19.9	+35.6	27.8	2 13.0	+35.9	27.9	3 06.0	+36.3	27.9	57
58	2 31.8	−33.6	153.0	1 38.3	−33.9	153.0	0 44.9	−34.4	153.0	0 08.6	+34.7	27.0	1 02.0	+35.1	27.0	1 55.5	+35.5	27.0	2 48.9	+35.9	27.1	3 42.3	+36.3	27.1	58
59	1 58.2	−33.6	153.8	1 04.4	−34.0	153.8	0 10.5	−34.3	153.8	0 43.3	+34.7	26.2	1 37.1	+35.2	26.2	2 31.0	+35.4	26.2	3 24.8	+35.8	26.2	4 18.6	+36.2	26.3	59
60	1 24.6	−33.7	154.6	0 30.4	−34.0	154.6	0 23.8	+34.4	25.4	1 18.0	+34.8	25.4	2 12.3	+35.0	25.4	3 06.4	+35.5	25.4	4 00.6	+35.8	25.4	4 54.8	+36.2	25.5	60
61	0 50.9	−33.6	155.4	0 03.6	+34.0	24.6	0 58.2	+34.3	24.6	1 52.8	+34.7	24.6	2 47.3	+35.1	24.6	3 41.9	+35.4	24.6	4 36.4	+35.8	24.6	5 31.0	+36.1	24.7	61
62	0 17.3	−33.6	156.3	0 37.6	+34.0	23.7	1 32.5	+34.4	23.7	2 27.5	+34.6	23.8	3 22.4	+35.0	23.8	4 17.3	+35.3	23.8	5 12.2	+35.7	23.8	6 07.1	+36.0	23.9	62
63	0 16.3	+33.7	22.9	1 11.6	+34.0	22.9	2 06.9	+34.3	22.9	3 02.1	+34.7	22.9	3 57.4	+35.0	23.0	4 52.6	+35.3	23.0	5 47.9	+35.6	23.0	6 43.1	+35.9	23.1	63
64	0 50.0	+33.6	22.1	1 45.6	+33.9	22.1	2 41.2	+34.3	22.1	3 36.8	+34.6	22.1	4 32.4	+34.9	22.1	5 27.9	+35.2	22.2	6 23.5	+35.5	22.2	7 19.0	+35.9	22.3	64
65	1 23.6	+33.6	21.2	2 19.5	+34.0	21.3	3 15.5	+34.2	21.3	4 11.4	+34.5	21.3	5 07.3	+34.8	21.3	6 03.1	+35.2	21.4	6 59.0	+35.5	21.4	7 54.9	+35.7	21.5	65
66	1 57.2	+33.6	20.4	2 53.5	+33.9	20.4	3 49.7	+34.2	20.5	4 45.9	+34.5	20.5	5 42.1	+34.8	20.5	6 38.3	+35.1	20.5	7 34.5	+35.3	20.6	8 30.6	+35.7	20.6	66
67	2 30.8	+33.6	19.6	3 27.4	+33.8	19.6	4 23.9	+34.1	19.6	5 20.4	+34.4	19.7	6 16.9	+34.7	19.7	7 13.4	+34.9	19.7	8 09.8	+35.3	19.8	9 06.3	+35.5	19.8	67
68	3 04.4	+33.5	18.8	4 01.2	+33.8	18.8	4 58.0	+34.1	18.8	5 54.8	+34.3	18.8	6 51.6	+34.6	18.9	7 48.3	+34.9	18.9	8 45.1	+35.2	19.0	9 41.8	+35.5	19.0	68
69	3 37.9	+33.5	17.9	4 35.0	+33.7	17.9	5 32.1	+34.0	18.0	6 29.1	+34.3	18.0	7 26.2	+34.5	18.0	8 23.2	+34.8	18.1	9 20.3	+35.0	18.1	10 17.3	+35.3	18.2	69
70	4 11.4	+33.4	17.1	5 08.7	+33.7	17.1	6 06.1	+33.9	17.1	7 03.4	+34.2	17.2	8 00.7	+34.4	17.2	8 58.0	+34.7	17.3	9 55.3	+34.9	17.3	10 52.6	+35.2	17.4	70
71	4 44.8	+33.4	16.3	5 42.4	+33.6	16.3	6 40.0	+33.8	16.3	7 37.6	+34.0	16.4	8 35.1	+34.4	16.4	9 32.7	+34.5	16.4	10 30.2	+34.8	16.5	11 27.8	+35.0	16.5	71
72	5 18.2	+33.3	15.4	6 16.0	+33.5	15.5	7 13.8	+33.8	15.5	8 11.6	+34.0	15.5	9 09.5	+34.2	15.6	10 07.2	+34.5	15.6	11 05.0	+34.7	15.7	12 02.8	+34.9	15.7	72
73	5 51.5	+33.2	14.6	6 49.5	+33.5	14.6	7 47.6	+33.6	14.7	8 45.6	+33.9	14.7	9 43.7	+34.0	14.7	10 41.7	+34.3	14.8	11 39.7	+34.5	14.8	12 37.7	+34.7	14.9	73
74	6 24.7	+33.1	13.8	7 23.0	+33.3	13.8	8 21.2	+33.6	13.8	9 19.5	+33.7	13.9	10 17.7	+34.0	13.9	11 16.0	+34.1	13.9	12 14.2	+34.4	14.0	13 12.4	+34.6	14.0	74
75	6 57.8	+33.1	12.9	7 56.3	+33.2	12.9	8 54.8	+33.4	13.0	9 53.2	+33.7	13.0	10 51.7	+33.8	13.1	11 50.1	+34.0	13.1	12 48.6	+34.2	13.2	13 47.0	+34.4	13.2	75
76	7 30.9	+32.9	12.1	8 29.5	+33.2	12.1	9 28.2	+33.3	12.1	10 26.9	+33.5	12.2	11 25.5	+33.7	12.2	12 24.1	+33.9	12.3	13 22.8	+34.0	12.3	14 21.4	+34.2	12.4	76
77	8 03.8	+32.9	11.2	9 02.7	+33.0	11.3	10 01.5	+33.2	11.3	11 00.4	+33.3	11.3	11 59.2	+33.5	11.4	12 58.0	+33.7	11.4	13 56.8	+33.9	11.5	14 55.6	+34.0	11.5	77
78	8 36.7	+32.7	10.4	9 35.7	+32.9	10.4	10 34.7	+33.0	10.4	11 33.7	+33.2	10.5	12 32.7	+33.4	10.5	13 31.7	+33.5	10.6	14 30.7	+33.6	10.6	15 29.6	+33.9	10.7	78
79	9 09.4	+32.6	9.5	10 08.6	+32.7	9.6	11 07.7	+32.9	9.6	12 06.9	+33.0	9.6	13 06.1	+33.1	9.7	14 05.2	+33.3	9.7	15 04.3	+33.5	9.8	16 03.5	+33.6	9.8	79
80	9 42.0	+32.5	8.7	10 41.3	+32.7	8.7	11 40.6	+32.8	8.7	12 39.9	+32.9	8.8	13 39.2	+33.1	8.8	14 38.5	+33.2	8.8	15 37.8	+33.3	8.9	16 37.1	+33.4	8.9	80
81	10 14.5	+32.4	7.8	11 14.0	+32.4	7.9	12 13.4	+32.6	7.9	13 12.8	+32.7	7.9	14 12.3	+32.8	8.0	15 11.7	+32.9	8.0	16 11.1	+33.1	8.0	17 10.5	+33.2	8.1	81
82	10 46.9	+32.2	7.0	11 46.4	+32.4	7.0	12 46.0	+32.4	7.0	13 45.5	+32.6	7.1	14 45.1	+32.6	7.1	15 44.6	+32.8	7.1	16 44.2	+32.8	7.2	17 43.7	+32.9	7.2	82
83	11 19.1	+32.1	6.1	12 18.8	+32.1	6.1	13 18.4	+32.3	6.2	14 18.1	+32.3	6.2	15 17.7	+32.4	6.2	16 17.4	+32.5	6.2	17 17.0	+32.6	6.3	18 16.6	+32.8	6.3	83
84	11 51.2	+31.9	5.3	12 50.9	+32.0	5.3	13 50.7	+32.0	5.3	14 50.4	+32.2	5.3	15 50.1	+32.3	5.3	16 49.9	+32.3	5.4	17 49.6	+32.4	5.4	18 49.4	+32.4	5.4	84
85	12 23.1	+31.7	4.4	13 22.9	+31.8	4.4	14 22.7	+31.9	4.4	15 22.6	+31.9	4.4	16 22.4	+32.0	4.5	17 22.2	+32.1	4.5	18 22.0	+32.1	4.5	19 21.8	+32.2	4.5	85
86	12 54.8	+31.6	3.5	13 54.7	+31.6	3.5	14 54.6	+31.7	3.5	15 54.5	+31.7	3.6	16 54.4	+31.7	3.6	17 54.3	+31.8	3.6	18 54.1	+31.9	3.6	19 54.0	+31.9	3.6	86
87	13 26.4	+31.4	2.6	14 26.3	+31.5	2.7	15 26.3	+31.4	2.7	16 26.2	+31.5	2.7	17 26.1	+31.6	2.7	18 26.1	+31.5	2.7	19 26.0	+31.6	2.7	20 25.9	+31.7	2.7	87
88	13 57.8	+31.2	1.8	14 57.8	+31.2	1.8	15 57.7	+31.3	1.8	16 57.7	+31.3	1.8	17 57.7	+31.3	1.8	18 57.6	+31.4	1.8	19 57.6	+31.4	1.8	20 57.6	+31.3	1.8	88
89	14 29.0	+31.0	0.9	15 29.0	+31.0	0.9	16 29.0	+31.0	0.9	17 29.0	+31.0	0.9	18 29.0	+31.0	0.9	19 29.0	+31.0	0.9	20 29.0	+31.0	0.9	21 28.9	+31.1	0.9	89
90	15 00.0	+30.8	0.0	16 00.0	+30.8	0.0	17 00.0	+30.8	0.0	18 00.0	+30.8	0.0	19 00.0	+30.8	0.0	20 00.0	+30.8	0.0	21 00.0	+30.8	0.0	22 00.0	+30.7	0.0	90
	15°			16°			17°			18°			19°			20°			21°			22°			

S. Lat. {L.H.A. greater than 180° ....Zn=180°−Z; L.H.A. less than 180°...........Zn=180°+Z

LATITUDE **SAME** NAME AS DECLINATION L.H.A. 121°, 239°

121

60°, 300° L.H.A. LATITUDE SAME NAME AS DECLINATION

N. Lat. {L.H.A. greater than 180° .....Zn=Z
{L.H.A. less than 180°............Zn=360°–Z

Dec.	15° Hc	d	Z	16° Hc	d	Z	17° Hc	d	Z	18° Hc	d	Z
°	° ′	′	°	° ′	′	°	° ′	′	°	° ′	′	°
0	28 52.7	+17.5	98.5	28 43.6	+18.6	99.0	28 33.9	+19.7	99.6	28 23.6	+20.9	100.1
1	29 10.2	+16.9	97.4	29 02.2	+18.1	98.0	28 53.6	+19.2	98.5	28 44.5	+20.3	99.0
2	29 27.1	+16.4	96.3	29 20.3	+17.5	96.9	29 12.8	+18.7	97.4	29 04.8	+19.8	98.0
3	29 43.5	+15.9	95.2	29 37.8	+17.0	95.8	29 31.5	+18.1	96.3	29 24.6	+19.2	96.9
4	29 59.4	+15.2	94.1	29 54.8	+16.4	94.7	29 49.6	+17.6	95.2	29 43.8	+18.8	95.8
5	30 14.6	+14.7	93.0	30 11.2	+15.9	93.5	30 07.2	+17.0	94.1	30 02.6	+18.2	94.7
6	30 29.3	+14.1	91.8	30 27.1	+15.3	92.4	30 24.2	+16.5	93.0	30 20.8	+17.6	93.6
7	30 43.4	+13.6	90.7	30 42.4	+14.7	91.3	30 40.7	+15.9	91.9	30 38.4	+17.1	92.5
8	30 57.0	+12.9	89.6	30 57.1	+14.1	90.2	30 56.6	+15.3	90.8	30 55.5	+16.5	91.4
9	31 09.9	+12.3	88.4	31 11.2	+13.5	89.0	31 11.9	+14.7	89.7	31 12.0	+15.8	90.3
10	31 22.2	+11.7	87.3	31 24.7	+12.9	87.9	31 26.6	+14.1	88.5	31 27.8	+15.3	89.1
11	31 33.9	+11.1	86.1	31 37.6	+12.3	86.8	31 40.7	+13.5	87.4	31 43.1	+14.7	88.0
12	31 45.0	+10.5	85.0	31 49.9	+11.7	85.6	31 54.2	+12.9	86.2	31 57.8	+14.1	86.9
13	31 55.5	+9.8	83.8	32 01.6	+11.1	84.5	32 07.1	+12.2	85.1	32 11.9	+13.5	85.7
14	32 05.3	+9.2	82.7	32 12.7	+10.4	83.3	32 19.3	+11.6	83.9	32 25.4	+12.8	84.6
15	32 14.5	+8.6	81.5	32 23.1	+9.7	82.1	32 30.9	+11.0	82.8	32 38.2	+12.2	83.4
16	32 23.1	+7.8	80.3	32 32.8	+9.1	81.0	32 41.9	+10.3	81.6	32 50.4	+11.5	82.2
17	32 30.9	+7.3	79.2	32 41.9	+8.5	79.8	32 52.2	+9.7	80.4	33 01.9	+10.8	81.1
18	32 38.2	+6.6	78.0	32 50.4	+7.7	78.6	33 01.9	+9.0	79.2	33 12.7	+10.3	79.9
19	32 44.8	+5.9	76.8	32 58.1	+7.1	77.4	33 10.9	+8.3	78.1	33 23.0	+9.5	78.7
20	32 50.7	+5.2	75.6	33 05.2	+6.5	76.2	33 19.2	+7.6	76.9	33 32.5	+8.8	77.5
21	32 55.9	+4.6	74.4	33 11.7	+5.7	75.1	33 26.8	+7.0	75.7	33 41.3	+8.2	76.3
22	33 00.5	+3.8	73.2	33 17.4	+5.1	73.9	33 33.8	+6.3	74.5	33 49.5	+7.5	75.1
23	33 04.3	+3.3	72.0	33 22.5	+4.4	72.7	33 40.1	+5.6	73.3	33 57.0	+6.8	73.9
24	33 07.6	+2.5	70.9	33 26.9	+3.7	71.5	33 45.7	+4.9	72.1	34 03.8	+6.1	72.7
25	33 10.1	+1.8	69.7	33 30.6	+3.0	70.3	33 50.6	+4.2	70.9	34 09.9	+5.4	71.5
26	33 11.9	+1.2	68.5	33 33.6	+2.4	69.1	33 54.8	+3.5	69.7	34 15.3	+4.6	70.3
27	33 13.1	+0.4	67.3	33 36.0	+1.6	67.9	33 58.3	+2.7	68.5	34 19.9	+4.0	69.1
28	33 13.5	−0.2	66.1	33 37.6	+0.9	66.7	34 01.0	+2.1	67.3	34 23.9	+3.2	67.9
29	33 13.3	−0.9	64.9	33 38.5	+0.2	65.5	34 03.1	+1.4	66.1	34 27.1	+2.6	66.7
30	33 12.4	−1.6	63.7	33 38.7	−0.4	64.3	34 04.5	+0.7	64.9	34 29.7	+1.8	65.5
31	33 10.8	−2.2	62.5	33 38.3	−1.2	63.1	34 05.2	−0.1	63.7	34 31.5	+1.1	64.3
32	33 08.6	−3.0	61.3	33 37.1	−1.8	61.9	34 05.1	−0.7	62.5	34 32.6	+0.4	63.1
33	33 05.6	−3.6	60.1	33 35.3	−2.6	60.7	34 04.4	−1.5	61.3	34 33.0	−0.4	61.9
34	33 02.0	−4.3	58.9	33 32.7	−3.2	59.5	34 02.9	−2.1	60.1	34 32.6	−1.1	60.6
35	32 57.7	−5.0	57.7	33 29.5	−4.0	58.3	34 00.8	−2.9	58.9	34 31.5	−1.8	59.4
36	32 52.7	−5.7	56.5	33 25.5	−4.6	57.1	33 57.9	−3.6	57.6	34 29.7	−2.5	58.2
37	32 47.0	−6.3	55.4	33 20.9	−5.3	55.9	33 54.3	−4.2	56.4	34 27.2	−3.2	57.0
38	32 40.7	−7.0	54.2	33 15.6	−6.0	54.7	33 50.1	−5.0	55.2	34 24.0	−3.9	55.8
39	32 33.7	−7.6	53.0	33 09.6	−6.6	53.5	33 45.1	−5.7	54.0	34 20.1	−4.7	54.6
40	32 26.1	−8.3	51.8	33 03.0	−7.4	52.3	33 39.4	−6.3	52.8	34 15.4	−5.3	53.4
41	32 17.8	−9.0	50.6	32 55.6	−8.0	51.1	33 33.1	−7.1	51.7	34 10.1	−6.1	52.2
42	32 08.8	−9.6	49.5	32 47.6	−8.6	50.0	33 26.0	−7.7	50.5	34 04.0	−6.8	51.0
43	31 59.2	−10.2	48.3	32 39.0	−9.4	48.8	33 18.3	−8.4	49.3	33 57.2	−7.4	49.8
44	31 49.0	−10.8	47.1	32 29.6	−9.9	47.6	33 09.9	−9.1	48.1	33 49.8	−8.2	48.6
45	31 38.2	−11.5	46.0	32 19.7	−10.6	46.4	33 00.8	−9.7	46.9	33 41.6	−8.8	47.4
46	31 26.7	−12.1	44.8	32 09.1	−11.3	45.3	32 51.1	−10.4	45.7	33 32.8	−9.5	46.2
47	31 14.6	−12.7	43.7	31 57.8	−11.9	44.1	32 40.7	−11.0	44.6	33 23.3	−10.2	45.0
48	31 01.9	−13.3	42.6	31 45.9	−12.5	43.0	32 29.7	−11.7	43.4	33 13.1	−10.8	43.8
49	30 48.6	−13.9	41.4	31 33.4	−13.1	41.8	32 18.0	−12.3	42.2	33 02.3	−11.5	42.7
50	30 34.7	−14.5	40.3	31 20.3	−13.7	40.7	32 05.7	−13.0	41.1	32 50.8	−12.2	41.5
51	30 20.2	−15.1	39.2	31 06.6	−14.3	39.5	31 52.7	−13.5	39.9	32 38.6	−12.8	40.3
52	30 05.1	−15.6	38.0	30 52.3	−14.9	38.4	31 39.2	−14.2	38.8	32 25.8	−13.4	39.2
53	29 49.5	−16.2	36.9	30 37.4	−15.5	37.3	31 25.0	−14.8	37.6	32 12.4	−14.1	38.0
54	29 33.3	−16.7	35.8	30 21.9	−16.1	36.2	31 10.2	−15.3	36.5	31 58.3	−14.6	36.9
55	29 16.6	−17.3	34.7	30 05.8	−16.6	35.0	30 54.9	−16.0	35.4	31 43.7	−15.3	35.7
56	28 59.3	−17.8	33.6	29 49.2	−17.2	33.9	30 38.9	−16.5	34.3	31 28.4	−15.9	34.6
57	28 41.5	−18.3	32.5	29 32.0	−17.7	32.8	30 22.4	−17.1	33.1	31 12.5	−16.5	33.5
58	28 23.2	−18.8	31.4	29 14.3	−18.2	31.7	30 05.3	−17.7	32.0	30 56.0	−17.0	32.3
59	28 04.4	−19.4	30.4	28 56.1	−18.8	30.6	29 47.6	−18.2	30.9	30 39.0	−17.6	31.2
60	27 45.0	−19.8	29.3	28 37.3	−19.3	29.6	29 29.4	−18.7	29.8	30 21.4	−18.2	30.1
61	27 25.2	−20.3	28.2	28 18.0	−19.8	28.5	29 10.7	−19.3	28.7	30 03.2	−18.7	29.0
62	27 04.9	−20.8	27.2	27 58.2	−20.3	27.4	28 51.4	−19.7	27.7	29 44.5	−19.2	27.9
63	26 44.1	−21.2	26.1	27 37.9	−20.7	26.3	28 31.7	−20.3	26.6	29 25.3	−19.8	26.8
64	26 22.9	−21.7	25.1	27 17.2	−21.3	25.3	28 11.4	−20.8	25.5	29 05.5	−20.3	25.8
65	26 01.2	−22.2	24.0	26 55.9	−21.7	24.2	27 50.6	−21.3	24.5	28 45.2	−20.8	24.7
66	25 39.0	−22.5	23.0	26 34.2	−22.1	23.2	27 29.3	−21.7	23.4	28 24.4	−21.3	23.6
67	25 16.5	−23.0	22.0	26 12.1	−22.6	22.2	27 07.6	−22.2	22.3	28 03.1	−21.8	22.5
68	24 53.5	−23.4	21.0	25 49.5	−23.1	21.1	26 45.4	−22.7	21.3	27 41.3	−22.3	21.5
69	24 30.1	−23.9	19.9	25 26.4	−23.4	20.1	26 22.7	−23.1	20.3	27 19.0	−22.7	20.4
70	24 06.2	−24.2	18.9	25 03.0	−23.9	19.1	25 59.6	−23.5	19.2	26 56.3	−23.2	19.4
71	23 42.0	−24.6	17.9	24 39.1	−24.3	18.1	25 36.1	−23.9	18.2	26 33.1	−23.7	18.4
72	23 17.4	−24.9	16.9	24 14.8	−24.7	17.1	25 12.2	−24.4	17.2	26 09.4	−24.0	17.3
73	22 52.5	−25.4	16.0	23 50.1	−25.0	16.1	24 47.8	−24.8	16.2	25 45.4	−24.5	16.3
74	22 27.1	−25.6	15.0	23 25.1	−25.4	15.1	24 23.0	−25.2	15.2	25 20.9	−24.9	15.3
75	22 01.5	−26.1	14.0	22 59.7	−25.8	14.1	23 57.8	−25.5	14.2	24 56.0	−25.3	14.3
76	21 35.4	−26.3	13.0	22 33.9	−26.2	13.1	23 32.3	−25.9	13.2	24 30.7	−25.7	13.3
77	21 09.1	−26.7	12.1	22 07.7	−26.5	12.1	23 06.4	−26.3	12.2	24 05.0	−26.1	12.3
78	20 42.4	−27.0	11.1	21 41.2	−26.8	11.2	22 40.1	−26.6	11.3	23 38.9	−26.4	11.3
79	20 15.4	−27.3	10.1	21 14.4	−27.1	10.2	22 13.5	−27.0	10.3	23 12.5	−26.8	10.4
80	19 48.1	−27.7	9.2	20 47.3	−27.5	9.3	21 46.5	−27.3	9.3	22 45.7	−27.2	9.4
81	19 20.4	−27.9	8.3	20 19.8	−27.8	8.3	21 19.2	−27.6	8.4	22 18.5	−27.5	8.4
82	18 52.5	−28.1	7.3	19 52.0	−28.0	7.4	20 51.6	−28.0	7.4	21 51.0	−27.8	7.5
83	18 24.4	−28.5	6.4	19 24.0	−28.4	6.4	20 23.6	−28.2	6.5	21 23.2	−28.1	6.5
84	17 55.9	−28.7	5.5	18 55.6	−28.6	5.5	19 55.4	−28.6	5.5	20 55.1	−28.5	5.6
85	17 27.2	−29.0	4.5	18 27.0	−28.9	4.6	19 26.8	−28.8	4.6	20 26.6	−28.7	4.6
86	16 58.2	−29.2	3.6	17 58.1	−29.2	3.6	18 58.0	−29.1	3.7	19 57.9	−29.1	3.7
87	16 29.0	−29.4	2.7	17 28.9	−29.4	2.7	18 28.9	−29.4	2.7	19 28.8	−29.3	2.8
88	15 59.6	−29.7	1.8	16 59.5	−29.6	1.8	17 59.5	−29.6	1.8	18 59.5	−29.6	1.8
89	15 29.9	−29.9	0.9	16 29.9	−29.9	0.9	17 29.9	−29.9	0.9	18 29.9	−29.9	0.9
90	15 00.0	−30.1	0.0	16 00.0	−30.1	0.0	17 00.0	−30.1	0.0	18 00.0	−30.1	0.0
	15°			16°			17°			18°		

19° Hc	d	Z	20° Hc	d	Z	21° Hc	d	Z	22° Hc	d	Z	Dec.
° ′	′	°	° ′	′	°	° ′	′	°	° ′	′	°	°
28 12.8	+21.9	100.6	28 01.5	+23.0	101.2	27 49.6	+24.0	101.7	27 37.1	+25.2	102.2	0
28 34.7	+21.5	99.6	28 24.5	+22.5	100.1	28 13.6	+23.7	100.7	28 02.3	+24.7	101.2	1
28 56.2	+20.9	98.5	28 47.0	+22.0	99.1	28 37.3	+23.1	99.6	28 27.0	+24.2	100.1	2
29 17.1	+20.4	97.4	29 09.0	+21.5	98.0	29 00.4	+22.6	98.6	28 51.2	+23.7	99.1	3
29 37.5	+19.9	96.4	29 30.5	+21.0	96.9	29 23.0	+22.1	97.5	29 14.9	+23.2	98.0	4
29 57.4	+19.3	95.3	29 51.5	+20.5	95.9	29 45.1	+21.6	96.4	29 38.1	+22.7	97.0	5
30 16.7	+18.8	94.2	30 12.0	+19.9	94.8	30 06.7	+21.1	95.3	30 00.8	+22.2	95.9	6
30 35.5	+18.2	93.1	30 31.9	+19.4	93.7	30 27.8	+20.5	94.3	30 23.0	+21.7	94.8	7
30 53.7	+17.7	92.0	30 51.3	+18.8	92.6	30 48.3	+20.0	93.2	30 44.7	+21.1	93.8	8
31 11.4	+17.0	90.9	31 10.1	+18.3	91.5	31 08.3	+19.4	92.1	31 05.8	+20.6	92.7	9
31 28.4	+16.5	89.7	31 28.4	+17.7	90.4	31 27.7	+18.8	91.0	31 26.4	+20.0	91.6	10
31 44.9	+15.9	88.6	31 46.1	+17.0	89.2	31 46.5	+18.3	89.8	31 46.4	+19.4	90.5	11
32 00.8	+15.3	87.5	32 03.1	+16.5	88.1	32 04.8	+17.6	88.7	32 05.8	+18.8	89.4	12
32 16.1	+14.6	86.3	32 19.6	+15.8	87.0	32 22.4	+17.1	87.6	32 24.6	+18.2	88.2	13
32 30.7	+14.1	85.2	32 35.4	+15.3	85.8	32 39.5	+16.4	86.5	32 42.8	+17.7	87.1	14
32 44.8	+13.3	84.0	32 50.7	+14.5	84.7	32 55.9	+15.8	85.3	33 00.5	+16.9	86.0	15
32 58.1	+12.8	82.9	33 05.2	+14.0	83.5	33 11.7	+15.1	84.2	33 17.4	+16.4	84.8	16
33 10.9	+12.1	81.7	33 19.2	+13.3	82.4	33 26.8	+14.5	83.0	33 33.8	+15.7	83.7	17
33 23.0	+11.4	80.5	33 32.5	+12.6	81.2	33 41.3	+13.9	81.8	33 49.5	+15.1	82.5	18
33 34.4	+10.7	79.4	33 45.1	+12.0	80.0	33 55.2	+13.2	80.7	34 04.6	+14.4	81.3	19
33 45.1	+10.1	78.2	33 57.1	+11.3	78.8	34 08.4	+12.5	79.5	34 19.0	+13.7	80.2	20
33 55.2	+9.4	77.0	34 08.4	+10.6	77.6	34 20.9	+11.8	78.3	34 32.7	+13.0	79.0	21
34 04.6	+8.7	75.8	34 19.0	+9.9	76.5	34 32.7	+11.1	77.1	34 45.7	+12.3	77.8	22
34 13.3	+8.0	74.6	34 28.9	+9.2	75.3	34 43.8	+10.4	75.9	34 58.0	+11.7	76.6	23
34 21.3	+7.2	73.4	34 38.1	+8.5	74.1	34 54.2	+9.7	74.7	35 09.7	+10.9	75.4	24
34 28.5	+6.6	72.2	34 46.6	+7.7	72.9	35 03.9	+9.0	73.5	35 20.6	+10.2	74.2	25
34 35.1	+5.9	71.0	34 54.3	+7.1	71.6	35 12.9	+8.3	72.3	35 30.8	+9.5	73.0	26
34 41.0	+5.1	69.8	35 01.4	+6.3	70.4	35 21.2	+7.5	71.1	35 40.3	+8.7	71.8	27
34 46.1	+4.5	68.6	35 07.7	+5.6	69.2	35 28.7	+6.8	69.9	35 49.0	+8.0	70.6	28
34 50.6	+3.7	67.4	35 13.3	+4.9	68.0	35 35.5	+6.1	68.7	35 57.0	+7.3	69.3	29
34 54.3	+2.9	66.1	35 18.2	+4.2	66.8	35 41.6	+5.3	67.4	36 04.3	+6.5	68.1	30
34 57.2	+2.3	64.9	35 22.4	+3.3	65.6	35 46.9	+4.5	66.2	36 10.8	+5.7	66.9	31
34 59.5	+1.5	63.7	35 25.7	+2.7	64.3	35 51.4	+3.8	65.0	36 16.5	+5.0	65.6	32
35 01.0	+0.7	62.5	35 28.4	+1.9	63.1	35 55.2	+3.1	63.7	36 21.5	+4.2	64.4	33
35 01.7	+0.1	61.3	35 30.3	+1.2	61.9	35 58.3	+2.3	62.5	36 25.7	+3.4	63.2	34
35 01.8	−0.7	60.0	35 31.5	+0.4	60.7	36 00.6	+1.5	61.3	36 29.1	+2.7	61.9	35
35 01.1	−1.4	58.8	35 31.9	−0.4	59.4	36 02.1	+0.8	60.0	36 31.8	+1.9	60.7	36
34 59.7	−2.2	57.6	35 31.5	−1.0	58.2	36 02.9	0.0	58.8	36 33.7	+1.1	59.4	37
34 57.5	−2.9	56.4	35 30.5	−1.9	57.0	36 02.9	−0.7	57.6	36 34.8	+0.3	58.2	38
34 54.6	−3.6	55.2	35 28.6	−2.5	55.7	36 02.2	−1.6	56.3	36 35.1	−0.4	56.9	39
34 51.0	−4.4	53.9	35 26.1	−3.4	54.5	36 00.6	−2.2	55.1	36 34.7	−1.2	55.7	40
34 46.6	−5.0	52.7	35 22.7	−4.0	53.3	35 58.4	−3.1	53.9	36 33.5	−2.0	54.5	41
34 41.6	−5.8	51.5	35 18.7	−4.8	52.1	35 55.3	−3.7	52.6	36 31.5	−2.7	53.2	42
34 35.8	−6.5	50.3	35 13.9	−5.5	50.8	35 51.6	−4.6	51.4	36 28.8	−3.6	52.0	43
34 29.3	−7.2	49.1	35 08.4	−6.3	49.6	35 47.0	−5.3	50.2	36 25.2	−4.3	50.7	44
34 22.1	−8.0	47.9	35 02.1	−7.0	48.4	35 41.7	−6.0	48.9	36 20.9	−5.1	49.5	45
34 14.1	−8.6	46.7	34 55.1	−7.7	47.2	35 35.7	−6.8	47.7	36 15.8	−5.8	48.3	46
34 05.5	−9.3	45.5	34 47.4	−8.4	46.0	35 28.9	−7.5	46.5	36 10.0	−6.6	47.0	47
33 56.2	−10.0	44.3	34 39.0	−9.1	44.8	35 21.4	−8.2	45.3	36 03.4	−7.3	45.8	48
33 46.2	−10.6	43.1	34 29.9	−9.9	43.6	35 13.2	−9.0	44.1	35 56.1	−8.1	44.6	49
33 35.6	−11.4	41.9	34 20.0	−10.5	42.4	35 04.2	−9.7	42.9	35 48.0	−8.8	43.3	50
33 24.2	−12.0	40.8	34 09.5	−11.2	41.2	34 54.5	−10.4	41.7	35 39.2	−9.6	42.1	51
33 12.2	−12.7	39.6	33 58.3	−11.9	40.0	34 44.1	−11.1	40.5	35 29.6	−10.3	40.9	52
32 59.5	−13.3	38.4	33 46.4	−12.6	38.8	34 33.0	−11.8	39.3	35 19.3	−11.0	39.7	53
32 46.2	−13.9	37.3	33 33.8	−13.2	37.7	34 21.2	−12.5	38.1	35 08.3	−11.7	38.5	54
32 32.3	−14.6	36.1	33 20.6	−13.9	36.5	34 08.7	−13.1	36.9	34 56.6	−12.4	37.3	55
32 17.7	−15.2	35.0	33 06.7	−14.5	35.3	33 55.6	−13.8	35.7	34 44.2	−13.1	36.1	56
32 02.5	−15.9	33.8	32 52.2	−15.1	34.2	33 41.8	−14.5	34.5	34 31.1	−13.8	34.9	57
31 46.6	−16.4	32.7	32 37.1	−15.8	33.0	33 27.3	−15.2	33.4	34 17.3	−14.5	33.7	58
31 30.2	−17.0	31.5	32 21.3	−16.4	31.9	33 12.1	−15.7	32.2	34 02.8	−15.1	32.6	59
31 13.2	−17.6	30.4	32 04.9	−17.0	30.7	32 56.4	−16.4	31.1	33 47.7	−15.8	31.4	60
30 55.6	−18.1	29.3	31 47.9	−17.6	29.6	32 40.0	−17.1	29.9	33 31.9	−16.5	30.2	61
30 37.5	−18.8	28.2	31 30.3	−18.2	28.5	32 22.9	−17.6	28.8	33 15.4	−17.0	29.1	62
30 18.7	−19.2	27.1	31 12.1	−18.8	27.4	32 05.3	−18.2	27.6	32 58.4	−17.7	27.9	63
29 59.5	−19.9	26.0	30 53.3	−19.3	26.3	31 47.1	−18.8	26.5	32 40.7	−18.3	26.8	64
29 39.6	−20.3	24.9	30 34.0	−19.9	25.2	31 28.3	−19.4	25.4	32 22.4	−18.9	25.7	65
29 19.3	−20.9	23.8	30 14.1	−20.4	24.1	31 08.9	−20.0	24.3	32 03.5	−19.5	24.6	66
28 58.4	−21.3	22.8	29 53.7	−20.9	23.0	30 48.9	−20.5	23.2	31 44.0	−20.1	23.4	67
28 37.1	−21.9	21.7	29 32.8	−21.5	21.9	30 28.4	−21.1	22.1	31 23.9	−20.6	22.3	68
28 15.2	−22.4	20.6	29 11.3	−22.0	20.8	30 07.3	−21.5	21.0	31 03.3	−21.2	21.2	69
27 52.8	−22.8	19.6	28 49.3	−22.4	19.8	29 45.8	−22.1	20.0	30 42.1	−21.7	20.2	70
27 30.0	−23.3	18.5	28 26.9	−23.0	18.7	29 23.7	−22.7	18.9	30 20.4	−22.3	19.1	71
27 06.7	−23.8	17.5	28 03.9	−23.4	17.7	29 01.0	−23.1	17.8	29 58.1	−22.7	18.0	72
26 42.9	−24.2	16.5	27 40.5	−23.9	16.6	28 37.9	−23.6	16.8	29 35.4	−23.3	16.9	73
26 18.7	−24.6	15.4	27 16.6	−24.4	15.6	28 14.3	−24.0	15.7	29 12.1	−23.8	15.9	74
25 54.1	−25.0	14.4	26 52.2	−24.8	14.6	27 50.3	−24.6	14.7	28 48.3	−24.3	14.8	75
25 29.1	−25.5	13.4	26 27.4	−25.2	13.5	27 25.7	−24.9	13.7	28 24.0	−24.7	13.8	76
25 03.6	−25.8	12.4	26 02.2	−25.6	12.5	27 00.8	−25.5	12.6	27 59.3	−25.2	12.7	77
24 37.8	−26.3	11.4	25 36.6	−26.1	11.5	26 35.3	−25.8	11.6	27 34.1	−25.6	11.7	78
24 11.5	−26.6	10.4	25 10.5	−26.4	10.5	26 09.5	−26.3	10.6	27 08.5	−26.1	10.7	79
23 44.9	−27.0	9.5	24 44.1	−26.9	9.5	25 43.2	−26.6	9.6	26 42.4	−26.5	9.7	80
23 17.9	−27.4	8.5	24 17.2	−27.2	8.5	25 16.6	−27.1	8.6	26 15.9	−26.9	8.7	81
22 50.5	−27.7	7.5	23 50.0	−27.6	7.6	24 49.5	−27.5	7.6	25 49.0	−27.4	7.7	82
22 22.8	−28.0	6.6	23 22.4	−27.9	6.6	24 22.0	−27.8	6.7	25 21.6	−27.7	6.7	83
21 54.8	−28.4	5.6	22 54.5	−28.3	5.6	23 54.2	−28.2	5.7	24 53.9	−28.1	5.7	84
21 26.4	−28.7	4.7	22 26.2	−28.6	4.7	23 26.0	−28.5	4.7	24 25.8	−28.4	4.8	85
20 57.7	−29.0	3.7	21 57.6	−28.9	3.7	22 57.5	−28.9	3.8	23 57.4	−28.9	3.8	86
20 28.7	−29.3	2.8	21 28.7	−29.3	2.8	22 28.6	−29.2	2.8	23 28.5	−29.1	2.8	87
19 59.4	−29.5	1.8	20 59.4	−29.5	1.9	21 59.4	−29.6	1.9	22 59.4	−29.6	1.9	88
19 29.9	−29.9	0.9	20 29.9	−29.9	0.9	21 29.8	−29.8	0.9	22 29.8	−29.8	0.9	89
19 00.0	−30.1	0.0	20 00.0	−30.1	0.0	21 00.0	−30.1	0.0	22 00.0	−30.2	0.0	90
19°			20°			21°			22°			

LATITUDE **CONTRARY** NAME TO DECLINATION — L.H.A. 60°, 300°

Dec.	15° Hc	d	Z	16° Hc	d	Z	17° Hc	d	Z	18° Hc	d	Z	19° Hc	d	Z	20° Hc	d	Z	21° Hc	d	Z	22° Hc	d	Z	Dec.
°	° ′	′	°	° ′	′	°	° ′	′	°	° ′	′	°	° ′	′	°	° ′	′	°	° ′	′	°	° ′	′	°	°
0	28 52.7	-18.0	98.5	28 43.6	-19.1	99.0	28 33.9	-20.2	99.6	28 23.6	-21.3	100.1	28 12.8	-22.4	100.6	28 01.5	-23.5	101.2	27 49.6	-24.6	101.7	27 37.1	-25.5	102.2	0
1	28 34.7	-18.5	99.6	28 24.5	-19.6	100.1	28 13.7	-20.8	100.7	28 02.3	-21.8	101.2	27 50.4	-22.9	101.7	27 38.0	-24.0	102.2	27 25.0	-25.0	102.7	27 11.6	-26.1	103.2	1
2	28 16.2	-19.0	100.7	28 04.9	-20.2	101.2	27 52.9	-21.2	101.7	27 40.5	-22.3	102.2	27 27.5	-23.3	102.7	27 14.0	-24.4	103.2	27 00.0	-25.4	103.7	26 45.5	-26.4	104.2	2
3	27 57.2	-19.5	101.7	27 44.7	-20.6	102.3	27 31.7	-21.7	102.8	27 18.2	-22.7	103.3	27 04.2	-23.8	103.8	26 49.6	-24.8	104.3	26 34.6	-25.9	104.8	26 19.1	-26.9	105.2	3
4	27 37.7	-20.0	102.8	27 24.1	-21.1	103.3	27 10.0	-22.1	103.8	26 55.5	-23.2	104.3	26 40.4	-24.3	104.8	26 24.8	-25.3	105.3	26 08.7	-26.2	105.8	25 52.2	-27.3	106.2	4
5	27 17.7	-20.5	103.9	27 03.0	-21.5	104.4	26 47.9	-22.6	104.9	26 32.3	-23.7	105.3	26 16.1	-24.6	105.8	25 59.5	-25.7	106.3	25 42.5	-26.7	106.8	25 24.9	-27.6	107.2	5
6	26 57.2	-21.0	104.9	26 41.5	-22.0	105.4	26 25.3	-23.1	105.9	26 08.6	-24.1	106.4	25 51.5	-25.1	106.8	25 33.8	-26.0	107.3	25 15.8	-27.1	107.8	24 57.3	-28.1	108.2	6
7	26 36.2	-21.4	106.0	26 19.5	-22.5	106.5	26 02.2	-23.4	106.9	25 44.5	-24.5	107.4	25 26.4	-25.5	107.8	25 07.8	-26.5	108.3	24 48.7	-27.5	108.7	24 29.2	-28.4	109.2	7
8	26 14.8	-21.8	107.0	25 57.0	-22.9	107.5	25 38.8	-24.0	108.0	25 20.0	-24.9	108.4	25 00.9	-25.9	108.9	24 41.3	-26.9	109.3	24 21.2	-27.8	109.7	24 00.8	-28.8	110.1	8
9	25 53.0	-22.3	108.1	25 34.1	-23.3	108.5	25 14.8	-24.3	109.0	24 55.1	-25.3	109.4	24 35.0	-26.3	109.8	24 14.4	-27.3	110.3	23 53.4	-28.2	110.7	23 32.0	-29.1	111.1	9
10	25 30.7	-22.8	109.1	25 10.8	-23.7	109.5	24 50.5	-24.7	110.0	24 29.8	-25.7	110.4	24 08.7	-26.7	110.8	23 47.1	-27.6	111.2	23 25.2	-28.5	111.7	23 02.9	-29.5	112.1	10
11	25 07.9	-23.1	110.1	24 47.1	-24.2	110.6	24 25.8	-25.1	111.0	24 04.1	-26.1	111.4	23 42.0	-27.0	111.8	23 19.5	-27.9	112.2	22 56.7	-28.9	112.6	22 33.4	-29.8	113.0	11
12	24 44.8	-23.6	111.1	24 22.9	-24.5	111.6	24 00.7	-25.5	112.0	23 38.0	-26.4	112.4	23 15.0	-27.4	112.8	22 51.6	-28.4	113.2	22 27.8	-29.3	113.6	22 03.6	-30.1	113.9	12
13	24 21.2	-24.0	112.1	23 58.4	-24.9	112.6	23 35.2	-25.9	113.0	23 11.6	-26.8	113.4	22 47.6	-27.7	113.8	22 23.2	-28.6	114.1	21 58.5	-29.5	114.5	21 33.5	-30.5	114.9	13
14	23 57.2	-24.3	113.1	23 33.5	-25.3	113.6	23 09.3	-26.2	113.9	22 44.8	-27.2	114.3	22 19.9	-28.1	114.7	21 54.6	-29.0	115.1	21 29.0	-29.9	115.4	21 03.0	-30.7	115.8	14
15	23 32.9	-24.7	114.1	23 08.2	-25.7	114.5	22 43.1	-26.6	114.9	22 17.6	-27.5	115.3	21 51.8	-28.4	115.7	21 25.6	-29.3	116.0	20 59.1	-30.1	116.4	20 32.3	-31.0	116.7	15
16	23 08.2	-25.1	115.1	22 42.5	-26.0	115.5	22 16.5	-27.0	115.9	21 50.1	-27.9	116.3	21 23.4	-28.7	116.6	20 56.3	-29.6	117.0	20 29.0	-30.5	117.3	20 01.3	-31.3	117.6	16
17	22 43.1	-25.5	116.1	22 16.5	-26.4	116.5	21 49.5	-27.3	116.9	21 22.2	-28.1	117.2	20 54.7	-29.1	117.6	20 26.7	-29.8	117.9	19 58.5	-30.7	118.2	19 30.0	-31.5	118.5	17
18	22 17.6	-25.8	117.1	21 50.1	-26.7	117.5	21 22.2	-27.5	117.8	20 54.1	-28.5	118.2	20 25.6	-29.3	118.5	19 56.9	-30.2	118.8	19 27.8	-31.0	119.1	18 58.5	-31.9	119.4	18
19	21 51.8	-26.2	118.1	21 23.4	-27.1	118.4	20 54.7	-28.0	118.8	20 25.6	-28.7	119.1	19 56.3	-29.6	119.4	19 26.7	-30.5	119.7	18 56.8	-31.3	120.0	18 26.6	-32.0	120.3	19
20	21 25.6	-26.5	119.0	20 56.3	-27.3	119.4	20 26.7	-28.2	119.7	19 56.9	-29.1	120.0	19 26.7	-29.9	120.3	18 56.2	-30.7	120.6	18 25.5	-31.5	120.9	17 54.6	-32.4	121.2	20
21	20 59.1	-26.8	120.0	20 29.0	-27.7	120.3	19 58.5	-28.5	120.7	19 27.8	-29.3	121.0	18 56.8	-30.2	121.3	18 25.5	-30.9	121.5	17 54.0	-31.8	121.8	17 22.2	-32.5	122.1	21
22	20 32.3	-27.1	121.0	20 01.3	-28.0	121.3	19 30.0	-28.8	121.6	18 58.5	-29.7	121.9	18 26.6	-30.4	122.2	17 54.6	-31.3	122.5	17 22.2	-32.0	122.7	16 49.7	-32.8	123.0	22
23	20 05.2	-27.4	121.9	19 33.3	-28.2	122.2	19 01.2	-29.1	122.5	18 28.8	-29.8	122.8	17 56.2	-30.7	123.1	17 23.3	-31.4	123.3	16 50.2	-32.2	123.6	16 16.9	-33.0	123.9	23
24	19 37.8	-27.7	122.9	19 05.1	-28.6	123.2	18 32.1	-29.3	123.4	17 59.0	-30.2	123.7	17 25.5	-30.9	124.0	16 51.9	-31.7	124.2	16 18.0	-32.4	124.5	15 43.9	-33.1	124.7	24
25	19 10.1	-28.1	123.8	18 36.5	-28.8	124.1	18 02.8	-29.6	124.4	17 28.8	-30.4	124.6	16 54.6	-31.1	124.9	16 20.2	-31.9	125.1	15 45.6	-32.7	125.4	15 10.8	-33.4	125.6	25
26	18 42.0	-28.2	124.7	18 07.7	-29.0	125.0	17 33.2	-29.9	125.3	16 58.4	-30.6	125.5	16 23.5	-31.4	125.8	15 48.3	-32.1	126.0	15 12.9	-32.8	126.2	14 37.4	-33.6	126.4	26
27	18 13.8	-28.6	125.7	17 38.7	-29.4	125.9	17 03.3	-30.0	126.2	16 27.8	-30.8	126.4	15 52.1	-31.6	126.7	15 16.2	-32.3	126.9	14 40.1	-33.1	127.1	14 03.8	-33.7	127.3	27
28	17 45.2	-28.8	126.6	17 09.3	-29.5	126.8	16 33.3	-30.4	127.1	15 57.0	-31.1	127.3	15 20.5	-31.8	127.5	14 43.9	-32.6	127.8	14 07.0	-33.2	128.0	13 30.1	-34.0	128.2	28
29	17 16.4	-29.1	127.5	16 39.8	-29.8	127.8	16 02.9	-30.5	128.0	15 25.9	-31.3	128.2	14 48.7	-32.0	128.4	14 11.3	-32.7	128.6	13 33.8	-33.4	128.8	12 56.1	-34.1	129.0	29
30	16 47.3	-29.3	128.4	16 10.0	-30.1	128.7	15 32.4	-30.8	128.9	14 54.6	-31.4	129.1	14 16.7	-32.2	129.3	13 38.6	-32.8	129.5	13 00.4	-33.6	129.7	12 22.0	-34.2	129.8	30
31	16 18.0	-29.5	129.3	15 39.9	-30.2	129.6	15 01.6	-31.0	129.8	14 23.2	-31.7	130.0	13 44.5	-32.3	130.2	13 05.8	-33.1	130.3	12 26.8	-33.7	130.5	11 47.8	-34.4	130.7	31
32	15 48.5	-29.7	130.2	15 09.7	-30.5	130.5	14 30.6	-31.1	130.7	13 51.5	-31.9	130.8	13 12.2	-32.6	131.0	12 32.7	-33.2	131.2	11 53.1	-33.9	131.4	11 13.4	-34.5	131.5	32
33	15 18.8	-30.0	131.1	14 39.2	-30.7	131.3	13 59.5	-31.4	131.5	13 19.6	-32.0	131.7	12 39.6	-32.7	131.9	11 59.5	-33.4	132.1	11 19.2	-34.0	132.2	10 38.9	-34.7	132.4	33
34	14 48.8	-30.2	132.0	14 08.5	-30.8	132.2	13 28.1	-31.5	132.4	12 47.6	-32.2	132.6	12 06.9	-32.8	132.7	11 26.1	-33.5	132.9	10 45.2	-34.1	133.0	10 04.2	-34.8	133.2	34
35	14 18.6	-30.4	132.9	13 37.7	-31.1	133.1	12 56.6	-31.7	133.3	12 15.4	-32.4	133.5	11 34.1	-33.1	133.6	10 52.6	-33.6	133.7	10 11.1	-34.3	133.9	9 29.4	-34.9	134.0	35
36	13 48.2	-30.6	133.8	13 06.6	-31.2	134.0	12 24.9	-31.9	134.2	11 43.0	-32.5	134.3	11 01.0	-33.1	134.5	10 19.0	-33.8	134.6	9 36.8	-34.4	134.7	8 54.5	-35.0	134.8	36
37	13 17.6	-30.7	134.7	12 35.4	-31.4	134.9	11 53.0	-32.1	135.0	11 10.5	-32.7	135.2	10 27.9	-33.3	135.3	9 45.2	-33.9	135.4	9 02.4	-34.5	135.5	8 19.5	-35.1	135.7	37
38	12 46.9	-30.9	135.6	12 04.0	-31.6	135.7	11 20.9	-32.1	135.9	10 37.8	-32.8	136.0	9 54.6	-33.4	136.1	9 11.3	-34.0	136.3	8 27.9	-34.6	136.4	7 44.4	-35.2	136.5	38
39	12 16.0	-31.1	136.5	11 32.4	-31.7	136.6	10 48.8	-32.4	136.7	10 05.0	-32.9	136.9	9 21.2	-33.6	137.0	8 37.3	-34.2	137.1	7 53.3	-34.7	137.2	7 09.2	-35.3	137.3	39
40	11 44.9	-31.3	137.3	11 00.7	-31.9	137.5	10 16.4	-32.4	137.6	9 32.1	-33.1	137.7	8 47.6	-33.6	137.8	8 03.1	-34.2	137.9	7 18.6	-34.8	138.0	6 33.9	-35.3	138.1	40
41	11 13.6	-31.4	138.2	10 28.8	-32.0	138.3	9 44.0	-32.6	138.5	8 59.0	-33.2	138.6	8 14.0	-33.8	138.7	7 28.9	-34.3	138.8	6 43.8	-34.9	138.8	5 58.6	-35.5	138.9	41
42	10 42.2	-31.5	139.1	9 56.8	-32.1	139.2	9 11.4	-32.7	139.3	8 25.8	-33.2	139.4	7 40.2	-33.8	139.5	6 54.6	-34.4	139.6	6 08.9	-35.0	139.7	5 23.1	-35.5	139.7	42
43	10 10.7	-31.7	139.9	9 24.7	-32.3	140.1	8 38.7	-32.9	140.2	7 52.6	-33.4	140.3	7 06.4	-33.9	140.3	6 20.2	-34.5	140.4	5 33.9	-35.0	140.5	4 47.6	-35.5	140.5	43
44	9 39.0	-31.8	140.8	8 52.4	-32.3	140.9	8 05.8	-32.9	141.0	7 19.2	-33.5	141.1	6 32.5	-34.1	141.2	5 45.7	-34.5	141.2	4 58.9	-35.1	141.3	4 12.1	-35.6	141.3	44
45	9 07.2	-32.0	141.7	8 20.1	-32.5	141.8	7 32.9	-33.0	141.8	6 45.7	-33.6	141.9	5 58.4	-34.0	142.0	5 11.2	-34.7	142.1	4 23.8	-35.1	142.1	3 36.5	-35.7	142.2	45
46	8 35.2	-32.0	142.5	7 47.6	-32.6	142.6	6 59.9	-33.1	142.7	6 12.1	-33.6	142.8	5 24.4	-34.2	142.8	4 36.5	-34.6	142.9	3 48.7	-35.2	142.9	3 00.8	-35.7	143.0	46
47	8 03.2	-32.2	143.4	7 15.0	-32.7	143.5	6 26.8	-33.2	143.5	5 38.5	-33.7	143.6	4 50.2	-34.2	143.6	4 01.9	-34.8	143.7	3 13.5	-35.2	143.7	2 25.1	-35.7	143.8	47
48	7 31.0	-32.2	144.2	6 42.3	-32.7	144.3	5 53.6	-33.3	144.4	5 04.8	-33.8	144.4	4 16.0	-34.3	144.5	3 27.1	-34.7	144.5	2 38.3	-35.3	144.5	1 49.4	-35.7	144.6	48
49	6 58.8	-32.4	145.1	6 09.6	-32.9	145.1	5 20.3	-33.3	145.2	4 31.0	-33.8	145.3	3 41.7	-34.3	145.3	2 52.4	-34.8	145.3	2 03.0	-35.3	145.4	1 13.7	-35.8	145.4	49
50	6 26.4	-32.4	145.9	5 36.7	-32.9	146.0	4 47.0	-33.4	146.0	3 57.2	-33.9	146.1	3 07.4	-34.4	146.1	2 17.6	-34.9	146.1	1 27.7	-35.3	146.2	0 37.9	-35.8	146.2	50
51	5 54.0	-32.5	146.8	5 03.8	-33.0	146.8	4 13.6	-33.5	146.9	3 23.3	-33.9	146.9	2 33.0	-34.3	146.9	1 42.7	-34.8	147.0	0 52.4	-35.3	147.0	0 02.1	-35.7	147.0	51
52	5 21.5	-32.6	147.6	4 30.8	-33.0	147.7	3 40.1	-33.5	147.7	2 49.4	-34.0	147.7	1 58.7	-34.5	147.8	1 07.9	-34.9	147.8	0 17.1	-35.3	147.8	0 33.6	+35.8	32.2	52
53	4 48.9	-32.6	148.5	3 57.8	-33.1	148.5	3 06.6	-33.6	148.5	2 15.4	-33.9	148.6	1 24.2	-34.4	148.6	0 33.0	-34.8	148.6	0 18.2	+35.3	31.4	1 09.4	+35.7	31.4	53
54	4 16.3	-32.7	149.3	3 24.7	-33.1	149.3	2 33.1	-33.6	149.4	1 41.5	-34.0	149.4	0 49.8	-34.4	149.4	0 01.8	+34.9	30.6	0 53.5	+35.3	30.6	1 45.1	+35.7	30.6	54
55	3 43.6	-32.7	150.1	2 51.6	-33.2	150.2	1 59.5	-33.6	150.2	1 07.5	-34.1	150.2	0 15.4	-34.5	150.2	0 36.7	+34.9	29.8	1 28.8	+35.2	29.8	2 20.8	+35.7	29.8	55
56	3 10.9	-32.8	151.0	2 18.4	-33.2	151.0	1 25.9	-33.6	151.0	0 33.4	-34.0	151.0	0 19.1	+34.4	29.0	1 11.6	+34.8	29.0	2 04.0	+35.3	29.0	2 56.5	+35.7	29.0	56
57	2 38.1	-32.8	151.8	1 45.2	-33.2	151.8	0 52.3	-33.6	151.9	0 00.6	+34.0	28.1	0 53.5	+34.4	28.1	1 46.4	+34.8	28.2	2 39.3	+35.2	28.2	3 32.2	+35.6	28.2	57
58	2 05.3	-32.8	152.7	1 12.0	-33.2	152.7	0 18.7	-33.6	152.7	0 34.6	+34.0	27.3	1 27.9	+34.4	27.3	2 21.2	+34.8	27.3	3 14.5	+35.2	27.4	4 07.8	+35.6	27.4	58
59	1 32.5	-32.9	153.5	0 38.8	-33.3	153.5	0 14.9	+33.7	26.5	1 08.6	+34.0	26.5	2 02.3	+34.4	26.5	2 56.0	+34.8	26.5	3 49.7	+35.1	26.6	4 43.4	+35.5	26.6	59
60	0 59.6	-32.9	154.3	0 05.5	-33.2	154.3	0 48.6	+33.6	25.7	1 42.6	+34.0	25.7	2 36.7	+34.4	25.7	3 30.8	+34.7	25.7	4 24.8	+35.1	25.7	5 18.9	+35.4	25.8	60
61	0 26.7	-32.8	155.2	0 27.7	+33.3	24.8	1 22.2	+33.6	24.8	2 16.6	+34.0	24.8	3 11.1	+34.3	24.9	4 05.5	+34.7	24.9	4 59.9	+35.0	24.9	5 54.3	+35.4	25.0	61
62	0 06.1	+32.9	24.0	1 01.0	+33.2	24.0	1 55.8	+33.5	24.0	2 50.6	+33.9	24.0	3 45.4	+34.2	24.0	4 40.2	+34.6	24.1	5 34.9	+35.0	24.1	6 29.7	+35.3	24.2	62
63	0 39.0	+32.9	23.2	1 34.2	+33.2	23.2	2 29.3	+33.6	23.2	3 24.5	+33.9	23.2	4 19.6	+34.3	23.2	5 14.8	+34.5	23.3	6 09.9	+34.9	23.3	7 05.0	+35.2	23.3	63
64	1 11.9	+32.8	22.3	2 07.4	+33.2	22.3	3 02.9	+33.5	22.3	3 58.4	+33.8	22.4	4 53.9	+34.1	22.4	5 49.3	+34.5	22.4	6 44.8	+34.8	22.5	7 40.2	+35.1	22.5	64
65	1 44.7	+32.9	21.5	2 40.6	+33.1	21.5	3 36.4	+33.4	21.5	4 32.2	+33.8	21.5	5 28.0	+34.1	21.6	6 23.8	+34.4	21.6	7 19.6	+34.7	21.7	8 15.3	+35.0	21.7	65
66	2 17.6	+32.8	20.6	3 13.7	+33.1	20.7	4 09.8	+33.4	20.7	5 06.0	+33.7	20.7	6 02.1	+34.0	20.7	6 58.2	+34.3	20.8	7 54.3	+34.6	20.8	8 50.3	+35.0	20.9	66
67	2 50.4	+32.7	19.8	3 46.8	+33.1	19.8	4 43.2	+33.4	19.8	5 39.7	+33.6	19.9	6 36.1	+33.9	19.9	7 32.5	+34.2	20.0	8 28.9	+34.5	20.0	9 25.3	+34.8	20.1	67
68	3 23.1	+32.7	19.0	4 19.9	+33.0	19.0	5 16.6	+33.3	19.0	6 13.3	+33.6	19.0	7 10.0	+33.9	19.1	8 06.7	+34.1	19.1	9 03.4	+34.4	19.2	10 00.1	+34.6	19.2	68
69	3 55.8	+32.7	18.1	4 52.9	+32.9	18.1	5 49.9	+33.2	18.2	6 46.9	+33.4	18.2	7 43.9	+33.7	18.3	8 40.8	+34.0	18.3	9 37.8	+34.3	18.3	10 34.7	+34.6	18.4	69
70	4 28.5	+32.6	17.3	5 25.8	+32.9	17.3	6 23.1	+33.1	17.3	7 20.3	+33.4	17.4	8 17.6	+33.6	17.4	9 14.8	+33.9	17.5	10 12.1	+34.1	17.5	11 09.3	+34.4	17.6	70
71	5 01.1	+32.6	16.4	5 58.7	+32.8	16.5	6 56.2	+33.0	16.5	7 53.7	+33.3	16.5	8 51.2	+33.6	16.6	9 48.7	+33.8	16.6	10 46.2	+34.0	16.7	11 43.7	+34.2	16.7	71
72	5 33.7	+32.4	15.6	6 31.5	+32.7	15.6	7 29.2	+33.0	15.7	8 27.0	+33.2	15.7	9 24.8	+33.4	15.7	10 22.5	+33.6	15.8	11 20.2	+33.9	15.8	12 17.9	+34.1	15.9	72
73	6 06.1	+32.4	14.8	7 04.2	+32.6	14.8	8 02.2	+32.8	14.8	9 00.2	+33.0	14.9	9 58.2	+33.2	14.9	10 56.1	+33.5	14.9	11 54.1	+33.7	15.0	12 52.0	+34.0	15.1	73
74	6 38.5	+32.3	13.9	7 36.8	+32.5	13.9	8 35.0	+32.7	14.0	9 33.2	+33.0	14.0	10 31.4	+33.2	14.1	11 29.6	+33.4	14.1	12 27.8	+33.6	14.2	13 26.0	+33.8	14.2	74
75	7 10.8	+32.3	13.1	8 09.3	+32.4	13.1	9 07.7	+32.6	13.1	10 06.2	+32.8	13.2	11 04.6	+33.0	13.2	12 03.0	+33.2	13.2	13 01.4	+33.4	13.3	13 59.8	+33.6	13.4	75
76	7 43.1	+32.1	12.2	8 41.7	+32.3	12.2	9 40.3	+32.5	12.3	10 39.0	+32.6	12.3	11 37.6	+32.8	12.4	12 36.2	+33.0	12.4	13 34.8	+33.2	12.4	14 33.4	+33.4	12.5	76
77	8 15.2	+32.0	11.4	9 14.0	+32.2	11.4	10 12.8	+32.4	11.4	11 11.6	+32.5	11.5	12 10.4	+32.7	11.5	13 09.2	+32.9	11.5	14 08.0	+33.0	11.6	15 06.8	+33.2	11.6	77
78	8 47.2	+31.9	10.5	9 46.2	+32.0	10.5	10 45.2	+32.2	10.6	11 44.1	+32.4	10.6	12 43.1	+32.5	10.6	13 42.1	+32.7	10.7	14 41.0	+32.9	10.7	15 40.0	+33.0	10.8	78
79	9 19.1	+31.7	9.6	10 18.2	+31.9	9.7	11 17.4	+32.0	9.7	12 16.5	+32.2	9.7	13 15.6	+32.4	9.8	14 14.8	+32.5	9.8	15 13.9	+32.6	9.9	16 13.0	+32.8	9.9	79
80	9 50.8	+31.7	8.8	10 50.1	+31.8	8.8	11 49.4	+31.9	8.8	12 48.7	+32.0	8.9	13 48.0	+32.1	8.9	14 47.3	+32.3	8.9	15 46.5	+32.5	9.0	16 45.8	+32.6	9.0	80
81	10 22.5	+31.5	7.9	11 21.9	+31.6	7.9	12 21.3	+31.7	8.0	13 20.7	+31.9	8.0	14 20.1	+32.0	8.0	15 19.6	+32.0	8.1	16 19.0	+32.2	8.1	17 18.4	+32.3	8.2	81
82	10 54.0	+31.3	7.1	11 53.5	+31.5	7.1	12 53.0	+31.6	7.1	13 52.6	+31.7	7.1	14 52.1	+31.8	7.2	15 51.6	+31.9	7.2	16 51.2	+32.0	7.2	17 50.7	+32.1	7.3	82
83	11 25.3	+31.2	6.2	12 25.0	+31.2	6.2	13 24.6	+31.4	6.2	14 24.3	+31.4	6.3	15 23.9	+31.6	6.3	16 23.5	+31.7	6.3	17 23.2	+31.7	6.3	18 22.8	+31.8	6.4	83
84	11 56.5	+31.0	5.3	12 56.2	+31.2	5.3	13 56.0	+31.2	5.4	14 55.7	+31.3	5.4	15 55.5	+31.3	5.4	16 55.2	+31.4	5.4	17 54.9	+31.5	5.5	18 54.6	+31.6	5.5	84
85	12 27.5	+30.9	4.4	13 27.4	+30.9	4.5	14 27.2	+31.0	4.5	15 27.0	+31.1	4.5	16 26.8	+31.1	4.5	17 26.6	+31.2	4.5	18 26.4	+31.3	4.6	19 26.2	+31.4	4.6	85
86	12 58.4	+30.7	3.6	13 58.3	+30.7	3.6	14 58.2	+30.8	3.6	15 58.1	+30.8	3.6	16 57.9	+30.9	3.6	17 57.8	+31.0	3.6	18 57.7	+31.0	3.6	19 57.6	+31.0	3.7	86
87	13 29.1	+30.5	2.7	14 29.0	+30.6	2.7	15 29.0	+30.5	2.7	16 28.9	+30.6	2.7	17 28.8	+30.7	2.7	18 28.8	+30.6	2.7	19 28.7	+30.7	2.8	20 28.6	+30.8	2.8	87
88	13 59.6	+30.3	1.8	14 59.6	+30.3	1.8	15 59.5	+30.4	1.8	16 59.5	+30.4	1.8	17 59.5	+30.4	1.8	18 59.4	+30.5	1.8	19 59.4	+30.5	1.8	20 59.4	+30.4	1.9	88
89	14 29.9	+30.1	0.9	15 29.9	+30.1	0.9	16 29.9	+30.1	0.9	17 29.9	+30.1	0.9	18 29.9	+30.1	0.9	19 29.9	+30.1	0.9	20 29.9	+30.1	0.9	21 29.8	+30.2	0.9	89
90	15 00.0	+29.9	0.0	16 00.0	+29.9	0.0	17 00.0	+29.9	0.0	18 00.0	+29.9	0.0	19 00.0	+29.9	0.0	20 00.0	+29.9	0.0	21 00.0	+29.8	0.0	22 00.0	+29.8	0.0	90
	15°			16°			17°			18°			19°			20°			21°			22°			

S. Lat. { L.H.A. greater than 180° ....Zn=180°−Z
L.H.A. less than 180°...........Zn=180°+Z

LATITUDE **SAME** NAME AS DECLINATION — L.H.A. 120°, 240°

61°, 299° L.H.A. LATITUDE SAME NAME AS DECLINATION

N. Lat. {L.H.A. greater than 180° .....Zn=Z; L.H.A. less than 180°............Zn=360°−Z}

Dec.	15° Hc	15° d	15° Z	16° Hc	16° d	16° Z	17° Hc	17° d	17° Z	18° Hc	18° d	18° Z
°	° ′	′	°	° ′	′	°	° ′	′	°	° ′	′	°
0	27 55.4	+17.3	98.2	27 46.6	+18.5	98.7	27 37.3	+19.5	99.2	27 27.4	+20.7	99.7
1	28 12.7	+16.8	97.1	28 05.1	+17.9	97.6	27 56.8	+19.1	98.1	27 48.1	+20.1	98.7
2	28 29.5	+16.3	96.0	28 23.0	+17.4	96.5	28 15.9	+18.5	97.1	28 08.2	+19.7	97.6
3	28 45.8	+15.7	94.9	28 40.4	+16.9	95.4	28 34.4	+18.1	96.0	28 27.9	+19.2	96.5
4	29 01.5	+15.3	93.8	28 57.3	+16.4	94.3	28 52.5	+17.5	94.9	28 47.1	+18.6	95.4
5	29 16.8	+14.6	92.7	29 13.7	+15.8	93.2	29 10.0	+16.9	93.8	29 05.7	+18.1	94.4
6	29 31.4	+14.1	91.6	29 29.5	+15.2	92.1	29 26.9	+16.5	92.7	29 23.8	+17.6	93.3
7	29 45.5	+13.5	90.5	29 44.7	+14.7	91.0	29 43.4	+15.8	91.6	29 41.4	+17.0	92.2
8	29 59.0	+13.0	89.3	29 59.4	+14.2	89.9	29 59.2	+15.3	90.5	29 58.4	+16.5	91.1
9	30 12.0	+12.3	88.2	30 13.6	+13.5	88.8	30 14.5	+14.8	89.4	30 14.9	+15.9	89.9
10	30 24.3	+11.8	87.1	30 27.1	+13.0	87.7	30 29.3	+14.1	88.2	30 30.8	+15.3	88.8
11	30 36.1	+11.2	85.9	30 40.1	+12.3	86.5	30 43.4	+13.6	87.1	30 46.1	+14.8	87.7
12	30 47.3	+10.6	84.8	30 52.4	+11.8	85.4	30 57.0	+12.9	86.0	31 00.9	+14.1	86.6
13	30 57.9	+9.9	83.6	31 04.2	+11.2	84.2	31 09.9	+12.4	84.8	31 15.0	+13.6	85.4
14	31 07.8	+9.4	82.5	31 15.4	+10.5	83.1	31 22.3	+11.7	83.7	31 28.6	+12.9	84.3
15	31 17.2	+8.7	81.3	31 25.9	+10.0	81.9	31 34.0	+11.2	82.5	31 41.5	+12.3	83.2
16	31 25.9	+8.1	80.2	31 35.9	+9.3	80.8	31 45.2	+10.5	81.4	31 53.8	+11.7	82.0
17	31 34.0	+7.5	79.0	31 45.2	+8.6	79.6	31 55.7	+9.8	80.2	32 05.5	+11.1	80.8
18	31 41.5	+6.8	77.8	31 53.8	+8.1	78.5	32 05.5	+9.3	79.1	32 16.6	+10.4	79.7
19	31 48.3	+6.2	76.7	32 01.9	+7.3	77.3	32 14.8	+8.5	77.9	32 27.0	+9.8	78.5
20	31 54.5	+5.6	75.5	32 09.2	+6.8	76.1	32 23.3	+8.0	76.7	32 36.8	+9.1	77.3
21	32 00.1	+4.9	74.3	32 16.0	+6.1	74.9	32 31.3	+7.2	75.6	32 45.9	+8.5	76.2
22	32 05.0	+4.2	73.2	32 22.1	+5.4	73.8	32 38.5	+6.6	74.4	32 54.4	+7.8	75.0
23	32 09.2	+3.6	72.0	32 27.5	+4.7	72.6	32 45.1	+6.0	73.2	33 02.2	+7.1	73.8
24	32 12.8	+2.9	70.8	32 32.2	+4.1	71.4	32 51.1	+5.3	72.0	33 09.3	+6.5	72.6
25	32 15.7	+2.3	69.6	32 36.3	+3.5	70.2	32 56.4	+4.6	70.8	33 15.8	+5.7	71.4
26	32 18.0	+1.6	68.4	32 39.8	+2.7	69.0	33 01.0	+3.9	69.6	33 21.5	+5.1	70.2
27	32 19.6	+1.0	67.3	32 42.5	+2.1	67.8	33 04.9	+3.2	68.4	33 26.6	+4.4	69.1
28	32 20.6	+0.3	66.1	32 44.6	+1.4	66.7	33 08.1	+2.6	67.3	33 31.0	+3.7	67.9
29	32 20.9	−0.4	64.9	32 46.0	+0.8	65.5	33 10.7	+1.9	66.1	33 34.7	+3.1	66.7
30	32 20.5	−1.1	63.7	32 46.8	+0.1	64.3	33 12.6	+1.1	64.9	33 37.8	+2.3	65.5
31	32 19.4	−1.7	62.5	32 46.9	−0.6	63.1	33 13.7	+0.5	63.7	33 40.1	+1.6	64.3
32	32 17.7	−2.3	61.3	32 46.3	−1.3	61.9	33 14.2	−0.1	62.5	33 41.7	+0.9	63.1
33	32 15.4	−3.1	60.2	32 45.0	−2.0	60.7	33 14.1	−0.9	61.3	33 42.6	+0.3	61.9
34	32 12.3	−3.6	59.0	32 43.0	−2.6	59.5	33 13.2	−1.6	60.1	33 42.9	−0.5	60.7
35	32 08.7	−4.4	57.8	32 40.4	−3.3	58.3	33 11.6	−2.2	58.9	33 42.4	−1.2	59.5
36	32 04.3	−5.0	56.6	32 37.1	−4.0	57.1	33 09.4	−2.9	57.7	33 41.2	−1.8	58.3
37	31 59.3	−5.6	55.4	32 33.1	−4.6	56.0	33 06.5	−3.6	56.5	33 39.4	−2.6	57.1
38	31 53.7	−6.3	54.3	32 28.5	−5.3	54.8	33 02.9	−4.3	55.3	33 36.8	−3.2	55.9
39	31 47.4	−6.9	53.1	32 23.2	−5.9	53.6	32 58.6	−4.9	54.1	33 33.6	−4.0	54.7
40	31 40.5	−7.6	51.9	32 17.3	−6.6	52.4	32 53.7	−5.7	52.9	33 29.6	−4.6	53.5
41	31 32.9	−8.2	50.8	32 10.7	−7.3	51.2	32 48.0	−6.3	51.7	33 25.0	−5.4	52.3
42	31 24.7	−8.8	49.6	32 03.4	−7.9	50.1	32 41.7	−6.9	50.6	33 19.6	−6.0	51.1
43	31 15.9	−9.4	48.4	31 55.5	−8.5	48.9	32 34.8	−7.6	49.4	33 13.6	−6.6	49.9
44	31 06.5	−10.1	47.3	31 47.0	−9.2	47.7	32 27.2	−8.3	48.2	33 07.0	−7.4	48.7
45	30 56.4	−10.7	46.1	31 37.8	−9.8	46.6	32 18.9	−8.9	47.0	32 59.6	−8.0	47.5
46	30 45.7	−11.2	45.0	31 28.0	−10.4	45.4	32 10.0	−9.6	45.9	32 51.6	−8.7	46.3
47	30 34.5	−11.9	43.9	31 17.6	−11.0	44.3	32 00.4	−10.2	44.7	32 42.9	−9.4	45.1
48	30 22.6	−12.4	42.7	31 06.6	−11.7	43.1	31 50.2	−10.8	43.5	32 33.5	−10.0	44.0
49	30 10.2	−13.1	41.6	30 54.9	−12.2	42.0	31 39.4	−11.5	42.4	32 23.5	−10.6	42.8
50	29 57.1	−13.6	40.5	30 42.7	−12.9	40.8	31 27.9	−12.1	41.2	32 12.9	−11.3	41.6
51	29 43.5	−14.1	39.3	30 29.8	−13.4	39.7	31 15.8	−12.6	40.1	32 01.6	−11.9	40.5
52	29 29.4	−14.8	38.2	30 16.4	−14.0	38.6	31 03.2	−13.3	38.9	31 49.7	−12.5	39.3
53	29 14.6	−15.3	37.1	30 02.4	−14.6	37.4	30 49.9	−13.9	37.8	31 37.2	−13.2	38.2
54	28 59.3	−15.8	36.0	29 47.8	−15.2	36.3	30 36.0	−14.4	36.7	31 24.0	−13.7	37.0
55	28 43.5	−16.3	34.9	29 32.6	−15.7	35.2	30 21.6	−15.1	35.5	31 10.3	−14.4	35.9
56	28 27.2	−16.9	33.8	29 16.9	−16.2	34.1	30 06.5	−15.6	34.4	30 55.9	−14.9	34.8
57	28 10.3	−17.4	32.7	29 00.7	−16.8	33.0	29 50.9	−16.1	33.3	30 41.0	−15.6	33.6
58	27 52.9	−17.9	31.6	28 43.9	−17.3	31.9	29 34.8	−16.7	32.2	30 25.4	−16.0	32.5
59	27 35.0	−18.4	30.5	28 26.6	−17.8	30.8	29 18.1	−17.3	31.1	30 09.4	−16.7	31.4
60	27 16.6	−18.9	29.5	28 08.8	−18.4	29.7	29 00.8	−17.8	30.0	29 52.7	−17.2	30.3
61	26 57.7	−19.3	28.4	27 50.4	−18.8	28.7	28 43.0	−18.3	28.9	29 35.5	−17.8	29.2
62	26 38.4	−19.9	27.3	27 31.6	−19.3	27.6	28 24.7	−18.8	27.8	29 17.7	−18.3	28.1
63	26 18.5	−20.3	26.3	27 12.3	−19.8	26.5	28 05.9	−19.3	26.8	28 59.4	−18.8	27.0
64	25 58.2	−20.7	25.2	26 52.5	−20.3	25.5	27 46.6	−19.8	25.7	28 40.6	−19.3	25.9
65	25 37.5	−21.2	24.2	26 32.2	−20.8	24.4	27 26.8	−20.3	24.6	28 21.3	−19.9	24.8
66	25 16.3	−21.6	23.2	26 11.4	−21.2	23.4	27 06.5	−20.8	23.6	28 01.4	−20.3	23.8
67	24 54.7	−22.0	22.1	25 50.2	−21.6	22.3	26 45.7	−21.2	22.5	27 41.1	−20.8	22.7
68	24 32.7	−22.5	21.1	25 28.6	−22.1	21.3	26 24.5	−21.7	21.5	27 20.3	−21.3	21.6
69	24 10.2	−22.8	20.1	25 06.5	−22.5	20.3	26 02.8	−22.1	20.4	26 59.0	−21.8	20.6
70	23 47.4	−23.3	19.1	24 44.0	−22.9	19.2	25 40.7	−22.6	19.4	26 37.2	−22.2	19.5
71	23 24.1	−23.6	18.1	24 21.1	−23.3	18.2	25 18.1	−23.0	18.4	26 15.0	−22.6	18.5
72	23 00.5	−24.0	17.1	23 57.8	−23.7	17.2	24 55.1	−23.4	17.3	25 52.4	−23.1	17.5
73	22 36.5	−24.4	16.1	23 34.1	−24.1	16.2	24 31.7	−23.8	16.3	25 29.3	−23.5	16.5
74	22 12.1	−24.7	15.1	23 10.0	−24.4	15.2	24 07.9	−24.2	15.3	25 05.8	−24.0	15.4
75	21 47.4	−25.1	14.1	22 45.6	−24.9	14.2	23 43.7	−24.6	14.3	24 41.8	−24.3	14.4
76	21 22.3	−25.4	13.1	22 20.7	−25.1	13.2	23 19.1	−24.9	13.3	24 17.5	−24.7	13.4
77	20 56.9	−25.7	12.2	21 55.6	−25.6	12.2	22 54.2	−25.3	12.3	23 52.8	−25.1	12.4
78	20 31.2	−26.1	11.2	21 30.0	−25.8	11.3	22 28.9	−25.7	11.3	23 27.7	−25.5	11.4
79	20 05.1	−26.4	10.2	21 04.2	−26.2	10.3	22 03.2	−26.0	10.4	23 02.2	−25.9	10.4
80	19 38.7	−26.6	9.3	20 38.0	−26.6	9.3	21 37.2	−26.4	9.4	22 36.3	−26.2	9.5
81	19 12.1	−27.0	8.3	20 11.4	−26.8	8.4	21 10.8	−26.7	8.4	22 10.1	−26.5	8.5
82	18 45.1	−27.2	7.4	19 44.6	−27.1	7.4	20 44.1	−27.0	7.5	21 43.6	−26.9	7.5
83	18 17.9	−27.5	6.4	19 17.5	−27.4	6.5	20 17.1	−27.3	6.5	21 16.7	−27.2	6.6
84	17 50.4	−27.8	5.5	18 50.1	−27.7	5.5	19 49.8	−27.6	5.6	20 49.5	−27.5	5.6
85	17 22.6	−28.1	4.6	18 22.4	−28.0	4.6	19 22.2	−27.9	4.6	20 22.0	−27.8	4.7
86	16 54.5	−28.2	3.7	17 54.4	−28.2	3.7	18 54.3	−28.2	3.7	19 54.2	−28.1	3.7
87	16 26.3	−28.6	2.7	17 26.2	−28.5	2.8	18 26.1	−28.4	2.8	19 26.1	−28.5	2.8
88	15 57.7	−28.7	1.8	16 57.7	−28.7	1.8	17 57.7	−28.7	1.8	18 57.6	−28.6	1.8
89	15 29.0	−29.0	0.9	16 29.0	−29.0	0.9	17 29.0	−29.0	0.9	18 29.0	−29.0	0.9
90	15 00.0	−29.2	0.0	16 00.0	−29.2	0.0	17 00.0	−29.2	0.0	18 00.0	−29.2	0.0
	15°			16°			17°			18°		

19° Hc	19° d	19° Z	20° Hc	20° d	20° Z	21° Hc	21° d	21° Z	22° Hc	22° d	22° Z	Dec.
° ′	′	°	° ′	′	°	° ′	′	°	° ′	′	°	°
27 17.0	+21.8	100.2	27 06.1	+22.8	100.7	26 54.7	+23.9	101.2	26 42.7	+25.0	101.7	0
27 38.8	+21.2	99.2	27 28.9	+22.4	99.7	27 18.6	+23.4	100.2	27 07.7	+24.5	100.7	1
28 00.0	+20.8	98.1	27 51.3	+21.9	98.6	27 42.0	+23.0	99.2	27 32.2	+24.0	99.7	2
28 20.8	+20.3	97.1	28 13.2	+21.3	97.6	28 05.0	+22.4	98.1	27 56.2	+23.6	98.6	3
28 41.1	+19.8	96.0	28 34.5	+20.9	96.5	28 27.4	+22.0	97.1	28 19.8	+23.1	97.6	4
29 00.9	+19.2	94.9	28 55.4	+20.4	95.5	28 49.4	+21.5	96.0	28 42.9	+22.6	96.6	5
29 20.1	+18.7	93.8	29 15.8	+19.9	94.4	29 10.9	+21.0	94.9	29 05.5	+22.1	95.5	6
29 38.8	+18.2	92.7	29 35.7	+19.3	93.3	29 31.9	+20.5	93.9	29 27.6	+21.6	94.4	7
29 57.0	+17.6	91.6	29 55.0	+18.8	92.2	29 52.4	+19.9	92.8	29 49.2	+21.0	93.4	8
30 14.6	+17.1	90.5	30 13.8	+18.2	91.1	30 12.3	+19.4	91.7	30 10.2	+20.6	92.3	9
30 31.7	+16.5	89.4	30 32.0	+17.7	90.0	30 31.7	+18.8	90.6	30 30.8	+19.9	91.2	10
30 48.2	+15.9	88.3	30 49.7	+17.1	88.9	30 50.5	+18.3	89.5	30 50.7	+19.5	90.1	11
31 04.1	+15.4	87.2	31 06.8	+16.5	87.8	31 08.8	+17.7	88.4	31 10.2	+18.8	89.0	12
31 19.5	+14.7	86.0	31 23.3	+15.9	86.7	31 26.5	+17.1	87.3	31 29.0	+18.3	87.9	13
31 34.2	+14.1	84.9	31 39.2	+15.3	85.5	31 43.6	+16.5	86.1	31 47.3	+17.7	86.8	14
31 48.3	+13.6	83.8	31 54.5	+14.7	84.4	32 00.1	+15.9	85.0	32 05.0	+17.1	85.6	15
32 01.9	+12.9	82.6	32 09.2	+14.1	83.2	32 16.0	+15.3	83.9	32 22.1	+16.4	84.5	16
32 14.8	+12.2	81.5	32 23.3	+13.5	82.1	32 31.3	+14.6	82.7	32 38.5	+15.9	83.4	17
32 27.0	+11.6	80.3	32 36.8	+12.8	80.9	32 45.9	+14.0	81.6	32 54.4	+15.2	82.2	18
32 38.6	+11.0	79.1	32 49.6	+12.2	79.8	32 59.9	+13.4	80.4	33 09.6	+14.6	81.1	19
32 49.6	+10.3	78.0	33 01.8	+11.5	78.6	33 13.3	+12.7	79.2	33 24.2	+13.9	79.9	20
32 59.9	+9.7	76.8	33 13.3	+10.9	77.4	33 26.0	+12.1	78.1	33 38.1	+13.3	78.7	21
33 09.6	+9.0	75.6	33 24.2	+10.2	76.3	33 38.1	+11.4	76.9	33 51.4	+12.5	77.6	22
33 18.6	+8.3	74.4	33 34.4	+9.5	75.1	33 49.5	+10.7	75.7	34 03.9	+12.0	76.4	23
33 26.9	+7.6	73.3	33 43.9	+8.8	73.9	34 00.2	+10.0	74.5	34 15.9	+11.2	75.2	24
33 34.5	+7.0	72.1	33 52.7	+8.1	72.7	34 10.2	+9.4	73.3	34 27.1	+10.5	74.0	25
33 41.5	+6.3	70.9	34 00.8	+7.5	71.5	34 19.6	+8.6	72.2	34 37.6	+9.8	72.8	26
33 47.8	+5.5	69.7	34 08.3	+6.7	70.3	34 28.2	+7.9	71.0	34 47.4	+9.2	71.6	27
33 53.3	+4.9	68.5	34 15.0	+6.1	69.1	34 36.1	+7.2	69.8	34 56.6	+8.4	70.4	28
33 58.2	+4.2	67.3	34 21.1	+5.3	67.9	34 43.3	+6.5	68.5	35 05.0	+7.7	69.2	29
34 02.4	+3.4	66.1	34 26.4	+4.6	66.7	34 49.8	+5.8	67.3	35 12.7	+6.9	68.0	30
34 05.8	+2.8	64.9	34 31.0	+3.9	65.5	34 55.6	+5.1	66.1	35 19.6	+6.2	66.8	31
34 08.6	+2.1	63.7	34 34.9	+3.2	64.3	35 00.7	+4.3	64.9	35 25.8	+5.5	65.5	32
34 10.7	+1.3	62.5	34 38.1	+2.5	63.1	35 05.0	+3.6	63.7	35 31.3	+4.8	64.3	33
34 12.0	+0.6	61.2	34 40.6	+1.7	61.8	35 08.6	+2.9	62.5	35 36.1	+4.0	63.1	34
34 12.6	−0.1	60.0	34 42.3	+1.0	60.6	35 11.5	+2.1	61.2	35 40.1	+3.2	61.9	35
34 12.5	−0.7	58.8	34 43.3	+0.3	59.4	35 13.6	+1.4	60.0	35 43.3	+2.5	60.6	36
34 11.8	−1.6	57.6	34 43.6	−0.4	58.2	35 15.0	+0.6	58.8	35 45.8	+1.7	59.4	37
34 10.2	−2.2	56.4	34 43.2	−1.2	57.0	35 15.6	−0.1	57.6	35 47.5	+1.0	58.2	38
34 08.0	−2.9	55.2	34 42.0	−1.9	55.8	35 15.5	−0.8	56.3	35 48.5	+0.3	56.9	39
34 05.1	−3.6	54.0	34 40.1	−2.6	54.6	35 14.7	−1.6	55.1	35 48.8	−0.6	55.7	40
34 01.5	−4.4	52.8	34 37.5	−3.3	53.3	35 13.1	−2.3	53.9	35 48.2	−1.2	54.5	41
33 57.1	−5.0	51.6	34 34.2	−4.1	52.1	35 10.8	−3.0	52.7	35 47.0	−2.1	53.2	42
33 52.1	−5.7	50.4	34 30.1	−4.7	50.9	35 07.8	−3.8	51.5	35 44.9	−2.8	52.0	43
33 46.4	−6.5	49.2	34 25.4	−5.5	49.7	35 04.0	−4.5	50.2	35 42.1	−3.5	50.8	44
33 39.9	−7.1	48.0	34 19.9	−6.2	48.5	34 59.5	−5.3	49.0	35 38.6	−4.3	49.6	45
33 32.8	−7.8	46.8	34 13.7	−6.9	47.3	34 54.2	−6.0	47.8	35 34.3	−5.0	48.3	46
33 25.0	−8.4	45.6	34 06.8	−7.6	46.1	34 48.2	−6.6	46.6	35 29.3	−5.8	47.1	47
33 16.6	−9.2	44.4	33 59.2	−8.3	44.9	34 41.6	−7.4	45.4	35 23.5	−6.5	45.9	48
33 07.4	−9.8	43.2	33 50.9	−8.9	43.7	34 34.2	−8.2	44.2	35 17.0	−7.2	44.7	49
32 57.6	−10.5	42.1	33 42.0	−9.7	42.5	34 26.0	−8.8	43.0	35 09.8	−8.0	43.4	50
32 47.1	−11.1	40.9	33 32.3	−10.3	41.3	34 17.2	−9.5	41.8	35 01.8	−8.7	42.2	51
32 36.0	−11.8	39.7	33 22.0	−11.0	40.1	34 07.7	−10.2	40.6	34 53.1	−9.4	41.0	52
32 24.2	−12.4	38.6	33 11.0	−11.7	39.0	33 57.5	−10.9	39.4	34 43.7	−10.1	39.8	53
32 11.8	−13.0	37.4	32 59.3	−12.3	37.8	33 46.6	−11.5	38.2	34 33.6	−10.8	38.6	54
31 58.8	−13.7	36.3	32 47.0	−12.9	36.6	33 35.1	−12.3	37.0	34 22.8	−11.5	37.4	55
31 45.1	−14.3	35.1	32 34.1	−13.6	35.5	33 22.8	−12.9	35.9	34 11.3	−12.1	36.2	56
31 30.8	−14.8	34.0	32 20.5	−14.2	34.3	33 09.9	−13.5	34.7	33 59.2	−12.9	35.1	57
31 16.0	−15.5	32.8	32 06.3	−14.9	33.2	32 56.4	−14.2	33.5	33 46.3	−13.5	33.9	58
31 00.5	−16.1	31.7	31 51.4	−15.4	32.0	32 42.2	−14.8	32.4	33 32.8	−14.2	32.7	59
30 44.4	−16.6	30.6	31 36.0	−16.1	30.9	32 27.4	−15.4	31.2	33 18.6	−14.8	31.6	60
30 27.8	−17.2	29.5	31 19.9	−16.6	29.8	32 12.0	−16.1	30.1	33 03.8	−15.5	30.4	61
30 10.6	−17.8	28.4	31 03.3	−17.2	28.6	31 55.9	−16.7	28.9	32 48.3	−16.1	29.2	62
29 52.8	−18.3	27.3	30 46.1	−17.8	27.5	31 39.2	−17.2	27.8	32 32.2	−16.7	28.1	63
29 34.5	−18.8	26.2	30 28.3	−18.3	26.4	31 22.0	−17.9	26.7	32 15.5	−17.3	27.0	64
29 15.7	−19.4	25.1	30 10.0	−18.9	25.3	31 04.1	−18.4	25.6	31 58.2	−17.9	25.8	65
28 56.3	−19.9	24.0	29 51.1	−19.5	24.2	30 45.7	−18.5	24.5	31 40.3	−18.5	24.7	66
28 36.4	−20.4	22.9	29 31.6	−19.9	23.1	30 26.8	−19.6	23.4	31 21.8	−19.1	23.6	67
28 16.0	−20.9	21.8	29 11.7	−20.5	22.0	30 07.2	−20.0	22.3	31 02.7	−19.6	22.5	68
27 55.1	−21.4	20.8	28 51.2	−21.0	21.0	29 47.2	−20.6	21.2	30 43.1	−20.2	21.4	69
27 33.7	−21.8	19.7	28 30.2	−21.5	19.9	29 26.6	−21.1	20.1	30 22.9	−20.7	20.3	70
27 11.9	−22.3	18.7	28 08.7	−22.0	18.8	29 05.5	−21.7	19.0	30 02.2	−21.3	19.2	71
26 49.6	−22.8	17.6	27 46.7	−22.4	17.8	28 43.8	−22.1	18.0	29 40.9	−21.8	18.1	72
26 26.8	−23.2	16.6	27 24.3	−22.9	16.7	28 21.7	−22.6	16.9	29 19.1	−22.3	17.1	73
26 03.6	−23.7	15.6	27 01.4	−23.4	15.7	27 59.1	−23.1	15.8	28 56.8	−22.8	16.0	74
25 39.9	−24.0	14.5	26 38.0	−23.8	14.7	27 36.0	−23.5	14.8	28 34.0	−23.3	14.9	75
25 15.9	−24.5	13.5	26 14.2	−24.3	13.6	27 12.5	−24.0	13.8	28 10.7	−23.7	13.9	76
24 51.4	−24.9	12.5	25 49.9	−24.6	12.6	26 48.5	−24.5	12.7	27 47.0	−24.2	12.8	77
24 26.5	−25.3	11.5	25 25.3	−25.1	11.6	26 24.0	−24.9	11.7	27 22.8	−24.7	11.8	78
24 01.2	−25.7	10.5	25 00.2	−25.5	10.6	25 59.1	−25.3	10.7	26 58.1	−25.1	10.8	79
23 35.5	−26.0	9.5	24 34.7	−25.9	9.6	25 33.8	−25.7	9.7	26 33.0	−25.6	9.8	80
23 09.5	−26.4	8.6	24 08.8	−26.2	8.6	25 08.1	−26.1	8.7	26 07.4	−25.9	8.8	81
22 43.1	−26.8	7.6	23 42.6	−26.7	7.6	24 42.0	−26.5	7.7	25 41.5	−26.4	7.8	82
22 16.3	−27.1	6.6	23 15.9	−27.0	6.7	24 15.5	−26.9	6.7	25 15.1	−26.8	6.8	83
21 49.2	−27.4	5.7	22 48.9	−27.3	5.7	23 48.6	−27.2	5.7	24 48.3	−27.1	5.8	84
21 21.8	−27.8	4.7	22 21.6	−27.7	4.7	23 21.4	−27.6	4.8	24 21.2	−27.5	4.8	85
20 54.0	−28.0	3.7	21 53.9	−28.0	3.8	22 53.8	−28.0	3.8	23 53.7	−27.9	3.8	86
20 26.0	−28.4	2.8	21 25.9	−28.3	2.8	22 25.8	−28.3	2.8	23 25.8	−28.3	2.9	87
19 57.6	−28.7	1.9	20 57.6	−28.7	1.9	21 57.5	−28.6	1.9	22 57.5	−28.6	1.9	88
19 28.9	−28.9	0.9	20 28.9	−28.9	0.9	21 28.9	−28.9	0.9	22 28.9	−28.9	0.9	89
19 00.0	−29.2	0.0	20 00.0	−29.2	0.0	21 00.0	−29.2	0.0	22 00.0	−29.2	0.0	90
19°			20°			21°			22°			

61°, 299° L.H.A. LATITUDE SAME NAME AS DECLINATION

LATITUDE CONTRARY NAME TO DECLINATION   L.H.A. 61°, 299°

Dec.	15° Hc	d	Z	16° Hc	d	Z	17° Hc	d	Z	18° Hc	d	Z
°	° ′	′	°	° ′	′	°	° ′	′	°	° ′	′	°
0	27 55.4	−17.8	98.2	27 46.6	−18.9	98.7	27 37.3	−20.1	99.2	27 27.4	−21.1	99.7
1	27 37.6	−18.4	99.2	27 27.7	−19.5	99.8	27 17.2	−20.5	100.3	27 06.3	−21.6	100.8
2	27 19.2	−18.8	100.3	27 08.2	−19.9	100.8	26 56.7	−21.0	101.3	26 44.7	−22.1	101.8
3	27 00.4	−19.3	101.4	26 48.3	−20.3	101.9	26 35.7	−21.4	102.4	26 22.6	−22.5	102.9
4	26 41.1	−19.7	102.4	26 28.0	−20.9	102.9	26 14.3	−21.9	103.4	26 00.1	−22.9	103.9
5	26 21.4	−20.3	103.5	26 07.1	−21.3	104.0	25 52.4	−22.3	104.5	25 37.2	−23.4	104.9
6	26 01.1	−20.6	104.5	25 45.8	−21.7	105.0	25 30.1	−22.8	105.5	25 13.8	−23.8	105.9
7	25 40.5	−21.2	105.6	25 24.1	−22.2	106.1	25 07.3	−23.2	106.5	24 50.0	−24.2	107.0
8	25 19.3	−21.5	106.6	25 01.9	−22.5	107.1	24 44.1	−23.6	107.5	24 25.8	−24.6	108.0
9	24 57.8	−22.0	107.7	24 39.4	−23.0	108.1	24 20.5	−24.0	108.5	24 01.2	−24.9	109.0
10	24 35.8	−22.4	108.7	24 16.4	−23.4	109.1	23 56.5	−24.4	109.5	23 36.3	−25.4	110.0
11	24 13.4	−22.8	109.7	23 53.0	−23.8	110.1	23 32.1	−24.7	110.5	23 10.9	−25.7	110.9
12	23 50.6	−23.2	110.7	23 29.2	−24.2	111.1	23 07.4	−25.1	111.5	22 45.2	−26.1	111.9
13	23 27.4	−23.5	111.7	23 05.0	−24.5	112.1	22 42.3	−25.5	112.5	22 19.1	−26.4	112.9
14	23 03.9	−24.0	112.7	22 40.5	−24.9	113.1	22 16.8	−25.9	113.5	21 52.7	−26.8	113.9
15	22 39.9	−24.3	113.7	22 15.6	−25.3	114.1	21 50.9	−26.2	114.5	21 25.9	−27.1	114.8
16	22 15.6	−24.7	114.7	21 50.3	−25.6	115.1	21 24.7	−26.5	115.4	20 58.8	−27.4	115.8
17	21 50.9	−25.0	115.7	21 24.7	−25.9	116.0	20 58.2	−26.8	116.4	20 31.4	−27.7	116.7
18	21 25.9	−25.4	116.7	20 58.8	−26.3	117.0	20 31.4	−27.2	117.4	20 03.7	−28.1	117.7
19	21 00.5	−25.7	117.6	20 32.5	−26.5	118.0	20 04.2	−27.4	118.3	19 35.6	−28.3	118.6
20	20 34.8	−26.0	118.6	20 06.0	−26.9	118.9	19 36.8	−27.8	119.3	19 07.3	−28.6	119.6
21	20 08.8	−26.3	119.6	19 39.1	−27.2	119.9	19 09.0	−28.0	120.2	18 38.7	−28.8	120.5
22	19 42.5	−26.6	120.5	19 11.9	−27.5	120.8	18 41.0	−28.3	121.1	18 09.9	−29.2	121.4
23	19 15.9	−26.9	121.5	18 44.4	−27.7	121.8	18 12.7	−28.6	122.1	17 40.7	−29.3	122.3
24	18 49.0	−27.2	122.4	18 16.7	−28.0	122.7	17 44.1	−28.8	123.0	17 11.4	−29.7	123.2
25	18 21.8	−27.5	123.4	17 48.7	−28.3	123.6	17 15.3	−29.1	123.9	16 41.7	−29.8	124.2
26	17 54.3	−27.8	124.3	17 20.4	−28.6	124.6	16 46.2	−29.3	124.8	16 11.9	−30.1	125.1
27	17 26.5	−28.0	125.2	16 51.8	−28.8	125.5	16 16.9	−29.6	125.7	15 41.8	−30.3	126.0
28	16 58.5	−28.2	126.2	16 23.0	−29.0	126.4	15 47.3	−29.7	126.6	15 11.5	−30.6	126.9
29	16 30.3	−28.5	127.1	15 54.0	−29.2	127.3	15 17.6	−30.0	127.5	14 40.9	−30.7	127.7
30	16 01.8	−28.7	128.0	15 24.8	−29.5	128.2	14 47.6	−30.2	128.4	14 10.2	−30.9	128.6
31	15 33.1	−29.0	128.9	14 55.3	−29.7	129.1	14 17.4	−30.4	129.3	13 39.3	−31.1	129.5
32	15 04.1	−29.1	129.8	14 25.6	−29.9	130.0	13 47.0	−30.6	130.2	13 08.2	−31.3	130.4
33	14 35.0	−29.4	130.7	13 55.7	−30.0	130.9	13 16.4	−30.8	131.1	12 36.9	−31.5	131.3
34	14 05.6	−29.6	131.6	13 25.7	−30.3	131.8	12 45.6	−30.9	132.0	12 05.4	−31.6	132.1
35	13 36.0	−29.7	132.5	12 55.4	−30.4	132.7	12 14.7	−31.1	132.9	11 33.8	−31.8	133.0
36	13 06.3	−30.0	133.4	12 25.0	−30.6	133.6	11 43.6	−31.3	133.7	11 02.0	−31.9	133.9
37	12 36.3	−30.1	134.3	11 54.4	−30.8	134.5	11 12.3	−31.4	134.6	10 30.1	−32.1	134.7
38	12 06.2	−30.3	135.2	11 23.6	−31.0	135.3	10 40.9	−31.6	135.5	9 58.0	−32.2	135.6
39	11 35.9	−30.4	136.1	10 52.6	−31.0	136.2	10 09.3	−31.7	136.3	9 25.8	−32.3	136.4
40	11 05.5	−30.7	136.9	10 21.6	−31.3	137.1	9 37.6	−31.8	137.2	8 53.5	−32.4	137.3
41	10 34.8	−30.7	137.8	9 50.3	−31.3	137.9	9 05.8	−32.0	138.0	8 21.1	−32.5	138.2
42	10 04.1	−30.9	138.7	9 19.0	−31.5	138.8	8 33.8	−32.0	138.9	7 48.6	−32.7	139.0
43	9 33.2	−31.0	139.6	8 47.5	−31.6	139.7	8 01.8	−32.2	139.8	7 15.9	−32.7	139.8
44	9 02.2	−31.1	140.4	8 15.9	−31.7	140.5	7 29.6	−32.3	140.6	6 43.2	−32.8	140.7
45	8 31.1	−31.3	141.3	7 44.2	−31.8	141.4	6 57.3	−32.3	141.5	6 10.4	−32.9	141.5
46	7 59.8	−31.3	142.2	7 12.4	−31.9	142.2	6 25.0	−32.5	142.3	5 37.5	−33.0	142.4
47	7 28.5	−31.5	143.0	6 40.5	−32.0	143.1	5 52.5	−32.5	143.2	5 04.5	−33.1	143.2
48	6 57.0	−31.5	143.9	6 08.5	−32.0	143.9	5 20.0	−32.6	144.0	4 31.4	−33.0	144.1
49	6 25.5	−31.7	144.7	5 36.5	−32.2	144.8	4 47.4	−32.6	144.8	3 58.4	−33.2	144.9
50	5 53.8	−31.7	145.6	5 04.3	−32.2	145.6	4 14.8	−32.7	145.7	3 25.2	−33.2	145.7
51	5 22.1	−31.8	146.4	4 32.1	−32.3	146.5	3 42.1	−32.8	146.5	2 52.0	−33.2	146.6
52	4 50.3	−31.8	147.3	3 59.8	−32.3	147.3	3 09.3	−32.8	147.4	2 18.8	−33.3	147.4
53	4 18.5	−31.9	148.1	3 27.5	−32.3	148.2	2 36.5	−32.8	148.2	1 45.5	−33.2	148.2
54	3 46.6	−32.0	149.0	2 55.2	−32.4	149.0	2 03.7	−32.8	149.0	1 12.3	−33.3	149.1
55	3 14.6	−32.0	149.8	2 22.8	−32.5	149.9	1 30.9	−32.9	149.9	0 39.0	−33.3	149.9
56	2 42.6	−32.0	150.7	1 50.3	−32.4	150.7	0 58.0	−32.9	150.7	0 05.7	−33.3	150.7
57	2 10.6	−32.0	151.5	1 17.9	−32.5	151.5	0 25.1	−32.9	151.6	0 27.6	+33.3	28.4
58	1 38.6	−32.1	152.4	0 45.4	−32.5	152.4	0 07.8	+32.9	27.6	1 00.9	+33.3	27.6
59	1 06.5	−32.1	153.2	0 12.9	−32.5	153.2	0 40.7	+32.8	26.8	1 34.2	+33.3	26.8
60	0 34.4	−32.1	154.1	0 19.6	+32.5	25.9	1 13.5	+32.9	25.9	2 07.5	+33.2	26.0
61	0 02.3	−32.1	154.9	0 52.1	+32.4	25.1	1 46.4	+32.8	25.1	2 40.7	+33.2	25.1
62	0 29.8	+32.1	24.2	1 24.5	+32.5	24.3	2 19.2	+32.8	24.3	3 13.9	+33.2	24.3
63	1 01.9	+32.1	23.4	1 57.0	+32.4	23.4	2 52.0	+32.8	23.4	3 47.1	+33.1	23.4
64	1 34.0	+32.1	22.6	2 29.4	+32.4	22.6	3 24.8	+32.7	22.6	4 20.2	+33.1	22.6
65	2 06.1	+32.0	21.7	3 01.8	+32.4	21.7	3 57.5	+32.7	21.7	4 53.3	+33.0	21.8
66	2 38.1	+32.0	20.9	3 34.2	+32.3	20.9	4 30.2	+32.6	20.9	5 26.3	+32.9	20.9
67	3 10.1	+32.0	20.0	4 06.5	+32.2	20.0	5 02.8	+32.6	20.1	5 59.2	+32.8	20.1
68	3 42.1	+31.9	19.2	4 38.7	+32.2	19.2	5 35.4	+32.5	19.2	6 32.0	+32.8	19.3
69	4 14.0	+31.8	18.3	5 10.9	+32.1	18.3	6 07.9	+32.4	18.4	7 04.8	+32.7	18.4
70	4 45.8	+31.8	17.5	5 43.0	+32.1	17.5	6 40.3	+32.3	17.5	7 37.5	+32.6	17.6
71	5 17.6	+31.7	16.6	6 15.1	+32.0	16.6	7 12.6	+32.2	16.7	8 10.1	+32.4	16.7
72	5 49.3	+31.7	15.8	6 47.1	+31.9	15.8	7 44.8	+32.1	15.8	8 42.5	+32.4	15.9
73	6 21.0	+31.5	14.9	7 19.0	+31.7	14.9	8 16.9	+32.0	15.0	9 14.9	+32.2	15.0
74	6 52.5	+31.5	14.1	7 50.7	+31.7	14.1	8 48.9	+31.9	14.1	9 47.1	+32.1	14.2
75	7 24.0	+31.4	13.2	8 22.4	+31.6	13.2	9 20.8	+31.8	13.3	10 19.2	+32.0	13.3
76	7 55.4	+31.2	12.3	8 54.0	+31.4	12.4	9 52.6	+31.6	12.4	10 51.2	+31.8	12.4
77	8 26.6	+31.2	11.5	9 25.4	+31.4	11.5	10 24.2	+31.5	11.5	11 23.0	+31.7	11.6
78	8 57.8	+31.0	10.6	9 56.8	+31.2	10.6	10 55.7	+31.4	10.7	11 54.7	+31.5	10.7
79	9 28.8	+30.9	9.7	10 28.0	+31.0	9.8	11 27.1	+31.2	9.8	12 26.2	+31.3	9.8
80	9 59.7	+30.8	8.9	10 59.0	+30.9	8.9	11 58.3	+31.0	8.9	12 57.5	+31.2	9.0
81	10 30.5	+30.6	8.0	11 29.9	+30.7	8.0	12 29.3	+30.9	8.1	13 28.7	+31.0	8.1
82	11 01.1	+30.5	7.1	12 00.6	+30.6	7.1	13 00.2	+30.7	7.2	13 59.7	+30.8	7.2
83	11 31.6	+30.3	6.2	12 31.2	+30.4	6.3	13 30.9	+30.5	6.3	14 30.5	+30.6	6.3
84	12 01.9	+30.1	5.4	13 01.6	+30.3	5.4	14 01.4	+30.3	5.4	15 01.1	+30.4	5.4
85	12 32.0	+30.0	4.5	13 31.9	+30.0	4.5	14 31.7	+30.1	4.5	15 31.5	+30.2	4.5
86	13 02.0	+29.8	3.6	14 01.9	+29.8	3.6	15 01.8	+29.9	3.6	16 01.7	+29.9	3.6
87	13 31.8	+29.6	2.7	14 31.7	+29.7	2.7	15 31.7	+29.6	2.7	16 31.6	+29.7	2.7
88	14 01.4	+29.4	1.8	15 01.4	+29.4	1.8	16 01.3	+29.5	1.8	17 01.3	+29.5	1.8
89	14 30.8	+29.2	0.9	15 30.8	+29.2	0.9	16 30.8	+29.2	0.9	17 30.8	+29.2	0.9
90	15 00.0	+29.0	0.0	16 00.0	+29.0	0.0	17 00.0	+29.0	0.0	18 00.0	+29.0	0.0
	15°			16°			17°			18°		

19° Hc	d	Z	20° Hc	d	Z	21° Hc	d	Z	22° Hc	d	Z	Dec.
° ′	′	°	° ′	′	°	° ′	′	°	° ′	′	°	°
27 17.0	−22.2	100.2	27 06.1	−23.3	100.7	26 54.7	−24.4	101.2	26 42.7	−25.4	101.7	0
26 54.8	−22.7	101.3	26 42.8	−23.7	101.8	26 30.3	−24.7	102.3	26 17.3	−25.8	102.7	1
26 32.1	−23.1	102.3	26 19.1	−24.2	102.8	26 05.6	−25.2	103.3	25 51.5	−26.2	103.7	2
26 09.0	−23.5	103.3	25 54.9	−24.5	103.8	25 40.4	−25.6	104.3	25 25.3	−26.6	104.7	3
25 45.5	−24.0	104.4	25 30.4	−25.0	104.8	25 14.8	−26.0	105.3	24 58.7	−27.0	105.7	4
25 21.5	−24.4	105.4	25 05.4	−25.4	105.8	24 48.8	−26.4	106.3	24 31.7	−27.4	106.7	5
24 57.1	−24.8	106.4	24 40.0	−25.8	106.8	24 22.4	−26.8	107.3	24 04.3	−27.7	107.7	6
24 32.3	−25.2	107.4	24 14.2	−26.2	107.8	23 55.6	−27.2	108.2	23 36.6	−28.1	108.7	7
24 07.1	−25.6	108.4	23 48.0	−26.6	108.8	23 28.4	−27.5	109.2	23 08.5	−28.5	109.6	8
23 41.5	−25.9	109.4	23 21.4	−26.9	109.8	23 00.9	−27.9	110.2	22 40.0	−28.8	110.6	9
23 15.6	−26.3	110.4	22 54.5	−27.3	110.8	22 33.0	−28.2	111.1	22 11.2	−29.1	111.5	10
22 49.3	−26.7	111.3	22 27.2	−27.6	111.7	22 04.8	−28.5	112.1	21 42.1	−29.5	112.5	11
22 22.6	−27.0	112.3	21 59.6	−27.9	112.7	21 36.3	−28.8	113.1	21 12.6	−29.7	113.4	12
21 55.6	−27.4	113.3	21 31.7	−28.3	113.6	21 07.5	−29.2	114.0	20 42.9	−30.1	114.3	13
21 28.2	−27.7	114.2	21 03.4	−28.6	114.6	20 38.3	−29.5	114.9	20 12.8	−30.3	115.3	14
21 00.5	−28.0	115.2	20 34.8	−28.8	115.5	20 08.8	−29.7	115.9	19 42.5	−30.6	116.2	15
20 32.5	−28.3	116.1	20 06.0	−29.2	116.5	19 39.1	−30.1	116.8	19 11.9	−30.9	117.1	16
20 04.2	−28.6	117.1	19 36.8	−29.5	117.4	19 09.0	−30.3	117.7	18 41.0	−31.1	118.0	17
19 35.6	−28.8	118.0	19 07.3	−29.7	118.3	18 38.7	−30.5	118.6	18 09.9	−31.4	118.9	18
19 06.8	−29.2	118.9	18 37.6	−30.0	119.2	18 08.2	−30.9	119.5	17 38.5	−31.7	119.8	19
18 37.6	−29.4	119.9	18 07.6	−30.3	120.1	17 37.3	−31.0	120.4	17 06.8	−31.8	120.7	20
18 08.2	−29.7	120.8	17 37.3	−30.5	121.0	17 06.3	−31.3	121.3	16 35.0	−32.1	121.6	21
17 38.5	−30.0	121.7	17 06.8	−30.7	122.0	16 35.0	−31.5	122.2	16 02.9	−32.3	122.5	22
17 08.5	−30.1	122.6	16 36.1	−31.0	122.8	16 03.5	−31.8	123.1	15 30.6	−32.5	123.3	23
16 38.4	−30.5	123.5	16 05.1	−31.2	123.7	15 31.7	−31.9	124.0	14 58.1	−32.7	124.2	24
16 07.9	−30.6	124.4	15 33.9	−31.4	124.6	14 59.8	−32.2	124.9	14 25.4	−32.9	125.1	25
15 37.3	−30.9	125.3	15 02.5	−31.6	125.5	14 27.6	−32.3	125.7	13 52.5	−33.1	125.9	26
15 06.4	−31.0	126.2	14 30.9	−31.8	126.4	13 55.3	−32.6	126.6	13 19.4	−33.2	126.8	27
14 35.4	−31.3	127.1	13 59.1	−32.0	127.3	13 22.7	−32.7	127.5	12 46.2	−33.5	127.6	28
14 04.1	−31.4	127.9	13 27.1	−32.1	128.1	12 50.0	−32.9	128.3	12 12.7	−33.5	128.5	29
13 32.7	−31.7	128.8	12 55.0	−32.4	129.0	12 17.1	−33.0	129.2	11 39.2	−33.7	129.3	30
13 01.0	−31.8	129.7	12 22.6	−32.5	129.9	11 44.1	−33.2	130.0	11 05.5	−33.9	130.2	31
12 29.2	−32.0	130.6	11 50.1	−32.6	130.7	11 10.9	−33.3	130.9	10 31.6	−34.0	131.0	32
11 57.2	−32.1	131.4	11 17.5	−32.8	131.6	10 37.6	−33.5	131.7	9 57.6	−34.1	131.9	33
11 25.1	−32.3	132.3	10 44.7	−33.0	132.4	10 04.1	−33.6	132.6	9 23.5	−34.2	132.7	34
10 52.8	−32.4	133.2	10 11.7	−33.0	133.3	9 30.5	−33.7	133.4	8 49.3	−34.4	133.5	35
10 20.4	−32.6	134.0	9 38.7	−33.2	134.1	8 56.8	−33.8	134.3	8 14.9	−34.4	134.4	36
9 47.8	−32.7	134.9	9 05.5	−33.4	135.0	8 23.0	−33.9	135.1	7 40.5	−34.6	135.2	37
9 15.1	−32.8	135.7	8 32.1	−33.4	135.8	7 49.1	−34.0	135.9	7 05.9	−34.6	136.0	38
8 42.3	−32.9	136.6	7 58.7	−33.5	136.7	7 15.1	−34.2	136.7	6 31.3	−34.7	136.8	39
8 09.4	−33.0	137.4	7 25.2	−33.6	137.5	6 40.9	−34.2	137.6	5 56.6	−34.8	137.7	40
7 36.4	−33.2	138.2	6 51.6	−33.7	138.3	6 06.7	−34.2	138.4	5 21.8	−34.8	138.5	41
7 03.2	−33.2	139.1	6 17.9	−33.8	139.2	5 32.5	−34.4	139.2	4 47.0	−34.9	139.3	42
6 30.0	−33.3	139.9	5 44.1	−33.9	140.0	4 58.1	−34.4	140.1	4 12.1	−34.9	140.1	43
5 56.7	−33.3	140.8	5 10.2	−33.9	140.8	4 23.7	−34.4	140.9	3 37.2	−35.0	140.9	44
5 23.4	−33.5	141.6	4 36.3	−34.0	141.7	3 49.3	−34.6	141.7	3 02.2	−35.1	141.7	45
4 49.9	−33.5	142.4	4 02.3	−34.0	142.5	3 14.7	−34.5	142.5	2 27.1	−35.0	142.5	46
4 16.4	−33.5	143.3	3 28.3	−34.0	143.3	2 40.2	−34.6	143.3	1 52.1	−35.1	143.4	47
3 42.9	−33.6	144.1	2 54.3	−34.2	144.1	2 05.6	−34.6	144.2	1 17.0	−35.1	144.2	48
3 09.3	−33.7	144.9	2 20.1	−34.1	145.0	1 31.0	−34.6	145.0	0 41.9	−35.1	145.0	49
2 35.6	−33.7	145.8	1 46.0	−34.1	145.8	0 56.4	−34.6	145.8	0 06.8	−35.1	145.8	50
2 01.9	−33.7	146.6	1 11.9	−34.2	146.6	0 21.8	−34.7	146.6	0 28.3	+35.1	33.4	51
1 28.2	−33.7	147.4	0 37.7	−34.2	147.4	0 12.9	+34.6	32.6	1 03.4	+35.1	32.6	52
0 54.5	−33.7	148.2	0 03.5	−34.2	148.2	0 47.5	+34.6	31.8	1 38.5	+35.1	31.8	53
0 20.8	−33.7	149.1	0 30.7	+34.1	30.9	1 22.1	+34.6	30.9	2 13.6	+35.0	31.0	54
0 12.9	+33.8	30.1	1 04.8	+34.2	30.1	1 56.7	+34.6	30.1	2 48.6	+35.0	30.1	55
0 46.7	+33.7	29.3	1 39.0	+34.1	29.3	2 31.3	+34.6	29.3	3 23.6	+35.0	29.3	56
1 20.4	+33.7	28.5	2 13.1	+34.2	28.5	3 05.9	+34.5	28.5	3 58.6	+34.9	28.5	57
1 54.1	+33.7	27.6	2 47.3	+34.0	27.6	3 40.4	+34.5	27.7	4 33.5	+34.9	27.7	58
2 27.8	+33.6	26.8	3 21.3	+34.1	26.8	4 14.9	+34.4	26.9	5 08.4	+34.8	26.9	59
3 01.4	+33.6	26.0	3 55.4	+34.0	26.0	4 49.3	+34.3	26.0	5 43.2	+34.7	26.1	60
3 35.0	+33.6	25.1	4 29.4	+33.9	25.2	5 23.6	+34.3	25.2	6 17.9	+34.7	25.3	61
4 08.6	+33.5	24.3	5 03.3	+33.9	24.3	5 57.9	+34.3	24.4	6 52.6	+34.6	24.4	62
4 42.1	+33.5	23.5	5 37.2	+33.8	23.5	6 32.2	+34.1	23.6	7 27.2	+34.4	23.6	63
5 15.6	+33.4	22.6	6 11.0	+33.7	22.7	7 06.3	+34.1	22.7	8 01.6	+34.4	22.8	64
5 49.0	+33.3	21.8	6 44.7	+33.6	21.9	7 40.4	+33.9	21.9	8 36.0	+34.3	22.0	65
6 22.3	+33.2	21.0	7 18.3	+33.6	21.0	8 14.3	+33.9	21.1	9 10.3	+34.1	21.1	66
6 55.5	+33.2	20.1	7 51.9	+33.4	20.2	8 48.2	+33.7	20.2	9 44.4	+34.1	20.3	67
7 28.7	+33.0	19.3	8 25.3	+33.3	19.3	9 21.9	+33.6	19.4	10 18.5	+33.9	19.5	68
8 01.7	+33.0	18.5	8 58.6	+33.3	18.5	9 55.5	+33.5	18.6	10 52.4	+33.8	18.6	69
8 34.7	+32.8	17.6	9 31.9	+33.1	17.7	10 29.0	+33.4	17.7	11 26.2	+33.6	17.8	70
9 07.5	+32.7	16.8	10 05.0	+32.9	16.8	11 02.4	+33.2	16.9	11 59.8	+33.5	16.9	71
9 40.2	+32.6	15.9	10 37.9	+32.9	16.0	11 35.6	+33.1	16.0	12 33.3	+33.3	16.1	72
10 12.8	+32.5	15.1	11 10.8	+32.6	15.1	12 08.7	+32.9	15.2	13 06.6	+33.1	15.2	73
10 45.3	+32.3	14.2	11 43.4	+32.6	14.3	12 41.6	+32.7	14.3	13 39.7	+33.0	14.4	74
11 17.6	+32.2	13.3	12 16.0	+32.4	13.4	13 14.3	+32.6	13.4	14 12.7	+32.8	13.5	75
11 49.8	+32.0	12.5	12 48.4	+32.2	12.5	13 46.9	+32.4	12.6	14 45.5	+32.6	12.6	76
12 21.8	+31.8	11.6	13 20.6	+32.0	11.7	14 19.3	+32.2	11.7	15 18.1	+32.3	11.8	77
12 53.6	+31.7	10.8	13 52.6	+31.8	10.8	14 51.5	+32.0	10.8	15 50.4	+32.2	10.9	78
13 25.3	+31.5	9.9	14 24.4	+31.7	9.9	15 23.5	+31.8	10.0	16 22.6	+32.0	10.0	79
13 56.8	+31.3	9.0	14 56.1	+31.4	9.0	15 55.3	+31.6	9.1	16 54.6	+31.7	9.1	80
14 28.1	+31.1	8.1	15 27.5	+31.3	8.2	16 26.9	+31.4	8.2	17 26.3	+31.5	8.2	81
14 59.2	+30.9	7.2	15 58.8	+31.0	7.3	16 58.3	+31.1	7.3	17 57.8	+31.2	7.4	82
15 30.1	+30.7	6.4	16 29.8	+30.8	6.4	17 29.4	+30.9	6.4	18 29.0	+31.0	6.5	83
16 00.8	+30.5	5.5	17 00.6	+30.5	5.5	18 00.3	+30.6	5.5	19 00.0	+30.7	5.5	84
16 31.3	+30.2	4.6	17 31.1	+30.3	4.6	18 30.9	+30.4	4.6	19 30.7	+30.5	4.6	85
17 01.5	+30.0	3.7	18 01.4	+30.1	3.7	19 01.3	+30.1	3.7	20 01.2	+30.1	3.7	86
17 31.5	+29.8	2.8	18 31.5	+29.8	2.8	19 31.4	+29.8	2.8	20 31.3	+29.9	2.8	87
18 01.3	+29.5	1.8	19 01.3	+29.5	1.9	20 01.2	+29.6	1.9	21 01.2	+29.6	1.9	88
18 30.8	+29.2	0.9	19 30.8	+29.2	0.9	20 30.8	+29.2	0.9	21 30.8	+29.2	0.9	89
19 00.0	+28.9	0.0	20 00.0	+28.9	0.0	21 00.0	+28.9	0.0	22 00.0	+28.9	0.0	90
19°			20°			21°			22°			

S. Lat. {L.H.A. greater than 180° ....Zn=180°−Z; L.H.A. less than 180°...........Zn=180°+Z}

LATITUDE SAME NAME AS DECLINATION   L.H.A. 119°, 241°

62°, 298° L.H.A. LATITUDE SAME NAME AS DECLINATION

N. Lat. {L.H.A. greater than 180° .....Zn=Z; L.H.A. less than 180°............Zn=360°−Z}

Dec.	15° Hc	15° d	15° Z	16° Hc	16° d	16° Z	17° Hc	17° d	17° Z	18° Hc	18° d	18° Z	19° Hc	19° d	19° Z	20° Hc	20° d	20° Z	21° Hc	21° d	21° Z	22° Hc	22° d	22° Z	Dec.
°	° ′	′	°	° ′	′	°	° ′	′	°	° ′	′	°	° ′	′	°	° ′	′	°	° ′	′	°	° ′	′	°	°
0	26 58.0	+17.2	97.8	26 49.6	+18.3	98.3	26 40.6	+19.4	98.8	26 31.1	+20.5	99.3	26 21.2	+21.5	99.8	26 10.7	+22.6	100.3	25 59.7	+23.7	100.8	25 48.2	+24.8	101.3	0
1	27 15.2	+16.7	96.8	27 07.9	+17.8	97.3	27 00.0	+18.9	97.8	26 51.6	+20.0	98.3	26 42.7	+21.1	98.8	26 33.3	+22.2	99.3	26 23.4	+23.3	99.8	26 13.0	+24.3	100.3	1
2	27 31.9	+16.1	95.7	27 25.7	+17.3	96.2	27 18.9	+18.5	96.7	27 11.6	+19.6	97.2	27 03.8	+20.7	97.7	26 55.5	+21.7	98.2	26 46.7	+22.8	98.7	26 37.3	+23.9	99.2	2
3	27 48.0	+15.7	94.6	27 43.0	+16.8	95.1	27 37.4	+17.9	95.6	27 31.2	+19.0	96.2	27 24.5	+20.1	96.7	27 17.2	+21.3	97.2	27 09.5	+22.3	97.7	27 01.2	+23.4	98.2	3
4	28 03.7	+15.2	93.5	27 59.8	+16.3	94.0	27 55.3	+17.4	94.6	27 50.2	+18.6	95.1	27 44.6	+19.7	95.6	27 38.5	+20.8	96.1	27 31.8	+21.9	96.7	27 24.6	+23.0	97.2	4
5	28 18.9	+14.6	92.4	28 16.1	+15.7	92.9	28 12.7	+16.9	93.5	28 08.8	+18.0	94.0	28 04.3	+19.2	94.5	27 59.3	+20.3	95.1	27 53.7	+21.4	95.6	27 47.6	+22.5	96.1	5
6	28 33.5	+14.0	91.3	28 31.8	+15.3	91.8	28 29.6	+16.4	92.4	28 26.8	+17.6	92.9	28 23.5	+18.7	93.5	28 19.6	+19.8	94.0	28 15.1	+20.9	94.5	28 10.1	+22.0	95.1	6
7	28 47.5	+13.6	90.2	28 47.1	+14.6	90.7	28 46.0	+15.8	91.3	28 44.4	+17.0	91.8	28 42.2	+18.1	92.4	28 39.4	+19.2	92.9	28 36.0	+20.4	93.5	28 32.1	+21.5	94.0	7
8	29 01.1	+12.9	89.1	29 01.7	+14.2	89.6	29 01.8	+15.4	90.2	29 01.4	+16.4	90.7	29 00.3	+17.6	91.3	28 58.6	+18.8	91.8	28 56.4	+19.9	92.4	28 53.6	+21.0	93.0	8
9	29 14.0	+12.5	88.0	29 15.9	+13.6	88.5	29 17.2	+14.7	89.1	29 17.8	+15.9	89.6	29 17.9	+17.1	90.2	29 17.4	+18.2	90.8	29 16.3	+19.4	91.3	29 14.6	+20.5	91.9	9
10	29 26.5	+11.8	86.8	29 29.5	+13.0	87.4	29 31.9	+14.2	88.0	29 33.7	+15.4	88.5	29 35.0	+16.5	89.1	29 35.6	+17.7	89.7	29 35.7	+18.8	90.2	29 35.1	+20.0	90.8	10
11	29 38.3	+11.3	85.7	29 42.5	+12.5	86.3	29 46.1	+13.6	86.8	29 49.1	+14.8	87.4	29 51.5	+16.0	88.0	29 53.3	+17.1	88.6	29 54.5	+18.3	89.1	29 55.1	+19.4	89.7	11
12	29 49.6	+10.7	84.6	29 55.0	+11.8	85.2	29 59.7	+13.1	85.7	30 03.9	+14.2	86.3	30 07.5	+15.4	86.9	30 10.4	+16.6	87.5	30 12.8	+17.7	88.0	30 14.5	+18.9	88.6	12
13	30 00.3	+10.1	83.4	30 06.8	+11.3	84.0	30 12.8	+12.5	84.6	30 18.1	+13.7	85.2	30 22.9	+14.8	85.8	30 27.0	+16.0	86.3	30 30.5	+17.2	86.9	30 33.4	+18.4	87.5	13
14	30 10.4	+9.5	82.3	30 18.1	+10.7	82.9	30 25.3	+11.9	83.5	30 31.8	+13.1	84.0	30 37.7	+14.3	84.6	30 43.0	+15.4	85.2	30 47.7	+16.6	85.8	30 51.8	+17.7	86.4	14
15	30 19.9	+8.9	81.2	30 28.8	+10.1	81.7	30 37.2	+11.2	82.3	30 44.9	+12.4	82.9	30 52.0	+13.6	83.5	30 58.4	+14.9	84.1	31 04.3	+16.0	84.7	31 09.5	+17.2	85.3	15
16	30 28.8	+8.4	80.0	30 38.9	+9.5	80.6	30 48.4	+10.7	81.2	30 57.3	+11.9	81.8	31 05.6	+13.1	82.4	31 13.3	+14.2	83.0	31 20.3	+15.4	83.6	31 26.7	+16.6	84.2	16
17	30 37.2	+7.7	78.9	30 48.4	+8.9	79.4	30 59.1	+10.1	80.0	31 09.2	+11.3	80.6	31 18.7	+12.4	81.2	31 27.5	+13.6	81.8	31 35.7	+14.8	82.4	31 43.3	+16.0	83.1	17
18	30 44.9	+7.1	77.7	30 57.3	+8.3	78.3	31 09.2	+9.5	78.9	31 20.5	+10.6	79.5	31 31.1	+11.8	80.1	31 41.1	+13.0	80.7	31 50.5	+14.2	81.3	31 59.3	+15.4	81.9	18
19	30 52.0	+6.4	76.6	31 05.6	+7.7	77.1	31 18.7	+8.8	77.7	31 31.1	+10.0	78.3	31 42.9	+11.2	78.9	31 54.1	+12.4	79.5	32 04.7	+13.6	80.2	32 14.7	+14.7	80.8	19
20	30 58.4	+5.9	75.4	31 13.3	+7.0	76.0	31 27.5	+8.2	76.6	31 41.1	+9.4	77.2	31 54.1	+10.6	77.8	32 06.5	+11.8	78.4	32 18.3	+12.9	79.0	32 29.4	+14.2	79.6	20
21	31 04.3	+5.2	74.2	31 20.3	+6.4	74.8	31 35.7	+7.6	75.4	31 50.5	+8.8	76.0	32 04.7	+10.0	76.6	32 18.3	+11.1	77.2	32 31.2	+12.4	77.8	32 43.6	+13.5	78.5	21
22	31 09.5	+4.6	73.1	31 26.7	+5.8	73.7	31 43.3	+6.9	74.2	31 59.3	+8.1	74.8	32 14.7	+9.3	75.4	32 29.4	+10.5	76.1	32 43.6	+11.6	76.7	32 57.1	+12.8	77.3	22
23	31 14.1	+4.0	71.9	31 32.5	+5.1	72.5	31 50.2	+6.3	73.1	32 07.4	+7.5	73.7	32 24.0	+8.6	74.3	32 39.9	+9.8	74.9	32 55.2	+11.0	75.5	33 09.9	+12.2	76.1	23
24	31 18.1	+3.3	70.7	31 37.6	+4.5	71.3	31 56.5	+5.7	71.9	32 14.9	+6.8	72.5	32 32.6	+8.0	73.1	32 49.7	+9.2	73.7	33 06.2	+10.4	74.3	33 22.1	+11.5	75.0	24
25	31 21.4	+2.7	69.6	31 42.1	+3.8	70.1	32 02.2	+5.0	70.7	32 21.7	+6.1	71.3	32 40.6	+7.3	71.9	32 58.9	+8.5	72.5	33 16.6	+9.7	73.2	33 33.6	+10.9	73.8	25
26	31 24.1	+2.1	68.4	31 45.9	+3.2	69.0	32 07.2	+4.3	69.6	32 27.8	+5.5	70.1	32 47.9	+6.7	70.8	33 07.4	+7.8	71.4	33 26.3	+9.0	72.0	33 44.5	+10.2	72.6	26
27	31 26.2	+1.4	67.2	31 49.1	+2.6	67.8	32 11.5	+3.7	68.4	32 33.3	+4.9	69.0	32 54.6	+6.0	69.6	33 15.2	+7.2	70.2	33 35.3	+8.3	70.8	33 54.7	+9.5	71.4	27
28	31 27.6	+0.8	66.1	31 51.7	+1.9	66.6	32 15.2	+3.0	67.2	32 38.2	+4.2	67.8	33 00.6	+5.3	68.4	33 22.4	+6.5	69.0	33 43.6	+7.6	69.6	34 04.2	+8.8	70.2	28
29	31 28.4	+0.1	64.9	31 53.6	+1.2	65.4	32 18.2	+2.4	66.0	32 42.4	+3.5	66.6	33 05.9	+4.6	67.2	33 28.9	+5.8	67.8	33 51.2	+7.0	68.4	34 13.0	+8.1	69.0	29
30	31 28.5	−0.5	63.7	31 54.8	+0.6	64.3	32 20.6	+1.7	64.8	32 45.9	+2.8	65.4	33 10.5	+4.0	66.0	33 34.7	+5.1	66.6	33 58.2	+6.2	67.2	34 21.1	+7.4	67.8	30
31	31 28.0	−1.1	62.5	31 55.4	0.0	63.1	32 22.3	+1.1	63.6	32 48.7	+2.1	64.2	33 14.5	+3.3	64.8	33 39.8	+4.4	65.4	34 04.4	+5.6	66.0	34 28.5	+6.7	66.6	31
32	31 26.9	−1.8	61.4	31 55.4	−0.7	61.9	32 23.4	+0.3	62.5	32 50.8	+1.5	63.0	33 17.8	+2.6	63.6	33 44.2	+3.7	64.2	34 10.0	+4.8	64.8	34 35.2	+6.0	65.4	32
33	31 25.1	−2.4	60.2	31 54.7	−1.4	60.7	32 23.7	−0.2	61.3	32 52.3	+0.8	61.8	33 20.4	+1.9	62.4	33 47.9	+3.0	63.0	34 14.8	+4.2	63.6	34 41.2	+5.3	64.2	33
34	31 22.7	−3.1	59.0	31 53.3	−2.0	59.6	32 23.5	−1.0	60.1	32 53.1	+0.2	60.7	33 22.3	+1.2	61.2	33 50.9	+2.3	61.8	34 19.0	+3.4	62.4	34 46.5	+4.5	63.0	34
35	31 19.6	−3.7	57.9	31 51.3	−2.7	58.4	32 22.5	−1.6	58.9	32 53.3	−0.6	59.5	33 23.5	+0.5	60.0	33 53.2	+1.6	60.6	34 22.4	+2.7	61.2	34 51.0	+3.8	61.8	35
36	31 15.9	−4.3	56.7	31 48.6	−3.3	57.2	32 20.9	−2.3	57.7	32 52.7	−1.2	58.3	33 24.0	−0.2	58.8	33 54.8	+0.9	59.4	34 25.1	+2.0	60.0	34 54.8	+3.1	60.6	36
37	31 11.6	−5.0	55.5	31 45.3	−3.9	56.0	32 18.6	−2.9	56.5	32 51.5	−1.9	57.1	33 23.8	−0.8	57.6	33 55.7	+0.2	58.2	34 27.1	+1.2	58.8	34 57.9	+2.4	59.4	37
38	31 06.6	−5.6	54.4	31 41.4	−4.6	54.9	32 15.7	−3.6	55.4	32 49.6	−2.6	55.9	33 23.0	−1.6	56.4	33 55.9	−0.5	57.0	34 28.3	+0.6	57.6	35 00.3	+1.6	58.1	38
39	31 01.0	−6.2	53.2	31 36.8	−5.3	53.7	32 12.1	−4.2	54.2	32 47.0	−3.3	54.7	33 21.4	−2.2	55.2	33 55.4	−1.2	55.8	34 28.9	−0.2	56.3	35 01.9	+0.9	56.9	39
40	30 54.8	−6.8	52.0	31 31.5	−5.8	52.5	32 07.9	−5.0	53.0	32 43.7	−3.9	53.5	33 19.2	−2.9	54.0	33 54.2	−1.9	54.6	34 28.7	−0.8	55.1	35 02.8	+0.1	55.7	40
41	30 48.0	−7.4	50.9	31 25.7	−6.5	51.3	32 02.9	−5.5	51.8	32 39.8	−4.6	52.3	33 16.3	−3.6	52.8	33 52.3	−2.6	53.4	34 27.9	−1.6	53.9	35 02.9	−0.5	54.5	41
42	30 40.6	−8.1	49.7	31 19.2	−7.2	50.2	31 57.4	−6.2	50.7	32 35.2	−5.2	51.1	33 12.7	−4.3	51.7	33 49.7	−3.3	52.2	34 26.3	−2.4	52.7	35 02.4	−1.3	53.3	42
43	30 32.5	−8.7	48.6	31 12.0	−7.7	49.0	31 51.2	−6.9	49.5	32 30.0	−5.9	50.0	33 08.4	−5.0	50.5	33 46.4	−4.0	51.0	34 23.9	−3.0	51.5	35 01.1	−2.1	52.0	43
44	30 23.8	−9.2	47.4	31 04.3	−8.4	47.9	31 44.3	−7.4	48.3	32 24.1	−6.6	48.8	33 03.4	−5.6	49.3	33 42.4	−4.7	49.8	34 20.9	−3.7	50.3	34 59.0	−2.8	50.8	44
45	30 14.6	−9.9	46.3	30 55.9	−9.0	46.7	31 36.9	−8.2	47.2	32 17.5	−7.2	47.6	32 57.8	−6.4	48.1	33 37.7	−5.4	48.6	34 17.2	−4.5	49.1	34 56.2	−3.5	49.6	45
46	30 04.7	−10.4	45.1	30 46.9	−9.6	45.6	31 28.7	−8.7	46.0	32 10.3	−7.9	46.4	32 51.4	−6.9	46.9	33 32.3	−6.1	47.4	34 12.7	−5.2	47.9	34 52.7	−4.2	48.4	46
47	29 54.3	−11.1	44.0	30 37.3	−10.2	44.4	31 20.0	−9.4	44.8	32 02.4	−8.5	45.3	32 44.5	−7.7	45.7	33 26.2	−6.8	46.2	34 07.5	−5.9	46.7	34 48.5	−4.9	47.2	47
48	29 43.2	−11.6	42.9	30 27.1	−10.8	43.3	31 10.6	−10.0	43.7	31 53.9	−9.2	44.1	32 36.8	−8.3	44.5	33 19.4	−7.4	45.0	34 01.7	−6.6	45.5	34 43.6	−5.7	46.0	48
49	29 31.6	−12.1	41.7	30 16.3	−11.4	42.1	31 00.6	−10.6	42.5	31 44.7	−9.8	42.9	32 28.5	−9.0	43.4	33 12.0	−8.2	43.8	33 55.1	−7.3	44.3	34 37.9	−6.4	44.7	49
50	29 19.5	−12.8	40.6	30 04.9	−12.0	41.0	30 50.0	−11.2	41.4	31 34.9	−10.4	41.8	32 19.5	−9.6	42.2	33 03.8	−8.8	42.6	33 47.8	−7.9	43.1	34 31.5	−7.1	43.5	50
51	29 06.7	−13.3	39.5	29 52.9	−12.5	39.9	30 38.8	−11.8	40.2	31 24.5	−11.0	40.6	32 09.9	−10.2	41.0	32 55.0	−9.4	41.4	33 39.9	−8.7	41.9	34 24.4	−7.8	42.3	51
52	28 53.4	−13.8	38.4	29 40.4	−13.2	38.7	30 27.0	−12.3	39.1	31 13.5	−11.7	39.5	31 59.7	−10.9	39.9	32 45.6	−10.1	40.3	33 31.2	−9.3	40.7	34 16.6	−8.5	41.1	52
53	28 39.6	−14.4	37.3	29 27.2	−13.6	37.6	30 14.7	−13.0	38.0	31 01.8	−12.2	38.3	31 48.8	−11.5	38.7	32 35.5	−10.8	39.1	33 21.9	−10.0	39.5	34 08.1	−9.2	39.9	53
54	28 25.2	−14.9	36.2	29 13.6	−14.3	36.5	30 01.7	−13.6	36.8	30 49.6	−12.8	37.2	31 37.3	−12.1	37.6	32 24.7	−11.4	37.9	33 11.9	−10.6	38.3	33 58.9	−9.9	38.7	54
55	28 10.3	−15.4	35.1	28 59.3	−14.8	35.4	29 48.1	−14.1	35.7	30 36.8	−13.5	36.0	31 25.2	−12.8	36.4	32 13.3	−12.0	36.8	33 01.3	−11.3	37.2	33 49.0	−10.6	37.6	55
56	27 54.9	−16.0	34.0	28 44.5	−15.3	34.3	29 34.0	−14.7	34.6	30 23.3	−14.0	34.9	31 12.4	−13.3	35.3	32 01.3	−12.7	35.6	32 50.0	−12.0	36.0	33 38.4	−11.2	36.4	56
57	27 38.9	−16.5	32.9	28 29.2	−15.8	33.2	29 19.3	−15.2	33.5	30 09.3	−14.6	33.8	30 59.1	−14.0	34.1	31 48.6	−13.2	34.5	32 38.0	−12.6	34.8	33 27.2	−12.0	35.2	57
58	27 22.4	−16.9	31.8	28 13.4	−16.4	32.1	29 04.1	−15.8	32.4	29 54.7	−15.1	32.7	30 45.1	−14.5	33.0	31 35.4	−13.9	33.3	32 25.4	−13.2	33.7	33 15.2	−12.5	34.0	58
59	27 05.5	−17.5	30.7	27 57.0	−16.9	31.0	28 48.3	−16.3	31.3	29 39.6	−15.8	31.6	30 30.6	−15.1	31.9	31 21.5	−14.5	32.2	32 12.2	−13.9	32.5	33 02.7	−13.3	32.9	59
60	26 48.0	−17.9	29.6	27 40.1	−17.4	29.9	28 32.0	−16.8	30.2	29 23.8	−16.2	30.4	30 15.5	−15.7	30.7	31 07.0	−15.1	31.0	31 58.3	−14.5	31.4	32 49.4	−13.8	31.7	60
61	26 30.1	−18.4	28.6	27 22.7	−17.9	28.8	28 15.2	−17.3	29.1	29 07.6	−16.8	29.3	29 59.8	−16.2	29.6	30 51.9	−15.7	29.9	31 43.8	−15.1	30.2	32 35.6	−14.5	30.5	61
62	26 11.7	−18.9	27.5	27 04.8	−18.4	27.7	27 57.9	−17.9	28.0	28 50.8	−17.4	28.2	29 43.6	−16.8	28.5	30 36.2	−16.2	28.8	31 28.7	−15.7	29.1	32 21.1	−15.1	29.4	62
63	25 52.8	−19.4	26.5	26 46.4	−18.8	26.7	27 40.0	−18.4	26.9	28 33.4	−17.8	27.2	29 26.8	−17.4	27.4	30 20.0	−16.8	27.7	31 13.0	−16.2	28.0	32 06.0	−15.8	28.2	63
64	25 33.4	−19.7	25.4	26 27.6	−19.3	25.6	27 21.6	−18.8	25.8	28 15.6	−18.4	26.1	29 09.4	−17.8	26.3	30 03.2	−17.4	26.6	30 56.8	−16.9	26.8	31 50.2	−16.3	27.1	64
65	25 13.7	−20.3	24.4	26 08.3	−19.8	24.6	27 02.8	−19.3	24.8	27 57.2	−18.8	25.0	28 51.6	−18.4	25.2	29 45.8	−17.9	25.5	30 39.9	−17.4	25.7	31 33.9	−16.9	26.0	65
66	24 53.4	−20.6	23.3	25 48.5	−20.2	23.5	26 43.5	−19.8	23.7	27 38.4	−19.4	23.9	28 33.2	−18.9	24.1	29 27.9	−18.5	24.4	30 22.5	−18.0	24.6	31 17.0	−17.5	24.8	66
67	24 32.8	−21.1	22.3	25 28.3	−20.7	22.5	26 23.7	−20.3	22.7	27 19.0	−19.8	22.8	28 14.3	−19.5	23.1	29 09.4	−19.0	23.3	30 04.5	−18.5	23.5	30 59.5	−18.1	23.7	67
68	24 11.7	−21.5	21.3	25 07.6	−21.1	21.4	26 03.4	−20.7	21.6	26 59.2	−20.3	21.8	27 54.8	−19.9	22.0	28 50.4	−19.5	22.2	29 46.0	−19.1	22.4	30 41.4	−18.7	22.6	68
69	23 50.2	−21.9	20.2	24 46.5	−21.5	20.4	25 42.7	−21.1	20.6	26 38.9	−20.8	20.7	27 34.9	−20.4	20.9	28 30.9	−20.0	21.1	29 26.9	−19.6	21.3	30 22.7	−19.2	21.5	69
70	23 28.3	−22.2	19.2	24 25.0	−22.0	19.4	25 21.6	−21.6	19.5	26 18.1	−21.3	19.7	27 14.5	−20.8	19.9	28 10.9	−20.5	20.0	29 07.3	−20.2	20.2	30 03.5	−19.7	20.4	70
71	23 06.1	−22.7	18.2	24 03.0	−22.3	18.3	25 00.0	−22.0	18.5	25 56.8	−21.6	18.6	26 53.7	−21.4	18.8	27 50.4	−21.0	19.0	28 47.1	−20.6	19.1	29 43.8	−20.3	19.3	71
72	22 43.4	−23.0	17.2	23 40.7	−22.7	17.3	24 38.0	−22.5	17.5	25 35.2	−22.1	17.6	26 32.3	−21.8	17.8	27 29.4	−21.4	17.9	28 26.5	−21.1	18.1	29 23.5	−20.8	18.2	72
73	22 20.4	−23.4	16.2	23 18.0	−23.2	16.3	24 15.5	−22.8	16.4	25 13.1	−22.6	16.6	26 10.5	−22.2	16.7	27 08.0	−22.0	16.9	28 05.4	−21.6	17.0	29 02.7	−21.3	17.2	73
74	21 57.0	−23.8	15.2	22 54.8	−23.4	15.3	23 52.7	−23.2	15.4	24 50.5	−22.9	15.6	25 48.3	−22.7	15.7	26 46.0	−22.3	15.8	27 43.8	−22.1	16.0	28 41.4	−21.8	16.1	74
75	21 33.2	−24.1	14.2	22 31.4	−23.9	14.3	23 29.5	−23.6	14.4	24 27.6	−23.4	14.5	25 25.6	−23.1	14.7	26 23.7	−22.9	14.8	27 21.7	−22.6	14.9	28 19.6	−22.3	15.0	75
76	21 09.1	−24.5	13.2	22 07.5	−24.2	13.3	23 05.9	−24.0	13.4	24 04.2	−23.7	13.5	25 02.5	−23.5	13.6	26 00.8	−23.2	13.7	26 59.1	−23.0	13.9	27 57.3	−22.7	14.0	76
77	20 44.6	−24.7	12.3	21 43.3	−24.6	12.3	22 41.9	−24.4	12.4	23 40.5	−24.2	12.5	24 39.0	−23.9	12.6	25 37.6	−23.7	12.7	26 36.1	−23.5	12.8	27 34.6	−23.3	12.9	77
78	20 19.9	−25.1	11.3	21 18.7	−24.9	11.4	22 17.5	−24.7	11.4	23 16.3	−24.5	11.5	24 15.1	−24.3	11.6	25 13.9	−24.2	11.7	26 12.6	−23.9	11.8	27 11.3	−23.7	11.9	78
79	19 54.8	−25.4	10.3	20 53.8	−25.2	10.4	21 52.8	−25.1	10.5	22 51.8	−24.9	10.5	23 50.8	−24.7	10.6	24 49.7	−24.5	10.7	25 48.7	−24.3	10.8	26 47.6	−24.1	10.9	79
80	19 29.4	−25.8	9.4	20 28.6	−25.6	9.4	21 27.7	−25.4	9.5	22 26.9	−25.2	9.5	23 26.1	−25.1	9.6	24 25.2	−24.9	9.7	25 24.4	−24.8	9.8	26 23.5	−24.6	9.9	80
81	19 03.6	−26.0	8.4	20 03.0	−25.9	8.5	21 02.3	−25.7	8.5	22 01.7	−25.6	8.6	23 01.0	−25.4	8.6	24 00.3	−25.3	8.7	24 59.6	−25.1	8.8	25 58.9	−25.0	8.8	81
82	18 37.6	−26.3	7.5	19 37.1	−26.1	7.5	20 36.6	−26.0	7.5	21 36.1	−25.9	7.6	22 35.6	−25.8	7.6	23 35.0	−25.6	7.7	24 34.5	−25.6	7.8	25 33.9	−25.4	7.8	82
83	18 11.3	−26.5	6.5	19 11.0	−26.5	6.5	20 10.6	−26.4	6.6	21 10.2	−26.3	6.6	22 09.8	−26.2	6.7	23 09.4	−26.1	6.7	24 08.9	−25.9	6.8	25 08.5	−25.8	6.8	83
84	17 44.8	−26.9	5.6	18 44.5	−26.8	5.6	19 44.2	−26.7	5.6	20 43.9	−26.6	5.7	21 43.6	−26.5	5.7	22 43.3	−26.4	5.7	23 43.0	−26.3	5.8	24 42.7	−26.2	5.8	84
85	17 17.9	−27.1	4.6	18 17.7	−27.0	4.6	19 17.5	−26.9	4.7	20 17.3	−26.8	4.7	21 17.1	−26.8	4.7	22 16.9	−26.7	4.8	23 16.7	−26.6	4.8	24 16.5	−26.6	4.8	85
86	16 50.8	−27.3	3.7	17 50.7	−27.3	3.7	18 50.6	−27.3	3.7	19 50.5	−27.2	3.8	20 50.3	−27.1	3.8	21 50.2	−27.1	3.8	22 50.1	−27.0	3.8	23 49.9	−26.9	3.9	86
87	16 23.5	−27.6	2.8	17 23.4	−27.5	2.8	18 23.3	−27.5	2.8	19 23.3	−27.5	2.8	20 23.2	−27.4	2.8	21 23.1	−27.4	2.8	22 23.1	−27.4	2.9	23 23.0	−27.3	2.9	87
88	15 55.9	−27.8	1.8	16 55.9	−27.9	1.8	17 55.8	−27.8	1.9	18 55.8	−27.8	1.9	19 55.8	−27.8	1.9	20 55.7	−27.7	1.9	21 55.7	−27.7	1.9	22 55.7	−27.7	1.9	88
89	15 28.1	−28.1	0.9	16 28.0	−28.0	0.9	17 28.0	−28.0	0.9	18 28.0	−28.0	0.9	19 28.0	−28.0	0.9	20 28.0	−28.0	0.9	21 28.0	−28.0	0.9	22 28.0	−28.0	1.0	89
90	15 00.0	−28.3	0.0	16 00.0	−28.3	0.0	17 00.0	−28.3	0.0	18 00.0	−28.3	0.0	19 00.0	−28.3	0.0	20 00.0	−28.3	0.0	21 00.0	−28.3	0.0	22 00.0	−28.3	0.0	90
	15°			16°			17°			18°			19°			20°			21°			22°			

62°, 298° L.H.A. LATITUDE SAME NAME AS DECLINATION

LATITUDE CONTRARY NAME TO DECLINATION L.H.A. 62°, 298°

Dec.	15° Hc	d	Z	16° Hc	d	Z	17° Hc	d	Z	18° Hc	d	Z	19° Hc	d	Z	20° Hc	d	Z	21° Hc	d	Z	22° Hc	d	Z	Dec.
°	° ′	′	°	° ′	′	°	° ′	′	°	° ′	′	°	° ′	′	°	° ′	′	°	° ′	′	°	° ′	′	°	°
0	26 58.0	-17.7	97.8	26 49.6	-18.8	98.3	26 40.6	-19.9	98.8	26 31.1	-20.9	99.3	26 21.2	-22.1	99.8	26 10.7	-23.1	100.3	25 59.7	-24.1	100.8	25 48.2	-25.2	101.3	0
1	26 40.3	-18.1	98.9	26 30.8	-19.2	99.4	26 20.7	-20.3	99.9	26 10.2	-21.4	100.4	25 59.1	-22.4	100.9	25 47.6	-23.5	101.3	25 35.6	-24.6	101.8	25 23.0	-25.5	102.3	1
2	26 22.2	-18.6	100.0	26 11.6	-19.7	100.5	26 00.4	-20.8	100.9	25 48.8	-21.9	101.4	25 36.7	-22.9	101.9	25 24.1	-24.0	102.4	25 11.0	-25.0	102.8	24 57.5	-26.0	103.3	2
3	26 03.6	-19.1	101.0	25 51.9	-20.2	101.5	25 39.6	-21.2	102.0	25 26.9	-22.2	102.4	25 13.8	-23.3	102.9	25 00.1	-24.3	103.4	24 46.0	-25.3	103.8	24 31.5	-26.4	104.3	3
4	25 44.5	-19.5	102.1	25 31.7	-20.6	102.6	25 18.4	-21.6	103.0	25 04.7	-22.7	103.5	24 50.5	-23.8	103.9	24 35.8	-24.7	104.4	24 20.7	-25.8	104.8	24 05.1	-26.7	105.2	4
5	25 25.0	-20.0	103.1	25 11.1	-21.0	103.6	24 56.8	-22.1	104.0	24 42.0	-23.1	104.5	24 26.7	-24.1	104.9	24 11.1	-25.2	105.4	23 54.9	-26.1	105.8	23 38.4	-27.1	106.2	5
6	25 05.0	-20.4	104.2	24 50.1	-21.5	104.6	24 34.7	-22.5	105.1	24 18.9	-23.5	105.5	24 02.6	-24.5	105.9	23 45.9	-25.5	106.4	23 28.8	-26.5	106.8	23 11.3	-27.5	107.2	6
7	24 44.6	-20.8	105.2	24 28.6	-21.8	105.7	24 12.2	-22.9	106.1	23 55.4	-23.9	106.5	23 38.1	-24.9	106.9	23 20.4	-25.9	107.4	23 02.3	-26.8	107.8	22 43.8	-27.8	108.2	7
8	24 23.8	-21.3	106.2	24 06.8	-22.3	106.7	23 49.3	-23.3	107.1	23 31.5	-24.3	107.5	23 13.2	-25.3	107.9	22 54.5	-26.2	108.3	22 35.5	-27.2	108.7	22 16.0	-28.2	109.1	8
9	24 02.5	-21.6	107.3	23 44.5	-22.7	107.7	23 26.0	-23.6	108.1	23 07.2	-24.7	108.5	22 47.9	-25.6	108.9	22 28.3	-26.6	109.3	22 08.3	-27.6	109.7	21 47.8	-28.4	110.1	9
10	23 40.9	-22.1	108.3	23 21.8	-23.0	108.7	23 02.4	-24.1	109.1	22 42.5	-25.0	109.5	22 22.3	-26.0	109.9	22 01.7	-26.9	110.3	21 40.7	-27.8	110.7	21 19.4	-28.8	111.0	10
11	23 18.8	-22.4	109.3	22 58.8	-23.5	109.7	22 38.3	-24.4	110.1	22 17.5	-25.3	110.5	21 56.3	-26.3	110.9	21 34.8	-27.3	111.2	21 12.9	-28.2	111.6	20 50.6	-29.1	112.0	11
12	22 56.4	-22.9	110.3	22 35.3	-23.8	110.7	22 13.9	-24.7	111.1	21 52.2	-25.8	111.5	21 30.0	-26.6	111.8	21 07.5	-27.6	112.2	20 44.7	-28.5	112.6	20 21.5	-29.4	112.9	12
13	22 33.5	-23.2	111.3	22 11.5	-24.1	111.7	21 49.2	-25.1	112.1	21 26.4	-26.0	112.4	21 03.4	-27.0	112.8	20 39.9	-27.8	113.1	20 16.2	-28.8	113.5	19 52.1	-29.7	113.8	13
14	22 10.3	-23.5	112.3	21 47.4	-24.5	112.7	21 24.1	-25.5	113.0	21 00.4	-26.4	113.4	20 36.4	-27.3	113.8	20 12.1	-28.2	114.1	19 47.4	-29.1	114.4	19 22.4	-29.9	114.7	14
15	21 46.8	-23.9	113.3	21 22.9	-24.9	113.7	20 58.6	-25.8	114.0	20 34.0	-26.7	114.4	20 09.1	-27.6	114.7	19 43.9	-28.5	115.0	19 18.3	-29.3	115.4	18 52.5	-30.2	115.7	15
16	21 22.9	-24.3	114.3	20 58.0	-25.2	114.6	20 32.8	-26.1	115.0	20 07.3	-27.0	115.3	19 41.5	-27.9	115.6	19 15.4	-28.8	116.0	18 49.0	-29.7	116.3	18 22.3	-30.5	116.6	16
17	20 58.6	-24.6	115.3	20 32.8	-25.5	115.6	20 06.7	-26.4	115.9	19 40.3	-27.3	116.3	19 13.6	-28.2	116.6	18 46.6	-29.0	116.9	18 19.3	-29.9	117.2	17 51.8	-30.7	117.5	17
18	20 34.0	-24.9	116.2	20 07.3	-25.8	116.6	19 40.3	-26.7	116.9	19 13.0	-27.6	117.2	18 45.4	-28.4	117.5	18 17.6	-29.3	117.8	17 49.4	-30.1	118.1	17 21.1	-31.0	118.4	18
19	20 09.1	-25.2	117.2	19 41.5	-26.1	117.5	19 13.6	-27.0	117.9	18 45.4	-27.8	118.2	18 17.0	-28.7	118.5	17 48.3	-29.6	118.7	17 19.3	-30.4	119.0	16 50.1	-31.2	119.3	19
20	19 43.9	-25.6	118.2	19 15.4	-26.4	118.5	18 46.6	-27.3	118.8	18 17.6	-28.2	119.1	17 48.3	-29.0	119.4	17 18.7	-29.8	119.6	16 48.9	-30.6	119.9	16 18.9	-31.4	120.2	20
21	19 18.3	-25.8	119.1	18 49.0	-26.7	119.4	18 19.3	-27.5	119.7	17 49.4	-28.3	120.0	17 19.3	-29.2	120.3	16 48.9	-30.0	120.6	16 18.3	-30.8	120.8	15 47.5	-31.7	121.1	21
22	18 52.5	-26.2	120.1	18 22.3	-27.0	120.4	17 51.8	-27.8	120.7	17 21.1	-28.7	120.9	16 50.1	-29.5	121.2	16 18.9	-30.3	121.5	15 47.5	-31.1	121.7	15 15.8	-31.8	121.9	22
23	18 26.3	-26.4	121.0	17 55.3	-27.3	121.3	17 24.0	-28.1	121.6	16 52.4	-28.9	121.9	16 20.6	-29.7	122.1	15 48.6	-30.5	122.4	15 16.4	-31.3	122.6	14 44.0	-32.1	122.8	23
24	17 59.9	-26.7	122.0	17 28.0	-27.5	122.3	16 55.9	-28.3	122.5	16 23.5	-29.1	122.8	15 50.9	-29.9	123.0	15 18.1	-30.7	123.3	14 45.1	-31.5	123.5	14 11.9	-32.2	123.7	24
25	17 33.2	-26.9	122.9	17 00.5	-27.8	123.2	16 27.6	-28.6	123.4	15 54.4	-29.4	123.7	15 21.0	-30.1	123.9	14 47.4	-30.9	124.1	14 13.6	-31.6	124.4	13 39.7	-32.4	124.6	25
26	17 06.3	-27.2	123.9	16 32.7	-28.0	124.1	15 59.0	-28.8	124.4	15 25.0	-29.6	124.6	14 50.9	-30.4	124.8	14 16.5	-31.1	125.0	13 42.0	-31.9	125.2	13 07.3	-32.6	125.4	26
27	16 39.1	-27.5	124.8	16 04.7	-28.2	125.0	15 30.2	-29.0	125.3	14 55.4	-29.7	125.5	14 20.5	-30.5	125.7	13 45.4	-31.3	125.9	13 10.1	-32.0	126.1	12 34.7	-32.7	126.3	27
28	16 11.6	-27.7	125.7	15 36.5	-28.5	126.0	15 01.2	-29.3	126.2	14 25.7	-30.0	126.4	13 50.0	-30.8	126.6	13 14.1	-31.4	126.8	12 38.1	-32.2	127.0	12 02.0	-32.9	127.1	28
29	15 43.9	-27.9	126.6	15 08.0	-28.7	126.9	14 31.9	-29.4	127.1	13 55.7	-30.2	127.3	13 19.2	-30.9	127.5	12 42.7	-31.7	127.7	12 05.9	-32.3	127.8	11 29.1	-33.1	128.0	29
30	15 16.0	-28.2	127.6	14 39.3	-28.9	127.8	14 02.5	-29.7	128.0	13 25.5	-30.4	128.2	12 48.3	-31.1	128.4	12 11.0	-31.8	128.5	11 33.6	-32.5	128.7	10 56.0	-33.2	128.8	30
31	14 47.8	-28.3	128.5	14 10.4	-29.1	128.7	13 32.8	-29.8	128.9	12 55.1	-30.5	129.1	12 17.2	-31.2	129.2	11 39.2	-31.9	129.4	11 01.1	-32.7	129.6	10 22.8	-33.3	129.7	31
32	14 19.5	-28.6	129.4	13 41.3	-29.3	129.6	13 03.0	-30.0	129.8	12 24.6	-30.8	129.9	11 46.0	-31.4	130.1	11 07.3	-32.1	130.3	10 28.4	-32.8	130.4	9 49.5	-33.5	130.5	32
33	13 50.9	-28.8	130.3	13 12.0	-29.5	130.5	12 33.0	-30.2	130.7	11 53.8	-30.8	130.8	11 14.6	-31.6	131.0	10 35.2	-32.3	131.1	9 55.6	-32.9	131.3	9 16.0	-33.5	131.4	33
34	13 22.1	-28.9	131.2	12 42.5	-29.6	131.4	12 02.8	-30.3	131.5	11 23.0	-31.1	131.7	10 43.0	-31.7	131.8	10 02.9	-32.4	132.0	9 22.7	-33.0	132.1	8 42.5	-33.7	132.2	34
35	12 53.2	-29.2	132.1	12 12.9	-29.9	132.3	11 32.5	-30.6	132.4	10 51.9	-31.2	132.6	10 11.3	-31.9	132.7	9 30.5	-32.5	132.8	8 49.7	-33.1	133.0	8 08.8	-33.8	133.1	35
36	12 24.0	-29.3	133.0	11 43.0	-30.0	133.2	11 01.9	-30.6	133.3	10 20.7	-31.3	133.4	9 39.4	-31.9	133.6	8 58.0	-32.6	133.7	8 16.6	-33.3	133.8	7 35.0	-33.9	133.9	36
37	11 54.7	-29.5	133.9	11 13.0	-30.1	134.0	10 31.3	-30.8	134.2	9 49.4	-31.4	134.3	9 07.5	-32.1	134.4	8 25.4	-32.7	134.5	7 43.3	-33.3	134.6	7 01.1	-33.9	134.7	37
38	11 25.2	-29.7	134.8	10 42.9	-30.3	134.9	10 00.5	-31.0	135.0	9 18.0	-31.6	135.2	8 35.4	-32.2	135.3	7 52.7	-32.8	135.4	7 10.0	-33.5	135.5	6 27.2	-34.1	135.6	38
39	10 55.5	-29.8	135.7	10 12.6	-30.5	135.8	9 29.5	-31.1	135.9	8 46.4	-31.7	136.0	8 03.2	-32.3	136.1	7 19.9	-32.9	136.2	6 36.5	-33.5	136.3	5 53.1	-34.1	136.4	39
40	10 25.7	-29.9	136.5	9 42.1	-30.5	136.7	8 58.4	-31.1	136.8	8 14.7	-31.8	136.9	7 30.9	-32.5	137.0	6 47.0	-33.1	137.1	6 03.0	-33.6	137.1	5 19.0	-34.2	137.2	40
41	9 55.8	-30.1	137.4	9 11.6	-30.7	137.5	8 27.3	-31.4	137.6	7 42.9	-31.9	137.7	6 58.4	-32.5	137.8	6 13.9	-33.0	137.9	5 29.4	-33.7	138.0	4 44.8	-34.2	138.0	41
42	9 25.7	-30.2	138.3	8 40.9	-30.9	138.4	7 55.9	-31.4	138.5	7 11.0	-32.0	138.6	6 25.9	-32.5	138.7	5 40.9	-33.2	138.7	4 55.7	-33.7	138.8	4 10.6	-34.3	138.9	42
43	8 55.5	-30.4	139.2	8 10.0	-30.9	139.3	7 24.5	-31.5	139.4	6 39.0	-32.1	139.4	5 53.4	-32.7	139.5	5 07.7	-33.2	139.6	4 22.0	-33.8	139.6	3 36.3	-34.4	139.7	43
44	8 25.1	-30.4	140.1	7 39.1	-31.0	140.1	6 53.0	-31.6	140.2	6 06.9	-32.2	140.3	5 20.7	-32.7	140.4	4 34.5	-33.3	140.4	3 48.2	-33.8	140.5	3 01.9	-34.4	140.5	44
45	7 54.7	-30.6	140.9	7 08.1	-31.1	141.0	6 21.4	-31.7	141.1	5 34.7	-32.2	141.1	4 48.0	-32.8	141.2	4 01.2	-33.3	141.3	3 14.4	-33.9	141.3	2 27.5	-34.4	141.3	45
46	7 24.1	-30.6	141.8	6 37.0	-31.3	141.9	5 49.7	-31.7	141.9	5 02.5	-32.3	142.0	4 15.2	-32.9	142.0	3 27.9	-33.4	142.1	2 40.5	-33.9	142.1	1 53.1	-34.4	142.1	46
47	6 53.5	-30.8	142.7	6 05.7	-31.3	142.7	5 18.0	-31.9	142.8	4 30.2	-32.4	142.8	3 42.3	-32.9	142.9	2 54.5	-33.4	142.9	2 06.6	-33.9	142.9	1 18.7	-34.4	143.0	47
48	6 22.7	-30.8	143.5	5 34.4	-31.3	143.6	4 46.1	-31.9	143.6	3 57.8	-32.4	143.7	3 09.4	-32.9	143.7	2 21.1	-33.5	143.8	1 32.7	-34.0	143.8	0 44.3	-34.5	143.8	48
49	5 51.9	-31.0	144.4	5 03.1	-31.5	144.4	4 14.2	-31.9	144.5	3 25.4	-32.5	144.5	2 36.5	-33.0	144.6	1 47.6	-33.4	144.6	0 58.7	-33.9	144.6	0 09.8	-34.4	144.6	49
50	5 20.9	-31.0	145.2	4 31.6	-31.5	145.3	3 42.3	-32.0	145.3	2 52.9	-32.5	145.4	2 03.5	-32.9	145.4	1 14.2	-33.5	145.4	0 24.8	-34.0	145.4	0 24.6	+34.5	34.6	50
51	4 49.9	-31.0	146.1	4 00.1	-31.5	146.2	3 10.3	-32.1	146.2	2 20.4	-32.5	146.2	1 30.6	-33.1	146.2	0 40.7	-33.5	146.2	0 09.2	+34.0	33.8	0 59.1	+34.4	33.8	51
52	4 18.9	-31.1	147.0	3 28.6	-31.6	147.0	2 38.2	-32.0	147.0	1 47.9	-32.6	147.1	0 57.5	-33.0	147.1	0 07.2	-33.5	147.1	0 43.2	+33.9	32.9	1 33.5	+34.5	32.9	52
53	3 47.8	-31.2	147.8	2 57.0	-31.7	147.9	2 06.2	-32.1	147.9	1 15.3	-32.5	147.9	0 24.5	-33.0	147.9	0 26.3	+33.5	32.1	1 17.1	+34.0	32.1	2 08.0	+34.3	32.1	53
54	3 16.6	-31.2	148.7	2 25.3	-31.6	148.7	1 34.1	-32.2	148.7	0 42.8	-32.6	148.7	0 08.5	+33.0	31.3	0 59.8	+33.5	31.3	1 51.1	+33.9	31.3	2 42.3	+34.4	31.3	54
55	2 45.4	-31.3	149.5	1 53.7	-31.7	149.6	1 01.9	-32.1	149.6	0 10.2	-32.6	149.6	0 41.5	+33.1	30.4	1 33.3	+33.4	30.4	2 25.0	+33.9	30.5	3 16.7	+34.3	30.5	55
56	2 14.1	-31.2	150.4	1 22.0	-31.7	150.4	0 29.8	-32.1	150.4	0 22.4	+32.6	29.6	1 14.6	+33.0	29.6	2 06.7	+33.5	29.6	2 58.9	+33.8	29.6	3 51.0	+34.3	29.7	56
57	1 42.9	-31.3	151.2	0 50.3	-31.8	151.3	0 02.3	+32.2	28.7	0 55.0	+32.5	28.7	1 47.6	+32.9	28.8	2 40.2	+33.3	28.8	3 32.7	+33.8	28.8	4 25.3	+34.2	28.8	57
58	1 11.6	-31.4	152.1	0 18.5	-31.7	152.1	0 34.5	+32.1	27.9	1 27.5	+32.6	27.9	2 20.5	+33.0	27.9	3 13.5	+33.4	27.9	4 06.5	+33.8	28.0	4 59.5	+34.2	28.0	58
59	0 40.2	-31.3	152.9	0 13.2	+31.7	27.0	1 06.6	+32.2	27.1	2 00.1	+32.5	27.1	2 53.5	+32.9	27.1	3 46.9	+33.3	27.1	4 40.3	+33.7	27.1	5 33.7	+34.1	27.2	59
60	0 08.9	-31.3	153.8	0 44.9	+31.7	26.2	1 38.8	+32.1	26.2	2 32.6	+32.5	26.2	3 26.4	+32.9	26.2	4 20.2	+33.3	26.3	5 14.0	+33.6	26.3	6 07.8	+34.0	26.4	60
61	0 22.4	+31.3	25.3	1 16.6	+31.7	25.4	2 10.9	+32.0	25.4	3 05.1	+32.4	25.4	3 59.3	+32.8	25.4	4 53.5	+33.1	25.4	5 47.6	+33.6	25.5	6 41.8	+33.9	25.5	61
62	0 53.7	+31.3	24.5	1 48.3	+31.7	24.5	2 42.9	+32.1	24.5	3 37.5	+32.4	24.5	4 32.1	+32.7	24.6	5 26.6	+33.2	24.6	6 21.2	+33.5	24.7	7 15.7	+33.8	24.7	62
63	1 25.0	+31.3	23.6	2 20.0	+31.7	23.7	3 15.0	+32.0	23.7	4 09.9	+32.4	23.7	5 04.8	+32.7	23.7	5 59.8	+33.0	23.8	6 54.7	+33.4	23.8	7 49.5	+33.8	23.9	63
64	1 56.3	+31.3	22.8	2 51.7	+31.6	22.8	3 47.0	+31.9	22.8	4 42.3	+32.2	22.9	5 37.5	+32.7	22.9	6 32.8	+33.0	22.9	7 28.1	+33.3	23.0	8 23.3	+33.6	23.0	64
65	2 27.6	+31.2	21.9	3 23.3	+31.5	22.0	4 18.9	+31.9	22.0	5 14.5	+32.3	22.0	6 10.2	+32.5	22.0	7 05.8	+32.8	22.1	8 01.4	+33.1	22.1	8 56.9	+33.5	22.2	65
66	2 58.8	+31.2	21.1	3 54.8	+31.5	21.1	4 50.8	+31.8	21.1	5 46.8	+32.1	21.2	6 42.7	+32.5	21.2	7 38.6	+32.8	21.2	8 34.5	+33.1	21.3	9 30.4	+33.4	21.4	66
67	3 30.0	+31.2	20.2	4 26.3	+31.5	20.2	5 22.6	+31.8	20.3	6 18.9	+32.0	20.3	7 15.2	+32.3	20.4	8 11.4	+32.7	20.4	9 07.6	+33.0	20.5	10 03.8	+33.3	20.5	67
68	4 01.2	+31.1	19.4	4 57.8	+31.4	19.4	5 54.4	+31.6	19.4	6 50.9	+32.0	19.5	7 47.5	+32.3	19.5	8 44.1	+32.5	19.6	9 40.6	+32.8	19.6	10 37.1	+33.1	19.7	68
69	4 32.3	+31.0	18.5	5 29.2	+31.3	18.5	6 26.0	+31.6	18.6	7 22.9	+31.9	18.6	8 19.8	+32.1	18.7	9 16.6	+32.4	18.7	10 13.4	+32.7	18.8	11 10.2	+33.0	18.8	69
70	5 03.3	+31.0	17.6	6 00.5	+31.2	17.7	6 57.6	+31.5	17.7	7 54.8	+31.8	17.8	8 51.9	+32.1	17.8	9 49.0	+32.3	17.8	10 46.1	+32.6	17.9	11 43.2	+32.9	18.0	70
71	5 34.3	+30.9	16.8	6 31.7	+31.1	16.8	7 29.1	+31.4	16.9	8 26.6	+31.6	16.9	9 24.0	+31.9	16.9	10 21.3	+32.2	17.0	11 18.7	+32.4	17.0	12 16.1	+32.6	17.1	71
72	6 05.2	+30.8	15.9	7 02.8	+31.1	16.0	8 00.5	+31.3	16.0	8 58.2	+31.5	16.0	9 55.9	+31.7	16.1	10 53.5	+32.0	16.1	11 51.1	+32.3	16.2	12 48.7	+32.6	16.2	72
73	6 36.0	+30.7	15.1	7 33.9	+30.9	15.1	8 31.8	+31.2	15.1	9 29.7	+31.4	15.2	10 27.6	+31.6	15.2	11 25.5	+31.9	15.3	12 23.4	+32.1	15.3	13 21.3	+32.3	15.4	73
74	7 06.7	+30.6	14.2	8 04.8	+30.9	14.2	9 03.0	+31.1	14.3	10 01.1	+31.3	14.3	10 59.3	+31.5	14.4	11 57.4	+31.7	14.4	12 55.5	+31.9	14.5	13 53.6	+32.1	14.5	74
75	7 37.3	+30.5	13.3	8 35.7	+30.7	13.4	9 34.1	+30.9	13.4	10 32.4	+31.1	13.4	11 30.8	+31.3	13.5	12 29.1	+31.5	13.5	13 27.4	+31.8	13.6	14 25.7	+32.0	13.6	75
76	8 07.8	+30.4	12.5	9 06.4	+30.6	12.5	10 05.0	+30.8	12.5	11 03.5	+31.0	12.6	12 02.1	+31.2	12.6	13 00.6	+31.4	12.7	13 59.2	+31.5	12.7	14 57.7	+31.8	12.8	76
77	8 38.2	+30.3	11.6	9 37.0	+30.5	11.6	10 35.8	+30.6	11.7	11 34.5	+30.8	11.7	12 33.3	+31.0	11.7	13 32.0	+31.2	11.8	14 30.7	+31.4	11.8	15 29.5	+31.5	11.9	77
78	9 08.5	+30.2	10.7	10 07.5	+30.3	10.7	11 06.4	+30.5	10.8	12 05.3	+30.7	10.8	13 04.3	+30.8	10.9	14 03.2	+31.0	10.9	15 02.1	+31.2	11.0	16 01.0	+31.3	11.0	78
79	9 38.7	+30.0	9.8	10 37.8	+30.2	9.9	11 36.9	+30.3	9.9	12 36.0	+30.5	9.9	13 35.1	+30.6	10.0	14 34.2	+30.8	10.0	15 33.3	+30.9	10.1	16 32.3	+31.1	10.1	79
80	10 08.7	+29.9	9.0	11 08.0	+30.0	9.0	12 07.2	+30.2	9.0	13 06.5	+30.3	9.1	14 05.7	+30.5	9.1	15 05.0	+30.6	9.1	16 04.2	+30.7	9.2	17 03.4	+30.9	9.2	80
81	10 38.6	+29.7	8.1	11 38.0	+29.9	8.1	12 37.4	+30.0	8.1	13 36.8	+30.1	8.2	14 36.2	+30.2	8.2	15 35.6	+30.3	8.2	16 34.9	+30.5	8.3	17 34.3	+30.6	8.3	81
82	11 08.3	+29.6	7.2	12 07.9	+29.7	7.2	13 07.4	+29.8	7.2	14 06.9	+29.9	7.3	15 06.4	+30.0	7.3	16 05.9	+30.2	7.3	17 05.4	+30.3	7.4	18 04.9	+30.4	7.4	82
83	11 37.9	+29.4	6.3	12 37.6	+29.5	6.3	13 37.2	+29.6	6.4	14 36.8	+29.7	6.4	15 36.4	+29.9	6.4	16 36.1	+29.9	6.4	17 35.7	+30.0	6.5	18 35.3	+30.1	6.5	83
84	12 07.3	+29.3	5.4	13 07.1	+29.3	5.4	14 06.8	+29.4	5.5	15 06.5	+29.5	5.5	16 06.3	+29.5	5.5	17 06.0	+29.6	5.5	18 05.7	+29.7	5.6	19 05.4	+29.8	5.6	84
85	12 36.6	+29.1	4.5	13 36.4	+29.1	4.5	14 36.2	+29.2	4.6	15 36.0	+29.3	4.6	16 35.8	+29.4	4.6	17 35.6	+29.4	4.6	18 35.4	+29.5	4.7	19 35.2	+29.6	4.7	85
86	13 05.7	+28.8	3.6	14 05.5	+29.0	3.6	15 05.4	+29.0	3.7	16 05.3	+29.0	3.7	17 05.2	+29.1	3.7	18 05.0	+29.2	3.7	19 04.9	+29.2	3.7	20 04.8	+29.3	3.8	86
87	13 34.5	+28.7	2.7	14 34.5	+28.7	2.7	15 34.4	+28.8	2.7	16 34.3	+28.8	2.8	17 34.3	+28.8	2.8	18 34.2	+28.9	2.8	19 34.1	+28.9	2.8	20 34.1	+28.9	2.8	87
88	14 03.2	+28.5	1.8	15 03.2	+28.5	1.8	16 03.2	+28.5	1.8	17 03.1	+28.6	1.8	18 03.1	+28.6	1.9	19 03.1	+28.6	1.9	20 03.0	+28.7	1.9	21 03.0	+28.7	1.9	88
89	14 31.7	+28.3	0.9	15 31.7	+28.3	0.9	16 31.7	+28.3	0.9	17 31.7	+28.3	0.9	18 31.7	+28.3	0.9	19 31.7	+28.3	0.9	20 31.7	+28.3	0.9	21 31.7	+28.3	0.9	89
90	15 00.0	+28.1	0.0	16 00.0	+28.0	0.0	17 00.0	+28.0	0.0	18 00.0	+28.0	0.0	19 00.0	+28.0	0.0	20 00.0	+28.0	0.0	21 00.0	+28.0	0.0	22 00.0	+28.0	0.0	90
	15°			16°			17°			18°			19°			20°			21°			22°			

S. Lat. {L.H.A. greater than 180° ....Zn=180°–Z; L.H.A. less than 180°...........Zn=180°+Z}

LATITUDE SAME NAME AS DECLINATION L.H.A. 118°, 242°

127

63°, 297° L.H.A. LATITUDE SAME NAME AS DECLINATION N. Lat. {L.H.A. greater than 180° .....Zn=Z; L.H.A. less than 180°............Zn=360°-Z}

Dec.	15° Hc	15° d	15° Z	16° Hc	16° d	16° Z	17° Hc	17° d	17° Z	18° Hc	18° d	18° Z	19° Hc	19° d	19° Z	20° Hc	20° d	20° Z	21° Hc	21° d	21° Z	22° Hc	22° d	22° Z	Dec.
°	° ′	′	°	° ′	′	°	° ′	′	°	° ′	′	°	° ′	′	°	° ′	′	°	° ′	′	°	° ′	′	°	°
0	26 00.6	+17.0	97.5	25 52.5	+18.1	98.0	25 43.9	+19.2	98.5	25 34.8	+20.3	98.9	25 25.2	+21.4	99.4	25 15.2	+22.4	99.9	25 04.6	+23.6	100.3	24 53.6	+24.6	100.8	0
1	26 17.6	+16.6	96.4	26 10.6	+17.7	96.9	26 03.1	+18.8	97.4	25 55.1	+19.9	97.9	25 46.6	+21.0	98.4	25 37.6	+22.1	98.9	25 28.2	+23.1	99.3	25 18.2	+24.1	99.8	1
2	26 34.2	+16.1	95.4	26 28.3	+17.2	95.9	26 21.9	+18.3	96.4	26 15.0	+19.4	96.9	26 07.6	+20.5	97.3	25 59.7	+21.6	97.8	25 51.3	+22.6	98.3	25 42.3	+23.8	98.8	2
3	26 50.3	+15.6	94.3	26 45.5	+16.7	94.8	26 40.2	+17.9	95.3	26 34.4	+19.0	95.8	26 28.1	+20.1	96.3	26 21.3	+21.1	96.8	26 13.9	+22.3	97.3	26 06.1	+23.3	97.8	3
4	27 05.9	+15.0	93.2	27 02.2	+16.3	93.7	26 58.1	+17.3	94.2	26 53.4	+18.5	94.7	26 48.2	+19.6	95.2	26 42.4	+20.7	95.7	26 36.2	+21.7	96.2	26 29.4	+22.8	96.7	4
5	27 20.9	+14.6	92.1	27 18.5	+15.7	92.6	27 15.4	+16.9	93.2	27 11.9	+17.9	93.7	27 07.8	+19.1	94.2	27 03.1	+20.2	94.7	26 57.9	+21.4	95.2	26 52.2	+22.5	95.7	5
6	27 35.5	+14.1	91.0	27 34.2	+15.2	91.5	27 32.3	+16.3	92.1	27 29.8	+17.5	92.6	27 26.9	+18.6	93.1	27 23.3	+19.8	93.6	27 19.3	+20.8	94.1	27 14.7	+21.9	94.7	6
7	27 49.6	+13.5	89.9	27 49.4	+14.7	90.5	27 48.6	+15.9	91.0	27 47.3	+17.0	91.5	27 45.5	+18.1	92.0	27 43.1	+19.2	92.6	27 40.1	+20.3	93.1	27 36.6	+21.5	93.6	7
8	28 03.1	+13.0	88.8	28 04.1	+14.1	89.4	28 04.5	+15.3	89.9	28 04.3	+16.5	90.4	28 03.6	+17.6	91.0	28 02.3	+18.7	91.5	28 00.4	+19.9	92.0	27 58.1	+20.9	92.6	8
9	28 16.1	+12.5	87.7	28 18.2	+13.7	88.3	28 19.8	+14.8	88.8	28 20.8	+15.9	89.3	28 21.2	+17.1	89.9	28 21.0	+18.2	90.4	28 20.3	+19.4	91.0	28 19.0	+20.5	91.5	9
10	28 28.6	+11.9	86.6	28 31.9	+13.1	87.1	28 34.6	+14.2	87.7	28 36.7	+15.4	88.2	28 38.3	+16.5	88.8	28 39.2	+17.8	89.3	28 39.7	+18.8	89.9	28 39.5	+20.0	90.4	10
11	28 40.5	+11.4	85.5	28 45.0	+12.5	86.0	28 48.8	+13.7	86.6	28 52.1	+14.9	87.1	28 54.8	+16.0	87.7	28 57.0	+17.1	88.2	28 58.5	+18.3	88.8	28 59.5	+19.4	89.3	11
12	28 51.9	+10.8	84.4	28 57.5	+12.0	84.9	29 02.5	+13.2	85.5	29 07.0	+14.3	86.0	29 10.8	+15.5	86.6	29 14.1	+16.7	87.1	29 16.8	+17.8	87.7	29 18.9	+19.0	88.3	12
13	29 02.7	+10.3	83.2	29 09.5	+11.4	83.8	29 15.7	+12.6	84.4	29 21.3	+13.8	84.9	29 26.3	+14.9	85.5	29 30.8	+16.0	86.0	29 34.6	+17.2	86.6	29 37.9	+18.3	87.2	13
14	29 13.0	+9.7	82.1	29 20.9	+10.9	82.7	29 28.3	+12.0	83.2	29 35.1	+13.2	83.8	29 41.2	+14.4	84.4	29 46.8	+15.6	84.9	29 51.8	+16.7	85.5	29 56.2	+17.9	86.1	14
15	29 22.7	+9.1	81.0	29 31.8	+10.3	81.5	29 40.3	+11.5	82.1	29 48.3	+12.6	82.7	29 55.6	+13.8	83.2	30 02.4	+14.9	83.8	30 08.5	+16.2	84.4	30 14.1	+17.3	85.0	15
16	29 31.8	+8.5	79.9	29 42.1	+9.7	80.4	29 51.8	+10.8	81.0	30 00.9	+12.0	81.5	30 09.4	+13.2	82.1	30 17.3	+14.4	82.7	30 24.7	+15.5	83.3	30 31.4	+16.7	83.9	16
17	29 40.3	+8.0	78.7	29 51.8	+9.1	79.3	30 02.6	+10.3	79.8	30 12.9	+11.5	80.4	30 22.6	+12.6	81.0	30 31.7	+13.8	81.6	30 40.2	+15.0	82.2	30 48.1	+16.1	82.7	17
18	29 48.3	+7.3	77.6	30 00.9	+8.5	78.1	30 12.9	+9.7	78.7	30 24.4	+10.8	79.3	30 35.2	+12.1	79.9	30 45.5	+13.2	80.4	30 55.2	+14.4	81.0	31 04.2	+15.6	81.6	18
19	29 55.6	+6.8	76.4	30 09.4	+7.9	77.0	30 22.6	+9.1	77.6	30 35.2	+10.3	78.1	30 47.3	+11.4	78.7	30 58.7	+12.6	79.3	31 09.6	+13.7	79.9	31 19.8	+14.9	80.5	19
20	30 02.4	+6.1	75.3	30 17.3	+7.4	75.8	30 31.7	+8.5	76.4	30 45.5	+9.7	77.0	30 58.7	+10.9	77.6	31 11.3	+12.0	78.2	31 23.3	+13.2	78.8	31 34.7	+14.4	79.4	20
21	30 08.5	+5.6	74.1	30 24.7	+6.7	74.7	30 40.2	+7.9	75.3	30 55.2	+9.0	75.8	31 09.6	+10.2	76.4	31 23.3	+11.4	77.0	31 36.5	+12.6	77.6	31 49.1	+13.7	78.2	21
22	30 14.1	+4.9	73.0	30 31.4	+6.1	73.5	30 48.1	+7.3	74.1	31 04.2	+8.5	74.7	31 19.8	+9.6	75.3	31 34.7	+10.8	75.9	31 49.1	+11.9	76.5	32 02.8	+13.1	77.1	22
23	30 19.0	+4.4	71.8	30 37.5	+5.5	72.4	30 55.4	+6.6	73.0	31 12.7	+7.8	73.5	31 29.4	+8.9	74.1	31 45.5	+10.1	74.7	32 01.0	+11.3	75.3	32 15.9	+12.5	75.9	23
24	30 23.4	+3.7	70.7	30 43.0	+4.9	71.2	31 02.0	+6.0	71.8	31 20.5	+7.1	72.4	31 38.3	+8.4	73.0	31 55.6	+9.5	73.5	32 12.3	+10.7	74.2	32 28.4	+11.8	74.8	24
25	30 27.1	+3.1	69.5	30 47.9	+4.2	70.1	31 08.0	+5.4	70.6	31 27.6	+6.6	71.2	31 46.7	+7.7	71.8	32 05.1	+8.9	72.4	32 23.0	+10.0	73.0	32 40.2	+11.2	73.6	25
26	30 30.2	+2.5	68.4	30 52.1	+3.6	68.9	31 13.4	+4.8	69.5	31 34.2	+5.9	70.0	31 54.4	+7.0	70.6	32 14.0	+8.2	71.2	32 33.0	+9.4	71.8	32 51.4	+10.6	72.4	26
27	30 32.7	+1.9	67.2	30 55.7	+3.0	67.7	31 18.2	+4.1	68.3	31 40.1	+5.3	68.9	32 01.4	+6.5	69.5	32 22.2	+7.6	70.0	32 42.4	+8.7	70.6	33 02.0	+9.9	71.3	27
28	30 34.6	+1.3	66.0	30 58.7	+2.4	66.6	31 22.3	+3.5	67.1	31 45.4	+4.6	67.7	32 07.9	+5.7	68.3	32 29.8	+6.9	68.9	32 51.1	+8.1	69.5	33 11.9	+9.2	70.1	28
29	30 35.9	+0.7	64.9	31 01.1	+1.8	65.4	31 25.8	+2.9	66.0	31 50.0	+4.0	66.5	32 13.6	+5.1	67.1	32 36.7	+6.2	67.7	32 59.2	+7.4	68.3	33 21.1	+8.5	68.9	29
30	30 36.6	0.0	63.7	31 02.9	+1.1	64.2	31 28.7	+2.2	64.8	31 54.0	+3.3	65.4	32 18.7	+4.5	65.9	32 42.9	+5.6	66.5	33 06.6	+6.7	67.1	33 29.6	+7.9	67.7	30
31	30 36.6	-0.6	62.5	31 04.0	+0.5	63.1	31 30.9	+1.6	63.6	31 57.3	+2.7	64.2	32 23.2	+3.8	64.7	32 48.5	+4.9	65.3	33 13.3	+6.0	65.9	33 37.5	+7.1	66.5	31
32	30 36.0	-1.2	61.4	31 04.5	-0.2	61.9	31 32.5	+0.9	62.4	32 00.0	+2.0	63.0	32 27.0	+3.1	63.6	32 53.4	+4.2	64.1	33 19.3	+5.4	64.7	33 44.6	+6.5	65.3	32
33	30 34.8	-1.8	60.2	31 04.3	-0.7	60.7	31 33.4	+0.3	61.3	32 02.0	+1.4	61.8	32 30.1	+2.5	62.4	32 57.6	+3.6	63.0	33 24.7	+4.6	63.5	33 51.1	+5.8	64.1	33
34	30 33.0	-2.5	59.1	31 03.6	-1.4	59.6	31 33.7	-0.3	60.1	32 03.4	+0.7	60.6	32 32.6	+1.7	61.2	33 01.2	+2.9	61.8	33 29.3	+4.0	62.3	33 56.9	+5.1	62.9	34
35	30 30.5	-3.0	57.9	31 02.2	-2.1	58.4	31 33.4	-1.0	58.9	32 04.1	+0.1	59.5	32 34.3	+1.2	60.0	33 04.1	+2.2	60.6	33 33.3	+3.3	61.1	34 02.0	+4.4	61.7	35
36	30 27.5	-3.7	56.7	31 00.1	-2.6	57.2	31 32.4	-1.7	57.8	32 04.2	-0.6	58.3	32 35.5	+0.4	58.8	33 06.3	+1.5	59.4	33 36.6	+2.6	59.9	34 06.4	+3.7	60.5	36
37	30 23.8	-4.3	55.6	30 57.5	-3.3	56.1	31 30.7	-2.2	56.6	32 03.6	-1.3	57.1	32 35.9	-0.2	57.6	33 07.8	+0.8	58.2	33 39.2	+1.9	58.7	34 10.1	+2.9	59.3	37
38	30 19.5	-4.9	54.4	30 54.2	-3.9	54.9	31 28.5	-2.9	55.4	32 02.3	-1.9	55.9	32 35.7	-0.9	56.4	33 08.6	+0.2	57.0	33 41.1	+1.2	57.5	34 13.0	+2.3	58.1	38
39	30 14.6	-5.5	53.3	30 50.3	-4.5	53.8	31 25.6	-3.6	54.2	32 00.4	-2.6	54.7	32 34.8	-1.5	55.3	33 08.8	-0.6	55.8	33 42.3	+0.5	56.3	34 15.3	+1.5	56.9	39
40	30 09.1	-6.1	52.1	30 45.8	-5.2	52.6	31 22.0	-4.2	53.1	31 57.8	-3.2	53.6	32 33.3	-2.3	54.1	33 08.2	-1.2	54.6	33 42.8	-0.2	55.1	34 16.8	+0.9	55.7	40
41	30 03.0	-6.7	51.0	30 40.6	-5.8	51.4	31 17.8	-4.8	51.9	31 54.6	-3.8	52.4	32 31.0	-2.8	52.9	33 07.0	-1.9	53.4	33 42.6	-0.9	53.9	34 17.7	+0.1	54.5	41
42	29 56.3	-7.3	49.8	30 34.8	-6.4	50.3	31 13.0	-5.5	50.7	31 50.8	-4.5	51.2	32 28.2	-3.6	51.7	33 05.1	-2.5	52.2	33 41.7	-1.6	52.7	34 17.8	-0.6	53.3	42
43	29 49.0	-7.9	48.7	30 28.4	-6.9	49.1	31 07.5	-6.0	49.6	31 46.3	-5.2	50.0	32 24.6	-4.2	50.5	33 02.6	-3.3	51.0	33 40.1	-2.3	51.5	34 17.2	-1.3	52.1	43
44	29 41.1	-8.5	47.5	30 21.5	-7.6	48.0	31 01.5	-6.7	48.4	31 41.1	-5.8	48.9	32 20.4	-4.9	49.3	32 59.3	-3.9	49.8	33 37.8	-3.0	50.3	34 15.9	-2.0	50.9	44
45	29 32.6	-9.0	46.4	30 13.9	-8.2	46.8	30 54.8	-7.4	47.3	31 35.3	-6.4	47.7	32 15.5	-5.5	48.2	32 55.4	-4.7	48.6	33 34.8	-3.7	49.1	34 13.9	-2.8	49.6	45
46	29 23.6	-9.6	45.3	30 05.7	-8.8	45.7	30 47.4	-7.9	46.1	31 28.9	-7.1	46.5	32 10.0	-6.2	47.0	32 50.7	-5.2	47.5	33 31.1	-4.3	47.9	34 11.1	-3.4	48.4	46
47	29 14.0	-10.2	44.1	29 56.9	-9.4	44.5	30 39.5	-8.5	44.9	31 21.8	-7.7	45.4	32 03.8	-6.8	45.8	32 45.5	-6.0	46.3	33 26.8	-5.1	46.7	34 07.7	-4.2	47.2	47
48	29 03.8	-10.8	43.0	29 47.5	-10.0	43.4	30 31.0	-9.2	43.8	31 14.1	-8.3	44.2	31 57.0	-7.5	44.6	32 39.5	-6.6	45.1	33 21.7	-5.7	45.5	34 03.5	-4.8	46.0	48
49	28 53.0	-11.3	41.9	29 37.5	-10.5	42.3	30 21.8	-9.7	42.6	31 05.8	-8.9	43.1	31 49.5	-8.1	43.5	32 32.9	-7.3	43.9	33 16.0	-6.5	44.4	33 58.7	-5.6	44.8	49
50	28 41.7	-11.9	40.8	29 27.0	-11.1	41.1	30 12.1	-10.4	41.5	30 56.9	-9.6	41.9	31 41.4	-8.8	42.3	32 25.6	-7.9	42.7	33 09.5	-7.1	43.2	33 53.1	-6.2	43.6	50
51	28 29.8	-12.4	39.6	29 15.9	-11.7	40.0	30 01.7	-10.9	40.4	30 47.3	-10.1	40.7	31 32.6	-9.3	41.1	32 17.7	-8.6	41.6	33 02.4	-7.7	42.0	33 46.9	-7.0	42.4	51
52	28 17.4	-13.0	38.5	29 04.2	-12.2	38.9	29 50.8	-11.5	39.2	30 37.2	-10.8	39.6	31 23.3	-10.0	40.0	32 09.1	-9.2	40.4	32 54.7	-8.5	40.8	33 39.9	-7.6	41.2	52
53	28 04.4	-13.5	37.4	28 52.0	-12.8	37.8	29 39.3	-12.1	38.1	30 26.4	-11.3	38.5	31 13.3	-10.6	38.8	31 59.9	-9.9	39.2	32 46.2	-9.1	39.6	33 32.3	-8.3	40.0	53
54	27 50.9	-14.0	36.3	28 39.2	-13.3	36.6	29 27.2	-12.6	37.0	30 15.1	-12.0	37.3	31 02.7	-11.3	37.7	31 50.0	-10.5	38.1	32 37.1	-9.7	38.4	33 24.0	-9.0	38.9	54
55	27 36.9	-14.5	35.2	28 25.9	-13.9	35.5	29 14.6	-13.2	35.9	30 03.1	-12.5	36.2	30 51.4	-11.8	36.5	31 39.5	-11.1	36.9	32 27.4	-10.4	37.3	33 15.0	-9.6	37.7	55
56	27 22.4	-15.0	34.1	28 12.0	-14.4	34.4	29 01.4	-13.8	34.7	29 50.6	-13.1	35.1	30 39.6	-12.4	35.4	31 28.4	-11.7	35.7	32 17.0	-11.0	36.1	33 05.4	-10.4	36.5	56
57	27 07.4	-15.6	33.0	27 57.6	-14.9	33.3	28 47.6	-14.3	33.6	29 37.5	-13.7	33.9	30 27.2	-13.0	34.3	31 16.7	-12.4	34.6	32 06.0	-11.7	34.9	32 55.0	-10.9	35.3	57
58	26 51.8	-16.0	32.0	27 42.7	-15.5	32.2	28 33.3	-14.8	32.5	29 23.8	-14.2	32.8	30 14.2	-13.6	33.1	31 04.3	-12.9	33.5	31 54.3	-12.3	33.8	32 44.1	-11.7	34.1	58
59	26 35.8	-16.5	30.9	27 27.2	-15.9	31.1	28 18.5	-15.4	31.4	29 09.6	-14.7	31.7	30 00.6	-14.2	32.0	30 51.4	-13.6	32.3	31 42.0	-12.9	32.6	32 32.4	-12.2	33.0	59
60	26 19.3	-17.0	29.8	27 11.3	-16.5	30.1	28 03.1	-15.8	30.3	28 54.9	-15.3	30.6	29 46.4	-14.7	30.9	30 37.8	-14.1	31.2	31 29.1	-13.5	31.5	32 20.2	-12.9	31.8	60
61	26 02.3	-17.5	28.7	26 54.8	-16.9	29.0	27 47.3	-16.4	29.2	28 39.6	-15.9	29.5	29 31.7	-15.3	29.8	30 23.7	-14.7	30.1	31 15.6	-14.2	30.4	32 07.3	-13.6	30.7	61
62	25 44.8	-17.9	27.7	26 37.9	-17.4	27.9	27 30.9	-16.9	28.1	28 23.7	-16.4	28.4	29 16.4	-15.8	28.7	30 09.0	-15.3	28.9	31 01.4	-14.7	29.2	31 53.7	-14.1	29.5	62
63	25 26.9	-18.4	26.6	26 20.5	-17.9	26.8	27 14.0	-17.4	27.1	28 07.3	-16.8	27.3	29 00.6	-16.4	27.6	29 53.7	-15.8	27.8	30 46.7	-15.3	28.1	31 39.6	-14.8	28.4	63
64	25 08.5	-18.8	25.6	26 02.6	-18.4	25.8	26 56.6	-17.9	26.0	27 50.5	-17.4	26.2	28 44.2	-16.9	26.5	29 37.9	-16.4	26.7	30 31.4	-15.8	27.0	31 24.8	-15.3	27.2	64
65	24 49.7	-19.3	24.5	25 44.2	-18.8	24.7	26 38.7	-18.4	24.9	27 33.1	-17.9	25.1	28 27.3	-17.4	25.4	29 21.5	-16.9	25.6	30 15.6	-16.5	25.8	31 09.5	-16.0	26.1	65
66	24 30.4	-19.7	23.5	25 25.4	-19.2	23.6	26 20.3	-18.8	23.9	27 15.2	-18.4	24.1	28 09.9	-17.9	24.3	29 04.6	-17.5	24.5	29 59.1	-17.0	24.7	30 53.5	-16.5	25.0	66
67	24 10.7	-20.1	22.4	25 06.2	-19.7	22.6	26 01.5	-19.3	22.8	26 56.8	-18.9	23.0	27 52.0	-18.5	23.2	28 47.1	-18.0	23.4	29 42.1	-17.5	23.6	30 37.0	-17.1	23.9	67
68	23 50.6	-20.5	21.4	24 46.5	-20.2	21.6	25 42.2	-19.7	21.7	26 37.9	-19.3	21.9	27 33.5	-18.9	22.1	28 29.1	-18.5	22.3	29 24.6	-18.1	22.5	30 19.9	-17.6	22.8	68
69	23 30.1	-20.9	20.4	24 26.3	-20.5	20.5	25 22.5	-20.2	20.7	26 18.6	-19.8	20.9	27 14.6	-19.4	21.0	28 10.6	-19.0	21.2	29 06.5	-18.6	21.4	30 02.3	-18.2	21.6	69
70	23 09.2	-21.3	19.4	24 05.8	-21.0	19.5	25 02.3	-20.6	19.7	25 58.8	-20.3	19.8	26 55.2	-19.9	20.0	27 51.6	-19.5	20.2	28 47.9	-19.2	20.3	29 44.1	-18.8	20.5	70
71	22 47.9	-21.7	18.3	23 44.8	-21.3	18.5	24 41.7	-21.0	18.6	25 38.5	-20.7	18.8	26 35.3	-20.3	18.9	27 32.1	-20.1	19.1	28 28.7	-19.6	19.3	29 25.3	-19.3	19.5	71
72	22 26.2	-22.1	17.3	23 23.5	-21.8	17.5	24 20.7	-21.5	17.6	25 17.8	-21.1	17.7	26 15.0	-20.8	17.9	27 12.0	-20.4	18.0	28 09.1	-20.2	18.2	29 06.0	-19.8	18.4	72
73	22 04.1	-22.4	16.3	23 01.7	-22.1	16.4	23 59.2	-21.8	16.6	24 56.7	-21.5	16.7	25 54.2	-21.3	16.8	26 51.6	-21.0	17.0	27 48.9	-20.6	17.1	28 46.2	-20.3	17.3	73
74	21 41.7	-22.8	15.3	22 39.6	-22.6	15.4	23 37.4	-22.3	15.5	24 35.2	-22.0	15.7	25 32.9	-21.7	15.8	26 30.6	-21.4	15.9	27 28.3	-21.1	16.1	28 25.9	-20.8	16.2	74
75	21 18.9	-23.1	14.3	22 17.0	-22.9	14.4	23 15.1	-22.6	14.5	24 13.2	-22.4	14.6	25 11.2	-22.1	14.8	26 09.2	-21.8	14.9	27 07.2	-21.6	15.0	28 05.1	-21.3	15.2	75
76	20 55.8	-23.5	13.3	21 54.1	-23.2	13.4	22 52.5	-23.0	13.5	23 50.8	-22.8	13.6	24 49.1	-22.5	13.7	25 47.4	-22.3	13.9	26 45.6	-22.0	14.0	27 43.8	-21.8	14.1	76
77	20 32.3	-23.8	12.4	21 30.9	-23.6	12.4	22 29.5	-23.4	12.5	23 28.0	-23.1	12.6	24 26.6	-23.0	12.7	25 25.1	-22.7	12.8	26 23.6	-22.5	12.9	27 22.0	-22.2	13.0	77
78	20 08.5	-24.2	11.4	21 07.3	-23.9	11.5	22 06.1	-23.8	11.5	23 04.9	-23.6	11.6	24 03.6	-23.3	11.7	25 02.4	-23.2	11.8	26 01.1	-22.9	11.9	26 59.8	-22.7	12.0	78
79	19 44.3	-24.4	10.4	20 43.4	-24.3	10.5	21 42.3	-24.0	10.5	22 41.3	-23.9	10.6	23 40.3	-23.7	10.7	24 39.2	-23.5	10.8	25 38.2	-23.4	10.9	26 37.1	-23.2	11.0	79
80	19 19.9	-24.8	9.4	20 19.1	-24.6	9.5	21 18.3	-24.5	9.6	22 17.4	-24.3	9.6	23 16.6	-24.1	9.7	24 15.7	-23.9	9.8	25 14.8	-23.7	9.8	26 13.9	-23.6	9.9	80
81	18 55.1	-25.0	8.5	19 54.5	-24.9	8.5	20 53.8	-24.7	8.6	21 53.1	-24.6	8.6	22 52.5	-24.5	8.7	23 51.8	-24.4	8.8	24 51.1	-24.2	8.8	25 50.3	-24.0	8.9	81
82	18 30.1	-25.3	7.5	19 29.6	-25.2	7.6	20 29.1	-25.1	7.6	21 28.5	-24.9	7.7	22 28.0	-24.9	7.7	23 27.4	-24.7	7.8	24 26.9	-24.6	7.8	25 26.3	-24.4	7.9	82
83	18 04.8	-25.7	6.6	19 04.4	-25.6	6.6	20 04.0	-25.4	6.6	21 03.6	-25.3	6.7	22 03.1	-25.1	6.7	23 02.7	-25.0	6.8	24 02.3	-25.0	6.8	25 01.9	-24.9	6.9	83
84	17 39.1	-25.9	5.6	18 38.8	-25.8	5.6	19 38.6	-25.8	5.7	20 38.3	-25.7	5.7	21 38.0	-25.6	5.8	22 37.7	-25.5	5.8	23 37.3	-25.3	5.8	24 37.0	-25.2	5.9	84
85	17 13.2	-26.1	4.7	18 13.0	-26.0	4.7	19 12.8	-26.0	4.7	20 12.6	-25.9	4.7	21 12.4	-25.8	4.8	22 12.2	-25.8	4.8	23 12.0	-25.7	4.8	24 11.8	-25.6	4.9	85
86	16 47.1	-26.4	3.7	17 47.0	-26.4	3.7	18 46.8	-26.3	3.8	19 46.7	-26.2	3.8	20 46.6	-26.2	3.8	21 46.4	-26.1	3.8	22 46.3	-26.1	3.9	23 46.2	-26.0	3.9	86
87	16 20.7	-26.7	2.8	17 20.6	-26.6	2.8	18 20.5	-26.5	2.8	19 20.5	-26.6	2.8	20 20.4	-26.5	2.9	21 20.3	-26.4	2.9	22 20.2	-26.4	2.9	23 20.2	-26.4	2.9	87
88	15 54.0	-26.9	1.9	16 54.0	-26.9	1.9	17 54.0	-26.9	1.9	18 53.9	-26.8	1.9	19 53.9	-26.8	1.9	20 53.9	-26.8	1.9	21 53.8	-26.7	1.9	22 53.8	-26.7	1.9	88
89	15 27.1	-27.1	0.9	16 27.1	-27.1	0.9	17 27.1	-27.1	0.9	18 27.1	-27.1	0.9	19 27.1	-27.1	0.9	20 27.1	-27.1	1.0	21 27.1	-27.1	1.0	22 27.1	-27.1	1.0	89
90	15 00.0	-27.3	0.0	16 00.0	-27.4	0.0	17 00.0	-27.4	0.0	18 00.0	-27.4	0.0	19 00.0	-27.4	0.0	20 00.0	-27.4	0.0	21 00.0	-27.4	0.0	22 00.0	-27.4	0.0	90
	15°			16°			17°			18°			19°			20°			21°			22°			

63°, 297° L.H.A. LATITUDE SAME NAME AS DECLINATION

128

LATITUDE **CONTRARY** NAME TO DECLINATION L.H.A. 63°, 297°

Dec.	15° Hc	d	Z	16° Hc	d	Z	17° Hc	d	Z	18° Hc	d	Z	19° Hc	d	Z	20° Hc	d	Z	21° Hc	d	Z	22° Hc	d	Z	Dec.
°	° ′	′	°	° ′	′	°	° ′	′	°	° ′	′	°	° ′	′	°	° ′	′	°	° ′	′	°	° ′	′	°	°
0	26 00.6	−17.5	97.5	25 52.5	−18.6	98.0	25 43.9	−19.7	98.5	25 34.8	−20.8	98.9	25 25.2	−21.8	99.4	25 15.2	−22.9	99.9	25 04.6	−23.9	100.3	24 53.6	−25.0	100.8	0
1	25 43.1	−18.0	98.6	25 33.9	−19.1	99.0	25 24.2	−20.2	99.5	25 14.0	−21.2	100.0	25 03.4	−22.3	100.4	24 52.3	−23.3	100.9	24 40.7	−24.4	101.4	24 28.6	−25.3	101.8	1
2	25 25.1	−18.4	99.6	25 14.8	−19.5	100.1	25 04.0	−20.5	100.6	24 52.8	−21.6	101.0	24 41.1	−22.7	101.5	24 29.0	−23.8	101.9	24 16.3	−24.7	102.4	24 03.3	−25.8	102.8	2
3	25 06.7	−18.9	100.7	24 55.3	−19.9	101.1	24 43.5	−21.0	101.6	24 31.2	−22.1	102.0	24 18.4	−23.1	102.5	24 05.2	−24.1	102.9	23 51.6	−25.1	103.4	23 37.5	−26.1	103.8	3
4	24 47.8	−19.3	101.7	24 35.4	−20.4	102.2	24 22.5	−21.4	102.6	24 09.1	−22.4	103.1	23 55.3	−23.4	103.5	23 41.1	−24.5	103.9	23 26.5	−25.5	104.4	23 11.4	−26.5	104.8	4
5	24 28.5	−19.7	102.8	24 15.0	−20.8	103.2	24 01.1	−21.9	103.7	23 46.7	−22.9	104.1	23 31.9	−23.9	104.5	23 16.6	−24.8	104.9	23 01.0	−25.9	105.3	22 44.9	−26.8	105.7	5
6	24 08.8	−20.2	103.8	23 54.2	−21.2	104.2	23 39.2	−22.2	104.7	23 23.8	−23.2	105.1	23 08.0	−24.2	105.5	22 51.8	−25.3	105.9	22 35.1	−26.2	106.3	22 18.1	−27.2	106.7	6
7	23 48.6	−20.5	104.8	23 33.0	−21.5	105.3	23 17.0	−22.6	105.7	23 00.6	−23.6	106.1	22 43.8	−24.6	106.5	22 26.5	−25.6	106.9	22 08.9	−26.6	107.3	21 50.9	−27.5	107.7	7
8	23 28.1	−21.0	105.9	23 11.5	−22.0	106.3	22 54.4	−23.0	106.7	22 37.0	−24.0	107.1	22 19.2	−25.0	107.5	22 00.9	−25.9	107.9	21 42.3	−26.9	108.3	21 23.4	−27.9	108.6	8
9	23 07.1	−21.3	106.9	22 49.5	−22.4	107.3	22 31.4	−23.3	107.7	22 13.0	−24.3	108.1	21 54.2	−25.3	108.5	21 35.0	−26.3	108.8	21 15.4	−27.2	109.2	20 55.5	−28.1	109.6	9
10	22 45.8	−21.8	107.9	22 27.1	−22.7	108.3	22 08.1	−23.7	108.7	21 48.7	−24.7	109.1	21 28.9	−25.7	109.4	21 08.7	−26.6	109.8	20 48.2	−27.5	110.2	20 27.4	−28.5	110.5	10
11	22 24.0	−22.1	108.9	22 04.4	−23.1	109.3	21 44.4	−24.1	109.7	21 24.0	−25.0	110.0	21 03.2	−25.9	110.4	20 42.1	−26.9	110.8	20 20.7	−27.8	111.1	19 58.9	−28.7	111.5	11
12	22 01.9	−22.4	109.9	21 41.3	−23.4	110.3	21 20.3	−24.4	110.7	20 59.0	−25.4	111.0	20 37.3	−26.3	111.4	20 15.2	−27.2	111.7	19 52.9	−28.2	112.1	19 30.2	−29.1	112.4	12
13	21 39.5	−22.9	110.9	21 17.9	−23.8	111.3	20 55.9	−24.7	111.6	20 33.6	−25.7	112.0	20 11.0	−26.6	112.3	19 48.0	−27.5	112.7	19 24.7	−28.4	113.0	19 01.1	−29.3	113.3	13
14	21 16.6	−23.1	111.9	20 54.1	−24.2	112.3	20 31.2	−25.1	112.6	20 07.9	−26.0	113.0	19 44.4	−26.9	113.3	19 20.5	−27.8	113.6	18 56.3	−28.7	113.9	18 31.8	−29.6	114.2	14
15	20 53.5	−23.6	112.9	20 29.9	−24.4	113.2	20 06.1	−25.4	113.6	19 41.9	−26.3	113.9	19 17.5	−27.2	114.2	18 52.7	−28.1	114.6	18 27.6	−29.0	114.9	18 02.2	−29.8	115.2	15
16	20 29.9	−23.8	113.9	20 05.5	−24.8	114.2	19 40.7	−25.7	114.5	19 15.6	−26.5	114.9	18 50.3	−27.5	115.2	18 24.6	−28.4	115.5	17 58.6	−29.2	115.8	17 32.4	−30.1	116.1	16
17	20 06.1	−24.2	114.9	19 40.7	−25.1	115.2	19 15.0	−25.9	115.5	18 49.1	−26.9	115.8	18 22.8	−27.8	116.1	17 56.2	−28.6	116.4	17 29.4	−29.5	116.7	17 02.3	−30.3	117.0	17
18	19 41.9	−24.4	115.8	19 15.6	−25.3	116.2	18 49.1	−26.3	116.5	18 22.2	−27.2	116.8	17 55.0	−28.0	117.1	17 27.6	−28.9	117.3	16 59.9	−29.7	117.6	16 32.0	−30.6	117.9	18
19	19 17.5	−24.8	116.8	18 50.3	−25.7	117.1	18 22.8	−26.6	117.4	17 55.0	−27.4	117.7	17 27.0	−28.3	118.0	16 58.7	−29.1	118.3	16 30.2	−30.0	118.5	16 01.4	−30.7	118.8	19
20	18 52.7	−25.1	117.8	18 24.6	−26.0	118.1	17 56.2	−26.8	118.4	17 27.6	−27.7	118.6	16 58.7	−28.5	118.9	16 29.6	−29.4	119.2	16 00.2	−30.1	119.4	15 30.7	−31.0	119.7	20
21	18 27.6	−25.4	118.7	17 58.6	−26.2	119.0	17 29.4	−27.1	119.3	16 59.9	−27.9	119.6	16 30.2	−28.8	119.8	16 00.2	−29.5	120.1	15 30.1	−30.4	120.3	14 59.7	−31.2	120.6	21
22	18 02.2	−25.6	119.7	17 32.4	−26.5	120.0	17 02.3	−27.3	120.2	16 32.0	−28.2	120.5	16 01.4	−29.0	120.7	15 30.7	−29.8	121.0	14 59.7	−30.6	121.2	14 28.5	−31.4	121.4	22
23	17 36.6	−25.9	120.6	17 05.9	−26.8	120.9	16 35.0	−27.6	121.2	16 03.8	−28.4	121.4	15 32.4	−29.2	121.6	15 00.9	−30.1	121.9	14 29.1	−30.8	122.1	13 57.1	−31.6	122.3	23
24	17 10.7	−26.2	121.6	16 39.1	−27.0	121.8	16 07.4	−27.8	122.1	15 35.4	−28.6	122.3	15 03.2	−29.4	122.6	14 30.8	−30.2	122.8	13 58.3	−31.0	123.0	13 25.5	−31.8	123.2	24
25	16 44.5	−26.4	122.5	16 12.1	−27.2	122.8	15 39.6	−28.1	123.0	15 06.8	−28.9	123.2	14 33.8	−29.6	123.5	14 00.6	−30.4	123.7	13 27.3	−31.2	123.9	12 53.7	−31.9	124.1	25
26	16 18.1	−26.7	123.4	15 44.9	−27.5	123.7	15 11.5	−28.3	123.9	14 37.9	−29.0	124.1	14 04.2	−29.9	124.4	13 30.2	−30.6	124.6	12 56.1	−31.4	124.7	12 21.8	−32.1	124.9	26
27	15 51.4	−26.9	124.4	15 17.4	−27.7	124.6	14 43.2	−28.5	124.8	14 08.9	−29.3	125.0	13 34.3	−30.0	125.2	12 59.6	−30.8	125.4	12 24.7	−31.5	125.6	11 49.7	−32.2	125.8	27
28	15 24.5	−27.2	125.3	14 49.7	−28.0	125.5	14 14.7	−28.7	125.7	13 39.6	−29.5	125.9	13 04.3	−30.2	126.1	12 28.8	−30.9	126.3	11 53.2	−31.7	126.5	11 17.5	−32.4	126.7	28
29	14 57.3	−27.4	126.2	14 21.7	−28.1	126.4	13 46.0	−28.9	126.6	13 10.1	−29.6	126.8	12 34.1	−30.4	127.0	11 57.9	−31.1	127.2	11 21.5	−31.8	127.4	10 45.1	−32.6	127.5	29
30	14 29.9	−27.6	127.2	13 53.6	−28.3	127.4	13 17.1	−29.1	127.5	12 40.5	−29.8	127.7	12 03.7	−30.6	127.9	11 26.8	−31.3	128.1	10 49.7	−32.0	128.2	10 12.5	−32.6	128.4	30
31	14 02.3	−27.7	128.1	13 25.3	−28.6	128.3	12 48.0	−29.2	128.4	12 10.7	−30.0	128.6	11 33.1	−30.7	128.8	10 55.5	−31.4	128.9	10 17.7	−32.1	129.1	9 39.9	−32.8	129.2	31
32	13 34.6	−28.0	129.0	12 56.7	−28.7	129.2	12 18.8	−29.5	129.3	11 40.7	−30.2	129.5	11 02.4	−30.8	129.7	10 24.1	−31.6	129.8	9 45.6	−32.2	129.9	9 07.1	−33.0	130.1	32
33	13 06.6	−28.2	129.9	12 28.0	−28.9	130.1	11 49.3	−29.6	130.2	11 10.5	−30.3	130.4	10 31.6	−31.0	130.5	9 52.5	−31.7	130.7	9 13.4	−32.4	130.8	8 34.1	−33.0	130.9	33
34	12 38.4	−28.4	130.8	11 59.1	−29.1	131.0	11 19.7	−29.7	131.1	10 40.2	−30.4	131.3	10 00.6	−31.2	131.4	9 20.8	−31.8	131.5	8 41.0	−32.5	131.6	8 01.1	−33.1	131.8	34
35	12 10.0	−28.5	131.7	11 30.0	−29.2	131.9	10 50.0	−30.0	132.0	10 09.8	−30.6	132.1	9 29.4	−31.2	132.3	8 49.0	−31.9	132.4	8 08.5	−32.5	132.5	7 28.0	−33.2	132.6	35
36	11 41.5	−28.7	132.6	11 00.8	−29.4	132.7	10 20.0	−30.0	132.9	9 39.2	−30.8	133.0	8 58.2	−31.4	133.1	8 17.1	−32.0	133.2	7 36.0	−32.7	133.3	6 54.8	−33.4	133.4	36
37	11 12.8	−28.9	133.5	10 31.4	−29.5	133.6	9 50.0	−30.2	133.8	9 08.4	−30.8	133.9	8 26.8	−31.5	134.0	7 45.1	−32.2	134.1	7 03.3	−32.8	134.2	6 21.4	−33.4	134.3	37
38	10 43.9	−29.0	134.4	10 01.9	−29.7	134.5	9 19.8	−30.3	134.6	8 37.6	−31.0	134.8	7 55.3	−31.6	134.9	7 12.9	−32.2	134.9	6 30.5	−32.9	135.0	5 48.0	−33.4	135.1	38
39	10 14.9	−29.2	135.3	9 32.2	−29.8	135.4	8 49.5	−30.5	135.5	8 06.6	−31.1	135.6	7 23.7	−31.7	135.7	6 40.7	−32.3	135.8	5 57.7	−33.0	135.9	5 14.6	−33.6	135.9	39
40	9 45.7	−29.3	136.2	9 02.4	−29.9	136.3	8 19.0	−30.5	136.4	7 35.5	−31.1	136.5	6 52.0	−31.8	136.6	6 08.4	−32.4	136.6	5 24.7	−33.0	136.7	4 41.0	−33.6	136.8	40
41	9 16.4	−29.4	137.1	8 32.5	−30.1	137.2	7 48.5	−30.7	137.3	7 04.4	−31.3	137.3	6 20.2	−31.9	137.4	5 36.0	−32.5	137.5	4 51.7	−33.0	137.6	4 07.4	−33.6	137.6	41
42	8 47.0	−29.5	137.9	8 02.4	−30.1	138.0	7 17.8	−30.8	138.1	6 33.1	−31.4	138.2	5 48.3	−31.9	138.3	5 03.5	−32.5	138.3	4 18.7	−33.1	138.4	3 33.8	−33.7	138.4	42
43	8 17.5	−29.7	138.8	7 32.3	−30.3	138.9	6 47.0	−30.8	139.0	6 01.7	−31.4	139.1	5 16.4	−32.0	139.1	4 31.0	−32.6	139.2	3 45.6	−33.2	139.2	3 00.1	−33.7	139.3	43
44	7 47.8	−29.8	139.7	7 02.0	−30.4	139.8	6 16.2	−31.0	139.8	5 30.3	−31.5	139.9	4 44.4	−32.1	140.0	3 58.4	−32.6	140.0	3 12.4	−33.2	140.1	2 26.4	−33.8	140.1	44
45	7 18.0	−29.9	140.6	6 31.6	−30.4	140.6	5 45.2	−31.0	140.7	4 58.8	−31.6	140.8	4 12.3	−32.2	140.8	3 25.8	−32.7	140.9	2 39.2	−33.2	140.9	1 52.6	−33.7	140.9	45
46	6 48.1	−29.9	141.4	6 01.2	−30.5	141.5	5 14.2	−31.1	141.6	4 27.2	−31.6	141.6	3 40.1	−32.1	141.7	2 53.1	−32.8	141.7	2 06.0	−33.3	141.7	1 18.9	−33.8	141.7	46
47	6 18.2	−30.1	142.3	5 30.7	−30.6	142.4	4 43.1	−31.1	142.4	3 55.6	−31.7	142.5	3 08.0	−32.3	142.5	2 20.3	−32.7	142.5	1 32.7	−33.3	142.6	0 45.1	−33.9	142.6	47
48	5 48.1	−30.1	143.2	5 00.1	−30.7	143.2	4 12.0	−31.2	143.3	3 23.9	−31.8	143.3	2 35.7	−32.2	143.4	1 47.6	−32.8	143.4	0 59.4	−33.3	143.4	0 11.2	−33.8	143.4	48
49	5 18.0	−30.2	144.1	4 29.4	−30.8	144.1	3 40.8	−31.3	144.1	2 52.1	−31.7	144.2	2 03.5	−32.3	144.2	1 14.8	−32.8	144.2	0 26.1	−33.3	144.2	0 22.6	+33.8	35.8	49
50	4 47.8	−30.3	144.9	3 58.6	−30.7	145.0	3 09.5	−31.3	145.0	2 20.4	−31.8	145.0	1 31.2	−32.3	145.0	0 42.0	−32.8	145.1	0 07.2	+33.3	34.9	0 56.4	+33.8	34.9	50
51	4 17.5	−30.3	145.8	3 27.9	−30.9	145.8	2 38.2	−31.3	145.9	1 48.6	−31.9	145.9	0 58.9	−32.3	145.9	0 09.2	−32.8	145.9	0 40.5	+33.3	34.1	1 30.2	+33.7	34.1	51
52	3 47.2	−30.4	146.6	2 57.0	−30.8	146.7	2 06.9	−31.4	146.7	1 16.7	−31.8	146.7	0 26.6	−32.4	146.7	0 23.6	+32.8	33.3	1 13.8	+33.2	33.3	2 03.9	+33.8	33.3	52
53	3 16.8	−30.5	147.5	2 26.2	−31.0	147.5	1 35.5	−31.4	147.6	0 44.9	−31.9	147.6	0 05.8	+32.3	32.4	0 56.4	+32.8	32.4	1 47.0	+33.3	32.4	2 37.7	+33.7	32.5	53
54	2 46.3	−30.4	148.4	1 55.2	−30.9	148.4	1 04.1	−31.4	148.4	0 13.0	−31.8	148.4	0 38.1	+32.3	31.6	1 29.2	+32.8	31.6	2 20.3	+33.2	31.6	3 11.4	+33.7	31.6	54
55	2 15.9	−30.5	149.2	1 24.3	−30.9	149.3	0 32.7	−31.4	149.3	0 18.8	+31.9	30.7	1 10.4	+32.3	30.7	2 02.0	+32.7	30.8	2 53.5	+33.2	30.8	3 45.1	+33.6	30.8	55
56	1 45.4	−30.5	150.1	0 53.4	−31.0	150.1	0 01.3	−31.4	150.1	0 50.7	+31.8	29.9	1 42.7	+32.3	29.9	2 34.7	+32.7	29.9	3 26.7	+33.2	29.9	4 18.7	+33.6	30.0	56
57	1 14.9	−30.6	151.0	0 22.4	−31.0	151.0	0 30.1	+31.4	29.0	1 22.5	+31.9	29.0	2 15.0	+32.2	29.1	3 07.4	+32.7	29.1	3 59.9	+33.0	29.1	4 52.3	+33.5	29.1	57
58	0 44.3	−30.5	151.8	0 08.6	+30.9	28.2	1 01.5	+31.4	28.2	1 54.4	+31.8	28.2	2 47.2	+32.2	28.2	3 40.1	+32.6	28.2	4 32.9	+33.1	28.3	5 25.8	+33.4	28.3	58
59	0 13.8	−30.6	152.7	0 39.5	+31.0	27.3	1 32.9	+31.3	27.3	2 26.2	+31.7	27.3	3 19.4	+32.2	27.4	4 12.7	+32.6	27.4	5 06.0	+33.0	27.4	5 59.2	+33.4	27.5	59
60	0 16.8	+30.5	26.5	1 10.5	+30.9	26.5	2 04.2	+31.4	26.5	2 57.9	+31.7	26.5	3 51.6	+32.1	26.5	4 45.3	+32.5	26.6	5 39.0	+32.8	26.6	6 32.6	+33.3	26.6	60
61	0 47.3	+30.6	25.6	1 41.4	+31.0	25.6	2 35.6	+31.3	25.6	3 29.6	+31.7	25.6	4 23.7	+32.1	25.7	5 17.8	+32.4	25.7	6 11.8	+32.9	25.8	7 05.9	+33.2	25.8	61
62	1 17.9	+30.5	24.7	2 12.4	+30.9	24.7	3 06.9	+31.2	24.8	4 01.3	+31.7	24.8	4 55.8	+32.0	24.8	5 50.2	+32.4	24.9	6 44.7	+32.7	24.9	7 39.1	+33.1	25.0	62
63	1 48.4	+30.5	23.9	2 43.3	+30.8	23.9	3 38.1	+31.2	23.9	4 33.0	+31.5	23.9	5 27.8	+31.9	24.0	6 22.6	+32.3	24.0	7 17.4	+32.6	24.1	8 12.2	+33.0	24.1	63
64	2 18.9	+30.5	23.0	3 14.1	+30.8	23.0	4 09.3	+31.2	23.1	5 04.5	+31.5	23.1	5 59.7	+31.9	23.1	6 54.9	+32.2	23.2	7 50.0	+32.6	23.2	8 45.2	+32.8	23.3	64
65	2 49.4	+30.4	22.1	3 44.9	+30.8	22.2	4 40.5	+31.1	22.2	5 36.0	+31.5	22.2	6 31.6	+31.7	22.3	7 27.1	+32.1	22.3	8 22.6	+32.4	22.4	9 18.0	+32.8	22.4	65
66	3 19.8	+30.4	21.3	4 15.7	+30.7	21.3	5 11.6	+31.0	21.3	6 07.5	+31.3	21.4	7 03.3	+31.7	21.4	7 59.2	+32.0	21.5	8 55.0	+32.3	21.5	9 50.8	+32.6	21.6	66
67	3 50.2	+30.3	20.4	4 46.4	+30.6	20.4	5 42.6	+30.9	20.5	6 38.8	+31.3	20.5	7 35.0	+31.5	20.6	8 31.2	+31.8	20.6	9 27.3	+32.2	20.7	10 23.4	+32.5	20.7	67
68	4 20.5	+30.3	19.6	5 17.0	+30.6	19.6	6 13.5	+30.9	19.6	7 10.1	+31.1	19.7	8 06.5	+31.5	19.7	9 03.0	+31.8	19.8	9 59.5	+32.0	19.8	10 55.9	+32.4	19.9	68
69	4 50.8	+30.2	18.7	5 47.6	+30.5	18.7	6 44.4	+30.8	18.8	7 41.2	+31.1	18.8	8 38.0	+31.3	18.8	9 34.8	+31.6	18.9	10 31.5	+32.0	19.0	11 28.3	+32.2	19.0	69
70	5 21.0	+30.1	17.8	6 18.1	+30.4	17.9	7 15.2	+30.7	17.9	8 12.3	+30.9	17.9	9 09.3	+31.3	18.0	10 06.4	+31.5	18.0	11 03.5	+31.7	18.1	12 00.5	+32.0	18.2	70
71	5 51.1	+30.0	17.0	6 48.5	+30.3	17.0	7 45.9	+30.5	17.0	8 43.2	+30.8	17.1	9 40.6	+31.1	17.1	10 37.9	+31.4	17.2	11 35.2	+31.6	17.2	12 32.5	+31.9	17.3	71
72	6 21.1	+30.0	16.1	7 18.8	+30.2	16.1	8 16.4	+30.5	16.2	9 14.0	+30.7	16.2	10 11.7	+30.9	16.2	11 09.3	+31.2	16.3	12 06.8	+31.5	16.4	13 04.4	+31.7	16.4	72
73	6 51.1	+29.9	15.2	7 49.0	+30.1	15.2	8 46.9	+30.3	15.3	9 44.7	+30.6	15.3	10 42.6	+30.8	15.4	11 40.5	+31.0	15.4	12 38.3	+31.3	15.5	13 36.1	+31.5	15.5	73
74	7 21.0	+29.7	14.3	8 19.1	+30.0	14.4	9 17.2	+30.2	14.4	10 15.3	+30.4	14.5	11 13.4	+30.7	14.5	12 11.5	+30.9	14.6	13 09.6	+31.1	14.6	14 07.6	+31.3	14.7	74
75	7 50.7	+29.7	13.5	8 49.1	+29.8	13.5	9 47.4	+30.1	13.5	10 45.7	+30.3	13.6	11 44.1	+30.5	13.6	12 42.4	+30.7	13.7	13 40.7	+30.9	13.7	14 38.9	+31.2	13.8	75
76	8 20.4	+29.5	12.6	9 18.9	+29.8	12.6	10 17.5	+29.9	12.7	11 16.0	+30.2	12.7	12 14.6	+30.3	12.7	13 13.1	+30.5	12.8	14 11.6	+30.7	12.8	15 10.1	+30.9	12.9	76
77	8 49.9	+29.4	11.7	9 48.7	+29.6	11.7	10 47.4	+29.8	11.8	11 46.2	+29.9	11.8	12 44.9	+30.1	11.9	13 43.6	+30.3	11.9	14 42.3	+30.5	12.0	15 41.0	+30.7	12.0	77
78	9 19.3	+29.3	10.8	10 18.3	+29.4	10.9	11 17.2	+29.6	10.9	12 16.1	+29.8	10.9	13 15.0	+30.0	11.0	14 13.9	+30.2	11.0	15 12.8	+30.3	11.1	16 11.7	+30.5	11.1	78
79	9 48.6	+29.2	9.9	10 47.7	+29.3	10.0	11 46.8	+29.5	10.0	12 45.9	+29.6	10.0	13 45.0	+29.7	10.1	14 44.1	+29.9	10.1	15 43.1	+30.1	10.2	16 42.2	+30.2	10.2	79
80	10 17.8	+29.0	9.0	11 17.0	+29.2	9.1	12 16.3	+29.3	9.1	13 15.5	+29.4	9.1	14 14.7	+29.6	9.2	15 14.0	+29.7	9.2	16 13.2	+29.9	9.3	17 12.4	+30.0	9.3	80
81	10 46.8	+28.8	8.2	11 46.2	+28.9	8.2	12 45.6	+29.1	8.2	13 44.9	+29.3	8.3	14 44.3	+29.4	8.3	15 43.7	+29.5	8.3	16 43.1	+29.6	8.4	17 42.4	+29.8	8.4	81
82	11 15.6	+28.7	7.3	12 15.1	+28.8	7.3	13 14.7	+28.9	7.3	14 14.2	+29.0	7.4	15 13.7	+29.1	7.4	16 13.2	+29.2	7.4	17 12.7	+29.3	7.5	18 12.2	+29.4	7.5	82
83	11 44.3	+28.5	6.4	12 43.9	+28.7	6.4	13 43.6	+28.7	6.4	14 43.2	+28.8	6.4	15 42.8	+28.9	6.5	16 42.4	+29.0	6.5	17 42.0	+29.2	6.5	18 41.6	+29.3	6.6	83
84	12 12.8	+28.4	5.5	13 12.6	+28.4	5.5	14 12.3	+28.5	5.5	15 12.0	+28.6	5.5	16 11.7	+28.7	5.6	17 11.4	+28.8	5.6	18 11.2	+28.8	5.6	19 10.9	+28.9	5.7	84
85	12 41.2	+28.1	4.6	13 41.0	+28.2	4.6	14 40.8	+28.3	4.6	15 40.6	+28.4	4.6	16 40.4	+28.4	4.6	17 40.2	+28.5	4.7	18 40.0	+28.6	4.7	19 39.8	+28.7	4.7	85
86	13 09.3	+28.0	3.7	14 09.2	+28.0	3.7	15 09.1	+28.1	3.7	16 09.0	+28.1	3.7	17 08.8	+28.2	3.7	18 08.7	+28.3	3.8	19 08.6	+28.3	3.8	20 08.5	+28.3	3.8	86
87	13 37.3	+27.8	2.8	14 37.2	+27.9	2.8	15 37.2	+27.8	2.8	16 37.1	+27.9	2.8	17 37.0	+28.0	2.8	18 37.0	+27.9	2.8	19 36.9	+28.0	2.8	20 36.8	+28.1	2.9	87
88	14 05.1	+27.6	1.8	15 05.1	+27.5	1.8	16 05.0	+27.6	1.9	17 05.0	+27.6	1.9	18 05.0	+27.6	1.9	19 04.9	+27.7	1.9	20 04.9	+27.7	1.9	21 04.9	+27.7	1.9	88
89	14 32.7	+27.3	0.9	15 32.6	+27.4	0.9	16 32.6	+27.4	0.9	17 32.6	+27.4	0.9	18 32.6	+27.4	0.9	19 32.6	+27.4	0.9	20 32.6	+27.4	1.0	21 32.6	+27.4	1.0	89
90	15 00.0	+27.1	0.0	16 00.0	+27.1	0.0	17 00.0	+27.1	0.0	18 00.0	+27.1	0.0	19 00.0	+27.1	0.0	20 00.0	+27.1	0.0	21 00.0	+27.1	0.0	22 00.0	+27.1	0.0	90
	15°			16°			17°			18°			19°			20°			21°			22°			

S. Lat. {L.H.A. greater than 180° ....Zn=180°−Z; L.H.A. less than 180°...........Zn=180°+Z}

LATITUDE **SAME** NAME AS DECLINATION L.H.A. 117°, 243°

129

64°, 296° L.H.A. LATITUDE SAME NAME AS DECLINATION N. Lat. {L.H.A. greater than 180° .....Zn=Z; L.H.A. less than 180°............Zn=360°-Z}

Dec.	15° Hc	d	Z	16° Hc	d	Z	17° Hc	d	Z	18° Hc	d	Z	19° Hc	d	Z	20° Hc	d	Z	21° Hc	d	Z	22° Hc	d	Z	Dec.
°	° ′	′	°	° ′	′	°	° ′	′	°	° ′	′	°	° ′	′	°	° ′	′	°	° ′	′	°	° ′	′	°	°
0	25 03.1	+16.9	97.2	24 55.3	+18.1	97.7	24 47.1	+19.1	98.1	24 38.4	+20.2	98.6	24 29.2	+21.3	99.0	24 19.6	+22.3	99.5	24 09.5	+23.3	99.9	23 58.9	+24.4	100.4	0
1	25 20.0	+16.5	96.1	25 13.4	+17.5	96.6	25 06.2	+18.7	97.1	24 58.6	+19.7	97.5	24 50.5	+20.8	98.0	24 41.9	+21.9	98.5	24 32.8	+23.0	98.9	24 23.3	+24.0	99.4	1
2	25 36.5	+16.0	95.1	25 30.9	+17.1	95.5	25 24.9	+18.2	96.0	25 18.3	+19.3	96.5	25 11.3	+20.4	97.0	25 03.8	+21.5	97.4	24 55.8	+22.5	97.9	24 47.3	+23.6	98.3	2
3	25 52.5	+15.5	94.0	25 48.0	+16.7	94.5	25 43.1	+17.7	95.0	25 37.6	+18.9	95.4	25 31.7	+20.0	95.9	25 25.3	+21.0	96.4	25 18.3	+22.2	96.9	25 10.9	+23.2	97.3	3
4	26 08.0	+15.0	92.9	26 04.7	+16.1	93.4	26 00.8	+17.3	93.9	25 56.5	+18.4	94.4	25 51.7	+19.5	94.9	25 46.3	+20.6	95.4	25 40.5	+21.6	95.8	25 34.1	+22.8	96.3	4
5	26 23.0	+14.6	91.8	26 20.8	+15.7	92.3	26 18.1	+16.8	92.8	26 14.9	+17.9	93.3	26 11.2	+19.0	93.8	26 06.9	+20.1	94.3	26 02.1	+21.3	94.8	25 56.9	+22.3	95.3	5
6	26 37.6	+14.0	90.8	26 36.5	+15.2	91.3	26 34.9	+16.4	91.8	26 32.8	+17.5	92.3	26 30.2	+18.6	92.8	26 27.0	+19.7	93.3	26 23.4	+20.8	93.8	26 19.2	+21.9	94.2	6
7	26 51.6	+13.6	89.7	26 51.7	+14.7	90.2	26 51.3	+15.8	90.7	26 50.3	+16.9	91.2	26 48.8	+18.0	91.7	26 46.7	+19.2	92.2	26 44.2	+20.3	92.7	26 41.1	+21.4	93.2	7
8	27 05.2	+13.0	88.6	27 06.4	+14.2	89.1	27 07.1	+15.3	89.6	27 07.2	+16.5	90.1	27 06.8	+17.6	90.6	27 05.9	+18.7	91.1	27 04.5	+19.8	91.7	27 02.5	+20.9	92.2	8
9	27 18.2	+12.6	87.5	27 20.6	+13.7	88.0	27 22.4	+14.8	88.5	27 23.7	+16.0	89.0	27 24.4	+17.1	89.6	27 24.6	+18.3	90.1	27 24.3	+19.4	90.6	27 23.4	+20.5	91.1	9
10	27 30.8	+12.0	86.4	27 34.3	+13.1	86.9	27 37.2	+14.4	87.4	27 39.7	+15.4	87.9	27 41.5	+16.6	88.5	27 42.9	+17.7	89.0	27 43.7	+18.8	89.5	27 43.9	+20.0	90.0	10
11	27 42.8	+11.4	85.3	27 47.4	+12.7	85.8	27 51.6	+13.7	86.3	27 55.1	+15.0	86.9	27 58.1	+16.1	87.4	28 00.6	+17.2	87.9	28 02.5	+18.4	88.4	28 03.9	+19.4	89.0	11
12	27 54.2	+11.0	84.2	28 00.1	+12.1	84.7	28 05.3	+13.3	85.2	28 10.1	+14.4	85.8	28 14.2	+15.6	86.3	28 17.8	+16.7	86.8	28 20.9	+17.8	87.4	28 23.3	+19.0	87.9	12
13	28 05.2	+10.4	83.1	28 12.2	+11.5	83.6	28 18.6	+12.7	84.1	28 24.5	+13.8	84.7	28 29.8	+15.0	85.2	28 34.5	+16.2	85.7	28 38.7	+17.3	86.3	28 42.3	+18.5	86.8	13
14	28 15.6	+9.8	81.9	28 23.7	+11.0	82.5	28 31.3	+12.2	83.0	28 38.3	+13.4	83.5	28 44.8	+14.5	84.1	28 50.7	+15.6	84.6	28 56.0	+16.8	85.2	29 00.8	+17.9	85.7	14
15	28 25.4	+9.3	80.8	28 34.7	+10.5	81.3	28 43.5	+11.6	81.9	28 51.7	+12.8	82.4	28 59.3	+13.9	83.0	29 06.3	+15.1	83.5	29 12.8	+16.2	84.1	29 18.7	+17.4	84.6	15
16	28 34.7	+8.8	79.7	28 45.2	+9.9	80.2	28 55.1	+11.1	80.8	29 04.5	+12.2	81.3	29 13.2	+13.4	81.9	29 21.4	+14.6	82.4	29 29.0	+15.7	83.0	29 36.1	+16.8	83.5	16
17	28 43.5	+8.2	78.6	28 55.1	+9.4	79.1	29 06.2	+10.5	79.6	29 16.7	+11.6	80.2	29 26.6	+12.8	80.8	29 36.0	+13.9	81.3	29 44.7	+15.2	81.9	29 52.9	+16.3	82.4	17
18	28 51.7	+7.6	77.4	29 04.5	+8.7	78.0	29 16.7	+9.9	78.5	29 28.3	+11.1	79.1	29 39.4	+12.3	79.6	29 49.9	+13.4	80.2	29 59.9	+14.5	80.8	30 09.2	+15.7	81.3	18
19	28 59.3	+7.0	76.3	29 13.2	+8.2	76.8	29 26.6	+9.4	77.4	29 39.4	+10.5	77.9	29 51.7	+11.6	78.5	30 03.3	+12.9	79.1	30 14.4	+14.0	79.6	30 24.9	+15.2	80.2	19
20	29 06.3	+6.5	75.2	29 21.4	+7.6	75.7	29 36.0	+8.7	76.3	29 49.9	+10.0	76.8	30 03.3	+11.1	77.4	30 16.2	+12.2	77.9	30 28.4	+13.4	78.5	30 40.1	+14.5	79.1	20
21	29 12.8	+5.9	74.0	29 29.0	+7.1	74.6	29 44.7	+8.2	75.1	29 59.9	+9.3	75.7	30 14.4	+10.5	76.2	30 28.4	+11.7	76.8	30 41.8	+12.8	77.4	30 54.6	+14.0	78.0	21
22	29 18.7	+5.3	72.9	29 36.1	+6.4	73.4	29 52.9	+7.6	74.0	30 09.2	+8.8	74.5	30 24.9	+9.9	75.1	30 40.1	+11.0	75.7	30 54.6	+12.3	76.2	31 08.6	+13.4	76.8	22
23	29 24.0	+4.7	71.7	29 42.5	+5.9	72.3	30 00.5	+7.0	72.8	30 18.0	+8.1	73.4	30 34.8	+9.3	73.9	30 51.1	+10.5	74.5	31 06.9	+11.6	75.1	31 22.0	+12.8	75.7	23
24	29 28.7	+4.1	70.6	29 48.4	+5.2	71.1	30 07.5	+6.4	71.7	30 26.1	+7.5	72.2	30 44.1	+8.7	72.8	31 01.6	+9.8	73.4	31 18.5	+11.0	74.0	31 34.8	+12.1	74.5	24
25	29 32.8	+3.6	69.4	29 53.6	+4.7	70.0	30 13.9	+5.8	70.5	30 33.6	+7.0	71.1	30 52.8	+8.1	71.6	31 11.4	+9.2	72.2	31 29.5	+10.3	72.8	31 46.9	+11.5	73.4	25
26	29 36.4	+2.9	68.3	29 58.3	+4.1	68.8	30 19.7	+5.2	69.4	30 40.6	+6.3	69.9	31 00.9	+7.4	70.5	31 20.6	+8.6	71.1	31 39.8	+9.8	71.6	31 58.4	+10.9	72.2	26
27	29 39.3	+2.4	67.2	30 02.4	+3.4	67.7	30 24.9	+4.6	68.2	30 46.9	+5.7	68.8	31 08.3	+6.9	69.3	31 29.2	+8.0	69.9	31 49.6	+9.1	70.5	32 09.3	+10.3	71.1	27
28	29 41.7	+1.7	66.0	30 05.8	+2.9	66.5	30 29.5	+3.9	67.1	30 52.6	+5.1	67.6	31 15.2	+6.2	68.2	31 37.2	+7.4	68.7	31 58.7	+8.5	69.3	32 19.6	+9.6	69.9	28
29	29 43.4	+1.2	64.9	30 08.7	+2.2	65.4	30 33.4	+3.4	65.9	30 57.7	+4.4	66.5	31 21.4	+5.5	67.0	31 44.5	+6.7	67.6	32 07.2	+7.8	68.2	32 29.2	+9.0	68.7	29
30	29 44.6	+0.6	63.7	30 10.9	+1.7	64.2	30 36.8	+2.7	64.7	31 02.1	+3.9	65.3	31 26.9	+5.0	65.8	31 51.2	+6.1	66.4	32 15.0	+7.2	67.0	32 38.2	+8.3	67.6	30
31	29 45.2	-0.1	62.5	30 12.6	+1.0	63.1	30 39.5	+2.1	63.6	31 06.0	+3.2	64.1	31 31.9	+4.3	64.7	31 57.3	+5.4	65.2	32 22.2	+6.5	65.8	32 46.5	+7.6	66.4	31
32	29 45.1	-0.6	61.4	30 13.6	+0.4	61.9	30 41.6	+1.5	62.4	31 09.2	+2.5	63.0	31 36.2	+3.6	63.5	32 02.7	+4.7	64.1	32 28.7	+5.8	64.6	32 54.1	+7.0	65.2	32
33	29 44.5	-1.3	60.2	30 14.0	-0.2	60.7	30 43.1	+0.9	61.3	31 11.7	+2.0	61.8	31 39.8	+3.0	62.3	32 07.4	+4.1	62.9	32 34.5	+5.2	63.4	33 01.1	+6.3	64.0	33
34	29 43.2	-1.8	59.1	30 13.8	-0.8	59.6	30 44.0	+0.2	60.1	31 13.7	+1.3	60.6	31 42.8	+2.4	61.2	32 11.5	+3.5	61.7	32 39.7	+4.6	62.3	33 07.4	+5.6	62.8	34
35	29 41.4	-2.4	57.9	30 13.0	-1.4	58.4	30 44.2	-0.4	58.9	31 15.0	+0.6	59.5	31 45.2	+1.7	60.0	32 15.0	+2.8	60.5	32 44.3	+3.8	61.1	33 13.0	+5.0	61.6	35
36	29 39.0	-3.0	56.8	30 11.6	-2.0	57.3	30 43.8	-1.0	57.8	31 15.6	0.0	58.3	31 46.9	+1.1	58.8	32 17.8	+2.1	59.3	32 48.1	+3.2	59.9	33 18.0	+4.2	60.5	36
37	29 36.0	-3.7	55.6	30 09.6	-2.6	56.1	30 42.8	-1.6	56.6	31 15.6	-0.6	57.1	31 48.0	+0.4	57.6	32 19.9	+1.5	58.2	32 51.3	+2.5	58.7	33 22.2	+3.6	59.3	37
38	29 32.3	-4.2	54.5	30 07.0	-3.2	55.0	30 41.2	-2.2	55.4	31 15.0	-1.2	55.9	31 48.4	-0.2	56.5	32 21.4	+0.8	57.0	32 53.8	+1.9	57.5	33 25.8	+2.9	58.1	38
39	29 28.1	-4.8	53.3	30 03.8	-3.9	53.8	30 39.0	-2.9	54.3	31 13.8	-1.9	54.8	31 48.2	-0.9	55.3	32 22.2	+0.1	55.8	32 55.7	+1.1	56.3	33 28.7	+2.2	56.9	39
40	29 23.3	-5.3	52.2	29 59.9	-4.4	52.7	30 36.1	-3.5	53.1	31 11.9	-2.5	53.6	31 47.3	-1.5	54.1	32 22.3	-0.5	54.6	32 56.8	+0.5	55.1	33 30.9	+1.5	55.7	40
41	29 18.0	-6.0	51.1	29 55.5	-5.1	51.5	30 32.6	-4.1	52.0	31 09.4	-3.1	52.4	31 45.8	-2.2	52.9	32 21.8	-1.2	53.4	32 57.3	-0.2	53.9	33 32.4	+0.8	54.5	41
42	29 12.0	-6.6	49.9	29 50.4	-5.6	50.4	30 28.5	-4.7	50.8	31 06.3	-3.8	51.3	31 43.6	-2.8	51.7	32 20.6	-1.9	52.2	32 57.1	-0.9	52.7	33 33.2	+0.1	53.3	42
43	29 05.4	-7.1	48.8	29 44.8	-6.2	49.2	30 23.8	-5.3	49.6	31 02.5	-4.4	50.1	31 40.8	-3.5	50.6	32 18.7	-2.5	51.1	32 56.2	-1.5	51.6	33 33.3	-0.6	52.1	43
44	28 58.3	-7.7	47.6	29 38.6	-6.8	48.1	30 18.5	-5.9	48.5	30 58.1	-5.0	48.9	31 37.3	-4.1	49.4	32 16.2	-3.2	49.9	32 54.7	-2.3	50.4	33 32.7	-1.2	50.9	44
45	28 50.6	-8.2	46.5	29 31.8	-7.4	46.9	30 12.6	-6.5	47.3	30 53.1	-5.7	47.8	31 33.2	-4.7	48.2	32 13.0	-3.8	48.7	32 52.4	-2.9	49.2	33 31.5	-2.0	49.7	45
46	28 42.4	-8.8	45.4	29 24.4	-8.0	45.8	30 06.1	-7.2	46.2	30 47.4	-6.2	46.6	31 28.5	-5.4	47.1	32 09.2	-4.5	47.5	32 49.5	-3.6	48.0	33 29.5	-2.7	48.5	46
47	28 33.6	-9.4	44.3	29 16.4	-8.6	44.6	29 58.9	-7.7	45.0	30 41.2	-6.9	45.5	31 23.1	-6.0	45.9	32 04.7	-5.1	46.3	32 45.9	-4.2	46.8	33 26.8	-3.3	47.3	47
48	28 24.2	-9.9	43.1	29 07.8	-9.1	43.5	29 51.2	-8.3	43.9	30 34.3	-7.5	44.3	31 17.1	-6.7	44.7	31 59.6	-5.8	45.2	32 41.7	-4.9	45.6	33 23.5	-4.1	46.1	48
49	28 14.3	-10.5	42.0	28 58.7	-9.7	42.4	29 42.9	-8.9	42.8	30 26.8	-8.1	43.2	31 10.4	-7.2	43.6	31 53.8	-6.5	44.0	32 36.8	-5.6	44.4	33 19.4	-4.7	44.9	49
50	28 03.8	-11.0	40.9	28 49.0	-10.2	41.3	29 34.0	-9.5	41.6	30 18.7	-8.7	42.0	31 03.2	-7.9	42.4	31 47.3	-7.1	42.8	32 31.2	-6.3	43.2	33 14.7	-5.4	43.7	50
51	27 52.8	-11.6	39.8	28 38.8	-10.8	40.1	29 24.5	-10.0	40.5	30 10.0	-9.3	40.9	30 55.3	-8.5	41.2	31 40.2	-7.7	41.7	32 24.9	-6.9	42.1	33 09.3	-6.1	42.5	51
52	27 41.2	-12.0	38.7	28 28.0	-11.4	39.0	29 14.5	-10.6	39.4	30 00.7	-9.8	39.7	30 46.8	-9.1	40.1	31 32.5	-8.3	40.5	32 18.0	-7.5	40.9	33 03.2	-6.7	41.3	52
53	27 29.2	-12.6	37.6	28 16.6	-11.9	37.9	29 03.9	-11.2	38.2	29 50.9	-10.5	38.6	30 37.7	-9.8	38.9	31 24.2	-9.0	39.3	32 10.5	-8.2	39.7	32 56.5	-7.4	40.1	53
54	27 16.6	-13.2	36.5	28 04.7	-12.4	36.8	28 52.7	-11.8	37.1	29 40.4	-11.0	37.4	30 27.9	-10.3	37.8	31 15.2	-9.6	38.2	32 02.3	-8.9	38.6	32 49.1	-8.1	38.9	54
55	27 03.4	-13.6	35.4	27 52.3	-13.0	35.7	28 40.9	-12.3	36.0	29 29.4	-11.6	36.3	30 17.6	-10.9	36.7	31 05.6	-10.2	37.0	31 53.4	-9.5	37.4	32 41.0	-8.8	37.8	55
56	26 49.8	-14.1	34.3	27 39.3	-13.5	34.6	28 28.6	-12.8	34.9	29 17.8	-12.2	35.2	30 06.7	-11.5	35.5	30 55.4	-10.8	35.9	31 43.9	-10.1	36.2	32 32.2	-9.4	36.6	56
57	26 35.7	-14.6	33.2	27 25.8	-14.0	33.5	28 15.8	-13.4	33.8	29 05.6	-12.7	34.1	29 55.2	-12.1	34.4	30 44.6	-11.4	34.7	31 33.8	-10.7	35.1	32 22.8	-10.0	35.4	57
58	26 21.1	-15.1	32.1	27 11.8	-14.5	32.4	28 02.4	-13.9	32.7	28 52.9	-13.3	33.0	29 43.1	-12.6	33.3	30 33.2	-12.0	33.6	31 23.1	-11.4	33.9	32 12.8	-10.7	34.3	58
59	26 06.0	-15.6	31.0	26 57.3	-15.0	31.3	27 48.5	-14.4	31.6	28 39.6	-13.8	31.8	29 30.5	-13.2	32.1	30 21.2	-12.6	32.4	31 11.7	-11.9	32.8	32 02.1	-11.3	33.1	59
60	25 50.4	-16.0	30.0	26 42.3	-15.5	30.2	27 34.1	-14.9	30.5	28 25.8	-14.4	30.7	29 17.3	-13.8	31.0	30 08.6	-13.2	31.3	30 59.8	-12.6	31.6	31 50.8	-12.0	31.9	60
61	25 34.4	-16.6	28.9	26 26.8	-16.0	29.1	27 19.2	-15.5	29.4	28 11.4	-14.9	29.6	29 03.5	-14.3	29.9	29 55.4	-13.7	30.2	30 47.2	-13.1	30.5	31 38.8	-12.5	30.8	61
62	25 17.8	-16.9	27.8	26 10.8	-16.4	28.0	27 03.7	-15.9	28.3	27 56.5	-15.4	28.5	28 49.2	-14.9	28.8	29 41.7	-14.3	29.1	30 34.1	-13.8	29.3	31 26.3	-13.2	29.6	62
63	25 00.9	-17.5	26.8	25 54.4	-16.9	27.0	26 47.8	-16.4	27.2	27 41.1	-15.9	27.4	28 34.3	-15.4	27.7	29 27.4	-14.9	27.9	30 20.3	-14.3	28.2	31 13.1	-13.8	28.5	63
64	24 43.4	-17.8	25.7	25 37.5	-17.4	25.9	26 31.4	-16.9	26.1	27 25.2	-16.4	26.4	28 18.9	-15.9	26.6	29 12.5	-15.4	26.8	30 06.0	-14.9	27.1	30 59.3	-14.3	27.4	64
65	24 25.6	-18.3	24.7	25 20.1	-17.9	24.9	26 14.5	-17.4	25.1	27 08.8	-17.0	25.3	28 03.0	-16.5	25.5	28 57.1	-16.0	25.7	29 51.1	-15.5	26.0	30 45.0	-15.0	26.2	65
66	24 07.3	-18.7	23.6	25 02.2	-18.3	23.8	25 57.1	-17.9	24.0	26 51.8	-17.4	24.2	27 46.5	-16.9	24.4	28 41.1	-16.5	24.6	29 35.6	-16.0	24.9	30 30.0	-15.5	25.1	66
67	23 48.6	-19.2	22.6	24 43.9	-18.7	22.7	25 39.2	-18.3	22.9	26 34.4	-17.8	23.1	27 29.6	-17.5	23.3	28 24.6	-17.0	23.5	29 19.6	-16.6	23.8	30 14.5	-16.1	24.0	67
68	23 29.4	-19.5	21.5	24 25.2	-19.2	21.7	25 20.9	-18.7	21.9	26 16.6	-18.4	22.1	27 12.1	-17.9	22.2	28 07.6	-17.5	22.4	29 03.0	-17.1	22.7	29 58.4	-16.7	22.9	68
69	23 09.9	-20.0	20.5	24 06.0	-19.5	20.7	25 02.2	-19.2	20.8	25 58.2	-18.8	21.0	26 54.2	-18.4	21.2	27 50.1	-18.0	21.4	28 45.9	-17.6	21.6	29 41.7	-17.2	21.8	69
70	22 49.9	-20.3	19.5	23 46.5	-20.0	19.6	24 43.0	-19.7	19.8	25 39.4	-19.3	19.9	26 35.8	-18.9	20.1	27 32.1	-18.5	20.3	28 28.3	-18.1	20.5	29 24.5	-17.8	20.7	70
71	22 29.6	-20.7	18.5	23 26.5	-20.4	18.6	24 23.3	-20.0	18.7	25 20.1	-19.7	18.9	26 16.9	-19.4	19.0	27 13.6	-19.1	19.2	28 10.2	-18.7	19.4	29 06.7	-18.2	19.6	71
72	22 08.9	-21.1	17.4	23 06.1	-20.8	17.6	24 03.3	-20.5	17.7	25 00.4	-20.1	17.8	25 57.5	-19.8	18.0	26 54.5	-19.4	18.1	27 51.5	-19.1	18.3	28 48.5	-18.8	18.5	72
73	21 47.8	-21.5	16.4	22 45.3	-21.2	16.6	23 42.8	-20.9	16.7	24 40.3	-20.6	16.8	25 37.7	-20.3	16.9	26 35.1	-20.0	17.1	27 32.4	-19.7	17.2	28 29.7	-19.3	17.4	73
74	21 26.3	-21.8	15.4	22 24.1	-21.5	15.5	23 21.9	-21.2	15.7	24 19.7	-21.0	15.8	25 17.4	-20.7	15.9	26 15.1	-20.4	16.0	27 12.7	-20.1	16.2	28 10.4	-19.9	16.3	74
75	21 04.5	-22.2	14.4	22 02.6	-21.9	14.5	23 00.7	-21.7	14.6	23 58.7	-21.4	14.7	24 56.7	-21.1	14.9	25 54.7	-20.9	15.0	26 52.6	-20.6	15.1	27 50.5	-20.3	15.3	75
76	20 42.3	-22.5	13.4	21 40.7	-22.3	13.5	22 39.0	-22.0	13.6	23 37.3	-21.8	13.7	24 35.6	-21.6	13.8	25 33.8	-21.3	13.9	26 32.0	-21.0	14.1	27 30.2	-20.8	14.2	76
77	20 19.8	-22.8	12.5	21 18.4	-22.6	12.5	22 17.0	-22.4	12.6	23 15.5	-22.2	12.7	24 14.0	-21.9	12.8	25 12.5	-21.7	12.9	26 11.0	-21.5	13.0	27 09.4	-21.2	13.1	77
78	19 57.0	-23.2	11.5	20 55.8	-23.0	11.5	21 54.6	-22.8	11.6	22 53.3	-22.5	11.7	23 52.1	-22.4	11.8	24 50.8	-22.1	11.9	25 49.5	-21.9	12.0	26 48.2	-21.7	12.1	78
79	19 33.8	-23.4	10.5	20 32.8	-23.3	10.6	21 31.8	-23.1	10.6	22 30.8	-23.0	10.7	23 29.7	-22.7	10.8	24 28.7	-22.6	10.9	25 27.6	-22.4	10.9	26 26.5	-22.2	11.0	79
80	19 10.4	-23.8	9.5	20 09.5	-23.6	9.6	21 08.7	-23.5	9.6	22 07.8	-23.3	9.7	23 07.0	-23.2	9.8	24 06.1	-23.0	9.8	25 05.2	-22.8	9.9	26 04.3	-22.6	10.0	80
81	18 46.6	-24.1	8.5	19 45.9	-23.9	8.6	20 45.2	-23.8	8.6	21 44.5	-23.6	8.7	22 43.8	-23.5	8.8	23 43.1	-23.3	8.8	24 42.4	-23.2	8.9	25 41.7	-23.1	9.0	81
82	18 22.5	-24.4	7.6	19 22.0	-24.3	7.6	20 21.4	-24.1	7.7	21 20.9	-24.0	7.7	22 20.3	-23.8	7.8	23 19.8	-23.8	7.8	24 19.2	-23.6	7.9	25 18.6	-23.4	8.0	82
83	17 58.1	-24.7	6.6	18 57.7	-24.5	6.7	19 57.3	-24.4	6.7	20 56.9	-24.3	6.7	21 56.5	-24.2	6.8	22 56.0	-24.1	6.8	23 55.6	-24.0	6.9	24 55.2	-23.9	6.9	83
84	17 33.4	-24.9	5.7	18 33.2	-24.9	5.7	19 32.9	-24.8	5.7	20 32.6	-24.7	5.8	21 32.3	-24.6	5.8	22 31.9	-24.4	5.8	23 31.6	-24.3	5.9	24 31.3	-24.3	5.9	84
85	17 08.5	-25.2	4.7	18 08.3	-25.1	4.7	19 08.1	-25.0	4.8	20 07.9	-25.0	4.8	21 07.7	-24.9	4.8	22 07.5	-24.9	4.9	23 07.3	-24.8	4.9	24 07.0	-24.6	4.9	85
86	16 43.3	-25.4	3.8	17 43.2	-25.4	3.8	18 43.1	-25.4	3.8	19 42.9	-25.3	3.8	20 42.8	-25.2	3.8	21 42.6	-25.1	3.9	22 42.5	-25.1	3.9	23 42.4	-25.1	3.9	86
87	16 17.9	-25.8	2.8	17 17.8	-25.7	2.8	18 17.7	-25.6	2.8	19 17.6	-25.6	2.9	20 17.6	-25.6	2.9	21 17.5	-25.5	2.9	22 17.4	-25.5	2.9	23 17.3	-25.4	2.9	87
88	15 52.1	-25.9	1.9	16 52.1	-25.9	1.9	17 52.1	-25.9	1.9	18 52.0	-25.8	1.9	19 52.0	-25.8	1.9	20 52.0	-25.9	1.9	21 51.9	-25.8	1.9	22 51.9	-25.8	2.0	88
89	15 26.2	-26.2	0.9	16 26.2	-26.2	0.9	17 26.2	-26.2	0.9	18 26.2	-26.2	0.9	19 26.2	-26.2	1.0	20 26.1	-26.1	1.0	21 26.1	-26.1	1.0	22 26.1	-26.1	1.0	89
90	15 00.0	-26.4	0.0	16 00.0	-26.4	0.0	17 00.0	-26.4	0.0	18 00.0	-26.4	0.0	19 00.0	-26.4	0.0	20 00.0	-26.5	0.0	21 00.0	-26.5	0.0	22 00.0	-26.5	0.0	90
	15°			16°			17°			18°			19°			20°			21°			22°			

64°, 296° L.H.A. LATITUDE SAME NAME AS DECLINATION

130

LATITUDE **CONTRARY** NAME TO DECLINATION **L.H.A. 64°, 296°**

Dec.	15° Hc	d	Z	16° Hc	d	Z	17° Hc	d	Z	18° Hc	d	Z	19° Hc	d	Z	20° Hc	d	Z	21° Hc	d	Z	22° Hc	d	Z	Dec.
°	° ′	′	°	° ′	′	°	° ′	′	°	° ′	′	°	° ′	′	°	° ′	′	°	° ′	′	°	° ′	′	°	°
0	25 03.1	−17.4	97.2	24 55.3	−18.4	97.7	24 47.1	−19.5	98.1	24 38.4	−20.6	98.6	24 29.2	−21.6	99.0	24 19.6	−22.7	99.5	24 09.5	−23.8	99.9	23 58.9	−24.8	100.4	0
1	24 45.7	−17.8	98.3	24 36.9	−18.9	98.7	24 27.6	−20.0	99.2	24 17.8	−21.0	99.6	24 07.6	−22.1	100.0	23 56.9	−23.2	100.5	23 45.7	−24.1	100.9	23 34.1	−25.1	101.3	1
2	24 27.9	−18.2	99.3	24 18.0	−19.3	99.7	24 07.6	−20.4	100.2	23 56.8	−21.5	100.6	23 45.5	−22.5	101.1	23 33.7	−23.5	101.5	23 21.6	−24.6	101.9	23 09.0	−25.6	102.3	2
3	24 09.7	−18.7	100.3	23 58.7	−19.7	100.8	23 47.2	−20.8	101.2	23 35.3	−21.8	101.6	23 23.0	−22.9	102.1	23 10.2	−23.9	102.5	22 57.0	−24.9	102.9	22 43.4	−25.9	103.3	3
4	23 51.0	−19.1	101.4	23 39.0	−20.2	101.8	23 26.4	−21.1	102.2	23 13.5	−22.2	102.7	23 00.1	−23.2	103.1	22 46.3	−24.2	103.5	22 32.1	−25.2	103.9	22 17.5	−26.2	104.3	4
5	23 31.9	−19.5	102.4	23 18.8	−20.5	102.8	23 05.3	−21.6	103.3	22 51.3	−22.6	103.7	22 36.9	−23.6	104.1	22 22.1	−24.6	104.5	22 06.9	−25.6	104.9	21 51.3	−26.6	105.3	5
6	23 12.4	−19.8	103.5	22 58.3	−21.0	103.9	22 43.7	−22.0	104.3	22 28.7	−23.0	104.7	22 13.3	−24.0	105.1	21 57.5	−25.0	105.5	21 41.3	−26.0	105.9	21 24.7	−26.9	106.2	6
7	22 52.6	−20.3	104.5	22 37.3	−21.3	104.9	22 21.7	−22.3	105.3	22 05.7	−23.3	105.7	21 49.3	−24.3	106.1	21 32.5	−25.3	106.4	21 15.3	−26.2	106.8	20 57.8	−27.2	107.2	7
8	22 32.3	−20.7	105.5	22 16.0	−21.7	105.9	21 59.4	−22.7	106.3	21 42.4	−23.7	106.7	21 25.0	−24.7	107.0	21 07.2	−25.6	107.4	20 49.1	−26.6	107.8	20 30.6	−27.6	108.1	8
9	22 11.6	−21.0	106.5	21 54.3	−22.0	106.9	21 36.7	−23.0	107.3	21 18.7	−24.0	107.7	21 00.3	−25.0	108.0	20 41.6	−26.0	108.4	20 22.5	−26.9	108.7	20 03.0	−27.8	109.1	9
10	21 50.6	−21.5	107.5	21 32.3	−22.4	107.9	21 13.7	−23.4	108.3	20 54.7	−24.4	108.6	20 35.3	−25.3	109.0	20 15.6	−26.3	109.3	19 55.6	−27.2	109.7	19 35.2	−28.2	110.0	10
11	21 29.1	−21.7	108.5	21 09.9	−22.8	108.9	20 50.3	−23.7	109.3	20 30.3	−24.7	109.6	20 10.0	−25.6	110.0	19 49.3	−26.5	110.3	19 28.4	−27.5	110.6	19 07.0	−28.4	111.0	11
12	21 07.4	−22.1	109.5	20 47.1	−23.1	109.9	20 26.6	−24.1	110.2	20 05.6	−25.0	110.6	19 44.4	−26.0	110.9	19 22.8	−26.9	111.3	19 00.9	−27.8	111.6	18 38.6	−28.7	111.9	12
13	20 45.3	−22.5	110.5	20 24.0	−23.4	110.9	20 02.5	−24.4	111.2	19 40.6	−25.3	111.6	19 18.4	−26.2	111.9	18 55.9	−27.2	112.2	18 33.1	−28.1	112.5	18 09.9	−28.9	112.8	13
14	20 22.8	−22.8	111.5	20 00.6	−23.7	111.9	19 38.1	−24.7	112.2	19 15.3	−25.6	112.5	18 52.2	−26.6	112.8	18 28.7	−27.4	113.1	18 05.0	−28.3	113.4	17 41.0	−29.2	113.7	14
15	20 00.0	−23.1	112.5	19 36.9	−24.1	112.8	19 13.4	−25.0	113.2	18 49.7	−25.9	113.5	18 25.6	−26.8	113.8	18 01.3	−27.7	114.1	17 36.7	−28.6	114.4	17 11.8	−29.5	114.7	15
16	19 36.9	−23.5	113.5	19 12.8	−24.4	113.8	18 48.4	−25.2	114.1	18 23.8	−26.2	114.4	17 58.8	−27.1	114.7	17 33.6	−28.0	115.0	17 08.1	−28.8	115.3	16 42.3	−29.7	115.6	16
17	19 13.4	−23.7	114.5	18 48.4	−24.6	114.8	18 23.2	−25.6	115.1	17 57.6	−26.5	115.4	17 31.7	−27.3	115.7	17 05.6	−28.2	115.9	16 39.3	−29.1	116.2	16 12.6	−29.9	116.5	17
18	18 49.7	−24.1	115.4	18 23.8	−25.0	115.7	17 57.6	−25.9	116.0	17 31.1	−26.7	116.3	17 04.4	−27.6	116.6	16 37.4	−28.4	116.9	16 10.2	−29.3	117.1	15 42.7	−30.1	117.4	18
19	18 25.6	−24.3	116.4	17 58.8	−25.2	116.7	17 31.7	−26.1	117.0	17 04.4	−27.0	117.3	16 36.8	−27.8	117.5	16 09.0	−28.7	117.8	15 40.9	−29.6	118.0	15 12.6	−30.4	118.3	19
20	18 01.3	−24.6	117.4	17 33.6	−25.5	117.6	17 05.6	−26.3	117.9	16 37.4	−27.2	118.2	16 09.0	−28.1	118.4	15 40.3	−29.0	118.7	15 11.3	−29.7	118.9	14 42.2	−30.6	119.2	20
21	17 36.7	−24.9	118.3	17 08.1	−25.8	118.6	16 39.3	−26.7	118.9	16 10.2	−27.5	119.1	15 40.9	−28.3	119.4	15 11.3	−29.1	119.6	14 41.6	−30.0	119.8	14 11.6	−30.7	120.1	21
22	17 11.8	−25.2	119.3	16 42.3	−26.0	119.5	16 12.6	−26.8	119.8	15 42.7	−27.7	120.0	15 12.6	−28.6	120.3	14 42.2	−29.3	120.5	14 11.6	−30.1	120.7	13 40.9	−31.0	120.9	22
23	16 46.6	−25.4	120.2	16 16.3	−26.3	120.5	15 45.8	−27.2	120.7	15 15.0	−27.9	121.0	14 44.0	−28.7	121.2	14 12.9	−29.6	121.4	13 41.5	−30.3	121.6	13 09.9	−31.1	121.8	23
24	16 21.2	−25.7	121.2	15 50.0	−26.5	121.4	15 18.6	−27.3	121.6	14 47.1	−28.2	121.9	14 15.3	−29.0	122.1	13 43.3	−29.7	122.3	13 11.2	−30.6	122.5	12 38.8	−31.3	122.7	24
25	15 55.5	−25.9	122.1	15 23.5	−26.7	122.3	14 51.3	−27.5	122.6	14 18.9	−28.3	122.8	13 46.3	−29.1	123.0	13 13.6	−30.0	123.2	12 40.6	−30.7	123.4	12 07.5	−31.4	123.6	25
26	15 29.6	−26.2	123.0	14 56.8	−27.0	123.3	14 23.8	−27.8	123.5	13 50.6	−28.6	123.7	13 17.2	−29.3	123.9	12 43.6	−30.1	124.1	12 09.9	−30.8	124.3	11 36.1	−31.6	124.4	26
27	15 03.4	−26.4	124.0	14 29.8	−27.2	124.2	13 56.0	−28.0	124.4	13 22.0	−28.7	124.6	12 47.9	−29.6	124.8	12 13.5	−30.2	125.0	11 39.1	−31.1	125.1	11 04.5	−31.8	125.3	27
28	14 37.0	−26.6	124.9	14 02.6	−27.4	125.1	13 28.0	−28.1	125.3	12 53.3	−29.0	125.5	12 18.3	−29.7	125.7	11 43.3	−30.5	125.9	11 08.0	−31.1	126.0	10 32.7	−31.9	126.2	28
29	14 10.4	−26.8	125.8	13 35.2	−27.6	126.0	12 59.9	−28.4	126.2	12 24.3	−29.1	126.4	11 48.6	−29.8	126.6	11 12.8	−30.6	126.7	10 36.9	−31.3	126.9	10 00.8	−32.0	127.0	29
30	13 43.6	−27.0	126.7	13 07.6	−27.7	126.9	12 31.5	−28.5	127.1	11 55.2	−29.3	127.3	11 18.8	−30.0	127.5	10 42.2	−30.7	127.6	10 05.6	−31.5	127.8	9 28.8	−32.2	127.9	30
31	13 16.6	−27.2	127.7	12 39.9	−28.0	127.8	12 03.0	−28.7	128.0	11 25.9	−29.4	128.2	10 48.8	−30.2	128.3	10 11.5	−30.9	128.5	9 34.1	−31.6	128.6	8 56.6	−32.3	128.7	31
32	12 49.4	−27.4	128.6	12 11.9	−28.2	128.8	11 34.3	−28.9	128.9	10 56.5	−29.6	129.1	10 18.6	−30.3	129.2	9 40.6	−31.0	129.4	9 02.5	−31.7	129.5	8 24.3	−32.4	129.6	32
33	12 22.0	−27.6	129.5	11 43.7	−28.3	129.7	11 05.4	−29.0	129.8	10 26.9	−29.7	130.0	9 48.3	−30.4	130.1	9 09.6	−31.1	130.2	8 30.8	−31.8	130.3	7 51.9	−32.4	130.5	33
34	11 54.4	−27.8	130.4	11 15.4	−28.4	130.6	10 36.4	−29.2	130.7	9 57.2	−29.9	130.8	9 17.9	−30.6	131.0	8 38.5	−31.2	131.1	7 59.0	−31.9	131.2	7 19.5	−32.6	131.3	34
35	11 26.6	−27.9	131.3	10 47.0	−28.7	131.5	10 07.2	−29.3	131.6	9 27.3	−30.0	131.7	8 47.3	−30.7	131.8	8 07.3	−31.4	132.0	7 27.1	−32.0	132.1	6 46.9	−32.7	132.1	35
36	10 58.7	−28.1	132.2	10 18.3	−28.7	132.3	9 37.9	−29.5	132.5	8 57.3	−30.1	132.6	8 16.6	−30.8	132.7	7 35.9	−31.5	132.8	6 55.1	−32.1	132.9	6 14.2	−32.7	133.0	36
37	10 30.6	−28.2	133.1	9 49.6	−29.0	133.2	9 08.4	−29.6	133.4	8 27.2	−30.3	133.5	7 45.8	−30.9	133.6	7 04.4	−31.5	133.7	6 23.0	−32.2	133.8	5 41.5	−32.9	133.8	37
38	10 02.4	−28.4	134.0	9 20.6	−29.0	134.1	8 38.8	−29.7	134.2	7 56.9	−30.3	134.3	7 14.9	−31.0	134.4	6 32.9	−31.6	134.6	5 50.8	−32.3	134.6	5 08.6	−32.9	134.7	38
39	9 34.0	−28.5	134.9	8 51.6	−29.2	135.0	8 09.1	−29.8	135.1	7 26.6	−30.5	135.2	6 43.9	−31.1	135.3	6 01.3	−31.8	135.4	5 18.5	−32.3	135.5	4 35.7	−32.9	135.5	39
40	9 05.5	−28.7	135.8	8 22.4	−29.3	135.9	7 39.3	−29.9	136.0	6 56.1	−30.6	136.1	6 12.8	−31.1	136.2	5 29.5	−31.7	136.2	4 46.2	−32.4	136.3	4 02.8	−33.0	136.4	40
41	8 36.8	−28.8	136.7	7 53.1	−29.4	136.8	7 09.4	−30.1	136.9	6 25.5	−30.6	137.0	5 41.7	−31.3	137.0	4 57.8	−31.9	137.1	4 13.8	−32.5	137.1	3 29.8	−33.1	137.2	41
42	8 08.0	−28.8	137.6	7 23.7	−29.5	137.7	6 39.3	−30.1	137.7	5 54.9	−30.7	137.8	5 10.4	−31.3	137.9	4 25.9	−31.9	137.9	3 41.3	−32.5	138.0	2 56.7	−33.0	138.0	42
43	7 39.2	−29.0	138.5	6 54.2	−29.6	138.5	6 09.2	−30.2	138.6	5 24.2	−30.8	138.7	4 39.1	−31.4	138.7	3 54.0	−32.0	138.8	3 08.8	−32.5	138.8	2 23.7	−33.1	138.9	43
44	7 10.2	−29.1	139.3	6 24.6	−29.7	139.4	5 39.0	−30.2	139.5	4 53.4	−30.9	139.5	4 07.7	−31.4	139.6	3 22.0	−32.0	139.6	2 36.3	−32.6	139.7	1 50.6	−33.2	139.7	44
45	6 41.1	−29.2	140.2	5 54.9	−29.7	140.3	5 08.8	−30.4	140.3	4 22.5	−30.9	140.4	3 36.3	−31.5	140.4	2 50.0	−32.0	140.5	2 03.7	−32.6	140.5	1 17.4	−33.1	140.5	45
46	6 11.9	−29.3	141.1	5 25.2	−29.9	141.2	4 38.4	−30.4	141.2	3 51.6	−30.9	141.3	3 04.8	−31.5	141.3	2 18.0	−32.1	141.3	1 31.1	−32.6	141.3	0 44.3	−33.2	141.4	46
47	5 42.6	−29.4	142.0	4 55.3	−29.9	142.0	4 08.0	−30.5	142.1	3 20.7	−31.1	142.1	2 33.3	−31.6	142.2	1 45.9	−32.1	142.2	0 58.5	−32.6	142.2	0 11.1	−33.2	142.2	47
48	5 13.2	−29.4	142.8	4 25.4	−30.0	142.9	3 37.5	−30.5	142.9	2 49.6	−31.0	143.0	2 01.7	−31.6	143.0	1 13.8	−32.1	143.0	0 25.9	−32.7	143.0	0 22.1	+33.1	37.0	48
49	4 43.8	−29.5	143.7	3 55.4	−30.0	143.8	3 07.0	−30.5	143.8	2 18.6	−31.1	143.8	1 30.1	−31.6	143.9	0 41.7	−32.1	143.9	0 06.8	+32.6	36.1	0 55.2	+33.2	36.1	49
50	4 14.3	−29.5	144.6	3 25.4	−30.1	144.6	2 36.5	−30.6	144.7	1 47.5	−31.1	144.7	0 58.5	−31.6	144.7	0 09.6	−32.2	144.7	0 39.4	+32.6	35.3	1 28.4	+33.1	35.3	50
51	3 44.8	−29.6	145.5	2 55.3	−30.1	145.5	2 05.9	−30.7	145.5	1 16.4	−31.1	145.5	0 26.9	−31.6	145.6	0 22.6	+32.1	34.4	1 12.0	+32.6	34.5	2 01.5	+33.1	34.5	51
52	3 15.2	−29.7	146.3	2 25.2	−30.1	146.4	1 35.2	−30.6	146.4	0 45.3	−31.2	146.4	0 04.7	+31.6	33.6	0 54.7	+32.1	33.6	1 44.6	+32.6	33.6	2 34.6	+33.1	33.6	52
53	2 45.5	−29.7	147.2	1 55.1	−30.2	147.2	1 04.6	−30.6	147.2	0 14.1	−31.1	147.3	0 36.3	+31.6	32.7	1 26.8	+32.1	32.8	2 17.2	+32.6	32.8	3 07.7	+33.0	32.8	53
54	2 15.8	−29.7	148.1	1 24.9	−30.2	148.1	0 34.0	−30.7	148.1	0 17.0	+31.1	31.9	1 07.9	+31.6	31.9	1 58.9	+32.0	31.9	2 49.8	+32.5	31.9	3 40.7	+33.0	32.0	54
55	1 46.1	−29.7	149.0	0 54.7	−30.2	149.0	0 03.3	−30.7	149.0	0 48.1	+31.1	31.0	1 39.5	+31.6	31.0	2 30.9	+32.1	31.1	3 22.3	+32.5	31.1	4 13.7	+32.9	31.1	55
56	1 16.4	−29.8	149.8	0 24.5	−30.2	149.8	0 27.4	+30.6	30.2	1 19.2	+31.2	30.2	2 11.1	+31.6	30.2	3 03.0	+32.0	30.2	3 54.8	+32.4	30.2	4 46.6	+32.9	30.3	56
57	0 46.6	−29.8	150.7	0 05.7	+30.2	29.3	0 58.0	+30.7	29.3	1 50.4	+31.0	29.3	2 42.7	+31.5	29.3	3 35.0	+31.9	29.4	4 27.2	+32.4	29.4	5 19.5	+32.8	29.4	57
58	0 16.8	−29.7	151.6	0 35.9	+30.2	28.4	1 28.7	+30.6	28.5	2 21.4	+31.1	28.5	3 14.2	+31.4	28.5	4 06.9	+31.9	28.5	4 59.6	+32.3	28.6	5 52.3	+32.7	28.6	58
59	0 12.9	+29.8	27.6	1 06.1	+30.2	27.6	1 59.3	+30.6	27.6	2 52.5	+31.0	27.6	3 45.6	+31.5	27.6	4 38.8	+31.8	27.7	5 31.9	+32.2	27.7	6 25.0	+32.7	27.8	59
60	0 42.7	+29.8	26.7	1 36.3	+30.2	26.7	2 29.9	+30.6	26.7	3 23.5	+31.0	26.8	4 17.1	+31.3	26.8	5 10.6	+31.8	26.8	6 04.1	+32.2	26.9	6 57.7	+32.5	26.9	60
61	1 12.5	+29.7	25.8	2 06.5	+30.1	25.9	3 00.5	+30.5	25.9	3 54.5	+30.9	25.9	4 48.4	+31.3	25.9	5 42.4	+31.7	26.0	6 36.3	+32.1	26.0	7 30.2	+32.5	26.1	61
62	1 42.2	+29.8	25.0	2 36.6	+30.1	25.0	3 31.0	+30.5	25.0	4 25.4	+30.8	25.0	5 19.7	+31.2	25.1	6 14.1	+31.6	25.1	7 08.4	+31.9	25.2	8 02.7	+32.3	25.2	62
63	2 12.0	+29.6	24.1	3 06.7	+30.1	24.1	4 01.5	+30.4	24.1	4 56.2	+30.8	24.2	5 50.9	+31.2	24.2	6 45.7	+31.5	24.3	7 40.3	+31.9	24.3	8 35.0	+32.3	24.4	63
64	2 41.6	+29.7	23.2	3 36.8	+30.0	23.3	4 31.9	+30.4	23.3	5 27.0	+30.7	23.3	6 22.1	+31.1	23.4	7 17.2	+31.4	23.4	8 12.2	+31.8	23.5	9 07.3	+32.1	23.5	64
65	3 11.3	+29.6	22.4	4 06.8	+29.9	22.4	5 02.3	+30.3	22.4	5 57.7	+30.6	22.5	6 53.2	+30.9	22.5	7 48.6	+31.3	22.5	8 44.0	+31.6	22.6	9 39.4	+32.0	22.7	65
66	3 40.9	+29.6	21.5	4 36.7	+29.9	21.5	5 32.6	+30.2	21.5	6 28.3	+30.6	21.6	7 24.1	+30.9	21.6	8 19.9	+31.2	21.7	9 15.6	+31.6	21.7	10 11.4	+31.8	21.8	66
67	4 10.5	+29.5	20.6	5 06.6	+29.8	20.6	6 02.8	+30.1	20.7	6 58.9	+30.4	20.7	7 55.0	+30.8	20.8	8 51.1	+31.1	20.8	9 47.2	+31.4	20.9	10 43.2	+31.7	20.9	67
68	4 40.0	+29.4	19.7	5 36.4	+29.8	19.8	6 32.9	+30.0	19.8	7 29.3	+30.4	19.9	8 25.8	+30.6	19.9	9 22.2	+30.9	20.0	10 18.6	+31.2	20.0	11 14.9	+31.6	20.1	68
69	5 09.4	+29.4	18.9	6 06.2	+29.6	18.9	7 02.9	+30.0	18.9	7 59.7	+30.2	19.0	8 56.4	+30.5	19.0	9 53.1	+30.8	19.1	10 49.8	+31.1	19.1	11 46.5	+31.4	19.2	69
70	5 38.8	+29.3	18.0	6 35.8	+29.6	18.0	7 32.9	+29.8	18.1	8 29.9	+30.1	18.1	9 26.9	+30.4	18.2	10 23.9	+30.7	18.2	11 20.9	+31.0	18.3	12 17.9	+31.2	18.3	70
71	6 08.1	+29.2	17.1	7 05.4	+29.5	17.1	8 02.7	+29.8	17.2	9 00.0	+30.0	17.2	9 57.3	+30.3	17.3	10 54.6	+30.6	17.3	11 51.9	+30.8	17.4	12 49.1	+31.1	17.5	71
72	6 37.3	+29.1	16.2	7 34.9	+29.3	16.3	8 32.5	+29.6	16.3	9 30.0	+29.9	16.4	10 27.6	+30.1	16.4	11 25.2	+30.3	16.5	12 22.7	+30.6	16.5	13 20.2	+30.9	16.6	72
73	7 06.4	+29.0	15.4	8 04.2	+29.3	15.4	9 02.1	+29.5	15.4	9 59.9	+29.7	15.5	10 57.7	+30.0	15.5	11 55.5	+30.2	15.6	12 53.3	+30.5	15.6	13 51.1	+30.7	15.7	73
74	7 35.4	+28.9	14.5	8 33.5	+29.1	14.5	9 31.6	+29.3	14.5	10 29.6	+29.6	14.6	11 27.7	+29.8	14.6	12 25.7	+30.1	14.7	13 23.8	+30.2	14.8	14 21.8	+30.5	14.8	74
75	8 04.3	+28.8	13.6	9 02.6	+29.0	13.6	10 00.9	+29.2	13.7	10 59.2	+29.4	13.7	11 57.5	+29.6	13.8	12 55.8	+29.8	13.8	13 54.0	+30.1	13.9	14 52.3	+30.3	13.9	75
76	8 33.1	+28.6	12.7	9 31.6	+28.9	12.7	10 30.1	+29.1	12.8	11 28.6	+29.3	12.8	12 27.1	+29.5	12.9	13 25.6	+29.7	12.9	14 24.1	+29.9	13.0	15 22.6	+30.0	13.0	76
77	9 01.7	+28.6	11.8	10 00.5	+28.7	11.8	10 59.2	+28.9	11.9	11 57.9	+29.1	11.9	12 56.6	+29.3	12.0	13 55.3	+29.4	12.0	14 54.0	+29.6	12.1	15 52.6	+29.9	12.1	77
78	9 30.3	+28.4	10.9	10 29.2	+28.6	11.0	11 28.1	+28.7	11.0	12 27.0	+28.9	11.0	13 25.9	+29.1	11.1	14 24.7	+29.3	11.1	15 23.6	+29.5	11.2	16 22.5	+29.6	11.2	78
79	9 58.7	+28.2	10.0	10 57.8	+28.4	10.1	11 56.8	+28.6	10.1	12 55.9	+28.7	10.1	13 55.0	+28.8	10.2	14 54.0	+29.1	10.2	15 53.1	+29.2	10.3	16 52.1	+29.4	10.3	79
80	10 26.9	+28.1	9.1	11 26.2	+28.2	9.2	12 25.4	+28.4	9.2	13 24.6	+28.6	9.2	14 23.8	+28.7	9.3	15 23.1	+28.8	9.3	16 22.3	+28.9	9.4	17 21.5	+29.1	9.4	80
81	10 55.0	+28.0	8.2	11 54.4	+28.1	8.3	12 53.8	+28.2	8.3	13 53.2	+28.3	8.3	14 52.5	+28.5	8.4	15 51.9	+28.6	8.4	16 51.2	+28.8	8.4	17 50.6	+28.9	8.5	81
82	11 23.0	+27.8	7.3	12 22.5	+27.9	7.4	13 22.0	+28.0	7.4	14 21.5	+28.1	7.4	15 21.0	+28.2	7.5	16 20.5	+28.4	7.5	17 20.0	+28.5	7.5	18 19.5	+28.6	7.6	82
83	11 50.8	+27.6	6.4	12 50.4	+27.7	6.5	13 50.0	+27.8	6.5	14 49.6	+27.9	6.5	15 49.2	+28.1	6.5	16 48.9	+28.1	6.6	17 48.5	+28.2	6.6	18 48.1	+28.3	6.6	83
84	12 18.4	+27.4	5.5	13 18.1	+27.5	5.5	14 17.8	+27.6	5.6	15 17.5	+27.7	5.6	16 17.3	+27.7	5.6	17 17.0	+27.8	5.6	18 16.7	+27.9	5.7	19 16.4	+28.0	5.7	84
85	12 45.8	+27.3	4.6	13 45.6	+27.3	4.6	14 45.4	+27.4	4.6	15 45.2	+27.5	4.7	16 45.0	+27.6	4.7	17 44.8	+27.6	4.7	18 44.6	+27.7	4.7	19 44.4	+27.8	4.8	85
86	13 13.1	+27.0	3.7	14 12.9	+27.1	3.7	15 12.8	+27.2	3.7	16 12.7	+27.2	3.7	17 12.6	+27.2	3.8	18 12.4	+27.3	3.8	19 12.3	+27.4	3.8	20 12.2	+27.4	3.8	86
87	13 40.1	+26.9	2.8	14 40.0	+26.9	2.8	15 40.0	+26.9	2.8	16 39.9	+27.0	2.8	17 39.8	+27.0	2.8	18 39.7	+27.1	2.8	19 39.7	+27.1	2.9	20 39.6	+27.1	2.9	87
88	14 07.0	+26.6	1.9	15 06.9	+26.7	1.9	16 06.9	+26.7	1.9	17 06.9	+26.7	1.9	18 06.8	+26.8	1.9	19 06.8	+26.7	1.9	20 06.8	+26.7	1.9	21 06.7	+26.8	1.9	88
89	14 33.6	+26.4	0.9	15 33.6	+26.4	0.9	16 33.6	+26.4	0.9	17 33.6	+26.4	0.9	18 33.6	+26.4	0.9	19 33.5	+26.5	1.0	20 33.5	+26.5	1.0	21 33.5	+26.5	1.0	89
90	15 00.0	+26.2	0.0	16 00.0	+26.2	0.0	17 00.0	+26.2	0.0	18 00.0	+26.2	0.0	19 00.0	+26.2	0.0	20 00.0	+26.1	0.0	21 00.0	+26.1	0.0	22 00.0	+26.1	0.0	90
	15°			16°			17°			18°			19°			20°			21°			22°			

S. Lat. {L.H.A. greater than 180° ....Zn=180°−Z; L.H.A. less than 180°...........Zn=180°+Z}

LATITUDE **SAME** NAME AS DECLINATION **L.H.A. 116°, 244°**

131

65°, 295° L.H.A. LATITUDE SAME NAME AS DECLINATION

N. Lat. {L.H.A. greater than 180° .....Zn=Z ; L.H.A. less than 180°............Zn=360°−Z}

Dec.	15° Hc	d	Z	16° Hc	d	Z	17° Hc	d	Z	18° Hc	d	Z	19° Hc	d	Z	20° Hc	d	Z	21° Hc	d	Z	22° Hc	d	Z	Dec.
°	° ′	′	°	° ′	′	°	° ′	′	°	° ′	′	°	° ′	′	°	° ′	′	°	° ′	′	°	° ′	′	°	°
0	24 05.6	+16.8	96.9	23 58.2	+17.8	97.3	23 50.3	+18.9	97.8	23 41.9	+20.1	98.2	23 33.2	+21.1	98.6	23 23.9	+22.2	99.1	23 14.3	+23.2	99.5	23 04.2	+24.2	99.9	0
1	24 22.4	+16.3	95.8	24 16.0	+17.5	96.3	24 09.2	+18.6	96.7	24 02.0	+19.6	97.2	23 54.3	+20.7	97.6	23 46.1	+21.8	98.0	23 37.5	+22.8	98.5	23 28.4	+23.9	98.9	1
2	24 38.7	+15.9	94.8	24 33.5	+17.0	95.2	24 27.8	+18.1	95.7	24 21.6	+19.2	96.1	24 15.0	+20.3	96.6	24 07.9	+21.3	97.0	24 00.3	+22.4	97.5	23 52.3	+23.4	97.9	2
3	24 54.6	+15.5	93.7	24 50.5	+16.6	94.2	24 45.9	+17.7	94.6	24 40.8	+18.8	95.1	24 35.3	+19.8	95.5	24 29.2	+21.0	96.0	24 22.7	+22.0	96.5	24 15.7	+23.1	96.9	3
4	25 10.1	+15.0	92.6	25 07.1	+16.1	93.1	25 03.6	+17.2	93.6	24 59.6	+18.3	94.0	24 55.1	+19.4	94.5	24 50.2	+20.5	95.0	24 44.7	+21.6	95.4	24 38.8	+22.7	95.9	4
5	25 25.1	+14.5	91.6	25 23.2	+15.6	92.0	25 20.8	+16.8	92.5	25 17.9	+17.9	93.0	25 14.5	+19.0	93.5	25 10.7	+20.0	93.9	25 06.3	+21.2	94.4	25 01.5	+22.2	94.9	5
6	25 39.6	+14.1	90.5	25 38.8	+15.2	91.0	25 37.6	+16.3	91.5	25 35.8	+17.4	91.9	25 33.5	+18.6	92.4	25 30.7	+19.7	92.9	25 27.5	+20.7	93.4	25 23.7	+21.8	93.8	6
7	25 53.7	+13.6	89.4	25 54.0	+14.7	89.9	25 53.9	+15.8	90.4	25 53.2	+17.0	90.9	25 52.1	+18.0	91.4	25 50.4	+19.2	91.8	25 48.2	+20.3	92.3	25 45.5	+21.4	92.8	7
8	26 07.3	+13.0	88.3	26 08.7	+14.3	88.8	26 09.7	+15.4	89.3	26 10.2	+16.5	89.8	26 10.1	+17.6	90.3	26 09.6	+18.7	90.8	26 08.5	+19.8	91.3	26 06.9	+20.9	91.8	8
9	26 20.3	+12.6	87.2	26 23.0	+13.7	87.7	26 25.1	+14.8	88.2	26 26.7	+15.9	88.7	26 27.7	+17.1	89.2	26 28.3	+18.2	89.7	26 28.3	+19.3	90.2	26 27.8	+20.4	90.7	9
10	26 32.9	+12.1	86.2	26 36.7	+13.2	86.7	26 39.9	+14.4	87.2	26 42.6	+15.6	87.7	26 44.8	+16.7	88.2	26 46.5	+17.8	88.7	26 47.6	+18.9	89.2	26 48.2	+20.0	89.7	10
11	26 45.0	+11.6	85.1	26 49.9	+12.8	85.6	26 54.3	+13.9	86.1	26 58.2	+15.0	86.6	27 01.5	+16.1	87.1	27 04.3	+17.2	87.6	27 06.5	+18.4	88.1	27 08.2	+19.5	88.6	11
12	26 56.6	+11.1	84.0	27 02.7	+12.2	84.5	27 08.2	+13.3	85.0	27 13.2	+14.5	85.5	27 17.6	+15.7	86.0	27 21.5	+16.8	86.5	27 24.9	+17.9	87.0	27 27.7	+19.1	87.6	12
13	27 07.7	+10.5	82.9	27 14.9	+11.7	83.4	27 21.5	+12.9	83.9	27 27.7	+14.0	84.4	27 33.3	+15.1	84.9	27 38.3	+16.3	85.4	27 42.8	+17.4	86.0	27 46.8	+18.5	86.5	13
14	27 18.2	+10.0	81.7	27 26.6	+11.1	82.3	27 34.4	+12.3	82.8	27 41.7	+13.4	83.3	27 48.4	+14.6	83.8	27 54.6	+15.7	84.3	28 00.2	+16.9	84.9	28 05.3	+18.0	85.4	14
15	27 28.2	+9.5	80.6	27 37.7	+10.7	81.2	27 46.7	+11.8	81.7	27 55.1	+13.0	82.2	28 03.0	+14.1	82.7	28 10.3	+15.2	83.3	28 17.1	+16.4	83.8	28 23.3	+17.5	84.3	15
16	27 37.7	+9.0	79.5	27 48.4	+10.1	80.0	27 58.5	+11.2	80.6	28 08.1	+12.4	81.1	28 17.1	+13.5	81.6	28 25.5	+14.7	82.2	28 33.5	+15.8	82.7	28 40.8	+17.0	83.2	16
17	27 46.7	+8.4	78.4	27 58.5	+9.6	78.9	28 09.7	+10.8	79.4	28 20.5	+11.8	80.0	28 30.6	+13.0	80.5	28 40.2	+14.2	81.0	28 49.3	+15.3	81.6	28 57.8	+16.4	82.1	17
18	27 55.1	+7.9	77.3	28 08.1	+9.0	77.8	28 20.5	+10.1	78.3	28 32.3	+11.3	78.9	28 43.6	+12.5	79.4	28 54.4	+13.6	79.9	29 04.6	+14.8	80.5	29 14.2	+15.9	81.0	18
19	28 03.0	+7.3	76.2	28 17.1	+8.4	76.7	28 30.6	+9.6	77.2	28 43.6	+10.8	77.7	28 56.1	+11.9	78.3	29 08.0	+13.1	78.8	29 19.4	+14.2	79.4	29 30.1	+15.4	79.9	19
20	28 10.3	+6.8	75.0	28 25.5	+8.0	75.6	28 40.2	+9.1	76.1	28 54.4	+10.2	76.6	29 08.0	+11.4	77.2	29 21.1	+12.5	77.7	29 33.6	+13.6	78.3	29 45.5	+14.8	78.8	20
21	28 17.1	+6.2	73.9	28 33.5	+7.3	74.4	28 49.3	+8.5	75.0	29 04.6	+9.6	75.5	29 19.4	+10.7	76.0	29 33.6	+11.9	76.6	29 47.2	+13.1	77.1	30 00.3	+14.2	77.7	21
22	28 23.3	+5.7	72.8	28 40.8	+6.8	73.3	28 57.8	+7.9	73.8	29 14.2	+9.1	74.4	29 30.1	+10.2	74.9	29 45.5	+11.3	75.5	30 00.3	+12.5	76.0	30 14.5	+13.6	76.6	22
23	28 29.0	+5.1	71.6	28 47.6	+6.2	72.2	29 05.7	+7.4	72.7	29 23.3	+8.5	73.2	29 40.3	+9.7	73.8	29 56.8	+10.8	74.3	30 12.8	+11.9	74.9	30 28.1	+13.1	75.4	23
24	28 34.1	+4.5	70.5	28 53.8	+5.7	71.0	29 13.1	+6.7	71.6	29 31.8	+7.9	72.1	29 50.0	+9.0	72.6	30 07.6	+10.2	73.2	30 24.7	+11.3	73.7	30 41.2	+12.4	74.3	24
25	28 38.6	+3.9	69.4	28 59.5	+5.0	69.9	29 19.8	+6.2	70.4	29 39.7	+7.3	71.0	29 59.0	+8.4	71.5	30 17.8	+9.5	72.0	30 36.0	+10.7	72.6	30 53.6	+11.9	73.2	25
26	28 42.5	+3.4	68.2	29 04.5	+4.5	68.8	29 26.0	+5.6	69.3	29 47.0	+6.7	69.8	30 07.4	+7.9	70.4	30 27.3	+9.0	70.9	30 46.7	+10.1	71.5	31 05.5	+11.2	72.0	26
27	28 45.9	+2.8	67.1	29 09.0	+3.9	67.6	29 31.6	+5.0	68.1	29 53.7	+6.1	68.7	30 15.3	+7.2	69.2	30 36.3	+8.4	69.8	30 56.8	+9.5	70.3	31 16.7	+10.7	70.9	27
28	28 48.7	+2.3	66.0	29 12.9	+3.4	66.5	29 36.6	+4.5	67.0	29 59.8	+5.6	67.5	30 22.5	+6.7	68.1	30 44.7	+7.7	68.6	31 06.3	+8.9	69.2	31 27.4	+10.0	69.7	28
29	28 51.0	+1.6	64.8	29 16.3	+2.7	65.3	29 41.1	+3.8	65.8	30 05.4	+4.9	66.4	30 29.2	+6.0	66.9	30 52.4	+7.2	67.4	31 15.2	+8.2	68.0	31 37.4	+9.4	68.6	29
30	28 52.6	+1.1	63.7	29 19.0	+2.2	64.2	29 44.9	+3.2	64.7	30 10.3	+4.3	65.2	30 35.2	+5.4	65.7	30 59.6	+6.5	66.3	31 23.4	+7.7	66.8	31 46.8	+8.7	67.4	30
31	28 53.7	+0.5	62.5	29 21.2	+1.5	63.0	29 48.1	+2.7	63.5	30 14.6	+3.7	64.1	30 40.6	+4.8	64.6	31 06.1	+5.9	65.1	31 31.1	+7.0	65.7	31 55.5	+8.1	66.2	31
32	28 54.2	0.0	61.4	29 22.7	+1.0	61.9	29 50.8	+2.0	62.4	30 18.3	+3.1	62.9	30 45.4	+4.2	63.4	31 12.0	+5.3	64.0	31 38.1	+6.3	64.5	32 03.6	+7.5	65.1	32
33	28 54.2	-0.7	60.3	29 23.7	+0.4	60.7	29 52.8	+1.4	61.2	30 21.4	+2.5	61.7	30 49.6	+3.6	62.3	31 17.3	+4.6	62.8	31 44.4	+5.8	63.4	32 11.1	+6.8	63.9	33
34	28 53.5	-1.2	59.1	29 24.1	-0.2	59.6	29 54.2	+0.9	60.1	30 23.9	+1.9	60.6	30 53.2	+2.9	61.1	31 21.9	+4.0	61.6	31 50.2	+5.0	62.2	32 17.9	+6.2	62.7	34
35	28 52.3	-1.8	58.0	29 23.9	-0.8	58.4	29 55.1	+0.2	58.9	30 25.8	+1.3	59.4	30 56.1	+2.3	59.9	31 25.9	+3.4	60.5	31 55.2	+4.5	61.0	32 24.1	+5.5	61.6	35
36	28 50.5	-2.4	56.8	29 23.1	-1.4	57.3	29 55.3	-0.4	57.8	30 27.1	+0.6	58.3	30 58.4	+1.7	58.8	31 29.3	+2.7	59.3	31 59.7	+3.8	59.8	32 29.6	+4.8	60.4	36
37	28 48.1	-3.0	55.7	29 21.7	-2.0	56.1	29 54.9	-0.9	56.6	30 27.7	+0.1	57.1	31 00.1	+1.0	57.6	31 32.0	+2.1	58.1	32 03.5	+3.1	58.7	32 34.4	+4.2	59.2	37
38	28 45.1	-3.5	54.5	29 19.7	-2.5	55.0	29 54.0	-1.6	55.5	30 27.8	-0.6	56.0	31 01.1	+0.5	56.4	31 34.1	+1.4	57.0	32 06.6	+2.4	57.5	32 38.6	+3.5	58.0	38
39	28 41.6	-4.1	53.4	29 17.2	-3.2	53.9	29 52.4	-2.2	54.3	30 27.2	-1.2	54.8	31 01.6	-0.2	55.3	31 35.5	+0.8	55.8	32 09.0	+1.9	56.3	32 42.1	+2.9	56.8	39
40	28 37.5	-4.7	52.3	29 14.0	-3.7	52.7	29 50.2	-2.8	53.2	30 26.0	-1.8	53.6	31 01.4	-0.9	54.1	31 36.3	+0.2	54.6	32 10.9	+1.1	55.1	32 45.0	+2.1	55.6	40
41	28 32.8	-5.2	51.1	29 10.3	-4.3	51.6	29 47.4	-3.3	52.0	30 24.2	-2.5	52.5	31 00.5	-1.4	52.9	31 36.5	-0.5	53.4	32 12.0	+0.5	53.9	32 47.1	+1.5	54.4	41
42	28 27.6	-5.8	50.0	29 06.0	-4.9	50.4	29 44.1	-4.0	50.9	30 21.7	-3.0	51.3	30 59.1	-2.1	51.8	31 36.0	-1.2	52.3	32 12.5	-0.2	52.8	32 48.6	+0.8	53.3	42
43	28 21.8	-6.3	48.9	29 01.1	-5.4	49.3	29 40.1	-4.6	49.7	30 18.7	-3.6	50.2	30 57.0	-2.8	50.6	31 34.8	-1.7	51.1	32 12.3	-0.8	51.6	32 49.4	+0.2	52.1	43
44	28 15.5	-6.9	47.7	28 55.7	-6.1	48.1	29 35.5	-5.1	48.6	30 15.1	-4.3	49.0	30 54.2	-3.3	49.4	31 33.1	-2.5	49.9	32 11.5	-1.5	50.4	32 49.6	-0.6	50.9	44
45	28 08.6	-7.5	46.6	28 49.6	-6.6	47.0	29 30.4	-5.8	47.4	30 10.8	-4.9	47.8	30 50.9	-4.0	48.3	31 30.6	-3.0	48.7	32 10.0	-2.1	49.2	32 49.0	-1.2	49.7	45
46	28 01.1	-8.0	45.5	28 43.0	-7.2	45.9	29 24.6	-6.3	46.3	30 05.9	-5.4	46.7	30 46.9	-4.6	47.1	31 27.6	-3.7	47.6	32 07.9	-2.8	48.0	32 47.8	-1.8	48.5	46
47	27 53.1	-8.6	44.4	28 35.8	-7.7	44.7	29 18.3	-6.9	45.1	30 00.5	-6.1	45.5	30 42.3	-5.2	46.0	31 23.9	-4.4	46.4	32 05.1	-3.5	46.8	32 46.0	-2.6	47.3	47
48	27 44.5	-9.1	43.3	28 28.1	-8.3	43.6	29 11.4	-7.5	44.0	29 54.4	-6.7	44.4	30 37.1	-5.8	44.8	31 19.5	-4.9	45.2	32 01.6	-4.1	45.7	32 43.4	-3.2	46.1	48
49	27 35.4	-9.6	42.1	28 19.8	-8.9	42.5	29 03.9	-8.0	42.9	29 47.7	-7.2	43.2	30 31.3	-6.4	43.6	31 14.6	-5.6	44.1	31 57.5	-4.7	44.5	32 40.2	-3.9	44.9	49
50	27 25.8	-10.2	41.0	28 10.9	-9.3	41.4	28 55.9	-8.7	41.7	29 40.5	-7.8	42.1	30 24.9	-7.1	42.5	31 09.0	-6.3	42.9	31 52.8	-5.4	43.3	32 36.3	-4.6	43.8	50
51	27 15.6	-10.6	39.9	28 01.6	-10.0	40.3	28 47.2	-9.2	40.6	29 32.7	-8.5	41.0	30 17.8	-7.6	41.3	31 02.7	-6.8	41.7	31 47.4	-6.1	42.1	32 31.7	-5.2	42.6	51
52	27 05.0	-11.2	38.8	27 51.6	-10.5	39.1	28 38.0	-9.7	39.5	29 24.2	-9.0	39.8	30 10.2	-8.2	40.2	30 55.9	-7.5	40.6	31 41.3	-6.7	41.0	32 26.5	-5.9	41.4	52
53	26 53.8	-11.7	37.7	27 41.1	-11.0	38.0	28 28.3	-10.3	38.4	29 15.2	-9.5	38.7	30 02.0	-8.9	39.1	30 48.4	-8.1	39.4	31 34.6	-7.3	39.8	32 20.6	-6.5	40.2	53
54	26 42.1	-12.3	36.6	27 30.1	-11.5	36.9	28 18.0	-10.8	37.2	29 05.7	-10.2	37.6	29 53.1	-9.4	37.9	30 40.3	-8.7	38.3	31 27.3	-7.9	38.6	32 14.1	-7.2	39.0	54
55	26 29.8	-12.7	35.5	27 18.6	-12.1	35.8	28 07.2	-11.4	36.1	28 55.5	-10.7	36.4	29 43.7	-10.0	36.8	30 31.6	-9.2	37.1	31 19.4	-8.6	37.5	32 06.9	-7.9	37.9	55
56	26 17.1	-13.2	34.4	27 06.5	-12.5	34.7	27 55.8	-11.9	35.0	28 44.8	-11.2	35.3	29 33.7	-10.6	35.6	30 22.4	-9.9	36.0	31 10.8	-9.2	36.3	31 59.0	-8.5	36.7	56
57	26 03.9	-13.7	33.3	26 54.0	-13.1	33.6	27 43.9	-12.5	33.9	28 33.6	-11.8	34.2	29 23.1	-11.1	34.5	30 12.5	-10.5	34.8	31 01.6	-9.8	35.2	31 50.5	-9.1	35.5	57
58	25 50.2	-14.1	32.2	26 40.9	-13.6	32.5	27 31.4	-13.0	32.8	28 21.8	-12.4	33.1	29 12.0	-11.8	33.4	30 02.0	-11.1	33.7	30 51.8	-10.4	34.0	31 41.4	-9.7	34.4	58
59	25 36.1	-14.7	31.2	26 27.3	-14.0	31.4	27 18.4	-13.4	31.7	28 09.4	-12.9	32.0	29 00.2	-12.2	32.3	29 50.9	-11.6	32.6	30 41.4	-11.0	32.9	31 31.7	-10.4	33.2	59
60	25 21.4	-15.1	30.1	26 13.3	-14.6	30.3	27 05.0	-14.0	30.6	27 56.5	-13.4	30.9	28 48.0	-12.8	31.1	29 39.3	-12.3	31.4	30 30.4	-11.6	31.7	31 21.3	-11.0	32.0	60
61	25 06.3	-15.6	29.0	25 58.7	-15.0	29.3	26 51.0	-14.5	29.5	27 43.1	-13.9	29.8	28 35.2	-13.4	30.0	29 27.0	-12.8	30.3	30 18.8	-12.2	30.6	31 10.3	-11.6	30.9	61
62	24 50.7	-16.0	28.0	25 43.7	-15.5	28.2	26 36.5	-15.0	28.4	27 29.2	-14.4	28.7	28 21.8	-13.9	28.9	29 14.2	-13.3	29.2	30 06.6	-12.8	29.5	30 58.7	-12.2	29.8	62
63	24 34.7	-16.5	26.9	25 28.2	-16.0	27.1	26 21.5	-15.5	27.3	27 14.8	-15.0	27.6	28 07.9	-14.4	27.8	29 00.9	-13.9	28.1	29 53.8	-13.4	28.3	30 46.5	-12.8	28.6	63
64	24 18.2	-16.9	25.8	25 12.2	-16.4	26.0	26 06.0	-15.9	26.3	26 59.8	-15.5	26.5	27 53.5	-15.0	26.7	28 47.0	-14.5	27.0	29 40.4	-13.9	27.2	30 33.7	-13.4	27.5	64
65	24 01.3	-17.3	24.8	24 55.8	-16.9	25.0	25 50.1	-16.4	25.2	26 44.3	-15.9	25.4	27 38.5	-15.5	25.6	28 32.5	-14.9	25.8	29 26.5	-14.5	26.1	30 20.3	-14.0	26.3	65
66	23 44.0	-17.8	23.7	24 38.9	-17.3	23.9	25 33.7	-16.9	24.1	26 28.4	-16.4	24.3	27 23.0	-15.9	24.5	28 17.6	-15.5	24.7	29 12.0	-15.0	25.0	30 06.3	-14.5	25.2	66
67	23 26.2	-18.1	22.7	24 21.6	-17.8	22.9	25 16.8	-17.3	23.1	26 12.0	-16.9	23.2	27 07.1	-16.5	23.4	28 02.1	-16.1	23.7	28 57.0	-15.6	23.9	29 51.8	-15.1	24.1	67
68	23 08.1	-18.6	21.7	24 03.8	-18.2	21.8	24 59.5	-17.8	22.0	25 55.1	-17.4	22.2	26 50.6	-17.0	22.4	27 46.0	-16.5	22.6	28 41.4	-16.1	22.8	29 36.7	-15.7	23.0	68
69	22 49.5	-19.0	20.6	23 45.6	-18.6	20.8	24 41.7	-18.2	20.9	25 37.7	-17.8	21.1	26 33.6	-17.4	21.3	27 29.5	-17.0	21.5	28 25.3	-16.6	21.7	29 21.0	-16.2	21.9	69
70	22 30.5	-19.3	19.6	23 27.0	-19.0	19.7	24 23.5	-18.7	19.9	25 19.9	-18.3	20.1	26 16.2	-17.9	20.2	27 12.5	-17.6	20.4	28 08.7	-17.2	20.6	29 04.8	-16.7	20.8	70
71	22 11.2	-19.8	18.6	23 08.0	-19.4	18.7	24 04.8	-19.0	18.9	25 01.6	-18.7	19.0	25 58.3	-18.4	19.2	26 54.9	-18.0	19.3	27 51.5	-17.6	19.5	28 48.1	-17.3	19.7	71
72	21 51.4	-20.1	17.6	22 48.6	-19.8	17.7	23 45.8	-19.5	17.8	24 42.9	-19.2	18.0	25 39.9	-18.8	18.1	26 36.9	-18.5	18.3	27 33.9	-18.2	18.4	28 30.8	-17.8	18.6	72
73	21 31.3	-20.4	16.5	22 28.8	-20.2	16.7	23 26.3	-19.9	16.8	24 23.7	-19.6	16.9	25 21.1	-19.3	17.1	26 18.4	-18.9	17.2	27 15.7	-18.6	17.3	28 13.0	-18.3	17.5	73
74	21 10.9	-20.9	15.5	22 08.6	-20.5	15.6	23 06.4	-20.3	15.8	24 04.1	-20.0	15.9	25 01.8	-19.7	16.0	25 59.5	-19.4	16.1	26 57.1	-19.1	16.3	27 54.7	-18.8	16.4	74
75	20 50.0	-21.2	14.5	21 48.1	-21.0	14.6	22 46.1	-20.7	14.7	23 44.1	-20.4	14.8	24 42.1	-20.1	15.0	25 40.1	-19.9	15.1	26 38.0	-19.6	15.2	27 35.9	-19.3	15.3	75
76	20 28.8	-21.5	13.5	21 27.1	-21.2	13.6	22 25.4	-21.0	13.7	23 23.7	-20.8	13.8	24 22.0	-20.6	13.9	25 20.2	-20.3	14.0	26 18.4	-20.1	14.2	27 16.6	-19.8	14.3	76
77	20 07.3	-21.9	12.5	21 05.9	-21.7	12.6	22 04.4	-21.4	12.7	23 02.9	-21.2	12.8	24 01.4	-21.0	12.9	24 59.9	-20.7	13.0	25 58.3	-20.5	13.1	26 56.8	-20.3	13.2	77
78	19 45.4	-22.1	11.5	20 44.2	-22.0	11.6	21 43.0	-21.8	11.7	22 41.7	-21.6	11.8	23 40.4	-21.3	11.9	24 39.2	-21.2	12.0	25 37.8	-20.9	12.1	26 36.5	-20.7	12.2	78
79	19 23.3	-22.6	10.6	20 22.2	-22.3	10.6	21 21.2	-22.1	10.7	22 20.1	-21.9	10.8	23 19.1	-21.8	10.9	24 18.0	-21.6	10.9	25 16.9	-21.4	11.0	26 15.8	-21.2	11.1	79
80	19 00.7	-22.8	9.6	19 59.9	-22.6	9.6	20 59.1	-22.5	9.7	21 58.2	-22.3	9.8	22 57.3	-22.1	9.8	23 56.4	-22.0	9.9	24 55.5	-21.8	10.0	25 54.6	-21.6	10.1	80
81	18 37.9	-23.1	8.6	19 37.3	-23.0	8.7	20 36.6	-22.9	8.7	21 35.9	-22.7	8.8	22 35.2	-22.6	8.8	23 34.4	-22.3	8.9	24 33.7	-22.2	9.0	25 33.0	-22.1	9.0	81
82	18 14.8	-23.4	7.6	19 14.3	-23.3	7.7	20 13.7	-23.1	7.7	21 13.2	-23.0	7.8	22 12.6	-22.9	7.8	23 12.1	-22.8	7.9	24 11.5	-22.6	7.9	25 10.9	-22.5	8.0	82
83	17 51.4	-23.7	6.7	18 51.0	-23.6	6.7	19 50.6	-23.5	6.7	20 50.2	-23.4	6.8	21 49.7	-23.2	6.8	22 49.3	-23.1	6.9	23 48.9	-23.0	6.9	24 48.4	-22.9	7.0	83
84	17 27.7	-24.0	5.7	18 27.4	-23.9	5.7	19 27.1	-23.8	5.8	20 26.8	-23.7	5.8	21 26.5	-23.6	5.8	22 26.2	-23.5	5.9	23 25.9	-23.4	5.9	24 25.5	-23.3	6.0	84
85	17 03.7	-24.2	4.7	18 03.5	-24.1	4.8	19 03.3	-24.1	4.8	20 03.1	-24.0	4.8	21 02.9	-23.9	4.9	22 02.7	-23.9	4.9	23 02.5	-23.8	4.9	24 02.2	-23.7	5.0	85
86	16 39.5	-24.5	3.8	17 39.4	-24.5	3.8	18 39.2	-24.3	3.8	19 39.1	-24.3	3.8	20 39.0	-24.3	3.9	21 38.8	-24.2	3.9	22 38.7	-24.2	3.9	23 38.5	-24.0	4.0	86
87	16 15.0	-24.8	2.8	17 14.9	-24.7	2.8	18 14.9	-24.7	2.9	19 14.8	-24.7	2.9	20 14.7	-24.6	2.9	21 14.6	-24.5	2.9	22 14.5	-24.5	2.9	23 14.5	-24.5	3.0	87
88	15 50.2	-25.0	1.9	16 50.2	-25.0	1.9	17 50.2	-25.0	1.9	18 50.1	-24.9	1.9	19 50.1	-24.9	1.9	20 50.1	-24.9	1.9	21 50.0	-24.8	2.0	22 50.0	-24.8	2.0	88
89	15 25.2	-25.2	0.9	16 25.2	-25.2	0.9	17 25.2	-25.2	0.9	18 25.2	-25.2	1.0	19 25.2	-25.2	1.0	20 25.2	-25.2	1.0	21 25.2	-25.2	1.0	22 25.2	-25.2	1.0	89
90	15 00.0	-25.5	0.0	16 00.0	-25.5	0.0	17 00.0	-25.5	0.0	18 00.0	-25.5	0.0	19 00.0	-25.5	0.0	20 00.0	-25.5	0.0	21 00.0	-25.5	0.0	22 00.0	-25.5	0.0	90
	15°			16°			17°			18°			19°			20°			21°			22°			

65°, 295° L.H.A. LATITUDE SAME NAME AS DECLINATION

132

LATITUDE CONTRARY NAME TO DECLINATION L.H.A. 65°, 295°

Dec.	15° Hc	d	Z	16° Hc	d	Z	17° Hc	d	Z	18° Hc	d	Z
°	° ′	′	°	° ′	′	°	° ′	′	°	° ′	′	°
0	24 05.6	-17.2	96.9	23 58.2	-18.4	97.3	23 50.3	-19.4	97.8	23 41.9	-20.4	98.2
1	23 48.4	-17.7	97.9	23 39.8	-18.7	98.4	23 30.9	-19.8	98.8	23 21.5	-20.9	99.2
2	23 30.7	-18.1	99.0	23 21.1	-19.1	99.4	23 11.1	-20.2	99.8	23 00.6	-21.2	100.2
3	23 12.6	-18.4	100.0	23 02.0	-19.5	100.4	22 50.9	-20.6	100.8	22 39.4	-21.6	101.3
4	22 54.2	-18.9	101.0	22 42.5	-20.0	101.5	22 30.3	-20.9	101.9	22 17.8	-22.0	102.3
5	22 35.3	-19.3	102.1	22 22.5	-20.3	102.5	22 09.4	-21.4	102.9	21 55.8	-22.4	103.3
6	22 16.0	-19.6	103.1	22 02.2	-20.6	103.5	21 48.0	-21.7	103.9	21 33.4	-22.7	104.3
7	21 56.4	-20.0	104.1	21 41.6	-21.1	104.5	21 26.3	-22.0	104.9	21 10.7	-23.0	105.3
8	21 36.4	-20.4	105.1	21 20.5	-21.4	105.5	21 04.3	-22.4	105.9	20 47.7	-23.4	106.3
9	21 16.0	-20.8	106.1	20 59.1	-21.7	106.5	20 41.9	-22.8	106.9	20 24.3	-23.8	107.2
10	20 55.2	-21.1	107.2	20 37.4	-22.1	107.5	20 19.1	-23.1	107.9	20 00.5	-24.0	108.2
11	20 34.1	-21.4	108.2	20 15.3	-22.5	108.5	19 56.0	-23.4	108.9	19 36.5	-24.4	109.2
12	20 12.7	-21.8	109.1	19 52.8	-22.7	109.5	19 32.6	-23.7	109.8	19 12.1	-24.6	110.2
13	19 50.9	-22.1	110.1	19 30.1	-23.1	110.5	19 08.9	-24.0	110.8	18 47.5	-25.0	111.1
14	19 28.8	-22.4	111.1	19 07.0	-23.4	111.5	18 44.9	-24.3	111.8	18 22.5	-25.2	112.1
15	19 06.4	-22.8	112.1	18 43.6	-23.6	112.4	18 20.6	-24.6	112.7	17 57.3	-25.6	113.0
16	18 43.6	-23.0	113.1	18 20.0	-24.0	113.4	17 56.0	-24.9	113.7	17 31.7	-25.8	114.0
17	18 20.6	-23.3	114.1	17 56.0	-24.3	114.4	17 31.1	-25.2	114.7	17 05.9	-26.0	114.9
18	17 57.3	-23.7	115.0	17 31.7	-24.5	115.3	17 05.9	-25.4	115.6	16 39.9	-26.3	115.9
19	17 33.6	-23.9	116.0	17 07.2	-24.8	116.3	16 40.5	-25.7	116.5	16 13.6	-26.6	116.8
20	17 09.7	-24.1	117.0	16 42.4	-25.1	117.2	16 14.8	-25.9	117.5	15 47.0	-26.8	117.7
21	16 45.6	-24.5	117.9	16 17.3	-25.3	118.2	15 48.9	-26.2	118.4	15 20.2	-27.0	118.7
22	16 21.1	-24.7	118.9	15 52.0	-25.5	119.1	15 22.7	-26.4	119.4	14 53.2	-27.2	119.6
23	15 56.4	-24.9	119.8	15 26.5	-25.8	120.1	14 56.3	-26.6	120.3	14 26.0	-27.5	120.5
24	15 31.5	-25.2	120.8	15 00.7	-26.0	121.0	14 29.7	-26.9	121.2	13 58.5	-27.7	121.4
25	15 06.3	-25.4	121.7	14 34.7	-26.3	121.9	14 02.8	-27.0	122.1	13 30.8	-27.8	122.4
26	14 40.9	-25.7	122.6	14 08.4	-26.4	122.9	13 35.8	-27.3	123.1	13 03.0	-28.1	123.3
27	14 15.2	-25.8	123.6	13 42.0	-26.7	123.8	13 08.5	-27.4	124.0	12 34.9	-28.2	124.2
28	13 49.4	-26.1	124.5	13 15.3	-26.8	124.7	12 41.1	-27.7	124.9	12 06.7	-28.4	125.1
29	13 23.3	-26.2	125.4	12 48.5	-27.1	125.6	12 13.4	-27.8	125.8	11 38.3	-28.6	126.0
30	12 57.1	-26.5	126.4	12 21.4	-27.2	126.5	11 45.6	-28.0	126.7	11 09.7	-28.7	126.9
31	12 30.6	-26.7	127.3	11 54.2	-27.4	127.4	11 17.6	-28.1	127.6	10 41.0	-28.9	127.8
32	12 03.9	-26.8	128.2	11 26.8	-27.6	128.4	10 49.5	-28.3	128.5	10 12.1	-29.1	128.7
33	11 37.1	-27.0	129.1	10 59.2	-27.7	129.3	10 21.2	-28.5	129.4	9 43.0	-29.1	129.5
34	11 10.1	-27.1	130.0	10 31.5	-27.9	130.2	9 52.7	-28.6	130.3	9 13.9	-29.3	130.4
35	10 43.0	-27.4	130.9	10 03.6	-28.0	131.1	9 24.1	-28.7	131.2	8 44.6	-29.5	131.3
36	10 15.6	-27.4	131.8	9 35.6	-28.2	132.0	8 55.4	-28.9	132.1	8 15.1	-29.5	132.2
37	9 48.2	-27.7	132.7	9 07.4	-28.3	132.9	8 26.5	-28.9	133.0	7 45.6	-29.6	133.1
38	9 20.5	-27.7	133.6	8 39.1	-28.4	133.7	7 57.6	-29.1	133.9	7 16.0	-29.8	133.9
39	8 52.8	-27.9	134.5	8 10.7	-28.6	134.6	7 28.5	-29.2	134.7	6 46.2	-29.8	134.8
40	8 24.9	-28.0	135.4	7 42.1	-28.6	135.5	6 59.3	-29.3	135.6	6 16.4	-29.9	135.7
41	7 56.9	-28.1	136.3	7 13.5	-28.8	136.4	6 30.0	-29.4	136.5	5 46.5	-30.0	136.6
42	7 28.8	-28.2	137.2	6 44.7	-28.8	137.3	6 00.6	-29.4	137.4	5 16.5	-30.1	137.4
43	7 00.6	-28.3	138.1	6 15.9	-28.9	138.2	5 31.2	-29.6	138.2	4 46.4	-30.2	138.3
44	6 32.3	-28.5	139.0	5 47.0	-29.1	139.1	5 01.6	-29.6	139.1	4 16.2	-30.2	139.2
45	6 03.8	-28.5	139.9	5 17.9	-29.0	139.9	4 32.0	-29.7	140.0	3 46.0	-30.2	140.0
46	5 35.3	-28.5	140.8	4 48.9	-29.2	140.8	4 02.3	-29.7	140.9	3 15.8	-30.3	140.9
47	5 06.8	-28.7	141.6	4 19.7	-29.2	141.7	3 32.6	-29.8	141.7	2 45.5	-30.4	141.8
48	4 38.1	-28.7	142.5	3 50.5	-29.3	142.6	3 02.8	-29.8	142.6	2 15.1	-30.3	142.6
49	4 09.4	-28.8	143.4	3 21.2	-29.3	143.4	2 33.0	-29.9	143.5	1 44.8	-30.4	143.5
50	3 40.6	-28.8	144.3	2 51.9	-29.4	144.3	2 03.1	-29.8	144.3	1 14.4	-30.4	144.4
51	3 11.8	-28.9	145.2	2 22.5	-29.4	145.2	1 33.3	-29.9	145.2	0 44.0	-30.4	145.2
52	2 42.9	-28.9	146.0	1 53.1	-29.4	146.1	1 03.4	-30.0	146.1	0 13.6	-30.5	146.1
53	2 14.0	-28.9	146.9	1 23.7	-29.4	146.9	0 33.4	-29.9	146.9	0 16.9	+30.4	33.1
54	1 45.1	-29.0	147.8	0 54.3	-29.5	147.8	0 03.5	-29.9	147.8	0 47.3	+30.4	32.2
55	1 16.1	-29.0	148.7	0 24.8	-29.4	148.7	0 26.4	+29.9	31.3	1 17.7	+30.4	31.3
56	0 47.1	-29.0	149.5	0 04.6	+29.5	30.5	0 56.3	+30.0	30.5	1 48.1	+30.3	30.5
57	0 18.1	-29.0	150.4	0 34.1	+29.4	29.6	1 26.3	+29.8	29.6	2 18.4	+30.4	29.6
58	0 10.9	+29.0	28.7	1 03.5	+29.5	28.7	1 56.1	+29.9	28.7	2 48.8	+30.2	28.7
59	0 39.9	+29.0	27.8	1 33.0	+29.4	27.8	2 26.0	+29.8	27.9	3 19.0	+30.3	27.9
60	1 08.9	+29.0	27.0	2 02.4	+29.3	27.0	2 55.8	+29.8	27.0	3 49.3	+30.2	27.0
61	1 37.9	+28.9	26.1	2 31.7	+29.4	26.1	3 25.6	+29.8	26.1	4 19.5	+30.1	26.1
62	2 06.8	+28.9	25.2	3 01.1	+29.3	25.2	3 55.4	+29.7	25.2	4 49.6	+30.1	25.3
63	2 35.7	+28.9	24.3	3 30.4	+29.2	24.3	4 25.1	+29.6	24.4	5 19.7	+30.0	24.4
64	3 04.6	+28.8	23.4	3 59.6	+29.2	23.5	4 54.7	+29.5	23.5	5 49.7	+29.9	23.5
65	3 33.4	+28.8	22.6	4 28.8	+29.2	22.6	5 24.2	+29.5	22.6	6 19.6	+29.8	22.7
66	4 02.2	+28.8	21.7	4 58.0	+29.1	21.7	5 53.7	+29.4	21.8	6 49.4	+29.8	21.8
67	4 31.0	+28.6	20.8	5 27.1	+28.9	20.8	6 23.1	+29.3	20.9	7 19.2	+29.6	20.9
68	4 59.6	+28.6	19.9	5 56.0	+29.0	20.0	6 52.4	+29.2	20.0	7 48.8	+29.5	20.0
69	5 28.2	+28.6	19.0	6 25.0	+28.8	19.1	7 21.6	+29.2	19.1	8 18.3	+29.4	19.2
70	5 56.8	+28.4	18.2	6 53.8	+28.7	18.2	7 50.8	+29.0	18.2	8 47.7	+29.3	18.3
71	6 25.2	+28.3	17.3	7 22.5	+28.6	17.3	8 19.8	+28.8	17.4	9 17.0	+29.2	17.4
72	6 53.5	+28.3	16.4	7 51.1	+28.5	16.4	8 48.6	+28.8	16.5	9 46.2	+29.0	16.5
73	7 21.8	+28.1	15.5	8 19.6	+28.4	15.5	9 17.4	+28.6	15.6	10 15.2	+28.9	15.6
74	7 49.9	+28.1	14.6	8 48.0	+28.2	14.6	9 46.0	+28.5	14.7	10 44.1	+28.7	14.7
75	8 18.0	+27.9	13.7	9 16.2	+28.2	13.7	10 14.5	+28.4	13.8	11 12.8	+28.5	13.8
76	8 45.9	+27.8	12.8	9 44.4	+28.0	12.9	10 42.9	+28.2	12.9	11 41.3	+28.4	12.9
77	9 13.7	+27.6	11.9	10 12.4	+27.8	12.0	11 11.1	+28.0	12.0	12 09.7	+28.3	12.0
78	9 41.3	+27.5	11.0	10 40.2	+27.7	11.1	11 39.1	+27.8	11.1	12 38.0	+28.0	11.1
79	10 08.8	+27.4	10.1	11 07.9	+27.5	10.2	12 06.9	+27.7	10.2	13 06.0	+27.8	10.2
80	10 36.2	+27.2	9.2	11 35.4	+27.3	9.2	12 34.6	+27.5	9.3	13 33.8	+27.7	9.3
81	11 03.4	+27.0	8.3	12 02.7	+27.2	8.3	13 02.1	+27.3	8.4	14 01.5	+27.4	8.4
82	11 30.4	+26.9	7.4	12 29.9	+27.0	7.4	13 29.4	+27.1	7.5	14 28.9	+27.2	7.5
83	11 57.3	+26.7	6.5	12 56.9	+26.8	6.5	13 56.5	+26.9	6.5	14 56.1	+27.0	6.6
84	12 24.0	+26.5	5.6	13 23.7	+26.6	5.6	14 23.4	+26.7	5.6	15 23.1	+26.8	5.6
85	12 50.5	+26.3	4.6	13 50.3	+26.4	4.7	14 50.1	+26.5	4.7	15 49.9	+26.5	4.7
86	13 16.8	+26.1	3.7	14 16.7	+26.2	3.7	15 16.6	+26.2	3.8	16 16.4	+26.3	3.8
87	13 42.9	+25.9	2.8	14 42.9	+25.9	2.8	15 42.8	+26.0	2.8	16 42.7	+26.0	2.8
88	14 08.8	+25.7	1.9	15 08.8	+25.7	1.9	16 08.8	+25.7	1.9	17 08.7	+25.8	1.9
89	14 34.5	+25.5	0.9	15 34.5	+25.5	0.9	16 34.5	+25.5	0.9	17 34.5	+25.5	0.9
90	15 00.0	+25.2	0.0	16 00.0	+25.2	0.0	17 00.0	+25.2	0.0	18 00.0	+25.2	0.0
	15°			16°			17°			18°		

19° Hc	d	Z	20° Hc	d	Z	21° Hc	d	Z	22° Hc	d	Z	Dec.
° ′	′	°	° ′	′	°	° ′	′	°	° ′	′	°	°
23 33.2	-21.5	98.6	23 23.9	-22.5	99.1	23 14.3	-23.6	99.5	23 04.2	-24.7	99.9	0
23 11.7	-21.9	99.6	23 01.4	-23.0	100.1	22 50.7	-24.0	100.5	22 39.5	-24.9	100.9	1
22 49.8	-22.3	100.7	22 38.4	-23.3	101.1	22 26.7	-24.3	101.5	22 14.6	-25.4	101.9	2
22 27.5	-22.7	101.7	22 15.1	-23.6	102.1	22 02.4	-24.7	102.5	21 49.2	-25.6	102.9	3
22 04.8	-23.0	102.7	21 51.5	-24.0	103.1	21 37.7	-25.0	103.4	21 23.6	-26.0	103.8	4
21 41.8	-23.3	103.7	21 27.5	-24.4	104.0	21 12.7	-25.4	104.4	20 57.6	-26.4	104.8	5
21 18.5	-23.8	104.7	21 03.1	-24.7	105.0	20 47.3	-25.6	105.4	20 31.2	-26.6	105.8	6
20 54.7	-24.0	105.6	20 38.4	-25.1	106.0	20 21.7	-26.0	106.4	20 04.6	-27.0	106.7	7
20 30.7	-24.4	106.6	20 13.3	-25.3	107.0	19 55.7	-26.3	107.3	19 37.6	-27.2	107.7	8
20 06.3	-24.7	107.6	19 48.0	-25.7	107.9	19 29.4	-26.7	108.3	19 10.4	-27.6	108.6	9
19 41.6	-25.0	108.6	19 22.3	-25.9	108.9	19 02.7	-26.8	109.2	18 42.8	-27.8	109.5	10
19 16.6	-25.3	109.5	18 56.4	-26.3	109.9	18 35.9	-27.2	110.2	18 15.0	-28.1	110.5	11
18 51.3	-25.6	110.5	18 30.1	-26.5	110.8	18 08.7	-27.5	111.1	17 46.9	-28.3	111.4	12
18 25.7	-25.9	111.4	18 03.6	-26.8	111.7	17 41.2	-27.7	112.0	17 18.6	-28.6	112.3	13
17 59.8	-26.2	112.4	17 36.8	-27.1	112.7	17 13.5	-27.9	113.0	16 50.0	-28.9	113.3	14
17 33.6	-26.4	113.3	17 09.7	-27.3	113.6	16 45.6	-28.3	113.9	16 21.1	-29.1	114.2	15
17 07.2	-26.7	114.3	16 42.4	-27.6	114.6	16 17.3	-28.4	114.8	15 52.0	-29.3	115.1	16
16 40.5	-26.9	115.2	16 14.8	-27.8	115.5	15 48.9	-28.7	115.7	15 22.7	-29.5	116.0	17
16 13.6	-27.2	116.1	15 47.0	-28.0	116.4	15 20.2	-28.9	116.6	14 53.2	-29.7	116.9	18
15 46.4	-27.4	117.1	15 19.0	-28.3	117.3	14 51.3	-29.1	117.6	14 23.5	-30.0	117.8	19
15 19.0	-27.7	118.0	14 50.7	-28.5	118.2	14 22.2	-29.3	118.5	13 53.5	-30.1	118.7	20
14 51.3	-27.8	118.9	14 22.2	-28.7	119.1	13 52.9	-29.5	119.4	13 23.4	-30.3	119.6	21
14 23.5	-28.1	119.8	13 53.5	-28.9	120.0	13 23.4	-29.7	120.3	12 53.1	-30.5	120.5	22
13 55.4	-28.3	120.7	13 24.6	-29.1	120.9	12 53.7	-29.9	121.1	12 22.6	-30.7	121.3	23
13 27.1	-28.5	121.6	12 55.5	-29.2	121.8	12 23.8	-30.1	122.0	11 51.9	-30.8	122.2	24
12 58.6	-28.6	122.5	12 26.3	-29.5	122.7	11 53.7	-30.2	122.9	11 21.1	-31.0	123.1	25
12 30.0	-28.9	123.5	11 56.8	-29.6	123.6	11 23.5	-30.4	123.8	10 50.1	-31.2	124.0	26
12 01.1	-29.0	124.3	11 27.2	-29.8	124.5	10 53.1	-30.5	124.7	10 18.9	-31.2	124.8	27
11 32.1	-29.1	125.2	10 57.4	-29.9	125.4	10 22.6	-30.7	125.6	9 47.7	-31.4	125.7	28
11 03.0	-29.4	126.1	10 27.5	-30.1	126.3	9 51.9	-30.8	126.4	9 16.3	-31.6	126.6	29
10 33.6	-29.4	127.0	9 57.4	-30.2	127.2	9 21.1	-30.9	127.3	8 44.7	-31.6	127.4	30
10 04.2	-29.7	127.9	9 27.2	-30.3	128.0	8 50.2	-31.0	128.2	8 13.1	-31.8	128.3	31
9 34.5	-29.7	128.8	8 56.9	-30.5	128.9	8 19.2	-31.2	129.0	7 41.3	-31.8	129.1	32
9 04.8	-29.9	129.7	8 26.4	-30.5	129.8	7 48.0	-31.3	129.9	7 09.5	-32.0	130.0	33
8 34.9	-30.0	130.5	7 55.9	-30.7	130.7	7 16.7	-31.3	130.8	6 37.5	-32.0	130.9	34
8 04.9	-30.1	131.4	7 25.2	-30.8	131.5	6 45.4	-31.5	131.6	6 05.5	-32.1	131.7	35
7 34.8	-30.2	132.3	6 54.4	-30.9	132.4	6 13.9	-31.5	132.5	5 33.4	-32.2	132.6	36
7 04.6	-30.3	133.2	6 23.5	-30.9	133.3	5 42.4	-31.6	133.3	5 01.2	-32.3	133.4	37
6 34.3	-30.4	134.0	5 52.6	-31.1	134.1	5 10.8	-31.7	134.2	4 28.9	-32.3	134.2	38
6 03.9	-30.5	134.9	5 21.5	-31.1	135.0	4 39.1	-31.8	135.0	3 56.6	-32.4	135.1	39
5 33.4	-30.5	135.8	4 50.4	-31.2	135.8	4 07.3	-31.8	135.9	3 24.2	-32.4	135.9	40
5 02.9	-30.7	136.6	4 19.2	-31.2	136.7	3 35.5	-31.8	136.7	2 51.8	-32.4	136.8	41
4 32.2	-30.6	137.5	3 48.0	-31.3	137.5	3 03.7	-31.9	137.6	2 19.4	-32.5	137.6	42
4 01.6	-30.8	138.4	3 16.7	-31.3	138.4	2 31.8	-31.9	138.4	1 46.9	-32.5	138.5	43
3 30.8	-30.8	139.2	2 45.4	-31.4	139.3	1 59.9	-31.9	139.3	1 14.4	-32.5	139.3	44
3 00.0	-30.8	140.1	2 14.0	-31.4	140.1	1 28.0	-32.0	140.1	0 41.9	-32.5	140.1	45
2 29.2	-30.9	140.9	1 42.6	-31.4	141.0	0 56.0	-32.0	141.0	0 09.4	-32.5	141.0	46
1 58.3	-30.8	141.8	1 11.2	-31.5	141.8	0 24.0	-32.0	141.8	0 23.1	+32.6	38.2	47
1 27.5	-31.0	142.7	0 39.7	-31.4	142.7	0 08.0	+31.9	37.3	0 55.7	+32.5	37.3	48
0 56.5	-30.9	143.5	0 08.3	-31.4	143.5	0 39.9	+32.0	36.5	1 28.2	+32.5	36.5	49
0 25.6	-30.9	144.4	0 23.1	+31.5	35.6	1 11.9	+32.0	35.6	2 00.7	+32.4	35.7	50
0 05.3	+30.9	34.8	0 54.6	+31.4	34.8	1 43.9	+31.9	34.8	2 33.1	+32.5	34.8	51
0 36.2	+30.9	33.9	1 26.0	+31.4	33.9	2 15.8	+31.9	33.9	3 05.6	+32.3	34.0	52
1 07.1	+30.9	33.1	1 57.4	+31.4	33.1	2 47.7	+31.9	33.1	3 37.9	+32.4	33.1	53
1 38.0	+30.9	32.2	2 28.8	+31.4	32.2	3 19.6	+31.8	32.2	4 10.3	+32.3	32.3	54
2 08.9	+30.9	31.3	3 00.2	+31.3	31.4	3 51.4	+31.7	31.4	4 42.6	+32.2	31.4	55
2 39.8	+30.8	30.5	3 31.5	+31.2	30.5	4 23.1	+31.8	30.5	5 14.8	+32.2	30.6	56
3 10.6	+30.8	29.6	4 02.7	+31.2	29.7	4 54.9	+31.6	29.7	5 47.0	+32.1	29.7	57
3 41.4	+30.7	28.8	4 33.9	+31.2	28.8	5 26.5	+31.6	28.8	6 19.1	+32.0	28.9	58
4 12.1	+30.6	27.9	5 05.1	+31.1	27.9	5 58.1	+31.5	28.0	6 51.1	+31.9	28.0	59
4 42.7	+30.6	27.0	5 36.2	+31.0	27.1	6 29.6	+31.4	27.1	7 23.0	+31.8	27.2	60
5 13.3	+30.6	26.2	6 07.2	+30.9	26.2	7 01.0	+31.3	26.3	7 54.8	+31.7	26.3	61
5 43.9	+30.4	25.3	6 38.1	+30.8	25.4	7 32.3	+31.2	25.4	8 26.5	+31.6	25.5	62
6 14.3	+30.4	24.5	7 08.9	+30.8	24.5	8 03.5	+31.1	24.6	8 58.1	+31.5	24.6	63
6 44.7	+30.3	23.6	7 39.7	+30.6	23.6	8 34.6	+31.0	23.7	9 29.6	+31.3	23.8	64
7 15.0	+30.1	22.7	8 10.3	+30.5	22.8	9 05.6	+30.9	22.8	10 00.9	+31.2	22.9	65
7 45.1	+30.1	21.8	8 40.8	+30.4	21.9	9 36.5	+30.7	22.0	10 32.1	+31.1	22.0	66
8 15.2	+30.0	21.0	9 11.2	+30.3	21.0	10 07.2	+30.6	21.1	11 03.2	+30.9	21.2	67
8 45.2	+29.8	20.1	9 41.5	+30.1	20.1	10 37.8	+30.5	20.2	11 34.1	+30.8	20.3	68
9 15.0	+29.7	19.2	10 11.6	+30.1	19.3	11 08.3	+30.3	19.3	12 04.9	+30.6	19.4	69
9 44.7	+29.6	18.3	10 41.7	+29.8	18.4	11 38.6	+30.1	18.5	12 35.5	+30.4	18.5	70
10 14.3	+29.4	17.4	11 11.5	+29.7	17.5	12 08.7	+30.0	17.6	13 05.9	+30.3	17.6	71
10 43.7	+29.3	16.6	11 41.2	+29.5	16.6	12 38.7	+29.8	16.7	13 36.2	+30.0	16.7	72
11 13.0	+29.1	15.7	12 10.7	+29.4	15.7	13 08.5	+29.6	15.8	14 06.2	+29.9	15.9	73
11 42.1	+28.9	14.8	12 40.1	+29.2	14.8	13 38.1	+29.4	14.9	14 36.1	+29.6	15.0	74
12 11.0	+28.8	13.9	13 09.3	+29.0	13.9	14 07.5	+29.2	14.0	15 05.7	+29.5	14.1	75
12 39.8	+28.6	13.0	13 38.3	+28.8	13.0	14 36.7	+29.0	13.1	15 35.2	+29.2	13.2	76
13 08.4	+28.4	12.1	14 07.1	+28.6	12.1	15 05.7	+28.8	12.2	16 04.4	+29.0	12.2	77
13 36.8	+28.2	11.2	14 35.7	+28.4	11.2	15 34.5	+28.6	11.3	16 33.4	+28.7	11.3	78
14 05.0	+28.0	10.3	15 04.1	+28.1	10.3	16 03.1	+28.3	10.4	17 02.1	+28.5	10.4	79
14 33.0	+27.8	9.4	15 32.2	+28.0	9.4	16 31.4	+28.1	9.4	17 30.6	+28.2	9.5	80
15 00.8	+27.6	8.4	16 00.2	+27.7	8.5	16 59.5	+27.8	8.5	17 58.8	+28.0	8.6	81
15 28.4	+27.3	7.5	16 27.9	+27.4	7.6	17 27.3	+27.6	7.6	18 26.8	+27.7	7.6	82
15 55.7	+27.1	6.6	16 55.3	+27.2	6.6	17 54.9	+27.3	6.7	18 54.5	+27.4	6.7	83
16 22.8	+26.9	5.7	17 22.5	+27.0	5.7	18 22.2	+27.1	5.7	19 21.9	+27.2	5.8	84
16 49.7	+26.6	4.7	17 49.5	+26.7	4.8	18 49.3	+26.7	4.8	19 49.1	+26.8	4.8	85
17 16.3	+26.3	3.8	18 16.2	+26.4	3.8	19 16.0	+26.5	3.8	20 15.9	+26.5	3.9	86
17 42.6	+26.1	2.9	18 42.6	+26.1	2.9	19 42.5	+26.1	2.9	20 42.4	+26.2	2.9	87
18 08.7	+25.8	1.9	19 08.7	+25.8	1.9	20 08.6	+25.9	1.9	21 08.6	+25.9	1.9	88
18 34.5	+25.5	1.0	19 34.5	+25.5	1.0	20 34.5	+25.5	1.0	21 34.5	+25.5	1.0	89
19 00.0	+25.2	0.0	20 00.0	+25.2	0.0	21 00.0	+25.2	0.0	22 00.0	+25.2	0.0	90
19°			20°			21°			22°			

S. Lat. { L.H.A. greater than 180° ....Zn=180°–Z / L.H.A. less than 180°...........Zn=180°+Z

LATITUDE SAME NAME AS DECLINATION L.H.A. 115°, 245°

Dec.	15° Hc	d	Z	16° Hc	d	Z	17° Hc	d	Z	18° Hc	d	Z	19° Hc	d	Z	20° Hc	d	Z	21° Hc	d	Z	22° Hc	d	Z	Dec.
°	° ′	′	°	° ′	′	°	° ′	′	°	° ′	′	°	° ′	′	°	° ′	′	°	° ′	′	°	° ′	′	°	°
0	23 08.0	+16.7	96.6	23 00.9	+17.8	97.0	22 53.4	+18.8	97.4	22 45.4	+20.0	97.8	22 37.0	+21.0	98.2	22 28.2	+22.0	98.7	22 19.0	+23.0	99.1	22 09.3	+24.1	99.5	0
1	23 24.7	+16.3	95.5	23 18.7	+17.3	96.0	23 12.2	+18.5	96.4	23 05.4	+19.5	96.8	22 58.0	+20.6	97.2	22 50.2	+21.7	97.7	22 42.0	+22.7	98.1	22 33.4	+23.7	98.5	1
2	23 41.0	+15.8	94.5	23 36.0	+17.0	94.9	23 30.7	+18.0	95.3	23 24.9	+19.1	95.8	23 18.6	+20.2	96.2	23 11.9	+21.2	96.6	23 04.7	+22.3	97.1	22 57.1	+23.4	97.5	2
3	23 56.8	+15.4	93.4	23 53.0	+16.5	93.9	23 48.7	+17.6	94.3	23 44.0	+18.7	94.7	23 38.8	+19.7	95.2	23 33.1	+20.9	95.6	23 27.0	+21.9	96.1	23 20.5	+22.9	96.5	3
4	24 12.2	+15.0	92.4	24 09.5	+16.1	92.8	24 06.3	+17.2	93.3	24 02.7	+18.2	93.7	23 58.5	+19.4	94.2	23 54.0	+20.4	94.6	23 48.9	+21.5	95.0	23 43.4	+22.6	95.5	4
5	24 27.2	+14.5	91.3	24 25.6	+15.6	91.8	24 23.5	+16.7	92.2	24 20.9	+17.9	92.7	24 17.9	+18.9	93.1	24 14.4	+20.0	93.6	24 10.4	+21.1	94.0	24 06.0	+22.2	94.5	5
6	24 41.7	+14.0	90.2	24 41.2	+15.2	90.7	24 40.2	+16.3	91.2	24 38.8	+17.4	91.6	24 36.8	+18.5	92.1	24 34.4	+19.6	92.5	24 31.5	+20.7	93.0	24 28.2	+21.7	93.4	6
7	24 55.7	+13.6	89.2	24 56.4	+14.7	89.6	24 56.5	+15.8	90.1	24 56.2	+16.9	90.6	24 55.3	+18.1	91.0	24 54.0	+19.2	91.5	24 52.2	+20.3	92.0	24 49.9	+21.4	92.4	7
8	25 09.3	+13.2	88.1	25 11.1	+14.2	88.6	25 12.3	+15.4	89.0	25 13.1	+16.5	89.5	25 13.4	+17.6	90.0	25 13.2	+18.7	90.4	25 12.5	+19.8	90.9	25 11.3	+20.9	91.4	8
9	25 22.5	+12.6	87.0	25 25.3	+13.8	87.5	25 27.7	+14.9	88.0	25 29.6	+16.0	88.4	25 31.0	+17.1	88.9	25 31.9	+18.2	89.4	25 32.3	+19.3	89.9	25 32.2	+20.4	90.3	9
10	25 35.1	+12.2	85.9	25 39.1	+13.3	86.4	25 42.6	+14.5	86.9	25 45.6	+15.6	87.4	25 48.1	+16.7	87.8	25 50.1	+17.8	88.3	25 51.6	+18.9	88.8	25 52.6	+20.0	89.3	10
11	25 47.3	+11.7	84.8	25 52.4	+12.9	85.3	25 57.1	+13.9	85.8	26 01.2	+15.1	86.3	26 04.8	+16.2	86.8	26 07.9	+17.4	87.3	26 10.5	+18.5	87.8	26 12.6	+19.6	88.3	11
12	25 59.0	+11.2	83.8	26 05.3	+12.3	84.2	26 11.0	+13.5	84.7	26 16.3	+14.6	85.2	26 21.0	+15.8	85.7	26 25.3	+16.8	86.2	26 29.0	+17.9	86.7	26 32.2	+19.1	87.2	12
13	26 10.2	+10.7	82.7	26 17.6	+11.8	83.1	26 24.5	+13.0	83.6	26 30.9	+14.1	84.1	26 36.8	+15.2	84.6	26 42.1	+16.4	85.1	26 46.9	+17.5	85.6	26 51.3	+18.6	86.1	13
14	26 20.9	+10.2	81.6	26 29.4	+11.4	82.1	26 37.5	+12.4	82.5	26 45.0	+13.6	83.0	26 52.0	+14.7	83.5	26 58.5	+15.8	84.1	27 04.4	+17.0	84.6	27 09.9	+18.1	85.1	14
15	26 31.1	+9.7	80.5	26 40.8	+10.8	81.0	26 49.9	+12.0	81.5	26 58.6	+13.1	82.0	27 06.7	+14.3	82.5	27 14.3	+15.4	83.0	27 21.4	+16.5	83.5	27 28.0	+17.6	84.0	15
16	26 40.8	+9.1	79.4	26 51.6	+10.3	79.9	27 01.9	+11.5	80.4	27 11.7	+12.6	80.9	27 21.0	+13.7	81.4	27 29.7	+14.9	81.9	27 37.9	+16.0	82.4	27 45.6	+17.1	82.9	16
17	26 49.9	+8.7	78.2	27 01.9	+9.8	78.7	27 13.4	+10.9	79.2	27 24.3	+12.1	79.8	27 34.7	+13.2	80.3	27 44.6	+14.3	80.8	27 53.9	+15.5	81.3	28 02.7	+16.6	81.8	17
18	26 58.6	+8.1	77.1	27 11.7	+9.3	77.6	27 24.3	+10.4	78.1	27 36.4	+11.5	78.7	27 47.9	+12.7	79.2	27 58.9	+13.8	79.7	28 09.4	+14.9	80.2	28 19.3	+16.1	80.7	18
19	27 06.7	+7.6	76.0	27 21.0	+8.7	76.5	27 34.7	+9.9	77.0	27 47.9	+11.0	77.5	28 00.6	+12.1	78.1	28 12.7	+13.3	78.6	28 24.3	+14.4	79.1	28 35.4	+15.5	79.6	19
20	27 14.3	+7.1	74.9	27 29.7	+8.2	75.4	27 44.6	+9.3	75.9	27 58.9	+10.5	76.4	28 12.7	+11.6	77.0	28 26.0	+12.7	77.5	28 38.7	+13.9	78.0	28 50.9	+15.0	78.5	20
21	27 21.4	+6.6	73.8	27 37.9	+7.7	74.3	27 53.9	+8.8	74.8	28 09.4	+9.9	75.3	28 24.3	+11.1	75.8	28 38.7	+12.2	76.4	28 52.6	+13.3	76.9	29 05.9	+14.5	77.4	21
22	27 28.0	+6.0	72.7	27 45.6	+7.1	73.2	28 02.7	+8.3	73.7	28 19.3	+9.4	74.2	28 35.4	+10.5	74.7	28 50.9	+11.7	75.2	29 05.9	+12.8	75.8	29 20.4	+13.9	76.3	22
23	27 34.0	+5.4	71.6	27 52.7	+6.6	72.1	28 11.0	+7.7	72.6	28 28.7	+8.8	73.1	28 45.9	+9.9	73.6	29 02.6	+11.0	74.1	29 18.7	+12.2	74.7	29 34.3	+13.3	75.2	23
24	27 39.4	+5.0	70.4	27 59.3	+6.0	70.9	28 18.7	+7.1	71.4	28 37.5	+8.3	71.9	28 55.8	+9.4	72.5	29 13.6	+10.5	73.0	29 30.9	+11.6	73.5	29 47.6	+12.8	74.1	24
25	27 44.4	+4.3	69.3	28 05.3	+5.5	69.8	28 25.8	+6.6	70.3	28 45.8	+7.7	70.8	29 05.2	+8.8	71.3	29 24.1	+10.0	71.9	29 42.5	+11.1	72.4	30 00.4	+12.2	73.0	25
26	27 48.7	+3.9	68.2	28 10.8	+4.9	68.7	28 32.4	+6.0	69.2	28 53.5	+7.1	69.7	29 14.0	+8.3	70.2	29 34.1	+9.3	70.7	29 53.6	+10.5	71.3	30 12.6	+11.6	71.8	26
27	27 52.6	+3.2	67.0	28 15.7	+4.4	67.5	28 38.4	+5.4	68.0	29 00.6	+6.5	68.6	29 22.3	+7.6	69.1	29 43.4	+8.8	69.6	30 04.1	+9.9	70.1	30 24.2	+11.0	70.7	27
28	27 55.8	+2.7	65.9	28 20.1	+3.8	66.4	28 43.8	+4.9	66.9	29 07.1	+6.0	67.4	29 29.9	+7.1	67.9	29 52.2	+8.2	68.5	30 14.0	+9.3	69.0	30 35.2	+10.4	69.6	28
29	27 58.5	+2.2	64.8	28 23.9	+3.2	65.3	28 48.7	+4.3	65.8	29 13.1	+5.4	66.3	29 37.0	+6.5	66.8	30 00.4	+7.6	67.3	30 23.3	+8.7	67.9	30 45.6	+9.8	68.4	29
30	28 00.7	+1.6	63.7	28 27.1	+2.7	64.1	28 53.0	+3.8	64.6	29 18.5	+4.8	65.1	29 43.5	+5.9	65.6	30 08.0	+7.0	66.2	30 32.0	+8.1	66.7	30 55.4	+9.2	67.3	30
31	28 02.3	+1.1	62.5	28 29.8	+2.1	63.0	28 56.8	+3.1	63.5	29 23.3	+4.3	64.0	29 49.4	+5.3	64.5	30 15.0	+6.4	65.0	30 40.1	+7.4	65.6	31 04.6	+8.6	66.1	31
32	28 03.4	+0.4	61.4	28 31.9	+1.5	61.9	28 59.9	+2.6	62.3	29 27.6	+3.6	62.8	29 54.7	+4.7	63.4	30 21.4	+5.7	63.9	30 47.5	+6.9	64.4	31 13.2	+8.0	64.9	32
33	28 03.8	0.0	60.3	28 33.4	+1.0	60.7	29 02.5	+2.0	61.2	29 31.2	+3.0	61.7	29 59.4	+4.1	62.2	30 27.1	+5.2	62.7	30 54.4	+6.2	63.2	31 21.2	+7.3	63.8	33
34	28 03.8	-0.7	59.1	28 34.4	+0.3	59.6	29 04.5	+1.4	60.1	29 34.2	+2.5	60.6	30 03.5	+3.5	61.1	30 32.3	+4.6	61.6	31 00.6	+5.7	62.1	31 28.5	+6.7	62.6	34
35	28 03.1	-1.1	58.0	28 34.7	-0.1	58.4	29 05.9	+0.9	58.9	29 36.7	+1.9	59.4	30 07.0	+2.9	59.9	30 36.9	+3.9	60.4	31 06.3	+5.0	60.9	31 35.2	+6.0	61.5	35
36	28 02.0	-1.8	56.9	28 34.6	-0.8	57.3	29 06.8	+0.2	57.8	29 38.6	+1.2	58.3	30 09.9	+2.3	58.7	30 40.8	+3.3	59.2	31 11.3	+4.3	59.8	31 41.2	+5.5	60.3	36
37	28 00.2	-2.3	55.7	28 33.8	-1.3	56.2	29 07.0	-0.3	56.6	29 39.8	+0.7	57.1	30 12.2	+1.7	57.6	30 44.1	+2.7	58.1	31 15.6	+3.8	58.6	31 46.7	+4.7	59.1	37
38	27 57.9	-2.8	54.6	28 32.5	-1.9	55.0	29 06.7	-0.9	55.5	29 40.5	+0.1	55.9	30 13.9	+1.0	56.4	30 46.8	+2.1	56.9	31 19.4	+3.1	57.4	31 51.4	+4.2	57.9	38
39	27 55.1	-3.4	53.5	28 30.6	-2.5	53.9	29 05.8	-1.5	54.3	29 40.6	-0.6	54.8	30 14.9	+0.5	55.3	30 48.9	+1.5	55.8	31 22.5	+2.4	56.3	31 55.6	+3.4	56.8	39
40	27 51.7	-4.0	52.3	28 28.1	-3.0	52.8	29 04.3	-2.1	53.2	29 40.0	-1.1	53.6	30 15.4	-0.2	54.1	30 50.4	+0.8	54.6	31 24.9	+1.8	55.1	31 59.0	+2.9	55.6	40
41	27 47.7	-4.5	51.2	28 25.1	-3.6	51.6	29 02.2	-2.7	52.1	29 38.9	-1.7	52.5	30 15.2	-0.7	53.0	30 51.2	+0.2	53.4	31 26.7	+1.2	53.9	32 01.9	+2.1	54.4	41
42	27 43.2	-5.1	50.1	28 21.5	-4.1	50.5	28 59.5	-3.2	50.9	29 37.2	-2.3	51.3	30 14.5	-1.4	51.8	30 51.4	-0.4	52.3	31 27.9	+0.6	52.7	32 04.0	+1.6	53.2	42
43	27 38.1	-5.6	49.0	28 17.4	-4.7	49.4	28 56.3	-3.8	49.8	29 34.9	-2.9	50.2	30 13.1	-2.0	50.6	30 51.0	-1.1	51.1	31 28.5	-0.1	51.6	32 05.6	+0.8	52.1	43
44	27 32.5	-6.1	47.8	28 12.7	-5.3	48.2	28 52.5	-4.4	48.6	29 32.0	-3.5	49.0	30 11.1	-2.6	49.5	30 49.9	-1.6	49.9	31 28.4	-0.8	50.4	32 06.4	+0.2	50.9	44
45	27 26.4	-6.7	46.7	28 07.4	-5.8	47.1	28 48.1	-5.0	47.5	29 28.5	-4.1	47.9	30 08.5	-3.2	48.3	30 48.3	-2.3	48.8	31 27.6	-1.4	49.2	32 06.6	-0.4	49.7	45
46	27 19.7	-7.2	45.6	28 01.6	-6.4	46.0	28 43.1	-5.5	46.4	29 24.4	-4.7	46.8	30 05.3	-3.8	47.2	30 46.0	-3.0	47.6	31 26.2	-2.0	48.1	32 06.2	-1.1	48.5	46
47	27 12.5	-7.7	44.5	27 55.2	-6.9	44.8	28 37.6	-6.1	45.2	29 19.7	-5.2	45.6	30 01.5	-4.4	46.0	30 43.0	-3.5	46.4	31 24.2	-2.6	46.9	32 05.1	-1.8	47.3	47
48	27 04.8	-8.3	43.4	27 48.3	-7.5	43.7	28 31.5	-6.7	44.1	29 14.5	-5.9	44.5	29 57.1	-5.0	44.9	30 39.5	-4.2	45.3	31 21.6	-3.3	45.7	32 03.3	-2.4	46.2	48
49	26 56.5	-8.8	42.2	27 40.8	-8.0	42.6	28 24.8	-7.2	43.0	29 08.6	-6.4	43.3	29 52.1	-5.6	43.7	30 35.3	-4.7	44.1	31 18.3	-4.0	44.5	32 00.9	-3.1	45.0	49
50	26 47.7	-9.3	41.1	27 32.8	-8.6	41.5	28 17.6	-7.8	41.8	29 02.2	-7.0	42.2	29 46.5	-6.2	42.6	30 30.6	-5.4	43.0	31 14.3	-4.5	43.4	31 57.8	-3.7	43.8	50
51	26 38.4	-9.8	40.0	27 24.2	-9.0	40.4	28 09.8	-8.3	40.7	28 55.2	-7.5	41.1	29 40.3	-6.8	41.4	30 25.2	-6.0	41.8	31 09.8	-5.2	42.2	31 54.1	-4.4	42.6	51
52	26 28.6	-10.3	38.9	27 15.2	-9.6	39.2	28 01.5	-8.8	39.6	28 47.7	-8.2	39.9	29 33.5	-7.3	40.3	30 19.2	-6.6	40.7	31 04.6	-5.8	41.0	31 49.7	-5.0	41.5	52
53	26 18.3	-10.9	37.8	27 05.6	-10.2	38.1	27 52.7	-9.5	38.5	28 39.5	-8.7	38.8	29 26.2	-8.0	39.1	30 12.6	-7.2	39.5	30 58.8	-6.5	39.9	31 44.7	-5.7	40.3	53
54	26 07.4	-11.3	36.7	26 55.4	-10.6	37.0	27 43.2	-9.9	37.3	28 30.8	-9.2	37.7	29 18.2	-8.5	38.0	30 05.4	-7.8	38.4	30 52.3	-7.0	38.7	31 39.0	-6.3	39.1	54
55	25 56.1	-11.8	35.6	26 44.8	-11.2	35.9	27 33.3	-10.5	36.2	28 21.6	-9.8	36.5	29 09.7	-9.1	36.9	29 57.6	-8.4	37.2	30 45.3	-7.7	37.6	31 32.7	-6.9	37.9	55
56	25 44.3	-12.3	34.5	26 33.6	-11.6	34.8	27 22.8	-11.0	35.1	28 11.8	-10.3	35.4	29 00.6	-9.7	35.7	29 49.2	-9.0	36.1	30 37.6	-8.3	36.4	31 25.8	-7.6	36.8	56
57	25 32.0	-12.8	33.5	26 22.0	-12.2	33.7	27 11.8	-11.5	34.0	28 01.5	-10.9	34.3	28 50.9	-10.2	34.6	29 40.2	-9.5	34.9	30 29.3	-8.9	35.3	31 18.2	-8.2	35.6	57
58	25 19.2	-13.2	32.4	26 09.8	-12.6	32.6	27 00.3	-12.0	32.9	27 50.6	-11.4	33.2	28 40.7	-10.8	33.5	29 30.7	-10.2	33.8	30 20.4	-9.5	34.1	31 10.0	-8.8	34.5	58
59	25 06.0	-13.7	31.3	25 57.2	-13.1	31.6	26 48.3	-12.6	31.8	27 39.2	-12.0	32.1	28 29.9	-11.3	32.4	29 20.5	-10.7	32.7	30 10.9	-10.0	33.0	31 01.2	-9.5	33.3	59
60	24 52.3	-14.2	30.2	25 44.1	-13.7	30.5	26 35.7	-13.0	30.7	27 27.2	-12.4	31.0	28 18.6	-11.9	31.3	29 09.8	-11.3	31.5	30 00.9	-10.7	31.8	30 51.7	-10.0	32.1	60
61	24 38.1	-14.6	29.2	25 30.4	-14.0	29.4	26 22.7	-13.6	29.6	27 14.8	-13.0	29.9	28 06.7	-12.4	30.1	28 58.5	-11.8	30.4	29 50.2	-11.2	30.7	30 41.7	-10.6	31.0	61
62	24 23.5	-15.1	28.1	25 16.4	-14.6	28.3	26 09.1	-14.0	28.5	27 01.8	-13.5	28.8	27 54.3	-12.9	29.0	28 46.7	-12.4	29.3	29 39.0	-11.9	29.6	30 31.1	-11.3	29.9	62
63	24 08.4	-15.5	27.0	25 01.8	-15.0	27.2	25 55.1	-14.5	27.5	26 48.3	-14.0	27.7	27 41.4	-13.5	27.9	28 34.3	-12.9	28.2	29 27.1	-12.3	28.4	30 19.8	-11.8	28.7	63
64	23 52.9	-15.9	26.0	24 46.8	-15.5	26.2	25 40.6	-15.0	26.4	26 34.3	-14.5	26.6	27 27.9	-14.0	26.8	28 21.4	-13.5	27.1	29 14.8	-13.0	27.3	30 08.0	-12.4	27.6	64
65	23 37.0	-16.4	24.9	24 31.3	-15.9	25.1	25 25.6	-15.4	25.3	26 19.8	-14.9	25.5	27 13.9	-14.5	25.7	28 07.9	-14.0	26.0	29 01.8	-13.5	26.2	29 55.6	-13.0	26.5	65
66	23 20.6	-16.8	23.9	24 15.4	-16.3	24.1	25 10.2	-15.9	24.2	26 04.9	-15.5	24.4	26 59.4	-15.0	24.6	27 53.9	-14.5	24.9	28 48.3	-14.0	25.1	29 42.6	-13.6	25.3	66
67	23 03.8	-17.2	22.8	23 59.1	-16.8	23.0	24 54.3	-16.4	23.2	25 49.4	-15.9	23.4	26 44.4	-15.4	23.6	27 39.4	-15.0	23.8	28 34.3	-14.6	24.0	29 29.0	-14.1	24.2	67
68	22 46.6	-17.6	21.8	23 42.3	-17.2	21.9	24 37.9	-16.8	22.1	25 33.5	-16.4	22.3	26 29.0	-16.0	22.5	27 24.4	-15.6	22.7	28 19.7	-15.1	22.9	29 14.9	-14.7	23.1	68
69	22 29.0	-18.0	20.8	23 25.1	-17.6	20.9	24 21.1	-17.2	21.1	25 17.1	-16.8	21.2	26 13.0	-16.5	21.4	27 08.8	-16.0	21.6	28 04.6	-15.7	21.8	29 00.2	-15.2	22.0	69
70	22 11.0	-18.3	19.7	23 07.5	-18.0	19.9	24 03.9	-17.7	20.0	25 00.3	-17.3	20.2	25 56.5	-16.9	20.3	26 52.8	-16.6	20.5	27 48.9	-16.1	20.7	28 45.0	-15.7	20.9	70
71	21 52.7	-18.8	18.7	22 49.5	-18.4	18.8	23 46.2	-18.0	19.0	24 43.0	-17.8	19.1	25 39.6	-17.4	19.3	26 36.2	-17.0	19.4	27 32.8	-16.7	19.6	28 29.3	-16.3	19.8	71
72	21 33.9	-19.1	17.7	22 31.1	-18.9	17.8	23 28.2	-18.5	17.9	24 25.2	-18.1	18.1	25 22.2	-17.8	18.2	26 19.2	-17.5	18.4	27 16.1	-17.1	18.5	28 13.0	-16.8	18.7	72
73	21 14.8	-19.5	16.7	22 12.2	-19.2	16.8	23 09.7	-18.9	16.9	24 07.1	-18.6	17.0	25 04.4	-18.3	17.2	26 01.7	-17.9	17.3	26 59.0	-17.6	17.4	27 56.2	-17.3	17.6	73
74	20 55.3	-19.9	15.6	21 53.0	-19.5	15.7	22 50.8	-19.3	15.9	23 48.5	-19.0	16.0	24 46.1	-18.7	16.1	25 43.8	-18.5	16.2	26 41.4	-18.2	16.4	27 38.9	-17.8	16.5	74
75	20 35.4	-20.2	14.6	21 33.5	-20.0	14.7	22 31.5	-19.7	14.8	23 29.5	-19.5	14.9	24 27.4	-19.1	15.1	25 25.3	-18.8	15.2	26 23.2	-18.6	15.3	27 21.1	-18.3	15.4	75
76	20 15.2	-20.5	13.6	21 13.5	-20.3	13.7	22 11.8	-20.1	13.8	23 10.0	-19.8	13.9	24 08.3	-19.6	14.0	25 06.5	-19.3	14.1	26 04.6	-19.0	14.2	27 02.8	-18.8	14.4	76
77	19 54.7	-20.9	12.6	20 53.2	-20.6	12.7	21 51.7	-20.4	12.8	22 50.2	-20.2	12.9	23 48.7	-20.0	13.0	24 47.2	-19.8	13.1	25 45.6	-19.5	13.2	26 44.0	-19.3	13.3	77
78	19 33.8	-21.2	11.6	20 32.6	-21.0	11.7	21 31.3	-20.8	11.8	22 30.0	-20.6	11.9	23 28.7	-20.3	12.0	24 27.4	-20.1	12.0	25 26.1	-20.0	12.1	26 24.7	-19.7	12.2	78
79	19 12.6	-21.5	10.6	20 11.6	-21.4	10.7	21 10.5	-21.2	10.8	22 09.4	-20.9	10.8	23 08.4	-20.8	10.9	24 07.3	-20.6	11.0	25 06.1	-20.3	11.1	26 05.0	-20.2	11.2	79
80	18 51.1	-21.9	9.6	19 50.2	-21.7	9.7	20 49.3	-21.5	9.8	21 48.5	-21.4	9.8	22 47.6	-21.2	9.9	23 46.7	-21.0	10.0	24 45.8	-20.8	10.1	25 44.8	-20.6	10.1	80
81	18 29.2	-22.1	8.7	19 28.5	-22.0	8.7	20 27.8	-21.8	8.8	21 27.1	-21.7	8.8	22 26.4	-21.5	8.9	23 25.7	-21.4	9.0	24 25.0	-21.3	9.0	25 24.2	-21.1	9.1	81
82	18 07.1	-22.4	7.7	19 06.5	-22.3	7.7	20 06.0	-22.2	7.8	21 05.4	-22.0	7.8	22 04.9	-21.9	7.9	23 04.3	-21.8	7.9	24 03.7	-21.6	8.0	25 03.1	-21.5	8.1	82
83	17 44.7	-22.8	6.7	18 44.2	-22.6	6.8	19 43.8	-22.5	6.8	20 43.4	-22.4	6.8	21 43.0	-22.3	6.9	22 42.5	-22.1	6.9	23 42.1	-22.0	7.0	24 41.6	-21.9	7.0	83
84	17 21.9	-23.0	5.7	18 21.6	-22.9	5.8	19 21.3	-22.8	5.8	20 21.0	-22.7	5.8	21 20.7	-22.6	5.9	22 20.4	-22.5	5.9	23 20.1	-22.5	6.0	24 19.7	-22.3	6.0	84
85	16 58.9	-23.2	4.8	17 58.7	-23.2	4.8	18 58.5	-23.1	4.8	19 58.3	-23.0	4.9	20 58.1	-23.0	4.9	21 57.9	-22.9	4.9	22 57.6	-22.8	5.0	23 57.4	-22.7	5.0	85
86	16 35.7	-23.6	3.8	17 35.5	-23.5	3.8	18 35.4	-23.4	3.9	19 35.3	-23.4	3.9	20 35.1	-23.3	3.9	21 35.0	-23.3	3.9	22 34.8	-23.1	4.0	23 34.7	-23.1	4.0	86
87	16 12.1	-23.8	2.9	17 12.0	-23.7	2.9	18 12.0	-23.7	2.9	19 11.9	-23.7	2.9	20 11.8	-23.6	2.9	21 11.7	-23.5	2.9	22 11.7	-23.6	3.0	23 11.6	-23.5	3.0	87
88	15 48.3	-24.0	1.9	16 48.3	-24.0	1.9	17 48.3	-24.0	1.9	18 48.2	-23.9	1.9	19 48.2	-23.9	1.9	20 48.2	-24.0	2.0	21 48.1	-23.9	2.0	22 48.1	-23.9	2.0	88
89	15 24.3	-24.3	0.9	16 24.3	-24.3	1.0	17 24.3	-24.3	1.0	18 24.3	-24.3	1.0	19 24.3	-24.3	1.0	20 24.2	-24.2	1.0	21 24.2	-24.2	1.0	22 24.2	-24.2	1.0	89
90	15 00.0	-24.5	0.0	16 00.0	-24.5	0.0	17 00.0	-24.5	0.0	18 00.0	-24.5	0.0	19 00.0	-24.6	0.0	20 00.0	-24.6	0.0	21 00.0	-24.6	0.0	22 00.0	-24.6	0.0	90
	15°			16°			17°			18°			19°			20°			21°			22°			

LATITUDE CONTRARY NAME TO DECLINATION — L.H.A. 66°, 294°

Dec.	15° Hc	d	Z	16° Hc	d	Z	17° Hc	d	Z	18° Hc	d	Z	19° Hc	d	Z	20° Hc	d	Z	21° Hc	d	Z	22° Hc	d	Z	Dec.
°	° ′	′	°	° ′	′	°	° ′	′	°	° ′	′	°	° ′	′	°	° ′	′	°	° ′	′	°	° ′	′	°	°
0	23 08.0	−17.1	96.6	23 00.9	−18.1	97.0	22 53.4	−19.2	97.4	22 45.4	−20.3	97.8	22 37.0	−21.3	98.2	22 28.2	−22.4	98.7	22 19.0	−23.4	99.1	22 09.3	−24.4	99.5	0
1	22 50.9	−17.5	97.6	22 42.8	−18.6	98.0	22 34.2	−19.7	98.4	22 25.1	−20.6	98.9	22 15.7	−21.7	99.3	22 05.8	−22.7	99.7	21 55.6	−23.8	100.1	21 44.9	−24.8	100.5	1
2	22 33.4	−17.9	98.7	22 24.2	−19.0	99.1	22 14.5	−20.0	99.5	22 04.5	−21.1	99.9	21 54.0	−22.1	100.3	21 43.1	−23.1	100.7	21 31.8	−24.1	101.0	21 20.1	−25.1	101.4	2
3	22 15.5	−18.2	99.7	22 05.2	−19.3	100.1	21 54.5	−20.4	100.5	21 43.4	−21.4	100.9	21 31.9	−22.5	101.3	21 20.0	−23.5	101.7	21 07.7	−24.5	102.0	20 55.0	−25.5	102.4	3
4	21 57.3	−18.7	100.7	21 45.9	−19.7	101.1	21 34.1	−20.7	101.5	21 22.0	−21.8	101.9	21 09.4	−22.8	102.3	20 56.5	−23.8	102.6	20 43.2	−24.8	103.0	20 29.5	−25.8	103.4	4
5	21 38.6	−19.1	101.7	21 26.2	−20.1	102.1	21 13.4	−21.1	102.5	21 00.2	−22.1	102.9	20 46.6	−23.1	103.3	20 32.7	−24.1	103.6	20 18.4	−25.1	104.0	20 03.7	−26.1	104.3	5
6	21 19.5	−19.4	102.8	21 06.1	−20.4	103.1	20 52.3	−21.5	103.5	20 38.1	−22.5	103.9	20 23.5	−23.5	104.2	20 08.6	−24.5	104.6	19 53.3	−25.5	104.9	19 37.6	−26.4	105.3	6
7	21 00.1	−19.7	103.8	20 45.7	−20.8	104.1	20 30.8	−21.8	104.5	20 15.6	−22.8	104.9	20 00.0	−23.7	105.2	19 44.1	−24.7	105.6	19 27.8	−25.7	105.9	19 11.2	−26.7	106.2	7
8	20 40.4	−20.1	104.8	20 24.9	−21.1	105.1	20 09.0	−22.1	105.5	19 52.8	−23.1	105.8	19 36.3	−24.1	106.2	19 19.4	−25.1	106.5	19 02.1	−26.0	106.9	18 44.5	−26.9	107.2	8
9	20 20.3	−20.5	105.8	20 03.8	−21.5	106.1	19 46.9	−22.4	106.5	19 29.7	−23.4	106.8	19 12.2	−24.4	107.2	18 54.3	−25.4	107.5	18 36.1	−26.3	107.8	18 17.6	−27.3	108.1	9
10	19 59.8	−20.8	106.8	19 42.3	−21.8	107.1	19 24.5	−22.8	107.5	19 06.3	−23.8	107.8	18 47.8	−24.7	108.1	18 28.9	−25.6	108.5	18 09.8	−26.6	108.8	17 50.3	−27.5	109.1	10
11	19 39.0	−21.1	107.8	19 20.5	−22.1	108.1	19 01.7	−23.1	108.5	18 42.5	−24.0	108.8	18 23.1	−25.0	109.1	18 03.3	−25.9	109.4	17 43.2	−26.9	109.7	17 22.8	−27.8	110.0	11
12	19 17.9	−21.5	108.8	18 58.4	−22.4	109.1	18 38.6	−23.4	109.4	18 18.5	−24.3	109.7	17 58.1	−25.3	110.0	17 37.4	−26.2	110.4	17 16.3	−27.1	110.6	16 55.0	−28.0	110.9	12
13	18 56.4	−21.7	109.8	18 36.0	−22.7	110.1	18 15.2	−23.6	110.4	17 54.2	−24.6	110.7	17 32.8	−25.5	111.0	17 11.2	−26.5	111.3	16 49.2	−27.3	111.6	16 27.0	−28.2	111.9	13
14	18 34.7	−22.1	110.7	18 13.3	−23.1	111.1	17 51.6	−24.0	111.4	17 29.6	−24.9	111.7	17 07.3	−25.8	111.9	16 44.7	−26.7	112.2	16 21.9	−27.6	112.5	15 58.8	−28.5	112.8	14
15	18 12.6	−22.4	111.7	17 50.2	−23.3	112.0	17 27.6	−24.2	112.3	17 04.7	−25.2	112.6	16 41.5	−26.1	112.9	16 18.0	−27.0	113.2	15 54.3	−27.9	113.4	15 30.3	−28.7	113.7	15
16	17 50.2	−22.6	112.7	17 26.9	−23.5	113.0	17 03.4	−24.5	113.3	16 39.5	−25.4	113.6	16 15.4	−26.3	113.8	15 51.0	−27.2	114.1	15 26.4	−28.1	114.4	15 01.6	−29.0	114.6	16
17	17 27.6	−22.9	113.7	17 03.4	−23.9	114.0	16 38.9	−24.8	114.2	16 14.1	−25.7	114.5	15 49.1	−26.6	114.8	15 23.8	−27.4	115.0	14 58.3	−28.2	115.3	14 32.6	−29.1	115.5	17
18	17 04.7	−23.2	114.6	16 39.5	−24.1	114.9	16 14.1	−25.0	115.2	15 48.4	−25.9	115.4	15 22.5	−26.7	115.7	14 56.4	−27.6	115.9	14 30.1	−28.5	116.2	14 03.5	−29.4	116.4	18
19	16 41.5	−23.5	115.6	16 15.4	−24.4	115.9	15 49.1	−25.3	116.1	15 22.5	−26.1	116.4	14 55.8	−27.0	116.6	14 28.8	−27.9	116.9	14 01.6	−28.7	117.1	13 34.1	−29.5	117.3	19
20	16 18.0	−23.7	116.6	15 51.0	−24.6	116.8	15 23.8	−25.5	117.1	14 56.4	−26.3	117.3	14 28.8	−27.2	117.5	14 00.9	−28.0	117.8	13 32.9	−28.9	118.0	13 04.6	−29.7	118.2	20
21	15 54.3	−24.0	117.5	15 26.4	−24.8	117.8	14 58.3	−25.7	118.0	14 30.1	−26.6	118.2	14 01.6	−27.5	118.5	13 32.9	−28.3	118.7	13 04.0	−29.1	118.9	12 34.9	−29.9	119.1	21
22	15 30.3	−24.3	118.5	15 01.6	−25.1	118.7	14 32.6	−25.9	118.9	14 03.5	−26.8	119.2	13 34.1	−27.6	119.4	13 04.6	−28.4	119.6	12 34.9	−29.3	119.8	12 05.0	−30.1	120.0	22
23	15 06.0	−24.4	119.4	14 36.5	−25.4	119.7	14 06.7	−26.2	119.9	13 36.7	−27.0	120.1	13 06.5	−27.8	120.3	12 36.2	−28.7	120.5	12 05.6	−29.4	120.7	11 34.9	−30.2	120.9	23
24	14 41.6	−24.7	120.4	14 11.1	−25.5	120.6	13 40.5	−26.4	120.8	13 09.7	−27.2	121.0	12 38.7	−28.0	121.2	12 07.5	−28.8	121.4	11 36.2	−29.6	121.6	11 04.7	−30.4	121.7	24
25	14 16.9	−24.9	121.3	13 45.6	−25.7	121.5	13 14.1	−26.5	121.7	12 42.5	−27.4	121.9	12 10.7	−28.2	122.1	11 38.7	−28.9	122.3	11 06.6	−29.8	122.5	10 34.3	−30.5	122.6	25
26	13 52.0	−25.1	122.2	13 19.9	−26.0	122.5	12 47.6	−26.8	122.6	12 15.1	−27.5	122.8	11 42.5	−28.3	123.0	11 09.8	−29.2	123.2	10 36.8	−29.9	123.3	10 03.8	−30.7	123.5	26
27	13 26.9	−25.4	123.2	12 53.9	−26.1	123.4	12 20.8	−26.9	123.6	11 47.6	−27.7	123.7	11 14.2	−28.5	123.9	10 40.6	−29.2	124.1	10 06.9	−30.0	124.2	9 33.1	−30.7	124.4	27
28	13 01.5	−25.5	124.1	12 27.8	−26.3	124.3	11 53.9	−27.1	124.5	11 19.9	−27.9	124.6	10 45.7	−28.7	124.8	10 11.4	−29.5	125.0	9 36.9	−30.2	125.1	9 02.4	−31.0	125.2	28
29	12 36.0	−25.7	125.0	12 01.5	−26.5	125.2	11 26.8	−27.3	125.4	10 52.0	−28.1	125.6	10 17.0	−28.8	125.7	9 41.9	−29.5	125.8	9 06.7	−30.3	126.0	8 31.4	−31.0	126.1	29
30	12 10.3	−25.9	126.0	11 35.0	−26.7	126.1	10 59.5	−27.4	126.3	10 23.9	−28.2	126.5	9 48.2	−28.9	126.6	9 12.4	−29.7	126.7	8 36.4	−30.4	126.9	8 00.4	−31.1	127.0	30
31	11 44.4	−26.1	126.9	11 08.3	−26.9	127.1	10 32.1	−27.6	127.2	9 55.7	−28.3	127.3	9 19.3	−29.1	127.5	8 42.7	−29.8	127.6	8 06.0	−30.5	127.7	7 29.3	−31.3	127.8	31
32	11 18.3	−26.3	127.8	10 41.4	−27.0	128.0	10 04.5	−27.8	128.1	9 27.4	−28.5	128.2	8 50.2	−29.2	128.4	8 12.9	−29.9	128.5	7 35.5	−30.6	128.6	6 58.0	−31.3	128.7	32
33	10 52.0	−26.4	128.7	10 14.4	−27.1	128.9	9 36.7	−27.9	129.0	8 58.9	−28.6	129.1	8 21.0	−29.3	129.3	7 43.0	−30.0	129.4	7 04.9	−30.7	129.5	6 26.7	−31.4	129.6	33
34	10 25.6	−26.6	129.6	9 47.3	−27.3	129.8	9 08.8	−28.0	129.9	8 30.3	−28.7	130.0	7 51.7	−29.5	130.1	7 13.0	−30.2	130.2	6 34.2	−30.8	130.3	5 55.3	−31.5	130.4	34
35	9 59.0	−26.7	130.5	9 20.0	−27.4	130.7	8 40.8	−28.1	130.8	8 01.6	−28.9	130.9	7 22.2	−29.5	131.0	6 42.8	−30.2	131.1	6 03.4	−30.9	131.2	5 23.8	−31.6	131.3	35
36	9 32.3	−26.8	131.5	8 52.6	−27.6	131.6	8 12.7	−28.3	131.7	7 32.7	−28.9	131.8	6 52.7	−29.6	131.9	6 12.6	−30.3	132.0	5 32.5	−31.0	132.1	4 52.2	−31.6	132.1	36
37	9 05.5	−27.0	132.4	8 25.0	−27.7	132.5	7 44.4	−28.3	132.6	7 03.8	−29.0	132.7	6 23.1	−29.7	132.8	5 42.3	−30.4	132.8	5 01.5	−31.0	132.9	4 20.6	−31.7	133.0	37
38	8 38.5	−27.1	133.3	7 57.3	−27.8	133.4	7 16.1	−28.5	133.5	6 34.8	−29.2	133.6	5 53.4	−29.8	133.6	5 11.9	−30.4	133.7	4 30.5	−31.1	133.8	3 48.9	−31.7	133.8	38
39	8 11.4	−27.3	134.2	7 29.5	−27.9	134.3	6 47.6	−28.6	134.4	6 05.6	−29.2	134.4	5 23.6	−29.9	134.5	4 41.5	−30.5	134.6	3 59.4	−31.2	134.6	3 17.2	−31.8	134.7	39
40	7 44.1	−27.3	135.1	7 01.6	−28.0	135.2	6 19.0	−28.6	135.2	5 36.4	−29.3	135.3	4 53.7	−29.9	135.4	4 11.0	−30.6	135.4	3 28.2	−31.2	135.5	2 45.4	−31.8	135.5	40
41	7 16.8	−27.5	136.0	6 33.6	−28.1	136.1	5 50.4	−28.8	136.1	5 07.1	−29.4	136.2	4 23.8	−30.0	136.3	3 40.4	−30.6	136.3	2 57.0	−31.2	136.3	2 13.6	−31.8	136.4	41
42	6 49.3	−27.6	136.9	6 05.5	−28.2	136.9	5 21.6	−28.8	137.0	4 37.7	−29.4	137.1	3 53.8	−30.1	137.1	3 09.8	−30.7	137.2	2 25.8	−31.3	137.2	1 41.8	−31.9	137.2	42
43	6 21.7	−27.6	137.8	5 37.3	−28.3	137.8	4 52.8	−28.9	137.9	4 08.3	−29.5	137.9	3 23.7	−30.1	138.0	2 39.1	−30.7	138.0	1 54.5	−31.3	138.0	1 09.9	−31.9	138.1	43
44	5 54.1	−27.7	138.7	5 09.0	−28.3	138.7	4 23.9	−28.9	138.8	3 38.8	−29.6	138.8	2 53.6	−30.1	138.9	2 08.4	−30.7	138.9	1 23.2	−31.3	138.9	0 38.0	−31.9	138.9	44
45	5 26.4	−27.8	139.5	4 40.7	−28.4	139.6	3 55.0	−29.0	139.6	3 09.2	−29.5	139.7	2 23.5	−30.2	139.7	1 37.7	−30.7	139.7	0 51.9	−31.3	139.8	0 06.1	−31.9	139.8	45
46	4 58.6	−27.9	140.4	4 12.3	−28.5	140.5	3 26.0	−29.1	140.5	2 39.7	−29.7	140.6	1 53.3	−30.2	140.6	1 07.0	−30.8	140.6	0 20.6	−31.3	140.6	0 25.8	+31.9	39.4	46
47	4 30.7	−28.0	141.3	3 43.8	−28.5	141.4	2 56.9	−29.1	141.4	2 10.0	−29.6	141.4	1 23.1	−30.2	141.4	0 36.2	−30.8	141.5	0 10.7	+31.4	38.5	0 57.7	+31.8	38.5	47
48	4 02.7	−28.0	142.2	3 15.3	−28.6	142.2	2 27.8	−29.1	142.3	1 40.4	−29.7	142.3	0 52.9	−30.2	142.3	0 05.4	−30.8	142.3	0 42.1	+31.3	37.7	1 29.5	+31.9	37.7	48
49	3 34.7	−28.0	143.1	2 46.7	−28.6	143.1	1 58.7	−29.1	143.2	1 10.7	−29.7	143.2	0 22.7	−30.3	143.2	0 25.4	+30.7	36.8	1 13.4	+31.3	36.8	2 01.4	+31.8	36.8	49
50	3 06.7	−28.1	144.0	2 18.1	−28.6	144.0	1 29.6	−29.2	144.0	0 41.0	−29.7	144.0	0 07.6	+30.2	36.0	0 56.1	+30.8	36.0	1 44.7	+31.3	36.0	2 33.2	+31.8	36.0	50
51	2 38.6	−28.2	144.9	1 49.5	−28.7	144.9	1 00.4	−29.2	144.9	0 11.3	−29.7	144.9	0 37.8	+30.2	35.1	1 26.9	+30.7	35.1	2 16.0	+31.2	35.1	3 05.0	+31.8	35.2	51
52	2 10.4	−28.2	145.7	1 20.8	−28.7	145.8	0 31.2	−29.2	145.8	0 18.4	+29.7	34.2	1 08.0	+30.2	34.2	1 57.6	+30.7	34.2	2 47.2	+31.2	34.3	3 36.8	+31.7	34.3	52
53	1 42.2	−28.2	146.6	0 52.1	−28.7	146.6	0 02.0	−29.2	146.6	0 48.1	+29.7	33.4	1 38.2	+30.2	33.4	2 28.3	+30.7	33.4	3 18.4	+31.2	33.4	4 08.5	+31.6	33.5	53
54	1 14.0	−28.2	147.5	0 23.4	−28.7	147.5	0 27.2	+29.2	32.5	1 17.8	+29.7	32.5	2 08.4	+30.2	32.5	2 59.0	+30.6	32.5	3 49.6	+31.1	32.6	4 40.1	+31.6	32.6	54
55	0 45.8	−28.2	148.4	0 05.3	+28.7	31.6	0 56.4	+29.1	31.6	1 47.5	+29.6	31.6	2 38.6	+30.1	31.6	3 29.6	+30.6	31.7	4 20.7	+31.0	31.7	5 11.7	+31.5	31.7	55
56	0 17.6	−28.2	149.3	0 34.0	+28.7	30.7	1 25.5	+29.2	30.7	2 17.1	+29.6	30.7	3 08.7	+30.0	30.8	4 00.2	+30.6	30.8	4 51.7	+31.0	30.8	5 43.2	+31.5	30.9	56
57	0 10.6	+28.2	29.8	1 02.7	+28.6	29.8	1 54.7	+29.1	29.9	2 46.7	+29.6	29.9	3 38.7	+30.1	29.9	4 30.8	+30.4	29.9	5 22.7	+31.0	30.0	6 14.7	+31.4	30.0	57
58	0 38.8	+28.3	29.0	1 31.3	+28.7	29.0	2 23.8	+29.1	29.0	3 16.3	+29.5	29.0	4 08.8	+29.9	29.0	5 01.2	+30.4	29.1	5 53.7	+30.8	29.1	6 46.1	+31.2	29.2	58
59	1 07.1	+28.2	28.1	2 00.0	+28.6	28.1	2 52.9	+29.1	28.1	3 45.8	+29.5	28.1	4 38.7	+29.9	28.2	5 31.6	+30.4	28.2	6 24.5	+30.7	28.3	7 17.3	+31.2	28.3	59
60	1 35.3	+28.1	27.2	2 28.6	+28.6	27.2	3 22.0	+29.0	27.2	4 15.3	+29.4	27.3	5 08.6	+29.9	27.3	6 02.0	+30.2	27.3	6 55.2	+30.7	27.4	7 48.5	+31.1	27.5	60
61	2 03.4	+28.2	26.3	2 57.2	+28.6	26.3	3 51.0	+28.9	26.4	4 44.7	+29.4	26.4	5 38.5	+29.7	26.4	6 32.2	+30.2	26.5	7 25.9	+30.6	26.5	8 19.6	+30.9	26.6	61
62	2 31.6	+28.1	25.4	3 25.8	+28.5	25.4	4 19.9	+28.9	25.5	5 14.1	+29.3	25.5	6 08.2	+29.7	25.6	7 02.4	+30.0	25.6	7 56.5	+30.4	25.7	8 50.5	+30.9	25.7	62
63	2 59.7	+28.1	24.5	3 54.3	+28.4	24.6	4 48.8	+28.9	24.6	5 43.4	+29.2	24.6	6 37.9	+29.6	24.7	7 32.4	+30.0	24.7	8 26.9	+30.3	24.8	9 21.4	+30.7	24.9	63
64	3 27.8	+28.0	23.7	4 22.7	+28.4	23.7	5 17.7	+28.7	23.7	6 12.6	+29.1	23.8	7 07.5	+29.5	23.8	8 02.4	+29.8	23.9	8 57.2	+30.2	23.9	9 52.1	+30.5	24.0	64
65	3 55.8	+27.9	22.8	4 51.1	+28.3	22.8	5 46.4	+28.7	22.8	6 41.7	+29.0	22.9	7 37.0	+29.3	22.9	8 32.2	+29.7	23.0	9 27.4	+30.1	23.0	10 22.6	+30.5	23.1	65
66	4 23.7	+27.9	21.9	5 19.4	+28.3	21.9	6 15.1	+28.6	21.9	7 10.7	+28.9	22.0	8 06.3	+29.3	22.0	9 01.9	+29.6	22.1	9 57.5	+30.0	22.2	10 53.1	+30.3	22.2	66
67	4 51.6	+27.9	21.0	5 47.7	+28.1	21.0	6 43.7	+28.4	21.1	7 39.6	+28.8	21.1	8 35.6	+29.1	21.2	9 31.5	+29.5	21.2	10 27.5	+29.8	21.3	11 23.4	+30.1	21.4	67
68	5 19.5	+27.7	20.1	6 15.8	+28.1	20.1	7 12.1	+28.4	20.2	8 08.4	+28.7	20.2	9 04.7	+29.1	20.3	10 01.0	+29.3	20.3	10 57.3	+29.6	20.4	11 53.5	+29.9	20.5	68
69	5 47.2	+27.7	19.2	6 43.9	+28.0	19.2	7 40.5	+28.3	19.3	8 37.1	+28.6	19.3	9 33.8	+28.8	19.4	10 30.3	+29.2	19.4	11 26.9	+29.5	19.5	12 23.4	+29.8	19.6	69
70	6 14.9	+27.6	18.3	7 11.9	+27.8	18.4	8 08.8	+28.1	18.4	9 05.7	+28.5	18.4	10 02.6	+28.8	18.5	10 59.5	+29.0	18.6	11 56.4	+29.3	18.6	12 53.2	+29.6	18.7	70
71	6 42.5	+27.5	17.4	7 39.7	+27.8	17.5	8 36.9	+28.1	17.5	9 34.2	+28.3	17.6	10 31.4	+28.5	17.6	11 28.5	+28.9	17.7	12 25.7	+29.1	17.7	13 22.8	+29.5	17.8	71
72	7 10.0	+27.3	16.5	8 07.5	+27.6	16.6	9 05.0	+27.9	16.6	10 02.5	+28.1	16.7	10 59.9	+28.5	16.7	11 57.4	+28.7	16.8	12 54.8	+29.0	16.8	13 52.3	+29.2	16.9	72
73	7 37.3	+27.3	15.6	8 35.1	+27.5	15.7	9 32.9	+27.7	15.7	10 30.6	+28.0	15.8	11 28.4	+28.2	15.8	12 26.1	+28.5	15.9	13 23.8	+28.8	15.9	14 21.5	+29.0	16.0	73
74	8 04.6	+27.2	14.7	9 02.6	+27.4	14.8	10 00.6	+27.7	14.8	10 58.6	+27.9	14.9	11 56.6	+28.1	14.9	12 54.6	+28.3	15.0	13 52.6	+28.5	15.0	14 50.5	+28.8	15.1	74
75	8 31.8	+27.0	13.8	9 30.0	+27.3	13.9	10 28.3	+27.4	13.9	11 26.5	+27.7	14.0	12 24.7	+27.9	14.0	13 22.9	+28.2	14.1	14 21.1	+28.4	14.1	15 19.3	+28.6	14.2	75
76	8 58.8	+26.9	12.9	9 57.3	+27.1	13.0	10 55.7	+27.3	13.0	11 54.2	+27.5	13.1	12 52.6	+27.7	13.1	13 51.1	+27.9	13.2	14 49.5	+28.1	13.2	15 47.9	+28.3	13.3	76
77	9 25.7	+26.7	12.0	10 24.4	+26.9	12.1	11 23.0	+27.2	12.1	12 21.7	+27.3	12.1	13 20.3	+27.6	12.2	14 19.0	+27.7	12.2	15 17.6	+27.9	12.3	16 16.2	+28.1	12.4	77
78	9 52.4	+26.6	11.1	10 51.3	+26.8	11.2	11 50.2	+26.9	11.2	12 49.0	+27.2	11.2	13 47.9	+27.3	11.3	14 46.7	+27.5	11.3	15 45.5	+27.7	11.4	16 44.3	+27.9	11.4	78
79	10 19.0	+26.5	10.2	11 18.1	+26.6	10.2	12 17.1	+26.8	10.3	13 16.2	+26.9	10.3	14 15.2	+27.1	10.4	15 14.2	+27.3	10.4	16 13.2	+27.5	10.5	17 12.2	+27.6	10.5	79
80	10 45.5	+26.3	9.3	11 44.7	+26.4	9.3	12 43.9	+26.6	9.4	13 43.1	+26.7	9.4	14 42.3	+26.9	9.4	15 41.5	+27.0	9.5	16 40.7	+27.1	9.5	17 39.8	+27.4	9.6	80
81	11 11.8	+26.1	8.4	12 11.1	+26.3	8.4	13 10.5	+26.4	8.4	14 09.8	+26.6	8.5	15 09.2	+26.6	8.5	16 08.5	+26.8	8.6	17 07.8	+27.0	8.6	18 07.2	+27.0	8.6	81
82	11 37.9	+26.0	7.5	12 37.4	+26.1	7.5	13 36.9	+26.2	7.5	14 36.4	+26.3	7.5	15 35.8	+26.5	7.6	16 35.3	+26.6	7.6	17 34.8	+26.7	7.7	18 34.2	+26.8	7.7	82
83	12 03.9	+25.7	6.5	13 03.5	+25.8	6.6	14 03.1	+25.9	6.6	15 02.7	+26.1	6.6	16 02.3	+26.2	6.7	17 01.9	+26.3	6.7	18 01.5	+26.4	6.7	19 01.0	+26.5	6.8	83
84	12 29.6	+25.6	5.6	13 29.3	+25.7	5.6	14 29.0	+25.8	5.7	15 28.8	+25.8	5.7	16 28.5	+25.9	5.7	17 28.2	+26.0	5.7	18 27.9	+26.1	5.8	19 27.5	+26.3	5.8	84
85	12 55.2	+25.4	4.7	13 55.0	+25.5	4.7	14 54.8	+25.5	4.7	15 54.6	+25.6	4.7	16 54.4	+25.7	4.8	17 54.2	+25.7	4.8	18 54.0	+25.8	4.8	19 53.8	+25.9	4.9	85
86	13 20.6	+25.2	3.8	14 20.5	+25.2	3.8	15 20.3	+25.3	3.8	16 20.2	+25.3	3.8	17 20.1	+25.4	3.8	18 19.9	+25.5	3.8	19 19.8	+25.5	3.9	20 19.7	+25.5	3.9	86
87	13 45.8	+24.9	2.8	14 45.7	+25.0	2.8	15 45.6	+25.1	2.8	16 45.5	+25.1	2.9	17 45.5	+25.1	2.9	18 45.4	+25.2	2.9	19 45.3	+25.2	2.9	20 45.2	+25.3	2.9	87
88	14 10.7	+24.8	1.9	15 10.7	+24.8	1.9	16 10.7	+24.8	1.9	17 10.6	+24.9	1.9	18 10.6	+24.8	1.9	19 10.6	+24.8	1.9	20 10.5	+24.9	1.9	21 10.5	+24.9	2.0	88
89	14 35.5	+24.5	0.9	15 35.5	+24.5	0.9	16 35.5	+24.5	1.0	17 35.5	+24.5	1.0	18 35.4	+24.6	1.0	19 35.4	+24.6	1.0	20 35.4	+24.6	1.0	21 35.4	+24.6	1.0	89
90	15 00.0	+24.3	0.0	16 00.0	+24.3	0.0	17 00.0	+24.3	0.0	18 00.0	+24.3	0.0	19 00.0	+24.3	0.0	20 00.0	+24.2	0.0	21 00.0	+24.2	0.0	22 00.0	+24.2	0.0	90
	15°			16°			17°			18°			19°			20°			21°			22°			

S. Lat. {L.H.A. greater than 180° ....Zn=180°−Z; L.H.A. less than 180°...........Zn=180°+Z}

LATITUDE SAME NAME AS DECLINATION — L.H.A. 114°, 246°

67°, 293° L.H.A. LATITUDE SAME NAME AS DECLINATION

N. Lat. {L.H.A. greater than 180° .....Zn=Z / L.H.A. less than 180°.............Zn=360°-Z}

Dec.	15°			16°			17°			18°			19°			20°			21°			22°			Dec.
	Hc	d	Z	Hc	d	Z	Hc	d	Z	Hc	d	Z	Hc	d	Z	Hc	d	Z	Hc	d	Z	Hc	d	Z	
°	° ′	′	°	° ′	′	°	° ′	′	°	° ′	′	°	° ′	′	°	° ′	′	°	° ′	′	°	° ′	′	°	°
0	22 10.4	+16.6	96.3	22 03.7	+17.6	96.7	21 56.5	+18.7	97.1	21 48.9	+19.8	97.5	21 40.9	+20.8	97.9	21 32.5	+21.8	98.3	21 23.6	+23.0	98.6	21 14.4	+24.0	99.0	0
1	22 27.0	+16.2	95.2	22 21.3	+17.3	95.6	22 15.2	+18.3	96.0	22 08.7	+19.4	96.5	22 01.7	+20.5	96.9	21 54.3	+21.6	97.3	21 46.6	+22.5	97.7	21 38.4	+23.5	98.0	1
2	22 43.2	+15.7	94.2	22 38.6	+16.8	94.6	22 33.5	+18.0	95.0	22 28.1	+19.0	95.4	22 22.2	+20.1	95.8	22 15.9	+21.1	96.3	22 09.1	+22.2	96.7	22 01.9	+23.3	97.1	2
3	22 58.9	+15.4	93.1	22 55.4	+16.5	93.6	22 51.5	+17.5	94.0	22 47.1	+18.6	94.4	22 42.3	+19.7	94.8	22 37.0	+20.8	95.2	22 31.3	+21.8	95.7	22 25.2	+22.8	96.1	3
4	23 14.3	+14.9	92.1	23 11.9	+16.0	92.5	23 09.0	+17.1	92.9	23 05.7	+18.2	93.4	23 02.0	+19.2	93.8	22 57.8	+20.3	94.2	22 53.1	+21.5	94.6	22 48.0	+22.5	95.1	4
5	23 29.2	+14.5	91.0	23 27.9	+15.6	91.5	23 26.1	+16.7	91.9	23 23.9	+17.8	92.3	23 21.2	+18.9	92.8	23 18.1	+20.0	93.2	23 14.6	+21.0	93.6	23 10.5	+22.1	94.1	5
6	23 43.7	+14.1	90.0	23 43.5	+15.2	90.4	23 42.8	+16.3	90.9	23 41.7	+17.4	91.3	23 40.1	+18.5	91.7	23 38.1	+19.6	92.2	23 35.6	+20.6	92.6	23 32.6	+21.7	93.0	6
7	23 57.8	+13.6	88.9	23 58.7	+14.7	89.4	23 59.1	+15.9	89.8	23 59.1	+17.0	90.2	23 58.6	+18.1	90.7	23 57.7	+19.1	91.1	23 56.2	+20.3	91.6	23 54.3	+21.3	92.0	7
8	24 11.4	+13.2	87.8	24 13.4	+14.3	88.3	24 15.0	+15.4	88.7	24 16.1	+16.5	89.2	24 16.7	+17.6	89.6	24 16.8	+18.7	90.1	24 16.5	+19.8	90.5	24 15.6	+20.9	91.0	8
9	24 24.6	+12.7	86.8	24 27.7	+13.9	87.2	24 30.4	+14.9	87.7	24 32.6	+16.0	88.1	24 34.3	+17.2	88.6	24 35.5	+18.3	89.1	24 36.3	+19.3	89.5	24 36.5	+20.5	90.0	9
10	24 37.3	+12.3	85.7	24 41.6	+13.4	86.2	24 45.3	+14.6	86.6	24 48.6	+15.7	87.1	24 51.5	+16.7	87.5	24 53.8	+17.8	88.0	24 55.6	+19.0	88.5	24 57.0	+20.0	88.9	10
11	24 49.6	+11.8	84.6	24 55.0	+12.9	85.1	24 59.9	+14.0	85.5	25 04.3	+15.1	86.0	25 08.2	+16.3	86.5	25 11.6	+17.4	87.0	25 14.6	+18.5	87.4	25 17.0	+19.6	87.9	11
12	25 01.4	+11.3	83.5	25 07.9	+12.4	84.0	25 13.9	+13.6	84.5	25 19.4	+14.7	84.9	25 24.5	+15.8	85.4	25 29.0	+17.0	85.9	25 33.1	+18.0	86.4	25 36.6	+19.2	86.8	12
13	25 12.7	+10.9	82.5	25 20.3	+12.0	82.9	25 27.5	+13.1	83.4	25 34.1	+14.3	83.9	25 40.3	+15.3	84.3	25 46.0	+16.4	84.8	25 51.1	+17.6	85.3	25 55.8	+18.6	85.8	13
14	25 23.6	+10.3	81.4	25 32.3	+11.5	81.8	25 40.6	+12.6	82.3	25 48.4	+13.7	82.8	25 55.6	+14.9	83.3	26 02.4	+16.0	83.8	26 08.7	+17.1	84.2	26 14.4	+18.3	84.7	14
15	25 33.9	+9.9	80.3	25 43.8	+11.0	80.8	25 53.2	+12.2	81.2	26 02.1	+13.3	81.7	26 10.5	+14.4	82.2	26 18.4	+15.5	82.7	26 25.8	+16.6	83.2	26 32.7	+17.7	83.7	15
16	25 43.8	+9.4	79.2	25 54.8	+10.6	79.7	26 05.4	+11.6	80.1	26 15.4	+12.8	80.6	26 24.9	+13.9	81.1	26 33.9	+15.0	81.6	26 42.4	+16.2	82.1	26 50.4	+17.3	82.6	16
17	25 53.2	+8.9	78.1	26 05.4	+10.0	78.6	26 17.0	+11.2	79.0	26 28.2	+12.2	79.5	26 38.8	+13.4	80.0	26 48.9	+14.6	80.5	26 58.6	+15.6	81.0	27 07.7	+16.7	81.5	17
18	26 02.1	+8.4	77.0	26 15.4	+9.5	77.5	26 28.2	+10.6	78.0	26 40.4	+11.8	78.4	26 52.2	+12.9	78.9	27 03.5	+14.0	79.4	27 14.2	+15.1	79.9	27 24.4	+16.3	80.4	18
19	26 10.5	+7.9	75.9	26 24.9	+9.0	76.4	26 38.8	+10.1	76.9	26 52.2	+11.3	77.3	27 05.1	+12.4	77.8	27 17.5	+13.5	78.3	27 29.3	+14.7	78.8	27 40.7	+15.7	79.4	19
20	26 18.4	+7.4	74.8	26 33.9	+8.5	75.3	26 48.9	+9.7	75.7	27 03.5	+10.7	76.2	27 17.5	+11.8	76.7	27 31.0	+13.0	77.2	27 44.0	+14.1	77.8	27 56.4	+15.3	78.3	20
21	26 25.8	+6.9	73.7	26 42.4	+8.0	74.2	26 58.6	+9.1	74.6	27 14.2	+10.2	75.1	27 29.3	+11.4	75.6	27 44.0	+12.4	76.1	27 58.1	+13.6	76.7	28 11.7	+14.7	77.2	21
22	26 32.7	+6.3	72.6	26 50.4	+7.5	73.0	27 07.7	+8.5	73.5	27 24.4	+9.7	74.0	27 40.7	+10.8	74.5	27 56.4	+12.0	75.0	28 11.7	+13.0	75.6	28 26.4	+14.1	76.1	22
23	26 39.0	+5.8	71.5	26 57.9	+6.9	71.9	27 16.2	+8.1	72.4	27 34.1	+9.2	72.9	27 51.5	+10.3	73.4	28 08.4	+11.3	73.9	28 24.7	+12.5	74.4	28 40.5	+13.7	75.0	23
24	26 44.8	+5.4	70.3	27 04.8	+6.4	70.8	27 24.3	+7.5	71.3	27 43.3	+8.6	71.8	28 01.8	+9.7	72.3	28 19.7	+10.9	72.8	28 37.2	+12.0	73.3	28 54.2	+13.0	73.9	24
25	26 50.2	+4.7	69.2	27 11.2	+5.9	69.7	27 31.8	+7.0	70.2	27 51.9	+8.1	70.7	28 11.5	+9.2	71.2	28 30.6	+10.3	71.7	28 49.2	+11.4	72.2	29 07.2	+12.6	72.7	25
26	26 54.9	+4.3	68.1	27 17.1	+5.3	68.6	27 38.8	+6.4	69.1	28 00.0	+7.5	69.6	28 20.7	+8.6	70.1	28 40.9	+9.7	70.6	29 00.6	+10.8	71.1	29 19.8	+11.9	71.6	26
27	26 59.2	+3.7	67.0	27 22.4	+4.8	67.5	27 45.2	+5.9	67.9	28 07.5	+7.0	68.4	28 29.3	+8.1	68.9	28 50.6	+9.2	69.4	29 11.4	+10.3	70.0	29 31.7	+11.4	70.5	27
28	27 02.9	+3.2	65.9	27 27.2	+4.3	66.3	27 51.1	+5.3	66.8	28 14.5	+6.4	67.3	28 37.4	+7.5	67.8	28 59.8	+8.6	68.3	29 21.7	+9.7	68.8	29 43.1	+10.8	69.4	28
29	27 06.1	+2.7	64.7	27 31.5	+3.7	65.2	27 56.4	+4.8	65.7	28 20.9	+5.9	66.2	28 44.9	+6.9	66.7	29 08.4	+8.0	67.2	29 31.4	+9.1	67.7	29 53.9	+10.3	68.2	29
30	27 08.8	+2.1	63.6	27 35.2	+3.2	64.1	28 01.2	+4.2	64.6	28 26.8	+5.3	65.0	28 51.8	+6.4	65.5	29 16.4	+7.5	66.0	29 40.5	+8.6	66.6	30 04.2	+9.6	67.1	30
31	27 10.9	+1.6	62.5	27 38.4	+2.6	63.0	28 05.4	+3.7	63.4	28 32.1	+4.7	63.9	28 58.2	+5.8	64.4	29 23.9	+6.9	64.9	29 49.1	+7.9	65.4	30 13.8	+9.0	66.0	31
32	27 12.5	+1.0	61.4	27 41.0	+2.1	61.8	28 09.1	+3.1	62.3	28 36.8	+4.2	62.8	29 04.0	+5.2	63.3	29 30.8	+6.3	63.8	29 57.0	+7.4	64.3	30 22.8	+8.5	64.8	32
33	27 13.5	+0.5	60.2	27 43.1	+1.5	60.7	28 12.2	+2.6	61.2	28 41.0	+3.6	61.6	29 09.2	+4.7	62.1	29 37.1	+5.7	62.6	30 04.4	+6.8	63.1	30 31.3	+7.8	63.7	33
34	27 14.0	0.0	59.1	27 44.6	+1.0	59.6	28 14.8	+2.0	60.0	28 44.6	+3.0	60.5	29 13.9	+4.0	61.0	29 42.8	+5.1	61.5	30 11.2	+6.1	62.0	30 39.1	+7.2	62.5	34
35	27 14.0	-0.6	58.0	27 45.6	+0.4	58.4	28 16.8	+1.4	58.9	28 47.6	+2.4	59.4	29 17.9	+3.5	59.8	29 47.9	+4.5	60.3	30 17.3	+5.6	60.8	30 46.3	+6.6	61.4	35
36	27 13.4	-1.1	56.9	27 46.0	-0.1	57.3	28 18.2	+0.9	57.8	28 50.0	+1.9	58.2	29 21.4	+2.9	58.7	29 52.4	+3.9	59.2	30 22.9	+4.9	59.7	30 52.9	+6.0	60.2	36
37	27 12.3	-1.6	55.8	27 45.9	-0.7	56.2	28 19.1	+0.3	56.6	28 51.9	+1.3	57.1	29 24.3	+2.3	57.6	29 56.3	+3.3	58.0	30 27.8	+4.4	58.5	30 58.9	+5.4	59.0	37
38	27 10.7	-2.2	54.6	27 45.2	-1.2	55.1	28 19.4	-0.3	55.5	28 53.2	+0.7	55.9	29 26.6	+1.7	56.4	29 59.6	+2.7	56.9	30 32.2	+3.7	57.4	31 04.3	+4.7	57.9	38
39	27 08.5	-2.7	53.5	27 44.0	-1.8	53.9	28 19.1	-0.8	54.4	28 53.9	+0.2	54.8	29 28.3	+1.1	55.3	30 02.3	+2.1	55.7	30 35.9	+3.1	56.2	31 09.0	+4.2	56.7	39
40	27 05.8	-3.3	52.4	27 42.2	-2.3	52.8	28 18.3	-1.4	53.2	28 54.1	-0.5	53.7	29 29.4	+0.6	54.1	30 04.4	+1.5	54.6	30 39.0	+2.5	55.1	31 13.2	+3.4	55.5	40
41	27 02.5	-3.8	51.3	27 39.9	-2.9	51.7	28 16.9	-1.9	52.1	28 53.6	-1.0	52.5	29 30.0	-0.1	53.0	30 05.9	+0.9	53.4	30 41.5	+1.8	53.9	31 16.6	+2.9	54.4	41
42	26 58.7	-4.3	50.1	27 37.0	-3.4	50.5	28 15.0	-2.5	50.9	28 52.6	-1.6	51.4	29 29.9	-0.7	51.8	30 06.8	+0.3	52.3	30 43.3	+1.3	52.7	31 19.5	+2.2	53.2	42
43	26 54.4	-4.8	49.0	27 33.6	-4.0	49.4	28 12.5	-3.1	49.8	28 51.0	-2.1	50.2	29 29.2	-1.2	50.7	30 07.1	-0.3	51.1	30 44.6	+0.6	51.6	31 21.7	+1.6	52.0	43
44	26 49.6	-5.4	47.9	27 29.6	-4.5	48.3	28 09.4	-3.6	48.7	28 48.9	-2.8	49.1	29 28.0	-1.9	49.5	30 06.8	-1.0	49.9	30 45.2	0.0	50.4	31 23.3	+0.9	50.9	44
45	26 44.2	-5.9	46.8	27 25.1	-5.0	47.2	28 05.8	-4.2	47.5	28 46.1	-3.3	47.9	29 26.1	-2.4	48.4	30 05.8	-1.5	48.8	30 45.2	-0.6	49.2	31 24.2	+0.3	49.7	45
46	26 38.3	-6.4	45.7	27 20.1	-5.6	46.0	28 01.6	-4.8	46.4	28 42.8	-3.9	46.8	29 23.7	-3.0	47.2	30 04.3	-2.1	47.6	30 44.6	-1.3	48.1	31 24.5	-0.4	48.5	46
47	26 31.9	-7.0	44.6	27 14.5	-6.1	44.9	27 56.8	-5.2	45.3	28 38.9	-4.4	45.7	29 20.7	-3.6	46.1	30 02.2	-2.8	46.5	30 43.3	-1.9	46.9	31 24.1	-0.9	47.4	47
48	26 24.9	-7.4	43.5	27 08.4	-6.7	43.8	27 51.6	-5.9	44.2	28 34.5	-5.1	44.5	29 17.1	-4.2	44.9	29 59.4	-3.3	45.3	30 41.4	-2.4	45.7	31 23.2	-1.7	46.2	48
49	26 17.5	-8.0	42.3	27 01.7	-7.1	42.7	27 45.7	-6.4	43.0	28 29.4	-5.6	43.4	29 12.9	-4.8	43.8	29 56.1	-4.0	44.2	30 39.0	-3.2	44.6	31 21.5	-2.2	45.0	49
50	26 09.5	-8.4	41.2	26 54.6	-7.7	41.6	27 39.3	-6.9	41.9	28 23.8	-6.1	42.3	29 08.1	-5.3	42.6	29 52.1	-4.5	43.0	30 35.8	-3.7	43.4	31 19.3	-2.9	43.8	50
51	26 01.1	-9.0	40.1	26 46.9	-8.3	40.5	27 32.4	-7.5	40.8	28 17.7	-6.7	41.1	29 02.8	-6.0	41.5	29 47.6	-5.2	41.9	30 32.1	-4.3	42.3	31 16.4	-3.6	42.7	51
52	25 52.1	-9.4	39.0	26 38.6	-8.7	39.3	27 24.9	-8.0	39.7	28 11.0	-7.3	40.0	28 56.8	-6.5	40.4	29 42.4	-5.7	40.7	30 27.8	-5.0	41.1	31 12.8	-4.1	41.5	52
53	25 42.7	-10.0	37.9	26 29.9	-9.2	38.2	27 16.9	-8.5	38.6	28 03.7	-7.8	38.9	28 50.3	-7.0	39.2	29 36.7	-6.3	39.6	30 22.8	-5.6	40.0	31 08.7	-4.8	40.3	53
54	25 32.7	-10.4	36.8	26 20.7	-9.8	37.1	27 08.4	-9.1	37.4	27 55.9	-8.3	37.8	28 43.3	-7.7	38.1	29 30.4	-6.9	38.4	30 17.2	-6.1	38.8	31 03.9	-5.4	39.2	54
55	25 22.3	-10.9	35.8	26 10.9	-10.2	36.0	26 59.3	-9.5	36.3	27 47.6	-8.9	36.6	28 35.6	-8.2	37.0	29 23.5	-7.5	37.3	30 11.1	-6.8	37.6	30 58.5	-6.1	38.0	55
56	25 11.4	-11.4	34.7	26 00.7	-10.8	34.9	26 49.8	-10.1	35.2	27 38.7	-9.4	35.5	28 27.4	-8.7	35.8	29 16.0	-8.1	36.2	30 04.3	-7.4	36.5	30 52.4	-6.6	36.8	56
57	25 00.0	-11.9	33.6	25 49.9	-11.2	33.8	26 39.7	-10.6	34.1	27 29.3	-10.0	34.4	28 18.7	-9.3	34.7	29 07.9	-8.7	35.0	29 56.9	-7.9	35.4	30 45.8	-7.3	35.7	57
58	24 48.1	-12.3	32.5	25 38.7	-11.7	32.8	26 29.1	-11.1	33.0	27 19.3	-10.5	33.3	28 09.4	-9.9	33.6	28 59.2	-9.2	33.9	29 49.0	-8.6	34.2	30 38.5	-7.9	34.5	58
59	24 35.8	-12.8	31.4	25 27.0	-12.2	31.7	26 18.0	-11.7	31.9	27 08.8	-11.0	32.2	27 59.5	-10.4	32.5	28 50.0	-9.7	32.8	29 40.4	-9.1	33.1	30 30.6	-8.5	33.4	59
60	24 23.0	-13.2	30.4	25 14.8	-12.7	30.6	26 06.3	-12.1	30.8	26 57.8	-11.5	31.1	27 49.1	-10.9	31.4	28 40.3	-10.4	31.6	29 31.3	-9.7	31.9	30 22.1	-9.1	32.2	60
61	24 09.8	-13.7	29.3	25 02.1	-13.1	29.5	25 54.2	-12.5	29.7	26 46.3	-12.0	30.0	27 38.2	-11.5	30.2	28 29.9	-10.8	30.5	29 21.6	-10.3	30.8	30 13.0	-9.7	31.1	61
62	23 56.1	-14.1	28.2	24 49.0	-13.6	28.4	25 41.7	-13.1	28.7	26 34.3	-12.6	28.9	27 26.7	-12.0	29.1	28 19.1	-11.5	29.4	29 11.3	-10.9	29.7	30 03.3	-10.2	30.0	62
63	23 42.0	-14.5	27.2	24 35.4	-14.1	27.4	25 28.6	-13.5	27.6	26 21.7	-13.0	27.8	27 14.7	-12.5	28.0	28 07.6	-11.9	28.3	29 00.4	-11.4	28.5	29 53.1	-10.9	28.8	63
64	23 27.5	-15.0	26.1	24 21.3	-14.5	26.3	25 15.1	-14.1	26.5	26 08.7	-13.5	26.7	27 02.2	-13.0	26.9	27 55.7	-12.5	27.2	28 49.0	-12.0	27.4	29 42.2	-11.4	27.7	64
65	23 12.5	-15.4	25.0	24 06.8	-14.9	25.2	25 01.0	-14.4	25.4	25 55.2	-14.0	25.6	26 49.2	-13.5	25.8	27 43.2	-13.0	26.1	28 37.0	-12.5	26.3	29 30.8	-12.1	26.6	65
66	22 57.1	-15.8	24.0	23 51.9	-15.4	24.2	24 46.6	-15.0	24.4	25 41.2	-14.5	24.5	26 35.7	-14.0	24.8	27 30.2	-13.6	25.0	28 24.5	-13.0	25.2	29 18.7	-12.5	25.4	66
67	22 41.3	-16.2	22.9	23 36.5	-15.8	23.1	24 31.6	-15.3	23.3	25 26.7	-14.9	23.5	26 21.7	-14.5	23.7	27 16.6	-14.0	23.9	28 11.5	-13.6	24.1	29 06.2	-13.1	24.3	67
68	22 25.1	-16.7	21.9	23 20.7	-16.2	22.1	24 16.3	-15.8	22.2	25 11.8	-15.4	22.4	26 07.2	-15.0	22.6	27 02.6	-14.6	22.8	27 57.9	-14.2	23.0	28 53.1	-13.7	23.2	68
69	22 08.4	-17.0	20.9	23 04.5	-16.6	21.0	24 00.5	-16.3	21.2	24 56.4	-15.9	21.3	25 52.2	-15.4	21.5	26 48.0	-15.0	21.7	27 43.7	-14.6	21.9	28 39.4	-14.2	22.1	69
70	21 51.4	-17.4	19.8	22 47.9	-17.1	20.0	23 44.2	-16.7	20.1	24 40.5	-16.3	20.3	25 36.8	-15.9	20.4	26 33.0	-15.6	20.6	27 29.1	-15.1	20.8	28 25.2	-14.8	21.0	70
71	21 34.0	-17.7	18.8	22 30.8	-17.4	18.9	23 27.5	-17.0	19.1	24 24.2	-16.7	19.2	25 20.9	-16.4	19.4	26 17.4	-16.0	19.5	27 14.0	-15.7	19.7	28 10.4	-15.3	19.9	71
72	21 16.3	-18.2	17.8	22 13.4	-17.8	17.9	23 10.5	-17.5	18.0	24 07.5	-17.2	18.2	25 04.5	-16.9	18.3	26 01.4	-16.5	18.5	26 58.3	-16.1	18.6	27 55.1	-15.8	18.8	72
73	20 58.1	-18.5	16.8	21 55.6	-18.3	16.9	22 53.0	-18.0	17.0	23 50.3	-17.6	17.1	24 47.6	-17.2	17.2	25 44.9	-16.9	17.4	26 42.2	-16.7	17.5	27 39.3	-16.3	17.7	73
74	20 39.6	-18.9	15.7	21 37.3	-18.5	15.8	22 35.0	-18.3	15.9	23 32.7	-18.0	16.1	24 30.4	-17.8	16.2	25 28.0	-17.5	16.3	26 25.5	-17.1	16.5	27 23.0	-16.8	16.6	74
75	20 20.7	-19.2	14.7	21 18.8	-19.0	14.8	22 16.7	-18.6	14.9	23 14.7	-18.4	15.0	24 12.6	-18.1	15.1	25 10.5	-17.8	15.3	26 08.4	-17.6	15.4	27 06.2	-17.3	15.5	75
76	20 01.5	-19.5	13.7	20 59.8	-19.3	13.8	21 58.1	-19.1	13.9	22 56.3	-18.8	14.0	23 54.5	-18.6	14.1	24 52.7	-18.3	14.2	25 50.8	-18.0	14.3	26 48.9	-17.7	14.4	76
77	19 42.0	-19.9	12.7	20 40.5	-19.7	12.8	21 39.0	-19.5	12.9	22 37.5	-19.2	13.0	23 35.9	-18.9	13.1	24 34.4	-18.8	13.2	25 32.8	-18.5	13.3	26 31.2	-18.3	13.4	77
78	19 22.1	-20.2	11.7	20 20.8	-20.0	11.8	21 19.5	-19.8	11.9	22 18.3	-19.6	11.9	23 17.0	-19.4	12.0	24 15.6	-19.1	12.1	25 14.3	-19.0	12.2	26 12.9	-18.7	12.3	78
79	19 01.9	-20.6	10.7	20 00.8	-20.3	10.8	20 59.7	-20.1	10.8	21 58.7	-20.0	10.9	22 57.6	-19.8	11.0	23 56.5	-19.6	11.1	24 55.3	-19.4	11.2	25 54.2	-19.2	11.3	79
80	18 41.3	-20.8	9.7	19 40.5	-20.7	9.8	20 39.6	-20.5	9.8	21 38.7	-20.4	9.9	22 37.8	-20.2	10.0	23 36.9	-20.0	10.0	24 35.9	-19.8	10.1	25 35.0	-19.6	10.2	80
81	18 20.5	-21.2	8.7	19 19.8	-21.0	8.8	20 19.1	-20.9	8.8	21 18.3	-20.7	8.9	22 17.6	-20.5	9.0	23 16.9	-20.4	9.0	24 16.1	-20.2	9.1	25 15.4	-20.1	9.2	81
82	17 59.3	-21.4	7.7	18 58.8	-21.4	7.8	19 58.2	-21.2	7.8	20 57.6	-21.0	7.9	21 57.1	-20.9	7.9	22 56.5	-20.8	8.0	23 55.9	-20.6	8.1	24 55.3	-20.5	8.1	82
83	17 37.9	-21.8	6.8	18 37.4	-21.6	6.8	19 37.0	-21.5	6.8	20 36.6	-21.4	6.9	21 36.2	-21.3	6.9	22 35.7	-21.2	7.0	23 35.3	-21.1	7.0	24 34.8	-20.9	7.1	83
84	17 16.1	-22.0	5.8	18 15.8	-21.9	5.8	19 15.5	-21.8	5.8	20 15.2	-21.8	5.9	21 14.9	-21.7	5.9	22 14.5	-21.5	6.0	23 14.2	-21.4	6.0	24 13.9	-21.4	6.1	84
85	16 54.1	-22.3	4.8	17 53.9	-22.2	4.8	18 53.7	-22.2	4.9	19 53.4	-22.0	4.9	20 53.2	-22.0	4.9	21 53.0	-21.9	5.0	22 52.8	-21.8	5.0	23 52.5	-21.7	5.0	85
86	16 31.8	-22.6	3.8	17 31.7	-22.5	3.9	18 31.5	-22.4	3.9	19 31.4	-22.4	3.9	20 31.2	-22.3	3.9	21 31.1	-22.3	4.0	22 31.0	-22.2	4.0	23 30.8	-22.1	4.0	86
87	16 09.2	-22.8	2.9	17 09.2	-22.8	2.9	18 09.1	-22.8	2.9	19 09.0	-22.7	2.9	20 08.9	-22.6	2.9	21 08.8	-22.6	3.0	22 08.8	-22.6	3.0	23 08.7	-22.5	3.0	87
88	15 46.4	-23.1	1.9	16 46.4	-23.1	1.9	17 46.3	-23.0	1.9	18 46.3	-23.0	1.9	19 46.3	-23.0	2.0	20 46.2	-22.9	2.0	21 46.2	-22.9	2.0	22 46.2	-22.9	2.0	88
89	15 23.3	-23.3	1.0	16 23.3	-23.3	1.0	17 23.3	-23.3	1.0	18 23.3	-23.3	1.0	19 23.3	-23.3	1.0	20 23.3	-23.3	1.0	21 23.3	-23.3	1.0	22 23.3	-23.3	1.0	89
90	15 00.0	-23.6	0.0	16 00.0	-23.6	0.0	17 00.0	-23.6	0.0	18 00.0	-23.6	0.0	19 00.0	-23.6	0.0	20 00.0	-23.6	0.0	21 00.0	-23.6	0.0	22 00.0	-23.6	0.0	90
	15°			16°			17°			18°			19°			20°			21°			22°			

67°, 293° L.H.A. LATITUDE SAME NAME AS DECLINATION

136

LATITUDE **CONTRARY** NAME TO DECLINATION L.H.A. 67°, 293°

Dec.	15° Hc	d	Z	16° Hc	d	Z	17° Hc	d	Z	18° Hc	d	Z
°	° ′	′	°	° ′	′	°	° ′	′	°	° ′	′	°
0	22 10.4	-16.9	96.3	22 03.7	-18.1	96.7	21 56.5	-19.1	97.1	21 48.9	-20.2	97.5
1	21 53.5	-17.4	97.3	21 45.6	-18.4	97.7	21 37.4	-19.5	98.1	21 28.7	-20.5	98.5
2	21 36.1	-17.7	98.3	21 27.2	-18.8	98.7	21 17.9	-19.8	99.1	21 08.2	-20.9	99.5
3	21 18.4	-18.1	99.4	21 08.4	-19.1	99.7	20 58.1	-20.2	100.1	20 47.3	-21.2	100.5
4	21 00.3	-18.5	100.4	20 49.3	-19.5	100.8	20 37.9	-20.6	101.1	20 26.1	-21.6	101.5
5	20 41.8	-18.8	101.4	20 29.8	-19.9	101.8	20 17.3	-20.8	102.1	20 04.5	-21.9	102.5
6	20 23.0	-19.2	102.4	20 09.9	-20.2	102.8	19 56.5	-21.3	103.1	19 42.6	-22.2	103.5
7	20 03.8	-19.5	103.4	19 49.7	-20.5	103.8	19 35.2	-21.5	104.1	19 20.4	-22.5	104.5
8	19 44.3	-19.9	104.4	19 29.2	-20.9	104.8	19 13.7	-21.9	105.1	18 57.9	-22.9	105.4
9	19 24.4	-20.1	105.4	19 08.3	-21.2	105.8	18 51.8	-22.1	106.1	18 35.0	-23.1	106.4
10	19 04.3	-20.5	106.4	18 47.1	-21.5	106.8	18 29.7	-22.5	107.1	18 11.9	-23.5	107.4
11	18 43.8	-20.9	107.4	18 25.6	-21.8	107.7	18 07.2	-22.8	108.1	17 48.4	-23.7	108.4
12	18 22.9	-21.1	108.4	18 03.8	-22.1	108.7	17 44.4	-23.0	109.0	17 24.7	-24.0	109.3
13	18 01.8	-21.4	109.4	17 41.7	-22.3	109.7	17 21.4	-23.4	110.0	17 00.7	-24.3	110.3
14	17 40.4	-21.7	110.4	17 19.4	-22.7	110.7	16 58.0	-23.6	111.0	16 36.4	-24.5	111.2
15	17 18.7	-22.0	111.4	16 56.7	-22.9	111.6	16 34.4	-23.8	111.9	16 11.9	-24.8	112.2
16	16 56.7	-22.3	112.3	16 33.8	-23.2	112.6	16 10.6	-24.1	112.9	15 47.1	-25.0	113.1
17	16 34.4	-22.5	113.3	16 10.6	-23.5	113.6	15 46.5	-24.4	113.8	15 22.1	-25.3	114.1
18	16 11.9	-22.8	114.3	15 47.1	-23.7	114.5	15 22.1	-24.6	114.8	14 56.8	-25.5	115.0
19	15 49.1	-23.0	115.2	15 23.4	-23.9	115.5	14 57.5	-24.8	115.7	14 31.3	-25.7	116.0
20	15 26.1	-23.3	116.2	14 59.5	-24.2	116.4	14 32.7	-25.1	116.7	14 05.6	-25.9	116.9
21	15 02.8	-23.6	117.1	14 35.3	-24.4	117.4	14 07.6	-25.3	117.6	13 39.7	-26.2	117.8
22	14 39.2	-23.7	118.1	14 10.9	-24.7	118.3	13 42.3	-25.5	118.5	13 13.5	-26.3	118.7
23	14 15.5	-24.0	119.0	13 46.2	-24.8	119.3	13 16.8	-25.7	119.5	12 47.2	-26.5	119.7
24	13 51.5	-24.2	120.0	13 21.4	-25.1	120.2	12 51.1	-25.9	120.4	12 20.7	-26.7	120.6
25	13 27.3	-24.4	120.9	12 56.3	-25.2	121.1	12 25.2	-26.0	121.3	11 54.0	-26.9	121.5
26	13 02.9	-24.7	121.9	12 31.1	-25.4	122.1	11 59.2	-26.3	122.2	11 27.1	-27.1	122.4
27	12 38.2	-24.8	122.8	12 05.7	-25.7	123.0	11 32.9	-26.4	123.2	11 00.0	-27.2	123.3
28	12 13.4	-25.0	123.7	11 40.0	-25.8	123.9	11 06.5	-26.6	124.1	10 32.8	-27.4	124.2
29	11 48.4	-25.2	124.7	11 14.2	-25.9	124.8	10 39.9	-26.8	125.0	10 05.4	-27.5	125.1
30	11 23.2	-25.3	125.6	10 48.3	-26.2	125.8	10 13.1	-26.9	125.9	9 37.9	-27.7	126.0
31	10 57.9	-25.5	126.5	10 22.1	-26.3	126.7	9 46.2	-27.0	126.8	9 10.2	-27.8	126.9
32	10 32.4	-25.7	127.4	9 55.8	-26.4	127.6	9 19.2	-27.2	127.7	8 42.4	-27.9	127.8
33	10 06.7	-25.8	128.4	9 29.4	-26.6	128.5	8 52.0	-27.3	128.6	8 14.5	-28.0	128.7
34	9 40.9	-26.0	129.3	9 02.8	-26.7	129.4	8 24.7	-27.4	129.5	7 46.5	-28.2	129.6
35	9 14.9	-26.1	130.2	8 36.1	-26.8	130.3	7 57.3	-27.6	130.4	7 18.3	-28.2	130.5
36	8 48.8	-26.3	131.1	8 09.3	-27.0	131.2	7 29.7	-27.6	131.3	6 50.1	-28.4	131.4
37	8 22.5	-26.4	132.0	7 42.3	-27.0	132.1	7 02.1	-27.8	132.2	6 21.7	-28.4	132.3
38	7 56.1	-26.4	132.9	7 15.3	-27.2	133.0	6 34.3	-27.9	133.1	5 53.3	-28.6	133.2
39	7 29.7	-26.6	133.8	6 48.1	-27.3	133.9	6 06.4	-27.9	134.0	5 24.7	-28.6	134.1
40	7 03.1	-26.7	134.7	6 20.8	-27.4	134.8	5 38.5	-28.0	134.9	4 56.1	-28.6	134.9
41	6 36.4	-26.8	135.6	5 53.4	-27.4	135.7	5 10.5	-28.1	135.8	4 27.5	-28.8	135.8
42	6 09.6	-26.9	136.5	5 26.0	-27.5	136.6	4 42.4	-28.2	136.7	3 58.7	-28.8	136.7
43	5 42.7	-27.0	137.4	4 58.5	-27.6	137.5	4 14.2	-28.2	137.5	3 29.9	-28.8	137.6
44	5 15.7	-27.1	138.3	4 30.9	-27.7	138.4	3 46.0	-28.3	138.4	3 01.1	-28.9	138.5
45	4 48.6	-27.1	139.2	4 03.2	-27.7	139.3	3 17.7	-28.3	139.3	2 32.2	-28.9	139.3
46	4 21.5	-27.2	140.1	3 35.5	-27.8	140.2	2 49.4	-28.4	140.2	2 03.3	-29.0	140.2
47	3 54.3	-27.2	141.0	3 07.7	-27.8	141.0	2 21.0	-28.4	141.1	1 34.3	-28.9	141.1
48	3 27.1	-27.3	141.9	2 39.9	-27.9	141.9	1 52.6	-28.4	142.0	1 05.4	-29.0	142.0
49	2 59.8	-27.3	142.8	2 12.0	-27.9	142.8	1 24.2	-28.5	142.8	0 36.4	-29.0	142.8
50	2 32.5	-27.4	143.7	1 44.1	-27.9	143.7	0 55.7	-28.4	143.7	0 07.4	-29.0	143.7
51	2 05.1	-27.4	144.6	1 16.2	-28.0	144.6	0 27.3	-28.5	144.6	0 21.6	+29.0	35.4
52	1 37.7	-27.5	145.5	0 48.2	-27.9	145.5	0 01.2	+28.5	34.5	0 50.6	+29.0	34.5
53	1 10.2	-27.4	146.4	0 20.3	-28.0	146.4	0 29.7	+28.4	33.6	1 19.6	+29.0	33.7
54	0 42.8	-27.4	147.2	0 07.7	+27.9	32.8	0 58.1	+28.5	32.8	1 48.6	+28.9	32.8
55	0 15.4	-27.5	148.1	0 35.6	+27.9	31.9	1 26.6	+28.4	31.9	2 17.5	+28.9	31.9
56	0 12.1	+27.5	31.0	1 03.5	+28.0	31.0	1 55.0	+28.4	31.0	2 46.4	+28.9	31.0
57	0 39.6	+27.4	30.1	1 31.5	+27.9	30.1	2 23.4	+28.3	30.1	3 15.3	+28.8	30.1
58	1 07.0	+27.4	29.2	1 59.4	+27.9	29.2	2 51.7	+28.4	29.2	3 44.1	+28.8	29.3
59	1 34.4	+27.4	28.3	2 27.3	+27.8	28.3	3 20.1	+28.2	28.4	4 12.9	+28.7	28.4
60	2 01.8	+27.4	27.4	2 55.1	+27.8	27.4	3 48.3	+28.3	27.5	4 41.6	+28.6	27.5
61	2 29.2	+27.4	26.5	3 22.9	+27.7	26.6	4 16.6	+28.1	26.6	5 10.2	+28.6	26.6
62	2 56.6	+27.3	25.6	3 50.6	+27.7	25.7	4 44.7	+28.1	25.7	5 38.8	+28.5	25.7
63	3 23.9	+27.2	24.7	4 18.3	+27.7	24.8	5 12.8	+28.0	24.8	6 07.3	+28.4	24.9
64	3 51.1	+27.2	23.9	4 46.0	+27.5	23.9	5 40.8	+28.0	23.9	6 35.7	+28.3	24.0
65	4 18.3	+27.1	23.0	5 13.5	+27.5	23.0	6 08.8	+27.8	23.0	7 04.0	+28.2	23.1
66	4 45.4	+27.1	22.1	5 41.0	+27.4	22.1	6 36.6	+27.8	22.1	7 32.2	+28.1	22.2
67	5 12.5	+27.0	21.2	6 08.4	+27.4	21.2	7 04.4	+27.6	21.2	8 00.3	+28.0	21.3
68	5 39.5	+26.9	20.3	6 35.8	+27.2	20.3	7 32.0	+27.6	20.4	8 28.3	+27.8	20.4
69	6 06.4	+26.8	19.4	7 03.0	+27.1	19.4	7 59.6	+27.4	19.5	8 56.1	+27.8	19.5
70	6 33.2	+26.7	18.5	7 30.1	+27.0	18.5	8 27.0	+27.3	18.6	9 23.9	+27.5	18.6
71	6 59.9	+26.6	17.6	7 57.1	+26.9	17.6	8 54.3	+27.2	17.7	9 51.4	+27.5	17.7
72	7 26.5	+26.5	16.7	8 24.0	+26.8	16.7	9 21.5	+27.0	16.8	10 18.9	+27.3	16.8
73	7 53.0	+26.4	15.8	8 50.8	+26.6	15.8	9 48.5	+26.9	15.9	10 46.2	+27.1	15.9
74	8 19.4	+26.3	14.9	9 17.4	+26.5	14.9	10 15.4	+26.7	14.9	11 13.3	+27.0	15.0
75	8 45.7	+26.1	13.9	9 43.9	+26.4	14.0	10 42.1	+26.6	14.0	11 40.3	+26.8	14.1
76	9 11.8	+26.0	13.0	10 10.3	+26.2	13.1	11 08.7	+26.4	13.1	12 07.1	+26.6	13.2
77	9 37.8	+25.9	12.1	10 36.5	+26.0	12.2	11 35.1	+26.2	12.2	12 33.7	+26.5	12.2
78	10 03.7	+25.6	11.2	11 02.5	+25.9	11.2	12 01.3	+26.1	11.3	13 00.2	+26.2	11.3
79	10 29.3	+25.6	10.3	11 28.4	+25.7	10.3	12 27.4	+25.9	10.4	13 26.4	+26.1	10.4
80	10 54.9	+25.4	9.4	11 54.1	+25.5	9.4	12 53.3	+25.7	9.4	13 52.5	+25.8	9.5
81	11 20.3	+25.2	8.4	12 19.6	+25.3	8.5	13 19.0	+25.4	8.5	14 18.3	+25.6	8.5
82	11 45.5	+25.0	7.5	12 44.9	+25.2	7.5	13 44.4	+25.3	7.6	14 43.9	+25.4	7.6
83	12 10.5	+24.8	6.6	13 10.1	+24.9	6.6	14 09.7	+25.0	6.6	15 09.3	+25.1	6.7
84	12 35.3	+24.7	5.7	13 35.0	+24.8	5.7	14 34.7	+24.9	5.7	15 34.4	+24.9	5.7
85	13 00.0	+24.4	4.7	13 59.8	+24.5	4.7	14 59.6	+24.5	4.8	15 59.3	+24.7	4.8
86	13 24.4	+24.2	3.8	14 24.3	+24.3	3.8	15 24.1	+24.4	3.8	16 24.0	+24.4	3.8
87	13 48.6	+24.0	2.8	14 48.6	+24.0	2.9	15 48.5	+24.1	2.9	16 48.4	+24.1	2.9
88	14 12.6	+23.8	1.9	15 12.6	+23.8	1.9	16 12.6	+23.8	1.9	17 12.5	+23.9	1.9
89	14 36.4	+23.6	1.0	15 36.4	+23.6	1.0	16 36.4	+23.6	1.0	17 36.4	+23.6	1.0
90	15 00.0	+23.3	0.0	16 00.0	+23.3	0.0	17 00.0	+23.3	0.0	18 00.0	+23.3	0.0
	15°			16°			17°			18°		

19° Hc	d	Z	20° Hc	d	Z	21° Hc	d	Z	22° Hc	d	Z	Dec.
° ′	′	°	° ′	′	°	° ′	′	°	° ′	′	°	°
21 40.9	-21.2	97.9	21 32.5	-22.3	98.3	21 23.6	-23.2	98.6	21 14.4	-24.3	99.0	0
21 19.7	-21.6	98.9	21 10.2	-22.6	99.3	21 00.4	-23.6	99.6	20 50.1	-24.6	100.0	1
20 58.1	-21.9	99.9	20 47.6	-22.9	100.2	20 36.8	-24.0	100.6	20 25.5	-24.9	101.0	2
20 36.2	-22.2	100.9	20 24.7	-23.3	101.2	20 12.8	-24.2	101.6	20 00.6	-25.3	102.0	3
20 14.0	-22.6	101.9	20 01.4	-23.5	102.2	19 48.6	-24.6	102.6	19 35.3	-25.5	102.9	4
19 51.4	-22.9	102.8	19 37.9	-23.9	103.2	19 24.0	-24.9	103.5	19 09.8	-25.9	103.9	5
19 28.5	-23.2	103.8	19 14.0	-24.2	104.2	18 59.1	-25.2	104.5	18 43.9	-26.1	104.8	6
19 05.3	-23.6	104.8	18 49.8	-24.6	105.1	18 33.9	-25.5	105.5	18 17.8	-26.5	105.8	7
18 41.7	-23.8	105.8	18 25.2	-24.7	106.1	18 08.4	-25.7	106.4	17 51.3	-26.7	106.7	8
18 17.9	-24.1	106.7	18 00.5	-25.1	107.1	17 42.7	-26.0	107.4	17 24.6	-26.9	107.7	9
17 53.8	-24.4	107.7	17 35.4	-25.4	108.0	17 16.7	-26.3	108.3	16 57.7	-27.2	108.6	10
17 29.4	-24.7	108.7	17 10.0	-25.6	109.0	16 50.4	-26.6	109.3	16 30.5	-27.5	109.5	11
17 04.7	-24.9	109.6	16 44.4	-25.9	109.9	16 23.8	-26.7	110.2	16 03.0	-27.7	110.5	12
16 39.8	-25.2	110.6	16 18.5	-26.1	110.8	15 57.1	-27.1	111.1	15 35.3	-27.9	111.4	13
16 14.6	-25.5	111.5	15 52.4	-26.3	111.8	15 30.0	-27.2	112.0	15 07.4	-28.2	112.3	14
15 49.1	-25.7	112.5	15 26.1	-26.6	112.7	15 02.8	-27.5	113.0	14 39.2	-28.3	113.2	15
15 23.4	-25.9	113.4	14 59.5	-26.8	113.6	14 35.3	-27.7	113.9	14 10.9	-28.6	114.1	16
14 57.5	-26.2	114.3	14 32.7	-27.1	114.6	14 07.6	-27.9	114.8	13 42.3	-28.8	115.0	17
14 31.3	-26.3	115.3	14 05.6	-27.2	115.5	13 39.7	-28.1	115.7	13 13.5	-28.9	115.9	18
14 05.0	-26.6	116.2	13 38.4	-27.5	116.4	13 11.6	-28.3	116.6	12 44.6	-29.1	116.8	19
13 38.4	-26.8	117.1	13 10.9	-27.6	117.3	12 43.3	-28.5	117.5	12 15.5	-29.3	117.7	20
13 11.6	-27.0	118.0	12 43.3	-27.8	118.2	12 14.8	-28.6	118.4	11 46.2	-29.5	118.6	21
12 44.6	-27.2	119.0	12 15.5	-28.0	119.1	11 46.2	-28.9	119.3	11 16.7	-29.7	119.5	22
12 17.4	-27.3	119.9	11 47.5	-28.2	120.0	11 17.3	-29.0	120.2	10 47.0	-29.7	120.4	23
11 50.1	-27.6	120.8	11 19.3	-28.4	121.0	10 48.3	-29.1	121.1	10 17.3	-30.0	121.3	24
11 22.5	-27.7	121.7	10 50.9	-28.4	121.8	10 19.2	-29.3	122.0	9 47.3	-30.1	122.2	25
10 54.8	-27.8	122.6	10 22.5	-28.7	122.7	9 49.9	-29.4	122.9	9 17.3	-30.2	123.0	26
10 27.0	-28.0	123.5	9 53.8	-28.8	123.6	9 20.5	-29.5	123.8	8 47.1	-30.3	123.9	27
9 59.0	-28.2	124.4	9 25.0	-28.9	124.5	8 51.0	-29.7	124.7	8 16.8	-30.4	124.8	28
9 30.8	-28.3	125.3	8 56.1	-29.0	125.4	8 21.3	-29.8	125.5	7 46.4	-30.6	125.7	29
9 02.5	-28.4	126.2	8 27.1	-29.2	126.3	7 51.5	-29.9	126.4	7 15.8	-30.6	126.5	30
8 34.1	-28.5	127.1	7 57.9	-29.3	127.2	7 21.6	-30.0	127.3	6 45.2	-30.7	127.4	31
8 05.6	-28.7	128.0	7 28.6	-29.3	128.1	6 51.6	-30.1	128.2	6 14.5	-30.8	128.3	32
7 36.9	-28.7	128.8	6 59.3	-29.5	128.9	6 21.5	-30.2	129.0	5 43.7	-30.9	129.1	33
7 08.2	-28.9	129.7	6 29.8	-29.6	129.8	5 51.3	-30.2	129.9	5 12.8	-30.9	130.0	34
6 39.3	-29.0	130.6	6 00.2	-29.6	130.7	5 21.1	-30.4	130.8	4 41.9	-31.1	130.8	35
6 10.3	-29.0	131.5	5 30.6	-29.8	131.6	4 50.7	-30.4	131.6	4 10.8	-31.0	131.7	36
5 41.3	-29.1	132.4	5 00.8	-29.8	132.4	4 20.3	-30.4	132.5	3 39.8	-31.1	132.6	37
5 12.2	-29.2	133.3	4 31.0	-29.8	133.3	3 49.9	-30.5	133.4	3 08.7	-31.2	133.4	38
4 43.0	-29.3	134.1	4 01.2	-29.9	134.2	3 19.4	-30.6	134.2	2 37.5	-31.2	134.3	39
4 13.7	-29.3	135.0	3 31.3	-30.0	135.1	2 48.8	-30.6	135.1	2 06.3	-31.2	135.1	40
3 44.4	-29.4	135.9	3 01.3	-30.0	135.9	2 18.2	-30.6	136.0	1 35.1	-31.3	136.0	41
3 15.0	-29.4	136.8	2 31.3	-30.0	136.8	1 47.6	-30.7	136.8	1 03.8	-31.2	136.8	42
2 45.6	-29.4	137.6	2 01.3	-30.1	137.7	1 16.9	-30.6	137.7	0 32.6	-31.3	137.7	43
2 16.2	-29.5	138.5	1 31.2	-30.1	138.5	0 46.3	-30.7	138.5	0 01.3	-31.3	138.5	44
1 46.7	-29.5	139.4	1 01.1	-30.1	139.4	0 15.6	-30.7	139.4	0 30.0	+31.2	40.6	45
1 17.2	-29.6	140.2	0 31.0	-30.1	140.2	0 15.1	+30.7	39.8	1 01.2	+31.3	39.8	46
0 47.6	-29.5	141.1	0 00.9	-30.1	141.1	0 45.8	+30.6	38.9	1 32.5	+31.2	38.9	47
0 18.1	-29.6	142.0	0 29.2	+30.1	38.0	1 16.4	+30.7	38.0	2 03.7	+31.2	38.0	48
0 11.5	+29.5	37.2	0 59.3	+30.1	37.2	1 47.1	+30.6	37.2	2 34.9	+31.2	37.2	49
0 41.0	+29.5	36.3	1 29.4	+30.0	36.3	2 17.7	+30.6	36.3	3 06.1	+31.1	36.3	50
1 10.5	+29.5	35.4	1 59.4	+30.1	35.4	2 48.3	+30.6	35.4	3 37.2	+31.1	35.5	51
1 40.0	+29.5	34.5	2 29.5	+30.0	34.6	3 18.9	+30.5	34.6	4 08.3	+31.0	34.6	52
2 09.5	+29.5	33.7	2 59.5	+29.9	33.7	3 49.4	+30.4	33.7	4 39.3	+30.9	33.8	53
2 39.0	+29.4	32.8	3 29.4	+30.0	32.8	4 19.8	+30.4	32.9	5 10.2	+30.9	32.9	54
3 08.4	+29.4	31.9	3 59.4	+29.8	32.0	4 50.2	+30.4	32.0	5 41.1	+30.8	32.0	55
3 37.8	+29.3	31.0	4 29.2	+29.8	31.1	5 20.6	+30.2	31.1	6 11.9	+30.8	31.2	56
4 07.1	+29.3	30.2	4 59.0	+29.7	30.2	5 50.8	+30.2	30.3	6 42.7	+30.6	30.3	57
4 36.4	+29.2	29.3	5 28.7	+29.7	29.3	6 21.0	+30.1	29.4	7 13.3	+30.5	29.5	58
5 05.6	+29.2	28.4	5 58.4	+29.6	28.5	6 51.1	+30.0	28.5	7 43.8	+30.5	28.6	59
5 34.8	+29.0	27.5	6 28.0	+29.4	27.6	7 21.1	+29.9	27.6	8 14.3	+30.3	27.7	60
6 03.8	+29.0	26.7	6 57.4	+29.4	26.7	7 51.0	+29.8	26.8	8 44.6	+30.2	26.8	61
6 32.8	+28.9	25.8	7 26.8	+29.3	25.8	8 20.8	+29.7	25.9	9 14.8	+30.0	26.0	62
7 01.7	+28.8	24.9	7 56.1	+29.2	25.0	8 50.5	+29.5	25.0	9 44.8	+30.0	25.1	63
7 30.5	+28.7	24.0	8 25.3	+29.0	24.1	9 20.0	+29.5	24.1	10 14.8	+29.8	24.2	64
7 59.2	+28.5	23.1	8 54.3	+28.9	23.2	9 49.5	+29.2	23.3	10 44.6	+29.6	23.3	65
8 27.7	+28.5	22.2	9 23.2	+28.8	22.3	10 18.7	+29.2	22.4	11 14.2	+29.5	22.4	66
8 56.2	+28.3	21.4	9 52.0	+28.7	21.4	10 47.9	+29.0	21.5	11 43.7	+29.3	21.6	67
9 24.5	+28.2	20.5	10 20.7	+28.5	20.5	11 16.9	+28.8	20.6	12 13.0	+29.2	20.7	68
9 52.7	+28.0	19.6	10 49.2	+28.3	19.6	11 45.7	+28.7	19.7	12 42.2	+28.9	19.8	69
10 20.7	+27.9	18.7	11 17.5	+28.2	18.7	12 14.4	+28.4	18.8	13 11.1	+28.8	18.9	70
10 48.6	+27.7	17.8	11 45.7	+28.0	17.8	12 42.8	+28.3	17.9	13 39.9	+28.6	18.0	71
11 16.3	+27.6	16.9	12 13.7	+27.9	16.9	13 11.1	+28.1	17.0	14 08.5	+28.4	17.1	72
11 43.9	+27.4	16.0	12 41.6	+27.6	16.0	13 39.2	+27.9	16.1	14 36.9	+28.1	16.1	73
12 11.3	+27.2	15.0	13 09.2	+27.5	15.1	14 07.1	+27.7	15.2	15 05.0	+28.0	15.2	74
12 38.5	+27.0	14.1	13 36.7	+27.2	14.2	14 34.8	+27.5	14.3	15 33.0	+27.7	14.3	75
13 05.5	+26.9	13.2	14 03.9	+27.1	13.3	15 02.3	+27.3	13.3	16 00.7	+27.5	13.4	76
13 32.4	+26.6	12.3	14 31.0	+26.8	12.4	15 29.6	+27.0	12.4	16 28.2	+27.2	12.5	77
13 59.0	+26.4	11.4	14 57.8	+26.6	11.4	15 56.6	+26.8	11.5	16 55.4	+27.0	11.5	78
14 25.4	+26.2	10.4	15 24.4	+26.4	10.5	16 23.4	+26.6	10.5	17 22.4	+26.7	10.6	79
14 51.6	+26.0	9.5	15 50.8	+26.1	9.6	16 50.0	+26.3	9.6	17 49.1	+26.5	9.7	80
15 17.6	+25.8	8.6	16 16.9	+25.9	8.6	17 16.3	+26.0	8.7	18 15.6	+26.1	8.7	81
15 43.4	+25.5	7.6	16 42.8	+25.7	7.7	17 42.3	+25.7	7.7	18 41.7	+25.9	7.8	82
16 08.9	+25.2	6.7	17 08.5	+25.3	6.7	18 08.0	+25.5	6.8	19 07.6	+25.6	6.8	83
16 34.1	+25.0	5.8	17 33.8	+25.1	5.8	18 33.5	+25.2	5.8	19 33.2	+25.3	5.9	84
16 59.1	+24.8	4.8	17 58.9	+24.8	4.8	18 58.7	+24.9	4.9	19 58.5	+25.0	4.9	85
17 23.9	+24.4	3.9	18 23.7	+24.6	3.9	19 23.6	+24.6	3.9	20 23.5	+24.6	3.9	86
17 48.3	+24.2	2.9	18 48.3	+24.2	2.9	19 48.2	+24.2	2.9	20 48.1	+24.3	3.0	87
18 12.5	+23.9	1.9	19 12.5	+23.9	1.9	20 12.4	+24.0	2.0	21 12.4	+24.0	2.0	88
18 36.4	+23.6	1.0	19 36.4	+23.6	1.0	20 36.4	+23.6	1.0	21 36.4	+23.6	1.0	89
19 00.0	+23.3	0.0	20 00.0	+23.3	0.0	21 00.0	+23.3	0.0	22 00.0	+23.3	0.0	90
19°			20°			21°			22°			

S. Lat. { L.H.A. greater than 180° ....Zn=180°−Z; L.H.A. less than 180°...........Zn=180°+Z }

LATITUDE **SAME** NAME AS DECLINATION L.H.A. 113°, 247°

68°, 292° L.H.A. LATITUDE SAME NAME AS DECLINATION N. Lat. {L.H.A. greater than 180° .....Zn=Z; L.H.A. less than 180°............Zn=360°−Z}

Dec.	15° Hc	d	Z	16° Hc	d	Z	17° Hc	d	Z	18° Hc	d	Z	19° Hc	d	Z	20° Hc	d	Z	21° Hc	d	Z	22° Hc	d	Z	Dec.
°	° ′	′	°	° ′	′	°	° ′	′	°	° ′	′	°	° ′	′	°	° ′	′	°	° ′	′	°	° ′	′	°	°
0	21 12.8	+16.5	96.0	21 06.4	+17.5	96.4	20 59.5	+18.6	96.7	20 52.3	+19.6	97.1	20 44.7	+20.7	97.5	20 36.6	+21.8	97.9	20 28.2	+22.8	98.2	20 19.4	+23.8	98.6	0
1	21 29.3	+16.1	94.9	21 23.9	+17.2	95.3	21 18.1	+18.3	95.7	21 11.9	+19.4	96.1	21 05.4	+20.3	96.5	20 58.4	+21.4	96.9	20 51.0	+22.5	97.2	20 43.2	+23.5	97.6	1
2	21 45.4	+15.7	93.9	21 41.1	+16.8	94.3	21 36.4	+17.8	94.7	21 31.3	+18.9	95.1	21 25.7	+20.0	95.5	21 19.8	+21.0	95.9	21 13.5	+22.0	96.3	21 06.7	+23.1	96.6	2
3	22 01.1	+15.3	92.9	21 57.9	+16.3	93.3	21 54.2	+17.5	93.7	21 50.2	+18.5	94.1	21 45.7	+19.6	94.5	21 40.8	+20.7	94.9	21 35.5	+21.8	95.3	21 29.8	+22.8	95.7	3
4	22 16.4	+14.9	91.8	22 14.2	+16.0	92.2	22 11.7	+17.1	92.6	22 08.7	+18.2	93.0	22 05.3	+19.3	93.4	22 01.5	+20.3	93.9	21 57.3	+21.3	94.3	21 52.6	+22.4	94.7	4
5	22 31.3	+14.5	90.8	22 30.2	+15.6	91.2	22 28.8	+16.7	91.6	22 26.9	+17.8	92.0	22 24.6	+18.8	92.4	22 21.8	+19.9	92.8	22 18.6	+21.0	93.2	22 15.0	+22.1	93.7	5
6	22 45.8	+14.0	89.7	22 45.8	+15.2	90.1	22 45.5	+16.2	90.6	22 44.7	+17.3	91.0	22 43.4	+18.5	91.4	22 41.7	+19.6	91.8	22 39.6	+20.6	92.2	22 37.1	+21.6	92.6	6
7	22 59.8	+13.7	88.7	23 01.0	+14.8	89.1	23 01.7	+15.9	89.5	23 02.0	+17.0	89.9	23 01.9	+18.0	90.4	23 01.3	+19.1	90.8	23 00.2	+20.2	91.2	22 58.7	+21.3	91.6	7
8	23 13.5	+13.2	87.6	23 15.8	+14.3	88.0	23 17.6	+15.5	88.5	23 19.0	+16.5	88.9	23 19.9	+17.7	89.3	23 20.4	+18.7	89.8	23 20.4	+19.8	90.2	23 20.0	+20.9	90.6	8
9	23 26.7	+12.8	86.5	23 30.1	+13.9	87.0	23 33.1	+15.0	87.4	23 35.5	+16.2	87.8	23 37.6	+17.2	88.3	23 39.1	+18.3	88.7	23 40.2	+19.4	89.2	23 40.9	+20.5	89.6	9
10	23 39.5	+12.4	85.5	23 44.0	+13.5	85.9	23 48.1	+14.6	86.4	23 51.7	+15.7	86.8	23 54.8	+16.8	87.2	23 57.4	+17.9	87.7	23 59.6	+19.0	88.1	24 01.4	+20.0	88.6	10
11	23 51.9	+11.9	84.4	23 57.5	+13.0	84.8	24 02.7	+14.1	85.3	24 07.4	+15.2	85.7	24 11.6	+16.3	86.2	24 15.3	+17.5	86.6	24 18.6	+18.6	87.1	24 21.4	+19.7	87.5	11
12	24 03.8	+11.5	83.3	24 10.5	+12.6	83.8	24 16.8	+13.7	84.2	24 22.6	+14.8	84.7	24 27.9	+16.0	85.1	24 32.8	+17.0	85.6	24 37.2	+18.1	86.0	24 41.1	+19.2	86.5	12
13	24 15.3	+11.0	82.3	24 23.1	+12.1	82.7	24 30.5	+13.2	83.2	24 37.4	+14.4	83.6	24 43.9	+15.4	84.1	24 49.8	+16.6	84.5	24 55.3	+17.7	85.0	25 00.3	+18.8	85.5	13
14	24 26.3	+10.5	81.2	24 35.2	+11.7	81.6	24 43.7	+12.8	82.1	24 51.8	+13.9	82.5	24 59.3	+15.0	83.0	25 06.4	+16.1	83.5	25 13.0	+17.2	83.9	25 19.1	+18.3	84.4	14
15	24 36.8	+10.1	80.1	24 46.9	+11.2	80.6	24 56.5	+12.3	81.0	25 05.7	+13.4	81.5	25 14.3	+14.6	81.9	25 22.5	+15.7	82.4	25 30.2	+16.8	82.9	25 37.4	+17.9	83.3	15
16	24 46.9	+9.6	79.0	24 58.1	+10.7	79.5	25 08.8	+11.9	79.9	25 19.1	+13.0	80.4	25 28.9	+14.0	80.9	25 38.2	+15.1	81.3	25 47.0	+16.3	81.8	25 55.3	+17.4	82.3	16
17	24 56.5	+9.2	77.9	25 08.8	+10.3	78.4	25 20.7	+11.4	78.8	25 32.1	+12.4	79.3	25 42.9	+13.6	79.8	25 53.3	+14.8	80.3	26 03.3	+15.8	80.7	26 12.7	+16.9	81.2	17
18	25 05.7	+8.6	76.8	25 19.1	+9.8	77.3	25 32.1	+10.8	77.8	25 44.5	+12.0	78.2	25 56.5	+13.2	78.7	26 08.1	+14.2	79.2	26 19.1	+15.3	79.7	26 29.6	+16.4	80.2	18
19	25 14.3	+8.2	75.7	25 28.9	+9.3	76.2	25 42.9	+10.4	76.7	25 56.5	+11.6	77.1	26 09.7	+12.6	77.6	26 22.3	+13.7	78.1	26 34.4	+14.9	78.6	26 46.0	+16.0	79.1	19
20	25 22.5	+7.7	74.6	25 38.2	+8.8	75.1	25 53.3	+10.0	75.6	26 08.1	+11.0	76.0	26 22.3	+12.1	76.5	26 36.0	+13.3	77.0	26 49.3	+14.3	77.5	27 02.0	+15.4	78.0	20
21	25 30.2	+7.2	73.5	25 47.0	+8.3	74.0	26 03.3	+9.4	74.5	26 19.1	+10.5	74.9	26 34.4	+11.6	75.4	26 49.3	+12.7	75.9	27 03.6	+13.8	76.4	27 17.4	+15.0	76.9	21
22	25 37.4	+6.7	72.4	25 55.3	+7.8	72.9	26 12.7	+8.9	73.4	26 29.6	+10.0	73.9	26 46.0	+11.1	74.3	27 02.0	+12.2	74.8	27 17.4	+13.4	75.3	27 32.4	+14.4	75.8	22
23	25 44.1	+6.2	71.3	26 03.1	+7.2	71.8	26 21.6	+8.4	72.3	26 39.6	+9.5	72.7	26 57.1	+10.6	73.2	27 14.2	+11.7	73.7	27 30.8	+12.8	74.2	27 46.8	+14.0	74.7	23
24	25 50.3	+5.7	70.2	26 10.3	+6.8	70.7	26 30.0	+7.8	71.2	26 49.1	+9.0	71.6	27 07.7	+10.1	72.1	27 25.9	+11.2	72.6	27 43.6	+12.3	73.1	28 00.8	+13.4	73.6	24
25	25 56.0	+5.2	69.1	26 17.1	+6.3	69.6	26 37.8	+7.4	70.1	26 58.1	+8.4	70.5	27 17.8	+9.6	71.0	27 37.1	+10.6	71.5	27 55.9	+11.7	72.0	28 14.2	+12.8	72.5	25
26	26 01.2	+4.7	68.0	26 23.4	+5.8	68.5	26 45.2	+6.8	68.9	27 06.5	+7.9	69.4	27 27.4	+9.0	69.9	27 47.7	+10.2	70.4	28 07.6	+11.2	70.9	28 27.0	+12.3	71.4	26
27	26 05.9	+4.1	66.9	26 29.2	+5.2	67.4	26 52.0	+6.4	67.8	27 14.4	+7.4	68.3	27 36.4	+8.5	68.8	27 57.9	+9.5	69.3	28 18.8	+10.7	69.8	28 39.3	+11.8	70.3	27
28	26 10.0	+3.7	65.8	26 34.4	+4.7	66.3	26 58.4	+5.8	66.7	27 21.8	+6.9	67.2	27 44.9	+7.9	67.7	28 07.4	+9.1	68.2	28 29.5	+10.1	68.7	28 51.1	+11.2	69.2	28
29	26 13.7	+3.2	64.7	26 39.1	+4.3	65.1	27 04.2	+5.2	65.6	27 28.7	+6.3	66.1	27 52.8	+7.4	66.6	28 16.5	+8.4	67.0	28 39.6	+9.6	67.5	29 02.3	+10.6	68.1	29
30	26 16.9	+2.6	63.6	26 43.4	+3.6	64.0	27 09.4	+4.7	64.5	27 35.0	+5.8	65.0	28 00.2	+6.9	65.4	28 24.9	+8.0	65.9	28 49.2	+9.0	66.4	29 12.9	+10.1	66.9	30
31	26 19.5	+2.1	62.5	26 47.0	+3.2	62.9	27 14.1	+4.2	63.4	27 40.8	+5.3	63.8	28 07.1	+6.3	64.3	28 32.9	+7.3	64.8	28 58.2	+8.4	65.3	29 23.0	+9.5	65.8	31
32	26 21.6	+1.6	61.3	26 50.2	+2.6	61.8	27 18.3	+3.7	62.2	27 46.1	+4.7	62.7	28 13.4	+5.7	63.2	28 40.2	+6.8	63.7	29 06.6	+7.9	64.2	29 32.5	+9.0	64.7	32
33	26 23.2	+1.1	60.2	26 52.8	+2.1	60.7	27 22.0	+3.1	61.1	27 50.8	+4.1	61.6	28 19.1	+5.2	62.0	28 47.0	+6.2	62.5	29 14.5	+7.2	63.0	29 41.5	+8.3	63.5	33
34	26 24.3	+0.5	59.1	26 54.9	+1.6	59.5	27 25.1	+2.6	60.0	27 54.9	+3.6	60.4	28 24.3	+4.6	60.9	28 53.2	+5.7	61.4	29 21.7	+6.7	61.9	29 49.8	+7.7	62.4	34
35	26 24.8	+0.1	58.0	26 56.5	+1.0	58.4	27 27.7	+2.0	58.9	27 58.5	+3.0	59.3	28 28.9	+4.1	59.8	28 58.9	+5.1	60.3	29 28.4	+6.2	60.7	29 57.5	+7.2	61.2	35
36	26 24.9	−0.5	56.9	26 57.5	+0.5	57.3	27 29.7	+1.5	57.7	28 01.5	+2.5	58.2	28 33.0	+3.4	58.6	29 04.0	+4.5	59.1	29 34.6	+5.5	59.6	30 04.7	+6.6	60.1	36
37	26 24.4	−1.0	55.8	26 58.0	−0.1	56.2	27 31.2	+0.9	56.6	28 04.0	+1.9	57.1	28 36.4	+3.0	57.5	29 08.5	+3.9	58.0	29 40.1	+4.9	58.5	30 11.3	+5.9	58.9	37
38	26 23.4	−1.5	54.6	26 57.9	−0.5	55.1	27 32.1	+0.4	55.5	28 05.9	+1.4	55.9	28 39.4	+2.3	56.4	29 12.4	+3.3	56.8	29 45.0	+4.4	57.3	30 17.2	+5.4	57.8	38
39	26 21.9	−2.1	53.5	26 57.4	−1.1	53.9	27 32.5	−0.1	54.4	28 07.3	+0.8	54.8	28 41.7	+1.8	55.2	29 15.7	+2.8	55.7	29 49.4	+3.7	56.2	30 22.6	+4.7	56.6	39
40	26 19.8	−2.5	52.4	26 56.3	−1.7	52.8	27 32.4	−0.7	53.2	28 08.1	+0.3	53.7	28 43.5	+1.2	54.1	29 18.5	+2.1	54.5	29 53.1	+3.1	55.0	30 27.3	+4.1	55.5	40
41	26 17.3	−3.1	51.3	26 54.6	−2.1	51.7	27 31.7	−1.3	52.1	28 08.4	−0.4	52.5	28 44.7	+0.6	52.9	29 20.6	+1.6	53.4	29 56.2	+2.6	53.9	30 31.4	+3.5	54.3	41
42	26 14.2	−3.6	50.2	26 52.5	−2.7	50.6	27 30.4	−1.8	51.0	28 08.0	−0.8	51.4	28 45.3	+0.1	51.8	29 22.2	+1.0	52.2	29 58.8	+1.9	52.7	30 34.9	+2.9	53.2	42
43	26 10.6	−4.1	49.1	26 49.8	−3.2	49.5	27 28.6	−2.3	49.8	28 07.2	−1.5	50.3	28 45.4	−0.6	50.7	29 23.2	+0.4	51.1	30 00.7	+1.3	51.5	30 37.8	+2.3	52.0	43
44	26 06.5	−4.6	48.0	26 46.6	−3.8	48.3	27 26.3	−2.9	48.7	28 05.7	−2.0	49.1	28 44.8	−1.1	49.5	29 23.6	−0.2	50.4	30 02.0	+0.8	50.4	30 40.1	+1.7	50.8	44
45	26 01.9	−5.1	46.9	26 42.8	−4.3	47.2	27 23.4	−3.4	47.6	28 03.7	−2.5	48.0	28 43.7	−1.6	48.4	29 23.4	−0.8	48.8	30 02.8	+0.1	49.2	30 41.8	+1.0	49.7	45
46	25 56.8	−5.6	45.7	26 38.5	−4.8	46.1	27 20.0	−4.0	46.5	28 01.2	−3.1	46.9	28 42.1	−2.3	47.2	29 22.6	−1.3	47.7	30 02.9	−0.5	48.1	30 42.8	+0.4	48.5	46
47	25 51.2	−6.1	44.6	26 33.7	−5.3	45.0	27 16.0	−4.4	45.3	27 58.1	−3.7	45.7	28 39.8	−2.8	46.1	29 21.3	−2.0	46.5	30 02.4	−1.1	46.9	30 43.2	−0.2	47.4	47
48	25 45.1	−6.7	43.5	26 28.4	−5.8	43.9	27 11.6	−5.1	44.2	27 54.4	−4.2	44.6	28 37.0	−3.4	45.0	29 19.3	−2.5	45.4	30 01.3	−1.7	45.8	30 43.0	−0.8	46.2	48
49	25 38.4	−7.1	42.4	26 22.6	−6.3	42.8	27 06.5	−5.5	43.1	27 50.2	−4.8	43.5	28 33.6	−3.9	43.8	29 16.8	−3.2	44.2	29 59.6	−2.3	44.6	30 42.2	−1.5	45.0	49
50	25 31.3	−7.6	41.3	26 16.3	−6.9	41.7	27 01.0	−6.1	42.0	27 45.4	−5.3	42.3	28 29.7	−4.6	42.7	29 13.6	−3.7	43.1	29 57.3	−2.9	43.5	30 40.7	−2.0	43.9	50
51	25 23.7	−8.1	40.2	26 09.4	−7.4	40.5	26 54.9	−6.6	40.9	27 40.1	−5.8	41.2	28 25.1	−5.0	41.6	29 09.9	−4.3	41.9	29 54.4	−3.5	42.3	30 38.7	−2.7	42.7	51
52	25 15.6	−8.6	39.1	26 02.0	−7.8	39.4	26 48.3	−7.2	39.8	27 34.3	−6.4	40.1	28 20.1	−5.7	40.4	29 05.6	−4.9	40.8	29 50.9	−4.1	41.2	30 36.0	−3.4	41.5	52
53	25 07.0	−9.1	38.0	25 54.2	−8.4	38.3	26 41.1	−7.6	38.6	27 27.9	−7.0	39.0	28 14.4	−6.2	39.3	29 00.7	−5.4	39.6	29 46.8	−4.7	40.0	30 32.6	−3.9	40.4	53
54	24 57.9	−9.5	37.0	25 45.8	−8.9	37.2	26 33.5	−8.2	37.5	27 20.9	−7.4	37.8	28 08.2	−6.7	38.2	28 55.3	−6.0	38.5	29 42.1	−5.3	38.9	30 28.7	−4.5	39.2	54
55	24 48.4	−10.0	35.9	25 36.9	−9.3	36.1	26 25.3	−8.7	36.4	27 13.5	−8.0	36.7	28 01.5	−7.3	37.0	28 49.3	−6.6	37.4	29 36.8	−5.8	37.7	30 24.2	−5.2	38.1	55
56	24 38.4	−10.5	34.8	25 27.6	−9.9	35.0	26 16.6	−9.2	35.3	27 05.5	−8.5	35.6	27 54.2	−7.9	35.9	28 42.7	−7.2	36.2	29 31.0	−6.5	36.6	30 19.0	−5.7	36.9	56
57	24 27.9	−10.9	33.7	25 17.7	−10.3	34.0	26 07.4	−9.7	34.2	26 57.0	−9.1	34.5	27 46.3	−8.4	34.8	28 35.5	−7.7	35.1	29 24.5	−7.1	35.4	30 13.3	−6.4	35.8	57
58	24 17.0	−11.4	32.6	25 07.4	−10.8	32.9	25 57.7	−10.1	33.1	26 47.9	−9.5	33.4	27 37.9	−8.9	33.7	28 27.8	−8.3	34.0	29 17.4	−7.6	34.3	30 06.9	−6.9	34.6	58
59	24 05.6	−11.9	31.5	24 56.6	−11.2	31.8	25 47.6	−10.7	32.0	26 38.4	−10.1	32.3	27 29.0	−9.5	32.6	28 19.5	−8.8	32.9	29 09.8	−8.2	33.2	30 00.0	−7.6	33.5	59
60	23 53.7	−12.3	30.5	24 45.4	−11.8	30.7	25 36.9	−11.2	30.9	26 28.3	−10.6	31.2	27 19.5	−9.9	31.5	28 10.7	−9.4	31.7	29 01.6	−8.8	32.0	29 52.4	−8.2	32.3	60
61	23 41.4	−12.7	29.4	24 33.6	−12.2	29.6	25 25.7	−11.6	29.8	26 17.7	−11.1	30.1	27 09.6	−10.5	30.3	28 01.3	−10.0	30.6	28 52.8	−9.3	30.9	29 44.2	−8.7	31.2	61
62	23 28.7	−13.2	28.3	24 21.4	−12.6	28.5	25 14.1	−12.1	28.8	26 06.6	−11.5	29.0	26 59.1	−11.1	29.2	27 51.3	−10.4	29.5	28 43.5	−9.9	29.8	29 35.5	−9.3	30.0	62
63	23 15.5	−13.6	27.3	24 08.8	−13.1	27.5	25 02.0	−12.6	27.7	25 55.1	−12.1	27.9	26 48.0	−11.5	28.1	27 40.9	−11.0	28.4	28 33.6	−10.4	28.6	29 26.2	−9.9	28.9	63
64	23 01.9	−14.0	26.2	23 55.7	−13.5	26.4	24 49.4	−13.0	26.6	25 43.0	−12.5	26.8	26 36.5	−12.0	27.0	27 29.9	−11.5	27.3	28 23.2	−11.0	27.5	29 16.3	−10.5	27.8	64
65	22 47.9	−14.4	25.2	23 42.2	−14.0	25.3	24 36.4	−13.5	25.5	25 30.5	−13.1	25.7	26 24.5	−12.6	25.9	27 18.4	−12.1	26.2	28 12.2	−11.6	26.4	29 05.8	−11.0	26.6	65
66	22 33.5	−14.9	24.1	23 28.2	−14.4	24.3	24 22.9	−14.0	24.5	25 17.4	−13.5	24.7	26 11.9	−13.0	24.9	27 06.3	−12.5	25.1	28 00.6	−12.1	25.3	28 54.8	−11.6	25.5	66
67	22 18.6	−15.2	23.1	23 13.8	−14.8	23.2	24 08.9	−14.4	23.4	25 03.9	−13.9	23.6	25 58.9	−13.5	23.8	26 53.8	−13.1	24.0	27 48.5	−12.6	24.2	28 43.2	−12.1	24.4	67
68	22 03.4	−15.6	22.0	22 59.0	−15.2	22.2	23 54.5	−14.8	22.3	24 50.0	−14.4	22.5	25 45.4	−14.0	22.7	26 40.7	−13.6	22.9	27 35.9	−13.1	23.1	28 31.1	−12.7	23.3	68
69	21 47.8	−16.1	21.0	22 43.8	−15.7	21.1	23 39.7	−15.3	21.3	24 35.6	−14.9	21.4	25 31.4	−14.5	21.6	26 27.1	−14.0	21.8	27 22.8	−13.6	22.0	28 18.4	−13.2	22.2	69
70	21 31.7	−16.4	19.9	22 28.1	−16.0	20.1	23 24.4	−15.6	20.2	24 20.7	−15.3	20.4	25 16.9	−14.9	20.5	26 13.1	−14.6	20.7	27 09.2	−14.2	20.9	28 05.2	−13.7	21.1	70
71	21 15.3	−16.8	18.9	22 12.1	−16.5	19.0	23 08.8	−16.1	19.2	24 05.4	−15.7	19.3	25 02.0	−15.4	19.5	25 58.5	−15.0	19.6	26 55.0	−14.6	19.8	27 51.5	−14.3	20.0	71
72	20 58.5	−17.1	17.9	21 55.6	−16.8	18.0	22 52.7	−16.6	18.1	23 49.7	−16.2	18.3	24 46.6	−15.8	18.4	25 43.5	−15.5	18.5	26 40.4	−15.2	18.7	27 37.2	−14.8	18.9	72
73	20 41.4	−17.6	16.8	21 38.8	−17.2	17.0	22 36.1	−16.9	17.1	23 33.5	−16.6	17.2	24 30.8	−16.3	17.3	25 28.0	−15.9	17.5	26 25.2	−15.6	17.6	27 22.4	−15.3	17.8	73
74	20 23.8	−17.8	15.8	21 21.6	−17.6	15.9	22 19.2	−17.3	16.0	23 16.9	−17.0	16.2	24 14.5	−16.7	16.3	25 12.1	−16.4	16.4	26 09.6	−16.1	16.5	27 07.1	−15.8	16.7	74
75	20 06.0	−18.3	14.8	21 04.0	−18.0	14.9	22 01.9	−17.7	15.0	22 59.9	−17.4	15.1	23 57.8	−17.2	15.2	24 55.7	−16.9	15.3	25 53.5	−16.6	15.5	26 51.3	−16.3	15.6	75
76	19 47.7	−18.5	13.8	20 46.0	−18.3	13.9	21 44.2	−18.0	14.0	22 42.5	−17.9	14.1	23 40.6	−17.5	14.2	24 38.8	−17.3	14.3	25 36.9	−17.0	14.4	26 35.0	−16.7	14.5	76
77	19 29.2	−18.9	12.8	20 27.7	−18.7	12.9	21 26.2	−18.5	12.9	22 24.6	−18.2	13.0	23 23.1	−18.0	13.1	24 21.5	−17.7	13.2	25 19.9	−17.5	13.3	26 18.3	−17.3	13.5	77
78	19 10.3	−19.2	11.8	20 09.0	−19.0	11.8	21 07.7	−18.8	11.9	22 06.4	−18.6	12.0	23 05.1	−18.4	12.1	24 03.8	−18.2	12.2	25 02.4	−17.9	12.3	26 01.0	−17.7	12.4	78
79	18 51.1	−19.6	10.8	19 50.0	−19.4	10.8	20 48.9	−19.2	10.9	21 47.8	−19.0	11.0	22 46.7	−18.8	11.1	23 45.6	−18.6	11.1	24 44.5	−18.4	11.2	25 43.3	−18.2	11.3	79
80	18 31.5	−19.9	9.8	19 30.6	−19.7	9.8	20 29.7	−19.5	9.9	21 28.8	−19.3	10.0	22 27.9	−19.1	10.0	23 27.0	−19.0	10.1	24 26.1	−18.8	10.2	25 25.1	−18.6	10.3	80
81	18 11.6	−20.1	8.8	19 10.9	−20.0	8.8	20 10.2	−19.8	8.9	21 09.5	−19.7	8.9	22 08.8	−19.6	9.0	23 08.0	−19.4	9.1	24 07.3	−19.3	9.1	25 06.5	−19.1	9.2	81
82	17 51.5	−20.5	7.8	18 50.9	−20.3	7.8	19 50.4	−20.2	7.9	20 49.8	−20.1	7.9	21 49.2	−19.9	8.0	22 48.6	−19.8	8.0	23 48.0	−19.6	8.1	24 47.4	−19.5	8.2	82
83	17 31.0	−20.7	6.8	18 30.6	−20.7	6.8	19 30.2	−20.6	6.9	20 29.7	−20.4	6.9	21 29.3	−20.3	7.0	22 28.8	−20.1	7.0	23 28.4	−20.1	7.1	24 27.9	−19.9	7.1	83
84	17 10.3	−21.1	5.8	18 09.9	−20.9	5.9	19 09.6	−20.8	5.9	20 09.3	−20.7	5.9	21 09.0	−20.7	6.0	22 08.7	−20.6	6.0	23 08.3	−20.4	6.0	24 08.0	−20.3	6.1	84
85	16 49.2	−21.3	4.8	17 49.0	−21.2	4.9	18 48.8	−21.2	4.9	19 48.6	−21.1	4.9	20 48.3	−21.0	5.0	21 48.1	−20.9	5.0	22 47.9	−20.8	5.0	23 47.7	−20.8	5.1	85
86	16 27.9	−21.6	3.9	17 27.8	−21.6	3.9	18 27.6	−21.4	3.9	19 27.5	−21.4	3.9	20 27.3	−21.3	4.0	21 27.2	−21.3	4.0	22 27.1	−21.3	4.0	23 26.9	−21.1	4.0	86
87	16 06.3	−21.8	2.9	17 06.2	−21.8	2.9	18 06.2	−21.8	2.9	19 06.1	−21.7	2.9	20 06.0	−21.7	3.0	21 05.9	−21.6	3.0	22 05.8	−21.5	3.0	23 05.8	−21.6	3.0	87
88	15 44.5	−22.1	1.9	16 44.4	−22.1	1.9	17 44.4	−22.1	1.9	18 44.4	−22.1	2.0	19 44.3	−22.0	2.0	20 44.3	−22.0	2.0	21 44.3	−22.0	2.0	22 44.2	−21.9	2.0	88
89	15 22.4	−22.4	1.0	16 22.3	−22.3	1.0	17 22.3	−22.3	1.0	18 22.3	−22.3	1.0	19 22.3	−22.3	1.0	20 22.3	−22.3	1.0	21 22.3	−22.3	1.0	22 22.3	−22.3	1.0	89
90	15 00.0	−22.6	0.0	16 00.0	−22.6	0.0	17 00.0	−22.6	0.0	18 00.0	−22.6	0.0	19 00.0	−22.6	0.0	20 00.0	−22.6	0.0	21 00.0	−22.6	0.0	22 00.0	−22.7	0.0	90
	15°			16°			17°			18°			19°			20°			21°			22°			

68°, 292° L.H.A. LATITUDE SAME NAME AS DECLINATION

138

Dec.	15° Hc	15° d	15° Z	16° Hc	16° d	16° Z	17° Hc	17° d	17° Z	18° Hc	18° d	18° Z
°	° ′	′	°	° ′	′	°	° ′	′	°	° ′	′	°
0	21 12.8	-16.8	96.0	21 06.4	-17.9	96.4	20 59.5	-18.9	96.7	20 52.3	-20.0	97.1
1	20 56.0	-17.3	97.0	20 48.5	-18.3	97.4	20 40.6	-19.4	97.8	20 32.3	-20.4	98.1
2	20 38.7	-17.5	98.0	20 30.2	-18.6	98.4	20 21.2	-19.6	98.8	20 11.9	-20.7	99.1
3	20 21.2	-18.0	99.0	20 11.6	-19.0	99.4	20 01.6	-20.1	99.8	19 51.2	-21.0	100.1
4	20 03.2	-18.2	100.1	19 52.6	-19.3	100.4	19 41.5	-20.3	100.8	19 30.2	-21.4	101.1
5	19 45.0	-18.6	101.1	19 33.3	-19.7	101.4	19 21.2	-20.7	101.8	19 08.8	-21.7	102.1
6	19 26.4	-19.0	102.1	19 13.6	-20.0	102.4	19 00.5	-21.0	102.8	18 47.1	-22.0	103.1
7	19 07.4	-19.3	103.1	18 53.6	-20.2	103.4	18 39.5	-21.3	103.8	18 25.1	-22.3	104.1
8	18 48.1	-19.6	104.1	18 33.4	-20.6	104.4	18 18.2	-21.5	104.7	18 02.8	-22.6	105.1
9	18 28.5	-19.9	105.1	18 12.8	-21.0	105.4	17 56.7	-21.9	105.7	17 40.2	-22.8	106.0
10	18 08.6	-20.2	106.1	17 51.8	-21.2	106.4	17 34.8	-22.2	106.7	17 17.4	-23.2	107.0
11	17 48.4	-20.5	107.1	17 30.6	-21.4	107.4	17 12.6	-22.5	107.7	16 54.2	-23.4	108.0
12	17 27.9	-20.8	108.1	17 09.2	-21.8	108.4	16 50.1	-22.7	108.6	16 30.8	-23.7	108.9
13	17 07.1	-21.1	109.0	16 47.4	-22.1	109.3	16 27.4	-23.0	109.6	16 07.1	-23.9	109.9
14	16 46.0	-21.3	110.0	16 25.3	-22.3	110.3	16 04.4	-23.3	110.6	15 43.2	-24.2	110.8
15	16 24.7	-21.7	111.0	16 03.0	-22.5	111.3	15 41.1	-23.5	111.5	15 19.0	-24.4	111.8
16	16 03.0	-21.9	112.0	15 40.5	-22.9	112.2	15 17.6	-23.7	112.5	14 54.6	-24.7	112.7
17	15 41.1	-22.1	112.9	15 17.6	-23.0	113.2	14 53.9	-24.0	113.4	14 29.9	-24.9	113.7
18	15 19.0	-22.4	113.9	14 54.6	-23.3	114.1	14 29.9	-24.2	114.4	14 05.0	-25.1	114.6
19	14 56.6	-22.6	114.9	14 31.3	-23.6	115.1	14 05.7	-24.4	115.3	13 39.9	-25.3	115.5
20	14 34.0	-22.9	115.8	14 07.7	-23.7	116.0	13 41.3	-24.7	116.3	13 14.6	-25.5	116.5
21	14 11.1	-23.1	116.8	13 44.0	-24.0	117.0	13 16.6	-24.8	117.2	12 49.1	-25.7	117.4
22	13 48.0	-23.3	117.7	13 20.0	-24.2	117.9	12 51.8	-25.0	118.1	12 23.4	-25.9	118.3
23	13 24.7	-23.5	118.7	12 55.8	-24.4	118.9	12 26.8	-25.3	119.1	11 57.5	-26.0	119.3
24	13 01.2	-23.7	119.6	12 31.4	-24.5	119.8	12 01.5	-25.4	120.0	11 31.5	-26.3	120.2
25	12 37.5	-24.0	120.6	12 06.9	-24.8	120.7	11 36.1	-25.6	120.9	11 05.2	-26.4	121.1
26	12 13.5	-24.1	121.5	11 42.1	-24.9	121.7	11 10.5	-25.7	121.8	10 38.8	-26.6	122.0
27	11 49.4	-24.3	122.4	11 17.2	-25.1	122.6	10 44.8	-26.0	122.8	10 12.2	-26.7	122.9
28	11 25.1	-24.4	123.4	10 52.1	-25.3	123.5	10 18.8	-26.0	123.7	9 45.5	-26.9	123.8
29	11 00.7	-24.7	124.3	10 26.8	-25.5	124.5	9 52.8	-26.3	124.6	9 18.6	-27.0	124.7
30	10 36.0	-24.8	125.2	10 01.3	-25.5	125.4	9 26.5	-26.3	125.5	8 51.6	-27.1	125.6
31	10 11.2	-25.0	126.1	9 35.8	-25.8	126.3	9 00.2	-26.5	126.4	8 24.5	-27.2	126.5
32	9 46.2	-25.1	127.1	9 10.0	-25.9	127.2	8 33.7	-26.6	127.3	7 57.3	-27.4	127.4
33	9 21.1	-25.2	128.0	8 44.1	-26.0	128.1	8 07.1	-26.8	128.2	7 29.9	-27.5	128.3
34	8 55.9	-25.4	128.9	8 18.1	-26.1	129.0	7 40.3	-26.8	129.1	7 02.4	-27.6	129.2
35	8 30.5	-25.5	129.8	7 52.0	-26.2	129.9	7 13.5	-27.0	130.0	6 34.8	-27.7	130.1
36	8 05.0	-25.7	130.7	7 25.8	-26.4	130.8	6 46.5	-27.1	130.9	6 07.1	-27.7	131.0
37	7 39.3	-25.7	131.7	6 59.4	-26.4	131.8	6 19.4	-27.1	131.8	5 39.4	-27.9	131.9
38	7 13.6	-25.9	132.6	6 33.0	-26.6	132.7	5 52.3	-27.3	132.7	5 11.5	-27.9	132.8
39	6 47.7	-25.9	133.5	6 06.4	-26.6	133.6	5 25.0	-27.3	133.6	4 43.6	-28.0	133.7
40	6 21.8	-26.1	134.4	5 39.8	-26.8	134.5	4 57.7	-27.4	134.5	4 15.6	-28.0	134.6
41	5 55.7	-26.1	135.3	5 13.0	-26.8	135.4	4 30.3	-27.4	135.4	3 47.6	-28.1	135.5
42	5 29.6	-26.3	136.2	4 46.2	-26.8	136.3	4 02.9	-27.6	136.3	3 19.5	-28.2	136.4
43	5 03.3	-26.3	137.1	4 19.4	-27.0	137.2	3 35.3	-27.5	137.2	2 51.3	-28.2	137.2
44	4 37.0	-26.3	138.0	3 52.4	-27.0	138.0	3 07.8	-27.6	138.1	2 23.1	-28.2	138.1
45	4 10.7	-26.5	138.9	3 25.4	-27.0	138.9	2 40.2	-27.7	139.0	1 54.9	-28.3	139.0
46	3 44.2	-26.5	139.8	2 58.4	-27.1	139.8	2 12.5	-27.7	139.9	1 26.6	-28.2	139.9
47	3 17.7	-26.5	140.7	2 31.3	-27.1	140.7	1 44.8	-27.7	140.8	0 58.4	-28.3	140.8
48	2 51.2	-26.6	141.6	2 04.2	-27.2	141.6	1 17.1	-27.7	141.6	0 30.1	-28.3	141.7
49	2 24.6	-26.6	142.5	1 37.0	-27.2	142.5	0 49.4	-27.7	142.5	0 01.8	-28.3	142.5
50	1 58.0	-26.6	143.4	1 09.8	-27.2	143.4	0 21.7	-27.8	143.4	0 26.5	+28.3	36.6
51	1 31.4	-26.7	144.3	0 42.6	-27.2	144.3	0 06.1	+27.7	35.7	0 54.8	+28.3	35.7
52	1 04.7	-26.7	145.2	0 15.4	-27.2	145.2	0 33.8	+27.8	34.8	1 23.1	+28.2	34.8
53	0 38.0	-26.7	146.1	0 11.8	+27.2	33.9	1 01.6	+27.7	33.9	1 51.3	+28.3	33.9
54	0 11.3	-26.7	147.0	0 39.0	+27.2	33.0	1 29.3	+27.7	33.0	2 19.6	+28.2	33.1
55	0 15.4	+26.6	32.1	1 06.2	+27.2	32.1	1 57.0	+27.6	32.1	2 47.8	+28.1	32.2
56	0 42.0	+26.7	31.2	1 33.4	+27.1	31.2	2 24.6	+27.7	31.3	3 15.9	+28.1	31.3
57	1 08.7	+26.7	30.3	2 00.5	+27.1	30.4	2 52.3	+27.6	30.4	3 44.0	+28.1	30.4
58	1 35.4	+26.6	29.4	2 27.6	+27.1	29.5	3 19.9	+27.5	29.5	4 12.1	+28.0	29.5
59	2 02.0	+26.6	28.5	2 54.7	+27.1	28.6	3 47.4	+27.5	28.6	4 40.1	+27.9	28.6
60	2 28.6	+26.6	27.6	3 21.8	+27.0	27.7	4 14.9	+27.4	27.7	5 08.0	+27.9	27.7
61	2 55.2	+26.5	26.7	3 48.8	+26.9	26.8	4 42.3	+27.4	26.8	5 35.9	+27.8	26.9
62	3 21.7	+26.5	25.9	4 15.7	+26.9	25.9	5 09.7	+27.3	25.9	6 03.7	+27.6	26.0
63	3 48.2	+26.4	25.0	4 42.6	+26.8	25.0	5 37.0	+27.2	25.0	6 31.3	+27.6	25.1
64	4 14.6	+26.4	24.1	5 09.4	+26.8	24.1	6 04.2	+27.1	24.1	6 58.9	+27.5	24.2
65	4 41.0	+26.3	23.2	5 36.2	+26.6	23.2	6 31.3	+27.0	23.2	7 26.4	+27.4	23.3
66	5 07.3	+26.2	22.2	6 02.8	+26.6	22.3	6 58.3	+26.9	22.3	7 53.8	+27.3	22.4
67	5 33.5	+26.1	21.3	6 29.4	+26.5	21.4	7 25.2	+26.9	21.4	8 21.1	+27.1	21.5
68	5 59.6	+26.1	20.4	6 55.9	+26.3	20.5	7 52.1	+26.6	20.5	8 48.2	+27.1	20.6
69	6 25.7	+25.9	19.5	7 22.2	+26.3	19.6	8 18.7	+26.6	19.6	9 15.3	+26.8	19.7
70	6 51.6	+25.9	18.6	7 48.5	+26.1	18.7	8 45.3	+26.5	18.7	9 42.1	+26.8	18.8
71	7 17.5	+25.7	17.7	8 14.6	+26.0	17.8	9 11.8	+26.3	17.8	10 08.9	+26.6	17.9
72	7 43.2	+25.6	16.8	8 40.6	+25.9	16.8	9 38.1	+26.1	16.9	10 35.5	+26.4	16.9
73	8 08.8	+25.5	15.9	9 06.5	+25.8	15.9	10 04.2	+26.0	16.0	11 01.9	+26.3	16.0
74	8 34.3	+25.4	15.0	9 32.3	+25.6	15.0	10 30.2	+25.9	15.1	11 28.2	+26.1	15.1
75	8 59.7	+25.2	14.1	9 57.9	+25.5	14.1	10 56.1	+25.7	14.1	11 54.3	+25.9	14.2
76	9 24.9	+25.1	13.1	10 23.4	+25.3	13.2	11 21.8	+25.5	13.2	12 20.2	+25.7	13.3
77	9 50.0	+25.0	12.2	10 48.7	+25.1	12.3	11 47.3	+25.3	12.3	12 45.9	+25.5	12.3
78	10 15.0	+24.7	11.3	11 13.8	+25.0	11.3	12 12.6	+25.2	11.4	13 11.4	+25.4	11.4
79	10 39.7	+24.7	10.4	11 38.8	+24.7	10.4	12 37.8	+24.9	10.4	13 36.8	+25.1	10.5
80	11 04.4	+24.4	9.4	12 03.5	+24.6	9.5	13 02.7	+24.8	9.5	14 01.9	+24.9	9.6
81	11 28.8	+24.3	8.5	12 28.1	+24.5	8.5	13 27.5	+24.5	8.6	14 26.8	+24.7	8.6
82	11 53.1	+24.1	7.6	12 52.6	+24.2	7.6	13 52.0	+24.4	7.6	14 51.5	+24.4	7.7
83	12 17.2	+23.9	6.6	13 16.8	+24.0	6.7	14 16.4	+24.1	6.7	15 15.9	+24.3	6.7
84	12 41.1	+23.7	5.7	13 40.8	+23.7	5.7	14 40.5	+23.8	5.7	15 40.2	+23.9	5.8
85	13 04.8	+23.4	4.8	14 04.5	+23.6	4.8	15 04.3	+23.7	4.8	16 04.1	+23.7	4.8
86	13 28.2	+23.3	3.8	14 28.1	+23.3	3.8	15 28.0	+23.4	3.8	16 27.8	+23.5	3.9
87	13 51.5	+23.1	2.9	14 51.4	+23.1	2.9	15 51.4	+23.1	2.9	16 51.3	+23.2	2.9
88	14 14.6	+22.8	1.9	15 14.5	+22.9	1.9	16 14.5	+22.9	1.9	17 14.5	+22.9	1.9
89	14 37.4	+22.6	1.0	15 37.4	+22.6	1.0	16 37.4	+22.6	1.0	17 37.4	+22.6	1.0
90	15 00.0	+22.4	0.0	16 00.0	+22.3	0.0	17 00.0	+22.3	0.0	18 00.0	+22.3	0.0
	15°			16°			17°			18°		

19° Hc	19° d	19° Z	20° Hc	20° d	20° Z	21° Hc	21° d	21° Z	22° Hc	22° d	22° Z	Dec.
° ′	′	°	° ′	′	°	° ′	′	°	° ′	′	°	°
20 44.7	-21.1	97.5	20 36.6	-22.1	97.9	20 28.2	-23.1	98.2	20 19.4	-24.1	98.6	0
20 23.6	-21.4	98.5	20 14.5	-22.4	98.9	20 05.1	-23.4	99.2	19 55.3	-24.4	99.6	1
20 02.2	-21.7	99.5	19 52.1	-22.7	99.8	19 41.7	-23.8	100.2	19 30.9	-24.8	100.6	2
19 40.5	-22.1	100.5	19 29.4	-23.1	100.8	19 17.9	-24.1	101.2	19 06.1	-25.0	101.5	3
19 18.4	-22.4	101.5	19 06.3	-23.4	101.8	18 53.8	-24.3	102.1	18 41.1	-25.4	102.5	4
18 56.0	-22.7	102.4	18 42.9	-23.7	102.8	18 29.5	-24.7	103.1	18 15.7	-25.6	103.4	5
18 33.3	-22.9	103.4	18 19.2	-23.9	103.8	18 04.8	-24.9	104.1	17 50.1	-25.9	104.4	6
18 10.4	-23.3	104.4	17 55.3	-24.3	104.7	17 39.9	-25.2	105.0	17 24.2	-26.2	105.3	7
17 47.1	-23.6	105.4	17 31.0	-24.5	105.7	17 14.7	-25.5	106.0	16 58.0	-26.4	106.3	8
17 23.5	-23.8	106.3	17 06.5	-24.8	106.6	16 49.2	-25.8	106.9	16 31.6	-26.7	107.2	9
16 59.7	-24.1	107.3	16 41.7	-25.1	107.6	16 23.4	-26.0	107.9	16 04.9	-26.9	108.1	10
16 35.6	-24.4	108.3	16 16.6	-25.3	108.5	15 57.4	-26.2	108.8	15 38.0	-27.2	109.1	11
16 11.2	-24.6	109.2	15 51.3	-25.5	109.5	15 31.2	-26.5	109.7	15 10.8	-27.4	110.0	12
15 46.6	-24.9	110.2	15 25.8	-25.8	110.4	15 04.7	-26.7	110.7	14 43.4	-27.6	110.9	13
15 21.7	-25.1	111.1	15 00.0	-26.0	111.3	14 38.0	-26.9	111.6	14 15.8	-27.8	111.8	14
14 56.6	-25.3	112.0	14 34.0	-26.3	112.3	14 11.1	-27.1	112.5	13 48.0	-28.0	112.7	15
14 31.3	-25.6	113.0	14 07.7	-26.4	113.2	13 44.0	-27.4	113.4	13 20.0	-28.2	113.7	16
14 05.7	-25.8	113.9	13 41.3	-26.7	114.1	13 16.6	-27.5	114.4	12 51.8	-28.4	114.6	17
13 39.9	-25.9	114.8	13 14.6	-26.8	115.1	12 49.1	-27.7	115.3	12 23.4	-28.5	115.5	18
13 14.0	-26.2	115.8	12 47.8	-27.1	116.0	12 21.4	-27.9	116.2	11 54.9	-28.8	116.4	19
12 47.8	-26.4	116.7	12 20.7	-27.2	116.9	11 53.5	-28.1	117.1	11 26.1	-28.9	117.3	20
12 21.4	-26.5	117.6	11 53.5	-27.4	117.8	11 25.4	-28.2	118.0	10 57.2	-29.0	118.2	21
11 54.9	-26.8	118.5	11 26.1	-27.6	118.7	10 57.2	-28.4	118.9	10 28.2	-29.2	119.0	22
11 28.1	-26.9	119.4	10 58.5	-27.7	119.6	10 28.8	-28.5	119.8	9 59.0	-29.4	119.9	23
11 01.2	-27.1	120.4	10 30.8	-27.9	120.5	10 00.3	-28.7	120.7	9 29.6	-29.5	120.8	24
10 34.1	-27.2	121.3	10 02.9	-28.0	121.4	9 31.6	-28.8	121.6	9 00.1	-29.6	121.7	25
10 06.9	-27.3	122.2	9 34.9	-28.1	122.3	9 02.8	-29.0	122.5	8 30.5	-29.7	122.6	26
9 39.6	-27.6	123.1	9 06.8	-28.3	123.2	8 33.8	-29.0	123.3	8 00.8	-29.8	123.5	27
9 12.0	-27.6	124.0	8 38.5	-28.5	124.1	8 04.8	-29.2	124.2	7 31.0	-30.0	124.3	28
8 44.4	-27.8	124.9	8 10.0	-28.5	125.0	7 35.6	-29.3	125.1	7 01.0	-30.0	125.2	29
8 16.6	-27.9	125.8	7 41.5	-28.6	125.9	7 06.3	-29.4	126.0	6 31.0	-30.1	126.1	30
7 48.7	-28.0	126.7	7 12.9	-28.8	126.8	6 36.9	-29.5	126.9	6 00.9	-30.2	127.0	31
7 20.7	-28.1	127.6	6 44.1	-28.8	127.6	6 07.4	-29.5	127.7	5 30.7	-30.3	127.8	32
6 52.6	-28.2	128.4	6 15.3	-29.0	128.5	5 37.9	-29.7	128.6	5 00.4	-30.4	128.7	33
6 24.4	-28.3	129.3	5 46.3	-29.0	129.4	5 08.2	-29.7	129.5	4 30.0	-30.4	129.6	34
5 56.1	-28.4	130.2	5 17.3	-29.0	130.3	4 38.5	-29.8	130.4	3 59.6	-30.4	130.4	35
5 27.7	-28.4	131.1	4 48.3	-29.2	131.2	4 08.7	-29.8	131.2	3 29.2	-30.5	131.3	36
4 59.3	-28.6	132.0	4 19.1	-29.2	132.0	3 38.9	-29.9	132.1	2 58.7	-30.6	132.1	37
4 30.7	-28.6	132.9	3 49.9	-29.3	132.9	3 09.0	-29.9	133.0	2 28.1	-30.6	133.0	38
4 02.1	-28.6	133.8	3 20.6	-29.3	133.8	2 39.1	-30.0	133.8	1 57.5	-30.6	133.9	39
3 33.5	-28.7	134.6	2 51.3	-29.3	134.7	2 09.1	-30.0	134.7	1 26.9	-30.6	134.7	40
3 04.8	-28.8	135.5	2 22.0	-29.4	135.5	1 39.1	-30.0	135.6	0 56.3	-30.7	135.6	41
2 36.0	-28.8	136.4	1 52.6	-29.4	136.4	1 09.1	-30.0	136.4	0 25.6	-30.6	136.4	42
2 07.2	-28.8	137.3	1 23.2	-29.5	137.3	0 39.1	-30.1	137.3	0 05.0	+30.7	42.7	43
1 38.4	-28.8	138.1	0 53.7	-29.4	138.2	0 09.0	-30.0	138.2	0 35.7	+30.6	41.8	44
1 09.6	-28.9	139.0	0 24.3	-29.5	139.0	0 21.0	+30.0	41.0	1 06.3	+30.6	41.0	45
0 40.7	-28.8	139.9	0 05.2	+29.4	40.1	0 51.0	+30.1	40.1	1 36.9	+30.6	40.1	46
0 11.9	-28.9	140.8	0 34.6	+29.4	39.2	1 21.1	+30.0	39.2	2 07.5	+30.6	39.3	47
0 17.0	+28.8	38.3	1 04.0	+29.5	38.4	1 51.1	+30.0	38.4	2 38.1	+30.6	38.4	48
0 45.8	+28.9	37.5	1 33.5	+29.4	37.5	2 21.1	+29.9	37.5	3 08.7	+30.5	37.5	49
1 14.7	+28.8	36.6	2 02.9	+29.3	36.6	2 51.0	+29.9	36.6	3 39.2	+30.4	36.7	50
1 43.5	+28.8	35.7	2 32.2	+29.4	35.7	3 20.9	+29.9	35.8	4 09.6	+30.4	35.8	51
2 12.3	+28.8	34.8	3 01.6	+29.3	34.9	3 50.8	+29.8	34.9	4 40.0	+30.3	34.9	52
2 41.1	+28.8	34.0	3 30.9	+29.2	34.0	4 20.6	+29.8	34.0	5 10.3	+30.3	34.1	53
3 09.9	+28.6	33.1	4 00.1	+29.2	33.1	4 50.4	+29.6	33.2	5 40.6	+30.2	33.2	54
3 38.5	+28.7	32.2	4 29.3	+29.1	32.2	5 20.0	+29.7	32.3	6 10.8	+30.1	32.3	55
4 07.2	+28.6	31.3	4 58.4	+29.1	31.4	5 49.7	+29.5	31.4	6 40.9	+30.0	31.5	56
4 35.8	+28.5	30.4	5 27.5	+29.0	30.5	6 19.2	+29.4	30.5	7 10.9	+29.9	30.6	57
5 04.3	+28.4	29.6	5 56.5	+28.9	29.6	6 48.6	+29.4	29.7	7 40.8	+29.8	29.7	58
5 32.7	+28.4	28.7	6 25.4	+28.8	28.7	7 18.0	+29.2	28.8	8 10.6	+29.6	28.8	59
6 01.1	+28.3	27.8	6 54.2	+28.7	27.8	7 47.2	+29.2	27.9	8 40.2	+29.6	28.0	60
6 29.4	+28.2	26.9	7 22.9	+28.6	27.0	8 16.4	+29.0	27.0	9 09.8	+29.4	27.1	61
6 57.6	+28.1	26.0	7 51.5	+28.5	26.1	8 45.4	+28.9	26.1	9 39.2	+29.3	26.2	62
7 25.7	+28.0	25.1	8 20.0	+28.4	25.2	9 14.3	+28.7	25.2	10 08.5	+29.2	25.3	63
7 53.7	+27.8	24.2	8 48.4	+28.2	24.3	9 43.0	+28.7	24.3	10 37.7	+29.0	24.4	64
8 21.5	+27.8	23.3	9 16.6	+28.1	23.4	10 11.7	+28.5	23.5	11 06.7	+28.8	23.5	65
8 49.3	+27.6	22.4	9 44.7	+28.0	22.5	10 40.2	+28.3	22.6	11 35.5	+28.7	22.6	66
9 16.9	+27.5	21.5	10 12.7	+27.8	21.6	11 08.5	+28.2	21.7	12 04.2	+28.5	21.7	67
9 44.4	+27.3	20.6	10 40.5	+27.7	20.7	11 36.7	+28.0	20.8	12 32.7	+28.4	20.8	68
10 11.7	+27.2	19.7	11 08.2	+27.5	19.8	12 04.7	+27.8	19.9	13 01.1	+28.1	19.9	69
10 38.9	+27.1	18.8	11 35.7	+27.4	18.9	12 32.5	+27.6	19.0	13 29.2	+28.0	19.0	70
11 06.0	+26.9	17.9	12 03.1	+27.1	18.0	13 00.1	+27.5	18.0	13 57.2	+27.7	18.1	71
11 32.9	+26.7	17.0	12 30.2	+27.0	17.1	13 27.6	+27.2	17.1	14 24.9	+27.5	17.2	72
11 59.6	+26.5	16.1	12 57.2	+26.8	16.2	13 54.8	+27.1	16.2	14 52.4	+27.3	16.3	73
12 26.1	+26.3	15.2	13 24.0	+26.6	15.2	14 21.9	+26.8	15.3	15 19.7	+27.1	15.4	74
12 52.4	+26.2	14.3	13 50.6	+26.3	14.3	14 48.7	+26.6	14.4	15 46.8	+26.9	14.4	75
13 18.6	+25.9	13.3	14 16.9	+26.2	13.4	15 15.3	+26.4	13.4	16 13.7	+26.6	13.5	76
13 44.5	+25.7	12.4	14 43.1	+25.9	12.5	15 41.7	+26.1	12.5	16 40.3	+26.3	12.6	77
14 10.2	+25.6	11.5	15 09.0	+25.7	11.5	16 07.8	+25.9	11.6	17 06.6	+26.1	11.6	78
14 35.8	+25.3	10.5	15 34.7	+25.5	10.6	16 33.7	+25.7	10.6	17 32.7	+25.8	10.7	79
15 01.1	+25.0	9.6	16 00.2	+25.2	9.6	16 59.4	+25.3	9.7	17 58.5	+25.5	9.7	80
15 26.1	+24.8	8.7	16 25.4	+25.0	8.7	17 24.7	+25.2	8.7	18 24.0	+25.3	8.8	81
15 50.9	+24.6	7.7	16 50.4	+24.7	7.7	17 49.9	+24.8	7.8	18 49.3	+25.0	7.8	82
16 15.5	+24.3	6.8	17 15.1	+24.4	6.8	18 14.7	+24.5	6.8	19 14.3	+24.6	6.9	83
16 39.8	+24.1	5.8	17 39.5	+24.2	5.8	18 39.2	+24.3	5.9	19 38.9	+24.4	5.9	84
17 03.9	+23.8	4.8	18 03.7	+23.9	4.9	19 03.5	+23.9	4.9	20 03.3	+24.0	4.9	85
17 27.7	+23.5	3.9	18 27.6	+23.5	3.9	19 27.4	+23.7	3.9	20 27.3	+23.7	4.0	86
17 51.2	+23.2	2.9	18 51.1	+23.3	2.9	19 51.1	+23.3	3.0	20 51.0	+23.3	3.0	87
18 14.4	+23.0	2.0	19 14.4	+23.0	2.0	20 14.4	+23.0	2.0	21 14.3	+23.0	2.0	88
18 37.4	+22.6	1.0	19 37.4	+22.6	1.0	20 37.4	+22.6	1.0	21 37.3	+22.7	1.0	89
19 00.0	+22.3	0.0	20 00.0	+22.3	0.0	21 00.0	+22.3	0.0	22 00.0	+22.3	0.0	90
19°			20°			21°			22°			

S. Lat. {L.H.A. greater than 180° ....Zn=180°–Z; L.H.A. less than 180°...........Zn=180°+Z}

69°, 291° L.H.A. LATITUDE SAME NAME AS DECLINATION

N. Lat. {L.H.A. greater than 180° .....Zn=Z; L.H.A. less than 180°............Zn=360°−Z}

Dec.	15°			16°			17°			18°		
	Hc	d	Z	Hc	d	Z	Hc	d	Z	Hc	d	Z
°	° ′	′	°	° ′	′	°	° ′	′	°	° ′	′	°
0	20 15.1	+16.4	95.7	20 09.0	+17.5	96.0	20 02.5	+18.5	96.4	19 55.6	+19.6	96.8
1	20 31.5	+16.0	94.6	20 26.5	+17.0	95.0	20 21.0	+18.2	95.4	20 15.2	+19.2	95.8
2	20 47.5	+15.7	93.6	20 43.5	+16.8	94.0	20 39.2	+17.8	94.4	20 34.4	+18.8	94.7
3	21 03.2	+15.2	92.6	21 00.3	+16.3	93.0	20 57.0	+17.4	93.4	20 53.2	+18.5	93.7
4	21 18.4	+14.9	91.5	21 16.6	+16.0	91.9	21 14.4	+17.0	92.3	21 11.7	+18.2	92.7
5	21 33.3	+14.5	90.5	21 32.6	+15.6	90.9	21 31.4	+16.7	91.3	21 29.9	+17.7	91.7
6	21 47.8	+14.1	89.5	21 48.2	+15.1	89.9	21 48.1	+16.3	90.3	21 47.6	+17.4	90.7
7	22 01.9	+13.7	88.4	22 03.3	+14.8	88.8	22 04.4	+15.9	89.2	22 05.0	+16.9	89.6
8	22 15.6	+13.3	87.4	22 18.1	+14.4	87.8	22 20.3	+15.4	88.2	22 21.9	+16.6	88.6
9	22 28.9	+12.9	86.3	22 32.5	+14.0	86.7	22 35.7	+15.1	87.1	22 38.5	+16.2	87.6
10	22 41.8	+12.4	85.3	22 46.5	+13.6	85.7	22 50.8	+14.7	86.1	22 54.7	+15.8	86.5
11	22 54.2	+12.1	84.2	23 00.1	+13.1	84.6	23 05.5	+14.2	85.0	23 10.5	+15.3	85.5
12	23 06.3	+11.6	83.1	23 13.2	+12.7	83.5	23 19.7	+13.8	84.0	23 25.8	+14.9	84.4
13	23 17.9	+11.1	82.1	23 25.9	+12.3	82.5	23 33.5	+13.4	82.9	23 40.7	+14.5	83.4
14	23 29.0	+10.8	81.0	23 38.2	+11.8	81.4	23 46.9	+13.0	81.9	23 55.2	+14.1	82.3
15	23 39.8	+10.2	79.9	23 50.0	+11.4	80.3	23 59.9	+12.5	80.8	24 09.3	+13.6	81.2
16	23 50.0	+9.9	78.8	24 01.4	+11.0	79.3	24 12.4	+12.0	79.7	24 22.9	+13.1	80.2
17	23 59.9	+9.4	77.8	24 12.4	+10.5	78.2	24 24.4	+11.6	78.6	24 36.0	+12.7	79.1
18	24 09.3	+8.9	76.7	24 22.9	+10.0	77.1	24 36.0	+11.1	77.6	24 48.7	+12.2	78.0
19	24 18.2	+8.4	75.6	24 32.9	+9.5	76.0	24 47.1	+10.7	76.5	25 00.9	+11.8	76.9
20	24 26.6	+8.0	74.5	24 42.4	+9.1	74.9	24 57.8	+10.2	75.4	25 12.7	+11.3	75.8
21	24 34.6	+7.5	73.4	24 51.5	+8.6	73.9	25 08.0	+9.7	74.3	25 24.0	+10.8	74.8
22	24 42.1	+7.1	72.3	25 00.1	+8.2	72.8	25 17.7	+9.2	73.2	25 34.8	+10.3	73.7
23	24 49.2	+6.6	71.2	25 08.3	+7.6	71.7	25 26.9	+8.8	72.1	25 45.1	+9.9	72.6
24	24 55.8	+6.1	70.1	25 15.9	+7.2	70.6	25 35.7	+8.3	71.0	25 55.0	+9.3	71.5
25	25 01.9	+5.6	69.0	25 23.1	+6.7	69.5	25 43.9	+7.8	69.9	26 04.3	+8.8	70.4
26	25 07.5	+5.1	67.9	25 29.8	+6.2	68.4	25 51.7	+7.2	68.8	26 13.1	+8.4	69.3
27	25 12.6	+4.6	66.8	25 36.0	+5.6	67.3	25 58.9	+6.8	67.7	26 21.5	+7.8	68.2
28	25 17.2	+4.1	65.7	25 41.6	+5.2	66.2	26 05.7	+6.2	66.6	26 29.3	+7.3	67.1
29	25 21.3	+3.7	64.6	25 46.8	+4.7	65.1	26 11.9	+5.8	65.5	26 36.6	+6.8	66.0
30	25 25.0	+3.1	63.5	25 51.5	+4.2	64.0	26 17.7	+5.2	64.4	26 43.4	+6.2	64.8
31	25 28.1	+2.7	62.4	25 55.7	+3.7	62.8	26 22.9	+4.7	63.3	26 49.6	+5.8	63.7
32	25 30.8	+2.1	61.3	25 59.4	+3.1	61.7	26 27.6	+4.2	62.2	26 55.4	+5.2	62.6
33	25 32.9	+1.7	60.2	26 02.5	+2.7	60.6	26 31.8	+3.6	61.1	27 00.6	+4.7	61.5
34	25 34.6	+1.1	59.1	26 05.2	+2.1	59.5	26 35.4	+3.2	59.9	27 05.3	+4.1	60.4
35	25 35.7	+0.6	58.0	26 07.3	+1.7	58.4	26 38.6	+2.6	58.8	27 09.4	+3.7	59.3
36	25 36.3	+0.2	56.9	26 09.0	+1.1	57.3	26 41.2	+2.1	57.7	27 13.1	+3.0	58.1
37	25 36.5	−0.4	55.8	26 10.1	+0.6	56.2	26 43.3	+1.6	56.6	27 16.1	+2.6	57.0
38	25 36.1	−0.8	54.7	26 10.7	+0.1	55.1	26 44.9	+1.0	55.5	27 18.7	+2.0	55.9
39	25 35.3	−1.4	53.6	26 10.8	−0.5	53.9	26 45.9	+0.5	54.3	27 20.7	+1.4	54.8
40	25 33.9	−1.9	52.4	26 10.3	−0.9	52.8	26 46.4	0.0	53.2	27 22.1	+1.0	53.6
41	25 32.0	−2.3	51.3	26 09.4	−1.5	51.7	26 46.4	−0.6	52.1	27 23.1	+0.3	52.5
42	25 29.7	−2.9	50.2	26 07.9	−2.0	50.6	26 45.8	−1.0	51.0	27 23.4	−0.1	51.4
43	25 26.8	−3.3	49.1	26 05.9	−2.4	49.5	26 44.8	−1.6	49.9	27 23.3	−0.7	50.3
44	25 23.5	−3.9	48.0	26 03.5	−3.0	48.4	26 43.2	−2.2	48.8	27 22.6	−1.3	49.1
45	25 19.6	−4.3	46.9	26 00.5	−3.5	47.3	26 41.0	−2.6	47.6	27 21.3	−1.8	48.0
46	25 15.3	−4.9	45.8	25 57.0	−4.1	46.2	26 38.4	−3.2	46.5	27 19.5	−2.3	46.9
47	25 10.4	−5.3	44.7	25 52.9	−4.5	45.0	26 35.2	−3.7	45.4	27 17.2	−2.9	45.8
48	25 05.1	−5.8	43.6	25 48.4	−5.0	43.9	26 31.5	−4.2	44.3	27 14.3	−3.4	44.6
49	24 59.3	−6.3	42.5	25 43.4	−5.5	42.8	26 27.3	−4.7	43.2	27 10.9	−3.9	43.5
50	24 53.0	−6.8	41.4	25 37.9	−6.0	41.7	26 22.6	−5.3	42.1	27 07.0	−4.5	42.4
51	24 46.2	−7.2	40.3	25 31.9	−6.5	40.6	26 17.3	−5.8	40.9	27 02.5	−5.0	41.3
52	24 39.0	−7.7	39.2	25 25.4	−7.0	39.5	26 11.5	−6.2	39.8	26 57.5	−5.5	40.2
53	24 31.3	−8.2	38.1	25 18.4	−7.5	38.4	26 05.3	−6.8	38.7	26 52.0	−6.1	39.0
54	24 23.1	−8.7	37.0	25 10.9	−8.0	37.3	25 58.5	−7.3	37.6	26 45.9	−6.6	37.9
55	24 14.4	−9.1	36.0	25 02.9	−8.5	36.2	25 51.2	−7.8	36.5	26 39.3	−7.1	36.8
56	24 05.3	−9.6	34.9	24 54.4	−8.9	35.1	25 43.4	−8.3	35.4	26 32.2	−7.6	35.7
57	23 55.7	−10.0	33.8	24 45.5	−9.4	34.1	25 35.1	−8.7	34.3	26 24.6	−8.1	34.6
58	23 45.7	−10.5	32.7	24 36.1	−9.9	33.0	25 26.4	−9.3	33.2	26 16.5	−8.7	33.5
59	23 35.2	−10.9	31.6	24 26.2	−10.3	31.9	25 17.1	−9.7	32.1	26 07.8	−9.1	32.4
60	23 24.3	−11.4	30.6	24 15.9	−10.8	30.8	25 07.4	−10.3	31.0	25 58.7	−9.6	31.3
61	23 12.9	−11.8	29.5	24 05.1	−11.3	29.7	24 57.1	−10.7	29.9	25 49.1	−10.2	30.2
62	23 01.1	−12.2	28.4	23 53.8	−11.6	28.6	24 46.4	−11.1	28.9	25 38.9	−10.6	29.1
63	22 48.9	−12.6	27.4	23 42.2	−12.2	27.6	24 35.3	−11.6	27.8	25 28.3	−11.1	28.0
64	22 36.3	−13.1	26.3	23 30.0	−12.6	26.5	24 23.7	−12.1	26.7	25 17.2	−11.6	26.9
65	22 23.2	−13.4	25.3	23 17.4	−13.0	25.4	24 11.6	−12.5	25.6	25 05.6	−12.0	25.8
66	22 09.8	−13.9	24.2	23 04.4	−13.4	24.4	23 59.1	−13.0	24.6	24 53.6	−12.5	24.7
67	21 55.9	−14.3	23.2	22 51.0	−13.8	23.3	23 46.1	−13.4	23.5	24 41.1	−13.0	23.7
68	21 41.6	−14.6	22.1	22 37.2	−14.3	22.3	23 32.7	−13.9	22.4	24 28.1	−13.4	22.6
69	21 27.0	−15.1	21.1	22 22.9	−14.6	21.2	23 18.8	−14.2	21.4	24 14.7	−13.9	21.5
70	21 11.9	−15.4	20.0	22 08.3	−15.1	20.2	23 04.6	−14.7	20.3	24 00.8	−14.3	20.5
71	20 56.5	−15.8	19.0	21 53.2	−15.4	19.1	22 49.9	−15.1	19.3	23 46.5	−14.8	19.4
72	20 40.7	−16.2	18.0	21 37.8	−15.9	18.1	22 34.8	−15.5	18.2	23 31.7	−15.1	18.3
73	20 24.5	−16.5	16.9	21 21.9	−16.2	17.0	22 19.3	−16.0	17.2	23 16.6	−15.6	17.3
74	20 08.0	−16.9	15.9	21 05.7	−16.6	16.0	22 03.3	−16.3	16.1	23 01.0	−16.0	16.2
75	19 51.1	−17.2	14.9	20 49.1	−17.0	15.0	21 47.0	−16.7	15.1	22 45.0	−16.5	15.2
76	19 33.9	−17.6	13.9	20 32.1	−17.3	14.0	21 30.3	−17.0	14.0	22 28.5	−16.8	14.1
77	19 16.3	−17.9	12.9	20 14.8	−17.7	12.9	21 13.3	−17.5	13.0	22 11.7	−17.2	13.1
78	18 58.4	−18.2	11.8	19 57.1	−18.0	11.9	20 55.8	−17.8	12.0	21 54.5	−17.6	12.1
79	18 40.2	−18.6	10.8	19 39.1	−18.4	10.9	20 38.0	−18.1	11.0	21 36.9	−18.0	11.0
80	18 21.6	−18.8	9.8	19 20.7	−18.6	9.9	20 19.9	−18.6	10.0	21 18.9	−18.3	10.0
81	18 02.8	−19.2	8.8	19 02.1	−19.1	8.9	20 01.3	−18.8	8.9	21 00.6	−18.7	9.0
82	17 43.6	−19.5	7.8	18 43.0	−19.3	7.9	19 42.5	−19.2	7.9	20 41.9	−19.1	8.0
83	17 24.1	−19.7	6.8	18 23.7	−19.7	6.9	19 23.3	−19.6	6.9	20 22.8	−19.4	7.0
84	17 04.4	−20.1	5.9	18 04.0	−19.9	5.9	19 03.7	−19.8	5.9	20 03.4	−19.8	6.0
85	16 44.3	−20.3	4.9	17 44.1	−20.3	4.9	18 43.9	−20.2	4.9	19 43.6	−20.0	5.0
86	16 24.0	−20.6	3.9	17 23.8	−20.5	3.9	18 23.7	−20.5	3.9	19 23.6	−20.5	4.0
87	16 03.4	−20.9	2.9	17 03.3	−20.8	2.9	18 03.2	−20.8	2.9	19 03.1	−20.7	3.0
88	15 42.5	−21.1	1.9	16 42.5	−21.1	1.9	17 42.4	−21.0	2.0	18 42.4	−21.0	2.0
89	15 21.4	−21.4	1.0	16 21.4	−21.4	1.0	17 21.4	−21.4	1.0	18 21.4	−21.4	1.0
90	15 00.0	−21.6	0.0	16 00.0	−21.6	0.0	17 00.0	−21.6	0.0	18 00.0	−21.6	0.0
	15°			16°			17°			18°		

Dec.	19°			20°			21°			22°		
	Hc	d	Z	Hc	d	Z	Hc	d	Z	Hc	d	Z
°	° ′	′	°	° ′	′	°	° ′	′	°	° ′	′	°
0	19 48.4	+20.6	97.1	19 40.8	+21.6	97.5	19 32.8	+22.6	97.8	19 24.4	+23.7	98.2
1	20 09.0	+20.2	96.1	20 02.4	+21.3	96.5	19 55.4	+22.4	96.8	19 48.1	+23.3	97.2
2	20 29.2	+19.9	95.1	20 23.7	+20.9	95.5	20 17.8	+21.9	95.9	20 11.4	+23.1	96.2
3	20 49.1	+19.6	94.1	20 44.6	+20.7	94.5	20 39.7	+21.7	94.9	20 34.5	+22.7	95.2
4	21 08.7	+19.2	93.1	21 05.3	+20.2	93.5	21 01.4	+21.3	93.9	20 57.2	+22.3	94.3
5	21 27.9	+18.8	92.1	21 25.5	+19.9	92.5	21 22.7	+20.9	92.9	21 19.5	+22.0	93.3
6	21 46.7	+18.4	91.1	21 45.4	+19.5	91.5	21 43.6	+20.6	91.9	21 41.5	+21.6	92.3
7	22 05.1	+18.1	90.0	22 04.9	+19.1	90.4	22 04.2	+20.2	90.8	22 03.1	+21.3	91.3
8	22 23.2	+17.7	89.0	22 24.0	+18.8	89.4	22 24.4	+19.8	89.8	22 24.4	+20.9	90.2
9	22 40.9	+17.2	88.0	22 42.8	+18.3	88.4	22 44.2	+19.5	88.8	22 45.3	+20.5	89.2
10	22 58.1	+16.9	86.9	23 01.1	+18.0	87.4	23 03.7	+19.0	87.8	23 05.8	+20.1	88.2
11	23 15.0	+16.4	85.9	23 19.1	+17.5	86.3	23 22.7	+18.6	86.7	23 25.9	+19.7	87.2
12	23 31.4	+16.0	84.8	23 36.6	+17.1	85.3	23 41.3	+18.2	85.7	23 45.6	+19.2	86.1
13	23 47.4	+15.6	83.8	23 53.7	+16.7	84.2	23 59.5	+17.8	84.7	24 04.8	+18.9	85.1
14	24 03.0	+15.2	82.7	24 10.4	+16.2	83.2	24 17.3	+17.3	83.6	24 23.7	+18.4	84.1
15	24 18.2	+14.7	81.7	24 26.6	+15.8	82.1	24 34.6	+16.9	82.6	24 42.1	+18.0	83.0
16	24 32.9	+14.2	80.6	24 42.4	+15.4	81.1	24 51.5	+16.5	81.5	25 00.1	+17.6	82.0
17	24 47.1	+13.8	79.5	24 57.8	+14.9	80.0	25 08.0	+16.0	80.5	25 17.7	+17.1	80.9
18	25 00.9	+13.4	78.5	25 12.7	+14.4	78.9	25 24.0	+15.5	79.4	25 34.8	+16.6	79.9
19	25 14.3	+12.8	77.4	25 27.1	+14.0	77.9	25 39.5	+15.1	78.3	25 51.4	+16.2	78.8
20	25 27.1	+12.4	76.3	25 41.1	+13.5	76.8	25 54.6	+14.6	77.2	26 07.6	+15.7	77.7
21	25 39.5	+11.9	75.2	25 54.6	+13.0	75.7	26 09.2	+14.1	76.2	26 23.3	+15.2	76.6
22	25 51.4	+11.5	74.1	26 07.6	+12.5	74.6	26 23.3	+13.6	75.1	26 38.5	+14.7	75.6
23	26 02.9	+10.9	73.0	26 20.1	+12.0	73.5	26 36.9	+13.1	74.0	26 53.2	+14.2	74.5
24	26 13.8	+10.4	71.9	26 32.1	+11.6	72.4	26 50.0	+12.6	72.9	27 07.4	+13.7	73.4
25	26 24.2	+9.9	70.8	26 43.7	+11.0	71.3	27 02.6	+12.1	71.8	27 21.1	+13.2	72.3
26	26 34.1	+9.4	69.7	26 54.7	+10.5	70.2	27 14.7	+11.6	70.7	27 34.3	+12.7	71.2
27	26 43.5	+8.9	68.6	27 05.2	+9.9	69.1	27 26.3	+11.1	69.6	27 47.0	+12.1	70.1
28	26 52.4	+8.4	67.5	27 15.1	+9.5	68.0	27 37.4	+10.5	68.5	27 59.1	+11.6	69.0
29	27 00.8	+7.9	66.4	27 24.6	+8.9	66.9	27 47.9	+10.0	67.4	28 10.7	+11.1	67.9
30	27 08.7	+7.3	65.3	27 33.5	+8.4	65.8	27 57.9	+9.4	66.3	28 21.8	+10.5	66.8
31	27 16.0	+6.8	64.2	27 41.9	+7.8	64.7	28 07.3	+8.9	65.1	28 32.3	+10.0	65.6
32	27 22.8	+6.2	63.1	27 49.7	+7.3	63.5	28 16.2	+8.4	64.0	28 42.3	+9.4	64.5
33	27 29.0	+5.7	62.0	27 57.0	+6.8	62.4	28 24.6	+7.8	62.9	28 51.7	+8.8	63.4
34	27 34.7	+5.2	60.8	28 03.8	+6.2	61.3	28 32.4	+7.2	61.8	29 00.5	+8.3	62.3
35	27 39.9	+4.6	59.7	28 10.0	+5.6	60.2	28 39.6	+6.7	60.6	29 08.8	+7.7	61.1
36	27 44.5	+4.1	58.6	28 15.6	+5.1	59.0	28 46.3	+6.1	59.5	29 16.5	+7.1	60.0
37	27 48.6	+3.5	57.5	28 20.7	+4.5	57.9	28 52.4	+5.5	58.4	29 23.6	+6.6	58.8
38	27 52.1	+3.0	56.3	28 25.2	+4.0	56.8	28 57.9	+4.9	57.2	29 30.2	+5.9	57.7
39	27 55.1	+2.4	55.2	28 29.2	+3.4	55.6	29 02.8	+4.4	56.1	29 36.1	+5.4	56.6
40	27 57.5	+1.9	54.1	28 32.6	+2.8	54.5	29 07.2	+3.8	54.9	29 41.5	+4.8	55.4
41	27 59.4	+1.3	52.9	28 35.4	+2.3	53.4	29 11.0	+3.2	53.8	29 46.3	+4.1	54.3
42	28 00.7	+0.8	51.8	28 37.7	+1.6	52.2	29 14.2	+2.7	52.7	29 50.4	+3.6	53.1
43	28 01.5	+0.2	50.7	28 39.3	+1.2	51.1	29 16.9	+2.0	51.5	29 54.0	+3.0	52.0
44	28 01.7	−0.4	49.5	28 40.5	+0.5	49.9	29 18.9	+1.4	50.4	29 57.0	+2.4	50.8
45	28 01.3	−0.9	48.4	28 41.0	0.0	48.8	29 20.3	+0.9	49.2	29 59.4	+1.7	49.7
46	28 00.4	−1.5	47.3	28 41.0	−0.6	47.7	29 21.2	+0.3	48.1	30 01.1	+1.2	48.5
47	27 58.9	−2.0	46.1	28 40.4	−1.2	46.5	29 21.5	−0.3	46.9	30 02.3	+0.6	47.3
48	27 56.9	−2.6	45.0	28 39.2	−1.8	45.4	29 21.2	−0.9	45.8	30 02.9	−0.1	46.2
49	27 54.3	−3.1	43.9	28 37.4	−2.3	44.2	29 20.3	−1.5	44.6	30 02.8	−0.6	45.0
50	27 51.2	−3.7	42.7	28 35.1	−2.9	43.1	29 18.8	−2.1	43.5	30 02.2	−1.3	43.9
51	27 47.5	−4.2	41.6	28 32.2	−3.4	42.0	29 16.7	−2.7	42.3	30 00.9	−1.8	42.7
52	27 43.3	−4.8	40.5	28 28.8	−4.1	40.8	29 14.0	−3.2	41.2	29 59.1	−2.5	41.6
53	27 38.5	−5.4	39.4	28 24.7	−4.5	39.7	29 10.8	−3.8	40.1	29 56.6	−3.1	40.4
54	27 33.1	−5.8	38.2	28 20.2	−5.2	38.6	29 07.0	−4.5	38.9	29 53.5	−3.6	39.3
55	27 27.3	−6.4	37.1	28 15.0	−5.7	37.4	29 02.5	−4.9	37.8	29 49.9	−4.3	38.1
56	27 20.9	−7.0	36.0	28 09.3	−6.3	36.3	28 57.6	−5.6	36.6	29 45.6	−4.9	37.0
57	27 13.9	−7.5	34.9	28 03.0	−6.8	35.2	28 52.0	−6.1	35.5	29 40.7	−5.4	35.8
58	27 06.4	−8.0	33.8	27 56.2	−7.3	34.1	28 45.9	−6.8	34.4	29 35.3	−6.0	34.7
59	26 58.4	−8.5	32.7	27 48.9	−7.9	32.9	28 39.1	−7.2	33.2	29 29.3	−6.7	33.5
60	26 49.9	−9.0	31.5	27 41.0	−8.5	31.8	28 31.9	−7.9	32.1	29 22.6	−7.2	32.4
61	26 40.9	−9.6	30.4	27 32.5	−9.0	30.7	28 24.0	−8.3	31.0	29 15.4	−7.8	31.3
62	26 31.3	−10.1	29.3	27 23.5	−9.5	29.6	28 15.7	−9.0	29.8	29 07.6	−8.3	30.1
63	26 21.2	−10.5	28.2	27 14.0	−10.0	28.5	28 06.7	−9.5	28.7	28 59.3	−8.9	29.0
64	26 10.7	−11.1	27.1	27 04.0	−10.5	27.4	27 57.2	−10.0	27.6	28 50.4	−9.5	27.9
65	25 59.6	−11.6	26.0	26 53.5	−11.1	26.3	27 47.2	−10.5	26.5	28 40.9	−10.1	26.7
66	25 48.0	−12.0	24.9	26 42.4	−11.6	25.2	27 36.7	−11.1	25.4	28 30.8	−10.6	25.6
67	25 36.0	−12.5	23.9	26 30.8	−12.1	24.1	27 25.6	−11.6	24.3	28 20.2	−11.1	24.5
68	25 23.5	−13.0	22.8	26 18.7	−12.5	23.0	27 14.0	−12.2	23.2	28 09.1	−11.7	23.4
69	25 10.5	−13.5	21.7	26 06.2	−13.1	21.9	27 01.8	−12.6	22.1	27 57.4	−12.2	22.3
70	24 57.0	−13.9	20.6	25 53.1	−13.5	20.8	26 49.2	−13.2	21.0	27 45.2	−12.8	21.1
71	24 43.1	−14.4	19.5	25 39.6	−14.0	19.7	26 36.0	−13.6	19.9	27 32.4	−13.2	20.0
72	24 28.7	−14.9	18.5	25 25.6	−14.5	18.6	26 22.4	−14.2	18.8	27 19.2	−13.8	18.9
73	24 13.8	−15.2	17.4	25 11.1	−15.0	17.6	26 08.2	−14.6	17.7	27 05.4	−14.3	17.9
74	23 58.6	−15.8	16.4	24 56.1	−15.4	16.5	25 53.6	−15.1	16.6	26 51.1	−14.8	16.8
75	23 42.8	−16.1	15.3	24 40.7	−15.9	15.4	25 38.5	−15.5	15.5	26 36.3	−15.3	15.7
76	23 26.7	−16.6	14.3	24 24.8	−16.2	14.4	25 23.0	−16.1	14.5	26 21.0	−15.7	14.6
77	23 10.1	−16.9	13.2	24 08.6	−16.8	13.3	25 06.9	−16.5	13.4	26 05.3	−16.3	13.5
78	22 53.2	−17.4	12.2	23 51.8	−17.1	12.3	24 50.4	−16.9	12.4	25 49.0	−16.7	12.5
79	22 35.8	−17.8	11.1	23 34.7	−17.6	11.2	24 33.5	−17.4	11.3	25 32.3	−17.1	11.4
80	22 18.0	−18.1	10.1	23 17.1	−18.0	10.2	24 16.1	−17.8	10.2	25 15.2	−17.6	10.3
81	21 59.9	−18.6	9.1	22 59.1	−18.4	9.1	23 58.3	−18.2	9.2	24 57.6	−18.1	9.3
82	21 41.3	−18.9	8.0	22 40.7	−18.8	8.1	23 40.1	−18.6	8.2	24 39.5	−18.5	8.2
83	21 22.4	−19.3	7.0	22 21.9	−19.2	7.1	23 21.5	−19.1	7.1	24 21.0	−18.9	7.2
84	21 03.1	−19.7	6.0	22 02.7	−19.5	6.0	23 02.4	−19.4	6.1	24 02.1	−19.4	6.1
85	20 43.4	−20.0	5.0	21 43.2	−19.9	5.0	22 43.0	−19.9	5.1	23 42.7	−19.7	5.1
86	20 23.4	−20.3	4.0	21 23.3	−20.3	4.0	22 23.1	−20.2	4.0	23 23.0	−20.2	4.1
87	20 03.1	−20.7	3.0	21 03.0	−20.7	3.0	22 02.9	−20.6	3.0	23 02.8	−20.5	3.0
88	19 42.4	−21.1	2.0	20 42.3	−21.0	2.0	21 42.3	−21.0	2.0	22 42.3	−21.0	2.0
89	19 21.3	−21.3	1.0	20 21.3	−21.3	1.0	21 21.3	−21.3	1.0	22 21.3	−21.3	1.0
90	19 00.0	−21.7	0.0	20 00.0	−21.7	0.0	21 00.0	−21.7	0.0	22 00.0	−21.7	0.0
	19°			20°			21°			22°		

69°, 291° L.H.A. LATITUDE SAME NAME AS DECLINATION

140

Dec.	15°			16°			17°			18°		
°	Hc ° ′	d ′	Z °	Hc ° ′	d ′	Z °	Hc ° ′	d ′	Z °	Hc ° ′	d ′	Z °
0	20 15.1	−16.7	95.7	20 09.0	−17.8	96.0	20 02.5	−18.8	96.4	19 55.6	−19.8	96.8
1	19 58.4	−17.1	96.7	19 51.2	−18.1	97.1	19 43.7	−19.2	97.4	19 35.8	−20.3	97.8
2	19 41.3	−17.4	97.7	19 33.1	−18.5	98.1	19 24.5	−19.5	98.4	19 15.5	−20.5	98.8
3	19 23.9	−17.7	98.7	19 14.6	−18.8	99.1	19 05.0	−19.9	99.4	18 55.0	−20.9	99.8
4	19 06.2	−18.1	99.7	18 55.8	−19.1	100.1	18 45.1	−20.1	100.4	18 34.1	−21.1	100.8
5	18 48.1	−18.5	100.8	18 36.7	−19.4	101.1	18 25.0	−20.5	101.4	18 13.0	−21.5	101.7
6	18 29.6	−18.7	101.8	18 17.3	−19.8	102.1	18 04.5	−20.7	102.4	17 51.5	−21.8	102.7
7	18 10.9	−19.0	102.8	17 57.5	−20.1	103.1	17 43.8	−21.1	103.4	17 29.7	−22.0	103.7
8	17 51.9	−19.4	103.8	17 37.4	−20.3	104.1	17 22.7	−21.3	104.4	17 07.7	−22.4	104.7
9	17 32.5	−19.6	104.7	17 17.1	−20.6	105.1	17 01.4	−21.7	105.3	16 45.3	−22.6	105.6
10	17 12.9	−19.9	105.7	16 56.5	−21.0	106.0	16 39.7	−21.8	106.3	16 22.7	−22.8	106.6
11	16 53.0	−20.3	106.7	16 35.5	−21.1	107.0	16 17.9	−22.2	107.3	15 59.9	−23.1	107.6
12	16 32.7	−20.4	107.7	16 14.4	−21.5	108.0	15 55.7	−22.4	108.3	15 36.8	−23.4	108.5
13	16 12.3	−20.8	108.7	15 52.9	−21.7	109.0	15 33.3	−22.7	109.2	15 13.4	−23.6	109.5
14	15 51.5	−21.0	109.7	15 31.2	−22.0	109.9	15 10.6	−22.9	110.2	14 49.8	−23.9	110.4
15	15 30.5	−21.3	110.6	15 09.2	−22.2	110.9	14 47.7	−23.2	111.1	14 25.9	−24.0	111.4
16	15 09.2	−21.5	111.6	14 47.0	−22.5	111.9	14 24.5	−23.3	112.1	14 01.9	−24.3	112.3
17	14 47.7	−21.8	112.6	14 24.5	−22.6	112.8	14 01.2	−23.6	113.0	13 37.6	−24.5	113.3
18	14 25.9	−22.0	113.5	14 01.9	−22.9	113.8	13 37.6	−23.8	114.0	13 13.1	−24.7	114.2
19	14 03.9	−22.2	114.5	13 39.0	−23.2	114.7	13 13.8	−24.1	114.9	12 48.4	−24.9	115.1
20	13 41.7	−22.4	115.5	13 15.8	−23.3	115.7	12 49.7	−24.2	115.9	12 23.5	−25.1	116.1
21	13 19.3	−22.7	116.4	12 52.5	−23.5	116.6	12 25.5	−24.4	116.8	11 58.4	−25.3	117.0
22	12 56.6	−22.8	117.4	12 29.0	−23.8	117.6	12 01.1	−24.6	117.7	11 33.1	−25.5	117.9
23	12 33.8	−23.1	118.3	12 05.2	−23.9	118.5	11 36.5	−24.8	118.7	11 07.6	−25.6	118.9
24	12 10.7	−23.2	119.2	11 41.3	−24.1	119.4	11 11.7	−24.9	119.6	10 42.0	−25.8	119.8
25	11 47.5	−23.5	120.2	11 17.2	−24.3	120.4	10 46.8	−25.1	120.5	10 16.2	−25.9	120.7
26	11 24.0	−23.6	121.1	10 52.9	−24.4	121.3	10 21.7	−25.3	121.5	9 50.3	−26.1	121.6
27	11 00.4	−23.8	122.1	10 28.5	−24.6	122.2	9 56.4	−25.4	122.4	9 24.2	−26.2	122.5
28	10 36.6	−23.9	123.0	10 03.9	−24.8	123.2	9 31.0	−25.6	123.3	8 58.0	−26.4	123.4
29	10 12.7	−24.1	123.9	9 39.1	−24.9	124.1	9 05.4	−25.7	124.2	8 31.6	−26.4	124.3
30	9 48.6	−24.3	124.9	9 14.2	−25.0	125.0	8 39.7	−25.8	125.1	8 05.2	−26.7	125.3
31	9 24.3	−24.4	125.8	8 49.2	−25.2	125.9	8 13.9	−26.0	126.0	7 38.5	−26.7	126.2
32	8 59.9	−24.5	126.7	8 24.0	−25.3	126.8	7 47.9	−26.0	127.0	7 11.8	−26.8	127.1
33	8 35.4	−24.7	127.6	7 58.7	−25.5	127.8	7 21.9	−26.2	127.9	6 45.0	−26.9	128.0
34	8 10.7	−24.8	128.6	7 33.2	−25.5	128.7	6 55.7	−26.3	128.8	6 18.1	−27.0	128.9
35	7 45.9	−24.9	129.5	7 07.7	−25.7	129.6	6 29.4	−26.4	129.7	5 51.1	−27.1	129.8
36	7 21.0	−25.1	130.4	6 42.0	−25.7	130.5	6 03.0	−26.4	130.6	5 24.0	−27.2	130.7
37	6 55.9	−25.1	131.3	6 16.3	−25.9	131.4	5 36.6	−26.6	131.5	4 56.8	−27.3	131.5
38	6 30.8	−25.2	132.2	5 50.4	−25.9	132.3	5 10.0	−26.6	132.4	4 29.5	−27.3	132.4
39	6 05.6	−25.4	133.1	5 24.5	−26.0	133.2	4 43.4	−26.7	133.3	4 02.2	−27.3	133.3
40	5 40.2	−25.4	134.1	4 58.5	−26.1	134.1	4 16.7	−26.8	134.2	3 34.9	−27.5	134.2
41	5 14.8	−25.5	135.0	4 32.4	−26.2	135.0	3 49.9	−26.8	135.1	3 07.4	−27.4	135.1
42	4 49.3	−25.5	135.9	4 06.2	−26.2	135.9	3 23.1	−26.9	136.0	2 40.0	−27.6	136.0
43	4 23.8	−25.7	136.8	3 40.0	−26.3	136.8	2 56.2	−26.9	136.9	2 12.4	−27.5	136.9
44	3 58.1	−25.7	137.7	3 13.7	−26.3	137.7	2 29.3	−26.9	137.8	1 44.9	−27.6	137.8
45	3 32.4	−25.7	138.6	2 47.4	−26.3	138.6	2 02.4	−27.0	138.7	1 17.3	−27.6	138.7
46	3 06.7	−25.8	139.5	2 21.1	−26.4	139.5	1 35.4	−27.0	139.6	0 49.7	−27.5	139.6
47	2 40.9	−25.8	140.4	1 54.7	−26.5	140.4	1 08.4	−27.0	140.4	0 22.2	−27.7	140.5
48	2 15.1	−25.9	141.3	1 28.2	−26.4	141.3	0 41.4	−27.0	141.3	0 05.5	+27.6	38.7
49	1 49.2	−25.9	142.2	1 01.8	−26.5	142.2	0 14.4	−27.1	142.2	0 33.1	+27.5	37.8
50	1 23.3	−25.9	143.1	0 35.3	−26.4	143.1	0 12.7	+27.0	36.9	1 00.6	+27.6	36.9
51	0 57.4	−25.9	144.0	0 08.9	−26.5	144.0	0 39.7	+27.0	36.0	1 28.2	+27.6	36.0
52	0 31.5	−25.9	144.9	0 17.6	+26.5	35.1	1 06.7	+27.0	35.1	1 55.8	+27.5	35.1
53	0 05.6	−26.0	145.8	0 44.1	+26.4	34.2	1 33.7	+27.0	34.2	2 23.3	+27.5	34.2
54	0 20.4	+25.9	33.3	1 10.5	+26.5	33.3	2 00.7	+26.9	33.3	2 50.8	+27.5	33.3
55	0 46.3	+25.9	32.4	1 37.0	+26.4	32.4	2 27.6	+26.9	32.4	3 18.3	+27.4	32.4
56	1 12.2	+25.9	31.5	2 03.4	+26.4	31.5	2 54.5	+26.9	31.5	3 45.7	+27.3	31.5
57	1 38.1	+25.9	30.6	2 29.8	+26.3	30.6	3 21.4	+26.8	30.6	4 13.0	+27.3	30.7
58	2 04.0	+25.8	29.7	2 56.1	+26.3	29.7	3 48.2	+26.8	29.7	4 40.3	+27.2	29.8
59	2 29.8	+25.8	28.8	3 22.4	+26.3	28.8	4 15.0	+26.7	28.8	5 07.5	+27.2	28.9
60	2 55.6	+25.8	27.9	3 48.7	+26.2	27.9	4 41.7	+26.6	27.9	5 34.7	+27.1	28.0
61	3 21.4	+25.7	27.0	4 14.9	+26.1	27.0	5 08.3	+26.6	27.0	6 01.8	+26.9	27.1
62	3 47.1	+25.7	26.1	4 41.0	+26.1	26.1	5 34.9	+26.4	26.1	6 28.7	+26.9	26.2
63	4 12.8	+25.5	25.1	5 07.1	+25.9	25.2	6 01.3	+26.4	25.2	6 55.6	+26.8	25.3
64	4 38.3	+25.6	24.2	5 33.0	+26.0	24.3	6 27.7	+26.3	24.3	7 22.4	+26.7	24.4
65	5 03.9	+25.4	23.3	5 59.0	+25.8	23.4	6 54.0	+26.2	23.4	7 49.1	+26.5	23.5
66	5 29.3	+25.4	22.4	6 24.8	+25.7	22.5	7 20.2	+26.1	22.5	8 15.6	+26.5	22.6
67	5 54.7	+25.3	21.5	6 50.5	+25.6	21.6	7 46.3	+26.0	21.6	8 42.1	+26.3	21.7
68	6 20.0	+25.1	20.6	7 16.1	+25.5	20.6	8 12.3	+25.8	20.7	9 08.4	+26.1	20.7
69	6 45.1	+25.1	19.7	7 41.6	+25.4	19.7	8 38.1	+25.7	19.8	9 34.5	+26.1	19.8
70	7 10.2	+25.0	18.8	8 07.0	+25.3	18.8	9 03.8	+25.6	18.9	10 00.6	+25.8	18.9
71	7 35.2	+24.8	17.9	8 32.3	+25.1	17.9	9 29.4	+25.4	17.9	10 26.4	+25.8	18.0
72	8 00.0	+24.8	16.9	8 57.4	+25.0	17.0	9 54.8	+25.3	17.0	10 52.2	+25.5	17.1
73	8 24.8	+24.6	16.0	9 22.4	+24.9	16.1	10 20.1	+25.1	16.1	11 17.7	+25.4	16.2
74	8 49.4	+24.4	15.1	9 47.3	+24.7	15.1	10 45.2	+25.0	15.2	11 43.1	+25.2	15.2
75	9 13.8	+24.4	14.2	10 12.0	+24.6	14.2	11 10.2	+24.7	14.3	12 08.3	+25.0	14.3
76	9 38.2	+24.1	13.2	10 36.6	+24.4	13.3	11 34.9	+24.7	13.3	12 33.3	+24.9	13.4
77	10 02.3	+24.1	12.3	11 01.0	+24.2	12.4	11 59.6	+24.4	12.4	12 58.2	+24.6	12.4
78	10 26.4	+23.8	11.4	11 25.2	+24.0	11.4	12 24.0	+24.2	11.5	13 22.8	+24.4	11.5
79	10 50.2	+23.7	10.4	11 49.2	+23.9	10.5	12 48.2	+24.0	10.5	13 47.2	+24.2	10.6
80	11 13.9	+23.5	9.5	12 13.1	+23.6	9.5	13 12.2	+23.9	9.6	14 11.4	+24.0	9.6
81	11 37.4	+23.3	8.6	12 36.7	+23.5	8.6	13 36.1	+23.6	8.6	14 35.4	+23.7	8.7
82	12 00.7	+23.2	7.6	13 00.2	+23.3	7.7	13 59.7	+23.4	7.7	14 59.1	+23.5	7.7
83	12 23.9	+22.9	6.7	13 23.5	+23.0	6.7	14 23.1	+23.1	6.7	15 22.6	+23.3	6.8
84	12 46.8	+22.8	5.7	13 46.5	+22.9	5.8	14 46.2	+23.0	5.8	15 45.9	+23.0	5.8
85	13 09.6	+22.5	4.8	14 09.4	+22.6	4.8	15 09.2	+22.6	4.8	16 08.9	+22.8	4.9
86	13 32.1	+22.3	3.8	14 32.0	+22.3	3.9	15 31.8	+22.5	3.9	16 31.7	+22.5	3.9
87	13 54.4	+22.1	2.9	14 54.3	+22.2	2.9	15 54.3	+22.1	2.9	16 54.2	+22.2	2.9
88	14 16.5	+21.9	1.9	15 16.5	+21.9	1.9	16 16.4	+22.0	1.9	17 16.4	+22.0	2.0
89	14 38.4	+21.6	1.0	15 38.4	+21.6	1.0	16 38.4	+21.6	1.0	17 38.4	+21.6	1.0
90	15 00.0	+21.4	0.0	16 00.0	+21.4	0.0	17 00.0	+21.4	0.0	18 00.0	+21.4	0.0
	15°			16°			17°			18°		

Dec.	19°			20°			21°			22°		
°	Hc ° ′	d ′	Z °	Hc ° ′	d ′	Z °	Hc ° ′	d ′	Z °	Hc ° ′	d ′	Z °
0	19 48.4	−20.9	97.1	19 40.8	−22.0	97.5	19 32.8	−23.0	97.8	19 24.4	−24.0	98.2
1	19 27.5	−21.3	98.1	19 18.8	−22.3	98.5	19 09.8	−23.3	98.8	19 00.4	−24.3	99.2
2	19 06.2	−21.6	99.1	18 56.5	−22.5	99.4	18 46.5	−23.6	99.8	18 36.1	−24.5	100.1
3	18 44.6	−21.8	100.1	18 34.0	−22.9	100.4	18 22.9	−23.9	100.8	18 11.6	−24.9	101.1
4	18 22.8	−22.2	101.1	18 11.1	−23.2	101.4	17 59.0	−24.1	101.7	17 46.7	−25.2	102.0
5	18 00.6	−22.5	102.1	17 47.9	−23.5	102.4	17 34.9	−24.5	102.7	17 21.5	−25.4	103.0
6	17 38.1	−22.7	103.0	17 24.4	−23.7	103.3	17 10.4	−24.7	103.6	16 56.1	−25.6	103.9
7	17 15.4	−23.1	104.0	17 00.7	−24.0	104.3	16 45.7	−25.0	104.6	16 30.5	−26.0	104.9
8	16 52.3	−23.3	105.0	16 36.7	−24.3	105.3	16 20.7	−25.2	105.5	16 04.5	−26.1	105.8
9	16 29.0	−23.5	105.9	16 12.4	−24.5	106.2	15 55.5	−25.4	106.5	15 38.4	−26.4	106.8
10	16 05.5	−23.9	106.9	15 47.9	−24.8	107.2	15 30.1	−25.8	107.4	15 12.0	−26.7	107.7
11	15 41.6	−24.0	107.8	15 23.1	−25.0	108.1	15 04.3	−25.9	108.4	14 45.3	−26.8	108.6
12	15 17.6	−24.3	108.8	14 58.1	−25.2	109.0	14 38.4	−26.2	109.3	14 18.5	−27.1	109.5
13	14 53.3	−24.6	109.7	14 32.9	−25.5	110.0	14 12.2	−26.3	110.2	13 51.4	−27.3	110.5
14	14 28.7	−24.8	110.7	14 07.4	−25.7	110.9	13 45.9	−26.6	111.2	13 24.1	−27.5	111.4
15	14 03.9	−24.9	111.6	13 41.7	−25.9	111.9	13 19.3	−26.8	112.1	12 56.6	−27.6	112.3
16	13 39.0	−25.2	112.6	13 15.8	−26.1	112.8	12 52.5	−27.0	113.0	12 29.0	−27.9	113.2
17	13 13.8	−25.4	113.5	12 49.7	−26.2	113.7	12 25.5	−27.1	113.9	12 01.1	−28.0	114.1
18	12 48.4	−25.6	114.4	12 23.5	−26.5	114.6	11 58.4	−27.4	114.8	11 33.1	−28.2	115.0
19	12 22.8	−25.8	115.3	11 57.0	−26.6	115.5	11 31.0	−27.5	115.7	11 04.9	−28.3	115.9
20	11 57.0	−26.0	116.3	11 30.4	−26.9	116.5	11 03.5	−27.6	116.6	10 36.6	−28.5	116.8
21	11 31.0	−26.1	117.2	11 03.5	−26.9	117.4	10 35.9	−27.8	117.5	10 08.1	−28.7	117.7
22	11 04.9	−26.3	118.1	10 36.6	−27.2	118.3	10 08.1	−28.0	118.4	9 39.4	−28.8	118.6
23	10 38.6	−26.4	119.0	10 09.4	−27.3	119.2	9 40.1	−28.1	119.3	9 10.6	−28.9	119.5
24	10 12.2	−26.7	119.9	9 42.1	−27.4	120.1	9 12.0	−28.2	120.2	8 41.7	−29.0	120.4
25	9 45.5	−26.7	120.8	9 14.7	−27.5	121.0	8 43.8	−28.4	121.1	8 12.7	−29.2	121.3
26	9 18.8	−26.9	121.8	8 47.2	−27.7	121.9	8 15.4	−28.5	122.0	7 43.5	−29.2	122.1
27	8 51.9	−27.0	122.7	8 19.5	−27.6	122.8	7 46.9	−28.6	122.9	7 14.3	−29.4	123.0
28	8 24.9	−27.2	123.6	7 51.7	−28.0	123.7	7 18.3	−28.7	123.8	6 44.9	−29.4	123.9
29	7 57.7	−27.2	124.5	7 23.7	−28.0	124.6	6 49.6	−28.8	124.7	6 15.5	−29.6	124.8
30	7 30.5	−27.4	125.4	6 55.7	−28.1	125.5	6 20.8	−28.8	125.6	5 45.9	−29.6	125.6
31	7 03.1	−27.5	126.3	6 27.6	−28.2	126.4	5 52.0	−29.0	126.4	5 16.3	−29.7	126.5
32	6 35.6	−27.5	127.2	5 59.4	−28.4	127.2	5 23.0	−29.0	127.3	4 46.6	−29.8	127.4
33	6 08.1	−27.7	128.0	5 31.0	−28.3	128.1	4 54.0	−29.1	128.2	4 16.8	−29.8	128.3
34	5 40.4	−27.7	128.9	5 02.7	−28.5	129.0	4 24.9	−29.2	129.1	3 47.0	−29.9	129.1
35	5 12.7	−27.8	129.8	4 34.2	−28.5	129.9	3 55.7	−29.2	130.0	3 17.1	−29.9	130.0
36	4 44.9	−27.9	130.7	4 05.7	−28.6	130.8	3 26.5	−29.3	130.8	2 47.2	−29.9	130.9
37	4 17.0	−28.0	131.6	3 37.1	−28.6	131.7	2 57.2	−29.3	131.7	2 17.3	−30.0	131.7
38	3 49.0	−28.0	132.5	3 08.5	−28.7	132.5	2 27.9	−29.4	132.6	1 47.3	−30.0	132.6
39	3 21.0	−28.0	133.4	2 39.8	−28.7	133.4	1 58.5	−29.3	133.5	1 17.3	−30.1	133.5
40	2 53.0	−28.1	134.3	2 11.1	−28.8	134.3	1 29.2	−29.4	134.3	0 47.2	−30.0	134.3
41	2 24.9	−28.1	135.2	1 42.3	−28.7	135.2	0 59.8	−29.4	135.2	0 17.2	−30.0	135.2
42	1 56.8	−28.2	136.0	1 13.6	−28.8	136.1	0 30.4	−29.4	136.1	0 12.8	+30.1	43.9
43	1 28.6	−28.1	136.9	0 44.8	−28.8	136.9	0 01.0	−29.5	136.9	0 42.9	+30.0	43.1
44	1 00.5	−28.2	137.8	0 16.0	−28.8	137.8	0 28.5	+29.4	42.2	1 12.9	+30.0	42.2
45	0 32.3	−28.2	138.7	0 12.8	+28.8	41.3	0 57.9	+29.4	41.3	1 42.9	+30.0	41.3
46	0 04.1	−28.2	139.6	0 41.6	+28.8	40.4	1 27.3	+29.3	40.4	2 12.9	+30.0	40.5
47	0 24.1	+28.2	39.5	1 10.4	+28.8	39.6	1 56.6	+29.4	39.6	2 42.9	+29.9	39.6
48	0 52.3	+28.2	38.7	1 39.1	+28.8	38.7	2 26.0	+29.3	38.7	3 12.8	+29.9	38.7
49	1 20.5	+28.1	37.8	2 07.9	+28.7	37.8	2 55.3	+29.3	37.8	3 42.7	+29.8	37.9
50	1 48.6	+28.2	36.9	2 36.6	+28.7	36.9	3 24.6	+29.2	37.0	4 12.5	+29.7	37.0
51	2 16.8	+28.1	36.0	3 05.3	+28.6	36.0	3 53.8	+29.2	36.1	4 42.3	+29.7	36.1
52	2 44.9	+28.0	35.1	3 33.9	+28.6	35.2	4 23.0	+29.1	35.2	5 12.0	+29.6	35.2
53	3 12.9	+28.0	34.2	4 02.5	+28.5	34.3	4 52.1	+29.0	34.3	5 41.6	+29.6	34.4
54	3 40.9	+28.0	33.4	4 31.0	+28.5	33.4	5 21.1	+29.0	33.4	6 11.2	+29.4	33.5
55	4 08.9	+27.9	32.5	4 59.5	+28.4	32.5	5 50.1	+28.9	32.6	6 40.6	+29.4	32.6
56	4 36.8	+27.8	31.6	5 27.9	+28.3	31.6	6 19.0	+28.8	31.7	7 10.0	+29.3	31.7
57	5 04.6	+27.8	30.7	5 56.2	+28.2	30.7	6 47.8	+28.7	30.8	7 39.3	+29.1	30.9
58	5 32.4	+27.7	29.8	6 24.4	+28.2	29.9	7 16.5	+28.6	29.9	8 08.4	+29.1	30.0
59	6 00.1	+27.6	28.9	6 52.6	+28.0	29.0	7 45.1	+28.4	29.0	8 37.5	+28.9	29.1
60	6 27.7	+27.5	28.0	7 20.6	+28.0	28.1	8 13.5	+28.4	28.1	9 06.4	+28.8	28.2
61	6 55.2	+27.4	27.1	7 48.6	+27.8	27.2	8 41.9	+28.3	27.3	9 35.2	+28.7	27.3
62	7 22.6	+27.3	26.2	8 16.4	+27.7	26.3	9 10.2	+28.1	26.4	10 03.9	+28.5	26.4
63	7 49.9	+27.1	25.3	8 44.1	+27.6	25.4	9 38.3	+27.9	25.5	10 32.4	+28.4	25.5
64	8 17.0	+27.1	24.4	9 11.7	+27.4	24.5	10 06.2	+27.9	24.6	11 00.8	+28.2	24.6
65	8 44.1	+26.9	23.5	9 39.1	+27.3	23.6	10 34.1	+27.6	23.7	11 29.0	+28.1	23.7
66	9 11.0	+26.8	22.6	10 06.4	+27.1	22.7	11 01.7	+27.6	22.8	11 57.1	+27.8	22.8
67	9 37.8	+26.7	21.7	10 33.5	+27.0	21.8	11 29.3	+27.3	21.9	12 24.9	+27.7	21.9
68	10 04.5	+26.5	20.8	11 00.5	+26.9	20.9	11 56.6	+27.2	20.9	12 52.6	+27.5	21.0
69	10 31.0	+26.3	19.9	11 27.4	+26.6	20.0	12 23.8	+26.9	20.0	13 20.1	+27.3	20.1
70	10 57.3	+26.2	19.0	11 54.0	+26.5	19.0	12 50.7	+26.8	19.1	13 47.4	+27.1	19.2
71	11 23.5	+26.0	18.1	12 20.5	+26.3	18.1	13 17.5	+26.6	18.2	14 14.5	+26.9	18.3
72	11 49.5	+25.8	17.1	12 46.8	+26.1	17.2	13 44.1	+26.4	17.3	14 41.4	+26.7	17.4
73	12 15.3	+25.7	16.2	13 12.9	+26.0	16.3	14 10.5	+26.2	16.4	15 08.1	+26.4	16.4
74	12 41.0	+25.4	15.3	13 38.9	+25.7	15.4	14 36.7	+26.0	15.4	15 34.5	+26.2	15.5
75	13 06.4	+25.3	14.4	14 04.6	+25.4	14.4	15 02.7	+25.7	14.5	16 00.7	+26.0	14.6
76	13 31.7	+25.0	13.4	14 30.0	+25.3	13.5	15 28.4	+25.5	13.6	16 26.7	+25.7	13.6
77	13 56.7	+24.9	12.5	14 55.3	+25.0	12.6	15 53.9	+25.2	12.6	16 52.4	+25.5	12.7
78	14 21.6	+24.6	11.6	15 20.3	+24.8	11.6	16 19.1	+25.0	11.7	17 17.9	+25.1	11.7
79	14 46.2	+24.4	10.6	15 45.1	+24.6	10.7	16 44.1	+24.7	10.7	17 43.0	+25.0	10.8
80	15 10.6	+24.1	9.7	16 09.7	+24.3	9.7	17 08.8	+24.5	9.8	18 08.0	+24.6	9.8
81	15 34.7	+23.9	8.7	16 34.0	+24.0	8.8	17 33.3	+24.2	8.8	18 32.6	+24.3	8.9
82	15 58.6	+23.6	7.8	16 58.0	+23.8	7.8	17 57.5	+23.9	7.9	18 56.9	+24.0	7.9
83	16 22.2	+23.4	6.8	17 21.8	+23.5	6.8	18 21.4	+23.6	6.9	19 20.9	+23.8	6.9
84	16 45.6	+23.1	5.8	17 45.3	+23.2	5.9	18 45.0	+23.3	5.9	19 44.7	+23.4	6.0
85	17 08.7	+22.9	4.9	18 08.5	+22.9	4.9	19 08.3	+23.0	4.9	20 08.1	+23.0	5.0
86	17 31.6	+22.5	3.9	18 31.4	+22.6	3.9	19 31.3	+22.7	4.0	20 31.1	+22.8	4.0
87	17 54.1	+22.3	2.9	18 54.0	+22.3	3.0	19 54.0	+22.3	3.0	20 53.9	+22.4	3.0
88	18 16.4	+21.9	2.0	19 16.3	+22.0	2.0	20 16.3	+22.0	2.0	21 16.3	+22.0	2.0
89	18 38.3	+21.7	1.0	19 38.3	+21.7	1.0	20 38.3	+21.7	1.0	21 38.3	+21.7	1.0
90	19 00.0	+21.3	0.0	20 00.0	+21.3	0.0	21 00.0	+21.3	0.0	22 00.0	+21.3	0.0
	19°			20°			21°			22°		

S. Lat. {L.H.A. greater than 180° ....Zn=180°−Z; L.H.A. less than 180°...........Zn=180°+Z}

70°, 290° L.H.A. LATITUDE SAME NAME AS DECLINATION

N. Lat. {L.H.A. greater than 180° .....Zn=Z
{L.H.A. less than 180°............Zn=360°-Z

Dec.	15°			16°			17°			18°		
°	Hc ° ′	d ′	Z °	Hc ° ′	d ′	Z °	Hc ° ′	d ′	Z °	Hc ° ′	d ′	Z °
0	19 17.5	+16.2	95.4	19 11.7	+17.3	95.7	19 05.5	+18.4	96.1	18 59.0	+19.4	96.4
1	19 33.7	+16.0	94.4	19 29.0	+17.0	94.7	19 23.9	+18.0	95.1	19 18.4	+19.1	95.4
2	19 49.7	+15.6	93.3	19 46.0	+16.7	93.7	19 41.9	+17.8	94.1	19 37.5	+18.8	94.4
3	20 05.3	+15.2	92.3	20 02.7	+16.3	92.7	19 59.7	+17.3	93.0	19 56.3	+18.4	93.4
4	20 20.5	+14.9	91.3	20 19.0	+15.9	91.6	20 17.0	+17.1	92.0	20 14.7	+18.1	92.4
5	20 35.4	+14.5	90.2	20 34.9	+15.6	90.6	20 34.1	+16.6	91.0	20 32.8	+17.7	91.4
6	20 49.9	+14.1	89.2	20 50.5	+15.2	89.6	20 50.7	+16.3	90.0	20 50.5	+17.4	90.3
7	21 04.0	+13.7	88.2	21 05.7	+14.8	88.6	21 07.0	+15.9	88.9	21 07.9	+17.0	89.3
8	21 17.7	+13.4	87.1	21 20.5	+14.5	87.5	21 22.9	+15.5	87.9	21 24.9	+16.6	88.3
9	21 31.1	+12.9	86.1	21 35.0	+14.0	86.5	21 38.4	+15.2	86.9	21 41.5	+16.2	87.3
10	21 44.0	+12.6	85.0	21 49.0	+13.7	85.4	21 53.6	+14.7	85.8	21 57.7	+15.9	86.2
11	21 56.6	+12.1	84.0	22 02.7	+13.2	84.4	22 08.3	+14.4	84.8	22 13.6	+15.4	85.2
12	22 08.7	+11.8	82.9	22 15.9	+12.9	83.3	22 22.7	+13.9	83.7	22 29.0	+15.1	84.1
13	22 20.5	+11.3	81.9	22 28.8	+12.4	82.3	22 36.6	+13.5	82.7	22 44.1	+14.6	83.1
14	22 31.8	+10.9	80.8	22 41.2	+12.0	81.2	22 50.1	+13.2	81.6	22 58.7	+14.2	82.0
15	22 42.7	+10.5	79.7	22 53.2	+11.6	80.1	23 03.3	+12.6	80.6	23 12.9	+13.8	81.0
16	22 53.2	+10.1	78.7	23 04.8	+11.1	79.1	23 15.9	+12.3	79.5	23 26.7	+13.3	79.9
17	23 03.3	+9.6	77.6	23 15.9	+10.8	78.0	23 28.2	+11.8	78.4	23 40.0	+12.9	78.9
18	23 12.9	+9.2	76.5	23 26.7	+10.2	76.9	23 40.0	+11.4	77.4	23 52.9	+12.5	77.8
19	23 22.1	+8.7	75.4	23 36.9	+9.9	75.9	23 51.4	+10.9	76.3	24 05.4	+12.0	76.7
20	23 30.8	+8.3	74.4	23 46.8	+9.4	74.8	24 02.3	+10.5	75.2	24 17.4	+11.6	75.6
21	23 39.1	+7.8	73.3	23 56.2	+8.9	73.7	24 12.8	+10.0	74.1	24 29.0	+11.1	74.6
22	23 46.9	+7.4	72.2	24 05.1	+8.5	72.6	24 22.8	+9.5	73.1	24 40.1	+10.6	73.5
23	23 54.3	+7.0	71.1	24 13.6	+8.0	71.5	24 32.3	+9.1	72.0	24 50.7	+10.2	72.4
24	24 01.3	+6.4	70.0	24 21.6	+7.5	70.4	24 41.4	+8.6	70.9	25 00.9	+9.7	71.3
25	24 07.7	+6.1	68.9	24 29.1	+7.1	69.4	24 50.0	+8.2	69.8	25 10.6	+9.2	70.2
26	24 13.8	+5.5	67.8	24 36.2	+6.6	68.3	24 58.2	+7.7	68.7	25 19.8	+8.7	69.1
27	24 19.3	+5.1	66.8	24 42.8	+6.1	67.2	25 05.9	+7.1	67.6	25 28.5	+8.2	68.0
28	24 24.4	+4.6	65.7	24 48.9	+5.7	66.1	25 13.0	+6.7	66.5	25 36.7	+7.8	66.9
29	24 29.0	+4.1	64.6	24 54.6	+5.1	65.0	25 19.7	+6.2	65.4	25 44.5	+7.2	65.8
30	24 33.1	+3.7	63.5	24 59.7	+4.7	63.9	25 25.9	+5.7	64.3	25 51.7	+6.8	64.7
31	24 36.8	+3.1	62.4	25 04.4	+4.2	62.8	25 31.6	+5.3	63.2	25 58.5	+6.2	63.6
32	24 39.9	+2.7	61.3	25 08.6	+3.7	61.7	25 36.9	+4.7	62.1	26 04.7	+5.8	62.5
33	24 42.6	+2.2	60.2	25 12.3	+3.2	60.6	25 41.6	+4.2	61.0	26 10.5	+5.2	61.4
34	24 44.8	+1.8	59.1	25 15.5	+2.7	59.5	25 45.8	+3.7	59.9	26 15.7	+4.7	60.3
35	24 46.6	+1.2	58.0	25 18.2	+2.2	58.4	25 49.5	+3.2	58.8	26 20.4	+4.2	59.2
36	24 47.8	+0.8	56.9	25 20.4	+1.8	57.3	25 52.7	+2.7	57.7	26 24.6	+3.7	58.1
37	24 48.6	+0.3	55.8	25 22.2	+1.2	56.2	25 55.4	+2.2	56.6	26 28.3	+3.1	57.0
38	24 48.9	-0.3	54.7	25 23.4	+0.7	55.1	25 57.6	+1.7	55.4	26 31.4	+2.7	55.9
39	24 48.6	-0.6	53.6	25 24.1	+0.3	53.9	25 59.3	+1.1	54.3	26 34.1	+2.1	54.7
40	24 48.0	-1.2	52.5	25 24.4	-0.3	52.8	26 00.4	+0.7	53.2	26 36.2	+1.6	53.6
41	24 46.8	-1.7	51.4	25 24.1	-0.8	51.7	26 01.1	+0.2	52.1	26 37.8	+1.1	52.5
42	24 45.1	-2.1	50.3	25 23.3	-1.2	50.6	26 01.3	-0.4	51.0	26 38.9	+0.5	51.4
43	24 43.0	-2.6	49.2	25 22.1	-1.8	49.5	26 00.9	-0.9	49.9	26 39.4	0.0	50.3
44	24 40.4	-3.1	48.1	25 20.3	-2.2	48.4	26 00.0	-1.4	48.8	26 39.4	-0.5	49.1
45	24 37.3	-3.6	47.0	25 18.1	-2.8	47.3	25 58.6	-1.9	47.7	26 38.9	-1.0	48.0
46	24 33.7	-4.1	45.9	25 15.3	-3.2	46.2	25 56.7	-2.4	46.5	26 37.9	-1.6	46.9
47	24 29.6	-4.5	44.8	25 12.1	-3.7	45.1	25 54.3	-2.9	45.4	26 36.3	-2.1	45.8
48	24 25.1	-5.0	43.7	25 08.4	-4.2	44.0	25 51.4	-3.4	44.3	26 34.2	-2.6	44.7
49	24 20.1	-5.5	42.6	25 04.2	-4.7	42.9	25 48.0	-3.9	43.2	26 31.6	-3.1	43.6
50	24 14.6	-5.9	41.5	24 59.5	-5.2	41.8	25 44.1	-4.4	42.1	26 28.5	-3.6	42.4
51	24 08.7	-6.4	40.4	24 54.3	-5.7	40.7	25 39.7	-4.9	41.0	26 24.9	-4.2	41.3
52	24 02.3	-6.9	39.3	24 48.6	-6.1	39.6	25 34.8	-5.5	39.9	26 20.7	-4.7	40.2
53	23 55.4	-7.3	38.2	24 42.5	-6.6	38.5	25 29.3	-5.9	38.8	26 16.0	-5.2	39.1
54	23 48.1	-7.8	37.1	24 35.9	-7.1	37.4	25 23.4	-6.4	37.7	26 10.8	-5.7	38.0
55	23 40.3	-8.2	36.1	24 28.8	-7.6	36.3	25 17.0	-6.9	36.6	26 05.1	-6.2	36.9
56	23 32.1	-8.7	35.0	24 21.2	-8.0	35.2	25 10.1	-7.4	35.5	25 58.9	-6.7	35.8
57	23 23.4	-9.1	33.9	24 13.2	-8.5	34.1	25 02.7	-7.8	34.4	25 52.2	-7.2	34.7
58	23 14.3	-9.6	32.8	24 04.7	-9.0	33.1	24 54.9	-8.4	33.3	25 45.0	-7.8	33.6
59	23 04.7	-9.9	31.7	23 55.7	-9.4	32.0	24 46.5	-8.8	32.2	25 37.2	-8.2	32.5
60	22 54.8	-10.5	30.7	23 46.3	-9.8	30.9	24 37.7	-9.2	31.1	25 29.0	-8.7	31.4
61	22 44.3	-10.8	29.6	23 36.5	-10.3	29.8	24 28.5	-9.8	30.0	25 20.3	-9.1	30.3
62	22 33.5	-11.3	28.5	23 26.2	-10.8	28.7	24 18.7	-10.2	29.0	25 11.2	-9.7	29.2
63	22 22.2	-11.7	27.5	23 15.4	-11.2	27.7	24 08.5	-10.7	27.9	25 01.5	-10.2	28.1
64	22 10.5	-12.1	26.4	23 04.2	-11.6	26.6	23 57.8	-11.1	26.8	24 51.3	-10.6	27.0
65	21 58.4	-12.4	25.4	22 52.6	-12.0	25.5	23 46.7	-11.5	25.7	24 40.7	-11.0	25.9
66	21 46.0	-12.9	24.3	22 40.6	-12.4	24.5	23 35.2	-12.0	24.6	24 29.7	-11.6	24.8
67	21 33.1	-13.3	23.3	22 28.2	-12.9	23.4	23 23.2	-12.5	23.6	24 18.1	-12.0	23.8
68	21 19.8	-13.7	22.2	22 15.3	-13.3	22.4	23 10.7	-12.8	22.5	24 06.1	-12.4	22.7
69	21 06.1	-14.1	21.2	22 02.0	-13.7	21.3	22 57.9	-13.3	21.5	23 53.7	-12.9	21.6
70	20 52.0	-14.4	20.1	21 48.3	-14.0	20.3	22 44.6	-13.7	20.4	23 40.8	-13.3	20.5
71	20 37.6	-14.8	19.1	21 34.3	-14.5	19.2	22 30.9	-14.1	19.3	23 27.5	-13.7	19.5
72	20 22.8	-15.2	18.0	21 19.8	-14.8	18.2	22 16.8	-14.5	18.3	23 13.8	-14.2	18.4
73	20 07.6	-15.5	17.0	21 05.0	-15.3	17.1	22 02.3	-14.9	17.2	22 59.6	-14.6	17.4
74	19 52.1	-15.9	16.0	20 49.7	-15.6	16.1	21 47.4	-15.3	16.2	22 45.0	-15.0	16.3
75	19 36.2	-16.2	15.0	20 34.1	-15.9	15.1	21 32.1	-15.7	15.2	22 30.0	-15.4	15.3
76	19 20.0	-16.6	13.9	20 18.2	-16.3	14.0	21 16.4	-16.1	14.1	22 14.6	-15.9	14.2
77	19 03.4	-16.9	12.9	20 01.9	-16.7	13.0	21 00.3	-16.4	13.1	21 58.7	-16.2	13.2
78	18 46.5	-17.2	11.9	19 45.2	-17.0	12.0	20 43.9	-16.8	12.1	21 42.5	-16.5	12.1
79	18 29.3	-17.6	10.9	19 28.2	-17.4	11.0	20 27.1	-17.2	11.0	21 26.0	-17.0	11.1
80	18 11.7	-17.9	9.9	19 10.8	-17.7	9.9	20 09.9	-17.5	10.0	21 09.0	-17.4	10.1
81	17 53.8	-18.1	8.9	18 53.1	-18.0	8.9	19 52.4	-17.9	9.0	20 51.6	-17.7	9.1
82	17 35.7	-18.5	7.9	18 35.1	-18.3	7.9	19 34.5	-18.2	8.0	20 33.9	-18.0	8.0
83	17 17.2	-18.8	6.9	18 16.8	-18.7	6.9	19 16.3	-18.5	7.0	20 15.9	-18.4	7.0
84	16 58.4	-19.0	5.9	17 58.1	-19.0	5.9	18 57.8	-18.9	6.0	19 57.5	-18.8	6.0
85	16 39.4	-19.4	4.9	17 39.1	-19.2	4.9	18 38.9	-19.2	5.0	19 38.7	-19.1	5.0
86	16 20.0	-19.6	3.9	17 19.9	-19.6	3.9	18 19.7	-19.4	4.0	19 19.6	-19.4	4.0
87	16 00.4	-19.9	2.9	17 00.3	-19.8	2.9	18 00.3	-19.8	3.0	19 00.2	-19.8	3.0
88	15 40.5	-20.1	2.0	16 40.5	-20.1	2.0	17 40.5	-20.1	2.0	18 40.4	-20.0	2.0
89	15 20.4	-20.4	1.0	16 20.4	-20.4	1.0	17 20.4	-20.4	1.0	18 20.4	-20.4	1.0
90	15 00.0	-20.6	0.0	16 00.0	-20.7	0.0	17 00.0	-20.7	0.0	18 00.0	-20.7	0.0
	15°			16°			17°			18°		

19°			20°			21°			22°			Dec.
Hc ° ′	d ′	Z °	Hc ° ′	d ′	Z °	Hc ° ′	d ′	Z °	Hc ° ′	d ′	Z °	°
18 52.1	+20.5	96.8	18 44.8	+21.5	97.1	18 37.2	+22.6	97.4	18 29.3	+23.6	97.8	0
19 12.6	+20.1	95.8	19 06.3	+21.2	96.1	18 59.8	+22.2	96.5	18 52.9	+23.2	96.8	1
19 32.7	+19.8	94.8	19 27.5	+20.9	95.1	19 22.0	+21.9	95.5	19 16.1	+22.9	95.8	2
19 52.5	+19.5	93.8	19 48.4	+20.6	94.1	19 43.9	+21.6	94.5	19 39.0	+22.7	94.8	3
20 12.0	+19.2	92.8	20 09.0	+20.2	93.1	20 05.5	+21.3	93.5	20 01.7	+22.2	93.9	4
20 31.2	+18.8	91.7	20 29.2	+19.8	92.1	20 26.8	+20.9	92.5	20 23.9	+22.0	92.9	5
20 50.0	+18.4	90.7	20 49.0	+19.5	91.1	20 47.7	+20.5	91.5	20 45.9	+21.6	91.9	6
21 08.4	+18.1	89.7	21 08.5	+19.2	90.1	21 08.2	+20.2	90.5	21 07.5	+21.3	90.9	7
21 26.5	+17.7	88.7	21 27.7	+18.7	89.1	21 28.4	+19.8	89.5	21 28.8	+20.8	89.9	8
21 44.2	+17.3	87.7	21 46.4	+18.4	88.1	21 48.2	+19.5	88.5	21 49.6	+20.6	88.9	9
22 01.5	+16.9	86.6	22 04.8	+18.0	87.0	22 07.7	+19.1	87.4	22 10.2	+20.1	87.8	10
22 18.4	+16.5	85.6	22 22.8	+17.6	86.0	22 26.8	+18.7	86.4	22 30.3	+19.8	86.8	11
22 34.9	+16.2	84.6	22 40.4	+17.2	85.0	22 45.5	+18.2	85.4	22 50.1	+19.3	85.8	12
22 51.1	+15.7	83.5	22 57.6	+16.8	83.9	23 03.7	+17.9	84.4	23 09.4	+19.0	84.8	13
23 06.8	+15.3	82.5	23 14.4	+16.4	82.9	23 21.6	+17.5	83.3	23 28.4	+18.5	83.7	14
23 22.1	+14.8	81.4	23 30.8	+16.0	81.8	23 39.1	+17.1	82.3	23 46.9	+18.2	82.7	15
23 36.9	+14.5	80.4	23 46.8	+15.5	80.8	23 56.2	+16.6	81.2	24 05.1	+17.7	81.7	16
23 51.4	+14.0	79.3	24 02.3	+15.1	79.7	24 12.8	+16.2	80.2	24 22.8	+17.3	80.6	17
24 05.4	+13.5	78.2	24 17.4	+14.6	78.7	24 29.0	+15.7	79.1	24 40.1	+16.8	79.6	18
24 18.9	+13.1	77.2	24 32.0	+14.2	77.6	24 44.7	+15.3	78.0	24 56.9	+16.4	78.5	19
24 32.0	+12.7	76.1	24 46.2	+13.8	76.5	25 00.0	+14.8	77.0	25 13.3	+15.9	77.4	20
24 44.7	+12.2	75.0	25 00.0	+13.3	75.5	25 14.8	+14.4	75.9	25 29.2	+15.5	76.4	21
24 56.9	+11.7	73.9	25 13.3	+12.8	74.4	25 29.2	+13.9	74.8	25 44.7	+14.9	75.3	22
25 08.6	+11.3	72.8	25 26.1	+12.3	73.3	25 43.1	+13.4	73.8	25 59.6	+14.5	74.2	23
25 19.9	+10.7	71.8	25 38.4	+11.9	72.2	25 56.5	+12.9	72.7	26 14.1	+14.1	73.1	24
25 30.6	+10.3	70.7	25 50.3	+11.3	71.1	26 09.4	+12.5	71.6	26 28.2	+13.5	72.1	25
25 40.9	+9.8	69.6	26 01.6	+10.9	70.0	26 21.9	+11.9	70.5	26 41.7	+13.0	71.0	26
25 50.7	+9.3	68.5	26 12.5	+10.4	68.9	26 33.8	+11.5	69.4	26 54.7	+12.5	69.9	27
26 00.0	+8.8	67.4	26 22.9	+9.8	67.8	26 45.3	+10.9	68.3	27 07.2	+12.0	68.8	28
26 08.8	+8.3	66.3	26 32.7	+9.4	66.7	26 56.2	+10.4	67.2	27 19.2	+11.5	67.7	29
26 17.1	+7.8	65.2	26 42.1	+8.8	65.6	27 06.6	+9.9	66.1	27 30.7	+11.0	66.6	30
26 24.9	+7.3	64.1	26 50.9	+8.4	64.5	27 16.5	+9.4	65.0	27 41.7	+10.4	65.5	31
26 32.2	+6.8	63.0	26 59.3	+7.8	63.4	27 25.9	+8.8	63.9	27 52.1	+9.9	64.3	32
26 39.0	+6.2	61.9	27 07.1	+7.2	62.3	27 34.7	+8.3	62.8	28 02.0	+9.3	63.2	33
26 45.2	+5.7	60.7	27 14.3	+6.8	61.2	27 43.0	+7.8	61.6	28 11.3	+8.8	62.1	34
26 50.9	+5.2	59.6	27 21.1	+6.2	60.1	27 50.8	+7.2	60.5	28 20.1	+8.3	61.0	35
26 56.1	+4.7	58.5	27 27.3	+5.6	58.9	27 58.0	+6.7	59.4	28 28.4	+7.6	59.9	36
27 00.8	+4.1	57.4	27 32.9	+5.2	57.8	28 04.7	+6.1	58.3	28 36.0	+7.2	58.7	37
27 04.9	+3.7	56.3	27 38.1	+4.6	56.7	28 10.8	+5.6	57.1	28 43.2	+6.5	57.6	38
27 08.6	+3.0	55.2	27 42.7	+4.0	55.6	28 16.4	+5.0	56.0	28 49.7	+6.0	56.5	39
27 11.6	+2.6	54.0	27 46.7	+3.5	54.4	28 21.4	+4.4	54.9	28 55.7	+5.4	55.3	40
27 14.2	+1.9	52.9	27 50.2	+2.9	53.3	28 25.8	+3.9	53.8	29 01.1	+4.9	54.2	41
27 16.1	+1.5	51.8	27 53.1	+2.4	52.2	28 29.7	+3.3	52.6	29 06.0	+4.2	53.1	42
27 17.6	+0.9	50.7	27 55.5	+1.8	51.1	28 33.0	+2.8	51.5	29 10.2	+3.7	51.9	43
27 18.5	+0.4	49.5	27 57.3	+1.3	49.9	28 35.8	+2.1	50.3	29 13.9	+3.1	50.8	44
27 18.9	-0.2	48.4	27 58.6	+0.7	48.8	28 37.9	+1.6	49.2	29 17.0	+2.5	49.6	45
27 18.7	-0.7	47.3	27 59.3	+0.1	47.7	28 39.5	+1.1	48.1	29 19.5	+1.9	48.5	46
27 18.0	-1.2	46.2	27 59.4	-0.4	46.5	28 40.6	+0.4	46.9	29 21.4	+1.3	47.3	47
27 16.8	-1.8	45.0	27 59.0	-0.9	45.4	28 41.0	-0.1	45.8	29 22.7	+0.8	46.2	48
27 15.0	-2.3	43.9	27 58.1	-1.5	44.3	28 40.9	-0.7	44.6	29 23.5	+0.1	45.0	49
27 12.7	-2.9	42.8	27 56.6	-2.1	43.1	28 40.2	-1.2	43.5	29 23.6	-0.4	43.9	50
27 09.8	-3.4	41.7	27 54.5	-2.6	42.0	28 39.0	-1.9	42.4	29 23.2	-1.1	42.7	51
27 06.4	-3.9	40.5	27 51.9	-3.2	40.9	28 37.1	-2.4	41.2	29 22.1	-1.6	41.6	52
27 02.5	-4.5	39.4	27 48.7	-3.7	39.7	28 34.7	-2.9	40.1	29 20.5	-2.2	40.4	53
26 58.0	-5.0	38.3	27 45.0	-4.3	38.6	28 31.8	-3.6	39.0	29 18.3	-2.8	39.3	54
26 53.0	-5.5	37.2	27 40.7	-4.8	37.5	28 28.2	-4.1	37.8	29 15.5	-3.4	38.2	55
26 47.5	-6.1	36.1	27 35.9	-5.4	36.4	28 24.1	-4.7	36.7	29 12.1	-3.9	37.0	56
26 41.4	-6.5	34.9	27 30.5	-5.9	35.2	28 19.4	-5.2	35.5	29 08.2	-4.6	35.9	57
26 34.9	-7.1	33.8	27 24.6	-6.4	34.1	28 14.2	-5.8	34.4	29 03.6	-5.1	34.7	58
26 27.8	-7.6	32.7	27 18.2	-7.0	33.0	28 08.4	-6.3	33.3	28 58.5	-5.7	33.6	59
26 20.2	-8.1	31.6	27 11.2	-7.5	31.9	28 02.1	-6.9	32.2	28 52.8	-6.3	32.5	60
26 12.1	-8.6	30.5	27 03.7	-8.0	30.8	27 55.2	-7.4	31.0	28 46.5	-6.8	31.3	61
26 03.5	-9.1	29.4	26 55.7	-8.6	29.7	27 47.8	-8.0	29.9	28 39.7	-7.4	30.2	62
25 54.4	-9.6	28.3	26 47.1	-9.0	28.5	27 39.8	-8.5	28.8	28 32.3	-8.0	29.1	63
25 44.8	-10.1	27.2	26 38.1	-9.6	27.4	27 31.3	-9.1	27.7	28 24.3	-8.5	27.9	64
25 34.7	-10.6	26.1	26 28.5	-10.1	26.3	27 22.2	-9.6	26.6	28 15.8	-9.1	26.8	65
25 24.1	-11.1	25.0	26 18.4	-10.6	25.2	27 12.6	-10.1	25.5	28 06.7	-9.6	25.7	66
25 13.0	-11.5	23.9	26 07.8	-11.1	24.1	27 02.5	-10.6	24.3	27 57.1	-10.1	24.6	67
25 01.5	-12.0	22.9	25 56.7	-11.6	23.0	26 51.9	-11.2	23.2	27 47.0	-10.7	23.4	68
24 49.5	-12.5	21.8	25 45.1	-12.0	22.0	26 40.7	-11.6	22.1	27 36.3	-11.2	22.3	69
24 37.0	-13.0	20.7	25 33.1	-12.6	20.9	26 29.1	-12.1	21.0	27 25.1	-11.8	21.2	70
24 24.0	-13.3	19.6	25 20.5	-13.0	19.8	26 17.0	-12.7	20.0	27 13.3	-12.2	20.1	71
24 10.7	-13.9	18.6	25 07.5	-13.5	18.7	26 04.3	-13.1	18.9	27 01.1	-12.8	19.0	72
23 56.8	-14.3	17.5	24 54.0	-13.9	17.6	25 51.2	-13.6	17.8	26 48.3	-13.3	17.9	73
23 42.5	-14.7	16.4	24 40.1	-14.4	16.6	25 37.6	-14.1	16.7	26 35.0	-13.8	16.8	74
23 27.8	-15.1	15.4	24 25.7	-14.9	15.5	25 23.5	-14.6	15.6	26 21.2	-14.2	15.7	75
23 12.7	-15.5	14.3	24 10.8	-15.3	14.4	25 08.9	-15.0	14.5	26 07.0	-14.8	14.7	76
22 57.2	-16.0	13.3	23 55.5	-15.7	13.4	24 53.9	-15.5	13.5	25 52.2	-15.2	13.6	77
22 41.2	-16.4	12.2	23 39.8	-16.1	12.3	24 38.4	-15.9	12.4	25 37.0	-15.7	12.5	78
22 24.8	-16.7	11.2	23 23.7	-16.6	11.3	24 22.5	-16.4	11.4	25 21.3	-16.1	11.4	79
22 08.1	-17.2	10.1	23 07.1	-17.0	10.2	24 06.1	-16.7	10.3	25 05.2	-16.6	10.4	80
21 50.9	-17.6	9.1	22 50.1	-17.4	9.2	23 49.4	-17.3	9.2	24 48.6	-17.1	9.3	81
21 33.3	-17.9	8.1	22 32.7	-17.7	8.1	23 32.1	-17.6	8.2	24 31.5	-17.5	8.3	82
21 15.4	-18.3	7.1	22 15.0	-18.2	7.1	23 14.5	-18.0	7.2	24 14.0	-17.9	7.2	83
20 57.1	-18.6	6.0	21 56.8	-18.6	6.1	22 56.5	-18.5	6.1	23 56.1	-18.3	6.2	84
20 38.5	-19.0	5.0	21 38.2	-18.9	5.1	22 38.0	-18.8	5.1	23 37.8	-18.8	5.1	85
20 19.5	-19.4	4.0	21 19.3	-19.3	4.0	22 19.2	-19.3	4.1	23 19.0	-19.2	4.1	86
20 00.1	-19.7	3.0	21 00.0	-19.6	3.0	21 59.9	-19.6	3.0	22 59.8	-19.5	3.1	87
19 40.4	-20.0	2.0	20 40.4	-20.0	2.0	21 40.3	-20.0	2.0	22 40.3	-20.0	2.0	88
19 20.4	-20.4	1.0	20 20.4	-20.4	1.0	21 20.3	-20.3	1.0	22 20.3	-20.3	1.0	89
19 00.0	-20.7	0.0	20 00.0	-20.7	0.0	21 00.0	-20.7	0.0	22 00.0	-20.7	0.0	90
19°			20°			21°			22°			

70°, 290° L.H.A. LATITUDE SAME NAME AS DECLINATION

LATITUDE CONTRARY NAME TO DECLINATION L.H.A. 70°, 290°

Dec.	15° Hc	d	Z	16° Hc	d	Z	17° Hc	d	Z	18° Hc	d	Z	19° Hc	d	Z	20° Hc	d	Z	21° Hc	d	Z	22° Hc	d	Z	Dec.
°	° ′	′	°	° ′	′	°	° ′	′	°	° ′	′	°	° ′	′	°	° ′	′	°	° ′	′	°	° ′	′	°	°
0	19 17.5	-16.7	95.4	19 11.7	-17.7	95.7	19 05.5	-18.7	96.1	18 59.0	-19.8	96.4	18 52.1	-20.8	96.8	18 44.8	-21.8	97.1	18 37.2	-22.8	97.4	18 29.3	-23.8	97.8	0
1	19 00.8	-16.9	96.4	18 54.0	-18.0	96.7	18 46.8	-19.1	97.1	18 39.2	-20.1	97.4	18 31.3	-21.1	97.7	18 23.0	-22.1	98.1	18 14.4	-23.1	98.4	18 05.5	-24.2	98.7	1
2	18 43.9	-17.3	97.4	18 36.0	-18.4	97.7	18 27.7	-19.4	98.1	18 19.1	-20.4	98.4	18 10.2	-21.4	98.7	18 00.9	-22.4	99.1	17 51.3	-23.4	99.4	17 41.3	-24.4	99.7	2
3	18 26.6	-17.6	98.4	18 17.6	-18.6	98.8	18 08.3	-19.6	99.1	17 58.7	-20.7	99.4	17 48.8	-21.7	99.7	17 38.5	-22.7	100.0	17 27.9	-23.7	100.3	17 16.9	-24.7	100.7	3
4	18 09.0	-17.9	99.4	17 59.0	-18.9	99.8	17 48.7	-20.0	100.1	17 38.0	-21.0	100.4	17 27.1	-22.0	100.7	17 15.8	-23.0	101.0	17 04.2	-24.0	101.3	16 52.2	-24.9	101.6	4
5	17 51.1	-18.2	100.4	17 40.1	-19.3	100.7	17 28.7	-20.2	101.1	17 17.0	-21.2	101.4	17 05.1	-22.3	101.7	16 52.8	-23.3	102.0	16 40.2	-24.2	102.3	16 27.3	-25.2	102.6	5
6	17 32.9	-18.5	101.4	17 20.8	-19.5	101.7	17 08.5	-20.6	102.0	16 55.8	-21.6	102.3	16 42.8	-22.5	102.6	16 29.5	-23.5	102.9	16 16.0	-24.5	103.2	16 02.1	-25.5	103.5	6
7	17 14.4	-18.9	102.4	17 01.3	-19.8	102.7	16 47.9	-20.8	103.0	16 34.2	-21.8	103.3	16 20.3	-22.8	103.6	16 06.0	-23.8	103.9	15 51.5	-24.8	104.2	15 36.6	-25.7	104.4	7
8	16 55.5	-19.1	103.4	16 41.5	-20.1	103.7	16 27.1	-21.1	104.0	16 12.4	-22.1	104.3	15 57.5	-23.1	104.6	15 42.2	-24.0	104.8	15 26.7	-25.0	105.1	15 10.9	-25.9	105.4	8
9	16 36.4	-19.3	104.4	16 21.4	-20.4	104.7	16 06.0	-21.4	105.0	15 50.3	-22.3	105.3	15 34.4	-23.3	105.5	15 18.2	-24.2	105.8	15 01.8	-25.3	106.1	14 45.0	-26.1	106.3	9
10	16 17.1	-19.7	105.4	16 01.0	-20.7	105.7	15 44.6	-21.6	106.0	15 28.0	-22.6	106.2	15 11.1	-23.5	106.5	14 54.0	-24.5	106.7	14 36.5	-25.4	107.0	14 18.9	-26.4	107.2	10
11	15 57.4	-19.9	106.4	15 40.3	-20.9	106.7	15 23.0	-21.9	106.9	15 05.4	-22.8	107.2	14 47.6	-23.8	107.4	14 29.5	-24.8	107.7	14 11.1	-25.6	107.9	13 52.5	-26.5	108.2	11
12	15 37.5	-20.2	107.4	15 19.4	-21.1	107.6	15 01.1	-22.1	107.9	14 42.6	-23.1	108.1	14 23.8	-24.0	108.4	14 04.7	-24.9	108.6	13 45.5	-25.9	108.9	13 26.0	-26.8	109.1	12
13	15 17.3	-20.4	108.3	14 58.3	-21.4	108.6	14 39.0	-22.3	108.8	14 19.5	-23.3	109.1	13 59.8	-24.2	109.3	13 39.8	-25.1	109.6	13 19.6	-26.1	109.8	12 59.2	-27.0	110.0	13
14	14 56.9	-20.7	109.3	14 36.9	-21.6	109.6	14 16.7	-22.6	109.8	13 56.2	-23.5	110.0	13 35.6	-24.5	110.3	13 14.7	-25.4	110.5	12 53.5	-26.2	110.7	12 32.2	-27.1	110.9	14
15	14 36.2	-20.9	110.3	14 15.3	-21.9	110.5	13 54.1	-22.8	110.8	13 32.7	-23.7	111.0	13 11.1	-24.6	111.2	12 49.3	-25.5	111.4	12 27.3	-26.4	111.6	12 05.1	-27.4	111.8	15
16	14 15.3	-21.2	111.3	13 53.4	-22.1	111.5	13 31.3	-23.0	111.7	13 09.0	-23.9	111.9	12 46.5	-24.8	112.1	12 23.8	-25.8	112.4	12 00.9	-26.7	112.6	11 37.7	-27.5	112.7	16
17	13 54.1	-21.4	112.2	13 31.3	-22.3	112.4	13 08.3	-23.2	112.7	12 45.1	-24.2	112.9	12 21.7	-25.1	113.1	11 58.0	-25.9	113.3	11 34.2	-26.8	113.5	11 10.2	-27.6	113.7	17
18	13 32.7	-21.6	113.2	13 09.0	-22.5	113.4	12 45.1	-23.4	113.6	12 20.9	-24.3	113.8	11 56.6	-25.2	114.0	11 32.1	-26.1	114.2	11 07.4	-26.9	114.4	10 42.6	-27.8	114.6	18
19	13 11.1	-21.8	114.1	12 46.5	-22.7	114.3	12 21.7	-23.7	114.6	11 56.6	-24.5	114.7	11 31.4	-25.4	114.9	11 06.0	-26.2	115.1	10 40.5	-27.1	115.3	10 14.8	-28.0	115.5	19
20	12 49.3	-22.0	115.1	12 23.8	-22.9	115.3	11 58.0	-23.8	115.5	11 32.1	-24.7	115.7	11 06.0	-25.5	115.9	10 39.8	-26.4	116.0	10 13.4	-27.3	116.2	9 46.8	-28.1	116.4	20
21	12 27.3	-22.2	116.0	12 00.9	-23.2	116.2	11 34.2	-24.0	116.4	11 07.4	-24.8	116.6	10 40.5	-25.7	116.8	10 13.4	-26.6	116.9	9 46.1	-27.4	117.1	9 18.7	-28.2	117.3	21
22	12 05.1	-22.4	117.0	11 37.7	-23.2	117.2	11 10.2	-24.1	117.4	10 42.6	-25.0	117.5	10 14.8	-25.9	117.7	9 46.8	-26.7	117.9	9 18.7	-27.5	118.0	8 50.5	-28.4	118.1	22
23	11 42.7	-22.6	117.9	11 14.5	-23.5	118.1	10 46.1	-24.3	118.3	10 17.6	-25.2	118.5	9 48.9	-26.0	118.6	9 20.1	-26.8	118.8	8 51.2	-27.7	118.9	8 22.1	-28.5	119.0	23
24	11 20.1	-22.8	118.9	10 51.0	-23.6	119.1	10 21.8	-24.5	119.2	9 52.4	-25.3	119.4	9 22.9	-26.2	119.5	8 53.3	-27.0	119.7	8 23.5	-27.8	119.8	7 53.6	-28.6	119.9	24
25	10 57.3	-23.0	119.8	10 27.4	-23.8	120.0	9 57.3	-24.7	120.2	9 27.1	-25.5	120.3	8 56.7	-26.3	120.4	8 26.3	-27.1	120.6	7 55.7	-27.9	120.7	7 25.0	-28.7	120.8	25
26	10 34.3	-23.1	120.8	10 03.6	-24.0	120.9	9 32.6	-24.7	121.1	9 01.6	-25.6	121.2	8 30.4	-26.4	121.4	7 59.2	-27.2	121.5	7 27.8	-28.0	121.6	6 56.3	-28.8	121.7	26
27	10 11.2	-23.3	121.7	9 39.6	-24.1	121.9	9 07.9	-25.0	122.0	8 36.0	-25.7	122.1	8 04.0	-26.5	122.3	7 32.0	-27.4	122.4	6 59.8	-28.1	122.5	6 27.5	-28.9	122.6	27
28	9 47.9	-23.4	122.6	9 15.5	-24.3	122.8	8 42.9	-25.0	122.9	8 10.3	-25.9	123.0	7 37.5	-26.6	123.2	7 04.6	-27.4	123.3	6 31.7	-28.2	123.4	5 58.6	-29.0	123.5	28
29	9 24.5	-23.6	123.6	8 51.2	-24.3	123.7	8 17.9	-25.2	123.8	7 44.4	-26.0	124.0	7 10.9	-26.8	124.1	6 37.2	-27.5	124.2	6 03.5	-28.3	124.3	5 29.6	-29.0	124.3	29
30	9 00.9	-23.7	124.5	8 26.9	-24.6	124.6	7 52.7	-25.3	124.8	7 18.4	-26.0	124.9	6 44.1	-26.9	125.0	6 09.7	-27.6	125.1	5 35.2	-28.4	125.1	5 00.6	-29.1	125.2	30
31	8 37.2	-23.9	125.4	8 02.3	-24.6	125.6	7 27.4	-25.4	125.7	6 52.4	-26.2	125.8	6 17.2	-26.9	125.9	5 42.1	-27.7	126.0	5 06.8	-28.5	126.0	4 31.5	-29.2	126.1	31
32	8 13.3	-23.9	126.4	7 37.7	-24.7	126.5	7 02.0	-25.5	126.6	6 26.2	-26.3	126.7	5 50.3	-27.0	126.8	5 14.4	-27.8	126.8	4 38.3	-28.5	126.9	4 02.3	-29.3	127.0	32
33	7 49.4	-24.2	127.3	7 13.0	-24.9	127.4	6 36.5	-25.7	127.5	5 59.9	-26.4	127.6	5 23.3	-27.1	127.7	4 46.6	-27.9	127.7	4 09.8	-28.5	127.8	3 33.0	-29.3	127.9	33
34	7 25.2	-24.2	128.2	6 48.1	-25.0	128.3	6 10.8	-25.7	128.4	5 33.5	-26.4	128.5	4 56.2	-27.2	128.6	4 18.7	-27.9	128.6	3 41.3	-28.7	128.7	3 03.7	-29.3	128.7	34
35	7 01.0	-24.3	129.1	6 23.1	-25.0	129.2	5 45.1	-25.8	129.3	5 07.1	-26.5	129.4	4 29.0	-27.3	129.5	3 50.8	-27.9	129.5	3 12.6	-28.6	129.6	2 34.4	-29.4	129.6	35
36	6 36.7	-24.4	130.1	5 58.1	-25.2	130.1	5 19.3	-25.8	130.2	4 40.6	-26.6	130.3	4 01.7	-27.3	130.3	3 22.9	-28.0	130.4	2 44.0	-28.7	130.4	2 05.0	-29.4	130.5	36
37	6 12.3	-24.5	131.0	5 32.9	-25.2	131.1	4 53.5	-26.0	131.1	4 14.0	-26.7	131.2	3 34.4	-27.3	131.2	2 54.9	-28.1	131.3	2 15.3	-28.8	131.3	1 35.6	-29.4	131.3	37
38	5 47.8	-24.6	131.9	5 07.7	-25.4	132.0	4 27.5	-26.0	132.0	3 47.3	-26.7	132.1	3 07.1	-27.4	132.1	2 26.8	-28.1	132.2	1 46.5	-28.7	132.2	1 06.2	-29.4	132.2	38
39	5 23.2	-24.7	132.8	4 42.3	-25.3	132.9	4 01.5	-26.1	132.9	3 20.6	-26.8	133.0	2 39.7	-27.5	133.0	1 58.7	-28.1	133.1	1 17.8	-28.8	133.1	0 36.8	-29.5	133.1	39
40	4 58.5	-24.8	133.7	4 17.0	-25.5	133.8	3 35.4	-26.1	133.8	2 53.8	-26.8	133.9	2 12.2	-27.4	133.9	1 30.6	-28.1	133.9	0 49.0	-28.8	134.0	0 07.3	-29.4	134.0	40
41	4 33.7	-24.8	134.6	3 51.5	-25.5	134.7	3 09.3	-26.2	134.7	2 27.0	-26.8	134.8	1 44.8	-27.5	134.8	1 02.5	-28.2	134.8	0 20.2	-28.8	134.8	0 22.1	+29.5	45.2	41
42	4 08.9	-24.9	135.6	3 26.0	-25.6	135.6	2 43.1	-26.2	135.6	2 00.2	-26.9	135.7	1 17.3	-27.5	135.7	0 34.3	-28.1	135.7	0 08.6	+28.8	44.3	0 51.6	+29.4	44.3	42
43	3 44.0	-25.0	136.5	3 00.4	-25.6	136.5	2 16.9	-26.3	136.5	1 33.3	-26.9	136.6	0 49.8	-27.6	136.6	0 06.2	-28.2	136.6	0 37.4	+28.8	43.4	1 21.0	+29.4	43.4	43
44	3 19.0	-25.0	137.4	2 34.8	-25.6	137.4	1 50.6	-26.2	137.5	1 06.4	-26.9	137.5	0 22.2	-27.5	137.5	0 22.0	+28.1	42.5	1 06.2	+28.8	42.5	1 50.4	+29.4	42.6	44
45	2 54.0	-25.1	138.3	2 09.2	-25.7	138.3	1 24.4	-26.3	138.3	0 39.5	-26.9	138.4	0 05.3	+27.5	41.6	0 50.1	+28.2	41.6	1 35.0	+28.7	41.7	2 19.8	+29.3	41.7	45
46	2 28.9	-25.0	139.2	1 43.5	-25.7	139.2	0 58.1	-26.3	139.2	0 12.6	-26.9	139.2	0 32.8	+27.6	40.8	1 18.3	+28.1	40.8	2 03.7	+28.7	40.8	2 49.1	+29.4	40.8	46
47	2 03.9	-25.2	140.1	1 17.8	-25.7	140.1	0 31.8	-26.4	140.1	0 14.3	+26.9	39.9	1 00.4	+27.5	39.9	1 46.4	+28.1	39.9	2 32.4	+28.7	39.9	3 18.5	+29.2	39.9	47
48	1 38.7	-25.1	141.0	0 52.1	-25.7	141.0	0 05.4	-26.3	141.0	0 41.2	+26.9	39.0	1 27.9	+27.5	39.0	2 14.5	+28.1	39.0	3 01.1	+28.7	39.0	3 47.7	+29.2	39.1	48
49	1 13.6	-25.2	141.9	0 26.4	-25.8	141.9	0 20.9	+26.3	38.1	1 08.1	+26.9	38.1	1 55.4	+27.4	38.1	2 42.6	+28.0	38.1	3 29.8	+28.6	38.1	4 16.9	+29.2	38.2	49
50	0 48.4	-25.1	142.8	0 00.6	-25.7	142.8	0 47.2	+26.3	37.2	1 35.0	+26.9	37.2	2 22.8	+27.4	37.2	3 10.6	+28.0	37.2	3 58.4	+28.5	37.3	4 46.1	+29.1	37.3	50
51	0 23.3	-25.2	143.7	0 25.1	+25.8	36.3	1 13.5	+26.3	36.3	2 01.9	+26.8	36.3	2 50.2	+27.4	36.3	3 38.6	+27.9	36.3	4 26.9	+28.5	36.4	5 15.2	+29.0	36.4	51
52	0 01.9	+25.2	35.3	0 50.9	+25.7	35.4	1 39.8	+26.3	35.4	2 28.7	+26.8	35.4	3 17.6	+27.4	35.4	4 06.5	+27.9	35.5	4 55.4	+28.4	35.5	5 44.2	+28.9	35.6	52
53	0 27.1	+25.2	34.4	1 16.6	+25.7	34.4	2 06.1	+26.2	34.5	2 55.5	+26.8	34.5	3 45.0	+27.2	34.5	4 34.4	+27.8	34.6	5 23.8	+28.3	34.6	6 13.1	+28.9	34.7	53
54	0 52.3	+25.1	33.5	1 42.3	+25.7	33.5	2 32.3	+26.2	33.6	3 22.3	+26.7	33.6	4 12.2	+27.3	33.6	5 02.2	+27.7	33.7	5 52.1	+28.2	33.7	6 42.0	+28.7	33.8	54
55	1 17.4	+25.2	32.6	2 08.0	+25.6	32.6	2 58.5	+26.1	32.7	3 49.0	+26.6	32.7	4 39.5	+27.1	32.7	5 29.9	+27.7	32.8	6 20.3	+28.2	32.8	7 10.7	+28.7	32.9	55
56	1 42.6	+25.1	31.7	2 33.6	+25.6	31.7	3 24.6	+26.1	31.8	4 15.6	+26.6	31.8	5 06.6	+27.1	31.8	5 57.6	+27.5	31.9	6 48.5	+28.1	32.0	7 39.4	+28.5	32.0	56
57	2 07.7	+25.1	30.8	2 59.2	+25.6	30.8	3 50.7	+26.1	30.9	4 42.2	+26.5	30.9	5 33.7	+27.0	30.9	6 25.1	+27.5	31.0	7 16.6	+27.9	31.1	8 07.9	+28.5	31.1	57
58	2 32.8	+25.0	29.9	3 24.8	+25.5	29.9	4 16.8	+25.9	30.0	5 08.7	+26.5	30.0	6 00.7	+26.9	30.0	6 52.6	+27.4	30.1	7 44.5	+27.8	30.2	8 36.4	+28.3	30.2	58
59	2 57.8	+25.0	29.0	3 50.3	+25.4	29.0	4 42.7	+26.0	29.1	5 35.2	+26.3	29.1	6 27.6	+26.8	29.1	7 20.0	+27.3	29.2	8 12.3	+27.8	29.3	9 04.7	+28.1	29.3	59
60	3 22.8	+25.0	28.1	4 15.7	+25.4	28.1	5 08.7	+25.8	28.1	6 01.5	+26.3	28.2	6 54.4	+26.7	28.2	7 47.3	+27.1	28.3	8 40.1	+27.6	28.4	9 32.8	+28.1	28.5	60
61	3 47.8	+24.8	27.2	4 41.1	+25.4	27.2	5 34.5	+25.7	27.2	6 27.8	+26.2	27.3	7 21.1	+26.6	27.3	8 14.4	+27.0	27.4	9 07.7	+27.4	27.5	10 00.9	+27.9	27.6	61
62	4 12.6	+24.9	26.3	5 06.5	+25.2	26.3	6 00.2	+25.7	26.3	6 54.0	+26.1	26.4	7 47.7	+26.5	26.4	8 41.4	+26.9	26.5	9 35.1	+27.3	26.6	10 28.8	+27.7	26.7	62
63	4 37.5	+24.7	25.3	5 31.7	+25.2	25.4	6 25.9	+25.6	25.4	7 20.1	+25.9	25.5	8 14.2	+26.4	25.5	9 08.3	+26.8	25.6	10 02.4	+27.2	25.7	10 56.5	+27.6	25.8	63
64	5 02.2	+24.7	24.4	5 56.9	+25.0	24.5	6 51.5	+25.4	24.5	7 46.0	+25.9	24.6	8 40.6	+26.2	24.6	9 35.1	+26.6	24.7	10 29.6	+27.0	24.8	11 24.1	+27.4	24.8	64
65	5 26.9	+24.6	23.5	6 21.9	+25.0	23.6	7 16.9	+25.4	23.6	8 11.9	+25.7	23.7	9 06.8	+26.1	23.7	10 01.7	+26.5	23.8	10 56.6	+26.9	23.9	11 51.5	+27.2	23.9	65
66	5 51.5	+24.5	22.6	6 46.9	+24.9	22.6	7 42.3	+25.2	22.7	8 37.6	+25.6	22.7	9 32.9	+26.0	22.8	10 28.2	+26.4	22.9	11 23.5	+26.7	22.9	12 18.7	+27.1	23.0	66
67	6 16.0	+24.4	21.7	7 11.8	+24.7	21.7	8 07.5	+25.1	21.8	9 03.2	+25.5	21.8	9 58.9	+25.8	21.9	10 54.6	+26.1	22.0	11 50.2	+26.5	22.0	12 45.8	+26.9	22.1	67
68	6 40.4	+24.3	20.8	7 36.5	+24.7	20.8	8 32.6	+25.0	20.9	9 28.7	+25.3	20.9	10 24.7	+25.6	21.0	11 20.7	+26.0	21.0	12 16.7	+26.3	21.1	13 12.7	+26.6	21.2	68
69	7 04.7	+24.2	19.8	8 01.2	+24.5	19.9	8 57.6	+24.8	19.9	9 54.0	+25.1	20.0	10 50.3	+25.5	20.1	11 46.7	+25.8	20.1	12 43.0	+26.2	20.2	13 39.3	+26.5	20.3	69
70	7 28.9	+24.1	18.9	8 25.7	+24.4	19.0	9 22.4	+24.7	19.0	10 19.1	+25.0	19.1	11 15.8	+25.4	19.1	12 12.5	+25.6	19.2	13 09.2	+25.9	19.3	14 05.8	+26.2	19.4	70
71	7 53.0	+24.0	18.0	8 50.1	+24.2	18.0	9 47.1	+24.6	18.1	10 44.1	+24.9	18.1	11 41.2	+25.1	18.2	12 38.1	+25.5	18.3	13 35.1	+25.7	18.3	14 32.0	+26.1	18.4	71
72	8 17.0	+23.8	17.1	9 14.3	+24.1	17.1	10 11.7	+24.4	17.2	11 09.0	+24.7	17.2	12 06.3	+24.9	17.3	13 03.6	+25.2	17.3	14 00.8	+25.6	17.4	14 58.1	+25.8	17.5	72
73	8 40.8	+23.7	16.1	9 38.4	+24.0	16.2	10 36.1	+24.2	16.2	11 33.7	+24.5	16.3	12 31.2	+24.8	16.3	13 28.8	+25.0	16.4	14 26.4	+25.3	16.5	15 23.9	+25.5	16.6	73
74	9 04.5	+23.6	15.2	10 02.4	+23.8	15.3	11 00.3	+24.0	15.3	11 58.2	+24.3	15.4	12 56.0	+24.6	15.4	13 53.8	+24.9	15.5	14 51.7	+25.0	15.5	15 49.4	+25.4	15.6	74
75	9 28.1	+23.4	14.3	10 26.2	+23.7	14.3	11 24.3	+23.9	14.4	12 22.5	+24.1	14.4	13 20.6	+24.3	14.5	14 18.7	+24.5	14.5	15 16.7	+24.9	14.6	16 14.8	+25.1	14.7	75
76	9 51.5	+23.2	13.3	10 49.9	+23.4	13.4	11 48.2	+23.7	13.4	12 46.6	+23.9	13.5	13 44.9	+24.2	13.5	14 43.2	+24.4	13.6	15 41.6	+24.5	13.7	16 39.9	+24.8	13.7	76
77	10 14.7	+23.1	12.4	11 13.3	+23.3	12.4	12 11.9	+23.5	12.5	13 10.5	+23.7	12.5	14 09.1	+23.9	12.6	15 07.6	+24.1	12.6	16 06.1	+24.4	12.7	17 04.7	+24.5	12.8	77
78	10 37.8	+23.0	11.5	11 36.6	+23.2	11.5	12 35.4	+23.3	11.5	13 34.2	+23.5	11.6	14 33.0	+23.7	11.6	15 31.7	+23.9	11.7	16 30.5	+24.1	11.8	17 29.2	+24.3	11.8	78
79	11 00.8	+22.7	10.5	11 59.8	+22.9	10.6	12 58.7	+23.1	10.6	13 57.7	+23.3	10.6	14 56.7	+23.4	10.7	15 55.6	+23.6	10.7	16 54.6	+23.8	10.8	17 53.5	+24.0	10.9	79
80	11 23.5	+22.6	9.6	12 22.7	+22.7	9.6	13 21.8	+22.9	9.7	14 21.0	+23.0	9.7	15 20.1	+23.2	9.7	16 19.2	+23.4	9.8	17 18.4	+23.5	9.8	18 17.5	+23.7	9.9	80
81	11 46.1	+22.4	8.6	12 45.4	+22.5	8.7	13 44.7	+22.7	8.7	14 44.0	+22.8	8.7	15 43.3	+23.0	8.8	16 42.6	+23.1	8.8	17 41.9	+23.3	8.9	18 41.2	+23.4	8.9	81
82	12 08.5	+22.2	7.7	13 07.9	+22.3	7.7	14 07.4	+22.4	7.8	15 06.8	+22.6	7.8	16 06.3	+22.7	7.8	17 05.7	+22.8	7.9	18 05.2	+22.9	7.9	19 04.6	+23.1	8.0	82
83	12 30.7	+22.0	6.7	13 30.2	+22.1	6.8	14 29.8	+22.2	6.8	15 29.4	+22.3	6.8	16 29.0	+22.4	6.9	17 28.5	+22.6	6.9	18 28.1	+22.7	6.9	19 27.7	+22.7	7.0	83
84	12 52.7	+21.7	5.8	13 52.3	+21.9	5.8	14 52.0	+22.0	5.8	15 51.7	+22.1	5.9	16 51.4	+22.2	5.9	17 51.1	+22.2	5.9	18 50.8	+22.3	6.0	19 50.4	+22.5	6.0	84
85	13 14.4	+21.6	4.8	14 14.2	+21.7	4.8	15 14.0	+21.7	4.9	16 13.8	+21.8	4.9	17 13.6	+21.8	4.9	18 13.3	+22.0	4.9	19 13.1	+22.1	5.0	20 12.9	+22.1	5.0	85
86	13 36.0	+21.4	3.9	14 35.9	+21.4	3.9	15 35.7	+21.5	3.9	16 35.6	+21.5	3.9	17 35.4	+21.6	3.9	18 35.3	+21.7	4.0	19 35.2	+21.7	4.0	20 35.0	+21.8	4.0	86
87	13 57.4	+21.1	2.9	14 57.3	+21.1	2.9	15 57.2	+21.2	2.9	16 57.1	+21.3	2.9	17 57.0	+21.3	3.0	18 57.0	+21.3	3.0	19 56.9	+21.4	3.0	20 56.8	+21.4	3.0	87
88	14 18.5	+20.9	1.9	15 18.4	+20.9	1.9	16 18.4	+20.9	2.0	17 18.4	+20.9	2.0	18 18.3	+21.0	2.0	19 18.3	+21.0	2.0	20 18.3	+21.0	2.0	21 18.2	+21.1	2.0	88
89	14 39.4	+20.6	1.0	15 39.3	+20.7	1.0	16 39.3	+20.7	1.0	17 39.3	+20.7	1.0	18 39.3	+20.7	1.0	19 39.3	+20.7	1.0	20 39.3	+20.7	1.0	21 39.3	+20.7	1.0	89
90	15 00.0	+20.4	0.0	16 00.0	+20.4	0.0	17 00.0	+20.4	0.0	18 00.0	+20.4	0.0	19 00.0	+20.4	0.0	20 00.0	+20.4	0.0	21 00.0	+20.3	0.0	22 00.0	+20.3	0.0	90
	15°			16°			17°			18°			19°			20°			21°			22°			

S. Lat. {L.H.A. greater than 180° ....Zn=180°−Z; L.H.A. less than 180°...........Zn=180°+Z

LATITUDE SAME NAME AS DECLINATION L.H.A. 110°, 250°

143

71°, 289° L.H.A. LATITUDE SAME NAME AS DECLINATION N. Lat. {L.H.A. greater than 180° .....Zn=Z; L.H.A. less than 180°............Zn=360°−Z}

Dec.	15° Hc	d	Z	16° Hc	d	Z	17° Hc	d	Z	18° Hc	d	Z
°	° ′	′	°	° ′	′	°	° ′	′	°	° ′	′	°
0	18 19.7	+16.2	95.1	18 14.2	+17.3	95.4	18 08.4	+18.3	95.7	18 02.2	+19.4	96.1
1	18 35.9	+15.9	94.1	18 31.5	+16.9	94.4	18 26.7	+18.0	94.7	18 21.6	+19.0	95.1
2	18 51.8	+15.6	93.1	18 48.4	+16.6	93.4	18 44.7	+17.7	93.7	18 40.6	+18.7	94.1
3	19 07.4	+15.1	92.0	19 05.0	+16.3	92.4	19 02.4	+17.3	92.7	18 59.3	+18.4	93.1
4	19 22.5	+14.9	91.0	19 21.3	+15.9	91.4	19 19.7	+17.0	91.7	19 17.7	+18.1	92.1
5	19 37.4	+14.5	90.0	19 37.2	+15.6	90.3	19 36.7	+16.6	90.7	19 35.8	+17.7	91.1
6	19 51.9	+14.1	89.0	19 52.8	+15.2	89.3	19 53.3	+16.3	89.7	19 53.5	+17.4	90.0
7	20 06.0	+13.8	87.9	20 08.0	+14.9	88.3	20 09.6	+16.0	88.7	20 10.9	+17.0	89.0
8	20 19.8	+13.4	86.9	20 22.9	+14.5	87.3	20 25.6	+15.6	87.6	20 27.9	+16.6	88.0
9	20 33.2	+13.1	85.8	20 37.4	+14.1	86.2	20 41.2	+15.2	86.6	20 44.5	+16.3	87.0
10	20 46.3	+12.6	84.8	20 51.5	+13.8	85.2	20 56.4	+14.8	85.6	21 00.8	+15.9	85.9
11	20 58.9	+12.3	83.8	21 05.3	+13.3	84.1	21 11.2	+14.5	84.5	21 16.7	+15.6	84.9
12	21 11.2	+11.9	82.7	21 18.6	+13.0	83.1	21 25.7	+14.0	83.5	21 32.3	+15.1	83.9
13	21 23.1	+11.5	81.7	21 31.6	+12.6	82.0	21 39.7	+13.7	82.4	21 47.4	+14.8	82.8
14	21 34.6	+11.1	80.6	21 44.2	+12.2	81.0	21 53.4	+13.3	81.4	22 02.2	+14.3	81.8
15	21 45.7	+10.7	79.5	21 56.4	+11.8	79.9	22 06.7	+12.8	80.3	22 16.5	+14.0	80.7
16	21 56.4	+10.3	78.5	22 08.2	+11.3	78.9	22 19.5	+12.5	79.3	22 30.5	+13.5	79.7
17	22 06.7	+9.8	77.4	22 19.5	+11.0	77.8	22 32.0	+12.0	78.2	22 44.0	+13.2	78.6
18	22 16.5	+9.5	76.4	22 30.5	+10.5	76.8	22 44.0	+11.7	77.2	22 57.2	+12.7	77.6
19	22 26.0	+9.0	75.3	22 41.0	+10.1	75.7	22 55.7	+11.1	76.1	23 09.9	+12.2	76.5
20	22 35.0	+8.6	74.2	22 51.1	+9.7	74.6	23 06.8	+10.8	75.0	23 22.1	+11.9	75.4
21	22 43.6	+8.2	73.1	23 00.8	+9.3	73.5	23 17.6	+10.3	74.0	23 34.0	+11.4	74.4
22	22 51.8	+7.7	72.1	23 10.1	+8.8	72.5	23 27.9	+9.9	72.9	23 45.4	+10.9	73.3
23	22 59.5	+7.3	71.0	23 18.9	+8.3	71.4	23 37.8	+9.4	71.8	23 56.3	+10.5	72.2
24	23 06.8	+6.9	69.9	23 27.2	+8.0	70.3	23 47.2	+9.0	70.7	24 06.8	+10.1	71.1
25	23 13.7	+6.4	68.8	23 35.2	+7.4	69.2	23 56.2	+8.6	69.6	24 16.9	+9.6	70.1
26	23 20.1	+6.0	67.7	23 42.6	+7.0	68.2	24 04.8	+8.0	68.6	24 26.5	+9.1	69.0
27	23 26.1	+5.5	66.7	23 49.6	+6.6	67.1	24 12.8	+7.6	67.5	24 35.6	+8.7	67.9
28	23 31.6	+5.1	65.6	23 56.2	+6.1	66.0	24 20.4	+7.2	66.4	24 44.3	+8.1	66.8
29	23 36.7	+4.6	64.5	24 02.3	+5.6	64.9	24 27.6	+6.6	65.3	24 52.4	+7.8	65.7
30	23 41.3	+4.1	63.4	24 07.9	+5.2	63.8	24 34.2	+6.2	64.2	25 00.2	+7.2	64.6
31	23 45.4	+3.7	62.3	24 13.1	+4.7	62.7	24 40.4	+5.8	63.1	25 07.4	+6.7	63.5
32	23 49.1	+3.3	61.2	24 17.8	+4.3	61.6	24 46.2	+5.2	62.0	25 14.1	+6.3	62.4
33	23 52.4	+2.7	60.1	24 22.1	+3.7	60.5	24 51.4	+4.8	60.9	25 20.4	+5.7	61.3
34	23 55.1	+2.3	59.0	24 25.8	+3.3	59.4	24 56.2	+4.2	59.8	25 26.1	+5.3	60.2
35	23 57.4	+1.9	57.9	24 29.1	+2.8	58.3	25 00.4	+3.8	58.7	25 31.4	+4.8	59.1
36	23 59.3	+1.4	56.9	24 31.9	+2.4	57.2	25 04.2	+3.3	57.6	25 36.2	+4.3	58.0
37	24 00.7	+0.9	55.8	24 34.3	+1.8	56.1	25 07.5	+2.8	56.5	25 40.5	+3.7	56.9
38	24 01.6	+0.4	54.7	24 36.1	+1.4	55.0	25 10.3	+2.4	55.4	25 44.2	+3.3	55.8
39	24 02.0	0.0	53.6	24 37.5	+0.9	53.9	25 12.7	+1.8	54.3	25 47.5	+2.8	54.7
40	24 02.0	−0.5	52.5	24 38.4	+0.4	52.8	25 14.5	+1.3	53.2	25 50.3	+2.2	53.6
41	24 01.5	−0.9	51.4	24 38.8	0.0	51.7	25 15.8	+0.9	52.1	25 52.5	+1.8	52.5
42	24 00.6	−1.5	50.3	24 38.8	−0.6	50.6	25 16.7	+0.3	51.0	25 54.3	+1.2	51.4
43	23 59.1	−1.9	49.2	24 38.2	−1.0	49.5	25 17.0	−0.1	49.9	25 55.5	+0.8	50.3
44	23 57.2	−2.3	48.1	24 37.2	−1.5	48.4	25 16.9	−0.7	48.8	25 56.3	+0.2	49.1
45	23 54.9	−2.8	47.0	24 35.7	−2.0	47.3	25 16.2	−1.1	47.7	25 56.5	−0.3	48.0
46	23 52.1	−3.3	45.9	24 33.7	−2.5	46.2	25 15.1	−1.6	46.6	25 56.2	−0.8	46.9
47	23 48.8	−3.7	44.8	24 31.2	−2.9	45.1	25 13.5	−2.2	45.5	25 55.4	−1.3	45.8
48	23 45.1	−4.2	43.7	24 28.3	−3.4	44.0	25 11.3	−2.6	44.4	25 54.1	−1.8	44.7
49	23 40.9	−4.7	42.6	24 24.9	−3.9	42.9	25 08.7	−3.1	43.3	25 52.3	−2.3	43.6
50	23 36.2	−5.1	41.5	24 21.0	−4.3	41.8	25 05.6	−3.6	42.2	25 50.0	−2.8	42.5
51	23 31.1	−5.5	40.5	24 16.7	−4.9	40.8	25 02.0	−4.1	41.1	25 47.2	−3.4	41.4
52	23 25.6	−6.1	39.4	24 11.8	−5.3	39.7	24 57.9	−4.5	39.9	25 43.8	−3.8	40.3
53	23 19.5	−6.4	38.3	24 06.5	−5.7	38.6	24 53.4	−5.1	38.9	25 40.0	−4.3	39.1
54	23 13.1	−6.9	37.2	24 00.8	−6.2	37.5	24 48.3	−5.5	37.8	25 35.7	−4.9	38.0
55	23 06.2	−7.4	36.1	23 54.6	−6.7	36.4	24 42.8	−6.0	36.7	25 30.8	−5.3	36.9
56	22 58.8	−7.7	35.1	23 47.9	−7.1	35.3	24 36.8	−6.5	35.6	25 25.5	−5.8	35.8
57	22 51.1	−8.2	34.0	23 40.8	−7.6	34.2	24 30.3	−7.0	34.5	25 19.7	−6.3	34.7
58	22 42.9	−8.7	32.9	23 33.2	−8.1	33.1	24 23.3	−7.4	33.4	25 13.4	−6.8	33.6
59	22 34.2	−9.0	31.8	23 25.1	−8.4	32.1	24 15.9	−7.9	32.3	25 06.6	−7.3	32.5
60	22 25.2	−9.5	30.8	23 16.7	−9.0	31.0	24 08.0	−8.3	31.2	24 59.3	−7.8	31.4
61	22 15.7	−9.9	29.7	23 07.7	−9.3	29.9	23 59.7	−8.8	30.1	24 51.5	−8.2	30.3
62	22 05.8	−10.4	28.6	22 58.4	−9.8	28.8	23 50.9	−9.3	29.0	24 43.3	−8.7	29.3
63	21 55.4	−10.7	27.6	22 48.6	−10.2	27.8	23 41.6	−9.7	28.0	24 34.6	−9.2	28.2
64	21 44.7	−11.1	26.5	22 38.4	−10.7	26.7	23 31.9	−10.1	26.9	24 25.4	−9.6	27.1
65	21 33.6	−11.5	25.4	22 27.7	−11.0	25.6	23 21.8	−10.6	25.8	24 15.8	−10.1	26.0
66	21 22.1	−12.0	24.4	22 16.7	−11.5	24.6	23 11.2	−11.0	24.7	24 05.7	−10.6	24.9
67	21 10.1	−12.3	23.3	22 05.2	−11.9	23.5	23 00.2	−11.5	23.7	23 55.1	−11.0	23.8
68	20 57.8	−12.7	22.3	21 53.3	−12.3	22.4	22 48.7	−11.8	22.6	23 44.1	−11.5	22.8
69	20 45.1	−13.0	21.2	21 41.0	−12.7	21.4	22 36.9	−12.3	21.5	23 32.6	−11.8	21.7
70	20 32.1	−13.5	20.2	21 28.3	−13.0	20.3	22 24.6	−12.7	20.5	23 20.8	−12.4	20.6
71	20 18.6	−13.8	19.2	21 15.3	−13.5	19.3	22 11.9	−13.1	19.4	23 08.4	−12.7	19.6
72	20 04.8	−14.2	18.1	21 01.8	−13.9	18.2	21 58.8	−13.6	18.4	22 55.7	−13.2	18.5
73	19 50.6	−14.5	17.1	20 47.9	−14.2	17.2	21 45.2	−13.9	17.3	22 42.5	−13.6	17.4
74	19 36.1	−14.9	16.1	20 33.7	−14.6	16.2	21 31.3	−14.3	16.3	22 28.9	−14.0	16.4
75	19 21.2	−15.2	15.0	20 19.1	−14.9	15.1	21 17.0	−14.6	15.2	22 14.9	−14.4	15.3
76	19 06.0	−15.6	14.0	20 04.2	−15.3	14.1	21 02.4	−15.1	14.2	22 00.5	−14.8	14.3
77	18 50.4	−15.9	13.0	19 48.9	−15.7	13.1	20 47.3	−15.4	13.2	21 45.7	−15.2	13.2
78	18 34.5	−16.2	12.0	19 33.2	−16.0	12.0	20 31.9	−15.8	12.1	21 30.5	−15.6	12.2
79	18 18.3	−16.6	11.0	19 17.2	−16.4	11.0	20 16.1	−16.2	11.1	21 14.9	−15.9	11.2
80	18 01.7	−16.8	9.9	19 00.8	−16.7	10.0	19 59.9	−16.5	10.1	20 59.0	−16.4	10.1
81	17 44.9	−17.2	8.9	18 44.1	−17.0	9.0	19 43.4	−16.9	9.0	20 42.6	−16.7	9.1
82	17 27.7	−17.5	7.9	18 27.1	−17.3	8.0	19 26.5	−17.2	8.0	20 25.9	−17.0	8.1
83	17 10.2	−17.7	6.9	18 09.8	−17.7	7.0	19 09.3	−17.5	7.0	20 08.9	−17.4	7.1
84	16 52.5	−18.1	5.9	17 52.1	−17.9	6.0	18 51.8	−17.8	6.0	19 51.5	−17.8	6.0
85	16 34.4	−18.3	4.9	17 34.2	−18.3	5.0	18 34.0	−18.2	5.0	19 33.7	−18.1	5.0
86	16 16.1	−18.7	3.9	17 15.9	−18.5	4.0	18 15.8	−18.5	4.0	19 15.6	−18.4	4.0
87	15 57.4	−18.8	3.0	16 57.4	−18.9	3.0	17 57.3	−18.8	3.0	18 57.2	−18.7	3.0
88	15 38.6	−19.2	2.0	16 38.5	−19.1	2.0	17 38.5	−19.1	2.0	18 38.5	−19.1	2.0
89	15 19.4	−19.4	1.0	16 19.4	−19.4	1.0	17 19.4	−19.4	1.0	18 19.4	−19.4	1.0
90	15 00.0	−19.7	0.0	16 00.0	−19.7	0.0	17 00.0	−19.7	0.0	18 00.0	−19.7	0.0

Dec.	19° Hc	d	Z	20° Hc	d	Z	21° Hc	d	Z	22° Hc	d	Z
°	° ′	′	°	° ′	′	°	° ′	′	°	° ′	′	°
0	17 55.7	+20.4	96.4	17 48.9	+21.4	96.7	17 41.7	+22.4	97.0	17 34.2	+23.4	97.3
1	18 16.1	+20.1	95.4	18 10.3	+21.1	95.7	18 04.1	+22.1	96.1	17 57.6	+23.1	96.4
2	18 36.2	+19.7	94.4	18 31.4	+20.8	94.7	18 26.2	+21.9	95.1	18 20.7	+22.9	95.4
3	18 55.9	+19.5	93.4	18 52.2	+20.5	93.8	18 48.1	+21.5	94.1	18 43.6	+22.5	94.4
4	19 15.4	+19.1	92.4	19 12.7	+20.1	92.8	19 09.6	+21.2	93.1	19 06.1	+22.3	93.5
5	19 34.5	+18.8	91.4	19 32.8	+19.8	91.8	19 30.8	+20.9	92.1	19 28.4	+21.9	92.5
6	19 53.3	+18.4	90.4	19 52.6	+19.5	90.8	19 51.7	+20.5	91.1	19 50.3	+21.6	91.5
7	20 11.7	+18.1	89.4	20 12.1	+19.2	89.8	20 12.2	+20.2	90.1	20 11.9	+21.2	90.5
8	20 29.8	+17.7	88.4	20 31.3	+18.8	88.7	20 32.4	+19.9	89.1	20 33.1	+20.9	89.5
9	20 47.5	+17.4	87.4	20 50.1	+18.4	87.7	20 52.3	+19.4	88.1	20 54.0	+20.6	88.5
10	21 04.9	+17.0	86.3	21 08.5	+18.1	86.7	21 11.7	+19.2	87.1	21 14.6	+20.2	87.5
11	21 21.9	+16.6	85.3	21 26.6	+17.7	85.7	21 30.9	+18.7	86.1	21 34.8	+19.8	86.5
12	21 38.5	+16.2	84.3	21 44.3	+17.3	84.7	21 49.6	+18.4	85.1	21 54.6	+19.5	85.5
13	21 54.7	+15.8	83.2	22 01.6	+16.9	83.6	22 08.0	+18.0	84.0	22 14.1	+19.0	84.4
14	22 10.5	+15.5	82.2	22 18.5	+16.5	82.6	22 26.0	+17.6	83.0	22 33.1	+18.7	83.4
15	22 26.0	+15.0	81.1	22 35.0	+16.1	81.6	22 43.6	+17.2	82.0	22 51.8	+18.3	82.4
16	22 41.0	+14.7	80.1	22 51.1	+15.7	80.5	23 00.8	+16.8	80.9	23 10.1	+17.8	81.3
17	22 55.7	+14.2	79.0	23 06.8	+15.3	79.5	23 17.6	+16.4	79.9	23 27.9	+17.5	80.3
18	23 09.9	+13.7	78.0	23 22.1	+14.9	78.4	23 34.0	+15.9	78.8	23 45.4	+17.0	79.3
19	23 23.6	+13.4	76.9	23 37.0	+14.4	77.4	23 49.9	+15.5	77.8	24 02.4	+16.6	78.2
20	23 37.0	+12.9	75.9	23 51.4	+14.0	76.3	24 05.4	+15.1	76.7	24 19.0	+16.2	77.2
21	23 49.9	+12.5	74.8	24 05.4	+13.6	75.2	24 20.5	+14.7	75.7	24 35.2	+15.7	76.1
22	24 02.4	+12.0	73.7	24 19.0	+13.1	74.2	24 35.2	+14.1	74.6	24 50.9	+15.2	75.0
23	24 14.4	+11.6	72.7	24 32.1	+12.7	73.1	24 49.3	+13.8	73.5	25 06.1	+14.8	74.0
24	24 26.0	+11.1	71.6	24 44.8	+12.2	72.0	25 03.1	+13.2	72.5	25 20.9	+14.4	72.9
25	24 37.1	+10.7	70.5	24 57.0	+11.7	70.9	25 16.3	+12.8	71.4	25 35.3	+13.8	71.8
26	24 47.8	+10.2	69.4	25 08.7	+11.2	69.8	25 29.1	+12.3	70.3	25 49.1	+13.4	70.7
27	24 58.0	+9.7	68.3	25 19.9	+10.8	68.8	25 41.4	+11.9	69.2	26 02.5	+12.9	69.7
28	25 07.7	+9.2	67.2	25 30.7	+10.3	67.7	25 53.3	+11.3	68.1	26 15.4	+12.4	68.6
29	25 16.9	+8.8	66.1	25 41.0	+9.8	66.6	26 04.6	+10.9	67.0	26 27.8	+11.9	67.5
30	25 25.7	+8.2	65.0	25 50.8	+9.3	65.5	26 15.5	+10.3	65.9	26 39.7	+11.4	66.4
31	25 33.9	+7.8	64.0	26 00.1	+8.8	64.4	26 25.8	+9.8	64.8	26 51.1	+10.9	65.3
32	25 41.7	+7.3	62.9	26 08.9	+8.3	63.3	26 35.6	+9.4	63.7	27 02.0	+10.3	64.2
33	25 49.0	+6.7	61.8	26 17.2	+7.8	62.2	26 45.0	+8.8	62.6	27 12.3	+9.9	63.1
34	25 55.7	+6.3	60.6	26 25.0	+7.2	61.1	26 53.8	+8.3	61.5	27 22.2	+9.3	62.0
35	26 02.0	+5.8	59.5	26 32.2	+6.8	60.0	27 02.1	+7.7	60.4	27 31.5	+8.8	60.9
36	26 07.8	+5.2	58.4	26 39.0	+6.2	58.9	27 09.8	+7.3	59.3	27 40.3	+8.2	59.7
37	26 13.0	+4.8	57.3	26 45.2	+5.8	57.7	27 17.1	+6.7	58.2	27 48.5	+7.7	58.6
38	26 17.8	+4.2	56.2	26 51.0	+5.2	56.6	27 23.8	+6.2	57.1	27 56.2	+7.2	57.5
39	26 22.0	+3.7	55.1	26 56.2	+4.6	55.5	27 30.0	+5.6	55.9	28 03.4	+6.6	56.4
40	26 25.7	+3.2	54.0	27 00.8	+4.2	54.4	27 35.6	+5.1	54.8	28 10.0	+6.0	55.2
41	26 28.9	+2.7	52.9	27 05.0	+3.6	53.3	27 40.7	+4.5	53.7	28 16.0	+5.5	54.1
42	26 31.6	+2.1	51.8	27 08.6	+3.0	52.1	27 45.2	+4.0	52.6	28 21.5	+4.9	53.0
43	26 33.7	+1.7	50.6	27 11.6	+2.6	51.0	27 49.2	+3.4	51.4	28 26.4	+4.4	51.9
44	26 35.4	+1.1	49.5	27 14.2	+2.0	49.9	27 52.6	+2.9	50.3	28 30.8	+3.8	50.7
45	26 36.5	+0.5	48.4	27 16.2	+1.4	48.8	27 55.5	+2.4	49.2	28 34.6	+3.2	49.6
46	26 37.0	+0.1	47.3	27 17.6	+0.9	47.7	27 57.9	+1.8	48.0	28 37.8	+2.7	48.4
47	26 37.1	−0.5	46.2	27 18.5	+0.4	46.5	27 59.7	+1.2	46.9	28 40.5	+2.1	47.3
48	26 36.6	−1.0	45.0	27 18.9	−0.2	45.4	28 00.9	+0.6	45.8	28 42.6	+1.5	46.2
49	26 35.6	−1.5	43.9	27 18.7	−0.7	44.3	28 01.5	+0.2	44.6	28 44.1	+0.9	45.0
50	26 34.1	−2.0	42.8	27 18.0	−1.2	43.2	28 01.7	−0.5	43.5	28 45.0	+0.4	43.9
51	26 32.1	−2.6	41.7	27 16.8	−1.8	42.0	28 01.2	−1.0	42.4	28 45.4	−0.2	42.7
52	26 29.5	−3.1	40.6	27 15.0	−2.4	40.9	28 00.2	−1.6	41.2	28 45.2	−0.8	41.6
53	26 26.4	−3.6	39.5	27 12.6	−2.8	39.8	27 58.6	−2.1	40.1	28 44.4	−1.3	40.5
54	26 22.8	−4.1	38.3	27 09.8	−3.4	38.7	27 56.5	−2.6	39.0	28 43.1	−2.0	39.3
55	26 18.7	−4.6	37.2	27 06.4	−4.0	37.5	27 53.9	−3.3	37.9	28 41.1	−2.5	38.2
56	26 14.1	−5.2	36.1	27 02.4	−4.4	36.4	27 50.6	−3.7	36.7	28 38.6	−3.0	37.0
57	26 08.9	−5.6	35.0	26 58.0	−5.0	35.3	27 46.9	−4.4	35.6	28 35.6	−3.7	35.9
58	26 03.3	−6.2	33.9	26 53.0	−5.5	34.2	27 42.5	−4.8	34.5	28 31.9	−4.2	34.8
59	25 57.1	−6.7	32.8	26 47.5	−6.1	33.1	27 37.7	−5.5	33.3	28 27.7	−4.8	33.6
60	25 50.4	−7.1	31.7	26 41.4	−6.6	31.9	27 32.2	−5.9	32.2	28 22.9	−5.3	32.5
61	25 43.3	−7.7	30.6	26 34.8	−7.0	30.8	27 26.3	−6.5	31.1	28 17.6	−5.9	31.4
62	25 35.6	−8.2	29.5	26 27.8	−7.6	29.7	27 19.8	−7.0	30.0	28 11.7	−6.5	30.2
63	25 27.4	−8.6	28.4	26 20.2	−8.2	28.6	27 12.8	−7.6	28.9	28 05.2	−7.0	29.1
64	25 18.8	−9.2	27.3	26 12.0	−8.6	27.5	27 05.2	−8.1	27.7	27 58.2	−7.5	28.0
65	25 09.6	−9.6	26.2	26 03.4	−9.1	26.4	26 57.1	−8.6	26.6	27 50.7	−8.1	26.9
66	25 00.0	−10.1	25.1	25 54.3	−9.6	25.3	26 48.5	−9.1	25.5	27 42.6	−8.6	25.7
67	24 49.9	−10.5	24.0	25 44.7	−10.1	24.2	26 39.4	−9.7	24.4	27 34.0	−9.2	24.6
68	24 39.4	−11.0	22.9	25 34.6	−10.6	23.1	26 29.7	−10.1	23.3	27 24.8	−9.7	23.5
69	24 28.4	−11.5	21.9	25 24.0	−11.0	22.0	26 19.6	−10.6	22.2	27 15.1	−10.2	22.4
70	24 16.9	−12.0	20.8	25 13.0	−11.6	20.9	26 09.0	−11.2	21.1	27 04.9	−10.7	21.3
71	24 04.9	−12.3	19.7	25 01.4	−12.0	19.9	25 57.8	−11.6	20.0	26 54.2	−11.3	20.2
72	23 52.6	−12.9	18.6	24 49.4	−12.5	18.8	25 46.2	−12.2	18.9	26 42.9	−11.8	19.1
73	23 39.7	−13.2	17.6	24 36.9	−12.9	17.7	25 34.0	−12.6	17.8	26 31.1	−12.2	18.0
74	23 26.5	−13.7	16.5	24 24.0	−13.4	16.6	25 21.4	−13.0	16.8	26 18.9	−12.8	16.9
75	23 12.8	−14.2	15.4	24 10.6	−13.8	15.6	25 08.4	−13.6	15.7	26 06.1	−13.2	15.8
76	22 58.6	−14.5	14.4	23 56.8	−14.3	14.5	24 54.8	−14.0	14.6	25 52.9	−13.8	14.7
77	22 44.1	−14.9	13.3	23 42.5	−14.7	13.4	24 40.8	−14.4	13.5	25 39.1	−14.2	13.6
78	22 29.2	−15.4	12.3	23 27.8	−15.2	12.4	24 26.4	−14.9	12.5	25 24.9	−14.6	12.6
79	22 13.8	−15.8	11.2	23 12.6	−15.5	11.3	24 11.5	−15.4	11.4	25 10.3	−15.2	11.5
80	21 58.0	−16.1	10.2	22 57.1	−16.0	10.3	23 56.1	−15.8	10.3	24 55.1	−15.6	10.4
81	21 41.9	−16.6	9.2	22 41.1	−16.4	9.2	23 40.3	−16.2	9.3	24 39.5	−16.0	9.4
82	21 25.3	−16.9	8.1	22 24.7	−16.7	8.2	23 24.1	−16.6	8.2	24 23.5	−16.5	8.3
83	21 08.4	−17.3	7.1	22 08.0	−17.2	7.1	23 07.5	−17.0	7.2	24 07.0	−16.9	7.3
84	20 51.1	−17.6	6.1	21 50.8	−17.5	6.1	22 50.5	−17.5	6.2	23 50.1	−17.3	6.2
85	20 33.5	−18.0	5.0	21 33.3	−18.0	5.1	22 33.0	−17.8	5.1	23 32.8	−17.8	5.2
86	20 15.5	−18.4	4.0	21 15.3	−18.3	4.1	22 15.2	−18.2	4.1	23 15.0	−18.1	4.1
87	19 57.1	−18.7	3.0	20 57.0	−18.6	3.0	21 57.0	−18.7	3.1	22 56.9	−18.6	3.1
88	19 38.4	−19.0	2.0	20 38.4	−19.0	2.0	21 38.3	−18.9	2.0	22 38.3	−19.0	2.0
89	19 19.4	−19.4	1.0	20 19.4	−19.4	1.0	21 19.4	−19.4	1.0	22 19.3	−19.3	1.0
90	19 00.0	−19.7	0.0	20 00.0	−19.7	0.0	21 00.0	−19.7	0.0	22 00.0	−19.7	0.0

71°, 289° L.H.A. LATITUDE SAME NAME AS DECLINATION

144

LATITUDE **CONTRARY** NAME TO DECLINATION L.H.A. 71°, 289°

Dec.	15° Hc	d	Z	16° Hc	d	Z	17° Hc	d	Z	18° Hc	d	Z
°	° ′	′	°	° ′	′	°	° ′	′	°	° ′	′	°
0	18 19.7	−16.5	95.1	18 14.2	−17.5	95.4	18 08.4	−18.6	95.7	18 02.2	−19.6	96.1
1	18 03.2	−16.8	96.1	17 56.7	−17.9	96.4	17 49.8	−18.9	96.7	17 42.6	−20.0	97.1
2	17 46.4	−17.1	97.1	17 38.8	−18.2	97.4	17 30.9	−19.2	97.7	17 22.6	−20.2	98.1
3	17 29.3	−17.5	98.1	17 20.6	−18.5	98.4	17 11.7	−19.5	98.7	17 02.4	−20.5	99.0
4	17 11.8	−17.7	99.1	17 02.1	−18.7	99.4	16 52.2	−19.8	99.7	16 41.9	−20.8	100.0
5	16 54.1	−18.1	100.1	16 43.4	−19.1	100.4	16 32.4	−20.1	100.7	16 21.1	−21.1	101.0
6	16 36.0	−18.3	101.1	16 24.3	−19.3	101.4	16 12.3	−20.3	101.7	16 00.0	−21.3	102.0
7	16 17.7	−18.6	102.1	16 05.0	−19.6	102.4	15 52.0	−20.6	102.7	15 38.7	−21.6	102.9
8	15 59.1	−18.8	103.1	15 45.4	−19.9	103.4	15 31.4	−20.9	103.6	15 17.1	−21.9	103.9
9	15 40.3	−19.2	104.1	15 25.5	−20.1	104.4	15 10.5	−21.1	104.6	14 55.2	−22.0	104.9
10	15 21.1	−19.3	105.1	15 05.4	−20.4	105.3	14 49.4	−21.3	105.6	14 33.2	−22.4	105.8
11	15 01.8	−19.7	106.1	14 45.0	−20.6	106.3	14 28.1	−21.6	106.6	14 10.8	−22.5	106.8
12	14 42.1	−19.9	107.0	14 24.4	−20.8	107.3	14 06.5	−21.8	107.5	13 48.3	−22.8	107.8
13	14 22.2	−20.1	108.0	14 03.6	−21.1	108.2	13 44.7	−22.1	108.5	13 25.5	−22.9	108.7
14	14 02.1	−20.3	109.0	13 42.5	−21.3	109.2	13 22.6	−22.2	109.4	13 02.6	−23.2	109.7
15	13 41.8	−20.6	109.9	13 21.2	−21.5	110.2	13 00.4	−22.5	110.4	12 39.4	−23.4	110.6
16	13 21.2	−20.8	110.9	12 59.7	−21.8	111.1	12 37.9	−22.6	111.3	12 16.0	−23.6	111.5
17	13 00.4	−21.0	111.9	12 37.9	−21.9	112.1	12 15.3	−22.9	112.3	11 52.4	−23.7	112.5
18	12 39.4	−21.2	112.8	12 16.0	−22.1	113.0	11 52.4	−23.0	113.2	11 28.7	−24.0	113.4
19	12 18.2	−21.4	113.8	11 53.9	−22.4	114.0	11 29.4	−23.2	114.2	11 04.7	−24.1	114.4
20	11 56.8	−21.7	114.7	11 31.5	−22.5	114.9	11 06.2	−23.4	115.1	10 40.6	−24.3	115.3
21	11 35.1	−21.7	115.7	11 09.0	−22.6	115.9	10 42.8	−23.6	116.1	10 16.3	−24.4	116.2
22	11 13.4	−22.0	116.7	10 46.4	−22.9	116.8	10 19.2	−23.7	117.0	9 51.9	−24.6	117.1
23	10 51.4	−22.2	117.6	10 23.5	−23.0	117.8	9 55.5	−23.9	117.9	9 27.3	−24.7	118.1
24	10 29.2	−22.3	118.5	10 00.5	−23.2	118.7	9 31.6	−24.0	118.9	9 02.6	−24.9	119.0
25	10 06.9	−22.5	119.5	9 37.3	−23.3	119.6	9 07.6	−24.2	119.8	8 37.7	−25.0	119.9
26	9 44.4	−22.6	120.4	9 14.0	−23.5	120.6	8 43.4	−24.3	120.7	8 12.7	−25.1	120.8
27	9 21.8	−22.8	121.4	8 50.5	−23.6	121.5	8 19.1	−24.4	121.6	7 47.6	−25.3	121.8
28	8 59.0	−22.9	122.3	8 26.9	−23.7	122.4	7 54.7	−24.6	122.6	7 22.3	−25.3	122.7
29	8 36.1	−23.0	123.2	8 03.2	−23.9	123.4	7 30.1	−24.6	123.5	6 57.0	−25.5	123.6
30	8 13.1	−23.2	124.2	7 39.3	−24.0	124.3	7 05.5	−24.8	124.4	6 31.5	−25.5	124.5
31	7 49.9	−23.3	125.1	7 15.3	−24.1	125.2	6 40.7	−24.9	125.3	6 06.0	−25.7	125.4
32	7 26.6	−23.5	126.0	6 51.2	−24.2	126.1	6 15.8	−25.0	126.2	5 40.3	−25.7	126.3
33	7 03.1	−23.5	127.0	6 27.0	−24.3	127.1	5 50.8	−25.0	127.1	5 14.6	−25.8	127.2
34	6 39.6	−23.6	127.9	6 02.7	−24.4	128.0	5 25.8	−25.2	128.1	4 48.8	−25.9	128.1
35	6 16.0	−23.8	128.8	5 38.3	−24.4	128.9	5 00.6	−25.2	129.0	4 22.9	−26.0	129.0
36	5 52.2	−23.8	129.7	5 13.9	−24.6	129.8	4 35.4	−25.3	129.9	3 56.9	−26.0	129.9
37	5 28.4	−23.9	130.7	4 49.3	−24.6	130.7	4 10.1	−25.3	130.8	3 30.9	−26.0	130.8
38	5 04.5	−24.0	131.6	4 24.7	−24.7	131.6	3 44.8	−25.4	131.7	3 04.9	−26.2	131.7
39	4 40.5	−24.0	132.5	4 00.0	−24.8	132.6	3 19.4	−25.5	132.6	2 38.7	−26.1	132.6
40	4 16.5	−24.1	133.4	3 35.2	−24.8	133.5	2 53.9	−25.5	133.5	2 12.6	−26.2	133.5
41	3 52.4	−24.2	134.3	3 10.4	−24.9	134.4	2 28.4	−25.5	134.4	1 46.4	−26.2	134.4
42	3 28.2	−24.3	135.3	2 45.5	−24.9	135.3	2 02.9	−25.6	135.3	1 20.2	−26.2	135.3
43	3 03.9	−24.3	136.2	2 20.6	−24.9	136.2	1 37.3	−25.6	136.2	0 54.0	−26.3	136.2
44	2 39.6	−24.3	137.1	1 55.7	−25.0	137.1	1 11.7	−25.6	137.1	0 27.7	−26.2	137.1
45	2 15.3	−24.3	138.0	1 30.7	−25.0	138.0	0 46.1	−25.6	138.0	0 01.5	−26.2	138.0
46	1 51.0	−24.4	138.9	1 05.7	−25.0	138.9	0 20.5	−25.6	138.9	0 24.7	+26.3	41.1
47	1 26.6	−24.4	139.8	0 40.7	−25.0	139.8	0 05.1	+25.7	40.2	0 51.0	+26.2	40.2
48	1 02.2	−24.5	140.7	0 15.7	−25.0	140.8	0 30.8	+25.6	39.2	1 17.2	+26.2	39.3
49	0 37.7	−24.4	141.7	0 09.3	+25.0	38.3	0 56.4	+25.6	38.3	1 43.4	+26.2	38.4
50	0 13.3	−24.4	142.6	0 34.3	+25.0	37.4	1 22.0	+25.6	37.4	2 09.6	+26.2	37.5
51	0 11.1	+24.5	36.5	0 59.3	+25.0	36.5	1 47.6	+25.5	36.5	2 35.8	+26.1	36.6
52	0 35.6	+24.4	35.6	1 24.3	+25.0	35.6	2 13.1	+25.5	35.6	3 01.9	+26.0	35.7
53	1 00.0	+24.4	34.7	1 49.3	+25.0	34.7	2 38.6	+25.5	34.7	3 27.9	+26.1	34.8
54	1 24.4	+24.4	33.8	2 14.3	+24.9	33.8	3 04.1	+25.5	33.8	3 54.0	+25.9	33.9
55	1 48.8	+24.3	32.9	2 39.2	+24.8	32.9	3 29.6	+25.3	32.9	4 19.9	+25.9	32.9
56	2 13.1	+24.4	31.9	3 04.0	+24.9	32.0	3 54.9	+25.4	32.0	4 45.8	+25.8	32.0
57	2 37.5	+24.3	31.0	3 28.9	+24.7	31.1	4 20.3	+25.2	31.1	5 11.6	+25.8	31.1
58	3 01.8	+24.2	30.1	3 53.6	+24.8	30.1	4 45.5	+25.2	30.2	5 37.4	+25.6	30.2
59	3 26.0	+24.2	29.2	4 18.4	+24.6	29.2	5 10.7	+25.1	29.3	6 03.0	+25.6	29.3
60	3 50.2	+24.1	28.3	4 43.0	+24.6	28.3	5 35.8	+25.0	28.4	6 28.6	+25.5	28.4
61	4 14.3	+24.1	27.4	5 07.6	+24.5	27.4	6 00.8	+25.0	27.4	6 54.1	+25.3	27.5
62	4 38.4	+24.0	26.4	5 32.1	+24.4	26.5	6 25.8	+24.8	26.5	7 19.4	+25.3	26.6
63	5 02.4	+23.9	25.5	5 56.5	+24.3	25.6	6 50.6	+24.7	25.6	7 44.7	+25.1	25.7
64	5 26.3	+23.8	24.6	6 20.8	+24.2	24.6	7 15.3	+24.7	24.7	8 09.8	+25.1	24.8
65	5 50.1	+23.8	23.7	6 45.0	+24.2	23.7	7 40.0	+24.5	23.8	8 34.9	+24.8	23.8
66	6 13.9	+23.6	22.8	7 09.2	+24.0	22.8	8 04.5	+24.3	22.9	8 59.7	+24.8	22.9
67	6 37.5	+23.5	21.8	7 33.2	+23.9	21.9	8 28.8	+24.3	21.9	9 24.5	+24.6	22.0
68	7 01.0	+23.5	20.9	7 57.1	+23.7	21.0	8 53.1	+24.1	21.0	9 49.1	+24.5	21.1
69	7 24.5	+23.3	20.0	8 20.8	+23.7	20.0	9 17.2	+24.0	20.1	10 13.6	+24.2	20.1
70	7 47.8	+23.2	19.1	8 44.5	+23.5	19.1	9 41.2	+23.8	19.2	10 37.8	+24.2	19.2
71	8 11.0	+23.0	18.1	9 08.0	+23.4	18.2	10 05.0	+23.7	18.2	11 02.0	+23.9	18.3
72	8 34.0	+23.0	17.2	9 31.4	+23.2	17.2	10 28.7	+23.5	17.3	11 25.9	+23.8	17.3
73	8 57.0	+22.8	16.3	9 54.6	+23.0	16.3	10 52.2	+23.3	16.3	11 49.7	+23.6	16.4
74	9 19.8	+22.6	15.3	10 17.6	+22.9	15.4	11 15.5	+23.1	15.4	12 13.3	+23.4	15.5
75	9 42.4	+22.5	14.4	10 40.5	+22.8	14.4	11 38.6	+23.0	14.5	12 36.7	+23.2	14.5
76	10 04.9	+22.3	13.4	11 03.3	+22.5	13.5	12 01.6	+22.8	13.5	12 59.9	+23.0	13.6
77	10 27.2	+22.2	12.5	11 25.8	+22.4	12.5	12 24.4	+22.6	12.6	13 22.9	+22.8	12.6
78	10 49.4	+22.0	11.5	11 48.2	+22.2	11.6	12 47.0	+22.3	11.6	13 45.7	+22.6	11.7
79	11 11.4	+21.8	10.6	12 10.4	+21.9	10.6	13 09.3	+22.2	10.7	14 08.3	+22.3	10.7
80	11 33.2	+21.6	9.6	12 32.3	+21.8	9.7	13 31.5	+21.9	9.7	14 30.6	+22.1	9.8
81	11 54.8	+21.5	8.7	12 54.1	+21.6	8.7	13 53.4	+21.8	8.8	14 52.7	+21.9	8.8
82	12 16.3	+21.2	7.7	13 15.7	+21.4	7.8	14 15.2	+21.4	7.8	15 14.6	+21.6	7.8
83	12 37.5	+21.0	6.8	13 37.1	+21.1	6.8	14 36.6	+21.3	6.8	15 36.2	+21.4	6.9
84	12 58.5	+20.8	5.8	13 58.2	+20.9	5.8	14 57.9	+21.0	5.9	15 57.6	+21.1	5.9
85	13 19.3	+20.6	4.9	14 19.1	+20.7	4.9	15 18.9	+20.7	4.9	16 18.7	+20.8	4.9
86	13 39.9	+20.4	3.9	14 39.8	+20.4	3.9	15 39.6	+20.5	3.9	16 39.5	+20.6	3.9
87	14 00.3	+20.1	2.9	15 00.2	+20.2	2.9	16 00.1	+20.3	3.0	17 00.1	+20.2	3.0
88	14 20.4	+19.9	2.0	15 20.4	+19.9	2.0	16 20.4	+19.9	2.0	17 20.3	+20.0	2.0
89	14 40.3	+19.7	1.0	15 40.3	+19.7	1.0	16 40.3	+19.7	1.0	17 40.3	+19.7	1.0
90	15 00.0	+19.4	0.0	16 00.0	+19.4	0.0	17 00.0	+19.4	0.0	18 00.0	+19.4	0.0
	15°			16°			17°			18°		

Dec.	19° Hc	d	Z	20° Hc	d	Z	21° Hc	d	Z	22° Hc	d	Z	Dec.
°	° ′	′	°	° ′	′	°	° ′	′	°	° ′	′	°	°
0	17 55.7	−20.7	96.4	17 48.9	−21.7	96.7	17 41.7	−22.7	97.0	17 34.2	−23.7	97.3	0
1	17 35.0	−20.9	97.4	17 27.2	−22.0	97.7	17 19.0	−23.0	98.0	17 10.5	−24.0	98.3	1
2	17 14.1	−21.3	98.4	17 05.2	−22.3	98.7	16 56.0	−23.3	99.0	16 46.5	−24.3	99.3	2
3	16 52.8	−21.5	99.3	16 42.9	−22.5	99.6	16 32.7	−23.5	99.9	16 22.2	−24.5	100.2	3
4	16 31.3	−21.8	100.3	16 20.4	−22.8	100.6	16 09.2	−23.8	100.9	15 57.7	−24.8	101.2	4
5	16 09.5	−22.1	101.3	15 57.6	−23.1	101.6	15 45.4	−24.0	101.8	15 32.9	−25.0	102.1	5
6	15 47.4	−22.3	102.3	15 34.5	−23.3	102.5	15 21.4	−24.3	102.8	15 07.9	−25.2	103.1	6
7	15 25.1	−22.6	103.2	15 11.2	−23.5	103.5	14 57.1	−24.5	103.7	14 42.7	−25.4	104.0	7
8	15 02.5	−22.8	104.2	14 47.7	−23.8	104.4	14 32.6	−24.7	104.7	14 17.3	−25.7	104.9	8
9	14 39.7	−23.0	105.1	14 23.9	−24.0	105.4	14 07.9	−25.0	105.6	13 51.6	−25.9	105.9	9
10	14 16.7	−23.3	106.1	13 59.9	−24.2	106.3	13 42.9	−25.1	106.6	13 25.7	−26.1	106.8	10
11	13 53.4	−23.5	107.0	13 35.7	−24.4	107.3	13 17.8	−25.4	107.5	12 59.6	−26.3	107.7	11
12	13 29.9	−23.7	108.0	13 11.3	−24.7	108.2	12 52.4	−25.6	108.4	12 33.3	−26.5	108.6	12
13	13 06.2	−23.9	108.9	12 46.6	−24.8	109.1	12 26.8	−25.7	109.4	12 06.8	−26.6	109.6	13
14	12 42.3	−24.1	109.9	12 21.8	−25.0	110.1	12 01.1	−26.0	110.3	11 40.2	−26.8	110.5	14
15	12 18.2	−24.3	110.8	11 56.8	−25.3	111.0	11 35.1	−26.1	111.2	11 13.4	−27.0	111.4	15
16	11 53.9	−24.5	111.7	11 31.5	−25.3	111.9	11 09.0	−26.2	112.1	10 46.4	−27.2	112.3	16
17	11 29.4	−24.7	112.7	11 06.2	−25.6	112.9	10 42.8	−26.5	113.0	10 19.2	−27.3	113.2	17
18	11 04.7	−24.8	113.6	10 40.6	−25.7	113.8	10 16.3	−26.5	114.0	9 51.9	−27.4	114.1	18
19	10 39.9	−25.0	114.5	10 14.9	−25.9	114.7	9 49.8	−26.8	114.9	9 24.5	−27.6	115.0	19
20	10 14.9	−25.1	115.5	9 49.0	−26.0	115.6	9 23.0	−26.8	115.8	8 56.9	−27.7	115.9	20
21	9 49.8	−25.3	116.4	9 23.0	−26.1	116.5	8 56.2	−27.0	116.7	8 29.2	−27.9	116.8	21
22	9 24.5	−25.5	117.3	8 56.9	−26.3	117.4	8 29.2	−27.2	117.6	8 01.3	−27.9	117.7	22
23	8 59.0	−25.6	118.2	8 30.6	−26.4	118.4	8 02.0	−27.2	118.5	7 33.4	−28.1	118.6	23
24	8 33.4	−25.7	119.1	8 04.2	−26.6	119.3	7 34.8	−27.4	119.4	7 05.3	−28.2	119.5	24
25	8 07.7	−25.8	120.0	7 37.6	−26.6	120.2	7 07.4	−27.4	120.3	6 37.1	−28.2	120.4	25
26	7 41.9	−25.9	121.0	7 11.0	−26.8	121.1	6 40.0	−27.6	121.2	6 08.9	−28.4	121.3	26
27	7 16.0	−26.1	121.9	6 44.2	−26.8	122.0	6 12.4	−27.6	122.1	5 40.5	−28.4	122.2	27
28	6 49.9	−26.2	122.8	6 17.4	−27.0	122.9	5 44.8	−27.8	123.0	5 12.1	−28.5	123.0	28
29	6 23.7	−26.2	123.7	5 50.4	−27.0	123.8	5 17.0	−27.8	123.9	4 43.6	−28.6	123.9	29
30	5 57.5	−26.3	124.6	5 23.4	−27.1	124.7	4 49.2	−27.8	124.7	4 15.0	−28.6	124.8	30
31	5 31.2	−26.5	125.5	4 56.3	−27.2	125.6	4 21.4	−28.0	125.6	3 46.4	−28.7	125.7	31
32	5 04.7	−26.4	126.4	4 29.1	−27.2	126.5	3 53.4	−27.9	126.5	3 17.7	−28.7	126.6	32
33	4 38.3	−26.6	127.3	4 01.9	−27.3	127.3	3 25.5	−28.1	127.4	2 49.0	−28.8	127.4	33
34	4 11.7	−26.6	128.2	3 34.6	−27.4	128.2	2 57.4	−28.1	128.3	2 20.2	−28.8	128.3	34
35	3 45.1	−26.7	129.1	3 07.2	−27.4	129.1	2 29.3	−28.1	129.2	1 51.4	−28.8	129.2	35
36	3 18.4	−26.7	130.0	2 39.8	−27.4	130.0	2 01.2	−28.1	130.1	1 22.6	−28.9	130.1	36
37	2 51.7	−26.8	130.9	2 12.4	−27.5	130.9	1 33.1	−28.2	130.9	0 53.7	−28.8	131.0	37
38	2 24.9	−26.8	131.8	1 44.9	−27.5	131.8	1 04.9	−28.2	131.8	0 24.9	−28.9	131.8	38
39	1 58.1	−26.8	132.7	1 17.4	−27.5	132.7	0 36.7	−28.2	132.7	0 04.0	+28.8	47.3	39
40	1 31.3	−26.9	133.6	0 49.9	−27.5	133.6	0 08.5	−28.2	133.6	0 32.8	+28.9	46.4	40
41	1 04.4	−26.9	134.5	0 22.4	−27.6	134.5	0 19.7	+28.2	45.5	1 01.7	+28.8	45.5	41
42	0 37.5	−26.9	135.4	0 05.2	+27.5	44.6	0 47.9	+28.1	44.6	1 30.5	+28.9	44.7	42
43	0 10.6	−26.8	136.3	0 32.7	+27.5	43.8	1 16.0	+28.2	43.8	1 59.4	+28.8	43.8	43
44	0 16.2	+26.9	42.9	1 00.2	+27.5	42.9	1 44.2	+28.1	42.9	2 28.2	+28.7	42.9	44
45	0 43.1	+26.9	42.0	1 27.7	+27.5	42.0	2 12.3	+28.1	42.0	2 56.9	+28.7	42.0	45
46	1 10.0	+26.8	41.1	1 55.2	+27.5	41.1	2 40.4	+28.1	41.1	3 25.6	+28.7	41.1	46
47	1 36.8	+26.9	40.2	2 22.7	+27.4	40.2	3 08.5	+28.0	40.2	3 54.3	+28.6	40.3	47
48	2 03.7	+26.8	39.3	2 50.1	+27.4	39.3	3 36.5	+28.0	39.3	4 22.9	+28.6	39.4	48
49	2 30.5	+26.7	38.4	3 17.5	+27.3	38.4	4 04.5	+27.9	38.5	4 51.5	+28.4	38.5	49
50	2 57.2	+26.7	37.5	3 44.8	+27.3	37.5	4 32.4	+27.8	37.6	5 19.9	+28.4	37.6	50
51	3 23.9	+26.7	36.6	4 12.1	+27.2	36.6	5 00.2	+27.8	36.7	5 48.3	+28.4	36.7	51
52	3 50.6	+26.6	35.7	4 39.3	+27.2	35.7	5 28.0	+27.7	35.8	6 16.7	+28.2	35.8	52
53	4 17.2	+26.6	34.8	5 06.5	+27.1	34.8	5 55.7	+27.6	34.9	6 44.9	+28.1	35.0	53
54	4 43.8	+26.4	33.9	5 33.6	+27.0	33.9	6 23.3	+27.5	34.0	7 13.0	+28.1	34.1	54
55	5 10.2	+26.5	33.0	6 00.6	+26.9	33.0	6 50.8	+27.5	33.1	7 41.1	+27.9	33.2	55
56	5 36.7	+26.3	32.1	6 27.5	+26.8	32.1	7 18.3	+27.3	32.2	8 09.0	+27.8	32.3	56
57	6 03.0	+26.2	31.2	6 54.3	+26.7	31.2	7 45.6	+27.2	31.3	8 36.8	+27.7	31.4	57
58	6 29.2	+26.1	30.3	7 21.0	+26.6	30.3	8 12.8	+27.0	30.4	9 04.5	+27.5	30.5	58
59	6 55.3	+26.1	29.4	7 47.6	+26.5	29.4	8 39.8	+27.0	29.5	9 32.0	+27.4	29.6	59
60	7 21.4	+25.9	28.5	8 14.1	+26.4	28.5	9 06.8	+26.8	28.6	9 59.4	+27.3	28.7	60
61	7 47.3	+25.8	27.6	8 40.5	+26.2	27.6	9 33.6	+26.7	27.7	10 26.7	+27.1	27.8	61
62	8 13.1	+25.7	26.6	9 06.7	+26.1	26.7	10 00.3	+26.5	26.8	10 53.8	+27.0	26.9	62
63	8 38.8	+25.5	25.7	9 32.8	+26.0	25.8	10 26.8	+26.4	25.9	11 20.8	+26.7	26.0	63
64	9 04.3	+25.4	24.8	9 58.8	+25.8	24.9	10 53.2	+26.2	25.0	11 47.5	+26.7	25.1	64
65	9 29.7	+25.3	23.9	10 24.6	+25.6	24.0	11 19.4	+26.0	24.0	12 14.2	+26.4	24.1	65
66	9 55.0	+25.1	23.0	10 50.2	+25.5	23.1	11 45.4	+25.9	23.1	12 40.6	+26.2	23.2	66
67	10 20.1	+25.0	22.1	11 15.7	+25.3	22.1	12 11.3	+25.7	22.2	13 06.8	+26.0	22.3	67
68	10 45.1	+24.8	21.1	11 41.0	+25.2	21.2	12 37.0	+25.4	21.3	13 32.8	+25.9	21.4	68
69	11 09.9	+24.6	20.2	12 06.2	+24.9	20.3	13 02.4	+25.3	20.4	13 58.7	+25.6	20.4	69
70	11 34.5	+24.4	19.3	12 31.1	+24.8	19.3	13 27.7	+25.1	19.4	14 24.3	+25.4	19.5	70
71	11 58.9	+24.3	18.3	12 55.9	+24.6	18.4	13 52.8	+24.9	18.5	14 49.7	+25.2	18.6	71
72	12 23.2	+24.1	17.4	13 20.4	+24.4	17.5	14 17.7	+24.6	17.5	15 14.9	+24.9	17.6	72
73	12 47.3	+23.8	16.5	13 44.8	+24.1	16.5	14 42.3	+24.4	16.6	15 39.8	+24.7	16.7	73
74	13 11.1	+23.7	15.5	14 08.9	+24.0	15.6	15 06.7	+24.2	15.7	16 04.5	+24.4	15.7	74
75	13 34.8	+23.4	14.6	14 32.9	+23.6	14.6	15 30.9	+23.9	14.7	16 28.9	+24.2	14.8	75
76	13 58.2	+23.3	13.6	14 56.5	+23.5	13.7	15 54.8	+23.7	13.8	16 53.1	+23.9	13.8	76
77	14 21.5	+23.0	12.7	15 20.0	+23.2	12.7	16 18.5	+23.4	12.8	17 17.0	+23.7	12.9	77
78	14 44.5	+22.7	11.7	15 43.2	+23.0	11.8	16 41.9	+23.2	11.8	17 40.7	+23.3	11.9	78
79	15 07.2	+22.5	10.8	16 06.2	+22.7	10.8	17 05.1	+22.9	10.9	18 04.0	+23.1	10.9	79
80	15 29.7	+22.3	9.8	16 28.9	+22.4	9.9	17 28.0	+22.6	9.9	18 27.1	+22.7	10.0	80
81	15 52.0	+22.0	8.8	16 51.3	+22.2	8.9	17 50.6	+22.3	8.9	18 49.8	+22.5	9.0	81
82	16 14.0	+21.8	7.9	17 13.5	+21.8	7.9	18 12.9	+22.0	8.0	19 12.3	+22.1	8.0	82
83	16 35.8	+21.5	6.9	17 35.3	+21.6	6.9	18 34.9	+21.7	7.0	19 34.4	+21.9	7.0	83
84	16 57.3	+21.2	5.9	17 56.9	+21.3	6.0	18 56.6	+21.4	6.0	19 56.3	+21.5	6.0	84
85	17 18.5	+20.9	5.0	18 18.2	+21.0	5.0	19 18.0	+21.1	5.0	20 17.8	+21.1	5.0	85
86	17 39.4	+20.6	4.0	18 39.2	+20.7	4.0	19 39.1	+20.7	4.0	20 38.9	+20.8	4.0	86
87	18 00.0	+20.3	3.0	18 59.9	+20.4	3.0	19 59.8	+20.4	3.0	20 59.7	+20.5	3.0	87
88	18 20.3	+20.0	2.0	19 20.3	+20.0	2.0	20 20.2	+20.1	2.0	21 20.2	+20.1	2.0	88
89	18 40.3	+19.7	1.0	19 40.3	+19.7	1.0	20 40.3	+19.7	1.0	21 40.3	+19.7	1.0	89
90	19 00.0	+19.4	0.0	20 00.0	+19.4	0.0	21 00.0	+19.4	0.0	22 00.0	+19.3	0.0	90
	19°			20°			21°			22°			

S. Lat. {L.H.A. greater than 180° ....Zn=180°−Z
L.H.A. less than 180°...........Zn=180°+Z

LATITUDE **SAME** NAME AS DECLINATION L.H.A. 109°, 251°

	15°			16°			17°			18°			19°			20°			21°			22°			
Dec.	Hc	d	Z	Hc	d	Z	Hc	d	Z	Hc	d	Z	Hc	d	Z	Hc	d	Z	Hc	d	Z	Hc	d	Z	Dec.
°	° ′	′	°	° ′	′	°	° ′	′	°	° ′	′	°	° ′	′	°	° ′	′	°	° ′	′	°	° ′	′	°	°
0	17 22.0	+16.1	94.8	17 16.8	+17.2	95.1	17 11.3	+18.2	95.4	17 05.5	+19.2	95.7	16 59.3	+20.3	96.0	16 52.8	+21.4	96.3	16 46.1	+22.3	96.6	16 39.0	+23.3	96.9	0
1	17 38.1	+15.8	93.8	17 34.0	+16.9	94.1	17 29.5	+17.9	94.4	17 24.7	+19.0	94.7	17 19.6	+20.0	95.1	17 14.2	+21.0	95.4	17 08.4	+22.0	95.7	17 02.3	+23.0	96.0	1
2	17 53.9	+15.5	92.8	17 50.9	+16.5	93.1	17 47.4	+17.6	93.4	17 43.7	+18.6	93.7	17 39.6	+19.7	94.1	17 35.2	+20.7	94.4	17 30.4	+21.8	94.7	17 25.3	+22.8	95.0	2
3	18 09.4	+15.2	91.8	18 07.4	+16.2	92.1	18 05.0	+17.3	92.4	18 02.3	+18.4	92.7	17 59.3	+19.4	93.1	17 55.9	+20.4	93.4	17 52.2	+21.4	93.7	17 48.1	+22.5	94.0	3
4	18 24.6	+14.8	90.7	18 23.6	+16.0	91.1	18 22.3	+17.0	91.4	18 20.7	+18.0	91.7	18 18.7	+19.1	92.1	18 16.3	+20.2	92.4	18 13.6	+21.2	92.7	18 10.6	+22.2	93.1	4
5	18 39.4	+14.6	89.7	18 39.6	+15.5	90.1	18 39.3	+16.7	90.4	18 38.7	+17.7	90.7	18 37.8	+18.7	91.1	18 36.5	+19.8	91.4	18 34.8	+20.8	91.8	18 32.8	+21.9	92.1	5
6	18 54.0	+14.1	88.7	18 55.1	+15.3	89.0	18 56.0	+16.3	89.4	18 56.4	+17.4	89.7	18 56.5	+18.5	90.1	18 56.3	+19.5	90.4	18 55.6	+20.6	90.8	18 54.7	+21.5	91.1	6
7	19 08.1	+13.9	87.7	19 10.4	+14.9	88.0	19 12.3	+16.0	88.4	19 13.8	+17.0	88.7	19 15.0	+18.1	89.1	19 15.8	+19.1	89.4	19 16.2	+20.2	89.8	19 16.2	+21.3	90.1	7
8	19 22.0	+13.4	86.6	19 25.3	+14.6	87.0	19 28.3	+15.6	87.3	19 30.8	+16.8	87.7	19 33.1	+17.7	88.1	19 34.9	+18.8	88.4	19 36.4	+19.9	88.8	19 37.5	+20.9	89.1	8
9	19 35.4	+13.2	85.6	19 39.9	+14.2	86.0	19 43.9	+15.3	86.3	19 47.6	+16.3	86.7	19 50.8	+17.5	87.0	19 53.7	+18.5	87.4	19 56.3	+19.5	87.8	19 58.4	+20.6	88.1	9
10	19 48.6	+12.7	84.6	19 54.1	+13.8	84.9	19 59.2	+14.9	85.3	20 03.9	+16.0	85.7	20 08.3	+17.0	86.0	20 12.2	+18.2	86.4	20 15.8	+19.2	86.8	20 19.0	+20.3	87.1	10
11	20 01.3	+12.5	83.5	20 07.9	+13.5	83.9	20 14.1	+14.6	84.3	20 19.9	+15.6	84.6	20 25.3	+16.7	85.0	20 30.4	+17.7	85.4	20 35.0	+18.8	85.7	20 39.3	+19.9	86.1	11
12	20 13.8	+12.0	82.5	20 21.4	+13.1	82.9	20 28.7	+14.2	83.2	20 35.5	+15.3	83.6	20 42.0	+16.4	84.0	20 48.1	+17.5	84.4	20 53.8	+18.5	84.7	20 59.2	+19.5	85.1	12
13	20 25.8	+11.6	81.4	20 34.5	+12.8	81.8	20 42.9	+13.8	82.2	20 50.8	+14.9	82.6	20 58.4	+16.0	82.9	21 05.6	+17.0	83.3	21 12.3	+18.1	83.7	21 18.7	+19.2	84.1	13
14	20 37.4	+11.3	80.4	20 47.3	+12.3	80.8	20 56.7	+13.4	81.1	21 05.7	+14.5	81.5	21 14.4	+15.6	81.9	21 22.6	+16.7	82.3	21 30.4	+17.8	82.7	21 37.9	+18.8	83.1	14
15	20 48.7	+10.9	79.4	20 59.6	+12.0	79.7	21 10.1	+13.1	80.1	21 20.2	+14.2	80.5	21 30.0	+15.2	80.9	21 39.3	+16.2	81.3	21 48.2	+17.3	81.7	21 56.7	+18.4	82.1	15
16	20 59.6	+10.5	78.3	21 11.6	+11.6	78.7	21 23.2	+12.6	79.1	21 34.4	+13.7	79.4	21 45.2	+14.8	79.8	21 55.5	+15.9	80.2	22 05.5	+17.0	80.6	22 15.1	+18.0	81.0	16
17	21 10.1	+10.1	77.2	21 23.2	+11.2	77.6	21 35.8	+12.3	78.0	21 48.1	+13.4	78.4	22 00.0	+14.4	78.8	22 11.4	+15.5	79.2	22 22.5	+16.5	79.6	22 33.1	+17.6	80.0	17
18	21 20.2	+9.8	76.2	21 34.4	+10.8	76.6	21 48.1	+11.9	77.0	22 01.5	+12.9	77.3	22 14.4	+14.0	77.7	22 26.9	+15.1	78.1	22 39.0	+16.2	78.6	22 50.7	+17.3	79.0	18
19	21 30.0	+9.3	75.1	21 45.2	+10.3	75.5	22 00.0	+11.4	75.9	22 14.4	+12.5	76.3	22 28.4	+13.6	76.7	22 42.0	+14.7	77.1	22 55.2	+15.8	77.5	23 08.0	+16.8	77.9	19
20	21 39.3	+8.9	74.1	21 55.5	+10.0	74.4	22 11.4	+11.1	74.8	22 26.9	+12.1	75.2	22 42.0	+13.2	75.6	22 56.7	+14.3	76.0	23 11.0	+15.3	76.5	23 24.8	+16.4	76.9	20
21	21 48.2	+8.5	73.0	22 05.5	+9.6	73.4	22 22.5	+10.6	73.8	22 39.0	+11.7	74.2	22 55.2	+12.8	74.6	23 11.0	+13.8	75.0	23 26.3	+14.9	75.4	23 41.2	+16.0	75.8	21
22	21 56.7	+8.1	71.9	22 15.1	+9.1	72.3	22 33.1	+10.2	72.7	22 50.7	+11.3	73.1	23 08.0	+12.3	73.5	23 24.8	+13.4	73.9	23 41.2	+14.5	74.3	23 57.2	+15.5	74.8	22
23	22 04.8	+7.6	70.9	22 24.2	+8.8	71.2	22 43.3	+9.8	71.6	23 02.0	+10.9	72.0	23 20.3	+11.9	72.5	23 38.2	+13.0	72.9	23 55.7	+14.0	73.3	24 12.7	+15.1	73.7	23
24	22 12.4	+7.3	69.8	22 33.0	+8.2	70.2	22 53.1	+9.4	70.6	23 12.9	+10.4	71.0	23 32.2	+11.5	71.4	23 51.2	+12.5	71.8	24 09.7	+13.6	72.2	24 27.8	+14.7	72.7	24
25	22 19.7	+6.8	68.7	22 41.2	+7.9	69.1	23 02.5	+8.9	69.5	23 23.3	+9.9	69.9	23 43.7	+11.0	70.3	24 03.7	+12.1	70.7	24 23.3	+13.1	71.2	24 42.5	+14.2	71.6	25
26	22 26.5	+6.4	67.6	22 49.1	+7.4	68.0	23 11.4	+8.4	68.4	23 33.2	+9.6	68.8	23 54.7	+10.6	69.2	24 15.8	+11.6	69.7	24 36.4	+12.7	70.1	24 56.7	+13.7	70.5	26
27	22 32.9	+5.9	66.6	22 56.5	+7.0	67.0	23 19.8	+8.1	67.3	23 42.8	+9.0	67.7	24 05.3	+10.1	68.2	24 27.4	+11.2	68.6	24 49.1	+12.2	69.0	25 10.4	+13.3	69.4	27
28	22 38.8	+5.6	65.5	23 03.5	+6.6	65.9	23 27.9	+7.6	66.3	23 51.8	+8.7	66.7	24 15.4	+9.7	67.1	24 38.6	+10.7	67.5	25 01.3	+11.8	67.9	25 23.7	+12.8	68.4	28
29	22 44.4	+5.1	64.4	23 10.1	+6.1	64.8	23 35.5	+7.1	65.2	24 00.5	+8.1	65.6	24 25.1	+9.2	66.0	24 49.3	+10.2	66.4	25 13.1	+11.2	66.8	25 36.5	+12.3	67.3	29
30	22 49.5	+4.6	63.3	23 16.2	+5.7	63.7	23 42.6	+6.7	64.1	24 08.6	+7.7	64.5	24 34.3	+8.7	64.9	24 59.5	+9.8	65.3	25 24.3	+10.8	65.8	25 48.8	+11.8	66.2	30
31	22 54.1	+4.2	62.2	23 21.9	+5.2	62.6	23 49.3	+6.2	63.0	24 16.3	+7.3	63.4	24 43.0	+8.2	63.8	25 09.3	+9.2	64.2	25 35.1	+10.3	64.7	26 00.6	+11.3	65.1	31
32	22 58.3	+3.8	61.2	23 27.1	+4.8	61.5	23 55.5	+5.8	61.9	24 23.6	+6.7	62.3	24 51.2	+7.8	62.7	25 18.5	+8.8	63.1	25 45.4	+9.9	63.6	26 11.9	+10.9	64.0	32
33	23 02.1	+3.3	60.1	23 31.9	+4.3	60.5	24 01.3	+5.3	60.8	24 30.3	+6.3	61.2	24 59.0	+7.3	61.6	25 27.3	+8.3	62.1	25 55.3	+9.3	62.5	26 22.8	+10.3	62.9	33
34	23 05.4	+2.9	59.0	23 36.2	+3.8	59.4	24 06.6	+4.8	59.7	24 36.6	+5.9	60.1	25 06.3	+6.8	60.5	25 35.6	+7.9	61.0	26 04.6	+8.8	61.4	26 33.1	+9.8	61.8	34
35	23 08.3	+2.5	57.9	23 40.0	+3.4	58.3	24 11.4	+4.4	58.7	24 42.5	+5.3	59.0	25 13.1	+6.4	59.4	25 43.5	+7.3	59.9	26 13.4	+8.3	60.3	26 42.9	+9.4	60.7	35
36	23 10.8	+2.0	56.8	23 43.4	+3.0	57.2	24 15.8	+3.9	57.6	24 47.8	+4.9	57.9	25 19.5	+5.8	58.3	25 50.8	+6.8	58.8	26 21.7	+7.8	59.2	26 52.3	+8.8	59.6	36
37	23 12.8	+1.5	55.7	23 46.4	+2.5	56.1	24 19.7	+3.4	56.5	24 52.7	+4.3	56.8	25 25.3	+5.4	57.2	25 57.6	+6.3	57.6	26 29.5	+7.3	58.1	27 01.1	+8.2	58.5	37
38	23 14.3	+1.1	54.6	23 48.9	+2.0	55.0	24 23.1	+3.0	55.4	24 57.0	+3.9	55.7	25 30.7	+4.8	56.1	26 03.9	+5.8	56.5	26 36.8	+6.8	57.0	27 09.3	+7.8	57.4	38
39	23 15.4	+0.6	53.6	23 50.9	+1.5	53.9	24 26.1	+2.5	54.3	25 00.9	+3.5	54.6	25 35.5	+4.3	55.0	26 09.7	+5.3	55.4	26 43.6	+6.2	55.8	27 17.1	+7.2	56.3	39
40	23 16.0	+0.2	52.5	23 52.4	+1.1	52.8	24 28.6	+2.0	53.2	25 04.4	+2.9	53.5	25 39.8	+3.9	53.9	26 15.0	+4.8	54.3	26 49.8	+5.8	54.7	27 24.3	+6.7	55.1	40
41	23 16.2	−0.2	51.4	23 53.5	+0.7	51.7	24 30.6	+1.5	52.1	25 07.3	+2.4	52.4	25 43.7	+3.3	52.8	26 19.8	+4.3	53.2	26 55.6	+5.2	53.6	27 31.0	+6.1	54.0	41
42	23 16.0	−0.7	50.3	23 54.2	+0.1	50.6	24 32.1	+1.0	51.0	25 09.7	+2.0	51.3	25 47.0	+2.9	51.7	26 24.1	+3.7	52.1	27 00.8	+4.6	52.5	27 37.1	+5.6	52.9	42
43	23 15.3	−1.2	49.2	23 54.3	−0.3	49.5	24 33.1	+0.6	49.9	25 11.7	+1.4	50.2	25 49.9	+2.3	50.6	26 27.8	+3.2	51.0	27 05.4	+4.2	51.4	27 42.7	+5.1	51.8	43
44	23 14.1	−1.6	48.1	23 54.0	−0.7	48.4	24 33.7	+0.1	48.8	25 13.1	+1.0	49.1	25 52.2	+1.8	49.5	26 31.0	+2.8	49.9	27 09.6	+3.6	50.3	27 47.8	+4.5	50.7	44
45	23 12.5	−2.1	47.0	23 53.3	−1.3	47.3	24 33.8	−0.4	47.7	25 14.1	+0.4	48.0	25 54.0	+1.4	48.4	26 33.8	+2.1	48.8	27 13.2	+3.0	49.1	27 52.3	+3.9	49.5	45
46	23 10.4	−2.5	45.9	23 52.0	−1.6	46.3	24 33.4	−0.9	46.6	25 14.5	0.0	46.9	25 55.4	+0.8	47.3	26 35.9	+1.7	47.6	27 16.2	+2.6	48.0	27 56.2	+3.4	48.4	46
47	23 07.9	−2.9	44.9	23 50.4	−2.2	45.2	24 32.5	−1.3	45.5	25 14.5	−0.5	45.8	25 56.2	+0.3	46.2	26 37.6	+1.1	46.5	27 18.8	+1.9	46.9	27 59.6	+2.9	47.3	47
48	23 05.0	−3.4	43.8	23 48.2	−2.6	44.1	24 31.2	−1.8	44.4	25 14.0	−1.1	44.7	25 56.5	−0.2	45.0	26 38.7	+0.7	45.4	27 20.7	+1.5	45.8	28 02.5	+2.2	46.1	48
49	23 01.6	−3.8	42.7	23 45.6	−3.1	43.0	24 29.4	−2.3	43.3	25 12.9	−1.5	43.6	25 56.3	−0.7	43.9	26 39.4	0.0	44.3	27 22.2	+0.9	44.6	28 04.7	+1.8	45.0	49
50	22 57.8	−4.3	41.6	23 42.5	−3.5	41.9	24 27.1	−2.8	42.2	25 11.4	−2.0	42.5	25 55.6	−1.3	42.8	26 39.4	−0.4	43.2	27 23.1	+0.4	43.5	28 06.5	+1.1	43.9	50
51	22 53.5	−4.7	40.5	23 39.0	−4.0	40.8	24 24.3	−3.2	41.1	25 09.4	−2.5	41.4	25 54.3	−1.7	41.7	26 39.0	−1.0	42.0	27 23.5	−0.2	42.4	28 07.6	+0.7	42.7	51
52	22 48.8	−5.2	39.4	23 35.0	−4.4	39.7	24 21.1	−3.7	40.0	25 06.9	−2.9	40.3	25 52.6	−2.2	40.6	26 38.0	−1.4	40.9	27 23.3	−0.8	41.3	28 08.3	0.0	41.6	52
53	22 43.6	−5.6	38.4	23 30.6	−4.9	38.6	24 17.4	−4.2	38.9	25 04.0	−3.5	39.2	25 50.4	−2.8	39.5	26 36.6	−2.1	39.8	27 22.5	−1.2	40.1	28 08.3	−0.5	40.5	53
54	22 38.0	−6.0	37.3	23 25.7	−5.4	37.5	24 13.2	−4.7	37.8	25 00.5	−4.0	38.1	25 47.6	−3.2	38.4	26 34.5	−2.5	38.7	27 21.3	−1.8	39.0	28 07.8	−1.1	39.3	54
55	22 32.0	−6.5	36.2	23 20.3	−5.8	36.4	24 08.5	−5.1	36.7	24 56.5	−4.4	37.0	25 44.4	−3.8	37.3	26 32.0	−3.0	37.6	27 19.5	−2.4	37.9	28 06.7	−1.6	38.2	55
56	22 25.5	−6.8	35.1	23 14.5	−6.2	35.4	24 03.4	−5.6	35.6	24 52.1	−4.9	35.9	25 40.6	−4.2	36.2	26 29.0	−3.6	36.5	27 17.1	−2.9	36.8	28 05.1	−2.2	37.1	56
57	22 18.7	−7.4	34.0	23 08.3	−6.7	34.3	23 57.8	−6.0	34.5	24 47.2	−5.5	34.8	25 36.4	−4.8	35.1	26 25.4	−4.1	35.3	27 14.2	−3.4	35.6	28 02.9	−2.7	35.9	57
58	22 11.3	−7.7	33.0	23 01.6	−7.1	33.2	23 51.8	−6.6	33.4	24 41.7	−5.8	33.7	25 31.6	−5.3	34.0	26 21.3	−4.6	34.2	27 10.8	−3.9	34.5	28 00.2	−3.3	34.8	58
59	22 03.6	−8.1	31.9	22 54.5	−7.6	32.1	23 45.2	−6.9	32.4	24 35.9	−6.4	32.6	25 26.3	−5.7	32.8	26 16.7	−5.1	33.1	27 06.9	−4.5	33.4	27 56.9	−3.9	33.7	59
60	21 55.5	−8.6	30.8	22 46.9	−7.9	31.0	23 38.3	−7.4	31.3	24 29.5	−6.8	31.5	25 20.6	−6.2	31.7	26 11.6	−5.7	32.0	27 02.4	−5.1	32.3	27 53.0	−4.4	32.5	60
61	21 46.9	−8.9	29.8	22 39.0	−8.5	30.0	23 30.9	−7.9	30.2	24 22.7	−7.3	30.4	25 14.4	−6.8	30.6	26 05.9	−6.1	30.9	26 57.3	−5.5	31.1	27 48.6	−4.9	31.4	61
62	21 38.0	−9.4	28.7	22 30.5	−8.8	28.9	23 23.0	−8.3	29.1	24 15.4	−7.8	29.3	25 07.6	−7.2	29.5	25 59.8	−6.7	29.8	26 51.8	−6.1	30.0	27 43.7	−5.5	30.3	62
63	21 28.6	−9.8	27.6	22 21.7	−9.3	27.8	23 14.7	−8.7	28.0	24 07.6	−8.2	28.2	25 00.4	−7.7	28.5	25 53.1	−7.1	28.7	26 45.7	−6.6	28.9	27 38.2	−6.1	29.2	63
64	21 18.8	−10.1	26.6	22 12.4	−9.6	26.8	23 06.0	−9.2	27.0	23 59.4	−8.7	27.2	24 52.7	−8.1	27.4	25 46.0	−7.7	27.6	26 39.1	−7.1	27.8	27 32.1	−6.6	28.0	64
65	21 08.7	−10.6	25.5	22 02.8	−10.1	25.7	22 56.8	−9.6	25.9	23 50.7	−9.1	26.1	24 44.6	−8.7	26.3	25 38.3	−8.1	26.5	26 32.0	−7.7	26.7	27 25.5	−7.1	26.9	65
66	20 58.1	−11.0	24.5	21 52.7	−10.5	24.6	22 47.2	−10.1	24.8	23 41.6	−9.6	25.0	24 35.9	−9.1	25.2	25 30.2	−8.6	25.4	26 24.3	−8.1	25.6	27 18.4	−7.6	25.8	66
67	20 47.1	−11.3	23.4	21 42.2	−10.9	23.6	22 37.1	−10.4	23.7	23 32.0	−10.0	23.9	24 26.8	−9.6	24.1	25 21.6	−9.2	24.3	26 16.2	−8.6	24.5	27 10.8	−8.2	24.7	67
68	20 35.8	−11.7	22.4	21 31.3	−11.3	22.5	22 26.7	−10.9	22.7	23 22.0	−10.5	22.8	24 17.2	−10.0	23.0	25 12.4	−9.6	23.2	26 07.6	−9.2	23.4	27 02.6	−8.7	23.6	68
69	20 24.1	−12.1	21.3	21 20.0	−11.7	21.5	22 15.8	−11.3	21.6	23 11.5	−10.9	21.8	24 07.2	−10.5	21.9	25 02.8	−10.0	22.1	25 58.4	−9.7	22.3	26 53.9	−9.2	22.5	69
70	20 12.0	−12.5	20.3	21 08.3	−12.1	20.4	22 04.5	−11.7	20.5	23 00.6	−11.3	20.7	23 56.7	−10.9	20.8	24 52.8	−10.6	21.0	25 48.7	−10.1	21.2	26 44.7	−9.8	21.4	70
71	19 59.5	−12.8	19.2	20 56.2	−12.5	19.4	21 52.8	−12.2	19.5	22 49.3	−11.8	19.6	23 45.8	−11.4	19.8	24 42.2	−11.0	19.9	25 38.6	−10.6	20.1	26 34.9	−10.2	20.3	71
72	19 46.7	−13.2	18.2	20 43.7	−12.8	18.3	21 40.6	−12.5	18.4	22 37.5	−12.1	18.6	23 34.4	−11.8	18.7	24 31.2	−11.5	18.8	25 28.0	−11.1	19.0	26 24.7	−10.8	19.2	72
73	19 33.5	−13.5	17.2	20 30.9	−13.3	17.3	21 28.1	−12.9	17.4	22 25.4	−12.6	17.5	23 22.6	−12.3	17.6	24 19.7	−11.9	17.8	25 16.9	−11.6	17.9	26 13.9	−11.2	18.1	73
74	19 20.0	−13.9	16.1	20 17.6	−13.6	16.2	21 15.2	−13.3	16.3	22 12.8	−13.0	16.4	23 10.3	−12.7	16.6	24 07.8	−12.4	16.7	25 05.3	−12.1	16.8	26 02.7	−11.8	17.0	74
75	19 06.1	−14.2	15.1	20 04.0	−13.9	15.2	21 01.9	−13.6	15.3	21 59.8	−13.4	15.4	22 57.6	−13.1	15.5	23 55.4	−12.8	15.6	24 53.2	−12.5	15.7	25 50.9	−12.2	15.9	75
76	18 51.9	−14.6	14.1	19 50.1	−14.3	14.2	20 48.3	−14.1	14.2	21 46.4	−13.8	14.3	22 44.5	−13.5	14.4	23 42.6	−13.2	14.6	24 40.7	−13.0	14.7	25 38.7	−12.7	14.8	76
77	18 37.3	−14.8	13.0	19 35.8	−14.7	13.1	20 34.2	−14.4	13.2	21 32.6	−14.2	13.3	22 31.0	−13.9	13.4	23 29.4	−13.7	13.5	24 27.7	−13.5	13.6	25 26.0	−13.2	13.7	77
78	18 22.5	−15.3	12.0	19 21.1	−15.0	12.1	20 19.8	−14.8	12.2	21 18.4	−14.5	12.3	22 17.1	−14.4	12.3	23 15.7	−14.2	12.4	24 14.2	−13.8	12.5	25 12.8	−13.7	12.6	78
79	18 07.2	−15.5	11.0	19 06.1	−15.3	11.1	20 05.0	−15.1	11.1	21 03.9	−15.0	11.2	22 02.7	−14.7	11.3	23 01.5	−14.5	11.4	24 00.4	−14.4	11.5	24 59.1	−14.1	11.5	79
80	17 51.7	−15.9	10.0	18 50.8	−15.7	10.0	19 49.9	−15.5	10.1	20 48.9	−15.3	10.2	21 48.0	−15.2	10.2	22 47.0	−14.9	10.3	23 46.0	−14.7	10.4	24 45.0	−14.5	10.5	80
81	17 35.8	−16.1	9.0	18 35.1	−16.0	9.0	19 34.4	−15.9	9.1	20 33.6	−15.7	9.1	21 32.8	−15.5	9.2	22 32.1	−15.4	9.3	23 31.3	−15.2	9.3	24 30.5	−15.1	9.4	81
82	17 19.7	−16.5	8.0	18 19.1	−16.3	8.0	19 18.5	−16.2	8.1	20 17.9	−16.0	8.1	21 17.3	−15.9	8.2	22 16.7	−15.8	8.2	23 16.1	−15.6	8.3	24 15.4	−15.4	8.3	82
83	17 03.2	−16.7	7.0	18 02.8	−16.7	7.0	19 02.3	−16.5	7.0	20 01.9	−16.4	7.1	21 01.4	−16.3	7.1	22 00.9	−16.1	7.2	23 00.5	−16.1	7.2	24 00.0	−15.9	7.3	83
84	16 46.5	−17.1	6.0	17 46.1	−16.9	6.0	18 45.8	−16.9	6.0	19 45.5	−16.8	6.1	20 45.1	−16.6	6.1	21 44.8	−16.6	6.1	22 44.4	−16.4	6.2	23 44.1	−16.3	6.2	84
85	16 29.4	−17.3	5.0	17 29.2	−17.3	5.0	18 28.9	−17.1	5.0	19 28.7	−17.1	5.0	20 28.5	−17.0	5.1	21 28.2	−16.9	5.1	22 28.0	−16.8	5.1	23 27.8	−16.8	5.2	85
86	16 12.1	−17.6	4.0	17 11.9	−17.5	4.0	18 11.8	−17.5	4.0	19 11.6	−17.4	4.0	20 11.5	−17.4	4.1	21 11.3	−17.3	4.1	22 11.2	−17.2	4.1	23 11.0	−17.1	4.1	86
87	15 54.5	−17.9	3.0	16 54.4	−17.9	3.0	17 54.3	−17.8	3.0	18 54.2	−17.7	3.0	19 54.1	−17.7	3.0	20 54.0	−17.6	3.1	21 54.0	−17.7	3.1	22 53.9	−17.6	3.1	87
88	15 36.6	−18.2	2.0	16 36.5	−18.1	2.0	17 36.5	−18.1	2.0	18 36.5	−18.1	2.0	19 36.4	−18.0	2.0	20 36.4	−18.0	2.0	21 36.3	−17.9	2.0	22 36.3	−18.0	2.1	88
89	15 18.4	−18.4	1.0	16 18.4	−18.4	1.0	17 18.4	−18.4	1.0	18 18.4	−18.4	1.0	19 18.4	−18.4	1.0	20 18.4	−18.4	1.0	21 18.4	−18.4	1.0	22 18.3	−18.3	1.0	89
90	15 00.0	−18.7	0.0	16 00.0	−18.7	0.0	17 00.0	−18.7	0.0	18 00.0	−18.7	0.0	19 00.0	−18.7	0.0	20 00.0	−18.7	0.0	21 00.0	−18.7	0.0	22 00.0	−18.7	0.0	90
	15°			16°			17°			18°			19°			20°			21°			22°			

	15°			16°			17°			18°			19°			20°			21°			22°			
Dec.	Hc	d	Z	Hc	d	Z	Hc	d	Z	Hc	d	Z	Hc	d	Z	Hc	d	Z	Hc	d	Z	Hc	d	Z	Dec.
°	° ′	′	°	° ′	′	°	° ′	′	°	° ′	′	°	° ′	′	°	° ′	′	°	° ′	′	°	° ′	′	°	°
0	17 22.0	-16.4	94.8	17 16.8	-17.5	95.1	17 11.3	-18.5	95.4	17 05.5	-19.6	95.7	16 59.3	-20.6	96.0	16 52.8	-21.5	96.3	16 46.1	-22.6	96.6	16 39.0	-23.6	96.9	0
1	17 05.6	-16.7	95.8	16 59.3	-17.7	96.1	16 52.8	-18.8	96.4	16 45.9	-19.8	96.7	16 38.7	-20.8	97.0	16 31.3	-21.9	97.3	16 23.5	-22.9	97.6	16 15.4	-23.9	97.9	1
2	16 48.9	-17.0	96.8	16 41.6	-18.1	97.1	16 34.0	-19.1	97.4	16 26.1	-20.1	97.7	16 17.9	-21.1	98.0	16 09.4	-22.1	98.3	16 00.6	-23.1	98.6	15 51.5	-24.1	98.9	2
3	16 31.9	-17.3	97.8	16 23.5	-18.3	98.1	16 14.9	-19.3	98.4	16 06.0	-20.4	98.7	15 56.8	-21.4	99.0	15 47.3	-22.4	99.3	15 37.5	-23.4	99.5	15 27.4	-24.3	99.8	3
4	16 14.6	-17.6	98.8	16 05.2	-18.6	99.1	15 55.6	-19.6	99.4	15 45.6	-20.6	99.7	15 35.4	-21.6	99.9	15 24.9	-22.6	100.2	15 14.1	-23.6	100.5	15 03.1	-24.6	100.8	4
5	15 57.0	-17.9	99.8	15 46.6	-18.9	100.1	15 36.0	-19.9	100.4	15 25.0	-20.9	100.6	15 13.8	-21.9	100.9	15 02.3	-22.9	101.2	14 50.5	-23.8	101.4	14 38.5	-24.8	101.7	5
6	15 39.1	-18.1	100.8	15 27.7	-19.1	101.1	15 16.1	-20.2	101.3	15 04.1	-21.1	101.6	14 51.9	-22.1	101.9	14 39.4	-23.0	102.1	14 26.7	-24.1	102.4	14 13.7	-25.0	102.6	6
7	15 21.0	-18.4	101.8	15 08.6	-19.4	102.1	14 55.9	-20.3	102.3	14 43.0	-21.4	102.6	14 29.8	-22.3	102.8	14 16.4	-23.4	103.1	14 02.6	-24.2	103.3	13 48.7	-25.3	103.6	7
8	15 02.6	-18.6	102.8	14 49.2	-19.6	103.0	14 35.6	-20.7	103.3	14 21.6	-21.6	103.5	14 07.5	-22.6	103.8	13 53.0	-23.5	104.0	13 38.4	-24.5	104.3	13 23.4	-25.4	104.5	8
9	14 44.0	-18.9	103.8	14 29.6	-19.9	104.0	14 14.9	-20.8	104.3	14 00.0	-21.8	104.5	13 44.9	-22.8	104.7	13 29.5	-23.8	105.0	13 13.9	-24.7	105.2	12 58.0	-25.6	105.4	9
10	14 25.1	-19.1	104.7	14 09.7	-20.1	105.0	13 54.1	-21.1	105.2	13 38.2	-22.0	105.5	13 22.1	-23.0	105.7	13 05.7	-23.9	105.9	12 49.2	-24.9	106.1	12 32.4	-25.9	106.4	10
11	14 06.0	-19.3	105.7	13 49.6	-20.3	106.0	13 33.0	-21.3	106.2	13 16.2	-22.3	106.4	12 59.1	-23.2	106.6	12 41.8	-24.2	106.9	12 24.3	-25.1	107.1	12 06.5	-26.0	107.3	11
12	13 46.7	-19.6	106.7	13 29.3	-20.6	106.9	13 11.7	-21.5	107.2	12 53.9	-22.5	107.4	12 35.9	-23.4	107.6	12 17.6	-24.3	107.8	11 59.2	-25.3	108.0	11 40.5	-26.2	108.2	12
13	13 27.1	-19.8	107.7	13 08.7	-20.7	107.9	12 50.2	-21.7	108.1	12 31.4	-22.6	108.3	12 12.5	-23.6	108.5	11 53.3	-24.5	108.7	11 33.9	-25.4	108.9	11 14.3	-26.3	109.1	13
14	13 07.3	-20.1	108.6	12 48.0	-21.0	108.9	12 28.5	-22.0	109.1	12 08.8	-22.9	109.3	11 48.9	-23.8	109.5	11 28.8	-24.8	109.7	11 08.5	-25.6	109.9	10 48.0	-26.5	110.0	14
15	12 47.2	-20.2	109.6	12 27.0	-21.2	109.8	12 06.5	-22.1	110.0	11 45.9	-23.0	110.2	11 25.1	-24.0	110.4	11 04.0	-24.8	110.6	10 42.9	-25.8	110.8	10 21.5	-26.7	111.0	15
16	12 27.0	-20.5	110.6	12 05.8	-21.4	110.8	11 44.4	-22.3	111.0	11 22.9	-23.3	111.2	11 01.1	-24.1	111.3	10 39.2	-25.1	111.5	10 17.1	-26.0	111.7	9 54.8	-26.8	111.9	16
17	12 06.5	-20.6	111.5	11 44.4	-21.5	111.7	11 22.1	-22.5	111.9	10 59.6	-23.4	112.1	10 37.0	-24.3	112.3	10 14.1	-25.2	112.5	9 51.1	-26.0	112.6	9 28.0	-27.0	112.8	17
18	11 45.9	-20.8	112.5	11 22.9	-21.8	112.7	10 59.6	-22.6	112.9	10 36.2	-23.5	113.0	10 12.7	-24.5	113.2	9 48.9	-25.3	113.4	9 25.1	-26.3	113.5	9 01.0	-27.0	113.7	18
19	11 25.1	-21.1	113.5	11 01.1	-21.9	113.6	10 37.0	-22.9	113.8	10 12.7	-23.8	114.0	9 48.2	-24.6	114.1	9 23.6	-25.5	114.3	8 58.8	-26.3	114.4	8 34.0	-27.3	114.6	19
20	11 04.0	-21.1	114.4	10 39.2	-22.1	114.6	10 14.1	-23.0	114.7	9 48.9	-23.8	114.9	9 23.6	-24.8	115.1	8 58.1	-25.6	115.2	8 32.5	-26.5	115.3	8 06.7	-27.3	115.5	20
21	10 42.9	-21.4	115.4	10 17.1	-22.3	115.5	9 51.1	-23.1	115.7	9 25.1	-24.1	115.8	8 58.8	-24.8	116.0	8 32.5	-25.8	116.1	8 06.0	-26.6	116.3	7 39.4	-27.4	116.4	21
22	10 21.5	-21.6	116.3	9 54.8	-22.4	116.5	9 28.0	-23.3	116.6	9 01.0	-24.1	116.8	8 34.0	-25.1	116.9	8 06.7	-25.8	117.0	7 39.4	-26.7	117.2	7 12.0	-27.6	117.3	22
23	9 59.9	-21.7	117.3	9 32.4	-22.6	117.4	9 04.7	-23.4	117.6	8 36.9	-24.3	117.7	8 08.9	-25.1	117.8	7 40.9	-26.0	117.9	7 12.7	-26.8	118.1	6 44.4	-27.6	118.2	23
24	9 38.2	-21.8	118.2	9 09.8	-22.7	118.3	8 41.3	-23.6	118.5	8 12.6	-24.4	118.6	7 43.8	-25.3	118.7	7 14.9	-26.1	118.9	6 45.9	-26.9	119.0	6 16.8	-27.8	119.1	24
25	9 16.4	-22.0	119.1	8 47.1	-22.9	119.3	8 17.7	-23.7	119.4	7 48.2	-24.6	119.5	7 18.5	-25.4	119.7	6 48.8	-26.2	119.8	6 19.0	-27.1	119.9	5 49.0	-27.8	120.0	25
26	8 54.4	-22.2	120.1	8 24.2	-22.9	120.2	7 54.0	-23.8	120.3	7 23.6	-24.6	120.5	6 53.1	-25.4	120.6	6 22.6	-26.3	120.7	5 51.9	-27.1	120.8	5 21.2	-27.9	120.8	26
27	8 32.2	-22.2	121.0	8 01.3	-23.2	121.2	7 30.2	-24.0	121.3	6 59.0	-24.8	121.4	6 27.7	-25.6	121.5	5 56.3	-26.4	121.6	5 24.8	-27.1	121.7	4 53.3	-27.9	121.7	27
28	8 10.0	-22.5	122.0	7 38.1	-23.2	122.1	7 06.2	-24.0	122.2	6 34.2	-24.9	122.3	6 02.1	-25.7	122.4	5 29.9	-26.4	122.5	4 57.7	-27.3	122.6	4 25.4	-28.1	122.6	28
29	7 47.5	-22.5	122.9	7 14.9	-23.3	123.0	6 42.2	-24.2	123.1	6 09.3	-24.9	123.2	5 36.4	-25.7	123.3	5 03.5	-26.6	123.4	4 30.4	-27.3	123.4	3 57.3	-28.1	123.5	29
30	7 25.0	-22.6	123.8	6 51.6	-23.5	123.9	6 18.0	-24.2	124.0	5 44.4	-25.1	124.1	5 10.7	-25.8	124.2	4 36.9	-26.6	124.3	4 03.1	-27.4	124.3	3 29.2	-28.1	124.4	30
31	7 02.4	-22.8	124.8	6 28.1	-23.6	124.9	5 53.8	-24.4	125.0	5 19.3	-25.1	125.0	4 44.9	-25.9	125.1	4 10.3	-26.6	125.2	3 35.7	-27.4	125.2	3 01.1	-28.2	125.3	31
32	6 39.6	-22.9	125.7	6 04.5	-23.6	125.8	5 29.4	-24.4	125.9	4 54.2	-25.2	126.0	4 19.0	-26.0	126.0	3 43.7	-26.8	126.1	3 08.3	-27.5	126.1	2 32.9	-28.2	126.2	32
33	6 16.7	-22.9	126.6	5 40.9	-23.7	126.7	5 05.0	-24.5	126.8	4 29.0	-25.2	126.9	3 53.0	-26.0	126.9	3 16.9	-26.7	127.0	2 40.8	-27.5	127.0	2 04.7	-28.2	127.0	33
34	5 53.8	-23.1	127.6	5 17.2	-23.9	127.6	4 40.5	-24.5	127.7	4 03.8	-25.4	127.8	3 27.0	-26.1	127.8	2 50.2	-26.8	127.9	2 13.3	-27.5	127.9	1 36.5	-28.3	127.9	34
35	5 30.7	-23.1	128.5	4 53.3	-23.8	128.6	4 15.9	-24.6	128.6	3 38.4	-25.3	128.7	3 00.9	-26.1	128.7	2 23.4	-26.9	128.8	1 45.8	-27.6	128.8	1 08.2	-28.3	128.8	35
36	5 07.6	-23.2	129.4	4 29.5	-24.0	129.5	3 51.3	-24.7	129.5	3 13.1	-25.5	129.6	2 34.8	-26.1	129.6	1 56.5	-26.8	129.7	1 18.2	-27.6	129.7	0 39.9	-28.3	129.7	36
37	4 44.4	-23.3	130.3	4 05.5	-24.0	130.4	3 26.6	-24.8	130.5	2 47.6	-25.4	130.5	2 08.7	-26.2	130.5	1 29.7	-26.9	130.6	0 50.6	-27.6	130.6	0 11.6	-28.3	130.6	37
38	4 21.1	-23.4	131.3	3 41.5	-24.1	131.3	3 01.8	-24.8	131.4	2 22.2	-25.5	131.4	1 42.5	-26.2	131.4	1 02.8	-27.0	131.4	0 23.0	-27.6	131.5	0 16.7	+28.3	48.5	38
39	3 57.7	-23.4	132.2	3 17.4	-24.2	132.2	2 37.0	-24.8	132.3	1 56.7	-25.6	132.3	1 16.3	-26.3	132.3	0 35.8	-26.9	132.3	0 04.6	+27.6	47.7	0 45.0	+28.3	47.7	39
40	3 34.3	-23.5	133.1	2 53.2	-24.1	133.2	2 12.2	-24.9	133.2	1 31.1	-25.5	133.2	0 50.0	-26.2	133.2	0 08.9	-26.9	133.2	0 32.2	+27.6	46.8	1 13.3	+28.2	46.8	40
41	3 10.8	-23.5	134.0	2 29.1	-24.2	134.1	1 47.3	-24.9	134.1	1 05.6	-25.6	134.1	0 23.8	-26.3	134.1	0 18.0	+26.9	45.9	0 59.8	+27.5	45.9	1 41.5	+28.3	45.9	41
42	2 47.3	-23.6	135.0	2 04.9	-24.3	135.0	1 22.4	-24.9	135.0	0 40.0	-25.6	135.0	0 02.5	+26.2	45.0	0 44.9	+26.9	45.0	1 27.3	+27.6	45.0	2 09.8	+28.2	45.0	42
43	2 23.7	-23.6	135.9	1 40.6	-24.3	135.9	0 57.5	-24.9	135.9	0 14.4	-25.6	135.9	0 28.7	+26.2	44.1	1 11.8	+26.9	44.1	1 54.9	+27.5	44.1	2 38.0	+28.1	44.1	43
44	2 00.1	-23.7	136.8	1 16.3	-24.3	136.8	0 32.6	-25.0	136.8	0 11.2	+25.6	43.2	0 54.9	+26.3	43.2	1 38.7	+26.9	43.2	2 22.4	+27.5	43.2	3 06.1	+28.2	43.2	44
45	1 36.4	-23.6	137.7	0 52.0	-24.3	137.7	0 07.6	-24.9	137.7	0 36.8	+25.5	42.3	1 21.2	+26.2	42.3	2 05.6	+26.8	42.3	2 49.9	+27.5	42.3	3 34.3	+28.1	42.4	45
46	1 12.8	-23.7	138.6	0 27.7	-24.3	138.6	0 17.3	+24.9	41.4	1 02.3	+25.6	41.4	1 47.4	+26.1	41.4	2 32.4	+26.8	41.4	3 17.4	+27.4	41.4	4 02.4	+28.0	41.5	46
47	0 49.1	-23.7	139.6	0 03.4	-24.3	139.6	0 42.2	+25.0	40.4	1 27.9	+25.5	40.5	2 13.5	+26.2	40.5	2 59.2	+26.7	40.5	3 44.8	+27.3	40.5	4 30.4	+27.9	40.6	47
48	0 25.4	-23.7	140.5	0 20.9	+24.3	39.5	1 07.2	+24.9	39.5	1 53.4	+25.5	39.5	2 39.7	+26.1	39.6	3 25.9	+26.7	39.6	4 12.1	+27.3	39.7	4 58.3	+27.9	39.7	48
49	0 01.7	-23.7	141.4	0 45.2	+24.3	38.6	1 32.1	+24.9	38.6	2 18.9	+25.5	38.6	3 05.8	+26.1	38.7	3 52.6	+26.7	38.7	4 39.4	+27.3	38.8	5 26.2	+27.8	38.8	49
50	0 22.0	+23.7	37.7	1 09.5	+24.3	37.7	1 57.0	+24.8	37.7	2 44.4	+25.5	37.7	3 31.9	+26.0	37.8	4 19.3	+26.6	37.8	5 06.7	+27.1	37.9	5 54.0	+27.7	37.9	50
51	0 45.7	+23.7	36.8	1 33.8	+24.2	36.8	2 21.8	+24.8	36.8	3 09.9	+25.3	36.8	3 57.9	+25.9	36.9	4 45.9	+26.5	36.9	5 33.8	+27.1	37.0	6 21.7	+27.7	37.0	51
52	1 09.4	+23.7	35.8	1 58.0	+24.2	35.9	2 46.6	+24.8	35.9	3 35.2	+25.4	35.9	4 23.8	+25.9	36.0	5 12.4	+26.4	36.0	6 00.9	+27.0	36.1	6 49.4	+27.5	36.1	52
53	1 33.1	+23.6	34.9	2 22.2	+24.2	34.9	3 11.4	+24.8	35.0	4 00.6	+25.2	35.0	4 49.7	+25.8	35.1	5 38.8	+26.4	35.1	6 27.9	+26.9	35.2	7 16.9	+27.4	35.2	53
54	1 56.7	+23.6	34.0	2 46.4	+24.2	34.0	3 36.2	+24.6	34.1	4 25.8	+25.3	34.1	5 15.5	+25.7	34.2	6 05.2	+26.2	34.2	6 54.8	+26.7	34.3	7 44.3	+27.3	34.3	54
55	2 20.3	+23.6	33.1	3 10.6	+24.1	33.1	4 00.8	+24.6	33.2	4 51.1	+25.1	33.2	5 41.2	+25.7	33.2	6 31.4	+26.2	33.3	7 21.5	+26.7	33.4	8 11.6	+27.2	33.4	55
56	2 43.9	+23.5	32.2	3 34.7	+24.0	32.2	4 25.4	+24.6	32.2	5 16.2	+25.0	32.3	6 06.9	+25.5	32.3	6 57.6	+26.0	32.4	7 48.2	+26.6	32.5	8 38.8	+27.1	32.5	56
57	3 07.4	+23.5	31.2	3 58.7	+24.0	31.3	4 50.0	+24.5	31.3	5 41.2	+25.0	31.4	6 32.4	+25.5	31.4	7 23.6	+26.0	31.5	8 14.8	+26.4	31.6	9 05.9	+26.9	31.6	57
58	3 30.9	+23.5	30.3	4 22.7	+23.9	30.4	5 14.5	+24.4	30.4	6 06.2	+24.9	30.5	6 57.9	+25.4	30.5	7 49.6	+25.8	30.6	8 41.2	+26.3	30.7	9 32.8	+26.8	30.7	58
59	3 54.4	+23.3	29.4	4 46.6	+23.9	29.4	5 38.9	+24.3	29.5	6 31.1	+24.7	29.5	7 23.3	+25.2	29.6	8 15.4	+25.7	29.7	9 07.5	+26.2	29.7	9 59.6	+26.6	29.8	59
60	4 17.7	+23.3	28.5	5 10.5	+23.7	28.5	6 03.2	+24.2	28.6	6 55.8	+24.7	28.6	7 48.5	+25.1	28.7	8 41.1	+25.6	28.8	9 33.7	+26.0	28.8	10 26.2	+26.5	28.9	60
61	4 41.0	+23.3	27.6	5 34.2	+23.7	27.6	6 27.4	+24.1	27.6	7 20.5	+24.6	27.7	8 13.6	+25.0	27.8	9 06.7	+25.4	27.8	9 59.7	+25.9	27.9	10 52.7	+26.4	28.0	61
62	5 04.3	+23.1	26.6	5 57.9	+23.6	26.7	6 51.5	+24.0	26.7	7 45.1	+24.4	26.8	8 38.6	+24.9	26.8	9 32.1	+25.3	26.9	10 25.6	+25.7	27.0	11 19.1	+26.1	27.1	62
63	5 27.4	+23.1	25.7	6 21.5	+23.5	25.7	7 15.5	+23.9	25.8	8 09.5	+24.3	25.9	9 03.5	+24.7	25.9	9 57.4	+25.2	26.0	10 51.3	+25.6	26.1	11 45.2	+26.0	26.2	63
64	5 50.5	+23.0	24.8	6 45.0	+23.3	24.8	7 39.4	+23.8	24.9	8 33.8	+24.2	24.9	9 28.2	+24.6	25.0	10 22.6	+25.0	25.1	11 16.9	+25.4	25.2	12 11.2	+25.8	25.2	64
65	6 13.5	+22.8	23.8	7 08.3	+23.3	23.9	8 03.2	+23.6	23.9	8 58.0	+24.0	24.0	9 52.8	+24.4	24.1	10 47.6	+24.8	24.2	11 42.3	+25.2	24.2	12 37.0	+25.6	24.3	65
66	6 36.3	+22.8	22.9	7 31.6	+23.1	23.0	8 26.8	+23.6	23.0	9 22.0	+23.9	23.1	10 17.2	+24.3	23.2	11 12.4	+24.6	23.2	12 07.5	+25.0	23.3	13 02.6	+25.4	23.4	66
67	6 59.1	+22.7	22.0	7 54.7	+23.1	22.0	8 50.4	+23.3	22.1	9 45.9	+23.8	22.2	10 41.5	+24.1	22.2	11 37.0	+24.5	22.3	12 32.5	+24.9	22.4	13 28.0	+25.2	22.5	67
68	7 21.8	+22.5	21.1	8 17.8	+22.9	21.1	9 13.7	+23.3	21.2	10 09.7	+23.6	21.2	11 05.6	+23.9	21.3	12 01.5	+24.3	21.4	12 57.4	+24.6	21.4	13 53.2	+25.0	21.5	68
69	7 44.3	+22.5	20.1	8 40.7	+22.7	20.2	9 37.0	+23.1	20.2	10 33.3	+23.4	20.3	11 29.5	+23.8	20.4	12 25.8	+24.1	20.4	13 22.0	+24.4	20.5	14 18.2	+24.7	20.6	69
70	8 06.8	+22.3	19.2	9 03.4	+22.6	19.2	10 00.1	+22.9	19.3	10 56.7	+23.2	19.3	11 53.3	+23.6	19.4	12 49.9	+23.9	19.5	13 46.4	+24.2	19.6	14 42.9	+24.6	19.7	70
71	8 29.1	+22.1	18.2	9 26.0	+22.5	18.3	10 23.0	+22.8	18.3	11 19.9	+23.1	18.4	12 16.9	+23.3	18.5	13 13.8	+23.6	18.5	14 10.6	+24.0	18.6	15 07.5	+24.3	18.7	71
72	8 51.2	+22.1	17.3	9 48.5	+22.3	17.4	10 45.8	+22.6	17.4	11 43.0	+22.9	17.5	12 40.2	+23.2	17.5	13 37.4	+23.5	17.6	14 34.6	+23.8	17.7	15 31.8	+24.0	17.8	72
73	9 13.3	+21.8	16.4	10 10.8	+22.2	16.4	11 08.4	+22.4	16.5	12 05.9	+22.7	16.5	13 03.4	+23.0	16.6	14 00.9	+23.2	16.7	14 58.4	+23.5	16.7	15 55.8	+23.8	16.8	73
74	9 35.1	+21.8	15.4	10 33.0	+21.9	15.5	11 30.8	+22.2	15.5	12 28.6	+22.5	15.6	13 26.4	+22.7	15.6	14 24.1	+23.1	15.7	15 21.9	+23.3	15.8	16 19.6	+23.6	15.9	74
75	9 56.9	+21.5	14.5	10 54.9	+21.8	14.5	11 53.0	+22.1	14.6	12 51.1	+22.3	14.6	13 49.1	+22.6	14.7	14 47.2	+22.7	14.7	15 45.2	+23.0	14.8	16 43.2	+23.2	14.9	75
76	10 18.4	+21.4	13.5	11 16.7	+21.7	13.6	12 15.1	+21.8	13.6	13 13.4	+22.0	13.7	14 11.7	+22.3	13.7	15 09.9	+22.6	13.8	16 08.2	+22.8	13.9	17 06.4	+23.1	13.9	76
77	10 39.8	+21.2	12.6	11 38.4	+21.4	12.6	12 36.9	+21.7	12.7	13 35.4	+21.9	12.7	14 34.0	+22.0	12.8	15 32.5	+22.3	12.8	16 31.0	+22.5	12.9	17 29.5	+22.7	13.0	77
78	11 01.0	+21.1	11.6	11 59.8	+21.2	11.7	12 58.6	+21.4	11.7	13 57.3	+21.6	11.8	14 56.0	+21.9	11.8	15 54.8	+22.0	11.9	16 53.5	+22.2	11.9	17 52.2	+22.4	12.0	78
79	11 22.1	+20.8	10.7	12 21.0	+21.1	10.7	13 20.0	+21.2	10.7	14 18.9	+21.4	10.8	15 17.9	+21.5	10.8	16 16.8	+21.8	10.9	17 15.7	+22.0	11.0	18 14.6	+22.1	11.0	79
80	11 42.9	+20.7	9.7	12 42.1	+20.8	9.7	13 41.2	+21.0	9.8	14 40.3	+21.2	9.8	15 39.4	+21.4	9.9	16 38.6	+21.4	9.9	17 37.7	+21.6	10.0	18 36.7	+21.9	10.0	80
81	12 03.6	+20.5	8.8	13 02.9	+20.6	8.8	14 02.2	+20.8	8.8	15 01.5	+20.9	8.9	16 00.8	+21.0	8.9	17 00.0	+21.3	9.0	17 59.3	+21.4	9.0	18 58.6	+21.5	9.1	81
82	12 24.1	+20.3	7.8	13 23.5	+20.4	7.8	14 23.0	+20.5	7.9	15 22.4	+20.7	7.9	16 21.8	+20.8	7.9	17 21.3	+20.9	8.0	18 20.7	+21.0	8.0	19 20.1	+21.2	8.1	82
83	12 44.4	+20.0	6.8	13 43.9	+20.2	6.9	14 43.5	+20.3	6.9	15 43.1	+20.4	6.9	16 42.6	+20.5	7.0	17 42.2	+20.6	7.0	18 41.7	+20.8	7.0	19 41.3	+20.8	7.1	83
84	13 04.4	+19.9	5.9	14 04.1	+19.9	5.9	15 03.8	+20.0	5.9	16 03.5	+20.1	5.9	17 03.1	+20.3	6.0	18 02.8	+20.3	6.0	19 02.5	+20.4	6.0	20 02.1	+20.6	6.1	84
85	13 24.3	+19.6	4.9	14 24.0	+19.7	4.9	15 23.8	+19.8	4.9	16 23.6	+19.8	5.0	17 23.4	+19.9	5.0	18 23.1	+20.1	5.0	19 22.9	+20.1	5.0	20 22.7	+20.2	5.1	85
86	13 43.9	+19.4	3.9	14 43.7	+19.5	3.9	15 43.6	+19.5	4.0	16 43.4	+19.6	4.0	17 43.3	+19.6	4.0	18 43.2	+19.7	4.0	19 43.0	+19.8	4.0	20 42.9	+19.8	4.1	86
87	14 03.3	+19.1	2.9	15 03.2	+19.2	3.0	16 03.1	+19.2	3.0	17 03.0	+19.3	3.0	18 02.9	+19.4	3.0	19 02.9	+19.3	3.0	20 02.8	+19.4	3.0	21 02.7	+19.5	3.1	87
88	14 22.4	+18.9	2.0	15 22.4	+18.9	2.0	16 22.3	+19.0	2.0	17 22.3	+19.0	2.0	18 22.3	+19.0	2.0	19 22.2	+19.1	2.0	20 22.2	+19.1	2.0	21 22.2	+19.1	2.0	88
89	14 41.3	+18.7	1.0	15 41.3	+18.7	1.0	16 41.3	+18.7	1.0	17 41.3	+18.7	1.0	18 41.3	+18.7	1.0	19 41.3	+18.7	1.0	20 41.3	+18.7	1.0	21 41.3	+18.7	1.0	89
90	15 00.0	+18.4	0.0	16 00.0	+18.4	0.0	17 00.0	+18.4	0.0	18 00.0	+18.4	0.0	19 00.0	+18.4	0.0	20 00.0	+18.4	0.0	21 00.0	+18.4	0.0	22 00.0	+18.3	0.0	90
	15°			16°			17°			18°			19°			20°			21°			22°			

S. Lat. {L.H.A. greater than 180° ....Zn=180°−Z; L.H.A. less than 180°............Zn=180°+Z}

73°, 287° L.H.A. LATITUDE SAME NAME AS DECLINATION N. Lat. {L.H.A. greater than 180° .....Zn=Z; L.H.A. less than 180°............Zn=360°–Z}

Dec.	15° Hc	15° d	15° Z	16° Hc	16° d	16° Z	17° Hc	17° d	17° Z	18° Hc	18° d	18° Z	19° Hc	19° d	19° Z	20° Hc	20° d	20° Z	21° Hc	21° d	21° Z	22° Hc	22° d	22° Z	Dec.
°	° ′	′	°	° ′	′	°	° ′	′	°	° ′	′	°	° ′	′	°	° ′	′	°	° ′	′	°	° ′	′	°	°
0	16 24.2	+16.1	94.5	16 19.4	+17.0	94.8	16 14.2	+18.1	95.1	16 08.7	+19.1	95.4	16 02.9	+20.2	95.7	15 56.8	+21.2	96.0	15 50.4	+22.2	96.3	15 43.7	+23.2	96.5	0
1	16 40.3	+15.7	93.5	16 36.4	+16.9	93.8	16 32.3	+17.8	94.1	16 27.8	+18.9	94.4	16 23.1	+19.9	94.7	16 18.0	+20.9	95.0	16 12.6	+22.0	95.3	16 06.9	+23.0	95.6	1
2	16 56.0	+15.5	92.5	16 53.3	+16.5	92.8	16 50.1	+17.6	93.1	16 46.7	+18.6	93.4	16 43.0	+19.6	93.7	16 38.9	+20.7	94.0	16 34.6	+21.7	94.3	16 29.9	+22.7	94.6	2
3	17 11.5	+15.1	91.5	17 09.8	+16.2	91.8	17 07.7	+17.3	92.1	17 05.3	+18.3	92.4	17 02.6	+19.4	92.7	16 59.6	+20.4	93.0	16 56.3	+21.4	93.3	16 52.6	+22.4	93.6	3
4	17 26.6	+14.9	90.5	17 26.0	+15.9	90.8	17 25.0	+16.9	91.1	17 23.6	+18.1	91.4	17 22.0	+19.0	91.7	17 20.0	+20.1	92.1	17 17.7	+21.1	92.4	17 15.0	+22.2	92.7	4
5	17 41.5	+14.5	89.5	17 41.9	+15.6	89.8	17 41.9	+16.7	90.1	17 41.7	+17.7	90.4	17 41.0	+18.8	90.7	17 40.1	+19.8	91.1	17 38.8	+20.8	91.4	17 37.2	+21.9	91.7	5
6	17 56.0	+14.2	88.5	17 57.5	+15.3	88.8	17 58.6	+16.3	89.1	17 59.4	+17.4	89.4	17 59.8	+18.4	89.7	17 59.9	+19.5	90.1	17 59.6	+20.6	90.4	17 59.1	+21.5	90.7	6
7	18 10.2	+13.9	87.4	18 12.8	+14.9	87.8	18 14.9	+16.0	88.1	18 16.8	+17.0	88.4	18 18.2	+18.2	88.7	18 19.4	+19.2	89.1	18 20.2	+20.2	89.4	18 20.6	+21.3	89.7	7
8	18 24.1	+13.6	86.4	18 27.7	+14.6	86.7	18 30.9	+15.7	87.1	18 33.8	+16.8	87.4	18 36.4	+17.8	87.7	18 38.6	+18.8	88.1	18 40.4	+19.9	88.4	18 41.9	+20.9	88.8	8
9	18 37.7	+13.2	85.4	18 42.3	+14.3	85.7	18 46.6	+15.4	86.1	18 50.6	+16.4	86.4	18 54.2	+17.5	86.7	18 57.4	+18.6	87.1	19 00.3	+19.6	87.4	19 02.8	+20.7	87.8	9
10	18 50.9	+12.9	84.3	18 56.6	+14.0	84.7	19 02.0	+15.0	85.0	19 07.0	+16.1	85.4	19 11.7	+17.1	85.7	19 16.0	+18.2	86.1	19 19.9	+19.3	86.4	19 23.5	+20.3	86.8	10
11	19 03.8	+12.5	83.3	19 10.6	+13.6	83.7	19 17.0	+14.7	84.0	19 23.1	+15.8	84.4	19 28.8	+16.8	84.7	19 34.2	+17.8	85.1	19 39.2	+18.9	85.4	19 43.8	+19.9	85.8	11
12	19 16.3	+12.2	82.3	19 24.2	+13.2	82.6	19 31.7	+14.3	83.0	19 38.9	+15.4	83.3	19 45.6	+16.5	83.7	19 52.0	+17.6	84.0	19 58.1	+18.6	84.4	20 03.7	+19.7	84.8	12
13	19 28.5	+11.8	81.2	19 37.4	+12.9	81.6	19 46.0	+14.0	81.9	19 54.3	+15.0	82.3	20 02.1	+16.1	82.7	20 09.6	+17.1	83.0	20 16.7	+18.2	83.4	20 23.4	+19.3	83.8	13
14	19 40.3	+11.5	80.2	19 50.3	+12.6	80.6	20 00.0	+13.6	80.9	20 09.3	+14.7	81.3	20 18.2	+15.8	81.6	20 26.7	+16.9	82.0	20 34.9	+17.9	82.4	20 42.7	+18.9	82.8	14
15	19 51.8	+11.1	79.2	20 02.9	+12.2	79.5	20 13.6	+13.3	79.9	20 24.0	+14.3	80.2	20 34.0	+15.3	80.6	20 43.6	+16.4	81.0	20 52.8	+17.5	81.4	21 01.6	+18.6	81.7	15
16	20 02.9	+10.7	78.1	20 15.1	+11.8	78.5	20 26.9	+12.8	78.8	20 38.3	+13.9	79.2	20 49.3	+15.1	79.6	21 00.0	+16.1	80.0	21 10.3	+17.1	80.3	21 20.2	+18.2	80.7	16
17	20 13.6	+10.4	77.1	20 26.9	+11.4	77.4	20 39.7	+12.5	77.8	20 52.2	+13.6	78.2	21 04.4	+14.6	78.5	21 16.1	+15.7	78.9	21 27.4	+16.8	79.3	21 38.4	+17.8	79.7	17
18	20 24.0	+10.0	76.0	20 38.3	+11.0	76.4	20 52.2	+12.2	76.7	21 05.8	+13.2	77.1	21 19.0	+14.2	77.5	21 31.8	+15.3	77.9	21 44.2	+16.3	78.3	21 56.2	+17.4	78.7	18
19	20 34.0	+9.6	75.0	20 49.3	+10.7	75.3	21 04.4	+11.7	75.7	21 19.0	+12.8	76.1	21 33.2	+13.9	76.5	21 47.1	+14.9	76.8	22 00.5	+16.0	77.2	22 13.6	+17.0	77.6	19
20	20 43.6	+9.2	73.9	21 00.0	+10.3	74.3	21 16.1	+11.3	74.6	21 31.8	+12.4	75.0	21 47.1	+13.4	75.4	22 02.0	+14.5	75.8	22 16.5	+15.6	76.2	22 30.6	+16.7	76.6	20
21	20 52.8	+8.8	72.8	21 10.3	+9.9	73.2	21 27.4	+11.0	73.6	21 44.2	+12.0	74.0	22 00.5	+13.1	74.4	22 16.5	+14.1	74.8	22 32.1	+15.2	75.1	22 47.3	+16.2	75.6	21
22	21 01.6	+8.4	71.8	21 20.2	+9.4	72.2	21 38.4	+10.5	72.5	21 56.2	+11.6	72.9	22 13.6	+12.7	73.3	22 30.6	+13.8	73.7	22 47.3	+14.7	74.1	23 03.5	+15.8	74.5	22
23	21 10.0	+8.1	70.7	21 29.6	+9.1	71.1	21 48.9	+10.1	71.5	22 07.8	+11.1	71.9	22 26.3	+12.2	72.2	22 44.4	+13.2	72.6	23 02.0	+14.4	73.0	23 19.3	+15.4	73.5	23
24	21 18.1	+7.6	69.7	21 38.7	+8.7	70.0	21 59.0	+9.7	70.4	22 18.9	+10.8	70.8	22 38.5	+11.8	71.2	22 57.6	+12.9	71.6	23 16.4	+13.9	72.0	23 34.7	+15.0	72.4	24
25	21 25.7	+7.2	68.6	21 47.4	+8.3	69.0	22 08.7	+9.3	69.3	22 29.7	+10.4	69.7	22 50.3	+11.4	70.1	23 10.5	+12.4	70.5	23 30.3	+13.5	70.9	23 49.7	+14.5	71.3	25
26	21 32.9	+6.8	67.5	21 55.7	+7.8	67.9	22 18.0	+8.9	68.3	22 40.1	+9.9	68.7	23 01.7	+11.0	69.1	23 22.9	+12.0	69.5	23 43.8	+13.0	69.9	24 04.2	+14.1	70.3	26
27	21 39.7	+6.4	66.5	22 03.5	+7.4	66.8	22 26.9	+8.5	67.2	22 50.0	+9.5	67.6	23 12.7	+10.5	68.0	23 34.9	+11.6	68.4	23 56.8	+12.6	68.8	24 18.3	+13.7	69.2	27
28	21 46.1	+6.0	65.4	22 10.9	+7.0	65.8	22 35.4	+8.0	66.1	22 59.5	+9.0	66.5	23 23.2	+10.1	66.9	23 46.5	+11.1	67.3	24 09.4	+12.2	67.7	24 32.0	+13.2	68.1	28
29	21 52.1	+5.6	64.3	22 17.9	+6.6	64.7	22 43.4	+7.6	65.1	23 08.5	+8.6	65.4	23 33.3	+9.6	65.8	23 57.6	+10.7	66.2	24 21.6	+11.7	66.7	24 45.2	+12.7	67.1	29
30	21 57.7	+5.1	63.3	22 24.5	+6.2	63.6	22 51.0	+7.2	64.0	23 17.1	+8.2	64.4	23 42.9	+9.2	64.8	24 08.3	+10.2	65.2	24 33.3	+11.2	65.6	24 57.9	+12.3	66.0	30
31	22 02.8	+4.8	62.2	22 30.7	+5.7	62.5	22 58.2	+6.7	62.9	23 25.3	+7.8	63.3	23 52.1	+8.7	63.7	24 18.5	+9.8	64.1	24 44.5	+10.8	64.5	25 10.2	+11.8	64.9	31
32	22 07.6	+4.3	61.1	22 36.4	+5.3	61.5	23 04.9	+6.3	61.8	23 33.1	+7.2	62.2	24 00.8	+8.3	62.6	24 28.3	+9.3	63.0	24 55.3	+10.3	63.4	25 22.0	+11.3	63.8	32
33	22 11.9	+3.9	60.0	22 41.7	+4.9	60.4	23 11.2	+5.8	60.8	23 40.3	+6.9	61.1	24 09.1	+7.9	61.5	24 37.6	+8.8	61.9	25 05.6	+9.8	62.3	25 33.3	+10.8	62.7	33
34	22 15.8	+3.4	58.9	22 46.6	+4.4	59.3	23 17.0	+5.4	59.7	23 47.2	+6.3	60.0	24 17.0	+7.3	60.4	24 46.4	+8.3	60.8	25 15.4	+9.4	61.2	25 44.1	+10.4	61.7	34
35	22 19.2	+3.1	57.9	22 51.0	+4.0	58.2	23 22.4	+5.0	58.6	23 53.5	+6.0	59.0	24 24.3	+6.9	59.3	24 54.7	+7.9	59.7	25 24.8	+8.8	60.1	25 54.5	+9.8	60.6	35
36	22 22.3	+2.6	56.8	22 55.0	+3.5	57.1	23 27.4	+4.5	57.5	23 59.5	+5.4	57.9	24 31.2	+6.4	58.3	25 02.6	+7.4	58.6	25 33.6	+8.4	59.0	26 04.3	+9.4	59.5	36
37	22 24.9	+2.1	55.7	22 58.5	+3.1	56.1	23 31.9	+4.0	56.4	24 04.9	+5.0	56.8	24 37.6	+6.0	57.2	25 10.0	+6.9	57.5	25 42.0	+7.9	57.9	26 13.7	+8.8	58.4	37
38	22 27.0	+1.8	54.6	23 01.6	+2.7	55.0	23 35.9	+3.6	55.3	24 09.9	+4.5	55.7	24 43.6	+5.4	56.1	25 16.9	+6.4	56.4	25 49.9	+7.4	56.8	26 22.5	+8.3	57.3	38
39	22 28.8	+1.3	53.5	23 04.3	+2.2	53.9	23 39.5	+3.1	54.2	24 14.4	+4.1	54.6	24 49.0	+5.0	55.0	25 23.3	+5.9	55.3	25 57.3	+6.8	55.7	26 30.8	+7.9	56.2	39
40	22 30.1	+0.8	52.5	23 06.5	+1.8	52.8	23 42.6	+2.7	53.1	24 18.5	+3.6	53.5	24 54.0	+4.5	53.9	25 29.2	+5.5	54.2	26 04.1	+6.4	54.6	26 38.7	+7.3	55.0	40
41	22 30.9	+0.5	51.4	23 08.3	+1.3	51.7	23 45.3	+2.2	52.0	24 22.1	+3.1	52.4	24 58.5	+4.0	52.8	25 34.7	+4.9	53.1	26 10.5	+5.8	53.5	26 46.0	+6.8	53.9	41
42	22 31.4	0.0	50.3	23 09.6	+0.9	50.6	23 47.5	+1.8	51.0	24 25.2	+2.6	51.3	25 02.5	+3.6	51.7	25 39.6	+4.4	52.0	26 16.3	+5.4	52.4	26 52.8	+6.2	52.8	42
43	22 31.4	-0.4	49.2	23 10.5	+0.4	49.5	23 49.3	+1.2	49.9	24 27.8	+2.2	50.2	25 06.1	+3.0	50.6	25 44.0	+4.0	50.9	26 21.7	+4.8	51.3	26 59.0	+5.8	51.7	43
44	22 31.0	-0.9	48.1	23 10.9	-0.1	48.4	23 50.5	+0.9	48.8	24 30.0	+1.6	49.1	25 09.1	+2.5	49.5	25 48.0	+3.4	49.8	26 26.5	+4.3	50.2	27 04.8	+5.2	50.6	44
45	22 30.1	-1.3	47.0	23 10.8	-0.4	47.4	23 51.4	+0.3	47.7	24 31.6	+1.2	48.0	25 11.6	+2.1	48.4	25 51.4	+2.9	48.7	26 30.8	+3.8	49.1	27 10.0	+4.6	49.5	45
46	22 28.8	-1.7	46.0	23 10.4	-0.9	46.3	23 51.7	-0.1	46.6	24 32.8	+0.8	46.9	25 13.7	+1.6	47.3	25 54.3	+2.4	47.6	26 34.6	+3.3	48.0	27 14.6	+4.2	48.3	46
47	22 27.1	-2.2	44.9	23 09.5	-1.4	45.2	23 51.6	-0.5	45.5	24 33.6	+0.2	45.8	25 15.3	+1.0	46.1	25 56.7	+1.9	46.5	26 37.9	+2.7	46.9	27 18.8	+3.6	47.2	47
48	22 24.9	-2.6	43.8	23 08.1	-1.8	44.1	23 51.1	-1.1	44.4	24 33.8	-0.2	44.7	25 16.3	+0.6	45.0	25 58.6	+1.4	45.4	26 40.6	+2.2	45.7	27 22.4	+3.0	46.1	48
49	22 22.3	-3.0	42.7	23 06.3	-2.3	43.0	23 50.0	-1.5	43.3	24 33.6	-0.7	43.6	25 16.9	+0.1	43.9	26 00.0	+0.9	44.3	26 42.8	+1.7	44.6	27 25.4	+2.5	45.0	49
50	22 19.3	-3.5	41.6	23 04.0	-2.7	41.9	23 48.5	-1.9	42.2	24 32.9	-1.2	42.5	25 17.0	-0.4	42.8	26 00.9	+0.4	43.2	26 44.5	+1.2	43.5	27 27.9	+2.0	43.9	50
51	22 15.8	-3.9	40.6	23 01.3	-3.2	40.8	23 46.6	-2.4	41.1	24 31.7	-1.7	41.4	25 16.6	-0.9	41.7	26 01.3	-0.2	42.0	26 45.7	+0.6	42.4	27 29.9	+1.4	42.7	51
52	22 11.9	-4.3	39.5	22 58.1	-3.6	39.8	23 44.2	-2.9	40.0	24 30.0	-2.1	40.3	25 15.7	-1.4	40.6	26 01.1	-0.6	40.9	26 46.3	+0.1	41.3	27 31.3	+0.9	41.6	52
53	22 07.6	-4.7	38.4	22 54.5	-4.0	38.7	23 41.3	-3.3	38.9	24 27.9	-2.6	39.2	25 14.3	-1.9	39.5	26 00.5	-1.2	39.8	26 46.4	-0.4	40.1	27 32.2	+0.3	40.5	53
54	22 02.9	-5.2	37.3	22 50.5	-4.5	37.6	23 38.0	-3.8	37.8	24 25.3	-3.1	38.1	25 12.4	-2.4	38.4	25 59.3	-1.7	38.7	26 46.0	-0.9	39.0	27 32.5	-0.2	39.3	54
55	21 57.7	-5.5	36.3	22 46.0	-4.9	36.5	23 34.2	-4.3	36.8	24 22.2	-3.6	37.0	25 10.0	-2.9	37.3	25 57.6	-2.2	37.6	26 45.1	-1.5	37.9	27 32.3	-0.7	38.2	55
56	21 52.2	-6.0	35.2	22 41.1	-5.3	35.4	23 29.9	-4.6	35.7	24 18.6	-4.0	35.9	25 07.1	-3.4	36.2	25 55.4	-2.6	36.5	26 43.6	-2.0	36.8	27 31.6	-1.3	37.1	56
57	21 46.2	-6.4	34.1	22 35.8	-5.8	34.3	23 25.3	-5.2	34.6	24 14.6	-4.5	34.8	25 03.7	-3.8	35.1	25 52.8	-3.2	35.4	26 41.6	-2.5	35.7	27 30.3	-1.9	36.0	57
58	21 39.8	-6.8	33.0	22 30.0	-6.2	33.3	23 20.1	-5.6	33.5	24 10.1	-5.0	33.7	24 59.9	-4.3	34.0	25 49.6	-3.7	34.3	26 39.1	-3.1	34.5	27 28.4	-2.4	34.8	58
59	21 33.0	-7.3	32.0	22 23.8	-6.6	32.2	23 14.5	-6.0	32.4	24 05.1	-5.4	32.6	24 55.6	-4.9	32.9	25 45.9	-4.2	33.2	26 36.0	-3.6	33.4	27 26.0	-2.9	33.7	59
60	21 25.7	-7.6	30.9	22 17.2	-7.1	31.1	23 08.5	-6.5	31.3	23 59.7	-5.9	31.6	24 50.7	-5.3	31.8	25 41.7	-4.8	32.0	26 32.4	-4.1	32.3	27 23.1	-3.5	32.6	60
61	21 18.1	-8.0	29.8	22 10.1	-7.5	30.0	23 02.0	-6.9	30.3	23 53.8	-6.4	30.5	24 45.4	-5.8	30.7	25 36.9	-5.2	30.9	26 28.3	-4.6	31.2	27 19.6	-4.0	31.5	61
62	21 10.1	-8.4	28.8	22 02.6	-7.9	29.0	22 55.1	-7.4	29.2	23 47.4	-6.8	29.4	24 39.6	-6.2	29.6	25 31.7	-5.7	29.8	26 23.7	-5.1	30.1	27 15.6	-4.6	30.3	62
63	21 01.7	-8.9	27.7	21 54.7	-8.3	27.9	22 47.7	-7.8	28.1	23 40.6	-7.3	28.3	24 33.4	-6.8	28.5	25 26.0	-6.2	28.7	26 18.6	-5.7	29.0	27 11.0	-5.1	29.2	63
64	20 52.8	-9.2	26.7	21 46.4	-8.7	26.8	22 39.9	-8.2	27.0	23 33.3	-7.7	27.2	24 26.6	-7.2	27.4	25 19.8	-6.6	27.6	26 12.9	-6.1	27.9	27 05.9	-5.6	28.1	64
65	20 43.6	-9.6	25.6	21 37.7	-9.1	25.8	22 31.7	-8.6	25.9	23 25.6	-8.1	26.1	24 19.4	-7.6	26.3	25 13.2	-7.2	26.5	26 06.8	-6.7	26.7	27 00.3	-6.1	27.0	65
66	20 34.0	-9.9	24.5	21 28.6	-9.5	24.7	22 23.1	-9.1	24.9	23 17.5	-8.7	25.1	24 11.8	-8.2	25.2	25 06.0	-7.7	25.4	26 00.1	-7.1	25.6	26 54.2	-6.7	25.9	66
67	20 24.1	-10.4	23.5	21 19.1	-10.0	23.6	22 14.0	-9.5	23.8	23 08.8	-9.0	24.0	24 03.6	-8.6	24.2	24 58.3	-8.1	24.3	25 53.0	-7.7	24.5	26 47.5	-7.2	24.7	67
68	20 13.7	-10.7	22.4	21 09.1	-10.3	22.6	22 04.5	-9.9	22.7	22 59.8	-9.5	22.9	23 55.0	-9.0	23.1	24 50.2	-8.6	23.3	25 45.3	-8.2	23.4	26 40.3	-7.7	23.6	68
69	20 03.0	-11.1	21.4	20 58.8	-10.7	21.5	21 54.6	-10.3	21.7	22 50.3	-9.9	21.8	23 46.0	-9.5	22.0	24 41.6	-9.1	22.2	25 37.1	-8.6	22.3	26 32.6	-8.2	22.5	69
70	19 51.9	-11.5	20.4	20 48.1	-11.1	20.5	21 44.3	-10.7	20.6	22 40.4	-10.3	20.8	23 36.5	-9.9	20.9	24 32.5	-9.5	21.1	25 28.5	-9.2	21.2	26 24.4	-8.8	21.4	70
71	19 40.4	-11.8	19.3	20 37.0	-11.5	19.4	21 33.6	-11.1	19.6	22 30.1	-10.8	19.7	23 26.6	-10.4	19.8	24 23.0	-10.0	20.0	25 19.3	-9.6	20.1	26 15.6	-9.2	20.3	71
72	19 28.6	-12.2	18.3	20 25.5	-11.8	18.4	21 22.5	-11.5	18.5	22 19.3	-11.1	18.6	23 16.2	-10.8	18.8	24 13.0	-10.5	18.9	25 09.7	-10.1	19.1	26 06.4	-9.8	19.2	72
73	19 16.4	-12.5	17.2	20 13.7	-12.2	17.3	21 11.0	-11.9	17.4	22 08.2	-11.6	17.6	23 05.4	-11.3	17.7	24 02.5	-10.9	17.8	24 59.6	-10.6	18.0	25 56.6	-10.2	18.1	73
74	19 03.9	-12.9	16.2	20 01.5	-12.6	16.3	20 59.1	-12.3	16.4	21 56.6	-12.0	16.5	22 54.1	-11.7	16.6	23 51.6	-11.4	16.8	24 49.0	-11.0	16.9	25 46.4	-10.7	17.0	74
75	18 51.0	-13.2	15.2	19 48.9	-12.9	15.3	20 46.8	-12.7	15.4	21 44.6	-12.4	15.5	22 42.4	-12.1	15.6	23 40.2	-11.8	15.7	24 38.0	-11.5	15.8	25 35.7	-11.2	15.9	75
76	18 37.8	-13.6	14.1	19 36.0	-13.3	14.2	20 34.1	-13.0	14.3	21 32.2	-12.7	14.4	22 30.3	-12.5	14.5	23 28.4	-12.2	14.6	24 26.5	-12.0	14.7	25 24.5	-11.7	14.8	76
77	18 24.2	-13.8	13.1	19 22.7	-13.7	13.2	20 21.1	-13.4	13.3	21 19.5	-13.2	13.4	22 17.8	-12.9	13.4	23 16.2	-12.7	13.5	24 14.5	-12.4	13.6	25 12.8	-12.2	13.8	77
78	18 10.4	-14.3	12.1	19 09.0	-14.0	12.2	20 07.7	-13.8	12.2	21 06.3	-13.6	12.3	22 04.9	-13.3	12.4	23 03.5	-13.1	12.5	24 02.1	-12.9	12.6	25 00.6	-12.6	12.7	78
79	17 56.1	-14.5	11.1	18 55.0	-14.3	11.1	19 53.9	-14.1	11.2	20 52.7	-13.9	11.3	21 51.6	-13.7	11.3	22 50.4	-13.5	11.4	23 49.2	-13.3	11.5	24 48.0	-13.1	11.6	79
80	17 41.6	-14.8	10.0	18 40.7	-14.7	10.1	19 39.8	-14.5	10.2	20 38.8	-14.3	10.2	21 37.9	-14.2	10.3	22 36.9	-13.9	10.4	23 35.9	-13.7	10.4	24 34.9	-13.6	10.5	80
81	17 26.8	-15.2	9.0	18 26.0	-15.0	9.1	19 25.3	-14.9	9.1	20 24.5	-14.7	9.2	21 23.7	-14.5	9.2	22 23.0	-14.4	9.3	23 22.2	-14.2	9.4	24 21.3	-14.0	9.5	81
82	17 11.6	-15.4	8.0	18 11.0	-15.3	8.1	19 10.4	-15.1	8.1	20 09.8	-15.0	8.2	21 09.2	-14.9	8.2	22 08.6	-14.7	8.3	23 08.0	-14.6	8.3	24 07.3	-14.4	8.4	82
83	16 56.2	-15.8	7.0	17 55.7	-15.6	7.0	18 55.3	-15.5	7.1	19 54.8	-15.4	7.1	20 54.3	-15.2	7.2	21 53.9	-15.2	7.2	22 53.4	-15.0	7.3	23 52.9	-14.9	7.3	83
84	16 40.4	-16.0	6.0	17 40.1	-15.9	6.0	18 39.8	-15.9	6.1	19 39.4	-15.7	6.1	20 39.1	-15.6	6.1	21 38.7	-15.5	6.2	22 38.4	-15.4	6.2	23 38.0	-15.3	6.3	84
85	16 24.4	-16.3	5.0	17 24.2	-16.3	5.0	18 23.9	-16.1	5.0	19 23.7	-16.1	5.1	20 23.5	-16.0	5.1	21 23.2	-15.9	5.1	22 23.0	-15.8	5.2	23 22.7	-15.7	5.2	85
86	16 08.1	-16.7	4.0	17 07.9	-16.5	4.0	18 07.8	-16.5	4.0	19 07.6	-16.4	4.0	20 07.5	-16.4	4.1	21 07.3	-16.3	4.1	22 07.2	-16.3	4.1	23 07.0	-16.1	4.2	86
87	15 51.4	-16.8	3.0	16 51.4	-16.9	3.0	17 51.3	-16.8	3.0	18 51.2	-16.7	3.0	19 51.1	-16.7	3.1	20 51.0	-16.6	3.1	21 50.9	-16.6	3.1	22 50.9	-16.6	3.1	87
88	15 34.6	-17.2	2.0	16 34.5	-17.1	2.0	17 34.5	-17.1	2.0	18 34.5	-17.1	2.0	19 34.4	-17.0	2.0	20 34.4	-17.0	2.0	21 34.3	-16.9	2.1	22 34.3	-17.0	2.1	88
89	15 17.4	-17.4	1.0	16 17.4	-17.4	1.0	17 17.4	-17.4	1.0	18 17.4	-17.4	1.0	19 17.4	-17.4	1.0	20 17.4	-17.4	1.0	21 17.4	-17.4	1.0	22 17.3	-17.3	1.0	89
90	15 00.0	-17.7	0.0	16 00.0	-17.7	0.0	17 00.0	-17.7	0.0	18 00.0	-17.7	0.0	19 00.0	-17.7	0.0	20 00.0	-17.7	0.0	21 00.0	-17.7	0.0	22 00.0	-17.7	0.0	90
	15°			16°			17°			18°			19°			20°			21°			22°			

73°, 287° L.H.A. LATITUDE SAME NAME AS DECLINATION

148

LATITUDE **CONTRARY** NAME TO DECLINATION **L.H.A. 73°, 287°**

Dec.	15° Hc	d	Z	16° Hc	d	Z	17° Hc	d	Z	18° Hc	d	Z	19° Hc	d	Z	20° Hc	d	Z	21° Hc	d	Z	22° Hc	d	Z	Dec.
°	° ′	′	°	° ′	′	°	° ′	′	°	° ′	′	°	° ′	′	°	° ′	′	°	° ′	′	°	° ′	′	°	°
0	16 24.2	-16.3	94.5	16 19.4	-17.4	94.8	16 14.2	-18.4	95.1	16 08.7	-19.5	95.4	16 02.9	-20.5	95.7	15 56.8	-21.5	96.0	15 50.4	-22.5	96.3	15 43.7	-23.5	96.5	0
1	16 07.9	-16.6	95.5	16 02.0	-17.7	95.8	15 55.8	-18.7	96.1	15 49.2	-19.7	96.4	15 42.4	-20.7	96.7	15 35.3	-21.7	96.9	15 27.9	-22.7	97.2	15 20.2	-23.7	97.5	1
2	15 51.3	-16.9	96.5	15 44.3	-17.9	96.8	15 37.1	-19.0	97.1	15 29.5	-19.9	97.4	15 21.7	-21.0	97.6	15 13.6	-22.0	97.9	15 05.2	-23.0	98.2	14 56.5	-23.9	98.4	2
3	15 34.4	-17.1	97.5	15 26.4	-18.2	97.8	15 18.1	-19.2	98.1	15 09.6	-20.2	98.3	15 00.7	-21.2	98.6	14 51.6	-22.2	98.9	14 42.2	-23.2	99.1	14 32.6	-24.2	99.4	3
4	15 17.3	-17.4	98.5	15 08.2	-18.4	98.8	14 58.9	-19.4	99.1	14 49.4	-20.5	99.3	14 39.5	-21.4	99.6	14 29.4	-22.4	99.8	14 19.0	-23.4	100.1	14 08.4	-24.4	100.3	4
5	14 59.9	-17.7	99.5	14 49.8	-18.7	99.8	14 39.5	-19.7	100.0	14 28.9	-20.7	100.3	14 18.1	-21.7	100.5	14 07.0	-22.7	100.8	13 55.6	-23.6	101.0	13 44.0	-24.6	101.3	5
6	14 42.2	-17.9	100.5	14 31.1	-18.9	100.8	14 19.8	-19.9	101.0	14 08.2	-20.9	101.3	13 56.4	-21.9	101.5	13 44.3	-22.9	101.7	13 32.0	-23.9	102.0	13 19.4	-24.8	102.2	6
7	14 24.3	-18.2	101.5	14 12.2	-19.2	101.7	13 59.9	-20.2	102.0	13 47.3	-21.2	102.2	13 34.5	-22.2	102.5	13 21.4	-23.1	102.7	13 08.1	-24.1	102.9	12 54.6	-25.1	103.1	7
8	14 06.1	-18.4	102.5	13 53.0	-19.4	102.7	13 39.7	-20.4	102.9	13 26.1	-21.3	103.2	13 12.3	-22.3	103.4	12 58.3	-23.3	103.6	12 44.0	-24.2	103.9	12 29.5	-25.2	104.1	8
9	13 47.7	-18.7	103.4	13 33.6	-19.6	103.7	13 19.3	-20.6	103.9	13 04.8	-21.6	104.1	12 50.0	-22.6	104.4	12 35.0	-23.5	104.6	12 19.8	-24.5	104.8	12 04.3	-25.4	105.0	9
10	13 29.0	-18.8	104.4	13 14.0	-19.9	104.7	12 58.7	-20.8	104.9	12 43.2	-21.8	105.1	12 27.4	-22.7	105.3	12 11.5	-23.7	105.5	11 55.3	-24.6	105.7	11 38.9	-25.5	105.9	10
11	13 10.2	-19.1	105.4	12 54.1	-20.0	105.6	12 37.9	-21.1	105.8	12 21.4	-22.0	106.1	12 04.7	-23.0	106.3	11 47.8	-23.9	106.5	11 30.7	-24.9	106.7	11 13.4	-25.8	106.9	11
12	12 51.1	-19.3	106.4	12 34.1	-20.3	106.6	12 16.8	-21.2	106.8	11 59.4	-22.2	107.0	11 41.7	-23.1	107.2	11 23.9	-24.1	107.4	11 05.8	-24.9	107.6	10 47.6	-25.9	107.8	12
13	12 31.8	-19.5	107.3	12 13.8	-20.5	107.6	11 55.6	-21.4	107.8	11 37.2	-22.4	108.0	11 18.6	-23.3	108.1	10 59.8	-24.2	108.3	10 40.9	-25.2	108.5	10 21.7	-26.0	108.7	13
14	12 12.3	-19.7	108.3	11 53.3	-20.6	108.5	11 34.2	-21.6	108.7	11 14.8	-22.5	108.9	10 55.3	-23.5	109.1	10 35.6	-24.4	109.3	10 15.7	-25.3	109.4	9 55.7	-26.2	109.6	14
15	11 52.6	-19.9	109.3	11 32.7	-20.9	109.5	11 12.6	-21.8	109.7	10 52.3	-22.7	109.8	10 31.8	-23.6	110.0	10 11.2	-24.5	110.2	9 50.4	-25.4	110.4	9 29.5	-26.4	110.5	15
16	11 32.7	-20.1	110.2	11 11.8	-21.0	110.4	10 50.8	-22.0	110.6	10 29.6	-22.9	110.8	10 08.2	-23.8	111.0	9 46.7	-24.7	111.1	9 25.0	-25.6	111.3	9 03.1	-26.5	111.4	16
17	11 12.6	-20.3	111.2	10 50.8	-21.2	111.4	10 28.8	-22.1	111.6	10 06.7	-23.1	111.7	9 44.4	-24.0	111.9	9 22.0	-24.9	112.0	8 59.4	-25.8	112.2	8 36.6	-26.6	112.3	17
18	10 52.3	-20.5	112.2	10 29.6	-21.4	112.3	10 06.7	-22.3	112.5	9 43.6	-23.2	112.7	9 20.4	-24.0	112.8	8 57.1	-25.0	113.0	8 33.6	-25.8	113.1	8 10.0	-26.7	113.2	18
19	10 31.8	-20.6	113.1	10 08.2	-21.5	113.3	9 44.4	-22.4	113.4	9 20.4	-23.3	113.6	8 56.4	-24.3	113.7	8 32.1	-25.1	113.9	8 07.8	-26.0	114.0	7 43.3	-26.9	114.2	19
20	10 11.2	-20.8	114.1	9 46.7	-21.7	114.2	9 22.0	-22.6	114.4	8 57.1	-23.5	114.5	8 32.1	-24.3	114.7	8 07.0	-25.2	114.8	7 41.8	-26.1	114.9	7 16.4	-26.9	115.1	20
21	9 50.4	-20.9	115.0	9 25.0	-21.9	115.2	8 59.4	-22.8	115.3	8 33.6	-23.6	115.5	8 07.8	-24.5	115.6	7 41.8	-25.4	115.7	7 15.7	-26.2	115.8	6 49.5	-27.1	116.0	21
22	9 29.5	-21.2	116.0	9 03.1	-22.0	116.1	8 36.6	-22.9	116.3	8 10.0	-23.7	116.4	7 43.3	-24.6	116.5	7 16.4	-25.4	116.6	6 49.5	-26.3	116.7	6 22.4	-27.1	116.9	22
23	9 08.3	-21.2	116.9	8 41.1	-22.1	117.1	8 13.7	-23.0	117.2	7 46.3	-23.9	117.3	7 18.7	-24.7	117.4	6 51.0	-25.6	117.5	6 23.2	-26.4	117.7	5 55.3	-27.3	117.7	23
24	8 47.1	-21.4	117.9	8 19.0	-22.3	118.0	7 50.7	-23.1	118.1	7 22.4	-24.0	118.2	6 54.0	-24.8	118.4	6 25.4	-25.7	118.5	5 56.8	-26.5	118.6	5 28.0	-27.3	118.6	24
25	8 25.7	-21.5	118.8	7 56.7	-22.4	118.9	7 27.6	-23.2	119.1	6 58.4	-24.1	119.2	6 29.1	-24.9	119.3	5 59.7	-25.7	119.4	5 30.3	-26.6	119.5	5 00.7	-27.4	119.5	25
26	8 04.2	-21.7	119.8	7 34.3	-22.5	119.9	7 04.4	-23.4	120.0	6 34.3	-24.2	120.1	6 04.2	-25.0	120.2	5 34.0	-25.8	120.3	5 03.7	-26.6	120.4	4 33.3	-27.4	120.4	26
27	7 42.5	-21.8	120.7	7 11.8	-22.6	120.8	6 41.0	-23.4	120.9	6 10.1	-24.2	121.0	5 39.2	-25.1	121.1	5 08.2	-25.9	121.2	4 37.1	-26.8	121.3	4 05.9	-27.5	121.3	27
28	7 20.7	-21.9	121.6	6 49.2	-22.8	121.7	6 17.6	-23.6	121.8	5 45.9	-24.4	121.9	5 14.1	-25.2	122.0	4 42.3	-26.0	122.1	4 10.3	-26.7	122.2	3 38.4	-27.6	122.2	28
29	6 58.8	-22.0	122.6	6 26.4	-22.8	122.7	5 54.0	-23.6	122.8	5 21.5	-24.5	122.9	4 48.9	-25.2	122.9	4 16.3	-26.1	123.0	3 43.6	-26.9	123.1	3 10.8	-27.6	123.1	29
30	6 36.8	-22.1	123.5	6 03.6	-22.9	123.6	5 30.4	-23.8	123.7	4 57.0	-24.5	123.8	4 23.7	-25.3	123.8	3 50.2	-26.1	123.9	3 16.7	-26.8	123.9	2 43.2	-27.6	124.0	30
31	6 14.7	-22.3	124.5	5 40.7	-23.0	124.5	5 06.6	-23.8	124.6	4 32.5	-24.6	124.7	3 58.4	-25.4	124.7	3 24.1	-26.1	124.8	2 49.9	-26.9	124.8	2 15.6	-27.7	124.9	31
32	5 52.4	-22.3	125.4	5 17.7	-23.1	125.5	4 42.8	-23.9	125.5	4 07.9	-24.6	125.6	3 33.0	-25.5	125.7	2 58.0	-26.2	125.7	2 23.0	-27.0	125.7	1 47.9	-27.7	125.8	32
33	5 30.1	-22.4	126.3	4 54.6	-23.2	126.4	4 18.9	-23.9	126.5	3 43.3	-24.8	126.5	3 07.5	-25.4	126.6	2 31.8	-26.2	126.6	1 56.0	-27.0	126.6	1 20.2	-27.7	126.7	33
34	5 07.7	-22.4	127.3	4 31.4	-23.3	127.3	3 55.0	-24.0	127.4	3 18.5	-24.7	127.4	2 42.1	-25.5	127.5	2 05.6	-26.3	127.5	1 29.0	-27.0	127.5	0 52.5	-27.8	127.5	34
35	4 45.3	-22.6	128.2	4 08.1	-23.3	128.2	3 31.0	-24.1	128.3	2 53.8	-24.8	128.3	2 16.6	-25.6	128.4	1 39.3	-26.3	128.4	1 02.0	-27.0	128.4	0 24.7	-27.7	128.4	35
36	4 22.7	-22.6	129.1	3 44.8	-23.3	129.2	3 06.9	-24.1	129.2	2 29.0	-24.9	129.2	1 51.0	-25.6	129.3	1 13.0	-26.3	129.3	0 35.0	-27.0	129.3	0 03.0	+27.8	50.7	36
37	4 00.1	-22.7	130.0	3 21.5	-23.5	130.1	2 42.8	-24.1	130.1	2 04.1	-24.9	130.2	1 25.4	-25.6	130.2	0 46.7	-26.3	130.2	0 08.0	-27.1	130.2	0 30.8	+27.7	49.8	37
38	3 37.4	-22.7	131.0	2 58.0	-23.4	131.0	2 18.7	-24.2	131.0	1 39.2	-24.9	131.1	0 59.8	-25.6	131.1	0 20.4	-26.3	131.1	0 19.1	+27.0	48.9	0 58.5	+27.7	48.9	38
39	3 14.7	-22.8	131.9	2 34.6	-23.5	131.9	1 54.5	-24.2	132.0	1 14.3	-24.9	132.0	0 34.2	-25.6	132.0	0 05.9	+26.4	48.0	0 46.1	+27.0	48.0	1 26.2	+27.7	48.0	39
40	2 51.9	-22.9	132.8	2 11.1	-23.6	132.9	1 30.3	-24.3	132.9	0 49.4	-24.9	132.9	0 08.6	-25.6	132.9	0 32.3	+26.3	47.1	1 13.1	+27.0	47.1	1 53.9	+27.7	47.1	40
41	2 29.0	-22.9	133.7	1 47.5	-23.5	133.8	1 06.0	-24.2	133.8	0 24.5	-25.0	133.8	0 17.0	+25.7	46.2	0 58.6	+26.3	46.2	1 40.1	+27.0	46.2	2 21.6	+27.6	46.2	41
42	2 06.1	-22.9	134.7	1 24.0	-23.6	134.7	0 41.8	-24.3	134.7	0 00.5	+24.9	45.3	0 42.7	+25.6	45.3	1 24.9	+26.2	45.3	2 07.1	+26.9	45.3	2 49.2	+27.6	45.4	42
43	1 43.2	-22.9	135.6	1 00.4	-23.6	135.6	0 17.5	-24.3	135.6	0 25.4	+24.9	44.4	1 08.3	+25.6	44.4	1 51.1	+26.3	44.4	2 34.0	+26.9	44.4	3 16.8	+27.6	44.5	43
44	1 20.3	-23.0	136.5	0 36.8	-23.7	136.5	0 06.8	+24.3	43.5	0 50.3	+25.0	43.5	1 33.9	+25.5	43.5	2 17.4	+26.2	43.5	3 00.9	+26.9	43.5	3 44.4	+27.5	43.6	44
45	0 57.3	-22.9	137.4	0 13.1	-23.6	137.5	0 31.1	+24.2	42.6	1 15.3	+24.9	42.6	1 59.4	+25.6	42.6	2 43.6	+26.2	42.6	3 27.8	+26.8	42.6	4 11.9	+27.4	42.7	45
46	0 34.4	-23.0	138.4	0 10.5	+23.6	41.6	0 55.3	+24.3	41.6	1 40.2	+24.8	41.7	2 25.0	+25.5	41.7	3 09.8	+26.1	41.7	3 54.6	+26.7	41.7	4 39.3	+27.4	41.8	46
47	0 11.4	-23.0	139.3	0 34.1	+23.6	40.7	1 19.6	+24.2	40.7	2 05.0	+24.9	40.7	2 50.5	+25.4	40.8	3 35.9	+26.1	40.8	4 21.3	+26.7	40.9	5 06.7	+27.3	40.9	47
48	0 11.6	+23.0	39.8	0 57.7	+23.6	39.8	1 43.8	+24.2	39.8	2 29.9	+24.8	39.8	3 15.9	+25.5	39.9	4 02.0	+26.0	39.9	4 48.0	+26.6	40.0	5 34.0	+27.2	40.0	48
49	0 34.6	+22.9	38.9	1 21.3	+23.6	38.9	2 08.0	+24.2	38.9	2 54.7	+24.8	38.9	3 41.4	+25.3	39.0	4 28.0	+26.0	39.0	5 14.6	+26.6	39.1	6 01.2	+27.1	39.1	49
50	0 57.5	+23.0	37.9	1 44.9	+23.5	38.0	2 32.2	+24.1	38.0	3 19.5	+24.7	38.0	4 06.7	+25.3	38.0	4 54.0	+25.8	38.1	5 41.2	+26.4	38.2	6 28.3	+27.0	38.2	50
51	1 20.5	+22.9	37.0	2 08.4	+23.5	37.0	2 56.3	+24.1	37.1	3 44.2	+24.6	37.1	4 32.0	+25.2	37.1	5 19.8	+25.8	37.2	6 07.6	+26.4	37.2	6 55.3	+27.0	37.3	51
52	1 43.4	+22.9	36.1	2 31.9	+23.5	36.1	3 20.4	+24.0	36.1	4 08.8	+24.6	36.2	4 57.2	+25.2	36.2	5 45.6	+25.7	36.3	6 34.0	+26.2	36.3	7 22.3	+26.8	36.4	52
53	2 06.3	+22.9	35.2	2 55.4	+23.4	35.2	3 44.4	+24.0	35.2	4 33.4	+24.5	35.3	5 22.4	+25.1	35.3	6 11.3	+25.7	35.4	7 00.2	+26.2	35.4	7 49.1	+26.7	35.5	53
54	2 29.2	+22.9	34.2	3 18.8	+23.4	34.3	4 08.4	+23.9	34.3	4 57.9	+24.5	34.3	5 47.5	+24.9	34.4	6 37.0	+25.5	34.5	7 26.4	+26.1	34.5	8 15.8	+26.6	34.6	54
55	2 52.1	+22.8	33.3	3 42.2	+23.3	33.3	4 32.3	+23.8	33.4	5 22.4	+24.4	33.4	6 12.4	+24.9	33.5	7 02.5	+25.4	33.6	7 52.5	+25.9	33.6	8 42.4	+26.4	33.7	55
56	3 14.9	+22.7	32.4	4 05.5	+23.3	32.4	4 56.1	+23.8	32.5	5 46.8	+24.2	32.5	6 37.3	+24.8	32.6	7 27.9	+25.3	32.6	8 18.4	+25.8	32.7	9 08.8	+26.4	32.8	56
57	3 37.6	+22.7	31.5	4 28.8	+23.1	31.5	5 19.9	+23.7	31.5	6 11.0	+24.2	31.6	7 02.1	+24.7	31.7	7 53.2	+25.2	31.7	8 44.2	+25.7	31.8	9 35.2	+26.1	31.9	57
58	4 00.3	+22.6	30.5	4 51.9	+23.2	30.6	5 43.6	+23.6	30.6	6 35.2	+24.1	30.7	7 26.8	+24.6	30.7	8 18.4	+25.0	30.8	9 09.9	+25.5	30.9	10 01.3	+26.1	31.0	58
59	4 22.9	+22.6	29.6	5 15.1	+23.0	29.6	6 07.2	+23.5	29.7	6 59.3	+24.0	29.8	7 51.4	+24.4	29.8	8 43.4	+24.9	29.9	9 35.4	+25.4	30.0	10 27.4	+25.8	30.1	59
60	4 45.5	+22.4	28.7	5 38.1	+22.9	28.7	6 30.7	+23.4	28.8	7 23.3	+23.8	28.8	8 15.8	+24.3	28.9	9 08.3	+24.8	29.0	10 00.8	+25.3	29.0	10 53.2	+25.7	29.1	60
61	5 07.9	+22.4	27.7	6 01.0	+22.9	27.8	6 54.1	+23.3	27.8	7 47.1	+23.8	27.9	8 40.1	+24.2	28.0	9 33.1	+24.6	28.0	10 26.1	+25.0	28.1	11 18.9	+25.6	28.2	61
62	5 30.3	+22.3	26.8	6 23.9	+22.7	26.9	7 17.4	+23.2	26.9	8 10.9	+23.6	27.0	9 04.3	+24.1	27.0	9 57.7	+24.5	27.1	10 51.1	+25.0	27.2	11 44.5	+25.3	27.3	62
63	5 52.6	+22.3	25.9	6 46.6	+22.6	25.9	7 40.6	+23.0	26.0	8 34.5	+23.5	26.0	9 28.4	+23.9	26.1	10 22.2	+24.4	26.2	11 16.1	+24.7	26.3	12 09.8	+25.2	26.4	63
64	6 14.9	+22.1	24.9	7 09.2	+22.6	25.0	8 03.6	+22.9	25.0	8 58.0	+23.3	25.1	9 52.3	+23.7	25.2	10 46.6	+24.1	25.3	11 40.8	+24.6	25.3	12 35.0	+25.0	25.4	64
65	6 37.0	+22.0	24.0	7 31.8	+22.4	24.1	8 26.5	+22.8	24.1	9 21.3	+23.2	24.2	10 16.0	+23.6	24.3	11 10.7	+24.0	24.3	12 05.4	+24.3	24.4	13 00.0	+24.8	24.5	65
66	6 59.0	+21.9	23.1	7 54.2	+22.3	23.1	8 49.3	+22.7	23.2	9 44.5	+23.0	23.2	10 39.6	+23.4	23.3	11 34.7	+23.8	23.4	12 29.7	+24.2	23.5	13 24.8	+24.5	23.6	66
67	7 20.9	+21.8	22.1	8 16.5	+22.1	22.2	9 12.0	+22.5	22.2	10 07.5	+22.9	22.3	11 03.0	+23.3	22.4	11 58.5	+23.6	22.5	12 53.9	+24.0	22.5	13 49.3	+24.4	22.6	67
68	7 42.7	+21.6	21.2	8 38.6	+22.0	21.2	9 34.5	+22.4	21.3	10 30.4	+22.7	21.4	11 26.3	+23.0	21.4	12 22.1	+23.4	21.5	13 17.9	+23.8	21.6	14 13.7	+24.1	21.7	68
69	8 04.3	+21.6	20.3	9 00.6	+21.9	20.3	9 56.9	+22.2	20.4	10 53.1	+22.6	20.4	11 49.3	+22.9	20.5	12 45.5	+23.2	20.6	13 41.7	+23.5	20.7	14 37.8	+23.9	20.7	69
70	8 25.9	+21.4	19.3	9 22.5	+21.7	19.4	10 19.1	+22.0	19.4	11 15.7	+22.3	19.5	12 12.2	+22.7	19.6	13 08.7	+23.0	19.6	14 05.2	+23.4	19.7	15 01.7	+23.7	19.8	70
71	8 47.3	+21.2	18.4	9 44.2	+21.6	18.4	10 41.1	+21.9	18.5	11 38.0	+22.2	18.5	12 34.9	+22.5	18.6	13 31.7	+22.8	18.7	14 28.6	+23.1	18.8	15 25.4	+23.4	18.8	71
72	9 08.5	+21.1	17.4	10 05.8	+21.4	17.5	11 03.0	+21.7	17.5	12 00.2	+22.0	17.6	12 57.4	+22.3	17.7	13 54.5	+22.6	17.7	14 51.7	+22.9	17.8	15 48.8	+23.2	17.9	72
73	9 29.6	+21.0	16.5	10 27.2	+21.2	16.5	11 24.7	+21.5	16.6	12 22.2	+21.8	16.6	13 19.7	+22.0	16.7	14 17.1	+22.4	16.8	15 14.6	+22.6	16.8	16 12.0	+22.9	16.9	73
74	9 50.6	+20.8	15.5	10 48.4	+21.0	15.6	11 46.2	+21.3	15.6	12 44.0	+21.5	15.7	13 41.7	+21.9	15.7	14 39.5	+22.1	15.8	15 37.2	+22.4	15.9	16 34.9	+22.6	16.0	74
75	10 11.4	+20.6	14.6	11 09.4	+20.9	14.6	12 07.5	+21.1	14.7	13 05.5	+21.4	14.7	14 03.6	+21.6	14.8	15 01.6	+21.8	14.8	15 59.6	+22.1	14.9	16 57.5	+22.4	15.0	75
76	10 32.0	+20.5	13.6	11 30.3	+20.7	13.7	12 28.6	+20.9	13.7	13 26.9	+21.1	13.8	14 25.2	+21.3	13.8	15 23.4	+21.6	13.9	16 21.7	+21.8	14.0	17 19.9	+22.1	14.0	76
77	10 52.5	+20.2	12.7	11 51.0	+20.5	12.7	12 49.5	+20.7	12.7	13 48.0	+21.0	12.8	14 46.5	+21.2	12.9	15 45.0	+21.4	12.9	16 43.5	+21.6	13.0	17 42.0	+21.8	13.1	77
78	11 12.7	+20.1	11.7	12 11.5	+20.3	11.7	13 10.2	+20.5	11.8	14 09.0	+20.7	11.8	15 07.7	+20.9	11.9	16 06.4	+21.1	11.9	17 05.1	+21.3	12.0	18 03.8	+21.5	12.1	78
79	11 32.8	+19.9	10.7	12 31.8	+20.1	10.8	13 30.7	+20.3	10.8	14 29.7	+20.4	10.9	15 28.6	+20.6	10.9	16 27.5	+20.8	11.0	17 26.4	+21.0	11.0	18 25.3	+21.2	11.1	79
80	11 52.7	+19.8	9.8	12 51.9	+19.8	9.8	13 51.0	+20.0	9.8	14 50.1	+20.2	9.9	15 49.2	+20.4	9.9	16 48.3	+20.5	10.0	17 47.4	+20.7	10.0	18 46.5	+20.8	10.1	80
81	12 12.5	+19.5	8.8	13 11.7	+19.7	8.8	14 11.0	+19.8	8.9	15 10.3	+20.0	8.9	16 09.6	+20.1	9.0	17 08.8	+20.3	9.0	18 08.1	+20.4	9.1	19 07.3	+20.6	9.1	81
82	12 32.0	+19.3	7.8	13 31.4	+19.4	7.9	14 30.8	+19.6	7.9	15 30.3	+19.7	7.9	16 29.7	+19.8	8.0	17 29.1	+20.0	8.0	18 28.5	+20.1	8.1	19 27.9	+20.2	8.1	82
83	12 51.3	+19.0	6.9	13 50.8	+19.2	6.9	14 50.4	+19.3	6.9	15 50.0	+19.4	7.0	16 49.5	+19.6	7.0	17 49.1	+19.6	7.0	18 48.6	+19.8	7.1	19 48.1	+19.9	7.1	83
84	13 10.3	+18.9	5.9	14 10.0	+19.0	5.9	15 09.7	+19.1	5.9	16 09.4	+19.1	6.0	17 09.1	+19.2	6.0	18 08.7	+19.4	6.0	19 08.4	+19.4	6.1	20 08.0	+19.6	6.1	84
85	13 29.2	+18.6	4.9	14 29.0	+18.7	4.9	15 28.8	+18.8	5.0	16 28.5	+18.9	5.0	17 28.3	+19.0	5.0	18 28.1	+19.0	5.0	19 27.8	+19.2	5.1	20 27.6	+19.2	5.1	85
86	13 47.8	+18.4	3.9	14 47.7	+18.5	4.0	15 47.6	+18.5	4.0	16 47.4	+18.6	4.0	17 47.3	+18.6	4.0	18 47.1	+18.7	4.0	19 47.0	+18.8	4.1	20 46.8	+18.9	4.1	86
87	14 06.2	+18.2	3.0	15 06.2	+18.2	3.0	16 06.1	+18.2	3.0	17 06.0	+18.3	3.0	18 05.9	+18.4	3.0	19 05.8	+18.4	3.0	20 05.8	+18.4	3.1	21 05.7	+18.5	3.1	87
88	14 24.4	+17.9	2.0	15 24.4	+17.9	2.0	16 24.3	+18.0	2.0	17 24.3	+18.0	2.0	18 24.3	+18.0	2.0	19 24.2	+18.1	2.0	20 24.2	+18.1	2.0	21 24.2	+18.1	2.1	88
89	14 42.3	+17.7	1.0	15 42.3	+17.7	1.0	16 42.3	+17.7	1.0	17 42.3	+17.7	1.0	18 42.3	+17.7	1.0	19 42.3	+17.7	1.0	20 42.3	+17.7	1.0	21 42.3	+17.7	1.0	89
90	15 00.0	+17.4	0.0	16 00.0	+17.4	0.0	17 00.0	+17.4	0.0	18 00.0	+17.4	0.0	19 00.0	+17.4	0.0	20 00.0	+17.4	0.0	21 00.0	+17.4	0.0	22 00.0	+17.3	0.0	90
	15°			16°			17°			18°			19°			20°			21°			22°			

S. Lat. {L.H.A. greater than 180° ....Zn=180°–Z; L.H.A. less than 180°...........Zn=180°+Z}

LATITUDE **SAME** NAME AS DECLINATION **L.H.A. 107°, 253°**

149

Dec.	15° Hc	d	Z	16° Hc	d	Z	17° Hc	d	Z	18° Hc	d	Z	19° Hc	d	Z	20° Hc	d	Z	21° Hc	d	Z	22° Hc	d	Z	Dec.
°	° ′	′	°	° ′	′	°	° ′	′	°	° ′	′	°	° ′	′	°	° ′	′	°	° ′	′	°	° ′	′	°	°
0	15 26.5	+15.9	94.2	15 21.9	+17.0	94.5	15 17.0	+18.1	94.8	15 11.8	+19.1	95.1	15 06.4	+20.1	95.3	15 00.7	+21.1	95.6	14 54.7	+22.1	95.9	14 48.4	+23.2	96.1	0
1	15 42.4	+15.7	93.2	15 38.9	+16.7	93.5	15 35.1	+17.7	93.8	15 30.9	+18.9	94.1	15 26.5	+19.9	94.4	15 21.8	+20.9	94.6	15 16.8	+21.9	94.9	15 11.6	+22.8	95.2	1
2	15 58.1	+15.5	92.2	15 55.6	+16.5	92.5	15 52.8	+17.6	92.8	15 49.8	+18.5	93.1	15 46.4	+19.6	93.4	15 42.7	+20.6	93.7	15 38.7	+21.6	93.9	15 34.4	+22.7	94.2	2
3	16 13.6	+15.1	91.2	16 12.1	+16.2	91.5	16 10.4	+17.2	91.8	16 08.3	+18.3	92.1	16 06.0	+19.3	92.4	16 03.3	+20.3	92.7	16 00.3	+21.4	93.0	15 57.1	+22.4	93.3	3
4	16 28.7	+14.8	90.2	16 28.3	+15.9	90.5	16 27.6	+17.0	90.8	16 26.6	+18.0	91.1	16 25.3	+19.0	91.4	16 23.6	+20.1	91.7	16 21.7	+21.1	92.0	16 19.5	+22.1	92.3	4
5	16 43.5	+14.6	89.2	16 44.2	+15.6	89.5	16 44.6	+16.6	89.8	16 44.6	+17.7	90.1	16 44.3	+18.8	90.4	16 43.7	+19.8	90.7	16 42.8	+20.8	91.0	16 41.6	+21.8	91.3	5
6	16 58.1	+14.2	88.2	16 59.8	+15.3	88.5	17 01.2	+16.4	88.8	17 02.3	+17.4	89.1	17 03.1	+18.4	89.4	17 03.5	+19.5	89.7	17 03.6	+20.6	90.0	17 03.4	+21.6	90.3	6
7	17 12.3	+14.0	87.2	17 15.1	+15.0	87.5	17 17.6	+16.1	87.8	17 19.7	+17.1	88.1	17 21.5	+18.2	88.4	17 23.0	+19.2	88.7	17 24.2	+20.2	89.1	17 25.0	+21.3	89.4	7
8	17 26.3	+13.6	86.2	17 30.1	+14.7	86.5	17 33.7	+15.7	86.8	17 36.8	+16.9	87.1	17 39.7	+17.9	87.4	17 42.2	+18.9	87.7	17 44.4	+20.0	88.1	17 46.3	+20.9	88.4	8
9	17 39.9	+13.3	85.1	17 44.8	+14.4	85.5	17 49.4	+15.5	85.8	17 53.7	+16.5	86.1	17 57.6	+17.5	86.4	18 01.1	+18.6	86.8	18 04.4	+19.6	87.1	18 07.2	+20.7	87.4	9
10	17 53.2	+13.0	84.1	17 59.2	+14.1	84.4	18 04.9	+15.1	84.8	18 10.2	+16.1	85.1	18 15.1	+17.3	85.4	18 19.7	+18.3	85.8	18 24.0	+19.3	86.1	18 27.9	+20.4	86.4	10
11	18 06.2	+12.7	83.1	18 13.3	+13.7	83.4	18 20.0	+14.8	83.7	18 26.3	+15.9	84.1	18 32.4	+16.9	84.4	18 38.0	+18.0	84.7	18 43.3	+19.1	85.1	18 48.3	+20.1	85.4	11
12	18 18.9	+12.3	82.1	18 27.0	+13.4	82.4	18 34.8	+14.4	82.7	18 42.2	+15.5	83.1	18 49.3	+16.6	83.4	18 56.0	+17.6	83.7	19 02.4	+18.6	84.1	19 08.4	+19.7	84.4	12
13	18 31.2	+12.0	81.0	18 40.4	+13.1	81.4	18 49.2	+14.2	81.7	18 57.7	+15.2	82.0	19 05.9	+16.2	82.4	19 13.6	+17.3	82.7	19 21.0	+18.4	83.1	19 28.1	+19.4	83.4	13
14	18 43.2	+11.7	80.0	18 53.5	+12.7	80.3	19 03.4	+13.8	80.7	19 12.9	+14.9	81.0	19 22.1	+15.9	81.4	19 30.9	+17.0	81.7	19 39.4	+18.0	82.1	19 47.5	+19.1	82.4	14
15	18 54.9	+11.3	79.0	19 06.2	+12.4	79.3	19 17.2	+13.4	79.6	19 27.8	+14.5	80.0	19 38.0	+15.6	80.3	19 47.9	+16.6	80.7	19 57.4	+17.7	81.1	20 06.6	+18.7	81.4	15
16	19 06.2	+11.0	77.9	19 18.6	+12.0	78.3	19 30.6	+13.1	78.6	19 42.3	+14.1	79.0	19 53.6	+15.2	79.3	20 04.5	+16.3	79.7	20 15.1	+17.3	80.0	20 25.3	+18.4	80.4	16
17	19 17.2	+10.6	76.9	19 30.6	+11.7	77.2	19 43.7	+12.7	77.6	19 56.4	+13.8	77.9	20 08.8	+14.8	78.3	20 20.8	+15.9	78.6	20 32.4	+17.0	79.0	20 43.7	+18.0	79.4	17
18	19 27.8	+10.2	75.8	19 42.3	+11.3	76.2	19 56.4	+12.4	76.5	20 10.2	+13.4	76.9	20 23.6	+14.5	77.3	20 36.7	+15.5	77.6	20 49.4	+16.5	78.0	21 01.7	+17.6	78.4	18
19	19 38.0	+9.9	74.8	19 53.6	+10.9	75.1	20 08.8	+12.0	75.5	20 23.6	+13.1	75.9	20 38.1	+14.1	76.2	20 52.2	+15.2	76.6	21 05.9	+16.3	77.0	21 19.3	+17.3	77.3	19
20	19 47.9	+9.5	73.7	20 04.5	+10.6	74.1	20 20.8	+11.6	74.5	20 36.7	+12.7	74.8	20 52.2	+13.7	75.2	21 07.4	+14.8	75.5	21 22.2	+15.8	75.9	21 36.6	+16.8	76.3	20
21	19 57.4	+9.2	72.7	20 15.1	+10.2	73.0	20 32.4	+11.3	73.4	20 49.4	+12.3	73.8	21 05.9	+13.4	74.1	21 22.2	+14.4	74.5	21 38.0	+15.4	74.9	21 53.4	+16.5	75.3	21
22	20 06.6	+8.7	71.6	20 25.3	+9.8	72.0	20 43.7	+10.8	72.4	21 01.7	+11.9	72.7	21 19.3	+13.0	73.1	21 36.6	+14.0	73.5	21 53.4	+15.1	73.8	22 09.9	+16.1	74.2	22
23	20 15.3	+8.4	70.6	20 35.1	+9.4	70.9	20 54.5	+10.5	71.3	21 13.6	+11.5	71.7	21 32.3	+12.5	72.0	21 50.6	+13.6	72.4	22 08.5	+14.7	72.8	22 26.0	+15.7	73.2	23
24	20 23.7	+8.0	69.5	20 44.5	+9.1	69.9	21 05.0	+10.1	70.2	21 25.1	+11.1	70.6	21 44.8	+12.2	71.0	22 04.2	+13.2	71.4	22 23.2	+14.2	71.8	22 41.7	+15.3	72.1	24
25	20 31.7	+7.7	68.5	20 53.6	+8.6	68.8	21 15.1	+9.7	69.2	21 36.2	+10.7	69.6	21 57.0	+11.7	69.9	22 17.4	+12.8	70.3	22 37.4	+13.8	70.7	22 57.0	+14.9	71.1	25
26	20 39.4	+7.2	67.4	21 02.2	+8.3	67.8	21 24.8	+9.3	68.1	21 46.9	+10.4	68.5	22 08.7	+11.4	68.9	22 30.2	+12.4	69.3	22 51.2	+13.5	69.6	23 11.9	+14.5	70.0	26
27	20 46.6	+6.9	66.4	21 10.5	+7.9	66.7	21 34.1	+8.8	67.1	21 57.3	+9.9	67.4	22 20.1	+10.9	67.8	22 42.6	+11.9	68.2	23 04.7	+13.0	68.6	23 26.4	+14.0	69.0	27
28	20 53.5	+6.4	65.3	21 18.4	+7.4	65.6	21 42.9	+8.5	66.0	22 07.2	+9.5	66.4	22 31.0	+10.5	66.7	22 54.5	+11.6	67.1	23 17.7	+12.5	67.5	23 40.4	+13.6	67.9	28
29	20 59.9	+6.1	64.2	21 25.8	+7.1	64.6	21 51.4	+8.1	64.9	22 16.7	+9.0	65.3	22 41.5	+10.1	65.7	23 06.1	+11.1	66.1	23 30.2	+12.1	66.5	23 54.0	+13.1	66.9	29
30	21 06.0	+5.6	63.2	21 32.9	+6.6	63.5	21 59.5	+7.6	63.9	22 25.7	+8.7	64.2	22 51.6	+9.7	64.6	23 17.2	+10.6	65.0	23 42.3	+11.7	65.4	24 07.1	+12.7	65.8	30
31	21 11.6	+5.3	62.1	21 39.5	+6.3	62.4	22 07.1	+7.2	62.8	22 34.4	+8.2	63.2	23 01.3	+9.2	63.5	23 27.8	+10.3	63.9	23 54.0	+11.3	64.3	24 19.8	+12.3	64.7	31
32	21 16.9	+4.8	61.0	21 45.8	+5.8	61.4	22 14.3	+6.9	61.7	22 42.6	+7.8	62.1	23 10.5	+8.8	62.5	23 38.1	+9.7	62.9	24 05.3	+10.7	63.2	24 32.1	+11.8	63.7	32
33	21 21.7	+4.4	60.0	21 51.6	+5.4	60.3	22 21.2	+6.3	60.7	22 50.4	+7.4	61.0	23 19.3	+8.3	61.4	23 47.8	+9.4	61.8	24 16.0	+10.4	62.2	24 43.9	+11.3	62.6	33
34	21 26.1	+4.1	58.9	21 57.0	+5.0	59.2	22 27.5	+6.0	59.6	22 57.8	+6.9	59.9	23 27.6	+7.9	60.3	23 57.2	+8.9	60.7	24 26.4	+9.8	61.1	24 55.2	+10.9	61.5	34
35	21 30.2	+3.6	57.8	22 02.0	+4.5	58.2	22 33.5	+5.5	58.5	23 04.7	+6.5	58.9	23 35.5	+7.5	59.2	24 06.1	+8.4	59.6	24 36.2	+9.4	60.0	25 06.1	+10.3	60.4	35
36	21 33.8	+3.2	56.7	22 06.5	+4.2	57.1	22 39.0	+5.1	57.4	23 11.2	+6.0	57.8	23 43.0	+7.0	58.1	24 14.5	+7.9	58.5	24 45.6	+9.0	58.9	25 16.4	+9.9	59.3	36
37	21 37.0	+2.8	55.7	22 10.7	+3.7	56.0	22 44.1	+4.6	56.3	23 17.2	+5.6	56.7	23 50.0	+6.5	57.1	24 22.4	+7.5	57.4	24 54.6	+8.4	57.8	25 26.3	+9.4	58.2	37
38	21 39.8	+2.4	54.6	22 14.4	+3.3	54.9	22 48.7	+4.3	55.3	23 22.8	+5.1	55.6	23 56.5	+6.1	56.0	24 29.9	+7.1	56.3	25 03.0	+8.0	56.7	25 35.7	+9.0	57.1	38
39	21 42.2	+1.9	53.5	22 17.7	+2.9	53.8	22 53.0	+3.7	54.2	23 27.9	+4.7	54.5	24 02.6	+5.6	54.9	24 37.0	+6.5	55.3	25 11.0	+7.5	55.6	25 44.7	+8.4	56.0	39
40	21 44.1	+1.6	52.4	22 20.6	+2.4	52.8	22 56.7	+3.4	53.1	23 32.6	+4.3	53.4	24 08.2	+5.2	53.8	24 43.5	+6.1	54.2	25 18.5	+7.0	54.5	25 53.1	+7.9	54.9	40
41	21 45.7	+1.1	51.4	22 23.0	+2.0	51.7	23 00.1	+2.9	52.0	23 36.9	+3.7	52.4	24 13.4	+4.6	52.7	24 49.6	+5.6	53.1	25 25.5	+6.5	53.4	26 01.0	+7.5	53.8	41
42	21 46.8	+0.7	50.3	22 25.0	+1.6	50.6	23 03.0	+2.4	50.9	23 40.6	+3.4	51.3	24 18.0	+4.3	51.6	24 55.2	+5.1	52.0	25 32.0	+6.0	52.3	26 08.5	+6.9	52.7	42
43	21 47.5	+0.3	49.2	22 26.6	+1.1	49.5	23 05.4	+2.0	49.8	23 44.0	+2.8	50.2	24 22.3	+3.7	50.5	25 00.3	+4.6	50.9	25 38.0	+5.5	51.2	26 15.4	+6.4	51.6	43
44	21 47.8	−0.1	48.1	22 27.7	+0.7	48.4	23 07.4	+1.6	48.8	23 46.8	+2.4	49.1	24 26.0	+3.3	49.4	25 04.9	+4.1	49.8	25 43.5	+5.0	50.1	26 21.8	+5.9	50.5	44
45	21 47.7	−0.6	47.1	22 28.4	+0.3	47.4	23 09.0	+1.1	47.7	23 49.2	+2.0	48.0	24 29.3	+2.8	48.3	25 09.0	+3.7	48.7	25 48.5	+4.5	49.0	26 27.7	+5.4	49.4	45
46	21 47.1	−1.0	46.0	22 28.7	−0.2	46.3	23 10.1	+0.6	46.6	23 51.2	+1.5	46.9	24 32.1	+2.3	47.2	25 12.7	+3.1	47.6	25 53.0	+4.0	47.9	26 33.1	+4.8	48.3	46
47	21 46.1	−1.3	44.9	22 28.5	−0.6	45.2	23 10.7	+0.2	45.5	23 52.7	+1.0	45.8	24 34.4	+1.8	46.1	25 15.8	+2.7	46.5	25 57.0	+3.5	46.8	26 37.9	+4.4	47.2	47
48	21 44.8	−1.8	43.8	22 27.9	−1.0	44.1	23 10.9	−0.2	44.4	23 53.7	+0.5	44.7	24 36.2	+1.4	45.0	25 18.5	+2.1	45.4	26 00.5	+3.0	45.7	26 42.3	+3.8	46.1	48
49	21 43.0	−2.3	42.8	22 26.9	−1.4	43.0	23 10.7	−0.7	43.3	23 54.2	+0.1	43.6	24 37.6	+0.8	43.9	25 20.6	+1.7	44.3	26 03.5	+2.5	44.6	26 46.1	+3.3	44.9	49
50	21 40.7	−2.6	41.7	22 25.5	−1.9	41.9	23 10.0	−1.1	42.2	23 54.3	−0.4	42.5	24 38.4	+0.4	42.8	25 22.3	+1.2	43.1	26 06.0	+1.9	43.5	26 49.4	+2.8	43.8	50
51	21 38.1	−3.0	40.6	22 23.6	−2.4	40.9	23 08.9	−1.6	41.1	23 53.9	−0.8	41.4	24 38.8	−0.1	41.7	25 23.5	+0.7	42.0	26 07.9	+1.5	42.4	26 52.2	+2.2	42.7	51
52	21 35.1	−3.5	39.5	22 21.2	−2.7	39.8	23 07.3	−2.1	40.1	23 53.1	−1.3	40.3	24 38.7	−0.5	40.6	25 24.2	+0.2	40.9	26 09.4	+0.9	41.2	26 54.4	+1.7	41.6	52
53	21 31.6	−3.9	38.5	22 18.5	−3.2	38.7	23 05.2	−2.4	39.0	23 51.8	−1.8	39.2	24 38.2	−1.1	39.5	25 24.4	−0.4	39.8	26 10.3	+0.5	40.1	26 56.1	+1.2	40.5	53
54	21 27.7	−4.3	37.4	22 15.3	−3.6	37.6	23 02.8	−3.0	37.9	23 50.0	−2.2	38.1	24 37.1	−1.5	38.4	25 24.0	−0.8	38.7	26 10.8	−0.1	39.0	26 57.3	+0.6	39.3	54
55	21 23.4	−4.7	36.3	22 11.7	−4.0	36.5	22 59.8	−3.3	36.8	23 47.8	−2.7	37.1	24 35.6	−2.0	37.3	25 23.2	−1.3	37.6	26 10.7	−0.6	37.9	26 57.9	+0.1	38.2	55
56	21 18.7	−5.1	35.2	22 07.7	−4.5	35.5	22 56.5	−3.8	35.7	23 45.1	−3.1	36.0	24 33.6	−2.5	36.2	25 21.9	−1.8	36.5	26 10.1	−1.2	36.8	26 58.0	−0.4	37.1	56
57	21 13.6	−5.5	34.2	22 03.2	−4.9	34.4	22 52.7	−4.3	34.6	23 42.0	−3.6	34.9	24 31.1	−2.9	35.1	25 20.1	−2.3	35.4	26 08.9	−1.6	35.7	26 57.6	−1.0	36.0	57
58	21 08.1	−5.9	33.1	21 58.3	−5.2	33.3	22 48.4	−4.7	33.5	23 38.4	−4.1	33.8	24 28.2	−3.5	34.0	25 17.8	−2.8	34.3	26 07.3	−2.2	34.6	26 56.6	−1.5	34.8	58
59	21 02.2	−6.3	32.0	21 53.1	−5.8	32.2	22 43.7	−5.1	32.5	23 34.3	−4.5	32.7	24 24.7	−3.9	32.9	25 15.0	−3.3	33.2	26 05.1	−2.6	33.5	26 55.1	−2.0	33.7	59
60	20 55.9	−6.7	31.0	21 47.3	−6.1	31.2	22 38.6	−5.5	31.4	23 29.8	−5.0	31.6	24 20.8	−4.4	31.8	25 11.7	−3.8	32.1	26 02.5	−3.2	32.3	26 53.1	−2.6	32.6	60
61	20 49.2	−7.0	29.9	21 41.2	−6.5	30.1	22 33.1	−6.0	30.3	23 24.8	−5.4	30.5	24 16.4	−4.8	30.7	25 07.9	−4.2	31.0	25 59.3	−3.7	31.2	26 50.5	−3.0	31.5	61
62	20 42.2	−7.5	28.8	21 34.7	−7.0	29.0	22 27.1	−6.4	29.2	23 19.4	−5.9	29.4	24 11.6	−5.3	29.7	25 03.7	−4.8	29.9	25 55.6	−4.2	30.1	26 47.5	−3.6	30.4	62
63	20 34.7	−7.9	27.8	21 27.7	−7.3	28.0	22 20.7	−6.9	28.2	23 13.5	−6.3	28.4	24 06.3	−5.8	28.6	24 58.9	−5.2	28.8	25 51.4	−4.6	29.0	26 43.9	−4.2	29.3	63
64	20 26.8	−8.2	26.7	21 20.4	−7.8	26.9	22 13.8	−7.2	27.1	23 07.2	−6.7	27.3	24 00.5	−6.3	27.5	24 53.7	−5.7	27.7	25 46.8	−5.2	27.9	26 39.7	−4.6	28.1	64
65	20 18.6	−8.7	25.7	21 12.6	−8.2	25.8	22 06.6	−7.7	26.0	23 00.5	−7.2	26.2	23 54.2	−6.7	26.4	24 48.0	−6.2	26.6	25 41.6	−5.7	26.8	26 35.1	−5.2	27.0	65
66	20 09.9	−9.0	24.6	21 04.4	−8.5	24.8	21 58.9	−8.1	24.9	22 53.3	−7.7	25.1	23 47.5	−7.1	25.3	24 41.8	−6.7	25.5	25 35.9	−6.2	25.7	26 29.9	−5.7	25.9	66
67	20 00.9	−9.3	23.6	20 55.9	−8.9	23.7	21 50.8	−8.5	23.9	22 45.6	−8.0	24.0	23 40.4	−7.6	24.2	24 35.1	−7.2	24.4	25 29.7	−6.7	24.6	26 24.2	−6.2	24.8	67
68	19 51.6	−9.8	22.5	20 47.0	−9.4	22.7	21 42.3	−8.9	22.8	22 37.6	−8.5	23.0	23 32.8	−8.1	23.1	24 27.9	−7.6	23.3	25 23.0	−7.2	23.5	26 18.0	−6.7	23.7	68
69	19 41.8	−10.1	21.5	20 37.6	−9.7	21.6	21 33.4	−9.3	21.7	22 29.1	−8.9	21.9	23 24.7	−8.5	22.0	24 20.3	−8.1	22.2	25 15.8	−7.6	22.4	26 11.3	−7.3	22.6	69
70	19 31.7	−10.5	20.4	20 27.9	−10.1	20.5	21 24.1	−9.8	20.7	22 20.2	−9.4	20.8	23 16.2	−8.9	21.0	24 12.2	−8.5	21.1	25 08.2	−8.2	21.3	26 04.0	−7.7	21.5	70
71	19 21.2	−10.8	19.4	20 17.8	−10.5	19.5	21 14.3	−10.1	19.6	22 10.8	−9.7	19.8	23 07.3	−9.4	19.9	24 03.7	−9.0	20.0	25 00.0	−8.6	20.2	25 56.3	−8.2	20.4	71
72	19 10.4	−11.2	18.3	20 07.3	−10.8	18.4	21 04.2	−10.5	18.6	22 01.1	−10.2	18.7	22 57.9	−9.8	18.8	23 54.7	−9.5	19.0	24 51.4	−9.1	19.1	25 48.1	−8.8	19.3	72
73	18 59.2	−11.5	17.3	19 56.5	−11.2	17.4	20 53.7	−10.9	17.5	21 50.9	−10.5	17.6	22 48.1	−10.2	17.8	23 45.2	−9.9	17.9	24 42.3	−9.6	18.0	25 39.3	−9.2	18.2	73
74	18 47.7	−11.9	16.3	19 45.3	−11.6	16.4	20 42.8	−11.2	16.5	21 40.4	−11.0	16.6	22 37.9	−10.7	16.7	23 35.3	−10.3	16.8	24 32.7	−10.0	16.9	25 30.1	−9.7	17.1	74
75	18 35.8	−12.2	15.2	19 33.7	−11.9	15.3	20 31.6	−11.7	15.4	21 29.4	−11.4	15.5	22 27.2	−11.1	15.6	23 25.0	−10.8	15.7	24 22.7	−10.5	15.9	25 20.4	−10.2	16.0	75
76	18 23.6	−12.5	14.2	19 21.8	−12.3	14.3	20 19.9	−12.0	14.4	21 18.0	−11.7	14.5	22 16.1	−11.5	14.6	23 14.2	−11.3	14.7	24 12.2	−10.9	14.8	25 10.2	−10.7	14.9	76
77	18 11.1	−12.9	13.2	19 09.5	−12.6	13.2	20 07.9	−12.4	13.3	21 06.3	−12.2	13.4	22 04.6	−11.9	13.5	23 02.9	−11.6	13.6	24 01.3	−11.4	13.7	24 59.5	−11.1	13.8	77
78	17 58.2	−13.2	12.1	18 56.9	−13.0	12.2	19 55.5	−12.8	12.3	20 54.1	−12.5	12.4	21 52.7	−12.3	12.4	22 51.3	−12.1	12.5	23 49.9	−11.9	12.6	24 48.4	−11.6	12.7	78
79	17 45.0	−13.5	11.1	18 43.9	−13.3	11.2	19 42.7	−13.1	11.2	20 41.6	−12.9	11.3	21 40.4	−12.7	11.4	22 39.2	−12.5	11.5	23 38.0	−12.3	11.5	24 36.8	−12.1	11.6	79
80	17 31.5	−13.8	10.1	18 30.6	−13.7	10.1	19 29.6	−13.4	10.2	20 28.7	−13.3	10.3	21 27.7	−13.1	10.3	22 26.7	−12.9	10.4	23 25.7	−12.7	10.5	24 24.7	−12.5	10.6	80
81	17 17.7	−14.2	9.1	18 16.9	−14.0	9.1	19 16.2	−13.9	9.2	20 15.4	−13.7	9.2	21 14.6	−13.5	9.3	22 13.8	−13.3	9.3	23 13.0	−13.1	9.4	24 12.2	−13.0	9.5	81
82	17 03.5	−14.4	8.0	18 02.9	−14.3	8.1	19 02.3	−14.1	8.1	20 01.7	−14.0	8.2	21 01.1	−13.8	8.2	22 00.5	−13.7	8.3	22 59.9	−13.6	8.4	23 59.2	−13.4	8.4	82
83	16 49.1	−14.7	7.0	17 48.6	−14.6	7.1	18 48.2	−14.5	7.1	19 47.7	−14.3	7.2	20 47.3	−14.3	7.2	21 46.8	−14.1	7.2	22 46.3	−14.0	7.3	23 45.8	−13.9	7.4	83
84	16 34.4	−15.1	6.0	17 34.0	−14.9	6.0	18 33.7	−14.8	6.1	19 33.4	−14.8	6.1	20 33.0	−14.6	6.2	21 32.7	−14.5	6.2	22 32.3	−14.4	6.2	23 31.9	−14.2	6.3	84
85	16 19.3	−15.3	5.0	17 19.1	−15.2	5.0	18 18.9	−15.2	5.1	19 18.6	−15.0	5.1	20 18.4	−15.0	5.1	21 18.2	−14.9	5.2	22 17.9	−14.8	5.2	23 17.7	−14.7	5.2	85
86	16 04.0	−15.6	4.0	17 03.9	−15.6	4.0	18 03.7	−15.4	4.0	19 03.6	−15.4	4.1	20 03.4	−15.3	4.1	21 03.3	−15.3	4.1	22 03.1	−15.2	4.1	23 03.0	−15.2	4.2	86
87	15 48.4	−15.8	3.0	16 48.3	−15.8	3.0	17 48.3	−15.8	3.0	18 48.2	−15.8	3.0	19 48.1	−15.7	3.1	20 48.0	−15.6	3.1	21 47.9	−15.6	3.1	22 47.8	−15.5	3.1	87
88	15 32.6	−16.2	2.0	16 32.5	−16.1	2.0	17 32.5	−16.1	2.0	18 32.4	−16.0	2.0	19 32.4	−16.0	2.0	20 32.4	−16.0	2.1	21 32.3	−15.9	2.1	22 32.3	−16.0	2.1	88
89	15 16.4	−16.4	1.0	16 16.4	−16.4	1.0	17 16.4	−16.4	1.0	18 16.4	−16.4	1.0	19 16.4	−16.4	1.0	20 16.4	−16.4	1.0	21 16.4	−16.4	1.0	22 16.3	−16.3	1.0	89
90	15 00.0	−16.7	0.0	16 00.0	−16.7	0.0	17 00.0	−16.7	0.0	18 00.0	−16.7	0.0	19 00.0	−16.7	0.0	20 00.0	−16.7	0.0	21 00.0	−16.7	0.0	22 00.0	−16.7	0.0	90
	15°			16°			17°			18°			19°			20°			21°			22°			

LATITUDE **CONTRARY** NAME TO DECLINATION **L.H.A. 74°, 286°**

Dec.	15° Hc	d	Z	16° Hc	d	Z	17° Hc	d	Z	18° Hc	d	Z	Dec.
°	° ′	′	°	° ′	′	°	° ′	′	°	° ′	′	°	°
0	15 26.5	−16.3	94.2	15 21.9	−17.3	94.5	15 17.0	−18.3	94.8	15 11.8	−19.3	95.1	0
1	15 10.2	−16.5	95.2	15 04.6	−17.5	95.5	14 58.7	−18.6	95.8	14 52.5	−19.6	96.0	1
2	14 53.7	−16.8	96.2	14 47.1	−17.8	96.5	14 40.1	−18.8	96.8	14 32.9	−19.8	97.0	2
3	14 36.9	−17.0	97.2	14 29.3	−18.1	97.5	14 21.3	−19.1	97.7	14 13.1	−20.1	98.0	3
4	14 19.9	−17.2	98.2	14 11.2	−18.3	98.5	14 02.2	−19.2	98.7	13 53.0	−20.3	99.0	4
5	14 02.7	−17.5	99.2	13 52.9	−18.5	99.5	13 43.0	−19.6	99.7	13 32.7	−20.5	99.9	5
6	13 45.2	−17.8	100.2	13 34.4	−18.7	100.4	13 23.4	−19.7	100.7	13 12.2	−20.7	100.9	6
7	13 27.4	−17.9	101.2	13 15.7	−19.0	101.4	13 03.7	−20.0	101.6	12 51.5	−21.0	101.9	7
8	13 09.5	−18.2	102.2	12 56.7	−19.2	102.4	12 43.7	−20.1	102.6	12 30.5	−21.1	102.8	8
9	12 51.3	−18.4	103.1	12 37.5	−19.4	103.4	12 23.6	−20.4	103.6	12 09.4	−21.4	103.8	9
10	12 32.9	−18.6	104.1	12 18.1	−19.6	104.3	12 03.2	−20.6	104.5	11 48.0	−21.5	104.7	10
11	12 14.3	−18.9	105.1	11 58.5	−19.8	105.3	11 42.6	−20.7	105.5	11 26.5	−21.7	105.7	11
12	11 55.4	−19.0	106.1	11 38.7	−19.9	106.3	11 21.9	−21.0	106.5	11 04.8	−21.9	106.6	12
13	11 36.4	−19.2	107.0	11 18.8	−20.2	107.2	11 00.9	−21.1	107.4	10 42.9	−22.1	107.6	13
14	11 17.2	−19.4	108.0	10 58.6	−20.4	108.2	10 39.8	−21.3	108.4	10 20.8	−22.2	108.5	14
15	10 57.8	−19.6	109.0	10 38.2	−20.5	109.1	10 18.5	−21.5	109.3	9 58.6	−22.4	109.5	15
16	10 38.2	−19.7	109.9	10 17.7	−20.7	110.1	9 57.0	−21.6	110.3	9 36.2	−22.6	110.4	16
17	10 18.5	−19.9	110.9	9 57.0	−20.8	111.0	9 35.4	−21.8	111.2	9 13.6	−22.7	111.4	17
18	9 58.6	−20.1	111.8	9 36.2	−21.1	112.0	9 13.6	−21.9	112.2	8 50.9	−22.8	112.3	18
19	9 38.5	−20.3	112.8	9 15.1	−21.1	112.9	8 51.7	−22.1	113.1	8 28.1	−23.0	113.2	19
20	9 18.2	−20.4	113.7	8 54.0	−21.3	113.9	8 29.6	−22.2	114.0	8 05.1	−23.1	114.2	20
21	8 57.8	−20.5	114.7	8 32.7	−21.5	114.8	8 07.4	−22.3	115.0	7 42.0	−23.2	115.1	21
22	8 37.3	−20.7	115.7	8 11.2	−21.5	115.8	7 45.1	−22.5	115.9	7 18.8	−23.3	116.0	22
23	8 16.6	−20.8	116.6	7 49.7	−21.7	116.7	7 22.6	−22.5	116.8	6 55.5	−23.5	117.0	23
24	7 55.8	−21.0	117.5	7 28.0	−21.8	117.7	7 00.1	−22.7	117.8	6 32.0	−23.5	117.9	24
25	7 34.8	−21.0	118.5	7 06.2	−22.0	118.6	6 37.4	−22.8	118.7	6 08.5	−23.6	118.8	25
26	7 13.8	−21.2	119.4	6 44.2	−22.0	119.5	6 14.6	−22.9	119.6	5 44.9	−23.7	119.7	26
27	6 52.6	−21.3	120.4	6 22.2	−22.2	120.5	5 51.7	−23.0	120.6	5 21.2	−23.9	120.7	27
28	6 31.3	−21.4	121.3	6 00.0	−22.2	121.4	5 28.7	−23.0	121.5	4 57.3	−23.8	121.6	28
29	6 09.9	−21.5	122.3	5 37.8	−22.3	122.3	5 05.7	−23.2	122.4	4 33.5	−24.0	122.5	29
30	5 48.4	−21.6	123.2	5 15.5	−22.4	123.3	4 42.5	−23.2	123.4	4 09.5	−24.0	123.4	30
31	5 26.8	−21.7	124.1	4 53.1	−22.5	124.2	4 19.3	−23.3	124.3	3 45.5	−24.1	124.3	31
32	5 05.1	−21.8	125.1	4 30.6	−22.6	125.1	3 56.0	−23.3	125.2	3 21.4	−24.1	125.3	32
33	4 43.3	−21.8	126.0	4 08.0	−22.6	126.1	3 32.7	−23.4	126.1	2 57.3	−24.2	126.2	33
34	4 21.5	−21.9	126.9	3 45.4	−22.7	127.0	3 09.3	−23.4	127.0	2 33.1	−24.2	127.1	34
35	3 59.6	−22.0	127.9	3 22.7	−22.7	127.9	2 45.9	−23.5	128.0	2 08.9	−24.2	128.0	35
36	3 37.6	−22.0	128.8	3 00.0	−22.8	128.9	2 22.4	−23.6	128.9	1 44.7	−24.3	128.9	36
37	3 15.6	−22.1	129.7	2 37.2	−22.8	129.8	1 58.8	−23.5	129.8	1 20.4	−24.3	129.8	37
38	2 53.5	−22.1	130.7	2 14.4	−22.8	130.7	1 35.3	−23.6	130.7	0 56.1	−24.3	130.7	38
39	2 31.4	−22.1	131.6	1 51.6	−22.9	131.6	1 11.7	−23.6	131.7	0 31.8	−24.3	131.7	39
40	2 09.3	−22.2	132.5	1 28.7	−22.9	132.6	0 48.1	−23.6	132.6	0 07.5	−24.3	132.6	40
41	1 47.1	−22.3	133.5	1 05.8	−22.9	133.5	0 24.5	−23.6	133.5	0 16.8	+24.3	46.5	41
42	1 24.8	−22.2	134.4	0 42.9	−23.0	134.4	0 00.9	−23.6	134.4	0 41.1	+24.3	45.6	42
43	1 02.6	−22.3	135.3	0 19.9	−22.9	135.3	0 22.7	+23.7	44.7	1 05.4	+24.3	44.7	43
44	0 40.3	−22.2	136.2	0 03.0	+23.0	43.7	0 46.4	+23.6	43.8	1 29.7	+24.3	43.8	44
45	0 18.1	−22.3	137.2	0 26.0	+22.9	42.8	1 10.0	+23.5	42.8	1 54.0	+24.2	42.9	45
46	0 04.2	+22.3	41.9	0 48.9	+22.9	41.9	1 33.5	+23.6	41.9	2 18.2	+24.2	41.9	46
47	0 26.5	+22.3	41.0	1 11.8	+22.9	41.0	1 57.1	+23.5	41.0	2 42.4	+24.1	41.0	47
48	0 48.8	+22.2	40.0	1 34.7	+22.9	40.0	2 20.6	+23.5	40.1	3 06.5	+24.1	40.1	48
49	1 11.0	+22.3	39.1	1 57.6	+22.8	39.1	2 44.1	+23.5	39.2	3 30.6	+24.1	39.2	49
50	1 33.3	+22.2	38.2	2 20.4	+22.8	38.2	3 07.6	+23.4	38.2	3 54.7	+24.0	38.3	50
51	1 55.5	+22.2	37.2	2 43.2	+22.8	37.3	3 31.0	+23.3	37.3	4 18.7	+23.9	37.3	51
52	2 17.7	+22.1	36.3	3 06.0	+22.7	36.3	3 54.3	+23.3	36.4	4 42.6	+23.9	36.4	52
53	2 39.8	+22.1	35.4	3 28.7	+22.7	35.4	4 17.6	+23.2	35.5	5 06.5	+23.7	35.5	53
54	3 01.9	+22.1	34.5	3 51.4	+22.6	34.5	4 40.8	+23.2	34.5	5 30.2	+23.7	34.6	54
55	3 24.0	+22.0	33.5	4 14.0	+22.5	33.6	5 04.0	+23.0	33.6	5 53.9	+23.6	33.7	55
56	3 46.0	+21.9	32.6	4 36.5	+22.5	32.6	5 27.0	+23.0	32.7	6 17.5	+23.5	32.7	56
57	4 07.9	+21.9	31.7	4 59.0	+22.4	31.7	5 50.0	+22.9	31.8	6 41.0	+23.4	31.8	57
58	4 29.8	+21.8	30.7	5 21.4	+22.3	30.8	6 12.9	+22.8	30.8	7 04.4	+23.3	30.9	58
59	4 51.6	+21.7	29.8	5 43.7	+22.2	29.8	6 35.7	+22.7	29.9	7 27.7	+23.2	30.0	59
60	5 13.3	+21.7	28.9	6 05.9	+22.1	28.9	6 58.4	+22.6	29.0	7 50.9	+23.0	29.0	60
61	5 35.0	+21.5	27.9	6 28.0	+22.0	28.0	7 21.0	+22.4	28.0	8 13.9	+22.9	28.1	61
62	5 56.5	+21.5	27.0	6 50.0	+21.9	27.0	7 43.4	+22.4	27.1	8 36.8	+22.8	27.2	62
63	6 18.0	+21.4	26.0	7 11.9	+21.8	26.1	8 05.8	+22.2	26.2	8 59.6	+22.7	26.2	63
64	6 39.4	+21.2	25.1	7 33.7	+21.7	25.2	8 28.0	+22.1	25.2	9 22.3	+22.4	25.3	64
65	7 00.6	+21.2	24.2	7 55.4	+21.5	24.2	8 50.1	+21.9	24.3	9 44.7	+22.4	24.3	65
66	7 21.8	+21.0	23.2	8 16.9	+21.4	23.3	9 12.0	+21.8	23.3	10 07.1	+22.2	23.4	66
67	7 42.8	+20.9	22.3	8 38.3	+21.3	22.3	9 33.8	+21.6	22.4	10 29.3	+22.0	22.5	67
68	8 03.7	+20.8	21.3	8 59.6	+21.1	21.4	9 55.4	+21.5	21.4	10 51.3	+21.8	21.5	68
69	8 24.5	+20.6	20.4	9 20.7	+21.0	20.4	10 16.9	+21.3	20.5	11 13.1	+21.6	20.6	69
70	8 45.1	+20.5	19.4	9 41.7	+20.8	19.5	10 38.2	+21.2	19.5	11 34.7	+21.5	19.6	70
71	9 05.6	+20.3	18.5	10 02.5	+20.6	18.5	10 59.4	+20.9	18.6	11 56.2	+21.3	18.7	71
72	9 25.9	+20.2	17.5	10 23.1	+20.5	17.6	11 20.3	+20.8	17.6	12 17.5	+21.1	17.7	72
73	9 46.1	+20.0	16.6	10 43.6	+20.3	16.6	11 41.1	+20.6	16.7	12 38.6	+20.8	16.7	73
74	10 06.1	+19.9	15.6	11 03.9	+20.1	15.7	12 01.7	+20.4	15.7	12 59.4	+20.7	15.8	74
75	10 26.0	+19.7	14.7	11 24.0	+20.0	14.7	12 22.1	+20.2	14.8	13 20.1	+20.4	14.8	75
76	10 45.7	+19.5	13.7	11 44.0	+19.7	13.7	12 42.3	+19.9	13.8	13 40.5	+20.2	13.8	76
77	11 05.2	+19.3	12.7	12 03.7	+19.6	12.8	13 02.2	+19.8	12.8	14 00.7	+20.0	12.9	77
78	11 24.5	+19.2	11.8	12 23.3	+19.3	11.8	13 22.0	+19.5	11.9	14 20.7	+19.7	11.9	78
79	11 43.7	+18.9	10.8	12 42.6	+19.1	10.8	13 41.5	+19.3	10.9	14 40.4	+19.5	10.9	79
80	12 02.6	+18.8	9.8	13 01.7	+18.9	9.9	14 00.8	+19.1	9.9	14 59.9	+19.3	10.0	80
81	12 21.4	+18.5	8.9	13 20.6	+18.7	8.9	14 19.9	+18.8	8.9	15 19.2	+19.0	9.0	81
82	12 39.9	+18.3	7.9	13 39.3	+18.5	7.9	14 38.7	+18.6	7.9	15 38.2	+18.7	8.0	82
83	12 58.2	+18.1	6.9	13 57.8	+18.2	6.9	14 57.3	+18.4	7.0	15 56.9	+18.4	7.0	83
84	13 16.3	+17.9	5.9	14 16.0	+18.0	6.0	15 15.7	+18.0	6.0	16 15.3	+18.2	6.0	84
85	13 34.2	+17.6	4.9	14 34.0	+17.7	5.0	15 33.7	+17.8	5.0	16 33.5	+17.9	5.0	85
86	13 51.8	+17.4	4.0	14 51.7	+17.5	4.0	15 51.5	+17.6	4.0	16 51.4	+17.6	4.0	86
87	14 09.2	+17.2	3.0	15 09.2	+17.2	3.0	16 09.1	+17.2	3.0	17 09.0	+17.3	3.0	87
88	14 26.4	+16.9	2.0	15 26.4	+16.9	2.0	16 26.3	+17.0	2.0	17 26.3	+17.0	2.0	88
89	14 43.3	+16.7	1.0	15 43.3	+16.7	1.0	16 43.3	+16.7	1.0	17 43.3	+16.7	1.0	89
90	15 00.0	+16.4	0.0	16 00.0	+16.4	0.0	17 00.0	+16.4	0.0	18 00.0	+16.4	0.0	90
	15°			16°			17°			18°			

Dec.	19° Hc	d	Z	20° Hc	d	Z	21° Hc	d	Z	22° Hc	d	Z	Dec.
°	° ′	′	°	° ′	′	°	° ′	′	°	° ′	′	°	°
0	15 06.4	−20.3	95.3	15 00.7	−21.4	95.6	14 54.7	−22.4	95.9	14 48.4	−23.3	96.1	0
1	14 46.1	−20.6	96.3	14 39.3	−21.6	96.6	14 32.3	−22.6	96.8	14 25.1	−23.6	97.1	1
2	14 25.5	−20.9	97.3	14 17.7	−21.8	97.5	14 09.7	−22.8	97.8	14 01.5	−23.8	98.0	2
3	14 04.6	−21.1	98.2	13 55.9	−22.1	98.5	13 46.9	−23.1	98.7	13 37.7	−24.1	99.0	3
4	13 43.5	−21.2	99.2	13 33.8	−22.3	99.4	13 23.8	−23.2	99.7	13 13.6	−24.2	99.9	4
5	13 22.3	−21.6	100.2	13 11.5	−22.5	100.4	13 00.6	−23.5	100.6	12 49.4	−24.4	100.9	5
6	13 00.7	−21.7	101.1	12 49.0	−22.7	101.4	12 37.1	−23.6	101.6	12 25.0	−24.7	101.8	6
7	12 39.0	−21.9	102.1	12 26.3	−22.8	102.3	12 13.5	−23.9	102.5	12 00.3	−24.8	102.7	7
8	12 17.1	−22.1	103.0	12 03.5	−23.1	103.2	11 49.6	−24.0	103.5	11 35.5	−25.0	103.7	8
9	11 55.0	−22.3	104.0	11 40.4	−23.3	104.2	11 25.6	−24.3	104.4	11 10.5	−25.1	104.6	9
10	11 32.7	−22.5	104.9	11 17.1	−23.5	105.1	11 01.3	−24.4	105.3	10 45.4	−25.3	105.5	10
11	11 10.2	−22.7	105.9	10 53.6	−23.6	106.1	10 36.9	−24.5	106.3	10 20.1	−25.5	106.4	11
12	10 47.5	−22.9	106.8	10 30.0	−23.8	107.0	10 12.4	−24.7	107.2	9 54.6	−25.6	107.4	12
13	10 24.6	−23.0	107.8	10 06.2	−23.9	107.9	9 47.7	−24.9	108.1	9 29.0	−25.8	108.3	13
14	10 01.6	−23.1	108.7	9 42.3	−24.1	108.9	9 22.8	−25.0	109.0	9 03.2	−25.9	109.2	14
15	9 38.5	−23.4	109.6	9 18.2	−24.2	109.8	8 57.8	−25.1	110.0	8 37.3	−26.1	110.1	15
16	9 15.1	−23.4	110.6	8 54.0	−24.4	110.7	8 32.7	−25.3	110.9	8 11.2	−26.1	111.0	16
17	8 51.7	−23.6	111.5	8 29.6	−24.5	111.7	8 07.4	−25.4	111.8	7 45.1	−26.3	111.9	17
18	8 28.1	−23.7	112.4	8 05.1	−24.6	112.6	7 42.0	−25.5	112.7	7 18.8	−26.4	112.8	18
19	8 04.4	−23.9	113.4	7 40.5	−24.7	113.5	7 16.5	−25.6	113.6	6 52.4	−26.5	113.7	19
20	7 40.5	−24.0	114.3	7 15.8	−24.9	114.4	6 50.9	−25.7	114.5	6 25.9	−26.5	114.6	20
21	7 16.5	−24.1	115.2	6 50.9	−25.0	115.3	6 25.2	−25.8	115.4	5 59.4	−26.7	115.5	21
22	6 52.4	−24.2	116.1	6 25.9	−25.0	116.2	5 59.4	−25.9	116.3	5 32.7	−26.8	116.4	22
23	6 28.2	−24.3	117.1	6 00.9	−25.2	117.2	5 33.5	−26.0	117.2	5 05.9	−26.8	117.3	23
24	6 03.9	−24.3	118.0	5 35.7	−25.2	118.1	5 07.5	−26.1	118.2	4 39.1	−26.9	118.2	24
25	5 39.6	−24.5	118.9	5 10.5	−25.3	119.0	4 41.4	−26.1	119.1	4 12.2	−26.9	119.1	25
26	5 15.1	−24.6	119.8	4 45.2	−25.4	119.9	4 15.3	−26.2	120.0	3 45.3	−27.0	120.0	26
27	4 50.5	−24.6	120.7	4 19.8	−25.4	120.8	3 49.1	−26.3	120.9	3 18.3	−27.1	120.9	27
28	4 25.9	−24.7	121.6	3 54.4	−25.5	121.7	3 22.8	−26.3	121.8	2 51.2	−27.1	121.8	28
29	4 01.2	−24.8	122.6	3 28.9	−25.6	122.6	2 56.5	−26.3	122.7	2 24.1	−27.1	122.7	29
30	3 36.4	−24.8	123.5	3 03.3	−25.6	123.5	2 30.2	−26.4	123.6	1 57.0	−27.2	123.6	30
31	3 11.6	−24.8	124.4	2 37.7	−25.6	124.4	2 03.8	−26.4	124.5	1 29.8	−27.2	124.5	31
32	2 46.8	−24.9	125.3	2 12.1	−25.7	125.3	1 37.4	−26.5	125.4	1 02.6	−27.2	125.4	32
33	2 21.9	−25.0	126.2	1 46.4	−25.7	126.2	1 10.9	−26.4	126.3	0 35.4	−27.2	126.3	33
34	1 56.9	−24.9	127.1	1 20.7	−25.7	127.1	0 44.5	−26.5	127.2	0 08.2	−27.2	127.2	34
35	1 32.0	−25.0	128.0	0 55.0	−25.7	128.0	0 18.0	−26.5	128.1	0 19.0	+27.2	51.9	35
36	1 07.0	−25.0	128.9	0 29.3	−25.8	128.9	0 08.5	+26.4	51.0	0 46.2	+27.2	51.1	36
37	0 42.0	−25.0	129.8	0 03.5	−25.7	129.9	0 34.9	+26.5	50.2	1 13.4	+27.1	50.2	37
38	0 17.0	−25.1	130.8	0 22.2	+25.8	49.2	1 01.4	+26.4	49.3	1 40.5	+27.2	49.3	38
39	0 08.1	+25.0	48.3	0 48.0	+25.7	48.3	1 27.8	+26.5	48.4	2 07.7	+27.1	48.4	39
40	0 33.1	+25.0	47.4	1 13.7	+25.7	47.4	1 54.3	+26.3	47.5	2 34.8	+27.1	47.5	40
41	0 58.1	+25.0	46.5	1 39.4	+25.7	46.5	2 20.6	+26.4	46.6	3 01.9	+27.0	46.6	41
42	1 23.1	+25.0	45.6	2 05.1	+25.6	45.6	2 47.0	+26.3	45.7	3 28.9	+27.0	45.7	42
43	1 48.1	+24.9	44.7	2 30.7	+25.6	44.7	3 13.3	+26.3	44.8	3 55.9	+26.9	44.8	43
44	2 13.0	+24.9	43.8	2 56.3	+25.6	43.8	3 39.6	+26.2	43.9	4 22.8	+26.9	43.9	44
45	2 37.9	+24.9	42.9	3 21.9	+25.5	42.9	4 05.8	+26.2	43.0	4 49.7	+26.8	43.0	45
46	3 02.8	+24.8	42.0	3 47.4	+25.5	42.0	4 32.0	+26.1	42.1	5 16.5	+26.7	42.1	46
47	3 27.6	+24.8	41.1	4 12.9	+25.4	41.1	4 58.1	+26.0	41.2	5 43.2	+26.7	41.2	47
48	3 52.4	+24.7	40.1	4 38.3	+25.3	40.2	5 24.1	+25.9	40.2	6 09.9	+26.5	40.3	48
49	4 17.1	+24.7	39.2	5 03.6	+25.2	39.3	5 50.0	+25.9	39.3	6 36.4	+26.4	39.4	49
50	4 41.8	+24.6	38.3	5 28.8	+25.2	38.4	6 15.9	+25.7	38.4	7 02.8	+26.4	38.5	50
51	5 06.4	+24.5	37.4	5 54.0	+25.1	37.5	6 41.6	+25.7	37.5	7 29.2	+26.2	37.6	51
52	5 30.9	+24.4	36.5	6 19.1	+25.0	36.5	7 07.3	+25.5	36.6	7 55.4	+26.1	36.7	52
53	5 55.3	+24.3	35.6	6 44.1	+24.9	35.6	7 32.8	+25.5	35.7	8 21.5	+26.0	35.8	53
54	6 19.6	+24.2	34.6	7 09.0	+24.7	34.7	7 58.3	+25.3	34.8	8 47.5	+25.9	34.9	54
55	6 43.8	+24.2	33.7	7 33.7	+24.7	33.8	8 23.6	+25.2	33.9	9 13.4	+25.7	34.0	55
56	7 08.0	+24.0	32.8	7 58.4	+24.5	32.9	8 48.8	+25.0	33.0	9 39.1	+25.5	33.0	56
57	7 32.0	+23.9	31.9	8 22.9	+24.4	32.0	9 13.8	+24.9	32.0	10 04.6	+25.5	32.1	57
58	7 55.9	+23.8	31.0	8 47.3	+24.3	31.0	9 38.7	+24.8	31.1	10 30.1	+25.2	31.2	58
59	8 19.7	+23.6	30.0	9 11.6	+24.1	30.1	10 03.5	+24.6	30.2	10 55.3	+25.1	30.3	59
60	8 43.3	+23.5	29.1	9 35.7	+24.0	29.2	10 28.1	+24.4	29.3	11 20.4	+24.9	29.4	60
61	9 06.8	+23.4	28.2	9 59.7	+23.8	28.2	10 52.5	+24.3	28.3	11 45.3	+24.8	28.4	61
62	9 30.2	+23.2	27.2	10 23.5	+23.7	27.3	11 16.8	+24.1	27.4	12 10.1	+24.5	27.5	62
63	9 53.4	+23.1	26.3	10 47.2	+23.5	26.4	11 40.9	+24.0	26.5	12 34.6	+24.4	26.6	63
64	10 16.5	+22.9	25.4	11 10.7	+23.3	25.4	12 04.9	+23.7	25.5	12 59.0	+24.1	25.6	64
65	10 39.4	+22.7	24.4	11 34.0	+23.1	24.5	12 28.6	+23.5	24.6	13 23.1	+24.0	24.7	65
66	11 02.1	+22.6	23.5	11 57.1	+23.0	23.6	12 52.1	+23.4	23.6	13 47.1	+23.7	23.7	66
67	11 24.7	+22.4	22.5	12 20.1	+22.7	22.6	13 15.5	+23.1	22.7	14 10.8	+23.5	22.8	67
68	11 47.1	+22.2	21.6	12 42.8	+22.6	21.7	13 38.6	+22.9	21.7	14 34.3	+23.3	21.8	68
69	12 09.3	+22.0	20.6	13 05.4	+22.3	20.7	14 01.5	+22.7	20.8	14 57.6	+23.0	20.9	69
70	12 31.3	+21.8	19.7	13 27.7	+22.2	19.8	14 24.2	+22.4	19.8	15 20.6	+22.8	19.9	70
71	12 53.1	+21.5	18.7	13 49.9	+21.9	18.8	14 46.6	+22.3	18.9	15 43.4	+22.5	19.0	71
72	13 14.6	+21.4	17.8	14 11.8	+21.6	17.8	15 08.9	+21.9	17.9	16 05.9	+22.3	18.0	72
73	13 36.0	+21.2	16.8	14 33.4	+21.5	16.9	15 30.8	+21.8	17.0	16 28.2	+22.0	17.0	73
74	13 57.2	+20.9	15.8	14 54.9	+21.2	15.9	15 52.6	+21.4	16.0	16 50.2	+21.8	16.1	74
75	14 18.1	+20.7	14.9	15 16.1	+20.9	14.9	16 14.0	+21.2	15.0	17 12.0	+21.4	15.1	75
76	14 38.8	+20.4	13.9	15 37.0	+20.7	14.0	16 35.2	+20.9	14.0	17 33.4	+21.2	14.1	76
77	14 59.2	+20.2	12.9	15 57.7	+20.4	13.0	16 56.1	+20.7	13.1	17 54.6	+20.8	13.1	77
78	15 19.4	+19.9	12.0	16 18.1	+20.1	12.0	17 16.8	+20.3	12.1	18 15.4	+20.6	12.1	78
79	15 39.3	+19.7	11.0	16 38.2	+19.9	11.0	17 37.1	+20.1	11.1	18 36.0	+20.3	11.2	79
80	15 59.0	+19.4	10.0	16 58.1	+19.6	10.1	17 57.2	+19.7	10.1	18 56.3	+19.9	10.2	80
81	16 18.4	+19.2	9.0	17 17.7	+19.3	9.1	18 16.9	+19.5	9.1	19 16.2	+19.6	9.2	81
82	16 37.6	+18.8	8.0	17 37.0	+19.0	8.1	18 36.4	+19.1	8.1	19 35.8	+19.3	8.2	82
83	16 56.4	+18.6	7.0	17 56.0	+18.7	7.1	18 55.5	+18.8	7.1	19 55.1	+18.9	7.2	83
84	17 15.0	+18.3	6.0	18 14.7	+18.3	6.1	19 14.3	+18.5	6.1	20 14.0	+18.6	6.1	84
85	17 33.3	+17.9	5.0	18 33.0	+18.1	5.1	19 32.8	+18.1	5.1	20 32.6	+18.2	5.1	85
86	17 51.2	+17.7	4.0	18 51.1	+17.7	4.1	19 50.9	+17.8	4.1	20 50.8	+17.9	4.1	86
87	18 08.9	+17.4	3.0	19 08.8	+17.4	3.1	20 08.7	+17.5	3.1	21 08.7	+17.5	3.1	87
88	18 26.3	+17.0	2.0	19 26.2	+17.1	2.0	20 26.2	+17.1	2.1	21 26.2	+17.1	2.1	88
89	18 43.3	+16.7	1.0	19 43.3	+16.7	1.0	20 43.3	+16.7	1.0	21 43.3	+16.7	1.0	89
90	19 00.0	+16.4	0.0	20 00.0	+16.4	0.0	21 00.0	+16.4	0.0	22 00.0	+16.3	0.0	90
	19°			20°			21°			22°			

S. Lat. { L.H.A. greater than 180° ....Zn=180°−Z
L.H.A. less than 180°...........Zn=180°+Z

LATITUDE **SAME** NAME AS DECLINATION **L.H.A. 106°, 254°**

151

Dec.	15° Hc	d	Z	16° Hc	d	Z	17° Hc	d	Z	18° Hc	d	Z	19° Hc	d	Z	20° Hc	d	Z	21° Hc	d	Z	22° Hc	d	Z	Dec.
°	° ′	′	°	° ′	′	°	° ′	′	°	° ′	′	°	° ′	′	°	° ′	′	°	° ′	′	°	° ′	′	°	°
0	14 28.7	+15.9	94.0	14 24.4	+16.9	94.2	14 19.8	+18.0	94.5	14 15.0	+19.0	94.7	14 09.9	+20.0	95.0	14 04.6	+21.0	95.2	13 59.0	+22.0	95.5	13 53.1	+23.0	95.7	0
1	14 44.6	+15.6	93.0	14 41.3	+16.7	93.2	14 37.8	+17.7	93.5	14 34.0	+18.8	93.8	14 29.9	+19.8	94.0	14 25.6	+20.8	94.3	14 21.0	+21.8	94.5	14 16.1	+22.9	94.8	1
2	15 00.2	+15.4	92.0	14 58.0	+16.5	92.2	14 55.5	+17.5	92.5	14 52.8	+18.5	92.8	14 49.7	+19.6	93.0	14 46.4	+20.6	93.3	14 42.8	+21.6	93.6	14 39.0	+22.5	93.8	2
3	15 15.6	+15.1	91.0	15 14.5	+16.1	91.2	15 13.0	+17.2	91.5	15 11.3	+18.2	91.8	15 09.3	+19.3	92.1	15 07.0	+20.3	92.3	15 04.4	+21.3	92.6	15 01.5	+22.4	92.9	3
4	15 30.7	+14.9	90.0	15 30.6	+15.9	90.2	15 30.2	+17.0	90.5	15 29.5	+18.0	90.8	15 28.6	+19.0	91.1	15 27.3	+20.0	91.4	15 25.7	+21.1	91.6	15 23.9	+22.1	91.9	4
5	15 45.6	+14.6	89.0	15 46.5	+15.7	89.2	15 47.2	+16.7	89.5	15 47.5	+17.7	89.8	15 47.6	+18.7	90.1	15 47.3	+19.8	90.4	15 46.8	+20.8	90.7	15 46.0	+21.8	90.9	5
6	16 00.2	+14.3	88.0	16 02.2	+15.3	88.2	16 03.9	+16.4	88.5	16 05.2	+17.5	88.8	16 06.3	+18.5	89.1	16 07.1	+19.5	89.4	16 07.6	+20.6	89.7	16 07.8	+21.6	90.0	6
7	16 14.5	+14.0	86.9	16 17.5	+15.1	87.2	16 20.3	+16.1	87.5	16 22.7	+17.2	87.8	16 24.8	+18.2	88.1	16 26.6	+19.3	88.4	16 28.2	+20.2	88.7	16 29.4	+21.3	89.0	7
8	16 28.5	+13.7	85.9	16 32.6	+14.7	86.2	16 36.4	+15.8	86.5	16 39.9	+16.8	86.8	16 43.0	+17.9	87.1	16 45.9	+18.9	87.4	16 48.4	+20.0	87.7	16 50.7	+21.0	88.0	8
9	16 42.2	+13.4	84.9	16 47.3	+14.5	85.2	16 52.2	+15.5	85.5	16 56.7	+16.6	85.8	17 00.9	+17.7	86.1	17 04.8	+18.7	86.4	17 08.4	+19.7	86.7	17 11.7	+20.7	87.0	9
10	16 55.6	+13.1	83.9	17 01.8	+14.2	84.2	17 07.7	+15.3	84.5	17 13.3	+16.3	84.8	17 18.6	+17.3	85.1	17 23.5	+18.4	85.4	17 28.1	+19.4	85.7	17 32.4	+20.5	86.1	10
11	17 08.7	+12.8	82.9	17 16.0	+13.9	83.2	17 23.0	+14.9	83.5	17 29.6	+16.0	83.8	17 35.9	+17.0	84.1	17 41.9	+18.1	84.4	17 47.5	+19.2	84.8	17 52.9	+20.1	85.1	11
12	17 21.5	+12.5	81.9	17 29.9	+13.5	82.2	17 37.9	+14.6	82.5	17 45.6	+15.6	82.8	17 52.9	+16.7	83.1	18 00.0	+17.7	83.4	18 06.7	+18.8	83.8	18 13.0	+19.8	84.1	12
13	17 34.0	+12.2	80.8	17 43.4	+13.2	81.1	17 52.5	+14.3	81.5	18 01.2	+15.4	81.8	18 09.6	+16.4	82.1	18 17.7	+17.5	82.4	18 25.5	+18.4	82.8	18 32.8	+19.6	83.1	13
14	17 46.2	+11.8	79.8	17 56.6	+12.9	80.1	18 06.8	+13.9	80.4	18 16.6	+15.0	80.8	18 26.0	+16.1	81.1	18 35.2	+17.1	81.4	18 43.9	+18.2	81.8	18 52.4	+19.2	82.1	14
15	17 58.0	+11.5	78.8	18 09.5	+12.6	79.1	18 20.7	+13.7	79.4	18 31.6	+14.7	79.7	18 42.1	+15.8	80.1	18 52.3	+16.8	80.4	19 02.1	+17.8	80.7	19 11.6	+18.9	81.1	15
16	18 09.5	+11.2	77.7	18 22.1	+12.3	78.1	18 34.4	+13.3	78.4	18 46.3	+14.3	78.7	18 57.9	+15.4	79.1	19 09.1	+16.4	79.4	19 19.9	+17.5	79.7	19 30.5	+18.5	80.1	16
17	18 20.7	+10.9	76.7	18 34.4	+11.9	77.0	18 47.7	+12.9	77.4	19 00.6	+14.1	77.7	19 13.3	+15.0	78.0	19 25.5	+16.1	78.4	19 37.4	+17.2	78.7	19 49.0	+18.2	79.1	17
18	18 31.6	+10.5	75.7	18 46.3	+11.6	76.0	19 00.6	+12.7	76.3	19 14.7	+13.6	76.7	19 28.3	+14.7	77.0	19 41.6	+15.8	77.3	19 54.6	+16.8	77.7	20 07.2	+17.9	78.1	18
19	18 42.1	+10.2	74.6	18 57.9	+11.2	75.0	19 13.3	+12.2	75.3	19 28.3	+13.3	75.6	19 43.0	+14.4	76.0	19 57.4	+15.4	76.3	20 11.4	+16.5	76.7	20 25.1	+17.4	77.0	19
20	18 52.3	+9.8	73.6	19 09.1	+10.8	73.9	19 25.5	+11.9	74.3	19 41.6	+13.0	74.6	19 57.4	+14.0	74.9	20 12.8	+15.1	75.3	20 27.9	+16.1	75.7	20 42.5	+17.2	76.0	20
21	19 02.1	+9.5	72.5	19 19.9	+10.6	72.9	19 37.4	+11.6	73.2	19 54.6	+12.6	73.6	20 11.4	+13.7	73.9	20 27.9	+14.6	74.3	20 44.0	+15.7	74.6	20 59.7	+16.7	75.0	21
22	19 11.6	+9.1	71.5	19 30.5	+10.1	71.8	19 49.0	+11.2	72.2	20 07.2	+12.2	72.5	20 25.1	+13.2	72.9	20 42.5	+14.4	73.2	20 59.7	+15.3	73.6	21 16.4	+16.4	74.0	22
23	19 20.7	+8.8	70.4	19 40.6	+9.8	70.8	20 00.2	+10.8	71.1	20 19.4	+11.9	71.5	20 38.3	+12.9	71.8	20 56.9	+13.9	72.2	21 15.0	+15.0	72.6	21 32.8	+16.0	72.9	23
24	19 29.5	+8.4	69.4	19 50.4	+9.4	69.7	20 11.0	+10.5	70.1	20 31.3	+11.5	70.4	20 51.2	+12.5	70.8	21 10.8	+13.5	71.1	21 30.0	+14.6	71.5	21 48.8	+15.6	71.9	24
25	19 37.9	+8.0	68.3	19 59.8	+9.1	68.7	20 21.5	+10.0	69.0	20 42.8	+11.1	69.4	21 03.7	+12.2	69.7	21 24.3	+13.2	70.1	21 44.6	+14.2	70.5	22 04.4	+15.3	70.9	25
26	19 45.9	+7.6	67.3	20 08.9	+8.6	67.6	20 31.5	+9.7	68.0	20 53.9	+10.7	68.3	21 15.9	+11.7	68.7	21 37.5	+12.8	69.1	21 58.8	+13.7	69.4	22 19.7	+14.8	69.8	26
27	19 53.5	+7.3	66.2	20 17.5	+8.3	66.6	20 41.2	+9.3	66.9	21 04.6	+10.3	67.3	21 27.6	+11.3	67.6	21 50.3	+12.3	68.0	22 12.5	+13.4	68.4	22 34.5	+14.4	68.8	27
28	20 00.8	+6.9	65.2	20 25.8	+8.0	65.5	20 50.5	+9.0	65.9	21 14.9	+9.9	66.2	21 38.9	+11.0	66.6	22 02.6	+12.0	66.9	22 25.9	+13.0	67.3	22 48.9	+14.0	67.7	28
29	20 07.7	+6.6	64.1	20 33.8	+7.5	64.5	20 59.5	+8.5	64.8	21 24.8	+9.6	65.2	21 49.9	+10.5	65.5	22 14.6	+11.5	65.9	22 38.9	+12.5	66.3	23 02.9	+13.5	66.7	29
30	20 14.3	+6.1	63.1	20 41.3	+7.1	63.4	21 08.0	+8.1	63.7	21 34.4	+9.1	64.1	22 00.4	+10.1	64.5	22 26.1	+11.1	64.8	22 51.4	+12.2	65.2	23 16.4	+13.2	65.6	30
31	20 20.4	+5.8	62.0	20 48.4	+6.8	62.3	21 16.1	+7.7	62.7	21 43.5	+8.7	63.0	22 10.5	+9.7	63.4	22 37.2	+10.7	63.8	23 03.6	+11.7	64.1	23 29.6	+12.7	64.5	31
32	20 26.2	+5.4	60.9	20 55.2	+6.3	61.3	21 23.8	+7.4	61.6	21 52.2	+8.3	62.0	22 20.2	+9.3	62.3	22 47.9	+10.3	62.7	23 15.3	+11.2	63.1	23 42.3	+12.2	63.5	32
33	20 31.6	+4.9	59.9	21 01.5	+6.0	60.2	21 31.2	+6.9	60.6	22 00.5	+7.9	60.9	22 29.5	+8.9	61.3	22 58.2	+9.9	61.6	23 26.5	+10.9	62.0	23 54.5	+11.9	62.4	33
34	20 36.5	+4.6	58.8	21 07.5	+5.5	59.1	21 38.1	+6.5	59.5	22 08.4	+7.5	59.8	22 38.4	+8.4	60.2	23 08.1	+9.4	60.6	23 37.4	+10.4	60.9	24 06.4	+11.3	61.3	34
35	20 41.1	+4.2	57.8	21 13.0	+5.2	58.1	21 44.6	+6.1	58.4	22 15.9	+7.0	58.8	22 46.8	+8.0	59.1	23 17.5	+8.9	59.5	23 47.8	+9.9	59.9	24 17.7	+10.9	60.2	35
36	20 45.3	+3.9	56.7	21 18.2	+4.7	57.0	21 50.7	+5.7	57.3	22 22.9	+6.6	57.7	22 54.8	+7.6	58.0	23 26.4	+8.6	58.4	23 57.7	+9.5	58.8	24 28.6	+10.5	59.2	36
37	20 49.2	+3.4	55.6	21 22.9	+4.3	55.9	21 56.4	+5.2	56.3	22 29.5	+6.2	56.6	23 02.4	+7.1	57.0	23 35.0	+8.0	57.3	24 07.2	+9.0	57.7	24 39.1	+10.0	58.1	37
38	20 52.6	+3.0	54.6	21 27.2	+4.0	54.9	22 01.6	+4.9	55.2	22 35.7	+5.8	55.5	23 09.5	+6.7	55.9	23 43.0	+7.6	56.2	24 16.2	+8.6	56.6	24 49.1	+9.5	57.0	38
39	20 55.6	+2.6	53.5	21 31.2	+3.5	53.8	22 06.5	+4.4	54.1	22 41.5	+5.3	54.5	23 16.2	+6.3	54.8	23 50.6	+7.2	55.2	24 24.8	+8.1	55.5	24 58.6	+9.0	55.9	39
40	20 58.2	+2.2	52.4	21 34.7	+3.1	52.7	22 10.9	+4.0	53.0	22 46.8	+4.9	53.4	23 22.5	+5.8	53.7	23 57.8	+6.7	54.1	24 32.9	+7.6	54.4	25 07.6	+8.6	54.8	40
41	21 00.4	+1.8	51.3	21 37.8	+2.6	51.6	22 14.9	+3.5	52.0	22 51.7	+4.4	52.3	23 28.3	+5.3	52.6	24 04.5	+6.3	53.0	24 40.5	+7.2	53.3	25 16.2	+8.0	53.7	41
42	21 02.2	+1.4	50.3	21 40.4	+2.3	50.6	22 18.4	+3.2	50.9	22 56.1	+4.1	51.2	23 33.6	+4.9	51.5	24 10.8	+5.8	51.9	24 47.7	+6.6	52.3	25 24.2	+7.6	52.6	42
43	21 03.6	+1.0	49.2	21 42.7	+1.9	49.5	22 21.6	+2.7	49.8	23 00.2	+3.5	50.1	23 38.5	+4.4	50.5	24 16.6	+5.3	50.8	24 54.3	+6.2	51.2	25 31.8	+7.1	51.5	43
44	21 04.6	+0.6	48.1	21 44.6	+1.4	48.4	22 24.3	+2.2	48.7	23 03.7	+3.1	49.0	23 42.9	+4.0	49.4	24 21.9	+4.8	49.7	25 00.5	+5.7	50.1	25 38.9	+6.6	50.4	44
45	21 05.2	+0.2	47.1	21 46.0	+1.0	47.3	22 26.5	+1.9	47.6	23 06.8	+2.7	48.0	23 46.9	+3.5	48.3	24 26.7	+4.4	48.6	25 06.2	+5.3	49.0	25 45.5	+6.1	49.3	45
46	21 05.4	−0.2	46.0	21 47.0	+0.6	46.3	22 28.4	+1.4	46.6	23 09.5	+2.3	46.9	23 50.4	+3.1	47.2	24 31.1	+3.9	47.5	25 11.5	+4.7	47.9	25 51.6	+5.6	48.2	46
47	21 05.2	−0.6	44.9	21 47.6	+0.2	45.2	22 29.8	+1.0	45.5	23 11.8	+1.7	45.8	23 53.5	+2.6	46.1	24 35.0	+3.4	46.4	25 16.2	+4.2	46.8	25 57.2	+5.1	47.1	47
48	21 04.6	−1.0	43.8	21 47.8	−0.2	44.1	22 30.8	+0.5	44.4	23 13.5	+1.4	44.7	23 56.1	+2.1	45.0	24 38.4	+2.9	45.3	25 20.4	+3.8	45.7	26 02.3	+4.5	46.0	48
49	21 03.6	−1.4	42.8	21 47.6	−0.7	43.0	22 31.3	+0.1	43.3	23 14.9	+0.8	43.6	23 58.2	+1.7	43.9	24 41.3	+2.5	44.2	25 24.2	+3.3	44.6	26 06.8	+4.1	44.9	49
50	21 02.2	−1.8	41.7	21 46.9	−1.1	42.0	22 31.4	−0.3	42.2	23 15.7	+0.5	42.5	23 59.9	+1.2	42.8	24 43.8	+1.9	43.1	25 27.5	+2.7	43.4	26 10.9	+3.5	43.8	50
51	21 00.4	−2.2	40.6	21 45.8	−1.5	40.9	22 31.1	−0.8	41.2	23 16.2	0.0	41.4	24 01.1	+0.7	41.7	24 45.7	+1.5	42.0	25 30.2	+2.3	42.3	26 14.4	+3.1	42.7	51
52	20 58.2	−2.7	39.6	21 44.3	−1.9	39.8	22 30.3	−1.2	40.1	23 16.2	−0.5	40.3	24 01.8	+0.3	40.6	24 47.2	+1.0	40.9	25 32.5	+1.7	41.2	26 17.5	+2.5	41.6	52
53	20 55.5	−3.0	38.5	21 42.4	−2.3	38.7	22 29.1	−1.6	39.0	23 15.7	−0.9	39.3	24 02.1	−0.2	39.5	24 48.2	+0.6	39.8	25 34.2	+1.3	40.1	26 20.0	+2.0	40.4	53
54	20 52.5	−3.4	37.4	21 40.1	−2.7	37.7	22 27.5	−2.0	37.9	23 14.8	−1.4	38.2	24 01.9	−0.7	38.4	24 48.8	0.0	38.7	25 35.5	+0.7	39.0	26 22.0	+1.5	39.3	54
55	20 49.1	−3.8	36.4	21 37.4	−3.2	36.6	22 25.5	−2.5	36.8	23 13.4	−1.8	37.1	24 01.2	−1.1	37.3	24 48.8	−0.4	37.6	25 36.2	+0.3	37.9	26 23.5	+1.0	38.2	55
56	20 45.3	−4.2	35.3	21 34.2	−3.6	35.5	22 23.0	−3.0	35.7	23 11.6	−2.3	36.0	24 00.1	−1.6	36.2	24 48.4	−1.0	36.5	25 36.5	−0.2	36.8	26 24.5	+0.4	37.1	56
57	20 41.1	−4.6	34.2	21 30.6	−4.0	34.4	22 20.0	−3.3	34.7	23 09.3	−2.7	34.9	23 58.5	−2.1	35.2	24 47.4	−1.4	35.4	25 36.3	−0.8	35.7	26 24.9	−0.1	36.0	57
58	20 36.5	−5.0	33.2	21 26.6	−4.3	33.4	22 16.7	−3.8	33.6	23 06.6	−3.1	33.8	23 56.4	−2.5	34.1	24 46.0	−1.9	34.3	25 35.5	−1.2	34.6	26 24.8	−0.6	34.9	58
59	20 31.5	−5.4	32.1	21 22.3	−4.8	32.3	22 12.9	−4.2	32.5	23 03.5	−3.6	32.7	23 53.9	−3.0	33.0	24 44.1	−2.3	33.2	25 34.3	−1.8	33.5	26 24.2	−1.1	33.7	59
60	20 26.1	−5.8	31.0	21 17.5	−5.2	31.2	22 08.7	−4.6	31.4	22 59.9	−4.1	31.6	23 50.9	−3.5	31.9	24 41.8	−2.9	32.1	25 32.5	−2.2	32.4	26 23.1	−1.6	32.6	60
61	20 20.3	−6.1	30.0	21 12.3	−5.6	30.2	22 04.1	−5.1	30.4	22 55.8	−4.5	30.6	23 47.4	−3.9	30.8	24 38.9	−3.3	31.0	25 30.3	−2.8	31.3	26 21.5	−2.2	31.5	61
62	20 14.2	−6.6	28.9	21 06.7	−6.1	29.1	21 59.0	−5.4	29.3	22 51.3	−4.9	29.5	23 43.5	−4.4	29.7	24 35.6	−3.8	29.9	25 27.5	−3.2	30.1	26 19.3	−2.6	30.4	62
63	20 07.6	−6.9	27.8	21 00.6	−6.4	28.0	21 53.6	−5.9	28.2	22 46.4	−5.4	28.4	23 39.1	−4.8	28.6	24 31.8	−4.3	28.8	25 24.3	−3.8	29.0	26 16.7	−3.2	29.3	63
64	20 00.7	−7.3	26.8	20 54.2	−6.8	27.0	21 47.7	−6.3	27.1	22 41.0	−5.8	27.3	23 34.3	−5.3	27.5	24 27.5	−4.8	27.7	25 20.5	−4.2	27.9	26 13.5	−3.7	28.2	64
65	19 53.4	−7.6	25.7	20 47.4	−7.1	25.9	21 41.4	−6.7	26.1	22 35.2	−6.2	26.2	23 29.0	−5.7	26.4	24 22.7	−5.2	26.6	25 16.3	−4.7	26.8	26 09.8	−4.2	27.1	65
66	19 45.8	−8.1	24.7	20 40.3	−7.6	24.8	21 34.7	−7.1	25.0	22 29.0	−6.6	25.2	23 23.3	−6.2	25.3	24 17.5	−5.7	25.5	25 11.6	−5.3	25.7	26 05.6	−4.8	25.9	66
67	19 37.7	−8.4	23.6	20 32.7	−8.0	23.8	21 27.6	−7.6	23.9	22 22.4	−7.1	24.1	23 17.1	−6.6	24.3	24 11.8	−6.2	24.4	25 06.3	−5.7	24.6	26 00.8	−5.2	24.8	67
68	19 29.3	−8.7	22.6	20 24.7	−8.3	22.7	21 20.0	−7.9	22.9	22 15.3	−7.5	23.0	23 10.5	−7.1	23.2	24 05.6	−6.6	23.4	25 00.6	−6.1	23.5	25 55.6	−5.7	23.7	68
69	19 20.6	−9.2	21.5	20 16.4	−8.8	21.7	21 12.1	−8.3	21.8	22 07.8	−7.9	21.9	23 03.4	−7.5	22.1	23 59.0	−7.1	22.3	24 54.5	−6.7	22.4	25 49.9	−6.3	22.6	69
70	19 11.4	−9.4	20.5	20 07.6	−9.1	20.6	21 03.8	−8.7	20.7	21 59.9	−8.4	20.9	22 55.9	−7.9	21.0	23 51.9	−7.6	21.2	24 47.8	−7.2	21.3	25 43.6	−6.7	21.5	70
71	19 02.0	−9.9	19.4	19 58.5	−9.4	19.5	20 55.1	−9.2	19.7	21 51.5	−8.7	19.8	22 48.0	−8.4	19.9	23 44.3	−8.0	20.1	24 40.6	−7.6	20.2	25 36.9	−7.2	20.4	71
72	18 52.1	−10.1	18.4	19 49.1	−9.9	18.5	20 45.9	−9.5	18.6	21 42.8	−9.2	18.7	22 39.6	−8.8	18.9	23 36.3	−8.4	19.0	24 33.0	−8.1	19.2	25 29.7	−7.7	19.3	72
73	18 42.0	−10.6	17.3	19 39.2	−10.2	17.5	20 36.4	−9.8	17.6	21 33.6	−9.5	17.7	22 30.8	−9.3	17.8	23 27.9	−8.9	17.9	24 24.9	−8.5	18.1	25 22.0	−8.2	18.2	73
74	18 31.4	−10.8	16.3	19 29.0	−10.6	16.4	20 26.6	−10.3	16.5	21 24.1	−10.0	16.6	22 21.5	−9.6	16.7	23 19.0	−9.3	16.9	24 16.4	−9.0	17.0	25 13.8	−8.7	17.1	74
75	18 20.6	−11.2	15.3	19 18.4	−10.9	15.4	20 16.3	−10.6	15.5	21 14.1	−10.3	15.6	22 11.9	−10.1	15.7	23 09.7	−9.8	15.8	24 07.4	−9.5	15.9	25 05.1	−9.2	16.0	75
76	18 09.4	−11.5	14.2	19 07.5	−11.2	14.3	20 05.7	−11.1	14.4	21 03.8	−10.8	14.5	22 01.8	−10.4	14.6	22 59.9	−10.2	14.7	23 57.9	−9.9	14.8	24 55.9	−9.7	14.9	76
77	17 57.9	−11.9	13.2	18 56.3	−11.7	13.3	19 54.6	−11.3	13.4	20 53.0	−11.1	13.4	21 51.4	−10.9	13.5	22 49.7	−10.7	13.6	23 48.0	−10.4	13.7	24 46.2	−10.1	13.8	77
78	17 46.0	−12.2	12.2	18 44.6	−11.9	12.2	19 43.3	−11.8	12.3	20 41.9	−11.5	12.4	21 40.5	−11.3	12.5	22 39.0	−11.0	12.6	23 37.6	−10.8	12.7	24 36.1	−10.6	12.8	78
79	17 33.8	−12.5	11.1	18 32.7	−12.3	11.2	19 31.5	−12.1	11.3	20 30.4	−11.9	11.3	21 29.2	−11.7	11.4	22 28.0	−11.5	11.5	23 26.8	−11.3	11.6	24 25.5	−11.0	11.7	79
80	17 21.3	−12.8	10.1	18 20.4	−12.6	10.2	19 19.4	−12.4	10.2	20 18.5	−12.3	10.3	21 17.5	−12.1	10.4	22 16.5	−11.9	10.4	23 15.5	−11.7	10.5	24 14.5	−11.5	10.6	80
81	17 08.5	−13.1	9.1	18 07.8	−13.0	9.1	19 07.0	−12.8	9.2	20 06.2	−12.6	9.3	21 05.4	−12.4	9.3	22 04.6	−12.3	9.4	23 03.8	−12.1	9.5	24 03.0	−11.9	9.5	81
82	16 55.4	−13.4	8.1	17 54.8	−13.3	8.1	18 54.2	−13.1	8.2	19 53.6	−13.0	8.2	20 53.0	−12.9	8.3	21 52.3	−12.7	8.3	22 51.7	−12.5	8.4	23 51.1	−12.4	8.5	82
83	16 42.0	−13.7	7.1	17 41.5	−13.6	7.1	18 41.1	−13.5	7.1	19 40.6	−13.3	7.2	20 40.1	−13.2	7.2	21 39.6	−13.0	7.3	22 39.2	−13.0	7.3	23 38.7	−12.9	7.4	83
84	16 28.3	−14.0	6.0	17 27.9	−13.9	6.1	18 27.6	−13.8	6.1	19 27.3	−13.7	6.1	20 26.9	−13.6	6.2	21 26.6	−13.5	6.2	22 26.2	−13.4	6.3	23 25.8	−13.2	6.3	84
85	16 14.3	−14.3	5.0	17 14.0	−14.2	5.1	18 13.8	−14.1	5.1	19 13.6	−14.1	5.1	20 13.3	−13.9	5.1	21 13.1	−13.9	5.2	22 12.8	−13.8	5.2	23 12.6	−13.7	5.3	85
86	16 00.0	−14.6	4.0	16 59.8	−14.5	4.0	17 59.7	−14.5	4.1	18 59.5	−14.4	4.1	19 59.4	−14.4	4.1	20 59.2	−14.2	4.1	21 59.0	−14.1	4.2	22 58.9	−14.1	4.2	86
87	15 45.4	−14.9	3.0	16 45.3	−14.8	3.0	17 45.2	−14.7	3.0	18 45.1	−14.7	3.1	19 45.0	−14.6	3.1	20 45.0	−14.7	3.1	21 44.9	−14.6	3.1	22 44.8	−14.5	3.1	87
88	15 30.5	−15.1	2.0	16 30.5	−15.1	2.0	17 30.5	−15.1	2.0	18 30.4	−15.0	2.0	19 30.4	−15.0	2.0	20 30.3	−14.9	2.1	21 30.3	−15.0	2.1	22 30.3	−15.0	2.1	88
89	15 15.4	−15.4	1.0	16 15.4	−15.4	1.0	17 15.4	−15.4	1.0	18 15.4	−15.4	1.0	19 15.4	−15.4	1.0	20 15.4	−15.4	1.0	21 15.3	−15.3	1.0	22 15.3	−15.3	1.0	89
90	15 00.0	−15.7	0.0	16 00.0	−15.7	0.0	17 00.0	−15.7	0.0	18 00.0	−15.7	0.0	19 00.0	−15.7	0.0	20 00.0	−15.7	0.0	21 00.0	−15.7	0.0	22 00.0	−15.7	0.0	90
	15°			16°			17°			18°			19°			20°			21°			22°			

Dec.	15°			16°			17°			18°			Dec.
°	Hc ° ′	d ′	Z °	Hc ° ′	d ′	Z °	Hc ° ′	d ′	Z °	Hc ° ′	d ′	Z °	°
0	14 28.7	-16.2	94.0	14 24.4	-17.2	94.2	14 19.8	-18.2	94.5	14 15.0	-19.3	94.7	0
1	14 12.5	-16.4	95.0	14 07.2	-17.5	95.2	14 01.6	-18.5	95.5	13 55.7	-19.4	95.7	1
2	13 56.1	-16.7	96.0	13 49.7	-17.6	96.2	13 43.1	-18.7	96.4	13 36.3	-19.7	96.7	2
3	13 39.4	-16.9	96.9	13 32.1	-18.0	97.2	13 24.4	-18.9	97.4	13 16.6	-20.0	97.7	3
4	13 22.5	-17.1	97.9	13 14.1	-18.1	98.2	13 05.5	-19.1	98.4	12 56.6	-20.1	98.6	4
5	13 05.4	-17.3	98.9	12 56.0	-18.3	99.1	12 46.4	-19.4	99.4	12 36.5	-20.4	99.6	5
6	12 48.1	-17.6	99.9	12 37.7	-18.6	100.1	12 27.0	-19.5	100.3	12 16.1	-20.5	100.6	6
7	12 30.5	-17.7	100.9	12 19.1	-18.8	101.1	12 07.5	-19.8	101.3	11 55.6	-20.8	101.5	7
8	12 12.8	-18.0	101.9	12 00.3	-18.9	102.1	11 47.7	-20.0	102.3	11 34.8	-20.9	102.5	8
9	11 54.8	-18.2	102.8	11 41.4	-19.2	103.0	11 27.7	-20.1	103.2	11 13.9	-21.1	103.4	9
10	11 36.6	-18.3	103.8	11 22.2	-19.3	104.0	11 07.6	-20.3	104.2	10 52.8	-21.3	104.4	10
11	11 18.3	-18.6	104.8	11 02.9	-19.6	105.0	10 47.3	-20.5	105.2	10 31.5	-21.5	105.3	11
12	10 59.7	-18.7	105.7	10 43.3	-19.7	105.9	10 26.8	-20.7	106.1	10 10.0	-21.6	106.3	12
13	10 41.0	-19.0	106.7	10 23.6	-19.9	106.9	10 06.1	-20.8	107.1	9 48.4	-21.8	107.2	13
14	10 22.0	-19.0	107.7	10 03.7	-20.0	107.8	9 45.3	-21.0	108.0	9 26.6	-21.9	108.2	14
15	10 03.0	-19.3	108.6	9 43.7	-20.2	108.8	9 24.3	-21.2	109.0	9 04.7	-22.1	109.1	15
16	9 43.7	-19.4	109.6	9 23.5	-20.4	109.8	9 03.1	-21.3	109.9	8 42.6	-22.2	110.1	16
17	9 24.3	-19.6	110.6	9 03.1	-20.5	110.7	8 41.8	-21.4	110.9	8 20.4	-22.3	111.0	17
18	9 04.7	-19.7	111.5	8 42.6	-20.6	111.7	8 20.4	-21.6	111.8	7 58.1	-22.5	111.9	18
19	8 45.0	-19.9	112.5	8 22.0	-20.8	112.6	7 58.8	-21.7	112.7	7 35.6	-22.6	112.9	19
20	8 25.1	-20.0	113.4	8 01.2	-20.9	113.6	7 37.1	-21.8	113.7	7 13.0	-22.7	113.8	20
21	8 05.1	-20.1	114.4	7 40.3	-21.1	114.5	7 15.3	-21.9	114.6	6 50.3	-22.8	114.7	21
22	7 45.0	-20.3	115.3	7 19.2	-21.1	115.5	6 53.4	-22.0	115.6	6 27.5	-23.0	115.7	22
23	7 24.7	-20.4	116.3	6 58.1	-21.3	116.4	6 31.4	-22.2	116.5	6 04.5	-23.0	116.6	23
24	7 04.3	-20.5	117.2	6 36.8	-21.4	117.3	6 09.2	-22.2	117.4	5 41.5	-23.1	117.5	24
25	6 43.8	-20.6	118.2	6 15.4	-21.4	118.3	5 47.0	-22.4	118.4	5 18.4	-23.2	118.5	25
26	6 23.2	-20.7	119.1	5 54.0	-21.6	119.2	5 24.6	-22.4	119.3	4 55.2	-23.2	119.4	26
27	6 02.5	-20.8	120.1	5 32.4	-21.7	120.2	5 02.2	-22.5	120.2	4 32.0	-23.4	120.3	27
28	5 41.7	-20.9	121.0	5 10.7	-21.7	121.1	4 39.7	-22.5	121.2	4 08.6	-23.4	121.2	28
29	5 20.8	-21.0	122.0	4 49.0	-21.8	122.0	4 17.2	-22.7	122.1	3 45.2	-23.4	122.2	29
30	4 59.8	-21.1	122.9	4 27.2	-21.9	123.0	3 54.5	-22.7	123.0	3 21.8	-23.5	123.1	30
31	4 38.7	-21.1	123.8	4 05.3	-22.0	123.9	3 31.8	-22.7	123.9	2 58.3	-23.6	124.0	31
32	4 17.6	-21.2	124.8	3 43.3	-22.0	124.8	3 09.1	-22.8	124.9	2 34.7	-23.6	124.9	32
33	3 56.4	-21.3	125.7	3 21.3	-22.0	125.8	2 46.3	-22.9	125.8	2 11.1	-23.6	125.8	33
34	3 35.1	-21.3	126.6	2 59.3	-22.1	126.7	2 23.4	-22.9	126.7	1 47.5	-23.6	126.8	34
35	3 13.8	-21.4	127.6	2 37.2	-22.2	127.6	2 00.5	-22.9	127.7	1 23.9	-23.7	127.7	35
36	2 52.4	-21.4	128.5	2 15.0	-22.2	128.6	1 37.6	-22.9	128.6	1 00.2	-23.7	128.6	36
37	2 31.0	-21.5	129.5	1 52.8	-22.2	129.5	1 14.7	-23.0	129.5	0 36.5	-23.7	129.5	37
38	2 09.5	-21.5	130.4	1 30.6	-22.2	130.4	0 51.7	-23.0	130.4	0 12.8	-23.7	130.4	38
39	1 48.0	-21.5	131.3	1 08.4	-22.3	131.3	0 28.7	-23.0	131.3	0 10.9	+23.7	48.6	39
40	1 26.5	-21.6	132.3	0 46.1	-22.3	132.3	0 05.7	-22.9	132.3	0 34.6	+23.7	47.7	40
41	1 04.9	-21.6	133.2	0 23.8	-22.2	133.2	0 17.2	+23.0	46.8	0 58.3	+23.7	46.8	41
42	0 43.3	-21.6	134.1	0 01.6	-22.3	134.1	0 40.2	+23.0	45.9	1 22.0	+23.6	45.9	42
43	0 21.7	-21.5	135.1	0 20.7	+22.3	44.9	1 03.2	+22.9	45.0	1 45.6	+23.7	45.0	43
44	0 00.2	-21.6	136.0	0 43.0	+22.3	44.0	1 26.1	+23.0	44.0	2 09.3	+23.6	44.1	44
45	0 21.4	+21.6	43.1	1 05.3	+22.2	43.1	1 49.1	+22.9	43.1	2 32.9	+23.5	43.1	45
46	0 43.0	+21.6	42.1	1 27.5	+22.2	42.2	2 12.0	+22.8	42.2	2 56.4	+23.5	42.2	46
47	1 04.6	+21.5	41.2	1 49.7	+22.2	41.2	2 34.8	+22.9	41.3	3 19.9	+23.5	41.3	47
48	1 26.1	+21.6	40.3	2 11.9	+22.2	40.3	2 57.7	+22.7	40.3	3 43.4	+23.4	40.4	48
49	1 47.7	+21.5	39.3	2 34.1	+22.1	39.4	3 20.4	+22.8	39.4	4 06.8	+23.3	39.4	49
50	2 09.2	+21.5	38.4	2 56.2	+22.1	38.4	3 43.2	+22.6	38.5	4 30.1	+23.3	38.5	50
51	2 30.7	+21.4	37.5	3 18.3	+22.0	37.5	4 05.8	+22.7	37.5	4 53.4	+23.2	37.6	51
52	2 52.1	+21.4	36.5	3 40.3	+21.9	36.6	4 28.5	+22.5	36.6	5 16.6	+23.1	36.7	52
53	3 13.5	+21.3	35.6	4 02.2	+21.9	35.6	4 51.0	+22.4	35.7	5 39.7	+23.0	35.7	53
54	3 34.8	+21.3	34.7	4 24.1	+21.9	34.7	5 13.4	+22.4	34.8	6 02.7	+22.9	34.8	54
55	3 56.1	+21.2	33.7	4 46.0	+21.7	33.8	5 35.8	+22.3	33.8	6 25.6	+22.9	33.9	55
56	4 17.3	+21.1	32.8	5 07.7	+21.7	32.8	5 58.1	+22.2	32.9	6 48.5	+22.7	33.0	56
57	4 38.4	+21.1	31.9	5 29.4	+21.6	31.9	6 20.3	+22.1	32.0	7 11.2	+22.6	32.0	57
58	4 59.5	+21.0	30.9	5 51.0	+21.5	31.0	6 42.4	+22.0	31.0	7 33.8	+22.5	31.1	58
59	5 20.5	+20.9	30.0	6 12.5	+21.3	30.0	7 04.4	+21.9	30.1	7 56.3	+22.3	30.2	59
60	5 41.4	+20.8	29.0	6 33.8	+21.3	29.1	7 26.3	+21.7	29.1	8 18.6	+22.3	29.2	60
61	6 02.2	+20.7	28.1	6 55.1	+21.2	28.1	7 48.0	+21.6	28.2	8 40.9	+22.1	28.3	61
62	6 22.9	+20.6	27.1	7 16.3	+21.0	27.2	8 09.6	+21.5	27.3	9 03.0	+21.9	27.3	62
63	6 43.5	+20.5	26.2	7 37.3	+21.0	26.3	8 31.1	+21.4	26.3	9 24.9	+21.8	26.4	63
64	7 04.0	+20.4	25.3	7 58.3	+20.8	25.3	8 52.5	+21.2	25.4	9 46.7	+21.6	25.4	64
65	7 24.4	+20.3	24.3	8 19.1	+20.7	24.4	9 13.7	+21.1	24.4	10 08.3	+21.5	24.5	65
66	7 44.7	+20.1	23.4	8 39.8	+20.5	23.4	9 34.8	+20.9	23.5	10 29.8	+21.3	23.6	66
67	8 04.8	+20.0	22.4	9 00.3	+20.4	22.5	9 55.7	+20.8	22.5	10 51.1	+21.1	22.6	67
68	8 24.8	+19.9	21.5	9 20.7	+20.2	21.5	10 16.5	+20.6	21.6	11 12.2	+21.0	21.6	68
69	8 44.7	+19.7	20.5	9 40.9	+20.1	20.6	10 37.1	+20.4	20.6	11 33.2	+20.8	20.7	69
70	9 04.4	+19.6	19.5	10 01.0	+19.9	19.6	10 57.5	+20.2	19.7	11 54.0	+20.5	19.7	70
71	9 24.0	+19.4	18.6	10 20.9	+19.7	18.6	11 17.7	+20.1	18.7	12 14.5	+20.4	18.8	71
72	9 43.4	+19.3	17.6	10 40.6	+19.6	17.7	11 37.8	+19.8	17.7	12 34.9	+20.1	17.8	72
73	10 02.7	+19.1	16.7	11 00.2	+19.3	16.7	11 57.6	+19.7	16.8	12 55.0	+20.0	16.8	73
74	10 21.8	+18.9	15.7	11 19.5	+19.2	15.8	12 17.3	+19.4	15.8	13 15.0	+19.7	15.9	74
75	10 40.7	+18.7	14.7	11 38.7	+19.0	14.8	12 36.7	+19.3	14.8	13 34.7	+19.5	14.9	75
76	10 59.4	+18.6	13.8	11 57.7	+18.8	13.8	12 56.0	+19.0	13.9	13 54.2	+19.3	13.9	76
77	11 18.0	+18.4	12.8	12 16.5	+18.6	12.8	13 15.0	+18.8	12.9	14 13.5	+19.0	13.0	77
78	11 36.4	+18.2	11.8	12 35.1	+18.4	11.9	13 33.8	+18.6	11.9	14 32.5	+18.8	12.0	78
79	11 54.6	+17.9	10.9	12 53.5	+18.1	10.9	13 52.4	+18.3	10.9	14 51.3	+18.5	11.0	79
80	12 12.5	+17.8	9.9	13 11.6	+18.0	9.9	14 10.7	+18.1	10.0	15 09.8	+18.3	10.0	80
81	12 30.3	+17.6	8.9	13 29.6	+17.7	8.9	14 28.8	+17.9	9.0	15 28.1	+18.0	9.0	81
82	12 47.9	+17.3	7.9	13 47.3	+17.5	8.0	14 46.7	+17.6	8.0	15 46.1	+17.8	8.0	82
83	13 05.2	+17.1	6.9	14 04.8	+17.2	7.0	15 04.3	+17.4	7.0	16 03.9	+17.4	7.0	83
84	13 22.3	+16.9	6.0	14 22.0	+17.0	6.0	15 21.7	+17.0	6.0	16 21.3	+17.2	6.0	84
85	13 39.2	+16.6	5.0	14 39.0	+16.7	5.0	15 38.7	+16.9	5.0	16 38.5	+16.9	5.0	85
86	13 55.8	+16.5	4.0	14 55.7	+16.5	4.0	15 55.6	+16.5	4.0	16 55.4	+16.6	4.0	86
87	14 12.3	+16.1	3.0	15 12.2	+16.2	3.0	16 12.1	+16.3	3.0	17 12.0	+16.3	3.0	87
88	14 28.4	+15.9	2.0	15 28.4	+15.9	2.0	16 28.4	+15.9	2.0	17 28.3	+16.0	2.0	88
89	14 44.3	+15.7	1.0	15 44.3	+15.7	1.0	16 44.3	+15.7	1.0	17 44.3	+15.7	1.0	89
90	15 00.0	+15.4	0.0	16 00.0	+15.4	0.0	17 00.0	+15.4	0.0	18 00.0	+15.4	0.0	90
	15°			16°			17°			18°			

Dec.	19°			20°			21°			22°			Dec.
°	Hc ° ′	d ′	Z °	Hc ° ′	d ′	Z °	Hc ° ′	d ′	Z °	Hc ° ′	d ′	Z °	°
0	14 09.9	-20.3	95.0	14 04.6	-21.3	95.2	13 59.0	-22.3	95.5	13 53.1	-23.3	95.7	0
1	13 49.6	-20.4	96.0	13 43.3	-21.5	96.2	13 36.7	-22.5	96.4	13 29.8	-23.4	96.7	1
2	13 29.2	-20.8	96.9	13 21.8	-21.7	97.2	13 14.2	-22.7	97.4	13 06.4	-23.7	97.6	2
3	13 08.4	-20.9	97.9	13 00.1	-21.9	98.1	12 51.5	-22.9	98.3	12 42.7	-23.9	98.6	3
4	12 47.5	-21.1	98.8	12 38.2	-22.2	99.1	12 28.6	-23.1	99.3	12 18.8	-24.1	99.5	4
5	12 26.4	-21.4	99.8	12 16.0	-22.3	100.0	12 05.5	-23.3	100.2	11 54.7	-24.2	100.4	5
6	12 05.0	-21.5	100.8	11 53.7	-22.5	101.0	11 42.2	-23.5	101.2	11 30.5	-24.5	101.4	6
7	11 43.5	-21.7	101.7	11 31.2	-22.7	101.9	11 18.7	-23.6	102.1	11 06.0	-24.6	102.3	7
8	11 21.8	-21.9	102.7	11 08.5	-22.8	102.9	10 55.1	-23.9	103.1	10 41.4	-24.7	103.3	8
9	10 59.9	-22.1	103.6	10 45.7	-23.1	103.8	10 31.2	-23.9	104.0	10 16.7	-25.0	104.2	9
10	10 37.8	-22.3	104.6	10 22.6	-23.2	104.7	10 07.3	-24.2	104.9	9 51.7	-25.1	105.1	10
11	10 15.5	-22.4	105.5	9 59.4	-23.3	105.7	9 43.1	-24.3	105.8	9 26.6	-25.2	106.0	11
12	9 53.1	-22.5	106.5	9 36.1	-23.6	106.6	9 18.8	-24.4	106.8	9 01.4	-25.3	106.9	12
13	9 30.6	-22.8	107.4	9 12.5	-23.6	107.5	8 54.4	-24.6	107.7	8 36.1	-25.5	107.8	13
14	9 07.8	-22.8	108.3	8 48.9	-23.8	108.5	8 29.8	-24.7	108.6	8 10.6	-25.6	108.8	14
15	8 45.0	-23.0	109.3	8 25.1	-23.9	109.4	8 05.1	-24.8	109.5	7 45.0	-25.8	109.7	15
16	8 22.0	-23.2	110.2	8 01.2	-24.1	110.3	7 40.3	-25.0	110.5	7 19.2	-25.8	110.6	16
17	7 58.8	-23.2	111.1	7 37.1	-24.1	111.3	7 15.3	-25.0	111.4	6 53.4	-25.9	111.5	17
18	7 35.6	-23.4	112.1	7 13.0	-24.3	112.2	6 50.3	-25.2	112.3	6 27.5	-26.1	112.4	18
19	7 12.2	-23.5	113.0	6 48.7	-24.4	113.1	6 25.1	-25.2	113.2	6 01.4	-26.1	113.3	19
20	6 48.7	-23.6	113.9	6 24.3	-24.4	114.0	5 59.9	-25.4	114.1	5 35.3	-26.2	114.2	20
21	6 25.1	-23.7	114.8	5 59.9	-24.6	114.9	5 34.5	-25.4	115.0	5 09.1	-26.3	115.1	21
22	6 01.4	-23.8	115.8	5 35.3	-24.7	115.9	5 09.1	-25.5	115.9	4 42.8	-26.4	116.0	22
23	5 37.6	-23.8	116.7	5 10.6	-24.7	116.8	4 43.6	-25.6	116.9	4 16.4	-26.4	116.9	23
24	5 13.8	-24.0	117.6	4 45.9	-24.8	117.7	4 18.0	-25.6	117.8	3 50.0	-26.5	117.8	24
25	4 49.8	-24.0	118.5	4 21.1	-24.9	118.6	3 52.4	-25.7	118.7	3 23.5	-26.5	118.7	25
26	4 25.8	-24.1	119.5	3 56.2	-24.9	119.5	3 26.7	-25.8	119.6	2 57.0	-26.6	119.6	26
27	4 01.7	-24.2	120.4	3 31.3	-25.0	120.4	3 00.9	-25.8	120.5	2 30.4	-26.6	120.5	27
28	3 37.5	-24.2	121.3	3 06.3	-25.0	121.3	2 35.1	-25.8	121.4	2 03.8	-26.6	121.4	28
29	3 13.3	-24.3	122.2	2 41.3	-25.1	122.2	2 09.3	-25.9	122.3	1 37.2	-26.7	122.3	29
30	2 49.0	-24.3	123.1	2 16.2	-25.1	123.2	1 43.4	-25.9	123.2	1 10.5	-26.6	123.2	30
31	2 24.7	-24.3	124.0	1 51.1	-25.1	124.1	1 17.5	-25.9	124.1	0 43.9	-26.7	124.1	31
32	2 00.4	-24.4	124.9	1 26.0	-25.2	125.0	0 51.6	-25.9	125.0	0 17.2	-26.7	125.0	32
33	1 36.0	-24.4	125.9	1 00.8	-25.1	125.9	0 25.7	-26.0	125.9	0 09.5	+26.7	54.1	33
34	1 11.6	-24.4	126.8	0 35.7	-25.2	126.8	0 00.3	+25.9	53.2	0 36.2	+26.7	53.2	34
35	0 47.2	-24.5	127.7	0 10.5	-25.2	127.7	0 26.2	+25.9	52.3	1 02.9	+26.7	52.3	35
36	0 22.7	-24.4	128.6	0 14.7	+25.2	51.4	0 52.1	+25.9	51.4	1 29.6	+26.6	51.4	36
37	0 01.7	+24.4	50.5	0 39.9	+25.1	50.5	1 18.0	+25.9	50.5	1 56.2	+26.6	50.5	37
38	0 26.1	+24.5	49.6	1 05.0	+25.2	49.6	1 43.9	+25.9	49.6	2 22.8	+26.6	49.6	38
39	0 50.6	+24.4	48.7	1 30.2	+25.1	48.7	2 09.8	+25.8	48.7	2 49.4	+26.5	48.7	39
40	1 15.0	+24.4	47.7	1 55.3	+25.1	47.8	2 35.6	+25.8	47.8	3 15.9	+26.5	47.8	40
41	1 39.4	+24.3	46.8	2 20.4	+25.1	46.9	3 01.4	+25.8	46.9	3 42.4	+26.5	46.9	41
42	2 03.7	+24.4	45.9	2 45.5	+25.0	45.9	3 27.2	+25.7	46.0	4 08.9	+26.3	46.0	42
43	2 28.1	+24.3	45.0	3 10.5	+25.0	45.0	3 52.9	+25.6	45.1	4 35.2	+26.3	45.1	43
44	2 52.4	+24.2	44.1	3 35.5	+24.9	44.1	4 18.5	+25.6	44.2	5 01.5	+26.3	44.2	44
45	3 16.6	+24.3	43.2	4 00.4	+24.8	43.2	4 44.1	+25.5	43.3	5 27.8	+26.1	43.3	45
46	3 40.9	+24.1	42.3	4 25.2	+24.8	42.3	5 09.6	+25.4	42.4	5 53.9	+26.1	42.4	46
47	4 05.0	+24.1	41.3	4 50.0	+24.8	41.4	5 35.0	+25.4	41.4	6 20.0	+26.0	41.5	47
48	4 29.1	+24.0	40.4	5 14.8	+24.6	40.5	6 00.4	+25.2	40.5	6 46.0	+25.8	40.6	48
49	4 53.1	+24.0	39.5	5 39.4	+24.5	39.6	6 25.6	+25.2	39.6	7 11.8	+25.8	39.7	49
50	5 17.1	+23.8	38.6	6 03.9	+24.5	38.6	6 50.8	+25.0	38.7	7 37.6	+25.6	38.8	50
51	5 40.9	+23.8	37.7	6 28.4	+24.4	37.7	7 15.8	+25.0	37.8	8 03.2	+25.6	37.9	51
52	6 04.7	+23.7	36.7	6 52.8	+24.2	36.8	7 40.8	+24.8	36.9	8 28.8	+25.4	37.0	52
53	6 28.4	+23.6	35.8	7 17.0	+24.2	35.9	8 05.6	+24.7	36.0	8 54.2	+25.2	36.0	53
54	6 52.0	+23.4	34.9	7 41.2	+24.0	35.0	8 30.3	+24.6	35.0	9 19.4	+25.1	35.1	54
55	7 15.4	+23.4	34.0	8 05.2	+23.9	34.0	8 54.9	+24.4	34.1	9 44.5	+25.0	34.2	55
56	7 38.8	+23.2	33.0	8 29.1	+23.8	33.1	9 19.3	+24.3	33.2	10 09.5	+24.8	33.3	56
57	8 02.0	+23.2	32.1	8 52.9	+23.6	32.2	9 43.6	+24.2	32.3	10 34.3	+24.7	32.4	57
58	8 25.2	+22.9	31.2	9 16.5	+23.5	31.2	10 07.8	+23.9	31.3	10 59.0	+24.5	31.4	58
59	8 48.1	+22.9	30.2	9 40.0	+23.3	30.3	10 31.7	+23.9	30.4	11 23.5	+24.3	30.5	59
60	9 11.0	+22.7	29.3	10 03.3	+23.2	29.4	10 55.6	+23.6	29.5	11 47.8	+24.1	29.6	60
61	9 33.7	+22.5	28.4	10 26.5	+23.0	28.4	11 19.2	+23.5	28.5	12 11.9	+23.9	28.6	61
62	9 56.2	+22.4	27.4	10 49.5	+22.8	27.5	11 42.7	+23.3	27.6	12 35.8	+23.8	27.7	62
63	10 18.6	+22.3	26.5	11 12.3	+22.7	26.6	12 06.0	+23.1	26.6	12 59.6	+23.5	26.7	63
64	10 40.9	+22.0	25.5	11 35.0	+22.5	25.6	12 29.1	+22.9	25.7	13 23.1	+23.3	25.8	64
65	11 02.9	+21.9	24.6	11 57.5	+22.3	24.7	12 52.0	+22.7	24.8	13 46.4	+23.1	24.9	65
66	11 24.8	+21.7	23.6	12 19.8	+22.0	23.7	13 14.7	+22.5	23.8	14 09.5	+22.9	23.9	66
67	11 46.5	+21.5	22.7	12 41.8	+21.9	22.8	13 37.2	+22.2	22.9	14 32.4	+22.7	22.9	67
68	12 08.0	+21.3	21.7	13 03.7	+21.7	21.8	13 59.4	+22.1	21.9	14 55.1	+22.4	22.0	68
69	12 29.3	+21.1	20.8	13 25.4	+21.5	20.8	14 21.5	+21.8	20.9	15 17.5	+22.1	21.0	69
70	12 50.4	+20.9	19.8	13 46.9	+21.2	19.9	14 43.3	+21.5	20.0	15 39.6	+21.9	20.1	70
71	13 11.3	+20.7	18.8	14 08.1	+21.0	18.9	15 04.8	+21.4	19.0	16 01.5	+21.7	19.1	71
72	13 32.0	+20.5	17.9	14 29.1	+20.8	18.0	15 26.2	+21.0	18.0	16 23.2	+21.4	18.1	72
73	13 52.5	+20.2	16.9	14 49.9	+20.5	17.0	15 47.2	+20.8	17.1	16 44.6	+21.1	17.2	73
74	14 12.7	+20.0	15.9	15 10.4	+20.2	16.0	16 08.0	+20.6	16.1	17 05.7	+20.8	16.2	74
75	14 32.7	+19.7	15.0	15 30.6	+20.1	15.0	16 28.6	+20.2	15.1	17 26.5	+20.5	15.2	75
76	14 52.4	+19.5	14.0	15 50.7	+19.7	14.1	16 48.8	+20.0	14.1	17 47.0	+20.3	14.2	76
77	15 11.9	+19.3	13.0	16 10.4	+19.5	13.1	17 08.8	+19.7	13.1	18 07.3	+19.9	13.2	77
78	15 31.2	+19.0	12.0	16 29.9	+19.2	12.1	17 28.5	+19.4	12.2	18 27.2	+19.6	12.2	78
79	15 50.2	+18.7	11.0	16 49.1	+18.9	11.1	17 47.9	+19.1	11.2	18 46.8	+19.3	11.2	79
80	16 08.9	+18.5	10.1	17 08.0	+18.6	10.1	18 07.0	+18.8	10.2	19 06.1	+19.0	10.2	80
81	16 27.4	+18.1	9.1	17 26.6	+18.3	9.1	18 25.8	+18.5	9.2	19 25.1	+18.6	9.2	81
82	16 45.5	+17.9	8.1	17 44.9	+18.0	8.1	18 44.3	+18.2	8.2	19 43.7	+18.3	8.2	82
83	17 03.4	+17.6	7.1	18 02.9	+17.7	7.1	19 02.5	+17.8	7.2	20 02.0	+18.0	7.2	83
84	17 21.0	+17.3	6.1	18 20.6	+17.4	6.1	19 20.3	+17.5	6.1	20 20.0	+17.6	6.2	84
85	17 38.3	+17.0	5.1	18 38.0	+17.1	5.1	19 37.8	+17.2	5.1	20 37.6	+17.2	5.2	85
86	17 55.3	+16.6	4.1	18 55.1	+16.7	4.1	19 55.0	+16.8	4.1	20 54.8	+16.9	4.1	86
87	18 11.9	+16.4	3.1	19 11.8	+16.4	3.1	20 11.8	+16.4	3.1	21 11.7	+16.5	3.1	87
88	18 28.3	+16.0	2.0	19 28.2	+16.1	2.0	20 28.2	+16.1	2.1	21 28.2	+16.1	2.1	88
89	18 44.3	+15.7	1.0	19 44.3	+15.7	1.0	20 44.3	+15.7	1.0	21 44.3	+15.7	1.0	89
90	19 00.0	+15.4	0.0	20 00.0	+15.4	0.0	21 00.0	+15.3	0.0	22 00.0	+15.3	0.0	90
	19°			20°			21°			22°			

S. Lat. {L.H.A. greater than 180° ....Zn=180°–Z
{L.H.A. less than 180°...........Zn=180°+Z

76°, 284° L.H.A. LATITUDE SAME NAME AS DECLINATION

N. Lat. {L.H.A. greater than 180° .....Zn=Z; L.H.A. less than 180°............Zn=360°−Z}

Dec.	15°			16°			17°			18°			19°			20°			21°			22°			Dec.
	Hc	d	Z	Hc	d	Z	Hc	d	Z	Hc	d	Z	Hc	d	Z	Hc	d	Z	Hc	d	Z	Hc	d	Z	
°	° ′	′	°	° ′	′	°	° ′	′	°	° ′	′	°	° ′	′	°	° ′	′	°	° ′	′	°	° ′	′	°	°
0	13 30.8	+15.9	93.7	13 26.8	+16.9	93.9	13 22.6	+17.9	94.2	13 18.1	+19.0	94.4	13 13.4	+19.9	94.6	13 08.4	+21.0	94.9	13 03.2	+22.0	95.1	12 57.7	+23.0	95.3	0
1	13 46.7	+15.6	92.7	13 43.7	+16.7	92.9	13 40.5	+17.7	93.2	13 37.1	+18.7	93.4	13 33.3	+19.8	93.7	13 29.4	+20.7	93.9	13 25.2	+21.7	94.1	13 20.7	+22.7	94.4	1
2	14 02.3	+15.4	91.7	14 00.4	+16.4	92.0	13 58.2	+17.4	92.2	13 55.8	+18.4	92.5	13 53.1	+19.5	92.7	13 50.1	+20.5	92.9	13 46.9	+21.5	93.2	13 43.4	+22.6	93.4	2
3	14 17.7	+15.1	90.7	14 16.8	+16.2	91.0	14 15.6	+17.2	91.2	14 14.2	+18.3	91.5	14 12.6	+19.2	91.7	14 10.6	+20.3	92.0	14 08.4	+21.3	92.2	14 06.0	+22.3	92.5	3
4	14 32.8	+14.8	89.7	14 33.0	+15.9	90.0	14 32.8	+17.0	90.2	14 32.5	+18.0	90.5	14 31.8	+19.0	90.7	14 30.9	+20.1	91.0	14 29.7	+21.1	91.3	14 28.3	+22.0	91.5	4
5	14 47.6	+14.7	88.7	14 48.9	+15.6	89.0	14 49.8	+16.7	89.2	14 50.5	+17.7	89.5	14 50.8	+18.8	89.8	14 51.0	+19.7	90.0	14 50.8	+20.8	90.3	14 50.3	+21.9	90.6	5
6	15 02.3	+14.3	87.7	15 04.5	+15.4	88.0	15 06.5	+16.4	88.2	15 08.2	+17.5	88.5	15 09.6	+18.5	88.8	15 10.7	+19.6	89.1	15 11.6	+20.6	89.3	15 12.2	+21.5	89.6	6
7	15 16.6	+14.1	86.7	15 19.9	+15.1	87.0	15 22.9	+16.2	87.2	15 25.7	+17.2	87.5	15 28.1	+18.3	87.8	15 30.3	+19.3	88.1	15 32.2	+20.3	88.4	15 33.7	+21.4	88.6	7
8	15 30.7	+13.8	85.7	15 35.0	+14.9	86.0	15 39.1	+15.9	86.2	15 42.9	+16.9	86.5	15 46.4	+18.0	86.8	15 49.6	+19.0	87.1	15 52.5	+20.0	87.4	15 55.1	+21.0	87.7	8
9	15 44.5	+13.5	84.7	15 49.9	+14.5	85.0	15 55.0	+15.6	85.2	15 59.8	+16.7	85.5	16 04.4	+17.7	85.8	16 08.6	+18.7	86.1	16 12.5	+19.8	86.4	16 16.1	+20.8	86.7	9
10	15 58.0	+13.2	83.7	16 04.4	+14.3	84.0	16 10.6	+15.4	84.2	16 16.5	+16.4	84.5	16 22.1	+17.4	84.8	16 27.3	+18.5	85.1	16 32.3	+19.5	85.4	16 36.9	+20.6	85.7	10
11	16 11.2	+13.0	82.7	16 18.7	+14.0	82.9	16 26.0	+15.0	83.2	16 32.9	+16.1	83.5	16 39.5	+17.1	83.8	16 45.8	+18.2	84.1	16 51.8	+19.2	84.4	16 57.5	+20.2	84.7	11
12	16 24.2	+12.6	81.6	16 32.7	+13.7	81.9	16 41.0	+14.8	82.2	16 49.0	+15.8	82.5	16 56.6	+16.9	82.8	17 04.0	+17.8	83.1	17 11.0	+18.9	83.4	17 17.7	+19.9	83.7	12
13	16 36.8	+12.3	80.6	16 46.4	+13.4	80.9	16 55.8	+14.4	81.2	17 04.8	+15.5	81.5	17 13.5	+16.5	81.8	17 21.8	+17.6	82.1	17 29.9	+18.6	82.4	17 37.6	+19.7	82.8	13
14	16 49.1	+12.1	79.6	16 59.8	+13.1	79.9	17 10.2	+14.2	80.2	17 20.3	+15.2	80.5	17 30.0	+16.3	80.8	17 39.4	+17.3	81.1	17 48.5	+18.3	81.4	17 57.3	+19.3	81.8	14
15	17 01.2	+11.7	78.6	17 12.9	+12.8	78.9	17 24.4	+13.8	79.2	17 35.5	+14.8	79.5	17 46.3	+15.9	79.8	17 56.7	+17.0	80.1	18 06.8	+18.1	80.4	18 16.6	+19.1	80.8	15
16	17 12.9	+11.5	77.5	17 25.7	+12.5	77.8	17 38.2	+13.5	78.2	17 50.3	+14.6	78.5	18 02.2	+15.6	78.8	18 13.7	+16.6	79.1	18 24.9	+17.6	79.4	18 35.7	+18.7	79.8	16
17	17 24.4	+11.1	76.5	17 38.2	+12.1	76.8	17 51.7	+13.2	77.1	18 04.9	+14.3	77.4	18 17.8	+15.3	77.8	18 30.3	+16.4	78.1	18 42.5	+17.4	78.4	18 54.4	+18.4	78.8	17
18	17 35.5	+10.8	75.5	17 50.3	+11.9	75.8	18 04.9	+12.9	76.1	18 19.2	+13.9	76.4	18 33.1	+14.9	76.8	18 46.7	+16.0	77.1	18 59.9	+17.0	77.4	19 12.8	+18.1	77.8	18
19	17 46.3	+10.4	74.5	18 02.2	+11.5	74.8	18 17.8	+12.5	75.1	18 33.1	+13.6	75.4	18 48.0	+14.7	75.7	19 02.7	+15.6	76.1	19 16.9	+16.7	76.4	19 30.9	+17.7	76.7	19
20	17 56.7	+10.1	73.4	18 13.7	+11.2	73.7	18 30.3	+12.2	74.0	18 46.7	+13.2	74.4	19 02.7	+14.2	74.7	19 18.3	+15.3	75.0	19 33.6	+16.4	75.4	19 48.6	+17.4	75.7	20
21	18 06.8	+9.8	72.4	18 24.9	+10.8	72.7	18 42.5	+11.9	73.0	18 59.9	+12.9	73.3	19 16.9	+14.0	73.7	19 33.6	+15.0	74.0	19 50.0	+16.0	74.4	20 06.0	+17.0	74.7	21
22	18 16.6	+9.5	71.3	18 35.7	+10.5	71.7	18 54.4	+11.5	72.0	19 12.8	+12.6	72.3	19 30.9	+13.6	72.6	19 48.6	+14.6	73.0	20 06.0	+15.6	73.3	20 23.0	+16.7	73.7	22
23	18 26.1	+9.1	70.3	18 46.2	+10.1	70.6	19 05.9	+11.2	70.9	19 25.4	+12.2	71.3	19 44.5	+13.2	71.6	20 03.2	+14.3	72.0	20 21.6	+15.3	72.3	20 39.7	+16.3	72.7	23
24	18 35.2	+8.8	69.3	18 56.3	+9.8	69.6	19 17.1	+10.8	69.9	19 37.6	+11.8	70.2	19 57.7	+12.8	70.6	20 17.5	+13.9	70.9	20 36.9	+14.9	71.3	20 56.0	+15.9	71.6	24
25	18 44.0	+8.4	68.2	19 06.1	+9.5	68.5	19 27.9	+10.5	68.9	19 49.4	+11.5	69.2	20 10.5	+12.5	69.5	20 31.4	+13.5	69.9	20 51.8	+14.6	70.2	21 11.9	+15.6	70.6	25
26	18 52.4	+8.1	67.2	19 15.6	+9.1	67.5	19 38.4	+10.1	67.8	20 00.9	+11.1	68.1	20 23.0	+12.2	68.5	20 44.9	+13.1	68.8	21 06.4	+14.1	69.2	21 27.5	+15.2	69.6	26
27	19 00.5	+7.7	66.1	19 24.7	+8.7	66.4	19 48.5	+9.7	66.8	20 12.0	+10.7	67.1	20 35.2	+11.7	67.4	20 58.0	+12.8	67.8	21 20.5	+13.8	68.2	21 42.7	+14.7	68.5	27
28	19 08.2	+7.4	65.1	19 33.4	+8.3	65.4	19 58.2	+9.4	65.7	20 22.7	+10.4	66.1	20 46.9	+11.4	66.4	21 10.8	+12.3	66.7	21 34.3	+13.4	67.1	21 57.4	+14.4	67.5	28
29	19 15.6	+7.0	64.0	19 41.7	+8.0	64.3	20 07.6	+9.0	64.7	20 33.1	+10.0	65.0	20 58.3	+11.0	65.3	21 23.1	+12.0	65.7	21 47.7	+12.9	66.1	22 11.8	+14.0	66.4	29
30	19 22.6	+6.7	63.0	19 49.7	+7.7	63.3	20 16.6	+8.6	63.6	20 43.1	+9.6	63.9	21 09.3	+10.5	64.3	21 35.1	+11.6	64.6	22 00.6	+12.6	65.0	22 25.8	+13.6	65.4	30
31	19 29.3	+6.2	61.9	19 57.4	+7.2	62.2	20 25.2	+8.2	62.6	20 52.7	+9.2	62.9	21 19.8	+10.2	63.2	21 46.7	+11.2	63.6	22 13.2	+12.2	64.0	22 39.4	+13.1	64.3	31
32	19 35.5	+5.9	60.9	20 04.6	+6.9	61.2	20 33.4	+7.8	61.5	21 01.9	+8.8	61.8	21 30.0	+9.8	62.2	21 57.9	+10.7	62.5	22 25.4	+11.7	62.9	22 52.5	+12.8	63.3	32
33	19 41.4	+5.6	59.8	20 11.5	+6.5	60.1	20 41.2	+7.5	60.4	21 10.7	+8.4	60.8	21 39.8	+9.4	61.1	22 08.6	+10.4	61.5	22 37.1	+11.4	61.8	23 05.3	+12.3	62.2	33
34	19 47.0	+5.1	58.7	20 18.0	+6.1	59.1	20 48.7	+7.0	59.4	21 19.1	+8.0	59.7	21 49.2	+9.0	60.1	22 19.0	+9.9	60.4	22 48.5	+10.9	60.8	23 17.6	+11.9	61.1	34
35	19 52.1	+4.8	57.7	20 24.1	+5.7	58.0	20 55.7	+6.7	58.3	21 27.1	+7.6	58.6	21 58.2	+8.5	59.0	22 28.9	+9.5	59.3	22 59.4	+10.4	59.7	23 29.5	+11.4	60.1	35
36	19 56.9	+4.4	56.6	20 29.8	+5.3	56.9	21 02.4	+6.3	57.3	21 34.7	+7.2	57.6	22 06.7	+8.2	57.9	22 38.4	+9.1	58.3	23 09.8	+10.1	58.6	23 40.9	+11.0	59.0	36
37	20 01.3	+4.1	55.6	20 35.1	+5.0	55.9	21 08.7	+5.8	56.2	21 41.9	+6.8	56.5	22 14.9	+7.7	56.8	22 47.5	+8.7	57.2	23 19.9	+9.6	57.6	23 51.9	+10.5	57.9	37
38	20 05.4	+3.6	54.5	20 40.1	+4.5	54.8	21 14.5	+5.5	55.1	21 48.7	+6.4	55.4	22 22.6	+7.3	55.8	22 56.2	+8.2	56.1	23 29.5	+9.1	56.5	24 02.4	+10.1	56.8	38
39	20 09.0	+3.3	53.4	20 44.6	+4.2	53.7	21 20.0	+5.0	54.0	21 55.1	+5.9	54.4	22 29.9	+6.9	54.7	23 04.4	+7.8	55.0	23 38.6	+8.7	55.4	24 12.5	+9.7	55.8	39
40	20 12.3	+2.9	52.4	20 48.8	+3.7	52.7	21 25.0	+4.7	53.0	22 01.0	+5.6	53.3	22 36.8	+6.4	53.6	23 12.2	+7.3	54.0	23 47.3	+8.3	54.3	24 22.2	+9.1	54.7	40
41	20 15.2	+2.5	51.3	20 52.5	+3.4	51.6	21 29.7	+4.2	51.9	22 06.6	+5.1	52.2	22 43.2	+6.0	52.6	23 19.5	+6.9	52.9	23 55.6	+7.8	53.2	24 31.3	+8.8	53.6	41
42	20 17.7	+2.1	50.2	20 55.9	+3.0	50.5	21 33.9	+3.8	50.8	22 11.7	+4.7	51.1	22 49.2	+5.6	51.5	23 26.4	+6.5	51.8	24 03.4	+7.3	52.2	24 40.1	+8.2	52.5	42
43	20 19.8	+1.7	49.2	20 58.9	+2.5	49.5	21 37.7	+3.5	49.8	22 16.4	+4.2	50.1	22 54.8	+5.1	50.4	23 32.9	+6.0	50.7	24 10.7	+6.9	51.1	24 48.3	+7.7	51.4	43
44	20 21.5	+1.3	48.1	21 01.4	+2.2	48.4	21 41.2	+3.0	48.7	22 20.6	+3.9	49.0	22 59.9	+4.7	49.3	23 38.9	+5.5	49.6	24 17.6	+6.4	50.0	24 56.0	+7.3	50.3	44
45	20 22.8	+1.0	47.0	21 03.6	+1.7	47.3	21 44.2	+2.5	47.6	22 24.5	+3.4	47.9	23 04.6	+4.2	48.2	23 44.4	+5.1	48.5	24 24.0	+5.9	48.9	25 03.3	+6.8	49.2	45
46	20 23.8	+0.5	46.0	21 05.3	+1.4	46.3	21 46.7	+2.2	46.5	22 27.9	+3.0	46.8	23 08.8	+3.8	47.1	23 49.5	+4.6	47.5	24 29.9	+5.5	47.8	25 10.1	+6.3	48.1	46
47	20 24.3	+0.2	44.9	21 06.7	+1.0	45.2	21 48.9	+1.7	45.5	22 30.9	+2.5	45.8	23 12.6	+3.4	46.1	23 54.1	+4.2	46.4	24 35.4	+5.0	46.7	25 16.4	+5.9	47.0	47
48	20 24.5	−0.3	43.8	21 07.7	+0.5	44.1	21 50.6	+1.4	44.4	22 33.4	+2.1	44.7	23 16.0	+2.9	45.0	23 58.3	+3.7	45.3	24 40.4	+4.5	45.6	25 22.3	+5.3	45.9	48
49	20 24.2	−0.6	42.8	21 08.2	+0.1	43.0	21 52.0	+0.9	43.3	22 35.5	+1.7	43.6	23 18.9	+2.4	43.9	24 02.0	+3.2	44.2	24 44.9	+4.0	44.5	25 27.6	+4.8	44.8	49
50	20 23.6	−1.0	41.7	21 08.3	−0.2	42.0	21 52.9	+0.4	42.2	22 37.2	+1.2	42.5	23 21.3	+2.0	42.8	24 05.2	+2.8	43.1	24 48.9	+3.6	43.4	25 32.4	+4.4	43.7	50
51	20 22.6	−1.4	40.6	21 08.1	−0.7	40.9	21 53.3	+0.1	41.2	22 38.4	+0.8	41.4	23 23.3	+1.6	41.7	24 08.0	+2.3	42.0	24 52.5	+3.1	42.3	25 36.8	+3.8	42.6	51
52	20 21.2	−1.7	39.6	21 07.4	−1.1	39.8	21 53.4	−0.4	40.1	22 39.2	+0.4	40.3	23 24.9	+1.1	40.6	24 10.3	+1.8	40.9	24 55.6	+2.5	41.2	25 40.6	+3.3	41.5	52
53	20 19.5	−2.2	38.5	21 06.3	−1.4	38.8	21 53.0	−0.7	39.0	22 39.6	−0.1	39.3	23 26.0	+0.6	39.5	24 12.1	+1.4	39.8	24 58.1	+2.1	40.1	25 43.9	+2.9	40.4	53
54	20 17.3	−2.6	37.4	21 04.9	−1.9	37.7	21 52.3	−1.2	37.9	22 39.5	−0.5	38.2	23 26.6	+0.2	38.4	24 13.5	+0.9	38.7	25 00.2	+1.6	39.0	25 46.8	+2.3	39.3	54
55	20 14.7	−2.9	36.4	21 03.0	−2.3	36.6	21 51.1	−1.7	36.8	22 39.0	−0.9	37.1	23 26.8	−0.3	37.3	24 14.4	+0.4	37.6	25 01.8	+1.2	37.9	25 49.1	+1.8	38.2	55
56	20 11.8	−3.3	35.3	21 00.7	−2.7	35.5	21 49.4	−2.0	35.8	22 38.1	−1.4	36.0	23 26.5	−0.7	36.3	24 14.8	0.0	36.5	25 03.0	+0.6	36.8	25 50.9	+1.3	37.1	56
57	20 08.5	−3.7	34.3	20 58.0	−3.1	34.5	21 47.4	−2.5	34.7	22 36.7	−1.9	34.9	23 25.8	−1.2	35.2	24 14.8	−0.6	35.4	25 03.6	+0.1	35.7	25 52.2	+0.8	36.0	57
58	20 04.8	−4.1	33.2	20 54.9	−3.5	33.4	21 44.9	−2.8	33.6	22 34.8	−2.2	33.8	23 24.6	−1.6	34.1	24 14.2	−1.0	34.3	25 03.7	−0.3	34.6	25 53.0	+0.3	34.9	58
59	20 00.7	−4.5	32.1	20 51.4	−3.9	32.3	21 42.1	−3.3	32.5	22 32.6	−2.7	32.8	23 23.0	−2.1	33.0	24 13.2	−1.4	33.2	25 03.4	−0.9	33.5	25 53.3	−0.2	33.7	59
60	19 56.2	−4.8	31.1	20 47.5	−4.2	31.3	21 38.8	−3.7	31.5	22 29.9	−3.1	31.7	23 20.9	−2.5	31.9	24 11.8	−2.0	32.1	25 02.5	−1.3	32.4	25 53.1	−0.7	32.6	60
61	19 51.4	−5.3	30.0	20 43.3	−4.7	30.2	21 35.1	−4.1	30.4	22 26.8	−3.6	30.6	23 18.4	−3.0	30.8	24 09.8	−2.4	31.0	25 01.2	−1.8	31.3	25 52.4	−1.2	31.5	61
62	19 46.1	−5.6	29.0	20 38.6	−5.1	29.1	21 31.0	−4.6	29.3	22 23.2	−4.0	29.5	23 15.4	−3.4	29.7	24 07.4	−2.8	29.9	24 59.4	−2.3	30.2	25 51.2	−1.8	30.4	62
63	19 40.5	−5.9	27.9	20 33.5	−5.4	28.1	21 26.4	−4.9	28.2	22 19.2	−4.4	28.4	23 12.0	−3.9	28.6	24 04.6	−3.4	28.8	24 57.1	−2.8	29.1	25 49.4	−2.2	29.3	63
64	19 34.6	−6.4	26.8	20 28.1	−5.9	27.0	21 21.5	−5.3	27.2	22 14.8	−4.8	27.4	23 08.1	−4.3	27.6	24 01.2	−3.8	27.8	24 54.3	−3.3	28.0	25 47.2	−2.7	28.2	64
65	19 28.2	−6.7	25.8	20 22.2	−6.2	25.9	21 16.2	−5.8	26.1	22 10.0	−5.3	26.3	23 03.8	−4.8	26.5	23 57.4	−4.3	26.7	24 51.0	−3.8	26.9	25 44.5	−3.3	27.1	65
66	19 21.5	−7.0	24.7	20 16.0	−6.6	24.9	21 10.4	−6.1	25.0	22 04.7	−5.6	25.2	22 59.0	−5.2	25.4	23 53.1	−4.7	25.6	24 47.2	−4.2	25.8	25 41.2	−3.7	26.0	66
67	19 14.5	−7.4	23.7	20 09.4	−7.0	23.8	21 04.3	−6.6	24.0	21 59.1	−6.1	24.1	22 53.8	−5.7	24.3	23 48.4	−5.2	24.5	24 43.0	−4.7	24.7	25 37.5	−4.3	24.9	67
68	19 07.1	−7.8	22.6	20 02.4	−7.3	22.8	20 57.7	−6.9	22.9	21 53.0	−6.6	23.1	22 48.1	−6.1	23.2	23 43.2	−5.6	23.4	24 38.3	−5.2	23.6	25 33.2	−4.7	23.8	68
69	18 59.3	−8.1	21.6	19 55.1	−7.8	21.7	20 50.8	−7.4	21.8	21 46.4	−6.9	22.0	22 42.0	−6.5	22.1	23 37.6	−6.1	22.3	24 33.1	−5.7	22.5	25 28.5	−5.3	22.7	69
70	18 51.2	−8.5	20.5	19 47.3	−8.1	20.7	20 43.4	−7.7	20.8	21 39.5	−7.3	20.9	22 35.5	−6.9	21.1	23 31.5	−6.6	21.2	24 27.4	−6.2	21.4	25 23.2	−5.7	21.6	70
71	18 42.7	−8.9	19.5	19 39.2	−8.5	19.6	20 35.7	−8.1	19.7	21 32.2	−7.8	19.9	22 28.6	−7.4	20.0	23 24.9	−7.0	20.1	24 21.2	−6.6	20.3	25 17.5	−6.2	20.4	71
72	18 33.8	−9.1	18.4	19 30.7	−8.8	18.5	20 27.6	−8.5	18.7	21 24.4	−8.1	18.8	22 21.2	−7.8	18.9	23 17.9	−7.4	19.1	24 14.6	−7.0	19.2	25 11.3	−6.7	19.4	72
73	18 24.7	−9.6	17.4	19 21.9	−9.2	17.5	20 19.1	−8.9	17.6	21 16.3	−8.6	17.7	22 13.4	−8.2	17.8	23 10.5	−7.9	18.0	24 07.6	−7.6	18.1	25 04.6	−7.2	18.3	73
74	18 15.1	−9.8	16.4	19 12.7	−9.6	16.5	20 10.2	−9.2	16.6	21 07.7	−8.9	16.7	22 05.2	−8.6	16.8	23 02.6	−8.3	16.9	24 00.0	−8.0	17.0	24 57.4	−7.7	17.2	74
75	18 05.3	−10.2	15.3	19 03.1	−9.9	15.4	20 01.0	−9.6	15.5	20 58.8	−9.4	15.6	21 56.6	−9.1	15.7	22 54.3	−8.8	15.8	23 52.0	−8.4	15.9	24 49.7	−8.2	16.1	75
76	17 55.1	−10.5	14.3	18 53.2	−10.2	14.4	19 51.4	−10.0	14.5	20 49.4	−9.7	14.5	21 47.5	−9.4	14.6	22 45.5	−9.1	14.7	23 43.6	−9.0	14.9	24 41.5	−8.6	15.0	76
77	17 44.6	−10.8	13.2	18 43.0	−10.6	13.3	19 41.4	−10.4	13.4	20 39.7	−10.1	13.5	21 38.1	−9.9	13.6	22 36.4	−9.6	13.7	23 34.6	−9.3	13.8	24 32.9	−9.1	13.9	77
78	17 33.8	−11.2	12.2	18 32.4	−10.9	12.3	19 31.0	−10.7	12.4	20 29.6	−10.5	12.4	21 28.2	−10.3	12.5	22 26.8	−10.1	12.6	23 25.3	−9.8	12.7	24 23.8	−9.5	12.8	78
79	17 22.6	−11.5	11.2	18 21.5	−11.3	11.2	19 20.3	−11.1	11.3	20 19.1	−10.8	11.4	21 17.9	−10.6	11.5	22 16.7	−10.4	11.5	23 15.5	−10.2	11.6	24 14.3	−10.0	11.7	79
80	17 11.1	−11.8	10.2	18 10.2	−11.6	10.2	19 09.2	−11.4	10.3	20 08.3	−11.3	10.3	21 07.3	−11.1	10.4	22 06.3	−10.9	10.5	23 05.3	−10.7	10.6	24 04.3	−10.5	10.6	80
81	16 59.3	−12.1	9.1	17 58.6	−12.0	9.2	18 57.8	−11.8	9.2	19 57.0	−11.6	9.3	20 56.2	−11.4	9.4	21 55.4	−11.2	9.4	22 54.6	−11.1	9.5	23 53.8	−10.9	9.6	81
82	16 47.2	−12.3	8.1	17 46.6	−12.2	8.2	18 46.0	−12.1	8.2	19 45.4	−11.9	8.2	20 44.8	−11.8	8.3	21 44.2	−11.7	8.4	22 43.5	−11.5	8.4	23 42.9	−11.4	8.5	82
83	16 34.9	−12.7	7.1	17 34.4	−12.6	7.1	18 33.9	−12.4	7.2	19 33.5	−12.4	7.2	20 33.0	−12.2	7.3	21 32.5	−12.1	7.3	22 32.0	−11.9	7.4	23 31.5	−11.8	7.4	83
84	16 22.2	−13.0	6.1	17 21.8	−12.9	6.1	18 21.5	−12.8	6.1	19 21.1	−12.6	6.2	20 20.8	−12.6	6.2	21 20.4	−12.4	6.3	22 20.1	−12.4	6.3	23 19.7	−12.2	6.3	84
85	16 09.2	−13.3	5.1	17 08.9	−13.2	5.1	18 08.7	−13.1	5.1	19 08.5	−13.1	5.1	20 08.2	−12.9	5.2	21 08.0	−12.9	5.2	22 07.7	−12.7	5.2	23 07.5	−12.7	5.3	85
86	15 55.9	−13.6	4.0	16 55.7	−13.4	4.1	17 55.6	−13.4	4.1	18 55.4	−13.3	4.1	19 55.3	−13.3	4.1	20 55.1	−13.2	4.2	21 55.0	−13.2	4.2	22 54.8	−13.1	4.2	86
87	15 42.3	−13.8	3.0	16 42.3	−13.8	3.0	17 42.2	−13.8	3.1	18 42.1	−13.7	3.1	19 42.0	−13.7	3.1	20 41.9	−13.6	3.1	21 41.8	−13.5	3.1	22 41.7	−13.5	3.2	87
88	15 28.5	−14.1	2.0	16 28.5	−14.1	2.0	17 28.4	−14.0	2.0	18 28.4	−14.0	2.0	19 28.3	−14.0	2.1	20 28.3	−14.0	2.1	21 28.3	−14.0	2.1	22 28.2	−13.9	2.1	88
89	15 14.4	−14.4	1.0	16 14.4	−14.4	1.0	17 14.4	−14.4	1.0	18 14.4	−14.4	1.0	19 14.3	−14.3	1.0	20 14.3	−14.3	1.0	21 14.3	−14.3	1.0	22 14.3	−14.3	1.0	89
90	15 00.0	−14.6	0.0	16 00.0	−14.7	0.0	17 00.0	−14.7	0.0	18 00.0	−14.7	0.0	19 00.0	−14.7	0.0	20 00.0	−14.7	0.0	21 00.0	−14.7	0.0	22 00.0	−14.7	0.0	90
	15°			16°			17°			18°			19°			20°			21°			22°			

76°, 284° L.H.A. LATITUDE SAME NAME AS DECLINATION

Dec.	15° Hc	d	Z	16° Hc	d	Z	17° Hc	d	Z	18° Hc	d	Z	19° Hc	d	Z	20° Hc	d	Z	21° Hc	d	Z	22° Hc	d	Z	Dec.
°	° ′	′	°	° ′	′	°	° ′	′	°	° ′	′	°	° ′	′	°	° ′	′	°	° ′	′	°	° ′	′	°	°
0	13 30.8	−16.1	93.7	13 26.8	−17.1	93.9	13 22.6	−18.1	94.2	13 18.1	−19.2	94.4	13 13.4	−20.2	94.6	13 08.4	−21.2	94.9	13 03.2	−22.2	95.1	12 57.7	−23.1	95.3	0
1	13 14.7	−16.3	94.7	13 09.7	−17.3	94.9	13 04.5	−18.4	95.1	12 58.9	−19.3	95.4	12 53.2	−20.4	95.6	12 47.2	−21.4	95.8	12 41.0	−22.4	96.1	12 34.6	−23.4	96.3	1
2	12 58.4	−16.5	95.7	12 52.4	−17.6	95.9	12 46.1	−18.6	96.1	12 39.6	−19.6	96.3	12 32.8	−20.6	96.6	12 25.8	−21.6	96.8	12 18.6	−22.5	97.0	12 11.2	−23.6	97.2	2
3	12 41.9	−16.8	96.7	12 34.8	−17.8	96.9	12 27.5	−18.8	97.1	12 20.0	−19.8	97.3	12 12.2	−20.8	97.5	12 04.2	−21.7	97.7	11 56.1	−22.8	98.0	11 47.6	−23.7	98.2	3
4	12 25.1	−16.9	97.6	12 17.0	−17.9	97.9	12 08.7	−19.0	98.1	12 00.2	−20.0	98.3	11 51.4	−21.0	98.5	11 42.5	−22.0	98.7	11 33.3	−23.0	98.9	11 23.9	−23.9	99.1	4
5	12 08.2	−17.2	98.6	11 59.1	−18.2	98.8	11 49.7	−19.2	99.0	11 40.2	−20.2	99.2	11 30.4	−21.1	99.4	11 20.5	−22.2	99.6	11 10.3	−23.1	99.8	11 00.0	−24.1	100.0	5
6	11 51.0	−17.4	99.6	11 40.9	−18.4	99.8	11 30.5	−19.3	100.0	11 20.0	−20.4	100.2	11 09.3	−21.4	100.4	10 58.3	−22.3	100.6	10 47.2	−23.3	100.8	10 35.9	−24.3	101.0	6
7	11 33.6	−17.6	100.6	11 22.5	−18.6	100.8	11 11.2	−19.6	101.0	10 59.6	−20.5	101.2	10 47.9	−21.5	101.4	10 36.0	−22.5	101.5	10 23.9	−23.4	101.7	10 11.6	−24.4	101.9	7
8	11 16.0	−17.7	101.6	11 03.9	−18.7	101.7	10 51.6	−19.7	101.9	10 39.1	−20.7	102.1	10 26.4	−21.7	102.3	10 13.5	−22.6	102.5	10 00.5	−23.7	102.7	9 47.2	−24.5	102.8	8
9	10 58.3	−18.0	102.5	10 45.2	−19.0	102.7	10 31.9	−20.0	102.9	10 18.4	−20.9	103.1	10 04.7	−21.9	103.3	9 50.9	−22.9	103.4	9 36.8	−23.7	103.6	9 22.7	−24.7	103.8	9
10	10 40.3	−18.1	103.5	10 26.2	−19.1	103.7	10 11.9	−20.0	103.9	9 57.5	−21.1	104.0	9 42.8	−22.0	104.2	9 28.0	−22.9	104.4	9 13.1	−23.9	104.5	8 58.0	−24.9	104.7	10
11	10 22.2	−18.3	104.5	10 07.1	−19.3	104.6	9 51.9	−20.3	104.8	9 36.4	−21.2	105.0	9 20.8	−22.1	105.1	9 05.1	−23.1	105.3	8 49.2	−24.1	105.4	8 33.1	−25.0	105.6	11
12	10 03.9	−18.5	105.4	9 47.8	−19.4	105.6	9 31.6	−20.4	105.8	9 15.2	−21.3	105.9	8 58.7	−22.3	106.1	8 42.0	−23.3	106.2	8 25.1	−24.1	106.4	8 08.1	−25.0	106.5	12
13	9 45.4	−18.6	106.4	9 28.4	−19.6	106.6	9 11.2	−20.5	106.7	8 53.9	−21.5	106.9	8 36.4	−22.5	107.0	8 18.7	−23.3	107.2	8 01.0	−24.3	107.3	7 43.1	−25.3	107.4	13
14	9 26.8	−18.8	107.4	9 08.8	−19.8	107.5	8 50.7	−20.7	107.7	8 32.4	−21.7	107.8	8 13.9	−22.5	108.0	7 55.4	−23.5	108.1	7 36.7	−24.5	108.2	7 17.8	−25.3	108.3	14
15	9 08.0	−19.0	108.3	8 49.0	−19.8	108.5	8 30.0	−20.9	108.6	8 10.7	−21.7	108.8	7 51.4	−22.7	108.9	7 31.9	−23.6	109.0	7 12.2	−24.5	109.1	6 52.5	−25.4	109.3	15
16	8 49.0	−19.0	109.3	8 29.2	−20.1	109.4	8 09.1	−20.9	109.6	7 49.0	−21.9	109.7	7 28.7	−22.8	109.8	7 08.3	−23.8	109.9	6 47.7	−24.6	110.1	6 27.1	−25.5	110.2	16
17	8 30.0	−19.3	110.2	8 09.1	−20.1	110.4	7 48.2	−21.1	110.5	7 27.1	−22.0	110.6	7 05.9	−23.0	110.8	6 44.5	−23.8	110.9	6 23.1	−24.7	111.0	6 01.6	−25.7	111.1	17
18	8 10.7	−19.3	111.2	7 49.0	−20.3	111.3	7 27.1	−21.2	111.5	7 05.1	−22.2	111.6	6 42.9	−23.0	111.7	6 20.7	−23.9	111.8	5 58.4	−24.8	111.9	5 35.9	−25.7	112.0	18
19	7 51.4	−19.5	112.2	7 28.7	−20.4	112.3	7 05.9	−21.4	112.4	6 42.9	−22.2	112.5	6 19.9	−23.1	112.6	5 56.8	−24.0	112.7	5 33.6	−24.9	112.8	5 10.2	−25.7	112.9	19
20	7 31.9	−19.7	113.1	7 08.3	−20.6	113.2	6 44.5	−21.4	113.3	6 20.7	−22.3	113.5	5 56.8	−23.2	113.5	5 32.8	−24.1	113.6	5 08.7	−25.0	113.7	4 44.5	−25.9	113.8	20
21	7 12.2	−19.7	114.1	6 47.7	−20.6	114.2	6 23.1	−21.5	114.3	5 58.4	−22.5	114.4	5 33.6	−23.4	114.5	5 08.7	−24.2	114.6	4 43.7	−25.1	114.6	4 18.6	−25.9	114.7	21
22	6 52.5	−19.8	115.0	6 27.1	−20.8	115.1	6 01.6	−21.7	115.2	5 35.9	−22.5	115.3	5 10.2	−23.3	115.4	4 44.5	−24.3	115.5	4 18.6	−25.1	115.6	3 52.7	−26.0	115.6	22
23	6 32.7	−20.0	116.0	6 06.3	−20.8	116.1	5 39.9	−21.7	116.2	5 13.4	−22.6	116.2	4 46.9	−23.5	116.3	4 20.2	−24.3	116.4	3 53.5	−25.2	116.5	3 26.7	−26.0	116.5	23
24	6 12.7	−20.0	116.9	5 45.5	−20.9	117.0	5 18.2	−21.8	117.1	4 50.8	−22.6	117.2	4 23.4	−23.5	117.2	3 55.9	−24.4	117.3	3 28.3	−25.2	117.4	3 00.7	−26.0	117.4	24
25	5 52.7	−20.2	117.9	5 24.6	−21.1	118.0	4 56.4	−21.9	118.0	4 28.2	−22.8	118.1	3 59.9	−23.6	118.2	3 31.5	−24.4	118.2	3 03.1	−25.3	118.3	2 34.7	−26.1	118.3	25
26	5 32.5	−20.2	118.8	5 03.5	−21.1	118.9	4 34.5	−21.9	119.0	4 05.4	−22.8	119.0	3 36.3	−23.7	119.1	3 07.1	−24.5	119.1	2 37.8	−25.3	119.2	2 08.6	−26.2	119.2	26
27	5 12.3	−20.4	119.8	4 42.4	−21.1	119.8	4 12.6	−22.1	119.9	3 42.6	−22.8	120.0	3 12.6	−23.7	120.0	2 42.6	−24.5	120.1	2 12.5	−25.3	120.1	1 42.4	−26.1	120.1	27
28	4 51.9	−20.4	120.7	4 21.3	−21.3	120.8	3 50.5	−22.0	120.8	3 19.8	−23.0	120.9	2 48.9	−23.7	120.9	2 18.1	−24.6	121.0	1 47.2	−25.4	121.0	1 16.3	−26.2	121.0	28
29	4 31.5	−20.5	121.6	4 00.0	−21.3	121.7	3 28.5	−22.2	121.8	2 56.8	−22.9	121.8	2 25.2	−23.8	121.9	1 53.5	−24.6	121.9	1 21.8	−25.4	121.9	0 50.1	−26.2	121.9	29
30	4 11.0	−20.5	122.6	3 38.7	−21.4	122.6	3 06.3	−22.2	122.7	2 33.9	−23.0	122.7	2 01.4	−23.8	122.8	1 28.9	−24.6	122.8	0 56.4	−25.4	122.8	0 23.9	−26.2	122.8	30
31	3 50.5	−20.6	123.5	3 17.3	−21.4	123.6	2 44.1	−22.2	123.6	2 10.9	−23.1	123.7	1 37.6	−23.8	123.7	1 04.3	−24.6	123.7	0 31.0	−25.4	123.7	0 02.3	+26.2	56.3	31
32	3 29.9	−20.7	124.5	2 55.9	−21.5	124.5	2 21.9	−22.3	124.6	1 47.8	−23.0	124.6	1 13.8	−23.9	124.6	0 39.7	−24.6	124.6	0 05.6	−25.4	124.6	0 28.5	+26.2	55.4	32
33	3 09.2	−20.7	125.4	2 34.4	−21.5	125.5	1 59.6	−22.3	125.5	1 24.8	−23.1	125.5	0 49.9	−23.8	125.5	0 15.1	−24.7	125.5	0 19.8	+25.4	54.5	0 54.7	+26.2	54.5	33
34	2 48.5	−20.7	126.4	2 12.9	−21.5	126.4	1 37.3	−22.3	126.4	1 01.7	−23.1	126.4	0 26.1	−23.8	126.4	0 09.6	+24.6	53.6	0 45.2	+25.4	53.6	1 20.9	+26.1	53.6	34
35	2 27.8	−20.8	127.3	1 51.4	−21.6	127.3	1 15.0	−22.3	127.3	0 38.6	−23.1	127.4	0 02.2	−23.9	127.4	0 34.2	+24.7	52.6	1 10.6	+25.4	52.7	1 47.0	+26.1	52.7	35
36	2 07.0	−20.9	128.2	1 29.8	−21.6	128.3	0 52.7	−22.4	128.3	0 15.5	−23.1	128.3	0 21.7	+23.9	51.7	0 58.9	+24.6	51.7	1 36.0	+25.4	51.7	2 13.1	+26.1	51.8	36
37	1 46.1	−20.8	129.2	1 08.2	−21.6	129.2	0 30.3	−22.4	129.2	0 07.6	+23.1	50.8	0 45.6	+23.8	50.8	1 23.5	+24.6	50.8	2 01.4	+25.3	50.8	2 39.2	+26.1	50.9	37
38	1 25.3	−20.9	130.1	0 46.6	−21.6	130.1	0 07.9	−22.3	130.1	0 30.7	+23.2	49.9	1 09.4	+23.8	49.9	1 48.1	+24.5	49.9	2 26.7	+25.3	49.9	3 05.3	+26.0	50.0	38
39	1 04.4	−20.9	131.0	0 25.0	−21.7	131.1	0 14.4	+22.4	48.9	0 53.9	+23.0	49.0	1 33.2	+23.9	49.0	2 12.6	+24.6	49.0	2 52.0	+25.2	49.0	3 31.3	+26.0	49.1	39
40	0 43.5	−21.0	132.0	0 03.3	−21.6	132.0	0 36.8	+22.4	48.0	1 16.9	+23.1	48.0	1 57.1	+23.7	48.0	2 37.2	+24.5	48.1	3 17.2	+25.2	48.1	3 57.3	+25.9	48.2	40
41	0 22.5	−20.9	132.9	0 18.3	+21.6	47.1	0 59.2	+22.3	47.1	1 40.0	+23.1	47.1	2 20.8	+23.8	47.2	3 01.7	+24.4	47.2	3 42.4	+25.2	47.2	4 23.2	+25.8	47.3	41
42	0 01.6	−20.9	133.9	0 39.9	+21.7	46.1	1 21.5	+22.3	46.2	2 03.1	+23.0	46.2	2 44.6	+23.7	46.2	3 26.1	+24.4	46.3	4 07.6	+25.0	46.3	4 49.0	+25.8	46.4	42
43	0 19.3	+20.9	45.2	1 01.6	+21.6	45.2	1 43.8	+22.3	45.2	2 26.1	+22.9	45.3	3 08.3	+23.7	45.3	3 50.5	+24.3	45.3	4 32.6	+25.1	45.4	5 14.8	+25.7	45.4	43
44	0 40.2	+20.9	44.3	1 23.2	+21.6	44.3	2 06.1	+22.3	44.3	2 49.0	+23.0	44.3	3 32.0	+23.6	44.4	4 14.8	+24.3	44.4	4 57.7	+24.9	44.5	5 40.5	+25.5	44.5	44
45	1 01.1	+20.9	43.3	1 44.8	+21.5	43.3	2 28.4	+22.2	43.4	3 12.0	+22.9	43.4	3 55.6	+23.5	43.4	4 39.1	+24.2	43.5	5 22.6	+24.9	43.6	6 06.0	+25.6	43.6	45
46	1 22.0	+20.9	42.4	2 06.3	+21.5	42.4	2 50.6	+22.2	42.4	3 34.9	+22.8	42.5	4 19.1	+23.5	42.5	5 03.3	+24.1	42.6	5 47.5	+24.7	42.6	6 31.6	+25.4	42.7	46
47	1 42.9	+20.8	41.5	2 27.8	+21.5	41.5	3 12.8	+22.1	41.5	3 57.7	+22.8	41.6	4 42.6	+23.4	41.6	5 27.4	+24.1	41.7	6 12.2	+24.7	41.7	6 57.0	+25.3	41.8	47
48	2 03.7	+20.8	40.5	2 49.3	+21.5	40.5	3 34.9	+22.1	40.6	4 20.5	+22.6	40.6	5 06.0	+23.3	40.7	5 51.5	+23.9	40.7	6 36.9	+24.6	40.8	7 22.3	+25.2	40.9	48
49	2 24.5	+20.8	39.6	3 10.8	+21.3	39.6	3 57.0	+22.0	39.6	4 43.1	+22.7	39.7	5 29.3	+23.2	39.8	6 15.4	+23.9	39.8	7 01.5	+24.4	39.9	7 47.5	+25.0	40.0	49
50	2 45.3	+20.7	38.6	3 32.1	+21.4	38.7	4 19.0	+21.9	38.7	5 05.8	+22.5	38.8	5 52.5	+23.2	38.8	6 39.3	+23.7	38.9	7 25.9	+24.4	39.0	8 12.5	+25.0	39.1	50
51	3 06.0	+20.7	37.7	3 53.5	+21.2	37.7	4 40.9	+21.9	37.8	5 28.3	+22.5	37.8	6 15.7	+23.0	37.9	7 03.0	+23.6	38.0	7 50.3	+24.2	38.1	8 37.5	+24.8	38.1	51
52	3 26.7	+20.6	36.8	4 14.7	+21.2	36.8	5 02.8	+21.8	36.8	5 50.8	+22.3	36.9	6 38.7	+23.0	37.0	7 26.6	+23.6	37.0	8 14.5	+24.1	37.1	9 02.3	+24.7	37.2	52
53	3 47.3	+20.6	35.8	4 35.9	+21.2	35.9	5 24.6	+21.6	35.9	6 13.1	+22.3	36.0	7 01.7	+22.8	36.0	7 50.2	+23.4	36.1	8 38.6	+24.0	36.2	9 27.0	+24.5	36.3	53
54	4 07.9	+20.4	34.9	4 57.1	+21.0	34.9	5 46.2	+21.7	35.0	6 35.4	+22.2	35.0	7 24.5	+22.7	35.1	8 13.6	+23.2	35.2	9 02.6	+23.8	35.3	9 51.5	+24.4	35.4	54
55	4 28.3	+20.5	33.9	5 18.1	+21.0	34.0	6 07.9	+21.5	34.0	6 57.6	+22.0	34.1	7 47.2	+22.6	34.2	8 36.8	+23.2	34.3	9 26.4	+23.7	34.3	10 15.9	+24.2	34.4	55
56	4 48.8	+20.3	33.0	5 39.1	+20.8	33.0	6 29.4	+21.4	33.1	7 19.6	+21.9	33.2	8 09.8	+22.5	33.2	9 00.0	+23.0	33.3	9 50.1	+23.5	33.4	10 40.1	+24.1	33.5	56
57	5 09.1	+20.3	32.0	5 59.9	+20.8	32.1	6 50.8	+21.3	32.2	7 41.5	+21.8	32.2	8 32.3	+22.3	32.3	9 23.0	+22.8	32.4	10 13.6	+23.4	32.5	11 04.2	+23.9	32.6	57
58	5 29.4	+20.1	31.1	6 20.7	+20.7	31.2	7 12.1	+21.1	31.2	8 03.3	+21.7	31.3	8 54.6	+22.2	31.4	9 45.8	+22.7	31.4	10 37.0	+23.2	31.5	11 28.1	+23.7	31.6	58
59	5 49.5	+20.1	30.2	6 41.4	+20.6	30.2	7 33.2	+21.1	30.3	8 25.0	+21.6	30.3	9 16.8	+22.0	30.4	10 08.5	+22.5	30.5	11 00.2	+23.0	30.6	11 51.8	+23.5	30.7	59
60	6 09.6	+20.0	29.2	7 02.0	+20.4	29.3	7 54.3	+20.9	29.3	8 46.6	+21.4	29.4	9 38.8	+21.9	29.5	10 31.0	+22.4	29.6	11 23.2	+22.8	29.7	12 15.3	+23.3	29.8	60
61	6 29.6	+19.8	28.3	7 22.4	+20.3	28.3	8 15.2	+20.8	28.4	9 08.0	+21.2	28.5	10 00.7	+21.7	28.5	10 53.4	+22.2	28.6	11 46.0	+22.7	28.7	12 38.6	+23.2	28.8	61
62	6 49.4	+19.8	27.3	7 42.7	+20.2	27.4	8 36.0	+20.7	27.4	9 29.2	+21.1	27.5	10 22.4	+21.6	27.6	11 15.6	+22.0	27.7	12 08.7	+22.5	27.8	13 01.8	+22.9	27.9	62
63	7 09.2	+19.6	26.4	8 02.9	+20.1	26.4	8 56.7	+20.5	26.5	9 50.3	+21.0	26.6	10 44.0	+21.4	26.6	11 37.6	+21.8	26.7	12 31.2	+22.2	26.8	13 24.7	+22.7	26.9	63
64	7 28.8	+19.5	25.4	8 23.0	+19.9	25.5	9 17.2	+20.3	25.5	10 11.3	+20.8	25.6	11 05.4	+21.2	25.7	11 59.4	+21.7	25.8	12 53.4	+22.1	25.9	13 47.4	+22.5	26.0	64
65	7 48.3	+19.4	24.5	8 42.9	+19.8	24.5	9 37.5	+20.2	24.6	10 32.1	+20.6	24.7	11 26.6	+21.0	24.7	12 21.1	+21.4	24.8	13 15.5	+21.8	24.9	14 09.9	+22.3	25.0	65
66	8 07.7	+19.3	23.5	9 02.7	+19.7	23.6	9 57.7	+20.1	23.6	10 52.7	+20.4	23.7	11 47.6	+20.8	23.8	12 42.5	+21.2	23.9	13 37.3	+21.7	24.0	14 32.2	+22.0	24.1	66
67	8 27.0	+19.1	22.5	9 22.4	+19.5	22.6	10 17.8	+19.8	22.7	11 13.1	+20.3	22.7	12 08.4	+20.7	22.8	13 03.7	+21.0	22.9	13 59.0	+21.4	23.0	14 54.2	+21.8	23.1	67
68	8 46.1	+19.0	21.6	9 41.9	+19.3	21.6	10 37.6	+19.7	21.7	11 33.4	+20.0	21.8	12 29.1	+20.4	21.9	13 24.7	+20.8	21.9	14 20.4	+21.1	22.0	15 16.0	+21.5	22.1	68
69	9 05.1	+18.8	20.6	10 01.2	+19.2	20.7	10 57.3	+19.5	20.7	11 53.4	+19.9	20.8	12 49.5	+20.2	20.9	13 45.5	+20.6	21.0	14 41.5	+21.0	21.1	15 37.5	+21.3	21.2	69
70	9 23.9	+18.6	19.7	10 20.4	+19.0	19.7	11 16.8	+19.4	19.8	12 13.3	+19.6	19.8	13 09.7	+20.0	19.9	14 06.1	+20.3	20.0	15 02.5	+20.6	20.1	15 58.8	+21.0	20.2	70
71	9 42.5	+18.5	18.7	10 39.4	+18.8	18.8	11 36.2	+19.1	18.8	12 32.9	+19.5	18.9	13 29.7	+19.8	19.0	14 26.4	+20.1	19.0	15 23.1	+20.5	19.1	16 19.8	+20.8	19.2	71
72	10 01.0	+18.4	17.7	10 58.2	+18.6	17.8	11 55.3	+18.9	17.8	12 52.4	+19.2	17.9	13 49.5	+19.5	18.0	14 46.5	+19.9	18.1	15 43.6	+20.1	18.1	16 40.6	+20.4	18.2	72
73	10 19.4	+18.1	16.8	11 16.8	+18.4	16.8	12 14.2	+18.7	16.9	13 11.6	+19.0	16.9	14 09.0	+19.3	17.0	15 06.4	+19.6	17.1	16 03.7	+19.9	17.2	17 01.0	+20.2	17.3	73
74	10 37.5	+18.0	15.8	11 35.2	+18.3	15.8	12 32.9	+18.6	15.9	13 30.6	+18.8	16.0	14 28.3	+19.1	16.0	15 26.0	+19.3	16.1	16 23.6	+19.6	16.2	17 21.2	+19.9	16.3	74
75	10 55.5	+17.8	14.8	11 53.5	+18.0	14.9	12 51.5	+18.3	14.9	13 49.4	+18.6	15.0	14 47.4	+18.8	15.1	15 45.3	+19.1	15.1	16 43.2	+19.4	15.2	17 41.1	+19.6	15.3	75
76	11 13.3	+17.6	13.8	12 11.5	+17.9	13.9	13 09.8	+18.0	13.9	14 08.0	+18.3	14.0	15 06.2	+18.6	14.1	16 04.4	+18.8	14.1	17 02.6	+19.0	14.2	18 00.7	+19.3	14.3	76
77	11 30.9	+17.4	12.9	12 29.4	+17.6	12.9	13 27.8	+17.9	13.0	14 26.3	+18.1	13.0	15 24.8	+18.3	13.1	16 23.2	+18.5	13.2	17 21.6	+18.8	13.2	18 20.0	+19.0	13.3	77
78	11 48.3	+17.2	11.9	12 47.0	+17.4	11.9	13 45.7	+17.6	12.0	14 44.4	+17.8	12.0	15 43.1	+18.0	12.1	16 41.7	+18.3	12.2	17 40.4	+18.4	12.2	18 39.0	+18.7	12.3	78
79	12 05.5	+17.0	10.9	13 04.4	+17.2	11.0	14 03.3	+17.4	11.0	15 02.2	+17.6	11.1	16 01.1	+17.7	11.1	17 00.0	+17.9	11.2	17 58.8	+18.2	11.2	18 57.7	+18.3	11.3	79
80	12 22.5	+16.8	9.9	13 21.6	+17.0	10.0	14 20.7	+17.1	10.0	15 19.8	+17.3	10.1	16 18.8	+17.5	10.1	17 17.9	+17.7	10.2	18 17.0	+17.8	10.2	19 16.0	+18.0	10.3	80
81	12 39.3	+16.6	8.9	13 38.6	+16.7	9.0	14 37.8	+16.9	9.0	15 37.1	+17.0	9.1	16 36.3	+17.2	9.1	17 35.6	+17.3	9.2	18 34.8	+17.5	9.2	19 34.0	+17.7	9.3	81
82	12 55.9	+16.3	8.0	13 55.3	+16.5	8.0	14 54.7	+16.6	8.0	15 54.1	+16.8	8.1	16 53.5	+16.9	8.1	17 52.9	+17.0	8.2	18 52.3	+17.2	8.2	19 51.7	+17.3	8.3	82
83	13 12.2	+16.1	7.0	14 11.8	+16.2	7.0	15 11.3	+16.4	7.0	16 10.9	+16.4	7.1	17 10.4	+16.6	7.1	18 09.9	+16.8	7.1	19 09.5	+16.8	7.2	20 09.0	+17.0	7.2	83
84	13 28.3	+15.9	6.0	14 28.0	+16.0	6.0	15 27.7	+16.1	6.0	16 27.3	+16.2	6.1	17 27.0	+16.3	6.1	18 26.7	+16.4	6.1	19 26.3	+16.5	6.2	20 26.0	+16.6	6.2	84
85	13 44.2	+15.7	5.0	14 44.0	+15.7	5.0	15 43.8	+15.8	5.0	16 43.5	+15.9	5.1	17 43.3	+16.0	5.1	18 43.1	+16.0	5.1	19 42.8	+16.2	5.2	20 42.6	+16.2	5.2	85
86	13 59.9	+15.4	4.0	14 59.7	+15.5	4.0	15 59.6	+15.5	4.0	16 59.4	+15.6	4.1	17 59.3	+15.7	4.1	18 59.1	+15.8	4.1	19 59.0	+15.8	4.1	20 58.8	+15.9	4.2	86
87	14 15.3	+15.1	3.0	15 15.2	+15.2	3.0	16 15.1	+15.3	3.0	17 15.0	+15.3	3.0	18 15.0	+15.3	3.1	19 14.9	+15.4	3.1	20 14.8	+15.4	3.1	21 14.7	+15.5	3.1	87
88	14 30.4	+15.0	2.0	15 30.4	+14.9	2.0	16 30.4	+14.9	2.0	17 30.3	+15.0	2.0	18 30.3	+15.0	2.0	19 30.3	+15.0	2.1	20 30.2	+15.1	2.1	21 30.2	+15.1	2.1	88
89	14 45.4	+14.6	1.0	15 45.3	+14.7	1.0	16 45.3	+14.7	1.0	17 45.3	+14.7	1.0	18 45.3	+14.7	1.0	19 45.3	+14.7	1.0	20 45.3	+14.7	1.0	21 45.3	+14.7	1.0	89
90	15 00.0	+14.4	0.0	16 00.0	+14.4	0.0	17 00.0	+14.4	0.0	18 00.0	+14.4	0.0	19 00.0	+14.3	0.0	20 00.0	+14.3	0.0	21 00.0	+14.3	0.0	22 00.0	+14.3	0.0	90
	15°			16°			17°			18°			19°			20°			21°			22°			

S. Lat. {L.H.A. greater than 180° ....Zn=180°−Z
L.H.A. less than 180°...........Zn=180°+Z

Dec.	15°			16°			17°			18°			19°			20°			21°			22°			Dec.
Dec.	Hc	d	Z	Hc	d	Z	Hc	d	Z	Hc	d	Z	Hc	d	Z	Hc	d	Z	Hc	d	Z	Hc	d	Z	Dec.
°	° ′	′	°	° ′	′	°	° ′	′	°	° ′	′	°	° ′	′	°	° ′	′	°	° ′	′	°	° ′	′	°	°
0	12 33.0	+15.8	93.4	12 29.3	+16.8	93.6	12 25.4	+17.8	93.9	12 21.2	+18.9	94.1	12 16.8	+19.9	94.3	12 12.2	+20.9	94.5	12 07.4	+21.9	94.7	12 02.3	+22.9	94.9	0
1	12 48.8	+15.6	92.4	12 46.1	+16.6	92.7	12 43.2	+17.7	92.9	12 40.1	+18.6	93.1	12 36.7	+19.7	93.3	12 33.1	+20.7	93.6	12 29.3	+21.7	93.8	12 25.2	+22.7	94.0	1
2	13 04.4	+15.3	91.4	13 02.7	+16.4	91.7	13 00.9	+17.4	91.9	12 58.7	+18.5	92.1	12 56.4	+19.5	92.4	12 53.8	+20.5	92.6	12 51.0	+21.4	92.8	12 47.9	+22.5	93.0	2
3	13 19.7	+15.1	90.4	13 19.1	+16.2	90.7	13 18.3	+17.2	90.9	13 17.2	+18.2	91.2	13 15.9	+19.2	91.4	13 14.3	+20.2	91.6	13 12.4	+21.3	91.9	13 10.4	+22.2	92.1	3
4	13 34.8	+14.9	89.5	13 35.3	+15.9	89.7	13 35.5	+16.9	89.9	13 35.4	+18.0	90.2	13 35.1	+19.0	90.4	13 34.5	+20.1	90.7	13 33.7	+21.1	90.9	13 32.6	+22.1	91.1	4
5	13 49.7	+14.7	88.5	13 51.2	+15.7	88.7	13 52.4	+16.8	88.9	13 53.4	+17.8	89.2	13 54.1	+18.8	89.4	13 54.6	+19.8	89.7	13 54.8	+20.8	89.9	13 54.7	+21.8	90.2	5
6	14 04.4	+14.3	87.5	14 06.9	+15.4	87.7	14 09.2	+16.4	88.0	14 11.2	+17.5	88.2	14 12.9	+18.5	88.5	14 14.4	+19.5	88.7	14 15.6	+20.6	89.0	14 16.5	+21.6	89.2	6
7	14 18.7	+14.2	86.5	14 22.3	+15.2	86.7	14 25.6	+16.3	87.0	14 28.7	+17.2	87.2	14 31.4	+18.3	87.5	14 33.9	+19.4	87.7	14 36.2	+20.3	88.0	14 38.1	+21.4	88.3	7
8	14 32.9	+13.9	85.5	14 37.5	+14.9	85.7	14 41.9	+15.9	86.0	14 45.9	+17.1	86.2	14 49.7	+18.1	86.5	14 53.3	+19.0	86.8	14 56.5	+20.1	87.0	14 59.5	+21.1	87.3	8
9	14 46.8	+13.6	84.4	14 52.4	+14.7	84.7	14 57.8	+15.7	85.0	15 03.0	+16.7	85.2	15 07.8	+17.8	85.5	15 12.3	+18.9	85.8	15 16.6	+19.9	86.1	15 20.6	+20.9	86.3	9
10	15 00.4	+13.3	83.4	15 07.1	+14.4	83.7	15 13.5	+15.5	84.0	15 19.7	+16.5	84.2	15 25.6	+17.5	84.5	15 31.2	+18.5	84.8	15 36.5	+19.5	85.1	15 41.5	+20.6	85.4	10
11	15 13.7	+13.1	82.4	15 21.5	+14.1	82.7	15 29.0	+15.2	83.0	15 36.2	+16.2	83.2	15 43.1	+17.3	83.5	15 49.7	+18.3	83.8	15 56.0	+19.4	84.1	16 02.1	+20.3	84.4	11
12	15 26.8	+12.8	81.4	15 35.6	+13.9	81.7	15 44.2	+14.9	82.0	15 52.4	+16.0	82.2	16 00.4	+16.9	82.5	16 08.0	+18.0	82.8	16 15.4	+19.0	83.1	16 22.4	+20.1	83.4	12
13	15 39.6	+12.6	80.4	15 49.5	+13.6	80.7	15 59.1	+14.6	81.0	16 08.4	+15.6	81.2	16 17.3	+16.7	81.5	16 26.0	+17.7	81.8	16 34.4	+18.8	82.1	16 42.5	+19.8	82.4	13
14	15 52.2	+12.2	79.4	16 03.1	+13.3	79.7	16 13.7	+14.3	80.0	16 24.0	+15.4	80.2	16 34.0	+16.4	80.5	16 43.7	+17.5	80.8	16 53.2	+18.4	81.1	17 02.3	+19.5	81.4	14
15	16 04.4	+12.0	78.4	16 16.4	+13.0	78.7	16 28.0	+14.1	78.9	16 39.4	+15.1	79.2	16 50.4	+16.2	79.5	17 01.2	+17.1	79.8	17 11.6	+18.2	80.1	17 21.8	+19.2	80.4	15
16	16 16.4	+11.6	77.3	16 29.4	+12.7	77.6	16 42.1	+13.7	77.9	16 54.5	+14.7	78.2	17 06.6	+15.8	78.5	17 18.3	+16.9	78.8	17 29.8	+17.9	79.1	17 41.0	+18.9	79.4	16
17	16 28.0	+11.4	76.3	16 42.1	+12.4	76.6	16 55.8	+13.4	76.9	17 09.2	+14.5	77.2	17 22.4	+15.5	77.5	17 35.2	+16.5	77.8	17 47.7	+17.6	78.1	17 59.9	+18.6	78.4	17
18	16 39.4	+11.0	75.3	16 54.5	+12.1	75.6	17 09.2	+13.2	75.9	17 23.7	+14.2	76.2	17 37.9	+15.2	76.5	17 51.7	+16.3	76.8	18 05.3	+17.2	77.1	18 18.5	+18.3	77.4	18
19	16 50.4	+10.8	74.3	17 06.6	+11.7	74.6	17 22.4	+12.8	74.9	17 37.9	+13.8	75.2	17 53.1	+14.9	75.5	18 08.0	+15.9	75.8	18 22.5	+17.0	76.1	18 36.8	+17.9	76.4	19
20	17 01.2	+10.4	73.2	17 18.3	+11.5	73.5	17 35.2	+12.5	73.8	17 51.7	+13.6	74.1	18 08.0	+14.5	74.5	18 23.9	+15.6	74.8	18 39.5	+16.6	75.1	18 54.7	+17.7	75.4	20
21	17 11.6	+10.2	72.2	17 29.8	+11.2	72.5	17 47.7	+12.2	72.8	18 05.3	+13.2	73.1	18 22.5	+14.3	73.4	18 39.5	+15.2	73.8	18 56.1	+16.3	74.1	19 12.4	+17.3	74.4	21
22	17 21.8	+9.8	71.2	17 41.0	+10.8	71.5	17 59.9	+11.8	71.8	18 18.5	+12.8	72.1	18 36.8	+13.9	72.4	18 54.7	+14.9	72.7	19 12.4	+15.9	73.1	19 29.7	+16.9	73.4	22
23	17 31.6	+9.5	70.1	17 51.8	+10.5	70.4	18 11.7	+11.5	70.8	18 31.3	+12.6	71.1	18 50.7	+13.5	71.4	19 09.6	+14.6	71.7	19 28.3	+15.6	72.0	19 46.6	+16.6	72.4	23
24	17 41.1	+9.1	69.1	18 02.3	+10.2	69.4	18 23.2	+11.2	69.7	18 43.9	+12.2	70.0	19 04.2	+13.2	70.4	19 24.2	+14.3	70.7	19 43.9	+15.2	71.0	20 03.2	+16.3	71.4	24
25	17 50.2	+8.9	68.1	18 12.5	+9.8	68.4	18 34.4	+10.9	68.7	18 56.1	+11.8	69.0	19 17.4	+12.9	69.3	19 38.5	+13.8	69.7	19 59.1	+14.9	70.0	20 19.5	+15.9	70.3	25
26	17 59.1	+8.4	67.0	18 22.3	+9.5	67.3	18 45.3	+10.5	67.6	19 07.9	+11.6	68.0	19 30.3	+12.5	68.3	19 52.3	+13.6	68.6	20 14.0	+14.6	69.0	20 35.4	+15.5	69.3	26
27	18 07.5	+8.2	66.0	18 31.8	+9.2	66.3	18 55.8	+10.1	66.6	19 19.5	+11.1	66.9	19 42.8	+12.2	67.3	20 05.9	+13.1	67.6	20 28.6	+14.1	67.9	20 50.9	+15.2	68.3	27
28	18 15.7	+7.8	65.0	18 41.0	+8.8	65.3	19 05.9	+9.8	65.6	19 30.6	+10.8	65.9	19 55.0	+11.8	66.2	20 19.0	+12.8	66.5	20 42.7	+13.8	66.9	21 06.1	+14.8	67.2	28
29	18 23.5	+7.5	63.9	18 49.8	+8.4	64.2	19 15.7	+9.5	64.5	19 41.4	+10.4	64.8	20 06.8	+11.4	65.2	20 31.8	+12.4	65.5	20 56.5	+13.4	65.9	21 20.9	+14.4	66.2	29
30	18 31.0	+7.2	62.9	18 58.2	+8.2	63.2	19 25.2	+9.1	63.5	19 51.8	+10.1	63.8	20 18.2	+11.0	64.1	20 44.2	+12.0	64.5	21 09.9	+13.0	64.8	21 35.3	+14.0	65.2	30
31	18 38.2	+6.7	61.8	19 06.4	+7.7	62.1	19 34.3	+8.7	62.4	20 01.9	+9.7	62.7	20 29.2	+10.7	63.1	20 56.2	+11.7	63.4	21 22.9	+12.7	63.8	21 49.3	+13.6	64.1	31
32	18 44.9	+6.5	60.8	19 14.1	+7.4	61.1	19 43.0	+8.3	61.4	20 11.6	+9.3	61.7	20 39.9	+10.3	62.0	21 07.9	+11.2	62.4	21 35.6	+12.2	62.7	22 02.9	+13.2	63.1	32
33	18 51.4	+6.1	59.7	19 21.5	+7.0	60.0	19 51.3	+8.0	60.3	20 20.9	+8.9	60.6	20 50.2	+9.9	61.0	21 19.1	+10.9	61.3	21 47.8	+11.8	61.7	22 16.1	+12.8	62.0	33
34	18 57.5	+5.7	58.7	19 28.5	+6.7	59.0	19 59.3	+7.6	59.3	20 29.8	+8.6	59.6	21 00.1	+9.5	59.9	21 30.0	+10.5	60.3	21 59.6	+11.4	60.6	22 28.9	+12.4	61.0	34
35	19 03.2	+5.3	57.6	19 35.2	+6.3	57.9	20 06.9	+7.3	58.2	20 38.4	+8.2	58.5	21 09.6	+9.1	58.9	21 40.5	+10.0	59.2	22 11.0	+11.0	59.5	22 41.3	+12.0	59.9	35
36	19 08.5	+5.1	56.6	19 41.5	+5.9	56.9	20 14.2	+6.8	57.2	20 46.6	+7.7	57.5	21 18.7	+8.7	57.8	21 50.5	+9.7	58.1	22 22.0	+10.6	58.5	22 53.3	+11.5	58.8	36
37	19 13.6	+4.6	55.5	19 47.4	+5.6	55.8	20 21.0	+6.5	56.1	20 54.3	+7.4	56.4	21 27.4	+8.3	56.7	22 00.2	+9.2	57.1	22 32.6	+10.2	57.4	23 04.8	+11.1	57.8	37
38	19 18.2	+4.3	54.4	19 53.0	+5.1	54.7	20 27.5	+6.1	55.0	21 01.7	+7.0	55.3	21 35.7	+7.9	55.7	22 09.4	+8.8	56.0	22 42.8	+9.8	56.3	23 15.9	+10.7	56.7	38
39	19 22.5	+3.9	53.4	19 58.1	+4.8	53.7	20 33.6	+5.6	54.0	21 08.7	+6.6	54.3	21 43.6	+7.5	54.6	22 18.2	+8.4	54.9	22 52.6	+9.3	55.3	23 26.6	+10.2	55.6	39
40	19 26.4	+3.5	52.3	20 02.9	+4.5	52.6	20 39.2	+5.3	52.9	21 15.3	+6.2	53.2	21 51.1	+7.1	53.5	22 26.6	+8.0	53.9	23 01.9	+8.8	54.2	23 36.8	+9.8	54.5	40
41	19 29.9	+3.2	51.3	20 07.4	+4.0	51.6	20 44.5	+5.0	51.8	21 21.5	+5.8	52.1	21 58.2	+6.6	52.5	22 34.6	+7.5	52.8	23 10.7	+8.5	53.1	23 46.6	+9.3	53.5	41
42	19 33.1	+2.8	50.2	20 11.4	+3.6	50.5	20 49.5	+4.5	50.8	21 27.3	+5.3	51.1	22 04.8	+6.3	51.4	22 42.1	+7.2	51.7	23 19.2	+8.0	52.0	23 55.9	+8.9	52.4	42
43	19 35.9	+2.4	49.2	20 15.0	+3.3	49.4	20 54.0	+4.1	49.7	21 32.6	+5.0	50.0	22 11.1	+5.8	50.3	22 49.3	+6.6	50.6	23 27.2	+7.5	51.0	24 04.8	+8.5	51.3	43
44	19 38.3	+2.1	48.1	20 18.3	+2.9	48.4	20 58.1	+3.7	48.6	21 37.6	+4.5	48.9	22 16.9	+5.4	49.2	22 55.9	+6.3	49.6	23 34.7	+7.1	49.9	24 13.3	+7.9	50.2	44
45	19 40.4	+1.7	47.0	20 21.2	+2.5	47.3	21 01.8	+3.3	47.6	21 42.1	+4.2	47.9	22 22.3	+5.0	48.2	23 02.2	+5.8	48.5	23 41.8	+6.7	48.8	24 21.2	+7.5	49.1	45
46	19 42.1	+1.3	46.0	20 23.7	+2.1	46.2	21 05.1	+2.9	46.5	21 46.3	+3.7	46.8	22 27.3	+4.5	47.1	23 08.0	+5.3	47.4	23 48.5	+6.2	47.7	24 28.7	+7.1	48.0	46
47	19 43.4	+0.9	44.9	20 25.8	+1.7	45.2	21 08.0	+2.5	45.4	21 50.0	+3.3	45.7	22 31.8	+4.1	46.0	23 13.3	+5.0	46.3	23 54.7	+5.7	46.6	24 35.8	+6.5	47.0	47
48	19 44.3	+0.6	43.8	20 27.5	+1.3	44.1	21 10.5	+2.1	44.4	21 53.3	+2.9	44.6	22 35.9	+3.7	44.9	23 18.3	+4.4	45.2	24 00.4	+5.3	45.5	24 42.3	+6.1	45.9	48
49	19 44.9	+0.2	42.8	20 28.8	+1.0	43.0	21 12.6	+1.7	43.3	21 56.2	+2.4	43.6	22 39.6	+3.2	43.8	23 22.7	+4.0	44.1	24 05.7	+4.8	44.4	24 48.4	+5.6	44.8	49
50	19 45.1	−0.2	41.7	20 29.8	+0.5	42.0	21 14.3	+1.3	42.2	21 58.6	+2.1	42.5	22 42.8	+2.8	42.8	23 26.7	+3.6	43.1	24 10.5	+4.3	43.4	24 54.0	+5.1	43.7	50
51	19 44.9	−0.6	40.7	20 30.3	+0.2	40.9	21 15.6	+0.9	41.1	22 00.7	+1.6	41.4	22 45.6	+2.3	41.7	23 30.3	+3.1	42.0	24 14.8	+3.9	42.3	24 59.1	+4.6	42.6	51
52	19 44.3	−0.9	39.6	20 30.5	−0.3	39.8	21 16.5	+0.4	40.1	22 02.3	+1.2	40.3	22 47.9	+2.0	40.6	23 33.4	+2.7	40.9	24 18.7	+3.4	41.2	25 03.7	+4.2	41.5	52
53	19 43.4	−1.4	38.5	20 30.2	−0.6	38.8	21 16.9	+0.1	39.0	22 03.5	+0.7	39.2	22 49.9	+1.4	39.5	23 36.1	+2.2	39.8	24 22.1	+2.9	40.1	25 07.9	+3.6	40.4	53
54	19 42.0	−1.7	37.5	20 29.6	−1.0	37.7	21 17.0	−0.3	37.9	22 04.2	+0.4	38.2	22 51.3	+1.1	38.4	23 38.3	+1.7	38.7	24 25.0	+2.4	39.0	25 11.5	+3.2	39.3	54
55	19 40.3	−2.0	36.4	20 28.6	−1.4	36.6	21 16.7	−0.8	36.9	22 04.6	−0.1	37.1	22 52.4	+0.6	37.3	23 40.0	+1.3	37.6	24 27.4	+2.0	37.9	25 14.7	+2.7	38.2	55
56	19 38.3	−2.5	35.3	20 27.2	−1.9	35.6	21 15.9	−1.2	35.8	22 04.5	−0.5	36.0	22 53.0	+0.1	36.3	23 41.3	+0.8	36.5	24 29.4	+1.5	36.8	25 17.4	+2.2	37.1	56
57	19 35.8	−2.8	34.3	20 25.3	−2.1	34.5	21 14.7	−1.5	34.7	22 04.0	−0.9	34.9	22 53.1	−0.3	35.2	23 42.1	+0.3	35.4	24 30.9	+1.0	35.7	25 19.6	+1.6	36.0	57
58	19 33.0	−3.2	33.2	20 23.2	−2.6	33.4	21 13.2	−2.0	33.6	22 03.1	−1.4	33.9	22 52.8	−0.7	34.1	23 42.4	−0.1	34.3	24 31.9	+0.6	34.6	25 21.2	+1.2	34.8	58
59	19 29.8	−3.5	32.2	20 20.6	−3.0	32.4	21 11.2	−2.4	32.6	22 01.7	−1.8	32.8	22 52.1	−1.2	33.0	23 42.3	−0.5	33.2	24 32.5	0.0	33.5	25 22.4	+0.7	33.7	59
60	19 26.3	−3.9	31.1	20 17.6	−3.4	31.3	21 08.8	−2.8	31.5	21 59.9	−2.2	31.7	22 50.9	−1.6	31.9	23 41.8	−1.0	32.1	24 32.5	−0.4	32.4	25 23.1	+0.2	32.6	60
61	19 22.4	−4.3	30.0	20 14.2	−3.7	30.2	21 06.0	−3.1	30.4	21 57.7	−2.6	30.6	22 49.3	−2.1	30.8	23 40.8	−1.5	31.1	24 32.1	−0.9	31.3	25 23.3	−0.3	31.5	61
62	19 18.1	−4.7	29.0	20 10.5	−4.1	29.2	21 02.9	−3.6	29.3	21 55.1	−3.0	29.5	22 47.2	−2.4	29.7	23 39.3	−1.9	30.0	24 31.2	−1.4	30.2	25 23.0	−0.8	30.4	62
63	19 13.4	−5.0	27.9	20 06.4	−4.5	28.1	20 59.3	−4.0	28.3	21 52.1	−3.5	28.5	22 44.8	−3.0	28.7	23 37.4	−2.4	28.9	24 29.8	−1.8	29.1	25 22.2	−1.3	29.3	63
64	19 08.4	−5.4	26.9	20 01.9	−4.9	27.0	20 55.3	−4.4	27.2	21 48.6	−3.9	27.4	22 41.8	−3.3	27.6	23 35.0	−2.9	27.8	24 28.0	−2.3	28.0	25 20.9	−1.8	28.2	64
65	19 03.0	−5.7	25.8	19 57.0	−5.3	26.0	20 50.9	−4.8	26.1	21 44.7	−4.3	26.3	22 38.5	−3.9	26.5	23 32.1	−3.3	26.7	24 25.7	−2.8	26.9	25 19.1	−2.3	27.1	65
66	18 57.3	−6.1	24.8	19 51.7	−5.6	24.9	20 46.1	−5.2	25.1	21 40.4	−4.7	25.2	22 34.6	−4.2	25.4	23 28.8	−3.8	25.6	24 22.9	−3.3	25.8	25 16.8	−2.7	26.0	66
67	18 51.2	−6.5	23.7	19 46.1	−6.0	23.9	20 40.9	−5.5	24.0	21 35.7	−5.1	24.2	22 30.4	−4.7	24.3	23 25.0	−4.2	24.5	24 19.6	−3.8	24.7	25 14.1	−3.3	24.9	67
68	18 44.7	−6.8	22.7	19 40.1	−6.4	22.8	20 35.4	−6.0	22.9	21 30.6	−5.5	23.1	22 25.7	−5.1	23.3	23 20.8	−4.6	23.4	24 15.8	−4.2	23.6	25 10.8	−3.8	23.8	68
69	18 37.9	−7.1	21.6	19 33.7	−6.7	21.8	20 29.4	−6.3	21.9	21 25.1	−6.0	22.0	22 20.6	−5.5	22.2	23 16.2	−5.1	22.3	24 11.6	−4.6	22.5	25 07.0	−4.2	22.7	69
70	18 30.8	−7.5	20.6	19 27.0	−7.2	20.7	20 23.1	−6.8	20.8	21 19.1	−6.3	21.0	22 15.1	−5.9	21.1	23 11.1	−5.6	21.3	24 07.0	−5.2	21.4	25 02.8	−4.8	21.6	70
71	18 23.3	−7.8	19.5	19 19.8	−7.4	19.6	20 16.3	−7.1	19.8	21 12.8	−6.8	19.9	22 09.2	−6.4	20.0	23 05.5	−6.0	20.2	24 01.8	−5.6	20.3	24 58.0	−5.2	20.5	71
72	18 15.5	−8.2	18.5	19 12.4	−7.9	18.6	20 09.2	−7.5	18.7	21 06.0	−7.1	18.8	22 02.8	−6.8	19.0	22 59.5	−6.4	19.1	23 56.2	−6.1	19.2	24 52.8	−5.7	19.4	72
73	18 07.3	−8.5	17.4	19 04.5	−8.2	17.5	20 01.7	−7.8	17.7	20 58.9	−7.6	17.8	21 56.0	−7.2	17.9	22 53.1	−6.9	18.0	23 50.1	−6.5	18.1	24 47.1	−6.2	18.3	73
74	17 58.8	−8.8	16.4	18 56.3	−8.5	16.5	19 53.9	−8.3	16.6	20 51.3	−7.9	16.7	21 48.8	−7.6	16.8	22 46.2	−7.3	16.9	23 43.6	−7.0	17.1	24 40.9	−6.6	17.2	74
75	17 50.0	−9.2	15.4	18 47.8	−8.9	15.4	19 45.6	−8.6	15.5	20 43.4	−8.3	15.6	21 41.2	−8.1	15.7	22 38.9	−7.7	15.9	23 36.6	−7.4	16.0	24 34.3	−7.2	16.1	75
76	17 40.8	−9.5	14.3	18 38.9	−9.2	14.4	19 37.0	−9.0	14.5	20 35.1	−8.7	14.6	21 33.1	−8.4	14.7	22 31.2	−8.2	14.8	23 29.2	−7.9	14.9	24 27.1	−7.6	15.0	76
77	17 31.3	−9.8	13.3	18 29.7	−9.6	13.4	19 28.0	−9.3	13.4	20 26.4	−9.1	13.5	21 24.7	−8.8	13.6	22 23.0	−8.6	13.7	23 21.3	−8.3	13.8	24 19.5	−8.0	13.9	77
78	17 21.5	−10.2	12.3	18 20.1	−9.9	12.3	19 18.7	−9.7	12.4	20 17.3	−9.5	12.5	21 15.9	−9.3	12.6	22 14.4	−9.0	12.6	23 13.0	−8.8	12.7	24 11.5	−8.5	12.8	78
79	17 11.3	−10.4	11.2	18 10.2	−10.3	11.3	19 09.0	−10.0	11.4	20 07.8	−9.8	11.4	21 06.6	−9.6	11.5	22 05.4	−9.4	11.6	23 04.2	−9.2	11.7	24 03.0	−9.0	11.7	79
80	17 00.9	−10.8	10.2	17 59.9	−10.5	10.2	18 59.0	−10.4	10.3	19 58.0	−10.2	10.4	20 57.0	−10.0	10.4	21 56.0	−9.8	10.5	22 55.0	−9.6	10.6	23 54.0	−9.5	10.7	80
81	16 50.1	−11.0	9.2	17 49.4	−10.9	9.2	18 48.6	−10.8	9.3	19 47.8	−10.6	9.3	20 47.0	−10.4	9.4	21 46.2	−10.3	9.4	22 45.4	−10.1	9.5	23 44.5	−9.9	9.6	81
82	16 39.1	−11.4	8.1	17 38.5	−11.3	8.2	18 37.8	−11.0	8.2	19 37.2	−10.9	8.3	20 36.6	−10.8	8.3	21 35.9	−10.6	8.4	22 35.3	−10.5	8.4	23 34.6	−10.3	8.5	82
83	16 27.7	−11.7	7.1	17 27.2	−11.5	7.2	18 26.8	−11.5	7.2	19 26.3	−11.3	7.2	20 25.8	−11.2	7.3	21 25.3	−11.0	7.3	22 24.8	−10.9	7.4	23 24.3	−10.8	7.4	83
84	16 16.0	−11.9	6.1	17 15.7	−11.9	6.1	18 15.3	−11.7	6.2	19 15.0	−11.7	6.2	20 14.6	−11.5	6.2	21 14.3	−11.4	6.3	22 13.9	−11.3	6.3	23 13.5	−11.2	6.4	84
85	16 04.1	−12.3	5.1	17 03.8	−12.1	5.1	18 03.6	−12.1	5.1	19 03.3	−11.9	5.2	20 03.1	−11.9	5.2	21 02.9	−11.9	5.2	22 02.6	−11.7	5.3	23 02.3	−11.6	5.3	85
86	15 51.8	−12.5	4.1	16 51.7	−12.5	4.1	17 51.5	−12.4	4.1	18 51.4	−12.4	4.1	19 51.2	−12.3	4.1	20 51.0	−12.2	4.2	21 50.9	−12.2	4.2	22 50.7	−12.0	4.2	86
87	15 39.3	−12.8	3.0	16 39.2	−12.8	3.1	17 39.1	−12.7	3.1	18 39.0	−12.7	3.1	19 38.9	−12.6	3.1	20 38.8	−12.5	3.1	21 38.7	−12.5	3.1	22 38.7	−12.5	3.2	87
88	15 26.5	−13.1	2.0	16 26.4	−13.0	2.0	17 26.4	−13.1	2.0	18 26.3	−13.0	2.1	19 26.3	−13.0	2.1	20 26.3	−13.0	2.1	21 26.2	−12.9	2.1	22 26.2	−12.9	2.1	88
89	15 13.4	−13.4	1.0	16 13.4	−13.4	1.0	17 13.3	−13.3	1.0	18 13.3	−13.3	1.0	19 13.3	−13.3	1.0	20 13.3	−13.3	1.0	21 13.3	−13.3	1.0	22 13.3	−13.3	1.1	89
90	15 00.0	−13.6	0.0	16 00.0	−13.6	0.0	17 00.0	−13.6	0.0	18 00.0	−13.7	0.0	19 00.0	−13.7	0.0	20 00.0	−13.7	0.0	21 00.0	−13.7	0.0	22 00.0	−13.7	0.0	90
	15°			16°			17°			18°			19°			20°			21°			22°			

LATITUDE CONTRARY NAME TO DECLINATION — L.H.A. 77°, 283°

Dec.	15° Hc	15° d	15° Z	16° Hc	16° d	16° Z	17° Hc	17° d	17° Z	18° Hc	18° d	18° Z
°	° ′	′	°	° ′	′	°	° ′	′	°	° ′	′	°
0	12 33.0	-16.0	93.4	12 29.3	-17.1	93.6	12 25.4	-18.1	93.9	12 21.2	-19.1	94.1
1	12 17.0	-16.3	94.4	12 12.2	-17.2	94.6	12 07.3	-18.3	94.8	12 02.1	-19.3	95.1
2	12 00.7	-16.4	95.4	11 55.0	-17.5	95.6	11 49.0	-18.4	95.8	11 42.8	-19.4	96.0
3	11 44.3	-16.6	96.4	11 37.5	-17.6	96.6	11 30.6	-18.7	96.8	11 23.4	-19.7	97.0
4	11 27.7	-16.9	97.4	11 19.9	-17.9	97.6	11 11.9	-18.9	97.8	11 03.7	-19.9	97.9
5	11 10.8	-17.0	98.3	11 02.0	-18.0	98.5	10 53.0	-19.0	98.7	10 43.8	-20.0	98.9
6	10 53.8	-17.2	99.3	10 44.0	-18.2	99.5	10 34.0	-19.2	99.7	10 23.8	-20.2	99.9
7	10 36.6	-17.4	100.3	10 25.8	-18.4	100.5	10 14.8	-19.4	100.6	10 03.6	-20.3	100.8
8	10 19.2	-17.5	101.3	10 07.4	-18.5	101.4	9 55.4	-19.5	101.6	9 43.3	-20.6	101.8
9	10 01.7	-17.8	102.2	9 48.9	-18.8	102.4	9 35.9	-19.7	102.6	9 22.7	-20.6	102.7
10	9 43.9	-17.9	103.2	9 30.1	-18.8	103.4	9 16.2	-19.9	103.5	9 02.1	-20.8	103.7
11	9 26.0	-18.0	104.2	9 11.3	-19.1	104.3	8 56.3	-20.0	104.5	8 41.3	-21.0	104.6
12	9 08.0	-18.2	105.1	8 52.2	-19.1	105.3	8 36.3	-20.1	105.4	8 20.3	-21.1	105.6
13	8 49.8	-18.4	106.1	8 33.1	-19.4	106.2	8 16.2	-20.3	106.4	7 59.2	-21.2	106.5
14	8 31.4	-18.5	107.1	8 13.7	-19.4	107.2	7 55.9	-20.4	107.3	7 38.0	-21.4	107.5
15	8 12.9	-18.6	108.0	7 54.3	-19.6	108.2	7 35.5	-20.5	108.3	7 16.6	-21.4	108.4
16	7 54.3	-18.8	109.0	7 34.7	-19.7	109.1	7 15.0	-20.6	109.2	6 55.2	-21.6	109.4
17	7 35.5	-18.9	109.9	7 15.0	-19.8	110.1	6 54.4	-20.8	110.2	6 33.6	-21.7	110.3
18	7 16.6	-19.0	110.9	6 55.2	-20.0	111.0	6 33.6	-20.9	111.1	6 11.9	-21.7	111.2
19	6 57.6	-19.1	111.9	6 35.2	-20.0	112.0	6 12.7	-20.9	112.1	5 50.2	-21.9	112.2
20	6 38.5	-19.2	112.8	6 15.2	-20.2	112.9	5 51.8	-21.1	113.0	5 28.3	-22.0	113.1
21	6 19.3	-19.4	113.8	5 55.0	-20.2	113.9	5 30.7	-21.1	114.0	5 06.3	-22.0	114.0
22	5 59.9	-19.4	114.7	5 34.8	-20.3	114.8	5 09.6	-21.2	114.9	4 44.3	-22.1	115.0
23	5 40.5	-19.5	115.7	5 14.5	-20.5	115.8	4 48.4	-21.3	115.8	4 22.2	-22.2	115.9
24	5 21.0	-19.7	116.6	4 54.0	-20.5	116.7	4 27.1	-21.4	116.8	4 00.0	-22.2	116.8
25	5 01.3	-19.7	117.6	4 33.5	-20.5	117.6	4 05.7	-21.5	117.7	3 37.8	-22.3	117.8
26	4 41.6	-19.7	118.5	4 13.0	-20.7	118.6	3 44.2	-21.5	118.6	3 15.5	-22.4	118.7
27	4 21.9	-19.9	119.5	3 52.3	-20.7	119.5	3 22.7	-21.5	119.6	2 53.1	-22.4	119.6
28	4 02.0	-19.9	120.4	3 31.6	-20.7	120.5	3 01.2	-21.6	120.5	2 30.7	-22.4	120.6
29	3 42.1	-20.0	121.4	3 10.9	-20.8	121.4	2 39.6	-21.7	121.4	2 08.3	-22.5	121.5
30	3 22.1	-20.0	122.3	2 50.1	-20.9	122.3	2 17.9	-21.6	122.4	1 45.8	-22.5	122.4
31	3 02.1	-20.1	123.2	2 29.2	-20.9	123.3	1 56.3	-21.7	123.3	1 23.3	-22.5	123.3
32	2 42.0	-20.1	124.2	2 08.3	-20.9	124.2	1 34.6	-21.8	124.2	1 00.8	-22.6	124.3
33	2 21.9	-20.1	125.1	1 47.4	-21.0	125.2	1 12.8	-21.7	125.2	0 38.2	-22.5	125.2
34	2 01.8	-20.2	126.1	1 26.4	-21.0	126.1	0 51.1	-21.8	126.1	0 15.7	-22.6	126.1
35	1 41.6	-20.3	127.0	1 05.4	-21.0	127.0	0 29.3	-21.8	127.0	0 06.9	+22.5	53.0
36	1 21.3	-20.2	128.0	0 44.4	-21.0	128.0	0 07.5	-21.8	128.0	0 29.4	+22.5	52.0
37	1 01.1	-20.3	128.9	0 23.4	-21.0	128.9	0 14.3	+21.7	51.1	0 51.9	+22.6	51.1
38	0 40.8	-20.2	129.8	0 02.4	-21.0	129.8	0 36.0	+21.8	50.2	1 14.5	+22.5	50.2
39	0 20.6	-20.3	130.8	0 18.6	+21.0	49.2	0 57.8	+21.8	49.2	1 37.0	+22.5	49.2
40	0 00.3	-20.3	131.7	0 39.6	+21.0	48.3	1 19.6	+21.7	48.3	1 59.5	+22.4	48.3
41	0 20.0	+20.3	47.3	1 00.6	+21.0	47.3	1 41.3	+21.7	47.4	2 21.9	+22.4	47.4
42	0 40.3	+20.2	46.4	1 21.6	+21.0	46.4	2 03.0	+21.7	46.4	2 44.3	+22.4	46.5
43	1 00.5	+20.3	45.5	1 42.6	+20.9	45.5	2 24.7	+21.6	45.5	3 06.7	+22.3	45.5
44	1 20.8	+20.2	44.5	2 03.5	+20.9	44.5	2 46.3	+21.6	44.6	3 29.0	+22.3	44.6
45	1 41.0	+20.2	43.6	2 24.4	+20.9	43.6	3 07.9	+21.5	43.6	3 51.3	+22.2	43.7
46	2 01.2	+20.1	42.6	2 45.3	+20.8	42.7	3 29.4	+21.5	42.7	4 13.5	+22.1	42.7
47	2 21.3	+20.2	41.7	3 06.1	+20.8	41.7	3 50.9	+21.4	41.8	4 35.6	+22.1	41.8
48	2 41.5	+20.0	40.7	3 26.9	+20.7	40.8	4 12.3	+21.4	40.8	4 57.7	+22.0	40.9
49	3 01.5	+20.1	39.8	3 47.6	+20.7	39.8	4 33.7	+21.2	39.9	5 19.7	+21.9	39.9
50	3 21.6	+19.9	38.9	4 08.3	+20.6	38.9	4 54.9	+21.3	38.9	5 41.6	+21.8	39.0
51	3 41.5	+20.0	37.9	4 28.9	+20.5	38.0	5 16.2	+21.1	38.0	6 03.4	+21.7	38.1
52	4 01.5	+19.8	37.0	4 49.4	+20.4	37.0	5 37.3	+21.0	37.1	6 25.1	+21.6	37.1
53	4 21.3	+19.8	36.0	5 09.8	+20.4	36.1	5 58.3	+20.9	36.1	6 46.7	+21.5	36.2
54	4 41.1	+19.7	35.1	5 30.2	+20.2	35.1	6 19.2	+20.9	35.2	7 08.2	+21.4	35.3
55	5 00.8	+19.6	34.1	5 50.4	+20.2	34.2	6 40.1	+20.7	34.2	7 29.6	+21.3	34.3
56	5 20.4	+19.5	33.2	6 10.6	+20.1	33.2	7 00.8	+20.6	33.3	7 50.9	+21.1	33.4
57	5 39.9	+19.5	32.2	6 30.7	+19.9	32.3	7 21.4	+20.5	32.3	8 12.0	+21.1	32.4
58	5 59.4	+19.3	31.3	6 50.6	+19.9	31.3	7 41.9	+20.3	31.4	8 33.1	+20.8	31.5
59	6 18.7	+19.3	30.3	7 10.5	+19.7	30.4	8 02.2	+20.3	30.5	8 53.9	+20.8	30.5
60	6 38.0	+19.1	29.4	7 30.2	+19.6	29.4	8 22.5	+20.1	29.5	9 14.7	+20.5	29.6
61	6 57.1	+19.0	28.4	7 49.8	+19.5	28.5	8 42.6	+19.9	28.5	9 35.2	+20.5	28.6
62	7 16.1	+18.9	27.5	8 09.3	+19.4	27.5	9 02.5	+19.8	27.6	9 55.7	+20.2	27.7
63	7 35.0	+18.8	26.5	8 28.7	+19.2	26.6	9 22.3	+19.7	26.6	10 15.9	+20.1	26.7
64	7 53.8	+18.6	25.5	8 47.9	+19.0	25.6	9 42.0	+19.5	25.7	10 36.0	+19.9	25.8
65	8 12.4	+18.5	24.6	9 06.9	+18.9	24.6	10 01.5	+19.3	24.7	10 55.9	+19.8	24.8
66	8 30.9	+18.3	23.6	9 25.8	+18.8	23.7	10 20.8	+19.1	23.8	11 15.7	+19.5	23.8
67	8 49.2	+18.3	22.7	9 44.6	+18.6	22.7	10 39.9	+19.0	22.8	11 35.2	+19.4	22.9
68	9 07.5	+18.0	21.7	10 03.2	+18.4	21.8	10 58.9	+18.8	21.8	11 54.6	+19.2	21.9
69	9 25.5	+17.9	20.7	10 21.6	+18.3	20.8	11 17.7	+18.6	20.9	12 13.8	+18.9	20.9
70	9 43.4	+17.7	19.8	10 39.9	+18.0	19.8	11 36.3	+18.4	19.9	12 32.7	+18.8	20.0
71	10 01.1	+17.6	18.8	10 57.9	+17.9	18.9	11 54.7	+18.2	18.9	12 51.5	+18.5	19.0
72	10 18.7	+17.4	17.8	11 15.8	+17.7	17.9	12 12.9	+18.0	17.9	13 10.0	+18.3	18.0
73	10 36.1	+17.2	16.8	11 33.5	+17.5	16.9	12 30.9	+17.8	17.0	13 28.3	+18.1	17.0
74	10 53.3	+17.0	15.9	11 51.0	+17.3	15.9	12 48.7	+17.6	16.0	13 46.4	+17.8	16.1
75	11 10.3	+16.9	14.9	12 08.3	+17.1	14.9	13 06.3	+17.3	15.0	14 04.2	+17.6	15.1
76	11 27.2	+16.6	13.9	12 25.4	+16.9	14.0	13 23.6	+17.2	14.0	14 21.8	+17.4	14.1
77	11 43.8	+16.5	12.9	12 42.3	+16.7	13.0	13 40.8	+16.8	13.0	14 39.2	+17.1	13.1
78	12 00.3	+16.2	12.0	12 59.0	+16.4	12.0	13 57.6	+16.7	12.0	14 56.3	+16.9	12.1
79	12 16.5	+16.0	11.0	13 15.4	+16.2	11.0	14 14.3	+16.4	11.1	15 13.2	+16.6	11.1
80	12 32.5	+15.8	10.0	13 31.6	+16.0	10.0	14 30.7	+16.1	10.1	15 29.8	+16.3	10.1
81	12 48.3	+15.6	9.0	13 47.6	+15.7	9.0	14 46.8	+15.9	9.1	15 46.1	+16.0	9.1
82	13 03.9	+15.4	8.0	14 03.3	+15.5	8.0	15 02.7	+15.7	8.1	16 02.1	+15.8	8.1
83	13 19.3	+15.1	7.0	14 18.8	+15.3	7.0	15 18.4	+15.3	7.1	16 17.9	+15.5	7.1
84	13 34.4	+14.9	6.0	14 34.1	+15.0	6.0	15 33.7	+15.1	6.1	16 33.4	+15.2	6.1
85	13 49.3	+14.6	5.0	14 49.1	+14.7	5.0	15 48.8	+14.8	5.1	16 48.6	+14.9	5.1
86	14 03.9	+14.4	4.0	15 03.8	+14.4	4.0	16 03.6	+14.6	4.1	17 03.5	+14.6	4.1
87	14 18.3	+14.2	3.0	15 18.2	+14.2	3.0	16 18.2	+14.2	3.0	17 18.1	+14.3	3.1
88	14 32.5	+13.9	2.0	15 32.4	+14.0	2.0	16 32.4	+14.0	2.0	17 32.4	+13.9	2.0
89	14 46.4	+13.6	1.0	15 46.4	+13.6	1.0	16 46.4	+13.6	1.0	17 46.3	+13.7	1.0
90	15 00.0	+13.4	0.0	16 00.0	+13.4	0.0	17 00.0	+13.3	0.0	18 00.0	+13.3	0.0
	15°			16°			17°			18°		

Dec.	19° Hc	19° d	19° Z	20° Hc	20° d	20° Z	21° Hc	21° d	21° Z	22° Hc	22° d	22° Z
°	° ′	′	°	° ′	′	°	° ′	′	°	° ′	′	°
0	12 16.8	-20.1	94.3	12 12.2	-21.1	94.5	12 07.4	-22.1	94.7	12 02.3	-23.1	94.9
1	11 56.7	-20.3	95.3	11 51.1	-21.3	95.5	11 45.3	-22.3	95.7	11 39.2	-23.2	95.9
2	11 36.4	-20.4	96.2	11 29.8	-21.4	96.4	11 23.0	-22.4	96.6	11 16.0	-23.5	96.8
3	11 16.0	-20.7	97.2	11 08.4	-21.7	97.4	11 00.6	-22.7	97.6	10 52.5	-23.6	97.8
4	10 55.3	-20.8	98.1	10 46.7	-21.8	98.3	10 37.9	-22.8	98.5	10 28.9	-23.7	98.7
5	10 34.5	-21.1	99.1	10 24.9	-22.0	99.3	10 15.1	-22.9	99.5	10 05.2	-24.0	99.6
6	10 13.4	-21.1	100.0	10 02.9	-22.2	100.2	9 52.2	-23.2	100.4	9 41.2	-24.0	100.6
7	9 52.3	-21.4	101.0	9 40.7	-22.3	101.2	9 29.0	-23.2	101.3	9 17.2	-24.3	101.5
8	9 30.9	-21.5	101.9	9 18.4	-22.4	102.1	9 05.8	-23.4	102.3	8 52.9	-24.3	102.4
9	9 09.4	-21.6	102.9	8 56.0	-22.6	103.0	8 42.4	-23.6	103.2	8 28.6	-24.5	103.3
10	8 47.8	-21.8	103.8	8 33.4	-22.7	104.0	8 18.8	-23.7	104.1	8 04.1	-24.6	104.3
11	8 26.0	-21.9	104.8	8 10.7	-22.9	104.9	7 55.1	-23.8	105.1	7 39.5	-24.7	105.2
12	8 04.1	-22.0	105.7	7 47.8	-23.0	105.9	7 31.3	-23.9	106.0	7 14.8	-24.9	106.1
13	7 42.1	-22.2	106.7	7 24.8	-23.1	106.8	7 07.4	-24.0	106.9	6 49.9	-24.9	107.0
14	7 19.9	-22.3	107.6	7 01.7	-23.2	107.7	6 43.4	-24.1	107.8	6 25.0	-25.1	107.9
15	6 57.6	-22.4	108.5	6 38.5	-23.3	108.6	6 19.3	-24.3	108.8	5 59.9	-25.1	108.9
16	6 35.2	-22.5	109.5	6 15.2	-23.4	109.6	5 55.0	-24.3	109.7	5 34.8	-25.2	109.8
17	6 12.7	-22.5	110.4	5 51.8	-23.5	110.5	5 30.7	-24.4	110.6	5 09.6	-25.3	110.7
18	5 50.2	-22.7	111.3	5 28.3	-23.6	111.4	5 06.3	-24.4	111.5	4 44.3	-25.4	111.6
19	5 27.5	-22.8	112.3	5 04.7	-23.7	112.3	4 41.9	-24.6	112.4	4 18.9	-25.4	112.5
20	5 04.7	-22.8	113.2	4 41.0	-23.7	113.3	4 17.3	-24.6	113.3	3 53.5	-25.5	113.4
21	4 41.9	-23.0	114.1	4 17.3	-23.8	114.2	3 52.7	-24.7	114.3	3 28.0	-25.5	114.3
22	4 18.9	-23.0	115.0	3 53.5	-23.9	115.1	3 28.0	-24.7	115.2	3 02.5	-25.6	115.2
23	3 55.9	-23.0	116.0	3 29.6	-23.9	116.0	3 03.3	-24.8	116.1	2 36.9	-25.6	116.1
24	3 32.9	-23.1	116.9	3 05.7	-23.9	116.9	2 38.5	-24.8	117.0	2 11.3	-25.7	117.0
25	3 09.8	-23.2	117.8	2 41.8	-24.0	117.9	2 13.7	-24.9	117.9	1 45.6	-25.7	117.9
26	2 46.6	-23.2	118.7	2 17.8	-24.1	118.8	1 48.8	-24.8	118.8	1 19.9	-25.7	118.8
27	2 23.4	-23.2	119.7	1 53.7	-24.1	119.7	1 24.0	-24.9	119.7	0 54.2	-25.7	119.7
28	2 00.2	-23.3	120.6	1 29.6	-24.0	120.6	0 59.1	-24.9	120.6	0 28.5	-25.7	120.6
29	1 36.9	-23.3	121.5	1 05.6	-24.2	121.5	0 34.2	-25.0	121.5	0 02.8	-25.7	121.5
30	1 13.6	-23.3	122.4	0 41.4	-24.1	122.4	0 09.2	-24.9	122.5	0 22.9	+25.8	57.5
31	0 50.3	-23.3	123.4	0 17.3	-24.1	123.4	0 15.7	+24.9	56.6	0 48.7	+25.7	56.6
32	0 27.0	-23.3	124.3	0 06.8	+24.1	55.7	0 40.6	+24.9	55.7	1 14.4	+25.7	55.7
33	0 03.7	-23.4	125.2	0 30.9	+24.1	54.8	1 05.5	+24.9	54.8	1 40.1	+25.6	54.8
34	0 19.7	+23.3	53.9	0 55.0	+24.1	53.9	1 30.4	+24.9	53.9	2 05.7	+25.7	53.9
35	0 43.0	+23.3	53.0	1 19.1	+24.1	53.0	1 55.3	+24.8	53.0	2 31.4	+25.6	53.0
36	1 06.3	+23.3	52.0	1 43.2	+24.1	52.1	2 20.1	+24.8	52.1	2 57.0	+25.5	52.1
37	1 29.6	+23.3	51.1	2 07.3	+24.0	51.1	2 44.9	+24.8	51.2	3 22.5	+25.5	51.2
38	1 52.9	+23.2	50.2	2 31.3	+24.0	50.2	3 09.7	+24.7	50.3	3 48.0	+25.4	50.3
39	2 16.1	+23.3	49.3	2 55.3	+23.9	49.3	3 34.4	+24.6	49.3	4 13.4	+25.4	49.4
40	2 39.4	+23.1	48.3	3 19.2	+23.9	48.4	3 59.0	+24.6	48.4	4 38.8	+25.3	48.5
41	3 02.5	+23.1	47.4	3 43.1	+23.8	47.5	4 23.6	+24.6	47.5	5 04.1	+25.3	47.6
42	3 25.6	+23.1	46.5	4 06.9	+23.8	46.5	4 48.2	+24.4	46.6	5 29.4	+25.1	46.7
43	3 48.7	+23.0	45.6	4 30.7	+23.7	45.6	5 12.6	+24.4	45.7	5 54.5	+25.1	45.8
44	4 11.7	+23.0	44.7	4 54.4	+23.6	44.7	5 37.0	+24.3	44.8	6 19.6	+24.9	44.8
45	4 34.7	+22.8	43.7	5 18.0	+23.5	43.8	6 01.3	+24.2	43.9	6 44.5	+24.9	43.9
46	4 57.5	+22.8	42.8	5 41.5	+23.5	42.9	6 25.5	+24.1	42.9	7 09.4	+24.8	43.0
47	5 20.3	+22.7	41.9	6 05.0	+23.4	41.9	6 49.6	+24.0	42.0	7 34.2	+24.6	42.1
48	5 43.0	+22.7	40.9	6 28.4	+23.2	41.0	7 13.6	+23.9	41.1	7 58.8	+24.5	41.2
49	6 05.7	+22.5	40.0	6 51.6	+23.2	40.1	7 37.5	+23.8	40.2	8 23.3	+24.4	40.3
50	6 28.2	+22.4	39.1	7 14.8	+23.0	39.2	8 01.3	+23.6	39.2	8 47.7	+24.2	39.3
51	6 50.6	+22.3	38.1	7 37.8	+22.9	38.2	8 24.9	+23.5	38.3	9 11.9	+24.2	38.4
52	7 12.9	+22.2	37.2	8 00.7	+22.8	37.3	8 48.4	+23.4	37.4	9 36.1	+23.9	37.5
53	7 35.1	+22.1	36.3	8 23.5	+22.6	36.4	9 11.8	+23.2	36.4	10 00.0	+23.8	36.5
54	7 57.2	+22.0	35.3	8 46.1	+22.6	35.4	9 35.0	+23.1	35.5	10 23.8	+23.7	35.6
55	8 19.2	+21.8	34.4	9 08.7	+22.3	34.5	9 58.1	+22.9	34.6	10 47.5	+23.4	34.7
56	8 41.0	+21.7	33.4	9 31.0	+22.2	33.5	10 21.0	+22.8	33.6	11 10.9	+23.3	33.7
57	9 02.7	+21.5	32.5	9 53.2	+22.1	32.6	10 43.8	+22.6	32.7	11 34.2	+23.2	32.8
58	9 24.2	+21.4	31.6	10 15.3	+21.9	31.6	11 06.4	+22.4	31.7	11 57.4	+22.9	31.9
59	9 45.6	+21.2	30.6	10 37.2	+21.7	30.7	11 28.8	+22.2	30.8	12 20.3	+22.7	30.9
60	10 06.8	+21.1	29.7	10 58.9	+21.6	29.8	11 51.0	+22.0	29.9	12 43.0	+22.5	30.0
61	10 27.9	+20.9	28.7	11 20.5	+21.4	28.8	12 13.0	+21.9	28.9	13 05.5	+22.4	29.0
62	10 48.8	+20.7	27.8	11 41.9	+21.1	27.8	12 34.9	+21.6	27.9	13 27.9	+22.1	28.1
63	11 09.5	+20.5	26.8	12 03.0	+21.0	26.9	12 56.5	+21.5	27.0	13 50.0	+21.8	27.1
64	11 30.0	+20.4	25.8	12 24.0	+20.8	25.9	13 18.0	+21.2	26.0	14 11.8	+21.7	26.1
65	11 50.4	+20.1	24.9	12 44.8	+20.6	25.0	13 39.2	+21.0	25.1	14 33.5	+21.4	25.2
66	12 10.5	+20.0	23.9	13 05.4	+20.3	24.0	14 00.2	+20.7	24.1	14 54.9	+21.2	24.2
67	12 30.5	+19.7	23.0	13 25.7	+20.2	23.0	14 20.9	+20.5	23.1	15 16.1	+20.9	23.2
68	12 50.2	+19.6	22.0	13 45.9	+19.9	22.1	14 41.4	+20.3	22.2	15 37.0	+20.7	22.3
69	13 09.8	+19.3	21.0	14 05.8	+19.6	21.1	15 01.7	+20.1	21.2	15 57.7	+20.3	21.3
70	13 29.1	+19.1	20.0	14 25.4	+19.5	20.1	15 21.8	+19.7	20.2	16 18.0	+20.2	20.3
71	13 48.2	+18.8	19.1	14 44.9	+19.2	19.1	15 41.5	+19.6	19.2	16 38.2	+19.8	19.3
72	14 07.0	+18.7	18.1	15 04.1	+18.9	18.2	16 01.1	+19.2	18.3	16 58.0	+19.6	18.3
73	14 25.7	+18.3	17.1	15 23.0	+18.7	17.2	16 20.3	+19.0	17.3	17 17.6	+19.2	17.4
74	14 44.0	+18.2	16.1	15 41.7	+18.4	16.2	16 39.3	+18.7	16.3	17 36.8	+19.0	16.4
75	15 02.2	+17.8	15.1	16 00.1	+18.1	15.2	16 58.0	+18.4	15.3	17 55.8	+18.7	15.4
76	15 20.0	+17.6	14.1	16 18.2	+17.9	14.2	17 16.4	+18.1	14.3	18 14.5	+18.3	14.4
77	15 37.6	+17.4	13.2	16 36.1	+17.5	13.2	17 34.5	+17.8	13.3	18 32.8	+18.1	13.4
78	15 55.0	+17.0	12.2	16 53.6	+17.3	12.2	17 52.3	+17.4	12.3	18 50.9	+17.7	12.4
79	16 12.0	+16.8	11.2	17 10.9	+17.0	11.2	18 09.7	+17.2	11.3	19 08.6	+17.4	11.3
80	16 28.8	+16.5	10.2	17 27.9	+16.7	10.2	18 26.9	+16.9	10.3	19 26.0	+17.0	10.3
81	16 45.3	+16.2	9.2	17 44.6	+16.3	9.2	18 43.8	+16.5	9.3	19 43.0	+16.7	9.3
82	17 01.5	+15.9	8.2	18 00.9	+16.1	8.2	19 00.3	+16.2	8.2	19 59.7	+16.3	8.3
83	17 17.4	+15.7	7.1	18 17.0	+15.7	7.2	19 16.5	+15.9	7.2	20 16.0	+16.0	7.3
84	17 33.1	+15.2	6.1	18 32.7	+15.4	6.2	19 32.4	+15.5	6.2	20 32.0	+15.6	6.2
85	17 48.3	+15.0	5.1	18 48.1	+15.1	5.1	19 47.9	+15.1	5.2	20 47.6	+15.3	5.2
86	18 03.3	+14.7	4.1	19 03.2	+14.7	4.1	20 03.0	+14.8	4.1	21 02.9	+14.8	4.2
87	18 18.0	+14.3	3.1	19 17.9	+14.4	3.1	20 17.8	+14.5	3.1	21 17.7	+14.5	3.1
88	18 32.3	+14.0	2.1	19 32.3	+14.0	2.1	20 32.3	+14.0	2.1	21 32.2	+14.1	2.1
89	18 46.3	+13.7	1.0	19 46.3	+13.7	1.0	20 46.3	+13.7	1.0	21 46.3	+13.7	1.0
90	19 00.0	+13.3	0.0	20 00.0	+13.3	0.0	21 00.0	+13.3	0.0	22 00.0	+13.3	0.0
	19°			20°			21°			22°		

S. Lat. { L.H.A. greater than 180° ....Zn=180°−Z ; L.H.A. less than 180°..........Zn=180°+Z

LATITUDE SAME NAME AS DECLINATION — L.H.A. 103°, 257°

78°, 282° L.H.A. LATITUDE **SAME** NAME AS DECLINATION N. Lat. {L.H.A. greater than 180° .....Zn=Z; L.H.A. less than 180°............Zn=360°–Z

Dec.	15°			16°			17°			18°			19°			20°			21°			22°			Dec.
	Hc	d	Z	Hc	d	Z	Hc	d	Z	Hc	d	Z	Hc	d	Z	Hc	d	Z	Hc	d	Z	Hc	d	Z	
°	° ′	′	°	° ′	′	°	° ′	′	°	° ′	′	°	° ′	′	°	° ′	′	°	° ′	′	°	° ′	′	°	°
0	11 35.1	+15.8	93.1	11 31.7	+16.8	93.4	11 28.1	+17.8	93.6	11 24.3	+18.8	93.8	11 20.2	+19.9	94.0	11 16.0	+20.8	94.2	11 11.5	+21.9	94.4	11 06.9	+22.8	94.6	0
1	11 50.9	+15.5	92.2	11 48.5	+16.6	92.4	11 45.9	+17.6	92.6	11 43.1	+18.6	92.8	11 40.1	+19.6	93.0	11 36.8	+20.7	93.2	11 33.4	+21.6	93.4	11 29.7	+22.6	93.6	1
2	12 06.4	+15.4	91.2	12 05.1	+16.3	91.4	12 03.5	+17.4	91.6	12 01.7	+18.4	91.8	11 59.7	+19.4	92.0	11 57.5	+20.4	92.2	11 55.0	+21.5	92.5	11 52.3	+22.5	92.7	2
3	12 21.8	+15.1	90.2	12 21.4	+16.2	90.4	12 20.9	+17.2	90.6	12 20.1	+18.2	90.8	12 19.1	+19.3	91.1	12 17.9	+20.3	91.3	12 16.5	+21.2	91.5	12 14.8	+22.2	91.7	3
4	12 36.9	+14.9	89.2	12 37.6	+15.9	89.4	12 38.1	+17.0	89.6	12 38.3	+18.0	89.9	12 38.4	+19.0	90.1	12 38.2	+20.0	90.3	12 37.7	+21.1	90.5	12 37.0	+22.1	90.8	4
5	12 51.8	+14.7	88.2	12 53.5	+15.8	88.4	12 55.1	+16.7	88.7	12 56.3	+17.8	88.9	12 57.4	+18.8	89.1	12 58.2	+19.8	89.3	12 58.8	+20.8	89.6	12 59.1	+21.8	89.8	5
6	13 06.5	+14.4	87.2	13 09.3	+15.4	87.4	13 11.8	+16.5	87.7	13 14.1	+17.6	87.9	13 16.2	+18.6	88.1	13 18.0	+19.6	88.4	13 19.6	+20.6	88.6	13 20.9	+21.6	88.9	6
7	13 20.9	+14.2	86.2	13 24.7	+15.3	86.4	13 28.3	+16.3	86.7	13 31.7	+17.3	86.9	13 34.8	+18.3	87.2	13 37.6	+19.4	87.4	13 40.2	+20.4	87.7	13 42.5	+21.4	87.9	7
8	13 35.1	+14.0	85.2	13 40.0	+15.0	85.5	13 44.6	+16.1	85.7	13 49.0	+17.1	85.9	13 53.1	+18.1	86.2	13 57.0	+19.1	86.4	14 00.6	+20.1	86.7	14 03.9	+21.2	86.9	8
9	13 49.1	+13.7	84.2	13 55.0	+14.8	84.5	14 00.7	+15.8	84.7	14 06.1	+16.8	85.0	14 11.2	+17.9	85.2	14 16.1	+18.9	85.5	14 20.7	+20.0	85.7	14 25.1	+20.9	86.0	9
10	14 02.8	+13.5	83.2	14 09.8	+14.5	83.5	14 16.5	+15.6	83.7	14 22.9	+16.6	84.0	14 29.1	+17.6	84.2	14 35.0	+18.7	84.5	14 40.7	+19.6	84.7	14 46.0	+20.7	85.0	10
11	14 16.3	+13.2	82.2	14 24.3	+14.3	82.5	14 32.1	+15.3	82.7	14 39.5	+16.4	83.0	14 46.7	+17.4	83.2	14 53.7	+18.4	83.5	15 00.3	+19.5	83.8	15 06.7	+20.5	84.0	11
12	14 29.5	+13.0	81.2	14 38.6	+14.0	81.5	14 47.4	+15.0	81.7	14 55.9	+16.1	82.0	15 04.1	+17.1	82.2	15 12.1	+18.1	82.5	15 19.8	+19.1	82.8	15 27.2	+20.2	83.1	12
13	14 42.5	+12.7	80.2	14 52.6	+13.8	80.4	15 02.4	+14.8	80.7	15 12.0	+15.8	81.0	15 21.2	+16.9	81.2	15 30.2	+17.9	81.5	15 38.9	+18.9	81.8	15 47.4	+19.9	82.1	13
14	14 55.2	+12.5	79.2	15 06.4	+13.4	79.4	15 17.2	+14.5	79.7	15 27.8	+15.5	80.0	15 38.1	+16.6	80.3	15 48.1	+17.6	80.5	15 57.8	+18.7	80.8	16 07.3	+19.6	81.1	14
15	15 07.7	+12.1	78.2	15 19.8	+13.2	78.4	15 31.7	+14.3	78.7	15 43.3	+15.3	79.0	15 54.7	+16.3	79.3	16 05.7	+17.4	79.5	16 16.5	+18.3	79.8	16 26.9	+19.4	80.1	15
16	15 19.8	+11.9	77.1	15 33.0	+13.0	77.4	15 46.0	+13.9	77.7	15 58.6	+15.0	78.0	16 11.0	+16.0	78.3	16 23.1	+17.0	78.5	16 34.8	+18.1	78.8	16 46.3	+19.1	79.1	16
17	15 31.7	+11.6	76.1	15 46.0	+12.6	76.4	15 59.9	+13.7	76.7	16 13.6	+14.7	77.0	16 27.0	+15.7	77.2	16 40.1	+16.8	77.5	16 52.9	+17.8	77.8	17 05.4	+18.8	78.1	17
18	15 43.3	+11.4	75.1	15 58.6	+12.4	75.4	16 13.6	+13.4	75.7	16 28.3	+14.4	76.0	16 42.7	+15.5	76.2	16 56.9	+16.4	76.5	17 10.7	+17.5	76.8	17 24.2	+18.5	77.1	18
19	15 54.7	+11.0	74.1	16 11.0	+12.1	74.4	16 27.0	+13.1	74.7	16 42.7	+14.2	74.9	16 58.2	+15.1	75.2	17 13.3	+16.2	75.5	17 28.2	+17.2	75.8	17 42.7	+18.2	76.1	19
20	16 05.7	+10.8	73.1	16 23.1	+11.7	73.3	16 40.1	+12.8	73.6	16 56.9	+13.8	73.9	17 13.3	+14.9	74.2	17 29.5	+15.9	74.5	17 45.4	+16.8	74.8	18 00.9	+17.9	75.1	20
21	16 16.5	+10.4	72.0	16 34.8	+11.5	72.3	16 52.9	+12.5	72.6	17 10.7	+13.5	72.9	17 28.2	+14.5	73.2	17 45.4	+15.5	73.5	18 02.2	+16.6	73.8	18 18.8	+17.6	74.1	21
22	16 26.9	+10.2	71.0	16 46.3	+11.2	71.3	17 05.4	+12.2	71.6	17 24.2	+13.2	71.9	17 42.7	+14.2	72.2	18 00.9	+15.2	72.5	18 18.8	+16.3	72.8	18 36.4	+17.2	73.1	22
23	16 37.1	+9.8	70.0	16 57.5	+10.8	70.3	17 17.6	+11.9	70.6	17 37.4	+12.9	70.9	17 56.9	+13.9	71.2	18 16.1	+15.0	71.5	18 35.1	+15.9	71.8	18 53.6	+17.0	72.1	23
24	16 46.9	+9.6	69.0	17 08.3	+10.6	69.2	17 29.5	+11.5	69.5	17 50.3	+12.6	69.8	18 10.8	+13.6	70.1	18 31.1	+14.5	70.5	18 51.0	+15.6	70.8	19 10.6	+16.6	71.1	24
25	16 56.5	+9.2	67.9	17 18.9	+10.2	68.2	17 41.0	+11.2	68.5	18 02.9	+12.2	68.8	18 24.4	+13.2	69.1	18 45.6	+14.3	69.4	19 06.6	+15.2	69.8	19 27.2	+16.2	70.1	25
26	17 05.7	+8.9	66.9	17 29.1	+9.9	67.2	17 52.2	+11.0	67.5	18 15.1	+11.9	67.8	18 37.6	+12.9	68.1	18 59.9	+13.9	68.4	19 21.8	+14.9	68.7	19 43.4	+15.9	69.1	26
27	17 14.6	+8.6	65.9	17 39.0	+9.6	66.1	18 03.2	+10.5	66.4	18 27.0	+11.6	66.7	18 50.5	+12.6	67.1	19 13.8	+13.5	67.4	19 36.7	+14.5	67.7	19 59.3	+15.5	68.0	27
28	17 23.2	+8.3	64.8	17 48.6	+9.3	65.1	18 13.7	+10.3	65.4	18 38.6	+11.2	65.7	19 03.1	+12.2	66.0	19 27.3	+13.2	66.3	19 51.2	+14.2	66.7	20 14.8	+15.2	67.0	28
29	17 31.5	+8.0	63.8	17 57.9	+8.9	64.1	18 24.0	+9.9	64.4	18 49.8	+10.9	64.7	19 15.3	+11.9	65.0	19 40.5	+12.9	65.3	20 05.4	+13.9	65.6	20 30.0	+14.8	66.0	29
30	17 39.5	+7.6	62.7	18 06.8	+8.6	63.0	18 33.9	+9.5	63.3	19 00.7	+10.5	63.6	19 27.2	+11.5	63.9	19 53.4	+12.5	64.3	20 19.3	+13.4	64.6	20 44.8	+14.5	64.9	30
31	17 47.1	+7.3	61.7	18 15.4	+8.3	62.0	18 43.4	+9.3	62.3	19 11.2	+10.2	62.6	19 38.7	+11.1	62.9	20 05.9	+12.1	63.2	20 32.7	+13.1	63.6	20 59.3	+14.1	63.9	31
32	17 54.4	+7.0	60.7	18 23.7	+7.9	60.9	18 52.7	+8.8	61.2	19 21.4	+9.8	61.5	19 49.8	+10.8	61.9	20 18.0	+11.7	62.2	20 45.8	+12.7	62.5	21 13.4	+13.6	62.9	32
33	18 01.4	+6.6	59.6	18 31.6	+7.5	59.9	19 01.5	+8.5	60.2	19 31.2	+9.5	60.5	20 00.6	+10.4	60.8	20 29.7	+11.4	61.1	20 58.5	+12.4	61.5	21 27.0	+13.3	61.8	33
34	18 08.0	+6.3	58.6	18 39.1	+7.3	58.9	19 10.0	+8.2	59.2	19 40.7	+9.1	59.5	20 11.0	+10.1	59.8	20 41.1	+11.0	60.1	21 10.9	+11.9	60.4	21 40.3	+12.9	60.8	34
35	18 14.3	+5.9	57.5	18 46.4	+6.8	57.8	19 18.2	+7.8	58.1	19 49.8	+8.7	58.4	20 21.1	+9.6	58.7	20 52.1	+10.6	59.0	21 22.8	+11.5	59.4	21 53.2	+12.5	59.7	35
36	18 20.2	+5.6	56.5	18 53.2	+6.5	56.8	19 26.0	+7.4	57.0	19 58.5	+8.3	57.4	20 30.7	+9.3	57.7	21 02.7	+10.2	58.0	21 34.3	+11.2	58.3	22 05.7	+12.1	58.7	36
37	18 25.8	+5.3	55.4	18 59.7	+6.2	55.7	19 33.4	+7.1	56.0	20 06.8	+8.0	56.3	20 40.0	+8.9	56.6	21 12.9	+9.8	56.9	21 45.5	+10.7	57.3	22 17.8	+11.7	57.6	37
38	18 31.1	+4.9	54.4	19 05.9	+5.8	54.7	19 40.5	+6.7	54.9	20 14.8	+7.6	55.2	20 48.9	+8.5	55.5	21 22.7	+9.4	55.9	21 56.2	+10.4	56.2	22 29.5	+11.2	56.5	38
39	18 36.0	+4.5	53.3	19 11.7	+5.4	53.6	19 47.2	+6.3	53.9	20 22.4	+7.2	54.2	20 57.4	+8.1	54.5	21 32.1	+9.0	54.8	22 06.6	+9.9	55.1	22 40.7	+10.8	55.5	39
40	18 40.5	+4.2	52.3	19 17.1	+5.1	52.5	19 53.5	+5.9	52.8	20 29.6	+6.9	53.1	21 05.5	+7.7	53.4	21 41.1	+8.6	53.7	22 16.5	+9.5	54.1	22 51.5	+10.4	54.4	40
41	18 44.7	+3.9	51.2	19 22.2	+4.7	51.5	19 59.4	+5.6	51.8	20 36.5	+6.4	52.1	21 13.2	+7.3	52.4	21 49.7	+8.2	52.7	22 26.0	+9.1	53.0	23 01.9	+10.0	53.3	41
42	18 48.6	+3.5	50.2	19 26.9	+4.4	50.4	20 05.0	+5.2	50.7	20 42.9	+6.0	51.0	21 20.5	+6.9	51.3	21 57.9	+7.8	51.6	22 35.1	+8.6	51.9	23 11.9	+9.5	52.3	42
43	18 52.1	+3.1	49.1	19 31.3	+3.9	49.4	20 10.2	+4.8	49.7	20 48.9	+5.7	49.9	21 27.4	+6.5	50.2	22 05.7	+7.4	50.5	22 43.7	+8.2	50.9	23 21.4	+9.1	51.2	43
44	18 55.2	+2.8	48.1	19 35.2	+3.6	48.3	20 15.0	+4.4	48.6	20 54.6	+5.3	48.9	21 33.9	+6.1	49.2	22 13.1	+6.9	49.5	22 51.9	+7.8	49.8	23 30.5	+8.7	50.1	44
45	18 58.0	+2.4	47.0	19 38.8	+3.3	47.3	20 19.4	+4.1	47.5	20 59.9	+4.8	47.8	21 40.0	+5.7	48.1	22 20.0	+6.5	48.4	22 59.7	+7.4	48.7	23 39.2	+8.2	49.0	45
46	19 00.4	+2.1	45.9	19 42.1	+2.8	46.2	20 23.5	+3.6	46.5	21 04.7	+4.5	46.7	21 45.7	+5.3	47.0	22 26.5	+6.1	47.3	23 07.1	+6.9	47.6	23 47.4	+7.7	48.0	46
47	19 02.5	+1.7	44.9	19 44.9	+2.5	45.1	20 27.1	+3.3	45.4	21 09.2	+4.0	45.7	21 51.0	+4.8	45.9	22 32.6	+5.7	46.2	23 14.0	+6.4	46.5	23 55.1	+7.3	46.9	47
48	19 04.2	+1.3	43.8	19 47.4	+2.1	44.1	20 30.4	+2.9	44.3	21 13.2	+3.7	44.6	21 55.8	+4.5	44.9	22 38.3	+5.2	45.2	23 20.4	+6.1	45.5	24 02.4	+6.8	45.8	48
49	19 05.5	+1.0	42.8	19 49.5	+1.7	43.0	20 33.3	+2.4	43.3	21 16.9	+3.2	43.5	22 00.3	+4.0	43.8	22 43.5	+4.8	44.1	23 26.5	+5.5	44.4	24 09.2	+6.4	44.7	49
50	19 06.5	+0.6	41.7	19 51.2	+1.4	41.9	20 35.7	+2.1	42.2	21 20.1	+2.8	42.5	22 04.3	+3.6	42.7	22 48.3	+4.3	43.0	23 32.0	+5.2	43.3	24 15.6	+5.9	43.6	50
51	19 07.1	+0.3	40.7	19 52.6	+0.9	40.9	20 37.8	+1.7	41.1	21 22.9	+2.5	41.4	22 07.9	+3.1	41.6	22 52.6	+3.9	41.9	23 37.2	+4.6	42.2	24 21.5	+5.4	42.5	51
52	19 07.4	−0.1	39.6	19 53.5	+0.6	39.8	20 39.5	+1.3	40.1	21 25.4	+2.0	40.3	22 11.0	+2.8	40.6	22 56.5	+3.5	40.8	23 41.8	+4.2	41.1	24 26.9	+5.0	41.4	52
53	19 07.3	−0.5	38.5	19 54.1	+0.2	38.8	20 40.8	+0.9	39.0	21 27.4	+1.6	39.2	22 13.8	+2.3	39.5	23 00.0	+3.0	39.8	23 46.0	+3.8	40.0	24 31.9	+4.4	40.3	53
54	19 06.8	−0.9	37.5	19 54.3	−0.1	37.7	20 41.7	+0.5	37.9	21 29.0	+1.2	38.2	22 16.1	+1.9	38.4	23 03.0	+2.6	38.7	23 49.8	+3.3	38.9	24 36.3	+4.0	39.2	54
55	19 05.9	−1.2	36.4	19 54.2	−0.6	36.6	20 42.2	+0.1	36.9	21 30.2	+0.8	37.1	22 18.0	+1.4	37.3	23 05.6	+2.1	37.6	23 53.1	+2.8	37.8	24 40.3	+3.6	38.1	55
56	19 04.7	−1.5	35.4	19 53.6	−0.9	35.6	20 42.3	−0.2	35.8	21 31.0	+0.3	36.0	22 19.4	+1.0	36.2	23 07.7	+1.7	36.5	23 55.9	+2.3	36.8	24 43.9	+3.0	37.0	56
57	19 03.2	−1.9	34.3	19 52.7	−1.3	34.5	20 42.1	−0.7	34.7	21 31.3	0.0	34.9	22 20.4	+0.6	35.2	23 09.4	+1.3	35.4	23 58.2	+1.9	35.7	24 46.9	+2.6	35.9	57
58	19 01.3	−2.3	33.2	19 51.4	−1.7	33.4	20 41.4	−1.1	33.6	21 31.3	−0.5	33.9	22 21.0	+0.2	34.1	23 10.7	+0.7	34.3	24 00.1	+1.5	34.6	24 49.5	+2.0	34.8	58
59	18 59.0	−2.7	32.2	19 49.7	−2.1	32.4	20 40.3	−1.5	32.6	21 30.8	−0.9	32.8	22 21.2	−0.3	33.0	23 11.4	+0.4	33.2	24 01.6	+0.9	33.5	24 51.5	+1.6	33.7	59
60	18 56.3	−3.0	31.1	19 47.6	−2.4	31.3	20 38.8	−1.8	31.5	21 29.9	−1.2	31.7	22 20.9	−0.7	31.9	23 11.8	−0.1	32.1	24 02.5	+0.5	32.4	24 53.1	+1.1	32.6	60
61	18 53.3	−3.3	30.1	19 45.2	−2.8	30.3	20 37.0	−2.3	30.4	21 28.7	−1.7	30.6	22 20.2	−1.1	30.8	23 11.7	−0.6	31.1	24 03.0	0.0	31.3	24 54.2	+0.6	31.5	61
62	18 50.0	−3.8	29.0	19 42.4	−3.2	29.2	20 34.7	−2.6	29.4	21 27.0	−2.2	29.6	22 19.1	−1.6	29.8	23 11.1	−1.0	30.0	24 03.0	−0.4	30.2	24 54.8	+0.2	30.4	62
63	18 46.2	−4.0	28.0	19 39.2	−3.6	28.1	20 32.1	−3.1	28.3	21 24.8	−2.5	28.5	22 17.5	−2.0	28.7	23 10.1	−1.4	28.9	24 02.6	−0.9	29.1	24 55.0	−0.4	29.3	63
64	18 42.2	−4.4	26.9	19 35.6	−3.9	27.1	20 29.0	−3.4	27.2	21 22.3	−2.9	27.4	22 15.5	−2.4	27.6	23 08.7	−1.9	27.8	24 01.7	−1.4	28.0	24 54.6	−0.8	28.2	64
65	18 37.8	−4.8	25.9	19 31.7	−4.3	26.0	20 25.6	−3.8	26.2	21 19.4	−3.3	26.3	22 13.1	−2.8	26.5	23 06.8	−2.4	26.7	24 00.3	−1.8	26.9	24 53.8	−1.3	27.1	65
66	18 33.0	−5.1	24.8	19 27.4	−4.7	25.0	20 21.8	−4.2	25.1	21 16.1	−3.8	25.3	22 10.3	−3.3	25.4	23 04.4	−2.8	25.6	23 58.5	−2.3	25.8	24 52.5	−1.9	26.0	66
67	18 27.9	−5.5	23.8	19 22.7	−5.0	23.9	20 17.6	−4.6	24.0	21 12.3	−4.1	24.2	22 07.0	−3.7	24.4	23 01.6	−3.2	24.5	23 56.2	−2.8	24.7	24 50.6	−2.3	24.9	67
68	18 22.4	−5.8	22.7	19 17.7	−5.4	22.8	20 13.0	−5.0	23.0	21 08.2	−4.6	23.1	22 03.3	−4.1	23.3	22 58.4	−3.7	23.5	23 53.4	−3.2	23.6	24 48.3	−2.7	23.8	68
69	18 16.6	−6.2	21.7	19 12.3	−5.7	21.8	20 08.0	−5.4	21.9	21 03.6	−4.9	22.1	21 59.2	−4.5	22.2	22 54.7	−4.1	22.4	23 50.2	−3.7	22.5	24 45.6	−3.3	22.7	69
70	18 10.4	−6.5	20.6	19 06.6	−6.2	20.7	20 02.6	−5.7	20.9	20 58.7	−5.4	21.0	21 54.7	−5.0	21.1	22 50.6	−4.5	21.3	23 46.5	−4.2	21.4	24 42.3	−3.7	21.6	70
71	18 03.9	−6.8	19.6	19 00.4	−6.4	19.7	19 56.9	−6.1	19.8	20 53.3	−5.7	19.9	21 49.7	−5.4	20.1	22 46.1	−5.0	20.2	23 42.3	−4.6	20.4	24 38.6	−4.3	20.5	71
72	17 57.1	−7.2	18.5	18 54.0	−6.9	18.6	19 50.8	−6.5	18.7	20 47.6	−6.1	18.9	21 44.3	−5.7	19.0	22 41.1	−5.5	19.1	23 37.7	−5.0	19.3	24 34.3	−4.7	19.4	72
73	17 49.9	−7.5	17.5	18 47.1	−7.2	17.6	19 44.3	−6.8	17.7	20 41.5	−6.6	17.8	21 38.6	−6.2	17.9	22 35.6	−5.8	18.0	23 32.7	−5.6	18.2	24 29.6	−5.1	18.3	73
74	17 42.4	−7.8	16.4	18 39.9	−7.5	16.5	19 37.5	−7.3	16.6	20 34.9	−6.9	16.7	21 32.4	−6.6	16.8	22 29.8	−6.3	17.0	23 27.1	−5.9	17.1	24 24.5	−5.7	17.2	74
75	17 34.6	−8.2	15.4	18 32.4	−7.9	15.5	19 30.2	−7.6	15.6	20 28.0	−7.3	15.7	21 25.8	−7.0	15.8	22 23.5	−6.7	15.9	23 21.2	−6.4	16.0	24 18.8	−6.1	16.1	75
76	17 26.4	−8.4	14.4	18 24.5	−8.2	14.4	19 22.6	−7.9	14.5	20 20.7	−7.7	14.6	21 18.8	−7.5	14.7	22 16.8	−7.2	14.8	23 14.8	−6.9	14.9	24 12.7	−6.6	15.0	76
77	17 18.0	−8.8	13.3	18 16.3	−8.5	13.4	19 14.7	−8.3	13.5	20 13.0	−8.0	13.6	21 11.3	−7.8	13.6	22 09.6	−7.5	13.7	23 07.9	−7.3	13.8	24 06.1	−7.0	13.9	77
78	17 09.2	−9.2	12.3	18 07.8	−8.9	12.4	19 06.4	−8.7	12.4	20 05.0	−8.5	12.5	21 03.5	−8.2	12.6	22 02.1	−8.0	12.7	23 00.6	−7.7	12.8	23 59.1	−7.5	12.9	78
79	17 00.0	−9.4	11.3	17 58.9	−9.2	11.3	18 57.7	−9.0	11.4	19 56.5	−8.8	11.5	20 55.3	−8.6	11.5	21 54.1	−8.4	11.6	22 52.9	−8.2	11.7	23 51.6	−7.9	11.8	79
80	16 50.6	−9.7	10.2	17 49.7	−9.6	10.3	18 48.7	−9.4	10.3	19 47.7	−9.2	10.4	20 46.7	−9.0	10.5	21 45.7	−8.8	10.5	22 44.7	−8.6	10.6	23 43.7	−8.4	10.7	80
81	16 40.9	−10.1	9.2	17 40.1	−9.9	9.2	18 39.3	−9.7	9.3	19 38.5	−9.5	9.4	20 37.7	−9.3	9.4	21 36.9	−9.2	9.5	22 36.1	−9.0	9.5	23 35.3	−8.9	9.6	81
82	16 30.8	−10.3	8.2	17 30.2	−10.2	8.2	18 29.6	−10.0	8.3	19 29.0	−9.9	8.3	20 28.4	−9.8	8.4	21 27.7	−9.6	8.4	22 27.1	−9.5	8.5	23 26.4	−9.3	8.5	82
83	16 20.5	−10.6	7.1	17 20.0	−10.5	7.2	18 19.6	−10.4	7.2	19 19.1	−10.3	7.3	20 18.6	−10.1	7.3	21 18.1	−10.0	7.4	22 17.6	−9.9	7.4	23 17.1	−9.7	7.5	83
84	16 09.9	−11.0	6.1	17 09.5	−10.8	6.1	18 09.2	−10.8	6.2	19 08.8	−10.6	6.2	20 08.5	−10.5	6.3	21 08.1	−10.4	6.3	22 07.7	−10.2	6.3	23 07.4	−10.2	6.4	84
85	15 58.9	−11.2	5.1	16 58.7	−11.1	5.1	17 58.4	−11.0	5.1	18 58.2	−11.0	5.2	19 58.0	−10.9	5.2	20 57.7	−10.8	5.2	21 57.5	−10.7	5.3	22 57.2	−10.6	5.3	85
86	15 47.7	−11.5	4.1	16 47.6	−11.5	4.1	17 47.4	−11.4	4.1	18 47.2	−11.3	4.1	19 47.1	−11.3	4.2	20 46.9	−11.1	4.2	21 46.8	−11.1	4.2	22 46.6	−11.0	4.2	86
87	15 36.2	−11.8	3.0	16 36.1	−11.7	3.1	17 36.0	−11.7	3.1	18 35.9	−11.6	3.1	19 35.8	−11.5	3.1	20 35.8	−11.6	3.1	21 35.7	−11.5	3.2	22 35.6	−11.5	3.2	87
88	15 24.4	−12.1	2.0	16 24.4	−12.1	2.0	17 24.3	−12.0	2.1	18 24.3	−12.0	2.1	19 24.3	−12.0	2.1	20 24.2	−11.9	2.1	21 24.2	−11.9	2.1	22 24.1	−11.8	2.1	88
89	15 12.3	−12.3	1.0	16 12.3	−12.3	1.0	17 12.3	−12.3	1.0	18 12.3	−12.3	1.0	19 12.3	−12.3	1.0	20 12.3	−12.3	1.0	21 12.3	−12.3	1.0	22 12.3	−12.3	1.1	89
90	15 00.0	−12.6	0.0	16 00.0	−12.6	0.0	17 00.0	−12.6	0.0	18 00.0	−12.6	0.0	19 00.0	−12.6	0.0	20 00.0	−12.7	0.0	21 00.0	−12.7	0.0	22 00.0	−12.7	0.0	90
	15°			16°			17°			18°			19°			20°			21°			22°			

Dec.	15° Hc	15° d	15° Z	16° Hc	16° d	16° Z	17° Hc	17° d	17° Z	18° Hc	18° d	18° Z
°	° ′	′	°	° ′	′	°	° ′	′	°	° ′	′	°
0	11 35.1	−15.9	93.1	11 31.7	−17.0	93.4	11 28.1	−18.0	93.6	11 24.3	−19.0	93.8
1	11 19.2	−16.2	94.1	11 14.7	−17.1	94.3	11 10.1	−18.2	94.5	11 05.3	−19.2	94.7
2	11 03.0	−16.3	95.1	10 57.6	−17.4	95.3	10 51.9	−18.3	95.5	10 46.1	−19.4	95.7
3	10 46.7	−16.5	96.1	10 40.2	−17.5	96.3	10 33.6	−18.6	96.5	10 26.7	−19.5	96.7
4	10 30.2	−16.7	97.1	10 22.7	−17.7	97.3	10 15.0	−18.7	97.4	10 07.2	−19.8	97.6
5	10 13.5	−16.9	98.0	10 05.0	−17.9	98.2	9 56.3	−18.9	98.4	9 47.4	−19.8	98.6
6	9 56.6	−17.0	99.0	9 47.1	−18.0	99.2	9 37.4	−19.0	99.4	9 27.6	−20.1	99.5
7	9 39.6	−17.3	100.0	9 29.1	−18.2	100.2	9 18.4	−19.2	100.3	9 07.5	−20.1	100.5
8	9 22.3	−17.3	101.0	9 10.9	−18.4	101.1	8 59.2	−19.4	101.3	8 47.4	−20.4	101.4
9	9 05.0	−17.5	101.9	8 52.5	−18.5	102.1	8 39.8	−19.4	102.2	8 27.0	−20.4	102.4
10	8 47.5	−17.7	102.9	8 34.0	−18.7	103.1	8 20.4	−19.7	103.2	8 06.6	−20.6	103.3
11	8 29.8	−17.8	103.9	8 15.3	−18.7	104.0	8 00.7	−19.7	104.2	7 46.0	−20.7	104.3
12	8 12.0	−18.0	104.8	7 56.6	−19.0	105.0	7 41.0	−19.9	105.1	7 25.3	−20.8	105.2
13	7 54.0	−18.0	105.8	7 37.6	−19.0	105.9	7 21.1	−20.0	106.1	7 04.5	−21.0	106.2
14	7 36.0	−18.2	106.8	7 18.6	−19.2	106.9	7 01.1	−20.1	107.0	6 43.5	−21.1	107.1
15	7 17.8	−18.4	107.7	6 59.4	−19.2	107.8	6 41.0	−20.2	108.0	6 22.4	−21.1	108.1
16	6 59.4	−18.4	108.7	6 40.2	−19.4	108.8	6 20.8	−20.4	108.9	6 01.3	−21.3	109.0
17	6 41.0	−18.6	109.6	6 20.8	−19.5	109.8	6 00.4	−20.4	109.9	5 40.0	−21.3	109.9
18	6 22.4	−18.6	110.6	6 01.3	−19.6	110.7	5 40.0	−20.5	110.8	5 18.7	−21.5	110.9
19	6 03.8	−18.8	111.6	5 41.7	−19.7	111.7	5 19.5	−20.6	111.7	4 57.2	−21.5	111.8
20	5 45.0	−18.8	112.5	5 22.0	−19.8	112.6	4 58.9	−20.7	112.7	4 35.7	−21.6	112.8
21	5 26.2	−19.0	113.5	5 02.2	−19.8	113.5	4 38.2	−20.7	113.6	4 14.1	−21.6	113.7
22	5 07.2	−19.0	114.4	4 42.4	−19.9	114.5	4 17.5	−20.9	114.6	3 52.5	−21.7	114.6
23	4 48.2	−19.1	115.4	4 22.5	−20.1	115.4	3 56.6	−20.8	115.5	3 30.8	−21.8	115.6
24	4 29.1	−19.2	116.3	4 02.4	−20.0	116.4	3 35.8	−21.0	116.4	3 09.0	−21.8	116.5
25	4 09.9	−19.2	117.3	3 42.4	−20.1	117.3	3 14.8	−21.0	117.4	2 47.2	−21.9	117.4
26	3 50.7	−19.4	118.2	3 22.3	−20.2	118.3	2 53.8	−21.0	118.3	2 25.3	−21.9	118.4
27	3 31.3	−19.3	119.2	3 02.1	−20.3	119.2	2 32.8	−21.1	119.3	2 03.4	−21.9	119.3
28	3 12.0	−19.5	120.1	2 41.8	−20.2	120.2	2 11.7	−21.1	120.2	1 41.5	−22.0	120.2
29	2 52.5	−19.4	121.1	2 21.6	−20.3	121.1	1 50.6	−21.2	121.1	1 19.5	−22.0	121.2
30	2 33.1	−19.5	122.0	2 01.3	−20.4	122.0	1 29.4	−21.2	122.1	0 57.5	−22.0	122.1
31	2 13.6	−19.6	123.0	1 40.9	−20.4	123.0	1 08.2	−21.2	123.0	0 35.5	−22.0	123.0
32	1 54.0	−19.6	123.9	1 20.5	−20.4	123.9	0 47.0	−21.2	123.9	0 13.5	−22.0	124.0
33	1 34.4	−19.6	124.8	1 00.1	−20.4	124.9	0 25.8	−21.2	124.9	0 08.5	+22.0	55.1
34	1 14.8	−19.6	125.8	0 39.7	−20.4	125.8	0 04.6	−21.2	125.8	0 30.5	+22.0	54.2
35	0 55.2	−19.6	126.7	0 19.3	−20.4	126.7	0 16.6	+21.2	53.3	0 52.5	+22.0	53.3
36	0 35.6	−19.7	127.7	0 01.1	+20.5	52.3	0 37.8	+21.2	52.3	1 14.5	+21.9	52.3
37	0 15.9	−19.7	128.6	0 21.6	+20.4	51.4	0 59.0	+21.2	51.4	1 36.4	+22.0	51.4
38	0 03.8	+19.6	50.4	0 42.0	+20.4	50.4	1 20.2	+21.2	50.4	1 58.4	+21.9	50.5
39	0 23.4	+19.7	49.5	1 02.4	+20.4	49.5	1 41.4	+21.1	49.5	2 20.3	+21.9	49.5
40	0 43.1	+19.6	48.5	1 22.8	+20.3	48.5	2 02.5	+21.1	48.6	2 42.2	+21.8	48.6
41	1 02.7	+19.6	47.6	1 43.1	+20.4	47.6	2 23.6	+21.1	47.6	3 04.0	+21.8	47.7
42	1 22.3	+19.6	46.6	2 03.5	+20.3	46.7	2 44.7	+21.0	46.7	3 25.8	+21.7	46.7
43	1 41.9	+19.6	45.7	2 23.8	+20.3	45.7	3 05.7	+20.9	45.8	3 47.5	+21.7	45.8
44	2 01.5	+19.5	44.8	2 44.1	+20.2	44.8	3 26.6	+21.0	44.8	4 09.2	+21.6	44.9
45	2 21.0	+19.5	43.8	3 04.3	+20.2	43.8	3 47.6	+20.8	43.9	4 30.8	+21.5	43.9
46	2 40.5	+19.5	42.9	3 24.5	+20.1	42.9	4 08.4	+20.8	42.9	4 52.3	+21.5	43.0
47	3 00.0	+19.4	41.9	3 44.6	+20.1	42.0	4 29.2	+20.7	42.0	5 13.8	+21.3	42.1
48	3 19.4	+19.3	41.0	4 04.7	+20.0	41.0	4 49.9	+20.7	41.1	5 35.1	+21.3	41.1
49	3 38.7	+19.3	40.0	4 24.7	+19.9	40.1	5 10.6	+20.5	40.1	5 56.4	+21.2	40.2
50	3 58.0	+19.2	39.1	4 44.6	+19.8	39.1	5 31.1	+20.5	39.2	6 17.6	+21.1	39.2
51	4 17.2	+19.2	38.1	5 04.4	+19.8	38.2	5 51.6	+20.3	38.2	6 38.7	+21.0	38.3
52	4 36.4	+19.1	37.2	5 24.2	+19.7	37.2	6 11.9	+20.3	37.3	6 59.7	+20.8	37.4
53	4 55.5	+19.0	36.2	5 43.9	+19.5	36.3	6 32.2	+20.2	36.3	7 20.5	+20.8	36.4
54	5 14.5	+18.9	35.3	6 03.4	+19.5	35.3	6 52.4	+20.0	35.4	7 41.3	+20.6	35.5
55	5 33.4	+18.8	34.3	6 22.9	+19.4	34.4	7 12.4	+20.0	34.4	8 01.9	+20.5	34.5
56	5 52.2	+18.7	33.4	6 42.3	+19.3	33.4	7 32.4	+19.8	33.5	8 22.4	+20.3	33.6
57	6 10.9	+18.6	32.4	7 01.6	+19.1	32.5	7 52.2	+19.6	32.5	8 42.7	+20.2	32.6
58	6 29.5	+18.5	31.4	7 20.7	+19.0	31.5	8 11.8	+19.6	31.6	9 02.9	+20.1	31.7
59	6 48.0	+18.4	30.5	7 39.7	+18.9	30.6	8 31.4	+19.4	30.6	9 23.0	+19.9	30.7
60	7 06.4	+18.3	29.5	7 58.6	+18.8	29.6	8 50.8	+19.2	29.7	9 42.9	+19.8	29.7
61	7 24.7	+18.2	28.6	8 17.4	+18.6	28.6	9 10.0	+19.2	28.7	10 02.7	+19.5	28.8
62	7 42.9	+18.0	27.6	8 36.0	+18.5	27.7	9 29.2	+18.9	27.7	10 22.2	+19.4	27.8
63	8 00.9	+17.9	26.6	8 54.5	+18.4	26.7	9 48.1	+18.8	26.8	10 41.6	+19.3	26.9
64	8 18.8	+17.8	25.7	9 12.9	+18.2	25.7	10 06.9	+18.6	25.8	11 00.9	+19.0	25.9
65	8 36.6	+17.6	24.7	9 31.1	+18.0	24.8	10 25.5	+18.5	24.9	11 19.9	+18.9	24.9
66	8 54.2	+17.4	23.7	9 49.1	+17.8	23.8	10 44.0	+18.2	23.9	11 38.8	+18.7	24.0
67	9 11.6	+17.3	22.8	10 06.9	+17.7	22.8	11 02.2	+18.1	22.9	11 57.5	+18.4	23.0
68	9 28.9	+17.2	21.8	10 24.6	+17.5	21.9	11 20.3	+17.9	21.9	12 15.9	+18.3	22.0
69	9 46.1	+17.0	20.8	10 42.1	+17.4	20.9	11 38.2	+17.7	21.0	12 34.2	+18.0	21.0
70	10 03.1	+16.8	19.9	10 59.5	+17.1	19.9	11 55.9	+17.5	20.0	12 52.2	+17.9	20.1
71	10 19.9	+16.6	18.9	11 16.6	+17.0	18.9	12 13.4	+17.2	19.0	13 10.1	+17.6	19.1
72	10 36.5	+16.4	17.9	11 33.6	+16.7	18.0	12 30.6	+17.1	18.0	13 27.7	+17.4	18.1
73	10 52.9	+16.3	16.9	11 50.3	+16.6	17.0	12 47.7	+16.9	17.1	13 45.1	+17.1	17.1
74	11 09.2	+16.1	16.0	12 06.9	+16.3	16.0	13 04.6	+16.6	16.1	14 02.2	+16.9	16.1
75	11 25.3	+15.9	15.0	12 23.2	+16.2	15.0	13 21.2	+16.4	15.1	14 19.1	+16.7	15.1
76	11 41.2	+15.6	14.0	12 39.4	+15.9	14.0	13 37.6	+16.1	14.1	14 35.8	+16.4	14.2
77	11 56.8	+15.5	13.0	12 55.3	+15.7	13.0	13 53.7	+15.9	13.1	14 52.2	+16.1	13.2
78	12 12.3	+15.3	12.0	13 11.0	+15.4	12.1	14 09.6	+15.7	12.1	15 08.3	+15.9	12.2
79	12 27.6	+15.0	11.0	13 26.4	+15.3	11.1	14 25.3	+15.4	11.1	15 24.2	+15.6	11.2
80	12 42.6	+14.8	10.0	13 41.7	+15.0	10.1	14 40.7	+15.2	10.1	15 39.8	+15.3	10.2
81	12 57.4	+14.6	9.0	13 56.7	+14.7	9.1	14 55.9	+14.9	9.1	15 55.1	+15.1	9.2
82	13 12.0	+14.4	8.0	14 11.4	+14.5	8.1	15 10.8	+14.6	8.1	16 10.2	+14.8	8.1
83	13 26.4	+14.1	7.0	14 25.9	+14.2	7.1	15 25.4	+14.4	7.1	16 25.0	+14.5	7.1
84	13 40.5	+13.9	6.0	14 40.1	+14.0	6.1	15 39.8	+14.1	6.1	16 39.5	+14.2	6.1
85	13 54.4	+13.6	5.0	14 54.1	+13.8	5.1	15 53.9	+13.8	5.1	16 53.7	+13.8	5.1
86	14 08.0	+13.4	4.0	15 07.9	+13.4	4.1	16 07.7	+13.5	4.1	17 07.5	+13.6	4.1
87	14 21.4	+13.1	3.0	15 21.3	+13.2	3.0	16 21.2	+13.2	3.1	17 21.1	+13.3	3.1
88	14 34.5	+12.9	2.0	15 34.5	+12.9	2.0	16 34.4	+13.0	2.0	17 34.4	+13.0	2.1
89	14 47.4	+12.6	1.0	15 47.4	+12.6	1.0	16 47.4	+12.6	1.0	17 47.4	+12.6	1.0
90	15 00.0	+12.3	0.0	16 00.0	+12.3	0.0	17 00.0	+12.3	0.0	18 00.0	+12.3	0.0
	15°			16°			17°			18°		

19° Hc	19° d	19° Z	20° Hc	20° d	20° Z	21° Hc	21° d	21° Z	22° Hc	22° d	22° Z	Dec.
° ′	′	°	° ′	′	°	° ′	′	°	° ′	′	°	°
11 20.2	−20.0	94.0	11 16.0	−21.0	94.2	11 11.5	−22.0	94.4	11 06.9	−23.0	94.6	0
11 00.2	−20.2	94.9	10 55.0	−21.2	95.1	10 49.5	−22.2	95.3	10 43.9	−23.2	95.5	1
10 40.0	−20.3	95.9	10 33.8	−21.4	96.1	10 27.3	−22.3	96.2	10 20.7	−23.3	96.4	2
10 19.7	−20.6	96.8	10 12.4	−21.5	97.0	10 05.0	−22.5	97.2	9 57.4	−23.5	97.4	3
9 59.1	−20.7	97.8	9 50.9	−21.7	98.0	9 42.5	−22.7	98.1	9 33.9	−23.6	98.3	4
9 38.4	−20.8	98.7	9 29.2	−21.8	98.9	9 19.8	−22.8	99.1	9 10.3	−23.8	99.2	5
9 17.6	−21.1	99.7	9 07.4	−22.0	99.9	8 57.0	−22.9	100.0	8 46.5	−23.9	100.2	6
8 56.5	−21.1	100.6	8 45.4	−22.1	100.8	8 34.1	−23.1	100.9	8 22.6	−24.0	101.1	7
8 35.4	−21.3	101.6	8 23.3	−22.3	101.7	8 11.0	−23.2	101.9	7 58.6	−24.2	102.0	8
8 14.1	−21.4	102.5	8 01.0	−22.4	102.7	7 47.8	−23.4	102.8	7 34.4	−24.3	102.9	9
7 52.7	−21.6	103.5	7 38.6	−22.5	103.6	7 24.4	−23.4	103.7	7 10.1	−24.4	103.9	10
7 31.1	−21.6	104.4	7 16.1	−22.6	104.5	7 01.0	−23.6	104.7	6 45.7	−24.4	104.8	11
7 09.5	−21.8	105.4	6 53.5	−22.7	105.5	6 37.4	−23.6	105.6	6 21.3	−24.6	105.7	12
6 47.7	−21.9	106.3	6 30.8	−22.9	106.4	6 13.8	−23.8	106.5	5 56.7	−24.7	106.6	13
6 25.8	−22.0	107.2	6 07.9	−22.9	107.3	5 50.0	−23.8	107.4	5 32.0	−24.8	107.5	14
6 03.8	−22.1	108.2	5 45.0	−23.0	108.3	5 26.2	−24.0	108.4	5 07.2	−24.8	108.4	15
5 41.7	−22.2	109.1	5 22.0	−23.1	109.2	5 02.2	−24.0	109.3	4 42.4	−24.9	109.4	16
5 19.5	−22.3	110.0	4 58.9	−23.2	110.1	4 38.2	−24.1	110.2	4 17.5	−25.0	110.3	17
4 57.2	−22.3	111.0	4 35.7	−23.2	111.0	4 14.1	−24.1	111.1	3 52.5	−25.0	111.2	18
4 34.9	−22.4	111.9	4 12.5	−23.3	112.0	3 50.0	−24.2	112.0	3 27.5	−25.1	112.1	19
4 12.5	−22.5	112.8	3 49.2	−23.4	112.9	3 25.8	−24.3	113.0	3 02.4	−25.2	113.0	20
3 50.0	−22.5	113.8	3 25.8	−23.4	113.8	3 01.5	−24.3	113.9	2 37.2	−25.1	113.9	21
3 27.5	−22.6	114.7	3 02.4	−23.5	114.7	2 37.2	−24.3	114.8	2 12.1	−25.2	114.8	22
3 04.9	−22.7	115.6	2 38.9	−23.5	115.7	2 12.9	−24.4	115.7	1 46.9	−25.3	115.7	23
2 42.2	−22.7	116.5	2 15.4	−23.6	116.6	1 48.5	−24.4	116.6	1 21.6	−25.2	116.6	24
2 19.5	−22.7	117.5	1 51.8	−23.5	117.5	1 24.1	−24.4	117.5	0 56.4	−25.3	117.5	25
1 56.8	−22.8	118.4	1 28.3	−23.7	118.4	0 59.7	−24.5	118.4	0 31.1	−25.3	118.5	26
1 34.0	−22.7	119.3	1 04.6	−23.6	119.3	0 35.2	−24.4	119.4	0 05.8	−25.3	119.4	27
1 11.3	−22.8	120.2	0 41.0	−23.6	120.3	0 10.8	−24.5	120.3	0 19.5	+25.2	59.7	28
0 48.5	−22.8	121.2	0 17.4	−23.6	121.2	0 13.7	+24.4	58.8	0 44.7	+25.3	58.8	29
0 25.7	−22.9	122.1	0 06.2	+23.7	57.9	0 38.1	+24.5	57.9	1 10.0	+25.2	57.9	30
0 02.8	−22.8	123.0	0 29.9	+23.6	57.0	1 02.6	+24.4	57.0	1 35.2	+25.3	57.0	31
0 20.0	+22.8	56.1	0 53.5	+23.6	56.1	1 27.0	+24.4	56.1	2 00.5	+25.1	56.1	32
0 42.8	+22.8	55.1	1 17.1	+23.6	55.1	1 51.4	+24.4	55.2	2 25.6	+25.2	55.2	33
1 05.6	+22.8	54.2	1 40.7	+23.5	54.2	2 15.8	+24.3	54.2	2 50.8	+25.1	54.3	34
1 28.4	+22.7	53.3	2 04.2	+23.6	53.3	2 40.1	+24.3	53.3	3 15.9	+25.1	53.4	35
1 51.1	+22.8	52.3	2 27.8	+23.5	52.4	3 04.4	+24.2	52.4	3 41.0	+25.0	52.5	36
2 13.9	+22.7	51.4	2 51.3	+23.4	51.5	3 28.6	+24.2	51.5	4 06.0	+24.9	51.6	37
2 36.6	+22.6	50.5	3 14.7	+23.4	50.5	3 52.8	+24.2	50.6	4 30.9	+24.9	50.6	38
2 59.2	+22.6	49.6	3 38.1	+23.4	49.6	4 17.0	+24.1	49.7	4 55.8	+24.8	49.7	39
3 21.8	+22.6	48.6	4 01.5	+23.2	48.7	4 41.1	+24.0	48.7	5 20.6	+24.7	48.8	40
3 44.4	+22.5	47.7	4 24.7	+23.3	47.8	5 05.1	+23.9	47.8	5 45.3	+24.6	47.9	41
4 06.9	+22.4	46.8	4 48.0	+23.1	46.8	5 29.0	+23.8	46.9	6 09.9	+24.6	47.0	42
4 29.3	+22.4	45.9	5 11.1	+23.1	45.9	5 52.8	+23.8	46.0	6 34.5	+24.4	46.1	43
4 51.7	+22.3	44.9	5 34.2	+22.9	45.0	6 16.6	+23.6	45.1	6 58.9	+24.3	45.1	44
5 14.0	+22.2	44.0	5 57.1	+22.9	44.1	6 40.2	+23.6	44.1	7 23.2	+24.3	44.2	45
5 36.2	+22.1	43.1	6 20.0	+22.8	43.1	7 03.8	+23.4	43.2	7 47.5	+24.1	43.3	46
5 58.3	+22.0	42.1	6 42.8	+22.6	42.2	7 27.2	+23.3	42.3	8 11.6	+23.9	42.4	47
6 20.3	+21.9	41.2	7 05.4	+22.6	41.3	7 50.5	+23.2	41.4	8 35.5	+23.9	41.4	48
6 42.2	+21.8	40.3	7 28.0	+22.4	40.3	8 13.7	+23.1	40.4	8 59.4	+23.7	40.5	49
7 04.0	+21.7	39.3	7 50.4	+22.4	39.4	8 36.8	+22.9	39.5	9 23.1	+23.5	39.6	50
7 25.7	+21.6	38.4	8 12.8	+22.1	38.5	8 59.7	+22.8	38.6	9 46.6	+23.4	38.7	51
7 47.3	+21.5	37.4	8 34.9	+22.1	37.5	9 22.5	+22.6	37.6	10 10.0	+23.2	37.7	52
8 08.8	+21.3	36.5	8 57.0	+21.9	36.6	9 45.1	+22.5	36.7	10 33.2	+23.1	36.8	53
8 30.1	+21.2	35.5	9 18.9	+21.8	35.6	10 07.6	+22.4	35.7	10 56.3	+22.9	35.8	54
8 51.3	+21.0	34.6	9 40.7	+21.6	34.7	10 30.0	+22.1	34.8	11 19.2	+22.7	34.9	55
9 12.3	+20.9	33.6	10 02.3	+21.4	33.7	10 52.1	+22.0	33.8	11 41.9	+22.6	34.0	56
9 33.2	+20.8	32.7	10 23.7	+21.3	32.8	11 14.1	+21.8	32.9	12 04.5	+22.3	33.0	57
9 54.0	+20.6	31.7	10 45.0	+21.1	31.8	11 35.9	+21.6	31.9	12 26.8	+22.1	32.1	58
10 14.6	+20.4	30.8	11 06.1	+20.9	30.9	11 57.5	+21.5	31.0	12 48.9	+22.0	31.1	59
10 35.0	+20.2	29.8	11 27.0	+20.7	29.9	12 19.0	+21.2	30.0	13 10.9	+21.7	30.2	60
10 55.2	+20.1	28.9	11 47.7	+20.6	29.0	12 40.2	+21.0	29.1	13 32.6	+21.5	29.2	61
11 15.3	+19.9	27.9	12 08.3	+20.3	28.0	13 01.2	+20.8	28.1	13 54.1	+21.3	28.2	62
11 35.2	+19.6	27.0	12 28.6	+20.1	27.1	13 22.0	+20.6	27.2	14 15.4	+21.0	27.3	63
11 54.8	+19.5	26.0	12 48.7	+20.0	26.1	13 42.6	+20.4	26.2	14 36.4	+20.8	26.3	64
12 14.3	+19.3	25.0	13 08.7	+19.7	25.1	14 03.0	+20.1	25.2	14 57.2	+20.6	25.3	65
12 33.6	+19.1	24.1	13 28.4	+19.5	24.1	14 23.1	+19.9	24.3	15 17.8	+20.3	24.4	66
12 52.7	+18.8	23.1	13 47.9	+19.2	23.2	14 43.0	+19.6	23.3	15 38.1	+20.0	23.4	67
13 11.5	+18.7	22.1	14 07.1	+19.0	22.2	15 02.6	+19.4	22.3	15 58.1	+19.8	22.4	68
13 30.2	+18.4	21.1	14 26.1	+18.8	21.2	15 22.0	+19.2	21.3	16 17.9	+19.5	21.4	69
13 48.6	+18.2	20.2	14 44.9	+18.5	20.2	15 41.2	+18.8	20.3	16 37.4	+19.2	20.4	70
14 06.8	+17.9	19.2	15 03.4	+18.3	19.3	16 00.0	+18.6	19.3	16 56.6	+19.0	19.4	71
14 24.7	+17.7	18.2	15 21.7	+18.0	18.3	16 18.6	+18.4	18.4	17 15.6	+18.6	18.5	72
14 42.4	+17.4	17.2	15 39.7	+17.7	17.3	16 37.0	+18.0	17.4	17 34.2	+18.4	17.5	73
14 59.8	+17.2	16.2	15 57.4	+17.5	16.3	16 55.0	+17.8	16.4	17 52.6	+18.0	16.5	74
15 17.0	+16.9	15.2	16 14.9	+17.2	15.3	17 12.8	+17.4	15.4	18 10.6	+17.7	15.5	75
15 33.9	+16.7	14.2	16 32.1	+16.9	14.3	17 30.2	+17.2	14.4	18 28.3	+17.4	14.4	76
15 50.6	+16.4	13.2	16 49.0	+16.6	13.3	17 47.4	+16.8	13.4	18 45.7	+17.1	13.4	77
16 07.0	+16.1	12.2	17 05.6	+16.3	12.3	18 04.2	+16.5	12.4	19 02.8	+16.8	12.4	78
16 23.1	+15.8	11.2	17 21.9	+16.0	11.3	18 20.7	+16.2	11.3	19 19.6	+16.4	11.4	79
16 38.9	+15.5	10.2	17 37.9	+15.7	10.3	18 36.9	+15.9	10.3	19 36.0	+16.0	10.4	80
16 54.4	+15.2	9.2	17 53.6	+15.4	9.3	18 52.8	+15.6	9.3	19 52.0	+15.7	9.4	81
17 09.6	+14.9	8.2	18 09.0	+15.0	8.2	19 08.4	+15.2	8.3	20 07.7	+15.4	8.3	82
17 24.5	+14.6	7.2	18 24.0	+14.8	7.2	19 23.6	+14.8	7.3	20 23.1	+15.0	7.3	83
17 39.1	+14.3	6.2	18 38.8	+14.4	6.2	19 38.4	+14.5	6.2	20 38.1	+14.6	6.3	84
17 53.4	+14.0	5.1	18 53.2	+14.0	5.2	19 52.9	+14.2	5.2	20 52.7	+14.2	5.2	85
18 07.4	+13.6	4.1	19 07.2	+13.8	4.1	20 07.1	+13.8	4.2	21 06.9	+13.9	4.2	86
18 21.0	+13.4	3.1	19 21.0	+13.3	3.1	20 20.9	+13.4	3.1	21 20.8	+13.4	3.2	87
18 34.4	+13.0	2.1	19 34.3	+13.0	2.1	20 34.3	+13.0	2.1	21 34.2	+13.1	2.1	88
18 47.4	+12.6	1.0	19 47.3	+12.7	1.0	20 47.3	+12.7	1.0	21 47.3	+12.7	1.1	89
19 00.0	+12.3	0.0	20 00.0	+12.3	0.0	21 00.0	+12.3	0.0	22 00.0	+12.3	0.0	90
19°			20°			21°			22°			

S. Lat. { L.H.A. greater than 180° ....Zn=180°−Z; L.H.A. less than 180°...........Zn=180°+Z

LATITUDE **SAME** NAME AS DECLINATION — L.H.A. 102°, 258°

Dec.	15° Hc	d	Z	16° Hc	d	Z	17° Hc	d	Z	18° Hc	d	Z	19° Hc	d	Z	20° Hc	d	Z	21° Hc	d	Z	22° Hc	d	Z	Dec.
°	° ′	′	°	° ′	′	°	° ′	′	°	° ′	′	°	° ′	′	°	° ′	′	°	° ′	′	°	° ′	′	°	°
0	10 37.2	+15.8	92.9	10 34.1	+16.8	93.1	10 30.8	+17.8	93.3	10 27.3	+18.8	93.4	10 23.6	+19.8	93.6	10 19.7	+20.8	93.8	10 15.7	+21.7	94.0	10 11.4	+22.8	94.2	0
1	10 53.0	+15.5	91.9	10 50.9	+16.5	92.1	10 48.6	+17.5	92.3	10 46.1	+18.6	92.5	10 43.4	+19.6	92.7	10 40.5	+20.6	92.8	10 37.4	+21.6	93.0	10 34.2	+22.5	93.2	1
2	11 08.5	+15.3	90.9	11 07.4	+16.4	91.1	11 06.1	+17.4	91.3	11 04.7	+18.4	91.5	11 03.0	+19.4	91.7	11 01.1	+20.4	91.9	10 59.0	+21.5	92.1	10 56.7	+22.5	92.3	2
3	11 23.8	+15.1	89.9	11 23.8	+16.1	90.1	11 23.5	+17.2	90.3	11 23.1	+18.2	90.5	11 22.4	+19.2	90.7	11 21.5	+20.3	90.9	11 20.5	+21.2	91.1	11 19.2	+22.2	91.3	3
4	11 38.9	+15.0	88.9	11 39.9	+16.0	89.1	11 40.7	+17.0	89.4	11 41.3	+18.0	89.6	11 41.6	+19.1	89.8	11 41.8	+20.0	90.0	11 41.7	+21.0	90.2	11 41.4	+22.0	90.4	4
5	11 53.9	+14.7	88.0	11 55.9	+15.7	88.2	11 57.7	+16.8	88.4	11 59.3	+17.8	88.6	12 00.7	+18.8	88.8	12 01.8	+19.9	89.0	12 02.7	+20.9	89.2	12 03.4	+21.9	89.4	5
6	12 08.6	+14.5	87.0	12 11.6	+15.6	87.2	12 14.5	+16.6	87.4	12 17.1	+17.6	87.6	12 19.5	+18.6	87.8	12 21.7	+19.6	88.0	12 23.6	+20.6	88.3	12 25.3	+21.6	88.5	6
7	12 23.1	+14.3	86.0	12 27.2	+15.3	86.2	12 31.1	+16.3	86.4	12 34.7	+17.4	86.6	12 38.1	+18.4	86.9	12 41.3	+19.4	87.1	12 44.2	+20.5	87.3	12 46.9	+21.5	87.5	7
8	12 37.4	+14.0	85.0	12 42.5	+15.1	85.2	12 47.4	+16.2	85.4	12 52.1	+17.2	85.6	12 56.5	+18.2	85.9	13 00.7	+19.2	86.1	13 04.7	+20.2	86.3	13 08.4	+21.2	86.6	8
9	12 51.4	+13.9	84.0	12 57.6	+14.9	84.2	13 03.6	+15.9	84.4	13 09.3	+16.9	84.7	13 14.7	+18.0	84.9	13 19.9	+19.0	85.1	13 24.9	+20.0	85.4	13 29.6	+21.0	85.6	9
10	13 05.3	+13.6	83.0	13 12.5	+14.7	83.2	13 19.5	+15.7	83.4	13 26.2	+16.7	83.7	13 32.7	+17.7	83.9	13 38.9	+18.8	84.2	13 44.9	+19.8	84.4	13 50.6	+20.8	84.6	10
11	13 18.9	+13.4	82.0	13 27.2	+14.4	82.2	13 35.2	+15.4	82.5	13 42.9	+16.5	82.7	13 50.4	+17.5	82.9	13 57.7	+18.5	83.2	14 04.7	+19.5	83.4	14 11.4	+20.6	83.7	11
12	13 32.3	+13.1	81.0	13 41.6	+14.1	81.2	13 50.6	+15.2	81.5	13 59.4	+16.2	81.7	14 07.9	+17.3	81.9	14 16.2	+18.3	82.2	14 24.2	+19.3	82.5	14 32.0	+20.3	82.7	12
13	13 45.4	+12.9	80.0	13 55.7	+14.0	80.2	14 05.8	+15.0	80.5	14 15.6	+16.0	80.7	14 25.2	+17.0	81.0	14 34.5	+18.0	81.2	14 43.5	+19.1	81.5	14 52.3	+20.0	81.7	13
14	13 58.3	+12.7	79.0	14 09.7	+13.7	79.2	14 20.8	+14.7	79.5	14 31.6	+15.8	79.7	14 42.2	+16.8	80.0	14 52.5	+17.8	80.2	15 02.6	+18.8	80.5	15 12.3	+19.9	80.8	14
15	14 11.0	+12.4	78.0	14 23.4	+13.4	78.2	14 35.5	+14.4	78.5	14 47.4	+15.4	78.7	14 59.0	+16.5	79.0	15 10.3	+17.5	79.2	15 21.4	+18.5	79.5	15 32.2	+19.5	79.8	15
16	14 23.4	+12.1	76.9	14 36.8	+13.1	77.2	14 49.9	+14.2	77.5	15 02.8	+15.3	77.7	15 15.5	+16.2	78.0	15 27.8	+17.3	78.2	15 39.9	+18.3	78.5	15 51.7	+19.3	78.8	16
17	14 35.5	+11.9	75.9	14 49.9	+12.9	76.2	15 04.1	+14.0	76.4	15 18.1	+14.9	76.7	15 31.7	+16.0	77.0	15 45.1	+17.0	77.3	15 58.2	+18.0	77.5	16 11.0	+19.0	77.8	17
18	14 47.4	+11.6	74.9	15 02.8	+12.7	75.2	15 18.1	+13.6	75.4	15 33.0	+14.7	75.7	15 47.7	+15.7	76.0	16 02.1	+16.7	76.3	16 16.2	+17.7	76.5	16 30.0	+18.7	76.8	18
19	14 59.0	+11.3	73.9	15 15.5	+12.3	74.2	15 31.7	+13.4	74.4	15 47.7	+14.4	74.7	16 03.4	+15.4	75.0	16 18.8	+16.4	75.3	16 33.9	+17.4	75.5	16 48.7	+18.5	75.8	19
20	15 10.3	+11.1	72.9	15 27.8	+12.1	73.2	15 45.1	+13.1	73.4	16 02.1	+14.1	73.7	16 18.8	+15.1	74.0	16 35.2	+16.1	74.3	16 51.3	+17.2	74.5	17 07.2	+18.1	74.8	20
21	15 21.4	+10.8	71.9	15 39.9	+11.8	72.1	15 58.2	+12.8	72.4	16 16.2	+13.8	72.7	16 33.9	+14.8	73.0	16 51.3	+15.9	73.2	17 08.5	+16.8	73.5	17 25.3	+17.9	73.8	21
22	15 32.2	+10.5	70.9	15 51.7	+11.5	71.1	16 11.0	+12.5	71.4	16 30.0	+13.5	71.7	16 48.7	+14.6	72.0	17 07.2	+15.5	72.2	17 25.3	+16.6	72.5	17 43.2	+17.5	72.8	22
23	15 42.7	+10.2	69.8	16 03.2	+11.2	70.1	16 23.5	+12.2	70.4	16 43.5	+13.3	70.6	17 03.3	+14.2	70.9	17 22.7	+15.3	71.2	17 41.9	+16.2	71.5	18 00.7	+17.3	71.8	23
24	15 52.9	+9.9	68.8	16 14.4	+11.0	69.1	16 35.7	+12.0	69.3	16 56.8	+12.9	69.6	17 17.5	+13.9	69.9	17 38.0	+14.9	70.2	17 58.1	+15.9	70.5	18 18.0	+16.9	70.8	24
25	16 02.8	+9.6	67.8	16 25.4	+10.6	68.0	16 47.7	+11.6	68.3	17 09.7	+12.6	68.6	17 31.4	+13.6	68.9	17 52.9	+14.6	69.2	18 14.0	+15.6	69.5	18 34.9	+16.6	69.8	25
26	16 12.4	+9.4	66.8	16 36.0	+10.3	67.0	16 59.3	+11.3	67.3	17 22.3	+12.3	67.6	17 45.0	+13.3	67.9	18 07.5	+14.3	68.2	18 29.6	+15.3	68.5	18 51.5	+16.3	68.8	26
27	16 21.8	+9.0	65.7	16 46.3	+10.0	66.0	17 10.6	+11.0	66.3	17 34.6	+12.0	66.6	17 58.3	+13.0	66.9	18 21.8	+13.9	67.2	18 44.9	+15.0	67.5	19 07.8	+15.9	67.8	27
28	16 30.8	+8.7	64.7	16 56.3	+9.7	65.0	17 21.6	+10.7	65.2	17 46.6	+11.6	65.5	18 11.3	+12.6	65.8	18 35.7	+13.6	66.1	18 59.9	+14.6	66.4	19 23.7	+15.6	66.8	28
29	16 39.5	+8.5	63.7	17 06.0	+9.4	63.9	17 32.3	+10.3	64.2	17 58.2	+11.4	64.5	18 23.9	+12.3	64.8	18 49.3	+13.3	65.1	19 14.5	+14.2	65.4	19 39.3	+15.2	65.7	29
30	16 48.0	+8.1	62.6	17 15.4	+9.1	62.9	17 42.6	+10.1	63.2	18 09.6	+11.0	63.5	18 36.2	+12.0	63.8	19 02.6	+13.0	64.1	19 28.7	+13.9	64.4	19 54.5	+14.9	64.7	30
31	16 56.1	+7.8	61.6	17 24.5	+8.8	61.9	17 52.7	+9.7	62.1	18 20.6	+10.6	62.4	18 48.2	+11.6	62.7	19 15.6	+12.6	63.0	19 42.6	+13.6	63.4	20 09.4	+14.5	63.7	31
32	17 03.9	+7.5	60.6	17 33.3	+8.4	60.8	18 02.4	+9.4	61.1	18 31.2	+10.4	61.4	18 59.8	+11.3	61.7	19 28.2	+12.2	62.0	19 56.2	+13.2	62.3	20 23.9	+14.1	62.6	32
33	17 11.4	+7.1	59.5	17 41.7	+8.1	59.8	18 11.8	+9.0	60.1	18 41.6	+10.0	60.4	19 11.1	+10.9	60.7	19 40.4	+11.9	61.0	20 09.4	+12.8	61.3	20 38.0	+13.8	61.6	33
34	17 18.5	+6.9	58.5	17 49.8	+7.8	58.7	18 20.8	+8.7	59.0	18 51.6	+9.6	59.3	19 22.0	+10.6	59.6	19 52.3	+11.5	59.9	20 22.2	+12.4	60.2	20 51.8	+13.4	60.6	34
35	17 25.4	+6.5	57.4	17 57.6	+7.4	57.7	18 29.5	+8.4	58.0	19 01.2	+9.3	58.3	19 32.6	+10.2	58.6	20 03.8	+11.1	58.9	20 34.6	+12.1	59.2	21 05.2	+13.0	59.5	35
36	17 31.9	+6.2	56.4	18 05.0	+7.1	56.7	18 37.9	+8.0	56.9	19 10.5	+8.9	57.2	19 42.8	+9.9	57.5	20 14.9	+10.8	57.8	20 46.7	+11.7	58.1	21 18.2	+12.7	58.5	36
37	17 38.1	+5.9	55.3	18 12.1	+6.8	55.6	18 45.9	+7.6	55.9	19 19.4	+8.6	56.2	19 52.7	+9.4	56.5	20 25.7	+10.4	56.8	20 58.4	+11.3	57.1	21 30.9	+12.2	57.4	37
38	17 44.0	+5.5	54.3	18 18.9	+6.4	54.6	18 53.5	+7.4	54.8	19 28.0	+8.2	55.1	20 02.1	+9.2	55.4	20 36.1	+10.0	55.7	21 09.7	+10.9	56.0	21 43.1	+11.8	56.4	38
39	17 49.5	+5.2	53.3	18 25.3	+6.1	53.5	19 00.9	+6.9	53.8	19 36.2	+7.8	54.1	20 11.3	+8.7	54.4	20 46.1	+9.6	54.7	21 20.6	+10.6	55.0	21 54.9	+11.4	55.3	39
40	17 54.7	+4.9	52.2	18 31.4	+5.7	52.5	19 07.8	+6.6	52.7	19 44.0	+7.5	53.0	20 20.0	+8.3	53.3	20 55.7	+9.2	53.6	21 31.2	+10.1	53.9	22 06.3	+11.1	54.3	40
41	17 59.6	+4.5	51.2	18 37.1	+5.4	51.4	19 14.4	+6.2	51.7	19 51.5	+7.1	52.0	20 28.3	+8.0	52.3	21 04.9	+8.9	52.6	21 41.3	+9.7	52.9	22 17.4	+10.6	53.2	41
42	18 04.1	+4.2	50.1	18 42.5	+5.0	50.4	19 20.6	+5.9	50.6	19 58.6	+6.7	50.9	20 36.3	+7.6	51.2	21 13.8	+8.4	51.5	21 51.0	+9.3	51.8	22 28.0	+10.1	52.1	42
43	18 08.3	+3.8	49.1	18 47.5	+4.7	49.3	19 26.5	+5.5	49.6	20 05.3	+6.3	49.9	20 43.9	+7.2	50.1	21 22.2	+8.0	50.4	22 00.3	+8.9	50.7	22 38.1	+9.8	51.1	43
44	18 12.1	+3.5	48.0	18 52.2	+4.3	48.3	19 32.0	+5.1	48.5	20 11.6	+6.0	48.8	20 51.1	+6.7	49.1	21 30.2	+7.7	49.4	22 09.2	+8.5	49.7	22 47.9	+9.3	50.0	44
45	18 15.6	+3.2	47.0	18 56.5	+3.9	47.2	19 37.1	+4.8	47.5	20 17.6	+5.6	47.7	20 57.8	+6.4	48.0	21 37.9	+7.2	48.3	22 17.7	+8.0	48.6	22 57.2	+8.9	48.9	45
46	18 18.8	+2.8	45.9	19 00.4	+3.6	46.2	19 41.9	+4.4	46.4	20 23.2	+5.2	46.7	21 04.2	+6.0	46.9	21 45.1	+6.8	47.2	22 25.7	+7.6	47.5	23 06.1	+8.5	47.8	46
47	18 21.6	+2.5	44.9	19 04.0	+3.3	45.1	19 46.3	+4.0	45.3	20 28.4	+4.8	45.6	21 10.2	+5.6	45.9	21 51.9	+6.4	46.2	22 33.3	+7.2	46.5	23 14.6	+8.0	46.8	47
48	18 24.1	+2.1	43.8	19 07.3	+2.9	44.0	19 50.3	+3.7	44.3	20 33.2	+4.4	44.5	21 15.8	+5.2	44.8	21 58.3	+6.0	45.1	22 40.5	+6.8	45.4	23 22.6	+7.5	45.7	48
49	18 26.2	+1.7	42.8	19 10.2	+2.5	43.0	19 54.0	+3.2	43.2	20 37.6	+4.0	43.5	21 21.0	+4.8	43.7	22 04.3	+5.5	44.0	22 47.3	+6.3	44.3	23 30.1	+7.2	44.6	49
50	18 27.9	+1.5	41.7	19 12.7	+2.1	41.9	19 57.2	+2.9	42.2	20 41.6	+3.6	42.4	21 25.8	+4.4	42.7	22 09.8	+5.2	42.9	22 53.6	+5.9	43.2	23 37.3	+6.6	43.5	50
51	18 29.4	+1.0	40.6	19 14.8	+1.8	40.9	20 00.1	+2.5	41.1	20 45.2	+3.3	41.3	21 30.2	+4.0	41.6	22 15.0	+4.7	41.9	22 59.5	+5.5	42.1	23 43.9	+6.2	42.4	51
52	18 30.4	+0.7	39.6	19 16.6	+1.4	39.8	20 02.6	+2.1	40.0	20 48.5	+2.8	40.3	21 34.2	+3.5	40.5	22 19.7	+4.2	40.8	23 05.0	+5.0	41.1	23 50.1	+5.8	41.4	52
53	18 31.1	+0.4	38.5	19 18.0	+1.1	38.8	20 04.7	+1.8	39.0	20 51.3	+2.4	39.2	21 37.7	+3.1	39.5	22 23.9	+3.9	39.7	23 10.0	+4.6	40.0	23 55.9	+5.3	40.3	53
54	18 31.5	0.0	37.5	19 19.1	+0.6	37.7	20 06.5	+1.3	37.9	20 53.7	+2.1	38.1	21 40.8	+2.8	38.4	22 27.8	+3.4	38.6	23 14.6	+4.1	38.9	24 01.2	+4.8	39.2	54
55	18 31.5	−0.3	36.4	19 19.7	+0.4	36.6	20 07.8	+1.0	36.8	20 55.8	+1.6	37.1	21 43.6	+2.3	37.3	22 31.2	+3.0	37.6	23 18.7	+3.7	37.8	24 06.0	+4.4	38.1	55
56	18 31.2	−0.7	35.4	19 20.1	−0.1	35.6	20 08.8	+0.6	35.8	20 57.4	+1.2	36.0	21 45.9	+1.9	36.2	22 34.2	+2.6	36.5	23 22.4	+3.2	36.7	24 10.4	+3.9	37.0	56
57	18 30.5	−1.0	34.3	19 20.0	−0.4	34.5	20 09.4	+0.2	34.7	20 58.6	+0.9	34.9	21 47.8	+1.4	35.2	22 36.8	+2.1	35.4	23 25.6	+2.8	35.6	24 14.3	+3.4	35.9	57
58	18 29.5	−1.4	33.3	19 19.6	−0.8	33.5	20 09.6	−0.2	33.7	20 59.5	+0.4	33.9	21 49.2	+1.1	34.1	22 38.9	+1.6	34.3	23 28.4	+2.3	34.5	24 17.7	+3.0	34.8	58
59	18 28.1	−1.8	32.2	19 18.8	−1.2	32.4	20 09.4	−0.6	32.6	20 59.9	0.0	32.8	21 50.3	+0.6	33.0	22 40.5	+1.3	33.2	23 30.7	+1.8	33.5	24 20.7	+2.4	33.7	59
60	18 26.3	−2.0	31.2	19 17.6	−1.5	31.3	20 08.8	−0.9	31.5	20 59.9	−0.3	31.7	21 50.9	+0.2	31.9	22 41.8	+0.8	32.1	23 32.5	+1.4	32.4	24 23.1	+2.0	32.6	60
61	18 24.3	−2.5	30.1	19 16.1	−1.9	30.3	20 07.9	−1.3	30.5	20 59.6	−0.8	30.6	21 51.1	−0.2	30.8	22 42.6	+0.4	31.1	23 33.9	+1.0	31.3	24 25.1	+1.6	31.5	61
62	18 21.8	−2.7	29.1	19 14.2	−2.2	29.2	20 06.6	−1.8	29.4	20 58.8	−1.2	29.6	21 50.9	−0.6	29.8	22 43.0	−0.1	30.0	23 34.9	+0.5	30.2	24 26.7	+1.0	30.4	62
63	18 19.1	−3.2	28.0	19 12.0	−2.6	28.2	20 04.8	−2.0	28.3	20 57.6	−1.6	28.5	21 50.3	−1.0	28.7	22 42.9	−0.5	28.9	23 35.4	0.0	29.1	24 27.7	+0.6	29.3	63
64	18 15.9	−3.4	26.9	19 09.4	−3.0	27.1	20 02.8	−2.5	27.3	20 56.0	−1.9	27.4	21 49.3	−1.5	27.6	22 42.4	−1.0	27.8	23 35.4	−0.4	28.0	24 28.3	+0.1	28.2	64
65	18 12.5	−3.9	25.9	19 06.4	−3.3	26.0	20 00.3	−2.9	26.2	20 54.1	−2.4	26.4	21 47.8	−1.9	26.5	22 41.4	−1.4	26.7	23 35.0	−0.9	26.9	24 28.4	−0.3	27.1	65
66	18 08.6	−4.1	24.8	19 03.1	−3.7	25.0	19 57.4	−3.2	25.1	20 51.7	−2.8	25.3	21 45.9	−2.3	25.5	22 40.0	−1.8	25.6	23 34.1	−1.4	25.8	24 28.1	−0.9	26.0	66
67	18 04.5	−4.5	23.8	18 59.4	−4.1	23.9	19 54.2	−3.6	24.1	20 48.9	−3.1	24.2	21 43.6	−2.7	24.4	22 38.2	−2.2	24.6	23 32.7	−1.7	24.7	24 27.2	−1.3	24.9	67
68	18 00.0	−4.8	22.7	18 55.3	−4.4	22.9	19 50.6	−4.0	23.0	20 45.8	−3.6	23.2	21 40.9	−3.1	23.3	22 36.0	−2.7	23.5	23 31.0	−2.3	23.6	24 25.9	−1.8	23.8	68
69	17 55.2	−5.2	21.7	18 50.9	−4.8	21.8	19 46.6	−4.4	22.0	20 42.2	−4.0	22.1	21 37.8	−3.6	22.2	22 33.3	−3.2	22.4	23 28.7	−2.7	22.6	24 24.1	−2.3	22.7	69
70	17 50.0	−5.5	20.7	18 46.1	−5.1	20.8	19 42.2	−4.7	20.9	20 38.2	−4.3	21.0	21 34.2	−4.0	21.2	22 30.1	−3.5	21.3	23 26.0	−3.2	21.5	24 21.8	−2.7	21.6	70
71	17 44.5	−5.8	19.6	18 41.0	−5.5	19.7	19 37.5	−5.2	19.8	20 33.9	−4.8	20.0	21 30.2	−4.3	20.1	22 26.6	−4.0	20.2	23 22.8	−3.6	20.4	24 19.1	−3.3	20.5	71
72	17 38.7	−6.2	18.6	18 35.5	−5.8	18.7	19 32.3	−5.4	18.8	20 29.1	−5.1	18.9	21 25.9	−4.8	19.0	22 22.6	−4.4	19.1	23 19.2	−4.0	19.3	24 15.8	−3.6	19.4	72
73	17 32.5	−6.5	17.5	18 29.7	−6.2	17.6	19 26.9	−5.9	17.7	20 24.0	−5.5	17.8	21 21.1	−5.2	17.9	22 18.2	−4.9	18.1	23 15.2	−4.5	18.2	24 12.2	−4.2	18.3	73
74	17 26.0	−6.8	16.5	18 23.5	−6.5	16.6	19 21.0	−6.2	16.7	20 18.5	−5.9	16.8	21 15.9	−5.6	16.9	22 13.3	−5.3	17.0	23 10.7	−5.0	17.1	24 08.0	−4.6	17.2	74
75	17 19.2	−7.2	15.4	18 17.0	−6.9	15.5	19 14.8	−6.6	15.6	20 12.6	−6.3	15.7	21 10.3	−6.0	15.8	22 08.0	−5.7	15.9	23 05.7	−5.4	16.0	24 03.4	−5.1	16.2	75
76	17 12.0	−7.4	14.4	18 10.1	−7.2	14.5	19 08.2	−6.9	14.6	20 06.3	−6.7	14.6	21 04.3	−6.4	14.7	22 02.3	−6.1	14.8	23 00.3	−5.8	15.0	23 58.3	−5.6	15.1	76
77	17 04.6	−7.8	13.4	18 02.9	−7.5	13.4	19 01.3	−7.3	13.5	19 59.6	−7.0	13.6	20 57.9	−6.7	13.7	21 56.2	−6.5	13.8	22 54.5	−6.3	13.9	23 52.7	−6.0	14.0	77
78	16 56.8	−8.1	12.3	17 55.4	−7.8	12.4	18 54.0	−7.6	12.5	19 52.6	−7.4	12.5	20 51.2	−7.2	12.6	21 49.7	−7.0	12.7	22 48.2	−6.7	12.8	23 46.7	−6.5	12.9	78
79	16 48.7	−8.4	11.3	17 47.6	−8.2	11.3	18 46.4	−8.0	11.4	19 45.2	−7.8	11.5	20 44.0	−7.6	11.6	21 42.7	−7.3	11.6	22 41.5	−7.1	11.7	23 40.2	−6.9	11.8	79
80	16 40.3	−8.7	10.2	17 39.4	−8.6	10.3	18 38.4	−8.4	10.4	19 37.4	−8.2	10.4	20 36.4	−8.0	10.5	21 35.4	−7.8	10.6	22 34.4	−7.6	10.6	23 33.3	−7.3	10.7	80
81	16 31.6	−9.0	9.2	17 30.8	−8.8	9.3	18 30.0	−8.6	9.3	19 29.2	−8.5	9.4	20 28.4	−8.3	9.4	21 27.6	−8.1	9.5	22 26.8	−8.0	9.6	23 26.0	−7.9	9.6	81
82	16 22.6	−9.3	8.2	17 22.0	−9.2	8.2	18 21.4	−9.1	8.3	19 20.7	−8.8	8.3	20 20.1	−8.7	8.4	21 19.5	−8.6	8.4	22 18.8	−8.4	8.5	23 18.1	−8.2	8.6	82
83	16 13.3	−9.6	7.2	17 12.8	−9.5	7.2	18 12.3	−9.3	7.2	19 11.9	−9.3	7.3	20 11.4	−9.1	7.3	21 10.9	−9.0	7.4	22 10.4	−8.8	7.4	23 09.9	−8.7	7.5	83
84	16 03.7	−9.9	6.1	17 03.3	−9.8	6.2	18 03.0	−9.7	6.2	19 02.6	−9.5	6.2	20 02.3	−9.5	6.3	21 01.9	−9.3	6.3	22 01.6	−9.3	6.4	23 01.2	−9.2	6.4	84
85	15 53.8	−10.2	5.1	16 53.5	−10.1	5.1	17 53.3	−10.0	5.2	18 53.1	−10.0	5.2	19 52.8	−9.8	5.2	20 52.6	−9.8	5.3	21 52.3	−9.7	5.3	22 52.0	−9.5	5.3	85
86	15 43.6	−10.5	4.1	16 43.4	−10.4	4.1	17 43.3	−10.4	4.1	18 43.1	−10.2	4.1	19 43.0	−10.2	4.2	20 42.8	−10.1	4.2	21 42.6	−10.0	4.2	22 42.5	−10.0	4.3	86
87	15 33.1	−10.7	3.1	16 33.0	−10.7	3.1	17 32.9	−10.6	3.1	18 32.9	−10.7	3.1	19 32.8	−10.6	3.1	20 32.7	−10.5	3.1	21 32.6	−10.5	3.2	22 32.5	−10.4	3.2	87
88	15 22.4	−11.1	2.0	16 22.3	−11.0	2.0	17 22.3	−11.0	2.1	18 22.2	−10.9	2.1	19 22.2	−10.9	2.1	20 22.2	−10.9	2.1	21 22.1	−10.8	2.1	22 22.1	−10.9	2.1	88
89	15 11.3	−11.3	1.0	16 11.3	−11.3	1.0	17 11.3	−11.3	1.0	18 11.3	−11.3	1.0	19 11.3	−11.3	1.0	20 11.3	−11.3	1.0	21 11.3	−11.3	1.1	22 11.2	−11.2	1.1	89
90	15 00.0	−11.6	0.0	16 00.0	−11.6	0.0	17 00.0	−11.6	0.0	18 00.0	−11.6	0.0	19 00.0	−11.6	0.0	20 00.0	−11.6	0.0	21 00.0	−11.6	0.0	22 00.0	−11.7	0.0	90
	15°			16°			17°			18°			19°			20°			21°			22°			

LATITUDE **CONTRARY** NAME TO DECLINATION — L.H.A. 79°, 281°

Dec.	15°			16°			17°			18°			19°			20°			21°			22°			Dec.
	Hc	d	Z	Hc	d	Z	Hc	d	Z	Hc	d	Z	Hc	d	Z	Hc	d	Z	Hc	d	Z	Hc	d	Z	
°	° ′	′	°	° ′	′	°	° ′	′	°	° ′	′	°	° ′	′	°	° ′	′	°	° ′	′	°	° ′	′	°	°
0	10 37.2	−15.8	92.9	10 34.1	−16.9	93.1	10 30.8	−17.9	93.3	10 27.3	−18.9	93.4	10 23.6	−19.9	93.6	10 19.7	−20.9	93.8	10 15.7	−22.0	94.0	10 11.4	−22.9	94.2	0
1	10 21.4	−16.1	93.9	10 17.2	−17.1	94.0	10 12.9	−18.1	94.2	10 08.4	−19.1	94.4	10 03.7	−20.1	94.6	9 58.8	−21.1	94.8	9 53.7	−22.1	94.9	9 48.5	−23.1	95.1	1
2	10 05.3	−16.3	94.8	10 00.1	−17.2	95.0	9 54.8	−18.3	95.2	9 49.3	−19.3	95.4	9 43.6	−20.3	95.5	9 37.7	−21.3	95.7	9 31.6	−22.2	95.9	9 25.4	−23.2	96.0	2
3	9 49.0	−16.4	95.8	9 42.9	−17.4	96.0	9 36.5	−18.4	96.2	9 30.0	−19.4	96.3	9 23.3	−20.4	96.5	9 16.4	−21.4	96.7	9 09.4	−22.4	96.8	9 02.2	−23.4	97.0	3
4	9 32.6	−16.5	96.8	9 25.5	−17.6	97.0	9 18.1	−18.6	97.1	9 10.6	−19.6	97.3	9 02.9	−20.6	97.4	8 55.0	−21.5	97.6	8 47.0	−22.5	97.8	8 38.8	−23.5	97.9	4
5	9 16.1	−16.8	97.8	9 07.9	−17.8	97.9	8 59.5	−18.7	98.1	8 51.0	−19.7	98.2	8 42.3	−20.7	98.4	8 33.5	−21.7	98.5	8 24.5	−22.7	98.7	8 15.3	−23.6	98.8	5
6	8 59.3	−16.8	98.7	8 50.1	−17.8	98.9	8 40.8	−18.9	99.0	8 31.3	−19.9	99.2	8 21.6	−20.8	99.3	8 11.8	−21.8	99.5	8 01.8	−22.8	99.6	7 51.7	−23.7	99.8	6
7	8 42.5	−17.1	99.7	8 32.3	−18.1	99.9	8 21.9	−19.0	100.0	8 11.4	−20.0	100.1	8 00.8	−21.0	100.3	7 50.0	−22.0	100.4	7 39.0	−22.9	100.6	7 28.0	−23.9	100.7	7
8	8 25.4	−17.1	100.7	8 14.2	−18.1	100.8	8 02.9	−19.2	101.0	7 51.4	−20.1	101.1	7 39.8	−21.1	101.2	7 28.0	−22.0	101.4	7 16.1	−23.0	101.5	7 04.1	−24.0	101.6	8
9	8 08.3	−17.4	101.6	7 56.1	−18.3	101.8	7 43.7	−19.2	101.9	7 31.3	−20.3	102.1	7 18.7	−21.2	102.2	7 06.0	−22.2	102.3	6 53.1	−23.1	102.4	6 40.1	−24.0	102.5	9
10	7 50.9	−17.4	102.6	7 37.8	−18.5	102.7	7 24.5	−19.4	102.9	7 11.0	−20.3	103.0	6 57.5	−21.4	103.1	6 43.8	−22.3	103.2	6 30.0	−23.2	103.4	6 16.1	−24.2	103.5	10
11	7 33.5	−17.6	103.6	7 19.3	−18.5	103.7	7 05.1	−19.5	103.8	6 50.7	−20.5	103.9	6 36.1	−21.4	104.1	6 21.5	−22.4	104.2	6 06.8	−23.4	104.3	5 51.9	−24.3	104.4	11
12	7 15.9	−17.7	104.5	7 00.8	−18.7	104.7	6 45.6	−19.7	104.8	6 30.2	−20.6	104.9	6 14.7	−21.5	105.0	5 59.1	−22.5	105.1	5 43.4	−23.4	105.2	5 27.6	−24.3	105.3	12
13	6 58.2	−17.8	105.5	6 42.1	−18.7	105.6	6 25.9	−19.7	105.7	6 09.6	−20.7	105.8	5 53.2	−21.7	105.9	5 36.6	−22.5	106.0	5 20.0	−23.5	106.1	5 03.3	−24.4	106.2	13
14	6 40.4	−17.9	106.5	6 23.4	−18.9	106.6	6 06.2	−19.8	106.7	5 48.9	−20.8	106.8	5 31.5	−21.7	106.9	5 14.1	−22.7	107.0	4 56.5	−23.6	107.1	4 38.9	−24.5	107.1	14
15	6 22.5	−18.0	107.4	6 04.5	−19.0	107.5	5 46.4	−20.0	107.6	5 28.1	−20.8	107.7	5 09.8	−21.8	107.8	4 51.4	−22.7	107.9	4 32.9	−23.6	108.0	4 14.4	−24.6	108.1	15
16	6 04.5	−18.1	108.4	5 45.5	−19.1	108.5	5 26.4	−20.0	108.6	5 07.3	−21.0	108.7	4 48.0	−21.8	108.8	4 28.7	−22.8	108.8	4 09.3	−23.7	108.9	3 49.8	−24.6	109.0	16
17	5 46.4	−18.3	109.3	5 26.4	−19.1	109.4	5 06.4	−20.1	109.5	4 46.3	−21.0	109.6	4 26.2	−22.0	109.7	4 05.9	−22.9	109.8	3 45.6	−23.8	109.8	3 25.2	−24.6	109.9	17
18	5 28.1	−18.3	110.3	5 07.3	−19.3	110.4	4 46.3	−20.1	110.5	4 25.3	−21.1	110.5	4 04.2	−22.0	110.6	3 43.0	−22.9	110.7	3 21.8	−23.8	110.7	3 00.6	−24.8	110.8	18
19	5 09.8	−18.4	111.3	4 48.0	−19.3	111.3	4 26.2	−20.3	111.4	4 04.2	−21.2	111.5	3 42.2	−22.1	111.6	3 20.1	−22.9	111.6	2 58.0	−23.9	111.7	2 35.8	−24.7	111.7	19
20	4 51.4	−18.5	112.2	4 28.7	−19.4	112.3	4 05.9	−20.3	112.4	3 43.0	−21.2	112.4	3 20.1	−22.1	112.5	2 57.2	−23.1	112.5	2 34.1	−23.9	112.6	2 11.1	−24.8	112.6	20
21	4 32.9	−18.5	113.2	4 09.3	−19.5	113.2	3 45.6	−20.4	113.3	3 21.8	−21.2	113.4	2 58.0	−22.2	113.4	2 34.1	−23.0	113.5	2 10.2	−23.9	113.5	1 46.3	−24.8	113.5	21
22	4 14.4	−18.6	114.1	3 49.8	−19.5	114.2	3 25.2	−20.4	114.2	3 00.6	−21.4	114.3	2 35.8	−22.2	114.3	2 11.1	−23.1	114.4	1 46.3	−24.0	114.4	1 21.5	−24.8	114.4	22
23	3 55.8	−18.7	115.1	3 30.3	−19.6	115.1	3 04.8	−20.5	115.2	2 39.2	−21.3	115.2	2 13.6	−22.2	115.3	1 48.0	−23.1	115.3	1 22.3	−23.9	115.3	0 56.7	−24.9	115.3	23
24	3 37.1	−18.8	116.0	3 10.7	−19.6	116.1	2 44.3	−20.5	116.1	2 17.9	−21.4	116.2	1 51.4	−22.3	116.2	1 24.9	−23.2	116.2	0 58.4	−24.0	116.2	0 31.8	−24.8	116.3	24
25	3 18.3	−18.8	117.0	2 51.1	−19.7	117.0	2 23.8	−20.6	117.1	1 56.5	−21.5	117.1	1 29.1	−22.3	117.1	1 01.7	−23.1	117.2	0 34.4	−24.1	117.2	0 07.0	−24.9	117.2	25
26	2 59.5	−18.8	117.9	2 31.4	−19.7	118.0	2 03.2	−20.6	118.0	1 35.0	−21.4	118.0	1 06.8	−22.3	118.1	0 38.6	−23.2	118.1	0 10.3	−24.0	118.1	0 17.9	+24.9	61.9	26
27	2 40.7	−18.9	118.9	2 11.7	−19.8	118.9	1 42.6	−20.6	119.0	1 13.6	−21.5	119.0	0 44.5	−22.3	119.0	0 15.4	−23.2	119.0	0 13.7	+24.0	61.0	0 42.8	+24.8	61.0	27
28	2 21.8	−19.0	119.8	1 51.9	−19.8	119.9	1 22.0	−20.6	119.9	0 52.1	−21.5	119.9	0 22.2	−22.4	119.9	0 07.8	+23.1	60.1	0 37.7	+24.0	60.1	1 07.6	+24.8	60.1	28
29	2 02.8	−18.9	120.8	1 32.1	−19.8	120.8	1 01.4	−20.7	120.8	0 30.6	−21.5	120.8	0 00.2	+22.3	59.2	0 30.9	+23.2	59.2	1 01.7	+24.0	59.2	1 32.4	+24.8	59.2	29
30	1 43.9	−19.0	121.7	1 12.3	−19.9	121.8	0 40.7	−20.7	121.8	0 09.1	−21.5	121.8	0 22.5	+22.3	58.2	0 54.1	+23.1	58.2	1 25.7	+23.9	58.3	1 57.2	+24.8	58.3	30
31	1 24.9	−19.1	122.7	0 52.4	−19.8	122.7	0 20.0	−20.6	122.7	0 12.4	+21.5	57.3	0 44.8	+22.3	57.3	1 17.2	+23.2	57.3	1 49.6	+24.0	57.3	2 22.0	+24.7	57.4	31
32	1 05.8	−19.0	123.6	0 32.6	−19.9	123.6	0 00.6	+20.7	56.4	0 33.9	+21.5	56.4	1 07.1	+22.3	56.4	1 40.4	+23.0	56.4	2 13.6	+23.8	56.4	2 46.7	+24.7	56.5	32
33	0 46.8	−19.1	124.6	0 12.7	−19.8	124.6	0 21.3	+20.7	55.4	0 55.4	+21.5	55.4	1 29.4	+22.3	55.4	2 03.4	+23.1	55.5	2 37.4	+23.9	55.5	3 11.4	+24.7	55.5	33
34	0 27.7	−19.0	125.5	0 07.1	+19.9	54.5	0 42.0	+20.7	54.5	1 16.9	+21.4	54.5	1 51.7	+22.2	54.5	2 26.5	+23.0	54.5	3 01.3	+23.8	54.6	3 36.1	+24.6	54.6	34
35	0 08.7	−19.1	126.5	0 27.0	+19.9	53.5	1 02.7	+20.6	53.5	1 38.3	+21.4	53.6	2 13.9	+22.3	53.6	2 49.5	+23.0	53.6	3 25.1	+23.8	53.7	4 00.7	+24.5	53.7	35
36	0 10.4	+19.1	52.6	0 46.9	+19.8	52.6	1 23.3	+20.6	52.6	1 59.7	+21.4	52.6	2 36.2	+22.1	52.7	3 12.5	+23.0	52.7	3 48.9	+23.7	52.7	4 25.2	+24.4	52.8	36
37	0 29.5	+19.0	51.6	1 06.7	+19.8	51.6	1 43.9	+20.6	51.7	2 21.1	+21.4	51.7	2 58.3	+22.1	51.7	3 35.5	+22.8	51.8	4 12.6	+23.6	51.8	4 49.6	+24.4	51.9	37
38	0 48.5	+19.0	50.7	1 26.5	+19.8	50.7	2 04.5	+20.6	50.7	2 42.5	+21.3	50.8	3 20.4	+22.1	50.8	3 58.3	+22.9	50.8	4 36.2	+23.6	50.9	5 14.0	+24.3	51.0	38
39	1 07.5	+19.1	49.7	1 46.3	+19.8	49.8	2 25.1	+20.5	49.8	3 03.8	+21.3	49.8	3 42.5	+22.0	49.9	4 21.2	+22.7	49.9	4 59.8	+23.5	50.0	5 38.3	+24.3	50.0	39
40	1 26.6	+19.0	48.8	2 06.1	+19.7	48.8	2 45.6	+20.5	48.8	3 25.1	+21.2	48.9	4 04.5	+22.0	48.9	4 43.9	+22.7	49.0	5 23.3	+23.4	49.1	6 02.6	+24.1	49.1	40
41	1 45.6	+18.9	47.8	2 25.8	+19.7	47.9	3 06.1	+20.4	47.9	3 46.3	+21.1	47.9	4 26.5	+21.8	48.0	5 06.6	+22.6	48.1	5 46.7	+23.3	48.1	6 26.7	+24.0	48.2	41
42	2 04.5	+19.0	46.9	2 45.5	+19.7	46.9	3 26.5	+20.4	47.0	4 07.4	+21.1	47.0	4 48.3	+21.8	47.1	5 29.2	+22.5	47.1	6 10.0	+23.2	47.2	6 50.7	+23.9	47.3	42
43	2 23.5	+18.9	45.9	3 05.2	+19.6	46.0	3 46.9	+20.3	46.0	4 28.5	+21.0	46.1	5 10.1	+21.7	46.1	5 51.7	+22.4	46.2	6 33.2	+23.1	46.3	7 14.6	+23.8	46.4	43
44	2 42.4	+18.8	45.0	3 24.8	+19.5	45.0	4 07.2	+20.2	45.1	4 49.5	+21.0	45.1	5 31.8	+21.7	45.2	6 14.1	+22.3	45.3	6 56.3	+23.0	45.3	7 38.4	+23.7	45.4	44
45	3 01.2	+18.8	44.0	3 44.3	+19.5	44.1	4 27.4	+20.2	44.1	5 10.5	+20.8	44.2	5 53.5	+21.5	44.3	6 36.4	+22.2	44.3	7 19.3	+22.9	44.4	8 02.1	+23.6	44.5	45
46	3 20.0	+18.8	43.1	4 03.8	+19.4	43.1	4 47.6	+20.1	43.2	5 31.3	+20.8	43.2	6 15.0	+21.4	43.3	6 58.6	+22.1	43.4	7 42.2	+22.8	43.5	8 25.7	+23.4	43.6	46
47	3 38.8	+18.6	42.1	4 23.2	+19.4	42.2	5 07.7	+20.0	42.2	5 52.1	+20.7	42.3	6 36.4	+21.4	42.4	7 20.7	+22.0	42.5	8 05.0	+22.6	42.5	8 49.1	+23.3	42.6	47
48	3 57.4	+18.7	41.2	4 42.6	+19.3	41.2	5 27.7	+19.9	41.3	6 12.8	+20.5	41.4	6 57.8	+21.2	41.4	7 42.7	+21.9	41.5	8 27.6	+22.5	41.6	9 12.4	+23.2	41.7	48
49	4 16.1	+18.5	40.2	5 01.9	+19.1	40.3	5 47.6	+19.8	40.3	6 33.3	+20.5	40.4	7 19.0	+21.1	40.5	8 04.6	+21.7	40.6	8 50.1	+22.4	40.7	9 35.6	+23.0	40.8	49
50	4 34.6	+18.5	39.3	5 21.0	+19.1	39.3	6 07.4	+19.8	39.4	6 53.8	+20.3	39.5	7 40.1	+21.0	39.5	8 26.3	+21.6	39.6	9 12.5	+22.2	39.7	9 58.6	+22.8	39.8	50
51	4 53.1	+18.4	38.3	5 40.1	+19.0	38.4	6 27.2	+19.6	38.4	7 14.1	+20.3	38.5	8 01.1	+20.8	38.6	8 47.9	+21.5	38.7	9 34.7	+22.1	38.8	10 21.4	+22.7	38.9	51
52	5 11.5	+18.3	37.4	5 59.1	+19.0	37.4	6 46.8	+19.5	37.5	7 34.4	+20.1	37.6	8 21.9	+20.7	37.7	9 09.4	+21.3	37.7	9 56.8	+21.9	37.8	10 44.1	+22.5	38.0	52
53	5 29.8	+18.2	36.4	6 18.1	+18.8	36.5	7 06.3	+19.4	36.5	7 54.5	+20.0	36.6	8 42.6	+20.6	36.7	9 30.7	+21.1	36.8	10 18.7	+21.7	36.9	11 06.6	+22.4	37.0	53
54	5 48.0	+18.1	35.4	6 36.9	+18.7	35.5	7 25.7	+19.2	35.6	8 14.5	+19.8	35.7	9 03.2	+20.4	35.8	9 51.8	+21.0	35.8	10 40.4	+21.6	36.0	11 29.0	+22.1	36.1	54
55	6 06.1	+18.0	34.5	6 55.6	+18.5	34.6	7 44.9	+19.2	34.6	8 34.3	+19.7	34.7	9 23.6	+20.3	34.8	10 12.8	+20.9	34.9	11 02.0	+21.4	35.0	11 51.1	+22.0	35.1	55
56	6 24.1	+17.9	33.5	7 14.1	+18.5	33.6	8 04.1	+19.0	33.7	8 54.0	+19.6	33.8	9 43.9	+20.1	33.8	10 33.7	+20.6	33.9	11 23.4	+21.2	34.1	12 13.1	+21.7	34.2	56
57	6 42.0	+17.8	32.6	7 32.6	+18.3	32.6	8 23.1	+18.9	32.7	9 13.6	+19.4	32.8	10 04.0	+19.9	32.9	10 54.3	+20.5	33.0	11 44.6	+21.0	33.1	12 34.8	+21.6	33.2	57
58	6 59.8	+17.7	31.6	7 50.9	+18.2	31.7	8 42.0	+18.7	31.8	9 33.0	+19.2	31.8	10 23.9	+19.8	31.9	11 14.8	+20.3	32.0	12 05.6	+20.9	32.1	12 56.4	+21.4	32.3	58
59	7 17.5	+17.6	30.6	8 09.1	+18.1	30.7	9 00.7	+18.6	30.8	9 52.2	+19.1	30.9	10 43.7	+19.6	31.0	11 35.1	+20.1	31.1	12 26.5	+20.6	31.2	13 17.8	+21.1	31.3	59
60	7 35.1	+17.4	29.7	8 27.2	+17.9	29.7	9 19.3	+18.4	29.8	10 11.3	+18.9	29.9	11 03.3	+19.4	30.0	11 55.2	+19.9	30.1	12 47.1	+20.4	30.2	13 38.9	+20.9	30.3	60
61	7 52.5	+17.3	28.7	8 45.1	+17.8	28.8	9 37.7	+18.2	28.9	10 30.2	+18.7	28.9	11 22.7	+19.2	29.0	12 15.1	+19.7	29.1	13 07.5	+20.2	29.3	13 59.8	+20.7	29.4	61
62	8 09.8	+17.2	27.7	9 02.9	+17.6	27.8	9 55.9	+18.1	27.9	10 48.9	+18.6	28.0	11 41.9	+19.0	28.1	12 34.8	+19.5	28.2	13 27.7	+20.0	28.3	14 20.5	+20.4	28.4	62
63	8 27.0	+17.0	26.8	9 20.5	+17.5	26.8	10 14.0	+17.9	26.9	11 07.5	+18.4	27.0	12 00.9	+18.9	27.1	12 54.3	+19.3	27.2	13 47.7	+19.7	27.3	14 40.9	+20.2	27.4	63
64	8 44.0	+16.8	25.8	9 38.0	+17.3	25.9	10 31.9	+17.8	26.0	11 25.9	+18.2	26.0	12 19.8	+18.6	26.1	13 13.6	+19.1	26.2	14 07.4	+19.5	26.3	15 01.1	+20.0	26.5	64
65	9 00.8	+16.8	24.8	9 55.3	+17.1	24.9	10 49.7	+17.5	25.0	11 44.1	+17.9	25.1	12 38.4	+18.4	25.2	13 32.7	+18.8	25.3	14 26.9	+19.3	25.4	15 21.1	+19.7	25.5	65
66	9 17.6	+16.5	23.9	10 12.4	+17.0	23.9	11 07.2	+17.4	24.0	12 02.0	+17.8	24.1	12 56.8	+18.2	24.2	13 51.5	+18.6	24.3	14 46.2	+19.0	24.4	15 40.8	+19.4	24.5	66
67	9 34.1	+16.4	22.9	10 29.4	+16.8	23.0	11 24.6	+17.2	23.0	12 19.8	+17.6	23.1	13 15.0	+17.9	23.2	14 10.1	+18.4	23.3	15 05.2	+18.8	23.4	16 00.2	+19.2	23.5	67
68	9 50.5	+16.2	21.9	10 46.2	+16.6	22.0	11 41.8	+17.0	22.1	12 37.4	+17.3	22.1	13 32.9	+17.8	22.2	14 28.5	+18.1	22.3	15 24.0	+18.5	22.4	16 19.4	+18.9	22.5	68
69	10 06.7	+16.1	20.9	11 02.8	+16.4	21.0	11 58.8	+16.7	21.1	12 54.7	+17.2	21.2	13 50.7	+17.5	21.2	14 46.6	+17.8	21.3	15 42.5	+18.2	21.4	16 38.3	+18.6	21.5	69
70	10 22.8	+15.9	20.0	11 19.2	+16.2	20.0	12 15.5	+16.6	20.1	13 11.9	+16.9	20.2	14 08.2	+17.2	20.3	15 04.4	+17.7	20.3	16 00.7	+18.0	20.4	16 56.9	+18.3	20.5	70
71	10 38.7	+15.7	19.0	11 35.4	+16.0	19.0	12 32.1	+16.3	19.1	13 28.8	+16.7	19.2	14 25.4	+17.0	19.3	15 22.1	+17.3	19.4	16 18.7	+17.6	19.5	17 15.2	+18.0	19.6	71
72	10 54.4	+15.5	18.0	11 51.4	+15.8	18.1	12 48.4	+16.2	18.1	13 45.5	+16.4	18.2	14 42.4	+16.8	18.3	15 39.4	+17.1	18.4	16 36.3	+17.4	18.5	17 33.2	+17.8	18.6	72
73	11 09.9	+15.3	17.0	12 07.2	+15.6	17.1	13 04.6	+15.9	17.1	14 01.9	+16.2	17.2	14 59.2	+16.5	17.3	15 56.5	+16.8	17.4	16 53.7	+17.1	17.5	17 51.0	+17.4	17.5	73
74	11 25.2	+15.1	16.0	12 22.8	+15.4	16.1	13 20.5	+15.6	16.1	14 18.1	+15.9	16.2	15 15.7	+16.2	16.3	16 13.3	+16.5	16.4	17 10.8	+16.8	16.5	18 08.4	+17.1	16.5	74
75	11 40.3	+14.9	15.0	12 38.2	+15.2	15.1	13 36.1	+15.5	15.2	14 34.0	+15.7	15.2	15 31.9	+16.0	15.3	16 29.8	+16.2	15.4	17 27.6	+16.5	15.4	18 25.5	+16.7	15.5	75
76	11 55.2	+14.7	14.0	12 53.4	+14.9	14.1	13 51.6	+15.2	14.2	14 49.7	+15.5	14.2	15 47.9	+15.7	14.3	16 46.0	+16.0	14.4	17 44.1	+16.2	14.4	18 42.2	+16.5	14.5	76
77	12 09.9	+14.5	13.1	13 08.3	+14.8	13.1	14 06.8	+14.9	13.2	15 05.2	+15.2	13.2	16 03.6	+15.4	13.3	17 02.0	+15.6	13.4	18 00.3	+15.9	13.4	18 58.7	+16.1	13.5	77
78	12 24.4	+14.3	12.1	13 23.1	+14.4	12.1	14 21.7	+14.7	12.2	15 20.4	+14.9	12.2	16 19.0	+15.1	12.3	17 17.6	+15.3	12.3	18 16.2	+15.6	12.4	19 14.8	+15.8	12.5	78
79	12 38.7	+14.0	11.1	13 37.5	+14.3	11.1	14 36.4	+14.4	11.2	15 35.3	+14.6	11.2	16 34.1	+14.8	11.3	17 32.9	+15.1	11.3	18 31.8	+15.2	11.4	19 30.6	+15.4	11.5	79
80	12 52.7	+13.8	10.1	13 51.8	+14.0	10.1	14 50.8	+14.2	10.2	15 49.9	+14.3	10.2	16 48.9	+14.6	10.3	17 48.0	+14.7	10.3	18 47.0	+14.9	10.4	19 46.0	+15.1	10.4	80
81	13 06.5	+13.6	9.1	14 05.8	+13.7	9.1	15 05.0	+13.9	9.2	16 04.2	+14.1	9.2	17 03.5	+14.2	9.2	18 02.7	+14.4	9.3	19 01.9	+14.5	9.3	20 01.1	+14.7	9.4	81
82	13 20.1	+13.4	8.1	14 19.5	+13.5	8.1	15 18.9	+13.7	8.1	16 18.3	+13.8	8.2	17 17.7	+13.9	8.2	18 17.1	+14.0	8.3	19 16.4	+14.3	8.3	20 15.8	+14.4	8.4	82
83	13 33.5	+13.1	7.1	14 33.0	+13.3	7.1	15 32.6	+13.3	7.1	16 32.1	+13.5	7.2	17 31.6	+13.6	7.2	18 31.1	+13.8	7.2	19 30.7	+13.8	7.3	20 30.2	+14.0	7.3	83
84	13 46.6	+12.9	6.1	14 46.3	+12.9	6.1	15 45.9	+13.1	6.1	16 45.6	+13.2	6.2	17 45.2	+13.3	6.2	18 44.9	+13.4	6.2	19 44.5	+13.5	6.3	20 44.2	+13.6	6.3	84
85	13 59.5	+12.6	5.1	14 59.2	+12.7	5.1	15 59.0	+12.8	5.1	16 58.8	+12.8	5.1	17 58.5	+13.0	5.2	18 58.3	+13.0	5.2	19 58.0	+13.2	5.2	20 57.8	+13.2	5.3	85
86	14 12.1	+12.4	4.1	15 11.9	+12.5	4.1	16 11.8	+12.5	4.1	17 11.6	+12.6	4.1	18 11.5	+12.6	4.1	19 11.3	+12.7	4.2	20 11.2	+12.7	4.2	21 11.0	+12.8	4.2	86
87	14 24.5	+12.1	3.0	15 24.4	+12.1	3.1	16 24.3	+12.2	3.1	17 24.2	+12.3	3.1	18 24.1	+12.3	3.1	19 24.0	+12.4	3.1	20 23.9	+12.4	3.1	21 23.8	+12.5	3.2	87
88	14 36.6	+11.8	2.0	15 36.5	+11.9	2.0	16 36.5	+11.9	2.0	17 36.5	+11.9	2.1	18 36.4	+12.0	2.1	19 36.4	+12.0	2.1	20 36.3	+12.1	2.1	21 36.3	+12.0	2.1	88
89	14 48.4	+11.6	1.0	15 48.4	+11.6	1.0	16 48.4	+11.6	1.0	17 48.4	+11.6	1.0	18 48.4	+11.6	1.0	19 48.4	+11.6	1.0	20 48.4	+11.6	1.1	21 48.3	+11.7	1.1	89
90	15 00.0	+11.3	0.0	16 00.0	+11.3	0.0	17 00.0	+11.3	0.0	18 00.0	+11.3	0.0	19 00.0	+11.3	0.0	20 00.0	+11.3	0.0	21 00.0	+11.3	0.0	22 00.0	+11.2	0.0	90
	15°			16°			17°			18°			19°			20°			21°			22°			

S. Lat. { L.H.A. greater than 180° ....Zn=180°−Z; L.H.A. less than 180°...........Zn=180°+Z

LATITUDE **SAME** NAME AS DECLINATION — L.H.A. 101°, 259°

80°, 280° L.H.A. — LATITUDE SAME NAME AS DECLINATION

N. Lat. {L.H.A. greater than 180° .....Zn=Z; L.H.A. less than 180°............Zn=360°-Z

Dec.	15°			16°			17°			18°			19°			20°			21°			22°			Dec.
	Hc	d	Z	Hc	d	Z	Hc	d	Z	Hc	d	Z	Hc	d	Z	Hc	d	Z	Hc	d	Z	Hc	d	Z	
°	° ′	′	°	° ′	′	°	° ′	′	°	° ′	′	°	° ′	′	°	° ′	′	°	° ′	′	°	° ′	′	°	°
0	9 39.4	+15.6	92.6	9 36.5	+16.7	92.8	9 33.5	+17.7	93.0	9 30.4	+18.7	93.1	9 27.0	+19.7	93.3	9 23.5	+20.7	93.5	9 19.8	+21.7	93.6	9 15.9	+22.7	93.8	0
1	9 55.0	+15.5	91.6	9 53.2	+16.5	91.8	9 51.2	+17.6	92.0	9 49.1	+18.5	92.2	9 46.7	+19.6	92.3	9 44.2	+20.6	92.5	9 41.5	+21.6	92.7	9 38.6	+22.6	92.8	1
2	10 10.5	+15.3	90.7	10 09.7	+16.4	90.8	10 08.8	+17.4	91.0	10 07.6	+18.4	91.2	10 06.3	+19.4	91.4	10 04.8	+20.4	91.5	10 03.1	+21.4	91.7	10 01.2	+22.3	91.9	2
3	10 25.8	+15.2	89.7	10 26.1	+16.2	89.9	10 26.2	+17.1	90.0	10 26.0	+18.2	90.2	10 25.7	+19.2	90.4	10 25.2	+20.2	90.6	10 24.5	+21.2	90.8	10 23.5	+22.3	91.0	3
4	10 41.0	+14.9	88.7	10 42.3	+16.0	88.9	10 43.3	+17.1	89.1	10 44.2	+18.1	89.3	10 44.9	+19.1	89.4	10 45.4	+20.0	89.6	10 45.7	+21.0	89.8	10 45.8	+22.0	90.0	4
5	10 55.9	+14.8	87.7	10 58.3	+15.7	87.9	11 00.4	+16.8	88.1	11 02.3	+17.8	88.3	11 04.0	+18.8	88.5	11 05.4	+19.9	88.7	11 06.7	+20.9	88.9	11 07.8	+21.9	89.1	5
6	11 10.7	+14.6	86.7	11 14.0	+15.7	86.9	11 17.2	+16.6	87.1	11 20.1	+17.7	87.3	11 22.8	+18.7	87.5	11 25.3	+19.7	87.7	11 27.6	+20.7	87.9	11 29.7	+21.7	88.1	6
7	11 25.3	+14.4	85.7	11 29.7	+15.4	85.9	11 33.8	+16.4	86.1	11 37.8	+17.4	86.3	11 41.5	+18.5	86.5	11 45.0	+19.5	86.7	11 48.3	+20.5	87.0	11 51.4	+21.5	87.2	7
8	11 39.7	+14.1	84.7	11 45.1	+15.2	84.9	11 50.2	+16.3	85.1	11 55.2	+17.3	85.4	12 00.0	+18.2	85.6	12 04.5	+19.3	85.8	12 08.8	+20.3	86.0	12 12.9	+21.3	86.2	8
9	11 53.8	+14.0	83.7	12 00.3	+15.0	83.9	12 06.5	+16.0	84.2	12 12.5	+17.0	84.4	12 18.2	+18.1	84.6	12 23.8	+19.1	84.8	12 29.1	+20.1	85.0	12 34.2	+21.1	85.3	9
10	12 07.8	+13.7	82.7	12 15.3	+14.7	83.0	12 22.5	+15.8	83.2	12 29.5	+16.8	83.4	12 36.3	+17.8	83.6	12 42.9	+18.8	83.8	12 49.2	+19.9	84.1	12 55.3	+20.8	84.3	10
11	12 21.5	+13.6	81.7	12 30.0	+14.6	82.0	12 38.3	+15.6	82.2	12 46.3	+16.7	82.4	12 54.1	+17.7	82.6	13 01.7	+18.7	82.9	13 09.1	+19.6	83.1	13 16.1	+20.7	83.3	11
12	12 35.1	+13.3	80.8	12 44.6	+14.3	81.0	12 53.9	+15.4	81.2	13 03.0	+16.3	81.4	13 11.8	+17.4	81.7	13 20.4	+18.4	81.9	13 28.7	+19.4	82.1	13 36.8	+20.4	82.4	12
13	12 48.4	+13.1	79.8	12 58.9	+14.1	80.0	13 09.3	+15.1	80.2	13 19.3	+16.2	80.4	13 29.2	+17.2	80.7	13 38.8	+18.2	80.9	13 48.1	+19.3	81.2	13 57.2	+20.3	81.4	13
14	13 01.5	+12.8	78.8	13 13.0	+13.9	79.0	13 24.4	+14.9	79.2	13 35.5	+15.9	79.4	13 46.4	+16.9	79.7	13 57.0	+17.9	79.9	14 07.4	+18.9	80.2	14 17.5	+19.9	80.4	14
15	13 14.3	+12.6	77.7	13 26.9	+13.7	78.0	13 39.3	+14.7	78.2	13 51.4	+15.7	78.5	14 03.3	+16.7	78.7	14 14.9	+17.8	78.9	14 26.3	+18.7	79.2	14 37.4	+19.8	79.5	15
16	13 26.9	+12.4	76.7	13 40.6	+13.4	77.0	13 54.0	+14.4	77.2	14 07.1	+15.4	77.5	14 20.0	+16.5	77.7	14 32.7	+17.4	78.0	14 45.0	+18.5	78.2	14 57.2	+19.4	78.5	16
17	13 39.3	+12.1	75.7	13 54.0	+13.1	76.0	14 08.4	+14.1	76.2	14 22.5	+15.2	76.5	14 36.5	+16.2	76.7	14 50.1	+17.2	77.0	15 03.5	+18.2	77.2	15 16.6	+19.3	77.5	17
18	13 51.4	+11.9	74.7	14 07.1	+12.9	75.0	14 22.5	+14.0	75.2	14 37.7	+15.0	75.5	14 52.7	+15.9	75.7	15 07.3	+17.0	76.0	15 21.7	+18.0	76.2	15 35.9	+18.9	76.5	18
19	14 03.3	+11.6	73.7	14 20.0	+12.7	74.0	14 36.5	+13.6	74.2	14 52.7	+14.6	74.5	15 08.6	+15.7	74.7	15 24.3	+16.7	75.0	15 39.7	+17.7	75.3	15 54.8	+18.7	75.5	19
20	14 14.9	+11.4	72.7	14 32.7	+12.3	73.0	14 50.1	+13.4	73.2	15 07.3	+14.4	73.5	15 24.3	+15.4	73.7	15 41.0	+16.4	74.0	15 57.4	+17.4	74.3	16 13.5	+18.4	74.5	20
21	14 26.3	+11.1	71.7	14 45.0	+12.2	71.9	15 03.5	+13.1	72.2	15 21.7	+14.2	72.5	15 39.7	+15.1	72.7	15 57.4	+16.1	73.0	16 14.8	+17.1	73.3	16 31.9	+18.2	73.5	21
22	14 37.4	+10.9	70.7	14 57.2	+11.8	70.9	15 16.6	+12.9	71.2	15 35.9	+13.8	71.4	15 54.8	+14.9	71.7	16 13.5	+15.9	72.0	16 31.9	+16.9	72.3	16 50.1	+17.8	72.6	22
23	14 48.3	+10.6	69.7	15 09.0	+11.6	69.9	15 29.5	+12.6	70.2	15 49.7	+13.6	70.4	16 09.7	+14.6	70.7	16 29.4	+15.5	71.0	16 48.8	+16.6	71.3	17 07.9	+17.6	71.6	23
24	14 58.9	+10.3	68.6	15 20.6	+11.3	68.9	15 42.1	+12.3	69.2	16 03.3	+13.3	69.4	16 24.3	+14.2	69.7	16 44.9	+15.3	70.0	17 05.4	+16.2	70.3	17 25.5	+17.2	70.6	24
25	15 09.2	+10.0	67.6	15 31.9	+11.0	67.9	15 54.4	+12.0	68.1	16 16.6	+13.0	68.4	16 38.5	+14.0	68.7	17 00.2	+15.0	69.0	17 21.6	+16.0	69.3	17 42.7	+17.0	69.5	25
26	15 19.2	+9.8	66.6	15 42.9	+10.8	66.9	16 06.4	+11.7	67.1	16 29.6	+12.7	67.4	16 52.5	+13.7	67.7	17 15.2	+14.7	67.9	17 37.6	+15.6	68.2	17 59.7	+16.6	68.5	26
27	15 29.0	+9.4	65.6	15 53.7	+10.4	65.8	16 18.1	+11.4	66.1	16 42.3	+12.4	66.4	17 06.2	+13.4	66.6	17 29.9	+14.3	66.9	17 53.2	+15.4	67.2	18 16.3	+16.3	67.5	27
28	15 38.4	+9.2	64.6	16 04.1	+10.2	64.8	16 29.5	+11.2	65.1	16 54.7	+12.1	65.3	17 19.6	+13.0	65.6	17 44.2	+14.0	65.9	18 08.6	+15.0	66.2	18 32.6	+16.0	66.5	28
29	15 47.6	+8.9	63.5	16 14.3	+9.8	63.8	16 40.7	+10.8	64.0	17 06.8	+11.8	64.3	17 32.6	+12.8	64.6	17 58.2	+13.8	64.9	18 23.6	+14.6	65.2	18 48.6	+15.6	65.5	29
30	15 56.5	+8.6	62.5	16 24.1	+9.6	62.8	16 51.5	+10.5	63.0	17 18.6	+11.4	63.3	17 45.4	+12.4	63.6	18 12.0	+13.4	63.9	18 38.2	+14.4	64.2	19 04.2	+15.4	64.5	30
31	16 05.1	+8.4	61.5	16 33.7	+9.2	61.7	17 02.0	+10.2	62.0	17 30.0	+11.2	62.3	17 57.8	+12.1	62.5	18 25.4	+13.0	62.8	18 52.6	+14.0	63.1	19 19.6	+14.9	63.5	31
32	16 13.5	+8.0	60.4	16 42.9	+9.0	60.7	17 12.2	+9.9	61.0	17 41.2	+10.8	61.2	18 09.9	+11.8	61.5	18 38.4	+12.7	61.8	19 06.6	+13.7	62.1	19 34.5	+14.7	62.4	32
33	16 21.5	+7.7	59.4	16 51.9	+8.6	59.7	17 22.1	+9.5	59.9	17 52.0	+10.5	60.2	18 21.7	+11.4	60.5	18 51.1	+12.4	60.8	19 20.3	+13.3	61.1	19 49.2	+14.2	61.4	33
34	16 29.2	+7.4	58.4	17 00.5	+8.4	58.6	17 31.6	+9.3	58.9	18 02.5	+10.2	59.2	18 33.1	+11.1	59.5	19 03.5	+12.0	59.7	19 33.6	+13.0	60.0	20 03.4	+13.9	60.4	34
35	16 36.6	+7.1	57.3	17 08.9	+8.0	57.6	17 40.9	+8.9	57.9	18 12.7	+9.8	58.1	18 44.2	+10.8	58.4	19 15.5	+11.7	58.7	19 46.6	+12.6	59.0	20 17.3	+13.6	59.3	35
36	16 43.7	+6.8	56.3	17 16.9	+7.6	56.6	17 49.8	+8.6	56.8	18 22.5	+9.5	57.1	18 55.0	+10.4	57.4	19 27.2	+11.4	57.7	19 59.2	+12.2	58.0	20 30.9	+13.1	58.3	36
37	16 50.5	+6.4	55.3	17 24.5	+7.4	55.5	17 58.4	+8.3	55.8	18 32.0	+9.2	56.0	19 05.4	+10.1	56.3	19 38.6	+10.9	56.6	20 11.4	+11.9	56.9	20 44.0	+12.8	57.2	37
38	16 56.9	+6.2	54.2	17 31.9	+7.0	54.5	18 06.7	+7.9	54.7	18 41.2	+8.8	55.0	19 15.5	+9.7	55.3	19 49.5	+10.6	55.6	20 23.3	+11.5	55.9	20 56.8	+12.4	56.2	38
39	17 03.1	+5.8	53.2	17 38.9	+6.8	53.4	18 14.6	+7.6	53.7	18 50.0	+8.5	54.0	19 25.2	+9.3	54.2	20 00.1	+10.2	54.5	20 34.8	+11.1	54.8	21 09.2	+12.0	55.1	39
40	17 08.9	+5.6	52.1	17 45.7	+6.3	52.4	18 22.2	+7.2	52.6	18 58.5	+8.1	52.9	19 34.5	+9.0	53.2	20 10.3	+9.9	53.5	20 45.9	+10.8	53.8	21 21.2	+11.7	54.1	40
41	17 14.5	+5.1	51.1	17 52.0	+6.1	51.3	18 29.4	+6.9	51.6	19 06.6	+7.7	51.9	19 43.5	+8.6	52.1	20 20.2	+9.5	52.4	20 56.7	+10.3	52.7	21 32.9	+11.2	53.0	41
42	17 19.6	+4.9	50.1	17 58.1	+5.7	50.3	18 36.3	+6.5	50.6	19 14.3	+7.4	50.8	19 52.1	+8.3	51.1	20 29.7	+9.1	51.4	21 07.0	+10.0	51.7	21 44.1	+10.8	52.0	42
43	17 24.5	+4.6	49.0	18 03.8	+5.3	49.3	18 42.8	+6.2	49.5	19 21.7	+7.0	49.8	20 00.4	+7.8	50.0	20 38.8	+8.7	50.3	21 17.0	+9.5	50.6	21 54.9	+10.4	50.9	43
44	17 29.1	+4.2	48.0	18 09.1	+5.1	48.2	18 49.0	+5.9	48.5	19 28.7	+6.7	48.7	20 08.2	+7.5	49.0	20 47.5	+8.3	49.3	21 26.5	+9.2	49.6	22 05.3	+10.0	49.9	44
45	17 33.3	+3.9	46.9	18 14.2	+4.7	47.2	18 54.9	+5.5	47.4	19 35.4	+6.3	47.7	20 15.7	+7.1	47.9	20 55.8	+7.9	48.2	21 35.7	+8.7	48.5	22 15.3	+9.6	48.8	45
46	17 37.2	+3.5	45.9	18 18.9	+4.3	46.1	19 00.4	+5.1	46.3	19 41.7	+5.9	46.6	20 22.8	+6.7	46.9	21 03.7	+7.6	47.1	21 44.4	+8.4	47.4	22 24.9	+9.2	47.7	46
47	17 40.7	+3.3	44.8	18 23.2	+4.0	45.1	19 05.5	+4.8	45.3	19 47.6	+5.6	45.5	20 29.5	+6.4	45.8	21 11.3	+7.1	46.1	21 52.8	+7.9	46.4	22 34.1	+8.7	46.7	47
48	17 44.0	+2.8	43.8	18 27.2	+3.6	44.0	19 10.3	+4.4	44.2	19 53.2	+5.1	44.5	20 35.9	+5.9	44.7	21 18.4	+6.7	45.0	22 00.7	+7.5	45.3	22 42.8	+8.3	45.6	48
49	17 46.8	+2.6	42.7	18 30.8	+3.3	42.9	19 14.7	+4.0	43.2	19 58.3	+4.8	43.4	20 41.8	+5.6	43.7	21 25.1	+6.3	43.9	22 08.2	+7.1	44.2	22 51.1	+7.9	44.5	49
50	17 49.4	+2.2	41.7	18 34.1	+3.0	41.9	19 18.7	+3.7	42.1	20 03.1	+4.5	42.4	20 47.4	+5.1	42.6	21 31.4	+5.9	42.9	22 15.3	+6.7	43.2	22 59.0	+7.4	43.4	50
51	17 51.6	+1.9	40.6	18 37.1	+2.6	40.8	19 22.4	+3.3	41.1	20 07.6	+4.0	41.3	20 52.5	+4.8	41.6	21 37.3	+5.6	41.8	22 22.0	+6.2	42.1	23 06.4	+7.0	42.4	51
52	17 53.5	+1.5	39.6	18 39.7	+2.2	39.8	19 25.7	+2.9	40.0	20 11.6	+3.6	40.2	20 57.3	+4.4	40.5	21 42.9	+5.0	40.7	22 28.2	+5.8	41.0	23 13.4	+6.6	41.3	52
53	17 55.0	+1.2	38.5	18 41.9	+1.9	38.7	19 28.6	+2.6	39.0	20 15.2	+3.3	39.2	21 01.7	+3.9	39.4	21 47.9	+4.7	39.7	22 34.0	+5.4	39.9	23 20.0	+6.1	40.2	53
54	17 56.2	+0.9	37.5	18 43.8	+1.5	37.7	19 31.2	+2.2	37.9	20 18.5	+2.9	38.1	21 05.6	+3.6	38.3	21 52.6	+4.3	38.6	22 39.4	+5.0	38.8	23 26.1	+5.6	39.1	54
55	17 57.1	+0.5	36.4	18 45.3	+1.2	36.6	19 33.4	+1.9	36.8	20 21.4	+2.5	37.0	21 09.2	+3.2	37.3	21 56.9	+3.8	37.5	22 44.4	+4.5	37.8	23 31.7	+5.2	38.0	55
56	17 57.6	+0.2	35.4	18 46.5	+0.8	35.6	19 35.3	+1.4	35.8	20 23.9	+2.1	36.0	21 12.4	+2.7	36.2	22 00.7	+3.4	36.4	22 48.9	+4.1	36.7	23 36.9	+4.8	36.9	56
57	17 57.8	-0.1	34.3	18 47.3	+0.5	34.5	19 36.7	+1.1	34.7	20 26.0	+1.7	34.9	21 15.1	+2.4	35.1	22 04.1	+3.0	35.4	22 53.0	+3.6	35.6	23 41.7	+4.3	35.9	57
58	17 57.7	-0.5	33.3	18 47.8	+0.1	33.5	19 37.8	+0.7	33.6	20 27.7	+1.3	33.8	21 17.5	+1.9	34.1	22 07.1	+2.6	34.3	22 56.6	+3.2	34.5	23 46.0	+3.8	34.8	58
59	17 57.2	-0.8	32.2	18 47.9	-0.2	32.4	19 38.5	+0.3	32.6	20 29.0	+0.9	32.8	21 19.4	+1.5	33.0	22 09.7	+2.1	33.2	22 59.8	+2.7	33.4	23 49.8	+3.4	33.7	59
60	17 56.4	-1.2	31.2	18 47.7	-0.7	31.3	19 38.8	0.0	31.5	20 29.9	+0.6	31.7	21 20.9	+1.1	31.9	22 11.8	+1.7	32.1	23 02.5	+2.4	32.4	23 53.2	+2.9	32.6	60
61	17 55.2	-1.5	30.1	18 47.0	-0.9	30.3	19 38.8	-0.4	30.5	20 30.5	+0.1	30.6	21 22.0	+0.8	30.8	22 13.5	+1.3	31.0	23 04.9	+1.8	31.3	23 56.1	+2.4	31.5	61
62	17 53.7	-1.9	29.1	18 46.1	-1.3	29.2	19 38.4	-0.8	29.4	20 30.6	-0.2	29.6	21 22.8	+0.3	29.8	22 14.8	+0.8	30.0	23 06.7	+1.4	30.2	23 58.5	+2.0	30.4	62
63	17 51.8	-2.1	28.0	18 44.8	-1.7	28.2	19 37.6	-1.1	28.3	20 30.4	-0.6	28.5	21 23.1	-0.1	28.7	22 15.6	+0.5	28.9	23 08.1	+1.0	29.1	24 00.5	+1.5	29.3	63
64	17 49.7	-2.6	27.0	18 43.1	-2.0	27.1	19 36.5	-1.6	27.3	20 29.8	-1.1	27.4	21 23.0	-0.6	27.6	22 16.1	0.0	27.8	23 09.1	+0.5	28.0	24 02.0	+1.1	28.2	64
65	17 47.1	-2.8	25.9	18 41.1	-2.4	26.1	19 34.9	-1.9	26.2	20 28.7	-1.4	26.4	21 22.4	-0.9	26.5	22 16.1	-0.5	26.7	23 09.6	+0.1	26.9	24 03.1	+0.5	27.1	65
66	17 44.3	-3.2	24.9	18 38.7	-2.7	25.0	19 33.0	-2.2	25.2	20 27.3	-1.8	25.3	21 21.5	-1.3	25.5	22 15.6	-0.8	25.6	23 09.7	-0.4	25.8	24 03.6	+0.2	26.0	66
67	17 41.1	-3.5	23.8	18 36.0	-3.1	24.0	19 30.8	-2.7	24.1	20 25.5	-2.2	24.2	21 20.2	-1.8	24.4	22 14.8	-1.3	24.6	23 09.3	-0.8	24.7	24 03.8	-0.4	24.9	67
68	17 37.6	-3.9	22.8	18 32.9	-3.5	22.9	19 28.1	-3.0	23.0	20 23.3	-2.6	23.2	21 18.4	-2.1	23.3	22 13.5	-1.7	23.5	23 08.5	-1.3	23.7	24 03.4	-0.8	23.8	68
69	17 33.7	-4.2	21.7	18 29.4	-3.7	21.8	19 25.1	-3.4	22.0	20 20.7	-3.0	22.1	21 16.3	-2.6	22.3	22 11.8	-2.2	22.4	23 07.2	-1.7	22.6	24 02.6	-1.3	22.7	69
70	17 29.5	-4.5	20.7	18 25.7	-4.2	20.8	19 21.7	-3.7	20.9	20 17.7	-3.3	21.0	21 13.7	-3.0	21.2	22 09.6	-2.5	21.3	23 05.5	-2.2	21.5	24 01.3	-1.8	21.6	70
71	17 25.0	-4.8	19.6	18 21.5	-4.5	19.7	19 18.0	-4.1	19.9	20 14.4	-3.8	20.0	21 10.7	-3.3	20.1	22 07.1	-3.0	20.2	23 03.3	-2.6	20.4	23 59.5	-2.2	20.5	71
72	17 20.2	-5.2	18.6	18 17.0	-4.8	18.7	19 13.9	-4.5	18.8	20 10.6	-4.1	18.9	21 07.4	-3.8	19.0	22 04.1	-3.4	19.2	23 00.7	-3.0	19.3	23 57.3	-2.7	19.5	72
73	17 15.0	-5.5	17.5	18 12.2	-5.1	17.6	19 09.4	-4.9	17.7	20 06.5	-4.5	17.9	21 03.6	-4.2	18.0	22 00.7	-3.9	18.1	22 57.7	-3.5	18.2	23 54.6	-3.1	18.4	73
74	17 09.5	-5.8	16.5	18 07.1	-5.5	16.6	19 04.5	-5.2	16.7	20 02.0	-4.9	16.8	20 59.4	-4.5	16.9	21 56.8	-4.2	17.0	22 54.2	-4.0	17.1	23 51.5	-3.6	17.3	74
75	17 03.7	-6.1	15.5	18 01.6	-5.9	15.5	18 59.3	-5.5	15.6	19 57.1	-5.3	15.7	20 54.9	-5.0	15.8	21 52.6	-4.7	15.9	22 50.2	-4.3	16.1	23 47.9	-4.1	16.2	75
76	16 57.6	-6.4	14.4	17 55.7	-6.2	14.5	18 53.8	-5.9	14.6	19 51.8	-5.6	14.7	20 49.9	-5.4	14.8	21 47.9	-5.1	14.9	22 45.9	-4.9	15.0	23 43.8	-4.5	15.1	76
77	16 51.2	-6.8	13.4	17 49.5	-6.5	13.5	18 47.9	-6.3	13.5	19 46.2	-6.0	13.6	20 44.5	-5.8	13.7	21 42.8	-5.5	13.8	22 41.0	-5.2	13.9	23 39.3	-5.0	14.0	77
78	16 44.4	-7.0	12.3	17 43.0	-6.8	12.4	18 41.6	-6.6	12.5	19 40.2	-6.4	12.6	20 38.7	-6.1	12.6	21 37.3	-5.9	12.7	22 35.8	-5.7	12.8	23 34.3	-5.4	12.9	78
79	16 37.4	-7.4	11.3	17 36.2	-7.2	11.4	18 35.0	-7.0	11.4	19 33.8	-6.7	11.5	20 32.6	-6.5	11.6	21 31.4	-6.4	11,7	22 30.1	-6.1	11.7	23 28.9	-5.9	11.8	79
80	16 30.0	-7.7	10.3	17 29.0	-7.5	10.3	18 28.0	-7.3	10.4	19 27.1	-7.2	10.4	20 26.1	-7.0	10.5	21 25.0	-6.7	10.6	22 24.0	-6.5	10.7	23 23.0	-6.4	10.7	80
81	16 22.3	-8.0	9.2	17 21.5	-7.8	9.3	18 20.7	-7.6	9.3	19 19.9	-7.4	9.4	20 19.1	-7.3	9.5	21 18.3	-7.1	9.5	22 17.5	-7.0	9.6	23 16.6	-6.7	9.7	81
82	16 14.3	-8.2	8.2	17 13.7	-8.1	8.3	18 13.1	-8.0	8.3	19 12.5	-7.9	8.3	20 11.8	-7.7	8.4	21 11.2	-7.6	8.5	22 10.5	-7.4	8.5	23 09.9	-7.3	8.6	82
83	16 06.1	-8.6	7.2	17 05.6	-8.5	7.2	18 05.1	-8.3	7.3	19 04.6	-8.2	7.3	20 04.1	-8.0	7.3	21 03.6	-7.9	7.4	22 03.1	-7.8	7.4	23 02.6	-7.6	7.5	83
84	15 57.5	-8.9	6.1	16 57.1	-8.7	6.2	17 56.8	-8.7	6.2	18 56.4	-8.5	6.2	19 56.1	-8.5	6.3	20 55.7	-8.3	6.3	21 55.3	-8.2	6.4	22 55.0	-8.1	6.4	84
85	15 48.6	-9.1	5.1	16 48.4	-9.1	5.1	17 48.1	-8.9	5.2	18 47.9	-8.9	5.2	19 47.6	-8.8	5.2	20 47.4	-8.7	5.3	21 47.1	-8.6	5.3	22 46.9	-8.6	5.3	85
86	15 39.5	-9.5	4.1	16 39.3	-9.4	4.1	17 39.2	-9.4	4.1	18 39.0	-9.2	4.2	19 38.8	-9.1	4.2	20 38.7	-9.1	4.2	21 38.5	-9.0	4.2	22 38.3	-8.9	4.3	86
87	15 30.0	-9.7	3.1	16 29.9	-9.6	3.1	17 29.8	-9.6	3.1	18 29.8	-9.6	3.1	19 29.7	-9.6	3.1	20 29.6	-9.5	3.2	21 29.5	-9.4	3.2	22 29.4	-9.4	3.2	87
88	15 20.3	-10.0	2.0	16 20.3	-10.0	2.1	17 20.2	-9.9	2.1	18 20.2	-9.9	2.1	19 20.1	-9.9	2.1	20 20.1	-9.9	2.1	21 20.1	-9.9	2.1	22 20.0	-9.8	2.1	88
89	15 10.3	-10.3	1.0	16 10.3	-10.3	1.0	17 10.3	-10.3	1.0	18 10.3	-10.3	1.0	19 10.2	-10.2	1.0	20 10.2	-10.2	1.0	21 10.2	-10.2	1.1	22 10.2	-10.2	1.1	89
90	15 00.0	-10.6	0.0	16 00.0	-10.6	0.0	17 00.0	-10.6	0.0	18 00.0	-10.6	0.0	19 00.0	-10.6	0.0	20 00.0	-10.6	0.0	21 00.0	-10.6	0.0	22 00.0	-10.6	0.0	90
	15°			16°			17°			18°			19°			20°			21°			22°			

80°, 280° L.H.A. LATITUDE SAME NAME AS DECLINATION

162

LATITUDE CONTRARY NAME TO DECLINATION L.H.A. 80°, 280°

Dec.	15°			16°			17°			18°			19°			20°			21°			22°			Dec.
	Hc	d	Z	Hc	d	Z	Hc	d	Z	Hc	d	Z	Hc	d	Z	Hc	d	Z	Hc	d	Z	Hc	d	Z	
°	° ′	′	°	° ′	′	°	° ′	′	°	° ′	′	°	° ′	′	°	° ′	′	°	° ′	′	°	° ′	′	°	°
0	9 39.4	-15.9	92.6	9 36.5	-16.8	92.8	9 33.5	-17.8	93.0	9 30.4	-18.9	93.1	9 27.0	-19.9	93.3	9 23.5	-20.9	93.5	9 19.8	-21.9	93.6	9 15.9	-22.8	93.8	0
1	9 23.5	-16.0	93.6	9 19.7	-17.0	93.8	9 15.7	-18.1	93.9	9 11.5	-19.1	94.1	9 07.1	-20.0	94.2	9 02.6	-21.0	94.4	8 57.9	-22.0	94.6	8 53.1	-23.0	94.7	1
2	9 07.5	-16.1	94.6	9 02.7	-17.2	94.7	8 57.6	-18.1	94.9	8 52.4	-19.1	95.0	8 47.1	-20.2	95.2	8 41.6	-21.2	95.3	8 35.9	-22.1	95.5	8 30.1	-23.1	95.6	2
3	8 51.4	-16.3	95.5	8 45.5	-17.3	95.7	8 39.5	-18.4	95.8	8 33.3	-19.3	96.0	8 26.9	-20.3	96.1	8 20.4	-21.3	96.3	8 13.8	-22.3	96.4	8 07.0	-23.3	96.6	3
4	8 35.1	-16.5	96.5	8 28.2	-17.5	96.7	8 21.1	-18.4	96.8	8 14.0	-19.5	97.0	8 06.6	-20.4	97.1	7 59.1	-21.4	97.2	7 51.5	-22.4	97.4	7 43.7	-23.4	97.5	4
5	8 18.6	-16.6	97.5	8 10.7	-17.6	97.6	8 02.7	-18.6	97.8	7 54.5	-19.6	97.9	7 46.2	-20.6	98.0	7 37.7	-21.5	98.2	7 29.1	-22.5	98.3	7 20.3	-23.4	98.4	5
6	8 02.0	-16.7	98.5	7 53.1	-17.7	98.6	7 44.1	-18.7	98.7	7 34.9	-19.7	98.9	7 25.6	-20.7	99.0	7 16.2	-21.7	99.1	7 06.6	-22.7	99.2	6 56.9	-23.6	99.4	6
7	7 45.3	-16.9	99.4	7 35.4	-17.8	99.6	7 25.4	-18.9	99.7	7 15.2	-19.8	99.8	7 04.9	-20.8	99.9	6 54.5	-21.8	100.1	6 43.9	-22.7	100.2	6 33.3	-23.7	100.3	7
8	7 28.4	-16.9	100.4	7 17.6	-18.0	100.5	7 06.5	-18.9	100.6	6 55.4	-20.0	100.8	6 44.1	-20.9	100.9	6 32.7	-21.9	101.0	6 21.2	-22.8	101.1	6 09.6	-23.8	101.2	8
9	7 11.5	-17.1	101.4	6 59.6	-18.1	101.5	6 47.6	-19.1	101.6	6 35.4	-20.0	101.7	6 23.2	-21.0	101.8	6 10.8	-21.9	101.9	5 58.4	-23.0	102.0	5 45.8	-23.9	102.1	9
10	6 54.4	-17.3	102.3	6 41.5	-18.2	102.4	6 28.5	-19.2	102.6	6 15.4	-20.2	102.7	6 02.2	-21.1	102.8	5 48.9	-22.1	102.9	5 35.4	-23.0	103.0	5 21.9	-23.9	103.1	10
11	6 37.1	-17.3	103.3	6 23.3	-18.3	103.4	6 09.3	-19.3	103.5	5 55.2	-20.2	103.6	5 41.1	-21.2	103.7	5 26.8	-22.2	103.8	5 12.4	-23.1	103.9	4 58.0	-24.1	104.0	11
12	6 19.8	-17.4	104.3	6 05.0	-18.4	104.4	5 50.0	-19.3	104.5	5 35.0	-20.3	104.6	5 19.9	-21.3	104.7	5 04.6	-22.2	104.7	4 49.3	-23.1	104.8	4 33.9	-24.1	104.9	12
13	6 02.4	-17.6	105.2	5 46.6	-18.6	105.3	5 30.7	-19.5	105.4	5 14.7	-20.5	105.5	4 58.6	-21.4	105.6	4 42.4	-22.3	105.7	4 26.2	-23.3	105.8	4 09.8	-24.1	105.8	13
14	5 44.8	-17.6	106.2	5 28.0	-18.6	106.3	5 11.2	-19.6	106.4	4 54.2	-20.5	106.5	4 37.2	-21.4	106.5	4 20.1	-22.4	106.6	4 02.9	-23.3	106.7	3 45.7	-24.3	106.7	14
15	5 27.2	-17.8	107.1	5 09.4	-18.6	107.2	4 51.6	-19.6	107.3	4 33.7	-20.5	107.4	4 15.8	-21.5	107.5	3 57.7	-22.4	107.5	3 39.6	-23.4	107.6	3 21.4	-24.2	107.7	15
16	5 09.4	-17.8	108.1	4 50.8	-18.8	108.2	4 32.0	-19.7	108.3	4 13.2	-20.7	108.3	3 54.3	-21.6	108.4	3 35.3	-22.5	108.5	3 16.2	-23.4	108.5	2 57.2	-24.4	108.6	16
17	4 51.6	-17.9	109.1	4 32.0	-18.8	109.1	4 12.3	-19.8	109.2	3 52.5	-20.7	109.3	3 32.7	-21.6	109.3	3 12.8	-22.6	109.4	2 52.8	-23.4	109.4	2 32.8	-24.3	109.5	17
18	4 33.7	-17.9	110.0	4 13.2	-18.9	110.1	3 52.5	-19.8	110.2	3 31.8	-20.7	110.2	3 11.1	-21.7	110.3	2 50.2	-22.6	110.3	2 29.4	-23.5	110.4	2 08.5	-24.4	110.4	18
19	4 15.8	-18.1	111.0	3 54.3	-19.0	111.0	3 32.7	-19.9	111.1	3 11.1	-20.9	111.2	2 49.4	-21.8	111.2	2 27.6	-22.6	111.2	2 05.9	-23.5	111.3	1 44.1	-24.4	111.3	19
20	3 57.7	-18.1	111.9	3 35.3	-19.1	112.0	3 12.8	-20.0	112.0	2 50.2	-20.8	112.1	2 27.6	-21.7	112.1	2 05.0	-22.6	112.2	1 42.4	-23.6	112.2	1 19.7	-24.5	112.2	20
21	3 39.6	-18.2	112.9	3 16.2	-19.0	112.9	2 52.8	-20.0	113.0	2 29.4	-20.9	113.0	2 05.9	-21.8	113.1	1 42.4	-22.7	113.1	1 18.8	-23.6	113.1	0 55.2	-24.4	113.1	21
22	3 21.4	-18.2	113.8	2 57.2	-19.2	113.9	2 32.8	-20.0	113.9	2 08.5	-21.0	114.0	1 44.1	-21.8	114.0	1 19.7	-22.7	114.0	0 55.2	-23.6	114.0	0 30.8	-24.5	114.1	22
23	3 03.2	-18.3	114.8	2 38.0	-19.2	114.8	2 12.8	-20.1	114.9	1 47.5	-20.9	114.9	1 22.3	-21.9	114.9	0 57.0	-22.8	115.0	0 31.6	-23.6	115.0	0 06.3	-24.5	115.0	23
24	2 44.9	-18.3	115.7	2 18.8	-19.2	115.8	1 52.7	-20.1	115.8	1 26.6	-21.0	115.8	1 00.4	-21.9	115.9	0 34.2	-22.7	115.9	0 08.0	-23.6	115.9	0 18.2	+24.4	64.1	24
25	2 26.6	-18.4	116.7	1 59.6	-19.2	116.7	1 32.6	-20.1	116.8	1 05.6	-21.0	116.8	0 38.5	-21.8	116.8	0 11.5	-22.7	116.8	0 15.6	+23.6	63.2	0 42.6	+24.5	63.2	25
26	2 08.2	-18.4	117.7	1 40.4	-19.3	117.7	1 12.5	-20.2	117.7	0 44.6	-21.0	117.7	0 16.7	-21.9	117.7	0 11.2	+22.8	62.3	0 39.2	+23.5	62.3	1 07.1	+24.4	62.3	26
27	1 49.8	-18.4	118.6	1 21.1	-19.3	118.6	0 52.3	-20.1	118.6	0 23.6	-21.0	118.7	0 05.2	+21.9	61.3	0 34.0	+22.7	61.3	1 02.7	+23.6	61.4	1 31.5	+24.4	61.4	27
28	1 31.4	-18.4	119.6	1 01.8	-19.3	119.6	0 32.2	-20.2	119.6	0 02.6	-21.1	119.6	0 27.1	+21.8	60.4	0 56.7	+22.7	60.4	1 26.3	+23.6	60.4	1 55.9	+24.4	60.5	28
29	1 13.0	-18.5	120.5	0 42.5	-19.3	120.5	0 12.0	-20.2	120.5	0 18.5	+21.0	59.5	0 48.9	+21.9	59.5	1 19.4	+22.7	59.5	1 49.9	+23.5	59.5	2 20.3	+24.3	59.5	29
30	0 54.5	-18.5	121.5	0 23.2	-19.4	121.5	0 08.2	+20.1	58.5	0 39.5	+21.0	58.5	1 10.8	+21.8	58.5	1 42.1	+22.7	58.6	2 13.4	+23.5	58.6	2 44.6	+24.3	58.6	30
31	0 36.0	-18.5	122.4	0 03.8	-19.3	122.4	0 28.3	+20.2	57.6	1 00.5	+21.0	57.6	1 32.6	+21.8	57.6	2 04.8	+22.6	57.6	2 36.9	+23.4	57.7	3 08.9	+24.3	57.7	31
32	0 17.5	-18.5	123.4	0 15.5	+19.3	56.6	0 48.5	+20.1	56.6	1 21.5	+20.9	56.7	1 54.4	+21.8	56.7	2 27.4	+22.6	56.7	3 00.3	+23.4	56.8	3 33.2	+24.2	56.8	32
33	0 01.0	+18.5	55.7	0 34.8	+19.3	55.7	1 08.6	+20.2	55.7	1 42.4	+21.0	55.7	2 16.2	+21.8	55.7	2 50.0	+22.5	55.8	3 23.7	+23.3	55.8	3 57.4	+24.1	55.9	33
34	0 19.5	+18.5	54.7	0 54.1	+19.4	54.7	1 28.8	+20.1	54.8	2 03.4	+20.9	54.8	2 38.0	+21.7	54.8	3 12.5	+22.5	54.9	3 47.0	+23.3	54.9	4 21.5	+24.1	55.0	34
35	0 38.0	+18.5	53.8	1 13.5	+19.2	53.8	1 48.9	+20.1	53.8	2 24.3	+20.9	53.8	2 59.7	+21.6	53.9	3 35.0	+22.5	53.9	4 10.3	+23.3	54.0	4 45.6	+24.0	54.0	35
36	0 56.5	+18.5	52.8	1 32.7	+19.3	52.8	2 09.0	+20.0	52.9	2 45.2	+20.8	52.9	3 21.3	+21.6	52.9	3 57.5	+22.3	53.0	4 33.6	+23.1	53.1	5 09.6	+23.9	53.1	36
37	1 15.0	+18.4	51.9	1 52.0	+19.2	51.9	2 29.0	+20.0	51.9	3 06.0	+20.8	52.0	3 42.9	+21.6	52.0	4 19.8	+22.4	52.1	4 56.7	+23.1	52.1	5 33.5	+23.8	52.2	37
38	1 33.4	+18.4	50.9	2 11.2	+19.2	51.0	2 49.0	+20.0	51.0	3 26.8	+20.7	51.0	4 04.5	+21.5	51.1	4 42.2	+22.2	51.1	5 19.8	+23.0	51.2	5 57.3	+23.8	51.3	38
39	1 51.8	+18.4	50.0	2 30.4	+19.2	50.0	3 09.0	+19.9	50.0	3 47.5	+20.6	50.1	4 26.0	+21.4	50.1	5 04.4	+22.1	50.2	5 42.8	+22.9	50.3	6 21.1	+23.6	50.4	39
40	2 10.2	+18.4	49.0	2 49.6	+19.1	49.1	3 28.9	+19.8	49.1	4 08.1	+20.6	49.1	4 47.4	+21.3	49.2	5 26.5	+22.1	49.3	6 05.7	+22.8	49.3	6 44.7	+23.6	49.4	40
41	2 28.6	+18.3	48.1	3 08.7	+19.0	48.1	3 48.7	+19.8	48.1	4 28.7	+20.6	48.2	5 08.7	+21.3	48.3	5 48.6	+22.0	48.3	6 28.5	+22.7	48.4	7 08.3	+23.4	48.5	41
42	2 46.9	+18.3	47.1	3 27.7	+19.0	47.2	4 08.5	+19.7	47.2	4 49.3	+20.4	47.3	5 30.0	+21.1	47.3	6 10.6	+21.9	47.4	6 51.2	+22.6	47.5	7 31.7	+23.3	47.6	42
43	3 05.2	+18.2	46.2	3 46.7	+19.0	46.2	4 28.2	+19.7	46.3	5 09.7	+20.4	46.3	5 51.1	+21.1	46.4	6 32.5	+21.7	46.5	7 13.8	+22.4	46.6	7 55.0	+23.2	46.6	43
44	3 23.4	+18.2	45.2	4 05.7	+18.8	45.3	4 47.9	+19.6	45.3	5 30.1	+20.2	45.4	6 12.2	+20.9	45.4	6 54.2	+21.7	45.5	7 36.2	+22.4	45.6	8 18.2	+23.0	45.7	44
45	3 41.6	+18.1	44.3	4 24.5	+18.8	44.3	5 07.5	+19.4	44.4	5 50.3	+20.2	44.4	6 33.1	+20.9	44.5	7 15.9	+21.6	44.6	7 58.6	+22.2	44.7	8 41.2	+23.0	44.8	45
46	3 59.7	+18.0	43.3	4 43.3	+18.7	43.3	5 26.9	+19.4	43.4	6 10.5	+20.1	43.5	6 54.0	+20.8	43.6	7 37.5	+21.4	43.6	8 20.8	+22.1	43.7	9 04.2	+22.7	43.8	46
47	4 17.7	+18.0	42.3	5 02.0	+18.7	42.4	5 46.3	+19.3	42.5	6 30.6	+19.9	42.5	7 14.8	+20.6	42.6	7 58.9	+21.3	42.7	8 42.9	+22.0	42.8	9 26.9	+22.7	42.9	47
48	4 35.7	+17.9	41.4	5 20.7	+18.5	41.4	6 05.6	+19.2	41.5	6 50.5	+19.9	41.6	7 35.4	+20.5	41.7	8 20.2	+21.1	41.8	9 04.9	+21.8	41.9	9 49.6	+22.4	42.0	48
49	4 53.6	+17.8	40.4	5 39.2	+18.5	40.5	6 24.8	+19.1	40.6	7 10.4	+19.7	40.6	7 55.9	+20.4	40.7	8 41.3	+21.1	40.8	9 26.7	+21.7	40.9	10 12.0	+22.3	41.0	49
50	5 11.4	+17.7	39.5	5 57.7	+18.3	39.5	6 43.9	+19.0	39.6	7 30.1	+19.6	39.7	8 16.3	+20.2	39.8	9 02.4	+20.8	39.9	9 48.4	+21.5	40.0	10 34.3	+22.2	40.1	50
51	5 29.1	+17.6	38.5	6 16.0	+18.3	38.6	7 02.9	+18.9	38.6	7 49.7	+19.5	38.7	8 36.5	+20.1	38.8	9 23.2	+20.8	38.9	10 09.9	+21.3	39.0	10 56.5	+21.9	39.1	51
52	5 46.7	+17.6	37.5	6 34.3	+18.1	37.6	7 21.8	+18.7	37.7	8 09.2	+19.4	37.8	8 56.6	+20.0	37.9	9 44.0	+20.5	38.0	10 31.2	+21.2	38.1	11 18.4	+21.8	38.2	52
53	6 04.3	+17.4	36.6	6 52.4	+18.0	36.7	7 40.5	+18.6	36.7	8 28.6	+19.2	36.8	9 16.6	+19.8	36.9	10 04.5	+20.4	37.0	10 52.4	+21.0	37.1	11 40.2	+21.6	37.2	53
54	6 21.7	+17.3	35.6	7 10.4	+17.9	35.7	7 59.1	+18.5	35.8	8 47.8	+19.1	35.9	9 36.4	+19.6	36.0	10 24.9	+20.3	36.1	11 13.4	+20.8	36.2	12 01.8	+21.4	36.3	54
55	6 39.0	+17.2	34.7	7 28.3	+17.8	34.7	8 17.6	+18.4	34.8	9 06.9	+18.9	34.9	9 56.0	+19.5	35.0	10 45.2	+20.0	35.1	11 34.2	+20.7	35.2	12 23.2	+21.2	35.3	55
56	6 56.2	+17.1	33.7	7 46.1	+17.7	33.8	8 36.0	+18.2	33.8	9 25.8	+18.7	33.9	10 15.5	+19.3	34.0	11 05.2	+19.9	34.1	11 54.9	+20.4	34.3	12 44.4	+21.0	34.4	56
57	7 13.3	+17.0	32.7	8 03.8	+17.5	32.8	8 54.2	+18.0	32.9	9 44.5	+18.6	33.0	10 34.8	+19.2	33.1	11 25.1	+19.7	33.2	12 15.3	+20.2	33.3	13 05.4	+20.8	33.4	57
58	7 30.3	+16.8	31.8	8 21.3	+17.3	31.8	9 12.2	+17.9	31.9	10 03.1	+18.5	32.0	10 54.0	+18.9	32.1	11 44.8	+19.5	32.2	12 35.5	+20.0	32.3	13 26.2	+20.5	32.4	58
59	7 47.1	+16.7	30.8	8 38.6	+17.3	30.9	9 30.1	+17.8	30.9	10 21.6	+18.2	31.0	11 12.9	+18.8	31.1	12 04.3	+19.3	31.2	12 55.5	+19.8	31.4	13 46.7	+20.4	31.5	59
60	8 03.8	+16.6	29.8	8 55.9	+17.0	29.9	9 47.9	+17.5	30.0	10 39.8	+18.1	30.1	11 31.7	+18.6	30.2	12 23.6	+19.0	30.3	13 15.3	+19.6	30.4	14 07.1	+20.1	30.5	60
61	8 20.4	+16.4	28.9	9 12.9	+17.0	28.9	10 05.4	+17.4	29.0	10 57.9	+17.9	29.1	11 50.3	+18.4	29.2	12 42.6	+18.9	29.3	13 34.9	+19.4	29.4	14 27.2	+19.8	29.5	61
62	8 36.8	+16.3	27.9	9 29.9	+16.7	28.0	10 22.8	+17.3	28.0	11 15.8	+17.7	28.1	12 08.7	+18.1	28.2	13 01.5	+18.7	28.3	13 54.3	+19.1	28.4	14 47.0	+19.6	28.6	62
63	8 53.1	+16.2	26.9	9 46.6	+16.6	27.0	10 40.1	+17.0	27.1	11 33.5	+17.5	27.2	12 26.8	+18.0	27.2	13 20.2	+18.4	27.4	14 13.4	+18.9	27.5	15 06.6	+19.4	27.6	63
64	9 09.3	+15.9	25.9	10 03.2	+16.4	26.0	10 57.1	+16.9	26.1	11 51.0	+17.3	26.2	12 44.8	+17.8	26.3	13 38.6	+18.2	26.4	14 32.3	+18.7	26.5	15 26.0	+19.1	26.6	64
65	9 25.2	+15.9	25.0	10 19.6	+16.3	25.0	11 14.0	+16.6	25.1	12 08.3	+17.1	25.2	13 02.6	+17.5	25.3	13 56.8	+17.9	25.4	14 51.0	+18.4	25.5	15 45.1	+18.8	25.6	65
66	9 41.1	+15.6	24.0	10 35.9	+16.0	24.0	11 30.6	+16.5	24.1	12 25.4	+16.9	24.2	13 20.1	+17.3	24.3	14 14.7	+17.8	24.4	15 09.4	+18.1	24.5	16 03.9	+18.6	24.6	66
67	9 56.7	+15.5	23.0	10 51.9	+15.9	23.1	11 47.1	+16.3	23.1	12 42.3	+16.6	23.2	13 37.4	+17.1	23.3	14 32.5	+17.4	23.4	15 27.5	+17.9	23.5	16 22.5	+18.3	23.6	67
68	10 12.2	+15.3	22.0	11 07.8	+15.7	22.1	12 03.4	+16.0	22.2	12 58.9	+16.5	22.2	13 54.5	+16.8	22.3	14 49.9	+17.2	22.4	15 45.4	+17.6	22.5	16 40.8	+18.0	22.7	68
69	10 27.5	+15.1	21.0	11 23.5	+15.5	21.1	12 19.4	+15.9	21.2	13 15.4	+16.2	21.3	14 11.3	+16.6	21.3	15 07.1	+17.0	21.4	16 03.0	+17.3	21.5	16 58.8	+17.7	21.7	69
70	10 42.6	+15.0	20.0	11 39.0	+15.3	20.1	12 35.3	+15.6	20.2	13 31.6	+16.0	20.3	14 27.9	+16.3	20.4	15 24.1	+16.7	20.4	16 20.3	+17.0	20.5	17 16.5	+17.4	20.7	70
71	10 57.6	+14.7	19.1	11 54.3	+15.0	19.1	12 50.9	+15.4	19.2	13 47.6	+15.7	19.3	14 44.2	+16.1	19.4	15 40.8	+16.4	19.5	16 37.3	+16.8	19.5	17 33.9	+17.1	19.7	71
72	11 12.3	+14.6	18.1	12 09.3	+14.9	18.1	13 06.3	+15.2	18.2	14 03.3	+15.5	18.3	15 00.3	+15.8	18.4	15 57.2	+16.1	18.5	16 54.1	+16.5	18.5	17 51.0	+16.8	18.6	72
73	11 26.9	+14.3	17.1	12 24.2	+14.6	17.1	13 21.5	+15.0	17.2	14 18.8	+15.3	17.3	15 16.1	+15.5	17.4	16 13.3	+15.9	17.4	17 10.6	+16.1	17.5	18 07.8	+16.4	17.6	73
74	11 41.2	+14.1	16.1	12 38.8	+14.5	16.2	13 36.5	+14.7	16.2	14 34.1	+15.0	16.3	15 31.6	+15.3	16.4	16 29.2	+15.6	16.4	17 26.7	+15.9	16.5	18 24.2	+16.2	16.6	74
75	11 55.3	+14.0	15.1	12 53.3	+14.2	15.2	13 51.2	+14.4	15.2	14 49.1	+14.7	15.3	15 46.9	+15.0	15.4	16 44.8	+15.2	15.4	17 42.6	+15.5	15.5	18 40.4	+15.8	15.6	75
76	12 09.3	+13.7	14.1	13 07.5	+13.9	14.2	14 05.6	+14.3	14.2	15 03.8	+14.5	14.3	16 01.9	+14.7	14.4	17 00.0	+15.0	14.4	17 58.1	+15.3	14.5	18 56.2	+15.5	14.6	76
77	12 23.0	+13.5	13.1	13 21.4	+13.8	13.2	14 19.9	+13.9	13.2	15 18.3	+14.2	13.3	16 16.6	+14.5	13.3	17 15.0	+14.7	13.4	18 13.4	+14.9	13.5	19 11.7	+15.2	13.6	77
78	12 36.5	+13.3	12.1	13 35.2	+13.5	12.2	14 33.8	+13.7	12.2	15 32.5	+13.9	12.3	16 31.1	+14.1	12.3	17 29.7	+14.3	12.4	18 28.3	+14.6	12.5	19 26.9	+14.8	12.5	78
79	12 49.8	+13.1	11.1	13 48.7	+13.2	11.2	14 47.5	+13.5	11.2	15 46.4	+13.6	11.3	16 45.2	+13.9	11.3	17 44.0	+14.1	11.4	18 42.9	+14.2	11.4	19 41.7	+14.4	11.5	79
80	13 02.9	+12.8	10.1	14 01.9	+13.0	10.2	15 01.0	+13.2	10.2	16 00.0	+13.4	10.2	16 59.1	+13.5	10.3	17 58.1	+13.7	10.4	18 57.1	+13.9	10.4	19 56.1	+14.1	10.5	80
81	13 15.7	+12.6	9.1	14 14.9	+12.8	9.1	15 14.2	+12.9	9.2	16 13.4	+13.1	9.2	17 12.6	+13.2	9.3	18 11.8	+13.4	9.3	19 11.0	+13.6	9.4	20 10.2	+13.7	9.4	81
82	13 28.3	+12.3	8.1	14 27.7	+12.5	8.1	15 27.1	+12.6	8.2	16 26.5	+12.7	8.2	17 25.8	+12.9	8.3	18 25.2	+13.1	8.3	19 24.6	+13.2	8.4	20 23.9	+13.4	8.4	82
83	13 40.6	+12.1	7.1	14 40.2	+12.2	7.1	15 39.7	+12.3	7.2	16 39.2	+12.5	7.2	17 38.7	+12.6	7.2	18 38.3	+12.7	7.3	19 37.8	+12.8	7.3	20 37.3	+13.0	7.4	83
84	13 52.7	+11.9	6.1	14 52.4	+11.9	6.1	15 52.0	+12.1	6.1	16 51.7	+12.2	6.2	17 51.3	+12.3	6.2	18 51.0	+12.4	6.2	19 50.6	+12.5	6.3	20 50.3	+12.6	6.3	84
85	14 04.6	+11.6	5.1	15 04.3	+11.7	5.1	16 04.1	+11.8	5.1	17 03.9	+11.8	5.2	18 03.6	+12.0	5.2	19 03.4	+12.0	5.2	20 03.1	+12.2	5.2	21 02.9	+12.2	5.3	85
86	14 16.2	+11.3	4.1	15 16.0	+11.5	4.1	16 15.9	+11.5	4.1	17 15.7	+11.6	4.1	18 15.6	+11.6	4.1	19 15.4	+11.7	4.2	20 15.3	+11.7	4.2	21 15.1	+11.8	4.2	86
87	14 27.5	+11.1	3.1	15 27.5	+11.1	3.1	16 27.4	+11.1	3.1	17 27.3	+11.2	3.1	18 27.2	+11.3	3.1	19 27.1	+11.3	3.1	20 27.0	+11.4	3.2	21 26.9	+11.4	3.2	87
88	14 38.6	+10.8	2.0	15 38.6	+10.8	2.0	16 38.5	+10.9	2.1	17 38.5	+10.9	2.1	18 38.5	+10.9	2.1	19 38.4	+11.0	2.1	20 38.4	+11.0	2.1	21 38.3	+11.1	2.1	88
89	14 49.4	+10.6	1.0	15 49.4	+10.6	1.0	16 49.4	+10.6	1.0	17 49.4	+10.6	1.0	18 49.4	+10.6	1.0	19 49.4	+10.6	1.0	20 49.4	+10.6	1.1	21 49.4	+10.6	1.1	89
90	15 00.0	+10.3	0.0	16 00.0	+10.3	0.0	17 00.0	+10.3	0.0	18 00.0	+10.3	0.0	19 00.0	+10.2	0.0	20 00.0	+10.2	0.0	21 00.0	+10.2	0.0	22 00.0	+10.2	0.0	90
	15°			16°			17°			18°			19°			20°			21°			22°			

S. Lat. {L.H.A. greater than 180° ....Zn=180°−Z; L.H.A. less than 180°...........Zn=180°+Z}

LATITUDE SAME NAME AS DECLINATION L.H.A. 100°, 260°

LATITUDE SAME NAME AS DECLINATION

N. Lat. { L.H.A. greater than 180° .....Zn=Z
{ L.H.A. less than 180°............Zn=360°–Z

Dec.	15° Hc	d	Z	16° Hc	d	Z	17° Hc	d	Z	18° Hc	d	Z	19° Hc	d	Z	20° Hc	d	Z	21° Hc	d	Z	22° Hc	d	Z	Dec.
0	8 41.5	+15.6	92.3	8 38.9	+16.7	92.5	8 36.2	+17.7	92.7	8 33.4	+18.6	92.8	8 30.4	+19.6	93.0	8 27.2	+20.7	93.1	8 23.9	+21.6	93.2	8 20.4	+22.6	93.4	0
1	8 57.1	+15.5	91.4	8 55.6	+16.5	91.5	8 53.9	+17.5	91.7	8 52.0	+18.6	91.8	8 50.0	+19.6	92.0	8 47.9	+20.5	92.2	8 45.5	+21.6	92.3	8 43.0	+22.5	92.5	1
2	9 12.6	+15.3	90.4	9 12.1	+16.3	90.6	9 11.4	+17.4	90.7	9 10.6	+18.4	90.9	9 09.6	+19.4	91.0	9 08.4	+20.4	91.2	9 07.1	+21.3	91.4	9 05.5	+22.4	91.5	2
3	9 27.9	+15.1	89.4	9 28.4	+16.2	89.6	9 28.8	+17.2	89.7	9 29.0	+18.2	89.9	9 29.0	+19.2	90.1	9 28.8	+20.2	90.2	9 28.4	+21.3	90.4	9 27.9	+22.2	90.6	3
4	9 43.0	+15.0	88.4	9 44.6	+16.0	88.6	9 46.0	+17.0	88.8	9 47.2	+18.0	88.9	9 48.2	+19.0	89.1	9 49.0	+20.1	89.3	9 49.7	+21.0	89.5	9 50.1	+22.1	89.6	4
5	9 58.0	+14.9	87.4	10 00.6	+15.9	87.6	10 03.0	+16.9	87.8	10 05.2	+17.9	88.0	10 07.2	+18.9	88.2	10 09.1	+19.9	88.3	10 10.7	+20.9	88.5	10 12.2	+21.9	88.7	5
6	10 12.9	+14.6	86.5	10 16.5	+15.6	86.6	10 19.9	+16.7	86.8	10 23.1	+17.7	87.0	10 26.1	+18.8	87.2	10 29.0	+19.7	87.4	10 31.6	+20.8	87.6	10 34.1	+21.7	87.7	6
7	10 27.5	+14.5	85.5	10 32.1	+15.5	85.7	10 36.6	+16.5	85.8	10 40.8	+17.5	86.0	10 44.9	+18.5	86.2	10 48.7	+19.6	86.4	10 52.4	+20.5	86.5	10 55.8	+21.6	86.8	7
8	10 42.0	+14.2	84.5	10 47.6	+15.3	84.7	10 53.1	+16.3	84.9	10 58.3	+17.4	85.1	11 03.4	+18.4	85.3	11 08.3	+19.3	85.5	11 12.9	+20.4	85.6	11 17.4	+21.3	85.8	8
9	10 56.2	+14.1	83.5	11 02.9	+15.1	83.7	11 09.4	+16.1	83.9	11 15.7	+17.1	84.1	11 21.8	+18.1	84.3	11 27.6	+19.2	84.5	11 33.3	+20.2	84.7	11 38.7	+21.2	84.9	9
10	11 10.3	+13.9	82.5	11 18.0	+14.9	82.7	11 25.5	+16.0	82.9	11 32.8	+17.0	83.1	11 39.9	+18.0	83.3	11 46.8	+19.0	83.5	11 53.5	+20.0	83.7	11 59.9	+21.0	83.9	10
11	11 24.2	+13.7	81.5	11 32.9	+14.8	81.7	11 41.5	+15.7	81.9	11 49.8	+16.8	82.1	11 57.9	+17.8	82.3	12 05.8	+18.8	82.6	12 13.5	+19.7	82.8	12 20.9	+20.8	83.0	11
12	11 37.9	+13.5	80.5	11 47.7	+14.5	80.7	11 57.2	+15.5	80.9	12 06.6	+16.5	81.1	12 15.7	+17.5	81.4	12 24.6	+18.5	81.6	12 33.2	+19.6	81.8	12 41.7	+20.6	82.0	12
13	11 51.4	+13.2	79.5	12 02.2	+14.3	79.7	12 12.7	+15.3	80.0	12 23.1	+16.3	80.2	12 33.2	+17.4	80.4	12 43.1	+18.4	80.6	12 52.8	+19.4	80.8	13 02.3	+20.3	81.1	13
14	12 04.6	+13.1	78.5	12 16.5	+14.0	78.7	12 28.1	+15.1	79.0	12 39.4	+16.1	79.2	12 50.6	+17.1	79.4	13 01.5	+18.1	79.6	13 12.2	+19.1	79.9	13 22.6	+20.2	80.1	14
15	12 17.7	+12.8	77.5	12 30.5	+13.9	77.7	12 43.2	+14.8	78.0	12 55.5	+15.9	78.2	13 07.7	+16.9	78.4	13 19.6	+17.9	78.6	13 31.3	+18.9	78.9	13 42.8	+19.9	79.1	15
16	12 30.5	+12.7	76.5	12 44.4	+13.6	76.8	12 58.0	+14.7	77.0	13 11.4	+15.7	77.2	13 24.6	+16.7	77.4	13 37.5	+17.7	77.7	13 50.2	+18.7	77.9	14 02.7	+19.7	78.1	16
17	12 43.2	+12.3	75.5	12 58.0	+13.4	75.8	13 12.7	+14.4	76.0	13 27.1	+15.4	76.2	13 41.3	+16.4	76.4	13 55.2	+17.5	76.7	14 08.9	+18.5	76.9	14 22.4	+19.4	77.2	17
18	12 55.5	+12.2	74.5	13 11.4	+13.2	74.8	13 27.1	+14.2	75.0	13 42.5	+15.2	75.2	13 57.7	+16.2	75.5	14 12.7	+17.2	75.7	14 27.4	+18.2	75.9	14 41.8	+19.2	76.2	18
19	13 07.7	+11.9	73.5	13 24.6	+12.9	73.8	13 41.3	+13.9	74.0	13 57.7	+15.0	74.2	14 13.9	+16.0	74.5	14 29.9	+16.9	74.7	14 45.6	+17.9	75.0	15 01.0	+18.9	75.2	19
20	13 19.6	+11.7	72.5	13 37.5	+12.7	72.7	13 55.2	+13.7	73.0	14 12.7	+14.7	73.2	14 29.9	+15.7	73.5	14 46.8	+16.7	73.7	15 03.5	+17.7	74.0	15 19.9	+18.7	74.2	20
21	13 31.3	+11.5	71.5	13 50.2	+12.5	71.7	14 08.9	+13.5	72.0	14 27.4	+14.4	72.3	14 45.6	+15.4	72.5	15 03.5	+16.4	72.7	15 21.2	+17.4	73.0	15 38.6	+18.4	73.2	21
22	13 42.8	+11.2	70.5	14 02.7	+12.2	70.7	14 22.4	+13.2	71.0	14 41.8	+14.2	71.2	15 01.0	+15.2	71.5	15 19.9	+16.2	71.7	15 38.6	+17.2	72.0	15 57.0	+18.2	72.3	22
23	13 54.0	+10.9	69.5	14 14.9	+11.9	69.7	14 35.6	+12.9	70.0	14 56.0	+13.9	70.2	15 16.2	+14.9	70.5	15 36.1	+15.9	70.7	15 55.8	+16.9	71.0	16 15.2	+17.9	71.3	23
24	14 04.9	+10.7	68.5	14 26.8	+11.7	68.7	14 48.5	+12.7	69.0	15 09.9	+13.7	69.2	15 31.1	+14.6	69.5	15 52.0	+15.6	69.7	16 12.7	+16.6	70.0	16 33.1	+17.6	70.3	24
25	14 15.6	+10.5	67.5	14 38.5	+11.4	67.7	15 01.2	+12.4	67.9	15 23.6	+13.3	68.2	15 45.7	+14.4	68.5	16 07.6	+15.4	68.7	16 29.3	+16.3	69.0	16 50.7	+17.2	69.3	25
26	14 26.1	+10.1	66.4	14 49.9	+11.2	66.7	15 13.6	+12.1	66.9	15 36.9	+13.1	67.2	16 00.1	+14.1	67.4	16 23.0	+15.0	67.7	16 45.6	+16.0	68.0	17 07.9	+17.0	68.3	26
27	14 36.2	+9.9	65.4	15 01.1	+10.9	65.7	15 25.7	+11.8	65.9	15 50.0	+12.9	66.2	16 14.2	+13.7	66.4	16 38.0	+14.8	66.7	17 01.6	+15.7	67.0	17 24.9	+16.7	67.3	27
28	14 46.1	+9.7	64.4	15 12.0	+10.6	64.6	15 37.5	+11.6	64.9	16 02.9	+12.5	65.2	16 27.9	+13.5	65.4	16 52.8	+14.4	65.7	17 17.3	+15.5	66.0	17 41.6	+16.4	66.3	28
29	14 55.8	+9.4	63.4	15 22.6	+10.3	63.6	15 49.1	+11.3	63.9	16 15.4	+12.2	64.1	16 41.4	+13.2	64.4	17 07.2	+14.2	64.7	17 32.8	+15.1	65.0	17 58.0	+16.1	65.2	29
30	15 05.2	+9.1	62.4	15 32.9	+10.0	62.6	16 00.4	+11.0	62.9	16 27.6	+12.0	63.1	16 54.6	+12.9	63.4	17 21.4	+13.8	63.7	17 47.9	+14.8	63.9	18 14.1	+15.7	64.2	30
31	15 14.3	+8.8	61.3	15 42.9	+9.8	61.6	16 11.4	+10.7	61.8	16 39.6	+11.6	62.1	17 07.5	+12.6	62.4	17 35.2	+13.6	62.6	18 02.7	+14.5	62.9	18 29.8	+15.5	63.2	31
32	15 23.1	+8.5	60.3	15 52.7	+9.4	60.6	16 22.1	+10.4	60.8	16 51.2	+11.3	61.1	17 20.1	+12.3	61.3	17 48.8	+13.2	61.6	18 17.2	+14.1	61.9	18 45.3	+15.1	62.2	32
33	15 31.6	+8.3	59.3	16 02.1	+9.2	59.5	16 32.5	+10.1	59.8	17 02.5	+11.1	60.0	17 32.4	+11.9	60.3	18 02.0	+12.9	60.6	18 31.3	+13.8	60.9	19 00.4	+14.7	61.2	33
34	15 39.9	+7.9	58.3	16 11.3	+8.9	58.5	16 42.6	+9.7	58.8	17 13.6	+10.7	59.0	17 44.3	+11.7	59.3	18 14.9	+12.5	59.6	18 45.1	+13.5	59.9	19 15.1	+14.4	60.2	34
35	15 47.8	+7.7	57.2	16 20.2	+8.6	57.5	16 52.3	+9.5	57.7	17 24.3	+10.4	58.0	17 56.0	+11.3	58.3	18 27.4	+12.2	58.5	18 58.6	+13.1	58.8	19 29.5	+14.1	59.1	35
36	15 55.5	+7.4	56.2	16 28.8	+8.2	56.4	17 01.8	+9.2	56.7	17 34.7	+10.0	56.9	18 07.3	+10.9	57.2	18 39.6	+11.9	57.5	19 11.7	+12.8	57.8	19 43.6	+13.7	58.1	36
37	16 02.9	+7.0	55.2	16 37.0	+8.0	55.4	17 11.0	+8.8	55.7	17 44.7	+9.8	55.9	18 18.2	+10.7	56.2	18 51.5	+11.5	56.5	19 24.5	+12.5	56.8	19 57.3	+13.3	57.1	37
38	16 09.9	+6.8	54.1	16 45.0	+7.7	54.4	17 19.8	+8.6	54.6	17 54.5	+9.4	54.9	18 28.9	+10.3	55.1	19 03.0	+11.2	55.4	19 37.0	+12.1	55.7	20 10.6	+13.0	56.0	38
39	16 16.7	+6.5	53.1	16 52.7	+7.3	53.3	17 28.4	+8.2	53.6	18 03.9	+9.1	53.8	18 39.2	+9.9	54.1	19 14.2	+10.9	54.4	19 49.1	+11.7	54.7	20 23.6	+12.6	55.0	39
40	16 23.2	+6.2	52.1	17 00.0	+7.0	52.3	17 36.6	+7.9	52.5	18 13.0	+8.7	52.8	18 49.1	+9.6	53.1	19 25.1	+10.4	53.3	20 00.8	+11.3	53.6	20 36.2	+12.3	53.9	40
41	16 29.4	+5.8	51.0	17 07.0	+6.7	51.3	17 44.5	+7.5	51.5	18 21.7	+8.4	51.8	18 58.7	+9.3	52.0	19 35.5	+10.2	52.3	20 12.1	+11.0	52.6	20 48.5	+11.8	52.9	41
42	16 35.2	+5.6	50.0	17 13.7	+6.4	50.2	17 52.0	+7.2	50.5	18 30.1	+8.1	50.7	19 08.0	+8.9	51.0	19 45.7	+9.7	51.3	20 23.1	+10.6	51.5	21 00.3	+11.5	51.8	42
43	16 40.8	+5.2	48.9	17 20.1	+6.1	49.2	17 59.2	+6.9	49.4	18 38.2	+7.7	49.7	19 16.9	+8.5	49.9	19 55.4	+9.4	50.2	20 33.7	+10.2	50.5	21 11.8	+11.0	50.8	43
44	16 46.0	+5.0	47.9	17 26.2	+5.7	48.1	18 06.1	+6.6	48.4	18 45.9	+7.3	48.6	19 25.4	+8.2	48.9	20 04.8	+9.0	49.2	20 43.9	+9.9	49.4	21 22.8	+10.7	49.7	44
45	16 51.0	+4.6	46.9	17 31.9	+5.4	47.1	18 12.7	+6.2	47.3	18 53.2	+7.1	47.6	19 33.6	+7.8	47.8	20 13.8	+8.6	48.1	20 53.8	+9.4	48.4	21 33.5	+10.3	48.7	45
46	16 55.6	+4.3	45.8	17 37.3	+5.1	46.0	18 18.9	+5.9	46.3	19 00.3	+6.6	46.5	19 41.4	+7.5	46.8	20 22.4	+8.3	47.0	21 03.2	+9.1	47.3	21 43.8	+9.8	47.6	46
47	16 59.9	+4.0	44.8	17 42.4	+4.7	45.0	18 24.7	+5.6	45.2	19 06.9	+6.3	45.5	19 48.9	+7.1	45.7	20 30.7	+7.8	46.0	21 12.3	+8.6	46.3	21 53.6	+9.5	46.5	47
48	17 03.9	+3.6	43.7	17 47.1	+4.5	44.0	18 30.3	+5.1	44.2	19 13.2	+5.9	44.4	19 56.0	+6.7	44.7	20 38.5	+7.5	44.9	21 20.9	+8.3	45.2	22 03.1	+9.0	45.5	48
49	17 07.5	+3.4	42.7	17 51.6	+4.0	42.9	18 35.4	+4.8	43.1	19 19.1	+5.6	43.4	20 02.7	+6.3	43.6	20 46.0	+7.1	43.9	21 29.2	+7.8	44.1	22 12.1	+8.7	44.4	49
50	17 10.9	+3.0	41.6	17 55.6	+3.8	41.9	18 40.2	+4.5	42.1	19 24.7	+5.2	42.3	20 09.0	+5.9	42.6	20 53.1	+6.7	42.8	21 37.0	+7.5	43.1	22 20.8	+8.2	43.3	50
51	17 13.9	+2.7	40.6	17 59.4	+3.4	40.8	18 44.7	+4.1	41.0	19 29.9	+4.8	41.3	20 14.9	+5.6	41.5	20 59.8	+6.3	41.7	21 44.5	+7.0	42.0	22 29.0	+7.7	42.3	51
52	17 16.6	+2.4	39.6	18 02.8	+3.0	39.8	18 48.8	+3.8	40.0	19 34.7	+4.5	40.2	20 20.5	+5.2	40.4	21 06.1	+5.9	40.7	21 51.5	+6.6	40.9	22 36.7	+7.4	41.2	52
53	17 19.0	+2.1	38.5	18 05.8	+2.8	38.7	18 52.6	+3.4	38.9	19 39.2	+4.1	39.1	20 25.7	+4.8	39.4	21 12.0	+5.5	39.6	21 58.1	+6.2	39.9	22 44.1	+6.9	40.1	53
54	17 21.0	+1.7	37.5	18 08.6	+2.3	37.7	18 56.0	+3.0	37.9	19 43.3	+3.7	38.1	20 30.5	+4.4	38.3	21 17.5	+5.0	38.5	22 04.3	+5.8	38.8	22 51.0	+6.5	39.0	54
55	17 22.7	+1.4	36.4	18 10.9	+2.1	36.6	18 59.0	+2.7	36.8	19 47.0	+3.4	37.0	20 34.9	+4.0	37.2	21 22.5	+4.7	37.5	22 10.1	+5.3	37.7	22 57.5	+6.0	38.0	55
56	17 24.1	+1.1	35.4	18 13.0	+1.7	35.6	19 01.7	+2.3	35.7	19 50.4	+2.9	36.0	20 38.9	+3.6	36.2	21 27.2	+4.3	36.4	22 15.4	+5.0	36.6	23 03.5	+5.6	36.9	56
57	17 25.2	+0.7	34.3	18 14.7	+1.3	34.5	19 04.0	+2.0	34.7	19 53.3	+2.6	34.9	20 42.5	+3.2	35.1	21 31.5	+3.8	35.3	22 20.4	+4.5	35.6	23 09.1	+5.2	35.8	57
58	17 25.9	+0.4	33.3	18 16.0	+1.0	33.4	19 06.0	+1.6	33.6	19 55.9	+2.2	33.8	20 45.7	+2.8	34.0	21 35.3	+3.5	34.3	22 24.9	+4.0	34.5	23 14.3	+4.7	34.7	58
59	17 26.3	+0.1	32.2	18 17.0	+0.7	32.4	19 07.6	+1.2	32.6	19 58.1	+1.8	32.8	20 48.5	+2.4	33.0	21 38.8	+3.0	33.2	22 28.9	+3.7	33.4	23 19.0	+4.2	33.6	59
60	17 26.4	-0.3	31.2	18 17.7	+0.3	31.3	19 08.8	+0.9	31.5	19 59.9	+1.5	31.7	20 50.9	+2.1	31.9	21 41.8	+2.6	32.1	22 32.6	+3.2	32.3	23 23.2	+3.8	32.6	60
61	17 26.1	-0.6	30.1	18 18.0	-0.1	30.3	19 09.7	+0.5	30.5	20 01.4	+1.1	30.6	20 53.0	+1.6	30.8	21 44.4	+2.2	31.0	22 35.8	+2.8	31.2	23 27.0	+3.4	31.5	61
62	17 25.5	-0.9	29.1	18 17.9	-0.4	29.2	19 10.2	+0.2	29.4	20 02.5	+0.6	29.6	20 54.6	+1.2	29.8	21 46.6	+1.8	30.0	22 38.6	+2.3	30.2	23 30.4	+2.9	30.4	62
63	17 24.6	-1.2	28.0	18 17.5	-0.7	28.2	19 10.4	-0.2	28.3	20 03.1	+0.3	28.5	20 55.8	+0.9	28.7	21 48.4	+1.4	28.9	22 40.9	+1.9	29.1	23 33.3	+2.4	29.3	63
64	17 23.4	-1.6	27.0	18 16.8	-1.1	27.1	19 10.2	-0.6	27.3	20 03.4	0.0	27.4	20 56.7	+0.4	27.6	21 49.8	+0.9	27.8	22 42.8	+1.5	28.0	23 35.7	+2.0	28.2	64
65	17 21.8	-1.9	25.9	18 15.7	-1.4	26.1	19 09.6	-1.0	26.2	20 03.4	-0.5	26.4	20 57.1	0.0	26.5	21 50.7	+0.5	26.7	22 44.3	+1.0	26.9	23 37.7	+1.5	27.1	65
66	17 19.9	-2.2	24.9	18 14.3	-1.8	25.0	19 08.6	-1.3	25.2	20 02.9	-0.8	25.3	20 57.1	-0.4	25.5	21 51.2	+0.1	25.6	22 45.3	+0.6	25.8	23 39.2	+1.1	26.0	66
67	17 17.7	-2.6	23.8	18 12.5	-2.1	24.0	19 07.3	-1.6	24.1	20 02.1	-1.3	24.3	20 56.7	-0.7	24.4	21 51.3	-0.3	24.6	22 45.9	+0.1	24.7	23 40.3	+0.6	24.9	67
68	17 15.1	-2.8	22.8	18 10.4	-2.4	22.9	19 05.7	-2.1	23.1	20 00.8	-1.6	23.2	20 56.0	-1.2	23.3	21 51.0	-0.7	23.5	22 46.0	-0.3	23.7	23 40.9	+0.2	23.8	68
69	17 12.3	-3.2	21.7	18 08.0	-2.8	21.9	19 03.6	-2.4	22.0	19 59.2	-2.0	22.1	20 54.8	-1.6	22.3	21 50.3	-1.2	22.4	22 45.7	-0.7	22.6	23 41.1	-0.3	22.7	69
70	17 09.1	-3.6	20.7	18 05.2	-3.2	20.8	19 01.2	-2.7	20.9	19 57.2	-2.3	21.1	20 53.2	-2.0	21.2	21 49.1	-1.6	21.3	22 45.0	-1.2	21.5	23 40.8	-0.8	21.6	70
71	17 05.5	-3.8	19.7	18 02.0	-3.5	19.8	18 58.5	-3.1	19.9	19 54.9	-2.8	20.0	20 51.2	-2.3	20.1	21 47.5	-1.9	20.3	22 43.8	-1.6	20.4	23 40.0	-1.1	20.6	71
72	17 01.7	-4.2	18.6	17 58.5	-3.8	18.7	18 55.4	-3.5	18.8	19 52.1	-3.1	18.9	20 48.9	-2.8	19.1	21 45.6	-2.5	19.2	22 42.2	-2.1	19.3	23 38.9	-1.7	19.5	72
73	16 57.5	-4.4	17.6	17 54.7	-4.1	17.7	18 51.9	-3.8	17.8	19 49.0	-3.5	17.9	20 46.1	-3.2	18.0	21 43.1	-2.8	18.1	22 40.1	-2.4	18.2	23 37.1	-2.1	18.4	73
74	16 53.1	-4.8	16.5	17 50.6	-4.5	16.6	18 48.1	-4.2	16.7	19 45.5	-3.9	16.8	20 42.9	-3.5	16.9	21 40.3	-3.2	17.0	22 37.7	-3.0	17.2	23 35.0	-2.6	17.3	74
75	16 48.3	-5.1	15.5	17 46.1	-4.8	15.6	18 43.9	-4.6	15.7	19 41.6	-4.2	15.8	20 39.4	-4.0	15.9	21 37.1	-3.7	16.0	22 34.7	-3.3	16.1	23 32.4	-3.1	16.2	75
76	16 43.2	-5.4	14.4	17 41.3	-5.2	14.5	18 39.3	-4.9	14.6	19 37.4	-4.6	14.7	20 35.4	-4.3	14.8	21 33.4	-4.1	14.9	22 31.4	-3.8	15.0	23 29.3	-3.5	15.1	76
77	16 37.8	-5.8	13.4	17 36.1	-5.5	13.5	18 34.4	-5.2	13.6	19 32.8	-5.0	13.6	20 31.1	-4.8	13.7	21 29.3	-4.4	13.8	22 27.6	-4.2	13.9	23 25.8	-3.9	14.0	77
78	16 32.0	-6.0	12.4	17 30.6	-5.8	12.4	18 29.2	-5.6	12.5	19 27.8	-5.4	12.6	20 26.3	-5.1	12.7	21 24.9	-4.9	12.7	22 23.4	-4.7	12.8	23 21.9	-4.4	12.9	78
79	16 26.0	-6.4	11.3	17 24.8	-6.1	11.4	18 23.6	-5.9	11.5	19 22.4	-5.7	11.5	20 21.2	-5.5	11.6	21 20.0	-5.3	11.7	22 18.7	-5.1	11.8	23 17.5	-4.9	11.8	79
80	16 19.6	-6.6	10.3	17 18.7	-6.5	10.3	18 17.7	-6.3	10.4	19 16.7	-6.1	10.5	20 15.7	-5.9	10.5	21 14.7	-5.7	10.6	22 13.6	-5.5	10.7	23 12.6	-5.3	10.8	80
81	16 13.0	-6.9	9.3	17 12.2	-6.8	9.3	18 11.4	-6.6	9.4	19 10.6	-6.4	9.5	20 09.8	-6.3	9.5	21 09.0	-6.1	9.5	22 08.1	-5.9	9.6	23 07.3	-5.7	9.7	81
82	16 06.1	-7.3	8.2	17 05.4	-7.1	8.3	18 04.8	-6.9	8.3	19 04.2	-6.8	8.4	20 03.5	-6.6	8.4	21 02.9	-6.5	8.5	22 02.2	-6.3	8.5	23 01.6	-6.2	8.6	82
83	15 58.8	-7.5	7.2	16 58.3	-7.4	7.2	17 57.9	-7.3	7.3	18 57.4	-7.2	7.3	19 56.9	-7.0	7.4	20 56.4	-6.9	7.4	21 55.9	-6.8	7.5	22 55.4	-6.7	7.5	83
84	15 51.3	-7.9	6.2	16 50.9	-7.7	6.2	17 50.6	-7.6	6.2	18 50.2	-7.5	6.3	19 49.9	-7.4	6.3	20 49.5	-7.3	6.3	21 49.1	-7.2	6.4	22 48.7	-7.0	6.4	84
85	15 43.4	-8.1	5.1	16 43.2	-8.0	5.2	17 43.0	-8.0	5.2	18 42.7	-7.8	5.2	19 42.5	-7.8	5.2	20 42.2	-7.7	5.3	21 41.9	-7.5	5.3	22 41.7	-7.5	5.4	85
86	15 35.3	-8.4	4.1	16 35.2	-8.4	4.1	17 35.0	-8.3	4.1	18 34.9	-8.3	4.2	19 34.7	-8.1	4.2	20 34.5	-8.0	4.2	21 34.4	-8.0	4.2	22 34.2	-7.9	4.3	86
87	15 26.9	-8.7	3.1	16 26.8	-8.6	3.1	17 26.7	-8.6	3.1	18 26.6	-8.5	3.1	19 26.6	-8.5	3.1	20 26.5	-8.5	3.2	21 26.4	-8.4	3.2	22 26.3	-8.4	3.2	87
88	15 18.2	-9.0	2.0	16 18.2	-9.0	2.1	17 18.1	-8.9	2.1	18 18.1	-8.9	2.1	19 18.1	-8.9	2.1	20 18.0	-8.8	2.1	21 18.0	-8.8	2.1	22 17.9	-8.7	2.1	88
89	15 09.2	-9.2	1.0	16 09.2	-9.2	1.0	17 09.2	-9.2	1.0	18 09.2	-9.2	1.0	19 09.2	-9.2	1.0	20 09.2	-9.2	1.1	21 09.2	-9.2	1.1	22 09.2	-9.2	1.1	89
90	15 00.0	-9.5	0.0	16 00.0	-9.5	0.0	17 00.0	-9.5	0.0	18 00.0	-9.6	0.0	19 00.0	-9.6	0.0	20 00.0	-9.6	0.0	21 00.0	-9.6	0.0	22 00.0	-9.6	0.0	90
	15°			16°			17°			18°			19°			20°			21°			22°			

81°, 279° L.H.A.

LATITUDE SAME NAME AS DECLINATION

LATITUDE **CONTRARY** NAME TO DECLINATION **L.H.A. 81°, 279°**

Dec. °	15° Hc ° ′	d ′	Z °	16° Hc ° ′	d ′	Z °	17° Hc ° ′	d ′	Z °	18° Hc ° ′	d ′	Z °	Dec. °
0	8 41.5	-15.8	92.3	8 38.9	-16.8	92.5	8 36.2	-17.8	92.7	8 33.4	-18.9	92.8	0
1	8 25.7	-16.0	93.3	8 22.1	-16.9	93.5	8 18.4	-17.9	93.6	8 14.5	-18.9	93.8	1
2	8 09.7	-16.0	94.3	8 05.2	-17.1	94.4	8 00.5	-18.1	94.6	7 55.6	-19.1	94.7	2
3	7 53.7	-16.2	95.3	7 48.1	-17.2	95.4	7 42.4	-18.2	95.5	7 36.5	-19.2	95.7	3
4	7 37.5	-16.4	96.2	7 30.9	-17.4	96.4	7 24.2	-18.4	96.5	7 17.3	-19.3	96.6	4
5	7 21.1	-16.4	97.2	7 13.5	-17.4	97.3	7 05.8	-18.4	97.5	6 58.0	-19.5	97.6	5
6	7 04.7	-16.6	98.2	6 56.1	-17.6	98.3	6 47.4	-18.6	98.4	6 38.5	-19.5	98.5	6
7	6 48.1	-16.7	99.2	6 38.5	-17.7	99.3	6 28.8	-18.7	99.4	6 19.0	-19.7	99.5	7
8	6 31.4	-16.8	100.1	6 20.8	-17.8	100.2	6 10.1	-18.8	100.3	5 59.3	-19.8	100.4	8
9	6 14.6	-16.9	101.1	6 03.0	-17.9	101.2	5 51.3	-18.8	101.3	5 39.5	-19.8	101.4	9
10	5 57.7	-17.0	102.0	5 45.1	-18.0	102.1	5 32.5	-19.0	102.2	5 19.7	-20.0	102.3	10
11	5 40.7	-17.1	103.0	5 27.1	-18.0	103.1	5 13.5	-19.1	103.2	4 59.7	-20.0	103.3	11
12	5 23.6	-17.2	104.0	5 09.1	-18.2	104.1	4 54.4	-19.1	104.1	4 39.7	-20.1	104.2	12
13	5 06.4	-17.3	104.9	4 50.9	-18.3	105.0	4 35.3	-19.2	105.1	4 19.6	-20.1	105.2	13
14	4 49.1	-17.3	105.9	4 32.6	-18.3	106.0	4 16.1	-19.3	106.1	3 59.5	-20.3	106.1	14
15	4 31.8	-17.5	106.9	4 14.3	-18.4	106.9	3 56.8	-19.3	107.0	3 39.2	-20.3	107.1	15
16	4 14.3	-17.5	107.8	3 55.9	-18.4	107.9	3 37.5	-19.4	107.9	3 18.9	-20.3	108.0	16
17	3 56.8	-17.6	108.8	3 37.5	-18.6	108.8	3 18.1	-19.5	108.9	2 58.6	-20.4	108.9	17
18	3 39.2	-17.6	109.7	3 18.9	-18.5	109.8	2 58.6	-19.5	109.8	2 38.2	-20.4	109.9	18
19	3 21.6	-17.7	110.7	3 00.4	-18.7	110.7	2 39.1	-19.6	110.8	2 17.8	-20.5	110.8	19
20	3 03.9	-17.7	111.7	2 41.7	-18.6	111.7	2 19.5	-19.5	111.7	1 57.3	-20.5	111.8	20
21	2 46.2	-17.8	112.6	2 23.1	-18.7	112.6	2 00.0	-19.7	112.7	1 36.8	-20.5	112.7	21
22	2 28.4	-17.9	113.6	2 04.4	-18.8	113.6	1 40.3	-19.6	113.6	1 16.3	-20.6	113.7	22
23	2 10.5	-17.8	114.5	1 45.6	-18.7	114.5	1 20.7	-19.7	114.6	0 55.7	-20.5	114.6	23
24	1 52.7	-17.9	115.5	1 26.9	-18.8	115.5	1 01.0	-19.7	115.5	0 35.2	-20.6	115.5	24
25	1 34.8	-18.0	116.4	1 08.1	-18.9	116.4	0 41.3	-19.7	116.5	0 14.6	-20.6	116.5	25
26	1 16.8	-17.9	117.4	0 49.2	-18.8	117.4	0 21.6	-19.7	117.4	0 06.0	+20.6	62.6	26
27	0 58.9	-18.0	118.3	0 30.4	-18.8	118.3	0 01.9	-19.7	118.4	0 26.6	+20.5	61.6	27
28	0 40.9	-17.9	119.3	0 11.6	-18.9	119.3	0 17.8	+19.7	60.7	0 47.1	+20.6	60.7	28
29	0 23.0	-18.0	120.2	0 07.3	+18.8	59.8	0 37.5	+19.7	59.8	1 07.7	+20.5	59.8	29
30	0 05.0	-18.0	121.2	0 26.1	+18.8	58.8	0 57.2	+19.6	58.8	1 28.2	+20.5	58.8	30
31	0 13.0	+18.0	57.8	0 44.9	+18.8	57.9	1 16.8	+19.7	57.9	1 48.7	+20.5	57.9	31
32	0 31.0	+17.9	56.9	1 03.7	+18.8	56.9	1 36.5	+19.6	56.9	2 09.2	+20.5	57.0	32
33	0 48.9	+18.0	55.9	1 22.5	+18.8	56.0	1 56.1	+19.6	56.0	2 29.7	+20.4	56.0	33
34	1 06.9	+17.9	55.0	1 41.3	+18.8	55.0	2 15.7	+19.6	55.0	2 50.1	+20.4	55.1	34
35	1 24.8	+17.9	54.0	2 00.1	+18.7	54.1	2 35.3	+19.5	54.1	3 10.5	+20.3	54.1	35
36	1 42.7	+17.9	53.1	2 18.8	+18.7	53.1	2 54.8	+19.5	53.1	3 30.8	+20.2	53.2	36
37	2 00.6	+17.9	52.1	2 37.5	+18.6	52.2	3 14.3	+19.4	52.2	3 51.0	+20.2	52.2	37
38	2 18.5	+17.8	51.2	2 56.1	+18.6	51.2	3 33.7	+19.3	51.2	4 11.2	+20.1	51.3	38
39	2 36.3	+17.8	50.2	3 14.7	+18.5	50.2	3 53.0	+19.3	50.3	4 31.3	+20.1	50.4	39
40	2 54.1	+17.7	49.3	3 33.2	+18.5	49.3	4 12.3	+19.3	49.3	4 51.4	+20.0	49.4	40
41	3 11.8	+17.7	48.3	3 51.7	+18.4	48.3	4 31.6	+19.1	48.4	5 11.4	+19.9	48.5	41
42	3 29.5	+17.6	47.3	4 10.1	+18.3	47.4	4 50.7	+19.1	47.4	5 31.3	+19.8	47.5	42
43	3 47.1	+17.5	46.4	4 28.4	+18.3	46.4	5 09.8	+19.0	46.5	5 51.1	+19.7	46.6	43
44	4 04.6	+17.5	45.4	4 46.7	+18.2	45.5	5 28.8	+18.9	45.5	6 10.8	+19.6	45.6	44
45	4 22.1	+17.4	44.5	5 04.9	+18.1	44.5	5 47.7	+18.8	44.6	6 30.4	+19.5	44.7	45
46	4 39.5	+17.3	43.5	5 23.0	+18.0	43.6	6 06.5	+18.6	43.6	6 49.9	+19.3	43.7	46
47	4 56.8	+17.3	42.5	5 41.0	+17.9	42.6	6 25.1	+18.6	42.7	7 09.2	+19.3	42.8	47
48	5 14.1	+17.1	41.6	5 58.9	+17.8	41.6	6 43.7	+18.5	41.7	7 28.5	+19.1	41.8	48
49	5 31.2	+17.1	40.6	6 16.7	+17.8	40.7	7 02.2	+18.4	40.8	7 47.6	+19.0	40.8	49
50	5 48.3	+17.0	39.7	6 34.5	+17.6	39.7	7 20.6	+18.2	39.8	8 06.6	+18.9	39.9	50
51	6 05.3	+16.8	38.7	6 52.1	+17.4	38.8	7 38.8	+18.1	38.8	8 25.5	+18.8	38.9	51
52	6 22.1	+16.8	37.7	7 09.5	+17.4	37.8	7 56.9	+18.0	37.9	8 44.3	+18.6	38.0	52
53	6 38.9	+16.6	36.8	7 26.9	+17.3	36.8	8 14.9	+17.9	36.9	9 02.9	+18.4	37.0	53
54	6 55.5	+16.5	35.8	7 44.2	+17.1	35.9	8 32.8	+17.7	35.9	9 21.3	+18.3	36.0	54
55	7 12.0	+16.4	34.8	8 01.3	+16.9	34.9	8 50.5	+17.5	35.0	9 39.6	+18.1	35.1	55
56	7 28.4	+16.3	33.9	8 18.2	+16.9	33.9	9 08.0	+17.4	34.0	9 57.7	+18.0	34.1	56
57	7 44.7	+16.2	32.9	8 35.1	+16.7	33.0	9 25.4	+17.2	33.0	10 15.7	+17.7	33.1	57
58	8 00.9	+16.0	31.9	8 51.8	+16.5	32.0	9 42.6	+17.1	32.1	10 33.4	+17.7	32.2	58
59	8 16.9	+15.8	30.9	9 08.3	+16.4	31.0	9 59.7	+16.9	31.1	10 51.1	+17.4	31.2	59
60	8 32.7	+15.7	30.0	9 24.7	+16.2	30.0	10 16.6	+16.7	30.1	11 08.5	+17.2	30.2	60
61	8 48.4	+15.6	29.0	9 40.9	+16.1	29.1	10 33.3	+16.6	29.1	11 25.7	+17.0	29.2	61
62	9 04.0	+15.4	28.0	9 57.0	+15.8	28.1	10 49.9	+16.3	28.2	11 42.7	+16.9	28.3	62
63	9 19.4	+15.3	27.0	10 12.8	+15.8	27.1	11 06.2	+16.2	27.2	11 59.6	+16.6	27.3	63
64	9 34.7	+15.0	26.0	10 28.6	+15.5	26.1	11 22.4	+16.0	26.2	12 16.2	+16.4	26.3	64
65	9 49.7	+15.0	25.1	10 44.1	+15.3	25.1	11 38.4	+15.8	25.2	12 32.6	+16.2	25.3	65
66	10 04.7	+14.7	24.1	10 59.4	+15.2	24.2	11 54.2	+15.5	24.2	12 48.8	+16.0	24.3	66
67	10 19.4	+14.6	23.1	11 14.6	+14.9	23.2	12 09.7	+15.4	23.3	13 04.8	+15.8	23.3	67
68	10 34.0	+14.3	22.1	11 29.5	+14.8	22.2	12 25.1	+15.1	22.3	13 20.6	+15.5	22.3	68
69	10 48.3	+14.2	21.1	11 44.3	+14.5	21.2	12 40.2	+14.9	21.3	13 36.1	+15.3	21.4	69
70	11 02.5	+14.0	20.1	11 58.8	+14.4	20.2	12 55.1	+14.7	20.3	13 51.4	+15.1	20.4	70
71	11 16.5	+13.8	19.1	12 13.2	+14.1	19.2	13 09.8	+14.5	19.3	14 06.5	+14.8	19.4	71
72	11 30.3	+13.6	18.1	12 27.3	+13.9	18.2	13 24.3	+14.2	18.3	14 21.3	+14.5	18.4	72
73	11 43.9	+13.4	17.2	12 41.2	+13.7	17.2	13 38.5	+14.0	17.3	14 35.8	+14.3	17.4	73
74	11 57.3	+13.2	16.2	12 54.9	+13.5	16.2	13 52.5	+13.8	16.3	14 50.1	+14.0	16.4	74
75	12 10.5	+12.9	15.2	13 08.4	+13.2	15.2	14 06.3	+13.5	15.3	15 04.1	+13.8	15.4	75
76	12 23.4	+12.8	14.2	13 21.6	+13.0	14.2	14 19.8	+13.2	14.3	15 17.9	+13.5	14.3	76
77	12 36.2	+12.5	13.2	13 34.6	+12.7	13.2	14 33.0	+13.0	13.3	15 31.4	+13.2	13.3	77
78	12 48.7	+12.3	12.2	13 47.3	+12.6	12.2	14 46.0	+12.7	12.3	15 44.6	+12.9	12.3	78
79	13 01.0	+12.0	11.2	13 59.9	+12.2	11.2	14 58.7	+12.5	11.2	15 57.5	+12.7	11.3	79
80	13 13.0	+11.9	10.1	14 12.1	+12.0	10.2	15 11.2	+12.1	10.2	16 10.2	+12.4	10.3	80
81	13 24.9	+11.6	9.1	14 24.1	+11.7	9.2	15 23.3	+11.9	9.2	16 22.6	+12.0	9.3	81
82	13 36.5	+11.3	8.1	14 35.8	+11.5	8.2	15 35.2	+11.7	8.2	16 34.6	+11.8	8.2	82
83	13 47.8	+11.1	7.1	14 47.3	+11.2	7.2	15 46.9	+11.3	7.2	16 46.4	+11.4	7.2	83
84	13 58.9	+10.8	6.1	14 58.5	+11.0	6.1	15 58.2	+11.0	6.2	16 57.8	+11.2	6.2	84
85	14 09.7	+10.6	5.1	15 09.5	+10.7	5.1	16 09.2	+10.8	5.1	17 09.0	+10.8	5.2	85
86	14 20.3	+10.3	4.1	15 20.2	+10.3	4.1	16 20.0	+10.5	4.1	17 19.8	+10.6	4.1	86
87	14 30.6	+10.1	3.1	15 30.5	+10.1	3.1	16 30.5	+10.1	3.1	17 30.4	+10.2	3.1	87
88	14 40.7	+9.8	2.0	15 40.6	+9.9	2.1	16 40.6	+9.9	2.1	17 40.6	+9.8	2.1	88
89	14 50.5	+9.5	1.0	15 50.5	+9.5	1.0	16 50.5	+9.5	1.0	17 50.4	+9.6	1.0	89
90	15 00.0	+9.2	0.0	16 00.0	+9.2	0.0	17 00.0	+9.2	0.0	18 00.0	+9.2	0.0	90
	15°			16°			17°			18°			

Dec. °	19° Hc ° ′	d ′	Z °	20° Hc ° ′	d ′	Z °	21° Hc ° ′	d ′	Z °	22° Hc ° ′	d ′	Z °	Dec. °
0	8 30.4	-19.9	93.0	8 27.2	-20.8	93.1	8 23.9	-21.8	93.2	8 20.4	-22.8	93.4	0
1	8 10.5	-19.9	93.9	8 06.4	-21.0	94.0	8 02.1	-22.0	94.2	7 57.6	-22.9	94.3	1
2	7 50.6	-20.1	94.9	7 45.4	-21.0	95.0	7 40.1	-22.0	95.1	7 34.7	-23.0	95.3	2
3	7 30.5	-20.2	95.8	7 24.4	-21.2	95.9	7 18.1	-22.2	96.1	7 11.7	-23.2	96.2	3
4	7 10.3	-20.3	96.8	7 03.2	-21.3	96.9	6 55.9	-22.3	97.0	6 48.5	-23.2	97.1	4
5	6 50.0	-20.5	97.7	6 41.9	-21.4	97.8	6 33.6	-22.3	97.9	6 25.3	-23.4	98.1	5
6	6 29.5	-20.5	98.7	6 20.5	-21.6	98.8	6 11.3	-22.5	98.9	6 01.9	-23.4	99.0	6
7	6 09.0	-20.6	99.6	5 58.9	-21.6	99.7	5 48.8	-22.6	99.8	5 38.5	-23.5	99.9	7
8	5 48.4	-20.8	100.5	5 37.3	-21.7	100.6	5 26.2	-22.6	100.7	5 15.0	-23.6	100.8	8
9	5 27.6	-20.8	101.5	5 15.6	-21.7	101.6	5 03.6	-22.8	101.7	4 51.4	-23.7	101.8	9
10	5 06.8	-20.9	102.4	4 53.9	-21.9	102.5	4 40.8	-22.8	102.6	4 27.7	-23.8	102.7	10
11	4 45.9	-21.0	103.4	4 32.0	-21.9	103.4	4 18.0	-22.9	103.5	4 03.9	-23.8	103.6	11
12	4 24.9	-21.0	104.3	4 10.1	-22.0	104.4	3 55.1	-22.9	104.4	3 40.1	-23.8	104.5	12
13	4 03.9	-21.1	105.2	3 48.1	-22.1	105.3	3 32.2	-23.0	105.4	3 16.3	-24.0	105.4	13
14	3 42.8	-21.2	106.2	3 26.0	-22.1	106.2	3 09.2	-23.0	106.3	2 52.3	-23.9	106.4	14
15	3 21.6	-21.2	107.1	3 03.9	-22.2	107.2	2 46.2	-23.1	107.2	2 28.4	-24.0	107.3	15
16	3 00.4	-21.3	108.1	2 41.7	-22.2	108.1	2 23.1	-23.1	108.1	2 04.4	-24.1	108.2	16
17	2 39.1	-21.3	109.0	2 19.5	-22.2	109.0	2 00.0	-23.2	109.1	1 40.3	-24.0	109.1	17
18	2 17.8	-21.4	109.9	1 57.3	-22.3	110.0	1 36.8	-23.2	110.0	1 16.3	-24.1	110.0	18
19	1 56.4	-21.4	110.9	1 35.0	-22.3	110.9	1 13.6	-23.2	110.9	0 52.2	-24.1	110.9	19
20	1 35.0	-21.4	111.8	1 12.7	-22.3	111.8	0 50.4	-23.2	111.8	0 28.1	-24.1	111.9	20
21	1 13.6	-21.4	112.7	0 50.4	-22.3	112.8	0 27.2	-23.2	112.8	0 04.0	-24.1	112.8	21
22	0 52.2	-21.5	113.7	0 28.1	-22.3	113.7	0 04.0	-23.2	113.7	0 20.1	+24.1	66.3	22
23	0 30.7	-21.4	114.6	0 05.8	-22.4	114.6	0 19.2	+23.2	65.4	0 44.2	+24.1	65.4	23
24	0 09.3	-21.5	115.5	0 16.6	+22.3	64.5	0 42.4	+23.2	64.5	1 08.3	+24.1	64.5	24
25	0 12.2	+21.4	63.5	0 38.9	+22.3	63.5	1 05.6	+23.2	63.5	1 32.4	+24.0	63.6	25
26	0 33.6	+21.5	62.6	1 01.2	+22.3	62.6	1 28.8	+23.2	62.6	1 56.4	+24.0	62.7	26
27	0 55.1	+21.4	61.7	1 23.5	+22.3	61.7	1 52.0	+23.1	61.7	2 20.4	+24.0	61.7	27
28	1 16.5	+21.4	60.7	1 45.8	+22.3	60.7	2 15.1	+23.1	60.8	2 44.4	+23.9	60.8	28
29	1 37.9	+21.4	59.8	2 08.1	+22.2	59.8	2 38.2	+23.1	59.9	3 08.3	+23.9	59.9	29
30	1 59.3	+21.3	58.9	2 30.3	+22.2	58.9	3 01.3	+23.0	58.9	3 32.2	+23.8	59.0	30
31	2 20.6	+21.3	57.9	2 52.5	+22.1	58.0	3 24.3	+22.9	58.0	3 56.0	+23.8	58.1	31
32	2 41.9	+21.3	57.0	3 14.6	+22.1	57.0	3 47.2	+22.9	57.1	4 19.8	+23.7	57.1	32
33	3 03.2	+21.2	56.0	3 36.7	+22.0	56.1	4 10.1	+22.9	56.2	4 43.5	+23.7	56.2	33
34	3 24.4	+21.2	55.1	3 58.7	+22.0	55.2	4 33.0	+22.7	55.2	5 07.2	+23.5	55.3	34
35	3 45.6	+21.1	54.2	4 20.7	+21.9	54.2	4 55.7	+22.7	54.3	5 30.7	+23.5	54.4	35
36	4 06.7	+21.0	53.2	4 42.6	+21.8	53.3	5 18.4	+22.6	53.4	5 54.2	+23.4	53.4	36
37	4 27.7	+21.0	52.3	5 04.4	+21.7	52.4	5 41.0	+22.5	52.4	6 17.6	+23.2	52.5	37
38	4 48.7	+20.9	51.4	5 26.1	+21.7	51.4	6 03.5	+22.4	51.5	6 40.8	+23.2	51.6	38
39	5 09.6	+20.8	50.4	5 47.8	+21.6	50.5	6 25.9	+22.4	50.6	7 04.0	+23.1	50.7	39
40	5 30.4	+20.7	49.5	6 09.4	+21.4	49.6	6 48.3	+22.2	49.6	7 27.1	+22.9	49.7	40
41	5 51.1	+20.7	48.5	6 30.8	+21.4	48.6	7 10.5	+22.1	48.7	7 50.0	+22.8	48.8	41
42	6 11.8	+20.5	47.6	6 52.2	+21.2	47.7	7 32.6	+21.9	47.8	8 12.8	+22.7	47.9	42
43	6 32.3	+20.4	46.6	7 13.4	+21.2	46.7	7 54.5	+21.9	46.8	8 35.5	+22.6	46.9	43
44	6 52.7	+20.3	45.7	7 34.6	+21.0	45.8	8 16.4	+21.7	45.9	8 58.1	+22.4	46.0	44
45	7 13.0	+20.2	44.7	7 55.6	+20.9	44.8	8 38.1	+21.6	44.9	9 20.5	+22.3	45.1	45
46	7 33.2	+20.1	43.8	8 16.5	+20.7	43.9	8 59.7	+21.4	44.0	9 42.8	+22.1	44.1	46
47	7 53.3	+19.9	42.8	8 37.2	+20.6	42.9	9 21.1	+21.3	43.1	10 04.9	+21.9	43.2	47
48	8 13.2	+19.8	41.9	8 57.8	+20.5	42.0	9 42.4	+21.1	42.1	10 26.8	+21.8	42.2	48
49	8 33.0	+19.7	40.9	9 18.3	+20.3	41.0	10 03.5	+21.0	41.2	10 48.6	+21.6	41.3	49
50	8 52.7	+19.5	40.0	9 38.6	+20.1	40.1	10 24.5	+20.8	40.2	11 10.2	+21.5	40.3	50
51	9 12.2	+19.3	39.0	9 58.7	+20.0	39.1	10 45.3	+20.6	39.2	11 31.7	+21.2	39.4	51
52	9 31.5	+19.2	38.1	10 18.7	+19.9	38.2	11 05.9	+20.4	38.3	11 52.9	+21.1	38.4	52
53	9 50.7	+19.1	37.1	10 38.6	+19.6	37.2	11 26.3	+20.3	37.3	12 14.0	+20.8	37.5	53
54	10 09.8	+18.9	36.1	10 58.2	+19.5	36.3	11 46.6	+20.0	36.4	12 34.8	+20.7	36.5	54
55	10 28.7	+18.7	35.2	11 17.7	+19.2	35.3	12 06.6	+19.9	35.4	12 55.5	+20.4	35.5	55
56	10 47.4	+18.5	34.2	11 36.9	+19.1	34.3	12 26.5	+19.6	34.4	13 15.9	+20.2	34.6	56
57	11 05.9	+18.3	33.2	11 56.0	+18.9	33.4	12 46.1	+19.4	33.5	13 36.1	+20.0	33.6	57
58	11 24.2	+18.1	32.3	12 14.9	+18.7	32.4	13 05.5	+19.3	32.5	13 56.1	+19.8	32.6	58
59	11 42.3	+18.0	31.3	12 33.6	+18.5	31.4	13 24.8	+19.0	31.5	14 15.9	+19.5	31.7	59
60	12 00.3	+17.7	30.3	12 52.1	+18.2	30.4	13 43.8	+18.7	30.6	14 35.4	+19.3	30.7	60
61	12 18.0	+17.6	29.3	13 10.3	+18.0	29.5	14 02.5	+18.5	29.6	14 54.7	+19.0	29.7	61
62	12 35.6	+17.3	28.4	13 28.3	+17.8	28.5	14 21.0	+18.3	28.6	15 13.7	+18.8	28.7	62
63	12 52.9	+17.1	27.4	13 46.1	+17.6	27.5	14 39.3	+18.1	27.6	15 32.5	+18.5	27.7	63
64	13 10.0	+16.9	26.4	14 03.7	+17.3	26.5	14 57.4	+17.7	26.6	15 51.0	+18.2	26.7	64
65	13 26.9	+16.6	25.4	14 21.0	+17.1	25.5	15 15.1	+17.6	25.6	16 09.2	+18.0	25.8	65
66	13 43.5	+16.4	24.4	14 38.1	+16.8	24.5	15 32.7	+17.2	24.6	16 27.2	+17.6	24.8	66
67	13 59.9	+16.2	23.4	14 54.9	+16.6	23.5	15 49.9	+17.0	23.6	16 44.8	+17.4	23.8	67
68	14 16.1	+15.9	22.4	15 11.5	+16.3	22.5	16 06.9	+16.7	22.7	17 02.2	+17.1	22.8	68
69	14 32.0	+15.6	21.4	15 27.8	+16.0	21.5	16 23.6	+16.4	21.7	17 19.3	+16.8	21.8	69
70	14 47.6	+15.4	20.5	15 43.8	+15.8	20.5	16 40.0	+16.1	20.6	17 36.1	+16.5	20.8	70
71	15 03.0	+15.2	19.4	15 59.6	+15.5	19.5	16 56.1	+15.9	19.6	17 52.6	+16.2	19.7	71
72	15 18.2	+14.9	18.4	16 15.1	+15.2	18.5	17 12.0	+15.5	18.6	18 08.8	+15.9	18.7	72
73	15 33.1	+14.6	17.4	16 30.3	+14.9	17.5	17 27.5	+15.2	17.6	18 24.7	+15.5	17.7	73
74	15 47.7	+14.3	16.4	16 45.2	+14.6	16.5	17 42.7	+14.9	16.6	18 40.2	+15.2	16.7	74
75	16 02.0	+14.0	15.4	16 59.8	+14.3	15.5	17 57.6	+14.6	15.6	18 55.4	+14.9	15.7	75
76	16 16.0	+13.8	14.4	17 14.1	+14.0	14.5	18 12.2	+14.3	14.6	19 10.3	+14.5	14.7	76
77	16 29.8	+13.4	13.4	17 28.1	+13.7	13.5	18 26.5	+13.9	13.5	19 24.8	+14.2	13.6	77
78	16 43.2	+13.2	12.4	17 41.8	+13.4	12.4	18 40.4	+13.6	12.5	19 39.0	+13.8	12.6	78
79	16 56.4	+12.8	11.4	17 55.2	+13.0	11.4	18 54.0	+13.3	11.5	19 52.8	+13.5	11.6	79
80	17 09.2	+12.6	10.3	18 08.2	+12.8	10.4	19 07.3	+12.9	10.5	20 06.3	+13.1	10.5	80
81	17 21.8	+12.2	9.3	18 21.0	+12.4	9.4	19 20.2	+12.5	9.4	20 19.4	+12.7	9.5	81
82	17 34.0	+11.9	8.3	18 33.4	+12.0	8.3	19 32.7	+12.2	8.4	20 32.1	+12.3	8.4	82
83	17 45.9	+11.6	7.3	18 45.4	+11.7	7.3	19 44.9	+11.9	7.3	20 44.4	+12.0	7.4	83
84	17 57.5	+11.3	6.2	18 57.1	+11.4	6.3	19 56.8	+11.5	6.3	20 56.4	+11.6	6.3	84
85	18 08.8	+10.9	5.2	19 08.5	+11.0	5.2	20 08.3	+11.1	5.3	21 08.0	+11.2	5.3	85
86	18 19.7	+10.6	4.2	19 19.5	+10.7	4.2	20 19.4	+10.7	4.2	21 19.2	+10.8	4.2	86
87	18 30.3	+10.2	3.1	19 30.2	+10.3	3.1	20 30.1	+10.3	3.2	21 30.0	+10.4	3.2	87
88	18 40.5	+9.9	2.1	19 40.5	+9.9	2.1	20 40.4	+10.0	2.1	21 40.4	+10.0	2.1	88
89	18 50.4	+9.6	1.0	19 50.4	+9.6	1.1	20 50.4	+9.6	1.1	21 50.4	+9.6	1.1	89
90	19 00.0	+9.2	0.0	20 00.0	+9.2	0.0	21 00.0	+9.2	0.0	22 00.0	+9.2	0.0	90
	19°			20°			21°			22°			

S. Lat. { L.H.A. greater than 180° ....Zn=180°−Z; L.H.A. less than 180°...........Zn=180°+Z

LATITUDE **SAME** NAME AS DECLINATION **L.H.A. 99°, 261°**

165

82°, 278° L.H.A. LATITUDE SAME NAME AS DECLINATION

N. Lat. {L.H.A. greater than 180° .....Zn=Z
L.H.A. less than 180°............Zn=360°–Z

Dec.	15°			16°			17°			18°			19°			20°			21°			22°			Dec.
	Hc	d	Z	Hc	d	Z	Hc	d	Z	Hc	d	Z	Hc	d	Z	Hc	d	Z	Hc	d	Z	Hc	d	Z	
°	° ′	′	°	° ′	′	°	° ′	′	°	° ′	′	°	° ′	′	°	° ′	′	°	° ′	′	°	° ′	′	°	°
0	7 43.5	+15.6	92.1	7 41.3	+16.6	92.2	7 38.9	+17.6	92.4	7 36.4	+18.6	92.5	7 33.7	+19.6	92.6	7 30.9	+20.6	92.8	7 27.9	+21.7	92.9	7 24.8	+22.7	93.0	0
1	7 59.1	+15.5	91.1	7 57.9	+16.5	91.2	7 56.5	+17.5	91.4	7 55.0	+18.5	91.5	7 53.3	+19.5	91.7	7 51.5	+20.5	91.8	7 49.6	+21.5	91.9	7 47.5	+22.4	92.1	1
2	8 14.6	+15.3	90.1	8 14.4	+16.3	90.3	8 14.0	+17.4	90.4	8 13.5	+18.4	90.6	8 12.8	+19.4	90.7	8 12.0	+20.4	90.9	8 11.1	+21.3	91.0	8 09.9	+22.4	91.1	2
3	8 29.9	+15.2	89.2	8 30.7	+16.2	89.3	8 31.4	+17.2	89.5	8 31.9	+18.2	89.6	8 32.2	+19.3	89.8	8 32.4	+20.2	89.9	8 32.4	+21.3	90.1	8 32.3	+22.2	90.2	3
4	8 45.1	+15.0	88.2	8 46.9	+16.1	88.3	8 48.6	+17.1	88.5	8 50.1	+18.1	88.6	8 51.5	+19.1	88.8	8 52.6	+20.1	89.0	8 53.7	+21.0	89.1	8 54.5	+22.1	89.3	4
5	9 00.1	+14.9	87.2	9 03.0	+15.9	87.4	9 05.7	+16.9	87.5	9 08.2	+17.9	87.7	9 10.6	+18.9	87.8	9 12.7	+20.0	88.0	9 14.7	+21.0	88.2	9 16.6	+21.9	88.3	5
6	9 15.0	+14.7	86.2	9 18.9	+15.7	86.4	9 22.6	+16.8	86.5	9 26.1	+17.8	86.7	9 29.5	+18.8	86.9	9 32.7	+19.8	87.0	9 35.7	+20.8	87.2	9 38.5	+21.8	87.4	6
7	9 29.7	+14.6	85.2	9 34.6	+15.6	85.4	9 39.4	+16.5	85.6	9 43.9	+17.6	85.7	9 48.3	+18.6	85.9	9 52.5	+19.6	86.1	9 56.5	+20.6	86.3	10 00.3	+21.6	86.4	7
8	9 44.3	+14.4	84.2	9 50.2	+15.4	84.4	9 55.9	+16.5	84.6	10 01.5	+17.4	84.8	10 06.9	+18.4	84.9	10 12.1	+19.4	85.1	10 17.1	+20.4	85.3	10 21.9	+21.4	85.5	8
9	9 58.7	+14.2	83.3	10 05.6	+15.2	83.4	10 12.4	+16.2	83.6	10 18.9	+17.3	83.8	10 25.3	+18.3	84.0	10 31.5	+19.3	84.2	10 37.5	+20.3	84.3	10 43.3	+21.3	84.5	9
10	10 12.9	+14.0	82.3	10 20.8	+15.1	82.5	10 28.6	+16.1	82.6	10 36.2	+17.1	82.8	10 43.6	+18.1	83.0	10 50.8	+19.1	83.2	10 57.8	+20.1	83.4	11 04.6	+21.1	83.6	10
11	10 26.9	+13.8	81.3	10 35.9	+14.8	81.5	10 44.7	+15.9	81.7	10 53.3	+16.9	81.8	11 01.7	+17.9	82.0	11 09.9	+18.9	82.2	11 17.9	+19.9	82.4	11 25.7	+20.9	82.6	11
12	10 40.7	+13.7	80.3	10 50.7	+14.7	80.5	11 00.6	+15.7	80.7	11 10.2	+16.7	80.9	11 19.6	+17.7	81.1	11 28.8	+18.7	81.3	11 37.8	+19.7	81.5	11 46.6	+20.7	81.7	12
13	10 54.4	+13.5	79.3	11 05.4	+14.5	79.5	11 16.3	+15.5	79.7	11 26.9	+16.5	79.9	11 37.3	+17.5	80.1	11 47.5	+18.6	80.3	11 57.5	+19.6	80.5	12 07.3	+20.6	80.7	13
14	11 07.9	+13.2	78.3	11 19.9	+14.3	78.5	11 31.8	+15.3	78.7	11 43.4	+16.3	78.9	11 54.8	+17.4	79.1	12 06.1	+18.3	79.3	12 17.1	+19.3	79.5	12 27.9	+20.3	79.8	14
15	11 21.1	+13.1	77.3	11 34.2	+14.1	77.5	11 47.1	+15.1	77.7	11 59.7	+16.1	77.9	12 12.2	+17.1	78.1	12 24.4	+18.1	78.3	12 36.4	+19.1	78.6	12 48.2	+20.1	78.8	15
16	11 34.2	+12.9	76.3	11 48.3	+13.9	76.5	12 02.2	+14.8	76.7	12 15.8	+15.9	76.9	12 29.3	+16.9	77.2	12 42.5	+17.9	77.4	12 55.5	+18.9	77.6	13 08.3	+19.9	77.8	16
17	11 47.1	+12.6	75.3	12 02.2	+13.6	75.5	12 17.0	+14.7	75.7	12 31.7	+15.7	76.0	12 46.2	+16.6	76.2	13 00.4	+17.7	76.4	13 14.4	+18.7	76.6	13 28.2	+19.6	76.9	17
18	11 59.7	+12.5	74.3	12 15.8	+13.5	74.5	12 31.7	+14.5	74.7	12 47.4	+15.4	75.0	13 02.8	+16.5	75.2	13 18.1	+17.4	75.4	13 33.1	+18.4	75.6	13 47.8	+19.5	75.9	18
19	12 12.2	+12.2	73.3	12 29.3	+13.2	73.5	12 46.2	+14.2	73.8	13 02.8	+15.3	74.0	13 19.3	+16.2	74.2	13 35.5	+17.2	74.4	13 51.5	+18.2	74.7	14 07.3	+19.1	74.9	19
20	12 24.4	+12.0	72.3	12 42.5	+13.0	72.5	13 00.4	+14.0	72.8	13 18.1	+15.0	73.0	13 35.5	+16.0	73.2	13 52.7	+17.0	73.4	14 09.7	+18.0	73.7	14 26.4	+19.0	73.9	20
21	12 36.4	+11.8	71.3	12 55.5	+12.8	71.5	13 14.4	+13.8	71.8	13 33.1	+14.7	72.0	13 51.5	+15.8	72.2	14 09.7	+16.7	72.5	14 27.7	+17.7	72.7	14 45.4	+18.7	72.9	21
22	12 48.2	+11.5	70.3	13 08.3	+12.5	70.5	13 28.2	+13.5	70.8	13 47.8	+14.5	71.0	14 07.3	+15.5	71.2	14 26.4	+16.5	71.5	14 45.4	+17.5	71.7	15 04.1	+18.5	72.0	22
23	12 59.7	+11.3	69.3	13 20.8	+12.3	69.5	13 41.7	+13.3	69.8	14 02.3	+14.3	70.0	14 22.8	+15.2	70.2	14 42.9	+16.3	70.5	15 02.9	+17.2	70.7	15 22.6	+18.1	71.0	23
24	13 11.0	+11.1	68.3	13 33.1	+12.1	68.5	13 55.0	+13.0	68.8	14 16.6	+14.0	69.0	14 38.0	+15.0	69.2	14 59.2	+15.9	69.5	15 20.1	+16.9	69.7	15 40.7	+18.0	70.0	24
25	13 22.1	+10.9	67.3	13 45.2	+11.8	67.5	14 08.0	+12.8	67.7	14 30.6	+13.8	68.0	14 53.0	+14.7	68.2	15 15.1	+15.7	68.5	15 37.0	+16.7	68.7	15 58.7	+17.6	69.0	25
26	13 33.0	+10.6	66.3	13 57.0	+11.6	66.5	14 20.8	+12.5	66.7	14 44.4	+13.5	67.0	15 07.7	+14.5	67.2	15 30.8	+15.5	67.5	15 53.7	+16.4	67.7	16 16.3	+17.4	68.0	26
27	13 43.6	+10.3	65.3	14 08.6	+11.3	65.5	14 33.3	+12.3	65.7	14 57.9	+13.2	66.0	15 22.2	+14.2	66.2	15 46.3	+15.1	66.5	16 10.1	+16.1	66.7	16 33.7	+17.1	67.0	27
28	13 53.9	+10.1	64.3	14 19.9	+11.0	64.5	14 45.6	+12.0	64.7	15 11.1	+13.0	65.0	15 36.4	+13.9	65.2	16 01.4	+14.9	65.5	16 26.2	+15.9	65.7	16 50.8	+16.8	66.0	28
29	14 04.0	+9.9	63.2	14 30.9	+10.8	63.5	14 57.6	+11.8	63.7	15 24.1	+12.7	63.9	15 50.3	+13.7	64.2	16 16.3	+14.6	64.5	16 42.1	+15.5	64.7	17 07.6	+16.4	65.0	29
30	14 13.9	+9.5	62.2	14 41.7	+10.5	62.4	15 09.4	+11.4	62.7	15 36.8	+12.4	62.9	16 04.0	+13.3	63.2	16 30.9	+14.3	63.4	16 57.6	+15.3	63.7	17 24.0	+16.2	64.0	30
31	14 23.4	+9.4	61.2	14 52.2	+10.3	61.4	15 20.8	+11.2	61.7	15 49.2	+12.1	61.9	16 17.3	+13.1	62.2	16 45.2	+14.0	62.4	17 12.9	+14.9	62.7	17 40.2	+15.9	63.0	31
32	14 32.8	+9.0	60.2	15 02.5	+10.0	60.4	15 32.0	+10.9	60.6	16 01.3	+11.8	60.9	16 30.4	+12.7	61.2	16 59.2	+13.7	61.4	17 27.8	+14.6	61.7	17 56.1	+15.6	62.0	32
33	14 41.8	+8.8	59.2	15 12.5	+9.7	59.4	15 42.9	+10.6	59.6	16 13.1	+11.6	59.9	16 43.1	+12.5	60.1	17 12.9	+13.4	60.4	17 42.4	+14.3	60.7	18 11.7	+15.2	61.0	33
34	14 50.6	+8.5	58.1	15 22.2	+9.4	58.4	15 53.5	+10.4	58.6	16 24.7	+11.2	58.9	16 55.6	+12.2	59.1	17 26.3	+13.1	59.4	17 56.7	+14.0	59.6	18 26.9	+14.9	59.9	34
35	14 59.1	+8.3	57.1	15 31.6	+9.1	57.3	16 03.9	+10.0	57.6	16 35.9	+11.0	57.8	17 07.8	+11.8	58.1	17 39.4	+12.7	58.4	18 10.7	+13.7	58.6	18 41.8	+14.6	58.9	35
36	15 07.4	+7.9	56.1	15 40.7	+8.9	56.3	16 13.9	+9.8	56.6	16 46.9	+10.6	56.8	17 19.6	+11.6	57.1	17 52.1	+12.5	57.3	18 24.4	+13.3	57.6	18 56.4	+14.3	57.9	36
37	15 15.3	+7.7	55.1	15 49.6	+8.6	55.3	16 23.7	+9.4	55.5	16 57.5	+10.3	55.8	17 31.2	+11.2	56.0	18 04.6	+12.1	56.3	18 37.7	+13.0	56.6	19 10.7	+13.9	56.9	37
38	15 23.0	+7.4	54.0	15 58.2	+8.2	54.3	16 33.1	+9.1	54.5	17 07.8	+10.1	54.7	17 42.4	+10.9	55.0	18 16.7	+11.7	55.3	18 50.7	+12.7	55.5	19 24.6	+13.5	55.8	38
39	15 30.4	+7.1	53.0	16 06.4	+8.0	53.2	16 42.2	+8.9	53.5	17 17.9	+9.7	53.7	17 53.3	+10.5	54.0	18 28.4	+11.5	54.2	19 03.4	+12.3	54.5	19 38.1	+13.2	54.8	39
40	15 37.5	+6.8	52.0	16 14.4	+7.7	52.2	16 51.1	+8.5	52.4	17 27.6	+9.3	52.7	18 03.8	+10.3	52.9	18 39.9	+11.1	53.2	19 15.7	+12.0	53.5	19 51.3	+12.8	53.8	40
41	15 44.3	+6.6	50.9	16 22.1	+7.3	51.2	16 59.6	+8.2	51.4	17 36.9	+9.1	51.6	18 14.1	+9.9	51.9	18 51.0	+10.7	52.2	19 27.7	+11.6	52.4	20 04.1	+12.5	52.7	41
42	15 50.9	+6.2	49.9	16 29.4	+7.1	50.1	17 07.8	+7.9	50.4	17 46.0	+8.7	50.6	18 24.0	+9.5	50.9	19 01.7	+10.4	51.1	19 39.3	+11.2	51.4	20 16.6	+12.1	51.7	42
43	15 57.1	+6.0	48.9	16 36.5	+6.7	49.1	17 15.7	+7.6	49.3	17 54.7	+8.4	49.6	18 33.5	+9.2	49.8	19 12.1	+10.1	50.1	19 50.5	+10.9	50.3	20 28.7	+11.7	50.6	43
44	16 03.1	+5.6	47.8	16 43.2	+6.5	48.1	17 23.3	+7.2	48.3	18 03.1	+8.1	48.5	18 42.7	+8.9	48.8	19 22.2	+9.7	49.0	20 01.4	+10.5	49.3	20 40.4	+11.4	49.6	44
45	16 08.7	+5.3	46.8	16 49.7	+6.1	47.0	17 30.5	+6.9	47.2	18 11.2	+7.7	47.5	18 51.6	+8.5	47.7	19 31.9	+9.3	48.0	20 11.9	+10.2	48.3	20 51.8	+10.9	48.5	45
46	16 14.0	+5.1	45.8	16 55.8	+5.8	46.0	17 37.4	+6.6	46.2	18 18.9	+7.4	46.4	19 00.1	+8.2	46.7	19 41.2	+9.0	46.9	20 22.1	+9.7	47.2	21 02.7	+10.6	47.5	46
47	16 19.1	+4.7	44.7	17 01.6	+5.5	44.9	17 44.0	+6.3	45.2	18 26.3	+7.0	45.4	19 08.3	+7.8	45.6	19 50.2	+8.6	45.9	20 31.8	+9.4	46.2	21 13.3	+10.2	46.4	47
48	16 23.8	+4.5	43.7	17 07.1	+5.2	43.9	17 50.3	+5.9	44.1	18 33.3	+6.7	44.3	19 16.1	+7.5	44.6	19 58.8	+8.2	44.8	20 41.2	+9.0	45.1	21 23.5	+9.7	45.4	48
49	16 28.3	+4.1	42.6	17 12.3	+4.9	42.9	17 56.2	+5.6	43.1	18 40.0	+6.3	43.3	19 23.6	+7.0	43.5	20 07.0	+7.8	43.8	20 50.2	+8.6	44.0	21 33.2	+9.4	44.3	49
50	16 32.4	+3.8	41.6	17 17.2	+4.5	41.8	18 01.8	+5.3	42.0	18 46.3	+6.0	42.2	19 30.6	+6.8	42.5	20 14.8	+7.5	42.7	20 58.8	+8.2	43.0	21 42.6	+9.0	43.2	50
51	16 36.2	+3.5	40.6	17 21.7	+4.2	40.8	18 07.1	+4.9	41.0	18 52.3	+5.6	41.2	19 37.4	+6.3	41.4	20 22.3	+7.1	41.7	21 07.0	+7.8	41.9	21 51.6	+8.5	42.2	51
52	16 39.7	+3.2	39.5	17 25.9	+3.9	39.7	18 12.0	+4.6	39.9	18 57.9	+5.3	40.1	19 43.7	+6.0	40.4	20 29.4	+6.6	40.6	21 14.8	+7.4	40.9	22 00.1	+8.2	41.1	52
53	16 42.9	+2.9	38.5	17 29.8	+3.5	38.7	18 16.6	+4.2	38.9	19 03.2	+4.9	39.1	19 49.7	+5.6	39.3	20 36.0	+6.4	39.5	21 22.2	+7.0	39.8	22 08.3	+7.7	40.0	53
54	16 45.8	+2.5	37.4	17 33.3	+3.3	37.6	18 20.8	+3.9	37.8	19 08.1	+4.6	38.0	19 55.3	+5.2	38.3	20 42.4	+5.9	38.5	21 29.2	+6.6	38.7	22 16.0	+7.3	39.0	54
55	16 48.3	+2.3	36.4	17 36.6	+2.8	36.6	18 24.7	+3.5	36.8	19 12.7	+4.2	37.0	20 00.5	+4.9	37.2	20 48.3	+5.5	37.4	21 35.8	+6.2	37.7	22 23.3	+6.8	37.9	55
56	16 50.6	+1.9	35.3	17 39.4	+2.6	35.5	18 28.2	+3.2	35.7	19 16.9	+3.8	35.9	20 05.4	+4.5	36.1	20 53.8	+5.1	36.4	21 42.0	+5.8	36.6	22 30.1	+6.5	36.8	56
57	16 52.5	+1.6	34.3	17 42.0	+2.2	34.5	18 31.4	+2.8	34.7	19 20.7	+3.4	34.9	20 09.9	+4.0	35.1	20 58.9	+4.7	35.3	21 47.8	+5.4	35.5	22 36.6	+6.0	35.7	57
58	16 54.1	+1.3	33.3	17 44.2	+1.9	33.4	18 34.2	+2.5	33.6	19 24.1	+3.1	33.8	20 13.9	+3.8	34.0	21 03.6	+4.3	34.2	21 53.2	+4.9	34.4	22 42.6	+5.6	34.7	58
59	16 55.4	+1.0	32.2	17 46.1	+1.6	32.4	18 36.7	+2.2	32.6	19 27.2	+2.8	32.7	20 17.7	+3.3	32.9	21 07.9	+4.0	33.1	21 58.1	+4.5	33.4	22 48.2	+5.1	33.6	59
60	16 56.4	+0.6	31.2	17 47.7	+1.2	31.3	18 38.9	+1.7	31.5	19 30.0	+2.3	31.7	20 21.0	+2.9	31.9	21 11.9	+3.5	32.1	22 02.6	+4.2	32.3	22 53.3	+4.7	32.5	60
61	16 57.0	+0.4	30.1	17 48.9	+0.9	30.3	18 40.6	+1.5	30.4	19 32.3	+2.0	30.6	20 23.9	+2.5	30.8	21 15.4	+3.1	31.0	22 06.8	+3.6	31.2	22 58.0	+4.3	31.4	61
62	16 57.4	0.0	29.1	17 49.8	+0.5	29.2	18 42.1	+1.0	29.4	19 34.3	+1.6	29.6	20 26.4	+2.2	29.7	21 18.5	+2.7	29.9	22 10.4	+3.3	30.1	23 02.3	+3.8	30.3	62
63	16 57.4	-0.3	28.0	17 50.3	+0.2	28.2	18 43.1	+0.8	28.3	19 35.9	+1.2	28.5	20 28.6	+1.8	28.7	21 21.2	+2.3	28.9	22 13.7	+2.8	29.1	23 06.1	+3.4	29.3	63
64	16 57.1	-0.7	27.0	17 50.5	-0.1	27.1	18 43.9	+0.3	27.3	19 37.1	+0.9	27.4	20 30.4	+1.3	27.6	21 23.5	+1.9	27.8	22 16.5	+2.4	28.0	23 09.5	+2.9	28.2	64
65	16 56.4	-0.9	25.9	17 50.4	-0.5	26.1	18 44.2	0.0	26.2	19 38.0	+0.5	26.4	20 31.7	+1.0	26.5	21 25.4	+1.4	26.7	22 18.9	+2.0	26.9	23 12.4	+2.5	27.1	65
66	16 55.5	-1.3	24.9	17 49.9	-0.8	25.0	18 44.2	-0.3	25.2	19 38.5	+0.1	25.3	20 32.7	+0.6	25.5	21 26.8	+1.1	25.6	22 20.9	+1.5	25.8	23 14.9	+2.0	26.0	66
67	16 54.2	-1.5	23.9	17 49.1	-1.1	24.0	18 43.9	-0.7	24.1	19 38.6	-0.2	24.3	20 33.3	+0.2	24.4	21 27.9	+0.6	24.6	22 22.4	+1.1	24.7	23 16.9	+1.6	24.9	67
68	16 52.7	-1.9	22.8	17 48.0	-1.5	22.9	18 43.2	-1.1	23.1	19 38.4	-0.7	23.2	20 33.5	-0.2	23.3	21 28.5	+0.3	23.5	22 23.5	+0.7	23.7	23 18.5	+1.1	23.8	68
69	16 50.8	-2.2	21.8	17 46.5	-1.8	21.9	18 42.1	-1.4	22.0	19 37.7	-1.0	22.1	20 33.3	-0.6	22.3	21 28.8	-0.2	22.4	22 24.2	+0.3	22.6	23 19.6	+0.7	22.7	69
70	16 48.6	-2.6	20.7	17 44.7	-2.2	20.8	18 40.7	-1.7	20.9	19 36.7	-1.3	21.1	20 32.7	-1.0	21.2	21 28.6	-0.6	21.3	22 24.5	-0.2	21.5	23 20.3	+0.2	21.6	70
71	16 46.0	-2.8	19.7	17 42.5	-2.5	19.8	18 39.0	-2.2	19.9	19 35.4	-1.8	20.0	20 31.7	-1.4	20.1	21 28.0	-1.0	20.3	22 24.3	-0.6	20.4	23 20.5	-0.2	20.6	71
72	16 43.2	-3.2	18.6	17 40.0	-2.8	18.7	18 36.8	-2.4	18.8	19 33.6	-2.1	19.0	20 30.3	-1.7	19.1	21 27.0	-1.4	19.2	22 23.7	-1.1	19.3	23 20.3	-0.7	19.5	72
73	16 40.0	-3.4	17.6	17 37.2	-3.1	17.7	18 34.4	-2.9	17.8	19 31.5	-2.5	17.9	20 28.6	-2.2	18.0	21 25.6	-1.8	18.1	22 22.6	-1.5	18.2	23 19.6	-1.2	18.4	73
74	16 36.6	-3.8	16.5	17 34.1	-3.5	16.6	18 31.5	-3.1	16.7	19 29.0	-2.9	16.8	20 26.4	-2.5	16.9	21 23.8	-2.2	17.0	22 21.1	-1.9	17.2	23 18.4	-1.5	17.3	74
75	16 32.8	-4.1	15.5	17 30.6	-3.8	15.6	18 28.4	-3.5	15.7	19 26.1	-3.2	15.8	20 23.9	-3.0	15.9	21 21.6	-2.7	16.0	22 19.2	-2.3	16.1	23 16.9	-2.1	16.2	75
76	16 28.7	-4.4	14.5	17 26.8	-4.1	14.5	18 24.9	-3.9	14.6	19 22.9	-3.6	14.7	20 20.9	-3.3	14.8	21 18.9	-3.0	14.9	22 16.9	-2.8	15.0	23 14.8	-2.5	15.1	76
77	16 24.3	-4.7	13.4	17 22.7	-4.5	13.5	18 21.0	-4.2	13.6	19 19.3	-4.0	13.7	20 17.6	-3.7	13.7	21 15.9	-3.5	13.8	22 14.1	-3.2	13.9	23 12.3	-2.9	14.0	77
78	16 19.6	-5.0	12.4	17 18.2	-4.8	12.5	18 16.8	-4.6	12.5	19 15.3	-4.3	12.6	20 13.9	-4.1	12.7	21 12.4	-3.8	12.8	22 10.9	-3.6	12.8	23 09.4	-3.4	12.9	78
79	16 14.6	-5.3	11.4	17 13.4	-5.1	11.4	18 12.2	-4.9	11.5	19 11.0	-4.7	11.5	20 09.8	-4.5	11.6	21 08.6	-4.3	11.7	22 07.3	-4.0	11.8	23 06.0	-3.8	11.9	79
80	16 09.3	-5.6	10.3	17 08.3	-5.4	10.4	18 07.3	-5.2	10.4	19 06.3	-5.0	10.5	20 05.3	-4.8	10.6	21 04.3	-4.7	10.6	22 03.3	-4.5	10.7	23 02.2	-4.3	10.8	80
81	16 03.7	-5.9	9.3	17 02.9	-5.8	9.3	18 02.1	-5.6	9.4	19 01.3	-5.4	9.4	20 00.5	-5.3	9.5	20 59.6	-5.0	9.6	21 58.8	-4.9	9.6	22 57.9	-4.7	9.7	81
82	15 57.8	-6.3	8.2	16 57.1	-6.0	8.3	17 56.5	-5.9	8.3	18 55.9	-5.8	8.4	19 55.2	-5.6	8.4	20 54.6	-5.5	8.5	21 53.9	-5.3	8.5	22 53.2	-5.1	8.6	82
83	15 51.5	-6.5	7.2	16 51.1	-6.4	7.2	17 50.6	-6.3	7.3	18 50.1	-6.1	7.3	19 49.6	-6.0	7.4	20 49.1	-5.8	7.4	21 48.6	-5.7	7.5	22 48.1	-5.6	7.5	83
84	15 45.0	-6.7	6.2	16 44.7	-6.7	6.2	17 44.3	-6.5	6.2	18 44.0	-6.5	6.3	19 43.6	-6.3	6.3	20 43.3	-6.3	6.4	21 42.9	-6.1	6.4	22 42.5	-6.0	6.4	84
85	15 38.3	-7.1	5.1	16 38.0	-7.0	5.2	17 37.8	-6.9	5.2	18 37.5	-6.8	5.2	19 37.3	-6.8	5.3	20 37.0	-6.6	5.3	21 36.8	-6.6	5.3	22 36.5	-6.5	5.4	85
86	15 31.2	-7.4	4.1	16 31.0	-7.3	4.1	17 30.9	-7.3	4.2	18 30.7	-7.2	4.2	19 30.5	-7.1	4.2	20 30.4	-7.0	4.2	21 30.2	-6.9	4.3	22 30.0	-6.8	4.3	86
87	15 23.8	-7.7	3.1	16 23.7	-7.6	3.1	17 23.6	-7.5	3.1	18 23.5	-7.5	3.1	19 23.4	-7.4	3.1	20 23.4	-7.5	3.2	21 23.3	-7.4	3.2	22 23.2	-7.3	3.2	87
88	15 16.1	-7.9	2.1	16 16.1	-7.9	2.1	17 16.1	-7.9	2.1	18 16.0	-7.8	2.1	19 16.0	-7.8	2.1	20 15.9	-7.7	2.1	21 15.9	-7.7	2.1	22 15.9	-7.8	2.1	88
89	15 08.2	-8.2	1.0	16 08.2	-8.2	1.0	17 08.2	-8.2	1.0	18 08.2	-8.2	1.0	19 08.2	-8.2	1.0	20 08.2	-8.2	1.1	21 08.2	-8.2	1.1	22 08.1	-8.1	1.1	89
90	15 00.0	-8.5	0.0	16 00.0	-8.5	0.0	17 00.0	-8.5	0.0	18 00.0	-8.5	0.0	19 00.0	-8.5	0.0	20 00.0	-8.5	0.0	21 00.0	-8.5	0.0	22 00.0	-8.6	0.0	90
	15°			16°			17°			18°			19°			20°			21°			22°			

82°, 278° L.H.A. LATITUDE SAME NAME AS DECLINATION

LATITUDE CONTRARY NAME TO DECLINATION L.H.A. 82°, 278°

Dec.	15°			16°			17°			18°		
°	Hc ° ′	d ′	Z °	Hc ° ′	d ′	Z °	Hc ° ′	d ′	Z °	Hc ° ′	d ′	Z °
0	7 43.5	−15.7	92.1	7 41.3	−16.8	92.2	7 38.9	−17.8	92.4	7 36.4	−18.8	92.5
1	7 27.8	−15.9	93.1	7 24.5	−16.8	93.2	7 21.1	−17.9	93.3	7 17.6	−18.9	93.4
2	7 11.9	−15.9	94.0	7 07.7	−17.0	94.2	7 03.2	−18.0	94.3	6 58.7	−19.0	94.4
3	6 56.0	−16.2	95.0	6 50.7	−17.2	95.1	6 45.2	−18.1	95.2	6 39.7	−19.1	95.4
4	6 39.8	−16.2	96.0	6 33.5	−17.2	96.1	6 27.1	−18.2	96.2	6 20.6	−19.2	96.3
5	6 23.6	−16.3	96.9	6 16.3	−17.3	97.0	6 08.9	−18.3	97.2	6 01.4	−19.3	97.3
6	6 07.3	−16.4	97.9	5 59.0	−17.4	98.0	5 50.6	−18.4	98.1	5 42.1	−19.5	98.2
7	5 50.9	−16.6	98.9	5 41.6	−17.6	99.0	5 32.2	−18.6	99.1	5 22.6	−19.5	99.2
8	5 34.3	−16.6	99.8	5 24.0	−17.6	99.9	5 13.6	−18.6	100.0	5 03.1	−19.5	100.1
9	5 17.7	−16.7	100.8	5 06.4	−17.7	100.9	4 55.0	−18.7	101.0	4 43.6	−19.7	101.1
10	5 01.0	−16.8	101.8	4 48.7	−17.8	101.9	4 36.3	−18.7	101.9	4 23.9	−19.7	102.0
11	4 44.2	−16.9	102.7	4 30.9	−17.8	102.8	4 17.6	−18.8	102.9	4 04.2	−19.8	103.0
12	4 27.3	−16.9	103.7	4 13.1	−18.0	103.8	3 58.8	−18.9	103.8	3 44.4	−19.9	103.9
13	4 10.4	−17.1	104.7	3 55.1	−17.9	104.7	3 39.9	−19.0	104.8	3 24.5	−19.9	104.9
14	3 53.3	−17.1	105.6	3 37.2	−18.1	105.7	3 20.9	−19.0	105.7	3 04.6	−20.0	105.8
15	3 36.2	−17.1	106.6	3 19.1	−18.1	106.6	3 01.9	−19.1	106.7	2 44.6	−20.0	106.7
16	3 19.1	−17.2	107.5	3 01.0	−18.2	107.6	2 42.8	−19.1	107.6	2 24.6	−20.0	107.7
17	3 01.9	−17.3	108.5	2 42.8	−18.2	108.5	2 23.7	−19.1	108.6	2 04.6	−20.1	108.6
18	2 44.6	−17.3	109.5	2 24.6	−18.2	109.5	2 04.6	−19.2	109.5	1 44.5	−20.1	109.6
19	2 27.3	−17.3	110.4	2 06.4	−18.3	110.5	1 45.4	−19.2	110.5	1 24.4	−20.1	110.5
20	2 10.0	−17.4	111.4	1 48.1	−18.3	111.4	1 26.2	−19.2	111.4	1 04.3	−20.2	111.5
21	1 52.6	−17.4	112.3	1 29.8	−18.3	112.4	1 07.0	−19.3	112.4	0 44.1	−20.2	112.4
22	1 35.2	−17.4	113.3	1 11.5	−18.4	113.3	0 47.7	−19.3	113.3	0 23.9	−20.1	113.3
23	1 17.8	−17.5	114.2	0 53.1	−18.4	114.3	0 28.4	−19.2	114.3	0 03.8	−20.2	114.3
24	1 00.3	−17.5	115.2	0 34.7	−18.3	115.2	0 09.2	−19.3	115.2	0 16.4	+20.2	64.8
25	0 42.8	−17.5	116.2	0 16.4	−18.4	116.2	0 10.1	+19.3	63.8	0 36.6	+20.1	63.8
26	0 25.3	−17.5	117.1	0 02.0	+18.4	62.9	0 29.4	+19.2	62.9	0 56.7	+20.2	62.9
27	0 07.8	−17.5	118.1	0 20.4	+18.4	61.9	0 48.6	+19.3	61.9	1 16.9	+20.1	62.0
28	0 09.7	+17.5	61.0	0 38.8	+18.3	61.0	1 07.9	+19.2	61.0	1 37.0	+20.1	61.0
29	0 27.2	+17.5	60.0	0 57.1	+18.4	60.0	1 27.1	+19.2	60.0	1 57.1	+20.0	60.1
30	0 44.7	+17.4	59.1	1 15.5	+18.3	59.1	1 46.3	+19.2	59.1	2 17.1	+20.1	59.1
31	1 02.1	+17.5	58.1	1 33.8	+18.3	58.1	2 05.5	+19.2	58.1	2 37.2	+19.9	58.2
32	1 19.6	+17.4	57.1	1 52.1	+18.3	57.2	2 24.7	+19.1	57.2	2 57.1	+20.0	57.2
33	1 37.0	+17.4	56.2	2 10.4	+18.2	56.2	2 43.8	+19.0	56.2	3 17.1	+19.9	56.3
34	1 54.4	+17.4	55.2	2 28.6	+18.2	55.3	3 02.8	+19.0	55.3	3 37.0	+19.8	55.3
35	2 11.8	+17.4	54.3	2 46.8	+18.2	54.3	3 21.8	+19.0	54.3	3 56.8	+19.7	54.4
36	2 29.2	+17.3	53.3	3 05.0	+18.1	53.4	3 40.8	+18.9	53.4	4 16.5	+19.7	53.5
37	2 46.5	+17.2	52.4	3 23.1	+18.0	52.4	3 59.7	+18.8	52.4	4 36.2	+19.6	52.5
38	3 03.7	+17.2	51.4	3 41.1	+18.0	51.4	4 18.5	+18.8	51.5	4 55.8	+19.6	51.6
39	3 20.9	+17.1	50.4	3 59.1	+17.9	50.5	4 37.3	+18.6	50.5	5 15.4	+19.4	50.6
40	3 38.0	+17.1	49.5	4 17.0	+17.9	49.5	4 55.9	+18.6	49.6	5 34.8	+19.4	49.7
41	3 55.1	+17.1	48.5	4 34.9	+17.7	48.6	5 14.5	+18.5	48.6	5 54.2	+19.2	48.7
42	4 12.2	+16.9	47.6	4 52.6	+17.7	47.6	5 33.0	+18.5	47.7	6 13.4	+19.2	47.8
43	4 29.1	+16.9	46.6	5 10.3	+17.6	46.7	5 51.5	+18.3	46.7	6 32.6	+19.0	46.8
44	4 46.0	+16.8	45.6	5 27.9	+17.5	45.7	6 09.8	+18.2	45.8	6 51.6	+18.9	45.8
45	5 02.8	+16.7	44.7	5 45.4	+17.4	44.7	6 28.0	+18.1	44.8	7 10.5	+18.9	44.9
46	5 19.5	+16.6	43.7	6 02.8	+17.3	43.8	6 46.1	+18.0	43.8	7 29.4	+18.7	43.9
47	5 36.1	+16.5	42.7	6 20.1	+17.2	42.8	7 04.1	+17.9	42.9	7 48.1	+18.5	43.0
48	5 52.6	+16.4	41.8	6 37.3	+17.1	41.8	7 22.0	+17.8	41.9	8 06.6	+18.4	42.0
49	6 09.0	+16.3	40.8	6 54.4	+17.0	40.9	7 39.8	+17.6	41.0	8 25.0	+18.3	41.1
50	6 25.3	+16.2	39.8	7 11.4	+16.8	39.9	7 57.4	+17.5	40.0	8 43.3	+18.2	40.1
51	6 41.5	+16.1	38.9	7 28.2	+16.8	38.9	8 14.9	+17.3	39.0	9 01.5	+17.9	39.1
52	6 57.6	+16.0	37.9	7 45.0	+16.6	38.0	8 32.2	+17.2	38.1	9 19.4	+17.9	38.2
53	7 13.6	+15.9	36.9	8 01.6	+16.4	37.0	8 49.4	+17.1	37.1	9 37.3	+17.6	37.2
54	7 29.5	+15.7	35.9	8 18.0	+16.3	36.0	9 06.5	+16.9	36.1	9 54.9	+17.5	36.2
55	7 45.2	+15.6	35.0	8 34.3	+16.2	35.1	9 23.4	+16.8	35.1	10 12.4	+17.4	35.2
56	8 00.8	+15.4	34.0	8 50.5	+16.0	34.1	9 40.2	+16.5	34.2	10 29.8	+17.1	34.3
57	8 16.2	+15.3	33.0	9 06.5	+15.9	33.1	9 56.7	+16.5	33.2	10 46.9	+17.0	33.3
58	8 31.5	+15.2	32.0	9 22.4	+15.7	32.1	10 13.2	+16.2	32.2	11 03.9	+16.8	32.3
59	8 46.7	+15.0	31.1	9 38.1	+15.5	31.2	10 29.4	+16.1	31.2	11 20.7	+16.6	31.3
60	9 01.7	+14.9	30.1	9 53.6	+15.4	30.2	10 45.5	+15.8	30.3	11 37.3	+16.3	30.4
61	9 16.6	+14.7	29.1	10 09.0	+15.2	29.2	11 01.3	+15.7	29.3	11 53.6	+16.2	29.4
62	9 31.3	+14.5	28.1	10 24.2	+15.0	28.2	11 17.0	+15.5	28.3	12 09.8	+16.0	28.4
63	9 45.8	+14.4	27.1	10 39.2	+14.8	27.2	11 32.5	+15.3	27.3	12 25.8	+15.8	27.4
64	10 00.2	+14.1	26.2	10 54.0	+14.6	26.2	11 47.8	+15.1	26.3	12 41.6	+15.5	26.4
65	10 14.3	+14.1	25.2	11 08.6	+14.5	25.2	12 02.9	+14.9	25.3	12 57.1	+15.3	25.4
66	10 28.4	+13.8	24.2	11 23.1	+14.2	24.3	12 17.8	+14.6	24.3	13 12.4	+15.1	24.4
67	10 42.2	+13.6	23.2	11 37.3	+14.1	23.3	12 32.4	+14.5	23.4	13 27.5	+14.8	23.4
68	10 55.8	+13.5	22.2	11 51.4	+13.8	22.3	12 46.9	+14.2	22.4	13 42.3	+14.6	22.4
69	11 09.3	+13.2	21.2	12 05.2	+13.6	21.3	13 01.1	+14.0	21.4	13 56.9	+14.4	21.4
70	11 22.5	+13.1	20.2	12 18.8	+13.4	20.3	13 15.1	+13.7	20.4	14 11.3	+14.1	20.4
71	11 35.6	+12.8	19.2	12 32.2	+13.2	19.3	13 28.8	+13.5	19.4	14 25.4	+13.9	19.4
72	11 48.4	+12.6	18.2	12 45.4	+12.9	18.3	13 42.3	+13.3	18.4	14 39.3	+13.6	18.4
73	12 01.0	+12.5	17.2	12 58.3	+12.8	17.3	13 55.6	+13.0	17.4	14 52.9	+13.3	17.4
74	12 13.5	+12.2	16.2	13 11.1	+12.4	16.3	14 08.6	+12.8	16.3	15 06.2	+13.1	16.4
75	12 25.7	+11.9	15.2	13 23.5	+12.3	15.3	14 21.4	+12.5	15.3	15 19.3	+12.8	15.4
76	12 37.6	+11.8	14.2	13 35.8	+12.0	14.3	14 33.9	+12.3	14.3	15 32.1	+12.5	14.4
77	12 49.4	+11.5	13.2	13 47.8	+11.8	13.3	14 46.2	+12.0	13.3	15 44.6	+12.2	13.4
78	13 00.9	+11.3	12.2	13 59.6	+11.5	12.3	14 58.2	+11.7	12.3	15 56.8	+12.0	12.4
79	13 12.2	+11.1	11.2	14 11.1	+11.2	11.2	15 09.9	+11.5	11.3	16 08.8	+11.6	11.3
80	13 23.3	+10.8	10.2	14 22.3	+11.0	10.2	15 21.4	+11.1	10.3	16 20.4	+11.4	10.3
81	13 34.1	+10.6	9.2	14 33.3	+10.8	9.2	15 32.5	+10.9	9.3	16 31.8	+11.0	9.3
82	13 44.7	+10.3	8.2	14 44.1	+10.4	8.2	15 43.4	+10.6	8.2	16 42.8	+10.8	8.3
83	13 55.0	+10.1	7.1	14 54.5	+10.2	7.2	15 54.0	+10.4	7.2	16 53.6	+10.4	7.2
84	14 05.1	+9.8	6.1	15 04.7	+9.9	6.2	16 04.4	+10.0	6.2	17 04.0	+10.1	6.2
85	14 14.9	+9.5	5.1	15 14.6	+9.7	5.1	16 14.4	+9.7	5.2	17 14.1	+9.9	5.2
86	14 24.4	+9.3	4.1	15 24.3	+9.3	4.1	16 24.1	+9.5	4.1	17 24.0	+9.5	4.2
87	14 33.7	+9.1	3.1	15 33.6	+9.1	3.1	16 33.6	+9.1	3.1	17 33.5	+9.1	3.1
88	14 42.8	+8.7	2.0	15 42.7	+8.8	2.1	16 42.7	+8.8	2.1	17 42.6	+8.9	2.1
89	14 51.5	+8.5	1.0	15 51.5	+8.5	1.0	16 51.5	+8.5	1.0	17 51.5	+8.5	1.0
90	15 00.0	+8.2	0.0	16 00.0	+8.2	0.0	17 00.0	+8.2	0.0	18 00.0	+8.2	0.0
	15°			16°			17°			18°		

Dec.	19°			20°			21°			22°		
°	Hc ° ′	d ′	Z °	Hc ° ′	d ′	Z °	Hc ° ′	d ′	Z °	Hc ° ′	d ′	Z °
0	7 33.7	−19.8	92.6	7 30.9	−20.8	92.8	7 27.9	−21.7	92.9	7 24.8	−22.7	93.0
1	7 13.9	−19.9	93.6	7 10.1	−20.9	93.7	7 06.2	−21.9	93.8	7 02.1	−22.8	93.9
2	6 54.0	−20.0	94.5	6 49.2	−20.9	94.6	6 44.3	−21.9	94.8	6 39.3	−23.0	94.9
3	6 34.0	−20.1	95.5	6 28.3	−21.1	95.6	6 22.4	−22.1	95.7	6 16.3	−23.0	95.8
4	6 13.9	−20.2	96.4	6 07.2	−21.2	96.5	6 00.3	−22.2	96.6	5 53.3	−23.1	96.7
5	5 53.7	−20.3	97.4	5 46.0	−21.3	97.5	5 38.1	−22.2	97.6	5 30.2	−23.2	97.7
6	5 33.4	−20.4	98.3	5 24.7	−21.4	98.4	5 15.9	−22.3	98.5	5 07.0	−23.3	98.6
7	5 13.0	−20.4	99.3	5 03.3	−21.4	99.3	4 53.6	−22.5	99.4	4 43.7	−23.4	99.5
8	4 52.6	−20.6	100.2	4 41.9	−21.5	100.3	4 31.1	−22.4	100.4	4 20.3	−23.4	100.4
9	4 32.0	−20.6	101.1	4 20.4	−21.6	101.2	4 08.7	−22.6	101.3	3 56.9	−23.5	101.4
10	4 11.4	−20.7	102.1	3 58.8	−21.7	102.2	3 46.1	−22.6	102.2	3 33.4	−23.6	102.3
11	3 50.7	−20.8	103.0	3 37.1	−21.7	103.1	3 23.5	−22.7	103.1	3 09.8	−23.6	103.2
12	3 29.9	−20.8	104.0	3 15.4	−21.8	104.0	3 00.8	−22.7	104.1	2 46.2	−23.6	104.1
13	3 09.1	−20.9	104.9	2 53.6	−21.8	105.0	2 38.1	−22.7	105.0	2 22.6	−23.7	105.0
14	2 48.2	−20.9	105.8	2 31.8	−21.8	105.9	2 15.4	−22.8	105.9	1 58.9	−23.7	106.0
15	2 27.3	−20.9	106.8	2 10.0	−21.9	106.8	1 52.6	−22.8	106.9	1 35.2	−23.7	106.9
16	2 06.4	−21.0	107.7	1 48.1	−21.9	107.8	1 29.8	−22.8	107.8	1 11.5	−23.8	107.8
17	1 45.4	−21.0	108.7	1 26.2	−21.9	108.7	1 07.0	−22.9	108.7	0 47.7	−23.8	108.7
18	1 24.4	−21.0	109.6	1 04.3	−22.0	109.6	0 44.1	−22.9	109.6	0 23.9	−23.7	109.6
19	1 03.4	−21.1	110.5	0 42.3	−22.0	110.5	0 21.2	−22.8	110.6	0 00.2	−23.8	110.6
20	0 42.3	−21.1	111.5	0 20.3	−21.9	111.5	0 01.6	+22.9	68.5	0 23.6	+23.8	68.5
21	0 21.2	−21.0	112.4	0 01.6	+22.0	67.6	0 24.5	+22.9	67.6	0 47.4	+23.7	67.6
22	0 00.2	−21.1	113.3	0 23.6	+22.0	66.7	0 47.4	+22.8	66.7	1 11.1	+23.8	66.7
23	0 20.9	+21.1	65.7	0 45.6	+21.9	65.7	1 10.2	+22.9	65.7	1 34.9	+23.7	65.8
24	0 42.0	+21.0	64.8	1 07.5	+22.0	64.8	1 33.1	+22.8	64.8	1 58.6	+23.6	64.8
25	1 03.0	+21.0	63.8	1 29.5	+21.9	63.9	1 55.9	+22.7	63.9	2 22.2	+23.7	63.9
26	1 24.0	+21.1	62.9	1 51.4	+21.8	62.9	2 18.6	+22.8	63.0	2 45.9	+23.6	63.0
27	1 45.1	+20.9	62.0	2 13.2	+21.9	62.0	2 41.4	+22.7	62.0	3 09.5	+23.5	62.1
28	2 06.0	+21.0	61.0	2 35.1	+21.8	61.1	3 04.1	+22.6	61.1	3 33.0	+23.5	61.2
29	2 27.0	+20.9	60.1	2 56.9	+21.7	60.1	3 26.7	+22.6	60.2	3 56.5	+23.5	60.2
30	2 47.9	+20.9	59.2	3 18.6	+21.7	59.2	3 49.3	+22.6	59.3	4 20.0	+23.3	59.3
31	3 08.8	+20.8	58.2	3 40.3	+21.7	58.3	4 11.9	+22.4	58.3	4 43.3	+23.3	58.4
32	3 29.6	+20.7	57.3	4 02.0	+21.6	57.3	4 34.3	+22.4	57.4	5 06.6	+23.3	57.5
33	3 50.3	+20.7	56.3	4 23.6	+21.5	56.4	4 56.7	+22.4	56.5	5 29.9	+23.1	56.5
34	4 11.0	+20.7	55.4	4 45.1	+21.4	55.5	5 19.1	+22.2	55.5	5 53.0	+23.0	55.6
35	4 31.7	+20.5	54.5	5 06.5	+21.4	54.5	5 41.3	+22.2	54.6	6 16.0	+23.0	54.7
36	4 52.2	+20.5	53.5	5 27.9	+21.2	53.6	6 03.5	+22.0	53.7	6 39.0	+22.8	53.8
37	5 12.7	+20.4	52.6	5 49.1	+21.2	52.7	6 25.5	+22.0	52.7	7 01.8	+22.7	52.8
38	5 33.1	+20.3	51.6	6 10.3	+21.1	51.7	6 47.5	+21.8	51.8	7 24.5	+22.6	51.9
39	5 53.4	+20.2	50.7	6 31.4	+21.0	50.8	7 09.3	+21.7	50.9	7 47.1	+22.5	51.0
40	6 13.6	+20.1	49.7	6 52.4	+20.8	49.8	7 31.0	+21.6	49.9	8 09.6	+22.4	50.0
41	6 33.7	+20.0	48.8	7 13.2	+20.8	48.9	7 52.6	+21.5	49.0	8 32.0	+22.2	49.1
42	6 53.7	+19.9	47.8	7 34.0	+20.6	47.9	8 14.1	+21.4	48.0	8 54.2	+22.1	48.1
43	7 13.6	+19.8	46.9	7 54.6	+20.5	47.0	8 35.5	+21.2	47.1	9 16.3	+21.9	47.2
44	7 33.4	+19.6	45.9	8 15.1	+20.3	46.0	8 56.7	+21.0	46.1	9 38.2	+21.8	46.3
45	7 53.0	+19.5	45.0	8 35.4	+20.2	45.1	9 17.7	+21.0	45.2	10 00.0	+21.6	45.3
46	8 12.5	+19.4	44.0	8 55.6	+20.1	44.1	9 38.7	+20.7	44.2	10 21.6	+21.4	44.4
47	8 31.9	+19.3	43.1	9 15.7	+19.9	43.2	9 59.4	+20.6	43.3	10 43.0	+21.3	43.4
48	8 51.2	+19.0	42.1	9 35.6	+19.8	42.2	10 20.0	+20.4	42.4	11 04.3	+21.1	42.5
49	9 10.2	+19.0	41.2	9 55.4	+19.6	41.3	10 40.4	+20.3	41.4	11 25.4	+20.9	41.5
50	9 29.2	+18.8	40.2	10 15.0	+19.4	40.3	11 00.7	+20.1	40.4	11 46.3	+20.7	40.6
51	9 48.0	+18.6	39.2	10 34.4	+19.3	39.3	11 20.8	+19.9	39.5	12 07.0	+20.6	39.6
52	10 06.6	+18.4	38.3	10 53.7	+19.0	38.4	11 40.7	+19.7	38.5	12 27.6	+20.3	38.6
53	10 25.0	+18.3	37.3	11 12.7	+18.9	37.4	12 00.4	+19.4	37.5	12 47.9	+20.1	37.7
54	10 43.3	+18.1	36.3	11 31.6	+18.7	36.4	12 19.8	+19.3	36.6	13 08.0	+19.9	36.7
55	11 01.4	+17.9	35.4	11 50.3	+18.5	35.5	12 39.1	+19.1	35.6	13 27.9	+19.6	35.7
56	11 19.3	+17.7	34.4	12 08.8	+18.3	34.5	12 58.2	+18.9	34.6	13 47.5	+19.5	34.8
57	11 37.0	+17.6	33.4	12 27.1	+18.1	33.5	13 17.1	+18.6	33.7	14 07.0	+19.2	33.8
58	11 54.6	+17.3	32.4	12 45.2	+17.8	32.5	13 35.7	+18.4	32.7	14 26.2	+18.9	32.8
59	12 11.9	+17.1	31.5	13 03.0	+17.7	31.6	13 54.1	+18.2	31.7	14 45.1	+18.7	31.8
60	12 29.0	+16.9	30.5	13 20.7	+17.4	30.6	14 12.3	+17.9	30.7	15 03.8	+18.5	30.8
61	12 45.9	+16.7	29.5	13 38.1	+17.2	29.6	14 30.2	+17.7	29.7	15 22.3	+18.2	29.9
62	13 02.6	+16.4	28.5	13 55.3	+16.9	28.6	14 47.9	+17.4	28.7	15 40.5	+17.9	28.9
63	13 19.0	+16.3	27.5	14 12.2	+16.7	27.6	15 05.3	+17.2	27.8	15 58.4	+17.7	27.9
64	13 35.3	+16.0	26.5	14 28.9	+16.5	26.6	15 22.5	+16.9	26.8	16 16.1	+17.3	26.9
65	13 51.3	+15.7	25.5	14 45.4	+16.2	25.6	15 39.4	+16.7	25.8	16 33.4	+17.1	25.9
66	14 07.0	+15.5	24.5	15 01.6	+15.9	24.6	15 56.1	+16.3	24.8	16 50.5	+16.8	24.9
67	14 22.5	+15.3	23.5	15 17.5	+15.7	23.6	16 12.4	+16.1	23.8	17 07.3	+16.5	23.9
68	14 37.8	+15.0	22.5	15 33.2	+15.4	22.6	16 28.5	+15.8	22.8	17 23.8	+16.2	22.9
69	14 52.8	+14.7	21.5	15 48.6	+15.1	21.6	16 44.3	+15.5	21.8	17 40.0	+15.9	21.9
70	15 07.5	+14.5	20.5	16 03.7	+14.8	20.6	16 59.8	+15.2	20.7	17 55.9	+15.6	20.9
71	15 22.0	+14.2	19.5	16 18.5	+14.6	19.6	17 15.0	+14.9	19.7	18 11.5	+15.2	19.8
72	15 36.2	+13.9	18.5	16 33.1	+14.2	18.6	17 29.9	+14.6	18.7	18 26.7	+14.9	18.8
73	15 50.1	+13.6	17.5	16 47.3	+14.0	17.6	17 44.5	+14.3	17.7	18 41.6	+14.6	17.8
74	16 03.7	+13.4	16.5	17 01.3	+13.6	16.6	17 58.8	+13.9	16.7	18 56.2	+14.3	16.8
75	16 17.1	+13.1	15.5	17 14.9	+13.4	15.6	18 12.7	+13.6	15.7	19 10.5	+13.9	15.7
76	16 30.2	+12.7	14.5	17 28.3	+13.0	14.5	18 26.3	+13.3	14.6	19 24.4	+13.5	14.7
77	16 42.9	+12.5	13.4	17 41.3	+12.7	13.5	18 39.6	+13.0	13.6	19 37.9	+13.2	13.7
78	16 55.4	+12.2	12.4	17 54.0	+12.4	12.5	18 52.6	+12.6	12.6	19 51.1	+12.9	12.6
79	17 07.6	+11.8	11.4	18 06.4	+12.0	11.5	19 05.2	+12.2	11.5	20 04.0	+12.4	11.6
80	17 19.4	+11.6	10.4	18 18.4	+11.8	10.4	19 17.4	+12.0	10.5	20 16.4	+12.1	10.6
81	17 31.0	+11.2	9.3	18 30.2	+11.4	9.4	19 29.4	+11.5	9.5	20 28.5	+11.8	9.5
82	17 42.2	+10.9	8.3	18 41.6	+11.0	8.4	19 40.9	+11.2	8.4	20 40.3	+11.3	8.5
83	17 53.1	+10.6	7.3	18 52.6	+10.7	7.3	19 52.1	+10.8	7.4	20 51.6	+11.0	7.4
84	18 03.7	+10.2	6.3	19 03.3	+10.4	6.3	20 02.9	+10.5	6.3	21 02.6	+10.5	6.4
85	18 13.9	+9.9	5.2	19 13.7	+9.9	5.2	20 13.4	+10.1	5.3	21 13.1	+10.2	5.3
86	18 23.8	+9.6	4.2	19 23.6	+9.7	4.2	20 23.5	+9.7	4.2	21 23.3	+9.8	4.3
87	18 33.4	+9.2	3.1	19 33.3	+9.3	3.2	20 33.2	+9.3	3.2	21 33.1	+9.4	3.2
88	18 42.6	+8.9	2.1	19 42.6	+8.9	2.1	20 42.5	+9.0	2.1	21 42.5	+8.9	2.1
89	18 51.5	+8.5	1.0	19 51.5	+8.5	1.1	20 51.5	+8.5	1.1	21 51.4	+8.6	1.1
90	19 00.0	+8.2	0.0	20 00.0	+8.2	0.0	21 00.0	+8.2	0.0	22 00.0	+8.1	0.0
	19°			20°			21°			22°		

S. Lat. {L.H.A. greater than 180° ....Zn=180°−Z; L.H.A. less than 180°...........Zn=180°+Z}

LATITUDE SAME NAME AS DECLINATION L.H.A. 98°, 262°

83°, 277° L.H.A. LATITUDE SAME NAME AS DECLINATION N. Lat. {L.H.A. greater than 180° .....Zn=Z; L.H.A. less than 180°............Zn=360°–Z

Dec.	15°			16°			17°			18°			19°			20°			21°			22°			Dec.
	Hc	d	Z	Hc	d	Z	Hc	d	Z	Hc	d	Z	Hc	d	Z	Hc	d	Z	Hc	d	Z	Hc	d	Z	
°	° ′	′	°	° ′	′	°	° ′	′	°	° ′	′	°	° ′	′	°	° ′	′	°	° ′	′	°	° ′	′	°	°
0	6 45.6	+15.6	91.8	6 43.7	+16.5	91.9	6 41.6	+17.6	92.1	6 39.3	+18.7	92.2	6 37.0	+19.6	92.3	6 34.6	+20.6	92.4	6 32.0	+21.6	92.5	6 29.3	+22.5	92.6	0
1	7 01.2	+15.5	90.8	7 00.2	+16.5	91.0	6 59.2	+17.5	91.1	6 58.0	+18.5	91.2	6 56.6	+19.5	91.3	6 55.2	+20.4	91.5	6 53.6	+21.4	91.6	6 51.8	+22.5	91.7	1
2	7 16.7	+15.3	89.9	7 16.7	+16.4	90.0	7 16.7	+17.3	90.1	7 16.5	+18.3	90.3	7 16.1	+19.4	90.4	7 15.6	+20.4	90.5	7 15.0	+21.4	90.6	7 14.3	+22.4	90.8	2
3	7 32.0	+15.2	88.9	7 33.1	+16.2	89.0	7 34.0	+17.3	89.2	7 34.8	+18.3	89.3	7 35.5	+19.2	89.4	7 36.0	+20.3	89.6	7 36.4	+21.3	89.7	7 36.7	+22.2	89.8	3
4	7 47.2	+15.1	87.9	7 49.3	+16.1	88.1	7 51.3	+17.1	88.2	7 53.1	+18.1	88.3	7 54.7	+19.2	88.5	7 56.3	+20.1	88.6	7 57.7	+21.1	88.8	7 58.9	+22.1	88.9	4
5	8 02.3	+14.9	86.9	8 05.4	+15.9	87.1	8 08.4	+16.9	87.2	8 11.2	+18.0	87.4	8 13.9	+19.0	87.5	8 16.4	+20.0	87.7	8 18.8	+20.9	87.8	8 21.0	+21.9	88.0	5
6	8 17.2	+14.8	86.0	8 21.3	+15.9	86.1	8 25.3	+16.9	86.3	8 29.2	+17.8	86.4	8 32.9	+18.8	86.6	8 36.4	+19.8	86.7	8 39.7	+20.9	86.9	8 42.9	+21.9	87.0	6
7	8 32.0	+14.6	85.0	8 37.2	+15.6	85.1	8 42.2	+16.6	85.3	8 47.0	+17.7	85.4	8 51.7	+18.7	85.6	8 56.2	+19.7	85.8	9 00.6	+20.7	85.9	9 04.8	+21.7	86.1	7
8	8 46.6	+14.5	84.0	8 52.8	+15.5	84.2	8 58.8	+16.6	84.3	9 04.7	+17.5	84.5	9 10.4	+18.5	84.6	9 15.9	+19.6	84.8	9 21.3	+20.5	85.0	9 26.5	+21.5	85.1	8
9	9 01.1	+14.4	83.0	9 08.3	+15.4	83.2	9 15.4	+16.3	83.3	9 22.2	+17.4	83.5	9 28.9	+18.4	83.7	9 35.5	+19.3	83.8	9 41.8	+20.4	84.0	9 48.0	+21.4	84.2	9
10	9 15.5	+14.1	82.0	9 23.7	+15.2	82.2	9 31.7	+16.2	82.4	9 39.6	+17.2	82.5	9 47.3	+18.2	82.7	9 54.8	+19.3	82.9	10 02.2	+20.2	83.1	10 09.4	+21.2	83.2	10
11	9 29.6	+14.0	81.1	9 38.9	+15.0	81.2	9 47.9	+16.1	81.4	9 56.8	+17.1	81.6	10 05.5	+18.1	81.7	10 14.1	+19.0	81.9	10 22.4	+20.1	82.1	10 30.6	+21.0	82.3	11
12	9 43.6	+13.9	80.1	9 53.9	+14.8	80.2	10 04.0	+15.8	80.4	10 13.9	+16.8	80.6	10 23.6	+17.9	80.8	10 33.1	+18.9	81.0	10 42.5	+19.8	81.1	10 51.6	+20.9	81.3	12
13	9 57.5	+13.6	79.1	10 08.7	+14.7	79.3	10 19.8	+15.7	79.4	10 30.7	+16.7	79.6	10 41.5	+17.7	79.8	10 52.0	+18.7	80.0	11 02.3	+19.7	80.2	11 12.5	+20.6	80.4	13
14	10 11.1	+13.5	78.1	10 23.4	+14.5	78.3	10 35.5	+15.5	78.5	10 47.4	+16.5	78.6	10 59.2	+17.5	78.8	11 10.7	+18.5	79.0	11 22.0	+19.5	79.2	11 33.1	+20.5	79.4	14
15	10 24.6	+13.3	77.1	10 37.9	+14.3	77.3	10 51.0	+15.3	77.5	11 03.9	+16.4	77.7	11 16.7	+17.3	77.9	11 29.2	+18.3	78.0	11 41.5	+19.3	78.2	11 53.6	+20.3	78.5	15
16	10 37.9	+13.1	76.1	10 52.2	+14.1	76.3	11 06.3	+15.2	76.5	11 20.3	+16.1	76.7	11 34.0	+17.1	76.9	11 47.5	+18.1	77.1	12 00.8	+19.1	77.3	12 13.9	+20.1	77.5	16
17	10 51.0	+12.9	75.1	11 06.3	+14.0	75.3	11 21.5	+14.9	75.5	11 36.4	+15.9	75.7	11 51.1	+16.9	75.9	12 05.6	+17.9	76.1	12 19.9	+18.9	76.3	12 34.0	+19.9	76.5	17
18	11 03.9	+12.8	74.1	11 20.3	+13.7	74.3	11 36.4	+14.7	74.5	11 52.3	+15.7	74.7	12 08.0	+16.7	74.9	12 23.5	+17.7	75.1	12 38.8	+18.7	75.3	12 53.9	+19.7	75.6	18
19	11 16.7	+12.5	73.1	11 34.0	+13.5	73.3	11 51.1	+14.5	73.5	12 08.0	+15.5	73.7	12 24.7	+16.5	73.9	12 41.2	+17.5	74.1	12 57.5	+18.5	74.4	13 13.6	+19.4	74.6	19
20	11 29.2	+12.3	72.1	11 47.5	+13.3	72.3	12 05.6	+14.3	72.5	12 23.5	+15.3	72.7	12 41.2	+16.3	72.9	12 58.7	+17.3	73.2	13 16.0	+18.2	73.4	13 33.0	+19.3	73.6	20
21	11 41.5	+12.1	71.1	12 00.8	+13.1	71.3	12 19.9	+14.1	71.5	12 38.8	+15.1	71.7	12 57.5	+16.1	72.0	13 16.0	+17.0	72.2	13 34.2	+18.1	72.4	13 52.3	+19.0	72.6	21
22	11 53.6	+11.9	70.1	12 13.9	+12.9	70.3	12 34.0	+13.9	70.5	12 53.9	+14.9	70.8	13 13.6	+15.8	71.0	13 33.0	+16.8	71.2	13 52.3	+17.7	71.4	14 11.3	+18.7	71.7	22
23	12 05.5	+11.7	69.1	12 26.8	+12.7	69.3	12 47.9	+13.6	69.5	13 08.8	+14.6	69.8	13 29.4	+15.6	70.0	13 49.8	+16.6	70.2	14 10.0	+17.6	70.4	14 30.0	+18.5	70.7	23
24	12 17.2	+11.5	68.1	12 39.5	+12.4	68.3	13 01.5	+13.5	68.5	13 23.4	+14.4	68.8	13 45.0	+15.4	69.0	14 06.4	+16.3	69.2	14 27.6	+17.3	69.5	14 48.5	+18.3	69.7	24
25	12 28.7	+11.2	67.1	12 51.9	+12.2	67.3	13 15.0	+13.1	67.5	13 37.8	+14.1	67.8	14 00.4	+15.1	68.0	14 22.7	+16.1	68.2	14 44.9	+17.0	68.5	15 06.8	+18.0	68.7	25
26	12 39.9	+11.1	66.1	13 04.1	+12.0	66.3	13 28.1	+13.0	66.5	13 51.9	+13.9	66.8	14 15.5	+14.8	67.0	14 38.8	+15.8	67.2	15 01.9	+16.8	67.5	15 24.8	+17.7	67.7	26
27	12 51.0	+10.7	65.1	13 16.1	+11.8	65.3	13 41.1	+12.7	65.5	14 05.8	+13.7	65.8	14 30.3	+14.6	66.0	14 54.6	+15.6	66.2	15 18.7	+16.5	66.5	15 42.5	+17.5	66.7	27
28	13 01.7	+10.6	64.1	13 27.9	+11.5	64.3	13 53.8	+12.4	64.5	14 19.5	+13.4	64.8	14 44.9	+14.4	65.0	15 10.2	+15.3	65.2	15 35.2	+16.3	65.5	16 00.0	+17.2	65.7	28
29	13 12.3	+10.3	63.1	13 39.4	+11.2	63.3	14 06.2	+12.2	63.5	14 32.9	+13.1	63.7	14 59.3	+14.1	64.0	15 25.5	+15.0	64.2	15 51.5	+15.9	64.5	16 17.2	+16.9	64.7	29
30	13 22.6	+10.1	62.1	13 50.6	+11.0	62.3	14 18.4	+12.0	62.5	14 46.0	+12.9	62.7	15 13.4	+13.8	63.0	15 40.5	+14.8	63.2	16 07.4	+15.7	63.5	16 34.1	+16.6	63.7	30
31	13 32.7	+9.8	61.1	14 01.6	+10.8	61.3	14 30.4	+11.6	61.5	14 58.9	+12.6	61.7	15 27.2	+13.5	62.0	15 55.3	+14.4	62.2	16 23.1	+15.4	62.5	16 50.7	+16.4	62.7	31
32	13 42.5	+9.6	60.0	14 12.4	+10.5	60.3	14 42.0	+11.5	60.5	15 11.5	+12.3	60.7	15 40.7	+13.3	61.0	16 09.7	+14.2	61.2	16 38.5	+15.1	61.5	17 07.1	+16.0	61.7	32
33	13 52.1	+9.3	59.0	14 22.9	+10.2	59.2	14 53.5	+11.1	59.5	15 23.8	+12.1	59.7	15 54.0	+13.0	59.9	16 23.9	+13.9	60.2	16 53.6	+14.8	60.5	17 23.1	+15.7	60.7	33
34	14 01.4	+9.1	58.0	14 33.1	+10.0	58.2	15 04.6	+10.9	58.5	15 35.9	+11.8	58.7	16 07.0	+12.7	58.9	16 37.8	+13.6	59.2	17 08.4	+14.6	59.4	17 38.8	+15.4	59.7	34
35	14 10.5	+8.8	57.0	14 43.1	+9.7	57.2	15 15.5	+10.6	57.4	15 47.7	+11.5	57.7	16 19.7	+12.3	57.9	16 51.4	+13.3	58.2	17 23.0	+14.2	58.4	17 54.2	+15.2	58.7	35
36	14 19.3	+8.5	56.0	14 52.8	+9.4	56.2	15 26.1	+10.3	56.4	15 59.2	+11.2	56.6	16 32.0	+12.1	56.9	17 04.7	+13.0	57.1	17 37.2	+13.8	57.4	18 09.4	+14.7	57.7	36
37	14 27.8	+8.3	54.9	15 02.2	+9.2	55.2	15 36.4	+10.0	55.4	16 10.4	+10.9	55.6	16 44.1	+11.8	55.9	17 17.7	+12.7	56.1	17 51.0	+13.6	56.4	18 24.1	+14.5	56.7	37
38	14 36.1	+8.1	53.9	15 11.4	+8.9	54.1	15 46.4	+9.8	54.4	16 21.3	+10.6	54.6	16 55.9	+11.5	54.8	17 30.4	+12.3	55.1	18 04.6	+13.2	55.4	18 38.6	+14.1	55.6	38
39	14 44.2	+7.7	52.9	15 20.3	+8.6	53.1	15 56.2	+9.4	53.3	16 31.9	+10.3	53.6	17 07.4	+11.2	53.8	17 42.7	+12.1	54.1	18 17.8	+12.9	54.3	18 52.7	+13.8	54.6	39
40	14 51.9	+7.5	51.9	15 28.9	+8.3	52.1	16 05.6	+9.2	52.3	16 42.2	+10.0	52.5	17 18.6	+10.9	52.8	17 54.8	+11.7	53.0	18 30.7	+12.6	53.3	19 06.5	+13.4	53.6	40
41	14 59.4	+7.2	50.8	15 37.2	+8.0	51.1	16 14.8	+8.9	51.3	16 52.2	+9.7	51.5	17 29.5	+10.5	51.8	18 06.5	+11.4	52.0	18 43.3	+12.3	52.3	19 19.9	+13.1	52.5	41
42	15 06.6	+6.9	49.8	15 45.2	+7.7	50.0	16 23.7	+8.5	50.3	17 01.9	+9.4	50.5	17 40.0	+10.2	50.7	18 17.9	+11.0	51.0	18 55.6	+11.8	51.2	19 33.0	+12.7	51.5	42
43	15 13.5	+6.6	48.8	15 52.9	+7.5	49.0	16 32.2	+8.3	49.2	17 11.3	+9.1	49.4	17 50.2	+9.9	49.7	18 28.9	+10.8	49.9	19 07.4	+11.6	50.2	19 45.7	+12.4	50.5	43
44	15 20.1	+6.4	47.8	16 00.4	+7.1	48.0	16 40.5	+7.9	48.2	17 20.4	+8.7	48.4	18 00.1	+9.6	48.7	18 39.7	+10.3	48.9	19 19.0	+11.2	49.2	19 58.1	+12.0	49.4	44
45	15 26.5	+6.0	46.7	16 07.5	+6.9	46.9	16 48.4	+7.7	47.2	17 29.1	+8.5	47.4	18 09.7	+9.2	47.6	18 50.0	+10.0	47.9	19 30.2	+10.8	48.1	20 10.1	+11.7	48.4	45
46	15 32.5	+5.8	45.7	16 14.4	+6.5	45.9	16 56.1	+7.3	46.1	17 37.6	+8.1	46.3	18 18.9	+8.9	46.6	19 00.0	+9.7	46.8	19 41.0	+10.5	47.1	20 21.8	+11.2	47.3	46
47	15 38.3	+5.5	44.7	16 20.9	+6.3	44.9	17 03.4	+7.0	45.1	17 45.7	+7.7	45.3	18 27.8	+8.5	45.5	19 09.7	+9.3	45.8	19 51.5	+10.1	46.0	20 33.0	+10.9	46.3	47
48	15 43.8	+5.2	43.6	16 27.2	+5.9	43.8	17 10.4	+6.7	44.0	17 53.4	+7.5	44.3	18 36.3	+8.2	44.5	19 19.0	+9.0	44.7	20 01.6	+9.7	45.0	20 43.9	+10.5	45.2	48
49	15 49.0	+4.9	42.6	16 33.1	+5.6	42.8	17 17.1	+6.3	43.0	18 00.9	+7.1	43.2	18 44.5	+7.9	43.4	19 28.0	+8.6	43.7	20 11.3	+9.4	43.9	20 54.4	+10.1	44.2	49
50	15 53.9	+4.6	41.6	16 38.7	+5.4	41.8	17 23.4	+6.1	42.0	18 08.0	+6.7	42.2	18 52.4	+7.5	42.4	19 36.6	+8.2	42.6	20 20.7	+8.9	42.9	21 04.5	+9.7	43.1	50
51	15 58.5	+4.3	40.5	16 44.1	+5.0	40.7	17 29.5	+5.7	40.9	18 14.7	+6.5	41.1	18 59.9	+7.1	41.3	19 44.8	+7.9	41.6	20 29.6	+8.6	41.8	21 14.2	+9.4	42.1	51
52	16 02.8	+4.0	39.5	16 49.1	+4.7	39.7	17 35.2	+5.4	39.9	18 21.2	+6.0	40.1	19 07.0	+6.8	40.3	19 52.7	+7.5	40.5	20 38.2	+8.2	40.8	21 23.6	+8.9	41.0	52
53	16 06.8	+3.7	38.4	16 53.8	+4.3	38.6	17 40.6	+5.0	38.8	18 27.2	+5.8	39.0	19 13.8	+6.4	39.2	20 00.2	+7.1	39.5	20 46.4	+7.8	39.7	21 32.5	+8.5	40.0	53
54	16 10.5	+3.4	37.4	16 58.1	+4.1	37.6	17 45.6	+4.7	37.8	18 33.0	+5.4	38.0	19 20.2	+6.1	38.2	20 07.3	+6.7	38.4	20 54.2	+7.5	38.6	21 41.0	+8.1	38.9	54
55	16 13.9	+3.1	36.4	17 02.2	+3.7	36.5	17 50.3	+4.4	36.7	18 38.4	+5.0	36.9	19 26.3	+5.7	37.1	20 14.0	+6.4	37.4	21 01.7	+7.0	37.6	21 49.1	+7.7	37.8	55
56	16 17.0	+2.8	35.3	17 05.9	+3.5	35.5	17 54.7	+4.1	35.7	18 43.4	+4.7	35.9	19 32.0	+5.3	36.1	20 20.4	+6.0	36.3	21 08.7	+6.6	36.5	21 56.8	+7.3	36.8	56
57	16 19.8	+2.5	34.3	17 09.4	+3.0	34.5	17 58.8	+3.7	34.6	18 48.1	+4.3	34.8	19 37.3	+4.9	35.0	20 26.4	+5.5	35.2	21 15.3	+6.2	35.5	22 04.1	+6.9	35.7	57
58	16 22.3	+2.2	33.2	17 12.4	+2.8	33.4	18 02.5	+3.4	33.6	18 52.4	+4.0	33.8	19 42.2	+4.6	34.0	20 31.9	+5.2	34.2	21 21.5	+5.8	34.4	22 11.0	+6.4	34.6	58
59	16 24.5	+1.9	32.2	17 15.2	+2.5	32.4	18 05.9	+3.0	32.5	18 56.4	+3.6	32.7	19 46.8	+4.2	32.9	20 37.1	+4.8	33.1	21 27.3	+5.4	33.3	22 17.4	+6.0	33.5	59
60	16 26.4	+1.5	31.2	17 17.7	+2.1	31.3	18 08.9	+2.7	31.5	19 00.0	+3.3	31.7	19 51.0	+3.9	31.8	20 41.9	+4.4	32.0	21 32.7	+5.0	32.2	22 23.4	+5.6	32.5	60
61	16 27.9	+1.3	30.1	17 19.8	+1.8	30.3	18 11.6	+2.3	30.4	19 03.3	+2.9	30.6	19 54.9	+3.4	30.8	20 46.3	+4.1	31.0	21 37.7	+4.6	31.2	22 29.0	+5.2	31.4	61
62	16 29.2	+0.9	29.1	17 21.6	+1.5	29.2	18 13.9	+2.0	29.4	19 06.2	+2.5	29.5	19 58.3	+3.1	29.7	20 50.4	+3.6	29.9	21 42.3	+4.2	30.1	22 34.2	+4.7	30.3	62
63	16 30.1	+0.7	28.0	17 23.1	+1.1	28.2	18 15.9	+1.7	28.3	19 08.7	+2.2	28.5	20 01.4	+2.7	28.7	20 54.0	+3.2	28.8	21 46.5	+3.7	29.0	22 38.9	+4.3	29.2	63
64	16 30.8	+0.3	27.0	17 24.2	+0.8	27.1	18 17.6	+1.3	27.3	19 10.9	+1.8	27.4	20 04.1	+2.3	27.6	20 57.2	+2.8	27.8	21 50.2	+3.4	28.0	22 43.2	+3.9	28.1	64
65	16 31.1	0.0	25.9	17 25.0	+0.5	26.1	18 18.9	+0.9	26.2	19 12.7	+1.4	26.4	20 06.4	+1.9	26.5	21 00.0	+2.4	26.7	21 53.6	+2.9	26.9	22 47.1	+3.4	27.1	65
66	16 31.1	−0.3	24.9	17 25.5	+0.2	25.0	18 19.8	+0.6	25.2	19 14.1	+1.1	25.3	20 08.3	+1.5	25.5	21 02.4	+2.1	25.6	21 56.5	+2.5	25.8	22 50.5	+3.0	26.0	66
67	16 30.8	−0.6	23.9	17 25.7	−0.2	24.0	18 20.4	+0.3	24.1	19 15.2	+0.7	24.3	20 09.8	+1.2	24.4	21 04.5	+1.6	24.6	21 59.0	+2.1	24.7	22 53.5	+2.5	24.9	67
68	16 30.2	−0.9	22.8	17 25.5	−0.5	22.9	18 20.7	−0.1	23.1	19 15.9	+0.3	23.2	20 11.0	+0.8	23.3	21 06.1	+1.2	23.5	22 01.1	+1.6	23.6	22 56.0	+2.1	23.8	68
69	16 29.3	−1.2	21.8	17 25.0	−0.9	21.9	18 20.6	−0.4	22.0	19 16.2	0.0	22.1	20 11.8	+0.4	22.3	21 07.3	+0.8	22.4	22 02.7	+1.2	22.6	22 58.1	+1.6	22.7	69
70	16 28.1	−1.6	20.7	17 24.1	−1.1	20.8	18 20.2	−0.8	21.0	19 16.2	−0.4	21.1	20 12.2	0.0	21.2	21 08.1	+0.4	21.3	22 03.9	+0.8	21.5	22 59.7	+1.2	21.6	70
71	16 26.5	−1.8	19.7	17 23.0	−1.5	19.8	18 19.4	−1.1	19.9	19 15.8	−0.7	20.0	20 12.2	−0.4	20.1	21 08.5	0.0	20.3	22 04.7	+0.4	20.4	23 00.9	+0.8	20.6	71
72	16 24.7	−2.2	18.6	17 21.5	−1.8	18.7	18 18.3	−1.5	18.8	19 15.1	−1.2	19.0	20 11.8	−0.8	19.1	21 08.5	−0.4	19.2	22 05.1	0.0	19.3	23 01.7	+0.3	19.5	72
73	16 22.5	−2.4	17.6	17 19.7	−2.1	17.7	18 16.8	−1.8	17.8	19 13.9	−1.4	17.9	20 11.0	−1.1	18.0	21 08.1	−0.8	18.1	22 05.1	−0.5	18.3	23 02.0	−0.1	18.4	73
74	16 20.1	−2.8	16.6	17 17.6	−2.5	16.7	18 15.0	−2.1	16.7	19 12.5	−1.9	16.8	20 09.9	−1.6	16.9	21 07.3	−1.3	17.1	22 04.6	−0.9	17.2	23 01.9	−0.6	17.3	74
75	16 17.3	−3.1	15.5	17 15.1	−2.8	15.6	18 12.9	−2.5	15.7	19 10.6	−2.2	15.8	20 08.3	−1.9	15.9	21 06.0	−1.6	16.0	22 03.7	−1.3	16.1	23 01.3	−1.0	16.2	75
76	16 14.2	−3.4	14.5	17 12.3	−3.1	14.6	18 10.4	−2.9	14.6	19 08.4	−2.6	14.7	20 06.4	−2.3	14.8	21 04.4	−2.0	14.9	22 02.4	−1.8	15.0	23 00.3	−1.4	15.1	76
77	16 10.8	−3.6	13.4	17 09.2	−3.5	13.5	18 07.5	−3.2	13.6	19 05.8	−2.9	13.7	20 04.1	−2.7	13.8	21 02.4	−2.4	13.8	22 00.6	−2.1	13.9	22 58.9	−2.0	14.0	77
78	16 07.2	−4.0	12.4	17 05.7	−3.7	12.5	18 04.3	−3.5	12.5	19 02.9	−3.3	12.6	20 01.4	−3.0	12.7	21 00.0	−2.9	12.8	21 58.5	−2.6	12.9	22 56.9	−2.3	12.9	78
79	16 03.2	−4.3	11.4	17 02.0	−4.1	11.4	18 00.8	−3.9	11.5	18 59.6	−3.7	11.6	19 58.4	−3.5	11.6	20 57.1	−3.2	11.7	21 55.9	−3.0	11.8	22 54.6	−2.8	11.9	79
80	15 58.9	−4.6	10.3	16 57.9	−4.4	10.4	17 56.9	−4.2	10.4	18 55.9	−4.0	10.5	19 54.9	−3.8	10.6	20 53.9	−3.6	10.6	21 52.9	−3.5	10.7	22 51.8	−3.2	10.8	80
81	15 54.3	−4.9	9.3	16 53.5	−4.7	9.3	17 52.7	−4.5	9.4	18 51.9	−4.4	9.4	19 51.1	−4.2	9.5	20 50.3	−4.1	9.6	21 49.4	−3.8	9.6	22 48.6	−3.7	9.7	81
82	15 49.4	−5.1	8.3	16 48.8	−5.0	8.3	17 48.2	−4.9	8.3	18 47.5	−4.7	8.4	19 46.9	−4.6	8.4	20 46.2	−4.4	8.5	21 45.6	−4.3	8.6	22 44.9	−4.1	8.6	82
83	15 44.3	−5.5	7.2	16 43.8	−5.3	7.3	17 43.3	−5.2	7.3	18 42.8	−5.1	7.3	19 42.3	−4.9	7.4	20 41.8	−4.8	7.4	21 41.3	−4.7	7.5	22 40.8	−4.5	7.5	83
84	15 38.8	−5.7	6.2	16 38.5	−5.7	6.2	17 38.1	−5.5	6.2	18 37.7	−5.4	6.3	19 37.4	−5.3	6.3	20 37.0	−5.2	6.4	21 36.6	−5.1	6.4	22 36.3	−5.0	6.5	84
85	15 33.1	−6.1	5.2	16 32.8	−5.9	5.2	17 32.6	−5.9	5.2	18 32.3	−5.8	5.2	19 32.1	−5.7	5.3	20 31.8	−5.6	5.3	21 31.5	−5.5	5.3	22 31.3	−5.4	5.4	85
86	15 27.0	−6.3	4.1	16 26.9	−6.3	4.1	17 26.7	−6.2	4.2	18 26.5	−6.1	4.2	19 26.4	−6.1	4.2	20 26.2	−6.0	4.2	21 26.0	−5.9	4.3	22 25.9	−5.9	4.3	86
87	15 20.7	−6.6	3.1	16 20.6	−6.6	3.1	17 20.5	−6.5	3.1	18 20.4	−6.4	3.1	19 20.3	−6.4	3.2	20 20.2	−6.3	3.2	21 20.1	−6.3	3.2	22 20.0	−6.2	3.2	87
88	15 14.1	−6.9	2.1	16 14.0	−6.8	2.1	17 14.0	−6.8	2.1	18 14.0	−6.9	2.1	19 13.9	−6.8	2.1	20 13.9	−6.8	2.1	21 13.8	−6.7	2.1	22 13.8	−6.7	2.1	88
89	15 07.2	−7.2	1.0	16 07.2	−7.2	1.0	17 07.2	−7.2	1.0	18 07.1	−7.1	1.0	19 07.1	−7.1	1.1	20 07.1	−7.1	1.1	21 07.1	−7.1	1.1	22 07.1	−7.1	1.1	89
90	15 00.0	−7.4	0.0	16 00.0	−7.5	0.0	17 00.0	−7.5	0.0	18 00.0	−7.5	0.0	19 00.0	−7.5	0.0	20 00.0	−7.5	0.0	21 00.0	−7.5	0.0	22 00.0	−7.5	0.0	90
	15°			16°			17°			18°			19°			20°			21°			22°			

83°, 277° L.H.A. LATITUDE SAME NAME AS DECLINATION

168

LATITUDE **CONTRARY** NAME TO DECLINATION **L.H.A. 83°, 277°**

Dec.	15°			16°			17°			18°			19°			20°			21°			22°			Dec.
	Hc	d	Z	Hc	d	Z	Hc	d	Z	Hc	d	Z	Hc	d	Z	Hc	d	Z	Hc	d	Z	Hc	d	Z	
°	° ′	′	°	° ′	′	°	° ′	′	°	° ′	′	°	° ′	′	°	° ′	′	°	° ′	′	°	° ′	′	°	°
0	6 45.6	−15.7	91.8	6 43.7	−16.8	91.9	6 41.6	−17.8	92.1	6 39.3	−18.7	92.2	6 37.0	−19.7	92.3	6 34.6	−20.8	92.4	6 32.0	−21.7	92.5	6 29.3	−22.7	92.6	**0**
1	6 29.9	−15.8	92.8	6 26.9	−16.8	92.9	6 23.8	−17.8	93.0	6 20.6	−18.8	93.1	6 17.3	−19.8	93.2	6 13.8	−20.8	93.3	6 10.3	−21.8	93.5	6 06.6	−22.8	93.6	**1**
2	6 14.1	−15.9	93.8	6 10.1	−16.9	93.9	6 06.0	−17.9	94.0	6 01.8	−18.9	94.1	5 57.5	−19.9	94.2	5 53.0	−20.9	94.3	5 48.5	−21.9	94.4	5 43.8	−22.8	94.5	**2**
3	5 58.2	−16.0	94.7	5 53.2	−17.0	94.8	5 48.1	−18.0	94.9	5 42.9	−19.0	95.0	5 37.6	−20.1	95.1	5 32.1	−21.0	95.2	5 26.6	−22.0	95.3	5 21.0	−23.0	95.4	**3**
4	5 42.2	−16.1	95.7	5 36.2	−17.1	95.8	5 30.1	−18.1	95.9	5 23.9	−19.2	96.0	5 17.5	−20.1	96.1	5 11.1	−21.0	96.2	5 04.6	−22.0	96.3	4 58.0	−23.0	96.4	**4**
5	5 26.1	−16.2	96.7	5 19.1	−17.2	96.8	5 12.0	−18.2	96.9	5 04.7	−19.1	96.9	4 57.4	−20.1	97.0	4 50.1	−21.2	97.1	4 42.6	−22.1	97.2	4 35.0	−23.1	97.3	**5**
6	5 09.9	−16.3	97.6	5 01.9	−17.3	97.7	4 53.8	−18.3	97.8	4 45.6	−19.3	97.9	4 37.3	−20.3	98.0	4 28.9	−21.2	98.1	4 20.5	−22.2	98.1	4 11.9	−23.1	98.2	**6**
7	4 53.6	−16.4	98.6	4 44.6	−17.4	98.7	4 35.5	−18.4	98.8	4 26.3	−19.4	98.8	4 17.0	−20.3	98.9	4 07.7	−21.3	99.0	3 58.3	−22.3	99.1	3 48.8	−23.2	99.1	**7**
8	4 37.2	−16.4	99.6	4 27.2	−17.4	99.6	4 17.1	−18.4	99.7	4 06.9	−19.4	99.8	3 56.7	−20.4	99.9	3 46.4	−21.4	99.9	3 36.0	−22.3	100.0	3 25.6	−23.3	100.1	**8**
9	4 20.8	−16.6	100.5	4 09.8	−17.6	100.6	3 58.7	−18.5	100.7	3 47.5	−19.4	100.7	3 36.3	−20.4	100.8	3 25.0	−21.4	100.9	3 13.7	−22.4	100.9	3 02.3	−23.3	101.0	**9**
10	4 04.2	−16.6	101.5	3 52.2	−17.5	101.6	3 40.2	−18.6	101.6	3 28.1	−19.6	101.7	3 15.9	−20.5	101.7	3 03.6	−21.4	101.8	2 51.3	−22.4	101.9	2 39.0	−23.4	101.9	**10**
11	3 47.6	−16.6	102.5	3 34.7	−17.7	102.5	3 21.6	−18.6	102.6	3 08.5	−19.6	102.6	2 55.4	−20.6	102.7	2 42.2	−21.5	102.7	2 28.9	−22.4	102.8	2 15.6	−23.4	102.8	**11**
12	3 31.0	−16.7	103.4	3 17.0	−17.7	103.5	3 03.0	−18.7	103.5	2 48.9	−19.6	103.6	2 34.8	−20.6	103.6	2 20.7	−21.6	103.7	2 06.5	−22.5	103.7	1 52.2	−23.4	103.7	**12**
13	3 14.3	−16.8	104.4	2 59.3	−17.7	104.4	2 44.3	−18.7	104.5	2 29.3	−19.7	104.5	2 14.2	−20.6	104.6	1 59.1	−21.5	104.6	1 44.0	−22.5	104.6	1 28.8	−23.4	104.7	**13**
14	2 57.5	−16.8	105.3	2 41.6	−17.8	105.4	2 25.6	−18.7	105.4	2 09.6	−19.7	105.5	1 53.6	−20.6	105.5	1 37.6	−21.6	105.5	1 21.5	−22.6	105.6	1 05.4	−23.5	105.6	**14**
15	2 40.7	−16.9	106.3	2 23.8	−17.8	106.3	2 06.9	−18.8	106.4	1 49.9	−19.7	106.4	1 33.0	−20.7	106.4	1 16.0	−21.6	106.5	0 58.9	−22.5	106.5	0 41.9	−23.5	106.5	**15**
16	2 23.8	−16.9	107.3	2 06.0	−17.9	107.3	1 48.1	−18.8	107.3	1 30.2	−19.7	107.4	1 12.3	−20.7	107.4	0 54.4	−21.7	107.4	0 36.4	−22.6	107.4	0 18.4	−23.4	107.4	**16**
17	2 06.9	−17.0	108.2	1 48.1	−17.9	108.3	1 29.3	−18.8	108.3	1 10.5	−19.8	108.3	0 51.6	−20.7	108.3	0 32.7	−21.6	108.3	0 13.8	−22.5	108.3	0 05.0	+23.5	71.7	**17**
18	1 49.9	−16.9	109.2	1 30.2	−17.9	109.2	1 10.5	−18.9	109.2	0 50.7	−19.8	109.3	0 30.9	−20.6	109.3	0 11.1	−21.7	109.3	0 08.7	+22.6	70.7	0 28.5	+23.5	70.7	**18**
19	1 33.0	−17.0	110.1	1 12.3	−17.9	110.2	0 51.6	−18.9	110.2	0 30.9	−19.8	110.2	0 10.2	−20.8	110.2	0 10.6	+21.6	69.8	0 31.3	+22.5	69.8	0 52.0	+23.4	69.8	**19**
20	1 16.0	−17.1	111.1	0 54.4	−18.0	111.1	0 32.7	−18.9	111.1	0 11.1	−19.8	111.1	0 10.6	+20.7	68.9	0 32.2	+21.6	68.9	0 53.8	+22.6	68.9	1 15.4	+23.5	68.9	**20**
21	0 58.9	−17.0	112.1	0 36.4	−18.0	112.1	0 13.8	−18.8	112.1	0 08.7	+19.8	67.9	0 31.3	+20.7	67.9	0 53.8	+21.6	67.9	1 16.4	+22.5	67.9	1 38.9	+23.4	68.0	**21**
22	0 41.9	−17.0	113.0	0 18.4	−17.9	113.0	0 05.0	+18.9	67.0	0 28.5	+19.8	67.0	0 52.0	+20.7	67.0	1 15.4	+21.6	67.0	1 38.9	+22.5	67.0	2 02.3	+23.4	67.1	**22**
23	0 24.9	−17.1	114.0	0 00.5	−18.0	114.0	0 23.9	+18.9	66.0	0 48.3	+19.8	66.0	1 12.7	+20.7	66.0	1 37.0	+21.6	66.1	2 01.4	+22.4	66.1	2 25.7	+23.3	66.1	**23**
24	0 07.8	−17.1	114.9	0 17.5	+18.0	65.1	0 42.8	+18.9	65.1	1 08.1	+19.7	65.1	1 33.4	+20.6	65.1	1 58.6	+21.5	65.1	2 23.8	+22.4	65.2	2 49.0	+23.3	65.2	**24**
25	0 09.3	+17.0	64.1	0 35.5	+17.9	64.1	1 01.7	+18.8	64.1	1 27.8	+19.8	64.1	1 54.0	+20.6	64.2	2 20.1	+21.5	64.2	2 46.2	+22.4	64.2	3 12.3	+23.2	64.3	**25**
26	0 26.3	+17.1	63.1	0 53.4	+18.0	63.2	1 20.5	+18.8	63.2	1 47.6	+19.7	63.2	2 14.6	+20.6	63.2	2 41.6	+21.5	63.3	3 08.6	+22.3	63.3	3 35.5	+23.2	63.4	**26**
27	0 43.4	+17.0	62.2	1 11.4	+17.9	62.2	1 39.3	+18.8	62.2	2 07.3	+19.7	62.2	2 35.2	+20.6	62.3	3 03.1	+21.4	62.3	3 30.9	+22.3	62.4	3 58.7	+23.2	62.4	**27**
28	1 00.4	+17.0	61.2	1 29.3	+17.9	61.2	1 58.1	+18.8	61.3	2 27.0	+19.6	61.3	2 55.8	+20.5	61.3	3 24.5	+21.4	61.4	3 53.2	+22.2	61.4	4 21.9	+23.0	61.5	**28**
29	1 17.4	+17.0	60.3	1 47.2	+17.8	60.3	2 16.9	+18.7	60.3	2 46.6	+19.6	60.4	3 16.3	+20.4	60.4	3 45.9	+21.3	60.5	4 15.4	+22.2	60.5	4 44.9	+23.0	60.6	**29**
30	1 34.4	+17.0	59.3	2 05.0	+17.9	59.3	2 35.6	+18.7	59.4	3 06.2	+19.5	59.4	3 36.7	+20.4	59.5	4 07.2	+21.2	59.5	4 37.6	+22.0	59.6	5 07.9	+22.9	59.7	**30**
31	1 51.4	+16.9	58.3	2 22.9	+17.8	58.4	2 54.3	+18.7	58.4	3 25.7	+19.5	58.5	3 57.1	+20.3	58.5	4 28.4	+21.1	58.6	4 59.6	+22.0	58.7	5 30.8	+22.8	58.7	**31**
32	2 08.3	+16.9	57.4	2 40.7	+17.7	57.4	3 13.0	+18.5	57.5	3 45.2	+19.4	57.5	4 17.4	+20.3	57.6	4 49.5	+21.1	57.6	5 21.6	+21.9	57.7	5 53.6	+22.8	57.8	**32**
33	2 25.2	+16.9	56.4	2 58.4	+17.7	56.5	3 31.5	+18.6	56.5	4 04.6	+19.4	56.6	4 37.7	+20.1	56.6	5 10.6	+21.0	56.7	5 43.5	+21.8	56.8	6 16.4	+22.6	56.9	**33**
34	2 42.1	+16.8	55.5	3 16.1	+17.6	55.5	3 50.1	+18.4	55.6	4 24.0	+19.3	55.6	4 57.8	+20.1	55.7	5 31.6	+20.9	55.8	6 05.3	+21.8	55.8	6 39.0	+22.5	55.9	**34**
35	2 58.9	+16.8	54.5	3 33.7	+17.6	54.5	4 08.5	+18.4	54.6	4 43.3	+19.2	54.7	5 17.9	+20.0	54.7	5 52.5	+20.8	54.8	6 27.1	+21.6	54.9	7 01.5	+22.4	55.0	**35**
36	3 15.7	+16.7	53.5	3 51.3	+17.5	53.6	4 26.9	+18.3	53.7	5 02.5	+19.1	53.7	5 37.9	+19.9	53.8	6 13.3	+20.7	53.9	6 48.7	+21.5	54.0	7 23.9	+22.3	54.1	**36**
37	3 32.4	+16.7	52.6	4 08.8	+17.5	52.6	4 45.2	+18.3	52.7	5 21.6	+19.0	52.8	5 57.8	+19.9	52.8	6 34.0	+20.7	52.9	7 10.2	+21.4	53.0	7 46.2	+22.2	53.1	**37**
38	3 49.1	+16.6	51.6	4 26.3	+17.4	51.7	5 03.5	+18.1	51.7	5 40.6	+18.9	51.8	6 17.7	+19.7	51.9	6 54.7	+20.4	52.0	7 31.6	+21.2	52.1	8 08.4	+22.0	52.2	**38**
39	4 05.7	+16.5	50.7	4 43.7	+17.3	50.7	5 21.6	+18.1	50.8	5 59.5	+18.9	50.9	6 37.4	+19.6	50.9	7 15.1	+20.4	51.0	7 52.8	+21.2	51.1	8 30.4	+21.9	51.3	**39**
40	4 22.2	+16.4	49.7	5 01.0	+17.2	49.8	5 39.7	+18.0	49.8	6 18.4	+18.7	49.9	6 57.0	+19.5	50.0	7 35.5	+20.3	50.1	8 14.0	+21.0	50.2	8 52.3	+21.8	50.3	**40**
41	4 38.6	+16.4	48.7	5 18.2	+17.1	48.8	5 57.7	+17.8	48.9	6 37.1	+18.6	48.9	7 16.5	+19.4	49.0	7 55.8	+20.1	49.1	8 35.0	+20.9	49.3	9 14.1	+21.6	49.4	**41**
42	4 55.0	+16.3	47.8	5 35.3	+17.0	47.8	6 15.5	+17.8	47.9	6 55.7	+18.5	48.0	7 35.9	+19.2	48.1	8 15.9	+20.0	48.2	8 55.9	+20.7	48.3	9 35.7	+21.5	48.4	**42**
43	5 11.3	+16.2	46.8	5 52.3	+17.0	46.9	6 33.3	+17.7	46.9	7 14.2	+18.4	47.0	7 55.1	+19.1	47.1	8 35.9	+19.8	47.2	9 16.6	+20.6	47.4	9 57.2	+21.3	47.5	**43**
44	5 27.5	+16.1	45.8	6 09.3	+16.8	45.9	6 51.0	+17.5	46.0	7 32.6	+18.3	46.1	8 14.2	+19.0	46.2	8 55.7	+19.7	46.3	9 37.2	+20.4	46.4	10 18.5	+21.1	46.5	**44**
45	5 43.6	+16.0	44.9	6 26.1	+16.7	44.9	7 08.5	+17.4	45.0	7 50.9	+18.1	45.1	8 33.2	+18.8	45.2	9 15.4	+19.6	45.3	9 57.6	+20.2	45.4	10 39.6	+21.0	45.6	**45**
46	5 59.6	+15.9	43.9	6 42.8	+16.6	44.0	7 25.9	+17.3	44.1	8 09.0	+18.0	44.1	8 52.0	+18.7	44.3	9 35.0	+19.4	44.4	10 17.8	+20.1	44.5	11 00.6	+20.8	44.6	**46**
47	6 15.5	+15.8	42.9	6 59.4	+16.5	43.0	7 43.2	+17.2	43.1	8 27.0	+17.9	43.2	9 10.7	+18.6	43.3	9 54.4	+19.2	43.4	10 37.9	+19.9	43.5	11 21.4	+20.6	43.7	**47**
48	6 31.3	+15.7	41.9	7 15.9	+16.3	42.0	8 00.4	+17.0	42.1	8 44.9	+17.7	42.2	9 29.3	+18.4	42.3	10 13.6	+19.1	42.4	10 57.8	+19.8	42.6	11 42.0	+20.4	42.7	**48**
49	6 47.0	+15.5	41.0	7 32.2	+16.3	41.1	8 17.4	+16.9	41.2	9 02.6	+17.5	41.3	9 47.7	+18.2	41.4	10 32.7	+18.8	41.5	11 17.6	+19.5	41.6	12 02.4	+20.2	41.7	**49**
50	7 02.5	+15.5	40.0	7 48.5	+16.1	40.1	8 34.3	+16.8	40.2	9 20.1	+17.4	40.3	10 05.9	+18.0	40.4	10 51.5	+18.7	40.5	11 37.1	+19.4	40.6	12 22.6	+20.0	40.8	**50**
51	7 18.0	+15.3	39.0	8 04.6	+15.9	39.1	8 51.1	+16.6	39.2	9 37.5	+17.3	39.3	10 23.9	+17.9	39.4	11 10.2	+18.5	39.5	11 56.5	+19.1	39.7	12 42.6	+19.8	39.8	**51**
52	7 33.3	+15.2	38.1	8 20.5	+15.8	38.1	9 07.7	+16.4	38.2	9 54.8	+17.0	38.3	10 41.8	+17.7	38.5	11 28.7	+18.4	38.6	12 15.6	+19.0	38.7	13 02.4	+19.6	38.8	**52**
53	7 48.5	+15.1	37.1	8 36.3	+15.7	37.2	9 24.1	+16.3	37.3	10 11.8	+16.9	37.4	10 59.5	+17.5	37.5	11 47.1	+18.1	37.6	12 34.6	+18.7	37.7	13 22.0	+19.3	37.9	**53**
54	8 03.6	+14.9	36.1	8 52.0	+15.5	36.2	9 40.4	+16.1	36.3	10 28.7	+16.7	36.4	11 17.0	+17.3	36.5	12 05.2	+17.9	36.6	12 53.3	+18.5	36.8	13 41.3	+19.1	36.9	**54**
55	8 18.5	+14.8	35.1	9 07.5	+15.4	35.2	9 56.5	+16.0	35.3	10 45.4	+16.6	35.4	11 34.3	+17.1	35.5	12 23.1	+17.7	35.7	13 11.8	+18.3	35.8	14 00.4	+18.9	35.9	**55**
56	8 33.3	+14.6	34.1	9 22.9	+15.2	34.2	10 12.5	+15.7	34.3	11 02.0	+16.3	34.4	11 51.4	+16.9	34.6	12 40.8	+17.5	34.7	13 30.1	+18.1	34.8	14 19.3	+18.7	34.9	**56**
57	8 47.9	+14.5	33.2	9 38.1	+15.0	33.3	10 28.2	+15.6	33.3	11 18.3	+16.2	33.5	12 08.3	+16.8	33.6	12 58.3	+17.3	33.7	13 48.2	+17.8	33.8	14 38.0	+18.4	34.0	**57**
58	9 02.4	+14.3	32.2	9 53.1	+14.9	32.3	10 43.8	+15.4	32.4	11 34.5	+15.9	32.5	12 25.1	+16.5	32.6	13 15.6	+17.0	32.7	14 06.0	+17.6	32.8	14 56.4	+18.1	33.0	**58**
59	9 16.7	+14.1	31.2	10 08.0	+14.7	31.3	10 59.2	+15.2	31.4	11 50.4	+15.8	31.5	12 41.6	+16.2	31.6	13 32.6	+16.8	31.7	14 23.6	+17.4	31.9	15 14.5	+17.9	32.0	**59**
60	9 30.8	+14.0	30.2	10 22.7	+14.5	30.3	11 14.4	+15.1	30.4	12 06.2	+15.5	30.5	12 57.8	+16.1	30.6	13 49.4	+16.6	30.7	14 41.0	+17.1	30.9	15 32.4	+17.7	31.0	**60**
61	9 44.8	+13.8	29.2	10 37.2	+14.3	29.3	11 29.5	+14.8	29.4	12 21.7	+15.3	29.5	13 13.9	+15.8	29.6	14 06.0	+16.3	29.7	14 58.1	+16.8	29.9	15 50.1	+17.3	30.0	**61**
62	9 58.6	+13.7	28.2	10 51.5	+14.1	28.3	11 44.3	+14.6	28.4	12 37.0	+15.1	28.5	13 29.7	+15.6	28.6	14 22.3	+16.1	28.8	15 14.9	+16.6	28.9	16 07.4	+17.1	29.0	**62**
63	10 12.3	+13.5	27.2	11 05.6	+13.9	27.3	11 58.9	+14.4	27.4	12 52.1	+14.9	27.5	13 45.3	+15.3	27.6	14 38.4	+15.9	27.8	15 31.5	+16.3	27.9	16 24.5	+16.8	28.0	**63**
64	10 25.8	+13.2	26.3	11 19.5	+13.8	26.3	12 13.3	+14.2	26.4	13 07.0	+14.6	26.5	14 00.6	+15.2	26.6	14 54.3	+15.5	26.8	15 47.8	+16.0	26.9	16 41.3	+16.5	27.0	**64**
65	10 39.0	+13.1	25.3	11 33.3	+13.5	25.3	12 27.5	+14.0	25.4	13 21.6	+14.5	25.5	14 15.8	+14.8	25.6	15 09.8	+15.3	25.8	16 03.8	+15.8	25.9	16 57.8	+16.2	26.0	**65**
66	10 52.1	+12.9	24.3	11 46.8	+13.3	24.4	12 41.5	+13.7	24.4	13 36.1	+14.1	24.5	14 30.6	+14.6	24.6	15 25.1	+15.1	24.8	16 19.6	+15.5	24.9	17 14.0	+15.9	25.0	**66**
67	11 05.0	+12.8	23.3	12 00.1	+13.2	23.4	12 55.2	+13.5	23.4	13 50.2	+14.0	23.5	14 45.2	+14.4	23.6	15 40.2	+14.7	23.8	16 35.1	+15.1	23.9	17 29.9	+15.6	24.0	**67**
68	11 17.8	+12.5	22.3	12 13.3	+12.9	22.4	13 08.7	+13.3	22.4	14 04.2	+13.6	22.5	14 59.6	+14.0	22.6	15 54.9	+14.5	22.7	16 50.2	+14.9	22.9	17 45.5	+15.3	23.0	**68**
69	11 30.3	+12.3	21.3	12 26.2	+12.6	21.4	13 22.0	+13.1	21.4	14 17.8	+13.5	21.5	15 13.6	+13.8	21.6	16 09.4	+14.2	21.7	17 05.1	+14.6	21.8	18 00.8	+14.9	22.0	**69**
70	11 42.6	+12.1	20.3	12 38.8	+12.5	20.4	13 35.1	+12.8	20.4	14 31.3	+13.1	20.5	15 27.4	+13.6	20.6	16 23.6	+13.9	20.7	17 19.7	+14.3	20.8	18 15.7	+14.7	20.9	**70**
71	11 54.7	+11.9	19.3	12 51.3	+12.2	19.4	13 47.9	+12.5	19.4	14 44.4	+13.0	19.5	15 41.0	+13.2	19.6	16 37.5	+13.6	19.7	17 34.0	+13.9	19.8	18 30.4	+14.3	19.9	**71**
72	12 06.6	+11.6	18.3	13 03.5	+12.0	18.4	14 00.4	+12.4	18.4	14 57.4	+12.6	18.5	15 54.2	+13.0	18.6	16 51.1	+13.3	18.7	17 47.9	+13.6	18.8	18 44.7	+14.0	18.9	**72**
73	12 18.2	+11.5	17.3	13 15.5	+11.8	17.3	14 12.8	+12.0	17.4	15 10.0	+12.4	17.5	16 07.2	+12.7	17.6	17 04.4	+13.0	17.7	18 01.5	+13.4	17.8	18 58.7	+13.6	17.9	**73**
74	12 29.7	+11.2	16.3	13 27.3	+11.5	16.3	14 24.8	+11.8	16.4	15 22.4	+12.1	16.5	16 19.9	+12.4	16.6	17 17.4	+12.7	16.7	18 14.9	+12.9	16.7	19 12.3	+13.3	16.8	**74**
75	12 40.9	+11.0	15.3	13 38.8	+11.2	15.3	14 36.6	+11.6	15.4	15 34.5	+11.8	15.5	16 32.3	+12.1	15.5	17 30.1	+12.3	15.6	18 27.8	+12.7	15.7	19 25.6	+12.9	15.8	**75**
76	12 51.9	+10.8	14.3	13 50.0	+11.1	14.3	14 48.2	+11.2	14.4	15 46.3	+11.5	14.4	16 44.4	+11.8	14.5	17 42.4	+12.1	14.6	18 40.5	+12.3	14.7	19 38.5	+12.6	14.8	**76**
77	13 02.7	+10.5	13.2	14 01.1	+10.7	13.3	14 59.4	+11.0	13.4	15 57.8	+11.2	13.4	16 56.2	+11.4	13.5	17 54.5	+11.7	13.6	18 52.8	+12.0	13.6	19 51.1	+12.2	13.7	**77**
78	13 13.2	+10.3	12.2	14 11.8	+10.5	12.3	15 10.4	+10.8	12.3	16 09.0	+11.0	12.4	17 07.6	+11.2	12.5	18 06.2	+11.4	12.5	19 04.8	+11.6	12.6	20 03.3	+11.9	12.7	**78**
79	13 23.5	+10.0	11.2	14 22.3	+10.3	11.3	15 21.2	+10.4	11.3	16 20.0	+10.6	11.4	17 18.8	+10.9	11.4	18 17.6	+11.1	11.5	19 16.4	+11.3	11.6	20 15.2	+11.4	11.6	**79**
80	13 33.5	+9.8	10.2	14 32.6	+10.0	10.3	15 31.6	+10.2	10.3	16 30.6	+10.4	10.4	17 29.7	+10.5	10.4	18 28.7	+10.7	10.5	19 27.7	+10.9	10.5	20 26.6	+11.2	10.6	**80**
81	13 43.3	+9.6	9.2	14 42.6	+9.7	9.2	15 41.8	+9.9	9.3	16 41.0	+10.0	9.3	17 40.2	+10.2	9.4	18 39.4	+10.4	9.4	19 38.6	+10.5	9.5	20 37.8	+10.7	9.5	**81**
82	13 52.9	+9.3	8.2	14 52.3	+9.4	8.2	15 51.7	+9.6	8.3	16 51.0	+9.8	8.3	17 50.4	+9.9	8.3	18 49.8	+10.0	8.4	19 49.1	+10.2	8.4	20 48.5	+10.3	8.5	**82**
83	14 02.2	+9.1	7.2	15 01.7	+9.2	7.2	16 01.3	+9.3	7.2	17 00.8	+9.4	7.3	18 00.3	+9.5	7.3	18 59.8	+9.7	7.3	19 59.3	+9.8	7.4	20 58.8	+10.0	7.4	**83**
84	14 11.3	+8.7	6.1	15 10.9	+8.9	6.2	16 10.6	+9.0	6.2	17 10.2	+9.1	6.2	18 09.8	+9.3	6.3	19 09.5	+9.3	6.3	20 09.1	+9.5	6.3	21 08.8	+9.5	6.4	**84**
85	14 20.0	+8.6	5.1	15 19.8	+8.6	5.1	16 19.6	+8.7	5.2	17 19.3	+8.8	5.2	18 19.1	+8.8	5.2	19 18.8	+9.0	5.3	20 18.6	+9.0	5.3	21 18.3	+9.2	5.3	**85**
86	14 28.6	+8.2	4.1	15 28.4	+8.3	4.1	16 28.3	+8.4	4.1	17 28.1	+8.5	4.2	18 27.9	+8.6	4.2	19 27.8	+8.6	4.2	20 27.6	+8.7	4.2	21 27.5	+8.7	4.3	**86**
87	14 36.8	+8.0	3.1	15 36.7	+8.1	3.1	16 36.7	+8.0	3.1	17 36.6	+8.1	3.1	18 36.5	+8.2	3.1	19 36.4	+8.2	3.2	20 36.3	+8.3	3.2	21 36.2	+8.3	3.2	**87**
88	14 44.8	+7.8	2.1	15 44.8	+7.7	2.1	16 44.7	+7.8	2.1	17 44.7	+7.8	2.1	18 44.7	+7.8	2.1	19 44.6	+7.9	2.1	20 44.6	+7.9	2.1	21 44.5	+8.0	2.1	**88**
89	14 52.6	+7.4	1.0	15 52.5	+7.5	1.0	16 52.5	+7.5	1.0	17 52.5	+7.5	1.0	18 52.5	+7.5	1.0	19 52.5	+7.5	1.1	20 52.5	+7.5	1.1	21 52.5	+7.5	1.1	**89**
90	15 00.0	+7.2	0.0	16 00.0	+7.2	0.0	17 00.0	+7.2	0.0	18 00.0	+7.1	0.0	19 00.0	+7.1	0.0	20 00.0	+7.1	0.0	21 00.0	+7.1	0.0	22 00.0	+7.1	0.0	**90**
	15°			16°			17°			18°			19°			20°			21°			22°			

S. Lat. {L.H.A. greater than 180° ....Zn=180°–Z; L.H.A. less than 180°...........Zn=180°+Z

LATITUDE **SAME** NAME AS DECLINATION **L.H.A. 97°, 263°**

169

Dec.	15° Hc	d	Z	16° Hc	d	Z	17° Hc	d	Z	18° Hc	d	Z	19° Hc	d	Z	20° Hc	d	Z	21° Hc	d	Z	22° Hc	d	Z	Dec.
°	° ′	′	°	° ′	′	°	° ′	′	°	° ′	′	°	° ′	′	°	° ′	′	°	° ′	′	°	° ′	′	°	°
0	5 47.7	+15.5	91.6	5 46.0	+16.6	91.7	5 44.2	+17.6	91.8	5 42.3	+18.6	91.9	5 40.3	+19.6	92.0	5 38.2	+20.6	92.1	5 36.0	+21.6	92.2	5 33.7	+22.5	92.3	0
1	6 03.2	+15.5	90.6	6 02.6	+16.4	90.7	6 01.8	+17.5	90.8	6 00.9	+18.5	90.9	5 59.9	+19.5	91.0	5 58.8	+20.5	91.1	5 57.6	+21.4	91.2	5 56.2	+22.5	91.3	1
2	6 18.7	+15.4	89.6	6 19.0	+16.4	89.7	6 19.3	+17.4	89.8	6 19.4	+18.4	89.9	6 19.4	+19.4	90.1	6 19.3	+20.3	90.2	6 19.0	+21.4	90.3	6 18.7	+22.3	90.4	2
3	6 34.1	+15.2	88.6	6 35.4	+16.3	88.8	6 36.7	+17.2	88.9	6 37.8	+18.2	89.0	6 38.8	+19.2	89.1	6 39.6	+20.3	89.2	6 40.4	+21.3	89.3	6 41.0	+22.3	89.5	3
4	6 49.3	+15.1	87.7	6 51.7	+16.1	87.8	6 53.9	+17.2	87.9	6 56.0	+18.2	88.0	6 58.0	+19.2	88.2	6 59.9	+20.2	88.3	7 01.7	+21.1	88.4	7 03.3	+22.1	88.5	4
5	7 04.4	+15.0	86.7	7 07.8	+16.0	86.8	7 11.1	+17.0	86.9	7 14.2	+18.0	87.1	7 17.2	+19.0	87.2	7 20.1	+20.0	87.3	7 22.8	+21.0	87.5	7 25.4	+22.0	87.6	5
6	7 19.4	+14.9	85.7	7 23.8	+15.9	85.8	7 28.1	+16.9	86.0	7 32.2	+17.9	86.1	7 36.2	+18.9	86.2	7 40.1	+19.9	86.4	7 43.8	+20.9	86.5	7 47.4	+21.9	86.6	6
7	7 34.3	+14.7	84.7	7 39.7	+15.8	84.9	7 45.0	+16.8	85.0	7 50.1	+17.8	85.1	7 55.1	+18.8	85.3	8 00.0	+19.8	85.4	8 04.7	+20.8	85.6	8 09.3	+21.7	85.7	7
8	7 49.0	+14.6	83.8	7 55.5	+15.6	83.9	8 01.8	+16.6	84.0	8 07.9	+17.7	84.2	8 13.9	+18.7	84.3	8 19.8	+19.6	84.5	8 25.5	+20.6	84.6	8 31.0	+21.7	84.8	8
9	8 03.6	+14.5	82.8	8 11.1	+15.4	82.9	8 18.4	+16.5	83.1	8 25.6	+17.4	83.2	8 32.6	+18.5	83.4	8 39.4	+19.5	83.5	8 46.1	+20.5	83.7	8 52.7	+21.4	83.8	9
10	8 18.1	+14.3	81.8	8 26.5	+15.4	81.9	8 34.9	+16.3	82.1	8 43.0	+17.4	82.2	8 51.1	+18.3	82.4	8 58.9	+19.4	82.6	9 06.6	+20.4	82.7	9 14.1	+21.4	82.9	10
11	8 32.4	+14.2	80.8	8 41.9	+15.2	81.0	8 51.2	+16.2	81.1	9 00.4	+17.2	81.3	9 09.4	+18.2	81.4	9 18.3	+19.2	81.6	9 27.0	+20.1	81.8	9 35.5	+21.1	81.9	11
12	8 46.6	+14.0	79.8	8 57.1	+15.0	80.0	9 07.4	+16.1	80.1	9 17.6	+17.0	80.3	9 27.6	+18.1	80.5	9 37.5	+19.0	80.6	9 47.1	+20.1	80.8	9 56.6	+21.0	81.0	12
13	9 00.6	+13.8	78.9	9 12.1	+14.9	79.0	9 23.5	+15.8	79.2	9 34.6	+16.9	79.3	9 45.7	+17.8	79.5	9 56.5	+18.9	79.7	10 07.2	+19.8	79.8	10 17.6	+20.9	80.0	13
14	9 14.4	+13.7	77.9	9 27.0	+14.7	78.0	9 39.3	+15.7	78.2	9 51.5	+16.7	78.4	10 03.5	+17.7	78.5	10 15.4	+18.7	78.7	10 27.0	+19.7	78.9	10 38.5	+20.7	79.1	14
15	9 28.1	+13.6	76.9	9 41.7	+14.5	77.0	9 55.0	+15.6	77.2	10 08.2	+16.6	77.4	10 21.2	+17.6	77.6	10 34.1	+18.5	77.7	10 46.7	+19.5	77.9	10 59.2	+20.5	78.1	15
16	9 41.7	+13.3	75.9	9 56.2	+14.4	76.1	10 10.6	+15.3	76.2	10 24.8	+16.3	76.4	10 38.8	+17.3	76.6	10 52.6	+18.3	76.8	11 06.2	+19.3	77.0	11 19.7	+20.3	77.2	16
17	9 55.0	+13.2	74.9	10 10.6	+14.2	75.1	10 25.9	+15.2	75.3	10 41.1	+16.2	75.4	10 56.1	+17.2	75.6	11 10.9	+18.2	75.8	11 25.5	+19.2	76.0	11 40.0	+20.1	76.2	17
18	10 08.2	+13.0	73.9	10 24.8	+14.0	74.1	10 41.1	+15.0	74.3	10 57.3	+16.0	74.5	11 13.3	+17.0	74.6	11 29.1	+17.9	74.8	11 44.7	+18.9	75.0	12 00.1	+19.9	75.2	18
19	10 21.2	+12.9	72.9	10 38.8	+13.8	73.1	10 56.1	+14.8	73.3	11 13.3	+15.8	73.5	11 30.3	+16.7	73.7	11 47.0	+17.8	73.9	12 03.6	+18.8	74.1	12 20.0	+19.7	74.3	19
20	10 34.1	+12.6	71.9	10 52.6	+13.6	72.1	11 10.9	+14.6	72.3	11 29.1	+15.6	72.5	11 47.0	+16.6	72.7	12 04.8	+17.6	72.9	12 22.4	+18.5	73.1	12 39.7	+19.5	73.3	20
21	10 46.7	+12.5	70.9	11 06.2	+13.5	71.1	11 25.5	+14.5	71.3	11 44.7	+15.4	71.5	12 03.6	+16.4	71.7	12 22.4	+17.3	71.9	12 40.9	+18.3	72.1	12 59.2	+19.3	72.3	21
22	10 59.2	+12.2	69.9	11 19.7	+13.2	70.1	11 40.0	+14.2	70.3	12 00.1	+15.2	70.5	12 20.0	+16.2	70.7	12 39.7	+17.1	70.9	12 59.2	+18.1	71.1	13 18.5	+19.1	71.4	22
23	11 11.4	+12.1	68.9	11 32.9	+13.0	69.1	11 54.2	+14.0	69.3	12 15.3	+14.9	69.5	12 36.2	+15.9	69.7	12 56.8	+16.9	69.9	13 17.3	+17.9	70.2	13 37.6	+18.8	70.4	23
24	11 23.5	+11.8	67.9	11 45.9	+12.8	68.1	12 08.2	+13.8	68.3	12 30.2	+14.8	68.5	12 52.1	+15.7	68.7	13 13.7	+16.7	69.0	13 35.2	+17.6	69.2	13 56.4	+18.6	69.4	24
25	11 35.3	+11.7	66.9	11 58.7	+12.7	67.1	12 22.0	+13.5	67.3	12 45.0	+14.5	67.5	13 07.8	+15.5	67.7	13 30.4	+16.5	68.0	13 52.8	+17.4	68.2	14 15.0	+18.4	68.4	25
26	11 47.0	+11.4	65.9	12 11.4	+12.4	66.1	12 35.5	+13.4	66.3	12 59.5	+14.3	66.5	13 23.3	+15.3	66.8	13 46.9	+16.2	67.0	14 10.2	+17.2	67.2	14 33.4	+18.1	67.4	26
27	11 58.4	+11.2	64.9	12 23.8	+12.1	65.1	12 48.9	+13.1	65.3	13 13.8	+14.1	65.5	13 38.6	+15.0	65.8	14 03.1	+16.0	66.0	14 27.4	+16.9	66.2	14 51.5	+17.8	66.5	27
28	12 09.6	+11.1	63.9	12 35.9	+12.0	64.1	13 02.0	+12.9	64.3	13 27.9	+13.8	64.5	13 53.6	+14.8	64.8	14 19.1	+15.7	65.0	14 44.3	+16.7	65.2	15 09.3	+17.6	65.5	28
29	12 20.7	+10.7	62.9	12 47.9	+11.7	63.1	13 14.9	+12.7	63.3	13 41.7	+13.6	63.5	14 08.4	+14.5	63.8	14 34.8	+15.4	64.0	15 01.0	+16.4	64.2	15 26.9	+17.4	64.5	29
30	12 31.4	+10.6	61.9	12 59.6	+11.5	62.1	13 27.6	+12.4	62.3	13 55.3	+13.4	62.5	14 22.9	+14.3	62.8	14 50.2	+15.2	63.0	15 17.4	+16.1	63.2	15 44.3	+17.0	63.5	30
31	12 42.0	+10.3	60.9	13 11.1	+11.2	61.1	13 40.0	+12.1	61.3	14 08.7	+13.1	61.5	14 37.2	+14.0	61.8	15 05.4	+15.0	62.0	15 33.5	+15.9	62.2	16 01.3	+16.8	62.5	31
32	12 52.3	+10.1	59.9	13 22.3	+11.0	60.1	13 52.1	+12.0	60.3	14 21.8	+12.8	60.5	14 51.2	+13.7	60.8	15 20.4	+14.7	61.0	15 49.4	+15.6	61.2	16 18.1	+16.5	61.5	32
33	13 02.4	+9.9	58.9	13 33.3	+10.8	59.1	14 04.1	+11.6	59.3	14 34.6	+12.6	59.5	15 04.9	+13.5	59.7	15 35.1	+14.4	60.0	16 05.0	+15.3	60.2	16 34.6	+16.2	60.5	33
34	13 12.3	+9.6	57.9	13 44.1	+10.5	58.1	14 15.7	+11.5	58.3	14 47.2	+12.3	58.5	15 18.4	+13.2	58.7	15 49.5	+14.1	59.0	16 20.3	+15.0	59.2	16 50.8	+16.0	59.5	34
35	13 21.9	+9.4	56.9	13 54.6	+10.3	57.1	14 27.2	+11.1	57.3	14 59.5	+12.0	57.5	15 31.6	+13.0	57.7	16 03.6	+13.8	58.0	16 35.3	+14.7	58.2	17 06.8	+15.6	58.5	35
36	13 31.3	+9.1	55.8	14 04.9	+10.0	56.0	14 38.3	+10.9	56.3	15 11.5	+11.8	56.5	15 44.6	+12.6	56.7	16 17.4	+13.5	57.0	16 50.0	+14.4	57.2	17 22.4	+15.3	57.5	36
37	13 40.4	+8.9	54.8	14 14.9	+9.8	55.0	14 49.2	+10.6	55.2	15 23.3	+11.5	55.5	15 57.2	+12.4	55.7	16 30.9	+13.3	55.9	17 04.4	+14.2	56.2	17 37.7	+15.0	56.4	37
38	13 49.3	+8.7	53.8	14 24.7	+9.5	54.0	14 59.8	+10.4	54.2	15 34.8	+11.2	54.4	16 09.6	+12.1	54.7	16 44.2	+12.9	54.9	17 18.6	+13.8	55.2	17 52.7	+14.7	55.4	38
39	13 58.0	+8.3	52.8	14 34.2	+9.2	53.0	15 10.2	+10.1	53.2	15 46.0	+11.0	53.4	16 21.7	+11.8	53.7	16 57.1	+12.7	53.9	17 32.4	+13.5	54.2	18 07.4	+14.4	54.4	39
40	14 06.3	+8.2	51.8	14 43.4	+8.9	52.0	15 20.3	+9.8	52.2	15 57.0	+10.6	52.4	16 33.5	+11.5	52.6	17 09.8	+12.3	52.9	17 45.9	+13.2	53.1	18 21.8	+14.0	53.4	40
41	14 14.5	+7.8	50.7	14 52.3	+8.7	50.9	15 30.1	+9.5	51.2	16 07.6	+10.3	51.4	16 45.0	+11.1	51.6	17 22.1	+12.0	51.9	17 59.1	+12.8	52.1	18 35.8	+13.7	52.4	41
42	14 22.3	+7.6	49.7	15 01.0	+8.4	49.9	15 39.6	+9.2	50.1	16 17.9	+10.1	50.4	16 56.1	+10.9	50.6	17 34.1	+11.7	50.8	18 11.9	+12.6	51.1	18 49.5	+13.4	51.3	42
43	14 29.9	+7.3	48.7	15 09.4	+8.2	48.9	15 48.8	+8.9	49.1	16 28.0	+9.7	49.3	17 07.0	+10.6	49.6	17 45.8	+11.4	49.8	18 24.5	+12.2	50.0	19 02.9	+13.0	50.3	43
44	14 37.2	+7.1	47.7	15 17.6	+7.8	47.9	15 57.7	+8.7	48.1	16 37.7	+9.5	48.3	17 17.6	+10.2	48.5	17 57.2	+11.1	48.8	18 36.7	+11.8	49.0	19 15.9	+12.7	49.3	44
45	14 44.3	+6.8	46.6	15 25.4	+7.6	46.8	16 06.4	+8.3	47.1	16 47.2	+9.1	47.3	17 27.8	+9.9	47.5	18 08.3	+10.7	47.7	18 48.5	+11.5	48.0	19 28.6	+12.3	48.2	45
46	14 51.1	+6.5	45.6	15 33.0	+7.3	45.8	16 14.7	+8.1	46.0	16 56.3	+8.8	46.2	17 37.7	+9.6	46.5	18 19.0	+10.4	46.7	19 00.0	+11.2	46.9	19 40.9	+12.0	47.2	46
47	14 57.6	+6.2	44.6	15 40.3	+7.0	44.8	16 22.8	+7.7	45.0	17 05.1	+8.5	45.2	17 47.3	+9.3	45.4	18 29.4	+10.0	45.7	19 11.2	+10.8	45.9	19 52.9	+11.6	46.2	47
48	15 03.8	+6.0	43.6	15 47.3	+6.7	43.8	16 30.5	+7.5	44.0	17 13.6	+8.2	44.2	17 56.6	+8.9	44.4	18 39.4	+9.7	44.6	19 22.0	+10.5	44.9	20 04.5	+11.2	45.1	48
49	15 09.8	+5.7	42.5	15 54.0	+6.4	42.7	16 38.0	+7.1	42.9	17 21.8	+7.9	43.1	18 05.5	+8.6	43.3	18 49.1	+9.3	43.6	19 32.5	+10.1	43.8	20 15.7	+10.8	44.1	49
50	15 15.5	+5.4	41.5	16 00.4	+6.1	41.7	16 45.1	+6.8	41.9	17 29.7	+7.5	42.1	18 14.1	+8.3	42.3	18 58.4	+9.0	42.5	19 42.6	+9.7	42.8	20 26.5	+10.5	43.0	50
51	15 20.9	+5.1	40.5	16 06.5	+5.8	40.7	16 51.9	+6.5	40.8	17 37.2	+7.3	41.0	18 22.4	+7.9	41.3	19 07.4	+8.7	41.5	19 52.3	+9.4	41.7	20 37.0	+10.1	42.0	51
52	15 26.0	+4.8	39.4	16 12.3	+5.5	39.6	16 58.4	+6.2	39.8	17 44.5	+6.8	40.0	18 30.3	+7.6	40.2	19 16.1	+8.3	40.4	20 01.7	+9.0	40.7	20 47.1	+9.7	40.9	52
53	15 30.8	+4.5	38.4	16 17.8	+5.2	38.6	17 04.6	+5.9	38.8	17 51.3	+6.6	39.0	18 37.9	+7.3	39.2	19 24.4	+7.9	39.4	20 10.7	+8.6	39.6	20 56.8	+9.3	39.9	53
54	15 35.3	+4.3	37.4	16 23.0	+4.9	37.5	17 10.5	+5.5	37.7	17 57.9	+6.2	37.9	18 45.2	+6.8	38.1	19 32.3	+7.5	38.3	20 19.3	+8.2	38.6	21 06.1	+8.9	38.8	54
55	15 39.6	+3.9	36.3	16 27.9	+4.6	36.5	17 16.0	+5.3	36.7	18 04.1	+5.9	36.9	18 52.0	+6.6	37.1	19 39.8	+7.2	37.3	20 27.5	+7.9	37.5	21 15.0	+8.6	37.7	55
56	15 43.5	+3.7	35.3	16 32.5	+4.2	35.5	17 21.3	+4.9	35.6	18 10.0	+5.5	35.8	18 58.6	+6.1	36.0	19 47.0	+6.9	36.2	20 35.4	+7.4	36.4	21 23.6	+8.1	36.7	56
57	15 47.2	+3.4	34.3	16 36.7	+4.0	34.4	17 26.2	+4.6	34.6	18 15.5	+5.2	34.8	19 04.7	+5.9	35.0	19 53.9	+6.4	35.2	20 42.8	+7.1	35.4	21 31.7	+7.7	35.6	57
58	15 50.6	+3.0	33.2	16 40.7	+3.7	33.4	17 30.8	+4.2	33.5	18 20.7	+4.9	33.7	19 10.6	+5.4	33.9	20 00.3	+6.1	34.1	20 49.9	+6.7	34.3	21 39.4	+7.3	34.5	58
59	15 53.6	+2.8	32.2	16 44.4	+3.3	32.3	17 35.0	+3.9	32.5	18 25.6	+4.5	32.7	19 16.0	+5.1	32.9	20 06.4	+5.6	33.1	20 56.6	+6.3	33.3	21 46.7	+6.9	33.5	59
60	15 56.4	+2.5	31.1	16 47.7	+3.0	31.3	17 38.9	+3.6	31.5	18 30.1	+4.1	31.6	19 21.1	+4.7	31.8	20 12.0	+5.3	32.0	21 02.9	+5.9	32.2	21 53.6	+6.5	32.4	60
61	15 58.9	+2.1	30.1	16 50.7	+2.7	30.2	17 42.5	+3.3	30.4	18 34.2	+3.8	30.6	19 25.8	+4.4	30.7	20 17.3	+5.0	30.9	21 08.8	+5.4	31.1	22 00.1	+6.0	31.3	61
62	16 01.0	+1.9	29.1	16 53.4	+2.4	29.2	17 45.8	+2.9	29.4	18 38.0	+3.5	29.5	19 30.2	+4.0	29.7	20 22.3	+4.5	29.9	21 14.2	+5.1	30.1	22 06.1	+5.7	30.3	62
63	16 02.9	+1.6	28.0	16 55.8	+2.1	28.2	17 48.7	+2.6	28.3	18 41.5	+3.1	28.5	19 34.2	+3.6	28.6	20 26.8	+4.1	28.8	21 19.3	+4.7	29.0	22 11.8	+5.2	29.2	63
64	16 04.5	+1.2	27.0	16 57.9	+1.8	27.1	17 51.3	+2.2	27.3	18 44.6	+2.7	27.4	19 37.8	+3.2	27.6	20 30.9	+3.8	27.7	21 24.0	+4.3	27.9	22 17.0	+4.8	28.1	64
65	16 05.7	+1.0	25.9	16 59.7	+1.4	26.1	17 53.5	+1.9	26.2	18 47.3	+2.4	26.4	19 41.0	+2.9	26.5	20 34.7	+3.4	26.7	21 28.3	+3.8	26.8	22 21.8	+4.3	27.0	65
66	16 06.7	+0.7	24.9	17 01.1	+1.1	25.0	17 55.4	+1.6	25.2	18 49.7	+2.0	25.3	19 43.9	+2.5	25.5	20 38.1	+2.9	25.6	21 32.1	+3.5	25.8	22 26.1	+3.9	26.0	66
67	16 07.4	+0.3	23.9	17 02.2	+0.8	24.0	17 57.0	+1.2	24.1	18 51.7	+1.7	24.2	19 46.4	+2.1	24.4	20 41.0	+2.6	24.5	21 35.6	+3.0	24.7	22 30.0	+3.5	24.9	67
68	16 07.7	+0.1	22.8	17 03.0	+0.5	22.9	17 58.2	+0.9	23.1	18 53.4	+1.3	23.2	19 48.5	+1.8	23.3	20 43.6	+2.2	23.5	21 38.6	+2.6	23.6	22 33.5	+3.1	23.8	68
69	16 07.8	−0.3	21.8	17 03.5	+0.1	21.9	17 59.1	+0.6	22.0	18 54.7	+1.0	22.1	19 50.3	+1.4	22.3	20 45.8	+1.8	22.4	21 41.2	+2.2	22.6	22 36.6	+2.6	22.7	69
70	16 07.5	−0.5	20.7	17 03.6	−0.1	20.8	17 59.7	+0.2	21.0	18 55.7	+0.6	21.1	19 51.7	+0.9	21.2	20 47.6	+1.3	21.3	21 43.4	+1.8	21.5	22 39.2	+2.2	21.6	70
71	16 07.0	−0.9	19.7	17 03.5	−0.5	19.8	17 59.9	−0.1	19.9	18 56.3	+0.2	20.0	19 52.6	+0.7	20.1	20 48.9	+1.0	20.3	21 45.2	+1.4	20.4	22 41.4	+1.8	20.5	71
72	16 06.1	−1.1	18.7	17 03.0	−0.8	18.8	17 59.8	−0.5	18.9	18 56.5	−0.1	19.0	19 53.3	+0.2	19.1	20 49.9	+0.6	19.2	21 46.6	+0.9	19.3	22 43.2	+1.3	19.5	72
73	16 05.0	−1.5	17.6	17 02.2	−1.2	17.7	17 59.3	−0.8	17.8	18 56.4	−0.5	17.9	19 53.5	−0.2	18.0	20 50.5	+0.2	18.1	21 47.5	+0.6	18.2	22 44.5	+0.9	18.4	73
74	16 03.5	−1.7	16.6	17 01.0	−1.4	16.7	17 58.5	−1.2	16.7	18 55.9	−0.8	16.8	19 53.3	−0.5	16.9	20 50.7	−0.2	17.1	21 48.1	+0.1	17.2	22 45.4	+0.4	17.3	74
75	16 01.8	−2.1	15.5	16 59.6	−1.8	15.6	17 57.3	−1.4	15.7	18 55.1	−1.2	15.8	19 52.8	−0.9	15.9	20 50.5	−0.6	16.0	21 48.2	−0.3	16.1	22 45.8	0.0	16.2	75
76	15 59.7	−2.3	14.5	16 57.8	−2.1	14.6	17 55.9	−1.9	14.6	18 53.9	−1.6	14.7	19 51.9	−1.3	14.8	20 49.9	−1.0	14.9	21 47.9	−0.8	15.0	22 45.8	−0.4	15.1	76
77	15 57.4	−2.7	13.5	16 55.7	−2.4	13.5	17 54.0	−2.1	13.6	18 52.3	−1.9	13.7	19 50.6	−1.6	13.8	20 48.9	−1.4	13.8	21 47.1	−1.1	13.9	22 45.4	−0.9	14.0	77
78	15 54.7	−3.0	12.4	16 53.3	−2.7	12.5	17 51.9	−2.5	12.5	18 50.4	−2.2	12.6	19 49.0	−2.1	12.7	20 47.5	−1.8	12.8	21 46.0	−1.6	12.9	22 44.5	−1.3	13.0	78
79	15 51.7	−3.2	11.4	16 50.6	−3.1	11.4	17 49.4	−2.9	11.5	18 48.2	−2.7	11.6	19 46.9	−2.4	11.6	20 45.7	−2.2	11.7	21 44.4	−1.9	11.8	22 43.2	−1.8	11.9	79
80	15 48.5	−3.5	10.3	16 47.5	−3.3	10.4	17 46.5	−3.1	10.4	18 45.5	−3.0	10.5	19 44.5	−2.8	10.6	20 43.5	−2.6	10.6	21 42.5	−2.4	10.7	22 41.4	−2.2	10.8	80
81	15 45.0	−3.9	9.3	16 44.2	−3.7	9.3	17 43.4	−3.5	9.4	18 42.5	−3.3	9.5	19 41.7	−3.1	9.5	20 40.9	−3.0	9.6	21 40.1	−2.9	9.6	22 39.2	−2.6	9.7	81
82	15 41.1	−4.1	8.3	16 40.5	−4.0	8.3	17 39.9	−3.9	8.4	18 39.2	−3.7	8.4	19 38.6	−3.6	8.5	20 37.9	−3.4	8.5	21 37.2	−3.2	8.6	22 36.6	−3.1	8.6	82
83	15 37.0	−4.4	7.2	16 36.5	−4.3	7.3	17 36.0	−4.2	7.3	18 35.5	−4.0	7.3	19 35.0	−3.9	7.4	20 34.5	−3.7	7.4	21 34.0	−3.6	7.5	22 33.5	−3.5	7.5	83
84	15 32.6	−4.8	6.2	16 32.2	−4.6	6.2	17 31.8	−4.4	6.3	18 31.5	−4.4	6.3	19 31.1	−4.2	6.3	20 30.8	−4.2	6.4	21 30.4	−4.1	6.4	22 30.0	−3.9	6.5	84
85	15 27.8	−5.0	5.2	16 27.6	−4.9	5.2	17 27.4	−4.9	5.2	18 27.1	−4.7	5.2	19 26.9	−4.7	5.3	20 26.6	−4.6	5.3	21 26.3	−4.4	5.3	22 26.1	−4.4	5.4	85
86	15 22.8	−5.2	4.1	16 22.7	−5.2	4.1	17 22.5	−5.1	4.2	18 22.4	−5.1	4.2	19 22.2	−5.0	4.2	20 22.0	−4.9	4.2	21 21.9	−4.9	4.3	22 21.7	−4.8	4.3	86
87	15 17.6	−5.6	3.1	16 17.5	−5.6	3.1	17 17.4	−5.5	3.1	18 17.3	−5.4	3.1	19 17.2	−5.4	3.2	20 17.1	−5.3	3.2	21 17.0	−5.3	3.2	22 16.9	−5.2	3.2	87
88	15 12.0	−5.9	2.1	16 11.9	−5.8	2.1	17 11.9	−5.8	2.1	18 11.9	−5.8	2.1	19 11.8	−5.7	2.1	20 11.8	−5.7	2.1	21 11.7	−5.6	2.1	22 11.7	−5.6	2.1	88
89	15 06.1	−6.1	1.0	16 06.1	−6.1	1.0	17 06.1	−6.1	1.0	18 06.1	−6.1	1.0	19 06.1	−6.1	1.1	20 06.1	−6.1	1.1	21 06.1	−6.1	1.1	22 06.1	−6.1	1.1	89
90	15 00.0	−6.4	0.0	16 00.0	−6.4	0.0	17 00.0	−6.4	0.0	18 00.0	−6.4	0.0	19 00.0	−6.4	0.0	20 00.0	−6.5	0.0	21 00.0	−6.5	0.0	22 00.0	−6.5	0.0	90
	15°			16°			17°			18°			19°			20°			21°			22°			

LATITUDE **CONTRARY** NAME TO DECLINATION — L.H.A. 84°, 276°

Dec.	15° Hc	d	Z	16° Hc	d	Z	17° Hc	d	Z	18° Hc	d	Z
°	° ′	′	°	° ′	′	°	° ′	′	°	° ′	′	°
0	5 47.7	-15.7	91.6	5 46.0	-16.7	91.7	5 44.2	-17.7	91.8	5 42.3	-18.7	91.9
1	5 32.0	-15.7	92.5	5 29.3	-16.7	92.6	5 26.5	-17.7	92.7	5 23.6	-18.7	92.8
2	5 16.3	-15.9	93.5	5 12.6	-16.9	93.6	5 08.8	-17.9	93.7	5 04.9	-18.9	93.8
3	5 00.4	-15.9	94.5	4 55.7	-16.9	94.6	4 50.9	-17.9	94.6	4 46.0	-18.9	94.7
4	4 44.5	-16.0	95.4	4 38.8	-17.0	95.5	4 33.0	-18.0	95.6	4 27.1	-19.0	95.7
5	4 28.5	-16.1	96.4	4 21.8	-17.1	96.5	4 15.0	-18.1	96.6	4 08.1	-19.1	96.6
6	4 12.4	-16.1	97.4	4 04.7	-17.2	97.4	3 56.9	-18.2	97.5	3 49.0	-19.1	97.6
7	3 56.3	-16.3	98.3	3 47.5	-17.2	98.4	3 38.7	-18.2	98.5	3 29.9	-19.2	98.5
8	3 40.0	-16.2	99.3	3 30.3	-17.3	99.4	3 20.5	-18.2	99.4	3 10.7	-19.3	99.5
9	3 23.8	-16.4	100.3	3 13.0	-17.3	100.3	3 02.3	-18.4	100.4	2 51.4	-19.3	100.4
10	3 07.4	-16.4	101.2	2 55.7	-17.4	101.3	2 43.9	-18.3	101.3	2 32.1	-19.3	101.4
11	2 51.0	-16.4	102.2	2 38.3	-17.4	102.2	2 25.6	-18.4	102.3	2 12.8	-19.4	102.3
12	2 34.6	-16.5	103.2	2 20.9	-17.5	103.2	2 07.2	-18.4	103.2	1 53.4	-19.4	103.3
13	2 18.1	-16.5	104.1	2 03.4	-17.5	104.2	1 48.8	-18.5	104.2	1 34.0	-19.4	104.2
14	2 01.6	-16.6	105.1	1 45.9	-17.5	105.1	1 30.3	-18.5	105.1	1 14.6	-19.4	105.2
15	1 45.0	-16.6	106.0	1 28.4	-17.5	106.1	1 11.8	-18.5	106.1	0 55.2	-19.5	106.1
16	1 28.4	-16.6	107.0	1 10.9	-17.6	107.0	0 53.3	-18.5	107.0	0 35.7	-19.5	107.1
17	1 11.8	-16.6	108.0	0 53.3	-17.6	108.0	0 34.8	-18.6	108.0	0 16.2	-19.4	108.0
18	0 55.2	-16.7	108.9	0 35.7	-17.6	108.9	0 16.2	-18.5	108.9	0 03.2	+19.5	71.1
19	0 38.5	-16.6	109.9	0 18.1	-17.6	109.9	0 02.3	+18.5	70.1	0 22.7	+19.5	70.1
20	0 21.9	-16.7	110.8	0 00.5	-17.6	110.8	0 20.8	+18.6	69.2	0 42.2	+19.4	69.2
21	0 05.2	-16.7	111.8	0 17.1	+17.6	68.2	0 39.4	+18.5	68.2	1 01.6	+19.5	68.2
22	0 11.5	+16.6	67.2	0 34.7	+17.6	67.2	0 57.9	+18.5	67.3	1 21.1	+19.4	67.3
23	0 28.1	+16.7	66.3	0 52.3	+17.6	66.3	1 16.4	+18.5	66.3	1 40.5	+19.4	66.3
24	0 44.8	+16.7	65.3	1 09.9	+17.5	65.3	1 34.9	+18.4	65.4	1 59.9	+19.4	65.4
25	1 01.5	+16.6	64.4	1 27.4	+17.5	64.4	1 53.3	+18.5	64.4	2 19.3	+19.3	64.4
26	1 18.1	+16.6	63.4	1 44.9	+17.5	63.4	2 11.8	+18.4	63.4	2 38.6	+19.3	63.5
27	1 34.7	+16.6	62.4	2 02.4	+17.5	62.5	2 30.2	+18.3	62.5	2 57.9	+19.2	62.5
28	1 51.3	+16.5	61.5	2 19.9	+17.4	61.5	2 48.5	+18.3	61.5	3 17.1	+19.2	61.6
29	2 07.8	+16.5	60.5	2 37.3	+17.4	60.5	3 06.8	+18.3	60.6	3 36.3	+19.1	60.6
30	2 24.3	+16.5	59.5	2 54.7	+17.4	59.6	3 25.1	+18.2	59.6	3 55.4	+19.0	59.7
31	2 40.8	+16.4	58.6	3 12.1	+17.2	58.6	3 43.3	+18.1	58.7	4 14.4	+19.0	58.7
32	2 57.2	+16.4	57.6	3 29.3	+17.3	57.7	4 01.4	+18.1	57.7	4 33.4	+18.9	57.8
33	3 13.6	+16.3	56.7	3 46.6	+17.1	56.7	4 19.5	+18.0	56.8	4 52.3	+18.8	56.8
34	3 29.9	+16.3	55.7	4 03.7	+17.1	55.7	4 37.5	+17.9	55.8	5 11.1	+18.8	55.9
35	3 46.2	+16.2	54.7	4 20.8	+17.0	54.8	4 55.4	+17.8	54.9	5 29.9	+18.6	54.9
36	4 02.4	+16.1	53.8	4 37.8	+17.0	53.8	5 13.2	+17.8	53.9	5 48.5	+18.6	54.0
37	4 18.5	+16.1	52.8	4 54.8	+16.8	52.9	5 31.0	+17.6	52.9	6 07.1	+18.4	53.0
38	4 34.6	+15.9	51.8	5 11.6	+16.8	51.9	5 48.6	+17.6	52.0	6 25.5	+18.4	52.1
39	4 50.5	+15.9	50.9	5 28.4	+16.7	50.9	6 06.2	+17.4	51.0	6 43.9	+18.2	51.1
40	5 06.4	+15.8	49.9	5 45.1	+16.5	50.0	6 23.6	+17.4	50.1	7 02.1	+18.1	50.1
41	5 22.2	+15.8	48.9	6 01.6	+16.5	49.0	6 41.0	+17.2	49.1	7 20.2	+18.0	49.2
42	5 38.0	+15.6	48.0	6 18.1	+16.4	48.0	6 58.2	+17.1	48.1	7 38.2	+17.9	48.2
43	5 53.6	+15.5	47.0	6 34.5	+16.2	47.1	7 15.3	+17.0	47.2	7 56.1	+17.7	47.3
44	6 09.1	+15.4	46.0	6 50.7	+16.2	46.1	7 32.3	+16.9	46.2	8 13.8	+17.6	46.3
45	6 24.5	+15.3	45.0	7 06.9	+16.0	45.1	7 49.2	+16.7	45.2	8 31.4	+17.5	45.3
46	6 39.8	+15.2	44.1	7 22.9	+15.9	44.2	8 05.9	+16.6	44.3	8 48.9	+17.3	44.4
47	6 55.0	+15.1	43.1	7 38.8	+15.8	43.2	8 22.5	+16.5	43.3	9 06.2	+17.1	43.4
48	7 10.1	+14.9	42.1	7 54.6	+15.6	42.2	8 39.0	+16.3	42.3	9 23.3	+17.0	42.4
49	7 25.0	+14.9	41.1	8 10.2	+15.5	41.2	8 55.3	+16.1	41.3	9 40.3	+16.8	41.4
50	7 39.9	+14.6	40.2	8 25.7	+15.3	40.3	9 11.4	+16.0	40.4	9 57.1	+16.7	40.5
51	7 54.5	+14.6	39.2	8 41.0	+15.2	39.3	9 27.4	+15.9	39.4	10 13.8	+16.4	39.5
52	8 09.1	+14.4	38.2	8 56.2	+15.0	38.3	9 43.3	+15.6	38.4	10 30.2	+16.3	38.5
53	8 23.5	+14.3	37.2	9 11.2	+14.9	37.3	9 58.9	+15.5	37.4	10 46.5	+16.2	37.5
54	8 37.8	+14.1	36.2	9 26.1	+14.7	36.3	10 14.4	+15.3	36.4	11 02.7	+15.9	36.6
55	8 51.9	+13.9	35.3	9 40.8	+14.6	35.4	10 29.7	+15.2	35.5	11 18.6	+15.7	35.6
56	9 05.8	+13.8	34.3	9 55.4	+14.4	34.4	10 44.9	+14.9	34.5	11 34.3	+15.5	34.6
57	9 19.6	+13.7	33.3	10 09.8	+14.2	33.4	10 59.8	+14.8	33.5	11 49.8	+15.4	33.6
58	9 33.3	+13.4	32.3	10 24.0	+14.0	32.4	11 14.6	+14.6	32.5	12 05.2	+15.1	32.6
59	9 46.7	+13.3	31.3	10 38.0	+13.8	31.4	11 29.2	+14.3	31.5	12 20.3	+14.9	31.6
60	10 00.0	+13.2	30.3	10 51.8	+13.6	30.4	11 43.5	+14.2	30.5	12 35.2	+14.7	30.6
61	10 13.2	+12.9	29.3	11 05.4	+13.5	29.4	11 57.7	+13.9	29.5	12 49.9	+14.4	29.6
62	10 26.1	+12.8	28.3	11 18.9	+13.2	28.4	12 11.6	+13.8	28.5	13 04.3	+14.2	28.6
63	10 38.9	+12.5	27.3	11 32.1	+13.1	27.4	12 25.4	+13.5	27.5	13 18.5	+14.0	27.6
64	10 51.4	+12.4	26.4	11 45.2	+12.8	26.4	12 38.9	+13.3	26.5	13 32.5	+13.8	26.6
65	11 03.8	+12.2	25.4	11 58.0	+12.6	25.4	12 52.2	+13.0	25.5	13 46.3	+13.5	25.6
66	11 16.0	+12.0	24.4	12 10.6	+12.4	24.4	13 05.2	+12.9	24.5	13 59.8	+13.3	24.6
67	11 28.0	+11.8	23.4	12 23.0	+12.2	23.4	13 18.1	+12.6	23.5	14 13.1	+13.0	23.6
68	11 39.8	+11.5	22.4	12 35.2	+12.0	22.4	13 30.7	+12.3	22.5	14 26.1	+12.7	22.6
69	11 51.3	+11.4	21.4	12 47.2	+11.7	21.4	13 43.0	+12.1	21.5	14 38.8	+12.5	21.6
70	12 02.7	+11.1	20.4	12 58.9	+11.5	20.4	13 55.1	+11.9	20.5	14 51.3	+12.2	20.6
71	12 13.8	+11.0	19.3	13 10.4	+11.3	19.4	14 07.0	+11.6	19.5	15 03.5	+12.0	19.6
72	12 24.8	+10.7	18.3	13 21.7	+11.0	18.4	14 18.6	+11.4	18.5	15 15.5	+11.7	18.6
73	12 35.5	+10.4	17.3	13 32.7	+10.8	17.4	14 30.0	+11.1	17.5	15 27.2	+11.4	17.6
74	12 45.9	+10.3	16.3	13 43.5	+10.5	16.4	14 41.1	+10.8	16.5	15 38.6	+11.1	16.5
75	12 56.2	+10.0	15.3	13 54.0	+10.3	15.4	14 51.9	+10.5	15.4	15 49.7	+10.8	15.5
76	13 06.2	+9.8	14.3	14 04.3	+10.0	14.4	15 02.4	+10.3	14.4	16 00.5	+10.6	14.5
77	13 16.0	+9.5	13.3	14 14.3	+9.8	13.3	15 12.7	+10.0	13.4	16 11.1	+10.2	13.5
78	13 25.5	+9.3	12.3	14 24.1	+9.5	12.3	15 22.7	+9.8	12.4	16 21.3	+10.0	12.4
79	13 34.8	+9.0	11.3	14 33.6	+9.3	11.3	15 32.5	+9.4	11.4	16 31.3	+9.6	11.4
80	13 43.8	+8.8	10.2	14 42.9	+8.9	10.3	15 41.9	+9.2	10.3	16 40.9	+9.4	10.4
81	13 52.6	+8.6	9.2	14 51.8	+8.7	9.3	15 51.1	+8.8	9.3	16 50.3	+9.0	9.4
82	14 01.2	+8.2	8.2	15 00.5	+8.5	8.2	15 59.9	+8.6	8.3	16 59.3	+8.7	8.3
83	14 09.4	+8.1	7.2	15 09.0	+8.1	7.2	16 08.5	+8.3	7.2	17 08.0	+8.4	7.3
84	14 17.5	+7.7	6.2	15 17.1	+7.9	6.2	16 16.8	+7.9	6.2	17 16.4	+8.1	6.2
85	14 25.2	+7.5	5.1	15 25.0	+7.6	5.2	16 24.7	+7.7	5.2	17 24.5	+7.7	5.2
86	14 32.7	+7.2	4.1	15 32.6	+7.3	4.1	16 32.4	+7.4	4.2	17 32.2	+7.5	4.2
87	14 39.9	+7.0	3.1	15 39.9	+7.0	3.1	16 39.8	+7.0	3.1	17 39.7	+7.1	3.1
88	14 46.9	+6.7	2.1	15 46.9	+6.7	2.1	16 46.8	+6.8	2.1	17 46.8	+6.8	2.1
89	14 53.6	+6.4	1.0	15 53.6	+6.4	1.0	16 53.6	+6.4	1.0	17 53.6	+6.4	1.0
90	15 00.0	+6.1	0.0	16 00.0	+6.1	0.0	17 00.0	+6.1	0.0	18 00.0	+6.1	0.0
	15°			16°			17°			18°		

Dec.	19° Hc	d	Z	20° Hc	d	Z	21° Hc	d	Z	22° Hc	d	Z
°	° ′	′	°	° ′	′	°	° ′	′	°	° ′	′	°
0	5 40.3	-19.7	92.0	5 38.2	-20.6	92.1	5 36.0	-21.6	92.2	5 33.7	-22.6	92.3
1	5 20.6	-19.7	92.9	5 17.6	-20.8	93.0	5 14.4	-21.8	93.1	5 11.1	-22.7	93.2
2	5 00.9	-19.9	93.9	4 56.8	-20.8	93.9	4 52.6	-21.8	94.0	4 48.4	-22.8	94.1
3	4 41.0	-19.9	94.8	4 36.0	-20.9	94.9	4 30.8	-21.9	95.0	4 25.6	-22.9	95.0
4	4 21.1	-20.0	95.8	4 15.1	-21.0	95.8	4 08.9	-21.9	95.9	4 02.7	-22.9	96.0
5	4 01.1	-20.0	96.7	3 54.1	-21.0	96.8	3 47.0	-22.0	96.8	3 39.8	-23.0	96.9
6	3 41.1	-20.2	97.6	3 33.1	-21.1	97.7	3 25.0	-22.1	97.8	3 16.8	-23.0	97.8
7	3 20.9	-20.1	98.6	3 12.0	-21.2	98.6	3 02.9	-22.1	98.7	2 53.8	-23.0	98.7
8	3 00.8	-20.2	99.5	2 50.8	-21.2	99.6	2 40.8	-22.1	99.6	2 30.8	-23.2	99.7
9	2 40.6	-20.3	100.5	2 29.6	-21.2	100.5	2 18.7	-22.2	100.6	2 07.6	-23.1	100.6
10	2 20.3	-20.3	101.4	2 08.4	-21.3	101.5	1 56.5	-22.2	101.5	1 44.5	-23.2	101.5
11	2 00.0	-20.3	102.4	1 47.1	-21.3	102.4	1 34.3	-22.3	102.4	1 21.3	-23.2	102.4
12	1 39.7	-20.4	103.3	1 25.8	-21.3	103.3	1 12.0	-22.3	103.3	0 58.1	-23.2	103.4
13	1 19.3	-20.4	104.2	1 04.5	-21.3	104.3	0 49.7	-22.2	104.3	0 34.9	-23.2	104.3
14	0 58.9	-20.4	105.2	0 43.2	-21.3	105.2	0 27.5	-22.3	105.2	0 11.7	-23.2	105.2
15	0 38.5	-20.4	106.1	0 21.9	-21.4	106.1	0 05.2	-22.3	106.1	0 11.5	+23.2	73.9
16	0 18.1	-20.4	107.1	0 00.5	-21.3	107.1	0 17.1	+22.3	72.9	0 34.7	+23.2	72.9
17	0 02.3	+20.4	72.0	0 20.8	+21.4	72.0	0 39.4	+22.2	72.0	0 57.9	+23.2	72.0
18	0 22.7	+20.4	71.1	0 42.2	+21.3	71.1	1 01.6	+22.3	71.1	1 21.1	+23.2	71.1
19	0 43.1	+20.4	70.1	1 03.5	+21.3	70.1	1 23.9	+22.2	70.2	1 44.3	+23.1	70.2
20	1 03.5	+20.4	69.2	1 24.8	+21.3	69.2	1 46.1	+22.2	69.2	2 07.4	+23.1	69.3
21	1 23.9	+20.4	68.2	1 46.1	+21.3	68.3	2 08.3	+22.2	68.3	2 30.5	+23.1	68.3
22	1 44.3	+20.3	67.3	2 07.4	+21.2	67.3	2 30.5	+22.1	67.4	2 53.6	+23.0	67.4
23	2 04.6	+20.3	66.4	2 28.6	+21.2	66.4	2 52.6	+22.1	66.4	3 16.6	+23.0	66.5
24	2 24.9	+20.2	65.4	2 49.8	+21.2	65.5	3 14.7	+22.1	65.5	3 39.6	+22.9	65.6
25	2 45.1	+20.2	64.5	3 11.0	+21.1	64.5	3 36.8	+21.9	64.6	4 02.5	+22.8	64.6
26	3 05.3	+20.2	63.5	3 32.1	+21.0	63.6	3 58.7	+21.9	63.6	4 25.3	+22.8	63.7
27	3 25.5	+20.1	62.6	3 53.1	+21.0	62.6	4 20.6	+21.9	62.7	4 48.1	+22.7	62.8
28	3 45.6	+20.1	61.6	4 14.1	+20.9	61.7	4 42.5	+21.8	61.8	5 10.8	+22.7	61.8
29	4 05.7	+19.9	60.7	4 35.0	+20.8	60.8	5 04.3	+21.6	60.8	5 33.5	+22.5	60.9
30	4 25.6	+19.9	59.8	4 55.8	+20.8	59.8	5 25.9	+21.6	59.9	5 56.0	+22.4	60.0
31	4 45.5	+19.9	58.8	5 16.6	+20.6	58.9	5 47.5	+21.6	59.0	6 18.4	+22.4	59.1
32	5 05.4	+19.7	57.9	5 37.2	+20.6	57.9	6 09.1	+21.4	58.0	6 40.8	+22.2	58.1
33	5 25.1	+19.7	56.9	5 57.8	+20.5	57.0	6 30.5	+21.3	57.1	7 03.0	+22.2	57.2
34	5 44.8	+19.5	56.0	6 18.3	+20.4	56.0	6 51.8	+21.2	56.1	7 25.2	+22.0	56.2
35	6 04.3	+19.5	55.0	6 38.7	+20.3	55.1	7 13.0	+21.1	55.2	7 47.2	+21.9	55.3
36	6 23.8	+19.3	54.1	6 59.0	+20.1	54.2	7 34.1	+20.9	54.3	8 09.1	+21.7	54.4
37	6 43.1	+19.3	53.1	7 19.1	+20.1	53.2	7 55.0	+20.8	53.3	8 30.8	+21.6	53.4
38	7 02.4	+19.1	52.2	7 39.2	+19.9	52.3	8 15.8	+20.7	52.4	8 52.4	+21.5	52.5
39	7 21.5	+19.0	51.2	7 59.1	+19.8	51.3	8 36.5	+20.6	51.4	9 13.9	+21.3	51.5
40	7 40.5	+18.9	50.2	8 18.9	+19.6	50.3	8 57.1	+20.4	50.5	9 35.2	+21.2	50.6
41	7 59.4	+18.8	49.3	8 38.5	+19.5	49.4	9 17.5	+20.3	49.5	9 56.4	+21.0	49.6
42	8 18.2	+18.6	48.3	8 58.0	+19.4	48.4	9 37.8	+20.1	48.6	10 17.4	+20.9	48.7
43	8 36.8	+18.4	47.4	9 17.4	+19.2	47.5	9 57.9	+19.9	47.6	10 38.3	+20.6	47.7
44	8 55.2	+18.3	46.4	9 36.6	+19.0	46.5	10 17.8	+19.8	46.6	10 58.9	+20.5	46.8
45	9 13.5	+18.2	45.4	9 55.6	+18.9	45.6	10 37.6	+19.6	45.7	11 19.4	+20.3	45.8
46	9 31.7	+18.0	44.5	10 14.5	+18.7	44.6	10 57.2	+19.4	44.7	11 39.7	+20.2	44.9
47	9 49.7	+17.9	43.5	10 33.2	+18.5	43.6	11 16.6	+19.2	43.8	11 59.9	+19.9	43.9
48	10 07.6	+17.6	42.5	10 51.7	+18.4	42.7	11 35.8	+19.0	42.8	12 19.8	+19.7	42.9
49	10 25.2	+17.5	41.6	11 10.1	+18.1	41.7	11 54.8	+18.9	41.8	12 39.5	+19.5	42.0
50	10 42.7	+17.3	40.6	11 28.2	+18.0	40.7	12 13.7	+18.6	40.9	12 59.0	+19.3	41.0
51	11 00.0	+17.1	39.6	11 46.2	+17.8	39.7	12 32.3	+18.4	39.9	13 18.3	+19.1	40.0
52	11 17.1	+17.0	38.6	12 04.0	+17.5	38.8	12 50.7	+18.2	38.9	13 37.4	+18.8	39.1
53	11 34.1	+16.7	37.7	12 21.5	+17.4	37.8	13 08.9	+18.0	37.9	13 56.2	+18.6	38.1
54	11 50.8	+16.5	36.7	12 38.9	+17.1	36.8	13 26.9	+17.7	36.9	14 14.8	+18.4	37.1
55	12 07.3	+16.4	35.7	12 56.0	+17.0	35.8	13 44.6	+17.6	36.0	14 33.2	+18.1	36.1
56	12 23.7	+16.1	34.7	13 13.0	+16.6	34.8	14 02.2	+17.2	35.0	14 51.3	+17.8	35.1
57	12 39.8	+15.9	33.7	13 29.6	+16.5	33.9	14 19.4	+17.1	34.0	15 09.1	+17.6	34.1
58	12 55.7	+15.6	32.7	13 46.1	+16.2	32.9	14 36.5	+16.7	33.0	15 26.7	+17.4	33.1
59	13 11.3	+15.5	31.7	14 02.3	+16.0	31.9	14 53.2	+16.6	32.0	15 44.1	+17.1	32.2
60	13 26.8	+15.2	30.7	14 18.3	+15.7	30.9	15 09.8	+16.2	31.0	16 01.2	+16.7	31.2
61	13 42.0	+14.9	29.8	14 34.0	+15.5	29.9	15 26.0	+16.0	30.0	16 17.9	+16.6	30.2
62	13 56.9	+14.8	28.8	14 49.5	+15.2	28.9	15 42.0	+15.7	29.0	16 34.5	+16.2	29.2
63	14 11.7	+14.4	27.8	15 04.7	+15.0	27.9	15 57.7	+15.5	28.0	16 50.7	+15.9	28.1
64	14 26.1	+14.3	26.8	15 19.7	+14.7	26.9	16 13.2	+15.1	27.0	17 06.6	+15.6	27.1
65	14 40.4	+13.9	25.8	15 34.4	+14.4	25.9	16 28.3	+14.9	26.0	17 22.2	+15.4	26.1
66	14 54.3	+13.7	24.7	15 48.8	+14.1	24.9	16 43.2	+14.6	25.0	17 37.6	+15.0	25.1
67	15 08.0	+13.4	23.7	16 02.9	+13.9	23.9	16 57.8	+14.2	24.0	17 52.6	+14.7	24.1
68	15 21.4	+13.2	22.7	16 16.8	+13.5	22.8	17 12.0	+14.0	23.0	18 07.3	+14.3	23.1
69	15 34.6	+12.9	21.7	16 30.3	+13.3	21.8	17 26.0	+13.6	21.9	18 21.6	+14.1	22.1
70	15 47.5	+12.6	20.7	16 43.6	+12.9	20.8	17 39.6	+13.4	20.9	18 35.7	+13.7	21.0
71	16 00.1	+12.3	19.7	16 56.5	+12.7	19.8	17 53.0	+13.0	19.9	18 49.4	+13.3	20.0
72	16 12.4	+12.0	18.7	17 09.2	+12.3	18.8	18 06.0	+12.7	18.9	19 02.7	+13.1	19.0
73	16 24.4	+11.7	17.6	17 21.5	+12.1	17.7	18 18.7	+12.3	17.8	19 15.8	+12.6	17.9
74	16 36.1	+11.4	16.6	17 33.6	+11.7	16.7	18 31.0	+12.0	16.8	19 28.4	+12.4	16.9
75	16 47.5	+11.1	15.6	17 45.3	+11.4	15.7	18 43.0	+11.7	15.8	19 40.8	+11.9	15.9
76	16 58.6	+10.8	14.6	17 56.7	+11.0	14.6	18 54.7	+11.3	14.7	19 52.7	+11.6	14.8
77	17 09.4	+10.5	13.5	18 07.7	+10.8	13.6	19 06.0	+11.0	13.7	20 04.3	+11.3	13.8
78	17 19.9	+10.2	12.5	18 18.5	+10.4	12.6	19 17.0	+10.7	12.7	20 15.6	+10.8	12.7
79	17 30.1	+9.8	11.5	18 28.9	+10.0	11.5	19 27.7	+10.2	11.6	20 26.4	+10.5	11.7
80	17 39.9	+9.6	10.4	18 38.9	+9.7	10.5	19 37.9	+9.9	10.6	20 36.9	+10.1	10.6
81	17 49.5	+9.2	9.4	18 48.6	+9.4	9.5	19 47.8	+9.6	9.5	20 47.0	+9.7	9.6
82	17 58.7	+8.8	8.4	18 58.0	+9.0	8.4	19 57.4	+9.1	8.5	20 56.7	+9.3	8.5
83	18 07.5	+8.5	7.3	19 07.0	+8.7	7.4	20 06.5	+8.8	7.4	21 06.0	+8.9	7.5
84	18 16.0	+8.2	6.3	19 15.7	+8.3	6.3	20 15.3	+8.4	6.4	21 14.9	+8.6	6.4
85	18 24.2	+7.9	5.2	19 24.0	+7.9	5.3	20 23.7	+8.1	5.3	21 23.5	+8.1	5.3
86	18 32.1	+7.5	4.2	19 31.9	+7.6	4.2	20 31.8	+7.6	4.3	21 31.6	+7.7	4.3
87	18 39.6	+7.1	3.1	19 39.5	+7.2	3.2	20 39.4	+7.3	3.2	21 39.3	+7.3	3.2
88	18 46.7	+6.9	2.1	19 46.7	+6.8	2.1	20 46.7	+6.8	2.1	21 46.6	+6.9	2.1
89	18 53.6	+6.4	1.1	19 53.5	+6.5	1.1	20 53.5	+6.5	1.1	21 53.5	+6.5	1.1
90	19 00.0	+6.1	0.0	20 00.0	+6.1	0.0	21 00.0	+6.1	0.0	22 00.0	+6.1	0.0
	19°			20°			21°			22°		

S. Lat. { L.H.A. greater than 180° ....Zn=180°–Z
L.H.A. less than 180°..........Zn=180°+Z

LATITUDE **SAME** NAME AS DECLINATION — L.H.A. 96°, 264°

85°, 275° L.H.A. LATITUDE SAME NAME AS DECLINATION N. Lat. {L.H.A. greater than 180° .....Zn=Z; L.H.A. less than 180°............Zn=360°–Z

Dec.	15° Hc	d	Z	16° Hc	d	Z	17° Hc	d	Z	18° Hc	d	Z	19° Hc	d	Z	20° Hc	d	Z	21° Hc	d	Z	22° Hc	d	Z	Dec.
°	° ′	′	°	° ′	′	°	° ′	′	°	° ′	′	°	° ′	′	°	° ′	′	°	° ′	′	°	° ′	′	°	°
0	4 49.8	+15.5	91.3	4 48.4	+16.5	91.4	4 46.9	+17.5	91.5	4 45.3	+18.5	91.5	4 43.6	+19.6	91.6	4 41.9	+20.5	91.7	4 40.0	+21.6	91.8	4 38.1	+22.5	91.9	0
1	5 05.3	+15.5	90.3	5 04.9	+16.5	90.4	5 04.4	+17.5	90.5	5 03.8	+18.5	90.6	5 03.2	+19.5	90.7	5 02.4	+20.5	90.8	5 01.6	+21.4	90.9	5 00.6	+22.5	90.9	1
2	5 20.8	+15.3	89.4	5 21.4	+16.4	89.5	5 21.9	+17.4	89.5	5 22.3	+18.4	89.6	5 22.7	+19.3	89.7	5 22.9	+20.4	89.8	5 23.0	+21.4	89.9	5 23.1	+22.3	90.0	2
3	5 36.1	+15.3	88.4	5 37.8	+16.2	88.5	5 39.3	+17.3	88.6	5 40.7	+18.3	88.7	5 42.0	+19.3	88.8	5 43.3	+20.3	88.9	5 44.4	+21.3	89.0	5 45.4	+22.3	89.1	3
4	5 51.4	+15.2	87.4	5 54.0	+16.2	87.5	5 56.6	+17.2	87.6	5 59.0	+18.2	87.7	6 01.3	+19.2	87.8	6 03.6	+20.2	87.9	6 05.7	+21.1	88.0	6 07.7	+22.1	88.1	4
5	6 06.6	+15.0	86.4	6 10.2	+16.1	86.5	6 13.8	+17.1	86.7	6 17.2	+18.1	86.8	6 20.5	+19.1	86.9	6 23.8	+20.0	87.0	6 26.8	+21.1	87.1	6 29.8	+22.1	87.2	5
6	6 21.6	+15.0	85.5	6 26.3	+16.0	85.6	6 30.9	+16.9	85.7	6 35.3	+18.0	85.8	6 39.6	+19.0	85.9	6 43.8	+20.0	86.0	6 47.9	+21.0	86.2	6 51.9	+21.9	86.3	6
7	6 36.6	+14.8	84.5	6 42.3	+15.8	84.6	6 47.8	+16.9	84.7	6 53.3	+17.9	84.8	6 58.6	+18.9	85.0	7 03.8	+19.9	85.1	7 08.9	+20.8	85.2	7 13.8	+21.9	85.3	7
8	6 51.4	+14.7	83.5	6 58.1	+15.8	83.6	7 04.7	+16.7	83.8	7 11.2	+17.7	83.9	7 17.5	+18.7	84.0	7 23.7	+19.7	84.1	7 29.7	+20.8	84.3	7 35.7	+21.7	84.4	8
9	7 06.1	+14.6	82.5	7 13.9	+15.6	82.7	7 21.4	+16.7	82.8	7 28.9	+17.6	82.9	7 36.2	+18.7	83.1	7 43.4	+19.6	83.2	7 50.5	+20.6	83.3	7 57.4	+21.6	83.5	9
10	7 20.7	+14.5	81.6	7 29.5	+15.4	81.7	7 38.1	+16.5	81.8	7 46.5	+17.5	82.0	7 54.9	+18.4	82.1	8 03.0	+19.5	82.2	8 11.1	+20.4	82.4	8 19.0	+21.4	82.5	10
11	7 35.2	+14.3	80.6	7 44.9	+15.3	80.7	7 54.6	+16.3	80.9	8 04.0	+17.4	81.0	8 13.3	+18.4	81.1	8 22.5	+19.4	81.3	8 31.5	+20.4	81.4	8 40.4	+21.3	81.6	11
12	7 49.5	+14.2	79.6	8 00.3	+15.2	79.7	8 10.9	+16.2	79.9	8 21.4	+17.2	80.0	8 31.7	+18.2	80.2	8 41.9	+19.2	80.3	8 51.9	+20.2	80.5	9 01.7	+21.2	80.6	12
13	8 03.7	+14.1	78.6	8 15.5	+15.1	78.8	8 27.1	+16.1	78.9	8 38.6	+17.1	79.1	8 49.9	+18.1	79.2	9 01.1	+19.0	79.4	9 12.1	+20.0	79.5	9 22.9	+21.0	79.7	13
14	8 17.8	+13.9	77.6	8 30.6	+14.9	77.8	8 43.2	+15.9	77.9	8 55.7	+16.9	78.1	9 08.0	+17.9	78.2	9 20.1	+18.9	78.4	9 32.1	+19.9	78.6	9 43.9	+20.9	78.7	14
15	8 31.7	+13.8	76.7	8 45.5	+14.8	76.8	8 59.1	+15.8	77.0	9 12.6	+16.7	77.1	9 25.9	+17.7	77.3	9 39.0	+18.7	77.4	9 52.0	+19.7	77.6	10 04.8	+20.7	77.8	15
16	8 45.5	+13.6	75.7	9 00.3	+14.6	75.8	9 14.9	+15.6	76.0	9 29.3	+16.6	76.1	9 43.6	+17.6	76.3	9 57.7	+18.6	76.5	10 11.7	+19.5	76.6	10 25.5	+20.5	76.8	16
17	8 59.1	+13.5	74.7	9 14.9	+14.4	74.8	9 30.5	+15.4	75.0	9 45.9	+16.5	75.2	10 01.2	+17.4	75.3	10 16.3	+18.4	75.5	10 31.2	+19.4	75.7	10 46.0	+20.3	75.9	17
18	9 12.6	+13.3	73.7	9 29.3	+14.3	73.9	9 45.9	+15.3	74.0	10 02.4	+16.2	74.2	10 18.6	+17.3	74.4	10 34.7	+18.2	74.5	10 50.6	+19.2	74.7	11 06.3	+20.2	74.9	18
19	9 25.9	+13.1	72.7	9 43.6	+14.1	72.9	10 01.2	+15.1	73.0	10 18.6	+16.1	73.2	10 35.9	+17.0	73.4	10 52.9	+18.1	73.6	11 09.8	+19.0	73.8	11 26.5	+20.0	73.9	19
20	9 39.0	+13.0	71.7	9 57.7	+14.0	71.9	10 16.3	+14.9	72.1	10 34.7	+15.9	72.2	10 52.9	+16.9	72.4	11 11.0	+17.8	72.6	11 28.8	+18.8	72.8	11 46.5	+19.7	73.0	20
21	9 52.0	+12.8	70.7	10 11.7	+13.8	70.9	10 31.2	+14.8	71.1	10 50.6	+15.7	71.3	11 09.8	+16.7	71.4	11 28.8	+17.7	71.6	11 47.6	+18.6	71.8	12 06.2	+19.6	72.0	21
22	10 04.8	+12.6	69.7	10 25.5	+13.5	69.9	10 46.0	+14.5	70.1	11 06.3	+15.5	70.3	11 26.5	+16.5	70.5	11 46.5	+17.4	70.6	12 06.2	+18.5	70.8	12 25.8	+19.4	71.1	22
23	10 17.4	+12.4	68.7	10 39.0	+13.4	68.9	11 00.5	+14.4	69.1	11 21.8	+15.4	69.3	11 43.0	+16.3	69.5	12 03.9	+17.3	69.7	12 24.7	+18.2	69.9	12 45.2	+19.2	70.1	23
24	10 29.8	+12.2	67.8	10 52.4	+13.2	67.9	11 14.9	+14.2	68.1	11 37.2	+15.1	68.3	11 59.3	+16.1	68.5	12 21.2	+17.0	68.7	12 42.9	+18.0	68.9	13 04.4	+18.9	69.1	24
25	10 42.0	+12.1	66.8	11 05.6	+13.1	66.9	11 29.1	+13.9	67.1	11 52.3	+14.9	67.3	12 15.4	+15.8	67.5	12 38.2	+16.8	67.7	13 00.9	+17.7	67.9	13 23.3	+18.7	68.1	25
26	10 54.1	+11.9	65.8	11 18.7	+12.8	65.9	11 43.0	+13.8	66.1	12 07.2	+14.7	66.3	12 31.2	+15.7	66.5	12 55.0	+16.6	66.7	13 18.6	+17.6	66.9	13 42.0	+18.5	67.2	26
27	11 06.0	+11.6	64.8	11 31.5	+12.6	64.9	11 56.8	+13.5	65.1	12 21.9	+14.5	65.3	12 46.9	+15.4	65.5	13 11.6	+16.4	65.7	13 36.2	+17.3	66.0	14 00.5	+18.3	66.2	27
28	11 17.6	+11.5	63.8	11 44.1	+12.4	63.9	12 10.3	+13.4	64.1	12 36.4	+14.3	64.3	13 02.3	+15.2	64.5	13 28.0	+16.1	64.8	13 53.5	+17.1	65.0	14 18.8	+18.0	65.2	28
29	11 29.1	+11.2	62.8	11 56.5	+12.2	62.9	12 23.7	+13.1	63.1	12 50.7	+14.0	63.3	13 17.5	+15.0	63.5	13 44.1	+16.0	63.8	14 10.6	+16.8	64.0	14 36.8	+17.7	64.2	29
30	11 40.3	+11.1	61.8	12 08.7	+11.9	61.9	12 36.8	+12.9	62.1	13 04.7	+13.9	62.3	13 32.5	+14.7	62.5	14 00.1	+15.6	62.8	14 27.4	+16.6	63.0	14 54.5	+17.6	63.2	30
31	11 51.4	+10.8	60.8	12 20.6	+11.8	60.9	12 49.7	+12.6	61.1	13 18.6	+13.5	61.3	13 47.2	+14.5	61.6	14 15.7	+15.4	61.8	14 44.0	+16.3	62.0	15 12.1	+17.2	62.2	31
32	12 02.2	+10.7	59.7	12 32.4	+11.5	59.9	13 02.3	+12.5	60.1	13 32.1	+13.4	60.3	14 01.7	+14.3	60.6	14 31.1	+15.2	60.8	15 00.3	+16.1	61.0	15 29.3	+17.0	61.2	32
33	12 12.9	+10.4	58.7	12 43.9	+11.3	58.9	13 14.8	+12.2	59.1	13 45.5	+13.1	59.3	14 16.0	+14.0	59.5	14 46.3	+14.9	59.8	15 16.4	+15.8	60.0	15 46.3	+16.7	60.2	33
34	12 23.3	+10.1	57.7	12 55.2	+11.1	57.9	13 27.0	+11.9	58.1	13 58.6	+12.8	58.3	14 30.0	+13.7	58.5	15 01.2	+14.6	58.8	15 32.2	+15.5	59.0	16 03.0	+16.4	59.2	34
35	12 33.4	+10.0	56.7	13 06.3	+10.8	56.9	13 38.9	+11.7	57.1	14 11.4	+12.6	57.3	14 43.7	+13.5	57.5	15 15.8	+14.4	57.8	15 47.7	+15.3	58.0	16 19.4	+16.2	58.2	35
36	12 43.4	+9.7	55.7	13 17.1	+10.6	55.9	13 50.6	+11.5	56.1	14 24.0	+12.4	56.3	14 57.2	+13.2	56.5	15 30.2	+14.1	56.8	16 03.0	+15.0	57.0	16 35.6	+15.8	57.2	36
37	12 53.1	+9.5	54.7	13 27.7	+10.3	54.9	14 02.1	+11.2	55.1	14 36.4	+12.0	55.3	15 10.4	+13.0	55.5	15 44.3	+13.8	55.7	16 18.0	+14.6	56.0	16 51.4	+15.6	56.2	37
38	13 02.6	+9.2	53.7	13 38.0	+10.1	53.9	14 13.3	+11.0	54.1	14 48.4	+11.8	54.3	15 23.4	+12.6	54.5	15 58.1	+13.5	54.7	16 32.6	+14.4	55.0	17 07.0	+15.2	55.2	38
39	13 11.8	+9.0	52.7	13 48.1	+9.9	52.9	14 24.3	+10.7	53.1	15 00.2	+11.6	53.3	15 36.0	+12.4	53.5	16 11.6	+13.3	53.7	16 47.0	+14.1	54.0	17 22.2	+15.0	54.2	39
40	13 20.8	+8.8	51.7	13 58.0	+9.6	51.8	14 35.0	+10.4	52.0	15 11.8	+11.3	52.3	15 48.4	+12.1	52.5	16 24.9	+12.9	52.7	17 01.1	+13.8	52.9	17 37.2	+14.6	53.2	40
41	13 29.6	+8.5	50.6	14 07.6	+9.3	50.8	14 45.4	+10.2	51.0	15 23.1	+10.9	51.2	16 00.5	+11.8	51.5	16 37.8	+12.7	51.7	17 14.9	+13.5	51.9	17 51.8	+14.3	52.2	41
42	13 38.1	+8.3	49.6	14 16.9	+9.1	49.8	14 55.6	+9.9	50.0	15 34.0	+10.8	50.2	16 12.3	+11.6	50.4	16 50.5	+12.3	50.7	17 28.4	+13.2	50.9	18 06.1	+14.0	51.2	42
43	13 46.4	+8.0	48.6	14 26.0	+8.8	48.8	15 05.5	+9.6	49.0	15 44.8	+10.4	49.2	16 23.9	+11.2	49.4	17 02.8	+12.1	49.6	17 41.6	+12.8	49.9	18 20.1	+13.7	50.1	43
44	13 54.4	+7.8	47.6	14 34.8	+8.6	47.8	15 15.1	+9.3	48.0	15 55.2	+10.1	48.2	16 35.1	+10.9	48.4	17 14.9	+11.7	48.6	17 54.4	+12.6	48.9	18 33.8	+13.3	49.1	44
45	14 02.2	+7.5	46.6	14 43.4	+8.3	46.7	15 24.4	+9.1	46.9	16 05.3	+9.8	47.1	16 46.0	+10.6	47.4	17 26.6	+11.4	47.6	18 07.0	+12.2	47.8	18 47.1	+13.0	48.1	45
46	14 09.7	+7.2	45.5	14 51.7	+8.0	45.7	15 33.5	+8.7	45.9	16 15.1	+9.6	46.1	16 56.6	+10.4	46.3	17 38.0	+11.1	46.6	18 19.2	+11.8	46.8	19 00.1	+12.7	47.0	46
47	14 16.9	+7.0	44.5	14 59.7	+7.7	44.7	15 42.2	+8.5	44.9	16 24.7	+9.2	45.1	17 07.0	+10.0	45.3	17 49.1	+10.7	45.5	18 31.0	+11.5	45.8	19 12.8	+12.3	46.0	47
48	14 23.9	+6.8	43.5	15 07.4	+7.5	43.7	15 50.7	+8.2	43.9	16 33.9	+9.0	44.1	17 17.0	+9.6	44.3	17 59.8	+10.5	44.5	18 42.5	+11.2	44.7	19 25.1	+11.9	45.0	48
49	14 30.7	+6.4	42.5	15 14.9	+7.1	42.6	15 58.9	+7.9	42.8	16 42.9	+8.6	43.0	17 26.6	+9.4	43.2	18 10.3	+10.1	43.5	18 53.7	+10.9	43.7	19 37.0	+11.6	43.9	49
50	14 37.1	+6.2	41.4	15 22.0	+6.9	41.6	16 06.8	+7.6	41.8	16 51.5	+8.3	42.0	17 36.0	+9.0	42.2	18 20.4	+9.7	42.4	19 04.6	+10.5	42.7	19 48.6	+11.2	42.9	50
51	14 43.3	+5.9	40.4	15 28.9	+6.6	40.6	16 14.4	+7.3	40.8	16 59.8	+8.0	41.0	17 45.0	+8.7	41.2	18 30.1	+9.5	41.4	19 15.1	+10.1	41.6	19 59.8	+10.9	41.8	51
52	14 49.2	+5.6	39.4	15 35.5	+6.3	39.5	16 21.7	+7.0	39.7	17 07.8	+7.7	39.9	17 53.7	+8.4	40.1	18 39.6	+9.0	40.3	19 25.2	+9.8	40.6	20 10.7	+10.5	40.8	52
53	14 54.8	+5.4	38.3	15 41.8	+6.1	38.5	16 28.7	+6.7	38.7	17 15.5	+7.4	38.9	18 02.1	+8.1	39.1	18 48.6	+8.8	39.3	19 35.0	+9.4	39.5	20 21.2	+10.1	39.8	53
54	15 00.2	+5.1	37.3	15 47.9	+5.7	37.5	16 35.4	+6.4	37.7	17 22.9	+7.0	37.8	18 10.2	+7.7	38.0	18 57.4	+8.3	38.3	19 44.4	+9.0	38.5	20 31.3	+9.7	38.7	54
55	15 05.3	+4.8	36.3	15 53.6	+5.4	36.4	16 41.8	+6.1	36.6	17 29.9	+6.7	36.8	18 17.9	+7.3	37.0	19 05.7	+8.0	37.2	19 53.4	+8.7	37.4	20 41.0	+9.4	37.6	55
56	15 10.1	+4.5	35.3	15 59.0	+5.2	35.4	16 47.9	+5.7	35.6	17 36.6	+6.4	35.8	18 25.2	+7.1	36.0	19 13.7	+7.7	36.2	20 02.1	+8.3	36.4	20 50.4	+8.9	36.6	56
57	15 14.6	+4.2	34.2	16 04.2	+4.8	34.4	16 53.6	+5.5	34.5	17 43.0	+6.1	34.7	18 32.3	+6.6	34.9	19 21.4	+7.3	35.1	20 10.4	+8.0	35.3	20 59.3	+8.6	35.5	57
58	15 18.8	+4.0	33.2	16 09.0	+4.5	33.3	16 59.1	+5.1	33.5	17 49.1	+5.7	33.7	18 38.9	+6.4	33.9	19 28.7	+6.9	34.1	20 18.4	+7.5	34.3	21 07.9	+8.1	34.5	58
59	15 22.8	+3.6	32.1	16 13.5	+4.3	32.3	17 04.2	+4.8	32.5	17 54.8	+5.4	32.6	18 45.3	+5.9	32.8	19 35.6	+6.6	33.0	20 25.9	+7.2	33.2	21 16.0	+7.8	33.4	59
60	15 26.4	+3.4	31.1	16 17.8	+3.9	31.3	17 09.0	+4.5	31.4	18 00.2	+5.0	31.6	18 51.2	+5.6	31.8	19 42.2	+6.2	31.9	20 33.1	+6.7	32.1	21 23.8	+7.4	32.3	60
61	15 29.8	+3.1	30.1	16 21.7	+3.6	30.2	17 13.5	+4.2	30.4	18 05.2	+4.7	30.5	18 56.8	+5.3	30.7	19 48.4	+5.8	30.9	20 39.8	+6.4	31.1	21 31.2	+6.9	31.3	61
62	15 32.9	+2.8	29.0	16 25.3	+3.3	29.2	17 17.7	+3.8	29.3	18 09.9	+4.4	29.5	19 02.1	+4.9	29.7	19 54.2	+5.4	29.8	20 46.2	+6.0	30.0	21 38.1	+6.6	30.2	62
63	15 35.7	+2.5	28.0	16 28.6	+3.0	28.1	17 21.5	+3.5	28.3	18 14.3	+4.0	28.4	19 07.0	+4.6	28.6	19 59.6	+5.1	28.8	20 52.2	+5.6	28.9	21 44.7	+6.1	29.1	63
64	15 38.2	+2.2	27.0	16 31.6	+2.7	27.1	17 25.0	+3.2	27.2	18 18.3	+3.7	27.4	19 11.6	+4.1	27.5	20 04.7	+4.7	27.7	20 57.8	+5.2	27.9	21 50.8	+5.7	28.1	64
65	15 40.4	+1.9	25.9	16 34.3	+2.4	26.1	17 28.2	+2.8	26.2	18 22.0	+3.3	26.3	19 15.7	+3.8	26.5	20 09.4	+4.3	26.6	21 03.0	+4.8	26.8	21 56.5	+5.3	27.0	65
66	15 42.3	+1.6	24.9	16 36.7	+2.1	25.0	17 31.0	+2.6	25.1	18 25.3	+3.0	25.3	19 19.5	+3.5	25.4	20 13.7	+3.9	25.6	21 07.8	+4.4	25.7	22 01.8	+4.9	25.9	66
67	15 43.9	+1.3	23.9	16 38.8	+1.7	24.0	17 33.6	+2.2	24.1	18 28.3	+2.7	24.2	19 23.0	+3.1	24.4	20 17.6	+3.6	24.5	21 12.2	+4.0	24.7	22 06.7	+4.4	24.8	67
68	15 45.2	+1.1	22.8	16 40.5	+1.5	22.9	17 35.8	+1.8	23.0	18 31.0	+2.2	23.2	19 26.1	+2.7	23.3	20 21.2	+3.1	23.5	21 16.2	+3.5	23.6	22 11.1	+4.0	23.8	68
69	15 46.3	+0.7	21.8	16 42.0	+1.1	21.9	17 37.6	+1.6	22.0	18 33.2	+2.0	22.1	19 28.8	+2.3	22.3	20 24.3	+2.8	22.4	21 19.7	+3.2	22.5	22 15.1	+3.6	22.7	69
70	15 47.0	+0.5	20.7	16 43.1	+0.8	20.8	17 39.2	+1.2	21.0	18 35.2	+1.6	21.1	19 31.1	+2.0	21.2	20 27.1	+2.3	21.3	21 22.9	+2.8	21.5	22 18.7	+3.2	21.6	70
71	15 47.5	+0.1	19.7	16 43.9	+0.5	19.8	17 40.4	+0.8	19.9	18 36.8	+1.2	20.0	19 33.1	+1.6	20.1	20 29.4	+2.0	20.3	21 25.7	+2.3	20.4	22 21.9	+2.7	20.5	71
72	15 47.6	-0.2	18.7	16 44.4	+0.2	18.8	17 41.2	+0.6	18.9	18 38.0	+0.9	19.0	19 34.7	+1.2	19.1	20 31.4	+1.6	19.2	21 28.0	+2.0	19.3	22 24.6	+2.4	19.5	72
73	15 47.4	-0.4	17.6	16 44.6	-0.1	17.7	17 41.8	+0.2	17.8	18 38.9	+0.5	17.9	19 35.9	+0.9	18.0	20 33.0	+1.2	18.1	21 30.0	+1.5	18.2	22 27.0	+1.8	18.4	73
74	15 47.0	-0.8	16.6	16 44.5	-0.5	16.7	17 42.0	-0.2	16.8	18 39.4	+0.2	16.8	19 36.8	+0.5	16.9	20 34.2	+0.8	17.1	21 31.5	+1.1	17.2	22 28.8	+1.5	17.3	74
75	15 46.2	-1.0	15.5	16 44.0	-0.7	15.6	17 41.8	-0.5	15.7	18 39.6	-0.2	15.8	19 37.3	+0.1	15.9	20 35.0	+0.4	16.0	21 32.6	+0.7	16.1	22 30.3	+1.0	16.2	75
76	15 45.2	-1.3	14.5	16 43.3	-1.1	14.6	17 41.3	-0.8	14.7	18 39.4	-0.6	14.7	19 37.4	-0.3	14.8	20 35.4	0.0	14.9	21 33.3	+0.3	15.0	22 31.3	+0.6	15.1	76
77	15 43.9	-1.7	13.5	16 42.2	-1.4	13.5	17 40.5	-1.1	13.6	18 38.8	-0.8	13.7	19 37.1	-0.6	13.8	20 35.4	-0.4	13.9	21 33.6	-0.1	13.9	22 31.9	+0.1	14.0	77
78	15 42.2	-1.9	12.4	16 40.8	-1.7	12.5	17 39.4	-1.5	12.6	18 38.0	-1.3	12.6	19 36.5	-1.0	12.7	20 35.0	-0.8	12.8	21 33.5	-0.5	12.9	22 32.0	-0.3	13.0	78
79	15 40.3	-2.2	11.4	16 39.1	-2.0	11.4	17 37.9	-1.8	11.5	18 36.7	-1.6	11.6	19 35.5	-1.4	11.6	20 34.2	-1.1	11.7	21 33.0	-1.0	11.8	22 31.7	-0.7	11.9	79
80	15 38.1	-2.5	10.3	16 37.1	-2.3	10.4	17 36.1	-2.1	10.5	18 35.1	-1.9	10.5	19 34.1	-1.7	10.6	20 33.1	-1.6	10.6	21 32.0	-1.3	10.7	22 31.0	-1.2	10.8	80
81	15 35.6	-2.8	9.3	16 34.8	-2.7	9.4	17 34.0	-2.5	9.4	18 33.2	-2.3	9.5	19 32.4	-2.2	9.5	20 31.5	-1.9	9.6	21 30.7	-1.8	9.6	22 29.8	-1.6	9.7	81
82	15 32.8	-3.1	8.3	16 32.1	-2.9	8.3	17 31.5	-2.8	8.4	18 30.9	-2.7	8.4	19 30.2	-2.5	8.5	20 29.6	-2.4	8.5	21 28.9	-2.2	8.6	22 28.2	-2.0	8.6	82
83	15 29.7	-3.4	7.2	16 29.2	-3.3	7.3	17 28.7	-3.1	7.3	18 28.2	-3.0	7.4	19 27.7	-2.8	7.4	20 27.2	-2.7	7.4	21 26.7	-2.6	7.5	22 26.2	-2.5	7.5	83
84	15 26.3	-3.7	6.2	16 25.9	-3.5	6.2	17 25.6	-3.5	6.3	18 25.2	-3.3	6.3	19 24.9	-3.3	6.3	20 24.5	-3.1	6.4	21 24.1	-3.0	6.4	22 23.7	-2.8	6.5	84
85	15 22.6	-3.9	5.2	16 22.4	-3.9	5.2	17 22.1	-3.7	5.2	18 21.9	-3.7	5.2	19 21.6	-3.6	5.3	20 21.4	-3.5	5.3	21 21.1	-3.4	5.3	22 20.9	-3.4	5.4	85
86	15 18.7	-4.3	4.1	16 18.5	-4.2	4.2	17 18.4	-4.2	4.2	18 18.2	-4.0	4.2	19 18.0	-3.9	4.2	20 17.9	-3.9	4.2	21 17.7	-3.8	4.3	22 17.5	-3.7	4.3	86
87	15 14.4	-4.5	3.1	16 14.3	-4.4	3.1	17 14.2	-4.4	3.1	18 14.2	-4.4	3.1	19 14.1	-4.4	3.2	20 14.0	-4.3	3.2	21 13.9	-4.2	3.2	22 13.8	-4.2	3.2	87
88	15 09.9	-4.8	2.1	16 09.9	-4.8	2.1	17 09.8	-4.7	2.1	18 09.8	-4.7	2.1	19 09.7	-4.6	2.1	20 09.7	-4.7	2.1	21 09.7	-4.7	2.1	22 09.6	-4.6	2.2	88
89	15 05.1	-5.1	1.0	16 05.1	-5.1	1.0	17 05.1	-5.1	1.0	18 05.1	-5.1	1.0	19 05.1	-5.1	1.1	20 05.0	-5.0	1.1	21 05.0	-5.0	1.1	22 05.0	-5.0	1.1	89
90	15 00.0	-5.4	0.0	16 00.0	-5.4	0.0	17 00.0	-5.4	0.0	18 00.0	-5.4	0.0	19 00.0	-5.4	0.0	20 00.0	-5.4	0.0	21 00.0	-5.4	0.0	22 00.0	-5.4	0.0	90
	15°			16°			17°			18°			19°			20°			21°			22°			

85°, 275° L.H.A. LATITUDE SAME NAME AS DECLINATION

172

LATITUDE **CONTRARY** NAME TO DECLINATION **L.H.A. 85°, 275°**

Dec.	15°			16°			17°			18°			19°			20°			21°			22°			Dec.
°	Hc ° ′	d ′	Z °	Hc ° ′	d ′	Z °	Hc ° ′	d ′	Z °	Hc ° ′	d ′	Z °	Hc ° ′	d ′	Z °	Hc ° ′	d ′	Z °	Hc ° ′	d ′	Z °	Hc ° ′	d ′	Z °	°
0	4 49.8	−15.7	91.3	4 48.4	−16.7	91.4	4 46.9	−17.7	91.5	4 45.3	−18.7	91.5	4 43.6	−19.6	91.6	4 41.9	−20.7	91.7	4 40.0	−21.6	91.8	4 38.1	−22.6	91.9	0
1	4 34.1	−15.7	92.3	4 31.7	−16.7	92.3	4 29.2	−17.7	92.4	4 26.6	−18.7	92.5	4 24.0	−19.7	92.6	4 21.2	−20.7	92.7	4 18.4	−21.7	92.7	4 15.5	−22.6	92.8	1
2	4 18.4	−15.8	93.2	4 15.0	−16.8	93.3	4 11.5	−17.8	93.4	4 07.9	−18.8	93.5	4 04.3	−19.8	93.5	4 00.5	−20.7	93.6	3 56.7	−21.7	93.7	3 52.9	−22.7	93.7	2
3	4 02.6	−15.8	94.2	3 58.2	−16.8	94.3	3 53.7	−17.8	94.3	3 49.1	−18.8	94.4	3 44.5	−19.8	94.5	3 39.8	−20.8	94.5	3 35.0	−21.8	94.6	3 30.2	−22.8	94.7	3
4	3 46.8	−15.9	95.2	3 41.4	−16.9	95.2	3 35.9	−18.0	95.3	3 30.3	−18.9	95.4	3 24.7	−19.9	95.4	3 19.0	−20.9	95.5	3 13.2	−21.8	95.5	3 07.4	−22.8	95.6	4
5	3 30.9	−16.0	96.1	3 24.5	−17.0	96.2	3 17.9	−17.9	96.3	3 11.4	−19.0	96.3	3 04.8	−20.0	96.4	2 58.1	−20.9	96.4	2 51.4	−21.9	96.5	2 44.6	−22.9	96.5	5
6	3 14.9	−16.0	97.1	3 07.5	−17.0	97.2	3 00.0	−18.0	97.2	2 52.4	−19.0	97.3	2 44.8	−20.0	97.3	2 37.2	−21.0	97.4	2 29.5	−22.0	97.4	2 21.7	−22.9	97.4	6
7	2 58.9	−16.1	98.1	2 50.5	−17.1	98.1	2 42.0	−18.1	98.2	2 33.4	−19.0	98.2	2 24.8	−20.0	98.3	2 16.2	−21.0	98.3	2 07.5	−21.9	98.3	1 58.8	−22.9	98.4	7
8	2 42.8	−16.1	99.0	2 33.4	−17.1	99.1	2 23.9	−18.1	99.1	2 14.4	−19.1	99.2	2 04.8	−20.1	99.2	1 55.2	−21.0	99.2	1 45.6	−22.0	99.3	1 35.9	−23.0	99.3	8
9	2 26.7	−16.2	100.0	2 16.3	−17.2	100.0	2 05.8	−18.1	100.1	1 55.3	−19.1	100.1	1 44.7	−20.1	100.1	1 34.2	−21.1	100.2	1 23.6	−22.1	100.2	1 12.9	−22.9	100.2	9
10	2 10.5	−16.2	101.0	1 59.1	−17.2	101.0	1 47.7	−18.2	101.0	1 36.2	−19.2	101.1	1 24.6	−20.1	101.1	1 13.1	−21.1	101.1	1 01.5	−22.0	101.1	0 50.0	−23.0	101.1	10
11	1 54.3	−16.2	101.9	1 41.9	−17.2	102.0	1 29.5	−18.2	102.0	1 17.0	−19.1	102.0	1 04.5	−20.1	102.0	0 52.0	−21.1	102.0	0 39.5	−22.0	102.1	0 27.0	−23.0	102.1	11
12	1 38.1	−16.3	102.9	1 24.7	−17.2	102.9	1 11.3	−18.2	102.9	0 57.9	−19.2	103.0	0 44.4	−20.1	103.0	0 30.9	−21.1	103.0	0 17.5	−22.1	103.0	0 04.0	−23.0	103.0	12
13	1 21.8	−16.2	103.8	1 07.5	−17.3	103.9	0 53.1	−18.2	103.9	0 38.7	−19.2	103.9	0 24.3	−20.2	103.9	0 09.8	−21.1	103.9	0 04.6	+22.0	76.1	0 19.0	+23.0	76.1	13
14	1 05.6	−16.3	104.8	0 50.2	−17.3	104.8	0 34.9	−18.3	104.8	0 19.5	−19.2	104.8	0 04.1	−20.1	104.8	0 11.3	+21.1	75.2	0 26.6	+22.1	75.2	0 42.0	+23.0	75.2	14
15	0 49.3	−16.4	105.8	0 32.9	−17.2	105.8	0 16.6	−18.2	105.8	0 00.3	−19.2	105.8	0 16.0	+20.2	74.2	0 32.4	+21.0	74.2	0 48.7	+22.0	74.2	1 05.0	+22.9	74.2	15
16	0 32.9	−16.3	106.7	0 15.7	−17.3	106.7	0 01.6	+18.3	73.3	0 18.9	+19.2	73.3	0 36.2	+20.1	73.3	0 53.4	+21.1	73.3	1 10.7	+22.0	73.3	1 27.9	+23.0	73.3	16
17	0 16.6	−16.3	107.7	0 01.6	+17.3	72.3	0 19.9	+18.2	72.3	0 38.1	+19.2	72.3	0 56.3	+20.1	72.3	1 14.5	+21.1	72.3	1 32.7	+22.0	72.4	1 50.9	+22.9	72.4	17
18	0 00.3	−16.3	108.7	0 18.9	+17.3	71.3	0 38.1	+18.2	71.4	0 57.3	+19.1	71.4	1 16.4	+20.1	71.4	1 35.6	+21.0	71.4	1 54.7	+21.9	71.4	2 13.8	+22.9	71.5	18
19	0 16.0	+16.4	70.4	0 36.2	+17.2	70.4	0 56.3	+18.2	70.4	1 16.4	+19.2	70.4	1 36.5	+20.1	70.4	1 56.6	+21.0	70.5	2 16.6	+22.0	70.5	2 36.7	+22.8	70.5	19
20	0 32.4	+16.3	69.4	0 53.4	+17.3	69.4	1 14.5	+18.2	69.4	1 35.6	+19.1	69.5	1 56.6	+20.0	69.5	2 17.6	+21.0	69.5	2 38.6	+21.8	69.6	2 59.5	+22.8	69.6	20
21	0 48.7	+16.3	68.5	1 10.7	+17.2	68.5	1 32.7	+18.2	68.5	1 54.7	+19.1	68.5	2 16.6	+20.1	68.6	2 38.6	+20.9	68.6	3 00.4	+21.9	68.6	3 22.3	+22.7	68.7	21
22	1 05.0	+16.3	67.5	1 27.9	+17.2	67.5	1 50.9	+18.1	67.5	2 13.8	+19.0	67.6	2 36.7	+19.9	67.6	2 59.5	+20.9	67.7	3 22.3	+21.7	67.7	3 45.0	+22.7	67.8	22
23	1 21.3	+16.2	66.5	1 45.1	+17.2	66.6	2 09.0	+18.1	66.6	2 32.8	+19.0	66.6	2 56.6	+19.9	66.7	3 20.4	+20.8	66.7	3 44.0	+21.8	66.8	4 07.7	+22.6	66.8	23
24	1 37.5	+16.3	65.6	2 02.3	+17.2	65.6	2 27.1	+18.1	65.6	2 51.8	+19.0	65.7	3 16.5	+19.9	65.7	3 41.2	+20.7	65.8	4 05.8	+21.6	65.8	4 30.3	+22.5	65.9	24
25	1 53.8	+16.2	64.6	2 19.5	+17.1	64.6	2 45.2	+18.0	64.7	3 10.8	+18.9	64.7	3 36.4	+19.8	64.8	4 01.9	+20.7	64.8	4 27.4	+21.6	64.9	4 52.8	+22.5	65.0	25
26	2 10.0	+16.1	63.6	2 36.6	+17.0	63.7	3 03.2	+17.9	63.7	3 29.7	+18.9	63.8	3 56.2	+19.7	63.8	4 22.6	+20.6	63.9	4 49.0	+21.5	64.0	5 15.3	+22.4	64.0	26
27	2 26.1	+16.1	62.7	2 53.6	+17.1	62.7	3 21.1	+17.9	62.8	3 48.6	+18.7	62.8	4 15.9	+19.7	62.9	4 43.2	+20.6	63.0	5 10.5	+21.4	63.0	5 37.7	+22.3	63.1	27
28	2 42.2	+16.1	61.7	3 10.7	+16.9	61.8	3 39.0	+17.9	61.8	4 07.3	+18.8	61.9	4 35.6	+19.6	61.9	5 03.8	+20.5	62.0	5 31.9	+21.3	62.1	6 00.0	+22.2	62.2	28
29	2 58.3	+16.0	60.7	3 27.6	+16.9	60.8	3 56.9	+17.7	60.9	4 26.1	+18.6	60.9	4 55.2	+19.5	61.0	5 24.3	+20.3	61.1	5 53.2	+21.3	61.2	6 22.2	+22.0	61.2	29
30	3 14.3	+16.0	59.8	3 44.5	+16.9	59.8	4 14.6	+17.7	59.9	4 44.7	+18.6	60.0	5 14.7	+19.4	60.0	5 44.6	+20.3	60.1	6 14.5	+21.1	60.2	6 44.2	+22.0	60.3	30
31	3 30.3	+15.9	58.8	4 01.4	+16.7	58.9	4 32.3	+17.7	58.9	5 03.3	+18.5	59.0	5 34.1	+19.4	59.1	6 04.9	+20.2	59.2	6 35.6	+21.1	59.3	7 06.2	+21.9	59.4	31
32	3 46.2	+15.9	57.8	4 18.1	+16.7	57.9	4 50.0	+17.5	58.0	5 21.8	+18.4	58.1	5 53.5	+19.2	58.1	6 25.1	+20.1	58.2	6 56.7	+20.9	58.3	7 28.1	+21.8	58.4	32
33	4 02.1	+15.8	56.9	4 34.8	+16.7	56.9	5 07.5	+17.5	57.0	5 40.2	+18.3	57.1	6 12.7	+19.1	57.2	6 45.2	+20.0	57.3	7 17.6	+20.8	57.4	7 49.9	+21.6	57.5	33
34	4 17.9	+15.7	55.9	4 51.5	+16.5	56.0	5 25.0	+17.4	56.1	5 58.5	+18.2	56.1	6 31.8	+19.1	56.2	7 05.2	+19.8	56.3	7 38.4	+20.7	56.4	8 11.5	+21.5	56.6	34
35	4 33.6	+15.6	54.9	5 08.0	+16.4	55.0	5 42.4	+17.2	55.1	6 16.7	+18.1	55.2	6 50.9	+18.9	55.3	7 25.0	+19.7	55.4	7 59.1	+20.5	55.5	8 33.0	+21.4	55.6	35
36	4 49.2	+15.5	54.0	5 24.4	+16.4	54.1	5 59.6	+17.2	54.1	6 34.8	+17.9	54.2	7 09.8	+18.8	54.3	7 44.7	+19.6	54.4	8 19.6	+20.4	54.5	8 54.4	+21.2	54.7	36
37	5 04.7	+15.5	53.0	5 40.8	+16.3	53.1	6 16.8	+17.1	53.2	6 52.7	+17.9	53.3	7 28.6	+18.7	53.4	8 04.3	+19.5	53.5	8 40.0	+20.3	53.6	9 15.6	+21.0	53.7	37
38	5 20.2	+15.4	52.0	5 57.1	+16.1	52.1	6 33.9	+16.9	52.2	7 10.6	+17.8	52.3	7 47.3	+18.5	52.4	8 23.8	+19.4	52.5	9 00.3	+20.1	52.6	9 36.6	+21.0	52.8	38
39	5 35.6	+15.2	51.1	6 13.2	+16.1	51.1	6 50.8	+16.9	51.2	7 28.4	+17.6	51.3	8 05.8	+18.4	51.4	8 43.2	+19.1	51.6	9 20.4	+20.0	51.7	9 57.6	+20.7	51.8	39
40	5 50.8	+15.2	50.1	6 29.3	+15.9	50.2	7 07.7	+16.7	50.3	7 46.0	+17.5	50.4	8 24.2	+18.3	50.5	9 02.3	+19.1	50.6	9 40.4	+19.8	50.7	10 18.3	+20.6	50.9	40
41	6 06.0	+15.1	49.1	6 45.2	+15.9	49.2	7 24.4	+16.6	49.3	8 03.5	+17.3	49.4	8 42.5	+18.1	49.5	9 21.4	+18.9	49.6	10 00.2	+19.6	49.8	10 38.9	+20.4	49.9	41
42	6 21.1	+14.9	48.1	7 01.1	+15.7	48.2	7 41.0	+16.5	48.3	8 20.8	+17.3	48.4	9 00.6	+18.0	48.6	9 40.3	+18.7	48.7	10 19.8	+19.5	48.8	10 59.3	+20.2	49.0	42
43	6 36.0	+14.9	47.2	7 16.8	+15.6	47.3	7 57.5	+16.3	47.4	8 38.1	+17.0	47.5	9 18.6	+17.8	47.6	9 59.0	+18.6	47.7	10 39.3	+19.3	47.8	11 19.5	+20.1	48.0	43
44	6 50.9	+14.7	46.2	7 32.4	+15.4	46.3	8 13.8	+16.2	46.4	8 55.1	+17.0	46.5	9 36.4	+17.6	46.6	10 17.6	+18.3	46.7	10 58.6	+19.1	46.9	11 39.6	+19.8	47.0	44
45	7 05.6	+14.6	45.2	7 47.8	+15.3	45.3	8 30.0	+16.0	45.4	9 12.1	+16.7	45.5	9 54.0	+17.5	45.6	10 35.9	+18.2	45.8	11 17.7	+19.0	45.9	11 59.4	+19.7	46.1	45
46	7 20.2	+14.5	44.2	8 03.1	+15.2	44.3	8 46.0	+15.9	44.4	9 28.8	+16.6	44.6	10 11.5	+17.3	44.7	10 54.1	+18.1	44.8	11 36.7	+18.7	44.9	12 19.1	+19.4	45.1	46
47	7 34.7	+14.3	43.3	8 18.3	+15.1	43.4	9 01.9	+15.8	43.5	9 45.4	+16.5	43.6	10 28.8	+17.2	43.7	11 12.2	+17.8	43.8	11 55.4	+18.5	44.0	12 38.5	+19.3	44.1	47
48	7 49.0	+14.2	42.3	8 33.4	+14.9	42.4	9 17.7	+15.5	42.5	10 01.9	+16.2	42.6	10 46.0	+16.9	42.7	11 30.0	+17.6	42.9	12 13.9	+18.4	43.0	12 57.8	+19.0	43.2	48
49	8 03.2	+14.1	41.3	8 48.3	+14.7	41.4	9 33.2	+15.4	41.5	10 18.1	+16.1	41.6	11 02.9	+16.8	41.8	11 47.6	+17.5	41.9	12 32.3	+18.1	42.0	13 16.8	+18.8	42.2	49
50	8 17.3	+13.9	40.3	9 03.0	+14.6	40.4	9 48.6	+15.3	40.5	10 34.2	+15.9	40.6	11 19.7	+16.6	40.8	12 05.1	+17.2	40.9	12 50.4	+17.9	41.1	13 35.6	+18.5	41.2	50
51	8 31.2	+13.8	39.3	9 17.6	+14.4	39.4	10 03.9	+15.1	39.5	10 50.1	+15.7	39.7	11 36.3	+16.3	39.8	12 22.3	+17.0	39.9	13 08.3	+17.7	40.1	13 54.1	+18.4	40.2	51
52	8 45.0	+13.6	38.4	9 32.0	+14.3	38.5	10 19.0	+14.9	38.6	11 05.8	+15.6	38.7	11 52.6	+16.2	38.8	12 39.3	+16.9	38.9	13 26.0	+17.4	39.1	14 12.5	+18.1	39.2	52
53	8 58.6	+13.5	37.4	9 46.3	+14.1	37.5	10 33.9	+14.7	37.6	11 21.4	+15.3	37.7	12 08.8	+16.0	37.8	12 56.2	+16.5	38.0	13 43.4	+17.2	38.1	14 30.6	+17.8	38.3	53
54	9 12.1	+13.3	36.4	10 00.4	+13.9	36.5	10 48.6	+14.5	36.6	11 36.7	+15.1	36.7	12 24.8	+15.7	36.8	13 12.7	+16.4	37.0	14 00.6	+17.0	37.1	14 48.4	+17.6	37.3	54
55	9 25.4	+13.1	35.4	10 14.3	+13.7	35.5	11 03.1	+14.3	35.6	11 51.8	+15.0	35.7	12 40.5	+15.5	35.9	13 29.1	+16.1	36.0	14 17.6	+16.7	36.1	15 06.0	+17.4	36.3	55
56	9 38.5	+13.0	34.4	10 28.0	+13.6	34.5	11 17.4	+14.1	34.6	12 06.8	+14.7	34.7	12 56.0	+15.3	34.9	13 45.2	+15.9	35.0	14 34.3	+16.5	35.1	15 23.4	+17.0	35.3	56
57	9 51.5	+12.8	33.4	10 41.6	+13.3	33.5	11 31.5	+14.0	33.6	12 21.5	+14.5	33.7	13 11.3	+15.1	33.9	14 01.1	+15.7	34.0	14 50.8	+16.2	34.1	15 40.4	+16.8	34.3	57
58	10 04.3	+12.6	32.4	10 54.9	+13.2	32.5	11 45.5	+13.7	32.6	12 36.0	+14.3	32.7	13 26.4	+14.8	32.9	14 16.8	+15.4	33.0	15 07.0	+16.0	33.1	15 57.2	+16.6	33.3	58
59	10 16.9	+12.5	31.4	11 08.1	+13.0	31.5	11 59.2	+13.5	31.6	12 50.3	+14.0	31.8	13 41.2	+14.6	31.9	14 32.2	+15.1	32.0	15 23.0	+15.7	32.2	16 13.8	+16.2	32.3	59
60	10 29.4	+12.2	30.4	11 21.1	+12.7	30.5	12 12.7	+13.3	30.6	13 04.3	+13.8	30.8	13 55.8	+14.4	30.9	14 47.3	+14.9	31.0	15 38.7	+15.4	31.1	16 30.0	+16.0	31.3	60
61	10 41.6	+12.1	29.4	11 33.8	+12.6	29.5	12 26.0	+13.1	29.6	13 18.1	+13.6	29.8	14 10.2	+14.1	29.9	15 02.2	+14.6	30.0	15 54.1	+15.1	30.1	16 46.0	+15.6	30.3	61
62	10 53.7	+11.8	28.4	11 46.4	+12.4	28.5	12 39.1	+12.8	28.6	13 31.7	+13.4	28.8	14 24.3	+13.8	28.9	15 16.8	+14.3	29.0	16 09.2	+14.9	29.1	17 01.6	+15.4	29.3	62
63	11 05.5	+11.7	27.4	11 58.8	+12.1	27.5	12 51.9	+12.7	27.6	13 45.1	+13.1	27.7	14 38.1	+13.6	27.9	15 31.1	+14.1	28.0	16 24.1	+14.6	28.1	17 17.0	+15.0	28.3	63
64	11 17.2	+11.5	26.4	12 10.9	+11.9	26.5	13 04.6	+12.4	26.6	13 58.2	+12.8	26.7	14 51.7	+13.4	26.9	15 45.2	+13.8	27.0	16 38.7	+14.2	27.1	17 32.0	+14.8	27.3	64
65	11 28.7	+11.2	25.4	12 22.8	+11.7	25.5	13 17.0	+12.1	25.6	14 11.0	+12.6	25.7	15 05.1	+13.0	25.9	15 59.0	+13.5	26.0	16 52.9	+14.0	26.1	17 46.8	+14.4	26.2	65
66	11 39.9	+11.1	24.4	12 34.5	+11.5	24.5	13 29.1	+11.9	24.6	14 23.6	+12.4	24.7	15 18.1	+12.8	24.8	16 12.5	+13.3	25.0	17 06.9	+13.7	25.1	18 01.2	+14.1	25.2	66
67	11 51.0	+10.8	23.4	12 46.0	+11.3	23.5	13 41.0	+11.7	23.6	14 36.0	+12.1	23.7	15 30.9	+12.5	23.8	16 25.8	+12.9	23.9	17 20.6	+13.3	24.1	18 15.3	+13.8	24.2	67
68	12 01.8	+10.7	22.4	12 57.3	+11.0	22.5	13 52.7	+11.4	22.6	14 48.1	+11.8	22.7	15 43.4	+12.2	22.8	16 38.7	+12.6	22.9	17 33.9	+13.1	23.0	18 29.1	+13.5	23.2	68
69	12 12.5	+10.4	21.4	13 08.3	+10.8	21.5	14 04.1	+11.2	21.6	14 59.9	+11.5	21.7	15 55.6	+12.0	21.8	16 51.3	+12.3	21.9	17 47.0	+12.7	22.0	18 42.6	+13.1	22.1	69
70	12 22.9	+10.2	20.4	13 19.1	+10.5	20.5	14 15.3	+10.9	20.6	15 11.4	+11.3	20.7	16 07.6	+11.6	20.8	17 03.6	+12.1	20.9	17 59.7	+12.4	21.0	18 55.7	+12.7	21.1	70
71	12 33.1	+9.9	19.4	13 29.6	+10.3	19.5	14 26.2	+10.6	19.6	15 22.7	+11.0	19.7	16 19.2	+11.3	19.8	17 15.7	+11.7	19.9	18 12.1	+12.0	20.0	19 08.4	+12.5	20.1	71
72	12 43.0	+9.8	18.4	13 39.9	+10.1	18.5	14 36.8	+10.4	18.6	15 33.7	+10.7	18.6	16 30.5	+11.1	18.7	17 27.4	+11.3	18.8	18 24.1	+11.8	18.9	19 20.9	+12.0	19.0	72
73	12 52.8	+9.4	17.4	13 50.0	+9.8	17.5	14 47.2	+10.1	17.5	15 44.4	+10.5	17.6	16 41.6	+10.7	17.7	17 38.7	+11.1	17.8	18 35.9	+11.3	17.9	19 32.9	+11.7	18.0	73
74	13 02.2	+9.3	16.4	13 59.8	+9.6	16.4	14 57.3	+9.9	16.5	15 54.9	+10.1	16.6	16 52.3	+10.5	16.7	17 49.8	+10.7	16.8	18 47.2	+11.1	16.9	19 44.6	+11.4	17.0	74
75	13 11.5	+9.0	15.4	14 09.4	+9.2	15.4	15 07.2	+9.6	15.5	16 05.0	+9.8	15.6	17 02.8	+10.1	15.6	18 00.5	+10.5	15.7	18 58.3	+10.7	15.8	19 56.0	+11.0	15.9	75
76	13 20.5	+8.8	14.3	14 18.6	+9.1	14.4	15 16.8	+9.2	14.5	16 14.8	+9.6	14.5	17 12.9	+9.8	14.6	18 11.0	+10.0	14.7	19 09.0	+10.3	14.8	20 07.0	+10.6	14.9	76
77	13 29.3	+8.5	13.3	14 27.7	+8.7	13.4	15 26.0	+9.1	13.4	16 24.4	+9.2	13.5	17 22.7	+9.5	13.6	18 21.0	+9.8	13.7	19 19.3	+10.0	13.7	20 17.6	+10.2	13.8	77
78	13 37.8	+8.3	12.3	14 36.4	+8.5	12.4	15 35.1	+8.7	12.4	16 33.6	+9.0	12.5	17 32.2	+9.2	12.5	18 30.8	+9.4	12.6	19 29.3	+9.6	12.7	20 27.8	+9.9	12.8	78
79	13 46.1	+8.0	11.3	14 44.9	+8.3	11.3	15 43.8	+8.4	11.4	16 42.6	+8.6	11.4	17 41.4	+8.8	11.5	18 40.2	+9.0	11.6	19 38.9	+9.3	11.6	20 37.7	+9.5	11.7	79
80	13 54.1	+7.8	10.3	14 53.2	+7.9	10.3	15 52.2	+8.1	10.4	16 51.2	+8.3	10.4	17 50.2	+8.5	10.5	18 49.2	+8.7	10.5	19 48.2	+8.9	10.6	20 47.2	+9.1	10.7	80
81	14 01.9	+7.5	9.2	15 01.1	+7.7	9.3	16 00.3	+7.9	9.3	16 59.5	+8.1	9.4	17 58.7	+8.2	9.4	18 57.9	+8.4	9.5	19 57.1	+8.5	9.5	20 56.3	+8.7	9.6	81
82	14 09.4	+7.3	8.2	15 08.8	+7.4	8.3	16 08.2	+7.5	8.3	17 07.6	+7.7	8.3	18 06.9	+7.9	8.4	19 06.3	+8.0	8.4	20 05.6	+8.2	8.5	21 05.0	+8.3	8.5	82
83	14 16.7	+7.0	7.2	15 16.2	+7.1	7.2	16 15.7	+7.3	7.3	17 15.3	+7.3	7.3	18 14.8	+7.5	7.3	19 14.3	+7.6	7.4	20 13.8	+7.7	7.4	21 13.3	+7.9	7.5	83
84	14 23.7	+6.7	6.2	15 23.3	+6.9	6.2	16 23.0	+6.9	6.2	17 22.6	+7.1	6.3	18 22.3	+7.1	6.3	19 21.9	+7.3	6.3	20 21.5	+7.4	6.4	21 21.2	+7.5	6.4	84
85	14 30.4	+6.5	5.1	15 30.2	+6.5	5.2	16 29.9	+6.7	5.2	17 29.7	+6.7	5.2	18 29.4	+6.8	5.3	19 29.2	+6.9	5.3	20 28.9	+7.0	5.3	21 28.7	+7.1	5.4	85
86	14 36.9	+6.2	4.1	15 36.7	+6.3	4.1	16 36.6	+6.3	4.2	17 36.4	+6.4	4.2	18 36.2	+6.5	4.2	19 36.1	+6.5	4.2	20 35.9	+6.6	4.3	21 35.8	+6.6	4.3	86
87	14 43.1	+5.9	3.1	15 43.0	+5.9	3.1	16 42.9	+6.0	3.1	17 42.8	+6.1	3.1	18 42.7	+6.1	3.2	19 42.6	+6.2	3.2	20 42.5	+6.2	3.2	21 42.4	+6.3	3.2	87
88	14 49.0	+5.6	2.1	15 48.9	+5.7	2.1	16 48.9	+5.7	2.1	17 48.9	+5.7	2.1	18 48.8	+5.8	2.1	19 48.8	+5.8	2.1	20 48.7	+5.9	2.1	21 48.7	+5.9	2.1	88
89	14 54.6	+5.4	1.0	15 54.6	+5.4	1.0	16 54.6	+5.4	1.0	17 54.6	+5.4	1.0	18 54.6	+5.4	1.1	19 54.6	+5.4	1.1	20 54.6	+5.4	1.1	21 54.6	+5.4	1.1	89
90	15 00.0	+5.1	0.0	16 00.0	+5.1	0.0	17 00.0	+5.1	0.0	18 00.0	+5.1	0.0	19 00.0	+5.1	0.0	20 00.0	+5.0	0.0	21 00.0	+5.0	0.0	22 00.0	+5.0	0.0	90
	15°			16°			17°			18°			19°			20°			21°			22°			

S. Lat. {L.H.A. greater than 180° ....Zn=180°−Z; L.H.A. less than 180°...........Zn=180°+Z

LATITUDE **SAME** NAME AS DECLINATION **L.H.A. 95°, 265°**

173

86°, 274° L.H.A. LATITUDE SAME NAME AS DECLINATION N. Lat. {L.H.A. greater than 180° .....Zn=Z
{L.H.A. less than 180°............Zn=360°–Z

Dec.	15°			16°			17°			18°			19°			20°			21°			22°			Dec.
	Hc	d	Z	Hc	d	Z	Hc	d	Z	Hc	d	Z	Hc	d	Z	Hc	d	Z	Hc	d	Z	Hc	d	Z	
°	° ′	′	°	° ′	′	°	° ′	′	°	° ′	′	°	° ′	′	°	° ′	′	°	° ′	′	°	° ′	′	°	°
0	3 51.8	+15.5	91.0	3 50.7	+16.5	91.1	3 49.5	+17.5	91.2	3 48.2	+18.6	91.2	3 46.9	+19.5	91.3	3 45.5	+20.5	91.4	3 44.0	+21.6	91.4	3 42.5	+22.5	91.5	0
1	4 07.3	+15.5	90.1	4 07.2	+16.5	90.1	4 07.0	+17.5	90.2	4 06.8	+18.5	90.3	4 06.4	+19.5	90.4	4 06.0	+20.5	90.4	4 05.6	+21.4	90.5	4 05.0	+22.4	90.6	1
2	4 22.8	+15.4	89.1	4 23.7	+16.4	89.2	4 24.5	+17.4	89.3	4 25.3	+18.4	89.3	4 25.9	+19.4	89.4	4 26.5	+20.4	89.5	4 27.0	+21.4	89.6	4 27.4	+22.4	89.6	2
3	4 38.2	+15.3	88.1	4 40.1	+16.3	88.2	4 41.9	+17.4	88.3	4 43.7	+18.3	88.4	4 45.3	+19.4	88.5	4 46.9	+20.3	88.5	4 48.4	+21.3	88.6	4 49.8	+22.3	88.7	3
4	4 53.5	+15.2	87.2	4 56.4	+16.3	87.2	4 59.3	+17.2	87.3	5 02.0	+18.3	87.4	5 04.7	+19.2	87.5	5 07.2	+20.3	87.6	5 09.7	+21.2	87.7	5 12.1	+22.2	87.8	4
5	5 08.7	+15.1	86.2	5 12.7	+16.1	86.3	5 16.5	+17.2	86.4	5 20.3	+18.1	86.5	5 23.9	+19.2	86.6	5 27.5	+20.1	86.7	5 30.9	+21.1	86.7	5 34.3	+22.1	86.8	5
6	5 23.8	+15.1	85.2	5 28.8	+16.1	85.3	5 33.7	+17.0	85.4	5 38.4	+18.1	85.5	5 43.1	+19.0	85.6	5 47.6	+20.1	85.7	5 52.0	+21.1	85.8	5 56.4	+22.0	85.9	6
7	5 38.9	+14.9	84.2	5 44.9	+15.9	84.3	5 50.7	+17.0	84.4	5 56.5	+17.9	84.5	6 02.1	+19.0	84.7	6 07.7	+19.9	84.8	6 13.1	+20.9	84.9	6 18.4	+21.9	85.0	7
8	5 53.8	+14.9	83.3	6 00.8	+15.9	83.4	6 07.7	+16.8	83.5	6 14.4	+17.9	83.6	6 21.1	+18.8	83.7	6 27.6	+19.9	83.8	6 34.0	+20.9	83.9	6 40.3	+21.8	84.0	8
9	6 08.7	+14.7	82.3	6 16.7	+15.7	82.4	6 24.5	+16.8	82.5	6 32.3	+17.7	82.6	6 39.9	+18.8	82.7	6 47.5	+19.7	82.9	6 54.9	+20.7	83.0	7 02.1	+21.7	83.1	9
10	6 23.4	+14.6	81.3	6 32.4	+15.6	81.4	6 41.3	+16.6	81.5	6 50.0	+17.7	81.7	6 58.7	+18.6	81.8	7 07.2	+19.6	81.9	7 15.6	+20.6	82.0	7 23.8	+21.6	82.2	10
11	6 38.0	+14.6	80.3	6 48.0	+15.6	80.5	6 57.9	+16.5	80.6	7 07.7	+17.5	80.7	7 17.3	+18.5	80.8	7 26.8	+19.5	81.0	7 36.2	+20.5	81.1	7 45.4	+21.5	81.2	11
12	6 52.6	+14.3	79.4	7 03.6	+15.4	79.5	7 14.4	+16.4	79.6	7 25.2	+17.4	79.7	7 35.8	+18.4	79.9	7 46.3	+19.4	80.0	7 56.7	+20.3	80.1	8 06.9	+21.3	80.3	12
13	7 06.9	+14.3	78.4	7 19.0	+15.2	78.5	7 30.8	+16.3	78.6	7 42.6	+17.2	78.8	7 54.2	+18.3	78.9	8 05.7	+19.2	79.0	8 17.0	+20.2	79.2	8 28.2	+21.2	79.3	13
14	7 21.2	+14.2	77.4	7 34.2	+15.2	77.5	7 47.1	+16.1	77.7	7 59.8	+17.2	77.8	8 12.5	+18.1	77.9	8 24.9	+19.1	78.1	8 37.2	+20.1	78.2	8 49.4	+21.0	78.4	14
15	7 35.4	+14.0	76.4	7 49.4	+15.0	76.6	8 03.2	+16.0	76.7	8 17.0	+17.0	76.8	8 30.6	+17.9	77.0	8 44.0	+19.0	77.1	8 57.3	+19.9	77.3	9 10.4	+20.9	77.4	15
16	7 49.4	+13.8	75.4	8 04.4	+14.8	75.6	8 19.2	+15.9	75.7	8 34.0	+16.8	75.9	8 48.5	+17.9	76.0	9 03.0	+18.8	76.2	9 17.2	+19.8	76.3	9 31.3	+20.8	76.5	16
17	8 03.2	+13.8	74.5	8 19.2	+14.8	74.6	8 35.1	+15.7	74.7	8 50.8	+16.7	74.9	9 06.4	+17.6	75.1	9 21.8	+18.6	75.2	9 37.0	+19.6	75.4	9 52.1	+20.6	75.5	17
18	8 17.0	+13.6	73.5	8 34.0	+14.5	73.6	8 50.8	+15.6	73.8	9 07.5	+16.5	73.9	9 24.0	+17.5	74.1	9 40.4	+18.5	74.2	9 56.6	+19.5	74.4	10 12.7	+20.4	74.6	18
19	8 30.6	+13.4	72.5	8 48.5	+14.5	72.6	9 06.4	+15.4	72.8	9 24.0	+16.4	73.0	9 41.5	+17.4	73.1	9 58.9	+18.3	73.3	10 16.1	+19.2	73.4	10 33.1	+20.2	73.6	19
20	8 44.0	+13.3	71.5	9 03.0	+14.2	71.7	9 21.8	+15.2	71.8	9 40.4	+16.2	72.0	9 58.9	+17.2	72.1	10 17.2	+18.1	72.3	10 35.3	+19.2	72.5	10 53.3	+20.1	72.7	20
21	8 57.3	+13.1	70.5	9 17.2	+14.1	70.7	9 37.0	+15.1	70.8	9 56.6	+16.1	71.0	10 16.1	+17.0	71.2	10 35.3	+18.0	71.3	10 54.5	+18.9	71.5	11 13.4	+19.9	71.7	21
22	9 10.4	+13.0	69.5	9 31.3	+14.0	69.7	9 52.1	+14.9	69.9	10 12.7	+15.8	70.0	10 33.1	+16.8	70.2	10 53.3	+17.8	70.4	11 13.4	+18.7	70.6	11 33.3	+19.7	70.7	22
23	9 23.4	+12.8	68.5	9 45.3	+13.7	68.7	10 07.0	+14.7	68.9	10 28.5	+15.7	69.0	10 49.9	+16.6	69.2	11 11.1	+17.6	69.4	11 32.1	+18.6	69.6	11 53.0	+19.4	69.8	23
24	9 36.2	+12.6	67.6	9 59.0	+13.6	67.7	10 21.7	+14.5	67.9	10 44.2	+15.5	68.1	11 06.5	+16.5	68.2	11 28.7	+17.4	68.4	11 50.7	+18.3	68.6	12 12.4	+19.3	68.8	24
25	9 48.8	+12.5	66.6	10 12.6	+13.4	66.7	10 36.2	+14.4	66.9	10 59.7	+15.3	67.1	11 23.0	+16.2	67.3	11 46.1	+17.2	67.4	12 09.0	+18.2	67.6	12 31.7	+19.1	67.8	25
26	10 01.3	+12.3	65.6	10 26.0	+13.3	65.7	10 50.6	+14.2	65.9	11 15.0	+15.1	66.1	11 39.2	+16.1	66.3	12 03.3	+17.0	66.5	12 27.2	+17.9	66.7	12 50.8	+18.9	66.9	26
27	10 13.6	+12.1	64.6	10 39.3	+13.0	64.7	11 04.8	+14.0	64.9	11 30.1	+14.9	65.1	11 55.3	+15.8	65.3	12 20.3	+16.8	65.5	12 45.1	+17.7	65.7	13 09.7	+18.6	65.9	27
28	10 25.7	+11.9	63.6	10 52.3	+12.8	63.8	11 18.8	+13.7	63.9	11 45.0	+14.7	64.1	12 11.1	+15.7	64.3	12 37.1	+16.5	64.5	13 02.8	+17.5	64.7	13 28.3	+18.5	64.9	28
29	10 37.6	+11.7	62.6	11 05.1	+12.7	62.8	11 32.5	+13.6	62.9	11 59.7	+14.5	63.1	12 26.8	+15.4	63.3	12 53.6	+16.4	63.5	13 20.3	+17.3	63.7	13 46.8	+18.1	63.9	29
30	10 49.3	+11.6	61.6	11 17.8	+12.5	61.8	11 46.1	+13.4	61.9	12 14.2	+14.3	62.1	12 42.2	+15.2	62.3	13 10.0	+16.1	62.5	13 37.6	+17.0	62.7	14 04.9	+18.0	63.0	30
31	11 00.9	+11.3	60.6	11 30.3	+12.2	60.8	11 59.5	+13.1	60.9	12 28.5	+14.1	61.1	12 57.4	+15.0	61.3	13 26.1	+15.9	61.5	13 54.6	+16.8	61.8	14 22.9	+17.7	62.0	31
32	11 12.2	+11.2	59.6	11 42.5	+12.0	59.8	12 12.6	+13.0	59.9	12 42.6	+13.8	60.1	13 12.4	+14.7	60.3	13 42.0	+15.6	60.5	14 11.4	+16.5	60.8	14 40.6	+17.4	61.0	32
33	11 23.4	+10.9	58.6	11 54.5	+11.9	58.8	12 25.6	+12.7	58.9	12 56.4	+13.7	59.1	13 27.1	+14.5	59.3	13 57.6	+15.4	59.6	14 27.9	+16.3	59.8	14 58.0	+17.2	60.0	33
34	11 34.3	+10.7	57.6	12 06.4	+11.6	57.8	12 38.3	+12.5	57.9	13 10.1	+13.3	58.1	13 41.6	+14.3	58.3	14 13.0	+15.2	58.6	14 44.2	+16.1	58.8	15 15.2	+17.0	59.0	34
35	11 45.0	+10.5	56.6	12 18.0	+11.4	56.8	12 50.8	+12.3	56.9	13 23.4	+13.2	57.1	13 55.9	+14.0	57.3	14 28.2	+14.9	57.6	15 00.3	+15.8	57.8	15 32.2	+16.6	58.0	35
36	11 55.5	+10.3	55.6	12 29.4	+11.1	55.8	13 03.1	+12.0	55.9	13 36.6	+12.9	56.1	14 09.9	+13.8	56.3	14 43.1	+14.6	56.6	15 16.1	+15.5	56.8	15 48.8	+16.4	57.0	36
37	12 05.8	+10.1	54.6	12 40.5	+11.0	54.7	13 15.1	+11.8	54.9	13 49.5	+12.6	55.1	14 23.7	+13.5	55.3	14 57.7	+14.4	55.6	15 31.6	+15.2	55.8	16 05.2	+16.1	56.0	37
38	12 15.9	+9.9	53.6	12 51.5	+10.7	53.7	13 26.9	+11.6	53.9	14 02.1	+12.5	54.1	14 37.2	+13.3	54.3	15 12.1	+14.1	54.5	15 46.8	+15.0	54.8	16 21.3	+15.9	55.0	38
39	12 25.8	+9.6	52.5	13 02.2	+10.5	52.7	13 38.5	+11.3	52.9	14 14.6	+12.1	53.1	14 50.5	+13.0	53.3	15 26.2	+13.9	53.5	16 01.8	+14.7	53.8	16 37.2	+15.5	54.0	39
40	12 35.4	+9.4	51.5	13 12.7	+10.2	51.7	13 49.8	+11.0	51.9	14 26.7	+11.9	52.1	15 03.5	+12.7	52.3	15 40.1	+13.5	52.5	16 16.5	+14.4	52.8	16 52.7	+15.2	53.0	40
41	12 44.8	+9.2	50.5	13 22.9	+10.0	50.7	14 00.8	+10.9	50.9	14 38.6	+11.6	51.1	15 16.2	+12.5	51.3	15 53.6	+13.3	51.5	16 30.9	+14.1	51.7	17 07.9	+15.0	52.0	41
42	12 54.0	+9.0	49.5	13 32.9	+9.8	49.7	14 11.7	+10.5	49.9	14 50.2	+11.4	50.1	15 28.7	+12.1	50.3	16 06.9	+13.0	50.5	16 45.0	+13.8	50.7	17 22.9	+14.6	51.0	42
43	13 03.0	+8.7	48.5	13 42.7	+9.5	48.7	14 22.2	+10.3	48.9	15 01.6	+11.1	49.1	15 40.8	+11.9	49.3	16 19.9	+12.7	49.5	16 58.8	+13.5	49.7	17 37.5	+14.3	50.0	43
44	13 11.7	+8.4	47.5	13 52.2	+9.2	47.7	14 32.5	+10.0	47.8	15 12.7	+10.8	48.0	15 52.7	+11.6	48.2	16 32.6	+12.4	48.5	17 12.3	+13.2	48.7	17 51.8	+14.0	48.9	44
45	13 20.1	+8.3	46.5	14 01.4	+9.0	46.6	14 42.5	+9.8	46.8	15 23.5	+10.6	47.0	16 04.3	+11.4	47.2	16 45.0	+12.1	47.4	17 25.5	+12.9	47.7	18 05.8	+13.7	47.9	45
46	13 28.4	+7.9	45.4	14 10.4	+8.7	45.6	14 52.3	+9.5	45.8	15 34.1	+10.2	46.0	16 15.7	+11.0	46.2	16 57.1	+11.8	46.4	17 38.4	+12.5	46.6	18 19.5	+13.3	46.9	46
47	13 36.3	+7.8	44.4	14 19.1	+8.5	44.6	15 01.8	+9.2	44.8	15 44.3	+10.0	45.0	16 26.7	+10.7	45.2	17 08.9	+11.5	45.4	17 50.9	+12.3	45.6	18 32.8	+13.0	45.9	47
48	13 44.1	+7.5	43.4	14 27.6	+8.2	43.6	15 11.0	+9.0	43.8	15 54.3	+9.7	44.0	16 37.4	+10.4	44.2	17 20.4	+11.1	44.4	18 03.2	+11.9	44.6	18 45.8	+12.7	44.8	48
49	13 51.6	+7.2	42.4	14 35.8	+8.0	42.6	15 20.0	+8.6	42.7	16 04.0	+9.3	42.9	16 47.8	+10.1	43.1	17 31.5	+10.9	43.3	18 15.1	+11.6	43.6	18 58.5	+12.3	43.8	49
50	13 58.8	+6.9	41.4	14 43.8	+7.6	41.5	15 28.6	+8.4	41.7	16 13.3	+9.1	41.9	16 57.9	+9.8	42.1	17 42.4	+10.5	42.3	18 26.7	+11.2	42.5	19 10.8	+12.0	42.8	50
51	14 05.7	+6.8	40.3	14 51.4	+7.4	40.5	15 37.0	+8.1	40.7	16 22.4	+8.8	40.9	17 07.7	+9.5	41.1	17 52.9	+10.2	41.3	18 37.9	+10.9	41.5	19 22.8	+11.6	41.7	51
52	14 12.5	+6.4	39.3	14 58.8	+7.1	39.5	15 45.1	+7.8	39.7	16 31.2	+8.5	39.8	17 17.2	+9.2	40.0	18 03.1	+9.9	40.2	18 48.8	+10.6	40.5	19 34.4	+11.3	40.7	52
53	14 18.9	+6.2	38.3	15 05.9	+6.9	38.4	15 52.9	+7.5	38.6	16 39.7	+8.2	38.8	17 26.4	+8.8	39.0	18 13.0	+9.5	39.2	18 59.4	+10.2	39.4	19 45.7	+10.9	39.6	53
54	14 25.1	+5.9	37.3	15 12.8	+6.5	37.4	16 00.4	+7.2	37.6	16 47.9	+7.8	37.8	17 35.2	+8.6	38.0	18 22.5	+9.2	38.2	19 09.6	+9.8	38.4	19 56.6	+10.5	38.6	54
55	14 31.0	+5.6	36.2	15 19.3	+6.3	36.4	16 07.6	+6.9	36.6	16 55.7	+7.6	36.7	17 43.8	+8.2	36.9	18 31.7	+8.8	37.1	19 19.4	+9.5	37.3	20 07.1	+10.1	37.5	55
56	14 36.6	+5.4	35.2	15 25.6	+6.0	35.4	16 14.5	+6.6	35.5	17 03.3	+7.2	35.7	17 52.0	+7.8	35.9	18 40.5	+8.5	36.1	19 28.9	+9.2	36.3	20 17.2	+9.8	36.5	56
57	14 42.0	+5.1	34.2	15 31.6	+5.7	34.3	16 21.1	+6.3	34.5	17 10.5	+6.9	34.7	17 59.8	+7.5	34.8	18 49.0	+8.2	35.0	19 38.1	+8.8	35.2	20 27.0	+9.4	35.4	57
58	14 47.1	+4.8	33.1	15 37.3	+5.4	33.3	16 27.4	+6.0	33.5	17 17.4	+6.6	33.6	18 07.3	+7.2	33.8	18 57.2	+7.7	34.0	19 46.9	+8.4	34.2	20 36.4	+9.0	34.4	58
59	14 51.9	+4.6	32.1	15 42.7	+5.1	32.3	16 33.4	+5.7	32.4	17 24.0	+6.3	32.6	18 14.5	+6.9	32.7	19 04.9	+7.5	32.9	19 55.3	+8.0	33.1	20 45.4	+8.7	33.3	59
60	14 56.5	+4.3	31.1	15 47.8	+4.9	31.2	16 39.1	+5.4	31.4	17 30.3	+5.9	31.5	18 21.4	+6.5	31.7	19 12.4	+7.1	31.9	20 03.3	+7.6	32.1	20 54.1	+8.2	32.3	60
61	15 00.8	+4.0	30.0	15 52.7	+4.5	30.2	16 44.5	+5.1	30.3	17 36.2	+5.7	30.5	18 27.9	+6.2	30.7	19 19.5	+6.7	30.8	20 10.9	+7.3	31.0	21 02.3	+7.8	31.2	61
62	15 04.8	+3.7	29.0	15 57.2	+4.2	29.1	16 49.6	+4.7	29.3	17 41.9	+5.2	29.4	18 34.1	+5.8	29.6	19 26.2	+6.3	29.8	20 18.2	+6.9	30.0	21 10.1	+7.5	30.1	62
63	15 08.5	+3.4	28.0	16 01.4	+4.0	28.1	16 54.3	+4.5	28.3	17 47.1	+5.0	28.4	18 39.9	+5.4	28.6	19 32.5	+6.0	28.7	20 25.1	+6.5	28.9	21 17.6	+7.0	29.1	63
64	15 11.9	+3.2	26.9	16 05.4	+3.6	27.1	16 58.8	+4.1	27.2	17 52.1	+4.6	27.4	18 45.3	+5.1	27.5	19 38.5	+5.6	27.7	20 31.6	+6.1	27.8	21 24.6	+6.7	28.0	64
65	15 15.1	+2.8	25.9	16 09.0	+3.3	26.0	17 02.9	+3.8	26.2	17 56.7	+4.3	26.3	18 50.4	+4.8	26.5	19 44.1	+5.3	26.6	20 37.7	+5.8	26.8	21 31.3	+6.2	26.9	65
66	15 17.9	+2.6	24.9	16 12.3	+3.0	25.0	17 06.7	+3.5	25.1	18 01.0	+3.9	25.3	18 55.2	+4.4	25.4	19 49.4	+4.8	25.6	20 43.5	+5.3	25.7	21 37.5	+5.8	25.9	66
67	15 20.5	+2.3	23.8	16 15.3	+2.8	24.0	17 10.2	+3.1	24.1	18 04.9	+3.6	24.2	18 59.6	+4.0	24.3	19 54.2	+4.5	24.5	20 48.8	+4.9	24.6	21 43.3	+5.4	24.8	67
68	15 22.8	+2.0	22.8	16 18.1	+2.4	22.9	17 13.3	+2.8	23.0	18 08.5	+3.3	23.2	19 03.6	+3.7	23.3	19 58.7	+4.1	23.4	20 53.7	+4.6	23.6	21 48.7	+5.0	23.7	68
69	15 24.8	+1.7	21.8	16 20.5	+2.1	21.9	17 16.1	+2.5	22.0	18 11.8	+2.9	22.1	19 07.3	+3.3	22.2	20 02.8	+3.8	22.4	20 58.3	+4.1	22.5	21 53.7	+4.6	22.7	69
70	15 26.5	+1.4	20.7	16 22.6	+1.8	20.8	17 18.6	+2.2	20.9	18 14.7	+2.5	21.1	19 10.6	+3.0	21.2	20 06.6	+3.3	21.3	21 02.4	+3.8	21.4	21 58.3	+4.1	21.6	70
71	15 27.9	+1.2	19.7	16 24.4	+1.5	19.8	17 20.8	+1.9	19.9	18 17.2	+2.3	20.0	19 13.6	+2.6	20.1	20 09.9	+3.0	20.2	21 06.2	+3.3	20.4	22 02.4	+3.7	20.5	71
72	15 29.1	+0.8	18.7	16 25.9	+1.2	18.7	17 22.7	+1.5	18.8	18 19.5	+1.8	18.9	19 16.2	+2.2	19.1	20 12.9	+2.6	19.2	21 09.5	+3.0	19.3	22 06.1	+3.3	19.4	72
73	15 29.9	+0.6	17.6	16 27.1	+0.8	17.7	17 24.2	+1.2	17.8	18 21.3	+1.6	17.9	19 18.4	+1.9	18.0	20 15.5	+2.1	18.1	21 12.5	+2.5	18.2	22 09.4	+2.9	18.4	73
74	15 30.5	+0.2	16.6	16 27.9	+0.6	16.7	17 25.4	+0.9	16.7	18 22.9	+1.1	16.8	19 20.3	+1.5	16.9	20 17.6	+1.9	17.0	21 15.0	+2.1	17.2	22 12.3	+2.5	17.3	74
75	15 30.7	0.0	15.5	16 28.5	+0.3	15.6	17 26.3	+0.5	15.7	18 24.0	+0.9	15.8	19 21.8	+1.1	15.9	20 19.5	+1.4	16.0	21 17.1	+1.7	16.1	22 14.8	+2.0	16.2	75
76	15 30.7	−0.3	14.5	16 28.8	−0.1	14.6	17 26.8	+0.2	14.7	18 24.9	+0.4	14.7	19 22.9	+0.7	14.8	20 20.9	+1.0	14.9	21 18.8	+1.3	15.0	22 16.8	+1.6	15.1	76
77	15 30.4	−0.6	13.5	16 28.7	−0.3	13.5	17 27.0	−0.1	13.6	18 25.3	+0.2	13.7	19 23.6	+0.4	13.8	20 21.9	+0.6	13.8	21 20.1	+0.9	13.9	22 18.4	+1.1	14.0	77
78	15 29.8	−0.9	12.4	16 28.4	−0.7	12.5	17 26.9	−0.4	12.6	18 25.5	−0.2	12.6	19 24.0	0.0	12.7	20 22.5	+0.3	12.8	21 21.0	+0.5	12.9	22 19.5	+0.8	13.0	78
79	15 28.9	−1.2	11.4	16 27.7	−1.0	11.4	17 26.5	−0.8	11.5	18 25.3	−0.6	11.6	19 24.0	−0.3	11.6	20 22.8	−0.1	11.7	21 21.5	+0.1	11.8	22 20.3	+0.3	11.9	79
80	15 27.7	−1.5	10.4	16 26.7	−1.3	10.4	17 25.7	−1.1	10.5	18 24.7	−0.9	10.5	19 23.7	−0.7	10.6	20 22.7	−0.6	10.6	21 21.6	−0.3	10.7	22 20.6	−0.2	10.8	80
81	15 26.2	−1.8	9.3	16 25.4	−1.6	9.4	17 24.6	−1.4	9.4	18 23.8	−1.3	9.5	19 23.0	−1.1	9.5	20 22.1	−0.9	9.6	21 21.3	−0.7	9.6	22 20.4	−0.5	9.7	81
82	15 24.4	−2.0	8.3	16 23.8	−1.9	8.3	17 23.2	−1.8	8.4	18 22.5	−1.6	8.4	19 21.9	−1.5	8.5	20 21.2	−1.3	8.5	21 20.6	−1.2	8.6	22 19.9	−1.0	8.6	82
83	15 22.4	−2.4	7.2	16 21.9	−2.2	7.3	17 21.4	−2.1	7.3	18 20.9	−1.9	7.4	19 20.4	−1.8	7.4	20 19.9	−1.7	7.4	21 19.4	−1.5	7.5	22 18.9	−1.4	7.6	83
84	15 20.0	−2.6	6.2	16 19.7	−2.5	6.2	17 19.3	−2.4	6.3	18 19.0	−2.3	6.3	19 18.6	−2.2	6.3	20 18.2	−2.0	6.4	21 17.9	−2.0	6.4	22 17.5	−1.9	6.5	84
85	15 17.4	−2.9	5.2	16 17.2	−2.9	5.2	17 16.9	−2.7	5.2	18 16.7	−2.7	5.3	19 16.4	−2.5	5.3	20 16.2	−2.5	5.3	21 15.9	−2.4	5.4	22 15.6	−2.2	5.4	85
86	15 14.5	−3.2	4.1	16 14.3	−3.1	4.2	17 14.2	−3.1	4.2	18 14.0	−3.0	4.2	19 13.9	−3.0	4.2	20 13.7	−2.9	4.3	21 13.5	−2.8	4.3	22 13.4	−2.7	4.3	86
87	15 11.3	−3.5	3.1	16 11.2	−3.4	3.1	17 11.1	−3.4	3.1	18 11.0	−3.3	3.2	19 10.9	−3.2	3.2	20 10.8	−3.2	3.2	21 10.7	−3.1	3.2	22 10.7	−3.2	3.2	87
88	15 07.8	−3.8	2.1	16 07.8	−3.8	2.1	17 07.7	−3.7	2.1	18 07.7	−3.7	2.1	19 07.7	−3.7	2.1	20 07.6	−3.6	2.1	21 07.6	−3.6	2.1	22 07.5	−3.5	2.2	88
89	15 04.0	−4.0	1.0	16 04.0	−4.0	1.0	17 04.0	−4.0	1.0	18 04.0	−4.0	1.0	19 04.0	−4.0	1.1	20 04.0	−4.0	1.1	21 04.0	−4.0	1.1	22 04.0	−4.0	1.1	89
90	15 00.0	−4.3	0.0	16 00.0	−4.3	0.0	17 00.0	−4.3	0.0	18 00.0	−4.4	0.0	19 00.0	−4.4	0.0	20 00.0	−4.4	0.0	21 00.0	−4.4	0.0	22 00.0	−4.4	0.0	90
	15°			16°			17°			18°			19°			20°			21°			22°			

86°, 274° L.H.A. LATITUDE SAME NAME AS DECLINATION

174

LATITUDE **CONTRARY** NAME TO DECLINATION **L.H.A. 86°, 274°**

Dec.	15° Hc	d	Z	16° Hc	d	Z	17° Hc	d	Z	18° Hc	d	Z
°	° ′	′	°	° ′	′	°	° ′	′	°	° ′	′	°
0	3 51.8	−15.6	91.0	3 50.7	−16.6	91.1	3 49.5	−17.6	91.2	3 48.2	−18.6	91.2
1	3 36.2	−15.6	92.0	3 34.1	−16.7	92.1	3 31.9	−17.7	92.1	3 29.6	−18.6	92.2
2	3 20.6	−15.8	93.0	3 17.4	−16.7	93.0	3 14.2	−17.7	93.1	3 11.0	−18.8	93.1
3	3 04.8	−15.7	93.9	3 00.7	−16.8	94.0	2 56.5	−17.8	94.0	2 52.2	−18.7	94.1
4	2 49.1	−15.8	94.9	2 43.9	−16.8	95.0	2 38.7	−17.8	95.0	2 33.5	−18.9	95.0
5	2 33.3	−15.9	95.9	2 27.1	−16.9	95.9	2 20.9	−17.9	96.0	2 14.6	−18.8	96.0
6	2 17.4	−15.9	96.8	2 10.2	−16.9	96.9	2 03.0	−17.9	96.9	1 55.8	−18.9	96.9
7	2 01.5	−15.9	97.8	1 53.3	−16.9	97.8	1 45.1	−17.9	97.9	1 36.9	−18.9	97.9
8	1 45.6	−16.0	98.8	1 36.4	−16.9	98.8	1 27.2	−17.9	98.8	1 18.0	−18.9	98.8
9	1 29.6	−16.0	99.7	1 19.5	−17.0	99.8	1 09.3	−18.0	99.8	0 59.1	−19.0	99.8
10	1 13.6	−16.0	100.7	1 02.5	−17.0	100.7	0 51.3	−18.0	100.7	0 40.1	−18.9	100.7
11	0 57.6	−16.0	101.7	0 45.5	−17.0	101.7	0 33.3	−18.0	101.7	0 21.2	−19.0	101.7
12	0 41.6	−16.1	102.6	0 28.5	−17.0	102.6	0 15.3	−17.9	102.6	0 02.2	−18.9	102.6
13	0 25.5	−16.0	103.6	0 11.5	−17.1	103.6	0 02.6	+18.0	76.4	0 16.7	+19.0	76.4
14	0 09.5	−16.0	104.5	0 05.6	+17.0	75.5	0 20.6	+18.0	75.5	0 35.7	+19.0	75.5
15	0 06.5	+16.1	74.5	0 22.6	+17.0	74.5	0 38.6	+18.0	74.5	0 54.7	+18.9	74.5
16	0 22.6	+16.0	73.5	0 39.6	+17.0	73.5	0 56.6	+18.0	73.5	1 13.6	+18.9	73.6
17	0 38.6	+16.1	72.6	0 56.6	+17.0	72.6	1 14.6	+17.9	72.6	1 32.5	+18.9	72.6
18	0 54.7	+16.0	71.6	1 13.6	+17.0	71.6	1 32.5	+17.9	71.6	1 51.4	+18.8	71.7
19	1 10.7	+16.0	70.6	1 30.6	+16.9	70.7	1 50.4	+17.9	70.7	2 10.2	+18.9	70.7
20	1 26.7	+15.9	69.7	1 47.5	+16.9	69.7	2 08.3	+17.8	69.7	2 29.1	+18.7	69.8
21	1 42.6	+16.0	68.7	2 04.4	+16.9	68.7	2 26.1	+17.9	68.8	2 47.8	+18.8	68.8
22	1 58.6	+15.9	67.7	2 21.3	+16.8	67.8	2 44.0	+17.7	67.8	3 06.6	+18.7	67.9
23	2 14.5	+15.8	66.8	2 38.1	+16.8	66.8	3 01.7	+17.7	66.9	3 25.3	+18.6	66.9
24	2 30.3	+15.9	65.8	2 54.9	+16.7	65.9	3 19.4	+17.7	65.9	3 43.9	+18.6	66.0
25	2 46.2	+15.7	64.8	3 11.6	+16.7	64.9	3 37.1	+17.6	64.9	4 02.5	+18.5	65.0
26	3 01.9	+15.8	63.9	3 28.3	+16.7	63.9	3 54.7	+17.5	64.0	4 21.0	+18.4	64.1
27	3 17.7	+15.6	62.9	3 45.0	+16.5	63.0	4 12.2	+17.5	63.0	4 39.4	+18.3	63.1
28	3 33.3	+15.6	61.9	4 01.5	+16.5	62.0	4 29.7	+17.3	62.1	4 57.7	+18.3	62.1
29	3 48.9	+15.6	61.0	4 18.0	+16.4	61.0	4 47.0	+17.3	61.1	5 16.0	+18.2	61.2
30	4 04.5	+15.5	60.0	4 34.4	+16.4	60.1	5 04.3	+17.3	60.1	5 34.2	+18.1	60.2
31	4 20.0	+15.4	59.0	4 50.8	+16.3	59.1	5 21.6	+17.1	59.2	5 52.3	+17.9	59.3
32	4 35.4	+15.3	58.1	5 07.1	+16.1	58.1	5 38.7	+17.0	58.2	6 10.2	+17.9	58.3
33	4 50.7	+15.2	57.1	5 23.2	+16.1	57.2	5 55.7	+17.0	57.3	6 28.1	+17.8	57.4
34	5 05.9	+15.2	56.1	5 39.3	+16.0	56.2	6 12.7	+16.8	56.3	6 45.9	+17.7	56.4
35	5 21.1	+15.0	55.2	5 55.3	+15.9	55.2	6 29.5	+16.7	55.3	7 03.6	+17.5	55.4
36	5 36.1	+15.0	54.2	6 11.2	+15.8	54.3	6 46.2	+16.6	54.4	7 21.1	+17.4	54.5
37	5 51.1	+14.8	53.2	6 27.0	+15.7	53.3	7 02.8	+16.5	53.4	7 38.5	+17.3	53.5
38	6 05.9	+14.8	52.2	6 42.7	+15.5	52.3	7 19.3	+16.3	52.4	7 55.8	+17.2	52.5
39	6 20.7	+14.7	51.3	6 58.2	+15.5	51.4	7 35.6	+16.3	51.5	8 13.0	+17.0	51.6
40	6 35.4	+14.5	50.3	7 13.7	+15.3	50.4	7 51.9	+16.1	50.5	8 30.0	+16.9	50.6
41	6 49.9	+14.4	49.3	7 29.0	+15.2	49.4	8 08.0	+15.9	49.5	8 46.9	+16.7	49.6
42	7 04.3	+14.3	48.3	7 44.2	+15.0	48.4	8 23.9	+15.8	48.5	9 03.6	+16.6	48.7
43	7 18.6	+14.2	47.4	7 59.2	+14.9	47.5	8 39.7	+15.7	47.6	9 20.2	+16.4	47.7
44	7 32.8	+14.0	46.4	8 14.1	+14.8	46.5	8 55.4	+15.5	46.6	9 36.6	+16.2	46.7
45	7 46.8	+13.9	45.4	8 28.9	+14.6	45.5	9 10.9	+15.4	45.6	9 52.8	+16.1	45.7
46	8 00.7	+13.8	44.4	8 43.5	+14.5	44.5	9 26.3	+15.2	44.6	10 08.9	+15.9	44.7
47	8 14.5	+13.6	43.4	8 58.0	+14.3	43.5	9 41.5	+15.0	43.6	10 24.8	+15.8	43.8
48	8 28.1	+13.4	42.4	9 12.3	+14.2	42.5	9 56.5	+14.8	42.7	10 40.6	+15.5	42.8
49	8 41.5	+13.4	41.5	9 26.5	+14.0	41.6	10 11.3	+14.7	41.7	10 56.1	+15.3	41.8
50	8 54.9	+13.1	40.5	9 40.5	+13.8	40.6	10 26.0	+14.5	40.7	11 11.4	+15.2	40.8
51	9 08.0	+13.0	39.5	9 54.3	+13.6	39.6	10 40.5	+14.3	39.7	11 26.6	+15.0	39.8
52	9 21.0	+12.8	38.5	10 07.9	+13.5	38.6	10 54.8	+14.1	38.7	11 41.6	+14.7	38.8
53	9 33.8	+12.7	37.5	10 21.4	+13.3	37.6	11 08.9	+13.9	37.7	11 56.3	+14.6	37.9
54	9 46.5	+12.5	36.5	10 34.7	+13.1	36.6	11 22.8	+13.7	36.7	12 10.9	+14.3	36.9
55	9 59.0	+12.3	35.5	10 47.8	+12.9	35.6	11 36.5	+13.6	35.7	12 25.2	+14.1	35.9
56	10 11.3	+12.2	34.5	11 00.7	+12.8	34.6	11 50.1	+13.3	34.7	12 39.3	+13.9	34.9
57	10 23.5	+11.9	33.5	11 13.5	+12.5	33.6	12 03.4	+13.1	33.7	12 53.2	+13.7	33.9
58	10 35.4	+11.8	32.5	11 26.0	+12.3	32.6	12 16.5	+12.8	32.8	13 06.9	+13.4	32.9
59	10 47.2	+11.6	31.5	11 38.3	+12.1	31.6	12 29.3	+12.7	31.8	13 20.3	+13.2	31.9
60	10 58.8	+11.3	30.5	11 50.4	+11.9	30.6	12 42.0	+12.4	30.7	13 33.5	+13.0	30.9
61	11 10.1	+11.2	29.5	12 02.3	+11.7	29.6	12 54.4	+12.2	29.7	13 46.5	+12.7	29.9
62	11 21.3	+11.0	28.5	12 14.0	+11.5	28.6	13 06.6	+12.0	28.7	13 59.2	+12.5	28.9
63	11 32.3	+10.8	27.5	12 25.5	+11.2	27.6	13 18.6	+11.7	27.7	14 11.7	+12.2	27.8
64	11 43.1	+10.5	26.5	12 36.7	+11.0	26.6	13 30.3	+11.5	26.7	14 23.9	+11.9	26.8
65	11 53.6	+10.4	25.5	12 47.7	+10.8	25.6	13 41.8	+11.3	25.7	14 35.8	+11.7	25.8
66	12 04.0	+10.1	24.5	12 58.5	+10.6	24.6	13 53.1	+10.9	24.7	14 47.5	+11.5	24.8
67	12 14.1	+9.9	23.5	13 09.1	+10.3	23.6	14 04.0	+10.8	23.7	14 59.0	+11.1	23.8
68	12 24.0	+9.7	22.5	13 19.4	+10.1	22.6	14 14.8	+10.5	22.7	15 10.1	+10.9	22.8
69	12 33.7	+9.4	21.5	13 29.5	+9.8	21.6	14 25.3	+10.2	21.7	15 21.0	+10.6	21.8
70	12 43.1	+9.2	20.5	13 39.3	+9.6	20.6	14 35.5	+9.9	20.6	15 31.6	+10.3	20.7
71	12 52.3	+9.0	19.5	13 48.9	+9.3	19.5	14 45.4	+9.7	19.6	15 41.9	+10.1	19.7
72	13 01.3	+8.8	18.4	13 58.2	+9.1	18.5	14 55.1	+9.4	18.6	15 52.0	+9.7	18.7
73	13 10.1	+8.5	17.4	14 07.3	+8.8	17.5	15 04.5	+9.2	17.6	16 01.7	+9.5	17.7
74	13 18.6	+8.3	16.4	14 16.1	+8.6	16.5	15 13.7	+8.8	16.6	16 11.2	+9.1	16.6
75	13 26.9	+8.0	15.4	14 24.7	+8.3	15.5	15 22.5	+8.6	15.5	16 20.3	+8.9	15.6
76	13 34.9	+7.8	14.4	14 33.0	+8.0	14.4	15 31.1	+8.3	14.5	16 29.2	+8.5	14.6
77	13 42.7	+7.5	13.4	14 41.0	+7.8	13.4	15 39.4	+8.0	13.5	16 37.7	+8.3	13.5
78	13 50.2	+7.3	12.3	14 48.8	+7.5	12.4	15 47.4	+7.7	12.4	16 46.0	+7.9	12.5
79	13 57.5	+7.0	11.3	14 56.3	+7.2	11.4	15 55.1	+7.4	11.4	16 53.9	+7.6	11.5
80	14 04.5	+6.7	10.3	15 03.5	+7.0	10.3	16 02.5	+7.2	10.4	17 01.5	+7.4	10.4
81	14 11.2	+6.5	9.3	15 10.5	+6.6	9.3	16 09.7	+6.8	9.4	17 08.9	+6.9	9.4
82	14 17.7	+6.3	8.2	15 17.1	+6.4	8.3	16 16.5	+6.5	8.3	17 15.8	+6.7	8.4
83	14 24.0	+5.9	7.2	15 23.5	+6.1	7.2	16 23.0	+6.2	7.3	17 22.5	+6.4	7.3
84	14 29.9	+5.7	6.2	15 29.6	+5.8	6.2	16 29.2	+5.9	6.2	17 28.9	+6.0	6.3
85	14 35.6	+5.4	5.2	15 35.4	+5.5	5.2	16 35.1	+5.6	5.2	17 34.9	+5.7	5.2
86	14 41.0	+5.2	4.1	15 40.9	+5.2	4.1	16 40.7	+5.3	4.2	17 40.6	+5.3	4.2
87	14 46.2	+4.9	3.1	15 46.1	+4.9	3.1	16 46.0	+5.0	3.1	17 45.9	+5.1	3.1
88	14 51.1	+4.6	2.1	15 51.0	+4.7	2.1	16 51.0	+4.7	2.1	17 51.0	+4.6	2.1
89	14 55.7	+4.3	1.0	15 55.7	+4.3	1.0	16 55.7	+4.3	1.0	17 55.6	+4.4	1.0
90	15 00.0	+4.0	0.0	16 00.0	+4.0	0.0	17 00.0	+4.0	0.0	18 00.0	+4.0	0.0
	15°			16°			17°			18°		

Dec.	19° Hc	d	Z	20° Hc	d	Z	21° Hc	d	Z	22° Hc	d	Z
°	° ′	′	°	° ′	′	°	° ′	′	°	° ′	′	°
0	3 46.9	−19.6	91.3	3 45.5	−20.6	91.4	3 44.0	−21.5	91.4	3 42.5	−22.6	91.5
1	3 27.3	−19.7	92.3	3 24.9	−20.6	92.3	3 22.5	−21.7	92.4	3 19.9	−22.6	92.4
2	3 07.6	−19.7	93.2	3 04.3	−20.7	93.3	3 00.8	−21.6	93.3	2 57.3	−22.6	93.4
3	2 47.9	−19.7	94.1	2 43.6	−20.8	94.2	2 39.2	−21.8	94.2	2 34.7	−22.7	94.3
4	2 28.2	−19.8	95.1	2 22.8	−20.8	95.1	2 17.4	−21.7	95.2	2 12.0	−22.7	95.2
5	2 08.4	−19.9	96.0	2 02.0	−20.8	96.1	1 55.7	−21.8	96.1	1 49.3	−22.8	96.1
6	1 48.5	−19.8	97.0	1 41.2	−20.8	97.0	1 33.9	−21.8	97.0	1 26.5	−22.8	97.1
7	1 28.7	−19.9	97.9	1 20.4	−20.9	97.9	1 12.1	−21.9	98.0	1 03.7	−22.7	98.0
8	1 08.8	−19.9	98.9	0 59.5	−20.9	98.9	0 50.2	−21.8	98.9	0 41.0	−22.9	98.9
9	0 48.9	−20.0	99.8	0 38.6	−20.9	99.8	0 28.4	−21.9	99.8	0 18.1	−22.8	99.8
10	0 28.9	−19.9	100.8	0 17.7	−20.8	100.8	0 06.5	−21.8	100.8	0 04.7	+22.8	79.2
11	0 09.0	−19.9	101.7	0 03.1	+20.9	78.3	0 15.3	+21.9	78.3	0 27.5	+22.8	78.3
12	0 10.9	+19.9	77.4	0 24.0	+20.9	77.4	0 37.2	+21.8	77.4	0 50.3	+22.8	77.4
13	0 30.8	+20.0	76.4	0 44.9	+20.9	76.4	0 59.0	+21.8	76.4	1 13.1	+22.7	76.5
14	0 50.8	+19.9	75.5	1 05.8	+20.9	75.5	1 20.8	+21.8	75.5	1 35.8	+22.8	75.5
15	1 10.7	+19.9	74.5	1 26.7	+20.8	74.6	1 42.6	+21.8	74.6	1 58.6	+22.7	74.6
16	1 30.6	+19.8	73.6	1 47.5	+20.8	73.6	2 04.4	+21.7	73.6	2 21.3	+22.7	73.7
17	1 50.4	+19.8	72.6	2 08.3	+20.8	72.7	2 26.1	+21.7	72.7	2 44.0	+22.6	72.8
18	2 10.2	+19.8	71.7	2 29.1	+20.7	71.7	2 47.8	+21.7	71.8	3 06.6	+22.6	71.8
19	2 30.0	+19.8	70.8	2 49.8	+20.7	70.8	3 09.5	+21.6	70.8	3 29.2	+22.5	70.9
20	2 49.8	+19.7	69.8	3 10.5	+20.6	69.9	3 31.1	+21.6	69.9	3 51.7	+22.5	70.0
21	3 09.5	+19.7	68.9	3 31.1	+20.6	68.9	3 52.7	+21.5	69.0	4 14.2	+22.4	69.0
22	3 29.2	+19.6	67.9	3 51.7	+20.5	68.0	4 14.2	+21.4	68.0	4 36.6	+22.3	68.1
23	3 48.8	+19.5	67.0	4 12.2	+20.5	67.0	4 35.6	+21.3	67.1	4 58.9	+22.2	67.2
24	4 08.3	+19.5	66.0	4 32.7	+20.3	66.1	4 56.9	+21.3	66.2	5 21.1	+22.2	66.2
25	4 27.8	+19.4	65.1	4 53.0	+20.3	65.1	5 18.2	+21.2	65.2	5 43.3	+22.1	65.3
26	4 47.2	+19.3	64.1	5 13.3	+20.2	64.2	5 39.4	+21.1	64.3	6 05.4	+22.0	64.4
27	5 06.5	+19.2	63.2	5 33.5	+20.2	63.3	6 00.5	+21.0	63.3	6 27.4	+21.8	63.4
28	5 25.7	+19.2	62.2	5 53.7	+20.0	62.3	6 21.5	+20.9	62.4	6 49.2	+21.8	62.5
29	5 44.9	+19.0	61.3	6 13.7	+19.9	61.4	6 42.4	+20.8	61.5	7 11.0	+21.7	61.6
30	6 03.9	+19.0	60.3	6 33.6	+19.8	60.4	7 03.2	+20.6	60.5	7 32.7	+21.5	60.6
31	6 22.9	+18.8	59.4	6 53.4	+19.7	59.5	7 23.8	+20.6	59.6	7 54.2	+21.4	59.7
32	6 41.7	+18.8	58.4	7 13.1	+19.6	58.5	7 44.4	+20.4	58.6	8 15.6	+21.3	58.7
33	7 00.5	+18.6	57.5	7 32.7	+19.5	57.6	8 04.8	+20.3	57.7	8 36.9	+21.1	57.8
34	7 19.1	+18.5	56.5	7 52.2	+19.3	56.6	8 25.1	+20.2	56.7	8 58.0	+21.0	56.9
35	7 37.6	+18.3	55.5	8 11.5	+19.2	55.6	8 45.3	+20.0	55.8	9 19.0	+20.8	55.9
36	7 55.9	+18.3	54.6	8 30.7	+19.0	54.7	9 05.3	+19.9	54.8	9 39.8	+20.7	55.0
37	8 14.2	+18.1	53.6	8 49.7	+18.9	53.7	9 25.2	+19.7	53.9	10 00.5	+20.5	54.0
38	8 32.3	+17.9	52.6	9 08.6	+18.8	52.8	9 44.9	+19.5	52.9	10 21.0	+20.4	53.0
39	8 50.2	+17.8	51.7	9 27.4	+18.6	51.8	10 04.4	+19.4	51.9	10 41.4	+20.1	52.1
40	9 08.0	+17.7	50.7	9 46.0	+18.4	50.8	10 23.8	+19.2	51.0	11 01.5	+20.0	51.1
41	9 25.7	+17.5	49.7	10 04.4	+18.3	49.9	10 43.0	+19.1	50.0	11 21.5	+19.8	50.2
42	9 43.2	+17.3	48.8	10 22.7	+18.1	48.9	11 02.1	+18.8	49.1	11 41.3	+19.6	49.2
43	10 00.5	+17.2	47.8	10 40.8	+17.9	47.9	11 20.9	+18.7	48.1	12 00.9	+19.5	48.2
44	10 17.7	+17.0	46.8	10 58.7	+17.7	47.0	11 39.6	+18.4	47.1	12 20.4	+19.2	47.3
45	10 34.7	+16.8	45.9	11 16.4	+17.6	46.0	11 58.0	+18.3	46.1	12 39.6	+19.0	46.3
46	10 51.5	+16.6	44.9	11 34.0	+17.3	45.0	12 16.3	+18.1	45.2	12 58.6	+18.7	45.3
47	11 08.1	+16.4	43.9	11 51.3	+17.1	44.0	12 34.4	+17.8	44.2	13 17.3	+18.6	44.4
48	11 24.5	+16.3	42.9	12 08.4	+17.0	43.1	12 52.2	+17.6	43.2	13 35.9	+18.3	43.4
49	11 40.8	+16.0	41.9	12 25.4	+16.7	42.1	13 09.8	+17.4	42.2	13 54.2	+18.1	42.4
50	11 56.8	+15.8	41.0	12 42.1	+16.5	41.1	13 27.2	+17.2	41.2	14 12.3	+17.8	41.4
51	12 12.6	+15.7	40.0	12 58.6	+16.3	40.1	13 44.4	+17.0	40.3	14 30.1	+17.6	40.4
52	12 28.3	+15.4	39.0	13 14.9	+16.0	39.1	14 01.4	+16.7	39.3	14 47.7	+17.4	39.4
53	12 43.7	+15.1	38.0	13 30.9	+15.8	38.1	14 18.1	+16.4	38.3	15 05.1	+17.1	38.4
54	12 58.8	+15.0	37.0	13 46.7	+15.6	37.1	14 34.5	+16.2	37.3	15 22.2	+16.8	37.5
55	13 13.8	+14.7	36.0	14 02.3	+15.3	36.1	14 50.7	+15.9	36.3	15 39.0	+16.6	36.5
56	13 28.5	+14.5	35.0	14 17.6	+15.1	35.1	15 06.6	+15.7	35.3	15 55.6	+16.2	35.5
57	13 43.0	+14.3	34.0	14 32.7	+14.8	34.1	15 22.3	+15.4	34.3	16 11.8	+16.0	34.5
58	13 57.3	+14.0	33.0	14 47.5	+14.6	33.1	15 37.7	+15.2	33.3	16 27.8	+15.7	33.5
59	14 11.3	+13.7	32.0	15 02.1	+14.3	32.1	15 52.9	+14.8	32.3	16 43.5	+15.5	32.4
60	14 25.0	+13.5	31.0	15 16.4	+14.0	31.1	16 07.7	+14.6	31.3	16 59.0	+15.1	31.4
61	14 38.5	+13.2	30.0	15 30.4	+13.8	30.1	16 22.3	+14.3	30.3	17 14.1	+14.8	30.4
62	14 51.7	+13.0	29.0	15 44.2	+13.5	29.1	16 36.6	+14.0	29.3	17 28.9	+14.5	29.4
63	15 04.7	+12.7	28.0	15 57.7	+13.2	28.1	16 50.6	+13.6	28.2	17 43.4	+14.2	28.4
64	15 17.4	+12.4	27.0	16 10.9	+12.9	27.1	17 04.2	+13.4	27.2	17 57.6	+13.8	27.4
65	15 29.8	+12.2	25.9	16 23.8	+12.6	26.1	17 17.6	+13.1	26.2	18 11.4	+13.6	26.3
66	15 42.0	+11.8	24.9	16 36.4	+12.3	25.0	17 30.7	+12.7	25.2	18 25.0	+13.2	25.3
67	15 53.8	+11.6	23.9	16 48.7	+12.0	24.0	17 43.4	+12.5	24.2	18 38.2	+12.8	24.3
68	16 05.4	+11.3	22.9	17 00.7	+11.7	23.0	17 55.9	+12.1	23.1	18 51.0	+12.6	23.3
69	16 16.7	+11.0	21.9	17 12.4	+11.4	22.0	18 08.0	+11.8	22.1	19 03.6	+12.1	22.2
70	16 27.7	+10.7	20.8	17 23.8	+11.0	20.9	18 19.8	+11.4	21.1	19 15.7	+11.9	21.2
71	16 38.4	+10.4	19.8	17 34.8	+10.8	19.9	18 31.2	+11.1	20.0	19 27.6	+11.4	20.1
72	16 48.8	+10.1	18.8	17 45.6	+10.4	18.9	18 42.3	+10.8	19.0	19 39.0	+11.2	19.1
73	16 58.9	+9.7	17.8	17 56.0	+10.1	17.9	18 53.1	+10.4	18.0	19 50.2	+10.7	18.1
74	17 08.6	+9.5	16.7	18 06.1	+9.8	16.8	19 03.5	+10.1	16.9	20 00.9	+10.4	17.0
75	17 18.1	+9.1	15.7	18 15.9	+9.4	15.8	19 13.6	+9.7	15.9	20 11.3	+10.0	16.0
76	17 27.2	+8.9	14.7	18 25.3	+9.1	14.7	19 23.3	+9.4	14.8	20 21.3	+9.6	14.9
77	17 36.1	+8.5	13.6	18 34.4	+8.7	13.7	19 32.7	+8.9	13.8	20 30.9	+9.3	13.9
78	17 44.6	+8.1	12.6	18 43.1	+8.4	12.6	19 41.6	+8.7	12.7	20 40.2	+8.8	12.8
79	17 52.7	+7.8	11.5	18 51.5	+8.0	11.6	19 50.3	+8.2	11.7	20 49.0	+8.5	11.7
80	18 00.5	+7.5	10.5	18 59.5	+7.7	10.6	19 58.5	+7.9	10.6	20 57.5	+8.1	10.7
81	18 08.0	+7.2	9.5	19 07.2	+7.4	9.5	20 06.4	+7.5	9.6	21 05.6	+7.6	9.6
82	18 15.2	+6.8	8.4	19 14.6	+6.9	8.5	20 13.9	+7.1	8.5	21 13.2	+7.3	8.6
83	18 22.0	+6.5	7.4	19 21.5	+6.6	7.4	20 21.0	+6.8	7.5	21 20.5	+6.9	7.5
84	18 28.5	+6.1	6.3	19 28.1	+6.3	6.3	20 27.8	+6.3	6.4	21 27.4	+6.5	6.4
85	18 34.6	+5.8	5.3	19 34.4	+5.8	5.3	20 34.1	+6.0	5.3	21 33.9	+6.0	5.4
86	18 40.4	+5.4	4.2	19 40.2	+5.5	4.2	20 40.1	+5.6	4.3	21 39.9	+5.7	4.3
87	18 45.8	+5.1	3.2	19 45.7	+5.2	3.2	20 45.7	+5.1	3.2	21 45.6	+5.2	3.2
88	18 50.9	+4.7	2.1	19 50.9	+4.7	2.1	20 50.8	+4.8	2.1	21 50.8	+4.8	2.1
89	18 55.6	+4.4	1.1	19 55.6	+4.4	1.1	20 55.6	+4.4	1.1	21 55.6	+4.4	1.1
90	19 00.0	+4.0	0.0	20 00.0	+4.0	0.0	21 00.0	+4.0	0.0	22 00.0	+4.0	0.0
	19°			20°			21°			22°		

S. Lat. {L.H.A. greater than 180° ....Zn=180°−Z; L.H.A. less than 180°...........Zn=180°+Z}

LATITUDE **SAME** NAME AS DECLINATION **L.H.A. 94°, 266°**

175

Dec.	15°			16°			17°			18°		
	Hc	d	Z	Hc	d	Z	Hc	d	Z	Hc	d	Z
°	° ′	′	°	° ′	′	°	° ′	′	°	° ′	′	°
0	2 53.9	+15.5	90.8	2 53.0	+16.6	90.8	2 52.1	+17.6	90.9	2 51.2	+18.5	90.9
1	3 09.4	+15.5	89.8	3 09.6	+16.4	89.9	3 09.7	+17.5	89.9	3 09.7	+18.5	90.0
2	3 24.9	+15.4	88.8	3 26.0	+16.5	88.9	3 27.2	+17.4	89.0	3 28.2	+18.4	89.0
3	3 40.3	+15.3	87.9	3 42.5	+16.3	87.9	3 44.6	+17.3	88.0	3 46.6	+18.4	88.1
4	3 55.6	+15.3	86.9	3 58.8	+16.3	87.0	4 01.9	+17.3	87.0	4 05.0	+18.3	87.1
5	4 10.9	+15.2	85.9	4 15.1	+16.2	86.0	4 19.2	+17.3	86.1	4 23.3	+18.2	86.2
6	4 26.1	+15.1	85.0	4 31.3	+16.2	85.0	4 36.5	+17.1	85.1	4 41.5	+18.2	85.2
7	4 41.2	+15.1	84.0	4 47.5	+16.0	84.1	4 53.6	+17.1	84.2	4 59.7	+18.0	84.2
8	4 56.3	+15.0	83.0	5 03.5	+16.0	83.1	5 10.7	+17.0	83.2	5 17.7	+18.0	83.3
9	5 11.3	+14.8	82.1	5 19.5	+15.9	82.1	5 27.7	+16.9	82.2	5 35.7	+17.9	82.3
10	5 26.1	+14.8	81.1	5 35.4	+15.8	81.2	5 44.6	+16.7	81.3	5 53.6	+17.8	81.4
11	5 40.9	+14.7	80.1	5 51.2	+15.7	80.2	6 01.3	+16.7	80.3	6 11.4	+17.7	80.4
12	5 55.6	+14.6	79.1	6 06.9	+15.6	79.2	6 18.0	+16.6	79.3	6 29.1	+17.5	79.5
13	6 10.2	+14.5	78.2	6 22.5	+15.4	78.3	6 34.6	+16.5	78.4	6 46.6	+17.5	78.5
14	6 24.7	+14.3	77.2	6 37.9	+15.4	77.3	6 51.1	+16.3	77.4	7 04.1	+17.3	77.5
15	6 39.0	+14.3	76.2	6 53.3	+15.2	76.3	7 07.4	+16.3	76.4	7 21.4	+17.3	76.6
16	6 53.3	+14.1	75.2	7 08.5	+15.2	75.3	7 23.7	+16.1	75.5	7 38.7	+17.0	75.6
17	7 07.4	+14.0	74.2	7 23.7	+15.0	74.4	7 39.8	+15.9	74.5	7 55.7	+17.0	74.6
18	7 21.4	+13.9	73.3	7 38.7	+14.8	73.4	7 55.7	+15.9	73.5	8 12.7	+16.8	73.7
19	7 35.3	+13.8	72.3	7 53.5	+14.7	72.4	8 11.6	+15.7	72.5	8 29.5	+16.7	72.7
20	7 49.1	+13.6	71.3	8 08.2	+14.6	71.4	8 27.3	+15.5	71.6	8 46.2	+16.5	71.7
21	8 02.7	+13.5	70.3	8 22.8	+14.5	70.5	8 42.8	+15.4	70.6	9 02.7	+16.4	70.7
22	8 16.2	+13.3	69.3	8 37.3	+14.3	69.5	8 58.2	+15.3	69.6	9 19.1	+16.2	69.8
23	8 29.5	+13.2	68.3	8 51.6	+14.1	68.5	9 13.5	+15.1	68.6	9 35.3	+16.0	68.8
24	8 42.7	+13.0	67.4	9 05.7	+14.0	67.5	9 28.6	+14.9	67.7	9 51.3	+15.9	67.8
25	8 55.7	+12.9	66.4	9 19.7	+13.8	66.5	9 43.5	+14.8	66.7	10 07.2	+15.7	66.8
26	9 08.6	+12.7	65.4	9 33.5	+13.6	65.5	9 58.3	+14.6	65.7	10 22.9	+15.5	65.9
27	9 21.3	+12.5	64.4	9 47.1	+13.5	64.5	10 12.9	+14.4	64.7	10 38.4	+15.3	64.9
28	9 33.8	+12.4	63.4	10 00.6	+13.3	63.6	10 27.3	+14.2	63.7	10 53.7	+15.2	63.9
29	9 46.2	+12.2	62.4	10 13.9	+13.1	62.6	10 41.5	+14.0	62.7	11 08.9	+14.9	62.9
30	9 58.4	+12.0	61.4	10 27.0	+13.0	61.6	10 55.5	+13.9	61.7	11 23.8	+14.8	61.9
31	10 10.4	+11.9	60.4	10 40.0	+12.7	60.6	11 09.4	+13.6	60.7	11 38.6	+14.6	60.9
32	10 22.3	+11.6	59.4	10 52.7	+12.6	59.6	11 23.0	+13.5	59.8	11 53.2	+14.3	59.9
33	10 33.9	+11.5	58.4	11 05.3	+12.3	58.6	11 36.5	+13.2	58.8	12 07.5	+14.1	58.9
34	10 45.4	+11.3	57.4	11 17.6	+12.2	57.6	11 49.7	+13.1	57.8	12 21.6	+14.0	57.9
35	10 56.7	+11.1	56.4	11 29.8	+11.9	56.6	12 02.8	+12.8	56.8	12 35.6	+13.7	56.9
36	11 07.8	+10.9	55.4	11 41.7	+11.8	55.6	12 15.6	+12.6	55.8	12 49.3	+13.4	56.0
37	11 18.7	+10.6	54.4	11 53.5	+11.5	54.6	12 28.2	+12.4	54.8	13 02.7	+13.3	55.0
38	11 29.3	+10.5	53.4	12 05.0	+11.3	53.6	12 40.6	+12.1	53.8	13 16.0	+13.0	54.0
39	11 39.8	+10.3	52.4	12 16.3	+11.1	52.6	12 52.7	+12.0	52.8	13 29.0	+12.7	52.9
40	11 50.1	+10.0	51.4	12 27.4	+10.9	51.6	13 04.7	+11.7	51.8	13 41.7	+12.6	51.9
41	12 00.1	+9.9	50.4	12 38.3	+10.7	50.6	13 16.4	+11.4	50.7	13 54.3	+12.2	50.9
42	12 10.0	+9.6	49.4	12 49.0	+10.4	49.6	13 27.8	+11.2	49.7	14 06.5	+12.0	49.9
43	12 19.6	+9.4	48.4	12 59.4	+10.2	48.5	13 39.0	+11.0	48.7	14 18.5	+11.8	48.9
44	12 29.0	+9.2	47.4	13 09.6	+9.9	47.5	13 50.0	+10.7	47.7	14 30.3	+11.5	47.9
45	12 38.2	+8.9	46.4	13 19.5	+9.7	46.5	14 00.7	+10.5	46.7	14 41.8	+11.2	46.9
46	12 47.1	+8.7	45.3	13 29.2	+9.5	45.5	14 11.2	+10.2	45.7	14 53.0	+11.0	45.9
47	12 55.8	+8.5	44.3	13 38.7	+9.2	44.5	14 21.4	+10.0	44.7	15 04.0	+10.7	44.9
48	13 04.3	+8.2	43.3	13 47.9	+8.9	43.5	14 31.4	+9.7	43.7	15 14.7	+10.4	43.8
49	13 12.5	+8.0	42.3	13 56.8	+8.8	42.5	14 41.1	+9.4	42.6	15 25.1	+10.2	42.8
50	13 20.5	+7.8	41.3	14 05.6	+8.4	41.4	14 50.5	+9.1	41.6	15 35.3	+9.8	41.8
51	13 28.3	+7.5	40.3	14 14.0	+8.2	40.4	14 59.6	+8.9	40.6	15 45.1	+9.6	40.8
52	13 35.8	+7.2	39.2	14 22.2	+7.9	39.4	15 08.5	+8.6	39.6	15 54.7	+9.3	39.7
53	13 43.0	+7.0	38.2	14 30.1	+7.7	38.4	15 17.1	+8.3	38.5	16 04.0	+9.0	38.7
54	13 50.0	+6.8	37.2	14 37.8	+7.4	37.3	15 25.4	+8.0	37.5	16 13.0	+8.6	37.7
55	13 56.8	+6.5	36.2	14 45.2	+7.1	36.3	15 33.4	+7.8	36.5	16 21.6	+8.4	36.7
56	14 03.3	+6.2	35.1	14 52.3	+6.8	35.3	15 41.2	+7.5	35.5	16 30.0	+8.1	35.6
57	14 09.5	+5.9	34.1	14 59.1	+6.6	34.3	15 48.7	+7.1	34.4	16 38.1	+7.8	34.6
58	14 15.4	+5.8	33.1	15 05.7	+6.3	33.2	15 55.8	+6.9	33.4	16 45.9	+7.4	33.6
59	14 21.2	+5.4	32.1	15 12.0	+6.0	32.2	16 02.7	+6.6	32.4	16 53.3	+7.2	32.5
60	14 26.6	+5.2	31.0	15 18.0	+5.7	31.2	16 09.3	+6.2	31.3	17 00.5	+6.8	31.5
61	14 31.8	+4.9	30.0	15 23.7	+5.4	30.1	16 15.5	+6.0	30.3	17 07.3	+6.5	30.4
62	14 36.7	+4.6	29.0	15 29.1	+5.2	29.1	16 21.5	+5.7	29.2	17 13.8	+6.2	29.4
63	14 41.3	+4.4	27.9	15 34.3	+4.8	28.1	16 27.2	+5.3	28.2	17 20.0	+5.9	28.4
64	14 45.7	+4.0	26.9	15 39.1	+4.6	27.0	16 32.5	+5.1	27.2	17 25.9	+5.5	27.3
65	14 49.7	+3.8	25.9	15 43.7	+4.3	26.0	16 37.6	+4.7	26.1	17 31.4	+5.2	26.3
66	14 53.5	+3.6	24.9	15 48.0	+3.9	25.0	16 42.3	+4.5	25.1	17 36.6	+4.9	25.2
67	14 57.1	+3.2	23.8	15 51.9	+3.7	23.9	16 46.8	+4.1	24.1	17 41.5	+4.6	24.2
68	15 00.3	+3.0	22.8	15 55.6	+3.4	22.9	16 50.9	+3.8	23.0	17 46.1	+4.2	23.1
69	15 03.3	+2.7	21.8	15 59.0	+3.1	21.9	16 54.7	+3.5	22.0	17 50.3	+3.9	22.1
70	15 06.0	+2.4	20.7	16 02.1	+2.8	20.8	16 58.2	+3.1	20.9	17 54.2	+3.5	21.0
71	15 08.4	+2.1	19.7	16 04.9	+2.5	19.8	17 01.3	+2.9	19.9	17 57.7	+3.2	20.0
72	15 10.5	+1.9	18.6	16 07.4	+2.1	18.7	17 04.2	+2.5	18.8	18 00.9	+2.9	18.9
73	15 12.4	+1.5	17.6	16 09.5	+1.9	17.7	17 06.7	+2.2	17.8	18 03.8	+2.5	17.9
74	15 13.9	+1.3	16.6	16 11.4	+1.6	16.7	17 08.9	+1.9	16.7	18 06.3	+2.2	16.8
75	15 15.2	+1.0	15.5	16 13.0	+1.3	15.6	17 10.8	+1.5	15.7	18 08.5	+1.9	15.8
76	15 16.2	+0.7	14.5	16 14.3	+0.9	14.6	17 12.3	+1.2	14.6	18 10.4	+1.5	14.7
77	15 16.9	+0.4	13.5	16 15.2	+0.7	13.5	17 13.5	+0.9	13.6	18 11.9	+1.1	13.7
78	15 17.3	+0.1	12.4	16 15.9	+0.3	12.5	17 14.4	+0.6	12.6	18 13.0	+0.8	12.6
79	15 17.4	-0.1	11.4	16 16.2	+0.1	11.4	17 15.0	+0.3	11.5	18 13.8	+0.5	11.6
80	15 17.3	-0.5	10.4	16 16.3	-0.3	10.4	17 15.3	-0.1	10.5	18 14.3	+0.1	10.5
81	15 16.8	-0.7	9.3	16 16.0	-0.5	9.4	17 15.2	-0.4	9.4	18 14.4	-0.2	9.5
82	15 16.1	-1.0	8.3	16 15.5	-0.9	8.3	17 14.8	-0.7	8.4	18 14.2	-0.6	8.4
83	15 15.1	-1.3	7.2	16 14.6	-1.2	7.3	17 14.1	-1.0	7.3	18 13.6	-0.9	7.4
84	15 13.8	-1.6	6.2	16 13.4	-1.5	6.2	17 13.1	-1.4	6.3	18 12.7	-1.3	6.3
85	15 12.2	-1.9	5.2	16 11.9	-1.7	5.2	17 11.7	-1.7	5.2	18 11.4	-1.6	5.3
86	15 10.3	-2.1	4.1	16 10.2	-2.1	4.2	17 10.0	-2.0	4.2	18 09.8	-1.9	4.2
87	15 08.2	-2.5	3.1	16 08.1	-2.4	3.1	17 08.0	-2.4	3.1	18 07.9	-2.3	3.2
88	15 05.7	-2.7	2.1	16 05.7	-2.7	2.1	17 05.6	-2.6	2.1	18 05.6	-2.6	2.1
89	15 03.0	-3.0	1.0	16 03.0	-3.0	1.0	17 03.0	-3.0	1.0	18 03.0	-3.0	1.1
90	15 00.0	-3.3	0.0	16 00.0	-3.3	0.0	17 00.0	-3.3	0.0	18 00.0	-3.3	0.0
	15°			16°			17°			18°		

19°			20°			21°			22°			Dec.
Hc	d	Z	Hc	d	Z	Hc	d	Z	Hc	d	Z	
° ′	′	°	° ′	′	°	° ′	′	°	° ′	′	°	°
2 50.2	+19.5	91.0	2 49.1	+20.6	91.0	2 48.0	+21.5	91.1	2 46.9	+22.5	91.1	0
3 09.7	+19.5	90.0	3 09.7	+20.4	90.1	3 09.5	+21.5	90.1	3 09.4	+22.4	90.2	1
3 29.2	+19.4	89.1	3 30.1	+20.4	89.1	3 31.0	+21.4	89.2	3 31.8	+22.4	89.3	2
3 48.6	+19.4	88.1	3 50.5	+20.4	88.2	3 52.4	+21.3	88.3	3 54.2	+22.3	88.3	3
4 08.0	+19.3	87.2	4 10.9	+20.3	87.3	4 13.7	+21.3	87.3	4 16.5	+22.2	87.4	4
4 27.3	+19.2	86.2	4 31.2	+20.2	86.3	4 35.0	+21.2	86.4	4 38.7	+22.2	86.5	5
4 46.5	+19.1	85.3	4 51.4	+20.1	85.4	4 56.2	+21.1	85.5	5 00.9	+22.1	85.5	6
5 05.6	+19.1	84.3	5 11.5	+20.1	84.4	5 17.3	+21.0	84.5	5 23.0	+22.0	84.6	7
5 24.7	+19.0	83.4	5 31.6	+19.9	83.5	5 38.3	+21.0	83.6	5 45.0	+21.9	83.7	8
5 43.7	+18.9	82.4	5 51.5	+19.9	82.5	5 59.3	+20.8	82.6	6 06.9	+21.8	82.7	9
6 02.6	+18.7	81.5	6 11.4	+19.8	81.6	6 20.1	+20.8	81.7	6 28.7	+21.8	81.8	10
6 21.3	+18.7	80.5	6 31.2	+19.6	80.6	6 40.9	+20.6	80.7	6 50.5	+21.6	80.9	11
6 40.0	+18.6	79.6	6 50.8	+19.6	79.7	7 01.5	+20.5	79.8	7 12.1	+21.4	79.9	12
6 58.6	+18.4	78.6	7 10.4	+19.4	78.7	7 22.0	+20.4	78.9	7 33.5	+21.4	79.0	13
7 17.0	+18.3	77.6	7 29.8	+19.3	77.8	7 42.4	+20.3	77.9	7 54.9	+21.3	78.0	14
7 35.3	+18.2	76.7	7 49.1	+19.1	76.8	8 02.7	+20.1	77.0	8 16.2	+21.1	77.1	15
7 53.5	+18.1	75.7	8 08.2	+19.1	75.9	8 22.8	+20.0	76.0	8 37.3	+20.9	76.1	16
8 11.6	+17.9	74.8	8 27.3	+18.9	74.9	8 42.8	+19.9	75.0	8 58.2	+20.9	75.2	17
8 29.5	+17.8	73.8	8 46.2	+18.7	73.9	9 02.7	+19.7	74.1	9 19.1	+20.6	74.2	18
8 47.3	+17.6	72.8	9 04.9	+18.6	73.0	9 22.4	+19.6	73.1	9 39.7	+20.6	73.3	19
9 04.9	+17.5	71.9	9 23.5	+18.5	72.0	9 42.0	+19.4	72.2	10 00.3	+20.3	72.3	20
9 22.4	+17.3	70.9	9 42.0	+18.3	71.1	10 01.4	+19.2	71.2	10 20.6	+20.2	71.4	21
9 39.7	+17.2	69.9	10 00.3	+18.1	70.1	10 20.6	+19.1	70.3	10 40.8	+20.0	70.4	22
9 56.9	+17.0	69.0	10 18.4	+17.9	69.1	10 39.7	+18.9	69.3	11 00.8	+19.8	69.5	23
10 13.9	+16.8	68.0	10 36.3	+17.8	68.1	10 58.6	+18.7	68.3	11 20.6	+19.7	68.5	24
10 30.7	+16.7	67.0	10 54.1	+17.5	67.2	11 17.3	+18.5	67.4	11 40.3	+19.4	67.5	25
10 47.4	+16.4	66.0	11 11.6	+17.4	66.2	11 35.8	+18.3	66.4	11 59.7	+19.3	66.6	26
11 03.8	+16.3	65.0	11 29.0	+17.2	65.2	11 54.1	+18.1	65.4	12 19.0	+19.0	65.6	27
11 20.1	+16.0	64.1	11 46.2	+17.0	64.2	12 12.2	+17.9	64.4	12 38.0	+18.8	64.6	28
11 36.1	+15.9	63.1	12 03.2	+16.8	63.3	12 30.1	+17.7	63.5	12 56.8	+18.6	63.7	29
11 52.0	+15.7	62.1	12 20.0	+16.6	62.3	12 47.8	+17.5	62.5	13 15.4	+18.4	62.7	30
12 07.7	+15.4	61.1	12 36.6	+16.3	61.3	13 05.3	+17.3	61.5	13 33.8	+18.2	61.7	31
12 23.1	+15.3	60.1	12 52.9	+16.2	60.3	13 22.6	+17.0	60.5	13 52.0	+17.9	60.7	32
12 38.4	+15.0	59.1	13 09.1	+15.9	59.3	13 39.6	+16.8	59.5	14 09.9	+17.7	59.7	33
12 53.4	+14.8	58.1	13 25.0	+15.7	58.3	13 56.4	+16.5	58.5	14 27.6	+17.4	58.8	34
13 08.2	+14.6	57.1	13 40.7	+15.4	57.3	14 12.9	+16.4	57.6	14 45.0	+17.2	57.8	35
13 22.8	+14.3	56.1	13 56.1	+15.2	56.3	14 29.3	+16.0	56.6	15 02.2	+17.0	56.8	36
13 37.1	+14.1	55.1	14 11.3	+14.9	55.3	14 45.3	+15.8	55.6	15 19.2	+16.6	55.8	37
13 51.2	+13.8	54.1	14 26.2	+14.7	54.3	15 01.1	+15.6	54.6	15 35.8	+16.4	54.8	38
14 05.0	+13.6	53.1	14 40.9	+14.5	53.3	15 16.7	+15.2	53.6	15 52.2	+16.1	53.8	39
14 18.6	+13.4	52.1	14 55.4	+14.2	52.3	15 31.9	+15.0	52.6	16 08.3	+15.9	52.8	40
14 32.0	+13.1	51.1	15 09.6	+13.9	51.3	15 46.9	+14.8	51.6	16 24.2	+15.5	51.8	41
14 45.1	+12.8	50.1	15 23.5	+13.6	50.3	16 01.7	+14.4	50.5	16 39.7	+15.3	50.8	42
14 57.9	+12.6	49.1	15 37.1	+13.3	49.3	16 16.1	+14.2	49.5	16 55.0	+14.9	49.8	43
15 10.5	+12.2	48.1	15 50.4	+13.1	48.3	16 30.3	+13.8	48.5	17 09.9	+14.7	48.8	44
15 22.7	+12.0	47.1	16 03.5	+12.8	47.3	16 44.1	+13.6	47.5	17 24.6	+14.3	47.7	45
15 34.7	+11.8	46.1	16 16.3	+12.5	46.3	16 57.7	+13.2	46.5	17 38.9	+14.0	46.7	46
15 46.5	+11.4	45.0	16 28.8	+12.2	45.3	17 10.9	+13.0	45.5	17 52.9	+13.8	45.7	47
15 57.9	+11.2	44.0	16 41.0	+11.9	44.2	17 23.9	+12.6	44.4	18 06.7	+13.3	44.7	48
16 09.1	+10.8	43.0	16 52.9	+11.6	43.2	17 36.5	+12.4	43.4	18 20.0	+13.1	43.6	49
16 19.9	+10.6	42.0	17 04.5	+11.2	42.2	17 48.9	+12.0	42.4	18 33.1	+12.7	42.6	50
16 30.5	+10.3	41.0	17 15.7	+11.0	41.2	18 00.9	+11.6	41.4	18 45.8	+12.4	41.6	51
16 40.8	+9.9	39.9	17 26.7	+10.7	40.1	18 12.5	+11.4	40.3	18 58.2	+12.0	40.6	52
16 50.7	+9.7	38.9	17 37.4	+10.3	39.1	18 23.9	+11.0	39.3	19 10.2	+11.7	39.5	53
17 00.4	+9.3	37.9	17 47.7	+10.0	38.1	18 34.9	+10.6	38.3	19 21.9	+11.3	38.5	54
17 09.7	+9.0	36.8	17 57.7	+9.6	37.0	18 45.5	+10.3	37.2	19 33.2	+11.0	37.4	55
17 18.7	+8.7	35.8	18 07.3	+9.4	36.0	18 55.8	+10.0	36.2	19 44.2	+10.6	36.4	56
17 27.4	+8.4	34.8	18 16.7	+9.0	34.9	19 05.8	+9.6	35.1	19 54.8	+10.2	35.3	57
17 35.8	+8.1	33.7	18 25.7	+8.6	33.9	19 15.4	+9.3	34.1	20 05.0	+9.9	34.3	58
17 43.9	+7.7	32.7	18 34.3	+8.3	32.9	19 24.7	+8.9	33.0	20 14.9	+9.5	33.2	59
17 51.6	+7.4	31.6	18 42.6	+8.0	31.8	19 33.6	+8.5	32.0	20 24.4	+9.1	32.2	60
17 59.0	+7.1	30.6	18 50.6	+7.6	30.8	19 42.1	+8.2	30.9	20 33.5	+8.7	31.1	61
18 06.1	+6.7	29.6	18 58.2	+7.3	29.7	19 50.3	+7.8	29.9	20 42.2	+8.4	30.1	62
18 12.8	+6.4	28.5	19 05.5	+6.9	28.7	19 58.1	+7.4	28.8	20 50.6	+7.9	29.0	63
18 19.2	+6.0	27.5	19 12.4	+6.5	27.6	20 05.5	+7.0	27.8	20 58.5	+7.6	28.0	64
18 25.2	+5.7	26.4	19 18.9	+6.2	26.6	20 12.5	+6.7	26.7	21 06.1	+7.1	26.9	65
18 30.9	+5.3	25.4	19 25.1	+5.8	25.5	20 19.2	+6.3	25.7	21 13.2	+6.8	25.8	66
18 36.2	+5.0	24.3	19 30.9	+5.4	24.5	20 25.5	+5.9	24.6	21 20.0	+6.3	24.8	67
18 41.2	+4.7	23.3	19 36.3	+5.1	23.4	20 31.4	+5.5	23.5	21 26.3	+6.0	23.7	68
18 45.9	+4.3	22.2	19 41.4	+4.7	22.3	20 36.9	+5.1	22.5	21 32.3	+5.5	22.6	69
18 50.2	+3.9	21.2	19 46.1	+4.3	21.3	20 42.0	+4.7	21.4	21 37.8	+5.1	21.6	70
18 54.1	+3.6	20.1	19 50.4	+4.0	20.2	20 46.7	+4.3	20.3	21 42.9	+4.7	20.5	71
18 57.7	+3.2	19.0	19 54.4	+3.5	19.2	20 51.0	+3.9	19.3	21 47.6	+4.3	19.4	72
19 00.9	+2.8	18.0	19 57.9	+3.2	18.1	20 54.9	+3.6	18.2	21 51.9	+3.9	18.3	73
19 03.7	+2.5	16.9	20 01.1	+2.8	17.0	20 58.5	+3.1	17.1	21 55.8	+3.4	17.3	74
19 06.2	+2.2	15.9	20 03.9	+2.5	16.0	21 01.6	+2.7	16.1	21 59.2	+3.1	16.2	75
19 08.4	+1.7	14.8	20 06.4	+2.0	14.9	21 04.3	+2.4	15.0	22 02.3	+2.6	15.1	76
19 10.1	+1.4	13.8	20 08.4	+1.7	13.8	21 06.7	+1.9	13.9	22 04.9	+2.2	14.0	77
19 11.5	+1.1	12.7	20 10.1	+1.2	12.8	21 08.6	+1.5	12.9	22 07.1	+1.7	13.0	78
19 12.6	+0.7	11.6	20 11.3	+0.9	11.7	21 10.1	+1.1	11.8	22 08.8	+1.3	11.9	79
19 13.3	+0.3	10.6	20 12.2	+0.5	10.6	21 11.2	+0.7	10.7	22 10.1	+1.0	10.8	80
19 13.6	-0.1	9.5	20 12.7	+0.2	9.6	21 11.9	+0.3	9.6	22 11.1	+0.4	9.7	81
19 13.5	-0.4	8.5	20 12.9	-0.3	8.5	21 12.2	-0.1	8.6	22 11.5	+0.1	8.6	82
19 13.1	-0.8	7.4	20 12.6	-0.6	7.5	21 12.1	-0.5	7.5	22 11.6	-0.4	7.6	83
19 12.3	-1.1	6.3	20 12.0	-1.1	6.4	21 11.6	-0.9	6.4	22 11.2	-0.8	6.5	84
19 11.2	-1.5	5.3	20 10.9	-1.4	5.3	21 10.7	-1.4	5.4	22 10.4	-1.2	5.4	85
19 09.7	-1.9	4.2	20 09.5	-1.8	4.3	21 09.3	-1.7	4.3	22 09.2	-1.7	4.3	86
19 07.8	-2.2	3.2	20 07.7	-2.2	3.2	21 07.6	-2.1	3.2	22 07.5	-2.1	3.2	87
19 05.6	-2.6	2.1	20 05.5	-2.6	2.1	21 05.5	-2.6	2.1	22 05.4	-2.5	2.2	88
19 03.0	-3.0	1.1	20 02.9	-2.9	1.1	21 02.9	-2.9	1.1	22 02.9	-2.9	1.1	89
19 00.0	-3.3	0.0	20 00.0	-3.3	0.0	21 00.0	-3.3	0.0	22 00.0	-3.4	0.0	90
19°			20°			21°			22°			

LATITUDE CONTRARY NAME TO DECLINATION L.H.A. 87°, 273°

Dec.	15° Hc	d	Z	16° Hc	d	Z	17° Hc	d	Z	18° Hc	d	Z	19° Hc	d	Z	20° Hc	d	Z	21° Hc	d	Z	22° Hc	d	Z	Dec.
°	° ′	′	°	° ′	′	°	° ′	′	°	° ′	′	°	° ′	′	°	° ′	′	°	° ′	′	°	° ′	′	°	°
0	2 53.9	-15.6	90.8	2 53.0	-16.6	90.8	2 52.1	-17.6	90.9	2 51.2	-18.6	90.9	2 50.2	-19.6	91.0	2 49.1	-20.5	91.0	2 48.0	-21.5	91.1	2 46.9	-22.5	91.1	0
1	2 38.3	-15.6	91.7	2 36.4	-16.6	91.8	2 34.5	-17.6	91.8	2 32.6	-18.6	91.9	2 30.6	-19.6	91.9	2 28.6	-20.6	92.0	2 26.5	-21.6	92.0	2 24.4	-22.6	92.1	1
2	2 22.7	-15.7	92.7	2 19.8	-16.7	92.8	2 16.9	-17.7	92.8	2 14.0	-18.7	92.8	2 11.0	-19.7	92.9	2 08.0	-20.7	92.9	2 04.9	-21.6	92.9	2 01.8	-22.6	93.0	2
3	2 07.0	-15.7	93.7	2 03.1	-16.7	93.7	1 59.2	-17.7	93.7	1 55.3	-18.7	93.8	1 51.3	-19.7	93.8	1 47.3	-20.7	93.8	1 43.3	-21.7	93.9	1 39.2	-22.6	93.9	3
4	1 51.3	-15.7	94.6	1 46.4	-16.7	94.7	1 41.5	-17.7	94.7	1 36.6	-18.7	94.7	1 31.6	-19.7	94.8	1 26.6	-20.6	94.8	1 21.6	-21.6	94.8	1 16.6	-22.7	94.8	4
5	1 35.6	-15.8	95.6	1 29.7	-16.7	95.6	1 23.8	-17.7	95.7	1 17.9	-18.8	95.7	1 11.9	-19.7	95.7	1 06.0	-20.8	95.7	1 00.0	-21.7	95.7	0 53.9	-22.6	95.8	5
6	1 19.8	-15.7	96.6	1 13.0	-16.8	96.6	1 06.1	-17.8	96.6	0 59.1	-18.7	96.6	0 52.2	-19.8	96.6	0 45.2	-20.7	96.7	0 38.3	-21.7	96.7	0 31.3	-22.7	96.7	6
7	1 04.1	-15.8	97.5	0 56.2	-16.8	97.6	0 48.3	-17.8	97.6	0 40.4	-18.8	97.6	0 32.4	-19.7	97.6	0 24.5	-20.7	97.6	0 16.6	-21.7	97.6	0 08.6	-22.6	97.6	7
8	0 48.3	-15.8	98.5	0 39.4	-16.8	98.5	0 30.5	-17.8	98.5	0 21.6	-18.8	98.5	0 12.7	-19.8	98.5	0 03.8	-20.7	98.5	0 05.1	+21.7	81.5	0 14.0	+22.7	81.5	8
9	0 32.5	-15.9	99.5	0 22.6	-16.8	99.5	0 12.7	-17.8	99.5	0 02.8	-18.8	99.5	0 07.1	+19.7	80.5	0 16.9	+20.8	80.5	0 26.8	+21.7	80.5	0 36.7	+22.6	80.5	9
10	0 16.6	-15.8	100.4	0 05.8	-16.8	100.4	0 05.1	+17.8	79.6	0 16.0	+18.7	79.6	0 26.8	+19.8	79.6	0 37.7	+20.7	79.6	0 48.5	+21.7	79.6	0 59.3	+22.7	79.6	10
11	0 00.8	-15.8	101.4	0 11.0	+16.8	78.6	0 22.9	+17.8	78.6	0 34.7	+18.7	78.6	0 46.6	+19.7	78.6	0 58.4	+20.7	78.6	1 10.2	+21.7	78.7	1 22.0	+22.6	78.7	11
12	0 15.0	+15.8	77.6	0 27.8	+16.8	77.6	0 40.7	+17.8	77.7	0 53.5	+18.7	77.7	1 06.3	+19.7	77.7	1 19.1	+20.7	77.7	1 31.9	+21.6	77.7	1 44.6	+22.6	77.8	12
13	0 30.8	+15.8	76.7	0 44.6	+16.8	76.7	0 58.5	+17.7	76.7	1 12.2	+18.8	76.7	1 26.0	+19.7	76.7	1 39.8	+20.6	76.8	1 53.5	+21.6	76.8	2 07.2	+22.5	76.8	13
14	0 46.6	+15.8	75.7	1 01.4	+16.8	75.7	1 16.2	+17.8	75.7	1 31.0	+18.7	75.8	1 45.7	+19.7	75.8	2 00.4	+20.6	75.8	2 15.1	+21.6	75.9	2 29.7	+22.5	75.9	14
15	1 02.4	+15.8	74.7	1 18.2	+16.7	74.8	1 34.0	+17.7	74.8	1 49.7	+18.7	74.8	2 05.4	+19.6	74.8	2 21.0	+20.6	74.9	2 36.7	+21.5	74.9	2 52.2	+22.5	75.0	15
16	1 18.2	+15.8	73.8	1 34.9	+16.8	73.8	1 51.7	+17.7	73.8	2 08.4	+18.6	73.9	2 25.0	+19.6	73.9	2 41.6	+20.6	73.9	2 58.2	+21.5	74.0	3 14.7	+22.4	74.0	16
17	1 34.0	+15.7	72.8	1 51.7	+16.7	72.8	2 09.4	+17.6	72.9	2 27.0	+18.6	72.9	2 44.6	+19.6	73.0	3 02.2	+20.5	73.0	3 19.7	+21.4	73.1	3 37.1	+22.4	73.1	17
18	1 49.7	+15.7	71.8	2 08.4	+16.6	71.9	2 27.0	+17.6	71.9	2 45.6	+18.6	72.0	3 04.2	+19.5	72.0	3 22.7	+20.4	72.1	3 41.1	+21.4	72.1	3 59.5	+22.3	72.2	18
19	2 05.4	+15.6	70.9	2 25.0	+16.6	70.9	2 44.6	+17.6	71.0	3 04.2	+18.5	71.0	3 23.7	+19.4	71.1	3 43.1	+20.4	71.1	4 02.5	+21.3	71.2	4 21.8	+22.2	71.3	19
20	2 21.0	+15.7	69.9	2 41.6	+16.6	70.0	3 02.2	+17.5	70.0	3 22.7	+18.4	70.1	3 43.1	+19.4	70.1	4 03.5	+20.3	70.2	4 23.8	+21.2	70.2	4 44.0	+22.2	70.3	20
21	2 36.7	+15.5	69.0	2 58.2	+16.5	69.0	3 19.7	+17.4	69.0	3 41.1	+18.4	69.1	4 02.5	+19.3	69.2	4 23.8	+20.2	69.2	4 45.0	+21.2	69.3	5 06.2	+22.0	69.4	21
22	2 52.2	+15.6	68.0	3 14.7	+16.5	68.0	3 37.1	+17.4	68.1	3 59.5	+18.3	68.2	4 21.8	+19.2	68.2	4 44.0	+20.2	68.3	5 06.2	+21.1	68.4	5 28.2	+22.0	68.5	22
23	3 07.8	+15.5	67.0	3 31.2	+16.4	67.1	3 54.5	+17.4	67.1	4 17.8	+18.3	67.2	4 41.0	+19.2	67.3	5 04.2	+20.1	67.3	5 27.3	+20.9	67.4	5 50.2	+21.9	67.5	23
24	3 23.3	+15.4	66.0	3 47.6	+16.3	66.1	4 11.9	+17.2	66.2	4 36.1	+18.1	66.2	5 00.2	+19.1	66.3	5 24.3	+20.0	66.4	5 48.2	+20.9	66.5	6 12.1	+21.8	66.6	24
25	3 38.7	+15.3	65.1	4 03.9	+16.3	65.1	4 29.1	+17.2	65.2	4 54.2	+18.1	65.3	5 19.3	+19.0	65.4	5 44.3	+19.9	65.5	6 09.1	+20.8	65.5	6 33.9	+21.7	65.6	25
26	3 54.0	+15.3	64.1	4 20.2	+16.2	64.2	4 46.3	+17.1	64.2	5 12.3	+18.0	64.3	5 38.3	+18.9	64.4	6 04.2	+19.7	64.5	6 29.9	+20.7	64.6	6 55.6	+21.6	64.7	26
27	4 09.3	+15.2	63.1	4 36.4	+16.1	63.2	5 03.4	+17.0	63.3	5 30.3	+17.9	63.4	5 57.2	+18.8	63.5	6 23.9	+19.7	63.6	6 50.6	+20.6	63.7	7 17.2	+21.5	63.8	27
28	4 24.5	+15.2	62.2	4 52.5	+16.0	62.2	5 20.4	+16.9	62.3	5 48.2	+17.9	62.4	6 16.0	+18.7	62.5	6 43.6	+19.6	62.6	7 11.2	+20.5	62.7	7 38.7	+21.3	62.8	28
29	4 39.7	+15.0	61.2	5 08.5	+16.0	61.3	5 37.3	+16.9	61.4	6 06.1	+17.7	61.4	6 34.7	+18.6	61.5	7 03.2	+19.5	61.7	7 31.7	+20.3	61.8	8 00.0	+21.2	61.9	29
30	4 54.7	+15.0	60.2	5 24.5	+15.8	60.3	5 54.2	+16.7	60.4	6 23.8	+17.6	60.5	6 53.3	+18.5	60.6	7 22.7	+19.3	60.7	7 52.0	+20.2	60.8	8 21.2	+21.1	60.9	30
31	5 09.7	+14.9	59.3	5 40.3	+15.8	59.3	6 10.9	+16.6	59.4	6 41.4	+17.5	59.5	7 11.8	+18.3	59.6	7 42.0	+19.3	59.7	8 12.2	+20.1	59.9	8 42.3	+20.9	60.0	31
32	5 24.6	+14.8	58.3	5 56.1	+15.7	58.4	6 27.5	+16.5	58.5	6 58.9	+17.3	58.6	7 30.1	+18.2	58.7	8 01.3	+19.0	58.8	8 32.3	+19.9	58.9	9 03.2	+20.8	59.0	32
33	5 39.4	+14.7	57.3	6 11.8	+15.5	57.4	6 44.0	+16.5	57.5	7 16.2	+17.3	57.6	7 48.3	+18.1	57.7	8 20.3	+19.0	57.8	8 52.2	+19.8	58.0	9 24.0	+20.6	58.1	33
34	5 54.1	+14.6	56.3	6 27.3	+15.5	56.4	7 00.5	+16.2	56.5	7 33.5	+17.1	56.6	8 06.4	+18.0	56.7	8 39.3	+18.8	56.9	9 12.0	+19.7	57.0	9 44.6	+20.5	57.1	34
35	6 08.7	+14.5	55.4	6 42.8	+15.3	55.5	7 16.7	+16.2	55.6	7 50.6	+17.0	55.7	8 24.4	+17.8	55.8	8 58.1	+18.7	55.9	9 31.7	+19.5	56.0	10 05.1	+20.3	56.2	35
36	6 23.2	+14.4	54.4	6 58.1	+15.2	54.5	7 32.9	+16.0	54.6	8 07.6	+16.9	54.7	8 42.2	+17.7	54.8	9 16.8	+18.5	54.9	9 51.2	+19.3	55.1	10 25.4	+20.2	55.2	36
37	6 37.6	+14.2	53.4	7 13.3	+15.1	53.5	7 48.9	+15.9	53.6	8 24.5	+16.7	53.7	8 59.9	+17.5	53.9	9 35.3	+18.3	54.0	10 10.5	+19.1	54.1	10 45.6	+19.9	54.3	37
38	6 51.8	+14.2	52.4	7 28.4	+14.9	52.5	8 04.8	+15.8	52.6	8 41.2	+16.6	52.8	9 17.4	+17.4	52.9	9 53.6	+18.2	53.0	10 29.6	+19.0	53.2	11 05.5	+19.8	53.3	38
39	7 06.0	+14.0	51.5	7 43.3	+14.8	51.6	8 20.6	+15.6	51.7	8 57.8	+16.4	51.8	9 34.8	+17.2	51.9	10 11.8	+18.0	52.0	10 48.6	+18.8	52.2	11 25.3	+19.6	52.4	39
40	7 20.0	+13.9	50.5	7 58.1	+14.7	50.6	8 36.2	+15.5	50.7	9 14.2	+16.2	50.8	9 52.0	+17.1	50.9	10 29.8	+17.8	51.1	11 07.4	+18.6	51.2	11 44.9	+19.4	51.4	40
41	7 33.9	+13.8	49.5	8 12.8	+14.6	49.6	8 51.7	+15.3	49.7	9 30.4	+16.1	49.8	10 09.1	+16.8	50.0	10 47.6	+17.7	50.1	11 26.0	+18.4	50.3	12 04.3	+19.2	50.4	41
42	7 47.7	+13.6	48.5	8 27.4	+14.4	48.6	9 07.0	+15.1	48.7	9 46.5	+15.9	48.9	10 25.9	+16.7	49.0	11 05.3	+17.4	49.1	11 44.4	+18.3	49.3	12 23.5	+19.0	49.4	42
43	8 01.3	+13.5	47.5	8 41.8	+14.2	47.6	9 22.1	+15.0	47.8	10 02.4	+15.8	47.9	10 42.6	+16.5	48.0	11 22.7	+17.3	48.2	12 02.7	+18.0	48.3	12 42.5	+18.8	48.5	43
44	8 14.8	+13.3	46.5	8 56.0	+14.1	46.7	9 37.1	+14.9	46.8	10 18.2	+15.6	46.9	10 59.1	+16.4	47.0	11 40.0	+17.0	47.2	12 20.7	+17.8	47.3	13 01.3	+18.6	47.5	44
45	8 28.1	+13.2	45.6	9 10.1	+13.9	45.7	9 52.0	+14.6	45.8	10 33.8	+15.4	45.9	11 15.5	+16.1	46.1	11 57.0	+16.9	46.2	12 38.5	+17.6	46.4	13 19.9	+18.3	46.5	45
46	8 41.3	+13.1	44.6	9 24.0	+13.8	44.7	10 06.6	+14.5	44.8	10 49.2	+15.2	44.9	11 31.6	+15.9	45.1	12 13.9	+16.7	45.2	12 56.1	+17.4	45.4	13 38.2	+18.1	45.5	46
47	8 54.4	+12.8	43.6	9 37.8	+13.6	43.7	10 21.1	+14.3	43.8	11 04.4	+15.0	43.9	11 47.5	+15.7	44.1	12 30.6	+16.4	44.2	13 13.5	+17.1	44.4	13 56.3	+17.9	44.6	47
48	9 07.2	+12.8	42.6	9 51.4	+13.4	42.7	10 35.4	+14.1	42.8	11 19.4	+14.8	43.0	12 03.2	+15.6	43.1	12 47.0	+16.2	43.3	13 30.6	+17.0	43.4	14 14.2	+17.6	43.6	48
49	9 20.0	+12.5	41.6	10 04.8	+13.2	41.7	10 49.5	+14.0	41.8	11 34.2	+14.6	42.0	12 18.8	+15.3	42.1	13 03.2	+16.0	42.3	13 47.6	+16.6	42.4	14 31.8	+17.4	42.6	49
50	9 32.5	+12.4	40.6	10 18.0	+13.1	40.7	11 03.5	+13.7	40.8	11 48.8	+14.4	41.0	12 34.1	+15.0	41.1	13 19.2	+15.8	41.3	14 04.2	+16.5	41.4	14 49.2	+17.1	41.6	50
51	9 44.9	+12.2	39.6	10 31.1	+12.9	39.7	11 17.2	+13.5	39.9	12 03.2	+14.2	40.0	12 49.1	+14.9	40.1	13 35.0	+15.5	40.3	14 20.7	+16.2	40.4	15 06.3	+16.9	40.6	51
52	9 57.1	+12.1	38.6	10 44.0	+12.7	38.7	11 30.7	+13.4	38.9	12 17.4	+14.0	39.0	13 04.0	+14.6	39.1	13 50.5	+15.3	39.3	14 36.9	+15.9	39.4	15 23.2	+16.6	39.6	52
53	10 09.2	+11.8	37.6	10 56.7	+12.5	37.7	11 44.1	+13.1	37.9	12 31.4	+13.8	38.0	13 18.6	+14.4	38.1	14 05.8	+15.0	38.3	14 52.8	+15.7	38.5	15 39.8	+16.3	38.6	53
54	10 21.0	+11.7	36.6	11 09.2	+12.3	36.7	11 57.2	+12.9	36.9	12 45.2	+13.5	37.0	13 33.0	+14.2	37.1	14 20.8	+14.8	37.3	15 08.5	+15.4	37.5	15 56.1	+16.0	37.6	54
55	10 32.7	+11.5	35.6	11 21.5	+12.1	35.7	12 10.1	+12.7	35.9	12 58.7	+13.3	36.0	13 47.2	+13.9	36.1	14 35.6	+14.5	36.3	15 23.9	+15.2	36.4	16 12.1	+15.8	36.6	55
56	10 44.2	+11.3	34.6	11 33.6	+11.8	34.7	12 22.8	+12.5	34.9	13 12.0	+13.1	35.0	14 01.1	+13.7	35.1	14 50.1	+14.3	35.3	15 39.1	+14.8	35.4	16 27.9	+15.5	35.6	56
57	10 55.5	+11.1	33.6	11 45.4	+11.7	33.7	12 35.3	+12.3	33.9	13 25.1	+12.8	34.0	14 14.8	+13.4	34.1	15 04.4	+14.0	34.3	15 53.9	+14.6	34.4	16 43.4	+15.2	34.6	57
58	11 06.6	+10.9	32.6	11 57.1	+11.5	32.7	12 47.6	+12.0	32.9	13 37.9	+12.6	33.0	14 28.2	+13.2	33.1	15 18.4	+13.7	33.3	16 08.5	+14.3	33.4	16 58.6	+14.8	33.6	58
59	11 17.5	+10.7	31.6	12 08.6	+11.2	31.7	12 59.6	+11.8	31.9	13 50.5	+12.4	32.0	14 41.4	+12.9	32.1	15 32.1	+13.5	32.3	16 22.8	+14.1	32.4	17 13.4	+14.6	32.6	59
60	11 28.2	+10.5	30.6	12 19.8	+11.1	30.7	13 11.4	+11.5	30.9	14 02.9	+12.1	31.0	14 54.3	+12.6	31.1	15 45.6	+13.2	31.3	16 36.9	+13.7	31.4	17 28.0	+14.3	31.6	60
61	11 38.7	+10.3	29.6	12 30.9	+10.8	29.7	13 22.9	+11.4	29.8	14 15.0	+11.8	30.0	15 06.9	+12.4	30.1	15 58.8	+12.9	30.2	16 50.6	+13.4	30.4	17 42.3	+13.9	30.5	61
62	11 49.0	+10.1	28.6	12 41.7	+10.6	28.7	13 34.3	+11.0	28.8	14 26.8	+11.6	29.0	15 19.3	+12.1	29.1	16 11.7	+12.6	29.2	17 04.0	+13.1	29.4	17 56.2	+13.7	29.5	62
63	11 59.1	+9.9	27.6	12 52.3	+10.3	27.7	13 45.3	+10.9	27.8	14 38.4	+11.3	27.9	15 31.4	+11.8	28.1	16 24.3	+12.3	28.2	17 17.1	+12.8	28.3	18 09.9	+13.3	28.5	63
64	12 09.0	+9.6	26.6	13 02.6	+10.1	26.7	13 56.2	+10.6	26.8	14 49.7	+11.0	26.9	15 43.2	+11.5	27.1	16 36.6	+12.0	27.2	17 29.9	+12.5	27.3	18 23.2	+13.0	27.5	64
65	12 18.6	+9.4	25.6	13 12.7	+9.9	25.7	14 06.8	+10.3	25.8	15 00.7	+10.8	25.9	15 54.7	+11.2	26.0	16 48.6	+11.7	26.2	17 42.4	+12.2	26.3	18 36.2	+12.6	26.4	65
66	12 28.0	+9.2	24.6	13 22.6	+9.6	24.7	14 17.1	+10.0	24.8	15 11.5	+10.5	24.9	16 05.9	+11.0	25.0	17 00.3	+11.4	25.1	17 54.6	+11.8	25.3	18 48.8	+12.3	25.4	66
67	12 37.2	+9.0	23.6	13 32.2	+9.4	23.7	14 27.1	+9.8	23.8	15 22.0	+10.3	23.9	16 16.9	+10.6	24.0	17 11.7	+11.0	24.1	18 06.4	+11.5	24.2	19 01.1	+11.9	24.4	67
68	12 46.2	+8.7	22.6	13 41.6	+9.1	22.6	14 36.9	+9.6	22.7	15 32.3	+9.9	22.8	16 27.5	+10.4	23.0	17 22.7	+10.8	23.1	18 17.9	+11.2	23.2	19 13.0	+11.6	23.3	68
69	12 54.9	+8.5	21.5	13 50.7	+8.9	21.6	14 46.5	+9.2	21.7	15 42.2	+9.6	21.8	16 37.9	+10.0	21.9	17 33.5	+10.4	22.0	18 29.1	+10.8	22.2	19 24.6	+11.3	22.3	69
70	13 03.4	+8.3	20.5	13 59.6	+8.6	20.6	14 55.7	+9.0	20.7	15 51.8	+9.4	20.8	16 47.9	+9.8	20.9	17 43.9	+10.2	21.0	18 39.9	+10.5	21.1	19 35.9	+10.9	21.3	70
71	13 11.7	+8.0	19.5	14 08.2	+8.4	19.6	15 04.7	+8.7	19.7	16 01.2	+9.1	19.8	16 57.7	+9.4	19.9	17 54.1	+9.8	20.0	18 50.4	+10.2	20.1	19 46.8	+10.5	20.2	71
72	13 19.7	+7.8	18.5	14 16.6	+8.1	18.6	15 13.4	+8.5	18.7	16 10.3	+8.8	18.7	17 07.1	+9.1	18.8	18 03.9	+9.4	18.9	19 00.6	+9.8	19.1	19 57.3	+10.1	19.2	72
73	13 27.5	+7.5	17.5	14 24.7	+7.8	17.5	15 21.9	+8.1	17.6	16 19.1	+8.4	17.7	17 16.2	+8.8	17.8	18 13.3	+9.1	17.9	19 10.4	+9.4	18.0	20 07.4	+9.8	18.1	73
74	13 35.0	+7.3	16.5	14 32.5	+7.6	16.5	15 30.0	+7.9	16.6	16 27.5	+8.2	16.7	17 25.0	+8.5	16.8	18 22.4	+8.8	16.9	19 19.8	+9.1	17.0	20 17.2	+9.4	17.1	74
75	13 42.3	+7.0	15.4	14 40.1	+7.3	15.5	15 37.9	+7.6	15.6	16 35.7	+7.9	15.6	17 33.5	+8.1	15.7	18 31.2	+8.4	15.8	19 28.9	+8.7	15.9	20 26.6	+9.0	16.0	75
76	13 49.3	+6.8	14.4	14 47.4	+7.0	14.5	15 45.5	+7.3	14.5	16 43.6	+7.5	14.6	17 41.6	+7.8	14.7	18 39.6	+8.1	14.8	19 37.6	+8.4	14.9	20 35.6	+8.7	15.0	76
77	13 56.1	+6.5	13.4	14 54.4	+6.8	13.4	15 52.8	+7.0	13.5	16 51.1	+7.3	13.6	17 49.4	+7.5	13.6	18 47.7	+7.8	13.7	19 46.0	+8.0	13.8	20 44.3	+8.2	13.9	77
78	14 02.6	+6.2	12.4	15 01.2	+6.5	12.4	15 59.8	+6.7	12.5	16 58.4	+6.9	12.5	17 56.9	+7.2	12.6	18 55.5	+7.4	12.7	19 54.0	+7.6	12.8	20 52.5	+7.9	12.8	78
79	14 08.8	+6.0	11.3	15 07.7	+6.2	11.4	16 06.5	+6.4	11.4	17 05.3	+6.6	11.5	18 04.1	+6.8	11.6	19 02.9	+7.0	11.6	20 01.6	+7.3	11.7	21 00.4	+7.4	11.8	79
80	14 14.8	+5.8	10.3	15 13.9	+5.9	10.4	16 12.9	+6.1	10.4	17 11.9	+6.3	10.5	18 10.9	+6.5	10.5	19 09.9	+6.6	10.6	20 08.9	+6.8	10.6	21 07.8	+7.1	10.7	80
81	14 20.6	+5.4	9.3	15 19.8	+5.6	9.3	16 19.0	+5.8	9.4	17 18.2	+5.9	9.4	18 17.4	+6.1	9.5	19 16.5	+6.4	9.5	20 15.7	+6.5	9.6	21 14.9	+6.6	9.6	81
82	14 26.0	+5.2	8.3	15 25.4	+5.4	8.3	16 24.8	+5.5	8.3	17 24.1	+5.7	8.4	18 23.5	+5.8	8.4	19 22.9	+5.9	8.5	20 22.2	+6.1	8.5	21 21.5	+6.3	8.6	82
83	14 31.2	+5.0	7.2	15 30.8	+5.0	7.3	16 30.3	+5.2	7.3	17 29.8	+5.3	7.3	18 29.3	+5.4	7.4	19 28.8	+5.6	7.4	20 28.3	+5.7	7.5	21 27.8	+5.8	7.5	83
84	14 36.2	+4.6	6.2	15 35.8	+4.8	6.2	16 35.5	+4.8	6.3	17 35.1	+5.0	6.3	18 34.7	+5.1	6.3	19 34.4	+5.2	6.4	20 34.0	+5.3	6.4	21 33.6	+5.5	6.4	84
85	14 40.8	+4.4	5.2	15 40.6	+4.5	5.2	16 40.3	+4.6	5.2	17 40.1	+4.6	5.2	18 39.8	+4.8	5.3	19 39.6	+4.8	5.3	20 39.3	+4.9	5.3	21 39.1	+5.0	5.4	85
86	14 45.2	+4.1	4.1	15 45.1	+4.1	4.2	16 44.9	+4.2	4.2	17 44.7	+4.4	4.2	18 44.6	+4.4	4.2	19 44.4	+4.5	4.2	20 44.2	+4.6	4.3	21 44.1	+4.6	4.3	86
87	14 49.3	+3.9	3.1	15 49.2	+3.9	3.1	16 49.1	+4.0	3.1	17 49.1	+3.9	3.1	18 49.0	+4.0	3.2	19 48.9	+4.1	3.2	20 48.8	+4.1	3.2	21 48.7	+4.2	3.2	87
88	14 53.2	+3.5	2.1	15 53.1	+3.6	2.1	16 53.1	+3.6	2.1	17 53.0	+3.7	2.1	18 53.0	+3.7	2.1	19 53.0	+3.7	2.1	20 52.9	+3.8	2.1	21 52.9	+3.7	2.2	88
89	14 56.7	+3.3	1.0	15 56.7	+3.3	1.0	16 56.7	+3.3	1.0	17 56.7	+3.3	1.0	18 56.7	+3.3	1.1	19 56.7	+3.3	1.1	20 56.7	+3.3	1.1	21 56.6	+3.4	1.1	89
90	15 00.0	+3.0	0.0	16 00.0	+3.0	0.0	17 00.0	+3.0	0.0	18 00.0	+3.0	0.0	19 00.0	+3.0	0.0	20 00.0	+2.9	0.0	21 00.0	+2.9	0.0	22 00.0	+2.9	0.0	90
	15°			16°			17°			18°			19°			20°			21°			22°			

S. Lat. {L.H.A. greater than 180° ....Zn=180°−Z; L.H.A. less than 180°...........Zn=180°+Z}

LATITUDE SAME NAME AS DECLINATION L.H.A. 93°, 267°

Dec.	15°			16°			17°			18°			19°			20°			21°			22°			Dec.
	Hc	d	Z	Hc	d	Z	Hc	d	Z	Hc	d	Z	Hc	d	Z	Hc	d	Z	Hc	d	Z	Hc	d	Z	
°	° ′	′	°	° ′	′	°	° ′	′	°	° ′	′	°	° ′	′	°	° ′	′	°	° ′	′	°	° ′	′	°	°
0	1 55.9	+15.5	90.5	1 55.3	+16.6	90.6	1 54.8	+17.5	90.6	1 54.1	+18.6	90.6	1 53.5	+19.5	90.7	1 52.8	+20.5	90.7	1 52.0	+21.5	90.7	1 51.3	+22.4	90.7	0
1	2 11.4	+15.5	89.6	2 11.9	+16.5	89.6	2 12.3	+17.5	89.6	2 12.7	+18.5	89.7	2 13.0	+19.5	89.7	2 13.3	+20.5	89.7	2 13.5	+21.5	89.8	2 13.7	+22.5	89.8	1
2	2 26.9	+15.5	88.6	2 28.4	+16.4	88.6	2 29.8	+17.4	88.7	2 31.2	+18.4	88.7	2 32.5	+19.4	88.8	2 33.8	+20.4	88.8	2 35.0	+21.4	88.8	2 36.2	+22.4	88.9	2
3	2 42.4	+15.4	87.6	2 44.8	+16.4	87.7	2 47.2	+17.5	87.7	2 49.6	+18.4	87.8	2 51.9	+19.4	87.8	2 54.2	+20.4	87.9	2 56.4	+21.4	87.9	2 58.6	+22.3	88.0	3
4	2 57.8	+15.3	86.6	3 01.2	+16.4	86.7	3 04.7	+17.3	86.8	3 08.0	+18.4	86.8	3 11.3	+19.4	86.9	3 14.6	+20.3	86.9	3 17.8	+21.3	87.0	3 20.9	+22.3	87.0	4
5	3 13.1	+15.3	85.7	3 17.6	+16.3	85.7	3 22.0	+17.3	85.8	3 26.4	+18.3	85.9	3 30.7	+19.3	85.9	3 34.9	+20.3	86.0	3 39.1	+21.3	86.0	3 43.2	+22.3	86.1	5
6	3 28.4	+15.2	84.7	3 33.9	+16.2	84.8	3 39.3	+17.3	84.8	3 44.7	+18.2	84.9	3 50.0	+19.2	85.0	3 55.2	+20.2	85.0	4 00.4	+21.2	85.1	4 05.5	+22.1	85.2	6
7	3 43.6	+15.2	83.7	3 50.1	+16.2	83.8	3 56.6	+17.1	83.9	4 02.9	+18.2	83.9	4 09.2	+19.2	84.0	4 15.4	+20.2	84.1	4 21.6	+21.1	84.2	4 27.6	+22.1	84.2	7
8	3 58.8	+15.1	82.8	4 06.3	+16.1	82.8	4 13.7	+17.1	82.9	4 21.1	+18.1	83.0	4 28.4	+19.1	83.1	4 35.6	+20.0	83.1	4 42.7	+21.0	83.2	4 49.7	+22.1	83.3	8
9	4 13.9	+15.0	81.8	4 22.4	+16.0	81.9	4 30.8	+17.1	82.0	4 39.2	+18.0	82.0	4 47.5	+19.0	82.1	4 55.6	+20.0	82.2	5 03.7	+21.0	82.3	5 11.8	+21.9	82.4	9
10	4 28.9	+15.0	80.8	4 38.4	+16.0	80.9	4 47.9	+16.9	81.0	4 57.2	+17.9	81.1	5 06.5	+18.9	81.2	5 15.6	+20.0	81.3	5 24.7	+20.9	81.3	5 33.7	+21.9	81.4	10
11	4 43.9	+14.8	79.9	4 54.4	+15.8	79.9	5 04.8	+16.9	80.0	5 15.1	+17.9	80.1	5 25.4	+18.8	80.2	5 35.6	+19.8	80.3	5 45.6	+20.8	80.4	5 55.6	+21.7	80.5	11
12	4 58.7	+14.8	78.9	5 10.2	+15.8	79.0	5 21.7	+16.7	79.1	5 33.0	+17.8	79.2	5 44.2	+18.8	79.3	5 55.4	+19.7	79.4	6 06.4	+20.7	79.5	6 17.3	+21.7	79.6	12
13	5 13.5	+14.7	77.9	5 26.0	+15.7	78.0	5 38.4	+16.7	78.1	5 50.8	+17.6	78.2	6 03.0	+18.6	78.3	6 15.1	+19.6	78.4	6 27.1	+20.6	78.5	6 39.0	+21.5	78.6	13
14	5 28.2	+14.6	76.9	5 41.7	+15.6	77.0	5 55.1	+16.6	77.1	6 08.4	+17.6	77.2	6 21.6	+18.6	77.3	6 34.7	+19.5	77.5	6 47.7	+20.5	77.6	7 00.5	+21.5	77.7	14
15	5 42.8	+14.5	76.0	5 57.3	+15.5	76.1	6 11.7	+16.5	76.2	6 26.0	+17.4	76.3	6 40.2	+18.4	76.4	6 54.2	+19.4	76.5	7 08.2	+20.3	76.6	7 22.0	+21.3	76.7	15
16	5 57.3	+14.4	75.0	6 12.8	+15.4	75.1	6 28.2	+16.3	75.2	6 43.4	+17.4	75.3	6 58.6	+18.3	75.4	7 13.6	+19.3	75.6	7 28.5	+20.3	75.7	7 43.3	+21.2	75.8	16
17	6 11.7	+14.3	74.0	6 28.2	+15.2	74.1	6 44.5	+16.3	74.2	7 00.8	+17.2	74.3	7 16.9	+18.2	74.5	7 32.9	+19.1	74.6	7 48.8	+20.1	74.7	8 04.5	+21.1	74.9	17
18	6 26.0	+14.2	73.0	6 43.4	+15.2	73.1	7 00.8	+16.1	73.3	7 18.0	+17.1	73.4	7 35.1	+18.0	73.5	7 52.0	+19.1	73.6	8 08.9	+20.0	73.8	8 25.6	+20.9	73.9	18
19	6 40.2	+14.0	72.1	6 58.6	+15.0	72.2	7 16.9	+16.0	72.3	7 35.1	+16.9	72.4	7 53.1	+18.0	72.5	8 11.1	+18.8	72.7	8 28.9	+19.8	72.8	8 46.5	+20.8	73.0	19
20	6 54.2	+14.0	71.1	7 13.6	+14.9	71.2	7 32.9	+15.9	71.3	7 52.0	+16.9	71.4	8 11.1	+17.8	71.6	8 29.9	+18.8	71.7	8 48.7	+19.7	71.9	9 07.3	+20.6	72.0	20
21	7 08.2	+13.8	70.1	7 28.5	+14.8	70.2	7 48.8	+15.7	70.3	8 08.9	+16.7	70.5	8 28.9	+17.6	70.6	8 48.7	+18.6	70.8	9 08.4	+19.5	70.9	9 27.9	+20.5	71.1	21
22	7 22.0	+13.7	69.1	7 43.3	+14.6	69.2	8 04.5	+15.6	69.4	8 25.6	+16.5	69.5	8 46.5	+17.5	69.7	9 07.3	+18.4	69.8	9 27.9	+19.4	70.0	9 48.4	+20.4	70.1	22
23	7 35.7	+13.5	68.1	7 57.9	+14.6	68.3	8 20.1	+15.5	68.4	8 42.1	+16.4	68.5	9 04.0	+17.4	68.7	9 25.7	+18.3	68.8	9 47.3	+19.3	69.0	10 08.8	+20.1	69.2	23
24	7 49.2	+13.4	67.2	8 12.5	+14.3	67.3	8 35.6	+15.3	67.4	8 58.5	+16.3	67.6	9 21.4	+17.1	67.7	9 44.0	+18.2	67.9	10 06.6	+19.0	68.0	10 28.9	+20.0	68.2	24
25	8 02.6	+13.3	66.2	8 26.8	+14.2	66.3	8 50.9	+15.1	66.4	9 14.8	+16.1	66.6	9 38.5	+17.1	66.7	10 02.2	+17.9	66.9	10 25.6	+18.9	67.1	10 48.9	+19.8	67.2	25
26	8 15.9	+13.2	65.2	8 41.0	+14.1	65.3	9 06.0	+15.0	65.5	9 30.9	+15.9	65.6	9 55.6	+16.8	65.8	10 20.1	+17.8	65.9	10 44.5	+18.7	66.1	11 08.7	+19.7	66.3	26
27	8 29.1	+12.9	64.2	8 55.1	+13.9	64.3	9 21.0	+14.9	64.5	9 46.8	+15.8	64.6	10 12.4	+16.7	64.8	10 37.9	+17.6	65.0	11 03.2	+18.5	65.1	11 28.4	+19.4	65.3	27
28	8 42.0	+12.9	63.2	9 09.0	+13.8	63.4	9 35.9	+14.6	63.5	10 02.6	+15.5	63.7	10 29.1	+16.5	63.8	10 55.5	+17.4	64.0	11 21.7	+18.4	64.2	11 47.8	+19.2	64.3	28
29	8 54.9	+12.7	62.2	9 22.8	+13.6	62.4	9 50.5	+14.5	62.5	10 18.1	+15.5	62.7	10 45.6	+16.3	62.8	11 12.9	+17.3	63.0	11 40.1	+18.1	63.2	12 07.0	+19.1	63.4	29
30	9 07.6	+12.5	61.2	9 36.4	+13.4	61.4	10 05.0	+14.4	61.5	10 33.6	+15.2	61.7	11 01.9	+16.2	61.9	11 30.2	+17.0	62.0	11 58.2	+17.9	62.2	12 26.1	+18.8	62.4	30
31	9 20.1	+12.3	60.2	9 49.8	+13.2	60.4	10 19.4	+14.1	60.5	10 48.8	+15.0	60.7	11 18.1	+15.9	60.9	11 47.2	+16.8	61.1	12 16.1	+17.8	61.2	12 44.9	+18.6	61.4	31
32	9 32.4	+12.2	59.3	10 03.0	+13.1	59.4	10 33.5	+14.0	59.6	11 03.8	+14.9	59.7	11 34.0	+15.7	59.9	12 04.0	+16.6	60.1	12 33.9	+17.5	60.3	13 03.5	+18.4	60.5	32
33	9 44.6	+12.0	58.3	10 16.1	+12.9	58.4	10 47.5	+13.7	58.6	11 18.7	+14.6	58.7	11 49.7	+15.6	58.9	12 20.6	+16.5	59.1	12 51.4	+17.3	59.3	13 21.9	+18.2	59.5	33
34	9 56.6	+11.8	57.3	10 29.0	+12.7	57.4	11 01.2	+13.6	57.6	11 33.3	+14.5	57.7	12 05.3	+15.3	57.9	12 37.1	+16.2	58.1	13 08.7	+17.0	58.3	13 40.1	+18.0	58.5	34
35	10 08.4	+11.7	56.3	10 41.7	+12.5	56.4	11 14.8	+13.4	56.6	11 47.8	+14.2	56.8	12 20.6	+15.1	56.9	12 53.3	+15.9	57.1	13 25.7	+16.9	57.3	13 58.1	+17.7	57.5	35
36	10 20.1	+11.5	55.3	10 54.2	+12.3	55.4	11 28.2	+13.2	55.6	12 02.0	+14.1	55.8	12 35.7	+14.9	55.9	13 09.2	+15.8	56.1	13 42.6	+16.6	56.3	14 15.8	+17.4	56.5	36
37	10 31.6	+11.2	54.3	11 06.5	+12.2	54.4	11 41.4	+12.9	54.6	12 16.1	+13.8	54.8	12 50.6	+14.7	54.9	13 25.0	+15.5	55.1	13 59.2	+16.3	55.3	14 33.2	+17.2	55.5	37
38	10 42.8	+11.1	53.3	11 18.7	+11.9	53.4	11 54.3	+12.8	53.6	12 29.9	+13.6	53.8	13 05.3	+14.4	54.0	13 40.5	+15.3	54.1	14 15.5	+16.2	54.3	14 50.4	+17.0	54.6	38
39	10 53.9	+10.9	52.3	11 30.6	+11.7	52.4	12 07.1	+12.5	52.6	12 43.5	+13.4	52.8	13 19.7	+14.2	53.0	13 55.8	+15.0	53.1	14 31.7	+15.8	53.4	15 07.4	+16.7	53.6	39
40	11 04.8	+10.7	51.3	11 42.3	+11.5	51.4	12 19.6	+12.4	51.6	12 56.9	+13.1	51.8	13 33.9	+14.0	52.0	14 10.8	+14.8	52.2	14 47.5	+15.6	52.4	15 24.1	+16.4	52.6	40
41	11 15.5	+10.5	50.3	11 53.8	+11.3	50.4	12 32.0	+12.1	50.6	13 10.0	+12.9	50.8	13 47.9	+13.7	51.0	14 25.6	+14.5	51.2	15 03.1	+15.4	51.4	15 40.5	+16.2	51.6	41
42	11 26.0	+10.3	49.3	12 05.1	+11.1	49.4	12 44.1	+11.9	49.6	13 22.9	+12.7	49.8	14 01.6	+13.5	50.0	14 40.1	+14.3	50.1	15 18.5	+15.1	50.4	15 56.7	+15.9	50.6	42
43	11 36.3	+10.1	48.3	12 16.2	+10.9	48.4	12 56.0	+11.6	48.6	13 35.6	+12.4	48.8	14 15.1	+13.2	48.9	14 54.4	+14.0	49.1	15 33.6	+14.8	49.4	16 12.6	+15.6	49.6	43
44	11 46.4	+9.9	47.3	12 27.1	+10.6	47.4	13 07.6	+11.4	47.6	13 48.0	+12.2	47.8	14 28.3	+12.9	47.9	15 08.4	+13.7	48.1	15 48.4	+14.5	48.3	16 28.2	+15.3	48.6	44
45	11 56.3	+9.6	46.2	12 37.7	+10.4	46.4	13 19.0	+11.2	46.6	14 00.2	+11.9	46.7	14 41.2	+12.7	46.9	15 22.1	+13.5	47.1	16 02.9	+14.2	47.3	16 43.5	+15.0	47.6	45
46	12 05.9	+9.5	45.2	12 48.1	+10.2	45.4	13 30.2	+10.9	45.6	14 12.1	+11.7	45.7	14 53.9	+12.5	45.9	15 35.6	+13.2	46.1	16 17.1	+14.0	46.3	16 58.5	+14.7	46.5	46
47	12 15.4	+9.2	44.2	12 58.3	+9.9	44.4	13 41.1	+10.7	44.5	14 23.8	+11.4	44.7	15 06.4	+12.1	44.9	15 48.8	+12.9	45.1	16 31.1	+13.6	45.3	17 13.2	+14.4	45.5	47
48	12 24.6	+9.0	43.2	13 08.2	+9.7	43.4	13 51.8	+10.4	43.5	14 35.2	+11.2	43.7	15 18.5	+11.9	43.9	16 01.7	+12.6	44.1	16 44.7	+13.4	44.3	17 27.6	+14.1	44.5	48
49	12 33.6	+8.7	42.2	13 17.9	+9.5	42.4	14 02.2	+10.2	42.5	14 46.4	+10.9	42.7	15 30.4	+11.6	42.9	16 14.3	+12.4	43.1	16 58.1	+13.0	43.3	17 41.7	+13.8	43.5	49
50	12 42.3	+8.5	41.2	13 27.4	+9.2	41.3	14 12.4	+9.9	41.5	14 57.3	+10.6	41.7	15 42.0	+11.4	41.9	16 26.7	+12.0	42.1	17 11.1	+12.8	42.3	17 55.5	+13.4	42.5	50
51	12 50.8	+8.3	40.2	13 36.6	+9.0	40.3	14 22.3	+9.7	40.5	15 07.9	+10.4	40.7	15 53.4	+11.0	40.8	16 38.7	+11.7	41.0	17 23.9	+12.4	41.2	18 08.9	+13.2	41.4	51
52	12 59.1	+8.1	39.2	13 45.6	+8.7	39.3	14 32.0	+9.4	39.5	15 18.3	+10.0	39.6	16 04.4	+10.7	39.8	16 50.4	+11.4	40.0	17 36.3	+12.1	40.2	18 22.1	+12.8	40.4	52
53	13 07.2	+7.8	38.1	13 54.3	+8.5	38.3	14 41.4	+9.1	38.4	15 28.3	+9.8	38.6	16 15.1	+10.5	38.8	17 01.8	+11.2	39.0	17 48.4	+11.8	39.2	18 34.9	+12.4	39.4	53
54	13 15.0	+7.6	37.1	14 02.8	+8.2	37.3	14 50.5	+8.9	37.4	15 38.1	+9.5	37.6	16 25.6	+10.1	37.8	17 13.0	+10.8	38.0	18 00.2	+11.5	38.1	18 47.3	+12.2	38.4	54
55	13 22.6	+7.3	36.1	14 11.0	+8.0	36.2	14 59.4	+8.5	36.4	15 47.6	+9.2	36.6	16 35.7	+9.9	36.7	17 23.8	+10.5	36.9	18 11.7	+11.1	37.1	18 59.5	+11.7	37.3	55
56	13 29.9	+7.1	35.1	14 19.0	+7.7	35.2	15 07.9	+8.3	35.4	15 56.8	+8.9	35.5	16 45.6	+9.5	35.7	17 34.3	+10.1	35.9	18 22.8	+10.8	36.1	19 11.2	+11.5	36.3	56
57	13 37.0	+6.8	34.1	14 26.7	+7.4	34.2	15 16.2	+8.1	34.3	16 05.7	+8.7	34.5	16 55.1	+9.3	34.7	17 44.4	+9.9	34.9	18 33.6	+10.5	35.0	19 22.7	+11.0	35.2	57
58	13 43.8	+6.6	33.0	14 34.1	+7.1	33.2	15 24.3	+7.7	33.3	16 14.4	+8.3	33.5	17 04.4	+8.9	33.6	17 54.3	+9.5	33.8	18 44.1	+10.1	34.0	19 33.7	+10.8	34.2	58
59	13 50.4	+6.3	32.0	14 41.2	+6.9	32.1	15 32.0	+7.5	32.3	16 22.7	+8.0	32.4	17 13.3	+8.6	32.6	18 03.8	+9.1	32.8	18 54.2	+9.7	33.0	19 44.5	+10.3	33.2	59
60	13 56.7	+6.1	31.0	14 48.1	+6.6	31.1	15 39.5	+7.1	31.3	16 30.7	+7.7	31.4	17 21.9	+8.2	31.6	18 12.9	+8.9	31.7	19 03.9	+9.4	31.9	19 54.8	+10.0	32.1	60
61	14 02.8	+5.8	30.0	14 54.7	+6.4	30.1	15 46.6	+6.9	30.2	16 38.4	+7.4	30.4	17 30.1	+8.0	30.5	18 21.8	+8.5	30.7	19 13.3	+9.1	30.9	20 04.8	+9.6	31.1	61
62	14 08.6	+5.5	28.9	15 01.1	+6.0	29.1	15 53.5	+6.6	29.2	16 45.8	+7.1	29.3	17 38.1	+7.6	29.5	18 30.3	+8.1	29.7	19 22.4	+8.7	29.8	20 14.4	+9.2	30.0	62
63	14 14.1	+5.3	27.9	15 07.1	+5.8	28.0	16 00.1	+6.2	28.2	16 52.9	+6.8	28.3	17 45.7	+7.3	28.5	18 38.4	+7.8	28.6	19 31.1	+8.3	28.8	20 23.6	+8.9	29.0	63
64	14 19.4	+5.0	26.9	15 12.9	+5.5	27.0	16 06.3	+6.0	27.1	16 59.7	+6.5	27.3	17 53.0	+7.0	27.4	18 46.2	+7.5	27.6	19 39.4	+8.0	27.7	20 32.5	+8.4	27.9	64
65	14 24.4	+4.8	25.9	15 18.4	+5.2	26.0	16 12.3	+5.7	26.1	17 06.2	+6.1	26.2	18 00.0	+6.6	26.4	18 53.7	+7.1	26.5	19 47.4	+7.5	26.7	20 40.9	+8.1	26.8	65
66	14 29.2	+4.5	24.8	15 23.6	+5.0	24.9	16 18.0	+5.4	25.1	17 12.3	+5.9	25.2	18 06.6	+6.3	25.3	19 00.8	+6.8	25.5	19 54.9	+7.3	25.6	20 49.0	+7.7	25.8	66
67	14 33.7	+4.2	23.8	15 28.6	+4.6	23.9	16 23.4	+5.1	24.0	17 18.2	+5.5	24.1	18 12.9	+5.9	24.3	19 07.6	+6.3	24.4	20 02.2	+6.8	24.6	20 56.7	+7.3	24.7	67
68	14 37.9	+3.9	22.8	15 33.2	+4.3	22.9	16 28.5	+4.7	23.0	17 23.7	+5.2	23.1	18 18.8	+5.6	23.2	19 13.9	+6.1	23.4	20 09.0	+6.5	23.5	21 04.0	+6.9	23.7	68
69	14 41.8	+3.7	21.7	15 37.5	+4.1	21.8	16 33.2	+4.5	21.9	17 28.9	+4.8	22.1	18 24.4	+5.3	22.2	19 20.0	+5.6	22.3	20 15.5	+6.0	22.4	21 10.9	+6.5	22.6	69
70	14 45.5	+3.4	20.7	15 41.6	+3.8	20.8	16 37.7	+4.1	20.9	17 33.7	+4.5	21.0	18 29.7	+4.9	21.1	19 25.6	+5.3	21.3	20 21.5	+5.7	21.4	21 17.4	+6.1	21.5	70
71	14 48.9	+3.1	19.7	15 45.4	+3.4	19.8	16 41.8	+3.8	19.9	17 38.2	+4.2	20.0	18 34.6	+4.6	20.1	19 30.9	+5.0	20.2	20 27.2	+5.3	20.3	21 23.5	+5.7	20.5	71
72	14 52.0	+2.8	18.6	15 48.8	+3.2	18.7	16 45.6	+3.6	18.8	17 42.4	+3.9	18.9	18 39.2	+4.2	19.0	19 35.9	+4.5	19.1	20 32.5	+4.9	19.3	21 29.2	+5.2	19.4	72
73	14 54.8	+2.6	17.6	15 52.0	+2.9	17.7	16 49.2	+3.2	17.8	17 46.3	+3.5	17.9	18 43.4	+3.8	18.0	19 40.4	+4.2	18.1	20 37.4	+4.6	18.2	21 34.4	+4.9	18.3	73
74	14 57.4	+2.3	16.6	15 54.9	+2.6	16.6	16 52.4	+2.8	16.7	17 49.8	+3.2	16.8	18 47.2	+3.5	16.9	19 44.6	+3.8	17.0	20 42.0	+4.1	17.1	21 39.3	+4.4	17.2	74
75	14 59.7	+2.0	15.5	15 57.5	+2.2	15.6	16 55.2	+2.6	15.7	17 53.0	+2.8	15.8	18 50.7	+3.2	15.9	19 48.4	+3.5	16.0	20 46.1	+3.7	16.1	21 43.7	+4.1	16.2	75
76	15 01.7	+1.7	14.5	15 59.7	+2.0	14.6	16 57.8	+2.3	14.6	17 55.8	+2.6	14.7	18 53.9	+2.8	14.8	19 51.9	+3.0	14.9	20 49.8	+3.4	15.0	21 47.8	+3.6	15.1	76
77	15 03.4	+1.4	13.5	16 01.7	+1.7	13.5	17 00.1	+1.9	13.6	17 58.4	+2.1	13.7	18 56.7	+2.4	13.8	19 54.9	+2.7	13.8	20 53.2	+2.9	13.9	21 51.4	+3.2	14.0	77
78	15 04.8	+1.2	12.4	16 03.4	+1.4	12.5	17 02.0	+1.6	12.6	18 00.5	+1.9	12.6	18 59.1	+2.0	12.7	19 57.6	+2.3	12.8	20 56.1	+2.5	12.9	21 54.6	+2.8	12.9	78
79	15 06.0	+0.8	11.4	16 04.8	+1.1	11.4	17 03.6	+1.3	11.5	18 02.4	+1.5	11.6	19 01.1	+1.8	11.6	19 59.9	+1.9	11.7	20 58.6	+2.2	11.8	21 57.4	+2.3	11.9	79
80	15 06.8	+0.6	10.4	16 05.9	+0.7	10.4	17 04.9	+0.9	10.5	18 03.9	+1.1	10.5	19 02.9	+1.3	10.6	20 01.8	+1.6	10.6	21 00.8	+1.7	10.7	21 59.7	+2.0	10.8	80
81	15 07.4	+0.3	9.3	16 06.6	+0.5	9.4	17 05.8	+0.7	9.4	18 05.0	+0.8	9.5	19 04.2	+1.0	9.5	20 03.4	+1.1	9.6	21 02.5	+1.4	9.6	22 01.7	+1.5	9.7	81
82	15 07.7	+0.1	8.3	16 07.1	+0.2	8.3	17 06.5	+0.3	8.4	18 05.8	+0.5	8.4	19 05.2	+0.6	8.5	20 04.5	+0.8	8.5	21 03.9	+0.9	8.6	22 03.2	+1.1	8.6	82
83	15 07.8	−0.3	7.2	16 07.3	−0.2	7.3	17 06.8	0.0	7.3	18 06.3	+0.1	7.4	19 05.8	+0.3	7.4	20 05.3	+0.4	7.5	21 04.8	+0.5	7.5	22 04.3	+0.6	7.6	83
84	15 07.5	−0.5	6.2	16 07.1	−0.4	6.2	17 06.8	−0.3	6.3	18 06.4	−0.2	6.3	19 06.1	−0.1	6.3	20 05.7	0.0	6.4	21 05.3	+0.1	6.4	22 04.9	+0.3	6.5	84
85	15 07.0	−0.9	5.2	16 06.7	−0.7	5.2	17 06.5	−0.7	5.2	18 06.2	−0.6	5.3	19 06.0	−0.5	5.3	20 05.7	−0.4	5.3	21 05.4	−0.2	5.4	22 05.2	−0.2	5.4	85
86	15 06.1	−1.1	4.1	16 06.0	−1.1	4.2	17 05.8	−1.0	4.2	18 05.6	−0.9	4.2	19 05.5	−0.8	4.2	20 05.3	−0.7	4.3	21 05.2	−0.7	4.3	22 05.0	−0.6	4.3	86
87	15 05.0	−1.4	3.1	16 04.9	−1.3	3.1	17 04.8	−1.3	3.1	18 04.7	−1.2	3.2	19 04.7	−1.2	3.2	20 04.6	−1.2	3.2	21 04.5	−1.1	3.2	22 04.4	−1.1	3.2	87
88	15 03.6	−1.6	2.1	16 03.6	−1.7	2.1	17 03.5	−1.6	2.1	18 03.5	−1.6	2.1	19 03.5	−1.6	2.1	20 03.4	−1.5	2.1	21 03.4	−1.5	2.1	22 03.3	−1.4	2.2	88
89	15 02.0	−2.0	1.0	16 01.9	−1.9	1.0	17 01.9	−1.9	1.0	18 01.9	−1.9	1.1	19 01.9	−1.9	1.1	20 01.9	−1.9	1.1	21 01.9	−1.9	1.1	22 01.9	−1.9	1.1	89
90	15 00.0	−2.2	0.0	16 00.0	−2.2	0.0	17 00.0	−2.3	0.0	18 00.0	−2.3	0.0	19 00.0	−2.3	0.0	20 00.0	−2.3	0.0	21 00.0	−2.3	0.0	22 00.0	−2.3	0.0	90
	15°			16°			17°			18°			19°			20°			21°			22°			

LATITUDE **CONTRARY** NAME TO DECLINATION **L.H.A. 88°, 272°**

Dec.	15° Hc	d	Z	16° Hc	d	Z	17° Hc	d	Z	18° Hc	d	Z	19° Hc	d	Z	20° Hc	d	Z	21° Hc	d	Z	22° Hc	d	Z	Dec.
°	° ′	′	°	° ′	′	°	° ′	′	°	° ′	′	°	° ′	′	°	° ′	′	°	° ′	′	°	° ′	′	°	°
0	1 55.9	−15.5	90.5	1 55.3	−16.5	90.6	1 54.8	−17.6	90.6	1 54.1	−18.5	90.6	1 53.5	−19.6	90.7	1 52.8	−20.6	90.7	1 52.0	−21.5	90.7	1 51.3	−22.5	90.7	0
1	1 40.4	−15.6	91.5	1 38.8	−16.6	91.5	1 37.2	−17.6	91.5	1 35.6	−18.6	91.6	1 33.9	−19.6	91.6	1 32.2	−20.6	91.6	1 30.5	−21.6	91.7	1 28.8	−22.6	91.7	1
2	1 24.8	−15.6	92.5	1 22.2	−16.6	92.5	1 19.6	−17.6	92.5	1 17.0	−18.6	92.5	1 14.3	−19.6	92.5	1 11.6	−20.5	92.6	1 08.9	−21.5	92.6	1 06.2	−22.5	92.6	2
3	1 09.2	−15.7	93.4	1 05.6	−16.7	93.4	1 02.0	−17.7	93.5	0 58.4	−18.7	93.5	0 54.7	−19.6	93.5	0 51.1	−20.7	93.5	0 47.4	−21.6	93.5	0 43.7	−22.6	93.5	3
4	0 53.5	−15.6	94.4	0 48.9	−16.6	94.4	0 44.3	−17.6	94.4	0 39.7	−18.6	94.4	0 35.1	−19.6	94.4	0 30.4	−20.6	94.4	0 25.8	−21.6	94.5	0 21.1	−22.5	94.5	4
5	0 37.9	−15.7	95.3	0 32.3	−16.7	95.4	0 26.7	−17.7	95.4	0 21.1	−18.7	95.4	0 15.5	−19.7	95.4	0 09.8	−20.6	95.4	0 04.2	−21.6	95.4	0 01.4	+22.6	84.6	5
6	0 22.2	−15.6	96.3	0 15.6	−16.6	96.3	0 09.0	−17.6	96.3	0 02.4	−18.6	96.3	0 04.2	+19.6	83.7	0 10.8	+20.6	83.7	0 17.4	+21.6	83.7	0 24.0	+22.5	83.7	6
7	0 06.6	−15.7	97.3	0 01.0	+16.7	82.7	0 08.6	+17.7	82.7	0 16.2	+18.7	82.7	0 23.8	+19.6	82.7	0 31.4	+20.6	82.7	0 39.0	+21.5	82.8	0 46.5	+22.6	82.8	7
8	0 09.1	+15.6	81.8	0 17.7	+16.6	81.8	0 26.3	+17.6	81.8	0 34.9	+18.6	81.8	0 43.4	+19.6	81.8	0 52.0	+20.6	81.8	1 00.5	+21.5	81.8	1 09.1	+22.5	81.8	8
9	0 24.7	+15.7	80.8	0 34.3	+16.7	80.8	0 43.9	+17.6	80.8	0 53.5	+18.6	80.8	1 03.0	+19.6	80.8	1 12.6	+20.6	80.9	1 22.1	+21.5	80.9	1 31.6	+22.5	80.9	9
10	0 40.4	+15.6	79.8	0 51.0	+16.6	79.8	1 01.5	+17.7	79.9	1 12.1	+18.6	79.9	1 22.6	+19.6	79.9	1 33.2	+20.5	79.9	1 43.6	+21.6	79.9	1 54.1	+22.5	80.0	10
11	0 56.0	+15.6	78.9	1 07.6	+16.6	78.9	1 19.2	+17.6	78.9	1 30.7	+18.6	78.9	1 42.2	+19.6	79.0	1 53.7	+20.5	79.0	2 05.2	+21.4	79.0	2 16.6	+22.4	79.1	11
12	1 11.6	+15.6	77.9	1 24.2	+16.6	77.9	1 36.8	+17.5	77.9	1 49.3	+18.5	78.0	2 01.8	+19.5	78.0	2 14.2	+20.5	78.0	2 26.6	+21.5	78.1	2 39.0	+22.4	78.1	12
13	1 27.2	+15.6	76.9	1 40.8	+16.6	77.0	1 54.3	+17.6	77.0	2 07.8	+18.5	77.0	2 21.3	+19.5	77.1	2 34.7	+20.4	77.1	2 48.1	+21.4	77.1	3 01.4	+22.3	77.2	13
14	1 42.8	+15.6	76.0	1 57.4	+16.5	76.0	2 11.9	+17.5	76.0	2 26.3	+18.5	76.1	2 40.8	+19.4	76.1	2 55.1	+20.4	76.2	3 09.5	+21.3	76.2	3 23.7	+22.3	76.3	14
15	1 58.4	+15.5	75.0	2 13.9	+16.5	75.0	2 29.4	+17.4	75.1	2 44.8	+18.4	75.1	3 00.2	+19.4	75.2	3 15.5	+20.4	75.2	3 30.8	+21.3	75.3	3 46.0	+22.3	75.3	15
16	2 13.9	+15.5	74.0	2 30.4	+16.4	74.1	2 46.8	+17.4	74.1	3 03.2	+18.4	74.2	3 19.6	+19.3	74.2	3 35.9	+20.2	74.3	3 52.1	+21.2	74.3	4 08.3	+22.1	74.4	16
17	2 29.4	+15.4	73.1	2 46.8	+16.4	73.1	3 04.2	+17.4	73.2	3 21.6	+18.3	73.2	3 38.9	+19.3	73.3	3 56.1	+20.3	73.3	4 13.3	+21.2	73.4	4 30.4	+22.1	73.5	17
18	2 44.8	+15.4	72.1	3 03.2	+16.4	72.1	3 21.6	+17.3	72.2	3 39.9	+18.3	72.3	3 58.2	+19.2	72.3	4 16.4	+20.1	72.4	4 34.5	+21.1	72.5	4 52.5	+22.0	72.5	18
19	3 00.2	+15.3	71.1	3 19.6	+16.3	71.2	3 38.9	+17.2	71.2	3 58.2	+18.2	71.3	4 17.4	+19.1	71.4	4 36.5	+20.1	71.4	4 55.6	+21.0	71.5	5 14.5	+22.0	71.6	19
20	3 15.5	+15.3	70.2	3 35.9	+16.2	70.2	3 56.1	+17.2	70.3	4 16.4	+18.1	70.3	4 36.5	+19.1	70.4	4 56.6	+20.0	70.5	5 16.6	+20.9	70.6	5 36.5	+21.8	70.7	20
21	3 30.8	+15.2	69.2	3 52.1	+16.2	69.3	4 13.3	+17.1	69.3	4 34.5	+18.0	69.4	4 55.6	+18.9	69.5	5 16.6	+19.9	69.6	5 37.5	+20.8	69.6	5 58.3	+21.8	69.7	21
22	3 46.0	+15.2	68.2	4 08.3	+16.0	68.3	4 30.4	+17.0	68.4	4 52.5	+18.0	68.4	5 14.5	+18.9	68.5	5 36.5	+19.8	68.6	5 58.3	+20.7	68.7	6 20.1	+21.6	68.8	22
23	4 01.2	+15.1	67.3	4 24.3	+16.1	67.3	4 47.4	+17.0	67.4	5 10.5	+17.8	67.5	5 33.4	+18.8	67.6	5 56.3	+19.7	67.7	6 19.0	+20.7	67.8	6 41.7	+21.5	67.9	23
24	4 16.3	+15.0	66.3	4 40.4	+15.9	66.4	5 04.4	+16.9	66.4	5 28.3	+17.8	66.5	5 52.2	+18.7	66.6	6 16.0	+19.6	66.7	6 39.7	+20.5	66.8	7 03.2	+21.5	66.9	24
25	4 31.3	+14.9	65.3	4 56.3	+15.9	65.4	5 21.3	+16.7	65.5	5 46.1	+17.7	65.6	6 10.9	+18.6	65.7	6 35.6	+19.5	65.8	7 00.2	+20.4	65.9	7 24.7	+21.3	66.0	25
26	4 46.2	+14.9	64.3	5 12.2	+15.7	64.4	5 38.0	+16.7	64.5	6 03.8	+17.6	64.6	6 29.5	+18.5	64.7	6 55.1	+19.4	64.8	7 20.6	+20.3	64.9	7 46.0	+21.2	65.0	26
27	5 01.1	+14.7	63.4	5 27.9	+15.7	63.4	5 54.7	+16.6	63.5	6 21.4	+17.5	63.6	6 48.0	+18.4	63.7	7 14.5	+19.3	63.8	7 40.9	+20.2	64.0	8 07.2	+21.0	64.1	27
28	5 15.8	+14.7	62.4	5 43.6	+15.6	62.5	6 11.3	+16.5	62.6	6 38.9	+17.3	62.7	7 06.4	+18.2	62.8	7 33.8	+19.1	62.9	8 01.1	+20.0	63.0	8 28.2	+20.9	63.1	28
29	5 30.5	+14.6	61.4	5 59.2	+15.4	61.5	6 27.8	+16.3	61.6	6 56.2	+17.3	61.7	7 24.6	+18.2	61.8	7 52.9	+19.0	61.9	8 21.1	+19.9	62.1	8 49.1	+20.8	62.2	29
30	5 45.1	+14.5	60.4	6 14.6	+15.4	60.5	6 44.1	+16.3	60.6	7 13.5	+17.1	60.7	7 42.8	+18.0	60.9	8 11.9	+18.9	61.0	8 41.0	+19.7	61.1	9 09.9	+20.6	61.2	30
31	5 59.6	+14.4	59.5	6 30.0	+15.3	59.6	7 00.4	+16.1	59.7	7 30.6	+17.0	59.8	8 00.8	+17.8	59.9	8 30.8	+18.8	60.0	9 00.7	+19.6	60.2	9 30.5	+20.5	60.3	31
32	6 14.0	+14.2	58.5	6 45.3	+15.1	58.6	7 16.5	+16.0	58.7	7 47.6	+16.9	58.8	8 18.6	+17.8	58.9	8 49.6	+18.5	59.1	9 20.3	+19.5	59.2	9 51.0	+20.3	59.3	32
33	6 28.2	+14.2	57.5	7 00.4	+15.0	57.6	7 32.5	+15.9	57.7	8 04.5	+16.7	57.8	8 36.4	+17.6	58.0	9 08.1	+18.5	58.1	9 39.8	+19.3	58.2	10 11.3	+20.2	58.4	33
34	6 42.4	+14.0	56.5	7 15.4	+14.9	56.6	7 48.4	+15.7	56.7	8 21.2	+16.6	56.9	8 54.0	+17.4	57.0	9 26.6	+18.3	57.1	9 59.1	+19.1	57.3	10 31.5	+19.9	57.4	34
35	6 56.4	+14.0	55.6	7 30.3	+14.8	55.7	8 04.1	+15.6	55.8	8 37.8	+16.5	55.9	9 11.4	+17.3	56.0	9 44.9	+18.1	56.2	10 18.2	+19.0	56.3	10 51.4	+19.8	56.5	35
36	7 10.4	+13.8	54.6	7 45.1	+14.6	54.7	8 19.7	+15.5	54.8	8 54.3	+16.2	54.9	9 28.7	+17.1	55.1	10 03.0	+17.9	55.2	10 37.2	+18.7	55.3	11 11.2	+19.6	55.5	36
37	7 24.2	+13.6	53.6	7 59.7	+14.5	53.7	8 35.2	+15.3	53.8	9 10.5	+16.2	53.9	9 45.8	+17.0	54.1	10 20.9	+17.8	54.2	10 55.9	+18.6	54.4	11 30.8	+19.4	54.5	37
38	7 37.8	+13.6	52.6	8 14.2	+14.4	52.7	8 50.5	+15.2	52.8	9 26.7	+16.0	53.0	10 02.8	+16.7	53.1	10 38.7	+17.6	53.3	11 14.5	+18.4	53.4	11 50.2	+19.3	53.6	38
39	7 51.4	+13.4	51.6	8 28.6	+14.2	51.7	9 05.7	+15.0	51.9	9 42.7	+15.8	52.0	10 19.5	+16.6	52.1	10 56.3	+17.4	52.3	11 32.9	+18.3	52.4	12 09.5	+19.0	52.6	39
40	8 04.8	+13.2	50.6	8 42.8	+14.0	50.8	9 20.7	+14.8	50.9	9 58.5	+15.6	51.0	10 36.1	+16.5	51.2	11 13.7	+17.2	51.3	11 51.2	+18.0	51.5	12 28.5	+18.8	51.6	40
41	8 18.0	+13.1	49.7	8 56.8	+13.9	49.8	9 35.5	+14.7	49.9	10 14.1	+15.4	50.0	10 52.6	+16.2	50.2	11 30.9	+17.1	50.3	12 09.2	+17.8	50.5	12 47.3	+18.6	50.7	41
42	8 31.1	+13.0	48.7	9 10.7	+13.7	48.8	9 50.2	+14.5	48.9	10 29.5	+15.3	49.1	11 08.8	+16.1	49.2	11 48.0	+16.8	49.4	12 27.0	+17.6	49.5	13 05.9	+18.3	49.7	42
43	8 44.1	+12.8	47.7	9 24.4	+13.6	47.8	10 04.7	+14.3	47.9	10 44.8	+15.1	48.1	11 24.9	+15.8	48.2	12 04.8	+16.6	48.4	12 44.6	+17.4	48.5	13 24.2	+18.2	48.7	43
44	8 56.9	+12.6	46.7	9 38.0	+13.4	46.8	10 19.0	+14.2	46.9	10 59.9	+14.9	47.1	11 40.7	+15.7	47.2	12 21.4	+16.4	47.4	13 02.0	+17.1	47.6	13 42.4	+17.9	47.7	44
45	9 09.5	+12.5	45.7	9 51.4	+13.2	45.8	10 33.2	+13.9	46.0	11 14.8	+14.7	46.1	11 56.4	+15.4	46.2	12 37.8	+16.2	46.4	13 19.1	+16.9	46.6	14 00.3	+17.7	46.7	45
46	9 22.0	+12.4	44.7	10 04.6	+13.1	44.8	10 47.1	+13.8	45.0	11 29.5	+14.5	45.1	12 11.8	+15.2	45.3	12 54.0	+16.0	45.4	13 36.0	+16.7	45.6	14 18.0	+17.4	45.8	46
47	9 34.4	+12.1	43.7	10 17.7	+12.8	43.8	11 00.9	+13.6	44.0	11 44.0	+14.3	44.1	12 27.0	+15.1	44.3	13 10.0	+15.7	44.4	13 52.7	+16.5	44.6	14 35.4	+17.2	44.8	47
48	9 46.5	+12.0	42.7	10 30.5	+12.7	42.9	11 14.5	+13.4	43.0	11 58.3	+14.1	43.1	12 42.1	+14.8	43.3	13 25.7	+15.5	43.4	14 09.2	+16.2	43.6	14 52.6	+16.9	43.8	48
49	9 58.5	+11.8	41.7	10 43.2	+12.5	41.9	11 27.9	+13.2	42.0	12 12.4	+13.9	42.1	12 56.9	+14.5	42.3	13 41.2	+15.3	42.4	14 25.4	+16.0	42.6	15 09.5	+16.7	42.8	49
50	10 10.3	+11.6	40.7	10 55.7	+12.3	40.9	11 41.1	+12.9	41.0	12 26.3	+13.6	41.1	13 11.4	+14.4	41.3	13 56.5	+15.0	41.4	14 41.4	+15.7	41.6	15 26.2	+16.4	41.8	50
51	10 21.9	+11.5	39.7	11 08.0	+12.1	39.9	11 54.0	+12.8	40.0	12 39.9	+13.5	40.1	13 25.8	+14.1	40.3	14 11.5	+14.8	40.4	14 57.1	+15.4	40.6	15 42.6	+16.1	40.8	51
52	10 33.4	+11.2	38.7	11 20.1	+11.9	38.9	12 06.8	+12.5	39.0	12 53.4	+13.2	39.1	13 39.9	+13.8	39.3	14 26.3	+14.5	39.4	15 12.5	+15.2	39.6	15 58.7	+15.8	39.8	52
53	10 44.6	+11.1	37.7	11 32.0	+11.7	37.9	12 19.3	+12.4	38.0	13 06.6	+13.0	38.1	13 53.7	+13.6	38.3	14 40.8	+14.2	38.4	15 27.7	+14.9	38.6	16 14.5	+15.6	38.8	53
54	10 55.7	+10.8	36.7	11 43.7	+11.5	36.9	12 31.7	+12.1	37.0	13 19.6	+12.7	37.1	14 07.3	+13.4	37.3	14 55.0	+14.0	37.4	15 42.6	+14.7	37.6	16 30.1	+15.3	37.8	54
55	11 06.5	+10.7	35.7	11 55.2	+11.3	35.9	12 43.8	+11.9	36.0	13 32.3	+12.5	36.1	14 20.7	+13.1	36.3	15 09.0	+13.8	36.4	15 57.3	+14.3	36.6	16 45.4	+14.9	36.8	55
56	11 17.2	+10.5	34.7	12 06.5	+11.0	34.9	12 55.7	+11.6	35.0	13 44.8	+12.2	35.1	14 33.8	+12.9	35.3	15 22.8	+13.4	35.4	16 11.6	+14.1	35.6	17 00.3	+14.7	35.8	56
57	11 27.7	+10.2	33.7	12 17.5	+10.9	33.9	13 07.3	+11.4	34.0	13 57.0	+12.0	34.1	14 46.7	+12.6	34.3	15 36.2	+13.2	34.4	16 25.7	+13.7	34.6	17 15.0	+14.4	34.7	57
58	11 37.9	+10.1	32.7	12 28.4	+10.6	32.8	13 18.7	+11.2	33.0	14 09.0	+11.8	33.1	14 59.3	+12.3	33.2	15 49.4	+12.9	33.4	16 39.4	+13.5	33.6	17 29.4	+14.0	33.7	58
59	11 48.0	+9.8	31.7	12 39.0	+10.4	31.8	13 29.9	+11.0	32.0	14 20.8	+11.5	32.1	15 11.6	+12.0	32.2	16 02.3	+12.6	32.4	16 52.9	+13.2	32.5	17 43.4	+13.8	32.7	59
60	11 57.8	+9.6	30.7	12 49.4	+10.1	30.8	13 40.9	+10.6	30.9	14 32.3	+11.2	31.1	15 23.6	+11.8	31.2	16 14.9	+12.3	31.4	17 06.1	+12.9	31.5	17 57.2	+13.4	31.7	60
61	12 07.4	+9.4	29.7	12 59.5	+9.9	29.8	13 51.5	+10.5	29.9	14 43.5	+11.0	30.1	15 35.4	+11.5	30.2	16 27.2	+12.0	30.3	17 19.0	+12.5	30.5	18 10.6	+13.1	30.7	61
62	12 16.8	+9.2	28.7	13 09.4	+9.7	28.8	14 02.0	+10.2	28.9	14 54.5	+10.7	29.0	15 46.9	+11.2	29.2	16 39.2	+11.8	29.3	17 31.5	+12.2	29.5	18 23.7	+12.8	29.6	62
63	12 26.0	+9.0	27.7	13 19.1	+9.4	27.8	14 12.2	+9.9	27.9	15 05.2	+10.4	28.0	15 58.1	+10.9	28.2	16 51.0	+11.4	28.3	17 43.7	+12.0	28.4	18 36.5	+12.4	28.6	63
64	12 35.0	+8.7	26.7	13 28.5	+9.2	26.8	14 22.1	+9.7	26.9	15 15.6	+10.1	27.0	16 09.0	+10.6	27.1	17 02.4	+11.1	27.3	17 55.7	+11.6	27.4	18 48.9	+12.1	27.6	64
65	12 43.7	+8.5	25.7	13 37.7	+9.0	25.8	14 31.8	+9.4	25.9	15 25.7	+9.9	26.0	16 19.6	+10.3	26.1	17 13.5	+10.8	26.2	18 07.3	+11.2	26.4	19 01.0	+11.7	26.5	65
66	12 52.2	+8.2	24.6	13 46.7	+8.7	24.7	14 41.2	+9.1	24.8	15 35.6	+9.6	25.0	16 29.9	+10.1	25.1	17 24.3	+10.4	25.2	18 18.5	+10.9	25.4	19 12.7	+11.4	25.5	66
67	13 00.4	+8.0	23.6	13 55.4	+8.4	23.7	14 50.3	+8.8	23.8	15 45.2	+9.2	23.9	16 40.0	+9.7	24.1	17 34.7	+10.2	24.2	18 29.4	+10.6	24.3	19 24.1	+11.0	24.5	67
68	13 08.4	+7.8	22.6	14 03.8	+8.2	22.7	14 59.1	+8.6	22.8	15 54.4	+9.0	22.9	16 49.7	+9.4	23.0	17 44.9	+9.8	23.1	18 40.0	+10.3	23.3	19 35.1	+10.7	23.4	68
69	13 16.2	+7.6	21.6	14 12.0	+7.9	21.7	15 07.7	+8.3	21.8	16 03.4	+8.7	21.9	16 59.1	+9.1	22.0	17 54.7	+9.5	22.1	18 50.3	+9.9	22.2	19 45.8	+10.3	22.4	69
70	13 23.8	+7.3	20.6	14 19.9	+7.7	20.7	15 16.0	+8.1	20.8	16 12.1	+8.4	20.9	17 08.2	+8.8	21.0	18 04.2	+9.2	21.1	19 00.2	+9.5	21.2	19 56.1	+9.9	21.3	70
71	13 31.1	+7.0	19.6	14 27.6	+7.4	19.6	15 24.1	+7.7	19.7	16 20.5	+8.1	19.8	17 17.0	+8.4	19.9	18 13.4	+8.8	20.0	19 09.7	+9.2	20.1	20 06.0	+9.6	20.3	71
72	13 38.1	+6.8	18.5	14 35.0	+7.1	18.6	15 31.8	+7.5	18.7	16 28.6	+7.8	18.8	17 25.4	+8.2	18.9	18 22.2	+8.5	19.0	19 18.9	+8.8	19.1	20 15.6	+9.2	19.2	72
73	13 44.9	+6.5	17.5	14 42.1	+6.8	17.6	15 39.3	+7.2	17.7	16 36.4	+7.5	17.8	17 33.6	+7.8	17.8	18 30.7	+8.1	17.9	19 27.7	+8.5	18.1	20 24.8	+8.8	18.2	73
74	13 51.4	+6.3	16.5	14 48.9	+6.6	16.6	15 46.5	+6.8	16.6	16 43.9	+7.2	16.7	17 41.4	+7.5	16.8	18 38.8	+7.8	16.9	19 36.2	+8.1	17.0	20 33.6	+8.4	17.1	74
75	13 57.7	+6.0	15.5	14 55.5	+6.3	15.5	15 53.3	+6.6	15.6	16 51.1	+6.9	15.7	17 48.9	+7.1	15.8	18 46.6	+7.4	15.9	19 44.3	+7.7	16.0	20 42.0	+8.0	16.1	75
76	14 03.7	+5.8	14.4	15 01.8	+6.1	14.5	15 59.9	+6.3	14.6	16 58.0	+6.5	14.6	17 56.0	+6.8	14.7	18 54.0	+7.1	14.8	19 52.0	+7.4	14.9	20 50.0	+7.6	15.0	76
77	14 09.5	+5.5	13.4	15 07.9	+5.7	13.5	16 06.2	+6.0	13.5	17 04.5	+6.3	13.6	18 02.8	+6.5	13.7	19 01.1	+6.8	13.8	19 59.4	+7.0	13.8	20 57.6	+7.3	13.9	77
78	14 15.0	+5.2	12.4	15 13.6	+5.5	12.4	16 12.2	+5.7	12.5	17 10.8	+5.9	12.6	18 09.3	+6.2	12.6	19 07.9	+6.3	12.7	20 06.4	+6.6	12.8	21 04.9	+6.8	12.9	78
79	14 20.2	+5.0	11.4	15 19.1	+5.1	11.4	16 17.9	+5.4	11.5	17 16.7	+5.6	11.5	18 15.5	+5.8	11.6	19 14.2	+6.0	11.7	20 13.0	+6.2	11.7	21 11.7	+6.5	11.8	79
80	14 25.2	+4.7	10.3	15 24.2	+4.9	10.4	16 23.3	+5.0	10.4	17 22.3	+5.2	10.5	18 21.3	+5.4	10.5	19 20.2	+5.7	10.6	20 19.2	+5.9	10.7	21 18.2	+6.0	10.7	80
81	14 29.9	+4.5	9.3	15 29.1	+4.6	9.3	16 28.3	+4.8	9.4	17 27.5	+5.0	9.4	18 26.7	+5.1	9.5	19 25.9	+5.3	9.5	20 25.1	+5.4	9.6	21 24.2	+5.6	9.7	81
82	14 34.4	+4.1	8.3	15 33.7	+4.4	8.3	16 33.1	+4.5	8.3	17 32.5	+4.6	8.4	18 31.8	+4.8	8.4	19 31.2	+4.9	8.5	20 30.5	+5.1	8.5	21 29.8	+5.3	8.6	82
83	14 38.5	+3.9	7.2	15 38.1	+4.0	7.3	16 37.6	+4.1	7.3	17 37.1	+4.3	7.3	18 36.6	+4.4	7.4	19 36.1	+4.5	7.4	20 35.6	+4.7	7.5	21 35.1	+4.8	7.5	83
84	14 42.4	+3.6	6.2	15 42.1	+3.7	6.2	16 41.7	+3.9	6.3	17 41.4	+3.9	6.3	18 41.0	+4.1	6.3	19 40.6	+4.2	6.4	20 40.3	+4.2	6.4	21 39.9	+4.4	6.5	84
85	14 46.0	+3.4	5.2	15 45.8	+3.4	5.2	16 45.6	+3.5	5.2	17 45.3	+3.6	5.2	18 45.1	+3.7	5.3	19 44.8	+3.8	5.3	20 44.5	+3.9	5.3	21 44.3	+4.0	5.4	85
86	14 49.4	+3.1	4.1	15 49.2	+3.2	4.2	16 49.1	+3.2	4.2	17 48.9	+3.3	4.2	18 48.8	+3.3	4.2	19 48.6	+3.4	4.2	20 48.4	+3.5	4.3	21 48.3	+3.5	4.3	86
87	14 52.5	+2.8	3.1	15 52.4	+2.8	3.1	16 52.3	+2.9	3.1	17 52.2	+2.9	3.2	18 52.1	+3.0	3.2	19 52.0	+3.1	3.2	20 51.9	+3.1	3.2	21 51.8	+3.2	3.2	87
88	14 55.3	+2.5	2.1	15 55.2	+2.6	2.1	16 55.2	+2.5	2.1	17 55.1	+2.6	2.1	18 55.1	+2.6	2.1	19 55.1	+2.6	2.1	20 55.0	+2.7	2.1	21 55.0	+2.7	2.2	88
89	14 57.8	+2.2	1.0	15 57.8	+2.2	1.0	16 57.7	+2.3	1.0	17 57.7	+2.3	1.1	18 57.7	+2.3	1.1	19 57.7	+2.3	1.1	20 57.7	+2.3	1.1	21 57.7	+2.3	1.1	89
90	15 00.0	+2.0	0.0	16 00.0	+1.9	0.0	17 00.0	+1.9	0.0	18 00.0	+1.9	0.0	19 00.0	+1.9	0.0	20 00.0	+1.9	0.0	21 00.0	+1.9	0.0	22 00.0	+1.9	0.0	90
	15°			16°			17°			18°			19°			20°			21°			22°			

S. Lat. {L.H.A. greater than 180° ....Zn=180°−Z; L.H.A. less than 180°...........Zn=180°+Z

LATITUDE **SAME** NAME AS DECLINATION **L.H.A. 92°, 268°**

179

89°, 271° L.H.A. LATITUDE SAME NAME AS DECLINATION N. Lat. {L.H.A. greater than 180° .....Zn=Z
L.H.A. less than 180°............Zn=360°−Z

Dec.	15°			16°			17°			18°			19°			20°			21°			22°			Dec.
	Hc	d	Z	Hc	d	Z	Hc	d	Z	Hc	d	Z	Hc	d	Z	Hc	d	Z	Hc	d	Z	Hc	d	Z	
°	° ′	′	°	° ′	′	°	° ′	′	°	° ′	′	°	° ′	′	°	° ′	′	°	° ′	′	°	° ′	′	°	°
0	0 58.0	+15.5	90.3	0 57.7	+16.5	90.3	0 57.4	+17.5	90.3	0 57.1	+18.5	90.3	0 56.7	+19.6	90.3	0 56.4	+20.5	90.3	0 56.0	+21.5	90.4	0 55.6	+22.5	90.4	0
1	1 13.5	+15.5	89.3	1 14.2	+16.5	89.3	1 14.9	+17.5	89.3	1 15.6	+18.5	89.4	1 16.3	+19.5	89.4	1 16.9	+20.5	89.4	1 17.5	+21.5	89.4	1 18.1	+22.5	89.4	1
2	1 29.0	+15.5	88.3	1 30.7	+16.5	88.4	1 32.4	+17.5	88.4	1 34.1	+18.5	88.4	1 35.8	+19.4	88.4	1 37.4	+20.5	88.5	1 39.0	+21.4	88.5	1 40.6	+22.4	88.5	2
3	1 44.5	+15.4	87.4	1 47.2	+16.5	87.4	1 49.9	+17.5	87.4	1 52.6	+18.5	87.5	1 55.2	+19.5	87.5	1 57.9	+20.4	87.5	2 00.4	+21.5	87.6	2 03.0	+22.4	87.6	3
4	1 59.9	+15.4	86.4	2 03.7	+16.4	86.4	2 07.4	+17.4	86.5	2 11.1	+18.4	86.5	2 14.7	+19.4	86.5	2 18.3	+20.4	86.6	2 21.9	+21.3	86.6	2 25.4	+22.3	86.7	4
5	2 15.3	+15.4	85.4	2 20.1	+16.4	85.5	2 24.8	+17.4	85.5	2 29.5	+18.4	85.5	2 34.1	+19.4	85.6	2 38.7	+20.4	85.6	2 43.2	+21.4	85.7	2 47.7	+22.3	85.7	5
6	2 30.7	+15.3	84.5	2 36.5	+16.3	84.5	2 42.2	+17.3	84.5	2 47.9	+18.3	84.6	2 53.5	+19.3	84.6	2 59.1	+20.3	84.7	3 04.6	+21.3	84.8	3 10.0	+22.3	84.8	6
7	2 46.0	+15.3	83.5	2 52.8	+16.3	83.5	2 59.5	+17.3	83.6	3 06.2	+18.3	83.6	3 12.8	+19.3	83.7	3 19.4	+20.2	83.8	3 25.9	+21.2	83.8	3 32.3	+22.2	83.9	7
8	3 01.3	+15.2	82.5	3 09.1	+16.2	82.6	3 16.8	+17.2	82.6	3 24.5	+18.2	82.7	3 32.1	+19.2	82.7	3 39.6	+20.2	82.8	3 47.1	+21.2	82.9	3 54.5	+22.1	82.9	8
9	3 16.5	+15.2	81.6	3 25.3	+16.2	81.6	3 34.0	+17.2	81.7	3 42.7	+18.2	81.7	3 51.3	+19.1	81.8	3 59.8	+20.1	81.9	4 08.3	+21.1	81.9	4 16.6	+22.1	82.0	9
10	3 31.7	+15.1	80.6	3 41.5	+16.1	80.6	3 51.2	+17.1	80.7	4 00.9	+18.1	80.8	4 10.4	+19.1	80.9	4 19.9	+20.1	80.9	4 29.4	+21.0	81.0	4 38.7	+22.0	81.1	10
11	3 46.8	+15.1	79.6	3 57.6	+16.1	79.7	4 08.3	+17.1	79.8	4 19.0	+18.0	79.8	4 29.5	+19.0	79.9	4 40.0	+20.0	80.0	4 50.4	+21.0	80.1	5 00.7	+21.9	80.1	11
12	4 01.9	+15.0	78.6	4 13.7	+15.9	78.7	4 25.4	+16.9	78.8	4 37.0	+17.9	78.9	4 48.5	+19.0	78.9	5 00.0	+19.9	79.0	5 11.4	+20.8	79.1	5 22.6	+21.9	79.2	12
13	4 16.9	+14.9	77.7	4 29.6	+15.9	77.7	4 42.3	+16.9	77.8	4 54.9	+17.9	77.9	5 07.5	+18.8	78.0	5 19.9	+19.8	78.1	5 32.2	+20.8	78.2	5 44.5	+21.7	78.3	13
14	4 31.8	+14.8	76.7	4 45.5	+15.8	76.8	4 59.2	+16.8	76.9	5 12.8	+17.8	77.0	5 26.3	+18.7	77.0	5 39.7	+19.7	77.1	5 53.0	+20.7	77.2	6 06.2	+21.7	77.3	14
15	4 46.6	+14.7	75.7	5 01.3	+15.8	75.8	5 16.0	+16.7	75.9	5 30.6	+17.7	76.0	5 45.0	+18.7	76.1	5 59.4	+19.7	76.2	6 13.7	+20.6	76.3	6 27.9	+21.5	76.4	15
16	5 01.3	+14.7	74.8	5 17.1	+15.6	74.8	5 32.7	+16.6	74.9	5 48.3	+17.6	75.0	6 03.7	+18.6	75.1	6 19.1	+19.5	75.2	6 34.3	+20.5	75.3	6 49.4	+21.4	75.5	16
17	5 16.0	+14.6	73.8	5 32.7	+15.6	73.9	5 49.3	+16.6	74.0	6 05.9	+17.4	74.1	6 22.3	+18.4	74.2	6 38.6	+19.4	74.3	6 54.8	+20.3	74.4	7 10.8	+21.4	74.5	17
18	5 30.6	+14.4	72.8	5 48.3	+15.4	72.9	6 05.9	+16.4	73.0	6 23.3	+17.4	73.1	6 40.7	+18.4	73.2	6 58.0	+19.3	73.3	7 15.1	+20.3	73.5	7 32.2	+21.2	73.6	18
19	5 45.0	+14.4	71.8	6 03.7	+15.4	71.9	6 22.3	+16.3	72.0	6 40.7	+17.3	72.1	6 59.1	+18.2	72.3	7 17.3	+19.2	72.4	7 35.4	+20.1	72.5	7 53.4	+21.0	72.6	19
20	5 59.4	+14.3	70.9	6 19.1	+15.2	71.0	6 38.6	+16.2	71.1	6 58.0	+17.1	71.2	7 17.3	+18.1	71.3	7 36.5	+19.0	71.4	7 55.5	+20.0	71.6	8 14.4	+21.0	71.7	20
21	6 13.7	+14.2	69.9	6 34.3	+15.1	70.0	6 54.8	+16.0	70.1	7 15.1	+17.1	70.2	7 35.4	+18.0	70.3	7 55.5	+18.9	70.5	8 15.5	+19.9	70.6	8 35.4	+20.8	70.7	21
22	6 27.9	+14.0	68.9	6 49.4	+15.0	69.0	7 10.8	+16.0	69.1	7 32.2	+16.9	69.2	7 53.4	+17.8	69.4	8 14.4	+18.8	69.5	8 35.4	+19.7	69.6	8 56.2	+20.6	69.8	22
23	6 41.9	+14.0	67.9	7 04.4	+14.9	68.0	7 26.8	+15.8	68.2	7 49.1	+16.7	68.3	8 11.2	+17.7	68.4	8 33.2	+18.7	68.5	8 55.1	+19.6	68.7	9 16.8	+20.5	68.8	23
24	6 55.9	+13.8	66.9	7 19.3	+14.7	67.1	7 42.6	+15.7	67.2	8 05.8	+16.7	67.3	8 28.9	+17.6	67.4	8 51.9	+18.4	67.6	9 14.7	+19.4	67.7	9 37.3	+20.4	67.9	24
25	7 09.7	+13.7	66.0	7 34.0	+14.7	66.1	7 58.3	+15.6	66.2	8 22.5	+16.4	66.3	8 46.5	+17.4	66.5	9 10.3	+18.4	66.6	9 34.1	+19.2	66.8	9 57.7	+20.2	66.9	25
26	7 23.4	+13.5	65.0	7 48.7	+14.5	65.1	8 13.9	+15.4	65.2	8 38.9	+16.4	65.4	9 03.9	+17.2	65.5	9 28.7	+18.2	65.7	9 53.3	+19.1	65.8	10 17.9	+20.0	66.0	26
27	7 36.9	+13.4	64.0	8 03.2	+14.3	64.1	8 29.3	+15.3	64.3	8 55.3	+16.2	64.4	9 21.1	+17.2	64.5	9 46.9	+18.0	64.7	10 12.4	+19.0	64.8	10 37.9	+19.8	65.0	27
28	7 50.3	+13.3	63.0	8 17.5	+14.2	63.1	8 44.6	+15.1	63.3	9 11.5	+16.0	63.4	9 38.3	+16.9	63.6	10 04.9	+17.8	63.7	10 31.4	+18.7	63.9	10 57.7	+19.7	64.1	28
29	8 03.6	+13.2	62.0	8 31.7	+14.1	62.2	8 59.7	+14.9	62.3	9 27.5	+15.9	62.4	9 55.2	+16.8	62.6	10 22.7	+17.7	62.8	10 50.1	+18.6	62.9	11 17.4	+19.4	63.1	29
30	8 16.8	+13.0	61.0	8 45.8	+13.9	61.2	9 14.6	+14.8	61.3	9 43.4	+15.7	61.5	10 12.0	+16.6	61.6	10 40.4	+17.5	61.8	11 08.7	+18.4	61.9	11 36.8	+19.3	62.1	30
31	8 29.8	+12.9	60.1	8 59.7	+13.7	60.2	9 29.4	+14.7	60.3	9 59.1	+15.5	60.5	10 28.6	+16.4	60.6	10 57.9	+17.3	60.8	11 27.1	+18.2	61.0	11 56.1	+19.1	61.2	31
32	8 42.7	+12.7	59.1	9 13.4	+13.6	59.2	9 44.1	+14.5	59.4	10 14.6	+15.4	59.5	10 45.0	+16.2	59.7	11 15.2	+17.1	59.8	11 45.3	+18.0	60.0	12 15.2	+18.9	60.2	32
33	8 55.4	+12.5	58.1	9 27.0	+13.4	58.2	9 58.6	+14.3	58.4	10 30.0	+15.1	58.5	11 01.2	+16.1	58.7	11 32.3	+16.9	58.9	12 03.3	+17.8	59.0	12 34.1	+18.6	59.2	33
34	9 07.9	+12.4	57.1	9 40.4	+13.3	57.2	10 12.9	+14.1	57.4	10 45.1	+15.0	57.5	11 17.3	+15.8	57.7	11 49.2	+16.8	57.9	12 21.1	+17.6	58.1	12 52.7	+18.5	58.2	34
35	9 20.3	+12.2	56.1	9 53.7	+13.1	56.2	10 27.0	+13.9	56.4	11 00.1	+14.8	56.5	11 33.1	+15.7	56.7	12 06.0	+16.5	56.9	12 38.7	+17.3	57.1	13 11.2	+18.2	57.3	35
36	9 32.5	+12.1	55.1	10 06.8	+12.9	55.3	10 40.9	+13.8	55.4	11 14.9	+14.6	55.6	11 48.8	+15.4	55.7	12 22.5	+16.3	55.9	12 56.0	+17.2	56.1	13 29.4	+18.0	56.3	36
37	9 44.6	+11.8	54.1	10 19.7	+12.7	54.3	10 54.7	+13.5	54.4	11 29.5	+14.4	54.6	12 04.2	+15.3	54.7	12 38.8	+16.1	54.9	13 13.2	+16.9	55.1	13 47.4	+17.8	55.3	37
38	9 56.4	+11.7	53.1	10 32.4	+12.5	53.3	11 08.2	+13.4	53.4	11 43.9	+14.2	53.6	12 19.5	+15.0	53.8	12 54.9	+15.8	53.9	13 30.1	+16.7	54.1	14 05.2	+17.5	54.3	38
39	10 08.1	+11.6	52.1	10 44.9	+12.4	52.3	11 21.6	+13.1	52.4	11 58.1	+14.0	52.6	12 34.5	+14.8	52.8	13 10.7	+15.6	52.9	13 46.8	+16.4	53.1	14 22.7	+17.3	53.3	39
40	10 19.7	+11.3	51.1	10 57.3	+12.1	51.3	11 34.7	+13.0	51.4	12 12.1	+13.7	51.6	12 49.3	+14.6	51.8	13 26.3	+15.4	52.0	14 03.2	+16.2	52.1	14 40.0	+17.0	52.3	40
41	10 31.0	+11.2	50.1	11 09.4	+12.0	50.3	11 47.7	+12.7	50.4	12 25.8	+13.6	50.6	13 03.9	+14.3	50.8	13 41.7	+15.2	51.0	14 19.4	+16.0	51.2	14 57.0	+16.8	51.4	41
42	10 42.2	+10.9	49.1	11 21.4	+11.7	49.3	12 00.4	+12.6	49.4	12 39.4	+13.3	49.6	13 18.2	+14.1	49.8	13 56.9	+14.9	50.0	14 35.4	+15.7	50.2	15 13.8	+16.5	50.4	42
43	10 53.1	+10.8	48.1	11 33.1	+11.5	48.3	12 13.0	+12.3	48.4	12 52.7	+13.1	48.6	13 32.3	+13.9	48.8	14 11.8	+14.7	49.0	14 51.1	+15.5	49.2	15 30.3	+16.2	49.4	43
44	11 03.9	+10.5	47.1	11 44.6	+11.4	47.3	12 25.3	+12.1	47.4	13 05.8	+12.9	47.6	13 46.2	+13.7	47.8	14 26.5	+14.4	48.0	15 06.6	+15.2	48.2	15 46.5	+16.0	48.4	44
45	11 14.4	+10.4	46.1	11 56.0	+11.1	46.3	12 37.4	+11.9	46.4	13 18.7	+12.6	46.6	13 59.9	+13.3	46.8	14 40.9	+14.1	47.0	15 21.8	+14.9	47.2	16 02.5	+15.7	47.4	45
46	11 24.8	+10.2	45.1	12 07.1	+10.9	45.3	12 49.3	+11.6	45.4	13 31.3	+12.4	45.6	14 13.2	+13.2	45.8	14 55.0	+13.9	46.0	15 36.7	+14.6	46.1	16 18.2	+15.4	46.4	46
47	11 35.0	+9.9	44.1	12 18.0	+10.7	44.3	13 00.9	+11.4	44.4	13 43.7	+12.2	44.6	14 26.4	+12.9	44.8	15 08.9	+13.6	44.9	15 51.3	+14.4	45.1	16 33.6	+15.1	45.3	47
48	11 44.9	+9.8	43.1	12 28.7	+10.4	43.3	13 12.3	+11.2	43.4	13 55.9	+11.8	43.6	14 39.3	+12.6	43.8	15 22.5	+13.4	43.9	16 05.7	+14.0	44.1	16 48.7	+14.8	44.3	48
49	11 54.7	+9.5	42.1	12 39.1	+10.3	42.2	13 23.5	+10.9	42.4	14 07.7	+11.7	42.6	14 51.9	+12.3	42.7	15 35.9	+13.0	42.9	16 19.7	+13.8	43.1	17 03.5	+14.5	43.3	49
50	12 04.2	+9.3	41.1	12 49.4	+10.0	41.2	13 34.4	+10.7	41.4	14 19.4	+11.4	41.6	15 04.2	+12.1	41.7	15 48.9	+12.8	41.9	16 33.5	+13.5	42.1	17 18.0	+14.2	42.3	50
51	12 13.5	+9.1	40.1	12 59.4	+9.7	40.2	13 45.1	+10.5	40.4	14 30.8	+11.1	40.5	15 16.3	+11.8	40.7	16 01.7	+12.5	40.9	16 47.0	+13.2	41.1	17 32.2	+13.9	41.3	51
52	12 22.6	+8.8	39.1	13 09.1	+9.5	39.2	13 55.6	+10.1	39.4	14 41.9	+10.8	39.5	15 28.1	+11.5	39.7	16 14.2	+12.2	39.9	17 00.2	+12.9	40.1	17 46.1	+13.5	40.3	52
53	12 31.4	+8.7	38.1	13 18.6	+9.3	38.2	14 05.7	+10.0	38.3	14 52.7	+10.6	38.5	15 39.6	+11.3	38.7	16 26.4	+11.9	38.9	17 13.1	+12.6	39.0	17 59.6	+13.3	39.2	53
54	12 40.1	+8.4	37.0	13 27.9	+9.1	37.2	14 15.7	+9.6	37.3	15 03.3	+10.3	37.5	15 50.9	+11.0	37.7	16 38.3	+11.6	37.8	17 25.7	+12.2	38.0	18 12.9	+12.9	38.2	54
55	12 48.5	+8.1	36.0	13 37.0	+8.7	36.2	14 25.3	+9.5	36.3	15 13.6	+10.1	36.5	16 01.9	+10.6	36.6	16 49.9	+11.3	36.8	17 37.9	+12.0	37.0	18 25.8	+12.6	37.2	55
56	12 56.6	+8.0	35.0	13 45.7	+8.6	35.1	14 34.8	+9.1	35.3	15 23.7	+9.7	35.4	16 12.5	+10.4	35.6	17 01.2	+11.0	35.8	17 49.9	+11.6	36.0	18 38.4	+12.2	36.2	56
57	13 04.6	+7.7	34.0	13 54.3	+8.3	34.1	14 43.9	+8.9	34.3	15 33.4	+9.5	34.4	16 22.9	+10.1	34.6	17 12.2	+10.7	34.8	18 01.5	+11.3	34.9	18 50.6	+11.9	35.1	57
58	13 12.3	+7.4	33.0	14 02.6	+8.0	33.1	14 52.8	+8.6	33.2	15 42.9	+9.2	33.4	16 33.0	+9.7	33.6	17 22.9	+10.4	33.7	18 12.8	+10.9	33.9	19 02.5	+11.6	34.1	58
59	13 19.7	+7.2	32.0	14 10.6	+7.7	32.1	15 01.4	+8.3	32.2	15 52.1	+8.9	32.4	16 42.7	+9.5	32.5	17 33.3	+10.0	32.7	18 23.7	+10.6	32.9	19 14.1	+11.2	33.1	59
60	13 26.9	+7.0	30.9	14 18.3	+7.6	31.1	15 09.7	+8.1	31.2	16 01.0	+8.6	31.3	16 52.2	+9.2	31.5	17 43.3	+9.7	31.7	18 34.3	+10.3	31.8	19 25.3	+10.8	32.0	60
61	13 33.9	+6.7	29.9	14 25.9	+7.2	30.0	15 17.8	+7.7	30.2	16 09.6	+8.3	30.3	17 01.4	+8.8	30.5	17 53.0	+9.4	30.6	18 44.6	+10.0	30.8	19 36.1	+10.5	31.0	61
62	13 40.6	+6.4	28.9	14 33.1	+7.0	29.0	15 25.5	+7.5	29.1	16 17.9	+8.0	29.3	17 10.2	+8.5	29.4	18 02.4	+9.1	29.6	18 54.6	+9.5	29.7	19 46.6	+10.1	29.9	62
63	13 47.0	+6.2	27.9	14 40.1	+6.7	28.0	15 33.0	+7.2	28.1	16 25.9	+7.7	28.2	17 18.7	+8.2	28.4	18 11.5	+8.7	28.5	19 04.1	+9.3	28.7	19 56.7	+9.8	28.9	63
64	13 53.2	+6.0	26.8	14 46.8	+6.4	27.0	15 40.2	+6.9	27.1	16 33.6	+7.4	27.2	17 26.9	+7.9	27.4	18 20.2	+8.4	27.5	19 13.4	+8.8	27.7	20 06.5	+9.3	27.8	64
65	13 59.2	+5.7	25.8	14 53.2	+6.1	25.9	15 47.1	+6.6	26.0	16 41.0	+7.1	26.2	17 34.8	+7.6	26.3	18 28.6	+8.0	26.5	19 22.2	+8.5	26.6	20 15.8	+9.0	26.8	65
66	14 04.9	+5.4	24.8	14 59.3	+5.9	24.9	15 53.7	+6.3	25.0	16 48.1	+6.7	25.1	17 42.4	+7.2	25.3	18 36.6	+7.7	25.4	19 30.7	+8.2	25.6	20 24.8	+8.7	25.7	66
67	14 10.3	+5.2	23.8	15 05.2	+5.6	23.9	16 00.0	+6.1	24.0	16 54.8	+6.5	24.1	17 49.6	+6.9	24.2	18 44.3	+7.3	24.4	19 38.9	+7.8	24.5	20 33.5	+8.2	24.7	67
68	14 15.5	+4.9	22.7	15 10.8	+5.3	22.8	16 06.1	+5.7	22.9	17 01.3	+6.1	23.1	17 56.5	+6.5	23.2	18 51.6	+7.0	23.3	19 46.7	+7.4	23.5	20 41.7	+7.8	23.6	68
69	14 20.4	+4.6	21.7	15 16.1	+5.0	21.8	16 11.8	+5.4	21.9	17 07.4	+5.9	22.0	18 03.0	+6.3	22.1	18 58.6	+6.6	22.3	19 54.1	+7.0	22.4	20 49.5	+7.5	22.5	69
70	14 25.0	+4.4	20.7	15 21.1	+4.8	20.8	16 17.2	+5.1	20.9	17 13.3	+5.5	21.0	18 09.3	+5.8	21.1	19 05.2	+6.3	21.2	20 01.1	+6.7	21.3	20 57.0	+7.0	21.5	70
71	14 29.4	+4.1	19.6	15 25.9	+4.4	19.7	16 22.3	+4.8	19.8	17 18.8	+5.1	19.9	18 15.1	+5.6	20.0	19 11.5	+5.9	20.2	20 07.8	+6.3	20.3	21 04.0	+6.7	20.4	71
72	14 33.5	+3.8	18.6	15 30.3	+4.2	18.7	16 27.1	+4.6	18.8	17 23.9	+4.9	18.9	18 20.7	+5.2	19.0	19 17.4	+5.5	19.1	20 14.1	+5.9	19.2	21 10.7	+6.3	19.4	72
73	14 37.3	+3.6	17.6	15 34.5	+3.9	17.7	16 31.7	+4.1	17.8	17 28.8	+4.5	17.8	18 25.9	+4.8	17.9	19 22.9	+5.2	18.1	20 20.0	+5.5	18.2	21 17.0	+5.8	18.3	73
74	14 40.9	+3.3	16.6	15 38.4	+3.6	16.6	16 35.8	+3.9	16.7	17 33.3	+4.2	16.8	18 30.7	+4.5	16.9	19 28.1	+4.8	17.0	20 25.5	+5.1	17.1	21 22.8	+5.5	17.2	74
75	14 44.2	+3.0	15.5	15 42.0	+3.2	15.6	16 39.7	+3.6	15.7	17 37.5	+3.9	15.8	18 35.2	+4.2	15.8	19 32.9	+4.5	15.9	20 30.6	+4.7	16.0	21 28.3	+5.0	16.1	75
76	14 47.2	+2.7	14.5	15 45.2	+3.0	14.6	16 43.3	+3.3	14.6	17 41.4	+3.5	14.7	18 39.4	+3.8	14.8	19 37.4	+4.0	14.9	20 35.3	+4.4	15.0	21 33.3	+4.6	15.1	76
77	14 49.9	+2.4	13.5	15 48.2	+2.7	13.5	16 46.6	+2.9	13.6	17 44.9	+3.2	13.7	18 43.2	+3.4	13.7	19 41.4	+3.7	13.8	20 39.7	+4.0	13.9	21 37.9	+4.2	14.0	77
78	14 52.3	+2.2	12.4	15 50.9	+2.4	12.5	16 49.5	+2.6	12.5	17 48.1	+2.8	12.6	18 46.6	+3.1	12.7	19 45.1	+3.4	12.8	20 43.7	+3.5	12.8	21 42.1	+3.8	12.9	78
79	14 54.5	+1.9	11.4	15 53.3	+2.1	11.4	16 52.1	+2.4	11.5	17 50.9	+2.6	11.6	18 49.7	+2.7	11.6	19 48.5	+2.9	11.7	20 47.2	+3.2	11.8	21 45.9	+3.4	11.9	79
80	14 56.4	+1.6	10.4	15 55.4	+1.8	10.4	16 54.5	+1.9	10.5	17 53.5	+2.1	10.5	18 52.4	+2.4	10.6	19 51.4	+2.6	10.6	20 50.4	+2.7	10.7	21 49.3	+3.0	10.8	80
81	14 58.0	+1.4	9.3	15 57.2	+1.6	9.4	16 56.4	+1.7	9.4	17 55.6	+1.9	9.5	18 54.8	+2.0	9.5	19 54.0	+2.2	9.6	20 53.1	+2.4	9.6	21 52.3	+2.5	9.7	81
82	14 59.4	+1.0	8.3	15 58.8	+1.2	8.3	16 58.1	+1.4	8.4	17 57.5	+1.5	8.4	18 56.8	+1.7	8.5	19 56.2	+1.8	8.5	20 55.5	+2.0	8.6	21 54.8	+2.2	8.6	82
83	15 00.4	+0.8	7.2	16 00.0	+0.9	7.3	16 59.5	+1.0	7.3	17 59.0	+1.2	7.4	18 58.5	+1.3	7.4	19 58.0	+1.4	7.4	20 57.5	+1.5	7.5	21 57.0	+1.7	7.5	83
84	15 01.2	+0.5	6.2	16 00.9	+0.6	6.2	17 00.5	+0.7	6.3	18 00.2	+0.8	6.3	18 59.8	+0.9	6.3	19 59.4	+1.1	6.4	20 59.0	+1.2	6.4	21 58.7	+1.2	6.5	84
85	15 01.7	+0.2	5.2	16 01.5	+0.3	5.2	17 01.2	+0.4	5.2	18 01.0	+0.5	5.3	19 00.7	+0.6	5.3	20 00.5	+0.6	5.3	21 00.2	+0.8	5.4	21 59.9	+0.9	5.4	85
86	15 01.9	0.0	4.1	16 01.8	0.0	4.2	17 01.6	+0.1	4.2	18 01.5	+0.1	4.2	19 01.3	+0.2	4.2	20 01.1	+0.3	4.3	21 01.0	+0.3	4.3	22 00.8	+0.4	4.3	86
87	15 01.9	−0.4	3.1	16 01.8	−0.3	3.1	17 01.7	−0.2	3.1	18 01.6	−0.2	3.2	19 01.5	−0.1	3.2	20 01.4	−0.1	3.2	21 01.3	0.0	3.2	22 01.2	0.0	3.2	87
88	15 01.5	−0.6	2.1	16 01.5	−0.6	2.1	17 01.5	−0.6	2.1	18 01.4	−0.5	2.1	19 01.4	−0.5	2.1	20 01.3	−0.4	2.1	21 01.3	−0.5	2.1	22 01.2	−0.4	2.2	88
89	15 00.9	−0.9	1.0	16 00.9	−0.9	1.0	17 00.9	−0.9	1.0	18 00.9	−0.9	1.1	19 00.9	−0.9	1.1	20 00.9	−0.9	1.1	21 00.8	−0.8	1.1	22 00.8	−0.8	1.1	89
90	15 00.0	−1.2	0.0	16 00.0	−1.2	0.0	17 00.0	−1.2	0.0	18 00.0	−1.2	0.0	19 00.0	−1.2	0.0	20 00.0	−1.2	0.0	21 00.0	−1.2	0.0	22 00.0	−1.3	0.0	90
	15°			16°			17°			18°			19°			20°			21°			22°			

89°, 271° L.H.A. LATITUDE SAME NAME AS DECLINATION

180

LATITUDE **CONTRARY** NAME TO DECLINATION **L.H.A. 89°, 271°**

Dec.	15° Hc	d	Z	16° Hc	d	Z	17° Hc	d	Z	18° Hc	d	Z	19° Hc	d	Z	20° Hc	d	Z	21° Hc	d	Z	22° Hc	d	Z	Dec.
°	° ′	′	°	° ′	′	°	° ′	′	°	° ′	′	°	° ′	′	°	° ′	′	°	° ′	′	°	° ′	′	°	°
0	0 58.0	−15.6	90.3	0 57.7	−16.6	90.3	0 57.4	−17.6	90.3	0 57.1	−18.6	90.3	0 56.7	−19.5	90.3	0 56.4	−20.5	90.3	0 56.0	−21.5	90.4	0 55.6	−22.5	90.4	0
1	0 42.4	−15.5	91.2	0 41.1	−16.5	91.2	0 39.8	−17.5	91.2	0 38.5	−18.5	91.3	0 37.2	−19.6	91.3	0 35.9	−20.6	91.3	0 34.5	−21.5	91.3	0 33.1	−22.4	91.3	1
2	0 26.9	−15.6	92.2	0 24.6	−16.6	92.2	0 22.3	−17.6	92.2	0 20.0	−18.6	92.2	0 17.6	−19.5	92.2	0 15.3	−20.5	92.2	0 13.0	−21.5	92.2	0 10.7	−22.5	92.2	2
3	0 11.3	−15.6	93.2	0 08.0	−16.6	93.2	0 04.7	−17.6	93.2	0 01.4	−18.6	93.2	0 01.9	+19.6	86.8	0 05.2	+20.6	86.8	0 08.5	+21.6	86.8	0 11.8	+22.5	86.8	3
4	0 04.3	+15.5	85.9	0 08.6	+16.5	85.9	0 12.9	+17.5	85.9	0 17.2	+18.5	85.9	0 21.5	+19.5	85.9	0 25.8	+20.5	85.9	0 30.1	+21.5	85.9	0 34.3	+22.5	85.9	4
5	0 19.8	+15.6	84.9	0 25.1	+16.6	84.9	0 30.4	+17.6	84.9	0 35.7	+18.6	84.9	0 41.0	+19.6	84.9	0 46.3	+20.5	85.0	0 51.6	+21.5	85.0	0 56.8	+22.5	85.0	5
6	0 35.4	+15.5	83.9	0 41.7	+16.6	84.0	0 48.0	+17.5	84.0	0 54.3	+18.5	84.0	1 00.6	+19.5	84.0	1 06.8	+20.5	84.0	1 13.1	+21.5	84.0	1 19.3	+22.4	84.1	6
7	0 50.9	+15.5	83.0	0 58.2	+16.6	83.0	1 05.5	+17.6	83.0	1 12.8	+18.6	83.0	1 20.1	+19.5	83.1	1 27.3	+20.5	83.1	1 34.6	+21.4	83.1	1 41.7	+22.5	83.1	7
8	1 06.4	+15.6	82.0	1 14.8	+16.5	82.0	1 23.1	+17.5	82.1	1 31.4	+18.4	82.1	1 39.6	+19.5	82.1	1 47.8	+20.5	82.1	1 56.0	+21.4	82.2	2 04.2	+22.4	82.2	8
9	1 22.0	+15.4	81.0	1 31.3	+16.5	81.1	1 40.6	+17.5	81.1	1 49.8	+18.5	81.1	1 59.1	+19.4	81.2	2 08.3	+20.4	81.2	2 17.4	+21.4	81.2	2 26.6	+22.3	81.3	9
10	1 37.4	+15.5	80.1	1 47.8	+16.4	80.1	1 58.1	+17.4	80.1	2 08.3	+18.4	80.2	2 18.5	+19.4	80.2	2 28.7	+20.4	80.3	2 38.8	+21.4	80.3	2 48.9	+22.3	80.3	10
11	1 52.9	+15.4	79.1	2 04.2	+16.4	79.1	2 15.5	+17.4	79.2	2 26.7	+18.4	79.2	2 37.9	+19.4	79.3	2 49.1	+20.3	79.3	3 00.2	+21.3	79.4	3 11.2	+22.3	79.4	11
12	2 08.3	+15.4	78.1	2 20.6	+16.4	78.2	2 32.9	+17.4	78.2	2 45.1	+18.4	78.3	2 57.3	+19.3	78.3	3 09.4	+20.3	78.4	3 21.5	+21.2	78.4	3 33.5	+22.2	78.5	12
13	2 23.7	+15.4	77.2	2 37.0	+16.4	77.2	2 50.3	+17.3	77.3	3 03.5	+18.2	77.3	3 16.6	+19.3	77.4	3 29.7	+20.2	77.4	3 42.7	+21.2	77.5	3 55.7	+22.1	77.6	13
14	2 39.1	+15.3	76.2	2 53.4	+16.2	76.3	3 07.6	+17.2	76.3	3 21.7	+18.3	76.4	3 35.9	+19.2	76.4	3 49.9	+20.2	76.5	4 03.9	+21.1	76.6	4 17.8	+22.1	76.6	14
15	2 54.4	+15.2	75.2	3 09.6	+16.3	75.3	3 24.8	+17.2	75.4	3 40.0	+18.2	75.4	3 55.1	+19.1	75.5	4 10.1	+20.1	75.5	4 25.0	+21.1	75.6	4 39.9	+22.0	75.7	15
16	3 09.6	+15.2	74.3	3 25.9	+16.1	74.3	3 42.0	+17.2	74.4	3 58.2	+18.1	74.5	4 14.2	+19.1	74.5	4 30.2	+20.0	74.6	4 46.1	+20.9	74.7	5 01.9	+21.9	74.8	16
17	3 24.8	+15.2	73.3	3 42.0	+16.2	73.4	3 59.2	+17.1	73.4	4 16.3	+18.0	73.5	4 33.3	+19.0	73.6	4 50.2	+19.9	73.7	5 07.0	+20.9	73.7	5 23.8	+21.8	73.8	17
18	3 40.0	+15.1	72.3	3 58.2	+16.0	72.4	4 16.3	+17.0	72.5	4 34.3	+18.0	72.5	4 52.3	+18.9	72.6	5 10.1	+19.9	72.7	5 27.9	+20.8	72.8	5 45.6	+21.8	72.9	18
19	3 55.1	+15.0	71.4	4 14.2	+16.0	71.4	4 33.3	+16.9	71.5	4 52.3	+17.8	71.6	5 11.2	+18.8	71.7	5 30.0	+19.8	71.8	5 48.7	+20.7	71.9	6 07.4	+21.6	72.0	19
20	4 10.1	+14.9	70.4	4 30.2	+15.9	70.5	4 50.2	+16.8	70.5	5 10.1	+17.8	70.6	5 30.0	+18.7	70.7	5 49.8	+19.6	70.8	6 09.4	+20.6	70.9	6 29.0	+21.5	71.0	20
21	4 25.0	+14.9	69.4	4 46.1	+15.8	69.5	5 07.0	+16.8	69.6	5 27.9	+17.7	69.7	5 48.7	+18.7	69.8	6 09.4	+19.6	69.9	6 30.0	+20.5	70.0	6 50.5	+21.5	70.1	21
22	4 39.9	+14.8	68.5	5 01.9	+15.7	68.5	5 23.8	+16.7	68.6	5 45.6	+17.6	68.7	6 07.4	+18.5	68.8	6 29.0	+19.5	68.9	6 50.5	+20.4	69.0	7 12.0	+21.3	69.1	22
23	4 54.7	+14.7	67.5	5 17.6	+15.6	67.6	5 40.5	+16.5	67.7	6 03.2	+17.5	67.7	6 25.9	+18.4	67.8	6 48.5	+19.3	68.0	7 10.9	+20.3	68.1	7 33.3	+21.2	68.2	23
24	5 09.4	+14.6	66.5	5 33.2	+15.6	66.6	5 57.0	+16.5	66.7	6 20.7	+17.4	66.8	6 44.3	+18.4	66.9	7 07.8	+19.3	67.0	7 31.2	+20.2	67.1	7 54.5	+21.0	67.2	24
25	5 24.0	+14.5	65.5	5 48.8	+15.4	65.6	6 13.5	+16.4	65.7	6 38.1	+17.3	65.8	7 02.7	+18.2	65.9	7 27.1	+19.1	66.0	7 51.4	+20.0	66.2	8 15.5	+21.0	66.3	25
26	5 38.5	+14.4	64.6	6 04.2	+15.4	64.7	6 29.9	+16.2	64.8	6 55.4	+17.2	64.9	7 20.9	+18.0	65.0	7 46.2	+19.0	65.1	8 11.4	+19.9	65.2	8 36.5	+20.8	65.4	26
27	5 52.9	+14.3	63.6	6 19.6	+15.2	63.7	6 46.1	+16.2	63.8	7 12.6	+17.0	63.9	7 38.9	+18.0	64.0	8 05.2	+18.8	64.1	8 31.3	+19.7	64.3	8 57.3	+20.6	64.4	27
28	6 07.2	+14.3	62.6	6 34.8	+15.1	62.7	7 02.3	+16.0	62.8	7 29.6	+16.9	62.9	7 56.9	+17.8	63.0	8 24.0	+18.7	63.2	8 51.0	+19.6	63.3	9 17.9	+20.5	63.5	28
29	6 21.5	+14.1	61.6	6 49.9	+15.0	61.7	7 18.3	+15.9	61.8	7 46.5	+16.8	62.0	8 14.7	+17.7	62.1	8 42.7	+18.6	62.2	9 10.6	+19.5	62.4	9 38.4	+20.3	62.5	29
30	6 35.6	+14.0	60.7	7 04.9	+14.9	60.8	7 34.2	+15.7	60.9	8 03.3	+16.7	61.0	8 32.4	+17.5	61.1	9 01.3	+18.4	61.3	9 30.1	+19.3	61.4	9 58.7	+20.2	61.5	30
31	6 49.6	+13.8	59.7	7 19.8	+14.8	59.8	7 49.9	+15.7	59.9	8 20.0	+16.5	60.0	8 49.9	+17.4	60.1	9 19.7	+18.3	60.3	9 49.4	+19.1	60.4	10 18.9	+20.0	60.6	31
32	7 03.4	+13.8	58.7	7 34.6	+14.6	58.8	8 05.6	+15.5	58.9	8 36.5	+16.4	59.0	9 07.3	+17.2	59.2	9 38.0	+18.1	59.3	10 08.5	+19.0	59.5	10 38.9	+19.9	59.6	32
33	7 17.2	+13.6	57.7	7 49.2	+14.5	57.8	8 21.1	+15.3	57.9	8 52.9	+16.2	58.1	9 24.5	+17.1	58.2	9 56.1	+17.9	58.4	10 27.5	+18.8	58.5	10 58.8	+19.6	58.7	33
34	7 30.8	+13.5	56.7	8 03.7	+14.3	56.8	8 36.4	+15.2	57.0	9 09.1	+16.0	57.1	9 41.6	+16.9	57.2	10 14.0	+17.8	57.4	10 46.3	+18.6	57.5	11 18.4	+19.5	57.7	34
35	7 44.3	+13.3	55.7	8 18.0	+14.2	55.9	8 51.6	+15.1	56.0	9 25.1	+15.9	56.1	9 58.5	+16.7	56.3	10 31.8	+17.5	56.4	11 04.9	+18.4	56.6	11 37.9	+19.2	56.7	35
36	7 57.6	+13.3	54.8	8 32.2	+14.1	54.9	9 06.7	+14.9	55.0	9 41.0	+15.7	55.1	10 15.2	+16.6	55.3	10 49.3	+17.4	55.4	11 23.3	+18.2	55.6	11 57.1	+19.1	55.8	36
37	8 10.9	+13.0	53.8	8 46.3	+13.9	53.9	9 21.6	+14.7	54.0	9 56.7	+15.6	54.2	10 31.8	+16.4	54.3	11 06.7	+17.3	54.5	11 41.5	+18.1	54.6	12 16.2	+18.9	54.8	37
38	8 23.9	+12.9	52.8	9 00.2	+13.7	52.9	9 36.3	+14.5	53.0	10 12.3	+15.4	53.2	10 48.2	+16.2	53.3	11 24.0	+17.0	53.5	11 59.6	+17.8	53.7	12 35.1	+18.6	53.8	38
39	8 36.8	+12.8	51.8	9 13.9	+13.6	51.9	9 50.8	+14.4	52.1	10 27.7	+15.2	52.2	11 04.4	+16.0	52.4	11 41.0	+16.8	52.5	12 17.4	+17.6	52.7	12 53.7	+18.5	52.9	39
40	8 49.6	+12.6	50.8	9 27.5	+13.4	50.9	10 05.2	+14.2	51.1	10 42.9	+15.0	51.2	11 20.4	+15.8	51.4	11 57.8	+16.6	51.5	12 35.0	+17.5	51.7	13 12.2	+18.2	51.9	40
41	9 02.2	+12.5	49.8	9 40.9	+13.2	50.0	10 19.4	+14.1	50.1	10 57.9	+14.8	50.2	11 36.2	+15.6	50.4	12 14.4	+16.4	50.5	12 52.5	+17.2	50.7	13 30.4	+18.0	50.9	41
42	9 14.7	+12.3	48.8	9 54.1	+13.1	49.0	10 33.5	+13.8	49.1	11 12.7	+14.6	49.2	11 51.8	+15.4	49.4	12 30.8	+16.2	49.6	13 09.7	+16.9	49.7	13 48.4	+17.7	49.9	42
43	9 27.0	+12.1	47.8	10 07.2	+12.9	48.0	10 47.3	+13.7	48.1	11 27.3	+14.5	48.3	12 07.2	+15.2	48.4	12 47.0	+16.0	48.6	13 26.6	+16.8	48.8	14 06.1	+17.5	48.9	43
44	9 39.1	+12.0	46.8	10 20.1	+12.7	47.0	11 01.0	+13.5	47.1	11 41.8	+14.2	47.3	12 22.4	+15.0	47.4	13 03.0	+15.7	47.6	13 43.4	+16.5	47.8	14 23.6	+17.3	47.9	44
45	9 51.1	+11.8	45.9	10 32.8	+12.5	46.0	11 14.5	+13.2	46.1	11 56.0	+14.0	46.3	12 37.4	+14.8	46.4	13 18.7	+15.5	46.6	13 59.9	+16.2	46.8	14 40.9	+17.0	47.0	45
46	10 02.9	+11.6	44.9	10 45.3	+12.4	45.0	11 27.7	+13.1	45.1	12 10.0	+13.8	45.3	12 52.2	+14.5	45.4	13 34.2	+15.3	45.6	14 16.1	+16.0	45.8	14 57.9	+16.8	46.0	46
47	10 14.5	+11.4	43.9	10 57.7	+12.1	44.0	11 40.8	+12.9	44.1	12 23.8	+13.6	44.3	13 06.7	+14.3	44.4	13 49.5	+15.0	44.6	14 32.1	+15.8	44.8	15 14.7	+16.4	45.0	47
48	10 25.9	+11.2	42.9	11 09.8	+12.0	43.0	11 53.7	+12.6	43.1	12 37.4	+13.4	43.3	13 21.0	+14.1	43.4	14 04.5	+14.8	43.6	14 47.9	+15.5	43.8	15 31.1	+16.3	44.0	48
49	10 37.1	+11.1	41.9	11 21.8	+11.7	42.0	12 06.3	+12.4	42.1	12 50.8	+13.1	42.3	13 35.1	+13.8	42.4	14 19.3	+14.5	42.6	15 03.4	+15.2	42.8	15 47.4	+15.9	43.0	49
50	10 48.2	+10.8	40.9	11 33.5	+11.5	41.0	12 18.7	+12.3	41.1	13 03.9	+12.9	41.3	13 48.9	+13.6	41.4	14 33.8	+14.3	41.6	15 18.6	+15.0	41.8	16 03.3	+15.7	42.0	50
51	10 59.0	+10.7	39.9	11 45.0	+11.4	40.0	12 31.0	+12.0	40.1	13 16.8	+12.7	40.3	14 02.5	+13.3	40.4	14 48.1	+14.0	40.6	15 33.6	+14.7	40.8	16 19.0	+15.4	41.0	51
52	11 09.7	+10.4	38.9	11 56.4	+11.1	39.0	12 43.0	+11.7	39.1	13 29.5	+12.4	39.3	14 15.8	+13.1	39.4	15 02.1	+13.8	39.6	15 48.3	+14.4	39.8	16 34.4	+15.1	40.0	52
53	11 20.1	+10.3	37.9	12 07.5	+10.9	38.0	12 54.7	+11.6	38.1	13 41.9	+12.2	38.3	14 28.9	+12.9	38.4	15 15.9	+13.5	38.6	16 02.7	+14.2	38.8	16 49.5	+14.7	38.9	53
54	11 30.4	+10.0	36.9	12 18.4	+10.6	37.0	13 06.3	+11.3	37.1	13 54.1	+11.9	37.3	14 41.8	+12.5	37.4	15 29.4	+13.2	37.6	16 16.9	+13.8	37.8	17 04.2	+14.5	37.9	54
55	11 40.4	+9.9	35.8	12 29.0	+10.5	36.0	13 17.6	+11.0	36.1	14 06.0	+11.7	36.2	14 54.3	+12.3	36.4	15 42.6	+12.9	36.6	16 30.7	+13.6	36.7	17 18.7	+14.2	36.9	55
56	11 50.3	+9.6	34.8	12 39.5	+10.2	35.0	13 28.6	+10.8	35.1	14 17.7	+11.4	35.2	15 06.6	+12.1	35.4	15 55.5	+12.6	35.6	16 44.3	+13.2	35.7	17 32.9	+13.9	35.9	56
57	11 59.9	+9.4	33.8	12 49.7	+10.0	34.0	13 39.4	+10.6	34.1	14 29.1	+11.2	34.2	15 18.7	+11.7	34.4	16 08.1	+12.4	34.5	16 57.5	+13.0	34.7	17 46.8	+13.5	34.9	57
58	12 09.3	+9.2	32.8	12 59.7	+9.7	32.9	13 50.0	+10.3	33.1	14 40.3	+10.8	33.2	15 30.4	+11.5	33.4	16 20.5	+12.0	33.5	17 10.5	+12.6	33.7	18 00.3	+13.3	33.9	58
59	12 18.5	+8.9	31.8	13 09.4	+9.6	31.9	14 00.3	+10.1	32.1	14 51.1	+10.7	32.2	15 41.9	+11.2	32.3	16 32.5	+11.8	32.5	17 23.1	+12.3	32.7	18 13.6	+12.9	32.8	59
60	12 27.4	+8.8	30.8	13 19.0	+9.2	30.9	14 10.4	+9.8	31.0	15 01.8	+10.3	31.2	15 53.1	+10.9	31.3	16 44.3	+11.4	31.5	17 35.4	+12.0	31.6	18 26.5	+12.5	31.8	60
61	12 36.2	+8.5	29.8	13 28.2	+9.1	29.9	14 20.2	+9.6	30.0	15 12.1	+10.1	30.2	16 04.0	+10.6	30.3	16 55.7	+11.2	30.4	17 47.4	+11.7	30.6	18 39.0	+12.3	30.8	61
62	12 44.7	+8.3	28.8	13 37.3	+8.7	28.9	14 29.8	+9.3	29.0	15 22.2	+9.8	29.1	16 14.6	+10.3	29.3	17 06.9	+10.8	29.4	17 59.1	+11.4	29.6	18 51.3	+11.8	29.7	62
63	12 53.0	+8.0	27.8	13 46.0	+8.6	27.9	14 39.1	+9.0	28.0	15 32.0	+9.5	28.1	16 24.9	+10.0	28.2	17 17.7	+10.5	28.4	18 10.5	+11.0	28.5	19 03.1	+11.6	28.7	63
64	13 01.0	+7.8	26.7	13 54.6	+8.2	26.8	14 48.1	+8.7	27.0	15 41.5	+9.2	27.1	16 34.9	+9.7	27.2	17 28.2	+10.2	27.4	18 21.5	+10.7	27.5	19 14.7	+11.2	27.7	64
65	13 08.8	+7.6	25.7	14 02.8	+8.1	25.8	14 56.8	+8.5	25.9	15 50.7	+9.0	26.1	16 44.6	+9.4	26.2	17 38.4	+9.9	26.3	18 32.2	+10.3	26.5	19 25.9	+10.8	26.6	65
66	13 16.4	+7.3	24.7	14 10.9	+7.7	24.8	15 05.3	+8.2	24.9	15 59.7	+8.6	25.0	16 54.0	+9.1	25.2	17 48.3	+9.6	25.3	18 42.5	+10.0	25.4	19 36.7	+10.4	25.6	66
67	13 23.7	+7.1	23.7	14 18.6	+7.5	23.8	15 13.5	+7.9	23.9	16 08.3	+8.4	24.0	17 03.1	+8.8	24.1	17 57.9	+9.2	24.2	18 52.5	+9.7	24.4	19 47.1	+10.1	24.5	67
68	13 30.8	+6.8	22.7	14 26.1	+7.2	22.8	15 21.4	+7.6	22.9	16 16.7	+8.0	23.0	17 11.9	+8.5	23.1	18 07.1	+8.8	23.2	19 02.2	+9.3	23.3	19 57.2	+9.8	23.5	68
69	13 37.6	+6.5	21.6	14 33.3	+7.0	21.7	15 29.0	+7.4	21.8	16 24.7	+7.8	21.9	17 20.4	+8.1	22.0	18 15.9	+8.6	22.2	19 11.5	+8.9	22.3	20 07.0	+9.3	22.4	69
70	13 44.1	+6.4	20.6	14 40.3	+6.7	20.7	15 36.4	+7.1	20.8	16 32.5	+7.4	20.9	17 28.5	+7.8	21.0	18 24.5	+8.2	21.1	19 20.4	+8.6	21.2	20 16.3	+9.0	21.4	70
71	13 50.5	+6.0	19.6	14 47.0	+6.4	19.7	15 43.5	+6.7	19.8	16 39.9	+7.1	19.9	17 36.3	+7.5	20.0	18 32.7	+7.8	20.1	19 29.0	+8.2	20.2	20 25.3	+8.6	20.3	71
72	13 56.5	+5.8	18.6	14 53.4	+6.1	18.6	15 50.2	+6.5	18.7	16 47.0	+6.9	18.8	17 43.8	+7.2	18.9	18 40.5	+7.6	19.0	19 37.2	+7.9	19.1	20 33.9	+8.2	19.3	72
73	14 02.3	+5.6	17.5	14 59.5	+5.9	17.6	15 56.7	+6.2	17.7	16 53.9	+6.5	17.8	17 51.0	+6.8	17.9	18 48.1	+7.1	18.0	19 45.1	+7.5	18.1	20 42.1	+7.8	18.2	73
74	14 07.9	+5.3	16.5	15 05.4	+5.6	16.6	16 02.9	+5.9	16.7	17 00.4	+6.1	16.8	17 57.8	+6.5	16.8	18 55.2	+6.8	16.9	19 52.6	+7.1	17.0	20 49.9	+7.5	17.1	74
75	14 13.2	+5.0	15.5	15 11.0	+5.3	15.6	16 08.8	+5.6	15.6	17 06.5	+5.9	15.7	18 04.3	+6.1	15.8	19 02.0	+6.5	15.9	19 59.7	+6.7	16.0	20 57.4	+7.0	16.1	75
76	14 18.2	+4.7	14.5	15 16.3	+5.0	14.5	16 14.4	+5.2	14.6	17 12.4	+5.6	14.7	18 10.4	+5.9	14.7	19 08.5	+6.0	14.8	20 06.4	+6.4	14.9	21 04.4	+6.6	15.0	76
77	14 22.9	+4.5	13.4	15 21.3	+4.7	13.5	16 19.6	+5.0	13.6	17 18.0	+5.2	13.6	18 16.3	+5.4	13.7	19 14.5	+5.8	13.8	20 12.8	+6.0	13.9	21 11.0	+6.3	14.0	77
78	14 27.4	+4.3	12.4	15 26.0	+4.5	12.5	16 24.6	+4.7	12.5	17 23.2	+4.9	12.6	18 21.7	+5.2	12.7	19 20.3	+5.3	12.7	20 18.8	+5.6	12.8	21 17.3	+5.8	12.9	78
79	14 31.7	+3.9	11.4	15 30.5	+4.1	11.4	16 29.3	+4.3	11.5	17 28.1	+4.5	11.5	18 26.9	+4.7	11.6	19 25.6	+5.0	11.7	20 24.4	+5.2	11.7	21 23.1	+5.4	11.8	79
80	14 35.6	+3.7	10.3	15 34.6	+3.9	10.4	16 33.6	+4.1	10.4	17 32.6	+4.3	10.5	18 31.6	+4.5	10.6	19 30.6	+4.6	10.6	20 29.6	+4.8	10.7	21 28.5	+5.1	10.8	80
81	14 39.3	+3.4	9.3	15 38.5	+3.6	9.3	16 37.7	+3.7	9.4	17 36.9	+3.9	9.4	18 36.1	+4.0	9.5	19 35.2	+4.3	9.6	20 34.4	+4.4	9.6	21 33.6	+4.6	9.7	81
82	14 42.7	+3.1	8.3	15 42.1	+3.2	8.3	16 41.4	+3.5	8.4	17 40.8	+3.6	8.4	18 40.1	+3.8	8.4	19 39.5	+3.9	8.5	20 38.8	+4.1	8.6	21 38.2	+4.2	8.6	82
83	14 45.8	+2.9	7.2	15 45.3	+3.0	7.3	16 44.9	+3.1	7.3	17 44.4	+3.2	7.4	18 43.9	+3.4	7.4	19 43.4	+3.5	7.4	20 42.9	+3.6	7.5	21 42.4	+3.7	7.5	83
84	14 48.7	+2.6	6.2	15 48.3	+2.7	6.2	16 48.0	+2.8	6.3	17 47.6	+2.9	6.3	18 47.3	+3.0	6.3	19 46.9	+3.1	6.4	20 46.5	+3.3	6.4	21 46.1	+3.4	6.5	84
85	14 51.3	+2.3	5.2	15 51.0	+2.4	5.2	16 50.8	+2.5	5.2	17 50.5	+2.6	5.3	18 50.3	+2.6	5.3	19 50.0	+2.8	5.3	20 49.8	+2.8	5.3	21 49.5	+2.9	5.4	85
86	14 53.6	+2.0	4.1	15 53.4	+2.1	4.2	16 53.3	+2.1	4.2	17 53.1	+2.2	4.2	18 52.9	+2.3	4.2	19 52.8	+2.3	4.3	20 52.6	+2.5	4.3	21 52.4	+2.6	4.3	86
87	14 55.6	+1.7	3.1	15 55.5	+1.8	3.1	16 55.4	+1.9	3.1	17 55.3	+1.9	3.2	18 55.2	+2.0	3.2	19 55.1	+2.0	3.2	20 55.1	+2.0	3.2	21 55.0	+2.1	3.2	87
88	14 57.3	+1.5	2.1	15 57.3	+1.5	2.1	16 57.3	+1.5	2.1	17 57.2	+1.6	2.1	18 57.2	+1.6	2.1	19 57.1	+1.7	2.1	20 57.1	+1.7	2.1	21 57.1	+1.6	2.2	88
89	14 58.8	+1.2	1.0	15 58.8	+1.2	1.0	16 58.8	+1.2	1.0	17 58.8	+1.2	1.1	18 58.8	+1.2	1.1	19 58.8	+1.2	1.1	20 58.8	+1.2	1.1	21 58.7	+1.3	1.1	89
90	15 00.0	+0.9	0.0	16 00.0	+0.9	0.0	17 00.0	+0.9	0.0	18 00.0	+0.9	0.0	19 00.0	+0.9	0.0	20 00.0	+0.9	0.0	21 00.0	+0.8	0.0	22 00.0	+0.8	0.0	90
	15°			16°			17°			18°			19°			20°			21°			22°			

S. Lat. { L.H.A. greater than 180° ....Zn=180°−Z
{ L.H.A. less than 180°...........Zn=180°+Z

LATITUDE **SAME** NAME AS DECLINATION **L.H.A. 91°, 269°**

181

LATITUDE **SAME** NAME AS DECLINATION N. Lat. { L.H.A. greater than 180° .....Zn=Z / L.H.A. less than 180°.............Zn=360°–Z

Dec.	15° Hc	d	Z	16° Hc	d	Z	17° Hc	d	Z	18° Hc	d	Z	19° Hc	d	Z	20° Hc	d	Z	21° Hc	d	Z	22° Hc	d	Z	Dec.
0	0 00.0	+15.5	90.0	0 00.0	+16.5	90.0	0 00.0	+17.5	90.0	0 00.0	+18.5	90.0	0 00.0	+19.5	90.0	0 00.0	+20.5	90.0	0 00.0	+21.5	90.0	0 00.0	+22.5	90.0	0
1	0 15.5	+15.6	89.0	0 16.5	+16.6	89.0	0 17.5	+17.6	89.0	0 18.5	+18.6	89.0	0 19.5	+19.6	89.1	0 20.5	+20.5	89.1	0 21.5	+21.5	89.1	0 22.5	+22.4	89.1	1
2	0 31.1	+15.5	88.1	0 33.1	+16.5	88.1	0 35.1	+17.5	88.1	0 37.1	+18.5	88.1	0 39.1	+19.5	88.1	0 41.0	+20.5	88.1	0 43.0	+21.5	88.1	0 44.9	+22.5	88.1	2
3	0 46.6	+15.5	87.1	0 49.6	+16.5	87.1	0 52.6	+17.5	87.1	0 55.6	+18.5	87.1	0 58.6	+19.5	87.2	1 01.5	+20.5	87.2	1 04.5	+21.4	87.2	1 07.4	+22.5	87.2	3
4	1 02.1	+15.5	86.1	1 06.1	+16.5	86.2	1 10.1	+17.5	86.2	1 14.1	+18.5	86.2	1 18.1	+19.5	86.2	1 22.0	+20.5	86.2	1 25.9	+21.5	86.3	1 29.8	+22.5	86.3	4
5	1 17.6	+15.4	85.2	1 22.6	+16.5	85.2	1 27.6	+17.5	85.2	1 32.6	+18.5	85.2	1 37.6	+19.4	85.3	1 42.5	+20.4	85.3	1 47.4	+21.4	85.3	1 52.3	+22.3	85.4	5
6	1 33.0	+15.5	84.2	1 39.1	+16.4	84.2	1 45.1	+17.4	84.3	1 51.1	+18.4	84.3	1 57.0	+19.4	84.3	2 02.9	+20.4	84.4	2 08.8	+21.4	84.4	2 14.6	+22.4	84.4	6
7	1 48.5	+15.3	83.2	1 55.5	+16.4	83.3	2 02.5	+17.4	83.3	2 09.5	+18.4	83.3	2 16.4	+19.4	83.4	2 23.3	+20.4	83.4	2 30.2	+21.3	83.5	2 37.0	+22.3	83.5	7
8	2 03.9	+15.3	82.3	2 11.9	+16.4	82.3	2 19.9	+17.4	82.3	2 27.9	+18.3	82.4	2 35.8	+19.4	82.4	2 43.7	+20.3	82.5	2 51.5	+21.3	82.5	2 59.3	+22.3	82.6	8
9	2 19.2	+15.4	81.3	2 28.3	+16.3	81.3	2 37.3	+17.3	81.4	2 46.2	+18.4	81.4	2 55.2	+19.3	81.5	3 04.0	+20.3	81.5	3 12.8	+21.3	81.6	3 21.6	+22.2	81.6	9
10	2 34.6	+15.2	80.3	2 44.6	+16.3	80.4	2 54.6	+17.3	80.4	3 04.6	+18.2	80.5	3 14.5	+19.2	80.5	3 24.3	+20.2	80.6	3 34.1	+21.2	80.7	3 43.8	+22.1	80.7	10
11	2 49.8	+15.3	79.4	3 00.9	+16.2	79.4	3 11.9	+17.2	79.5	3 22.8	+18.2	79.5	3 33.7	+19.2	79.6	3 44.5	+20.2	79.6	3 55.3	+21.1	79.7	4 05.9	+22.1	79.8	11
12	3 05.1	+15.2	78.4	3 17.1	+16.2	78.5	3 29.1	+17.2	78.5	3 41.0	+18.2	78.6	3 52.9	+19.1	78.6	4 04.7	+20.1	78.7	4 16.4	+21.0	78.8	4 28.0	+22.0	78.9	12
13	3 20.3	+15.1	77.4	3 33.3	+16.1	77.5	3 46.3	+17.1	77.5	3 59.2	+18.0	77.6	4 12.0	+19.0	77.7	4 24.8	+20.0	77.8	4 37.4	+21.0	77.8	4 50.0	+22.0	77.9	13
14	3 35.4	+15.1	76.5	3 49.4	+16.1	76.5	4 03.4	+17.0	76.6	4 17.2	+18.0	76.7	4 31.0	+19.0	76.7	4 44.8	+19.9	76.8	4 58.4	+20.9	76.9	5 12.0	+21.8	77.0	14
15	3 50.5	+15.0	75.5	4 05.5	+15.9	75.6	4 20.4	+16.9	75.6	4 35.2	+18.0	75.7	4 50.0	+18.9	75.8	5 04.7	+19.9	75.9	5 19.3	+20.8	76.0	5 33.8	+21.8	76.0	15
16	4 05.5	+14.8	74.5	4 21.4	+15.9	74.6	4 37.3	+16.9	74.7	4 53.2	+17.8	74.7	5 08.9	+18.8	74.8	5 24.6	+19.7	74.9	5 40.1	+20.8	75.0	5 55.6	+21.7	75.1	16
17	4 20.4	+14.8	73.5	4 37.3	+15.9	73.6	4 54.2	+16.8	73.7	5 11.0	+17.8	73.8	5 27.7	+18.7	73.9	5 44.3	+19.7	74.0	6 00.9	+20.6	74.1	6 17.3	+21.5	74.2	17
18	4 35.2	+14.8	72.6	4 53.2	+15.7	72.7	5 11.0	+16.7	72.7	5 28.8	+17.6	72.8	5 46.4	+18.7	72.9	6 04.0	+19.6	73.0	6 21.5	+20.5	73.1	6 38.8	+21.5	73.2	18
19	4 50.0	+14.7	71.6	5 08.9	+15.7	71.7	5 27.7	+16.6	71.8	5 46.4	+17.6	71.9	6 05.1	+18.5	72.0	6 23.6	+19.5	72.1	6 42.0	+20.4	72.2	7 00.3	+21.4	72.3	19
20	5 04.7	+14.6	70.6	5 24.6	+15.5	70.7	5 44.3	+16.6	70.8	6 04.0	+17.5	70.9	6 23.6	+18.4	71.0	6 43.1	+19.3	71.1	7 02.4	+20.3	71.2	7 21.7	+21.2	71.4	20
21	5 19.3	+14.5	69.7	5 40.1	+15.4	69.8	6 00.9	+16.4	69.8	6 21.5	+17.3	69.9	6 42.0	+18.3	70.1	7 02.4	+19.3	70.2	7 22.7	+20.2	70.3	7 42.9	+21.1	70.4	21
22	5 33.8	+14.4	68.7	5 55.5	+15.4	68.8	6 17.3	+16.3	68.9	6 38.8	+17.2	69.0	7 00.3	+18.2	69.1	7 21.7	+19.1	69.2	7 42.9	+20.1	69.3	8 04.0	+21.0	69.5	22
23	5 48.2	+14.4	67.7	6 11.0	+15.2	67.8	6 33.6	+16.2	67.9	6 56.1	+17.1	68.0	7 18.5	+18.1	68.1	7 40.8	+19.0	68.3	8 03.0	+19.9	68.4	8 25.0	+20.8	68.5	23
24	6 02.6	+14.2	66.7	6 26.2	+15.2	66.8	6 49.8	+16.1	66.9	7 13.2	+17.0	67.1	7 36.6	+17.9	67.2	7 59.8	+18.9	67.3	8 22.9	+19.8	67.4	8 45.8	+20.7	67.6	24
25	6 16.8	+14.1	65.8	6 41.4	+15.0	65.9	7 05.9	+15.9	66.0	7 30.2	+16.9	66.1	7 54.5	+17.8	66.2	8 18.7	+18.7	66.3	8 42.7	+19.6	66.5	9 06.5	+20.6	66.6	25
26	6 30.9	+14.0	64.8	6 56.4	+14.9	64.9	7 21.8	+15.9	65.0	7 47.1	+16.8	65.1	8 12.3	+17.7	65.2	8 37.4	+18.6	65.4	9 02.3	+19.5	65.5	9 27.1	+20.4	65.7	26
27	6 44.9	+13.8	63.8	7 11.3	+14.8	63.9	7 37.7	+15.7	64.0	8 03.9	+16.6	64.1	8 30.0	+17.5	64.3	8 56.0	+18.4	64.4	9 21.8	+19.3	64.6	9 47.5	+20.2	64.7	27
28	6 58.7	+13.8	62.8	7 26.1	+14.7	62.9	7 53.4	+15.5	63.0	8 20.5	+16.5	63.2	8 47.5	+17.4	63.3	9 14.4	+18.3	63.5	9 41.1	+19.2	63.6	10 07.7	+20.1	63.8	28
29	7 12.5	+13.6	61.8	7 40.8	+14.5	62.0	8 08.9	+15.5	62.1	8 37.0	+16.3	62.2	9 04.9	+17.2	62.3	9 32.7	+18.1	62.5	10 00.3	+19.0	62.7	10 27.8	+19.9	62.8	29
30	7 26.1	+13.5	60.9	7 55.3	+14.4	61.0	8 24.4	+15.2	61.1	8 53.3	+16.2	61.2	9 22.1	+17.1	61.4	9 50.8	+17.9	61.5	10 19.3	+18.9	61.7	10 47.7	+19.8	61.8	30
31	7 39.6	+13.4	59.9	8 09.7	+14.2	60.0	8 39.6	+15.2	60.1	9 09.5	+16.0	60.3	9 39.2	+16.9	60.4	10 08.7	+17.8	60.5	10 38.2	+18.6	60.7	11 07.5	+19.5	60.9	31
32	7 53.0	+13.2	58.9	8 23.9	+14.1	59.0	8 54.8	+15.0	59.1	9 25.5	+15.8	59.3	9 56.1	+16.7	59.4	10 26.5	+17.6	59.6	10 56.8	+18.5	59.7	11 27.0	+19.3	59.9	32
33	8 06.2	+13.1	57.9	8 38.0	+14.0	58.0	9 09.8	+14.8	58.2	9 41.3	+15.7	58.3	10 12.8	+16.6	58.4	10 44.1	+17.5	58.6	11 15.3	+18.3	58.8	11 46.3	+19.2	58.9	33
34	8 19.3	+12.9	56.9	8 52.0	+13.8	57.0	9 24.6	+14.6	57.2	9 57.0	+15.6	57.3	10 29.4	+16.3	57.5	11 01.6	+17.2	57.6	11 33.6	+18.1	57.8	12 05.5	+19.0	58.0	34
35	8 32.2	+12.8	55.9	9 05.8	+13.6	56.1	9 39.2	+14.5	56.2	10 12.6	+15.3	56.3	10 45.7	+16.2	56.5	11 18.8	+17.0	56.7	11 51.7	+17.9	56.8	12 24.5	+18.7	57.0	35
36	8 45.0	+12.7	54.9	9 19.4	+13.5	55.1	9 53.7	+14.3	55.2	10 27.9	+15.2	55.4	11 01.9	+16.0	55.5	11 35.8	+16.9	55.7	12 09.6	+17.7	55.9	12 43.2	+18.5	56.0	36
37	8 57.7	+12.4	53.9	9 32.9	+13.3	54.1	10 08.0	+14.2	54.2	10 43.1	+14.9	54.4	11 17.9	+15.9	54.5	11 52.7	+16.6	54.7	12 27.3	+17.5	54.9	13 01.7	+18.4	55.1	37
38	9 10.1	+12.3	53.0	9 46.2	+13.2	53.1	10 22.2	+14.0	53.2	10 58.0	+14.8	53.5	11 33.8	+15.6	53.5	12 09.3	+16.5	53.7	12 44.8	+17.2	53.9	13 20.1	+18.0	54.1	38
39	9 22.4	+12.2	52.0	9 59.4	+12.9	52.1	10 36.2	+13.7	52.2	11 12.8	+14.6	52.4	11 49.4	+15.4	52.6	12 25.8	+16.2	52.7	13 02.0	+17.1	52.9	13 38.1	+17.9	53.1	39
40	9 34.6	+12.0	51.0	10 12.3	+12.8	51.1	10 49.9	+13.6	51.3	11 27.4	+14.4	51.4	12 04.8	+15.2	51.6	12 42.0	+16.0	51.7	13 19.1	+16.8	51.9	13 56.0	+17.6	52.1	40
41	9 46.6	+11.8	50.0	10 25.1	+12.6	50.1	11 03.5	+13.4	50.3	11 41.8	+14.2	50.4	12 20.0	+15.0	50.6	12 58.0	+15.8	50.8	13 35.9	+16.6	50.9	14 13.6	+17.4	51.1	41
42	9 58.4	+11.6	49.0	10 37.7	+12.4	49.1	11 16.9	+13.2	49.3	11 56.0	+14.0	49.4	12 35.0	+14.7	49.6	13 13.8	+15.5	49.8	13 52.5	+16.3	49.9	14 31.0	+17.1	50.1	42
43	10 10.0	+11.5	48.0	10 50.1	+12.2	48.1	11 30.1	+13.0	48.3	12 10.0	+13.7	48.4	12 49.7	+14.6	48.6	13 29.3	+15.4	48.8	14 08.8	+16.1	49.0	14 48.1	+16.9	49.2	43
44	10 21.5	+11.2	47.0	11 02.3	+12.1	47.1	11 43.1	+12.8	47.3	12 23.7	+13.6	47.4	13 04.3	+14.3	47.6	13 44.7	+15.0	47.8	14 24.9	+15.8	48.0	15 05.0	+16.6	48.2	44
45	10 32.7	+11.1	46.0	11 14.4	+11.8	46.1	11 55.9	+12.5	46.3	12 37.3	+13.3	46.4	13 18.6	+14.0	46.6	13 59.7	+14.9	46.8	14 40.7	+15.6	47.0	15 21.6	+16.4	47.2	45
46	10 43.8	+10.9	45.0	11 26.2	+11.6	45.1	12 08.4	+12.4	45.3	12 50.6	+13.1	45.4	13 32.6	+13.9	45.6	14 14.6	+14.5	45.8	14 56.3	+15.4	46.0	15 38.0	+16.0	46.2	46
47	10 54.7	+10.7	44.0	11 37.8	+11.4	44.1	12 20.8	+12.1	44.3	13 03.7	+12.9	44.4	13 46.5	+13.6	44.6	14 29.1	+14.4	44.8	15 11.7	+15.0	45.0	15 54.0	+15.8	45.2	47
48	11 05.4	+10.5	43.0	11 49.2	+11.2	43.2	12 32.9	+12.0	43.3	13 16.6	+12.6	43.4	14 00.1	+13.3	43.6	14 43.5	+14.0	43.8	15 26.7	+14.8	44.0	16 09.8	+15.6	44.2	48
49	11 15.9	+10.2	42.0	12 00.4	+11.0	42.1	12 44.9	+11.6	42.3	13 29.2	+12.4	42.5	14 13.4	+13.1	42.6	14 57.5	+13.8	42.8	15 41.5	+14.5	43.0	16 25.4	+15.3	43.2	49
50	11 26.1	+10.1	41.0	12 11.4	+10.8	41.1	12 56.5	+11.5	41.3	13 41.6	+12.1	41.4	14 26.5	+12.9	41.6	15 11.3	+13.6	41.8	15 56.0	+14.3	41.9	16 40.6	+14.9	42.1	50
51	11 36.2	+9.9	40.0	12 22.2	+10.5	40.1	13 08.0	+11.2	40.3	13 53.7	+11.9	40.4	14 39.4	+12.5	40.6	15 24.9	+13.2	40.8	16 10.3	+13.9	40.9	16 55.5	+14.7	41.1	51
52	11 46.1	+9.6	39.0	12 32.7	+10.3	39.1	13 19.2	+11.0	39.2	14 05.6	+11.7	39.4	14 51.9	+12.3	39.6	15 38.1	+13.0	39.7	16 24.2	+13.7	39.9	17 10.2	+14.3	40.1	52
53	11 55.7	+9.5	38.0	12 43.0	+10.1	38.1	13 30.2	+10.7	38.2	14 17.3	+11.4	38.4	15 04.2	+12.1	38.6	15 51.1	+12.7	38.7	16 37.9	+13.3	38.9	17 24.5	+14.0	39.1	53
54	12 05.2	+9.2	36.9	12 53.1	+9.9	37.1	13 40.9	+10.5	37.2	14 28.7	+11.1	37.4	15 16.3	+11.7	37.5	16 03.8	+12.4	37.7	16 51.2	+13.1	37.9	17 38.5	+13.7	38.1	54
55	12 14.4	+9.0	35.9	13 03.0	+9.6	36.1	13 51.4	+10.2	36.2	14 39.8	+10.8	36.4	15 28.0	+11.5	36.5	16 16.2	+12.1	36.7	17 04.3	+12.7	36.9	17 52.2	+13.4	37.1	55
56	12 23.4	+8.8	34.9	13 12.6	+9.4	35.1	14 01.6	+10.0	35.2	14 50.6	+10.6	35.3	15 39.5	+11.2	35.5	16 28.3	+11.8	35.7	17 17.0	+12.4	35.8	18 05.6	+13.0	36.0	56
57	12 32.2	+8.5	33.9	13 22.0	+9.1	34.0	14 11.6	+9.8	34.1	15 01.2	+10.3	34.3	15 50.7	+10.9	34.5	16 40.1	+11.6	34.6	17 29.4	+12.2	34.8	18 18.6	+12.8	35.0	57
58	12 40.7	+8.4	32.9	13 31.1	+8.9	33.0	14 21.4	+9.4	33.2	15 11.5	+10.1	33.3	16 01.6	+10.7	33.5	16 51.7	+11.2	33.6	17 41.6	+11.8	33.8	18 31.4	+12.4	34.0	58
59	12 49.1	+8.1	31.9	13 40.0	+8.6	32.0	14 30.8	+9.2	32.1	15 21.6	+9.7	32.3	16 12.3	+10.3	32.4	17 02.9	+10.9	32.6	17 53.4	+11.4	32.8	18 43.8	+12.0	32.9	59
60	12 57.2	+7.8	30.9	13 48.6	+8.4	31.0	14 40.0	+9.0	31.1	15 31.3	+9.5	31.3	16 22.6	+10.0	31.4	17 13.8	+10.5	31.6	18 04.8	+11.2	31.7	18 55.8	+11.7	31.9	60
61	13 05.0	+7.6	29.8	13 57.0	+8.1	30.0	14 49.0	+8.6	30.1	15 40.8	+9.2	30.2	16 32.6	+9.8	30.4	17 24.3	+10.3	30.5	18 16.0	+10.8	30.7	19 07.5	+11.4	30.9	61
62	13 12.6	+7.4	28.8	14 05.1	+7.9	28.9	14 57.6	+8.4	29.2	15 50.0	+8.9	29.2	16 42.4	+9.4	29.3	17 34.6	+10.0	29.5	18 26.8	+10.5	29.7	19 18.9	+11.0	29.8	62
63	13 20.0	+7.1	27.8	14 13.0	+7.6	27.9	15 06.0	+8.1	28.0	15 58.9	+8.6	28.2	16 51.8	+9.1	28.3	17 44.6	+9.6	28.5	18 37.3	+10.1	28.6	19 29.9	+10.6	28.8	63
64	13 27.1	+6.9	26.8	14 20.6	+7.4	26.9	15 14.1	+7.8	27.0	16 07.5	+8.3	27.2	17 00.9	+8.8	27.3	17 54.2	+9.3	27.4	18 47.4	+9.8	27.6	19 40.5	+10.3	27.7	64
65	13 34.0	+6.6	25.8	14 28.0	+7.1	25.9	15 21.9	+7.6	26.1	16 15.8	+8.1	26.1	17 09.7	+8.5	26.3	18 03.5	+8.9	26.4	18 57.2	+9.4	26.5	19 50.8	+9.9	26.7	65
66	13 40.6	+6.4	24.7	14 35.1	+6.8	24.9	15 29.5	+7.2	25.0	16 23.9	+7.7	25.1	17 18.2	+8.1	25.2	18 12.4	+8.6	25.4	19 06.6	+9.1	25.5	20 00.7	+9.6	25.7	66
67	13 47.0	+6.1	23.7	14 41.9	+6.5	23.8	15 36.7	+7.0	24.0	16 31.6	+7.4	24.1	17 26.3	+7.9	24.2	18 21.0	+8.3	24.3	19 15.7	+8.7	24.5	20 10.3	+9.1	24.6	67
68	13 53.1	+5.9	22.7	14 48.4	+6.3	22.8	15 43.7	+6.7	22.9	16 39.0	+7.1	23.0	17 34.2	+7.5	23.1	18 29.3	+7.9	23.3	19 24.4	+8.4	23.4	20 19.4	+8.8	23.5	68
69	13 59.0	+5.6	21.7	14 54.7	+6.0	21.8	15 50.4	+6.4	21.9	16 46.1	+6.7	22.0	17 41.7	+7.2	22.1	18 37.2	+7.6	22.2	19 32.8	+8.0	22.4	20 28.2	+8.4	22.5	69
70	14 04.6	+5.3	20.6	15 00.7	+5.7	20.7	15 56.8	+6.1	20.9	16 52.8	+6.5	20.9	17 48.9	+6.8	21.1	18 44.8	+7.3	21.2	19 40.8	+7.6	21.3	20 36.6	+8.1	21.4	70
71	14 09.9	+5.1	19.6	15 06.4	+5.4	19.7	16 02.9	+5.8	19.8	16 59.3	+6.2	19.9	17 55.7	+6.5	20.0	18 52.1	+6.9	20.1	19 48.4	+7.2	20.2	20 44.7	+7.6	20.4	71
72	14 15.0	+4.8	18.6	15 11.8	+5.2	18.7	16 08.7	+5.5	18.8	17 05.5	+5.8	18.9	18 02.2	+6.2	19.0	18 59.0	+6.5	19.1	19 55.6	+6.9	19.2	20 52.3	+7.2	19.3	72
73	14 19.8	+4.6	17.6	15 17.0	+4.9	17.7	16 14.2	+5.2	17.7	17 11.3	+5.5	17.8	18 08.4	+5.8	17.9	19 05.5	+6.2	18.0	20 02.5	+6.5	18.1	20 59.5	+6.9	18.2	73
74	14 24.4	+4.3	16.5	15 21.9	+4.6	16.6	16 19.4	+4.9	16.7	17 16.8	+5.2	16.8	18 14.2	+5.5	16.9	19 11.7	+5.8	17.0	20 09.0	+6.1	17.1	21 06.4	+6.4	17.2	74
75	14 28.7	+4.0	15.5	15 26.5	+4.3	15.6	16 24.2	+4.6	15.7	17 22.0	+4.9	15.7	18 19.7	+5.2	15.8	19 17.5	+5.4	15.9	20 15.1	+5.8	16.0	21 12.8	+6.0	16.1	75
76	14 32.7	+3.7	14.5	15 30.8	+4.0	14.5	16 28.8	+4.3	14.6	17 26.9	+4.5	14.7	18 24.9	+4.8	14.8	19 22.9	+5.1	14.9	20 20.9	+5.3	15.0	21 18.8	+5.7	15.1	76
77	14 36.4	+3.5	13.4	15 34.8	+3.7	13.5	16 33.1	+4.0	13.6	17 31.4	+4.2	13.6	18 29.7	+4.5	13.7	19 28.0	+4.7	13.8	20 26.2	+5.0	13.9	21 24.5	+5.2	14.0	77
78	14 39.9	+3.2	12.4	15 38.5	+3.4	12.5	16 37.1	+3.6	12.5	17 35.6	+3.9	12.6	18 34.2	+4.1	12.7	19 32.7	+4.3	12.7	20 31.2	+4.6	12.8	21 29.7	+4.8	12.9	78
79	14 43.1	+2.9	11.4	15 41.9	+3.1	11.4	16 40.7	+3.3	11.5	17 39.5	+3.5	11.6	18 38.3	+3.7	11.6	19 37.0	+4.0	11.7	20 35.8	+4.2	11.8	21 34.5	+4.4	11.8	79
80	14 46.0	+2.7	10.3	15 45.0	+2.9	10.4	16 44.0	+3.1	10.4	17 43.0	+3.3	10.5	18 42.0	+3.4	10.6	19 41.0	+3.6	10.6	20 40.0	+3.8	10.7	21 38.9	+4.0	10.8	80
81	14 48.7	+2.3	9.3	15 47.9	+2.5	9.4	16 47.1	+2.7	9.4	17 46.3	+2.8	9.5	18 45.4	+3.1	9.5	19 44.6	+3.2	9.6	20 43.8	+3.4	9.6	21 42.9	+3.6	9.7	81
82	14 51.0	+2.1	8.3	15 50.4	+2.3	8.3	16 49.8	+2.4	8.4	17 49.1	+2.6	8.4	18 48.5	+2.7	8.5	19 47.8	+2.9	8.5	20 47.2	+3.0	8.6	21 46.5	+3.2	8.6	82
83	14 53.1	+1.9	7.2	15 52.7	+1.9	7.3	16 52.2	+2.0	7.3	17 51.7	+2.2	7.4	18 51.2	+2.3	7.4	19 50.7	+2.4	7.4	20 50.2	+2.6	7.5	21 49.7	+2.7	7.5	83
84	14 55.0	+1.5	6.2	15 54.6	+1.6	6.2	16 54.2	+1.8	6.3	17 53.9	+1.8	6.3	18 53.5	+2.0	6.3	19 53.1	+2.1	6.4	20 52.8	+2.2	6.4	21 52.4	+2.3	6.5	84
85	14 56.5	+1.3	5.2	15 56.2	+1.4	5.2	16 56.0	+1.4	5.2	17 55.8	+1.5	5.3	18 55.5	+1.6	5.3	19 55.2	+1.8	5.3	20 55.0	+1.8	5.4	21 54.7	+1.9	5.4	85
86	14 57.8	+0.9	4.1	15 57.6	+1.0	4.2	16 57.4	+1.2	4.2	17 57.3	+1.2	4.2	18 57.1	+1.3	4.2	19 57.0	+1.3	4.3	20 56.8	+1.4	4.3	21 56.6	+1.5	4.3	86
87	14 58.7	+0.7	3.1	15 58.6	+0.8	3.1	16 58.6	+0.8	3.1	17 58.5	+0.8	3.2	18 58.4	+0.9	3.2	19 58.3	+0.9	3.2	20 58.2	+1.0	3.2	21 58.1	+1.1	3.2	87
88	14 59.4	+0.3	2.1	15 59.4	+0.4	2.1	16 59.4	+0.4	2.1	17 59.3	+0.5	2.1	18 59.3	+0.5	2.1	19 59.2	+0.6	2.1	20 59.2	+0.6	2.1	21 59.2	+0.6	2.2	88
89	14 59.9	+0.1	1.0	15 59.8	+0.2	1.0	16 59.8	+0.2	1.0	17 59.8	+0.2	1.1	18 59.8	+0.2	1.1	19 59.8	+0.2	1.1	20 59.8	+0.2	1.1	21 59.8	+0.2	1.1	89
90	15 00.0	–0.1	0.0	16 00.0	–0.2	0.0	17 00.0	–0.2	0.0	18 00.0	–0.2	0.0	19 00.0	–0.2	0.0	20 00.0	–0.2	0.0	21 00.0	–0.2	0.0	22 00.0	–0.2	0.0	90

| | 15° | | | 16° | | | 17° | | | 18° | | | 19° | | | 20° | | | 21° | | | 22° | | | |

Dec.	15° Hc	d	Z	16° Hc	d	Z	17° Hc	d	Z	18° Hc	d	Z	19° Hc	d	Z	20° Hc	d	Z	21° Hc	d	Z	22° Hc	d	Z	Dec.
0	0 00.0	+15.5	90.0	0 00.0	+16.5	90.0	0 00.0	+17.5	90.0	0 00.0	+18.5	90.0	0 00.0	+19.5	90.0	0 00.0	+20.5	90.0	0 00.0	+21.5	90.0	0 00.0	+22.5	90.0	0
1	0 15.5	+15.6	89.0	0 16.5	+16.6	89.0	0 17.5	+17.6	89.0	0 18.5	+18.6	89.0	0 19.5	+19.6	89.1	0 20.5	+20.5	89.1	0 21.5	+21.5	89.1	0 22.5	+22.4	89.1	1
2	0 31.1	+15.5	88.1	0 33.1	+16.5	88.1	0 35.1	+17.5	88.1	0 37.1	+18.5	88.1	0 39.1	+19.5	88.1	0 41.0	+20.5	88.1	0 43.0	+21.5	88.1	0 44.9	+22.5	88.1	2
3	0 46.6	+15.5	87.1	0 49.6	+16.5	87.1	0 52.6	+17.5	87.1	0 55.6	+18.5	87.1	0 58.6	+19.5	87.2	1 01.5	+20.5	87.2	1 04.5	+21.4	87.2	1 07.4	+22.4	87.2	3
4	1 02.1	+15.5	86.1	1 06.1	+16.5	86.2	1 10.1	+17.5	86.2	1 14.1	+18.5	86.2	1 18.1	+19.5	86.2	1 22.0	+20.5	86.2	1 25.9	+21.5	86.3	1 29.8	+22.5	86.3	4
5	1 17.6	+15.4	85.2	1 22.6	+16.5	85.2	1 27.6	+17.5	85.2	1 32.6	+18.5	85.2	1 37.6	+19.4	85.3	1 42.5	+20.4	85.3	1 47.4	+21.5	85.3	1 52.3	+22.3	85.4	5
6	1 33.0	+15.5	84.2	1 39.1	+16.4	84.2	1 45.1	+17.4	84.3	1 51.1	+18.4	84.3	1 57.0	+19.4	84.3	2 02.9	+20.4	84.4	2 08.8	+21.4	84.4	2 14.6	+22.4	84.4	6
7	1 48.5	+15.4	83.2	1 55.5	+16.4	83.3	2 02.5	+17.4	83.3	2 09.5	+18.3	83.3	2 16.4	+19.4	83.4	2 23.3	+20.4	83.4	2 30.2	+21.3	83.5	2 37.0	+22.3	83.5	7
8	2 03.9	+15.3	82.3	2 11.9	+16.4	82.3	2 19.9	+17.4	82.3	2 27.9	+18.3	82.4	2 35.8	+19.4	82.4	2 43.7	+20.3	82.5	2 51.5	+21.3	82.5	2 59.3	+22.3	82.6	8
9	2 19.2	+15.4	81.3	2 28.3	+16.3	81.3	2 37.3	+17.3	81.4	2 46.2	+18.4	81.4	2 55.2	+19.3	81.5	3 04.0	+20.3	81.5	3 12.8	+21.3	81.6	3 21.6	+22.2	81.6	9
10	2 34.6	+15.2	80.3	2 44.6	+16.3	80.4	2 54.6	+17.3	80.4	3 04.6	+18.2	80.5	3 14.5	+19.2	80.5	3 24.3	+20.2	80.6	3 34.1	+21.2	80.7	3 43.8	+22.1	80.7	10
11	2 49.8	+15.3	79.4	3 00.9	+16.2	79.4	3 11.9	+17.2	79.5	3 22.8	+18.2	79.5	3 33.7	+19.2	79.6	3 44.5	+20.2	79.6	3 55.3	+21.1	79.7	4 05.9	+22.1	79.8	11
12	3 05.1	+15.2	78.4	3 17.1	+16.2	78.5	3 29.1	+17.2	78.5	3 41.0	+18.2	78.6	3 52.9	+19.1	78.6	4 04.7	+20.1	78.7	4 16.4	+21.1	78.8	4 28.0	+22.0	78.9	12
13	3 20.3	+15.1	77.4	3 33.3	+16.1	77.5	3 46.3	+17.1	77.5	3 59.2	+18.0	77.6	4 12.0	+19.0	77.7	4 24.8	+20.0	77.8	4 37.4	+21.0	77.8	4 50.0	+22.0	77.9	13
14	3 35.4	+15.1	76.5	3 49.4	+16.1	76.5	4 03.4	+17.0	76.6	4 17.2	+18.0	76.7	4 31.0	+19.0	76.7	4 44.8	+19.9	76.8	4 58.4	+20.9	76.9	5 12.0	+21.8	77.0	14
15	3 50.5	+15.0	75.5	4 05.5	+15.9	75.6	4 20.4	+16.9	75.6	4 35.2	+18.0	75.7	4 50.0	+18.9	75.8	5 04.7	+19.9	75.9	5 19.3	+20.8	76.0	5 33.8	+21.8	76.0	15
16	4 05.5	+14.9	74.5	4 21.4	+15.9	74.6	4 37.3	+16.9	74.7	4 53.2	+17.8	74.7	5 08.9	+18.8	74.8	5 24.6	+19.7	74.9	5 40.1	+20.8	75.0	5 55.6	+21.7	75.1	16
17	4 20.4	+14.8	73.5	4 37.3	+15.9	73.6	4 54.2	+16.8	73.7	5 11.0	+17.8	73.8	5 27.7	+18.7	73.9	5 44.3	+19.7	74.0	6 00.9	+20.6	74.1	6 17.3	+21.5	74.2	17
18	4 35.2	+14.8	72.6	4 53.2	+15.7	72.7	5 11.0	+16.7	72.7	5 28.8	+17.6	72.9	5 46.4	+18.7	72.9	6 04.0	+19.6	73.0	6 21.5	+20.5	73.1	6 38.8	+21.5	73.2	18
19	4 50.0	+14.7	71.6	5 08.9	+15.7	71.7	5 27.7	+16.6	71.8	5 46.4	+17.6	71.9	6 05.1	+18.5	72.0	6 23.6	+19.5	72.1	6 42.0	+20.4	72.2	7 00.3	+21.4	72.3	19
20	5 04.7	+14.6	70.6	5 24.6	+15.5	70.7	5 44.3	+16.6	70.8	6 04.0	+17.5	70.9	6 23.6	+18.5	71.0	6 43.1	+19.3	71.1	7 02.4	+20.4	71.2	7 21.7	+21.2	71.4	20
21	5 19.3	+14.5	69.7	5 40.1	+15.5	69.7	6 00.9	+16.4	69.8	6 21.5	+17.3	69.9	6 42.0	+18.3	70.1	7 02.4	+19.3	70.2	7 22.7	+20.2	70.3	7 42.9	+21.1	70.4	21
22	5 33.8	+14.5	68.7	5 55.6	+15.4	68.8	6 17.3	+16.3	68.9	6 38.8	+17.3	69.0	7 00.3	+18.2	69.1	7 21.7	+19.1	69.2	7 42.9	+20.1	69.3	8 04.0	+21.0	69.5	22
23	5 48.3	+14.3	67.7	6 11.0	+15.2	67.8	6 33.6	+16.2	67.9	6 56.1	+17.1	68.0	7 18.5	+18.1	68.1	7 40.8	+19.0	68.3	8 03.0	+19.9	68.4	8 25.0	+20.8	68.5	23
24	6 02.6	+14.2	66.7	6 26.2	+15.2	66.8	6 49.8	+16.1	66.9	7 13.2	+17.0	67.1	7 36.6	+17.9	67.2	7 59.8	+18.9	67.3	8 22.9	+19.8	67.4	8 45.8	+20.7	67.6	24
25	6 16.8	+14.1	65.8	6 41.4	+15.0	65.9	7 05.9	+15.9	66.0	7 30.2	+16.9	66.1	7 54.5	+17.8	66.2	8 18.7	+18.7	66.3	8 42.7	+19.6	66.5	9 06.5	+20.6	66.6	25
26	6 30.9	+14.0	64.9	6 56.4	+14.9	64.9	7 21.8	+15.9	65.0	7 47.1	+16.8	65.1	8 12.3	+17.7	65.2	8 37.4	+18.6	65.4	9 02.3	+19.5	65.5	9 27.1	+20.4	65.7	26
27	6 44.9	+13.8	63.8	7 11.3	+14.8	63.9	7 37.7	+15.7	64.0	8 03.9	+16.6	64.1	8 30.0	+17.5	64.3	8 56.0	+18.4	64.4	9 21.8	+19.3	64.6	9 47.5	+20.2	64.7	27
28	6 58.7	+13.8	62.8	7 26.1	+14.7	62.9	7 53.4	+15.5	63.0	8 20.5	+16.5	63.2	8 47.5	+17.4	63.3	9 14.4	+18.3	63.5	9 41.1	+19.2	63.6	10 07.7	+20.1	63.8	28
29	7 12.5	+13.6	61.9	7 40.8	+14.5	61.9	8 08.9	+15.5	62.1	8 37.0	+16.3	62.2	9 04.9	+17.2	62.3	9 32.7	+18.1	62.5	10 00.3	+19.0	62.6	10 27.8	+19.9	62.8	29
30	7 26.1	+13.5	60.9	7 55.3	+14.4	61.0	8 24.4	+15.2	61.1	8 53.3	+16.2	61.2	9 22.1	+17.1	61.4	9 50.8	+17.9	61.5	10 19.3	+18.9	61.7	10 47.7	+19.8	61.8	30
31	7 39.6	+13.4	59.9	8 09.7	+14.2	60.0	8 39.6	+15.2	60.1	9 09.5	+16.0	60.3	9 39.2	+16.9	60.4	10 08.7	+17.8	60.5	10 38.2	+18.6	60.7	11 07.5	+19.5	60.9	31
32	7 53.0	+13.2	58.9	8 23.9	+14.1	59.0	8 54.8	+15.0	59.1	9 25.5	+15.8	59.3	9 56.1	+16.7	59.4	10 26.5	+17.6	59.6	10 56.8	+18.5	59.7	11 27.0	+19.3	59.9	32
33	8 06.2	+13.1	57.9	8 38.0	+14.0	58.0	9 09.8	+14.8	58.2	9 41.3	+15.7	58.3	10 12.8	+16.6	58.4	10 44.1	+17.5	58.6	11 15.3	+18.3	58.8	11 46.3	+19.2	58.9	33
34	8 19.3	+12.9	56.9	8 52.0	+13.8	57.0	9 24.6	+14.6	57.2	9 57.0	+15.6	57.3	10 29.4	+16.3	57.5	11 01.6	+17.2	57.6	11 33.6	+18.1	57.8	12 05.5	+19.0	58.0	34
35	8 32.2	+12.8	55.9	9 05.8	+13.6	56.1	9 39.2	+14.5	56.2	10 12.6	+15.3	56.4	10 45.7	+16.2	56.5	11 18.8	+17.0	56.7	11 51.7	+17.9	56.8	12 24.5	+18.7	57.0	35
36	8 45.0	+12.7	54.9	9 19.4	+13.5	55.1	9 53.7	+14.3	55.2	10 27.9	+15.2	55.4	11 01.9	+16.0	55.5	11 35.8	+16.9	55.7	12 09.6	+17.7	55.9	12 43.2	+18.5	56.0	36
37	8 57.7	+12.4	53.9	9 32.9	+13.3	54.1	10 08.0	+14.2	54.2	10 43.1	+14.9	54.4	11 17.9	+15.9	54.5	11 52.7	+16.6	54.7	12 27.3	+17.5	54.9	13 01.7	+18.4	55.1	37
38	9 10.1	+12.3	53.0	9 46.2	+13.2	53.1	10 22.2	+14.0	53.2	10 58.0	+14.8	53.4	11 33.8	+15.6	53.5	12 09.3	+16.5	53.7	12 44.8	+17.2	53.9	13 20.1	+18.0	54.1	38
39	9 22.4	+12.2	52.0	9 59.4	+12.9	52.1	10 36.2	+13.7	52.2	11 12.8	+14.6	52.4	11 49.4	+15.4	52.6	12 25.8	+16.2	52.7	13 02.0	+17.1	52.9	13 38.1	+17.9	53.1	39
40	9 34.6	+12.0	51.0	10 12.3	+12.8	51.1	10 49.9	+13.6	51.3	11 27.4	+14.4	51.4	12 04.8	+15.2	51.6	12 42.0	+16.0	51.7	13 19.1	+16.8	51.9	13 56.0	+17.6	52.1	40
41	9 46.6	+11.8	50.0	10 25.1	+12.6	50.1	11 03.5	+13.4	50.3	11 41.8	+14.2	50.4	12 20.0	+15.0	50.6	12 58.0	+15.8	50.8	13 35.9	+16.6	50.9	14 13.6	+17.4	51.1	41
42	9 58.4	+11.6	49.0	10 37.7	+12.4	49.1	11 16.9	+13.2	49.3	11 56.0	+14.0	49.4	12 35.0	+14.7	49.6	13 13.8	+15.5	49.8	13 52.5	+16.3	49.9	14 31.0	+17.1	50.1	42
43	10 10.0	+11.5	48.0	10 50.1	+12.2	48.1	11 30.1	+13.0	48.3	12 10.0	+13.7	48.4	12 49.7	+14.6	48.6	13 29.3	+15.4	48.8	14 08.8	+16.1	49.0	14 48.1	+16.9	49.2	43
44	10 21.5	+11.2	47.0	11 02.3	+12.1	47.1	11 43.1	+12.8	47.3	12 23.7	+13.6	47.4	13 04.3	+14.3	47.6	13 44.7	+15.0	47.8	14 24.9	+15.8	48.0	15 05.0	+16.6	48.2	44
45	10 32.7	+11.1	46.0	11 14.4	+11.8	46.1	11 55.9	+12.5	46.3	12 37.3	+13.3	46.4	13 18.6	+14.0	46.6	13 59.7	+14.9	46.8	14 40.7	+15.6	47.0	15 21.6	+16.4	47.2	45
46	10 43.8	+10.9	45.0	11 26.2	+11.6	45.1	12 08.4	+12.4	45.3	12 50.6	+13.1	45.4	13 32.6	+13.9	45.6	14 14.6	+14.5	45.8	14 56.3	+15.4	46.0	15 38.0	+16.0	46.2	46
47	10 54.7	+10.7	44.0	11 37.8	+11.4	44.1	12 20.8	+12.1	44.3	13 03.7	+12.9	44.4	13 46.5	+13.6	44.6	14 29.1	+14.4	44.8	15 11.7	+15.0	45.0	15 54.0	+15.8	45.2	47
48	11 05.4	+10.5	43.0	11 49.2	+11.2	43.1	12 32.9	+12.0	43.3	13 16.6	+12.6	43.4	14 00.1	+13.3	43.6	14 43.5	+14.0	43.8	15 26.7	+14.8	44.0	16 09.8	+15.5	44.2	48
49	11 15.9	+10.3	42.0	12 00.4	+11.0	42.1	12 44.9	+11.6	42.3	13 29.2	+12.4	42.4	14 13.4	+13.1	42.6	14 57.5	+13.8	42.8	15 41.5	+14.5	43.0	16 25.4	+15.2	43.2	49
50	11 26.1	+10.1	41.0	12 11.4	+10.8	41.1	12 56.5	+11.5	41.3	13 41.6	+12.1	41.4	14 26.5	+12.9	41.6	15 11.3	+13.6	41.8	15 56.0	+14.3	41.9	16 40.6	+14.9	42.1	50
51	11 36.2	+9.9	40.0	12 22.2	+10.5	40.1	13 08.0	+11.2	40.3	13 53.7	+11.9	40.4	14 39.4	+12.5	40.6	15 24.9	+13.2	40.8	16 10.3	+13.9	40.9	16 55.5	+14.7	41.1	51
52	11 46.1	+9.6	39.0	12 32.7	+10.3	39.1	13 19.2	+10.9	39.2	14 05.6	+11.7	39.4	14 51.9	+12.3	39.6	15 38.1	+13.0	39.7	16 24.2	+13.7	39.9	17 10.2	+14.3	40.1	52
53	11 55.7	+9.5	38.0	12 43.0	+10.1	38.1	13 30.2	+10.7	38.2	14 17.3	+11.4	38.4	15 04.2	+12.1	38.6	15 51.1	+12.7	38.7	16 37.9	+13.3	38.9	17 24.5	+14.0	39.1	53
54	12 05.2	+9.2	36.9	12 53.1	+9.9	37.1	13 40.9	+10.5	37.2	14 28.7	+11.1	37.4	15 16.3	+11.7	37.5	16 03.8	+12.4	37.7	16 51.2	+13.1	37.9	17 38.5	+13.7	38.1	54
55	12 14.4	+8.9	35.9	13 03.0	+9.6	36.1	13 51.4	+10.2	36.2	14 39.8	+10.8	36.4	15 28.0	+11.5	36.5	16 16.2	+12.1	36.7	17 04.3	+12.7	36.9	17 52.2	+13.4	37.1	55
56	12 23.4	+8.8	34.9	13 12.6	+9.4	35.1	14 01.6	+10.0	35.2	14 50.6	+10.6	35.3	15 39.5	+11.2	35.5	16 28.3	+11.8	35.7	17 17.0	+12.4	35.8	18 05.6	+13.0	36.0	56
57	12 32.2	+8.5	33.9	13 22.0	+9.1	34.0	14 11.6	+9.8	34.1	15 01.2	+10.3	34.3	15 50.7	+10.9	34.5	16 40.1	+11.6	34.6	17 29.4	+12.2	34.8	18 18.6	+12.8	35.0	57
58	12 40.7	+8.4	32.9	13 31.1	+8.9	33.0	14 21.4	+9.4	33.2	15 11.5	+10.1	33.3	16 01.6	+10.7	33.5	16 51.7	+11.2	33.6	17 41.6	+11.8	33.8	18 31.4	+12.4	34.0	58
59	12 49.1	+8.1	31.9	13 40.0	+8.6	32.0	14 30.8	+9.2	32.1	15 21.6	+9.7	32.3	16 12.3	+10.3	32.4	17 02.9	+10.9	32.6	17 53.4	+11.4	32.8	18 43.8	+12.0	32.9	59
60	12 57.2	+7.8	30.9	13 48.6	+8.4	31.0	14 40.0	+9.0	31.1	15 31.3	+9.5	31.3	16 22.6	+10.0	31.4	17 13.8	+10.5	31.6	18 04.8	+11.2	31.7	18 55.8	+11.7	31.9	60
61	13 05.0	+7.6	29.8	13 57.0	+8.1	30.0	14 49.0	+8.6	30.1	15 40.8	+9.2	30.2	16 32.6	+9.8	30.4	17 24.3	+10.3	30.5	18 16.0	+10.8	30.7	19 07.5	+11.4	30.9	61
62	13 12.6	+7.4	28.8	14 05.1	+7.9	28.9	14 57.6	+8.4	29.1	15 50.0	+8.9	29.2	16 42.4	+9.4	29.4	17 34.6	+10.0	29.5	18 26.8	+10.5	29.7	19 18.9	+11.0	29.8	62
63	13 20.0	+7.1	27.8	14 13.0	+7.6	27.9	15 06.0	+8.1	28.0	15 58.9	+8.6	28.2	16 51.8	+9.1	28.3	17 44.6	+9.6	28.5	18 37.3	+10.1	28.6	19 29.9	+10.6	28.8	63
64	13 27.1	+6.9	26.8	14 20.6	+7.4	26.9	15 14.1	+7.8	27.0	16 07.5	+8.3	27.2	17 00.9	+8.8	27.3	17 54.2	+9.3	27.4	18 47.4	+9.8	27.6	19 40.5	+10.3	27.7	64
65	13 34.0	+6.6	25.8	14 28.0	+7.1	25.9	15 21.9	+7.6	26.0	16 15.8	+8.1	26.2	17 09.7	+8.5	26.3	18 03.5	+8.9	26.4	18 57.2	+9.4	26.5	19 50.8	+9.9	26.7	65
66	13 40.6	+6.4	24.7	14 35.1	+6.8	24.9	15 29.5	+7.2	25.0	16 23.9	+7.7	25.1	17 18.2	+8.1	25.2	18 12.4	+8.6	25.4	19 06.6	+9.1	25.5	20 00.7	+9.6	25.7	66
67	13 47.0	+6.1	23.7	14 41.9	+6.5	23.8	15 36.7	+7.0	23.9	16 31.6	+7.4	24.1	17 26.3	+7.9	24.2	18 21.0	+8.3	24.3	19 15.7	+8.7	24.5	20 10.3	+9.1	24.6	67
68	13 53.1	+5.9	22.7	14 48.4	+6.3	22.8	15 43.7	+6.7	22.9	16 39.0	+7.1	23.0	17 34.2	+7.5	23.1	18 29.3	+7.9	23.3	19 24.4	+8.4	23.4	20 19.4	+8.8	23.5	68
69	13 59.0	+5.6	21.7	14 54.7	+6.0	21.8	15 50.4	+6.4	21.9	16 46.1	+6.7	22.0	17 41.7	+7.2	22.1	18 37.2	+7.6	22.2	19 32.8	+8.0	22.4	20 28.2	+8.4	22.5	69
70	14 04.6	+5.3	20.7	15 00.7	+5.7	20.7	15 56.8	+6.1	20.8	16 52.8	+6.5	20.9	17 48.9	+6.8	21.1	18 44.8	+7.3	21.2	19 40.8	+7.6	21.3	20 36.6	+8.1	21.4	70
71	14 09.9	+5.1	19.6	15 06.4	+5.4	19.7	16 02.9	+5.8	19.8	16 59.3	+6.2	19.9	17 55.7	+6.5	20.0	18 52.1	+6.9	20.1	19 48.4	+7.2	20.2	20 44.7	+7.6	20.4	71
72	14 15.0	+4.8	18.6	15 11.8	+5.2	18.7	16 08.7	+5.5	18.8	17 05.5	+5.8	18.9	18 02.2	+6.2	19.0	18 59.0	+6.5	19.1	19 55.6	+6.9	19.2	20 52.3	+7.2	19.3	72
73	14 19.8	+4.6	17.6	15 17.0	+4.9	17.6	16 14.2	+5.2	17.7	17 11.3	+5.5	17.8	18 08.4	+5.8	17.9	19 05.5	+6.2	18.0	20 02.5	+6.5	18.1	20 59.5	+6.9	18.2	73
74	14 24.4	+4.3	16.5	15 21.9	+4.6	16.6	16 19.4	+4.8	16.7	17 16.8	+5.2	16.8	18 14.2	+5.5	16.9	19 11.7	+5.8	17.0	20 09.0	+6.1	17.1	21 06.4	+6.4	17.2	74
75	14 28.7	+4.0	15.5	15 26.5	+4.3	15.6	16 24.2	+4.6	15.7	17 22.0	+4.9	15.7	18 19.7	+5.2	15.8	19 17.5	+5.4	15.9	20 15.1	+5.8	16.0	21 12.8	+6.0	16.1	75
76	14 32.7	+3.7	14.5	15 30.8	+4.0	14.5	16 28.8	+4.3	14.6	17 26.9	+4.5	14.7	18 24.9	+4.8	14.8	19 22.9	+5.1	14.9	20 20.9	+5.3	15.0	21 18.8	+5.5	15.1	76
77	14 36.4	+3.5	13.4	15 34.8	+3.7	13.5	16 33.1	+4.0	13.6	17 31.4	+4.2	13.6	18 29.7	+4.5	13.7	19 28.0	+4.7	13.8	20 26.2	+5.0	13.9	21 24.5	+5.2	14.0	77
78	14 39.9	+3.2	12.4	15 38.5	+3.4	12.5	16 37.1	+3.6	12.5	17 35.6	+3.9	12.6	18 34.2	+4.1	12.7	19 32.7	+4.3	12.7	20 31.2	+4.6	12.8	21 29.7	+4.8	12.9	78
79	14 43.1	+2.9	11.4	15 41.9	+3.1	11.4	16 40.7	+3.3	11.5	17 39.5	+3.5	11.6	18 38.3	+3.7	11.6	19 37.0	+4.0	11.7	20 35.8	+4.2	11.8	21 34.5	+4.4	11.8	79
80	14 46.0	+2.7	10.3	15 45.0	+2.9	10.4	16 44.0	+3.1	10.4	17 43.0	+3.3	10.5	18 42.0	+3.4	10.6	19 41.0	+3.6	10.6	20 40.0	+3.8	10.7	21 38.9	+4.0	10.8	80
81	14 48.7	+2.3	9.3	15 47.9	+2.5	9.4	16 47.1	+2.7	9.4	17 46.3	+2.8	9.5	18 45.4	+3.1	9.5	19 44.6	+3.2	9.6	20 43.8	+3.4	9.6	21 42.9	+3.6	9.7	81
82	14 51.0	+2.1	8.3	15 50.4	+2.3	8.3	16 49.8	+2.4	8.4	17 49.1	+2.6	8.4	18 48.5	+2.7	8.5	19 47.8	+2.9	8.5	20 47.2	+3.0	8.6	21 46.5	+3.2	8.6	82
83	14 53.1	+1.9	7.2	15 52.7	+1.9	7.3	16 52.2	+2.0	7.3	17 51.7	+2.2	7.4	18 51.2	+2.3	7.4	19 50.7	+2.4	7.4	20 50.2	+2.6	7.5	21 49.7	+2.7	7.5	83
84	14 55.0	+1.5	6.2	15 54.6	+1.6	6.2	16 54.2	+1.8	6.3	17 53.9	+1.9	6.3	18 53.5	+2.0	6.3	19 53.1	+2.1	6.4	20 52.8	+2.2	6.4	21 52.4	+2.3	6.5	84
85	14 56.5	+1.3	5.2	15 56.2	+1.4	5.2	16 56.0	+1.4	5.2	17 55.8	+1.5	5.3	18 55.5	+1.6	5.3	19 55.2	+1.8	5.3	20 55.0	+1.8	5.4	21 54.7	+1.9	5.4	85
86	14 57.8	+0.9	4.1	15 57.6	+1.0	4.2	16 57.4	+1.2	4.2	17 57.3	+1.2	4.2	18 57.1	+1.3	4.2	19 57.0	+1.3	4.3	20 56.8	+1.4	4.3	21 56.6	+1.5	4.3	86
87	14 58.7	+0.7	3.1	15 58.6	+0.8	3.1	16 58.6	+0.8	3.1	17 58.5	+0.8	3.2	18 58.4	+0.9	3.2	19 58.3	+0.9	3.2	20 58.2	+1.0	3.2	21 58.1	+1.1	3.2	87
88	14 59.4	+0.5	2.1	15 59.4	+0.4	2.1	16 59.4	+0.4	2.1	17 59.3	+0.5	2.1	18 59.3	+0.5	2.1	19 59.2	+0.6	2.1	20 59.2	+0.6	2.1	21 59.2	+0.6	2.2	88
89	14 59.9	+0.1	1.0	15 59.8	+0.2	1.0	16 59.8	+0.2	1.0	17 59.8	+0.2	1.1	18 59.8	+0.2	1.1	19 59.8	+0.2	1.1	20 59.8	+0.2	1.1	21 59.8	+0.2	1.1	89
90	15 00.0	-0.1	0.0	16 00.0	-0.2	0.0	17 00.0	-0.2	0.0	18 00.0	-0.2	0.0	19 00.0	-0.2	0.0	20 00.0	-0.2	0.0	21 00.0	-0.2	0.0	22 00.0	-0.2	0.0	90
	15°			**16°**			**17°**			**18°**			**19°**			**20°**			**21°**			**22°**			

S. Lat. { L.H.A. greater than 180° ....Zn=180°−Z ; L.H.A. less than 180°............Zn=180°+Z }   **LATITUDE SAME NAME AS DECLINATION**   **L.H.A. 90°, 270°**

*No entries for contrary name appear on this page.

183

Dec.	23° Hc	d	Z	24° Hc	d	Z	25° Hc	d	Z	26° Hc	d	Z	27° Hc	d	Z	28° Hc	d	Z	29° Hc	d	Z	30° Hc	d	Z	Dec.
0	67 00.0	+60.0	180.0	66 00.0	+60.0	180.0	65 00.0	+60.0	180.0	64 00.0	+60.0	180.0	63 00.0	+60.0	180.0	62 00.0	+60.0	180.0	61 00.0	+60.0	180.0	60 00.0	+60.0	180.0	0
1	68 00.0	+60.0	180.0	67 00.0	+60.0	180.0	66 00.0	+60.0	180.0	65 00.0	+60.0	180.0	64 00.0	+60.0	180.0	63 00.0	+60.0	180.0	62 00.0	+60.0	180.0	61 00.0	+60.0	180.0	1
2	69 00.0	+60.0	180.0	68 00.0	+60.0	180.0	67 00.0	+60.0	180.0	66 00.0	+60.0	180.0	65 00.0	+60.0	180.0	64 00.0	+60.0	180.0	63 00.0	+60.0	180.0	62 00.0	+60.0	180.0	2
3	70 00.0	+60.0	180.0	69 00.0	+60.0	180.0	68 00.0	+60.0	180.0	67 00.0	+60.0	180.0	66 00.0	+60.0	180.0	65 00.0	+60.0	180.0	64 00.0	+60.0	180.0	63 00.0	+60.0	180.0	3
4	71 00.0	+60.0	180.0	70 00.0	+60.0	180.0	69 00.0	+60.0	180.0	68 00.0	+60.0	180.0	67 00.0	+60.0	180.0	66 00.0	+60.0	180.0	65 00.0	+60.0	180.0	64 00.0	+60.0	180.0	4
5	72 00.0	+60.0	180.0	71 00.0	+60.0	180.0	70 00.0	+60.0	180.0	69 00.0	+60.0	180.0	68 00.0	+60.0	180.0	67 00.0	+60.0	180.0	66 00.0	+60.0	180.0	65 00.0	+60.0	180.0	5
6	73 00.0	+60.0	180.0	72 00.0	+60.0	180.0	71 00.0	+60.0	180.0	70 00.0	+60.0	180.0	69 00.0	+60.0	180.0	68 00.0	+60.0	180.0	67 00.0	+60.0	180.0	66 00.0	+60.0	180.0	6
7	74 00.0	+60.0	180.0	73 00.0	+60.0	180.0	72 00.0	+60.0	180.0	71 00.0	+60.0	180.0	70 00.0	+60.0	180.0	69 00.0	+60.0	180.0	68 00.0	+60.0	180.0	67 00.0	+60.0	180.0	7
8	75 00.0	+60.0	180.0	74 00.0	+60.0	180.0	73 00.0	+60.0	180.0	72 00.0	+60.0	180.0	71 00.0	+60.0	180.0	70 00.0	+60.0	180.0	69 00.0	+60.0	180.0	68 00.0	+60.0	180.0	8
9	76 00.0	+60.0	180.0	75 00.0	+60.0	180.0	74 00.0	+60.0	180.0	73 00.0	+60.0	180.0	72 00.0	+60.0	180.0	71 00.0	+60.0	180.0	70 00.0	+60.0	180.0	69 00.0	+60.0	180.0	9
10	77 00.0	+60.0	180.0	76 00.0	+60.0	180.0	75 00.0	+60.0	180.0	74 00.0	+60.0	180.0	73 00.0	+60.0	180.0	72 00.0	+60.0	180.0	71 00.0	+60.0	180.0	70 00.0	+60.0	180.0	10
11	78 00.0	+60.0	180.0	77 00.0	+60.0	180.0	76 00.0	+60.0	180.0	75 00.0	+60.0	180.0	74 00.0	+60.0	180.0	73 00.0	+60.0	180.0	72 00.0	+60.0	180.0	71 00.0	+60.0	180.0	11
12	79 00.0	+60.0	180.0	78 00.0	+60.0	180.0	77 00.0	+60.0	180.0	76 00.0	+60.0	180.0	75 00.0	+60.0	180.0	74 00.0	+60.0	180.0	73 00.0	+60.0	180.0	72 00.0	+60.0	180.0	12
13	80 00.0	+60.0	180.0	79 00.0	+60.0	180.0	78 00.0	+60.0	180.0	77 00.0	+60.0	180.0	76 00.0	+60.0	180.0	75 00.0	+60.0	180.0	74 00.0	+60.0	180.0	73 00.0	+60.0	180.0	13
14	81 00.0	+60.0	180.0	80 00.0	+60.0	180.0	79 00.0	+60.0	180.0	78 00.0	+60.0	180.0	77 00.0	+60.0	180.0	76 00.0	+60.0	180.0	75 00.0	+60.0	180.0	74 00.0	+60.0	180.0	14
15	82 00.0	+60.0	180.0	81 00.0	+60.0	180.0	80 00.0	+60.0	180.0	79 00.0	+60.0	180.0	78 00.0	+60.0	180.0	77 00.0	+60.0	180.0	76 00.0	+60.0	180.0	75 00.0	+60.0	180.0	15
16	83 00.0	+60.0	180.0	82 00.0	+60.0	180.0	81 00.0	+60.0	180.0	80 00.0	+60.0	180.0	79 00.0	+60.0	180.0	78 00.0	+60.0	180.0	77 00.0	+60.0	180.0	76 00.0	+60.0	180.0	16
17	84 00.0	+60.0	180.0	83 00.0	+60.0	180.0	82 00.0	+60.0	180.0	81 00.0	+60.0	180.0	80 00.0	+60.0	180.0	79 00.0	+60.0	180.0	78 00.0	+60.0	180.0	77 00.0	+60.0	180.0	17
18	85 00.0	+60.0	180.0	84 00.0	+60.0	180.0	83 00.0	+60.0	180.0	82 00.0	+60.0	180.0	81 00.0	+60.0	180.0	80 00.0	+60.0	180.0	79 00.0	+60.0	180.0	78 00.0	+60.0	180.0	18
19	86 00.0	+60.0	180.0	85 00.0	+60.0	180.0	84 00.0	+60.0	180.0	83 00.0	+60.0	180.0	82 00.0	+60.0	180.0	81 00.0	+60.0	180.0	80 00.0	+60.0	180.0	79 00.0	+60.0	180.0	19
20	87 00.0	+60.0	180.0	86 00.0	+60.0	180.0	85 00.0	+60.0	180.0	84 00.0	+60.0	180.0	83 00.0	+60.0	180.0	82 00.0	+60.0	180.0	81 00.0	+60.0	180.0	80 00.0	+60.0	180.0	20
21	88 00.0	+60.0	180.0	87 00.0	+60.0	180.0	86 00.0	+60.0	180.0	85 00.0	+60.0	180.0	84 00.0	+60.0	180.0	83 00.0	+60.0	180.0	82 00.0	+60.0	180.0	81 00.0	+60.0	180.0	21
22	89 00.0	+60.0	180.0	88 00.0	+60.0	180.0	87 00.0	+60.0	180.0	86 00.0	+60.0	180.0	85 00.0	+60.0	180.0	84 00.0	+60.0	180.0	83 00.0	+60.0	180.0	82 00.0	+60.0	180.0	22
23	90 00.0	–60.0	90.0	89 00.0	+60.0	180.0	88 00.0	+60.0	180.0	87 00.0	+60.0	180.0	86 00.0	+60.0	180.0	85 00.0	+60.0	180.0	84 00.0	+60.0	180.0	83 00.0	+60.0	180.0	23
24	89 00.0	–60.0	0.0	90 00.0	–60.0	90.0	89 00.0	+60.0	180.0	88 00.0	+60.0	180.0	87 00.0	+60.0	180.0	86 00.0	+60.0	180.0	85 00.0	+60.0	180.0	84 00.0	+60.0	180.0	24
25	88 00.0	–60.0	0.0	89 00.0	–60.0	0.0	90 00.0	–60.0	90.0	89 00.0	+60.0	180.0	88 00.0	+60.0	180.0	87 00.0	+60.0	180.0	86 00.0	+60.0	180.0	85 00.0	+60.0	180.0	25
26	87 00.0	–60.0	0.0	88 00.0	–60.0	0.0	89 00.0	–60.0	0.0	90 00.0	–60.0	90.0	89 00.0	+60.0	180.0	88 00.0	+60.0	180.0	87 00.0	+60.0	180.0	86 00.0	+60.0	180.0	26
27	86 00.0	–60.0	0.0	87 00.0	–60.0	0.0	88 00.0	–60.0	0.0	89 00.0	–60.0	0.0	90 00.0	–60.0	90.0	89 00.0	+60.0	180.0	88 00.0	+60.0	180.0	87 00.0	+60.0	180.0	27
28	85 00.0	–60.0	0.0	86 00.0	–60.0	0.0	87 00.0	–60.0	0.0	88 00.0	–60.0	0.0	89 00.0	–60.0	0.0	90 00.0	–60.0	90.0	89 00.0	+60.0	180.0	88 00.0	+60.0	180.0	28
29	84 00.0	–60.0	0.0	85 00.0	–60.0	0.0	86 00.0	–60.0	0.0	87 00.0	–60.0	0.0	88 00.0	–60.0	0.0	89 00.0	–60.0	0.0	90 00.0	–60.0	90.0	89 00.0	+60.0	180.0	29
30	83 00.0	–60.0	0.0	84 00.0	–60.0	0.0	85 00.0	–60.0	0.0	86 00.0	–60.0	0.0	87 00.0	–60.0	0.0	88 00.0	–60.0	0.0	89 00.0	–60.0	0.0	90 00.0	–60.0	90.0	30
31	82 00.0	–60.0	0.0	83 00.0	–60.0	0.0	84 00.0	–60.0	0.0	85 00.0	–60.0	0.0	86 00.0	–60.0	0.0	87 00.0	–60.0	0.0	88 00.0	–60.0	0.0	89 00.0	–60.0	0.0	31
32	81 00.0	–60.0	0.0	82 00.0	–60.0	0.0	83 00.0	–60.0	0.0	84 00.0	–60.0	0.0	85 00.0	–60.0	0.0	86 00.0	–60.0	0.0	87 00.0	–60.0	0.0	88 00.0	–60.0	0.0	32
33	80 00.0	–60.0	0.0	81 00.0	–60.0	0.0	82 00.0	–60.0	0.0	83 00.0	–60.0	0.0	84 00.0	–60.0	0.0	85 00.0	–60.0	0.0	86 00.0	–60.0	0.0	87 00.0	–60.0	0.0	33
34	79 00.0	–60.0	0.0	80 00.0	–60.0	0.0	81 00.0	–60.0	0.0	82 00.0	–60.0	0.0	83 00.0	–60.0	0.0	84 00.0	–60.0	0.0	85 00.0	–60.0	0.0	86 00.0	–60.0	0.0	34
35	78 00.0	–60.0	0.0	79 00.0	–60.0	0.0	80 00.0	–60.0	0.0	81 00.0	–60.0	0.0	82 00.0	–60.0	0.0	83 00.0	–60.0	0.0	84 00.0	–60.0	0.0	85 00.0	–60.0	0.0	35
36	77 00.0	–60.0	0.0	78 00.0	–60.0	0.0	79 00.0	–60.0	0.0	80 00.0	–60.0	0.0	81 00.0	–60.0	0.0	82 00.0	–60.0	0.0	83 00.0	–60.0	0.0	84 00.0	–60.0	0.0	36
37	76 00.0	–60.0	0.0	77 00.0	–60.0	0.0	78 00.0	–60.0	0.0	79 00.0	–60.0	0.0	80 00.0	–60.0	0.0	81 00.0	–60.0	0.0	82 00.0	–60.0	0.0	83 00.0	–60.0	0.0	37
38	75 00.0	–60.0	0.0	76 00.0	–60.0	0.0	77 00.0	–60.0	0.0	78 00.0	–60.0	0.0	79 00.0	–60.0	0.0	80 00.0	–60.0	0.0	81 00.0	–60.0	0.0	82 00.0	–60.0	0.0	38
39	74 00.0	–60.0	0.0	75 00.0	–60.0	0.0	76 00.0	–60.0	0.0	77 00.0	–60.0	0.0	78 00.0	–60.0	0.0	79 00.0	–60.0	0.0	80 00.0	–60.0	0.0	81 00.0	–60.0	0.0	39
40	73 00.0	–60.0	0.0	74 00.0	–60.0	0.0	75 00.0	–60.0	0.0	76 00.0	–60.0	0.0	77 00.0	–60.0	0.0	78 00.0	–60.0	0.0	79 00.0	–60.0	0.0	80 00.0	–60.0	0.0	40
41	72 00.0	–60.0	0.0	73 00.0	–60.0	0.0	74 00.0	–60.0	0.0	75 00.0	–60.0	0.0	76 00.0	–60.0	0.0	77 00.0	–60.0	0.0	78 00.0	–60.0	0.0	79 00.0	–60.0	0.0	41
42	71 00.0	–60.0	0.0	72 00.0	–60.0	0.0	73 00.0	–60.0	0.0	74 00.0	–60.0	0.0	75 00.0	–60.0	0.0	76 00.0	–60.0	0.0	77 00.0	–60.0	0.0	78 00.0	–60.0	0.0	42
43	70 00.0	–60.0	0.0	71 00.0	–60.0	0.0	72 00.0	–60.0	0.0	73 00.0	–60.0	0.0	74 00.0	–60.0	0.0	75 00.0	–60.0	0.0	76 00.0	–60.0	0.0	77 00.0	–60.0	0.0	43
44	69 00.0	–60.0	0.0	70 00.0	–60.0	0.0	71 00.0	–60.0	0.0	72 00.0	–60.0	0.0	73 00.0	–60.0	0.0	74 00.0	–60.0	0.0	75 00.0	–60.0	0.0	76 00.0	–60.0	0.0	44
45	68 00.0	–60.0	0.0	69 00.0	–60.0	0.0	70 00.0	–60.0	0.0	71 00.0	–60.0	0.0	72 00.0	–60.0	0.0	73 00.0	–60.0	0.0	74 00.0	–60.0	0.0	75 00.0	–60.0	0.0	45
46	67 00.0	–60.0	0.0	68 00.0	–60.0	0.0	69 00.0	–60.0	0.0	70 00.0	–60.0	0.0	71 00.0	–60.0	0.0	72 00.0	–60.0	0.0	73 00.0	–60.0	0.0	74 00.0	–60.0	0.0	46
47	66 00.0	–60.0	0.0	67 00.0	–60.0	0.0	68 00.0	–60.0	0.0	69 00.0	–60.0	0.0	70 00.0	–60.0	0.0	71 00.0	–60.0	0.0	72 00.0	–60.0	0.0	73 00.0	–60.0	0.0	47
48	65 00.0	–60.0	0.0	66 00.0	–60.0	0.0	67 00.0	–60.0	0.0	68 00.0	–60.0	0.0	69 00.0	–60.0	0.0	70 00.0	–60.0	0.0	71 00.0	–60.0	0.0	72 00.0	–60.0	0.0	48
49	64 00.0	–60.0	0.0	65 00.0	–60.0	0.0	66 00.0	–60.0	0.0	67 00.0	–60.0	0.0	68 00.0	–60.0	0.0	69 00.0	–60.0	0.0	70 00.0	–60.0	0.0	71 00.0	–60.0	0.0	49
50	63 00.0	–60.0	0.0	64 00.0	–60.0	0.0	65 00.0	–60.0	0.0	66 00.0	–60.0	0.0	67 00.0	–60.0	0.0	68 00.0	–60.0	0.0	69 00.0	–60.0	0.0	70 00.0	–60.0	0.0	50
51	62 00.0	–60.0	0.0	63 00.0	–60.0	0.0	64 00.0	–60.0	0.0	65 00.0	–60.0	0.0	66 00.0	–60.0	0.0	67 00.0	–60.0	0.0	68 00.0	–60.0	0.0	69 00.0	–60.0	0.0	51
52	61 00.0	–60.0	0.0	62 00.0	–60.0	0.0	63 00.0	–60.0	0.0	64 00.0	–60.0	0.0	65 00.0	–60.0	0.0	66 00.0	–60.0	0.0	67 00.0	–60.0	0.0	68 00.0	–60.0	0.0	52
53	60 00.0	–60.0	0.0	61 00.0	–60.0	0.0	62 00.0	–60.0	0.0	63 00.0	–60.0	0.0	64 00.0	–60.0	0.0	65 00.0	–60.0	0.0	66 00.0	–60.0	0.0	67 00.0	–60.0	0.0	53
54	59 00.0	–60.0	0.0	60 00.0	–60.0	0.0	61 00.0	–60.0	0.0	62 00.0	–60.0	0.0	63 00.0	–60.0	0.0	64 00.0	–60.0	0.0	65 00.0	–60.0	0.0	66 00.0	–60.0	0.0	54
55	58 00.0	–60.0	0.0	59 00.0	–60.0	0.0	60 00.0	–60.0	0.0	61 00.0	–60.0	0.0	62 00.0	–60.0	0.0	63 00.0	–60.0	0.0	64 00.0	–60.0	0.0	65 00.0	–60.0	0.0	55
56	57 00.0	–60.0	0.0	58 00.0	–60.0	0.0	59 00.0	–60.0	0.0	60 00.0	–60.0	0.0	61 00.0	–60.0	0.0	62 00.0	–60.0	0.0	63 00.0	–60.0	0.0	64 00.0	–60.0	0.0	56
57	56 00.0	–60.0	0.0	57 00.0	–60.0	0.0	58 00.0	–60.0	0.0	59 00.0	–60.0	0.0	60 00.0	–60.0	0.0	61 00.0	–60.0	0.0	62 00.0	–60.0	0.0	63 00.0	–60.0	0.0	57
58	55 00.0	–60.0	0.0	56 00.0	–60.0	0.0	57 00.0	–60.0	0.0	58 00.0	–60.0	0.0	59 00.0	–60.0	0.0	60 00.0	–60.0	0.0	61 00.0	–60.0	0.0	62 00.0	–60.0	0.0	58
59	54 00.0	–60.0	0.0	55 00.0	–60.0	0.0	56 00.0	–60.0	0.0	57 00.0	–60.0	0.0	58 00.0	–60.0	0.0	59 00.0	–60.0	0.0	60 00.0	–60.0	0.0	61 00.0	–60.0	0.0	59
60	53 00.0	–60.0	0.0	54 00.0	–60.0	0.0	55 00.0	–60.0	0.0	56 00.0	–60.0	0.0	57 00.0	–60.0	0.0	58 00.0	–60.0	0.0	59 00.0	–60.0	0.0	60 00.0	–60.0	0.0	60
61	52 00.0	–60.0	0.0	53 00.0	–60.0	0.0	54 00.0	–60.0	0.0	55 00.0	–60.0	0.0	56 00.0	–60.0	0.0	57 00.0	–60.0	0.0	58 00.0	–60.0	0.0	59 00.0	–60.0	0.0	61
62	51 00.0	–60.0	0.0	52 00.0	–60.0	0.0	53 00.0	–60.0	0.0	54 00.0	–60.0	0.0	55 00.0	–60.0	0.0	56 00.0	–60.0	0.0	57 00.0	–60.0	0.0	58 00.0	–60.0	0.0	62
63	50 00.0	–60.0	0.0	51 00.0	–60.0	0.0	52 00.0	–60.0	0.0	53 00.0	–60.0	0.0	54 00.0	–60.0	0.0	55 00.0	–60.0	0.0	56 00.0	–60.0	0.0	57 00.0	–60.0	0.0	63
64	49 00.0	–60.0	0.0	50 00.0	–60.0	0.0	51 00.0	–60.0	0.0	52 00.0	–60.0	0.0	53 00.0	–60.0	0.0	54 00.0	–60.0	0.0	55 00.0	–60.0	0.0	56 00.0	–60.0	0.0	64
65	48 00.0	–60.0	0.0	49 00.0	–60.0	0.0	50 00.0	–60.0	0.0	51 00.0	–60.0	0.0	52 00.0	–60.0	0.0	53 00.0	–60.0	0.0	54 00.0	–60.0	0.0	55 00.0	–60.0	0.0	65
66	47 00.0	–60.0	0.0	48 00.0	–60.0	0.0	49 00.0	–60.0	0.0	50 00.0	–60.0	0.0	51 00.0	–60.0	0.0	52 00.0	–60.0	0.0	53 00.0	–60.0	0.0	54 00.0	–60.0	0.0	66
67	46 00.0	–60.0	0.0	47 00.0	–60.0	0.0	48 00.0	–60.0	0.0	49 00.0	–60.0	0.0	50 00.0	–60.0	0.0	51 00.0	–60.0	0.0	52 00.0	–60.0	0.0	53 00.0	–60.0	0.0	67
68	45 00.0	–60.0	0.0	46 00.0	–60.0	0.0	47 00.0	–60.0	0.0	48 00.0	–60.0	0.0	49 00.0	–60.0	0.0	50 00.0	–60.0	0.0	51 00.0	–60.0	0.0	52 00.0	–60.0	0.0	68
69	44 00.0	–60.0	0.0	45 00.0	–60.0	0.0	46 00.0	–60.0	0.0	47 00.0	–60.0	0.0	48 00.0	–60.0	0.0	49 00.0	–60.0	0.0	50 00.0	–60.0	0.0	51 00.0	–60.0	0.0	69
70	43 00.0	–60.0	0.0	44 00.0	–60.0	0.0	45 00.0	–60.0	0.0	46 00.0	–60.0	0.0	47 00.0	–60.0	0.0	48 00.0	–60.0	0.0	49 00.0	–60.0	0.0	50 00.0	–60.0	0.0	70
71	42 00.0	–60.0	0.0	43 00.0	–60.0	0.0	44 00.0	–60.0	0.0	45 00.0	–60.0	0.0	46 00.0	–60.0	0.0	47 00.0	–60.0	0.0	48 00.0	–60.0	0.0	49 00.0	–60.0	0.0	71
72	41 00.0	–60.0	0.0	42 00.0	–60.0	0.0	43 00.0	–60.0	0.0	44 00.0	–60.0	0.0	45 00.0	–60.0	0.0	46 00.0	–60.0	0.0	47 00.0	–60.0	0.0	48 00.0	–60.0	0.0	72
73	40 00.0	–60.0	0.0	41 00.0	–60.0	0.0	42 00.0	–60.0	0.0	43 00.0	–60.0	0.0	44 00.0	–60.0	0.0	45 00.0	–60.0	0.0	46 00.0	–60.0	0.0	47 00.0	–60.0	0.0	73
74	39 00.0	–60.0	0.0	40 00.0	–60.0	0.0	41 00.0	–60.0	0.0	42 00.0	–60.0	0.0	43 00.0	–60.0	0.0	44 00.0	–60.0	0.0	45 00.0	–60.0	0.0	46 00.0	–60.0	0.0	74
75	38 00.0	–60.0	0.0	39 00.0	–60.0	0.0	40 00.0	–60.0	0.0	41 00.0	–60.0	0.0	42 00.0	–60.0	0.0	43 00.0	–60.0	0.0	44 00.0	–60.0	0.0	45 00.0	–60.0	0.0	75
76	37 00.0	–60.0	0.0	38 00.0	–60.0	0.0	39 00.0	–60.0	0.0	40 00.0	–60.0	0.0	41 00.0	–60.0	0.0	42 00.0	–60.0	0.0	43 00.0	–60.0	0.0	44 00.0	–60.0	0.0	76
77	36 00.0	–60.0	0.0	37 00.0	–60.0	0.0	38 00.0	–60.0	0.0	39 00.0	–60.0	0.0	40 00.0	–60.0	0.0	41 00.0	–60.0	0.0	42 00.0	–60.0	0.0	43 00.0	–60.0	0.0	77
78	35 00.0	–60.0	0.0	36 00.0	–60.0	0.0	37 00.0	–60.0	0.0	38 00.0	–60.0	0.0	39 00.0	–60.0	0.0	40 00.0	–60.0	0.0	41 00.0	–60.0	0.0	42 00.0	–60.0	0.0	78
79	34 00.0	–60.0	0.0	35 00.0	–60.0	0.0	36 00.0	–60.0	0.0	37 00.0	–60.0	0.0	38 00.0	–60.0	0.0	39 00.0	–60.0	0.0	40 00.0	–60.0	0.0	41 00.0	–60.0	0.0	79
80	33 00.0	–60.0	0.0	34 00.0	–60.0	0.0	35 00.0	–60.0	0.0	36 00.0	–60.0	0.0	37 00.0	–60.0	0.0	38 00.0	–60.0	0.0	39 00.0	–60.0	0.0	40 00.0	–60.0	0.0	80
81	32 00.0	–60.0	0.0	33 00.0	–60.0	0.0	34 00.0	–60.0	0.0	35 00.0	–60.0	0.0	36 00.0	–60.0	0.0	37 00.0	–60.0	0.0	38 00.0	–60.0	0.0	39 00.0	–60.0	0.0	81
82	31 00.0	–60.0	0.0	32 00.0	–60.0	0.0	33 00.0	–60.0	0.0	34 00.0	–60.0	0.0	35 00.0	–60.0	0.0	36 00.0	–60.0	0.0	37 00.0	–60.0	0.0	38 00.0	–60.0	0.0	82
83	30 00.0	–60.0	0.0	31 00.0	–60.0	0.0	32 00.0	–60.0	0.0	33 00.0	–60.0	0.0	34 00.0	–60.0	0.0	35 00.0	–60.0	0.0	36 00.0	–60.0	0.0	37 00.0	–60.0	0.0	83
84	29 00.0	–60.0	0.0	30 00.0	–60.0	0.0	31 00.0	–60.0	0.0	32 00.0	–60.0	0.0	33 00.0	–60.0	0.0	34 00.0	–60.0	0.0	35 00.0	–60.0	0.0	36 00.0	–60.0	0.0	84
85	28 00.0	–60.0	0.0	29 00.0	–60.0	0.0	30 00.0	–60.0	0.0	31 00.0	–60.0	0.0	32 00.0	–60.0	0.0	33 00.0	–60.0	0.0	34 00.0	–60.0	0.0	35 00.0	–60.0	0.0	85
86	27 00.0	–60.0	0.0	28 00.0	–60.0	0.0	29 00.0	–60.0	0.0	30 00.0	–60.0	0.0	31 00.0	–60.0	0.0	32 00.0	–60.0	0.0	33 00.0	–60.0	0.0	34 00.0	–60.0	0.0	86
87	26 00.0	–60.0	0.0	27 00.0	–60.0	0.0	28 00.0	–60.0	0.0	29 00.0	–60.0	0.0	30 00.0	–60.0	0.0	31 00.0	–60.0	0.0	32 00.0	–60.0	0.0	33 00.0	–60.0	0.0	87
88	25 00.0	–60.0	0.0	26 00.0	–60.0	0.0	27 00.0	–60.0	0.0	28 00.0	–60.0	0.0	29 00.0	–60.0	0.0	30 00.0	–60.0	0.0	31 00.0	–60.0	0.0	32 00.0	–60.0	0.0	88
89	24 00.0	–60.0	0.0	25 00.0	–60.0	0.0	26 00.0	–60.0	0.0	27 00.0	–60.0	0.0	28 00.0	–60.0	0.0	29 00.0	–60.0	0.0	30 00.0	–60.0	0.0	31 00.0	–60.0	0.0	89
90	23 00.0	–60.0	0.0	24 00.0	–60.0	0.0	25 00.0	–60.0	0.0	26 00.0	–60.0	0.0	27 00.0	–60.0	0.0	28 00.0	–60.0	0.0	29 00.0	–60.0	0.0	30 00.0	–60.0	0.0	90

| | 23° | | | 24° | | | 25° | | | 26° | | | 27° | | | 28° | | | 29° | | | 30° | | | |

Dec.	23°			24°			25°			26°			27°			28°			29°			30°			Dec.
°	Hc ° ′	d ′	Z °	Hc ° ′	d ′	Z °	Hc ° ′	d ′	Z °	Hc ° ′	d ′	Z °	Hc ° ′	d ′	Z °	Hc ° ′	d ′	Z °	Hc ° ′	d ′	Z °	Hc ° ′	d ′	Z °	°
0	67 00.0	-60.0	180.0	66 00.0	-60.0	180.0	65 00.0	-60.0	180.0	64 00.0	-60.0	180.0	63 00.0	-60.0	180.0	62 00.0	-60.0	180.0	61 00.0	-60.0	180.0	60 00.0	-60.0	180.0	0
1	66 00.0	-60.0	180.0	65 00.0	-60.0	180.0	64 00.0	-60.0	180.0	63 00.0	-60.0	180.0	62 00.0	-60.0	180.0	61 00.0	-60.0	180.0	60 00.0	-60.0	180.0	59 00.0	-60.0	180.0	1
2	65 00.0	-60.0	180.0	64 00.0	-60.0	180.0	63 00.0	-60.0	180.0	62 00.0	-60.0	180.0	61 00.0	-60.0	180.0	60 00.0	-60.0	180.0	59 00.0	-60.0	180.0	58 00.0	-60.0	180.0	2
3	64 00.0	-60.0	180.0	63 00.0	-60.0	180.0	62 00.0	-60.0	180.0	61 00.0	-60.0	180.0	60 00.0	-60.0	180.0	59 00.0	-60.0	180.0	58 00.0	-60.0	180.0	57 00.0	-60.0	180.0	3
4	63 00.0	-60.0	180.0	62 00.0	-60.0	180.0	61 00.0	-60.0	180.0	60 00.0	-60.0	180.0	59 00.0	-60.0	180.0	58 00.0	-60.0	180.0	57 00.0	-60.0	180.0	56 00.0	-60.0	180.0	4
5	62 00.0	-60.0	180.0	61 00.0	-60.0	180.0	60 00.0	-60.0	180.0	59 00.0	-60.0	180.0	58 00.0	-60.0	180.0	57 00.0	-60.0	180.0	56 00.0	-60.0	180.0	55 00.0	-60.0	180.0	5
6	61 00.0	-60.0	180.0	60 00.0	-60.0	180.0	59 00.0	-60.0	180.0	58 00.0	-60.0	180.0	57 00.0	-60.0	180.0	56 00.0	-60.0	180.0	55 00.0	-60.0	180.0	54 00.0	-60.0	180.0	6
7	60 00.0	-60.0	180.0	59 00.0	-60.0	180.0	58 00.0	-60.0	180.0	57 00.0	-60.0	180.0	56 00.0	-60.0	180.0	55 00.0	-60.0	180.0	54 00.0	-60.0	180.0	53 00.0	-60.0	180.0	7
8	59 00.0	-60.0	180.0	58 00.0	-60.0	180.0	57 00.0	-60.0	180.0	56 00.0	-60.0	180.0	55 00.0	-60.0	180.0	54 00.0	-60.0	180.0	53 00.0	-60.0	180.0	52 00.0	-60.0	180.0	8
9	58 00.0	-60.0	180.0	57 00.0	-60.0	180.0	56 00.0	-60.0	180.0	55 00.0	-60.0	180.0	54 00.0	-60.0	180.0	53 00.0	-60.0	180.0	52 00.0	-60.0	180.0	51 00.0	-60.0	180.0	9
10	57 00.0	-60.0	180.0	56 00.0	-60.0	180.0	55 00.0	-60.0	180.0	54 00.0	-60.0	180.0	53 00.0	-60.0	180.0	52 00.0	-60.0	180.0	51 00.0	-60.0	180.0	50 00.0	-60.0	180.0	10
11	56 00.0	-60.0	180.0	55 00.0	-60.0	180.0	54 00.0	-60.0	180.0	53 00.0	-60.0	180.0	52 00.0	-60.0	180.0	51 00.0	-60.0	180.0	50 00.0	-60.0	180.0	49 00.0	-60.0	180.0	11
12	55 00.0	-60.0	180.0	54 00.0	-60.0	180.0	53 00.0	-60.0	180.0	52 00.0	-60.0	180.0	51 00.0	-60.0	180.0	50 00.0	-60.0	180.0	49 00.0	-60.0	180.0	48 00.0	-60.0	180.0	12
13	54 00.0	-60.0	180.0	53 00.0	-60.0	180.0	52 00.0	-60.0	180.0	51 00.0	-60.0	180.0	50 00.0	-60.0	180.0	49 00.0	-60.0	180.0	48 00.0	-60.0	180.0	47 00.0	-60.0	180.0	13
14	53 00.0	-60.0	180.0	52 00.0	-60.0	180.0	51 00.0	-60.0	180.0	50 00.0	-60.0	180.0	49 00.0	-60.0	180.0	48 00.0	-60.0	180.0	47 00.0	-60.0	180.0	46 00.0	-60.0	180.0	14
15	52 00.0	-60.0	180.0	51 00.0	-60.0	180.0	50 00.0	-60.0	180.0	49 00.0	-60.0	180.0	48 00.0	-60.0	180.0	47 00.0	-60.0	180.0	46 00.0	-60.0	180.0	45 00.0	-60.0	180.0	15
16	51 00.0	-60.0	180.0	50 00.0	-60.0	180.0	49 00.0	-60.0	180.0	48 00.0	-60.0	180.0	47 00.0	-60.0	180.0	46 00.0	-60.0	180.0	45 00.0	-60.0	180.0	44 00.0	-60.0	180.0	16
17	50 00.0	-60.0	180.0	49 00.0	-60.0	180.0	48 00.0	-60.0	180.0	47 00.0	-60.0	180.0	46 00.0	-60.0	180.0	45 00.0	-60.0	180.0	44 00.0	-60.0	180.0	43 00.0	-60.0	180.0	17
18	49 00.0	-60.0	180.0	48 00.0	-60.0	180.0	47 00.0	-60.0	180.0	46 00.0	-60.0	180.0	45 00.0	-60.0	180.0	44 00.0	-60.0	180.0	43 00.0	-60.0	180.0	42 00.0	-60.0	180.0	18
19	48 00.0	-60.0	180.0	47 00.0	-60.0	180.0	46 00.0	-60.0	180.0	45 00.0	-60.0	180.0	44 00.0	-60.0	180.0	43 00.0	-60.0	180.0	42 00.0	-60.0	180.0	41 00.0	-60.0	180.0	19
20	47 00.0	-60.0	180.0	46 00.0	-60.0	180.0	45 00.0	-60.0	180.0	44 00.0	-60.0	180.0	43 00.0	-60.0	180.0	42 00.0	-60.0	180.0	41 00.0	-60.0	180.0	40 00.0	-60.0	180.0	20
21	46 00.0	-60.0	180.0	45 00.0	-60.0	180.0	44 00.0	-60.0	180.0	43 00.0	-60.0	180.0	42 00.0	-60.0	180.0	41 00.0	-60.0	180.0	40 00.0	-60.0	180.0	39 00.0	-60.0	180.0	21
22	45 00.0	-60.0	180.0	44 00.0	-60.0	180.0	43 00.0	-60.0	180.0	42 00.0	-60.0	180.0	41 00.0	-60.0	180.0	40 00.0	-60.0	180.0	39 00.0	-60.0	180.0	38 00.0	-60.0	180.0	22
23	44 00.0	-60.0	180.0	43 00.0	-60.0	180.0	42 00.0	-60.0	180.0	41 00.0	-60.0	180.0	40 00.0	-60.0	180.0	39 00.0	-60.0	180.0	38 00.0	-60.0	180.0	37 00.0	-60.0	180.0	23
24	43 00.0	-60.0	180.0	42 00.0	-60.0	180.0	41 00.0	-60.0	180.0	40 00.0	-60.0	180.0	39 00.0	-60.0	180.0	38 00.0	-60.0	180.0	37 00.0	-60.0	180.0	36 00.0	-60.0	180.0	24
25	42 00.0	-60.0	180.0	41 00.0	-60.0	180.0	40 00.0	-60.0	180.0	39 00.0	-60.0	180.0	38 00.0	-60.0	180.0	37 00.0	-60.0	180.0	36 00.0	-60.0	180.0	35 00.0	-60.0	180.0	25
26	41 00.0	-60.0	180.0	40 00.0	-60.0	180.0	39 00.0	-60.0	180.0	38 00.0	-60.0	180.0	37 00.0	-60.0	180.0	36 00.0	-60.0	180.0	35 00.0	-60.0	180.0	34 00.0	-60.0	180.0	26
27	40 00.0	-60.0	180.0	39 00.0	-60.0	180.0	38 00.0	-60.0	180.0	37 00.0	-60.0	180.0	36 00.0	-60.0	180.0	35 00.0	-60.0	180.0	34 00.0	-60.0	180.0	33 00.0	-60.0	180.0	27
28	39 00.0	-60.0	180.0	38 00.0	-60.0	180.0	37 00.0	-60.0	180.0	36 00.0	-60.0	180.0	35 00.0	-60.0	180.0	34 00.0	-60.0	180.0	33 00.0	-60.0	180.0	32 00.0	-60.0	180.0	28
29	38 00.0	-60.0	180.0	37 00.0	-60.0	180.0	36 00.0	-60.0	180.0	35 00.0	-60.0	180.0	34 00.0	-60.0	180.0	33 00.0	-60.0	180.0	32 00.0	-60.0	180.0	31 00.0	-60.0	180.0	29
30	37 00.0	-60.0	180.0	36 00.0	-60.0	180.0	35 00.0	-60.0	180.0	34 00.0	-60.0	180.0	33 00.0	-60.0	180.0	32 00.0	-60.0	180.0	31 00.0	-60.0	180.0	30 00.0	-60.0	180.0	30
31	36 00.0	-60.0	180.0	35 00.0	-60.0	180.0	34 00.0	-60.0	180.0	33 00.0	-60.0	180.0	32 00.0	-60.0	180.0	31 00.0	-60.0	180.0	30 00.0	-60.0	180.0	29 00.0	-60.0	180.0	31
32	35 00.0	-60.0	180.0	34 00.0	-60.0	180.0	33 00.0	-60.0	180.0	32 00.0	-60.0	180.0	31 00.0	-60.0	180.0	30 00.0	-60.0	180.0	29 00.0	-60.0	180.0	28 00.0	-60.0	180.0	32
33	34 00.0	-60.0	180.0	33 00.0	-60.0	180.0	32 00.0	-60.0	180.0	31 00.0	-60.0	180.0	30 00.0	-60.0	180.0	29 00.0	-60.0	180.0	28 00.0	-60.0	180.0	27 00.0	-60.0	180.0	33
34	33 00.0	-60.0	180.0	32 00.0	-60.0	180.0	31 00.0	-60.0	180.0	30 00.0	-60.0	180.0	29 00.0	-60.0	180.0	28 00.0	-60.0	180.0	27 00.0	-60.0	180.0	26 00.0	-60.0	180.0	34
35	32 00.0	-60.0	180.0	31 00.0	-60.0	180.0	30 00.0	-60.0	180.0	29 00.0	-60.0	180.0	28 00.0	-60.0	180.0	27 00.0	-60.0	180.0	26 00.0	-60.0	180.0	25 00.0	-60.0	180.0	35
36	31 00.0	-60.0	180.0	30 00.0	-60.0	180.0	29 00.0	-60.0	180.0	28 00.0	-60.0	180.0	27 00.0	-60.0	180.0	26 00.0	-60.0	180.0	25 00.0	-60.0	180.0	24 00.0	-60.0	180.0	36
37	30 00.0	-60.0	180.0	29 00.0	-60.0	180.0	28 00.0	-60.0	180.0	27 00.0	-60.0	180.0	26 00.0	-60.0	180.0	25 00.0	-60.0	180.0	24 00.0	-60.0	180.0	23 00.0	-60.0	180.0	37
38	29 00.0	-60.0	180.0	28 00.0	-60.0	180.0	27 00.0	-60.0	180.0	26 00.0	-60.0	180.0	25 00.0	-60.0	180.0	24 00.0	-60.0	180.0	23 00.0	-60.0	180.0	22 00.0	-60.0	180.0	38
39	28 00.0	-60.0	180.0	27 00.0	-60.0	180.0	26 00.0	-60.0	180.0	25 00.0	-60.0	180.0	24 00.0	-60.0	180.0	23 00.0	-60.0	180.0	22 00.0	-60.0	180.0	21 00.0	-60.0	180.0	39
40	27 00.0	-60.0	180.0	26 00.0	-60.0	180.0	25 00.0	-60.0	180.0	24 00.0	-60.0	180.0	23 00.0	-60.0	180.0	22 00.0	-60.0	180.0	21 00.0	-60.0	180.0	20 00.0	-60.0	180.0	40
41	26 00.0	-60.0	180.0	25 00.0	-60.0	180.0	24 00.0	-60.0	180.0	23 00.0	-60.0	180.0	22 00.0	-60.0	180.0	21 00.0	-60.0	180.0	20 00.0	-60.0	180.0	19 00.0	-60.0	180.0	41
42	25 00.0	-60.0	180.0	24 00.0	-60.0	180.0	23 00.0	-60.0	180.0	22 00.0	-60.0	180.0	21 00.0	-60.0	180.0	20 00.0	-60.0	180.0	19 00.0	-60.0	180.0	18 00.0	-60.0	180.0	42
43	24 00.0	-60.0	180.0	23 00.0	-60.0	180.0	22 00.0	-60.0	180.0	21 00.0	-60.0	180.0	20 00.0	-60.0	180.0	19 00.0	-60.0	180.0	18 00.0	-60.0	180.0	17 00.0	-60.0	180.0	43
44	23 00.0	-60.0	180.0	22 00.0	-60.0	180.0	21 00.0	-60.0	180.0	20 00.0	-60.0	180.0	19 00.0	-60.0	180.0	18 00.0	-60.0	180.0	17 00.0	-60.0	180.0	16 00.0	-60.0	180.0	44
45	22 00.0	-60.0	180.0	21 00.0	-60.0	180.0	20 00.0	-60.0	180.0	19 00.0	-60.0	180.0	18 00.0	-60.0	180.0	17 00.0	-60.0	180.0	16 00.0	-60.0	180.0	15 00.0	-60.0	180.0	45
46	21 00.0	-60.0	180.0	20 00.0	-60.0	180.0	19 00.0	-60.0	180.0	18 00.0	-60.0	180.0	17 00.0	-60.0	180.0	16 00.0	-60.0	180.0	15 00.0	-60.0	180.0	14 00.0	-60.0	180.0	46
47	20 00.0	-60.0	180.0	19 00.0	-60.0	180.0	18 00.0	-60.0	180.0	17 00.0	-60.0	180.0	16 00.0	-60.0	180.0	15 00.0	-60.0	180.0	14 00.0	-60.0	180.0	13 00.0	-60.0	180.0	47
48	19 00.0	-60.0	180.0	18 00.0	-60.0	180.0	17 00.0	-60.0	180.0	16 00.0	-60.0	180.0	15 00.0	-60.0	180.0	14 00.0	-60.0	180.0	13 00.0	-60.0	180.0	12 00.0	-60.0	180.0	48
49	18 00.0	-60.0	180.0	17 00.0	-60.0	180.0	16 00.0	-60.0	180.0	15 00.0	-60.0	180.0	14 00.0	-60.0	180.0	13 00.0	-60.0	180.0	12 00.0	-60.0	180.0	11 00.0	-60.0	180.0	49
50	17 00.0	-60.0	180.0	16 00.0	-60.0	180.0	15 00.0	-60.0	180.0	14 00.0	-60.0	180.0	13 00.0	-60.0	180.0	12 00.0	-60.0	180.0	11 00.0	-60.0	180.0	10 00.0	-60.0	180.0	50
51	16 00.0	-60.0	180.0	15 00.0	-60.0	180.0	14 00.0	-60.0	180.0	13 00.0	-60.0	180.0	12 00.0	-60.0	180.0	11 00.0	-60.0	180.0	10 00.0	-60.0	180.0	9 00.0	-60.0	180.0	51
52	15 00.0	-60.0	180.0	14 00.0	-60.0	180.0	13 00.0	-60.0	180.0	12 00.0	-60.0	180.0	11 00.0	-60.0	180.0	10 00.0	-60.0	180.0	9 00.0	-60.0	180.0	8 00.0	-60.0	180.0	52
53	14 00.0	-60.0	180.0	13 00.0	-60.0	180.0	12 00.0	-60.0	180.0	11 00.0	-60.0	180.0	10 00.0	-60.0	180.0	9 00.0	-60.0	180.0	8 00.0	-60.0	180.0	7 00.0	-60.0	180.0	53
54	13 00.0	-60.0	180.0	12 00.0	-60.0	180.0	11 00.0	-60.0	180.0	10 00.0	-60.0	180.0	9 00.0	-60.0	180.0	8 00.0	-60.0	180.0	7 00.0	-60.0	180.0	6 00.0	-60.0	180.0	54
55	12 00.0	-60.0	180.0	11 00.0	-60.0	180.0	10 00.0	-60.0	180.0	9 00.0	-60.0	180.0	8 00.0	-60.0	180.0	7 00.0	-60.0	180.0	6 00.0	-60.0	180.0	5 00.0	-60.0	180.0	55
56	11 00.0	-60.0	180.0	10 00.0	-60.0	180.0	9 00.0	-60.0	180.0	8 00.0	-60.0	180.0	7 00.0	-60.0	180.0	6 00.0	-60.0	180.0	5 00.0	-60.0	180.0	4 00.0	-60.0	180.0	56
57	10 00.0	-60.0	180.0	9 00.0	-60.0	180.0	8 00.0	-60.0	180.0	7 00.0	-60.0	180.0	6 00.0	-60.0	180.0	5 00.0	-60.0	180.0	4 00.0	-60.0	180.0	3 00.0	-60.0	180.0	57
58	9 00.0	-60.0	180.0	8 00.0	-60.0	180.0	7 00.0	-60.0	180.0	6 00.0	-60.0	180.0	5 00.0	-60.0	180.0	4 00.0	-60.0	180.0	3 00.0	-60.0	180.0	2 00.0	-60.0	180.0	58
59	8 00.0	-60.0	180.0	7 00.0	-60.0	180.0	6 00.0	-60.0	180.0	5 00.0	-60.0	180.0	4 00.0	-60.0	180.0	3 00.0	-60.0	180.0	2 00.0	-60.0	180.0	1 00.0	-60.0	180.0	59
60	7 00.0	-60.0	180.0	6 00.0	-60.0	180.0	5 00.0	-60.0	180.0	4 00.0	-60.0	180.0	3 00.0	-60.0	180.0	2 00.0	-60.0	180.0	1 00.0	-60.0	180.0	0 00.0	+60.0	0.0	60
61	6 00.0	-60.0	180.0	5 00.0	-60.0	180.0	4 00.0	-60.0	180.0	3 00.0	-60.0	180.0	2 00.0	-60.0	180.0	1 00.0	-60.0	180.0	0 00.0	+60.0	0.0	1 00.0	+60.0	0.0	61
62	5 00.0	-60.0	180.0	4 00.0	-60.0	180.0	3 00.0	-60.0	180.0	2 00.0	-60.0	180.0	1 00.0	-60.0	180.0	0 00.0	+60.0	0.0	1 00.0	+60.0	0.0	2 00.0	+60.0	0.0	62
63	4 00.0	-60.0	180.0	3 00.0	-60.0	180.0	2 00.0	-60.0	180.0	1 00.0	-60.0	180.0	0 00.0	+60.0	0.0	1 00.0	+60.0	0.0	2 00.0	+60.0	0.0	3 00.0	+60.0	0.0	63
64	3 00.0	-60.0	180.0	2 00.0	-60.0	180.0	1 00.0	-60.0	180.0	0 00.0	+60.0	0.0	1 00.0	+60.0	0.0	2 00.0	+60.0	0.0	3 00.0	+60.0	0.0	4 00.0	+60.0	0.0	64
65	2 00.0	-60.0	180.0	1 00.0	-60.0	180.0	0 00.0	+60.0	0.0	1 00.0	+60.0	0.0	2 00.0	+60.0	0.0	3 00.0	+60.0	0.0	4 00.0	+60.0	0.0	5 00.0	+60.0	0.0	65
66	1 00.0	-60.0	180.0	0 00.0	+60.0	0.0	1 00.0	+60.0	0.0	2 00.0	+60.0	0.0	3 00.0	+60.0	0.0	4 00.0	+60.0	0.0	5 00.0	+60.0	0.0	6 00.0	+60.0	0.0	66
67	0 00.0	+60.0	0.0	1 00.0	+60.0	0.0	2 00.0	+60.0	0.0	3 00.0	+60.0	0.0	4 00.0	+60.0	0.0	5 00.0	+60.0	0.0	6 00.0	+60.0	0.0	7 00.0	+60.0	0.0	67
68	1 00.0	+60.0	0.0	2 00.0	+60.0	0.0	3 00.0	+60.0	0.0	4 00.0	+60.0	0.0	5 00.0	+60.0	0.0	6 00.0	+60.0	0.0	7 00.0	+60.0	0.0	8 00.0	+60.0	0.0	68
69	2 00.0	+60.0	0.0	3 00.0	+60.0	0.0	4 00.0	+60.0	0.0	5 00.0	+60.0	0.0	6 00.0	+60.0	0.0	7 00.0	+60.0	0.0	8 00.0	+60.0	0.0	9 00.0	+60.0	0.0	69
70	3 00.0	+60.0	0.0	4 00.0	+60.0	0.0	5 00.0	+60.0	0.0	6 00.0	+60.0	0.0	7 00.0	+60.0	0.0	8 00.0	+60.0	0.0	9 00.0	+60.0	0.0	10 00.0	+60.0	0.0	70
71	4 00.0	+60.0	0.0	5 00.0	+60.0	0.0	6 00.0	+60.0	0.0	7 00.0	+60.0	0.0	8 00.0	+60.0	0.0	9 00.0	+60.0	0.0	10 00.0	+60.0	0.0	11 00.0	+60.0	0.0	71
72	5 00.0	+60.0	0.0	6 00.0	+60.0	0.0	7 00.0	+60.0	0.0	8 00.0	+60.0	0.0	9 00.0	+60.0	0.0	10 00.0	+60.0	0.0	11 00.0	+60.0	0.0	12 00.0	+60.0	0.0	72
73	6 00.0	+60.0	0.0	7 00.0	+60.0	0.0	8 00.0	+60.0	0.0	9 00.0	+60.0	0.0	10 00.0	+60.0	0.0	11 00.0	+60.0	0.0	12 00.0	+60.0	0.0	13 00.0	+60.0	0.0	73
74	7 00.0	+60.0	0.0	8 00.0	+60.0	0.0	9 00.0	+60.0	0.0	10 00.0	+60.0	0.0	11 00.0	+60.0	0.0	12 00.0	+60.0	0.0	13 00.0	+60.0	0.0	14 00.0	+60.0	0.0	74
75	8 00.0	+60.0	0.0	9 00.0	+60.0	0.0	10 00.0	+60.0	0.0	11 00.0	+60.0	0.0	12 00.0	+60.0	0.0	13 00.0	+60.0	0.0	14 00.0	+60.0	0.0	15 00.0	+60.0	0.0	75
76	9 00.0	+60.0	0.0	10 00.0	+60.0	0.0	11 00.0	+60.0	0.0	12 00.0	+60.0	0.0	13 00.0	+60.0	0.0	14 00.0	+60.0	0.0	15 00.0	+60.0	0.0	16 00.0	+60.0	0.0	76
77	10 00.0	+60.0	0.0	11 00.0	+60.0	0.0	12 00.0	+60.0	0.0	13 00.0	+60.0	0.0	14 00.0	+60.0	0.0	15 00.0	+60.0	0.0	16 00.0	+60.0	0.0	17 00.0	+60.0	0.0	77
78	11 00.0	+60.0	0.0	12 00.0	+60.0	0.0	13 00.0	+60.0	0.0	14 00.0	+60.0	0.0	15 00.0	+60.0	0.0	16 00.0	+60.0	0.0	17 00.0	+60.0	0.0	18 00.0	+60.0	0.0	78
79	12 00.0	+60.0	0.0	13 00.0	+60.0	0.0	14 00.0	+60.0	0.0	15 00.0	+60.0	0.0	16 00.0	+60.0	0.0	17 00.0	+60.0	0.0	18 00.0	+60.0	0.0	19 00.0	+60.0	0.0	79
80	13 00.0	+60.0	0.0	14 00.0	+60.0	0.0	15 00.0	+60.0	0.0	16 00.0	+60.0	0.0	17 00.0	+60.0	0.0	18 00.0	+60.0	0.0	19 00.0	+60.0	0.0	20 00.0	+60.0	0.0	80
81	14 00.0	+60.0	0.0	15 00.0	+60.0	0.0	16 00.0	+60.0	0.0	17 00.0	+60.0	0.0	18 00.0	+60.0	0.0	19 00.0	+60.0	0.0	20 00.0	+60.0	0.0	21 00.0	+60.0	0.0	81
82	15 00.0	+60.0	0.0	16 00.0	+60.0	0.0	17 00.0	+60.0	0.0	18 00.0	+60.0	0.0	19 00.0	+60.0	0.0	20 00.0	+60.0	0.0	21 00.0	+60.0	0.0	22 00.0	+60.0	0.0	82
83	16 00.0	+60.0	0.0	17 00.0	+60.0	0.0	18 00.0	+60.0	0.0	19 00.0	+60.0	0.0	20 00.0	+60.0	0.0	21 00.0	+60.0	0.0	22 00.0	+60.0	0.0	23 00.0	+60.0	0.0	83
84	17 00.0	+60.0	0.0	18 00.0	+60.0	0.0	19 00.0	+60.0	0.0	20 00.0	+60.0	0.0	21 00.0	+60.0	0.0	22 00.0	+60.0	0.0	23 00.0	+60.0	0.0	24 00.0	+60.0	0.0	84
85	18 00.0	+60.0	0.0	19 00.0	+60.0	0.0	20 00.0	+60.0	0.0	21 00.0	+60.0	0.0	22 00.0	+60.0	0.0	23 00.0	+60.0	0.0	24 00.0	+60.0	0.0	25 00.0	+60.0	0.0	85
86	19 00.0	+60.0	0.0	20 00.0	+60.0	0.0	21 00.0	+60.0	0.0	22 00.0	+60.0	0.0	23 00.0	+60.0	0.0	24 00.0	+60.0	0.0	25 00.0	+60.0	0.0	26 00.0	+60.0	0.0	86
87	20 00.0	+60.0	0.0	21 00.0	+60.0	0.0	22 00.0	+60.0	0.0	23 00.0	+60.0	0.0	24 00.0	+60.0	0.0	25 00.0	+60.0	0.0	26 00.0	+60.0	0.0	27 00.0	+60.0	0.0	87
88	21 00.0	+60.0	0.0	22 00.0	+60.0	0.0	23 00.0	+60.0	0.0	24 00.0	+60.0	0.0	25 00.0	+60.0	0.0	26 00.0	+60.0	0.0	27 00.0	+60.0	0.0	28 00.0	+60.0	0.0	88
89	22 00.0	+60.0	0.0	23 00.0	+60.0	0.0	24 00.0	+60.0	0.0	25 00.0	+60.0	0.0	26 00.0	+60.0	0.0	27 00.0	+60.0	0.0	28 00.0	+60.0	0.0	29 00.0	+60.0	0.0	89
90	23 00.0	+60.0	0.0	24 00.0	+60.0	0.0	25 00.0	+60.0	0.0	26 00.0	+60.0	0.0	27 00.0	+60.0	0.0	28 00.0	+60.0	0.0	29 00.0	+60.0	0.0	30 00.0	+60.0	0.0	90
	23°			24°			25°			26°			27°			28°			29°			30°			

S. Lat. {L.H.A. greater than 180° ....Zn=180°−Z; L.H.A. less than 180°............Zn=180°+Z}

1°, 359° L.H.A.

LATITUDE SAME NAME AS DECLINATION N. Lat. {L.H.A. greater than 180° .....Zn=Z; L.H.A. less than 180°.............Zn=360°–Z}

Dec.	23° Hc	23° d	23° Z	24° Hc	24° d	24° Z	25° Hc	25° d	25° Z	26° Hc	26° d	26° Z
°	° ′	′	°	° ′	′	°	° ′	′	°	° ′	′	°
0	66 58.8	+59.9	177.4	65 58.8	+60.0	177.5	64 58.9	+59.9	177.6	63 58.9	+60.0	177.7
1	67 58.7	+60.0	177.3	66 58.8	+59.9	177.4	65 58.8	+60.0	177.5	64 58.9	+59.9	177.6
2	68 58.7	+59.9	177.2	67 58.7	+60.0	177.3	66 58.8	+59.9	177.4	65 58.8	+60.0	177.5
3	69 58.6	+59.9	177.1	68 58.7	+59.9	177.2	67 58.7	+60.0	177.3	66 58.8	+59.9	177.4
4	70 58.5	+59.9	176.9	69 58.6	+59.9	177.1	68 58.7	+59.9	177.2	67 58.7	+60.0	177.3
5	71 58.4	+60.0	176.8	70 58.5	+60.0	176.9	69 58.6	+60.0	177.1	68 58.7	+59.9	177.2
6	72 58.4	+59.9	176.6	71 58.5	+59.9	176.8	70 58.6	+59.9	176.9	69 58.6	+60.0	177.1
7	73 58.3	+59.9	176.4	72 58.4	+59.9	176.6	71 58.5	+59.9	176.8	70 58.6	+59.9	177.0
8	74 58.2	+59.8	176.2	73 58.3	+59.9	176.4	72 58.4	+59.9	176.6	71 58.5	+59.9	176.8
9	75 58.0	+59.9	175.9	74 58.2	+59.9	176.2	73 58.3	+59.9	176.4	72 58.4	+59.9	176.6
10	76 57.9	+59.8	175.6	75 58.1	+59.8	175.9	74 58.2	+59.9	176.2	73 58.3	+59.9	176.4
11	77 57.7	+59.8	175.3	76 57.9	+59.9	175.6	75 58.1	+59.8	175.9	74 58.2	+59.9	176.2
12	78 57.5	+59.8	174.9	77 57.8	+59.8	175.3	76 57.9	+59.9	175.7	75 58.1	+59.9	176.0
13	79 57.3	+59.7	174.4	78 57.6	+59.7	174.9	77 57.8	+59.8	175.3	76 58.0	+59.8	175.7
14	80 57.0	+59.7	173.8	79 57.3	+59.8	174.4	78 57.6	+59.8	174.9	77 57.8	+59.8	175.3
15	81 56.7	+59.5	173.1	80 57.1	+59.6	173.8	79 57.4	+59.7	174.5	78 57.6	+59.8	174.9
16	82 56.2	+59.4	172.2	81 56.7	+59.6	173.1	80 57.1	+59.7	173.9	79 57.4	+59.7	174.5
17	83 55.6	+59.2	170.9	82 56.3	+59.4	172.2	81 56.8	+59.5	173.2	80 57.1	+59.7	173.9
18	84 54.8	+58.8	169.2	83 55.7	+59.2	171.0	82 56.3	+59.4	172.2	81 56.8	+59.6	173.2
19	85 53.6	+57.9	166.7	84 54.9	+58.7	169.3	83 55.7	+59.2	171.0	82 56.4	+59.4	172.3
20	86 51.5	+56.2	•162.6	85 53.6	+58.1	166.8	84 54.9	+58.8	169.3	83 55.8	+59.2	171.1
21	87 47.7	+50.6	•154.9	86 51.7	+56.2	•162.7	85 53.7	+58.1	166.8	84 55.0	+58.8	169.4
22	88 38.3	+26.5	•137.1	87 47.9	+50.7	•155.1	86 51.8	+56.3	•162.8	85 53.8	+58.1	166.9
23	89 04.8	−26.2	• 89.8	88 38.6	+26.6	•137.3	87 48.1	+50.8	•155.2	86 51.9	+56.4	•162.9
24	88 38.6	−50.5	• 42.3	89 05.2	−26.3	• 89.8	88 38.9	+26.7	•137.5	87 48.3	+50.9	•155.4
25	87 48.1	−56.2	• 24.3	88 38.9	−50.6	• 42.1	89 05.6	−26.4	• 89.8	88 39.2	+26.9	•137.7
26	86 51.9	−58.0	16.7	87 48.3	−56.3	• 24.2	88 39.2	−50.8	• 41.9	89 06.1	−26.6	• 89.8
27	85 53.9	−58.7	12.6	86 52.0	−58.0	16.5	87 48.4	−56.2	• 24.0	88 39.5	−50.9	• 41.6
28	84 55.2	−59.2	10.0	85 54.0	−58.8	12.4	86 52.2	−58.1	16.4	87 48.6	−56.3	• 23.8
29	83 56.0	−59.4	8.3	84 55.2	−59.1	9.9	85 54.1	−58.8	12.3	86 52.3	−58.1	16.2
30	82 56.6	−59.6	7.1	83 56.1	−59.5	8.2	84 55.3	−59.2	9.8	85 54.2	−58.8	12.2
31	81 57.0	−59.6	6.1	82 56.6	−59.5	7.0	83 56.1	−59.4	8.1	84 55.4	−59.2	9.7
32	80 57.4	−59.7	5.4	81 57.1	−59.7	6.1	82 56.7	−59.6	6.9	83 56.2	−59.4	8.1
33	79 57.7	−59.8	4.8	80 57.4	−59.7	5.3	81 57.1	−59.6	6.0	82 56.8	−59.6	6.8
34	78 57.9	−59.8	4.3	79 57.7	−59.8	4.8	80 57.5	−59.7	5.3	81 57.2	−59.7	5.9
35	77 58.1	−59.8	3.9	78 57.9	−59.8	4.3	79 57.8	−59.8	4.7	80 57.5	−59.7	5.2
36	76 58.3	−59.9	3.6	77 58.1	−59.8	3.9	78 58.0	−59.8	4.2	79 57.8	−59.8	4.6
37	75 58.4	−59.9	3.3	76 58.3	−59.9	3.5	77 58.2	−59.9	3.8	78 58.0	−59.8	4.2
38	74 58.5	−59.9	3.0	75 58.4	−59.8	3.3	76 58.3	−59.8	3.5	77 58.2	−59.8	3.8
39	73 58.6	−59.9	2.8	74 58.6	−59.9	3.0	75 58.5	−59.9	3.2	76 58.4	−59.9	3.4
40	72 58.7	−59.9	2.6	73 58.7	−59.9	2.8	74 58.6	−59.9	3.0	75 58.5	−59.9	3.2
41	71 58.8	−59.9	2.4	72 58.8	−59.9	2.6	73 58.7	−59.9	2.7	74 58.6	−59.9	2.9
42	70 58.9	−59.9	2.3	71 58.9	−60.0	2.4	72 58.8	−59.9	2.5	73 58.7	−59.9	2.7
43	69 59.0	−60.0	2.1	70 58.9	−59.9	2.2	71 58.9	−59.9	2.4	72 58.8	−59.9	2.5
44	68 59.0	−59.9	2.0	69 59.0	−59.9	2.1	70 59.0	−60.0	2.2	71 58.9	−59.9	2.3
45	67 59.1	−60.0	1.9	68 59.1	−60.0	2.0	69 59.0	−59.9	2.1	70 59.0	−60.0	2.2
46	66 59.1	−59.9	1.8	67 59.1	−59.9	1.9	68 59.1	−60.0	1.9	69 59.0	−59.9	2.0
47	65 59.2	−60.0	1.7	66 59.2	−60.0	1.7	67 59.1	−59.9	1.8	68 59.1	−59.9	1.9
48	64 59.2	−59.9	1.6	65 59.2	−59.9	1.6	66 59.2	−60.0	1.7	67 59.2	−60.0	1.8
49	63 59.3	−60.0	1.5	64 59.3	−60.0	1.6	65 59.2	−59.9	1.6	66 59.2	−59.9	1.7
50	62 59.3	−59.9	1.4	63 59.3	−60.0	1.5	64 59.3	−60.0	1.5	65 59.3	−60.0	1.6
51	61 59.4	−60.0	1.3	62 59.3	−59.9	1.4	63 59.3	−59.9	1.4	64 59.3	−60.0	1.5
52	60 59.4	−60.0	1.3	61 59.4	−60.0	1.3	62 59.4	−60.0	1.4	63 59.3	−59.9	1.4
53	59 59.4	−59.9	1.2	60 59.4	−60.0	1.2	61 59.4	−60.0	1.3	62 59.4	−60.0	1.3
54	58 59.5	−60.0	1.1	59 59.4	−59.9	1.2	60 59.4	−59.9	1.2	61 59.4	−60.0	1.3
55	57 59.5	−60.0	1.1	58 59.5	−60.0	1.1	59 59.5	−60.0	1.1	60 59.4	−59.9	1.2
56	56 59.5	−60.0	1.0	57 59.5	−60.0	1.1	58 59.5	−60.0	1.1	59 59.5	−60.0	1.1
57	55 59.5	−59.9	1.0	56 59.5	−60.0	1.0	57 59.5	−60.0	1.0	58 59.5	−60.0	1.1
58	54 59.6	−60.0	0.9	55 59.5	−59.9	0.9	56 59.5	−59.9	1.0	57 59.5	−59.9	1.0
59	53 59.6	−60.0	0.9	54 59.6	−60.0	0.9	55 59.6	−60.0	0.9	56 59.6	−60.0	0.9
60	52 59.6	−60.0	0.8	53 59.6	−60.0	0.9	54 59.6	−60.0	0.9	55 59.6	−60.0	0.9
61	51 59.6	−60.0	0.8	52 59.6	−60.0	0.8	53 59.6	−60.0	0.8	54 59.6	−60.0	0.8
62	50 59.6	−59.9	0.7	51 59.6	−59.9	0.8	52 59.6	−59.9	0.8	53 59.6	−60.0	0.8
63	49 59.7	−60.0	0.7	50 59.7	−60.0	0.7	51 59.7	−60.0	0.7	52 59.6	−59.9	0.8
64	48 59.7	−60.0	0.7	49 59.7	−60.0	0.7	50 59.7	−60.0	0.7	51 59.7	−60.0	0.7
65	47 59.7	−60.0	0.6	48 59.7	−60.0	0.6	49 59.7	−60.0	0.7	50 59.7	−60.0	0.7
66	46 59.7	−60.0	0.6	47 59.7	−60.0	0.6	48 59.7	−60.0	0.6	49 59.7	−60.0	0.6
67	45 59.7	−60.0	0.6	46 59.7	−60.0	0.6	47 59.7	−60.0	0.6	48 59.7	−60.0	0.6
68	44 59.7	−59.9	0.5	45 59.7	−59.9	0.5	46 59.7	−59.9	0.5	47 59.7	−59.9	0.6
69	43 59.8	−60.0	0.5	44 59.8	−60.0	0.5	45 59.8	−60.0	0.5	46 59.8	−60.0	0.5
70	42 59.8	−60.0	0.5	43 59.8	−60.0	0.5	44 59.8	−60.0	0.5	45 59.8	−60.0	0.5
71	41 59.8	−60.0	0.4	42 59.8	−60.0	0.4	43 59.8	−60.0	0.5	44 59.8	−60.0	0.5
72	40 59.8	−60.0	0.4	41 59.8	−60.0	0.4	42 59.8	−60.0	0.4	43 59.8	−60.0	0.4
73	39 59.8	−60.0	0.4	40 59.8	−60.0	0.4	41 59.8	−60.0	0.4	42 59.8	−60.0	0.4
74	38 59.8	−60.0	0.4	39 59.8	−60.0	0.4	40 59.8	−60.0	0.4	41 59.8	−60.0	0.4
75	37 59.8	−59.9	0.3	38 59.8	−59.9	0.3	39 59.8	−59.9	0.3	40 59.8	−59.9	0.3
76	36 59.9	−60.0	0.3	37 59.9	−60.0	0.3	38 59.9	−60.0	0.3	39 59.9	−60.0	0.3
77	35 59.9	−60.0	0.3	36 59.9	−60.0	0.3	37 59.9	−60.0	0.3	38 59.9	−60.0	0.3
78	34 59.9	−60.0	0.3	35 59.9	−60.0	0.3	36 59.9	−60.0	0.3	37 59.9	−60.0	0.3
79	33 59.9	−60.0	0.2	34 59.9	−60.0	0.2	35 59.9	−60.0	0.2	36 59.9	−60.0	0.2
80	32 59.9	−60.0	0.2	33 59.9	−60.0	0.2	34 59.9	−60.0	0.2	35 59.9	−60.0	0.2
81	31 59.9	−60.0	0.2	32 59.9	−60.0	0.2	33 59.9	−60.0	0.2	34 59.9	−60.0	0.2
82	30 59.9	−60.0	0.2	31 59.9	−60.0	0.2	32 59.9	−60.0	0.2	33 59.9	−60.0	0.2
83	29 59.9	−60.0	0.1	30 59.9	−60.0	0.1	31 59.9	−60.0	0.1	32 59.9	−60.0	0.1
84	28 59.9	−59.9	0.1	29 59.9	−59.9	0.1	30 59.9	−59.9	0.1	31 59.9	−59.9	0.1
85	28 00.0	−60.0	0.1	29 00.0	−60.0	0.1	30 00.0	−60.0	0.1	31 00.0	−60.0	0.1
86	27 00.0	−60.0	0.1	28 00.0	−60.0	0.1	29 00.0	−60.0	0.1	30 00.0	−60.0	0.1
87	26 00.0	−60.0	0.1	27 00.0	−60.0	0.1	28 00.0	−60.0	0.1	29 00.0	−60.0	0.1
88	25 00.0	−60.0	0.0	26 00.0	−60.0	0.0	27 00.0	−60.0	0.0	28 00.0	−60.0	0.0
89	24 00.0	−60.0	0.0	25 00.0	−60.0	0.0	26 00.0	−60.0	0.0	27 00.0	−60.0	0.0
90	23 00.0	−60.0	0.0	24 00.0	−60.0	0.0	25 00.0	−60.0	0.0	26 00.0	−60.0	0.0
	23°			24°			25°			26°		

27° Hc	27° d	27° Z	28° Hc	28° d	28° Z	29° Hc	29° d	29° Z	30° Hc	30° d	30° Z	Dec.
° ′	′	°	° ′	′	°	° ′	′	°	° ′	′	°	°
62 59.0	+59.9	177.8	61 59.0	+60.0	177.9	60 59.1	+59.9	177.9	59 59.1	+60.0	178.0	0
63 58.9	+60.0	177.7	62 59.0	+59.9	177.8	61 59.0	+60.0	177.9	60 59.1	+59.9	177.9	1
64 58.9	+60.0	177.6	63 58.9	+60.0	177.7	62 59.0	+60.0	177.8	61 59.0	+60.0	177.9	2
65 58.9	+59.9	177.5	64 58.9	+60.0	177.6	63 59.0	+59.9	177.7	62 59.0	+60.0	177.8	3
66 58.8	+60.0	177.4	65 58.9	+59.9	177.5	64 58.9	+60.0	177.6	63 59.0	+59.9	177.7	4
67 58.8	+59.9	177.3	66 58.8	+60.0	177.5	65 58.9	+59.9	177.6	64 58.9	+60.0	177.6	5
68 58.7	+59.9	177.2	67 58.8	+59.9	177.3	66 58.8	+60.0	177.5	65 58.9	+59.9	177.6	6
69 58.6	+60.0	177.1	68 58.7	+60.0	177.2	67 58.8	+59.9	177.4	66 58.8	+60.0	177.5	7
70 58.6	+59.9	177.0	69 58.7	+59.9	177.1	68 58.7	+60.0	177.2	67 58.8	+60.0	177.4	8
71 58.5	+59.9	176.8	70 58.6	+59.9	177.0	69 58.7	+59.9	177.1	68 58.8	+59.9	177.2	9
72 58.4	+59.9	176.6	71 58.5	+59.9	176.8	70 58.6	+59.9	177.0	69 58.7	+59.9	177.1	10
73 58.3	+59.9	176.4	72 58.4	+60.0	176.6	71 58.5	+60.0	176.8	70 58.6	+60.0	177.0	11
74 58.2	+59.9	176.2	73 58.4	+59.9	176.5	72 58.5	+59.9	176.7	71 58.6	+59.9	176.8	12
75 58.1	+59.9	176.0	74 58.3	+59.8	176.2	73 58.4	+59.9	176.5	72 58.5	+59.9	176.7	13
76 58.0	+59.8	175.7	75 58.1	+59.9	176.0	74 58.3	+59.9	176.3	73 58.4	+59.9	176.5	14
77 57.8	+59.9	175.4	76 58.0	+59.9	175.7	75 58.2	+59.8	176.0	74 58.3	+59.9	176.3	15
78 57.7	+59.7	175.0	77 57.9	+59.8	175.4	76 58.0	+59.9	175.7	75 58.2	+59.9	176.0	16
79 57.4	+59.8	174.5	78 57.7	+59.8	175.0	77 57.9	+59.8	175.4	76 58.1	+59.8	175.8	17
80 57.2	+59.6	173.9	79 57.5	+59.7	174.5	78 57.7	+59.8	175.0	77 57.9	+59.9	175.4	18
81 56.8	+59.6	173.2	80 57.2	+59.7	174.0	79 57.5	+59.8	174.6	78 57.8	+59.8	175.1	19
82 56.4	+59.5	172.3	81 56.9	+59.6	173.3	80 57.3	+59.6	174.0	79 57.6	+59.7	174.6	20
83 55.9	+59.2	171.1	82 56.5	+59.4	172.4	81 56.9	+59.6	173.3	80 57.3	+59.7	174.1	21
84 55.1	+58.8	169.5	83 55.9	+59.3	171.2	82 56.5	+59.5	172.4	81 57.0	+59.6	173.4	22
85 53.9	+58.1	167.0	84 55.2	+58.8	169.5	83 56.0	+59.2	171.3	82 56.6	+59.5	172.5	23
86 52.0	+56.4	•163.0	85 54.0	+58.2	167.1	84 55.2	+58.9	169.6	83 56.1	+59.2	171.3	24
87 48.4	+51.1	•155.6	86 52.2	+56.4	•163.2	85 54.1	+58.2	167.2	84 55.3	+58.9	169.7	25
88 39.5	+27.0	•137.9	87 48.6	+51.2	•155.8	86 52.3	+56.5	•163.3	85 54.2	+58.2	167.3	26
89 06.5	−26.7	• 89.8	88 39.8	+27.2	•138.2	87 48.8	+51.3	•155.9	86 52.4	+56.6	•163.4	27
88 39.8	−51.0	• 41.3	89 07.0	−26.9	• 89.8	88 40.1	+27.4	•138.5	87 49.0	+51.5	•156.1	28
87 48.8	−56.4	• 23.6	88 40.1	−51.1	• 41.1	89 07.5	−27.0	• 89.8	88 40.5	+27.5	•138.7	29
86 52.4	−58.1	16.1	87 49.0	−56.4	• 23.4	88 40.5	−51.3	• 40.8	89 08.0	−27.2	• 89.8	30
85 54.3	−58.8	12.1	86 52.6	−58.2	15.9	87 49.2	−56.5	• 23.2	88 40.8	−51.4	• 40.5	31
84 55.5	−59.2	9.6	85 54.4	−58.8	12.0	86 52.7	−58.1	15.8	87 49.4	−56.5	• 22.9	32
83 56.3	−59.5	8.0	84 55.6	−59.2	9.5	85 54.6	−58.9	11.8	86 52.9	−58.2	15.6	33
82 56.8	−59.5	6.8	83 56.4	−59.5	7.9	84 55.7	−59.3	9.4	85 54.7	−58.9	11.7	34
81 57.3	−59.7	5.9	82 56.9	−59.6	6.7	83 56.4	−59.4	7.8	84 55.8	−59.3	9.3	35
80 57.6	−59.7	5.2	81 57.3	−59.7	5.8	82 57.0	−59.6	6.6	83 56.5	−59.5	7.7	36
79 57.9	−59.8	4.6	80 57.6	−59.7	5.1	81 57.4	−59.7	5.7	82 57.0	−59.6	6.5	37
78 58.1	−59.8	4.1	79 57.9	−59.8	4.5	80 57.7	−59.7	5.0	81 57.4	−59.6	5.6	38
77 58.3	−59.9	3.7	78 58.1	−59.8	4.1	79 58.0	−59.8	4.5	80 57.8	−59.8	5.0	39
76 58.4	−59.9	3.4	77 58.3	−59.8	3.7	78 58.2	−59.9	4.0	79 58.0	−59.8	4.4	40
75 58.5	−59.8	3.1	76 58.5	−59.9	3.4	77 58.3	−59.8	3.6	78 58.2	−59.8	3.9	41
74 58.7	−59.9	2.9	75 58.6	−59.9	3.1	76 58.5	−59.9	3.3	77 58.4	−59.9	3.6	42
73 58.8	−59.9	2.7	74 58.7	−59.9	2.8	75 58.6	−59.9	3.0	76 58.5	−59.8	3.2	43
72 58.9	−60.0	2.5	73 58.8	−59.9	2.6	74 58.7	−59.9	2.8	75 58.7	−59.9	3.0	44
71 58.9	−59.9	2.3	72 58.9	−59.9	2.4	73 58.8	−59.9	2.6	74 58.8	−59.9	2.7	45
70 59.0	−59.9	2.1	71 59.0	−60.0	2.2	72 58.9	−59.9	2.4	73 58.9	−60.0	2.5	46
69 59.1	−60.0	2.0	70 59.0	−59.9	2.1	71 59.0	−59.9	2.2	72 58.9	−59.9	2.3	47
68 59.1	−59.9	1.9	69 59.1	−59.9	2.0	70 59.1	−60.0	2.1	71 59.0	−59.9	2.2	48
67 59.2	−60.0	1.8	68 59.2	−60.0	1.8	69 59.1	−59.9	1.9	70 59.1	−60.0	2.0	49
66 59.2	−59.9	1.6	67 59.2	−59.9	1.7	68 59.2	−60.0	1.8	69 59.1	−59.9	1.9	50
65 59.3	−60.0	1.5	66 59.3	−60.0	1.6	67 59.2	−59.9	1.7	68 59.2	−59.9	1.8	51
64 59.3	−59.9	1.5	65 59.3	−60.0	1.5	66 59.3	−60.0	1.6	67 59.3	−60.0	1.6	52
63 59.4	−60.0	1.4	64 59.3	−59.9	1.4	65 59.3	−59.9	1.5	66 59.3	−60.0	1.5	53
62 59.4	−60.0	1.3	63 59.4	−60.0	1.3	64 59.4	−60.0	1.4	65 59.3	−59.9	1.4	54
61 59.4	−59.9	1.2	62 59.4	−60.0	1.3	63 59.4	−60.0	1.3	64 59.4	−60.0	1.4	55
60 59.5	−60.0	1.2	61 59.4	−59.9	1.2	62 59.4	−59.9	1.2	63 59.4	−59.9	1.3	56
59 59.5	−60.0	1.1	60 59.5	−60.0	1.1	61 59.5	−60.0	1.2	62 59.5	−60.0	1.2	57
58 59.5	−60.0	1.0	59 59.5	−60.0	1.1	60 59.5	−60.0	1.1	61 59.5	−60.0	1.1	58
57 59.5	−59.9	1.0	58 59.5	−59.9	1.0	59 59.5	−59.9	1.0	60 59.5	−60.0	1.1	59
56 59.6	−60.0	0.9	57 59.6	−60.0	0.9	58 59.6	−60.0	1.0	59 59.5	−59.9	1.0	60
55 59.6	−60.0	0.9	56 59.6	−60.0	0.9	57 59.6	−60.0	0.9	58 59.6	−60.0	0.9	61
54 59.6	−60.0	0.8	55 59.6	−60.0	0.8	56 59.6	−60.0	0.9	57 59.6	−60.0	0.9	62
53 59.6	−59.9	0.8	54 59.6	−59.9	0.8	55 59.6	−60.0	0.8	56 59.6	−60.0	0.8	63
52 59.7	−60.0	0.7	53 59.7	−60.0	0.7	54 59.6	−59.9	0.8	55 59.6	−59.9	0.8	64
51 59.7	−60.0	0.7	52 59.7	−60.0	0.7	53 59.7	−60.0	0.7	54 59.7	−60.0	0.7	65
50 59.7	−60.0	0.6	51 59.7	−60.0	0.7	52 59.7	−60.0	0.7	53 59.7	−60.0	0.7	66
49 59.7	−60.0	0.6	50 59.7	−60.0	0.6	51 59.7	−60.0	0.6	52 59.7	−60.0	0.6	67
48 59.7	−59.9	0.6	49 59.7	−60.0	0.6	50 59.7	−60.0	0.6	51 59.7	−60.0	0.6	68
47 59.8	−60.0	0.5	48 59.7	−59.9	0.5	49 59.7	−59.9	0.6	50 59.7	−59.9	0.6	69
46 59.8	−60.0	0.5	47 59.8	−60.0	0.5	48 59.8	−60.0	0.5	49 59.8	−60.0	0.5	70
45 59.8	−60.0	0.5	46 59.8	−60.0	0.5	47 59.8	−60.0	0.5	48 59.8	−60.0	0.5	71
44 59.8	−60.0	0.4	45 59.8	−60.0	0.4	46 59.8	−60.0	0.5	47 59.8	−60.0	0.5	72
43 59.8	−60.0	0.4	44 59.8	−60.0	0.4	45 59.8	−60.0	0.4	46 59.8	−60.0	0.4	73
42 59.8	−60.0	0.4	43 59.8	−60.0	0.4	44 59.8	−60.0	0.4	45 59.8	−60.0	0.4	74
41 59.8	−59.9	0.3	42 59.8	−60.0	0.4	43 59.8	−60.0	0.4	44 59.8	−60.0	0.4	75
40 59.9	−60.0	0.3	41 59.8	−59.9	0.3	42 59.8	−59.9	0.3	43 59.8	−59.9	0.3	76
39 59.9	−60.0	0.3	40 59.9	−60.0	0.3	41 59.9	−60.0	0.3	42 59.9	−60.0	0.3	77
38 59.9	−60.0	0.3	39 59.9	−60.0	0.3	40 59.9	−60.0	0.3	41 59.9	−60.0	0.3	78
37 59.9	−60.0	0.2	38 59.9	−60.0	0.2	39 59.9	−60.0	0.2	40 59.9	−60.0	0.3	79
36 59.9	−60.0	0.2	37 59.9	−60.0	0.2	38 59.9	−60.0	0.2	39 59.9	−60.0	0.2	80
35 59.9	−60.0	0.2	36 59.9	−60.0	0.2	37 59.9	−60.0	0.2	38 59.9	−60.0	0.2	81
34 59.9	−60.0	0.2	35 59.9	−60.0	0.2	36 59.9	−60.0	0.2	37 59.9	−60.0	0.2	82
33 59.9	−60.0	0.1	34 59.9	−60.0	0.1	35 59.9	−60.0	0.2	36 59.9	−60.0	0.2	83
32 59.9	−59.9	0.1	33 59.9	−59.9	0.1	34 59.9	−59.9	0.1	35 59.9	−59.9	0.1	84
32 00.0	−60.0	0.1	33 00.0	−60.0	0.1	34 00.0	−60.0	0.1	35 00.0	−60.0	0.1	85
31 00.0	−60.0	0.1	32 00.0	−60.0	0.1	33 00.0	−60.0	0.1	34 00.0	−60.0	0.1	86
30 00.0	−60.0	0.1	31 00.0	−60.0	0.1	32 00.0	−60.0	0.1	33 00.0	−60.0	0.1	87
29 00.0	−60.0	0.0	30 00.0	−60.0	0.0	31 00.0	−60.0	0.0	32 00.0	−60.0	0.0	88
28 00.0	−60.0	0.0	29 00.0	−60.0	0.0	30 00.0	−60.0	0.0	31 00.0	−60.0	0.0	89
27 00.0	−60.0	0.0	28 00.0	−60.0	0.0	29 00.0	−60.0	0.0	30 00.0	−60.0	0.0	90
27°			28°			29°			30°			

1°, 359° L.H.A. LATITUDE SAME NAME AS DECLINATION

186

LATITUDE **CONTRARY** NAME TO DECLINATION L.H.A. 1°, 359°

Dec.	23° Hc	d	Z	24° Hc	d	Z	25° Hc	d	Z	26° Hc	d	Z	27° Hc	d	Z	28° Hc	d	Z	29° Hc	d	Z	30° Hc	d	Z	Dec.
°	° ′	′	°	° ′	′	°	° ′	′	°	° ′	′	°	° ′	′	°	° ′	′	°	° ′	′	°	° ′	′	°	°
0	66 58.8	-60.0	177.4	65 58.8	-59.9	177.5	64 58.9	-60.0	177.6	63 58.9	-59.9	177.7	62 59.0	-60.0	177.8	61 59.0	-60.0	177.9	60 59.1	-60.0	177.9	59 59.1	-60.0	178.0	0
1	65 58.8	-59.9	177.5	64 58.9	-60.0	177.6	63 58.9	-59.9	177.7	62 59.0	-60.0	177.8	61 59.0	-60.0	177.9	60 59.0	-59.9	177.9	59 59.1	-60.0	178.0	58 59.1	-60.0	178.1	1
2	64 58.9	-60.0	177.6	63 58.9	-60.0	177.7	62 59.0	-60.0	177.8	61 59.0	-60.0	177.9	60 59.0	-59.9	177.9	59 59.1	-60.0	178.0	58 59.1	-60.0	178.1	57 59.1	-59.9	178.1	2
3	63 58.9	-60.0	177.7	62 58.9	-59.9	177.8	61 59.0	-60.0	177.9	60 59.0	-59.9	177.9	59 59.1	-60.0	178.0	58 59.1	-60.0	178.1	57 59.1	-59.9	178.1	56 59.2	-60.0	178.2	3
4	62 58.9	-59.9	177.8	61 59.0	-60.0	177.9	60 59.0	-59.9	177.9	59 59.1	-60.0	178.0	58 59.1	-60.0	178.1	57 59.1	-59.9	178.1	56 59.2	-60.0	178.2	55 59.2	-60.0	178.2	4
5	61 59.0	-60.0	177.9	60 59.0	-60.0	177.9	59 59.1	-60.0	178.0	58 59.1	-60.0	178.1	57 59.1	-60.0	178.1	56 59.2	-60.0	178.2	55 59.2	-60.0	178.2	54 59.2	-60.0	178.3	5
6	60 59.0	-60.0	177.9	59 59.0	-59.9	178.0	58 59.1	-60.0	178.1	57 59.1	-60.0	178.1	56 59.1	-59.9	178.2	55 59.2	-60.0	178.2	54 59.2	-60.0	178.3	53 59.2	-59.9	178.3	6
7	59 59.0	-59.9	178.0	58 59.1	-60.0	178.1	57 59.1	-60.0	178.1	56 59.1	-59.9	178.2	55 59.2	-60.0	178.2	54 59.2	-60.0	178.3	53 59.2	-60.0	178.3	52 59.3	-60.0	178.4	7
8	58 59.1	-60.0	178.1	57 59.1	-60.0	178.1	56 59.1	-59.9	178.2	55 59.2	-60.0	178.2	54 59.2	-60.0	178.3	53 59.2	-60.0	178.3	52 59.2	-59.9	178.4	51 59.3	-60.0	178.4	8
9	57 59.1	-60.0	178.1	56 59.1	-59.9	178.2	55 59.2	-60.0	178.2	54 59.2	-60.0	178.3	53 59.2	-60.0	178.3	52 59.2	-59.9	178.4	51 59.3	-60.0	178.4	50 59.3	-60.0	178.4	9
10	56 59.1	-59.9	178.2	55 59.2	-60.0	178.2	54 59.2	-60.0	178.3	53 59.2	-60.0	178.3	52 59.2	-59.9	178.4	51 59.3	-60.0	178.4	50 59.3	-60.0	178.4	49 59.3	-60.0	178.5	10
11	55 59.2	-60.0	178.2	54 59.2	-60.0	178.3	53 59.2	-60.0	178.3	52 59.2	-59.9	178.4	51 59.3	-60.0	178.4	50 59.3	-60.0	178.4	49 59.3	-60.0	178.5	48 59.3	-60.0	178.5	11
12	54 59.2	-60.0	178.3	53 59.2	-60.0	178.3	52 59.2	-60.0	178.4	51 59.3	-60.0	178.4	50 59.3	-60.0	178.4	49 59.3	-60.0	178.5	48 59.3	-60.0	178.5	47 59.3	-59.9	178.5	12
13	53 59.2	-60.0	178.3	52 59.2	-60.0	178.4	51 59.2	-59.9	178.4	50 59.3	-60.0	178.5	49 59.3	-60.0	178.5	48 59.3	-60.0	178.5	47 59.3	-60.0	178.5	46 59.4	-60.0	178.6	13
14	52 59.2	-60.0	178.4	51 59.2	-59.9	178.4	50 59.3	-60.0	178.5	49 59.3	-60.0	178.5	48 59.3	-60.0	178.5	47 59.3	-60.0	178.6	46 59.3	-59.9	178.6	45 59.4	-60.0	178.6	14
15	51 59.2	-59.9	178.4	50 59.3	-60.0	178.5	49 59.3	-60.0	178.5	48 59.3	-60.0	178.5	47 59.3	-60.0	178.6	46 59.3	-59.9	178.6	45 59.4	-60.0	178.6	44 59.4	-60.0	178.6	15
16	50 59.3	-60.0	178.5	49 59.3	-60.0	178.5	48 59.3	-60.0	178.5	47 59.3	-60.0	178.6	46 59.3	-59.9	178.6	45 59.4	-60.0	178.6	44 59.4	-60.0	178.6	43 59.4	-60.0	178.7	16
17	49 59.3	-60.0	178.5	48 59.3	-60.0	178.6	47 59.3	-60.0	178.6	46 59.3	-59.9	178.6	45 59.4	-60.0	178.6	44 59.4	-60.0	178.6	43 59.4	-60.0	178.7	42 59.4	-60.0	178.7	17
18	48 59.3	-60.0	178.6	47 59.3	-60.0	178.6	46 59.3	-59.9	178.6	45 59.4	-60.0	178.6	44 59.4	-60.0	178.7	43 59.4	-60.0	178.7	42 59.4	-60.0	178.7	41 59.4	-60.0	178.7	18
19	47 59.3	-60.0	178.6	46 59.3	-59.9	178.6	45 59.4	-60.0	178.6	44 59.4	-60.0	178.7	43 59.4	-60.0	178.7	42 59.4	-60.0	178.7	41 59.4	-60.0	178.7	40 59.4	-60.0	178.7	19
20	46 59.3	-59.9	178.6	45 59.4	-60.0	178.6	44 59.4	-60.0	178.7	43 59.4	-60.0	178.7	42 59.4	-60.0	178.7	41 59.4	-60.0	178.7	40 59.4	-60.0	178.8	39 59.4	-59.9	178.8	20
21	45 59.4	-60.0	178.7	44 59.4	-60.0	178.7	43 59.4	-60.0	178.7	42 59.4	-60.0	178.8	41 59.4	-60.0	178.8	40 59.4	-60.0	178.8	39 59.4	-59.9	178.8	38 59.5	-60.0	178.8	21
22	44 59.4	-60.0	178.7	43 59.4	-60.0	178.7	42 59.4	-60.0	178.7	41 59.4	-60.0	178.8	40 59.4	-60.0	178.8	39 59.4	-59.9	178.8	38 59.5	-60.0	178.8	37 59.5	-60.0	178.8	22
23	43 59.4	-60.0	178.7	42 59.4	-60.0	178.7	41 59.4	-60.0	178.8	40 59.4	-60.0	178.8	39 59.4	-59.9	178.8	38 59.5	-60.0	178.8	37 59.5	-60.0	178.8	36 59.5	-60.0	178.8	23
24	42 59.4	-60.0	178.8	41 59.4	-60.0	178.8	40 59.4	-60.0	178.8	39 59.4	-59.9	178.8	38 59.5	-60.0	178.8	37 59.5	-60.0	178.8	36 59.5	-60.0	178.9	35 59.5	-60.0	178.9	24
25	41 59.4	-60.0	178.8	40 59.4	-60.0	178.8	39 59.4	-59.9	178.8	38 59.5	-60.0	178.8	37 59.5	-60.0	178.8	36 59.5	-60.0	178.9	35 59.5	-60.0	178.9	34 59.5	-60.0	178.9	25
26	40 59.4	-60.0	178.8	39 59.4	-59.9	178.8	38 59.5	-60.0	178.8	37 59.5	-60.0	178.9	36 59.5	-60.0	178.9	35 59.5	-60.0	178.9	34 59.5	-60.0	178.9	33 59.5	-60.0	178.9	26
27	39 59.4	-59.9	178.8	38 59.5	-60.0	178.9	37 59.5	-60.0	178.9	36 59.5	-60.0	178.9	35 59.5	-60.0	178.9	34 59.5	-60.0	178.9	33 59.5	-60.0	178.9	32 59.5	-60.0	178.9	27
28	38 59.5	-60.0	178.9	37 59.5	-60.0	178.9	36 59.5	-60.0	178.9	35 59.5	-60.0	178.9	34 59.5	-60.0	178.9	33 59.5	-60.0	178.9	32 59.5	-60.0	178.9	31 59.5	-60.0	179.0	28
29	37 59.5	-60.0	178.9	36 59.5	-60.0	178.9	35 59.5	-60.0	178.9	34 59.5	-60.0	178.9	33 59.5	-60.0	178.9	32 59.5	-60.0	179.0	31 59.5	-60.0	179.0	30 59.5	-60.0	179.0	29
30	36 59.5	-60.0	178.9	35 59.5	-60.0	178.9	34 59.5	-60.0	178.9	33 59.5	-60.0	179.0	32 59.5	-60.0	179.0	31 59.5	-60.0	179.0	30 59.5	-60.0	179.0	29 59.5	-59.9	179.0	30
31	35 59.5	-60.0	178.9	34 59.5	-60.0	179.0	33 59.5	-60.0	179.0	32 59.5	-60.0	179.0	31 59.5	-60.0	179.0	30 59.5	-60.0	179.0	29 59.5	-59.9	179.0	28 59.6	-60.0	179.0	31
32	34 59.5	-60.0	179.0	33 59.5	-60.0	179.0	32 59.5	-60.0	179.0	31 59.5	-60.0	179.0	30 59.5	-60.0	179.0	29 59.5	-59.9	179.0	28 59.6	-60.0	179.0	27 59.6	-60.0	179.0	32
33	33 59.5	-60.0	179.0	32 59.5	-60.0	179.0	31 59.5	-60.0	179.0	30 59.5	-60.0	179.0	29 59.5	-59.9	179.0	28 59.6	-60.0	179.0	27 59.6	-60.0	179.1	26 59.6	-60.0	179.1	33
34	32 59.5	-60.0	179.0	31 59.5	-60.0	179.0	30 59.5	-59.9	179.0	29 59.5	-59.9	179.0	28 59.6	-60.0	179.1	27 59.6	-60.0	179.1	26 59.6	-60.0	179.1	25 59.6	-60.0	179.1	34
35	31 59.5	-60.0	179.0	30 59.5	-59.9	179.0	29 59.6	-60.0	179.1	28 59.6	-60.0	179.1	27 59.6	-60.0	179.1	26 59.6	-60.0	179.1	25 59.6	-60.0	179.1	24 59.6	-60.0	179.1	35
36	30 59.5	-59.9	179.1	29 59.6	-60.0	179.1	28 59.6	-60.0	179.1	27 59.6	-60.0	179.1	26 59.6	-60.0	179.1	25 59.6	-60.0	179.1	24 59.6	-60.0	179.1	23 59.6	-60.0	179.1	36
37	29 59.6	-60.0	179.1	28 59.6	-60.0	179.1	27 59.6	-60.0	179.1	26 59.6	-60.0	179.1	25 59.6	-60.0	179.1	24 59.6	-60.0	179.1	23 59.6	-60.0	179.1	22 59.6	-60.0	179.1	37
38	28 59.6	-60.0	179.1	27 59.6	-60.0	179.1	26 59.6	-60.0	179.1	25 59.6	-60.0	179.1	24 59.6	-60.0	179.1	23 59.6	-60.0	179.1	22 59.6	-60.0	179.1	21 59.6	-60.0	179.2	38
39	27 59.6	-60.0	179.1	26 59.6	-60.0	179.1	25 59.6	-60.0	179.1	24 59.6	-60.0	179.1	23 59.6	-60.0	179.1	22 59.6	-60.0	179.2	21 59.6	-60.0	179.2	20 59.6	-60.0	179.2	39
40	26 59.6	-60.0	179.1	25 59.6	-60.0	179.1	24 59.6	-60.0	179.2	23 59.6	-60.0	179.2	22 59.6	-60.0	179.2	21 59.6	-60.0	179.2	20 59.6	-60.0	179.2	19 59.6	-60.0	179.2	40
41	25 59.6	-60.0	179.2	24 59.6	-60.0	179.2	23 59.6	-60.0	179.2	22 59.6	-60.0	179.2	21 59.6	-60.0	179.2	20 59.6	-60.0	179.2	19 59.6	-60.0	179.2	18 59.6	-60.0	179.2	41
42	24 59.6	-60.0	179.2	23 59.6	-60.0	179.2	22 59.6	-60.0	179.2	21 59.6	-60.0	179.2	20 59.6	-60.0	179.2	19 59.6	-60.0	179.2	18 59.6	-60.0	179.2	17 59.6	-59.9	179.2	42
43	23 59.6	-60.0	179.2	22 59.6	-60.0	179.2	21 59.6	-60.0	179.2	20 59.6	-60.0	179.2	19 59.6	-60.0	179.2	18 59.6	-59.9	179.2	17 59.6	-59.9	179.2	16 59.7	-60.0	179.2	43
44	22 59.6	-60.0	179.2	21 59.6	-60.0	179.2	20 59.6	-60.0	179.2	19 59.6	-60.0	179.2	18 59.6	-59.9	179.2	17 59.7	-60.0	179.2	16 59.7	-60.0	179.2	15 59.7	-60.0	179.3	44
45	21 59.6	-60.0	179.2	20 59.6	-60.0	179.2	19 59.6	-59.9	179.2	18 59.6	-59.9	179.3	17 59.7	-60.0	179.3	16 59.7	-60.0	179.3	15 59.7	-60.0	179.3	14 59.7	-60.0	179.3	45
46	20 59.6	-59.9	179.3	19 59.6	-59.9	179.3	18 59.7	-60.0	179.3	17 59.7	-60.0	179.3	16 59.7	-60.0	179.3	15 59.7	-60.0	179.3	14 59.7	-60.0	179.3	13 59.7	-60.0	179.3	46
47	19 59.7	-60.0	179.3	18 59.7	-60.0	179.3	17 59.7	-60.0	179.3	16 59.7	-60.0	179.3	15 59.7	-60.0	179.3	14 59.7	-60.0	179.3	13 59.7	-60.0	179.3	12 59.7	-60.0	179.3	47
48	18 59.7	-60.0	179.3	17 59.7	-60.0	179.3	16 59.7	-60.0	179.3	15 59.7	-60.0	179.3	14 59.7	-60.0	179.3	13 59.7	-60.0	179.3	12 59.7	-60.0	179.3	11 59.7	-60.0	179.3	48
49	17 59.7	-60.0	179.3	16 59.7	-60.0	179.3	15 59.7	-60.0	179.3	14 59.7	-60.0	179.3	13 59.7	-60.0	179.3	12 59.7	-60.0	179.3	11 59.7	-60.0	179.3	10 59.7	-60.0	179.3	49
50	16 59.7	-60.0	179.3	15 59.7	-60.0	179.3	14 59.7	-60.0	179.3	13 59.7	-60.0	179.3	12 59.7	-60.0	179.3	11 59.7	-60.0	179.3	10 59.7	-60.0	179.3	9 59.7	-60.0	179.3	50
51	15 59.7	-60.0	179.3	14 59.7	-60.0	179.3	13 59.7	-60.0	179.4	12 59.7	-60.0	179.4	11 59.7	-60.0	179.4	10 59.7	-60.0	179.4	9 59.7	-60.0	179.4	8 59.7	-60.0	179.4	51
52	14 59.7	-60.0	179.4	13 59.7	-60.0	179.4	12 59.7	-60.0	179.4	11 59.7	-60.0	179.4	10 59.7	-60.0	179.4	9 59.7	-60.0	179.4	8 59.7	-60.0	179.4	7 59.7	-60.0	179.4	52
53	13 59.7	-60.0	179.4	12 59.7	-60.0	179.4	11 59.7	-60.0	179.4	10 59.7	-60.0	179.4	9 59.7	-60.0	179.4	8 59.7	-60.0	179.4	7 59.7	-60.0	179.4	6 59.7	-60.0	179.4	53
54	12 59.7	-60.0	179.4	11 59.7	-60.0	179.4	10 59.7	-60.0	179.4	9 59.7	-60.0	179.4	8 59.7	-60.0	179.4	7 59.7	-60.0	179.4	6 59.7	-60.0	179.4	5 59.7	-60.0	179.4	54
55	11 59.7	-60.0	179.4	10 59.7	-60.0	179.4	9 59.7	-60.0	179.4	8 59.7	-60.0	179.4	7 59.7	-60.0	179.4	6 59.7	-60.0	179.4	5 59.7	-60.0	179.4	4 59.7	-60.0	179.4	55
56	10 59.7	-60.0	179.4	9 59.7	-60.0	179.4	8 59.7	-60.0	179.4	7 59.7	-60.0	179.4	6 59.7	-60.0	179.4	5 59.7	-60.0	179.4	4 59.7	-60.0	179.4	3 59.7	-59.9	179.4	56
57	9 59.7	-60.0	179.4	8 59.7	-60.0	179.4	7 59.7	-60.0	179.5	6 59.7	-60.0	179.5	5 59.7	-59.9	179.5	4 59.7	-59.9	179.5	3 59.7	-59.9	179.5	2 59.8	-60.0	179.5	57
58	8 59.7	-60.0	179.5	7 59.7	-59.9	179.5	6 59.7	-59.9	179.5	5 59.7	-59.9	179.5	4 59.8	-60.0	179.5	3 59.8	-60.0	179.5	2 59.8	-60.0	179.5	1 59.8	-60.0	179.5	58
59	7 59.7	-59.9	179.5	6 59.8	-60.0	179.5	5 59.8	-60.0	179.5	4 59.8	-60.0	179.5	3 59.8	-60.0	179.5	2 59.8	-60.0	179.5	1 59.8	-60.0	179.5	0 59.8	-60.0	179.5	59
60	6 59.8	-60.0	179.5	5 59.8	-60.0	179.5	4 59.8	-60.0	179.5	3 59.8	-60.0	179.5	2 59.8	-60.0	179.5	1 59.8	-60.0	179.5	0 59.8	-60.0	179.5	0 00.2	+60.0	0.5	60
61	5 59.8	-60.0	179.5	4 59.8	-60.0	179.5	3 59.8	-60.0	179.5	2 59.8	-60.0	179.5	1 59.8	-60.0	179.5	0 59.8	-60.0	179.5	0 00.2	+60.0	0.5	1 00.2	+60.0	0.5	61
62	4 59.8	-60.0	179.5	3 59.8	-60.0	179.5	2 59.8	-60.0	179.5	1 59.8	-60.0	179.5	0 59.8	-60.0	179.5	0 00.2	+60.0	0.5	1 00.2	+60.0	0.5	2 00.2	+60.0	0.5	62
63	3 59.8	-60.0	179.5	2 59.8	-60.0	179.5	1 59.8	-60.0	179.5	0 59.8	-60.0	179.5	0 00.2	+60.0	0.5	1 00.2	+60.0	0.5	2 00.2	+60.0	0.5	3 00.2	+60.0	0.5	63
64	2 59.8	-60.0	179.6	1 59.8	-60.0	179.6	0 59.8	-60.0	179.6	0 00.2	+60.0	0.4	1 00.2	+60.0	0.4	2 00.2	+60.0	0.4	3 00.2	+60.0	0.4	4 00.2	+60.0	0.4	64
65	1 59.8	-60.0	179.6	0 59.8	-60.0	179.6	0 00.2	+60.0	0.4	1 00.2	+60.0	0.4	2 00.2	+60.0	0.4	3 00.2	+60.0	0.4	4 00.2	+60.0	0.4	5 00.2	+60.0	0.4	65
66	0 59.8	-60.0	179.6	0 00.2	+60.0	0.4	1 00.2	+60.0	0.4	2 00.2	+60.0	0.4	3 00.2	+60.0	0.4	4 00.2	+60.0	0.4	5 00.2	+60.0	0.4	6 00.2	+60.0	0.4	66
67	0 00.2	+60.0	0.4	1 00.2	+60.0	0.4	2 00.2	+60.0	0.4	3 00.2	+60.0	0.4	4 00.2	+60.0	0.4	5 00.2	+60.0	0.4	6 00.2	+60.0	0.4	7 00.2	+60.0	0.4	67
68	1 00.2	+60.0	0.4	2 00.2	+60.0	0.4	3 00.2	+60.0	0.4	4 00.2	+60.0	0.4	5 00.2	+60.0	0.4	6 00.2	+60.0	0.4	7 00.2	+60.0	0.4	8 00.2	+60.0	0.4	68
69	2 00.2	+60.0	0.4	3 00.2	+60.0	0.4	4 00.2	+60.0	0.4	5 00.2	+60.0	0.4	6 00.2	+60.0	0.4	7 00.2	+60.0	0.4	8 00.2	+60.0	0.4	9 00.2	+60.0	0.4	69
70	3 00.2	+60.0	0.3	4 00.2	+60.0	0.3	5 00.2	+60.0	0.3	6 00.2	+60.0	0.3	7 00.2	+60.0	0.3	8 00.2	+60.0	0.3	9 00.2	+60.0	0.3	10 00.2	+60.0	0.3	70
71	4 00.2	+59.9	0.3	5 00.2	+59.9	0.3	6 00.2	+59.9	0.3	7 00.2	+59.9	0.3	8 00.2	+59.9	0.3	9 00.2	+59.9	0.3	10 00.2	+59.9	0.3	11 00.2	+59.9	0.3	71
72	5 00.1	+60.0	0.3	6 00.1	+60.0	0.3	7 00.1	+60.0	0.3	8 00.1	+60.0	0.3	9 00.1	+60.0	0.3	10 00.1	+60.0	0.3	11 00.1	+60.0	0.3	12 00.1	+60.0	0.3	72
73	6 00.1	+60.0	0.3	7 00.1	+60.0	0.3	8 00.1	+60.0	0.3	9 00.1	+60.0	0.3	10 00.1	+60.0	0.3	11 00.1	+60.0	0.3	12 00.1	+60.0	0.3	13 00.1	+60.0	0.3	73
74	7 00.1	+60.0	0.3	8 00.1	+60.0	0.3	9 00.1	+60.0	0.3	10 00.1	+60.0	0.3	11 00.1	+60.0	0.3	12 00.1	+60.0	0.3	13 00.1	+60.0	0.3	14 00.1	+60.0	0.3	74
75	8 00.1	+60.0	0.3	9 00.1	+60.0	0.3	10 00.1	+60.0	0.3	11 00.1	+60.0	0.3	12 00.1	+60.0	0.3	13 00.1	+60.0	0.3	14 00.1	+60.0	0.3	15 00.1	+60.0	0.3	75
76	9 00.1	+60.0	0.2	10 00.1	+60.0	0.2	11 00.1	+60.0	0.2	12 00.1	+60.0	0.2	13 00.1	+60.0	0.2	14 00.1	+60.0	0.2	15 00.1	+60.0	0.3	16 00.1	+60.0	0.3	76
77	10 00.1	+60.0	0.2	11 00.1	+60.0	0.2	12 00.1	+60.0	0.2	13 00.1	+60.0	0.2	14 00.1	+60.0	0.2	15 00.1	+60.0	0.2	16 00.1	+60.0	0.2	17 00.1	+60.0	0.2	77
78	11 00.1	+60.0	0.2	12 00.1	+60.0	0.2	13 00.1	+60.0	0.2	14 00.1	+60.0	0.2	15 00.1	+60.0	0.2	16 00.1	+60.0	0.2	17 00.1	+60.0	0.2	18 00.1	+60.0	0.2	78
79	12 00.1	+60.0	0.2	13 00.1	+60.0	0.2	14 00.1	+60.0	0.2	15 00.1	+60.0	0.2	16 00.1	+60.0	0.2	17 00.1	+60.0	0.2	18 00.1	+60.0	0.2	19 00.1	+60.0	0.2	79
80	13 00.1	+60.0	0.2	14 00.1	+60.0	0.2	15 00.1	+60.0	0.2	16 00.1	+60.0	0.2	17 00.1	+60.0	0.2	18 00.1	+60.0	0.2	19 00.1	+60.0	0.2	20 00.1	+60.0	0.2	80
81	14 00.1	+60.0	0.2	15 00.1	+60.0	0.2	16 00.1	+60.0	0.2	17 00.1	+60.0	0.2	18 00.1	+60.0	0.2	19 00.1	+60.0	0.2	20 00.1	+60.0	0.2	21 00.1	+60.0	0.2	81
82	15 00.1	+60.0	0.1	16 00.1	+60.0	0.1	17 00.1	+60.0	0.1	18 00.1	+60.0	0.1	19 00.1	+60.0	0.1	20 00.1	+60.0	0.1	21 00.1	+60.0	0.1	22 00.1	+60.0	0.2	82
83	16 00.1	+60.0	0.1	17 00.1	+60.0	0.1	18 00.1	+60.0	0.1	19 00.1	+60.0	0.1	20 00.1	+60.0	0.1	21 00.1	+60.0	0.1	22 00.1	+60.0	0.1	23 00.1	+60.0	0.1	83
84	17 00.1	+59.9	0.1	18 00.1	+59.9	0.1	19 00.1	+59.9	0.1	20 00.1	+59.9	0.1	21 00.1	+59.9	0.1	22 00.1	+59.9	0.1	23 00.1	+59.9	0.1	24 00.1	+59.9	0.1	84
85	18 00.0	+60.0	0.1	19 00.0	+60.0	0.1	20 00.0	+60.0	0.1	21 00.0	+60.0	0.1	22 00.0	+60.0	0.1	23 00.0	+60.0	0.1	24 00.0	+60.0	0.1	25 00.0	+60.0	0.1	85
86	19 00.0	+60.0	0.1	20 00.0	+60.0	0.1	21 00.0	+60.0	0.1	22 00.0	+60.0	0.1	23 00.0	+60.0	0.1	24 00.0	+60.0	0.1	25 00.0	+60.0	0.1	26 00.0	+60.0	0.1	86
87	20 00.0	+60.0	0.1	21 00.0	+60.0	0.1	22 00.0	+60.0	0.1	23 00.0	+60.0	0.1	24 00.0	+60.0	0.1	25 00.0	+60.0	0.1	26 00.0	+60.0	0.1	27 00.0	+60.0	0.1	87
88	21 00.0	+60.0	0.0	22 00.0	+60.0	0.0	23 00.0	+60.0	0.0	24 00.0	+60.0	0.0	25 00.0	+60.0	0.0	26 00.0	+60.0	0.0	27 00.0	+60.0	0.0	28 00.0	+60.0	0.0	88
89	22 00.0	+60.0	0.0	23 00.0	+60.0	0.0	24 00.0	+60.0	0.0	25 00.0	+60.0	0.0	26 00.0	+60.0	0.0	27 00.0	+60.0	0.0	28 00.0	+60.0	0.0	29 00.0	+60.0	0.0	89
90	23 00.0	+60.0	0.0	24 00.0	+60.0	0.0	25 00.0	+60.0	0.0	26 00.0	+60.0	0.0	27 00.0	+60.0	0.0	28 00.0	+60.0	0.0	29 00.0	+60.0	0.0	30 00.0	+60.0	0.0	90
	23°			24°			25°			26°			27°			28°			29°			30°			

S. Lat. { L.H.A. greater than 180° ....Zn=180°–Z; L.H.A. less than 180°..........Zn=180°+Z

LATITUDE **SAME** NAME AS DECLINATION L.H.A. 179°, 181°

187

Dec.	23° Hc	d	Z	24° Hc	d	Z	25° Hc	d	Z	26° Hc	d	Z	27° Hc	d	Z	28° Hc	d	Z	29° Hc	d	Z	30° Hc	d	Z	Dec.
°	° ′	′	°	° ′	′	°	° ′	′	°	° ′	′	°	° ′	′	°	° ′	′	°	° ′	′	°	° ′	′	°	°
0	66 55.1	+59.8	174.9	65 55.3	+59.8	175.1	64 55.5	+59.8	175.3	63 55.7	+59.9	175.4	62 55.9	+59.8	175.6	61 56.1	+59.8	175.7	60 56.2	+59.9	175.9	59 56.4	+59.9	176.0	0
1	67 54.9	+59.7	174.7	66 55.1	+59.8	174.9	65 55.3	+59.9	175.1	64 55.6	+59.8	175.3	63 55.7	+59.9	175.4	62 55.9	+59.9	175.6	61 56.1	+59.9	175.7	60 56.3	+59.8	175.9	1
2	68 54.6	+59.8	174.4	67 54.9	+59.8	174.7	66 55.2	+59.7	174.9	65 55.4	+59.8	175.1	64 55.6	+59.8	175.3	63 55.8	+59.8	175.4	62 56.0	+59.8	175.6	61 56.1	+59.9	175.7	2
3	69 54.4	+59.7	174.2	68 54.7	+59.7	174.4	67 54.9	+59.8	174.7	66 55.2	+59.8	174.9	65 55.4	+59.8	175.1	64 55.6	+59.9	175.3	63 55.8	+59.9	175.5	62 56.0	+59.9	175.6	3
4	70 54.1	+59.7	173.9	69 54.4	+59.8	174.2	68 54.7	+59.8	174.4	67 55.0	+59.8	174.7	66 55.2	+59.8	174.9	65 55.5	+59.8	175.1	64 55.7	+59.8	175.3	63 55.9	+59.8	175.5	4
5	71 53.8	+59.7	173.6	70 54.2	+59.7	173.9	69 54.5	+59.7	174.2	68 54.8	+59.7	174.5	67 55.0	+59.8	174.7	66 55.3	+59.8	174.9	65 55.5	+59.8	175.1	64 55.7	+59.9	175.3	5
6	72 53.5	+59.6	173.2	71 53.9	+59.6	173.6	70 54.2	+59.7	173.9	69 54.5	+59.8	174.2	68 54.8	+59.8	174.5	67 55.1	+59.8	174.7	66 55.3	+59.9	174.9	65 55.6	+59.8	175.1	6
7	73 53.1	+59.6	172.8	72 53.5	+59.7	173.2	71 53.9	+59.7	173.6	70 54.3	+59.7	173.9	69 54.6	+59.7	174.2	68 54.9	+59.8	174.5	67 55.2	+59.7	174.7	66 55.4	+59.8	174.9	7
8	74 52.7	+59.5	172.4	73 53.2	+59.5	172.8	72 53.6	+59.6	173.3	71 54.0	+59.7	173.6	70 54.3	+59.8	173.9	69 54.7	+59.7	174.2	68 54.9	+59.8	174.5	67 55.2	+59.8	174.7	8
9	75 52.2	+59.4	171.9	74 52.7	+59.5	172.4	73 53.2	+59.6	172.9	72 53.7	+59.6	173.3	71 54.1	+59.6	173.6	70 54.4	+59.7	174.0	69 54.7	+59.8	174.2	68 55.0	+59.8	174.5	9
10	76 51.6	+59.4	171.3	75 52.2	+59.5	171.9	74 52.8	+59.5	172.4	73 53.3	+59.6	172.9	72 53.7	+59.7	173.3	71 54.1	+59.7	173.6	70 54.5	+59.7	174.0	69 54.8	+59.7	174.3	10
11	77 51.0	+59.2	170.6	76 51.7	+59.4	171.3	75 52.3	+59.5	171.9	74 52.9	+59.5	172.5	73 53.4	+59.6	172.9	72 53.8	+59.7	173.3	71 54.2	+59.7	173.7	70 54.5	+59.8	174.0	11
12	78 50.2	+59.1	169.8	77 51.1	+59.2	170.7	76 51.8	+59.4	171.4	75 52.4	+59.5	172.0	74 53.0	+59.5	172.5	73 53.5	+59.6	172.9	72 53.9	+59.6	173.3	71 54.3	+59.7	173.7	12
13	79 49.3	+58.9	168.9	78 50.3	+59.1	169.9	77 51.2	+59.2	170.7	76 51.9	+59.4	171.4	75 52.5	+59.5	172.0	74 53.1	+59.5	172.5	73 53.5	+59.7	173.0	72 54.0	+59.6	173.4	13
14	80 48.2	+58.6	167.8	79 49.4	+58.9	169.0	78 50.4	+59.1	169.9	77 51.3	+59.2	170.7	76 52.0	+59.4	171.4	75 52.6	+59.5	172.0	74 53.2	+59.5	172.5	73 53.6	+59.7	173.0	14
15	81 46.8	+58.3	166.4	80 48.3	+58.7	167.8	79 49.5	+59.0	169.0	78 50.5	+59.2	170.0	77 51.4	+59.3	170.8	76 52.1	+59.4	171.5	75 52.7	+59.5	172.1	74 53.3	+59.5	172.6	15
16	82 45.1	+57.7	164.6	81 47.0	+58.2	166.4	80 48.5	+58.6	167.9	79 49.7	+58.9	169.0	78 50.7	+59.1	170.0	77 51.5	+59.3	170.8	76 52.2	+59.4	171.5	75 52.8	+59.5	172.1	16
17	83 42.8	+56.9	162.3	82 45.2	+57.8	164.7	81 47.1	+58.3	166.5	80 48.6	+58.7	167.9	79 49.8	+59.0	169.1	78 50.8	+59.2	170.1	77 51.6	+59.3	170.9	76 52.3	+59.5	171.6	17
18	84 39.7	+55.5	159.1	83 43.0	+56.9	162.3	82 45.4	+57.8	164.7	81 47.3	+58.3	166.6	80 48.8	+58.7	168.0	79 50.0	+58.9	169.2	78 50.9	+59.2	170.1	77 51.8	+59.3	170.9	18
19	85 35.2	+53.0•	154.6	84 39.9	+55.6	159.2	83 43.2	+57.0	162.4	82 45.6	+57.9	164.8	81 47.5	+58.3	166.6	80 48.9	+58.8	168.1	79 50.1	+59.0	169.2	78 51.1	+59.2	170.2	19
20	86 28.2	+48.2•	147.8	85 35.5	+53.1•	154.7	84 40.2	+55.6	159.3	83 43.5	+57.0	162.5	82 45.8	+57.9	164.9	81 47.7	+58.4	166.7	80 49.1	+58.8	168.1	79 50.3	+59.0	169.3	20
21	87 16.4	+37.5•	136.8	86 28.6	+48.3•	148.0	85 35.8	+53.2•	154.9	84 40.5	+55.7	159.4	83 43.7	+57.1	162.6	82 46.1	+57.9	165.0	81 47.9	+58.4	166.8	80 49.3	+58.8	168.2	21
22	87 53.9	+15.6•	118.0	87 16.9	+37.8•	137.0	86 29.0	+48.5•	148.2	85 36.2	+53.3•	155.0	84 40.8	+55.7	159.6	83 44.0	+57.1	162.8	82 46.3	+57.9	165.1	81 48.1	+58.4	166.9	22
23	88 09.5	-14.8•	89.6	87 54.7	+15.7•	118.2	87 17.5	+37.9•	137.2	86 29.5	+48.6•	148.3	85 36.5	+53.4•	155.2	84 41.1	+55.8	159.7	83 44.2	+57.2	162.9	82 46.5	+58.0	165.2	23
24	87 54.7	-37.2•	61.0	88 10.4	-15.0•	89.6	87 55.4	+15.8•	118.4	87 18.1	+38.1•	137.4	86 29.9	+48.8•	148.5	85 36.9	+53.5•	155.4	84 41.4	+55.9	159.8	83 44.5	+57.2	163.0	24
25	87 17.5	-48.0•	42.0	87 55.4	-37.3•	60.8	88 11.2	-15.0•	89.6	87 56.2	+15.9•	118.6	87 18.7	+38.3•	137.6	86 30.4	+48.9•	148.7	85 37.3	+53.6•	155.5	84 41.7	+56.0	160.0	25
26	86 29.5	-53.0•	30.8	87 18.1	-48.2•	41.8	87 56.2	-37.5•	60.6	88 12.1	-15.1•	89.6	87 57.0	+16.1•	118.7	87 19.3	+38.5•	137.8	86 30.9	+49.0•	148.9	85 37.7	+53.7•	155.7	26
27	85 36.5	-55.4	24.0	86 29.9	-53.0•	30.6	87 18.7	-48.3•	41.5	87 57.0	-37.7•	60.4	88 13.1	-15.3•	89.5	87 57.8	+16.2•	118.9	87 19.9	+38.8•	138.1	86 31.4	+49.2•	149.2	27
28	84 41.1	-56.9	19.4	85 36.9	-55.5	23.8	86 30.4	-53.1•	30.4	87 19.3	-48.4•	41.3	87 57.8	-37.9•	60.1	88 14.0	-15.3•	89.5	87 58.7	+16.3•	119.2	87 20.6	+39.0•	138.3	28
29	83 44.2	-57.7	16.2	84 41.4	-56.9	19.3	85 37.3	-55.6	23.6	86 30.9	-53.2•	30.1	87 19.9	-48.5•	41.0	87 58.7	-38.1•	59.9	88 15.0	-15.4•	89.5	87 59.6	+16.5•	119.4	29
30	82 46.5	-58.2	13.9	83 44.5	-57.7	16.1	84 41.7	-56.9	19.1	85 37.7	-55.7	23.4	86 31.4	-53.3•	29.9	87 20.6	-48.7•	40.7	87 59.6	-38.3•	59.6	88 16.1	-15.6•	89.5	30
31	81 48.3	-58.7	12.1	82 46.8	-58.3	13.8	83 44.8	-57.8	15.9	84 42.0	-57.0	18.9	85 38.1	-55.7	23.1	86 31.9	-53.4•	29.6	87 21.3	-48.9•	40.4	88 00.5	-38.5•	59.4	31
32	80 49.6	-58.8	10.7	81 48.5	-58.7	12.0	82 47.0	-58.3	13.6	83 45.0	-57.8	15.8	84 42.4	-57.1	18.7	85 38.5	-55.8	22.9	86 32.4	-53.5•	29.4	87 22.0	-49.0•	40.1	32
33	79 50.8	-59.1	9.6	80 49.8	-58.9	10.6	81 48.7	-58.7	11.9	82 47.2	-58.3	13.5	83 45.3	-57.8	15.6	84 42.7	-57.1	18.5	85 38.9	-55.8	22.7	86 33.0	-53.7•	29.1	33
34	78 51.7	-59.3	8.6	79 50.9	-59.1	9.4	80 50.0	-58.9	10.5	81 48.9	-58.7	11.7	82 47.5	-58.4	13.3	83 45.6	-57.9	15.4	84 43.1	-57.2	18.3	85 39.3	-55.9	22.5	34
35	77 52.4	-59.3	7.8	78 51.8	-59.2	8.5	79 51.1	-59.1	9.3	80 50.2	-58.9	10.3	81 49.1	-58.7	11.6	82 47.7	-58.3	13.2	83 45.9	-57.9	15.3	84 43.4	-57.2	18.1	35
36	76 53.1	-59.4	7.1	77 52.6	-59.4	7.7	78 52.0	-59.3	8.4	79 51.3	-59.1	9.2	80 50.4	-58.9	10.2	81 49.4	-58.8	11.4	82 48.0	-58.4	13.0	83 46.2	-57.9	15.1	36
37	75 53.7	-59.6	6.6	76 53.2	-59.4	7.1	77 52.7	-59.3	7.6	78 52.2	-59.3	8.3	79 51.5	-59.2	9.1	80 50.6	-58.9	10.1	81 49.6	-58.7	11.3	82 48.3	-58.5	12.9	37
38	74 54.1	-59.5	6.1	75 53.8	-59.5	6.5	76 53.4	-59.5	7.0	77 52.9	-59.4	7.5	78 52.3	-59.2	8.2	79 51.7	-59.2	9.0	80 50.9	-59.0	10.0	81 49.8	-58.7	11.2	38
39	73 54.6	-59.6	5.6	74 54.3	-59.6	6.0	75 53.9	-59.5	6.4	76 53.5	-59.4	6.9	77 53.1	-59.4	7.4	78 52.5	-59.3	8.1	79 51.9	-59.2	8.9	80 51.1	-59.0	9.8	39
40	72 55.0	-59.7	5.2	73 54.7	-59.6	5.5	74 54.4	-59.6	5.9	75 54.1	-59.6	6.3	76 53.7	-59.5	6.8	77 53.2	-59.4	7.3	78 52.7	-59.3	8.0	79 52.1	-59.2	8.7	40
41	71 55.3	-59.7	4.9	72 55.1	-59.7	5.1	73 54.8	-59.6	5.5	74 54.5	-59.6	5.8	75 54.2	-59.5	6.2	76 53.8	-59.5	6.7	77 53.4	-59.4	7.2	78 52.9	-59.4	7.9	41
42	70 55.6	-59.7	4.6	71 55.4	-59.7	4.8	72 55.2	-59.7	5.1	73 54.9	-59.6	5.4	74 54.7	-59.6	5.7	75 54.3	-59.5	6.1	76 54.0	-59.5	6.6	77 53.5	-59.4	7.1	42
43	69 55.9	-59.8	4.3	70 55.7	-59.7	4.5	71 55.5	-59.7	4.7	72 55.3	-59.7	5.0	73 55.1	-59.7	5.3	74 54.8	-59.6	5.6	75 54.5	-59.6	6.0	76 54.1	-59.5	6.5	43
44	68 56.1	-59.7	4.0	69 56.0	-59.8	4.2	70 55.8	-59.7	4.4	71 55.6	-59.7	4.6	72 55.4	-59.7	4.9	73 55.2	-59.7	5.2	74 54.9	-59.6	5.5	75 54.6	-59.5	5.9	44
45	67 56.4	-59.8	3.8	68 56.2	-59.7	3.9	69 56.1	-59.8	4.1	70 55.9	-59.7	4.3	71 55.7	-59.7	4.6	72 55.5	-59.6	4.8	73 55.3	-59.6	5.1	74 55.1	-59.7	5.4	45
46	66 56.6	-59.8	3.5	67 56.5	-59.8	3.7	68 56.3	-59.8	3.9	69 56.2	-59.8	4.1	70 56.0	-59.7	4.3	71 55.9	-59.8	4.5	72 55.7	-59.7	4.7	73 55.4	-59.6	5.0	46
47	65 56.8	-59.8	3.3	66 56.7	-59.8	3.5	67 56.5	-59.7	3.6	68 56.4	-59.8	3.8	69 56.3	-59.8	4.0	70 56.1	-59.7	4.2	71 56.0	-59.8	4.4	72 55.8	-59.7	4.7	47
48	64 57.0	-59.9	3.2	65 56.9	-59.9	3.3	66 56.8	-59.9	3.4	67 56.6	-59.8	3.6	68 56.5	-59.8	3.7	69 56.4	-59.8	3.9	70 56.2	-59.7	4.1	71 56.1	-59.7	4.3	48
49	63 57.1	-59.8	3.0	64 57.0	-59.8	3.1	65 56.9	-59.8	3.2	66 56.8	-59.8	3.4	67 56.7	-59.8	3.5	68 56.6	-59.8	3.7	69 56.5	-59.8	3.8	70 56.4	-59.8	4.0	49
50	62 57.3	-59.9	2.8	63 57.2	-59.8	2.9	64 57.1	-59.8	3.0	65 57.0	-59.8	3.2	66 56.9	-59.8	3.3	67 56.8	-59.8	3.4	68 56.7	-59.8	3.6	69 56.6	-59.8	3.8	50
51	61 57.4	-59.8	2.7	62 57.4	-59.9	2.8	63 57.3	-59.9	2.9	64 57.2	-59.8	3.0	65 57.1	-59.8	3.1	66 57.0	-59.8	3.2	67 56.9	-59.8	3.4	68 56.8	-59.8	3.5	51
52	60 57.6	-59.9	2.5	61 57.5	-59.9	2.6	62 57.4	-59.8	2.7	63 57.4	-59.9	2.8	64 57.3	-59.9	2.9	65 57.2	-59.8	3.0	66 57.1	-59.8	3.1	67 57.0	-59.8	3.3	52
53	59 57.7	-59.9	2.4	60 57.6	-59.8	2.5	61 57.6	-59.9	2.6	62 57.5	-59.9	2.6	63 57.4	-59.8	2.7	64 57.4	-59.9	2.8	65 57.3	-59.8	3.0	66 57.2	-59.8	3.1	53
54	58 57.8	-59.9	2.3	59 57.8	-59.9	2.3	60 57.7	-59.9	2.4	61 57.6	-59.8	2.5	62 57.6	-59.9	2.6	63 57.5	-59.8	2.7	64 57.5	-59.9	2.8	65 57.4	-59.9	2.9	54
55	57 57.9	-59.9	2.2	58 57.9	-59.9	2.2	59 57.8	-59.9	2.3	60 57.8	-59.9	2.4	61 57.7	-59.9	2.4	62 57.7	-59.9	2.5	63 57.6	-59.9	2.6	64 57.5	-59.8	2.7	55
56	56 58.0	-59.9	2.1	57 58.0	-59.9	2.1	58 57.9	-59.8	2.2	59 57.9	-59.9	2.2	60 57.8	-59.8	2.3	61 57.8	-59.9	2.4	62 57.7	-59.8	2.5	63 57.7	-59.9	2.5	56
57	55 58.1	-59.9	1.9	56 58.1	-59.9	2.0	57 58.1	-59.9	2.1	58 58.0	-59.9	2.1	59 58.0	-59.9	2.2	60 57.9	-59.9	2.2	61 57.9	-59.9	2.3	62 57.8	-59.8	2.4	57
58	54 58.2	-59.9	1.8	55 58.2	-59.9	1.9	56 58.2	-59.9	1.9	57 58.1	-59.9	2.0	58 58.1	-59.9	2.1	59 58.0	-59.8	2.1	60 58.0	-59.9	2.2	61 58.0	-59.9	2.3	58
59	53 58.3	-59.9	1.8	54 58.3	-59.9	1.8	55 58.3	-60.0	1.8	56 58.2	-59.9	1.9	57 58.2	-59.9	1.9	58 58.2	-59.9	2.0	59 58.1	-59.9	2.1	60 58.1	-59.9	2.1	59
60	52 58.4	-59.9	1.7	53 58.4	-59.9	1.7	54 58.3	-59.9	1.7	55 58.3	-59.9	1.8	56 58.3	-59.9	1.8	57 58.3	-59.9	1.9	58 58.2	-59.9	1.9	59 58.2	-59.9	2.0	60
61	51 58.5	-59.9	1.6	52 58.5	-60.0	1.6	53 58.4	-59.9	1.6	54 58.4	-59.9	1.7	55 58.4	-59.9	1.7	56 58.4	-60.0	1.8	57 58.3	-59.9	1.8	58 58.3	-59.9	1.9	61
62	50 58.6	-60.0	1.5	51 58.5	-59.9	1.5	52 58.5	-59.9	1.6	53 58.5	-59.9	1.6	54 58.5	-59.9	1.6	55 58.4	-59.9	1.7	56 58.4	-59.9	1.7	57 58.4	-59.9	1.8	62
63	49 58.6	-59.9	1.4	50 58.6	-59.9	1.4	51 58.6	-59.9	1.5	52 58.6	-59.9	1.5	53 58.6	-60.0	1.5	54 58.5	-59.9	1.6	55 58.5	-59.9	1.6	56 58.5	-59.9	1.7	63
64	48 58.7	-59.9	1.3	49 58.7	-59.9	1.4	50 58.7	-59.9	1.4	51 58.7	-60.0	1.4	52 58.6	-59.9	1.5	53 58.6	-59.9	1.5	54 58.6	-59.9	1.5	55 58.6	-59.9	1.6	64
65	47 58.8	-59.9	1.3	48 58.8	-60.0	1.3	49 58.8	-60.0	1.3	50 58.7	-59.9	1.3	51 58.7	-59.9	1.4	52 58.7	-59.9	1.4	53 58.7	-59.9	1.4	54 58.7	-60.0	1.5	65
66	46 58.9	-60.0	1.2	47 58.8	-59.9	1.2	48 58.8	-59.9	1.2	49 58.8	-59.9	1.3	50 58.8	-59.9	1.3	51 58.8	-59.9	1.3	52 58.8	-60.0	1.4	53 58.7	-59.9	1.4	66
67	45 58.9	-59.9	1.1	46 58.9	-59.9	1.1	47 58.9	-59.9	1.2	48 58.9	-60.0	1.2	49 58.8	-59.9	1.2	50 58.9	-60.0	1.2	51 58.8	-59.9	1.3	52 58.8	-59.9	1.3	67
68	44 59.0	-60.0	1.1	45 59.0	-60.0	1.1	46 59.0	-60.0	1.1	47 58.9	-59.9	1.1	48 58.9	-59.9	1.1	49 58.9	-59.9	1.2	50 58.9	-59.9	1.2	51 58.9	-59.9	1.2	68
69	43 59.0	-59.9	1.0	44 59.0	-59.9	1.0	45 59.0	-59.9	1.0	46 59.0	-59.9	1.1	47 59.0	-59.9	1.1	48 59.0	-59.9	1.1	49 59.0	-60.0	1.1	50 59.0	-60.0	1.1	69
70	42 59.1	-59.9	0.9	43 59.1	-60.0	1.0	44 59.1	-60.0	1.0	45 59.1	-60.0	1.0	46 59.1	-60.0	1.0	47 59.1	-60.0	1.0	48 59.0	-59.9	1.0	49 59.0	-59.9	1.1	70
71	41 59.2	-60.0	0.9	42 59.1	-59.9	0.9	43 59.1	-59.9	0.9	44 59.1	-59.9	0.9	45 59.1	-59.9	0.9	46 59.1	-59.9	1.0	47 59.1	-59.9	1.0	48 59.1	-59.9	1.0	71
72	40 59.2	-59.9	0.8	41 59.2	-59.9	0.8	42 59.2	-59.9	0.8	43 59.2	-60.0	0.9	44 59.2	-60.0	0.9	45 59.2	-60.0	0.9	46 59.2	-60.0	0.9	47 59.2	-60.0	0.9	72
73	39 59.3	-60.0	0.8	40 59.3	-60.0	0.8	41 59.3	-60.0	0.8	42 59.2	-59.9	0.8	43 59.2	-59.9	0.8	44 59.2	-59.9	0.8	45 59.2	-59.9	0.8	46 59.2	-59.9	0.9	73
74	38 59.3	-59.9	0.7	39 59.3	-59.9	0.7	40 59.3	-59.9	0.7	41 59.3	-59.9	0.7	42 59.3	-59.9	0.8	43 59.3	-60.0	0.8	44 59.3	-60.0	0.8	45 59.3	-60.0	0.8	74
75	37 59.4	-60.0	0.7	38 59.4	-60.0	0.7	39 59.4	-60.0	0.7	40 59.4	-60.0	0.7	41 59.4	-60.0	0.7	42 59.3	-59.9	0.7	43 59.3	-59.9	0.7	44 59.3	-59.9	0.7	75
76	36 59.4	-59.9	0.6	37 59.4	-59.9	0.6	38 59.4	-59.9	0.6	39 59.4	-59.9	0.6	40 59.4	-59.9	0.6	41 59.4	-60.0	0.7	42 59.4	-60.0	0.7	43 59.4	-60.0	0.7	76
77	35 59.5	-60.0	0.6	36 59.5	-60.0	0.6	37 59.5	-60.0	0.6	38 59.5	-60.0	0.6	39 59.5	-60.0	0.6	40 59.4	-59.9	0.6	41 59.4	-59.9	0.6	42 59.4	-59.9	0.6	77
78	34 59.5	-59.9	0.5	35 59.5	-59.9	0.5	36 59.5	-59.9	0.5	37 59.5	-59.9	0.5	38 59.5	-60.0	0.5	39 59.5	-60.0	0.5	40 59.5	-60.0	0.6	41 59.5	-60.0	0.6	78
79	33 59.6	-60.0	0.5	34 59.6	-60.0	0.5	35 59.6	-60.0	0.5	36 59.6	-60.0	0.5	37 59.5	-59.9	0.5	38 59.5	-59.9	0.5	39 59.5	-59.9	0.5	40 59.5	-59.9	0.5	79
80	32 59.6	-60.0	0.4	33 59.6	-60.0	0.4	34 59.6	-60.0	0.4	35 59.6	-60.0	0.4	36 59.6	-60.0	0.4	37 59.6	-60.0	0.4	38 59.6	-60.0	0.4	39 59.6	-60.0	0.5	80
81	31 59.6	-59.9	0.4	32 59.6	-59.9	0.4	33 59.6	-59.9	0.4	34 59.6	-59.9	0.4	35 59.6	-59.9	0.4	36 59.6	-59.9	0.4	37 59.6	-59.9	0.4	38 59.6	-59.9	0.4	81
82	30 59.7	-60.0	0.3	31 59.7	-60.0	0.3	32 59.7	-60.0	0.3	33 59.7	-60.0	0.3	34 59.7	-60.0	0.3	35 59.7	-60.0	0.3	36 59.7	-60.0	0.3	37 59.7	-60.0	0.4	82
83	29 59.7	-59.9	0.3	30 59.7	-59.9	0.3	31 59.7	-59.9	0.3	32 59.7	-59.9	0.3	33 59.7	-59.9	0.3	34 59.7	-59.9	0.3	35 59.7	-59.9	0.3	36 59.7	-59.9	0.3	83
84	28 59.8	-60.0	0.2	29 59.8	-60.0	0.2	30 59.8	-60.0	0.2	31 59.8	-60.0	0.2	32 59.8	-60.0	0.2	33 59.8	-60.0	0.3	34 59.8	-60.0	0.3	35 59.8	-60.0	0.3	84
85	27 59.8	-60.0	0.2	28 59.8	-60.0	0.2	29 59.8	-60.0	0.2	30 59.8	-60.0	0.2	31 59.8	-60.0	0.2	32 59.8	-60.0	0.2	33 59.8	-60.0	0.2	34 59.8	-60.0	0.2	85
86	26 59.8	-59.9	0.2	27 59.8	-59.9	0.2	28 59.8	-59.9	0.2	29 59.8	-59.9	0.2	30 59.8	-59.9	0.2	31 59.8	-59.9	0.2	32 59.8	-59.9	0.2	33 59.8	-59.9	0.2	86
87	25 59.9	-60.0	0.1	26 59.9	-60.0	0.1	27 59.9	-60.0	0.1	28 59.9	-60.0	0.1	29 59.9	-60.0	0.1	30 59.9	-60.0	0.1	31 59.9	-60.0	0.1	32 59.9	-60.0	0.1	87
88	24 59.9	-59.9	0.1	25 59.9	-59.9	0.1	26 59.9	-59.9	0.1	27 59.9	-59.9	0.1	28 59.9	-59.9	0.1	29 59.9	-59.9	0.1	30 59.9	-59.9	0.1	31 59.9	-59.9	0.1	88
89	24 00.0	-60.0	0.0	25 00.0	-60.0	0.0	26 00.0	-60.0	0.0	27 00.0	-60.0	0.0	28 00.0	-60.0	0.0	29 00.0	-60.0	0.0	30 00.0	-60.0	0.0	31 00.0	-60.0	0.0	89
90	23 00.0	-60.0	0.0	24 00.0	-60.0	0.0	25 00.0	-60.0	0.0	26 00.0	-60.0	0.0	27 00.0	-60.0	0.0	28 00.0	-60.0	0.0	29 00.0	-60.0	0.0	30 00.0	-60.0	0.0	90
	23°			24°			25°			26°			27°			28°			29°			30°			

Dec.	23°			24°			25°			26°			27°			28°			29°			30°			Dec.
°	Hc ° ′	d ′	Z °	Hc ° ′	d ′	Z °	Hc ° ′	d ′	Z °	Hc ° ′	d ′	Z °	Hc ° ′	d ′	Z °	Hc ° ′	d ′	Z °	Hc ° ′	d ′	Z °	Hc ° ′	d ′	Z °	°
0	66 55.1	-59.8	174.9	65 55.3	-59.8	175.1	64 55.5	-59.8	175.3	63 55.7	-59.8	175.4	62 55.9	-59.9	175.6	61 56.1	-59.9	175.7	60 56.2	-59.9	175.9	59 56.4	-59.9	176.0	0
1	65 55.3	-59.9	175.1	64 55.5	-59.9	175.3	63 55.7	-59.9	175.4	62 55.9	-59.9	175.6	61 56.0	-59.8	175.7	60 56.2	-59.9	175.9	59 56.3	-59.9	176.0	58 56.5	-59.9	176.1	1
2	64 55.4	-59.8	175.3	63 55.6	-59.8	175.4	62 55.8	-59.8	175.6	61 56.0	-59.9	175.7	60 56.2	-59.9	175.9	59 56.3	-59.9	176.0	58 56.4	-59.8	176.1	57 56.6	-59.9	176.2	2
3	63 55.6	-59.8	175.5	62 55.8	-59.9	175.6	61 56.0	-59.9	175.8	60 56.1	-59.9	175.9	59 56.3	-59.9	176.0	58 56.4	-59.9	176.1	57 56.6	-60.0	176.2	56 56.7	-59.9	176.3	3
4	62 55.8	-59.9	175.6	61 55.9	-59.8	175.8	60 56.1	-59.9	175.9	59 56.2	-59.8	176.0	58 56.4	-59.9	176.1	57 56.5	-59.9	176.2	56 56.6	-59.9	176.3	55 56.8	-59.9	176.4	4
5	61 55.9	-59.9	175.8	60 56.1	-59.9	175.9	59 56.2	-59.9	176.0	58 56.4	-59.9	176.1	57 56.5	-59.9	176.2	56 56.6	-59.9	176.3	55 56.7	-59.9	176.4	54 56.9	-60.0	176.5	5
6	60 56.0	-59.8	175.9	59 56.2	-59.9	176.0	58 56.3	-59.9	176.1	57 56.5	-59.9	176.3	56 56.6	-59.9	176.4	55 56.7	-59.9	176.4	54 56.8	-59.9	176.5	53 56.9	-60.0	176.6	6
7	59 56.2	-59.9	176.0	58 56.3	-59.9	176.2	57 56.4	-59.8	176.3	56 56.6	-59.9	176.4	55 56.7	-59.9	176.5	54 56.8	-59.9	176.5	53 56.9	-59.9	176.6	52 57.0	-59.9	176.7	7
8	58 56.3	-59.9	176.2	57 56.4	-59.9	176.3	56 56.6	-59.9	176.4	55 56.7	-59.9	176.5	54 56.8	-59.9	176.6	53 56.9	-59.9	176.6	52 57.0	-59.9	176.7	51 57.1	-60.0	176.8	8
9	57 56.4	-59.9	176.3	56 56.5	-59.9	176.4	55 56.7	-60.0	176.5	54 56.8	-60.0	176.6	53 56.9	-60.0	176.6	52 57.0	-60.0	176.7	51 57.1	-60.0	176.8	50 57.2	-60.0	176.9	9
10	56 56.5	-59.9	176.4	55 56.6	-59.9	176.5	54 56.7	-59.9	176.6	53 56.8	-59.9	176.7	52 56.9	-59.9	176.7	51 57.0	-59.9	176.8	50 57.1	-59.9	176.9	49 57.2	-59.9	176.9	10
11	55 56.6	-59.9	176.5	54 56.7	-59.9	176.6	53 56.8	-59.9	176.7	52 56.9	-59.9	176.7	51 57.0	-59.9	176.8	50 57.1	-59.9	176.9	49 57.2	-59.9	176.9	48 57.3	-60.0	177.0	11
12	54 56.7	-59.9	176.6	53 56.8	-59.9	176.7	52 56.9	-59.9	176.8	51 57.0	-59.9	176.8	50 57.1	-59.9	176.9	49 57.2	-59.9	177.0	48 57.3	-60.0	177.0	47 57.3	-59.9	177.1	12
13	53 56.8	-59.9	176.7	52 56.9	-59.9	176.8	51 57.0	-59.9	176.8	50 57.1	-59.9	176.9	49 57.2	-60.0	177.0	48 57.3	-60.0	177.0	47 57.3	-59.9	177.1	46 57.4	-59.9	177.1	13
14	52 56.9	-59.9	176.8	51 57.0	-59.9	176.9	50 57.1	-60.0	176.9	49 57.2	-60.0	177.0	48 57.2	-59.9	177.0	47 57.3	-59.9	177.1	46 57.4	-59.9	177.2	45 57.5	-60.0	177.2	14
15	51 57.0	-59.9	176.9	50 57.1	-60.0	176.9	49 57.1	-59.9	177.0	48 57.2	-59.9	177.1	47 57.3	-59.9	177.1	46 57.4	-60.0	177.2	45 57.5	-60.0	177.2	44 57.5	-59.9	177.3	15
16	50 57.1	-60.0	176.9	49 57.1	-59.9	177.0	48 57.2	-59.9	177.1	47 57.3	-59.9	177.1	46 57.4	-60.0	177.2	45 57.4	-59.9	177.2	44 57.5	-59.9	177.3	43 57.6	-60.0	177.3	16
17	49 57.1	-59.9	177.0	48 57.2	-59.9	177.1	47 57.3	-59.9	177.1	46 57.4	-60.0	177.2	45 57.4	-59.9	177.2	44 57.5	-59.9	177.3	43 57.6	-60.0	177.3	42 57.6	-59.9	177.4	17
18	48 57.2	-59.9	177.1	47 57.3	-60.0	177.2	46 57.4	-60.0	177.2	45 57.4	-59.9	177.3	44 57.5	-60.0	177.3	43 57.6	-60.0	177.4	42 57.6	-59.9	177.4	41 57.7	-60.0	177.4	18
19	47 57.3	-60.0	177.2	46 57.3	-59.9	177.2	45 57.4	-59.9	177.3	44 57.5	-60.0	177.3	43 57.5	-59.9	177.4	42 57.6	-59.9	177.4	41 57.7	-60.0	177.5	40 57.7	-59.9	177.5	19
20	46 57.3	-59.9	177.2	45 57.4	-59.9	177.3	44 57.5	-60.0	177.3	43 57.5	-59.9	177.4	42 57.6	-59.9	177.4	41 57.7	-60.0	177.5	40 57.7	-59.9	177.5	39 57.8	-60.0	177.5	20
21	45 57.4	-59.9	177.3	44 57.5	-60.0	177.4	43 57.5	-59.9	177.4	42 57.6	-59.9	177.4	41 57.7	-60.0	177.5	40 57.7	-59.9	177.5	39 57.8	-60.0	177.6	38 57.8	-59.9	177.6	21
22	44 57.5	-60.0	177.4	43 57.5	-59.9	177.4	42 57.6	-60.0	177.5	41 57.7	-60.0	177.5	40 57.7	-59.9	177.5	39 57.8	-60.0	177.6	38 57.8	-59.9	177.6	37 57.9	-60.0	177.6	22
23	43 57.5	-59.9	177.4	42 57.6	-60.0	177.5	41 57.6	-59.9	177.5	40 57.7	-59.9	177.6	39 57.8	-60.0	177.6	38 57.8	-59.9	177.6	37 57.9	-60.0	177.7	36 57.9	-59.9	177.7	23
24	42 57.6	-60.0	177.5	41 57.6	-59.9	177.5	40 57.7	-59.9	177.6	39 57.8	-60.0	177.6	38 57.8	-59.9	177.6	37 57.9	-60.0	177.7	36 57.9	-60.0	177.7	35 58.0	-60.0	177.7	24
25	41 57.6	-59.9	177.6	40 57.7	-59.9	177.6	39 57.8	-60.0	177.6	38 57.8	-59.9	177.7	37 57.9	-60.0	177.7	36 57.9	-60.0	177.7	35 57.9	-59.9	177.8	34 58.0	-60.0	177.8	25
26	40 57.7	-59.9	177.6	39 57.8	-60.0	177.7	38 57.8	-59.9	177.7	37 57.9	-60.0	177.7	36 57.9	-60.0	177.8	35 57.9	-59.9	177.8	34 58.0	-60.0	177.8	33 58.0	-59.9	177.8	26
27	39 57.8	-60.0	177.7	38 57.8	-59.9	177.7	37 57.9	-60.0	177.7	36 57.9	-60.0	177.8	35 57.9	-59.9	177.8	34 58.0	-60.0	177.8	33 58.0	-59.9	177.9	32 58.1	-60.0	177.9	27
28	38 57.8	-59.9	177.7	37 57.9	-60.0	177.8	36 57.9	-60.0	177.8	35 57.9	-59.9	177.8	34 58.0	-60.0	177.8	33 58.0	-59.9	177.9	32 58.1	-60.0	177.9	31 58.1	-60.0	177.9	28
29	37 57.9	-60.0	177.8	36 57.9	-59.9	177.8	35 57.9	-59.9	177.8	34 58.0	-60.0	177.9	33 58.0	-59.9	177.9	32 58.1	-60.0	177.9	31 58.1	-60.0	177.9	30 58.1	-59.9	178.0	29
30	36 57.9	-59.9	177.8	35 58.0	-60.0	177.9	34 58.0	-60.0	177.9	33 58.0	-59.9	177.9	32 58.1	-60.0	177.9	31 58.1	-59.9	178.0	30 58.1	-59.9	178.0	29 58.2	-60.0	178.0	30
31	35 58.0	-60.0	177.9	34 58.0	-60.0	177.9	33 58.0	-59.9	177.9	32 58.1	-60.0	178.0	31 58.1	-59.9	178.0	30 58.2	-60.0	178.0	29 58.2	-60.0	178.0	28 58.2	-59.9	178.0	31
32	34 58.0	-59.9	177.9	33 58.0	-59.9	178.0	32 58.1	-60.0	178.0	31 58.1	-59.9	178.0	30 58.2	-60.0	178.0	29 58.2	-60.0	178.0	28 58.2	-59.9	178.1	27 58.3	-60.0	178.1	32
33	33 58.1	-60.0	178.0	32 58.1	-60.0	178.0	31 58.1	-59.9	178.0	30 58.2	-60.0	178.0	29 58.2	-60.0	178.1	28 58.2	-59.9	178.1	27 58.3	-60.0	178.1	26 58.3	-60.0	178.1	33
34	32 58.1	-60.0	178.0	31 58.1	-59.9	178.0	30 58.2	-60.0	178.1	29 58.2	-60.0	178.1	28 58.2	-59.9	178.1	27 58.3	-60.0	178.1	26 58.3	-60.0	178.1	25 58.3	-59.9	178.2	34
35	31 58.1	-59.9	178.1	30 58.2	-60.0	178.1	29 58.2	-60.0	178.1	28 58.2	-59.9	178.1	27 58.3	-60.0	178.1	26 58.3	-60.0	178.2	25 58.3	-59.9	178.2	24 58.4	-60.0	178.2	35
36	30 58.2	-60.0	178.1	29 58.2	-59.9	178.1	28 58.2	-59.9	178.2	27 58.3	-60.0	178.2	26 58.3	-60.0	178.2	25 58.3	-59.9	178.2	24 58.4	-60.0	178.2	23 58.4	-60.0	178.2	36
37	29 58.2	-59.9	178.2	28 58.3	-60.0	178.2	27 58.3	-60.0	178.2	26 58.3	-60.0	178.2	25 58.3	-59.9	178.2	24 58.4	-60.0	178.2	23 58.4	-60.0	178.3	22 58.4	-59.9	178.3	37
38	28 58.3	-60.0	178.2	27 58.3	-60.0	178.2	26 58.3	-59.9	178.2	25 58.3	-59.9	178.2	24 58.4	-60.0	178.3	23 58.4	-60.0	178.3	22 58.4	-59.9	178.3	21 58.5	-60.0	178.3	38
39	27 58.3	-60.0	178.2	26 58.3	-59.9	178.3	25 58.4	-60.0	178.3	24 58.4	-60.0	178.3	23 58.4	-60.0	178.3	22 58.4	-59.9	178.3	21 58.5	-60.0	178.3	20 58.5	-60.0	178.3	39
40	26 58.3	-59.9	178.3	25 58.4	-60.0	178.3	24 58.4	-60.0	178.3	23 58.4	-59.9	178.3	22 58.4	-59.9	178.3	21 58.5	-60.0	178.3	20 58.5	-60.0	178.4	19 58.5	-59.9	178.4	40
41	25 58.4	-60.0	178.3	24 58.4	-60.0	178.3	23 58.4	-59.9	178.3	22 58.5	-60.0	178.4	21 58.5	-60.0	178.4	20 58.5	-60.0	178.4	19 58.5	-59.9	178.4	18 58.6	-60.0	178.4	41
42	24 58.4	-59.9	178.4	23 58.4	-59.9	178.4	22 58.5	-60.0	178.4	21 58.5	-60.0	178.4	20 58.5	-60.0	178.4	19 58.5	-59.9	178.4	18 58.6	-60.0	178.4	17 58.6	-60.0	178.4	42
43	23 58.5	-60.0	178.4	22 58.5	-60.0	178.4	21 58.5	-60.0	178.4	20 58.5	-59.9	178.4	19 58.5	-59.9	178.4	18 58.6	-60.0	178.5	17 58.6	-60.0	178.5	16 58.6	-60.0	178.5	43
44	22 58.5	-60.0	178.4	21 58.5	-59.9	178.4	20 58.5	-59.9	178.5	19 58.6	-60.0	178.5	18 58.6	-60.0	178.5	17 58.6	-60.0	178.5	16 58.6	-59.9	178.5	15 58.6	-59.9	178.5	44
45	21 58.5	-59.9	178.5	20 58.6	-60.0	178.5	19 58.6	-60.0	178.5	18 58.6	-60.0	178.5	17 58.6	-60.0	178.5	16 58.6	-59.9	178.5	15 58.7	-60.0	178.5	14 58.7	-60.0	178.5	45
46	20 58.6	-60.0	178.5	19 58.6	-60.0	178.5	18 58.6	-60.0	178.5	17 58.6	-59.9	178.5	16 58.6	-59.9	178.5	15 58.7	-60.0	178.6	14 58.7	-60.0	178.6	13 58.7	-60.0	178.6	46
47	19 58.6	-60.0	178.5	18 58.6	-59.9	178.6	17 58.6	-59.9	178.6	16 58.7	-60.0	178.6	15 58.7	-60.0	178.6	14 58.7	-60.0	178.6	13 58.7	-60.0	178.6	12 58.7	-59.9	178.6	47
48	18 58.6	-59.9	178.6	17 58.7	-60.0	178.6	16 58.7	-60.0	178.6	15 58.7	-60.0	178.6	14 58.7	-60.0	178.6	13 58.7	-59.9	178.6	12 58.7	-59.9	178.6	11 58.8	-60.0	178.6	48
49	17 58.7	-60.0	178.6	16 58.7	-60.0	178.6	15 58.7	-60.0	178.6	14 58.7	-59.9	178.6	13 58.7	-59.9	178.6	12 58.8	-60.0	178.7	11 58.8	-60.0	178.7	10 58.8	-60.0	178.7	49
50	16 58.7	-60.0	178.7	15 58.7	-59.9	178.7	14 58.7	-59.9	178.7	13 58.8	-60.0	178.7	12 58.8	-60.0	178.7	11 58.8	-60.0	178.7	10 58.8	-60.0	178.7	9 58.8	-60.0	178.7	50
51	15 58.7	-59.9	178.7	14 58.8	-60.0	178.7	13 58.8	-60.0	178.7	12 58.8	-60.0	178.7	11 58.8	-60.0	178.7	10 58.8	-60.0	178.7	9 58.8	-59.9	178.7	8 58.8	-59.9	178.7	51
52	14 58.8	-60.0	178.7	13 58.8	-60.0	178.7	12 58.8	-60.0	178.7	11 58.8	-60.0	178.7	10 58.8	-59.9	178.7	9 58.8	-59.9	178.7	8 58.9	-60.0	178.8	7 58.9	-60.0	178.8	52
53	13 58.8	-60.0	178.8	12 58.8	-59.9	178.8	11 58.8	-59.9	178.8	10 58.8	-59.9	178.8	9 58.9	-60.0	178.8	8 58.9	-60.0	178.8	7 58.9	-60.0	178.8	6 58.9	-60.0	178.8	53
54	12 58.8	-59.9	178.8	11 58.9	-60.0	178.8	10 58.9	-60.0	178.8	9 58.9	-60.0	178.8	8 58.9	-60.0	178.8	7 58.9	-60.0	178.8	6 58.9	-60.0	178.8	5 58.9	-59.9	178.8	54
55	11 58.9	-60.0	178.8	10 58.9	-60.0	178.8	9 58.9	-60.0	178.8	8 58.9	-60.0	178.8	7 58.9	-60.0	178.8	6 58.9	-59.9	178.8	5 58.9	-59.9	178.8	4 59.0	-60.0	178.8	55
56	10 58.9	-60.0	178.9	9 58.9	-60.0	178.9	8 58.9	-59.9	178.9	7 58.9	-59.9	178.9	6 58.9	-59.9	178.9	5 59.0	-60.0	178.9	4 59.0	-60.0	178.9	3 59.0	-60.0	178.9	56
57	9 58.9	-59.9	178.9	8 58.9	-59.9	178.9	7 59.0	-60.0	178.9	6 59.0	-60.0	178.9	5 59.0	-60.0	178.9	4 59.0	-60.0	178.9	3 59.0	-60.0	178.9	2 59.0	-60.0	178.9	57
58	8 59.0	-60.0	178.9	7 59.0	-60.0	178.9	6 59.0	-60.0	178.9	5 59.0	-60.0	178.9	4 59.0	-60.0	178.9	3 59.0	-60.0	178.9	2 59.0	-59.9	178.9	1 59.0	-59.9	178.9	58
59	7 59.0	-60.0	179.0	6 59.0	-60.0	179.0	5 59.0	-60.0	179.0	4 59.0	-59.9	179.0	3 59.0	-59.9	179.0	2 59.0	-59.9	179.0	1 59.1	-60.0	179.0	0 59.1	-60.0	179.0	59
60	6 59.0	-59.9	179.0	5 59.0	-60.0	179.0	4 59.0	-59.9	179.0	3 59.1	-60.0	179.0	2 59.1	-60.0	179.0	1 59.1	-60.0	179.0	0 59.1	-60.0	179.0	0 00.9	+60.0	1.0	60
61	5 59.1	-60.0	179.0	4 59.1	-60.0	179.0	3 59.1	-60.0	179.0	2 59.1	-60.0	179.0	1 59.1	-60.0	179.0	0 59.1	-60.0	179.0	0 00.9	+60.0	1.0	1 00.9	+60.0	1.0	61
62	4 59.1	-60.0	179.1	3 59.1	-60.0	179.1	2 59.1	-60.0	179.1	1 59.1	-60.0	179.1	0 59.1	-59.9	179.1	0 00.9	+59.9	0.9	1 00.9	+59.9	0.9	2 00.9	+59.9	0.9	62
63	3 59.1	-59.9	179.1	2 59.1	-59.9	179.1	1 59.1	-59.9	179.1	0 59.1	-59.9	179.1	0 00.8	+60.0	0.9	1 00.8	+60.0	0.9	2 00.8	+60.0	0.9	3 00.8	+60.0	0.9	63
64	2 59.2	-60.0	179.1	1 59.2	-60.0	179.1	0 59.2	-60.0	179.1	0 00.8	+60.0	0.9	1 00.8	+60.0	0.9	2 00.8	+60.0	0.9	3 00.8	+60.0	0.9	4 00.8	+60.0	0.9	64
65	1 59.2	-60.0	179.2	0 59.2	-60.0	179.2	0 00.8	+60.0	0.8	1 00.8	+60.0	0.8	2 00.8	+60.0	0.8	3 00.8	+60.0	0.8	4 00.8	+59.9	0.8	5 00.8	+59.9	0.8	65
66	0 59.2	-60.0	179.2	0 00.8	+59.9	0.8	1 00.8	+59.9	0.8	2 00.8	+59.9	0.8	3 00.8	+59.9	0.8	4 00.8	+59.9	0.8	5 00.7	+60.0	0.8	6 00.7	+60.0	0.8	66
67	0 00.8	+59.9	0.8	1 00.7	+60.0	0.8	2 00.7	+60.0	0.8	3 00.7	+60.0	0.8	4 00.7	+60.0	0.8	5 00.7	+60.0	0.8	6 00.7	+60.0	0.8	7 00.7	+60.0	0.8	67
68	1 00.7	+60.0	0.7	2 00.7	+60.0	0.7	3 00.7	+60.0	0.8	4 00.7	+60.0	0.8	5 00.7	+60.0	0.8	6 00.7	+60.0	0.8	7 00.7	+60.0	0.8	8 00.7	+60.0	0.8	68
69	2 00.7	+60.0	0.7	3 00.7	+60.0	0.7	4 00.7	+60.0	0.7	5 00.7	+59.9	0.7	6 00.7	+59.9	0.7	7 00.7	+59.9	0.7	8 00.7	+59.9	0.7	9 00.7	+59.9	0.7	69
70	3 00.7	+59.9	0.7	4 00.7	+59.9	0.7	5 00.7	+59.9	0.7	6 00.6	+60.0	0.7	7 00.6	+60.0	0.7	8 00.6	+60.0	0.7	9 00.6	+60.0	0.7	10 00.6	+60.0	0.7	70
71	4 00.6	+60.0	0.7	5 00.6	+60.0	0.7	6 00.6	+60.0	0.7	7 00.6	+60.0	0.7	8 00.6	+60.0	0.7	9 00.6	+60.0	0.7	10 00.6	+60.0	0.7	11 00.6	+60.0	0.7	71
72	5 00.6	+60.0	0.6	6 00.6	+60.0	0.6	7 00.6	+60.0	0.6	8 00.6	+60.0	0.6	9 00.6	+60.0	0.6	10 00.6	+60.0	0.6	11 00.6	+59.9	0.6	12 00.6	+59.9	0.6	72
73	6 00.6	+59.9	0.6	7 00.6	+59.9	0.6	8 00.6	+59.9	0.6	9 00.6	+59.9	0.6	10 00.6	+59.9	0.6	11 00.6	+59.9	0.6	12 00.5	+60.0	0.6	13 00.5	+60.0	0.6	73
74	7 00.5	+60.0	0.6	8 00.5	+60.0	0.6	9 00.5	+60.0	0.6	10 00.5	+60.0	0.6	11 00.5	+60.0	0.6	12 00.5	+60.0	0.6	13 00.5	+60.0	0.6	14 00.5	+60.0	0.6	74
75	8 00.5	+60.0	0.5	9 00.5	+60.0	0.5	10 00.5	+60.0	0.5	11 00.5	+60.0	0.5	12 00.5	+60.0	0.5	13 00.5	+60.0	0.5	14 00.5	+60.0	0.5	15 00.5	+60.0	0.5	75
76	9 00.5	+59.9	0.5	10 00.5	+59.9	0.5	11 00.5	+59.9	0.5	12 00.5	+59.9	0.5	13 00.5	+59.9	0.5	14 00.5	+59.9	0.5	15 00.5	+59.9	0.5	16 00.5	+59.9	0.5	76
77	10 00.4	+60.0	0.5	11 00.4	+60.0	0.5	12 00.4	+60.0	0.5	13 00.4	+60.0	0.5	14 00.4	+60.0	0.5	15 00.4	+60.0	0.5	16 00.4	+60.0	0.5	17 00.4	+60.0	0.5	77
78	11 00.4	+60.0	0.4	12 00.4	+60.0	0.4	13 00.4	+60.0	0.4	14 00.4	+60.0	0.4	15 00.4	+60.0	0.4	16 00.4	+60.0	0.4	17 00.4	+60.0	0.4	18 00.4	+60.0	0.4	78
79	12 00.4	+59.9	0.4	13 00.4	+59.9	0.4	14 00.4	+59.9	0.4	15 00.4	+59.9	0.4	16 00.4	+59.9	0.4	17 00.4	+59.9	0.4	18 00.4	+59.9	0.4	19 00.4	+59.9	0.4	79
80	13 00.3	+60.0	0.4	14 00.3	+60.0	0.4	15 00.3	+60.0	0.4	16 00.3	+60.0	0.4	17 00.3	+60.0	0.4	18 00.3	+60.0	0.4	19 00.3	+60.0	0.4	20 00.3	+60.0	0.4	80
81	14 00.3	+60.0	0.3	15 00.3	+60.0	0.3	16 00.3	+60.0	0.3	17 00.3	+60.0	0.3	18 00.3	+60.0	0.3	19 00.3	+60.0	0.3	20 00.3	+60.0	0.3	21 00.3	+60.0	0.3	81
82	15 00.3	+59.9	0.3	16 00.3	+59.9	0.3	17 00.3	+59.9	0.3	18 00.3	+59.9	0.3	19 00.3	+59.9	0.3	20 00.3	+59.9	0.3	21 00.3	+59.9	0.3	22 00.3	+59.9	0.3	82
83	16 00.2	+60.0	0.3	17 00.2	+60.0	0.3	18 00.2	+60.0	0.3	19 00.2	+60.0	0.3	20 00.2	+60.0	0.3	21 00.2	+60.0	0.3	22 00.2	+60.0	0.3	23 00.2	+60.0	0.3	83
84	17 00.2	+60.0	0.2	18 00.2	+60.0	0.2	19 00.2	+60.0	0.2	20 00.2	+60.0	0.2	21 00.2	+60.0	0.2	22 00.2	+60.0	0.2	23 00.2	+60.0	0.2	24 00.2	+60.0	0.2	84
85	18 00.2	+59.9	0.2	19 00.2	+59.9	0.2	20 00.2	+59.9	0.2	21 00.2	+59.9	0.2	22 00.2	+59.9	0.2	23 00.2	+59.9	0.2	24 00.2	+59.9	0.2	25 00.2	+59.9	0.2	85
86	19 00.1	+60.0	0.1	20 00.1	+60.0	0.1	21 00.1	+60.0	0.1	22 00.1	+60.0	0.2	23 00.1	+60.0	0.2	24 00.1	+60.0	0.2	25 00.1	+60.0	0.2	26 00.1	+60.0	0.2	86
87	20 00.1	+60.0	0.1	21 00.1	+60.0	0.1	22 00.1	+60.0	0.1	23 00.1	+60.0	0.1	24 00.1	+60.0	0.1	25 00.1	+60.0	0.1	26 00.1	+60.0	0.1	27 00.1	+60.0	0.1	87
88	21 00.1	+59.9	0.1	22 00.1	+59.9	0.1	23 00.1	+59.9	0.1	24 00.1	+59.9	0.1	25 00.1	+59.9	0.1	26 00.1	+59.9	0.1	27 00.1	+59.9	0.1	28 00.1	+59.9	0.1	88
89	22 00.0	+60.0	0.0	23 00.0	+60.0	0.0	24 00.0	+60.0	0.0	25 00.0	+60.0	0.0	26 00.0	+60.0	0.0	27 00.0	+60.0	0.0	28 00.0	+60.0	0.0	29 00.0	+60.0	0.0	89
90	23 00.0	+60.0	0.0	24 00.0	+60.0	0.0	25 00.0	+60.0	0.0	26 00.0	+60.0	0.0	27 00.0	+60.0	0.0	28 00.0	+60.0	0.0	29 00.0	+60.0	0.0	30 00.0	+60.0	0.0	90
	23°			24°			25°			26°			27°			28°			29°			30°			

S. Lat. { L.H.A. greater than 180° ....Zn=180°–Z
L.H.A. less than 180°...........Zn=180°+Z

3°, 357° L.H.A. LATITUDE SAME NAME AS DECLINATION N. Lat. {L.H.A. greater than 180° .....Zn=Z
L.H.A. less than 180°............Zn=360°-Z

Dec.	23° Hc	d	Z	24° Hc	d	Z	25° Hc	d	Z	26° Hc	d	Z	27° Hc	d	Z	28° Hc	d	Z	29° Hc	d	Z	30° Hc	d	Z	Dec.
°	° ′	′	°	° ′	′	°	° ′	′	°	° ′	′	°	° ′	′	°	° ′	′	°	° ′	′	°	° ′	′	°	°
0	66 48.9	+59.6	172.4	65 49.5	+59.5	172.7	64 49.9	+59.6	172.9	63 50.4	+59.6	173.2	62 50.8	+59.7	173.4	61 51.2	+59.7	173.6	60 51.5	+59.7	173.8	59 51.9	+59.7	174.0	0
1	67 48.5	+59.5	172.0	66 49.0	+59.6	172.4	65 49.5	+59.6	172.7	64 50.0	+59.6	172.9	63 50.5	+59.6	173.2	62 50.9	+59.6	173.4	61 51.2	+59.8	173.6	60 51.6	+59.7	173.8	1
2	68 48.0	+59.4	171.7	67 48.6	+59.5	172.0	66 49.1	+59.6	172.4	65 49.6	+59.6	172.7	64 50.1	+59.6	172.9	63 50.5	+59.7	173.2	62 51.0	+59.6	173.4	61 51.3	+59.7	173.6	2
3	69 47.4	+59.4	171.3	68 48.1	+59.4	171.7	67 48.7	+59.5	172.0	66 49.2	+59.6	172.4	65 49.7	+59.6	172.7	64 50.2	+59.6	172.9	63 50.6	+59.7	173.2	62 51.0	+59.7	173.4	3
4	70 46.8	+59.3	170.9	69 47.5	+59.4	171.3	68 48.2	+59.4	171.7	67 48.8	+59.5	172.1	66 49.3	+59.6	172.4	65 49.8	+59.6	172.7	64 50.3	+59.6	172.9	63 50.7	+59.7	173.2	4
5	71 46.1	+59.3	170.4	70 46.9	+59.3	170.9	69 47.6	+59.4	171.3	68 48.3	+59.4	171.7	67 48.9	+59.5	172.1	66 49.4	+59.6	172.4	65 49.9	+59.6	172.7	64 50.4	+59.7	173.0	5
6	72 45.4	+59.1	169.9	71 46.2	+59.3	170.4	70 47.0	+59.4	170.9	69 47.7	+59.5	171.3	68 48.4	+59.5	171.7	67 49.0	+59.5	172.1	66 49.5	+59.6	172.4	65 50.1	+59.6	172.7	6
7	73 44.5	+59.1	169.3	72 45.5	+59.2	169.9	71 46.4	+59.2	170.4	70 47.2	+59.3	170.9	69 47.9	+59.4	171.3	68 48.5	+59.5	171.7	67 49.1	+59.6	172.1	66 49.7	+59.6	172.4	7
8	74 43.6	+58.9	168.7	73 44.7	+59.0	169.3	72 45.6	+59.2	169.9	71 46.5	+59.3	170.5	70 47.3	+59.4	170.9	69 48.0	+59.4	171.4	68 48.7	+59.5	171.8	67 49.3	+59.5	172.1	8
9	75 42.5	+58.7	167.9	74 43.7	+59.0	168.7	73 44.8	+59.1	169.4	72 45.8	+59.2	170.0	71 46.7	+59.3	170.5	70 47.4	+59.4	171.0	69 48.2	+59.4	171.4	68 48.8	+59.5	171.8	9
10	76 41.2	+58.6	167.1	75 42.7	+58.7	167.9	74 43.9	+58.9	168.7	73 45.0	+59.1	169.4	72 46.0	+59.2	170.0	71 46.8	+59.3	170.5	70 47.6	+59.4	171.0	69 48.3	+59.5	171.4	10
11	77 39.8	+58.3	166.1	76 41.4	+58.6	167.1	75 42.8	+58.8	168.0	74 44.1	+58.9	168.7	73 45.2	+59.1	169.4	72 46.1	+59.2	170.0	71 47.0	+59.3	170.5	70 47.8	+59.4	171.0	11
12	78 38.1	+58.0	164.9	77 40.0	+58.4	166.1	76 41.6	+58.7	167.1	75 43.0	+58.9	168.0	74 44.3	+59.0	168.8	73 45.3	+59.2	169.5	72 46.3	+59.2	170.0	71 47.2	+59.3	170.6	12
13	79 36.1	+57.6	163.6	78 38.4	+58.0	165.0	77 40.3	+58.3	166.2	76 41.9	+58.6	167.2	75 43.3	+58.8	168.1	74 44.5	+59.0	168.8	73 45.5	+59.2	169.5	72 46.5	+59.2	170.1	13
14	80 33.7	+57.1	162.0	79 36.4	+57.6	163.7	78 38.6	+58.1	165.1	77 40.5	+58.4	166.2	76 42.1	+58.7	167.2	75 43.5	+58.8	168.1	74 44.7	+59.0	168.9	73 45.7	+59.2	169.5	14
15	81 30.8	+56.3	160.0	80 34.0	+57.1	162.0	79 36.7	+57.7	163.7	78 38.9	+58.1	165.1	77 40.8	+58.4	166.3	76 42.3	+58.7	167.3	75 43.7	+58.9	168.2	74 44.9	+59.0	168.9	15
16	82 27.1	+55.2	157.5	81 31.1	+56.4	160.1	80 34.4	+57.1	162.1	79 37.0	+57.7	163.8	78 39.2	+58.1	165.2	77 41.0	+58.5	166.4	76 42.6	+58.7	167.4	75 43.9	+58.9	168.2	16
17	83 22.3	+53.6•	154.3	82 27.5	+55.3	157.6	81 31.5	+56.4	160.1	80 34.7	+57.2	162.2	79 37.3	+57.8	163.9	78 39.5	+58.1	165.3	77 41.3	+58.5	166.4	76 42.8	+58.8	167.4	17
18	84 15.9	+51.1•	150.1	83 22.8	+53.7•	154.4	82 27.9	+55.3	157.7	81 31.9	+56.4	160.2	80 35.1	+57.2	162.3	79 37.6	+57.8	164.0	78 39.8	+58.2	165.3	77 41.6	+58.5	166.5	18
19	85 07.0	+47.2•	144.5	84 16.5	+51.2•	150.3	83 23.2	+53.8	154.6	82 28.3	+55.5	157.8	81 32.3	+56.5	160.3	80 35.4	+57.3	162.4	79 38.0	+57.8	164.0	78 40.1	+58.2	165.4	19
20	85 54.2	+40.3•	136.5	85 07.7	+47.3•	144.6	84 17.0	+51.4•	150.4	83 23.8	+53.8•	154.7	82 28.8	+55.5	157.9	81 32.7	+56.6	160.5	80 35.8	+57.3	162.5	79 38.3	+57.9	164.1	20
21	86 34.5	+28.7•	125.1	85 55.0	+40.4•	136.7	85 08.4	+47.4•	144.8	84 17.6	+51.5•	150.6	83 24.3	+53.9	154.8	82 29.3	+55.5	158.1	81 33.1	+56.6	160.6	80 36.2	+57.3	162.6	21
22	87 03.2	+11.1•	109.3	86 35.4	+29.0•	125.3	85 55.8	+40.6•	136.9	85 09.1	+47.6•	145.0	84 18.2	+51.6•	150.7	83 24.8	+54.1	155.0	82 29.7	+55.7	158.2	81 33.5	+56.7	160.7	22
23	87 14.3	-9.9•	89.4	87 04.4	+11.2•	109.4	86 36.4	+29.2•	125.5	85 56.7	+40.8•	137.1	85 09.8	+47.7•	145.1	84 18.9	+51.7•	150.9	83 25.4	+54.1	155.1	82 30.2	+55.7	158.3	23
24	87 04.4	-28.0•	69.4	87 15.6	-10.0•	89.4	87 05.6	+11.3•	109.5	86 37.5	+29.3•	125.7	85 57.5	+41.1•	137.3	85 10.6	+47.9•	145.3	84 19.5	+51.9•	151.1	83 25.9	+54.3	155.3	24
25	86 36.4	-39.7•	53.3	87 05.6	-28.1•	69.3	87 16.9	-10.1•	89.4	87 06.8	+11.4•	109.6	86 38.6	+29.5•	125.9	85 58.5	+41.2•	137.5	85 11.4	+48.0•	145.6	84 20.2	+52.0•	151.3	25
26	85 56.7	-46.9•	41.7	86 37.5	-40.0•	53.0	87 06.8	-28.2•	69.1	87 18.2	-10.1•	89.3	87 08.1	+11.5•	109.8	86 39.7	+29.7•	126.1	85 59.4	+41.5•	137.7	85 12.2	+48.2•	145.8	26
27	85 09.8	-50.9•	33.6	85 57.5	-46.9•	41.4	86 38.6	-40.1•	52.8	87 08.1	-28.4•	68.9	87 19.6	-10.2•	89.3	87 09.4	+11.7•	109.9	86 40.9	+29.9•	126.3	86 00.4	+41.7•	138.0	27
28	84 18.9	-53.5•	27.8	85 10.6	-51.1•	33.3	85 58.5	-47.1•	41.2	86 39.7	-40.3•	52.5	87 09.4	-28.5•	68.7	87 21.1	-10.3•	89.3	87 10.8	+11.8•	110.1	86 42.1	+30.1•	126.6	28
29	83 25.4	-55.2	23.6	84 19.5	-53.6•	27.6	85 11.4	-51.2•	33.1	85 59.4	-47.2•	40.9	86 40.9	-40.5•	52.2	87 10.8	-28.7•	68.5	87 22.6	-10.4•	89.3	87 12.2	+11.9•	110.2	29
30	82 30.2	-56.2	20.3	83 25.9	-55.2	23.3	84 20.2	-53.7•	27.3	85 12.2	-51.3•	32.8	86 00.4	-47.4•	40.6	86 42.1	-40.7•	52.0	87 12.2	-28.9•	68.3	87 24.1	-10.4•	89.2	30
31	81 34.0	-57.0	17.8	82 30.7	-56.3	20.1	83 26.5	-55.2	23.1	84 20.9	-53.8•	27.1	85 13.0	-51.4•	32.5	86 01.4	-47.5•	40.3	86 43.3	-40.9•	51.7	87 13.7	-29.1•	68.1	31
32	80 37.0	-57.6	15.8	81 34.4	-57.0	17.6	82 31.3	-56.4	19.9	83 27.1	-55.3	22.9	84 21.6	-53.8•	26.8	85 13.9	-51.6•	32.3	86 02.4	-47.7•	40.0	86 44.6	-41.1•	51.4	32
33	79 39.4	-58.0	14.2	80 37.4	-57.6	15.6	81 34.9	-57.1	17.4	82 31.8	-56.4	19.7	83 27.8	-55.5	22.7	84 22.3	-53.9	26.6	85 14.7	-51.6•	32.0	86 03.5	-47.9•	39.7	33
34	78 41.4	-58.3	12.8	79 39.8	-58.0	14.0	80 37.8	-57.6	15.5	81 35.4	-57.1	17.3	82 32.3	-56.4	19.5	83 28.4	-55.5	22.4	84 23.1	-54.1	26.3	85 15.6	-51.8•	31.7	34
35	77 43.1	-58.5	11.6	78 41.8	-58.4	12.6	79 40.2	-58.1	13.8	80 38.3	-57.7	15.3	81 35.9	-57.2	17.1	82 32.9	-56.5	19.3	83 29.0	-55.5	22.2	84 23.8	-54.1	26.0	35
36	76 44.6	-58.8	10.6	77 43.4	-58.5	11.5	78 42.1	-58.3	12.5	79 40.6	-58.1	13.7	80 38.7	-57.7	15.1	81 36.4	-57.2	16.9	82 33.5	-56.6	19.1	83 29.7	-55.6	21.9	36
37	75 45.8	-58.9	9.8	76 44.9	-58.8	10.5	77 43.8	-58.6	11.3	78 42.5	-58.4	12.3	79 41.0	-58.1	13.5	80 39.2	-57.8	14.9	81 36.9	-57.3	16.7	82 34.1	-56.7	18.9	37
38	74 46.9	-59.1	9.0	75 46.1	-58.9	9.7	76 45.2	-58.8	10.4	77 44.1	-58.6	11.2	78 42.9	-58.4	12.2	79 41.4	-58.1	13.3	80 39.6	-57.8	14.7	81 37.4	-57.3	16.4	38
39	73 47.8	-59.1	8.4	74 47.2	-59.1	8.9	75 46.4	-59.0	9.5	76 45.5	-58.8	10.2	77 44.5	-58.7	11.0	78 43.3	-58.5	12.0	79 41.8	-58.1	13.1	80 40.1	-57.8	14.5	39
40	72 48.7	-59.2	7.8	73 48.1	-59.2	8.3	74 47.4	-59.0	8.8	75 46.7	-59.0	9.4	76 45.8	-58.8	10.1	77 44.8	-58.6	10.9	78 43.7	-58.5	11.8	79 42.3	-58.2	13.0	40
41	71 49.5	-59.4	7.3	72 48.9	-59.2	7.7	73 48.4	-59.2	8.1	74 47.7	-59.1	8.7	75 47.0	-59.0	9.3	76 46.2	-58.9	9.9	77 45.2	-58.7	10.7	78 44.1	-58.5	11.7	41
42	70 50.1	-59.3	6.8	71 49.7	-59.3	7.2	72 49.2	-59.3	7.6	73 48.6	-59.1	8.0	74 48.0	-59.1	8.5	75 47.3	-59.0	9.1	76 46.5	-58.9	9.8	77 45.6	-58.8	10.6	42
43	69 50.8	-59.5	6.4	70 50.4	-59.4	6.7	71 49.9	-59.3	7.1	72 49.5	-59.3	7.4	73 48.9	-59.2	7.9	74 48.3	-59.1	8.4	75 47.6	-59.0	9.0	76 46.8	-58.8	9.6	43
44	68 51.3	-59.5	6.0	69 51.0	-59.5	6.3	70 50.6	-59.4	6.6	71 50.2	-59.4	6.9	72 49.7	-59.3	7.3	73 49.2	-59.2	7.8	74 48.6	-59.1	8.3	75 48.0	-59.1	8.8	44
45	67 51.8	-59.5	5.6	68 51.5	-59.5	5.9	69 51.2	-59.5	6.2	70 50.8	-59.4	6.5	71 50.4	-59.3	6.8	72 50.0	-59.3	7.2	73 49.5	-59.2	7.6	74 48.9	-59.1	8.1	45
46	66 52.3	-59.6	5.3	67 52.0	-59.5	5.5	68 51.7	-59.5	5.8	69 51.4	-59.4	6.1	70 51.1	-59.4	6.4	71 50.7	-59.4	6.7	72 50.3	-59.4	7.1	73 49.8	-59.3	7.5	46
47	65 52.7	-59.6	5.0	66 52.5	-59.6	5.2	67 52.2	-59.5	5.4	68 52.0	-59.5	5.7	69 51.7	-59.5	6.0	70 51.3	-59.4	6.2	71 50.9	-59.3	6.6	72 50.5	-59.3	6.9	47
48	64 53.1	-59.6	4.7	65 52.9	-59.6	4.9	66 52.7	-59.6	5.1	67 52.5	-59.6	5.3	68 52.2	-59.5	5.6	69 51.9	-59.5	5.8	70 51.6	-59.5	6.1	71 51.2	-59.4	6.5	48
49	63 53.5	-59.6	4.5	64 53.3	-59.6	4.6	65 53.1	-59.6	4.8	66 52.9	-59.6	5.0	67 52.7	-59.6	5.2	68 52.4	-59.5	5.5	69 52.1	-59.5	5.7	70 51.8	-59.4	6.0	49
50	62 53.9	-59.7	4.2	63 53.7	-59.7	4.4	64 53.5	-59.6	4.5	65 53.3	-59.6	4.7	66 53.1	-59.6	4.9	67 52.9	-59.6	5.1	68 52.6	-59.5	5.4	69 52.4	-59.5	5.6	50
51	61 54.2	-59.7	4.0	62 54.0	-59.6	4.1	63 53.9	-59.7	4.3	64 53.7	-59.6	4.5	65 53.5	-59.6	4.6	66 53.3	-59.6	4.8	67 53.1	-59.6	5.0	68 52.9	-59.6	5.2	51
52	60 54.5	-59.7	3.8	61 54.4	-59.7	3.9	62 54.2	-59.7	4.1	63 54.1	-59.7	4.2	64 53.9	-59.7	4.4	65 53.7	-59.6	4.5	66 53.5	-59.6	4.7	67 53.3	-59.6	4.9	52
53	59 54.8	-59.7	3.6	60 54.7	-59.8	3.7	61 54.5	-59.7	3.8	62 54.4	-59.7	4.0	63 54.2	-59.6	4.1	64 54.1	-59.7	4.3	65 53.9	-59.6	4.4	66 53.7	-59.6	4.6	53
54	58 55.1	-59.8	3.4	59 54.9	-59.7	3.5	60 54.8	-59.7	3.6	61 54.7	-59.7	3.7	62 54.6	-59.7	3.9	63 54.4	-59.6	4.0	64 54.3	-59.7	4.2	65 54.1	-59.6	4.3	54
55	57 55.3	-59.7	3.2	58 55.2	-59.7	3.3	59 55.1	-59.7	3.4	60 55.0	-59.7	3.5	61 54.9	-59.7	3.7	62 54.8	-59.7	3.8	63 54.6	-59.7	3.9	64 54.5	-59.7	4.1	55
56	56 55.6	-59.8	3.1	57 55.5	-59.8	3.2	58 55.4	-59.8	3.3	59 55.3	-59.8	3.3	60 55.2	-59.8	3.5	61 55.1	-59.8	3.6	62 54.9	-59.7	3.7	63 54.8	-59.7	3.8	56
57	55 55.8	-59.8	2.9	56 55.7	-59.8	3.0	57 55.6	-59.8	3.1	58 55.5	-59.7	3.2	59 55.4	-59.7	3.3	60 55.3	-59.7	3.4	61 55.2	-59.7	3.5	62 55.1	-59.7	3.6	57
58	54 56.0	-59.8	2.8	55 55.9	-59.8	2.8	56 55.8	-59.7	2.9	57 55.8	-59.8	3.0	58 55.7	-59.8	3.1	59 55.6	-59.8	3.2	60 55.5	-59.7	3.3	61 55.4	-59.7	3.4	58
59	53 56.2	-59.8	2.6	54 56.1	-59.8	2.7	55 56.1	-59.8	2.8	56 56.0	-59.8	2.8	57 55.9	-59.8	2.9	58 55.8	-59.7	3.0	59 55.8	-59.8	3.1	60 55.7	-59.8	3.2	59
60	52 56.4	-59.8	2.5	53 56.3	-59.8	2.5	54 56.3	-59.8	2.6	55 56.2	-59.8	2.7	56 56.1	-59.7	2.7	57 56.1	-59.8	2.8	58 56.0	-59.8	2.9	59 55.9	-59.7	3.0	60
61	51 56.6	-59.8	2.4	52 56.5	-59.8	2.4	53 56.5	-59.8	2.5	54 56.4	-59.8	2.5	55 56.4	-59.8	2.6	56 56.3	-59.8	2.7	57 56.2	-59.7	2.7	58 56.2	-59.8	2.8	61
62	50 56.8	-59.9	2.2	51 56.7	-59.8	2.3	52 56.7	-59.8	2.3	53 56.6	-59.8	2.4	54 56.6	-59.8	2.5	55 56.5	-59.8	2.5	56 56.5	-59.8	2.6	57 56.4	-59.8	2.7	62
63	49 56.9	-59.8	2.1	50 56.9	-59.8	2.2	51 56.9	-59.9	2.2	52 56.8	-59.8	2.3	53 56.8	-59.9	2.3	54 56.7	-59.8	2.4	55 56.7	-59.8	2.4	56 56.6	-59.8	2.5	63
64	48 57.1	-59.8	2.0	49 57.1	-59.9	2.0	50 57.0	-59.8	2.1	51 57.0	-59.8	2.1	52 56.9	-59.8	2.2	53 56.9	-59.8	2.2	54 56.9	-59.9	2.3	55 56.8	-59.8	2.3	64
65	47 57.3	-59.9	1.9	48 57.2	-59.8	1.9	49 57.2	-59.8	2.0	50 57.2	-59.9	2.0	51 57.1	-59.8	2.1	52 57.1	-59.8	2.1	53 57.0	-59.8	2.2	54 57.0	-59.8	2.2	65
66	46 57.4	-59.8	1.8	47 57.4	-59.9	1.8	48 57.4	-59.9	1.9	49 57.3	-59.8	1.9	50 57.3	-59.9	1.9	51 57.3	-59.9	2.0	52 57.2	-59.8	2.0	53 57.2	-59.8	2.1	66
67	45 57.6	-59.9	1.7	46 57.5	-59.8	1.7	47 57.5	-59.8	1.7	48 57.5	-59.9	1.8	49 57.4	-59.8	1.8	50 57.4	-59.8	1.9	51 57.4	-59.9	1.9	52 57.4	-59.9	1.9	67
68	44 57.7	-59.9	1.6	45 57.7	-59.9	1.6	46 57.7	-59.9	1.6	47 57.6	-59.8	1.7	48 57.6	-59.8	1.7	49 57.6	-59.9	1.7	50 57.5	-59.8	1.8	51 57.5	-59.8	1.8	68
69	43 57.8	-59.8	1.5	44 57.8	-59.8	1.5	45 57.8	-59.9	1.5	46 57.8	-59.9	1.6	47 57.8	-59.9	1.6	48 57.7	-59.8	1.6	49 57.7	-59.8	1.7	50 57.7	-59.9	1.7	69
70	42 58.0	-59.9	1.4	43 58.0	-59.9	1.4	44 57.9	-59.8	1.4	45 57.9	-59.8	1.5	46 57.9	-59.9	1.5	47 57.9	-59.9	1.5	48 57.9	-59.9	1.6	49 57.8	-59.8	1.6	70
71	41 58.1	-59.9	1.3	42 58.1	-59.9	1.3	43 58.1	-59.9	1.4	44 58.1	-59.9	1.4	45 58.0	-59.8	1.4	46 58.0	-59.9	1.4	47 58.0	-59.9	1.5	48 58.0	-59.9	1.5	71
72	40 58.2	-59.9	1.2	41 58.2	-59.9	1.2	42 58.2	-59.9	1.3	43 58.2	-59.9	1.3	44 58.2	-59.9	1.3	45 58.1	-59.8	1.3	46 58.1	-59.8	1.4	47 58.1	-59.8	1.4	72
73	39 58.3	-59.8	1.1	40 58.3	-59.8	1.2	41 58.3	-59.9	1.2	42 58.3	-59.9	1.2	43 58.3	-59.9	1.2	44 58.3	-59.9	1.2	45 58.3	-59.9	1.3	46 58.3	-59.9	1.3	73
74	38 58.5	-59.9	1.1	39 58.5	-59.9	1.1	40 58.4	-59.8	1.1	41 58.4	-59.9	1.1	42 58.4	-59.9	1.1	43 58.4	-59.9	1.1	44 58.4	-59.9	1.2	45 58.4	-59.9	1.2	74
75	37 58.6	-59.9	1.0	38 58.6	-59.9	1.0	39 58.6	-59.9	1.0	40 58.5	-59.8	1.0	41 58.5	-59.8	1.0	42 58.5	-59.9	1.1	43 58.5	-59.9	1.1	44 58.5	-59.9	1.1	75
76	36 58.7	-59.9	0.9	37 58.7	-59.9	0.9	38 58.7	-59.9	0.9	39 58.7	-59.9	0.9	40 58.7	-59.9	1.0	41 58.6	-59.8	1.0	42 58.6	-59.8	1.0	43 58.6	-59.9	1.0	76
77	35 58.8	-59.9	0.8	36 58.8	-59.9	0.8	37 58.8	-59.9	0.9	38 58.8	-59.9	0.9	39 58.8	-59.9	0.9	40 58.8	-59.9	0.9	41 58.8	-59.9	0.9	42 58.7	-59.8	0.9	77
78	34 58.9	-59.9	0.8	35 58.9	-59.9	0.8	36 58.9	-59.9	0.8	37 58.9	-59.9	0.8	38 58.9	-59.9	0.8	39 58.9	-59.9	0.8	40 58.9	-59.9	0.8	41 58.9	-59.9	0.8	78
79	33 59.0	-59.9	0.7	34 59.0	-59.9	0.7	35 59.0	-59.9	0.7	36 59.0	-59.9	0.7	37 59.0	-59.9	0.7	38 59.0	-59.9	0.7	39 59.0	-59.9	0.7	40 59.0	-59.9	0.8	79
80	32 59.1	-59.9	0.6	33 59.1	-59.9	0.6	34 59.1	-59.9	0.6	35 59.1	-59.9	0.6	36 59.1	-59.9	0.7	37 59.1	-59.9	0.7	38 59.1	-59.9	0.7	39 59.1	-59.9	0.7	80
81	31 59.2	-59.9	0.6	32 59.2	-59.9	0.6	33 59.2	-59.9	0.6	34 59.2	-59.9	0.6	35 59.2	-59.9	0.6	36 59.2	-59.9	0.6	37 59.2	-59.9	0.6	38 59.2	-59.9	0.6	81
82	30 59.3	-59.9	0.5	31 59.3	-59.9	0.5	32 59.3	-59.9	0.5	33 59.3	-59.9	0.5	34 59.3	-59.9	0.5	35 59.3	-59.9	0.5	36 59.3	-59.9	0.5	37 59.3	-59.9	0.5	82
83	29 59.4	-59.9	0.4	30 59.4	-59.9	0.4	31 59.4	-59.9	0.4	32 59.4	-59.9	0.4	33 59.4	-59.9	0.4	34 59.4	-59.9	0.4	35 59.4	-59.9	0.5	36 59.4	-59.9	0.5	83
84	28 59.5	-59.9	0.4	29 59.5	-59.9	0.4	30 59.5	-59.9	0.4	31 59.5	-59.9	0.4	32 59.5	-59.9	0.4	33 59.5	-59.9	0.4	34 59.5	-59.9	0.4	35 59.5	-59.9	0.4	84
85	27 59.6	-59.9	0.3	28 59.6	-59.9	0.3	29 59.6	-59.9	0.3	30 59.6	-59.9	0.3	31 59.6	-59.9	0.3	32 59.6	-59.9	0.3	33 59.6	-59.9	0.3	34 59.6	-59.9	0.3	85
86	26 59.7	-60.0	0.2	27 59.7	-60.0	0.2	28 59.7	-60.0	0.2	29 59.7	-60.0	0.2	30 59.7	-60.0	0.2	31 59.7	-60.0	0.2	32 59.7	-60.0	0.2	33 59.7	-60.0	0.2	86
87	25 59.7	-59.9	0.2	26 59.7	-59.9	0.2	27 59.7	-59.9	0.2	28 59.7	-59.9	0.2	29 59.7	-59.9	0.2	30 59.7	-59.9	0.2	31 59.7	-59.9	0.2	32 59.7	-59.9	0.2	87
88	24 59.8	-59.9	0.1	25 59.8	-59.9	0.1	26 59.8	-59.9	0.1	27 59.8	-59.9	0.1	28 59.8	-59.9	0.1	29 59.8	-59.9	0.1	30 59.8	-59.9	0.1	31 59.8	-59.9	0.1	88
89	23 59.9	-59.9	0.1	24 59.9	-59.9	0.1	25 59.9	-59.9	0.1	26 59.9	-59.9	0.1	27 59.9	-59.9	0.1	28 59.9	-59.9	0.1	29 59.9	-59.9	0.1	30 59.9	-59.9	0.1	89
90	23 00.0	-59.9	0.0	24 00.0	-59.9	0.0	25 00.0	-59.9	0.0	26 00.0	-59.9	0.0	27 00.0	-59.9	0.0	28 00.0	-59.9	0.0	29 00.0	-59.9	0.0	30 00.0	-59.9	0.0	90
	23°			24°			25°			26°			27°			28°			29°			30°			

3°, 357° L.H.A. LATITUDE SAME NAME AS DECLINATION

190

LATITUDE **CONTRARY** NAME TO DECLINATION L.H.A. 3°, 357°

Dec.	23° Hc	d	Z	24° Hc	d	Z	25° Hc	d	Z	26° Hc	d	Z	27° Hc	d	Z	28° Hc	d	Z	29° Hc	d	Z	30° Hc	d	Z	Dec.
°	° ′	′	°	° ′	′	°	° ′	′	°	° ′	′	°	° ′	′	°	° ′	′	°	° ′	′	°	° ′	′	°	°
0	66 48.9	−59.5	172.4	65 49.5	−59.7	172.7	64 49.9	−59.6	172.9	63 50.4	−59.7	173.2	62 50.8	−59.7	173.4	61 51.2	−59.8	173.6	60 51.5	−59.8	173.8	59 51.9	−59.8	174.0	0
1	65 49.4	−59.6	172.7	64 49.8	−59.6	172.9	63 50.3	−59.7	173.2	62 50.7	−59.7	173.4	61 51.1	−59.7	173.6	60 51.4	−59.8	173.8	59 51.8	−59.8	174.0	58 52.1	−59.8	174.2	1
2	64 49.8	−59.7	172.9	63 50.2	−59.6	173.2	62 50.6	−59.7	173.4	61 51.0	−59.7	173.6	60 51.4	−59.8	173.8	59 51.7	−59.7	174.0	58 52.0	−59.8	174.2	57 52.3	−59.8	174.4	2
3	63 50.1	−59.6	173.2	62 50.6	−59.7	173.4	61 50.9	−59.7	173.6	60 51.3	−59.7	173.8	59 51.6	−59.7	174.0	58 52.0	−59.8	174.2	57 52.2	−59.7	174.4	56 52.5	−59.8	174.5	3
4	62 50.5	−59.7	173.4	61 50.9	−59.7	173.6	60 51.2	−59.7	173.8	59 51.6	−59.8	174.0	58 51.9	−59.8	174.2	57 52.2	−59.8	174.4	56 52.5	−59.8	174.5	55 52.7	−59.8	174.7	4
5	61 50.8	−59.7	173.7	60 51.2	−59.7	173.9	59 51.5	−59.7	174.0	58 51.8	−59.7	174.2	57 52.1	−59.8	174.4	56 52.4	−59.8	174.5	55 52.7	−59.8	174.7	54 52.9	−59.8	174.8	5
6	60 51.1	−59.7	173.9	59 51.5	−59.8	174.1	58 51.8	−59.8	174.2	57 52.1	−59.8	174.4	56 52.3	−59.7	174.5	55 52.6	−59.8	174.7	54 52.9	−59.8	174.8	53 53.1	−59.8	174.9	6
7	59 51.4	−59.7	174.1	58 51.7	−59.7	174.2	57 52.0	−59.8	174.4	56 52.3	−59.8	174.5	55 52.6	−59.8	174.7	54 52.8	−59.8	174.8	53 53.1	−59.9	174.9	52 53.3	−59.9	175.1	7
8	58 51.7	−59.8	174.2	57 52.0	−59.8	174.4	56 52.2	−59.7	174.6	55 52.5	−59.8	174.7	54 52.8	−59.8	174.8	53 53.0	−59.8	175.0	52 53.2	−59.8	175.1	51 53.4	−59.8	175.2	8
9	57 51.9	−59.7	174.4	56 52.2	−59.8	174.6	55 52.5	−59.8	174.7	54 52.7	−59.8	174.8	53 53.0	−59.9	175.0	52 53.2	−59.8	175.1	51 53.4	−59.8	175.2	50 53.6	−59.8	175.3	9
10	56 52.2	−59.8	174.6	55 52.4	−59.8	174.7	54 52.7	−59.8	174.9	53 52.9	−59.8	175.0	52 53.1	−59.8	175.1	51 53.4	−59.9	175.2	50 53.6	−59.9	175.3	49 53.8	−59.9	175.4	10
11	55 52.4	−59.8	174.7	54 52.6	−59.8	174.9	53 52.9	−59.8	175.0	52 53.1	−59.8	175.1	51 53.3	−59.8	175.2	50 53.5	−59.8	175.3	49 53.7	−59.8	175.4	48 53.9	−59.9	175.5	11
12	54 52.6	−59.8	174.9	53 52.8	−59.8	175.0	52 53.1	−59.8	175.1	51 53.3	−59.8	175.2	50 53.5	−59.9	175.3	49 53.7	−59.9	175.4	48 53.9	−59.9	175.5	47 54.0	−59.8	175.6	12
13	53 52.8	−59.8	175.0	52 53.0	−59.8	175.2	51 53.3	−59.9	175.3	50 53.5	−59.9	175.4	49 53.6	−59.8	175.5	48 53.8	−59.8	175.6	47 54.0	−59.9	175.6	46 54.2	−59.9	175.7	13
14	52 53.0	−59.8	175.2	51 53.2	−59.8	175.3	50 53.4	−59.8	175.4	49 53.6	−59.8	175.5	48 53.8	−59.9	175.6	47 54.0	−59.9	175.7	46 54.1	−59.8	175.7	45 54.3	−59.9	175.8	14
15	51 53.2	−59.8	175.3	50 53.4	−59.8	175.4	49 53.6	−59.8	175.5	48 53.8	−59.9	175.6	47 53.9	−59.8	175.7	46 54.1	−59.9	175.8	45 54.3	−59.9	175.8	44 54.4	−59.8	175.9	15
16	50 53.4	−59.8	175.4	49 53.6	−59.9	175.5	48 53.8	−59.9	175.6	47 53.9	−59.8	175.7	46 54.1	−59.9	175.8	45 54.2	−59.8	175.9	44 54.4	−59.9	175.9	43 54.6	−59.9	176.0	16
17	49 53.6	−59.9	175.5	48 53.7	−59.8	175.6	47 53.9	−59.8	175.7	46 54.1	−59.9	175.8	45 54.2	−59.8	175.9	44 54.4	−59.9	175.9	43 54.5	−59.9	176.0	42 54.7	−59.9	176.1	17
18	48 53.7	−59.8	175.7	47 53.9	−59.9	175.7	46 54.1	−59.9	175.8	45 54.2	−59.9	175.9	44 54.4	−59.9	176.0	43 54.5	−59.9	176.0	42 54.6	−59.8	176.1	41 54.8	−59.9	176.2	18
19	47 53.9	−59.9	175.8	46 54.0	−59.8	175.8	45 54.2	−59.9	175.9	44 54.3	−59.8	176.0	43 54.5	−59.9	176.1	42 54.6	−59.9	176.1	41 54.8	−59.9	176.2	40 54.9	−59.9	176.2	19
20	46 54.0	−59.8	175.9	45 54.2	−59.9	175.9	44 54.3	−59.8	176.0	43 54.5	−59.9	176.1	42 54.6	−59.9	176.1	41 54.7	−59.8	176.2	40 54.9	−59.9	176.3	39 55.0	−59.9	176.3	20
21	45 54.2	−59.9	176.0	44 54.3	−59.8	176.0	43 54.5	−59.9	176.1	42 54.6	−59.9	176.2	41 54.7	−59.9	176.2	40 54.9	−59.9	176.3	39 55.0	−59.9	176.3	38 55.1	−59.9	176.4	21
22	44 54.3	−59.8	176.1	43 54.5	−59.9	176.1	42 54.6	−59.9	176.2	41 54.7	−59.9	176.3	40 54.8	−59.8	176.3	39 55.0	−59.9	176.4	38 55.1	−59.9	176.4	37 55.2	−59.9	176.5	22
23	43 54.5	−59.9	176.2	42 54.6	−59.9	176.2	41 54.7	−59.9	176.3	40 54.8	−59.8	176.3	39 55.0	−59.9	176.4	38 55.1	−59.9	176.5	37 55.2	−59.9	176.5	36 55.3	−59.9	176.5	23
24	42 54.6	−59.9	176.3	41 54.7	−59.9	176.3	40 54.8	−59.8	176.4	39 55.0	−59.9	176.4	38 55.1	−59.9	176.5	37 55.2	−59.9	176.5	36 55.3	−59.9	176.6	35 55.4	−59.9	176.6	24
25	41 54.7	−59.9	176.3	40 54.8	−59.8	176.4	39 55.0	−59.9	176.5	38 55.1	−59.9	176.5	37 55.2	−59.9	176.6	36 55.3	−59.9	176.6	35 55.4	−59.9	176.6	34 55.5	−59.9	176.7	25
26	40 54.8	−59.8	176.4	39 55.0	−59.9	176.5	38 55.1	−59.9	176.5	37 55.2	−59.9	176.6	36 55.3	−59.9	176.6	35 55.4	−59.9	176.7	34 55.5	−59.9	176.7	33 55.6	−59.9	176.8	26
27	39 55.0	−59.9	176.5	38 55.1	−59.9	176.6	37 55.2	−59.9	176.6	36 55.3	−59.9	176.7	35 55.4	−59.9	176.7	34 55.5	−59.9	176.7	33 55.6	−59.9	176.8	32 55.7	−59.9	176.8	27
28	38 55.1	−59.9	176.6	37 55.2	−59.9	176.6	36 55.3	−59.9	176.7	35 55.4	−59.9	176.7	34 55.5	−59.9	176.8	33 55.6	−59.9	176.8	32 55.7	−59.9	176.8	31 55.8	−60.0	176.9	28
29	37 55.2	−59.9	176.7	36 55.3	−59.9	176.7	35 55.4	−59.9	176.8	34 55.5	−59.8	176.8	33 55.6	−59.9	176.8	32 55.7	−59.9	176.9	31 55.8	−60.0	176.9	30 55.8	−59.9	176.9	29
30	36 55.3	−59.9	176.7	35 55.4	−59.9	176.8	34 55.5	−59.9	176.8	33 55.6	−59.9	176.9	32 55.7	−59.9	176.9	31 55.8	−60.0	176.9	30 55.8	−59.9	177.0	29 55.9	−59.9	177.0	30
31	35 55.4	−59.9	176.8	34 55.5	−59.9	176.9	33 55.6	−59.9	176.9	32 55.7	−59.9	176.9	31 55.8	−60.0	177.0	30 55.8	−59.9	177.0	29 55.9	−59.9	177.0	28 56.0	−59.9	177.1	31
32	34 55.5	−59.9	176.9	33 55.6	−59.9	176.9	32 55.7	−59.9	177.0	31 55.8	−59.9	177.0	30 55.8	−59.9	177.0	29 55.9	−59.9	177.1	28 56.0	−59.9	177.1	27 56.1	−59.9	177.1	32
33	33 55.6	−59.9	177.0	32 55.7	−59.9	177.0	31 55.8	−59.9	177.0	30 55.9	−60.0	177.1	29 55.9	−59.9	177.1	28 56.0	−59.9	177.1	27 56.1	−59.9	177.2	26 56.2	−60.0	177.2	33
34	32 55.7	−59.9	177.0	31 55.8	−59.9	177.1	30 55.9	−59.9	177.1	29 55.9	−59.9	177.1	28 56.0	−59.9	177.2	27 56.1	−59.9	177.2	26 56.2	−60.0	177.2	25 56.2	−59.9	177.2	34
35	31 55.8	−59.9	177.1	30 55.9	−59.9	177.1	29 56.0	−59.9	177.2	28 56.0	−59.9	177.2	27 56.1	−59.9	177.2	26 56.2	−59.9	177.2	25 56.2	−59.9	177.3	24 56.3	−59.9	177.3	35
36	30 55.9	−59.9	177.2	29 56.0	−59.9	177.2	28 56.1	−60.0	177.2	27 56.1	−59.9	177.3	26 56.2	−59.9	177.3	25 56.3	−60.0	177.3	24 56.3	−59.9	177.3	23 56.4	−59.9	177.3	36
37	29 56.0	−59.9	177.2	28 56.1	−59.9	177.3	27 56.1	−59.9	177.3	26 56.2	−59.9	177.3	25 56.3	−59.9	177.3	24 56.3	−59.9	177.4	23 56.4	−59.9	177.4	22 56.5	−60.0	177.4	37
38	28 56.1	−59.9	177.3	27 56.2	−60.0	177.3	26 56.2	−59.9	177.3	25 56.3	−59.9	177.4	24 56.4	−60.0	177.4	23 56.4	−59.9	177.4	22 56.5	−60.0	177.4	21 56.5	−59.9	177.5	38
39	27 56.2	−59.9	177.4	26 56.2	−59.9	177.4	25 56.3	−59.9	177.4	24 56.4	−59.9	177.4	23 56.4	−59.9	177.4	22 56.5	−59.9	177.5	21 56.5	−59.9	177.5	20 56.6	−59.9	177.5	39
40	26 56.3	−59.9	177.4	25 56.3	−59.9	177.4	24 56.4	−59.9	177.5	23 56.5	−60.0	177.5	22 56.5	−59.9	177.5	21 56.6	−60.0	177.5	20 56.6	−59.9	177.5	19 56.7	−60.0	177.6	40
41	25 56.4	−60.0	177.5	24 56.4	−59.9	177.5	23 56.5	−59.9	177.5	22 56.5	−59.9	177.5	21 56.6	−59.9	177.6	20 56.6	−59.9	177.6	19 56.7	−59.9	177.6	18 56.7	−59.9	177.6	41
42	24 56.4	−59.9	177.5	23 56.5	−59.9	177.6	22 56.6	−60.0	177.6	21 56.6	−59.9	177.6	20 56.7	−60.0	177.6	19 56.7	−59.9	177.6	18 56.8	−60.0	177.6	17 56.8	−59.9	177.7	42
43	23 56.5	−59.9	177.6	22 56.6	−59.9	177.6	21 56.6	−59.9	177.6	20 56.7	−59.9	177.7	19 56.7	−59.9	177.7	18 56.8	−59.9	177.7	17 56.8	−59.9	177.7	16 56.9	−60.0	177.7	43
44	22 56.6	−59.9	177.7	21 56.7	−60.0	177.7	20 56.7	−59.9	177.7	19 56.8	−60.0	177.7	18 56.8	−59.9	177.7	17 56.9	−60.0	177.7	16 56.9	−59.9	177.7	15 56.9	−59.9	177.8	44
45	21 56.7	−59.9	177.7	20 56.7	−59.9	177.7	19 56.8	−59.9	177.7	18 56.8	−59.9	177.8	17 56.9	−59.9	177.8	16 56.9	−59.9	177.8	15 57.0	−60.0	177.8	14 57.0	−59.9	177.8	45
46	20 56.8	−59.9	177.8	19 56.8	−59.9	177.8	18 56.9	−60.0	177.8	17 56.9	−59.9	177.8	16 57.0	−60.0	177.8	15 57.0	−59.9	177.8	14 57.0	−59.9	177.8	13 57.1	−60.0	177.9	46
47	19 56.9	−60.0	177.8	18 56.9	−59.9	177.8	17 56.9	−59.9	177.8	16 57.0	−59.9	177.9	15 57.0	−59.9	177.9	14 57.1	−60.0	177.9	13 57.1	−59.9	177.9	12 57.1	−59.9	177.9	47
48	18 56.9	−59.9	177.9	17 57.0	−60.0	177.9	16 57.0	−59.9	177.9	15 57.1	−60.0	177.9	14 57.1	−59.9	177.9	13 57.1	−59.9	177.9	12 57.2	−60.0	177.9	11 57.2	−59.9	177.9	48
49	17 57.0	−59.9	177.9	16 57.0	−59.9	177.9	15 57.1	−59.9	178.0	14 57.1	−59.9	178.0	13 57.2	−60.0	178.0	12 57.2	−59.9	178.0	11 57.2	−59.9	178.0	10 57.3	−60.0	178.0	49
50	16 57.1	−59.9	178.0	15 57.1	−59.9	178.0	14 57.2	−60.0	178.0	13 57.2	−59.9	178.0	12 57.2	−59.9	178.0	11 57.3	−60.0	178.0	10 57.3	−59.9	178.0	9 57.3	−59.9	178.0	50
51	15 57.2	−60.0	178.0	14 57.2	−59.9	178.0	13 57.2	−59.9	178.1	12 57.3	−60.0	178.1	11 57.3	−59.9	178.1	10 57.3	−59.9	178.1	9 57.4	−60.0	178.1	8 57.4	−59.9	178.1	51
52	14 57.2	−59.9	178.1	13 57.3	−60.0	178.1	12 57.3	−59.9	178.1	11 57.3	−59.9	178.1	10 57.4	−60.0	178.1	9 57.4	−59.9	178.1	8 57.4	−59.9	178.1	7 57.5	−60.0	178.1	52
53	13 57.3	−59.9	178.1	12 57.3	−59.9	178.1	11 57.4	−60.0	178.2	10 57.4	−59.9	178.2	9 57.4	−59.9	178.2	8 57.5	−60.0	178.2	7 57.5	−59.9	178.2	6 57.5	−59.9	178.2	53
54	12 57.4	−59.9	178.2	11 57.4	−59.9	178.2	10 57.4	−59.9	178.2	9 57.5	−60.0	178.2	8 57.5	−59.9	178.2	7 57.5	−59.9	178.2	6 57.6	−60.0	178.2	5 57.6	−59.9	178.2	54
55	11 57.5	−60.0	178.2	10 57.5	−59.9	178.2	9 57.5	−59.9	178.3	8 57.5	−59.9	178.3	7 57.6	−60.0	178.3	6 57.6	−59.9	178.3	5 57.6	−59.9	178.3	4 57.7	−60.0	178.3	55
56	10 57.5	−59.9	178.3	9 57.6	−60.0	178.3	8 57.6	−59.9	178.3	7 57.6	−59.9	178.3	6 57.6	−59.9	178.3	5 57.7	−60.0	178.3	4 57.7	−59.9	178.3	3 57.7	−59.9	178.3	56
57	9 57.6	−59.9	178.3	8 57.6	−59.9	178.3	7 57.7	−60.0	178.4	6 57.7	−60.0	178.4	5 57.7	−59.9	178.4	4 57.7	−59.9	178.4	3 57.8	−60.0	178.4	2 57.8	−60.0	178.4	57
58	8 57.7	−60.0	178.4	7 57.7	−59.9	178.4	6 57.7	−59.9	178.4	5 57.7	−59.9	178.4	4 57.8	−60.0	178.4	3 57.8	−59.9	178.4	2 57.8	−59.9	178.4	1 57.8	−59.9	178.4	58
59	7 57.7	−59.9	178.4	6 57.8	−60.0	178.4	5 57.8	−59.9	178.4	4 57.8	−59.9	178.4	3 57.8	−59.9	178.5	2 57.9	−60.0	178.5	1 57.9	−60.0	178.5	0 57.9	−59.9	178.5	59
60	6 57.8	−59.9	178.5	5 57.8	−59.9	178.5	4 57.9	−60.0	178.5	3 57.9	−60.0	178.5	2 57.9	−59.9	178.5	1 57.9	−59.9	178.5	0 57.9	−59.9	178.5	0 02.0	+60.0	1.5	60
61	5 57.9	−59.9	178.5	4 57.9	−59.9	178.5	3 57.9	−59.9	178.5	2 57.9	−59.9	178.5	1 58.0	−60.0	178.5	0 58.0	−60.0	178.5	0 02.0	+59.9	1.5	1 02.0	+59.9	1.5	61
62	4 58.0	−60.0	178.6	3 58.0	−60.0	178.6	2 58.0	−59.9	178.6	1 58.0	−59.9	178.6	0 58.0	−59.9	178.6	0 02.0	+59.9	1.4	1 01.9	+60.0	1.4	2 01.9	+60.0	1.4	62
63	3 58.0	−59.9	178.6	2 58.0	−59.9	178.6	1 58.1	−60.0	178.6	0 58.1	−60.0	178.6	0 01.9	+59.9	1.4	1 01.9	+59.9	1.4	2 01.9	+59.9	1.4	3 01.9	+59.9	1.4	63
64	2 58.1	−59.9	178.7	1 58.1	−59.9	178.7	0 58.1	−59.9	178.7	0 01.9	+59.9	1.3	1 01.8	+60.0	1.3	2 01.8	+60.0	1.3	3 01.8	+59.9	1.3	4 01.8	+59.9	1.3	64
65	1 58.2	−60.0	178.7	0 58.2	−60.0	178.7	0 01.8	+59.9	1.3	1 01.8	+59.9	1.3	2 01.8	+59.9	1.3	3 01.8	+59.9	1.3	4 01.7	+60.0	1.3	5 01.7	+60.0	1.3	65
66	0 58.2	−59.9	178.8	0 01.8	+59.9	1.2	1 01.7	+60.0	1.2	2 01.7	+60.0	1.2	3 01.7	+59.9	1.2	4 01.7	+59.9	1.2	5 01.7	+59.9	1.2	6 01.7	+59.9	1.2	66
67	0 01.7	+59.9	1.2	1 01.7	+59.9	1.2	2 01.7	+59.9	1.2	3 01.7	+59.9	1.2	4 01.6	+60.0	1.2	5 01.6	+60.0	1.2	6 01.6	+60.0	1.2	7 01.6	+59.9	1.2	67
68	1 01.6	+60.0	1.1	2 01.6	+59.9	1.1	3 01.6	+59.9	1.1	4 01.6	+59.9	1.1	5 01.6	+59.9	1.1	6 01.6	+59.9	1.1	7 01.6	+59.9	1.1	8 01.5	+60.0	1.1	68
69	2 01.6	+59.9	1.1	3 01.5	+60.0	1.1	4 01.5	+60.0	1.1	5 01.5	+60.0	1.1	6 01.5	+59.9	1.1	7 01.5	+59.9	1.1	8 01.5	+59.9	1.1	9 01.5	+59.9	1.1	69
70	3 01.5	+59.9	1.0	4 01.5	+59.9	1.0	5 01.5	+59.9	1.0	6 01.5	+59.9	1.0	7 01.4	+60.0	1.0	8 01.4	+60.0	1.0	9 01.4	+60.0	1.0	10 01.4	+60.0	1.0	70
71	4 01.4	+59.9	1.0	5 01.4	+59.9	1.0	6 01.4	+59.9	1.0	7 01.4	+59.9	1.0	8 01.4	+59.9	1.0	9 01.4	+59.9	1.0	10 01.4	+59.9	1.0	11 01.4	+59.9	1.0	71
72	5 01.3	+60.0	0.9	6 01.3	+60.0	0.9	7 01.3	+60.0	0.9	8 01.3	+60.0	0.9	9 01.3	+59.9	0.9	10 01.3	+59.9	0.9	11 01.3	+59.9	0.9	12 01.3	+59.9	0.9	72
73	6 01.3	+59.9	0.9	7 01.3	+59.9	0.9	8 01.3	+59.9	0.9	9 01.3	+59.9	0.9	10 01.2	+60.0	0.9	11 01.2	+60.0	0.9	12 01.2	+60.0	0.9	13 01.2	+60.0	0.9	73
74	7 01.2	+59.9	0.8	8 01.2	+59.9	0.8	9 01.2	+59.9	0.8	10 01.2	+59.9	0.8	11 01.2	+59.9	0.8	12 01.2	+59.9	0.8	13 01.2	+59.9	0.8	14 01.2	+59.9	0.9	74
75	8 01.1	+60.0	0.8	9 01.1	+60.0	0.8	10 01.1	+60.0	0.8	11 01.1	+59.9	0.8	12 01.1	+59.9	0.8	13 01.1	+59.9	0.8	14 01.1	+59.9	0.8	15 01.1	+59.9	0.8	75
76	9 01.1	+59.9	0.7	10 01.1	+59.9	0.7	11 01.1	+59.9	0.7	12 01.0	+60.0	0.7	13 01.0	+60.0	0.7	14 01.0	+60.0	0.7	15 01.0	+60.0	0.8	16 01.0	+60.0	0.8	76
77	10 01.0	+59.9	0.7	11 01.0	+59.9	0.7	12 01.0	+59.9	0.7	13 01.0	+59.9	0.7	14 01.0	+59.9	0.7	15 01.0	+59.9	0.7	16 01.0	+59.9	0.7	17 01.0	+59.9	0.7	77
78	11 00.9	+59.9	0.6	12 00.9	+59.9	0.6	13 00.9	+59.9	0.6	14 00.9	+59.9	0.6	15 00.9	+59.9	0.6	16 00.9	+59.9	0.6	17 00.9	+59.9	0.7	18 00.9	+59.9	0.7	78
79	12 00.8	+60.0	0.6	13 00.8	+60.0	0.6	14 00.8	+60.0	0.6	15 00.8	+60.0	0.6	16 00.8	+60.0	0.6	17 00.8	+60.0	0.6	18 00.8	+60.0	0.6	19 00.8	+60.0	0.6	79
80	13 00.8	+59.9	0.5	14 00.8	+59.9	0.5	15 00.8	+59.9	0.5	16 00.8	+59.9	0.5	17 00.8	+59.9	0.5	18 00.8	+59.9	0.5	19 00.8	+59.9	0.6	20 00.8	+59.9	0.6	80
81	14 00.7	+59.9	0.5	15 00.7	+59.9	0.5	16 00.7	+59.9	0.5	17 00.7	+59.9	0.5	18 00.7	+59.9	0.5	19 00.7	+59.9	0.5	20 00.7	+59.9	0.5	21 00.7	+59.9	0.5	81
82	15 00.6	+59.9	0.4	16 00.6	+59.9	0.4	17 00.6	+59.9	0.4	18 00.6	+59.9	0.4	19 00.6	+59.9	0.4	20 00.6	+59.9	0.4	21 00.6	+59.9	0.4	22 00.6	+59.9	0.5	82
83	16 00.5	+60.0	0.4	17 00.5	+60.0	0.4	18 00.5	+60.0	0.4	19 00.5	+60.0	0.4	20 00.5	+60.0	0.4	21 00.5	+60.0	0.4	22 00.5	+60.0	0.4	23 00.5	+60.0	0.4	83
84	17 00.5	+59.9	0.3	18 00.5	+59.9	0.3	19 00.5	+59.9	0.3	20 00.5	+59.9	0.3	21 00.5	+59.9	0.3	22 00.5	+59.9	0.3	23 00.5	+59.9	0.3	24 00.5	+59.9	0.3	84
85	18 00.4	+59.9	0.3	19 00.4	+59.9	0.3	20 00.4	+59.9	0.3	21 00.4	+59.9	0.3	22 00.4	+59.9	0.3	23 00.4	+59.9	0.3	24 00.4	+59.9	0.3	25 00.4	+59.9	0.3	85
86	19 00.3	+59.9	0.2	20 00.3	+59.9	0.2	21 00.3	+59.9	0.2	22 00.3	+59.9	0.2	23 00.3	+59.9	0.2	24 00.3	+59.9	0.2	25 00.3	+59.9	0.2	26 00.3	+59.9	0.2	86
87	20 00.2	+60.0	0.2	21 00.2	+60.0	0.2	22 00.2	+60.0	0.2	23 00.2	+60.0	0.2	24 00.2	+60.0	0.2	25 00.2	+60.0	0.2	26 00.2	+60.0	0.2	27 00.2	+60.0	0.2	87
88	21 00.2	+59.9	0.1	22 00.2	+59.9	0.1	23 00.2	+59.9	0.1	24 00.2	+59.9	0.1	25 00.2	+59.9	0.1	26 00.2	+59.9	0.1	27 00.2	+59.9	0.1	28 00.2	+59.9	0.1	88
89	22 00.1	+59.9	0.1	23 00.1	+59.9	0.1	24 00.1	+59.9	0.1	25 00.1	+59.9	0.1	26 00.1	+59.9	0.1	27 00.1	+59.9	0.1	28 00.1	+59.9	0.1	29 00.1	+59.9	0.1	89
90	23 00.0	+59.9	0.0	24 00.0	+59.9	0.0	25 00.0	+59.9	0.0	26 00.0	+59.9	0.0	27 00.0	+59.9	0.0	28 00.0	+59.9	0.0	29 00.0	+59.9	0.0	30 00.0	+59.9	0.0	90
	23°			24°			25°			26°			27°			28°			29°			30°			

S. Lat. {L.H.A. greater than 180° ....Zn=180°−Z; L.H.A. less than 180°...........Zn=180°+Z

LATITUDE **SAME** NAME AS DECLINATION L.H.A. 177°, 183°

191

4°, 356° L.H.A. LATITUDE SAME NAME AS DECLINATION

N. Lat. {L.H.A. greater than 180° .....Zn=Z / L.H.A. less than 180°............Zn=360°−Z}

Dec.	23° Hc	23° d	23° Z	24° Hc	24° d	24° Z	25° Hc	25° d	25° Z	26° Hc	26° d	26° Z
°	° ′	′	°	° ′	′	°	° ′	′	°	° ′	′	°
0	66 40.4	+59.2	169.9	65 41.3	+59.3	170.2	64 42.1	+59.4	170.6	63 42.9	+59.4	170.9
1	67 39.6	+59.1	169.4	66 40.6	+59.1	169.9	65 41.5	+59.2	170.2	64 42.3	+59.3	170.6
2	68 38.7	+59.0	169.0	67 39.7	+59.2	169.4	66 40.7	+59.2	169.9	65 41.6	+59.3	170.2
3	69 37.7	+58.9	168.5	68 38.9	+59.0	169.0	67 39.9	+59.1	169.4	66 40.9	+59.2	169.9
4	70 36.6	+58.8	167.9	69 37.9	+58.9	168.5	68 39.0	+59.1	169.0	67 40.1	+59.1	169.4
5	71 35.4	+58.7	167.3	70 36.8	+58.8	167.9	69 38.1	+58.9	168.5	68 39.2	+59.1	169.0
6	72 34.1	+58.5	166.6	71 35.6	+58.7	167.3	70 37.0	+58.9	167.9	69 38.3	+59.0	168.5
7	73 32.6	+58.4	165.9	72 34.3	+58.6	166.6	71 35.9	+58.7	167.3	70 37.3	+58.8	168.0
8	74 31.0	+58.1	165.0	73 32.9	+58.4	165.9	72 34.6	+58.6	166.7	71 36.1	+58.8	167.4
9	75 29.1	+57.8	164.0	74 31.3	+58.1	165.0	73 33.2	+58.4	165.9	72 34.9	+58.6	166.7
10	76 26.9	+57.6	163.0	75 29.4	+57.9	164.1	74 31.6	+58.1	165.1	73 33.5	+58.4	166.0
11	77 24.5	+57.1	161.7	76 27.3	+57.6	163.0	75 29.7	+58.0	164.1	74 31.9	+58.2	165.1
12	78 21.6	+56.6	160.2	77 24.9	+57.1	161.8	76 27.7	+57.6	163.1	75 30.1	+57.9	164.2
13	79 18.2	+55.9	158.5	78 22.0	+56.7	160.3	77 25.3	+57.2	161.8	76 28.0	+57.7	163.1
14	80 14.1	+55.1	156.5	79 18.7	+56.0	158.6	78 22.5	+56.7	160.4	77 25.7	+57.2	161.9
15	81 09.2	+53.8	154.0	80 14.7	+55.1	156.6	79 19.2	+56.0	158.7	78 22.9	+56.8	160.5
16	82 03.0	+52.3	151.0	81 09.8	+53.9	154.1	80 15.2	+55.2	156.7	79 19.7	+56.1	158.8
17	82 55.3	+49.9•	147.2	82 03.7	+52.3	151.1	81 10.4	+54.0	154.2	80 15.8	+55.2	156.8
18	83 45.2	+46.5•	142.4	82 56.0	+50.1•	147.4	82 04.4	+52.5	151.2	81 11.0	+54.2	154.3
19	84 31.7	+41.5•	136.2	83 46.1	+46.7•	142.6	82 56.9	+50.1•	147.5	82 05.2	+52.5	151.4
20	85 13.2	+34.0•	128.1	84 32.8	+41.6•	136.4	83 47.0	+46.9•	142.7	82 57.7	+50.3•	147.7
21	85 47.2	+23.1•	117.6	85 14.4	+34.2•	128.3	84 33.9	+41.8•	136.6	83 48.0	+47.0•	142.9
22	86 10.3	+8.8•	104.4	85 48.6	+23.3•	117.7	85 15.7	+34.4•	128.5	84 35.0	+42.0•	136.8
23	86 19.1	-7.2•	89.2	86 11.9	+8.9•	104.4	85 50.1	+23.4•	117.9	85 17.0	+34.6•	128.7
24	86 11.9	-21.8•	74.0	86 20.8	-7.3•	89.2	86 13.5	+9.0•	104.5	85 51.6	+23.6•	118.0
25	85 50.1	-33.1•	60.5	86 13.5	-21.9•	73.8	86 22.5	-7.3•	89.2	86 15.2	+9.1•	104.6
26	85 17.0	-40.8•	49.7	85 51.6	-33.2•	60.3	86 15.2	-22.0•	73.7	86 24.3	-7.3•	89.1
27	84 36.2	-46.2•	41.4	85 18.4	-41.0•	49.4	85 53.2	-33.4•	60.0	86 17.0	-22.2•	73.5
28	83 50.0	-49.6•	35.0	84 37.4	-46.3•	41.1	85 19.8	-41.2•	49.2	85 54.8	-33.5•	59.8
29	83 00.4	-52.0•	30.1	83 51.1	-49.7•	34.7	84 38.6	-46.4•	40.8	85 21.3	-41.4•	48.9
30	82 08.4	-53.7	26.2	83 01.4	-52.2•	29.8	83 52.2	-49.8•	34.5	84 39.9	-46.5•	40.5
31	81 14.7	-55.0	23.1	82 09.2	-53.8	26.0	83 02.4	-52.3•	29.6	83 53.4	-50.0•	34.2
32	80 19.7	-55.9	20.6	81 15.4	-55.0	22.9	82 10.1	-53.9	25.7	83 03.4	-52.4	29.3
33	79 23.8	-56.5	18.5	80 20.4	-55.9	20.4	81 16.2	-55.0	22.7	82 11.0	-53.9	25.5
34	78 27.3	-57.1	16.8	79 24.5	-56.6	18.3	80 21.2	-56.0	20.2	81 17.1	-55.2	22.4
35	77 30.2	-57.5	15.3	78 27.9	-57.1	16.6	79 25.2	-56.6	18.1	80 21.9	-56.0	20.0
36	76 32.7	-57.8	14.0	77 30.8	-57.5	15.1	78 28.6	-57.2	16.4	79 25.9	-56.7	17.9
37	75 34.9	-58.1	12.9	76 33.3	-57.9	13.9	77 31.4	-57.6	14.9	78 29.2	-57.2	16.2
38	74 36.8	-58.3	12.0	75 35.4	-58.1	12.8	76 33.8	-57.8	13.7	77 32.0	-57.6	14.8
39	73 38.5	-58.5	11.1	74 37.3	-58.3	11.8	75 36.0	-58.2	12.6	76 34.4	-57.9	13.5
40	72 40.0	-58.7	10.3	73 39.0	-58.6	10.9	74 37.8	-58.4	11.6	75 36.5	-58.2	12.4
41	71 41.3	-58.8	9.6	72 40.4	-58.6	10.2	73 39.4	-58.5	10.8	74 38.3	-58.4	11.5
42	70 42.5	-58.9	9.0	71 41.8	-58.9	9.5	72 40.9	-58.7	10.0	73 39.9	-58.6	10.6
43	69 43.6	-59.0	8.5	70 42.9	-58.9	8.9	71 42.2	-58.9	9.4	72 41.3	-58.7	9.9
44	68 44.6	-59.1	8.0	69 44.0	-59.0	8.3	70 43.3	-58.9	8.7	71 42.6	-58.8	9.2
45	67 45.5	-59.1	7.5	68 45.0	-59.1	7.8	69 44.4	-59.0	8.2	70 43.8	-59.0	8.6
46	66 46.4	-59.3	7.1	67 45.9	-59.2	7.4	68 45.4	-59.1	7.7	69 44.8	-59.0	8.0
47	65 47.1	-59.3	6.7	66 46.7	-59.2	6.9	67 46.3	-59.2	7.2	68 45.8	-59.2	7.5
48	64 47.8	-59.3	6.3	65 47.5	-59.3	6.5	66 47.1	-59.3	6.8	67 46.6	-59.2	7.1
49	63 48.5	-59.4	6.0	64 48.2	-59.4	6.2	65 47.8	-59.3	6.4	66 47.4	-59.2	6.7
50	62 49.1	-59.4	5.6	63 48.8	-59.4	5.8	64 48.5	-59.4	6.0	65 48.2	-59.4	6.3
51	61 49.7	-59.5	5.3	62 49.4	-59.4	5.5	63 49.1	-59.4	5.7	64 48.8	-59.3	5.9
52	60 50.2	-59.5	5.1	61 50.0	-59.5	5.2	62 49.7	-59.4	5.4	63 49.5	-59.4	5.6
53	59 50.7	-59.5	4.8	60 50.5	-59.5	4.9	61 50.3	-59.5	5.1	62 50.1	-59.5	5.3
54	58 51.2	-59.5	4.5	59 51.0	-59.5	4.7	60 50.8	-59.5	4.8	61 50.6	-59.5	5.0
55	57 51.7	-59.6	4.3	58 51.5	-59.6	4.4	59 51.3	-59.5	4.6	60 51.1	-59.5	4.7
56	56 52.1	-59.6	4.1	57 51.9	-59.5	4.2	58 51.8	-59.6	4.3	59 51.6	-59.5	4.5
57	55 52.5	-59.6	3.9	56 52.4	-59.6	4.0	57 52.2	-59.6	4.1	58 52.1	-59.6	4.2
58	54 52.9	-59.6	3.7	55 52.8	-59.7	3.8	56 52.6	-59.6	3.9	57 52.5	-59.6	4.0
59	53 53.3	-59.7	3.5	54 53.1	-59.6	3.6	55 53.0	-59.6	3.7	56 52.9	-59.6	3.8
60	52 53.6	-59.7	3.3	53 53.5	-59.7	3.4	54 53.4	-59.7	3.5	55 53.3	-59.7	3.6
61	51 53.9	-59.6	3.1	52 53.8	-59.6	3.2	53 53.7	-59.6	3.3	54 53.6	-59.6	3.4
62	50 54.3	-59.7	3.0	51 54.2	-59.7	3.0	52 54.1	-59.7	3.1	53 54.0	-59.7	3.2
63	49 54.6	-59.7	2.8	50 54.5	-59.7	2.9	51 54.4	-59.7	2.9	52 54.3	-59.7	3.0
64	48 54.9	-59.8	2.7	49 54.8	-59.7	2.7	50 54.7	-59.7	2.8	51 54.6	-59.7	2.8
65	47 55.1	-59.7	2.5	48 55.1	-59.7	2.6	49 55.0	-59.7	2.6	50 54.9	-59.7	2.7
66	46 55.4	-59.7	2.4	47 55.4	-59.8	2.4	48 55.3	-59.7	2.5	49 55.2	-59.7	2.5
67	45 55.7	-59.8	2.2	46 55.6	-59.7	2.3	47 55.6	-59.8	2.3	48 55.5	-59.7	2.4
68	44 55.9	-59.7	2.1	45 55.9	-59.8	2.2	46 55.8	-59.7	2.2	47 55.8	-59.8	2.2
69	43 56.2	-59.8	2.0	44 56.1	-59.7	2.0	45 56.1	-59.8	2.1	46 56.0	-59.7	2.1
70	42 56.4	-59.8	1.9	43 56.4	-59.8	1.9	44 56.3	-59.7	1.9	45 56.3	-59.8	2.0
71	41 56.6	-59.8	1.7	42 56.6	-59.8	1.8	43 56.6	-59.8	1.8	44 56.5	-59.7	1.8
72	40 56.8	-59.7	1.6	41 56.8	-59.8	1.7	42 56.8	-59.8	1.7	43 56.8	-59.8	1.7
73	39 57.1	-59.8	1.5	40 57.0	-59.8	1.5	41 57.0	-59.8	1.6	42 57.0	-59.8	1.6
74	38 57.3	-59.8	1.4	39 57.2	-59.7	1.4	40 57.2	-59.8	1.5	41 57.2	-59.8	1.5
75	37 57.5	-59.8	1.3	38 57.5	-59.8	1.3	39 57.4	-59.8	1.3	40 57.4	-59.8	1.4
76	36 57.7	-59.8	1.2	37 57.7	-59.9	1.2	38 57.6	-59.8	1.2	39 57.6	-59.8	1.3
77	35 57.9	-59.9	1.1	36 57.8	-59.8	1.1	37 57.8	-59.8	1.1	38 57.8	-59.8	1.2
78	34 58.0	-59.8	1.0	35 58.0	-59.8	1.0	36 58.0	-59.8	1.0	37 58.0	-59.8	1.1
79	33 58.2	-59.8	0.9	34 58.2	-59.8	0.9	35 58.2	-59.8	0.9	36 58.2	-59.8	1.0
80	32 58.4	-59.8	0.8	33 58.4	-59.8	0.8	34 58.4	-59.8	0.8	35 58.4	-59.8	0.9
81	31 58.6	-59.9	0.7	32 58.6	-59.9	0.7	33 58.6	-59.9	0.8	34 58.6	-59.9	0.8
82	30 58.7	-59.8	0.6	31 58.7	-59.8	0.7	32 58.7	-59.8	0.7	33 58.7	-59.8	0.7
83	29 58.9	-59.8	0.6	30 58.9	-59.8	0.6	31 58.9	-59.8	0.6	32 58.9	-59.8	0.6
84	28 59.1	-59.9	0.5	29 59.1	-59.9	0.5	30 59.1	-59.9	0.5	31 59.1	-59.9	0.5
85	27 59.2	-59.8	0.4	28 59.2	-59.8	0.4	29 59.2	-59.8	0.4	30 59.2	-59.8	0.4
86	26 59.4	-59.8	0.3	27 59.4	-59.8	0.3	28 59.4	-59.8	0.3	29 59.4	-59.9	0.3
87	25 59.6	-59.9	0.2	26 59.6	-59.9	0.2	27 59.6	-59.9	0.2	28 59.5	-59.8	0.2
88	24 59.7	-59.8	0.2	25 59.7	-59.8	0.2	26 59.7	-59.8	0.2	27 59.7	-59.8	0.2
89	23 59.9	-59.9	0.1	24 59.9	-59.9	0.1	25 59.9	-59.9	0.1	26 59.9	-59.9	0.1
90	23 00.0	-59.9	0.0	24 00.0	-59.9	0.0	25 00.0	-59.9	0.0	26 00.0	-59.9	0.0
	23°			24°			25°			26°		

27° Hc	27° d	27° Z	28° Hc	28° d	28° Z	29° Hc	29° d	29° Z	30° Hc	30° d	30° Z	Dec.
° ′	′	°	° ′	′	°	° ′	′	°	° ′	′	°	°
62 43.6	+59.5	171.2	61 44.3	+59.5	171.5	60 45.0	+59.5	171.8	59 45.5	+59.6	172.0	0
63 43.1	+59.4	170.9	62 43.8	+59.4	171.2	61 44.5	+59.5	171.5	60 45.1	+59.5	171.8	1
64 42.5	+59.3	170.6	63 43.2	+59.4	170.9	62 44.0	+59.4	171.2	61 44.6	+59.5	171.5	2
65 41.8	+59.3	170.3	64 42.6	+59.4	170.6	63 43.4	+59.4	170.9	62 44.1	+59.5	171.3	3
66 41.1	+59.2	169.9	65 42.0	+59.3	170.3	64 42.8	+59.4	170.6	63 43.6	+59.4	171.0	4
67 40.3	+59.2	169.5	66 41.3	+59.2	169.9	65 42.2	+59.3	170.3	64 43.0	+59.4	170.6	5
68 39.5	+59.0	169.0	67 40.5	+59.2	169.5	66 41.5	+59.2	169.9	65 42.4	+59.3	170.3	6
69 38.5	+59.0	168.5	68 39.7	+59.1	169.0	67 40.7	+59.2	169.5	66 41.7	+59.3	169.9	7
70 37.5	+58.9	168.0	69 38.8	+59.0	168.5	68 39.9	+59.1	169.1	67 41.0	+59.2	169.5	8
71 36.4	+58.8	167.4	70 37.8	+58.9	168.0	69 39.0	+59.0	168.6	68 40.2	+59.1	169.1	9
72 35.2	+58.6	166.7	71 36.7	+58.8	167.4	70 38.0	+59.0	168.0	69 39.3	+59.0	168.6	10
73 33.8	+58.4	166.0	72 35.5	+58.6	166.8	71 37.0	+58.8	167.5	70 38.3	+59.0	168.1	11
74 32.2	+58.3	165.2	73 34.1	+58.5	166.0	72 35.8	+58.6	166.8	71 37.3	+58.8	167.5	12
75 30.5	+57.9	164.2	74 32.6	+58.2	165.2	73 34.4	+58.5	166.1	72 36.1	+58.7	166.9	13
76 28.4	+57.7	163.2	75 30.8	+58.1	164.3	74 32.9	+58.3	165.3	73 34.8	+58.5	166.1	14
77 26.1	+57.3	162.0	76 28.9	+57.7	163.2	75 31.2	+58.1	164.4	74 33.3	+58.4	165.3	15
78 23.4	+56.8	160.5	77 26.6	+57.3	162.0	76 29.3	+57.8	163.3	75 31.7	+58.0	164.4	16
79 20.2	+56.2	158.9	78 23.9	+56.9	160.6	77 27.1	+57.3	162.1	76 29.7	+57.8	163.4	17
80 16.4	+55.3	156.9	79 20.8	+56.2	159.0	78 24.4	+57.0	160.7	77 27.5	+57.5	162.2	18
81 11.7	+54.2	154.5	80 17.0	+55.4	157.0	79 21.4	+56.2	159.1	78 25.0	+56.9	160.8	19
82 05.9	+52.7	151.5	81 12.4	+54.3	154.6	80 17.6	+55.5	157.1	79 21.9	+56.4	159.2	20
82 58.6	+50.4•	147.8	82 06.7	+52.8	151.7	81 13.1	+54.4	154.7	80 18.3	+55.6	157.2	21
83 49.0	+47.2•	143.1	82 59.5	+50.5•	148.0	82 07.5	+52.9	151.8	81 13.9	+54.5	154.9	22
84 36.2	+42.2•	137.0	83 50.0	+47.4•	143.3	83 00.4	+50.7•	148.2	82 08.4	+53.0	152.0	23
85 18.4	+34.8•	128.8	84 37.4	+42.4•	137.2	83 51.1	+47.5•	143.5	83 01.4	+50.8•	148.4	24
85 53.2	+23.8•	118.2	85 19.8	+35.0•	129.1	84 38.6	+42.7•	137.4	83 52.2	+47.7•	143.7	25
86 17.0	+9.2•	104.7	85 54.8	+24.0•	118.4	85 21.3	+35.2•	129.3	84 39.9	+42.9•	137.6	26
86 26.2	-7.4•	89.1	86 18.8	+9.3•	104.8	85 56.5	+24.2•	118.6	85 22.8	+35.4•	129.5	27
86 18.8	-22.3•	73.3	86 28.1	-7.4•	89.1	86 20.7	+9.4•	104.9	85 58.2	+24.5•	118.8	28
85 56.5	-33.7•	59.5	86 20.7	-22.5•	73.2	86 30.1	-7.4•	89.0	86 22.7	+9.5•	105.0	29
85 22.8	-41.6•	48.6	85 58.2	-33.9•	59.3	86 22.7	-22.7•	73.0	86 32.2	-7.5•	89.0	30
84 41.2	-46.7•	40.2	85 24.3	-41.7•	48.3	86 00.0	-34.1•	59.0	86 24.7	-22.8•	72.8	31
83 54.5	-50.1•	33.9	84 42.6	-46.9•	39.9	85 25.9	-41.9•	48.0	86 01.9	-34.4•	58.7	32
83 04.4	-52.4•	29.0	83 55.7	-50.2•	33.6	84 44.0	-47.1•	39.6	85 27.5	-42.1•	47.6	33
82 12.0	-54.1	25.2	83 05.5	-52.6	28.7	83 56.9	-50.3•	33.3	84 45.4	-47.2•	39.3	34
81 17.9	-55.2	22.2	82 12.9	-54.1	25.0	83 06.6	-52.7	28.4	83 58.2	-50.5•	33.0	35
80 22.7	-56.1	19.7	81 18.8	-55.3	21.9	82 13.9	-54.2	24.7	83 07.7	-52.8	28.1	36
79 26.6	-56.7	17.7	80 23.5	-56.2	19.5	81 19.7	-55.4	21.7	82 14.9	-54.4	24.4	37
78 29.9	-57.3	16.0	79 27.3	-56.8	17.5	80 24.3	-56.2	19.3	81 20.5	-55.4	21.4	38
77 32.6	-57.6	14.6	78 30.5	-57.3	15.8	79 28.1	-56.9	17.3	80 25.1	-56.3	19.0	39
76 35.0	-58.0	13.3	77 33.2	-57.6	14.4	78 31.2	-57.3	15.6	79 28.8	-56.9	17.0	40
75 37.0	-58.2	12.2	76 35.6	-58.0	13.1	77 33.9	-57.7	14.2	78 31.9	-57.4	15.4	41
74 38.8	-58.4	11.3	75 37.6	-58.3	12.1	76 36.2	-58.1	12.9	77 34.5	-57.7	13.9	42
73 40.4	-58.6	10.5	74 39.3	-58.4	11.1	75 38.1	-58.2	11.9	76 36.8	-58.1	12.7	43
72 41.8	-58.7	9.7	73 40.9	-58.6	10.3	74 39.9	-58.5	10.9	75 38.7	-58.3	11.7	44
71 43.1	-58.9	9.0	72 42.3	-58.8	9.6	73 41.4	-58.7	10.1	74 40.4	-58.5	10.8	45
70 44.2	-59.0	8.4	71 43.5	-58.9	8.9	72 42.7	-58.7	9.4	73 41.9	-58.7	9.9	46
69 45.2	-59.1	7.9	70 44.6	-59.0	8.3	71 44.0	-59.0	8.7	72 43.2	-58.8	9.2	47
68 46.1	-59.1	7.4	69 45.6	-59.1	7.8	70 45.0	-59.0	8.1	71 44.4	-58.9	8.6	48
67 47.0	-59.2	7.0	68 46.5	-59.1	7.3	69 46.0	-59.1	7.6	70 45.5	-59.1	8.0	49
66 47.8	-59.3	6.5	67 47.4	-59.3	6.8	68 46.9	-59.2	7.1	69 46.4	-59.1	7.5	50
65 48.5	-59.3	6.1	66 48.1	-59.3	6.4	67 47.7	-59.2	6.7	68 47.3	-59.2	7.0	51
64 49.2	-59.4	5.8	65 48.8	-59.3	6.0	66 48.5	-59.3	6.3	67 48.1	-59.2	6.5	52
63 49.8	-59.4	5.5	64 49.5	-59.4	5.7	65 49.2	-59.4	5.9	66 48.9	-59.3	6.1	53
62 50.4	-59.5	5.2	63 50.1	-59.4	5.3	64 49.8	-59.4	5.5	65 49.6	-59.4	5.7	54
61 50.9	-59.5	4.9	62 50.7	-59.5	5.0	63 50.4	-59.4	5.2	64 50.2	-59.4	5.4	55
60 51.4	-59.5	4.6	61 51.2	-59.5	4.7	62 51.0	-59.5	4.9	63 50.8	-59.5	5.1	56
59 51.9	-59.6	4.3	60 51.7	-59.5	4.5	61 51.5	-59.5	4.6	62 51.3	-59.5	4.8	57
58 52.3	-59.5	4.1	59 52.2	-59.6	4.2	60 52.0	-59.5	4.4	61 51.8	-59.5	4.5	58
57 52.8	-59.6	3.9	58 52.6	-59.6	4.0	59 52.5	-59.6	4.1	60 52.3	-59.5	4.2	59
56 53.2	-59.7	3.7	57 53.0	-59.6	3.8	58 52.9	-59.6	3.9	59 52.8	-59.6	4.0	60
55 53.5	-59.6	3.5	56 53.4	-59.6	3.5	57 53.3	-59.6	3.6	58 53.2	-59.6	3.8	61
54 53.9	-59.7	3.3	55 53.8	-59.6	3.3	56 53.7	-59.6	3.4	57 53.6	-59.6	3.5	62
53 54.2	-59.6	3.1	54 54.2	-59.7	3.2	55 54.1	-59.7	3.2	56 54.0	-59.7	3.3	63
52 54.6	-59.7	2.9	53 54.5	-59.7	3.0	54 54.4	-59.7	3.0	55 54.3	-59.6	3.1	64
51 54.9	-59.7	2.7	52 54.8	-59.7	2.8	53 54.7	-59.6	2.9	54 54.7	-59.7	2.9	65
50 55.2	-59.7	2.6	51 55.1	-59.7	2.6	52 55.1	-59.7	2.7	53 55.0	-59.7	2.8	66
49 55.5	-59.8	2.4	50 55.4	-59.7	2.5	51 55.4	-59.8	2.5	52 55.3	-59.7	2.6	67
48 55.7	-59.7	2.3	49 55.7	-59.8	2.3	50 55.6	-59.7	2.4	51 55.6	-59.7	2.4	68
47 56.0	-59.7	2.1	48 56.0	-59.8	2.2	49 55.9	-59.7	2.2	50 55.9	-59.8	2.3	69
46 56.3	-59.8	2.0	47 56.2	-59.7	2.0	48 56.2	-59.8	2.1	49 56.1	-59.7	2.1	70
45 56.5	-59.8	1.9	46 56.5	-59.8	1.9	47 56.4	-59.7	1.9	48 56.4	-59.7	2.0	71
44 56.7	-59.7	1.7	45 56.7	-59.8	1.8	46 56.7	-59.8	1.8	47 56.7	-59.8	1.8	72
43 57.0	-59.8	1.6	44 56.9	-59.7	1.7	45 56.9	-59.8	1.7	46 56.9	-59.8	1.7	73
42 57.2	-59.8	1.5	43 57.2	-59.8	1.5	44 57.1	-59.7	1.6	45 57.1	-59.8	1.6	74
41 57.4	-59.8	1.4	42 57.4	-59.8	1.4	43 57.4	-59.8	1.4	44 57.3	-59.7	1.5	75
40 57.6	-59.8	1.3	41 57.6	-59.8	1.3	42 57.6	-59.8	1.3	43 57.6	-59.8	1.3	76
39 57.8	-59.8	1.2	40 57.8	-59.8	1.2	41 57.8	-59.8	1.2	42 57.8	-59.8	1.2	77
38 58.0	-59.8	1.1	39 58.0	-59.8	1.1	40 58.0	-59.8	1.1	41 58.0	-59.8	1.1	78
37 58.2	-59.8	1.0	38 58.2	-59.8	1.0	39 58.2	-59.8	1.0	40 58.2	-59.8	1.0	79
36 58.4	-59.8	0.9	37 58.4	-59.8	0.9	38 58.4	-59.9	0.9	39 58.4	-59.8	0.9	80
35 58.6	-59.9	0.8	36 58.6	-59.9	0.8	37 58.5	-59.8	0.8	38 58.5	-59.8	0.8	81
34 58.7	-59.8	0.7	35 58.7	-59.8	0.7	36 58.7	-59.8	0.7	37 58.7	-59.8	0.7	82
33 58.9	-59.8	0.6	34 58.9	-59.8	0.6	35 58.9	-59.8	0.6	36 58.9	-59.8	0.6	83
32 59.1	-59.9	0.5	33 59.1	-59.9	0.5	34 59.1	-59.9	0.5	35 59.1	-59.9	0.5	84
31 59.2	-59.8	0.4	32 59.2	-59.8	0.4	33 59.2	-59.8	0.4	34 59.2	-59.8	0.4	85
30 59.4	-59.9	0.3	31 59.4	-59.8	0.3	32 59.4	-59.8	0.3	33 59.4	-59.9	0.3	86
29 59.5	-59.8	0.2	30 59.5	-59.8	0.2	31 59.5	-59.8	0.2	32 59.5	-59.8	0.2	87
28 59.7	-59.8	0.2	29 59.7	-59.8	0.2	30 59.7	-59.8	0.2	31 59.7	-59.8	0.2	88
27 59.9	-59.9	0.1	28 59.9	-59.9	0.1	29 59.9	-59.9	0.1	30 59.9	-59.9	0.1	89
27 00.0	-59.9	0.0	28 00.0	-59.9	0.0	29 00.0	-59.9	0.0	30 00.0	-59.9	0.0	90
27°			28°			29°			30°			

4°, 356° L.H.A. LATITUDE SAME NAME AS DECLINATION

Dec.	23° Hc	23° d	23° Z	24° Hc	24° d	24° Z	25° Hc	25° d	25° Z	26° Hc	26° d	26° Z
°	° ′	′	°	° ′	′	°	° ′	′	°	° ′	′	°
0	66 40.4	−59.2	169.9	65 41.3	−59.3	170.2	64 42.1	−59.3	170.6	63 42.9	−59.4	170.9
1	65 41.2	−59.3	170.2	64 42.0	−59.4	170.6	63 42.8	−59.4	170.9	62 43.5	−59.5	171.2
2	64 41.9	−59.4	170.6	63 42.6	−59.3	170.9	62 43.4	−59.5	171.3	61 44.0	−59.4	171.5
3	63 42.5	−59.4	171.0	62 43.3	−59.5	171.3	61 43.9	−59.5	171.5	60 44.6	−59.6	171.8
4	62 43.1	−59.4	171.3	61 43.8	−59.5	171.6	60 44.4	−59.5	171.8	59 45.0	−59.5	172.1
5	61 43.7	−59.4	171.6	60 44.3	−59.5	171.8	59 44.9	−59.5	172.1	58 45.5	−59.6	172.3
6	60 44.3	−59.5	171.8	59 44.8	−59.5	172.1	58 45.4	−59.6	172.3	57 45.9	−59.6	172.5
7	59 44.8	−59.6	172.1	58 45.3	−59.5	172.3	57 45.8	−59.6	172.5	56 46.3	−59.6	172.7
8	58 45.2	−59.5	172.3	57 45.8	−59.6	172.6	56 46.2	−59.6	172.8	55 46.7	−59.6	172.9
9	57 45.7	−59.6	172.6	56 46.2	−59.6	172.8	55 46.6	−59.6	173.0	54 47.1	−59.7	173.1
10	56 46.1	−59.6	172.8	55 46.6	−59.7	173.0	54 47.0	−59.6	173.2	53 47.4	−59.6	173.3
11	55 46.5	−59.6	173.0	54 46.9	−59.6	173.2	53 47.4	−59.7	173.3	52 47.8	−59.7	173.5
12	54 46.9	−59.6	173.2	53 47.3	−59.7	173.4	52 47.7	−59.7	173.5	51 48.1	−59.7	173.7
13	53 47.3	−59.7	173.4	52 47.6	−59.6	173.5	51 48.0	−59.7	173.7	50 48.4	−59.7	173.8
14	52 47.6	−59.7	173.6	51 48.0	−59.7	173.7	50 48.3	−59.7	173.9	49 48.7	−59.8	174.0
15	51 47.9	−59.6	173.7	50 48.3	−59.7	173.9	49 48.6	−59.7	174.0	48 48.9	−59.7	174.1
16	50 48.3	−59.7	173.9	49 48.6	−59.7	174.0	48 48.9	−59.7	174.2	47 49.2	−59.7	174.3
17	49 48.6	−59.8	174.1	48 48.9	−59.8	174.2	47 49.2	−59.8	174.3	46 49.5	−59.8	174.4
18	48 48.8	−59.7	174.2	47 49.1	−59.7	174.3	46 49.4	−59.7	174.4	45 49.7	−59.7	174.5
19	47 49.1	−59.7	174.4	46 49.4	−59.7	174.5	45 49.7	−59.8	174.6	44 50.0	−59.8	174.7
20	46 49.4	−59.7	174.5	45 49.7	−59.8	174.6	44 49.9	−59.7	174.7	43 50.2	−59.8	174.8
21	45 49.7	−59.8	174.6	44 49.9	−59.7	174.7	43 50.2	−59.8	174.8	42 50.4	−59.8	174.9
22	44 49.9	−59.8	174.8	43 50.2	−59.8	174.9	42 50.4	−59.8	174.9	41 50.6	−59.8	175.0
23	43 50.1	−59.7	174.9	42 50.4	−59.8	175.0	41 50.6	−59.8	175.1	40 50.8	−59.8	175.1
24	42 50.4	−59.8	175.0	41 50.6	−59.8	175.1	40 50.8	−59.8	175.2	39 51.0	−59.8	175.2
25	41 50.6	−59.8	175.1	40 50.8	−59.8	175.2	39 51.0	−59.8	175.3	38 51.2	−59.8	175.3
26	40 50.8	−59.8	175.2	39 51.0	−59.8	175.3	38 51.2	−59.8	175.4	37 51.4	−59.8	175.4
27	39 51.0	−59.7	175.4	38 51.2	−59.8	175.4	37 51.4	−59.8	175.5	36 51.6	−59.8	175.5
28	38 51.3	−59.8	175.5	37 51.4	−59.8	175.5	36 51.6	−59.8	175.6	35 51.8	−59.8	175.6
29	37 51.5	−59.9	175.6	36 51.6	−59.8	175.6	35 51.8	−59.8	175.7	34 52.0	−59.9	175.7
30	36 51.6	−59.8	175.7	35 51.8	−59.8	175.7	34 52.0	−59.8	175.8	33 52.1	−59.8	175.8
31	35 51.8	−59.8	175.8	34 52.0	−59.8	175.8	33 52.2	−59.9	175.9	32 52.3	−59.8	175.9
32	34 52.0	−59.8	175.9	33 52.2	−59.8	175.9	32 52.3	−59.8	176.0	31 52.5	−59.9	176.0
33	33 52.2	−59.8	176.0	32 52.4	−59.9	176.0	31 52.5	−59.8	176.0	30 52.6	−59.8	176.1
34	32 52.4	−59.8	176.1	31 52.5	−59.8	176.1	30 52.7	−59.9	176.1	29 52.8	−59.8	176.2
35	31 52.6	−59.9	176.1	30 52.7	−59.8	176.2	29 52.8	−59.8	176.2	28 53.0	−59.9	176.3
36	30 52.7	−59.8	176.2	29 52.9	−59.9	176.3	28 53.0	−59.9	176.3	27 53.1	−59.8	176.3
37	29 52.9	−59.8	176.3	28 53.0	−59.8	176.4	27 53.1	−59.8	176.4	26 53.3	−59.9	176.4
38	28 53.1	−59.9	176.4	27 53.2	−59.9	176.4	26 53.3	−59.9	176.5	25 53.4	−59.9	176.5
39	27 53.2	−59.8	176.5	26 53.3	−59.8	176.5	25 53.4	−59.8	176.5	24 53.5	−59.8	176.6
40	26 53.4	−59.9	176.6	25 53.5	−59.9	176.6	24 53.6	−59.9	176.6	23 53.7	−59.9	176.6
41	25 53.5	−59.8	176.6	24 53.6	−59.8	176.7	23 53.7	−59.8	176.7	22 53.8	−59.8	176.7
42	24 53.7	−59.9	176.7	23 53.8	−59.9	176.7	22 53.9	−59.9	176.8	21 54.0	−59.9	176.8
43	23 53.8	−59.8	176.8	22 53.9	−59.8	176.8	21 54.0	−59.8	176.8	20 54.1	−59.9	176.9
44	22 54.0	−59.9	176.9	21 54.1	−59.9	176.9	20 54.2	−59.9	176.9	19 54.2	−59.8	176.9
45	21 54.1	−59.8	177.0	20 54.2	−59.9	177.0	19 54.3	−59.9	177.0	18 54.4	−59.9	177.0
46	20 54.3	−59.9	177.0	19 54.3	−59.8	177.0	18 54.4	−59.8	177.1	17 54.5	−59.9	177.1
47	19 54.4	−59.9	177.1	18 54.5	−59.9	177.1	17 54.6	−59.9	177.1	16 54.6	−59.8	177.1
48	18 54.5	−59.8	177.2	17 54.6	−59.8	177.2	16 54.7	−59.9	177.2	15 54.8	−59.9	177.2
49	17 54.7	−59.9	177.2	16 54.8	−59.9	177.3	15 54.8	−59.8	177.3	14 54.9	−59.9	177.3
50	16 54.8	−59.8	177.3	15 54.9	−59.9	177.3	14 55.0	−59.9	177.3	13 55.0	−59.9	177.4
51	15 55.0	−59.9	177.4	14 55.0	−59.9	177.4	13 55.1	−59.9	177.4	12 55.1	−59.8	177.4
52	14 55.1	−59.9	177.5	13 55.1	−59.8	177.5	12 55.2	−59.9	177.5	11 55.3	−59.9	177.5
53	13 55.2	−59.8	177.5	12 55.3	−59.9	177.5	11 55.3	−59.8	177.5	10 55.4	−59.9	177.5
54	12 55.4	−59.9	177.6	11 55.4	−59.9	177.6	10 55.5	−59.9	177.6	9 55.5	−59.9	177.6
55	11 55.5	−59.9	177.7	10 55.5	−59.8	177.7	9 55.6	−59.9	177.7	8 55.6	−59.8	177.7
56	10 55.6	−59.9	177.7	9 55.7	−59.9	177.7	8 55.7	−59.9	177.7	7 55.8	−59.9	177.7
57	9 55.7	−59.8	177.8	8 55.8	−59.9	177.8	7 55.8	−59.9	177.8	6 55.9	−59.9	177.8
58	8 55.9	−59.9	177.9	7 55.9	−59.9	177.9	6 55.9	−59.8	177.9	5 56.0	−59.9	177.9
59	7 56.0	−59.9	177.9	6 56.0	−59.8	177.9	5 56.1	−59.9	177.9	4 56.1	−59.9	177.9
60	6 56.1	−59.9	178.0	5 56.2	−59.9	178.0	4 56.2	−59.9	178.0	3 56.2	−59.9	178.0
61	5 56.2	−59.8	178.1	4 56.3	−59.9	178.1	3 56.3	−59.9	178.1	2 56.3	−59.8	178.1
62	4 56.4	−59.9	178.1	3 56.4	−59.9	178.1	2 56.4	−59.8	178.1	1 56.5	−59.9	178.1
63	3 56.5	−59.9	178.2	2 56.5	−59.9	178.2	1 56.6	−59.9	178.2	0 56.6	−59.9	178.2
64	2 56.6	−59.9	178.2	1 56.6	−59.8	178.2	0 56.7	−59.9	178.2	0 03.3	+59.9	1.8
65	1 56.7	−59.8	178.3	0 56.8	−59.9	178.3	0 03.2	+59.9	1.7	1 03.2	+59.9	1.7
66	0 56.9	−59.9	178.4	0 03.1	+59.9	1.6	1 03.1	+59.9	1.6	2 03.1	+59.8	1.6
67	0 03.0	+59.9	1.6	1 03.0	+59.9	1.6	2 03.0	+59.8	1.6	3 02.9	+59.9	1.6
68	1 02.9	+59.9	1.5	2 02.9	+59.8	1.5	3 02.8	+59.9	1.5	4 02.8	+59.9	1.5
69	2 02.8	+59.8	1.4	3 02.7	+59.9	1.4	4 02.7	+59.9	1.4	5 02.7	+59.9	1.4
70	3 02.6	+59.9	1.4	4 02.6	+59.9	1.4	5 02.6	+59.9	1.4	6 02.6	+59.9	1.4
71	4 02.5	+59.9	1.3	5 02.5	+59.9	1.3	6 02.5	+59.9	1.3	7 02.5	+59.8	1.3
72	5 02.4	+59.9	1.2	6 02.4	+59.9	1.2	7 02.4	+59.8	1.2	8 02.3	+59.9	1.2
73	6 02.3	+59.8	1.2	7 02.3	+59.8	1.2	8 02.2	+59.9	1.2	9 02.2	+59.9	1.2
74	7 02.1	+59.9	1.1	8 02.1	+59.9	1.1	9 02.1	+59.9	1.1	10 02.1	+59.9	1.1
75	8 02.0	+59.9	1.0	9 02.0	+59.9	1.0	10 02.0	+59.9	1.1	11 02.0	+59.9	1.1
76	9 01.9	+59.9	1.0	10 01.9	+59.9	1.0	11 01.9	+59.8	1.0	12 01.9	+59.8	1.0
77	10 01.8	+59.8	0.9	11 01.8	+59.8	0.9	12 01.7	+59.9	0.9	13 01.7	+59.9	0.9
78	11 01.6	+59.9	0.8	12 01.6	+59.9	0.8	13 01.6	+59.9	0.9	14 01.6	+59.9	0.9
79	12 01.5	+59.9	0.8	13 01.5	+59.9	0.8	14 01.5	+59.9	0.8	15 01.5	+59.9	0.8
80	13 01.4	+59.8	0.7	14 01.4	+59.8	0.7	15 01.4	+59.8	0.7	16 01.4	+59.8	0.7
81	14 01.2	+59.9	0.6	15 01.2	+59.9	0.6	16 01.2	+59.9	0.7	17 01.2	+59.9	0.7
82	15 01.1	+59.9	0.6	16 01.1	+59.9	0.6	17 01.1	+59.9	0.6	18 01.1	+59.9	0.6
83	16 01.0	+59.8	0.5	17 01.0	+59.8	0.5	18 01.0	+59.8	0.5	19 01.0	+59.8	0.5
84	17 00.8	+59.9	0.4	18 00.8	+59.9	0.4	19 00.8	+59.9	0.4	20 00.8	+59.9	0.4
85	18 00.7	+59.9	0.4	19 00.7	+59.9	0.4	20 00.7	+59.9	0.4	21 00.7	+59.9	0.4
86	19 00.6	+59.8	0.3	20 00.6	+59.8	0.3	21 00.6	+59.8	0.3	22 00.6	+59.8	0.3
87	20 00.4	+59.9	0.2	21 00.4	+59.9	0.2	22 00.4	+59.9	0.2	23 00.4	+59.9	0.2
88	21 00.3	+59.8	0.1	22 00.3	+59.8	0.2	23 00.3	+59.8	0.2	24 00.3	+59.8	0.2
89	22 00.1	+59.9	0.1	23 00.1	+59.9	0.1	24 00.1	+59.9	0.1	25 00.1	+59.9	0.1
90	23 00.0	+59.9	0.0	24 00.0	+59.9	0.0	25 00.0	+59.9	0.0	26 00.0	+59.9	0.0
	23°			24°			25°			26°		

27° Hc	27° d	27° Z	28° Hc	28° d	28° Z	29° Hc	29° d	29° Z	30° Hc	30° d	30° Z	Dec.
° ′	′	°	° ′	′	°	° ′	′	°	° ′	′	°	°
62 43.6	−59.4	171.2	61 44.3	−59.5	171.5	60 45.0	−59.6	171.8	59 45.5	−59.5	172.0	0
61 44.2	−59.5	171.5	60 44.8	−59.5	171.8	59 45.4	−59.6	172.0	58 46.0	−59.6	172.3	1
60 44.7	−59.5	171.8	59 45.3	−59.6	172.0	58 45.8	−59.6	172.3	57 46.4	−59.7	172.5	2
59 45.2	−59.6	172.1	58 45.7	−59.6	172.3	57 46.2	−59.6	172.5	56 46.7	−59.6	172.7	3
58 45.6	−59.6	172.3	57 46.1	−59.6	172.5	56 46.6	−59.6	172.7	55 47.1	−59.7	172.9	4
57 46.0	−59.6	172.5	56 46.5	−59.6	172.7	55 47.0	−59.7	172.9	54 47.4	−59.6	173.1	5
56 46.4	−59.6	172.7	55 46.9	−59.7	172.9	54 47.3	−59.6	173.1	53 47.8	−59.7	173.3	6
55 46.8	−59.6	172.9	54 47.2	−59.6	173.1	53 47.7	−59.7	173.3	52 48.1	−59.7	173.4	7
54 47.2	−59.7	173.1	53 47.6	−59.7	173.3	52 48.0	−59.7	173.4	51 48.4	−59.8	173.6	8
53 47.5	−59.7	173.3	52 47.9	−59.7	173.5	51 48.3	−59.7	173.6	50 48.6	−59.7	173.7	9
52 47.8	−59.7	173.5	51 48.2	−59.7	173.6	50 48.6	−59.8	173.8	49 48.9	−59.7	173.9	10
51 48.1	−59.7	173.6	50 48.5	−59.7	173.8	49 48.8	−59.7	173.9	48 49.2	−59.8	174.0	11
50 48.4	−59.7	173.8	49 48.8	−59.8	173.9	48 49.1	−59.7	174.1	47 49.4	−59.7	174.2	12
49 48.7	−59.7	174.0	48 49.0	−59.7	174.1	47 49.4	−59.8	174.2	46 49.7	−59.8	174.3	13
48 49.0	−59.8	174.1	47 49.3	−59.8	174.2	46 49.6	−59.8	174.3	45 49.9	−59.8	174.4	14
47 49.2	−59.7	174.2	46 49.5	−59.7	174.3	45 49.8	−59.7	174.5	44 50.1	−59.8	174.5	15
46 49.5	−59.8	174.4	45 49.8	−59.8	174.5	44 50.1	−59.8	174.6	43 50.3	−59.8	174.7	16
45 49.7	−59.7	174.5	44 50.0	−59.8	174.6	43 50.3	−59.8	174.7	42 50.5	−59.8	174.8	17
44 50.0	−59.8	174.6	43 50.2	−59.7	174.7	42 50.5	−59.8	174.8	41 50.7	−59.8	174.9	18
43 50.2	−59.8	174.8	42 50.5	−59.8	174.8	41 50.7	−59.8	174.9	40 50.9	−59.8	175.0	19
42 50.4	−59.8	174.9	41 50.7	−59.8	175.0	40 50.9	−59.8	175.0	39 51.1	−59.8	175.1	20
41 50.6	−59.8	175.0	40 50.9	−59.8	175.1	39 51.1	−59.8	175.1	38 51.3	−59.8	175.2	21
40 50.8	−59.8	175.1	39 51.1	−59.8	175.2	38 51.3	−59.8	175.2	37 51.5	−59.9	175.3	22
39 51.0	−59.8	175.2	38 51.3	−59.9	175.3	37 51.5	−59.9	175.3	36 51.6	−59.8	175.4	23
38 51.2	−59.8	175.3	37 51.4	−59.8	175.4	36 51.6	−59.8	175.4	35 51.8	−59.8	175.5	24
37 51.4	−59.8	175.4	36 51.6	−59.8	175.5	35 51.8	−59.8	175.5	34 52.0	−59.9	175.6	25
36 51.6	−59.8	175.5	35 51.8	−59.8	175.6	34 52.0	−59.9	175.6	33 52.1	−59.8	175.7	26
35 51.8	−59.8	175.6	34 52.0	−59.9	175.7	33 52.1	−59.8	175.7	32 52.3	−59.8	175.8	27
34 52.0	−59.9	175.7	33 52.1	−59.8	175.7	32 52.3	−59.8	175.8	31 52.5	−59.9	175.8	28
33 52.1	−59.8	175.8	32 52.3	−59.8	175.8	31 52.5	−59.9	175.9	30 52.6	−59.8	175.9	29
32 52.3	−59.8	175.9	31 52.5	−59.9	175.9	30 52.6	−59.8	176.0	29 52.8	−59.9	176.0	30
31 52.5	−59.9	176.0	30 52.6	−59.8	176.0	29 52.8	−59.9	176.0	28 52.9	−59.9	176.1	31
30 52.6	−59.8	176.0	29 52.8	−59.9	176.1	28 52.9	−59.9	176.1	27 53.0	−59.8	176.2	32
29 52.8	−59.9	176.1	28 52.9	−59.8	176.2	27 53.0	−59.8	176.2	26 53.2	−59.9	176.2	33
28 52.9	−59.8	176.2	27 53.1	−59.9	176.2	26 53.2	−59.9	176.3	25 53.3	−59.9	176.3	34
27 53.1	−59.9	176.3	26 53.2	−59.9	176.3	25 53.3	−59.8	176.4	24 53.4	−59.8	176.4	35
26 53.2	−59.8	176.4	25 53.3	−59.8	176.4	24 53.5	−59.9	176.4	23 53.6	−59.9	176.5	36
25 53.4	−59.9	176.4	24 53.5	−59.9	176.5	23 53.6	−59.9	176.5	22 53.7	−59.9	176.5	37
24 53.5	−59.8	176.5	23 53.6	−59.8	176.6	22 53.7	−59.8	176.6	21 53.8	−59.8	176.6	38
23 53.7	−59.9	176.6	22 53.8	−59.9	176.6	21 53.9	−59.9	176.7	20 54.0	−59.9	176.7	39
22 53.8	−59.9	176.7	21 53.9	−59.9	176.7	20 54.0	−59.9	176.7	19 54.1	−59.9	176.7	40
21 53.9	−59.8	176.7	20 54.0	−59.8	176.8	19 54.1	−59.9	176.8	18 54.2	−59.9	176.8	41
20 54.1	−59.9	176.8	19 54.2	−59.9	176.8	18 54.2	−59.8	176.9	17 54.3	−59.8	176.9	42
19 54.2	−59.9	176.9	18 54.3	−59.9	176.9	17 54.4	−59.9	176.9	16 54.5	−59.9	176.9	43
18 54.3	−59.8	177.0	17 54.4	−59.9	177.0	16 54.5	−59.9	177.0	15 54.6	−59.9	177.0	44
17 54.5	−59.9	177.0	16 54.5	−59.8	177.0	15 54.6	−59.9	177.1	14 54.7	−59.9	177.1	45
16 54.6	−59.9	177.1	15 54.7	−59.9	177.1	14 54.7	−59.8	177.1	13 54.8	−59.9	177.1	46
15 54.7	−59.9	177.2	14 54.8	−59.9	177.2	13 54.9	−59.9	177.2	12 54.9	−59.9	177.2	47
14 54.8	−59.8	177.2	13 54.9	−59.9	177.2	12 55.0	−59.9	177.3	11 55.0	−59.8	177.3	48
13 55.0	−59.9	177.3	12 55.0	−59.9	177.3	11 55.1	−59.9	177.3	10 55.2	−59.9	177.3	49
12 55.1	−59.9	177.4	11 55.1	−59.8	177.4	10 55.2	−59.9	177.4	9 55.3	−59.9	177.4	50
11 55.2	−59.9	177.4	10 55.3	−59.9	177.4	9 55.3	−59.9	177.4	8 55.4	−59.9	177.5	51
10 55.3	−59.9	177.5	9 55.4	−59.9	177.5	8 55.4	−59.9	177.5	7 55.5	−59.9	177.5	52
9 55.4	−59.8	177.6	8 55.5	−59.9	177.6	7 55.5	−59.8	177.6	6 55.6	−59.9	177.6	53
8 55.6	−59.9	177.6	7 55.6	−59.9	177.6	6 55.7	−59.9	177.6	5 55.7	−59.9	177.6	54
7 55.7	−59.9	177.7	6 55.7	−59.9	177.7	5 55.8	−59.9	177.7	4 55.8	−59.9	177.7	55
6 55.8	−59.9	177.7	5 55.8	−59.8	177.8	4 55.9	−59.9	177.8	3 55.9	−59.9	177.8	56
5 55.9	−59.9	177.8	4 56.0	−59.9	177.8	3 56.0	−59.9	177.8	2 56.0	−59.8	177.8	57
4 56.0	−59.9	177.9	3 56.1	−59.9	177.9	2 56.1	−59.9	177.9	1 56.2	−59.9	177.9	58
3 56.1	−59.8	177.9	2 56.2	−59.9	177.9	1 56.2	−59.9	177.9	0 56.3	−59.9	177.9	59
2 56.3	−59.9	178.0	1 56.3	−59.9	178.0	0 56.3	−59.9	178.0	0 03.6	+59.9	2.0	60
1 56.4	−59.9	178.1	0 56.4	−59.9	178.1	0 03.6	+59.8	1.9	1 03.5	+59.9	1.9	61
0 56.5	−59.9	178.1	0 03.5	+59.9	1.9	1 03.4	+59.9	1.9	2 03.4	+59.9	1.9	62
0 03.4	+59.9	1.8	1 03.4	+59.8	1.8	2 03.3	+59.9	1.8	3 03.3	+59.9	1.8	63
1 03.3	+59.9	1.8	2 03.2	+59.9	1.8	3 03.2	+59.9	1.8	4 03.2	+59.9	1.8	64
2 03.2	+59.8	1.7	3 03.1	+59.9	1.7	4 03.1	+59.9	1.7	5 03.1	+59.9	1.7	65
3 03.0	+59.9	1.6	4 03.0	+59.9	1.6	5 03.0	+59.9	1.6	6 03.0	+59.9	1.6	66
4 02.9	+59.9	1.6	5 02.9	+59.9	1.6	6 02.9	+59.9	1.6	7 02.9	+59.8	1.6	67
5 02.8	+59.9	1.5	6 02.8	+59.9	1.5	7 02.8	+59.9	1.5	8 02.7	+59.9	1.5	68
6 02.7	+59.9	1.4	7 02.7	+59.9	1.4	8 02.7	+59.8	1.4	9 02.6	+59.9	1.5	69
7 02.6	+59.9	1.4	8 02.6	+59.8	1.4	9 02.5	+59.9	1.4	10 02.5	+59.9	1.4	70
8 02.5	+59.8	1.3	9 02.4	+59.9	1.3	10 02.4	+59.9	1.3	11 02.4	+59.9	1.3	71
9 02.3	+59.9	1.3	10 02.3	+59.9	1.3	11 02.3	+59.9	1.3	12 02.3	+59.9	1.3	72
10 02.2	+59.9	1.2	11 02.2	+59.9	1.2	12 02.2	+59.9	1.2	13 02.2	+59.9	1.2	73
11 02.1	+59.9	1.1	12 02.1	+59.9	1.1	13 02.1	+59.9	1.1	14 02.1	+59.8	1.1	74
12 02.0	+59.9	1.1	13 02.0	+59.8	1.1	14 02.0	+59.8	1.1	15 01.9	+59.9	1.1	75
13 01.9	+59.8	1.0	14 01.8	+59.9	1.0	15 01.8	+59.9	1.0	16 01.8	+59.9	1.0	76
14 01.7	+59.9	0.9	15 01.7	+59.9	0.9	16 01.7	+59.9	0.9	17 01.7	+59.9	0.9	77
15 01.6	+59.9	0.9	16 01.6	+59.9	0.9	17 01.6	+59.9	0.9	18 01.6	+59.9	0.9	78
16 01.5	+59.9	0.8	17 01.5	+59.8	0.8	18 01.5	+59.8	0.8	19 01.5	+59.8	0.8	79
17 01.4	+59.8	0.7	18 01.3	+59.9	0.7	19 01.3	+59.9	0.7	20 01.3	+59.9	0.7	80
18 01.2	+59.9	0.7	19 01.2	+59.9	0.7	20 01.2	+59.9	0.7	21 01.2	+59.9	0.7	81
19 01.1	+59.9	0.6	20 01.1	+59.9	0.6	21 01.1	+59.9	0.6	22 01.1	+59.9	0.6	82
20 01.0	+59.8	0.5	21 01.0	+59.8	0.5	22 01.0	+59.8	0.5	23 01.0	+59.8	0.5	83
21 00.8	+59.9	0.4	22 00.8	+59.9	0.5	23 00.8	+59.9	0.5	24 00.8	+59.9	0.5	84
22 00.7	+59.9	0.4	23 00.7	+59.9	0.4	24 00.7	+59.9	0.4	25 00.7	+59.9	0.4	85
23 00.6	+59.8	0.3	24 00.6	+59.8	0.3	25 00.6	+59.8	0.3	26 00.6	+59.8	0.3	86
24 00.4	+59.9	0.2	25 00.4	+59.9	0.2	26 00.4	+59.9	0.2	27 00.4	+59.9	0.2	87
25 00.3	+59.8	0.2	26 00.3	+59.8	0.2	27 00.3	+59.8	0.2	28 00.3	+59.8	0.2	88
26 00.1	+59.9	0.1	27 00.1	+59.9	0.1	28 00.1	+59.9	0.1	29 00.1	+59.9	0.1	89
27 00.0	+59.9	0.0	28 00.0	+59.9	0.0	29 00.0	+59.9	0.0	30 00.0	+59.9	0.0	90
27°			28°			29°			30°			

S. Lat. {L.H.A. greater than 180° ....Zn=180°−Z; L.H.A. less than 180°...........Zn=180°+Z}

5°, 355° L.H.A. LATITUDE **SAME** NAME AS DECLINATION N. Lat. {L.H.A. greater than 180° .....Zn=Z; L.H.A. less than 180°............Zn=360°−Z

Dec.	23°			24°			25°			26°			27°			28°			29°			30°			Dec.
°	Hc ° ′	d ′	Z °	Hc ° ′	d ′	Z °	Hc ° ′	d ′	Z °	Hc ° ′	d ′	Z °	Hc ° ′	d ′	Z °	Hc ° ′	d ′	Z °	Hc ° ′	d ′	Z °	Hc ° ′	d ′	Z °	°
0	66 29.5	+58.7	167.4	65 30.9	+58.8	167.9	64 32.2	+58.9	168.3	63 33.4	+59.0	168.7	62 34.5	+59.1	169.1	61 35.6	+59.1	169.4	60 36.5	+59.3	169.8	59 37.5	+59.3	170.1	0
1	67 28.2	+58.6	166.9	66 29.7	+58.8	167.4	65 31.1	+58.9	167.9	64 32.4	+59.0	168.3	63 33.6	+59.1	168.7	62 34.7	+59.2	169.1	61 35.8	+59.2	169.4	60 36.8	+59.2	169.8	1
2	68 26.8	+58.5	166.3	67 28.5	+58.6	166.9	66 30.0	+58.7	167.4	65 31.4	+58.9	167.9	64 32.7	+58.9	168.3	63 33.9	+59.0	168.7	62 35.0	+59.1	169.1	61 36.0	+59.3	169.4	2
3	69 25.3	+58.4	165.7	68 27.1	+58.5	166.3	67 28.7	+58.7	166.9	66 30.3	+58.7	167.4	65 31.6	+58.9	167.9	64 32.9	+59.0	168.3	63 34.1	+59.1	168.7	62 35.3	+59.1	169.1	3
4	70 23.7	+58.1	165.0	69 25.6	+58.4	165.7	68 27.4	+58.5	166.3	67 29.0	+58.7	166.9	66 30.5	+58.8	167.4	65 31.9	+58.9	167.9	64 33.2	+59.0	168.3	63 34.4	+59.1	168.7	4
5	71 21.8	+58.0	164.2	70 24.0	+58.2	165.0	69 25.9	+58.4	165.7	68 27.7	+58.6	166.3	67 29.3	+58.7	166.9	66 30.8	+58.9	167.4	65 32.2	+59.0	167.9	64 33.5	+59.0	168.3	5
6	72 19.8	+57.8	163.4	71 22.2	+58.0	164.3	70 24.3	+58.2	165.0	69 26.3	+58.4	165.7	68 28.0	+58.6	166.3	67 29.7	+58.7	166.9	66 31.2	+58.8	167.4	65 32.5	+59.0	167.9	6
7	73 17.6	+57.4	162.5	72 20.2	+57.8	163.4	71 22.5	+58.1	164.3	70 24.7	+58.2	165.0	69 26.6	+58.5	165.7	68 28.4	+58.6	166.4	67 30.0	+58.8	166.9	66 31.5	+58.9	167.5	7
8	74 15.0	+57.2	161.5	73 18.0	+57.5	162.5	72 20.6	+57.8	163.5	71 22.9	+58.1	164.3	70 25.1	+58.2	165.1	69 27.0	+58.5	165.8	68 28.8	+58.6	166.4	67 30.4	+58.7	167.0	8
9	75 12.2	+56.7	160.3	74 15.5	+57.2	161.5	73 18.4	+57.5	162.6	72 21.0	+57.8	163.5	71 23.3	+58.1	164.4	70 25.5	+58.3	165.1	69 27.4	+58.5	165.8	68 29.1	+58.7	166.4	9
10	76 08.9	+56.3	159.0	75 12.7	+56.8	160.4	74 15.9	+57.3	161.5	73 18.8	+57.6	162.6	72 21.4	+57.9	163.5	71 23.8	+58.1	164.4	70 25.9	+58.3	165.2	69 27.8	+58.5	165.8	10
11	77 05.2	+55.7	157.5	76 09.5	+56.3	159.0	75 13.2	+56.8	160.4	74 16.4	+57.3	161.6	73 19.3	+57.7	162.7	72 21.9	+57.9	163.6	71 24.2	+58.2	164.4	70 26.3	+58.4	165.2	11
12	78 00.9	+54.9	155.8	77 05.8	+55.7	157.6	76 10.0	+56.4	159.1	75 13.7	+56.9	160.5	74 17.0	+57.3	161.7	73 19.8	+57.7	162.7	72 22.4	+58.0	163.6	71 24.7	+58.2	164.5	12
13	78 55.8	+54.0	153.7	78 01.5	+55.0	155.8	77 06.4	+55.8	157.6	76 10.6	+56.4	159.2	75 14.3	+56.9	160.5	74 17.5	+57.4	161.7	73 20.4	+57.7	162.8	72 22.9	+58.0	163.7	13
14	79 49.8	+52.8	151.4	78 56.5	+54.1	153.8	78 02.2	+55.1	155.9	77 07.0	+55.9	157.7	76 11.2	+56.5	159.3	75 14.9	+57.0	160.6	74 18.1	+57.4	161.8	73 20.9	+57.7	162.8	14
15	80 42.6	+51.2	148.6	79 50.6	+52.9	151.5	78 57.3	+54.2	153.9	78 02.9	+55.2	156.0	77 07.7	+56.0	157.8	76 11.9	+56.5	159.3	75 15.5	+57.0	160.7	74 18.6	+57.5	161.9	15
16	81 33.8	+49.1•	145.2	80 43.5	+51.3	148.7	79 51.5	+52.9	151.6	78 58.1	+54.2	154.0	78 03.7	+55.2	156.1	77 08.4	+56.0	157.9	76 12.5	+56.6	159.4	75 16.1	+57.1	160.8	16
17	82 22.9	+46.1•	141.0	81 34.8	+49.2•	145.3	80 44.4	+51.5	148.8	79 52.3	+53.1	151.7	78 58.9	+54.3	154.1	78 04.4	+55.3	156.2	77 09.1	+56.1	158.0	76 13.2	+56.7	159.5	17
18	83 09.0	+42.2•	136.0	82 24.0	+46.3•	141.2	81 35.9	+49.3•	145.4	80 45.4	+51.5	148.9	79 53.2	+53.2	151.8	78 59.7	+54.5	154.3	78 05.2	+55.4	156.3	77 09.9	+56.1	158.1	18
19	83 51.2	+36.7•	129.7	83 10.3	+42.4•	136.1	82 25.2	+46.5•	141.3	81 36.9	+49.5•	145.6	80 46.4	+51.7	149.1	79 54.2	+53.3	152.0	79 00.6	+54.5	154.4	78 06.0	+55.5	156.4	19
20	84 27.9	+29.2•	121.9	83 52.7	+36.9•	129.8	83 11.7	+42.5•	136.3	82 26.4	+46.7•	141.5	81 38.1	+49.6•	145.7	80 47.5	+51.7	149.2	79 55.1	+53.4	152.1	79 01.5	+54.6	154.5	20
21	84 57.1	+19.3•	112.4	84 29.6	+29.3•	122.0	83 54.2	+37.1•	130.0	83 13.1	+42.7•	136.5	82 27.7	+46.8•	141.7	81 39.2	+49.8•	145.9	80 48.5	+51.9	149.4	79 56.1	+53.5	152.3	21
22	85 16.4	+7.5•	101.2	84 58.9	+19.5•	112.5	84 31.3	+29.5•	122.2	83 55.8	+37.3•	130.2	83 14.5	+42.9•	136.6	82 29.0	+47.0•	141.8	81 40.4	+50.0•	146.1	80 49.6	+52.1	149.5	22
23	85 23.9	−5.5•	89.0	85 18.4	+7.6•	101.3	85 00.8	+19.7•	112.6	84 33.1	+29.7•	122.3	83 57.4	+37.5•	130.4	83 16.0	+43.1•	136.8	82 30.4	+47.1•	142.0	81 41.7	+50.1•	146.3	23
24	85 18.4	−17.6•	76.7	85 26.0	−5.5•	89.0	85 20.5	+7.6•	101.4	85 02.8	+19.9•	112.7	84 34.9	+30.0•	122.5	83 59.1	+37.7•	130.6	83 17.5	+43.3•	137.0	82 31.8	+47.3•	142.2	24
25	85 00.8	−27.7•	65.4	85 20.5	−17.7•	76.6	85 28.1	−5.4•	88.9	85 22.7	+7.7•	101.4	85 04.9	+20.0•	112.9	84 36.8	+30.2•	122.7	84 00.8	+38.0•	130.8	83 19.1	+43.5•	137.2	25
26	84 33.1	−35.7•	55.6	85 02.8	−27.9•	65.1	85 22.7	−17.8•	76.4	85 30.4	−5.5•	88.9	85 24.9	+7.8•	101.5	85 07.0	+20.2•	113.0	84 38.8	+30.4•	122.9	84 02.6	+38.2•	131.0	26
27	83 57.4	−41.4•	47.5	84 34.9	−35.8•	55.3	85 04.9	−28.1•	64.9	85 24.9	−17.9•	76.3	85 32.7	−5.5•	88.9	85 27.2	+7.9•	101.5	85 09.2	+20.4•	113.2	84 40.8	+30.7•	123.1	27
28	83 16.0	−45.6•	41.0	83 59.1	−41.6•	47.3	84 36.8	−36.0•	55.1	85 07.0	−28.2•	64.7	85 27.2	−18.0•	76.1	85 35.1	−5.5•	88.8	85 29.6	+8.0•	101.6	85 11.5	+20.6•	113.3	28
29	82 30.4	−48.7•	35.8	83 17.5	−45.7•	40.7	84 00.8	−41.7•	47.0	84 38.8	−36.2•	54.8	85 09.2	−28.4•	64.5	85 29.6	−18.1•	76.0	85 37.6	−5.5•	88.8	85 32.1	+8.1•	101.7	29
30	81 41.7	−50.9	31.5	82 31.8	−48.8•	35.5	83 19.1	−45.9•	40.4	84 02.6	−41.9•	46.7	84 40.8	−36.3•	54.5	85 11.5	−28.6•	64.2	85 32.1	−18.2•	75.8	85 40.2	−5.5•	88.7	30
31	80 50.8	−52.6	28.0	81 43.0	−51.0	31.2	82 33.2	−48.9•	35.2	83 20.7	−46.0•	40.1	84 04.5	−42.1•	46.4	84 42.9	−36.5•	54.2	85 13.9	−28.8•	64.0	85 34.7	−18.4•	75.7	31
32	79 58.2	−53.8	25.1	80 52.0	−52.7	27.7	81 44.3	−51.1	31.0	82 34.7	−49.1•	34.9	83 22.4	−46.2•	39.8	84 06.4	−42.3•	46.0	84 45.1	−36.8•	53.9	85 16.3	−29.0•	63.7	32
33	79 04.4	−54.8	22.7	79 59.3	−53.9	24.9	80 53.2	−52.8	27.5	81 45.6	−51.2	30.7	82 36.2	−49.2•	34.6	83 24.1	−46.4•	39.5	84 08.3	−42.4•	45.7	84 47.3	−37.0•	53.6	33
34	78 09.6	−55.6	20.6	79 05.4	−54.9	22.4	80 00.4	−54.0	24.6	80 54.4	−52.8	27.2	81 47.0	−51.3	30.4	82 37.7	−49.3•	34.3	83 25.9	−46.6•	39.2	84 10.3	−42.6•	45.4	34
35	77 14.0	−56.2	18.8	78 10.5	−55.6	20.4	79 06.4	−54.9	22.2	80 01.6	−54.1	24.3	80 55.7	−53.0	26.9	81 48.4	−51.4	30.1	82 39.3	−49.4•	34.0	83 27.7	−46.7•	38.8	35
36	76 17.8	−56.7	17.3	77 14.9	−56.3	18.6	78 11.5	−55.7	20.2	79 07.5	−55.0	21.9	80 02.7	−54.1	24.1	80 57.0	−53.1	26.6	81 49.9	−51.6	29.8	82 41.0	−49.7•	33.6	36
37	75 21.1	−57.1	16.0	76 18.6	−56.7	17.1	77 15.8	−56.3	18.4	78 12.5	−55.8	19.9	79 08.6	−55.1	21.7	80 03.9	−54.2	23.8	80 58.3	−53.2	26.3	81 51.3	−51.7	29.4	37
38	74 24.0	−57.4	14.8	75 21.9	−57.1	15.8	76 19.5	−56.8	16.9	77 16.7	−56.3	18.2	78 13.5	−55.8	19.7	79 09.7	−55.2	21.4	80 05.1	−54.3	23.5	80 59.6	−53.2	26.0	38
39	73 26.6	−57.7	13.8	74 24.8	−57.5	14.6	75 22.7	−57.1	15.6	76 20.4	−56.9	16.7	77 17.7	−56.4	17.9	78 14.5	−55.9	19.4	79 10.8	−55.3	21.1	80 06.4	−54.5	23.2	39
40	72 28.9	−57.9	12.8	73 27.3	−57.7	13.6	74 25.6	−57.5	14.4	75 23.5	−57.2	15.4	76 21.3	−56.9	16.4	77 18.6	−56.4	17.7	78 15.5	−55.9	19.2	79 11.9	−55.3	20.9	40
41	71 31.0	−58.2	12.0	72 29.6	−58.0	12.6	73 28.1	−57.8	13.4	74 26.3	−57.5	14.2	75 24.4	−57.3	15.1	76 22.2	−57.0	16.2	77 19.6	−56.5	17.4	78 16.6	−56.0	18.9	41
42	70 32.8	−58.3	11.2	71 31.6	−58.1	11.8	72 30.3	−58.0	12.4	73 28.8	−57.8	13.2	74 27.1	−57.6	14.0	75 25.2	−57.3	14.9	76 23.1	−57.0	16.0	77 20.6	−56.6	17.2	42
43	69 34.5	−58.5	10.5	70 33.5	−58.4	11.0	71 32.3	−58.2	11.6	72 31.0	−58.0	12.2	73 29.5	−57.8	13.0	74 27.9	−57.6	13.8	75 26.1	−57.4	14.7	76 24.0	−57.0	15.7	43
44	68 36.0	−58.5	9.9	69 35.1	−58.5	10.4	70 34.1	−58.4	10.9	71 33.0	−58.3	11.4	72 31.7	−58.1	12.1	73 30.3	−57.9	12.8	74 28.7	−57.6	13.5	75 27.0	−57.4	14.5	44
45	67 37.5	−58.8	9.3	68 36.6	−58.6	9.7	69 35.7	−58.5	10.2	70 34.7	−58.4	10.7	71 33.6	−58.2	11.2	72 32.4	−58.1	11.9	73 31.1	−57.9	12.5	74 29.6	−57.7	13.3	45
46	66 38.7	−58.8	8.8	67 38.0	−58.7	9.2	68 37.2	−58.6	9.6	69 36.3	−58.5	10.0	70 35.4	−58.4	10.5	71 34.3	−58.3	11.0	72 33.2	−58.2	11.6	73 31.9	−58.0	12.3	46
47	65 39.9	−58.9	8.3	66 39.3	−58.8	8.6	67 38.6	−58.8	9.0	68 37.8	−58.6	9.4	69 37.0	−58.6	9.8	70 36.0	−58.4	10.3	71 35.0	−58.3	10.8	72 33.9	−58.2	11.4	47
48	64 41.0	−58.9	7.8	65 40.5	−58.9	8.1	66 39.8	−58.8	8.5	67 39.2	−58.8	8.8	68 38.4	−58.7	9.2	69 37.6	−58.6	9.6	70 36.7	−58.5	10.1	71 35.7	−58.3	10.6	48
49	63 42.1	−59.1	7.4	64 41.6	−59.0	7.7	65 41.0	−58.9	8.0	66 40.4	−58.9	8.3	67 39.7	−58.8	8.7	68 39.0	−58.7	9.0	69 38.2	−58.6	9.5	70 37.4	−58.5	9.9	49
50	62 43.0	−59.1	7.0	63 42.6	−59.1	7.3	64 42.1	−59.0	7.5	65 41.5	−58.9	7.8	66 40.9	−58.8	8.1	67 40.3	−58.8	8.5	68 39.6	−58.7	8.9	69 38.9	−58.6	9.3	50
51	61 43.9	−59.1	6.7	62 43.5	−59.1	6.9	63 43.1	−59.1	7.1	64 42.6	−59.0	7.4	65 42.1	−59.0	7.7	66 41.5	−58.9	8.0	67 40.9	−58.8	8.3	68 40.3	−58.8	8.7	51
52	60 44.8	−59.2	6.3	61 44.4	−59.2	6.5	62 44.0	−59.1	6.7	63 43.6	−59.1	7.0	64 43.1	−59.0	7.2	65 42.6	−59.0	7.5	66 42.1	−58.9	7.8	67 41.5	−58.8	8.1	52
53	59 45.6	−59.3	6.0	60 45.2	−59.2	6.2	61 44.9	−59.2	6.4	62 44.5	−59.2	6.6	63 44.1	−59.1	6.8	64 43.6	−59.0	7.1	65 43.2	−59.0	7.3	66 42.7	−59.0	7.6	53
54	58 46.3	−59.3	5.7	59 46.0	−59.3	5.8	60 45.7	−59.3	6.0	61 45.3	−59.2	6.2	62 45.0	−59.2	6.4	63 44.6	−59.1	6.6	64 44.2	−59.1	6.9	65 43.7	−59.0	7.2	54
55	57 47.0	−59.3	5.4	58 46.7	−59.3	5.5	59 46.4	−59.2	5.7	60 46.1	−59.2	5.9	61 45.8	−59.2	6.1	62 45.5	−59.2	6.3	63 45.1	−59.1	6.5	64 44.7	−59.1	6.7	55
56	56 47.7	−59.4	5.1	57 47.4	−59.3	5.2	58 47.2	−59.4	5.4	59 46.9	−59.3	5.6	60 46.6	−59.3	5.7	61 46.3	−59.2	5.9	62 46.0	−59.2	6.1	63 45.6	−59.1	6.3	56
57	55 48.3	−59.4	4.8	56 48.1	−59.4	5.0	57 47.8	−59.3	5.1	58 47.6	−59.3	5.3	59 47.3	−59.3	5.4	60 47.1	−59.3	5.6	61 46.8	−59.3	5.8	62 46.5	−59.2	6.0	57
58	54 48.9	−59.4	4.6	55 48.7	−59.4	4.7	56 48.5	−59.4	4.8	57 48.3	−59.4	5.0	58 48.0	−59.3	5.1	59 47.8	−59.3	5.3	60 47.5	−59.3	5.4	61 47.3	−59.3	5.6	58
59	53 49.5	−59.5	4.4	54 49.3	−59.4	4.5	55 49.1	−59.4	4.6	56 48.9	−59.4	4.7	57 48.7	−59.4	4.8	58 48.5	−59.4	5.0	59 48.2	−59.3	5.1	60 48.0	−59.3	5.3	59
60	52 50.0	−59.5	4.1	53 49.9	−59.5	4.2	54 49.7	−59.5	4.3	55 49.5	−59.4	4.4	56 49.3	−59.4	4.6	57 49.1	−59.4	4.7	58 48.9	−59.3	4.8	59 48.7	−59.3	5.0	60
61	51 50.5	−59.5	3.9	52 50.4	−59.5	4.0	53 50.2	−59.4	4.1	54 50.1	−59.5	4.2	55 49.9	−59.4	4.3	56 49.7	−59.4	4.4	57 49.6	−59.4	4.6	58 49.4	−59.4	4.7	61
62	50 51.0	−59.5	3.7	51 50.9	−59.5	3.8	52 50.8	−59.5	3.9	53 50.6	−59.5	4.0	54 50.5	−59.5	4.1	55 50.3	−59.4	4.2	56 50.2	−59.5	4.3	57 50.0	−59.4	4.4	62
63	49 51.5	−59.5	3.5	50 51.4	−59.5	3.6	51 51.3	−59.5	3.7	52 51.1	−59.5	3.8	53 51.0	−59.5	3.8	54 50.9	−59.5	3.9	55 50.7	−59.4	4.0	56 50.6	−59.5	4.1	63
64	48 52.0	−59.6	3.3	49 51.9	−59.6	3.4	50 51.8	−59.6	3.5	51 51.6	−59.5	3.5	52 51.5	−59.5	3.6	53 51.4	−59.5	3.7	54 51.3	−59.5	3.8	55 51.1	−59.4	3.9	64
65	47 52.4	−59.6	3.1	48 52.3	−59.6	3.2	49 52.2	−59.5	3.3	50 52.1	−59.5	3.3	51 52.0	−59.5	3.4	52 51.9	−59.5	3.5	53 51.8	−59.5	3.6	54 51.7	−59.5	3.7	65
66	46 52.8	−59.6	3.0	47 52.7	−59.5	3.0	48 52.7	−59.6	3.1	49 52.6	−59.6	3.2	50 52.5	−59.6	3.2	51 52.4	−59.6	3.3	52 52.3	−59.6	3.4	53 52.2	−59.5	3.4	66
67	45 53.2	−59.6	2.8	46 53.2	−59.6	2.9	47 53.1	−59.6	2.9	48 53.0	−59.6	3.0	49 52.9	−59.5	3.0	50 52.8	−59.5	3.1	51 52.7	−59.5	3.2	52 52.7	−59.6	3.2	67
68	44 53.6	−59.6	2.6	45 53.6	−59.7	2.7	46 53.5	−59.6	2.7	47 53.4	−59.6	2.8	48 53.4	−59.6	2.8	49 53.3	−59.6	2.9	50 53.2	−59.6	3.0	51 53.1	−59.5	3.0	68
69	43 54.0	−59.6	2.5	44 53.9	−59.6	2.5	45 53.9	−59.6	2.6	46 53.8	−59.6	2.6	47 53.8	−59.6	2.7	48 53.7	−59.6	2.7	49 53.6	−59.6	2.8	50 53.6	−59.6	2.8	69
70	42 54.4	−59.7	2.3	43 54.3	−59.6	2.4	44 54.3	−59.7	2.4	45 54.2	−59.6	2.5	46 54.2	−59.7	2.5	47 54.1	−59.6	2.5	48 54.0	−59.6	2.6	49 54.0	−59.6	2.7	70
71	41 54.7	−59.6	2.2	42 54.7	−59.7	2.2	43 54.6	−59.6	2.3	44 54.6	−59.6	2.3	45 54.5	−59.6	2.3	46 54.5	−59.6	2.4	47 54.4	−59.6	2.4	48 54.4	−59.6	2.5	71
72	40 55.1	−59.7	2.0	41 55.0	−59.6	2.1	42 55.0	−59.7	2.1	43 55.0	−59.7	2.1	44 54.9	−59.6	2.2	45 54.9	−59.7	2.2	46 54.8	−59.6	2.3	47 54.8	−59.7	2.3	72
73	39 55.4	−59.7	1.9	40 55.4	−59.7	1.9	41 55.3	−59.6	2.0	42 55.3	−59.7	2.0	43 55.3	−59.7	2.0	44 55.2	−59.6	2.1	45 55.2	−59.7	2.1	46 55.1	−59.6	2.1	73
74	38 55.7	−59.7	1.8	39 55.7	−59.7	1.8	40 55.7	−59.7	1.8	41 55.6	−59.6	1.9	42 55.6	−59.7	1.9	43 55.6	−59.7	1.9	44 55.5	−59.6	1.9	45 55.5	−59.6	2.0	74
75	37 56.0	−59.6	1.6	38 56.0	−59.7	1.7	39 56.0	−59.7	1.7	40 56.0	−59.7	1.7	41 55.9	−59.6	1.7	42 55.9	−59.7	1.8	43 55.9	−59.7	1.8	44 55.9	−59.7	1.8	75
76	36 56.4	−59.7	1.5	37 56.3	−59.7	1.5	38 56.3	−59.7	1.6	39 56.3	−59.7	1.6	40 56.3	−59.7	1.6	41 56.2	−59.6	1.6	42 56.2	−59.7	1.7	43 56.2	−59.7	1.7	76
77	35 56.7	−59.8	1.4	36 56.6	−59.7	1.4	37 56.6	−59.7	1.4	38 56.6	−59.7	1.4	39 56.6	−59.7	1.5	40 56.6	−59.7	1.5	41 56.5	−59.7	1.5	42 56.5	−59.7	1.5	77
78	34 56.9	−59.7	1.3	35 56.9	−59.7	1.3	36 56.9	−59.7	1.3	37 56.9	−59.7	1.3	38 56.9	−59.7	1.3	39 56.9	−59.7	1.4	40 56.8	−59.6	1.4	41 56.8	−59.7	1.4	78
79	33 57.2	−59.7	1.1	34 57.2	−59.7	1.2	35 57.2	−59.7	1.2	36 57.2	−59.7	1.2	37 57.2	−59.7	1.2	38 57.2	−59.7	1.2	39 57.2	−59.8	1.2	40 57.1	−59.7	1.3	79
80	32 57.5	−59.7	1.0	33 57.5	−59.7	1.0	34 57.5	−59.7	1.1	35 57.5	−59.7	1.1	36 57.5	−59.8	1.1	37 57.5	−59.8	1.1	38 57.4	−59.7	1.1	39 57.4	−59.7	1.1	80
81	31 57.8	−59.8	0.9	32 57.8	−59.8	0.9	33 57.8	−59.8	0.9	34 57.8	−59.8	1.0	35 57.7	−59.7	1.0	36 57.7	−59.7	1.0	37 57.7	−59.7	1.0	38 57.7	−59.7	1.0	81
82	30 58.0	−59.7	0.8	31 58.0	−59.7	0.8	32 58.0	−59.7	0.8	33 58.0	−59.7	0.8	34 58.0	−59.7	0.8	35 58.0	−59.7	0.9	36 58.0	−59.7	0.9	37 58.0	−59.7	0.9	82
83	29 58.3	−59.7	0.7	30 58.3	−59.7	0.7	31 58.3	−59.7	0.7	32 58.3	−59.8	0.7	33 58.3	−59.8	0.7	34 58.3	−59.8	0.7	35 58.3	−59.8	0.8	36 58.3	−59.8	0.8	83
84	28 58.6	−59.8	0.6	29 58.6	−59.8	0.6	30 58.6	−59.8	0.6	31 58.6	−59.8	0.6	32 58.5	−59.7	0.6	33 58.5	−59.7	0.6	34 58.5	−59.7	0.6	35 58.5	−59.7	0.6	84
85	27 58.8	−59.7	0.5	28 58.8	−59.7	0.5	29 58.8	−59.7	0.5	30 58.8	−59.7	0.5	31 58.8	−59.7	0.5	32 58.8	−59.7	0.5	33 58.8	−59.8	0.5	34 58.8	−59.8	0.5	85
86	26 59.1	−59.8	0.4	27 59.1	−59.8	0.4	28 59.1	−59.8	0.4	29 59.1	−59.8	0.4	30 59.1	−59.8	0.4	31 59.1	−59.8	0.4	32 59.0	−59.7	0.4	33 59.0	−59.7	0.4	86
87	25 59.3	−59.8	0.3	26 59.3	−59.8	0.3	27 59.3	−59.8	0.3	28 59.3	−59.8	0.3	29 59.3	−59.8	0.3	30 59.3	−59.8	0.3	31 59.3	−59.8	0.3	32 59.3	−59.8	0.3	87
88	24 59.5	−59.7	0.2	25 59.5	−59.7	0.2	26 59.5	−59.7	0.2	27 59.5	−59.7	0.2	28 59.5	−59.7	0.2	29 59.5	−59.7	0.2	30 59.5	−59.7	0.2	31 59.5	−59.7	0.2	88
89	23 59.8	−59.8	0.1	24 59.8	−59.8	0.1	25 59.8	−59.8	0.1	26 59.8	−59.8	0.1	27 59.8	−59.8	0.1	28 59.8	−59.8	0.1	29 59.8	−59.8	0.1	30 59.8	−59.8	0.1	89
90	23 00.0	−59.8	0.0	24 00.0	−59.8	0.0	25 00.0	−59.8	0.0	26 00.0	−59.8	0.0	27 00.0	−59.8	0.0	28 00.0	−59.8	0.0	29 00.0	−59.8	0.0	30 00.0	−59.8	0.0	90
	23°			24°			25°			26°			27°			28°			29°			30°			

5°, 355° L.H.A. LATITUDE **SAME** NAME AS DECLINATION

194

LATITUDE **CONTRARY** NAME TO DECLINATION **L.H.A. 5°, 355°**

Dec.	23° Hc	d	Z	24° Hc	d	Z	25° Hc	d	Z	26° Hc	d	Z	27° Hc	d	Z	28° Hc	d	Z	29° Hc	d	Z	30° Hc	d	Z	Dec.
°	° ′	′	°	° ′	′	°	° ′	′	°	° ′	′	°	° ′	′	°	° ′	′	°	° ′	′	°	° ′	′	°	°
0	66 29.5	-58.8	167.4	65 30.9	-58.9	167.9	64 32.2	-59.0	168.3	63 33.4	-59.1	168.7	62 34.5	-59.2	169.1	61 35.6	-59.3	169.4	60 36.5	-59.2	169.8	59 37.5	-59.4	170.1	0
1	65 30.7	-58.9	167.9	64 32.0	-59.0	168.3	63 33.2	-59.1	168.7	62 34.3	-59.2	169.1	61 35.3	-59.2	169.4	60 36.3	-59.3	169.8	59 37.3	-59.4	170.1	58 38.1	-59.4	170.4	1
2	64 31.8	-59.0	168.3	63 33.0	-59.1	168.7	62 34.1	-59.1	169.1	61 35.1	-59.2	169.5	60 36.1	-59.2	169.8	59 37.0	-59.3	170.1	58 37.9	-59.4	170.4	57 38.7	-59.4	170.6	2
3	63 32.8	-59.1	168.7	62 33.9	-59.1	169.1	61 35.0	-59.2	169.5	60 35.9	-59.2	169.8	59 36.9	-59.4	170.1	58 37.7	-59.3	170.4	57 38.5	-59.4	170.6	56 39.3	-59.4	170.9	3
4	62 33.7	-59.1	169.1	61 34.8	-59.2	169.5	60 35.8	-59.3	169.8	59 36.7	-59.3	170.1	58 37.5	-59.3	170.4	57 38.4	-59.4	170.7	56 39.1	-59.4	170.9	55 39.9	-59.5	171.1	4
5	61 34.6	-59.1	169.5	60 35.6	-59.2	169.8	59 36.5	-59.3	170.1	58 37.4	-59.4	170.4	57 38.2	-59.4	170.7	56 39.0	-59.5	170.9	55 39.7	-59.5	171.1	54 40.4	-59.5	171.4	5
6	60 35.5	-59.3	169.8	59 36.4	-59.3	170.1	58 37.2	-59.3	170.4	57 38.0	-59.3	170.7	56 38.8	-59.4	170.9	55 39.5	-59.4	171.2	54 40.2	-59.4	171.4	53 40.9	-59.5	171.6	6
7	59 36.2	-59.2	170.2	58 37.1	-59.3	170.4	57 37.9	-59.4	170.7	56 38.7	-59.4	170.9	55 39.4	-59.4	171.2	54 40.1	-59.5	171.4	53 40.8	-59.6	171.6	52 41.4	-59.6	171.8	7
8	58 37.0	-59.3	170.5	57 37.8	-59.4	170.7	56 38.5	-59.3	171.0	55 39.3	-59.5	171.2	54 40.0	-59.5	171.4	53 40.6	-59.5	171.6	52 41.2	-59.5	171.8	51 41.8	-59.5	172.0	8
9	57 37.7	-59.4	170.7	56 38.4	-59.4	171.0	55 39.2	-59.5	171.2	54 39.8	-59.4	171.4	53 40.5	-59.5	171.6	52 41.1	-59.5	171.8	51 41.7	-59.5	172.0	50 42.3	-59.6	172.2	9
10	56 38.3	-59.3	171.0	55 39.0	-59.4	171.3	54 39.7	-59.4	171.5	53 40.4	-59.5	171.7	52 41.0	-59.5	171.9	51 41.6	-59.6	172.0	50 42.2	-59.6	172.2	49 42.7	-59.6	172.4	10
11	55 39.0	-59.4	171.3	54 39.6	-59.4	171.5	53 40.3	-59.5	171.7	52 40.9	-59.5	171.9	51 41.5	-59.6	172.1	50 42.0	-59.5	172.2	49 42.6	-59.6	172.4	48 43.1	-59.6	172.5	11
12	54 39.6	-59.5	171.5	53 40.2	-59.5	171.7	52 40.8	-59.5	171.9	51 41.4	-59.5	172.1	50 41.9	-59.5	172.3	49 42.5	-59.6	172.4	48 43.0	-59.6	172.6	47 43.5	-59.6	172.7	12
13	53 40.1	-59.4	171.8	52 40.7	-59.5	171.9	51 41.3	-59.5	172.1	50 41.9	-59.6	172.3	49 42.4	-59.6	172.5	48 42.9	-59.6	172.6	47 43.4	-59.6	172.7	46 43.9	-59.7	172.9	13
14	52 40.7	-59.5	172.0	51 41.2	-59.5	172.2	50 41.8	-59.6	172.3	49 42.3	-59.6	172.5	48 42.8	-59.6	172.6	47 43.3	-59.6	172.8	46 43.8	-59.7	172.9	45 44.2	-59.6	173.0	14
15	51 41.2	-59.5	172.2	50 41.7	-59.5	172.4	49 42.2	-59.5	172.5	48 42.7	-59.5	172.7	47 43.2	-59.6	172.8	46 43.7	-59.6	172.9	45 44.1	-59.6	173.1	44 44.6	-59.7	173.2	15
16	50 41.7	-59.6	172.4	49 42.2	-59.6	172.6	48 42.7	-59.6	172.7	47 43.2	-59.6	172.8	46 43.6	-59.6	173.0	45 44.1	-59.7	173.1	44 44.5	-59.7	173.2	43 44.9	-59.7	173.3	16
17	49 42.1	-59.5	172.6	48 42.6	-59.5	172.7	47 43.1	-59.6	172.9	46 43.6	-59.7	173.0	45 44.0	-59.6	173.1	44 44.4	-59.6	173.3	43 44.8	-59.6	173.4	42 45.2	-59.7	173.5	17
18	48 42.6	-59.6	172.8	47 43.1	-59.6	172.9	46 43.5	-59.6	173.1	45 43.9	-59.6	173.2	44 44.4	-59.7	173.3	43 44.8	-59.7	173.4	42 45.2	-59.7	173.5	41 45.5	-59.7	173.6	18
19	47 43.0	-59.5	173.0	46 43.5	-59.6	173.1	45 43.9	-59.6	173.2	44 44.3	-59.6	173.3	43 44.7	-59.6	173.4	42 45.1	-59.7	173.6	41 45.5	-59.7	173.7	40 45.8	-59.7	173.8	19
20	46 43.5	-59.6	173.1	45 43.9	-59.6	173.3	44 44.3	-59.7	173.4	43 44.7	-59.7	173.5	42 45.1	-59.7	173.6	41 45.4	-59.7	173.7	40 45.8	-59.7	173.8	39 46.1	-59.7	173.9	20
21	45 43.9	-59.7	173.3	44 44.3	-59.7	173.4	43 44.6	-59.6	173.5	42 45.0	-59.6	173.6	41 45.4	-59.7	173.7	40 45.7	-59.7	173.7	39 46.1	-59.7	173.9	38 46.4	-59.7	174.0	21
22	44 44.2	-59.6	173.5	43 44.6	-59.6	173.6	42 45.0	-59.7	173.7	41 45.4	-59.7	173.8	40 45.7	-59.7	173.9	39 46.0	-59.7	174.0	38 46.4	-59.7	174.1	37 46.7	-59.7	174.1	22
23	43 44.6	-59.6	173.6	42 45.0	-59.7	173.7	41 45.3	-59.6	173.8	40 45.7	-59.7	173.9	39 46.0	-59.7	174.0	38 46.3	-59.7	174.1	37 46.7	-59.8	174.2	36 47.0	-59.8	174.3	23
24	42 45.0	-59.7	173.8	41 45.3	-59.6	173.9	40 45.7	-59.7	174.0	39 46.0	-59.7	174.1	38 46.3	-59.7	174.1	37 46.6	-59.7	174.2	36 46.9	-59.7	174.3	35 47.2	-59.7	174.4	24
25	41 45.3	-59.6	173.9	40 45.7	-59.7	174.0	39 46.0	-59.7	174.1	38 46.3	-59.7	174.2	37 46.6	-59.7	174.3	36 46.9	-59.7	174.3	35 47.2	-59.7	174.4	34 47.5	-59.8	174.5	25
26	40 45.7	-59.7	174.1	39 46.0	-59.7	174.2	38 46.3	-59.7	174.2	37 46.6	-59.7	174.3	36 46.9	-59.7	174.4	35 47.2	-59.7	174.5	34 47.5	-59.8	174.5	33 47.7	-59.7	174.6	26
27	39 46.0	-59.7	174.2	38 46.3	-59.7	174.3	37 46.6	-59.7	174.4	36 46.9	-59.7	174.4	35 47.2	-59.7	174.5	34 47.5	-59.8	174.6	33 47.7	-59.7	174.6	32 48.0	-59.8	174.7	27
28	38 46.3	-59.6	174.3	37 46.6	-59.7	174.4	36 46.9	-59.7	174.5	35 47.2	-59.7	174.6	34 47.5	-59.8	174.6	33 47.7	-59.7	174.7	32 48.0	-59.8	174.7	31 48.2	-59.7	174.8	28
29	37 46.7	-59.7	174.5	36 46.9	-59.7	174.5	35 47.2	-59.7	174.6	34 47.5	-59.8	174.7	33 47.7	-59.7	174.7	32 48.0	-59.8	174.8	31 48.2	-59.7	174.9	30 48.5	-59.8	174.9	29
30	36 47.0	-59.7	174.6	35 47.2	-59.7	174.7	34 47.5	-59.7	174.7	33 47.7	-59.7	174.8	32 48.0	-59.8	174.8	31 48.2	-59.7	174.9	30 48.5	-59.8	175.0	29 48.7	-59.8	175.0	30
31	35 47.3	-59.8	174.7	34 47.5	-59.7	174.8	33 47.8	-59.8	174.8	32 48.0	-59.7	174.9	31 48.2	-59.7	175.0	30 48.5	-59.8	175.0	29 48.7	-59.8	175.1	28 48.9	-59.8	175.1	31
32	34 47.5	-59.7	174.8	33 47.8	-59.7	174.9	32 48.0	-59.7	175.0	31 48.3	-59.8	175.0	30 48.5	-59.8	175.1	29 48.7	-59.8	175.1	28 48.9	-59.8	175.2	27 49.1	-59.8	175.2	32
33	33 47.8	-59.7	175.0	32 48.1	-59.8	175.0	31 48.3	-59.8	175.1	30 48.5	-59.7	175.1	29 48.7	-59.7	175.2	28 48.9	-59.7	175.2	27 49.1	-59.7	175.3	26 49.3	-59.7	175.3	33
34	32 48.1	-59.7	175.1	31 48.3	-59.7	175.1	30 48.5	-59.7	175.2	29 48.8	-59.8	175.2	28 49.0	-59.8	175.3	27 49.2	-59.8	175.3	26 49.4	-59.8	175.4	25 49.6	-59.8	175.4	34
35	31 48.4	-59.8	175.2	30 48.6	-59.8	175.2	29 48.8	-59.8	175.3	28 49.0	-59.8	175.3	27 49.2	-59.8	175.4	26 49.4	-59.8	175.4	25 49.6	-59.8	175.5	24 49.8	-59.8	175.5	35
36	30 48.6	-59.7	175.3	29 48.8	-59.7	175.3	28 49.0	-59.8	175.4	27 49.2	-59.7	175.4	26 49.4	-59.7	175.5	25 49.6	-59.8	175.5	24 49.8	-59.8	175.5	23 50.0	-59.8	175.6	36
37	29 48.9	-59.7	175.4	28 49.1	-59.8	175.4	27 49.3	-59.8	175.5	26 49.5	-59.8	175.5	25 49.7	-59.8	175.6	24 49.8	-59.8	175.6	23 50.0	-59.8	175.6	22 50.2	-59.8	175.7	37
38	28 49.2	-59.8	175.5	27 49.3	-59.7	175.5	26 49.5	-59.7	175.6	25 49.7	-59.8	175.6	24 49.9	-59.8	175.7	23 50.0	-59.7	175.7	22 50.2	-59.7	175.7	21 50.4	-59.8	175.8	38
39	27 49.4	-59.7	175.6	26 49.6	-59.8	175.6	25 49.8	-59.8	175.7	24 49.9	-59.8	175.7	23 50.1	-59.8	175.8	22 50.3	-59.8	175.8	21 50.4	-59.8	175.8	20 50.6	-59.8	175.8	39
40	26 49.7	-59.8	175.7	25 49.8	-59.7	175.7	24 50.0	-59.8	175.8	23 50.1	-59.7	175.8	22 50.3	-59.8	175.8	21 50.5	-59.8	175.9	20 50.6	-59.8	175.9	19 50.8	-59.8	175.9	40
41	25 49.9	-59.8	175.8	24 50.1	-59.8	175.8	23 50.2	-59.8	175.9	22 50.4	-59.8	175.9	21 50.5	-59.8	175.9	20 50.7	-59.8	176.0	19 50.8	-59.8	176.0	18 51.0	-59.8	176.0	41
42	24 50.1	-59.7	175.9	23 50.3	-59.8	175.9	22 50.4	-59.7	176.0	21 50.6	-59.8	176.0	20 50.7	-59.8	176.0	19 50.9	-59.8	176.1	18 51.0	-59.8	176.1	17 51.2	-59.9	176.1	42
43	23 50.4	-59.8	176.0	22 50.5	-59.8	176.0	21 50.7	-59.8	176.1	20 50.8	-59.8	176.1	19 50.9	-59.8	176.1	18 51.1	-59.8	176.1	17 51.2	-59.8	176.2	16 51.3	-59.8	176.2	43
44	22 50.6	-59.8	176.1	21 50.7	-59.7	176.1	20 50.9	-59.8	176.2	19 51.0	-59.8	176.2	18 51.1	-59.8	176.2	17 51.3	-59.8	176.2	16 51.4	-59.8	176.2	15 51.5	-59.8	176.3	44
45	21 50.8	-59.8	176.2	20 51.0	-59.8	176.2	19 51.1	-59.8	176.2	18 51.2	-59.8	176.3	17 51.3	-59.8	176.3	16 51.5	-59.8	176.3	15 51.6	-59.8	176.3	14 51.7	-59.8	176.3	45
46	20 51.0	-59.7	176.3	19 51.2	-59.8	176.3	18 51.3	-59.8	176.3	17 51.4	-59.8	176.4	16 51.5	-59.8	176.4	15 51.7	-59.9	176.4	14 51.8	-59.8	176.4	13 51.9	-59.8	176.4	46
47	19 51.3	-59.8	176.4	18 51.4	-59.8	176.4	17 51.5	-59.8	176.4	16 51.6	-59.8	176.4	15 51.7	-59.8	176.5	14 51.8	-59.8	176.5	13 52.0	-59.9	176.5	12 52.1	-59.8	176.5	47
48	18 51.5	-59.8	176.5	17 51.6	-59.8	176.5	16 51.7	-59.8	176.5	15 51.8	-59.8	176.5	14 51.9	-59.8	176.5	13 52.0	-59.8	176.6	12 52.1	-59.8	176.6	11 52.3	-59.9	176.6	48
49	17 51.7	-59.8	176.6	16 51.8	-59.8	176.6	15 51.9	-59.8	176.6	14 52.0	-59.8	176.6	13 52.1	-59.8	176.6	12 52.2	-59.8	176.6	11 52.3	-59.8	176.7	10 52.4	-59.8	176.7	49
50	16 51.9	-59.8	176.6	15 52.0	-59.8	176.7	14 52.1	-59.8	176.7	13 52.2	-59.8	176.7	12 52.3	-59.8	176.7	11 52.4	-59.8	176.7	10 52.5	-59.8	176.7	9 52.6	-59.8	176.7	50
51	15 52.1	-59.8	176.7	14 52.2	-59.8	176.7	13 52.3	-59.8	176.8	12 52.4	-59.8	176.8	11 52.5	-59.8	176.8	10 52.6	-59.8	176.8	9 52.7	-59.8	176.8	8 52.8	-59.8	176.8	51
52	14 52.3	-59.8	176.8	13 52.4	-59.8	176.8	12 52.5	-59.8	176.8	11 52.6	-59.8	176.9	10 52.7	-59.8	176.9	9 52.8	-59.8	176.9	8 52.9	-59.9	176.9	7 53.0	-59.9	176.9	52
53	13 52.5	-59.8	176.9	12 52.6	-59.8	176.9	11 52.7	-59.8	176.9	10 52.8	-59.8	176.9	9 52.9	-59.8	176.9	8 53.0	-59.9	177.0	7 53.0	-59.8	177.0	6 53.1	-59.8	177.0	53
54	12 52.7	-59.8	177.0	11 52.8	-59.8	177.0	10 52.9	-59.8	177.0	9 53.0	-59.8	177.0	8 53.1	-59.9	177.0	7 53.1	-59.8	177.0	6 53.2	-59.8	177.0	5 53.3	-59.8	177.0	54
55	11 52.9	-59.8	177.1	10 53.0	-59.8	177.1	9 53.1	-59.8	177.1	8 53.2	-59.8	177.1	7 53.2	-59.8	177.1	6 53.3	-59.8	177.1	5 53.4	-59.8	177.1	4 53.5	-59.9	177.1	55
56	10 53.1	-59.8	177.2	9 53.2	-59.8	177.2	8 53.3	-59.8	177.2	7 53.4	-59.9	177.2	6 53.4	-59.8	177.2	5 53.5	-59.8	177.2	4 53.6	-59.8	177.2	3 53.6	-59.8	177.2	56
57	9 53.3	-59.8	177.2	8 53.4	-59.8	177.2	7 53.5	-59.8	177.3	6 53.5	-59.8	177.3	5 53.6	-59.8	177.3	4 53.7	-59.8	177.3	3 53.8	-59.9	177.3	2 53.8	-59.8	177.3	57
58	8 53.5	-59.8	177.3	7 53.6	-59.8	177.3	6 53.7	-59.8	177.3	5 53.7	-59.8	177.3	4 53.8	-59.8	177.3	3 53.9	-59.9	177.3	2 53.9	-59.8	177.3	1 54.0	-59.8	177.4	58
59	7 53.7	-59.8	177.4	6 53.8	-59.8	177.4	5 53.9	-59.9	177.4	4 53.9	-59.8	177.4	3 54.0	-59.8	177.4	2 54.0	-59.8	177.4	1 54.1	-59.8	177.4	0 54.2	-59.9	177.4	59
60	6 53.9	-59.8	177.5	5 54.0	-59.8	177.5	4 54.0	-59.8	177.5	3 54.1	-59.8	177.5	2 54.2	-59.9	177.5	1 54.2	-59.8	177.5	0 54.3	-59.8	177.5	0 05.7	+59.8	2.5	60
61	5 54.1	-59.8	177.6	4 54.2	-59.8	177.6	3 54.2	-59.8	177.6	2 54.3	-59.8	177.6	1 54.3	-59.8	177.6	0 54.4	-59.8	177.6	0 05.5	+59.9	2.4	1 05.5	+59.8	2.4	61
62	4 54.3	-59.8	177.6	3 54.4	-59.8	177.6	2 54.4	-59.8	177.7	1 54.5	-59.8	177.7	0 54.5	-59.8	177.7	0 05.4	+59.8	2.3	1 05.4	+59.8	2.3	2 05.3	+59.9	2.3	62
63	3 54.5	-59.8	177.7	2 54.6	-59.8	177.7	1 54.6	-59.8	177.7	0 54.7	-59.9	177.7	0 05.3	+59.8	2.3	1 05.2	+59.9	2.3	2 05.2	+59.8	2.3	3 05.2	+59.8	2.3	63
64	2 54.7	-59.8	177.8	1 54.8	-59.9	177.8	0 54.8	-59.8	177.8	0 05.2	+59.8	2.2	1 05.1	+59.8	2.2	2 05.1	+59.8	2.2	3 05.0	+59.8	2.2	4 05.0	+59.8	2.2	64
65	1 54.9	-59.8	177.9	0 54.9	-59.8	177.9	0 05.0	+59.8	2.1	1 05.0	+59.8	2.1	2 04.9	+59.8	2.1	3 04.9	+59.8	2.1	4 04.8	+59.9	2.1	5 04.8	+59.8	2.1	65
66	0 55.1	-59.8	178.0	0 04.9	+59.8	2.0	1 04.8	+59.8	2.0	2 04.8	+59.8	2.0	3 04.7	+59.9	2.0	4 04.7	+59.8	2.0	5 04.7	+59.8	2.0	6 04.6	+59.9	2.0	66
67	0 04.7	+59.8	2.0	1 04.7	+59.8	2.0	2 04.6	+59.8	2.0	3 04.6	+59.8	2.0	4 04.6	+59.8	2.0	5 04.5	+59.9	2.0	6 04.5	+59.8	2.0	7 04.5	+59.8	2.0	67
68	1 04.5	+59.8	1.9	2 04.5	+59.8	1.9	3 04.4	+59.9	1.9	4 04.4	+59.8	1.9	5 04.4	+59.8	1.9	6 04.4	+59.8	1.9	7 04.3	+59.8	1.9	8 04.3	+59.8	1.9	68
69	2 04.3	+59.8	1.8	3 04.3	+59.8	1.8	4 04.3	+59.8	1.8	5 04.2	+59.8	1.8	6 04.2	+59.8	1.8	7 04.2	+59.8	1.8	8 04.1	+59.9	1.8	9 04.1	+59.8	1.8	69
70	3 04.1	+59.8	1.7	4 04.1	+59.8	1.7	5 04.1	+59.8	1.7	6 04.0	+59.9	1.7	7 04.0	+59.8	1.7	8 04.0	+59.8	1.7	9 04.0	+59.8	1.7	10 03.9	+59.9	1.7	70
71	4 03.9	+59.8	1.6	5 03.9	+59.8	1.6	6 03.9	+59.8	1.6	7 03.9	+59.8	1.6	8 03.8	+59.8	1.6	9 03.8	+59.8	1.6	10 03.8	+59.8	1.7	11 03.8	+59.8	1.7	71
72	5 03.7	+59.8	1.5	6 03.7	+59.8	1.6	7 03.7	+59.8	1.6	8 03.7	+59.8	1.6	9 03.6	+59.9	1.6	10 03.6	+59.8	1.6	11 03.6	+59.8	1.6	12 03.6	+59.8	1.6	72
73	6 03.5	+59.8	1.5	7 03.5	+59.8	1.5	8 03.5	+59.8	1.5	9 03.5	+59.8	1.5	10 03.5	+59.8	1.5	11 03.4	+59.9	1.5	12 03.4	+59.8	1.5	13 03.4	+59.8	1.5	73
74	7 03.3	+59.8	1.4	8 03.3	+59.8	1.4	9 03.3	+59.8	1.4	10 03.3	+59.8	1.4	11 03.3	+59.8	1.4	12 03.3	+59.8	1.4	13 03.2	+59.9	1.4	14 03.2	+59.8	1.4	74
75	8 03.1	+59.8	1.3	9 03.1	+59.8	1.3	10 03.1	+59.8	1.3	11 03.1	+59.8	1.3	12 03.1	+59.8	1.3	13 03.1	+59.8	1.3	14 03.1	+59.8	1.3	15 03.0	+59.9	1.3	75
76	9 02.9	+59.9	1.2	10 02.9	+59.8	1.2	11 02.9	+59.8	1.2	12 02.9	+59.8	1.2	13 02.9	+59.8	1.2	14 02.9	+59.8	1.2	15 02.9	+59.8	1.3	16 02.9	+59.8	1.3	76
77	10 02.8	+59.8	1.1	11 02.7	+59.8	1.1	12 02.7	+59.8	1.2	13 02.7	+59.8	1.2	14 02.7	+59.8	1.2	15 02.7	+59.8	1.2	16 02.7	+59.8	1.2	17 02.7	+59.8	1.2	77
78	11 02.6	+59.7	1.1	12 02.5	+59.8	1.1	13 02.5	+59.8	1.1	14 02.5	+59.8	1.1	15 02.5	+59.8	1.1	16 02.5	+59.8	1.1	17 02.5	+59.8	1.1	18 02.5	+59.8	1.1	78
79	12 02.3	+59.8	1.0	13 02.3	+59.8	1.0	14 02.3	+59.8	1.0	15 02.3	+59.8	1.0	16 02.3	+59.8	1.0	17 02.3	+59.8	1.0	18 02.3	+59.8	1.0	19 02.3	+59.8	1.0	79
80	13 02.1	+59.8	0.9	14 02.1	+59.8	0.9	15 02.1	+59.8	0.9	16 02.1	+59.8	0.9	17 02.1	+59.8	0.9	18 02.1	+59.8	0.9	19 02.1	+59.8	0.9	20 02.1	+59.8	0.9	80
81	14 01.9	+59.8	0.8	15 01.9	+59.8	0.8	16 01.9	+59.8	0.8	17 01.9	+59.8	0.8	18 01.9	+59.8	0.8	19 01.9	+59.8	0.8	20 01.9	+59.8	0.8	21 01.9	+59.8	0.8	81
82	15 01.7	+59.8	0.7	16 01.7	+59.8	0.7	17 01.7	+59.8	0.7	18 01.7	+59.8	0.7	19 01.7	+59.8	0.7	20 01.7	+59.8	0.7	21 01.7	+59.8	0.7	22 01.7	+59.8	0.7	82
83	16 01.5	+59.8	0.6	17 01.5	+59.8	0.6	18 01.5	+59.8	0.6	19 01.5	+59.8	0.6	20 01.5	+59.8	0.6	21 01.5	+59.8	0.7	22 01.5	+59.8	0.7	23 01.5	+59.8	0.7	83
84	17 01.3	+59.8	0.5	18 01.3	+59.8	0.5	19 01.3	+59.8	0.6	20 01.3	+59.8	0.6	21 01.3	+59.8	0.6	22 01.3	+59.8	0.6	23 01.3	+59.8	0.6	24 01.3	+59.8	0.6	84
85	18 01.1	+59.8	0.5	19 01.1	+59.8	0.5	20 01.1	+59.8	0.5	21 01.1	+59.8	0.5	22 01.1	+59.8	0.5	23 01.1	+59.8	0.5	24 01.1	+59.8	0.5	25 01.1	+59.8	0.5	85
86	19 00.9	+59.8	0.4	20 00.9	+59.8	0.4	21 00.9	+59.8	0.4	22 00.9	+59.8	0.4	23 00.9	+59.7	0.4	24 00.9	+59.8	0.4	25 00.9	+59.8	0.4	26 00.9	+59.8	0.4	86
87	20 00.7	+59.8	0.3	21 00.7	+59.7	0.3	22 00.7	+59.7	0.3	23 00.7	+59.7	0.3	24 00.7	+59.7	0.3	25 00.7	+59.7	0.3	26 00.7	+59.7	0.3	27 00.7	+59.7	0.3	87
88	21 00.5	+59.7	0.2	22 00.4	+59.8	0.2	23 00.4	+59.8	0.2	24 00.4	+59.8	0.2	25 00.4	+59.8	0.2	26 00.4	+59.8	0.2	27 00.4	+59.8	0.2	28 00.4	+59.8	0.2	88
89	22 00.2	+59.8	0.1	23 00.2	+59.8	0.1	24 00.2	+59.8	0.1	25 00.2	+59.8	0.1	26 00.2	+59.8	0.1	27 00.2	+59.8	0.1	28 00.2	+59.8	0.1	29 00.2	+59.8	0.1	89
90	23 00.0	+59.8	0.0	24 00.0	+59.8	0.0	25 00.0	+59.8	0.0	26 00.0	+59.8	0.0	27 00.0	+59.8	0.0	28 00.0	+59.8	0.0	29 00.0	+59.8	0.0	30 00.0	+59.8	0.0	90
	23°			24°			25°			26°			27°			28°			29°			30°			

S. Lat. {L.H.A. greater than 180° ....Zn=180°−Z; L.H.A. less than 180°...........Zn=180°+Z

LATITUDE **SAME** NAME AS DECLINATION **L.H.A. 175°, 185°**

195

6°, 354° L.H.A. LATITUDE SAME NAME AS DECLINATION N. Lat. {L.H.A. greater than 180° .....Zn=Z; L.H.A. less than 180°............Zn=360°−Z

Dec.	23°			24°			25°			26°			27°			28°			29°			30°			Dec.
	Hc	d	Z	Hc	d	Z	Hc	d	Z	Hc	d	Z	Hc	d	Z	Hc	d	Z	Hc	d	Z	Hc	d	Z	
°	° ′	′	°	° ′	′	°	° ′	′	°	° ′	′	°	° ′	′	°	° ′	′	°	° ′	′	°	° ′	′	°	°
0	66 16.3	+58.2	164.9	65 18.3	+58.3	165.5	64 20.1	+58.5	166.0	63 21.8	+58.6	166.5	62 23.4	+58.8	167.0	61 24.9	+58.9	167.4	60 26.3	+59.0	167.8	59 27.6	+59.1	168.1	0
1	67 14.5	+58.0	164.3	66 16.6	+58.2	164.9	65 18.6	+58.4	165.5	64 20.4	+58.6	166.0	63 22.2	+58.6	166.5	62 23.8	+58.7	167.0	61 25.3	+58.8	167.4	60 26.7	+58.9	167.8	1
2	68 12.5	+57.9	163.7	67 14.8	+58.1	164.3	66 17.0	+58.2	164.9	65 19.0	+58.4	165.5	64 20.8	+58.5	166.0	63 22.5	+58.7	166.5	62 24.1	+58.8	167.0	61 25.6	+58.9	167.4	2
3	69 10.4	+57.6	162.9	68 12.9	+57.9	163.7	67 15.2	+58.1	164.3	66 17.4	+58.2	165.0	65 19.3	+58.5	165.5	64 21.2	+58.5	166.0	63 22.9	+58.7	166.5	62 24.5	+58.8	167.0	3
4	70 08.0	+57.4	162.1	69 10.8	+57.7	162.9	68 13.3	+57.9	163.7	67 15.6	+58.2	164.3	66 17.8	+58.3	165.0	65 19.7	+58.5	165.5	64 21.6	+58.6	166.1	63 23.3	+58.7	166.5	4
5	71 05.4	+57.2	161.3	70 08.5	+57.4	162.1	69 11.2	+57.8	163.0	68 13.8	+57.9	163.7	67 16.1	+58.1	164.4	66 18.2	+58.3	165.0	65 20.2	+58.5	165.5	64 22.0	+58.6	166.1	5
6	72 02.6	+56.8	160.3	71 05.9	+57.2	161.3	70 09.0	+57.5	162.2	69 11.7	+57.8	163.0	68 14.2	+58.0	163.7	67 16.5	+58.2	164.4	66 18.7	+58.3	165.0	65 20.6	+58.5	165.6	6
7	72 59.4	+56.5	159.2	72 03.1	+56.9	160.3	71 06.5	+57.2	161.3	70 09.5	+57.5	162.2	69 12.2	+57.8	163.0	68 14.7	+58.0	163.7	67 17.0	+58.2	164.4	66 19.1	+58.4	165.0	7
8	73 55.9	+56.0	158.0	73 00.0	+56.5	159.3	72 03.7	+56.9	160.4	71 07.0	+57.3	161.3	70 10.0	+57.6	162.2	69 12.7	+57.9	163.0	68 15.2	+58.1	163.8	67 17.5	+58.3	164.4	8
9	74 51.9	+55.5	156.7	73 56.5	+56.1	158.1	73 00.6	+56.6	159.3	72 04.3	+57.0	160.4	71 07.6	+57.3	161.4	70 10.6	+57.6	162.3	69 13.3	+57.9	163.1	68 15.8	+58.1	163.8	9
10	75 47.4	+54.9	155.2	74 52.6	+55.6	156.8	73 57.2	+56.1	158.1	73 01.3	+56.6	159.4	72 04.9	+57.0	160.5	71 08.2	+57.4	161.4	70 11.2	+57.6	162.3	69 13.9	+57.9	163.1	10
11	76 42.3	+54.1	153.5	75 48.2	+54.9	155.3	74 53.3	+55.7	156.8	73 57.9	+56.2	158.2	73 01.9	+56.7	159.4	72 05.6	+57.1	160.5	71 08.8	+57.5	161.5	70 11.8	+57.7	162.4	11
12	77 36.4	+53.1	151.6	76 43.1	+54.2	153.6	75 49.0	+55.0	155.3	74 54.1	+55.7	156.9	73 58.6	+56.3	158.3	73 02.7	+56.7	159.5	72 06.3	+57.1	160.6	71 09.5	+57.5	161.5	12
13	78 29.5	+51.9	149.3	77 37.3	+53.2	151.6	76 44.0	+54.2	153.7	75 49.8	+55.1	155.4	74 54.9	+55.7	157.0	73 59.4	+56.3	158.3	73 03.4	+56.8	159.5	72 07.0	+57.2	160.6	13
14	79 21.4	+50.4	146.7	78 30.5	+52.0	149.4	77 38.2	+53.3	151.7	76 44.9	+54.3	153.7	75 50.6	+55.2	155.5	74 55.7	+55.8	157.0	74 00.2	+56.4	158.4	73 04.2	+56.8	159.6	14
15	80 11.8	+48.4•	143.6	79 22.5	+50.5	146.8	78 31.5	+52.1	149.5	77 39.2	+53.4	151.8	76 45.8	+54.4	153.8	75 51.5	+55.3	155.6	74 56.6	+55.9	157.1	74 01.0	+56.5	158.5	15
16	81 00.2	+46.0•	140.0	80 13.0	+48.6•	143.7	79 23.6	+50.7	146.9	78 32.6	+52.2	149.6	77 40.2	+53.5	151.9	76 46.8	+54.5	153.9	75 52.5	+55.3	155.7	74 57.5	+56.0	157.2	16
17	81 46.2	+42.6•	135.7	81 01.6	+46.1•	140.1	80 14.3	+48.7•	143.9	79 24.8	+50.8	147.0	78 33.7	+52.4	149.7	77 41.3	+53.6	152.0	76 47.8	+54.6	154.0	75 53.5	+55.4	155.8	17
18	82 28.8	+38.3•	130.6	81 47.7	+42.8•	135.9	81 03.0	+46.2•	140.3	80 15.6	+48.9•	144.0	79 26.1	+50.9	147.2	78 34.9	+52.5	149.9	77 42.4	+53.7	152.2	76 48.9	+54.6	154.2	18
19	83 07.1	+32.7•	124.4	82 30.5	+38.5•	130.7	81 49.2	+43.0•	136.0	81 04.5	+46.4•	140.4	80 17.0	+49.0•	144.2	79 27.4	+51.0	147.3	78 36.1	+52.6	150.0	77 43.5	+53.9	152.3	19
20	83 39.8	+25.5•	117.1	83 09.0	+32.9•	124.6	82 32.2	+38.7•	130.9	81 50.9	+43.2•	136.2	81 06.0	+46.6•	140.6	80 18.4	+49.2•	144.3	79 28.7	+51.2	147.5	78 37.4	+52.7	150.1	20
21	84 05.3	+16.8•	108.6	83 41.9	+25.7•	117.2	83 10.9	+33.1•	124.7	82 34.1	+38.9•	131.0	81 52.6	+43.3•	136.3	81 07.6	+46.7•	140.8	80 19.9	+49.3•	144.5	79 30.1	+51.3	147.6	21
22	84 22.1	+6.5•	99.1	84 07.6	+16.9•	108.7	83 44.0	+26.0•	117.4	83 13.0	+33.3•	124.9	82 35.9	+39.2•	131.2	81 54.3	+43.6•	136.5	81 09.2	+46.9•	140.9	80 21.4	+49.5•	144.7	22
23	84 28.6	−4.1•	88.8	84 24.5	+6.6•	99.1	84 10.0	+17.0•	108.8	83 46.3	+26.1•	117.5	83 15.1	+33.5•	125.0	82 37.9	+39.4•	131.4	81 56.1	+43.8•	136.7	81 10.9	+47.1•	141.1	23
24	84 24.5	−14.5•	78.5	84 31.1	−4.1•	88.8	84 27.0	+6.8•	99.1	84 12.4	+17.2•	108.9	83 48.6	+26.4•	117.7	83 17.3	+33.7•	125.2	82 39.9	+39.6•	131.6	81 58.0	+44.0•	136.9	24
25	84 10.0	−23.7•	68.8	84 27.0	−14.6•	78.4	84 33.8	−4.2•	88.7	84 29.6	+6.9•	99.2	84 15.0	+17.3•	109.0	83 51.0	+26.6•	117.8	83 19.5	+34.0•	125.4	82 42.0	+39.8•	131.8	25
26	83 46.3	−31.2•	60.0	84 12.4	−23.8•	68.6	84 29.6	−14.6•	78.3	84 36.5	−4.2•	88.7	84 32.3	+7.0•	99.2	84 17.6	+17.5•	109.1	83 53.5	+26.8•	118.0	83 21.8	+34.3•	125.6	26
27	83 15.1	−37.2•	52.4	83 48.6	−31.3•	59.7	84 15.0	−24.0•	68.4	84 32.3	−14.7•	78.1	84 39.3	−4.2•	88.6	84 35.1	+7.1•	99.2	84 20.3	+17.7•	109.3	83 56.1	+27.0•	118.2	27
28	82 37.9	−41.8•	46.0	83 17.3	−37.4•	52.1	83 51.0	−31.5•	59.5	84 17.6	−24.1•	68.1	84 35.1	−14.8•	78.0	84 42.2	−4.2•	88.6	84 38.0	+7.2•	99.3	84 23.1	+17.9•	109.4	28
29	81 56.1	−45.2•	40.7	82 39.9	−41.9•	45.7	83 19.5	−37.5•	51.9	83 53.5	−31.7•	59.2	84 20.3	−24.2•	67.9	84 38.0	−14.9•	77.8	84 45.2	−4.2•	88.5	84 41.0	+7.3•	99.4	29
30	81 10.9	−47.9•	36.2	81 58.0	−45.4•	40.4	82 42.0	−42.0•	45.4	83 21.8	−37.6•	51.6	83 56.1	−31.9•	59.0	84 23.1	−24.4•	67.7	84 41.0	−15.0•	77.7	84 48.3	−4.2•	88.5	30
31	80 23.0	−50.0	32.4	81 12.6	−48.0•	35.9	82 00.0	−45.6•	40.1	82 44.2	−42.3•	45.1	83 24.2	−37.8•	51.3	83 58.7	−32.0•	58.7	84 26.0	−24.5•	67.5	84 44.1	−15.1•	77.5	31
32	79 33.0	−51.6	29.3	80 24.6	−50.1	32.1	81 14.4	−48.2•	35.6	82 01.9	−45.6•	39.8	82 46.4	−42.4•	44.8	83 26.7	−38.1•	50.9	84 01.5	−32.3•	58.4	84 29.0	−24.7•	67.2	32
33	78 41.4	−52.9	26.6	79 34.5	−51.7	29.0	80 26.2	−50.2	31.8	81 16.3	−48.4•	35.3	82 04.0	−45.9•	39.4	82 48.6	−42.5•	44.5	83 29.2	−38.2•	50.6	84 04.3	−32.5•	58.1	33
34	77 48.5	−53.9	24.2	78 42.8	−53.0	26.3	79 36.0	−51.8	28.7	80 27.9	−50.3	31.5	81 18.1	−48.4•	35.0	82 06.1	−46.0•	39.1	82 51.0	−42.8•	44.1	83 31.8	−38.5•	50.3	34
35	76 54.6	−54.7	22.2	77 49.8	−53.9	24.0	78 44.2	−53.0	26.0	79 37.6	−51.9	28.4	80 29.7	−50.5	31.2	81 20.1	−48.7•	34.6	82 08.2	−46.2•	38.7	82 53.3	−42.9•	43.8	35
36	75 59.9	−55.3	20.5	76 55.9	−54.8	22.0	77 51.2	−54.1	23.7	78 45.7	−53.1	25.7	79 39.2	−52.0	28.1	80 31.4	−50.5	30.9	81 22.0	−48.7•	34.3	82 10.4	−46.4•	38.4	36
37	75 04.6	−56.0	18.9	76 01.1	−55.4	20.2	76 57.1	−54.8	21.7	77 52.6	−54.2	23.4	78 47.2	−53.2	25.4	79 40.9	−52.2	27.8	80 33.3	−50.8	30.6	81 24.0	−48.9•	33.9	37
38	74 08.6	−56.3	17.5	75 05.7	−56.0	18.7	76 02.3	−55.5	20.0	76 58.4	−54.9	21.4	77 54.0	−54.2	23.1	78 48.7	−53.3	25.1	79 42.5	−52.2	27.5	80 35.1	−50.9	30.2	38
39	73 12.3	−56.8	16.3	74 09.7	−56.4	17.3	75 06.8	−56.0	18.4	76 03.5	−55.5	19.7	76 59.8	−55.0	21.2	77 55.4	−54.3	22.8	78 50.3	−53.4	24.8	79 44.2	−52.3	27.1	39
40	72 15.5	−57.1	15.2	73 13.3	−56.8	16.1	74 10.8	−56.5	17.1	75 08.0	−56.1	18.2	76 04.8	−55.6	19.4	77 01.1	−55.1	20.9	77 56.9	−54.4	22.5	78 51.9	−53.6	24.5	40
41	71 18.4	−57.3	14.2	72 16.5	−57.1	15.0	73 14.3	−56.8	15.9	74 11.9	−56.5	16.8	75 09.2	−56.2	17.9	76 06.0	−55.6	19.2	77 02.2	−55.2	20.6	77 58.3	−54.4	22.2	41
42	70 21.1	−57.6	13.4	71 19.4	−57.4	14.0	72 17.5	−57.2	14.8	73 15.4	−56.9	15.6	74 13.0	−56.6	16.6	75 10.4	−56.2	17.7	76 07.3	−55.7	18.9	77 03.9	−55.3	20.3	42
43	69 23.5	−57.9	12.5	70 22.0	−57.7	13.2	71 20.3	−57.4	13.8	72 18.5	−57.2	14.6	73 16.4	−56.9	15.4	74 14.2	−56.7	16.3	75 11.6	−56.3	17.4	76 08.6	−55.8	18.6	43
44	68 25.6	−57.9	11.8	69 24.3	−57.8	12.3	70 22.9	−57.7	12.9	71 21.3	−57.5	13.6	72 19.5	−57.3	14.3	73 17.5	−57.0	15.2	74 15.3	−56.7	16.1	75 12.8	−56.3	17.1	44
45	67 27.7	−58.2	11.1	68 26.5	−58.0	11.6	69 25.2	−57.9	12.1	70 23.8	−57.7	12.7	71 22.2	−57.5	13.4	72 20.5	−57.3	14.1	73 18.6	−57.0	14.9	74 16.5	−56.8	15.8	45
46	66 29.5	−58.3	10.5	67 28.5	−58.2	10.9	68 27.3	−58.0	11.4	69 26.1	−57.9	11.9	70 24.7	−57.7	12.5	71 23.2	−57.5	13.1	72 21.6	−57.4	13.9	73 19.7	−57.1	14.7	46
47	65 31.2	−58.4	9.9	66 30.3	−58.3	10.3	67 29.3	−58.2	10.7	68 28.2	−58.1	11.2	69 27.0	−58.0	11.7	70 25.7	−57.8	12.3	71 24.2	−57.6	12.9	72 22.6	−57.4	13.6	47
48	64 32.8	−58.5	9.4	65 32.0	−58.5	9.7	66 31.1	−58.4	10.1	67 30.1	−58.2	10.5	68 29.0	−58.1	11.0	69 27.9	−58.0	11.5	70 26.6	−57.8	12.1	71 25.2	−57.6	12.7	48
49	63 34.3	−58.7	8.9	64 33.5	−58.5	9.2	65 32.7	−58.5	9.5	66 31.9	−58.4	9.9	67 30.9	−58.2	10.3	68 29.9	−58.1	10.8	69 28.8	−58.0	11.3	70 27.6	−57.9	11.8	49
50	62 35.6	−58.7	8.4	63 35.0	−58.7	8.7	64 34.2	−58.5	9.0	65 33.5	−58.5	9.3	66 32.7	−58.4	9.7	67 31.8	−58.3	10.1	68 30.8	−58.2	10.6	69 29.7	−58.0	11.1	50
51	61 36.9	−58.8	8.0	62 36.3	−58.7	8.2	63 35.7	−58.7	8.5	64 35.0	−58.6	8.8	65 34.3	−58.6	9.2	66 33.5	−58.5	9.5	67 32.6	−58.3	9.9	68 31.7	−58.3	10.4	51
52	60 38.1	−58.9	7.5	61 37.6	−58.8	7.8	62 37.0	−58.8	8.0	63 36.4	−58.7	8.3	64 35.7	−58.6	8.6	65 35.0	−58.5	9.0	66 34.3	−58.5	9.3	67 33.4	−58.3	9.7	52
53	59 39.2	−58.9	7.2	60 38.8	−58.9	7.4	61 38.2	−58.8	7.6	62 37.7	−58.8	7.9	63 37.1	−58.7	8.1	64 36.5	−58.6	8.4	65 35.8	−58.5	8.8	66 35.1	−58.5	9.1	53
54	58 40.3	−59.0	6.8	59 39.9	−59.0	7.0	60 39.4	−58.9	7.2	61 38.9	−58.8	7.4	62 38.4	−58.8	7.7	63 37.9	−58.8	8.0	64 37.3	−58.7	8.2	65 36.6	−58.6	8.6	54
55	57 41.3	−59.0	6.4	58 40.9	−59.0	6.6	59 40.5	−58.9	6.8	60 40.1	−58.9	7.0	61 39.6	−58.9	7.3	62 39.1	−58.8	7.5	63 38.6	−58.8	7.8	64 38.0	−58.7	8.0	55
56	56 42.3	−59.1	6.1	57 41.9	−59.0	6.3	58 41.6	−59.1	6.5	59 41.2	−59.0	6.7	60 40.7	−58.9	6.9	61 40.3	−58.9	7.1	62 39.8	−58.8	7.3	63 39.3	−58.8	7.6	56
57	55 43.2	−59.2	5.8	56 42.9	−59.1	6.0	57 42.5	−59.0	6.1	58 42.2	−59.1	6.3	59 41.8	−59.0	6.5	60 41.4	−58.9	6.7	61 41.0	−58.9	6.9	62 40.5	−58.8	7.1	57
58	54 44.0	−59.1	5.5	55 43.8	−59.2	5.6	56 43.5	−59.2	5.8	57 43.1	−59.0	6.0	58 42.8	−59.0	6.1	59 42.5	−59.1	6.3	60 42.1	−59.0	6.5	61 41.7	−58.9	6.7	58
59	53 44.9	−59.3	5.2	54 44.6	−59.2	5.4	55 44.3	−59.1	5.5	56 44.1	−59.2	5.6	57 43.8	−59.2	5.8	58 43.4	−59.0	6.0	59 43.1	−59.0	6.1	60 42.8	−59.0	6.3	59
60	52 45.6	−59.2	5.0	53 45.4	−59.2	5.1	54 45.2	−59.2	5.2	55 44.9	−59.2	5.3	56 44.6	−59.1	5.5	57 44.4	−59.2	5.6	58 44.1	−59.1	5.8	59 43.8	−59.1	6.0	60
61	51 46.4	−59.3	4.7	52 46.2	−59.3	4.8	53 46.0	−59.3	4.9	54 45.7	−59.2	5.0	55 45.5	−59.2	5.2	56 45.2	−59.1	5.3	57 45.0	−59.2	5.4	58 44.7	−59.1	5.6	61
62	50 47.1	−59.3	4.5	51 46.9	−59.3	4.5	52 46.7	−59.3	4.7	53 46.5	−59.2	4.8	54 46.3	−59.2	4.9	55 46.1	−59.2	5.0	56 45.8	−59.1	5.1	57 45.6	−59.2	5.3	62
63	49 47.8	−59.4	4.2	50 47.6	−59.3	4.3	51 47.4	−59.3	4.4	52 47.3	−59.3	4.5	53 47.1	−59.3	4.6	54 46.9	−59.3	4.7	55 46.7	−59.3	4.8	56 46.4	−59.2	5.0	63
64	48 48.4	−59.3	4.0	49 48.3	−59.4	4.1	50 48.1	−59.3	4.2	51 48.0	−59.3	4.2	52 47.8	−59.3	4.3	53 47.6	−59.3	4.4	54 47.4	−59.2	4.6	55 47.2	−59.2	4.7	64
65	47 49.1	−59.4	3.8	48 48.9	−59.3	3.8	49 48.8	−59.4	3.9	50 48.7	−59.4	4.0	51 48.5	−59.3	4.1	52 48.3	−59.3	4.2	53 48.2	−59.3	4.3	54 48.0	−59.3	4.4	65
66	46 49.7	−59.4	3.6	47 49.6	−59.4	3.6	48 49.4	−59.4	3.7	49 49.3	−59.4	3.8	50 49.2	−59.4	3.9	51 49.0	−59.3	3.9	52 48.9	−59.3	4.0	53 48.7	−59.3	4.1	66
67	45 50.3	−59.5	3.4	46 50.2	−59.5	3.4	47 50.0	−59.4	3.5	48 49.9	−59.4	3.6	49 49.8	−59.4	3.6	50 49.7	−59.4	3.7	51 49.6	−59.4	3.8	52 49.4	−59.3	3.9	67
68	44 50.8	−59.4	3.2	45 50.7	−59.4	3.2	46 50.6	−59.4	3.3	47 50.5	−59.4	3.3	48 50.4	−59.4	3.4	49 50.3	−59.4	3.5	50 50.2	−59.4	3.6	51 50.1	−59.4	3.6	68
69	43 51.4	−59.5	3.0	44 51.3	−59.5	3.0	45 51.2	−59.4	3.1	46 51.1	−59.4	3.1	47 51.0	−59.4	3.2	48 50.9	−59.4	3.3	49 50.8	−59.4	3.3	50 50.7	−59.4	3.4	69
70	42 51.9	−59.5	2.8	43 51.8	−59.5	2.8	44 51.8	−59.5	2.9	45 51.7	−59.5	2.9	46 51.6	−59.5	3.0	47 51.5	−59.4	3.1	48 51.4	−59.4	3.1	49 51.3	−59.4	3.2	70
71	41 52.4	−59.5	2.6	42 52.3	−59.4	2.7	43 52.3	−59.5	2.7	44 52.2	−59.5	2.8	45 52.1	−59.4	2.8	46 52.1	−59.5	2.9	47 52.0	−59.5	2.9	48 51.9	−59.4	3.0	71
72	40 52.9	−59.5	2.4	41 52.9	−59.6	2.5	42 52.8	−59.5	2.5	43 52.7	−59.5	2.6	44 52.7	−59.5	2.6	45 52.6	−59.5	2.7	46 52.5	−59.4	2.7	47 52.5	−59.5	2.8	72
73	39 53.4	−59.5	2.3	40 53.3	−59.5	2.3	41 53.3	−59.5	2.4	42 53.2	−59.5	2.4	43 53.2	−59.5	2.4	44 53.1	−59.5	2.5	45 53.1	−59.5	2.5	46 53.0	−59.5	2.6	73
74	38 53.9	−59.6	2.1	39 53.8	−59.5	2.2	40 53.8	−59.6	2.2	41 53.7	−59.5	2.2	42 53.7	−59.5	2.3	43 53.6	−59.5	2.3	44 53.6	−59.5	2.3	45 53.5	−59.5	2.4	74
75	37 54.3	−59.5	2.0	38 54.3	−59.6	2.0	39 54.2	−59.5	2.0	40 54.2	−59.5	2.1	41 54.2	−59.6	2.1	42 54.1	−59.5	2.1	43 54.1	−59.5	2.2	44 54.0	−59.5	2.2	75
76	36 54.8	−59.6	1.8	37 54.7	−59.5	1.8	38 54.7	−59.6	1.9	39 54.7	−59.6	1.9	40 54.6	−59.5	1.9	41 54.6	−59.6	1.9	42 54.6	−59.6	2.0	43 54.5	−59.5	2.0	76
77	35 55.2	−59.6	1.7	36 55.2	−59.6	1.7	37 55.1	−59.5	1.7	38 55.1	−59.6	1.7	39 55.1	−59.6	1.8	40 55.0	−59.5	1.8	41 55.0	−59.5	1.8	42 55.0	−59.6	1.8	77
78	34 55.6	−59.6	1.5	35 55.6	−59.6	1.5	36 55.6	−59.6	1.6	37 55.5	−59.5	1.6	38 55.5	−59.6	1.6	39 55.5	−59.6	1.6	40 55.5	−59.6	1.6	41 55.4	−59.5	1.7	78
79	33 56.0	−59.6	1.4	34 56.0	−59.6	1.4	35 56.0	−59.6	1.4	36 56.0	−59.6	1.4	37 55.9	−59.5	1.4	38 55.9	−59.6	1.5	39 55.9	−59.6	1.5	40 55.9	−59.6	1.5	79
80	32 56.4	−59.6	1.2	33 56.4	−59.6	1.3	34 56.4	−59.6	1.3	35 56.4	−59.6	1.3	36 56.4	−59.6	1.3	37 56.3	−59.6	1.3	38 56.3	−59.6	1.3	39 56.3	−59.6	1.4	80
81	31 56.8	−59.6	1.1	32 56.8	−59.6	1.1	33 56.8	−59.6	1.1	34 56.8	−59.6	1.1	35 56.8	−59.7	1.2	36 56.7	−59.6	1.2	37 56.7	−59.6	1.2	38 56.7	−59.6	1.2	81
82	30 57.2	−59.6	1.0	31 57.2	−59.6	1.0	32 57.2	−59.7	1.0	33 57.2	−59.7	1.0	34 57.1	−59.6	1.0	35 57.1	−59.6	1.0	36 57.1	−59.6	1.0	37 57.1	−59.6	1.1	82
83	29 57.6	−59.7	0.8	30 57.6	−59.7	0.9	31 57.5	−59.6	0.9	32 57.5	−59.6	0.9	33 57.5	−59.6	0.9	34 57.5	−59.6	0.9	35 57.5	−59.6	0.9	36 57.5	−59.6	0.9	83
84	28 57.9	−59.6	0.7	29 57.9	−59.6	0.7	30 57.9	−59.6	0.7	31 57.9	−59.6	0.7	32 57.9	−59.6	0.7	33 57.9	−59.6	0.8	34 57.9	−59.6	0.8	35 57.9	−59.6	0.8	84
85	27 58.3	−59.7	0.6	28 58.3	−59.7	0.6	29 58.3	−59.7	0.6	30 58.3	−59.7	0.6	31 58.3	−59.7	0.6	32 58.3	−59.7	0.6	33 58.3	−59.7	0.6	34 58.3	−59.7	0.6	85
86	26 58.6	−59.6	0.5	27 58.6	−59.6	0.5	28 58.6	−59.6	0.5	29 58.6	−59.6	0.5	30 58.6	−59.6	0.5	31 58.6	−59.6	0.5	32 58.6	−59.6	0.5	33 58.6	−59.6	0.5	86
87	25 59.0	−59.7	0.3	26 59.0	−59.7	0.4	27 59.0	−59.7	0.4	28 59.0	−59.7	0.4	29 59.0	−59.7	0.4	30 59.0	−59.7	0.4	31 59.0	−59.7	0.4	32 59.0	−59.7	0.4	87
88	24 59.3	−59.6	0.2	25 59.3	−59.6	0.2	26 59.3	−59.6	0.2	27 59.3	−59.6	0.2	28 59.3	−59.6	0.2	29 59.3	−59.6	0.2	30 59.3	−59.6	0.2	31 59.3	−59.6	0.2	88
89	23 59.7	−59.7	0.1	24 59.7	−59.7	0.1	25 59.7	−59.7	0.1	26 59.7	−59.7	0.1	27 59.7	−59.7	0.1	28 59.7	−59.7	0.1	29 59.7	−59.7	0.1	30 59.7	−59.7	0.1	89
90	23 00.0	−59.7	0.0	24 00.0	−59.7	0.0	25 00.0	−59.7	0.0	26 00.0	−59.7	0.0	27 00.0	−59.7	0.0	28 00.0	−59.7	0.0	29 00.0	−59.7	0.0	30 00.0	−59.7	0.0	90
	23°			24°			25°			26°			27°			28°			29°			30°			

6°, 354° L.H.A. LATITUDE SAME NAME AS DECLINATION

196

Dec.	23° Hc	d	Z	24° Hc	d	Z	25° Hc	d	Z	26° Hc	d	Z	27° Hc	d	Z	28° Hc	d	Z	29° Hc	d	Z	30° Hc	d	Z	Dec.
°	° ′	′	°	° ′	′	°	° ′	′	°	° ′	′	°	° ′	′	°	° ′	′	°	° ′	′	°	° ′	′	°	°
0	66 16.3	−58.3	164.9	65 18.3	−58.5	165.5	64 20.1	−58.6	166.0	63 21.8	−58.7	166.5	62 23.4	−58.8	167.0	61 24.9	−58.9	167.4	60 26.3	−59.0	167.8	59 27.6	−59.0	168.1	0
1	65 18.0	−58.5	165.5	64 19.8	−58.6	166.0	63 21.5	−58.7	166.5	62 23.1	−58.8	167.0	61 24.6	−58.9	167.4	60 26.0	−59.0	167.8	59 27.3	−59.0	168.1	58 28.6	−59.1	168.5	1
2	64 19.5	−58.5	166.0	63 21.2	−58.6	166.5	62 22.8	−58.8	167.0	61 24.3	−58.9	167.4	60 25.7	−58.9	167.8	59 27.0	−59.0	168.1	58 28.3	−59.1	168.5	57 29.5	−59.2	168.8	2
3	63 21.0	−58.7	166.5	62 22.6	−58.8	167.0	61 24.0	−58.8	167.4	60 25.4	−58.9	167.8	59 26.8	−59.0	168.2	58 28.0	−59.1	168.5	57 29.2	−59.2	168.8	56 30.3	−59.2	169.1	3
4	62 22.3	−58.7	167.0	61 23.8	−58.8	167.4	60 25.2	−58.9	167.8	59 26.5	−59.0	168.2	58 27.8	−59.1	168.5	57 28.9	−59.1	168.8	56 30.0	−59.2	169.1	55 31.1	−59.3	169.4	4
5	61 23.6	−58.8	167.4	60 25.0	−58.9	167.8	59 26.3	−59.0	168.2	58 27.5	−59.0	168.5	57 28.7	−59.1	168.8	56 29.8	−59.2	169.1	55 30.8	−59.2	169.4	54 31.8	−59.2	169.7	5
6	60 24.8	−58.9	167.8	59 26.1	−59.0	168.2	58 27.3	−59.0	168.5	57 28.5	−59.1	168.9	56 29.6	−59.2	169.1	55 30.6	−59.2	169.4	54 31.6	−59.3	169.7	53 32.6	−59.4	169.9	6
7	59 25.9	−59.0	168.2	58 27.1	−59.0	168.6	57 28.3	−59.1	168.9	56 29.4	−59.2	169.2	55 30.4	−59.2	169.4	54 31.4	−59.3	169.7	53 32.3	−59.3	169.9	52 33.2	−59.3	170.2	7
8	58 26.9	−59.0	168.6	57 28.1	−59.1	168.9	56 29.2	−59.2	169.2	55 30.2	−59.2	169.5	54 31.2	−59.2	169.7	53 32.1	−59.2	170.0	52 33.0	−59.3	170.2	51 33.9	−59.4	170.4	8
9	57 27.9	−59.0	168.9	56 29.0	−59.1	169.2	55 30.0	−59.1	169.5	54 31.0	−59.2	169.8	53 32.0	−59.3	170.0	52 32.9	−59.4	170.2	51 33.7	−59.4	170.4	50 34.5	−59.4	170.6	9
10	56 28.9	−59.1	169.3	55 29.9	−59.2	169.5	54 30.9	−59.2	169.8	53 31.8	−59.3	170.0	52 32.7	−59.3	170.3	51 33.5	−59.3	170.5	50 34.3	−59.3	170.7	49 35.1	−59.4	170.9	10
11	55 29.8	−59.2	169.6	54 30.7	−59.2	169.8	53 31.7	−59.3	170.1	52 32.5	−59.3	170.3	51 33.4	−59.4	170.5	50 34.2	−59.4	170.7	49 35.0	−59.5	170.9	48 35.7	−59.5	171.1	11
12	54 30.6	−59.2	169.9	53 31.5	−59.2	170.1	52 32.4	−59.3	170.3	51 33.2	−59.3	170.5	50 34.0	−59.3	170.7	49 34.8	−59.4	170.9	48 35.5	−59.4	171.1	47 36.2	−59.4	171.3	12
13	53 31.4	−59.2	170.1	52 32.3	−59.3	170.4	51 33.1	−59.3	170.6	50 33.9	−59.3	170.8	49 34.7	−59.4	171.0	48 35.4	−59.4	171.1	47 36.1	−59.4	171.3	46 36.8	−59.5	171.5	13
14	52 32.2	−59.3	170.4	51 33.0	−59.3	170.6	50 33.8	−59.3	170.8	49 34.6	−59.4	171.0	48 35.3	−59.4	171.2	47 36.0	−59.5	171.3	46 36.7	−59.5	171.5	45 37.3	−59.5	171.7	14
15	51 32.9	−59.3	170.7	50 33.7	−59.3	170.9	49 34.5	−59.4	171.0	48 35.2	−59.4	171.2	47 35.9	−59.5	171.4	46 36.5	−59.4	171.5	45 37.2	−59.5	171.7	44 37.8	−59.5	171.8	15
16	50 33.6	−59.3	170.9	49 34.4	−59.4	171.1	48 35.1	−59.4	171.3	47 35.8	−59.4	171.4	46 36.4	−59.4	171.6	45 37.1	−59.5	171.7	44 37.7	−59.5	171.9	43 38.3	−59.6	172.0	16
17	49 34.3	−59.3	171.1	48 35.0	−59.4	171.3	47 35.7	−59.4	171.5	46 36.4	−59.5	171.6	45 37.0	−59.5	171.8	44 37.6	−59.5	171.9	43 38.2	−59.6	172.1	42 38.7	−59.5	172.2	17
18	48 35.0	−59.4	171.4	47 35.6	−59.4	171.5	46 36.3	−59.5	171.7	45 36.9	−59.5	171.8	44 37.5	−59.5	172.0	43 38.1	−59.5	172.1	42 38.6	−59.5	172.2	41 39.2	−59.6	172.4	18
19	47 35.6	−59.4	171.6	46 36.2	−59.4	171.7	45 36.8	−59.4	171.9	44 37.4	−59.4	172.0	43 38.0	−59.5	172.2	42 38.6	−59.6	172.3	41 39.1	−59.6	172.4	40 39.6	−59.6	172.5	19
20	46 36.2	−59.4	171.8	45 36.8	−59.4	171.9	44 37.4	−59.5	172.1	43 38.0	−59.5	172.2	42 38.5	−59.5	172.3	41 39.0	−59.5	172.4	40 39.5	−59.5	172.6	39 40.0	−59.5	172.7	20
21	45 36.8	−59.5	172.0	44 37.4	−59.5	172.1	43 37.9	−59.5	172.3	42 38.5	−59.6	172.4	41 39.0	−59.6	172.5	40 39.5	−59.6	172.6	39 40.0	−59.6	172.7	38 40.5	−59.6	172.8	21
22	44 37.3	−59.4	172.2	43 37.9	−59.5	172.3	42 38.4	−59.5	172.4	41 38.9	−59.5	172.5	40 39.4	−59.5	172.7	39 39.9	−59.5	172.8	38 40.4	−59.6	172.9	37 40.9	−59.7	173.0	22
23	43 37.9	−59.5	172.4	42 38.4	−59.5	172.5	41 38.9	−59.5	172.6	40 39.4	−59.5	172.7	39 39.9	−59.6	172.8	38 40.4	−59.6	172.9	37 40.8	−59.6	173.0	36 41.2	−59.6	173.1	23
24	42 38.4	−59.5	172.5	41 38.9	−59.5	172.7	40 39.4	−59.5	172.8	39 39.9	−59.6	172.9	38 40.3	−59.6	173.0	37 40.8	−59.6	173.1	36 41.2	−59.6	173.2	35 41.6	−59.6	173.2	24
25	41 38.9	−59.5	172.7	40 39.4	−59.5	172.8	39 39.9	−59.6	172.9	38 40.3	−59.6	173.0	37 40.7	−59.5	173.1	36 41.2	−59.6	173.2	35 41.6	−59.6	173.3	34 42.0	−59.7	173.4	25
26	40 39.4	−59.5	172.9	39 39.9	−59.6	173.0	38 40.3	−59.6	173.1	37 40.7	−59.5	173.2	36 41.2	−59.6	173.3	35 41.6	−59.7	173.4	34 42.0	−59.7	173.4	33 42.3	−59.6	173.5	26
27	39 39.9	−59.5	173.1	38 40.3	−59.5	173.1	37 40.7	−59.5	173.2	36 41.2	−59.6	173.3	35 41.6	−59.7	173.4	34 41.9	−59.6	173.5	33 42.3	−59.6	173.6	32 42.7	−59.7	173.6	27
28	38 40.4	−59.6	173.2	37 40.8	−59.6	173.3	36 41.2	−59.6	173.4	35 41.6	−59.6	173.5	34 41.9	−59.6	173.6	33 42.3	−59.6	173.6	32 42.7	−59.7	173.7	31 43.0	−59.6	173.8	28
29	37 40.8	−59.6	173.4	36 41.2	−59.6	173.5	35 41.6	−59.6	173.5	34 42.0	−59.7	173.6	33 42.3	−59.6	173.7	32 42.7	−59.7	173.8	31 43.0	−59.6	173.8	30 43.4	−59.7	173.9	29
30	36 41.2	−59.5	173.5	35 41.6	−59.6	173.6	34 42.0	−59.6	173.7	33 42.3	−59.6	173.8	32 42.7	−59.6	173.8	31 43.0	−59.6	173.9	30 43.4	−59.7	174.0	29 43.7	−59.7	174.0	30
31	35 41.7	−59.6	173.7	34 42.0	−59.6	173.7	33 42.4	−59.6	173.8	32 42.7	−59.6	173.9	31 43.1	−59.7	174.0	30 43.4	−59.7	174.0	29 43.7	−59.7	174.1	28 44.0	−59.6	174.1	31
32	34 42.1	−59.6	173.8	33 42.4	−59.6	173.9	32 42.8	−59.7	174.0	31 43.1	−59.6	174.0	30 43.4	−59.6	174.1	29 43.7	−59.6	174.1	28 44.0	−59.6	174.2	27 44.4	−59.7	174.3	32
33	33 42.5	−59.6	174.0	32 42.8	−59.6	174.0	31 43.1	−59.6	174.1	30 43.5	−59.7	174.1	29 43.8	−59.7	174.2	28 44.1	−59.7	174.3	27 44.4	−59.7	174.3	26 44.7	−59.7	174.4	33
34	32 42.9	−59.6	174.1	31 43.2	−59.6	174.2	30 43.5	−59.6	174.2	29 43.8	−59.6	174.3	28 44.1	−59.6	174.3	27 44.4	−59.7	174.4	26 44.7	−59.7	174.4	25 45.0	−59.7	174.5	34
35	31 43.3	−59.6	174.2	30 43.6	−59.7	174.3	29 43.9	−59.7	174.3	28 44.2	−59.7	174.4	27 44.5	−59.7	174.4	26 44.7	−59.7	174.5	25 45.0	−59.7	174.5	24 45.3	−59.7	174.6	35
36	30 43.7	−59.7	174.4	29 43.9	−59.6	174.4	28 44.2	−59.6	174.5	27 44.5	−59.7	174.5	26 44.8	−59.7	174.6	25 45.0	−59.6	174.6	24 45.3	−59.7	174.7	23 45.6	−59.7	174.7	36
37	29 44.0	−59.6	174.5	28 44.3	−59.6	174.5	27 44.6	−59.7	174.6	26 44.8	−59.6	174.6	25 45.1	−59.7	174.7	24 45.4	−59.7	174.7	23 45.6	−59.7	174.8	22 45.9	−59.7	174.8	37
38	28 44.4	−59.6	174.6	27 44.7	−59.7	174.7	26 44.9	−59.6	174.7	25 45.2	−59.7	174.8	24 45.4	−59.7	174.8	23 45.7	−59.7	174.8	22 45.9	−59.7	174.9	21 46.2	−59.8	174.9	38
39	27 44.8	−59.7	174.7	26 45.0	−59.6	174.8	25 45.3	−59.7	174.8	24 45.5	−59.7	174.9	23 45.7	−59.7	174.9	22 46.0	−59.7	174.9	21 46.2	−59.7	175.0	20 46.4	−59.7	175.0	39
40	26 45.1	−59.6	174.9	25 45.4	−59.7	174.9	24 45.6	−59.7	174.9	23 45.8	−59.7	175.0	22 46.0	−59.6	175.0	21 46.3	−59.7	175.1	20 46.5	−59.7	175.1	19 46.7	−59.7	175.1	40
41	25 45.5	−59.7	175.0	24 45.7	−59.7	175.0	23 45.9	−59.7	175.1	22 46.1	−59.7	175.1	21 46.4	−59.7	175.1	20 46.6	−59.7	175.2	19 46.8	−59.7	175.2	18 47.0	−59.7	175.2	41
42	24 45.8	−59.7	175.1	23 46.0	−59.7	175.1	22 46.2	−59.7	175.2	21 46.4	−59.7	175.2	20 46.7	−59.8	175.2	19 46.9	−59.8	175.3	18 47.1	−59.8	175.3	17 47.3	−59.8	175.3	42
43	23 46.1	−59.6	175.2	22 46.3	−59.6	175.2	21 46.5	−59.6	175.3	20 46.7	−59.6	175.3	19 46.9	−59.7	175.3	18 47.1	−59.7	175.4	17 47.3	−59.7	175.4	16 47.5	−59.7	175.4	43
44	22 46.5	−59.7	175.3	21 46.7	−59.7	175.4	20 46.9	−59.7	175.4	19 47.1	−59.8	175.4	18 47.2	−59.7	175.4	17 47.4	−59.7	175.5	16 47.6	−59.7	175.5	15 47.8	−59.7	175.5	44
45	21 46.8	−59.7	175.4	20 47.0	−59.7	175.5	19 47.2	−59.7	175.5	18 47.3	−59.7	175.5	17 47.5	−59.7	175.5	16 47.7	−59.7	175.6	15 47.9	−59.7	175.6	14 48.1	−59.8	175.6	45
46	20 47.1	−59.7	175.5	19 47.3	−59.7	175.6	18 47.5	−59.7	175.6	17 47.6	−59.7	175.6	16 47.8	−59.7	175.7	15 48.0	−59.7	175.7	14 48.2	−59.8	175.7	13 48.3	−59.7	175.7	46
47	19 47.4	−59.7	175.7	18 47.6	−59.7	175.7	17 47.8	−59.7	175.7	16 47.9	−59.7	175.7	15 48.1	−59.7	175.8	14 48.3	−59.8	175.8	13 48.4	−59.7	175.8	12 48.6	−59.8	175.8	47
48	18 47.7	−59.7	175.8	17 47.9	−59.7	175.8	16 48.1	−59.7	175.8	15 48.2	−59.7	175.8	14 48.4	−59.7	175.9	13 48.5	−59.7	175.9	12 48.7	−59.7	175.9	11 48.8	−59.7	175.9	48
49	17 48.0	−59.6	175.9	16 48.2	−59.7	175.9	15 48.4	−59.8	175.9	14 48.5	−59.7	175.9	13 48.7	−59.8	176.0	12 48.8	−59.7	176.0	11 49.0	−59.8	176.0	10 49.1	−59.7	176.0	49
50	16 48.4	−59.7	176.0	15 48.5	−59.7	176.0	14 48.6	−59.7	176.0	13 48.8	−59.7	176.0	12 48.9	−59.7	176.0	11 49.1	−59.8	176.1	10 49.2	−59.7	176.1	9 49.4	−59.8	176.1	50
51	15 48.7	−59.7	176.1	14 48.8	−59.7	176.1	13 48.9	−59.7	176.1	12 49.1	−59.8	176.1	11 49.2	−59.8	176.1	10 49.3	−59.7	176.2	9 49.5	−59.8	176.2	8 49.6	−59.7	176.2	51
52	14 49.0	−59.7	176.2	13 49.1	−59.7	176.2	12 49.2	−59.7	176.2	11 49.3	−59.7	176.2	10 49.5	−59.8	176.2	9 49.6	−59.7	176.3	8 49.7	−59.7	176.3	7 49.9	−59.8	176.3	52
53	13 49.3	−59.8	176.3	12 49.4	−59.8	176.3	11 49.5	−59.7	176.3	10 49.6	−59.7	176.3	9 49.7	−59.7	176.3	8 49.9	−59.8	176.3	7 50.0	−59.8	176.4	6 50.1	−59.7	176.4	53
54	12 49.5	−59.7	176.4	11 49.7	−59.7	176.4	10 49.8	−59.7	176.4	9 49.9	−59.7	176.4	8 50.0	−59.7	176.4	7 50.1	−59.7	176.5	6 50.2	−59.7	176.5	5 50.4	−59.8	176.5	54
55	11 49.8	−59.7	176.5	10 50.0	−59.8	176.5	9 50.1	−59.8	176.5	8 50.2	−59.8	176.5	7 50.3	−59.8	176.5	6 50.4	−59.7	176.5	5 50.5	−59.7	176.5	4 50.6	−59.7	176.6	55
56	10 50.1	−59.7	176.6	9 50.2	−59.7	176.6	8 50.3	−59.7	176.6	7 50.4	−59.7	176.6	6 50.5	−59.7	176.6	5 50.7	−59.8	176.6	4 50.8	−59.8	176.6	3 50.9	−59.8	176.6	56
57	9 50.4	−59.7	176.7	8 50.5	−59.7	176.7	7 50.6	−59.7	176.7	6 50.7	−59.7	176.7	5 50.8	−59.7	176.7	4 50.9	−59.7	176.7	3 51.0	−59.7	176.7	2 51.1	−59.7	176.7	57
58	8 50.7	−59.7	176.8	7 50.8	−59.7	176.8	6 50.9	−59.7	176.8	5 51.0	−59.8	176.8	4 51.1	−59.8	176.8	3 51.2	−59.8	176.8	2 51.3	−59.8	176.8	1 51.4	−59.8	176.8	58
59	7 51.0	−59.7	176.9	6 51.1	−59.7	176.9	5 51.2	−59.8	176.9	4 51.2	−59.7	176.9	3 51.3	−59.7	176.9	2 51.4	−59.7	176.9	1 51.5	−59.7	176.9	0 51.6	−59.8	176.9	59
60	6 51.3	−59.7	177.0	5 51.4	−59.8	177.0	4 51.4	−59.7	177.0	3 51.5	−59.7	177.0	2 51.6	−59.7	177.0	1 51.7	−59.8	177.0	0 51.8	−59.8	177.0	0 08.2	+59.7	3.0	60
61	5 51.6	−59.8	177.1	4 51.6	−59.7	177.1	3 51.7	−59.7	177.1	2 51.8	−59.8	177.1	1 51.9	−59.8	177.1	0 51.9	−59.7	177.1	0 08.0	+59.7	2.9	1 07.9	+59.8	2.9	61
62	4 51.8	−59.7	177.2	3 51.9	−59.7	177.2	2 52.0	−59.8	177.2	1 52.0	−59.7	177.2	0 52.1	−59.7	177.2	0 07.8	+59.8	2.8	1 07.7	+59.8	2.8	2 07.7	+59.7	2.8	62
63	3 52.1	−59.7	177.3	2 52.2	−59.7	177.3	1 52.2	−59.7	177.3	0 52.3	−59.7	177.3	0 07.6	+59.8	2.7	1 07.6	+59.7	2.7	2 07.5	+59.7	2.7	3 07.4	+59.8	2.7	63
64	2 52.4	−59.7	177.4	1 52.5	−59.8	177.4	0 52.5	−59.7	177.4	0 07.4	+59.8	2.6	1 07.4	+59.7	2.6	2 07.3	+59.7	2.6	3 07.2	+59.8	2.6	4 07.2	+59.7	2.6	64
65	1 52.7	−59.8	177.5	0 52.7	−59.7	177.5	0 07.2	+59.7	2.5	1 07.2	+59.7	2.5	2 07.1	+59.7	2.5	3 07.0	+59.8	2.5	4 07.0	+59.7	2.5	5 06.9	+59.8	2.5	65
66	0 52.9	−59.7	177.6	0 07.0	+59.7	2.4	1 06.9	+59.8	2.4	2 06.9	+59.7	2.4	3 06.8	+59.8	2.4	4 06.8	+59.7	2.4	5 06.7	+59.8	2.4	6 06.7	+59.7	2.5	66
67	0 06.8	+59.7	2.3	1 06.7	+59.7	2.3	2 06.7	+59.7	2.3	3 06.6	+59.8	2.3	4 06.6	+59.7	2.3	5 06.5	+59.8	2.4	6 06.5	+59.7	2.4	7 06.4	+59.8	2.4	67
68	1 06.5	+59.7	2.2	2 06.4	+59.8	2.2	3 06.4	+59.7	2.2	4 06.4	+59.7	2.2	5 06.3	+59.7	2.3	6 06.3	+59.7	2.3	7 06.2	+59.8	2.3	8 06.2	+59.7	2.3	68
69	2 06.2	+59.7	2.1	3 06.2	+59.7	2.1	4 06.1	+59.8	2.2	5 06.1	+59.7	2.2	6 06.0	+59.8	2.2	7 06.0	+59.7	2.2	8 06.0	+59.7	2.2	9 05.9	+59.8	2.2	69
70	3 05.9	+59.8	2.1	4 05.9	+59.7	2.1	5 05.9	+59.7	2.1	6 05.8	+59.8	2.1	7 05.8	+59.7	2.1	8 05.7	+59.8	2.1	9 05.7	+59.7	2.1	10 05.7	+59.7	2.1	70
71	4 05.7	+59.7	2.0	5 05.6	+59.7	2.0	6 05.6	+59.7	2.0	7 05.6	+59.7	2.0	8 05.5	+59.8	2.0	9 05.5	+59.7	2.0	10 05.4	+59.8	2.0	11 05.4	+59.8	2.0	71
72	5 05.4	+59.7	1.9	6 05.3	+59.8	1.9	7 05.3	+59.7	1.9	8 05.3	+59.7	1.9	9 05.3	+59.7	1.9	10 05.2	+59.8	1.9	11 05.2	+59.7	1.9	12 05.2	+59.7	1.9	72
73	6 05.1	+59.7	1.8	7 05.1	+59.7	1.8	8 05.0	+59.8	1.8	9 05.0	+59.7	1.8	10 05.0	+59.7	1.8	11 05.0	+59.7	1.8	12 04.9	+59.8	1.8	13 04.9	+59.7	1.8	73
74	7 04.8	+59.7	1.7	8 04.8	+59.7	1.7	9 04.8	+59.7	1.7	10 04.7	+59.8	1.7	11 04.7	+59.7	1.7	12 04.7	+59.7	1.7	13 04.7	+59.7	1.7	14 04.6	+59.8	1.7	74
75	8 04.5	+59.7	1.6	9 04.5	+59.7	1.6	10 04.5	+59.7	1.6	11 04.5	+59.7	1.6	12 04.4	+59.8	1.6	13 04.4	+59.7	1.6	14 04.4	+59.7	1.6	15 04.4	+59.7	1.6	75
76	9 04.2	+59.8	1.5	10 04.2	+59.7	1.5	11 04.2	+59.7	1.5	12 04.2	+59.7	1.5	13 04.2	+59.7	1.5	14 04.1	+59.8	1.5	15 04.1	+59.8	1.5	16 04.1	+59.7	1.5	76
77	10 04.0	+59.7	1.4	11 03.9	+59.8	1.4	12 03.9	+59.7	1.4	13 03.9	+59.7	1.4	14 03.9	+59.7	1.4	15 03.9	+59.7	1.4	16 03.9	+59.7	1.4	17 03.8	+59.8	1.4	77
78	11 03.7	+59.7	1.3	12 03.7	+59.7	1.3	13 03.6	+59.8	1.3	14 03.6	+59.7	1.3	15 03.6	+59.7	1.3	16 03.6	+59.7	1.3	17 03.6	+59.7	1.3	18 03.6	+59.7	1.3	78
79	12 03.4	+59.7	1.2	13 03.4	+59.7	1.2	14 03.4	+59.7	1.2	15 03.3	+59.8	1.2	16 03.3	+59.7	1.2	17 03.3	+59.7	1.2	18 03.3	+59.7	1.2	19 03.3	+59.7	1.2	79
80	13 03.1	+59.7	1.1	14 03.1	+59.7	1.1	15 03.1	+59.7	1.1	16 03.1	+59.7	1.1	17 03.0	+59.8	1.1	18 03.0	+59.8	1.1	19 03.0	+59.7	1.1	20 03.0	+59.7	1.1	80
81	14 02.8	+59.7	1.0	15 02.8	+59.7	1.0	16 02.8	+59.7	1.0	17 02.8	+59.7	1.0	18 02.8	+59.7	1.0	19 02.8	+59.7	1.0	20 02.7	+59.8	1.0	21 02.7	+59.7	1.0	81
82	15 02.5	+59.7	0.9	16 02.5	+59.7	0.9	17 02.5	+59.7	0.9	18 02.5	+59.7	0.9	19 02.5	+59.7	0.9	20 02.5	+59.7	0.9	21 02.5	+59.7	0.9	22 02.4	+59.8	0.9	82
83	16 02.2	+59.7	0.8	17 02.2	+59.7	0.8	18 02.2	+59.7	0.8	19 02.2	+59.7	0.8	20 02.2	+59.7	0.8	21 02.2	+59.7	0.8	22 02.2	+59.7	0.8	23 02.2	+59.7	0.8	83
84	17 01.9	+59.7	0.7	18 01.9	+59.7	0.7	19 01.9	+59.7	0.7	20 01.9	+59.7	0.7	21 01.9	+59.7	0.7	22 01.9	+59.7	0.7	23 01.9	+59.7	0.7	24 01.9	+59.7	0.7	84
85	18 01.6	+59.7	0.5	19 01.6	+59.7	0.6	20 01.6	+59.7	0.6	21 01.6	+59.7	0.6	22 01.6	+59.7	0.6	23 01.6	+59.7	0.6	24 01.6	+59.7	0.6	25 01.6	+59.7	0.6	85
86	19 01.3	+59.7	0.4	20 01.3	+59.7	0.4	21 01.3	+59.7	0.4	22 01.3	+59.7	0.5	23 01.3	+59.7	0.5	24 01.3	+59.7	0.5	25 01.3	+59.7	0.5	26 01.3	+59.7	0.5	86
87	20 01.0	+59.6	0.3	21 01.0	+59.6	0.3	22 01.0	+59.6	0.3	23 01.0	+59.6	0.3	24 01.0	+59.6	0.3	25 01.0	+59.6	0.3	26 01.0	+59.6	0.3	27 01.0	+59.6	0.4	87
88	21 00.6	+59.7	0.2	22 00.6	+59.7	0.2	23 00.6	+59.7	0.2	24 00.6	+59.7	0.2	25 00.6	+59.7	0.2	26 00.6	+59.7	0.2	27 00.6	+59.7	0.2	28 00.6	+59.7	0.2	88
89	22 00.3	+59.7	0.1	23 00.3	+59.7	0.1	24 00.3	+59.7	0.1	25 00.3	+59.7	0.1	26 00.3	+59.7	0.1	27 00.3	+59.7	0.1	28 00.3	+59.7	0.1	29 00.3	+59.7	0.1	89
90	23 00.0	+59.7	0.0	24 00.0	+59.7	0.0	25 00.0	+59.7	0.0	26 00.0	+59.7	0.0	27 00.0	+59.7	0.0	28 00.0	+59.7	0.0	29 00.0	+59.7	0.0	30 00.0	+59.7	0.0	90
	23°			24°			25°			26°			27°			28°			29°			30°			

S. Lat. {L.H.A. greater than 180° ....Zn=180°−Z; L.H.A. less than 180°...........Zn=180°+Z}

7°, 353° L.H.A. LATITUDE SAME NAME AS DECLINATION N. Lat. {L.H.A. greater than 180° .....Zn=Z / L.H.A. less than 180°............Zn=360°−Z}

Dec.	23° Hc	d	Z	24° Hc	d	Z	25° Hc	d	Z	26° Hc	d	Z	27° Hc	d	Z	28° Hc	d	Z	29° Hc	d	Z	30° Hc	d	Z	Dec.
°	° ′	′	°	° ′	′	°	° ′	′	°	° ′	′	°	° ′	′	°	° ′	′	°	° ′	′	°	° ′	′	°	°
0	66 00.8	+57.6	162.6	65 03.5	+57.8	163.2	64 06.0	+57.9	163.8	63 08.3	+58.1	164.4	62 10.4	+58.3	164.9	61 12.4	+58.5	165.3	60 14.3	+58.6	165.8	59 16.1	+58.7	166.2	0
1	66 58.4	+57.4	161.8	66 01.3	+57.6	162.6	65 03.9	+57.9	163.2	64 06.4	+58.0	163.8	63 08.7	+58.2	164.4	62 10.9	+58.3	164.9	61 12.9	+58.4	165.3	60 14.8	+58.6	165.8	1
2	67 55.8	+57.1	161.1	66 58.9	+57.4	161.9	66 01.8	+57.6	162.6	65 04.4	+57.9	163.2	64 06.9	+58.0	163.8	63 09.2	+58.2	164.4	62 11.3	+58.4	164.9	61 13.4	+58.4	165.3	2
3	68 52.9	+56.9	160.3	67 56.3	+57.2	161.1	66 59.4	+57.5	161.9	66 02.3	+57.7	162.6	65 04.9	+57.9	163.2	64 07.4	+58.1	163.8	63 09.7	+58.2	164.4	62 11.8	+58.4	164.9	3
4	69 49.8	+56.6	159.4	68 53.5	+56.9	160.3	67 56.9	+57.2	161.1	67 00.0	+57.5	161.9	66 02.8	+57.8	162.6	65 05.5	+57.9	163.2	64 07.9	+58.2	163.8	63 10.2	+58.3	164.4	4
5	70 46.4	+56.2	158.4	69 50.4	+56.6	159.4	68 54.1	+57.0	160.3	67 57.5	+57.2	161.1	67 00.6	+57.5	161.9	66 03.4	+57.8	162.6	65 06.1	+57.9	163.2	64 08.5	+58.2	163.8	5
6	71 42.6	+55.8	157.3	70 47.0	+56.3	158.4	69 51.1	+56.6	159.4	68 54.7	+57.0	160.3	67 58.1	+57.3	161.1	67 01.2	+57.6	161.9	66 04.0	+57.8	162.6	65 06.7	+58.0	163.3	6
7	72 38.4	+55.4	156.1	71 43.3	+55.9	157.3	70 47.7	+56.4	158.4	69 51.7	+56.8	159.4	68 55.4	+57.1	160.3	67 58.8	+57.3	161.2	67 01.8	+57.7	161.9	66 04.7	+57.8	162.6	7
8	73 33.8	+54.8	154.8	72 39.2	+55.4	156.1	71 44.1	+55.9	157.4	70 48.5	+56.4	158.5	69 52.5	+56.8	159.5	68 56.1	+57.1	160.4	67 59.5	+57.4	161.2	67 02.5	+57.7	162.0	8
9	74 28.6	+54.1	153.3	73 34.6	+54.9	154.8	72 40.0	+55.5	156.2	71 44.9	+56.0	157.4	70 49.3	+56.4	158.5	69 53.2	+56.9	159.5	68 56.9	+57.1	160.4	68 00.2	+57.5	161.3	9
10	75 22.7	+53.3	151.6	74 29.5	+54.2	153.3	73 35.5	+54.9	154.9	72 40.9	+55.5	156.2	71 45.7	+56.1	157.5	70 50.1	+56.5	158.6	69 54.0	+56.9	159.6	68 57.7	+57.2	160.5	10
11	76 16.0	+52.4	149.7	75 23.7	+53.4	151.7	74 30.4	+54.3	153.4	73 36.4	+55.0	154.9	72 41.8	+55.6	156.3	71 46.6	+56.1	157.5	70 50.9	+56.6	158.6	69 54.9	+56.9	159.6	11
12	77 08.4	+51.2	147.6	76 17.1	+52.5	149.8	75 24.7	+53.5	151.8	74 31.4	+54.4	153.5	73 37.4	+55.1	155.0	72 42.7	+55.7	156.4	71 47.5	+56.2	157.6	70 51.8	+56.7	158.7	12
13	77 59.6	+49.7	145.2	77 09.6	+51.3	147.7	76 18.2	+52.6	149.9	75 25.8	+53.6	151.8	74 32.5	+54.5	153.5	73 38.4	+55.2	155.1	72 43.7	+55.8	156.4	71 48.5	+56.2	157.6	13
14	78 49.3	+48.0	142.4	78 00.9	+49.9	145.3	77 10.8	+51.4	147.8	76 19.4	+52.7	150.0	75 27.0	+53.7	151.9	74 33.6	+54.6	153.6	73 39.5	+55.2	155.1	72 44.7	+55.9	156.5	14
15	79 37.3	+45.8	•139.2	78 50.8	+48.1	•142.5	78 02.2	+50.1	145.4	77 12.1	+51.6	147.9	76 20.7	+52.8	150.1	75 28.2	+53.8	152.0	74 34.7	+54.7	153.7	73 40.6	+55.3	155.2	15
16	80 23.1	+42.9	•135.5	79 38.9	+45.9	•139.3	78 52.3	+48.2	•142.6	78 03.7	+50.1	145.5	77 13.5	+51.6	148.0	76 22.0	+52.9	150.2	75 29.4	+53.9	152.1	74 35.9	+54.8	153.8	16
17	81 06.0	+39.4	•131.1	80 24.8	+43.1	•135.6	79 40.5	+46.1	•139.4	78 53.8	+48.4	142.8	78 05.1	+50.3	145.6	77 14.9	+51.8	148.1	76 23.3	+53.0	150.3	75 30.7	+54.0	152.2	17
18	81 45.4	+35.0	•126.1	81 07.9	+39.6	•131.2	80 26.6	+43.3	•135.7	79 42.2	+46.3	•139.6	78 55.4	+48.6	142.9	78 06.7	+50.4	145.8	77 16.3	+51.9	148.3	76 24.7	+53.1	150.4	18
19	82 20.4	+29.5	•120.2	81 47.5	+35.2	•126.2	81 09.9	+39.8	•131.4	80 28.5	+43.5	•135.9	79 44.0	+46.4	•139.7	78 57.1	+48.7	143.0	78 08.2	+50.6	145.9	77 17.8	+52.1	148.4	19
20	82 49.9	+22.7	•113.4	82 22.7	+29.6	•120.3	81 49.7	+35.4	•126.3	81 12.0	+40.0	•131.5	80 30.4	+43.7	•136.0	79 45.8	+46.6	•139.9	78 58.8	+48.9	143.2	78 09.9	+50.7	146.1	20
21	83 12.6	+14.8	•105.8	82 52.3	+23.0	•113.5	82 25.1	+29.8	•120.4	81 52.0	+35.6	•126.5	81 14.1	+40.2	•131.7	80 32.4	+43.9	•136.2	79 47.7	+46.8	•140.0	79 00.6	+49.1	143.4	21
22	83 27.4	+6.0	• 97.4	83 15.3	+14.9	•105.9	82 54.9	+23.2	•113.6	82 27.6	+30.1	•120.6	81 54.3	+35.9	•126.6	81 16.3	+40.5	•131.9	80 34.5	+44.1	•136.4	79 49.7	+47.0	•140.2	22
23	83 33.4	-3.2	• 88.6	83 30.2	+6.2	• 97.4	83 18.1	+15.1	•105.9	82 57.7	+23.3	•113.7	82 30.2	+30.3	•120.7	81 56.8	+36.0	•126.8	81 18.6	+40.7	•132.1	80 36.7	+44.3	•136.6	23
24	83 30.2	-12.1	• 79.8	83 36.4	-3.2	• 88.6	83 33.2	+6.2	• 97.5	83 21.0	+15.2	•106.0	83 00.5	+23.5	•113.9	82 32.8	+30.6	•120.9	81 59.3	+36.3	•127.0	81 21.0	+40.9	•132.2	24
25	83 18.1	-20.4	• 71.2	83 33.2	-12.2	• 79.6	83 39.4	-3.2	• 88.5	83 36.2	+6.4	• 97.5	83 24.0	+15.4	•106.1	83 03.4	+23.7	•114.0	82 35.6	+30.8	•121.0	82 01.9	+36.5	•127.2	25
26	82 57.7	-27.5	• 63.4	83 21.0	-20.5	• 71.0	83 36.2	-12.2	• 79.5	83 42.6	-3.2	• 88.5	83 39.4	+6.4	• 97.5	83 27.1	+15.6	•106.2	83 06.4	+23.9	•114.1	82 38.4	+31.1	•121.2	26
27	82 30.2	-33.4	• 56.3	83 00.5	-27.7	• 63.1	83 24.0	-20.6	• 70.9	83 39.4	-12.3	• 79.4	83 45.8	-3.1	• 88.4	83 42.7	+6.5	• 97.5	83 30.3	+15.8	•106.3	83 09.5	+24.1	•114.3	27
28	81 56.8	-38.2	• 50.2	82 32.8	-33.5	• 56.1	83 03.4	-27.8	• 62.9	83 27.1	-20.7	• 70.7	83 42.7	-12.4	• 79.2	83 49.2	-3.1	• 88.4	83 46.1	+6.6	• 97.5	83 33.6	+16.0	•106.4	28
29	81 18.6	-41.9	• 44.9	81 59.3	-38.3	• 49.9	82 35.6	-33.7	• 55.8	83 06.4	-28.0	• 62.6	83 30.3	-20.8	• 70.4	83 46.1	-12.5	• 79.1	83 52.7	-3.1	• 88.3	83 49.6	+6.7	• 97.6	29
30	80 36.7	-45.0	• 40.3	81 21.0	-42.1	• 44.6	82 01.9	-38.5	• 49.6	82 38.4	-33.8	• 55.5	83 09.5	-28.1	• 62.4	83 33.6	-20.9	• 70.2	83 49.6	-12.5	• 79.0	83 56.3	-3.1	• 88.2	30
31	79 51.7	-47.3	• 36.4	80 38.9	-45.1	• 40.0	81 23.4	-42.2	• 44.3	82 04.6	-38.7	• 49.3	82 41.4	-34.1	• 55.2	83 12.7	-28.3	• 62.1	83 37.1	-21.2	• 70.0	83 53.2	-12.6	• 78.8	31
32	79 04.4	-49.3	33.0	79 53.8	-47.5	• 36.1	80 41.2	-45.3	• 39.7	81 25.9	-42.4	• 43.9	82 07.3	-38.8	• 48.9	82 44.4	-34.2	• 54.9	83 15.9	-28.4	• 61.8	83 40.6	-21.3	• 69.8	32
33	78 15.1	-50.8	30.1	79 06.3	-49.3	32.7	79 55.9	-47.5	• 35.8	80 43.5	-45.4	• 39.4	81 28.5	-42.6	• 43.6	82 10.2	-39.0	• 48.6	82 47.5	-34.4	• 54.5	83 19.3	-28.6	• 61.5	33
34	77 24.3	-52.0	27.6	78 17.0	-50.9	29.8	79 08.4	-49.5	32.4	79 58.1	-47.7	• 35.5	80 45.9	-45.5	• 39.0	81 31.2	-42.8	• 43.2	82 13.1	-39.2	• 48.3	82 50.7	-34.7	• 54.2	34
35	76 32.3	-53.0	25.4	77 26.1	-52.1	27.3	78 18.9	-51.0	29.5	79 10.4	-49.6	32.1	80 00.4	-47.9	• 35.1	80 48.4	-45.7	• 38.7	81 33.9	-43.0	• 42.9	82 16.0	-39.4	• 47.9	35
36	75 39.3	-53.9	23.4	76 34.0	-53.2	25.1	77 27.9	-52.2	27.0	78 20.8	-51.1	29.2	79 12.5	-49.7	31.8	80 02.7	-48.0	• 34.8	80 50.9	-45.9	• 38.3	81 36.6	-43.1	• 42.5	36
37	74 45.4	-54.6	21.7	75 40.8	-53.9	23.2	76 35.7	-53.3	24.8	77 29.7	-52.3	26.7	78 22.8	-51.2	28.9	79 14.7	-49.9	31.4	80 05.0	-48.1	• 34.4	80 53.5	-46.1	• 37.9	37
38	73 50.8	-55.2	20.2	74 46.9	-54.7	21.5	75 42.4	-54.0	22.9	76 37.4	-53.3	24.5	77 31.6	-52.5	26.4	78 24.8	-51.4	28.6	79 16.9	-50.1	31.1	80 07.4	-48.3	• 34.0	38
39	72 55.6	-55.7	18.8	73 52.2	-55.2	19.9	74 48.4	-54.8	21.2	75 44.1	-54.2	22.6	76 39.1	-53.4	24.2	77 33.4	-52.5	26.1	78 26.8	-51.4	28.2	79 19.1	-50.2	30.7	39
40	71 59.9	-56.1	17.6	72 57.0	-55.8	18.6	73 53.6	-55.3	19.7	74 49.9	-54.8	20.9	75 45.7	-54.2	22.3	76 40.9	-53.5	23.9	77 35.4	-52.7	25.7	78 28.9	-51.6	27.9	40
41	71 03.8	-56.5	16.5	72 01.2	-56.1	17.3	72 58.3	-55.8	18.3	73 55.1	-55.4	19.4	74 51.5	-54.9	20.6	75 47.4	-54.3	22.0	76 42.7	-53.6	23.6	77 37.3	-52.7	25.4	41
42	70 07.3	-56.8	15.4	71 05.1	-56.6	16.2	72 02.5	-56.2	17.1	72 59.7	-55.8	18.0	73 56.6	-55.4	19.1	74 53.1	-55.0	20.3	75 49.1	-54.4	21.7	76 44.6	-53.7	23.3	42
43	69 10.5	-57.0	14.5	70 08.5	-56.8	15.2	71 06.3	-56.5	16.0	72 03.9	-56.3	16.8	73 01.2	-56.0	17.8	73 58.1	-55.5	18.8	74 54.7	-55.0	20.0	75 50.9	-54.5	21.4	43
44	68 13.5	-57.3	13.7	69 11.7	-57.1	14.3	70 09.8	-56.9	15.0	71 07.6	-56.6	15.7	72 05.2	-56.3	16.6	73 02.6	-56.0	17.5	73 59.7	-55.6	18.5	74 56.4	-55.2	19.7	44
45	67 16.2	-57.5	12.9	68 14.6	-57.4	13.4	69 12.9	-57.2	14.1	70 11.0	-56.9	14.7	71 08.9	-56.7	15.5	72 06.6	-56.4	16.3	73 04.1	-56.1	17.2	74 01.2	-55.6	18.2	45
46	66 18.7	-57.8	12.2	67 17.2	-57.5	12.7	68 15.7	-57.4	13.2	69 14.1	-57.2	13.8	70 12.2	-56.9	14.5	71 10.2	-56.7	15.2	72 08.0	-56.4	16.0	73 05.6	-56.2	16.9	46
47	65 20.9	-57.8	11.5	66 19.7	-57.7	11.9	67 18.3	-57.5	12.4	68 16.9	-57.4	13.0	69 15.3	-57.3	13.6	70 13.5	-57.0	14.2	71 11.6	-56.8	14.9	72 09.4	-56.5	15.7	47
48	64 23.1	-58.0	10.9	65 22.0	-57.9	11.3	66 20.8	-57.8	11.7	67 19.5	-57.7	12.2	68 18.0	-57.4	12.7	69 16.5	-57.3	13.3	70 14.8	-57.1	14.0	71 12.9	-56.8	14.7	48
49	63 25.1	-58.2	10.3	64 24.1	-58.1	10.7	65 23.0	-57.9	11.1	66 21.8	-57.8	11.5	67 20.6	-57.7	12.0	68 19.2	-57.5	12.5	69 17.7	-57.3	13.1	70 16.1	-57.1	13.7	49
50	62 26.9	-58.3	9.8	63 26.0	-58.2	10.1	64 25.1	-58.1	10.5	65 24.0	-57.9	10.8	66 22.9	-57.8	11.3	67 21.7	-57.7	11.7	68 20.4	-57.6	12.3	69 19.0	-57.4	12.8	50
51	61 28.6	-58.3	9.2	62 27.8	-58.2	9.5	63 27.0	-58.2	9.9	64 26.1	-58.1	10.2	65 25.1	-58.0	10.6	66 24.0	-57.9	11.0	67 22.8	-57.7	11.5	68 21.6	-57.6	12.0	51
52	60 30.3	-58.5	8.8	61 29.6	-58.4	9.0	62 28.8	-58.3	9.3	63 28.0	-58.3	9.7	64 27.1	-58.2	10.0	65 26.1	-58.0	10.4	66 25.1	-57.9	10.8	67 24.0	-57.8	11.3	52
53	59 31.8	-58.5	8.3	60 31.2	-58.5	8.6	61 30.5	-58.5	8.8	62 29.7	-58.3	9.1	63 28.9	-58.2	9.5	64 28.1	-58.2	9.8	65 27.2	-58.1	10.2	66 26.2	-57.9	10.6	53
54	58 33.3	-58.7	7.9	59 32.7	-58.6	8.1	60 32.0	-58.5	8.4	61 31.4	-58.5	8.6	62 30.7	-58.4	8.9	63 29.9	-58.3	9.2	64 29.1	-58.2	9.6	65 28.3	-58.1	9.9	54
55	57 34.6	-58.7	7.5	58 34.1	-58.7	7.7	59 33.5	-58.6	7.9	60 32.9	-58.5	8.2	61 32.3	-58.5	8.4	62 31.6	-58.4	8.7	63 30.9	-58.3	9.0	64 30.2	-58.3	9.3	55
56	56 35.9	-58.8	7.1	57 35.4	-58.7	7.3	58 34.9	-58.6	7.5	59 34.4	-58.6	7.7	60 33.8	-58.5	8.0	61 33.2	-58.5	8.2	62 32.6	-58.4	8.5	63 31.9	-58.3	8.8	56
57	55 37.1	-58.8	6.8	56 36.7	-58.8	6.9	57 36.3	-58.8	7.1	58 35.8	-58.7	7.3	59 35.3	-58.7	7.5	60 34.7	-58.5	7.8	61 34.2	-58.5	8.0	62 33.6	-58.5	8.3	57
58	54 38.3	-58.9	6.4	55 37.9	-58.8	6.6	56 37.5	-58.8	6.7	57 37.1	-58.8	6.9	58 36.6	-58.7	7.1	59 36.2	-58.7	7.3	60 35.7	-58.7	7.6	61 35.1	-58.5	7.8	58
59	53 39.4	-58.9	6.1	54 39.1	-58.9	6.2	55 38.7	-58.9	6.4	56 38.3	-58.8	6.6	57 37.9	-58.8	6.7	58 37.5	-58.7	6.9	59 37.0	-58.6	7.1	60 36.6	-58.7	7.3	59
60	52 40.5	-59.0	5.8	53 40.2	-59.0	5.9	54 39.8	-58.9	6.0	55 39.5	-58.9	6.2	56 39.1	-58.8	6.4	57 38.8	-58.8	6.5	58 38.4	-58.8	6.7	59 37.9	-58.7	6.9	60
61	51 41.5	-59.0	5.5	52 41.2	-59.0	5.6	53 40.9	-59.0	5.7	54 40.6	-58.9	5.9	55 40.3	-58.9	6.0	56 40.0	-58.9	6.2	57 39.6	-58.8	6.3	58 39.2	-58.8	6.5	61
62	50 42.5	-59.1	5.2	51 42.2	-59.0	5.3	52 41.9	-59.0	5.4	53 41.7	-59.0	5.5	54 41.4	-59.0	5.7	55 41.1	-58.9	5.8	56 40.8	-58.9	6.0	57 40.4	-58.8	6.1	62
63	49 43.4	-59.1	4.9	50 43.2	-59.1	5.0	51 42.9	-59.0	5.1	52 42.7	-59.0	5.2	53 42.4	-59.0	5.4	54 42.2	-59.0	5.5	55 41.9	-59.0	5.6	56 41.6	-58.9	5.8	63
64	48 44.3	-59.2	4.6	49 44.1	-59.1	4.7	50 43.9	-59.1	4.8	51 43.7	-59.1	4.9	52 43.4	-59.0	5.1	53 43.2	-59.0	5.2	54 42.9	-59.0	5.3	55 42.7	-59.0	5.4	64
65	47 45.1	-59.1	4.4	48 45.0	-59.2	4.5	49 44.8	-59.2	4.6	50 44.6	-59.1	4.7	51 44.4	-59.1	4.8	52 44.2	-59.1	4.9	53 43.9	-59.0	5.0	54 43.7	-59.0	5.1	65
66	46 46.0	-59.2	4.1	47 45.8	-59.2	4.2	48 45.6	-59.1	4.3	49 45.5	-59.2	4.4	50 45.3	-59.1	4.5	51 45.1	-59.1	4.6	52 44.9	-59.1	4.7	53 44.7	-59.1	4.8	66
67	45 46.8	-59.3	3.9	46 46.6	-59.2	4.0	47 46.5	-59.2	4.1	48 46.3	-59.2	4.1	49 46.2	-59.2	4.2	50 46.0	-59.2	4.3	51 45.8	-59.1	4.4	52 45.6	-59.1	4.5	67
68	44 47.5	-59.2	3.7	45 47.4	-59.2	3.8	46 47.3	-59.3	3.8	47 47.1	-59.2	3.9	48 47.0	-59.2	4.0	49 46.8	-59.1	4.1	50 46.7	-59.2	4.1	51 46.5	-59.1	4.2	68
69	43 48.3	-59.3	3.5	44 48.2	-59.3	3.5	45 48.0	-59.2	3.6	46 47.9	-59.2	3.7	47 47.8	-59.2	3.7	48 47.7	-59.2	3.8	49 47.5	-59.2	3.9	50 47.4	-59.2	4.0	69
70	42 49.0	-59.3	3.3	43 48.9	-59.3	3.3	44 48.8	-59.3	3.4	45 48.7	-59.3	3.4	46 48.6	-59.3	3.5	47 48.5	-59.3	3.6	48 48.3	-59.2	3.6	49 48.2	-59.2	3.7	70
71	41 49.7	-59.3	3.1	42 49.6	-59.3	3.1	43 49.5	-59.3	3.2	44 49.4	-59.3	3.2	45 49.3	-59.3	3.3	46 49.2	-59.2	3.3	47 49.1	-59.2	3.4	48 49.0	-59.2	3.5	71
72	40 50.4	-59.4	2.9	41 50.3	-59.4	2.9	42 50.2	-59.3	2.9	43 50.1	-59.3	3.0	44 50.0	-59.3	3.0	45 50.0	-59.3	3.1	46 49.9	-59.3	3.2	47 49.8	-59.3	3.2	72
73	39 51.0	-59.4	2.7	40 50.9	-59.3	2.7	41 50.9	-59.4	2.7	42 50.8	-59.3	2.8	43 50.7	-59.3	2.8	44 50.7	-59.4	2.9	45 50.6	-59.3	2.9	46 50.5	-59.3	3.0	73
74	38 51.6	-59.3	2.5	39 51.6	-59.4	2.5	40 51.5	-59.3	2.5	41 51.5	-59.4	2.6	42 51.4	-59.3	2.6	43 51.3	-59.3	2.7	44 51.3	-59.4	2.7	45 51.2	-59.3	2.8	74
75	37 52.3	-59.4	2.3	38 52.2	-59.4	2.3	39 52.2	-59.4	2.4	40 52.1	-59.4	2.4	41 52.1	-59.4	2.4	42 52.0	-59.4	2.5	43 51.9	-59.3	2.5	44 51.9	-59.4	2.6	75
76	36 52.9	-59.5	2.1	37 52.8	-59.4	2.1	38 52.8	-59.4	2.2	39 52.7	-59.4	2.2	40 52.7	-59.4	2.2	41 52.6	-59.3	2.3	42 52.6	-59.4	2.3	43 52.5	-59.3	2.3	76
77	35 53.4	-59.4	1.9	36 53.4	-59.4	2.0	37 53.4	-59.4	2.0	38 53.3	-59.4	2.0	39 53.3	-59.4	2.0	40 53.3	-59.4	2.1	41 53.2	-59.4	2.1	42 53.2	-59.4	2.1	77
78	34 54.0	-59.4	1.8	35 54.0	-59.4	1.8	36 54.0	-59.5	1.8	37 53.9	-59.4	1.8	38 53.9	-59.4	1.9	39 53.9	-59.5	1.9	40 53.8	-59.4	1.9	41 53.8	-59.4	2.0	78
79	33 54.6	-59.5	1.6	34 54.6	-59.5	1.6	35 54.5	-59.4	1.6	36 54.5	-59.4	1.7	37 54.5	-59.5	1.7	38 54.4	-59.4	1.7	39 54.4	-59.4	1.7	40 54.4	-59.4	1.8	79
80	32 55.1	-59.4	1.4	33 55.1	-59.5	1.5	34 55.1	-59.5	1.5	35 55.1	-59.5	1.5	36 55.0	-59.4	1.5	37 55.0	-59.4	1.5	38 55.0	-59.5	1.6	39 55.0	-59.5	1.6	80
81	31 55.7	-59.5	1.3	32 55.6	-59.4	1.3	33 55.6	-59.5	1.3	34 55.6	-59.5	1.3	35 55.6	-59.5	1.3	36 55.6	-59.5	1.4	37 55.6	-59.5	1.4	38 55.5	-59.4	1.4	81
82	30 56.2	-59.5	1.1	31 56.2	-59.5	1.1	32 56.1	-59.4	1.2	33 56.1	-59.4	1.2	34 56.1	-59.5	1.2	35 56.1	-59.5	1.2	36 56.1	-59.5	1.2	37 56.1	-59.5	1.2	82
83	29 56.7	-59.5	1.0	30 56.7	-59.5	1.0	31 56.7	-59.5	1.0	32 56.7	-59.5	1.0	33 56.6	-59.4	1.0	34 56.6	-59.5	1.0	35 56.6	-59.5	1.1	36 56.6	-59.5	1.1	83
84	28 57.2	-59.5	0.8	29 57.2	-59.5	0.8	30 57.2	-59.5	0.9	31 57.2	-59.5	0.9	32 57.2	-59.5	0.9	33 57.1	-59.5	0.9	34 57.1	-59.5	0.9	35 57.1	-59.5	0.9	84
85	27 57.7	-59.5	0.7	28 57.7	-59.5	0.7	29 57.7	-59.6	0.7	30 57.7	-59.6	0.7	31 57.7	-59.6	0.7	32 57.6	-59.5	0.7	33 57.6	-59.5	0.7	34 57.6	-59.5	0.7	85
86	26 58.2	-59.6	0.5	27 58.2	-59.6	0.6	28 58.1	-59.5	0.6	29 58.1	-59.5	0.6	30 58.1	-59.6	0.6	31 58.1	-59.5	0.6	32 58.1	-59.5	0.6	33 58.1	-59.5	0.6	86
87	25 58.6	-59.5	0.4	26 58.6	-59.5	0.4	27 58.6	-59.5	0.4	28 58.6	-59.5	0.4	29 58.6	-59.5	0.4	30 58.6	-59.5	0.4	31 58.6	-59.5	0.4	32 58.6	-59.5	0.4	87
88	24 59.1	-59.6	0.3	25 59.1	-59.6	0.3	26 59.1	-59.6	0.3	27 59.1	-59.6	0.3	28 59.1	-59.6	0.3	29 59.1	-59.6	0.3	30 59.1	-59.6	0.3	31 59.1	-59.6	0.3	88
89	23 59.5	-59.5	0.1	24 59.5	-59.5	0.1	25 59.5	-59.5	0.1	26 59.5	-59.5	0.1	27 59.5	-59.5	0.1	28 59.5	-59.5	0.1	29 59.5	-59.5	0.1	30 59.5	-59.5	0.1	89
90	23 00.0	-59.6	0.0	24 00.0	-59.6	0.0	25 00.0	-59.6	0.0	26 00.0	-59.6	0.0	27 00.0	-59.6	0.0	28 00.0	-59.6	0.0	29 00.0	-59.6	0.0	30 00.0	-59.6	0.0	90
	23°			24°			25°			26°			27°			28°			29°			30°			

7°, 353° L.H.A. LATITUDE SAME NAME AS DECLINATION

198

LATITUDE **CONTRARY** NAME TO DECLINATION **L.H.A. 7°, 353°**

Dec.	23° Hc	d	Z	24° Hc	d	Z	25° Hc	d	Z	26° Hc	d	Z
°	° ′	′	°	° ′	′	°	° ′	′	°	° ′	′	°
0	66 00.8	−57.7	162.6	65 03.5	−58.0	163.2	64 06.0	−58.2	163.8	63 08.3	−58.3	164.4
1	65 03.1	−57.9	163.2	64 05.5	−58.0	163.8	63 07.8	−58.2	164.4	62 10.0	−58.4	164.9
2	64 05.2	−58.1	163.8	63 07.5	−58.3	164.4	62 09.6	−58.4	164.9	61 11.6	−58.5	165.4
3	63 07.1	−58.2	164.4	62 09.2	−58.3	164.9	61 11.2	−58.4	165.4	60 13.1	−58.5	165.8
4	62 08.9	−58.3	164.9	61 10.9	−58.4	165.4	60 12.8	−58.5	165.8	59 14.6	−58.7	166.2
5	61 10.6	−58.4	165.4	60 12.5	−58.5	165.9	59 14.3	−58.7	166.3	58 15.9	−58.7	166.7
6	60 12.2	−58.5	165.9	59 14.0	−58.6	166.3	58 15.6	−58.7	166.7	57 17.2	−58.8	167.0
7	59 13.7	−58.6	166.3	58 15.4	−58.7	166.7	57 16.9	−58.7	167.1	56 18.4	−58.8	167.4
8	58 15.1	−58.6	166.7	57 16.7	−58.8	167.1	56 18.2	−58.9	167.4	55 19.6	−58.9	167.8
9	57 16.5	−58.8	167.1	56 17.9	−58.8	167.5	55 19.3	−58.8	167.8	54 20.7	−59.0	168.1
10	56 17.7	−58.7	167.5	55 19.1	−58.8	167.8	54 20.5	−59.0	168.1	53 21.7	−59.0	168.4
11	55 19.0	−58.9	167.9	54 20.3	−59.0	168.2	53 21.5	−59.0	168.4	52 22.7	−59.0	168.7
12	54 20.1	−58.9	168.2	53 21.3	−58.9	168.5	52 22.5	−59.0	168.7	51 23.7	−59.1	169.0
13	53 21.2	−59.0	168.5	52 22.4	−59.0	168.8	51 23.5	−59.1	169.0	50 24.6	−59.2	169.3
14	52 22.2	−59.0	168.8	51 23.4	−59.1	169.1	50 24.4	−59.1	169.3	49 25.4	−59.1	169.5
15	51 23.2	−59.0	169.1	50 24.3	−59.1	169.4	49 25.3	−59.1	169.6	48 26.3	−59.2	169.8
16	50 24.2	−59.1	169.4	49 25.2	−59.1	169.6	48 26.2	−59.2	169.8	47 27.1	−59.2	170.0
17	49 25.1	−59.1	169.7	48 26.1	−59.2	169.9	47 27.0	−59.2	170.1	46 27.9	−59.3	170.3
18	48 26.0	−59.2	169.9	47 26.9	−59.2	170.1	46 27.8	−59.3	170.3	45 28.6	−59.3	170.5
19	47 26.8	−59.1	170.2	46 27.7	−59.2	170.4	45 28.5	−59.2	170.5	44 29.3	−59.3	170.7
20	46 27.7	−59.3	170.4	45 28.5	−59.3	170.6	44 29.3	−59.3	170.8	43 30.0	−59.3	170.9
21	45 28.4	−59.2	170.7	44 29.2	−59.2	170.8	43 30.0	−59.3	171.0	42 30.7	−59.3	171.1
22	44 29.2	−59.3	170.9	43 30.0	−59.3	171.0	42 30.7	−59.4	171.2	41 31.4	−59.4	171.3
23	43 29.9	−59.2	171.1	42 30.7	−59.4	171.2	41 31.3	−59.3	171.4	40 32.0	−59.4	171.5
24	42 30.7	−59.4	171.3	41 31.3	−59.3	171.4	40 32.0	−59.4	171.6	39 32.6	−59.4	171.7
25	41 31.3	−59.3	171.5	40 32.0	−59.4	171.6	39 32.6	−59.4	171.8	38 33.2	−59.4	171.9
26	40 32.0	−59.3	171.7	39 32.6	−59.4	171.8	38 33.2	−59.4	171.9	37 33.8	−59.4	172.1
27	39 32.7	−59.4	171.9	38 33.2	−59.4	172.0	37 33.8	−59.4	172.1	36 34.4	−59.4	172.2
28	38 33.3	−59.4	172.1	37 33.8	−59.4	172.2	36 34.4	−59.4	172.3	35 34.9	−59.4	172.4
29	37 33.9	−59.4	172.3	36 34.4	−59.4	172.4	35 35.0	−59.5	172.5	34 35.5	−59.5	172.6
30	36 34.5	−59.4	172.4	35 35.0	−59.4	172.5	34 35.5	−59.5	172.6	33 36.0	−59.5	172.7
31	35 35.1	−59.5	172.6	34 35.6	−59.5	172.7	33 36.0	−59.4	172.8	32 36.5	−59.5	172.9
32	34 35.6	−59.4	172.8	33 36.1	−59.5	172.9	32 36.6	−59.5	173.0	31 37.0	−59.5	173.0
33	33 36.2	−59.5	173.0	32 36.6	−59.4	173.0	31 37.1	−59.5	173.1	30 37.5	−59.5	173.2
34	32 36.7	−59.4	173.1	31 37.2	−59.5	173.2	30 37.6	−59.5	173.3	29 38.0	−59.5	173.3
35	31 37.3	−59.5	173.3	30 37.7	−59.5	173.3	29 38.1	−59.5	173.4	28 38.5	−59.6	173.5
36	30 37.8	−59.5	173.4	29 38.2	−59.5	173.5	28 38.6	−59.6	173.5	27 38.9	−59.5	173.6
37	29 38.3	−59.5	173.6	28 38.7	−59.6	173.6	27 39.0	−59.5	173.7	26 39.4	−59.6	173.7
38	28 38.8	−59.5	173.7	27 39.1	−59.5	173.8	26 39.5	−59.6	173.8	25 39.8	−59.5	173.9
39	27 39.3	−59.5	173.9	26 39.6	−59.5	173.9	25 39.9	−59.5	174.0	24 40.3	−59.6	174.0
40	26 39.8	−59.6	174.0	25 40.1	−59.6	174.1	24 40.4	−59.6	174.1	23 40.7	−59.6	174.1
41	25 40.2	−59.5	174.1	24 40.5	−59.5	174.2	23 40.8	−59.5	174.2	22 41.1	−59.5	174.3
42	24 40.7	−59.6	174.3	23 41.0	−59.6	174.3	22 41.3	−59.6	174.4	21 41.6	−59.6	174.4
43	23 41.1	−59.5	174.4	22 41.4	−59.5	174.5	21 41.7	−59.6	174.5	20 42.0	−59.6	174.5
44	22 41.6	−59.6	174.5	21 41.9	−59.6	174.6	20 42.1	−59.6	174.6	19 42.4	−59.6	174.7
45	21 42.0	−59.5	174.7	20 42.3	−59.6	174.7	19 42.5	−59.5	174.7	18 42.8	−59.6	174.8
46	20 42.5	−59.6	174.8	19 42.7	−59.6	174.8	18 43.0	−59.6	174.9	17 43.2	−59.6	174.9
47	19 42.9	−59.6	174.9	18 43.1	−59.6	175.0	17 43.4	−59.6	175.0	16 43.6	−59.6	175.0
48	18 43.3	−59.6	175.1	17 43.5	−59.6	175.1	16 43.8	−59.6	175.1	15 44.0	−59.6	175.1
49	17 43.7	−59.5	175.2	16 44.0	−59.6	175.2	15 44.2	−59.6	175.2	14 44.4	−59.6	175.3
50	16 44.2	−59.6	175.3	15 44.4	−59.6	175.3	14 44.6	−59.7	175.4	13 44.8	−59.7	175.4
51	15 44.6	−59.6	175.4	14 44.8	−59.6	175.5	13 44.9	−59.6	175.5	12 45.1	−59.6	175.5
52	14 45.0	−59.6	175.6	13 45.2	−59.7	175.6	12 45.3	−59.6	175.6	11 45.5	−59.6	175.6
53	13 45.4	−59.6	175.7	12 45.5	−59.6	175.7	11 45.7	−59.6	175.7	10 45.9	−59.6	175.7
54	12 45.8	−59.6	175.8	11 45.9	−59.6	175.8	10 46.1	−59.6	175.8	9 46.3	−59.7	175.8
55	11 46.2	−59.6	175.9	10 46.3	−59.6	175.9	9 46.5	−59.6	175.9	8 46.6	−59.6	175.9
56	10 46.6	−59.6	176.0	9 46.7	−59.6	176.0	8 46.9	−59.7	176.0	7 47.0	−59.6	176.1
57	9 47.0	−59.7	176.1	8 47.1	−59.6	176.1	7 47.2	−59.6	176.2	6 47.4	−59.7	176.2
58	8 47.3	−59.6	176.3	7 47.5	−59.6	176.3	6 47.6	−59.6	176.3	5 47.7	−59.6	176.3
59	7 47.7	−59.6	176.4	6 47.9	−59.7	176.4	5 48.0	−59.7	176.4	4 48.1	−59.6	176.4
60	6 48.1	−59.6	176.5	5 48.2	−59.6	176.5	4 48.3	−59.6	176.5	3 48.5	−59.7	176.5
61	5 48.5	−59.6	176.6	4 48.6	−59.6	176.6	3 48.7	−59.6	176.6	2 48.8	−59.6	176.6
62	4 48.9	−59.6	176.7	3 49.0	−59.6	176.7	2 49.1	−59.6	176.7	1 49.2	−59.7	176.7
63	3 49.3	−59.7	176.8	2 49.4	−59.7	176.8	1 49.5	−59.7	176.8	0 49.5	−59.6	176.8
64	2 49.6	−59.6	176.9	1 49.7	−59.6	176.9	0 49.8	−59.6	176.9	0 10.1	+59.6	3.1
65	1 50.0	−59.6	177.0	0 50.1	−59.6	177.0	0 09.8	+59.6	3.0	1 09.7	+59.7	3.0
66	0 50.4	−59.6	177.2	0 09.5	+59.6	2.8	1 09.4	+59.7	2.8	2 09.4	+59.6	2.8
67	0 09.2	+59.6	2.7	1 09.1	+59.7	2.7	2 09.1	+59.6	2.7	3 09.0	+59.6	2.7
68	1 08.8	+59.7	2.6	2 08.8	+59.6	2.6	3 08.7	+59.6	2.6	4 08.6	+59.7	2.6
69	2 08.5	+59.6	2.5	3 08.4	+59.6	2.5	4 08.3	+59.7	2.5	5 08.3	+59.6	2.5
70	3 08.1	+59.6	2.4	4 08.0	+59.7	2.4	5 08.0	+59.6	2.4	6 07.9	+59.7	2.4
71	4 07.7	+59.6	2.3	5 07.7	+59.6	2.3	6 07.6	+59.6	2.3	7 07.6	+59.6	2.3
72	5 07.3	+59.6	2.2	6 07.3	+59.6	2.2	7 07.2	+59.7	2.2	8 07.2	+59.6	2.2
73	6 06.9	+59.7	2.1	7 06.9	+59.6	2.1	8 06.9	+59.6	2.1	9 06.8	+59.6	2.1
74	7 06.6	+59.6	1.9	8 06.5	+59.6	1.9	9 06.5	+59.6	1.9	10 06.4	+59.7	2.0
75	8 06.2	+59.6	1.8	9 06.1	+59.7	1.8	10 06.1	+59.6	1.8	11 06.1	+59.6	1.8
76	9 05.8	+59.6	1.7	10 05.8	+59.6	1.7	11 05.7	+59.6	1.7	12 05.7	+59.6	1.7
77	10 05.4	+59.6	1.6	11 05.4	+59.6	1.6	12 05.3	+59.7	1.6	13 05.3	+59.6	1.6
78	11 05.0	+59.6	1.5	12 05.0	+59.6	1.5	13 05.0	+59.6	1.5	14 04.9	+59.7	1.5
79	12 04.6	+59.6	1.4	13 04.6	+59.6	1.4	14 04.6	+59.6	1.4	15 04.6	+59.6	1.4
80	13 04.2	+59.6	1.2	14 04.2	+59.6	1.3	15 04.2	+59.6	1.3	16 04.2	+59.6	1.3
81	14 03.8	+59.6	1.1	15 03.8	+59.6	1.1	16 03.8	+59.6	1.1	17 03.8	+59.6	1.1
82	15 03.4	+59.6	1.0	16 03.4	+59.6	1.0	17 03.4	+59.6	1.0	18 03.4	+59.6	1.0
83	16 03.0	+59.6	0.9	17 03.0	+59.6	0.9	18 03.0	+59.6	0.9	19 03.0	+59.6	0.9
84	17 02.6	+59.6	0.8	18 02.6	+59.6	0.8	19 02.6	+59.6	0.8	20 02.6	+59.6	0.8
85	18 02.2	+59.5	0.6	19 02.2	+59.5	0.6	20 02.2	+59.5	0.6	21 02.2	+59.5	0.7
86	19 01.7	+59.6	0.5	20 01.7	+59.6	0.5	21 01.7	+59.6	0.5	22 01.7	+59.6	0.5
87	20 01.3	+59.6	0.4	21 01.3	+59.6	0.4	22 01.3	+59.6	0.4	23 01.3	+59.6	0.4
88	21 00.9	+59.5	0.3	22 00.9	+59.5	0.3	23 00.9	+59.5	0.3	24 00.9	+59.5	0.3
89	22 00.4	+59.6	0.1	23 00.4	+59.6	0.1	24 00.4	+59.6	0.1	25 00.4	+59.6	0.1
90	23 00.0	+59.5	0.0	24 00.0	+59.5	0.0	25 00.0	+59.5	0.0	26 00.0	+59.6	0.0
	23°			24°			25°			26°		

Dec.	27° Hc	d	Z	28° Hc	d	Z	29° Hc	d	Z	30° Hc	d	Z
°	° ′	′	°	° ′	′	°	° ′	′	°	° ′	′	°
0	62 10.4	−58.4	164.9	61 12.4	−58.5	165.3	60 14.3	−58.6	165.8	59 16.1	−58.7	166.2
1	61 12.0	−58.5	165.3	60 13.9	−58.6	165.8	59 15.7	−58.7	166.2	58 17.4	−58.9	166.6
2	60 13.5	−58.6	165.8	59 15.3	−58.7	166.2	58 17.0	−58.8	166.6	57 18.5	−58.8	167.0
3	59 14.9	−58.7	166.2	58 16.6	−58.8	166.6	57 18.2	−58.9	167.0	56 19.7	−59.0	167.3
4	58 16.2	−58.7	166.6	57 17.8	−58.8	167.0	56 19.3	−58.9	167.3	55 20.7	−58.9	167.7
5	57 17.5	−58.8	167.0	56 19.0	−58.9	167.4	55 20.4	−59.0	167.7	54 21.8	−59.1	168.0
6	56 18.7	−58.9	167.4	55 20.1	−58.9	167.7	54 21.4	−59.0	168.0	53 22.7	−59.0	168.3
7	55 19.8	−58.9	167.7	54 21.2	−59.0	168.0	53 22.4	−59.0	168.3	52 23.7	−59.2	168.6
8	54 20.9	−59.0	168.1	53 22.2	−59.1	168.3	52 23.4	−59.1	168.6	51 24.5	−59.1	168.8
9	53 21.9	−59.0	168.4	52 23.1	−59.1	168.6	51 24.3	−59.2	168.9	50 25.4	−59.2	169.1
10	52 22.9	−59.1	168.7	51 24.0	−59.1	168.9	50 25.1	−59.1	169.1	49 26.2	−59.2	169.4
11	51 23.8	−59.1	168.9	50 24.9	−59.1	169.2	49 26.0	−59.2	169.4	48 27.0	−59.3	169.6
12	50 24.7	−59.1	169.2	49 25.8	−59.2	169.4	48 26.8	−59.3	169.6	47 27.7	−59.3	169.8
13	49 25.6	−59.2	169.5	48 26.6	−59.2	169.7	47 27.5	−59.2	169.9	46 28.4	−59.3	170.1
14	48 26.4	−59.2	169.7	47 27.4	−59.3	169.9	46 28.3	−59.3	170.1	45 29.1	−59.3	170.3
15	47 27.2	−59.2	170.0	46 28.1	−59.3	170.2	45 29.0	−59.3	170.3	44 29.8	−59.3	170.5
16	46 28.0	−59.3	170.2	45 28.8	−59.3	170.4	44 29.7	−59.4	170.5	43 30.5	−59.4	170.7
17	45 28.7	−59.3	170.4	44 29.5	−59.3	170.6	43 30.3	−59.3	170.8	42 31.1	−59.4	170.9
18	44 29.4	−59.3	170.6	43 30.2	−59.3	170.8	42 31.0	−59.4	171.0	41 31.7	−59.4	171.1
19	43 30.1	−59.3	170.9	42 30.9	−59.4	171.0	41 31.6	−59.4	171.1	40 32.3	−59.4	171.3
20	42 30.8	−59.4	171.1	41 31.5	−59.4	171.2	40 32.2	−59.4	171.3	39 32.9	−59.5	171.5
21	41 31.4	−59.4	171.3	40 32.1	−59.4	171.4	39 32.8	−59.5	171.5	38 33.4	−59.4	171.6
22	40 32.0	−59.3	171.4	39 32.7	−59.4	171.6	38 33.3	−59.4	171.7	37 34.0	−59.5	171.8
23	39 32.7	−59.5	171.6	38 33.3	−59.5	171.8	37 33.9	−59.5	171.9	36 34.5	−59.5	172.0
24	38 33.2	−59.4	171.8	37 33.8	−59.4	171.9	36 34.4	−59.4	172.0	35 35.0	−59.5	172.1
25	37 33.8	−59.4	172.0	36 34.4	−59.5	172.1	35 35.0	−59.5	172.2	34 35.5	−59.5	172.3
26	36 34.4	−59.5	172.2	35 34.9	−59.4	172.3	34 35.5	−59.5	172.4	33 36.0	−59.5	172.4
27	35 34.9	−59.4	172.3	34 35.5	−59.5	172.4	33 36.0	−59.5	172.5	32 36.5	−59.6	172.6
28	34 35.5	−59.5	172.5	33 36.0	−59.5	172.6	32 36.5	−59.6	172.7	31 36.9	−59.5	172.7
29	33 36.0	−59.5	172.6	32 36.5	−59.6	172.7	31 36.9	−59.5	172.8	30 37.4	−59.6	172.9
30	32 36.5	−59.5	172.8	31 36.9	−59.5	172.9	30 37.4	−59.5	173.0	29 37.8	−59.5	173.0
31	31 37.0	−59.5	173.0	30 37.4	−59.5	173.0	29 37.9	−59.6	173.1	28 38.3	−59.6	173.2
32	30 37.5	−59.6	173.1	29 37.9	−59.6	173.2	28 38.3	−59.6	173.2	27 38.7	−59.6	173.3
33	29 37.9	−59.5	173.2	28 38.3	−59.5	173.3	27 38.7	−59.5	173.4	26 39.1	−59.5	173.4
34	28 38.4	−59.5	173.4	27 38.8	−59.6	173.5	26 39.2	−59.6	173.5	25 39.6	−59.6	173.6
35	27 38.9	−59.6	173.5	26 39.2	−59.5	173.6	25 39.6	−59.6	173.6	24 40.0	−59.6	173.7
36	26 39.3	−59.6	173.7	25 39.7	−59.6	173.7	24 40.0	−59.6	173.8	23 40.4	−59.6	173.8
37	25 39.7	−59.5	173.8	24 40.1	−59.6	173.9	23 40.4	−59.6	173.9	22 40.8	−59.6	173.9
38	24 40.2	−59.6	173.9	23 40.5	−59.6	174.0	22 40.8	−59.6	174.0	21 41.2	−59.7	174.1
39	23 40.6	−59.6	174.1	22 40.9	−59.6	174.1	21 41.2	−59.6	174.1	20 41.5	−59.6	174.2
40	22 41.0	−59.6	174.2	21 41.3	−59.6	174.2	20 41.6	−59.6	174.3	19 41.9	−59.6	174.3
41	21 41.4	−59.6	174.3	20 41.7	−59.6	174.4	19 42.0	−59.6	174.4	18 42.3	−59.6	174.4
42	20 41.8	−59.6	174.4	19 42.1	−59.6	174.5	18 42.4	−59.6	174.5	17 42.7	−59.7	174.5
43	19 42.2	−59.6	174.6	18 42.5	−59.6	174.6	17 42.8	−59.6	174.6	16 43.0	−59.6	174.7
44	18 42.6	−59.6	174.7	17 42.9	−59.6	174.7	16 43.2	−59.7	174.7	15 43.4	−59.6	174.8
45	17 43.0	−59.6	174.8	16 43.3	−59.6	174.8	15 43.5	−59.6	174.9	14 43.8	−59.7	174.9
46	16 43.4	−59.6	174.9	15 43.7	−59.7	175.0	14 43.9	−59.6	175.0	13 44.1	−59.6	175.0
47	15 43.8	−59.6	175.0	14 44.0	−59.6	175.1	13 44.3	−59.7	175.1	12 44.5	−59.7	175.1
48	14 44.2	−59.6	175.2	13 44.4	−59.6	175.2	12 44.6	−59.6	175.2	11 44.8	−59.6	175.2
49	13 44.6	−59.7	175.3	12 44.8	−59.7	175.3	11 45.0	−59.7	175.3	10 45.2	−59.7	175.3
50	12 44.9	−59.6	175.4	11 45.1	−59.6	175.4	10 45.3	−59.6	175.4	9 45.5	−59.6	175.4
51	11 45.3	−59.6	175.5	10 45.5	−59.6	175.5	9 45.7	−59.7	175.5	8 45.9	−59.6	175.5
52	10 45.7	−59.6	175.6	9 45.9	−59.7	175.6	8 46.0	−59.6	175.6	7 46.2	−59.7	175.7
53	9 46.1	−59.7	175.7	8 46.2	−59.6	175.7	7 46.4	−59.7	175.8	6 46.5	−59.6	175.8
54	8 46.4	−59.6	175.8	7 46.6	−59.7	175.9	6 46.7	−59.6	175.9	5 46.9	−59.7	175.9
55	7 46.8	−59.7	176.0	6 46.9	−59.6	176.0	5 47.1	−59.7	176.0	4 47.2	−59.6	176.0
56	6 47.1	−59.6	176.1	5 47.3	−59.7	176.1	4 47.4	−59.6	176.1	3 47.6	−59.7	176.1
57	5 47.5	−59.6	176.2	4 47.6	−59.6	176.2	3 47.8	−59.7	176.2	2 47.9	−59.7	176.2
58	4 47.9	−59.7	176.3	3 48.0	−59.7	176.3	2 48.1	−59.6	176.3	1 48.2	−59.6	176.3
59	3 48.2	−59.6	176.4	2 48.3	−59.6	176.4	1 48.5	−59.7	176.4	0 48.6	−59.7	176.4
60	2 48.6	−59.7	176.5	1 48.7	−59.7	176.5	0 48.8	−59.7	176.5	0 11.1	+59.7	3.5
61	1 48.9	−59.6	176.6	0 49.0	−59.6	176.6	0 10.9	+59.6	3.4	1 10.8	+59.6	3.4
62	0 49.3	−59.7	176.7	0 10.6	+59.7	3.3	1 10.5	+59.7	3.3	2 10.4	+59.6	3.3
63	0 10.4	+59.6	3.2	1 10.3	+59.6	3.2	2 10.2	+59.6	3.2	3 10.1	+59.7	3.2
64	1 10.0	+59.7	3.1	2 09.9	+59.7	3.1	3 09.8	+59.7	3.1	4 09.8	+59.6	3.1
65	2 09.7	+59.6	3.0	3 09.6	+59.6	3.0	4 09.5	+59.7	3.0	5 09.4	+59.7	3.0
66	3 09.3	+59.6	2.8	4 09.2	+59.7	2.8	5 09.2	+59.6	2.9	6 09.1	+59.6	2.9
67	4 08.9	+59.7	2.7	5 08.9	+59.6	2.7	6 08.8	+59.7	2.7	7 08.7	+59.7	2.8
68	5 08.6	+59.6	2.6	6 08.5	+59.7	2.6	7 08.5	+59.6	2.6	8 08.4	+59.7	2.6
69	6 08.2	+59.7	2.5	7 08.2	+59.6	2.5	8 08.1	+59.7	2.5	9 08.1	+59.6	2.5
70	7 07.9	+59.6	2.4	8 07.8	+59.7	2.4	9 07.8	+59.6	2.4	10 07.7	+59.7	2.4
71	8 07.5	+59.6	2.3	9 07.5	+59.6	2.3	10 07.4	+59.7	2.3	11 07.4	+59.6	2.3
72	9 07.1	+59.7	2.2	10 07.1	+59.6	2.2	11 07.1	+59.6	2.2	12 07.0	+59.7	2.2
73	10 06.8	+59.6	2.1	11 06.7	+59.7	2.1	12 06.7	+59.6	2.1	13 06.7	+59.6	2.1
74	11 06.4	+59.6	2.0	12 06.4	+59.6	2.0	13 06.3	+59.7	2.0	14 06.3	+59.6	2.0
75	12 06.0	+59.7	1.8	13 06.0	+59.6	1.9	14 06.0	+59.6	1.9	15 05.9	+59.7	1.9
76	13 05.7	+59.6	1.7	14 05.6	+59.7	1.7	15 05.6	+59.6	1.7	16 05.6	+59.6	1.8
77	14 05.3	+59.6	1.6	15 05.3	+59.6	1.6	16 05.2	+59.6	1.6	17 05.2	+59.7	1.6
78	15 04.9	+59.6	1.5	16 04.9	+59.6	1.5	17 04.9	+59.6	1.5	18 04.9	+59.6	1.5
79	16 04.5	+59.6	1.4	17 04.5	+59.6	1.4	18 04.5	+59.6	1.4	19 04.5	+59.6	1.4
80	17 04.1	+59.7	1.3	18 04.1	+59.6	1.3	19 04.1	+59.6	1.3	20 04.1	+59.6	1.3
81	18 03.8	+59.6	1.1	19 03.7	+59.7	1.2	20 03.7	+59.7	1.2	21 03.7	+59.6	1.2
82	19 03.4	+59.6	1.0	20 03.4	+59.6	1.0	21 03.3	+59.6	1.0	22 03.3	+59.6	1.0
83	20 03.0	+59.6	0.9	21 03.0	+59.6	0.9	22 02.9	+59.6	0.9	23 02.9	+59.6	0.9
84	21 02.6	+59.5	0.8	22 02.6	+59.5	0.8	23 02.5	+59.6	0.8	24 02.5	+59.6	0.8
85	22 02.1	+59.6	0.7	23 02.1	+59.6	0.7	24 02.1	+59.6	0.7	25 02.1	+59.6	0.7
86	23 01.7	+59.6	0.5	24 01.7	+59.6	0.5	25 01.7	+59.6	0.5	26 01.7	+59.6	0.5
87	24 01.3	+59.6	0.4	25 01.3	+59.6	0.4	26 01.3	+59.6	0.4	27 01.3	+59.6	0.4
88	25 00.9	+59.5	0.3	26 00.9	+59.5	0.3	27 00.9	+59.5	0.3	28 00.9	+59.5	0.3
89	26 00.4	+59.6	0.1	27 00.4	+59.6	0.1	28 00.4	+59.6	0.1	29 00.4	+59.6	0.1
90	27 00.0	+59.5	0.0	28 00.0	+59.6	0.0	29 00.0	+59.5	0.0	30 00.0	+59.5	0.0
	27°			28°			29°			30°		

S. Lat. {L.H.A. greater than 180° ....Zn=180°−Z; L.H.A. less than 180°..........Zn=180°+Z}

LATITUDE **SAME** NAME AS DECLINATION **L.H.A. 173°, 187°**

199

8°, 352° L.H.A. LATITUDE SAME NAME AS DECLINATION

N. Lat. {L.H.A. greater than 180° .....Zn=Z / L.H.A. less than 180°............Zn=360°−Z

Dec.	23° Hc	d	Z	24° Hc	d	Z	25° Hc	d	Z	26° Hc	d	Z	27° Hc	d	Z	28° Hc	d	Z	29° Hc	d	Z	30° Hc	d	Z	Dec.
°	° ′	′	°	° ′	′	°	° ′	′	°	° ′	′	°	° ′	′	°	° ′	′	°	° ′	′	°	° ′	′	°	°
0	65 43.2	+56.9	160.2	64 46.6	+57.2	160.9	63 49.8	+57.4	161.6	62 52.7	+57.7	162.2	61 55.5	+57.8	162.8	60 58.1	+58.0	163.3	60 00.6	+58.1	163.8	59 02.9	+58.3	164.3	0
1	66 40.1	+56.6	159.4	65 43.8	+56.9	160.2	64 47.2	+57.2	160.9	63 50.4	+57.4	161.6	62 53.3	+57.7	162.2	61 56.1	+57.9	162.8	60 58.7	+58.0	163.3	60 01.2	+58.1	163.8	1
2	67 36.7	+56.4	158.6	66 40.7	+56.7	159.4	65 44.4	+57.0	160.2	64 47.8	+57.3	160.9	63 51.0	+57.5	161.6	62 54.0	+57.7	162.2	61 56.7	+57.9	162.8	60 59.3	+58.1	163.3	2
3	68 33.1	+56.0	157.7	67 37.4	+56.4	158.6	66 41.4	+56.7	159.4	65 45.1	+57.0	160.2	64 48.5	+57.3	160.9	63 51.7	+57.5	161.6	62 54.6	+57.8	162.2	61 57.4	+57.9	162.8	3
4	69 29.1	+55.7	156.7	68 33.8	+56.1	157.7	67 38.1	+56.5	158.6	66 42.1	+56.8	159.5	65 45.8	+57.1	160.2	64 49.2	+57.3	161.0	63 52.4	+57.5	161.6	62 55.3	+57.8	162.2	4
5	70 24.8	+55.2	155.6	69 29.9	+55.7	156.7	68 34.6	+56.1	157.7	67 38.9	+56.5	158.6	66 42.9	+56.8	159.5	65 46.5	+57.2	160.3	64 49.9	+57.4	161.0	63 53.1	+57.6	161.6	5
6	71 20.0	+54.7	154.4	70 25.6	+55.3	155.6	69 30.7	+55.8	156.7	68 35.4	+56.2	157.7	67 39.7	+56.6	158.6	66 43.7	+56.9	159.5	65 47.3	+57.2	160.3	64 50.7	+57.5	161.0	6
7	72 14.7	+54.2	153.1	71 20.9	+54.8	154.4	70 26.5	+55.4	155.6	69 31.6	+55.9	156.7	68 36.3	+56.3	157.7	67 40.6	+56.6	158.7	66 44.5	+57.0	159.5	65 48.2	+57.2	160.3	7
8	73 08.9	+53.4	151.6	72 15.7	+54.2	153.1	71 21.9	+54.8	154.5	70 27.5	+55.4	155.7	69 32.6	+55.9	156.8	68 37.2	+56.3	157.8	67 41.5	+56.7	158.7	66 45.4	+57.0	159.6	8
9	74 02.3	+52.7	150.0	73 09.9	+53.6	151.7	72 16.7	+54.4	153.2	71 22.9	+54.9	154.5	70 28.5	+55.5	155.7	69 33.5	+56.0	156.8	68 38.2	+56.4	157.8	67 42.4	+56.8	158.8	9
10	74 55.0	+51.7	148.2	74 03.5	+52.7	150.1	73 11.1	+53.6	151.7	72 17.8	+54.4	153.2	71 24.0	+55.0	154.6	70 29.5	+55.6	155.8	69 34.6	+56.0	156.9	68 39.2	+56.4	157.9	10
11	75 46.7	+50.6	146.2	74 56.2	+51.9	148.3	74 04.7	+52.9	150.1	73 12.2	+53.8	151.8	72 19.0	+54.5	153.3	71 25.1	+55.1	154.6	70 30.6	+55.7	155.8	69 35.6	+56.2	156.9	11
12	76 37.3	+49.3	144.0	75 48.1	+50.7	146.3	74 57.6	+51.9	148.4	74 06.0	+53.0	150.2	73 13.5	+53.8	151.9	72 20.2	+54.6	153.3	71 26.3	+55.2	154.7	70 31.8	+55.7	155.9	12
13	77 26.6	+47.6	141.4	76 38.8	+49.4	144.0	75 49.5	+50.9	146.4	74 59.0	+52.0	148.4	74 07.3	+53.1	150.3	73 14.8	+53.9	151.9	72 21.5	+54.6	153.4	71 27.5	+55.3	154.8	13
14	78 14.2	+45.6•	138.5	77 28.2	+47.7	141.5	76 40.4	+49.5	144.1	75 51.0	+51.0	146.5	75 00.4	+52.2	148.5	74 08.7	+53.2	150.4	73 16.1	+54.1	152.0	72 22.8	+54.8	153.5	14
15	78 59.8	+43.2•	135.2	78 15.9	+45.8•	138.6	77 29.9	+47.9	141.6	76 42.0	+49.6	144.2	75 52.6	+51.1	146.6	75 01.9	+52.3	148.6	74 10.2	+53.3	150.5	73 17.6	+54.1	152.1	15
16	79 43.0	+40.2•	131.5	79 01.7	+43.4•	135.3	78 17.8	+45.9•	138.7	77 31.6	+48.1	141.7	76 43.7	+49.8	144.4	75 54.2	+51.3	146.7	75 03.5	+52.4	148.7	74 11.7	+53.4	150.6	16
17	80 23.2	+36.5•	127.2	79 45.1	+40.4•	131.6	79 03.7	+43.6•	135.5	78 19.7	+46.1•	138.9	77 33.5	+48.2	141.8	76 45.5	+49.9	144.5	75 55.9	+51.4	146.8	75 05.1	+52.6	148.9	17
18	80 59.7	+32.1•	122.3	80 25.5	+36.7•	127.3	79 47.3	+40.6•	131.7	79 05.8	+43.8•	135.6	78 21.7	+46.3•	139.0	77 35.4	+48.4	142.0	76 47.3	+50.1	144.6	75 57.7	+51.5	146.9	18
19	81 31.8	+26.8•	116.7	81 02.2	+32.3•	122.4	80 27.9	+36.9•	127.4	79 49.6	+40.8•	131.8	79 08.0	+43.9•	135.7	78 23.8	+46.5•	139.1	77 37.4	+48.6	142.1	76 49.2	+50.3	144.8	19
20	81 58.6	+20.5•	110.4	81 34.5	+27.0•	116.8	81 04.8	+32.6•	122.5	80 30.4	+37.1•	127.5	79 51.9	+41.0•	132.0	79 10.3	+44.1•	135.9	78 26.0	+46.6•	139.3	77 39.5	+48.7	142.3	20
21	82 19.1	+13.5•	103.6	82 01.5	+20.7•	110.5	81 37.4	+27.2•	116.9	81 07.5	+32.8•	122.6	80 32.9	+37.5•	127.7	79 54.4	+41.2•	132.1	79 12.6	+44.4•	136.0	78 28.2	+46.9•	139.5	21
22	82 32.6	+5.6•	96.2	82 22.2	+13.6•	103.6	82 04.6	+20.9•	110.6	81 40.3	+27.4•	117.0	81 10.4	+32.9•	122.8	80 35.6	+37.7•	127.9	79 57.0	+41.4•	132.3	79 15.1	+44.5•	136.2	22
23	82 38.2	−2.4•	88.4	82 35.8	+5.8•	96.2	82 25.5	+13.7•	103.7	82 07.7	+21.1•	110.7	81 43.3	+27.7•	117.1	81 13.3	+33.2•	122.9	80 38.4	+37.9•	128.0	79 59.6	+41.7•	132.5	23
24	82 35.8	−10.3•	80.7	82 41.6	−2.4•	88.4	82 39.2	+5.8•	96.1	82 28.8	+13.9•	103.7	82 11.0	+21.3•	110.8	81 46.5	+27.9•	117.3	81 16.3	+33.5•	123.1	80 41.3	+38.1•	128.2	24
25	82 25.5	−17.8•	73.1	82 39.2	−10.4•	80.5	82 45.0	−2.3•	88.3	82 42.7	+5.9•	96.1	82 32.3	+14.0•	103.8	82 14.4	+21.5•	110.9	81 49.8	+28.1•	117.4	81 19.4	+33.8•	123.3	25
26	82 07.7	−24.4•	66.0	82 28.8	−17.8•	72.9	82 42.7	−10.4•	80.4	82 48.6	−2.3•	88.2	82 46.3	+6.1•	96.2	82 35.9	+14.2•	103.8	82 17.9	+21.7•	111.0	81 53.2	+28.3•	117.6	26
27	81 43.3	−30.0•	59.5	82 11.0	−24.5•	65.7	82 32.3	−17.9•	72.7	82 46.3	−10.4•	80.3	82 52.4	−2.3•	88.2	82 50.1	+6.2•	96.2	82 39.6	+14.4•	103.9	82 21.5	+22.0•	111.2	27
28	81 13.3	−34.9•	53.6	81 46.5	−30.2•	59.2	82 14.4	−24.6•	65.5	82 35.9	−18.0•	72.5	82 50.1	−10.5•	80.1	82 56.3	−2.3•	88.1	82 54.0	+6.3•	96.2	82 43.5	+14.5•	104.0	28
29	80 38.4	−38.8•	48.5	81 16.3	−35.0•	53.3	81 49.8	−30.4•	58.9	82 17.9	−24.7•	65.3	82 39.6	−18.1•	72.3	82 54.0	−10.5•	80.0	83 00.3	−2.3•	88.1	82 58.0	+6.4•	96.2	29
30	79 59.6	−42.0•	43.9	80 41.3	−39.0•	48.1	81 19.4	−35.1•	53.0	81 53.2	−30.6•	58.6	82 21.5	−24.9•	65.0	82 43.5	−18.2•	72.1	82 58.0	−10.5•	79.9	83 04.4	−2.2•	88.0	30
31	79 17.6	−44.7•	39.9	80 02.3	−42.2•	43.6	80 44.3	−39.2•	47.8	81 22.6	−35.3•	52.7	81 56.6	−30.6•	58.3	82 25.3	−25.1•	64.8	82 47.5	−18.4•	71.9	83 02.2	−10.7•	79.7	31
32	78 32.9	−46.9	36.5	79 20.1	−44.8•	39.6	80 05.1	−42.3•	43.3	80 47.3	−39.3•	47.5	81 26.0	−35.6•	52.4	82 00.2	−30.8•	58.0	82 29.1	−25.2•	64.5	82 51.5	−18.4•	71.7	32
33	77 46.0	−48.6	33.4	78 35.3	−47.0	36.2	79 22.8	−45.0•	39.3	80 08.0	−42.5•	42.9	80 50.4	−39.4•	47.2	81 29.4	−35.7•	52.1	82 03.9	−31.0•	57.7	82 33.1	−25.4•	64.2	33
34	76 57.4	−50.1	30.7	77 48.3	−48.7	33.1	78 37.8	−47.1	35.8	79 25.5	−45.1•	39.0	80 11.0	−42.7•	42.6	80 53.7	−39.7•	46.8	81 33.8	−35.9•	51.7	82 07.7	−31.3•	57.4	34
35	76 07.3	−51.3	28.4	76 59.6	−50.2	30.4	77 50.7	−48.8	32.8	78 40.4	−47.3	35.5	79 28.3	−45.3•	38.6	80 14.0	−42.8•	42.2	80 57.0	−39.9•	46.4	81 36.4	−36.1•	51.4	35
36	75 16.0	−52.3	26.3	76 09.4	−51.4	28.1	77 01.9	−50.3	30.1	77 53.1	−48.9	32.4	78 43.0	−47.4	35.1	79 31.2	−45.5•	38.2	80 17.1	−43.0•	41.9	81 00.3	−40.0•	46.1	36
37	74 23.7	−53.1	24.4	75 18.0	−52.4	26.0	76 11.6	−51.5	27.8	77 04.2	−50.5	29.8	77 55.6	−49.1	32.1	78 45.7	−47.5	34.8	79 34.1	−45.6•	37.9	80 20.3	−43.2•	41.5	37
38	73 30.6	−53.9	22.7	74 25.6	−53.2	24.1	75 20.1	−52.5	25.7	76 13.7	−51.6	27.4	77 06.5	−50.5	29.4	77 58.2	−49.3	31.7	78 48.5	−47.8	34.4	79 37.1	−45.8•	37.5	38
39	72 36.7	−54.5	21.2	73 32.4	−54.0	22.4	74 27.6	−53.4	23.8	75 22.1	−52.6	25.4	76 16.0	−51.7	27.1	77 08.9	−50.7	29.1	78 00.7	−49.4	31.4	78 51.3	−47.9	34.0	39
40	71 42.2	−55.0	19.9	72 38.4	−54.5	20.9	73 34.2	−54.0	22.1	74 29.5	−53.4	23.5	75 24.3	−52.7	25.0	76 18.2	−51.8	26.8	77 11.3	−50.8	28.7	78 03.4	−49.6	31.0	40
41	70 47.2	−55.5	18.6	71 43.9	−55.1	19.6	72 40.2	−54.6	20.6	73 36.1	−54.1	21.8	74 31.6	−53.6	23.2	75 26.4	−52.8	24.7	76 20.5	−51.9	26.4	77 13.8	−50.9	28.4	41
42	69 51.7	−55.9	17.5	70 48.8	−55.6	18.3	71 45.6	−55.2	19.3	72 42.0	−54.7	20.4	73 38.0	−54.2	21.5	74 33.6	−53.6	22.9	75 28.6	−52.9	24.4	76 22.9	−52.1	26.1	42
43	68 55.8	−56.2	16.4	69 53.2	−55.9	17.2	70 50.4	−55.6	18.1	71 47.3	−55.2	19.0	72 43.8	−54.8	20.1	73 40.0	−54.3	21.2	74 35.7	−53.7	22.5	75 30.8	−53.0	24.0	43
44	67 59.6	−56.6	15.5	68 57.3	−56.3	16.2	69 54.8	−56.0	16.9	70 52.1	−55.7	17.8	71 49.0	−55.3	18.7	72 45.7	−54.9	19.7	73 42.0	−54.4	20.9	74 37.8	−53.8	22.2	44
45	67 03.0	−56.8	14.6	68 01.0	−56.6	15.2	68 58.8	−56.3	15.9	69 56.4	−56.1	16.7	70 53.7	−55.7	17.5	71 50.8	−55.3	18.4	72 47.6	−55.0	19.4	73 44.0	−54.5	20.6	45
46	66 06.2	−57.0	13.8	67 04.4	−56.8	14.4	68 02.5	−56.6	15.0	69 00.3	−56.3	15.7	69 58.0	−56.1	16.4	70 55.5	−55.8	17.2	71 52.6	−55.4	18.1	72 49.5	−55.0	19.1	46
47	65 09.2	−57.2	13.1	66 07.6	−57.1	13.6	67 05.9	−56.9	14.1	68 04.0	−56.7	14.7	69 01.9	−56.4	15.4	69 59.7	−56.2	16.1	70 57.2	−55.9	16.9	71 54.5	−55.6	17.8	47
48	64 12.0	−57.5	12.4	65 10.5	−57.3	12.8	66 09.0	−57.2	13.3	67 07.3	−56.9	13.9	68 05.5	−56.8	14.5	69 03.5	−56.5	15.1	70 01.3	−56.2	15.8	70 58.9	−55.9	16.6	48
49	63 14.5	−57.6	11.7	64 13.2	−57.4	12.1	65 11.8	−57.3	12.6	66 10.4	−57.2	13.1	67 08.7	−56.9	13.6	68 07.0	−56.8	14.2	69 05.1	−56.6	14.8	70 03.0	−56.3	15.5	49
50	62 16.9	−57.7	11.1	63 15.8	−57.7	11.5	64 14.5	−57.5	11.9	65 13.2	−57.4	12.3	66 11.8	−57.2	12.8	67 10.2	−57.0	13.3	68 08.5	−56.8	13.9	69 06.7	−56.6	14.5	50
51	61 19.2	−57.9	10.5	62 18.1	−57.8	10.9	63 17.0	−57.6	11.2	64 15.8	−57.5	11.6	65 14.6	−57.5	12.1	66 13.2	−57.3	12.5	67 11.7	−57.1	13.1	68 10.1	−56.9	13.6	51
52	60 21.3	−58.0	10.0	61 20.3	−57.9	10.3	62 19.4	−57.9	10.6	63 18.3	−57.7	11.0	64 17.1	−57.5	11.4	65 15.9	−57.4	11.8	66 14.6	−57.3	12.3	67 13.2	−57.2	12.8	52
53	59 23.3	−58.2	9.5	60 22.4	−58.0	9.8	61 21.5	−57.9	10.1	62 20.6	−57.9	10.4	63 19.6	−57.8	10.8	64 18.5	−57.7	11.1	65 17.3	−57.5	11.6	66 16.0	−57.3	12.0	53
54	58 25.1	−58.2	9.0	59 24.4	−58.2	9.2	60 23.6	−58.1	9.5	61 22.7	−58.0	9.8	62 21.8	−57.9	10.2	63 20.8	−57.7	10.5	64 19.8	−57.7	10.9	65 18.7	−57.6	11.3	54
55	57 26.9	−58.3	8.5	58 26.2	−58.2	8.8	59 25.5	−58.2	9.0	60 24.7	−58.1	9.3	61 23.9	−58.0	9.6	62 23.1	−58.0	9.9	63 22.1	−57.8	10.3	64 21.1	−57.7	10.6	55
56	56 28.6	−58.4	8.1	57 28.0	−58.4	8.3	58 27.3	−58.2	8.6	59 26.6	−58.2	8.8	60 25.9	−58.1	9.1	61 25.1	−58.0	9.4	62 24.3	−57.9	9.7	63 23.4	−57.8	10.0	56
57	55 30.2	−58.5	7.7	56 29.6	−58.4	7.9	57 29.1	−58.4	8.1	58 28.4	−58.3	8.3	59 27.8	−58.2	8.6	60 27.1	−58.2	8.8	61 26.4	−58.1	9.1	62 25.6	−58.0	9.4	57
58	54 31.7	−58.5	7.3	55 31.2	−58.5	7.5	56 30.7	−58.5	7.7	57 30.1	−58.4	7.9	58 29.6	−58.4	8.1	59 28.9	−58.2	8.4	60 28.3	−58.2	8.6	61 27.6	−58.1	8.9	58
59	53 33.2	−58.7	6.9	54 32.7	−58.6	7.1	55 32.2	−58.5	7.3	56 31.7	−58.4	7.5	57 31.2	−58.4	7.7	58 30.7	−58.4	7.9	59 30.1	−58.3	8.1	60 29.5	−58.3	8.4	59
60	52 34.5	−58.6	6.6	53 34.1	−58.6	6.7	54 33.7	−58.6	6.9	55 33.3	−58.6	7.1	56 32.8	−58.5	7.3	57 32.3	−58.4	7.4	58 31.8	−58.4	7.7	59 31.2	−58.3	7.9	60
61	51 35.9	−58.8	6.2	52 35.5	−58.7	6.4	53 35.1	−58.6	6.5	54 34.7	−58.6	6.7	55 34.3	−58.6	6.9	56 33.9	−58.6	7.0	57 33.4	−58.5	7.2	58 32.9	−58.4	7.4	61
62	50 37.1	−58.8	5.9	51 36.8	−58.8	6.0	52 36.5	−58.8	6.2	53 36.1	−58.7	6.3	54 35.7	−58.6	6.5	55 35.3	−58.6	6.6	56 34.9	−58.5	6.8	57 34.5	−58.5	7.0	62
63	49 38.3	−58.8	5.6	50 38.0	−58.8	5.7	51 37.7	−58.7	5.8	52 37.4	−58.7	6.0	53 37.1	−58.7	6.1	54 36.7	−58.6	6.3	55 36.4	−58.7	6.4	56 36.0	−58.6	6.6	63
64	48 39.5	−58.9	5.3	49 39.2	−58.8	5.4	50 39.0	−58.8	5.5	51 38.7	−58.8	5.6	52 38.4	−58.8	5.8	53 38.1	−58.8	5.9	54 37.7	−58.7	6.0	55 37.4	−58.7	6.2	64
65	47 40.6	−58.9	5.0	48 40.4	−58.9	5.1	49 40.1	−58.8	5.2	50 39.9	−58.9	5.3	51 39.6	−58.8	5.4	52 39.3	−58.7	5.6	53 39.0	−58.7	5.7	54 38.7	−58.7	5.8	65
66	46 41.7	−59.0	4.7	47 41.5	−59.0	4.8	48 41.3	−59.0	4.9	49 41.0	−58.9	5.0	50 40.8	−58.9	5.1	51 40.6	−58.9	5.2	52 40.3	−58.8	5.4	53 40.0	−58.7	5.5	66
67	45 42.7	−59.0	4.5	46 42.5	−58.9	4.5	47 42.3	−58.9	4.6	48 42.1	−58.9	4.7	49 41.9	−58.9	4.8	50 41.7	−58.9	4.9	51 41.5	−58.9	5.0	52 41.3	−58.9	5.1	67
68	44 43.7	−59.0	4.2	45 43.6	−59.1	4.3	46 43.4	−59.0	4.4	47 43.2	−59.0	4.4	48 43.0	−58.9	4.5	49 42.8	−58.9	4.6	50 42.6	−58.9	4.7	51 42.4	−58.9	4.8	68
69	43 44.7	−59.1	4.0	44 44.5	−59.0	4.0	45 44.4	−59.0	4.1	46 44.2	−59.0	4.2	47 44.1	−59.0	4.3	48 43.9	−59.0	4.3	49 43.7	−58.9	4.4	50 43.5	−58.9	4.5	69
70	42 45.6	−59.1	3.7	43 45.5	−59.1	3.8	44 45.4	−59.1	3.8	45 45.2	−59.0	3.9	46 45.1	−59.0	4.0	47 44.9	−59.0	4.1	48 44.8	−59.0	4.1	49 44.6	−58.9	4.2	70
71	41 46.5	−59.1	3.5	42 46.4	−59.1	3.5	43 46.3	−59.1	3.6	44 46.2	−59.1	3.7	45 46.1	−59.1	3.7	46 45.9	−59.0	3.8	47 45.8	−59.0	3.9	48 45.7	−59.1	3.9	71
72	40 47.4	−59.1	3.3	41 47.3	−59.1	3.3	42 47.2	−59.1	3.4	43 47.1	−59.1	3.4	44 47.0	−59.1	3.5	45 46.9	−59.1	3.5	46 46.8	−59.1	3.6	47 46.6	−59.0	3.7	72
73	39 48.3	−59.2	3.0	40 48.2	−59.2	3.1	41 48.1	−59.2	3.1	42 48.0	−59.1	3.2	43 47.9	−59.1	3.2	44 47.8	−59.1	3.3	45 47.7	−59.1	3.3	46 47.6	−59.1	3.4	73
74	38 49.1	−59.2	2.8	39 49.0	−59.2	2.9	40 48.9	−59.1	2.9	41 48.9	−59.2	3.0	42 48.8	−59.2	3.0	43 48.7	−59.1	3.0	44 48.6	−59.1	3.1	45 48.5	−59.1	3.2	74
75	37 49.9	−59.2	2.6	38 49.8	−59.2	2.7	39 49.8	−59.2	2.7	40 49.7	−59.2	2.7	41 49.6	−59.1	2.8	42 49.6	−59.2	2.8	43 49.5	−59.2	2.9	44 49.4	−59.1	2.9	75
76	36 50.7	−59.3	2.4	37 50.6	−59.2	2.4	38 50.6	−59.2	2.5	39 50.5	−59.2	2.5	40 50.5	−59.2	2.6	41 50.4	−59.2	2.6	42 50.3	−59.1	2.6	43 50.3	−59.2	2.7	76
77	35 51.4	−59.2	2.2	36 51.4	−59.2	2.2	37 51.4	−59.3	2.3	38 51.3	−59.2	2.3	39 51.3	−59.3	2.3	40 51.2	−59.2	2.4	41 51.2	−59.3	2.4	42 51.1	−59.2	2.4	77
78	34 52.2	−59.3	2.0	35 52.2	−59.3	2.0	36 52.1	−59.2	2.1	37 52.1	−59.3	2.1	38 52.0	−59.2	2.1	39 52.0	−59.2	2.2	40 51.9	−59.2	2.2	41 51.9	−59.2	2.2	78
79	33 52.9	−59.3	1.8	34 52.9	−59.3	1.9	35 52.9	−59.3	1.9	36 52.8	−59.2	1.9	37 52.8	−59.3	1.9	38 52.8	−59.3	2.0	39 52.7	−59.2	2.0	40 52.7	−59.3	2.0	79
80	32 53.6	−59.3	1.6	33 53.6	−59.3	1.7	34 53.6	−59.3	1.7	35 53.6	−59.3	1.7	36 53.5	−59.3	1.7	37 53.5	−59.3	1.8	38 53.5	−59.3	1.8	39 53.4	−59.2	1.8	80
81	31 54.3	−59.3	1.5	32 54.3	−59.3	1.5	33 54.3	−59.3	1.5	34 54.3	−59.3	1.5	35 54.2	−59.3	1.5	36 54.2	−59.3	1.6	37 54.2	−59.3	1.6	38 54.2	−59.3	1.6	81
82	30 55.0	−59.3	1.3	31 55.0	−59.3	1.3	32 55.0	−59.4	1.3	33 55.0	−59.4	1.3	34 54.9	−59.3	1.4	35 54.9	−59.3	1.4	36 54.9	−59.3	1.4	37 54.9	−59.3	1.4	82
83	29 55.7	−59.4	1.1	30 55.7	−59.4	1.1	31 55.6	−59.3	1.1	32 55.6	−59.3	1.2	33 55.6	−59.3	1.2	34 55.6	−59.3	1.2	35 55.6	−59.3	1.2	36 55.6	−59.3	1.2	83
84	28 56.3	−59.3	1.0	29 56.3	−59.3	1.0	30 56.3	−59.4	1.0	31 56.3	−59.4	1.0	32 56.3	−59.4	1.0	33 56.3	−59.4	1.0	34 56.3	−59.4	1.0	35 56.3	−59.4	1.0	84
85	27 57.0	−59.4	0.8	28 57.0	−59.4	0.8	29 56.9	−59.3	0.8	30 56.9	−59.3	0.8	31 56.9	−59.3	0.8	32 56.9	−59.3	0.8	33 56.9	−59.3	0.8	34 56.9	−59.3	0.8	85
86	26 57.6	−59.4	0.6	27 57.6	−59.4	0.6	28 57.6	−59.4	0.6	29 57.6	−59.4	0.6	30 57.6	−59.4	0.6	31 57.6	−59.4	0.7	32 57.6	−59.4	0.7	33 57.6	−59.4	0.7	86
87	25 58.2	−59.4	0.5	26 58.2	−59.4	0.5	27 58.2	−59.4	0.5	28 58.2	−59.4	0.5	29 58.2	−59.4	0.5	30 58.2	−59.4	0.5	31 58.2	−59.4	0.5	32 58.2	−59.4	0.5	87
88	24 58.8	−59.4	0.3	25 58.8	−59.4	0.3	26 58.8	−59.4	0.3	27 58.8	−59.4	0.3	28 58.8	−59.4	0.3	29 58.8	−59.4	0.3	30 58.8	−59.4	0.3	31 58.8	−59.4	0.3	88
89	23 59.4	−59.4	0.2	24 59.4	−59.4	0.2	25 59.4	−59.4	0.2	26 59.4	−59.4	0.2	27 59.4	−59.4	0.2	28 59.4	−59.4	0.2	29 59.4	−59.4	0.2	30 59.4	−59.4	0.2	89
90	23 00.0	−59.4	0.0	24 00.0	−59.4	0.0	25 00.0	−59.4	0.0	26 00.0	−59.4	0.0	27 00.0	−59.4	0.0	28 00.0	−59.4	0.0	29 00.0	−59.4	0.0	30 00.0	−59.4	0.0	90
	23°			24°			25°			26°			27°			28°			29°			30°			

8°, 352° L.H.A. LATITUDE SAME NAME AS DECLINATION

200

LATITUDE **CONTRARY** NAME TO DECLINATION — L.H.A. 8°, 352°

Dec.	23° Hc	d	Z	24° Hc	d	Z	25° Hc	d	Z	26° Hc	d	Z
°	° ′	′	°	° ′	′	°	° ′	′	°	° ′	′	°
0	65 43.2	−57.1	160.2	64 46.6	−57.4	160.9	63 49.8	−57.6	161.6	62 52.7	−57.7	162.2
1	64 46.1	−57.3	160.9	63 49.2	−57.5	161.6	62 52.2	−57.7	162.2	61 55.0	−57.9	162.8
2	63 48.8	−57.6	161.6	62 51.7	−57.7	162.2	61 54.5	−57.9	162.8	60 57.1	−58.1	163.4
3	62 51.2	−57.6	162.3	61 54.0	−57.8	162.8	60 56.6	−58.0	163.4	59 59.0	−58.1	163.9
4	61 53.6	−57.8	162.9	60 56.2	−58.0	163.4	59 58.6	−58.1	163.9	59 00.9	−58.3	164.4
5	60 55.8	−58.0	163.4	59 58.2	−58.1	163.9	59 00.5	−58.2	164.4	58 02.6	−58.3	164.8
6	59 57.8	−58.0	163.9	59 00.1	−58.2	164.4	58 02.3	−58.4	164.8	57 04.3	−58.4	165.2
7	58 59.8	−58.2	164.4	58 01.9	−58.3	164.9	57 03.9	−58.4	165.3	56 05.9	−58.6	165.7
8	58 01.6	−58.3	164.9	57 03.6	−58.4	165.3	56 05.5	−58.5	165.7	55 07.3	−58.5	166.1
9	57 03.3	−58.3	165.4	56 05.2	−58.4	165.7	55 07.0	−58.5	166.1	54 08.8	−58.7	166.4
10	56 05.0	−58.4	165.8	55 06.8	−58.6	166.1	54 08.5	−58.6	166.5	53 10.1	−58.7	166.8
11	55 06.6	−58.6	166.2	54 08.2	−58.6	166.5	53 09.9	−58.7	166.8	52 11.4	−58.8	167.1
12	54 08.0	−58.5	166.6	53 09.6	−58.6	166.9	52 11.2	−58.8	167.2	51 12.6	−58.8	167.4
13	53 09.5	−58.7	166.9	52 11.0	−58.7	167.2	51 12.4	−58.8	167.5	50 13.8	−58.8	167.8
14	52 10.8	−58.7	167.3	51 12.3	−58.8	167.6	50 13.6	−58.8	167.8	49 15.0	−59.0	168.1
15	51 12.1	−58.8	167.6	50 13.5	−58.9	167.9	49 14.8	−58.9	168.1	48 16.0	−58.9	168.3
16	50 13.3	−58.8	167.9	49 14.6	−58.8	168.2	48 15.9	−58.9	168.4	47 17.1	−59.0	168.6
17	49 14.5	−58.8	168.2	48 15.8	−58.9	168.5	47 17.0	−59.0	168.7	46 18.1	−59.0	168.9
18	48 15.7	−58.9	168.5	47 16.9	−59.0	168.7	46 18.0	−59.0	169.0	45 19.1	−59.1	169.2
19	47 16.8	−59.0	168.8	46 17.9	−59.0	169.0	45 19.0	−59.1	169.2	44 20.0	−59.1	169.4
20	46 17.8	−58.9	169.1	45 18.9	−59.0	169.3	44 19.9	−59.0	169.5	43 20.9	−59.1	169.6
21	45 18.9	−59.0	169.4	44 19.9	−59.1	169.5	43 20.9	−59.1	169.7	42 21.8	−59.1	169.9
22	44 19.9	−59.1	169.6	43 20.8	−59.1	169.8	42 21.8	−59.2	169.9	41 22.7	−59.2	170.1
23	43 20.8	−59.1	169.9	42 21.7	−59.1	170.0	41 22.6	−59.1	170.2	40 23.5	−59.2	170.3
24	42 21.7	−59.1	170.1	41 22.6	−59.1	170.2	40 23.5	−59.2	170.4	39 24.3	−59.2	170.5
25	41 22.6	−59.1	170.3	40 23.5	−59.2	170.5	39 24.3	−59.2	170.6	38 25.1	−59.3	170.7
26	40 23.5	−59.2	170.5	39 24.3	−59.2	170.7	38 25.1	−59.3	170.8	37 25.8	−59.2	170.9
27	39 24.3	−59.1	170.8	38 25.1	−59.2	170.9	37 25.8	−59.2	171.0	36 26.6	−59.3	171.1
28	38 25.2	−59.2	171.0	37 25.9	−59.3	171.1	36 26.6	−59.3	171.2	35 27.3	−59.3	171.3
29	37 26.0	−59.3	171.2	36 26.6	−59.2	171.3	35 27.3	−59.3	171.4	34 28.0	−59.3	171.5
30	36 26.7	−59.2	171.4	35 27.4	−59.3	171.5	34 28.0	−59.3	171.6	33 28.7	−59.3	171.7
31	35 27.5	−59.3	171.6	34 28.1	−59.3	171.7	33 28.7	−59.3	171.8	32 29.4	−59.4	171.9
32	34 28.2	−59.3	171.8	33 28.8	−59.3	171.9	32 29.4	−59.3	172.0	31 30.0	−59.3	172.0
33	33 28.9	−59.3	172.0	32 29.5	−59.3	172.0	31 30.1	−59.4	172.1	30 30.7	−59.4	172.2
34	32 29.6	−59.3	172.1	31 30.2	−59.3	172.2	30 30.7	−59.3	172.3	29 31.3	−59.4	172.4
35	31 30.3	−59.3	172.3	30 30.9	−59.4	172.4	29 31.4	−59.4	172.5	28 31.9	−59.4	172.5
36	30 31.0	−59.3	172.5	29 31.5	−59.3	172.6	28 32.0	−59.4	172.6	27 32.5	−59.4	172.7
37	29 31.7	−59.4	172.7	28 32.2	−59.4	172.7	27 32.6	−59.4	172.8	26 33.1	−59.4	172.9
38	28 32.3	−59.3	172.8	27 32.8	−59.4	172.9	26 33.2	−59.4	173.0	25 33.7	−59.4	173.0
39	27 33.0	−59.4	173.0	26 33.4	−59.4	173.1	25 33.8	−59.4	173.1	24 34.3	−59.5	173.2
40	26 33.6	−59.4	173.2	25 34.0	−59.4	173.2	24 34.4	−59.4	173.3	23 34.8	−59.4	173.3
41	25 34.2	−59.4	173.3	24 34.6	−59.4	173.4	23 35.0	−59.4	173.4	22 35.4	−59.5	173.5
42	24 34.8	−59.4	173.5	23 35.2	−59.4	173.5	22 35.6	−59.5	173.6	21 35.9	−59.4	173.6
43	23 35.4	−59.4	173.6	22 35.8	−59.5	173.7	21 36.1	−59.4	173.7	20 36.5	−59.5	173.8
44	22 36.0	−59.5	173.8	21 36.3	−59.4	173.8	20 36.7	−59.5	173.9	19 37.0	−59.5	173.9
45	21 36.5	−59.4	173.9	20 36.9	−59.5	174.0	19 37.2	−59.5	174.0	18 37.5	−59.4	174.0
46	20 37.1	−59.4	174.1	19 37.4	−59.4	174.1	18 37.7	−59.4	174.1	17 38.1	−59.5	174.2
47	19 37.7	−59.5	174.2	18 38.0	−59.5	174.3	17 38.3	−59.5	174.3	16 38.6	−59.5	174.3
48	18 38.2	−59.4	174.4	17 38.5	−59.4	174.4	16 38.8	−59.5	174.4	15 39.1	−59.5	174.5
49	17 38.8	−59.5	174.5	16 39.1	−59.5	174.5	15 39.3	−59.5	174.6	14 39.6	−59.5	174.6
50	16 39.3	−59.4	174.6	15 39.6	−59.5	174.7	14 39.8	−59.5	174.7	13 40.1	−59.5	174.7
51	15 39.9	−59.5	174.8	14 40.1	−59.5	174.8	13 40.3	−59.4	174.8	12 40.6	−59.5	174.8
52	14 40.4	−59.5	174.9	13 40.6	−59.5	174.9	12 40.9	−59.5	175.0	11 41.1	−59.5	175.0
53	13 40.9	−59.5	175.1	12 41.1	−59.5	175.1	11 41.4	−59.5	175.1	10 41.6	−59.5	175.1
54	12 41.4	−59.4	175.2	11 41.6	−59.4	175.2	10 41.9	−59.6	175.2	9 42.1	−59.6	175.2
55	11 42.0	−59.5	175.3	10 42.2	−59.5	175.3	9 42.3	−59.5	175.4	8 42.5	−59.5	175.4
56	10 42.5	−59.5	175.5	9 42.7	−59.5	175.5	8 42.8	−59.5	175.5	7 43.0	−59.5	175.5
57	9 43.0	−59.5	175.6	8 43.2	−59.5	175.6	7 43.3	−59.5	175.6	6 43.5	−59.5	175.6
58	8 43.5	−59.5	175.7	7 43.7	−59.6	175.7	6 43.8	−59.5	175.7	5 44.0	−59.5	175.7
59	7 44.0	−59.5	175.9	6 44.1	−59.5	175.9	5 44.3	−59.5	175.9	4 44.5	−59.6	175.9
60	6 44.5	−59.5	176.0	5 44.6	−59.5	176.0	4 44.8	−59.5	176.0	3 44.9	−59.5	176.0
61	5 45.0	−59.5	176.1	4 45.1	−59.5	176.1	3 45.3	−59.6	176.1	2 45.4	−59.5	176.1
62	4 45.5	−59.5	176.2	3 45.6	−59.5	176.2	2 45.7	−59.5	176.2	1 45.9	−59.6	176.3
63	3 46.0	−59.5	176.4	2 46.1	−59.5	176.4	1 46.2	−59.5	176.4	0 46.3	−59.5	176.4
64	2 46.5	−59.5	176.5	1 46.6	−59.5	176.5	0 46.7	−59.5	176.5	0 13.2	+59.5	3.5
65	1 47.0	−59.5	176.6	0 47.1	−59.5	176.6	0 12.8	+59.5	3.4	1 12.7	+59.5	3.4
66	0 47.5	−59.5	176.8	0 12.4	+59.5	3.2	1 12.3	+59.6	3.2	2 12.2	+59.6	3.2
67	0 12.0	+59.5	3.1	1 11.9	+59.6	3.1	2 11.9	+59.5	3.1	3 11.8	+59.5	3.1
68	1 11.5	+59.5	3.0	2 11.5	+59.5	3.0	3 11.4	+59.5	3.0	4 11.3	+59.5	3.0
69	2 11.0	+59.5	2.9	3 11.0	+59.5	2.9	4 10.9	+59.5	2.9	5 10.8	+59.5	2.9
70	3 10.5	+59.6	2.7	4 10.5	+59.5	2.7	5 10.4	+59.5	2.7	6 10.3	+59.6	2.7
71	4 10.1	+59.5	2.6	5 10.0	+59.5	2.6	6 09.9	+59.5	2.6	7 09.9	+59.5	2.6
72	5 09.6	+59.5	2.5	6 09.5	+59.5	2.5	7 09.4	+59.6	2.5	8 09.4	+59.5	2.5
73	6 09.1	+59.5	2.3	7 09.0	+59.5	2.4	8 09.0	+59.5	2.4	9 08.9	+59.5	2.4
74	7 08.6	+59.5	2.2	8 08.5	+59.5	2.2	9 08.5	+59.5	2.2	10 08.4	+59.5	2.2
75	8 08.1	+59.4	2.1	9 08.0	+59.5	2.1	10 08.0	+59.5	2.1	11 07.9	+59.5	2.1
76	9 07.5	+59.5	2.0	10 07.5	+59.5	2.0	11 07.5	+59.5	2.0	12 07.4	+59.5	2.0
77	10 07.0	+59.5	1.8	11 07.0	+59.5	1.8	12 07.0	+59.5	1.8	13 06.9	+59.5	1.8
78	11 06.5	+59.5	1.7	12 06.5	+59.5	1.7	13 06.5	+59.5	1.7	14 06.4	+59.5	1.7
79	12 06.0	+59.5	1.6	13 06.0	+59.5	1.6	14 06.0	+59.5	1.6	15 05.9	+59.5	1.6
80	13 05.5	+59.5	1.4	14 05.5	+59.5	1.4	15 05.5	+59.4	1.4	16 05.4	+59.5	1.4
81	14 05.0	+59.4	1.3	15 05.0	+59.4	1.3	16 04.9	+59.5	1.3	17 04.9	+59.5	1.3
82	15 04.4	+59.5	1.1	16 04.4	+59.5	1.2	17 04.4	+59.5	1.2	18 04.4	+59.5	1.2
83	16 03.9	+59.5	1.0	17 03.9	+59.5	1.0	18 03.9	+59.5	1.0	19 03.9	+59.4	1.0
84	17 03.4	+59.4	0.9	18 03.4	+59.4	0.9	19 03.4	+59.4	0.9	20 03.3	+59.5	0.9
85	18 02.8	+59.5	0.7	19 02.8	+59.5	0.7	20 02.8	+59.5	0.7	21 02.8	+59.5	0.7
86	19 02.3	+59.4	0.6	20 02.3	+59.4	0.6	21 02.3	+59.4	0.6	22 02.3	+59.4	0.6
87	20 01.7	+59.5	0.4	21 01.7	+59.5	0.4	22 01.7	+59.4	0.5	23 01.7	+59.4	0.5
88	21 01.2	+59.4	0.3	22 01.2	+59.4	0.3	23 01.1	+59.5	0.3	24 01.1	+59.5	0.3
89	22 00.6	+59.4	0.2	23 00.6	+59.4	0.2	24 00.6	+59.4	0.2	25 00.6	+59.4	0.2
90	23 00.0	+59.4	0.0	24 00.0	+59.4	0.0	25 00.0	+59.4	0.0	26 00.0	+59.4	0.0
	23°			24°			25°			26°		

27° Hc	d	Z	28° Hc	d	Z	29° Hc	d	Z	30° Hc	d	Z	Dec.
° ′	′	°	° ′	′	°	° ′	′	°	° ′	′	°	°
61 55.5	−57.9	162.8	60 58.1	−58.1	163.3	60 00.6	−58.3	163.8	59 02.9	−58.4	164.3	0
60 57.6	−58.1	163.3	60 00.0	−58.2	163.8	59 02.3	−58.3	164.3	58 04.5	−58.5	164.7	1
59 59.5	−58.2	163.9	59 01.8	−58.3	164.3	58 04.0	−58.5	164.8	57 06.0	−58.5	165.2	2
59 01.3	−58.3	164.3	58 03.5	−58.4	164.8	57 05.5	−58.5	165.2	56 07.5	−58.6	165.6	3
58 03.0	−58.3	164.8	57 05.1	−58.5	165.2	56 07.0	−58.6	165.6	55 08.9	−58.7	165.9	4
57 04.7	−58.5	165.2	56 06.6	−58.6	165.6	55 08.4	−58.6	166.0	54 10.2	−58.8	166.3	5
56 06.2	−58.5	165.6	55 08.0	−58.6	166.0	54 09.8	−58.7	166.3	53 11.4	−58.8	166.6	6
55 07.7	−58.6	166.0	54 09.4	−58.7	166.4	53 11.1	−58.8	166.7	52 12.6	−58.8	167.0	7
54 09.1	−58.7	166.4	53 10.7	−58.7	166.7	52 12.3	−58.8	167.0	51 13.8	−58.8	167.3	8
53 10.4	−58.7	166.7	52 12.0	−58.8	167.0	51 13.5	−58.9	167.3	50 14.9	−59.0	167.6	9
52 11.7	−58.8	167.1	51 13.2	−58.9	167.4	50 14.6	−58.9	167.6	49 15.9	−58.9	167.9	10
51 12.9	−58.9	167.4	50 14.3	−58.9	167.7	49 15.7	−59.0	167.9	48 17.0	−59.1	168.2	11
50 14.0	−58.8	167.7	49 15.4	−59.0	168.0	48 16.7	−59.0	168.2	47 17.9	−59.0	168.4	12
49 15.2	−59.0	168.0	48 16.4	−58.9	168.2	47 17.7	−59.1	168.5	46 18.9	−59.1	168.7	13
48 16.2	−58.9	168.3	47 17.5	−59.1	168.5	46 18.6	−59.0	168.7	45 19.8	−59.2	168.9	14
47 17.3	−59.0	168.6	46 18.4	−59.0	168.8	45 19.6	−59.2	169.0	44 20.6	−59.1	169.2	15
46 18.3	−59.1	168.8	45 19.4	−59.1	169.0	44 20.4	−59.1	169.2	43 21.5	−59.2	169.4	16
45 19.2	−59.1	169.1	44 20.3	−59.1	169.3	43 21.3	−59.2	169.5	42 22.3	−59.2	169.6	17
44 20.1	−59.1	169.3	43 21.2	−59.2	169.5	42 22.1	−59.2	169.7	41 23.1	−59.2	169.8	18
43 21.0	−59.1	169.6	42 22.0	−59.2	169.7	41 22.9	−59.2	169.9	40 23.9	−59.3	170.0	19
42 21.9	−59.2	169.8	41 22.8	−59.2	170.0	40 23.7	−59.2	170.1	39 24.6	−59.3	170.3	20
41 22.7	−59.2	170.0	40 23.6	−59.2	170.2	39 24.5	−59.3	170.3	38 25.3	−59.3	170.5	21
40 23.5	−59.2	170.2	39 24.4	−59.2	170.4	38 25.2	−59.2	170.5	37 26.0	−59.3	170.6	22
39 24.3	−59.2	170.5	38 25.2	−59.3	170.6	37 26.0	−59.4	170.7	36 26.7	−59.3	170.8	23
38 25.1	−59.3	170.7	37 25.9	−59.3	170.8	36 26.6	−59.3	170.9	35 27.4	−59.4	171.0	24
37 25.8	−59.2	170.9	36 26.6	−59.3	171.0	35 27.3	−59.3	171.1	34 28.0	−59.3	171.2	25
36 26.6	−59.3	171.1	35 27.3	−59.3	171.2	34 28.0	−59.4	171.3	33 28.7	−59.4	171.4	26
35 27.3	−59.3	171.2	34 28.0	−59.4	171.3	33 28.6	−59.3	171.5	32 29.3	−59.4	171.5	27
34 28.0	−59.4	171.4	33 28.6	−59.3	171.5	32 29.3	−59.4	171.6	31 29.9	−59.4	171.7	28
33 28.6	−59.3	171.6	32 29.3	−59.4	171.7	31 29.9	−59.4	171.8	30 30.5	−59.4	171.9	29
32 29.3	−59.3	171.8	31 29.9	−59.4	171.9	30 30.5	−59.4	172.0	29 31.1	−59.4	172.0	30
31 30.0	−59.4	172.0	30 30.5	−59.4	172.0	29 31.1	−59.4	172.1	28 31.7	−59.5	172.2	31
30 30.6	−59.4	172.1	29 31.1	−59.4	172.2	28 31.7	−59.4	172.3	27 32.2	−59.4	172.4	32
29 31.2	−59.4	172.3	28 31.7	−59.4	172.4	27 32.3	−59.5	172.4	26 32.8	−59.5	172.5	33
28 31.8	−59.4	172.5	27 32.3	−59.4	172.5	26 32.8	−59.4	172.6	25 33.3	−59.4	172.7	34
27 32.4	−59.4	172.6	26 32.9	−59.4	172.7	25 33.4	−59.5	172.7	24 33.9	−59.5	172.8	35
26 33.0	−59.4	172.8	25 33.5	−59.5	172.8	24 33.9	−59.4	172.9	23 34.4	−59.5	172.9	36
25 33.6	−59.5	172.9	24 34.0	−59.4	173.0	23 34.5	−59.5	173.0	22 34.9	−59.5	173.1	37
24 34.1	−59.4	173.1	23 34.6	−59.5	173.1	22 35.0	−59.5	173.2	21 35.4	−59.5	173.2	38
23 34.7	−59.5	173.2	22 35.1	−59.5	173.3	21 35.5	−59.5	173.3	20 35.9	−59.5	173.4	39
22 35.2	−59.4	173.4	21 35.6	−59.4	173.4	20 36.0	−59.5	173.5	19 36.4	−59.5	173.5	40
21 35.8	−59.5	173.5	20 36.2	−59.5	173.6	19 36.5	−59.5	173.6	18 36.9	−59.5	173.6	41
20 36.3	−59.5	173.7	19 36.7	−59.5	173.7	18 37.0	−59.5	173.7	17 37.4	−59.5	173.8	42
19 36.8	−59.5	173.8	18 37.2	−59.5	173.8	17 37.5	−59.5	173.9	16 37.9	−59.6	173.9	43
18 37.3	−59.4	173.9	17 37.7	−59.5	174.0	16 38.0	−59.5	174.0	15 38.3	−59.5	174.0	44
17 37.9	−59.5	174.1	16 38.2	−59.5	174.1	15 38.5	−59.5	174.1	14 38.8	−59.5	174.2	45
16 38.4	−59.5	174.2	15 38.7	−59.5	174.2	14 39.0	−59.6	174.3	13 39.3	−59.6	174.3	46
15 38.9	−59.5	174.3	14 39.2	−59.6	174.4	13 39.4	−59.5	174.4	12 39.7	−59.5	174.4	47
14 39.4	−59.5	174.5	13 39.6	−59.5	174.5	12 39.9	−59.5	174.5	11 40.2	−59.6	174.5	48
13 39.9	−59.6	174.6	12 40.1	−59.5	174.6	11 40.4	−59.6	174.7	10 40.6	−59.5	174.7	49
12 40.3	−59.5	174.7	11 40.6	−59.5	174.8	10 40.8	−59.5	174.8	9 41.1	−59.6	174.8	50
11 40.8	−59.5	174.9	10 41.1	−59.6	174.9	9 41.3	−59.5	174.9	8 41.5	−59.5	174.9	51
10 41.3	−59.5	175.0	9 41.5	−59.5	175.0	8 41.8	−59.6	175.0	7 42.0	−59.6	175.0	52
9 41.8	−59.5	175.1	8 42.0	−59.5	175.1	7 42.2	−59.5	175.2	6 42.4	−59.5	175.2	53
8 42.3	−59.6	175.3	7 42.5	−59.6	175.3	6 42.7	−59.6	175.3	5 42.9	−59.6	175.3	54
7 42.7	−59.5	175.4	6 42.9	−59.5	175.4	5 43.1	−59.5	175.4	4 43.3	−59.5	175.4	55
6 43.2	−59.5	175.5	5 43.4	−59.5	175.5	4 43.6	−59.6	175.5	3 43.8	−59.6	175.5	56
5 43.7	−59.6	175.6	4 43.9	−59.6	175.6	3 44.0	−59.5	175.6	2 44.2	−59.6	175.6	57
4 44.1	−59.5	175.8	3 44.3	−59.5	175.8	2 44.5	−59.6	175.8	1 44.6	−59.5	175.8	58
3 44.6	−59.5	175.9	2 44.8	−59.6	175.9	1 44.9	−59.5	175.9	0 45.1	−59.6	175.9	59
2 45.1	−59.6	176.0	1 45.2	−59.5	176.0	0 45.4	−59.6	176.0	0 14.5	+59.5	4.0	60
1 45.5	−59.5	176.1	0 45.7	−59.6	176.1	0 14.2	+59.5	3.9	1 14.0	+59.6	3.9	61
0 46.0	−59.5	176.3	0 13.9	+59.5	3.7	1 13.7	+59.6	3.7	2 13.6	+59.6	3.7	62
0 13.5	+59.6	3.6	1 13.4	+59.6	3.6	2 13.3	+59.5	3.6	3 13.2	+59.5	3.6	63
1 13.1	+59.5	3.5	2 13.0	+59.5	3.5	3 12.8	+59.6	3.5	4 12.7	+59.6	3.5	64
2 12.6	+59.5	3.4	3 12.5	+59.5	3.4	4 12.4	+59.5	3.4	5 12.3	+59.6	3.4	65
3 12.1	+59.6	3.3	4 12.0	+59.6	3.3	5 11.9	+59.6	3.3	6 11.9	+59.5	3.3	66
4 11.7	+59.5	3.1	5 11.6	+59.5	3.1	6 11.5	+59.5	3.1	7 11.4	+59.6	3.1	67
5 11.2	+59.5	3.0	6 11.1	+59.6	3.0	7 11.0	+59.6	3.0	8 11.0	+59.5	3.0	68
6 10.7	+59.6	2.9	7 10.7	+59.5	2.9	8 10.6	+59.5	2.9	9 10.5	+59.6	2.9	69
7 10.3	+59.5	2.7	8 10.2	+59.5	2.8	9 10.1	+59.6	2.8	10 10.1	+59.5	2.8	70
8 09.8	+59.5	2.6	9 09.7	+59.6	2.6	10 09.7	+59.5	2.6	11 09.6	+59.6	2.6	71
9 09.3	+59.6	2.5	10 09.3	+59.5	2.5	11 09.2	+59.5	2.5	12 09.2	+59.5	2.5	72
10 08.9	+59.5	2.4	11 08.8	+59.5	2.4	12 08.7	+59.6	2.4	13 08.7	+59.5	2.4	73
11 08.4	+59.5	2.2	12 08.3	+59.5	2.2	13 08.3	+59.5	2.3	14 08.2	+59.6	2.3	74
12 07.9	+59.5	2.1	13 07.8	+59.6	2.1	14 07.8	+59.5	2.1	15 07.8	+59.5	2.1	75
13 07.4	+59.5	2.0	14 07.4	+59.5	2.0	15 07.3	+59.5	2.0	16 07.3	+59.5	2.0	76
14 06.9	+59.5	1.8	15 06.9	+59.5	1.9	16 06.8	+59.6	1.9	17 06.8	+59.5	1.9	77
15 06.4	+59.5	1.7	16 06.4	+59.5	1.7	17 06.4	+59.5	1.7	18 06.3	+59.5	1.7	78
16 05.9	+59.5	1.6	17 05.9	+59.5	1.6	18 05.9	+59.5	1.6	19 05.8	+59.6	1.6	79
17 05.4	+59.5	1.4	18 05.4	+59.5	1.5	19 05.4	+59.5	1.5	20 05.4	+59.5	1.5	80
18 04.9	+59.5	1.3	19 04.9	+59.5	1.3	20 04.9	+59.5	1.3	21 04.9	+59.5	1.3	81
19 04.4	+59.5	1.2	20 04.4	+59.5	1.2	21 04.4	+59.4	1.2	22 04.4	+59.4	1.2	82
20 03.9	+59.4	1.0	21 03.9	+59.4	1.0	22 03.8	+59.5	1.0	23 03.8	+59.5	1.1	83
21 03.3	+59.5	0.9	22 03.3	+59.5	0.9	23 03.3	+59.5	0.9	24 03.3	+59.5	0.9	84
22 02.8	+59.5	0.7	23 02.8	+59.5	0.8	24 02.8	+59.5	0.8	25 02.8	+59.4	0.8	85
23 02.3	+59.4	0.6	24 02.3	+59.4	0.6	25 02.3	+59.4	0.6	26 02.2	+59.5	0.6	86
24 01.7	+59.4	0.5	25 01.7	+59.4	0.5	26 01.7	+59.4	0.5	27 01.7	+59.4	0.5	87
25 01.1	+59.5	0.3	26 01.1	+59.5	0.3	27 01.1	+59.5	0.3	28 01.1	+59.5	0.3	88
26 00.6	+59.4	0.2	27 00.6	+59.4	0.2	28 00.6	+59.4	0.2	29 00.6	+59.4	0.2	89
27 00.0	+59.4	0.0	28 00.0	+59.4	0.0	29 00.0	+59.4	0.0	30 00.0	+59.4	0.0	90
27°			28°			29°			30°			

S. Lat. { L.H.A. greater than 180° ....Zn=180°−Z
{ L.H.A. less than 180°...........Zn=180°+Z

LATITUDE **SAME** NAME AS DECLINATION — L.H.A. 172°, 188°

9°, 351° L.H.A. LATITUDE SAME NAME AS DECLINATION

N. Lat. {L.H.A. greater than 180° .....Zn=Z; L.H.A. less than 180°............Zn=360°−Z}

Dec.	23° Hc	d	Z	24° Hc	d	Z	25° Hc	d	Z	26° Hc	d	Z	27° Hc	d	Z	28° Hc	d	Z	29° Hc	d	Z	30° Hc	d	Z	Dec.
°	° ′	′	°	° ′	′	°	° ′	′	°	° ′	′	°	° ′	′	°	° ′	′	°	° ′	′	°	° ′	′	°	°
0	65 23.5	+56.1	157.9	64 27.7	+56.5	158.7	63 31.7	+56.7	159.5	62 35.4	+57.0	160.1	61 38.8	+57.3	160.8	60 42.1	+57.4	161.4	59 45.1	+57.7	161.9	58 48.0	+57.8	162.4	0
1	66 19.6	+55.9	157.1	65 24.2	+56.2	157.9	64 28.4	+56.6	158.7	63 32.4	+56.8	159.4	62 36.1	+57.1	160.1	61 39.5	+57.4	160.8	60 42.8	+57.5	161.4	59 45.8	+57.8	161.9	1
2	67 15.5	+55.5	156.1	66 20.4	+55.9	157.1	65 25.0	+56.2	157.9	64 29.2	+56.6	158.7	63 33.2	+56.8	159.4	62 36.9	+57.1	160.1	61 40.3	+57.4	160.8	60 43.6	+57.5	161.4	2
3	68 11.0	+55.1	155.1	67 16.3	+55.6	156.2	66 21.2	+56.0	157.1	65 25.8	+56.3	157.9	64 30.0	+56.7	158.7	63 34.0	+56.9	159.5	62 37.7	+57.2	160.1	61 41.1	+57.5	160.8	3
4	69 06.1	+54.6	154.1	68 11.9	+55.2	155.2	67 17.2	+55.6	156.2	66 22.1	+56.1	157.1	65 26.7	+56.4	157.9	64 30.9	+56.7	158.7	63 34.9	+57.0	159.5	62 38.6	+57.2	160.1	4
5	70 00.7	+54.2	152.9	69 07.1	+54.7	154.1	68 12.8	+55.3	155.2	67 18.2	+55.7	156.2	66 23.1	+56.1	157.1	65 27.6	+56.5	158.0	64 31.9	+56.7	158.8	63 35.8	+57.0	159.5	5
6	70 54.9	+53.6	151.6	70 01.8	+54.2	152.9	69 08.1	+54.8	154.1	68 13.9	+55.3	155.2	67 19.2	+55.8	156.2	66 24.1	+56.2	157.1	65 28.6	+56.5	158.0	64 32.8	+56.9	158.8	6
7	71 48.5	+52.8	150.2	70 56.0	+53.7	151.6	70 02.9	+54.3	152.9	69 09.2	+54.9	154.1	68 15.0	+55.4	155.2	67 20.3	+55.8	156.2	66 25.1	+56.3	157.2	65 29.7	+56.6	158.0	7
8	72 41.3	+52.1	148.6	71 49.7	+53.0	150.2	70 57.2	+53.8	151.7	70 04.1	+54.4	153.0	69 10.4	+54.9	154.2	68 16.1	+55.5	155.3	67 21.4	+55.9	156.3	66 26.3	+56.3	157.2	8
9	73 33.4	+51.2	146.9	72 42.7	+52.1	148.7	71 51.0	+53.0	150.3	70 58.5	+53.8	151.7	70 05.3	+54.5	153.0	69 11.6	+55.0	154.2	68 17.3	+55.6	155.3	67 22.6	+56.0	156.3	9
10	74 24.6	+50.1	145.0	73 34.8	+51.3	147.0	72 44.0	+52.3	148.7	71 52.3	+53.2	150.3	70 59.8	+54.0	151.8	70 06.6	+54.6	153.1	69 12.9	+55.1	154.3	68 18.6	+55.6	155.4	10
11	75 14.7	+48.8	142.9	74 26.1	+50.3	145.1	73 36.3	+51.5	147.0	72 45.5	+52.4	148.8	71 53.8	+53.2	150.4	71 01.2	+54.1	151.8	70 08.0	+54.7	153.1	69 14.2	+55.2	154.3	11
12	76 03.5	+47.3	140.6	75 16.4	+48.9	143.0	74 27.8	+50.3	145.2	73 37.9	+51.6	147.1	72 47.0	+52.6	148.9	71 55.3	+53.3	150.5	71 02.7	+54.1	151.9	70 09.4	+54.8	153.2	12
13	76 50.8	+45.5	137.9	76 05.3	+47.5	140.7	75 18.1	+49.1	143.1	74 29.5	+50.4	145.2	73 39.6	+51.6	147.2	72 48.6	+52.7	149.0	71 56.8	+53.5	150.5	71 04.2	+54.2	152.0	13
14	77 36.3	+43.4•	135.0	76 52.8	+45.6	138.0	76 07.2	+47.6	140.7	75 19.9	+49.3	143.2	74 31.2	+50.7	145.3	73 41.3	+51.8	147.3	72 50.3	+52.8	149.0	71 58.4	+53.7	150.6	14
15	78 19.7	+40.8•	131.7	77 38.4	+43.6•	135.1	76 54.8	+45.9	138.1	76 09.2	+47.8	140.8	75 21.9	+49.4	143.3	74 33.1	+50.7	145.4	73 43.1	+51.9	147.4	72 52.1	+52.9	149.1	15
16	79 00.5	+37.6•	127.9	78 22.0	+40.9•	131.8	77 40.7	+43.7•	135.2	76 57.0	+46.0	138.2	76 11.3	+47.9	141.0	75 23.8	+49.6	143.4	74 35.0	+50.9	145.6	73 45.0	+52.0	147.5	16
17	79 38.1	+34.1•	123.7	79 02.9	+37.9•	128.0	78 24.4	+41.2•	131.9	77 43.0	+43.9•	135.3	76 59.2	+46.2	138.4	76 13.4	+48.1	141.1	75 25.9	+49.7	143.5	74 37.0	+51.1	145.7	17
18	80 12.2	+29.6•	119.0	79 40.8	+34.3•	123.8	79 05.6	+38.1•	128.2	78 26.9	+41.4•	132.0	77 45.4	+44.1•	135.4	77 01.5	+46.4	138.5	76 15.6	+48.3	141.2	75 28.1	+49.9	143.6	18
19	80 41.8	+24.6•	113.8	80 15.1	+29.9•	119.1	79 43.7	+34.4•	124.0	79 08.3	+38.3•	128.3	78 29.5	+41.6•	132.2	77 47.9	+44.3•	135.6	77 03.9	+46.6	138.6	76 18.0	+48.4	141.4	19
20	81 06.4	+18.8•	108.0	80 45.0	+24.8•	113.9	80 18.1	+30.1•	119.2	79 46.6	+34.7•	124.1	79 11.1	+38.6•	128.4	78 32.2	+41.8•	132.3	77 50.5	+44.5•	135.7	77 06.4	+46.8	138.8	20
21	81 25.2	+12.4•	101.8	81 09.8	+19.0•	108.1	80 48.2	+25.0•	114.0	80 21.3	+30.3•	119.3	79 49.7	+34.9•	124.2	79 14.0	+38.8•	128.6	78 35.0	+42.1•	132.5	77 53.2	+44.7•	135.9	21
22	81 37.6	+5.4•	95.1	81 28.8	+12.5•	101.8	81 13.2	+19.2•	108.1	80 51.6	+25.3•	114.1	80 24.6	+30.5•	119.5	79 52.8	+35.2•	124.4	79 17.1	+39.0•	128.7	78 37.9	+42.3•	132.6	22
23	81 43.0	−1.7•	88.2	81 41.3	+5.5•	95.1	81 32.4	+12.7•	101.8	81 16.9	+19.3•	108.2	80 55.1	+25.5•	114.2	80 28.0	+30.8•	119.6	79 56.1	+35.4•	124.5	79 20.2	+39.3•	128.9	23
24	81 41.3	−8.9•	81.3	81 46.8	−1.7•	88.2	81 45.1	+5.6•	95.1	81 36.2	+12.8•	101.8	81 20.6	+19.6•	108.3	80 58.8	+25.7•	114.3	80 31.5	+31.1•	119.8	79 59.5	+35.6•	124.7	24
25	81 32.4	−15.5•	74.5	81 45.1	−8.9•	81.2	81 50.7	−1.7•	88.1	81 49.0	+5.7•	95.1	81 40.2	+12.9•	101.9	81 24.5	+19.8•	108.4	81 02.6	+25.9•	114.4	80 35.1	+31.4•	119.9	25
26	81 16.9	−21.8•	68.1	81 36.2	−15.6•	74.3	81 49.0	−8.8•	81.1	81 54.7	−1.6•	88.0	81 53.1	+5.9•	95.1	81 44.3	+13.1•	101.9	81 28.5	+20.0•	108.5	81 06.5	+26.1•	114.5	26
27	80 55.1	−27.1•	62.0	81 20.6	−21.8•	67.8	81 40.2	−15.7•	74.2	81 53.1	−8.8•	80.9	81 59.0	−1.6•	88.0	81 57.4	+5.9•	95.0	81 48.5	+13.3•	102.0	81 32.6	+20.3•	108.6	27
28	80 28.0	−31.9•	56.5	80 58.8	−27.3•	61.8	81 24.5	−21.9•	67.6	81 44.3	−15.8•	74.0	81 57.4	−8.9•	80.8	82 03.3	−1.5•	87.9	82 01.8	+6.0•	95.0	81 52.9	+13.4•	102.0	28
29	79 56.1	−35.9•	51.5	80 31.5	−32.0•	56.2	81 02.6	−27.5•	61.5	81 28.5	−22.0•	67.4	81 48.5	−15.9•	73.8	82 01.8	−8.9•	80.7	82 07.8	−1.5•	87.8	82 06.3	+6.2•	95.0	29
30	79 20.2	−39.3•	47.1	79 59.5	−36.1•	51.2	80 35.1	−32.1•	55.9	81 06.5	−27.6•	61.2	81 32.6	−22.1•	67.1	81 52.9	−16.0•	73.6	82 06.3	−8.9•	80.5	82 12.5	−1.5•	87.7	30
31	78 40.9	−42.1•	43.1	79 23.4	−39.4•	46.7	80 03.0	−36.2•	50.9	80 38.9	−32.3•	55.6	81 10.5	−27.7•	60.9	81 36.9	−22.3•	66.9	81 57.4	−16.1•	73.4	82 11.0	−9.0•	80.4	31
32	77 58.8	−44.4•	39.6	78 44.0	−42.2•	42.8	79 26.8	−39.6•	46.4	80 06.6	−36.4•	50.6	80 42.8	−32.5•	55.3	81 14.6	−27.9•	60.6	81 41.3	−22.4•	66.6	82 02.0	−16.1•	73.2	32
33	77 14.4	−46.4	36.4	78 01.8	−44.6•	39.2	78 47.2	−42.4•	42.4	79 30.2	−39.7•	46.1	80 10.3	−36.6•	50.2	80 46.7	−32.6•	55.0	81 18.9	−28.1•	60.3	81 45.9	−22.6•	66.3	33
34	76 28.0	−48.1	33.7	77 17.2	−46.6	36.1	78 04.8	−44.7•	38.9	78 50.5	−42.6•	42.1	79 33.7	−39.9•	45.7	80 14.1	−36.8•	49.9	80 50.8	−32.8•	54.6	81 23.3	−28.3•	60.0	34
35	75 39.9	−49.5	31.2	76 30.6	−48.1	33.3	77 20.1	−46.7	35.8	78 07.9	−44.9•	38.5	78 53.8	−42.7•	41.7	79 37.3	−40.1•	45.3	80 18.0	−37.0•	49.5	80 55.0	−33.1•	54.3	35
36	74 50.4	−50.6	28.9	75 42.5	−49.6	30.8	76 33.4	−48.3	33.0	77 23.0	−46.8	35.4	78 11.1	−45.0•	38.2	78 57.2	−42.9•	41.3	79 41.0	−40.3•	45.0	80 21.9	−37.1•	49.1	36
37	73 59.8	−51.6	26.9	74 52.9	−50.8	28.6	75 45.1	−49.7	30.5	76 36.2	−48.4	32.6	77 26.1	−47.0	35.0	78 14.3	−45.2•	37.8	79 00.7	−43.0•	41.0	79 44.8	−40.5•	44.6	37
38	73 08.2	−52.5	25.1	74 02.1	−51.7	26.6	74 55.4	−50.9	28.3	75 47.8	−49.9	30.2	76 39.1	−48.6	32.3	77 29.1	−47.1	34.7	78 17.7	−45.4•	37.4	79 04.3	−43.3•	40.6	38
39	72 15.7	−53.3	23.5	73 10.4	−52.6	24.8	74 04.5	−51.8	26.3	74 57.9	−50.9	27.9	75 50.5	−50.0	29.8	76 42.0	−48.7	31.9	77 32.3	−47.3	34.3	78 21.0	−45.5•	37.0	39
40	71 22.4	−53.8	22.0	72 17.8	−53.3	23.2	73 12.7	−52.7	24.5	74 07.0	−52.0	26.0	75 00.5	−51.0	27.6	75 53.3	−50.1	29.4	76 45.0	−48.9	31.5	77 35.5	−47.5	33.9	40
41	70 28.6	−54.4	20.7	71 24.5	−53.9	21.7	72 20.0	−53.4	22.9	73 15.0	−52.7	24.2	74 09.5	−52.1	25.6	75 03.2	−51.2	27.2	75 56.1	−50.2	29.1	76 48.0	−49.0	31.1	41
42	69 34.2	−54.9	19.5	70 30.6	−54.5	20.4	71 26.6	−54.0	21.4	72 22.3	−53.5	22.6	73 17.4	−52.9	23.8	74 12.0	−52.2	25.3	75 05.9	−51.3	26.9	75 59.0	−50.4	28.7	42
43	68 39.3	−55.3	18.3	69 36.1	−54.9	19.2	70 32.6	−54.5	20.1	71 28.8	−54.1	21.1	72 24.5	−53.5	22.2	73 19.8	−52.9	23.5	74 14.6	−52.3	24.9	75 08.6	−51.4	26.5	43
44	67 44.0	−55.7	17.3	68 41.2	−55.4	18.0	69 38.1	−55.0	18.9	70 34.7	−54.6	19.8	71 31.0	−54.2	20.8	72 26.9	−53.7	21.9	73 22.3	−53.1	23.3	74 17.2	−52.4	24.6	44
45	66 48.3	−56.0	16.3	67 45.8	−55.7	17.0	68 43.1	−55.5	17.7	69 40.1	−55.1	18.6	70 36.8	−54.7	19.5	71 33.2	−54.3	20.5	72 29.2	−53.8	21.6	73 24.8	−53.2	22.8	45
46	65 52.3	−56.3	15.4	66 50.1	−56.1	16.0	67 47.6	−55.8	16.7	68 45.0	−55.5	17.4	69 42.1	−55.2	18.3	70 38.9	−54.8	19.1	71 35.4	−54.3	20.1	72 31.6	−53.9	21.2	46
47	64 56.0	−56.5	14.6	65 54.0	−56.3	15.1	66 51.8	−56.1	15.8	67 49.5	−55.9	16.4	68 46.9	−55.5	17.1	69 44.1	−55.2	17.9	70 41.1	−54.9	18.8	71 37.7	−54.4	19.8	47
48	63 59.5	−56.8	13.8	64 57.7	−56.6	14.3	65 55.7	−56.4	14.9	66 53.6	−56.1	15.5	67 51.4	−55.9	16.1	68 48.9	−55.6	16.8	69 46.2	−55.3	17.6	70 43.3	−55.0	18.5	48
49	63 02.7	−57.0	13.1	64 01.1	−56.9	13.5	64 59.3	−56.6	14.0	65 57.5	−56.5	14.6	66 55.5	−56.3	15.2	67 53.3	−56.0	15.8	68 50.9	−55.7	16.5	69 48.3	−55.4	17.3	49
50	62 05.7	−57.2	12.4	63 04.2	−57.0	12.8	64 02.7	−56.9	13.3	65 01.0	−56.7	13.8	65 59.2	−56.5	14.3	66 57.3	−56.3	14.9	67 55.2	−56.1	15.5	68 52.9	−55.8	16.2	50
51	61 08.5	−57.4	11.8	62 07.2	−57.2	12.2	63 05.8	−57.1	12.6	64 04.3	−56.9	13.0	65 02.7	−56.7	13.5	66 01.0	−56.6	14.0	66 59.1	−56.3	14.6	67 57.1	−56.1	15.2	51
52	60 11.1	−57.5	11.2	61 10.0	−57.4	11.5	62 08.7	−57.2	11.9	63 07.4	−57.1	12.3	64 06.0	−57.0	12.7	65 04.4	−56.8	13.2	66 02.8	−56.6	13.7	67 01.0	−56.4	14.3	52
53	59 13.6	−57.6	10.6	60 12.6	−57.5	10.9	61 11.5	−57.5	11.3	62 10.3	−57.3	11.6	63 09.0	−57.2	12.0	64 07.6	−57.0	12.5	65 06.2	−56.9	12.9	66 04.6	−56.7	13.4	53
54	58 16.0	−57.8	10.1	59 15.1	−57.7	10.4	60 14.0	−57.5	10.7	61 13.0	−57.5	11.0	62 11.8	−57.3	11.4	63 10.6	−57.2	11.8	64 09.3	−57.1	12.2	65 07.9	−56.9	12.6	54
55	57 18.2	−57.8	9.6	58 17.4	−57.8	9.8	59 16.5	−57.7	10.1	60 15.5	−57.6	10.4	61 14.5	−57.5	10.7	62 13.4	−57.4	11.1	63 12.2	−57.2	11.5	64 11.0	−57.1	11.9	55
56	56 20.4	−58.0	9.1	57 19.6	−57.9	9.3	58 18.8	−57.9	9.6	59 17.9	−57.7	9.9	60 17.0	−57.7	10.2	61 16.0	−57.5	10.5	62 15.0	−57.5	10.8	63 13.9	−57.3	11.2	56
57	55 22.4	−58.1	8.6	56 21.7	−58.1	8.8	57 20.9	−57.9	9.1	58 20.2	−57.9	9.3	59 19.3	−57.7	9.6	60 18.5	−57.7	9.9	61 17.5	−57.5	10.2	62 16.6	−57.5	10.6	57
58	54 24.3	−58.2	8.2	55 23.6	−58.1	8.4	56 23.0	−58.1	8.6	57 22.3	−58.0	8.8	58 21.6	−57.9	9.1	59 20.8	−57.8	9.4	60 20.0	−57.8	9.6	61 19.1	−57.7	9.9	58
59	53 26.1	−58.3	7.8	54 25.5	−58.2	8.0	55 24.9	−58.1	8.2	56 24.3	−58.1	8.4	57 23.7	−58.1	8.6	58 23.0	−58.0	8.8	59 22.2	−57.8	9.1	60 21.4	−57.7	9.4	59
60	52 27.8	−58.3	7.4	53 27.3	−58.3	7.5	54 26.8	−58.2	7.7	55 26.2	−58.1	7.9	56 25.6	−58.1	8.1	57 25.0	−58.0	8.4	58 24.4	−58.0	8.6	59 23.7	−57.9	8.8	60
61	51 29.5	−58.4	7.0	52 29.0	−58.3	7.2	53 28.6	−58.4	7.3	54 28.1	−58.3	7.5	55 27.5	−58.2	7.7	56 27.0	−58.2	7.9	57 26.4	−58.1	8.1	58 25.8	−58.0	8.3	61
62	50 31.1	−58.5	6.6	51 30.7	−58.5	6.8	52 30.2	−58.3	6.9	53 29.8	−58.3	7.1	54 29.3	−58.3	7.3	55 28.8	−58.2	7.4	56 28.3	−58.2	7.6	57 27.8	−58.1	7.8	62
63	49 32.6	−58.5	6.3	50 32.2	−58.4	6.4	51 31.9	−58.5	6.6	52 31.5	−58.5	6.7	53 31.0	−58.3	6.9	54 30.6	−58.3	7.0	55 30.1	−58.2	7.2	56 29.7	−58.3	7.4	63
64	48 34.1	−58.6	5.9	49 33.8	−58.6	6.1	50 33.4	−58.5	6.2	51 33.0	−58.4	6.3	52 32.7	−58.5	6.5	53 32.3	−58.4	6.6	54 31.9	−58.4	6.8	55 31.4	−58.3	7.0	64
65	47 35.5	−58.7	5.6	48 35.2	−58.6	5.7	49 34.9	−58.6	5.9	50 34.6	−58.6	6.0	51 34.2	−58.5	6.1	52 33.9	−58.5	6.2	53 33.5	−58.4	6.4	54 33.1	−58.3	6.5	65
66	46 36.8	−58.6	5.3	47 36.6	−58.7	5.4	48 36.3	−58.6	5.5	49 36.0	−58.6	5.6	50 35.7	−58.5	5.8	51 35.4	−58.5	5.9	52 35.1	−58.5	6.0	53 34.8	−58.5	6.2	66
67	45 38.2	−58.8	5.0	46 37.9	−58.7	5.1	47 37.7	−58.7	5.2	48 37.4	−58.6	5.3	49 37.2	−58.7	5.4	50 36.9	−58.6	5.5	51 36.6	−58.5	5.6	52 36.3	−58.5	5.8	67
68	44 39.4	−58.8	4.7	45 39.2	−58.7	4.8	46 39.0	−58.7	4.9	47 38.8	−58.7	5.0	48 38.5	−58.6	5.1	49 38.3	−58.6	5.2	50 38.1	−58.7	5.3	51 37.8	−58.6	5.4	68
69	43 40.6	−58.8	4.4	44 40.5	−58.8	4.5	45 40.3	−58.8	4.6	46 40.1	−58.8	4.7	47 39.9	−58.8	4.8	48 39.7	−58.7	4.9	49 39.4	−58.6	5.0	50 39.2	−58.6	5.1	69
70	42 41.8	−58.8	4.2	43 41.7	−58.9	4.2	44 41.5	−58.8	4.3	45 41.3	−58.8	4.4	46 41.1	−58.7	4.5	47 41.0	−58.8	4.6	48 40.8	−58.8	4.6	49 40.6	−58.7	4.7	70
71	41 43.0	−58.9	3.9	42 42.8	−58.8	4.0	43 42.7	−58.9	4.0	44 42.5	−58.8	4.1	45 42.4	−58.8	4.2	46 42.2	−58.8	4.2	47 42.0	−58.7	4.3	48 41.9	−58.8	4.4	71
72	40 44.1	−58.9	3.7	41 44.0	−59.0	3.7	42 43.8	−58.9	3.8	43 43.7	−58.9	3.8	44 43.6	−58.9	3.9	45 43.4	−58.8	4.0	46 43.3	−58.8	4.0	47 43.1	−58.8	4.1	72
73	39 45.2	−59.0	3.4	40 45.0	−58.9	3.5	41 44.9	−58.9	3.5	42 44.8	−58.9	3.6	43 44.7	−58.9	3.6	44 44.6	−58.9	3.7	45 44.5	−58.9	3.8	46 44.3	−58.8	3.8	73
74	38 46.2	−59.0	3.2	39 46.1	−59.0	3.2	40 46.0	−58.9	3.3	41 45.9	−58.9	3.3	42 45.8	−58.9	3.4	43 45.7	−58.9	3.4	44 45.6	−58.9	3.5	45 45.5	−58.9	3.5	74
75	37 47.2	−59.0	2.9	38 47.1	−59.0	3.0	39 47.1	−59.0	3.0	40 47.0	−59.0	3.1	41 46.9	−59.0	3.1	42 46.8	−58.9	3.2	43 46.7	−58.9	3.2	44 46.6	−58.9	3.3	75
76	36 48.2	−59.0	2.7	37 48.1	−59.0	2.7	38 48.1	−59.0	2.8	39 48.0	−59.0	2.8	40 47.9	−59.0	2.9	41 47.9	−59.0	2.9	42 47.8	−59.0	3.0	43 47.7	−59.0	3.0	76
77	35 49.2	−59.1	2.5	36 49.1	−59.0	2.5	37 49.1	−59.1	2.6	38 49.0	−59.0	2.6	39 48.9	−59.0	2.6	40 48.9	−59.0	2.7	41 48.8	−59.0	2.7	42 48.7	−58.9	2.7	77
78	34 50.1	−59.1	2.3	35 50.1	−59.1	2.3	36 50.0	−59.0	2.3	37 50.0	−59.1	2.4	38 49.9	−59.0	2.4	39 49.9	−59.1	2.4	40 49.8	−59.0	2.5	41 49.8	−59.1	2.5	78
79	33 51.0	−59.1	2.1	34 51.0	−59.1	2.1	35 51.0	−59.1	2.1	36 50.9	−59.1	2.1	37 50.9	−59.1	2.2	38 50.8	−59.0	2.2	39 50.8	−59.1	2.2	40 50.7	−59.0	2.3	79
80	32 51.9	−59.1	1.9	33 51.9	−59.1	1.9	34 51.9	−59.1	1.9	35 51.8	−59.1	1.9	36 51.8	−59.1	1.9	37 51.8	−59.1	2.0	38 51.7	−59.0	2.0	39 51.7	−59.1	2.0	80
81	31 52.8	−59.1	1.7	32 52.8	−59.1	1.7	33 52.8	−59.2	1.7	34 52.7	−59.1	1.7	35 52.7	−59.1	1.7	36 52.7	−59.1	1.8	37 52.7	−59.1	1.8	38 52.6	−59.1	1.8	81
82	30 53.7	−59.2	1.5	31 53.7	−59.2	1.5	32 53.6	−59.1	1.5	33 53.6	−59.1	1.5	34 53.6	−59.1	1.5	35 53.6	−59.2	1.5	36 53.6	−59.2	1.6	37 53.5	−59.1	1.6	82
83	29 54.5	−59.2	1.3	30 54.5	−59.2	1.3	31 54.5	−59.2	1.3	32 54.5	−59.2	1.3	33 54.5	−59.2	1.3	34 54.4	−59.1	1.3	35 54.4	−59.1	1.3	36 54.4	−59.1	1.4	83
84	28 55.3	−59.1	1.1	29 55.3	−59.2	1.1	30 55.3	−59.2	1.1	31 55.3	−59.2	1.1	32 55.3	−59.2	1.1	33 55.3	−59.2	1.1	34 55.3	−59.2	1.1	35 55.3	−59.2	1.2	84
85	27 56.2	−59.2	0.9	28 56.1	−59.2	0.9	29 56.1	−59.2	0.9	30 56.1	−59.2	0.9	31 56.1	−59.2	0.9	32 56.1	−59.2	0.9	33 56.1	−59.2	0.9	34 56.1	−59.2	1.0	85
86	26 57.0	−59.3	0.7	27 56.9	−59.2	0.7	28 56.9	−59.2	0.7	29 56.9	−59.2	0.7	30 56.9	−59.2	0.7	31 56.9	−59.2	0.7	32 56.9	−59.2	0.7	33 56.9	−59.2	0.8	86
87	25 57.7	−59.2	0.5	26 57.7	−59.2	0.5	27 57.7	−59.2	0.5	28 57.7	−59.2	0.5	29 57.7	−59.2	0.5	30 57.7	−59.2	0.5	31 57.7	−59.2	0.6	32 57.7	−59.2	0.6	87
88	24 58.5	−59.2	0.3	25 58.5	−59.2	0.3	26 58.5	−59.2	0.4	27 58.5	−59.2	0.4	28 58.5	−59.2	0.4	29 58.5	−59.2	0.4	30 58.5	−59.2	0.4	31 58.5	−59.2	0.4	88
89	23 59.3	−59.3	0.2	24 59.3	−59.3	0.2	25 59.3	−59.3	0.2	26 59.3	−59.3	0.2	27 59.3	−59.3	0.2	28 59.3	−59.3	0.2	29 59.3	−59.3	0.2	30 59.3	−59.3	0.2	89
90	23 00.0	−59.3	0.0	24 00.0	−59.3	0.0	25 00.0	−59.3	0.0	26 00.0	−59.3	0.0	27 00.0	−59.3	0.0	28 00.0	−59.3	0.0	29 00.0	−59.3	0.0	30 00.0	−59.3	0.0	90
	23°			24°			25°			26°			27°			28°			29°			30°			

9°, 351° L.H.A. LATITUDE SAME NAME AS DECLINATION

202

Dec. °	23° Hc ° ′	d ′	Z °	24° Hc ° ′	d ′	Z °	25° Hc ° ′	d ′	Z °	26° Hc ° ′	d ′	Z °	27° Hc ° ′	d ′	Z °	28° Hc ° ′	d ′	Z °	29° Hc ° ′	d ′	Z °	30° Hc ° ′	d ′	Z °	Dec. °
0	65 23.5	-56.5	157.9	64 27.7	-56.7	158.7	63 31.7	-57.0	159.5	62 35.4	-57.3	160.1	61 38.8	-57.4	160.8	60 42.1	-57.7	161.4	59 45.1	-57.8	161.9	58 48.0	-58.0	162.4	0
1	64 27.0	-56.6	158.7	63 31.0	-57.0	159.5	62 34.7	-57.2	160.1	61 38.1	-57.4	160.8	60 41.4	-57.6	161.4	59 44.4	-57.7	161.9	58 47.3	-57.9	162.4	57 50.0	-58.1	162.9	1
2	63 30.4	-56.9	159.5	62 34.0	-57.1	160.2	61 37.5	-57.4	160.8	60 40.7	-57.5	161.4	59 43.8	-57.7	161.9	58 46.7	-57.9	162.4	57 49.4	-58.1	162.9	56 51.9	-58.1	163.4	2
3	62 33.5	-57.1	160.2	61 36.9	-57.3	160.8	60 40.1	-57.5	161.4	59 43.2	-57.7	162.0	58 46.1	-57.9	162.5	57 48.8	-58.0	162.9	56 51.3	-58.1	163.4	55 53.8	-58.3	163.8	3
4	61 36.4	-57.3	160.8	60 39.6	-57.5	161.4	59 42.6	-57.6	162.0	58 45.5	-57.8	162.5	57 48.2	-58.0	163.0	56 50.8	-58.1	163.4	55 53.2	-58.2	163.8	54 55.5	-58.3	164.2	4
5	60 39.1	-57.4	161.5	59 42.1	-57.6	162.0	58 45.0	-57.8	162.5	57 47.7	-57.9	163.0	56 50.2	-58.0	163.4	55 52.7	-58.2	163.9	54 55.0	-58.4	164.3	53 57.2	-58.5	164.6	5
6	59 41.7	-57.6	162.0	58 44.5	-57.7	162.6	57 47.2	-57.9	163.0	56 49.8	-58.1	163.5	55 52.2	-58.2	163.9	54 54.5	-58.3	164.3	53 56.6	-58.3	164.7	52 58.7	-58.5	165.0	6
7	58 44.1	-57.7	162.6	57 46.8	-57.9	163.1	56 49.3	-58.0	163.5	55 51.7	-58.1	163.9	54 54.0	-58.3	164.3	53 56.2	-58.4	164.7	52 58.3	-58.5	165.1	52 00.2	-58.5	165.4	7
8	57 46.4	-57.8	163.1	56 48.9	-58.0	163.6	55 51.3	-58.1	164.0	54 53.6	-58.2	164.4	53 55.7	-58.3	164.7	52 57.8	-58.4	165.1	51 59.8	-58.5	165.4	51 01.7	-58.6	165.7	8
9	56 48.6	-58.0	163.6	55 50.9	-58.0	164.0	54 53.2	-58.2	164.4	53 55.4	-58.3	164.8	52 57.4	-58.4	165.1	51 59.4	-58.5	165.5	51 01.3	-58.6	165.8	50 03.1	-58.7	166.1	9
10	55 50.6	-58.0	164.1	54 52.9	-58.2	164.5	53 55.0	-58.3	164.8	52 57.1	-58.4	165.2	51 59.0	-58.5	165.5	51 00.9	-58.6	165.8	50 02.7	-58.7	166.1	49 04.4	-58.8	166.4	10
11	54 52.6	-58.2	164.5	53 54.7	-58.2	164.9	52 56.7	-58.3	165.2	51 58.7	-58.5	165.6	51 00.5	-58.5	165.9	50 02.3	-58.6	166.2	49 04.0	-58.7	166.4	48 05.6	-58.7	166.7	11
12	53 54.4	-58.2	164.9	52 56.5	-58.4	165.3	51 58.4	-58.4	165.6	51 00.2	-58.5	165.9	50 02.0	-58.6	166.2	49 03.7	-58.7	166.5	48 05.3	-58.7	166.8	47 06.9	-58.8	167.0	12
13	52 56.2	-58.3	165.4	51 58.1	-58.4	165.7	51 00.0	-58.5	166.0	50 01.7	-58.6	166.3	49 03.4	-58.7	166.5	48 05.0	-58.7	166.8	47 06.6	-58.8	167.1	46 08.1	-58.9	167.3	13
14	51 57.9	-58.3	165.7	50 59.7	-58.4	166.0	50 01.5	-58.6	166.3	49 03.1	-58.6	166.6	48 04.7	-58.7	166.9	47 06.3	-58.8	167.1	46 07.8	-58.9	167.3	45 09.2	-58.9	167.6	14
15	50 59.6	-58.5	166.1	50 01.3	-58.6	166.4	49 02.9	-58.6	166.7	48 04.5	-58.7	166.9	47 06.0	-58.7	167.2	46 07.5	-58.8	167.4	45 08.9	-58.9	167.6	44 10.3	-59.0	167.8	15
16	50 01.1	-58.5	166.5	49 02.7	-58.5	166.7	48 04.3	-58.6	167.0	47 05.8	-58.7	167.2	46 07.3	-58.8	167.5	45 08.7	-58.9	167.7	44 10.0	-58.9	167.9	43 11.3	-58.9	168.1	16
17	49 02.6	-58.6	166.8	48 04.2	-58.7	167.1	47 05.7	-58.8	167.3	46 07.1	-58.8	167.5	45 08.5	-58.9	167.8	44 09.8	-58.9	168.0	43 11.1	-58.9	168.2	42 12.4	-59.0	168.3	17
18	48 04.0	-58.6	167.1	47 05.5	-58.7	167.4	46 06.9	-58.7	167.6	45 08.3	-58.8	167.8	44 09.6	-58.8	168.0	43 10.9	-58.9	168.2	42 12.2	-59.0	168.4	41 13.4	-59.1	168.6	18
19	47 05.4	-58.6	167.5	46 06.8	-58.7	167.7	45 08.2	-58.8	167.9	44 09.5	-58.9	168.1	43 10.8	-58.9	168.3	42 12.0	-59.0	168.5	41 13.2	-59.0	168.7	40 14.3	-59.0	168.8	19
20	46 06.8	-58.8	167.8	45 08.1	-58.8	168.0	44 09.4	-58.8	168.2	43 10.6	-58.8	168.4	42 11.9	-59.0	168.6	41 13.0	-59.0	168.7	40 14.2	-59.1	168.9	39 15.3	-59.1	169.1	20
21	45 08.0	-58.7	168.1	44 09.3	-58.8	168.3	43 10.6	-58.9	168.4	42 11.8	-59.0	168.6	41 12.9	-59.0	168.8	40 14.0	-59.0	169.0	39 15.1	-59.0	169.1	38 16.2	-59.1	169.3	21
22	44 09.3	-58.8	168.3	43 10.5	-58.8	168.5	42 11.7	-58.9	168.7	41 12.8	-58.9	168.9	40 13.9	-59.0	169.0	39 15.0	-59.0	169.2	38 16.1	-59.1	169.4	37 17.1	-59.2	169.5	22
23	43 10.5	-58.8	168.6	42 11.7	-58.9	168.8	41 12.8	-59.0	169.0	40 13.9	-59.0	169.1	39 14.9	-59.0	169.3	38 16.0	-59.1	169.4	37 17.0	-59.2	169.6	36 17.9	-59.1	169.7	23
24	42 11.7	-58.9	168.9	41 12.8	-59.0	169.0	40 13.8	-58.9	169.2	39 14.9	-59.0	169.4	38 15.9	-59.1	169.5	37 16.9	-59.1	169.7	36 17.8	-59.1	169.8	35 18.8	-59.2	169.9	24
25	41 12.8	-58.9	169.1	40 13.8	-58.9	169.3	39 14.9	-59.0	169.5	38 15.9	-59.1	169.6	37 16.8	-59.0	169.7	36 17.8	-59.1	169.9	35 18.7	-59.2	170.0	34 19.6	-59.2	170.1	25
26	40 13.9	-59.0	169.4	39 14.9	-59.0	169.5	38 15.9	-59.1	169.7	37 16.8	-59.0	169.8	36 17.8	-59.2	170.0	35 18.7	-59.2	170.1	34 19.5	-59.1	170.2	33 20.4	-59.2	170.3	26
27	39 14.9	-58.9	169.6	38 15.9	-59.0	169.8	37 16.8	-59.0	169.9	36 17.8	-59.1	170.0	35 18.6	-59.1	170.2	34 19.5	-59.1	170.3	33 20.4	-59.2	170.4	32 21.2	-59.2	170.5	27
28	38 16.0	-59.0	169.9	37 16.9	-59.1	170.0	36 17.8	-59.1	170.1	35 18.7	-59.2	170.3	34 19.5	-59.1	170.4	33 20.4	-59.2	170.5	32 21.2	-59.2	170.6	31 22.0	-59.3	170.7	28
29	37 17.0	-59.1	170.1	36 17.8	-59.0	170.2	35 18.7	-59.1	170.3	34 19.5	-59.1	170.5	33 20.4	-59.2	170.6	32 21.2	-59.2	170.7	31 22.0	-59.3	170.8	30 22.7	-59.2	170.9	29
30	36 17.9	-59.0	170.3	35 18.8	-59.1	170.4	34 19.6	-59.1	170.6	33 20.4	-59.1	170.7	32 21.2	-59.2	170.8	31 22.0	-59.2	170.9	30 22.7	-59.2	171.0	29 23.5	-59.3	171.1	30
31	35 18.9	-59.1	170.5	34 19.7	-59.1	170.7	33 20.5	-59.1	170.8	32 21.3	-59.2	170.9	31 22.0	-59.2	171.0	30 22.8	-59.3	171.1	29 23.5	-59.3	171.1	28 24.2	-59.3	171.2	31
32	34 19.8	-59.1	170.8	33 20.6	-59.1	170.9	32 21.4	-59.2	171.0	31 22.1	-59.2	171.1	30 22.8	-59.2	171.2	29 23.5	-59.2	171.2	28 24.2	-59.3	171.3	27 24.9	-59.3	171.4	32
33	33 20.7	-59.1	171.0	32 21.5	-59.2	171.1	31 22.2	-59.2	171.2	30 22.9	-59.2	171.3	29 23.6	-59.2	171.3	28 24.3	-59.3	171.4	27 24.9	-59.3	171.5	26 25.6	-59.3	171.6	33
34	32 21.6	-59.1	171.2	31 22.3	-59.1	171.3	30 23.0	-59.2	171.4	29 23.7	-59.2	171.4	28 24.4	-59.3	171.5	27 25.0	-59.3	171.6	26 25.6	-59.3	171.7	25 26.3	-59.4	171.7	34
35	31 22.5	-59.2	171.4	30 23.2	-59.2	171.5	29 23.8	-59.2	171.5	28 24.5	-59.3	171.6	27 25.1	-59.3	171.7	26 25.7	-59.3	171.8	25 26.3	-59.3	171.8	24 26.9	-59.3	171.9	35
36	30 23.3	-59.1	171.6	29 24.0	-59.2	171.6	28 24.6	-59.2	171.7	27 25.2	-59.2	171.8	26 25.8	-59.2	171.9	25 26.4	-59.3	171.9	24 27.0	-59.3	172.0	23 27.6	-59.3	172.1	36
37	29 24.2	-59.2	171.8	28 24.8	-59.2	171.8	27 25.4	-59.2	171.9	26 26.0	-59.3	172.0	25 26.6	-59.3	172.0	24 27.1	-59.3	172.1	23 27.7	-59.3	172.2	22 28.3	-59.4	172.2	37
38	28 25.0	-59.2	171.9	27 25.6	-59.2	172.0	26 26.2	-59.3	172.1	25 26.7	-59.2	172.2	24 27.3	-59.3	172.2	23 27.8	-59.3	172.3	22 28.4	-59.4	172.3	21 28.9	-59.4	172.4	38
39	27 25.8	-59.2	172.1	26 26.4	-59.3	172.2	25 26.9	-59.3	172.3	24 27.5	-59.3	172.3	23 28.0	-59.3	172.4	22 28.5	-59.3	172.4	21 29.0	-59.3	172.5	20 29.5	-59.3	172.5	39
40	26 26.6	-59.2	172.3	25 27.1	-59.2	172.4	24 27.6	-59.2	172.4	23 28.2	-59.3	172.5	22 28.7	-59.3	172.5	21 29.2	-59.4	172.6	20 29.7	-59.4	172.6	19 30.2	-59.4	172.7	40
41	25 27.4	-59.3	172.5	24 27.9	-59.3	172.5	23 28.4	-59.3	172.6	22 28.9	-59.3	172.7	21 29.4	-59.3	172.7	20 29.8	-59.3	172.8	19 30.3	-59.4	172.8	18 30.8	-59.4	172.8	41
42	24 28.1	-59.2	172.7	23 28.6	-59.3	172.7	22 29.1	-59.3	172.8	21 29.6	-59.4	172.8	20 30.0	-59.3	172.9	19 30.5	-59.4	172.9	18 30.9	-59.3	173.0	17 31.4	-59.4	173.0	42
43	23 28.9	-59.3	172.8	22 29.3	-59.2	172.9	21 29.8	-59.3	172.9	20 30.2	-59.3	173.0	19 30.7	-59.3	173.0	18 31.1	-59.3	173.1	17 31.6	-59.4	173.1	16 32.0	-59.4	173.1	43
44	22 29.6	-59.3	173.0	21 30.1	-59.3	173.1	20 30.5	-59.3	173.1	19 30.9	-59.3	173.1	18 31.4	-59.4	173.2	17 31.8	-59.4	173.2	16 32.2	-59.4	173.3	15 32.6	-59.4	173.3	44
45	21 30.3	-59.2	173.2	20 30.8	-59.3	173.2	19 31.2	-59.3	173.3	18 31.6	-59.3	173.3	17 32.0	-59.4	173.3	16 32.4	-59.4	173.4	15 32.8	-59.4	173.4	14 33.2	-59.4	173.4	45
46	20 31.1	-59.3	173.3	19 31.5	-59.4	173.4	18 31.9	-59.4	173.4	17 32.3	-59.4	173.5	16 32.6	-59.3	173.5	15 33.0	-59.4	173.5	14 33.4	-59.4	173.6	13 33.8	-59.4	173.6	46
47	19 31.8	-59.3	173.5	18 32.1	-59.3	173.5	17 32.5	-59.3	173.6	16 32.9	-59.4	173.6	15 33.3	-59.4	173.6	14 33.6	-59.3	173.7	13 34.0	-59.4	173.7	12 34.4	-59.5	173.7	47
48	18 32.5	-59.3	173.7	17 32.8	-59.3	173.7	16 33.2	-59.4	173.7	15 33.5	-59.3	173.8	14 33.9	-59.4	173.8	13 34.3	-59.4	173.8	12 34.6	-59.4	173.8	11 34.9	-59.4	173.9	48
49	17 33.2	-59.4	173.8	16 33.5	-59.3	173.9	15 33.8	-59.3	173.9	14 34.2	-59.4	173.9	13 34.5	-59.4	173.9	12 34.9	-59.4	174.0	11 35.2	-59.4	174.0	10 35.5	-59.4	174.0	49
50	16 33.8	-59.3	174.0	15 34.2	-59.4	174.0	14 34.5	-59.4	174.0	13 34.8	-59.3	174.1	12 35.1	-59.3	174.1	11 35.5	-59.4	174.1	10 35.8	-59.4	174.1	9 36.1	-59.4	174.1	50
51	15 34.5	-59.3	174.1	14 34.8	-59.3	174.2	13 35.1	-59.3	174.2	12 35.5	-59.4	174.2	11 35.8	-59.4	174.2	10 36.1	-59.4	174.3	9 36.4	-59.5	174.3	8 36.7	-59.5	174.3	51
52	14 35.2	-59.3	174.3	13 35.5	-59.4	174.3	12 35.8	-59.4	174.3	11 36.1	-59.4	174.4	10 36.4	-59.4	174.4	9 36.7	-59.5	174.4	8 36.9	-59.4	174.4	7 37.2	-59.4	174.4	52
53	13 35.9	-59.4	174.4	12 36.1	-59.3	174.5	11 36.4	-59.4	174.5	10 36.7	-59.4	174.5	9 37.0	-59.4	174.5	8 37.2	-59.4	174.5	7 37.5	-59.4	174.5	6 37.8	-59.5	174.6	53
54	12 36.5	-59.3	174.6	11 36.8	-59.4	174.6	10 37.0	-59.3	174.6	9 37.3	-59.4	174.6	8 37.6	-59.4	174.7	7 37.8	-59.4	174.7	6 38.1	-59.4	174.7	5 38.3	-59.4	174.7	54
55	11 37.2	-59.4	174.7	10 37.4	-59.3	174.8	9 37.7	-59.4	174.8	8 37.9	-59.4	174.8	7 38.2	-59.4	174.8	6 38.4	-59.4	174.8	5 38.7	-59.5	174.8	4 38.9	-59.4	174.8	55
56	10 37.8	-59.3	174.9	9 38.1	-59.4	174.9	8 38.3	-59.4	174.9	7 38.5	-59.4	174.9	6 38.8	-59.4	174.9	5 39.0	-59.4	175.0	4 39.2	-59.4	175.0	3 39.5	-59.5	175.0	56
57	9 38.5	-59.4	175.0	8 38.7	-59.4	175.1	7 38.9	-59.4	175.1	6 39.1	-59.4	175.1	5 39.4	-59.5	175.1	4 39.6	-59.4	175.1	3 39.8	-59.4	175.1	2 40.0	-59.4	175.1	57
58	8 39.1	-59.4	175.2	7 39.3	-59.4	175.2	6 39.5	-59.4	175.2	5 39.7	-59.4	175.2	4 39.9	-59.4	175.2	3 40.2	-59.5	175.2	2 40.4	-59.5	175.2	1 40.6	-59.5	175.2	58
59	7 39.7	-59.3	175.3	6 39.9	-59.3	175.3	5 40.1	-59.3	175.4	4 40.3	-59.4	175.4	3 40.5	-59.4	175.4	2 40.7	-59.4	175.4	1 40.9	-59.4	175.4	0 41.1	-59.4	175.4	59
60	6 40.4	-59.4	175.5	5 40.6	-59.4	175.5	4 40.8	-59.4	175.5	3 40.9	-59.4	175.5	2 41.1	-59.4	175.5	1 41.3	-59.4	175.5	0 41.5	-59.4	175.5	0 18.3	+59.5	4.5	60
61	5 41.0	-59.4	175.6	4 41.2	-59.4	175.6	3 41.4	-59.4	175.6	2 41.5	-59.4	175.6	1 41.7	-59.4	175.6	0 41.9	-59.4	175.7	0 17.9	+59.5	4.3	1 17.8	+59.4	4.4	61
62	4 41.6	-59.3	175.8	3 41.8	-59.4	175.8	2 42.0	-59.4	175.8	1 42.1	-59.4	175.8	0 42.3	-59.4	175.8	0 17.5	+59.5	4.2	1 17.4	+59.4	4.2	2 17.2	+59.5	4.2	62
63	3 42.3	-59.4	175.9	2 42.4	-59.4	175.9	1 42.6	-59.4	175.9	0 42.7	-59.4	175.9	0 17.1	+59.4	4.1	1 17.0	+59.4	4.1	2 16.8	+59.5	4.1	3 16.7	+59.4	4.1	63
64	2 42.9	-59.4	176.1	1 43.0	-59.3	176.1	0 43.2	-59.4	176.1	0 16.7	+59.4	3.9	1 16.5	+59.4	3.9	2 16.4	+59.4	3.9	3 16.3	+59.4	3.9	4 16.1	+59.5	3.9	64
65	1 43.5	-59.3	176.2	0 43.7	-59.4	176.2	0 16.2	+59.4	3.8	1 16.1	+59.4	3.8	2 15.9	+59.5	3.8	3 15.8	+59.4	3.8	4 15.7	+59.4	3.8	5 15.6	+59.4	3.8	65
66	0 44.2	-59.4	176.4	0 15.7	+59.4	3.6	1 15.6	+59.4	3.6	2 15.5	+59.4	3.7	3 15.4	+59.4	3.7	4 15.2	+59.5	3.7	5 15.1	+59.4	3.7	6 15.0	+59.4	3.7	66
67	0 15.2	+59.4	3.5	1 15.1	+59.4	3.5	2 15.0	+59.4	3.5	3 14.9	+59.4	3.5	4 14.8	+59.4	3.5	5 14.7	+59.4	3.5	6 14.5	+59.5	3.5	7 14.4	+59.5	3.5	67
68	1 14.6	+59.4	3.4	2 14.5	+59.4	3.4	3 14.4	+59.4	3.4	4 14.3	+59.4	3.4	5 14.2	+59.4	3.4	6 14.1	+59.4	3.4	7 14.0	+59.4	3.4	8 13.9	+59.4	3.4	68
69	2 14.0	+59.3	3.2	3 13.9	+59.4	3.2	4 13.8	+59.4	3.2	5 13.7	+59.4	3.2	6 13.6	+59.4	3.2	7 13.5	+59.4	3.2	8 13.4	+59.4	3.2	9 13.3	+59.4	3.3	69
70	3 13.3	+59.4	3.1	4 13.3	+59.3	3.1	5 13.2	+59.4	3.1	6 13.1	+59.4	3.1	7 13.0	+59.4	3.1	8 12.9	+59.4	3.1	9 12.8	+59.4	3.1	10 12.7	+59.5	3.1	70
71	4 12.7	+59.4	2.9	5 12.6	+59.4	2.9	6 12.6	+59.3	2.9	7 12.5	+59.4	2.9	8 12.4	+59.4	2.9	9 12.3	+59.4	3.0	10 12.2	+59.5	3.0	11 12.2	+59.4	3.0	71
72	5 12.1	+59.4	2.8	6 12.0	+59.4	2.8	7 11.9	+59.4	2.8	8 11.9	+59.4	2.8	9 11.8	+59.4	2.8	10 11.7	+59.4	2.8	11 11.7	+59.4	2.8	12 11.6	+59.4	2.8	72
73	6 11.5	+59.3	2.6	7 11.4	+59.4	2.6	8 11.3	+59.4	2.6	9 11.3	+59.4	2.7	10 11.2	+59.4	2.7	11 11.1	+59.4	2.7	12 11.1	+59.4	2.7	13 11.0	+59.4	2.7	73
74	7 10.8	+59.4	2.5	8 10.8	+59.3	2.5	9 10.7	+59.4	2.5	10 10.7	+59.3	2.5	11 10.6	+59.4	2.5	12 10.5	+59.4	2.5	13 10.5	+59.4	2.5	14 10.4	+59.4	2.5	74
75	8 10.2	+59.3	2.3	9 10.1	+59.4	2.4	10 10.1	+59.4	2.4	11 10.0	+59.4	2.4	12 10.0	+59.4	2.4	13 09.9	+59.4	2.4	14 09.9	+59.4	2.4	15 09.8	+59.4	2.4	75
76	9 09.5	+59.4	2.2	10 09.5	+59.4	2.2	11 09.5	+59.3	2.2	12 09.4	+59.4	2.2	13 09.4	+59.3	2.2	14 09.3	+59.4	2.2	15 09.3	+59.4	2.2	16 09.2	+59.4	2.3	76
77	10 08.9	+59.4	2.0	11 08.9	+59.3	2.1	12 08.8	+59.4	2.1	13 08.8	+59.4	2.1	14 08.7	+59.4	2.1	15 08.7	+59.4	2.1	16 08.7	+59.4	2.1	17 08.6	+59.4	2.1	77
78	11 08.3	+59.3	1.9	12 08.2	+59.4	1.9	13 08.2	+59.3	1.9	14 08.2	+59.3	1.9	15 08.1	+59.4	1.9	16 08.1	+59.4	1.9	17 08.1	+59.3	2.0	18 08.0	+59.4	2.0	78
79	12 07.6	+59.3	1.7	13 07.6	+59.3	1.8	14 07.5	+59.4	1.8	15 07.5	+59.4	1.8	16 07.5	+59.3	1.8	17 07.5	+59.3	1.8	18 07.4	+59.4	1.8	19 07.4	+59.4	1.8	79
80	13 06.9	+59.4	1.6	14 06.9	+59.4	1.6	15 06.9	+59.3	1.6	16 06.9	+59.3	1.6	17 06.8	+59.4	1.6	18 06.8	+59.4	1.6	19 06.8	+59.4	1.6	20 06.8	+59.3	1.7	80
81	14 06.3	+59.3	1.4	15 06.3	+59.3	1.5	16 06.2	+59.4	1.5	17 06.2	+59.4	1.5	18 06.2	+59.4	1.5	19 06.2	+59.3	1.5	20 06.2	+59.3	1.5	21 06.1	+59.4	1.5	81
82	15 05.6	+59.3	1.3	16 05.6	+59.3	1.3	17 05.6	+59.3	1.3	18 05.6	+59.3	1.3	19 05.6	+59.3	1.3	20 05.5	+59.4	1.3	21 05.5	+59.4	1.3	22 05.5	+59.4	1.3	82
83	16 04.9	+59.4	1.1	17 04.9	+59.4	1.1	18 04.9	+59.3	1.1	19 04.9	+59.3	1.2	20 04.9	+59.3	1.2	21 04.9	+59.3	1.2	22 04.9	+59.3	1.2	23 04.9	+59.3	1.2	83
84	17 04.3	+59.3	1.0	18 04.3	+59.3	1.0	19 04.2	+59.4	1.0	20 04.2	+59.4	1.0	21 04.2	+59.3	1.0	22 04.2	+59.3	1.0	23 04.2	+59.3	1.0	24 04.2	+59.3	1.0	84
85	18 03.6	+59.3	0.8	19 03.6	+59.3	0.8	20 03.6	+59.3	0.8	21 03.6	+59.3	0.8	22 03.5	+59.4	0.8	23 03.5	+59.4	0.8	24 03.5	+59.3	0.9	25 03.5	+59.3	0.9	85
86	19 02.9	+59.3	0.7	20 02.9	+59.3	0.7	21 02.9	+59.3	0.7	22 02.9	+59.3	0.7	23 02.9	+59.3	0.7	24 02.9	+59.3	0.7	25 02.8	+59.4	0.7	26 02.8	+59.4	0.7	86
87	20 02.2	+59.3	0.5	21 02.2	+59.3	0.5	22 02.2	+59.3	0.5	23 02.2	+59.3	0.5	24 02.2	+59.3	0.5	25 02.2	+59.3	0.5	26 02.2	+59.3	0.5	27 02.2	+59.2	0.5	87
88	21 01.5	+59.2	0.3	22 01.5	+59.2	0.3	23 01.5	+59.2	0.3	24 01.5	+59.2	0.3	25 01.5	+59.2	0.3	26 01.5	+59.2	0.3	27 01.5	+59.2	0.4	28 01.4	+59.3	0.4	88
89	22 00.7	+59.3	0.2	23 00.7	+59.3	0.2	24 00.7	+59.3	0.2	25 00.7	+59.3	0.2	26 00.7	+59.3	0.2	27 00.7	+59.3	0.2	28 00.7	+59.3	0.2	29 00.7	+59.3	0.2	89
90	23 00.0	+59.3	0.0	24 00.0	+59.3	0.0	25 00.0	+59.3	0.0	26 00.0	+59.3	0.0	27 00.0	+59.3	0.0	28 00.0	+59.3	0.0	29 00.0	+59.3	0.0	30 00.0	+59.3	0.0	90
	23°			24°			25°			26°			27°			28°			29°			30°			

S. Lat. { L.H.A. greater than 180° ....Zn=180°−Z; L.H.A. less than 180°...........Zn=180°+Z

10°, 350° L.H.A. LATITUDE **SAME** NAME AS DECLINATION N. Lat. {L.H.A. greater than 180° .....Zn=Z / L.H.A. less than 180°............Zn=360°−Z

Dec.	23°			24°			25°			26°			27°			28°			29°			30°			Dec.
	Hc	d	Z	Hc	d	Z	Hc	d	Z	Hc	d	Z	Hc	d	Z	Hc	d	Z	Hc	d	Z	Hc	d	Z	Dec.
°	° ′	′	°	° ′	′	°	° ′	′	°	° ′	′	°	° ′	′	°	° ′	′	°	° ′	′	°	° ′	′	°	°
0	65 01.7	+55.4	155.7	64 06.9	+55.7	156.6	63 11.6	+56.1	157.4	62 16.1	+56.4	158.1	61 20.3	+56.7	158.8	60 24.3	+56.9	159.4	59 28.0	+57.2	160.0	58 31.5	+57.4	160.6	0
1	65 57.1	+55.0	154.8	65 02.6	+55.4	155.7	64 07.7	+55.9	156.6	63 12.5	+56.2	157.3	62 17.0	+56.5	158.1	61 21.2	+56.8	158.8	60 25.2	+57.0	159.4	59 28.9	+57.2	160.0	1
2	66 52.1	+54.6	153.8	65 58.0	+55.1	154.8	65 03.6	+55.5	155.7	64 08.7	+55.9	156.6	63 13.5	+56.2	157.3	62 18.0	+56.5	158.1	61 22.2	+56.8	158.8	60 26.1	+57.1	159.4	2
3	67 46.7	+54.1	152.7	66 53.1	+54.7	153.8	65 59.1	+55.1	154.8	65 04.6	+55.5	155.7	64 09.7	+56.0	156.6	63 14.5	+56.3	157.3	62 19.0	+56.6	158.1	61 23.2	+56.8	158.8	3
4	68 40.8	+53.7	151.5	67 47.8	+54.2	152.7	66 54.2	+54.8	153.8	66 00.1	+55.3	154.8	65 05.7	+55.6	155.7	64 10.8	+56.0	156.6	63 15.6	+56.3	157.4	62 20.0	+56.7	158.1	4
5	69 34.5	+53.0	150.3	68 42.0	+53.7	151.6	67 49.0	+54.3	152.7	66 55.4	+54.8	153.8	66 01.3	+55.3	154.8	65 06.8	+55.7	155.7	64 11.9	+56.1	156.6	63 16.7	+56.4	157.4	5
6	70 27.5	+52.3	148.9	69 35.7	+53.1	150.3	68 43.3	+53.8	151.6	67 50.2	+54.4	152.8	66 56.6	+54.9	153.8	66 02.5	+55.4	154.8	65 08.0	+55.8	155.8	64 13.1	+56.2	156.6	6
7	71 19.8	+51.6	147.4	70 28.8	+52.5	148.9	69 37.1	+53.2	150.3	68 44.6	+53.9	151.6	67 51.5	+54.5	152.8	66 57.9	+55.0	153.9	66 03.8	+55.5	154.9	65 09.3	+55.9	155.8	7
8	72 11.4	+50.7	145.8	71 21.3	+51.7	147.5	70 30.3	+52.6	149.0	69 38.5	+53.3	150.4	68 46.0	+54.0	151.7	67 52.9	+54.6	152.8	66 59.3	+55.1	153.9	66 05.2	+55.5	154.9	8
9	73 02.1	+49.7	144.0	72 13.0	+50.8	145.8	71 22.9	+51.8	147.5	70 31.8	+52.7	149.0	69 40.0	+53.4	150.4	68 47.5	+54.1	151.7	67 54.4	+54.6	152.9	67 00.7	+55.2	153.9	9
10	73 51.8	+48.4	142.0	73 03.8	+49.8	144.1	72 14.7	+50.9	145.9	71 24.5	+51.9	147.6	70 33.4	+52.8	149.1	69 41.6	+53.5	150.5	68 49.0	+54.2	151.8	67 55.9	+54.8	152.9	10
11	74 40.2	+47.1	139.9	73 53.6	+48.6	142.1	73 05.6	+49.9	144.1	72 16.4	+51.1	146.0	71 26.2	+52.1	147.6	70 35.1	+52.9	149.1	69 43.2	+53.7	150.5	68 50.7	+54.3	151.8	11
12	75 27.3	+45.4	137.4	74 42.2	+47.2	139.9	73 55.5	+48.8	142.2	73 07.5	+50.1	144.2	72 18.3	+51.2	146.0	71 28.0	+52.2	147.7	70 36.9	+53.0	149.2	69 45.0	+53.7	150.6	12
13	76 12.7	+43.5	•134.8	75 29.4	+45.6	137.5	74 44.3	+47.3	140.0	73 57.6	+48.9	142.2	73 09.5	+50.2	144.3	72 20.2	+51.3	146.1	71 29.9	+52.3	147.8	70 38.7	+53.2	149.3	13
14	76 56.2	+41.2	•131.8	76 15.0	+43.7	•134.9	75 31.6	+45.8	137.6	74 46.5	+47.5	140.1	73 59.7	+49.0	142.3	73 11.5	+50.4	144.4	72 22.2	+51.5	146.2	71 31.9	+52.4	147.9	14
15	77 37.4	+38.6	•128.5	76 58.7	+41.4	•131.9	76 17.4	+43.9	•135.0	75 34.0	+45.9	137.7	74 48.7	+47.7	140.2	74 01.9	+49.2	142.4	73 13.7	+50.5	144.5	72 24.3	+51.6	146.3	15
16	78 16.0	+35.4	•124.8	77 40.1	+38.8	•128.6	77 01.3	+41.6	•132.0	76 19.9	+44.1	•135.1	75 36.4	+46.2	137.8	74 51.1	+47.9	140.3	74 04.2	+49.4	142.5	73 15.9	+50.7	144.6	16
17	78 51.4	+31.8	•120.8	78 18.9	+35.6	•124.9	77 42.9	+39.0	•128.7	77 04.0	+41.8	•132.1	76 22.6	+44.2	•135.2	75 39.0	+46.3	137.9	74 53.6	+48.0	140.4	74 06.6	+49.5	142.7	17
18	79 23.2	+27.6	•116.3	78 54.5	+32.1	•120.9	78 21.9	+35.9	•125.0	77 45.8	+39.2	•128.8	77 06.8	+42.1	•132.2	76 25.3	+44.5	•135.3	75 41.6	+46.6	138.1	74 56.1	+48.3	140.5	18
19	79 50.8	+22.8	•111.3	79 26.6	+27.8	•116.3	78 57.8	+32.2	•120.9	78 25.0	+36.1	•125.1	77 48.9	+39.4	•128.9	77 09.8	+42.2	•132.4	76 28.2	+44.6	•135.4	75 44.4	+46.7	138.2	19
20	80 13.6	+17.4	•106.0	79 54.4	+23.0	•111.4	79 30.0	+28.1	•116.4	79 01.1	+32.5	•121.1	78 28.3	+36.4	•125.3	77 52.0	+39.7	•129.1	77 12.8	+42.5	•132.5	76 31.1	+44.9	•135.6	20
21	80 31.0	+11.5	•100.3	80 17.4	+17.6	•106.0	79 58.1	+23.2	•111.5	79 33.6	+28.3	•116.5	79 04.7	+32.7	•121.2	78 31.7	+36.6	•125.4	77 55.3	+39.9	•129.2	77 16.0	+42.7	•132.7	21
22	80 42.5	+5.3	• 94.2	80 35.0	+11.6	•100.3	80 21.3	+17.7	•106.1	80 01.9	+23.4	•111.5	79 37.4	+28.5	•116.6	79 08.3	+33.0	•121.3	78 35.2	+36.9	•125.5	77 58.7	+40.2	•129.4	22
23	80 47.8	−1.2	• 88.0	80 46.6	+5.4	• 94.2	80 39.0	+11.9	•100.3	80 25.3	+18.0	•106.1	80 05.9	+23.6	•111.6	79 41.3	+28.7	•116.8	79 12.1	+33.2	•121.4	78 38.9	+37.1	•125.7	23
24	80 46.6	−7.6	• 81.8	80 52.0	−1.1	• 88.0	80 50.9	+5.4	• 94.2	80 43.3	+12.0	•100.3	80 29.5	+18.2	•106.2	80 10.0	+23.9	•111.7	79 45.3	+29.0	•116.9	79 16.0	+33.5	•121.6	24
25	80 39.0	−13.7	• 75.6	80 50.9	−7.6	• 81.7	80 56.3	−1.0	• 87.9	80 55.3	+5.6	• 94.1	80 47.7	+12.1	•100.3	80 33.9	+18.4	•106.3	80 14.3	+24.1	•111.8	79 49.5	+29.2	•117.0	25
26	80 25.3	−19.4	• 69.7	80 43.3	−13.8	• 75.5	80 55.3	−7.6	• 81.5	81 00.9	−1.1	• 87.8	80 59.8	+5.7	• 94.1	80 52.3	+12.3	•100.3	80 38.4	+18.6	•106.3	80 18.7	+24.4	•112.0	26
27	80 05.9	−24.6	• 64.1	80 29.5	−19.5	• 69.5	80 47.7	−13.8	• 75.3	80 59.8	−7.5	• 81.4	81 05.5	−0.9	• 87.7	81 04.6	+5.8	• 94.1	80 57.0	+12.5	•100.4	80 43.1	+18.8	•106.4	27
28	79 41.3	−29.2	• 58.9	80 10.0	−24.7	• 63.9	80 33.9	−19.6	• 69.3	80 52.3	−13.9	• 75.1	81 04.6	−7.6	• 81.3	81 10.4	−0.9	• 87.6	81 09.5	+5.9	• 94.1	81 01.9	+12.6	•100.4	28
29	79 12.1	−33.2	• 54.2	79 45.3	−29.3	• 58.6	80 14.3	−24.8	• 63.6	80 38.4	−19.7	• 69.0	80 57.0	−13.9	• 74.9	81 09.5	−7.6	• 81.1	81 15.4	−0.9	• 87.6	81 14.5	+6.0	• 94.1	29
30	78 38.9	−36.7	• 49.8	79 16.0	−33.4	• 53.8	79 49.5	−29.5	• 58.3	80 18.7	−25.0	• 63.3	80 43.1	−19.8	• 68.8	81 01.9	−14.0	• 74.7	81 14.5	−7.6	• 81.0	81 20.5	−0.8	• 87.5	30
31	78 02.2	−39.6	• 45.9	78 42.6	−36.8	• 49.5	79 20.0	−33.5	• 53.5	79 53.2	−29.6	• 58.0	80 23.3	−25.1	• 63.1	80 47.9	−19.9	• 68.6	81 06.9	−14.0	• 74.5	81 19.7	−7.6	• 80.9	31
32	77 22.6	−42.1	• 42.4	78 05.8	−39.7	• 45.6	78 46.5	−37.0	• 49.2	79 24.1	−33.6	• 53.2	79 58.2	−29.8	• 57.7	80 28.0	−25.3	• 62.8	80 52.9	−20.1	• 68.3	81 12.1	−14.1	• 74.3	32
33	76 40.5	−44.2	• 39.2	77 26.1	−42.3	• 42.0	78 09.5	−39.9	• 45.2	78 50.5	−37.1	• 48.8	79 28.4	−33.8	• 52.9	80 02.7	−29.9	• 57.4	80 32.8	−25.4	• 62.5	80 58.0	−20.2	• 68.0	33
34	75 56.3	−46.1	36.3	76 43.8	−44.3	38.8	77 29.6	−42.4	• 41.7	78 13.4	−40.1	• 44.9	78 54.6	−37.3	• 48.5	79 32.8	−34.0	• 52.5	80 07.4	−30.1	• 57.1	80 37.8	−25.6	• 62.2	34
35	75 10.2	−47.6	33.8	75 59.5	−46.2	36.0	76 47.2	−44.5	38.5	77 33.3	−42.6	• 41.3	78 17.3	−40.3	• 44.5	78 58.8	−37.5	• 48.1	79 37.3	−34.2	• 52.1	80 12.2	−30.3	• 56.7	35
36	74 22.6	−48.9	31.4	75 13.3	−47.7	33.4	76 02.7	−46.3	35.6	76 50.7	−44.6	38.1	77 37.0	−42.7	• 40.9	78 21.3	−40.4	• 44.1	79 03.1	−37.7	• 47.7	79 41.9	−34.4	• 51.8	36
37	73 33.7	−50.0	29.3	74 25.6	−49.1	31.1	75 16.4	−47.8	33.1	76 06.1	−46.5	35.3	76 54.3	−44.8	37.7	77 40.9	−42.9	• 40.5	78 25.4	−40.6	• 43.7	79 07.5	−37.9	• 47.3	37
38	72 43.7	−51.0	27.4	73 36.5	−50.1	29.0	74 28.6	−49.2	30.7	75 19.6	−48.0	32.7	76 09.5	−46.6	34.9	76 58.0	−45.0	37.4	77 44.8	−43.1	• 40.1	78 29.6	−40.8	• 43.3	38
39	71 52.7	−51.9	25.7	72 46.4	−51.1	27.1	73 39.4	−50.2	28.7	74 31.6	−49.2	30.4	75 22.9	−48.1	32.3	76 13.0	−46.8	34.5	77 01.7	−45.2	37.0	77 48.8	−43.3	• 39.7	39
40	71 00.8	−52.6	24.1	71 55.3	−52.0	25.4	72 49.2	−51.3	26.8	73 42.4	−50.4	28.3	74 34.8	−49.4	30.0	75 26.2	−48.2	31.9	76 16.5	−46.9	34.1	77 05.5	−45.3	36.5	40
41	70 08.2	−53.3	22.7	71 03.3	−52.7	23.8	71 57.9	−52.0	25.0	72 52.0	−51.4	26.4	73 45.4	−50.5	27.9	74 38.0	−49.6	29.6	75 29.6	−48.4	31.5	76 20.2	−47.1	33.7	41
42	69 14.9	−53.8	21.4	70 10.6	−53.3	22.4	71 05.9	−52.8	23.5	72 00.6	−52.1	24.7	72 54.9	−51.5	26.1	73 48.4	−50.6	27.6	74 41.2	−49.7	29.3	75 33.1	−48.6	31.1	42
43	68 21.1	−54.3	20.1	69 17.3	−53.9	21.0	70 13.1	−53.4	22.0	71 08.5	−52.9	23.1	72 03.4	−52.3	24.3	72 57.8	−51.6	25.7	73 51.5	−50.8	27.2	74 44.5	−49.9	28.9	43
44	67 26.8	−54.8	19.0	68 23.4	−54.4	19.8	69 19.7	−54.0	20.7	70 15.6	−53.5	21.7	71 11.1	−53.0	22.8	72 06.2	−52.4	24.0	73 00.7	−51.7	25.3	73 54.6	−50.9	26.8	44
45	66 32.0	−55.1	18.0	67 29.0	−54.8	18.7	68 25.7	−54.5	19.5	69 22.1	−54.1	20.4	70 18.1	−53.6	21.4	71 13.8	−53.1	22.4	72 09.0	−52.5	23.6	73 03.7	−51.8	24.9	45
46	65 36.9	−55.5	17.0	66 34.2	−55.2	17.7	67 31.2	−54.9	18.4	68 28.0	−54.5	19.2	69 24.5	−54.1	20.1	70 20.7	−53.7	21.0	71 16.5	−53.1	22.1	72 11.9	−52.6	23.2	46
47	64 41.4	−55.8	16.1	65 39.0	−55.6	16.7	66 36.3	−55.2	17.4	67 33.5	−55.0	18.1	68 30.4	−54.6	18.9	69 27.0	−54.2	19.7	70 23.4	−53.8	20.7	71 19.3	−53.3	21.7	47
48	63 45.6	−56.1	15.2	64 43.4	−55.8	15.8	65 41.1	−55.6	16.4	66 38.5	−55.3	17.0	67 35.8	−55.0	17.8	68 32.8	−54.7	18.5	69 29.6	−54.4	19.4	70 26.0	−53.9	20.3	48
49	62 49.5	−56.3	14.4	63 47.6	−56.2	14.9	64 45.5	−56.0	15.5	65 43.2	−55.7	16.1	66 40.8	−55.5	16.7	67 38.1	−55.1	17.4	68 35.2	−54.7	18.2	69 32.1	−54.4	19.0	49
50	61 53.2	−56.6	13.7	62 51.4	−56.3	14.2	63 49.5	−56.1	14.7	64 47.5	−55.9	15.2	65 45.3	−55.7	15.8	66 43.0	−55.5	16.4	67 40.5	−55.2	17.1	68 37.7	−54.9	17.8	50
51	60 56.6	−56.7	13.0	61 55.1	−56.6	13.4	62 53.4	−56.5	13.9	63 51.6	−56.3	14.4	64 49.6	−56.0	14.9	65 47.5	−55.8	15.5	66 45.3	−55.6	16.1	67 42.8	−55.3	16.7	51
52	59 59.9	−56.9	12.3	60 58.5	−56.8	12.7	61 56.9	−56.6	13.1	62 55.3	−56.5	13.6	63 53.6	−56.3	14.1	64 51.7	−56.1	14.6	65 49.7	−55.9	15.1	66 47.5	−55.6	15.7	52
53	59 03.0	−57.2	11.7	60 01.7	−57.0	12.1	61 00.3	−56.9	12.5	61 58.8	−56.7	12.9	62 57.3	−56.5	13.3	63 55.6	−56.3	13.8	64 53.8	−56.1	14.3	65 51.9	−55.9	14.8	53
54	58 05.8	−57.2	11.1	59 04.7	−57.2	11.5	60 03.4	−57.0	11.8	61 02.1	−56.9	12.2	62 00.8	−56.8	12.6	62 59.3	−56.6	13.0	63 57.7	−56.4	13.4	64 56.0	−56.3	13.9	54
55	57 08.6	−57.4	10.6	58 07.5	−57.3	10.9	59 06.4	−57.2	11.2	60 05.2	−57.0	11.5	61 04.0	−56.9	11.9	62 02.7	−56.8	12.3	63 01.3	−56.7	12.7	63 59.7	−56.4	13.1	55
56	56 11.2	−57.6	10.0	57 10.2	−57.4	10.3	58 09.2	−57.3	10.6	59 08.2	−57.3	10.9	60 07.1	−57.2	11.2	61 05.9	−57.0	11.6	62 04.6	−56.8	12.0	63 03.3	−56.7	12.4	56
57	55 13.6	−57.6	9.5	56 12.8	−57.6	9.8	57 11.9	−57.5	10.1	58 10.9	−57.3	10.3	59 09.9	−57.2	10.6	60 08.9	−57.2	11.0	61 07.8	−57.1	11.3	62 06.6	−57.0	11.7	57
58	54 16.0	−57.8	9.1	55 15.2	−57.7	9.3	56 14.4	−57.6	9.5	57 13.6	−57.6	9.8	58 12.7	−57.5	10.1	59 11.7	−57.3	10.4	60 10.7	−57.2	10.7	61 09.6	−57.1	11.0	58
59	53 18.2	−57.8	8.6	54 17.5	−57.8	8.8	55 16.8	−57.7	9.0	56 16.0	−57.6	9.3	57 15.2	−57.5	9.5	58 14.4	−57.5	9.8	59 13.5	−57.4	10.1	60 12.5	−57.2	10.4	59
60	52 20.4	−58.0	8.2	53 19.7	−57.9	8.4	54 19.1	−57.8	8.6	55 18.4	−57.8	8.8	56 17.7	−57.7	9.0	57 16.9	−57.6	9.2	58 16.1	−57.5	9.5	59 15.3	−57.4	9.8	60
61	51 22.4	−58.0	7.8	52 21.8	−57.9	7.9	53 21.3	−58.0	8.1	54 20.6	−57.8	8.3	55 20.0	−57.8	8.5	56 19.3	−57.7	8.7	57 18.6	−57.6	9.0	58 17.9	−57.6	9.2	61
62	50 24.4	−58.2	7.3	51 23.9	−58.1	7.5	52 23.3	−58.0	7.7	53 22.8	−58.0	7.9	54 22.2	−57.9	8.0	55 21.6	−57.8	8.2	56 21.0	−57.8	8.5	57 20.3	−57.7	8.7	62
63	49 26.2	−58.2	7.0	50 25.8	−58.2	7.1	51 25.3	−58.1	7.3	52 24.8	−58.0	7.4	53 24.3	−58.0	7.6	54 23.8	−58.0	7.8	55 23.2	−57.9	8.0	56 22.6	−57.8	8.2	63
64	48 28.0	−58.2	6.6	49 27.6	−58.2	6.7	50 27.2	−58.2	6.9	51 26.8	−58.1	7.0	52 26.3	−58.1	7.2	53 25.8	−58.0	7.3	54 25.3	−57.9	7.5	55 24.8	−57.9	7.7	64
65	47 29.8	−58.3	6.2	48 29.4	−58.3	6.4	49 29.0	−58.2	6.5	50 28.7	−58.3	6.6	51 28.2	−58.1	6.8	52 27.8	−58.1	6.9	53 27.4	−58.1	7.1	54 26.9	−58.0	7.3	65
66	46 31.5	−58.4	5.9	47 31.1	−58.3	6.0	48 30.8	−58.3	6.1	49 30.4	−58.2	6.2	50 30.1	−58.3	6.4	51 29.7	−58.2	6.5	52 29.3	−58.1	6.7	53 28.9	−58.1	6.8	66
67	45 33.1	−58.5	5.6	46 32.8	−58.4	5.7	47 32.5	−58.4	5.8	48 32.2	−58.4	5.9	49 31.8	−58.3	6.0	50 31.5	−58.3	6.1	51 31.2	−58.3	6.3	52 30.8	−58.2	6.4	67
68	44 34.6	−58.5	5.2	45 34.4	−58.5	5.3	46 34.1	−58.4	5.4	47 33.8	−58.4	5.5	48 33.5	−58.3	5.6	49 33.2	−58.3	5.8	50 32.9	−58.3	5.9	51 32.6	−58.2	6.0	68
69	43 36.1	−58.5	4.9	44 35.9	−58.5	5.0	45 35.7	−58.5	5.1	46 35.4	−58.4	5.2	47 35.2	−58.5	5.3	48 34.9	−58.4	5.4	49 34.6	−58.3	5.5	50 34.4	−58.4	5.6	69
70	42 37.6	−58.6	4.6	43 37.4	−58.6	4.7	44 37.2	−58.6	4.8	45 37.0	−58.5	4.9	46 36.7	−58.4	5.0	47 36.5	−58.4	5.1	48 36.3	−58.4	5.2	49 36.0	−58.4	5.3	70
71	41 39.0	−58.6	4.3	42 38.8	−58.6	4.4	43 38.6	−58.6	4.5	44 38.5	−58.6	4.6	45 38.3	−58.6	4.6	46 38.1	−58.6	4.7	47 37.9	−58.5	4.8	48 37.6	−58.4	4.9	71
72	40 40.4	−58.7	4.1	41 40.2	−58.6	4.1	42 40.1	−58.7	4.2	43 39.9	−58.6	4.3	44 39.7	−58.6	4.3	45 39.5	−58.5	4.4	46 39.4	−58.6	4.5	47 39.2	−58.5	4.6	72
73	39 41.7	−58.7	3.8	40 41.6	−58.7	3.8	41 41.4	−58.6	3.9	42 41.3	−58.7	4.0	43 41.1	−58.6	4.0	44 41.0	−58.6	4.1	45 40.8	−58.6	4.2	46 40.7	−58.6	4.2	73
74	38 43.0	−58.8	3.5	39 42.9	−58.8	3.6	40 42.8	−58.8	3.6	41 42.6	−58.7	3.7	42 42.5	−58.7	3.7	43 42.4	−58.7	3.8	44 42.2	−58.6	3.9	45 42.1	−58.6	3.9	74
75	37 44.2	−58.7	3.3	38 44.1	−58.7	3.3	39 44.0	−58.7	3.4	40 43.9	−58.7	3.4	41 43.8	−58.7	3.5	42 43.7	−58.7	3.5	43 43.6	−58.7	3.6	44 43.5	−58.7	3.6	75
76	36 45.5	−58.8	3.0	37 45.4	−58.8	3.0	38 45.3	−58.8	3.1	39 45.2	−58.8	3.1	40 45.1	−58.7	3.2	41 45.0	−58.7	3.2	42 44.9	−58.7	3.3	43 44.8	−58.7	3.3	76
77	35 46.7	−58.9	2.8	36 46.6	−58.8	2.8	37 46.5	−58.8	2.8	38 46.4	−58.8	2.9	39 46.4	−58.8	2.9	40 46.3	−58.8	3.0	41 46.2	−58.8	3.0	42 46.1	−58.7	3.1	77
78	34 47.8	−58.9	2.5	35 47.8	−58.9	2.6	36 47.7	−58.9	2.6	37 47.6	−58.8	2.6	38 47.6	−58.9	2.7	39 47.5	−58.8	2.7	40 47.4	−58.8	2.7	41 47.4	−58.8	2.8	78
79	33 48.9	−58.8	2.3	34 48.9	−58.9	2.3	35 48.8	−58.8	2.3	36 48.8	−58.9	2.4	37 48.7	−58.8	2.4	38 48.7	−58.9	2.4	39 48.6	−58.8	2.5	40 48.6	−58.8	2.5	79
80	32 50.1	−59.0	2.1	33 50.0	−58.9	2.1	34 50.0	−58.9	2.1	35 49.9	−58.9	2.1	36 49.9	−58.9	2.2	37 49.8	−58.8	2.2	38 49.8	−58.9	2.2	39 49.8	−58.9	2.3	80
81	31 51.1	−58.9	1.8	32 51.1	−58.9	1.9	33 51.1	−58.9	1.9	34 51.0	−58.9	1.9	35 51.0	−58.9	1.9	36 51.0	−58.9	1.9	37 50.9	−58.9	2.0	38 50.9	−58.9	2.0	81
82	30 52.2	−59.0	1.6	31 52.2	−59.0	1.6	32 52.2	−59.0	1.6	33 52.1	−58.9	1.7	34 52.1	−58.9	1.7	35 52.1	−59.0	1.7	36 52.0	−58.9	1.7	37 52.0	−58.9	1.8	82
83	29 53.2	−58.9	1.4	30 53.2	−59.0	1.4	31 53.2	−59.0	1.4	32 53.2	−59.0	1.4	33 53.2	−59.0	1.5	34 53.1	−58.9	1.5	35 53.1	−58.9	1.5	36 53.1	−58.9	1.5	83
84	28 54.3	−59.0	1.2	29 54.2	−59.0	1.2	30 54.2	−59.0	1.2	31 54.2	−59.0	1.2	32 54.2	−59.0	1.2	33 54.2	−59.0	1.3	34 54.2	−59.0	1.3	35 54.2	−59.0	1.3	84
85	27 55.3	−59.1	1.0	28 55.2	−59.0	1.0	29 55.2	−59.0	1.0	30 55.2	−59.0	1.0	31 55.2	−59.0	1.0	32 55.2	−59.0	1.0	33 55.2	−59.0	1.0	34 55.2	−59.0	1.1	85
86	26 56.2	−59.0	0.8	27 56.2	−59.0	0.8	28 56.2	−59.0	0.8	29 56.2	−59.0	0.8	30 56.2	−59.0	0.8	31 56.2	−59.0	0.8	32 56.2	−59.0	0.8	33 56.2	−59.0	0.8	86
87	25 57.2	−59.1	0.6	26 57.2	−59.1	0.6	27 57.2	−59.1	0.6	28 57.2	−59.1	0.6	29 57.2	−59.1	0.6	30 57.2	−59.1	0.6	31 57.2	−59.1	0.6	32 57.2	−59.1	0.6	87
88	24 58.1	−59.0	0.4	25 58.1	−59.0	0.4	26 58.1	−59.0	0.4	27 58.1	−59.0	0.4	28 58.1	−59.0	0.4	29 58.1	−59.0	0.4	30 58.1	−59.0	0.4	31 58.1	−59.0	0.4	88
89	23 59.1	−59.1	0.2	24 59.1	−59.1	0.2	25 59.1	−59.1	0.2	26 59.1	−59.1	0.2	27 59.1	−59.1	0.2	28 59.1	−59.1	0.2	29 59.1	−59.1	0.2	30 59.1	−59.1	0.2	89
90	23 00.0	−59.1	0.0	24 00.0	−59.1	0.0	25 00.0	−59.1	0.0	26 00.0	−59.1	0.0	27 00.0	−59.1	0.0	28 00.0	−59.1	0.0	29 00.0	−59.1	0.0	30 00.0	−59.1	0.0	90
	23°			24°			25°			26°			27°			28°			29°			30°			

LATITUDE CONTRARY NAME TO DECLINATION L.H.A. 10°, 350°

Dec.	23° Hc	d	Z	24° Hc	d	Z	25° Hc	d	Z	26° Hc	d	Z
°	° ′	′	°	° ′	′	°	° ′	′	°	° ′	′	°
0	65 01.7	−55.7	155.7	64 06.9	−56.1	156.6	63 11.6	−56.3	157.4	62 16.1	−56.6	158.1
1	64 06.0	−55.9	156.6	63 10.8	−56.3	157.4	62 15.3	−56.6	158.1	61 19.5	−56.8	158.8
2	63 10.1	−56.3	157.4	62 14.5	−56.5	158.1	61 18.7	−56.8	158.8	60 22.7	−57.1	159.4
3	62 13.8	−56.4	158.1	61 18.0	−56.7	158.8	60 21.9	−56.9	159.5	59 25.6	−57.2	160.1
4	61 17.4	−56.7	158.9	60 21.3	−57.0	159.5	59 25.0	−57.2	160.1	58 28.4	−57.3	160.7
5	60 20.7	−56.9	159.5	59 24.3	−57.0	160.1	58 27.8	−57.3	160.7	57 31.1	−57.5	161.2
6	59 23.8	−57.1	160.2	58 27.3	−57.3	160.7	57 30.5	−57.4	161.2	56 33.6	−57.6	161.7
7	58 26.7	−57.2	160.8	57 30.0	−57.4	161.3	56 33.1	−57.6	161.8	55 36.0	−57.7	162.2
8	57 29.5	−57.3	161.3	56 32.6	−57.5	161.8	55 35.5	−57.7	162.3	54 38.3	−57.8	162.7
9	56 32.2	−57.5	161.9	55 35.1	−57.7	162.3	54 37.8	−57.7	162.8	53 40.5	−58.0	163.2
10	55 34.7	−57.6	162.4	54 37.4	−57.7	162.8	53 40.1	−57.9	163.2	52 42.5	−58.0	163.6
11	54 37.1	−57.7	162.9	53 39.7	−57.9	163.3	52 42.2	−58.0	163.7	51 44.5	−58.1	164.0
12	53 39.4	−57.9	163.3	52 41.8	−57.9	163.7	51 44.2	−58.1	164.1	50 46.4	−58.2	164.4
13	52 41.5	−57.9	163.8	51 43.9	−58.1	164.1	50 46.1	−58.2	164.5	49 48.2	−58.2	164.8
14	51 43.6	−58.0	164.2	50 45.8	−58.1	164.6	49 47.9	−58.2	164.9	48 50.0	−58.3	165.2
15	50 45.6	−58.1	164.6	49 47.7	−58.2	164.9	48 49.7	−58.3	165.2	47 51.7	−58.4	165.5
16	49 47.5	−58.2	165.0	48 49.5	−58.3	165.3	47 51.4	−58.3	165.6	46 53.3	−58.5	165.9
17	48 49.3	−58.2	165.4	47 51.2	−58.3	165.7	46 53.1	−58.4	165.9	45 54.8	−58.5	166.2
18	47 51.1	−58.3	165.8	46 52.9	−58.4	166.0	45 54.7	−58.5	166.3	44 56.3	−58.5	166.5
19	46 52.8	−58.4	166.1	45 54.5	−58.4	166.4	44 56.2	−58.5	166.6	43 57.8	−58.6	166.8
20	45 54.4	−58.4	166.4	44 56.1	−58.5	166.7	43 57.7	−58.6	166.9	42 59.2	−58.6	167.1
21	44 56.0	−58.5	166.8	43 57.6	−58.6	167.0	42 59.1	−58.6	167.2	42 00.6	−58.7	167.4
22	43 57.5	−58.5	167.1	42 59.0	−58.6	167.3	42 00.5	−58.7	167.5	41 01.9	−58.7	167.7
23	42 59.0	−58.6	167.4	42 00.4	−58.6	167.6	41 01.8	−58.7	167.8	40 03.2	−58.8	167.9
24	42 00.4	−58.6	167.7	41 01.8	−58.7	167.9	40 03.1	−58.7	168.0	39 04.4	−58.8	168.2
25	41 01.8	−58.6	168.0	40 03.1	−58.7	168.1	39 04.4	−58.8	168.3	38 05.6	−58.8	168.5
26	40 03.2	−58.7	168.2	39 04.4	−58.8	168.4	38 05.6	−58.8	168.6	37 06.8	−58.9	168.7
27	39 04.5	−58.8	168.5	38 05.6	−58.7	168.7	37 06.8	−58.8	168.8	36 07.9	−58.9	169.0
28	38 05.7	−58.7	168.8	37 06.9	−58.9	168.9	36 08.0	−58.9	169.1	35 09.0	−58.9	169.2
29	37 07.0	−58.8	169.0	36 08.0	−58.8	169.2	35 09.1	−58.9	169.3	34 10.1	−58.9	169.4
30	36 08.2	−58.9	169.3	35 09.2	−58.9	169.4	34 10.2	−58.9	169.5	33 11.2	−59.0	169.6
31	35 09.3	−58.8	169.5	34 10.3	−58.9	169.6	33 11.3	−59.0	169.8	32 12.2	−58.9	169.9
32	34 10.5	−58.9	169.7	33 11.4	−58.9	169.9	32 12.3	−58.9	170.0	31 13.3	−59.0	170.1
33	33 11.6	−58.9	170.0	32 12.5	−58.9	170.1	31 13.4	−59.0	170.2	30 14.3	−59.1	170.3
34	32 12.7	−58.9	170.2	31 13.6	−59.0	170.3	30 14.4	−59.0	170.4	29 15.2	−59.0	170.5
35	31 13.8	−59.0	170.4	30 14.6	−59.0	170.5	29 15.4	−59.0	170.6	28 16.2	−59.1	170.7
36	30 14.8	−59.0	170.6	29 15.6	−59.0	170.7	28 16.4	−59.1	170.8	27 17.1	−59.0	170.9
37	29 15.8	−59.0	170.9	28 16.6	−59.0	170.9	27 17.3	−59.0	171.0	26 18.1	−59.1	171.1
38	28 16.8	−59.0	171.1	27 17.6	−59.1	171.1	26 18.3	−59.1	171.2	25 19.0	−59.1	171.3
39	27 17.8	−59.0	171.3	26 18.5	−59.0	171.3	25 19.2	−59.1	171.4	24 19.9	−59.2	171.5
40	26 18.8	−59.1	171.5	25 19.5	−59.1	171.5	24 20.1	−59.1	171.6	23 20.7	−59.1	171.7
41	25 19.7	−59.0	171.7	24 20.4	−59.1	171.7	23 21.0	−59.1	171.8	22 21.6	−59.1	171.9
42	24 20.7	−59.1	171.9	23 21.3	−59.1	171.9	22 21.9	−59.2	172.0	21 22.5	−59.2	172.0
43	23 21.6	−59.1	172.0	22 22.2	−59.1	172.1	21 22.7	−59.1	172.2	20 23.3	−59.2	172.2
44	22 22.5	−59.1	172.2	21 23.1	−59.2	172.3	20 23.6	−59.2	172.3	19 24.1	−59.1	172.4
45	21 23.4	−59.1	172.4	20 23.9	−59.1	172.5	19 24.4	−59.1	172.5	18 25.0	−59.2	172.6
46	20 24.3	−59.1	172.6	19 24.8	−59.2	172.7	18 25.3	−59.2	172.7	17 25.8	−59.2	172.7
47	19 25.2	−59.2	172.8	18 25.6	−59.1	172.8	17 26.1	−59.2	172.9	16 26.6	−59.2	172.9
48	18 26.0	−59.1	173.0	17 26.5	−59.2	173.0	16 26.9	−59.2	173.0	15 27.4	−59.2	173.1
49	17 26.9	−59.2	173.1	16 27.3	−59.2	173.2	15 27.7	−59.2	173.2	14 28.2	−59.3	173.2
50	16 27.7	−59.1	173.3	15 28.1	−59.1	173.3	14 28.5	−59.2	173.4	13 28.9	−59.2	173.4
51	15 28.6	−59.2	173.5	14 29.0	−59.2	173.5	13 29.3	−59.2	173.5	12 29.7	−59.2	173.6
52	14 29.4	−59.2	173.7	13 29.8	−59.2	173.7	12 30.1	−59.2	173.7	11 30.5	−59.3	173.7
53	13 30.2	−59.2	173.8	12 30.6	−59.2	173.9	11 30.9	−59.2	173.9	10 31.2	−59.2	173.9
54	12 31.0	−59.2	174.0	11 31.4	−59.3	174.0	10 31.7	−59.2	174.0	9 32.0	−59.2	174.1
55	11 31.8	−59.2	174.2	10 32.1	−59.2	174.2	9 32.5	−59.3	174.2	8 32.8	−59.3	174.2
56	10 32.6	−59.2	174.3	9 32.9	−59.2	174.3	8 33.2	−59.2	174.4	7 33.5	−59.2	174.4
57	9 33.4	−59.2	174.5	8 33.7	−59.2	174.5	7 34.0	−59.3	174.5	6 34.3	−59.3	174.5
58	8 34.2	−59.2	174.7	7 34.5	−59.2	174.7	6 34.7	−59.2	174.7	5 35.0	−59.3	174.7
59	7 35.0	−59.2	174.8	6 35.3	−59.3	174.8	5 35.5	−59.3	174.8	4 35.7	−59.2	174.9
60	6 35.8	−59.2	175.0	5 36.0	−59.2	175.0	4 36.2	−59.2	175.0	3 36.5	−59.3	175.0
61	5 36.6	−59.2	175.1	4 36.8	−59.2	175.2	3 37.0	−59.2	175.2	2 37.2	−59.2	175.2
62	4 37.4	−59.3	175.3	3 37.6	−59.3	175.3	2 37.8	−59.3	175.3	1 38.0	−59.3	175.3
63	3 38.1	−59.2	175.5	2 38.3	−59.2	175.5	1 38.5	−59.3	175.5	0 38.7	−59.3	175.5
64	2 38.9	−59.2	175.6	1 39.1	−59.3	175.6	0 39.2	−59.2	175.6	0 20.6	+59.2	4.4
65	1 39.7	−59.3	175.8	0 39.8	−59.2	175.8	0 20.0	+59.3	4.2	1 19.8	+59.3	4.2
66	0 40.4	−59.2	175.9	0 19.4	+59.2	4.1	1 19.3	+59.2	4.1	2 19.1	+59.3	4.1
67	0 18.8	+59.2	3.9	1 18.6	+59.3	3.9	2 18.5	+59.3	3.9	3 18.4	+59.2	3.9
68	1 18.0	+59.2	3.7	2 17.9	+59.2	3.7	3 17.8	+59.2	3.7	4 17.6	+59.3	3.7
69	2 17.2	+59.3	3.6	3 17.1	+59.3	3.6	4 17.0	+59.3	3.6	5 16.9	+59.2	3.6
70	3 16.5	+59.2	3.4	4 16.4	+59.2	3.4	5 16.3	+59.2	3.4	6 16.1	+59.3	3.4
71	4 15.7	+59.2	3.2	5 15.6	+59.2	3.3	6 15.5	+59.2	3.3	7 15.4	+59.3	3.3
72	5 14.9	+59.2	3.1	6 14.8	+59.3	3.1	7 14.7	+59.3	3.1	8 14.7	+59.2	3.1
73	6 14.1	+59.3	2.9	7 14.1	+59.2	2.9	8 14.0	+59.2	2.9	9 13.9	+59.2	2.9
74	7 13.4	+59.2	2.8	8 13.3	+59.2	2.8	9 13.2	+59.2	2.8	10 13.1	+59.3	2.8
75	8 12.6	+59.2	2.6	9 12.5	+59.2	2.6	10 12.4	+59.3	2.6	11 12.4	+59.2	2.6
76	9 11.8	+59.2	2.4	10 11.7	+59.2	2.4	11 11.7	+59.2	2.5	12 11.6	+59.2	2.5
77	10 11.0	+59.2	2.3	11 10.9	+59.2	2.3	12 10.9	+59.2	2.3	13 10.8	+59.3	2.3
78	11 10.2	+59.2	2.1	12 10.1	+59.2	2.1	13 10.1	+59.2	2.1	14 10.1	+59.2	2.1
79	12 09.4	+59.2	1.9	13 09.3	+59.2	1.9	14 09.3	+59.2	2.0	15 09.3	+59.2	2.0
80	13 08.6	+59.2	1.8	14 08.5	+59.2	1.8	15 08.5	+59.2	1.8	16 08.5	+59.2	1.8
81	14 07.8	+59.1	1.6	15 07.7	+59.2	1.6	16 07.7	+59.2	1.6	17 07.7	+59.2	1.6
82	15 06.9	+59.2	1.4	16 06.9	+59.2	1.4	17 06.9	+59.2	1.4	18 06.9	+59.2	1.5
83	16 06.1	+59.2	1.3	17 06.1	+59.1	1.3	18 06.1	+59.1	1.3	19 06.1	+59.1	1.3
84	17 05.3	+59.1	1.1	18 05.2	+59.2	1.1	19 05.2	+59.2	1.1	20 05.2	+59.2	1.1
85	18 04.4	+59.1	0.9	19 04.4	+59.1	0.9	20 04.4	+59.1	0.9	21 04.4	+59.1	0.9
86	19 03.5	+59.2	0.7	20 03.5	+59.2	0.7	21 03.5	+59.2	0.7	22 03.5	+59.2	0.7
87	20 02.7	+59.1	0.6	21 02.7	+59.1	0.6	22 02.7	+59.1	0.6	23 02.7	+59.1	0.6
88	21 01.8	+59.1	0.4	22 01.8	+59.1	0.4	23 01.8	+59.1	0.4	24 01.8	+59.1	0.4
89	22 00.9	+59.1	0.2	23 00.9	+59.1	0.2	24 00.9	+59.1	0.2	25 00.9	+59.1	0.2
90	23 00.0	+59.1	0.0	24 00.0	+59.1	0.0	25 00.0	+59.1	0.0	26 00.0	+59.1	0.0
	23°			24°			25°			26°		

Dec.	27° Hc	d	Z	28° Hc	d	Z	29° Hc	d	Z	30° Hc	d	Z
°	° ′	′	°	° ′	′	°	° ′	′	°	° ′	′	°
0	61 20.3	−56.9	158.8	60 24.3	−57.2	159.4	59 28.0	−57.3	160.0	58 31.5	−57.5	160.6
1	60 23.4	−57.0	159.4	59 27.1	−57.2	160.0	58 30.7	−57.5	160.6	57 34.0	−57.7	161.1
2	59 26.4	−57.3	160.0	58 29.9	−57.5	160.6	57 33.2	−57.6	161.1	56 36.3	−57.8	161.6
3	58 29.1	−57.4	160.6	57 32.4	−57.5	161.1	56 35.6	−57.8	161.6	55 38.5	−57.8	162.1
4	57 31.7	−57.5	161.2	56 34.9	−57.7	161.7	55 37.8	−57.8	162.1	54 40.7	−58.0	162.6
5	56 34.2	−57.6	161.7	55 37.2	−57.8	162.2	54 40.0	−57.9	162.6	53 42.7	−58.1	163.0
6	55 36.6	−57.8	162.2	54 39.4	−57.9	162.6	53 42.1	−58.1	163.0	52 44.6	−58.2	163.4
7	54 38.8	−57.9	162.7	53 41.5	−58.0	163.1	52 44.0	−58.1	163.5	51 46.4	−58.2	163.8
8	53 40.9	−57.9	163.1	52 43.5	−58.1	163.5	51 45.9	−58.2	163.9	50 48.2	−58.3	164.2
9	52 43.0	−58.1	163.6	51 45.4	−58.2	163.9	50 47.7	−58.3	164.3	49 49.9	−58.4	164.6
10	51 44.9	−58.1	164.0	50 47.2	−58.2	164.3	49 49.4	−58.3	164.6	48 51.5	−58.4	164.9
11	50 46.8	−58.2	164.4	49 49.0	−58.3	164.7	48 51.1	−58.5	165.0	47 53.1	−58.5	165.3
12	49 48.6	−58.3	164.7	48 50.7	−58.4	165.0	47 52.6	−58.4	165.3	46 54.6	−58.6	165.6
13	48 50.3	−58.4	165.1	47 52.3	−58.5	165.4	46 54.2	−58.5	165.7	45 56.0	−58.6	165.9
14	47 51.9	−58.4	165.5	46 53.8	−58.5	165.7	45 55.7	−58.6	166.0	44 57.4	−58.6	166.2
15	46 53.5	−58.4	165.8	45 55.3	−58.5	166.0	44 57.1	−58.6	166.3	43 58.8	−58.7	166.5
16	45 55.1	−58.6	166.1	44 56.8	−58.6	166.4	43 58.5	−58.7	166.6	43 00.1	−58.8	166.8
17	44 56.5	−58.5	166.4	43 58.2	−58.7	166.7	42 59.8	−58.7	166.9	42 01.3	−58.8	167.1
18	43 58.0	−58.7	166.7	42 59.5	−58.6	167.0	42 01.1	−58.8	167.2	41 02.5	−58.8	167.4
19	42 59.3	−58.6	167.0	42 00.9	−58.8	167.2	41 02.3	−58.8	167.4	40 03.7	−58.8	167.6
20	42 00.7	−58.7	167.3	41 02.1	−58.7	167.5	40 03.5	−58.8	167.7	39 04.9	−58.9	167.9
21	41 02.0	−58.8	167.6	40 03.4	−58.8	167.8	39 04.7	−58.9	167.9	38 06.0	−58.9	168.1
22	40 03.2	−58.7	167.9	39 04.6	−58.9	168.0	38 05.8	−58.8	168.2	37 07.1	−58.9	168.4
23	39 04.5	−58.9	168.1	38 05.7	−58.8	168.3	37 07.0	−59.0	168.4	36 08.2	−59.0	168.6
24	38 05.6	−58.8	168.4	37 06.9	−58.9	168.5	36 08.0	−58.9	168.7	35 09.2	−59.0	168.8
25	37 06.8	−58.9	168.6	36 08.0	−59.0	168.8	35 09.1	−59.0	168.9	34 10.2	−59.0	169.0
26	36 07.9	−58.9	168.9	35 09.0	−58.9	169.0	34 10.1	−59.0	169.1	33 11.2	−59.0	169.3
27	35 09.0	−58.9	169.1	34 10.1	−59.0	169.2	33 11.1	−59.0	169.3	32 12.2	−59.1	169.5
28	34 10.1	−59.0	169.3	33 11.1	−59.0	169.4	32 12.1	−59.0	169.6	31 13.1	−59.1	169.7
29	33 11.1	−58.9	169.5	32 12.1	−59.0	169.7	31 13.1	−59.1	169.8	30 14.0	−59.1	169.9
30	32 12.2	−59.0	169.8	31 13.1	−59.0	169.9	30 14.0	−59.0	170.0	29 14.9	−59.1	170.1
31	31 13.2	−59.1	170.0	30 14.1	−59.1	170.1	29 15.0	−59.1	170.2	28 15.8	−59.1	170.3
32	30 14.1	−59.0	170.2	29 15.0	−59.1	170.3	28 15.9	−59.1	170.4	27 16.7	−59.1	170.5
33	29 15.1	−59.1	170.4	28 15.9	−59.1	170.5	27 16.8	−59.2	170.6	26 17.6	−59.2	170.7
34	28 16.0	−59.0	170.6	27 16.8	−59.1	170.7	26 17.6	−59.1	170.8	25 18.4	−59.2	170.8
35	27 17.0	−59.1	170.8	26 17.7	−59.1	170.9	25 18.5	−59.2	170.9	24 19.2	−59.2	171.0
36	26 17.9	−59.1	171.0	25 18.6	−59.1	171.1	24 19.3	−59.1	171.1	23 20.0	−59.1	171.2
37	25 18.8	−59.2	171.2	24 19.5	−59.2	171.2	23 20.2	−59.2	171.3	22 20.9	−59.3	171.4
38	24 19.6	−59.1	171.4	23 20.3	−59.1	171.4	22 21.0	−59.2	171.5	21 21.6	−59.2	171.6
39	23 20.5	−59.1	171.5	22 21.2	−59.2	171.6	21 21.8	−59.2	171.7	20 22.4	−59.2	171.7
40	22 21.4	−59.2	171.7	21 22.0	−59.2	171.8	20 22.6	−59.2	171.8	19 23.2	−59.2	171.9
41	21 22.2	−59.2	171.9	20 22.8	−59.2	172.0	19 23.4	−59.2	172.0	18 24.0	−59.3	172.1
42	20 23.0	−59.1	172.1	19 23.6	−59.2	172.1	18 24.2	−59.3	172.2	17 24.7	−59.2	172.2
43	19 23.9	−59.2	172.3	18 24.4	−59.2	172.3	17 24.9	−59.2	172.4	16 25.5	−59.3	172.4
44	18 24.7	−59.2	172.4	17 25.2	−59.2	172.5	16 25.7	−59.3	172.5	15 26.2	−59.3	172.6
45	17 25.5	−59.3	172.6	16 26.0	−59.3	172.6	15 26.4	−59.2	172.7	14 26.9	−59.2	172.7
46	16 26.2	−59.2	172.8	15 26.7	−59.2	172.8	14 27.2	−59.3	172.8	13 27.7	−59.3	172.9
47	15 27.0	−59.2	172.9	14 27.5	−59.3	173.0	13 27.9	−59.2	173.0	12 28.4	−59.3	173.0
48	14 27.8	−59.2	173.1	13 28.2	−59.2	173.1	12 28.7	−59.3	173.2	11 29.1	−59.3	173.2
49	13 28.6	−59.3	173.3	12 29.0	−59.3	173.3	11 29.4	−59.3	173.3	10 29.8	−59.3	173.3
50	12 29.3	−59.2	173.4	11 29.7	−59.2	173.5	10 30.1	−59.3	173.5	9 30.5	−59.3	173.5
51	11 30.1	−59.3	173.6	10 30.5	−59.3	173.6	9 30.8	−59.3	173.6	8 31.2	−59.3	173.7
52	10 30.8	−59.2	173.8	9 31.2	−59.3	173.8	8 31.5	−59.2	173.8	7 31.9	−59.3	173.8
53	9 31.6	−59.3	173.9	8 31.9	−59.3	173.9	7 32.3	−59.3	173.9	6 32.6	−59.3	174.0
54	8 32.3	−59.2	174.1	7 32.6	−59.2	174.1	6 33.0	−59.3	174.1	5 33.3	−59.3	174.1
55	7 33.1	−59.3	174.2	6 33.4	−59.3	174.2	5 33.7	−59.3	174.3	4 34.0	−59.3	174.3
56	6 33.8	−59.3	174.4	5 34.1	−59.3	174.4	4 34.4	−59.3	174.4	3 34.7	−59.4	174.4
57	5 34.5	−59.2	174.5	4 34.8	−59.3	174.6	3 35.1	−59.3	174.6	2 35.3	−59.3	174.6
58	4 35.3	−59.3	174.7	3 35.5	−59.3	174.7	2 35.8	−59.3	174.7	1 36.0	−59.3	174.7
59	3 36.0	−59.3	174.9	2 36.2	−59.3	174.9	1 36.5	−59.3	174.9	0 36.7	−59.3	174.9
60	2 36.7	−59.3	175.0	1 36.9	−59.3	175.0	0 37.2	−59.3	175.0	0 22.6	+59.3	5.0
61	1 37.4	−59.2	175.2	0 37.6	−59.2	175.2	0 22.1	+59.3	4.8	1 21.9	+59.3	4.8
62	0 38.2	−59.3	175.3	0 21.6	+59.3	4.7	1 21.4	+59.4	4.7	2 21.2	+59.4	4.7
63	0 21.1	+59.3	4.5	1 20.9	+59.3	4.5	2 20.8	+59.3	4.5	3 20.6	+59.3	4.5
64	1 20.4	+59.3	4.4	2 20.2	+59.3	4.4	3 20.1	+59.3	4.4	4 19.9	+59.3	4.4
65	2 19.7	+59.3	4.2	3 19.5	+59.3	4.2	4 19.4	+59.3	4.2	5 19.2	+59.3	4.2
66	3 19.0	+59.2	4.1	4 18.8	+59.3	4.1	5 18.7	+59.3	4.1	6 18.5	+59.3	4.1
67	4 18.2	+59.3	3.9	5 18.1	+59.3	3.9	6 18.0	+59.2	3.9	7 17.8	+59.3	3.9
68	5 17.5	+59.3	3.7	6 17.4	+59.3	3.8	7 17.2	+59.3	3.8	8 17.1	+59.3	3.8
69	6 16.8	+59.2	3.6	7 16.7	+59.2	3.6	8 16.5	+59.3	3.6	9 16.4	+59.3	3.6
70	7 16.0	+59.3	3.4	8 15.9	+59.3	3.4	9 15.8	+59.3	3.4	10 15.7	+59.3	3.5
71	8 15.3	+59.3	3.3	9 15.2	+59.3	3.3	10 15.1	+59.3	3.3	11 15.0	+59.3	3.3
72	9 14.6	+59.2	3.1	10 14.5	+59.2	3.1	11 14.4	+59.3	3.1	12 14.3	+59.3	3.1
73	10 13.8	+59.3	3.0	11 13.7	+59.3	3.0	12 13.7	+59.2	3.0	13 13.6	+59.3	3.0
74	11 13.1	+59.2	2.8	12 13.0	+59.3	2.8	13 12.9	+59.3	2.8	14 12.9	+59.2	2.8
75	12 12.3	+59.3	2.6	13 12.3	+59.2	2.6	14 12.2	+59.2	2.7	15 12.1	+59.3	2.7
76	13 11.6	+59.2	2.5	14 11.5	+59.2	2.5	15 11.4	+59.3	2.5	16 11.4	+59.2	2.5
77	14 10.8	+59.2	2.3	15 10.7	+59.3	2.3	16 10.7	+59.2	2.3	17 10.6	+59.3	2.3
78	15 10.0	+59.2	2.1	16 10.0	+59.2	2.2	17 09.9	+59.3	2.2	18 09.9	+59.2	2.2
79	16 09.2	+59.3	2.0	17 09.2	+59.2	2.0	18 09.2	+59.2	2.0	19 09.1	+59.3	2.0
80	17 08.5	+59.2	1.8	18 08.4	+59.2	1.8	19 08.4	+59.2	1.8	20 08.4	+59.2	1.8
81	18 07.7	+59.2	1.6	19 07.6	+59.2	1.6	20 07.6	+59.2	1.7	21 07.6	+59.2	1.7
82	19 06.9	+59.1	1.5	20 06.8	+59.2	1.5	21 06.8	+59.2	1.5	22 06.8	+59.2	1.5
83	20 06.0	+59.2	1.3	21 06.0	+59.2	1.3	22 06.0	+59.2	1.3	23 06.0	+59.2	1.3
84	21 05.2	+59.2	1.1	22 05.2	+59.2	1.1	23 05.2	+59.2	1.1	24 05.2	+59.2	1.1
85	22 04.4	+59.1	0.9	23 04.4	+59.1	0.9	24 04.4	+59.1	0.9	25 04.4	+59.1	1.0
86	23 03.5	+59.2	0.8	24 03.5	+59.2	0.8	25 03.5	+59.2	0.8	26 03.5	+59.2	0.8
87	24 02.7	+59.1	0.6	25 02.7	+59.1	0.6	26 02.7	+59.1	0.6	27 02.7	+59.1	0.6
88	25 01.8	+59.1	0.4	26 01.8	+59.1	0.4	27 01.8	+59.1	0.4	28 01.8	+59.1	0.4
89	26 00.9	+59.1	0.2	27 00.9	+59.1	0.2	28 00.9	+59.1	0.2	29 00.9	+59.1	0.2
90	27 00.0	+59.1	0.0	28 00.0	+59.1	0.0	29 00.0	+59.1	0.0	30 00.0	+59.1	0.0
	27°			28°			29°			30°		

S. Lat. { L.H.A. greater than 180° ....Zn=180°−Z
{ L.H.A. less than 180°...........Zn=180°+Z

LATITUDE SAME NAME AS DECLINATION L.H.A. 170°, 190°

11°, 349° L.H.A. **LATITUDE SAME NAME AS DECLINATION** N. Lat. {L.H.A. greater than 180° .....Zn=Z / L.H.A. less than 180°............Zn=360°−Z}

Dec.	23°			24°			25°			26°			27°			28°			29°			30°			Dec.
	Hc	d	Z	Hc	d	Z	Hc	d	Z	Hc	d	Z	Hc	d	Z	Hc	d	Z	Hc	d	Z	Hc	d	Z	
°	° ′	′	°	° ′	′	°	° ′	′	°	° ′	′	°	° ′	′	°	° ′	′	°	° ′	′	°	° ′	′	°	°
0	64 38.1	+54.5	153.6	63 44.1	+55.0	154.5	62 49.8	+55.4	155.3	61 55.1	+55.8	156.1	61 00.1	+56.1	156.8	60 04.8	+56.4	157.5	59 09.3	+56.6	158.2	58 13.4	+56.9	158.8	0
1	65 32.6	+54.1	152.6	64 39.1	+54.6	153.5	63 45.2	+55.0	154.4	62 50.9	+55.4	155.3	61 56.2	+55.8	156.1	61 01.2	+56.1	156.8	60 05.9	+56.4	157.5	59 10.3	+56.7	158.1	1
2	66 26.7	+53.7	151.5	65 33.7	+54.2	152.6	64 40.2	+54.7	153.5	63 46.3	+55.1	154.4	62 52.0	+55.5	155.3	61 57.3	+55.9	156.1	61 02.3	+56.2	156.8	60 07.0	+56.5	157.5	2
3	67 20.4	+53.1	150.4	66 27.9	+53.8	151.5	65 34.9	+54.3	152.6	64 41.4	+54.8	153.5	63 47.5	+55.2	154.4	62 53.2	+55.6	155.3	61 58.5	+56.0	156.1	61 03.5	+56.3	156.8	3
4	68 13.5	+52.5	149.1	67 21.7	+53.2	150.4	66 29.2	+53.9	151.5	65 36.2	+54.4	152.6	64 42.7	+54.9	153.5	63 48.8	+55.3	154.4	62 54.5	+55.7	155.3	61 59.8	+56.0	156.1	4
5	69 06.0	+51.9	147.8	68 14.9	+52.6	149.1	67 23.1	+53.3	150.4	66 30.6	+53.9	151.5	65 37.6	+54.5	152.6	64 44.1	+55.0	153.6	63 50.2	+55.4	154.5	62 55.8	+55.8	155.3	5
6	69 57.9	+51.1	146.4	69 07.5	+52.0	147.8	68 16.4	+52.7	149.2	67 24.5	+53.5	150.4	66 32.1	+54.0	151.5	65 39.1	+54.5	152.6	64 45.6	+55.0	153.6	63 51.6	+55.5	154.5	6
7	70 49.0	+50.3	144.8	69 59.5	+51.3	146.4	69 09.1	+52.1	147.8	68 18.0	+52.8	149.2	67 26.1	+53.5	150.4	66 33.6	+54.1	151.6	65 40.6	+54.6	152.6	64 47.1	+55.1	153.6	7
8	71 39.3	+49.3	143.1	70 50.8	+50.4	144.8	70 01.2	+51.4	146.4	69 10.8	+52.2	147.9	68 19.6	+53.0	149.2	67 27.7	+53.7	150.5	66 35.2	+54.3	151.6	65 42.2	+54.8	152.7	8
9	72 28.6	+48.1	141.3	71 41.2	+49.4	143.1	70 52.6	+50.5	144.9	70 03.0	+51.5	146.5	69 12.6	+52.3	147.9	68 21.4	+53.1	149.3	67 29.5	+53.7	150.5	66 37.0	+54.3	151.7	9
10	73 16.7	+46.9	139.2	72 30.6	+48.3	141.3	71 43.1	+49.6	143.2	70 54.5	+50.7	144.9	70 04.9	+51.7	146.5	69 14.5	+52.4	148.0	68 23.2	+53.2	149.3	67 31.3	+53.8	150.6	10
11	74 03.6	+45.3	137.0	73 18.9	+47.0	139.3	72 32.7	+48.4	141.4	71 45.2	+49.7	143.3	70 56.6	+50.8	145.0	70 06.9	+51.8	146.6	69 16.4	+52.6	148.0	68 25.1	+53.4	149.4	11
12	74 48.9	+43.6	134.6	74 05.9	+45.5	137.1	73 21.1	+47.2	139.3	72 34.9	+48.6	141.4	71 47.4	+49.8	143.3	70 58.7	+50.9	145.1	70 09.0	+51.9	146.7	69 18.5	+52.7	148.1	12
13	75 32.5	+41.6•	131.9	74 51.4	+43.8	134.6	74 08.3	+45.7	137.1	73 23.5	+47.3	139.4	72 37.2	+48.8	141.5	71 49.6	+50.0	143.4	71 00.9	+51.1	145.1	70 11.2	+52.0	146.7	13
14	76 14.1	+39.2•	128.9	75 35.2	+41.7•	131.9	74 54.0	+43.9	134.7	74 10.8	+45.9	137.2	73 26.0	+47.5	139.5	72 39.6	+49.0	141.6	71 52.0	+50.2	143.5	71 03.2	+51.3	145.2	14
15	76 53.3	+36.6•	125.7	76 16.9	+39.5•	129.0	75 37.9	+42.0•	132.0	74 56.7	+44.2	134.8	74 13.5	+46.0	137.3	73 28.6	+47.6	139.6	72 42.2	+49.1	141.7	71 54.5	+50.3	143.6	15
16	77 29.9	+33.4•	122.1	76 56.4	+36.8•	125.7	76 19.9	+39.7•	129.1	75 40.9	+42.2•	132.1	74 59.5	+44.4	134.9	74 16.2	+46.3	137.4	73 31.3	+47.8	139.7	72 44.8	+49.3	141.8	16
17	78 03.3	+29.9•	118.2	77 33.2	+33.6•	122.2	76 59.6	+37.0•	125.8	76 23.1	+39.9•	129.2	75 43.9	+42.4•	132.2	75 02.5	+44.6	135.0	74 19.1	+46.5	137.5	73 34.1	+48.0	139.8	17
18	78 33.2	+25.8•	113.9	78 06.8	+30.1•	118.2	77 36.6	+33.9•	122.2	77 03.0	+37.2•	125.9	76 26.3	+40.1•	129.3	75 47.1	+42.6•	132.4	75 05.6	+44.8	135.1	74 22.1	+46.7	137.7	18
19	78 59.0	+21.3•	109.2	78 36.9	+26.1•	113.9	78 10.5	+30.3•	118.3	77 40.2	+34.1•	122.3	77 06.4	+37.5•	126.0	76 29.7	+40.4•	129.4	75 50.4	+42.8•	132.5	75 08.8	+45.0	135.3	19
20	79 20.3	+16.3•	104.3	79 03.0	+21.5•	109.3	78 40.8	+26.3•	114.0	78 14.3	+30.6•	118.4	77 43.9	+34.4•	122.5	77 10.1	+37.7•	126.2	76 33.2	+40.6•	129.5	75 53.8	+43.1•	132.6	20
21	79 36.6	+10.8•	99.0	79 24.5	+16.4•	104.3	79 07.1	+21.7•	109.3	78 44.9	+26.5•	114.1	78 18.3	+30.8•	118.5	77 47.8	+34.6•	122.6	77 13.8	+38.0•	126.3	76 36.9	+40.8•	129.7	21
22	79 47.4	+5.2•	93.5	79 40.9	+11.0•	99.0	79 28.8	+16.6•	104.3	79 11.4	+21.9•	109.4	78 49.1	+26.7•	114.2	78 22.4	+31.1•	118.6	77 51.8	+34.9•	122.7	77 17.7	+38.2•	126.4	22
23	79 52.6	-0.7•	87.8	79 51.9	+5.3•	93.4	79 45.4	+11.2•	99.0	79 33.3	+16.8•	104.3	79 15.8	+22.2•	109.5	78 53.5	+26.9•	114.3	78 26.7	+31.3•	118.7	77 55.9	+35.2•	122.9	23
24	79 51.9	-6.5•	82.2	79 57.2	-0.6•	87.8	79 56.6	+5.4•	93.4	79 50.1	+11.4•	99.0	79 38.0	+17.0•	104.4	79 20.4	+22.4•	109.5	78 58.0	+27.2•	114.4	78 31.1	+31.6•	118.9	24
25	79 45.4	-12.1•	76.5	79 56.6	-6.5•	82.0	80 02.0	-0.5•	87.7	80 01.5	+5.5•	93.4	79 55.0	+11.5•	99.0	79 42.8	+17.3•	104.4	79 25.2	+22.6•	109.6	79 02.7	+27.5•	114.5	25
26	79 33.3	-17.5•	71.1	79 50.1	-12.1•	76.4	80 01.5	-6.5•	81.9	80 07.0	-0.5•	87.6	80 06.5	+5.6•	93.3	80 00.1	+11.6•	99.0	79 47.8	+17.5•	104.5	79 30.2	+22.8•	109.7	26
27	79 15.8	-22.3•	65.9	79 38.0	-17.6•	70.9	79 55.0	-12.2•	76.2	80 06.5	-6.4•	81.8	80 12.1	-0.4•	87.5	80 11.7	+5.8•	93.3	80 05.3	+11.8•	99.0	79 53.0	+17.7•	104.6	27
28	78 53.5	-26.8•	61.0	79 20.4	-22.4•	65.6	79 42.8	-17.6•	70.6	80 00.1	-12.3•	76.0	80 11.7	-6.4•	81.6	80 17.5	-0.4•	87.4	80 17.1	+5.9•	93.3	80 10.7	+12.0•	99.0	28
29	78 26.7	-30.8•	56.4	78 58.0	-26.9•	60.7	79 25.2	-22.5•	65.4	79 47.8	-17.6•	70.4	80 05.3	-12.3•	75.8	80 17.1	-6.4•	81.5	80 23.0	-0.3•	87.3	80 22.7	+5.9•	93.2	29
30	77 55.9	-34.2•	52.2	78 31.1	-30.9•	56.1	79 02.7	-27.1•	60.4	79 30.2	-22.7•	65.1	79 53.0	-17.8•	70.2	80 10.7	-12.3•	75.6	80 22.7	-6.5•	81.3	80 28.6	-0.2•	87.2	30
31	77 21.7	-37.2•	48.4	78 00.2	-34.3•	51.9	78 35.6	-31.0•	55.8	79 07.5	-27.2•	60.1	79 35.2	-22.7•	64.8	79 58.4	-17.9•	69.9	80 16.2	-12.3•	75.4	80 28.4	-6.4•	81.2	31
32	76 44.5	-39.8•	44.9	77 25.9	-37.4•	48.0	78 04.6	-34.5•	51.6	78 40.3	-31.2•	55.5	79 12.5	-27.4•	59.8	79 40.5	-22.9•	64.5	80 03.9	-18.0•	69.7	80 22.0	-12.5•	75.2	32
33	76 04.7	-42.1•	41.7	76 48.5	-40.0•	44.5	77 30.1	-37.5•	47.7	78 09.1	-34.6•	51.2	78 45.1	-31.3•	55.1	79 17.6	-27.5•	59.5	79 45.9	-23.1•	64.2	80 09.5	-18.0•	69.4	33
34	75 22.6	-44.0	38.8	76 08.5	-42.2•	41.3	76 52.6	-40.1•	44.2	77 34.5	-37.7•	47.3	78 13.8	-34.8•	50.9	78 50.1	-31.5•	54.8	79 22.8	-27.6•	59.1	79 51.5	-23.3•	63.9	34
35	74 38.6	-45.7	36.2	75 26.3	-44.2	38.4	76 12.5	-42.4•	41.0	76 56.8	-40.3•	43.8	77 39.0	-37.9•	47.0	78 18.6	-35.0•	50.5	78 55.2	-31.7•	54.4	79 28.2	-27.8•	58.8	35
36	73 52.9	-47.2	33.8	74 42.1	-45.8	35.8	75 30.1	-44.3	38.1	76 16.5	-42.5•	40.6	77 01.1	-40.4•	43.4	77 43.6	-38.0•	46.6	78 23.5	-35.2•	50.1	79 00.4	-31.9•	54.0	36
37	73 05.7	-48.4	31.6	73 56.3	-47.3	33.4	74 45.8	-46.0	35.4	75 34.0	-44.4	37.7	76 20.7	-42.7•	40.2	77 05.6	-40.7•	43.0	77 48.3	-38.2•	46.2	78 28.5	-35.4•	49.7	37
38	72 17.3	-49.5	29.6	73 09.0	-48.5	31.2	73 59.8	-47.4	33.1	74 49.6	-46.2	35.1	75 38.0	-44.6	37.3	76 24.9	-42.8•	39.8	77 10.1	-40.8•	42.6	77 53.1	-38.4•	45.8	38
39	71 27.8	-50.5	27.8	72 20.5	-49.6	29.3	73 12.4	-48.6	30.9	74 03.4	-47.5	32.7	74 53.4	-46.3	34.7	75 42.1	-44.8	36.9	76 29.3	-43.1•	39.4	77 14.7	-41.0•	42.2	39
40	70 37.3	-51.3	26.1	71 30.9	-50.6	27.5	72 23.8	-49.8	28.9	73 15.9	-48.8	30.5	74 07.1	-47.7	32.3	74 57.3	-46.4	34.3	75 46.2	-44.9	36.5	76 33.7	-43.3•	39.0	40
41	69 46.0	-52.0	24.6	70 40.3	-51.4	25.8	71 34.0	-50.7	27.1	72 27.1	-49.9	28.5	73 19.4	-48.9	30.1	74 10.9	-47.9	31.9	75 01.3	-46.6	33.9	75 50.4	-45.1	36.1	41
42	68 54.0	-52.7	23.2	69 48.9	-52.1	24.3	70 43.3	-51.5	25.4	71 37.2	-50.8	26.7	72 30.5	-50.0	28.1	73 23.0	-49.1	29.7	74 14.7	-48.0	31.5	75 05.3	-46.8	33.4	42
43	68 01.3	-53.3	21.9	68 56.8	-52.8	22.9	69 51.8	-52.2	23.9	70 46.4	-51.6	25.1	71 40.5	-50.9	26.3	72 33.9	-50.1	27.8	73 26.7	-49.2	29.3	74 18.5	-48.1	31.1	43
44	67 08.0	-53.7	20.7	68 04.0	-53.3	21.6	68 59.6	-52.8	22.5	69 54.8	-52.3	23.6	70 49.6	-51.7	24.7	71 43.8	-51.0	26.0	72 37.5	-50.3	27.4	73 30.4	-49.4	28.9	44
45	66 14.3	-54.3	19.6	67 10.7	-53.9	20.4	68 06.8	-53.5	21.2	69 02.5	-52.9	22.2	69 57.9	-52.5	23.2	70 52.8	-51.8	24.3	71 47.2	-51.2	25.6	72 41.0	-50.4	27.0	45
46	65 20.0	-54.6	18.5	66 16.8	-54.3	19.2	67 13.3	-53.9	20.0	68 09.6	-53.6	20.9	69 05.4	-53.0	21.8	70 01.0	-52.6	22.8	70 56.0	-51.9	23.9	71 50.6	-51.3	25.2	46
47	64 25.4	-55.0	17.5	65 22.5	-54.7	18.2	66 19.4	-54.4	18.9	67 16.0	-54.0	19.7	68 12.4	-53.6	20.5	69 08.4	-53.1	21.4	70 04.1	-52.7	22.4	70 59.3	-52.1	23.5	47
48	63 30.4	-55.3	16.6	64 27.8	-55.0	17.2	65 25.0	-54.7	17.9	66 22.0	-54.4	18.6	67 18.8	-54.1	19.3	68 15.3	-53.7	20.2	69 11.4	-53.2	21.1	70 07.2	-52.7	22.1	48
49	62 35.1	-55.6	15.8	63 32.8	-55.4	16.3	64 30.3	-55.1	16.9	65 27.6	-54.8	17.5	66 24.7	-54.5	18.2	67 21.6	-54.2	19.0	68 18.2	-53.8	19.8	69 14.5	-53.4	20.7	49
50	61 39.5	-55.8	15.0	62 37.4	-55.6	15.5	63 35.2	-55.5	16.0	64 32.8	-55.2	16.6	65 30.2	-54.9	17.2	66 27.4	-54.6	17.9	67 24.4	-54.3	18.6	68 21.1	-53.9	19.4	50
51	60 43.7	-56.2	14.2	61 41.8	-56.0	14.7	62 39.7	-55.7	15.2	63 37.6	-55.5	15.7	64 35.3	-55.3	16.2	65 32.8	-55.0	16.9	66 30.1	-54.7	17.5	67 27.2	-54.4	18.3	51
52	59 47.5	-56.3	13.5	60 45.8	-56.1	13.9	61 44.0	-56.0	14.4	62 42.1	-55.8	14.8	63 40.0	-55.6	15.4	64 37.8	-55.3	15.9	65 35.4	-55.1	16.5	66 32.8	-54.8	17.2	52
53	58 51.2	-56.5	12.8	59 49.7	-56.4	13.2	60 48.0	-56.2	13.6	61 46.3	-56.0	14.1	62 44.4	-55.8	14.5	63 42.5	-55.7	15.0	64 40.3	-55.4	15.6	65 38.0	-55.1	16.2	53
54	57 54.7	-56.7	12.2	58 53.3	-56.6	12.5	59 51.8	-56.4	12.9	60 50.3	-56.3	13.3	61 48.6	-56.1	13.7	62 46.8	-55.9	14.2	63 44.9	-55.7	14.7	64 42.9	-55.5	15.2	54
55	56 58.0	-56.9	11.6	57 56.7	-56.8	11.9	58 55.4	-56.6	12.2	59 54.0	-56.5	12.6	60 52.5	-56.3	13.0	61 50.9	-56.2	13.4	62 49.2	-56.0	13.9	63 47.4	-55.8	14.3	55
56	56 01.1	-57.1	11.0	56 59.9	-56.9	11.3	57 58.8	-56.9	11.6	58 57.5	-56.7	11.9	59 56.2	-56.6	12.3	60 54.7	-56.4	12.7	61 53.2	-56.2	13.1	62 51.6	-56.0	13.5	56
57	55 04.0	-57.1	10.5	56 03.0	-57.1	10.7	57 01.9	-56.9	11.0	58 00.8	-56.8	11.3	58 59.6	-56.7	11.6	59 58.3	-56.6	12.0	60 57.0	-56.5	12.4	61 55.6	-56.3	12.8	57
58	54 06.9	-57.3	9.9	55 05.9	-57.2	10.2	56 05.0	-57.1	10.4	57 04.0	-57.1	10.7	58 02.9	-56.9	11.0	59 01.7	-56.7	11.3	60 00.5	-56.6	11.7	60 59.3	-56.6	12.0	58
59	53 09.6	-57.5	9.4	54 08.7	-57.3	9.7	55 07.9	-57.3	9.9	56 06.9	-57.1	10.2	57 06.0	-57.1	10.4	58 05.0	-57.0	10.7	59 03.9	-56.9	11.0	60 02.7	-56.7	11.4	59
60	52 12.1	-57.5	9.0	53 11.4	-57.5	9.2	54 10.6	-57.4	9.4	55 09.8	-57.3	9.6	56 08.9	-57.2	9.9	57 08.0	-57.1	10.1	58 07.0	-57.0	10.4	59 06.0	-56.9	10.7	60
61	51 14.6	-57.6	8.5	52 13.9	-57.5	8.7	53 13.2	-57.5	8.9	54 12.5	-57.4	9.1	55 11.7	-57.3	9.3	56 10.9	-57.3	9.6	57 10.0	-57.1	9.8	58 09.1	-57.0	10.1	61
62	50 17.0	-57.8	8.1	51 16.4	-57.7	8.2	52 15.7	-57.6	8.4	53 15.1	-57.6	8.6	54 14.4	-57.5	8.8	55 13.6	-57.3	9.0	56 12.9	-57.3	9.3	57 12.1	-57.2	9.5	62
63	49 19.2	-57.8	7.6	50 18.7	-57.8	7.8	51 18.1	-57.7	8.0	52 17.5	-57.6	8.1	53 16.9	-57.6	8.3	54 16.3	-57.6	8.5	55 15.6	-57.5	8.7	56 14.9	-57.4	9.0	63
64	48 21.4	-57.9	7.2	49 20.9	-57.8	7.4	50 20.4	-57.8	7.5	51 19.9	-57.8	7.7	52 19.3	-57.7	7.9	53 18.7	-57.6	8.0	54 18.1	-57.5	8.2	55 17.5	-57.5	8.4	64
65	47 23.5	-58.0	6.8	48 23.1	-58.0	7.0	49 22.6	-57.9	7.1	50 22.1	-57.8	7.3	51 21.6	-57.7	7.4	52 21.1	-57.7	7.6	53 20.6	-57.7	7.8	54 20.0	-57.6	7.9	65
66	46 25.5	-58.0	6.5	47 25.1	-58.0	6.6	48 24.7	-57.9	6.7	49 24.3	-57.9	6.8	50 23.9	-57.9	7.0	51 23.4	-57.8	7.1	52 22.9	-57.7	7.3	53 22.4	-57.7	7.5	66
67	45 27.5	-58.2	6.1	46 27.1	-58.1	6.2	47 26.8	-58.1	6.3	48 26.4	-58.0	6.5	49 26.0	-58.0	6.6	50 25.6	-57.9	6.7	51 25.2	-57.9	6.9	52 24.7	-57.8	7.0	67
68	44 29.3	-58.1	5.8	45 29.0	-58.1	5.9	46 28.7	-58.1	6.0	47 28.4	-58.1	6.1	48 28.0	-58.0	6.2	49 27.7	-58.0	6.3	50 27.3	-57.9	6.4	51 26.9	-57.9	6.6	68
69	43 31.2	-58.3	5.4	44 30.9	-58.2	5.5	45 30.6	-58.2	5.6	46 30.3	-58.1	5.7	47 30.0	-58.1	5.8	48 29.7	-58.1	5.9	49 29.4	-58.1	6.0	50 29.0	-58.0	6.2	69
70	42 32.9	-58.3	5.1	43 32.7	-58.3	5.2	44 32.4	-58.2	5.3	45 32.2	-58.2	5.3	46 31.9	-58.2	5.4	47 31.6	-58.1	5.5	48 31.3	-58.1	5.7	49 31.0	-58.0	5.8	70
71	41 34.6	-58.3	4.8	42 34.4	-58.3	4.8	43 34.2	-58.3	4.9	44 34.0	-58.3	5.0	45 33.7	-58.2	5.1	46 33.5	-58.2	5.2	47 33.2	-58.1	5.3	48 33.0	-58.2	5.4	71
72	40 36.3	-58.4	4.5	41 36.1	-58.4	4.5	42 35.9	-58.4	4.6	43 35.7	-58.3	4.7	44 35.5	-58.3	4.7	45 35.3	-58.3	4.8	46 35.1	-58.3	4.9	47 34.8	-58.2	5.0	72
73	39 37.9	-58.5	4.2	40 37.7	-58.4	4.2	41 37.5	-58.4	4.3	42 37.4	-58.4	4.3	43 37.2	-58.3	4.4	44 37.0	-58.3	4.5	45 36.8	-58.3	4.6	46 36.6	-58.2	4.7	73
74	38 39.4	-58.5	3.9	39 39.3	-58.5	3.9	40 39.1	-58.4	4.0	41 39.0	-58.4	4.0	42 38.9	-58.4	4.1	43 38.7	-58.4	4.2	44 38.5	-58.3	4.2	45 38.4	-58.4	4.3	74
75	37 40.9	-58.5	3.6	38 40.8	-58.5	3.6	39 40.7	-58.5	3.7	40 40.6	-58.5	3.7	41 40.5	-58.5	3.8	42 40.3	-58.4	3.9	43 40.2	-58.4	3.9	44 40.0	-58.3	4.0	75
76	36 42.4	-58.5	3.3	37 42.3	-58.5	3.3	38 42.2	-58.5	3.4	39 42.1	-58.5	3.4	40 42.0	-58.5	3.5	41 41.9	-58.5	3.5	42 41.8	-58.5	3.6	43 41.7	-58.5	3.7	76
77	35 43.9	-58.6	3.0	36 43.8	-58.6	3.1	37 43.7	-58.6	3.1	38 43.6	-58.6	3.2	39 43.5	-58.5	3.2	40 43.4	-58.5	3.2	41 43.3	-58.5	3.3	42 43.2	-58.5	3.3	77
78	34 45.3	-58.7	2.8	35 45.2	-58.6	2.8	36 45.1	-58.6	2.8	37 45.0	-58.5	2.9	38 45.0	-58.6	2.9	39 44.9	-58.6	3.0	40 44.8	-58.5	3.0	41 44.7	-58.5	3.0	78
79	33 46.6	-58.6	2.5	34 46.6	-58.7	2.5	35 46.5	-58.6	2.6	36 46.5	-58.7	2.6	37 46.4	-58.6	2.6	38 46.3	-58.6	2.7	39 46.3	-58.6	2.7	40 46.2	-58.6	2.8	79
80	32 48.0	-58.7	2.3	33 47.9	-58.7	2.3	34 47.9	-58.7	2.3	35 47.8	-58.6	2.3	36 47.8	-58.7	2.4	37 47.7	-58.6	2.4	38 47.7	-58.7	2.4	39 47.6	-58.6	2.5	80
81	31 49.3	-58.7	2.0	32 49.2	-58.7	2.0	33 49.2	-58.7	2.1	34 49.2	-58.7	2.1	35 49.1	-58.7	2.1	36 49.1	-58.7	2.1	37 49.0	-58.6	2.2	38 49.0	-58.7	2.2	81
82	30 50.6	-58.8	1.8	31 50.5	-58.7	1.8	32 50.5	-58.7	1.8	33 50.5	-58.7	1.8	34 50.4	-58.7	1.9	35 50.4	-58.7	1.9	36 50.4	-58.7	1.9	37 50.3	-58.6	1.9	82
83	29 51.8	-58.7	1.5	30 51.8	-58.8	1.6	31 51.8	-58.8	1.6	32 51.8	-58.8	1.6	33 51.7	-58.7	1.6	34 51.7	-58.7	1.6	35 51.7	-58.7	1.6	36 51.7	-58.8	1.7	83
84	28 53.1	-58.8	1.3	29 53.0	-58.7	1.3	30 53.0	-58.8	1.3	31 53.0	-58.8	1.3	32 53.0	-58.8	1.4	33 53.0	-58.8	1.4	34 53.0	-58.8	1.4	35 52.9	-58.7	1.4	84
85	27 54.3	-58.9	1.1	28 54.3	-58.9	1.1	29 54.2	-58.8	1.1	30 54.2	-58.8	1.1	31 54.2	-58.8	1.1	32 54.2	-58.8	1.1	33 54.2	-58.8	1.1	34 54.2	-58.8	1.2	85
86	26 55.4	-58.8	0.9	27 55.4	-58.8	0.9	28 55.4	-58.8	0.9	29 55.4	-58.8	0.9	30 55.4	-58.8	0.9	31 55.4	-58.8	0.9	32 55.4	-58.8	0.9	33 55.4	-58.8	0.9	86
87	25 56.6	-58.8	0.6	26 56.6	-58.8	0.6	27 56.6	-58.8	0.6	28 56.6	-58.8	0.7	29 56.6	-58.8	0.7	30 56.6	-58.8	0.7	31 56.6	-58.8	0.7	32 56.6	-58.9	0.7	87
88	24 57.8	-58.9	0.4	25 57.8	-58.9	0.4	26 57.8	-58.9	0.4	27 57.8	-58.9	0.4	28 57.8	-58.9	0.4	29 57.8	-58.9	0.4	30 57.8	-58.9	0.4	31 57.7	-58.8	0.4	88
89	23 58.9	-58.9	0.2	24 58.9	-58.9	0.2	25 58.9	-58.9	0.2	26 58.9	-58.9	0.2	27 58.9	-58.9	0.2	28 58.9	-58.9	0.2	29 58.9	-58.9	0.2	30 58.9	-58.9	0.2	89
90	23 00.0	-58.9	0.0	24 00.0	-58.9	0.0	25 00.0	-58.9	0.0	26 00.0	-58.9	0.0	27 00.0	-58.9	0.0	28 00.0	-58.9	0.0	29 00.0	-58.9	0.0	30 00.0	-58.9	0.0	90
	23°			24°			25°			26°			27°			28°			29°			30°			

11°, 349° L.H.A. **LATITUDE SAME NAME AS DECLINATION**

206

LATITUDE **CONTRARY** NAME TO DECLINATION **L.H.A. 11°, 349°**

Dec.	23° Hc	d	Z	24° Hc	d	Z	25° Hc	d	Z	26° Hc	d	Z	27° Hc	d	Z	28° Hc	d	Z	29° Hc	d	Z	30° Hc	d	Z	Dec.
°	° ′	′	°	° ′	′	°	° ′	′	°	° ′	′	°	° ′	′	°	° ′	′	°	° ′	′	°	° ′	′	°	°
0	64 38.1	-54.9	153.6	63 44.1	-55.3	154.5	62 49.8	-55.7	155.3	61 55.1	-56.0	156.1	61 00.1	-56.3	156.8	60 04.8	-56.6	157.5	59 09.3	-56.9	158.2	58 13.4	-57.0	158.8	0
1	63 43.2	-55.3	154.5	62 48.8	-55.6	155.3	61 54.1	-55.9	156.1	60 59.1	-56.2	156.8	60 03.8	-56.5	157.5	59 08.2	-56.7	158.2	58 12.4	-57.0	158.8	57 16.4	-57.2	159.3	1
2	62 47.9	-55.5	155.3	61 53.2	-55.9	156.1	60 58.2	-56.2	156.9	60 02.9	-56.5	157.5	59 07.3	-56.7	158.2	58 11.5	-57.0	158.8	57 15.4	-57.1	159.4	56 19.2	-57.4	159.9	2
3	61 52.4	-55.8	156.2	60 57.3	-56.1	156.9	60 02.0	-56.4	157.6	59 06.4	-56.6	158.2	58 10.6	-56.9	158.8	57 14.5	-57.0	159.4	56 18.3	-57.3	159.9	55 21.8	-57.4	160.4	3
4	60 56.6	-56.1	156.9	60 01.2	-56.3	157.6	59 05.6	-56.6	158.2	58 09.8	-56.8	158.8	57 13.7	-57.0	159.4	56 17.5	-57.3	159.9	55 21.0	-57.4	160.4	54 24.4	-57.6	160.9	4
5	60 00.5	-56.3	157.6	59 04.9	-56.5	158.3	58 09.0	-56.7	158.9	57 13.0	-57.0	159.4	56 16.7	-57.2	160.0	55 20.2	-57.4	160.5	54 23.6	-57.6	160.9	53 26.8	-57.7	161.4	5
6	59 04.2	-56.5	158.3	58 08.4	-56.8	158.9	57 12.3	-57.0	159.5	56 16.0	-57.2	160.0	55 19.5	-57.3	160.5	54 22.8	-57.5	161.0	53 26.0	-57.6	161.4	52 29.1	-57.8	161.8	6
7	58 07.7	-56.6	159.0	57 11.6	-56.9	159.5	56 15.3	-57.1	160.1	55 18.8	-57.3	160.6	54 22.2	-57.5	161.0	53 25.3	-57.6	161.5	52 28.4	-57.8	161.9	51 31.3	-57.9	162.3	7
8	57 11.1	-56.9	159.6	56 14.7	-57.0	160.1	55 18.2	-57.2	160.6	54 21.5	-57.4	161.1	53 24.7	-57.6	161.5	52 27.7	-57.7	161.9	51 30.6	-57.8	162.3	50 33.4	-58.0	162.7	8
9	56 14.2	-57.0	160.2	55 17.7	-57.2	160.7	54 21.0	-57.4	161.1	53 24.1	-57.5	161.6	52 27.1	-57.6	162.0	51 30.0	-57.8	162.4	50 32.8	-58.0	162.7	49 35.4	-58.0	163.1	9
10	55 17.2	-57.1	160.7	54 20.5	-57.3	161.2	53 23.6	-57.4	161.6	52 26.6	-57.6	162.0	51 29.5	-57.8	162.4	50 32.2	-57.9	162.8	49 34.8	-58.0	163.2	48 37.4	-58.2	163.5	10
11	54 20.1	-57.3	161.3	53 23.2	-57.5	161.7	52 26.2	-57.6	162.1	51 29.0	-57.7	162.5	50 31.7	-57.8	162.9	49 34.3	-58.0	163.2	48 36.8	-58.1	163.5	47 39.2	-58.2	163.9	11
12	53 22.8	-57.4	161.8	52 25.7	-57.5	162.2	51 28.6	-57.7	162.6	50 31.3	-57.9	162.9	49 33.9	-58.0	163.3	48 36.3	-58.0	163.6	47 38.7	-58.1	163.9	46 41.0	-58.2	164.2	12
13	52 25.4	-57.5	162.2	51 28.2	-57.7	162.6	50 30.9	-57.8	163.0	49 33.4	-57.9	163.3	48 35.9	-58.0	163.7	47 38.3	-58.1	164.0	46 40.6	-58.3	164.3	45 42.8	-58.4	164.6	13
14	51 27.9	-57.6	162.7	50 30.5	-57.7	163.1	49 33.1	-57.9	163.4	48 35.5	-58.0	163.7	47 37.9	-58.1	164.1	46 40.2	-58.2	164.3	45 42.3	-58.3	164.6	44 44.4	-58.3	164.9	14
15	50 30.3	-57.7	163.2	49 32.8	-57.8	163.5	48 35.2	-57.9	163.8	47 37.5	-58.0	164.1	46 39.8	-58.2	164.4	45 42.0	-58.3	164.7	44 44.0	-58.3	165.0	43 46.1	-58.5	165.2	15
16	49 32.6	-57.8	163.6	48 35.0	-58.0	163.9	47 37.3	-58.1	164.2	46 39.5	-58.1	164.5	45 41.6	-58.2	164.8	44 43.7	-58.3	165.0	43 45.7	-58.4	165.3	42 47.6	-58.4	165.5	16
17	48 34.8	-57.9	164.0	47 37.0	-58.0	164.3	46 39.2	-58.1	164.6	45 41.4	-58.2	164.9	44 43.4	-58.3	165.1	43 45.4	-58.4	165.4	42 47.3	-58.5	165.6	41 49.2	-58.6	165.8	17
18	47 36.9	-58.0	164.4	46 39.0	-58.2	164.7	45 41.1	-58.1	164.9	44 43.2	-58.3	165.2	43 45.1	-58.3	165.4	42 47.0	-58.4	165.7	41 48.8	-58.5	165.9	40 50.6	-58.5	166.1	18
19	46 38.9	-58.0	164.8	45 41.0	-58.2	165.0	44 43.0	-58.3	165.3	43 44.9	-58.3	165.5	42 46.8	-58.4	165.8	41 48.6	-58.5	166.0	40 50.3	-58.5	166.2	39 52.1	-58.7	166.4	19
20	45 40.9	-58.1	165.1	44 42.8	-58.2	165.4	43 44.7	-58.2	165.6	42 46.6	-58.4	165.9	41 48.4	-58.5	166.1	40 50.1	-58.5	166.3	39 51.8	-58.6	166.5	38 53.4	-58.6	166.7	20
21	44 42.8	-58.2	165.5	43 44.6	-58.2	165.7	42 46.5	-58.4	166.0	41 48.2	-58.4	166.2	40 49.9	-58.4	166.4	39 51.6	-58.6	166.6	38 53.2	-58.6	166.8	37 54.8	-58.7	167.0	21
22	43 44.6	-58.2	165.8	42 46.4	-58.3	166.1	41 48.1	-58.4	166.3	40 49.8	-58.4	166.5	39 51.5	-58.6	166.7	38 53.0	-58.6	166.9	37 54.6	-58.7	167.0	36 56.1	-58.7	167.2	22
23	42 46.4	-58.3	166.2	41 48.1	-58.4	166.4	40 49.7	-58.4	166.6	39 51.4	-58.6	166.8	38 52.9	-58.6	167.0	37 54.4	-58.6	167.1	36 55.9	-58.7	167.3	35 57.4	-58.8	167.5	23
24	41 48.1	-58.4	166.5	40 49.7	-58.4	166.7	39 51.3	-58.5	166.9	38 52.8	-58.5	167.1	37 54.3	-58.6	167.2	36 55.8	-58.7	167.4	35 57.2	-58.7	167.6	34 58.6	-58.8	167.7	24
25	40 49.7	-58.3	166.8	39 51.3	-58.5	167.0	38 52.8	-58.5	167.2	37 54.3	-58.6	167.3	36 55.7	-58.6	167.5	35 57.1	-58.7	167.7	34 58.5	-58.7	167.8	33 59.8	-58.8	168.0	25
26	39 51.4	-58.5	167.1	38 52.8	-58.5	167.3	37 54.3	-58.6	167.4	36 55.7	-58.6	167.6	35 57.1	-58.7	167.8	34 58.4	-58.7	167.9	33 59.8	-58.8	168.1	33 01.0	-58.8	168.2	26
27	38 52.9	-58.5	167.4	37 54.3	-58.5	167.6	36 55.7	-58.6	167.7	35 57.1	-58.7	167.9	34 58.4	-58.7	168.0	33 59.7	-58.8	168.2	33 01.0	-58.8	168.3	32 02.2	-58.9	168.4	27
28	37 54.4	-58.5	167.7	36 55.8	-58.6	167.8	35 57.1	-58.6	168.0	34 58.4	-58.6	168.1	33 59.7	-58.7	168.3	33 00.9	-58.7	168.4	32 02.2	-58.9	168.5	31 03.3	-58.8	168.7	28
29	36 55.9	-58.5	167.9	35 57.2	-58.6	168.1	34 58.5	-58.7	168.2	33 59.8	-58.6	168.4	33 01.0	-58.8	168.5	32 02.2	-58.9	168.6	31 03.3	-58.8	168.8	30 04.5	-59.0	168.9	29
30	35 57.4	-58.6	168.2	34 58.6	-58.6	168.4	33 59.8	-58.6	168.5	33 01.0	-58.7	168.6	32 02.2	-58.8	168.8	31 03.3	-58.8	168.9	30 04.5	-58.9	169.0	29 05.5	-58.9	169.1	30
31	34 58.8	-58.6	168.5	34 00.0	-58.7	168.6	33 01.2	-58.8	168.8	32 02.3	-58.8	168.9	31 03.4	-58.8	169.0	30 04.5	-58.9	169.1	29 05.6	-58.9	169.2	28 06.6	-58.9	169.3	31
32	34 00.2	-58.7	168.7	33 01.3	-58.7	168.9	32 02.4	-58.7	169.0	31 03.5	-58.8	169.1	30 04.6	-58.9	169.2	29 05.6	-58.8	169.3	28 06.7	-59.0	169.4	27 07.7	-59.0	169.5	32
33	33 01.5	-58.7	169.0	32 02.6	-58.7	169.1	31 03.7	-58.8	169.2	30 04.7	-58.8	169.3	29 05.7	-58.8	169.4	28 06.8	-59.0	169.5	27 07.7	-58.9	169.6	26 08.7	-59.0	169.7	33
34	32 02.8	-58.7	169.2	31 03.9	-58.8	169.4	30 04.9	-58.8	169.5	29 05.9	-58.8	169.6	28 06.9	-58.9	169.7	27 07.8	-58.9	169.8	26 08.8	-59.0	169.9	25 09.7	-59.0	169.9	34
35	31 04.1	-58.7	169.5	30 05.1	-58.8	169.6	29 06.1	-58.8	169.7	28 07.1	-58.9	169.8	27 08.0	-58.9	169.9	26 08.9	-58.9	170.0	25 09.8	-58.9	170.1	24 10.7	-59.0	170.1	35
36	30 05.4	-58.8	169.7	29 06.3	-58.8	169.8	28 07.3	-58.9	169.9	27 08.2	-58.9	170.0	26 09.1	-58.9	170.1	25 10.0	-59.0	170.2	24 10.9	-59.0	170.3	23 11.7	-59.0	170.3	36
37	29 06.6	-58.8	170.0	28 07.5	-58.8	170.0	27 08.4	-58.8	170.1	26 09.3	-58.9	170.2	25 10.2	-59.0	170.3	24 11.0	-59.0	170.4	23 11.9	-59.1	170.5	22 12.7	-59.1	170.5	37
38	28 07.8	-58.8	170.2	27 08.7	-58.8	170.3	26 09.6	-58.8	170.4	25 10.4	-58.9	170.4	24 11.2	-58.9	170.5	23 12.0	-58.9	170.6	22 12.8	-59.0	170.7	21 13.6	-59.0	170.7	38
39	27 09.0	-58.8	170.4	26 09.9	-58.9	170.5	25 10.7	-58.9	170.6	24 11.5	-59.0	170.6	23 12.3	-59.0	170.7	22 13.1	-59.1	170.8	21 13.8	-59.0	170.8	20 14.6	-59.1	170.9	39
40	26 10.2	-58.9	170.6	25 11.0	-58.9	170.7	24 11.8	-58.9	170.8	23 12.5	-58.9	170.8	22 13.3	-59.0	170.9	21 14.0	-59.0	171.0	20 14.8	-59.1	171.0	19 15.5	-59.1	171.1	40
41	25 11.3	-58.8	170.8	24 12.1	-58.9	170.9	23 12.9	-59.0	171.0	22 13.6	-59.0	171.1	21 14.3	-59.0	171.1	20 15.0	-59.0	171.2	19 15.7	-59.0	171.2	18 16.4	-59.1	171.3	41
42	24 12.5	-58.9	171.1	23 13.2	-58.9	171.1	22 13.9	-58.9	171.2	21 14.6	-59.0	171.2	20 15.3	-59.0	171.3	19 16.0	-59.0	171.4	18 16.7	-59.1	171.4	17 17.3	-59.1	171.5	42
43	23 13.6	-58.9	171.3	22 14.3	-59.0	171.3	21 15.0	-59.0	171.4	20 15.6	-59.0	171.4	19 16.3	-59.0	171.5	18 17.0	-59.1	171.5	17 17.6	-59.1	171.6	16 18.2	-59.1	171.6	43
44	22 14.7	-58.9	171.5	21 15.3	-58.9	171.5	20 16.0	-59.0	171.6	19 16.6	-59.0	171.6	18 17.3	-59.1	171.7	17 17.9	-59.1	171.7	16 18.5	-59.1	171.8	15 19.1	-59.1	171.8	44
45	21 15.8	-59.0	171.7	20 16.4	-59.0	171.7	19 17.0	-59.0	171.8	18 17.6	-59.0	171.8	17 18.2	-59.0	171.9	16 18.8	-59.0	171.9	15 19.4	-59.1	172.0	14 20.0	-59.1	172.0	45
46	20 16.8	-58.9	171.9	19 17.4	-58.9	171.9	18 18.0	-59.0	172.0	17 18.6	-59.0	172.0	16 19.2	-59.1	172.1	15 19.8	-59.1	172.1	14 20.3	-59.1	172.1	13 20.9	-59.1	172.2	46
47	19 17.9	-59.0	172.1	18 18.5	-59.0	172.1	17 19.0	-59.0	172.2	16 19.6	-59.1	172.2	15 20.1	-59.0	172.2	14 20.7	-59.1	172.3	13 21.2	-59.1	172.3	12 21.8	-59.2	172.3	47
48	18 18.9	-58.9	172.3	17 19.5	-59.0	172.3	16 20.0	-59.0	172.4	15 20.5	-59.0	172.4	14 21.1	-59.1	172.4	13 21.6	-59.1	172.5	12 22.1	-59.1	172.5	11 22.6	-59.1	172.5	48
49	17 20.0	-59.0	172.5	16 20.5	-59.0	172.5	15 21.0	-59.0	172.5	14 21.5	-59.1	172.6	13 22.0	-59.1	172.6	12 22.5	-59.1	172.6	11 23.0	-59.1	172.7	10 23.5	-59.2	172.7	49
50	16 21.0	-59.0	172.7	15 21.5	-59.0	172.7	14 22.0	-59.1	172.7	13 22.4	-59.0	172.8	12 22.9	-59.1	172.8	11 23.4	-59.1	172.8	10 23.9	-59.2	172.8	9 24.3	-59.1	172.9	50
51	15 22.0	-59.0	172.8	14 22.5	-59.1	172.9	13 22.9	-59.0	172.9	12 23.4	-59.1	172.9	11 23.8	-59.1	173.0	10 24.3	-59.1	173.0	9 24.7	-59.1	173.0	8 25.2	-59.2	173.0	51
52	14 23.0	-59.0	173.0	13 23.4	-59.0	173.1	12 23.9	-59.1	173.1	11 24.3	-59.1	173.1	10 24.7	-59.1	173.1	9 25.2	-59.2	173.2	8 25.6	-59.1	173.2	7 26.0	-59.1	173.2	52
53	13 24.0	-59.0	173.2	12 24.4	-59.0	173.2	11 24.8	-59.0	173.3	10 25.2	-59.1	173.3	9 25.6	-59.1	173.3	8 26.0	-59.1	173.3	7 26.5	-59.2	173.3	6 26.9	-59.2	173.4	53
54	12 25.0	-59.1	173.4	11 25.4	-59.1	173.4	10 25.8	-59.1	173.5	9 26.1	-59.0	173.5	8 26.5	-59.1	173.5	7 26.9	-59.1	173.5	6 27.3	-59.1	173.5	5 27.7	-59.2	173.5	54
55	11 25.9	-59.0	173.6	10 26.3	-59.0	173.6	9 26.7	-59.1	173.6	8 27.1	-59.1	173.6	7 27.4	-59.1	173.7	6 27.8	-59.1	173.7	5 28.2	-59.2	173.7	4 28.5	-59.2	173.7	55
56	10 26.9	-59.0	173.8	9 27.3	-59.1	173.8	8 27.6	-59.1	173.8	7 28.0	-59.1	173.8	6 28.3	-59.1	173.8	5 28.7	-59.2	173.8	4 29.0	-59.2	173.9	3 29.3	-59.1	173.9	56
57	9 27.9	-59.1	174.0	8 28.2	-59.1	174.0	7 28.5	-59.1	174.0	6 28.9	-59.1	174.0	5 29.2	-59.1	174.0	4 29.5	-59.1	174.0	3 29.8	-59.1	174.0	2 30.2	-59.2	174.0	57
58	8 28.8	-59.0	174.1	7 29.1	-59.0	174.1	6 29.5	-59.1	174.2	5 29.8	-59.1	174.2	4 30.1	-59.1	174.2	3 30.4	-59.2	174.2	2 30.7	-59.2	174.2	1 31.0	-59.2	174.2	58
59	7 29.8	-59.1	174.3	6 30.1	-59.1	174.3	5 30.4	-59.1	174.3	4 30.7	-59.1	174.3	3 31.0	-59.2	174.3	2 31.2	-59.1	174.4	1 31.5	-59.1	174.4	0 31.8	-59.1	174.4	59
60	6 30.7	-59.0	174.5	5 31.0	-59.0	174.5	4 31.3	-59.1	174.5	3 31.6	-59.2	174.5	2 31.8	-59.1	174.5	1 32.1	-59.1	174.5	0 32.4	-59.2	174.5	0 27.3	+59.2	5.5	60
61	5 31.7	-59.1	174.7	4 31.9	-59.0	174.7	3 32.2	-59.1	174.7	2 32.4	-59.1	174.7	1 32.7	-59.1	174.7	0 33.0	-59.2	174.7	0 26.8	+59.1	5.3	1 26.5	+59.2	5.3	61
62	4 32.6	-59.1	174.8	3 32.9	-59.1	174.9	2 33.1	-59.1	174.9	1 33.3	-59.1	174.9	0 33.6	-59.1	174.9	0 26.2	+59.1	5.1	1 25.9	+59.2	5.1	2 25.7	+59.2	5.1	62
63	3 33.5	-59.0	175.0	2 33.8	-59.1	175.0	1 34.0	-59.1	175.0	0 34.2	-59.1	175.0	0 25.5	+59.2	5.0	1 25.3	+59.2	5.0	2 25.1	+59.2	5.0	3 24.9	+59.1	5.0	63
64	2 34.5	-59.1	175.2	1 34.7	-59.1	175.2	0 34.9	-59.1	175.2	0 24.9	+59.1	4.8	1 24.7	+59.1	4.8	2 24.5	+59.1	4.8	3 24.3	+59.1	4.8	4 24.0	+59.2	4.8	64
65	1 35.4	-59.1	175.4	0 35.6	-59.1	175.4	0 24.2	+59.1	4.6	1 24.0	+59.1	4.6	2 23.8	+59.1	4.6	3 23.6	+59.1	4.6	4 23.4	+59.2	4.6	5 23.2	+59.2	4.6	65
66	0 36.3	-59.0	175.5	0 23.5	+59.1	4.5	1 23.3	+59.1	4.5	2 23.1	+59.1	4.5	3 22.9	+59.1	4.5	4 22.7	+59.2	4.5	5 22.6	+59.1	4.5	6 22.4	+59.1	4.5	66
67	0 22.7	+59.1	4.3	1 22.6	+59.0	4.3	2 22.4	+59.1	4.3	3 22.2	+59.1	4.3	4 22.0	+59.2	4.3	5 21.9	+59.1	4.3	6 21.7	+59.2	4.3	7 21.5	+59.2	4.3	67
68	1 21.8	+59.1	4.1	2 21.6	+59.1	4.1	3 21.5	+59.1	4.1	4 21.3	+59.1	4.1	5 21.2	+59.1	4.1	6 21.0	+59.1	4.1	7 20.9	+59.1	4.1	8 20.7	+59.2	4.1	68
69	2 20.9	+59.0	3.9	3 20.7	+59.1	3.9	4 20.6	+59.1	3.9	5 20.4	+59.1	3.9	6 20.3	+59.1	3.9	7 20.1	+59.2	4.0	8 20.0	+59.1	4.0	9 19.9	+59.1	4.0	69
70	3 19.9	+59.1	3.7	4 19.8	+59.1	3.8	5 19.7	+59.0	3.8	6 19.5	+59.1	3.8	7 19.4	+59.1	3.8	8 19.3	+59.1	3.8	9 19.1	+59.2	3.8	10 19.0	+59.2	3.8	70
71	4 19.0	+59.0	3.6	5 18.9	+59.0	3.6	6 18.7	+59.1	3.6	7 18.6	+59.1	3.6	8 18.5	+59.1	3.6	9 18.4	+59.1	3.6	10 18.3	+59.1	3.6	11 18.2	+59.1	3.6	71
72	5 18.0	+59.1	3.4	6 17.9	+59.0	3.4	7 17.8	+59.1	3.4	8 17.7	+59.1	3.4	9 17.6	+59.1	3.4	10 17.5	+59.1	3.4	11 17.4	+59.1	3.4	12 17.3	+59.1	3.5	72
73	6 17.1	+59.1	3.2	7 17.0	+59.1	3.2	8 16.9	+59.1	3.2	9 16.8	+59.1	3.2	10 16.7	+59.1	3.3	11 16.6	+59.1	3.3	12 16.5	+59.1	3.3	13 16.4	+59.1	3.3	73
74	7 16.2	+59.0	3.0	8 16.1	+59.0	3.0	9 16.0	+59.0	3.1	10 15.9	+59.1	3.1	11 15.8	+59.1	3.1	12 15.7	+59.1	3.1	13 15.6	+59.1	3.1	14 15.5	+59.2	3.1	74
75	8 15.2	+59.0	2.9	9 15.1	+59.1	2.9	10 15.0	+59.1	2.9	11 15.0	+59.0	2.9	12 14.9	+59.1	2.9	13 14.8	+59.1	2.9	14 14.7	+59.1	2.9	15 14.7	+59.1	2.9	75
76	9 14.2	+59.1	2.7	10 14.2	+59.0	2.7	11 14.1	+59.1	2.7	12 14.0	+59.1	2.7	13 14.0	+59.1	2.7	14 13.9	+59.1	2.7	15 13.8	+59.1	2.7	16 13.8	+59.1	2.8	76
77	10 13.3	+59.0	2.5	11 13.2	+59.1	2.5	12 13.2	+59.0	2.5	13 13.1	+59.1	2.5	14 13.1	+59.0	2.5	15 13.0	+59.1	2.5	16 12.9	+59.1	2.6	17 12.9	+59.1	2.6	77
78	11 12.3	+59.0	2.3	12 12.3	+59.0	2.3	13 12.2	+59.1	2.3	14 12.2	+59.0	2.3	15 12.1	+59.1	2.4	16 12.1	+59.0	2.4	17 12.0	+59.1	2.4	18 12.0	+59.0	2.4	78
79	12 11.3	+59.1	2.1	13 11.3	+59.0	2.1	14 11.3	+59.0	2.2	15 11.2	+59.1	2.2	16 11.2	+59.0	2.2	17 11.1	+59.1	2.2	18 11.1	+59.1	2.2	19 11.0	+59.1	2.2	79
80	13 10.4	+59.0	2.0	14 10.3	+59.0	2.0	15 10.3	+59.0	2.0	16 10.3	+59.0	2.0	17 10.2	+59.1	2.0	18 10.2	+59.0	2.0	19 10.2	+59.0	2.0	20 10.1	+59.1	2.0	80
81	14 09.4	+59.0	1.8	15 09.3	+59.1	1.8	16 09.3	+59.0	1.8	17 09.3	+59.0	1.8	18 09.3	+59.0	1.8	19 09.2	+59.1	1.8	20 09.2	+59.0	1.8	21 09.2	+59.0	1.8	81
82	15 08.4	+59.0	1.6	16 08.4	+59.0	1.6	17 08.3	+59.0	1.6	18 08.3	+59.0	1.6	19 08.3	+59.0	1.6	20 08.3	+59.0	1.6	21 08.2	+59.1	1.6	22 08.2	+59.0	1.6	82
83	16 07.4	+59.0	1.4	17 07.4	+58.9	1.4	18 07.3	+59.0	1.4	19 07.3	+59.0	1.4	20 07.3	+59.0	1.4	21 07.3	+59.0	1.4	22 07.3	+59.0	1.4	23 07.2	+59.1	1.4	83
84	17 06.4	+58.9	1.2	18 06.3	+59.0	1.2	19 06.3	+59.0	1.2	20 06.3	+59.0	1.2	21 06.3	+59.0	1.2	22 06.3	+59.0	1.2	23 06.3	+59.0	1.2	24 06.3	+59.0	1.3	84
85	18 05.3	+59.0	1.0	19 05.3	+59.0	1.0	20 05.3	+59.0	1.0	21 05.3	+59.0	1.0	22 05.3	+59.0	1.0	23 05.3	+59.0	1.0	24 05.3	+59.0	1.0	25 05.3	+58.9	1.1	85
86	19 04.3	+58.9	0.8	20 04.3	+58.9	0.8	21 04.3	+58.9	0.8	22 04.3	+58.9	0.8	23 04.3	+58.9	0.8	24 04.3	+58.9	0.8	25 04.3	+58.9	0.8	26 04.2	+59.0	0.8	86
87	20 03.2	+59.0	0.6	21 03.2	+59.0	0.6	22 03.2	+59.0	0.6	23 03.2	+59.0	0.6	24 03.2	+59.0	0.6	25 03.2	+59.0	0.6	26 03.2	+59.0	0.6	27 03.2	+59.0	0.6	87
88	21 02.2	+58.9	0.4	22 02.2	+58.9	0.4	23 02.2	+58.9	0.4	24 02.2	+58.9	0.4	25 02.2	+58.9	0.4	26 02.2	+58.9	0.4	27 02.2	+58.9	0.4	28 02.2	+58.9	0.4	88
89	22 01.1	+58.9	0.2	23 01.1	+58.9	0.2	24 01.1	+58.9	0.2	25 01.1	+58.9	0.2	26 01.1	+58.9	0.2	27 01.1	+58.9	0.2	28 01.1	+58.9	0.2	29 01.1	+58.9	0.2	89
90	23 00.0	+58.9	0.0	24 00.0	+58.9	0.0	25 00.0	+58.9	0.0	26 00.0	+58.9	0.0	27 00.0	+58.9	0.0	28 00.0	+58.9	0.0	29 00.0	+58.9	0.0	30 00.0	+58.9	0.0	90
	23°			24°			25°			26°			27°			28°			29°			30°			

S. Lat. {L.H.A. greater than 180° ....Zn=180°−Z
{L.H.A. less than 180°...........Zn=180°+Z

LATITUDE **SAME** NAME AS DECLINATION **L.H.A. 169°, 191°**

207

12°, 348° L.H.A. LATITUDE SAME NAME AS DECLINATION

N. Lat. {L.H.A. greater than 180° .....Zn=Z
{L.H.A. less than 180°............Zn=360°–Z

Dec.	23° Hc	d	Z	24° Hc	d	Z	25° Hc	d	Z	26° Hc	d	Z	27° Hc	d	Z	28° Hc	d	Z	29° Hc	d	Z	30° Hc	d	Z	Dec.
°	° ′	′	°	° ′	′	°	° ′	′	°	° ′	′	°	° ′	′	°	° ′	′	°	° ′	′	°	° ′	′	°	°
0	64 12.6	+53.6	151.5	63 19.6	+54.2	152.4	62 26.2	+54.6	153.3	61 32.4	+55.1	154.1	60 38.3	+55.4	154.9	59 43.8	+55.7	155.6	58 48.9	+56.1	156.3	57 53.9	+56.3	157.0	0
1	65 06.2	+53.2	150.4	64 13.8	+53.7	151.4	63 20.8	+54.3	152.4	62 27.5	+54.7	153.3	61 33.7	+55.1	154.1	60 39.5	+55.5	154.9	59 45.0	+55.9	155.6	58 50.2	+56.2	156.3	1
2	65 59.4	+52.7	149.3	65 07.5	+53.3	150.4	64 15.1	+53.9	151.4	63 22.2	+54.3	152.4	62 28.8	+54.8	153.3	61 35.0	+55.2	154.1	60 40.9	+55.5	154.9	59 46.4	+55.9	155.6	2
3	66 52.1	+52.1	148.1	66 00.8	+52.8	149.3	65 09.0	+53.4	150.4	64 16.5	+54.0	151.4	63 23.6	+54.4	152.4	62 30.2	+54.9	153.3	61 36.4	+55.3	154.1	60 42.3	+55.6	154.9	3
4	67 44.2	+51.4	146.8	66 53.6	+52.2	148.1	66 02.4	+52.8	149.3	65 10.5	+53.5	150.4	64 18.0	+54.1	151.4	63 25.1	+54.5	152.4	62 31.7	+55.0	153.3	61 37.9	+55.4	154.1	4
5	68 35.6	+50.7	145.4	67 45.8	+51.6	146.8	66 55.2	+52.4	148.1	66 04.0	+53.0	149.3	65 12.1	+53.6	150.4	64 19.6	+54.2	151.4	63 26.7	+54.6	152.4	62 33.3	+55.1	153.3	5
6	69 26.3	+49.9	143.9	68 37.4	+50.8	145.4	67 47.6	+51.6	146.8	66 57.0	+52.4	148.1	66 05.7	+53.1	149.3	65 13.8	+53.7	150.4	64 21.3	+54.3	151.5	63 28.4	+54.7	152.4	6
7	70 16.2	+49.0	142.3	69 28.2	+50.0	144.0	68 39.2	+51.0	145.5	67 49.4	+51.8	146.9	66 58.8	+52.5	148.1	66 07.5	+53.2	149.3	65 15.6	+53.8	150.5	64 23.1	+54.4	151.5	7
8	71 05.2	+47.8	140.6	70 18.2	+49.1	142.3	69 30.2	+50.1	144.0	68 41.2	+51.1	145.5	67 51.3	+52.0	146.9	67 00.7	+52.7	148.2	66 09.4	+53.3	149.4	65 17.5	+53.9	150.5	8
9	71 53.0	+46.7	138.7	71 07.3	+48.0	140.6	70 20.3	+49.3	142.4	69 32.3	+50.3	144.0	68 43.3	+51.2	145.5	67 53.4	+52.0	146.9	67 02.7	+52.8	148.2	66 11.4	+53.5	149.4	9
10	72 39.7	+45.3	136.6	71 55.3	+46.8	138.7	71 09.6	+48.2	140.7	70 22.6	+49.4	142.4	69 34.5	+50.4	144.1	68 45.4	+51.4	145.6	67 55.5	+52.2	147.0	67 04.9	+52.9	148.3	10
11	73 25.0	+43.6	134.4	72 42.1	+45.5	136.7	71 57.8	+46.9	138.8	71 12.0	+48.3	140.7	70 24.9	+49.6	142.5	69 36.8	+50.6	144.1	68 47.7	+51.5	145.6	67 57.8	+52.3	147.0	11
12	74 08.6	+41.9	131.9	73 27.6	+43.9	134.4	72 44.7	+45.7	136.7	72 00.3	+47.2	138.8	71 14.5	+48.5	140.8	70 27.4	+49.7	142.6	69 39.2	+50.8	144.2	68 50.1	+51.7	145.7	12
13	74 50.5	+39.8•	129.2	74 11.5	+42.0	132.0	73 30.4	+44.0	134.5	72 47.5	+45.8	136.8	72 03.0	+47.3	138.9	71 17.1	+48.7	140.8	70 30.0	+49.8	142.6	69 41.8	+50.9	144.3	13
14	75 30.3	+37.4•	126.3	74 53.5	+40.0•	129.3	74 14.4	+42.3	132.0	73 33.3	+44.2	134.6	72 50.3	+46.0	136.9	72 05.8	+47.5	139.0	71 19.8	+48.9	140.9	70 32.7	+50.0	142.7	14
15	76 07.7	+34.8•	123.1	75 33.5	+37.7•	126.4	74 56.7	+40.2•	129.4	74 17.5	+42.5	132.1	73 36.3	+44.5	134.6	72 53.3	+46.2	137.0	72 08.7	+47.7	139.1	71 22.7	+49.0	141.0	15
16	76 42.5	+31.6•	119.6	76 11.2	+34.9•	123.2	75 36.9	+37.9•	126.4	75 00.0	+40.5•	129.4	74 20.8	+42.7	132.2	73 39.5	+44.7	134.7	72 56.4	+46.4	137.1	72 11.7	+47.9	139.2	16
17	77 14.1	+28.2•	115.9	76 46.1	+31.9•	119.7	76 14.8	+35.2•	123.2	75 40.5	+38.1•	126.5	75 03.5	+40.7•	129.5	74 24.2	+42.9	132.3	73 42.8	+44.9	134.8	72 59.6	+46.6	137.2	17
18	77 42.3	+24.3•	111.8	77 18.0	+28.4•	115.9	76 50.0	+32.1•	119.8	76 18.6	+35.4•	123.3	75 44.2	+38.3•	126.6	75 07.1	+40.9•	129.7	74 27.7	+43.1	132.4	73 46.2	+45.1	135.0	18
19	78 06.6	+20.0•	107.4	77 46.4	+24.5•	111.8	77 22.1	+28.6•	116.0	76 54.0	+32.3•	119.8	76 22.5	+35.7•	123.4	75 48.0	+38.6•	126.7	75 10.8	+41.2•	129.8	74 31.3	+43.4	132.6	19
20	78 26.6	+15.3•	102.8	78 10.9	+20.3•	107.4	77 50.7	+24.8•	111.9	77 26.3	+28.9•	116.1	76 58.2	+32.6•	119.9	76 26.6	+35.9•	123.5	75 52.0	+38.8•	126.9	75 14.7	+41.4•	129.9	20
21	78 41.9	+10.4•	97.9	78 31.2	+15.5•	102.8	78 15.5	+20.4•	107.5	77 55.2	+25.0•	111.9	77 30.8	+29.1•	116.1	77 02.5	+32.9•	120.1	76 30.8	+36.2•	123.7	75 56.1	+39.1•	127.0	21
22	78 52.3	+5.1•	92.8	78 46.7	+10.5•	97.9	78 35.9	+15.7•	102.8	78 20.2	+20.7•	107.5	77 59.9	+25.2•	112.0	77 35.4	+29.4•	116.2	77 07.0	+33.1•	120.2	76 35.2	+36.4•	123.8	22
23	78 57.4	−0.2•	87.6	78 57.2	+5.2•	92.8	78 51.6	+10.7•	97.9	78 40.9	+15.9•	102.8	78 25.1	+20.9•	107.6	78 04.8	+25.4•	112.1	77 40.1	+29.7•	116.3	77 11.6	+33.4•	120.3	23
24	78 57.2	−5.6•	82.4	79 02.4	−0.1•	87.6	79 02.3	+5.4•	92.7	78 56.8	+10.8•	97.8	78 46.0	+16.1•	102.8	78 30.2	+21.1•	107.6	78 09.8	+25.7•	112.2	77 45.0	+30.0•	116.5	24
25	78 51.6	−10.7•	77.2	79 02.3	−5.5•	82.3	79 07.7	−0.1•	87.5	79 07.6	+5.5•	92.7	79 02.1	+11.0•	97.8	78 51.3	+16.3•	102.9	78 35.5	+21.3•	107.7	78 15.0	+25.9•	112.3	25
26	78 40.9	−15.8•	72.2	78 56.8	−10.8•	77.1	79 07.6	−5.5•	82.2	79 13.1	0.0•	87.4	79 13.1	+5.6•	92.6	79 07.6	+11.2•	97.8	78 56.8	+16.6•	102.9	78 40.9	+21.6•	107.8	26
27	78 25.1	−20.3•	67.3	78 46.0	−15.8•	72.0	79 02.1	−10.8•	76.9	79 13.1	−5.5•	82.0	79 18.7	+0.1•	87.3	79 18.8	+5.7•	92.6	79 13.4	+11.3•	97.8	79 02.5	+16.8•	103.0	27
28	78 04.8	−24.7•	62.7	78 30.2	−20.4•	67.1	78 51.3	−15.8•	71.8	79 07.6	−10.8•	76.7	79 18.8	−5.4•	81.9	79 24.5	+0.2•	87.2	79 24.7	+5.8•	92.5	79 19.3	+11.5•	97.8	28
29	77 40.1	−28.5•	58.4	78 09.8	−24.8•	62.4	78 35.5	−20.5•	66.8	78 56.8	−15.9•	71.5	79 13.4	−10.9•	76.5	79 24.7	−5.4•	81.7	79 30.5	+0.3•	87.1	79 30.8	+5.9•	92.5	29
30	77 11.6	−31.9•	54.3	77 45.0	−28.6•	58.1	78 15.0	−24.9•	62.1	78 40.9	−20.6•	66.6	79 02.5	−15.9•	71.3	79 19.3	−10.9•	76.3	79 30.8	−5.4•	81.6	79 36.7	+0.3•	87.0	30
31	76 39.7	−34.9•	50.6	77 16.4	−32.0•	54.0	77 50.1	−28.7•	57.8	78 20.3	−24.9•	61.8	78 46.6	−20.8•	66.3	79 08.4	−16.0•	71.1	79 25.4	−10.9•	76.1	79 37.0	−5.4•	81.4	31
32	76 04.8	−37.7•	47.1	76 44.4	−35.1•	50.2	77 21.4	−32.2•	53.7	77 55.4	−28.9•	57.4	78 25.8	−25.1•	61.5	78 52.4	−20.9•	66.0	79 14.5	−16.2•	70.8	79 31.6	−10.9•	75.9	32
33	75 27.1	−40.0•	44.0	76 09.3	−37.8•	46.8	76 49.2	−35.3•	49.9	77 26.5	−32.4•	53.3	78 00.7	−29.0•	57.1	78 31.5	−25.2•	61.2	78 58.3	−20.9•	65.7	79 20.7	−16.2•	70.6	33
34	74 47.1	−42.0	41.1	75 31.5	−40.1•	43.6	76 13.9	−37.9•	46.4	76 54.1	−35.4•	49.5	77 31.7	−32.5•	53.0	78 06.3	−29.2•	56.7	78 37.4	−25.4•	60.9	79 04.5	−21.1•	65.4	34
35	74 05.1	−43.8	38.4	74 51.4	−42.2	40.7	75 36.0	−40.3•	43.2	76 18.7	−38.1•	46.0	76 59.2	−35.6•	49.1	77 37.1	−32.7•	52.6	78 12.0	−29.4•	56.4	78 43.4	−25.6•	60.6	35
36	73 21.3	−45.4	36.0	74 09.2	−43.9	38.0	74 55.7	−42.3	40.3	75 40.6	−40.4•	42.8	76 23.6	−38.2•	45.6	77 04.4	−35.7•	48.8	77 42.6	−32.9•	52.2	78 17.8	−29.5•	56.0	36
37	72 35.9	−46.8	33.7	73 25.3	−45.6	35.6	74 13.4	−44.1	37.6	75 00.2	−42.5	39.9	75 45.4	−40.6•	42.4	76 28.7	−38.5•	45.2	77 09.7	−35.9•	48.4	77 48.3	−33.1•	51.8	37
38	71 49.1	−47.9	31.7	72 39.7	−46.9	33.4	73 29.3	−45.6	35.2	74 17.7	−44.2	37.2	75 04.8	−42.7	39.5	75 50.2	−40.8•	42.0	76 33.8	−38.6•	44.8	77 15.2	−36.2•	47.9	38
39	71 01.2	−49.0	29.8	71 52.8	−48.0	31.3	72 43.7	−47.1	33.0	73 33.5	−45.8	34.8	74 22.1	−44.4	36.8	75 09.4	−42.8	39.1	75 55.2	−41.0•	41.6	76 39.0	−38.8•	44.4	39
40	70 12.2	−50.0	28.1	71 04.8	−49.2	29.4	71 56.6	−48.2	30.9	72 47.7	−47.2	32.6	73 37.7	−45.9	34.4	74 26.6	−44.6	36.4	75 14.2	−43.0	38.7	76 00.2	−41.2•	41.2	40
41	69 22.2	−50.8	26.4	70 15.6	−50.0	27.7	71 08.4	−49.2	29.0	72 00.5	−48.3	30.5	72 51.8	−47.3	32.2	73 42.0	−46.1	34.0	74 31.2	−44.8	36.0	75 19.0	−43.2	38.2	41
42	68 31.4	−51.5	25.0	69 25.6	−50.9	26.1	70 19.2	−50.2	27.3	71 12.2	−49.4	28.7	72 04.5	−48.5	30.1	72 55.9	−47.4	31.8	73 46.4	−46.2	33.6	74 35.8	−44.9	35.6	42
43	67 39.9	−52.1	23.6	68 34.7	−51.6	24.6	69 29.0	−51.0	25.7	70 22.8	−50.3	26.9	71 16.0	−49.5	28.3	72 08.5	−48.7	29.7	73 00.2	−47.7	31.3	73 50.9	−46.5	33.1	43
44	66 47.8	−52.7	22.3	67 43.1	−52.2	23.2	68 38.0	−51.7	24.2	69 32.5	−51.1	25.3	70 26.5	−50.4	26.5	71 19.8	−49.6	27.9	72 12.5	−48.7	29.3	73 04.4	−47.7	30.9	44
45	65 55.1	−53.3	21.1	66 50.9	−52.8	22.0	67 46.3	−52.3	22.9	68 41.4	−51.8	23.9	69 36.1	−51.2	24.9	70 30.2	−50.5	26.1	71 23.8	−49.8	27.4	72 16.7	−49.0	28.9	45
46	65 01.8	−53.7	20.0	65 58.1	−53.4	20.8	66 54.0	−52.9	21.6	67 49.6	−52.4	22.5	68 44.9	−51.9	23.5	69 39.7	−51.4	24.6	70 34.0	−50.7	25.7	71 27.7	−49.9	27.0	46
47	64 08.1	−54.1	19.0	65 04.7	−53.7	19.7	66 01.1	−53.4	20.4	66 57.2	−53.0	21.2	67 53.0	−52.6	22.1	68 48.3	−52.0	23.1	69 43.3	−51.4	24.2	70 37.8	−50.8	25.3	47
48	63 14.0	−54.5	18.0	64 11.0	−54.2	18.6	65 07.7	−53.9	19.3	66 04.2	−53.5	20.1	67 00.4	−53.1	20.9	67 56.3	−52.6	21.7	68 51.9	−52.2	22.7	69 47.0	−51.6	23.7	48
49	62 19.5	−54.8	17.1	63 16.8	−54.6	17.7	64 13.8	−54.2	18.3	65 10.7	−53.9	19.0	66 07.3	−53.6	19.7	67 03.7	−53.2	20.5	67 59.7	−52.7	21.3	68 55.4	−52.2	22.3	49
50	61 24.7	−55.2	16.2	62 22.2	−54.9	16.7	63 19.6	−54.7	17.3	64 16.8	−54.4	17.9	65 13.7	−54.0	18.6	66 10.5	−53.7	19.3	67 07.0	−53.3	20.1	68 03.2	−52.9	21.0	50
51	60 29.5	−55.4	15.4	61 27.3	−55.2	15.9	62 24.9	−54.9	16.4	63 22.4	−54.7	17.0	64 19.7	−54.4	17.6	65 16.8	−54.1	18.2	66 13.7	−53.8	18.9	67 10.3	−53.4	19.7	51
52	59 34.1	−55.7	14.6	60 32.1	−55.5	15.1	61 30.0	−55.3	15.6	62 27.7	−55.0	16.1	63 25.3	−54.8	16.6	64 22.7	−54.5	17.2	65 19.9	−54.2	17.9	66 16.9	−53.9	18.6	52
53	58 38.4	−55.9	13.9	59 36.6	−55.7	14.3	60 34.7	−55.5	14.8	61 32.7	−55.4	15.2	62 30.5	−55.1	15.7	63 28.2	−54.9	16.3	64 25.7	−54.6	16.9	65 23.0	−54.3	17.5	53
54	57 42.5	−56.1	13.2	58 40.9	−56.0	13.6	59 39.2	−55.8	14.0	60 37.3	−55.6	14.4	61 35.4	−55.4	14.9	62 33.3	−55.2	15.4	63 31.1	−55.0	15.9	64 28.7	−54.7	16.5	54
55	56 46.4	−56.3	12.6	57 44.9	−56.1	12.9	58 43.4	−56.0	13.3	59 41.7	−55.8	13.7	60 40.0	−55.7	14.1	61 38.1	−55.5	14.5	62 36.1	−55.2	15.0	63 34.0	−55.0	15.5	55
56	55 50.1	−56.5	11.9	56 48.8	−56.4	12.3	57 47.4	−56.3	12.6	58 45.9	−56.1	13.0	59 44.3	−55.9	13.3	60 42.6	−55.7	13.7	61 40.9	−55.6	14.2	62 39.0	−55.4	14.7	56
57	54 53.6	−56.7	11.4	55 52.4	−56.6	11.6	56 51.1	−56.4	12.0	57 49.8	−56.3	12.3	58 48.4	−56.2	12.6	59 46.9	−56.0	13.0	60 45.3	−55.8	13.4	61 43.6	−55.6	13.8	57
58	53 56.9	−56.8	10.8	54 55.8	−56.7	11.1	55 54.7	−56.6	11.3	56 53.5	−56.5	11.6	57 52.2	−56.3	12.0	58 50.9	−56.2	12.3	59 49.5	−56.1	12.7	60 48.0	−55.9	13.1	58
59	53 00.1	−56.9	10.2	53 59.1	−56.8	10.5	54 58.1	−56.7	10.8	55 57.0	−56.6	11.0	56 55.9	−56.5	11.3	57 54.7	−56.4	11.6	58 53.4	−56.2	12.0	59 52.1	−56.1	12.3	59
60	52 03.2	−57.1	9.7	53 02.3	−57.0	10.0	54 01.4	−56.9	10.2	55 00.4	−56.8	10.4	55 59.4	−56.7	10.7	56 58.3	−56.6	11.0	57 57.2	−56.5	11.3	58 56.0	−56.4	11.6	60
61	51 06.1	−57.2	9.2	52 05.3	−57.1	9.4	53 04.5	−57.1	9.7	54 03.6	−57.0	9.9	55 02.7	−56.9	10.1	56 01.7	−56.7	10.4	57 00.7	−56.6	10.7	57 59.6	−56.5	11.0	61
62	50 08.9	−57.3	8.8	51 08.2	−57.3	8.9	52 07.4	−57.1	9.1	53 06.6	−57.0	9.4	54 05.8	−57.0	9.6	55 05.0	−56.9	9.8	56 04.1	−56.8	10.1	57 03.1	−56.7	10.3	62
63	49 11.6	−57.5	8.3	50 10.9	−57.3	8.5	51 10.3	−57.3	8.7	52 09.6	−57.3	8.9	53 08.8	−57.1	9.1	54 08.1	−57.1	9.3	55 07.3	−57.0	9.5	56 06.4	−56.9	9.7	63
64	48 14.1	−57.5	7.9	49 13.6	−57.5	8.0	50 13.0	−57.4	8.2	51 12.3	−57.3	8.4	52 11.7	−57.3	8.6	53 11.0	−57.2	8.7	54 10.3	−57.1	9.0	55 09.5	−57.0	9.2	64
65	47 16.6	−57.6	7.4	48 16.1	−57.5	7.6	49 15.6	−57.5	7.7	50 15.0	−57.4	7.9	51 14.4	−57.3	8.1	52 13.8	−57.3	8.2	53 13.2	−57.2	8.4	54 12.5	−57.1	8.6	65
66	46 19.0	−57.7	7.0	47 18.6	−57.7	7.2	48 18.1	−57.6	7.3	49 17.6	−57.5	7.5	50 17.1	−57.5	7.6	51 16.5	−57.4	7.8	52 16.0	−57.4	7.9	53 15.4	−57.3	8.1	66
67	45 21.3	−57.7	6.6	46 20.9	−57.7	6.8	47 20.5	−57.7	6.9	48 20.1	−57.7	7.0	49 19.6	−57.6	7.2	50 19.1	−57.5	7.3	51 18.6	−57.4	7.5	52 18.1	−57.4	7.6	67
68	44 23.6	−57.9	6.3	45 23.2	−57.8	6.4	46 22.8	−57.7	6.5	47 22.4	−57.7	6.6	48 22.0	−57.6	6.7	49 21.6	−57.6	6.9	50 21.2	−57.6	7.0	51 20.7	−57.5	7.2	68
69	43 25.7	−57.9	5.9	44 25.4	−57.9	6.0	45 25.1	−57.9	6.1	46 24.7	−57.8	6.2	47 24.4	−57.8	6.3	48 24.0	−57.7	6.4	49 23.6	−57.7	6.6	50 23.2	−57.6	6.7	69
70	42 27.8	−58.0	5.5	43 27.5	−57.9	5.6	44 27.2	−57.9	5.7	45 26.9	−57.8	5.8	46 26.6	−57.8	5.9	47 26.3	−57.8	6.0	48 25.9	−57.7	6.2	49 25.6	−57.7	6.3	70
71	41 29.8	−58.0	5.2	42 29.6	−58.0	5.3	43 29.3	−58.0	5.4	44 29.1	−58.0	5.4	45 28.8	−57.9	5.5	46 28.5	−57.9	5.6	47 28.2	−57.8	5.7	48 27.9	−57.8	5.9	71
72	40 31.8	−58.1	4.8	41 31.6	−58.1	4.9	42 31.3	−58.0	5.0	43 31.1	−58.0	5.1	44 30.9	−58.0	5.2	45 30.6	−57.9	5.3	46 30.4	−57.9	5.4	47 30.1	−57.9	5.5	72
73	39 33.7	−58.2	4.5	40 33.5	−58.1	4.6	41 33.3	−58.1	4.7	42 33.1	−58.1	4.7	43 32.9	−58.0	4.8	44 32.7	−58.0	4.9	45 32.5	−58.0	5.0	46 32.2	−57.9	5.1	73
74	38 35.5	−58.2	4.2	39 35.4	−58.2	4.3	40 35.2	−58.1	4.3	41 35.0	−58.1	4.4	42 34.9	−58.1	4.5	43 34.7	−58.1	4.5	44 34.5	−58.1	4.6	45 34.3	−58.0	4.7	74
75	37 37.3	−58.2	3.9	38 37.2	−58.2	3.9	39 37.1	−58.2	4.0	40 36.9	−58.2	4.1	41 36.8	−58.2	4.1	42 36.6	−58.1	4.2	43 36.4	−58.1	4.3	44 36.3	−58.1	4.3	75
76	36 39.1	−58.3	3.6	37 39.0	−58.3	3.6	38 38.9	−58.3	3.7	39 38.7	−58.2	3.7	40 38.6	−58.2	3.8	41 38.5	−58.2	3.9	42 38.3	−58.1	3.9	43 38.2	−58.2	4.0	76
77	35 40.8	−58.3	3.3	36 40.7	−58.3	3.3	37 40.6	−58.3	3.4	38 40.5	−58.3	3.4	39 40.4	−58.3	3.5	40 40.3	−58.3	3.5	41 40.2	−58.3	3.6	42 40.0	−58.2	3.6	77
78	34 42.5	−58.4	3.0	35 42.4	−58.4	3.1	36 42.3	−58.3	3.1	37 42.2	−58.3	3.1	38 42.1	−58.3	3.2	39 42.0	−58.3	3.2	40 41.9	−58.2	3.3	41 41.8	−58.2	3.3	78
79	33 44.1	−58.4	2.7	34 44.0	−58.4	2.8	35 44.0	−58.4	2.8	36 43.9	−58.4	2.8	37 43.8	−58.3	2.9	38 43.7	−58.3	2.9	39 43.7	−58.4	3.0	40 43.6	−58.3	3.0	79
80	32 45.7	−58.4	2.5	33 45.6	−58.4	2.5	34 45.6	−58.4	2.5	35 45.5	−58.4	2.5	36 45.5	−58.4	2.6	37 45.4	−58.4	2.6	38 45.3	−58.3	2.7	39 45.3	−58.4	2.7	80
81	31 47.3	−58.5	2.2	32 47.2	−58.5	2.2	33 47.2	−58.5	2.2	34 47.1	−58.4	2.3	35 47.1	−58.5	2.3	36 47.0	−58.4	2.3	37 47.0	−58.4	2.4	38 46.9	−58.4	2.4	81
82	30 48.8	−58.5	1.9	31 48.7	−58.4	2.0	32 48.7	−58.5	2.0	33 48.7	−58.5	2.0	34 48.6	−58.4	2.0	35 48.6	−58.5	2.0	36 48.6	−58.5	2.1	37 48.5	−58.4	2.1	82
83	29 50.3	−58.6	1.7	30 50.3	−58.6	1.7	31 50.2	−58.5	1.7	32 50.2	−58.5	1.7	33 50.2	−58.5	1.7	34 50.1	−58.5	1.8	35 50.1	−58.5	1.8	36 50.1	−58.5	1.8	83
84	28 51.7	−58.5	1.4	29 51.7	−58.5	1.4	30 51.7	−58.5	1.5	31 51.7	−58.6	1.5	32 51.7	−58.6	1.5	33 51.6	−58.5	1.5	34 51.6	−58.5	1.5	35 51.6	−58.5	1.5	84
85	27 53.2	−58.6	1.2	28 53.2	−58.6	1.2	29 53.2	−58.6	1.2	30 53.1	−58.5	1.2	31 53.1	−58.5	1.2	32 53.1	−58.6	1.2	33 53.1	−58.6	1.3	34 53.1	−58.6	1.3	85
86	26 54.6	−58.6	0.9	27 54.6	−58.6	0.9	28 54.6	−58.6	0.9	29 54.6	−58.6	1.0	30 54.6	−58.6	1.0	31 54.5	−58.5	1.0	32 54.5	−58.6	1.0	33 54.5	−58.6	1.0	86
87	25 56.0	−58.7	0.7	26 56.0	−58.7	0.7	27 56.0	−58.7	0.7	28 56.0	−58.7	0.7	29 56.0	−58.7	0.7	30 56.0	−58.7	0.7	31 55.9	−58.6	0.7	32 55.9	−58.6	0.7	87
88	24 57.3	−58.6	0.5	25 57.3	−58.6	0.5	26 57.3	−58.6	0.5	27 57.3	−58.6	0.5	28 57.3	−58.6	0.5	29 57.3	−58.6	0.5	30 57.3	−58.6	0.5	31 57.3	−58.6	0.5	88
89	23 58.7	−58.7	0.2	24 58.7	−58.7	0.2	25 58.7	−58.7	0.2	26 58.7	−58.7	0.2	27 58.7	−58.7	0.2	28 58.7	−58.7	0.2	29 58.7	−58.7	0.2	30 58.7	−58.7	0.2	89
90	23 00.0	−58.7	0.0	24 00.0	−58.7	0.0	25 00.0	−58.7	0.0	26 00.0	−58.7	0.0	27 00.0	−58.7	0.0	28 00.0	−58.7	0.0	29 00.0	−58.7	0.0	30 00.0	−58.7	0.0	90
	23°			24°			25°			26°			27°			28°			29°			30°			

12°, 348° L.H.A. LATITUDE SAME NAME AS DECLINATION

208

LATITUDE **CONTRARY** NAME TO DECLINATION — L.H.A. 12°, 348°

Dec.	23° Hc	d	Z	24° Hc	d	Z	25° Hc	d	Z	26° Hc	d	Z	27° Hc	d	Z	28° Hc	d	Z	29° Hc	d	Z	30° Hc	d	Z	Dec.
°	° ′	′	°	° ′	′	°	° ′	′	°	° ′	′	°	° ′	′	°	° ′	′	°	° ′	′	°	° ′	′	°	°
0	64 12.6	-54.1	151.5	63 19.6	-54.5	152.4	62 26.2	-54.9	153.3	61 32.4	-55.3	154.1	60 38.3	-55.7	154.9	59 43.8	-56.0	155.6	58 48.9	-56.2	156.3	57 53.9	-56.6	157.0	0
1	63 18.5	-54.5	152.4	62 25.1	-54.9	153.3	61 31.3	-55.3	154.2	60 37.1	-55.6	154.9	59 42.6	-55.9	155.7	58 47.8	-56.3	156.3	57 52.7	-56.5	157.0	56 57.3	-56.7	157.6	1
2	62 24.0	-54.8	153.4	61 30.2	-55.2	154.2	60 36.0	-55.5	155.0	59 41.5	-55.9	155.7	58 46.7	-56.2	156.4	57 51.5	-56.4	157.0	56 56.2	-56.7	157.6	56 00.6	-56.9	158.2	2
3	61 29.2	-55.1	154.2	60 35.0	-55.5	155.0	59 40.5	-55.8	155.7	58 45.6	-56.1	156.4	57 50.5	-56.3	157.0	56 55.1	-56.6	157.6	55 59.5	-56.8	158.2	55 03.7	-57.0	158.7	3
4	60 34.1	-55.4	155.0	59 39.5	-55.7	155.8	58 44.7	-56.0	156.4	57 49.5	-56.2	157.1	56 54.2	-56.6	157.7	55 58.5	-56.7	158.2	55 02.7	-57.0	158.8	54 06.7	-57.2	159.3	4
5	59 38.7	-55.7	155.8	58 43.8	-55.9	156.5	57 48.7	-56.3	157.1	56 53.3	-56.5	157.7	55 57.6	-56.7	158.3	55 01.8	-56.9	158.8	54 05.7	-57.1	159.3	53 09.5	-57.3	159.8	5
6	58 43.0	-55.9	156.5	57 47.9	-56.2	157.2	56 52.4	-56.4	157.8	55 56.8	-56.7	158.3	55 00.9	-56.8	158.9	54 04.9	-57.1	159.4	53 08.6	-57.2	159.8	52 12.2	-57.4	160.3	6
7	57 47.1	-56.1	157.2	56 51.7	-56.4	157.8	55 56.0	-56.6	158.4	55 00.1	-56.8	158.9	54 04.1	-57.0	159.4	53 07.8	-57.2	159.9	52 11.4	-57.4	160.3	51 14.8	-57.5	160.8	7
8	56 51.0	-56.3	157.9	55 55.3	-56.5	158.4	54 59.4	-56.7	159.0	54 03.3	-56.9	159.5	53 07.1	-57.2	159.9	52 10.6	-57.3	160.4	51 14.0	-57.4	160.8	50 17.3	-57.6	161.2	8
9	55 54.7	-56.4	158.5	54 58.8	-56.7	159.0	54 02.7	-56.9	159.5	53 06.4	-57.1	160.0	52 09.9	-57.2	160.4	51 13.3	-57.4	160.9	50 16.6	-57.6	161.3	49 19.7	-57.7	161.6	9
10	54 58.3	-56.7	159.1	54 02.1	-56.8	159.6	53 05.8	-57.0	160.1	52 09.3	-57.2	160.5	51 12.7	-57.4	160.9	50 15.9	-57.5	161.3	49 19.0	-57.7	161.7	48 22.0	-57.8	162.0	10
11	54 01.6	-56.8	159.7	53 05.3	-57.0	160.1	52 08.8	-57.2	160.6	51 12.1	-57.3	161.0	50 15.3	-57.5	161.4	49 18.4	-57.6	161.8	48 21.3	-57.7	162.1	47 24.2	-57.9	162.5	11
12	53 04.8	-56.9	160.2	52 08.3	-57.1	160.6	51 11.6	-57.3	161.1	50 14.8	-57.5	161.5	49 17.8	-57.6	161.8	48 20.8	-57.8	162.2	47 23.6	-57.9	162.5	46 26.3	-57.9	162.8	12
13	52 07.9	-57.1	160.7	51 11.2	-57.3	161.1	50 14.3	-57.4	161.5	49 17.3	-57.5	161.9	48 20.2	-57.6	162.3	47 23.0	-57.7	162.6	46 25.7	-57.9	162.9	45 28.4	-58.1	163.2	13
14	51 10.8	-57.2	161.2	50 13.9	-57.3	161.6	49 16.9	-57.5	162.0	48 19.8	-57.6	162.3	47 22.6	-57.8	162.7	46 25.3	-57.9	163.0	45 27.8	-57.9	163.3	44 30.3	-58.1	163.6	14
15	50 13.6	-57.3	161.7	49 16.6	-57.5	162.1	48 19.4	-57.6	162.4	47 22.2	-57.7	162.8	46 24.8	-57.8	163.1	45 27.4	-58.0	163.4	44 29.9	-58.1	163.6	43 32.2	-58.1	163.9	15
16	49 16.3	-57.4	162.2	48 19.1	-57.5	162.5	47 21.8	-57.6	162.8	46 24.5	-57.8	163.2	45 27.0	-57.9	163.4	44 29.4	-58.0	163.7	43 31.8	-58.1	164.0	42 34.1	-58.2	164.3	16
17	48 18.9	-57.5	162.6	47 21.6	-57.7	162.9	46 24.2	-57.8	163.2	45 26.7	-57.9	163.5	44 29.1	-58.0	163.8	43 31.4	-58.1	164.1	42 33.7	-58.2	164.3	41 35.9	-58.3	164.6	17
18	47 21.4	-57.6	163.0	46 23.9	-57.7	163.3	45 26.4	-57.8	163.6	44 28.8	-57.9	163.9	43 31.1	-58.0	164.2	42 33.3	-58.1	164.4	41 35.5	-58.2	164.7	40 37.6	-58.3	164.9	18
19	46 23.8	-57.7	163.4	45 26.2	-57.8	163.7	44 28.6	-57.9	164.0	43 30.9	-58.0	164.3	42 33.1	-58.1	164.5	41 35.2	-58.2	164.8	40 37.3	-58.3	165.0	39 39.3	-58.4	165.2	19
20	45 26.1	-57.8	163.8	44 28.4	-57.9	164.1	43 30.7	-58.0	164.4	42 32.9	-58.1	164.6	41 35.0	-58.2	164.9	40 37.0	-58.2	165.1	39 39.0	-58.3	165.3	38 40.9	-58.4	165.5	20
21	44 28.3	-57.8	164.2	43 30.5	-57.9	164.5	42 32.7	-58.0	164.7	41 34.8	-58.1	165.0	40 36.8	-58.2	165.2	39 38.8	-58.3	165.4	38 40.7	-58.4	165.6	37 42.5	-58.4	165.8	21
22	43 30.5	-57.9	164.6	42 32.6	-58.0	164.8	41 34.7	-58.1	165.1	40 36.7	-58.2	165.3	39 38.6	-58.3	165.5	38 40.5	-58.4	165.7	37 42.3	-58.4	165.9	36 44.1	-58.5	166.1	22
23	42 32.6	-58.0	164.9	41 34.6	-58.1	165.2	40 36.6	-58.2	165.4	39 38.5	-58.3	165.6	38 40.3	-58.3	165.8	37 42.1	-58.3	166.0	36 43.9	-58.5	166.2	35 45.6	-58.5	166.4	23
24	41 34.6	-58.0	165.3	40 36.5	-58.1	165.5	39 38.4	-58.2	165.7	38 40.2	-58.2	165.9	37 42.0	-58.3	166.1	36 43.8	-58.5	166.3	35 45.4	-58.4	166.5	34 47.1	-58.6	166.6	24
25	40 36.6	-58.1	165.6	39 38.4	-58.2	165.8	38 40.2	-58.2	166.0	37 42.0	-58.4	166.2	36 43.7	-58.4	166.4	35 45.3	-58.4	166.6	34 47.0	-58.6	166.7	33 48.5	-58.6	166.9	25
26	39 38.5	-58.2	166.0	38 40.2	-58.2	166.2	37 42.0	-58.3	166.3	36 43.6	-58.3	166.5	35 45.3	-58.5	166.7	34 46.9	-58.5	166.8	33 48.4	-58.5	167.0	32 49.9	-58.6	167.2	26
27	38 40.3	-58.2	166.3	37 42.0	-58.2	166.5	36 43.7	-58.4	166.6	35 45.3	-58.4	166.8	34 46.8	-58.4	167.0	33 48.4	-58.6	167.1	32 49.9	-58.6	167.3	31 51.3	-58.6	167.4	27
28	37 42.1	-58.2	166.6	36 43.8	-58.4	166.8	35 45.3	-58.3	166.9	34 46.9	-58.5	167.1	33 48.4	-58.5	167.2	32 49.8	-58.5	167.4	31 51.3	-58.7	167.5	30 52.7	-58.7	167.6	28
29	36 43.9	-58.3	166.9	35 45.4	-58.3	167.1	34 47.0	-58.5	167.2	33 48.4	-58.5	167.4	32 49.9	-58.6	167.5	31 51.3	-58.6	167.6	30 52.6	-58.6	167.8	29 54.0	-58.7	167.9	29
30	35 45.6	-58.3	167.2	34 47.1	-58.4	167.3	33 48.5	-58.4	167.5	32 49.9	-58.5	167.6	31 51.3	-58.5	167.8	30 52.7	-58.7	167.9	29 54.0	-58.7	168.0	28 55.3	-58.7	168.1	30
31	34 47.3	-58.4	167.5	33 48.7	-58.4	167.6	32 50.1	-58.5	167.8	31 51.4	-58.5	167.9	30 52.8	-58.6	168.0	29 54.0	-58.6	168.1	28 55.3	-58.7	168.3	27 56.6	-58.8	168.4	31
32	33 48.9	-58.4	167.7	32 50.3	-58.5	167.9	31 51.6	-58.5	168.0	30 52.9	-58.6	168.1	29 54.2	-58.7	168.3	28 55.4	-58.7	168.4	27 56.6	-58.7	168.5	26 57.8	-58.8	168.6	32
33	32 50.5	-58.4	168.0	31 51.8	-58.5	168.2	30 53.1	-58.6	168.3	29 54.3	-58.6	168.4	28 55.5	-58.6	168.5	27 56.7	-58.7	168.6	26 57.9	-58.8	168.7	25 59.0	-58.8	168.8	33
34	31 52.1	-58.5	168.3	30 53.3	-58.5	168.4	29 54.5	-58.6	168.5	28 55.7	-58.6	168.6	27 56.9	-58.7	168.7	26 58.0	-58.7	168.8	25 59.1	-58.7	168.9	25 00.2	-58.8	169.0	34
35	30 53.6	-58.5	168.6	29 54.8	-58.6	168.7	28 55.9	-58.6	168.8	27 57.1	-58.7	168.9	26 58.2	-58.7	169.0	25 59.3	-58.8	169.1	25 00.4	-58.8	169.2	24 01.4	-58.8	169.3	35
36	29 55.1	-58.5	168.8	28 56.2	-58.6	168.9	27 57.3	-58.6	169.0	26 58.4	-58.7	169.1	25 59.5	-58.7	169.2	25 00.5	-58.7	169.3	24 01.6	-58.8	169.4	23 02.6	-58.9	169.5	36
37	28 56.6	-58.6	169.1	27 57.6	-58.6	169.2	26 58.7	-58.7	169.3	25 59.7	-58.7	169.4	25 00.8	-58.8	169.4	24 01.8	-58.8	169.5	23 02.8	-58.9	169.6	22 03.7	-58.8	169.7	37
38	27 58.0	-58.6	169.3	26 59.0	-58.6	169.4	26 00.0	-58.6	169.5	25 01.0	-58.7	169.6	24 02.0	-58.7	169.7	23 03.0	-58.8	169.7	22 03.9	-58.8	169.8	21 04.9	-58.9	169.9	38
39	26 59.4	-58.6	169.6	26 00.4	-58.7	169.6	25 01.4	-58.7	169.7	24 02.3	-58.7	169.8	23 03.3	-58.8	169.9	22 04.2	-58.8	170.0	21 05.1	-58.9	170.0	20 06.0	-58.9	170.1	39
40	26 00.8	-58.6	169.8	25 01.7	-58.6	169.9	24 02.7	-58.7	170.0	23 03.6	-58.8	170.0	22 04.5	-58.8	170.1	21 05.4	-58.9	170.2	20 06.2	-58.8	170.2	19 07.1	-58.9	170.3	40
41	25 02.2	-58.7	170.0	24 03.1	-58.7	170.1	23 04.0	-58.8	170.2	22 04.8	-58.7	170.3	21 05.7	-58.8	170.3	20 06.5	-58.8	170.4	19 07.4	-58.9	170.4	18 08.2	-58.9	170.5	41
42	24 03.5	-58.7	170.3	23 04.4	-58.7	170.3	22 05.2	-58.7	170.4	21 06.1	-58.8	170.5	20 06.9	-58.9	170.5	19 07.7	-58.9	170.6	18 08.5	-58.9	170.6	17 09.3	-58.9	170.7	42
43	23 04.8	-58.7	170.5	22 05.7	-58.8	170.6	21 06.5	-58.8	170.6	20 07.3	-58.8	170.7	19 08.0	-58.8	170.7	18 08.8	-58.9	170.8	17 09.6	-58.9	170.8	16 10.4	-59.0	170.9	43
44	22 06.1	-58.7	170.7	21 06.9	-58.7	170.8	20 07.7	-58.8	170.8	19 08.5	-58.9	170.9	18 09.2	-58.9	170.9	17 09.9	-58.8	171.0	16 10.7	-58.9	171.0	15 11.4	-58.9	171.1	44
45	21 07.4	-58.7	170.9	20 08.2	-58.8	171.0	19 08.9	-58.8	171.0	18 09.6	-58.8	171.1	17 10.3	-58.8	171.1	16 11.1	-58.9	171.2	15 11.8	-59.0	171.2	14 12.5	-59.0	171.3	45
46	20 08.7	-58.8	171.2	19 09.4	-58.8	171.2	18 10.1	-58.8	171.3	17 10.8	-58.9	171.3	16 11.5	-58.9	171.4	15 12.2	-58.9	171.4	14 12.8	-58.9	171.4	13 13.5	-59.0	171.5	46
47	19 09.9	-58.7	171.4	18 10.6	-58.8	171.4	17 11.3	-58.8	171.5	16 11.9	-58.8	171.5	15 12.6	-58.9	171.6	14 13.3	-59.0	171.6	13 13.9	-59.0	171.6	12 14.5	-58.9	171.7	47
48	18 11.2	-58.8	171.6	17 11.8	-58.8	171.6	16 12.5	-58.9	171.7	15 13.1	-58.9	171.7	14 13.7	-58.9	171.7	13 14.3	-58.9	171.8	12 14.9	-58.9	171.8	11 15.6	-59.0	171.8	48
49	17 12.4	-58.8	171.8	16 13.0	-58.8	171.8	15 13.6	-58.8	171.9	14 14.2	-58.9	171.9	13 14.8	-58.9	171.9	12 15.4	-58.9	172.0	11 16.0	-59.0	172.0	10 16.6	-59.0	172.0	49
50	16 13.6	-58.8	172.0	15 14.2	-58.8	172.0	14 14.8	-58.9	172.1	13 15.3	-58.8	172.1	12 15.9	-58.9	172.1	11 16.5	-59.0	172.2	10 17.0	-58.9	172.2	9 17.6	-59.0	172.2	50
51	15 14.8	-58.8	172.2	14 15.4	-58.9	172.2	13 15.9	-58.9	172.3	12 16.5	-58.9	172.3	11 17.0	-58.9	172.3	10 17.5	-58.9	172.4	9 18.1	-59.0	172.4	8 18.6	-59.0	172.4	51
52	14 16.0	-58.8	172.4	13 16.5	-58.8	172.4	12 17.0	-58.8	172.5	11 17.6	-58.9	172.5	10 18.1	-59.0	172.5	9 18.6	-59.0	172.5	8 19.1	-59.0	172.6	7 19.6	-59.0	172.6	52
53	13 17.2	-58.9	172.6	12 17.7	-58.9	172.6	11 18.2	-58.9	172.7	10 18.7	-59.0	172.7	9 19.1	-58.9	172.7	8 19.6	-58.9	172.7	7 20.1	-59.0	172.8	6 20.6	-59.0	172.8	53
54	12 18.3	-58.8	172.8	11 18.8	-58.9	172.8	10 19.3	-58.9	172.9	9 19.7	-58.9	172.9	8 20.2	-58.9	172.9	7 20.7	-59.0	172.9	6 21.1	-59.0	172.9	5 21.6	-59.0	172.9	54
55	11 19.5	-58.8	173.0	10 19.9	-58.8	173.0	9 20.4	-58.9	173.1	8 20.8	-58.9	173.1	7 21.3	-59.0	173.1	6 21.7	-59.0	173.1	5 22.1	-59.0	173.1	4 22.6	-59.1	173.1	55
56	10 20.7	-58.9	173.2	9 21.1	-58.9	173.2	8 21.5	-58.9	173.3	7 21.9	-58.9	173.3	6 22.3	-58.9	173.3	5 22.7	-58.9	173.3	4 23.1	-59.0	173.3	3 23.5	-59.0	173.3	56
57	9 21.8	-58.9	173.4	8 22.2	-58.9	173.4	7 22.6	-58.9	173.4	6 23.0	-59.0	173.5	5 23.4	-59.0	173.5	4 23.8	-59.0	173.5	3 24.1	-59.0	173.5	2 24.5	-59.0	173.5	57
58	8 22.9	-58.8	173.6	7 23.3	-58.9	173.6	6 23.7	-58.9	173.6	5 24.0	-58.9	173.6	4 24.4	-58.9	173.7	3 24.8	-59.0	173.7	2 25.1	-59.0	173.7	1 25.5	-59.0	173.7	58
59	7 24.1	-58.9	173.8	6 24.4	-58.9	173.8	5 24.8	-59.0	173.8	4 25.1	-58.9	173.8	3 25.5	-59.0	173.8	2 25.8	-59.0	173.8	1 26.1	-59.0	173.9	0 26.5	-59.0	173.9	59
60	6 25.2	-58.9	174.0	5 25.5	-58.9	174.0	4 25.8	-58.9	174.0	3 26.2	-59.0	174.0	2 26.5	-59.0	174.0	1 26.8	-59.0	174.0	0 27.1	-59.0	174.0	0 32.5	+59.0	6.0	60
61	5 26.3	-58.9	174.2	4 26.6	-58.9	174.2	3 26.9	-58.9	174.2	2 27.2	-58.9	174.2	1 27.5	-58.9	174.2	0 27.8	-58.9	174.2	0 31.9	+59.0	5.8	1 31.5	+59.1	5.8	61
62	4 27.4	-58.9	174.4	3 27.7	-58.9	174.4	2 28.0	-58.9	174.4	1 28.3	-59.0	174.4	0 28.6	-59.0	174.4	0 31.1	+59.0	5.6	1 30.9	+59.0	5.6	2 30.6	+59.0	5.6	62
63	3 28.5	-58.8	174.6	2 28.8	-58.9	174.6	1 29.1	-58.9	174.6	0 29.3	-58.9	174.6	0 30.4	+58.9	5.4	1 30.1	+58.9	5.4	2 29.9	+58.9	5.4	3 29.6	+59.0	5.4	63
64	2 29.7	-58.9	174.8	1 29.9	-58.8	174.8	0 30.2	-59.0	174.8	0 29.6	+58.9	5.2	1 29.3	+59.0	5.2	2 29.1	+59.0	5.2	3 28.8	+59.0	5.2	4 28.6	+59.0	5.2	64
65	1 30.8	-58.9	175.0	0 31.0	-58.9	175.0	0 28.8	+58.9	5.0	1 28.5	+59.0	5.0	2 28.3	+59.0	5.0	3 28.1	+59.0	5.1	4 27.8	+59.0	5.1	5 27.6	+59.0	5.1	65
66	0 31.9	-58.9	175.1	0 27.9	+58.9	4.9	1 27.7	+58.9	4.9	2 27.5	+58.9	4.9	3 27.3	+58.9	4.9	4 27.1	+58.9	4.9	5 26.8	+59.0	4.9	6 26.6	+59.0	4.9	66
67	0 27.0	+58.9	4.7	1 26.8	+58.9	4.7	2 26.6	+58.9	4.7	3 26.4	+59.0	4.7	4 26.2	+59.0	4.7	5 26.0	+59.0	4.7	6 25.8	+59.0	4.7	7 25.6	+59.0	4.7	67
68	1 25.9	+58.9	4.5	2 25.7	+58.9	4.5	3 25.5	+59.0	4.5	4 25.4	+58.9	4.5	5 25.2	+58.9	4.5	6 25.0	+59.0	4.5	7 24.8	+59.0	4.5	8 24.6	+59.0	4.5	68
69	2 24.8	+58.9	4.3	3 24.6	+58.9	4.3	4 24.5	+58.9	4.3	5 24.3	+58.9	4.3	6 24.1	+59.0	4.3	7 24.0	+58.9	4.3	8 23.8	+59.0	4.3	9 23.6	+59.0	4.3	69
70	3 23.7	+58.9	4.1	4 23.5	+58.9	4.1	5 23.4	+58.9	4.1	6 23.2	+59.0	4.1	7 23.1	+58.9	4.1	8 22.9	+59.0	4.1	9 22.8	+58.9	4.1	10 22.6	+59.0	4.1	70
71	4 22.6	+58.9	3.9	5 22.4	+58.9	3.9	6 22.3	+58.9	3.9	7 22.2	+58.9	3.9	8 22.0	+59.0	3.9	9 21.9	+58.9	3.9	10 21.7	+59.0	3.9	11 21.6	+59.0	4.0	71
72	5 21.5	+58.8	3.7	6 21.3	+58.9	3.7	7 21.2	+58.9	3.7	8 21.1	+58.9	3.7	9 21.0	+58.9	3.7	10 20.8	+59.0	3.7	11 20.7	+59.0	3.8	12 20.6	+58.9	3.8	72
73	6 20.3	+58.9	3.5	7 20.2	+58.9	3.5	8 20.1	+58.9	3.5	9 20.0	+58.9	3.5	10 19.9	+58.9	3.5	11 19.8	+58.9	3.6	12 19.7	+58.9	3.6	13 19.5	+59.0	3.6	73
74	7 19.2	+58.9	3.3	8 19.1	+58.9	3.3	9 19.0	+58.9	3.3	10 18.9	+58.9	3.3	11 18.8	+58.9	3.4	12 18.7	+58.9	3.4	13 18.6	+58.9	3.4	14 18.5	+58.9	3.4	74
75	8 18.1	+58.8	3.1	9 18.0	+58.9	3.1	10 17.9	+58.9	3.1	11 17.8	+58.9	3.1	12 17.7	+58.9	3.2	13 17.6	+58.9	3.2	14 17.5	+59.0	3.2	15 17.4	+59.0	3.2	75
76	9 16.9	+58.9	2.9	10 16.9	+58.8	2.9	11 16.8	+58.9	2.9	12 16.7	+58.9	3.0	13 16.6	+58.9	3.0	14 16.5	+59.0	3.0	15 16.5	+58.9	3.0	16 16.4	+58.9	3.0	76
77	10 15.8	+58.9	2.7	11 15.7	+58.9	2.7	12 15.7	+58.8	2.7	13 15.6	+58.9	2.8	14 15.5	+58.9	2.8	15 15.5	+58.8	2.8	16 15.4	+58.9	2.8	17 15.3	+58.9	2.8	77
78	11 14.7	+58.8	2.5	12 14.6	+58.8	2.5	13 14.5	+58.9	2.5	14 14.5	+58.8	2.6	15 14.4	+58.9	2.6	16 14.4	+58.8	2.6	17 14.3	+58.9	2.6	18 14.2	+58.9	2.6	78
79	12 13.5	+58.8	2.3	13 13.4	+58.9	2.3	14 13.4	+58.8	2.3	15 13.3	+58.9	2.4	16 13.3	+58.9	2.4	17 13.2	+58.9	2.4	18 13.2	+58.9	2.4	19 13.1	+58.9	2.4	79
80	13 12.3	+58.9	2.1	14 12.3	+58.8	2.1	15 12.2	+58.9	2.1	16 12.2	+58.9	2.2	17 12.2	+58.8	2.2	18 12.1	+58.9	2.2	19 12.1	+58.8	2.2	20 12.0	+58.9	2.2	80
81	14 11.2	+58.8	1.9	15 11.1	+58.8	1.9	16 11.1	+58.8	1.9	17 11.1	+58.8	2.0	18 11.0	+58.9	2.0	19 11.0	+58.8	2.0	20 10.9	+58.9	2.0	21 10.9	+58.9	2.0	81
82	15 10.0	+58.8	1.7	16 09.9	+58.8	1.7	17 09.9	+58.8	1.7	18 09.9	+58.8	1.7	19 09.9	+58.8	1.8	20 09.8	+58.9	1.8	21 09.8	+58.8	1.8	22 09.8	+58.8	1.8	82
83	16 08.8	+58.8	1.5	17 08.7	+58.8	1.5	18 08.7	+58.8	1.5	19 08.7	+58.8	1.5	20 08.7	+58.8	1.5	21 08.7	+58.8	1.6	22 08.6	+58.9	1.6	23 08.6	+58.8	1.6	83
84	17 07.6	+58.7	1.3	18 07.5	+58.8	1.3	19 07.5	+58.8	1.3	20 07.5	+58.8	1.3	21 07.5	+58.8	1.3	22 07.5	+58.8	1.3	23 07.5	+58.8	1.4	24 07.4	+58.9	1.4	84
85	18 06.3	+58.8	1.1	19 06.3	+58.8	1.1	20 06.3	+58.8	1.1	21 06.3	+58.8	1.1	22 06.3	+58.8	1.1	23 06.3	+58.8	1.1	24 06.3	+58.8	1.1	25 06.3	+58.8	1.1	85
86	19 05.1	+58.8	0.9	20 05.1	+58.7	0.9	21 05.1	+58.7	0.9	22 05.1	+58.7	0.9	23 05.1	+58.8	0.9	24 05.1	+58.7	0.9	25 05.1	+58.7	0.9	26 05.1	+58.7	0.9	86
87	20 03.9	+58.7	0.7	21 03.8	+58.8	0.7	22 03.8	+58.8	0.7	23 03.8	+58.8	0.7	24 03.8	+58.8	0.7	25 03.8	+58.8	0.7	26 03.8	+58.8	0.7	27 03.8	+58.8	0.7	87
88	21 02.6	+58.7	0.4	22 02.6	+58.7	0.4	23 02.6	+58.7	0.5	24 02.6	+58.7	0.5	25 02.6	+58.7	0.5	26 02.6	+58.7	0.5	27 02.6	+58.8	0.5	28 02.6	+58.7	0.5	88
89	22 01.3	+58.7	0.2	23 01.3	+58.7	0.2	24 01.3	+58.7	0.2	25 01.3	+58.7	0.2	26 01.3	+58.7	0.2	27 01.3	+58.7	0.2	28 01.3	+58.7	0.2	29 01.3	+58.7	0.2	89
90	23 00.0	+58.7	0.0	24 00.0	+58.7	0.0	25 00.0	+58.7	0.0	26 00.0	+58.7	0.0	27 00.0	+58.7	0.0	28 00.0	+58.7	0.0	29 00.0	+58.7	0.0	30 00.0	+58.7	0.0	90
	23°			24°			25°			26°			27°			28°			29°			30°			

S. Lat. {L.H.A. greater than 180° ....Zn=180°−Z
{L.H.A. less than 180°...........Zn=180°+Z

LATITUDE **SAME** NAME AS DECLINATION — L.H.A. 168°, 192°

209

Dec.	23° Hc	d	Z	24° Hc	d	Z	25° Hc	d	Z	26° Hc	d	Z	27° Hc	d	Z	28° Hc	d	Z	29° Hc	d	Z	30° Hc	d	Z	Dec.
°	° ′	′	°	° ′	′	°	° ′	′	°	° ′	′	°	° ′	′	°	° ′	′	°	° ′	′	°	° ′	′	°	°
0	63 45.3	+52.8	149.4	62 53.4	+53.3	150.4	62 01.0	+53.8	151.4	61 08.1	+54.3	152.2	60 14.8	+54.7	153.0	59 21.1	+55.2	153.8	58 27.1	+55.5	154.5	57 32.8	+55.8	155.2	0
1	64 38.1	+52.2	148.3	63 46.7	+52.9	149.4	62 54.8	+53.4	150.4	62 02.4	+53.9	151.3	61 09.5	+54.4	152.2	60 16.3	+54.8	153.0	59 22.6	+55.2	153.8	58 28.6	+55.6	154.5	1
2	65 30.3	+51.7	147.2	64 39.6	+52.4	148.3	63 48.2	+53.0	149.4	62 56.3	+53.6	150.4	62 03.9	+54.1	151.3	61 11.1	+54.5	152.2	60 17.8	+54.9	153.0	59 24.2	+55.3	153.8	2
3	66 22.0	+51.1	145.9	65 32.0	+51.8	147.2	64 41.2	+52.5	148.3	63 49.9	+53.1	149.4	62 58.0	+53.6	150.4	62 05.6	+54.1	151.3	61 12.7	+54.6	152.2	60 19.5	+55.0	153.0	3
4	67 13.1	+50.3	144.6	66 23.8	+51.1	145.9	65 33.7	+51.9	147.2	64 43.0	+52.6	148.3	63 51.6	+53.2	149.4	62 59.7	+53.8	150.4	62 07.3	+54.3	151.3	61 14.5	+54.7	152.2	4
5	68 03.4	+49.5	143.2	67 14.9	+50.5	144.6	66 25.6	+51.3	145.9	65 35.6	+52.0	147.2	64 44.8	+52.7	148.3	63 53.5	+53.3	149.4	63 01.6	+53.8	150.4	62 09.2	+54.3	151.3	5
6	68 52.9	+48.7	141.6	68 05.4	+49.7	143.2	67 16.9	+50.6	144.6	66 27.6	+51.4	145.9	65 37.5	+52.2	147.2	64 46.8	+52.8	148.3	63 55.4	+53.5	149.4	63 03.5	+54.0	150.4	6
7	69 41.6	+47.6	140.0	68 55.1	+48.7	141.6	68 07.5	+49.8	143.2	67 19.0	+50.8	144.6	66 29.7	+51.6	146.0	65 39.6	+52.3	147.2	64 48.9	+52.9	148.4	63 57.5	+53.5	149.4	7
8	70 29.2	+46.5	138.2	69 43.8	+47.8	140.0	68 57.3	+49.0	141.7	68 09.8	+49.9	143.2	67 21.3	+50.8	144.7	66 31.9	+51.7	146.0	65 41.8	+52.4	147.2	64 51.0	+53.1	148.4	8
9	71 15.7	+45.2	136.2	70 31.6	+46.7	138.2	69 46.3	+47.9	140.0	68 59.7	+49.1	141.7	68 12.1	+50.2	143.2	67 23.6	+51.0	144.7	66 34.2	+51.9	146.0	65 44.1	+52.6	147.3	9
10	72 00.9	+43.7	134.2	71 18.3	+45.4	136.3	70 34.2	+46.8	138.2	69 48.8	+48.1	140.1	69 02.3	+49.2	141.7	68 14.6	+50.3	143.3	67 26.1	+51.2	144.7	66 36.7	+52.0	146.1	10
11	72 44.6	+42.1	131.9	72 03.7	+43.9	134.2	71 21.0	+45.6	136.3	70 36.9	+47.0	138.3	69 51.5	+48.3	140.1	69 04.9	+49.4	141.8	68 17.3	+50.4	143.4	67 28.7	+51.3	144.8	11
12	73 26.7	+40.3•	129.4	72 47.6	+42.3	131.9	72 06.6	+44.1	134.3	71 23.9	+45.8	136.4	70 39.8	+47.2	138.4	69 54.3	+48.5	140.2	69 07.7	+49.6	141.9	68 20.0	+50.6	143.4	12
13	74 07.0	+38.1•	126.8	73 29.9	+40.5•	129.5	72 50.7	+42.6	132.0	72 09.7	+44.3	134.3	71 27.0	+45.9	136.5	70 42.8	+47.4	138.4	69 57.3	+48.6	140.2	69 10.6	+49.7	141.9	13
14	74 45.1	+35.8•	123.9	74 10.4	+38.3•	126.8	73 33.3	+40.6•	129.6	72 54.0	+42.8	132.1	72 12.9	+44.6	134.4	71 30.2	+46.1	136.5	70 45.9	+47.6	138.5	70 00.3	+48.8	140.3	14
15	75 20.9	+33.0•	120.8	74 48.7	+36.0•	124.0	74 13.9	+38.6•	126.9	73 36.8	+40.8	129.6	72 57.5	+42.9	132.1	72 16.3	+44.8	134.5	71 33.5	+46.3	136.6	70 49.1	+47.8	138.6	15
16	75 53.9	+30.1•	117.4	75 24.7	+33.3•	120.8	74 52.5	+36.2•	124.0	74 17.6	+38.9•	127.0	73 40.4	+41.1	129.7	73 01.1	+43.1	132.2	72 19.8	+45.0	134.6	71 36.9	+46.6	136.7	16
17	76 24.0	+26.7•	113.8	75 58.0	+30.3•	117.5	75 28.7	+33.6•	120.9	74 56.5	+36.4•	124.1	74 21.5	+39.1•	127.1	73 44.2	+41.4	129.8	73 04.8	+43.4	132.3	72 23.5	+45.2	134.7	17
18	76 50.7	+23.0•	109.9	76 28.3	+26.9•	113.9	76 02.3	+30.5•	117.5	75 32.9	+33.8•	121.0	75 00.6	+36.7•	124.2	74 25.6	+39.3•	127.2	73 48.2	+41.6	129.9	73 08.7	+43.6	132.5	18
19	77 13.7	+18.9•	105.8	76 55.2	+23.2•	110.0	76 32.8	+27.2•	113.9	76 06.7	+30.8•	117.6	75 37.3	+34.0•	121.1	75 04.9	+36.9•	124.3	74 29.8	+39.5•	127.3	73 52.3	+41.8	130.0	19
20	77 32.6	+14.6•	101.5	77 18.4	+19.2•	105.8	77 00.0	+23.4•	110.0	76 37.5	+27.4•	114.0	76 11.3	+31.0•	117.7	75 41.8	+34.3•	121.2	75 09.3	+37.2•	124.4	74 34.1	+39.8•	127.4	20
21	77 47.2	+9.9•	96.9	77 37.6	+14.7•	101.5	77 23.4	+19.4•	105.9	77 04.9	+23.7•	110.1	76 42.3	+27.7•	114.0	76 16.1	+31.3•	117.8	75 46.5	+34.6•	121.3	75 13.9	+37.5•	124.5	21
22	77 57.1	+5.1•	92.2	77 52.3	+10.1•	96.9	77 42.8	+14.9•	101.5	77 28.6	+19.5•	105.9	77 10.0	+23.9•	110.1	76 47.4	+27.9•	114.1	76 21.1	+31.6•	117.9	75 51.4	+34.8•	121.4	22
23	78 02.2	+0.2•	87.5	78 02.4	+5.3•	92.2	77 57.7	+10.3•	96.9	77 48.1	+15.2•	101.5	77 33.9	+19.8•	105.9	77 15.3	+24.2•	110.2	76 52.7	+28.1•	114.2	76 26.2	+31.9•	118.0	23
24	78 02.4	−4.7•	82.6	78 07.7	+0.3•	87.3	78 08.0	+5.4•	92.1	78 03.3	+10.4•	96.8	77 53.7	+15.4•	101.5	77 39.5	+20.0•	106.0	77 20.8	+24.5•	110.2	76 58.1	+28.4•	114.3	24
25	77 57.7	−9.6•	77.8	78 08.0	−4.7•	82.5	78 13.4	+0.3•	87.2	78 13.7	+5.5•	92.0	78 09.1	+10.6•	96.8	77 59.5	+15.6•	101.5	77 45.3	+20.2•	106.0	77 26.5	+24.7•	110.3	25
26	77 48.1	−14.2•	73.1	78 03.3	−9.6•	77.6	78 13.7	−4.6•	82.3	78 19.2	+0.5•	87.1	78 19.7	+5.6•	92.0	78 15.1	+10.8•	96.8	78 05.5	+15.8•	101.5	77 51.2	+20.6•	106.1	26
27	77 33.9	−18.6•	68.6	77 53.7	−14.2•	72.9	78 09.1	−9.6•	77.5	78 19.7	−4.6•	82.2	78 25.3	+0.6•	87.0	78 25.9	+5.7•	91.9	78 21.3	+11.0•	96.8	78 11.8	+15.9•	101.5	27
28	77 15.3	−22.6•	64.2	77 39.5	−18.7•	68.3	77 59.5	−14.2•	72.7	78 15.1	−9.6•	77.3	78 25.9	−4.6•	82.1	78 31.6	+0.7•	86.9	78 32.3	+5.8•	91.9	78 27.7	+11.1•	96.8	28
29	76 52.7	−26.5•	60.1	77 20.8	−22.7•	63.9	77 45.3	−18.8•	68.1	78 05.5	−14.3•	72.5	78 21.3	−9.5•	77.1	78 32.3	−4.6•	81.9	78 38.1	+0.7•	86.8	78 38.8	+6.1•	91.8	29
30	76 26.2	−29.8•	56.2	76 58.1	−26.5•	59.8	77 26.5	−22.8•	63.6	77 51.2	−18.8•	67.8	78 11.8	−14.4•	72.2	78 27.7	−9.5•	76.9	78 38.8	−4.5•	81.8	78 44.9	+0.7•	86.7	30
31	75 56.4	−32.8•	52.5	76 31.6	−29.9•	55.8	77 03.7	−26.6•	59.4	77 32.4	−22.9•	63.3	77 57.4	−18.9•	67.5	78 18.2	−14.5•	72.0	78 34.3	−9.5•	76.7	78 45.6	−4.4•	81.6	31
32	75 23.6	−35.5•	49.2	76 01.7	−33.0•	52.2	76 37.1	−30.1•	55.5	77 09.5	−26.8•	59.1	77 38.5	−23.1•	63.0	78 03.7	−18.9•	67.3	78 24.8	−14.5•	71.8	78 41.2	−9.7•	76.5	32
33	74 48.1	−38.0•	46.0	75 28.7	−35.7•	48.8	76 07.0	−33.1•	51.8	76 42.7	−30.2•	55.2	77 15.4	−26.9•	58.8	77 44.8	−23.3•	62.7	78 10.3	−19.1•	67.0	78 31.5	−14.5•	71.5	33
34	74 10.1	−40.1	43.1	74 53.0	−38.1•	45.7	75 33.9	−35.8•	48.4	76 12.5	−33.2•	51.5	76 48.5	−30.3•	54.8	77 21.5	−27.0•	58.5	77 51.2	−23.4•	62.4	78 17.0	−19.2•	66.7	34
35	73 30.0	−41.9	40.5	74 14.9	−40.2•	42.7	74 58.1	−38.3•	45.3	75 39.3	−36.0•	48.0	76 18.2	−33.4•	51.1	76 54.5	−30.5•	54.4	77 27.8	−27.2•	58.1	77 57.8	−23.5•	62.1	35
36	72 48.1	−43.7	38.0	73 34.7	−42.1	40.1	74 19.8	−40.4	42.4	75 03.3	−38.4•	44.9	75 44.8	−36.2•	47.7	76 24.0	−33.6•	50.7	77 00.6	−30.7•	54.1	77 34.3	−27.4•	57.7	36
37	72 04.4	−45.1	35.7	72 52.6	−43.8	37.6	73 39.4	−42.2	39.7	74 24.9	−40.6•	42.0	75 08.6	−38.6•	44.5	75 50.4	−36.4•	47.3	76 29.9	−33.8•	50.3	77 06.9	−30.9•	53.7	37
38	71 19.3	−46.4	33.6	72 08.8	−45.2	35.3	72 57.2	−43.9	37.2	73 44.3	−42.4	39.3	74 30.0	−40.7•	41.6	75 14.0	−38.7•	44.1	75 56.1	−36.5•	46.8	76 36.0	−34.0•	49.9	38
39	70 32.9	−47.5	31.7	71 23.6	−46.5	33.2	72 13.3	−45.4	34.9	73 01.9	−44.0	36.8	73 49.3	−42.6	38.9	74 35.3	−40.9•	41.1	75 19.6	−38.9•	43.6	76 02.0	−36.7•	46.4	39
40	69 45.4	−48.6	29.9	70 37.1	−47.7	31.3	71 27.9	−46.6	32.8	72 17.9	−45.6	34.5	73 06.7	−44.2	36.4	73 54.4	−42.7	38.4	74 40.7	−41.1•	40.7	75 25.3	−39.1•	43.2	40
41	68 56.8	−49.4	28.2	69 49.4	−48.7	29.5	70 41.3	−47.8	30.9	71 32.3	−46.7	32.4	72 22.5	−45.6	34.1	73 11.7	−44.4	36.0	73 59.6	−42.9	38.0	74 46.2	−41.3•	40.3	41
42	68 07.4	−50.3	26.7	69 00.7	−49.5	27.8	69 53.5	−48.8	29.1	70 45.6	−48.0	30.5	71 36.9	−47.0	32.0	72 27.3	−45.8	33.7	73 16.7	−44.6	35.5	74 04.9	−43.1	37.6	42
43	67 17.1	−51.0	25.2	68 11.2	−50.4	26.3	69 04.7	−49.7	27.4	69 57.6	−48.9	28.7	70 49.9	−48.0	30.1	71 41.5	−47.1	31.6	72 32.1	−46.0	33.2	73 21.8	−44.8	35.1	43
44	66 26.1	−51.6	23.9	67 20.8	−51.1	24.8	68 15.0	−50.5	25.9	69 08.7	−49.8	27.0	70 01.9	−49.1	28.3	70 54.4	−48.2	29.6	71 46.1	−47.2	31.1	72 37.0	−46.1	32.8	44
45	65 34.5	−52.2	22.6	66 29.7	−51.7	23.5	67 24.5	−51.2	24.5	68 18.9	−50.6	25.5	69 12.8	−49.9	26.6	70 06.2	−49.2	27.9	70 58.9	−48.4	29.2	71 50.9	−47.5	30.7	45
46	64 42.3	−52.8	21.5	65 38.0	−52.3	22.3	66 33.3	−51.8	23.1	67 28.3	−51.3	24.1	68 22.9	−50.8	25.1	69 17.0	−50.1	26.2	70 10.5	−49.3	27.4	71 03.4	−48.5	28.8	46
47	63 49.5	−53.2	20.4	64 45.7	−52.9	21.1	65 41.5	−52.4	21.9	66 37.0	−51.9	22.7	67 32.1	−51.4	23.7	68 26.9	−50.9	24.7	69 21.2	−50.2	25.8	70 14.9	−49.5	27.0	47
48	62 56.3	−53.6	19.3	63 52.8	−53.3	20.0	64 49.1	−52.9	20.7	65 45.1	−52.5	21.5	66 40.7	−52.0	22.3	67 36.0	−51.5	23.3	68 31.0	−51.0	24.3	69 25.4	−50.3	25.4	48
49	62 02.7	−54.0	18.4	62 59.5	−53.7	19.0	63 56.2	−53.4	19.6	64 52.6	−53.0	20.3	65 48.7	−52.6	21.1	66 44.5	−52.2	21.9	67 40.0	−51.7	22.9	68 35.1	−51.1	23.8	49
50	61 08.7	−54.4	17.4	62 05.8	−54.1	18.0	63 02.8	−53.8	18.6	63 59.6	−53.5	19.3	64 56.1	−53.1	20.0	65 52.3	−52.7	20.7	66 48.3	−52.3	21.5	67 44.0	−51.8	22.4	50
51	60 14.3	−54.7	16.6	61 11.7	−54.4	17.1	62 09.0	−54.2	17.6	63 06.1	−53.9	18.2	64 03.0	−53.6	18.9	64 59.6	−53.2	19.6	65 56.0	−52.8	20.3	66 52.2	−52.4	21.1	51
52	59 19.6	−54.9	15.8	60 17.3	−54.7	16.2	61 14.8	−54.5	16.7	62 12.2	−54.2	17.3	63 09.4	−53.9	17.9	64 06.4	−53.6	18.5	65 03.2	−53.3	19.2	65 59.8	−53.0	19.9	52
53	58 24.7	−55.3	15.0	59 22.6	−55.1	15.4	60 20.3	−54.8	15.9	61 18.0	−54.6	16.4	62 15.5	−54.4	16.9	63 12.8	−54.1	17.5	64 09.9	−53.7	18.1	65 06.8	−53.4	18.8	53
54	57 29.4	−55.5	14.2	58 27.5	−55.3	14.6	59 25.5	−55.1	15.1	60 23.4	−54.9	15.5	61 21.1	−54.6	16.0	62 18.7	−54.4	16.5	63 16.2	−54.2	17.1	64 13.4	−53.8	17.7	54
55	56 33.9	−55.7	13.5	57 32.2	−55.5	13.9	58 30.4	−55.4	14.3	59 28.5	−55.2	14.7	60 26.5	−55.0	15.2	61 24.3	−54.7	15.6	62 22.0	−54.5	16.2	63 19.6	−54.3	16.7	55
56	55 38.2	−55.9	12.9	56 36.7	−55.8	13.2	57 35.0	−55.6	13.6	58 33.3	−55.4	14.0	59 31.5	−55.3	14.4	60 29.6	−55.1	14.8	61 27.5	−54.8	15.3	62 25.3	−54.6	15.8	56
57	54 42.3	−56.1	12.2	55 40.9	−56.0	12.6	56 39.4	−55.8	12.9	57 37.9	−55.7	13.2	58 36.2	−55.5	13.6	59 34.5	−55.3	14.0	60 32.7	−55.2	14.4	61 30.7	−54.9	14.9	57
58	53 46.2	−56.3	11.6	54 44.9	−56.1	11.9	55 43.6	−56.0	12.2	56 42.2	−55.9	12.5	57 40.7	−55.7	12.9	58 39.2	−55.6	13.2	59 37.5	−55.4	13.6	60 35.8	−55.2	14.1	58
59	52 49.9	−56.4	11.1	53 48.8	−56.4	11.3	54 47.6	−56.2	11.6	55 46.3	−56.1	11.9	56 45.0	−55.9	12.2	57 43.6	−55.8	12.5	58 42.1	−55.6	12.9	59 40.6	−55.5	13.3	59
60	51 53.5	−56.6	10.5	52 52.4	−56.5	10.7	53 51.4	−56.4	11.0	54 50.2	−56.2	11.3	55 49.1	−56.2	11.5	56 47.8	−56.0	11.9	57 46.5	−55.9	12.2	58 45.1	−55.7	12.5	60
61	50 56.9	−56.8	10.0	51 55.9	−56.6	10.2	52 55.0	−56.6	10.4	53 54.0	−56.5	10.7	54 52.9	−56.3	10.9	55 51.8	−56.2	11.2	56 50.6	−56.1	11.5	57 49.4	−56.0	11.8	61
62	50 00.1	−56.8	9.5	50 59.3	−56.8	9.7	51 58.4	−56.7	9.9	52 57.5	−56.6	10.1	53 56.6	−56.5	10.3	54 55.6	−56.4	10.6	55 54.5	−56.2	10.9	56 53.4	−56.1	11.1	62
63	49 03.3	−57.0	9.0	50 02.5	−56.9	9.1	51 01.7	−56.8	9.3	52 00.9	−56.7	9.6	53 00.1	−56.7	9.8	53 59.2	−56.6	10.0	54 58.3	−56.5	10.2	55 57.3	−56.4	10.5	63
64	48 06.3	−57.1	8.5	49 05.6	−57.0	8.7	50 04.9	−56.9	8.8	51 04.2	−56.9	9.0	52 03.4	−56.8	9.2	53 02.6	−56.7	9.4	54 01.8	−56.6	9.7	55 00.9	−56.5	9.9	64
65	47 09.2	−57.2	8.0	48 08.6	−57.1	8.2	49 08.0	−57.1	8.4	50 07.3	−57.0	8.5	51 06.6	−56.9	8.7	52 05.9	−56.8	8.9	53 05.2	−56.8	9.1	54 04.4	−56.7	9.3	65
66	46 12.0	−57.3	7.6	47 11.5	−57.3	7.7	48 10.9	−57.2	7.9	49 10.3	−57.1	8.0	50 09.7	−57.0	8.2	51 09.1	−57.0	8.4	52 08.4	−56.9	8.6	53 07.7	−56.8	8.8	66
67	45 14.7	−57.4	7.2	46 14.2	−57.3	7.3	47 13.7	−57.3	7.4	48 13.2	−57.2	7.6	49 12.7	−57.2	7.7	50 12.1	−57.1	7.9	51 11.5	−57.0	8.1	52 10.9	−56.9	8.2	67
68	44 17.3	−57.5	6.8	45 16.9	−57.5	6.9	46 16.4	−57.3	7.0	47 16.0	−57.3	7.1	48 15.5	−57.3	7.3	49 15.0	−57.2	7.4	50 14.5	−57.1	7.6	51 14.0	−57.1	7.7	68
69	43 19.8	−57.5	6.4	44 19.4	−57.5	6.5	45 19.1	−57.5	6.6	46 18.7	−57.5	6.7	47 18.2	−57.3	6.8	48 17.8	−57.3	7.0	49 17.4	−57.3	7.1	50 16.9	−57.2	7.2	69
70	42 22.3	−57.7	6.0	43 21.9	−57.6	6.1	44 21.6	−57.6	6.2	45 21.2	−57.5	6.3	46 20.9	−57.5	6.4	47 20.5	−57.4	6.5	48 20.1	−57.4	6.6	49 19.7	−57.3	6.8	70
71	41 24.6	−57.7	5.6	42 24.3	−57.6	5.7	43 24.0	−57.6	5.8	44 23.7	−57.6	5.9	45 23.4	−57.5	6.0	46 23.1	−57.5	6.1	47 22.7	−57.4	6.2	48 22.4	−57.4	6.3	71
72	40 26.9	−57.7	5.2	41 26.7	−57.8	5.3	42 26.4	−57.7	5.4	43 26.1	−57.6	5.5	44 25.9	−57.7	5.6	45 25.6	−57.6	5.7	46 25.3	−57.6	5.8	47 25.0	−57.5	5.9	72
73	39 29.2	−57.9	4.9	40 28.9	−57.8	5.0	41 28.7	−57.8	5.0	42 28.5	−57.8	5.1	43 28.2	−57.7	5.2	44 28.0	−57.7	5.3	45 27.7	−57.6	5.4	46 27.5	−57.6	5.5	73
74	38 31.3	−57.9	4.5	39 31.1	−57.8	4.6	40 30.9	−57.8	4.7	41 30.7	−57.8	4.7	42 30.5	−57.7	4.8	43 30.3	−57.7	4.9	44 30.1	−57.7	5.0	45 29.9	−57.7	5.1	74
75	37 33.4	−57.9	4.2	38 33.3	−57.9	4.3	39 33.1	−57.9	4.3	40 32.9	−57.8	4.4	41 32.8	−57.9	4.5	42 32.6	−57.8	4.5	43 32.4	−57.8	4.6	44 32.2	−57.8	4.7	75
76	36 35.5	−58.0	3.9	37 35.4	−58.0	3.9	38 35.2	−57.9	4.0	39 35.1	−58.0	4.0	40 34.9	−57.9	4.1	41 34.8	−57.9	4.2	42 34.6	−57.9	4.2	43 34.4	−57.8	4.3	76
77	35 37.5	−58.0	3.6	36 37.4	−58.0	3.6	37 37.3	−58.0	3.7	38 37.1	−57.9	3.7	39 37.0	−58.0	3.8	40 36.9	−58.0	3.8	41 36.7	−57.9	3.9	42 36.6	−57.9	3.9	77
78	34 39.5	−58.1	3.3	35 39.4	−58.1	3.3	36 39.3	−58.1	3.3	37 39.2	−58.1	3.4	38 39.0	−58.0	3.4	39 38.9	−58.0	3.5	40 38.8	−58.0	3.5	41 38.7	−57.9	3.6	78
79	33 41.4	−58.2	3.0	34 41.3	−58.1	3.0	35 41.2	−58.1	3.0	36 41.1	−58.1	3.1	37 41.0	−58.0	3.1	38 40.9	−58.0	3.2	39 40.8	−58.0	3.2	40 40.8	−58.1	3.2	79
80	32 43.2	−58.1	2.7	33 43.2	−58.2	2.7	34 43.1	−58.1	2.7	35 43.0	−58.1	2.8	36 43.0	−58.2	2.8	37 42.9	−58.1	2.8	38 42.8	−58.1	2.9	39 42.7	−58.0	2.9	80
81	31 45.1	−58.3	2.4	32 45.0	−58.2	2.4	33 45.0	−58.2	2.4	34 44.9	−58.2	2.5	35 44.8	−58.1	2.5	36 44.8	−58.2	2.5	37 44.7	−58.1	2.6	38 44.7	−58.2	2.6	81
82	30 46.8	−58.2	2.1	31 46.8	−58.2	2.1	32 46.8	−58.3	2.1	33 46.7	−58.2	2.2	34 46.7	−58.2	2.2	35 46.6	−58.2	2.2	36 46.6	−58.2	2.2	37 46.5	−58.1	2.3	82
83	29 48.6	−58.3	1.8	30 48.6	−58.3	1.8	31 48.5	−58.2	1.8	32 48.5	−58.3	1.9	33 48.5	−58.3	1.9	34 48.4	−58.2	1.9	35 48.4	−58.2	1.9	36 48.4	−58.2	2.0	83
84	28 50.3	−58.3	1.5	29 50.3	−58.3	1.6	30 50.3	−58.3	1.6	31 50.2	−58.2	1.6	32 50.2	−58.3	1.6	33 50.2	−58.3	1.6	34 50.2	−58.3	1.6	35 50.2	−58.3	1.7	84
85	27 52.0	−58.3	1.3	28 52.0	−58.4	1.3	29 52.0	−58.4	1.3	30 52.0	−58.4	1.3	31 51.9	−58.3	1.3	32 51.9	−58.3	1.3	33 51.9	−58.3	1.4	34 51.9	−58.3	1.4	85
86	26 53.7	−58.4	1.0	27 53.6	−58.3	1.0	28 53.6	−58.3	1.0	29 53.6	−58.3	1.0	30 53.6	−58.3	1.0	31 53.6	−58.3	1.1	32 53.6	−58.4	1.1	33 53.6	−58.4	1.1	86
87	25 55.3	−58.4	0.8	26 55.3	−58.4	0.8	27 55.3	−58.4	0.8	28 55.3	−58.4	0.8	29 55.3	−58.4	0.8	30 55.3	−58.4	0.8	31 55.2	−58.3	0.8	32 55.2	−58.3	0.8	87
88	24 56.9	−58.4	0.5	25 56.9	−58.4	0.5	26 56.9	−58.5	0.5	27 56.9	−58.5	0.5	28 56.9	−58.5	0.5	29 56.9	−58.5	0.5	30 56.9	−58.5	0.5	31 56.9	−58.5	0.5	88
89	23 58.5	−58.5	0.2	24 58.5	−58.5	0.2	25 58.4	−58.4	0.3	26 58.4	−58.4	0.3	27 58.4	−58.4	0.3	28 58.4	−58.4	0.3	29 58.4	−58.4	0.3	30 58.4	−58.4	0.3	89
90	23 00.0	−58.5	0.0	24 00.0	−58.5	0.0	25 00.0	−58.5	0.0	26 00.0	−58.5	0.0	27 00.0	−58.5	0.0	28 00.0	−58.5	0.0	29 00.0	−58.5	0.0	30 00.0	−58.5	0.0	90
	23°			24°			25°			26°			27°			28°			29°			30°			

Dec.	23° Hc	d	Z	24° Hc	d	Z	25° Hc	d	Z	26° Hc	d	Z	27° Hc	d	Z	28° Hc	d	Z	29° Hc	d	Z	30° Hc	d	Z	Dec.
°	° ′	′	°	° ′	′	°	° ′	′	°	° ′	′	°	° ′	′	°	° ′	′	°	° ′	′	°	° ′	′	°	°
0	63 45.3	-53.2	149.4	62 53.4	-53.8	150.4	62 01.0	-54.3	151.4	61 08.1	-54.7	152.2	60 14.8	-55.0	153.0	59 21.1	-55.4	153.8	58 27.1	-55.7	154.5	57 32.8	-56.0	155.2	0
1	62 52.1	-53.7	150.4	61 59.6	-54.1	151.4	61 06.7	-54.5	152.3	60 13.4	-54.9	153.1	59 19.8	-55.3	153.8	58 25.7	-55.6	154.6	57 31.4	-55.9	155.2	56 36.8	-56.2	155.9	1
2	61 58.4	-54.0	151.4	61 05.5	-54.5	152.3	60 12.2	-54.9	153.1	59 18.5	-55.2	153.9	58 24.5	-55.6	154.6	57 30.1	-55.8	155.3	56 35.5	-56.2	155.9	55 40.6	-56.4	156.5	2
3	61 04.4	-54.4	152.3	60 11.0	-54.8	153.1	59 17.3	-55.1	153.9	58 23.3	-55.5	154.6	57 28.9	-55.8	155.3	56 34.3	-56.1	155.9	55 39.3	-56.3	156.5	54 44.2	-56.6	157.1	3
4	60 10.0	-54.7	153.2	59 16.2	-55.0	153.9	58 22.2	-55.4	154.7	57 27.8	-55.7	155.3	56 33.1	-56.0	156.0	55 38.2	-56.3	156.6	54 43.0	-56.5	157.1	53 47.6	-56.7	157.7	4
5	59 15.3	-55.0	154.0	58 21.2	-55.4	154.7	57 26.8	-55.7	155.4	56 32.1	-55.9	156.0	55 37.1	-56.2	156.6	54 41.9	-56.4	157.2	53 46.5	-56.6	157.7	52 50.9	-56.9	158.2	5
6	58 20.3	-55.3	154.8	57 25.8	-55.5	155.4	56 31.1	-55.8	156.1	55 36.2	-56.2	156.7	54 40.9	-56.3	157.2	53 45.5	-56.6	157.8	52 49.9	-56.8	158.3	51 54.0	-57.0	158.7	6
7	57 25.0	-55.5	155.5	56 30.3	-55.8	156.1	55 35.3	-56.1	156.7	54 40.0	-56.3	157.3	53 44.6	-56.6	157.8	52 48.9	-56.7	158.3	51 53.1	-57.0	158.8	50 57.0	-57.1	159.2	7
8	56 29.5	-55.7	156.2	55 34.5	-56.0	156.8	54 39.2	-56.2	157.4	53 43.7	-56.4	157.9	52 48.0	-56.6	158.4	51 52.2	-56.9	158.9	50 56.1	-57.0	159.3	49 59.9	-57.2	159.7	8
9	55 33.8	-56.0	156.9	54 38.5	-56.2	157.4	53 43.0	-56.4	157.9	52 47.3	-56.7	158.4	51 51.4	-56.9	158.9	50 55.3	-57.0	159.4	49 59.1	-57.2	159.8	49 02.7	-57.3	160.2	9
10	54 37.8	-56.1	157.5	53 42.3	-56.4	158.0	52 46.6	-56.6	158.5	51 50.6	-56.7	159.0	50 54.5	-56.9	159.4	49 58.3	-57.1	159.9	49 01.9	-57.3	160.3	48 05.4	-57.5	160.6	10
11	53 41.7	-56.3	158.1	52 45.9	-56.5	158.6	51 50.0	-56.7	159.1	50 53.9	-56.9	159.5	49 57.6	-57.1	159.9	49 01.2	-57.3	160.3	48 04.6	-57.4	160.7	47 07.9	-57.5	161.1	11
12	52 45.4	-56.4	158.7	51 49.4	-56.6	159.1	50 53.3	-56.9	159.6	49 57.0	-57.0	160.0	49 00.5	-57.2	160.4	48 03.9	-57.3	160.8	47 07.2	-57.5	161.1	46 10.4	-57.6	161.5	12
13	51 49.0	-56.6	159.2	50 52.8	-56.8	159.7	49 56.4	-56.9	160.1	49 00.0	-57.2	160.5	48 03.3	-57.3	160.9	47 06.6	-57.4	161.2	46 09.7	-57.5	161.6	45 12.8	-57.7	161.9	13
14	50 52.4	-56.8	159.8	49 56.0	-56.9	160.2	48 59.5	-57.1	160.6	48 02.8	-57.2	160.9	47 06.0	-57.3	161.3	46 09.2	-57.6	161.6	45 12.2	-57.7	162.0	44 15.1	-57.8	162.3	14
15	49 55.6	-56.9	160.3	48 59.1	-57.1	160.7	48 02.4	-57.2	161.0	47 05.6	-57.4	161.4	46 08.7	-57.5	161.7	45 11.6	-57.6	162.0	44 14.5	-57.7	162.3	43 17.3	-57.9	162.6	15
16	48 58.7	-57.0	160.8	48 02.0	-57.1	161.1	47 05.2	-57.3	161.5	46 08.2	-57.4	161.8	45 11.2	-57.6	162.1	44 14.0	-57.7	162.4	43 16.8	-57.8	162.7	42 19.4	-57.9	163.0	16
17	48 01.7	-57.1	161.2	47 04.9	-57.3	161.6	46 07.9	-57.4	161.9	45 10.8	-57.5	162.2	44 13.6	-57.6	162.5	43 16.3	-57.7	162.8	42 19.0	-57.9	163.1	41 21.5	-57.9	163.3	17
18	47 04.6	-57.2	161.7	46 07.6	-57.3	162.0	45 10.5	-57.5	162.3	44 13.3	-57.6	162.6	43 16.0	-57.8	162.9	42 18.6	-57.9	163.2	41 21.1	-57.9	163.4	40 23.6	-58.1	163.7	18
19	46 07.4	-57.3	162.1	45 10.3	-57.5	162.4	44 13.0	-57.5	162.7	43 15.7	-57.7	163.0	42 18.2	-57.7	163.3	41 20.7	-57.8	163.5	40 23.2	-58.0	163.8	39 25.5	-58.1	164.0	19
20	45 10.1	-57.4	162.6	44 12.8	-57.5	162.8	43 15.5	-57.7	163.1	42 18.0	-57.8	163.4	41 20.5	-57.9	163.6	40 22.9	-58.0	163.9	39 25.2	-58.1	164.1	38 27.4	-58.1	164.3	20
21	44 12.7	-57.5	163.0	43 15.3	-57.6	163.2	42 17.8	-57.7	163.5	41 20.2	-57.8	163.8	40 22.6	-57.9	164.0	39 24.9	-58.0	164.2	38 27.1	-58.1	164.4	37 29.3	-58.2	164.7	21
22	43 15.2	-57.5	163.4	42 17.7	-57.7	163.6	41 20.1	-57.8	163.9	40 22.4	-57.8	164.1	39 24.7	-58.0	164.3	38 26.9	-58.1	164.6	37 29.0	-58.1	164.8	36 31.1	-58.2	165.0	22
23	42 17.7	-57.7	163.7	41 20.0	-57.7	164.0	40 22.3	-57.8	164.2	39 24.6	-58.0	164.5	38 26.7	-58.0	164.7	37 28.8	-58.1	164.9	36 30.9	-58.2	165.1	35 32.9	-58.3	165.3	23
24	41 20.0	-57.7	164.1	40 22.3	-57.8	164.4	39 24.5	-57.9	164.6	38 26.6	-58.0	164.8	37 28.7	-58.1	165.0	36 30.7	-58.2	165.2	35 32.7	-58.3	165.4	34 34.6	-58.3	165.5	24
25	40 22.3	-57.7	164.5	39 24.5	-57.9	164.7	38 26.6	-58.0	164.9	37 28.6	-58.0	165.1	36 30.6	-58.1	165.3	35 32.5	-58.2	165.5	34 34.4	-58.2	165.7	33 36.3	-58.4	165.8	25
26	39 24.6	-57.9	164.8	38 26.6	-57.9	165.0	37 28.6	-58.0	165.2	36 30.6	-58.1	165.4	35 32.5	-58.2	165.6	34 34.3	-58.2	165.8	33 36.2	-58.4	166.0	32 37.9	-58.4	166.1	26
27	38 26.7	-57.9	165.2	37 28.7	-58.0	165.4	36 30.6	-58.1	165.6	35 32.5	-58.2	165.7	34 34.3	-58.2	165.9	33 36.1	-58.3	166.1	32 37.8	-58.3	166.2	31 39.5	-58.4	166.4	27
28	37 28.8	-57.9	165.5	36 30.7	-58.0	165.7	35 32.5	-58.1	165.9	34 34.3	-58.1	166.0	33 36.1	-58.3	166.2	32 37.8	-58.3	166.4	31 39.5	-58.4	166.5	30 41.1	-58.4	166.6	28
29	36 30.9	-58.0	165.8	35 32.7	-58.1	166.0	34 34.4	-58.1	166.2	33 36.2	-58.3	166.3	32 37.8	-58.3	166.5	31 39.5	-58.4	166.6	30 41.1	-58.4	166.8	29 42.7	-58.5	166.9	29
30	35 32.9	-58.1	166.1	34 34.6	-58.1	166.3	33 36.3	-58.2	166.5	32 37.9	-58.2	166.6	31 39.5	-58.3	166.8	30 41.1	-58.4	166.9	29 42.7	-58.5	167.0	28 44.2	-58.5	167.2	30
31	34 34.8	-58.1	166.5	33 36.5	-58.2	166.6	32 38.1	-58.2	166.8	31 39.7	-58.3	166.9	30 41.2	-58.4	167.0	29 42.7	-58.4	167.2	28 44.2	-58.5	167.3	27 45.7	-58.6	167.4	31
32	33 36.7	-58.1	166.8	32 38.3	-58.2	166.9	31 39.9	-58.3	167.0	30 41.4	-58.4	167.2	29 42.8	-58.4	167.3	28 44.3	-58.5	167.4	27 45.7	-58.5	167.6	26 47.1	-58.5	167.7	32
33	32 38.6	-58.2	167.1	31 40.1	-58.2	167.2	30 41.6	-58.3	167.3	29 43.0	-58.3	167.5	28 44.4	-58.4	167.6	27 45.8	-58.4	167.7	26 47.2	-58.5	167.8	25 48.6	-58.6	167.9	33
34	31 40.4	-58.2	167.3	30 41.9	-58.3	167.5	29 43.3	-58.4	167.6	28 44.7	-58.4	167.7	27 46.0	-58.4	167.8	26 47.4	-58.6	167.9	25 48.7	-58.6	168.0	24 50.0	-58.7	168.1	34
35	30 42.2	-58.2	167.6	29 43.6	-58.3	167.7	28 44.9	-58.3	167.9	27 46.3	-58.5	168.0	26 47.6	-58.5	168.1	25 48.8	-58.5	168.2	24 50.1	-58.6	168.3	23 51.3	-58.6	168.4	35
36	29 44.0	-58.3	167.9	28 45.3	-58.4	168.0	27 46.6	-58.4	168.1	26 47.8	-58.4	168.2	25 49.1	-58.5	168.3	24 50.3	-58.5	168.4	23 51.5	-58.6	168.5	22 52.7	-58.6	168.6	36
37	28 45.7	-58.4	168.2	27 46.9	-58.3	168.3	26 48.2	-58.5	168.4	25 49.4	-58.5	168.5	24 50.6	-58.6	168.6	23 51.8	-58.6	168.7	22 52.9	-58.6	168.8	21 54.1	-58.7	168.8	37
38	27 47.3	-58.3	168.4	26 48.6	-58.4	168.5	25 49.7	-58.4	168.6	24 50.9	-58.5	168.7	23 52.0	-58.5	168.8	22 53.2	-58.6	168.9	21 54.3	-58.7	169.0	20 55.4	-58.7	169.1	38
39	26 49.0	-58.4	168.7	25 50.2	-58.5	168.8	24 51.3	-58.5	168.9	23 52.4	-58.5	169.0	22 53.5	-58.6	169.1	21 54.6	-58.6	169.1	20 55.6	-58.6	169.2	19 56.7	-58.7	169.3	39
40	25 50.6	-58.4	169.0	24 51.7	-58.4	169.1	23 52.8	-58.5	169.1	22 53.9	-58.6	169.2	21 54.9	-58.6	169.3	20 56.0	-58.7	169.4	19 57.0	-58.7	169.4	18 58.0	-58.7	169.5	40
41	24 52.2	-58.4	169.2	23 53.3	-58.5	169.3	22 54.3	-58.5	169.4	21 55.3	-58.5	169.5	20 56.3	-58.6	169.5	19 57.3	-58.6	169.6	18 58.3	-58.7	169.7	17 59.3	-58.8	169.7	41
42	23 53.8	-58.5	169.5	22 54.8	-58.5	169.5	21 55.8	-58.6	169.6	20 56.8	-58.6	169.7	19 57.7	-58.6	169.8	18 58.7	-58.7	169.8	17 59.6	-58.7	169.9	17 00.5	-58.7	169.9	42
43	22 55.3	-58.4	169.7	21 56.3	-58.5	169.8	20 57.2	-58.5	169.9	19 58.2	-58.6	169.9	18 59.1	-58.7	170.0	18 00.0	-58.7	170.0	17 00.9	-58.7	170.1	16 01.8	-58.8	170.1	43
44	21 56.9	-58.5	170.0	20 57.8	-58.6	170.0	19 58.7	-58.6	170.1	18 59.6	-58.7	170.1	18 00.4	-58.6	170.2	17 01.3	-58.7	170.3	16 02.2	-58.8	170.3	15 03.0	-58.7	170.4	44
45	20 58.4	-58.5	170.2	19 59.2	-58.5	170.3	19 00.1	-58.6	170.3	18 00.9	-58.6	170.4	17 01.8	-58.7	170.4	16 02.6	-58.7	170.5	15 03.4	-58.7	170.5	14 04.3	-58.8	170.6	45
46	19 59.9	-58.6	170.4	19 00.7	-58.6	170.5	18 01.5	-58.6	170.5	17 02.3	-58.6	170.6	16 03.1	-58.7	170.6	15 03.9	-58.7	170.7	14 04.7	-58.8	170.7	13 05.5	-58.8	170.8	46
47	19 01.3	-58.5	170.7	18 02.1	-58.6	170.7	17 02.9	-58.6	170.8	16 03.7	-58.7	170.8	15 04.4	-58.7	170.9	14 05.2	-58.7	170.9	13 05.9	-58.7	170.9	12 06.7	-58.8	171.0	47
48	18 02.8	-58.6	170.9	17 03.5	-58.6	170.9	16 04.3	-58.7	171.0	15 05.0	-58.7	171.0	14 05.7	-58.7	171.1	13 06.5	-58.8	171.1	12 07.2	-58.8	171.1	11 07.9	-58.8	171.2	48
49	17 04.2	-58.6	171.1	16 04.9	-58.6	171.2	15 05.6	-58.6	171.2	14 06.3	-58.7	171.2	13 07.0	-58.7	171.3	12 07.7	-58.7	171.3	11 08.4	-58.8	171.3	10 09.1	-58.8	171.4	49
50	16 05.6	-58.6	171.3	15 06.3	-58.6	171.4	14 07.0	-58.7	171.4	13 07.6	-58.7	171.5	12 08.3	-58.7	171.5	11 09.0	-58.8	171.5	10 09.6	-58.8	171.6	9 10.3	-58.9	171.6	50
51	15 07.0	-58.6	171.6	14 07.7	-58.7	171.6	13 08.3	-58.7	171.6	12 08.9	-58.7	171.7	11 09.6	-58.8	171.7	10 10.2	-58.8	171.7	9 10.8	-58.8	171.8	8 11.4	-58.8	171.8	51
52	14 08.4	-58.6	171.8	13 09.0	-58.6	171.8	12 09.6	-58.7	171.9	11 10.2	-58.7	171.9	10 10.8	-58.7	171.9	9 11.4	-58.8	171.9	8 12.0	-58.8	172.0	7 12.6	-58.8	172.0	52
53	13 09.8	-58.6	172.0	12 10.4	-58.7	172.0	11 10.9	-58.7	172.1	10 11.5	-58.7	172.1	9 12.1	-58.8	172.1	8 12.6	-58.7	172.1	7 13.2	-58.8	172.2	6 13.8	-58.9	172.2	53
54	12 11.2	-58.7	172.2	11 11.7	-58.7	172.3	10 12.2	-58.7	172.3	9 12.8	-58.7	172.3	8 13.3	-58.7	172.3	7 13.9	-58.8	172.3	6 14.4	-58.8	172.4	5 14.9	-58.8	172.4	54
55	11 12.5	-58.6	172.4	10 13.0	-58.7	172.5	9 13.5	-58.7	172.5	8 14.1	-58.8	172.5	7 14.6	-58.8	172.5	6 15.1	-58.8	172.5	5 15.6	-58.8	172.6	4 16.1	-58.9	172.6	55
56	10 13.9	-58.7	172.7	9 14.3	-58.6	172.7	8 14.8	-58.7	172.7	7 15.3	-58.7	172.7	6 15.8	-58.8	172.7	5 16.3	-58.8	172.7	4 16.8	-58.9	172.8	3 17.2	-58.8	172.8	56
57	9 15.2	-58.7	172.9	8 15.7	-58.7	172.9	7 16.1	-58.7	172.9	6 16.6	-58.8	172.9	5 17.0	-58.7	172.9	4 17.5	-58.8	172.9	3 17.9	-58.8	173.0	2 18.4	-58.9	173.0	57
58	8 16.5	-58.6	173.1	7 17.0	-58.7	173.1	6 17.4	-58.7	173.1	5 17.8	-58.7	173.1	4 18.3	-58.8	173.1	3 18.7	-58.8	173.1	2 19.1	-58.8	173.1	1 19.5	-58.8	173.2	58
59	7 17.9	-58.7	173.3	6 18.3	-58.7	173.3	5 18.7	-58.8	173.3	4 19.1	-58.8	173.3	3 19.5	-58.8	173.3	2 19.9	-58.8	173.3	1 20.3	-58.8	173.3	0 20.7	-58.9	173.3	59
60	6 19.2	-58.7	173.5	5 19.6	-58.8	173.5	4 19.9	-58.7	173.5	3 20.3	-58.7	173.5	2 20.7	-58.8	173.5	1 21.1	-58.8	173.5	0 21.5	-58.9	173.5	0 38.2	+58.8	6.5	60
61	5 20.5	-58.7	173.7	4 20.8	-58.7	173.7	3 21.2	-58.7	173.7	2 21.6	-58.8	173.7	1 21.9	-58.8	173.7	0 22.3	-58.8	173.7	0 37.4	+58.8	6.3	1 37.0	+58.9	6.3	61
62	4 21.8	-58.7	173.9	3 22.1	-58.7	173.9	2 22.5	-58.8	173.9	1 22.8	-58.8	173.9	0 23.1	-58.7	173.9	0 36.5	+58.8	6.1	1 36.2	+58.8	6.1	2 35.9	+58.8	6.1	62
63	3 23.1	-58.7	174.1	2 23.4	-58.7	174.1	1 23.7	-58.7	174.1	0 24.0	-58.7	174.1	0 35.6	+58.8	5.9	1 35.3	+58.8	5.9	2 35.0	+58.8	5.9	3 34.7	+58.8	5.9	63
64	2 24.4	-58.7	174.3	1 24.7	-58.7	174.3	0 25.0	-58.7	174.3	0 34.7	+58.8	5.7	1 34.4	+58.8	5.7	2 34.1	+58.8	5.7	3 33.8	+58.9	5.7	4 33.5	+58.9	5.7	64
65	1 25.7	-58.7	174.5	0 26.0	-58.7	174.5	0 33.7	+58.8	5.5	1 33.5	+58.7	5.5	2 33.2	+58.8	5.5	3 32.9	+58.8	5.5	4 32.7	+58.8	5.5	5 32.4	+58.8	5.5	65
66	0 27.0	-58.7	174.8	0 32.7	+58.8	5.2	1 32.5	+58.7	5.3	2 32.2	+58.8	5.3	3 32.0	+58.8	5.3	4 31.7	+58.8	5.3	5 31.5	+58.8	5.3	6 31.2	+58.9	5.3	66
67	0 31.7	+58.7	5.0	1 31.5	+58.7	5.0	2 31.2	+58.8	5.0	3 31.0	+58.7	5.1	4 30.8	+58.7	5.1	5 30.5	+58.8	5.1	6 30.3	+58.8	5.1	7 30.1	+58.8	5.1	67
68	1 30.4	+58.7	4.8	2 30.2	+58.7	4.8	3 30.0	+58.7	4.8	4 29.7	+58.8	4.8	5 29.5	+58.8	4.9	6 29.3	+58.8	4.9	7 29.1	+58.8	4.9	8 28.9	+58.8	4.9	68
69	2 29.1	+58.7	4.6	3 28.9	+58.7	4.6	4 28.7	+58.7	4.6	5 28.5	+58.7	4.6	6 28.3	+58.8	4.7	7 28.1	+58.8	4.7	8 27.9	+58.8	4.7	9 27.7	+58.8	4.7	69
70	3 27.8	+58.7	4.4	4 27.6	+58.7	4.4	5 27.4	+58.8	4.4	6 27.2	+58.8	4.4	7 27.1	+58.7	4.5	8 26.9	+58.8	4.5	9 26.7	+58.8	4.5	10 26.5	+58.8	4.5	70
71	4 26.5	+58.7	4.2	5 26.3	+58.7	4.2	6 26.2	+58.7	4.2	7 26.0	+58.7	4.2	8 25.8	+58.8	4.2	9 25.7	+58.7	4.3	10 25.5	+58.8	4.3	11 25.3	+58.8	4.3	71
72	5 25.2	+58.7	4.0	6 25.0	+58.7	4.0	7 24.9	+58.7	4.0	8 24.7	+58.8	4.0	9 24.6	+58.7	4.0	10 24.4	+58.8	4.1	11 24.3	+58.8	4.1	12 24.1	+58.8	4.1	72
73	6 23.9	+58.6	3.8	7 23.7	+58.7	3.8	8 23.6	+58.7	3.8	9 23.5	+58.7	3.8	10 23.3	+58.8	3.8	11 23.2	+58.7	3.8	12 23.1	+58.7	3.9	13 22.9	+58.8	3.9	73
74	7 22.5	+58.7	3.6	8 22.4	+58.7	3.6	9 22.3	+58.7	3.6	10 22.2	+58.7	3.6	11 22.1	+58.7	3.6	12 21.9	+58.8	3.6	13 21.8	+58.8	3.7	14 21.7	+58.8	3.7	74
75	8 21.2	+58.7	3.4	9 21.1	+58.7	3.4	10 21.0	+58.7	3.4	11 20.9	+58.7	3.4	12 20.8	+58.7	3.4	13 20.7	+58.7	3.4	14 20.6	+58.7	3.4	15 20.5	+58.7	3.5	75
76	9 19.9	+58.6	3.2	10 19.8	+58.7	3.2	11 19.7	+58.7	3.2	12 19.6	+58.7	3.2	13 19.5	+58.7	3.2	14 19.4	+58.7	3.2	15 19.3	+58.7	3.2	16 19.2	+58.8	3.3	76
77	10 18.5	+58.7	2.9	11 18.5	+58.6	3.0	12 18.4	+58.6	3.0	13 18.3	+58.7	3.0	14 18.2	+58.7	3.0	15 18.1	+58.7	3.0	16 18.0	+58.8	3.0	17 18.0	+58.7	3.0	77
78	11 17.2	+58.6	2.7	12 17.1	+58.7	2.7	13 17.0	+58.7	2.8	14 17.0	+58.7	2.8	15 16.9	+58.7	2.8	16 16.8	+58.7	2.8	17 16.8	+58.7	2.8	18 16.7	+58.7	2.8	78
79	12 15.8	+58.7	2.5	13 15.8	+58.6	2.5	14 15.7	+58.7	2.5	15 15.7	+58.6	2.6	16 15.6	+58.7	2.6	17 15.5	+58.7	2.6	18 15.5	+58.7	2.6	19 15.4	+58.7	2.6	79
80	13 14.5	+58.6	2.3	14 14.4	+58.6	2.3	15 14.4	+58.6	2.3	16 14.3	+58.7	2.3	17 14.3	+58.6	2.3	18 14.2	+58.7	2.4	19 14.2	+58.6	2.4	20 14.1	+58.7	2.4	80
81	14 13.1	+58.6	2.1	15 13.0	+58.7	2.1	16 13.0	+58.6	2.1	17 13.0	+58.6	2.1	18 12.9	+58.7	2.1	19 12.9	+58.6	2.1	20 12.8	+58.7	2.1	21 12.8	+58.7	2.2	81
82	15 11.7	+58.6	1.9	16 11.7	+58.6	1.9	17 11.6	+58.6	1.9	18 11.6	+58.6	1.9	19 11.6	+58.6	1.9	20 11.5	+58.7	1.9	21 11.5	+58.6	1.9	22 11.5	+58.6	1.9	82
83	16 10.3	+58.6	1.6	17 10.3	+58.6	1.6	18 10.2	+58.6	1.7	19 10.2	+58.6	1.7	20 10.2	+58.6	1.7	21 10.2	+58.6	1.7	22 10.1	+58.7	1.7	23 10.1	+58.6	1.7	83
84	17 08.9	+58.5	1.4	18 08.9	+58.5	1.4	19 08.8	+58.6	1.4	20 08.8	+58.6	1.4	21 08.8	+58.6	1.4	22 08.8	+58.6	1.5	23 08.8	+58.6	1.5	24 08.7	+58.6	1.5	84
85	18 07.4	+58.6	1.2	19 07.4	+58.6	1.2	20 07.4	+58.6	1.2	21 07.4	+58.6	1.2	22 07.4	+58.6	1.2	23 07.4	+58.5	1.2	24 07.4	+58.5	1.2	25 07.3	+58.6	1.2	85
86	19 06.0	+58.5	1.0	20 06.0	+58.5	1.0	21 06.0	+58.5	1.0	22 06.0	+58.5	1.0	23 06.0	+58.5	1.0	24 05.9	+58.6	1.0	25 05.9	+58.6	1.0	26 05.9	+58.6	1.0	86
87	20 04.5	+58.5	0.7	21 04.5	+58.5	0.7	22 04.5	+58.5	0.7	23 04.5	+58.5	0.7	24 04.5	+58.5	0.7	25 04.5	+58.5	0.7	26 04.5	+58.5	0.8	27 04.5	+58.5	0.8	87
88	21 03.0	+58.5	0.5	22 03.0	+58.5	0.5	23 03.0	+58.5	0.5	24 03.0	+58.5	0.5	25 03.0	+58.5	0.5	26 03.0	+58.5	0.5	27 03.0	+58.5	0.5	28 03.0	+58.5	0.5	88
89	22 01.5	+58.5	0.2	23 01.5	+58.5	0.2	24 01.5	+58.5	0.2	25 01.5	+58.5	0.2	26 01.5	+58.5	0.3	27 01.5	+58.5	0.3	28 01.5	+58.5	0.3	29 01.5	+58.5	0.3	89
90	23 00.0	+58.5	0.0	24 00.0	+58.4	0.0	25 00.0	+58.4	0.0	26 00.0	+58.4	0.0	27 00.0	+58.4	0.0	28 00.0	+58.4	0.0	29 00.0	+58.4	0.0	30 00.0	+58.4	0.0	90
	23°			24°			25°			26°			27°			28°			29°			30°			

S. Lat. { L.H.A. greater than 180° ....Zn=180°–Z; L.H.A. less than 180°...........Zn=180°+Z

N. Lat. {L.H.A. greater than 180° .....Zn=Z
{L.H.A. less than 180°............Zn=360°−Z

	23°			24°			25°			26°			27°			28°			29°			30°			
Dec.	Hc	d	Z	Hc	d	Z	Hc	d	Z	Hc	d	Z	Hc	d	Z	Hc	d	Z	Hc	d	Z	Hc	d	Z	Dec.
°	° ′	′	°	° ′	′	°	° ′	′	°	° ′	′	°	° ′	′	°	° ′	′	°	° ′	′	°	° ′	′	°	°
0	63 16.4	+51.9	147.5	62 25.5	+52.5	148.5	61 34.1	+53.1	149.5	60 42.2	+53.5	150.4	59 49.8	+54.0	151.2	58 57.0	+54.5	152.0	58 03.8	+54.9	152.8	57 10.3	+55.2	153.5	0
1	64 08.3	+51.3	146.3	63 18.0	+52.0	147.4	62 27.2	+52.6	148.5	61 35.7	+53.2	149.4	60 43.8	+53.7	150.3	59 51.5	+54.1	151.2	58 58.7	+54.6	152.0	58 05.5	+55.0	152.8	1
2	64 59.6	+50.6	145.1	64 10.0	+51.4	146.3	63 19.8	+52.0	147.4	62 28.9	+52.7	148.4	61 37.5	+53.3	149.4	60 45.6	+53.8	150.3	59 53.3	+54.2	151.2	59 00.5	+54.6	152.0	2
3	65 50.2	+50.0	143.8	65 01.4	+50.8	145.1	64 11.8	+51.6	146.3	63 21.6	+52.2	147.4	62 30.8	+52.8	148.4	61 39.4	+53.4	149.4	60 47.5	+53.9	150.3	59 55.1	+54.4	151.2	3
4	66 40.2	+49.2	142.5	65 52.2	+50.1	143.8	65 03.4	+50.9	145.1	64 13.8	+51.7	146.3	63 23.6	+52.3	147.4	62 32.8	+52.9	148.4	61 41.4	+53.5	149.4	60 49.5	+54.0	150.3	4
5	67 29.4	+48.4	141.0	66 42.3	+49.4	142.5	65 54.3	+50.3	143.8	65 05.5	+51.1	145.1	64 15.9	+51.9	146.3	63 25.7	+52.5	147.4	62 34.9	+53.0	148.4	61 43.5	+53.6	149.4	5
6	68 17.8	+47.4	139.4	67 31.7	+48.5	141.0	66 44.6	+49.5	142.5	65 56.6	+50.4	143.8	65 07.8	+51.2	145.1	64 18.2	+51.9	146.3	63 27.9	+52.6	147.4	62 37.1	+53.2	148.5	6
7	69 05.2	+46.3	137.7	68 20.2	+47.6	139.4	67 34.1	+48.7	141.0	66 47.0	+49.7	142.5	65 59.0	+50.5	143.8	65 10.1	+51.4	145.1	64 20.5	+52.1	146.3	63 30.3	+52.7	147.4	7
8	69 51.5	+45.2	135.9	69 07.8	+46.5	137.7	68 22.8	+47.7	139.4	67 36.7	+48.8	141.0	66 49.5	+49.8	142.5	66 01.5	+50.7	143.9	65 12.6	+51.5	145.2	64 23.0	+52.2	146.4	8
9	70 36.7	+43.8	134.0	69 54.3	+45.3	135.9	69 10.5	+46.7	137.8	68 25.5	+47.9	139.5	67 39.3	+49.0	141.1	66 52.2	+50.0	142.5	66 04.1	+50.9	143.9	65 15.2	+51.7	145.2	9
10	71 20.5	+42.3	131.9	70 39.6	+44.0	134.0	69 57.2	+45.5	136.0	69 13.4	+46.9	137.8	68 28.3	+48.1	139.5	67 42.2	+49.1	141.1	66 55.0	+50.1	142.6	66 06.9	+51.0	144.0	10
11	72 02.8	+40.6	129.6	71 23.6	+42.5	131.9	70 42.7	+44.2	134.0	70 00.3	+45.7	136.0	69 16.4	+47.1	137.9	68 31.3	+48.3	139.6	67 45.1	+49.4	141.2	66 57.9	+50.3	142.6	11
12	72 43.4	+38.7•	127.2	72 06.1	+40.8	129.6	71 26.9	+42.7	131.9	70 46.0	+44.4	134.1	70 03.5	+45.9	136.1	69 19.6	+47.2	137.9	68 34.5	+48.4	139.6	67 48.2	+49.5	141.2	12
13	73 22.1	+36.6•	124.6	72 46.9	+39.0•	127.2	72 09.6	+41.0	129.7	71 30.4	+42.9	132.0	70 49.4	+44.6	134.1	70 06.8	+46.1	136.1	69 22.9	+47.4	138.0	68 37.7	+48.7	139.7	13
14	73 58.7	+34.2•	121.7	73 25.9	+36.8•	124.6	72 50.6	+39.2	127.3	72 13.3	+41.2	129.8	71 34.0	+43.1	132.1	70 52.9	+44.8	134.2	70 10.3	+46.4	136.2	69 26.4	+47.6	138.1	14
15	74 32.9	+31.6•	118.7	74 02.7	+34.4•	121.8	73 29.8	+37.1•	124.7	72 54.5	+39.4	127.3	72 17.1	+41.5	129.8	71 37.7	+43.4	132.1	70 56.7	+45.0	134.3	70 14.0	+46.5	136.3	15
16	75 04.5	+28.6•	115.5	74 37.1	+31.8•	118.7	74 06.9	+34.7•	121.8	73 33.9	+37.3•	124.7	72 58.6	+39.6	127.4	72 21.1	+41.7	129.9	71 41.7	+43.6	132.2	71 00.5	+45.3	134.4	16
17	75 33.1	+25.4•	112.0	75 08.9	+28.9•	115.5	74 41.6	+32.0•	118.8	74 11.2	+35.0•	121.9	73 38.2	+37.6•	124.8	73 02.8	+39.9	127.5	72 25.3	+41.9	130.0	71 45.8	+43.8	132.3	17
18	75 58.5	+21.8•	108.3	75 37.8	+25.6•	112.0	75 13.6	+29.1•	115.5	74 46.2	+32.3•	118.9	74 15.8	+35.2•	122.0	73 42.7	+37.8•	124.9	73 07.2	+40.2	127.6	72 29.6	+42.2	130.1	18
19	76 20.3	+18.1•	104.4	76 03.4	+22.1•	108.3	75 42.7	+25.9•	112.1	75 18.5	+29.3•	115.6	74 51.0	+32.5•	118.9	74 20.5	+35.5•	122.1	73 47.4	+38.0•	125.0	73 11.8	+40.4	127.7	19
20	76 38.4	+13.9•	100.3	76 25.5	+18.2•	104.4	76 08.6	+22.3•	108.3	75 47.8	+26.2•	112.1	75 23.5	+29.7•	115.7	74 56.0	+32.8•	119.0	74 25.4	+35.8•	122.2	73 52.2	+38.3•	125.1	20
21	76 52.3	+9.6•	96.1	76 43.7	+14.2•	100.3	76 30.9	+18.5•	104.4	76 14.0	+22.5•	108.4	75 53.2	+26.3•	112.1	75 28.8	+29.9•	115.7	75 01.2	+33.1•	119.1	74 30.5	+36.0•	122.3	21
22	77 01.9	+5.2•	91.7	76 57.9	+9.8•	96.0	76 49.4	+14.3•	100.3	76 36.5	+18.7•	104.4	76 19.5	+22.8•	108.4	75 58.7	+26.6•	112.2	75 34.3	+30.1•	115.8	75 06.5	+33.4•	119.2	22
23	77 07.1	+0.6•	87.3	77 07.7	+5.2•	91.6	77 03.7	+9.9•	96.0	76 55.2	+14.5•	100.3	76 42.3	+18.9•	104.4	76 25.3	+23.1•	108.5	76 04.4	+26.9•	112.3	75 39.9	+30.5•	115.9	23
24	77 07.7	-4.0•	82.8	77 12.9	+0.7•	87.1	77 13.6	+5.4•	91.6	77 09.7	+10.1•	95.9	77 01.2	+14.8•	100.3	76 48.4	+19.1•	104.5	76 31.3	+23.3•	108.5	76 10.4	+27.1•	112.4	24
25	77 03.7	-8.5•	78.3	77 13.6	-3.9•	82.6	77 19.0	+0.8•	87.0	77 19.8	+5.6•	91.5	77 16.0	+10.3•	95.9	77 07.5	+14.9•	100.3	76 54.6	+19.4•	104.5	76 37.5	+23.6•	108.6	25
26	76 55.2	-12.9•	73.9	77 09.7	-8.5•	78.1	77 19.8	-3.8•	82.5	77 25.4	+0.9•	86.9	77 26.3	+5.6•	91.4	77 22.4	+10.5•	95.9	77 14.0	+15.2•	100.3	77 01.1	+19.6•	104.5	26
27	76 42.3	-17.0•	69.6	77 01.2	-12.8•	73.7	77 16.0	-8.5•	77.9	77 26.3	-3.9•	82.3	77 31.9	+1.0•	86.8	77 32.9	+5.8•	91.3	77 29.2	+10.6•	95.8	77 20.7	+15.4•	100.3	27
28	76 25.3	-20.9•	65.5	76 48.4	-17.1•	69.4	77 07.5	-12.9•	73.5	77 22.4	-8.4•	77.7	77 32.9	-3.7•	82.2	77 38.7	+1.1•	86.7	77 39.8	+6.0•	91.3	77 36.1	+10.8•	95.8	28
29	76 04.4	-24.5•	61.5	76 31.3	-20.9•	65.2	76 54.6	-17.1•	69.1	77 14.0	-12.9•	73.2	77 29.2	-8.5•	77.6	77 39.8	-3.7•	82.0	77 45.8	+1.1•	86.6	77 46.9	+6.1•	91.2	29
30	75 39.9	-27.8•	57.8	76 10.4	-24.6•	61.2	76 37.5	-21.0•	64.9	77 01.1	-17.1•	68.9	77 20.7	-12.9•	73.0	77 36.1	-8.4•	77.4	77 46.9	-3.7•	81.9	77 53.0	+1.2•	86.5	30
31	75 12.1	-30.8•	54.3	75 45.8	-28.0•	57.5	76 16.5	-24.7•	60.9	76 44.0	-21.2•	64.6	77 07.8	-17.2•	68.6	77 27.7	-13.0•	72.8	77 43.2	-8.4•	77.2	77 54.2	-3.6•	81.7	31
32	74 41.3	-33.6•	51.0	75 17.8	-30.9•	53.9	75 51.8	-28.1•	57.1	76 22.8	-24.8•	60.6	76 50.6	-21.3•	64.3	77 14.7	-17.3•	68.3	77 34.8	-13.0•	72.5	77 50.6	-8.4•	77.0	32
33	74 07.7	-36.0•	47.9	74 46.9	-33.7•	50.6	75 23.7	-31.1•	53.6	75 58.0	-28.2•	56.8	76 29.3	-24.9•	60.3	76 57.4	-21.4•	64.0	77 21.8	-17.4•	68.0	77 42.2	-13.1•	72.3	33
34	73 31.7	-38.2•	45.0	74 13.2	-36.2•	47.5	74 52.6	-33.8•	50.2	75 29.8	-31.2•	53.2	76 04.4	-28.3•	56.4	76 36.0	-25.0•	59.9	77 04.4	-21.5•	63.7	77 29.1	-17.5•	67.7	34
35	72 53.5	-40.2	42.3	73 37.0	-38.3•	44.6	74 18.8	-36.3•	47.1	74 58.6	-34.0•	49.9	75 36.1	-31.4•	52.8	76 11.0	-28.5•	56.1	76 42.9	-25.2•	59.6	77 11.6	-21.6•	63.4	35
36	72 13.3	-41.8	39.9	72 58.7	-40.3	42.0	73 42.5	-38.5•	44.2	74 24.6	-36.5•	46.7	75 04.7	-34.2•	49.5	75 42.5	-31.6•	52.4	76 17.7	-28.7•	55.7	76 50.0	-25.4•	59.2	36
37	71 31.5	-43.5	37.6	72 18.4	-42.0	39.5	73 04.0	-40.4	41.6	73 48.1	-38.6•	43.8	74 30.5	-36.6•	46.3	75 10.9	-34.3•	49.1	75 49.0	-31.7•	52.1	76 24.6	-28.8•	55.3	37
38	70 48.0	-44.8	35.4	71 36.4	-43.6	37.2	72 23.6	-42.2	39.1	73 09.5	-40.6	41.1	73 53.9	-38.8•	43.4	74 36.6	-36.8•	45.9	75 17.3	-34.5•	48.6	75 55.8	-32.0•	51.6	38
39	70 03.2	-46.0	33.4	70 52.8	-44.9	35.0	71 41.4	-43.7	36.8	72 28.9	-42.3	38.7	73 15.1	-40.8	40.7	73 59.8	-39.0•	43.0	74 42.8	-37.0•	45.5	75 23.8	-34.7•	48.2	39
40	69 17.2	-47.2	31.6	70 07.9	-46.2	33.0	70 57.7	-45.1	34.6	71 46.6	-43.9	36.3	72 34.3	-42.5	38.2	73 20.8	-40.9	40.3	74 05.8	-39.2•	42.6	74 49.1	-37.2•	45.0	40
41	68 30.0	-48.1	29.9	69 21.7	-47.3	31.2	70 12.6	-46.3	32.6	71 02.7	-45.2	34.2	71 51.8	-44.0	35.9	72 39.9	-42.7	37.8	73 26.6	-41.1	39.8	74 11.9	-39.3•	42.1	41
42	67 41.9	-49.0	28.3	68 34.4	-48.2	29.5	69 26.3	-47.4	30.8	70 17.5	-46.5	32.2	71 07.8	-45.4	33.8	71 57.2	-44.2	35.5	72 45.5	-42.8	37.3	73 32.6	-41.4	39.4	42
43	66 52.9	-49.8	26.8	67 46.2	-49.1	27.9	68 38.9	-48.3	29.1	69 31.0	-47.5	30.4	70 22.4	-46.6	31.8	71 13.0	-45.5	33.3	72 02.7	-44.4	35.0	72 51.2	-43.0	36.9	43
44	66 03.1	-50.5	25.4	66 57.1	-49.9	26.4	67 50.6	-49.3	27.5	68 43.5	-48.5	28.7	69 35.8	-47.6	29.9	70 27.5	-46.8	31.3	71 18.3	-45.7	32.9	72 08.2	-44.6	34.6	44
45	65 12.6	-51.2	24.1	66 07.2	-50.6	25.0	67 01.3	-50.0	26.0	67 55.0	-49.3	27.1	68 48.2	-48.7	28.2	69 40.7	-47.8	29.5	70 32.6	-46.9	30.9	71 23.6	-45.8	32.4	45
46	64 21.4	-51.7	22.9	65 16.6	-51.3	23.7	66 11.3	-50.7	24.6	67 05.7	-50.2	25.6	67 59.5	-49.5	26.6	68 52.9	-48.8	27.8	69 45.7	-48.0	29.1	70 37.8	-47.1	30.4	46
47	63 29.7	-52.2	21.7	64 25.3	-51.8	22.5	65 20.6	-51.4	23.3	66 15.5	-50.8	24.2	67 10.0	-50.2	25.2	68 04.1	-49.6	26.2	68 57.7	-48.9	27.4	69 50.7	-48.2	28.6	47
48	62 37.5	-52.8	20.6	63 33.5	-52.3	21.3	64 29.2	-51.9	22.1	65 24.7	-51.5	22.9	66 19.8	-51.0	23.8	67 14.5	-50.4	24.7	68 08.8	-49.8	25.8	69 02.5	-49.1	26.9	48
49	61 44.7	-53.1	19.6	62 41.2	-52.9	20.2	63 37.3	-52.4	20.9	64 33.2	-52.0	21.7	65 28.8	-51.5	22.5	66 24.1	-51.1	23.4	67 19.0	-50.5	24.3	68 13.4	-49.9	25.3	49
50	60 51.6	-53.6	18.6	61 48.3	-53.2	19.2	62 44.9	-52.9	19.9	63 41.2	-52.5	20.5	64 37.3	-52.2	21.3	65 33.0	-51.7	22.1	66 28.5	-51.2	22.9	67 23.5	-50.6	23.9	50
51	59 58.0	-53.9	17.7	60 55.1	-53.6	18.3	61 52.0	-53.3	18.8	62 48.7	-53.0	19.5	63 45.1	-52.6	20.1	64 41.3	-52.2	20.9	65 37.3	-51.9	21.6	66 32.9	-51.4	22.5	51
52	59 04.1	-54.2	16.8	60 01.5	-54.0	17.3	60 58.7	-53.7	17.9	61 55.7	-53.4	18.5	62 52.5	-53.1	19.1	63 49.1	-52.8	19.7	64 45.4	-52.3	20.4	65 41.5	-51.9	21.2	52
53	58 09.9	-54.5	16.0	59 07.5	-54.3	16.5	60 05.0	-54.1	17.0	61 02.3	-53.8	17.5	61 59.4	-53.5	18.1	62 56.3	-53.1	18.7	63 53.1	-52.9	19.3	64 49.6	-52.5	20.0	53
54	57 15.4	-54.9	15.2	58 13.2	-54.6	15.7	59 10.9	-54.4	16.1	60 08.5	-54.2	16.6	61 05.9	-53.9	17.1	62 03.2	-53.6	17.7	63 00.2	-53.3	18.3	63 57.1	-53.0	18.9	54
55	56 20.5	-55.0	14.5	57 18.6	-54.9	14.9	58 16.5	-54.7	15.3	59 14.3	-54.4	15.7	60 12.0	-54.2	16.2	61 09.6	-54.0	16.7	62 06.9	-53.7	17.3	63 04.1	-53.4	17.8	55
56	55 25.5	-55.3	13.8	56 23.7	-55.1	14.1	57 21.8	-54.9	14.5	58 19.9	-54.8	14.9	59 17.8	-54.6	15.4	60 15.6	-54.3	15.8	61 13.2	-54.0	16.3	62 10.7	-53.8	16.8	56
57	54 30.2	-55.5	13.1	55 28.6	-55.4	13.4	56 26.9	-55.2	13.8	57 25.1	-55.0	14.2	58 23.2	-54.8	14.6	59 21.3	-54.7	15.0	60 19.2	-54.5	15.4	61 16.9	-54.1	15.9	57
58	53 34.7	-55.8	12.5	54 33.2	-55.6	12.8	55 31.7	-55.4	13.1	56 30.1	-55.3	13.4	57 28.4	-55.1	13.8	58 26.6	-54.9	14.2	59 24.7	-54.7	14.6	60 22.8	-54.6	15.0	58
59	52 38.9	-55.9	11.9	53 37.6	-55.7	12.1	54 36.3	-55.7	12.4	55 34.8	-55.5	12.7	56 33.3	-55.3	13.1	57 31.7	-55.2	13.4	58 30.0	-55.0	13.8	59 28.2	-54.8	14.2	59
60	51 43.0	-56.0	11.3	52 41.9	-56.0	11.5	53 40.6	-55.8	11.8	54 39.3	-55.7	12.1	55 38.0	-55.6	12.4	56 36.5	-55.4	12.7	57 35.0	-55.2	13.0	58 33.4	-55.0	13.4	60
61	50 47.0	-56.3	10.7	51 45.9	-56.1	10.9	52 44.8	-56.0	11.2	53 43.6	-55.9	11.4	54 42.4	-55.8	11.7	55 41.1	-55.6	12.0	56 39.8	-55.5	12.3	57 38.4	-55.4	12.7	61
62	49 50.7	-56.3	10.1	50 49.8	-56.3	10.4	51 48.8	-56.2	10.6	52 47.7	-56.0	10.8	53 46.6	-55.9	11.1	54 45.5	-55.8	11.4	55 44.3	-55.7	11.6	56 43.0	-55.5	11.9	62
63	48 54.4	-56.6	9.6	49 53.5	-56.4	9.8	50 52.6	-56.3	10.0	51 51.7	-56.3	10.2	52 50.7	-56.2	10.5	53 49.7	-56.1	10.7	54 48.6	-55.9	11.0	55 47.5	-55.8	11.3	63
64	47 57.8	-56.6	9.1	48 57.1	-56.6	9.3	49 56.3	-56.5	9.5	50 55.4	-56.4	9.7	51 54.5	-56.3	9.9	52 53.6	-56.2	10.1	53 52.7	-56.1	10.4	54 51.7	-56.0	10.6	64
65	47 01.2	-56.8	8.6	48 00.5	-56.7	8.8	48 59.8	-56.6	9.0	49 59.0	-56.5	9.1	50 58.2	-56.4	9.3	51 57.4	-56.3	9.5	52 56.6	-56.3	9.8	53 55.7	-56.2	10.0	65
66	46 04.4	-56.9	8.2	47 03.8	-56.8	8.3	48 03.2	-56.8	8.5	49 02.5	-56.7	8.6	50 01.8	-56.6	8.8	51 01.1	-56.5	9.0	52 00.3	-56.4	9.2	52 59.5	-56.3	9.4	66
67	45 07.5	-56.9	7.7	46 07.0	-56.9	7.8	47 06.4	-56.8	8.0	48 05.8	-56.8	8.1	49 05.2	-56.7	8.3	50 04.6	-56.7	8.5	51 03.9	-56.6	8.7	52 03.2	-56.5	8.8	67
68	44 10.6	-57.1	7.3	45 10.1	-57.1	7.4	46 09.6	-57.0	7.5	47 09.0	-56.9	7.7	48 08.5	-56.9	7.8	49 07.9	-56.8	8.0	50 07.3	-56.7	8.1	51 06.7	-56.6	8.3	68
69	43 13.5	-57.2	6.8	44 13.0	-57.1	6.9	45 12.6	-57.1	7.1	46 12.1	-57.0	7.2	47 11.6	-56.9	7.3	48 11.1	-56.8	7.5	49 10.6	-56.8	7.6	50 10.1	-56.8	7.8	69
70	42 16.3	-57.3	6.4	43 15.9	-57.2	6.5	44 15.5	-57.1	6.6	45 15.1	-57.1	6.7	46 14.7	-57.1	6.9	47 14.3	-57.1	7.0	48 13.8	-57.0	7.1	49 13.3	-56.9	7.3	70
71	41 19.0	-57.3	6.0	42 18.7	-57.3	6.1	43 18.4	-57.3	6.2	44 18.0	-57.2	6.3	45 17.6	-57.1	6.4	46 17.2	-57.1	6.5	47 16.8	-57.0	6.7	48 16.4	-57.0	6.8	71
72	40 21.7	-57.4	5.6	41 21.4	-57.4	5.7	42 21.1	-57.3	5.8	43 20.8	-57.3	5.9	44 20.5	-57.3	6.0	45 20.1	-57.2	6.1	46 19.8	-57.2	6.2	47 19.4	-57.1	6.3	72
73	39 24.3	-57.5	5.3	40 24.0	-57.4	5.3	41 23.8	-57.5	5.4	42 23.5	-57.4	5.5	43 23.2	-57.3	5.6	44 22.9	-57.3	5.7	45 22.6	-57.2	5.8	46 22.3	-57.2	5.9	73
74	38 26.8	-57.6	4.9	39 26.6	-57.6	5.0	40 26.3	-57.5	5.0	41 26.1	-57.5	5.1	42 25.9	-57.5	5.2	43 25.6	-57.4	5.3	44 25.4	-57.4	5.4	45 25.1	-57.3	5.5	74
75	37 29.2	-57.6	4.5	38 29.0	-57.5	4.6	39 28.8	-57.5	4.7	40 28.6	-57.5	4.7	41 28.4	-57.5	4.8	42 28.2	-57.4	4.9	43 28.0	-57.4	4.9	44 27.8	-57.4	5.0	75
76	36 31.6	-57.7	4.2	37 31.5	-57.7	4.2	38 31.3	-57.6	4.3	39 31.1	-57.6	4.4	40 30.9	-57.5	4.4	41 30.8	-57.6	4.5	42 30.6	-57.5	4.6	43 30.4	-57.5	4.6	76
77	35 33.9	-57.7	3.8	36 33.8	-57.7	3.9	37 33.7	-57.7	3.9	38 33.5	-57.6	4.0	39 33.4	-57.7	4.0	40 33.2	-57.6	4.1	41 33.1	-57.6	4.2	42 32.9	-57.6	4.2	77
78	34 36.2	-57.8	3.5	35 36.1	-57.8	3.5	36 36.0	-57.8	3.6	37 35.9	-57.8	3.6	38 35.7	-57.7	3.7	39 35.6	-57.7	3.7	40 35.5	-57.7	3.8	41 35.3	-57.6	3.9	78
79	33 38.4	-57.8	3.2	34 38.3	-57.8	3.2	35 38.2	-57.8	3.3	36 38.1	-57.8	3.3	37 38.0	-57.7	3.3	38 37.9	-57.7	3.4	39 37.8	-57.7	3.4	40 37.7	-57.7	3.5	79
80	32 40.6	-57.9	2.9	33 40.5	-57.9	2.9	34 40.4	-57.8	2.9	35 40.3	-57.8	3.0	36 40.3	-57.9	3.0	37 40.2	-57.8	3.0	38 40.1	-57.8	3.1	39 40.0	-57.8	3.1	80
81	31 42.7	-57.9	2.5	32 42.6	-57.9	2.6	33 42.6	-57.9	2.6	34 42.5	-57.9	2.6	35 42.4	-57.8	2.7	36 42.4	-57.9	2.7	37 42.3	-57.8	2.7	38 42.2	-57.8	2.8	81
82	30 44.8	-58.0	2.2	31 44.7	-57.9	2.3	32 44.7	-58.0	2.3	33 44.6	-57.9	2.3	34 44.6	-58.0	2.3	35 44.5	-57.9	2.4	36 44.5	-57.9	2.4	37 44.4	-57.9	2.4	82
83	29 46.8	-58.0	1.9	30 46.8	-58.0	2.0	31 46.7	-58.0	2.0	32 46.7	-58.0	2.0	33 46.6	-57.9	2.0	34 46.6	-58.0	2.1	35 46.6	-58.0	2.1	36 46.5	-57.9	2.1	83
84	28 48.8	-58.1	1.7	29 48.8	-58.1	1.7	30 48.7	-58.0	1.7	31 48.7	-58.0	1.7	32 48.7	-58.0	1.7	33 48.6	-58.0	1.7	34 48.6	-58.0	1.8	35 48.6	-58.0	1.8	84
85	27 50.7	-58.1	1.4	28 50.7	-58.1	1.4	29 50.7	-58.1	1.4	30 50.7	-58.1	1.4	31 50.7	-58.1	1.4	32 50.6	-58.0	1.4	33 50.6	-58.0	1.5	34 50.6	-58.0	1.5	85
86	26 52.6	-58.1	1.1	27 52.6	-58.1	1.1	28 52.6	-58.1	1.1	29 52.6	-58.1	1.1	30 52.6	-58.1	1.1	31 52.6	-58.1	1.1	32 52.6	-58.1	1.2	33 52.6	-58.1	1.2	86
87	25 54.5	-58.1	0.8	26 54.5	-58.1	0.8	27 54.5	-58.1	0.8	28 54.5	-58.1	0.8	29 54.5	-58.1	0.8	30 54.5	-58.1	0.8	31 54.5	-58.1	0.9	32 54.5	-58.1	0.9	87
88	24 56.4	-58.2	0.5	25 56.4	-58.2	0.5	26 56.4	-58.2	0.5	27 56.4	-58.2	0.5	28 56.4	-58.2	0.6	29 56.4	-58.2	0.6	30 56.4	-58.2	0.6	31 56.4	-58.2	0.6	88
89	23 58.2	-58.2	0.3	24 58.2	-58.2	0.3	25 58.2	-58.2	0.3	26 58.2	-58.2	0.3	27 58.2	-58.2	0.3	28 58.2	-58.2	0.3	29 58.2	-58.2	0.3	30 58.2	-58.2	0.3	89
90	23 00.0	-58.2	0.0	24 00.0	-58.2	0.0	25 00.0	-58.2	0.0	26 00.0	-58.2	0.0	27 00.0	-58.2	0.0	28 00.0	-58.2	0.0	29 00.0	-58.2	0.0	30 00.0	-58.2	0.0	90
	23°			24°			25°			26°			27°			28°			29°			30°			

Dec.	23° Hc	d	Z	24° Hc	d	Z	25° Hc	d	Z	26° Hc	d	Z	27° Hc	d	Z	28° Hc	d	Z	29° Hc	d	Z	30° Hc	d	Z	Dec.
°	° ′	′	°	° ′	′	°	° ′	′	°	° ′	′	°	° ′	′	°	° ′	′	°	° ′	′	°	° ′	′	°	°
0	63 16.4	−52.4	147.5	62 25.5	−52.9	148.5	61 34.1	−53.5	149.5	60 42.2	−53.9	150.4	59 49.8	−54.3	151.2	58 57.0	−54.7	152.0	58 03.8	−55.1	152.8	57 10.3	−55.4	153.5	0
1	62 24.0	−52.8	148.5	61 32.6	−53.4	149.5	60 40.6	−53.8	150.4	59 48.3	−54.3	151.3	58 55.5	−54.7	152.1	58 02.3	−55.1	152.8	57 08.7	−55.3	153.5	56 14.9	−55.7	154.2	1
2	61 31.2	−53.3	149.5	60 39.2	−53.7	150.4	59 46.8	−54.2	151.3	58 54.0	−54.6	152.1	58 00.8	−55.0	152.8	57 07.2	−55.3	153.6	56 13.4	−55.6	154.2	55 19.2	−55.9	154.9	2
3	60 37.9	−53.6	150.5	59 45.5	−54.1	151.3	58 52.6	−54.4	152.1	57 59.4	−54.8	152.9	57 05.8	−55.2	153.6	56 11.9	−55.5	154.3	55 17.8	−55.8	154.9	54 23.3	−56.1	155.5	3
4	59 44.3	−54.0	151.4	58 51.4	−54.4	152.2	57 58.2	−54.8	152.9	57 04.6	−55.2	153.6	56 10.6	−55.4	154.3	55 16.4	−55.7	154.9	54 22.0	−56.0	155.5	53 27.2	−56.2	156.1	4
5	58 50.3	−54.3	152.2	57 57.0	−54.7	153.0	57 03.4	−55.0	153.7	56 09.4	−55.3	154.4	55 15.2	−55.6	155.0	54 20.7	−55.9	155.6	53 26.0	−56.2	156.1	52 31.0	−56.4	156.7	5
6	57 56.0	−54.6	153.1	57 02.3	−54.9	153.8	56 08.4	−55.3	154.4	55 14.1	−55.6	155.0	54 19.6	−55.9	155.6	53 24.8	−56.1	156.2	52 29.8	−56.4	156.7	51 34.6	−56.6	157.2	6
7	57 01.4	−54.9	153.8	56 07.4	−55.2	154.5	55 13.1	−55.5	155.1	54 18.5	−55.8	155.7	53 23.7	−56.0	156.3	52 28.7	−56.3	156.8	51 33.4	−56.5	157.3	50 38.0	−56.7	157.8	7
8	56 06.5	−55.1	154.6	55 12.2	−55.5	155.2	54 17.6	−55.7	155.8	53 22.7	−55.9	156.3	52 27.7	−56.2	156.8	51 32.4	−56.4	157.3	50 36.9	−56.6	157.8	49 41.3	−56.8	158.3	8
9	55 11.4	−55.4	155.3	54 16.7	−55.6	155.8	53 21.9	−55.9	156.4	52 26.8	−56.2	156.9	51 31.5	−56.4	157.4	50 36.0	−56.6	157.9	49 40.3	−56.8	158.3	48 44.5	−57.0	158.8	9
10	54 16.0	−55.6	155.9	53 21.1	−55.8	156.5	52 26.0	−56.1	157.0	51 30.6	−56.3	157.5	50 35.1	−56.5	158.0	49 39.4	−56.7	158.4	48 43.5	−56.8	158.8	47 47.5	−57.0	159.2	10
11	53 20.4	−55.7	156.6	52 25.3	−56.0	157.1	51 29.9	−56.2	157.6	50 34.3	−56.4	158.0	49 38.6	−56.6	158.5	48 42.7	−56.8	158.9	47 46.7	−57.0	159.3	46 50.5	−57.2	159.7	11
12	52 24.7	−56.0	157.2	51 29.3	−56.2	157.7	50 33.7	−56.4	158.1	49 37.9	−56.6	158.6	48 42.0	−56.8	159.0	47 45.9	−57.0	159.4	46 49.7	−57.2	159.8	45 53.3	−57.3	160.1	12
13	51 28.7	−56.1	157.8	50 33.1	−56.3	158.2	49 37.3	−56.5	158.7	48 41.3	−56.7	159.1	47 45.2	−56.9	159.5	46 48.9	−57.0	159.9	45 52.5	−57.2	160.2	44 56.0	−57.3	160.6	13
14	50 32.6	−56.3	158.3	49 36.8	−56.5	158.8	48 40.8	−56.7	159.2	47 44.6	−56.8	159.6	46 48.3	−57.0	159.9	45 51.9	−57.2	160.3	44 55.3	−57.3	160.6	43 58.7	−57.5	161.0	14
15	49 36.3	−56.4	158.9	48 40.3	−56.6	159.3	47 44.1	−56.8	159.7	46 47.8	−57.0	160.0	45 51.3	−57.1	160.4	44 54.7	−57.2	160.7	43 58.0	−57.4	161.1	43 01.2	−57.5	161.4	15
16	48 39.9	−56.5	159.4	47 43.7	−56.8	159.8	46 47.3	−56.9	160.1	45 50.8	−57.0	160.5	44 54.2	−57.2	160.8	43 57.5	−57.4	161.2	43 00.6	−57.4	161.5	42 03.7	−57.6	161.7	16
17	47 43.4	−56.7	159.9	46 46.9	−56.8	160.3	45 50.4	−57.0	160.6	44 53.8	−57.2	160.9	43 57.0	−57.3	161.3	43 00.1	−57.4	161.6	42 03.2	−57.6	161.8	41 06.1	−57.7	162.1	17
18	46 46.7	−56.8	160.4	45 50.1	−57.0	160.7	44 53.4	−57.1	161.0	43 56.6	−57.2	161.4	42 59.7	−57.4	161.7	42 02.7	−57.5	162.0	41 05.6	−57.6	162.2	40 08.4	−57.7	162.5	18
19	45 49.9	−56.9	160.8	44 53.1	−57.0	161.2	43 56.3	−57.2	161.5	42 59.4	−57.4	161.8	42 02.3	−57.4	162.1	41 05.2	−57.6	162.3	40 08.0	−57.7	162.6	39 10.7	−57.8	162.8	19
20	44 53.0	−57.0	161.3	43 56.1	−57.2	161.6	42 59.1	−57.3	161.9	42 02.0	−57.4	162.2	41 04.9	−57.6	162.4	40 07.6	−57.6	162.7	39 10.3	−57.8	162.9	38 12.9	−57.9	163.2	20
21	43 56.0	−57.1	161.7	42 58.9	−57.2	162.0	42 01.8	−57.3	162.3	41 04.6	−57.5	162.6	40 07.3	−57.6	162.8	39 10.0	−57.7	163.1	38 12.5	−57.8	163.3	37 15.0	−57.9	163.5	21
22	42 58.9	−57.2	162.1	42 01.7	−57.3	162.4	41 04.5	−57.5	162.7	40 07.1	−57.5	162.9	39 09.7	−57.6	163.2	38 12.3	−57.8	163.4	37 14.7	−57.8	163.6	36 17.1	−57.9	163.8	22
23	42 01.7	−57.3	162.6	41 04.4	−57.4	162.8	40 07.0	−57.5	163.1	39 09.6	−57.6	163.3	38 12.1	−57.8	163.5	37 14.5	−57.8	163.8	36 16.9	−58.0	164.0	35 19.2	−58.0	164.2	23
24	41 04.4	−57.4	163.0	40 07.0	−57.5	163.2	39 09.5	−57.6	163.4	38 12.0	−57.7	163.7	37 14.3	−57.7	163.9	36 16.7	−57.9	164.1	35 18.9	−57.9	164.3	34 21.2	−58.1	164.5	24
25	40 07.0	−57.4	163.3	39 09.5	−57.5	163.6	38 11.9	−57.6	163.8	37 14.3	−57.8	164.0	36 16.6	−57.9	164.2	35 18.8	−57.9	164.4	34 21.0	−58.0	164.6	33 23.1	−58.1	164.8	25
26	39 09.6	−57.5	163.7	38 12.0	−57.7	163.9	37 14.3	−57.7	164.2	36 16.5	−57.8	164.4	35 18.7	−57.9	164.5	34 20.9	−58.0	164.7	33 23.0	−58.1	164.9	32 25.0	−58.1	165.1	26
27	38 12.1	−57.6	164.1	37 14.3	−57.6	164.3	36 16.6	−57.8	164.5	35 18.7	−57.8	164.7	34 20.8	−57.9	164.9	33 22.9	−58.0	165.0	32 24.9	−58.1	165.2	31 26.9	−58.2	165.4	27
28	37 14.5	−57.6	164.4	36 16.7	−57.8	164.6	35 18.8	−57.8	164.8	34 20.9	−57.9	165.0	33 22.9	−58.0	165.2	32 24.9	−58.1	165.3	31 26.8	−58.2	165.5	30 28.7	−58.2	165.6	28
29	36 16.9	−57.7	164.8	35 18.9	−57.7	165.0	34 21.0	−57.9	165.2	33 23.0	−58.0	165.3	32 24.9	−58.0	165.5	31 26.8	−58.1	165.6	30 28.6	−58.1	165.8	29 30.5	−58.3	165.9	29
30	35 19.2	−57.8	165.1	34 21.2	−57.9	165.3	33 23.1	−57.9	165.5	32 25.0	−58.0	165.6	31 26.9	−58.1	165.8	30 28.7	−58.2	165.9	29 30.5	−58.3	166.1	28 32.2	−58.3	166.2	30
31	34 21.4	−57.8	165.5	33 23.3	−57.9	165.6	32 25.2	−58.0	165.8	31 27.0	−58.0	165.9	30 28.8	−58.1	166.1	29 30.5	−58.2	166.2	28 32.2	−58.2	166.3	27 33.9	−58.3	166.5	31
32	33 23.6	−57.8	165.8	32 25.4	−57.9	165.9	31 27.2	−58.0	166.1	30 29.0	−58.1	166.2	29 30.7	−58.2	166.4	28 32.3	−58.2	166.5	27 34.0	−58.3	166.6	26 35.6	−58.3	166.7	32
33	32 25.8	−57.9	166.1	31 27.5	−58.0	166.2	30 29.2	−58.0	166.4	29 30.9	−58.1	166.5	28 32.5	−58.2	166.6	27 34.1	−58.2	166.8	26 35.7	−58.3	166.9	25 37.3	−58.4	167.0	33
34	31 27.9	−58.0	166.4	30 29.5	−58.0	166.5	29 31.2	−58.1	166.7	28 32.8	−58.2	166.8	27 34.3	−58.2	166.9	26 35.9	−58.3	167.0	25 37.4	−58.3	167.1	24 38.9	−58.4	167.3	34
35	30 29.9	−58.0	166.7	29 31.5	−58.0	166.8	28 33.1	−58.1	167.0	27 34.6	−58.2	167.1	26 36.1	−58.2	167.2	25 37.6	−58.3	167.3	24 39.1	−58.4	167.4	23 40.5	−58.4	167.5	35
36	29 31.9	−58.0	167.0	28 33.5	−58.1	167.1	27 35.0	−58.2	167.2	26 36.4	−58.2	167.4	25 37.9	−58.3	167.5	24 39.3	−58.3	167.6	23 40.7	−58.4	167.7	22 42.1	−58.5	167.8	36
37	28 33.9	−58.0	167.3	27 35.4	−58.1	167.4	26 36.8	−58.2	167.5	25 38.2	−58.2	167.6	24 39.6	−58.3	167.7	23 41.0	−58.4	167.8	22 42.3	−58.4	167.9	21 43.6	−58.4	168.0	37
38	27 35.9	−58.1	167.6	26 37.3	−58.2	167.7	25 38.6	−58.2	167.8	24 40.0	−58.3	167.9	23 41.3	−58.3	168.0	22 42.6	−58.4	168.1	21 43.9	−58.4	168.2	20 45.2	−58.5	168.2	38
39	26 37.8	−58.1	167.9	25 39.1	−58.2	168.0	24 40.4	−58.2	168.1	23 41.7	−58.3	168.2	22 43.0	−58.4	168.2	21 44.2	−58.4	168.3	20 45.5	−58.5	168.4	19 46.7	−58.5	168.5	39
40	25 39.7	−58.2	168.1	24 40.9	−58.2	168.2	23 42.2	−58.3	168.3	22 43.4	−58.3	168.4	21 44.6	−58.3	168.5	20 45.8	−58.4	168.6	19 47.0	−58.5	168.6	18 48.2	−58.5	168.7	40
41	24 41.5	−58.2	168.4	23 42.7	−58.2	168.5	22 43.9	−58.3	168.6	21 45.1	−58.4	168.7	20 46.3	−58.4	168.7	19 47.4	−58.4	168.8	18 48.5	−58.5	168.9	17 49.7	−58.6	168.9	41
42	23 43.3	−58.2	168.7	22 44.5	−58.3	168.8	21 45.6	−58.3	168.8	20 46.7	−58.3	168.9	19 47.9	−58.5	169.0	18 49.0	−58.5	169.1	17 50.0	−58.5	169.1	16 51.1	−58.5	169.2	42
43	22 45.1	−58.2	168.9	21 46.2	−58.3	169.0	20 47.3	−58.3	169.1	19 48.4	−58.4	169.2	18 49.4	−58.4	169.2	17 50.5	−58.5	169.3	16 51.5	−58.5	169.3	15 52.6	−58.6	169.4	43
44	21 46.9	−58.3	169.2	20 47.9	−58.3	169.3	19 49.0	−58.4	169.3	18 50.0	−58.4	169.4	17 51.0	−58.4	169.5	16 52.0	−58.5	169.5	15 53.0	−58.5	169.6	14 54.0	−58.6	169.6	44
45	20 48.6	−58.3	169.5	19 49.6	−58.3	169.5	18 50.6	−58.4	169.6	17 51.6	−58.4	169.6	16 52.6	−58.5	169.7	15 53.5	−58.5	169.8	14 54.5	−58.6	169.8	13 55.4	−58.6	169.8	45
46	19 50.3	−58.3	169.7	18 51.3	−58.4	169.8	17 52.2	−58.4	169.8	16 53.2	−58.5	169.9	15 54.1	−58.5	169.9	14 55.0	−58.5	170.0	13 55.9	−58.5	170.0	12 56.8	−58.6	170.1	46
47	18 52.0	−58.3	170.0	17 52.9	−58.3	170.0	16 53.8	−58.4	170.1	15 54.7	−58.4	170.1	14 55.6	−58.5	170.2	13 56.5	−58.5	170.2	12 57.4	−58.6	170.3	11 58.2	−58.6	170.3	47
48	17 53.7	−58.3	170.2	16 54.6	−58.4	170.3	15 55.4	−58.4	170.3	14 56.3	−58.5	170.4	13 57.1	−58.5	170.4	12 58.0	−58.6	170.4	11 58.8	−58.6	170.5	10 59.6	−58.6	170.5	48
49	16 55.4	−58.4	170.5	15 56.2	−58.4	170.5	14 57.0	−58.4	170.5	13 57.8	−58.5	170.6	12 58.6	−58.5	170.6	11 59.4	−58.5	170.7	11 00.2	−58.6	170.7	10 01.0	−58.6	170.7	49
50	15 57.0	−58.4	170.7	14 57.8	−58.4	170.7	13 58.6	−58.5	170.8	12 59.3	−58.5	170.8	12 00.1	−58.5	170.9	11 00.9	−58.6	170.9	10 01.6	−58.6	170.9	9 02.4	−58.7	170.9	50
51	14 58.6	−58.4	170.9	13 59.4	−58.5	171.0	13 00.1	−58.5	171.0	12 00.8	−58.5	171.0	11 01.6	−58.6	171.1	10 02.3	−58.6	171.1	9 03.0	−58.6	171.1	8 03.7	−58.6	171.2	51
52	14 00.2	−58.4	171.2	13 00.9	−58.4	171.2	12 01.6	−58.4	171.2	11 02.3	−58.5	171.3	10 03.0	−58.5	171.3	9 03.7	−58.6	171.3	8 04.4	−58.6	171.3	7 05.1	−58.7	171.4	52
53	13 01.8	−58.4	171.4	12 02.5	−58.5	171.4	11 03.2	−58.5	171.5	10 03.8	−58.5	171.5	9 04.5	−58.6	171.5	8 05.1	−58.6	171.5	7 05.8	−58.6	171.6	6 06.4	−58.6	171.6	53
54	12 03.4	−58.4	171.6	11 04.0	−58.4	171.7	10 04.7	−58.5	171.7	9 05.3	−58.5	171.7	8 05.9	−58.5	171.7	7 06.5	−58.6	171.8	6 07.2	−58.7	171.8	5 07.8	−58.7	171.8	54
55	11 05.0	−58.5	171.9	10 05.6	−58.5	171.9	9 06.2	−58.5	171.9	8 06.8	−58.6	171.9	7 07.4	−58.6	172.0	6 07.9	−58.6	172.0	5 08.5	−58.6	172.0	4 09.1	−58.6	172.0	55
56	10 06.5	−58.4	172.1	9 07.1	−58.5	172.1	8 07.7	−58.5	172.1	7 08.2	−58.6	172.2	6 08.8	−58.6	172.2	5 09.3	−58.6	172.2	4 09.9	−58.6	172.2	3 10.5	−58.7	172.2	56
57	9 08.1	−58.5	172.3	8 08.6	−58.5	172.4	7 09.2	−58.6	172.4	6 09.7	−58.6	172.4	5 10.2	−58.6	172.4	4 10.7	−58.6	172.4	3 11.3	−58.7	172.4	2 11.8	−58.7	172.4	57
58	8 09.6	−58.4	172.6	7 10.1	−58.5	172.6	6 10.6	−58.5	172.6	5 11.1	−58.5	172.6	4 11.6	−58.6	172.6	3 12.1	−58.6	172.6	2 12.6	−58.6	172.6	1 13.1	−58.7	172.6	58
59	7 11.2	−58.5	172.8	6 11.6	−58.5	172.8	5 12.1	−58.5	172.8	4 12.6	−58.6	172.8	3 13.0	−58.5	172.8	2 13.5	−58.6	172.8	1 14.0	−58.7	172.8	0 14.4	−58.6	172.8	59
60	6 12.7	−58.5	173.0	5 13.1	−58.5	173.0	4 13.6	−58.6	173.0	3 14.0	−58.5	173.0	2 14.5	−58.6	173.0	1 14.9	−58.6	173.1	0 15.3	−58.6	173.1	0 44.2	+58.7	6.9	60
61	5 14.2	−58.5	173.2	4 14.6	−58.5	173.2	3 15.0	−58.5	173.3	2 15.5	−58.6	173.3	1 15.9	−58.6	173.3	0 16.3	−58.6	173.3	0 43.3	+58.6	6.7	1 42.9	+58.7	6.7	61
62	4 15.7	−58.5	173.5	3 16.1	−58.5	173.5	2 16.5	−58.5	173.5	1 16.9	−58.6	173.5	0 17.3	−58.6	173.5	0 42.3	+58.6	6.5	1 41.9	+58.7	6.5	2 41.6	+58.6	6.5	62
63	3 17.2	−58.5	173.7	2 17.6	−58.5	173.7	1 18.0	−58.6	173.7	0 18.3	−58.5	173.7	0 41.3	+58.6	6.3	1 40.9	+58.7	6.3	2 40.6	+58.6	6.3	3 40.2	+58.7	6.3	63
64	2 18.7	−58.4	173.9	1 19.1	−58.5	173.9	0 19.4	−58.5	173.9	0 40.2	+58.6	6.1	1 39.9	+58.6	6.1	2 39.6	+58.6	6.1	3 39.2	+58.7	6.1	4 38.9	+58.6	6.1	64
65	1 20.3	−58.5	174.1	0 20.6	−58.5	174.1	0 39.1	+58.6	5.9	1 38.8	+58.6	5.9	2 38.5	+58.6	5.9	3 38.2	+58.6	5.9	4 37.9	+58.6	5.9	5 37.5	+58.7	5.9	65
66	0 21.8	−58.5	174.4	0 37.9	+58.6	5.6	1 37.7	+58.5	5.6	2 37.4	+58.5	5.7	3 37.1	+58.6	5.7	4 36.8	+58.6	5.7	5 36.5	+58.6	5.7	6 36.2	+58.6	5.7	66
67	0 36.7	+58.5	5.4	1 36.5	+58.5	5.4	2 36.2	+58.5	5.4	3 35.9	+58.6	5.4	4 35.7	+58.5	5.4	5 35.4	+58.6	5.5	6 35.1	+58.6	5.5	7 34.8	+58.7	5.5	67
68	1 35.2	+58.5	5.2	2 35.0	+58.5	5.2	3 34.7	+58.6	5.2	4 34.5	+58.5	5.2	5 34.2	+58.6	5.2	6 34.0	+58.6	5.2	7 33.7	+58.6	5.2	8 33.5	+58.6	5.3	68
69	2 33.7	+58.5	5.0	3 33.5	+58.5	5.0	4 33.3	+58.5	5.0	5 33.0	+58.6	5.0	6 32.8	+58.6	5.0	7 32.6	+58.6	5.0	8 32.3	+58.6	5.0	9 32.1	+58.6	5.0	69
70	3 32.2	+58.5	4.8	4 32.0	+58.5	4.8	5 31.8	+58.5	4.8	6 31.6	+58.5	4.8	7 31.4	+58.5	4.8	8 31.2	+58.5	4.8	9 30.9	+58.6	4.8	10 30.7	+58.7	4.8	70
71	4 30.7	+58.5	4.5	5 30.5	+58.5	4.5	6 30.3	+58.5	4.5	7 30.1	+58.6	4.6	8 29.9	+58.6	4.6	9 29.7	+58.6	4.6	10 29.5	+58.6	4.6	11 29.4	+58.6	4.6	71
72	5 29.2	+58.4	4.3	6 29.0	+58.5	4.3	7 28.8	+58.5	4.3	8 28.7	+58.5	4.3	9 28.5	+58.5	4.3	10 28.3	+58.6	4.4	11 28.1	+58.6	4.4	12 28.0	+58.6	4.4	72
73	6 27.6	+58.5	4.1	7 27.5	+58.5	4.1	8 27.3	+58.5	4.1	9 27.2	+58.5	4.1	10 27.0	+58.6	4.1	11 26.9	+58.5	4.1	12 26.7	+58.6	4.2	13 26.6	+58.5	4.2	73
74	7 26.1	+58.5	3.9	8 26.0	+58.5	3.9	9 25.8	+58.5	3.9	10 25.7	+58.5	3.9	11 25.6	+58.5	3.9	12 25.4	+58.6	3.9	13 25.3	+58.5	3.9	14 25.1	+58.6	3.9	74
75	8 24.6	+58.4	3.6	9 24.5	+58.4	3.6	10 24.3	+58.5	3.6	11 24.2	+58.5	3.7	12 24.1	+58.5	3.7	13 24.0	+58.5	3.7	14 23.8	+58.6	3.7	15 23.7	+58.6	3.7	75
76	9 23.0	+58.5	3.4	10 22.9	+58.5	3.4	11 22.8	+58.5	3.4	12 22.7	+58.5	3.4	13 22.6	+58.5	3.4	14 22.5	+58.5	3.5	15 22.4	+58.5	3.5	16 22.3	+58.5	3.5	76
77	10 21.5	+58.4	3.2	11 21.4	+58.4	3.2	12 21.3	+58.5	3.2	13 21.2	+58.5	3.2	14 21.1	+58.5	3.2	15 21.0	+58.5	3.2	16 20.9	+58.5	3.3	17 20.8	+58.6	3.3	77
78	11 19.9	+58.4	2.9	12 19.8	+58.5	3.0	13 19.8	+58.4	3.0	14 19.7	+58.4	3.0	15 19.6	+58.5	3.0	16 19.5	+58.5	3.0	17 19.4	+58.5	3.0	18 19.4	+58.5	3.0	78
79	12 18.3	+58.5	2.7	13 18.3	+58.4	2.7	14 18.2	+58.4	2.7	15 18.1	+58.5	2.7	16 18.1	+58.4	2.8	17 18.0	+58.5	2.8	18 17.9	+58.5	2.8	19 17.9	+58.5	2.8	79
80	13 16.8	+58.4	2.5	14 16.7	+58.4	2.5	15 16.6	+58.5	2.5	16 16.6	+58.4	2.5	17 16.5	+58.5	2.5	18 16.5	+58.4	2.5	19 16.4	+58.5	2.6	20 16.4	+58.4	2.6	80
81	14 15.2	+58.4	2.2	15 15.1	+58.4	2.2	16 15.1	+58.4	2.3	17 15.0	+58.4	2.3	18 15.0	+58.4	2.3	19 14.9	+58.5	2.3	20 14.9	+58.4	2.3	21 14.8	+58.5	2.3	81
82	15 13.6	+58.3	2.0	16 13.5	+58.4	2.0	17 13.5	+58.4	2.0	18 13.4	+58.4	2.0	19 13.4	+58.4	2.0	20 13.4	+58.4	2.1	21 13.3	+58.4	2.1	22 13.3	+58.4	2.1	82
83	16 11.9	+58.4	1.8	17 11.9	+58.4	1.8	18 11.9	+58.3	1.8	19 11.8	+58.4	1.8	20 11.8	+58.4	1.8	21 11.8	+58.4	1.8	22 11.7	+58.4	1.8	23 11.7	+58.4	1.8	83
84	17 10.3	+58.3	1.5	18 10.3	+58.3	1.5	19 10.2	+58.4	1.5	20 10.2	+58.4	1.5	21 10.2	+58.4	1.6	22 10.2	+58.3	1.6	23 10.1	+58.4	1.6	24 10.1	+58.4	1.6	84
85	18 08.6	+58.3	1.3	19 08.6	+58.3	1.3	20 08.6	+58.3	1.3	21 08.6	+58.3	1.3	22 08.6	+58.3	1.3	23 08.5	+58.4	1.3	24 08.5	+58.4	1.3	25 08.5	+58.4	1.3	85
86	19 06.9	+58.3	1.0	20 06.9	+58.3	1.0	21 06.9	+58.3	1.0	22 06.9	+58.3	1.0	23 06.9	+58.3	1.1	24 06.9	+58.3	1.1	25 06.9	+58.3	1.1	26 06.9	+58.3	1.1	86
87	20 05.2	+58.3	0.8	21 05.2	+58.3	0.8	22 05.2	+58.3	0.8	23 05.2	+58.3	0.8	24 05.2	+58.3	0.8	25 05.2	+58.3	0.8	26 05.2	+58.3	0.8	27 05.2	+58.3	0.8	87
88	21 03.5	+58.3	0.5	22 03.5	+58.3	0.5	23 03.5	+58.3	0.5	24 03.5	+58.3	0.5	25 03.5	+58.3	0.5	26 03.5	+58.3	0.5	27 03.5	+58.3	0.5	28 03.5	+58.3	0.5	88
89	22 01.8	+58.2	0.3	23 01.8	+58.2	0.3	24 01.8	+58.2	0.3	25 01.8	+58.2	0.3	26 01.8	+58.2	0.3	27 01.8	+58.2	0.3	28 01.8	+58.2	0.3	29 01.8	+58.2	0.3	89
90	23 00.0	+58.2	0.0	24 00.0	+58.2	0.0	25 00.0	+58.2	0.0	26 00.0	+58.2	0.0	27 00.0	+58.2	0.0	28 00.0	+58.2	0.0	29 00.0	+58.2	0.0	30 00.0	+58.2	0.0	90
	23°			24°			25°			26°			27°			28°			29°			30°			

S. Lat. {L.H.A. greater than 180° ....Zn=180°−Z; L.H.A. less than 180°...........Zn=180°+Z}

15°, 345° L.H.A. LATITUDE SAME NAME AS DECLINATION N. Lat. {L.H.A. greater than 180° .....Zn=Z, L.H.A. less than 180°............Zn=360°−Z}

Dec.	23° Hc	d	Z	24° Hc	d	Z	25° Hc	d	Z	26° Hc	d	Z	27° Hc	d	Z	28° Hc	d	Z	29° Hc	d	Z	30° Hc	d	Z	Dec.
°	° ′	′	°	° ′	′	°	° ′	′	°	° ′	′	°	° ′	′	°	° ′	′	°	° ′	′	°	° ′	′	°	°
0	62 45.9	+51.0	145.6	61 56.1	+51.6	146.6	61 05.7	+52.3	147.6	60 14.8	+52.8	148.6	59 23.4	+53.3	149.5	58 31.5	+53.7	150.3	57 39.1	+54.3	151.1	56 46.4	+54.7	151.8	0
1	63 36.9	+50.3	144.4	62 47.7	+51.1	145.5	61 58.0	+51.7	146.6	61 07.6	+52.3	147.6	60 16.7	+52.9	148.5	59 25.2	+53.5	149.4	58 33.4	+53.8	150.3	57 41.1	+54.3	151.0	1
2	64 27.2	+49.7	143.1	63 38.8	+50.5	144.4	62 49.7	+51.2	145.5	61 59.9	+51.9	146.6	61 09.6	+52.4	147.6	60 18.7	+53.0	148.5	59 27.2	+53.6	149.4	58 35.4	+54.0	150.2	2
3	65 16.9	+48.9	141.8	64 29.3	+49.8	143.1	63 40.9	+50.6	144.3	62 51.8	+51.3	145.5	62 02.0	+52.0	146.6	61 11.7	+52.6	147.6	60 20.8	+53.1	148.5	59 29.4	+53.6	149.4	3
4	66 05.8	+48.1	140.4	65 19.1	+49.1	141.8	64 31.5	+50.0	143.1	63 43.1	+50.8	144.3	62 54.0	+51.5	145.5	62 04.3	+52.1	146.5	61 13.9	+52.8	147.6	60 23.0	+53.3	148.5	4
5	66 53.9	+47.2	138.9	66 08.2	+48.2	140.4	65 21.5	+49.2	141.8	64 33.9	+50.1	143.1	63 45.5	+50.9	144.3	62 56.4	+51.6	145.5	62 06.7	+52.2	146.5	61 16.3	+52.9	147.6	5
6	67 41.1	+46.2	137.3	66 56.4	+47.4	138.9	66 10.7	+48.4	140.4	65 24.0	+49.4	141.8	64 36.4	+50.3	143.1	63 48.0	+51.1	144.3	62 58.9	+51.8	145.5	62 09.2	+52.4	146.6	6
7	68 27.3	+45.1	135.6	67 43.8	+46.4	137.3	66 59.1	+47.6	138.9	66 13.4	+48.6	140.4	65 26.7	+49.5	141.8	64 39.1	+50.4	143.1	63 50.7	+51.2	144.4	63 01.6	+51.9	145.5	7
8	69 12.4	+43.8	133.8	68 30.2	+45.2	135.6	67 46.7	+46.5	137.3	67 02.0	+47.7	138.9	66 16.2	+48.8	140.4	65 29.5	+49.7	141.8	64 41.9	+50.6	143.2	63 53.5	+51.3	144.4	8
9	69 56.2	+42.5	131.8	69 15.4	+44.1	133.8	68 33.2	+45.5	135.6	67 49.7	+46.7	137.4	67 05.0	+47.9	139.0	66 19.2	+48.9	140.5	65 32.5	+49.8	141.9	64 44.8	+50.8	143.2	9
10	70 38.7	+40.9	129.7	69 59.5	+42.6	131.8	69 18.7	+44.2	133.8	68 36.4	+45.7	135.7	67 52.9	+46.9	137.4	67 08.1	+48.1	139.0	66 22.3	+49.2	140.5	65 35.6	+50.0	141.9	10
11	71 19.6	+39.2	127.5	70 42.1	+41.2	129.8	70 02.9	+42.9	131.9	69 22.1	+44.4	133.9	68 39.8	+45.9	135.7	67 56.2	+47.1	137.4	67 11.5	+48.2	139.1	66 25.6	+49.3	140.6	11
12	71 58.8	+37.3	•125.1	71 23.3	+39.4	127.5	70 45.8	+41.3	129.8	70 06.5	+43.1	131.9	69 25.7	+44.6	133.9	68 43.3	+46.1	135.8	67 59.7	+47.3	137.5	67 14.9	+48.5	139.1	12
13	72 36.1	+35.1	•122.5	72 02.7	+37.5	•125.1	71 27.1	+39.7	127.6	70 49.6	+41.6	129.8	70 10.3	+43.3	132.0	69 29.4	+44.9	134.0	68 47.0	+46.3	135.8	68 03.4	+47.5	137.6	13
14	73 11.2	+32.8	•119.7	72 40.2	+35.4	•122.5	72 06.8	+37.7	•125.2	71 31.2	+39.9	127.6	70 53.6	+41.8	129.9	70 14.3	+43.5	132.0	69 33.3	+45.1	134.0	68 50.9	+46.5	135.9	14
15	73 44.0	+30.2	•116.8	73 15.6	+33.0	•119.8	72 44.5	+35.7	•122.6	72 11.1	+37.9	•125.2	71 35.4	+40.1	127.7	70 57.8	+42.0	130.0	70 18.4	+43.8	132.1	69 37.4	+45.3	134.1	15
16	74 14.2	+27.4	•113.7	73 48.6	+30.5	•116.8	73 20.2	+33.3	•119.8	72 49.0	+35.9	•122.6	72 15.5	+38.3	•125.3	71 39.8	+40.4	127.7	71 02.2	+42.2	130.0	70 22.7	+44.0	132.2	16
17	74 41.6	+24.2	•110.3	74 19.1	+27.6	•113.7	73 53.5	+30.7	•116.9	73 24.9	+33.6	•119.9	72 53.8	+36.1	•122.7	72 20.2	+38.5	•125.3	71 44.4	+40.7	127.8	71 06.7	+42.5	130.1	17
18	75 05.8	+20.9	•106.8	74 46.7	+24.5	•110.4	74 24.2	+27.8	•113.7	73 58.5	+31.0	•116.9	73 29.9	+33.9	•119.9	72 58.7	+36.4	•122.8	72 25.1	+38.7	•125.4	71 49.2	+40.9	127.9	18
19	75 26.7	+17.2	•103.1	75 11.2	+21.1	•106.8	74 52.0	+24.7	•110.4	74 29.5	+28.1	•113.8	74 03.8	+31.2	•117.0	73 35.1	+34.1	•120.0	73 03.8	+36.7	•122.9	72 30.1	+39.0	125.5	19
20	75 43.9	+13.4	•99.3	75 32.3	+17.4	•103.1	75 16.7	+21.4	•106.8	74 57.6	+25.0	•110.4	74 35.0	+28.4	•113.8	74 09.2	+31.5	•117.0	73 40.5	+34.4	•120.1	73 09.1	+37.0	•122.9	20
21	75 57.3	+9.4	•95.3	75 49.7	+13.6	•99.3	75 38.1	+17.7	•103.1	75 22.6	+21.5	•106.9	75 03.4	+25.2	•110.4	74 40.7	+28.7	•113.9	74 14.9	+31.8	•117.1	73 46.1	+34.6	•120.2	21
22	76 06.7	+5.2	•91.2	76 03.3	+9.6	•95.2	75 55.8	+13.8	•99.2	75 44.1	+17.9	•103.1	75 28.6	+21.8	•106.9	75 09.4	+25.5	•110.5	74 46.7	+28.9	•113.9	74 20.7	+32.1	•117.2	22
23	76 11.9	+1.0	•87.1	76 12.9	+5.3	•91.1	76 09.6	+9.7	•95.2	76 02.0	+14.0	•99.2	75 50.4	+18.1	•103.1	75 34.9	+22.0	•106.9	75 15.6	+25.8	•110.6	74 52.8	+29.2	•114.0	23
24	76 12.9	−3.3	•82.9	76 18.2	+1.1	•86.9	76 19.3	+5.4	•91.0	76 16.0	+9.9	•95.1	76 08.5	+14.2	•99.2	75 56.9	+18.4	•103.1	75 41.4	+22.3	•107.0	75 22.0	+26.1	•110.6	24
25	76 09.6	−7.6	•78.7	76 19.3	−3.3	•82.7	76 24.7	+1.2	•86.8	76 25.9	+5.6	•91.0	76 22.7	+10.1	•95.1	76 15.3	+14.4	•99.2	76 03.7	+18.6	•103.1	75 48.1	+22.6	•107.0	25
26	76 02.0	−11.6	•74.5	76 16.0	−7.5	•78.5	76 25.9	−3.2	•82.6	76 31.5	+1.3	•86.7	76 32.8	+5.8	•90.9	76 29.7	+10.2	•95.0	76 22.3	+14.6	•99.2	76 10.7	+18.8	•103.2	26
27	75 50.4	−15.5	•70.5	76 08.5	−11.6	•74.3	76 22.7	−7.4	•78.3	76 32.8	−3.1	•82.4	76 38.6	+1.3	•86.6	76 39.9	+6.0	•90.8	76 36.9	+10.4	•95.0	76 29.5	+14.8	•99.2	27
28	75 34.9	−19.3	•66.6	75 56.9	−15.5	•70.3	76 15.3	−11.6	•74.1	76 29.7	−7.4	•78.1	76 39.9	−3.0	•82.2	76 45.9	+1.4	•86.5	76 47.3	+6.1	•90.7	76 44.3	+10.6	•95.0	28
29	75 15.6	−22.8	•62.8	75 41.4	−19.4	•66.3	76 03.7	−15.6	•70.0	76 22.3	−11.6	•73.9	76 36.9	−7.4	•77.9	76 47.3	−3.0	•82.1	76 53.4	+1.5	•86.3	76 54.9	+6.2	•90.6	29
30	74 52.8	−26.0	•59.2	75 22.0	−22.8	•62.5	75 48.1	−19.4	•66.0	76 10.7	−15.7	•69.7	76 29.5	−11.6	•73.7	76 44.3	−7.3	•77.7	76 54.9	−2.9	•81.9	77 01.1	+1.7	•86.2	30
31	74 26.8	−29.0	•55.8	74 59.2	−26.1	•58.9	75 28.7	−23.0	•62.2	75 55.0	−19.5	•65.7	76 17.9	−15.7	•69.5	76 37.0	−11.7	•73.4	76 52.0	−7.3	•77.5	77 02.8	−2.9	•81.8	31
32	73 57.8	−31.6	•52.6	74 33.1	−29.1	•55.5	75 05.7	−26.2	•58.6	75 35.5	−23.0	•61.9	76 02.2	−19.6	•65.4	76 25.3	−15.8	•69.2	76 44.7	−11.7	•73.2	76 59.9	−7.3	•77.3	32
33	73 26.2	−34.2	•49.6	74 04.0	−31.8	•52.3	74 39.5	−29.2	•55.1	75 12.5	−26.3	•58.2	75 42.6	−23.1	•61.6	76 09.5	−19.6	•65.1	76 33.0	−15.9	•68.9	76 52.6	−11.8	•72.9	33
34	72 52.0	−36.3	•46.8	73 32.2	−34.3	•49.2	74 10.3	−31.9	•51.9	74 46.2	−29.3	•54.8	75 19.5	−26.5	•57.9	75 49.9	−23.3	•61.2	76 17.1	−19.7	•64.8	76 40.8	−15.9	•68.6	34
35	72 15.7	−38.4	44.1	72 57.9	−36.5	•46.4	73 38.4	−34.4	•48.8	74 16.9	−32.1	•51.5	74 53.0	−29.5	•54.4	75 26.6	−26.6	•57.5	75 57.4	−23.4	•60.9	76 24.9	−19.9	•64.5	35
36	71 37.3	−40.2	41.6	72 21.4	−38.5	43.7	73 04.0	−36.7	•46.0	73 44.8	−34.6	•48.4	74 23.5	−32.2	•51.1	75 00.0	−29.6	•54.0	75 34.0	−26.8	•57.1	76 05.0	−23.5	•60.5	36
37	70 57.1	−41.8	39.3	71 42.9	−40.3	41.2	72 27.3	−38.6	43.3	73 10.2	−36.8	•45.6	73 51.3	−34.7	•48.0	74 30.4	−32.4	•50.7	75 07.2	−29.8	•53.6	75 41.5	−26.9	•56.8	37
38	70 15.3	−43.2	37.1	71 02.6	−41.9	38.9	71 48.7	−40.5	40.8	72 33.4	−38.8	42.9	73 16.6	−37.0	•45.1	73 58.0	−34.9	•47.6	74 37.4	−32.6	•50.3	75 14.6	−30.0	•53.2	38
39	69 32.1	−44.5	35.1	70 20.7	−43.4	36.7	71 08.2	−42.0	38.5	71 54.6	−40.6	40.4	72 39.6	−39.0	42.4	73 23.1	−37.2	•44.7	74 04.8	−35.1	•47.2	74 44.6	−32.8	•49.9	39
40	68 47.6	−45.8	33.2	69 37.3	−44.7	34.7	70 26.2	−43.5	36.3	71 14.0	−42.2	38.0	72 00.6	−40.8	39.9	72 45.9	−39.1	42.0	73 29.7	−37.3	•44.3	74 11.8	−35.3	•46.7	40
41	68 01.8	−46.7	31.5	68 52.6	−45.8	32.8	69 42.7	−44.9	34.3	70 31.8	−43.7	35.9	71 19.8	−42.3	37.6	72 06.8	−41.0	39.5	72 52.4	−39.3	41.6	73 36.5	−37.5	•43.8	41
42	67 15.1	−47.7	29.8	68 06.8	−46.9	31.1	68 57.8	−45.9	32.4	69 48.1	−45.0	33.9	70 37.5	−43.9	35.4	71 25.8	−42.5	37.2	72 13.1	−41.2	39.0	72 59.0	−39.6	41.1	42
43	66 27.4	−48.6	28.3	67 19.9	−47.8	29.4	68 11.9	−47.1	30.6	69 03.1	−46.1	32.0	69 53.6	−45.1	33.4	70 43.3	−44.0	35.0	71 31.9	−42.7	36.7	72 19.4	−41.3	38.6	43
44	65 38.8	−49.4	26.8	66 32.1	−48.7	27.9	67 24.8	−47.9	29.0	68 17.0	−47.1	30.2	69 08.5	−46.3	31.5	69 59.3	−45.3	33.0	70 49.2	−44.2	34.5	71 38.1	−42.9	36.2	44
45	64 49.4	−50.0	25.5	65 43.4	−49.5	26.4	66 36.9	−48.8	27.5	67 29.9	−48.1	28.6	68 22.2	−47.3	29.8	69 14.0	−46.4	31.1	70 05.0	−45.5	32.5	70 55.2	−44.4	34.0	45
46	63 59.4	−50.7	24.2	64 53.9	−50.1	25.1	65 48.1	−49.6	26.0	66 41.8	−49.0	27.0	67 34.9	−48.2	28.1	68 27.6	−47.5	29.3	69 19.5	−46.6	30.6	70 10.8	−45.6	32.0	46
47	63 08.7	−51.2	23.0	64 03.8	−50.8	23.8	64 58.5	−50.3	24.7	65 52.8	−49.7	25.6	66 46.7	−49.1	26.6	67 40.1	−48.4	27.7	68 32.9	−47.6	28.9	69 25.2	−46.8	30.1	47
48	62 17.5	−51.8	21.9	63 13.0	−51.4	22.6	64 08.2	−50.9	23.4	65 03.1	−50.4	24.2	65 57.6	−49.8	25.2	66 51.7	−49.2	26.2	67 45.3	−48.5	27.2	68 38.4	−47.8	28.4	48
49	61 25.7	−52.3	20.8	62 21.6	−51.8	21.5	63 17.3	−51.4	22.2	64 12.7	−51.0	23.0	65 07.8	−50.5	23.8	66 02.5	−49.9	24.7	66 56.8	−49.4	25.7	67 50.6	−48.7	26.8	49
50	60 33.4	−52.7	19.8	61 29.8	−52.4	20.4	62 25.9	−52.0	21.1	63 21.7	−51.5	21.8	64 17.3	−51.1	22.5	65 12.6	−50.7	23.4	66 07.4	−50.1	24.3	67 01.9	−49.5	25.2	50
51	59 40.7	−53.1	18.8	60 37.4	−52.8	19.4	61 33.9	−52.4	20.0	62 30.2	−52.1	20.7	63 26.2	−51.7	21.4	64 21.9	−51.2	22.1	65 17.3	−50.7	22.9	66 12.4	−50.2	23.8	51
52	58 47.6	−53.4	17.9	59 44.6	−53.1	18.4	60 41.5	−52.9	19.0	61 38.1	−52.5	19.6	62 34.5	−52.2	20.2	63 30.7	−51.8	20.9	64 26.6	−51.4	21.7	65 22.2	−50.9	22.5	52
53	57 54.2	−53.8	17.0	58 51.5	−53.6	17.5	59 48.6	−53.3	18.0	60 45.6	−53.0	18.6	61 42.3	−52.6	19.2	62 38.9	−52.3	19.8	63 35.2	−51.9	20.5	64 31.3	−51.5	21.2	53
54	57 00.4	−54.1	16.2	57 57.9	−53.8	16.7	58 55.3	−53.6	17.1	59 52.6	−53.4	17.6	60 49.7	−53.1	18.2	61 46.6	−52.8	18.8	62 43.3	−52.4	19.4	63 39.8	−52.1	20.1	54
55	56 06.3	−54.4	15.4	57 04.1	−54.2	15.8	58 01.7	−53.9	16.3	58 59.2	−53.7	16.7	59 56.6	−53.4	17.2	60 53.8	−53.1	17.8	61 50.9	−52.9	18.3	62 47.7	−52.5	18.9	55
56	55 11.9	−54.7	14.7	56 09.9	−54.5	15.1	57 07.8	−54.3	15.5	58 05.5	−54.0	15.9	59 03.2	−53.8	16.3	60 00.7	−53.6	16.8	60 58.0	−53.2	17.4	61 55.2	−53.0	17.9	56
57	54 17.2	−54.9	14.0	55 15.4	−54.7	14.3	56 13.5	−54.5	14.7	57 11.5	−54.3	15.1	58 09.4	−54.1	15.5	59 07.1	−53.9	15.9	60 04.8	−53.7	16.4	61 02.2	−53.3	16.9	57
58	53 22.3	−55.1	13.3	54 20.7	−55.0	13.6	55 19.0	−54.8	13.9	56 17.2	−54.6	14.3	57 15.3	−54.5	14.7	58 13.2	−54.2	15.1	59 11.1	−54.0	15.5	60 08.9	−53.8	16.0	58
59	52 27.2	−55.3	12.6	53 25.7	−55.1	12.9	54 24.2	−55.0	13.2	55 22.6	−54.9	13.6	56 20.8	−54.7	13.9	57 19.0	−54.5	14.3	58 17.1	−54.3	14.7	59 15.1	−54.1	15.1	59
60	51 31.9	−55.5	12.0	52 30.6	−55.4	12.3	53 29.2	−55.3	12.6	54 27.7	−55.1	12.9	55 26.1	−54.9	13.2	56 24.5	−54.8	13.5	57 22.8	−54.6	13.9	58 21.0	−54.4	14.3	60
61	50 36.4	−55.7	11.4	51 35.2	−55.6	11.7	52 33.9	−55.4	11.9	53 32.6	−55.3	12.2	54 31.2	−55.2	12.5	55 29.7	−55.0	12.8	56 28.2	−54.8	13.1	57 26.6	−54.7	13.5	61
62	49 40.7	−55.9	10.8	50 39.6	−55.8	11.1	51 38.5	−55.7	11.3	52 37.3	−55.5	11.5	53 36.0	−55.4	11.8	54 34.7	−55.2	12.1	55 33.4	−55.1	12.4	56 31.9	−54.9	12.7	62
63	48 44.8	−56.0	10.3	49 43.8	−55.9	10.5	50 42.8	−55.8	10.7	51 41.8	−55.8	10.9	52 40.6	−55.5	11.2	53 39.5	−55.5	11.4	54 38.3	−55.4	11.7	55 37.0	−55.2	12.0	63
64	47 48.8	−56.2	9.7	48 47.9	−56.1	9.9	49 47.0	−56.0	10.1	50 46.0	−55.8	10.3	51 45.1	−55.8	10.6	52 44.0	−55.6	10.8	53 42.9	−55.5	11.1	54 41.8	−55.4	11.3	64
65	46 52.6	−56.3	9.2	47 51.8	−56.2	9.4	48 51.0	−56.1	9.6	49 50.2	−56.1	9.8	50 49.3	−56.0	10.0	51 48.4	−55.9	10.2	52 47.4	−55.7	10.4	53 46.4	−55.6	10.7	65
66	45 56.3	−56.4	8.7	46 55.6	−56.3	8.9	47 54.9	−56.3	9.0	48 54.1	−56.2	9.2	49 53.3	−56.1	9.4	50 52.5	−56.0	9.6	51 51.7	−56.0	9.8	52 50.8	−55.9	10.0	66
67	44 59.9	−56.6	8.2	45 59.3	−56.5	8.4	46 58.6	−56.4	8.5	47 57.9	−56.3	8.7	48 57.2	−56.2	8.9	49 56.5	−56.2	9.0	50 55.7	−56.0	9.2	51 54.9	−55.9	9.4	67
68	44 03.3	−56.6	7.8	45 02.8	−56.6	7.9	46 02.2	−56.5	8.0	47 01.6	−56.5	8.2	48 01.0	−56.4	8.3	49 00.3	−56.3	8.5	49 59.7	−56.3	8.7	50 59.0	−56.2	8.9	68
69	43 06.7	−56.8	7.3	44 06.2	−56.7	7.4	45 05.7	−56.7	7.5	46 05.1	−56.5	7.7	47 04.6	−56.5	7.8	48 04.0	−56.4	8.0	49 03.4	−56.3	8.1	50 02.8	−56.3	8.3	69
70	42 09.9	−56.9	6.9	43 09.5	−56.8	7.0	44 09.0	−56.7	7.1	45 08.6	−56.7	7.2	46 08.1	−56.7	7.3	47 07.6	−56.6	7.5	48 07.1	−56.6	7.6	49 06.5	−56.4	7.8	70
71	41 13.0	−56.9	6.4	42 12.7	−56.9	6.5	43 12.3	−56.9	6.6	44 11.9	−56.8	6.7	45 11.4	−56.7	6.9	46 11.0	−56.7	7.0	47 10.5	−56.6	7.1	48 10.1	−56.6	7.3	71
72	40 16.1	−57.1	6.0	41 15.8	−57.0	6.1	42 15.4	−56.9	6.2	43 15.1	−57.0	6.3	44 14.7	−56.9	6.4	45 14.3	−56.8	6.5	46 13.9	−56.7	6.6	47 13.5	−56.7	6.8	72
73	39 19.0	−57.1	5.6	40 18.8	−57.1	5.7	41 18.5	−57.1	5.8	42 18.1	−57.0	5.9	43 17.8	−56.9	6.0	44 17.5	−56.9	6.1	45 17.2	−56.9	6.2	46 16.8	−56.8	6.3	73
74	38 21.9	−57.2	5.2	39 21.7	−57.2	5.3	40 21.4	−57.1	5.4	41 21.1	−57.0	5.5	42 20.9	−57.1	5.5	43 20.6	−57.0	5.6	44 20.3	−57.0	5.7	45 20.0	−56.9	5.8	74
75	37 24.7	−57.2	4.8	38 24.5	−57.2	4.9	39 24.3	−57.2	5.0	40 24.1	−57.2	5.0	41 23.8	−57.1	5.1	42 23.6	−57.1	5.2	43 23.3	−57.0	5.3	44 23.1	−57.1	5.4	75
76	36 27.5	−57.4	4.5	37 27.3	−57.3	4.5	38 27.1	−57.3	4.6	39 26.9	−57.3	4.7	40 26.7	−57.2	4.7	41 26.5	−57.2	4.8	42 26.3	−57.2	4.9	43 26.0	−57.1	4.9	76
77	35 30.1	−57.4	4.1	36 30.0	−57.4	4.2	37 29.8	−57.4	4.2	38 29.6	−57.3	4.3	39 29.5	−57.3	4.3	40 29.3	−57.3	4.4	41 29.1	−57.2	4.5	42 28.9	−57.2	4.5	77
78	34 32.7	−57.5	3.7	35 32.6	−57.5	3.8	36 32.4	−57.4	3.8	37 32.3	−57.4	3.9	38 32.2	−57.4	3.9	39 32.0	−57.3	4.0	40 31.9	−57.3	4.1	41 31.7	−57.3	4.1	78
79	33 35.2	−57.5	3.4	34 35.1	−57.5	3.4	35 35.0	−57.5	3.5	36 34.9	−57.4	3.5	37 34.8	−57.4	3.6	38 34.7	−57.4	3.6	39 34.6	−57.4	3.7	40 34.4	−57.3	3.7	79
80	32 37.7	−57.6	3.1	33 37.6	−57.5	3.1	34 37.5	−57.5	3.1	35 37.5	−57.6	3.2	36 37.4	−57.5	3.2	37 37.3	−57.5	3.3	38 37.2	−57.5	3.3	39 37.1	−57.5	3.3	80
81	31 40.1	−57.6	2.7	32 40.1	−57.6	2.8	33 40.0	−57.6	2.8	34 39.9	−57.5	2.8	35 39.9	−57.6	2.9	36 39.8	−57.6	2.9	37 39.7	−57.5	2.9	38 39.6	−57.5	3.0	81
82	30 42.5	−57.7	2.4	31 42.5	−57.7	2.4	32 42.4	−57.6	2.5	33 42.4	−57.7	2.5	34 42.3	−57.6	2.5	35 42.2	−57.6	2.5	36 42.2	−57.6	2.6	37 42.1	−57.6	2.6	82
83	29 44.8	−57.7	2.1	30 44.8	−57.7	2.1	31 44.8	−57.7	2.1	32 44.7	−57.7	2.1	33 44.7	−57.7	2.2	34 44.6	−57.6	2.2	35 44.6	−57.7	2.2	36 44.5	−57.6	2.3	83
84	28 47.1	−57.7	1.8	29 47.1	−57.8	1.8	30 47.1	−57.8	1.8	31 47.0	−57.7	1.8	32 47.0	−57.7	1.8	33 47.0	−57.7	1.9	34 46.9	−57.7	1.9	35 46.9	−57.7	1.9	84
85	27 49.4	−57.8	1.5	28 49.3	−57.7	1.5	29 49.3	−57.8	1.5	30 49.3	−57.8	1.5	31 49.3	−57.8	1.5	32 49.3	−57.8	1.5	33 49.2	−57.7	1.6	34 49.2	−57.7	1.6	85
86	26 51.6	−57.9	1.2	27 51.6	−57.9	1.2	28 51.5	−57.8	1.2	29 51.5	−57.8	1.2	30 51.5	−57.8	1.2	31 51.5	−57.8	1.2	32 51.5	−57.8	1.2	33 51.5	−57.8	1.2	86
87	25 53.7	−57.9	0.9	26 53.7	−57.9	0.9	27 53.7	−57.9	0.9	28 53.7	−57.9	0.9	29 53.7	−57.9	0.9	30 53.7	−57.9	0.9	31 53.7	−57.9	0.9	32 53.7	−57.9	0.9	87
88	24 55.8	−57.9	0.6	25 55.8	−57.9	0.6	26 55.8	−57.9	0.6	27 55.8	−57.9	0.6	28 55.8	−57.9	0.6	29 55.8	−57.9	0.6	30 55.8	−57.9	0.6	31 55.8	−57.9	0.6	88
89	23 57.9	−57.9	0.3	24 57.9	−57.9	0.3	25 57.9	−57.9	0.3	26 57.9	−57.9	0.3	27 57.9	−57.9	0.3	28 57.9	−57.9	0.3	29 57.9	−57.9	0.3	30 57.9	−57.9	0.3	89
90	23 00.0	−58.0	0.0	24 00.0	−58.0	0.0	25 00.0	−58.0	0.0	26 00.0	−58.0	0.0	27 00.0	−58.0	0.0	28 00.0	−58.0	0.0	29 00.0	−58.0	0.0	30 00.0	−58.0	0.0	90
	23°			24°			25°			26°			27°			28°			29°			30°			

15°, 345° L.H.A. LATITUDE SAME NAME AS DECLINATION

214

LATITUDE CONTRARY NAME TO DECLINATION — L.H.A. 15°, 345°

Dec. (°)	23° Hc (° ′)	23° d (′)	23° Z (°)	24° Hc (° ′)	24° d (′)	24° Z (°)	25° Hc (° ′)	25° d (′)	25° Z (°)	26° Hc (° ′)	26° d (′)	26° Z (°)
0	62 45.9	−51.5	145.6	61 56.1	−52.1	146.6	61 05.7	−52.7	147.6	60 14.8	−53.2	148.6
1	61 54.4	−52.0	146.7	61 04.0	−52.6	147.7	60 13.0	−53.0	148.6	59 21.6	−53.6	149.5
2	61 02.4	−52.4	147.7	60 11.4	−52.9	148.6	59 20.0	−53.5	149.5	58 28.0	−53.9	150.4
3	60 10.0	−52.9	148.7	59 18.5	−53.4	149.6	58 26.5	−53.8	150.4	57 34.1	−54.2	151.2
4	59 17.1	−53.3	149.6	58 25.1	−53.7	150.5	57 32.7	−54.1	151.2	56 39.9	−54.5	152.0
5	58 23.8	−53.6	150.5	57 31.4	−54.0	151.3	56 38.6	−54.4	152.0	55 45.4	−54.7	152.7
6	57 30.2	−53.9	151.4	56 37.4	−54.3	152.1	55 44.2	−54.7	152.8	54 50.7	−55.0	153.4
7	56 36.3	−54.2	152.2	55 43.1	−54.6	152.9	54 49.5	−54.9	153.5	53 55.7	−55.3	154.1
8	55 42.1	−54.6	152.9	54 48.5	−54.9	153.6	53 54.6	−55.2	154.2	53 00.4	−55.4	154.8
9	54 47.5	−54.7	153.7	53 53.6	−55.0	154.3	52 59.4	−55.3	154.9	52 05.0	−55.6	155.4
10	53 52.8	−55.0	154.4	52 58.6	−55.3	155.0	52 04.1	−55.6	155.5	51 09.4	−55.8	156.0
11	52 57.8	−55.2	155.1	52 03.3	−55.5	155.6	51 08.5	−55.7	156.1	50 13.6	−56.0	156.6
12	52 02.6	−55.4	155.7	51 07.8	−55.7	156.2	50 12.8	−55.9	156.7	49 17.6	−56.2	157.2
13	51 07.2	−55.6	156.3	50 12.1	−55.8	156.8	49 16.9	−56.1	157.3	48 21.4	−56.2	157.7
14	50 11.6	−55.8	156.9	49 16.3	−56.0	157.4	48 20.8	−56.2	157.8	47 25.2	−56.4	158.2
15	49 15.8	−56.0	157.5	48 20.3	−56.2	157.9	47 24.6	−56.3	158.3	46 28.8	−56.6	158.7
16	48 19.8	−56.0	158.0	47 24.1	−56.3	158.4	46 28.3	−56.5	158.8	45 32.2	−56.6	159.2
17	47 23.8	−56.3	158.6	46 27.8	−56.4	158.9	45 31.8	−56.6	159.3	44 35.6	−56.8	159.7
18	46 27.5	−56.3	159.1	45 31.4	−56.5	159.4	44 35.2	−56.7	159.8	43 38.8	−56.8	160.1
19	45 31.2	−56.5	159.6	44 34.9	−56.7	159.9	43 38.5	−56.8	160.2	42 42.0	−57.0	160.5
20	44 34.7	−56.6	160.0	43 38.2	−56.7	160.4	42 41.7	−56.9	160.7	41 45.0	−57.1	161.0
21	43 38.1	−56.7	160.5	42 41.5	−56.9	160.8	41 44.8	−57.1	161.1	40 47.9	−57.1	161.4
22	42 41.4	−56.8	160.9	41 44.6	−56.9	161.2	40 47.7	−57.0	161.5	39 50.8	−57.2	161.8
23	41 44.6	−56.9	161.4	40 47.7	−57.1	161.7	39 50.7	−57.2	161.9	38 53.6	−57.3	162.2
24	40 47.7	−57.0	161.8	39 50.6	−57.1	162.1	38 53.5	−57.3	162.3	37 56.3	−57.4	162.6
25	39 50.7	−57.1	162.2	38 53.5	−57.2	162.5	37 56.2	−57.3	162.7	36 58.9	−57.4	162.9
26	38 53.6	−57.2	162.6	37 56.3	−57.3	162.8	36 58.9	−57.4	163.1	36 01.5	−57.5	163.3
27	37 56.4	−57.2	163.0	36 59.0	−57.3	163.2	36 01.5	−57.4	163.4	35 04.0	−57.6	163.6
28	36 59.2	−57.3	163.4	36 01.7	−57.4	163.6	35 04.1	−57.5	163.8	34 06.4	−57.6	164.0
29	36 01.9	−57.4	163.7	35 04.3	−57.5	163.9	34 06.6	−57.6	164.1	33 08.8	−57.6	164.3
30	35 04.5	−57.4	164.1	34 06.8	−57.5	164.3	33 09.0	−57.6	164.5	32 11.2	−57.8	164.6
31	34 07.1	−57.5	164.5	33 09.3	−57.6	164.6	32 11.4	−57.7	164.8	31 13.4	−57.7	165.0
32	33 09.6	−57.6	164.8	32 11.7	−57.7	165.0	31 13.7	−57.7	165.1	30 15.7	−57.8	165.3
33	32 12.0	−57.6	165.1	31 14.0	−57.7	165.3	30 16.0	−57.8	165.4	29 17.9	−57.9	165.6
34	31 14.4	−57.6	165.5	30 16.3	−57.7	165.6	29 18.2	−57.8	165.8	28 20.0	−57.8	165.9
35	30 16.8	−57.7	165.8	29 18.6	−57.8	165.9	28 20.4	−57.8	166.1	27 22.2	−58.0	166.2
36	29 19.1	−57.7	166.1	28 20.8	−57.8	166.2	27 22.6	−57.9	166.4	26 24.2	−57.9	166.5
37	28 21.4	−57.8	166.4	27 23.0	−57.8	166.5	26 24.7	−58.0	166.7	25 26.3	−58.0	166.8
38	27 23.6	−57.8	166.7	26 25.2	−57.9	166.8	25 26.7	−57.9	166.9	24 28.3	−58.0	167.1
39	26 25.8	−57.9	167.0	25 27.3	−57.9	167.1	24 28.8	−58.0	167.2	23 30.3	−58.1	167.3
40	25 27.9	−57.9	167.3	24 29.4	−58.0	167.4	23 30.8	−58.0	167.5	22 32.2	−58.1	167.6
41	24 30.0	−57.9	167.6	23 31.4	−58.0	167.7	22 32.8	−58.1	167.8	21 34.1	−58.1	167.9
42	23 32.1	−58.0	167.9	22 33.4	−58.0	168.0	21 34.7	−58.0	168.1	20 36.0	−58.1	168.1
43	22 34.1	−57.9	168.2	21 35.4	−58.0	168.3	20 36.7	−58.1	168.3	19 37.9	−58.2	168.4
44	21 36.2	−58.0	168.4	20 37.4	−58.1	168.5	19 38.6	−58.2	168.6	18 39.7	−58.1	168.7
45	20 38.2	−58.1	168.7	19 39.3	−58.1	168.8	18 40.4	−58.1	168.9	17 41.6	−58.2	168.9
46	19 40.1	−58.0	169.0	18 41.2	−58.1	169.1	17 42.3	−58.2	169.1	16 43.4	−58.2	169.2
47	18 42.1	−58.1	169.3	17 43.1	−58.1	169.3	16 44.1	−58.1	169.4	15 45.2	−58.3	169.4
48	17 44.0	−58.1	169.5	16 45.0	−58.2	169.6	15 46.0	−58.2	169.6	14 46.9	−58.2	169.7
49	16 45.9	−58.1	169.8	15 46.8	−58.2	169.8	14 47.8	−58.3	169.9	13 48.7	−58.3	169.9
50	15 47.8	−58.2	170.0	14 48.6	−58.1	170.1	13 49.5	−58.2	170.1	12 50.4	−58.2	170.2
51	14 49.6	−58.1	170.3	13 50.5	−58.2	170.3	12 51.3	−58.2	170.4	11 52.2	−58.3	170.4
52	13 51.5	−58.2	170.6	12 52.3	−58.3	170.6	11 53.1	−58.3	170.6	10 53.9	−58.3	170.7
53	12 53.3	−58.2	170.8	11 54.0	−58.2	170.8	10 54.8	−58.3	170.9	9 55.6	−58.3	170.9
54	11 55.1	−58.2	171.1	10 55.8	−58.2	171.1	9 56.5	−58.2	171.1	8 57.3	−58.4	171.1
55	10 56.9	−58.2	171.3	9 57.6	−58.3	171.3	8 58.3	−58.3	171.4	7 58.9	−58.3	171.4
56	9 58.7	−58.2	171.5	8 59.3	−58.2	171.6	8 00.0	−58.3	171.6	7 00.6	−58.3	171.6
57	9 00.5	−58.3	171.8	8 01.1	−58.3	171.8	7 01.7	−58.3	171.8	6 02.3	−58.4	171.9
58	8 02.2	−58.2	172.0	7 02.8	−58.3	172.1	6 03.4	−58.3	172.1	5 03.9	−58.3	172.1
59	7 04.0	−58.3	172.3	6 04.5	−58.3	172.3	5 05.1	−58.4	172.3	4 05.6	−58.3	172.3
60	6 05.7	−58.2	172.5	5 06.2	−58.2	172.5	4 06.7	−58.3	172.5	3 07.3	−58.4	172.6
61	5 07.5	−58.3	172.8	4 08.0	−58.2	172.8	3 08.4	−58.3	172.8	2 08.9	−58.3	172.8
62	4 09.2	−58.2	173.0	3 09.7	−58.3	173.0	2 10.1	−58.3	173.0	1 10.6	−58.4	173.0
63	3 11.0	−58.3	173.2	2 11.4	−58.2	173.2	1 11.8	−58.3	173.3	0 12.2	−58.4	173.3
64	2 12.7	−58.3	173.5	1 13.1	−58.3	173.5	0 13.5	−58.4	173.5	0 46.2	+58.5	6.5
65	1 14.4	−58.3	173.7	0 14.8	−58.3	173.7	0 44.9	+58.3	6.3	1 44.5	+58.4	6.3
66	0 16.1	−58.2	174.0	0 43.5	+58.3	6.0	1 43.2	+58.3	6.0	2 42.9	+58.3	6.0
67	0 42.1	+58.3	5.8	1 41.8	+58.3	5.8	2 41.5	+58.3	5.8	3 41.2	+58.4	5.8
68	1 40.4	+58.3	5.6	2 40.1	+58.3	5.6	3 39.8	+58.4	5.6	4 39.6	+58.3	5.6
69	2 38.7	+58.2	5.3	3 38.4	+58.3	5.3	4 38.2	+58.3	5.3	5 37.9	+58.3	5.3
70	3 36.9	+58.3	5.1	4 36.7	+58.3	5.1	5 36.5	+58.3	5.1	6 36.2	+58.4	5.1
71	4 35.2	+58.3	4.8	5 35.0	+58.3	4.9	6 34.8	+58.3	4.9	7 34.6	+58.3	4.9
72	5 33.5	+58.2	4.6	6 33.3	+58.2	4.6	7 33.1	+58.3	4.6	8 32.9	+58.3	4.6
73	6 31.7	+58.3	4.4	7 31.5	+58.3	4.4	8 31.4	+58.2	4.4	9 31.2	+58.3	4.4
74	7 30.0	+58.2	4.1	8 29.8	+58.3	4.1	9 29.6	+58.3	4.1	10 29.5	+58.3	4.2
75	8 28.2	+58.2	3.9	9 28.1	+58.2	3.9	10 27.9	+58.3	3.9	11 27.8	+58.3	3.9
76	9 26.4	+58.2	3.6	10 26.3	+58.2	3.7	11 26.2	+58.2	3.7	12 26.1	+58.2	3.7
77	10 24.6	+58.3	3.4	11 24.5	+58.3	3.4	12 24.4	+58.3	3.4	13 24.3	+58.3	3.4
78	11 22.9	+58.1	3.1	12 22.8	+58.2	3.2	13 22.7	+58.2	3.2	14 22.6	+58.2	3.2
79	12 21.0	+58.2	2.9	13 21.0	+58.2	2.9	14 20.9	+58.2	2.9	15 20.8	+58.2	2.9
80	13 19.2	+58.2	2.6	14 19.2	+58.1	2.7	15 19.1	+58.2	2.7	16 19.0	+58.2	2.7
81	14 17.4	+58.1	2.4	15 17.3	+58.2	2.4	16 17.3	+58.2	2.4	17 17.2	+58.2	2.4
82	15 15.5	+58.2	2.1	16 15.5	+58.1	2.2	17 15.5	+58.1	2.2	18 15.4	+58.2	2.2
83	16 13.7	+58.1	1.9	17 13.6	+58.2	1.9	18 13.6	+58.1	1.9	19 13.6	+58.0	1.9
84	17 11.8	+58.1	1.6	18 11.8	+58.1	1.6	19 11.7	+58.2	1.6	20 11.7	+58.1	1.7
85	18 09.9	+58.1	1.4	19 09.9	+58.0	1.4	20 09.9	+58.0	1.4	21 09.8	+58.1	1.4
86	19 08.0	+58.0	1.1	20 07.9	+58.1	1.1	21 07.9	+58.1	1.1	22 07.9	+58.1	1.1
87	20 06.0	+58.0	0.8	21 06.0	+58.0	0.8	22 06.0	+58.0	0.8	23 06.0	+58.0	0.8
88	21 04.0	+58.0	0.6	22 04.0	+58.0	0.6	23 04.0	+58.0	0.6	24 04.0	+58.0	0.6
89	22 02.0	+58.0	0.3	23 02.0	+58.0	0.3	24 02.0	+58.0	0.3	25 02.0	+58.0	0.3
90	23 00.0	+57.9	0.0	24 00.0	+57.9	0.0	25 00.0	+57.9	0.0	26 00.0	+57.9	0.0

Dec. (°)	27° Hc (° ′)	27° d (′)	27° Z (°)	28° Hc (° ′)	28° d (′)	28° Z (°)	29° Hc (° ′)	29° d (′)	29° Z (°)	30° Hc (° ′)	30° d (′)	30° Z (°)
0	59 23.4	−53.7	149.5	58 31.5	−54.1	150.3	57 39.1	−54.5	151.1	56 46.4	−54.8	151.8
1	58 29.7	−54.0	150.3	57 37.4	−54.5	151.1	56 44.6	−54.7	151.8	55 51.6	−55.2	152.5
2	57 35.7	−54.3	151.1	56 42.9	−54.6	151.9	55 49.9	−55.1	152.6	54 56.4	−55.3	153.2
3	56 41.4	−54.6	151.9	55 48.3	−55.0	152.6	54 54.8	−55.2	153.3	54 01.1	−55.6	153.9
4	55 46.8	−54.9	152.7	54 53.3	−55.2	153.3	53 59.6	−55.5	153.9	53 05.5	−55.7	154.5
5	54 51.9	−55.1	153.4	53 58.1	−55.3	154.0	53 04.1	−55.7	154.6	52 09.8	−56.0	155.1
6	53 56.8	−55.3	154.1	53 02.8	−55.6	154.6	52 08.4	−55.9	155.2	51 13.8	−56.1	155.7
7	53 01.5	−55.5	154.7	52 07.2	−55.8	155.3	51 12.5	−56.0	155.8	50 17.7	−56.2	156.3
8	52 06.0	−55.7	155.3	51 11.4	−56.0	155.9	50 16.5	−56.2	156.4	49 21.5	−56.5	156.8
9	51 10.3	−55.9	155.9	50 15.4	−56.1	156.4	49 20.3	−56.3	156.9	48 25.0	−56.5	157.3
10	50 14.4	−56.0	156.5	49 19.3	−56.3	157.0	48 24.0	−56.5	157.4	47 28.5	−56.7	157.8
11	49 18.4	−56.2	157.1	48 23.0	−56.4	157.5	47 27.5	−56.6	157.9	46 31.8	−56.7	158.3
12	48 22.2	−56.3	157.6	47 26.6	−56.5	158.0	46 30.9	−56.7	158.4	45 35.1	−56.9	158.8
13	47 25.9	−56.5	158.1	46 30.1	−56.7	158.5	45 34.2	−56.8	158.9	44 38.2	−57.0	159.2
14	46 29.4	−56.6	158.6	45 33.4	−56.7	159.0	44 37.4	−57.0	159.3	43 41.2	−57.1	159.7
15	45 32.8	−56.7	159.1	44 36.7	−56.9	159.4	43 40.4	−57.0	159.8	42 44.1	−57.2	160.1
16	44 36.1	−56.8	159.5	43 39.8	−57.0	159.9	42 43.4	−57.1	160.2	41 46.9	−57.3	160.5
17	43 39.3	−57.0	160.0	42 42.8	−57.0	160.3	41 46.3	−57.2	160.6	40 49.6	−57.3	160.9
18	42 42.3	−57.0	160.4	41 45.8	−57.2	160.7	40 49.1	−57.3	161.0	39 52.3	−57.4	161.3
19	41 45.3	−57.1	160.8	40 48.6	−57.2	161.1	39 51.8	−57.4	161.4	38 54.9	−57.5	161.7
20	40 48.2	−57.2	161.3	39 51.4	−57.4	161.5	38 54.4	−57.4	161.8	37 57.4	−57.6	162.0
21	39 51.0	−57.2	161.7	38 54.0	−57.4	161.9	37 57.0	−57.5	162.2	36 59.8	−57.6	162.4
22	38 53.8	−57.4	162.0	37 56.6	−57.4	162.3	36 59.5	−57.6	162.5	36 02.2	−57.7	162.7
23	37 56.4	−57.4	162.4	36 59.2	−57.5	162.6	36 01.9	−57.6	162.9	35 04.5	−57.7	163.1
24	36 59.0	−57.5	162.8	36 01.7	−57.6	163.0	35 04.3	−57.7	163.2	34 06.8	−57.8	163.4
25	36 01.5	−57.5	163.1	35 04.1	−57.7	163.3	34 06.6	−57.8	163.5	33 09.0	−57.8	163.7
26	35 04.0	−57.6	163.5	34 06.4	−57.7	163.7	33 08.8	−57.8	163.9	32 11.2	−57.9	164.0
27	34 06.4	−57.7	163.8	33 08.7	−57.7	164.0	32 11.0	−57.8	164.2	31 13.3	−57.9	164.4
28	33 08.7	−57.7	164.2	32 11.0	−57.8	164.3	31 13.2	−57.9	164.5	30 15.4	−58.0	164.7
29	32 11.0	−57.7	164.5	31 13.2	−57.8	164.7	30 15.3	−57.9	164.8	29 17.4	−58.0	165.0
30	31 13.3	−57.8	164.8	30 15.4	−57.9	165.0	29 17.4	−58.0	165.1	28 19.4	−58.0	165.2
31	30 15.5	−57.9	165.1	29 17.5	−57.9	165.3	28 19.4	−58.0	165.4	27 21.4	−58.1	165.5
32	29 17.6	−57.8	165.4	28 19.6	−58.0	165.6	27 21.4	−58.0	165.7	26 23.3	−58.1	165.8
33	28 19.8	−58.0	165.7	27 21.6	−58.0	165.9	26 23.4	−58.1	166.0	25 25.2	−58.2	166.1
34	27 21.8	−57.9	166.0	26 23.6	−58.0	166.1	25 25.3	−58.1	166.3	24 27.0	−58.1	166.4
35	26 23.9	−58.0	166.3	25 25.6	−58.1	166.4	24 27.2	−58.1	166.5	23 28.9	−58.2	166.6
36	25 25.9	−58.0	166.6	24 27.5	−58.1	166.7	23 29.1	−58.2	166.8	22 30.7	−58.3	166.9
37	24 27.9	−58.1	166.9	23 29.4	−58.1	167.0	22 30.9	−58.1	167.1	21 32.4	−58.2	167.2
38	23 29.8	−58.1	167.2	22 31.3	−58.2	167.2	21 32.8	−58.3	167.3	20 34.2	−58.3	167.4
39	22 31.7	−58.1	167.4	21 33.1	−58.1	167.5	20 34.5	−58.2	167.6	19 35.9	−58.2	167.7
40	21 33.6	−58.1	167.7	20 35.0	−58.2	167.8	19 36.3	−58.2	167.9	18 37.7	−58.4	167.9
41	20 35.5	−58.1	168.0	19 36.8	−58.3	168.0	18 38.1	−58.3	168.1	17 39.3	−58.3	168.2
42	19 37.3	−58.2	168.2	18 38.5	−58.2	168.3	17 39.8	−58.3	168.4	16 41.0	−58.3	168.4
43	18 39.1	−58.2	168.5	17 40.3	−58.2	168.5	16 41.5	−58.3	168.6	15 42.7	−58.4	168.7
44	17 40.9	−58.2	168.7	16 42.1	−58.3	168.8	15 43.2	−58.3	168.8	14 44.3	−58.4	168.9
45	16 42.7	−58.3	169.0	15 43.8	−58.3	169.0	14 44.9	−58.4	169.1	13 45.9	−58.3	169.1
46	15 44.4	−58.2	169.2	14 45.5	−58.3	169.3	13 46.5	−58.3	169.3	12 47.6	−58.4	169.4
47	14 46.2	−58.3	169.5	13 47.2	−58.3	169.5	12 48.2	−58.4	169.6	11 49.2	−58.5	169.6
48	13 47.9	−58.3	169.7	12 48.9	−58.4	169.8	11 49.8	−58.4	169.8	10 50.7	−58.4	169.8
49	12 49.6	−58.3	170.0	11 50.5	−58.3	170.0	10 51.4	−58.4	170.0	9 52.3	−58.4	170.1
50	11 51.3	−58.3	170.2	10 52.2	−58.4	170.2	9 53.0	−58.4	170.3	8 53.9	−58.4	170.3
51	10 53.0	−58.3	170.5	9 53.8	−58.4	170.5	8 54.6	−58.4	170.5	7 55.5	−58.5	170.5
52	9 54.7	−58.4	170.7	8 55.4	−58.3	170.7	7 56.2	−58.4	170.7	6 57.0	−58.4	170.8
53	8 56.3	−58.3	170.9	7 57.1	−58.4	171.0	6 57.8	−58.4	171.0	5 58.6	−58.5	171.0
54	7 58.0	−58.4	171.2	6 58.7	−58.4	171.2	5 59.4	−58.4	171.2	5 00.1	−58.5	171.2
55	6 59.6	−58.3	171.4	6 00.3	−58.4	171.4	5 01.0	−58.5	171.4	4 01.6	−58.4	171.4
56	6 01.3	−58.4	171.6	5 01.9	−58.4	171.6	4 02.5	−58.4	171.7	3 03.2	−58.5	171.7
57	5 02.9	−58.4	171.9	4 03.5	−58.4	171.9	3 04.1	−58.4	171.9	2 04.7	−58.5	171.9
58	4 04.5	−58.4	172.1	3 05.1	−58.4	172.1	2 05.7	−58.5	172.1	1 06.2	−58.5	172.1
59	3 06.1	−58.3	172.3	2 06.7	−58.4	172.3	1 07.2	−58.4	172.3	0 07.7	−58.4	172.3
60	2 07.8	−58.4	172.6	1 08.3	−58.4	172.6	0 08.8	−58.5	172.6	0 50.7	+58.5	7.4
61	1 09.4	−58.4	172.8	0 09.9	−58.5	172.8	0 49.7	+58.4	7.2	1 49.2	+58.5	7.2
62	0 11.0	−58.4	173.0	0 48.6	+58.4	7.0	1 48.1	+58.5	7.0	2 47.7	+58.4	7.0
63	0 47.4	+58.4	6.7	1 47.0	+58.4	6.8	2 46.6	+58.4	6.8	3 46.1	+58.5	6.8
64	1 45.8	+58.3	6.5	2 45.4	+58.4	6.5	3 45.0	+58.4	6.5	4 44.6	+58.5	6.5
65	2 44.1	+58.4	6.3	3 43.8	+58.4	6.3	4 43.4	+58.5	6.3	5 43.1	+58.4	6.3
66	3 42.5	+58.4	6.1	4 42.2	+58.4	6.1	5 41.9	+58.4	6.1	6 41.5	+58.5	6.1
67	4 40.9	+58.4	5.8	5 40.6	+58.4	5.8	6 40.3	+58.4	5.8	7 40.0	+58.4	5.9
68	5 39.3	+58.3	5.6	6 39.0	+58.4	5.6	7 38.7	+58.4	5.6	8 38.4	+58.4	5.6
69	6 37.6	+58.4	5.4	7 37.4	+58.3	5.4	8 37.1	+58.4	5.4	9 36.8	+58.5	5.4
70	7 36.0	+58.3	5.1	8 35.7	+58.4	5.1	9 35.5	+58.4	5.2	10 35.3	+58.4	5.2
71	8 34.3	+58.4	4.9	9 34.1	+58.4	4.9	10 33.9	+58.4	4.9	11 33.7	+58.4	4.9
72	9 32.7	+58.3	4.7	10 32.5	+58.3	4.7	11 32.3	+58.4	4.7	12 32.1	+58.4	4.7
73	10 31.0	+58.3	4.4	11 30.8	+58.4	4.4	12 30.7	+58.3	4.4	13 30.5	+58.3	4.5
74	11 29.3	+58.3	4.2	12 29.2	+58.3	4.2	13 29.0	+58.4	4.2	14 28.8	+58.4	4.2
75	12 27.6	+58.3	3.9	13 27.5	+58.3	3.9	14 27.4	+58.3	4.0	15 27.2	+58.4	4.0
76	13 25.9	+58.3	3.7	14 25.8	+58.3	3.7	15 25.7	+58.3	3.7	16 25.6	+58.3	3.7
77	14 24.2	+58.3	3.4	15 24.1	+58.3	3.5	16 24.0	+58.3	3.5	17 23.9	+58.3	3.5
78	15 22.5	+58.2	3.2	16 22.4	+58.3	3.2	17 22.3	+58.3	3.2	18 22.2	+58.3	3.3
79	16 20.7	+58.3	3.0	17 20.7	+58.2	3.0	18 20.6	+58.2	3.0	19 20.5	+58.3	3.0
80	17 19.0	+58.2	2.7	18 18.9	+58.2	2.7	19 18.8	+58.3	2.7	20 18.8	+58.2	2.7
81	18 17.2	+58.2	2.4	19 17.1	+58.2	2.5	20 17.1	+58.2	2.5	21 17.0	+58.2	2.5
82	19 15.4	+58.1	2.2	20 15.3	+58.2	2.2	21 15.3	+58.2	2.2	22 15.2	+58.2	2.2
83	20 13.5	+58.2	1.9	21 13.5	+58.2	1.9	22 13.5	+58.1	2.0	23 13.4	+58.2	2.0
84	21 11.7	+58.1	1.7	22 11.7	+58.1	1.7	23 11.6	+58.2	1.7	24 11.6	+58.2	1.7
85	22 09.8	+58.1	1.4	23 09.8	+58.1	1.4	24 09.8	+58.1	1.4	25 09.8	+58.1	1.4
86	23 07.9	+58.1	1.1	24 07.9	+58.1	1.1	25 07.9	+58.1	1.1	26 07.9	+58.1	1.2
87	24 06.0	+58.0	0.9	25 06.0	+58.0	0.9	26 06.0	+58.0	0.9	27 06.0	+58.0	0.9
88	25 04.0	+58.0	0.6	26 04.0	+58.0	0.6	27 04.0	+58.0	0.6	28 04.0	+58.0	0.6
89	26 02.0	+58.0	0.3	27 02.0	+58.0	0.3	28 02.0	+58.0	0.3	29 02.0	+58.0	0.3
90	27 00.0	+57.9	0.0	28 00.0	+57.9	0.0	29 00.0	+57.9	0.0	30 00.0	+57.9	0.0

S. Lat. { L.H.A. greater than 180° .... Zn=180°−Z; L.H.A. less than 180° .... Zn=180°+Z

LATITUDE SAME NAME AS DECLINATION — L.H.A. 165°, 195°

Dec.	23° Hc	d	Z	24° Hc	d	Z	25° Hc	d	Z	26° Hc	d	Z	27° Hc	d	Z	28° Hc	d	Z	29° Hc	d	Z	30° Hc	d	Z	Dec.
°	° ′	′	°	° ′	′	°	° ′	′	°	° ′	′	°	° ′	′	°	° ′	′	°	° ′	′	°	° ′	′	°	°
0	62 14.0	+50.0	143.7	61 25.2	+50.8	144.8	60 35.9	+51.4	145.8	59 46.0	+52.0	146.8	58 55.5	+52.6	147.7	58 04.5	+53.1	148.6	57 13.1	+53.5	149.4	56 21.2	+54.0	150.2	0
1	63 04.0	+49.3	142.5	62 16.0	+50.1	143.7	61 27.3	+50.9	144.8	60 38.0	+51.5	145.8	59 48.1	+52.1	146.8	58 57.6	+52.7	147.7	58 06.6	+53.3	148.6	57 15.2	+53.7	149.4	1
2	63 53.3	+48.7	141.3	63 06.1	+49.6	142.5	62 18.2	+50.3	143.7	61 29.5	+51.0	144.7	60 40.2	+51.7	145.8	59 50.3	+52.3	146.8	58 59.9	+52.8	147.7	58 08.9	+53.3	148.5	2
3	64 42.0	+47.9	139.9	63 55.7	+48.8	141.2	63 08.5	+49.6	142.5	62 20.5	+50.5	143.6	61 31.9	+51.1	144.7	60 42.6	+51.8	145.8	59 52.7	+52.4	146.7	59 02.2	+53.0	147.7	3
4	65 29.9	+47.0	138.5	64 44.5	+48.0	139.9	63 58.1	+49.0	141.2	63 11.0	+49.8	142.4	62 23.0	+50.6	143.6	61 34.4	+51.3	144.7	60 45.1	+51.9	145.8	59 55.2	+52.6	146.7	4
5	66 16.9	+46.1	136.9	65 32.5	+47.2	138.5	64 47.1	+48.2	139.9	64 00.8	+49.1	141.2	63 13.6	+50.0	142.4	62 25.7	+50.7	143.6	61 37.0	+51.5	144.7	60 47.8	+52.1	145.8	5
6	67 03.0	+45.0	135.3	66 19.7	+46.2	136.9	65 35.3	+47.4	138.4	64 49.9	+48.4	139.9	64 03.6	+49.3	141.2	63 16.4	+50.2	142.4	62 28.5	+50.9	143.6	61 39.9	+51.6	144.7	6
7	67 48.0	+43.8	133.6	67 05.9	+45.3	135.3	66 22.7	+46.4	136.9	65 38.3	+47.5	138.5	64 52.9	+48.6	139.9	64 06.6	+49.4	141.2	63 19.4	+50.3	142.5	62 31.5	+51.0	143.6	7
8	68 31.8	+42.6	131.8	67 51.2	+44.0	133.6	67 09.1	+45.4	135.3	66 25.8	+46.7	137.0	65 41.5	+47.7	138.5	64 56.0	+48.8	139.9	64 09.7	+49.7	141.2	63 22.5	+50.5	142.5	8
9	69 14.4	+41.2	129.8	68 35.2	+42.8	131.8	67 54.5	+44.3	133.6	67 12.5	+45.6	135.4	66 29.2	+46.8	137.0	65 44.8	+47.9	138.5	64 59.4	+48.9	139.9	64 13.0	+49.8	141.3	9
10	69 55.6	+39.6	127.7	69 18.0	+41.4	129.8	68 38.8	+43.0	131.8	67 58.1	+44.4	133.6	67 16.0	+45.8	135.4	66 32.7	+47.0	137.0	65 48.3	+48.1	138.5	65 02.8	+49.1	140.0	10
11	70 35.2	+37.8	125.5	69 59.4	+39.8	127.7	69 21.8	+41.6	129.9	68 42.5	+43.3	131.8	68 01.8	+44.7	133.7	67 19.7	+46.0	135.4	66 36.4	+47.2	137.0	65 51.9	+48.3	138.6	11
12	71 13.0	+36.0	•123.1	70 39.2	+38.1	125.5	70 03.4	+40.0	127.8	69 25.8	+41.8	129.9	68 46.5	+43.4	131.9	68 05.7	+44.9	133.7	67 23.6	+46.2	135.5	66 40.2	+47.4	137.1	12
13	71 49.0	+33.8	•120.6	71 17.3	+36.2	•123.2	70 43.4	+38.4	125.6	70 07.6	+40.3	127.8	69 29.9	+42.1	129.9	68 50.6	+43.7	131.9	68 09.8	+45.1	133.8	67 27.6	+46.5	135.5	13
14	72 22.8	+31.6	•117.9	71 53.5	+34.1	•120.6	71 21.8	+36.4	•123.2	70 47.9	+38.6	125.6	70 12.0	+40.5	127.9	69 34.3	+42.3	130.0	68 54.9	+43.9	132.0	68 14.1	+45.3	133.8	14
15	72 54.4	+29.0	•115.1	72 27.6	+31.8	•117.9	71 58.2	+34.3	•120.7	71 26.5	+36.6	•123.2	70 52.5	+38.9	125.6	70 16.6	+40.8	127.9	69 38.8	+42.6	130.0	68 59.4	+44.2	132.0	15
16	73 23.4	+26.2	•112.0	72 59.4	+29.2	•115.1	72 32.5	+32.1	•118.0	72 03.1	+34.6	•120.7	71 31.4	+36.9	•123.3	70 57.4	+39.1	125.7	70 21.4	+41.0	128.0	69 43.6	+42.8	130.1	16
17	73 49.6	+23.2	•108.9	73 28.6	+26.5	•112.1	73 04.6	+29.5	•115.1	72 37.7	+32.3	•118.0	72 08.3	+34.9	•120.8	71 36.5	+37.2	•123.3	71 02.4	+39.4	125.8	70 26.4	+41.3	128.1	17
18	74 12.8	+20.0	•105.5	73 55.1	+23.4	•108.9	73 34.1	+26.7	•112.1	73 10.0	+29.8	•115.1	72 43.2	+32.5	•118.1	72 13.7	+35.1	•120.8	71 41.8	+37.5	•123.4	71 07.7	+39.6	125.9	18
19	74 32.8	+16.6	•102.0	74 18.5	+20.3	•105.5	74 00.8	+23.7	•108.9	73 39.8	+27.0	•112.1	73 15.7	+30.1	•115.2	72 48.8	+32.8	•118.1	72 19.3	+35.4	•120.9	71 47.3	+37.7	123.5	19
20	74 49.4	+12.9	• 98.4	74 38.8	+16.8	•102.0	74 24.5	+20.5	•105.5	74 06.8	+24.0	•108.9	73 45.8	+27.2	•112.1	73 21.6	+30.4	•115.2	72 54.7	+33.1	•118.2	72 25.0	+35.7	•121.0	20
21	75 02.3	+9.2	• 94.6	74 55.6	+13.1	• 98.3	74 45.0	+17.0	•102.0	74 30.8	+20.7	•105.5	74 13.0	+24.3	•108.9	73 52.0	+27.5	•112.2	73 27.8	+30.6	•115.3	73 00.7	+33.5	•118.3	21
22	75 11.5	+5.3	• 90.8	75 08.7	+9.4	• 94.5	75 02.0	+13.4	• 98.3	74 51.5	+17.2	•101.9	74 37.3	+20.9	•105.5	74 19.5	+24.5	•108.9	73 58.4	+27.8	•112.2	73 34.2	+30.8	•115.4	22
23	75 16.8	+1.3	• 86.9	75 18.1	+5.4	• 90.7	75 15.4	+9.5	• 94.5	75 08.7	+13.6	• 98.2	74 58.2	+17.5	•101.9	74 44.0	+21.2	•105.5	74 26.2	+24.8	•109.0	74 05.0	+28.1	•112.3	23
24	75 18.1	-2.7	• 82.9	75 23.5	+1.4	• 86.7	75 24.9	+5.6	• 90.6	75 22.3	+9.7	• 94.4	75 15.7	+13.8	• 98.2	75 05.2	+17.7	•101.9	74 51.0	+21.5	•105.5	74 33.1	+25.1	•109.0	24
25	75 15.4	-6.7	• 79.0	75 24.9	-2.6	• 82.8	75 30.5	+1.5	• 86.6	75 32.0	+5.7	• 90.5	75 29.5	+9.8	• 94.3	75 22.9	+14.0	• 98.2	75 12.5	+17.9	•101.9	74 58.2	+21.7	•105.6	25
26	75 08.7	-10.5	• 75.1	75 22.3	-6.6	• 78.8	75 32.0	-2.5	• 82.6	75 37.7	+1.6	• 86.5	75 39.3	+5.9	• 90.4	75 36.9	+10.1	• 94.3	75 30.4	+14.2	• 98.1	75 19.9	+18.2	•101.9	26
27	74 58.2	-14.2	• 71.3	75 15.7	-10.5	• 74.9	75 29.5	-6.6	• 78.6	75 39.3	-2.4	• 82.4	75 45.2	+1.8	• 86.3	75 47.0	+6.0	• 90.3	75 44.6	+10.3	• 94.2	75 38.1	+14.5	• 98.1	27
28	74 44.0	-17.8	• 67.6	75 05.2	-14.2	• 71.0	75 22.9	-10.4	• 74.7	75 36.9	-6.5	• 78.4	75 47.0	-2.4	• 82.3	75 53.0	+1.9	• 86.2	75 54.9	+6.1	• 90.2	75 52.6	+10.4	• 94.2	28
29	74 26.2	-21.2	• 64.0	74 51.0	-17.9	• 67.3	75 12.5	-14.3	• 70.8	75 30.4	-10.5	• 74.4	75 44.6	-6.5	• 78.2	75 54.9	-2.3	• 82.1	76 01.0	+2.0	• 86.1	76 03.0	+6.3	• 90.1	29
30	74 05.0	-24.3	• 60.5	74 33.1	-21.2	• 63.7	74 58.2	-17.9	• 67.0	75 19.9	-14.2	• 70.5	75 38.1	-10.4	• 74.2	75 52.6	-6.5	• 78.0	76 03.0	-2.2	• 82.0	76 09.3	+2.1	• 86.0	30
31	73 40.7	-27.2	• 57.2	74 11.9	-24.4	• 60.2	74 40.3	-21.3	• 63.4	75 05.7	-18.0	• 66.7	75 27.7	-14.4	• 70.2	75 46.1	-10.5	• 74.0	76 00.8	-6.5	• 77.8	76 11.4	-2.2	• 81.8	31
32	73 13.5	-29.9	• 54.1	73 47.5	-27.3	• 56.9	74 19.0	-24.5	• 59.9	74 47.7	-21.4	• 63.0	75 13.3	-18.0	• 66.4	75 35.6	-14.3	• 70.0	75 54.3	-10.4	• 73.7	76 09.2	-6.4	• 77.6	32
33	72 43.6	-32.3	• 51.1	73 20.2	-30.0	• 53.7	73 54.5	-27.4	• 56.5	74 26.3	-24.5	• 59.5	74 55.3	-21.4	• 62.7	75 21.3	-18.1	• 66.1	75 43.9	-14.5	• 69.7	76 02.8	-10.5	• 73.5	33
34	72 11.3	-34.6	• 48.3	72 50.2	-32.5	• 50.7	73 27.1	-30.1	• 53.4	74 01.8	-27.6	• 56.2	74 33.9	-24.7	• 59.2	75 03.2	-21.6	• 62.4	75 29.4	-18.1	• 65.8	75 52.3	-14.5	• 69.4	34
35	71 36.7	-36.7	45.7	72 17.7	-34.7	• 47.9	72 57.0	-32.6	• 50.4	73 34.2	-30.3	• 53.0	74 09.2	-27.7	• 55.8	74 41.6	-24.8	• 58.8	75 11.3	-21.7	• 62.0	75 37.8	-18.3	• 65.5	35
36	71 00.0	-38.5	43.2	71 43.0	-36.8	45.3	72 24.4	-34.9	• 47.5	73 03.9	-32.7	• 50.0	73 41.5	-30.4	• 52.6	74 16.8	-27.8	• 55.4	74 49.6	-25.0	• 58.4	75 19.5	-21.8	• 61.7	36
37	70 21.5	-40.1	40.9	71 06.2	-38.6	42.8	71 49.5	-36.9	44.9	72 31.2	-35.0	• 47.1	73 11.1	-32.9	• 49.5	73 49.0	-30.6	• 52.2	74 24.6	-28.0	• 55.0	74 57.7	-25.1	• 58.0	37
38	69 41.4	-41.7	38.7	70 27.6	-40.3	40.5	71 12.6	-38.8	42.4	71 56.2	-37.1	44.5	72 38.2	-35.2	• 46.7	73 18.4	-33.1	• 49.1	73 56.6	-30.7	• 51.7	74 32.6	-28.2	• 54.6	38
39	68 59.7	-43.0	36.7	69 47.3	-41.8	38.3	70 33.8	-40.4	40.1	71 19.1	-38.9	42.0	72 03.0	-37.3	44.0	72 45.3	-35.4	• 46.3	73 25.9	-33.3	• 48.7	74 04.4	-30.9	• 51.3	39
40	68 16.7	-44.3	34.8	69 05.5	-43.2	36.3	69 53.4	-42.0	37.9	70 40.2	-40.6	39.6	71 25.7	-39.1	41.5	72 09.9	-37.4	43.6	72 52.6	-35.6	• 45.8	73 33.5	-33.5	• 48.2	40
41	67 32.4	-45.4	33.0	68 22.3	-44.4	34.4	69 11.4	-43.3	35.8	69 59.6	-42.2	37.4	70 46.6	-40.7	39.2	71 32.5	-39.3	41.1	72 17.0	-37.6	43.1	73 00.0	-35.7	• 45.4	41
42	66 47.0	-46.4	31.3	67 37.9	-45.5	32.6	68 28.1	-44.6	33.9	69 17.4	-43.4	35.4	70 05.9	-42.3	37.0	70 53.2	-40.9	38.7	71 39.4	-39.4	40.6	72 24.3	-37.8	• 42.7	42
43	66 00.6	-47.4	29.7	66 52.4	-46.6	30.9	67 43.5	-45.6	32.1	68 34.0	-44.7	33.5	69 23.6	-43.6	34.9	70 12.3	-42.4	36.5	71 00.0	-41.2	38.3	71 46.5	-39.7	40.1	43
44	65 13.2	-48.1	28.2	66 05.8	-47.4	29.3	66 57.9	-46.7	30.4	67 49.3	-45.8	31.7	68 40.0	-44.9	33.0	69 29.9	-43.8	34.5	70 18.8	-42.6	36.1	71 06.8	-41.3	37.8	44
45	64 25.1	-48.9	26.8	65 18.4	-48.3	27.8	66 11.2	-47.6	28.9	67 03.5	-46.8	30.0	67 55.1	-45.9	31.2	68 46.1	-45.1	32.6	69 36.2	-44.0	34.0	70 25.5	-42.8	35.6	45
46	63 36.2	-49.6	25.5	64 30.1	-49.0	26.4	65 23.6	-48.4	27.4	66 16.7	-47.7	28.4	67 09.2	-47.0	29.5	68 01.0	-46.1	30.8	68 52.2	-45.2	32.1	69 42.7	-44.2	33.5	46
47	62 46.6	-50.3	24.3	63 41.1	-49.7	25.1	64 35.2	-49.1	26.0	65 29.0	-48.6	26.9	66 22.2	-47.9	28.0	67 14.9	-47.1	29.1	68 07.0	-46.2	30.3	68 58.5	-45.4	31.6	47
48	61 56.3	-50.8	23.1	62 51.4	-50.4	23.8	63 46.1	-49.8	24.7	64 40.4	-49.3	25.5	65 34.3	-48.6	26.5	66 27.8	-48.0	27.5	67 20.8	-47.3	28.6	68 13.1	-46.4	29.8	48
49	61 05.5	-51.3	22.0	62 01.0	-50.9	22.7	62 56.3	-50.5	23.4	63 51.1	-49.9	24.2	64 45.7	-49.4	25.1	65 39.8	-48.8	26.0	66 33.5	-48.2	27.0	67 26.7	-47.5	28.1	49
50	60 14.2	-51.8	20.9	61 10.1	-51.4	21.6	62 05.8	-51.0	22.2	63 01.2	-50.6	23.0	63 56.3	-50.1	23.8	64 51.0	-49.5	24.6	65 45.3	-48.9	25.6	66 39.2	-48.3	26.6	50
51	59 22.4	-52.2	19.9	60 18.7	-51.9	20.5	61 14.8	-51.5	21.1	62 10.6	-51.1	21.8	63 06.2	-50.7	22.5	64 01.5	-50.2	23.3	64 56.4	-49.7	24.2	65 50.9	-49.1	25.1	51
52	58 30.2	-52.7	19.0	59 26.8	-52.3	19.5	60 23.3	-52.0	20.1	61 19.5	-51.6	20.7	62 15.5	-51.2	21.4	63 11.3	-50.9	22.1	64 06.7	-50.4	22.9	65 01.8	-49.8	23.7	52
53	57 37.5	-53.0	18.0	58 34.5	-52.7	18.6	59 31.3	-52.4	19.1	60 27.9	-52.1	19.7	61 24.3	-51.8	20.3	62 20.4	-51.3	20.9	63 16.3	-50.9	21.6	64 12.0	-50.5	22.4	53
54	56 44.5	-53.4	17.2	57 41.8	-53.1	17.6	58 38.9	-52.9	18.1	59 35.8	-52.5	18.7	60 32.5	-52.2	19.2	61 29.1	-51.9	19.8	62 25.4	-51.5	20.5	63 21.5	-51.1	21.2	54
55	55 51.1	-53.6	16.4	56 48.7	-53.5	16.8	57 46.0	-53.2	17.2	58 43.3	-53.0	17.7	59 40.3	-52.6	18.2	60 37.2	-52.3	18.8	61 33.9	-52.0	19.4	62 30.4	-51.6	20.0	55
56	54 57.5	-54.0	15.6	55 55.2	-53.7	16.0	56 52.8	-53.5	16.4	57 50.3	-53.2	16.8	58 47.7	-53.0	17.3	59 44.9	-52.7	17.8	60 41.9	-52.4	18.4	61 38.8	-52.1	18.9	56
57	54 03.5	-54.2	14.8	55 01.5	-54.1	15.2	55 59.3	-53.8	15.6	56 57.1	-53.7	16.0	57 54.7	-53.4	16.4	58 52.2	-53.2	16.9	59 49.5	-52.8	17.4	60 46.7	-52.6	17.9	57
58	53 09.3	-54.5	14.1	54 07.4	-54.3	14.4	55 05.5	-54.1	14.8	56 03.4	-53.9	15.2	57 01.3	-53.7	15.6	57 59.0	-53.4	16.0	58 56.7	-53.3	16.4	59 54.1	-52.9	16.9	58
59	52 14.8	-54.7	13.4	53 13.1	-54.5	13.7	54 11.4	-54.4	14.0	55 09.5	-54.2	14.4	56 07.6	-54.0	14.8	57 05.6	-53.8	15.1	58 03.4	-53.6	15.6	59 01.2	-53.4	16.0	59
60	51 20.1	-55.0	12.7	52 18.6	-54.8	13.0	53 17.0	-54.7	13.3	54 15.3	-54.4	13.6	55 13.6	-54.3	14.0	56 11.8	-54.1	14.3	57 09.8	-53.9	14.7	58 07.8	-53.7	15.1	60
61	50 25.1	-55.1	12.1	51 23.8	-55.0	12.4	52 22.3	-54.8	12.6	53 20.9	-54.7	12.9	54 19.3	-54.5	13.2	55 17.7	-54.4	13.6	56 15.9	-54.2	13.9	57 14.1	-54.0	14.3	61
62	49 30.0	-55.3	11.5	50 28.8	-55.2	11.7	51 27.5	-55.1	12.0	52 26.2	-55.0	12.3	53 24.8	-54.8	12.5	54 23.3	-54.6	12.8	55 21.7	-54.4	13.2	56 20.1	-54.3	13.5	62
63	48 34.7	-55.5	10.9	49 33.6	-55.4	11.1	50 32.4	-55.2	11.4	51 31.2	-55.1	11.6	52 30.0	-55.0	11.9	53 28.7	-54.9	12.1	54 27.3	-54.7	12.4	55 25.8	-54.5	12.7	63
64	47 39.2	-55.7	10.3	48 38.2	-55.6	10.5	49 37.2	-55.5	10.7	50 36.1	-55.4	11.0	51 35.0	-55.3	11.2	52 33.8	-55.1	11.5	53 32.6	-55.0	11.7	54 31.3	-54.8	12.0	64
65	46 43.5	-55.8	9.8	47 42.6	-55.7	10.0	48 41.7	-55.6	10.2	49 40.7	-55.5	10.4	50 39.7	-55.4	10.6	51 38.7	-55.3	10.8	52 37.6	-55.2	11.1	53 36.5	-55.1	11.3	65
66	45 47.7	-56.0	9.3	46 46.9	-55.9	9.4	47 46.1	-55.8	9.6	48 45.2	-55.7	9.8	49 44.3	-55.6	10.0	50 43.4	-55.5	10.2	51 42.4	-55.3	10.4	52 41.4	-55.2	10.7	66
67	44 51.7	-56.0	8.7	45 51.0	-56.0	8.9	46 50.3	-55.9	9.1	47 49.5	-55.8	9.2	48 48.7	-55.7	9.4	49 47.9	-55.6	9.6	50 47.1	-55.6	9.8	51 46.2	-55.5	10.0	67
68	43 55.7	-56.3	8.2	44 55.0	-56.1	8.4	45 54.4	-56.1	8.5	46 53.7	-56.0	8.7	47 53.0	-55.9	8.9	48 52.3	-55.9	9.0	49 51.5	-55.7	9.2	50 50.7	-55.6	9.4	68
69	42 59.4	-56.3	7.8	43 58.9	-56.3	7.9	44 58.3	-56.2	8.0	45 57.7	-56.1	8.2	46 57.1	-56.1	8.3	47 56.4	-55.9	8.5	48 55.8	-55.9	8.6	49 55.1	-55.8	8.8	69
70	42 03.1	-56.4	7.3	43 02.6	-56.4	7.4	44 02.1	-56.3	7.5	45 01.6	-56.3	7.7	46 01.0	-56.2	7.8	47 00.5	-56.2	7.9	47 59.9	-56.1	8.1	48 59.3	-56.0	8.3	70
71	41 06.7	-56.6	6.8	42 06.2	-56.5	6.9	43 05.8	-56.5	7.1	44 05.3	-56.4	7.2	45 04.8	-56.3	7.3	46 04.3	-56.2	7.4	47 03.8	-56.2	7.6	48 03.3	-56.1	7.7	71
72	40 10.1	-56.6	6.4	41 09.7	-56.6	6.5	42 09.3	-56.5	6.6	43 08.9	-56.4	6.7	44 08.5	-56.4	6.8	45 08.1	-56.4	6.9	46 07.6	-56.3	7.1	47 07.2	-56.3	7.2	72
73	39 13.5	-56.8	6.0	40 13.1	-56.6	6.1	41 12.8	-56.6	6.1	42 12.5	-56.6	6.2	43 12.1	-56.6	6.3	44 11.7	-56.5	6.5	45 11.3	-56.4	6.6	46 10.9	-56.4	6.7	73
74	38 16.7	-56.8	5.6	39 16.5	-56.8	5.6	40 16.2	-56.8	5.7	41 15.9	-56.7	5.8	42 15.5	-56.6	5.9	43 15.2	-56.6	6.0	44 14.9	-56.6	6.1	45 14.5	-56.5	6.2	74
75	37 19.9	-56.9	5.1	38 19.7	-56.9	5.2	39 19.4	-56.8	5.3	40 19.2	-56.8	5.4	41 18.9	-56.8	5.5	42 18.6	-56.7	5.5	43 18.3	-56.6	5.6	44 18.0	-56.6	5.7	75
76	36 23.0	-57.0	4.8	37 22.8	-56.9	4.8	38 22.6	-56.9	4.9	39 22.4	-56.9	4.9	40 22.1	-56.8	5.0	41 21.9	-56.8	5.1	42 21.7	-56.8	5.2	43 21.4	-56.7	5.3	76
77	35 26.0	-57.0	4.4	36 25.9	-57.1	4.4	37 25.7	-57.0	4.5	38 25.5	-57.0	4.5	39 25.3	-56.9	4.6	40 25.1	-56.9	4.7	41 24.9	-56.9	4.7	42 24.7	-56.8	4.8	77
78	34 29.0	-57.1	4.0	35 28.8	-57.1	4.0	36 28.7	-57.1	4.1	37 28.5	-57.0	4.1	38 28.4	-57.0	4.2	39 28.2	-57.0	4.3	40 28.0	-56.9	4.3	41 27.9	-57.0	4.4	78
79	33 31.9	-57.2	3.6	34 31.7	-57.1	3.7	35 31.6	-57.1	3.7	36 31.5	-57.1	3.8	37 31.4	-57.1	3.8	38 31.2	-57.0	3.9	39 31.1	-57.0	3.9	40 30.9	-57.0	4.0	79
80	32 34.7	-57.3	3.3	33 34.6	-57.2	3.3	34 34.5	-57.2	3.3	35 34.4	-57.2	3.4	36 34.3	-57.2	3.4	37 34.2	-57.2	3.5	38 34.1	-57.2	3.5	39 33.9	-57.1	3.6	80
81	31 37.4	-57.3	2.9	32 37.4	-57.4	2.9	33 37.3	-57.3	3.0	34 37.2	-57.3	3.0	35 37.1	-57.2	3.0	36 37.0	-57.2	3.1	37 36.9	-57.2	3.1	38 36.8	-57.1	3.2	81
82	30 40.1	-57.3	2.6	31 40.1	-57.4	2.6	32 40.0	-57.3	2.6	33 39.9	-57.3	2.6	34 39.9	-57.3	2.7	35 39.8	-57.3	2.7	36 39.7	-57.2	2.7	37 39.7	-57.3	2.8	82
83	29 42.8	-57.4	2.2	30 42.7	-57.4	2.2	31 42.7	-57.4	2.3	32 42.6	-57.3	2.3	33 42.6	-57.4	2.3	34 42.5	-57.3	2.3	35 42.5	-57.3	2.4	36 42.4	-57.3	2.4	83
84	28 45.4	-57.5	1.9	29 45.3	-57.4	1.9	30 45.3	-57.4	1.9	31 45.3	-57.5	1.9	32 45.2	-57.4	2.0	33 45.2	-57.4	2.0	34 45.2	-57.4	2.0	35 45.1	-57.4	2.0	84
85	27 47.9	-57.5	1.6	28 47.9	-57.5	1.6	29 47.9	-57.5	1.6	30 47.8	-57.4	1.6	31 47.8	-57.4	1.6	32 47.8	-57.5	1.6	33 47.8	-57.5	1.7	34 47.7	-57.4	1.7	85
86	26 50.4	-57.5	1.2	27 50.4	-57.5	1.2	28 50.4	-57.6	1.3	29 50.4	-57.6	1.3	30 50.4	-57.6	1.3	31 50.3	-57.5	1.3	32 50.3	-57.5	1.3	33 50.3	-57.5	1.3	86
87	25 52.9	-57.6	0.9	26 52.9	-57.6	0.9	27 52.8	-57.5	0.9	28 52.8	-57.5	0.9	29 52.8	-57.5	1.0	30 52.8	-57.5	1.0	31 52.8	-57.5	1.0	32 52.8	-57.5	1.0	87
88	24 55.3	-57.6	0.6	25 55.3	-57.6	0.6	26 55.3	-57.6	0.6	27 55.3	-57.6	0.6	28 55.3	-57.6	0.6	29 55.3	-57.6	0.6	30 55.3	-57.6	0.6	31 55.3	-57.6	0.6	88
89	23 57.7	-57.7	0.3	24 57.7	-57.7	0.3	25 57.7	-57.7	0.3	26 57.7	-57.7	0.3	27 57.7	-57.7	0.3	28 57.7	-57.7	0.3	29 57.7	-57.7	0.3	30 57.7	-57.7	0.3	89
90	23 00.0	-57.7	0.0	24 00.0	-57.7	0.0	25 00.0	-57.7	0.0	26 00.0	-57.7	0.0	27 00.0	-57.7	0.0	28 00.0	-57.7	0.0	29 00.0	-57.7	0.0	30 00.0	-57.7	0.0	90
	23°			24°			25°			26°			27°			28°			29°			30°			

LATITUDE **CONTRARY** NAME TO DECLINATION — L.H.A. 16°, 344°

Dec.	23°			24°			25°			26°			27°			28°			29°			30°			Dec.
	Hc	d	Z	Hc	d	Z	Hc	d	Z	Hc	d	Z	Hc	d	Z	Hc	d	Z	Hc	d	Z	Hc	d	Z	
°	° ′	′	°	° ′	′	°	° ′	′	°	° ′	′	°	° ′	′	°	° ′	′	°	° ′	′	°	° ′	′	°	°
0	62 14.0	-50.7	143.7	61 25.2	-51.2	144.8	60 35.9	-51.9	145.8	59 46.0	-52.5	146.8	58 55.5	-53.0	147.7	58 04.5	-53.4	148.6	57 13.1	-53.9	149.4	56 21.2	-54.2	150.2	0
1	61 23.3	-51.1	144.9	60 34.0	-51.8	145.9	59 44.0	-52.3	146.9	58 53.5	-52.8	147.8	58 02.5	-53.3	148.6	57 11.1	-53.8	149.4	56 19.2	-54.2	150.2	55 27.0	-54.6	150.9	1
2	60 32.2	-51.6	145.9	59 42.2	-52.2	146.9	58 51.7	-52.7	147.8	58 00.7	-53.2	148.7	57 09.2	-53.7	149.5	56 17.3	-54.1	150.2	55 25.0	-54.4	151.0	54 32.4	-54.8	151.7	2
3	59 40.6	-52.1	147.0	58 50.0	-52.6	147.9	57 59.0	-53.1	148.7	57 07.5	-53.6	149.5	56 15.5	-53.9	150.3	55 23.2	-54.3	151.0	54 30.6	-54.7	151.7	53 37.6	-55.0	152.3	3
4	58 48.5	-52.5	147.9	57 57.4	-53.0	148.8	57 05.9	-53.5	149.6	56 13.9	-53.9	150.4	55 21.6	-54.3	151.1	54 28.9	-54.6	151.8	53 35.9	-55.0	152.4	52 42.6	-55.3	153.0	4
5	57 56.0	-52.9	148.9	57 04.4	-53.4	149.7	56 12.4	-53.8	150.4	55 20.0	-54.1	151.1	54 27.3	-54.5	151.8	53 34.3	-54.9	152.5	52 40.9	-55.1	153.1	51 47.3	-55.4	153.6	5
6	57 03.1	-53.3	149.7	56 11.0	-53.6	150.5	55 18.6	-54.0	151.2	54 25.9	-54.4	151.9	53 32.8	-54.7	152.5	52 39.4	-55.0	153.1	51 45.8	-55.4	153.7	50 51.9	-55.7	154.3	6
7	56 09.8	-53.5	150.6	55 17.4	-54.0	151.3	54 24.6	-54.3	152.0	53 31.5	-54.7	152.6	52 38.1	-55.0	153.2	51 44.4	-55.3	153.8	50 50.4	-55.5	154.3	49 56.2	-55.8	154.8	7
8	55 16.3	-53.9	151.4	54 23.4	-54.2	152.0	53 30.3	-54.6	152.7	52 36.8	-54.9	153.3	51 43.1	-55.2	153.9	50 49.1	-55.5	154.4	49 54.9	-55.8	154.9	49 00.4	-55.9	155.4	8
9	54 22.4	-54.2	152.1	53 29.2	-54.5	152.8	52 35.7	-54.8	153.4	51 41.9	-55.1	153.9	50 47.9	-55.4	154.5	49 53.6	-55.6	155.0	48 59.1	-55.8	155.5	48 04.5	-56.2	156.0	9
10	53 28.2	-54.4	152.9	52 34.7	-54.7	153.5	51 40.9	-55.0	154.0	50 46.8	-55.3	154.6	49 52.5	-55.5	155.1	48 58.0	-55.8	155.6	48 03.3	-56.1	156.0	47 08.3	-56.2	156.5	10
11	52 33.8	-54.6	153.6	51 40.0	-55.0	154.1	50 45.9	-55.2	154.7	49 51.5	-55.5	155.2	48 57.0	-55.8	155.7	48 02.2	-56.0	156.1	47 07.2	-56.2	156.6	46 12.1	-56.4	157.0	11
12	51 39.2	-54.9	154.2	50 45.0	-55.1	154.8	49 50.7	-55.5	155.3	48 56.0	-55.6	155.8	48 01.2	-55.9	156.2	47 06.2	-56.1	156.7	46 11.0	-56.3	157.1	45 15.7	-56.5	157.5	12
13	50 44.3	-55.0	154.9	49 49.9	-55.3	155.4	48 55.2	-55.5	155.9	48 00.4	-55.8	156.3	47 05.3	-56.0	156.8	46 10.1	-56.2	157.2	45 14.7	-56.4	157.6	44 19.2	-56.6	158.0	13
14	49 49.3	-55.3	155.5	48 54.6	-55.5	156.0	47 59.7	-55.8	156.4	47 04.6	-56.0	156.9	46 09.3	-56.2	157.3	45 13.9	-56.4	157.7	44 18.3	-56.5	158.1	43 22.6	-56.7	158.4	14
15	48 54.0	-55.4	156.1	47 59.1	-55.7	156.6	47 03.9	-55.9	157.0	46 08.6	-56.1	157.4	45 13.1	-56.3	157.8	44 17.5	-56.5	158.2	43 21.8	-56.7	158.5	42 25.9	-56.9	158.9	15
16	47 58.6	-55.6	156.7	47 03.4	-55.8	157.1	46 08.0	-56.0	157.5	45 12.5	-56.2	157.9	44 16.8	-56.4	158.3	43 21.0	-56.6	158.6	42 25.1	-56.8	159.0	41 29.0	-56.9	159.3	16
17	47 03.0	-55.8	157.2	46 07.6	-56.0	157.6	45 12.0	-56.2	158.0	44 16.3	-56.4	158.4	43 20.4	-56.5	158.8	42 24.4	-56.7	159.1	41 28.3	-56.8	159.4	40 32.1	-57.0	159.7	17
18	46 07.2	-55.9	157.8	45 11.6	-56.1	158.2	44 15.8	-56.3	158.5	43 19.9	-56.4	158.9	42 23.9	-56.6	159.2	41 27.7	-56.8	159.5	40 31.5	-57.0	159.8	39 35.1	-57.1	160.1	18
19	45 11.3	-56.0	158.3	44 15.5	-56.2	158.7	43 19.5	-56.4	159.0	42 23.5	-56.6	159.3	41 27.3	-56.8	159.7	40 30.9	-56.8	160.0	39 34.5	-57.0	160.2	38 38.0	-57.1	160.5	19
20	44 15.3	-56.2	158.8	43 19.3	-56.4	159.1	42 23.1	-56.5	159.5	41 26.9	-56.7	159.8	40 30.5	-56.8	160.1	39 34.1	-57.0	160.4	38 37.5	-57.1	160.6	37 40.9	-57.3	160.9	20
21	43 19.1	-56.3	159.3	42 22.9	-56.5	159.6	41 26.6	-56.6	159.9	40 30.2	-56.8	160.2	39 33.7	-56.9	160.5	38 37.1	-57.1	160.8	37 40.4	-57.2	161.0	36 43.6	-57.3	161.3	21
22	42 22.8	-56.4	159.8	41 26.4	-56.5	160.1	40 30.0	-56.7	160.4	39 33.4	-56.8	160.6	38 36.8	-57.0	160.9	37 40.0	-57.1	161.2	36 43.2	-57.3	161.4	35 46.3	-57.4	161.6	22
23	41 26.4	-56.5	160.2	40 29.9	-56.7	160.5	39 33.3	-56.8	160.8	38 36.6	-57.0	161.1	37 39.8	-57.1	161.3	36 42.9	-57.2	161.5	35 45.9	-57.3	161.8	34 48.9	-57.4	162.0	23
24	40 29.9	-56.6	160.7	39 33.2	-56.7	160.9	38 36.5	-56.9	161.2	37 39.6	-57.0	161.5	36 42.7	-57.2	161.7	35 45.7	-57.3	161.9	34 48.6	-57.4	162.1	33 51.5	-57.5	162.3	24
25	39 33.3	-56.7	161.1	38 36.5	-56.9	161.4	37 39.6	-57.0	161.6	36 42.6	-57.1	161.8	35 45.5	-57.2	162.1	34 48.4	-57.3	162.3	33 51.2	-57.4	162.5	32 54.0	-57.6	162.7	25
26	38 36.6	-56.8	161.5	37 39.6	-56.9	161.8	36 42.6	-57.1	162.0	35 45.5	-57.2	162.2	34 48.3	-57.3	162.4	33 51.1	-57.4	162.6	32 53.8	-57.5	162.8	31 56.4	-57.6	163.0	26
27	37 39.8	-56.9	161.9	36 42.7	-57.0	162.2	35 45.5	-57.1	162.4	34 48.3	-57.2	162.6	33 51.0	-57.3	162.8	32 53.7	-57.5	163.0	31 56.3	-57.6	163.2	30 58.8	-57.6	163.4	27
28	36 42.9	-57.0	162.3	35 45.7	-57.1	162.5	34 48.4	-57.2	162.8	33 51.1	-57.3	163.0	32 53.7	-57.4	163.2	31 56.2	-57.5	163.3	30 58.7	-57.6	163.5	30 01.2	-57.7	163.7	28
29	35 45.9	-57.0	162.7	34 48.6	-57.1	162.9	33 51.2	-57.2	163.1	32 53.8	-57.4	163.3	31 56.3	-57.5	163.5	30 58.7	-57.5	163.7	30 01.1	-57.6	163.8	29 03.5	-57.8	164.0	29
30	34 48.9	-57.1	163.1	33 51.5	-57.2	163.3	32 54.0	-57.3	163.5	31 56.4	-57.4	163.7	30 58.8	-57.5	163.8	30 01.2	-57.6	164.0	29 03.5	-57.7	164.2	28 05.7	-57.7	164.3	30
31	33 51.8	-57.1	163.5	32 54.3	-57.3	163.7	31 56.7	-57.4	163.8	30 59.0	-57.4	164.0	30 01.3	-57.5	164.2	29 03.6	-57.7	164.3	28 05.8	-57.7	164.5	27 08.0	-57.9	164.6	31
32	32 54.7	-57.3	163.8	31 57.0	-57.3	164.0	30 59.3	-57.4	164.2	30 01.6	-57.6	164.3	29 03.8	-57.6	164.5	28 05.9	-57.7	164.6	27 08.1	-57.8	164.8	26 10.1	-57.8	164.9	32
33	31 57.4	-57.2	164.2	30 59.7	-57.4	164.4	30 01.9	-57.5	164.5	29 04.0	-57.5	164.7	28 06.2	-57.7	164.8	27 08.2	-57.7	164.9	26 10.3	-57.8	165.1	25 12.3	-57.9	165.2	33
34	31 00.2	-57.4	164.5	30 02.3	-57.4	164.7	29 04.4	-57.5	164.8	28 06.5	-57.6	165.0	27 08.5	-57.7	165.1	26 10.5	-57.8	165.2	25 12.5	-57.9	165.4	24 14.4	-57.9	165.5	34
35	30 02.8	-57.4	164.9	29 04.9	-57.5	165.0	28 06.9	-57.6	165.2	27 08.9	-57.7	165.3	26 10.8	-57.7	165.4	25 12.7	-57.8	165.5	24 14.6	-57.9	165.7	23 16.5	-58.0	165.8	35
36	29 05.4	-57.4	165.2	28 07.4	-57.5	165.4	27 09.3	-57.6	165.5	26 11.2	-57.7	165.6	25 13.1	-57.8	165.7	24 14.9	-57.8	165.8	23 16.7	-57.9	166.0	22 18.5	-58.0	166.1	36
37	28 08.0	-57.5	165.5	27 09.9	-57.6	165.7	26 11.7	-57.6	165.8	25 13.5	-57.7	165.9	24 15.3	-57.8	166.0	23 17.1	-57.9	166.1	22 18.8	-57.9	166.2	21 20.5	-58.0	166.3	37
38	27 10.5	-57.5	165.9	26 12.3	-57.6	166.0	25 14.1	-57.7	166.1	24 15.8	-57.7	166.2	23 17.5	-57.8	166.3	22 19.2	-57.9	166.4	21 20.9	-58.0	166.5	20 22.5	-58.0	166.6	38
39	26 13.0	-57.6	166.2	25 14.7	-57.7	166.3	24 16.4	-57.7	166.4	23 18.1	-57.8	166.5	22 19.7	-57.9	166.6	21 21.3	-57.9	166.7	20 22.9	-58.0	166.8	19 24.5	-58.1	166.9	39
40	25 15.4	-57.6	166.5	24 17.0	-57.6	166.6	23 18.7	-57.8	166.7	22 20.3	-57.9	166.8	21 21.8	-57.9	166.9	20 23.4	-58.0	167.0	19 24.9	-58.0	167.1	18 26.4	-58.0	167.1	40
41	24 17.8	-57.7	166.8	23 19.4	-57.8	166.9	22 20.9	-57.8	167.0	21 22.4	-57.8	167.1	20 23.9	-57.9	167.2	19 25.4	-57.9	167.3	18 26.9	-58.0	167.3	17 28.4	-58.1	167.4	41
42	23 20.1	-57.6	167.1	22 21.6	-57.7	167.2	21 23.1	-57.8	167.3	20 24.6	-57.9	167.4	19 26.0	-57.9	167.5	18 27.5	-58.1	167.5	17 28.9	-58.1	167.6	16 30.3	-58.2	167.7	42
43	22 22.5	-57.7	167.4	21 23.9	-57.8	167.5	20 25.3	-57.8	167.6	19 26.7	-57.9	167.7	18 28.1	-58.0	167.7	17 29.4	-58.0	167.8	16 30.8	-58.1	167.9	15 32.1	-58.1	167.9	43
44	21 24.8	-57.8	167.7	20 26.1	-57.8	167.8	19 27.5	-57.9	167.9	18 28.8	-57.9	167.9	17 30.1	-58.0	168.0	16 31.4	-58.0	168.1	15 32.7	-58.1	168.1	14 34.0	-58.2	168.2	44
45	20 27.0	-57.8	168.0	19 28.3	-57.8	168.1	18 29.6	-57.9	168.1	17 30.9	-58.0	168.2	16 32.1	-58.0	168.3	15 33.4	-58.1	168.3	14 34.6	-58.1	168.4	13 35.8	-58.1	168.4	45
46	19 29.2	-57.8	168.3	18 30.5	-57.9	168.4	17 31.7	-57.9	168.4	16 32.9	-57.9	168.5	15 34.1	-58.0	168.5	14 35.3	-58.1	168.6	13 36.5	-58.1	168.6	12 37.7	-58.2	168.7	46
47	18 31.4	-57.8	168.6	17 32.6	-57.9	168.6	16 33.8	-57.9	168.7	15 35.0	-58.0	168.7	14 36.1	-58.0	168.8	13 37.2	-58.1	168.8	12 38.4	-58.2	168.9	11 39.5	-58.2	168.9	47
48	17 33.6	-57.8	168.8	16 34.7	-57.9	168.9	15 35.9	-58.0	169.0	14 37.0	-58.0	169.0	13 38.1	-58.1	169.1	12 39.1	-58.1	169.1	11 40.2	-58.1	169.2	10 41.3	-58.2	169.2	48
49	16 35.8	-57.9	169.1	15 36.8	-57.9	169.2	14 37.9	-58.0	169.2	13 39.0	-58.1	169.3	12 40.0	-58.1	169.3	11 41.0	-58.1	169.4	10 42.1	-58.2	169.4	9 43.1	-58.2	169.4	49
50	15 37.9	-57.9	169.4	14 38.9	-57.9	169.4	13 39.9	-58.0	169.5	12 40.9	-58.0	169.5	11 41.9	-58.1	169.6	10 42.9	-58.1	169.6	9 43.9	-58.2	169.6	8 44.9	-58.3	169.7	50
51	14 40.0	-57.9	169.7	13 41.0	-58.0	169.7	12 41.9	-58.0	169.8	11 42.9	-58.1	169.8	10 43.8	-58.1	169.8	9 44.8	-58.2	169.9	8 45.7	-58.2	169.9	7 46.6	-58.2	169.9	51
52	13 42.1	-57.9	169.9	12 43.0	-58.0	170.0	11 43.9	-58.0	170.0	10 44.8	-58.1	170.1	9 45.7	-58.1	170.1	8 46.6	-58.1	170.1	7 47.5	-58.2	170.1	6 48.4	-58.2	170.2	52
53	12 44.2	-58.0	170.2	11 45.0	-57.9	170.2	10 45.9	-58.0	170.3	9 46.8	-58.1	170.3	8 47.6	-58.1	170.3	7 48.5	-58.2	170.4	6 49.3	-58.2	170.4	5 50.2	-58.3	170.4	53
54	11 46.2	-57.9	170.5	10 47.1	-58.0	170.5	9 47.9	-58.1	170.5	8 48.7	-58.1	170.6	7 49.5	-58.1	170.6	6 50.3	-58.2	170.6	5 51.1	-58.2	170.6	4 51.9	-58.3	170.6	54
55	10 48.3	-58.0	170.7	9 49.1	-58.1	170.8	8 49.8	-58.0	170.8	7 50.6	-58.1	170.8	6 51.4	-58.2	170.8	5 52.1	-58.2	170.9	4 52.9	-58.2	170.9	3 53.6	-58.2	170.9	55
56	9 50.3	-58.0	171.0	8 51.0	-58.0	171.0	7 51.8	-58.1	171.0	6 52.5	-58.1	171.1	5 53.2	-58.1	171.1	4 53.9	-58.1	171.1	3 54.7	-58.3	171.1	2 55.4	-58.3	171.1	56
57	8 52.3	-58.0	171.3	7 53.0	-58.0	171.3	6 53.7	-58.1	171.3	5 54.4	-58.1	171.3	4 55.1	-58.2	171.3	3 55.8	-58.2	171.3	2 56.4	-58.2	171.4	1 57.1	-58.2	171.4	57
58	7 54.3	-58.0	171.5	6 55.0	-58.1	171.5	5 55.6	-58.0	171.6	4 56.3	-58.1	171.6	3 56.9	-58.1	171.6	2 57.6	-58.2	171.6	1 58.2	-58.2	171.6	0 58.9	-58.3	171.6	58
59	6 56.3	-58.0	171.8	5 56.9	-58.0	171.8	4 57.6	-58.1	171.8	3 58.2	-58.2	171.8	2 58.8	-58.2	171.8	1 59.4	-58.2	171.8	1 00.0	-58.2	171.8	0 00.6	-58.3	171.8	59
60	5 58.3	-58.0	172.0	4 58.9	-58.1	172.0	3 59.5	-58.1	172.1	3 00.0	-58.1	172.1	2 00.6	-58.1	172.1	1 01.2	-58.2	172.1	0 01.8	-58.3	172.1	0 57.7	+58.2	7.9	60
61	5 00.3	-58.0	172.3	4 00.8	-58.0	172.3	3 01.4	-58.1	172.3	2 01.9	-58.1	172.3	1 02.5	-58.2	172.3	0 03.0	-58.2	172.3	0 56.5	+58.2	7.7	1 55.9	+58.3	7.7	61
62	4 02.3	-58.1	172.5	3 02.8	-58.1	172.6	2 03.3	-58.1	172.6	1 03.8	-58.1	172.6	0 04.3	-58.2	172.6	0 55.2	+58.2	7.4	1 54.7	+58.2	7.4	2 54.2	+58.3	7.4	62
63	3 04.2	-58.0	172.8	2 04.7	-58.1	172.8	1 05.2	-58.1	172.8	0 05.7	-58.2	172.8	0 53.9	+58.1	7.2	1 53.4	+58.2	7.2	2 52.9	+58.3	7.2	3 52.5	+58.2	7.2	63
64	2 06.2	-58.0	173.1	1 06.6	-58.0	173.1	0 07.1	-58.1	173.1	0 52.5	+58.1	6.9	1 52.0	+58.2	6.9	2 51.6	+58.2	6.9	3 51.2	+58.2	7.0	4 50.7	+58.3	7.0	64
65	1 08.2	-58.1	173.3	0 08.6	-58.1	173.3	0 51.0	+58.1	6.7	1 50.6	+58.1	6.7	2 50.2	+58.1	6.7	3 49.8	+58.2	6.7	4 49.4	+58.2	6.7	5 49.0	+58.2	6.7	65
66	0 10.1	-58.0	173.6	0 49.5	+58.1	6.4	1 49.1	+58.1	6.4	2 48.7	+58.2	6.4	3 48.3	+58.2	6.5	4 48.0	+58.1	6.5	5 47.6	+58.2	6.5	6 47.2	+58.2	6.5	66
67	0 47.9	+58.0	6.2	1 47.6	+58.0	6.2	2 47.2	+58.1	6.2	3 46.9	+58.1	6.2	4 46.5	+58.1	6.2	5 46.1	+58.2	6.2	6 45.8	+58.2	6.2	7 45.4	+58.3	6.2	67
68	1 45.9	+58.1	5.9	2 45.6	+58.1	5.9	3 45.3	+58.1	5.9	4 45.0	+58.1	5.9	5 44.6	+58.2	6.0	6 44.3	+58.2	6.0	7 44.0	+58.2	6.0	8 43.7	+58.2	6.0	68
69	2 44.0	+58.0	5.7	3 43.7	+58.0	5.7	4 43.4	+58.1	5.7	5 43.1	+58.1	5.7	6 42.8	+58.1	5.7	7 42.5	+58.1	5.7	8 42.2	+58.2	5.7	9 41.9	+58.2	5.8	69
70	3 42.0	+58.0	5.4	4 41.7	+58.1	5.4	5 41.5	+58.0	5.4	6 41.2	+58.1	5.4	7 40.9	+58.1	5.5	8 40.6	+58.2	5.5	9 40.4	+58.1	5.5	10 40.1	+58.2	5.5	70
71	4 40.0	+58.0	5.2	5 39.8	+58.0	5.2	6 39.5	+58.1	5.2	7 39.3	+58.1	5.2	8 39.0	+58.2	5.2	9 38.8	+58.1	5.2	10 38.5	+58.2	5.2	11 38.3	+58.2	5.3	71
72	5 38.0	+58.1	4.9	6 37.8	+58.1	4.9	7 37.6	+58.1	4.9	8 37.4	+58.1	4.9	9 37.2	+58.1	5.0	10 36.9	+58.2	5.0	11 36.7	+58.2	5.0	12 36.5	+58.1	5.0	72
73	6 36.1	+58.0	4.7	7 35.9	+58.0	4.7	8 35.7	+58.0	4.7	9 35.5	+58.0	4.7	10 35.3	+58.1	4.7	11 35.1	+58.1	4.7	12 34.9	+58.1	4.7	13 34.6	+58.2	4.8	73
74	7 34.1	+58.0	4.4	8 33.9	+58.0	4.4	9 33.7	+58.0	4.4	10 33.5	+58.1	4.4	11 33.4	+58.0	4.4	12 33.2	+58.1	4.5	13 33.0	+58.1	4.5	14 32.8	+58.1	4.5	74
75	8 32.1	+57.9	4.1	9 31.9	+58.0	4.1	10 31.7	+58.1	4.2	11 31.6	+58.0	4.2	12 31.4	+58.1	4.2	13 31.3	+58.0	4.2	14 31.1	+58.1	4.2	15 30.9	+58.2	4.2	75
76	9 30.0	+58.0	3.9	10 29.9	+58.0	3.9	11 29.8	+58.0	3.9	12 29.6	+58.1	3.9	13 29.5	+58.0	3.9	14 29.3	+58.1	3.9	15 29.2	+58.1	4.0	16 29.1	+58.1	4.0	76
77	10 28.0	+58.0	3.6	11 27.9	+58.0	3.6	12 27.8	+58.0	3.6	13 27.7	+58.0	3.7	14 27.5	+58.1	3.7	15 27.4	+58.1	3.7	16 27.3	+58.1	3.7	17 27.2	+58.0	3.7	77
78	11 26.0	+57.9	3.4	12 25.9	+57.9	3.4	13 25.8	+58.0	3.4	14 25.7	+58.0	3.4	15 25.6	+58.0	3.4	16 25.5	+58.0	3.4	17 25.4	+58.0	3.4	18 25.2	+58.1	3.5	78
79	12 23.9	+58.0	3.1	13 23.8	+58.0	3.1	14 23.8	+57.9	3.1	15 23.7	+57.9	3.1	16 23.6	+58.0	3.1	17 23.5	+58.0	3.2	18 23.4	+58.0	3.2	19 23.3	+58.0	3.2	79
80	13 21.9	+57.9	2.8	14 21.8	+57.9	2.8	15 21.7	+58.0	2.8	16 21.6	+58.0	2.9	17 21.6	+57.9	2.9	18 21.5	+58.0	2.9	19 21.4	+58.0	2.9	20 21.3	+58.0	2.9	80
81	14 19.8	+57.9	2.6	15 19.7	+57.9	2.6	16 19.7	+57.9	2.6	17 19.6	+57.9	2.6	18 19.5	+58.0	2.6	19 19.5	+57.9	2.6	20 19.4	+58.0	2.6	21 19.3	+58.0	2.7	81
82	15 17.7	+57.9	2.3	16 17.6	+57.9	2.3	17 17.6	+57.9	2.3	18 17.5	+57.9	2.3	19 17.5	+57.9	2.3	20 17.4	+58.0	2.3	21 17.4	+57.9	2.4	22 17.3	+58.0	2.4	82
83	16 15.6	+57.8	2.0	17 15.5	+57.9	2.0	18 15.5	+57.9	2.0	19 15.4	+57.9	2.0	20 15.4	+57.9	2.1	21 15.4	+57.9	2.1	22 15.3	+57.9	2.1	23 15.3	+57.9	2.1	83
84	17 13.4	+57.8	1.7	18 13.4	+57.8	1.7	19 13.4	+57.8	1.7	20 13.3	+57.9	1.8	21 13.3	+57.9	1.8	22 13.3	+57.8	1.8	23 13.2	+57.9	1.8	24 13.2	+57.9	1.8	84
85	18 11.2	+57.8	1.4	19 11.2	+57.8	1.5	20 11.2	+57.8	1.5	21 11.2	+57.8	1.5	22 11.2	+57.8	1.5	23 11.1	+57.9	1.5	24 11.1	+57.9	1.5	25 11.1	+57.9	1.5	85
86	19 09.0	+57.8	1.2	20 09.0	+57.8	1.2	21 09.0	+57.8	1.2	22 09.0	+57.8	1.2	23 09.0	+57.8	1.2	24 09.0	+57.8	1.2	25 09.0	+57.8	1.2	26 09.0	+57.8	1.2	86
87	20 06.8	+57.8	0.9	21 06.8	+57.8	0.9	22 06.8	+57.8	0.9	23 06.8	+57.8	0.9	24 06.8	+57.8	0.9	25 06.8	+57.8	0.9	26 06.8	+57.8	0.9	27 06.8	+57.8	0.9	87
88	21 04.6	+57.7	0.6	22 04.6	+57.7	0.6	23 04.6	+57.7	0.6	24 04.6	+57.7	0.6	25 04.6	+57.7	0.6	26 04.6	+57.7	0.6	27 04.6	+57.7	0.6	28 04.6	+57.7	0.6	88
89	22 02.3	+57.7	0.3	23 02.3	+57.7	0.3	24 02.3	+57.7	0.3	25 02.3	+57.7	0.3	26 02.3	+57.7	0.3	27 02.3	+57.7	0.3	28 02.3	+57.7	0.3	29 02.3	+57.7	0.3	89
90	23 00.0	+57.7	0.0	24 00.0	+57.7	0.0	25 00.0	+57.7	0.0	26 00.0	+57.7	0.0	27 00.0	+57.7	0.0	28 00.0	+57.7	0.0	29 00.0	+57.7	0.0	30 00.0	+57.7	0.0	90
	23°			24°			25°			26°			27°			28°			29°			30°			

S. Lat. { L.H.A. greater than 180° ....Zn=180°−Z; L.H.A. less than 180°...........Zn=180°+Z

LATITUDE **SAME** NAME AS DECLINATION — L.H.A. 164°, 196°

217

17°, 343° L.H.A. LATITUDE **SAME** NAME AS DECLINATION N. Lat. {L.H.A. greater than 180° .....Zn=Z; L.H.A. less than 180°............Zn=360°-Z}

Dec.	23° Hc	d	Z	24° Hc	d	Z	25° Hc	d	Z	26° Hc	d	Z	27° Hc	d	Z	28° Hc	d	Z	29° Hc	d	Z	30° Hc	d	Z	Dec.
°	° ′	′	°	° ′	′	°	° ′	′	°	° ′	′	°	° ′	′	°	° ′	′	°	° ′	′	°	° ′	′	°	°
0	61 40.6	+49.1	142.0	60 53.0	+49.8	143.1	60 04.7	+50.6	144.1	59 15.8	+51.2	145.1	58 26.3	+51.8	146.0	57 36.3	+52.3	146.9	56 45.7	+52.9	147.8	55 54.8	+53.3	148.6	0
1	62 29.7	+48.4	140.7	61 42.8	+49.3	141.9	60 55.3	+50.0	143.0	60 07.0	+50.7	144.1	59 18.1	+51.4	145.1	58 28.6	+52.0	146.0	57 38.6	+52.5	146.9	56 48.1	+53.0	147.7	1
2	63 18.1	+47.7	139.4	62 32.1	+48.6	140.7	61 45.3	+49.4	141.9	60 57.7	+50.2	143.0	60 09.5	+50.8	144.0	59 20.6	+51.5	145.0	58 31.1	+52.1	146.0	57 41.1	+52.7	146.9	2
3	64 05.8	+46.8	138.1	63 20.7	+47.8	139.4	62 34.7	+48.7	140.7	61 47.9	+49.5	141.8	61 00.3	+50.3	143.0	60 12.1	+51.0	144.0	59 23.2	+51.7	145.0	58 33.8	+52.2	146.0	3
4	64 52.6	+45.9	136.6	64 08.5	+47.0	138.0	63 23.4	+48.0	139.4	62 37.4	+48.9	140.6	61 50.6	+49.8	141.8	61 03.1	+50.5	142.9	60 14.9	+51.2	144.0	59 26.0	+51.9	145.0	4
5	65 38.5	+45.0	135.1	64 55.5	+46.1	136.6	64 11.4	+47.2	138.0	63 26.3	+48.2	139.4	62 40.4	+49.0	140.6	61 53.6	+49.9	141.8	61 06.1	+50.6	142.9	60 17.9	+51.3	144.0	5
6	66 23.5	+43.9	133.4	65 41.6	+45.2	135.1	64 58.6	+46.3	136.6	64 14.5	+47.4	138.0	63 29.4	+48.4	139.3	62 43.5	+49.2	140.6	61 56.7	+50.1	141.8	61 09.2	+50.8	142.9	6
7	67 07.4	+42.6	131.7	66 26.8	+44.0	133.4	65 44.9	+45.3	135.0	65 01.9	+46.5	136.6	64 17.8	+47.6	138.0	63 32.7	+48.6	139.4	62 46.8	+49.4	140.6	62 00.0	+50.2	141.8	7
8	67 50.0	+41.4	129.9	67 10.8	+42.9	131.7	66 30.2	+44.3	133.4	65 48.4	+45.5	135.1	65 05.4	+46.7	136.6	64 21.3	+47.7	138.0	63 36.2	+48.7	139.4	62 50.2	+49.6	140.6	8
9	68 31.4	+40.0	127.9	67 53.7	+41.6	129.9	67 14.5	+43.1	131.7	66 33.9	+44.5	133.4	65 52.1	+45.7	135.1	65 09.0	+46.9	136.6	64 24.9	+48.0	138.0	63 39.8	+48.9	139.4	9
10	69 11.4	+38.3	125.9	68 35.3	+40.2	127.9	67 57.6	+41.9	129.9	67 18.4	+43.3	131.7	66 37.8	+44.7	133.5	65 55.9	+46.0	135.1	65 12.9	+47.1	136.6	64 28.7	+48.2	138.1	10
11	69 49.7	+36.6	123.7	69 15.5	+38.6	125.9	68 39.5	+40.3	127.9	68 01.7	+42.1	129.9	67 22.5	+43.6	131.8	66 41.9	+44.9	133.5	66 00.0	+46.1	135.1	65 16.9	+47.3	136.7	11
12	70 26.3	+34.7	121.3	69 54.1	+36.8	123.7	69 19.8	+38.9	125.9	68 43.8	+40.6	128.0	68 06.1	+42.3	129.9	67 26.8	+43.8	131.8	66 46.1	+45.2	133.5	66 04.2	+46.4	135.2	12
13	71 01.0	+32.7•	118.9	70 30.9	+35.0	121.3	69 58.7	+37.1	123.7	69 24.4	+39.1	125.9	68 48.4	+40.8	128.0	68 10.6	+42.5	130.0	67 31.3	+44.0	131.8	66 50.6	+45.4	133.6	13
14	71 33.7	+30.3•	116.2	71 05.9	+32.9•	118.9	70 35.8	+35.2•	121.4	70 03.5	+37.4	123.7	69 29.2	+39.4	125.9	68 53.1	+41.1	128.0	68 15.3	+42.8	130.0	67 36.0	+44.2	131.9	14
15	72 04.0	+27.9•	113.5	71 38.8	+30.6•	116.2	71 11.0	+33.1•	118.9	70 40.9	+35.4	121.4	70 08.6	+37.6	123.8	69 34.2	+39.6	126.0	68 58.1	+41.4	128.1	68 20.2	+43.1	130.1	15
16	72 31.9	+25.2•	110.6	72 09.4	+28.1•	113.5	71 44.1	+30.9•	116.3	71 16.3	+33.5•	118.9	70 46.2	+35.7	121.4	70 13.8	+37.9	123.8	69 39.5	+39.8	126.1	69 03.3	+41.6	128.2	16
17	72 57.1	+22.3•	107.5	72 37.5	+25.5•	110.6	72 15.0	+28.4•	113.5	71 49.8	+31.1•	116.3	71 21.9	+33.7•	119.0	70 51.7	+36.0	121.5	70 19.3	+38.2	123.9	69 44.9	+40.1	126.1	17
18	73 19.4	+19.3•	104.3	73 03.0	+22.6•	107.5	72 43.4	+25.7•	110.6	72 20.9	+28.7•	113.5	71 55.6	+31.4•	116.3	71 27.7	+34.0•	119.0	70 57.5	+36.3•	121.5	70 25.0	+38.5	123.9	18
19	73 38.7	+16.0•	101.0	73 25.6	+19.4•	104.3	73 09.1	+22.9•	107.5	72 49.6	+25.9•	110.6	72 27.0	+29.0•	113.5	72 01.7	+31.7•	116.4	71 33.8	+34.2•	119.1	71 03.5	+36.6•	121.6	19
20	73 54.7	+12.5•	97.5	73 45.0	+16.3•	100.9	73 32.0	+19.7•	104.3	73 15.5	+23.1•	107.5	72 56.0	+26.2•	110.6	72 33.4	+29.2•	113.6	72 08.0	+32.0•	116.4	71 40.1	+34.5•	119.1	20
21	74 07.2	+9.1•	94.0	74 01.3	+12.7•	97.5	73 51.7	+16.4•	100.9	73 38.6	+20.0•	104.2	73 22.2	+23.4•	107.5	73 02.6	+26.6•	110.6	72 40.0	+29.5•	113.6	72 14.6	+32.3•	116.5	21
22	74 16.3	+5.3•	90.3	74 14.0	+9.2•	93.9	74 08.1	+13.0•	97.4	73 58.6	+16.7•	100.9	73 45.6	+20.2•	104.2	73 29.2	+23.6•	107.5	73 09.5	+26.9•	110.7	72 46.9	+29.8•	113.7	22
23	74 21.6	+1.6•	86.7	74 23.2	+5.6•	90.2	74 21.1	+9.4•	93.8	74 15.3	+13.2•	97.3	74 05.8	+16.9•	100.8	73 52.8	+20.5•	104.2	73 36.4	+23.9•	107.5	73 16.7	+27.1•	110.7	23
24	74 23.2	-2.1•	82.9	74 28.8	+1.7•	86.5	74 30.5	+5.7•	90.1	74 28.5	+9.6•	93.7	74 22.7	+13.4•	97.3	74 13.3	+17.1•	100.8	74 00.3	+20.7•	104.2	73 43.8	+24.2•	107.6	24
25	74 21.1	-5.8•	79.2	74 30.5	-2.0•	82.8	74 36.2	+1.9•	86.4	74 38.1	+5.8•	90.0	74 36.1	+9.8•	93.7	74 30.4	+13.7•	97.3	74 21.0	+17.4•	100.8	74 08.0	+21.0•	104.3	25
26	74 15.3	-9.5•	75.6	74 28.5	-5.8•	79.0	74 38.1	-2.0•	82.6	74 43.9	+2.0•	86.3	74 45.9	+6.0•	89.9	74 44.1	+9.9•	93.6	74 38.4	+13.8•	97.2	74 29.0	+17.6•	100.8	26
27	74 05.8	-13.0•	71.9	74 22.7	-9.4•	75.3	74 36.1	-5.7•	78.8	74 45.9	-1.8•	82.5	74 51.9	+2.1•	86.1	74 54.0	+6.1•	89.8	74 52.2	+10.2•	93.5	74 46.6	+14.1•	97.2	27
28	73 52.8	-16.4•	68.4	74 13.3	-13.0•	71.7	74 30.4	-9.4•	75.1	74 44.1	-5.7•	78.7	74 54.0	-1.8•	82.3	75 00.1	+2.3•	86.0	75 02.4	+6.3•	89.7	75 00.7	+10.3•	93.5	28
29	73 36.4	-19.7•	65.0	74 00.3	-16.5•	68.1	74 21.0	-13.0•	71.4	74 38.4	-9.4•	74.9	74 52.2	-5.6•	78.5	75 02.4	-1.7•	82.1	75 08.7	+2.3•	85.9	75 11.0	+6.5•	89.6	29
30	73 16.7	-22.7•	61.6	73 43.8	-19.7•	64.7	74 08.0	-16.5•	67.8	74 29.0	-13.0•	71.2	74 46.6	-9.3•	74.6	75 00.7	-5.6•	78.3	75 11.0	-1.6•	82.0	75 17.5	+2.4•	85.7	30
31	72 54.0	-25.6•	58.5	73 24.1	-22.8•	61.3	73 51.5	-19.8•	64.3	74 16.0	-16.6•	67.5	74 37.3	-13.1•	70.9	74 55.1	-9.3•	74.4	75 09.4	-5.5•	78.0	75 19.9	-1.5•	81.8	31
32	72 28.4	-28.2•	55.4	73 01.3	-25.6•	58.1	73 31.7	-22.8•	61.0	73 59.4	-19.8•	64.0	74 24.2	-16.6•	67.2	74 45.8	-13.1•	70.6	75 03.9	-9.4•	74.2	75 18.4	-5.5•	77.8	32
33	72 00.2	-30.7•	52.5	72 35.7	-28.4•	55.1	73 08.9	-25.8•	57.8	73 39.6	-23.0•	60.6	74 07.6	-19.9•	63.7	74 32.7	-16.7•	66.9	74 54.5	-13.1•	70.4	75 12.9	-9.4•	73.9	33
34	71 29.5	-32.9•	49.8	72 07.3	-30.7•	52.1	72 43.1	-28.2•	54.7	73 16.6	-25.8•	57.4	73 47.7	-23.1•	60.3	74 16.0	-20.0•	63.4	74 41.4	-16.7•	66.6	75 03.5	-13.1•	70.1	34
35	70 56.6	-34.9•	47.2	71 36.6	-33.1•	49.4	72 14.7	-30.9•	51.8	72 50.8	-28.6•	54.3	73 24.6	-25.9•	57.0	73 56.0	-23.1•	59.9	74 24.7	-20.1•	63.0	74 50.4	-16.8•	66.3	35
36	70 21.7	-36.9	44.7	71 03.5	-35.1	46.8	71 43.8	-33.2•	49.0	72 22.2	-31.0•	51.4	72 58.7	-28.7•	53.9	73 32.9	-26.2•	56.6	74 04.6	-23.3•	59.6	74 33.6	-20.3•	62.7	36
37	69 44.8	-38.5	42.4	70 28.4	-36.9	44.3	71 10.6	-35.2	46.4	71 51.2	-33.3•	48.6	72 30.0	-31.2•	50.9	73 06.7	-28.8•	53.5	73 41.3	-26.3•	56.2	74 13.3	-23.4•	59.2	37
38	69 06.3	-40.2	40.2	69 51.5	-38.7	42.0	70 35.4	-37.1	43.9	71 17.9	-35.4•	45.9	71 58.8	-33.5•	48.1	72 37.9	-31.3•	50.5	73 15.0	-29.0•	53.1	73 49.9	-26.4•	55.8	38
39	68 26.1	-41.5	38.2	69 12.8	-40.3	39.8	69 58.3	-38.9	41.6	70 42.5	-37.3	43.5	71 25.3	-35.5•	45.5	72 06.6	-33.7•	47.7	72 46.0	-31.5•	50.1	73 23.5	-29.2•	52.6	39
40	67 44.6	-42.9	36.3	68 32.5	-41.7	37.8	69 19.4	-40.4	39.4	70 05.2	-39.0	41.1	70 49.8	-37.5	43.0	71 32.9	-35.7	45.0	72 14.5	-33.8•	47.2	72 54.3	-31.7•	49.6	40
41	67 01.7	-44.0	34.4	67 50.8	-43.0	35.8	68 39.0	-41.8	37.3	69 26.2	-40.6	38.9	70 12.3	-39.1	40.7	70 57.2	-37.6	42.5	71 40.7	-35.9•	44.6	72 22.6	-34.0•	46.8	41
42	66 17.7	-45.1	32.7	67 07.8	-44.1	34.0	67 57.2	-43.2	35.4	68 45.6	-41.9	36.9	69 33.2	-40.8	38.5	70 19.6	-39.4	40.2	71 04.8	-37.8	42.1	71 48.6	-36.1•	44.1	42
43	65 32.6	-46.0	31.1	66 23.7	-45.2	32.3	67 14.0	-44.2	33.5	68 03.7	-43.3	34.9	68 52.4	-42.1	36.4	69 40.2	-40.9	38.0	70 27.0	-39.6	39.7	71 12.5	-38.0	41.6	43
44	64 46.6	-47.0	29.6	65 38.5	-46.2	30.7	66 29.8	-45.4	31.8	67 20.4	-44.5	33.1	68 10.3	-43.5	34.4	68 59.3	-42.3	35.9	69 47.4	-41.1	37.5	70 34.5	-39.8	39.2	44
45	63 59.6	-47.8	28.1	64 52.3	-47.1	29.1	65 44.4	-46.3	30.2	66 35.9	-45.5	31.4	67 26.8	-44.6	32.6	68 17.0	-43.6	34.0	69 06.3	-42.5	35.4	69 54.7	-41.3	37.0	45
46	63 11.8	-48.5	26.8	64 05.2	-47.9	27.7	64 58.1	-47.2	28.7	65 50.4	-46.4	29.8	66 42.2	-45.6	30.9	67 33.4	-44.8	32.1	68 23.8	-43.8	33.5	69 13.4	-42.7	34.9	46
47	62 23.3	-49.1	25.5	63 17.3	-48.6	26.3	64 10.9	-48.0	27.2	65 04.0	-47.4	28.2	65 56.6	-46.6	29.3	66 48.6	-45.8	30.4	67 40.0	-44.9	31.7	68 30.7	-43.9	33.0	47
48	61 34.2	-49.8	24.3	62 28.7	-49.3	25.0	63 22.9	-48.8	25.9	64 16.6	-48.1	26.8	65 10.0	-47.5	27.8	66 02.8	-46.8	28.8	66 55.1	-46.0	29.9	67 46.8	-45.1	31.2	48
49	60 44.4	-50.4	23.1	61 39.4	-49.9	23.8	62 34.1	-49.4	24.6	63 28.5	-48.9	25.4	64 22.5	-48.3	26.3	65 16.0	-47.6	27.3	66 09.1	-46.9	28.3	67 01.7	-46.2	29.4	49
50	59 54.0	-50.9	22.0	60 49.5	-50.5	22.7	61 44.7	-50.0	23.4	62 39.6	-49.5	24.2	63 34.2	-49.0	25.0	64 28.4	-48.4	25.9	65 22.2	-47.8	26.8	66 15.5	-47.1	27.8	50
51	59 03.1	-51.3	21.0	59 59.0	-50.9	21.6	60 54.7	-50.6	22.2	61 50.1	-50.1	22.9	62 45.2	-49.7	23.7	63 40.0	-49.2	24.5	64 34.4	-48.6	25.4	65 28.4	-48.0	26.3	51
52	58 11.8	-51.8	20.0	59 08.1	-51.5	20.5	60 04.1	-51.1	21.1	61 00.0	-50.7	21.8	61 55.5	-50.2	22.5	62 50.8	-49.8	23.2	63 45.8	-49.3	24.0	64 40.4	-48.7	24.9	52
53	57 20.0	-52.2	19.0	58 16.6	-51.9	19.5	59 13.0	-51.5	20.1	60 09.3	-51.2	20.7	61 05.3	-50.8	21.3	62 01.0	-50.4	22.0	62 56.5	-49.9	22.8	63 51.7	-49.5	23.5	53
54	56 27.8	-52.6	18.1	57 24.7	-52.3	18.6	58 21.5	-52.0	19.1	59 18.1	-51.7	19.7	60 14.5	-51.3	20.3	61 10.6	-50.9	20.9	62 06.6	-50.5	21.6	63 02.2	-50.0	22.3	54
55	55 35.2	-53.0	17.3	56 32.4	-52.7	17.7	57 29.5	-52.4	18.2	58 26.4	-52.1	18.7	59 23.2	-51.8	19.2	60 19.7	-51.4	19.8	61 16.1	-51.1	20.4	62 12.2	-50.7	21.1	55
56	54 42.2	-53.2	16.4	55 39.7	-53.0	16.8	56 37.1	-52.8	17.3	57 34.3	-52.5	17.8	58 31.4	-52.2	18.2	59 28.3	-51.9	18.8	60 25.0	-51.6	19.3	61 21.5	-51.2	19.9	56
57	53 49.0	-53.6	15.6	54 46.7	-53.3	16.0	55 44.3	-53.1	16.4	56 41.8	-52.8	16.9	57 39.2	-52.6	17.3	58 36.4	-52.3	17.8	59 33.4	-52.0	18.3	60 30.3	-51.7	18.9	57
58	52 55.4	-53.8	14.9	53 53.4	-53.6	15.2	54 51.2	-53.4	15.6	55 49.0	-53.2	16.0	56 46.6	-53.0	16.4	57 44.1	-52.8	16.9	58 41.4	-52.4	17.3	59 38.6	-52.2	17.9	58
59	52 01.6	-54.1	14.2	52 59.8	-53.9	14.5	53 57.8	-53.7	14.8	54 55.8	-53.6	15.2	55 53.6	-53.3	15.6	56 51.3	-53.0	16.0	57 49.0	-52.9	16.4	58 46.4	-52.5	16.9	59
60	51 07.5	-54.3	13.5	52 05.9	-54.2	13.8	53 04.1	-54.0	14.1	54 02.2	-53.8	14.4	55 00.3	-53.6	14.8	55 58.3	-53.4	15.1	56 56.1	-53.1	15.5	57 53.9	-52.9	16.0	60
61	50 13.2	-54.5	12.8	51 11.7	-54.4	13.1	52 10.1	-54.2	13.4	53 08.4	-54.0	13.7	54 06.7	-53.9	14.0	55 04.9	-53.7	14.3	56 03.0	-53.5	14.7	57 01.0	-53.3	15.1	61
62	49 18.7	-54.8	12.2	50 17.3	-54.6	12.4	51 15.9	-54.5	12.7	52 14.4	-54.3	13.0	53 12.8	-54.1	13.3	54 11.2	-54.0	13.6	55 09.5	-53.8	13.9	56 07.7	-53.6	14.3	62
63	48 23.9	-54.9	11.5	49 22.7	-54.8	11.8	50 21.4	-54.7	12.0	51 20.1	-54.6	12.3	52 18.7	-54.4	12.5	53 17.2	-54.2	12.8	54 15.7	-54.1	13.1	55 14.1	-53.9	13.5	63
64	47 29.0	-55.1	10.9	48 27.9	-55.0	11.1	49 26.7	-54.9	11.4	50 25.5	-54.7	11.6	51 24.3	-54.7	11.9	52 23.0	-54.5	12.1	53 21.6	-54.4	12.4	54 20.2	-54.2	12.7	64
65	46 33.9	-55.3	10.4	47 32.9	-55.2	10.5	48 31.8	-55.1	10.8	49 30.8	-55.0	11.0	50 29.6	-54.8	11.2	51 28.5	-54.7	11.4	52 27.2	-54.5	11.7	53 26.0	-54.5	12.0	65
66	45 38.6	-55.5	9.8	46 37.7	-55.4	10.0	47 36.7	-55.2	10.2	48 35.8	-55.2	10.4	49 34.8	-55.0	10.6	50 33.8	-55.0	10.8	51 32.7	-54.8	11.0	52 31.5	-54.6	11.3	66
67	44 43.1	-55.6	9.3	45 42.3	-55.5	9.4	46 41.5	-55.4	9.6	47 40.6	-55.3	9.8	48 39.8	-55.3	10.0	49 38.8	-55.1	10.2	50 37.9	-55.0	10.4	51 36.9	-54.9	10.6	67
68	43 47.5	-55.7	8.7	44 46.8	-55.7	8.9	45 46.1	-55.6	9.0	46 45.3	-55.5	9.2	47 44.5	-55.4	9.4	48 43.7	-55.3	9.6	49 42.9	-55.2	9.8	50 42.0	-55.1	10.0	68
69	42 51.8	-55.9	8.2	43 51.1	-55.8	8.4	44 50.5	-55.7	8.5	45 49.8	-55.6	8.6	46 49.1	-55.5	8.8	47 48.4	-55.5	9.0	48 47.7	-55.4	9.2	49 46.9	-55.3	9.3	69
70	41 55.9	-56.0	7.7	42 55.3	-55.9	7.8	43 54.8	-55.9	8.0	44 54.2	-55.8	8.1	45 53.6	-55.7	8.3	46 52.9	-55.6	8.4	47 52.3	-55.6	8.6	48 51.6	-55.5	8.7	70
71	40 59.9	-56.1	7.2	41 59.4	-56.0	7.4	42 58.9	-56.0	7.5	43 58.4	-55.9	7.6	44 57.9	-55.9	7.7	45 57.3	-55.8	7.9	46 56.7	-55.7	8.0	47 56.1	-55.6	8.2	71
72	40 03.8	-56.2	6.8	41 03.4	-56.2	6.9	42 02.9	-56.1	7.0	43 02.5	-56.1	7.1	44 02.0	-56.0	7.2	45 01.5	-55.9	7.3	46 01.0	-55.8	7.5	47 00.5	-55.8	7.6	72
73	39 07.6	-56.4	6.3	40 07.2	-56.3	6.4	41 06.8	-56.2	6.5	42 06.4	-56.2	6.6	43 06.0	-56.1	6.7	44 05.6	-56.1	6.8	45 05.2	-56.0	7.0	46 04.7	-55.9	7.1	73
74	38 11.2	-56.4	5.9	39 10.9	-56.4	6.0	40 10.6	-56.3	6.1	41 10.2	-56.2	6.2	42 09.9	-56.2	6.2	43 09.5	-56.1	6.3	44 09.2	-56.2	6.4	45 08.8	-56.1	6.6	74
75	37 14.8	-56.5	5.5	38 14.5	-56.4	5.5	39 14.3	-56.5	5.6	40 14.0	-56.4	5.7	41 13.7	-56.4	5.8	42 13.4	-56.3	5.9	43 13.0	-56.2	6.0	44 12.7	-56.2	6.1	75
76	36 18.3	-56.6	5.0	37 18.1	-56.6	5.1	38 17.8	-56.5	5.2	39 17.6	-56.5	5.2	40 17.3	-56.4	5.3	41 17.1	-56.4	5.4	42 16.8	-56.4	5.5	43 16.5	-56.3	5.6	76
77	35 21.7	-56.7	4.6	36 21.5	-56.6	4.7	37 21.3	-56.6	4.7	38 21.1	-56.6	4.8	39 20.9	-56.6	4.9	40 20.7	-56.5	5.0	41 20.4	-56.4	5.0	42 20.2	-56.4	5.1	77
78	34 25.0	-56.7	4.2	35 24.9	-56.8	4.3	36 24.7	-56.7	4.3	37 24.5	-56.6	4.4	38 24.3	-56.6	4.4	39 24.2	-56.6	4.5	40 24.0	-56.6	4.6	41 23.8	-56.6	4.6	78
79	33 28.3	-56.9	3.8	34 28.1	-56.8	3.9	35 28.0	-56.8	3.9	36 27.9	-56.8	4.0	37 27.7	-56.7	4.0	38 27.6	-56.7	4.1	39 27.4	-56.7	4.1	40 27.2	-56.6	4.2	79
80	32 31.4	-56.8	3.5	33 31.3	-56.8	3.5	34 31.2	-56.8	3.5	35 31.1	-56.8	3.6	36 31.0	-56.8	3.6	37 30.9	-56.8	3.7	38 30.7	-56.7	3.7	39 30.6	-56.7	3.8	80
81	31 34.6	-57.0	3.1	32 34.5	-57.0	3.1	33 34.4	-56.9	3.1	34 34.3	-56.9	3.2	35 34.2	-56.9	3.2	36 34.1	-56.9	3.3	37 34.0	-56.8	3.3	38 33.9	-56.8	3.4	81
82	30 37.6	-57.0	2.7	31 37.5	-57.0	2.7	32 37.5	-57.0	2.8	33 37.4	-57.0	2.8	34 37.3	-56.9	2.8	35 37.2	-56.9	2.9	36 37.2	-56.9	2.9	37 37.1	-56.9	2.9	82
83	29 40.6	-57.1	2.4	30 40.5	-57.0	2.4	31 40.5	-57.1	2.4	32 40.4	-57.0	2.4	33 40.4	-57.1	2.5	34 40.3	-57.0	2.5	35 40.3	-57.0	2.5	36 40.2	-57.0	2.5	83
84	28 43.5	-57.1	2.0	29 43.5	-57.2	2.0	30 43.4	-57.1	2.0	31 43.4	-57.1	2.1	32 43.3	-57.0	2.1	33 43.3	-57.1	2.1	34 43.3	-57.1	2.1	35 43.2	-57.0	2.2	84
85	27 46.4	-57.2	1.7	28 46.3	-57.1	1.7	29 46.3	-57.1	1.7	30 46.3	-57.2	1.7	31 46.3	-57.2	1.7	32 46.2	-57.1	1.7	33 46.2	-57.1	1.8	34 46.2	-57.1	1.8	85
86	26 49.2	-57.2	1.3	27 49.2	-57.3	1.3	28 49.2	-57.3	1.3	29 49.1	-57.2	1.3	30 49.1	-57.2	1.4	31 49.1	-57.2	1.4	32 49.1	-57.2	1.4	33 49.1	-57.2	1.4	86
87	25 52.0	-57.3	1.0	26 51.9	-57.2	1.0	27 51.9	-57.2	1.0	28 51.9	-57.2	1.0	29 51.9	-57.2	1.0	30 51.9	-57.2	1.0	31 51.9	-57.2	1.0	32 51.9	-57.3	1.0	87
88	24 54.7	-57.3	0.6	25 54.7	-57.3	0.6	26 54.7	-57.3	0.7	27 54.7	-57.3	0.7	28 54.7	-57.3	0.7	29 54.7	-57.3	0.7	30 54.7	-57.3	0.7	31 54.6	-57.2	0.7	88
89	23 57.4	-57.4	0.3	24 57.4	-57.4	0.3	25 57.4	-57.4	0.3	26 57.4	-57.4	0.3	27 57.4	-57.4	0.3	28 57.4	-57.4	0.3	29 57.4	-57.4	0.3	30 57.4	-57.4	0.3	89
90	23 00.0	-57.4	0.0	24 00.0	-57.4	0.0	25 00.0	-57.4	0.0	26 00.0	-57.4	0.0	27 00.0	-57.4	0.0	28 00.0	-57.4	0.0	29 00.0	-57.4	0.0	30 00.0	-57.4	0.0	90
	23°			24°			25°			26°			27°			28°			29°			30°			

17°, 343° L.H.A. LATITUDE **SAME** NAME AS DECLINATION

218

LATITUDE **CONTRARY** NAME TO DECLINATION — L.H.A. 17°, 343°

Dec.	23° Hc	d	Z	24° Hc	d	Z	25° Hc	d	Z	26° Hc	d	Z	27° Hc	d	Z	28° Hc	d	Z	29° Hc	d	Z	30° Hc	d	Z	Dec.
°	° ′	′	°	° ′	′	°	° ′	′	°	° ′	′	°	° ′	′	°	° ′	′	°	° ′	′	°	° ′	′	°	°
0	61 40.6	-49.7	142.0	60 53.0	-50.4	143.1	60 04.7	-51.1	144.1	59 15.8	-51.7	145.1	58 26.3	-52.3	146.0	57 36.3	-52.8	146.9	56 45.7	-53.2	147.8	55 54.8	-53.7	148.6	0
1	60 50.9	-50.3	143.1	60 02.6	-51.0	144.2	59 13.6	-51.6	145.2	58 24.1	-52.1	146.1	57 34.0	-52.6	147.0	56 43.5	-53.1	147.8	55 52.5	-53.6	148.6	55 01.1	-54.0	149.3	1
2	60 00.6	-50.8	144.2	59 11.6	-51.4	145.2	58 22.0	-51.9	146.1	57 32.0	-52.5	147.0	56 41.4	-53.0	147.9	55 50.4	-53.5	148.6	54 58.9	-53.8	149.4	54 07.1	-54.2	150.1	2
3	59 09.8	-51.3	145.3	58 20.2	-51.9	146.2	57 30.1	-52.4	147.1	56 39.5	-52.9	147.9	55 48.4	-53.3	148.7	54 56.9	-53.7	149.4	54 05.1	-54.2	150.1	53 12.9	-54.5	150.8	3
4	58 18.5	-51.8	146.3	57 28.3	-52.3	147.2	56 37.7	-52.8	148.0	55 46.6	-53.2	148.8	54 55.1	-53.7	149.5	54 03.2	-54.0	150.2	53 10.9	-54.3	150.9	52 18.4	-54.8	151.5	4
5	57 26.7	-52.1	147.2	56 36.0	-52.6	148.1	55 44.9	-53.1	148.8	54 53.4	-53.6	149.6	54 01.4	-53.9	150.3	53 09.2	-54.3	150.9	52 16.6	-54.7	151.6	51 23.6	-54.9	152.2	5
6	56 34.6	-52.6	148.1	55 43.4	-53.0	148.9	54 51.8	-53.4	149.7	53 59.8	-53.8	150.4	53 07.5	-54.2	151.0	52 14.9	-54.5	151.6	51 21.9	-54.8	152.2	50 28.7	-55.1	152.8	6
7	55 42.0	-52.9	149.0	54 50.4	-53.3	149.7	53 58.4	-53.7	150.4	53 06.0	-54.0	151.1	52 13.3	-54.4	151.7	51 20.4	-54.8	152.3	50 27.1	-55.1	152.9	49 33.6	-55.4	153.4	7
8	54 49.1	-53.2	149.8	53 57.1	-53.6	150.5	53 04.7	-54.0	151.2	52 12.0	-54.4	151.8	51 18.9	-54.6	152.4	50 25.6	-54.9	153.0	49 32.0	-55.2	153.5	48 38.2	-55.5	154.0	8
9	53 55.9	-53.5	150.6	53 03.5	-53.9	151.3	52 10.7	-54.2	151.9	51 17.6	-54.5	152.5	50 24.3	-54.9	153.1	49 30.7	-55.2	153.6	48 36.8	-55.4	154.1	47 42.7	-55.7	154.6	9
10	53 02.4	-53.8	151.4	52 09.6	-54.1	152.0	51 16.5	-54.5	152.6	50 23.1	-54.8	153.2	49 29.4	-55.1	153.7	48 35.5	-55.3	154.2	47 41.4	-55.6	154.7	46 47.0	-55.8	155.1	10
11	52 08.6	-54.0	152.1	51 15.5	-54.4	152.7	50 22.0	-54.7	153.3	49 28.3	-55.0	153.8	48 34.3	-55.2	154.3	47 40.2	-55.5	154.8	46 45.8	-55.7	155.2	45 51.2	-55.9	155.7	11
12	51 14.6	-54.3	152.8	50 21.1	-54.6	153.4	49 27.3	-54.9	153.9	48 33.3	-55.1	154.4	47 39.1	-55.4	154.9	46 44.7	-55.7	155.3	45 50.1	-55.9	155.8	44 55.3	-56.1	156.2	12
13	50 20.3	-54.5	153.5	49 26.5	-54.8	154.0	48 32.4	-55.0	154.5	47 38.2	-55.4	155.0	46 43.7	-55.6	155.4	45 49.0	-55.8	155.9	44 54.2	-56.0	156.3	43 59.2	-56.3	156.7	13
14	49 25.8	-54.7	154.1	48 31.7	-55.0	154.6	47 37.4	-55.3	155.1	46 42.8	-55.5	155.6	45 48.1	-55.7	156.0	44 53.2	-55.9	156.4	43 58.2	-56.2	156.8	43 02.9	-56.3	157.2	14
15	48 31.1	-55.0	154.8	47 36.7	-55.2	155.2	46 42.1	-55.4	155.7	45 47.3	-55.6	156.1	44 52.4	-55.9	156.5	43 57.3	-56.1	156.9	43 02.0	-56.3	157.3	42 06.6	-56.5	157.6	15
16	47 36.1	-55.1	155.4	46 41.5	-55.3	155.8	45 46.7	-55.6	156.2	44 51.7	-55.8	156.6	43 56.5	-56.0	157.0	43 01.2	-56.2	157.4	42 05.7	-56.3	157.7	41 10.1	-56.5	158.1	16
17	46 41.0	-55.2	155.9	45 46.2	-55.6	156.4	44 51.1	-55.7	156.8	43 55.9	-55.9	157.2	43 00.5	-56.1	157.5	42 05.0	-56.3	157.9	41 09.4	-56.5	158.2	40 13.6	-56.7	158.5	17
18	45 45.8	-55.5	156.5	44 50.6	-55.6	156.9	43 55.4	-55.9	157.3	43 00.0	-56.1	157.7	42 04.4	-56.2	158.0	41 08.7	-56.4	158.3	40 12.9	-56.6	158.6	39 16.9	-56.7	158.9	18
19	44 50.3	-55.6	157.1	43 55.0	-55.8	157.4	42 59.5	-56.0	157.8	42 03.9	-56.2	158.1	41 08.2	-56.4	158.5	40 12.3	-56.5	158.8	39 16.3	-56.7	159.1	38 20.2	-56.8	159.4	19
20	43 54.7	-55.7	157.6	42 59.2	-55.9	157.9	42 03.5	-56.1	158.3	41 07.7	-56.3	158.6	40 11.8	-56.5	158.9	39 15.8	-56.7	159.2	38 19.6	-56.8	159.5	37 23.4	-56.9	159.8	20
21	42 59.0	-55.8	158.1	42 03.3	-56.1	158.4	41 07.4	-56.2	158.8	40 11.4	-56.3	159.1	39 15.3	-56.5	159.4	38 19.1	-56.7	159.6	37 22.8	-56.8	159.9	36 26.5	-57.0	160.2	21
22	42 03.2	-56.0	158.6	41 07.2	-56.1	158.9	40 11.2	-56.3	159.2	39 15.1	-56.5	159.5	38 18.8	-56.6	159.8	37 22.4	-56.7	160.1	36 26.0	-56.9	160.3	35 29.5	-57.1	160.6	22
23	41 07.2	-56.1	159.1	40 11.1	-56.3	159.4	39 14.9	-56.5	159.7	38 18.6	-56.6	159.9	37 22.2	-56.8	160.2	36 25.7	-56.9	160.5	35 29.1	-57.0	160.7	34 32.4	-57.1	160.9	23
24	40 11.1	-56.2	159.5	39 14.8	-56.4	159.8	38 18.4	-56.5	160.1	37 22.0	-56.7	160.4	36 25.4	-56.8	160.6	35 28.8	-57.0	160.9	34 32.1	-57.1	161.1	33 35.3	-57.2	161.3	24
25	39 14.9	-56.3	160.0	38 18.4	-56.4	160.3	37 21.9	-56.6	160.5	36 25.3	-56.7	160.8	35 28.6	-56.9	161.0	34 31.8	-57.0	161.2	33 35.0	-57.1	161.5	32 38.1	-57.3	161.7	25
26	38 18.6	-56.4	160.4	37 22.0	-56.6	160.7	36 25.3	-56.7	160.9	35 28.6	-56.9	161.2	34 31.7	-56.9	161.4	33 34.8	-57.0	161.6	32 37.9	-57.2	161.8	31 40.8	-57.3	162.0	26
27	37 22.2	-56.5	160.9	36 25.4	-56.6	161.1	35 28.6	-56.8	161.3	34 31.7	-56.9	161.6	33 34.8	-57.0	161.8	32 37.8	-57.2	162.0	31 40.7	-57.3	162.2	30 43.5	-57.3	162.4	27
28	36 25.7	-56.6	161.3	35 28.8	-56.7	161.5	34 31.8	-56.8	161.7	33 34.8	-56.9	161.9	32 37.8	-57.1	162.2	31 40.6	-57.2	162.3	30 43.4	-57.3	162.5	29 46.2	-57.5	162.7	28
29	35 29.1	-56.7	161.7	34 32.1	-56.8	161.9	33 35.0	-56.9	162.1	32 37.9	-57.1	162.3	31 40.7	-57.2	162.5	30 43.4	-57.2	162.7	29 46.1	-57.4	162.9	28 48.7	-57.4	163.0	29
30	34 32.4	-56.7	162.1	33 35.3	-56.9	162.3	32 38.1	-57.0	162.5	31 40.8	-57.1	162.7	30 43.5	-57.2	162.9	29 46.2	-57.4	163.0	28 48.7	-57.4	163.2	27 51.3	-57.5	163.4	30
31	33 35.7	-56.9	162.5	32 38.4	-56.9	162.7	31 41.1	-57.1	162.9	30 43.7	-57.1	163.0	29 46.3	-57.3	163.2	28 48.8	-57.3	163.4	27 51.3	-57.4	163.5	26 53.8	-57.6	163.7	31
32	32 38.8	-56.8	162.9	31 41.5	-57.0	163.1	30 44.0	-57.1	163.2	29 46.6	-57.2	163.4	28 49.0	-57.3	163.6	27 51.5	-57.4	163.7	26 53.9	-57.5	163.9	25 56.2	-57.6	164.0	32
33	31 42.0	-57.0	163.2	30 44.5	-57.1	163.4	29 46.9	-57.1	163.6	28 49.4	-57.3	163.7	27 51.7	-57.3	163.9	26 54.1	-57.5	164.0	25 56.4	-57.6	164.2	24 58.6	-57.6	164.3	33
34	30 45.0	-57.0	163.6	29 47.4	-57.1	163.8	28 49.8	-57.2	163.9	27 52.1	-57.3	164.1	26 54.4	-57.4	164.2	25 56.6	-57.5	164.4	24 58.8	-57.6	164.5	24 01.0	-57.7	164.6	34
35	29 48.0	-57.1	164.0	28 50.3	-57.2	164.1	27 52.6	-57.3	164.3	26 54.8	-57.4	164.4	25 57.0	-57.5	164.6	24 59.1	-57.5	164.7	24 01.2	-57.6	164.8	23 03.3	-57.7	164.9	35
36	28 50.9	-57.1	164.3	27 53.1	-57.2	164.5	26 55.3	-57.3	164.6	25 57.4	-57.4	164.7	24 59.5	-57.5	164.9	24 01.6	-57.6	165.0	23 03.6	-57.6	165.1	22 05.6	-57.7	165.2	36
37	27 53.8	-57.2	164.7	26 55.9	-57.3	164.8	25 58.0	-57.4	164.9	25 00.0	-57.4	165.1	24 02.0	-57.5	165.2	23 04.0	-57.6	165.3	22 06.0	-57.7	165.4	21 07.9	-57.8	165.5	37
38	26 56.6	-57.2	165.0	25 58.6	-57.3	165.2	25 00.6	-57.4	165.3	24 02.6	-57.5	165.4	23 04.5	-57.6	165.5	22 06.4	-57.6	165.6	21 08.3	-57.7	165.7	20 10.1	-57.8	165.8	38
39	25 59.4	-57.3	165.4	25 01.3	-57.3	165.5	24 03.2	-57.4	165.6	23 05.1	-57.5	165.7	22 06.9	-57.5	165.8	21 08.8	-57.7	165.9	20 10.6	-57.8	166.0	19 12.3	-57.8	166.1	39
40	25 02.1	-57.3	165.7	24 04.0	-57.4	165.8	23 05.8	-57.5	165.9	22 07.6	-57.6	166.0	21 09.4	-57.7	166.1	20 11.1	-57.7	166.2	19 12.8	-57.7	166.3	18 14.5	-57.8	166.4	40
41	24 04.8	-57.3	166.0	23 06.6	-57.5	166.1	22 08.3	-57.5	166.2	21 10.0	-57.6	166.3	20 11.7	-57.6	166.4	19 13.4	-57.7	166.5	18 15.1	-57.8	166.6	17 16.7	-57.9	166.6	41
42	23 07.5	-57.4	166.3	22 09.1	-57.4	166.4	21 10.8	-57.5	166.5	20 12.4	-57.6	166.6	19 14.1	-57.7	166.7	18 15.7	-57.8	166.8	17 17.3	-57.9	166.8	16 18.8	-57.9	166.9	42
43	22 10.1	-57.5	166.7	21 11.7	-57.5	166.7	20 13.3	-57.6	166.8	19 14.8	-57.6	166.9	18 16.4	-57.7	167.0	17 17.9	-57.8	167.1	16 19.4	-57.8	167.1	15 20.9	-57.9	167.2	43
44	21 12.6	-57.4	167.0	20 14.2	-57.6	167.0	19 15.7	-57.6	167.1	18 17.2	-57.7	167.2	17 18.7	-57.8	167.3	16 20.1	-57.8	167.3	15 21.6	-57.9	167.4	14 23.0	-57.9	167.5	44
45	20 15.2	-57.5	167.3	19 16.6	-57.5	167.3	18 18.1	-57.6	167.4	17 19.5	-57.7	167.5	16 20.9	-57.7	167.6	15 22.3	-57.8	167.6	14 23.7	-57.8	167.7	13 25.1	-57.9	167.7	45
46	19 17.7	-57.5	167.6	18 19.1	-57.6	167.6	17 20.5	-57.7	167.7	16 21.8	-57.7	167.8	15 23.2	-57.8	167.8	14 24.5	-57.8	167.9	13 25.9	-57.9	167.9	12 27.2	-58.0	168.0	46
47	18 20.2	-57.6	167.9	17 21.5	-57.6	167.9	16 22.8	-57.7	168.0	15 24.1	-57.7	168.1	14 25.4	-57.8	168.1	13 26.7	-57.9	168.2	12 28.0	-58.0	168.2	11 29.2	-58.0	168.3	47
48	17 22.6	-57.6	168.2	16 23.9	-57.7	168.2	15 25.1	-57.7	168.3	14 26.4	-57.8	168.3	13 27.6	-57.8	168.4	12 28.8	-57.8	168.4	11 30.0	-57.9	168.5	10 31.2	-57.9	168.5	48
49	16 25.0	-57.6	168.5	15 26.2	-57.6	168.5	14 27.4	-57.7	168.6	13 28.6	-57.8	168.6	12 29.8	-57.8	168.7	11 31.0	-57.9	168.7	10 32.1	-57.9	168.7	9 33.3	-58.0	168.8	49
50	15 27.4	-57.6	168.8	14 28.6	-57.7	168.8	13 29.7	-57.7	168.9	12 30.8	-57.8	168.9	11 32.0	-57.9	168.9	10 33.1	-57.9	169.0	9 34.2	-58.0	169.0	8 35.3	-58.0	169.0	50
51	14 29.8	-57.6	169.0	13 30.9	-57.7	169.1	12 32.0	-57.8	169.1	11 33.0	-57.8	169.2	10 34.1	-57.9	169.2	9 35.2	-57.9	169.2	8 36.2	-57.9	169.3	7 37.3	-58.1	169.3	51
52	13 32.2	-57.7	169.3	12 33.2	-57.7	169.4	11 34.2	-57.8	169.4	10 35.2	-57.8	169.4	9 36.2	-57.8	169.5	8 37.3	-58.0	169.5	7 38.3	-58.0	169.5	6 39.2	-58.0	169.6	52
53	12 34.5	-57.7	169.6	11 35.5	-57.8	169.7	10 36.4	-57.7	169.7	9 37.4	-57.8	169.7	8 38.4	-57.9	169.7	7 39.3	-57.9	169.8	6 40.3	-58.0	169.8	5 41.2	-58.0	169.8	53
54	11 36.8	-57.7	169.9	10 37.7	-57.7	169.9	9 38.7	-57.8	170.0	8 39.6	-57.9	170.0	7 40.5	-57.9	170.0	6 41.4	-57.9	170.0	5 42.3	-58.0	170.1	4 43.2	-58.0	170.1	54
55	10 39.1	-57.7	170.2	9 40.0	-57.8	170.2	8 40.9	-57.8	170.2	7 41.7	-57.8	170.3	6 42.6	-57.9	170.3	5 43.5	-58.0	170.3	4 44.3	-58.0	170.3	3 45.2	-58.1	170.3	55
56	9 41.4	-57.7	170.5	8 42.2	-57.7	170.5	7 43.1	-57.9	170.5	6 43.9	-57.9	170.5	5 44.7	-57.9	170.5	4 45.5	-58.0	170.6	3 46.3	-58.0	170.6	2 47.1	-58.0	170.6	56
57	8 43.7	-57.8	170.7	7 44.5	-57.8	170.8	6 45.2	-57.8	170.8	5 46.0	-57.9	170.8	4 46.8	-57.9	170.8	3 47.5	-57.9	170.8	2 48.3	-58.0	170.8	1 49.1	-58.1	170.8	57
58	7 45.9	-57.7	171.0	6 46.7	-57.8	171.0	5 47.4	-57.8	171.0	4 48.1	-57.8	171.1	3 48.9	-58.0	171.1	2 49.6	-58.0	171.1	1 50.3	-58.0	171.1	0 51.0	-58.0	171.1	58
59	6 48.2	-57.8	171.3	5 48.9	-57.8	171.3	4 49.6	-57.9	171.3	3 50.3	-57.9	171.3	2 50.9	-57.9	171.3	1 51.6	-57.9	171.3	0 52.3	-58.0	171.3	0 07.0	+58.0	8.7	59
60	5 50.4	-57.7	171.5	4 51.1	-57.8	171.6	3 51.7	-57.8	171.6	2 52.4	-57.9	171.6	1 53.0	-57.8	171.6	0 53.7	-58.0	171.6	0 05.7	+58.0	8.4	1 05.0	+58.1	8.4	60
61	4 52.7	-57.8	171.8	3 53.3	-57.8	171.8	2 53.9	-57.9	171.8	1 54.5	-57.9	171.8	0 55.1	-57.9	171.9	0 04.3	+58.0	8.1	1 03.7	+58.0	8.2	2 03.1	+58.0	8.2	61
62	3 54.9	-57.8	172.1	2 55.5	-57.9	172.1	1 56.0	-57.8	172.1	0 56.6	-57.9	172.1	0 02.8	+58.0	7.9	1 02.3	+57.9	7.9	2 01.7	+58.0	7.9	3 01.1	+58.1	7.9	62
63	2 57.1	-57.8	172.4	1 57.6	-57.8	172.4	0 58.2	-57.9	172.4	0 01.3	+57.9	7.6	1 00.8	+57.9	7.6	2 00.2	+58.0	7.6	2 59.7	+58.0	7.6	3 59.2	+58.0	7.6	63
64	1 59.3	-57.8	172.6	0 59.8	-57.8	172.6	0 00.3	-57.8	172.6	0 59.2	+57.9	7.4	1 58.7	+57.9	7.4	2 58.2	+58.0	7.4	3 57.7	+58.0	7.4	4 57.2	+58.0	7.4	64
65	1 01.5	-57.7	172.9	0 02.0	-57.8	172.9	0 57.5	+57.9	7.1	1 57.1	+57.9	7.1	2 56.6	+57.9	7.1	3 56.2	+57.9	7.1	4 55.7	+58.0	7.1	5 55.2	+58.0	7.1	65
66	0 03.8	-57.8	173.2	0 55.8	+57.8	6.8	1 55.4	+57.8	6.8	2 55.0	+57.8	6.8	3 54.5	+58.0	6.8	4 54.1	+58.0	6.8	5 53.7	+58.0	6.9	6 53.2	+58.1	6.9	66
67	0 54.0	+57.8	6.6	1 53.6	+57.9	6.6	2 53.2	+57.9	6.6	3 52.8	+57.9	6.6	4 52.5	+57.9	6.6	5 52.1	+57.9	6.6	6 51.7	+57.9	6.6	7 51.3	+58.0	6.6	67
68	1 51.8	+57.8	6.3	2 51.5	+57.8	6.3	3 51.1	+57.8	6.3	4 50.7	+57.9	6.3	5 50.4	+57.9	6.3	6 50.0	+57.9	6.3	7 49.6	+58.0	6.3	8 49.3	+58.0	6.4	68
69	2 49.6	+57.8	6.0	3 49.3	+57.8	6.0	4 48.9	+57.9	6.0	5 48.6	+57.9	6.0	6 48.3	+57.9	6.1	7 47.9	+58.0	6.1	8 47.6	+57.9	6.1	9 47.3	+57.9	6.1	69
70	3 47.4	+57.7	5.8	4 47.1	+57.8	5.8	5 46.8	+57.8	5.8	6 46.5	+57.8	5.8	7 46.2	+57.8	5.8	8 45.9	+57.9	5.8	9 45.5	+58.0	5.8	10 45.2	+58.0	5.8	70
71	4 45.1	+57.8	5.5	5 44.9	+57.8	5.5	6 44.6	+57.8	5.5	7 44.3	+57.9	5.5	8 44.0	+57.9	5.5	9 43.8	+57.9	5.5	10 43.5	+57.9	5.6	11 43.2	+58.0	5.6	71
72	5 42.9	+57.8	5.2	6 42.7	+57.8	5.2	7 42.4	+57.8	5.2	8 42.2	+57.8	5.2	9 41.9	+57.9	5.3	10 41.7	+57.8	5.3	11 41.4	+57.9	5.3	12 41.2	+57.9	5.3	72
73	6 40.7	+57.7	4.9	7 40.5	+57.7	4.9	8 40.2	+57.8	5.0	9 40.0	+57.8	5.0	10 39.8	+57.8	5.0	11 39.5	+57.9	5.0	12 39.3	+57.9	5.0	13 39.1	+57.9	5.0	73
74	7 38.4	+57.8	4.7	8 38.2	+57.8	4.7	9 38.0	+57.8	4.7	10 37.8	+57.8	4.7	11 37.6	+57.9	4.7	12 37.4	+57.9	4.7	13 37.2	+57.9	4.8	14 37.0	+57.9	4.8	74
75	8 36.2	+57.7	4.4	9 36.0	+57.7	4.4	10 35.8	+57.8	4.4	11 35.6	+57.8	4.4	12 35.5	+57.8	4.4	13 35.3	+57.8	4.5	14 35.1	+57.8	4.5	15 34.9	+57.9	4.5	75
76	9 33.9	+57.7	4.1	10 33.7	+57.8	4.1	11 33.6	+57.7	4.1	12 33.4	+57.8	4.2	13 33.3	+57.8	4.2	14 33.1	+57.8	4.2	15 32.9	+57.9	4.2	16 32.8	+57.8	4.2	76
77	10 31.6	+57.7	3.8	11 31.5	+57.7	3.8	12 31.3	+57.8	3.9	13 31.2	+57.8	3.9	14 31.1	+57.7	3.9	15 30.9	+57.8	3.9	16 30.8	+57.8	3.9	17 30.6	+57.9	4.0	77
78	11 29.3	+57.7	3.6	12 29.2	+57.7	3.6	13 29.1	+57.7	3.6	14 29.0	+57.7	3.6	15 28.8	+57.8	3.6	16 28.7	+57.8	3.6	17 28.6	+57.8	3.7	18 28.5	+57.8	3.7	78
79	12 27.0	+57.7	3.3	13 26.9	+57.7	3.3	14 26.8	+57.7	3.3	15 26.7	+57.7	3.3	16 26.6	+57.7	3.3	17 26.5	+57.7	3.4	18 26.4	+57.8	3.4	19 26.3	+57.8	3.4	79
80	13 24.7	+57.6	3.0	14 24.6	+57.6	3.0	15 24.5	+57.7	3.0	16 24.4	+57.7	3.0	17 24.3	+57.7	3.0	18 24.2	+57.8	3.1	19 24.2	+57.7	3.1	20 24.1	+57.7	3.1	80
81	14 22.3	+57.6	2.7	15 22.2	+57.7	2.7	16 22.2	+57.6	2.7	17 22.1	+57.7	2.7	18 22.0	+57.7	2.8	19 22.0	+57.7	2.8	20 21.9	+57.7	2.8	21 21.8	+57.7	2.8	81
82	15 19.9	+57.6	2.4	16 19.9	+57.6	2.4	17 19.8	+57.7	2.4	18 19.8	+57.6	2.5	19 19.7	+57.7	2.5	20 19.7	+57.6	2.5	21 19.6	+57.7	2.5	22 19.5	+57.7	2.5	82
83	16 17.5	+57.6	2.1	17 17.5	+57.6	2.1	18 17.5	+57.6	2.2	19 17.4	+57.6	2.2	20 17.4	+57.6	2.2	21 17.3	+57.7	2.2	22 17.3	+57.6	2.2	23 17.2	+57.7	2.2	83
84	17 15.1	+57.6	1.8	18 15.1	+57.6	1.8	19 15.1	+57.5	1.9	20 15.0	+57.6	1.9	21 15.0	+57.6	1.9	22 15.0	+57.6	1.9	23 14.9	+57.6	1.9	24 14.9	+57.6	1.9	84
85	18 12.7	+57.5	1.5	19 12.7	+57.5	1.5	20 12.6	+57.6	1.6	21 12.6	+57.6	1.6	22 12.6	+57.5	1.6	23 12.6	+57.6	1.6	24 12.5	+57.6	1.6	25 12.5	+57.6	1.6	85
86	19 10.2	+57.5	1.2	20 10.2	+57.5	1.2	21 10.2	+57.5	1.3	22 10.2	+57.5	1.3	23 10.1	+57.6	1.3	24 10.1	+57.6	1.3	25 10.1	+57.6	1.3	26 10.1	+57.5	1.3	86
87	20 07.7	+57.5	0.9	21 07.7	+57.5	0.9	22 07.7	+57.5	0.9	23 07.7	+57.5	1.0	24 07.7	+57.5	1.0	25 07.7	+57.5	1.0	26 07.7	+57.4	1.0	27 07.6	+57.5	1.0	87
88	21 05.2	+57.4	0.6	22 05.2	+57.4	0.6	23 05.2	+57.4	0.6	24 05.2	+57.4	0.6	25 05.2	+57.4	0.6	26 05.2	+57.4	0.7	27 05.1	+57.5	0.7	28 05.1	+57.5	0.7	88
89	22 02.6	+57.4	0.3	23 02.6	+57.4	0.3	24 02.6	+57.4	0.3	25 02.6	+57.4	0.3	26 02.6	+57.4	0.3	27 02.6	+57.4	0.3	28 02.6	+57.4	0.3	29 02.6	+57.4	0.3	89
90	23 00.0	+57.4	0.0	24 00.0	+57.4	0.0	25 00.0	+57.4	0.0	26 00.0	+57.4	0.0	27 00.0	+57.4	0.0	28 00.0	+57.4	0.0	29 00.0	+57.4	0.0	30 00.0	+57.4	0.0	90
	23°			24°			25°			26°			27°			28°			29°			30°			

S. Lat. {L.H.A. greater than 180° ....Zn=180°−Z
{L.H.A. less than 180°...........Zn=180°+Z

LATITUDE **SAME** NAME AS DECLINATION — L.H.A. 163°, 197°

18°, 342° L.H.A. LATITUDE SAME NAME AS DECLINATION

N. Lat. {L.H.A. greater than 180° .....Zn=Z
{L.H.A. less than 180°............Zn=360°–Z

	23°			24°			25°			26°			27°			28°			29°			30°			
Dec.	Hc	d	Z	Hc	d	Z	Hc	d	Z	Hc	d	Z	Hc	d	Z	Hc	d	Z	Hc	d	Z	Hc	d	Z	Dec.
°	° ′	′	°	° ′	′	°	° ′	′	°	° ′	′	°	° ′	′	°	° ′	′	°	° ′	′	°	° ′	′	°	°
0	61 05.9	+48.2	140.3	60 19.4	+49.0	141.4	59 32.2	+49.7	142.4	58 44.3	+50.4	143.5	57 55.8	+51.1	144.4	57 06.7	+51.7	145.3	56 17.1	+52.2	146.2	55 27.0	+52.8	147.0	0
1	61 54.1	+47.4	139.0	61 08.4	+48.3	140.2	60 21.9	+49.2	141.3	59 34.7	+49.9	142.4	58 46.9	+50.5	143.4	57 58.4	+51.2	144.4	57 09.3	+51.9	145.3	56 19.8	+52.3	146.1	1
2	62 41.5	+46.7	137.7	61 56.7	+47.6	139.0	61 11.1	+48.5	140.2	60 24.6	+49.3	141.3	59 37.4	+50.1	142.4	58 49.6	+50.7	143.4	58 01.2	+51.3	144.3	57 12.1	+52.0	145.2	2
3	63 28.2	+45.8	136.3	62 44.3	+46.9	137.6	61 59.6	+47.8	138.9	61 13.9	+48.7	140.1	60 27.5	+49.5	141.3	59 40.3	+50.3	142.3	58 52.5	+50.9	143.3	58 04.1	+51.5	144.3	3
4	64 14.0	+44.9	134.8	63 31.2	+46.0	136.3	62 47.4	+47.0	137.6	62 02.6	+48.0	138.9	61 17.0	+48.8	140.1	60 30.6	+49.6	141.2	59 43.4	+50.4	142.3	58 55.6	+51.1	143.3	4
5	64 58.9	+43.9	133.3	64 17.2	+45.1	134.8	63 34.4	+46.2	136.2	62 50.6	+47.2	137.6	62 05.8	+48.2	138.9	61 20.2	+49.0	140.1	60 33.8	+49.8	141.2	59 46.7	+50.5	142.3	5
6	65 42.8	+42.8	131.7	65 02.3	+44.1	133.3	64 20.6	+45.3	134.8	63 37.8	+46.4	136.2	62 54.0	+47.4	137.6	62 09.2	+48.4	138.9	61 23.6	+49.2	140.1	60 37.2	+50.0	141.2	6
7	66 25.6	+41.5	129.9	65 46.4	+43.0	131.6	65 05.9	+44.3	133.2	64 24.2	+45.5	134.8	63 41.4	+46.6	136.2	62 57.6	+47.6	137.6	62 12.8	+48.6	138.9	61 27.2	+49.4	140.1	7
8	67 07.1	+40.2	128.1	66 29.4	+41.7	129.9	65 50.2	+43.2	131.6	65 09.7	+44.5	133.2	64 28.0	+45.7	134.8	63 45.2	+46.8	136.2	63 01.4	+47.8	137.6	62 16.6	+48.8	138.9	8
9	67 47.3	+38.8	126.2	67 11.1	+40.5	128.1	66 33.4	+42.0	129.9	65 54.2	+43.4	131.6	65 13.7	+44.7	133.2	64 32.0	+45.9	134.8	63 49.2	+47.0	136.2	63 05.4	+48.0	137.6	9
10	68 26.1	+37.2	124.1	67 51.6	+39.0	126.1	67 15.4	+40.7	128.1	66 37.6	+42.2	129.9	65 58.4	+43.7	131.6	65 17.9	+45.0	133.3	64 36.2	+46.1	134.8	63 53.4	+47.2	136.3	10
11	69 03.3	+35.4	121.9	68 30.6	+37.4	124.1	67 56.1	+39.2	126.2	67 19.8	+41.0	128.1	66 42.1	+42.4	129.9	66 02.9	+43.8	131.7	65 22.3	+45.2	133.3	64 40.6	+46.4	134.8	11
12	69 38.7	+33.6	119.7	69 08.0	+35.7	121.9	68 35.3	+37.7	124.1	68 00.8	+39.5	126.2	67 24.5	+41.2	128.1	66 46.7	+42.8	129.9	66 07.5	+44.1	131.7	65 27.0	+45.4	133.3	12
13	70 12.3	+31.5•	117.2	69 43.7	+33.8	119.7	69 13.0	+35.9	121.9	68 40.3	+37.9	124.1	68 05.7	+39.8	126.2	67 29.5	+41.4	128.1	66 51.6	+43.0	130.0	66 12.4	+44.3	131.7	13
14	70 43.8	+29.3•	114.7	70 17.5	+31.8•	117.2	69 48.9	+34.1	119.7	69 18.2	+36.2	122.0	68 45.5	+38.2	124.2	68 10.9	+40.0	126.2	67 34.6	+41.7	128.2	66 56.7	+43.3	130.0	14
15	71 13.1	+26.9•	112.0	70 49.3	+29.5•	114.7	70 23.0	+32.1•	117.2	69 54.4	+34.4	119.7	69 23.7	+36.4	122.0	68 50.9	+38.5	124.2	68 16.3	+40.3	126.3	67 40.0	+41.9	128.2	15
16	71 40.0	+24.2•	109.2	71 18.8	+27.2•	112.0	70 55.1	+29.8•	114.7	70 28.8	+32.3•	117.3	70 00.1	+34.7	119.7	69 29.4	+36.7	122.0	68 56.6	+38.7	124.2	68 21.9	+40.6	126.3	16
17	72 04.2	+21.6•	106.3	71 46.0	+24.5•	109.2	71 24.9	+27.4•	112.0	71 01.1	+30.1•	114.7	70 34.8	+32.6•	117.3	70 06.1	+34.9	119.7	69 35.3	+37.1	122.1	69 02.5	+39.0	124.3	17
18	72 25.8	+18.6•	103.2	72 10.5	+21.8•	106.2	71 52.3	+24.8•	109.2	71 31.2	+27.6•	112.0	71 07.4	+30.3•	114.7	70 41.0	+32.9•	117.3	70 12.4	+35.1	119.8	69 41.5	+37.3	122.1	18
19	72 44.4	+15.5•	100.0	72 32.3	+18.8•	103.2	72 17.1	+22.0•	106.2	71 58.8	+25.1•	109.2	71 37.7	+28.0•	112.0	71 13.9	+30.7•	114.8	70 47.5	+33.2•	117.4	70 18.8	+35.5	119.8	19
20	72 59.9	+12.2•	96.7	72 51.1	+15.8•	100.0	72 39.1	+19.1•	103.1	72 23.9	+22.3•	106.2	72 05.7	+25.4•	109.2	71 44.6	+28.2•	112.0	71 20.7	+31.0•	114.8	70 54.3	+33.5•	117.4	20
21	73 12.1	+8.9•	93.4	73 06.9	+12.4•	96.7	72 58.2	+16.0•	99.9	72 46.2	+19.4•	103.1	72 31.1	+22.5•	106.2	72 12.8	+25.7•	109.2	71 51.7	+28.5•	112.1	71 27.8	+31.2•	114.8	21
22	73 21.0	+5.5•	89.9	73 19.3	+9.1•	93.3	73 14.2	+12.7•	96.6	73 05.6	+16.2•	99.9	72 53.6	+19.6•	103.1	72 38.5	+22.8•	106.2	72 20.2	+25.9•	109.2	71 59.0	+28.9•	112.1	22
23	73 26.5	+1.9•	86.5	73 28.4	+5.6•	89.8	73 26.9	+9.2•	93.2	73 21.8	+12.9•	96.5	73 13.2	+16.4•	99.8	73 01.3	+19.9•	103.1	72 46.1	+23.2•	106.2	72 27.9	+26.2•	109.3	23
24	73 28.4	-1.5•	82.9	73 34.0	+2.1•	86.3	73 36.1	+5.8•	89.7	73 34.7	+9.4•	93.1	73 29.6	+13.2•	96.5	73 21.2	+16.6•	99.8	73 09.3	+20.1•	103.1	72 54.1	+23.4•	106.2	24
25	73 26.9	-5.1•	79.4	73 36.1	-1.4•	82.8	73 41.9	+2.2•	86.2	73 44.1	+6.0•	89.6	73 42.8	+9.6•	93.0	73 37.8	+13.4•	96.4	73 29.4	+16.9•	99.8	73 17.5	+20.4•	103.1	25
26	73 21.8	-8.6•	75.9	73 34.7	-5.1•	79.2	73 44.1	-1.3•	82.6	73 50.1	+2.3•	86.0	73 52.4	+6.1•	89.5	73 51.2	+9.8•	92.9	73 46.3	+13.5•	96.4	73 37.9	+17.1•	99.8	26
27	73 13.2	-11.9•	72.5	73 29.6	-8.4•	75.7	73 42.8	-5.0•	79.0	73 52.4	-1.2•	82.4	73 58.5	+2.5•	85.9	74 01.0	+6.3•	89.4	73 59.8	+10.1•	92.9	73 55.0	+13.8•	96.3	27
28	73 01.3	-15.2•	69.1	73 21.2	-11.9•	72.3	73 37.8	-8.4•	75.5	73 51.2	-4.9•	78.8	74 01.0	-1.2•	82.3	74 07.3	+2.6•	85.7	74 09.9	+6.4•	89.3	74 08.8	+10.3•	92.8	28
29	72 46.1	-18.2•	65.8	73 09.3	-15.2•	68.8	73 29.4	-11.9•	72.0	73 46.3	-8.4•	75.3	73 59.8	-4.8•	78.6	74 09.9	-1.1•	82.1	74 16.3	+2.8•	85.6	74 19.1	+6.6•	89.2	29
30	72 27.9	-21.3•	62.6	72 54.1	-18.3•	65.5	73 17.5	-15.2•	68.6	73 37.9	-11.9•	71.7	73 55.0	-8.4•	75.0	74 08.8	-4.7•	78.4	74 19.1	-1.0•	81.9	74 25.7	+2.8•	85.5	30
31	72 06.6	-24.0•	59.6	72 35.8	-21.3•	62.3	73 02.3	-18.4•	65.2	73 26.0	-15.2•	68.3	73 46.6	-11.8•	71.5	74 04.1	-8.4•	74.8	74 18.1	-4.7•	78.2	74 28.5	-0.9•	81.7	31
32	71 42.6	-26.6•	56.6	72 14.5	-24.1•	59.2	72 43.9	-21.3•	62.0	73 10.8	-18.4•	64.9	73 34.8	-15.3•	68.0	73 55.7	-11.9•	71.2	74 13.4	-8.4•	74.5	74 27.6	-4.6•	78.0	32
33	71 16.0	-29.0•	53.8	71 50.4	-26.7•	56.3	72 22.6	-24.2•	58.9	72 52.4	-21.5•	61.6	73 19.5	-18.5•	64.6	73 43.8	-15.3•	67.7	74 05.0	-11.9•	70.9	74 23.0	-8.4•	74.3	33
34	70 47.0	-31.3•	51.1	71 23.7	-29.2•	53.4	71 58.4	-26.8•	55.9	72 30.9	-24.2•	58.5	73 01.0	-21.5•	61.3	73 28.5	-18.6•	64.2	73 53.1	-15.4•	67.4	74 14.6	-12.0•	70.6	34
35	70 15.7	-33.4	48.5	70 54.5	-31.3•	50.7	71 31.6	-29.3•	53.0	72 06.7	-27.0•	55.5	72 39.5	-24.4•	58.1	73 09.9	-21.6•	60.9	73 37.7	-18.6•	63.9	74 02.6	-15.4•	67.0	35
36	69 42.3	-35.2	46.1	70 23.2	-33.5•	48.1	71 02.3	-31.5•	50.3	71 39.7	-29.3•	52.6	72 15.1	-27.0•	55.1	72 48.3	-24.5•	57.7	73 19.1	-21.7•	60.6	73 47.2	-18.7•	63.6	36
37	69 07.1	-37.0	43.8	69 49.7	-35.4	45.7	70 30.8	-33.6•	47.7	71 10.4	-31.7•	49.9	71 48.1	-29.5•	52.2	72 23.8	-27.2•	54.7	72 57.4	-24.7•	57.4	73 28.5	-21.9•	60.2	37
38	68 30.1	-38.7	41.6	69 14.3	-37.1	43.4	69 57.2	-35.5	45.3	70 38.7	-33.8	47.3	71 18.6	-31.8•	49.5	71 56.6	-29.6•	51.8	72 32.7	-27.3•	54.3	73 06.6	-24.7•	56.9	38
39	67 51.4	-40.0	39.6	68 37.2	-38.8	41.2	69 21.7	-37.3	42.9	70 04.9	-35.6	44.8	70 46.8	-34.0•	46.8	71 27.0	-32.0•	49.0	72 05.4	-29.8•	51.3	72 41.9	-27.6•	53.8	39
40	67 11.4	-41.4	37.6	67 58.4	-40.2	39.1	68 44.4	-38.9	40.8	69 29.3	-37.5	42.5	70 12.8	-35.8	44.4	70 55.0	-34.1•	46.4	71 35.6	-32.2•	48.6	72 14.3	-30.0•	50.9	40
41	66 30.0	-42.7	35.8	67 18.2	-41.6	37.2	68 05.5	-40.3	38.7	68 51.8	-39.0	40.3	69 37.0	-37.6	42.0	70 20.9	-36.0	43.9	71 03.4	-34.3•	45.9	71 44.3	-32.3•	48.1	41
42	65 47.3	-43.8	34.1	66 36.6	-42.7	35.3	67 25.2	-41.7	36.7	68 12.8	-40.5	38.2	68 59.4	-39.2	39.8	69 44.9	-37.8	41.6	70 29.1	-36.2	43.4	71 12.0	-34.5•	45.4	42
43	65 03.5	-44.7	32.4	65 53.9	-43.9	33.6	66 43.5	-43.0	34.9	67 32.3	-41.9	36.3	68 20.2	-40.7	37.7	69 07.1	-39.4	39.4	69 52.9	-37.9	41.1	70 37.5	-36.4	42.9	43
44	64 18.8	-45.8	30.9	65 10.0	-45.0	32.0	66 00.5	-44.0	33.1	66 50.4	-43.1	34.4	67 39.5	-42.0	35.8	68 27.7	-40.8	37.3	69 15.0	-39.6	38.9	70 01.1	-38.1	40.6	44
45	63 33.0	-46.6	29.4	64 25.0	-45.8	30.4	65 16.5	-45.0	31.5	66 07.3	-44.1	32.7	66 57.5	-43.2	33.9	67 46.9	-42.2	35.3	68 35.4	-41.0	36.8	69 23.0	-39.8	38.4	45
46	62 46.4	-47.3	28.0	63 39.2	-46.7	28.9	64 31.5	-46.0	29.9	65 23.2	-45.2	31.0	66 14.3	-44.4	32.2	67 04.7	-43.4	33.4	67 54.4	-42.4	34.8	68 43.2	-41.2	36.3	46
47	61 59.1	-48.1	26.7	62 52.5	-47.5	27.5	63 45.5	-46.9	28.5	64 38.0	-46.2	29.5	65 29.9	-45.3	30.5	66 21.3	-44.5	31.7	67 12.0	-43.6	32.9	68 02.0	-42.6	34.3	47
48	61 11.0	-48.8	25.4	62 05.0	-48.2	26.2	62 58.6	-47.6	27.1	63 51.8	-47.0	28.0	64 44.6	-46.3	29.0	65 36.8	-45.6	30.1	66 28.4	-44.7	31.2	67 19.4	-43.8	32.4	48
49	60 22.2	-49.4	24.2	61 16.8	-48.9	25.0	62 11.0	-48.3	25.8	63 04.8	-47.7	26.6	63 58.3	-47.2	27.5	64 51.2	-46.4	28.5	65 43.7	-45.7	29.6	66 35.6	-44.9	30.7	49
50	59 32.8	-49.9	23.1	60 27.9	-49.5	23.8	61 22.7	-49.0	24.5	62 17.1	-48.5	25.3	63 11.1	-47.9	26.1	64 04.8	-47.3	27.0	64 58.0	-46.6	28.0	65 50.7	-45.8	29.0	50
51	58 42.9	-50.4	22.0	59 38.4	-50.0	22.6	60 33.7	-49.6	23.3	61 28.6	-49.1	24.0	62 23.2	-48.6	24.8	63 17.5	-48.0	25.6	64 11.4	-47.4	26.5	65 04.9	-46.8	27.5	51
52	57 52.5	-51.0	21.0	58 48.4	-50.6	21.6	59 44.1	-50.2	22.2	60 39.5	-49.7	22.8	61 34.6	-49.2	23.6	62 29.5	-48.8	24.3	63 24.0	-48.2	25.1	64 18.1	-47.6	26.0	52
53	57 01.5	-51.3	20.0	57 57.8	-51.0	20.5	58 53.9	-50.7	21.1	59 49.8	-50.3	21.7	60 45.4	-49.9	22.4	61 40.7	-49.4	23.1	62 35.8	-48.9	23.8	63 30.5	-48.4	24.6	53
54	56 10.2	-51.8	19.0	57 06.8	-51.5	19.5	58 03.2	-51.1	20.1	58 59.5	-50.8	20.6	59 55.5	-50.4	21.3	60 51.3	-50.0	21.9	61 46.9	-49.6	22.6	62 42.1	-49.1	23.3	54
55	55 18.4	-52.2	18.1	56 15.3	-51.9	18.6	57 12.1	-51.6	19.1	58 08.7	-51.2	19.6	59 05.1	-50.9	20.2	60 01.3	-50.5	20.8	60 57.3	-50.1	21.4	61 53.0	-49.6	22.1	55
56	54 26.2	-52.5	17.3	55 23.4	-52.2	17.7	56 20.5	-51.9	18.2	57 17.5	-51.7	18.6	58 14.2	-51.3	19.2	59 10.8	-51.0	19.7	60 07.2	-50.7	20.3	61 03.4	-50.3	20.9	56
57	53 33.7	-52.8	16.5	54 31.2	-52.6	16.9	55 28.6	-52.4	17.3	56 25.8	-52.1	17.7	57 22.9	-51.8	18.2	58 19.8	-51.5	18.7	59 16.5	-51.1	19.2	60 13.1	-50.8	19.8	57
58	52 40.9	-53.1	15.7	53 38.6	-52.9	16.0	54 36.2	-52.7	16.4	55 33.7	-52.4	16.8	56 31.1	-52.2	17.3	57 28.3	-51.9	17.7	58 25.4	-51.6	18.2	59 22.3	-51.3	18.7	58
59	51 47.8	-53.5	14.9	52 45.7	-53.2	15.2	53 43.5	-53.0	15.6	54 41.3	-52.8	16.0	55 38.9	-52.6	16.4	56 36.4	-52.3	16.8	57 33.8	-52.1	17.3	58 31.0	-51.8	17.7	59
60	50 54.3	-53.6	14.2	51 52.5	-53.5	14.5	52 50.5	-53.3	14.8	53 48.5	-53.1	15.2	54 46.3	-52.9	15.5	55 44.1	-52.7	15.9	56 41.7	-52.4	16.3	57 39.2	-52.1	16.8	60
61	50 00.7	-54.0	13.5	50 59.0	-53.8	13.8	51 57.2	-53.6	14.1	52 55.4	-53.4	14.4	53 53.4	-53.2	14.7	54 51.4	-53.0	15.1	55 49.3	-52.8	15.5	56 47.1	-52.6	15.9	61
62	49 06.7	-54.1	12.8	50 05.2	-54.0	13.1	51 03.6	-53.8	13.3	52 02.0	-53.7	13.6	53 00.2	-53.4	14.0	53 58.4	-53.3	14.3	54 56.5	-53.1	14.6	55 54.5	-52.8	15.0	62
63	48 12.6	-54.4	12.2	49 11.2	-54.2	12.4	50 09.8	-54.1	12.7	51 08.3	-53.9	12.9	52 06.8	-53.8	13.2	53 05.1	-53.6	13.5	54 03.4	-53.4	13.8	55 01.7	-53.3	14.2	63
64	47 18.2	-54.5	11.5	48 17.0	-54.4	11.7	49 15.7	-54.3	12.0	50 14.4	-54.2	12.2	51 13.0	-54.0	12.5	52 11.5	-53.8	12.8	53 10.0	-53.7	13.1	54 08.4	-53.5	13.4	64
65	46 23.7	-54.8	10.9	47 22.6	-54.7	11.1	48 21.4	-54.5	11.3	49 20.2	-54.4	11.6	50 19.0	-54.3	11.8	51 17.7	-54.1	12.1	52 16.3	-53.9	12.3	53 14.9	-53.8	12.6	65
66	45 28.9	-54.9	10.3	46 27.9	-54.8	10.5	47 26.9	-54.7	10.7	48 25.8	-54.6	10.9	49 24.7	-54.4	11.1	50 23.6	-54.4	11.4	51 22.4	-54.2	11.6	52 21.1	-54.0	11.9	66
67	44 34.0	-55.1	9.8	45 33.1	-55.0	9.9	46 32.2	-54.9	10.1	47 31.2	-54.7	10.3	48 30.3	-54.7	10.5	49 29.2	-54.5	10.7	50 28.2	-54.5	10.9	51 27.1	-54.4	11.2	67
68	43 38.9	-55.2	9.2	44 38.1	-55.1	9.4	45 37.3	-55.1	9.5	46 36.5	-55.0	9.7	47 35.6	-54.9	9.9	48 34.7	-54.8	10.1	49 33.7	-54.6	10.3	50 32.7	-54.5	10.5	68
69	42 43.7	-55.4	8.7	43 43.0	-55.4	8.8	44 42.2	-55.2	9.0	45 41.5	-55.1	9.1	46 40.7	-55.0	9.3	47 39.9	-54.9	9.5	48 39.1	-54.9	9.6	49 38.2	-54.7	9.8	69
70	41 48.3	-55.6	8.2	42 47.6	-55.4	8.3	43 47.0	-55.4	8.4	44 46.4	-55.3	8.6	45 45.7	-55.2	8.7	46 45.0	-55.2	8.9	47 44.2	-55.0	9.0	48 43.5	-55.0	9.2	70
71	40 52.7	-55.6	7.6	41 52.2	-55.6	7.8	42 51.6	-55.5	7.9	43 51.1	-55.5	8.0	44 50.5	-55.4	8.2	45 49.8	-55.2	8.3	46 49.2	-55.2	8.5	47 48.5	-55.1	8.6	71
72	39 57.1	-55.8	7.2	40 56.6	-55.7	7.3	41 56.1	-55.6	7.4	42 55.6	-55.6	7.5	43 55.1	-55.5	7.6	44 54.6	-55.5	7.7	45 54.0	-55.4	7.9	46 53.4	-55.3	8.0	72
73	39 01.3	-55.9	6.7	40 00.9	-55.8	6.8	41 00.5	-55.8	6.9	42 00.0	-55.7	7.0	42 59.6	-55.7	7.1	43 59.1	-55.6	7.2	44 58.6	-55.5	7.3	45 58.1	-55.4	7.5	73
74	38 05.4	-56.0	6.2	39 05.1	-56.0	6.3	40 04.7	-55.9	6.4	41 04.3	-55.8	6.5	42 03.9	-55.8	6.6	43 03.5	-55.7	6.7	44 03.1	-55.7	6.8	45 02.7	-55.6	6.9	74
75	37 09.4	-56.1	5.8	38 09.1	-56.0	5.8	39 08.8	-56.0	5.9	40 08.5	-56.0	6.0	41 08.1	-55.9	6.1	42 07.8	-55.9	6.2	43 07.4	-55.8	6.3	44 07.1	-55.8	6.4	75
76	36 13.3	-56.2	5.3	37 13.1	-56.2	5.4	38 12.8	-56.1	5.5	39 12.5	-56.1	5.5	40 12.2	-56.0	5.6	41 11.9	-55.9	5.7	42 11.6	-55.9	5.8	43 11.3	-55.9	5.9	76
77	35 17.1	-56.3	4.9	36 16.9	-56.2	4.9	37 16.7	-56.2	5.0	38 16.4	-56.1	5.1	39 16.2	-56.1	5.2	40 16.0	-56.1	5.2	41 15.7	-56.0	5.3	42 15.4	-56.0	5.4	77
78	34 20.8	-56.3	4.5	35 20.7	-56.4	4.5	36 20.5	-56.3	4.6	37 20.3	-56.3	4.6	38 20.1	-56.3	4.7	39 19.9	-56.2	4.8	40 19.7	-56.2	4.8	41 19.4	-56.1	4.9	78
79	33 24.5	-56.5	4.1	34 24.3	-56.4	4.1	35 24.2	-56.4	4.1	36 24.0	-56.3	4.2	37 23.8	-56.3	4.3	38 23.7	-56.3	4.3	39 23.5	-56.3	4.4	40 23.3	-56.2	4.4	79
80	32 28.0	-56.5	3.6	33 27.9	-56.5	3.7	34 27.8	-56.5	3.7	35 27.7	-56.5	3.8	36 27.5	-56.4	3.8	37 27.4	-56.4	3.9	38 27.2	-56.3	3.9	39 27.1	-56.3	4.0	80
81	31 31.5	-56.6	3.3	32 31.4	-56.6	3.3	33 31.3	-56.5	3.3	34 31.2	-56.5	3.4	35 31.1	-56.5	3.4	36 31.0	-56.5	3.4	37 30.9	-56.5	3.5	38 30.8	-56.5	3.5	81
82	30 34.9	-56.7	2.9	31 34.8	-56.6	2.9	32 34.8	-56.7	2.9	33 34.7	-56.6	3.0	34 34.6	-56.6	3.0	35 34.5	-56.6	3.0	36 34.4	-56.5	3.1	37 34.3	-56.5	3.1	82
83	29 38.2	-56.7	2.5	30 38.2	-56.7	2.5	31 38.1	-56.7	2.5	32 38.1	-56.7	2.6	33 38.0	-56.7	2.6	34 37.9	-56.6	2.6	35 37.9	-56.6	2.7	36 37.8	-56.6	2.7	83
84	28 41.5	-56.8	2.1	29 41.5	-56.8	2.1	30 41.4	-56.7	2.2	31 41.4	-56.8	2.2	32 41.3	-56.7	2.2	33 41.3	-56.7	2.2	34 41.3	-56.7	2.3	35 41.2	-56.7	2.3	84
85	27 44.7	-56.8	1.7	28 44.7	-56.8	1.8	29 44.7	-56.9	1.8	30 44.6	-56.8	1.8	31 44.6	-56.8	1.8	32 44.6	-56.8	1.8	33 44.6	-56.8	1.9	34 44.5	-56.7	1.9	85
86	26 47.9	-56.9	1.4	27 47.9	-56.9	1.4	28 47.8	-56.8	1.4	29 47.8	-56.8	1.4	30 47.8	-56.9	1.4	31 47.8	-56.9	1.5	32 47.8	-56.9	1.5	33 47.8	-56.9	1.5	86
87	25 51.0	-57.0	1.0	26 51.0	-57.0	1.0	27 51.0	-57.0	1.0	28 51.0	-57.0	1.1	29 50.9	-56.9	1.1	30 50.9	-56.9	1.1	31 50.9	-56.9	1.1	32 50.9	-56.9	1.1	87
88	24 54.0	-57.0	0.7	25 54.0	-57.0	0.7	26 54.0	-57.0	0.7	27 54.0	-57.0	0.7	28 54.0	-57.0	0.7	29 54.0	-57.0	0.7	30 54.0	-57.0	0.7	31 54.0	-57.0	0.7	88
89	23 57.0	-57.0	0.3	24 57.0	-57.0	0.3	25 57.0	-57.0	0.3	26 57.0	-57.0	0.3	27 57.0	-57.0	0.3	28 57.0	-57.0	0.4	29 57.0	-57.0	0.4	30 57.0	-57.0	0.4	89
90	23 00.0	-57.1	0.0	24 00.0	-57.1	0.0	25 00.0	-57.1	0.0	26 00.0	-57.1	0.0	27 00.0	-57.1	0.0	28 00.0	-57.1	0.0	29 00.0	-57.1	0.0	30 00.0	-57.1	0.0	90
	23°			24°			25°			26°			27°			28°			29°			30°			

18°, 342° L.H.A. LATITUDE SAME NAME AS DECLINATION

220

Dec.	23°			24°			25°			26°			Dec.
	Hc	d	Z	Hc	d	Z	Hc	d	Z	Hc	d	Z	
°	° ′	′	°	° ′	′	°	° ′	′	°	° ′	′	°	°
0	61 05.9	−48.8	140.3	60 19.4	−49.6	141.4	59 32.2	−50.3	142.4	58 44.3	−50.9	143.5	0
1	60 17.1	−49.4	141.4	59 29.8	−50.1	142.5	58 41.9	−50.8	143.5	57 53.4	−51.4	144.5	1
2	59 27.7	−50.0	142.6	58 39.7	−50.7	143.6	57 51.1	−51.2	144.5	57 02.0	−51.8	145.4	2
3	58 37.7	−50.5	143.6	57 49.0	−51.1	144.6	56 59.9	−51.7	145.5	56 10.2	−52.2	146.3	3
4	57 47.2	−51.0	144.7	56 57.9	−51.5	145.6	56 08.2	−52.1	146.4	55 18.0	−52.6	147.2	4
5	56 56.2	−51.4	145.6	56 06.4	−51.9	146.5	55 16.1	−52.4	147.3	54 25.4	−52.8	148.1	5
6	56 04.8	−51.8	146.6	55 14.5	−52.3	147.4	54 23.7	−52.8	148.1	53 32.6	−53.2	148.9	6
7	55 13.0	−52.2	147.5	54 22.2	−52.7	148.2	53 30.9	−53.0	148.9	52 39.4	−53.5	149.6	7
8	54 20.8	−52.6	148.3	53 29.5	−53.0	149.0	52 37.9	−53.4	149.7	51 45.9	−53.8	150.4	8
9	53 28.2	−52.8	149.2	52 36.5	−53.2	149.8	51 44.5	−53.7	150.5	50 52.1	−54.0	151.1	9
10	52 35.4	−53.2	149.9	51 43.3	−53.6	150.6	50 50.8	−53.8	151.2	49 58.1	−54.2	151.8	10
11	51 42.2	−53.4	150.7	50 49.7	−53.8	151.3	49 57.0	−54.2	151.9	49 03.9	−54.4	152.4	11
12	50 48.8	−53.7	151.4	49 55.9	−54.0	152.0	49 02.8	−54.3	152.5	48 09.5	−54.7	153.1	12
13	49 55.1	−54.0	152.1	49 01.9	−54.3	152.7	48 08.5	−54.6	153.2	47 14.8	−54.8	153.7	13
14	49 01.1	−54.2	152.8	48 07.6	−54.4	153.3	47 13.9	−54.8	153.8	46 20.0	−55.1	154.3	14
15	48 06.9	−54.4	153.4	47 13.2	−54.7	153.9	46 19.1	−54.9	154.4	45 24.9	−55.1	154.8	15
16	47 12.5	−54.5	154.1	46 18.5	−54.9	154.5	45 24.2	−55.1	155.0	44 29.8	−55.4	155.4	16
17	46 18.0	−54.8	154.7	45 23.6	−55.0	155.1	44 29.1	−55.2	155.5	43 34.4	−55.5	155.9	17
18	45 23.2	−54.9	155.3	44 28.6	−55.2	155.7	43 33.9	−55.5	156.1	42 38.9	−55.6	156.4	18
19	44 28.3	−55.2	155.8	43 33.4	−55.3	156.2	42 38.4	−55.5	156.6	41 43.3	−55.8	157.0	19
20	43 33.1	−55.2	156.4	42 38.1	−55.5	156.8	41 42.9	−55.7	157.1	40 47.5	−55.8	157.4	20
21	42 37.9	−55.4	156.9	41 42.6	−55.6	157.3	40 47.2	−55.8	157.6	39 51.7	−56.0	157.9	21
22	41 42.5	−55.6	157.4	40 47.0	−55.7	157.8	39 51.4	−55.9	158.1	38 55.7	−56.1	158.4	22
23	40 46.9	−55.6	157.9	39 51.3	−55.9	158.3	38 55.5	−56.0	158.6	37 59.6	−56.2	158.8	23
24	39 51.3	−55.8	158.4	38 55.4	−55.9	158.7	37 59.5	−56.2	159.0	37 03.4	−56.3	159.3	24
25	38 55.5	−55.9	158.9	37 59.5	−56.1	159.2	37 03.3	−56.2	159.5	36 07.1	−56.4	159.7	25
26	37 59.6	−56.0	159.4	37 03.4	−56.2	159.6	36 07.1	−56.3	159.9	35 10.7	−56.5	160.1	26
27	37 03.6	−56.1	159.8	36 07.2	−56.2	160.1	35 10.8	−56.4	160.3	34 14.2	−56.5	160.5	27
28	36 07.5	−56.2	160.3	35 11.0	−56.4	160.5	34 14.4	−56.5	160.7	33 17.7	−56.7	160.9	28
29	35 11.3	−56.3	160.7	34 14.6	−56.4	160.9	33 17.9	−56.6	161.1	32 21.0	−56.7	161.3	29
30	34 15.0	−56.4	161.1	33 18.2	−56.5	161.3	32 21.3	−56.7	161.5	31 24.3	−56.7	161.7	30
31	33 18.6	−56.5	161.5	32 21.7	−56.6	161.7	31 24.6	−56.7	161.9	30 27.6	−56.8	162.1	31
32	32 22.1	−56.5	161.9	31 25.1	−56.7	162.1	30 27.9	−56.7	162.3	29 30.8	−56.9	162.5	32
33	31 25.6	−56.6	162.3	30 28.4	−56.7	162.5	29 31.2	−56.9	162.7	28 33.9	−57.0	162.8	33
34	30 29.0	−56.7	162.7	29 31.7	−56.8	162.9	28 34.3	−56.9	163.0	27 36.9	−57.0	163.2	34
35	29 32.3	−56.7	163.1	28 34.9	−56.8	163.2	27 37.4	−56.9	163.4	26 39.9	−57.0	163.5	35
36	28 35.6	−56.8	163.5	27 38.1	−56.9	163.6	26 40.5	−57.0	163.8	25 42.9	−57.1	163.9	36
37	27 38.8	−56.8	163.8	26 41.2	−57.0	164.0	25 43.5	−57.1	164.1	24 45.8	−57.2	164.2	37
38	26 42.0	−56.9	164.2	25 44.2	−57.0	164.3	24 46.4	−57.1	164.4	23 48.6	−57.2	164.6	38
39	25 45.1	−57.0	164.5	24 47.2	−57.0	164.7	23 49.3	−57.1	164.8	22 51.4	−57.2	164.9	39
40	24 48.1	−57.0	164.9	23 50.2	−57.1	165.0	22 52.2	−57.2	165.1	21 54.2	−57.3	165.2	40
41	23 51.1	−57.0	165.2	22 53.1	−57.2	165.3	21 55.0	−57.2	165.4	20 56.9	−57.3	165.5	41
42	22 54.1	−57.1	165.6	21 55.9	−57.1	165.7	20 57.8	−57.3	165.8	19 59.6	−57.3	165.9	42
43	21 57.0	−57.2	165.9	20 58.8	−57.3	166.0	20 00.5	−57.3	166.1	19 02.3	−57.4	166.2	43
44	20 59.8	−57.1	166.2	20 01.5	−57.2	166.3	19 03.2	−57.3	166.4	18 04.9	−57.4	166.5	44
45	20 02.7	−57.2	166.5	19 04.3	−57.3	166.6	18 05.9	−57.3	166.7	17 07.5	−57.4	166.8	45
46	19 05.5	−57.3	166.9	18 07.0	−57.3	166.9	17 08.6	−57.4	167.0	16 10.1	−57.5	167.1	46
47	18 08.2	−57.2	167.2	17 09.7	−57.3	167.3	16 11.2	−57.4	167.3	15 12.6	−57.4	167.4	47
48	17 11.0	−57.3	167.5	16 12.4	−57.4	167.6	15 13.8	−57.4	167.6	14 15.2	−57.5	167.7	48
49	16 13.7	−57.3	167.8	15 15.0	−57.4	167.9	14 16.4	−57.5	167.9	13 17.7	−57.5	168.0	49
50	15 16.4	−57.4	168.1	14 17.6	−57.4	168.2	13 18.9	−57.5	168.2	12 20.2	−57.6	168.3	50
51	14 19.0	−57.4	168.4	13 20.2	−57.4	168.5	12 21.4	−57.5	168.5	11 22.6	−57.5	168.6	51
52	13 21.6	−57.3	168.7	12 22.8	−57.4	168.8	11 23.9	−57.5	168.8	10 25.1	−57.6	168.8	52
53	12 24.3	−57.5	169.0	11 25.4	−57.5	169.1	10 26.4	−57.5	169.1	9 27.5	−57.6	169.1	53
54	11 26.8	−57.4	169.3	10 27.9	−57.5	169.4	9 28.9	−57.5	169.4	8 29.9	−57.6	169.4	54
55	10 29.4	−57.4	169.6	9 30.4	−57.5	169.6	8 31.4	−57.6	169.7	7 32.3	−57.6	169.7	55
56	9 32.0	−57.5	169.9	8 32.9	−57.5	169.9	7 33.8	−57.5	170.0	6 34.7	−57.6	170.0	56
57	8 34.5	−57.4	170.2	7 35.4	−57.5	170.2	6 36.3	−57.6	170.2	5 37.1	−57.6	170.3	57
58	7 37.1	−57.5	170.5	6 37.9	−57.6	170.5	5 38.7	−57.6	170.5	4 39.5	−57.6	170.5	58
59	6 39.6	−57.5	170.8	5 40.3	−57.5	170.8	4 41.1	−57.6	170.8	3 41.9	−57.6	170.8	59
60	5 42.1	−57.5	171.1	4 42.8	−57.5	171.1	3 43.5	−57.6	171.1	2 44.3	−57.7	171.1	60
61	4 44.6	−57.5	171.4	3 45.3	−57.6	171.4	2 45.9	−57.6	171.4	1 46.6	−57.6	171.4	61
62	3 47.1	−57.5	171.6	2 47.7	−57.5	171.6	1 48.3	−57.6	171.7	0 49.0	−57.7	171.7	62
63	2 49.6	−57.6	171.9	1 50.2	−57.6	171.9	0 50.7	−57.6	171.9	0 08.7	+57.6	8.1	63
64	1 52.0	−57.5	172.2	0 52.6	−57.6	172.2	0 06.9	+57.5	7.8	1 06.3	+57.6	7.8	64
65	0 54.5	−57.5	172.5	0 05.0	+57.5	7.5	1 04.4	+57.6	7.5	2 03.9	+57.7	7.5	65
66	0 03.0	+57.5	7.2	1 02.5	+57.6	7.2	2 02.0	+57.6	7.2	3 01.6	+57.6	7.2	66
67	1 00.5	+57.5	6.9	2 00.1	+57.5	6.9	2 59.6	+57.6	6.9	3 59.2	+57.6	7.0	67
68	1 58.0	+57.6	6.7	2 57.6	+57.6	6.7	3 57.2	+57.6	6.7	4 56.8	+57.6	6.7	68
69	2 55.6	+57.5	6.4	3 55.2	+57.5	6.4	4 54.8	+57.6	6.4	5 54.4	+57.7	6.4	69
70	3 53.1	+57.5	6.1	4 52.7	+57.6	6.1	5 52.4	+57.6	6.1	6 52.1	+57.6	6.1	70
71	4 50.6	+57.5	5.8	5 50.3	+57.5	5.8	6 50.0	+57.5	5.8	7 49.7	+57.5	5.8	71
72	5 48.1	+57.5	5.5	6 47.8	+57.5	5.5	7 47.5	+57.6	5.5	8 47.2	+57.6	5.5	72
73	6 45.6	+57.4	5.2	7 45.3	+57.5	5.2	8 45.1	+57.5	5.2	9 44.8	+57.6	5.3	73
74	7 43.0	+57.5	4.9	8 42.8	+57.5	4.9	9 42.6	+57.5	5.0	10 42.4	+57.5	5.0	74
75	8 40.5	+57.5	4.6	9 40.3	+57.5	4.7	10 40.1	+57.5	4.7	11 39.9	+57.5	4.7	75
76	9 38.0	+57.4	4.3	10 37.8	+57.5	4.4	11 37.6	+57.5	4.4	12 37.4	+57.6	4.4	76
77	10 35.4	+57.4	4.1	11 35.3	+57.4	4.1	12 35.1	+57.5	4.1	13 35.0	+57.4	4.1	77
78	11 32.8	+57.4	3.8	12 32.7	+57.4	3.8	13 32.6	+57.4	3.8	14 32.4	+57.5	3.8	78
79	12 30.2	+57.4	3.5	13 30.1	+57.4	3.5	14 30.0	+57.4	3.5	15 29.9	+57.4	3.5	79
80	13 27.6	+57.4	3.2	14 27.5	+57.4	3.2	15 27.4	+57.4	3.2	16 27.3	+57.5	3.2	80
81	14 25.0	+57.3	2.9	15 24.9	+57.4	2.9	16 24.8	+57.4	2.9	17 24.8	+57.4	2.9	81
82	15 22.3	+57.4	2.6	16 22.3	+57.3	2.6	17 22.2	+57.4	2.6	18 22.2	+57.3	2.6	82
83	16 19.7	+57.2	2.2	17 19.6	+57.3	2.3	18 19.6	+57.3	2.3	19 19.5	+57.3	2.3	83
84	17 16.9	+57.3	1.9	18 16.9	+57.3	1.9	19 16.9	+57.3	2.0	20 16.8	+57.3	2.0	84
85	18 14.2	+57.2	1.6	19 14.2	+57.2	1.6	20 14.2	+57.2	1.6	21 14.1	+57.3	1.7	85
86	19 11.4	+57.2	1.3	20 11.4	+57.2	1.3	21 11.4	+57.2	1.3	22 11.4	+57.2	1.3	86
87	20 08.6	+57.2	1.0	21 08.6	+57.2	1.0	22 08.6	+57.2	1.0	23 08.6	+57.2	1.0	87
88	21 05.8	+57.1	0.7	22 05.8	+57.1	0.7	23 05.8	+57.1	0.7	24 05.8	+57.1	0.7	88
89	22 02.9	+57.1	0.3	23 02.9	+57.1	0.3	24 02.9	+57.1	0.3	25 02.9	+57.1	0.3	89
90	23 00.0	+57.0	0.0	24 00.0	+57.0	0.0	25 00.0	+57.0	0.0	26 00.0	+57.0	0.0	90
	23°			24°			25°			26°			

Dec.	27°			28°			29°			30°			Dec.
	Hc	d	Z	Hc	d	Z	Hc	d	Z	Hc	d	Z	
°	° ′	′	°	° ′	′	°	° ′	′	°	° ′	′	°	°
0	57 55.8	−51.5	144.4	57 06.7	−52.1	145.3	56 17.1	−52.6	146.2	55 27.0	−53.0	147.0	0
1	57 04.3	−52.0	145.4	56 14.6	−52.4	146.2	55 24.5	−52.9	147.0	54 34.0	−53.4	147.8	1
2	56 12.3	−52.3	146.3	55 22.2	−52.8	147.1	54 31.6	−53.2	147.8	53 40.6	−53.7	148.6	2
3	55 20.0	−52.7	147.1	54 29.4	−53.1	147.9	53 38.4	−53.6	148.6	52 46.9	−53.9	149.3	3
4	54 27.3	−53.0	148.0	53 36.3	−53.5	148.7	52 44.8	−53.8	149.4	51 53.0	−54.2	150.0	4
5	53 34.3	−53.3	148.8	52 42.8	−53.7	149.5	51 51.0	−54.1	150.1	50 58.8	−54.4	150.7	5
6	52 41.0	−53.6	149.5	51 49.1	−53.9	150.2	50 56.9	−54.3	150.8	50 04.4	−54.7	151.4	6
7	51 47.4	−53.8	150.3	50 55.2	−54.2	150.9	50 02.6	−54.5	151.5	49 09.7	−54.8	152.0	7
8	50 53.6	−54.1	151.0	50 01.0	−54.5	151.6	49 08.1	−54.8	152.1	48 14.9	−55.0	152.6	8
9	49 59.5	−54.4	151.7	49 06.5	−54.6	152.2	48 13.3	−54.9	152.7	47 19.9	−55.3	153.2	9
10	49 05.1	−54.5	152.3	48 11.9	−54.9	152.8	47 18.4	−55.1	153.3	46 24.6	−55.3	153.8	10
11	48 10.6	−54.8	152.9	47 17.0	−55.0	153.4	46 23.3	−55.3	153.9	45 29.3	−55.6	154.4	11
12	47 15.8	−54.9	153.6	46 22.0	−55.2	154.0	45 28.0	−55.5	154.5	44 33.7	−55.6	154.9	12
13	46 20.9	−55.1	154.1	45 26.8	−55.3	154.6	44 32.5	−55.6	155.0	43 38.1	−55.9	155.4	13
14	45 25.8	−55.3	154.7	44 31.5	−55.5	155.1	43 36.9	−55.7	155.5	42 42.2	−55.9	155.9	14
15	44 30.5	−55.4	155.3	43 36.0	−55.7	155.7	42 41.2	−55.8	156.0	41 46.3	−56.1	156.4	15
16	43 35.1	−55.5	155.8	42 40.3	−55.8	156.2	41 45.4	−56.0	156.5	40 50.2	−56.1	156.9	16
17	42 39.6	−55.7	156.3	41 44.5	−55.9	156.7	40 49.4	−56.1	157.0	39 54.1	−56.3	157.3	17
18	41 43.9	−55.9	156.8	40 48.6	−56.0	157.2	39 53.3	−56.2	157.5	38 57.8	−56.4	157.8	18
19	40 48.0	−55.9	157.3	39 52.6	−56.1	157.6	38 57.1	−56.3	157.9	38 01.4	−56.5	158.2	19
20	39 52.1	−56.1	157.8	38 56.5	−56.3	158.1	38 00.8	−56.5	158.4	37 04.9	−56.5	158.7	20
21	38 56.0	−56.2	158.2	38 00.2	−56.3	158.5	37 04.3	−56.5	158.8	36 08.4	−56.7	159.1	21
22	37 59.8	−56.2	158.7	37 03.9	−56.4	159.0	36 07.8	−56.5	159.2	35 11.7	−56.7	159.5	22
23	37 03.6	−56.4	159.1	36 07.5	−56.5	159.4	35 11.3	−56.7	159.6	34 15.0	−56.8	159.9	23
24	36 07.2	−56.4	159.5	35 11.0	−56.6	159.8	34 14.6	−56.7	160.0	33 18.2	−56.9	160.3	24
25	35 10.8	−56.6	160.0	34 14.4	−56.7	160.2	33 17.9	−56.9	160.4	32 21.3	−57.0	160.6	25
26	34 14.2	−56.6	160.4	33 17.7	−56.8	160.6	32 21.0	−56.8	160.8	31 24.3	−57.0	161.0	26
27	33 17.6	−56.7	160.8	32 20.9	−56.8	161.0	31 24.2	−57.0	161.2	30 27.3	−57.0	161.4	27
28	32 20.9	−56.7	161.2	31 24.1	−56.9	161.4	30 27.2	−57.0	161.5	29 30.3	−57.1	161.7	28
29	31 24.2	−56.9	161.5	30 27.2	−56.9	161.7	29 30.2	−57.0	161.9	28 33.2	−57.2	162.1	29
30	30 27.3	−56.8	161.9	29 30.3	−57.0	162.1	28 33.2	−57.2	162.3	27 36.0	−57.2	162.4	30
31	29 30.5	−57.0	162.2	28 33.3	−57.1	162.4	27 36.0	−57.1	162.6	26 38.8	−57.3	162.8	31
32	28 33.5	−57.0	162.6	27 36.2	−57.1	162.8	26 38.9	−57.2	163.0	25 41.5	−57.3	163.1	32
33	27 36.5	−57.1	163.0	26 39.1	−57.2	163.1	25 41.7	−57.3	163.3	24 44.2	−57.4	163.4	33
34	26 39.4	−57.1	163.3	25 41.9	−57.2	163.5	24 44.4	−57.3	163.6	23 46.8	−57.4	163.7	34
35	25 42.3	−57.1	163.7	24 44.7	−57.2	163.8	23 47.1	−57.3	163.9	22 49.4	−57.4	164.1	35
36	24 45.2	−57.2	164.0	23 47.5	−57.3	164.1	22 49.8	−57.4	164.3	21 52.0	−57.5	164.4	36
37	23 48.0	−57.2	164.4	22 50.2	−57.3	164.5	21 52.4	−57.4	164.6	20 54.5	−57.5	164.7	37
38	22 50.8	−57.3	164.7	21 52.9	−57.4	164.8	20 55.0	−57.5	164.9	19 57.0	−57.5	165.0	38
39	21 53.5	−57.3	165.0	20 55.5	−57.4	165.1	19 57.5	−57.5	165.2	18 59.5	−57.6	165.3	39
40	20 56.2	−57.4	165.3	19 58.1	−57.4	165.4	19 00.0	−57.5	165.5	18 01.9	−57.6	165.6	40
41	19 58.8	−57.4	165.6	19 00.7	−57.5	165.7	18 02.5	−57.5	165.8	17 04.3	−57.6	165.9	41
42	19 01.4	−57.4	165.9	18 03.2	−57.5	166.0	17 05.0	−57.6	166.1	16 06.7	−57.6	166.2	42
43	18 04.0	−57.4	166.2	17 05.7	−57.5	166.3	16 07.4	−57.6	166.4	15 09.1	−57.7	166.5	43
44	17 06.6	−57.5	166.6	16 08.2	−57.5	166.6	15 09.8	−57.6	166.7	14 11.4	−57.6	166.7	44
45	16 09.1	−57.5	166.9	15 10.7	−57.6	166.9	14 12.2	−57.6	167.0	13 13.8	−57.7	167.0	45
46	15 11.6	−57.5	167.1	14 13.1	−57.6	167.2	13 14.6	−57.7	167.3	12 16.1	−57.8	167.3	46
47	14 14.1	−57.6	167.4	13 15.5	−57.6	167.5	12 16.9	−57.6	167.5	11 18.3	−57.7	167.6	47
48	13 16.5	−57.5	167.7	12 17.9	−57.6	167.8	11 19.3	−57.7	167.8	10 20.6	−57.7	167.9	48
49	12 19.0	−57.6	168.0	11 20.3	−57.6	168.1	10 21.6	−57.7	168.1	9 22.9	−57.8	168.1	49
50	11 21.4	−57.6	168.3	10 22.7	−57.7	168.3	9 23.9	−57.7	168.4	8 25.1	−57.8	168.4	50
51	10 23.8	−57.6	168.6	9 25.0	−57.7	168.6	8 26.2	−57.7	168.7	7 27.3	−57.7	168.7	51
52	9 26.2	−57.6	168.9	8 27.3	−57.6	168.9	7 28.5	−57.8	168.9	6 29.6	−57.8	169.0	52
53	8 28.6	−57.6	169.2	7 29.7	−57.7	169.2	6 30.7	−57.7	169.2	5 31.8	−57.8	169.2	53
54	7 31.0	−57.7	169.4	6 32.0	−57.7	169.5	5 33.0	−57.8	169.5	4 34.0	−57.8	169.5	54
55	6 33.3	−57.6	169.7	5 34.3	−57.7	169.7	4 35.2	−57.7	169.8	3 36.2	−57.8	169.8	55
56	5 35.7	−57.7	170.0	4 36.6	−57.7	170.0	3 37.5	−57.8	170.0	2 38.4	−57.8	170.0	56
57	4 38.0	−57.7	170.3	3 38.9	−57.8	170.3	2 39.7	−57.7	170.3	1 40.6	−57.8	170.3	57
58	3 40.3	−57.6	170.6	2 41.1	−57.7	170.6	1 42.0	−57.8	170.6	0 42.8	−57.9	170.6	58
59	2 42.7	−57.7	170.8	1 43.4	−57.7	170.8	0 44.2	−57.8	170.8	0 15.1	+57.8	9.2	59
60	1 45.0	−57.7	171.1	0 45.7	−57.7	171.1	0 13.6	+57.7	8.9	1 12.9	+57.8	8.9	60
61	0 47.3	−57.7	171.4	0 12.0	+57.7	8.6	1 11.3	+57.8	8.6	2 10.7	+57.8	8.6	61
62	0 10.4	+57.7	8.3	1 09.7	+57.8	8.3	2 09.1	+57.8	8.3	3 08.5	+57.8	8.4	62
63	1 08.1	+57.6	8.1	2 07.5	+57.7	8.1	3 06.9	+57.7	8.1	4 06.3	+57.8	8.1	63
64	2 05.7	+57.7	7.8	3 05.2	+57.7	7.8	4 04.6	+57.8	7.8	5 04.1	+57.8	7.8	64
65	3 03.4	+57.7	7.5	4 02.9	+57.7	7.5	5 02.4	+57.7	7.5	6 01.9	+57.8	7.5	65
66	4 01.1	+57.7	7.2	5 00.6	+57.7	7.2	6 00.1	+57.8	7.3	6 59.7	+57.7	7.3	66
67	4 58.8	+57.6	7.0	5 58.3	+57.7	7.0	6 57.9	+57.6	7.0	7 57.4	+57.8	7.0	67
68	5 56.4	+57.7	6.7	6 56.0	+57.7	6.7	7 55.6	+57.7	6.7	8 55.2	+57.7	6.7	68
69	6 54.1	+57.6	6.4	7 53.7	+57.7	6.4	8 53.3	+57.7	6.4	9 52.9	+57.8	6.5	69
70	7 51.7	+57.6	6.1	8 51.4	+57.6	6.1	9 51.0	+57.7	6.2	10 50.7	+57.7	6.2	70
71	8 49.3	+57.7	5.8	9 49.0	+57.7	5.9	10 48.7	+57.7	5.9	11 48.4	+57.7	5.9	71
72	9 47.0	+57.6	5.6	10 46.7	+57.6	5.6	11 46.4	+57.6	5.6	12 46.1	+57.7	5.6	72
73	10 44.6	+57.5	5.3	11 44.3	+57.6	5.3	12 44.0	+57.7	5.3	13 43.8	+57.7	5.3	73
74	11 42.1	+57.6	5.0	12 41.9	+57.6	5.0	13 41.7	+57.6	5.0	14 41.5	+57.6	5.1	74
75	12 39.7	+57.6	4.7	13 39.5	+57.6	4.7	14 39.3	+57.6	4.7	15 39.1	+57.6	4.8	75
76	13 37.3	+57.5	4.4	14 37.1	+57.5	4.4	15 36.9	+57.6	4.5	16 36.7	+57.6	4.5	76
77	14 34.8	+57.5	4.1	15 34.6	+57.6	4.1	16 34.5	+57.5	4.2	17 34.3	+57.6	4.2	77
78	15 32.3	+57.5	3.8	16 32.2	+57.5	3.8	17 32.0	+57.6	3.9	18 31.9	+57.5	3.9	78
79	16 29.8	+57.5	3.5	17 29.7	+57.5	3.5	18 29.6	+57.5	3.6	19 29.4	+57.6	3.6	79
80	17 27.3	+57.4	3.2	18 27.2	+57.4	3.2	19 27.1	+57.4	3.3	20 27.0	+57.4	3.3	80
81	18 24.7	+57.4	2.9	19 24.6	+57.4	2.9	20 24.5	+57.5	3.0	21 24.4	+57.5	3.0	81
82	19 22.1	+57.4	2.6	20 22.0	+57.4	2.6	21 22.0	+57.4	2.6	22 21.9	+57.4	2.7	82
83	20 19.5	+57.3	2.3	21 19.4	+57.4	2.3	22 19.4	+57.3	2.3	23 19.3	+57.4	2.4	83
84	21 16.8	+57.3	2.0	22 16.8	+57.3	2.0	23 16.7	+57.4	2.0	24 16.7	+57.3	2.0	84
85	22 14.1	+57.3	1.7	23 14.1	+57.3	1.7	24 14.1	+57.2	1.7	25 14.0	+57.3	1.7	85
86	23 11.4	+57.2	1.3	24 11.4	+57.2	1.4	25 11.3	+57.3	1.4	26 11.3	+57.3	1.4	86
87	24 08.6	+57.2	1.0	25 08.6	+57.2	1.0	26 08.6	+57.2	1.0	27 08.6	+57.2	1.0	87
88	25 05.8	+57.1	0.7	26 05.8	+57.1	0.7	27 05.8	+57.1	0.7	28 05.8	+57.1	0.7	88
89	26 02.9	+57.1	0.3	27 02.9	+57.1	0.3	28 02.9	+57.1	0.4	29 02.9	+57.1	0.4	89
90	27 00.0	+57.0	0.0	28 00.0	+57.0	0.0	29 00.0	+57.0	0.0	30 00.0	+57.0	0.0	90
	27°			28°			29°			30°			

S. Lat. { L.H.A. greater than 180° ....Zn=180°−Z
L.H.A. less than 180°...........Zn=180°+Z

19°, 341° L.H.A. LATITUDE SAME NAME AS DECLINATION

N. Lat. {L.H.A. greater than 180° .....Zn=Z
{L.H.A. less than 180°............Zn=360°−Z

Dec.	23° Hc	d	Z	24° Hc	d	Z	25° Hc	d	Z	26° Hc	d	Z
°	° ′	′	°	° ′	′	°	° ′	′	°	° ′	′	°
0	60 30.0	+47.2	138.6	59 44.6	+48.1	139.8	58 58.4	+48.9	140.8	58 11.6	+49.6	141.9
1	61 17.2	+46.6	137.3	60 32.7	+47.4	138.5	59 47.3	+48.3	139.7	59 01.2	+49.1	140.8
2	62 03.8	+45.7	136.0	61 20.1	+46.7	137.3	60 35.6	+47.6	138.5	59 50.3	+48.4	139.6
3	62 49.5	+44.8	134.6	62 06.8	+45.9	136.0	61 23.2	+46.9	137.2	60 38.7	+47.8	138.5
4	63 34.3	+43.9	133.1	62 52.7	+45.0	134.6	62 10.1	+46.1	135.9	61 26.5	+47.1	137.2
5	64 18.2	+42.8	131.6	63 37.7	+44.1	133.1	62 56.2	+45.2	134.5	62 13.6	+46.3	135.9
6	65 01.0	+41.7	129.9	64 21.8	+43.1	131.6	63 41.4	+44.3	133.1	62 59.9	+45.4	134.5
7	65 42.7	+40.4	128.2	65 04.9	+41.9	129.9	64 25.7	+43.3	131.5	63 45.3	+44.5	133.1
8	66 23.1	+39.2	126.4	65 46.8	+40.7	128.2	65 09.0	+42.1	129.9	64 29.8	+43.5	131.5
9	67 02.3	+37.6	124.5	66 27.5	+39.3	126.4	65 51.1	+41.0	128.2	65 13.3	+42.4	129.9
10	67 39.9	+36.1	122.5	67 06.8	+38.0	124.5	66 32.1	+39.6	126.4	65 55.7	+41.2	128.2
11	68 16.0	+34.4	120.3	67 44.8	+36.3	122.4	67 11.7	+38.1	124.5	66 36.9	+39.9	126.4
12	68 50.4	+32.5	•118.1	68 21.1	+34.6	120.3	67 49.8	+36.6	122.4	67 16.8	+38.4	124.5
13	69 22.9	+30.4	•115.7	68 55.7	+32.8	118.1	68 26.4	+34.9	120.3	67 55.2	+36.8	122.4
14	69 53.3	+28.3	•113.3	69 28.5	+30.7	•115.7	69 01.3	+33.0	118.1	68 32.0	+35.2	120.3
15	70 21.6	+26.0	•110.7	69 59.2	+28.6	•113.2	69 34.3	+31.1	•115.7	69 07.2	+33.3	118.1
16	70 47.6	+23.5	•108.0	70 27.8	+26.2	•110.6	70 05.4	+28.8	•113.2	69 40.5	+31.3	•115.7
17	71 11.1	+20.8	•105.1	70 54.0	+23.7	•107.9	70 34.2	+26.5	•110.6	70 11.8	+29.1	•113.2
18	71 31.9	+18.0	•102.2	71 17.7	+21.1	•105.1	71 00.7	+24.0	•107.9	70 40.9	+26.8	•110.6
19	71 49.9	+15.1	• 99.2	71 38.8	+18.3	•102.1	71 24.7	+21.4	•105.0	71 07.7	+24.3	•107.9
20	72 05.0	+12.0	• 96.0	71 57.1	+15.3	• 99.1	71 46.1	+18.5	•102.1	71 32.0	+21.6	•105.0
21	72 17.0	+8.8	• 92.8	72 12.4	+12.2	• 95.9	72 04.6	+15.5	• 99.0	71 53.6	+18.8	•102.0
22	72 25.8	+5.6	• 89.6	72 24.6	+9.0	• 92.7	72 20.1	+12.4	• 95.9	72 12.4	+15.7	• 99.0
23	72 31.4	+2.2	• 86.3	72 33.6	+5.8	• 89.4	72 32.5	+9.3	• 92.6	72 28.1	+12.7	• 95.8
24	72 33.6	-1.1	• 82.9	72 39.4	+2.4	• 86.1	72 41.8	+5.9	• 89.3	72 40.8	+9.4	• 92.5
25	72 32.5	-4.4	• 79.6	72 41.8	-1.0	• 82.8	72 47.7	+2.5	• 86.0	72 50.2	+6.1	• 89.2
26	72 28.1	-7.6	• 76.3	72 40.8	-4.3	• 79.4	72 50.2	-0.8	• 82.6	72 56.3	+2.7	• 85.8
27	72 20.5	-10.9	• 73.0	72 36.5	-7.6	• 76.0	72 49.4	-4.3	• 79.2	72 59.0	-0.8	• 82.4
28	72 09.6	-14.0	• 69.8	72 28.9	-10.9	• 72.7	72 45.1	-7.5	• 75.8	72 58.2	-4.1	• 79.0
29	71 55.6	-17.0	• 66.6	72 18.0	-14.0	• 69.5	72 37.6	-10.8	• 72.5	72 54.1	-7.5	• 75.6
30	71 38.6	-19.8	• 63.5	72 04.0	-17.0	• 66.3	72 26.8	-14.0	• 69.2	72 46.6	-10.8	• 72.2
31	71 18.8	-22.6	• 60.6	71 47.0	-19.9	• 63.2	72 12.8	-17.1	• 66.0	72 35.8	-14.0	• 68.9
32	70 56.2	-25.1	• 57.7	71 27.1	-22.6	• 60.2	71 55.7	-19.9	• 62.9	72 21.8	-17.1	• 65.7
33	70 31.1	-27.5	• 55.0	71 04.5	-25.2	• 57.3	71 35.8	-22.7	• 59.9	72 04.7	-20.0	• 62.5
34	70 03.6	-29.7	• 52.3	70 39.3	-27.5	• 54.6	71 13.1	-25.3	• 57.0	71 44.7	-22.8	• 59.5
35	69 33.9	-31.8	• 49.8	70 11.8	-29.9	• 51.9	70 47.8	-27.7	• 54.2	71 21.9	-25.3	• 56.6
36	69 02.1	-33.7	47.4	69 41.9	-31.9	49.4	70 20.1	-29.9	• 51.5	70 56.6	-27.9	• 53.8
37	68 28.4	-35.5	45.1	69 10.0	-33.8	47.0	69 50.2	-32.0	• 49.0	70 28.7	-30.0	• 51.1
38	67 52.9	-37.1	43.0	68 36.2	-35.6	44.7	69 18.2	-34.0	46.5	69 58.7	-32.2	• 48.5
39	67 15.8	-38.7	40.9	68 00.6	-37.3	42.5	68 44.2	-35.8	44.2	69 26.5	-34.1	46.1
40	66 37.1	-40.0	38.9	67 23.3	-38.7	40.4	68 08.4	-37.3	42.1	68 52.4	-35.9	43.8
41	65 57.1	-41.2	37.1	66 44.6	-40.2	38.5	67 31.1	-38.9	40.0	68 16.5	-37.6	41.6
42	65 15.9	-42.5	35.3	66 04.4	-41.4	36.6	66 52.2	-40.3	38.0	67 38.9	-39.0	39.5
43	64 33.4	-43.5	33.7	65 23.0	-42.5	34.9	66 11.9	-41.6	36.2	66 59.9	-40.4	37.5
44	63 49.9	-44.5	32.1	64 40.5	-43.7	33.2	65 30.3	-42.7	34.4	66 19.5	-41.8	35.7
45	63 05.4	-45.4	30.6	63 56.8	-44.6	31.6	64 47.6	-43.8	32.7	65 37.7	-42.8	33.9
46	62 20.0	-46.2	29.1	63 12.2	-45.5	30.1	64 03.8	-44.7	31.1	64 54.9	-44.0	32.2
47	61 33.8	-47.0	27.8	62 26.7	-46.4	28.7	63 19.1	-45.7	29.6	64 10.9	-44.9	30.7
48	60 46.8	-47.7	26.5	61 40.3	-47.1	27.3	62 33.4	-46.5	28.2	63 26.0	-45.8	29.2
49	59 59.1	-48.4	25.3	60 53.2	-47.9	26.0	61 46.9	-47.3	26.9	62 40.2	-46.6	27.7
50	59 10.7	-48.9	24.1	60 05.3	-48.4	24.8	60 59.6	-47.9	25.6	61 53.6	-47.4	26.4
51	58 21.8	-49.5	23.0	59 16.9	-49.1	23.6	60 11.7	-48.6	24.3	61 06.2	-48.1	25.1
52	57 32.3	-50.1	21.9	58 27.8	-49.6	22.5	59 23.1	-49.2	23.2	60 18.1	-48.7	23.9
53	56 42.2	-50.5	20.9	57 38.2	-50.2	21.5	58 33.9	-49.7	22.1	59 29.4	-49.3	22.7
54	55 51.7	-50.9	19.9	56 48.0	-50.6	20.5	57 44.2	-50.3	21.0	58 40.1	-49.9	21.6
55	55 00.8	-51.4	19.0	55 57.4	-51.0	19.5	56 53.9	-50.7	20.0	57 50.2	-50.4	20.5
56	54 09.4	-51.7	18.1	55 06.4	-51.5	18.6	56 03.2	-51.2	19.0	56 59.8	-50.8	19.5
57	53 17.7	-52.1	17.3	54 14.9	-51.8	17.7	55 12.0	-51.5	18.1	56 09.0	-51.3	18.6
58	52 25.6	-52.4	16.4	53 23.1	-52.2	16.8	54 20.5	-51.9	17.2	55 17.7	-51.6	17.6
59	51 33.2	-52.7	15.6	52 30.9	-52.5	16.0	53 28.6	-52.3	16.4	54 26.1	-52.1	16.8
60	50 40.5	-53.0	14.9	51 38.4	-52.8	15.2	52 36.3	-52.6	15.5	53 34.0	-52.3	15.9
61	49 47.5	-53.3	14.2	50 45.6	-53.1	14.4	51 43.7	-52.9	14.8	52 41.7	-52.7	15.1
62	48 54.2	-53.5	13.4	49 52.5	-53.3	13.7	50 50.8	-53.2	14.0	51 49.0	-53.0	14.3
63	48 00.7	-53.8	12.8	48 59.2	-53.6	13.0	49 57.6	-53.5	13.3	50 56.0	-53.3	13.6
64	47 06.9	-54.0	12.1	48 05.6	-53.9	12.3	49 04.1	-53.6	12.6	50 02.7	-53.6	12.8
65	46 12.9	-54.1	11.5	47 11.7	-54.0	11.7	48 10.5	-54.0	11.9	49 09.1	-53.7	12.1
66	45 18.8	-54.4	10.9	46 17.7	-54.3	11.0	47 16.5	-54.1	11.3	48 15.4	-54.0	11.5
67	44 24.4	-54.6	10.3	45 23.4	-54.4	10.4	46 22.4	-54.3	10.6	47 21.4	-54.3	10.8
68	43 29.8	-54.7	9.7	44 29.0	-54.7	9.8	45 28.1	-54.6	10.0	46 27.1	-54.4	10.2
69	42 35.1	-54.9	9.1	43 34.3	-54.8	9.3	44 33.5	-54.7	9.4	45 32.7	-54.6	9.6
70	41 40.2	-55.0	8.6	42 39.5	-54.9	8.7	43 38.8	-54.8	8.9	44 38.1	-54.8	9.0
71	40 45.2	-55.2	8.0	41 44.6	-55.1	8.2	42 44.0	-55.0	8.3	43 43.3	-54.9	8.4
72	39 50.0	-55.3	7.5	40 49.5	-55.2	7.6	41 49.0	-55.2	7.8	42 48.4	-55.1	7.9
73	38 54.7	-55.4	7.0	39 54.3	-55.4	7.1	40 53.8	-55.3	7.2	41 53.3	-55.2	7.3
74	37 59.3	-55.6	6.5	38 58.9	-55.5	6.6	39 58.5	-55.5	6.7	40 58.1	-55.4	6.8
75	37 03.7	-55.6	6.1	38 03.4	-55.6	6.1	39 03.0	-55.5	6.2	40 02.7	-55.5	6.3
76	36 08.1	-55.8	5.6	37 07.8	-55.7	5.7	38 07.5	-55.7	5.7	39 07.2	-55.7	5.8
77	35 12.3	-55.9	5.1	36 12.1	-55.8	5.2	37 11.8	-55.8	5.3	38 11.5	-55.7	5.3
78	34 16.4	-55.9	4.7	35 16.2	-55.9	4.8	36 16.0	-55.9	4.8	37 15.8	-55.8	4.9
79	33 20.5	-56.1	4.3	34 20.3	-56.0	4.3	35 20.1	-56.0	4.4	36 20.0	-56.0	4.4
80	32 24.4	-56.1	3.8	33 24.3	-56.1	3.9	34 24.1	-56.0	3.9	35 24.0	-56.0	4.0
81	31 28.3	-56.2	3.4	32 28.2	-56.2	3.5	33 28.1	-56.2	3.5	34 28.0	-56.2	3.5
82	30 32.1	-56.3	3.0	31 32.0	-56.3	3.0	32 31.9	-56.2	3.1	33 31.8	-56.2	3.1
83	29 35.8	-56.4	2.6	30 35.7	-56.3	2.6	31 35.7	-56.4	2.7	32 35.6	-56.3	2.7
84	28 39.4	-56.4	2.2	29 39.4	-56.4	2.2	30 39.3	-56.4	2.3	31 39.3	-56.4	2.3
85	27 43.0	-56.5	1.8	28 43.0	-56.5	1.9	29 42.9	-56.4	1.9	30 42.9	-56.4	1.9
86	26 46.5	-56.5	1.5	27 46.5	-56.5	1.5	28 46.5	-56.6	1.5	29 46.5	-56.6	1.5
87	25 50.0	-56.6	1.1	26 50.0	-56.6	1.1	27 49.9	-56.5	1.1	28 49.9	-56.6	1.1
88	24 53.4	-56.7	0.7	25 53.4	-56.7	0.7	26 53.4	-56.7	0.7	27 53.3	-56.6	0.7
89	23 56.7	-56.7	0.4	24 56.7	-56.7	0.4	25 56.7	-56.7	0.4	26 56.7	-56.7	0.4
90	23 00.0	-56.8	0.0	24 00.0	-56.8	0.0	25 00.0	-56.8	0.0	26 00.0	-56.8	0.0
	23°			24°			25°			26°		

27° Hc	d	Z	28° Hc	d	Z	29° Hc	d	Z	30° Hc	d	Z	Dec.
° ′	′	°	° ′	′	°	° ′	′	°	° ′	′	°	°
57 24.1	+50.3	142.8	56 36.0	+50.9	143.7	55 47.3	+51.6	144.6	54 58.1	+52.1	145.4	0
58 14.4	+49.8	141.8	57 26.9	+50.5	142.8	56 38.9	+51.1	143.7	55 50.2	+51.7	144.6	1
59 04.2	+49.2	140.7	58 17.4	+50.0	141.8	57 30.0	+50.6	142.7	56 41.9	+51.3	143.7	2
59 53.4	+48.7	139.6	59 07.4	+49.4	140.7	58 20.6	+50.1	141.7	57 33.2	+50.8	142.7	3
60 42.1	+48.0	138.4	59 56.8	+48.8	139.6	59 10.7	+49.6	140.7	58 24.0	+50.3	141.7	4
61 30.1	+47.2	137.2	60 45.6	+48.2	138.4	60 00.3	+49.1	139.6	59 14.3	+49.8	140.6	5
62 17.3	+46.5	135.9	61 33.8	+47.5	137.2	60 49.4	+48.3	138.4	60 04.1	+49.2	139.5	6
63 03.8	+45.7	134.5	62 21.3	+46.7	135.9	61 37.7	+47.7	137.2	60 53.3	+48.6	138.4	7
63 49.5	+44.7	133.0	63 08.0	+45.8	134.5	62 25.4	+46.9	135.9	61 41.9	+47.9	137.2	8
64 34.2	+43.7	131.5	63 53.8	+45.0	133.0	63 12.3	+46.1	134.5	62 29.8	+47.1	135.9	9
65 17.9	+42.6	129.9	64 38.8	+43.9	131.5	63 58.4	+45.2	133.1	63 16.9	+46.3	134.5	10
66 00.5	+41.5	128.2	65 22.7	+42.9	129.9	64 43.6	+44.2	131.5	64 03.2	+45.4	133.1	11
66 42.0	+40.1	126.4	66 05.6	+41.7	128.2	65 27.8	+43.1	129.9	64 48.6	+44.5	131.6	12
67 22.1	+38.7	124.5	66 47.3	+40.4	126.4	66 10.9	+42.0	128.2	65 33.1	+43.3	130.0	13
68 00.8	+37.1	122.5	67 27.7	+38.9	124.5	66 52.9	+40.6	126.4	66 16.4	+42.2	128.3	14
68 37.9	+35.4	120.3	68 06.6	+37.4	122.5	67 33.5	+39.2	124.5	66 58.6	+41.0	126.5	15
69 13.3	+33.6	118.1	68 44.0	+35.8	120.4	68 12.7	+37.7	122.5	67 39.6	+39.5	124.6	16
69 46.9	+31.6	•115.7	69 19.8	+33.8	118.1	68 50.4	+36.0	120.4	68 19.1	+38.0	122.6	17
70 18.5	+29.4	•113.2	69 53.6	+31.9	•115.7	69 26.4	+34.2	118.2	68 57.1	+36.3	120.4	18
70 47.9	+27.1	•110.6	70 25.5	+29.7	•113.2	70 00.6	+32.2	•115.8	69 33.4	+34.4	118.2	19
71 15.0	+24.6	•107.9	70 55.2	+27.4	•110.6	70 32.8	+30.0	•113.3	70 07.8	+32.5	•115.8	20
71 39.6	+21.8	•105.0	71 22.6	+24.8	•107.9	71 02.8	+27.7	•110.6	70 40.3	+30.3	•113.3	21
72 01.4	+19.1	•102.0	71 47.4	+22.2	•105.0	71 30.5	+25.1	•107.9	71 10.6	+28.0	•110.7	22
72 20.5	+16.0	• 98.9	72 09.6	+19.3	•102.0	71 55.6	+22.4	•105.0	71 38.6	+25.4	•107.9	23
72 36.5	+12.9	• 95.7	72 28.9	+16.2	• 98.9	72 18.0	+19.6	•102.0	72 04.0	+22.8	•105.0	24
72 49.4	+9.6	• 92.4	72 45.1	+13.1	• 95.6	72 37.6	+16.5	• 98.8	72 26.8	+19.8	•102.0	25
72 59.0	+6.2	• 89.1	72 58.2	+9.8	• 92.3	72 54.1	+13.3	• 95.6	72 46.6	+16.8	• 98.8	26
73 05.2	+2.8	• 85.7	73 08.0	+6.5	• 88.9	73 07.4	+10.0	• 92.2	73 03.4	+13.5	• 95.5	27
73 08.0	-0.6	• 82.2	73 14.5	+2.9	• 85.5	73 17.4	+6.6	• 88.8	73 16.9	+10.2	• 92.2	28
73 07.4	-4.0	• 78.8	73 17.4	-0.5	• 82.0	73 24.0	+3.1	• 85.4	73 27.1	+6.8	• 88.7	29
73 03.4	-7.5	• 75.3	73 16.9	-4.0	• 78.6	73 27.1	-0.4	• 81.9	73 33.9	+3.2	• 85.2	30
72 55.9	-10.8	• 71.9	73 12.9	-7.4	• 75.1	73 26.7	-3.9	• 78.3	73 37.1	-0.3	• 81.7	31
72 45.1	-14.0	• 68.6	73 05.5	-10.8	• 71.7	73 22.8	-7.4	• 74.9	73 36.8	-3.9	• 78.1	32
72 31.1	-17.2	• 65.4	72 54.7	-14.1	• 68.3	73 15.4	-10.9	• 71.4	73 32.9	-7.4	• 74.6	33
72 13.9	-20.0	• 62.2	72 40.6	-17.2	• 65.0	73 04.5	-14.1	• 68.0	73 25.5	-10.8	• 71.1	34
71 53.9	-22.9	• 59.1	72 23.4	-20.1	• 61.8	72 50.4	-17.2	• 64.7	73 14.7	-14.2	• 67.7	35
71 31.0	-25.5	• 56.2	72 03.3	-23.0	• 58.7	72 33.2	-20.3	• 61.5	73 00.5	-17.3	• 64.3	36
71 05.5	-27.9	• 53.4	71 40.3	-25.6	• 55.8	72 12.9	-23.1	• 58.4	72 43.2	-20.4	• 61.1	37
70 37.6	-30.2	• 50.7	71 14.7	-28.1	• 52.9	71 49.8	-25.7	• 55.4	72 22.8	-23.2	• 57.9	38
70 07.4	-32.4	• 48.1	70 46.6	-30.4	• 50.2	71 24.1	-28.3	• 52.5	71 59.6	-25.9	• 54.9	39
69 35.0	-34.2	45.6	70 16.2	-32.5	• 47.6	70 55.8	-30.5	• 49.8	71 33.7	-28.4	• 52.0	40
69 00.8	-36.1	43.3	69 43.7	-34.4	45.2	70 25.3	-32.7	• 47.2	71 05.3	-30.7	• 49.3	41
68 24.7	-37.7	41.1	69 09.3	-36.2	42.8	69 52.6	-34.6	44.7	70 34.6	-32.9	• 46.7	42
67 47.0	-39.2	39.0	68 33.1	-37.9	40.6	69 18.0	-36.4	42.3	70 01.7	-34.8	44.2	43
67 07.8	-40.6	37.1	67 55.2	-39.4	38.5	68 41.6	-38.1	40.1	69 26.9	-36.6	41.8	44
66 27.2	-41.9	35.2	67 15.8	-40.8	36.6	68 03.5	-39.6	38.0	68 50.3	-38.3	39.6	45
65 45.3	-43.0	33.4	66 35.0	-42.0	34.7	67 23.9	-40.9	36.0	68 12.0	-39.8	37.5	46
65 02.3	-44.1	31.7	65 53.0	-43.2	32.9	66 43.0	-42.3	34.2	67 32.2	-41.1	35.5	47
64 18.2	-45.1	30.2	65 09.8	-44.3	31.2	66 00.7	-43.3	32.4	66 51.1	-42.5	33.7	48
63 33.1	-46.0	28.7	64 25.5	-45.2	29.7	65 17.4	-44.5	30.7	66 08.6	-43.5	31.9	49
62 47.1	-46.7	27.2	63 40.3	-46.2	28.2	64 32.9	-45.4	29.1	65 25.1	-44.7	30.2	50
62 00.4	-47.6	25.9	62 54.1	-46.9	26.7	63 47.5	-46.3	27.6	64 40.4	-45.6	28.6	51
61 12.8	-48.2	24.6	62 07.2	-47.7	25.4	63 01.2	-47.1	26.2	63 54.8	-46.4	27.1	52
60 24.6	-48.9	23.4	61 19.5	-48.4	24.1	62 14.1	-47.8	24.9	63 08.4	-47.3	25.7	53
59 35.7	-49.4	22.2	60 31.1	-49.0	22.9	61 26.3	-48.6	23.6	62 21.1	-48.0	24.4	54
58 46.3	-50.0	21.1	59 42.1	-49.6	21.7	60 37.7	-49.1	22.4	61 33.1	-48.7	23.1	55
57 56.3	-50.5	20.1	58 52.5	-50.1	20.6	59 48.6	-49.7	21.2	60 44.4	-49.3	21.9	56
57 05.8	-51.0	19.1	58 02.4	-50.6	19.6	58 58.9	-50.3	20.1	59 55.1	-49.9	20.7	57
56 14.8	-51.3	18.1	57 11.8	-51.1	18.6	58 08.6	-50.8	19.1	59 05.2	-50.4	19.6	58
55 23.5	-51.8	17.2	56 20.7	-51.5	17.6	57 17.8	-51.2	18.1	58 14.8	-50.9	18.6	59
54 31.7	-52.2	16.3	55 29.2	-51.9	16.7	56 26.6	-51.6	17.1	57 23.9	-51.4	17.6	60
53 39.5	-52.5	15.4	54 37.3	-52.2	15.8	55 35.0	-52.0	16.2	56 32.5	-51.7	16.6	61
52 47.0	-52.8	14.6	53 45.1	-52.6	15.0	54 43.0	-52.4	15.3	55 40.8	-52.2	15.7	62
51 54.2	-53.1	13.9	52 52.5	-53.0	14.2	53 50.6	-52.7	14.5	54 48.6	-52.5	14.9	63
51 01.1	-53.3	13.1	51 59.5	-53.2	13.4	52 57.9	-53.0	13.7	53 56.1	-52.8	14.0	64
50 07.8	-53.7	12.4	51 06.3	-53.4	12.7	52 04.9	-53.4	12.9	53 03.3	-53.1	13.2	65
49 14.1	-53.8	11.7	50 12.9	-53.8	11.9	51 11.5	-53.5	12.2	52 10.2	-53.5	12.5	66
48 20.3	-54.1	11.0	49 19.1	-53.9	11.3	50 18.0	-53.9	11.5	51 16.7	-53.7	11.7	67
47 26.2	-54.3	10.4	48 25.2	-54.2	10.6	49 24.1	-54.0	10.8	50 23.0	-53.9	11.0	68
46 31.9	-54.5	9.8	47 31.0	-54.4	9.9	48 30.1	-54.3	10.1	49 29.1	-54.2	10.3	69
45 37.4	-54.7	9.2	46 36.6	-54.6	9.3	47 35.8	-54.5	9.5	48 34.9	-54.3	9.7	70
44 42.7	-54.9	8.6	45 42.0	-54.8	8.7	46 41.3	-54.7	8.9	47 40.6	-54.6	9.1	71
43 47.8	-55.0	8.0	44 47.2	-54.9	8.1	45 46.6	-54.8	8.3	46 46.0	-54.8	8.4	72
42 52.8	-55.2	7.5	43 52.3	-55.1	7.6	44 51.8	-55.1	7.7	45 51.2	-55.0	7.9	73
41 57.6	-55.3	6.9	42 57.2	-55.3	7.0	43 56.7	-55.2	7.2	44 56.2	-55.1	7.3	74
41 02.3	-55.4	6.4	42 01.9	-55.4	6.5	43 01.5	-55.3	6.6	44 01.1	-55.2	6.7	75
40 06.9	-55.6	5.9	41 06.5	-55.5	6.0	42 06.2	-55.5	6.1	43 05.9	-55.5	6.2	76
39 11.3	-55.7	5.4	40 11.0	-55.6	5.5	41 10.7	-55.6	5.6	42 10.4	-55.5	5.7	77
38 15.6	-55.8	4.9	39 15.4	-55.8	5.0	40 15.1	-55.7	5.1	41 14.9	-55.7	5.2	78
37 19.8	-55.9	4.5	38 19.6	-55.9	4.5	39 19.4	-55.8	4.6	40 19.2	-55.8	4.7	79
36 23.9	-56.1	4.0	37 23.7	-56.0	4.1	38 23.6	-56.0	4.1	39 23.4	-55.9	4.2	80
35 27.8	-56.1	3.6	36 27.7	-56.1	3.6	37 27.6	-56.1	3.7	38 27.5	-56.1	3.7	81
34 31.7	-56.2	3.2	35 31.6	-56.1	3.2	36 31.5	-56.1	3.2	37 31.4	-56.1	3.3	82
33 35.5	-56.3	2.7	34 35.5	-56.3	2.8	35 35.4	-56.3	2.8	36 35.3	-56.2	2.8	83
32 39.2	-56.3	2.3	33 39.2	-56.4	2.3	34 39.1	-56.3	2.4	35 39.1	-56.3	2.4	84
31 42.9	-56.5	1.9	32 42.8	-56.4	1.9	33 42.8	-56.4	2.0	34 42.8	-56.4	2.0	85
30 46.4	-56.5	1.5	31 46.4	-56.5	1.5	32 46.4	-56.6	1.5	33 46.4	-56.5	1.6	86
29 49.9	-56.6	1.1	30 49.9	-56.6	1.1	31 49.9	-56.6	1.1	32 49.9	-56.6	1.2	87
28 53.3	-56.6	0.7	29 53.3	-56.6	0.8	30 53.3	-56.6	0.8	31 53.3	-56.6	0.8	88
27 56.7	-56.7	0.4	28 56.7	-56.7	0.4	29 56.7	-56.8	0.4	30 56.7	-56.7	0.4	89
27 00.0	-56.8	0.0	28 00.0	-56.8	0.0	29 00.0	-56.8	0.0	30 00.0	-56.8	0.0	90
27°			28°			29°			30°			

LATITUDE **CONTRARY** NAME TO DECLINATION L.H.A. 19°, 341°

Dec.	23° Hc	23° d	23° Z	24° Hc	24° d	24° Z	25° Hc	25° d	25° Z	26° Hc	26° d	26° Z	Dec.
°	° ′	′	°	° ′	′	°	° ′	′	°	° ′	′	°	°
0	60 30.0	−48.0	138.6	59 44.6	−48.8	139.8	58 58.4	−49.5	140.8	58 11.6	−50.2	141.9	0
1	59 42.0	−48.5	139.8	58 55.8	−49.3	140.9	58 08.9	−50.0	141.9	57 21.4	−50.6	142.9	1
2	58 53.5	−49.2	141.0	58 06.5	−49.8	142.0	57 18.9	−50.4	142.9	56 30.8	−51.1	143.9	2
3	58 04.3	−49.7	142.1	57 16.7	−50.4	143.0	56 28.5	−51.0	143.9	55 39.7	−51.5	144.8	3
4	57 14.6	−50.2	143.1	56 26.3	−50.8	144.0	55 37.5	−51.3	144.9	54 48.2	−51.9	145.7	4
5	56 24.4	−50.6	144.1	55 35.5	−51.2	145.0	54 46.2	−51.8	145.8	53 56.3	−52.2	146.6	5
6	55 33.8	−51.1	145.1	54 44.3	−51.6	145.9	53 54.4	−52.1	146.7	53 04.1	−52.6	147.4	6
7	54 42.7	−51.5	146.0	53 52.7	−52.0	146.8	53 02.3	−52.4	147.5	52 11.5	−52.9	148.2	7
8	53 51.2	−51.9	146.9	53 00.7	−52.3	147.6	52 09.9	−52.8	148.3	51 18.6	−53.1	149.0	8
9	52 59.3	−52.2	147.7	52 08.4	−52.6	148.4	51 17.1	−53.0	149.1	50 25.5	−53.4	149.7	9
10	52 07.1	−52.5	148.5	51 15.8	−53.0	149.2	50 24.1	−53.4	149.8	49 32.1	−53.7	150.4	10
11	51 14.6	−52.8	149.3	50 22.8	−53.2	149.9	49 30.7	−53.5	150.5	48 38.4	−53.9	151.1	11
12	50 21.8	−53.1	150.1	49 29.6	−53.5	150.6	48 37.2	−53.8	151.2	47 44.5	−54.2	151.7	12
13	49 28.7	−53.4	150.8	48 36.1	−53.7	151.3	47 43.4	−54.1	151.9	46 50.3	−54.3	152.4	13
14	48 35.3	−53.6	151.5	47 42.4	−53.9	152.0	46 49.3	−54.2	152.5	45 56.0	−54.5	153.0	14
15	47 41.7	−53.9	152.1	46 48.5	−54.1	152.6	45 55.1	−54.4	153.1	45 01.5	−54.7	153.6	15
16	46 47.8	−54.0	152.8	45 54.4	−54.4	153.3	45 00.7	−54.6	153.7	44 06.8	−54.9	154.2	16
17	45 53.8	−54.3	153.4	45 00.0	−54.5	153.9	44 06.1	−54.8	154.3	43 11.9	−55.0	154.7	17
18	44 59.5	−54.4	154.0	44 05.5	−54.7	154.5	43 11.3	−55.0	154.9	42 16.9	−55.2	155.3	18
19	44 05.1	−54.6	154.6	43 10.8	−54.9	155.0	42 16.3	−55.1	155.4	41 21.7	−55.3	155.8	19
20	43 10.5	−54.8	155.2	42 15.9	−55.0	155.6	41 21.2	−55.2	155.9	40 26.4	−55.5	156.3	20
21	42 15.7	−54.9	155.8	41 20.9	−55.1	156.1	40 26.0	−55.4	156.5	39 30.9	−55.6	156.8	21
22	41 20.8	−55.1	156.3	40 25.8	−55.3	156.6	39 30.6	−55.5	157.0	38 35.3	−55.7	157.3	22
23	40 25.7	−55.2	156.8	39 30.5	−55.5	157.1	38 35.1	−55.6	157.5	37 39.6	−55.8	157.8	23
24	39 30.5	−55.4	157.3	38 35.0	−55.5	157.6	37 39.5	−55.7	157.9	36 43.8	−55.9	158.2	24
25	38 35.1	−55.5	157.8	37 39.5	−55.7	158.1	36 43.8	−55.9	158.4	35 47.9	−56.0	158.7	25
26	37 39.6	−55.5	158.3	36 43.8	−55.7	158.6	35 47.9	−55.9	158.9	34 51.9	−56.1	159.1	26
27	36 44.1	−55.8	158.8	35 48.1	−55.9	159.0	34 52.0	−56.0	159.3	33 55.8	−56.2	159.5	27
28	35 48.3	−55.8	159.2	34 52.2	−56.0	159.5	33 56.0	−56.2	159.7	32 59.6	−56.2	160.0	28
29	34 52.5	−55.9	159.7	33 56.2	−56.0	159.9	32 59.8	−56.2	160.2	32 03.4	−56.4	160.4	29
30	33 56.6	−55.9	160.1	33 00.2	−56.2	160.4	32 03.6	−56.3	160.6	31 07.0	−56.4	160.8	30
31	33 00.7	−56.1	160.6	32 04.0	−56.2	160.8	31 07.3	−56.3	161.0	30 10.6	−56.5	161.2	31
32	32 04.6	−56.2	161.0	31 07.8	−56.3	161.2	30 11.0	−56.4	161.4	29 14.1	−56.6	161.6	32
33	31 08.4	−56.2	161.4	30 11.5	−56.4	161.6	29 14.6	−56.5	161.8	28 17.5	−56.6	161.9	33
34	30 12.2	−56.3	161.8	29 15.1	−56.4	162.0	28 18.1	−56.6	162.1	27 20.9	−56.7	162.3	34
35	29 15.9	−56.4	162.2	28 18.7	−56.5	162.4	27 21.5	−56.6	162.5	26 24.2	−56.7	162.7	35
36	28 19.5	−56.5	162.6	27 22.2	−56.6	162.7	26 24.9	−56.7	162.9	25 27.5	−56.8	163.0	36
37	27 23.0	−56.5	163.0	26 25.6	−56.6	163.1	25 28.2	−56.7	163.3	24 30.7	−56.8	163.4	37
38	26 26.5	−56.6	163.3	25 29.0	−56.7	163.5	24 31.5	−56.8	163.6	23 33.9	−56.9	163.7	38
39	25 29.9	−56.6	163.7	24 32.3	−56.7	163.9	23 34.7	−56.8	164.0	22 37.0	−56.9	164.1	39
40	24 33.3	−56.7	164.1	23 35.6	−56.8	164.2	22 37.9	−56.9	164.3	21 40.1	−57.0	164.4	40
41	23 36.6	−56.7	164.4	22 38.8	−56.8	164.6	21 41.0	−56.9	164.7	20 43.1	−57.0	164.8	41
42	22 39.9	−56.7	164.8	21 42.0	−56.9	164.9	20 44.1	−57.0	165.0	19 46.1	−57.0	165.1	42
43	21 43.2	−56.9	165.1	20 45.1	−56.9	165.2	19 47.1	−57.0	165.3	18 49.1	−57.1	165.4	43
44	20 46.3	−56.8	165.5	19 48.2	−56.9	165.6	18 50.1	−57.0	165.7	17 52.0	−57.1	165.8	44
45	19 49.5	−56.9	165.8	18 51.3	−57.0	165.9	17 53.1	−57.1	166.0	16 54.9	−57.2	166.1	45
46	18 52.6	−56.9	166.2	17 54.3	−57.0	166.3	16 56.0	−57.1	166.3	15 57.7	−57.1	166.4	46
47	17 55.7	−57.0	166.5	16 57.3	−57.0	166.6	15 58.9	−57.1	166.6	15 00.6	−57.2	166.7	47
48	16 58.7	−57.0	166.8	16 00.3	−57.1	166.9	15 01.8	−57.1	167.0	14 03.4	−57.3	167.0	48
49	16 01.7	−57.0	167.2	15 03.2	−57.1	167.2	14 04.7	−57.2	167.3	13 06.1	−57.2	167.3	49
50	15 04.7	−57.1	167.5	14 06.1	−57.2	167.5	13 07.5	−57.2	167.6	12 08.9	−57.2	167.6	50
51	14 07.6	−57.0	167.8	13 09.0	−57.2	167.9	12 10.3	−57.2	167.9	11 11.7	−57.3	167.9	51
52	13 10.6	−57.1	168.1	12 11.8	−57.1	168.2	11 13.1	−57.2	168.2	10 14.4	−57.3	168.2	52
53	12 13.5	−57.2	168.4	11 14.7	−57.2	168.5	10 15.9	−57.3	168.5	9 17.1	−57.3	168.5	53
54	11 16.3	−57.1	168.7	10 17.5	−57.2	168.8	9 18.6	−57.2	168.8	8 19.8	−57.4	168.8	54
55	10 19.2	−57.2	169.1	9 20.3	−57.2	169.1	8 21.4	−57.3	169.1	7 22.4	−57.3	169.1	55
56	9 22.0	−57.1	169.4	8 23.1	−57.3	169.4	7 24.1	−57.3	169.4	6 25.1	−57.3	169.4	56
57	8 24.9	−57.2	169.7	7 25.8	−57.2	169.7	6 26.8	−57.3	169.7	5 27.8	−57.4	169.7	57
58	7 27.7	−57.2	170.0	6 28.6	−57.3	170.0	5 29.5	−57.3	170.0	4 30.4	−57.3	170.0	58
59	6 30.5	−57.2	170.3	5 31.3	−57.2	170.3	4 32.2	−57.3	170.3	3 33.1	−57.4	170.3	59
60	5 33.3	−57.2	170.6	4 34.1	−57.3	170.6	3 34.9	−57.3	170.6	2 35.7	−57.4	170.6	60
61	4 36.1	−57.3	170.9	3 36.8	−57.3	170.9	2 37.6	−57.4	170.9	1 38.3	−57.4	170.9	61
62	3 38.8	−57.2	171.2	2 39.5	−57.2	171.2	1 40.2	−57.3	171.2	0 40.9	−57.3	171.2	62
63	2 41.6	−57.2	171.5	1 42.3	−57.3	171.5	0 42.9	−57.3	171.5	0 16.4	+57.4	8.5	63
64	1 44.4	−57.3	171.8	0 45.0	−57.3	171.8	0 14.4	+57.3	8.2	1 13.8	+57.4	8.2	64
65	0 47.1	−57.2	172.1	0 12.3	+57.3	7.9	1 11.7	+57.4	7.9	2 11.2	+57.3	7.9	65
66	0 10.1	+57.3	7.6	1 09.6	+57.3	7.6	2 09.1	+57.3	7.6	3 08.5	+57.3	7.6	66
67	1 07.4	+57.2	7.3	2 06.9	+57.3	7.3	3 06.4	+57.3	7.3	4 05.9	+57.4	7.3	67
68	2 04.6	+57.2	7.0	3 04.2	+57.2	7.0	4 03.7	+57.3	7.0	5 03.3	+57.3	7.0	68
69	3 01.8	+57.3	6.7	4 01.4	+57.3	6.7	5 01.0	+57.3	6.7	6 00.6	+57.3	6.7	69
70	3 59.1	+57.2	6.4	4 58.7	+57.3	6.4	5 58.3	+57.3	6.4	6 57.9	+57.4	6.4	70
71	4 56.3	+57.2	6.1	5 56.0	+57.2	6.1	6 55.6	+57.3	6.1	7 55.3	+57.3	6.1	71
72	5 53.5	+57.2	5.8	6 53.2	+57.2	5.8	7 52.9	+57.3	5.8	8 52.6	+57.3	5.8	72
73	6 50.7	+57.2	5.5	7 50.4	+57.3	5.5	8 50.2	+57.2	5.5	9 49.9	+57.3	5.5	73
74	7 47.9	+57.2	5.2	8 47.7	+57.2	5.2	9 47.4	+57.3	5.2	10 47.2	+57.2	5.2	74
75	8 45.1	+57.2	4.9	9 44.9	+57.2	4.9	10 44.7	+57.2	4.9	11 44.4	+57.3	4.9	75
76	9 42.3	+57.1	4.6	10 42.1	+57.2	4.6	11 41.9	+57.2	4.6	12 41.7	+57.2	4.6	76
77	10 39.4	+57.2	4.3	11 39.3	+57.1	4.3	12 39.1	+57.2	4.3	13 38.9	+57.2	4.3	77
78	11 36.6	+57.1	4.0	12 36.4	+57.1	4.0	13 36.3	+57.1	4.0	14 36.1	+57.2	4.0	78
79	12 33.7	+57.1	3.6	13 33.5	+57.2	3.7	14 33.4	+57.2	3.7	15 33.3	+57.1	3.7	79
80	13 30.8	+57.0	3.3	14 30.7	+57.0	3.3	15 30.6	+57.1	3.4	16 30.4	+57.2	3.4	80
81	14 27.8	+57.1	3.0	15 27.7	+57.1	3.0	16 27.7	+57.0	3.0	17 27.6	+57.1	3.1	81
82	15 24.9	+57.0	2.7	16 24.8	+57.0	2.7	17 24.7	+57.1	2.7	18 24.7	+57.0	2.7	82
83	16 21.9	+57.0	2.4	17 21.8	+57.0	2.4	18 21.8	+57.0	2.4	19 21.7	+57.0	2.4	83
84	17 18.9	+56.9	2.0	18 18.8	+57.0	2.1	19 18.8	+57.0	2.1	20 18.7	+57.0	2.1	84
85	18 15.8	+56.9	1.7	19 15.8	+56.9	1.7	20 15.8	+56.9	1.7	21 15.7	+57.0	1.7	85
86	19 12.7	+56.9	1.4	20 12.7	+56.9	1.4	21 12.7	+56.9	1.4	22 12.7	+56.9	1.4	86
87	20 09.6	+56.8	1.0	21 09.6	+56.8	1.0	22 09.6	+56.8	1.1	23 09.6	+56.8	1.1	87
88	21 06.4	+56.8	0.7	22 06.4	+56.8	0.7	23 06.4	+56.8	0.7	24 06.4	+56.8	0.7	88
89	22 03.2	+56.8	0.4	23 03.2	+56.8	0.4	24 03.2	+56.8	0.4	25 03.2	+56.8	0.4	89
90	23 00.0	+56.7	0.0	24 00.0	+56.7	0.0	25 00.0	+56.7	0.0	26 00.0	+56.7	0.0	90
	23°			24°			25°			26°			

Dec.	27° Hc	27° d	27° Z	28° Hc	28° d	28° Z	29° Hc	29° d	29° Z	30° Hc	30° d	30° Z	Dec.
°	° ′	′	°	° ′	′	°	° ′	′	°	° ′	′	°	°
0	57 24.1	−50.8	142.8	56 36.0	−51.4	143.7	55 47.3	−51.9	144.6	54 58.1	−52.4	145.4	0
1	56 33.3	−51.3	143.8	55 44.6	−51.8	144.7	54 55.4	−52.3	145.5	54 05.7	−52.8	146.3	1
2	55 42.0	−51.6	144.7	54 52.8	−52.1	145.6	54 03.1	−52.6	146.3	53 12.9	−53.0	147.1	2
3	54 50.4	−52.0	145.6	54 00.7	−52.5	146.4	53 10.5	−53.0	147.2	52 19.9	−53.4	147.9	3
4	53 58.4	−52.4	146.5	53 08.2	−52.9	147.2	52 17.5	−53.2	147.9	51 26.5	−53.7	148.6	4
5	53 06.0	−52.7	147.3	52 15.3	−53.1	148.0	51 24.3	−53.6	148.7	50 32.8	−53.9	149.3	5
6	52 13.3	−53.0	148.1	51 22.2	−53.4	148.8	50 30.7	−53.7	149.4	49 38.9	−54.1	150.0	6
7	51 20.3	−53.2	148.9	50 28.8	−53.6	149.5	49 37.0	−54.0	150.1	48 44.8	−54.3	150.7	7
8	50 27.1	−53.6	149.6	49 35.2	−53.9	150.2	48 43.0	−54.3	150.7	47 50.5	−54.6	151.3	8
9	49 33.5	−53.8	150.3	48 41.3	−54.2	150.9	47 48.7	−54.4	151.4	46 55.9	−54.7	151.9	9
10	48 39.7	−54.0	151.0	47 47.1	−54.3	151.5	46 54.3	−54.6	152.0	46 01.2	−54.9	152.5	10
11	47 45.7	−54.2	151.6	46 52.8	−54.5	152.1	45 59.7	−54.9	152.6	45 06.3	−55.1	153.1	11
12	46 51.5	−54.4	152.2	45 58.3	−54.7	152.7	45 04.8	−55.0	153.2	44 11.2	−55.3	153.6	12
13	45 57.1	−54.7	152.9	45 03.6	−54.9	153.3	44 09.8	−55.1	153.8	43 15.9	−55.4	154.2	13
14	45 02.4	−54.8	153.4	44 08.7	−55.1	153.9	43 14.7	−55.3	154.3	42 20.5	−55.5	154.7	14
15	44 07.6	−54.9	154.0	43 13.6	−55.2	154.4	42 19.4	−55.4	154.8	41 25.0	−55.7	155.2	15
16	43 12.7	−55.1	154.6	42 18.4	−55.4	155.0	41 24.0	−55.6	155.3	40 29.3	−55.7	155.7	16
17	42 17.6	−55.3	155.1	41 23.0	−55.4	155.5	40 28.4	−55.7	155.8	39 33.6	−55.9	156.2	17
18	41 22.3	−55.4	155.6	40 27.6	−55.7	156.0	39 32.7	−55.8	156.3	38 37.7	−56.0	156.6	18
19	40 26.9	−55.5	156.1	39 31.9	−55.7	156.5	38 36.9	−56.0	156.8	37 41.7	−56.2	157.1	19
20	39 31.4	−55.7	156.6	38 36.2	−55.8	157.0	37 40.9	−56.0	157.3	36 45.5	−56.2	157.6	20
21	38 35.7	−55.8	157.1	37 40.4	−56.0	157.4	36 44.9	−56.1	157.7	35 49.3	−56.3	158.0	21
22	37 39.9	−55.8	157.6	36 44.4	−56.1	157.9	35 48.8	−56.3	158.1	34 53.0	−56.4	158.4	22
23	36 44.1	−56.0	158.0	35 48.3	−56.1	158.3	34 52.5	−56.3	158.6	33 56.6	−56.4	158.8	23
24	35 48.1	−56.1	158.5	34 52.2	−56.2	158.7	33 56.2	−56.4	159.0	33 00.2	−56.6	159.2	24
25	34 52.0	−56.2	158.9	33 56.0	−56.4	159.2	32 59.8	−56.4	159.4	32 03.6	−56.6	159.6	25
26	33 55.8	−56.2	159.3	32 59.6	−56.4	159.6	32 03.4	−56.6	159.8	31 07.0	−56.7	160.0	26
27	32 59.6	−56.4	159.8	32 03.2	−56.5	160.0	31 06.8	−56.6	160.2	30 10.3	−56.7	160.4	27
28	32 03.2	−56.4	160.2	31 06.7	−56.5	160.4	30 10.2	−56.7	160.6	29 13.6	−56.8	160.8	28
29	31 06.8	−56.5	160.6	30 10.2	−56.6	160.8	29 13.5	−56.7	161.0	28 16.8	−56.9	161.1	29
30	30 10.3	−56.5	161.0	29 13.6	−56.7	161.2	28 16.8	−56.8	161.3	27 19.9	−56.9	161.5	30
31	29 13.8	−56.6	161.4	28 16.9	−56.7	161.5	27 20.0	−56.9	161.7	26 23.0	−57.0	161.8	31
32	28 17.2	−56.7	161.7	27 20.2	−56.8	161.9	26 23.1	−56.9	162.0	25 26.0	−57.0	162.2	32
33	27 20.5	−56.8	162.1	26 23.4	−56.9	162.3	25 26.2	−57.0	162.4	24 29.0	−57.1	162.5	33
34	26 23.7	−56.8	162.5	25 26.5	−56.9	162.6	24 29.2	−57.0	162.7	23 31.9	−57.1	162.9	34
35	25 26.9	−56.8	162.8	24 29.6	−57.0	163.0	23 32.2	−57.0	163.1	22 34.8	−57.2	163.2	35
36	24 30.1	−56.9	163.2	23 32.6	−57.0	163.3	22 35.2	−57.1	163.4	21 37.6	−57.2	163.5	36
37	23 33.2	−56.9	163.5	22 35.6	−57.0	163.6	21 38.1	−57.2	163.8	20 40.4	−57.2	163.9	37
38	22 36.3	−57.0	163.9	21 38.6	−57.1	164.0	20 40.9	−57.1	164.1	19 43.2	−57.3	164.2	38
39	21 39.3	−57.0	164.2	20 41.5	−57.1	164.3	19 43.8	−57.3	164.4	18 45.9	−57.2	164.5	39
40	20 42.3	−57.1	164.5	19 44.4	−57.1	164.6	18 46.5	−57.2	164.7	17 48.7	−57.4	164.8	40
41	19 45.2	−57.1	164.9	18 47.3	−57.2	165.0	17 49.3	−57.3	165.0	16 51.3	−57.3	165.1	41
42	18 48.1	−57.1	165.2	17 50.1	−57.2	165.3	16 52.0	−57.3	165.4	15 54.0	−57.4	165.4	42
43	17 51.0	−57.2	165.5	16 52.9	−57.3	165.6	15 54.7	−57.3	165.7	14 56.6	−57.4	165.7	43
44	16 53.8	−57.2	165.8	15 55.6	−57.2	165.9	14 57.4	−57.3	166.0	13 59.2	−57.4	166.0	44
45	15 56.6	−57.2	166.1	14 58.4	−57.3	166.2	14 00.1	−57.4	166.3	13 01.8	−57.5	166.3	45
46	14 59.4	−57.2	166.5	14 01.1	−57.4	166.5	13 02.7	−57.4	166.6	12 04.3	−57.4	166.6	46
47	14 02.2	−57.3	166.8	13 03.7	−57.3	166.8	12 05.3	−57.4	166.9	11 06.9	−57.5	166.9	47
48	13 04.9	−57.3	167.1	12 06.4	−57.4	167.1	11 07.9	−57.4	167.2	10 09.4	−57.5	167.2	48
49	12 07.6	−57.3	167.4	11 09.0	−57.3	167.4	10 10.5	−57.5	167.5	9 11.9	−57.5	167.5	49
50	11 10.3	−57.3	167.7	10 11.7	−57.4	167.7	9 13.0	−57.4	167.8	8 14.4	−57.5	167.8	50
51	10 13.0	−57.4	168.0	9 14.3	−57.4	168.0	8 15.6	−57.5	168.1	7 16.9	−57.5	168.1	51
52	9 15.6	−57.3	168.3	8 16.9	−57.4	168.3	7 18.1	−57.5	168.3	6 19.4	−57.6	168.4	52
53	8 18.3	−57.4	168.6	7 19.5	−57.5	168.6	6 20.6	−57.5	168.6	5 21.8	−57.5	168.7	53
54	7 20.9	−57.4	168.9	6 22.0	−57.4	168.9	5 23.1	−57.5	168.9	4 24.3	−57.6	168.9	54
55	6 23.5	−57.4	169.2	5 24.6	−57.5	169.2	4 25.6	−57.5	169.2	3 26.7	−57.5	169.2	55
56	5 26.1	−57.4	169.5	4 27.1	−57.4	169.5	3 28.1	−57.5	169.5	2 29.2	−57.6	169.5	56
57	4 28.7	−57.4	169.8	3 29.7	−57.5	169.8	2 30.6	−57.5	169.8	1 31.6	−57.6	169.8	57
58	3 31.3	−57.4	170.0	2 32.2	−57.4	170.1	1 33.1	−57.5	170.1	0 34.0	−57.5	170.1	58
59	2 33.9	−57.4	170.3	1 34.8	−57.5	170.3	0 35.6	−57.5	170.3	0 23.5	+57.6	9.7	59
60	1 36.5	−57.4	170.6	0 37.3	−57.5	170.6	0 21.9	+57.5	9.4	1 21.1	+57.6	9.4	60
61	0 39.1	−57.4	170.9	0 20.2	+57.4	9.1	1 19.4	+57.5	9.1	2 18.7	+57.6	9.1	61
62	0 18.3	+57.5	8.8	1 17.6	+57.5	8.8	2 16.9	+57.5	8.8	3 16.2	+57.6	8.8	62
63	1 15.8	+57.4	8.5	2 15.1	+57.5	8.5	3 14.4	+57.6	8.5	4 13.8	+57.5	8.5	63
64	2 13.2	+57.4	8.2	3 12.6	+57.4	8.2	4 12.0	+57.5	8.2	5 11.3	+57.6	8.2	64
65	3 10.6	+57.4	7.9	4 10.0	+57.5	7.9	5 09.5	+57.4	7.9	6 08.9	+57.5	8.0	65
66	4 08.0	+57.4	7.6	5 07.5	+57.4	7.6	6 06.9	+57.5	7.7	7 06.4	+57.5	7.7	66
67	5 05.4	+57.4	7.3	6 04.9	+57.5	7.3	7 04.4	+57.5	7.4	8 03.9	+57.5	7.4	67
68	6 02.8	+57.4	7.0	7 02.4	+57.4	7.1	8 01.9	+57.5	7.1	9 01.4	+57.5	7.1	68
69	7 00.2	+57.4	6.8	7 59.8	+57.4	6.8	8 59.4	+57.4	6.8	9 58.9	+57.5	6.8	69
70	7 57.6	+57.3	6.5	8 57.2	+57.4	6.5	9 56.8	+57.4	6.5	10 56.4	+57.5	6.5	70
71	8 54.9	+57.4	6.2	9 54.6	+57.4	6.2	10 54.2	+57.4	6.2	11 53.9	+57.4	6.2	71
72	9 52.3	+57.3	5.9	10 52.0	+57.3	5.9	11 51.6	+57.4	5.9	12 51.3	+57.5	5.9	72
73	10 49.6	+57.3	5.6	11 49.3	+57.4	5.6	12 49.0	+57.4	5.6	13 48.8	+57.4	5.6	73
74	11 46.9	+57.3	5.3	12 46.7	+57.3	5.3	13 46.4	+57.4	5.3	14 46.2	+57.3	5.3	74
75	12 44.2	+57.3	5.0	13 44.0	+57.3	5.0	14 43.8	+57.3	5.0	15 43.5	+57.4	5.0	75
76	13 41.5	+57.2	4.6	14 41.3	+57.3	4.7	15 41.1	+57.3	4.7	16 40.9	+57.3	4.7	76
77	14 38.7	+57.3	4.3	15 38.6	+57.2	4.4	16 38.4	+57.3	4.4	17 38.2	+57.3	4.4	77
78	15 36.0	+57.2	4.0	16 35.8	+57.2	4.1	17 35.7	+57.2	4.1	18 35.5	+57.3	4.1	78
79	16 33.2	+57.1	3.7	17 33.0	+57.2	3.7	18 32.9	+57.2	3.8	19 32.8	+57.2	3.8	79
80	17 30.3	+57.2	3.4	18 30.2	+57.2	3.4	19 30.1	+57.2	3.4	20 30.0	+57.2	3.5	80
81	18 27.5	+57.1	3.1	19 27.4	+57.1	3.1	20 27.3	+57.2	3.1	21 27.2	+57.2	3.1	81
82	19 24.6	+57.1	2.8	20 24.5	+57.1	2.8	21 24.5	+57.1	2.8	22 24.4	+57.1	2.8	82
83	20 21.7	+57.0	2.4	21 21.6	+57.1	2.4	22 21.6	+57.0	2.5	23 21.5	+57.1	2.5	83
84	21 18.7	+57.0	2.1	22 18.7	+57.0	2.1	23 18.6	+57.0	2.1	24 18.6	+57.0	2.1	84
85	22 15.7	+57.0	1.8	23 15.7	+56.9	1.8	24 15.6	+57.0	1.8	25 15.6	+57.0	1.8	85
86	23 12.7	+56.9	1.4	24 12.6	+57.0	1.4	25 12.6	+56.9	1.4	26 12.6	+56.9	1.5	86
87	24 09.6	+56.8	1.1	25 09.6	+56.8	1.1	26 09.5	+56.9	1.1	27 09.5	+56.9	1.1	87
88	25 06.4	+56.8	0.7	26 06.4	+56.8	0.7	27 06.4	+56.8	0.7	28 06.4	+56.8	0.7	88
89	26 03.2	+56.8	0.4	27 03.2	+56.8	0.4	28 03.2	+56.8	0.4	29 03.2	+56.8	0.4	89
90	27 00.0	+56.7	0.0	28 00.0	+56.7	0.0	29 00.0	+56.7	0.0	30 00.0	+56.7	0.0	90
	27°			28°			29°			30°			

S. Lat. { L.H.A. greater than 180° ....Zn=180°−Z
{ L.H.A. less than 180°............Zn=180°+Z

LATITUDE **SAME** NAME AS DECLINATION L.H.A. 161°, 199°

223

20°, 340° L.H.A. LATITUDE SAME NAME AS DECLINATION

N. Lat. {L.H.A. greater than 180° .....Zn=Z
{L.H.A. less than 180°............Zn=360°−Z

Dec.	23° Hc	23° d	23° Z	24° Hc	24° d	24° Z	25° Hc	25° d	25° Z	26° Hc	26° d	26° Z
°	° ′	′	°	° ′	′	°	° ′	′	°	° ′	′	°
0	59 52.9	+46.4	137.0	59 08.6	+47.2	138.2	58 23.5	+48.1	139.3	57 37.7	+48.8	140.3
1	60 39.3	+45.5	135.8	59 55.8	+46.6	137.0	59 11.6	+47.4	138.1	58 26.5	+48.3	139.2
2	61 24.8	+44.8	134.4	60 42.4	+45.8	135.7	59 59.0	+46.7	136.9	59 14.8	+47.6	138.1
3	62 09.6	+43.9	133.0	61 28.2	+44.9	134.3	60 45.7	+46.0	135.6	60 02.4	+46.9	136.8
4	62 53.5	+42.8	131.5	62 13.1	+44.1	132.9	61 31.7	+45.2	134.3	60 49.3	+46.2	135.6
5	63 36.3	+41.8	130.0	62 57.2	+43.1	131.5	62 16.9	+44.3	132.9	61 35.5	+45.4	134.3
6	64 18.1	+40.7	128.3	63 40.3	+42.0	129.9	63 01.2	+43.3	131.4	62 20.9	+44.5	132.9
7	64 58.8	+39.4	126.6	64 22.3	+40.9	128.3	63 44.5	+42.3	129.9	63 05.4	+43.5	131.4
8	65 38.2	+38.1	124.8	65 03.2	+39.7	126.6	64 26.8	+41.1	128.3	63 48.9	+42.6	129.9
9	66 16.3	+36.6	122.9	65 42.9	+38.3	124.8	65 07.9	+39.9	126.6	64 31.5	+41.4	128.2
10	66 52.9	+35.1	120.9	66 21.2	+36.9	122.9	65 47.8	+38.6	124.8	65 12.9	+40.1	126.5
11	67 28.0	+33.3	118.8	66 58.1	+35.3	120.9	66 26.4	+37.1	122.9	65 53.0	+38.9	124.7
12	68 01.3	+31.5	116.6	67 33.4	+33.6	118.8	67 03.5	+35.6	120.9	66 31.9	+37.4	122.9
13	68 32.8	+29.5•	114.3	68 07.0	+31.8	116.6	67 39.1	+33.9	118.8	67 09.3	+35.8	120.9
14	69 02.3	+27.4•	111.9	68 38.8	+29.8•	114.3	68 13.0	+32.0	116.6	67 45.1	+34.2	118.8
15	69 29.7	+25.2•	109.4	69 08.6	+27.7•	111.9	68 45.0	+30.1•	114.3	68 19.3	+32.3	116.6
16	69 54.9	+22.7•	106.8	69 36.3	+25.4•	109.4	69 15.1	+28.0•	111.9	68 51.6	+30.4•	114.3
17	70 17.6	+20.2•	104.1	70 01.7	+23.0•	106.7	69 43.1	+25.7•	109.3	69 22.0	+28.2•	111.9
18	70 37.8	+17.5•	101.3	70 24.7	+20.4•	104.0	70 08.8	+23.3•	106.7	69 50.2	+26.0•	109.3
19	70 55.3	+14.7•	98.4	70 45.1	+17.8•	101.2	70 32.1	+20.7•	104.0	70 16.2	+23.6•	106.7
20	71 10.0	+11.8•	95.4	71 02.9	+14.9•	98.3	70 52.8	+18.0•	101.1	70 39.8	+21.0•	103.9
21	71 21.8	+8.8•	92.3	71 17.8	+12.0•	95.3	71 10.8	+15.2•	98.2	71 00.8	+18.2•	101.1
22	71 30.6	+5.7•	89.2	71 29.8	+9.0•	92.2	71 26.0	+12.2•	95.2	71 19.0	+15.5•	98.1
23	71 36.3	+2.5•	86.1	71 38.8	+5.9•	89.1	71 38.2	+9.2•	92.1	71 34.5	+12.4•	95.1
24	71 38.8	-0.6•	82.9	71 44.7	+2.7•	85.9	71 47.4	+6.0•	88.9	71 46.9	+9.4•	92.0
25	71 38.2	-3.7•	79.7	71 47.4	-0.5•	82.7	71 53.4	+2.9•	85.7	71 56.3	+6.2•	88.8
26	71 34.5	-6.9•	76.6	71 46.9	-3.6•	79.5	71 56.3	-0.4•	82.5	72 02.5	+3.0•	85.6
27	71 27.6	-9.9•	73.4	71 43.3	-6.8•	76.3	71 55.9	-3.5•	79.3	72 05.5	-0.2•	82.3
28	71 17.7	-12.9•	70.3	71 36.5	-9.9•	73.2	71 52.4	-6.7•	76.1	72 05.3	-3.5•	79.1
29	71 04.8	-15.8•	67.3	71 26.6	-12.9•	70.0	71 45.7	-9.9•	72.9	72 01.8	-6.6•	75.8
30	70 49.0	-18.6•	64.3	71 13.7	-15.8•	67.0	71 35.8	-12.8•	69.8	71 55.2	-9.8•	72.6
31	70 30.4	-21.1•	61.5	70 57.9	-18.5•	64.0	71 23.0	-15.8•	66.7	71 45.4	-12.9•	69.5
32	70 09.3	-23.7•	58.7	70 39.4	-21.3•	61.1	71 07.2	-18.7•	63.7	71 32.5	-15.8•	66.4
33	69 45.6	-26.0•	56.0	70 18.1	-23.7•	58.3	70 48.5	-21.2•	60.8	71 16.7	-18.7•	63.3
34	69 19.6	-28.3•	53.4	69 54.4	-26.1•	55.6	70 27.3	-23.9•	57.9	70 58.0	-21.3•	60.4
35	68 51.3	-30.3	51.0	69 28.3	-28.3•	53.0	70 03.4	-26.1•	55.2	70 36.7	-23.9•	57.6
36	68 21.0	-32.2	48.6	69 00.0	-30.4•	50.5	69 37.3	-28.5•	52.6	70 12.8	-26.3•	54.8
37	67 48.8	-34.0	46.3	68 29.6	-32.4	48.2	69 08.8	-30.5•	50.1	69 46.5	-28.6•	52.2
38	67 14.8	-35.6	44.2	67 57.2	-34.1	45.9	68 38.3	-32.5	47.7	69 17.9	-30.6•	49.7
39	66 39.2	-37.2	42.1	67 23.1	-35.8	43.7	68 05.8	-34.2	45.4	68 47.3	-32.6	47.3
40	66 02.0	-38.6	40.2	66 47.3	-37.3	41.7	67 31.6	-35.9	43.3	68 14.7	-34.4	45.0
41	65 23.4	-39.9	38.3	66 10.0	-38.7	39.7	66 55.7	-37.5	41.2	67 40.3	-36.1	42.8
42	64 43.5	-41.2	36.5	65 31.3	-40.1	37.8	66 18.2	-38.9	39.2	67 04.2	-37.6	40.7
43	64 02.3	-42.2	34.8	64 51.2	-41.2	36.1	65 39.3	-40.2	37.4	66 26.6	-39.1	38.7
44	63 20.1	-43.2	33.2	64 10.0	-42.4	34.4	64 59.1	-41.4	35.6	65 47.5	-40.3	36.9
45	62 36.9	-44.2	31.7	63 27.6	-43.4	32.8	64 17.7	-42.5	33.9	65 07.2	-41.6	35.1
46	61 52.7	-45.1	30.3	62 44.2	-44.3	31.2	63 35.2	-43.5	32.3	64 25.6	-42.6	33.4
47	61 07.6	-45.9	28.9	61 59.9	-45.2	29.8	62 51.7	-44.5	30.8	63 43.0	-43.7	31.8
48	60 21.7	-46.6	27.6	61 14.7	-46.0	28.4	62 07.2	-45.3	29.3	62 59.3	-44.6	30.3
49	59 35.1	-47.4	26.3	60 28.7	-46.8	27.1	61 21.9	-46.2	27.9	62 14.7	-45.5	28.8
50	58 47.7	-47.9	25.1	59 41.9	-47.4	25.8	60 35.7	-46.9	26.6	61 29.2	-46.3	27.4
51	57 59.8	-48.6	24.0	58 54.5	-48.1	24.6	59 48.8	-47.5	25.3	60 42.9	-47.0	26.1
52	57 11.2	-49.1	22.9	58 06.4	-48.7	23.5	59 01.3	-48.2	24.1	59 55.9	-47.8	24.9
53	56 22.1	-49.6	21.8	57 17.7	-49.2	22.4	58 13.1	-48.8	23.0	59 08.1	-48.3	23.7
54	55 32.5	-50.1	20.8	56 28.5	-49.7	21.3	57 24.3	-49.4	21.9	58 19.8	-48.9	22.5
55	54 42.4	-50.5	19.8	55 38.8	-50.2	20.3	56 34.9	-49.8	20.9	57 30.9	-49.5	21.4
56	53 51.9	-50.9	18.9	54 48.6	-50.7	19.4	55 45.1	-50.3	19.9	56 41.4	-49.9	20.4
57	53 01.0	-51.4	18.0	53 57.9	-51.0	18.5	54 54.8	-50.8	18.9	55 51.5	-50.5	19.4
58	52 09.6	-51.6	17.2	53 06.9	-51.4	17.6	54 04.0	-51.1	18.0	55 01.0	-50.8	18.4
59	51 18.0	-52.0	16.4	52 15.5	-51.8	16.7	53 12.9	-51.5	17.1	54 10.2	-51.3	17.5
60	50 26.0	-52.3	15.6	51 23.7	-52.1	15.9	52 21.4	-51.9	16.3	53 18.9	-51.6	16.6
61	49 33.7	-52.6	14.8	50 31.6	-52.4	15.1	51 29.5	-52.2	15.4	52 27.3	-52.0	15.8
62	48 41.1	-52.9	14.1	49 39.2	-52.7	14.4	50 37.3	-52.5	14.7	51 35.3	-52.3	15.0
63	47 48.2	-53.1	13.4	48 46.5	-52.9	13.6	49 44.8	-52.8	13.9	50 43.0	-52.6	14.2
64	46 55.1	-53.4	12.7	47 53.6	-53.2	12.9	48 52.0	-53.0	13.2	49 50.4	-52.9	13.4
65	46 01.7	-53.6	12.0	47 00.4	-53.5	12.2	47 59.0	-53.3	12.5	48 57.5	-53.1	12.7
66	45 08.1	-53.8	11.4	46 06.9	-53.6	11.6	47 05.7	-53.6	11.8	48 04.4	-53.4	12.0
67	44 14.3	-54.0	10.8	45 13.3	-53.9	10.9	46 12.1	-53.7	11.1	47 11.0	-53.6	11.3
68	43 20.3	-54.1	10.1	44 19.4	-54.1	10.3	45 18.4	-54.0	10.5	46 17.4	-53.9	10.7
69	42 26.2	-54.4	9.6	43 25.3	-54.3	9.7	44 24.4	-54.1	9.9	45 23.5	-54.0	10.1
70	41 31.8	-54.5	9.0	42 31.0	-54.4	9.1	43 30.3	-54.4	9.3	44 29.5	-54.3	9.4
71	40 37.3	-54.7	8.4	41 36.6	-54.6	8.6	42 35.9	-54.5	8.7	43 35.2	-54.4	8.8
72	39 42.6	-54.8	7.9	40 42.0	-54.7	8.0	41 41.4	-54.6	8.1	42 40.8	-54.6	8.3
73	38 47.8	-55.0	7.4	39 47.3	-54.9	7.5	40 46.8	-54.8	7.6	41 46.2	-54.7	7.7
74	37 52.8	-55.0	6.9	38 52.4	-55.0	7.0	39 52.0	-55.0	7.1	40 51.5	-54.9	7.2
75	36 57.8	-55.3	6.4	37 57.4	-55.2	6.4	38 57.0	-55.1	6.5	39 56.6	-55.0	6.6
76	36 02.5	-55.3	5.9	37 02.2	-55.2	5.9	38 01.9	-55.2	6.0	39 01.6	-55.2	6.1
77	35 07.2	-55.4	5.4	36 07.0	-55.4	5.5	37 06.7	-55.4	5.5	38 06.4	-55.3	5.6
78	34 11.8	-55.5	4.9	35 11.6	-55.5	5.0	36 11.3	-55.4	5.1	37 11.1	-55.4	5.1
79	33 16.3	-55.7	4.5	34 16.1	-55.6	4.5	35 15.9	-55.6	4.6	36 15.7	-55.5	4.6
80	32 20.6	-55.7	4.0	33 20.5	-55.7	4.1	34 20.3	-55.6	4.1	35 20.2	-55.7	4.2
81	31 24.9	-55.8	3.6	32 24.8	-55.8	3.6	33 24.7	-55.8	3.7	34 24.5	-55.7	3.7
82	30 29.1	-55.9	3.2	31 29.0	-55.9	3.2	32 28.9	-55.8	3.2	33 28.8	-55.8	3.3
83	29 33.2	-56.0	2.7	30 33.1	-55.9	2.8	31 33.1	-56.0	2.8	32 33.0	-55.9	2.8
84	28 37.2	-56.0	2.3	29 37.2	-56.0	2.4	30 37.1	-56.0	2.4	31 37.1	-56.0	2.4
85	27 41.2	-56.1	1.9	28 41.2	-56.1	1.9	29 41.1	-56.1	2.0	30 41.1	-56.1	2.0
86	26 45.1	-56.2	1.5	27 45.1	-56.2	1.5	28 45.0	-56.1	1.6	29 45.0	-56.1	1.6
87	25 48.9	-56.2	1.1	26 48.9	-56.3	1.1	27 48.9	-56.3	1.2	28 48.9	-56.3	1.2
88	24 52.7	-56.3	0.8	25 52.6	-56.2	0.8	26 52.6	-56.2	0.8	27 52.6	-56.2	0.8
89	23 56.4	-56.4	0.4	24 56.4	-56.4	0.4	25 56.4	-56.4	0.4	26 56.4	-56.4	0.4
90	23 00.0	-56.4	0.0	24 00.0	-56.4	0.0	25 00.0	-56.4	0.0	26 00.0	-56.4	0.0
	23°			24°			25°			26°		

27° Hc	27° d	27° Z	28° Hc	28° d	28° Z	29° Hc	29° d	29° Z	30° Hc	30° d	30° Z	Dec.
° ′	′	°	° ′	′	°	° ′	′	°	° ′	′	°	°
56 51.2	+49.6	141.3	56 04.1	+50.2	142.2	55 16.4	+50.8	143.1	54 28.1	+51.4	143.9	0
57 40.8	+49.0	140.2	56 54.3	+49.7	141.2	56 07.2	+50.4	142.2	55 19.5	+51.1	143.1	1
58 29.8	+48.4	139.1	57 44.0	+49.2	140.2	56 57.6	+49.9	141.2	56 10.6	+50.5	142.1	2
59 18.2	+47.8	138.0	58 33.2	+48.7	139.1	57 47.5	+49.4	140.1	57 01.1	+50.1	141.1	3
60 06.0	+47.2	136.8	59 21.9	+48.0	138.0	58 36.9	+48.8	139.1	57 51.2	+49.6	140.1	4
60 53.2	+46.4	135.6	60 09.9	+47.3	136.8	59 25.7	+48.3	137.9	58 40.8	+49.0	139.0	5
61 39.6	+45.6	134.2	60 57.2	+46.6	135.5	60 14.0	+47.5	136.8	59 29.8	+48.4	137.9	6
62 25.2	+44.7	132.8	61 43.8	+45.8	134.2	61 01.5	+46.8	135.5	60 18.2	+47.8	136.7	7
63 09.9	+43.8	131.4	62 29.6	+45.0	132.8	61 48.3	+46.1	134.2	61 06.0	+47.0	135.5	8
63 53.7	+42.7	129.9	63 14.6	+44.0	131.4	62 34.4	+45.1	132.8	61 53.0	+46.3	134.2	9
64 36.4	+41.7	128.2	63 58.6	+43.0	129.9	63 19.5	+44.3	131.4	62 39.3	+45.4	132.8	10
65 18.1	+40.4	126.5	64 41.6	+41.9	128.2	64 03.8	+43.3	129.9	63 24.7	+44.5	131.4	11
65 58.5	+39.1	124.7	65 23.5	+40.7	126.5	64 47.1	+42.1	128.3	64 09.2	+43.6	129.9	12
66 37.6	+37.7	122.9	66 04.2	+39.4	124.8	65 29.2	+41.0	126.6	64 52.8	+42.4	128.3	13
67 15.3	+36.1	120.9	66 43.6	+38.0	122.9	66 10.2	+39.6	124.8	65 35.2	+41.2	126.6	14
67 51.4	+34.5	118.8	67 21.6	+36.4	120.9	66 49.8	+38.3	122.9	66 16.4	+40.0	124.8	15
68 25.9	+32.6	116.6	67 58.0	+34.7	118.8	67 28.1	+36.7	120.9	66 56.4	+38.5	122.9	16
68 58.5	+30.6•	114.3	68 32.7	+32.9	116.6	68 04.8	+35.0	118.8	67 34.9	+37.0	120.9	17
69 29.1	+28.6•	111.8	69 05.6	+31.0•	114.3	68 39.8	+33.3	116.6	68 11.9	+35.4	118.9	18
69 57.7	+26.2•	109.3	69 36.6	+28.8•	111.8	69 13.1	+31.2•	114.3	68 47.3	+33.5	116.7	19
70 23.9	+23.9•	106.7	70 05.4	+26.6•	109.3	69 44.3	+29.2•	111.9	69 20.8	+31.6•	114.3	20
70 47.8	+21.3•	103.9	70 32.0	+24.1•	106.6	70 13.5	+26.8•	109.3	69 52.4	+29.4•	111.9	21
71 09.1	+18.5•	101.0	70 56.1	+21.6•	103.9	70 40.3	+24.5•	106.6	70 21.8	+27.2•	109.3	22
71 27.6	+15.7•	98.1	71 17.7	+18.8•	101.0	71 04.8	+21.8•	103.8	70 49.0	+24.7•	106.6	23
71 43.3	+12.6•	95.0	71 36.5	+15.9•	98.0	71 26.6	+19.1•	100.9	71 13.7	+22.1•	103.8	24
71 55.9	+9.6•	91.9	71 52.4	+12.9•	94.9	71 45.7	+16.1•	97.9	71 35.8	+19.4•	100.9	25
72 05.5	+6.4•	88.7	72 05.3	+9.8•	91.8	72 01.8	+13.2•	94.8	71 55.2	+16.4•	97.9	26
72 11.9	+3.2•	85.4	72 15.1	+6.6•	88.5	72 15.0	+10.0•	91.7	72 11.6	+13.4•	94.8	27
72 15.1	-0.1•	82.2	72 21.7	+3.3•	85.3	72 25.0	+6.7•	88.4	72 25.0	+10.2•	91.6	28
72 15.0	-3.4•	78.9	72 25.0	0.0•	82.0	72 31.7	+3.5•	85.1	72 35.2	+6.9•	88.3	29
72 11.6	-6.6•	75.6	72 25.0	-3.3•	78.7	72 35.2	+0.1•	81.8	72 42.1	+3.6•	85.0	30
72 05.0	-9.8•	72.4	72 21.7	-6.6•	75.4	72 35.3	-3.2•	78.4	72 45.7	+0.2•	81.6	31
71 55.2	-12.9•	69.2	72 15.1	-9.7•	72.1	72 32.1	-6.5•	75.1	72 45.9	-3.1•	78.2	32
71 42.3	-15.8•	66.0	72 05.4	-12.9•	68.9	72 25.6	-9.8•	71.8	72 42.8	-6.5•	74.9	33
71 26.5	-18.7•	63.0	71 52.5	-15.9•	65.7	72 15.8	-12.9•	68.6	72 36.3	-9.8•	71.5	34
71 07.8	-21.5•	60.0	71 36.6	-18.8•	62.6	72 02.9	-16.0•	65.4	72 26.5	-12.9•	68.2	35
70 46.3	-24.0•	57.2	71 17.8	-21.6•	59.6	71 46.9	-18.9•	62.3	72 13.6	-16.1•	65.0	36
70 22.3	-26.4•	54.4	70 56.2	-24.1•	56.8	71 28.0	-21.6•	59.2	71 57.5	-18.9•	61.9	37
69 55.9	-28.7•	51.8	70 32.1	-26.5•	54.0	71 06.4	-24.2•	56.3	71 38.6	-21.8•	58.8	38
69 27.2	-30.8•	49.2	70 05.6	-28.9•	51.3	70 42.2	-26.7•	53.5	71 16.8	-24.4•	55.9	39
68 56.4	-32.7	46.8	69 36.7	-30.9•	48.8	70 15.5	-29.0•	50.9	70 52.4	-26.8•	53.1	40
68 23.7	-34.6	44.5	69 05.8	-32.9	46.3	69 46.5	-31.1•	48.3	70 25.6	-29.2•	50.4	41
67 49.1	-36.2	42.3	68 32.9	-34.7	44.0	69 15.4	-33.1	45.9	69 56.4	-31.3•	47.8	42
67 12.9	-37.8	40.2	67 58.2	-36.5	41.8	68 42.3	-34.9	43.5	69 25.1	-33.3	45.4	43
66 35.1	-39.2	38.3	67 21.7	-37.9	39.7	68 07.4	-36.6	41.3	68 51.8	-35.1	43.0	44
65 55.9	-40.5	36.4	66 43.8	-39.4	37.7	67 30.8	-38.2	39.2	68 16.7	-36.8	40.8	45
65 15.4	-41.7	34.6	66 04.4	-40.7	35.9	66 52.6	-39.5	37.2	67 39.9	-38.3	38.7	46
64 33.7	-42.8	32.9	65 23.7	-41.9	34.1	66 13.1	-40.9	35.3	67 01.6	-39.8	36.7	47
63 50.9	-43.9	31.3	64 41.8	-43.0	32.4	65 32.2	-42.1	33.5	66 21.8	-41.0	34.8	48
63 07.0	-44.8	29.8	63 58.8	-44.0	30.8	64 50.1	-43.2	31.8	65 40.8	-42.3	33.0	49
62 22.2	-45.6	28.3	63 14.8	-44.9	29.2	64 06.9	-44.2	30.2	64 58.5	-43.4	31.3	50
61 36.6	-46.5	26.9	62 29.9	-45.8	27.8	63 22.7	-45.1	28.7	64 15.1	-44.4	29.7	51
60 50.1	-47.1	25.6	61 44.1	-46.6	26.4	62 37.6	-46.0	27.3	63 30.7	-45.3	28.2	52
60 03.0	-47.9	24.3	60 57.5	-47.4	25.1	61 51.6	-46.7	25.9	62 45.4	-46.1	26.7	53
59 15.1	-48.5	23.2	60 10.1	-48.0	23.8	61 04.9	-47.5	24.6	61 59.3	-47.0	25.3	54
58 26.6	-49.0	22.0	59 22.1	-48.6	22.6	60 17.4	-48.2	23.3	61 12.3	-47.6	24.0	55
57 37.6	-49.6	20.9	58 33.5	-49.2	21.5	59 29.2	-48.8	22.1	60 24.7	-48.4	22.8	56
56 48.0	-50.1	19.9	57 44.3	-49.7	20.4	58 40.4	-49.3	21.0	59 36.3	-48.9	21.6	57
55 57.9	-50.6	18.9	56 54.6	-50.3	19.4	57 51.1	-49.9	19.9	58 47.4	-49.5	20.5	58
55 07.3	-50.9	17.9	56 04.3	-50.6	18.4	57 01.2	-50.4	18.9	57 57.9	-50.1	19.4	59
54 16.4	-51.4	17.0	55 13.7	-51.1	17.4	56 10.8	-50.8	17.9	57 07.8	-50.5	18.4	60
53 25.0	-51.8	16.2	54 22.6	-51.5	16.5	55 20.0	-51.2	16.9	56 17.3	-50.9	17.4	61
52 33.2	-52.1	15.3	53 31.1	-51.9	15.7	54 28.8	-51.7	16.0	55 26.4	-51.4	16.4	62
51 41.1	-52.4	14.5	52 39.2	-52.2	14.8	53 37.1	-51.9	15.2	54 35.0	-51.8	15.5	63
50 48.7	-52.7	13.7	51 47.0	-52.5	14.0	52 45.2	-52.4	14.3	53 43.2	-52.1	14.7	64
49 56.0	-53.0	13.0	50 54.5	-52.9	13.3	51 52.8	-52.6	13.5	52 51.1	-52.4	13.8	65
49 03.0	-53.2	12.3	50 01.6	-53.0	12.5	51 00.2	-52.9	12.8	51 58.7	-52.8	13.1	66
48 09.8	-53.5	11.6	49 08.6	-53.4	11.8	50 07.3	-53.2	12.0	51 05.9	-53.0	12.3	67
47 16.3	-53.7	10.9	48 15.2	-53.6	11.1	49 14.1	-53.5	11.3	50 12.9	-53.3	11.5	68
46 22.6	-53.9	10.2	47 21.6	-53.8	10.4	48 20.6	-53.7	10.6	49 19.6	-53.6	10.8	69
45 28.7	-54.2	9.6	46 27.8	-54.0	9.8	47 26.9	-53.9	10.0	48 26.0	-53.8	10.2	70
44 34.5	-54.3	9.0	45 33.8	-54.3	9.2	46 33.0	-54.1	9.3	47 32.2	-54.0	9.5	71
43 40.2	-54.5	8.4	44 39.5	-54.4	8.5	45 38.9	-54.4	8.7	46 38.2	-54.3	8.9	72
42 45.7	-54.7	7.8	43 45.1	-54.6	8.0	44 44.5	-54.5	8.1	45 43.9	-54.4	8.2	73
41 51.0	-54.8	7.3	42 50.5	-54.7	7.4	43 50.0	-54.7	7.5	44 49.5	-54.6	7.6	74
40 56.2	-55.0	6.7	41 55.8	-54.9	6.8	42 55.3	-54.8	6.9	43 54.9	-54.8	7.1	75
40 01.2	-55.1	6.2	41 00.9	-55.1	6.3	42 00.5	-55.0	6.4	43 00.1	-54.9	6.5	76
39 06.1	-55.2	5.7	40 05.8	-55.2	5.8	41 05.5	-55.1	5.9	42 05.2	-55.1	6.0	77
38 10.9	-55.4	5.2	39 10.6	-55.3	5.3	40 10.4	-55.3	5.3	41 10.1	-55.2	5.4	78
37 15.5	-55.5	4.7	38 15.3	-55.5	4.8	39 15.1	-55.4	4.8	40 14.9	-55.4	4.9	79
36 20.0	-55.6	4.2	37 19.8	-55.5	4.3	38 19.7	-55.6	4.3	39 19.5	-55.5	4.4	80
35 24.4	-55.7	3.8	36 24.3	-55.7	3.8	37 24.1	-55.6	3.9	38 24.0	-55.6	3.9	81
34 28.7	-55.8	3.3	35 28.6	-55.8	3.4	36 28.5	-55.7	3.4	37 28.4	-55.7	3.4	82
33 32.9	-55.9	2.9	34 32.8	-55.8	2.9	35 32.8	-55.9	2.9	36 32.7	-55.8	3.0	83
32 37.0	-56.0	2.4	33 37.0	-56.0	2.5	34 36.9	-55.9	2.5	35 36.9	-56.0	2.5	84
31 41.0	-56.0	2.0	32 41.0	-56.0	2.0	33 41.0	-56.1	2.1	34 40.9	-56.0	2.1	85
30 45.0	-56.2	1.6	31 45.0	-56.2	1.6	32 44.9	-56.1	1.6	33 44.9	-56.1	1.6	86
29 48.8	-56.2	1.2	30 48.8	-56.2	1.2	31 48.8	-56.2	1.2	32 48.8	-56.2	1.2	87
28 52.6	-56.3	0.8	29 52.6	-56.3	0.8	30 52.6	-56.3	0.8	31 52.6	-56.3	0.8	88
27 56.3	-56.3	0.4	28 56.3	-56.3	0.4	29 56.3	-56.3	0.4	30 56.3	-56.3	0.4	89
27 00.0	-56.4	0.0	28 00.0	-56.4	0.0	29 00.0	-56.4	0.0	30 00.0	-56.4	0.0	90
27°			28°			29°			30°			

20°, 340° L.H.A. LATITUDE SAME NAME AS DECLINATION

LATITUDE **CONTRARY** NAME TO DECLINATION **L.H.A. 20°, 340°**

Dec.	23°			24°			25°			26°			27°			28°			29°			30°			Dec.
	Hc	d	Z	Hc	d	Z	Hc	d	Z	Hc	d	Z	Hc	d	Z	Hc	d	Z	Hc	d	Z	Hc	d	Z	
°	° ′	′	°	° ′	′	°	° ′	′	°	° ′	′	°	° ′	′	°	° ′	′	°	° ′	′	°	° ′	′	°	°
0	59 52.9	-47.1	137.0	59 08.6	-47.9	138.2	58 23.5	-48.7	139.3	57 37.7	-49.4	140.3	56 51.2	-50.1	141.3	56 04.1	-50.7	142.2	55 16.4	-51.3	143.1	54 28.1	-51.8	143.9	0
1	59 05.8	-47.7	138.3	58 20.7	-48.5	139.3	57 34.8	-49.2	140.4	56 48.3	-49.9	141.3	56 01.1	-50.5	142.3	55 13.4	-51.1	143.2	54 25.1	-51.6	144.0	53 36.3	-52.2	144.8	1
2	58 18.1	-48.3	139.4	57 32.2	-49.1	140.4	56 45.6	-49.7	141.4	55 58.4	-50.4	142.3	55 10.6	-50.9	143.2	54 22.3	-51.5	144.1	53 33.5	-52.1	144.9	52 44.1	-52.4	145.6	2
3	57 29.8	-48.9	140.5	56 43.1	-49.5	141.5	55 55.9	-50.2	142.4	55 08.0	-50.8	143.3	54 19.7	-51.4	144.1	53 30.8	-51.9	144.9	52 41.4	-52.3	145.7	51 51.7	-52.8	146.4	3
4	56 40.9	-49.4	141.6	55 53.6	-50.1	142.5	55 05.7	-50.7	143.4	54 17.2	-51.2	144.2	53 28.3	-51.7	145.0	52 38.9	-52.2	145.8	51 49.1	-52.7	146.5	50 58.9	-53.1	147.2	4
5	55 51.5	-49.9	142.6	55 03.5	-50.5	143.5	54 15.0	-51.0	144.3	53 26.0	-51.5	145.1	52 36.6	-52.1	145.9	51 46.7	-52.5	146.6	50 56.4	-52.9	147.3	50 05.8	-53.4	147.9	5
6	55 01.6	-50.4	143.6	54 13.0	-50.9	144.4	53 24.0	-51.5	145.2	52 34.5	-52.0	146.0	51 44.5	-52.4	146.7	50 54.2	-52.8	147.4	50 03.5	-53.2	148.0	49 12.4	-53.6	148.6	6
7	54 11.2	-50.8	144.5	53 22.1	-51.3	145.3	52 32.5	-51.8	146.1	51 42.5	-52.2	146.8	50 52.1	-52.7	147.5	50 01.4	-53.1	148.1	49 10.3	-53.5	148.7	48 18.8	-53.8	149.3	7
8	53 20.4	-51.2	145.4	52 30.8	-51.7	146.2	51 40.7	-52.1	146.9	50 50.3	-52.6	147.6	49 59.4	-52.9	148.2	49 08.3	-53.4	148.8	48 16.8	-53.7	149.4	47 25.0	-54.1	150.0	8
9	52 29.2	-51.5	146.3	51 39.1	-52.0	147.0	50 48.6	-52.4	147.7	49 57.7	-52.8	148.3	49 06.5	-53.3	148.9	48 14.9	-53.6	149.5	47 23.1	-54.0	150.1	46 30.9	-54.2	150.6	9
10	51 37.7	-51.9	147.1	50 47.1	-52.3	147.8	49 56.2	-52.8	148.4	49 04.9	-53.2	149.1	48 13.2	-53.4	149.6	47 21.3	-53.8	150.2	46 29.1	-54.1	150.7	45 36.7	-54.5	151.2	10
11	50 45.8	-52.2	147.9	49 54.8	-52.6	148.6	49 03.4	-53.0	149.2	48 11.7	-53.3	149.8	47 19.8	-53.7	150.3	46 27.5	-54.0	150.8	45 35.0	-54.3	151.3	44 42.2	-54.6	151.8	11
12	49 53.6	-52.5	148.7	49 02.2	-52.9	149.3	48 10.4	-53.2	149.9	47 18.4	-53.6	150.4	46 26.1	-54.0	151.0	45 33.5	-54.2	151.5	44 40.7	-54.6	151.9	43 47.6	-54.8	152.4	12
13	49 01.1	-52.7	149.5	48 09.3	-53.1	150.0	47 17.2	-53.5	150.6	46 24.8	-53.8	151.1	45 32.1	-54.1	151.6	44 39.3	-54.5	152.1	43 46.1	-54.7	152.5	42 52.8	-55.0	152.9	13
14	48 08.4	-53.1	150.2	47 16.2	-53.4	150.7	46 23.7	-53.7	151.2	45 31.0	-54.0	151.7	44 38.0	-54.3	152.2	43 44.8	-54.6	152.7	42 51.4	-54.8	153.1	41 57.8	-55.1	153.5	14
15	47 15.3	-53.2	150.9	46 22.8	-53.6	151.4	45 30.0	-53.9	151.9	44 37.0	-54.2	152.3	43 43.7	-54.5	152.8	42 50.2	-54.7	153.2	41 56.6	-55.0	153.6	41 02.7	-55.2	154.0	15
16	46 22.1	-53.5	151.5	45 29.2	-53.8	152.0	44 36.1	-54.1	152.5	43 42.8	-54.4	152.9	42 49.2	-54.6	153.4	41 55.5	-54.9	153.8	41 01.6	-55.2	154.2	40 07.5	-55.4	154.5	16
17	45 28.6	-53.8	152.2	44 35.4	-54.0	152.7	43 42.0	-54.3	153.1	42 48.4	-54.6	153.5	41 54.6	-54.9	153.9	41 00.6	-55.1	154.3	40 06.4	-55.3	154.7	39 12.1	-55.5	155.0	17
18	44 34.8	-53.9	152.8	43 41.4	-54.2	153.3	42 47.7	-54.5	153.7	41 53.8	-54.7	154.1	40 59.7	-54.9	154.5	40 05.5	-55.2	154.8	39 11.1	-55.4	155.2	38 16.6	-55.6	155.5	18
19	43 40.9	-54.1	153.4	42 47.2	-54.4	153.9	41 53.2	-54.6	154.3	40 59.1	-54.9	154.6	40 04.8	-55.1	155.0	39 10.3	-55.3	155.3	38 15.7	-55.5	155.7	37 21.0	-55.8	156.0	19
20	42 46.8	-54.3	154.0	41 52.8	-54.6	154.4	40 58.6	-54.8	154.8	40 04.2	-55.0	155.2	39 09.7	-55.3	155.5	38 15.0	-55.4	155.8	37 20.2	-55.7	156.2	36 25.2	-55.8	156.5	20
21	41 52.5	-54.4	154.6	40 58.2	-54.7	155.0	40 03.8	-54.9	155.3	39 09.2	-55.2	155.7	38 14.4	-55.3	156.0	37 19.6	-55.6	156.3	36 24.5	-55.7	156.6	35 29.4	-55.9	156.9	21
22	40 58.1	-54.6	155.2	40 03.5	-54.8	155.5	39 08.9	-55.1	155.9	38 14.0	-55.2	156.2	37 19.1	-55.5	156.5	36 24.0	-55.7	156.8	35 28.8	-55.9	157.1	34 33.5	-56.1	157.4	22
23	40 03.5	-54.8	155.7	39 08.7	-55.0	156.0	38 13.8	-55.2	156.4	37 18.8	-55.4	156.7	36 23.6	-55.6	157.0	35 28.3	-55.8	157.3	34 32.9	-55.9	157.5	33 37.4	-56.1	157.8	23
24	39 08.7	-54.9	156.2	38 13.7	-55.1	156.6	37 18.6	-55.3	156.9	36 23.4	-55.5	157.2	35 28.0	-55.7	157.4	34 32.5	-55.8	157.7	33 37.0	-56.1	158.0	32 41.3	-56.2	158.2	24
25	38 13.8	-55.0	156.8	37 18.6	-55.2	157.1	36 23.3	-55.4	157.4	35 27.9	-55.7	157.6	34 32.3	-55.8	157.9	33 36.7	-56.0	158.1	32 40.9	-56.1	158.4	31 45.1	-56.3	158.6	25
26	37 18.8	-55.2	157.3	36 23.4	-55.4	157.6	35 27.9	-55.6	157.8	34 32.2	-55.7	158.1	33 36.5	-55.9	158.3	32 40.7	-56.0	158.6	31 44.8	-56.2	158.8	30 48.8	-56.3	159.0	26
27	36 23.6	-55.3	157.8	35 28.0	-55.5	158.0	34 32.3	-55.6	158.3	33 36.5	-55.8	158.5	32 40.6	-55.9	158.8	31 44.7	-56.2	159.0	30 48.6	-56.3	159.2	29 52.5	-56.4	159.4	27
28	35 28.3	-55.4	158.2	34 32.5	-55.5	158.5	33 36.7	-55.8	158.7	32 40.7	-55.9	159.0	31 44.7	-56.1	159.2	30 48.5	-56.2	159.4	29 52.3	-56.3	159.6	28 56.1	-56.5	159.8	28
29	34 32.9	-55.5	158.7	33 37.0	-55.7	158.9	32 40.9	-55.8	159.2	31 44.8	-56.0	159.4	30 48.6	-56.1	159.6	29 52.3	-56.2	159.8	28 56.0	-56.4	160.0	27 59.6	-56.6	160.2	29
30	33 37.4	-55.6	159.2	32 41.3	-55.7	159.4	31 45.1	-55.9	159.6	30 48.8	-56.0	159.8	29 52.5	-56.2	160.0	28 56.1	-56.4	160.2	27 59.6	-56.5	160.4	27 03.0	-56.6	160.6	30
31	32 41.8	-55.6	159.6	31 45.6	-55.9	159.8	30 49.2	-56.0	160.0	29 52.8	-56.2	160.2	28 56.3	-56.3	160.4	27 59.7	-56.4	160.6	27 03.1	-56.6	160.8	26 06.4	-56.7	160.9	31
32	31 46.2	-55.8	160.1	30 49.7	-55.9	160.3	29 53.2	-56.1	160.5	28 56.6	-56.2	160.6	28 00.0	-56.4	160.8	27 03.3	-56.5	161.0	26 06.5	-56.6	161.2	25 09.7	-56.7	161.3	32
33	30 50.4	-55.9	160.5	29 53.8	-56.0	160.7	28 57.1	-56.1	160.9	28 00.4	-56.3	161.0	27 03.6	-56.4	161.2	26 06.8	-56.5	161.4	25 09.9	-56.6	161.5	24 13.0	-56.8	161.7	33
34	29 54.5	-55.9	160.9	28 57.8	-56.1	161.1	28 01.0	-56.2	161.3	27 04.1	-56.3	161.4	26 07.2	-56.4	161.6	25 10.3	-56.6	161.7	24 13.3	-56.7	161.9	23 16.2	-56.8	162.0	34
35	28 58.6	-56.0	161.3	28 01.7	-56.1	161.5	27 04.8	-56.3	161.7	26 07.8	-56.4	161.8	25 10.8	-56.6	162.0	24 13.7	-56.6	162.1	23 16.6	-56.8	162.2	22 19.4	-56.9	162.4	35
36	28 02.6	-56.1	161.7	27 05.6	-56.3	161.9	26 08.5	-56.3	162.0	25 11.4	-56.5	162.2	24 14.2	-56.5	162.3	23 17.1	-56.7	162.5	22 19.8	-56.8	162.6	21 22.5	-56.9	162.7	36
37	27 06.5	-56.2	162.1	26 09.3	-56.2	162.3	25 12.2	-56.4	162.4	24 14.9	-56.5	162.6	23 17.7	-56.7	162.7	22 20.4	-56.8	162.8	21 23.0	-56.8	162.9	20 25.6	-56.9	163.1	37
38	26 10.3	-56.2	162.5	25 13.1	-56.4	162.7	24 15.8	-56.5	162.8	23 18.4	-56.5	162.9	22 21.0	-56.6	163.1	21 23.6	-56.7	163.2	20 26.2	-56.9	163.3	19 28.7	-57.0	163.4	38
39	25 14.1	-56.3	162.9	24 16.7	-56.4	163.0	23 19.3	-56.5	163.2	22 21.9	-56.7	163.3	21 24.4	-56.7	163.4	20 26.9	-56.9	163.5	19 29.3	-56.9	163.6	18 31.7	-57.0	163.7	39
40	24 17.8	-56.3	163.3	23 20.3	-56.4	163.4	22 22.8	-56.5	163.5	21 25.2	-56.6	163.7	20 27.7	-56.8	163.8	19 30.0	-56.8	163.9	18 32.4	-57.0	164.0	17 34.7	-57.0	164.0	40
41	23 21.5	-56.4	163.7	22 23.9	-56.5	163.8	21 26.3	-56.6	163.9	20 28.6	-56.7	164.0	19 30.9	-56.8	164.1	18 33.2	-56.9	164.2	17 35.4	-57.0	164.3	16 37.7	-57.1	164.4	41
42	22 25.1	-56.4	164.0	21 27.4	-56.6	164.2	20 29.7	-56.7	164.3	19 31.9	-56.7	164.4	18 34.1	-56.8	164.4	17 36.3	-56.9	164.5	16 38.4	-57.0	164.6	15 40.6	-57.1	164.7	42
43	21 28.7	-56.5	164.4	20 30.8	-56.5	164.5	19 33.0	-56.7	164.6	18 35.2	-56.8	164.7	17 37.3	-56.9	164.8	16 39.4	-57.0	164.9	15 41.4	-57.0	164.9	14 43.5	-57.1	165.0	43
44	20 32.2	-56.6	164.8	19 34.3	-56.7	164.9	18 36.3	-56.7	165.0	17 38.4	-56.8	165.0	16 40.4	-56.9	165.1	15 42.4	-57.0	165.2	14 44.4	-57.1	165.3	13 46.4	-57.2	165.3	44
45	19 35.6	-56.5	165.1	18 37.6	-56.6	165.2	17 39.6	-56.7	165.3	16 41.6	-56.9	165.4	15 43.5	-56.9	165.4	14 45.4	-57.0	165.5	13 47.3	-57.1	165.6	12 49.2	-57.2	165.6	45
46	18 39.1	-56.6	165.5	17 41.0	-56.7	165.6	16 42.9	-56.8	165.6	15 44.7	-56.8	165.7	14 46.6	-57.0	165.8	13 48.4	-57.0	165.8	12 50.2	-57.1	165.9	11 52.0	-57.2	165.9	46
47	17 42.5	-56.7	165.8	16 44.3	-56.6	165.9	15 46.1	-56.8	166.0	14 47.9	-56.9	166.0	13 49.6	-57.0	166.1	12 51.4	-57.1	166.2	11 53.1	-57.1	166.2	10 54.8	-57.2	166.3	47
48	16 45.8	-56.7	166.2	15 47.5	-56.7	166.2	14 49.3	-56.9	166.3	13 51.0	-57.0	166.4	12 52.6	-57.0	166.4	11 54.3	-57.1	166.5	10 56.0	-57.2	166.5	9 57.6	-57.2	166.6	48
49	15 49.1	-56.7	166.5	14 50.8	-56.8	166.6	13 52.4	-56.9	166.6	12 54.0	-56.9	166.7	11 55.6	-57.0	166.7	10 57.2	-57.1	166.8	9 58.8	-57.2	166.8	9 00.4	-57.3	166.9	49
50	14 52.4	-56.7	166.9	13 54.0	-56.8	166.9	12 55.5	-56.9	167.0	11 57.1	-57.0	167.0	10 58.6	-57.0	167.1	10 00.1	-57.1	167.1	9 01.6	-57.2	167.1	8 03.1	-57.2	167.2	50
51	13 55.7	-56.8	167.2	12 57.2	-56.9	167.2	11 58.6	-56.9	167.3	11 00.1	-57.0	167.3	10 01.6	-57.1	167.4	9 03.0	-57.1	167.4	8 04.4	-57.2	167.4	7 05.9	-57.3	167.5	51
52	12 58.9	-56.8	167.5	12 00.3	-56.8	167.6	11 01.7	-56.9	167.6	10 03.1	-57.0	167.7	9 04.5	-57.1	167.7	8 05.9	-57.2	167.7	7 07.2	-57.2	167.7	6 08.6	-57.3	167.8	52
53	12 02.1	-56.8	167.9	11 03.5	-56.9	167.9	10 04.8	-57.0	167.9	9 06.1	-57.0	168.0	8 07.4	-57.1	168.0	7 08.7	-57.1	168.0	6 10.0	-57.2	168.1	5 11.3	-57.3	168.1	53
54	11 05.3	-56.8	168.2	10 06.6	-56.9	168.2	9 07.8	-56.9	168.3	8 09.1	-57.1	168.3	7 10.3	-57.1	168.3	6 11.6	-57.2	168.3	5 12.8	-57.2	168.4	4 14.0	-57.3	168.4	54
55	10 08.5	-56.9	168.5	9 09.7	-57.0	168.5	8 10.9	-57.0	168.6	7 12.0	-57.0	168.6	6 13.2	-57.1	168.6	5 14.4	-57.2	168.6	4 15.6	-57.3	168.7	3 16.7	-57.3	168.7	55
56	9 11.6	-56.9	168.8	8 12.7	-56.9	168.9	7 13.9	-57.0	168.9	6 15.0	-57.1	168.9	5 16.1	-57.1	168.9	4 17.2	-57.2	168.9	3 18.3	-57.2	169.0	2 19.4	-57.3	169.0	56
57	8 14.7	-56.9	169.2	7 15.8	-57.0	169.2	6 16.9	-57.1	169.2	5 17.9	-57.1	169.2	4 19.0	-57.2	169.2	3 20.0	-57.2	169.2	2 21.1	-57.3	169.3	1 22.1	-57.3	169.3	57
58	7 17.8	-56.9	169.5	6 18.8	-56.9	169.5	5 19.8	-57.0	169.5	4 20.8	-57.0	169.5	3 21.8	-57.1	169.5	2 22.8	-57.2	169.5	1 23.8	-57.2	169.6	0 24.8	-57.3	169.6	58
59	6 20.9	-56.9	169.8	5 21.9	-57.0	169.8	4 22.8	-57.0	169.8	3 23.8	-57.1	169.8	2 24.7	-57.1	169.8	1 25.6	-57.2	169.9	0 26.6	-57.3	169.9	0 32.5	+57.3	10.1	59
60	5 24.0	-56.9	170.1	4 24.9	-57.0	170.1	3 25.8	-57.0	170.1	2 26.7	-57.1	170.1	1 27.6	-57.2	170.2	0 28.4	-57.1	170.2	0 30.7	+57.2	9.8	1 29.8	+57.3	9.8	60
61	4 27.1	-56.9	170.4	3 27.9	-57.0	170.4	2 28.8	-57.1	170.4	1 29.6	-57.1	170.5	0 30.4	-57.1	170.5	0 28.7	+57.2	9.5	1 27.9	+57.3	9.5	2 27.1	+57.3	9.6	61
62	3 30.2	-57.0	170.7	2 30.9	-57.0	170.8	1 31.7	-57.0	170.8	0 32.5	-57.1	170.8	0 26.7	+57.2	9.2	1 25.9	+57.2	9.2	2 25.2	+57.2	9.2	3 24.4	+57.3	9.3	62
63	2 33.2	-56.9	171.1	1 33.9	-57.0	171.1	0 34.7	-57.1	171.1	0 24.6	+57.1	8.9	1 23.9	+57.1	8.9	2 23.1	+57.2	8.9	3 22.4	+57.3	8.9	4 21.7	+57.3	9.0	63
64	1 36.3	-57.0	171.4	0 36.9	-56.9	171.4	0 22.4	+57.0	8.6	1 21.7	+57.1	8.6	2 21.0	+57.2	8.6	3 20.3	+57.2	8.6	4 19.7	+57.2	8.6	5 19.0	+57.2	8.7	64
65	0 39.3	-56.9	171.7	0 20.0	+57.0	8.3	1 19.4	+57.1	8.3	2 18.8	+57.1	8.3	3 18.2	+57.1	8.3	4 17.5	+57.2	8.3	5 16.9	+57.2	8.3	6 16.2	+57.3	8.4	65
66	0 17.6	+57.0	8.0	1 17.0	+57.0	8.0	2 16.5	+57.0	8.0	3 15.9	+57.1	8.0	4 15.3	+57.1	8.0	5 14.7	+57.2	8.0	6 14.1	+57.2	8.0	7 13.5	+57.3	8.1	66
67	1 14.6	+56.9	7.7	2 14.0	+57.0	7.7	3 13.5	+57.0	7.7	4 13.0	+57.0	7.7	5 12.4	+57.1	7.7	6 11.9	+57.2	7.7	7 11.3	+57.2	7.7	8 10.8	+57.2	7.8	67
68	2 11.5	+57.0	7.4	3 11.0	+57.0	7.4	4 10.5	+57.1	7.4	5 10.0	+57.1	7.4	6 09.5	+57.1	7.4	7 09.0	+57.2	7.4	8 08.5	+57.2	7.4	9 08.0	+57.2	7.5	68
69	3 08.5	+56.9	7.1	4 08.0	+57.0	7.1	5 07.6	+57.0	7.1	6 07.1	+57.0	7.1	7 06.6	+57.1	7.1	8 06.2	+57.1	7.1	9 05.7	+57.2	7.1	10 05.2	+57.3	7.2	69
70	4 05.4	+56.9	6.7	5 05.0	+56.9	6.7	6 04.6	+57.0	6.8	7 04.1	+57.1	6.8	8 03.7	+57.1	6.8	9 03.3	+57.1	6.8	10 02.9	+57.1	6.8	11 02.5	+57.2	6.8	70
71	5 02.3	+56.9	6.4	6 01.9	+57.0	6.4	7 01.6	+57.0	6.4	8 01.2	+57.0	6.5	9 00.8	+57.1	6.5	10 00.4	+57.1	6.5	11 00.0	+57.2	6.5	11 59.7	+57.1	6.5	71
72	5 59.2	+57.0	6.1	6 58.9	+56.9	6.1	7 58.6	+56.9	6.1	8 58.2	+57.0	6.1	9 57.9	+57.0	6.2	10 57.5	+57.1	6.2	11 57.2	+57.1	6.2	12 56.8	+57.2	6.2	72
73	6 56.2	+56.8	5.8	7 55.8	+57.0	5.8	8 55.5	+57.0	5.8	9 55.2	+57.0	5.8	10 54.9	+57.0	5.8	11 54.6	+57.1	5.9	12 54.3	+57.1	5.9	13 54.0	+57.1	5.9	73
74	7 53.1	+56.8	5.5	8 52.8	+56.9	5.5	9 52.5	+56.9	5.5	10 52.2	+57.0	5.5	11 51.9	+57.1	5.5	12 51.7	+57.0	5.5	13 51.4	+57.1	5.6	14 51.1	+57.1	5.6	74
75	8 49.9	+56.9	5.1	9 49.7	+56.9	5.2	10 49.4	+57.0	5.2	11 49.2	+57.0	5.2	12 49.0	+56.9	5.2	13 48.7	+57.0	5.2	14 48.5	+57.0	5.3	15 48.2	+57.1	5.3	75
76	9 46.8	+56.8	4.8	10 46.6	+56.9	4.8	11 46.4	+56.9	4.8	12 46.2	+56.9	4.9	13 45.9	+57.0	4.9	14 45.7	+57.0	4.9	15 45.5	+57.0	4.9	16 45.3	+57.0	5.0	76
77	10 43.6	+56.9	4.5	11 43.5	+56.8	4.5	12 43.3	+56.8	4.5	13 43.1	+56.9	4.5	14 42.9	+56.9	4.6	15 42.7	+57.0	4.6	16 42.5	+57.0	4.6	17 42.3	+57.0	4.6	77
78	11 40.5	+56.8	4.2	12 40.3	+56.8	4.2	13 40.1	+56.9	4.2	14 40.0	+56.9	4.2	15 39.8	+56.9	4.2	16 39.7	+56.9	4.3	17 39.5	+56.9	4.3	18 39.3	+57.0	4.3	78
79	12 37.3	+56.8	3.8	13 37.1	+56.8	3.9	14 37.0	+56.8	3.9	15 36.9	+56.8	3.9	16 36.7	+56.9	3.9	17 36.6	+56.9	3.9	18 36.4	+57.0	3.9	19 36.3	+56.9	4.0	79
80	13 34.1	+56.7	3.5	14 33.9	+56.8	3.5	15 33.8	+56.8	3.5	16 33.7	+56.8	3.6	17 33.6	+56.8	3.6	18 33.5	+56.8	3.6	19 33.4	+56.8	3.6	20 33.2	+56.9	3.6	80
81	14 30.8	+56.7	3.2	15 30.7	+56.8	3.2	16 30.6	+56.8	3.2	17 30.5	+56.8	3.2	18 30.4	+56.8	3.2	19 30.3	+56.9	3.3	20 30.2	+56.9	3.3	21 30.1	+56.9	3.3	81
82	15 27.5	+56.7	2.8	16 27.5	+56.7	2.8	17 27.4	+56.7	2.9	18 27.3	+56.7	2.9	19 27.2	+56.8	2.9	20 27.2	+56.7	2.9	21 27.1	+56.8	2.9	22 27.0	+56.8	3.0	82
83	16 24.2	+56.7	2.5	17 24.2	+56.6	2.5	18 24.1	+56.7	2.5	19 24.0	+56.8	2.5	20 24.0	+56.7	2.5	21 23.9	+56.8	2.6	22 23.9	+56.7	2.6	23 23.8	+56.8	2.6	83
84	17 20.9	+56.6	2.1	18 20.8	+56.7	2.2	19 20.8	+56.6	2.2	20 20.8	+56.6	2.2	21 20.7	+56.7	2.2	22 20.7	+56.7	2.2	23 20.6	+56.7	2.2	24 20.6	+56.7	2.2	84
85	18 17.5	+56.6	1.8	19 17.5	+56.6	1.8	20 17.4	+56.7	1.8	21 17.4	+56.6	1.8	22 17.4	+56.6	1.8	23 17.4	+56.6	1.9	24 17.3	+56.7	1.9	25 17.3	+56.6	1.9	85
86	19 14.1	+56.5	1.4	20 14.1	+56.5	1.5	21 14.1	+56.5	1.5	22 14.0	+56.6	1.5	23 14.0	+56.6	1.5	24 14.0	+56.6	1.5	25 14.0	+56.6	1.5	26 13.9	+56.7	1.5	86
87	20 10.6	+56.5	1.1	21 10.6	+56.5	1.1	22 10.6	+56.5	1.1	23 10.6	+56.5	1.1	24 10.6	+56.5	1.1	25 10.6	+56.5	1.1	26 10.6	+56.5	1.1	27 10.6	+56.5	1.2	87
88	21 07.1	+56.5	0.7	22 07.1	+56.5	0.7	23 07.1	+56.5	0.7	24 07.1	+56.5	0.7	25 07.1	+56.5	0.8	26 07.1	+56.5	0.8	27 07.1	+56.5	0.8	28 07.1	+56.5	0.8	88
89	22 03.6	+56.4	0.4	23 03.6	+56.4	0.4	24 03.6	+56.4	0.4	25 03.6	+56.4	0.4	26 03.6	+56.4	0.4	27 03.6	+56.4	0.4	28 03.6	+56.4	0.4	29 03.6	+56.4	0.4	89
90	23 00.0	+56.4	0.0	24 00.0	+56.4	0.0	25 00.0	+56.4	0.0	26 00.0	+56.4	0.0	27 00.0	+56.3	0.0	28 00.0	+56.3	0.0	29 00.0	+56.3	0.0	30 00.0	+56.3	0.0	90
	23°			24°			25°			26°			27°			28°			29°			30°			

S. Lat. { L.H.A. greater than 180° ....Zn=180°−Z
L.H.A. less than 180°...........Zn=180°+Z

LATITUDE **SAME** NAME AS DECLINATION **L.H.A. 160°, 200°**

225

21°, 339° L.H.A. LATITUDE SAME NAME AS DECLINATION

N. Lat. {L.H.A. greater than 180° .....Zn=Z; L.H.A. less than 180°............Zn=360°–Z}

Dec.	23° Hc	d	Z	24° Hc	d	Z	25° Hc	d	Z	26° Hc	d	Z	27° Hc	d	Z	28° Hc	d	Z	29° Hc	d	Z	30° Hc	d	Z	Dec.
°	° ′	′	°	° ′	′	°	° ′	′	°	° ′	′	°	° ′	′	°	° ′	′	°	° ′	′	°	° ′	′	°	°
0	59 14.7	+45.5	135.5	58 31.5	+46.4	136.7	57 47.5	+47.2	137.8	57 02.7	+48.1	138.8	56 17.2	+48.8	139.8	55 31.1	+49.5	140.7	54 44.3	+50.2	141.6	53 57.0	+50.8	142.5	0
1	60 00.2	+44.7	134.2	59 17.9	+45.7	135.4	58 34.7	+46.6	136.6	57 50.8	+47.4	137.7	57 06.0	+48.3	138.7	56 20.6	+49.0	139.7	55 34.5	+49.7	140.7	54 47.8	+50.3	141.6	1
2	60 44.9	+43.8	132.9	60 03.6	+44.9	134.1	59 21.3	+45.9	135.4	58 38.2	+46.8	136.5	57 54.3	+47.6	137.6	57 09.6	+48.4	138.7	56 24.2	+49.2	139.7	55 38.1	+49.9	140.6	2
3	61 28.7	+42.9	131.5	60 48.5	+44.0	132.8	60 07.2	+45.1	134.1	59 25.0	+46.1	135.3	58 41.9	+47.0	136.5	57 58.0	+47.9	137.6	57 13.4	+48.6	138.6	56 28.0	+49.4	139.6	3
4	62 11.6	+41.9	130.0	61 32.5	+43.1	131.4	60 52.3	+44.3	132.7	60 11.1	+45.3	134.0	59 28.9	+46.3	135.3	58 45.9	+47.2	136.4	58 02.0	+48.1	137.5	57 17.4	+48.8	138.6	4
5	62 53.5	+40.9	128.4	62 15.6	+42.2	129.9	61 36.6	+43.3	131.3	60 56.4	+44.5	132.7	60 15.2	+45.5	134.0	59 33.1	+46.5	135.2	58 50.1	+47.4	136.4	58 06.2	+48.3	137.5	5
6	63 34.4	+39.6	126.8	62 57.8	+41.0	128.4	62 19.9	+42.4	129.9	61 40.9	+43.6	131.3	61 00.7	+44.8	132.7	60 19.6	+45.7	134.0	59 37.5	+46.7	135.2	58 54.5	+47.6	136.4	6
7	64 14.0	+38.5	125.1	63 38.8	+40.0	126.7	63 02.3	+41.3	128.3	62 24.5	+42.6	129.8	61 45.5	+43.8	131.3	61 05.3	+45.0	132.6	60 24.2	+46.0	133.9	59 42.1	+47.0	135.2	7
8	64 52.5	+37.1	123.3	64 18.8	+38.7	125.0	63 43.6	+40.2	126.7	63 07.1	+41.6	128.3	62 29.3	+42.8	129.8	61 50.3	+44.1	131.2	61 10.2	+45.2	132.6	60 29.1	+46.2	133.9	8
9	65 29.6	+35.6	121.4	64 57.5	+37.3	123.3	64 23.8	+38.9	125.0	63 48.7	+40.4	126.7	63 12.1	+41.9	128.3	62 34.4	+43.1	129.8	61 55.4	+44.3	131.2	61 15.3	+45.4	132.6	9
10	66 05.2	+34.1	119.5	65 34.8	+35.9	121.4	65 02.7	+37.6	123.2	64 29.1	+39.2	125.0	63 54.0	+40.7	126.7	63 17.5	+42.1	128.3	62 39.7	+43.4	129.8	62 00.7	+44.6	131.2	10
11	66 39.3	+32.3	117.4	66 10.7	+34.3	119.4	65 40.3	+36.2	121.4	65 08.3	+37.9	123.2	64 34.7	+39.4	125.0	63 59.6	+40.9	126.7	63 23.1	+42.3	128.3	62 45.3	+43.6	129.8	11
12	67 11.6	+30.6	115.3	66 45.0	+32.7	117.4	66 16.5	+34.6	119.4	65 46.2	+36.4	121.3	65 14.1	+38.2	123.2	64 40.5	+39.8	125.0	64 05.4	+41.2	126.7	63 28.9	+42.6	128.3	12
13	67 42.2	+28.7•	113.0	67 17.7	+30.9	115.2	66 51.1	+33.0	117.3	66 22.6	+34.9	119.4	65 52.3	+36.7	121.3	65 20.3	+38.4	123.2	64 46.6	+40.1	125.0	64 11.5	+41.5	126.7	13
14	68 10.9	+26.6•	110.7	67 48.6	+28.9•	113.0	67 24.1	+31.1	115.2	66 57.5	+33.3	117.3	66 29.0	+35.2	119.4	65 58.7	+37.0	121.3	65 26.7	+38.7	123.2	64 53.0	+40.3	125.0	14
15	68 37.5	+24.4•	108.2	68 17.5	+26.9•	110.6	67 55.2	+29.2	112.9	67 30.8	+31.4	115.2	67 04.2	+33.5	117.3	66 35.7	+35.5	119.4	66 05.4	+37.3	121.3	65 33.3	+39.1	123.2	15
16	69 01.9	+22.0•	105.7	68 44.4	+24.6•	108.2	68 24.4	+27.2•	110.6	68 02.2	+29.5	112.9	67 37.7	+31.8	115.2	67 11.2	+33.8	117.3	66 42.7	+35.8	119.4	66 12.4	+37.6	121.4	16
17	69 23.9	+19.7•	103.1	69 09.0	+22.4•	105.7	68 51.6	+25.0•	108.1	68 31.7	+27.5•	110.6	68 09.5	+29.8•	112.9	67 45.0	+32.1	115.2	67 18.5	+34.1	117.3	66 50.0	+36.1	119.4	17
18	69 43.6	+17.0•	100.4	69 31.4	+19.9•	103.0	69 16.6	+22.6•	105.6	68 59.2	+25.2•	108.1	68 39.3	+27.7•	110.5	68 17.1	+30.1•	112.9	67 52.6	+32.4	115.2	67 26.1	+34.4	117.4	18
19	70 00.6	+14.4•	97.6	69 51.3	+17.3•	100.3	69 39.2	+20.2•	103.0	69 24.4	+22.9•	105.6	69 07.0	+25.6•	108.1	68 47.2	+28.0•	110.5	68 25.0	+30.4•	112.9	68 00.5	+32.7	115.2	19
20	70 15.0	+11.6•	94.7	70 08.6	+14.6•	97.5	69 59.4	+17.5•	100.2	69 47.3	+20.5•	102.9	69 32.6	+23.2•	105.5	69 15.2	+25.9•	108.1	68 55.4	+28.4•	110.5	68 33.2	+30.7•	112.9	20
21	70 26.6	+8.8•	91.8	70 23.2	+11.9•	94.6	70 16.9	+14.9•	97.4	70 07.8	+17.8•	100.2	69 55.8	+20.7•	102.9	69 41.1	+23.5•	105.5	69 23.8	+26.1•	108.1	69 03.9	+28.7•	110.6	21
22	70 35.4	+5.8•	88.9	70 35.1	+8.9•	91.7	70 31.8	+12.1•	94.5	70 25.6	+15.1•	97.3	70 16.5	+18.1•	100.1	70 04.6	+21.0•	102.8	69 49.9	+23.8•	105.5	69 32.6	+26.4•	108.1	22
23	70 41.2	+2.8•	85.9	70 44.0	+6.0•	88.7	70 43.9	+9.1•	91.6	70 40.7	+12.3•	94.4	70 34.6	+15.4•	97.3	70 25.6	+18.4•	100.0	70 13.7	+21.3•	102.8	69 59.0	+24.1•	105.5	23
24	70 44.0	−0.1•	82.8	70 50.0	+3.0•	85.7	70 53.0	+6.2•	88.6	70 53.0	+9.4•	91.5	70 50.0	+12.5•	94.3	70 44.0	+15.6•	97.2	70 35.0	+18.6•	100.0	70 23.1	+21.6•	102.8	24
25	70 43.9	−3.2•	79.8	70 53.0	0.0•	82.6	70 59.2	+3.2•	85.5	71 02.4	+6.4•	88.4	71 02.5	+9.6•	91.3	70 59.6	+12.7•	94.2	70 53.6	+15.9•	97.1	70 44.7	+19.0•	100.0	25
26	70 40.7	−6.1•	76.8	70 53.0	−3.0•	79.6	71 02.4	+0.1•	82.5	71 08.8	+3.3•	85.4	71 12.1	+6.5•	88.3	71 12.3	+9.8•	91.2	71 09.5	+13.0•	94.2	71 03.7	+16.1•	97.1	26
27	70 34.6	−9.0•	73.8	70 50.0	−6.0•	76.5	71 02.5	−2.9•	79.4	71 12.1	+0.2•	82.3	71 18.6	+3.5•	85.2	71 22.1	+6.8•	88.1	71 22.5	+10.0•	91.1	71 19.8	+13.2•	94.1	27
28	70 25.6	−11.9•	70.8	70 44.0	−9.0•	73.5	70 59.6	−6.0•	76.3	71 12.3	−2.8•	79.2	71 22.1	+0.4•	82.1	71 28.9	+3.6•	85.0	71 32.5	+6.9•	88.0	71 33.0	+10.2•	91.0	28
29	70 13.7	−14.7•	67.9	70 35.0	−11.9•	70.5	70 53.6	−8.9•	73.3	71 09.5	−5.8•	76.1	71 22.5	−2.7•	78.9	71 32.5	+0.5•	81.9	71 39.4	+3.8•	84.9	71 43.2	+7.1•	87.9	29
30	69 59.0	−17.3•	65.1	70 23.1	−14.6•	67.6	70 44.7	−11.8•	70.2	71 03.7	−8.9•	73.0	71 19.8	−5.8•	75.8	71 33.0	−2.6•	78.7	71 43.2	+0.7•	81.7	71 50.3	+4.0•	84.7	30
31	69 41.7	−19.9•	62.3	70 08.5	−17.3•	64.7	70 32.9	−14.6•	67.3	70 54.8	−11.8•	69.9	71 14.0	−8.8•	72.7	71 30.4	−5.7•	75.6	71 43.9	−2.6•	78.5	71 54.3	+0.7•	81.5	31
32	69 21.8	−22.3•	59.6	69 51.2	−19.9•	61.9	70 18.3	−17.4•	64.4	70 43.0	−14.7•	67.0	71 05.2	−11.8•	69.6	71 24.7	−8.8•	72.4	71 41.3	−5.6•	75.3	71 55.0	−2.4•	78.3	32
33	68 59.5	−24.6•	57.0	69 31.3	−22.4•	59.2	70 00.9	−19.9•	61.6	70 28.3	−17.4•	64.0	70 53.4	−14.7•	66.6	71 15.9	−11.8•	69.3	71 35.7	−8.8•	72.2	71 52.6	−5.6•	75.1	33
34	68 34.9	−26.8•	54.4	69 08.9	−24.7•	56.6	69 41.0	−22.5•	58.8	70 10.9	−20.0•	61.2	70 38.7	−17.4•	63.7	71 04.1	−14.7•	66.3	71 26.9	−11.8•	69.0	71 47.0	−8.8•	71.9	34
35	68 08.1	−28.8•	52.0	68 44.2	−26.9•	54.0	69 18.5	−24.8•	56.2	69 50.9	−22.5•	58.4	70 21.3	−20.1•	60.8	70 49.4	−17.5•	63.3	71 15.1	−14.8•	66.0	71 38.2	−11.8•	68.7	35
36	67 39.3	−30.8	49.7	68 17.3	−28.9•	51.6	68 53.7	−26.9•	53.6	69 28.4	−24.8•	55.8	70 01.2	−22.6•	58.0	70 31.9	−20.2•	60.4	71 00.3	−17.5•	63.0	71 26.4	−14.8•	65.6	36
37	67 08.5	−32.6	47.5	67 48.4	−30.9	49.3	68 26.8	−29.1•	51.2	69 03.6	−27.1•	53.2	69 38.6	−25.0•	55.4	70 11.7	−22.7•	57.6	70 42.8	−20.3•	60.1	71 11.6	−17.7•	62.6	37
38	66 35.9	−34.2	45.3	67 17.5	−32.7	47.0	67 57.7	−31.0	48.8	68 36.5	−29.2•	50.7	69 13.6	−27.2•	52.8	69 49.0	−25.1•	54.9	70 22.5	−22.8•	57.2	70 53.9	−20.3•	59.7	38
39	66 01.7	−35.8	43.3	66 44.8	−34.3	44.9	67 26.7	−32.8	46.6	68 07.3	−31.1	48.4	68 46.4	−29.3•	50.3	69 23.9	−27.3•	52.3	69 59.7	−25.2•	54.5	70 33.6	−23.0•	56.8	39
40	65 25.9	−37.2	41.3	66 10.5	−35.9	42.8	66 53.9	−34.5	44.4	67 36.2	−33.0	46.1	68 17.1	−31.3	47.9	68 56.6	−29.5•	49.8	69 34.5	−27.5•	51.9	70 10.6	−25.4•	54.1	40
41	64 48.7	−38.6	39.5	65 34.6	−37.4	40.9	66 19.8	−36.0	42.3	67 03.2	−34.6	43.9	67 45.8	−33.1	45.6	68 27.1	−31.4	47.4	69 07.0	−29.6•	49.4	69 45.2	−27.6•	51.4	41
42	64 10.1	−39.8	37.7	64 57.2	−38.7	39.0	65 43.4	−37.5	40.4	66 28.6	−36.2	41.9	67 12.7	−34.7	43.4	67 55.7	−33.3	45.1	68 37.4	−31.6	46.9	69 17.6	−29.8•	48.9	42
43	63 30.3	−40.9	36.0	64 18.5	−39.9	37.2	65 05.9	−38.8	38.5	65 52.4	−37.6	39.9	66 38.0	−36.4	41.4	67 22.4	−34.9	42.9	68 05.8	−33.5	44.6	68 47.8	−31.8	46.4	43
44	62 49.4	−42.0	34.4	63 38.6	−41.1	35.5	64 27.1	−40.1	36.7	65 14.8	−39.0	38.0	66 01.6	−37.8	39.4	66 47.5	−36.5	40.9	67 32.3	−35.1	42.4	68 16.0	−33.6	44.1	44
45	62 07.4	−43.0	32.8	62 57.5	−42.2	33.9	63 47.0	−41.3	35.0	64 35.8	−40.3	36.2	65 23.8	−39.2	37.5	66 11.0	−38.0	38.9	66 57.2	−36.7	40.3	67 42.4	−35.3	41.9	45
46	61 24.4	−44.0	31.3	62 15.3	−43.1	32.3	63 05.7	−42.2	33.4	63 55.5	−41.4	34.5	64 44.6	−40.4	35.7	65 33.0	−39.4	37.0	66 20.5	−38.2	38.3	67 07.1	−37.0	39.8	46
47	60 40.4	−44.7	29.9	61 32.2	−44.0	30.9	62 23.5	−43.3	31.8	63 14.1	−42.4	32.9	64 04.2	−41.5	34.0	64 53.6	−40.6	35.2	65 42.3	−39.5	36.4	66 30.1	−38.3	37.8	47
48	59 55.7	−45.6	28.6	60 48.2	−44.9	29.4	61 40.2	−44.2	30.4	62 31.7	−43.4	31.3	63 22.7	−42.6	32.4	64 13.0	−41.7	33.5	65 02.8	−40.8	34.6	65 51.8	−39.8	35.9	48
49	59 10.1	−46.2	27.3	60 03.3	−45.7	28.1	60 56.0	−45.0	28.9	61 48.3	−44.4	29.8	62 40.1	−43.6	30.8	63 31.3	−42.8	31.8	64 22.0	−41.9	32.9	65 12.0	−40.9	34.1	49
50	58 23.9	−47.0	26.1	59 17.6	−46.4	26.8	60 11.0	−45.9	27.6	61 03.9	−45.2	28.4	61 56.5	−44.5	29.3	62 48.5	−43.7	30.3	63 40.1	−43.0	31.3	64 31.1	−42.1	32.4	50
51	57 36.9	−47.6	24.9	58 31.2	−47.1	25.6	59 25.1	−46.5	26.3	60 18.7	−45.9	27.1	61 12.0	−45.4	27.9	62 04.8	−44.7	28.8	62 57.1	−43.9	29.7	63 49.0	−43.2	30.7	51
52	56 49.3	−48.1	23.8	57 44.1	−47.7	24.4	58 38.6	−47.2	25.1	59 32.8	−46.7	25.8	60 26.6	−46.1	26.6	61 20.1	−45.5	27.4	62 13.2	−44.9	28.3	63 05.8	−44.1	29.2	52
53	56 01.2	−48.7	22.7	56 56.4	−48.3	23.3	57 51.4	−47.8	23.9	58 46.1	−47.3	24.6	59 40.5	−46.8	25.3	60 34.6	−46.3	26.0	61 28.3	−45.6	26.8	62 21.7	−45.1	27.7	53
54	55 12.5	−49.2	21.7	56 08.1	−48.8	22.2	57 03.6	−48.4	22.8	57 58.8	−48.0	23.4	58 53.7	−47.5	24.1	59 48.3	−47.0	24.8	60 42.7	−46.5	25.5	61 36.6	−45.8	26.3	54
55	54 23.3	−49.7	20.7	55 19.3	−49.3	21.2	56 15.2	−49.0	21.7	57 10.8	−48.5	22.3	58 06.2	−48.1	22.9	59 01.3	−47.6	23.5	59 56.2	−47.1	24.2	60 50.8	−46.6	25.0	55
56	53 33.6	−50.1	19.7	54 30.0	−49.8	20.2	55 26.2	−49.4	20.7	56 22.3	−49.1	21.2	57 18.1	−48.7	21.8	58 13.7	−48.3	22.4	59 09.1	−47.8	23.0	60 04.2	−47.4	23.7	56
57	52 43.5	−50.5	18.8	53 40.2	−50.2	19.2	54 36.8	−49.9	19.7	55 33.2	−49.6	20.2	56 29.4	−49.2	20.7	57 25.4	−48.8	21.3	58 21.3	−48.5	21.8	59 16.8	−47.9	22.5	57
58	51 53.0	−50.9	17.9	52 50.0	−50.6	18.3	53 46.9	−50.3	18.7	54 43.6	−50.0	19.2	55 40.2	−49.7	19.7	56 36.6	−49.3	20.2	57 32.8	−48.9	20.7	58 28.9	−48.6	21.3	58
59	51 02.1	−51.3	17.1	51 59.4	−51.0	17.4	52 56.6	−50.8	17.8	53 53.6	−50.4	18.3	54 50.5	−50.1	18.7	55 47.3	−49.9	19.2	56 43.9	−49.5	19.7	57 40.3	−49.2	20.2	59
60	50 10.8	−51.6	16.2	51 08.4	−51.4	16.6	52 05.8	−51.1	17.0	53 03.2	−50.9	17.3	54 00.4	−50.6	17.8	54 57.4	−50.2	18.2	55 54.4	−50.0	18.6	56 51.1	−49.6	19.1	60
61	49 19.2	−51.9	15.5	50 17.0	−51.7	15.8	51 14.7	−51.4	16.1	52 12.3	−51.2	16.5	53 09.8	−51.0	16.8	54 07.2	−50.8	17.2	55 04.4	−50.4	17.7	56 01.5	−50.1	18.1	61
62	48 27.3	−52.2	14.7	49 25.3	−52.0	15.0	50 23.3	−51.8	15.3	51 21.1	−51.6	15.6	52 18.8	−51.3	16.0	53 16.4	−51.1	16.3	54 14.0	−50.9	16.7	55 11.4	−50.6	17.1	62
63	47 35.1	−52.4	14.0	48 33.3	−52.2	14.2	49 31.5	−52.1	14.5	50 29.5	−51.9	14.8	51 27.5	−51.7	15.1	52 25.3	−51.4	15.5	53 23.1	−51.2	15.8	54 20.8	−51.0	16.2	63
64	46 42.7	−52.7	13.2	47 41.1	−52.6	13.5	48 39.4	−52.4	13.8	49 37.6	−52.2	14.0	50 35.8	−52.0	14.3	51 33.9	−51.8	14.6	52 31.9	−51.6	15.0	53 29.8	−51.4	15.3	64
65	45 50.0	−53.0	12.6	46 48.5	−52.8	12.8	47 47.0	−52.7	13.0	48 45.4	−52.5	13.3	49 43.8	−52.4	13.6	50 42.1	−52.2	13.8	51 40.3	−52.0	14.1	52 38.4	−51.7	14.5	65
66	44 57.0	−53.2	11.9	45 55.7	−53.1	12.1	46 54.3	−52.9	12.3	47 52.9	−52.7	12.6	48 51.4	−52.6	12.8	49 49.9	−52.4	13.1	50 48.3	−52.2	13.3	51 46.7	−52.1	13.6	66
67	44 03.8	−53.4	11.2	45 02.6	−53.3	11.4	46 01.4	−53.1	11.6	47 00.2	−53.1	11.8	47 58.8	−52.8	12.1	48 57.5	−52.7	12.3	49 56.1	−52.6	12.6	50 54.6	−52.4	12.8	67
68	43 10.4	−53.6	10.6	44 09.3	−53.5	10.8	45 08.3	−53.4	11.0	46 07.1	−53.2	11.2	47 06.0	−53.1	11.4	48 04.8	−53.0	11.6	49 03.5	−52.8	11.8	50 02.2	−52.6	12.1	68
69	42 16.8	−53.8	10.0	43 15.8	−53.6	10.2	44 14.9	−53.6	10.3	45 13.9	−53.5	10.5	46 12.9	−53.4	10.7	47 11.8	−53.2	10.9	48 10.7	−53.1	11.1	49 09.6	−53.0	11.3	69
70	41 23.0	−54.0	9.4	42 22.2	−53.9	9.5	43 21.3	−53.8	9.7	44 20.4	−53.6	9.9	45 19.5	−53.5	10.0	46 18.6	−53.5	10.2	47 17.6	−53.3	10.4	48 16.6	−53.2	10.6	70
71	40 29.0	−54.2	8.8	41 28.3	−54.1	9.0	42 27.5	−53.9	9.1	43 26.8	−53.9	9.2	44 26.0	−53.8	9.4	45 25.1	−53.6	9.6	46 24.3	−53.6	9.7	47 23.4	−53.4	9.9	71
72	39 34.8	−54.3	8.3	40 34.2	−54.2	8.4	41 33.6	−54.2	8.5	42 32.9	−54.1	8.6	43 32.2	−54.0	8.8	44 31.5	−53.9	8.9	45 30.7	−53.7	9.1	46 30.0	−53.7	9.3	72
73	38 40.5	−54.4	7.7	39 40.0	−54.4	7.8	40 39.4	−54.3	7.9	41 38.8	−54.2	8.1	42 38.2	−54.1	8.2	43 37.6	−54.0	8.3	44 37.0	−54.0	8.5	45 36.3	−53.9	8.6	73
74	37 46.1	−54.6	7.2	38 45.6	−54.5	7.3	39 45.1	−54.4	7.4	40 44.6	−54.4	7.5	41 44.1	−54.3	7.6	42 43.6	−54.3	7.7	43 43.0	−54.1	7.9	44 42.4	−54.0	8.0	74
75	36 51.5	−54.7	6.7	37 51.1	−54.7	6.7	38 50.7	−54.6	6.8	39 50.2	−54.5	6.9	40 49.8	−54.5	7.0	41 49.3	−54.4	7.1	42 48.9	−54.4	7.3	43 48.4	−54.3	7.4	75
76	35 56.8	−54.9	6.1	36 56.4	−54.8	6.2	37 56.1	−54.8	6.3	38 55.7	−54.7	6.4	39 55.3	−54.6	6.5	40 54.9	−54.5	6.6	41 54.5	−54.5	6.7	42 54.1	−54.4	6.8	76
77	35 01.9	−55.0	5.6	36 01.6	−54.9	5.7	37 01.3	−54.9	5.8	38 01.0	−54.8	5.9	39 00.7	−54.8	6.0	40 00.4	−54.8	6.0	41 00.0	−54.6	6.1	41 59.7	−54.6	6.2	77
78	34 06.9	−55.0	5.2	35 06.7	−55.1	5.2	36 06.4	−55.0	5.3	37 06.2	−55.0	5.4	38 05.9	−54.9	5.4	39 05.6	−54.8	5.5	40 05.4	−54.8	5.6	41 05.1	−54.8	5.7	78
79	33 11.9	−55.2	4.7	34 11.6	−55.1	4.7	35 11.4	−55.1	4.8	36 11.2	−55.0	4.9	37 11.0	−55.0	4.9	38 10.8	−55.0	5.0	39 10.6	−55.0	5.1	40 10.3	−54.9	5.1	79
80	32 16.7	−55.3	4.2	33 16.5	−55.3	4.3	34 16.3	−55.2	4.3	35 16.2	−55.2	4.4	36 16.0	−55.2	4.4	37 15.8	−55.1	4.5	38 15.6	−55.1	4.5	39 15.4	−55.0	4.6	80
81	31 21.4	−55.4	3.8	32 21.2	−55.3	3.8	33 21.1	−55.3	3.8	34 21.0	−55.3	3.9	35 20.8	−55.2	3.9	36 20.7	−55.3	4.0	37 20.5	−55.2	4.0	38 20.4	−55.2	4.1	81
82	30 26.0	−55.5	3.3	31 25.9	−55.5	3.4	32 25.8	−55.5	3.4	33 25.7	−55.4	3.4	34 25.6	−55.4	3.5	35 25.4	−55.3	3.5	36 25.3	−55.3	3.6	37 25.2	−55.3	3.6	82
83	29 30.5	−55.6	2.9	30 30.4	−55.5	2.9	31 30.3	−55.5	2.9	32 30.3	−55.5	3.0	33 30.2	−55.5	3.0	34 30.1	−55.5	3.0	35 30.0	−55.4	3.1	36 29.9	−55.4	3.1	83
84	28 34.9	−55.6	2.4	29 34.9	−55.7	2.5	30 34.8	−55.6	2.5	31 34.8	−55.6	2.5	32 34.7	−55.6	2.5	33 34.6	−55.5	2.6	34 34.6	−55.6	2.6	35 34.5	−55.5	2.6	84
85	27 39.3	−55.7	2.0	28 39.2	−55.7	2.0	29 39.2	−55.7	2.1	30 39.2	−55.7	2.1	31 39.1	−55.6	2.1	32 39.1	−55.7	2.1	33 39.0	−55.6	2.2	34 39.0	−55.6	2.2	85
86	26 43.6	−55.8	1.6	27 43.5	−55.7	1.6	28 43.5	−55.8	1.6	29 43.5	−55.8	1.6	30 43.5	−55.8	1.7	31 43.4	−55.7	1.7	32 43.4	−55.7	1.7	33 43.4	−55.7	1.7	86
87	25 47.8	−55.9	1.2	26 47.8	−55.9	1.2	27 47.7	−55.8	1.2	28 47.7	−55.8	1.2	29 47.7	−55.8	1.2	30 47.7	−55.8	1.3	31 47.7	−55.8	1.3	32 47.7	−55.8	1.3	87
88	24 51.9	−55.9	0.8	25 51.9	−55.9	0.8	26 51.9	−55.9	0.8	27 51.9	−55.9	0.8	28 51.9	−55.9	0.8	29 51.9	−55.9	0.8	30 51.9	−55.9	0.8	31 51.9	−55.9	0.8	88
89	23 56.0	−56.0	0.4	24 56.0	−56.0	0.4	25 56.0	−56.0	0.4	26 56.0	−56.0	0.4	27 56.0	−56.0	0.4	28 56.0	−56.0	0.4	29 56.0	−56.0	0.4	30 56.0	−56.0	0.4	89
90	23 00.0	−56.0	0.0	24 00.0	−56.0	0.0	25 00.0	−56.0	0.0	26 00.0	−56.0	0.0	27 00.0	−56.0	0.0	28 00.0	−56.0	0.0	29 00.0	−56.1	0.0	30 00.0	−56.1	0.0	90
	23°			24°			25°			26°			27°			28°			29°			30°			

21°, 339° L.H.A. LATITUDE SAME NAME AS DECLINATION

LATITUDE **CONTRARY** NAME TO DECLINATION **L.H.A. 21°, 339°**

Dec.	23°			24°			25°			26°			27°			28°			29°			30°			Dec.
	Hc	d	Z	Hc	d	Z	Hc	d	Z	Hc	d	Z	Hc	d	Z	Hc	d	Z	Hc	d	Z	Hc	d	Z	
°	° ′	′	°	° ′	′	°	° ′	′	°	° ′	′	°	° ′	′	°	° ′	′	°	° ′	′	°	° ′	′	°	°
0	59 14.7	−46.2	135.5	58 31.5	−47.1	136.7	57 47.5	−47.9	137.8	57 02.7	−48.6	138.8	56 17.2	−49.3	139.8	55 31.1	−50.0	140.7	54 44.3	−50.6	141.6	53 57.0	−51.2	142.5	0
1	58 28.5	−46.9	136.7	57 44.4	−47.7	137.8	56 59.6	−48.5	138.9	56 14.1	−49.2	139.9	55 27.9	−49.8	140.8	54 41.1	−50.4	141.7	53 53.7	−51.0	142.5	53 05.8	−51.5	143.4	1
2	57 41.6	−47.5	137.9	56 56.7	−48.2	139.0	56 11.1	−48.9	139.9	55 24.9	−49.6	140.9	54 38.1	−50.3	141.8	53 50.7	−50.9	142.6	53 02.7	−51.4	143.4	52 14.3	−51.9	144.2	2
3	56 54.1	−48.1	139.1	56 08.5	−48.8	140.0	55 22.2	−49.5	141.0	54 35.3	−50.1	141.9	53 47.8	−50.7	142.7	52 59.8	−51.2	143.5	52 11.3	−51.7	144.3	51 22.4	−52.2	145.0	3
4	56 06.0	−48.6	140.1	55 19.7	−49.4	141.1	54 32.7	−49.9	142.0	53 45.2	−50.6	142.8	52 57.1	−51.1	143.6	52 08.6	−51.6	144.4	51 19.6	−52.1	145.1	50 30.2	−52.5	145.8	4
5	55 17.4	−49.2	141.2	54 30.3	−49.7	142.1	53 42.8	−50.4	142.9	52 54.6	−50.9	143.7	52 06.0	−51.4	144.5	51 17.0	−51.9	145.2	50 27.5	−52.3	145.9	49 37.7	−52.8	146.6	5
6	54 28.2	−49.6	142.2	53 40.6	−50.3	143.0	52 52.4	−50.8	143.8	52 03.7	−51.3	144.6	51 14.6	−51.8	145.3	50 25.1	−52.2	146.0	49 35.2	−52.7	146.7	48 44.9	−53.1	147.3	6
7	53 38.6	−50.1	143.1	52 50.3	−50.6	143.9	52 01.6	−51.1	144.7	51 12.4	−51.6	145.4	50 22.8	−52.0	146.1	49 32.9	−52.6	146.8	48 42.5	−52.9	147.4	47 51.8	−53.3	148.0	7
8	52 48.5	−50.5	144.0	51 59.7	−51.0	144.8	51 10.5	−51.5	145.5	50 20.8	−51.9	146.2	49 30.8	−52.4	146.9	48 40.3	−52.8	147.5	47 49.6	−53.2	148.1	46 58.5	−53.6	148.7	8
9	51 58.0	−50.8	144.9	51 08.7	−51.3	145.7	50 19.0	−51.8	146.3	49 28.9	−52.3	147.0	48 38.4	−52.7	147.6	47 47.5	−53.0	148.2	46 56.4	−53.4	148.8	46 04.9	−53.7	149.3	9
10	51 07.2	−51.2	145.8	50 17.4	−51.7	146.5	49 27.2	−52.2	147.1	48 36.6	−52.5	147.7	47 45.7	−52.9	148.3	46 54.5	−53.3	148.9	46 03.0	−53.7	149.4	45 11.2	−54.0	150.0	10
11	50 16.0	−51.6	146.6	49 25.7	−52.0	147.3	48 35.0	−52.4	147.9	47 44.1	−52.8	148.5	46 52.8	−53.2	149.0	46 01.2	−53.5	149.6	45 09.3	−53.8	150.1	44 17.2	−54.2	150.6	11
12	49 24.4	−51.9	147.4	48 33.7	−52.3	148.0	47 42.6	−52.6	148.6	46 51.3	−53.1	149.2	45 59.6	−53.4	149.7	45 07.7	−53.8	150.2	44 15.5	−54.1	150.7	43 23.0	−54.3	151.2	12
13	48 32.5	−52.1	148.2	47 41.4	−52.6	148.8	46 50.0	−53.0	149.3	45 58.2	−53.3	149.8	45 06.2	−53.6	150.3	44 13.9	−53.9	150.8	43 21.4	−54.2	151.3	42 28.7	−54.5	151.7	13
14	47 40.4	−52.5	148.9	46 48.8	−52.8	149.5	45 57.0	−53.1	150.0	45 04.9	−53.5	150.5	44 12.6	−53.8	151.0	43 20.0	−54.1	151.4	42 27.2	−54.4	151.9	41 34.2	−54.7	152.3	14
15	46 47.9	−52.7	149.6	45 56.0	−53.0	150.2	45 03.9	−53.4	150.7	44 11.4	−53.7	151.1	43 18.8	−54.0	151.6	42 25.9	−54.3	152.0	41 32.8	−54.6	152.5	40 39.5	−54.8	152.9	15
16	45 55.2	−52.9	150.3	45 03.0	−53.3	150.8	44 10.5	−53.6	151.3	43 17.7	−53.9	151.8	42 24.8	−54.2	152.2	41 31.6	−54.5	152.6	40 38.2	−54.7	153.0	39 44.7	−55.0	153.4	16
17	45 02.3	−53.2	151.0	44 09.7	−53.5	151.5	43 16.9	−53.8	151.9	42 23.8	−54.1	152.4	41 30.6	−54.4	152.8	40 37.1	−54.6	153.2	39 43.5	−54.9	153.5	38 49.7	−55.1	153.9	17
18	44 09.1	−53.4	151.6	43 16.2	−53.7	152.1	42 23.1	−54.0	152.5	41 29.7	−54.2	152.9	40 36.2	−54.5	153.3	39 42.5	−54.7	153.7	38 48.6	−55.0	154.1	37 54.6	−55.2	154.4	18
19	43 15.7	−53.6	152.3	42 22.5	−53.9	152.7	41 29.1	−54.2	153.1	40 35.5	−54.4	153.5	39 41.7	−54.7	153.9	38 47.8	−54.9	154.2	37 53.6	−55.1	154.6	36 59.4	−55.4	154.9	19
20	42 22.1	−53.7	152.9	41 28.6	−54.0	153.3	40 34.9	−54.3	153.7	39 41.1	−54.6	154.0	38 47.0	−54.8	154.4	37 52.9	−55.1	154.7	36 58.5	−55.2	155.1	36 04.0	−55.4	155.4	20
21	41 28.4	−54.0	153.5	40 34.6	−54.2	153.9	39 40.6	−54.4	154.2	38 46.5	−54.7	154.6	37 52.2	−54.9	154.9	36 57.8	−55.1	155.2	36 03.3	−55.4	155.6	35 08.6	−55.6	155.8	21
22	40 34.4	−54.1	154.1	39 40.4	−54.4	154.4	38 46.2	−54.7	154.8	37 51.8	−54.8	155.1	36 57.3	−55.1	155.4	36 02.7	−55.3	155.7	35 07.9	−55.5	156.0	34 13.0	−55.6	156.3	22
23	39 40.3	−54.3	154.6	38 46.0	−54.6	155.0	37 51.5	−54.7	155.3	36 57.0	−55.0	155.6	36 02.2	−55.1	155.9	35 07.4	−55.4	156.2	34 12.4	−55.5	156.5	33 17.4	−55.8	156.8	23
24	38 46.0	−54.5	155.2	37 51.4	−54.6	155.5	36 56.8	−54.9	155.8	36 02.0	−55.1	156.1	35 07.1	−55.3	156.4	34 12.0	−55.5	156.7	33 16.9	−55.7	156.9	32 21.6	−55.8	157.2	24
25	37 51.5	−54.5	155.7	36 56.8	−54.8	156.0	36 01.9	−55.0	156.3	35 06.9	−55.2	156.6	34 11.8	−55.4	156.9	33 16.5	−55.6	157.1	32 21.2	−55.8	157.4	31 25.8	−56.0	157.6	25
26	36 57.0	−54.8	156.2	36 02.0	−54.9	156.5	35 06.9	−55.1	156.8	34 11.7	−55.3	157.1	33 16.4	−55.5	157.3	32 20.9	−55.6	157.6	31 25.4	−55.8	157.8	30 29.8	−56.0	158.0	26
27	36 02.2	−54.8	156.7	35 07.1	−55.1	157.0	34 11.8	−55.3	157.3	33 16.4	−55.5	157.5	32 20.9	−55.6	157.8	31 25.3	−55.8	158.0	30 29.6	−56.0	158.2	29 33.8	−56.1	158.5	27
28	35 07.4	−55.0	157.2	34 12.0	−55.1	157.5	33 16.5	−55.3	157.8	32 20.9	−55.5	158.0	31 25.3	−55.7	158.2	30 29.5	−55.9	158.5	29 33.6	−56.0	158.7	28 37.7	−56.1	158.9	28
29	34 12.4	−55.0	157.7	33 16.9	−55.3	158.0	32 21.2	−55.4	158.2	31 25.4	−55.6	158.5	30 29.6	−55.8	158.7	29 33.6	−55.9	158.9	28 37.6	−56.0	159.1	27 41.6	−56.3	159.3	29
30	33 17.4	−55.2	158.2	32 21.6	−55.4	158.4	31 25.8	−55.6	158.7	30 29.8	−55.7	158.9	29 33.8	−55.8	159.1	28 37.7	−56.0	159.3	27 41.6	−56.2	159.5	26 45.3	−56.3	159.7	30
31	32 22.2	−55.3	158.7	31 26.2	−55.4	158.9	30 30.2	−55.6	159.1	29 34.1	−55.7	159.3	28 38.0	−56.0	159.5	27 41.7	−56.1	159.7	26 45.4	−56.2	159.9	25 49.0	−56.3	160.0	31
32	31 26.9	−55.4	159.1	30 30.8	−55.6	159.3	29 34.6	−55.7	159.5	28 38.4	−55.9	159.7	27 42.0	−56.0	159.9	26 45.6	−56.1	160.1	25 49.2	−56.3	160.3	24 52.7	−56.4	160.4	32
33	30 31.5	−55.5	159.6	29 35.2	−55.6	159.8	28 38.9	−55.8	160.0	27 42.5	−55.9	160.2	26 46.0	−56.0	160.3	25 49.5	−56.2	160.5	24 52.9	−56.3	160.7	23 56.3	−56.5	160.8	33
34	29 36.0	−55.5	160.0	28 39.6	−55.7	160.2	27 43.1	−55.8	160.4	26 46.6	−56.0	160.6	25 50.0	−56.2	160.7	24 53.3	−56.3	160.9	23 56.6	−56.4	161.0	22 59.8	−56.5	161.2	34
35	28 40.5	−55.7	160.5	27 43.9	−55.8	160.6	26 47.3	−55.9	160.8	25 50.6	−56.1	161.0	24 53.8	−56.1	161.1	23 57.0	−56.3	161.3	23 00.2	−56.4	161.4	22 03.3	−56.5	161.5	35
36	27 44.8	−55.7	160.9	26 48.1	−55.8	161.0	25 51.4	−56.0	161.2	24 54.5	−56.1	161.4	23 57.7	−56.3	161.5	23 00.7	−56.3	161.6	22 03.8	−56.5	161.8	21 06.8	−56.7	161.9	36
37	26 49.1	−55.8	161.3	25 52.3	−55.9	161.5	24 55.4	−56.1	161.6	23 58.4	−56.2	161.7	23 01.4	−56.3	161.9	22 04.4	−56.5	162.0	21 07.3	−56.6	162.1	20 10.1	−56.6	162.2	37
38	25 53.3	−55.8	161.7	24 56.4	−56.0	161.9	23 59.3	−56.1	162.0	23 02.2	−56.2	162.1	22 05.1	−56.3	162.3	21 07.9	−56.4	162.4	20 10.7	−56.5	162.5	19 13.5	−56.7	162.6	38
39	24 57.5	−55.9	162.1	24 00.4	−56.1	162.2	23 03.2	−56.2	162.4	22 06.0	−56.3	162.5	21 08.8	−56.4	162.6	20 11.5	−56.5	162.7	19 14.2	−56.7	162.8	18 16.8	−56.7	162.9	39
40	24 01.6	−56.0	162.5	23 04.3	−56.1	162.6	22 07.0	−56.2	162.8	21 09.7	−56.3	162.9	20 12.4	−56.5	163.0	19 15.0	−56.6	163.1	18 17.5	−56.6	163.2	17 20.1	−56.8	163.3	40
41	23 05.6	−56.0	162.9	22 08.2	−56.1	163.0	21 10.8	−56.2	163.1	20 13.4	−56.4	163.2	19 15.9	−56.5	163.3	18 18.4	−56.6	163.4	17 20.9	−56.7	163.5	16 23.3	−56.8	163.6	41
42	22 09.6	−56.1	163.3	21 12.1	−56.2	163.4	20 14.6	−56.4	163.5	19 17.0	−56.4	163.6	18 19.4	−56.5	163.7	17 21.8	−56.6	163.8	16 24.2	−56.7	163.9	15 26.5	−56.8	164.0	42
43	21 13.5	−56.2	163.7	20 15.9	−56.3	163.8	19 18.2	−56.3	163.9	18 20.6	−56.5	164.0	17 22.9	−56.5	164.1	16 25.2	−56.7	164.1	15 27.5	−56.8	164.2	14 29.7	−56.8	164.3	43
44	20 17.3	−56.2	164.0	19 19.6	−56.3	164.1	18 21.9	−56.4	164.2	17 24.1	−56.5	164.3	16 26.4	−56.6	164.4	15 28.5	−56.6	164.5	14 30.7	−56.8	164.6	13 32.9	−56.9	164.6	44
45	19 21.1	−56.2	164.4	18 23.3	−56.3	164.5	17 25.5	−56.4	164.6	16 27.6	−56.5	164.7	15 29.8	−56.7	164.8	14 31.9	−56.8	164.8	13 33.9	−56.8	164.9	12 36.0	−56.9	165.0	45
46	18 24.9	−56.3	164.8	17 27.0	−56.4	164.9	16 29.1	−56.5	165.0	15 31.1	−56.6	165.0	14 33.1	−56.6	165.1	13 35.1	−56.7	165.2	12 37.1	−56.8	165.2	11 39.1	−56.9	165.3	46
47	17 28.6	−56.3	165.2	16 30.6	−56.4	165.2	15 32.6	−56.5	165.3	14 34.5	−56.6	165.4	13 36.5	−56.7	165.4	12 38.4	−56.8	165.5	11 40.3	−56.9	165.5	10 42.2	−56.9	165.6	47
48	16 32.3	−56.3	165.5	15 34.2	−56.4	165.6	14 36.1	−56.6	165.7	13 37.9	−56.6	165.7	12 39.8	−56.8	165.8	11 41.6	−56.8	165.8	10 43.4	−56.8	165.9	9 45.3	−57.0	165.9	48
49	15 36.0	−56.4	165.9	14 37.8	−56.5	165.9	13 39.5	−56.5	166.0	12 41.3	−56.6	166.1	11 43.1	−56.7	166.1	10 44.8	−56.8	166.2	9 46.6	−56.9	166.2	8 48.3	−57.0	166.2	49
50	14 39.6	−56.5	166.2	13 41.3	−56.5	166.3	12 43.0	−56.6	166.3	11 44.7	−56.7	166.4	10 46.4	−56.8	166.4	9 48.0	−56.8	166.5	8 49.7	−56.9	166.5	7 51.3	−57.0	166.6	50
51	13 43.1	−56.4	166.6	12 44.8	−56.6	166.6	11 46.4	−56.6	166.7	10 48.0	−56.7	166.7	9 49.6	−56.8	166.8	8 51.2	−56.9	166.8	7 52.8	−57.0	166.8	6 54.3	−57.0	166.9	51
52	12 46.7	−56.5	166.9	11 48.2	−56.5	167.0	10 49.8	−56.7	167.0	9 51.3	−56.7	167.1	8 52.8	−56.8	167.1	7 54.3	−56.8	167.1	6 55.8	−56.9	167.2	5 57.3	−57.0	167.2	52
53	11 50.2	−56.5	167.3	10 51.7	−56.6	167.3	9 53.1	−56.6	167.4	8 54.6	−56.7	167.4	7 56.0	−56.8	167.4	6 57.5	−56.9	167.5	5 58.9	−56.9	167.5	5 00.3	−57.0	167.5	53
54	10 53.7	−56.5	167.6	9 55.1	−56.6	167.7	8 56.5	−56.7	167.7	7 57.9	−56.8	167.7	6 59.2	−56.8	167.7	6 00.6	−56.9	167.8	5 02.0	−57.0	167.8	4 03.3	−57.0	167.8	54
55	9 57.2	−56.6	168.0	8 58.5	−56.6	168.0	7 59.8	−56.7	168.0	7 01.1	−56.7	168.0	6 02.4	−56.8	168.1	5 03.7	−56.9	168.1	4 05.0	−57.0	168.1	3 06.3	−57.0	168.1	55
56	9 00.6	−56.5	168.3	8 01.9	−56.6	168.3	7 03.1	−56.7	168.4	6 04.4	−56.8	168.4	5 05.6	−56.8	168.4	4 06.8	−56.9	168.4	3 08.0	−56.9	168.4	2 09.3	−57.1	168.4	56
57	8 04.1	−56.6	168.6	7 05.3	−56.7	168.7	6 06.4	−56.7	168.7	5 07.6	−56.8	168.7	4 08.8	−56.9	168.7	3 09.9	−56.9	168.7	2 11.1	−57.0	168.7	1 12.2	−57.0	168.7	57
58	7 07.5	−56.6	169.0	6 08.6	−56.6	169.0	5 09.7	−56.7	169.0	4 10.8	−56.8	169.0	3 11.9	−56.8	169.0	2 13.0	−56.9	169.0	1 14.1	−57.0	169.1	0 15.2	−57.0	169.1	58
59	6 10.9	−56.6	169.3	5 12.0	−56.7	169.3	4 13.0	−56.7	169.3	3 14.0	−56.8	169.3	2 15.1	−56.9	169.4	1 16.1	−56.9	169.4	0 17.1	−57.0	169.4	0 41.8	+57.1	10.6	59
60	5 14.3	−56.6	169.6	4 15.3	−56.6	169.6	3 16.3	−56.8	169.7	2 17.2	−56.8	169.7	1 18.2	−56.9	169.7	0 19.2	−56.9	169.7	0 39.9	+56.9	10.3	1 38.9	+57.0	10.3	60
61	4 17.7	−56.6	170.0	3 18.6	−56.7	170.0	2 19.5	−56.7	170.0	1 20.4	−56.8	170.0	0 21.3	−56.8	170.0	0 37.7	+57.0	10.0	1 36.8	+57.0	10.0	2 35.9	+57.0	10.0	61
62	3 21.1	−56.7	170.3	2 21.9	−56.7	170.3	1 22.8	−56.8	170.3	0 23.6	−56.8	170.3	0 35.5	+56.9	9.7	1 34.7	+56.9	9.7	2 33.8	+57.0	9.7	3 32.9	+57.1	9.7	62
63	2 24.4	−56.6	170.6	1 25.2	−56.7	170.6	0 26.0	−56.7	170.6	0 33.2	+56.8	9.4	1 32.4	+56.8	9.4	2 31.6	+56.9	9.4	3 30.8	+56.9	9.4	4 30.0	+57.0	9.4	63
64	1 27.8	−56.7	171.0	0 28.5	−56.7	171.0	0 30.7	+56.8	9.0	1 30.0	+56.8	9.0	2 29.2	+56.9	9.0	3 28.5	+56.9	9.1	4 27.7	+57.0	9.1	5 27.0	+57.0	9.1	64
65	0 31.1	−56.6	171.3	0 28.2	+56.7	8.7	1 27.5	+56.7	8.7	2 26.8	+56.8	8.7	3 26.1	+56.8	8.7	4 25.4	+56.9	8.7	5 24.7	+56.9	8.8	6 24.0	+57.0	8.8	65
66	0 25.5	+56.6	8.4	1 24.9	+56.6	8.4	2 24.2	+56.7	8.4	3 23.6	+56.8	8.4	4 22.9	+56.9	8.4	5 22.3	+56.9	8.4	6 21.6	+57.0	8.4	7 21.0	+57.0	8.5	66
67	1 22.1	+56.7	8.1	2 21.5	+56.7	8.1	3 20.9	+56.8	8.1	4 20.4	+56.7	8.1	5 19.8	+56.8	8.1	6 19.2	+56.8	8.1	7 18.6	+56.9	8.1	8 18.0	+56.9	8.1	67
68	2 18.8	+56.6	7.7	3 18.2	+56.7	7.7	4 17.7	+56.7	7.7	5 17.1	+56.8	7.7	6 16.6	+56.8	7.8	7 16.0	+56.9	7.8	8 15.5	+56.9	7.8	9 14.9	+57.0	7.8	68
69	3 15.4	+56.6	7.4	4 14.9	+56.7	7.4	5 14.4	+56.7	7.4	6 13.9	+56.8	7.4	7 13.4	+56.8	7.4	8 12.9	+56.8	7.5	9 12.4	+56.9	7.5	10 11.9	+56.9	7.5	69
70	4 12.0	+56.6	7.1	5 11.6	+56.6	7.1	6 11.1	+56.7	7.1	7 10.7	+56.7	7.1	8 10.2	+56.8	7.1	9 09.7	+56.9	7.1	10 09.3	+56.8	7.2	11 08.8	+56.9	7.2	70
71	5 08.6	+56.7	6.7	6 08.2	+56.7	6.7	7 07.8	+56.7	6.8	8 07.4	+56.7	6.8	9 07.0	+56.7	6.8	10 06.6	+56.8	6.8	11 06.1	+56.9	6.8	12 05.7	+56.9	6.9	71
72	6 05.3	+56.6	6.4	7 04.9	+56.6	6.4	8 04.5	+56.7	6.4	9 04.1	+56.7	6.4	10 03.7	+56.8	6.5	11 03.4	+56.8	6.5	12 03.0	+56.8	6.5	13 02.6	+56.9	6.5	72
73	7 01.9	+56.5	6.1	8 01.5	+56.6	6.1	9 01.2	+56.6	6.1	10 00.8	+56.7	6.1	11 00.5	+56.7	6.1	12 00.2	+56.7	6.1	12 59.8	+56.8	6.2	13 59.5	+56.8	6.2	73
74	7 58.4	+56.6	5.7	8 58.1	+56.6	5.7	9 57.8	+56.7	5.8	10 57.5	+56.7	5.8	11 57.2	+56.7	5.8	12 56.9	+56.8	5.8	13 56.6	+56.8	5.8	14 56.3	+56.8	5.9	74
75	8 55.0	+56.5	5.4	9 54.7	+56.6	5.4	10 54.5	+56.6	5.4	11 54.2	+56.6	5.4	12 53.9	+56.7	5.5	13 53.7	+56.7	5.5	14 53.4	+56.7	5.5	15 53.1	+56.8	5.5	75
76	9 51.5	+56.6	5.0	10 51.3	+56.6	5.1	11 51.1	+56.6	5.1	12 50.8	+56.7	5.1	13 50.6	+56.6	5.1	14 50.4	+56.6	5.1	15 50.1	+56.7	5.2	16 49.9	+56.7	5.2	76
77	10 48.1	+56.5	4.7	11 47.9	+56.5	4.7	12 47.7	+56.5	4.7	13 47.5	+56.5	4.8	14 47.2	+56.7	4.8	15 47.0	+56.7	4.8	16 46.8	+56.6	4.8	17 46.6	+56.7	4.9	77
78	11 44.6	+56.5	4.4	12 44.4	+56.5	4.4	13 44.2	+56.6	4.4	14 44.0	+56.6	4.4	15 43.9	+56.6	4.4	16 43.7	+56.6	4.5	17 43.5	+56.6	4.5	18 43.3	+56.7	4.5	78
79	12 41.1	+56.4	4.0	13 40.9	+56.5	4.0	14 40.8	+56.5	4.1	15 40.6	+56.5	4.1	16 40.5	+56.5	4.1	17 40.3	+56.6	4.1	18 40.1	+56.6	4.1	19 40.0	+56.6	4.2	79
80	13 37.5	+56.4	3.7	14 37.4	+56.4	3.7	15 37.3	+56.4	3.7	16 37.1	+56.5	3.7	17 37.0	+56.5	3.7	18 36.9	+56.5	3.8	19 36.7	+56.6	3.8	20 36.6	+56.6	3.8	80
81	14 33.9	+56.4	3.3	15 33.8	+56.4	3.3	16 33.7	+56.5	3.4	17 33.6	+56.5	3.4	18 33.5	+56.5	3.4	19 33.4	+56.5	3.4	20 33.3	+56.5	3.4	21 33.2	+56.5	3.5	81
82	15 30.3	+56.4	3.0	16 30.2	+56.4	3.0	17 30.2	+56.4	3.0	18 30.1	+56.4	3.0	19 30.0	+56.4	3.0	20 29.9	+56.5	3.1	21 29.8	+56.5	3.1	22 29.7	+56.5	3.1	82
83	16 26.7	+56.3	2.6	17 26.6	+56.4	2.6	18 26.6	+56.3	2.6	19 26.5	+56.4	2.7	20 26.4	+56.4	2.7	21 26.4	+56.4	2.7	22 26.3	+56.4	2.7	23 26.2	+56.5	2.7	83
84	17 23.0	+56.3	2.2	18 23.0	+56.2	2.3	19 22.9	+56.3	2.3	20 22.9	+56.3	2.3	21 22.8	+56.3	2.3	22 22.8	+56.3	2.3	23 22.7	+56.4	2.3	24 22.7	+56.3	2.4	84
85	18 19.3	+56.2	1.9	19 19.2	+56.3	1.9	20 19.2	+56.3	1.9	21 19.2	+56.3	1.9	22 19.1	+56.3	1.9	23 19.1	+56.3	1.9	24 19.1	+56.3	2.0	25 19.0	+56.4	2.0	85
86	19 15.5	+56.2	1.5	20 15.5	+56.2	1.5	21 15.5	+56.2	1.5	22 15.5	+56.2	1.5	23 15.4	+56.3	1.6	24 15.4	+56.3	1.6	25 15.4	+56.2	1.6	26 15.4	+56.2	1.6	86
87	20 11.7	+56.2	1.1	21 11.7	+56.2	1.2	22 11.7	+56.1	1.2	23 11.7	+56.1	1.2	24 11.7	+56.1	1.2	25 11.7	+56.1	1.2	26 11.6	+56.2	1.2	27 11.6	+56.2	1.2	87
88	21 07.9	+56.1	0.8	22 07.9	+56.1	0.8	23 07.8	+56.2	0.8	24 07.8	+56.2	0.8	25 07.8	+56.2	0.8	26 07.8	+56.2	0.8	27 07.8	+56.1	0.8	28 07.8	+56.1	0.8	88
89	22 04.0	+56.0	0.4	23 04.0	+56.0	0.4	24 04.0	+56.0	0.4	25 04.0	+56.0	0.4	26 04.0	+56.0	0.4	27 04.0	+56.0	0.4	28 03.9	+56.1	0.4	29 03.9	+56.1	0.4	89
90	23 00.0	+56.0	0.0	24 00.0	+56.0	0.0	25 00.0	+56.0	0.0	26 00.0	+56.0	0.0	27 00.0	+56.0	0.0	28 00.0	+56.0	0.0	29 00.0	+56.0	0.0	30 00.0	+56.0	0.0	90
	23°			24°			25°			26°			27°			28°			29°			30°			

S. Lat. {L.H.A. greater than 180° ....Zn=180°−Z
{L.H.A. less than 180°...........Zn=180°+Z

LATITUDE **SAME** NAME AS DECLINATION **L.H.A. 159°, 201°**

227

22°, 338° L.H.A. LATITUDE SAME NAME AS DECLINATION N. Lat. {L.H.A. greater than 180° .....Zn=Z {L.H.A. less than 180°............Zn=360°-Z

Dec.	23° Hc	d	Z	24° Hc	d	Z	25° Hc	d	Z	26° Hc	d	Z
°	° ′	′	°	° ′	′	°	° ′	′	°	° ′	′	°
0	58 35.5	+44.6	134.0	57 53.4	+45.5	135.2	57 10.4	+46.4	136.3	56 26.6	+47.3	137.3
1	59 20.1	+43.8	132.7	58 38.9	+44.8	134.0	57 56.8	+45.8	135.1	57 13.9	+46.7	136.2
2	60 03.9	+42.9	131.4	59 23.7	+44.1	132.7	58 42.6	+45.0	133.9	58 00.6	+46.0	135.0
3	60 46.8	+42.0	130.0	60 07.8	+43.1	131.3	59 27.6	+44.3	132.6	58 46.6	+45.2	133.8
4	61 28.8	+41.0	128.5	60 50.9	+42.2	129.9	60 11.9	+43.4	131.2	59 31.8	+44.5	132.5
5	62 09.8	+39.9	126.9	61 33.1	+41.3	128.4	60 55.3	+42.4	129.8	60 16.3	+43.6	131.2
6	62 49.7	+38.8	125.3	62 14.4	+40.1	126.9	61 37.7	+41.5	128.4	60 59.9	+42.7	129.8
7	63 28.5	+37.4	123.6	62 54.5	+39.0	125.3	62 19.2	+40.4	126.8	61 42.6	+41.7	128.3
8	64 05.9	+36.2	121.9	63 33.5	+37.8	123.6	62 59.6	+39.3	125.2	62 24.3	+40.7	126.8
9	64 42.1	+34.7	120.0	64 11.3	+36.4	121.8	63 38.9	+38.0	123.5	63 05.0	+39.5	125.2
10	65 16.8	+33.1	118.1	64 47.7	+34.9	120.0	64 16.9	+36.7	121.8	63 44.5	+38.3	123.5
11	65 49.9	+31.5	116.1	65 22.6	+33.5	118.0	64 53.6	+35.2	119.9	64 22.8	+37.0	121.7
12	66 21.4	+29.8	114.0	65 56.1	+31.8	116.0	65 28.8	+33.7	118.0	64 59.8	+35.5	119.9
13	66 51.2	+27.8	111.8	66 27.9	+30.0	113.9	66 02.5	+32.1	116.0	65 35.3	+34.0	118.0
14	67 19.0	+25.9•	109.5	66 57.9	+28.1	111.7	66 34.6	+30.3	113.9	66 09.3	+32.4	116.0
15	67 44.9	+23.7•	107.2	67 26.0	+26.1•	109.5	67 04.9	+28.4	111.7	66 41.7	+30.6	113.9
16	68 08.6	+21.5•	104.7	67 52.1	+24.0•	107.1	67 33.3	+26.5•	109.4	67 12.3	+28.7	111.7
17	68 30.1	+19.1•	102.2	68 16.1	+21.8•	104.6	67 59.8	+24.3•	107.0	67 41.0	+26.7•	109.4
18	68 49.2	+16.6•	99.6	68 37.9	+19.4•	102.1	68 24.1	+22.0•	104.6	68 07.7	+24.6•	107.0
19	69 05.8	+14.1•	96.9	68 57.3	+16.9•	99.5	68 46.1	+19.7•	102.0	68 32.3	+22.4•	104.5
20	69 19.9	+11.5•	94.2	69 14.2	+14.4•	96.8	69 05.8	+17.2•	99.4	68 54.7	+19.9•	102.0
21	69 31.4	+8.7•	91.4	69 28.6	+11.7•	94.0	69 23.0	+14.6•	96.7	69 14.6	+17.5•	99.3
22	69 40.1	+6.0•	88.5	69 40.3	+8.9•	91.2	69 37.6	+11.9•	93.9	69 32.1	+14.8•	96.6
23	69 46.1	+3.1•	85.7	69 49.2	+6.2•	88.4	69 49.5	+9.2•	91.1	69 46.9	+12.2•	93.8
24	69 49.2	+0.3•	82.8	69 55.4	+3.3•	85.5	69 58.7	+6.3•	88.2	69 59.1	+9.4•	91.0
25	69 49.5	-2.6•	79.9	69 58.7	+0.4•	82.6	70 05.0	+3.5•	85.3	70 08.5	+6.5•	88.1
26	69 46.9	-5.4•	77.0	69 59.1	-2.4•	79.6	70 08.5	+0.6•	82.4	70 15.0	+3.6•	85.1
27	69 41.5	-8.2•	74.1	69 56.7	-5.3•	76.7	70 09.1	-2.4•	79.4	70 18.6	+0.8•	82.2
28	69 33.3	-10.9•	71.3	69 51.4	-8.2•	73.8	70 06.7	-5.2•	76.5	70 19.4	-2.2•	79.2
29	69 22.4	-13.6•	68.4	69 43.2	-10.8•	71.0	70 01.5	-8.0•	73.6	70 17.2	-5.2•	76.2
30	69 08.8	-16.1•	65.7	69 32.4	-13.6•	68.1	69 53.5	-10.9•	70.7	70 12.0	-7.9•	73.3
31	68 52.7	-18.7•	63.0	69 18.8	-16.2•	65.4	69 42.6	-13.5•	67.8	70 04.1	-10.8•	70.4
32	68 34.0	-21.0•	60.4	69 02.6	-18.6•	62.7	69 29.1	-16.2•	65.0	69 53.3	-13.6•	67.5
33	68 13.0	-23.3•	57.8	68 44.0	-21.1•	60.0	69 12.9	-18.7•	62.3	69 39.7	-16.2•	64.7
34	67 49.7	-25.4•	55.4	68 22.9	-23.3•	57.5	68 54.2	-21.1•	59.6	69 23.5	-18.7•	61.9
35	67 24.3	-27.5	53.0	67 59.6	-25.5•	55.0	68 33.1	-23.4•	57.1	69 04.8	-21.2•	59.2
36	66 56.8	-29.3	50.7	67 34.1	-27.6	52.6	68 09.7	-25.6•	54.6	68 43.6	-23.5•	56.6
37	66 27.5	-31.2	48.5	67 06.5	-29.4	50.3	67 44.1	-27.6•	52.1	68 20.1	-25.7•	54.1
38	65 56.3	-32.8	46.4	66 37.1	-31.3	48.1	67 16.5	-29.6	49.8	67 54.4	-27.7•	51.7
39	65 23.5	-34.4	44.4	66 05.8	-33.0	45.9	66 46.9	-31.4	47.6	67 26.7	-29.7	49.4
40	64 49.1	-35.9	42.4	65 32.8	-34.5	43.9	66 15.5	-33.1	45.5	66 57.0	-31.5	47.1
41	64 13.2	-37.2	40.5	64 58.3	-36.0	41.9	65 42.4	-34.6	43.4	66 25.5	-33.3	45.0
42	63 36.0	-38.5	38.8	64 22.3	-37.3	40.1	65 07.8	-36.2	41.4	65 52.2	-34.8	42.9
43	62 57.5	-39.7	37.1	63 45.0	-38.7	38.3	64 31.6	-37.5	39.6	65 17.4	-36.2	41.0
44	62 17.8	-40.8	35.4	63 06.3	-39.8	36.6	63 54.1	-38.7	37.8	64 41.2	-37.7	39.1
45	61 37.0	-41.8	33.9	62 26.5	-40.9	34.9	63 15.4	-40.0	36.1	64 03.5	-38.9	37.3
46	60 55.2	-42.7	32.4	61 45.6	-41.9	33.4	62 35.4	-41.0	34.4	63 24.6	-40.1	35.5
47	60 12.5	-43.7	30.9	61 03.7	-42.9	31.9	61 54.4	-42.1	32.9	62 44.5	-41.2	33.9
48	59 28.8	-44.4	29.6	60 20.8	-43.8	30.4	61 12.3	-43.0	31.4	62 03.3	-42.3	32.3
49	58 44.4	-45.2	28.3	59 37.0	-44.5	29.1	60 29.3	-43.9	29.9	61 21.0	-43.2	30.8
50	57 59.2	-45.9	27.0	58 52.5	-45.4	27.8	59 45.4	-44.8	28.6	60 37.8	-44.0	29.4
51	57 13.3	-46.6	25.8	58 07.1	-46.0	26.5	59 00.6	-45.4	27.2	59 53.8	-44.8	28.0
52	56 26.7	-47.2	24.7	57 21.1	-46.7	25.3	58 15.2	-46.2	26.0	59 08.9	-45.6	26.7
53	55 39.5	-47.8	23.6	56 34.4	-47.3	24.2	57 29.0	-46.9	24.8	58 23.3	-46.3	25.5
54	54 51.7	-48.3	22.5	55 47.1	-47.9	23.1	56 42.1	-47.4	23.6	57 37.0	-47.0	24.3
55	54 03.4	-48.8	21.5	54 59.2	-48.5	22.0	55 54.7	-48.0	22.5	56 50.0	-47.6	23.1
56	53 14.6	-49.2	20.5	54 10.7	-48.9	21.0	55 06.7	-48.6	21.5	56 02.4	-48.2	22.0
57	52 25.4	-49.7	19.5	53 21.8	-49.4	20.0	54 18.1	-49.0	20.5	55 14.2	-48.6	21.0
58	51 35.7	-50.1	18.6	52 32.4	-49.8	19.1	53 29.1	-49.5	19.5	54 25.6	-49.2	20.0
59	50 45.6	-50.5	17.8	51 42.6	-50.2	18.1	52 39.6	-49.9	18.5	53 36.4	-49.6	19.0
60	49 55.1	-50.9	16.9	50 52.4	-50.6	17.3	51 49.7	-50.4	17.6	52 46.8	-50.1	18.0
61	49 04.2	-51.2	16.1	50 01.8	-50.9	16.4	50 59.3	-50.7	16.8	51 56.7	-50.4	17.1
62	48 13.0	-51.4	15.3	49 10.9	-51.3	15.6	50 08.6	-51.0	15.9	51 06.3	-50.9	16.3
63	47 21.6	-51.8	14.5	48 19.6	-51.6	14.8	49 17.6	-51.4	15.1	50 15.4	-51.1	15.4
64	46 29.8	-52.1	13.8	47 28.0	-51.9	14.1	48 26.2	-51.7	14.3	49 24.3	-51.5	14.6
65	45 37.7	-52.3	13.1	46 36.1	-52.2	13.3	47 34.5	-52.0	13.6	48 32.8	-51.9	13.8
66	44 45.4	-52.6	12.4	45 43.9	-52.4	12.6	46 42.5	-52.3	12.8	47 40.9	-52.1	13.1
67	43 52.8	-52.8	11.7	44 51.5	-52.6	11.9	45 50.2	-52.5	12.1	46 48.8	-52.3	12.3
68	43 00.0	-53.0	11.1	43 58.9	-52.9	11.2	44 57.7	-52.8	11.4	45 56.5	-52.6	11.6
69	42 07.0	-53.2	10.4	43 06.0	-53.1	10.6	44 04.9	-53.0	10.8	45 03.9	-52.9	11.0
70	41 13.8	-53.5	9.8	42 12.9	-53.3	10.0	43 11.9	-53.2	10.1	44 11.0	-53.1	10.3
71	40 20.3	-53.6	9.2	41 19.6	-53.5	9.3	42 18.7	-53.4	9.5	43 17.9	-53.3	9.6
72	39 26.7	-53.7	8.6	40 26.1	-53.7	8.7	41 25.3	-53.5	8.9	42 24.6	-53.5	9.0
73	38 33.0	-54.0	8.1	39 32.4	-53.9	8.2	40 31.8	-53.8	8.3	41 31.1	-53.7	8.4
74	37 39.0	-54.0	7.5	38 38.5	-54.0	7.6	39 38.0	-54.0	7.7	40 37.4	-53.8	7.8
75	36 45.0	-54.3	7.0	37 44.5	-54.2	7.0	38 44.0	-54.1	7.1	39 43.6	-54.1	7.2
76	35 50.7	-54.3	6.4	36 50.3	-54.3	6.5	37 49.9	-54.2	6.6	38 49.5	-54.1	6.7
77	34 56.4	-54.5	5.9	35 56.0	-54.4	6.0	36 55.7	-54.4	6.1	37 55.4	-54.4	6.1
78	34 01.9	-54.7	5.4	35 01.6	-54.6	5.5	36 01.3	-54.5	5.5	37 01.0	-54.4	5.6
79	33 07.2	-54.7	4.9	34 07.0	-54.7	5.0	35 06.8	-54.7	5.0	36 06.6	-54.6	5.1
80	32 12.5	-54.8	4.4	33 12.3	-54.8	4.5	34 12.1	-54.7	4.5	35 12.0	-54.8	4.6
81	31 17.7	-55.0	3.9	32 17.5	-54.9	4.0	33 17.4	-54.9	4.0	34 17.2	-54.8	4.1
82	30 22.7	-55.0	3.5	31 22.6	-55.0	3.5	32 22.5	-55.0	3.5	33 22.4	-55.0	3.6
83	29 27.7	-55.2	3.0	30 27.6	-55.1	3.0	31 27.5	-55.1	3.1	32 27.4	-55.1	3.1
84	28 32.5	-55.2	2.6	29 32.5	-55.2	2.6	30 32.4	-55.2	2.6	31 32.3	-55.1	2.6
85	27 37.3	-55.3	2.1	28 37.3	-55.3	2.1	29 37.2	-55.3	2.2	30 37.2	-55.3	2.2
86	26 42.0	-55.4	1.7	27 42.0	-55.4	1.7	28 41.9	-55.3	1.7	29 41.9	-55.3	1.7
87	25 46.6	-55.5	1.2	26 46.6	-55.5	1.3	27 46.6	-55.5	1.3	28 46.6	-55.5	1.3
88	24 51.1	-55.5	0.8	25 51.1	-55.5	0.8	26 51.1	-55.5	0.8	27 51.1	-55.5	0.8
89	23 55.6	-55.6	0.4	24 55.6	-55.6	0.4	25 55.6	-55.6	0.4	26 55.6	-55.6	0.4
90	23 00.0	-55.7	0.0	24 00.0	-55.7	0.0	25 00.0	-55.7	0.0	26 00.0	-55.7	0.0

Dec.	27° Hc	d	Z	28° Hc	d	Z	29° Hc	d	Z	30° Hc	d	Z	Dec.
°	° ′	′	°	° ′	′	°	° ′	′	°	° ′	′	°	°
0	55 42.2	+48.0	138.3	54 57.0	+48.8	139.3	54 11.2	+49.5	140.2	53 24.8	+50.2	141.1	0
1	56 30.2	+47.5	137.3	55 45.8	+48.3	138.3	55 00.7	+49.0	139.2	54 15.0	+49.6	140.1	1
2	57 17.7	+46.9	136.1	56 34.1	+47.7	137.2	55 49.7	+48.5	138.2	55 04.6	+49.2	139.2	2
3	58 04.6	+46.2	135.0	57 21.8	+47.0	136.1	56 38.2	+47.9	137.1	55 53.8	+48.7	138.1	3
4	58 50.8	+45.5	133.8	58 08.8	+46.5	134.9	57 26.1	+47.3	136.0	56 42.5	+48.1	137.1	4
5	59 36.3	+44.6	132.5	58 55.3	+45.7	133.7	58 13.4	+46.6	134.9	57 30.6	+47.5	136.0	5
6	60 20.9	+43.9	131.1	59 41.0	+44.9	132.4	59 00.0	+45.9	133.7	58 18.1	+46.9	134.8	6
7	61 04.8	+43.0	129.7	60 25.9	+44.1	131.1	59 45.9	+45.2	132.4	59 05.0	+46.2	133.6	7
8	61 47.8	+41.9	128.3	61 10.0	+43.2	129.7	60 31.1	+44.4	131.1	59 51.2	+45.4	132.4	8
9	62 29.7	+41.0	126.8	61 53.2	+42.2	128.3	61 15.5	+43.4	129.7	60 36.6	+44.6	131.1	9
10	63 10.7	+39.8	125.2	62 35.4	+41.2	126.7	61 58.9	+42.5	128.2	61 21.2	+43.7	129.7	10
11	63 50.5	+38.5	123.5	63 16.6	+40.1	125.1	62 41.4	+41.5	126.7	62 04.9	+42.8	128.2	11
12	64 29.0	+37.3	121.7	63 56.7	+38.9	123.5	63 22.9	+40.3	125.1	62 47.7	+41.7	126.7	12
13	65 06.3	+35.8	119.9	64 35.6	+37.5	121.7	64 03.2	+39.2	123.5	63 29.4	+40.7	125.1	13
14	65 42.1	+34.3	118.0	65 13.1	+36.1	119.9	64 42.4	+37.8	121.7	64 10.1	+39.4	123.5	14
15	66 16.4	+32.7	115.9	65 49.2	+34.7	117.9	65 20.2	+36.5	119.9	64 49.5	+38.2	121.7	15
16	66 49.1	+30.9	113.8	66 23.9	+32.9	115.9	65 56.7	+34.9	117.9	65 27.7	+36.7	119.9	16
17	67 20.0	+29.0	111.6	66 56.8	+31.2	113.8	66 31.6	+33.3	115.9	66 04.4	+35.2	118.0	17
18	67 49.0	+27.1•	109.3	67 28.0	+29.4	111.6	67 04.9	+31.5	113.8	66 39.6	+33.6	115.9	18
19	68 16.1	+24.8•	106.9	67 57.4	+27.3•	109.3	67 36.4	+29.7	111.6	67 13.2	+31.9	113.8	19
20	68 40.9	+22.7•	104.5	68 24.7	+25.2•	106.9	68 06.1	+27.6•	109.3	67 45.1	+30.0•	111.6	20
21	69 03.6	+20.2•	101.9	68 49.9	+22.9•	104.4	68 33.7	+25.5•	106.9	68 15.1	+27.9•	109.3	21
22	69 23.8	+17.7•	99.2	69 12.8	+20.5•	101.8	68 59.2	+23.2•	104.4	68 43.0	+25.8•	106.9	22
23	69 41.5	+15.2•	96.5	69 33.3	+18.1•	99.2	69 22.4	+20.8•	101.8	69 08.8	+23.6•	104.4	23
24	69 56.7	+12.4•	93.7	69 51.4	+15.3•	96.4	69 43.2	+18.3•	99.1	69 32.4	+21.1•	101.8	24
25	70 09.1	+9.5•	90.8	70 06.7	+12.7•	93.6	70 01.5	+15.7•	96.3	69 53.5	+18.5•	99.1	25
26	70 18.6	+6.8•	87.9	70 19.4	+9.8•	90.7	70 17.2	+12.8•	93.5	70 12.0	+15.9•	96.3	26
27	70 25.4	+3.8•	85.0	70 29.2	+6.9•	87.8	70 30.0	+10.1•	90.6	70 27.9	+13.2•	93.4	27
28	70 29.2	+0.8•	82.0	70 36.1	+4.0•	84.8	70 40.1	+7.1•	87.6	70 41.1	+10.2•	90.5	28
29	70 30.0	-2.1•	79.0	70 40.1	+1.0•	81.8	70 47.2	+4.1•	84.6	70 51.3	+7.3•	87.5	29
30	70 27.9	-5.0•	76.0	70 41.1	-2.0•	78.8	70 51.3	+1.1•	81.6	70 58.6	+4.3•	84.4	30
31	70 22.9	-7.9•	73.0	70 39.1	-5.0•	75.7	70 52.4	-1.8•	78.5	71 02.9	+1.3•	81.4	31
32	70 15.0	-10.8•	70.1	70 34.1	-7.9•	72.7	70 50.6	-4.9•	75.5	71 04.2	-1.8•	78.3	32
33	70 04.2	-13.6•	67.2	70 26.2	-10.7•	69.8	70 45.7	-7.9•	72.4	71 02.4	-4.9•	75.2	33
34	69 50.6	-16.2•	64.3	70 15.5	-13.6•	66.8	70 37.8	-10.8•	69.5	70 57.5	-7.8•	72.2	34
35	69 34.4	-18.8•	61.6	70 01.9	-16.3•	64.0	70 27.0	-13.6•	66.5	70 49.7	-10.8•	69.1	35
36	69 15.6	-21.2•	58.9	69 45.6	-18.8•	61.2	70 13.4	-16.3•	63.6	70 38.9	-13.6•	66.1	36
37	68 54.4	-23.6•	56.2	69 26.8	-21.4•	58.4	69 57.1	-18.9•	60.8	70 25.3	-16.4•	63.2	37
38	68 30.8	-25.8•	53.7	69 05.4	-23.7•	55.8	69 38.2	-21.5•	58.0	70 08.9	-19.0•	60.4	38
39	68 05.0	-27.9•	51.3	68 41.7	-25.9•	53.3	69 16.7	-23.8•	55.4	69 49.9	-21.6•	57.6	39
40	67 37.1	-29.8	48.9	68 15.8	-28.0•	50.8	68 52.9	-26.0•	52.8	69 28.3	-23.9•	54.9	40
41	67 07.3	-31.7	46.7	67 47.8	-30.0	48.4	68 26.9	-28.2•	50.3	69 04.4	-26.2•	52.3	41
42	66 35.6	-33.3	44.5	67 17.8	-31.8	46.2	67 58.7	-30.1	47.9	68 38.2	-28.4•	49.8	42
43	66 02.3	-35.0	42.4	66 46.0	-33.5	44.0	67 28.6	-32.0	45.7	68 09.8	-30.3	47.4	43
44	65 27.3	-36.5	40.4	66 12.5	-35.2	41.9	66 56.6	-33.8	43.5	67 39.5	-32.2	45.1	44
45	64 50.8	-37.8	38.6	65 37.3	-36.6	39.9	66 22.8	-35.3	41.4	67 07.3	-33.9	42.9	45
46	64 13.0	-39.1	36.7	65 00.7	-38.0	38.0	65 47.5	-36.8	39.4	66 33.4	-35.5	40.9	46
47	63 33.9	-40.2	35.0	64 22.7	-39.3	36.2	65 10.7	-38.2	37.5	65 57.9	-37.0	38.8	47
48	62 53.7	-41.4	33.4	63 43.4	-40.4	34.5	64 32.5	-39.4	35.7	65 20.9	-38.4	36.9	48
49	62 12.3	-42.4	31.8	63 03.0	-41.6	32.8	63 53.1	-40.7	33.9	64 42.5	-39.6	35.1	49
50	61 29.9	-43.4	30.3	62 21.4	-42.5	31.3	63 12.4	-41.7	32.3	64 02.9	-40.9	33.4	50
51	60 46.5	-44.2	28.9	61 38.9	-43.6	29.8	62 30.7	-42.8	30.7	63 22.0	-41.9	31.7	51
52	60 02.3	-45.0	27.5	60 55.3	-44.3	28.3	61 47.9	-43.7	29.2	62 40.1	-43.0	30.2	52
53	59 17.3	-45.8	26.2	60 11.0	-45.2	27.0	61 04.2	-44.5	27.8	61 57.1	-43.9	28.6	53
54	58 31.5	-46.5	24.9	59 25.8	-46.0	25.7	60 19.7	-45.4	26.4	61 13.2	-44.7	27.2	54
55	57 45.0	-47.1	23.7	58 39.8	-46.6	24.4	59 34.3	-46.1	25.1	60 28.5	-45.6	25.8	55
56	56 57.9	-47.7	22.6	57 53.2	-47.3	23.2	58 48.2	-46.8	23.9	59 42.9	-46.3	24.5	56
57	56 10.2	-48.3	21.5	57 05.9	-47.9	22.1	58 01.4	-47.5	22.7	58 56.6	-47.0	23.3	57
58	55 21.9	-48.8	20.4	56 18.0	-48.4	21.0	57 13.9	-48.0	21.5	58 09.6	-47.6	22.1	58
59	54 33.1	-49.3	19.4	55 29.6	-49.0	19.9	56 25.9	-48.6	20.4	57 22.0	-48.2	21.0	59
60	53 43.8	-49.8	18.5	54 40.6	-49.5	18.9	55 37.3	-49.1	19.4	56 33.8	-48.8	19.9	60
61	52 54.0	-50.2	17.5	53 51.1	-49.9	17.9	54 48.2	-49.6	18.4	55 45.0	-49.2	18.8	61
62	52 03.8	-50.6	16.6	53 01.2	-50.3	17.0	53 58.6	-50.1	17.4	54 55.8	-49.8	17.8	62
63	51 13.2	-50.9	15.8	52 10.9	-50.7	16.1	53 08.5	-50.4	16.5	54 06.0	-50.2	16.9	63
64	50 22.3	-51.3	14.9	51 20.2	-51.1	15.2	52 18.1	-50.9	15.6	53 15.8	-50.6	15.9	64
65	49 31.0	-51.6	14.1	50 29.1	-51.4	14.4	51 27.2	-51.2	14.7	52 25.2	-51.0	15.0	65
66	48 39.4	-52.0	13.3	49 37.7	-51.7	13.6	50 36.0	-51.6	13.9	51 34.2	-51.4	14.2	66
67	47 47.4	-52.2	12.6	48 46.0	-52.1	12.8	49 44.4	-51.8	13.1	50 42.8	-51.6	13.4	67
68	46 55.2	-52.5	11.9	47 53.9	-52.3	12.1	48 52.6	-52.2	12.3	49 51.2	-52.1	12.6	68
69	46 02.7	-52.7	11.2	47 01.6	-52.6	11.4	48 00.4	-52.5	11.6	48 59.1	-52.3	11.8	69
70	45 10.0	-53.0	10.5	46 09.0	-52.8	10.7	47 07.9	-52.7	10.9	48 06.8	-52.5	11.1	70
71	44 17.0	-53.1	9.8	45 16.2	-53.1	10.0	46 15.2	-52.9	10.2	47 14.3	-52.9	10.3	71
72	43 23.9	-53.4	9.2	44 23.1	-53.3	9.3	45 22.3	-53.2	9.5	46 21.4	-53.0	9.7	72
73	42 30.5	-53.6	8.5	43 29.8	-53.5	8.7	44 29.1	-53.4	8.8	45 28.4	-53.3	9.0	73
74	41 36.9	-53.8	7.9	42 36.3	-53.7	8.1	43 35.7	-53.6	8.2	44 35.1	-53.6	8.3	74
75	40 43.1	-54.0	7.3	41 42.6	-53.9	7.5	42 42.1	-53.8	7.6	43 41.5	-53.7	7.7	75
76	39 49.1	-54.1	6.8	40 48.7	-54.0	6.9	41 48.3	-54.0	7.0	42 47.8	-53.9	7.1	76
77	38 55.0	-54.3	6.2	39 54.7	-54.3	6.3	40 54.3	-54.2	6.4	41 53.9	-54.1	6.5	77
78	38 00.7	-54.4	5.7	39 00.4	-54.3	5.8	40 00.1	-54.3	5.8	40 59.8	-54.2	5.9	78
79	37 06.3	-54.5	5.1	38 06.1	-54.5	5.2	39 05.8	-54.4	5.3	40 05.6	-54.5	5.4	79
80	36 11.8	-54.7	4.6	37 11.6	-54.7	4.7	38 11.4	-54.7	4.7	39 11.1	-54.5	4.8	80
81	35 17.1	-54.8	4.1	36 16.9	-54.8	4.2	37 16.7	-54.7	4.2	38 16.6	-54.7	4.3	81
82	34 22.3	-55.0	3.6	35 22.1	-54.9	3.7	36 22.0	-54.9	3.7	37 21.9	-54.9	3.8	82
83	33 27.3	-55.0	3.1	34 27.2	-55.0	3.2	35 27.1	-55.0	3.2	36 27.0	-54.9	3.3	83
84	32 32.3	-55.2	2.7	33 32.2	-55.1	2.7	34 32.1	-55.1	2.7	35 32.1	-55.1	2.8	84
85	31 37.1	-55.2	2.2	32 37.1	-55.3	2.2	33 37.0	-55.2	2.2	34 37.0	-55.2	2.3	85
86	30 41.9	-55.4	1.7	31 41.8	-55.3	1.8	32 41.8	-55.3	1.8	33 41.8	-55.3	1.8	86
87	29 46.5	-55.4	1.3	30 46.5	-55.4	1.3	31 46.5	-55.4	1.3	32 46.5	-55.4	1.3	87
88	28 51.1	-55.5	0.9	29 51.1	-55.5	0.9	30 51.1	-55.5	0.9	31 51.1	-55.5	0.9	88
89	27 55.6	-55.6	0.4	28 55.6	-55.6	0.4	29 55.6	-55.6	0.4	30 55.6	-55.6	0.4	89
90	27 00.0	-55.7	0.0	28 00.0	-55.7	0.0	29 00.0	-55.7	0.0	30 00.0	-55.7	0.0	90

22°, 338° L.H.A. LATITUDE SAME NAME AS DECLINATION

228

LATITUDE CONTRARY NAME TO DECLINATION — L.H.A. 22°, 338°

Dec. °	23° Hc ° ′	d ′	Z °	24° Hc ° ′	d ′	Z °	25° Hc ° ′	d ′	Z °	26° Hc ° ′	d ′	Z °
0	58 35.5	−45.3	134.0	57 53.4	−46.3	135.2	57 10.4	−47.1	136.3	56 26.6	−47.8	137.3
1	57 50.2	−46.1	135.3	57 07.1	−46.9	136.4	56 23.3	−47.7	137.4	55 38.8	−48.4	138.4
2	57 04.1	−46.7	136.5	56 20.2	−47.5	137.5	55 35.6	−48.2	138.5	54 50.4	−49.0	139.5
3	56 17.4	−47.3	137.6	55 32.7	−48.0	138.6	54 47.4	−48.7	139.5	54 01.4	−49.4	140.4
4	55 30.1	−47.9	138.7	54 44.7	−48.6	139.7	53 58.7	−49.3	140.5	53 12.0	−49.8	141.4
5	54 42.2	−48.4	139.8	53 56.1	−49.0	140.7	53 09.4	−49.6	141.5	52 22.2	−50.3	142.3
6	53 53.8	−48.9	140.8	53 07.1	−49.6	141.6	52 19.8	−50.1	142.4	51 31.9	−50.6	143.2
7	53 04.9	−49.3	141.8	52 17.5	−49.9	142.6	51 29.7	−50.5	143.3	50 41.3	−51.0	144.1
8	52 15.6	−49.8	142.7	51 27.6	−50.3	143.5	50 39.2	−50.9	144.2	49 50.3	−51.3	144.9
9	51 25.8	−50.2	143.6	50 37.3	−50.7	144.3	49 48.3	−51.2	145.0	48 59.0	−51.7	145.7
10	50 35.6	−50.6	144.5	49 46.6	−51.1	145.2	48 57.1	−51.5	145.8	48 07.3	−52.0	146.5
11	49 45.0	−50.9	145.3	48 55.5	−51.4	146.0	48 05.6	−51.8	146.6	47 15.3	−52.2	147.2
12	48 54.1	−51.2	146.1	48 04.1	−51.6	146.7	47 13.8	−52.1	147.3	46 23.1	−52.5	147.9
13	48 02.9	−51.6	146.9	47 12.5	−52.0	147.5	46 21.7	−52.4	148.1	45 30.6	−52.7	148.6
14	47 11.3	−51.8	147.7	46 20.5	−52.3	148.2	45 29.3	−52.6	148.8	44 37.9	−53.0	149.3
15	46 19.5	−52.1	148.4	45 28.2	−52.5	148.9	44 36.7	−52.8	149.5	43 44.9	−53.2	149.9
16	45 27.4	−52.4	149.1	44 35.7	−52.7	149.6	43 43.9	−53.1	150.1	42 51.7	−53.4	150.6
17	44 35.0	−52.6	149.8	43 43.0	−52.9	150.3	42 50.8	−53.3	150.8	41 58.3	−53.6	151.2
18	43 42.4	−52.9	150.5	42 50.1	−53.2	150.9	41 57.5	−53.5	151.4	41 04.7	−53.7	151.8
19	42 49.5	−53.0	151.1	41 56.9	−53.4	151.6	41 04.0	−53.6	152.0	40 11.0	−54.0	152.4
20	41 56.5	−53.3	151.8	41 03.5	−53.5	152.2	40 10.4	−53.9	152.6	39 17.0	−54.1	152.9
21	41 03.2	−53.4	152.4	40 10.0	−53.8	152.8	39 16.5	−54.0	153.1	38 22.9	−54.3	153.5
22	40 09.8	−53.7	153.0	39 16.2	−53.9	153.3	38 22.5	−54.1	153.7	37 28.6	−54.4	154.0
23	39 16.1	−53.8	153.6	38 22.3	−54.0	153.9	37 28.4	−54.3	154.2	36 34.2	−54.5	154.6
24	38 22.3	−53.9	154.1	37 28.3	−54.2	154.5	36 34.1	−54.5	154.8	35 39.7	−54.7	155.1
25	37 28.4	−54.2	154.7	36 34.1	−54.4	155.0	35 39.6	−54.6	155.3	34 45.0	−54.8	155.6
26	36 34.2	−54.2	155.2	35 39.7	−54.5	155.5	34 45.0	−54.7	155.8	33 50.2	−54.9	156.1
27	35 40.0	−54.4	155.7	34 45.2	−54.6	156.0	33 50.3	−54.8	156.3	32 55.3	−55.0	156.6
28	34 45.6	−54.5	156.3	33 50.6	−54.7	156.5	32 55.5	−54.9	156.8	32 00.3	−55.1	157.0
29	33 51.1	−54.7	156.8	32 55.9	−54.9	157.0	32 00.6	−55.0	157.3	31 05.2	−55.2	157.5
30	32 56.4	−54.7	157.3	32 01.0	−54.9	157.5	31 05.6	−55.2	157.7	30 10.0	−55.3	158.0
31	32 01.7	−54.9	157.7	31 06.1	−55.1	158.0	30 10.4	−55.2	158.2	29 14.7	−55.4	158.4
32	31 06.8	−55.0	158.2	30 11.0	−55.1	158.4	29 15.2	−55.3	158.6	28 19.3	−55.5	158.8
33	30 11.8	−55.0	158.7	29 15.9	−55.2	158.9	28 19.9	−55.4	159.1	27 23.8	−55.5	159.3
34	29 16.8	−55.2	159.1	28 20.7	−55.4	159.3	27 24.5	−55.5	159.5	26 28.3	−55.7	159.7
35	28 21.6	−55.2	159.6	27 25.3	−55.4	159.8	26 29.0	−55.5	160.0	25 32.6	−55.7	160.1
36	27 26.4	−55.4	160.0	26 29.9	−55.4	160.2	25 33.5	−55.7	160.4	24 36.9	−55.7	160.5
37	26 31.0	−55.4	160.5	25 34.5	−55.6	160.6	24 37.8	−55.7	160.8	23 41.2	−55.9	160.9
38	25 35.6	−55.4	160.9	24 38.9	−55.6	161.0	23 42.1	−55.7	161.2	22 45.3	−55.9	161.3
39	24 40.2	−55.6	161.3	23 43.3	−55.7	161.5	22 46.4	−55.8	161.6	21 49.4	−55.9	161.7
40	23 44.6	−55.6	161.7	22 47.6	−55.7	161.9	21 50.6	−55.9	162.0	20 53.5	−56.0	162.1
41	22 49.0	−55.7	162.1	21 51.9	−55.8	162.3	20 54.7	−55.9	162.4	19 57.5	−56.0	162.5
42	21 53.3	−55.7	162.5	20 56.1	−55.9	162.7	19 58.8	−56.0	162.8	19 01.5	−56.1	162.9
43	20 57.6	−55.8	162.9	20 00.2	−55.9	163.0	19 02.8	−56.0	163.2	18 05.4	−56.2	163.2
44	20 01.8	−55.8	163.3	19 04.3	−55.9	163.4	18 06.8	−56.1	163.5	17 09.2	−56.1	163.6
45	19 06.0	−55.9	163.7	18 08.4	−56.0	163.8	17 10.7	−56.1	163.9	16 13.1	−56.2	164.0
46	18 10.1	−55.9	164.1	17 12.4	−56.1	164.2	16 14.6	−56.1	164.3	15 16.9	−56.3	164.3
47	17 14.2	−56.0	164.5	16 16.3	−56.0	164.6	15 18.5	−56.2	164.6	14 20.6	−56.3	164.7
48	16 18.2	−56.0	164.9	15 20.3	−56.2	164.9	14 22.3	−56.2	165.0	13 24.3	−56.3	165.1
49	15 22.2	−56.1	165.2	14 24.1	−56.1	165.3	13 26.1	−56.2	165.4	12 28.0	−56.3	165.4
50	14 26.1	−56.1	165.6	13 28.0	−56.2	165.7	12 29.9	−56.3	165.7	11 31.7	−56.4	165.8
51	13 30.0	−56.1	166.0	12 31.8	−56.2	166.0	11 33.6	−56.3	166.1	10 35.3	−56.3	166.1
52	12 33.9	−56.1	166.3	11 35.6	−56.2	166.4	10 37.3	−56.3	166.4	9 39.0	−56.4	166.5
53	11 37.8	−56.2	166.7	10 39.4	−56.3	166.7	9 41.0	−56.4	166.8	8 42.6	−56.5	166.8
54	10 41.6	−56.2	167.1	9 43.1	−56.3	167.1	8 44.6	−56.3	167.1	7 46.1	−56.4	167.2
55	9 45.4	−56.2	167.4	8 46.8	−56.3	167.4	7 48.3	−56.4	167.5	6 49.7	−56.4	167.5
56	8 49.2	−56.2	167.8	7 50.5	−56.3	167.8	6 51.9	−56.4	167.8	5 53.3	−56.5	167.8
57	7 53.0	−56.3	168.1	6 54.2	−56.3	168.1	5 55.5	−56.4	168.2	4 56.8	−56.5	168.2
58	6 56.7	−56.3	168.5	5 57.9	−56.3	168.5	4 59.1	−56.4	168.5	4 00.3	−56.5	168.5
59	6 00.4	−56.3	168.8	5 01.6	−56.4	168.8	4 02.7	−56.4	168.8	3 03.8	−56.5	168.9
60	5 04.1	−56.3	169.2	4 05.2	−56.4	169.2	3 06.3	−56.5	169.2	2 07.3	−56.5	169.2
61	4 07.8	−56.3	169.5	3 08.8	−56.3	169.5	2 09.8	−56.4	169.5	1 10.8	−56.5	169.5
62	3 11.5	−56.3	169.9	2 12.5	−56.4	169.9	1 13.4	−56.4	169.9	0 14.3	−56.4	169.9
63	2 15.2	−56.3	170.2	1 16.1	−56.4	170.2	0 17.0	−56.5	170.2	0 42.1	+56.5	9.8
64	1 18.9	−56.3	170.5	0 19.7	−56.3	170.5	0 39.5	+56.4	9.5	1 38.6	+56.5	9.5
65	0 22.6	−56.3	170.9	0 36.6	+56.4	9.1	1 35.9	+56.4	9.1	2 35.1	+56.5	9.1
66	0 33.7	+56.3	8.8	1 33.0	+56.4	8.8	2 32.3	+56.4	8.8	3 31.6	+56.5	8.8
67	1 30.0	+56.4	8.4	2 29.4	+56.4	8.4	3 28.7	+56.5	8.4	4 28.1	+56.5	8.4
68	2 26.4	+56.3	8.1	3 25.8	+56.3	8.1	4 25.2	+56.4	8.1	5 24.6	+56.4	8.1
69	3 22.7	+56.3	7.7	4 22.1	+56.4	7.7	5 21.6	+56.4	7.7	6 21.0	+56.5	7.8
70	4 19.0	+56.3	7.4	5 18.5	+56.3	7.4	6 18.0	+56.4	7.4	7 17.5	+56.4	7.4
71	5 15.3	+56.2	7.0	6 14.8	+56.3	7.0	7 14.4	+56.3	7.1	8 13.9	+56.4	7.1
72	6 11.5	+56.3	6.7	7 11.1	+56.3	6.7	8 10.7	+56.4	6.7	9 10.3	+56.4	6.7
73	7 07.8	+56.3	6.3	8 07.4	+56.3	6.4	9 07.1	+56.3	6.4	10 06.7	+56.4	6.4
74	8 04.1	+56.2	6.0	9 03.7	+56.3	6.0	10 03.4	+56.3	6.0	11 03.1	+56.3	6.0
75	9 00.3	+56.2	5.6	10 00.0	+56.3	5.6	10 59.7	+56.3	5.7	11 59.4	+56.3	5.7
76	9 56.5	+56.2	5.3	10 56.3	+56.2	5.3	11 56.0	+56.3	5.3	12 55.7	+56.3	5.3
77	10 52.7	+56.2	4.9	11 52.5	+56.2	4.9	12 52.3	+56.2	5.0	13 52.0	+56.3	5.0
78	11 48.9	+56.1	4.6	12 48.7	+56.2	4.6	13 48.5	+56.2	4.6	14 48.3	+56.2	4.6
79	12 45.0	+56.1	4.2	13 44.9	+56.1	4.2	14 44.7	+56.2	4.2	15 44.5	+56.2	4.3
80	13 41.1	+56.1	3.8	14 41.0	+56.1	3.9	15 40.9	+56.1	3.9	16 40.7	+56.2	3.9
81	14 37.2	+56.0	3.5	15 37.1	+56.1	3.5	16 37.0	+56.1	3.5	17 36.9	+56.1	3.5
82	15 33.2	+56.0	3.1	16 33.2	+56.0	3.1	17 33.1	+56.0	3.1	18 33.0	+56.0	3.2
83	16 29.2	+56.0	2.7	17 29.2	+56.0	2.7	18 29.1	+56.0	2.8	19 29.0	+56.1	2.8
84	17 25.2	+55.9	2.4	18 25.2	+55.9	2.4	19 25.1	+56.0	2.4	20 25.1	+55.9	2.4
85	18 21.1	+55.9	2.0	19 21.1	+55.9	2.0	20 21.1	+55.9	2.0	21 21.0	+55.9	2.0
86	19 17.0	+55.8	1.6	20 17.0	+55.8	1.6	21 17.0	+55.8	1.6	22 16.9	+55.9	1.6
87	20 12.8	+55.8	1.2	21 12.8	+55.8	1.2	22 12.8	+55.8	1.2	23 12.8	+55.8	1.2
88	21 08.6	+55.7	0.8	22 08.6	+55.7	0.8	23 08.6	+55.7	0.8	24 08.6	+55.7	0.8
89	22 04.3	+55.7	0.4	23 04.3	+55.7	0.4	24 04.3	+55.7	0.4	25 04.3	+55.7	0.4
90	23 00.0	+55.6	0.0	24 00.0	+55.6	0.0	25 00.0	+55.6	0.0	26 00.0	+55.6	0.0
	23°			24°			25°			26°		

Dec. °	27° Hc ° ′	d ′	Z °	28° Hc ° ′	d ′	Z °	29° Hc ° ′	d ′	Z °	30° Hc ° ′	d ′	Z °
0	55 42.2	−48.6	138.3	54 57.0	−49.3	139.3	54 11.2	−49.9	140.2	53 24.8	−50.5	141.1
1	54 53.6	−49.1	139.4	54 07.7	−49.7	140.3	53 21.3	−50.4	141.1	52 34.3	−50.9	142.0
2	54 04.5	−49.6	140.4	53 18.0	−50.2	141.2	52 30.9	−50.7	142.0	51 43.4	−51.3	142.8
3	53 14.9	−50.0	141.3	52 27.8	−50.6	142.1	51 40.2	−51.1	142.9	50 52.1	−51.6	143.6
4	52 24.9	−50.4	142.2	51 37.2	−51.0	143.0	50 49.1	−51.5	143.7	50 00.5	−52.0	144.4
5	51 34.5	−50.8	143.1	50 46.2	−51.3	143.8	49 57.6	−51.8	144.5	49 08.5	−52.2	145.2
6	50 43.7	−51.2	143.9	49 54.9	−51.6	144.6	49 05.8	−52.1	145.3	48 16.3	−52.6	146.0
7	49 52.5	−51.5	144.8	49 03.3	−52.0	145.4	48 13.7	−52.4	146.1	47 23.7	−52.8	146.7
8	49 01.0	−51.8	145.6	48 11.3	−52.2	146.2	47 21.3	−52.6	146.8	46 30.9	−53.0	147.4
9	48 09.2	−52.1	146.3	47 19.1	−52.5	146.9	46 28.7	−52.9	147.5	45 37.9	−53.3	148.1
10	47 17.1	−52.3	147.1	46 26.6	−52.8	147.6	45 35.8	−53.2	148.2	44 44.6	−53.4	148.7
11	46 24.8	−52.7	147.8	45 33.8	−53.0	148.3	44 42.6	−53.3	148.8	43 51.2	−53.7	149.3
12	45 32.1	−52.8	148.5	44 40.8	−53.2	149.0	43 49.3	−53.6	149.5	42 57.5	−53.9	150.0
13	44 39.3	−53.1	149.1	43 47.6	−53.4	149.6	42 55.7	−53.7	150.1	42 03.6	−54.1	150.6
14	43 46.2	−53.3	149.8	42 54.2	−53.6	150.3	42 02.0	−54.0	150.7	41 09.5	−54.2	151.1
15	42 52.9	−53.6	150.4	42 00.6	−53.9	150.9	41 08.0	−54.1	151.3	40 15.3	−54.4	151.7
16	41 59.3	−53.7	151.0	41 06.7	−54.0	151.4	40 13.9	−54.2	151.9	39 20.9	−54.5	152.2
17	41 05.6	−53.8	151.6	40 12.7	−54.1	152.0	39 19.7	−54.5	152.4	38 26.4	−54.7	152.8
18	40 11.8	−54.1	152.2	39 18.6	−54.3	152.6	38 25.2	−54.5	153.0	37 31.7	−54.8	153.3
19	39 17.7	−54.2	152.8	38 24.3	−54.5	153.1	37 30.7	−54.7	153.5	36 36.9	−54.9	153.8
20	38 23.5	−54.4	153.3	37 29.8	−54.6	153.7	36 36.0	−54.9	154.0	35 42.0	−55.1	154.3
21	37 29.1	−54.5	153.8	36 35.2	−54.7	154.2	35 41.1	−55.0	154.5	34 46.9	−55.2	154.8
22	36 34.6	−54.6	154.4	35 40.5	−54.9	154.7	34 46.1	−55.0	155.0	33 51.7	−55.3	155.3
23	35 40.0	−54.8	154.9	34 45.6	−55.0	155.2	33 51.1	−55.2	155.5	32 56.4	−55.4	155.7
24	34 45.2	−54.9	155.4	33 50.6	−55.1	155.7	32 55.9	−55.3	155.9	32 01.0	−55.4	156.2
25	33 50.3	−55.0	155.9	32 55.5	−55.2	156.1	32 00.6	−55.4	156.4	31 05.6	−55.6	156.6
26	32 55.3	−55.1	156.4	32 00.3	−55.3	156.6	31 05.2	−55.5	156.8	30 10.0	−55.7	157.1
27	32 00.2	−55.2	156.8	31 05.0	−55.4	157.1	30 09.7	−55.5	157.3	29 14.3	−55.7	157.5
28	31 05.0	−55.3	157.3	30 09.6	−55.4	157.5	29 14.2	−55.7	157.7	28 18.6	−55.8	157.9
29	30 09.7	−55.4	157.7	29 14.2	−55.6	157.9	28 18.5	−55.7	158.2	27 22.8	−55.9	158.3
30	29 14.3	−55.4	158.2	28 18.6	−55.7	158.4	27 22.8	−55.8	158.6	26 26.9	−56.0	158.8
31	28 18.9	−55.6	158.6	27 22.9	−55.7	158.8	26 27.0	−55.9	159.0	25 30.9	−56.0	159.2
32	27 23.3	−55.6	159.0	26 27.2	−55.8	159.2	25 31.1	−55.9	159.4	24 34.9	−56.1	159.6
33	26 27.7	−55.8	159.5	25 31.4	−55.8	159.6	24 35.2	−56.0	159.8	23 38.8	−56.1	159.9
34	25 31.9	−55.7	159.9	24 35.6	−55.9	160.0	23 39.2	−56.1	160.2	22 42.7	−56.2	160.3
35	24 36.2	−55.9	160.3	23 39.7	−56.0	160.4	22 43.1	−56.1	160.6	21 46.5	−56.2	160.7
36	23 40.3	−55.9	160.7	22 43.7	−56.1	160.8	21 47.0	−56.2	161.0	20 50.3	−56.3	161.1
37	22 44.4	−55.9	161.1	21 47.6	−56.0	161.2	20 50.8	−56.2	161.3	19 54.0	−56.4	161.4
38	21 48.5	−56.1	161.5	20 51.6	−56.2	161.6	19 54.6	−56.3	161.7	18 57.6	−56.4	161.8
39	20 52.4	−56.0	161.8	19 55.4	−56.2	162.0	18 58.3	−56.3	162.1	18 01.2	−56.4	162.2
40	19 56.4	−56.1	162.2	18 59.2	−56.2	162.3	18 02.0	−56.3	162.4	17 04.8	−56.4	162.5
41	19 00.3	−56.2	162.6	18 03.0	−56.3	162.7	17 05.7	−56.4	162.8	16 08.4	−56.5	162.9
42	18 04.1	−56.2	163.0	17 06.7	−56.3	163.1	16 09.3	−56.4	163.2	15 11.9	−56.5	163.2
43	17 07.9	−56.2	163.3	16 10.4	−56.3	163.4	15 12.9	−56.5	163.5	14 15.4	−56.6	163.6
44	16 11.7	−56.3	163.7	15 14.1	−56.4	163.8	14 16.4	−56.4	163.9	13 18.8	−56.6	163.9
45	15 15.4	−56.3	164.1	14 17.7	−56.4	164.1	13 20.0	−56.6	164.2	12 22.2	−56.6	164.3
46	14 19.1	−56.4	164.4	13 21.3	−56.5	164.5	12 23.4	−56.5	164.5	11 25.6	−56.6	164.6
47	13 22.7	−56.3	164.8	12 24.8	−56.4	164.8	11 26.9	−56.5	164.9	10 29.0	−56.7	164.9
48	12 26.4	−56.4	165.1	11 28.4	−56.5	165.2	10 30.4	−56.6	165.2	9 32.3	−56.6	165.3
49	11 30.0	−56.5	165.5	10 31.9	−56.5	165.5	9 33.8	−56.6	165.6	8 35.7	−56.7	165.6
50	10 33.5	−56.4	165.8	9 35.4	−56.6	165.9	8 37.2	−56.6	165.9	7 39.0	−56.7	165.9
51	9 37.1	−56.5	166.2	8 38.8	−56.5	166.2	7 40.6	−56.7	166.2	6 42.3	−56.7	166.3
52	8 40.6	−56.5	166.5	7 42.3	−56.6	166.5	6 43.9	−56.6	166.6	5 45.6	−56.8	166.6
53	7 44.1	−56.5	166.8	6 45.7	−56.6	166.9	5 47.3	−56.7	166.9	4 48.8	−56.7	166.9
54	6 47.6	−56.5	167.2	5 49.1	−56.6	167.2	4 50.6	−56.7	167.2	3 52.1	−56.7	167.3
55	5 51.1	−56.5	167.5	4 52.5	−56.6	167.5	3 53.9	−56.6	167.6	2 55.4	−56.8	167.6
56	4 54.6	−56.5	167.9	3 55.9	−56.6	167.9	2 57.3	−56.7	167.9	1 58.6	−56.7	167.9
57	3 58.1	−56.6	168.2	2 59.3	−56.6	168.2	2 00.6	−56.7	168.2	1 01.9	−56.8	168.2
58	3 01.5	−56.5	168.5	2 02.7	−56.6	168.5	1 03.9	−56.7	168.5	0 05.1	−56.8	168.6
59	2 05.0	−56.6	168.9	1 06.1	−56.6	168.9	0 07.2	−56.7	168.9	0 51.7	+56.7	11.1
60	1 08.4	−56.6	169.2	0 09.5	−56.7	169.2	0 49.5	+56.7	10.8	1 48.4	+56.8	10.8
61	0 11.8	−56.5	169.5	0 47.2	+56.6	10.5	1 46.2	+56.6	10.5	2 45.2	+56.7	10.5
62	0 44.7	+56.6	10.1	1 43.8	+56.6	10.1	2 42.8	+56.7	10.1	3 41.9	+56.7	10.2
63	1 41.3	+56.6	9.8	2 40.4	+56.6	9.8	3 39.5	+56.7	9.8	4 38.6	+56.8	9.8
64	2 37.8	+56.6	9.5	3 37.0	+56.6	9.5	4 36.2	+56.7	9.5	5 35.4	+56.7	9.5
65	3 34.4	+56.5	9.1	4 33.6	+56.6	9.1	5 32.9	+56.6	9.2	6 32.1	+56.7	9.2
66	4 30.9	+56.5	8.8	5 30.2	+56.6	8.8	6 29.5	+56.6	8.8	7 28.8	+56.7	8.8
67	5 27.4	+56.6	8.5	6 26.8	+56.6	8.5	7 26.1	+56.7	8.5	8 25.5	+56.7	8.5
68	6 24.0	+56.5	8.1	7 23.4	+56.5	8.1	8 22.8	+56.6	8.2	9 22.2	+56.6	8.2
69	7 20.5	+56.5	7.8	8 19.9	+56.6	7.8	9 19.4	+56.6	7.8	10 18.8	+56.6	7.8
70	8 17.0	+56.4	7.4	9 16.5	+56.5	7.5	10 16.0	+56.5	7.5	11 15.4	+56.7	7.5
71	9 13.4	+56.5	7.1	10 13.0	+56.5	7.1	11 12.5	+56.6	7.1	12 12.1	+56.5	7.2
72	10 09.9	+56.4	6.8	11 09.5	+56.5	6.8	12 09.1	+56.5	6.8	13 08.6	+56.6	6.8
73	11 06.3	+56.4	6.4	12 06.0	+56.4	6.4	13 05.6	+56.5	6.5	14 05.2	+56.5	6.5
74	12 02.7	+56.4	6.1	13 02.4	+56.4	6.1	14 02.1	+56.4	6.1	15 01.7	+56.5	6.1
75	12 59.1	+56.4	5.7	13 58.8	+56.4	5.7	14 58.5	+56.5	5.8	15 58.2	+56.5	5.8
76	13 55.5	+56.3	5.4	14 55.2	+56.4	5.4	15 55.0	+56.3	5.4	16 54.7	+56.4	5.4
77	14 51.8	+56.3	5.0	15 51.6	+56.3	5.0	16 51.3	+56.4	5.1	17 51.1	+56.4	5.1
78	15 48.1	+56.3	4.6	16 47.9	+56.3	4.7	17 47.7	+56.3	4.7	18 47.5	+56.3	4.7
79	16 44.4	+56.2	4.3	17 44.2	+56.2	4.3	18 44.0	+56.3	4.3	19 43.8	+56.3	4.4
80	17 40.6	+56.2	3.9	18 40.4	+56.2	3.9	19 40.3	+56.2	4.0	20 40.1	+56.3	4.0
81	18 36.8	+56.1	3.5	19 36.6	+56.2	3.6	20 36.5	+56.2	3.6	21 36.4	+56.2	3.6
82	19 32.9	+56.1	3.2	20 32.8	+56.1	3.2	21 32.7	+56.1	3.2	22 32.6	+56.2	3.2
83	20 29.0	+56.0	2.8	21 28.9	+56.1	2.8	22 28.8	+56.1	2.8	23 28.8	+56.0	2.9
84	21 25.0	+56.0	2.4	22 25.0	+56.0	2.4	23 24.9	+56.0	2.4	24 24.8	+56.1	2.5
85	22 21.0	+55.9	2.0	23 21.0	+55.9	2.0	24 20.9	+56.0	2.1	25 20.9	+55.9	2.1
86	23 16.9	+55.9	1.6	24 16.9	+55.9	1.6	25 16.9	+55.8	1.7	26 16.8	+55.9	1.7
87	24 12.8	+55.8	1.2	25 12.8	+55.8	1.2	26 12.8	+55.8	1.3	27 12.7	+55.9	1.3
88	25 08.6	+55.7	0.8	26 08.6	+55.7	0.8	27 08.6	+55.7	0.8	28 08.6	+55.7	0.8
89	26 04.3	+55.7	0.4	27 04.3	+55.7	0.4	28 04.3	+55.7	0.4	29 04.3	+55.7	0.4
90	27 00.0	+55.6	0.0	28 00.0	+55.6	0.0	29 00.0	+55.6	0.0	30 00.0	+55.6	0.0
	27°			28°			29°			30°		

S. Lat. {L.H.A. greater than 180° ....Zn=180°−Z
{L.H.A. less than 180°............Zn=180°+Z

LATITUDE SAME NAME AS DECLINATION — L.H.A. 158°, 202°

229

23°, 337° L.H.A. LATITUDE SAME NAME AS DECLINATION

N. Lat. {L.H.A. greater than 180° .....Zn=Z
L.H.A. less than 180°............Zn=360°−Z

Dec.	23°			24°			25°			26°			27°			28°			29°			30°			Dec.
	Hc	d	Z	Hc	d	Z	Hc	d	Z	Hc	d	Z	Hc	d	Z	Hc	d	Z	Hc	d	Z	Hc	d	Z	
°	° ′	′	°	° ′	′	°	° ′	′	°	° ′	′	°	° ′	′	°	° ′	′	°	° ′	′	°	° ′	′	°	
0	57 55.3	+43.8	132.6	57 14.3	+44.7	133.8	56 32.3	+45.7	134.9	55 49.6	+46.5	135.9	55 06.1	+47.4	136.9	54 22.0	+48.1	137.9	53 37.1	+48.8	138.8	52 51.7	+49.5	139.7	0
1	58 39.1	+42.9	131.3	57 59.0	+44.0	132.5	57 18.0	+44.9	133.7	56 36.1	+45.9	134.8	55 53.5	+46.7	135.8	55 10.1	+47.5	136.8	54 25.9	+48.3	137.8	53 41.2	+49.0	138.7	1
2	59 22.0	+42.1	130.0	58 43.0	+43.1	131.2	58 02.9	+44.2	132.4	57 22.0	+45.2	133.6	56 40.2	+46.1	134.7	55 57.6	+46.9	135.8	55 14.2	+47.8	136.8	54 30.2	+48.5	137.7	2
3	60 04.1	+41.1	128.6	59 26.1	+42.3	129.9	58 47.1	+43.4	131.2	58 07.2	+44.4	132.4	57 26.3	+45.4	133.5	56 44.5	+46.4	134.6	56 02.0	+47.2	135.7	55 18.7	+47.9	136.7	3
4	60 45.2	+40.1	127.1	60 08.4	+41.4	128.5	59 30.5	+42.6	129.8	58 51.6	+43.6	131.1	58 11.7	+44.7	132.3	57 30.9	+45.6	133.5	56 49.2	+46.5	134.6	56 06.6	+47.4	135.6	4
5	61 25.3	+39.0	125.5	60 49.8	+40.3	127.0	60 13.1	+41.6	128.4	59 35.2	+42.8	129.7	58 56.4	+43.8	131.0	58 16.5	+44.9	132.2	57 35.7	+45.9	133.4	56 54.0	+46.8	134.5	5
6	62 04.3	+37.8	123.9	61 30.1	+39.3	125.5	60 54.7	+40.6	126.9	60 18.0	+41.9	128.3	59 40.2	+43.1	129.7	59 01.4	+44.1	131.0	58 21.6	+45.1	132.2	57 40.8	+46.1	133.4	6
7	62 42.1	+36.6	122.3	62 09.4	+38.1	123.9	61 35.3	+39.5	125.4	60 59.9	+40.8	126.9	60 23.3	+42.1	128.3	59 45.5	+43.3	129.6	59 06.7	+44.4	130.9	58 26.9	+45.4	132.2	7
8	63 18.7	+35.2	120.5	62 47.5	+36.8	122.2	62 14.8	+38.4	123.8	61 40.7	+39.8	125.4	61 05.4	+41.1	126.8	60 28.8	+42.4	128.3	59 51.1	+43.5	129.6	59 12.3	+44.7	130.9	8
9	63 53.9	+33.9	118.7	63 24.3	+35.6	120.5	62 53.2	+37.1	122.1	62 20.5	+38.7	123.8	61 46.5	+40.1	125.3	61 11.2	+41.4	126.8	60 34.6	+42.7	128.2	59 57.0	+43.8	129.6	9
10	64 27.8	+32.3	116.8	63 59.9	+34.1	118.6	63 30.3	+35.8	120.4	62 59.2	+37.4	122.1	62 26.6	+38.9	123.7	61 52.6	+40.3	125.3	61 17.3	+41.7	126.8	60 40.8	+42.9	128.2	10
11	65 00.1	+30.6	114.8	64 34.0	+32.6	116.7	64 06.1	+34.4	118.6	63 36.6	+36.1	120.4	63 05.5	+37.7	122.1	62 32.9	+39.2	123.7	61 59.0	+40.6	125.3	61 23.7	+41.9	126.8	11
12	65 30.7	+29.0	112.8	65 06.6	+30.9	114.8	64 40.5	+32.9	116.7	64 12.7	+34.7	118.5	63 43.2	+36.4	120.3	63 12.1	+38.1	122.0	62 39.6	+39.5	123.7	62 05.6	+41.0	125.3	12
13	65 59.7	+27.1	110.6	65 37.5	+29.3	112.7	65 13.4	+31.2	114.7	64 47.4	+33.2	116.6	64 19.6	+35.0	118.5	63 50.2	+36.7	120.3	63 19.1	+38.3	122.0	62 46.6	+39.8	123.7	13
14	66 26.8	+25.1•	108.4	66 06.8	+27.3	110.6	65 44.6	+29.6	112.7	65 20.6	+31.5	114.7	64 54.6	+33.5	116.6	64 26.9	+35.2	118.5	63 57.4	+37.0	120.3	63 26.4	+38.6	122.0	14
15	66 51.9	+23.1•	106.1	66 34.1	+25.5	108.4	66 14.2	+27.7	110.5	65 52.1	+29.9	112.6	65 28.1	+31.9	114.6	65 02.1	+33.8	116.6	64 34.4	+35.6	118.5	64 05.0	+37.3	120.3	15
16	67 15.0	+21.0•	103.8	66 59.6	+23.4•	106.1	66 41.9	+25.7•	108.3	66 22.0	+28.0	110.5	66 00.0	+30.1	112.6	65 35.9	+32.2	114.6	65 10.0	+34.1	116.6	64 42.3	+35.9	118.5	16
17	67 36.0	+18.7•	101.3	67 23.0	+21.2•	103.7	67 07.6	+23.7•	106.0	66 50.0	+26.0•	108.2	66 30.1	+28.3	110.4	66 08.1	+30.5	112.5	65 44.1	+32.5	114.6	65 18.2	+34.4	116.6	17
18	67 54.7	+16.3•	98.8	67 44.2	+19.0•	101.2	67 31.3	+21.5•	103.6	67 16.0	+24.0•	105.9	66 58.4	+26.4•	108.2	66 38.6	+28.6	110.4	66 16.6	+30.8	112.5	65 52.6	+32.9	114.6	18
19	68 11.0	+13.8•	96.2	68 03.2	+16.6•	98.7	67 52.8	+19.3•	101.1	67 40.0	+21.8•	103.5	67 24.8	+24.3•	105.9	67 07.2	+26.7•	108.2	66 47.4	+29.0	110.4	66 25.5	+31.1	112.5	19
20	68 24.8	+11.4•	93.6	68 19.8	+14.1•	96.1	68 12.1	+16.8•	98.6	68 01.8	+19.5•	101.1	67 49.1	+22.1•	103.5	67 33.9	+24.6•	105.8	67 16.4	+26.9•	108.1	66 56.6	+29.2	110.4	20
21	68 36.2	+8.7•	90.9	68 33.9	+11.6•	93.5	68 28.9	+14.4•	96.0	68 21.3	+17.2•	98.5	68 11.2	+19.8•	101.0	67 58.5	+22.4•	103.4	67 43.3	+25.0•	105.8	67 25.8	+27.4•	108.1	21
22	68 44.9	+6.1•	88.2	68 45.5	+8.9•	90.8	68 43.3	+11.8•	93.3	68 38.5	+14.6•	95.9	68 31.0	+17.4•	98.4	68 20.9	+20.1•	100.9	68 08.3	+22.7•	103.4	67 53.2	+25.2•	105.8	22
23	68 51.0	+3.4•	85.5	68 54.4	+6.3•	88.0	68 55.1	+9.2•	90.6	68 53.1	+12.1•	93.2	68 48.4	+14.9•	95.8	68 41.0	+17.7•	98.4	68 31.0	+20.4•	100.9	68 18.4	+23.0•	103.3	23
24	68 54.4	+0.7•	82.7	69 00.7	+3.6•	85.3	69 04.3	+6.5•	87.9	69 05.2	+9.4•	90.5	69 03.3	+12.3•	93.1	68 58.7	+15.1•	95.7	68 51.4	+17.9•	98.3	68 41.4	+20.7•	100.8	24
25	68 55.1	−2.0•	79.9	69 04.3	+0.9•	82.5	69 10.8	+3.8•	85.1	69 14.6	+6.7•	87.7	69 15.6	+9.6•	90.4	69 13.8	+12.6•	93.0	69 09.3	+15.5•	95.6	69 02.1	+18.3•	98.2	25
26	68 53.1	−4.7•	77.1	69 05.2	−1.9•	79.7	69 14.6	+1.0•	82.3	69 21.3	+3.9•	84.9	69 25.2	+6.9•	87.6	69 26.4	+9.9•	90.2	69 24.8	+12.8•	92.9	69 20.4	+15.7•	95.5	26
27	68 48.4	−7.4•	74.4	69 03.3	−4.6•	76.9	69 15.6	−1.8•	79.5	69 25.2	+1.2•	82.1	69 32.1	+4.2•	84.7	69 36.3	+7.1•	87.4	69 37.6	+10.1•	90.1	69 36.1	+13.0•	92.8	27
28	68 41.0	−10.0•	71.6	68 58.7	−7.3•	74.1	69 13.8	−4.5•	76.6	69 26.4	−1.6•	79.2	69 36.3	+1.3•	81.9	69 43.4	+4.3•	84.5	69 47.7	+7.3•	87.2	69 49.1	+10.3•	90.0	28
29	68 31.0	−12.6•	68.9	68 51.4	−10.0•	71.3	69 09.3	−7.2•	73.8	69 24.8	−4.4•	76.4	69 37.6	−1.5•	79.0	69 47.7	+1.4•	81.7	69 55.0	+4.4•	84.4	69 59.4	+7.5•	87.1	29
30	68 18.4	−15.1•	66.3	68 41.4	−12.5•	68.6	69 02.1	−9.9•	71.0	69 20.4	−7.2•	73.5	69 36.1	−4.4•	76.1	69 49.1	−1.4•	78.8	69 59.4	+1.6•	81.5	70 06.9	+4.6•	84.2	30
31	68 03.3	−17.5•	63.7	68 28.9	−15.1•	65.9	68 52.2	−12.5•	68.3	69 13.2	−9.9•	70.7	69 31.7	−7.0•	73.3	69 47.7	−4.2•	75.9	70 01.0	−1.3•	78.5	70 11.5	+1.8•	81.3	31
32	67 45.8	−19.8•	61.1	68 13.8	−17.5•	63.3	68 39.7	−15.1•	65.6	69 03.3	−12.4•	68.0	69 24.7	−9.9•	70.4	69 43.5	−7.0•	73.0	69 59.7	−4.1•	75.6	70 13.3	−1.2•	78.3	32
33	67 26.0	−22.0•	58.6	67 56.3	−19.8•	60.7	68 24.6	−17.5•	62.9	68 50.9	−15.1•	65.2	69 14.8	−12.5•	67.6	69 36.5	−9.8•	70.1	69 55.6	−7.0•	72.7	70 12.1	−4.1•	75.3	33
34	67 04.0	−24.1•	56.2	67 36.5	−22.1•	58.3	68 07.1	−19.8•	60.4	68 35.8	−17.5•	62.6	69 02.3	−15.0•	64.9	69 26.7	−12.5•	67.3	69 48.6	−9.8•	69.8	70 08.0	−6.9•	72.4	34
35	66 39.9	−26.1	53.9	67 14.4	−24.1•	55.8	67 47.3	−22.1•	57.8	68 18.3	−20.0•	60.0	68 47.3	−17.6•	62.2	69 14.2	−15.1•	64.5	69 38.8	−12.5•	67.0	70 01.1	−9.8•	69.5	35
36	66 13.8	−28.0	51.7	66 50.3	−26.2•	53.5	67 25.2	−24.3•	55.4	67 58.3	−22.1•	57.4	68 29.7	−20.0•	59.6	68 59.1	−17.7•	61.8	69 26.3	−15.1•	64.2	69 51.3	−12.5•	66.6	36
37	65 45.8	−29.8	49.5	66 24.1	−28.1	51.2	67 00.9	−26.3	53.0	67 36.2	−24.4•	55.0	68 09.7	−22.2•	57.0	68 41.4	−20.0•	59.2	69 11.2	−17.7•	61.4	69 38.8	−15.2•	63.8	37
38	65 16.0	−31.5	47.4	65 56.0	−29.9	49.0	66 34.6	−28.2	50.8	67 11.8	−26.3•	52.6	67 47.5	−24.5•	54.5	68 21.4	−22.4•	56.6	68 53.5	−20.1•	58.8	69 23.6	−17.8•	61.0	38
39	64 44.5	−33.1	45.4	65 26.1	−31.6	46.9	66 06.4	−30.0	48.6	66 45.5	−28.4	50.3	67 23.0	−26.5	52.2	67 59.0	−24.5•	54.1	68 33.4	−22.5•	56.2	69 05.8	−20.2•	58.3	39
40	64 11.4	−34.5	43.4	64 54.5	−33.2	44.9	65 36.4	−31.7	46.4	66 17.1	−30.1	48.1	66 56.5	−28.4	49.8	67 34.5	−26.6•	51.7	68 10.9	−24.7•	53.6	68 45.6	−22.6•	55.7	40
41	63 36.9	−35.9	41.6	64 21.3	−34.6	43.0	65 04.7	−33.3	44.4	65 47.0	−31.8	46.0	66 28.1	−30.3	47.6	67 07.9	−28.6	49.4	67 46.2	−26.8•	51.2	68 23.0	−24.8•	53.2	41
42	63 01.0	−37.2	39.8	63 46.7	−36.1	41.1	64 31.4	−34.8	42.5	65 15.2	−33.5	43.9	65 57.8	−32.0	45.5	66 39.3	−30.4	47.1	67 19.4	−28.7	48.9	67 58.2	−26.9•	50.7	42
43	62 23.8	−38.4	38.1	63 10.6	−37.3	39.3	63 56.6	−36.1	40.6	64 41.7	−34.9	42.0	65 25.8	−33.5	43.4	66 08.9	−32.2	45.0	66 50.7	−30.6	46.6	67 31.3	−28.9	48.4	43
44	61 45.4	−39.6	36.4	62 33.3	−38.6	37.6	63 20.5	−37.5	38.8	64 06.8	−36.3	40.1	64 52.3	−35.1	41.4	65 36.7	−33.7	42.9	66 20.1	−32.3	44.4	67 02.4	−30.8	46.1	44
45	61 05.8	−40.6	34.9	61 54.7	−39.6	35.9	62 43.0	−38.7	37.1	63 30.5	−37.7	38.3	64 17.2	−36.5	39.6	65 03.0	−35.3	40.9	65 47.8	−33.9	42.4	66 31.6	−32.5	43.9	45
46	60 25.2	−41.5	33.4	61 15.1	−40.8	34.4	62 04.3	−39.8	35.4	62 52.8	−38.8	36.5	63 40.7	−37.8	37.7	64 27.7	−36.7	39.0	65 13.9	−35.5	40.4	65 59.1	−34.1	41.8	46
47	59 43.7	−42.5	31.9	60 34.3	−41.7	32.8	61 24.5	−40.9	33.8	62 14.0	−40.0	34.9	63 02.9	−39.0	36.0	63 51.0	−37.9	37.2	64 38.4	−36.8	38.5	65 25.0	−35.7	39.8	47
48	59 01.2	−43.4	30.5	59 52.6	−42.6	31.4	60 43.6	−41.9	32.3	61 34.0	−41.0	33.3	62 23.9	−40.2	34.4	63 13.1	−39.2	35.5	64 01.6	−38.2	36.7	64 49.3	−37.0	37.9	48
49	58 17.8	−44.1	29.2	59 10.0	−43.5	30.0	60 01.7	−42.7	30.9	60 53.0	−42.0	31.8	61 43.7	−41.2	32.8	62 33.9	−40.3	33.8	63 23.4	−39.4	34.9	64 12.3	−38.4	36.1	49
50	57 33.7	−44.9	27.9	58 26.5	−44.2	28.7	59 19.0	−43.6	29.5	60 11.0	−42.9	30.3	61 02.5	−42.1	31.2	61 53.6	−41.4	32.2	62 44.0	−40.5	33.2	63 33.9	−39.6	34.3	50
51	56 48.8	−45.5	26.7	57 42.3	−45.0	27.4	58 35.4	−44.5	28.2	59 28.1	−43.8	28.9	60 20.4	−43.1	29.8	61 12.2	−42.4	30.7	62 03.5	−41.5	31.7	62 54.3	−40.7	32.7	51
52	56 03.3	−46.2	25.5	56 57.3	−45.7	26.2	57 50.9	−45.1	26.9	58 44.3	−44.6	27.6	59 37.3	−44.0	28.4	60 29.8	−43.2	29.2	61 22.0	−42.6	30.1	62 13.6	−41.8	31.1	52
53	55 17.1	−46.9	24.4	56 11.6	−46.4	25.0	57 05.8	−45.8	25.7	57 59.7	−45.3	26.3	58 53.3	−44.7	27.1	59 46.6	−44.1	27.8	60 39.4	−43.4	28.7	61 31.8	−42.7	29.6	53
54	54 30.2	−47.3	23.3	55 25.2	−46.9	23.9	56 20.0	−46.5	24.5	57 14.4	−45.9	25.1	58 08.6	−45.4	25.8	59 02.5	−44.9	26.5	59 56.0	−44.3	27.3	60 49.1	−43.6	28.1	54
55	53 42.9	−47.9	22.3	54 38.3	−47.5	22.8	55 33.5	−47.1	23.3	56 28.5	−46.7	23.9	57 23.2	−46.2	24.6	58 17.6	−45.6	25.2	59 11.7	−45.1	26.0	60 05.5	−44.5	26.7	55
56	52 55.0	−48.4	21.2	53 50.8	−48.0	21.7	54 46.4	−47.6	22.3	55 41.8	−47.2	22.8	56 37.0	−46.8	23.4	57 32.0	−46.3	24.0	58 26.6	−45.8	24.7	59 21.0	−45.3	25.4	56
57	52 06.6	−48.9	20.3	53 02.8	−48.6	20.7	53 58.8	−48.2	21.2	54 54.6	−47.8	21.7	55 50.2	−47.3	22.3	56 45.7	−47.0	22.8	57 40.8	−46.4	23.5	58 35.7	−45.9	24.1	57
58	51 17.7	−49.3	19.3	52 14.2	−48.9	19.8	53 10.6	−48.6	20.2	54 06.8	−48.3	20.7	55 02.9	−47.9	21.2	55 58.7	−47.5	21.7	56 54.4	−47.1	22.3	57 49.8	−46.7	22.9	58
59	50 28.4	−49.7	18.4	51 25.3	−49.5	18.8	52 22.0	−49.1	19.2	53 18.5	−48.7	19.7	54 15.0	−48.5	20.1	55 11.2	−48.1	20.6	56 07.3	−47.7	21.2	57 03.1	−47.3	21.7	59
60	49 38.7	−50.1	17.6	50 35.8	−49.8	17.9	51 32.9	−49.6	18.3	52 29.8	−49.3	18.7	53 26.5	−48.9	19.1	54 23.1	−48.6	19.6	55 19.6	−48.3	20.1	56 15.8	−47.8	20.6	60
61	48 48.6	−50.4	16.7	49 46.0	−50.2	17.1	50 43.3	−49.9	17.4	51 40.5	−49.6	17.8	52 37.6	−49.4	18.2	53 34.5	−49.0	18.6	54 31.3	−48.7	19.0	55 28.0	−48.4	19.5	61
62	47 58.2	−50.8	15.9	48 55.8	−50.5	16.2	49 53.4	−50.3	16.5	50 50.9	−50.1	16.9	51 48.2	−49.8	17.3	52 45.5	−49.5	17.6	53 42.6	−49.2	18.1	54 39.6	−48.9	18.5	62
63	47 07.4	−51.1	15.1	48 05.3	−50.9	15.4	49 03.1	−50.7	15.7	50 00.8	−50.4	16.0	50 58.4	−50.1	16.4	51 56.0	−50.0	16.7	52 53.4	−49.7	17.1	53 50.7	−49.4	17.5	63
64	46 16.3	−51.4	14.3	47 14.4	−51.2	14.6	48 12.4	−50.9	14.9	49 10.4	−50.8	15.2	50 08.3	−50.6	15.5	51 06.0	−50.3	15.8	52 03.7	−50.1	16.2	53 01.3	−49.8	16.5	64
65	45 24.9	−51.6	13.6	46 23.2	−51.5	13.9	47 21.5	−51.3	14.1	48 19.6	−51.1	14.4	49 17.7	−50.9	14.7	50 15.7	−50.7	15.0	51 13.6	−50.4	15.3	52 11.5	−50.3	15.6	65
66	44 33.3	−51.9	12.9	45 31.7	−51.7	13.1	46 30.2	−51.6	13.3	47 28.5	−51.4	13.6	48 26.8	−51.2	13.9	49 25.0	−51.0	14.1	50 23.2	−50.9	14.4	51 21.2	−50.6	14.7	66
67	43 41.4	−52.2	12.2	44 40.0	−52.0	12.4	45 38.6	−51.9	12.6	46 37.1	−51.7	12.8	47 35.6	−51.6	13.1	48 34.0	−51.4	13.3	49 32.3	−51.2	13.6	50 30.6	−51.0	13.9	67
68	42 49.2	−52.4	11.5	43 48.0	−52.3	11.7	44 46.7	−52.1	11.9	45 45.4	−52.0	12.1	46 44.0	−51.8	12.3	47 42.6	−51.7	12.6	48 41.1	−51.4	12.8	49 39.6	−51.3	13.1	68
69	41 56.8	−52.6	10.9	42 55.7	−52.5	11.0	43 54.6	−52.4	11.2	44 53.4	−52.2	11.4	45 52.2	−52.1	11.6	46 50.9	−51.9	11.8	47 49.7	−51.8	12.0	48 48.3	−51.6	12.3	69
70	41 04.2	−52.9	10.2	42 03.2	−52.7	10.4	43 02.2	−52.6	10.5	44 01.2	−52.5	10.7	45 00.1	−52.3	10.9	45 59.0	−52.2	11.1	46 57.9	−52.1	11.3	47 56.7	−51.9	11.5	70
71	40 11.3	−53.0	9.6	41 10.5	−53.0	9.7	42 09.6	−52.8	9.9	43 08.7	−52.7	10.0	44 07.8	−52.6	10.2	45 06.8	−52.5	10.4	46 05.8	−52.3	10.6	47 04.8	−52.3	10.8	71
72	39 18.3	−53.2	9.0	40 17.5	−53.1	9.1	41 16.8	−53.0	9.2	42 16.0	−52.9	9.4	43 15.2	−52.8	9.5	44 14.3	−52.7	9.7	45 13.5	−52.6	9.9	46 12.5	−52.4	10.0	72
73	38 25.1	−53.4	8.4	39 24.4	−53.3	8.5	40 23.8	−53.3	8.6	41 23.1	−53.2	8.8	42 22.4	−53.1	8.9	43 21.6	−52.9	9.0	44 20.9	−52.9	9.2	45 20.1	−52.7	9.4	73
74	37 31.7	−53.6	7.8	38 31.1	−53.5	7.9	39 30.5	−53.4	8.0	40 29.9	−53.3	8.1	41 29.3	−53.2	8.3	42 28.7	−53.1	8.4	43 28.0	−53.0	8.5	44 27.4	−53.0	8.7	74
75	36 38.1	−53.7	7.2	37 37.6	−53.6	7.3	38 37.1	−53.5	7.4	39 36.6	−53.5	7.5	40 36.1	−53.4	7.7	41 35.6	−53.4	7.8	42 35.0	−53.2	7.9	43 34.4	−53.1	8.0	75
76	35 44.4	−53.8	6.7	36 44.0	−53.8	6.8	37 43.6	−53.8	6.9	38 43.1	−53.6	7.0	39 42.7	−53.6	7.1	40 42.2	−53.5	7.2	41 41.8	−53.5	7.3	42 41.3	−53.4	7.4	76
77	34 50.6	−54.0	6.1	35 50.2	−53.9	6.2	36 49.8	−53.8	6.3	37 49.5	−53.8	6.4	38 49.1	−53.8	6.5	39 48.7	−53.7	6.6	40 48.3	−53.6	6.7	41 47.9	−53.6	6.8	77
78	33 56.6	−54.2	5.6	34 56.3	−54.1	5.7	35 56.0	−54.1	5.8	36 55.7	−54.0	5.8	37 55.3	−53.9	5.9	38 55.0	−53.8	6.0	39 54.7	−53.8	6.1	40 54.3	−53.7	6.2	78
79	33 02.4	−54.2	5.1	34 02.2	−54.2	5.2	35 01.9	−54.1	5.2	36 01.7	−54.1	5.3	37 01.4	−54.0	5.4	38 01.2	−54.1	5.4	39 00.9	−54.0	5.5	40 00.6	−53.9	5.6	79
80	32 08.2	−54.4	4.6	33 08.0	−54.4	4.6	34 07.8	−54.3	4.7	35 07.6	−54.3	4.8	36 07.4	−54.3	4.8	37 07.1	−54.1	4.9	38 06.9	−54.1	4.9	39 06.7	−54.1	5.0	80
81	31 13.8	−54.5	4.1	32 13.6	−54.4	4.1	33 13.5	−54.4	4.2	34 13.3	−54.4	4.2	35 13.1	−54.3	4.3	36 13.0	−54.3	4.3	37 12.8	−54.3	4.4	38 12.6	−54.2	4.5	81
82	30 19.3	−54.6	3.6	31 19.2	−54.6	3.6	32 19.1	−54.6	3.7	33 18.9	−54.5	3.7	34 18.8	−54.5	3.8	35 18.7	−54.5	3.8	36 18.5	−54.4	3.9	37 18.4	−54.4	3.9	82
83	29 24.7	−54.7	3.1	30 24.6	−54.7	3.2	31 24.5	−54.6	3.2	32 24.4	−54.6	3.2	33 24.3	−54.6	3.3	34 24.2	−54.5	3.3	35 24.1	−54.5	3.3	36 24.0	−54.5	3.4	83
84	28 30.0	−54.8	2.7	29 29.9	−54.7	2.7	30 29.9	−54.8	2.7	31 29.8	−54.7	2.7	32 29.7	−54.7	2.8	33 29.7	−54.7	2.8	34 29.6	−54.7	2.8	35 29.5	−54.6	2.9	84
85	27 35.2	−54.9	2.2	28 35.2	−54.9	2.2	29 35.1	−54.8	2.2	30 35.1	−54.9	2.3	31 35.0	−54.8	2.3	32 35.0	−54.8	2.3	33 34.9	−54.7	2.3	34 34.9	−54.8	2.4	85
86	26 40.3	−54.9	1.7	27 40.3	−54.9	1.8	28 40.3	−55.0	1.8	29 40.2	−54.9	1.8	30 40.2	−54.9	1.8	31 40.2	−54.9	1.8	32 40.2	−54.9	1.9	33 40.1	−54.8	1.9	86
87	25 45.4	−55.1	1.3	26 45.4	−55.1	1.3	27 45.3	−55.0	1.3	28 45.3	−55.0	1.3	29 45.3	−55.0	1.3	30 45.3	−55.0	1.4	31 45.3	−55.0	1.4	32 45.3	−55.0	1.4	87
88	24 50.3	−55.1	0.9	25 50.3	−55.1	0.9	26 50.3	−55.1	0.9	27 50.3	−55.1	0.9	28 50.3	−55.1	0.9	29 50.3	−55.1	0.9	30 50.3	−55.1	0.9	31 50.3	−55.1	0.9	88
89	23 55.2	−55.2	0.4	24 55.2	−55.2	0.4	25 55.2	−55.2	0.4	26 55.2	−55.2	0.4	27 55.2	−55.2	0.4	28 55.2	−55.2	0.4	29 55.2	−55.2	0.5	30 55.2	−55.2	0.5	89
90	23 00.0	−55.3	0.0	24 00.0	−55.3	0.0	25 00.0	−55.3	0.0	26 00.0	−55.3	0.0	27 00.0	−55.3	0.0	28 00.0	−55.3	0.0	29 00.0	−55.3	0.0	30 00.0	−55.3	0.0	90
	23°			24°			25°			26°			27°			28°			29°			30°			

23°, 337° L.H.A. LATITUDE SAME NAME AS DECLINATION

230

LATITUDE CONTRARY NAME TO DECLINATION L.H.A. 23°, 337°

Dec.	23° Hc	d	Z	24° Hc	d	Z	25° Hc	d	Z	26° Hc	d	Z	27° Hc	d	Z	28° Hc	d	Z	29° Hc	d	Z	30° Hc	d	Z	Dec.
°	° ′	′	°	° ′	′	°	° ′	′	°	° ′	′	°	° ′	′	°	° ′	′	°	° ′	′	°	° ′	′	°	°
0	57 55.3	−44.5	132.6	57 14.3	−45.5	133.8	56 32.3	−46.3	134.9	55 49.6	−47.1	135.9	55 06.1	−47.8	136.9	54 22.0	−48.6	137.9	53 37.1	−49.2	138.8	52 51.7	−49.9	139.7	0
1	57 10.8	−45.2	133.9	56 28.8	−46.1	135.0	55 46.0	−46.9	136.0	55 02.5	−47.7	137.0	54 18.3	−48.4	138.0	53 33.4	−49.1	138.9	52 47.9	−49.7	139.7	52 01.8	−50.3	140.6	1
2	56 25.6	−45.9	135.1	55 42.7	−46.7	136.1	54 59.1	−47.5	137.1	54 14.8	−48.2	138.1	53 29.9	−48.9	139.0	52 44.3	−49.5	139.8	51 58.2	−50.2	140.7	51 11.5	−50.7	141.5	2
3	55 39.7	−46.5	136.2	54 56.0	−47.3	137.2	54 11.6	−48.0	138.2	53 26.6	−48.7	139.1	52 41.0	−49.4	139.9	51 54.8	−50.0	140.8	51 08.0	−50.5	141.6	50 20.8	−51.0	142.3	3
4	54 53.2	−47.1	137.3	54 08.7	−47.8	138.3	53 23.6	−48.5	139.2	52 37.9	−49.2	140.0	51 51.6	−49.7	140.9	51 04.8	−50.3	141.7	50 17.5	−50.8	142.4	49 29.8	−51.4	143.1	4
5	54 06.1	−47.7	138.4	53 20.9	−48.4	139.3	52 35.1	−49.0	140.2	51 48.7	−49.6	141.0	51 01.9	−50.2	141.8	50 14.5	−50.7	142.5	49 26.7	−51.3	143.2	48 38.4	−51.7	143.9	5
6	53 18.4	−48.2	139.4	52 32.5	−48.8	140.3	51 46.1	−49.4	141.1	50 59.1	−49.9	141.9	50 11.7	−50.5	142.6	49 23.8	−51.1	143.3	48 35.4	−51.5	144.0	47 46.7	−52.0	144.7	6
7	52 30.2	−48.6	140.4	51 43.7	−49.2	141.2	50 56.7	−49.8	142.0	50 09.2	−50.4	142.8	49 21.2	−50.9	143.5	48 32.7	−51.3	144.1	47 43.9	−51.8	144.8	46 54.7	−52.2	145.4	7
8	51 41.6	−49.1	141.4	50 54.5	−49.7	142.1	50 06.9	−50.3	142.9	49 18.8	−50.7	143.6	48 30.3	−51.2	144.3	47 41.4	−51.7	144.9	46 52.1	−52.1	145.5	46 02.5	−52.6	146.1	8
9	50 52.5	−49.5	142.3	50 04.8	−50.0	143.0	49 16.6	−50.5	143.7	48 28.1	−51.1	144.4	47 39.1	−51.5	145.0	46 49.7	−51.9	145.7	46 00.0	−52.4	146.3	45 09.9	−52.7	146.8	9
10	50 03.0	−49.9	143.2	49 14.8	−50.5	143.9	48 26.1	−50.9	144.6	47 37.0	−51.4	145.2	46 47.6	−51.8	145.8	45 57.8	−52.3	146.4	45 07.6	−52.6	146.9	44 17.2	−53.0	147.5	10
11	49 13.1	−50.3	144.0	48 24.3	−50.7	144.7	47 35.2	−51.2	145.3	46 45.6	−51.6	146.0	45 55.8	−52.1	146.5	45 05.5	−52.4	147.1	44 15.0	−52.8	147.6	43 24.2	−53.2	148.1	11
12	48 22.8	−50.6	144.9	47 33.6	−51.1	145.5	46 44.0	−51.6	146.1	45 54.0	−52.0	146.7	45 03.7	−52.4	147.2	44 13.1	−52.7	147.8	43 22.2	−53.1	148.3	42 31.0	−53.4	148.8	12
13	47 32.2	−50.9	145.7	46 42.5	−51.4	146.3	45 52.4	−51.8	146.9	45 02.0	−52.1	147.4	44 11.3	−52.5	147.9	43 20.4	−53.0	148.4	42 29.1	−53.3	148.9	41 37.6	−53.6	149.4	13
14	46 41.3	−51.2	146.4	45 51.1	−51.6	147.0	45 00.6	−52.0	147.6	44 09.9	−52.5	148.1	43 18.8	−52.8	148.6	42 27.4	−53.1	149.1	41 35.8	−53.4	149.5	40 44.0	−53.8	150.0	14
15	45 50.1	−51.6	147.2	44 59.5	−52.0	147.7	44 08.6	−52.3	148.3	43 17.4	−52.7	148.8	42 26.0	−53.0	149.2	41 34.3	−53.3	149.7	40 42.4	−53.7	150.1	39 50.2	−53.9	150.6	15
16	44 58.5	−51.8	147.9	44 07.5	−52.1	148.4	43 16.3	−52.6	148.9	42 24.7	−52.8	149.4	41 33.0	−53.2	149.9	40 41.0	−53.6	150.3	39 48.7	−53.8	150.7	38 56.3	−54.1	151.1	16
17	44 06.7	−52.0	148.6	43 15.4	−52.5	149.1	42 23.7	−52.7	149.6	41 31.9	−53.1	150.1	40 39.8	−53.4	150.5	39 47.4	−53.7	150.9	38 54.9	−54.0	151.3	38 02.2	−54.3	151.7	17
18	43 14.7	−52.3	149.3	42 22.9	−52.6	149.8	41 31.0	−53.0	150.2	40 38.8	−53.3	150.7	39 46.4	−53.6	151.1	38 53.7	−53.8	151.5	38 00.9	−54.1	151.9	37 07.9	−54.4	152.2	18
19	42 22.4	−52.5	150.0	41 30.3	−52.8	150.4	40 38.0	−53.2	150.9	39 45.5	−53.5	151.3	38 52.8	−53.8	151.7	37 59.9	−54.0	152.0	37 06.8	−54.3	152.4	36 13.5	−54.5	152.7	19
20	41 29.9	−52.8	150.6	40 37.5	−53.1	151.1	39 44.8	−53.3	151.5	38 52.0	−53.6	151.9	37 59.0	−53.9	152.2	37 05.9	−54.2	152.6	36 12.5	−54.4	152.9	35 19.0	−54.7	153.3	20
21	40 37.1	−52.9	151.3	39 44.4	−53.2	151.7	38 51.5	−53.5	152.1	37 58.4	−53.8	152.4	37 05.1	−54.0	152.8	36 11.7	−54.3	153.1	35 18.1	−54.6	153.5	34 24.3	−54.7	153.8	21
22	39 44.2	−53.1	151.9	38 51.2	−53.4	152.3	37 58.0	−53.7	152.6	37 04.6	−53.9	153.0	36 11.1	−54.2	153.3	35 17.4	−54.5	153.7	34 23.5	−54.6	154.0	33 29.6	−54.9	154.3	22
23	38 51.1	−53.3	152.5	37 57.8	−53.6	152.9	37 04.3	−53.9	153.2	36 10.7	−54.1	153.5	35 16.9	−54.4	153.9	34 22.9	−54.5	154.2	33 28.9	−54.8	154.5	32 34.7	−55.0	154.7	23
24	37 57.8	−53.5	153.1	37 04.2	−53.8	153.4	36 10.4	−53.9	153.8	35 16.6	−54.3	154.1	34 22.5	−54.4	154.4	33 28.4	−54.7	154.7	32 34.1	−54.9	154.9	31 39.7	−55.1	155.2	24
25	37 04.3	−53.6	153.7	36 10.4	−53.8	154.0	35 16.5	−54.2	154.3	34 22.3	−54.3	154.6	33 28.1	−54.6	154.9	32 33.7	−54.8	155.2	31 39.2	−55.0	155.4	30 44.6	−55.2	155.7	25
26	36 10.7	−53.8	154.2	35 16.6	−54.1	154.5	34 22.3	−54.2	154.8	33 28.0	−54.5	155.1	32 33.5	−54.7	155.4	31 38.9	−54.9	155.6	30 44.2	−55.1	155.9	29 49.4	−55.3	156.1	26
27	35 16.9	−54.0	154.8	34 22.5	−54.1	155.1	33 28.1	−54.4	155.3	32 33.5	−54.6	155.6	31 38.8	−54.8	155.9	30 44.0	−55.0	156.1	29 49.1	−55.2	156.3	28 54.1	−55.4	156.6	27
28	34 22.9	−54.0	155.3	33 28.4	−54.3	155.6	32 33.7	−54.5	155.8	31 38.9	−54.7	156.1	30 44.0	−54.9	156.3	29 49.0	−55.1	156.6	28 53.9	−55.3	156.8	27 58.7	−55.5	157.0	28
29	33 28.9	−54.2	155.8	32 34.1	−54.4	156.1	31 39.2	−54.6	156.3	30 44.2	−54.8	156.6	29 49.1	−55.0	156.8	28 53.9	−55.2	157.0	27 58.6	−55.4	157.2	27 03.2	−55.5	157.4	29
30	32 34.7	−54.4	156.3	31 39.7	−54.6	156.6	30 44.6	−54.8	156.8	29 49.4	−55.0	157.0	28 54.1	−55.1	157.3	27 58.7	−55.3	157.5	27 03.2	−55.4	157.7	26 07.7	−55.6	157.9	30
31	31 40.3	−54.4	156.8	30 45.1	−54.6	157.1	29 49.8	−54.8	157.3	28 54.4	−55.0	157.5	27 59.0	−55.2	157.7	27 03.4	−55.3	157.9	26 07.8	−55.5	158.1	25 12.1	−55.7	158.3	31
32	30 45.9	−54.5	157.3	29 50.5	−54.7	157.5	28 55.0	−54.9	157.8	27 59.4	−55.1	158.0	27 03.8	−55.3	158.2	26 08.1	−55.5	158.3	25 12.3	−55.6	158.5	24 16.4	−55.8	158.7	32
33	29 51.4	−54.7	157.8	28 55.8	−54.9	158.0	28 00.1	−55.0	158.2	27 04.3	−55.1	158.4	26 08.5	−55.3	158.6	25 12.6	−55.5	158.8	24 16.7	−55.7	158.9	23 20.6	−55.8	159.1	33
34	28 56.7	−54.7	158.3	28 00.9	−54.9	158.5	27 05.1	−55.1	158.7	26 09.2	−55.3	158.8	25 13.2	−55.4	159.0	24 17.1	−55.5	159.2	23 21.0	−55.7	159.3	22 24.8	−55.8	159.5	34
35	28 02.0	−54.9	158.7	27 06.0	−55.0	158.9	26 10.0	−55.2	159.1	25 13.9	−55.3	159.3	24 17.8	−55.5	159.4	23 21.6	−55.7	159.6	22 25.3	−55.8	159.7	21 29.0	−55.9	159.9	35
36	27 07.1	−54.9	159.2	26 11.0	−55.1	159.4	25 14.8	−55.2	159.5	24 18.6	−55.4	159.7	23 22.3	−55.6	159.9	22 25.9	−55.7	160.0	21 29.5	−55.8	160.1	20 33.1	−56.0	160.3	36
37	26 12.2	−55.0	159.6	25 15.9	−55.1	159.8	24 19.6	−55.3	160.0	23 23.2	−55.5	160.1	22 26.7	−55.6	160.3	21 30.2	−55.7	160.4	20 33.7	−55.9	160.5	19 37.1	−56.0	160.7	37
38	25 17.2	−55.1	160.1	24 20.8	−55.3	160.2	23 24.3	−55.4	160.4	22 27.7	−55.5	160.5	21 31.1	−55.7	160.7	20 34.5	−55.8	160.8	19 37.8	−55.9	160.9	18 41.1	−56.1	161.0	38
39	24 22.1	−55.2	160.5	23 25.5	−55.3	160.7	22 28.9	−55.5	160.8	21 32.2	−55.6	160.9	20 35.4	−55.7	161.1	19 38.7	−55.9	161.2	18 41.9	−56.0	161.3	17 45.0	−56.1	161.4	39
40	23 26.9	−55.2	161.0	22 30.2	−55.4	161.1	21 33.4	−55.5	161.2	20 36.6	−55.7	161.4	19 39.7	−55.8	161.5	18 42.8	−55.9	161.6	17 45.9	−56.1	161.7	16 48.9	−56.1	161.8	40
41	22 31.7	−55.3	161.4	21 34.8	−55.4	161.5	20 37.9	−55.6	161.6	19 40.9	−55.6	161.7	18 43.9	−55.8	161.9	17 46.9	−55.9	162.0	16 49.8	−56.0	162.1	15 52.8	−56.2	162.1	41
42	21 36.4	−55.3	161.8	20 39.4	−55.5	161.9	19 42.3	−55.6	162.0	18 45.3	−55.8	162.1	17 48.1	−55.8	162.2	16 51.0	−56.0	162.3	15 53.8	−56.1	162.4	14 56.6	−56.2	162.5	42
43	20 41.1	−55.5	162.2	19 43.9	−55.5	162.3	18 46.7	−55.6	162.4	17 49.5	−55.8	162.5	16 52.3	−55.9	162.6	15 55.0	−56.0	162.7	14 57.7	−56.2	162.8	14 00.4	−56.3	162.9	43
44	19 45.6	−55.4	162.6	18 48.4	−55.6	162.7	17 51.1	−55.8	162.8	16 53.7	−55.8	162.9	15 56.4	−56.0	163.0	14 59.0	−56.1	163.1	14 01.5	−56.1	163.2	13 04.1	−56.3	163.2	44
45	18 50.2	−55.6	163.0	17 52.8	−55.7	163.1	16 55.3	−55.7	163.2	15 57.9	−55.9	163.3	15 00.4	−56.0	163.4	14 02.9	−56.1	163.5	13 05.4	−56.2	163.5	12 07.8	−56.3	163.6	45
46	17 54.6	−55.5	163.4	16 57.1	−55.7	163.5	15 59.6	−55.8	163.6	15 02.0	−55.9	163.7	14 04.4	−56.0	163.8	13 06.8	−56.1	163.8	12 09.2	−56.3	163.9	11 11.5	−56.3	163.9	46
47	16 59.1	−55.6	163.8	16 01.4	−55.7	163.9	15 03.8	−55.9	164.0	14 06.1	−55.9	164.1	13 08.4	−56.1	164.1	12 10.7	−56.2	164.2	11 12.9	−56.2	164.2	10 15.2	−56.4	164.3	47
48	16 03.5	−55.7	164.2	15 05.7	−55.8	164.3	14 07.9	−55.8	164.4	13 10.2	−56.0	164.4	12 12.3	−56.0	164.5	11 14.5	−56.2	164.5	10 16.7	−56.3	164.6	9 18.8	−56.3	164.6	48
49	15 07.8	−55.7	164.6	14 09.9	−55.8	164.7	13 12.1	−55.9	164.7	12 14.2	−56.0	164.8	11 16.3	−56.1	164.8	10 18.3	−56.2	164.9	9 20.4	−56.3	164.9	8 22.5	−56.4	165.0	49
50	14 12.1	−55.7	165.0	13 14.1	−55.8	165.0	12 16.2	−56.0	165.1	11 18.2	−56.1	165.2	10 20.2	−56.2	165.2	9 22.1	−56.2	165.3	8 24.1	−56.3	165.3	7 26.1	−56.4	165.3	50
51	13 16.4	−55.8	165.4	12 18.3	−55.9	165.4	11 20.2	−55.9	165.5	10 22.1	−56.0	165.5	9 24.0	−56.1	165.6	8 25.9	−56.2	165.6	7 27.8	−56.3	165.6	6 29.7	−56.4	165.7	51
52	12 20.6	−55.8	165.7	11 22.4	−55.9	165.8	10 24.3	−56.0	165.8	9 26.1	−56.1	165.9	8 27.9	−56.2	165.9	7 29.7	−56.3	166.0	6 31.5	−56.4	166.0	5 33.3	−56.5	166.0	52
53	11 24.8	−55.8	166.1	10 26.5	−55.9	166.2	9 28.3	−56.0	166.2	8 30.0	−56.1	166.2	7 31.7	−56.2	166.3	6 33.4	−56.2	166.3	5 35.1	−56.3	166.3	4 36.8	−56.4	166.4	53
54	10 29.0	−55.9	166.5	9 30.6	−55.9	166.5	8 32.3	−56.1	166.6	7 33.9	−56.1	166.6	6 35.5	−56.2	166.6	5 37.2	−56.3	166.7	4 38.8	−56.4	166.7	3 40.4	−56.5	166.7	54
55	9 33.1	−55.9	166.9	8 34.7	−56.0	166.9	7 36.2	−56.0	166.9	6 37.8	−56.1	167.0	5 39.3	−56.2	167.0	4 40.9	−56.3	167.0	3 42.4	−56.4	167.0	2 43.9	−56.4	167.0	55
56	8 37.2	−55.9	167.2	7 38.7	−56.0	167.3	6 40.2	−56.1	167.3	5 41.7	−56.2	167.3	4 43.1	−56.2	167.3	3 44.6	−56.3	167.4	2 46.0	−56.4	167.4	1 47.5	−56.5	167.4	56
57	7 41.3	−55.9	167.6	6 42.7	−56.0	167.6	5 44.1	−56.1	167.7	4 45.5	−56.1	167.7	3 46.9	−56.2	167.7	2 48.3	−56.3	167.7	1 49.6	−56.3	167.7	0 51.0	−56.4	167.7	57
58	6 45.4	−55.9	168.0	5 46.7	−56.0	168.0	4 48.0	−56.0	168.0	3 49.4	−56.2	168.0	2 50.7	−56.3	168.0	1 52.0	−56.4	168.0	0 53.3	−56.4	168.0	0 05.4	+56.5	11.9	58
59	5 49.5	−56.0	168.3	4 50.7	−56.0	168.3	3 52.0	−56.1	168.4	2 53.2	−56.2	168.4	1 54.4	−56.2	168.4	0 55.6	−56.3	168.4	0 03.1	+56.4	11.6	1 01.9	+56.5	11.6	59
60	4 53.5	−55.9	168.7	3 54.7	−56.0	168.7	2 55.9	−56.1	168.7	1 57.0	−56.2	168.7	0 58.2	−56.3	168.7	0 00.7	+56.3	11.3	0 59.5	+56.4	11.3	1 58.4	+56.4	11.3	60
61	3 57.6	−56.0	169.1	2 58.7	−56.1	169.1	1 59.8	−56.2	169.1	1 00.8	−56.1	169.1	0 01.9	−56.2	169.1	0 57.0	+56.3	10.9	1 55.9	+56.4	10.9	2 54.8	+56.5	10.9	61
62	3 01.6	−56.0	169.4	2 02.6	−56.0	169.4	1 03.6	−56.1	169.4	0 04.7	−56.2	169.4	0 54.3	+56.3	10.6	1 53.3	+56.3	10.6	2 52.3	+56.4	10.6	3 51.3	+56.4	10.6	62
63	2 05.6	−56.0	169.8	1 06.6	−56.1	169.8	0 07.5	−56.1	169.8	0 51.5	+56.2	10.2	1 50.6	+56.2	10.2	2 49.6	+56.3	10.2	3 48.7	+56.3	10.2	4 47.7	+56.4	10.3	63
64	1 09.6	−55.9	170.1	0 10.5	−56.0	170.1	0 48.6	+56.1	9.9	1 47.7	+56.2	9.9	2 46.8	+56.2	9.9	3 45.9	+56.3	9.9	4 45.0	+56.4	9.9	5 44.1	+56.4	9.9	64
65	0 13.7	−56.0	170.5	0 45.5	+56.1	9.5	1 44.7	+56.1	9.5	2 43.9	+56.1	9.5	3 43.0	+56.3	9.5	4 42.2	+56.3	9.5	5 41.4	+56.3	9.6	6 40.5	+56.4	9.6	65
66	0 42.3	+56.0	9.1	1 41.6	+56.0	9.1	2 40.8	+56.1	9.2	3 40.0	+56.2	9.2	4 39.3	+56.2	9.2	5 38.5	+56.3	9.2	6 37.7	+56.4	9.2	7 36.9	+56.4	9.2	66
67	1 38.3	+56.0	8.8	2 37.6	+56.0	8.8	3 36.9	+56.1	8.8	4 36.2	+56.1	8.8	5 35.5	+56.2	8.8	6 34.8	+56.2	8.8	7 34.1	+56.3	8.9	8 33.3	+56.4	8.9	67
68	2 34.3	+56.0	8.4	3 33.6	+56.1	8.4	4 33.0	+56.1	8.4	5 32.3	+56.2	8.5	6 31.7	+56.2	8.5	7 31.0	+56.3	8.5	8 30.4	+56.3	8.5	9 29.7	+56.4	8.5	68
69	3 30.3	+55.9	8.1	4 29.7	+56.0	8.1	5 29.1	+56.0	8.1	6 28.5	+56.1	8.1	7 27.9	+56.1	8.1	8 27.3	+56.2	8.1	9 26.7	+56.2	8.2	10 26.1	+56.3	8.2	69
70	4 26.2	+56.0	7.7	5 25.7	+56.0	7.7	6 25.1	+56.1	7.7	7 24.6	+56.1	7.7	8 24.0	+56.2	7.8	9 23.5	+56.2	7.8	10 22.9	+56.3	7.8	11 22.4	+56.3	7.8	70
71	5 22.2	+55.9	7.3	6 21.7	+56.0	7.4	7 21.2	+56.0	7.4	8 20.7	+56.1	7.4	9 20.2	+56.1	7.4	10 19.7	+56.2	7.4	11 19.2	+56.2	7.5	12 18.7	+56.2	7.5	71
72	6 18.1	+55.9	7.0	7 17.7	+55.9	7.0	8 17.2	+56.0	7.0	9 16.8	+56.0	7.0	10 16.3	+56.1	7.0	11 15.9	+56.1	7.1	12 15.4	+56.2	7.1	13 14.9	+56.3	7.1	72
73	7 14.0	+56.0	6.6	8 13.6	+56.0	6.6	9 13.2	+56.0	6.6	10 12.8	+56.1	6.7	11 12.4	+56.1	6.7	12 12.0	+56.1	6.7	13 11.6	+56.2	6.7	14 11.2	+56.2	6.8	73
74	8 10.0	+55.8	6.2	9 09.6	+55.9	6.3	10 09.2	+56.0	6.3	11 08.9	+56.0	6.3	12 08.5	+56.1	6.3	13 08.1	+56.1	6.3	14 07.8	+56.1	6.4	15 07.4	+56.2	6.4	74
75	9 05.8	+55.9	5.9	10 05.5	+55.9	5.9	11 05.2	+55.9	5.9	12 04.9	+56.0	5.9	13 04.6	+56.0	6.0	14 04.2	+56.1	6.0	15 03.9	+56.1	6.0	16 03.6	+56.1	6.0	75
76	10 01.7	+55.8	5.5	11 01.4	+55.9	5.5	12 01.1	+56.0	5.5	13 00.9	+55.9	5.6	14 00.6	+56.0	5.6	15 00.3	+56.0	5.6	16 00.0	+56.1	5.6	16 59.7	+56.1	5.7	76
77	10 57.5	+55.9	5.1	11 57.3	+55.9	5.2	12 57.1	+55.8	5.2	13 56.8	+55.9	5.2	14 56.6	+55.9	5.2	15 56.3	+56.0	5.2	16 56.1	+56.0	5.3	17 55.8	+56.1	5.3	77
78	11 53.4	+55.7	4.8	12 53.2	+55.8	4.8	13 52.9	+55.9	4.8	14 52.7	+55.9	4.8	15 52.5	+55.9	4.8	16 52.3	+56.0	4.9	17 52.1	+56.0	4.9	18 51.9	+56.0	4.9	78
79	12 49.1	+55.8	4.4	13 49.0	+55.8	4.4	14 48.8	+55.8	4.4	15 48.6	+55.9	4.4	16 48.4	+55.9	4.5	17 48.3	+55.9	4.5	18 48.1	+55.9	4.5	19 47.9	+55.9	4.5	79
80	13 44.9	+55.7	4.0	14 44.8	+55.7	4.0	15 44.6	+55.8	4.0	16 44.5	+55.8	4.1	17 44.3	+55.8	4.1	18 44.2	+55.8	4.1	19 44.0	+55.9	4.1	20 43.8	+55.9	4.2	80
81	14 40.6	+55.7	3.6	15 40.5	+55.7	3.6	16 40.4	+55.7	3.7	17 40.3	+55.7	3.7	18 40.1	+55.8	3.7	19 40.0	+55.8	3.7	20 39.9	+55.8	3.7	21 39.7	+55.9	3.8	81
82	15 36.3	+55.6	3.2	16 36.2	+55.7	3.3	17 36.1	+55.7	3.3	18 36.0	+55.7	3.3	19 35.9	+55.7	3.3	20 35.8	+55.8	3.3	21 35.7	+55.8	3.4	22 35.6	+55.8	3.4	82
83	16 31.9	+55.6	2.8	17 31.9	+55.6	2.9	18 31.8	+55.6	2.9	19 31.7	+55.7	2.9	20 31.6	+55.7	2.9	21 31.6	+55.6	2.9	22 31.5	+55.7	3.0	23 31.4	+55.7	3.0	83
84	17 27.5	+55.6	2.5	18 27.5	+55.5	2.5	19 27.4	+55.6	2.5	20 27.4	+55.6	2.5	21 27.3	+55.6	2.5	22 27.2	+55.7	2.5	23 27.2	+55.6	2.6	24 27.1	+55.7	2.6	84
85	18 23.1	+55.5	2.1	19 23.0	+55.6	2.1	20 23.0	+55.5	2.1	21 23.0	+55.5	2.1	22 22.9	+55.6	2.1	23 22.9	+55.5	2.1	24 22.8	+55.6	2.1	25 22.8	+55.6	2.2	85
86	19 18.6	+55.4	1.7	20 18.6	+55.4	1.7	21 18.5	+55.5	1.7	22 18.5	+55.5	1.7	23 18.5	+55.5	1.7	24 18.4	+55.5	1.7	25 18.4	+55.5	1.7	26 18.4	+55.5	1.7	86
87	20 14.0	+55.4	1.2	21 14.0	+55.4	1.3	22 14.0	+55.4	1.3	23 14.0	+55.4	1.3	24 14.0	+55.4	1.3	25 13.9	+55.5	1.3	26 13.9	+55.5	1.3	27 13.9	+55.5	1.3	87
88	21 09.4	+55.3	0.8	22 09.4	+55.3	0.8	23 09.4	+55.3	0.8	24 09.4	+55.3	0.9	25 09.4	+55.3	0.9	26 09.4	+55.3	0.9	27 09.4	+55.3	0.9	28 09.4	+55.3	0.9	88
89	22 04.7	+55.3	0.4	23 04.7	+55.3	0.4	24 04.7	+55.3	0.4	25 04.7	+55.3	0.4	26 04.7	+55.3	0.4	27 04.7	+55.3	0.4	28 04.7	+55.3	0.4	29 04.7	+55.3	0.4	89
90	23 00.0	+55.2	0.0	24 00.0	+55.2	0.0	25 00.0	+55.2	0.0	26 00.0	+55.2	0.0	27 00.0	+55.2	0.0	28 00.0	+55.2	0.0	29 00.0	+55.2	0.0	30 00.0	+55.2	0.0	90
	23°			24°			25°			26°			27°			28°			29°			30°			

S. Lat. { L.H.A. greater than 180° ....Zn=180°−Z
L.H.A. less than 180°...........Zn=180°+Z

LATITUDE SAME NAME AS DECLINATION L.H.A. 157°, 203°

N. Lat. {L.H.A. greater than 180° .....Zn=Z; L.H.A. less than 180°............Zn=360°–Z}

Dec.	23° Hc	d	Z	24° Hc	d	Z	25° Hc	d	Z	26° Hc	d	Z	27° Hc	d	Z	28° Hc	d	Z	29° Hc	d	Z	30° Hc	d	Z	Dec.
°	° ′	′	°	° ′	′	°	° ′	′	°	° ′	′	°	° ′	′	°	° ′	′	°	° ′	′	°	° ′	′	°	°
0	57 14.3	+42.9	131.3	56 34.2	+44.0	132.4	55 53.3	+44.9	133.5	55 11.6	+45.8	134.6	54 29.2	+46.6	135.6	53 46.0	+47.4	136.5	53 02.1	+48.1	137.4	52 17.6	+48.8	138.3	0
1	57 57.2	+42.1	130.0	57 18.2	+43.1	131.2	56 38.2	+44.2	132.3	55 57.4	+45.1	133.4	55 15.8	+46.0	134.5	54 33.4	+46.8	135.5	53 50.2	+47.6	136.4	53 06.4	+48.4	137.4	1
2	58 39.3	+41.2	128.6	58 01.3	+42.4	129.9	57 22.4	+43.4	131.1	56 42.5	+44.4	132.2	56 01.8	+45.3	133.3	55 20.2	+46.2	134.4	54 37.8	+47.1	135.4	53 54.8	+47.8	136.4	2
3	59 20.5	+40.2	127.2	58 43.7	+41.4	128.5	58 05.8	+42.5	129.8	57 26.9	+43.6	131.0	56 47.1	+44.6	132.1	56 06.4	+45.6	133.2	55 24.9	+46.4	134.3	54 42.6	+47.3	135.3	3
4	60 00.7	+39.3	125.7	59 25.1	+40.5	127.1	58 48.3	+41.7	128.4	58 10.5	+42.9	129.7	57 31.7	+43.9	130.9	56 52.0	+44.9	132.1	56 11.3	+45.8	133.2	55 29.9	+46.7	134.2	4
5	60 40.0	+38.1	124.2	60 05.6	+39.5	125.6	59 30.0	+40.8	127.0	58 53.4	+41.9	128.4	58 15.6	+43.1	129.6	57 36.9	+44.1	130.8	56 57.1	+45.2	132.0	56 16.6	+46.0	133.1	5
6	61 18.1	+37.0	122.6	60 45.1	+38.4	124.1	60 10.8	+39.8	125.6	59 35.3	+41.0	127.0	58 58.7	+42.2	128.3	58 21.0	+43.3	129.6	57 42.3	+44.4	130.8	57 02.6	+45.4	132.0	6
7	61 55.1	+35.7	121.0	61 23.5	+37.3	122.5	60 50.6	+38.6	124.0	60 16.3	+40.1	125.5	59 40.9	+41.3	126.9	59 04.3	+42.5	128.2	58 26.7	+43.6	129.5	57 48.0	+44.6	130.7	7
8	62 30.8	+34.4	119.2	62 00.8	+36.0	120.9	61 29.2	+37.6	122.5	60 56.4	+38.9	124.0	60 22.2	+40.3	125.4	59 46.8	+41.6	126.8	59 10.3	+42.7	128.2	58 32.6	+43.9	129.5	8
9	63 05.2	+33.0	117.4	62 36.8	+34.7	119.2	62 06.8	+36.3	120.8	61 35.3	+37.9	122.4	61 02.5	+39.3	123.9	60 28.4	+40.6	125.4	59 53.0	+41.9	126.8	59 16.5	+43.0	128.2	9
10	63 38.2	+31.5	115.6	63 11.5	+33.3	117.4	62 43.1	+35.0	119.1	62 13.2	+36.5	120.8	61 41.8	+38.1	122.4	61 09.0	+39.5	123.9	60 34.9	+40.8	125.4	59 59.5	+42.2	126.8	10
11	64 09.7	+29.9	113.6	63 44.8	+31.7	115.5	63 18.1	+33.6	117.3	62 49.7	+35.3	119.0	62 19.9	+36.9	120.7	61 48.5	+38.4	122.3	61 15.7	+39.9	123.9	60 41.7	+41.1	125.3	11
12	64 39.6	+28.2	111.6	64 16.5	+30.2	113.6	63 51.7	+32.1	115.4	63 25.0	+33.9	117.2	62 56.8	+35.5	119.0	62 26.9	+37.2	120.7	61 55.6	+38.7	122.3	61 22.8	+40.2	123.8	12
13	65 07.8	+26.4	109.6	64 46.7	+28.6	111.6	64 23.8	+30.5	113.5	63 58.9	+32.4	115.4	63 32.3	+34.2	117.2	63 04.1	+35.9	119.0	62 34.3	+37.5	120.6	62 03.0	+39.0	122.3	13
14	65 34.2	+24.6	107.4	65 15.3	+26.7	109.5	64 54.3	+28.8	111.5	64 31.3	+30.8	113.4	64 06.5	+32.8	115.3	63 40.0	+34.5	117.2	63 11.8	+36.2	118.9	62 42.0	+37.8	120.6	14
15	65 58.8	+22.5•	105.2	65 42.0	+24.8	107.3	65 23.1	+27.0	109.4	65 02.1	+29.2	111.4	64 39.3	+31.1	113.4	64 14.5	+33.0	115.3	63 48.0	+34.8	117.1	63 19.8	+36.5	118.9	15
16	66 21.3	+20.4•	102.9	66 06.8	+22.8•	105.1	65 50.1	+25.1	107.2	65 31.3	+27.3	109.3	65 10.4	+29.4	111.4	64 47.5	+31.5	113.4	64 22.8	+33.4	115.3	63 56.3	+35.2	117.1	16
17	66 41.7	+18.3•	100.5	66 29.6	+20.8•	102.8	66 15.2	+23.2•	105.0	65 58.6	+25.4	107.2	65 39.8	+27.7	109.3	65 19.0	+29.7	111.3	64 56.2	+31.7	113.3	64 31.5	+33.7	115.3	17
18	67 00.0	+16.0•	98.1	66 50.4	+18.5•	100.4	66 38.4	+21.0•	102.7	66 24.0	+23.5•	104.9	66 07.5	+25.7	107.1	65 48.7	+28.0	109.2	65 27.9	+30.1	111.3	65 05.2	+32.1	113.3	18
19	67 16.0	+13.7•	95.6	67 08.9	+16.3•	98.0	66 59.4	+18.8•	100.3	66 47.5	+21.3•	102.6	66 33.2	+23.8•	104.9	66 16.7	+26.1•	107.1	65 58.0	+28.3	109.2	65 37.3	+30.4	111.3	19
20	67 29.7	+11.3•	93.1	67 25.2	+14.0•	95.5	67 18.2	+16.6•	97.9	67 08.8	+19.1•	100.2	66 57.0	+21.6•	102.5	66 42.8	+24.0•	104.8	66 26.3	+26.4	107.0	66 07.7	+28.6	109.2	20
21	67 41.0	+8.7•	90.5	67 39.2	+11.5•	92.9	67 34.8	+14.2•	95.4	67 27.9	+16.9•	97.8	67 18.6	+19.4•	100.1	67 06.8	+22.0•	102.5	66 52.7	+24.4•	104.8	66 36.3	+26.7	107.0	21
22	67 49.7	+6.3•	87.9	67 50.7	+9.0•	90.3	67 49.0	+11.7•	92.8	67 44.8	+14.4•	95.2	67 38.0	+17.2•	97.7	67 28.8	+19.7•	100.1	67 17.1	+22.3•	102.4	67 03.0	+24.7•	104.7	22
23	67 56.0	+3.7•	85.3	67 59.7	+6.4•	87.7	68 00.7	+9.3•	90.2	67 59.2	+12.0•	92.7	67 55.2	+14.7•	95.1	67 48.5	+17.4•	97.6	67 39.4	+20.0•	100.0	67 27.7	+22.6•	102.4	23
24	67 59.7	+1.0•	82.6	68 06.1	+3.9•	85.1	68 10.0	+6.6•	87.5	68 11.2	+9.5•	90.0	68 09.9	+12.2•	92.5	68 05.9	+15.0•	95.0	67 59.4	+17.7•	97.5	67 50.3	+20.3•	99.9	24
25	68 00.7	-1.5•	79.9	68 10.0	+1.2•	82.4	68 16.6	+4.1•	84.9	68 20.7	+6.9•	87.4	68 22.1	+9.7•	89.9	68 20.9	+12.5•	92.4	68 17.1	+15.2•	94.9	68 10.6	+18.0•	97.4	25
26	67 59.2	-4.0•	77.3	68 11.2	-1.3•	79.7	68 20.7	+1.4•	82.2	68 27.6	+4.2•	84.7	68 31.8	+7.1•	87.2	68 33.4	+9.9•	89.8	68 32.3	+12.8•	92.3	68 28.6	+15.6•	94.8	26
27	67 55.2	-6.7•	74.6	68 09.9	-4.0•	77.0	68 22.1	-1.2•	79.5	68 31.8	+1.6•	82.0	68 38.9	+4.4•	84.5	68 43.3	+7.3•	87.0	68 45.1	+10.1•	89.6	68 44.2	+12.9•	92.2	27
28	67 48.5	-9.1•	72.0	68 05.9	-6.5•	74.3	68 20.9	-3.8•	76.7	68 33.4	-1.1•	79.2	68 43.3	+1.8•	81.7	68 50.6	+4.6•	84.3	68 55.2	+7.5•	86.9	68 57.1	+10.4•	89.5	28
29	67 39.4	-11.7•	69.3	67 59.4	-9.1•	71.7	68 17.1	-6.5•	74.0	68 32.3	-3.7•	76.5	68 45.1	-0.9•	79.0	68 55.2	+1.9•	81.5	69 02.7	+4.8•	84.1	69 07.5	+7.7•	86.7	29
30	67 27.7	-14.0•	66.8	67 50.3	-11.6•	69.0	68 10.6	-9.0•	71.4	68 28.6	-6.4•	73.8	68 44.2	-3.7•	76.2	68 57.1	-0.8•	78.8	69 07.5	+2.1•	81.3	69 15.2	+5.0•	83.9	30
31	67 13.7	-16.4•	64.3	67 38.7	-14.0•	66.4	68 01.6	-11.5•	68.7	68 22.2	-8.9•	71.1	68 40.5	-6.3•	73.5	68 56.3	-3.5•	76.0	69 09.6	-0.7•	78.5	69 20.2	+2.2•	81.1	31
32	66 57.3	-18.6•	61.8	67 24.7	-16.4•	63.9	67 50.1	-14.0•	66.1	68 13.3	-11.5•	68.4	68 34.2	-8.9•	70.8	68 52.8	-6.2•	73.2	69 08.9	-3.4•	75.7	69 22.4	-0.6•	78.3	32
33	66 38.7	-20.8•	59.4	67 08.3	-18.6•	61.4	67 36.1	-16.4•	63.5	68 01.8	-14.0•	65.8	68 25.3	-11.5•	68.1	68 46.6	-8.9•	70.4	69 05.5	-6.2•	72.9	69 21.8	-3.3•	75.4	33
34	66 17.9	-22.9•	57.0	66 49.7	-20.8•	59.0	67 19.7	-18.7•	61.0	67 47.8	-16.4•	63.2	68 13.8	-14.0•	65.4	68 37.7	-11.5•	67.7	68 59.3	-8.8•	70.1	69 18.5	-6.1•	72.6	34
35	65 55.0	-24.8	54.7	66 28.9	-22.9•	56.6	67 01.0	-20.8•	58.6	67 31.4	-18.7•	60.6	67 59.8	-16.4•	62.8	68 26.2	-14.0•	65.0	68 50.5	-11.5•	67.4	69 12.4	-8.9•	69.8	35
36	65 30.2	-26.7	52.5	66 06.0	-24.9	54.3	66 40.2	-23.0•	56.2	67 12.7	-20.9•	58.2	67 43.4	-18.7•	60.2	68 12.2	-16.4•	62.4	68 39.0	-14.0•	64.7	69 03.5	-11.4•	67.0	36
37	65 03.5	-28.5	50.4	65 41.1	-26.8	52.1	66 17.2	-25.0	53.9	66 51.8	-23.0•	55.8	67 24.7	-21.0•	57.7	67 55.8	-18.8•	59.8	68 25.0	-16.5•	62.0	68 52.1	-14.1•	64.3	37
38	64 35.0	-30.1	48.3	65 14.3	-28.6	49.9	65 52.2	-26.8	51.6	66 28.8	-25.1•	53.4	67 03.7	-23.1•	55.3	67 37.0	-21.1•	57.3	68 08.5	-18.9•	59.4	68 38.0	-16.6•	61.6	38
39	64 04.9	-31.8	46.3	64 45.7	-30.2	47.8	65 25.4	-28.7	49.5	66 03.7	-27.0	51.2	66 40.6	-25.2•	53.0	67 15.9	-23.2•	54.9	67 49.6	-21.2•	56.9	68 21.4	-18.9•	59.0	39
40	63 33.1	-33.2	44.4	64 15.5	-31.9	45.8	64 56.7	-30.4	47.4	65 36.7	-28.8	49.0	66 15.4	-27.1	50.7	66 52.7	-25.3•	52.5	67 28.4	-23.3•	54.4	68 02.5	-21.3•	56.4	40
41	62 59.9	-34.6	42.5	63 43.6	-33.3	43.9	64 26.3	-31.9	45.4	65 07.9	-30.5	46.9	65 48.3	-28.9	48.5	66 27.4	-27.2	50.2	67 05.1	-25.4•	52.0	67 41.2	-23.5•	54.0	41
42	62 25.3	-35.9	40.8	63 10.3	-34.7	42.0	63 54.4	-33.5	43.4	64 37.4	-32.1	44.9	65 19.4	-30.6	46.4	66 00.2	-29.1	48.0	66 39.7	-27.4	49.7	67 17.7	-25.5•	51.5	42
43	61 49.4	-37.2	39.0	62 35.6	-36.1	40.3	63 20.9	-34.9	41.5	64 05.3	-33.6	42.9	64 48.8	-32.3	44.3	65 31.1	-30.7	45.9	66 12.3	-29.2	47.5	66 52.2	-27.6	49.2	43
44	61 12.2	-38.3	37.4	61 59.5	-37.3	38.5	62 46.0	-36.2	39.7	63 31.7	-35.0	41.0	64 16.5	-33.7	42.4	65 00.4	-32.5	43.8	65 43.1	-31.0	45.4	66 24.6	-29.3	47.0	44
45	60 33.9	-39.4	35.8	61 22.2	-38.4	36.9	62 09.8	-37.4	38.0	62 56.7	-36.3	39.2	63 42.8	-35.2	40.5	64 27.9	-33.9	41.9	65 12.1	-32.5	43.3	65 55.3	-31.2	44.8	45
46	59 54.5	-40.4	34.3	60 43.8	-39.6	35.3	61 32.4	-38.6	36.4	62 20.4	-37.6	37.5	63 07.6	-36.5	38.7	63 54.0	-35.3	40.0	64 39.6	-34.2	41.3	65 24.1	-32.7	42.7	46
47	59 14.1	-41.4	32.8	60 04.2	-40.5	33.8	60 53.8	-39.7	34.8	61 42.8	-38.8	35.8	62 31.1	-37.8	36.9	63 18.7	-36.7	38.1	64 05.4	-35.5	39.4	64 51.4	-34.3	40.8	47
48	58 32.7	-42.2	31.4	59 23.7	-41.5	32.3	60 14.1	-40.6	33.2	61 04.0	-39.8	34.2	61 53.3	-38.9	35.3	62 42.0	-37.9	36.4	63 29.9	-36.9	37.6	64 17.1	-35.8	38.8	48
49	57 50.5	-43.0	30.1	58 42.2	-42.3	30.9	59 33.5	-41.7	31.8	60 24.2	-40.8	32.7	61 14.4	-40.0	33.7	62 04.1	-39.1	34.7	62 53.0	-38.1	35.8	63 41.3	-37.1	37.0	49
50	57 07.5	-43.8	28.8	57 59.9	-43.2	29.6	58 51.8	-42.5	30.4	59 43.4	-41.8	31.2	60 34.4	-41.0	32.2	61 25.0	-40.2	33.1	62 14.9	-39.3	34.2	63 04.2	-38.3	35.3	50
51	56 23.7	-44.6	27.5	57 16.7	-44.0	28.3	58 09.3	-43.3	29.0	59 01.6	-42.7	29.8	59 53.4	-41.9	30.7	60 44.8	-41.2	31.6	61 35.6	-40.3	32.6	62 25.9	-39.5	33.6	51
52	55 39.1	-45.2	26.3	56 32.7	-44.7	27.0	57 26.0	-44.1	27.7	58 18.9	-43.4	28.5	59 11.5	-42.8	29.3	60 03.6	-42.1	30.1	60 55.3	-41.4	31.0	61 46.4	-40.5	32.0	52
53	54 53.9	-45.9	25.2	55 48.0	-45.3	25.8	56 41.9	-44.8	26.5	57 35.5	-44.3	27.2	58 28.7	-43.7	27.9	59 21.5	-43.0	28.7	60 13.9	-42.3	29.5	61 05.9	-41.6	30.4	53
54	54 08.0	-46.4	24.1	55 02.7	-46.0	24.7	55 57.1	-45.5	25.3	56 51.2	-45.0	25.9	57 45.0	-44.4	26.6	58 38.5	-43.8	27.3	59 31.6	-43.2	28.1	60 24.3	-42.5	29.0	54
55	53 21.6	-47.0	23.0	54 16.7	-46.5	23.6	55 11.6	-46.1	24.1	56 06.2	-45.6	24.7	57 00.6	-45.1	25.4	57 54.7	-44.6	26.0	58 48.4	-44.0	26.8	59 41.8	-43.4	27.5	55
56	52 34.6	-47.5	22.0	53 30.2	-47.2	22.5	54 25.5	-46.7	23.0	55 20.6	-46.3	23.6	56 15.5	-45.8	24.2	57 10.1	-45.3	24.8	58 04.4	-44.8	25.5	58 58.4	-44.2	26.2	56
57	51 47.1	-48.0	21.0	52 43.0	-47.6	21.5	53 38.8	-47.3	21.9	54 34.3	-46.8	22.5	55 29.7	-46.5	23.0	56 24.8	-46.0	23.6	57 19.6	-45.5	24.2	58 14.2	-45.0	24.9	57
58	50 59.1	-48.5	20.0	51 55.4	-48.1	20.5	52 51.5	-47.7	20.9	53 47.5	-47.4	21.4	54 43.2	-47.0	21.9	55 38.8	-46.6	22.5	56 34.1	-46.1	23.0	57 29.2	-45.6	23.6	58
59	50 10.6	-48.9	19.1	51 07.3	-48.6	19.5	52 03.8	-48.3	19.9	53 00.1	-47.9	20.4	53 56.2	-47.5	20.8	54 52.2	-47.1	21.3	55 48.0	-46.8	21.9	56 43.6	-46.4	22.4	59
60	49 21.7	-49.2	18.2	50 18.7	-49.0	18.6	51 15.5	-48.7	19.0	52 12.2	-48.4	19.4	53 08.7	-48.1	19.8	54 05.1	-47.7	20.3	55 01.2	-47.3	20.8	55 57.2	-46.9	21.3	60
61	48 32.5	-49.7	17.3	49 29.7	-49.4	17.7	50 26.8	-49.1	18.0	51 23.8	-48.9	18.4	52 20.6	-48.5	18.8	53 17.4	-48.3	19.3	54 13.9	-47.9	19.7	55 10.3	-47.5	20.2	61
62	47 42.8	-50.0	16.5	48 40.3	-49.8	16.8	49 37.7	-49.6	17.1	50 34.9	-49.2	17.5	51 32.1	-49.0	17.9	52 29.1	-48.7	18.3	53 26.0	-48.3	18.7	54 22.8	-48.0	19.1	62
63	46 52.8	-50.4	15.7	47 50.5	-50.2	16.0	48 48.1	-49.9	16.3	49 45.7	-49.7	16.6	50 43.1	-49.4	17.0	51 40.4	-49.1	17.3	52 37.7	-48.9	17.7	53 34.8	-48.6	18.1	63
64	46 02.4	-50.7	14.9	47 00.3	-50.4	15.2	47 58.2	-50.2	15.4	48 56.0	-50.0	15.7	49 53.7	-49.8	16.1	50 51.3	-49.5	16.4	51 48.8	-49.3	16.8	52 46.2	-49.0	17.1	64
65	45 11.7	-51.0	14.1	46 09.9	-50.8	14.4	47 08.0	-50.6	14.6	48 06.0	-50.4	14.9	49 03.9	-50.2	15.2	50 01.8	-50.0	15.5	50 59.5	-49.7	15.8	51 57.2	-49.4	16.2	65
66	44 20.7	-51.2	13.4	45 19.1	-51.1	13.6	46 17.4	-50.9	13.9	47 15.6	-50.7	14.1	48 13.7	-50.5	14.4	49 11.8	-50.3	14.7	50 09.8	-50.1	15.0	51 07.8	-49.9	15.3	66
67	43 29.5	-51.5	12.7	44 28.0	-51.4	12.9	45 26.5	-51.2	13.1	46 24.9	-51.0	13.3	47 23.2	-50.8	13.6	48 21.5	-50.6	13.8	49 19.7	-50.4	14.1	50 17.9	-50.2	14.4	67
68	42 38.0	-51.8	12.0	43 36.6	-51.6	12.1	44 35.3	-51.5	12.4	45 33.9	-51.4	12.6	46 32.4	-51.2	12.8	47 30.9	-51.0	13.0	48 29.3	-50.8	13.3	49 27.7	-50.6	13.6	68
69	41 46.2	-52.0	11.3	42 45.0	-51.9	11.4	43 43.8	-51.7	11.6	44 42.5	-51.5	11.8	45 41.2	-51.4	12.0	46 39.9	-51.3	12.3	47 38.5	-51.1	12.5	48 37.1	-51.0	12.7	69
70	40 54.2	-52.3	10.6	41 53.1	-52.1	10.8	42 52.1	-52.0	10.9	43 51.0	-51.9	11.1	44 49.8	-51.7	11.3	45 48.6	-51.5	11.5	46 47.4	-51.4	11.7	47 46.1	-51.2	11.9	70
71	40 01.9	-52.4	10.0	41 01.0	-52.3	10.1	42 00.1	-52.2	10.3	42 59.1	-52.1	10.4	43 58.1	-52.0	10.6	44 57.1	-51.9	10.8	45 56.0	-51.7	11.0	46 54.9	-51.6	11.2	71
72	39 09.5	-52.6	9.3	40 08.7	-52.5	9.5	41 07.9	-52.5	9.6	42 07.0	-52.3	9.8	43 06.1	-52.2	9.9	44 05.2	-52.1	10.1	45 04.3	-52.0	10.3	46 03.3	-51.8	10.4	72
73	38 16.9	-52.9	8.7	39 16.2	-52.8	8.8	40 15.4	-52.6	9.0	41 14.7	-52.5	9.1	42 13.9	-52.4	9.2	43 13.1	-52.3	9.4	44 12.3	-52.2	9.5	45 11.5	-52.1	9.7	73
74	37 24.0	-53.0	8.1	38 23.4	-52.9	8.2	39 22.8	-52.8	8.3	40 22.2	-52.8	8.5	41 21.5	-52.7	8.6	42 20.8	-52.5	8.7	43 20.1	-52.4	8.9	44 19.4	-52.4	9.0	74
75	36 31.0	-53.1	7.5	37 30.5	-53.1	7.6	38 30.0	-53.0	7.7	39 29.4	-52.9	7.8	40 28.8	-52.8	8.0	41 28.3	-52.8	8.1	42 27.7	-52.7	8.2	43 27.0	-52.5	8.3	75
76	35 37.9	-53.4	7.0	36 37.4	-53.3	7.0	37 37.0	-53.2	7.1	38 36.5	-53.1	7.2	39 36.0	-53.0	7.3	40 35.5	-53.0	7.4	41 35.0	-52.9	7.6	42 34.5	-52.8	7.7	76
77	34 44.5	-53.5	6.4	35 44.1	-53.4	6.5	36 43.8	-53.4	6.6	37 43.4	-53.3	6.6	38 43.0	-53.3	6.7	39 42.5	-53.1	6.8	40 42.1	-53.1	6.9	41 41.7	-53.0	7.0	77
78	33 51.0	-53.6	5.8	34 50.7	-53.5	5.9	35 50.4	-53.5	6.0	36 50.1	-53.5	6.1	37 49.7	-53.4	6.1	38 49.4	-53.4	6.2	39 49.0	-53.2	6.3	40 48.7	-53.3	6.4	78
79	32 57.4	-53.7	5.3	33 57.2	-53.8	5.4	34 56.9	-53.7	5.4	35 56.6	-53.6	5.5	36 56.3	-53.5	5.6	37 56.0	-53.5	5.6	38 55.8	-53.5	5.7	39 55.4	-53.3	5.8	79
80	32 03.7	-53.9	4.8	33 03.4	-53.8	4.8	34 03.2	-53.8	4.9	35 03.0	-53.8	4.9	36 02.8	-53.7	5.0	37 02.5	-53.6	5.1	38 02.3	-53.6	5.1	39 02.1	-53.6	5.2	80
81	31 09.8	-54.1	4.3	32 09.6	-54.0	4.3	33 09.4	-53.9	4.4	34 09.2	-53.8	4.4	35 09.1	-53.9	4.5	36 08.9	-53.8	4.5	37 08.7	-53.8	4.6	38 08.5	-53.7	4.6	81
82	30 15.7	-54.1	3.8	31 15.6	-54.1	3.8	32 15.5	-54.1	3.8	33 15.4	-54.1	3.9	34 15.2	-54.0	3.9	35 15.1	-54.0	4.0	36 14.9	-53.9	4.0	37 14.8	-53.9	4.1	82
83	29 21.6	-54.2	3.3	30 21.5	-54.2	3.3	31 21.4	-54.2	3.3	32 21.3	-54.1	3.4	33 21.2	-54.1	3.4	34 21.1	-54.1	3.4	35 21.0	-54.1	3.5	36 20.9	-54.0	3.5	83
84	28 27.4	-54.3	2.8	29 27.3	-54.3	2.8	30 27.2	-54.2	2.8	31 27.2	-54.3	2.9	32 27.1	-54.2	2.9	33 27.0	-54.2	2.9	34 26.9	-54.2	3.0	35 26.9	-54.2	3.0	84
85	27 33.1	-54.5	2.3	28 33.0	-54.4	2.3	29 33.0	-54.4	2.3	30 32.9	-54.4	2.4	31 32.9	-54.4	2.4	32 32.8	-54.3	2.4	33 32.7	-54.3	2.4	34 32.7	-54.3	2.5	85
86	26 38.6	-54.5	1.8	27 38.6	-54.5	1.8	28 38.6	-54.5	1.9	29 38.5	-54.5	1.9	30 38.5	-54.5	1.9	31 38.5	-54.5	1.9	32 38.4	-54.4	1.9	33 38.4	-54.4	2.0	86
87	25 44.1	-54.6	1.4	26 44.1	-54.6	1.4	27 44.1	-54.6	1.4	28 44.0	-54.6	1.4	29 44.0	-54.6	1.4	30 44.0	-54.6	1.4	31 44.0	-54.6	1.4	32 44.0	-54.6	1.5	87
88	24 49.5	-54.7	0.9	25 49.5	-54.7	0.9	26 49.5	-54.7	0.9	27 49.4	-54.6	0.9	28 49.4	-54.6	0.9	29 49.4	-54.6	0.9	30 49.4	-54.6	0.9	31 49.4	-54.6	1.0	88
89	23 54.8	-54.8	0.4	24 54.8	-54.8	0.4	25 54.8	-54.8	0.5	26 54.8	-54.8	0.5	27 54.8	-54.8	0.5	28 54.8	-54.8	0.5	29 54.8	-54.8	0.5	30 54.8	-54.8	0.5	89
90	23 00.0	-54.8	0.0	24 00.0	-54.9	0.0	25 00.0	-54.9	0.0	26 00.0	-54.9	0.0	27 00.0	-54.9	0.0	28 00.0	-54.9	0.0	29 00.0	-54.9	0.0	30 00.0	-54.9	0.0	90
	23°			24°			25°			26°			27°			28°			29°			30°			

Dec.	23° Hc	d	Z	24° Hc	d	Z	25° Hc	d	Z	26° Hc	d	Z	27° Hc	d	Z	28° Hc	d	Z	29° Hc	d	Z	30° Hc	d	Z	Dec.
°	° ′	′	°	° ′	′	°	° ′	′	°	° ′	′	°	° ′	′	°	° ′	′	°	° ′	′	°	° ′	′	°	°
0	57 14.3	-43.7	131.3	56 34.2	-44.6	132.4	55 53.3	-45.5	133.5	55 11.6	-46.3	134.6	54 29.2	-47.2	135.6	53 46.0	-47.9	136.5	53 02.1	-48.6	137.4	52 17.6	-49.3	138.3	0
1	56 30.6	-44.5	132.5	55 49.6	-45.3	133.6	55 07.8	-46.2	134.7	54 25.3	-47.0	135.7	53 42.0	-47.7	136.6	52 58.1	-48.4	137.5	52 13.5	-49.1	138.4	51 28.3	-49.7	139.2	1
2	55 46.1	-45.1	133.7	55 04.3	-46.0	134.8	54 21.6	-46.7	135.8	53 38.3	-47.5	136.7	52 54.3	-48.2	137.6	52 09.7	-48.9	138.5	51 24.4	-49.5	139.3	50 38.6	-50.0	140.1	2
3	55 01.0	-45.7	134.9	54 18.3	-46.5	135.9	53 34.9	-47.3	136.8	52 50.8	-48.0	137.7	52 06.1	-48.7	138.6	51 20.8	-49.3	139.4	50 34.9	-49.9	140.2	49 48.6	-50.5	141.0	3
4	54 15.3	-46.4	136.0	53 31.8	-47.2	137.0	52 47.6	-47.8	137.9	52 02.8	-48.5	138.7	51 17.4	-49.1	139.5	50 31.5	-49.7	140.3	49 45.0	-50.2	141.1	48 58.1	-50.8	141.8	4
5	53 28.9	-46.9	137.1	52 44.6	-47.6	138.0	51 59.8	-48.3	138.8	51 14.3	-48.9	139.7	50 28.3	-49.5	140.5	49 41.8	-50.1	141.2	48 54.8	-50.7	141.9	48 07.3	-51.1	142.6	5
6	52 42.0	-47.4	138.1	51 57.0	-48.1	139.0	51 11.5	-48.8	139.8	50 25.4	-49.4	140.6	49 38.8	-49.9	141.3	48 51.7	-50.5	142.1	48 04.1	-50.9	142.7	47 16.2	-51.5	143.4	6
7	51 54.6	-48.0	139.1	51 08.9	-48.5	139.9	50 22.7	-49.1	140.7	49 36.0	-49.7	141.5	48 48.9	-50.3	142.2	48 01.2	-50.7	142.9	47 13.2	-51.3	143.5	46 24.7	-51.7	144.2	7
8	51 06.6	-48.3	140.1	50 20.4	-49.0	140.9	49 33.6	-49.6	141.6	48 46.3	-50.1	142.3	47 58.6	-50.6	143.0	47 10.5	-51.1	143.7	46 21.9	-51.5	144.3	45 33.0	-52.0	144.9	8
9	50 18.3	-48.9	141.0	49 31.4	-49.4	141.8	48 44.0	-49.9	142.5	47 56.2	-50.5	143.2	47 08.0	-51.0	143.8	46 19.4	-51.4	144.4	45 30.4	-51.9	145.0	44 41.0	-52.2	145.6	9
10	49 29.4	-49.2	141.9	48 42.0	-49.8	142.6	47 54.1	-50.3	143.3	47 05.7	-50.7	144.0	46 17.0	-51.2	144.6	45 28.0	-51.7	145.2	44 38.5	-52.0	145.7	43 48.8	-52.5	146.3	10
11	48 40.2	-49.6	142.8	47 52.2	-50.1	143.5	47 03.8	-50.6	144.1	46 15.0	-51.1	144.7	45 25.8	-51.5	145.3	44 36.3	-51.9	145.9	43 46.5	-52.4	146.4	42 56.3	-52.7	146.9	11
12	47 50.6	-50.0	143.6	47 02.1	-50.5	144.3	46 13.2	-51.0	144.9	45 23.9	-51.4	145.5	44 34.3	-51.8	146.0	43 44.4	-52.2	146.6	42 54.1	-52.5	147.1	42 03.6	-52.9	147.6	12
13	47 00.6	-50.3	144.5	46 11.6	-50.8	145.1	45 22.2	-51.2	145.7	44 32.5	-51.6	146.2	43 42.5	-52.0	146.8	42 52.2	-52.4	147.3	42 01.6	-52.8	147.8	41 10.7	-53.1	148.2	13
14	46 10.3	-50.6	145.3	45 20.8	-51.1	145.8	44 31.0	-51.5	146.4	43 40.9	-51.9	146.9	42 50.5	-52.3	147.4	41 59.8	-52.7	147.9	41 08.8	-53.0	148.4	40 17.6	-53.4	148.8	14
15	45 19.7	-51.0	146.0	44 29.7	-51.3	146.6	43 39.5	-51.7	147.1	42 49.0	-52.1	147.6	41 58.2	-52.5	148.1	41 07.1	-52.8	148.6	40 15.8	-53.2	149.0	39 24.2	-53.4	149.4	15
16	44 28.7	-51.2	146.8	43 38.4	-51.6	147.3	42 47.8	-52.0	147.8	41 56.9	-52.4	148.3	41 05.7	-52.7	148.7	40 14.3	-53.1	149.2	39 22.6	-53.3	149.6	38 30.8	-53.7	150.0	16
17	43 37.5	-51.5	147.5	42 46.8	-51.9	148.0	41 55.8	-52.3	148.5	41 04.5	-52.6	148.9	40 13.0	-52.9	149.4	39 21.2	-53.2	149.8	38 29.3	-53.6	150.2	37 37.1	-53.8	150.6	17
18	42 46.0	-51.7	148.2	41 54.9	-52.1	148.7	41 03.5	-52.4	149.1	40 11.9	-52.8	149.6	39 20.1	-53.1	150.0	38 28.0	-53.4	150.4	37 35.7	-53.7	150.8	36 43.3	-54.0	151.1	18
19	41 54.3	-52.0	148.9	41 02.8	-52.3	149.3	40 11.1	-52.7	149.8	39 19.1	-52.9	150.2	38 27.0	-53.3	150.6	37 34.6	-53.6	151.0	36 42.0	-53.8	151.3	35 49.3	-54.1	151.7	19
20	41 02.3	-52.2	149.6	40 10.5	-52.5	150.0	39 18.4	-52.8	150.4	38 26.2	-53.2	150.8	37 33.7	-53.5	151.2	36 41.0	-53.7	151.5	35 48.2	-54.0	151.9	34 55.2	-54.3	152.2	20
21	40 10.1	-52.4	150.2	39 18.0	-52.8	150.6	38 25.6	-53.1	151.0	37 33.0	-53.3	151.4	36 40.2	-53.6	151.7	35 47.3	-53.9	152.1	34 54.2	-54.1	152.4	34 00.9	-54.3	152.7	21
22	39 17.7	-52.6	150.8	38 25.2	-52.9	151.2	37 32.5	-53.2	151.6	36 39.7	-53.5	152.0	35 46.6	-53.7	152.3	34 53.4	-54.0	152.6	34 00.1	-54.3	152.9	33 06.6	-54.5	153.2	22
23	38 25.1	-52.8	151.5	37 32.3	-53.1	151.8	36 39.3	-53.3	152.2	35 46.2	-53.6	152.5	34 52.9	-53.9	152.8	33 59.4	-54.1	153.2	33 05.8	-54.4	153.5	32 12.1	-54.6	153.7	23
24	37 32.3	-53.0	152.1	36 39.2	-53.2	152.4	35 46.0	-53.6	152.7	34 52.6	-53.8	153.1	33 59.0	-54.0	153.4	33 05.3	-54.3	153.7	32 11.4	-54.5	154.0	31 17.5	-54.8	154.2	24
25	36 39.3	-53.1	152.6	35 46.0	-53.4	153.0	34 52.4	-53.6	153.3	33 58.8	-54.0	153.6	33 05.0	-54.2	153.9	32 11.0	-54.4	154.2	31 16.9	-54.6	154.4	30 22.7	-54.8	154.7	25
26	35 46.2	-53.3	153.2	34 52.6	-53.6	153.5	33 58.8	-53.8	153.8	33 04.8	-54.0	154.1	32 10.8	-54.3	154.4	31 16.6	-54.5	154.7	30 22.3	-54.7	154.9	29 27.9	-54.9	155.2	26
27	34 52.9	-53.5	153.8	33 59.0	-53.7	154.1	33 05.0	-54.0	154.4	32 10.8	-54.2	154.6	31 16.5	-54.4	154.9	30 22.1	-54.6	155.2	29 27.6	-54.8	155.4	28 33.0	-55.0	155.6	27
28	33 59.4	-53.6	154.3	33 05.3	-53.9	154.6	32 11.0	-54.1	154.9	31 16.6	-54.3	155.2	30 22.1	-54.5	155.4	29 27.5	-54.7	155.6	28 32.8	-54.9	155.9	27 38.0	-55.1	156.1	28
29	33 05.8	-53.7	154.9	32 11.4	-53.9	155.1	31 16.9	-54.2	155.4	30 22.3	-54.4	155.6	29 27.6	-54.6	155.9	28 32.8	-54.8	156.1	27 37.9	-55.0	156.3	26 42.9	-55.2	156.5	29
30	32 12.1	-53.9	155.4	31 17.5	-54.1	155.7	30 22.7	-54.3	155.9	29 27.9	-54.5	156.1	28 33.0	-54.7	156.4	27 38.0	-54.9	156.6	26 42.9	-55.1	156.8	25 47.7	-55.2	157.0	30
31	31 18.2	-54.0	155.9	30 23.4	-54.2	156.2	29 28.4	-54.4	156.4	28 33.4	-54.6	156.6	27 38.3	-54.8	156.8	26 43.1	-55.0	157.0	25 47.8	-55.1	157.2	24 52.5	-55.4	157.4	31
32	30 24.2	-54.1	156.4	29 29.2	-54.3	156.7	28 34.0	-54.5	156.9	27 38.8	-54.7	157.1	26 43.5	-54.9	157.3	25 48.1	-55.0	157.5	24 52.7	-55.3	157.7	23 57.1	-55.4	157.8	32
33	29 30.1	-54.2	156.9	28 34.9	-54.5	157.1	27 39.5	-54.6	157.3	26 44.1	-54.8	157.5	25 48.6	-54.9	157.7	24 53.1	-55.2	157.9	23 57.4	-55.3	158.1	23 01.7	-55.4	158.2	33
34	28 35.9	-54.3	157.4	27 40.4	-54.5	157.6	26 44.9	-54.7	157.8	25 49.3	-54.8	158.0	24 53.7	-55.1	158.2	23 57.9	-55.2	158.3	23 02.1	-55.3	158.5	22 06.3	-55.5	158.7	34
35	27 41.6	-54.5	157.9	26 45.9	-54.6	158.1	25 50.2	-54.7	158.3	24 54.5	-55.0	158.4	23 58.6	-55.1	158.6	23 02.7	-55.3	158.8	22 06.8	-55.5	158.9	21 10.8	-55.6	159.1	35
36	26 47.1	-54.5	158.4	25 51.3	-54.7	158.6	24 55.5	-54.9	158.7	23 59.5	-55.0	158.9	23 03.5	-55.2	159.0	22 07.4	-55.3	159.2	21 11.3	-55.5	159.3	20 15.2	-55.7	159.5	36
37	25 52.6	-54.6	158.8	24 56.6	-54.7	159.0	24 00.6	-54.9	159.2	23 04.5	-55.1	159.3	22 08.3	-55.2	159.5	21 12.1	-55.4	159.6	20 15.8	-55.5	159.7	19 19.5	-55.7	159.9	37
38	24 58.0	-54.7	159.3	24 01.9	-54.9	159.5	23 05.7	-55.0	159.6	22 09.4	-55.2	159.8	21 13.1	-55.3	159.9	20 16.7	-55.4	160.0	19 20.3	-55.6	160.1	18 23.8	-55.7	160.3	38
39	24 03.3	-54.7	159.7	23 07.0	-54.9	159.9	22 10.7	-55.1	160.0	21 14.2	-55.2	160.2	20 17.8	-55.4	160.3	19 21.3	-55.6	160.4	18 24.7	-55.6	160.5	17 28.1	-55.8	160.6	39
40	23 08.6	-54.9	160.2	22 12.1	-55.0	160.3	21 15.6	-55.2	160.5	20 19.0	-55.3	160.6	19 22.4	-55.4	160.7	18 25.7	-55.5	160.8	17 29.1	-55.7	160.9	16 32.3	-55.8	161.0	40
41	22 13.7	-54.9	160.6	21 17.1	-55.0	160.8	20 20.4	-55.2	160.9	19 23.7	-55.3	161.0	18 27.0	-55.5	161.1	17 30.2	-55.6	161.2	16 33.4	-55.8	161.3	15 36.5	-55.9	161.4	41
42	21 18.8	-54.9	161.1	20 22.1	-55.2	161.2	19 25.2	-55.2	161.3	18 28.4	-55.4	161.4	17 31.5	-55.5	161.5	16 34.6	-55.7	161.6	15 37.6	-55.7	161.7	14 40.6	-55.9	161.8	42
43	20 23.9	-55.1	161.5	19 26.9	-55.1	161.6	18 30.0	-55.3	161.7	17 33.0	-55.4	161.8	16 36.0	-55.6	161.9	15 38.9	-55.7	162.0	14 41.9	-55.9	162.1	13 44.7	-55.9	162.2	43
44	19 28.8	-55.1	161.9	18 31.8	-55.3	162.0	17 34.7	-55.4	162.1	16 37.6	-55.5	162.2	15 40.4	-55.6	162.3	14 43.2	-55.7	162.4	13 46.0	-55.8	162.5	12 48.8	-56.0	162.5	44
45	18 33.7	-55.1	162.3	17 36.5	-55.2	162.4	16 39.3	-55.4	162.5	15 42.1	-55.5	162.6	14 44.8	-55.6	162.7	13 47.5	-55.8	162.8	12 50.2	-55.9	162.8	11 52.8	-55.9	162.9	45
46	17 38.6	-55.2	162.8	16 41.3	-55.4	162.8	15 43.9	-55.4	162.9	14 46.6	-55.6	163.0	13 49.2	-55.7	163.1	12 51.7	-55.8	163.2	11 54.3	-55.9	163.2	10 56.9	-56.1	163.3	46
47	16 43.4	-55.3	163.2	15 45.9	-55.3	163.2	14 48.5	-55.5	163.3	13 51.0	-55.6	163.4	12 53.5	-55.7	163.5	11 55.9	-55.8	163.6	10 58.4	-55.9	163.6	10 00.8	-56.0	163.6	47
48	15 48.1	-55.3	163.6	14 50.6	-55.4	163.6	13 53.0	-55.5	163.7	12 55.4	-55.7	163.8	11 57.8	-55.8	163.8	11 00.1	-55.8	163.9	10 02.5	-56.0	164.0	9 04.8	-56.1	164.0	48
49	14 52.8	-55.3	164.0	13 55.2	-55.5	164.0	12 57.5	-55.6	164.1	11 59.7	-55.6	164.2	11 02.0	-55.8	164.2	10 04.3	-55.9	164.3	9 06.5	-56.0	164.3	8 08.7	-56.0	164.4	49
50	13 57.5	-55.4	164.4	12 59.7	-55.5	164.4	12 01.9	-55.6	164.5	11 04.1	-55.7	164.5	10 06.2	-55.8	164.6	9 08.4	-55.9	164.6	8 10.5	-56.0	164.7	7 12.7	-56.1	164.7	50
51	13 02.1	-55.4	164.8	12 04.2	-55.5	164.8	11 06.3	-55.6	164.9	10 08.4	-55.7	164.9	9 10.4	-55.8	165.0	8 12.5	-55.9	165.0	7 14.5	-56.0	165.0	6 16.6	-56.2	165.1	51
52	12 06.7	-55.4	165.2	11 08.7	-55.5	165.2	10 10.7	-55.7	165.3	9 12.7	-55.8	165.3	8 14.6	-55.8	165.3	7 16.6	-56.0	165.4	6 18.5	-56.0	165.4	5 20.4	-56.1	165.4	52
53	11 11.3	-55.5	165.6	10 13.2	-55.6	165.6	9 15.0	-55.6	165.6	8 16.9	-55.7	165.7	7 18.8	-55.9	165.7	6 20.6	-55.9	165.7	5 22.5	-56.1	165.8	4 24.3	-56.1	165.8	53
54	10 15.8	-55.5	165.9	9 17.6	-55.6	166.0	8 19.4	-55.7	166.0	7 21.2	-55.8	166.1	6 22.9	-55.9	166.1	5 24.7	-56.0	166.1	4 26.4	-56.0	166.1	3 28.2	-56.2	166.1	54
55	9 20.3	-55.5	166.3	8 22.0	-55.6	166.4	7 23.7	-55.7	166.4	6 25.4	-55.8	166.4	5 27.0	-55.8	166.4	4 28.7	-56.0	166.5	3 30.4	-56.1	166.5	2 32.0	-56.1	166.5	55
56	8 24.8	-55.6	166.7	7 26.4	-55.7	166.7	6 28.0	-55.8	166.8	5 29.6	-55.8	166.8	4 31.2	-55.9	166.8	3 32.7	-56.0	166.8	2 34.3	-56.1	166.8	1 35.9	-56.2	166.8	56
57	7 29.2	-55.5	167.1	6 30.7	-55.6	167.1	5 32.3	-55.8	167.1	4 33.8	-55.9	167.2	3 35.3	-56.0	167.2	2 36.7	-55.9	167.2	1 38.2	-56.0	167.2	0 39.7	-56.1	167.2	57
58	6 33.7	-55.6	167.5	5 35.1	-55.7	167.5	4 36.5	-55.7	167.5	3 37.9	-55.8	167.5	2 39.3	-55.9	167.5	1 40.8	-56.0	167.5	0 42.2	-56.1	167.6	0 16.4	+56.2	12.4	58
59	5 38.1	-55.6	167.8	4 39.4	-55.7	167.9	3 40.8	-55.8	167.9	2 42.1	-55.8	167.9	1 43.4	-55.9	167.9	0 44.8	-56.0	167.9	0 13.9	+56.1	12.1	1 12.6	+56.1	12.1	59
60	4 42.5	-55.6	168.2	3 43.7	-55.6	168.2	2 45.0	-55.8	168.3	1 46.3	-55.9	168.3	0 47.5	-55.9	168.3	0 11.2	+56.0	11.7	1 10.0	+56.1	11.7	2 08.7	+56.2	11.7	60
61	3 46.9	-55.6	168.6	2 48.1	-55.7	168.6	1 49.2	-55.7	168.6	0 50.4	-55.8	168.6	0 08.4	+55.9	11.4	1 07.2	+56.0	11.4	2 06.1	+56.0	11.4	3 04.9	+56.1	11.4	61
62	2 51.3	-55.7	169.0	1 52.4	-55.7	169.0	0 53.5	-55.8	169.0	0 05.4	+55.9	11.0	1 04.3	+55.9	11.0	2 03.2	+56.0	11.0	3 02.1	+56.1	11.0	4 01.0	+56.1	11.0	62
63	1 55.6	-55.6	169.4	0 56.7	-55.7	169.4	0 02.3	+55.8	10.6	1 01.3	+55.8	10.6	2 00.2	+56.0	10.6	2 59.2	+56.0	10.7	3 58.2	+56.0	10.7	4 57.1	+56.2	10.7	63
64	1 00.0	-55.6	169.7	0 01.0	-55.8	169.7	0 58.1	+55.8	10.3	1 57.1	+55.9	10.3	2 56.2	+55.9	10.3	3 55.2	+56.0	10.3	4 54.2	+56.1	10.3	5 53.3	+56.1	10.3	64
65	0 04.4	-55.7	170.1	0 54.8	+55.7	9.9	1 53.9	+55.7	9.9	2 53.0	+55.8	9.9	3 52.1	+55.9	9.9	4 51.2	+55.9	9.9	5 50.3	+56.0	10.0	6 49.4	+56.1	10.0	65
66	0 51.3	+55.6	9.5	1 50.5	+55.7	9.5	2 49.6	+55.8	9.5	3 48.8	+55.8	9.5	4 48.0	+55.8	9.6	5 47.1	+56.0	9.6	6 46.3	+56.0	9.6	7 45.5	+56.0	9.6	66
67	1 46.9	+55.6	9.1	2 46.2	+55.6	9.2	3 45.4	+55.7	9.2	4 44.6	+55.6	9.2	5 43.8	+55.9	9.2	6 43.1	+55.9	9.2	7 42.3	+56.0	9.2	8 41.5	+56.1	9.3	67
68	2 42.5	+55.7	8.8	3 41.8	+55.7	8.8	4 41.1	+55.8	8.8	5 40.4	+55.8	8.8	6 39.7	+55.9	8.8	7 39.0	+55.9	8.8	8 38.3	+56.0	8.9	9 37.6	+56.0	8.9	68
69	3 38.2	+55.6	8.4	4 37.5	+55.7	8.4	5 36.9	+55.7	8.4	6 36.2	+55.8	8.4	7 35.6	+55.8	8.5	8 34.9	+55.9	8.5	9 34.3	+55.9	8.5	10 33.6	+56.0	8.5	69
70	4 33.8	+55.6	8.0	5 33.2	+55.6	8.0	6 32.6	+55.7	8.0	7 32.0	+55.8	8.1	8 31.4	+55.8	8.1	9 30.8	+55.9	8.1	10 30.2	+55.9	8.1	11 29.6	+56.0	8.2	70
71	5 29.4	+55.6	7.6	6 28.8	+55.7	7.7	7 28.3	+55.7	7.7	8 27.8	+55.7	7.7	9 27.2	+55.8	7.7	10 26.7	+55.8	7.7	11 26.1	+55.9	7.8	12 25.6	+55.9	7.8	71
72	6 25.0	+55.5	7.3	7 24.5	+55.6	7.3	8 24.0	+55.7	7.3	9 23.5	+55.7	7.3	10 23.0	+55.8	7.3	11 22.5	+55.8	7.4	12 22.0	+55.9	7.4	13 21.5	+55.9	7.4	72
73	7 20.5	+55.6	6.9	8 20.1	+55.6	6.9	9 19.7	+55.6	6.9	10 19.2	+55.7	6.9	11 18.8	+55.7	7.0	12 18.3	+55.8	7.0	13 17.9	+55.8	7.0	14 17.4	+55.9	7.0	73
74	8 16.1	+55.5	6.5	9 15.7	+55.6	6.5	10 15.3	+55.6	6.5	11 14.9	+55.7	6.6	12 14.5	+55.7	6.6	13 14.1	+55.8	6.6	14 13.7	+55.8	6.6	15 13.3	+55.9	6.7	74
75	9 11.6	+55.5	6.1	10 11.3	+55.5	6.1	11 10.9	+55.6	6.2	12 10.6	+55.6	6.2	13 10.2	+55.7	6.2	14 09.9	+55.7	6.2	15 09.5	+55.8	6.3	16 09.2	+55.8	6.3	75
76	10 07.1	+55.5	5.7	11 06.8	+55.5	5.8	12 06.5	+55.6	5.8	13 06.2	+55.6	5.8	14 05.9	+55.6	5.8	15 05.6	+55.7	5.8	16 05.3	+55.7	5.9	17 05.0	+55.7	5.9	76
77	11 02.6	+55.4	5.3	12 02.3	+55.5	5.4	13 02.1	+55.5	5.4	14 01.8	+55.6	5.4	15 01.5	+55.6	5.4	16 01.3	+55.6	5.5	17 01.0	+55.7	5.5	18 00.7	+55.7	5.5	77
78	11 58.0	+55.5	5.0	12 57.8	+55.5	5.0	13 57.6	+55.5	5.0	14 57.4	+55.5	5.0	15 57.1	+55.6	5.0	16 56.9	+55.6	5.1	17 56.7	+55.6	5.1	18 56.4	+55.7	5.1	78
79	12 53.5	+55.3	4.6	13 53.3	+55.4	4.6	14 53.1	+55.4	4.6	15 52.9	+55.5	4.6	16 52.7	+55.5	4.7	17 52.5	+55.5	4.7	18 52.3	+55.6	4.7	19 52.1	+55.6	4.7	79
80	13 48.8	+55.4	4.2	14 48.7	+55.3	4.2	15 48.5	+55.4	4.2	16 48.4	+55.4	4.2	17 48.2	+55.4	4.3	18 48.0	+55.5	4.3	19 47.9	+55.5	4.3	20 47.7	+55.5	4.3	80
81	14 44.2	+55.3	3.8	15 44.0	+55.4	3.8	16 43.9	+55.4	3.8	17 43.8	+55.4	3.8	18 43.6	+55.5	3.9	19 43.5	+55.4	3.9	20 43.4	+55.4	3.9	21 43.2	+55.5	3.9	81
82	15 39.5	+55.2	3.4	16 39.4	+55.3	3.4	17 39.3	+55.3	3.4	18 39.2	+55.3	3.4	19 39.1	+55.3	3.4	20 38.9	+55.4	3.5	21 38.8	+55.4	3.5	22 38.7	+55.4	3.5	82
83	16 34.7	+55.2	3.0	17 34.7	+55.2	3.0	18 34.6	+55.2	3.0	19 34.5	+55.3	3.0	20 34.4	+55.3	3.0	21 34.3	+55.3	3.1	22 34.2	+55.4	3.1	23 34.1	+55.4	3.1	83
84	17 29.9	+55.2	2.6	18 29.9	+55.2	2.6	19 29.8	+55.2	2.6	20 29.8	+55.2	2.6	21 29.7	+55.2	2.6	22 29.6	+55.3	2.6	23 29.6	+55.2	2.7	24 29.5	+55.3	2.7	84
85	18 25.1	+55.1	2.1	19 25.1	+55.1	2.2	20 25.0	+55.1	2.2	21 25.0	+55.1	2.2	22 24.9	+55.2	2.2	23 24.9	+55.2	2.2	24 24.8	+55.2	2.2	25 24.8	+55.2	2.2	85
86	19 20.2	+55.0	1.7	20 20.2	+55.0	1.7	21 20.1	+55.1	1.7	22 20.1	+55.1	1.8	23 20.1	+55.1	1.8	24 20.1	+55.1	1.8	25 20.0	+55.2	1.8	26 20.0	+55.1	1.8	86
87	20 15.2	+55.0	1.3	21 15.2	+55.0	1.3	22 15.2	+55.0	1.3	23 15.2	+55.0	1.3	24 15.2	+55.0	1.3	25 15.2	+55.0	1.3	26 15.2	+55.0	1.4	27 15.1	+55.1	1.4	87
88	21 10.2	+55.0	0.9	22 10.2	+54.9	0.9	23 10.2	+54.9	0.9	24 10.2	+54.9	0.9	25 10.2	+54.9	0.9	26 10.2	+54.9	0.9	27 10.2	+54.9	0.9	28 10.2	+54.9	0.9	88
89	22 05.2	+54.8	0.4	23 05.1	+54.9	0.4	24 05.1	+54.9	0.4	25 05.1	+54.9	0.4	26 05.1	+54.9	0.5	27 05.1	+54.9	0.5	28 05.1	+54.9	0.5	29 05.1	+54.9	0.5	89
90	23 00.0	+54.8	0.0	24 00.0	+54.8	0.0	25 00.0	+54.8	0.0	26 00.0	+54.8	0.0	27 00.0	+54.8	0.0	28 00.0	+54.8	0.0	29 00.0	+54.8	0.0	30 00.0	+54.8	0.0	90
	23°			24°			25°			26°			27°			28°			29°			30°			

S. Lat. { L.H.A. greater than 180° ....Zn=180°–Z; L.H.A. less than 180°...........Zn=180°+Z

N. Lat. {L.H.A. greater than 180° .....Zn=Z; L.H.A. less than 180°............Zn=360°−Z}

Dec.	23° Hc	d	Z	24° Hc	d	Z	25° Hc	d	Z	26° Hc	d	Z	27° Hc	d	Z	28° Hc	d	Z	29° Hc	d	Z	30° Hc	d	Z	Dec.
°	° ′	′	°	° ′	′	°	° ′	′	°	° ′	′	°	° ′	′	°	° ′	′	°	° ′	′	°	° ′	′	°	°
0	56 32.3	+42.2	130.0	55 53.3	+43.2	131.1	55 13.5	+44.1	132.2	54 32.8	+45.0	133.2	53 51.3	+45.9	134.2	53 09.1	+46.7	135.2	52 26.2	+47.4	136.1	51 42.6	+48.2	137.0	0
1	57 14.5	+41.2	128.7	56 36.5	+42.3	129.8	55 57.6	+43.4	131.0	55 17.8	+44.3	132.1	54 37.2	+45.2	133.1	53 55.8	+46.1	134.1	53 13.6	+47.0	135.1	52 30.8	+47.7	136.0	1
2	57 55.7	+40.4	127.3	57 18.8	+41.6	128.5	56 41.0	+42.6	129.7	56 02.1	+43.7	130.9	55 22.4	+44.6	132.0	54 41.9	+45.5	133.0	54 00.6	+46.3	134.1	53 18.5	+47.1	135.0	2
3	58 36.1	+39.4	125.9	58 00.4	+40.6	127.2	57 23.6	+41.8	128.4	56 45.8	+42.8	129.6	56 07.0	+43.9	130.8	55 27.4	+44.8	131.9	54 46.9	+45.7	133.0	54 05.6	+46.6	134.0	3
4	59 15.5	+38.4	124.4	58 41.0	+39.7	125.8	58 05.4	+40.9	127.1	57 28.6	+42.1	128.4	56 50.9	+43.1	129.6	56 12.2	+44.2	130.7	55 32.6	+45.1	131.8	54 52.2	+46.0	132.9	4
5	59 53.9	+37.3	122.9	59 20.7	+38.7	124.3	58 46.3	+39.9	125.7	58 10.7	+41.2	127.0	57 34.0	+42.3	128.3	56 56.4	+43.3	129.5	56 17.7	+44.4	130.6	55 38.2	+45.4	131.8	5
6	60 31.2	+36.2	121.3	59 59.4	+37.6	122.8	59 26.2	+39.0	124.3	58 51.9	+40.2	125.6	58 16.3	+41.5	126.9	57 39.7	+42.6	128.2	57 02.1	+43.7	129.4	56 23.6	+44.6	130.6	6
7	61 07.4	+34.9	119.7	60 37.0	+36.4	121.3	60 05.2	+37.8	122.7	59 32.1	+39.2	124.2	58 57.8	+40.5	125.6	58 22.3	+41.7	126.9	57 45.8	+42.8	128.2	57 08.2	+43.9	129.4	7
8	61 42.3	+33.6	118.0	61 13.4	+35.2	119.6	60 43.0	+36.8	121.2	60 11.3	+38.2	122.7	59 38.3	+39.5	124.1	59 04.0	+40.8	125.5	58 28.6	+42.0	126.8	57 52.1	+43.2	128.1	8
9	62 15.9	+32.2	116.2	61 48.6	+33.9	117.9	61 19.8	+35.5	119.5	60 49.5	+37.0	121.1	60 17.8	+38.5	122.6	59 44.8	+39.8	124.1	59 10.6	+41.1	125.4	58 35.3	+42.3	126.8	9
10	62 48.1	+30.8	114.4	62 22.5	+32.5	116.2	61 55.3	+34.2	117.8	61 26.5	+35.8	119.5	60 56.3	+37.3	121.0	60 24.6	+38.8	122.6	59 51.7	+40.1	124.0	59 17.6	+41.3	125.4	10
11	63 18.9	+29.2	112.5	62 55.0	+31.1	114.3	62 29.5	+32.8	116.1	62 02.3	+34.5	117.8	61 33.6	+36.1	119.4	61 03.4	+37.6	121.0	60 31.8	+39.1	122.5	59 58.9	+40.4	124.0	11
12	63 48.1	+27.5	110.6	63 26.1	+29.5	112.4	63 02.3	+31.4	114.3	62 36.8	+33.2	116.0	62 09.7	+34.8	117.7	61 41.0	+36.5	119.4	61 10.9	+37.9	121.0	60 39.3	+39.4	122.5	12
13	64 15.6	+25.8	108.5	63 55.6	+27.8	110.5	63 33.7	+29.8	112.4	63 10.0	+31.6	114.2	62 44.5	+33.5	116.0	62 17.5	+35.1	117.7	61 48.8	+36.8	119.3	61 18.7	+38.3	120.9	13
14	64 41.4	+23.9	106.4	64 23.4	+26.1	108.4	64 03.5	+28.1	110.4	63 41.6	+30.1	112.3	63 18.0	+32.0	114.1	62 52.6	+33.8	115.9	62 25.6	+35.4	117.6	61 57.0	+37.0	119.3	14
15	65 05.3	+22.1	104.3	64 49.5	+24.3	106.3	64 31.6	+26.4	108.4	64 11.7	+28.5	110.3	63 50.0	+30.4	112.2	63 26.4	+32.3	114.1	63 01.0	+34.1	115.9	62 34.0	+35.8	117.6	15
16	65 27.4	+20.0•	102.0	65 13.8	+22.3•	104.2	64 58.0	+24.6	106.2	64 40.2	+26.7	108.3	64 20.4	+28.8	110.3	63 58.7	+30.8	112.2	63 35.1	+32.7	114.0	63 09.8	+34.4	115.9	16
17	65 47.4	+17.9•	99.8	65 36.1	+20.3•	101.9	65 22.6	+22.6•	104.1	65 06.9	+24.9	106.2	64 49.2	+27.0	108.2	64 29.5	+29.1	110.2	64 07.8	+31.1	112.1	63 44.2	+33.0	114.0	17
18	66 05.3	+15.7•	97.4	65 56.4	+18.2•	99.6	65 45.2	+20.6•	101.8	65 31.8	+23.0•	104.0	65 16.2	+25.2	106.1	64 58.6	+27.3	108.2	64 38.9	+29.4	110.2	64 17.2	+31.5	112.1	18
19	66 21.0	+13.5•	95.0	66 14.6	+16.0•	97.3	66 05.8	+18.5•	99.5	65 54.8	+20.9•	101.7	65 41.4	+23.3•	103.9	65 25.9	+25.6	106.0	65 08.3	+27.7	108.1	64 48.7	+29.7	110.1	19
20	66 34.5	+11.2•	92.6	66 30.6	+13.8•	94.9	66 24.3	+16.3•	97.2	66 15.7	+18.8•	99.4	66 04.7	+21.2•	101.7	65 51.5	+23.5•	103.8	65 36.0	+25.9	106.0	65 18.4	+28.1	108.1	20
21	66 45.7	+8.8•	90.1	66 44.4	+11.4•	92.4	66 40.6	+14.1•	94.8	66 34.5	+16.6•	97.1	66 25.9	+19.1•	99.3	66 15.0	+21.6•	101.6	66 01.9	+23.9•	103.8	65 46.5	+26.2	105.9	21
22	66 54.5	+6.4•	87.6	66 55.8	+9.1•	89.9	66 54.7	+11.7•	92.3	66 51.1	+14.3•	94.6	66 45.0	+16.9•	96.9	66 36.6	+19.4•	99.2	66 25.8	+21.8•	101.5	66 12.7	+24.2•	103.7	22
23	67 00.9	+4.0•	85.0	67 04.9	+6.6•	87.4	67 06.4	+9.3•	89.8	67 05.4	+11.9•	92.1	67 01.9	+14.6•	94.5	66 56.0	+17.1•	96.8	66 47.6	+19.7•	99.2	66 36.9	+22.2•	101.4	23
24	67 04.9	+1.5•	82.5	67 11.5	+4.2•	84.8	67 15.7	+6.8•	87.2	67 17.3	+9.5•	89.6	67 16.5	+12.2•	92.0	67 13.1	+14.9•	94.4	67 07.3	+17.5•	96.7	66 59.1	+20.0•	99.1	24
25	67 06.4	−1.0•	79.9	67 15.7	+1.6•	82.3	67 22.5	+4.3•	84.6	67 26.8	+7.1•	87.0	67 28.7	+9.7•	89.5	67 28.0	+12.4•	91.9	67 24.8	+15.1•	94.3	67 19.1	+17.7•	96.7	25
26	67 05.4	−3.5•	77.4	67 17.3	−0.8•	79.7	67 26.8	+1.9•	82.1	67 33.9	+4.5•	84.4	67 38.4	+7.3•	86.9	67 40.4	+10.0•	89.3	67 39.9	+12.7•	91.7	67 36.8	+15.4•	94.2	26
27	67 01.9	−5.9•	74.8	67 16.5	−3.4•	77.1	67 28.7	−0.7•	79.4	67 38.4	+2.0•	81.8	67 45.7	+4.7•	84.3	67 50.4	+7.5•	86.7	67 52.6	+10.3•	89.2	67 52.2	+13.0•	91.6	27
28	66 56.0	−8.4•	72.2	67 13.1	−5.8•	74.5	67 28.0	−3.2•	76.8	67 40.4	−0.5•	79.2	67 50.4	+2.2•	81.6	67 57.9	+5.0•	84.1	68 02.9	+7.7•	86.5	68 05.2	+10.5•	89.0	28
29	66 47.6	−10.7•	69.7	67 07.3	−8.2•	71.9	67 24.8	−5.7•	74.2	67 39.9	−3.1•	76.6	67 52.6	−0.4•	79.0	68 02.9	+2.3•	81.4	68 10.6	+5.1•	83.9	68 15.7	+7.9•	86.4	29
30	66 36.9	−13.1•	67.2	66 59.1	−10.7•	69.4	67 19.1	−8.2•	71.6	67 36.8	−5.6•	73.9	67 52.2	−3.0•	76.3	68 05.2	−0.3•	78.7	68 15.7	+2.5•	81.2	68 23.6	+5.3•	83.7	30
31	66 23.8	−15.3•	64.8	66 48.4	−13.0•	66.9	67 10.9	−10.6•	69.1	67 31.2	−8.1•	71.3	67 49.2	−5.5•	73.7	68 04.9	−2.8•	76.0	68 18.2	−0.2•	78.5	68 28.9	+2.6•	81.0	31
32	66 08.5	−17.5•	62.4	66 35.4	−15.3•	64.4	67 00.3	−13.0•	66.6	67 23.1	−10.6•	68.8	67 43.7	−8.0•	71.0	68 02.1	−5.5•	73.4	68 18.0	−2.7•	75.8	68 31.5	0.0•	78.2	32
33	65 51.0	−19.6•	60.0	66 20.1	−17.5•	62.0	66 47.3	−15.3•	64.1	67 12.5	−12.9•	66.2	67 35.7	−10.6•	68.4	67 56.6	−8.0•	70.7	68 15.3	−5.4•	73.1	68 31.5	−2.6•	75.5	33
34	65 31.4	−21.7•	57.7	66 02.6	−19.7•	59.6	66 32.0	−17.5•	61.6	66 59.6	−15.3•	63.7	67 25.1	−12.9•	65.8	67 48.6	−10.5•	68.1	68 09.9	−7.9•	70.4	68 28.9	−5.3•	72.8	34
35	65 09.7	−23.6	55.5	65 42.9	−21.7	57.3	66 14.5	−19.7•	59.2	66 44.3	−17.6•	61.2	67 12.2	−15.3•	63.3	67 38.1	−12.9•	65.5	68 02.0	−10.5•	67.7	68 23.6	−8.0•	70.1	35
36	64 46.1	−25.4	53.3	65 21.2	−23.6	55.1	65 54.8	−21.7•	56.9	66 26.7	−19.7•	58.8	66 56.9	−17.6•	60.8	67 25.2	−15.3•	62.9	67 51.5	−13.0•	65.1	68 15.6	−10.4•	67.4	36
37	64 20.7	−27.2	51.2	64 57.6	−25.5	52.9	65 33.1	−23.7	54.6	66 07.0	−21.8•	56.5	66 39.3	−19.7•	58.4	67 09.9	−17.7•	60.4	67 38.5	−15.4•	62.5	68 05.2	−13.0•	64.7	37
38	63 53.5	−28.9	49.2	64 32.1	−27.3	50.8	65 09.4	−25.6	52.4	65 45.2	−23.8	54.2	66 19.6	−21.9•	56.0	66 52.2	−19.8•	58.0	67 23.1	−17.6•	60.0	67 52.2	−15.4•	62.1	38
39	63 24.6	−30.4	47.2	64 04.8	−28.9	48.7	64 43.8	−27.4	50.3	65 21.4	−25.6	52.0	65 57.7	−23.9	53.7	66 32.4	−22.0•	55.6	67 05.5	−20.0•	57.5	67 36.8	−17.8•	59.6	39
40	62 54.2	−32.0	45.3	63 35.9	−30.6	46.7	64 16.4	−29.0	48.2	64 55.8	−27.5	49.8	65 33.8	−25.8	51.5	66 10.4	−23.9	53.3	66 45.5	−22.0•	55.1	67 19.0	−20.0•	57.1	40
41	62 22.2	−33.3	43.5	63 05.3	−32.0	44.8	63 47.4	−30.7	46.2	64 28.3	−29.2	47.7	65 08.0	−27.6	49.3	65 46.5	−25.9	51.0	66 23.5	−24.1•	52.8	66 59.0	−22.2•	54.7	41
42	61 48.9	−34.7	41.7	62 33.3	−33.5	43.0	63 16.7	−32.2	44.3	63 59.1	−30.8	45.7	64 40.4	−29.3	47.2	65 20.6	−27.8	48.8	65 59.4	−26.1	50.5	66 36.8	−24.2•	52.3	42
43	61 14.2	−35.9	40.0	61 59.8	−34.8	41.2	62 44.5	−33.6	42.4	63 28.3	−32.3	43.8	64 11.1	−30.9	45.2	64 52.8	−29.4	46.7	65 33.3	−27.8	48.3	66 12.6	−26.2	50.0	43
44	60 38.3	−37.1	38.3	61 25.0	−36.0	39.5	62 10.9	−34.9	40.7	62 56.0	−33.7	41.9	63 40.2	−32.5	43.3	64 23.4	−31.1	44.7	65 05.5	−29.6	46.2	65 46.4	−28.0	47.8	44
45	60 01.2	−38.2	36.7	60 49.0	−37.3	37.8	61 36.0	−36.2	38.9	62 22.3	−35.1	40.1	63 07.7	−33.8	41.4	63 52.3	−32.6	42.7	64 35.9	−31.3	44.2	65 18.4	−29.8	45.7	45
46	59 23.0	−39.2	35.2	60 11.7	−38.3	36.2	60 59.8	−37.3	37.3	61 47.2	−36.3	38.4	62 33.9	−35.3	39.6	63 19.7	−34.1	40.8	64 04.6	−32.8	42.2	64 48.6	−31.5	43.6	46
47	58 43.8	−40.2	33.7	59 33.4	−39.4	34.7	60 22.5	−38.5	35.7	61 10.9	−37.5	36.7	61 58.6	−36.5	37.8	62 45.6	−35.4	39.0	63 31.8	−34.2	40.3	64 17.1	−32.9	41.6	47
48	58 03.6	−41.1	32.3	58 54.0	−40.3	33.2	59 44.0	−39.5	34.1	60 33.4	−38.7	35.1	61 22.1	−37.7	36.2	62 10.2	−36.7	37.3	62 57.6	−35.6	38.5	63 44.2	−34.5	39.7	48
49	57 22.5	−42.0	30.9	58 13.7	−41.2	31.8	59 04.5	−40.5	32.6	59 54.7	−39.6	33.6	60 44.4	−38.8	34.6	61 33.5	−37.8	35.6	62 22.0	−36.9	36.7	63 09.7	−35.8	37.9	49
50	56 40.5	−42.7	29.6	57 32.5	−42.1	30.4	58 24.0	−41.4	31.2	59 15.1	−40.7	32.1	60 05.6	−39.8	33.0	60 55.7	−39.0	34.0	61 45.1	−38.0	35.0	62 33.9	−37.0	36.1	50
51	55 57.8	−43.6	28.4	56 50.4	−42.9	29.1	57 42.6	−42.2	29.9	58 34.4	−41.5	30.7	59 25.8	−40.8	31.5	60 16.7	−40.0	32.4	61 07.1	−39.2	33.4	61 56.9	−38.3	34.4	51
52	55 14.2	−44.2	27.2	56 07.5	−43.7	27.8	57 00.4	−43.1	28.5	57 52.9	−42.4	29.3	58 45.0	−41.7	30.1	59 36.7	−41.0	31.0	60 27.9	−40.2	31.9	61 18.6	−39.4	32.8	52
53	54 30.0	−44.8	26.0	55 23.8	−44.3	26.6	56 17.3	−43.8	27.3	57 10.5	−43.2	28.0	58 03.3	−42.6	28.7	58 55.7	−41.9	29.5	59 47.7	−41.2	30.4	60 39.2	−40.4	31.3	53
54	53 45.2	−45.5	24.8	54 39.5	−45.0	25.4	55 33.5	−44.5	26.1	56 27.3	−44.0	26.7	57 20.7	−43.3	27.4	58 13.8	−42.7	28.2	59 06.5	−42.1	28.9	59 58.8	−41.4	29.8	54
55	52 59.7	−46.1	23.7	53 54.5	−45.6	24.3	54 49.0	−45.1	24.9	55 43.3	−44.6	25.5	56 37.4	−44.1	26.1	57 31.1	−43.6	26.8	58 24.4	−42.9	27.6	59 17.4	−42.3	28.3	55
56	52 13.6	−46.6	22.7	53 08.9	−46.2	23.2	54 03.9	−45.8	23.7	54 58.7	−45.3	24.3	55 53.3	−44.9	24.9	56 47.5	−44.3	25.6	57 41.5	−43.7	26.2	58 35.1	−43.1	27.0	56
57	51 27.0	−47.1	21.7	52 22.7	−46.8	22.2	53 18.1	−46.3	22.7	54 13.4	−45.9	23.2	55 08.4	−45.4	23.7	56 03.2	−44.9	24.3	56 57.8	−44.5	25.0	57 52.0	−43.9	25.6	57
58	50 39.9	−47.6	20.7	51 35.9	−47.2	21.1	52 31.8	−46.9	21.6	53 27.5	−46.5	22.1	54 23.0	−46.1	22.6	55 18.3	−45.7	23.2	56 13.3	−45.2	23.8	57 08.1	−44.7	24.4	58
59	49 52.3	−48.1	19.7	50 48.7	−47.8	20.1	51 44.9	−47.4	20.6	52 41.0	−47.0	21.0	53 36.9	−46.6	21.5	54 32.6	−46.2	22.0	55 28.1	−45.8	22.6	56 23.4	−45.3	23.2	59
60	49 04.2	−48.5	18.8	50 00.9	−48.1	19.2	50 57.5	−47.8	19.6	51 54.0	−47.5	20.0	52 50.3	−47.2	20.5	53 46.4	−46.8	21.0	54 42.3	−46.4	21.5	55 38.1	−46.0	22.0	60
61	48 15.7	−48.9	17.9	49 12.8	−48.6	18.3	50 09.7	−48.3	18.7	51 06.5	−48.1	19.0	52 03.1	−47.7	19.5	52 59.6	−47.3	19.9	53 55.9	−46.9	20.4	54 52.1	−46.6	20.9	61
62	47 26.8	−49.2	17.1	48 24.2	−49.1	17.4	49 21.4	−48.8	17.7	50 18.4	−48.4	18.1	51 15.4	−48.1	18.5	52 12.3	−47.9	18.9	53 09.0	−47.6	19.3	54 05.5	−47.2	19.8	62
63	46 37.6	−49.6	16.2	47 35.1	−49.3	16.5	48 32.6	−49.1	16.8	49 30.0	−48.9	17.2	50 27.3	−48.6	17.5	51 24.4	−48.3	17.9	52 21.4	−48.0	18.3	53 18.3	−47.7	18.7	63
64	45 48.0	−50.0	15.4	46 45.8	−49.8	15.7	47 43.5	−49.5	16.0	48 41.1	−49.2	16.3	49 38.7	−49.1	16.6	50 36.1	−48.7	17.0	51 33.4	−48.4	17.3	52 30.6	−48.1	17.7	64
65	44 58.0	−50.3	14.6	45 56.0	−50.0	14.9	46 54.0	−49.9	15.2	47 51.9	−49.7	15.4	48 49.6	−49.4	15.7	49 47.4	−49.2	16.1	50 45.0	−48.9	16.4	51 42.5	−48.7	16.8	65
66	44 07.7	−50.5	13.9	45 06.0	−50.4	14.1	46 04.1	−50.2	14.3	47 02.2	−50.0	14.6	48 00.2	−49.7	14.9	48 58.2	−49.6	15.2	49 56.1	−49.4	15.5	50 53.8	−49.1	15.8	66
67	43 17.2	−50.9	13.1	44 15.6	−50.7	13.3	45 13.9	−50.5	13.6	46 12.2	−50.3	13.8	47 10.5	−50.2	14.1	48 08.6	−49.9	14.3	49 06.7	−49.7	14.6	50 04.7	−49.4	14.9	67
68	42 26.3	−51.1	12.4	43 24.9	−51.0	12.6	44 23.4	−50.8	12.8	45 21.9	−50.6	13.0	46 20.3	−50.4	13.3	47 18.7	−50.3	13.5	48 17.0	−50.0	13.8	49 15.3	−49.9	14.0	68
69	41 35.2	−51.4	11.7	42 33.9	−51.2	11.9	43 32.6	−51.0	12.1	44 31.3	−50.9	12.3	45 29.9	−50.8	12.5	46 28.4	−50.5	12.7	47 27.0	−50.5	12.9	48 25.4	−50.2	13.2	69
70	40 43.8	−51.6	11.0	41 42.7	−51.5	11.2	42 41.6	−51.4	11.3	43 40.4	−51.2	11.5	44 39.1	−51.0	11.7	45 37.9	−50.9	11.9	46 36.5	−50.7	12.1	47 35.2	−50.6	12.4	70
71	39 52.2	−51.8	10.3	40 51.2	−51.7	10.5	41 50.2	−51.6	10.6	42 49.2	−51.5	10.8	43 48.1	−51.3	11.0	44 47.0	−51.2	11.2	45 45.8	−51.0	11.4	46 44.6	−50.9	11.6	71
72	39 00.4	−52.1	9.7	39 59.5	−51.9	9.8	40 58.6	−51.8	10.0	41 57.7	−51.7	10.1	42 56.8	−51.6	10.3	43 55.8	−51.5	10.4	44 54.8	−51.3	10.6	45 53.7	−51.2	10.8	72
73	38 08.3	−52.2	9.0	39 07.6	−52.2	9.2	40 06.8	−52.0	9.3	41 06.0	−51.9	9.4	42 05.2	−51.8	9.6	43 04.3	−51.7	9.7	44 03.5	−51.6	9.9	45 02.5	−51.4	10.1	73
74	37 16.1	−52.4	8.4	38 15.4	−52.3	8.5	39 14.8	−52.3	8.7	40 14.1	−52.2	8.8	41 13.4	−52.1	8.9	42 12.6	−51.9	9.0	43 11.9	−51.9	9.2	44 11.1	−51.7	9.3	74
75	36 23.7	−52.7	7.8	37 23.1	−52.5	7.9	38 22.5	−52.4	8.0	39 21.9	−52.3	8.1	40 21.3	−52.3	8.3	41 20.7	−52.2	8.4	42 20.0	−52.0	8.5	43 19.4	−52.0	8.6	75
76	35 31.0	−52.7	7.2	36 30.6	−52.7	7.3	37 30.1	−52.7	7.4	38 29.6	−52.6	7.5	39 29.0	−52.4	7.6	40 28.5	−52.4	7.7	41 28.0	−52.3	7.8	42 27.4	−52.2	8.0	76
77	34 38.3	−53.0	6.6	35 37.9	−52.9	6.7	36 37.4	−52.8	6.8	37 37.0	−52.7	6.9	38 36.6	−52.7	7.0	39 36.1	−52.6	7.1	40 35.7	−52.6	7.2	41 35.2	−52.5	7.3	77
78	33 45.3	−53.1	6.1	34 45.0	−53.1	6.1	35 44.6	−53.0	6.2	36 44.3	−53.0	6.3	37 43.9	−52.9	6.4	38 43.5	−52.8	6.5	39 43.1	−52.7	6.6	40 42.7	−52.6	6.7	78
79	32 52.2	−53.2	5.5	33 51.9	−53.2	5.6	34 51.6	−53.1	5.6	35 51.3	−53.0	5.7	36 51.0	−53.0	5.8	37 50.7	−52.9	5.8	38 50.4	−52.9	5.9	39 50.1	−52.9	6.0	79
80	31 59.0	−53.4	5.0	32 58.7	−53.3	5.0	33 58.5	−53.3	5.1	34 58.3	−53.3	5.1	35 58.0	−53.2	5.2	36 57.8	−53.2	5.3	37 57.5	−53.1	5.3	38 57.2	−53.0	5.4	80
81	31 05.6	−53.5	4.4	32 05.4	−53.5	4.5	33 05.2	−53.4	4.5	34 05.0	−53.4	4.6	35 04.8	−53.3	4.6	36 04.6	−53.3	4.7	37 04.4	−53.2	4.8	38 04.2	−53.2	4.8	81
82	30 12.1	−53.7	3.9	31 11.9	−53.6	3.9	32 11.8	−53.6	4.0	33 11.6	−53.5	4.0	34 11.5	−53.5	4.1	35 11.3	−53.4	4.1	36 11.2	−53.4	4.2	37 11.0	−53.4	4.2	82
83	29 18.4	−53.7	3.4	30 18.3	−53.7	3.4	31 18.2	−53.7	3.5	32 18.1	−53.7	3.5	33 18.0	−53.6	3.5	34 17.9	−53.6	3.6	35 17.8	−53.6	3.6	36 17.6	−53.5	3.7	83
84	28 24.7	−53.9	2.9	29 24.6	−53.9	2.9	30 24.5	−53.8	2.9	31 24.4	−53.8	3.0	32 24.4	−53.8	3.0	33 24.3	−53.8	3.0	34 24.2	−53.7	3.1	35 24.1	−53.7	3.1	84
85	27 30.8	−54.0	2.4	28 30.7	−53.9	2.4	29 30.7	−53.9	2.4	30 30.6	−53.9	2.5	31 30.6	−53.9	2.5	32 30.5	−53.8	2.5	33 30.5	−53.9	2.5	34 30.4	−53.8	2.6	85
86	26 36.8	−54.0	1.9	27 36.8	−54.1	1.9	28 36.8	−54.1	1.9	29 36.7	−54.0	1.9	30 36.7	−54.0	2.0	31 36.7	−54.0	2.0	32 36.6	−54.0	2.0	33 36.6	−54.0	2.0	86
87	25 42.8	−54.2	1.4	26 42.7	−54.1	1.4	27 42.7	−54.1	1.4	28 42.7	−54.1	1.4	29 42.7	−54.1	1.5	30 42.7	−54.1	1.5	31 42.6	−54.1	1.5	32 42.6	−54.1	1.5	87
88	24 48.6	−54.3	0.9	25 48.6	−54.3	0.9	26 48.6	−54.3	0.9	27 48.6	−54.3	1.0	28 48.6	−54.3	1.0	29 48.6	−54.3	1.0	30 48.5	−54.2	1.0	31 48.5	−54.2	1.0	88
89	23 54.3	−54.3	0.5	24 54.3	−54.3	0.5	25 54.3	−54.3	0.5	26 54.3	−54.3	0.5	27 54.3	−54.3	0.5	28 54.3	−54.3	0.5	29 54.3	−54.3	0.5	30 54.3	−54.3	0.5	89
90	23 00.0	−54.4	0.0	24 00.0	−54.4	0.0	25 00.0	−54.4	0.0	26 00.0	−54.4	0.0	27 00.0	−54.4	0.0	28 00.0	−54.4	0.0	29 00.0	−54.4	0.0	30 00.0	−54.4	0.0	90
	23°			24°			25°			26°			27°			28°			29°			30°			

25°, 335° L.H.A. LATITUDE SAME NAME AS DECLINATION

LATITUDE **CONTRARY** NAME TO DECLINATION L.H.A. 25°, 335°

Dec.	23° Hc	d	Z	24° Hc	d	Z	25° Hc	d	Z	26° Hc	d	Z	27° Hc	d	Z	28° Hc	d	Z	29° Hc	d	Z	30° Hc	d	Z	Dec.
°	° ′	′	°	° ′	′	°	° ′	′	°	° ′	′	°	° ′	′	°	° ′	′	°	° ′	′	°	° ′	′	°	°
0	56 32.3	-42.9	130.0	55 53.3	-43.8	131.1	55 13.5	-44.8	132.2	54 32.8	-45.7	133.2	53 51.3	-46.5	134.2	53 09.1	-47.3	135.2	52 26.2	-48.0	136.1	51 42.6	-48.6	137.0	0
1	55 49.4	-43.6	131.2	55 09.5	-44.6	132.3	54 28.7	-45.4	133.3	53 47.1	-46.2	134.3	53 04.8	-47.0	135.3	52 21.8	-47.7	136.2	51 38.2	-48.4	137.1	50 54.0	-49.1	137.9	1
2	55 05.8	-44.4	132.4	54 24.9	-45.2	133.5	53 43.3	-46.1	134.5	53 00.9	-46.8	135.4	52 17.8	-47.5	136.3	51 34.1	-48.2	137.2	50 49.8	-48.9	138.0	50 04.9	-49.5	138.8	2
3	54 21.4	-44.9	133.6	53 39.7	-45.8	134.6	52 57.2	-46.6	135.5	52 14.1	-47.3	136.4	51 30.3	-48.0	137.3	50 45.9	-48.7	138.1	50 00.9	-49.3	138.9	49 15.4	-49.9	139.7	3
4	53 36.5	-45.6	134.7	52 53.9	-46.4	135.7	52 10.6	-47.1	136.6	51 26.8	-47.9	137.4	50 42.3	-48.5	138.3	49 57.2	-49.1	139.1	49 11.6	-49.6	139.8	48 25.5	-50.2	140.6	4
5	52 50.9	-46.2	135.8	52 07.5	-46.9	136.7	51 23.5	-47.6	137.6	50 38.9	-48.2	138.4	49 53.8	-48.9	139.2	49 08.1	-49.4	139.9	48 22.0	-50.1	140.7	47 35.3	-50.5	141.4	5
6	52 04.7	-46.7	136.9	51 20.6	-47.4	137.7	50 35.9	-48.1	138.5	49 50.7	-48.7	139.3	49 04.9	-49.3	140.1	48 18.7	-49.9	140.8	47 31.9	-50.4	141.5	46 44.8	-50.9	142.2	6
7	51 18.0	-47.3	137.9	50 33.2	-47.9	138.7	49 47.8	-48.5	139.5	49 02.0	-49.1	140.2	48 15.6	-49.6	140.9	47 28.8	-50.2	141.6	46 41.5	-50.7	142.3	45 53.9	-51.2	142.9	7
8	50 30.7	-47.7	138.8	49 45.3	-48.3	139.6	48 59.3	-48.9	140.4	48 12.9	-49.5	141.1	47 26.0	-50.1	141.8	46 38.6	-50.5	142.4	45 50.8	-51.0	143.1	45 02.7	-51.5	143.7	8
9	49 43.0	-48.1	139.8	48 57.0	-48.8	140.5	48 10.4	-49.3	141.2	47 23.4	-49.8	141.9	46 35.9	-50.3	142.6	45 48.1	-50.8	143.2	44 59.8	-51.2	143.8	44 11.2	-51.7	144.4	9
10	48 54.9	-48.6	140.7	48 08.2	-49.1	141.4	47 21.1	-49.7	142.1	46 33.6	-50.2	142.8	45 45.6	-50.7	143.4	44 57.3	-51.2	144.0	44 08.6	-51.6	144.6	43 19.5	-52.0	145.1	10
11	48 06.3	-48.9	141.6	47 19.1	-49.5	142.3	46 31.4	-50.0	142.9	45 43.4	-50.5	143.5	44 54.9	-50.9	144.1	44 06.1	-51.4	144.7	43 17.0	-51.8	145.3	42 27.5	-52.2	145.8	11
12	47 17.4	-49.4	142.5	46 29.6	-49.8	143.1	45 41.4	-50.3	143.7	44 52.9	-50.8	144.3	44 04.0	-51.3	144.9	43 14.7	-51.6	145.4	42 25.2	-52.1	145.9	41 35.3	-52.4	146.4	12
13	46 28.0	-49.6	143.3	45 39.8	-50.2	143.9	44 51.1	-50.6	144.5	44 02.1	-51.1	145.1	43 12.7	-51.5	145.6	42 23.1	-51.9	146.1	41 33.1	-52.3	146.6	40 42.9	-52.7	147.1	13
14	45 38.4	-50.1	144.1	44 49.6	-50.5	144.7	44 00.5	-51.0	145.2	43 11.0	-51.3	145.8	42 21.2	-51.7	146.3	41 31.2	-52.2	146.8	40 40.8	-52.5	147.3	39 50.2	-52.8	147.7	14
15	44 48.3	-50.3	144.9	43 59.1	-50.8	145.4	43 09.5	-51.2	146.0	42 19.7	-51.6	146.5	41 29.5	-52.0	147.0	40 39.0	-52.3	147.4	39 48.3	-52.7	147.9	38 57.4	-53.0	148.3	15
16	43 58.0	-50.6	145.6	43 08.3	-51.0	146.2	42 18.3	-51.4	146.7	41 28.1	-51.9	147.2	40 37.5	-52.2	147.6	39 46.7	-52.6	148.1	38 55.6	-52.8	148.5	38 04.4	-53.2	148.9	16
17	43 07.4	-50.9	146.4	42 17.3	-51.3	146.9	41 26.9	-51.7	147.4	40 36.2	-52.0	147.8	39 45.3	-52.4	148.3	38 54.1	-52.7	148.7	38 02.8	-53.1	149.1	37 11.2	-53.4	149.5	17
18	42 16.5	-51.2	147.1	41 26.0	-51.6	147.6	40 35.2	-51.9	148.0	39 44.2	-52.3	148.5	38 52.9	-52.6	148.9	38 01.4	-52.9	149.3	37 09.7	-53.2	149.7	36 17.8	-53.6	150.1	18
19	41 25.3	-51.4	147.8	40 34.4	-51.8	148.3	39 43.3	-52.2	148.7	38 51.9	-52.5	149.1	38 00.3	-52.8	149.5	37 08.5	-53.1	149.9	36 16.5	-53.5	150.3	35 24.2	-53.6	150.6	19
20	40 33.9	-51.6	148.5	39 42.6	-52.0	148.9	38 51.1	-52.3	149.3	37 59.4	-52.7	149.7	37 07.5	-53.0	150.1	36 15.4	-53.3	150.5	35 23.0	-53.5	150.8	34 30.6	-53.9	151.2	20
21	39 42.3	-51.9	149.1	38 50.6	-52.2	149.6	37 58.8	-52.5	150.0	37 06.7	-52.8	150.3	36 14.5	-53.1	150.7	35 22.1	-53.4	151.1	34 29.5	-53.7	151.4	33 36.7	-53.9	151.7	21
22	38 50.4	-52.1	149.8	37 58.4	-52.4	150.2	37 06.3	-52.8	150.6	36 13.9	-53.0	150.9	35 21.4	-53.3	151.3	34 28.7	-53.6	151.6	33 35.8	-53.8	151.9	32 42.8	-54.1	152.2	22
23	37 58.3	-52.3	150.4	37 06.0	-52.6	150.8	36 13.5	-52.9	151.2	35 20.9	-53.2	151.5	34 28.1	-53.5	151.8	33 35.1	-53.7	152.2	32 42.0	-54.0	152.5	31 48.7	-54.2	152.8	23
24	37 06.0	-52.5	151.0	36 13.4	-52.8	151.4	35 20.6	-53.0	151.8	34 27.7	-53.3	152.1	33 34.6	-53.6	152.4	32 41.4	-53.9	152.7	31 48.0	-54.1	153.0	30 54.5	-54.3	153.3	24
25	36 13.5	-52.6	151.7	35 20.6	-52.9	152.0	34 27.6	-53.2	152.3	33 34.4	-53.5	152.6	32 41.0	-53.7	152.9	31 47.5	-53.9	153.2	30 53.9	-54.2	153.5	30 00.2	-54.5	153.8	25
26	35 20.9	-52.8	152.2	34 27.7	-53.1	152.6	33 34.4	-53.4	152.9	32 40.9	-53.6	153.2	31 47.3	-53.9	153.5	30 53.6	-54.1	153.7	29 59.7	-54.3	154.0	29 05.7	-54.5	154.2	26
27	34 28.1	-53.0	152.8	33 34.6	-53.2	153.1	32 41.0	-53.5	153.4	31 47.3	-53.7	153.7	30 53.4	-53.9	154.0	29 59.5	-54.2	154.2	29 05.4	-54.4	154.5	28 11.2	-54.6	154.7	27
28	33 35.1	-53.1	153.4	32 41.4	-53.4	153.7	31 47.5	-53.6	154.0	30 53.6	-53.9	154.2	29 59.5	-54.1	154.5	29 05.3	-54.3	154.7	28 11.0	-54.6	155.0	27 16.6	-54.8	155.2	28
29	32 42.0	-53.3	153.9	31 48.0	-53.5	154.2	30 53.9	-53.7	154.5	29 59.7	-54.0	154.7	29 05.4	-54.2	155.0	28 11.0	-54.4	155.2	27 16.4	-54.6	155.4	26 21.8	-54.8	155.6	29
30	31 48.7	-53.4	154.5	30 54.5	-53.7	154.7	30 00.2	-53.9	155.0	29 05.7	-54.1	155.2	28 11.2	-54.3	155.5	27 16.6	-54.5	155.7	26 21.8	-54.7	155.9	25 27.0	-54.9	156.1	30
31	30 55.3	-53.6	155.0	30 00.8	-53.7	155.3	29 06.3	-54.0	155.5	28 11.6	-54.2	155.7	27 16.9	-54.4	155.9	26 22.1	-54.6	156.2	25 27.1	-54.7	156.3	24 32.1	-54.9	156.5	31
32	30 01.7	-53.6	155.5	29 07.1	-53.9	155.8	28 12.3	-54.1	156.0	27 17.4	-54.3	156.2	26 22.5	-54.5	156.4	25 27.5	-54.7	156.6	24 32.4	-54.9	156.8	23 37.2	-55.1	157.0	32
33	29 08.1	-53.8	156.1	28 13.2	-54.0	156.3	27 18.2	-54.2	156.5	26 23.1	-54.3	156.7	25 28.0	-54.6	156.9	24 32.8	-54.8	157.1	23 37.5	-54.9	157.2	22 42.1	-55.1	157.4	33
34	28 14.3	-53.9	156.6	27 19.2	-54.1	156.8	26 24.0	-54.3	157.0	25 28.8	-54.5	157.2	24 33.4	-54.6	157.3	23 38.0	-54.8	157.5	22 42.6	-55.1	157.7	21 47.0	-55.2	157.8	34
35	27 20.4	-54.0	157.1	26 25.1	-54.2	157.3	25 29.7	-54.3	157.4	24 34.3	-54.6	157.6	23 38.8	-54.8	157.8	22 43.2	-54.9	158.0	21 47.5	-55.0	158.1	20 51.8	-55.2	158.3	35
36	26 26.4	-54.1	157.6	25 30.9	-54.2	157.7	24 35.4	-54.5	157.9	23 39.7	-54.6	158.1	22 44.0	-54.8	158.2	21 48.3	-55.0	158.4	20 52.5	-55.2	158.5	19 56.6	-55.3	158.7	36
37	25 32.3	-54.2	158.0	24 36.7	-54.4	158.2	23 40.9	-54.5	158.4	22 45.1	-54.7	158.5	21 49.2	-54.8	158.7	20 53.3	-55.0	158.8	19 57.3	-55.2	159.0	19 01.3	-55.3	159.1	37
38	24 38.1	-54.2	158.5	23 42.3	-54.5	158.7	22 46.4	-54.6	158.8	21 50.4	-54.8	159.0	20 54.4	-55.0	159.1	19 58.3	-55.1	159.2	19 02.1	-55.2	159.4	18 06.0	-55.4	159.5	38
39	23 43.9	-54.4	159.0	22 47.8	-54.5	159.1	21 51.8	-54.7	159.3	20 55.6	-54.8	159.4	19 59.4	-55.0	159.5	19 03.2	-55.2	159.7	18 06.9	-55.3	159.8	17 10.6	-55.5	159.9	39
40	22 49.5	-54.4	159.4	21 53.3	-54.6	159.6	20 57.1	-54.8	159.7	20 00.8	-54.9	159.8	19 04.4	-55.0	160.0	18 08.0	-55.2	160.1	17 11.6	-55.4	160.2	16 15.1	-55.5	160.3	40
41	21 55.1	-54.5	159.9	20 58.7	-54.6	160.0	20 02.3	-54.8	160.2	19 05.9	-55.0	160.3	18 09.4	-55.2	160.4	17 12.8	-55.2	160.5	16 16.2	-55.4	160.6	15 19.6	-55.5	160.7	41
42	21 00.6	-54.6	160.3	20 04.1	-54.8	160.5	19 07.5	-54.9	160.6	18 10.9	-55.0	160.7	17 14.2	-55.1	160.8	16 17.6	-55.3	160.9	15 20.8	-55.4	161.0	14 24.1	-55.6	161.1	42
43	20 06.0	-54.6	160.8	19 09.3	-54.8	160.9	18 12.6	-54.9	161.0	17 15.9	-55.1	161.1	16 19.1	-55.2	161.2	15 22.3	-55.4	161.3	14 25.4	-55.5	161.4	13 28.5	-55.6	161.5	43
44	19 11.4	-54.7	161.2	18 14.5	-54.8	161.3	17 17.7	-55.0	161.4	16 20.8	-55.1	161.5	15 23.9	-55.3	161.6	14 26.9	-55.4	161.7	13 29.9	-55.5	161.8	12 32.9	-55.6	161.9	44
45	18 16.7	-54.8	161.7	17 19.7	-54.9	161.8	16 22.7	-55.0	161.9	15 25.7	-55.2	161.9	14 28.6	-55.3	162.0	13 31.5	-55.4	162.1	12 34.4	-55.5	162.2	11 37.3	-55.7	162.2	45
46	17 21.9	-54.8	162.1	16 24.8	-55.0	162.2	15 27.7	-55.1	162.3	14 30.5	-55.2	162.3	13 33.3	-55.3	162.4	12 36.1	-55.5	162.5	11 38.9	-55.6	162.6	10 41.6	-55.7	162.6	46
47	16 27.1	-54.9	162.5	15 29.8	-55.0	162.6	14 32.6	-55.1	162.7	13 35.3	-55.3	162.8	12 38.0	-55.4	162.8	11 40.6	-55.4	162.9	10 43.3	-55.6	162.9	9 45.9	-55.7	163.0	47
48	15 32.2	-54.9	162.9	14 34.8	-55.0	163.0	13 37.5	-55.2	163.1	12 40.0	-55.2	163.2	11 42.6	-55.4	163.2	10 45.2	-55.6	163.3	9 47.7	-55.6	163.3	8 50.2	-55.7	163.4	48
49	14 37.3	-55.0	163.3	13 39.8	-55.1	163.4	12 42.3	-55.2	163.5	11 44.8	-55.4	163.5	10 47.2	-55.4	163.6	9 49.6	-55.5	163.7	8 52.1	-55.7	163.7	7 54.5	-55.8	163.7	49
50	13 42.3	-55.0	163.8	12 44.7	-55.1	163.8	11 47.1	-55.2	163.9	10 49.4	-55.3	163.9	9 51.8	-55.5	164.0	8 54.1	-55.6	164.0	7 56.4	-55.7	164.1	6 58.7	-55.8	164.1	50
51	12 47.3	-55.0	164.2	11 49.6	-55.1	164.2	10 51.9	-55.3	164.3	9 54.1	-55.4	164.3	8 56.3	-55.5	164.4	7 58.5	-55.6	164.4	7 00.7	-55.7	164.5	6 02.9	-55.8	164.5	51
52	11 52.3	-55.1	164.6	10 54.5	-55.2	164.6	9 56.6	-55.3	164.7	8 58.7	-55.4	164.7	8 00.8	-55.5	164.8	7 02.9	-55.6	164.8	6 05.0	-55.7	164.8	5 07.1	-55.8	164.9	52
53	10 57.2	-55.1	165.0	9 59.3	-55.2	165.0	9 01.3	-55.3	165.1	8 03.3	-55.4	165.1	7 05.3	-55.5	165.1	6 07.3	-55.6	165.2	5 09.3	-55.7	165.2	4 11.3	-55.8	165.2	53
54	10 02.1	-55.1	165.4	9 04.1	-55.3	165.4	8 06.0	-55.4	165.5	7 07.9	-55.4	165.5	6 09.8	-55.5	165.5	5 11.7	-55.6	165.6	4 13.6	-55.7	165.6	3 15.5	-55.8	165.6	54
55	9 07.0	-55.2	165.8	8 08.8	-55.2	165.8	7 10.6	-55.3	165.9	6 12.5	-55.5	165.9	5 14.3	-55.6	165.9	4 16.1	-55.7	165.9	3 17.9	-55.8	165.9	2 19.7	-55.9	166.0	55
56	8 11.8	-55.1	166.2	7 13.6	-55.3	166.2	6 15.3	-55.4	166.2	5 17.0	-55.5	166.3	4 18.7	-55.6	166.3	3 20.4	-55.6	166.3	2 22.1	-55.7	166.3	1 23.8	-55.8	166.3	56
57	7 16.7	-55.2	166.6	6 18.3	-55.3	166.6	5 19.9	-55.4	166.6	4 21.5	-55.5	166.7	3 23.2	-55.6	166.7	2 24.8	-55.7	166.7	1 26.4	-55.8	166.7	0 28.0	-55.8	166.7	57
58	6 21.5	-55.3	167.0	5 23.0	-55.3	167.0	4 24.5	-55.4	167.0	3 26.1	-55.5	167.0	2 27.6	-55.6	167.0	1 29.1	-55.7	167.1	0 30.6	-55.7	167.1	0 27.8	+55.9	12.9	58
59	5 26.2	-55.2	167.4	4 27.7	-55.3	167.4	3 29.1	-55.4	167.4	2 30.6	-55.5	167.4	1 32.0	-55.6	167.4	0 33.4	-55.6	167.4	0 25.1	+55.8	12.6	1 23.7	+55.8	12.6	59
60	4 31.0	-55.3	167.8	3 32.4	-55.4	167.8	2 33.7	-55.4	167.8	1 35.1	-55.5	167.8	0 36.4	-55.6	167.8	0 22.2	+55.7	12.2	1 20.9	+55.7	12.2	2 19.5	+55.8	12.2	60
61	3 35.7	-55.2	168.2	2 37.0	-55.3	168.2	1 38.3	-55.4	168.2	0 39.6	-55.5	168.2	0 19.2	+55.5	11.8	1 17.9	+55.6	11.8	2 16.6	+55.8	11.8	3 15.3	+55.9	11.8	61
62	2 40.5	-55.3	168.5	1 41.7	-55.4	168.6	0 42.9	-55.4	168.6	0 15.9	+55.5	11.4	1 14.7	+55.6	11.4	2 13.5	+55.7	11.5	3 12.4	+55.7	11.5	4 11.2	+55.8	11.5	62
63	1 45.2	-55.3	168.9	0 46.3	-55.3	168.9	0 12.5	+55.5	11.1	1 11.4	+55.5	11.1	2 10.3	+55.6	11.1	3 09.2	+55.7	11.1	4 08.1	+55.7	11.1	5 07.0	+55.8	11.1	63
64	0 49.9	-55.2	169.3	0 09.0	+55.4	10.7	1 08.0	+55.4	10.7	2 06.9	+55.5	10.7	3 05.9	+55.6	10.7	4 04.9	+55.6	10.7	5 03.8	+55.7	10.7	6 02.8	+55.7	10.7	64
65	0 05.3	+55.3	10.3	1 04.4	+55.3	10.3	2 03.4	+55.4	10.3	3 02.4	+55.5	10.3	4 01.5	+55.5	10.3	5 00.5	+55.6	10.3	5 59.5	+55.7	10.3	6 58.5	+55.8	10.4	65
66	1 00.6	+55.3	9.9	1 59.7	+55.3	9.9	2 58.8	+55.4	9.9	3 57.9	+55.5	9.9	4 57.0	+55.6	9.9	5 56.1	+55.6	10.0	6 55.2	+55.7	10.0	7 54.3	+55.7	10.0	66
67	1 55.9	+55.2	9.5	2 55.0	+55.4	9.5	3 54.2	+55.4	9.5	4 53.4	+55.4	9.5	5 52.6	+55.5	9.6	6 51.7	+55.6	9.6	7 50.9	+55.6	9.6	8 50.0	+55.8	9.6	67
68	2 51.1	+55.3	9.1	3 50.4	+55.3	9.1	4 49.6	+55.4	9.1	5 48.8	+55.5	9.2	6 48.1	+55.5	9.2	7 47.3	+55.6	9.2	8 46.5	+55.7	9.2	9 45.8	+55.7	9.2	68
69	3 46.4	+55.2	8.7	4 45.7	+55.3	8.7	5 45.0	+55.4	8.8	6 44.3	+55.4	8.8	7 43.6	+55.5	8.8	8 42.9	+55.5	8.8	9 42.2	+55.6	8.8	10 41.5	+55.6	8.9	69
70	4 41.6	+55.3	8.3	5 41.0	+55.3	8.4	6 40.4	+55.3	8.4	7 39.7	+55.4	8.4	8 39.1	+55.4	8.4	9 38.4	+55.6	8.4	10 37.8	+55.6	8.5	11 37.1	+55.7	8.5	70
71	5 36.9	+55.2	7.9	6 36.3	+55.3	8.0	7 35.7	+55.3	8.0	8 35.1	+55.4	8.0	9 34.5	+55.5	8.0	10 34.0	+55.5	8.0	11 33.4	+55.5	8.1	12 32.8	+55.6	8.1	71
72	6 32.1	+55.2	7.6	7 31.6	+55.2	7.6	8 31.0	+55.3	7.6	9 30.5	+55.4	7.6	10 30.0	+55.4	7.6	11 29.5	+55.4	7.7	12 28.9	+55.5	7.7	13 28.4	+55.5	7.7	72
73	7 27.3	+55.2	7.2	8 26.8	+55.2	7.2	9 26.3	+55.3	7.2	10 25.9	+55.3	7.2	11 25.4	+55.4	7.2	12 24.9	+55.4	7.3	13 24.4	+55.5	7.3	14 23.9	+55.6	7.3	73
74	8 22.5	+55.1	6.8	9 22.0	+55.2	6.8	10 21.6	+55.3	6.8	11 21.2	+55.3	6.8	12 20.8	+55.3	6.8	13 20.3	+55.4	6.9	14 19.9	+55.5	6.9	15 19.5	+55.5	6.9	74
75	9 17.6	+55.1	6.4	10 17.2	+55.2	6.4	11 16.9	+55.2	6.4	12 16.5	+55.3	6.4	13 16.1	+55.3	6.5	14 15.7	+55.4	6.5	15 15.4	+55.4	6.5	16 15.0	+55.4	6.5	75
76	10 12.7	+55.1	6.0	11 12.4	+55.2	6.0	12 12.1	+55.2	6.0	13 11.8	+55.2	6.0	14 11.4	+55.3	6.1	15 11.1	+55.3	6.1	16 10.8	+55.3	6.1	17 10.4	+55.4	6.1	76
77	11 07.8	+55.1	5.6	12 07.6	+55.1	5.6	13 07.3	+55.1	5.6	14 07.0	+55.2	5.6	15 06.7	+55.2	5.7	16 06.4	+55.3	5.7	17 06.1	+55.3	5.7	18 05.8	+55.4	5.7	77
78	12 02.9	+55.0	5.2	13 02.7	+55.0	5.2	14 02.4	+55.1	5.2	15 02.2	+55.1	5.2	16 01.9	+55.2	5.2	17 01.7	+55.2	5.3	18 01.4	+55.3	5.3	19 01.2	+55.3	5.3	78
79	12 57.9	+55.0	4.7	13 57.7	+55.1	4.8	14 57.5	+55.1	4.8	15 57.3	+55.1	4.8	16 57.1	+55.1	4.8	17 56.9	+55.2	4.9	18 56.7	+55.2	4.9	19 56.5	+55.2	4.9	79
80	13 52.9	+55.0	4.3	14 52.8	+54.9	4.4	15 52.6	+55.0	4.4	16 52.4	+55.1	4.4	17 52.2	+55.1	4.4	18 52.1	+55.1	4.4	19 51.9	+55.1	4.5	20 51.7	+55.2	4.5	80
81	14 47.9	+54.9	3.9	15 47.7	+55.0	3.9	16 47.6	+55.0	4.0	17 47.5	+54.9	4.0	18 47.3	+55.0	4.0	19 47.2	+55.0	4.0	20 47.0	+55.1	4.1	21 46.9	+55.1	4.1	81
82	15 42.8	+54.8	3.5	16 42.7	+54.9	3.5	17 42.6	+54.9	3.5	18 42.4	+55.0	3.6	19 42.3	+55.0	3.6	20 42.2	+55.0	3.6	21 42.1	+55.0	3.6	22 42.0	+55.0	3.7	82
83	16 37.6	+54.9	3.1	17 37.6	+54.8	3.1	18 37.5	+54.8	3.1	19 37.4	+54.9	3.1	20 37.3	+54.9	3.2	21 37.2	+54.9	3.2	22 37.1	+55.0	3.2	23 37.0	+55.0	3.2	83
84	17 32.5	+54.7	2.7	18 32.4	+54.8	2.7	19 32.3	+54.8	2.7	20 32.3	+54.8	2.7	21 32.2	+54.8	2.7	22 32.1	+54.9	2.7	23 32.1	+54.8	2.8	24 32.0	+54.9	2.8	84
85	18 27.2	+54.7	2.2	19 27.2	+54.7	2.2	20 27.1	+54.7	2.3	21 27.1	+54.7	2.3	22 27.0	+54.8	2.3	23 27.0	+54.7	2.3	24 26.9	+54.8	2.3	25 26.9	+54.8	2.3	85
86	19 21.9	+54.6	1.8	20 21.9	+54.6	1.8	21 21.8	+54.7	1.8	22 21.8	+54.7	1.8	23 21.8	+54.7	1.8	24 21.7	+54.7	1.9	25 21.7	+54.7	1.9	26 21.7	+54.7	1.9	86
87	20 16.5	+54.6	1.4	21 16.5	+54.6	1.4	22 16.5	+54.6	1.4	23 16.5	+54.6	1.4	24 16.5	+54.6	1.4	25 16.4	+54.7	1.4	26 16.4	+54.6	1.4	27 16.4	+54.6	1.4	87
88	21 11.1	+54.5	0.9	22 11.1	+54.5	0.9	23 11.1	+54.5	0.9	24 11.1	+54.5	0.9	25 11.1	+54.5	0.9	26 11.1	+54.5	0.9	27 11.0	+54.6	1.0	28 11.0	+54.6	1.0	88
89	22 05.6	+54.4	0.5	23 05.6	+54.4	0.5	24 05.6	+54.4	0.5	25 05.6	+54.4	0.5	26 05.6	+54.4	0.5	27 05.6	+54.4	0.5	28 05.6	+54.4	0.5	29 05.6	+54.4	0.5	89
90	23 00.0	+54.3	0.0	24 00.0	+54.3	0.0	25 00.0	+54.3	0.0	26 00.0	+54.3	0.0	27 00.0	+54.3	0.0	28 00.0	+54.3	0.0	29 00.0	+54.3	0.0	30 00.0	+54.3	0.0	90
	23°			24°			25°			26°			27°			28°			29°			30°			

S. Lat. { L.H.A. greater than 180° ....Zn=180°−Z
L.H.A. less than 180°...........Zn=180°+Z

LATITUDE **SAME** NAME AS DECLINATION L.H.A. 155°, 205°

235

26°, 334° L.H.A. LATITUDE SAME NAME AS DECLINATION

N. Lat. {L.H.A. greater than 180° .....Zn=Z; L.H.A. less than 180°............Zn=360°-Z}

Dec.	23° Hc	d	Z	24° Hc	d	Z	25° Hc	d	Z	26° Hc	d	Z	Dec.
°	° ′	′	°	° ′	′	°	° ′	′	°	° ′	′	°	°
0	55 49.6	+41.3	128.7	55 11.6	+42.4	129.8	54 32.8	+43.3	130.9	53 53.1	+44.3	131.9	0
1	56 30.9	+40.5	127.4	55 54.0	+41.6	128.6	55 16.1	+42.7	129.7	54 37.4	+43.6	130.8	1
2	57 11.4	+39.6	126.0	56 35.6	+40.7	127.3	55 58.8	+41.8	128.5	55 21.0	+42.9	129.6	2
3	57 51.0	+38.6	124.6	57 16.3	+39.9	125.9	56 40.6	+41.0	127.2	56 03.9	+42.1	128.4	3
4	58 29.6	+37.6	123.2	57 56.2	+38.9	124.5	57 21.6	+40.2	125.8	56 46.0	+41.3	127.1	4
5	59 07.2	+36.6	121.7	58 35.1	+37.9	123.1	58 01.8	+39.1	124.4	57 27.3	+40.4	125.7	5
6	59 43.8	+35.3	120.1	59 13.0	+36.8	121.6	58 40.9	+38.2	123.0	58 07.7	+39.4	124.3	6
7	60 19.1	+34.2	118.5	59 49.8	+35.7	120.0	59 19.1	+37.1	121.5	58 47.1	+38.5	122.9	7
8	60 53.3	+32.8	116.8	60 25.5	+34.4	118.4	59 56.2	+36.0	119.9	59 25.6	+37.4	121.4	8
9	61 26.1	+31.5	115.1	60 59.9	+33.2	116.7	60 32.2	+34.7	118.3	60 03.0	+36.3	119.9	9
10	61 57.6	+30.1	113.3	61 33.1	+31.8	115.0	61 06.9	+33.5	116.7	60 39.3	+35.0	118.2	10
11	62 27.7	+28.5	111.5	62 04.9	+30.3	113.2	61 40.4	+32.1	114.9	61 14.3	+33.8	116.6	11
12	62 56.2	+26.9	109.5	62 35.2	+28.8	111.4	62 12.5	+30.7	113.1	61 48.1	+32.4	114.8	12
13	63 23.1	+25.2	107.6	63 04.0	+27.3	109.4	62 43.2	+29.1	111.3	62 20.5	+31.0	113.0	13
14	63 48.3	+23.4	105.5	63 31.3	+25.5	107.5	63 12.3	+27.6	109.3	62 51.5	+29.5	111.2	14
15	64 11.7	+21.6	103.4	63 56.8	+23.7	105.4	63 39.9	+25.8	107.4	63 21.0	+27.9	109.3	15
16	64 33.3	+19.6•	101.3	64 20.5	+21.9	103.3	64 05.7	+24.0	105.3	63 48.9	+26.1	107.3	16
17	64 52.9	+17.6•	99.0	64 42.4	+19.9•	101.1	64 29.7	+22.2	103.2	64 15.0	+24.4	105.2	17
18	65 10.5	+15.5•	96.8	65 02.3	+17.9•	98.9	64 51.9	+20.2•	101.0	64 39.4	+22.5	103.1	18
19	65 26.0	+13.4•	94.5	65 20.2	+15.8•	96.6	65 12.1	+18.2•	98.8	65 01.9	+20.5•	100.9	19
20	65 39.4	+11.1•	92.1	65 36.0	+13.6•	94.3	65 30.3	+16.1•	96.5	65 22.4	+18.5•	98.7	20
21	65 50.5	+8.9•	89.7	65 49.6	+11.4•	91.9	65 46.4	+13.9•	94.2	65 40.9	+16.4•	96.4	21
22	65 59.4	+6.5•	87.3	66 01.0	+9.1•	89.5	66 00.3	+11.7•	91.8	65 57.3	+14.2•	94.0	22
23	66 05.9	+4.2•	84.8	66 10.1	+6.8•	87.1	66 12.0	+9.4•	89.4	66 11.5	+11.9•	91.6	23
24	66 10.1	+1.9•	82.4	66 16.9	+4.5•	84.6	66 21.4	+7.0•	86.9	66 23.4	+9.6•	89.2	24
25	66 12.0	-0.5•	79.9	66 21.4	+2.0•	82.2	66 28.4	+4.6•	84.4	66 33.0	+7.2•	86.7	25
26	66 11.5	-2.9•	77.4	66 23.4	-0.4•	79.7	66 33.0	+2.2•	81.9	66 40.2	+4.9•	84.2	26
27	66 08.6	-5.3•	75.0	66 23.0	-2.7•	77.2	66 35.2	-0.2•	79.4	66 45.1	+2.4•	81.7	27
28	66 03.3	-7.6•	72.5	66 20.3	-5.1•	74.7	66 35.0	-2.6•	76.9	66 47.5	-0.1•	79.2	28
29	65 55.7	-9.8•	70.1	66 15.2	-7.5•	72.2	66 32.4	-5.0•	74.4	66 47.4	-2.4•	76.6	29
30	65 45.9	-12.1•	67.6	66 07.7	-9.8•	69.7	66 27.4	-7.4•	71.9	66 45.0	-4.9•	74.1	30
31	65 33.8	-14.4•	65.3	65 57.9	-12.1•	67.3	66 20.0	-9.7•	69.4	66 40.1	-7.3•	71.6	31
32	65 19.4	-16.4•	62.9	65 45.8	-14.3•	64.9	66 10.3	-12.0•	67.0	66 32.8	-9.7•	69.1	32
33	65 03.0	-18.5•	60.6	65 31.5	-16.4•	62.6	65 58.3	-14.3•	64.5	66 23.1	-12.0•	66.6	33
34	64 44.5	-20.5	58.4	65 15.1	-18.5•	60.2	65 44.0	-16.4•	62.2	66 11.1	-14.2•	64.2	34
35	64 24.0	-22.4	56.2	64 56.6	-20.5	58.0	65 27.6	-18.5•	59.8	65 56.9	-16.5•	61.8	35
36	64 01.6	-24.2	54.1	64 36.1	-22.4	55.8	65 09.1	-20.6	57.6	65 40.4	-18.5•	59.4	36
37	63 37.4	-25.9	52.0	64 13.7	-24.3	53.6	64 48.5	-22.4	55.3	65 21.9	-20.6•	57.1	37
38	63 11.5	-27.7	50.0	63 49.4	-26.0	51.5	64 26.1	-24.4	53.2	65 01.3	-22.5	54.9	38
39	62 43.8	-29.2	48.0	63 23.4	-27.7	49.5	64 01.7	-26.1	51.1	64 38.8	-24.5	52.7	39
40	62 14.6	-30.6	46.1	62 55.7	-29.3	47.6	63 35.6	-27.8	49.0	64 14.3	-26.2	50.6	40
41	61 44.0	-32.1	44.3	62 26.4	-30.8	45.6	63 07.8	-29.4	47.1	63 48.1	-27.9	48.5	41
42	61 11.9	-33.5	42.5	61 55.6	-32.2	43.8	62 38.4	-30.9	45.1	63 20.2	-29.5	46.5	42
43	60 38.4	-34.7	40.8	61 23.4	-33.5	42.0	62 07.5	-32.3	43.3	62 50.7	-31.0	44.6	43
44	60 03.7	-35.9	39.2	60 49.9	-34.9	40.3	61 35.2	-33.7	41.5	62 19.7	-32.5	42.8	44
45	59 27.8	-37.0	37.6	60 15.0	-36.0	38.7	61 01.5	-34.9	39.8	61 47.2	-33.8	41.0	45
46	58 50.8	-38.0	36.1	59 39.0	-37.1	37.1	60 26.6	-36.2	38.1	61 13.4	-35.1	39.2	46
47	58 12.8	-39.1	34.6	59 01.9	-38.2	35.5	59 50.4	-37.3	36.5	60 38.3	-36.3	37.6	47
48	57 33.7	-40.0	33.2	58 23.7	-39.2	34.0	59 13.1	-38.3	35.0	60 02.0	-37.4	36.0	48
49	56 53.7	-40.8	31.8	57 44.5	-40.1	32.6	58 34.8	-39.3	33.5	59 24.6	-38.5	34.4	49
50	56 12.9	-41.7	30.4	57 04.4	-41.0	31.2	57 55.5	-40.3	32.0	58 46.1	-39.5	32.9	50
51	55 31.2	-42.5	29.2	56 23.4	-41.8	29.9	57 15.2	-41.1	30.7	58 06.6	-40.4	31.5	51
52	54 48.7	-43.2	27.9	55 41.6	-42.6	28.6	56 34.1	-42.0	29.3	57 26.2	-41.3	30.1	52
53	54 05.5	-43.9	26.7	54 59.0	-43.4	27.4	55 52.1	-42.8	28.0	56 44.9	-42.2	28.8	53
54	53 21.6	-44.5	25.6	54 15.6	-44.0	26.2	55 09.3	-43.4	26.8	56 02.7	-42.9	27.5	54
55	52 37.1	-45.1	24.5	53 31.6	-44.6	25.0	54 25.9	-44.2	25.6	55 19.8	-43.6	26.2	55
56	51 52.0	-45.7	23.4	52 47.0	-45.3	23.9	53 41.7	-44.8	24.5	54 36.2	-44.3	25.0	56
57	51 06.3	-46.2	22.3	52 01.7	-45.8	22.8	52 56.9	-45.4	23.3	53 51.9	-45.0	23.9	57
58	50 20.1	-46.8	21.3	51 15.9	-46.4	21.8	52 11.5	-46.0	22.3	53 06.9	-45.5	22.8	58
59	49 33.3	-47.2	20.4	50 29.5	-46.9	20.8	51 25.5	-46.5	21.2	52 21.4	-46.2	21.7	59
60	48 46.1	-47.6	19.4	49 42.6	-47.3	19.8	50 39.0	-47.0	20.2	51 35.2	-46.6	20.7	60
61	47 58.5	-48.1	18.5	48 55.3	-47.8	18.9	49 52.0	-47.5	19.3	50 48.6	-47.2	19.7	61
62	47 10.4	-48.5	17.6	48 07.5	-48.2	18.0	49 04.5	-47.9	18.3	50 01.4	-47.6	18.7	62
63	46 21.9	-48.9	16.8	47 19.3	-48.6	17.1	48 16.6	-48.3	17.4	49 13.8	-48.1	17.7	63
64	45 33.0	-49.2	15.9	46 30.7	-49.0	16.2	47 28.3	-48.8	16.5	48 25.7	-48.4	16.8	64
65	44 43.8	-49.5	15.1	45 41.7	-49.3	15.4	46 39.5	-49.1	15.7	47 37.3	-48.9	16.0	65
66	43 54.3	-49.9	14.3	44 52.4	-49.7	14.6	45 50.4	-49.4	14.8	46 48.4	-49.3	15.1	66
67	43 04.4	-50.1	13.6	44 02.7	-50.0	13.8	45 01.0	-49.8	14.0	45 59.1	-49.5	14.3	67
68	42 14.3	-50.5	12.8	43 12.7	-50.2	13.0	44 11.2	-50.1	13.2	45 09.6	-50.0	13.5	68
69	41 23.8	-50.7	12.1	42 22.5	-50.6	12.3	43 21.1	-50.4	12.5	44 19.6	-50.2	12.7	69
70	40 33.1	-51.0	11.4	41 31.9	-50.8	11.6	42 30.7	-50.7	11.7	43 29.4	-50.5	11.9	70
71	39 42.1	-51.2	10.7	40 41.1	-51.1	10.8	41 40.0	-50.9	11.0	42 38.9	-50.8	11.2	71
72	38 50.9	-51.4	10.0	39 50.0	-51.3	10.2	40 49.1	-51.2	10.3	41 48.1	-51.1	10.5	72
73	37 59.5	-51.6	9.4	38 58.7	-51.5	9.5	39 57.9	-51.5	9.6	40 57.0	-51.3	9.8	73
74	37 07.9	-51.9	8.7	38 07.2	-51.8	8.8	39 06.4	-51.6	9.0	40 05.7	-51.5	9.1	74
75	36 16.0	-52.0	8.1	37 15.4	-51.9	8.2	38 14.8	-51.9	8.3	39 14.2	-51.8	8.4	75
76	35 24.0	-52.2	7.5	36 23.5	-52.2	7.6	37 22.9	-52.0	7.7	38 22.4	-52.0	7.8	76
77	34 31.8	-52.4	6.9	35 31.3	-52.3	7.0	36 30.9	-52.3	7.0	37 30.4	-52.2	7.1	77
78	33 39.4	-52.6	6.3	34 39.0	-52.5	6.4	35 38.6	-52.4	6.4	36 38.2	-52.3	6.5	78
79	32 46.8	-52.7	5.7	33 46.5	-52.6	5.8	34 46.2	-52.6	5.8	35 45.9	-52.6	5.9	79
80	31 54.1	-52.9	5.1	32 53.9	-52.9	5.2	33 53.6	-52.8	5.3	34 53.3	-52.7	5.3	80
81	31 01.2	-53.0	4.6	32 01.0	-52.9	4.6	33 00.8	-52.9	4.7	34 00.6	-52.8	4.7	81
82	30 08.2	-53.1	4.0	31 08.1	-53.1	4.1	32 07.9	-53.0	4.1	33 07.8	-53.0	4.2	82
83	29 15.1	-53.3	3.5	30 15.0	-53.2	3.5	31 14.9	-53.2	3.6	32 14.8	-53.2	3.6	83
84	28 21.8	-53.3	3.0	29 21.8	-53.4	3.0	30 21.7	-53.3	3.0	31 21.6	-53.3	3.1	84
85	27 28.5	-53.5	2.5	28 28.4	-53.5	2.5	29 28.4	-53.5	2.5	30 28.3	-53.4	2.5	85
86	26 35.0	-53.6	2.0	27 34.9	-53.5	2.0	28 34.9	-53.6	2.0	29 34.9	-53.6	2.0	86
87	25 41.4	-53.7	1.5	26 41.4	-53.7	1.5	27 41.3	-53.6	1.5	28 41.3	-53.6	1.5	87
88	24 47.7	-53.8	1.0	25 47.7	-53.8	1.0	26 47.7	-53.8	1.0	27 47.7	-53.8	1.0	88
89	23 53.9	-53.9	0.5	24 53.9	-53.9	0.5	25 53.9	-53.9	0.5	26 53.9	-53.9	0.5	89
90	23 00.0	-54.0	0.0	24 00.0	-54.0	0.0	25 00.0	-54.0	0.0	26 00.0	-54.0	0.0	90
	23°			24°			25°			26°			

Dec.	27° Hc	d	Z	28° Hc	d	Z	29° Hc	d	Z	30° Hc	d	Z	Dec.
°	° ′	′	°	° ′	′	°	° ′	′	°	° ′	′	°	°
0	53 12.6	+45.2	132.9	52 31.3	+46.0	133.9	51 49.4	+46.8	134.8	51 06.7	+47.6	135.7	0
1	53 57.8	+44.5	131.8	53 17.3	+45.5	132.8	52 36.2	+46.2	133.8	51 54.3	+47.0	134.7	1
2	54 42.3	+43.9	130.7	54 02.8	+44.8	131.7	53 22.4	+45.7	132.7	52 41.3	+46.5	133.7	2
3	55 26.2	+43.1	129.5	54 47.6	+44.1	130.6	54 08.1	+45.0	131.7	53 27.8	+45.9	132.7	3
4	56 09.3	+42.4	128.3	55 31.7	+43.4	129.4	54 53.1	+44.4	130.5	54 13.7	+45.4	131.6	4
5	56 51.7	+41.6	127.0	56 15.1	+42.6	128.2	55 37.5	+43.7	129.3	54 59.1	+44.6	130.4	5
6	57 33.3	+40.6	125.6	56 57.7	+41.9	126.9	56 21.2	+42.9	128.1	55 43.7	+44.0	129.3	6
7	58 13.9	+39.8	124.3	57 39.6	+41.0	125.6	57 04.1	+42.2	126.8	56 27.7	+43.2	128.0	7
8	58 53.7	+38.8	122.8	58 20.6	+40.0	124.2	57 46.3	+41.2	125.5	57 10.9	+42.4	126.8	8
9	59 32.5	+37.7	121.3	59 00.6	+39.1	122.8	58 27.5	+40.4	124.1	57 53.3	+41.6	125.5	9
10	60 10.2	+36.5	119.8	59 39.7	+38.0	121.3	59 07.9	+39.4	122.7	58 34.9	+40.6	124.1	10
11	60 46.7	+35.4	118.2	60 17.7	+36.9	119.7	59 47.3	+38.3	121.2	59 15.5	+39.7	122.7	11
12	61 22.1	+34.1	116.5	60 54.6	+35.7	118.1	60 25.6	+37.2	119.7	59 55.2	+38.6	121.2	12
13	61 56.2	+32.8	114.8	61 30.3	+34.4	116.5	61 02.8	+36.0	118.1	60 33.8	+37.6	119.6	13
14	62 29.0	+31.3	113.0	62 04.7	+33.1	114.7	61 38.8	+34.8	116.4	61 11.4	+36.3	118.0	14
15	63 00.3	+29.8	111.1	62 37.8	+31.6	112.9	62 13.6	+33.4	114.7	61 47.7	+35.1	116.4	15
16	63 30.1	+28.2	109.2	63 09.4	+30.2	111.1	62 47.0	+32.0	112.9	62 22.8	+33.8	114.6	16
17	63 58.3	+26.4	107.2	63 39.6	+28.5	109.1	63 19.0	+30.4	111.0	62 56.6	+32.3	112.8	17
18	64 24.7	+24.7	105.1	64 08.1	+26.8	107.1	63 49.4	+28.9	109.1	63 28.9	+30.8	111.0	18
19	64 49.4	+22.9	103.0	64 34.9	+25.0	105.1	64 18.3	+27.1	107.1	63 59.7	+29.2	109.0	19
20	65 12.3	+20.8•	100.8	64 59.9	+23.2	102.9	64 45.4	+25.4	105.0	64 28.9	+27.5	107.0	20
21	65 33.1	+18.8•	98.6	65 23.1	+21.1•	100.7	65 10.8	+23.5•	102.9	64 56.4	+25.7	104.9	21
22	65 51.9	+16.7•	96.3	65 44.2	+19.1•	98.5	65 34.3	+21.4•	100.6	65 22.1	+23.8	102.8	22
23	66 08.6	+14.4•	93.9	66 03.3	+17.0•	96.1	65 55.7	+19.5•	98.4	65 45.9	+21.8•	100.6	23
24	66 23.0	+12.2•	91.5	66 20.3	+14.7•	93.8	66 15.2	+17.2•	96.0	66 07.7	+19.7•	98.3	24
25	66 35.2	+9.9•	89.0	66 35.0	+12.5•	91.3	66 32.4	+15.0•	93.6	66 27.4	+17.6•	95.9	25
26	66 45.1	+7.4•	86.5	66 47.5	+10.1•	88.9	66 47.4	+12.7•	91.2	66 45.0	+15.3•	93.5	26
27	66 52.5	+5.1•	84.0	66 57.6	+7.6•	86.4	67 00.1	+10.4•	88.7	67 00.3	+12.9•	91.1	27
28	66 57.6	+2.5•	81.5	67 05.2	+5.3•	83.8	67 10.5	+7.9•	86.2	67 13.2	+10.6•	88.6	28
29	67 00.1	+0.2•	78.9	67 10.5	+2.7•	81.3	67 18.4	+5.4•	83.6	67 23.8	+8.1•	86.0	29
30	67 00.3	-2.4•	76.4	67 13.2	+0.3•	78.7	67 23.8	+2.9•	81.0	67 31.9	+5.7•	83.4	30
31	66 57.9	-4.8•	73.8	67 13.5	-2.2•	76.1	67 26.7	+0.5•	78.4	67 37.6	+3.1•	80.8	31
32	66 53.1	-7.2•	71.3	67 11.3	-4.7•	73.5	67 27.2	-2.1•	75.8	67 40.7	+0.5•	78.2	32
33	66 45.9	-9.6•	68.7	67 06.6	-7.2•	70.9	67 25.1	-4.7•	73.2	67 41.2	-2.0•	75.5	33
34	66 36.3	-12.0•	66.2	66 59.4	-9.6•	68.4	67 20.4	-7.1•	70.6	67 39.2	-4.5•	72.9	34
35	66 24.3	-14.2•	63.8	66 49.8	-11.9•	65.9	67 13.3	-9.5•	68.0	67 34.7	-7.1•	70.3	35
36	66 10.1	-16.5•	61.4	66 37.9	-14.2•	63.4	67 03.8	-12.0•	65.5	67 27.6	-9.5•	67.7	36
37	65 53.6	-18.6•	59.0	66 23.7	-16.5•	61.0	66 51.8	-14.2•	63.0	67 18.1	-12.0•	65.1	37
38	65 35.0	-20.6•	56.7	66 07.2	-18.7•	58.6	66 37.6	-16.6•	60.5	67 06.1	-14.3•	62.6	38
39	65 14.4	-22.6•	54.4	65 48.5	-20.7•	56.2	66 21.0	-18.7•	58.1	66 51.8	-16.6•	60.1	39
40	64 51.8	-24.6	52.2	65 27.8	-22.7•	54.0	66 02.3	-20.8•	55.8	66 35.2	-18.8•	57.7	40
41	64 27.2	-26.3	50.1	65 05.1	-24.7	51.8	65 41.5	-22.8•	53.5	66 16.4	-20.9•	55.3	41
42	64 00.9	-28.0	48.0	64 40.4	-26.4	49.6	65 18.7	-24.8	51.3	65 55.5	-22.9•	53.0	42
43	63 32.9	-29.6	46.0	64 14.0	-28.2	47.5	64 53.9	-26.6	49.1	65 32.6	-24.9	50.7	43
44	63 03.3	-31.2	44.1	63 45.8	-29.7	45.5	64 27.3	-28.3	47.0	65 07.7	-26.8	48.6	44
45	62 32.1	-32.6	42.2	63 16.1	-31.4	43.6	63 59.0	-29.9	45.0	64 40.9	-28.4	46.5	45
46	61 59.5	-34.0	40.4	62 44.7	-32.7	41.7	63 29.1	-31.5	43.0	64 12.5	-30.2	44.4	46
47	61 25.5	-35.2	38.7	62 12.0	-34.2	39.9	62 57.6	-33.0	41.1	63 42.3	-31.6	42.4	47
48	60 50.3	-36.5	37.0	61 37.8	-35.4	38.1	62 24.6	-34.3	39.3	63 10.7	-33.2	40.5	48
49	60 13.8	-37.6	35.4	61 02.4	-36.7	36.4	61 50.3	-35.6	37.5	62 37.5	-34.5	38.7	49
50	59 36.2	-38.7	33.8	60 25.7	-37.7	34.8	61 14.7	-36.8	35.9	62 03.0	-35.8	37.0	50
51	58 57.5	-39.6	32.3	59 48.0	-38.9	33.3	60 37.9	-38.0	34.2	61 27.2	-37.1	35.3	51
52	58 17.9	-40.6	30.9	59 09.1	-39.8	31.8	59 59.9	-39.1	32.7	60 50.1	-38.2	33.6	52
53	57 37.3	-41.5	29.5	58 29.3	-40.8	30.3	59 20.8	-40.0	31.2	60 11.9	-39.2	32.1	53
54	56 55.8	-42.3	28.2	57 48.5	-41.7	28.9	58 40.8	-41.0	29.7	59 32.7	-40.2	30.6	54
55	56 13.5	-43.1	26.9	57 06.8	-42.4	27.6	57 59.8	-41.8	28.3	58 52.5	-41.2	29.1	55
56	55 30.4	-43.8	25.6	56 24.4	-43.3	26.3	57 18.0	-42.7	27.0	58 11.3	-42.1	27.7	56
57	54 46.6	-44.5	24.5	55 41.1	-44.0	25.1	56 35.3	-43.4	25.7	57 29.2	-42.8	26.4	57
58	54 02.1	-45.1	23.3	54 57.1	-44.6	23.9	55 51.9	-44.2	24.5	56 46.4	-43.7	25.1	58
59	53 17.0	-45.7	22.2	54 12.5	-45.3	22.7	55 07.7	-44.8	23.3	56 02.7	-44.4	23.8	59
60	52 31.3	-46.3	21.1	53 27.2	-45.9	21.6	54 22.9	-45.5	22.1	55 18.3	-45.0	22.6	60
61	51 45.0	-46.8	20.1	52 41.3	-46.5	20.5	53 37.4	-46.1	21.0	54 33.3	-45.6	21.5	61
62	50 58.2	-47.3	19.1	51 54.8	-46.9	19.5	52 51.3	-46.6	19.9	53 47.7	-46.3	20.4	62
63	50 10.9	-47.8	18.1	51 07.9	-47.5	18.5	52 04.7	-47.1	18.9	53 01.4	-46.8	19.3	63
64	49 23.1	-48.2	17.2	50 20.4	-47.9	17.5	51 17.6	-47.7	17.9	52 14.6	-47.3	18.3	64
65	48 34.9	-48.6	16.3	49 32.5	-48.4	16.6	50 29.9	-48.1	16.9	51 27.3	-47.9	17.3	65
66	47 46.3	-49.0	15.4	48 44.1	-48.8	15.7	49 41.8	-48.5	16.0	50 39.4	-48.2	16.3	66
67	46 57.3	-49.4	14.5	47 55.3	-49.2	14.8	48 53.3	-49.0	15.1	49 51.2	-48.7	15.4	67
68	46 07.9	-49.8	13.7	47 06.1	-49.5	14.0	48 04.3	-49.3	14.2	49 02.5	-49.2	14.5	68
69	45 18.1	-50.0	12.9	46 16.6	-49.9	13.1	47 15.0	-49.7	13.4	48 13.3	-49.5	13.6	69
70	44 28.1	-50.4	12.1	45 26.7	-50.2	12.3	46 25.3	-50.0	12.6	47 23.8	-49.8	12.8	70
71	43 37.7	-50.6	11.4	44 36.5	-50.5	11.6	45 35.3	-50.4	11.8	46 34.0	-50.2	12.0	71
72	42 47.1	-51.0	10.6	43 46.0	-50.8	10.8	44 44.9	-50.6	11.0	45 43.8	-50.5	11.2	72
73	41 56.1	-51.2	9.9	42 55.2	-51.0	10.1	43 54.3	-51.0	10.2	44 53.3	-50.8	10.4	73
74	41 04.9	-51.4	9.2	42 04.2	-51.4	9.4	43 03.3	-51.2	9.5	44 02.5	-51.1	9.7	74
75	40 13.5	-51.7	8.5	41 12.8	-51.5	8.7	42 12.1	-51.4	8.8	43 11.4	-51.3	9.0	75
76	39 21.8	-51.9	7.9	40 21.3	-51.8	8.0	41 20.7	-51.7	8.1	42 20.1	-51.7	8.2	76
77	38 29.9	-52.0	7.2	39 29.5	-52.1	7.3	40 29.0	-52.0	7.4	41 28.4	-51.8	7.6	77
78	37 37.9	-52.3	6.6	38 37.4	-52.2	6.7	39 37.0	-52.1	6.8	40 36.6	-52.1	6.9	78
79	36 45.6	-52.5	6.0	37 45.2	-52.4	6.1	38 44.9	-52.4	6.2	39 44.5	-52.2	6.2	79
80	35 53.1	-52.7	5.4	36 52.8	-52.6	5.5	37 52.5	-52.5	5.5	38 52.3	-52.5	5.6	80
81	35 00.4	-52.8	4.8	36 00.2	-52.8	4.9	37 00.0	-52.7	4.9	37 59.8	-52.7	5.0	81
82	34 07.6	-53.0	4.2	35 07.4	-52.9	4.3	36 07.3	-52.9	4.3	37 07.1	-52.9	4.4	82
83	33 14.6	-53.1	3.7	34 14.5	-53.1	3.7	35 14.4	-53.1	3.8	36 14.2	-53.0	3.8	83
84	32 21.5	-53.3	3.1	33 21.4	-53.2	3.1	34 21.3	-53.2	3.2	35 21.2	-53.2	3.2	84
85	31 28.2	-53.4	2.6	32 28.2	-53.4	2.6	33 28.1	-53.3	2.6	34 28.0	-53.3	2.7	85
86	30 34.8	-53.5	2.0	31 34.8	-53.5	2.1	32 34.8	-53.5	2.1	33 34.7	-53.5	2.1	86
87	29 41.3	-53.7	1.5	30 41.3	-53.7	1.5	31 41.3	-53.7	1.5	32 41.2	-53.6	1.6	87
88	28 47.6	-53.7	1.0	29 47.6	-53.7	1.0	30 47.6	-53.7	1.0	31 47.6	-53.7	1.0	88
89	27 53.9	-53.9	0.5	28 53.9	-53.9	0.5	29 53.9	-53.9	0.5	30 53.9	-53.9	0.5	89
90	27 00.0	-54.0	0.0	28 00.0	-54.0	0.0	29 00.0	-54.0	0.0	30 00.0	-54.0	0.0	90
	27°			28°			29°			30°			

26°, 334° L.H.A. LATITUDE SAME NAME AS DECLINATION

236

LATITUDE CONTRARY NAME TO DECLINATION L.H.A. 26°, 334°

Dec.	23° Hc	d	Z	24° Hc	d	Z	25° Hc	d	Z	26° Hc	d	Z	27° Hc	d	Z	28° Hc	d	Z	29° Hc	d	Z	30° Hc	d	Z	Dec.
°	° ′	′	°	° ′	′	°	° ′	′	°	° ′	′	°	° ′	′	°	° ′	′	°	° ′	′	°	° ′	′	°	°
0	55 49.6	−42.1	128.7	55 11.6	−43.1	129.8	54 32.8	−44.1	130.9	53 53.1	−45.0	131.9	53 12.6	−45.8	132.9	52 31.3	−46.5	133.9	51 49.4	−47.3	134.8	51 06.7	−48.0	135.7	0
1	55 07.5	−42.9	130.0	54 28.5	−43.8	131.0	53 48.7	−44.7	132.1	53 08.1	−45.5	133.1	52 26.8	−46.3	134.0	51 44.8	−47.1	134.9	51 02.1	−47.8	135.8	50 18.7	−48.4	136.7	1
2	54 24.6	−43.6	131.2	53 44.7	−44.5	132.2	53 04.0	−45.3	133.2	52 22.6	−46.1	134.1	51 40.5	−46.9	135.1	50 57.7	−47.6	135.9	50 14.3	−48.3	136.8	49 30.3	−48.9	137.6	2
3	53 41.0	−44.2	132.3	53 00.2	−45.0	133.3	52 18.7	−45.9	134.3	51 36.5	−46.7	135.2	50 53.6	−47.3	136.0	50 10.1	−48.0	136.9	49 26.0	−48.7	137.7	48 41.4	−49.3	138.5	3
4	52 56.8	−44.9	133.5	52 15.2	−45.7	134.4	51 32.8	−46.4	135.3	50 49.8	−47.1	136.2	50 06.3	−47.9	137.0	49 22.1	−48.5	137.8	48 37.3	−49.0	138.6	47 52.1	−49.7	139.3	4
5	52 11.9	−45.4	134.6	51 29.5	−46.2	135.5	50 46.4	−46.9	136.3	50 02.7	−47.6	137.2	49 18.4	−48.2	137.9	48 33.6	−48.9	138.7	47 48.3	−49.5	139.4	47 02.4	−50.0	140.1	5
6	51 26.5	−46.0	135.6	50 43.3	−46.7	136.5	49 59.5	−47.4	137.3	49 15.1	−48.1	138.1	48 30.2	−48.7	138.9	47 44.7	−49.2	139.6	46 58.8	−49.8	140.3	46 12.4	−50.3	141.0	6
7	50 40.5	−46.5	136.6	49 56.6	−47.2	137.5	49 12.1	−47.9	138.2	48 27.0	−48.4	139.0	47 41.5	−49.0	139.7	46 55.5	−49.6	140.4	46 09.0	−50.1	141.1	45 22.1	−50.6	141.7	7
8	49 54.0	−47.0	137.6	49 09.4	−47.7	138.4	48 24.2	−48.3	139.2	47 38.6	−48.9	139.9	46 52.5	−49.5	140.6	46 05.9	−50.0	141.2	45 18.9	−50.5	141.9	44 31.5	−50.9	142.5	8
9	49 07.0	−47.5	138.6	48 21.7	−48.1	139.3	47 35.9	−48.6	140.1	46 49.7	−49.2	140.7	46 03.0	−49.7	141.4	45 15.9	−50.2	142.0	44 28.4	−50.7	142.6	43 40.6	−51.3	143.2	9
10	48 19.5	−47.9	139.5	47 33.6	−48.5	140.2	46 47.3	−49.1	140.9	46 00.5	−49.6	141.6	45 13.3	−50.1	142.2	44 25.7	−50.6	142.8	43 37.7	−51.0	143.4	42 49.3	−51.4	143.9	10
11	47 31.6	−48.3	140.4	46 45.1	−48.9	141.1	45 58.2	−49.4	141.7	45 10.9	−49.9	142.4	44 23.2	−50.4	143.0	43 35.1	−50.9	143.6	42 46.7	−51.3	144.1	41 57.9	−51.7	144.6	11
12	46 43.3	−48.7	141.3	45 56.2	−49.2	141.9	45 08.8	−49.7	142.6	44 21.0	−50.2	143.2	43 32.8	−50.7	143.7	42 44.2	−51.1	144.3	41 55.4	−51.6	144.8	41 06.2	−52.0	145.3	12
13	45 54.6	−49.1	142.1	45 07.0	−49.5	142.7	44 19.1	−50.1	143.3	43 30.8	−50.6	143.9	42 42.1	−51.0	144.5	41 53.1	−51.4	145.0	41 03.8	−51.8	145.5	40 14.2	−52.1	146.0	13
14	45 05.5	−49.4	143.0	44 17.5	−49.9	143.5	43 29.0	−50.3	144.1	42 40.2	−50.8	144.7	41 51.1	−51.2	145.2	41 01.7	−51.6	145.7	40 12.0	−52.0	146.2	39 22.1	−52.4	146.6	14
15	44 16.1	−49.7	143.7	43 27.6	−50.2	144.3	42 38.7	−50.7	144.9	41 49.4	−51.0	145.4	40 59.9	−51.4	145.9	40 10.1	−51.8	146.3	39 20.0	−52.2	146.8	38 29.7	−52.6	147.2	15
16	43 26.4	−50.0	144.5	42 37.4	−50.5	145.1	41 48.0	−50.9	145.6	40 58.4	−51.3	146.1	40 08.5	−51.7	146.5	39 18.3	−52.1	147.0	38 27.8	−52.4	147.4	37 37.1	−52.7	147.9	16
17	42 36.4	−50.4	145.3	41 46.9	−50.7	145.8	40 57.1	−51.1	146.3	40 07.1	−51.6	146.8	39 16.8	−51.9	147.2	38 26.2	−52.3	147.6	37 35.4	−52.6	148.1	36 44.4	−52.9	148.5	17
18	41 46.0	−50.5	146.0	40 56.2	−51.0	146.5	40 06.0	−51.4	147.0	39 15.5	−51.7	147.4	38 24.9	−52.1	147.9	37 33.9	−52.4	148.3	36 42.8	−52.8	148.7	35 51.5	−53.1	149.0	18
19	40 55.5	−50.9	146.7	40 05.2	−51.3	147.2	39 14.6	−51.6	147.6	38 23.8	−52.0	148.1	37 32.8	−52.4	148.5	36 41.5	−52.6	148.9	35 50.0	−52.9	149.3	34 58.4	−53.3	149.6	19
20	40 04.6	−51.1	147.4	39 13.9	−51.5	147.9	38 23.0	−51.8	148.3	37 31.8	−52.2	148.7	36 40.4	−52.5	149.1	35 48.9	−52.9	149.5	34 57.1	−53.1	149.8	34 05.1	−53.4	150.2	20
21	39 13.5	−51.3	148.1	38 22.4	−51.7	148.5	37 31.2	−52.1	148.9	36 39.6	−52.3	149.3	35 47.9	−52.6	149.7	34 56.0	−52.9	150.1	34 04.0	−53.3	150.4	33 11.7	−53.5	150.7	21
22	38 22.2	−51.6	148.8	37 30.7	−51.8	149.2	36 39.1	−52.2	149.6	35 47.3	−52.5	149.9	34 55.3	−52.9	150.3	34 03.1	−53.1	150.6	33 10.7	−53.4	150.9	32 18.2	−53.7	151.3	22
23	37 30.6	−51.7	149.4	36 38.9	−52.1	149.8	35 46.9	−52.4	150.2	34 54.8	−52.7	150.5	34 02.4	−53.0	150.9	33 10.0	−53.3	151.2	32 17.3	−53.5	151.5	31 24.5	−53.8	151.8	23
24	36 38.9	−52.0	150.1	35 46.8	−52.3	150.4	34 54.5	−52.6	150.8	34 02.1	−52.9	151.1	33 09.4	−53.1	151.4	32 16.7	−53.4	151.7	31 23.8	−53.7	152.0	30 30.7	−53.9	152.3	24
25	35 46.9	−52.1	150.7	34 54.5	−52.4	151.0	34 01.9	−52.7	151.4	33 09.2	−53.0	151.7	32 16.3	−53.3	152.0	31 23.3	−53.6	152.3	30 30.1	−53.8	152.5	29 36.8	−54.0	152.8	25
26	34 54.8	−52.4	151.3	34 02.1	−52.7	151.6	33 09.2	−52.9	151.9	32 16.2	−53.2	152.2	31 23.0	−53.4	152.5	30 29.7	−53.6	152.8	29 36.3	−53.9	153.1	28 42.8	−54.2	153.3	26
27	34 02.4	−52.4	151.9	33 09.4	−52.7	152.2	32 16.3	−53.0	152.5	31 23.0	−53.3	152.8	30 29.6	−53.5	153.0	29 36.1	−53.8	153.3	28 42.4	−54.0	153.6	27 48.6	−54.2	153.8	27
28	33 10.0	−52.7	152.5	32 16.7	−52.9	152.8	31 23.3	−53.2	153.0	30 29.7	−53.4	153.3	29 36.1	−53.7	153.6	28 42.3	−53.9	153.8	27 48.4	−54.1	154.0	26 54.4	−54.4	154.3	28
29	32 17.3	−52.8	153.0	31 23.8	−53.1	153.3	30 30.1	−53.3	153.6	29 36.3	−53.5	153.8	28 42.4	−53.8	154.1	27 48.4	−54.0	154.3	26 54.3	−54.3	154.5	26 00.0	−54.4	154.7	29
30	31 24.5	−52.9	153.6	30 30.7	−53.2	153.9	29 36.8	−53.4	154.1	28 42.8	−53.7	154.4	27 48.6	−53.9	154.6	26 54.4	−54.1	154.8	26 00.0	−54.3	155.0	25 05.6	−54.5	155.2	30
31	30 31.6	−53.1	154.1	29 37.5	−53.3	154.4	28 43.4	−53.6	154.6	27 49.1	−53.8	154.9	26 54.7	−54.0	155.1	26 00.3	−54.2	155.3	25 05.7	−54.4	155.5	24 11.1	−54.6	155.7	31
32	29 38.5	−53.2	154.7	28 44.2	−53.4	154.9	27 49.8	−53.6	155.1	26 55.3	−53.9	155.4	26 00.7	−54.0	155.6	25 06.1	−54.3	155.8	24 11.3	−54.5	155.9	23 16.5	−54.7	156.1	32
33	28 45.3	−53.3	155.2	27 50.8	−53.6	155.4	26 56.2	−53.8	155.6	26 01.4	−53.9	155.8	25 06.7	−54.2	156.0	24 11.8	−54.4	156.2	23 16.8	−54.5	156.4	22 21.8	−54.7	156.6	33
34	27 52.0	−53.5	155.7	26 57.2	−53.6	155.9	26 02.4	−53.9	156.1	25 07.5	−54.1	156.3	24 12.5	−54.3	156.5	23 17.4	−54.4	156.7	22 22.3	−54.7	156.9	21 27.1	−54.8	157.0	34
35	26 58.5	−53.5	156.2	26 03.6	−53.8	156.4	25 08.5	−53.9	156.6	24 13.4	−54.1	156.8	23 18.2	−54.3	157.0	22 23.0	−54.6	157.1	21 27.6	−54.7	157.3	20 32.3	−54.9	157.5	35
36	26 05.0	−53.7	156.7	25 09.8	−53.8	156.9	24 14.6	−54.1	157.1	23 19.3	−54.3	157.3	22 23.9	−54.4	157.4	21 28.4	−54.6	157.6	20 32.9	−54.7	157.7	19 37.4	−55.0	157.9	36
37	25 11.3	−53.7	157.2	24 16.0	−54.0	157.4	23 20.5	−54.1	157.6	22 25.0	−54.3	157.7	21 29.5	−54.5	157.9	20 33.8	−54.6	158.0	19 38.2	−54.9	158.2	18 42.4	−55.0	158.3	37
38	24 17.6	−53.9	157.7	23 22.0	−54.0	157.9	22 26.4	−54.2	158.1	21 30.7	−54.4	158.2	20 35.0	−54.6	158.3	19 39.2	−54.8	158.5	18 43.3	−54.8	158.6	17 47.4	−55.0	158.7	38
39	23 23.7	−53.9	158.2	22 28.0	−54.1	158.4	21 32.2	−54.3	158.5	20 36.3	−54.4	158.7	19 40.4	−54.6	158.8	18 44.4	−54.7	158.9	17 48.4	−54.9	159.0	16 52.4	−55.1	159.1	39
40	22 29.8	−54.0	158.7	21 33.9	−54.2	158.8	20 37.9	−54.4	159.0	19 41.9	−54.6	159.1	18 45.8	−54.7	159.2	17 49.7	−54.9	159.3	16 53.5	−55.0	159.5	15 57.3	−55.2	159.6	40
41	21 35.8	−54.1	159.2	20 39.7	−54.3	159.3	19 43.5	−54.4	159.4	18 47.3	−54.6	159.5	17 51.1	−54.8	159.7	16 54.8	−54.9	159.8	15 58.5	−55.1	159.9	15 02.1	−55.2	160.0	41
42	20 41.7	−54.2	159.6	19 45.4	−54.3	159.7	18 49.1	−54.5	159.9	17 52.7	−54.6	160.0	16 56.3	−54.8	160.1	15 59.9	−54.9	160.2	15 03.4	−55.0	160.3	14 06.9	−55.2	160.4	42
43	19 47.5	−54.2	160.1	18 51.1	−54.4	160.2	17 54.6	−54.5	160.3	16 58.1	−54.7	160.4	16 01.5	−54.8	160.5	15 05.0	−55.0	160.6	14 08.4	−55.2	160.7	13 11.7	−55.3	160.8	43
44	18 53.3	−54.3	160.5	17 56.7	−54.5	160.6	17 00.1	−54.6	160.7	16 03.4	−54.8	160.8	15 06.7	−54.9	160.9	14 10.0	−55.1	161.0	13 13.2	−55.1	161.1	12 16.4	−55.3	161.2	44
45	17 59.0	−54.4	161.0	17 02.2	−54.5	161.1	16 05.5	−54.7	161.2	15 08.6	−54.8	161.3	14 11.8	−54.9	161.4	13 14.9	−55.0	161.4	12 18.1	−55.2	161.5	11 21.1	−55.3	161.6	45
46	17 04.6	−54.4	161.4	16 07.7	−54.5	161.5	15 10.8	−54.7	161.6	14 13.8	−54.8	161.7	13 16.9	−55.0	161.8	12 19.9	−55.1	161.8	11 22.9	−55.3	161.9	10 25.8	−55.4	162.0	46
47	16 10.2	−54.5	161.9	15 13.2	−54.7	162.0	14 16.1	−54.8	162.0	13 19.0	−54.9	162.1	12 21.9	−55.0	162.2	11 24.8	−55.2	162.2	10 27.6	−55.2	162.3	9 30.4	−55.3	162.4	47
48	15 15.7	−54.5	162.3	14 18.5	−54.6	162.4	13 21.3	−54.7	162.5	12 24.1	−54.9	162.5	11 26.9	−55.1	162.6	10 29.6	−55.1	162.6	9 32.4	−55.3	162.7	8 35.1	−55.5	162.7	48
49	14 21.2	−54.6	162.7	13 23.9	−54.7	162.8	12 26.6	−54.9	162.9	11 29.2	−54.9	162.9	10 31.8	−55.0	163.0	9 34.5	−55.2	163.0	8 37.1	−55.4	163.1	7 39.6	−55.4	163.1	49
50	13 26.6	−54.6	163.2	12 29.2	−54.8	163.2	11 31.7	−54.8	163.3	10 34.3	−55.0	163.3	9 36.8	−55.1	163.4	8 39.3	−55.3	163.4	7 41.7	−55.3	163.5	6 44.2	−55.4	163.5	50
51	12 32.0	−54.6	163.6	11 34.4	−54.7	163.6	10 36.9	−54.9	163.7	9 39.3	−55.0	163.7	8 41.7	−55.2	163.8	7 44.0	−55.2	163.8	6 46.4	−55.4	163.9	5 48.8	−55.5	163.9	51
52	11 37.4	−54.7	164.0	10 39.7	−54.8	164.1	9 42.0	−55.0	164.1	8 44.3	−55.1	164.2	7 46.5	−55.1	164.2	6 48.8	−55.3	164.2	5 51.0	−55.3	164.3	4 53.3	−55.5	164.3	52
53	10 42.7	−54.8	164.4	9 44.9	−54.9	164.5	8 47.0	−54.9	164.5	7 49.2	−55.0	164.6	6 51.4	−55.2	164.6	5 53.5	−55.2	164.6	4 55.7	−55.4	164.6	3 57.8	−55.5	164.7	53
54	9 47.9	−54.7	164.8	8 50.0	−54.8	164.9	7 52.1	−55.0	164.9	6 54.2	−55.1	165.0	5 56.2	−55.2	165.0	4 58.3	−55.3	165.0	4 00.3	−55.4	165.0	3 02.3	−55.5	165.0	54
55	8 53.2	−54.8	165.3	7 55.2	−54.9	165.3	6 57.1	−55.0	165.3	5 59.1	−55.1	165.4	5 01.0	−55.2	165.4	4 03.0	−55.3	165.4	3 04.9	−55.4	165.4	2 06.8	−55.5	165.4	55
56	7 58.4	−54.8	165.7	7 00.3	−54.9	165.7	6 02.1	−55.0	165.7	5 04.0	−55.1	165.8	4 05.8	−55.2	165.8	3 07.7	−55.4	165.8	2 09.5	−55.4	165.8	1 11.3	−55.5	165.8	56
57	7 03.6	−54.8	166.1	6 05.4	−55.0	166.1	5 07.1	−55.0	166.1	4 08.9	−55.2	166.1	3 10.6	−55.2	166.2	2 12.3	−55.3	166.2	1 14.1	−55.4	166.2	0 15.8	−55.5	166.2	57
58	6 08.8	−54.9	166.5	5 10.4	−54.9	166.5	4 12.1	−55.1	166.5	3 13.7	−55.1	166.5	2 15.4	−55.2	166.6	1 17.0	−55.3	166.6	0 18.7	−55.5	166.6	0 39.7	+55.5	13.4	58
59	5 13.9	−54.8	166.9	4 15.5	−55.0	166.9	3 17.0	−55.0	166.9	2 18.6	−55.1	166.9	1 20.2	−55.3	166.9	0 21.7	−55.3	167.0	0 36.8	+55.4	13.0	1 35.2	+55.5	13.1	59
60	4 19.1	−54.9	167.3	3 20.5	−54.9	167.3	2 22.0	−55.1	167.3	1 23.5	−55.2	167.3	0 24.9	−55.2	167.3	0 33.6	+55.3	12.7	1 32.2	+55.4	12.7	2 30.7	+55.5	12.7	60
61	3 24.2	−54.9	167.7	2 25.6	−55.0	167.7	1 26.9	−55.0	167.7	0 28.3	−55.1	167.7	0 30.3	+55.2	12.3	1 28.9	+55.4	12.3	2 27.6	+55.4	12.3	3 26.2	+55.5	12.3	61
62	2 29.3	−54.9	168.1	1 30.6	−55.0	168.1	0 31.9	−55.1	168.1	0 26.8	+55.2	11.9	1 25.5	+55.3	11.9	2 24.3	+55.3	11.9	3 23.0	+55.4	11.9	4 21.7	+55.5	11.9	62
63	1 34.4	−54.9	168.5	0 35.6	−55.0	168.5	0 23.2	+55.0	11.5	1 22.0	+55.1	11.5	2 20.8	+55.2	11.5	3 19.6	+55.3	11.5	4 18.4	+55.3	11.5	5 17.2	+55.4	11.5	63
64	0 39.5	−54.9	168.9	0 19.4	+54.9	11.1	1 18.2	+55.1	11.1	2 17.1	+55.2	11.1	3 16.0	+55.2	11.1	4 14.9	+55.3	11.1	5 13.7	+55.4	11.1	6 12.6	+55.5	11.1	64
65	0 15.4	+54.9	10.7	1 14.3	+55.0	10.7	2 13.3	+55.0	10.7	3 12.3	+55.1	10.7	4 11.2	+55.2	10.7	5 10.2	+55.2	10.7	6 09.1	+55.4	10.7	7 08.1	+55.4	10.8	65
66	1 10.3	+54.9	10.3	2 09.7	+55.0	10.3	3 08.3	+55.1	10.3	4 07.4	+55.1	10.3	5 06.4	+55.2	10.3	6 05.4	+55.3	10.3	7 04.5	+55.3	10.4	8 03.5	+55.4	10.4	66
67	2 05.2	+54.9	9.9	3 04.3	+54.9	9.9	4 03.4	+55.0	9.9	5 02.5	+55.1	9.9	6 01.6	+55.2	9.9	7 00.7	+55.2	9.9	7 59.8	+55.3	10.0	8 58.9	+55.4	10.0	67
68	3 00.1	+54.8	9.5	3 59.2	+55.0	9.5	4 58.4	+55.0	9.5	5 57.6	+55.1	9.5	6 56.8	+55.1	9.5	7 55.9	+55.3	9.5	8 55.1	+55.3	9.6	9 54.3	+55.3	9.6	68
69	3 54.9	+54.9	9.1	4 54.2	+54.9	9.1	5 53.4	+55.0	9.1	6 52.7	+55.0	9.1	7 51.9	+55.1	9.1	8 51.2	+55.1	9.1	9 50.4	+55.2	9.2	10 49.6	+55.3	9.2	69
70	4 49.8	+54.8	8.7	5 49.1	+54.9	8.7	6 48.4	+55.0	8.7	7 47.7	+55.1	8.7	8 47.0	+55.1	8.7	9 46.3	+55.2	8.8	10 45.6	+55.3	8.8	11 44.9	+55.3	8.8	70
71	5 44.6	+54.9	8.2	6 44.0	+54.9	8.3	7 43.4	+55.0	8.3	8 42.8	+55.0	8.3	9 42.1	+55.1	8.3	10 41.5	+55.1	8.4	11 40.9	+55.2	8.4	12 40.2	+55.3	8.4	71
72	6 39.5	+54.8	7.8	7 38.9	+54.9	7.9	8 38.4	+54.9	7.9	9 37.8	+55.0	7.9	10 37.2	+55.1	7.9	11 36.6	+55.1	7.9	12 36.1	+55.1	8.0	13 35.5	+55.2	8.0	72
73	7 34.3	+54.8	7.4	8 33.8	+54.8	7.4	9 33.3	+54.9	7.5	10 32.8	+54.9	7.5	11 32.3	+55.0	7.5	12 31.7	+55.1	7.5	13 31.2	+55.1	7.6	14 30.7	+55.2	7.6	73
74	8 29.1	+54.8	7.0	9 28.6	+54.9	7.0	10 28.2	+54.9	7.1	11 27.7	+55.0	7.1	12 27.3	+54.9	7.1	13 26.8	+55.0	7.1	14 26.3	+55.1	7.2	15 25.9	+55.1	7.2	74
75	9 23.9	+54.7	6.6	10 23.5	+54.7	6.6	11 23.1	+54.8	6.6	12 22.7	+54.8	6.7	13 22.2	+55.0	6.7	14 21.8	+55.0	6.7	15 21.4	+55.0	6.8	16 21.0	+55.1	6.8	75
76	10 18.6	+54.7	6.2	11 18.2	+54.8	6.2	12 17.9	+54.8	6.2	13 17.5	+54.9	6.3	14 17.2	+54.9	6.3	15 16.8	+54.9	6.3	16 16.4	+55.0	6.3	17 16.1	+55.0	6.4	76
77	11 13.3	+54.7	5.8	12 13.0	+54.7	5.8	13 12.7	+54.7	5.8	14 12.4	+54.8	5.8	15 12.1	+54.8	5.9	16 11.7	+54.9	5.9	17 11.4	+55.0	5.9	18 11.1	+55.0	6.0	77
78	12 08.0	+54.6	5.3	13 07.7	+54.7	5.4	14 07.4	+54.8	5.4	15 07.2	+54.7	5.4	16 06.9	+54.8	5.4	17 06.6	+54.9	5.5	18 06.4	+54.8	5.5	19 06.1	+54.9	5.5	78
79	13 02.6	+54.6	4.9	14 02.4	+54.6	4.9	15 02.2	+54.6	5.0	16 01.9	+54.7	5.0	17 01.7	+54.7	5.0	18 01.5	+54.7	5.0	19 01.2	+54.8	5.1	20 01.0	+54.8	5.1	79
80	13 57.2	+54.5	4.5	14 57.0	+54.6	4.5	15 56.8	+54.6	4.5	16 56.6	+54.7	4.6	17 56.4	+54.7	4.6	18 56.2	+54.8	4.6	19 56.0	+54.8	4.6	20 55.8	+54.8	4.7	80
81	14 51.7	+54.5	4.1	15 51.6	+54.5	4.1	16 51.4	+54.6	4.1	17 51.3	+54.6	4.1	18 51.1	+54.6	4.2	19 51.0	+54.6	4.2	20 50.8	+54.7	4.2	21 50.6	+54.7	4.2	81
82	15 46.2	+54.5	3.6	16 46.1	+54.5	3.7	17 46.0	+54.5	3.7	18 45.9	+54.5	3.7	19 45.7	+54.6	3.7	20 45.6	+54.6	3.7	21 45.5	+54.6	3.8	22 45.3	+54.7	3.8	82
83	16 40.7	+54.4	3.2	17 40.6	+54.4	3.2	18 40.5	+54.4	3.2	19 40.4	+54.4	3.3	20 40.3	+54.5	3.3	21 40.2	+54.5	3.3	22 40.1	+54.5	3.3	23 40.0	+54.6	3.3	83
84	17 35.1	+54.3	2.8	18 35.0	+54.3	2.8	19 34.9	+54.4	2.8	20 34.8	+54.4	2.8	21 34.8	+54.4	2.8	22 34.7	+54.4	2.8	23 34.6	+54.5	2.9	24 34.6	+54.4	2.9	84
85	18 29.4	+54.3	2.3	19 29.3	+54.3	2.3	20 29.3	+54.3	2.3	21 29.2	+54.4	2.4	22 29.2	+54.3	2.4	23 29.1	+54.4	2.4	24 29.1	+54.4	2.4	25 29.0	+54.4	2.4	85
86	19 23.7	+54.2	1.9	20 23.6	+54.2	1.9	21 23.6	+54.2	1.9	22 23.6	+54.2	1.9	23 23.5	+54.3	1.9	24 23.5	+54.3	1.9	25 23.5	+54.2	1.9	26 23.4	+54.3	2.0	86
87	20 17.9	+54.1	1.4	21 17.8	+54.2	1.4	22 17.8	+54.2	1.4	23 17.8	+54.2	1.4	24 17.8	+54.1	1.4	25 17.8	+54.1	1.5	26 17.7	+54.2	1.5	27 17.7	+54.2	1.5	87
88	21 12.0	+54.0	0.9	22 12.0	+54.0	0.9	23 12.0	+54.0	1.0	24 12.0	+54.0	1.0	25 11.9	+54.1	1.0	26 11.9	+54.1	1.0	27 11.9	+54.1	1.0	28 11.9	+54.1	1.0	88
89	22 06.0	+54.0	0.5	23 06.0	+54.0	0.5	24 06.0	+54.0	0.5	25 06.0	+54.0	0.5	26 06.0	+54.0	0.5	27 06.0	+54.0	0.5	28 06.0	+54.0	0.5	29 06.0	+54.0	0.5	89
90	23 00.0	+53.9	0.0	24 00.0	+53.9	0.0	25 00.0	+53.9	0.0	26 00.0	+53.9	0.0	27 00.0	+53.9	0.0	28 00.0	+53.9	0.0	29 00.0	+53.9	0.0	30 00.0	+53.9	0.0	90
	23°			24°			25°			26°			27°			28°			29°			30°			

S. Lat. { L.H.A. greater than 180° ....Zn=180°−Z; L.H.A. less than 180°............Zn=180°+Z

LATITUDE SAME NAME AS DECLINATION L.H.A. 154°, 206°

Dec.	23°			24°			25°			26°			27°			28°			29°			30°			Dec.
	Hc	d	Z	Hc	d	Z	Hc	d	Z	Hc	d	Z	Hc	d	Z	Hc	d	Z	Hc	d	Z	Hc	d	Z	
°	° ′	′	°	° ′	′	°	° ′	′	°	° ′	′	°	° ′	′	°	° ′	′	°	° ′	′	°	° ′	′	°	°
0	55 06.1	+40.6	127.5	54 29.2	+41.6	128.6	53 51.3	+42.6	129.7	53 12.6	+43.6	130.7	52 33.0	+44.5	131.7	51 52.8	+45.3	132.7	51 11.7	+46.2	133.6	50 30.1	+46.9	134.5	0
1	55 46.7	+39.7	126.2	55 10.8	+40.8	127.3	54 33.9	+41.9	128.5	53 56.2	+42.9	129.5	53 17.5	+43.9	130.6	52 38.1	+44.7	131.6	51 57.9	+45.6	132.5	51 17.0	+46.4	133.5	1
2	56 26.4	+38.8	124.8	55 51.6	+40.0	126.1	55 15.8	+41.1	127.2	54 39.1	+42.1	128.4	54 01.4	+43.1	129.4	53 22.8	+44.2	130.5	52 43.5	+45.0	131.5	52 03.4	+45.8	132.4	2
3	57 05.2	+37.9	123.4	56 31.6	+39.1	124.7	55 56.9	+40.3	125.9	55 21.2	+41.4	127.1	54 44.5	+42.5	128.2	54 07.0	+43.4	129.3	53 28.5	+44.4	130.4	52 49.2	+45.3	131.4	3
4	57 43.1	+36.9	122.0	57 10.7	+38.2	123.3	56 37.2	+39.4	124.6	56 02.6	+40.5	125.8	55 27.0	+41.6	127.0	54 50.4	+42.7	128.1	54 12.9	+43.7	129.2	53 34.5	+44.6	130.3	4
5	58 20.0	+35.7	120.5	57 48.9	+37.1	121.9	57 16.6	+38.4	123.2	56 43.1	+39.7	124.5	56 08.6	+40.9	125.7	55 33.1	+41.9	126.9	54 56.6	+43.0	128.1	54 19.1	+44.0	129.2	5
6	58 55.7	+34.6	119.0	58 26.0	+36.1	120.4	57 55.0	+37.4	121.8	57 22.8	+38.7	123.1	56 49.5	+39.9	124.4	56 15.0	+41.2	125.6	55 39.6	+42.2	126.8	55 03.1	+43.3	128.0	6
7	59 30.3	+33.5	117.4	59 02.1	+34.9	118.9	58 32.4	+36.4	120.3	58 01.5	+37.8	121.7	57 29.4	+39.1	123.0	56 56.2	+40.2	124.3	56 21.8	+41.4	125.6	55 46.4	+42.5	126.8	7
8	60 03.8	+32.1	115.7	59 37.0	+33.7	117.3	59 08.8	+35.2	118.8	58 39.3	+36.7	120.2	58 08.5	+38.0	121.6	57 36.4	+39.4	122.9	57 03.2	+40.6	124.2	56 28.9	+41.7	125.5	8
9	60 35.9	+30.8	114.0	60 10.7	+32.5	115.6	59 44.0	+34.1	117.2	59 16.0	+35.5	118.7	58 46.5	+37.0	120.1	58 15.8	+38.3	121.5	57 43.8	+39.6	122.9	57 10.6	+40.9	124.2	9
10	61 06.7	+29.4	112.3	60 43.2	+31.1	113.9	60 18.1	+32.8	115.5	59 51.5	+34.4	117.1	59 23.5	+35.9	118.6	58 54.1	+37.3	120.0	58 23.4	+38.7	121.5	57 51.5	+40.0	122.8	10
11	61 36.1	+27.9	110.4	61 14.3	+29.7	112.2	60 50.9	+31.4	113.8	60 25.9	+33.1	115.4	59 59.4	+34.6	117.0	59 31.4	+36.2	118.5	59 02.1	+37.6	120.0	58 31.5	+38.9	121.4	11
12	62 04.0	+26.3	108.6	61 44.0	+28.2	110.3	61 22.3	+30.0	112.1	60 59.0	+31.7	113.7	60 34.0	+33.5	115.4	60 07.6	+35.0	116.9	59 39.7	+36.5	118.5	59 10.4	+38.0	119.9	12
13	62 30.3	+24.7	106.6	62 12.2	+26.6	108.5	61 52.3	+28.6	110.2	61 30.7	+30.4	112.0	61 07.5	+32.1	113.6	60 42.6	+33.8	115.3	60 16.2	+35.4	116.9	59 48.4	+36.8	118.4	13
14	62 55.0	+22.9	104.6	62 38.8	+25.0	106.5	62 20.9	+26.9	108.4	62 01.1	+28.8	110.1	61 39.6	+30.6	111.9	61 16.4	+32.4	113.6	60 51.6	+34.1	115.2	60 25.2	+35.7	116.8	14
15	63 17.9	+21.1	102.6	63 03.8	+23.3	104.5	62 47.8	+25.3	106.4	62 29.9	+27.3	108.3	62 10.2	+29.2	110.1	61 48.8	+31.0	111.8	61 25.7	+32.7	113.5	61 00.9	+34.5	115.2	15
16	63 39.0	+19.3	100.5	63 27.1	+21.4	102.5	63 13.1	+23.6	104.4	62 57.2	+25.7	106.3	62 39.4	+27.7	108.2	62 19.8	+29.6	110.0	61 58.4	+31.4	111.8	61 35.4	+33.1	113.5	16
17	63 58.3	+17.3•	98.4	63 48.5	+19.6	100.4	63 36.7	+21.8	102.4	63 22.9	+23.9	104.3	63 07.1	+25.9	106.2	62 49.4	+27.9	108.1	62 29.8	+29.9	109.9	62 08.5	+31.7	111.7	17
18	64 15.6	+15.3•	96.2	64 08.1	+17.6•	98.2	63 58.5	+19.9	100.2	63 46.8	+22.1	102.2	63 33.0	+24.3	104.2	63 17.3	+26.3	106.1	62 59.7	+28.3	108.0	62 40.2	+30.2	109.9	18
19	64 30.9	+13.3•	93.9	64 25.7	+15.6•	96.0	64 18.4	+17.9•	98.1	64 08.9	+20.2	100.1	63 57.3	+22.4	102.1	63 43.6	+24.6	104.1	63 28.0	+26.6	106.1	63 10.4	+28.7	108.0	19
20	64 44.2	+11.1•	91.7	64 41.3	+13.5•	93.8	64 36.3	+15.9•	95.9	64 29.1	+18.2•	98.0	64 19.7	+20.5	100.0	64 08.2	+22.7	102.1	63 54.6	+24.9	104.1	63 39.1	+27.0	106.0	20
21	64 55.3	+8.9•	89.3	64 54.8	+11.4•	91.5	64 52.2	+13.8•	93.6	64 47.3	+16.2•	95.7	64 40.2	+18.5•	97.8	64 30.9	+20.9	99.9	64 19.5	+23.1	102.0	64 06.1	+25.2	104.0	21
22	65 04.2	+6.7•	87.0	65 06.2	+9.2•	89.2	65 06.0	+11.6•	91.3	65 03.5	+14.1•	93.5	64 58.7	+16.5•	95.6	64 51.8	+18.8•	97.7	64 42.6	+21.2•	99.8	64 31.3	+23.4	101.9	22
23	65 10.9	+4.5•	84.6	65 15.4	+7.0•	86.8	65 17.6	+9.5•	89.0	65 17.6	+11.9•	91.1	65 15.2	+14.4•	93.3	65 10.6	+16.8•	95.5	65 03.8	+19.1•	97.6	64 54.7	+21.5	99.7	23
24	65 15.4	+2.2•	82.3	65 22.4	+4.7•	84.4	65 27.1	+7.2•	86.6	65 29.5	+9.7•	88.8	65 29.6	+12.2•	91.0	65 27.4	+14.7•	93.2	65 22.9	+17.1•	95.4	65 16.2	+19.5•	97.5	24
25	65 17.6	0.0•	79.9	65 27.1	+2.4•	82.0	65 34.3	+4.9•	84.2	65 39.2	+7.4•	86.4	65 41.8	+9.9•	88.6	65 42.1	+12.4•	90.8	65 40.0	+15.0•	93.0	65 35.7	+17.4•	95.2	25
26	65 17.6	-2.4•	77.5	65 29.5	+0.1•	79.6	65 39.2	+2.6•	81.8	65 46.6	+5.1•	84.0	65 51.7	+7.7•	86.2	65 54.5	+10.2•	88.4	65 55.0	+12.7•	90.7	65 53.1	+15.2•	92.9	26
27	65 15.2	-4.6•	75.1	65 29.6	-2.2•	77.2	65 41.8	+0.3•	79.4	65 51.7	+2.8•	81.6	65 59.4	+5.3•	83.8	66 04.7	+7.9•	86.0	66 07.7	+10.4•	88.3	66 08.3	+13.0•	90.5	27
28	65 10.6	-6.8•	72.7	65 27.4	-4.5•	74.8	65 42.1	-2.1•	76.9	65 54.5	+0.5•	79.1	66 04.7	+3.0•	81.3	66 12.6	+5.5•	83.6	66 18.1	+8.1•	85.8	66 21.3	+10.7•	88.1	28
29	65 03.8	-9.1•	70.4	65 22.9	-6.7•	72.4	65 40.0	-4.3•	74.5	65 55.0	-1.9•	76.7	66 07.7	+0.6•	78.9	66 18.1	+3.2•	81.1	66 26.2	+5.8•	83.4	66 32.0	+8.3•	85.6	29
30	64 54.7	-11.2•	68.0	65 16.2	-8.9•	70.0	65 35.7	-6.6•	72.1	65 53.1	-4.2•	74.2	66 08.3	-1.7•	76.4	66 21.3	+0.8•	78.6	66 32.0	+3.3•	80.9	66 40.3	+6.0•	83.2	30
31	64 43.5	-13.3•	65.7	65 07.3	-11.2•	67.7	65 29.1	-8.9•	69.7	65 48.9	-6.6•	71.8	66 06.6	-4.1•	73.9	66 22.1	-1.6•	76.1	66 35.3	+1.0•	78.4	66 46.3	+3.5•	80.6	31
32	64 30.2	-15.5•	63.4	64 56.1	-13.3•	65.3	65 20.2	-11.1•	67.3	65 42.3	-8.8•	69.4	66 02.5	-6.5•	71.5	66 20.5	-4.0•	73.6	66 36.3	-1.5•	75.8	66 49.8	+1.1•	78.1	32
33	64 14.7	-17.4	61.2	64 42.8	-15.4•	63.0	65 09.1	-13.3•	65.0	65 33.5	-11.0•	67.0	65 56.0	-8.7•	69.0	66 16.5	-6.4•	71.1	66 34.8	-3.9•	73.3	66 50.9	-1.4•	75.6	33
34	63 57.3	-19.4	59.0	64 27.4	-17.4•	60.8	64 55.8	-15.3•	62.7	65 22.5	-13.2•	64.6	65 47.3	-11.0•	66.6	66 10.1	-8.7•	68.7	66 30.9	-6.3•	70.8	66 49.5	-3.8•	73.0	34
35	63 37.9	-21.2	56.9	64 10.0	-19.4	58.6	64 40.5	-17.5•	60.4	65 09.3	-15.4•	62.3	65 36.3	-13.2•	64.2	66 01.4	-11.0•	66.2	66 24.6	-8.6•	68.3	66 45.7	-6.2•	70.5	35
36	63 16.7	-23.0	54.8	63 50.6	-21.3	56.4	64 23.0	-19.4	58.2	64 53.9	-17.5•	60.0	65 23.1	-15.4•	61.9	65 50.4	-13.2•	63.8	66 16.0	-11.0•	65.9	66 39.5	-8.6•	68.0	36
37	62 53.7	-24.8	52.7	63 29.3	-23.0	54.3	64 03.6	-21.3	56.0	64 36.4	-19.4	57.7	65 07.7	-17.5•	59.5	65 37.2	-15.4•	61.4	66 05.0	-13.2•	63.4	66 30.9	-11.0•	65.5	37
38	62 28.9	-26.4	50.7	63 06.3	-24.8	52.3	63 42.3	-23.1	53.9	64 17.0	-21.3	55.5	64 50.2	-19.5	57.3	65 21.8	-17.5•	59.1	65 51.8	-15.5•	61.0	66 19.9	-13.2•	63.0	38
39	62 02.5	-27.9	48.8	62 41.5	-26.5	50.3	63 19.2	-24.9	51.8	63 55.7	-23.3	53.4	64 30.7	-21.4	55.1	65 04.3	-19.5•	56.8	65 36.3	-17.5•	58.7	66 06.7	-15.5•	60.6	39
40	61 34.6	-29.5	46.9	62 15.0	-28.1	48.3	62 54.3	-26.5	49.8	63 32.4	-24.9	51.3	64 09.3	-23.3	52.9	64 44.8	-21.5	54.6	65 18.8	-19.7•	56.4	65 51.2	-17.6•	58.2	40
41	61 05.1	-30.9	45.1	61 46.9	-29.5	46.4	62 27.8	-28.2	47.8	63 07.5	-26.7	49.3	63 46.0	-25.1	50.8	64 23.3	-23.4	52.4	64 59.1	-21.6	54.1	65 33.6	-19.8•	55.9	41
42	60 34.2	-32.2	43.4	61 17.4	-31.0	44.6	61 59.6	-29.6	45.9	62 40.8	-28.2	47.3	63 20.9	-26.7	48.8	63 59.9	-25.2	50.3	64 37.5	-23.5	51.9	65 13.8	-21.7	53.6	42
43	60 02.0	-33.5	41.7	60 46.4	-32.3	42.8	61 30.0	-31.1	44.1	62 12.6	-29.8	45.4	62 54.2	-28.4	46.8	63 34.7	-26.9	48.3	64 14.0	-25.3	49.8	64 52.1	-23.6	51.4	43
44	59 28.5	-34.7	40.0	60 14.1	-33.6	41.1	60 58.9	-32.5	42.3	61 42.8	-31.2	43.6	62 25.8	-29.9	44.9	63 07.8	-28.5	46.3	63 48.7	-27.0	47.7	64 28.5	-25.5	49.3	44
45	58 53.8	-35.8	38.4	59 40.5	-34.8	39.5	60 26.4	-33.7	40.6	61 11.6	-32.6	41.8	61 55.9	-31.4	43.0	62 39.3	-30.1	44.3	63 21.7	-28.7	45.7	64 03.0	-27.2	47.2	45
46	58 18.0	-36.9	36.9	59 05.7	-36.0	37.9	59 52.7	-35.0	38.9	60 39.0	-33.9	40.0	61 24.5	-32.7	41.2	62 09.2	-31.5	42.5	62 53.0	-30.2	43.8	63 35.8	-28.8	45.2	46
47	57 41.1	-37.9	35.4	58 29.7	-37.0	36.3	59 17.7	-36.0	37.3	60 05.1	-35.1	38.4	60 51.8	-34.0	39.5	61 37.7	-32.9	40.7	62 22.8	-31.7	41.9	63 07.0	-30.4	43.2	47
48	57 03.2	-38.9	34.0	57 52.7	-38.1	34.8	58 41.7	-37.2	35.8	59 30.0	-36.2	36.8	60 17.8	-35.3	37.8	61 04.8	-34.2	38.9	61 51.1	-33.1	40.1	62 36.6	-31.9	41.3	48
49	56 24.3	-39.7	32.6	57 14.6	-39.0	33.4	58 04.5	-38.2	34.3	58 53.8	-37.3	35.2	59 42.5	-36.4	36.2	60 30.6	-35.4	37.2	61 18.0	-34.3	38.3	62 04.7	-33.2	39.5	49
50	55 44.6	-40.7	31.2	56 35.6	-39.9	32.0	57 26.3	-39.2	32.8	58 16.5	-38.4	33.7	59 06.1	-37.5	34.6	59 55.2	-36.6	35.6	60 43.7	-35.7	36.6	61 31.5	-34.6	37.7	50
51	55 03.9	-41.4	29.9	55 55.7	-40.7	30.7	56 47.1	-40.0	31.4	57 38.1	-39.3	32.3	58 28.6	-38.5	33.1	59 18.6	-37.7	34.0	60 08.0	-36.7	35.0	60 56.9	-35.8	36.0	51
52	54 22.5	-42.1	28.7	55 15.0	-41.6	29.4	56 07.1	-40.9	30.1	56 58.8	-40.2	30.9	57 50.1	-39.5	31.7	58 40.9	-38.7	32.5	59 31.3	-37.9	33.4	60 21.1	-37.0	34.4	52
53	53 40.4	-42.9	27.5	54 33.4	-42.3	28.1	55 26.2	-41.7	28.8	56 18.6	-41.1	29.5	57 10.6	-40.4	30.3	58 02.2	-39.6	31.1	58 53.4	-38.9	31.9	59 44.1	-38.1	32.8	53
54	52 57.5	-43.6	26.3	53 51.1	-43.0	26.9	54 44.5	-42.5	27.5	55 37.5	-41.8	28.2	56 30.2	-41.2	28.9	57 22.6	-40.6	29.7	58 14.5	-39.9	30.5	59 06.0	-39.1	31.3	54
55	52 13.9	-44.1	25.2	53 08.1	-43.7	25.7	54 02.0	-43.1	26.3	54 55.7	-42.6	26.9	55 49.0	-42.0	27.6	56 42.0	-41.4	28.3	57 34.6	-40.7	29.1	58 26.9	-40.1	29.8	55
56	51 29.8	-44.8	24.1	52 24.4	-44.3	24.6	53 18.9	-43.8	25.1	54 13.1	-43.4	25.7	55 07.0	-42.8	26.4	56 00.6	-42.2	27.0	56 53.9	-41.6	27.7	57 46.8	-40.9	28.4	56
57	50 45.0	-45.3	23.0	51 40.1	-44.9	23.5	52 35.1	-44.5	24.0	53 29.7	-43.9	24.6	54 24.2	-43.5	25.1	55 18.4	-43.0	25.7	56 12.3	-42.4	26.4	57 05.9	-41.9	27.1	57
58	49 59.7	-45.9	22.0	50 55.2	-45.4	22.4	51 50.6	-45.0	22.9	52 45.8	-44.7	23.4	53 40.7	-44.2	24.0	54 35.4	-43.7	24.5	55 29.9	-43.2	25.1	56 24.0	-42.6	25.8	58
59	49 13.8	-46.3	21.0	50 09.8	-46.0	21.4	51 05.6	-45.7	21.9	52 01.1	-45.2	22.3	52 56.5	-44.7	22.8	53 51.7	-44.3	23.4	54 46.7	-43.9	23.9	55 41.4	-43.3	24.5	59
60	48 27.5	-46.8	20.0	49 23.8	-46.5	20.4	50 19.9	-46.1	20.8	51 15.9	-45.7	21.3	52 11.8	-45.4	21.7	53 07.4	-44.9	22.2	54 02.8	-44.5	22.7	54 58.1	-44.1	23.3	60
61	47 40.7	-47.3	19.1	48 37.3	-46.9	19.4	49 33.8	-46.6	19.8	50 30.2	-46.3	20.2	51 26.4	-45.9	20.7	52 22.5	-45.6	21.1	53 18.3	-45.1	21.6	54 14.0	-44.7	22.1	61
62	46 53.4	-47.7	18.2	47 50.4	-47.4	18.5	48 47.2	-47.1	18.9	49 43.9	-46.8	19.3	50 40.5	-46.5	19.7	51 36.9	-46.1	20.1	52 33.2	-45.7	20.5	53 29.3	-45.3	21.0	62
63	46 05.7	-48.0	17.3	47 03.0	-47.8	17.6	48 00.1	-47.5	17.9	48 57.1	-47.2	18.3	49 54.0	-46.9	18.7	50 50.8	-46.6	19.1	51 47.5	-46.3	19.5	52 44.0	-46.0	19.9	63
64	45 17.7	-48.5	16.4	46 15.2	-48.2	16.7	47 12.6	-48.0	17.0	48 09.9	-47.7	17.4	49 07.1	-47.4	17.7	50 04.2	-47.1	18.1	51 01.2	-46.8	18.4	51 58.0	-46.4	18.8	64
65	44 29.2	-48.8	15.6	45 27.0	-48.6	15.9	46 24.6	-48.3	16.2	47 22.2	-48.1	16.5	48 19.7	-47.8	16.8	49 17.1	-47.6	17.1	50 14.4	-47.3	17.5	51 11.6	-47.0	17.8	65
66	43 40.4	-49.1	14.8	44 38.4	-48.9	15.0	45 36.3	-48.7	15.3	46 34.1	-48.5	15.6	47 31.9	-48.3	15.9	48 29.5	-47.9	16.2	49 27.1	-47.7	16.5	50 24.6	-47.5	16.8	66
67	42 51.3	-49.5	14.0	43 49.5	-49.3	14.2	44 47.6	-49.1	14.5	45 45.6	-48.8	14.7	46 43.6	-48.6	15.0	47 41.6	-48.4	15.3	48 39.4	-48.2	15.6	49 37.1	-47.9	15.9	67
68	42 01.8	-49.7	13.2	43 00.2	-49.6	13.4	43 58.5	-49.4	13.7	44 56.8	-49.2	13.9	45 55.0	-49.0	14.1	46 53.2	-48.8	14.4	47 51.2	-48.5	14.7	48 49.2	-48.3	15.0	68
69	41 12.1	-50.1	12.5	42 10.6	-49.8	12.7	43 09.1	-49.7	12.9	44 07.6	-49.5	13.1	45 06.0	-49.3	13.3	46 04.4	-49.2	13.6	47 02.7	-49.0	13.8	48 00.9	-48.7	14.1	69
70	40 22.0	-50.3	11.8	41 20.8	-50.2	11.9	42 19.4	-50.0	12.1	43 18.1	-49.9	12.3	44 16.7	-49.7	12.5	45 15.2	-49.5	12.7	46 13.7	-49.3	13.0	47 12.2	-49.2	13.2	70
71	39 31.7	-50.5	11.0	40 30.6	-50.4	11.2	41 29.4	-50.2	11.4	42 28.2	-50.1	11.6	43 27.0	-50.0	11.7	44 25.7	-49.8	11.9	45 24.4	-49.6	12.2	46 23.0	-49.4	12.4	71
72	38 41.2	-50.8	10.4	39 40.2	-50.7	10.5	40 39.2	-50.6	10.7	41 38.1	-50.4	10.8	42 37.0	-50.2	11.0	43 35.9	-50.1	11.2	44 34.8	-50.0	11.4	45 33.6	-49.9	11.6	72
73	37 50.4	-51.0	9.7	38 49.5	-50.9	9.8	39 48.6	-50.8	10.0	40 47.7	-50.7	10.1	41 46.8	-50.6	10.3	42 45.8	-50.4	10.4	43 44.8	-50.3	10.6	44 43.7	-50.1	10.8	73
74	36 59.4	-51.3	9.0	37 58.6	-51.1	9.1	38 57.8	-51.0	9.3	39 57.0	-50.9	9.4	40 56.2	-50.8	9.5	41 55.4	-50.7	9.7	42 54.5	-50.5	9.8	43 53.6	-50.4	10.0	74
75	36 08.1	-51.4	8.4	37 07.5	-51.4	8.5	38 06.8	-51.2	8.6	39 06.1	-51.1	8.7	40 05.4	-51.0	8.8	41 04.7	-50.9	9.0	42 04.0	-50.9	9.1	43 03.2	-50.7	9.3	75
76	35 16.7	-51.7	7.7	36 16.1	-51.5	7.8	37 15.6	-51.5	7.9	38 15.0	-51.4	8.0	39 14.4	-51.3	8.2	40 13.8	-51.2	8.3	41 13.1	-51.1	8.4	42 12.5	-51.0	8.5	76
77	34 25.0	-51.8	7.1	35 24.6	-51.8	7.2	36 24.1	-51.7	7.3	37 23.6	-51.6	7.4	38 23.1	-51.5	7.5	39 22.6	-51.4	7.6	40 22.0	-51.3	7.7	41 21.5	-51.2	7.8	77
78	33 33.2	-52.0	6.5	34 32.8	-51.9	6.6	35 32.4	-51.8	6.7	36 32.0	-51.8	6.7	37 31.6	-51.7	6.8	38 31.2	-51.7	6.9	39 30.7	-51.5	7.0	40 30.3	-51.5	7.1	78
79	32 41.2	-52.1	5.9	33 40.9	-52.1	6.0	34 40.6	-52.1	6.0	35 40.2	-51.9	6.1	36 39.9	-51.9	6.2	37 39.5	-51.8	6.3	38 39.2	-51.8	6.4	39 38.8	-51.7	6.5	79
80	31 49.1	-52.4	5.3	32 48.8	-52.3	5.4	33 48.5	-52.2	5.4	34 48.3	-52.2	5.5	35 48.0	-52.1	5.6	36 47.7	-52.1	5.6	37 47.4	-52.0	5.7	38 47.1	-51.9	5.8	80
81	30 56.7	-52.4	4.7	31 56.5	-52.4	4.8	32 56.3	-52.4	4.9	33 56.1	-52.3	4.9	34 55.9	-52.3	5.0	35 55.6	-52.2	5.0	36 55.4	-52.2	5.1	37 55.2	-52.1	5.2	81
82	30 04.3	-52.6	4.2	31 04.1	-52.6	4.2	32 03.9	-52.5	4.3	33 03.8	-52.5	4.3	34 03.6	-52.4	4.4	35 03.4	-52.4	4.4	36 03.2	-52.3	4.5	37 03.1	-52.4	4.5	82
83	29 11.7	-52.8	3.6	30 11.5	-52.7	3.7	31 11.4	-52.7	3.7	32 11.3	-52.7	3.7	33 11.2	-52.6	3.8	34 11.0	-52.5	3.8	35 10.9	-52.5	3.9	36 10.7	-52.4	3.9	83
84	28 18.9	-52.9	3.1	29 18.8	-52.8	3.1	30 18.7	-52.8	3.2	31 18.6	-52.7	3.2	32 18.6	-52.8	3.2	33 18.5	-52.8	3.3	34 18.4	-52.7	3.3	35 18.3	-52.7	3.3	84
85	27 26.0	-52.9	2.6	28 26.0	-53.0	2.6	29 25.9	-52.9	2.6	30 25.9	-53.0	2.6	31 25.8	-52.9	2.7	32 25.7	-52.8	2.7	33 25.7	-52.9	2.7	34 25.6	-52.8	2.7	85
86	26 33.1	-53.2	2.0	27 33.0	-53.1	2.0	28 33.0	-53.1	2.1	29 32.9	-53.0	2.1	30 32.9	-53.0	2.1	31 32.9	-53.1	2.1	32 32.8	-53.0	2.2	33 32.8	-53.0	2.2	86
87	25 39.9	-53.2	1.5	26 39.9	-53.2	1.5	27 39.9	-53.2	1.5	28 39.9	-53.2	1.6	29 39.9	-53.2	1.6	30 39.8	-53.1	1.6	31 39.8	-53.1	1.6	32 39.8	-53.1	1.6	87
88	24 46.7	-53.3	1.0	25 46.7	-53.3	1.0	26 46.7	-53.3	1.0	27 46.7	-53.3	1.0	28 46.7	-53.3	1.0	29 46.7	-53.3	1.0	30 46.7	-53.3	1.1	31 46.7	-53.3	1.1	88
89	23 53.4	-53.4	0.5	24 53.4	-53.4	0.5	25 53.4	-53.4	0.5	26 53.4	-53.4	0.5	27 53.4	-53.4	0.5	28 53.4	-53.4	0.5	29 53.4	-53.4	0.5	30 53.4	-53.4	0.5	89
90	23 00.0	-53.5	0.0	24 00.0	-53.5	0.0	25 00.0	-53.5	0.0	26 00.0	-53.5	0.0	27 00.0	-53.5	0.0	28 00.0	-53.5	0.0	29 00.0	-53.5	0.0	30 00.0	-53.5	0.0	90
	23°			24°			25°			26°			27°			28°			29°			30°			

27°, 333° L.H.A. LATITUDE SAME NAME AS DECLINATION

238

LATITUDE **CONTRARY** NAME TO DECLINATION L.H.A. 27°, 333°

Dec.	23° Hc	d	Z	24° Hc	d	Z	25° Hc	d	Z	26° Hc	d	Z	27° Hc	d	Z	28° Hc	d	Z	29° Hc	d	Z	30° Hc	d	Z	Dec.
°	° ′	′	°	° ′	′	°	° ′	′	°	° ′	′	°	° ′	′	°	° ′	′	°	° ′	′	°	° ′	′	°	°
0	55 06.1	-41.3	127.5	54 29.2	-42.4	128.6	53 51.3	-43.3	129.7	53 12.6	-44.3	130.7	52 33.0	-45.0	131.7	51 52.8	-45.9	132.7	51 11.7	-46.6	133.6	50 30.1	-47.5	134.5	0
1	54 24.8	-42.2	128.7	53 46.8	-43.1	129.8	53 08.0	-44.0	130.8	52 28.3	-44.8	131.8	51 48.0	-45.7	132.8	51 06.9	-46.5	133.7	50 25.1	-47.2	134.6	49 42.6	-47.8	135.4	1
2	53 42.6	-42.8	130.0	53 03.7	-43.7	131.0	52 24.0	-44.6	132.0	51 43.5	-45.4	132.9	51 02.3	-46.2	133.8	50 20.4	-46.9	134.7	49 37.9	-47.6	135.5	48 54.8	-48.3	136.3	2
3	52 59.8	-43.5	131.1	52 20.0	-44.4	132.1	51 39.4	-45.2	133.0	50 58.1	-46.0	134.0	50 16.1	-46.7	134.8	49 33.5	-47.4	135.7	48 50.3	-48.1	136.5	48 06.5	-48.7	137.2	3
4	52 16.3	-44.1	132.3	51 35.6	-45.0	133.2	50 54.2	-45.8	134.1	50 12.1	-46.5	135.0	49 29.4	-47.2	135.8	48 46.1	-47.9	136.6	48 02.2	-48.5	137.4	47 17.8	-49.1	138.1	4
5	51 32.2	-44.8	133.4	50 50.6	-45.5	134.3	50 08.4	-46.2	135.1	49 25.6	-46.9	135.9	48 42.2	-47.6	136.7	47 58.2	-48.2	137.5	47 13.7	-48.8	138.2	46 28.7	-49.4	138.9	5
6	50 47.4	-45.3	134.4	50 05.1	-46.0	135.3	49 22.2	-46.8	136.1	48 38.7	-47.5	136.9	47 54.6	-48.1	137.7	47 10.0	-48.7	138.4	46 24.9	-49.3	139.1	45 39.3	-49.8	139.8	6
7	50 02.1	-45.8	135.4	49 19.1	-46.6	136.3	48 35.4	-47.2	137.1	47 51.2	-47.8	137.8	47 06.5	-48.4	138.5	46 21.3	-49.0	139.2	45 35.6	-49.5	139.9	44 49.5	-50.1	140.6	7
8	49 16.3	-46.3	136.4	48 32.5	-46.9	137.2	47 48.2	-47.6	138.0	47 03.4	-48.2	138.7	46 18.1	-48.8	139.4	45 32.3	-49.4	140.1	44 46.1	-49.9	140.7	43 59.4	-50.4	141.3	8
9	48 30.0	-46.8	137.4	47 45.6	-47.5	138.2	47 00.6	-48.0	138.9	46 15.2	-48.7	139.6	45 29.3	-49.2	140.2	44 42.9	-49.7	140.9	43 56.2	-50.2	141.5	43 09.0	-50.7	142.1	9
10	47 43.2	-47.2	138.4	46 58.1	-47.8	139.1	46 12.6	-48.5	139.8	45 26.5	-49.0	140.4	44 40.1	-49.5	141.0	43 53.2	-50.0	141.7	43 06.0	-50.5	142.2	42 18.3	-50.9	142.8	10
11	46 56.0	-47.7	139.3	46 10.3	-48.3	139.9	45 24.1	-48.8	140.6	44 37.5	-49.3	141.2	43 50.6	-49.9	141.8	43 03.2	-50.3	142.4	42 15.5	-50.8	143.0	41 27.4	-51.2	143.5	11
12	46 08.3	-48.1	140.1	45 22.0	-48.6	140.8	44 35.3	-49.1	141.4	43 48.2	-49.6	142.0	43 00.7	-50.1	142.6	42 12.9	-50.6	143.2	41 24.7	-51.0	143.7	40 36.2	-51.5	144.2	12
13	45 20.2	-48.4	141.0	44 33.4	-48.9	141.6	43 46.2	-49.5	142.2	42 58.6	-50.0	142.8	42 10.6	-50.4	143.4	41 22.3	-50.9	143.9	40 33.7	-51.3	144.4	39 44.7	-51.6	144.9	13
14	44 31.8	-48.8	141.8	43 44.5	-49.3	142.4	42 56.7	-49.8	143.0	42 08.6	-50.2	143.6	41 20.2	-50.7	144.1	40 31.4	-51.1	144.6	39 42.4	-51.5	145.1	38 53.1	-51.9	145.5	14
15	43 43.0	-49.1	142.6	42 55.2	-49.6	143.2	42 06.9	-50.0	143.8	41 18.4	-50.5	144.3	40 29.5	-50.9	144.8	39 40.3	-51.3	145.3	38 50.9	-51.7	145.7	38 01.2	-52.1	146.2	15
16	42 53.9	-49.4	143.4	42 05.6	-49.9	144.0	41 16.9	-50.4	144.5	40 27.9	-50.8	145.0	39 38.6	-51.2	145.5	38 49.0	-51.6	145.9	37 59.2	-52.0	146.4	37 09.1	-52.3	146.8	16
17	42 04.5	-49.8	144.2	41 15.7	-50.2	144.7	40 26.5	-50.6	145.2	39 37.1	-51.0	145.7	38 47.4	-51.4	146.2	37 57.4	-51.7	146.6	37 07.2	-52.1	147.0	36 16.8	-52.5	147.4	17
18	41 14.7	-50.0	145.0	40 25.5	-50.5	145.4	39 35.9	-50.8	145.9	38 46.1	-51.2	146.4	37 56.0	-51.6	146.8	37 05.7	-52.0	147.2	36 15.1	-52.3	147.6	35 24.3	-52.6	148.0	18
19	40 24.7	-50.3	145.7	39 35.0	-50.7	146.2	38 45.1	-51.1	146.6	37 54.9	-51.5	147.0	37 04.4	-51.8	147.5	36 13.7	-52.2	147.9	35 22.8	-52.5	148.2	34 31.7	-52.8	148.6	19
20	39 34.4	-50.5	146.4	38 44.3	-50.9	146.8	37 54.0	-51.3	147.3	37 03.4	-51.7	147.7	36 12.6	-52.0	148.1	35 21.5	-52.3	148.5	34 30.3	-52.6	148.8	33 38.9	-53.0	149.2	20
21	38 43.9	-50.8	147.1	37 53.4	-51.1	147.5	37 02.7	-51.5	147.9	36 11.7	-51.8	148.3	35 20.6	-52.2	148.7	34 29.2	-52.5	149.1	33 37.7	-52.9	149.4	32 45.9	-53.1	149.7	21
22	37 53.1	-51.0	147.8	37 02.3	-51.4	148.2	36 11.2	-51.8	148.6	35 19.9	-52.1	148.9	34 28.4	-52.4	149.3	33 36.7	-52.7	149.6	32 44.8	-52.9	150.0	31 52.8	-53.2	150.3	22
23	37 02.1	-51.2	148.4	36 10.9	-51.6	148.8	35 19.4	-51.9	149.2	34 27.8	-52.2	149.5	33 36.0	-52.5	149.9	32 44.0	-52.8	150.2	31 51.9	-53.1	150.5	30 59.6	-53.4	150.8	23
24	36 10.9	-51.5	149.1	35 19.3	-51.8	149.4	34 27.5	-52.0	149.8	33 35.6	-52.4	150.1	32 43.5	-52.7	150.5	31 51.2	-53.0	150.8	30 58.8	-53.3	151.1	30 06.2	-53.5	151.4	24
25	35 19.4	-51.6	149.7	34 27.5	-51.9	150.1	33 35.5	-52.3	150.4	32 43.2	-52.5	150.7	31 50.8	-52.8	151.0	30 58.2	-53.1	151.3	30 05.5	-53.4	151.6	29 12.7	-53.7	151.9	25
26	34 27.8	-51.8	150.3	33 35.6	-52.1	150.7	32 43.2	-52.4	151.0	31 50.7	-52.7	151.3	30 58.0	-53.0	151.6	30 05.1	-53.2	151.9	29 12.1	-53.4	152.1	28 19.0	-53.7	152.4	26
27	33 36.0	-52.0	150.9	32 43.5	-52.3	151.3	31 50.8	-52.6	151.6	30 58.0	-52.9	151.9	30 05.0	-53.1	152.1	29 11.9	-53.4	152.4	28 18.7	-53.7	152.6	27 25.3	-53.8	152.9	27
28	32 44.0	-52.1	151.5	31 51.2	-52.4	151.8	30 58.2	-52.7	152.1	30 05.1	-53.0	152.4	29 11.9	-53.2	152.7	28 18.5	-53.5	152.9	27 25.0	-53.7	153.2	26 31.5	-54.0	153.4	28
29	31 51.9	-52.3	152.1	30 58.8	-52.6	152.4	30 05.5	-52.8	152.7	29 12.1	-53.1	152.9	28 18.7	-53.4	153.2	27 25.0	-53.5	153.4	26 31.3	-53.8	153.7	25 37.5	-54.0	153.9	29
30	30 59.6	-52.5	152.7	30 06.2	-52.7	153.0	29 12.7	-53.0	153.2	28 19.0	-53.2	153.5	27 25.3	-53.5	153.7	26 31.5	-53.7	153.9	25 37.5	-53.9	154.1	24 43.5	-54.2	154.4	30
31	30 07.1	-52.6	153.3	29 13.5	-52.9	153.5	28 19.7	-53.1	153.8	27 25.8	-53.3	154.0	26 31.8	-53.5	154.2	25 37.8	-53.8	154.4	24 43.6	-54.0	154.6	23 49.3	-54.2	154.8	31
32	29 14.5	-52.7	153.8	28 20.6	-53.0	154.1	27 26.6	-53.2	154.3	26 32.5	-53.5	154.5	25 38.3	-53.7	154.7	24 44.0	-53.9	154.9	23 49.6	-54.1	155.1	22 55.1	-54.3	155.3	32
33	28 21.8	-52.9	154.4	27 27.6	-53.1	154.6	26 33.4	-53.4	154.8	25 39.0	-53.5	155.0	24 44.6	-53.8	155.2	23 50.1	-54.0	155.4	22 55.5	-54.2	155.6	22 00.8	-54.4	155.8	33
34	27 28.9	-53.0	154.9	26 34.5	-53.2	155.1	25 40.0	-53.4	155.3	24 45.5	-53.7	155.5	23 50.8	-53.8	155.7	22 56.1	-54.1	155.9	22 01.3	-54.2	156.0	21 06.4	-54.4	156.2	34
35	26 35.9	-53.1	155.4	25 41.3	-53.3	155.6	24 46.6	-53.5	155.8	23 51.8	-53.7	156.0	22 57.0	-54.0	156.2	22 02.0	-54.1	156.3	21 07.1	-54.4	156.5	20 12.0	-54.5	156.7	35
36	25 42.8	-53.2	155.9	24 48.0	-53.4	156.1	23 53.1	-53.7	156.3	22 58.1	-53.8	156.5	22 03.0	-54.0	156.7	21 07.9	-54.2	156.8	20 12.7	-54.4	157.0	19 17.5	-54.6	157.1	36
37	24 49.6	-53.3	156.5	23 54.6	-53.6	156.6	22 59.4	-53.7	156.8	22 04.3	-54.0	157.0	21 09.0	-54.1	157.1	20 13.7	-54.3	157.3	19 18.3	-54.4	157.4	18 22.9	-54.6	157.5	37
38	23 56.3	-53.4	157.0	23 01.0	-53.6	157.1	22 05.7	-53.8	157.3	21 10.3	-53.9	157.4	20 14.9	-54.2	157.6	19 19.4	-54.3	157.7	18 23.9	-54.6	157.9	17 28.3	-54.7	158.0	38
39	23 02.9	-53.5	157.5	22 07.4	-53.7	157.6	21 11.9	-53.9	157.8	20 16.4	-54.1	157.9	19 20.7	-54.2	158.0	18 25.1	-54.5	158.2	17 29.3	-54.5	158.3	16 33.6	-54.8	158.4	39
40	22 09.4	-53.6	157.9	21 13.7	-53.7	158.1	20 18.0	-53.9	158.2	19 22.3	-54.1	158.4	18 26.5	-54.3	158.5	17 30.6	-54.4	158.6	16 34.8	-54.7	158.7	15 38.8	-54.8	158.8	40
41	21 15.8	-53.7	158.4	20 20.0	-53.9	158.6	19 24.1	-54.0	158.7	18 28.2	-54.2	158.8	17 32.2	-54.4	158.9	16 36.2	-54.5	159.1	15 40.1	-54.7	159.2	14 44.0	-54.8	159.3	41
42	20 22.1	-53.7	158.9	19 26.1	-53.9	159.0	18 30.1	-54.1	159.2	17 34.0	-54.3	159.3	16 37.8	-54.4	159.4	15 41.7	-54.6	159.5	14 45.4	-54.7	159.6	13 49.2	-54.9	159.7	42
43	19 28.4	-53.8	159.4	18 32.2	-54.0	159.5	17 36.0	-54.2	159.6	16 39.7	-54.3	159.7	15 43.4	-54.5	159.8	14 47.1	-54.6	159.9	13 50.7	-54.8	160.0	12 54.3	-54.9	160.1	43
44	18 34.6	-53.9	159.8	17 38.2	-54.0	160.0	16 41.8	-54.2	160.1	15 45.4	-54.4	160.2	14 48.9	-54.5	160.3	13 52.5	-54.7	160.3	12 55.9	-54.8	160.4	11 59.4	-55.0	160.5	44
45	17 40.7	-54.0	160.3	16 44.2	-54.2	160.4	15 47.6	-54.3	160.5	14 51.0	-54.4	160.6	13 54.4	-54.5	160.7	12 57.8	-54.7	160.8	12 01.1	-54.8	160.8	11 04.4	-55.0	160.9	45
46	16 46.7	-54.0	160.8	15 50.0	-54.1	160.9	14 53.3	-54.3	161.0	13 56.6	-54.4	161.0	12 59.9	-54.6	161.1	12 03.1	-54.8	161.2	11 06.3	-54.9	161.3	10 09.4	-55.0	161.3	46
47	15 52.7	-54.1	161.2	14 55.9	-54.2	161.3	13 59.0	-54.3	161.4	13 02.2	-54.6	161.5	12 05.3	-54.7	161.5	11 08.3	-54.8	161.6	10 11.4	-54.9	161.7	9 14.4	-55.0	161.7	47
48	14 58.6	-54.1	161.7	14 01.7	-54.3	161.8	13 04.7	-54.4	161.8	12 07.6	-54.5	161.9	11 10.6	-54.7	162.0	10 13.5	-54.8	162.0	9 16.5	-55.0	162.1	8 19.4	-55.1	162.1	48
49	14 04.5	-54.2	162.1	13 07.4	-54.3	162.2	12 10.3	-54.5	162.3	11 13.1	-54.6	162.3	10 15.9	-54.7	162.4	9 18.7	-54.8	162.4	8 21.5	-54.9	162.5	7 24.3	-55.1	162.5	49
50	13 10.3	-54.2	162.6	12 13.1	-54.4	162.6	11 15.8	-54.5	162.7	10 18.5	-54.6	162.7	9 21.2	-54.7	162.8	8 23.9	-54.9	162.8	7 26.6	-55.0	162.9	6 29.2	-55.1	162.9	50
51	12 16.1	-54.2	163.0	11 18.7	-54.3	163.1	10 21.3	-54.5	163.1	9 23.9	-54.6	163.2	8 26.5	-54.8	163.2	7 29.0	-54.9	163.3	6 31.6	-55.0	163.3	5 34.1	-55.1	163.3	51
52	11 21.9	-54.3	163.4	10 24.4	-54.5	163.5	9 26.8	-54.5	163.5	8 29.3	-54.7	163.6	7 31.7	-54.8	163.6	6 34.1	-54.9	163.7	5 36.6	-55.1	163.7	4 39.0	-55.2	163.7	52
53	10 27.6	-54.4	163.9	9 29.9	-54.4	163.9	8 32.3	-54.6	164.0	7 34.6	-54.7	164.0	6 36.9	-54.8	164.0	5 39.2	-54.9	164.1	4 41.5	-55.0	164.1	3 43.8	-55.1	164.1	53
54	9 33.2	-54.3	164.3	8 35.5	-54.5	164.3	7 37.7	-54.6	164.4	6 39.9	-54.7	164.4	5 42.1	-54.8	164.4	4 44.3	-54.9	164.5	3 46.5	-55.1	164.5	2 48.7	-55.2	164.5	54
55	8 38.9	-54.4	164.7	7 41.0	-54.5	164.8	6 43.1	-54.6	164.8	5 45.2	-54.7	164.8	4 47.3	-54.9	164.9	3 49.4	-55.0	164.9	2 51.4	-55.0	164.9	1 53.5	-55.1	164.9	55
56	7 44.5	-54.4	165.2	6 46.5	-54.5	165.2	5 48.5	-54.7	165.2	4 50.5	-54.8	165.2	3 52.4	-54.8	165.3	2 54.4	-54.9	165.3	1 56.4	-55.1	165.3	0 58.4	-55.2	165.3	56
57	6 50.1	-54.5	165.6	5 52.0	-54.6	165.6	4 53.8	-54.6	165.6	3 55.7	-54.7	165.7	2 57.6	-54.9	165.7	1 59.5	-55.0	165.7	1 01.3	-55.0	165.7	0 03.2	-55.2	165.7	57
58	5 55.6	-54.4	166.0	4 57.4	-54.5	166.0	3 59.2	-54.7	166.0	3 01.0	-54.8	166.1	2 02.7	-54.8	166.1	1 04.5	-55.0	166.1	0 06.3	-55.1	166.1	0 52.0	+55.1	13.9	58
59	5 01.2	-54.5	166.4	4 02.9	-54.6	166.4	3 04.5	-54.6	166.5	2 06.2	-54.8	166.5	1 07.9	-54.9	166.5	0 09.5	-54.9	166.5	0 48.8	+55.1	13.5	1 47.1	+55.2	13.5	59
60	4 06.7	-54.5	166.8	3 08.3	-54.6	166.9	2 09.9	-54.7	166.9	1 11.4	-54.8	166.9	0 13.0	-54.9	166.9	0 45.4	+55.0	13.1	1 43.9	+55.0	13.1	2 42.3	+55.2	13.1	60
61	3 12.2	-54.5	167.3	2 13.7	-54.6	167.3	1 15.2	-54.7	167.3	0 16.6	-54.7	167.3	0 41.9	+54.9	12.7	1 40.4	+55.0	12.7	2 38.9	+55.1	12.7	3 37.5	+55.1	12.7	61
62	2 17.7	-54.5	167.7	1 19.1	-54.6	167.7	0 20.5	-54.7	167.7	0 38.1	+54.8	12.3	1 36.8	+54.8	12.3	2 35.4	+54.9	12.3	3 34.0	+55.0	12.3	4 32.6	+55.1	12.3	62
63	1 23.2	-54.5	168.1	0 24.5	-54.6	168.1	0 34.2	+54.7	11.9	1 32.9	+54.8	11.9	2 31.6	+54.9	11.9	3 30.3	+55.0	11.9	4 29.0	+55.1	11.9	5 27.7	+55.1	11.9	63
64	0 28.7	-54.5	168.5	0 30.1	+54.6	11.5	1 28.9	+54.7	11.5	2 27.7	+54.7	11.5	3 26.5	+54.8	11.5	4 25.3	+54.9	11.5	5 24.1	+55.0	11.5	6 22.8	+55.1	11.6	64
65	0 25.8	+54.5	11.1	1 24.7	+54.6	11.1	2 23.6	+54.6	11.1	3 22.4	+54.8	11.1	4 21.3	+54.9	11.1	5 20.2	+54.9	11.1	6 19.1	+55.0	11.1	7 17.9	+55.1	11.2	65
66	1 20.3	+54.5	10.6	2 19.3	+54.5	10.6	3 18.2	+54.7	10.7	4 17.2	+54.7	10.7	5 16.2	+54.8	10.7	6 15.1	+54.9	10.7	7 14.1	+54.9	10.7	8 13.0	+55.1	10.8	66
67	2 14.8	+54.5	10.2	3 13.8	+54.6	10.2	4 12.9	+54.6	10.2	5 11.9	+54.8	10.3	6 11.0	+54.8	10.3	7 10.0	+54.9	10.3	8 09.0	+55.0	10.3	9 08.1	+55.0	10.4	67
68	3 09.3	+54.5	9.8	4 08.4	+54.6	9.8	5 07.5	+54.7	9.8	6 06.7	+54.7	9.8	7 05.8	+54.7	9.9	8 04.9	+54.8	9.9	9 04.0	+54.9	9.9	10 03.1	+55.0	9.9	68
69	4 03.8	+54.5	9.4	5 03.0	+54.5	9.4	6 02.2	+54.6	9.4	7 01.4	+54.6	9.4	8 00.5	+54.8	9.5	8 59.7	+54.9	9.5	9 58.9	+54.9	9.5	10 58.1	+54.9	9.5	69
70	4 58.3	+54.4	9.0	5 57.5	+54.5	9.0	6 56.8	+54.6	9.0	7 56.0	+54.7	9.0	8 55.3	+54.7	9.0	9 54.6	+54.7	9.1	10 53.8	+54.9	9.1	11 53.0	+55.0	9.1	70
71	5 52.7	+54.5	8.5	6 52.0	+54.5	8.6	7 51.4	+54.5	8.6	8 50.7	+54.6	8.6	9 50.0	+54.7	8.6	10 49.3	+54.8	8.7	11 48.7	+54.8	8.7	12 48.0	+54.9	8.7	71
72	6 47.2	+54.4	8.1	7 46.5	+54.5	8.1	8 45.9	+54.6	8.2	9 45.3	+54.6	8.2	10 44.7	+54.7	8.2	11 44.1	+54.7	8.2	12 43.5	+54.8	8.3	13 42.9	+54.8	8.3	72
73	7 41.6	+54.4	7.7	8 41.0	+54.5	7.7	9 40.5	+54.5	7.7	10 39.9	+54.6	7.8	11 39.4	+54.6	7.8	12 38.8	+54.7	7.8	13 38.3	+54.7	7.9	14 37.7	+54.8	7.9	73
74	8 36.0	+54.3	7.3	9 35.5	+54.4	7.3	10 35.0	+54.5	7.3	11 34.5	+54.5	7.3	12 34.0	+54.6	7.4	13 33.5	+54.6	7.4	14 33.0	+54.7	7.4	15 32.5	+54.8	7.5	74
75	9 30.3	+54.4	6.8	10 29.9	+54.4	6.9	11 29.5	+54.4	6.9	12 29.0	+54.5	6.9	13 28.6	+54.5	6.9	14 28.1	+54.6	7.0	15 27.7	+54.6	7.0	16 27.3	+54.7	7.0	75
76	10 24.7	+54.3	6.4	11 24.3	+54.3	6.4	12 23.9	+54.4	6.5	13 23.5	+54.5	6.5	14 23.1	+54.5	6.5	15 22.7	+54.6	6.5	16 22.3	+54.6	6.6	17 22.0	+54.6	6.6	76
77	11 19.0	+54.2	6.0	12 18.6	+54.3	6.0	13 18.3	+54.3	6.0	14 18.0	+54.4	6.0	15 17.6	+54.5	6.1	16 17.3	+54.5	6.1	17 16.9	+54.6	6.1	18 16.6	+54.6	6.2	77
78	12 13.2	+54.2	5.5	13 12.9	+54.3	5.6	14 12.6	+54.3	5.6	15 12.4	+54.3	5.6	16 12.1	+54.4	5.6	17 11.8	+54.4	5.7	18 11.5	+54.5	5.7	19 11.2	+54.5	5.7	78
79	13 07.4	+54.2	5.1	14 07.2	+54.2	5.1	15 06.9	+54.3	5.1	16 06.7	+54.3	5.2	17 06.5	+54.3	5.2	18 06.2	+54.4	5.2	19 06.0	+54.4	5.3	20 05.7	+54.5	5.3	79
80	14 01.6	+54.1	4.7	15 01.4	+54.2	4.7	16 01.2	+54.2	4.7	17 01.0	+54.2	4.7	18 00.8	+54.3	4.8	19 00.6	+54.3	4.8	20 00.4	+54.3	4.8	21 00.2	+54.3	4.8	80
81	14 55.7	+54.1	4.2	15 55.6	+54.1	4.2	16 55.4	+54.1	4.3	17 55.2	+54.2	4.3	18 55.1	+54.2	4.3	19 54.9	+54.2	4.3	20 54.7	+54.3	4.4	21 54.5	+54.3	4.4	81
82	15 49.8	+54.0	3.8	16 49.7	+54.0	3.8	17 49.5	+54.1	3.8	18 49.4	+54.1	3.8	19 49.3	+54.1	3.9	20 49.1	+54.2	3.9	21 49.0	+54.2	3.9	22 48.8	+54.3	3.9	82
83	16 43.8	+54.0	3.3	17 43.7	+54.0	3.3	18 43.6	+54.0	3.3	19 43.5	+54.0	3.4	20 43.4	+54.1	3.4	21 43.3	+54.1	3.4	22 43.2	+54.1	3.4	23 43.1	+54.1	3.5	83
84	17 37.8	+53.9	2.9	18 37.7	+53.9	2.9	19 37.6	+53.9	2.9	20 37.5	+54.0	2.9	21 37.5	+53.9	2.9	22 37.4	+54.0	2.9	23 37.3	+54.0	3.0	24 37.2	+54.1	3.0	84
85	18 31.7	+53.8	2.4	19 31.6	+53.8	2.4	20 31.5	+53.9	2.4	21 31.5	+53.9	2.4	22 31.4	+53.9	2.5	23 31.4	+53.9	2.5	24 31.3	+54.0	2.5	25 31.3	+53.9	2.5	85
86	19 25.5	+53.7	1.9	20 25.4	+53.8	1.9	21 25.4	+53.8	1.9	22 25.4	+53.8	2.0	23 25.3	+53.8	2.0	24 25.3	+53.8	2.0	25 25.3	+53.8	2.0	26 25.2	+53.9	2.0	86
87	20 19.2	+53.7	1.5	21 19.2	+53.7	1.5	22 19.2	+53.7	1.5	23 19.2	+53.7	1.5	24 19.1	+53.8	1.5	25 19.1	+53.8	1.5	26 19.1	+53.7	1.5	27 19.1	+53.7	1.5	87
88	21 12.9	+53.6	1.0	22 12.9	+53.6	1.0	23 12.9	+53.6	1.0	24 12.9	+53.6	1.0	25 12.9	+53.6	1.0	26 12.9	+53.6	1.0	27 12.8	+53.7	1.0	28 12.8	+53.7	1.0	88
89	22 06.5	+53.5	0.5	23 06.5	+53.5	0.5	24 06.5	+53.5	0.5	25 06.5	+53.5	0.5	26 06.5	+53.5	0.5	27 06.5	+53.5	0.5	28 06.5	+53.5	0.5	29 06.5	+53.5	0.5	89
90	23 00.0	+53.4	0.0	24 00.0	+53.4	0.0	25 00.0	+53.4	0.0	26 00.0	+53.4	0.0	27 00.0	+53.4	0.0	28 00.0	+53.4	0.0	29 00.0	+53.4	0.0	30 00.0	+53.4	0.0	90
	23°			24°			25°			26°			27°			28°			29°			30°			

S. Lat. {L.H.A. greater than 180° ....Zn=180°–Z; L.H.A. less than 180°...........Zn=180°+Z}

LATITUDE **SAME** NAME AS DECLINATION L.H.A. 153°, 207°

239

28°, 332° L.H.A. LATITUDE SAME NAME AS DECLINATION

N. Lat. {L.H.A. greater than 180° .....Zn=Z; L.H.A. less than 180°............Zn=360°–Z}

Dec.	23° Hc	d	Z	24° Hc	d	Z	25° Hc	d	Z	26° Hc	d	Z	27° Hc	d	Z	28° Hc	d	Z	29° Hc	d	Z	30° Hc	d	Z	Dec.
°	° ′	′	°	° ′	′	°	° ′	′	°	° ′	′	°	° ′	′	°	° ′	′	°	° ′	′	°	° ′	′	°	°
0	54 22.0	+39.8	126.3	53 46.0	+40.9	127.4	53 09.1	+41.9	128.5	52 31.3	+42.9	129.5	51 52.8	+43.8	130.5	51 13.4	+44.7	131.4	50 33.3	+45.6	132.4	49 52.6	+46.3	133.2	0
1	55 01.8	+39.0	125.0	54 26.9	+40.1	126.2	53 51.0	+41.2	127.3	53 14.2	+42.2	128.3	52 36.6	+43.1	129.4	51 58.1	+44.1	130.4	51 18.9	+44.9	131.3	50 38.9	+45.8	132.2	1
2	55 40.8	+38.1	123.7	55 07.0	+39.2	124.9	54 32.2	+40.4	126.0	53 56.4	+41.5	127.1	53 19.7	+42.5	128.2	52 42.2	+43.4	129.3	52 03.8	+44.4	130.3	51 24.7	+45.2	131.2	2
3	56 18.9	+37.1	122.3	55 46.2	+38.4	123.5	55 12.6	+39.5	124.7	54 37.9	+40.6	125.9	54 02.2	+41.7	127.0	53 25.6	+42.8	128.1	52 48.2	+43.7	129.2	52 09.9	+44.6	130.2	3
4	56 56.0	+36.1	120.9	56 24.6	+37.4	122.2	55 52.1	+38.7	123.4	55 18.5	+39.9	124.6	54 43.9	+41.0	125.8	54 08.4	+42.0	126.9	53 31.9	+43.0	128.0	52 54.5	+44.0	129.1	4
5	57 32.1	+35.0	119.4	57 02.0	+36.5	120.7	56 30.8	+37.7	122.0	55 58.4	+38.9	123.3	55 24.9	+40.1	124.5	54 50.4	+41.3	125.7	54 14.9	+42.3	126.8	53 38.5	+43.3	127.9	5
6	58 07.1	+34.0	117.9	57 38.5	+35.3	119.3	57 08.5	+36.7	120.6	56 37.3	+38.1	121.9	56 05.0	+39.3	123.2	55 31.7	+40.4	124.4	54 57.2	+41.6	125.6	54 21.8	+42.6	126.7	6
7	58 41.1	+32.7	116.3	58 13.8	+34.2	117.7	57 45.2	+35.7	119.2	57 15.4	+37.0	120.5	56 44.3	+38.3	121.8	56 12.1	+39.6	123.1	55 38.8	+40.7	124.3	55 04.4	+41.9	125.5	7
8	59 13.8	+31.5	114.7	58 48.0	+33.1	116.2	58 20.9	+34.5	117.6	57 52.4	+36.0	119.0	57 22.6	+37.4	120.4	56 51.7	+38.6	121.7	56 19.5	+39.9	123.0	55 46.3	+41.0	124.3	8
9	59 45.3	+30.1	113.0	59 21.1	+31.8	114.5	58 55.4	+33.4	116.1	58 28.4	+34.9	117.5	58 00.0	+36.3	119.0	57 30.3	+37.7	120.3	56 59.4	+39.0	121.7	56 27.3	+40.2	123.0	9
10	60 15.4	+28.8	111.3	59 52.9	+30.5	112.9	59 28.8	+32.1	114.4	59 03.3	+33.6	116.0	58 36.3	+35.2	117.4	58 08.0	+36.6	118.9	57 38.4	+38.0	120.3	57 07.5	+39.3	121.6	10
11	60 44.2	+27.3	109.5	60 23.4	+29.0	111.1	60 00.9	+30.8	112.8	59 36.9	+32.5	114.3	59 11.5	+34.0	115.9	58 44.6	+35.5	117.4	58 16.4	+36.9	118.8	57 46.8	+38.3	120.2	11
12	61 11.5	+25.8	107.6	60 52.4	+27.7	109.4	60 31.7	+29.4	111.0	60 09.4	+31.1	112.7	59 45.5	+32.8	114.2	59 20.1	+34.4	115.8	58 53.3	+35.9	117.3	58 25.1	+37.3	118.7	12
13	61 37.3	+24.1	105.8	61 20.1	+26.1	107.5	61 01.1	+28.0	109.2	60 40.5	+29.8	110.9	60 18.3	+31.5	112.6	59 54.5	+33.1	114.2	59 29.2	+34.7	115.7	59 02.4	+36.2	117.2	13
14	62 01.4	+22.5	103.8	61 46.2	+24.5	105.6	61 29.1	+26.4	107.4	61 10.3	+28.3	109.1	60 49.8	+30.1	110.8	60 27.6	+31.8	112.5	60 03.9	+33.5	114.1	59 38.6	+35.1	115.7	14
15	62 23.9	+20.8	101.8	62 10.7	+22.8	103.7	61 55.5	+24.9	105.5	61 38.6	+26.8	107.3	61 19.9	+28.6	109.0	60 59.4	+30.5	110.8	60 37.4	+32.1	112.4	60 13.7	+33.8	114.0	15
16	62 44.7	+18.9	99.8	62 33.5	+21.1	101.7	62 20.4	+23.1	103.6	62 05.4	+25.1	105.4	61 48.5	+27.1	107.2	61 29.9	+29.0	109.0	61 09.5	+30.8	110.7	60 47.5	+32.5	112.4	16
17	63 03.6	+17.1	97.7	62 54.6	+19.2	99.7	62 43.5	+21.4	101.6	62 30.5	+23.5	103.4	62 15.6	+25.5	105.3	61 58.9	+27.4	107.1	61 40.3	+29.3	108.9	61 20.0	+31.2	110.6	17
18	63 20.7	+15.1•	95.6	63 13.8	+17.4	97.6	63 04.9	+19.6	99.5	62 54.0	+21.7	101.4	62 41.1	+23.8	103.3	62 26.3	+25.9	105.2	62 09.6	+27.8	107.0	61 51.2	+29.7	108.8	18
19	63 35.8	+13.1•	93.4	63 31.2	+15.4•	95.4	63 24.5	+17.7	97.4	63 15.7	+19.9	99.4	63 04.9	+22.1	101.3	62 52.2	+24.1	103.2	62 37.4	+26.2	105.1	62 20.9	+28.1	107.0	19
20	63 48.9	+11.1•	91.2	63 46.6	+13.4•	93.2	63 42.2	+15.7•	95.3	63 35.6	+18.0	97.3	63 27.0	+20.2	99.3	63 16.3	+22.4	101.2	63 03.6	+24.5	103.2	62 49.0	+26.6	105.1	20
21	64 00.0	+9.1•	89.0	64 00.0	+11.4•	91.0	63 57.9	+13.7•	93.1	63 53.6	+16.0•	95.1	63 47.2	+18.3	97.1	63 38.7	+20.5	99.1	63 28.1	+22.8	101.1	63 15.6	+24.8	103.1	21
22	64 09.1	+6.8•	86.7	64 11.4	+9.3•	88.8	64 11.6	+11.7•	90.9	64 09.6	+14.0•	92.9	64 05.5	+16.3•	95.0	63 59.2	+18.7	97.0	63 50.9	+20.8	99.0	63 40.4	+23.1	101.0	22
23	64 15.9	+4.8•	84.4	64 20.7	+7.1•	86.5	64 23.3	+9.5•	88.6	64 23.6	+12.0•	90.7	64 21.8	+14.3•	92.8	64 17.9	+16.6•	94.8	64 11.7	+19.0	96.9	64 03.5	+21.2	98.9	23
24	64 20.7	+2.6•	82.1	64 27.8	+5.0•	84.2	64 32.8	+7.4•	86.3	64 35.6	+9.8•	88.4	64 36.1	+12.2•	90.5	64 34.5	+14.6•	92.6	64 30.7	+16.9•	94.7	64 24.7	+19.2	96.8	24
25	64 23.3	+0.3•	79.8	64 32.8	+2.8•	81.9	64 40.2	+5.2•	84.0	64 45.4	+7.6•	86.1	64 48.3	+10.1•	88.2	64 49.1	+12.5•	90.3	64 47.6	+14.9•	92.5	64 43.9	+17.3•	94.6	25
26	64 23.6	-1.8•	77.5	64 35.6	+0.5•	79.6	64 45.4	+2.9•	81.7	64 53.0	+5.4•	83.8	64 58.4	+7.8•	85.9	65 01.6	+10.3•	88.0	65 02.5	+12.7•	90.2	65 01.2	+15.2•	92.3	26
27	64 21.8	-3.9•	75.2	64 36.1	-1.6•	77.2	64 48.3	+0.8•	79.3	64 58.4	+3.2•	81.4	65 06.2	+5.7•	83.5	65 11.9	+8.1•	85.7	65 15.2	+10.6•	87.9	65 16.4	+13.0•	90.0	27
28	64 17.9	-6.2•	72.9	64 34.5	-3.8•	74.9	64 49.1	-1.5•	77.0	65 01.6	+0.9•	79.0	65 11.9	+3.3•	81.2	65 20.0	+5.8•	83.3	65 25.8	+8.3•	85.5	65 29.4	+10.8•	87.7	28
29	64 11.7	-8.2•	70.6	64 30.7	-6.0•	72.6	64 47.6	-3.7•	74.6	65 02.5	-1.3•	76.7	65 15.2	+1.2•	78.8	65 25.8	+3.6•	80.9	65 34.1	+6.1•	83.1	65 40.2	+8.6•	85.3	29
30	64 03.5	-10.4•	68.3	64 24.7	-8.2•	70.3	64 43.9	-5.9•	72.3	65 01.2	-3.6•	74.3	65 16.4	-1.2•	76.4	65 29.4	+1.3•	78.5	65 40.2	+3.8•	80.7	65 48.8	+6.2•	82.9	30
31	63 53.1	-12.4•	66.1	64 16.5	-10.3•	68.0	64 38.0	-8.0•	69.9	64 57.6	-5.8•	72.0	65 15.2	-3.4•	74.0	65 30.7	-1.1•	76.1	65 44.0	+1.4•	78.3	65 55.0	+4.0•	80.5	31
32	63 40.7	-14.5•	63.9	64 06.2	-12.4•	65.7	64 30.0	-10.3•	67.6	64 51.8	-7.9•	69.6	65 11.8	-5.7•	71.6	65 29.6	-3.3•	73.7	65 45.4	-0.9•	75.8	65 59.0	+1.6•	78.0	32
33	63 26.2	-16.4	61.7	63 53.8	-14.4	63.5	64 19.7	-12.3•	65.4	64 43.9	-10.2•	67.3	65 06.1	-7.9•	69.3	65 26.3	-5.6•	71.3	65 44.5	-3.2•	73.4	66 00.6	-0.8•	75.6	33
34	63 09.8	-18.3	59.6	63 39.4	-16.3	61.3	64 07.4	-14.3•	63.1	64 33.7	-12.3•	65.0	64 58.2	-10.1•	66.9	65 20.7	-7.8•	68.9	65 41.3	-5.5•	71.0	65 59.8	-3.1•	73.1	34
35	62 51.5	-20.1	57.5	63 23.1	-18.3	59.1	63 53.1	-16.4•	60.9	64 21.4	-14.3•	62.7	64 48.1	-12.3•	64.6	65 12.9	-10.1•	66.5	65 35.8	-7.8•	68.6	65 56.7	-5.4•	70.6	35
36	62 31.4	-21.9	55.4	63 04.8	-20.2	57.0	63 36.7	-18.3	58.7	64 07.1	-16.4•	60.5	64 35.8	-14.3•	62.3	65 02.8	-12.2•	64.2	65 28.0	-10.0•	66.2	65 51.3	-7.8•	68.2	36
37	62 09.5	-23.6	53.4	62 44.6	-21.9	55.0	63 18.4	-20.2	56.6	63 50.7	-18.3	58.3	64 21.5	-16.4•	60.0	64 50.6	-14.4•	61.9	65 18.0	-12.2•	63.8	65 43.5	-10.0•	65.8	37
38	61 45.9	-25.2	51.4	62 22.7	-23.6	52.9	62 58.2	-21.9	54.5	63 32.4	-20.2	56.1	64 05.1	-18.4	57.8	64 36.2	-16.4•	59.6	65 05.8	-14.4•	61.5	65 33.5	-12.2•	63.4	38
39	61 20.7	-26.7	49.5	61 59.1	-25.3	51.0	62 36.3	-23.7	52.5	63 12.2	-22.0	54.0	63 46.7	-20.2	55.7	64 19.8	-18.4	57.4	64 51.4	-16.5•	59.2	65 21.3	-14.4•	61.0	39
40	60 54.0	-28.3	47.7	61 33.8	-26.8	49.0	62 12.6	-25.4	50.5	62 50.2	-23.8	52.0	63 26.5	-22.1	53.5	64 01.4	-20.3	55.2	64 34.9	-18.4•	56.9	65 06.9	-16.5•	58.7	40
41	60 25.7	-29.7	45.9	61 07.0	-28.4	47.2	61 47.2	-26.9	48.5	62 26.4	-25.4	50.0	63 04.4	-23.9	51.5	63 41.1	-22.2	53.1	64 16.5	-20.5	54.7	64 50.4	-18.6•	56.4	41
42	59 56.0	-31.0	44.1	60 38.6	-29.7	45.4	61 20.3	-28.4	46.7	62 01.0	-27.1	48.0	62 40.5	-25.5	49.5	63 18.9	-23.9	51.0	63 56.0	-22.2	52.6	64 31.8	-20.5	54.2	42
43	59 25.0	-32.3	42.4	60 08.9	-31.1	43.6	60 51.9	-29.9	44.8	61 33.9	-28.5	46.1	62 15.0	-27.2	47.5	62 55.0	-25.7	48.9	63 33.8	-24.1	50.5	64 11.3	-22.4	52.1	43
44	58 52.7	-33.5	40.8	59 37.8	-32.5	41.9	60 22.0	-31.2	43.1	61 05.4	-30.0	44.3	61 47.8	-28.6	45.6	62 29.3	-27.3	47.0	63 09.7	-25.8	48.4	63 48.9	-24.2	49.9	44
45	58 19.2	-34.7	39.2	59 05.3	-33.6	40.3	59 50.8	-32.6	41.4	60 35.4	-31.4	42.5	61 19.2	-30.2	43.8	62 02.0	-28.8	45.1	62 43.9	-27.4	46.4	63 24.7	-25.9	47.9	45
46	57 44.5	-35.7	37.7	58 31.7	-34.8	38.7	59 18.2	-33.7	39.7	60 04.0	-32.6	40.8	60 49.0	-31.5	42.0	61 33.2	-30.3	43.2	62 16.5	-29.0	44.5	62 58.8	-27.6	45.9	46
47	57 08.8	-36.8	36.2	57 56.9	-35.8	37.1	58 44.5	-34.9	38.1	59 31.4	-33.9	39.1	60 17.5	-32.8	40.2	61 02.9	-31.6	41.4	61 47.5	-30.4	42.6	62 31.2	-29.2	43.9	47
48	56 32.0	-37.7	34.7	57 21.1	-36.9	35.6	58 09.6	-36.0	36.5	58 57.5	-35.1	37.5	59 44.7	-34.0	38.6	60 31.3	-33.0	39.7	61 17.1	-31.9	40.8	62 02.0	-30.6	42.1	48
49	55 54.3	-38.7	33.3	56 44.2	-37.9	34.2	57 33.6	-37.1	35.0	58 22.4	-36.2	36.0	59 10.7	-35.3	37.0	59 58.3	-34.2	38.0	60 45.2	-33.1	39.1	61 31.4	-32.0	40.2	49
50	55 15.6	-39.5	32.0	56 06.3	-38.8	32.8	56 56.5	-38.0	33.6	57 46.2	-37.2	34.5	58 35.4	-36.3	35.4	59 24.1	-35.4	36.4	60 12.1	-34.5	37.4	60 59.4	-33.4	38.5	50
51	54 36.1	-40.4	30.7	55 27.5	-39.7	31.4	56 18.5	-39.0	32.2	57 09.0	-38.1	33.0	57 59.1	-37.4	33.9	58 48.7	-36.5	34.8	59 37.6	-35.5	35.8	60 26.0	-34.6	36.8	51
52	53 55.7	-41.1	29.4	54 47.8	-40.5	30.1	55 39.5	-39.8	30.8	56 30.9	-39.2	31.6	57 21.7	-38.3	32.4	58 12.2	-37.6	33.3	59 02.1	-36.7	34.2	59 51.4	-35.8	35.1	52
53	53 14.6	-41.9	28.2	54 07.3	-41.3	28.8	54 59.7	-40.6	29.5	55 51.7	-39.9	30.2	56 43.4	-39.3	31.0	57 34.6	-38.5	31.8	58 25.4	-37.8	32.7	59 15.6	-36.9	33.6	53
54	52 32.7	-42.5	27.0	53 26.0	-42.0	27.6	54 19.1	-41.5	28.2	55 11.8	-40.8	28.9	56 04.1	-40.2	29.6	56 56.1	-39.5	30.4	57 47.6	-38.7	31.2	58 38.7	-37.9	32.0	54
55	51 50.2	-43.2	25.8	52 44.0	-42.7	26.4	53 37.6	-42.1	27.0	54 31.0	-41.6	27.6	55 23.9	-40.9	28.3	56 16.6	-40.4	29.0	57 08.9	-39.7	29.8	58 00.8	-39.0	30.6	55
56	51 07.0	-43.9	24.7	52 01.3	-43.3	25.3	52 55.5	-42.9	25.8	53 49.4	-42.4	26.4	54 43.0	-41.8	27.0	55 36.2	-41.1	27.7	56 29.2	-40.5	28.4	57 21.8	-39.9	29.1	56
57	50 23.1	-44.4	23.6	51 18.0	-44.0	24.1	52 12.6	-43.5	24.7	53 07.0	-43.0	25.2	54 01.2	-42.5	25.8	54 55.1	-42.0	26.4	55 48.7	-41.4	27.1	56 41.9	-40.7	27.8	57
58	49 38.7	-44.9	22.6	50 34.0	-44.5	23.1	51 29.1	-44.1	23.5	52 24.0	-43.6	24.1	53 18.7	-43.2	24.6	54 13.1	-42.6	25.2	55 07.3	-42.1	25.8	56 01.2	-41.6	26.4	58
59	48 53.8	-45.5	21.6	49 49.5	-45.1	22.0	50 45.0	-44.7	22.5	51 40.4	-44.3	22.9	52 35.5	-43.8	23.5	53 30.5	-43.4	24.0	54 25.2	-42.9	24.6	55 19.6	-42.3	25.2	59
60	48 08.3	-45.9	20.6	49 04.4	-45.6	21.0	50 00.3	-45.2	21.4	50 56.1	-44.8	21.9	51 51.7	-44.4	22.3	52 47.1	-44.0	22.8	53 42.3	-43.6	23.4	54 37.3	-43.1	23.9	60
61	47 22.4	-46.5	19.6	48 18.8	-46.1	20.0	49 15.1	-45.7	20.4	50 11.3	-45.4	20.8	51 07.3	-45.0	21.3	52 03.1	-44.6	21.7	52 58.7	-44.2	22.2	53 54.2	-43.8	22.7	61
62	46 35.9	-46.8	18.7	47 32.7	-46.6	19.1	48 29.4	-46.3	19.4	49 25.9	-45.9	19.8	50 22.3	-45.6	20.2	51 18.5	-45.2	20.6	52 14.5	-44.8	21.1	53 10.4	-44.4	21.6	62
63	45 49.1	-47.3	17.8	46 46.1	-46.9	18.1	47 43.1	-46.7	18.5	48 40.0	-46.4	18.8	49 36.7	-46.1	19.2	50 33.3	-45.8	19.6	51 29.7	-45.3	20.0	52 26.0	-45.0	20.5	63
64	45 01.8	-47.7	16.9	45 59.2	-47.5	17.2	46 56.4	-47.1	17.5	47 53.6	-46.9	17.9	48 50.6	-46.5	18.2	49 47.5	-46.2	18.6	50 44.4	-46.0	19.0	51 41.0	-45.6	19.4	64
65	44 14.1	-48.0	16.1	45 11.7	-47.8	16.4	46 09.3	-47.6	16.6	47 06.7	-47.3	16.9	48 04.1	-47.1	17.3	49 01.3	-46.7	17.6	49 58.4	-46.4	18.0	50 55.4	-46.1	18.3	65
66	43 26.1	-48.4	15.2	44 23.9	-48.1	15.5	45 21.7	-47.9	15.8	46 19.4	-47.7	16.1	47 17.0	-47.4	16.3	48 14.6	-47.2	16.7	49 12.0	-46.9	17.0	50 09.3	-46.6	17.3	66
67	42 37.7	-48.7	14.4	43 35.8	-48.5	14.7	44 33.8	-48.3	14.9	45 31.7	-48.1	15.2	46 29.6	-47.9	15.5	47 27.4	-47.6	15.7	48 25.1	-47.4	16.0	49 22.7	-47.1	16.4	67
68	41 49.0	-49.1	13.6	42 47.3	-48.9	13.9	43 45.5	-48.7	14.1	44 43.6	-48.4	14.3	45 41.7	-48.2	14.6	46 39.8	-48.0	14.8	47 37.7	-47.8	15.1	48 35.6	-47.5	15.4	68
69	40 59.9	-49.3	12.9	41 58.4	-49.2	13.1	42 56.8	-49.0	13.3	43 55.2	-48.8	13.5	44 53.5	-48.6	13.7	45 51.8	-48.4	14.0	46 49.9	-48.1	14.2	47 48.1	-48.0	14.5	69
70	40 10.6	-49.6	12.1	41 09.2	-49.4	12.3	42 07.8	-49.3	12.5	43 06.4	-49.1	12.7	44 04.9	-48.9	12.9	45 03.4	-48.8	13.1	46 01.8	-48.6	13.4	47 00.1	-48.4	13.6	70
71	39 21.0	-49.9	11.4	40 19.8	-49.8	11.6	41 18.5	-49.5	11.7	42 17.3	-49.5	11.9	43 16.0	-49.3	12.1	44 14.6	-49.1	12.3	45 13.2	-48.9	12.5	46 11.7	-48.7	12.8	71
72	38 31.1	-50.2	10.7	39 30.0	-50.0	10.8	40 29.0	-49.9	11.0	41 27.8	-49.7	11.2	42 26.7	-49.6	11.3	43 25.5	-49.4	11.5	44 24.3	-49.3	11.7	45 23.0	-49.1	11.9	72
73	37 40.9	-50.3	10.0	38 40.0	-50.2	10.1	39 39.1	-50.2	10.3	40 38.1	-50.0	10.4	41 37.1	-49.9	10.6	42 36.1	-49.8	10.7	43 35.0	-49.6	10.9	44 33.9	-49.4	11.1	73
74	36 50.6	-50.6	9.3	37 49.8	-50.5	9.4	38 48.9	-50.3	9.6	39 48.1	-50.3	9.7	40 47.2	-50.1	9.8	41 46.3	-50.0	10.0	42 45.4	-49.9	10.2	43 44.5	-49.8	10.3	74
75	36 00.0	-50.9	8.6	36 59.3	-50.8	8.7	37 58.6	-50.7	8.9	38 57.8	-50.5	9.0	39 57.1	-50.4	9.1	40 56.3	-50.3	9.3	41 55.5	-50.2	9.4	42 54.7	-50.1	9.5	75
76	35 09.1	-51.0	8.0	36 08.5	-50.9	8.1	37 07.9	-50.8	8.2	38 07.3	-50.7	8.3	39 06.7	-50.7	8.4	40 06.0	-50.5	8.5	41 05.3	-50.4	8.7	42 04.6	-50.3	8.8	76
77	34 18.1	-51.2	7.3	35 17.6	-51.2	7.4	36 17.1	-51.1	7.5	37 16.6	-51.0	7.6	38 16.0	-50.9	7.7	39 15.5	-50.8	7.8	40 14.9	-50.7	8.0	41 14.3	-50.6	8.1	77
78	33 26.9	-51.5	6.7	34 26.4	-51.3	6.8	35 26.0	-51.3	6.9	36 25.6	-51.2	7.0	37 25.1	-51.1	7.1	38 24.7	-51.1	7.2	39 24.2	-51.0	7.3	40 23.7	-50.9	7.4	78
79	32 35.4	-51.6	6.1	33 35.1	-51.5	6.2	34 34.7	-51.4	6.2	35 34.4	-51.4	6.3	36 34.0	-51.3	6.4	37 33.6	-51.2	6.5	38 33.2	-51.1	6.6	39 32.8	-51.1	6.7	79
80	31 43.8	-51.7	5.5	32 43.6	-51.7	5.6	33 43.3	-51.7	5.6	34 43.0	-51.6	5.7	35 42.7	-51.5	5.8	36 42.4	-51.5	5.8	37 42.1	-51.4	5.9	38 41.7	-51.3	6.0	80
81	30 52.1	-51.9	4.9	31 51.9	-51.9	5.0	32 51.6	-51.8	5.0	33 51.4	-51.8	5.1	34 51.2	-51.7	5.1	35 50.9	-51.6	5.2	36 50.7	-51.6	5.3	37 50.4	-51.5	5.3	81
82	30 00.2	-52.1	4.3	31 00.0	-52.0	4.4	31 59.8	-52.0	4.4	32 59.6	-51.9	4.5	33 59.5	-51.9	4.5	34 59.3	-51.9	4.6	35 59.1	-51.8	4.6	36 58.9	-51.8	4.7	82
83	29 08.1	-52.2	3.8	30 08.0	-52.2	3.8	31 07.8	-52.1	3.8	32 07.7	-52.1	3.9	33 07.6	-52.1	3.9	34 07.4	-52.0	4.0	35 07.3	-52.0	4.0	36 07.1	-51.9	4.1	83
84	28 15.9	-52.4	3.2	29 15.8	-52.3	3.2	30 15.7	-52.3	3.3	31 15.6	-52.3	3.3	32 15.5	-52.2	3.3	33 15.4	-52.2	3.4	34 15.3	-52.2	3.4	35 15.2	-52.1	3.4	84
85	27 23.5	-52.4	2.6	28 23.5	-52.5	2.7	29 23.4	-52.4	2.7	30 23.3	-52.4	2.7	31 23.3	-52.4	2.7	32 23.2	-52.3	2.8	33 23.1	-52.3	2.8	34 23.1	-52.3	2.8	85
86	26 31.1	-52.6	2.1	27 31.0	-52.6	2.1	28 31.0	-52.6	2.1	29 30.9	-52.5	2.2	30 30.9	-52.5	2.2	31 30.9	-52.6	2.2	32 30.8	-52.5	2.2	33 30.8	-52.5	2.3	86
87	25 38.5	-52.7	1.6	26 38.4	-52.7	1.6	27 38.4	-52.7	1.6	28 38.4	-52.7	1.6	29 38.4	-52.7	1.6	30 38.3	-52.6	1.6	31 38.3	-52.6	1.7	32 38.3	-52.6	1.7	87
88	24 45.8	-52.9	1.0	25 45.7	-52.8	1.0	26 45.7	-52.8	1.1	27 45.7	-52.8	1.1	28 45.7	-52.8	1.1	29 45.7	-52.8	1.1	30 45.7	-52.8	1.1	31 45.7	-52.8	1.1	88
89	23 52.9	-52.9	0.5	24 52.9	-52.9	0.5	25 52.9	-52.9	0.5	26 52.9	-52.9	0.5	27 52.9	-52.9	0.5	28 52.9	-52.9	0.5	29 52.9	-52.9	0.5	30 52.9	-52.9	0.5	89
90	23 00.0	-53.0	0.0	24 00.0	-53.0	0.0	25 00.0	-53.0	0.0	26 00.0	-53.0	0.0	27 00.0	-53.0	0.0	28 00.0	-53.0	0.0	29 00.0	-53.0	0.0	30 00.0	-53.0	0.0	90
	23°			24°			25°			26°			27°			28°			29°			30°			

28°, 332° L.H.A. LATITUDE SAME NAME AS DECLINATION

240

Dec.	23° Hc	23° d	23° Z	24° Hc	24° d	24° Z	25° Hc	25° d	25° Z	26° Hc	26° d	26° Z	27° Hc	27° d	27° Z	28° Hc	28° d	28° Z	29° Hc	29° d	29° Z	30° Hc	30° d	30° Z	Dec.
°	° ′	′	°	° ′	′	°	° ′	′	°	° ′	′	°	° ′	′	°	° ′	′	°	° ′	′	°	° ′	′	°	°
0	54 22.0	-40.7	126.3	53 46.0	-41.7	127.4	53 09.1	-42.6	128.5	52 31.3	-43.5	129.5	51 52.8	-44.5	130.5	51 13.4	-45.2	131.4	50 33.3	-46.0	132.4	49 52.6	-46.8	133.2	0
1	53 41.3	-41.4	127.6	53 04.3	-42.3	128.6	52 26.5	-43.3	129.6	51 47.8	-44.2	130.6	51 08.3	-45.0	131.6	50 28.2	-45.8	132.5	49 47.3	-46.5	133.4	49 05.8	-47.3	134.2	1
2	52 59.9	-42.1	128.8	52 22.0	-43.1	129.8	51 43.2	-44.0	130.8	51 03.6	-44.7	131.7	50 23.3	-45.5	132.6	49 42.4	-46.3	133.5	49 00.8	-47.1	134.3	48 18.5	-47.7	135.1	2
3	52 17.8	-42.8	130.0	51 38.9	-43.7	130.9	50 59.2	-44.5	131.9	50 18.9	-45.4	132.8	49 37.8	-46.1	133.6	48 56.1	-46.8	134.5	48 13.7	-47.4	135.3	47 30.8	-48.1	136.0	3
4	51 35.0	-43.4	131.1	50 55.2	-44.2	132.0	50 14.7	-45.0	132.9	49 33.5	-45.8	133.8	48 51.7	-46.5	134.6	48 09.3	-47.3	135.4	47 26.3	-47.9	136.2	46 42.7	-48.5	136.9	4
5	50 51.6	-44.0	132.2	50 11.0	-44.8	133.1	49 29.7	-45.6	133.9	48 47.7	-46.3	134.8	48 05.2	-47.0	135.6	47 22.0	-47.6	136.3	46 38.4	-48.3	137.1	45 54.2	-48.9	137.8	5
6	50 07.6	-44.6	133.3	49 26.2	-45.4	134.1	48 44.1	-46.1	134.9	48 01.4	-46.8	135.7	47 18.2	-47.5	136.5	46 34.4	-48.1	137.2	45 50.1	-48.7	137.9	45 05.3	-49.2	138.6	6
7	49 23.0	-45.1	134.3	48 40.8	-45.9	135.1	47 58.0	-46.6	135.9	47 14.6	-47.2	136.7	46 30.7	-47.8	137.4	45 46.3	-48.4	138.1	45 01.4	-49.0	138.8	44 16.1	-49.5	139.4	7
8	48 37.9	-45.7	135.3	47 54.9	-46.3	136.1	47 11.4	-47.0	136.8	46 27.4	-47.6	137.6	45 42.9	-48.2	138.3	44 57.9	-48.8	138.9	44 12.4	-49.3	139.6	43 26.6	-49.9	140.2	8
9	47 52.2	-46.1	136.3	47 08.6	-46.8	137.0	46 24.4	-47.4	137.7	45 39.8	-48.0	138.4	44 54.7	-48.6	139.1	44 09.1	-49.2	139.7	43 23.1	-49.7	140.4	42 36.7	-50.2	140.9	9
10	47 06.1	-46.6	137.2	46 21.8	-47.2	137.9	45 37.0	-47.8	138.6	44 51.8	-48.4	139.3	44 06.1	-49.0	139.9	43 19.9	-49.4	140.5	42 33.4	-49.9	141.1	41 46.5	-50.4	141.7	10
11	46 19.5	-47.0	138.1	45 34.6	-47.6	138.8	44 49.2	-48.2	139.5	44 03.4	-48.8	140.1	43 17.1	-49.2	140.7	42 30.5	-49.8	141.3	41 43.5	-50.3	141.9	40 56.1	-50.7	142.4	11
12	45 32.5	-47.4	139.0	44 47.0	-48.0	139.7	44 01.0	-48.5	140.3	43 14.6	-49.0	140.9	42 27.9	-49.6	141.5	41 40.7	-50.0	142.1	40 53.2	-50.5	142.6	40 05.4	-50.9	143.1	12
13	44 45.1	-47.8	139.9	43 59.0	-48.4	140.5	43 12.5	-48.9	141.1	42 25.6	-49.4	141.7	41 38.3	-49.9	142.3	40 50.7	-50.4	142.8	40 02.7	-50.7	143.3	39 14.5	-51.2	143.8	13
14	43 57.3	-48.2	140.7	43 10.6	-48.7	141.3	42 23.6	-49.2	141.9	41 36.2	-49.7	142.5	40 48.4	-50.1	143.0	40 00.3	-50.5	143.5	39 12.0	-51.1	144.0	38 23.3	-51.4	144.5	14
15	43 09.1	-48.5	141.6	42 21.9	-49.0	142.1	41 34.4	-49.5	142.7	40 46.5	-50.0	143.2	39 58.3	-50.4	143.7	39 09.8	-50.9	144.2	38 20.9	-51.2	144.7	37 31.9	-51.7	145.1	15
16	42 20.6	-48.8	142.4	41 32.9	-49.3	142.9	40 44.9	-49.8	143.4	39 56.5	-50.2	143.9	39 07.9	-50.7	144.4	38 18.9	-51.0	144.9	37 29.7	-51.4	145.3	36 40.2	-51.8	145.8	16
17	41 31.8	-49.2	143.2	40 43.6	-49.6	143.7	39 55.1	-50.1	144.2	39 06.3	-50.5	144.7	38 17.2	-50.9	145.1	37 27.9	-51.3	145.6	36 38.3	-51.7	146.0	35 48.4	-52.0	146.4	17
18	40 42.6	-49.4	143.9	39 54.0	-49.9	144.4	39 05.0	-50.3	144.9	38 15.8	-50.7	145.3	37 26.3	-51.1	145.8	36 36.6	-51.5	146.2	35 46.6	-51.8	146.6	34 56.4	-52.2	147.0	18
19	39 53.2	-49.7	144.7	39 04.1	-50.1	145.1	38 14.7	-50.5	145.6	37 25.1	-50.9	146.0	36 35.2	-51.3	146.4	35 45.1	-51.7	146.8	34 54.8	-52.0	147.2	34 04.2	-52.3	147.6	19
20	39 03.5	-50.0	145.4	38 14.0	-50.4	145.8	37 24.2	-50.8	146.3	36 34.2	-51.2	146.7	35 43.9	-51.5	147.1	34 53.4	-51.8	147.5	34 02.8	-52.2	147.8	33 11.9	-52.6	148.2	20
21	38 13.5	-50.2	146.1	37 23.6	-50.7	146.5	36 33.4	-51.0	146.9	35 43.0	-51.3	147.3	34 52.4	-51.7	147.7	34 01.6	-52.1	148.1	33 10.6	-52.4	148.4	32 19.3	-52.6	148.8	21
22	37 23.3	-50.5	146.8	36 32.9	-50.8	147.2	35 42.4	-51.2	147.6	34 51.7	-51.6	148.0	34 00.7	-51.9	148.3	33 09.5	-52.2	148.7	32 18.2	-52.5	149.0	31 26.7	-52.8	149.3	22
23	36 32.8	-50.7	147.5	35 42.1	-51.0	147.8	34 51.2	-51.4	148.2	34 00.1	-51.7	148.6	33 08.8	-52.1	148.9	32 17.3	-52.3	149.3	31 25.7	-52.7	149.6	30 33.9	-53.0	149.9	23
24	35 42.1	-50.9	148.1	34 51.1	-51.3	148.5	33 59.8	-51.6	148.8	33 08.4	-51.9	149.2	32 16.7	-52.2	149.5	31 25.0	-52.6	149.8	30 33.0	-52.8	150.1	29 40.9	-53.1	150.4	24
25	34 51.2	-51.1	148.8	33 59.8	-51.4	149.1	33 08.2	-51.7	149.5	32 16.5	-52.1	149.8	31 24.5	-52.4	150.1	30 32.4	-52.6	150.4	29 40.2	-53.0	150.7	28 47.8	-53.2	151.0	25
26	34 00.1	-51.3	149.4	33 08.4	-51.7	149.7	32 16.5	-52.0	150.1	31 24.4	-52.3	150.4	30 32.1	-52.5	150.7	29 39.8	-52.8	150.9	28 47.2	-53.0	151.2	27 54.6	-53.3	151.5	26
27	33 08.8	-51.5	150.0	32 16.7	-51.7	150.3	31 24.5	-52.1	150.7	30 32.1	-52.3	150.9	29 39.6	-52.6	151.2	28 47.0	-53.0	151.5	27 54.2	-53.2	151.7	27 01.3	-53.5	152.0	27
28	32 17.3	-51.6	150.6	31 25.0	-52.0	150.9	30 32.4	-52.2	151.2	29 39.8	-52.6	151.5	28 47.0	-52.8	151.8	27 54.0	-53.0	152.0	27 01.0	-53.3	152.3	26 07.8	-53.5	152.5	28
29	31 25.7	-51.8	151.2	30 33.0	-52.1	151.5	29 40.2	-52.4	151.8	28 47.2	-52.6	152.1	27 54.2	-52.9	152.3	27 01.0	-53.2	152.6	26 07.7	-53.4	152.8	25 14.3	-53.7	153.0	29
30	30 33.9	-52.0	151.8	29 40.9	-52.3	152.1	28 47.8	-52.5	152.4	27 54.6	-52.8	152.6	27 01.3	-53.1	152.8	26 07.8	-53.3	153.1	25 14.3	-53.5	153.3	24 20.6	-53.7	153.5	30
31	29 41.9	-52.1	152.4	28 48.6	-52.3	152.7	27 55.3	-52.7	152.9	27 01.8	-52.9	153.1	26 08.2	-53.1	153.4	25 14.5	-53.3	153.6	24 20.8	-53.6	153.8	23 26.9	-53.8	154.0	31
32	28 49.8	-52.3	153.0	27 56.3	-52.6	153.2	27 02.6	-52.7	153.4	26 08.9	-53.0	153.7	25 15.1	-53.3	153.9	24 21.2	-53.5	154.1	23 27.2	-53.7	154.3	22 33.1	-54.0	154.5	32
33	27 57.5	-52.4	153.5	27 03.7	-52.6	153.8	26 09.9	-52.9	154.0	25 15.9	-53.1	154.2	24 21.8	-53.3	154.4	23 27.7	-53.6	154.6	22 33.5	-53.8	154.8	21 39.1	-54.0	154.9	33
34	27 05.1	-52.5	154.1	26 11.1	-52.8	154.3	25 17.0	-53.0	154.5	24 22.8	-53.2	154.7	23 28.5	-53.5	154.9	22 34.1	-53.6	155.1	21 39.7	-53.9	155.2	20 45.1	-54.0	155.4	34
35	26 12.6	-52.7	154.6	25 18.3	-52.8	154.8	24 24.0	-53.1	155.0	23 29.6	-53.4	155.2	22 35.0	-53.5	155.4	21 40.5	-53.8	155.6	20 45.8	-53.9	155.7	19 51.1	-54.2	155.9	35
36	25 19.9	-52.7	155.2	24 25.5	-53.0	155.3	23 30.9	-53.2	155.5	22 36.2	-53.4	155.7	21 41.5	-53.6	155.9	20 46.7	-53.8	156.0	19 51.9	-54.1	156.2	18 56.9	-54.2	156.3	36
37	24 27.2	-52.9	155.7	23 32.5	-53.1	155.9	22 37.7	-53.3	156.0	21 42.8	-53.5	156.2	20 47.9	-53.7	156.4	19 52.9	-53.9	156.5	18 57.8	-54.0	156.6	18 02.7	-54.2	156.8	37
38	23 34.3	-52.9	156.2	22 39.4	-53.2	156.4	21 44.4	-53.4	156.5	20 49.3	-53.6	156.7	19 54.2	-53.8	156.8	18 59.0	-54.0	157.0	18 03.8	-54.2	157.1	17 08.5	-54.4	157.2	38
39	22 41.4	-53.1	156.7	21 46.2	-53.2	156.9	20 51.0	-53.4	157.0	19 55.7	-53.6	157.2	19 00.4	-53.8	157.3	18 05.0	-54.0	157.4	17 09.6	-54.2	157.6	16 14.1	-54.3	157.7	39
40	21 48.3	-53.1	157.2	20 53.0	-53.4	157.4	19 57.6	-53.6	157.5	19 02.1	-53.7	157.6	18 06.6	-53.9	157.8	17 11.0	-54.1	157.9	16 15.4	-54.3	158.0	15 19.8	-54.5	158.1	40
41	20 55.2	-53.3	157.7	19 59.6	-53.4	157.8	19 04.0	-53.6	158.0	18 08.4	-53.8	158.1	17 12.7	-54.0	158.2	16 16.9	-54.1	158.3	15 21.1	-54.3	158.4	14 25.3	-54.5	158.5	41
42	20 01.9	-53.3	158.2	19 06.2	-53.5	158.3	18 10.4	-53.7	158.5	17 14.6	-53.9	158.6	16 18.7	-54.0	158.7	15 22.8	-54.2	158.8	14 26.8	-54.3	158.9	13 30.8	-54.5	159.0	42
43	19 08.6	-53.4	158.7	18 12.7	-53.6	158.8	17 16.7	-53.7	158.9	16 20.7	-53.9	159.0	15 24.7	-54.1	159.1	14 28.6	-54.3	159.2	13 32.5	-54.4	159.3	12 36.3	-54.5	159.4	43
44	18 15.2	-53.4	159.2	17 19.1	-53.6	159.3	16 23.0	-53.8	159.4	15 26.8	-54.0	159.5	14 30.6	-54.1	159.6	13 34.3	-54.3	159.7	12 38.1	-54.5	159.8	11 41.8	-54.6	159.8	44
45	17 21.8	-53.6	159.6	16 25.5	-53.7	159.8	15 29.2	-53.9	159.9	14 32.8	-54.0	159.9	13 36.5	-54.2	160.0	12 40.0	-54.3	160.1	11 43.6	-54.5	160.2	10 47.2	-54.7	160.2	45
46	16 28.2	-53.6	160.1	15 31.8	-53.8	160.2	14 35.3	-53.9	160.3	13 38.8	-54.1	160.4	12 42.3	-54.3	160.5	11 45.7	-54.4	160.5	10 49.1	-54.5	160.6	9 52.5	-54.7	160.7	46
47	15 34.6	-53.6	160.6	14 38.0	-53.8	160.7	13 41.4	-54.0	160.8	12 44.7	-54.1	160.8	11 48.0	-54.2	160.9	10 51.3	-54.4	161.0	9 54.6	-54.6	161.0	8 57.8	-54.6	161.1	47
48	14 41.0	-53.7	161.1	13 44.2	-53.8	161.1	12 47.4	-54.0	161.2	11 50.6	-54.1	161.3	10 53.8	-54.3	161.3	9 56.9	-54.4	161.4	9 00.0	-54.5	161.5	8 03.2	-54.8	161.5	48
49	13 47.3	-53.8	161.5	12 50.4	-53.9	161.6	11 53.4	-54.0	161.7	10 56.5	-54.2	161.7	9 59.5	-54.4	161.8	9 02.5	-54.5	161.8	8 05.5	-54.6	161.9	7 08.4	-54.7	161.9	49
50	12 53.5	-53.8	162.0	11 56.5	-54.0	162.0	10 59.4	-54.1	162.1	10 02.3	-54.3	162.2	9 05.1	-54.3	162.2	8 08.0	-54.5	162.3	7 10.9	-54.7	162.3	6 13.7	-54.8	162.3	50
51	11 59.7	-53.8	162.4	11 02.5	-54.0	162.5	10 05.3	-54.1	162.5	9 08.0	-54.2	162.6	8 10.8	-54.4	162.6	7 13.5	-54.5	162.7	6 16.2	-54.6	162.7	5 18.9	-54.7	162.7	51
52	11 05.9	-53.9	162.9	10 08.5	-54.0	162.9	9 11.2	-54.2	163.0	8 13.8	-54.3	163.0	7 16.4	-54.4	163.1	6 19.0	-54.6	163.1	5 21.6	-54.7	163.1	4 24.2	-54.8	163.1	52
53	10 12.0	-53.9	163.3	9 14.5	-54.1	163.4	8 17.0	-54.2	163.4	7 19.5	-54.3	163.4	6 22.0	-54.5	163.5	5 24.4	-54.5	163.5	4 26.9	-54.7	163.5	3 29.4	-54.8	163.6	53
54	9 18.1	-54.0	163.8	8 20.4	-54.0	163.8	7 22.8	-54.2	163.8	6 25.2	-54.4	163.9	5 27.5	-54.4	163.9	4 29.9	-54.6	163.9	3 32.2	-54.7	164.0	2 34.6	-54.8	164.0	54
55	8 24.1	-54.0	164.2	7 26.4	-54.2	164.2	6 28.6	-54.2	164.3	5 30.8	-54.3	164.3	4 33.1	-54.5	164.3	3 35.3	-54.6	164.3	2 37.5	-54.7	164.4	1 39.8	-54.9	164.4	55
56	7 30.1	-54.0	164.6	6 32.2	-54.1	164.7	5 34.4	-54.3	164.7	4 36.5	-54.4	164.7	3 38.6	-54.5	164.7	2 40.7	-54.6	164.8	1 42.8	-54.7	164.8	0 44.9	-54.8	164.8	56
57	6 36.1	-54.0	165.1	5 38.1	-54.1	165.1	4 40.1	-54.2	165.1	3 42.1	-54.3	165.2	2 44.1	-54.5	165.2	1 46.1	-54.6	165.2	0 48.1	-54.7	165.2	0 09.9	+54.8	14.8	57
58	5 42.1	-54.1	165.5	4 44.0	-54.2	165.5	3 45.9	-54.3	165.6	2 47.8	-54.4	165.6	1 49.6	-54.5	165.6	0 51.5	-54.6	165.6	0 06.6	+54.7	14.4	1 04.7	+54.8	14.4	58
59	4 48.0	-54.1	166.0	3 49.8	-54.2	166.0	2 51.6	-54.3	166.0	1 53.4	-54.4	166.0	0 55.1	-54.5	166.0	0 03.1	+54.6	14.0	1 01.3	+54.7	14.0	1 59.5	+54.8	14.0	59
60	3 53.9	-54.1	166.4	2 55.6	-54.2	166.4	1 57.3	-54.3	166.4	0 59.0	-54.4	166.4	0 00.6	-54.4	166.4	0 57.7	+54.6	13.6	1 56.0	+54.7	13.6	2 54.3	+54.8	13.6	60
61	2 59.8	-54.0	166.8	2 01.4	-54.2	166.8	1 03.0	-54.3	166.8	0 04.6	-54.4	166.8	0 53.8	+54.5	13.2	1 52.3	+54.6	13.2	2 50.7	+54.7	13.2	3 49.1	+54.8	13.2	61
62	2 05.8	-54.2	167.3	1 07.2	-54.2	167.3	0 08.7	-54.3	167.3	0 49.8	+54.4	12.7	1 48.3	+54.5	12.7	2 46.9	+54.6	12.7	3 45.4	+54.7	12.8	4 43.9	+54.8	12.8	62
63	1 11.6	-54.1	167.7	0 13.0	-54.2	167.7	0 45.6	+54.3	12.3	1 44.2	+54.4	12.3	2 42.8	+54.5	12.3	3 41.5	+54.5	12.3	4 40.1	+54.6	12.3	5 38.7	+54.7	12.4	63
64	0 17.5	-54.1	168.1	0 41.2	+54.2	11.9	1 39.9	+54.3	11.9	2 38.6	+54.4	11.9	3 37.3	+54.5	11.9	4 36.0	+54.6	11.9	5 34.7	+54.7	11.9	6 33.4	+54.8	12.0	64
65	0 36.6	+54.1	11.4	1 35.4	+54.2	11.4	2 34.2	+54.3	11.5	3 33.0	+54.4	11.5	4 31.8	+54.4	11.5	5 30.6	+54.5	11.5	6 29.4	+54.6	11.5	7 28.2	+54.7	11.5	65
66	1 30.7	+54.1	11.0	2 29.6	+54.2	11.0	3 28.5	+54.2	11.0	4 27.4	+54.3	11.0	5 26.2	+54.5	11.1	6 25.1	+54.5	11.1	7 24.0	+54.6	11.1	8 22.9	+54.7	11.1	66
67	2 24.8	+54.1	10.6	3 23.8	+54.1	10.6	4 22.7	+54.3	10.6	5 21.7	+54.3	10.6	6 20.7	+54.4	10.6	7 19.6	+54.5	10.7	8 18.6	+54.6	10.7	9 17.6	+54.6	10.7	67
68	3 18.9	+54.0	10.1	4 17.9	+54.2	10.2	5 17.0	+54.2	10.2	6 16.0	+54.4	10.2	7 15.1	+54.4	10.2	8 14.1	+54.5	10.2	9 13.2	+54.5	10.3	10 12.2	+54.6	10.3	68
69	4 12.9	+54.1	9.7	5 12.1	+54.1	9.7	6 11.2	+54.2	9.7	7 10.4	+54.2	9.8	8 09.5	+54.3	9.8	9 08.6	+54.4	9.8	10 07.7	+54.5	9.8	11 06.8	+54.6	9.9	69
70	5 07.0	+54.1	9.3	6 06.2	+54.1	9.3	7 05.4	+54.2	9.3	8 04.6	+54.3	9.3	9 03.8	+54.4	9.4	10 03.0	+54.5	9.4	11 02.2	+54.5	9.4	12 01.4	+54.6	9.4	70
71	6 01.1	+54.0	8.8	7 00.3	+54.1	8.9	7 59.6	+54.2	8.9	8 58.9	+54.2	8.9	9 58.2	+54.3	8.9	10 57.5	+54.3	9.0	11 56.7	+54.5	9.0	12 56.0	+54.5	9.0	71
72	6 55.1	+54.0	8.4	7 54.4	+54.1	8.4	8 53.8	+54.1	8.4	9 53.1	+54.2	8.5	10 52.5	+54.3	8.5	11 51.8	+54.4	8.5	12 51.2	+54.4	8.6	13 50.5	+54.5	8.6	72
73	7 49.1	+54.0	8.0	8 48.5	+54.1	8.0	9 47.9	+54.1	8.0	10 47.3	+54.2	8.0	11 46.8	+54.2	8.1	12 46.2	+54.2	8.1	13 45.6	+54.3	8.1	14 45.0	+54.4	8.2	73
74	8 43.1	+53.9	7.5	9 42.6	+54.0	7.5	10 42.0	+54.1	7.6	11 41.5	+54.1	7.6	12 41.0	+54.2	7.6	13 40.4	+54.3	7.7	14 39.9	+54.3	7.7	15 39.4	+54.3	7.7	74
75	9 37.0	+53.9	7.1	10 36.6	+53.9	7.1	11 36.1	+54.0	7.1	12 35.6	+54.1	7.2	13 35.2	+54.1	7.2	14 34.7	+54.2	7.2	15 34.2	+54.3	7.2	16 33.7	+54.3	7.3	75
76	10 30.9	+53.9	6.6	11 30.5	+54.0	6.7	12 30.1	+54.0	6.7	13 29.7	+54.0	6.7	14 29.3	+54.1	6.7	15 28.9	+54.1	6.8	16 28.5	+54.2	6.8	17 28.0	+54.3	6.8	76
77	11 24.8	+53.8	6.2	12 24.5	+53.8	6.2	13 24.1	+53.9	6.2	14 23.7	+54.0	6.3	15 23.4	+54.0	6.3	16 23.0	+54.1	6.3	17 22.7	+54.1	6.4	18 22.3	+54.2	6.4	77
78	12 18.6	+53.8	5.7	13 18.3	+53.9	5.8	14 18.0	+53.9	5.8	15 17.7	+54.0	5.8	16 17.4	+54.0	5.8	17 17.1	+54.0	5.9	18 16.8	+54.1	5.9	19 16.5	+54.1	5.9	78
79	13 12.4	+53.8	5.3	14 12.2	+53.8	5.3	15 11.9	+53.8	5.3	16 11.7	+53.8	5.4	17 11.4	+53.9	5.4	18 11.1	+54.0	5.4	19 10.9	+54.0	5.4	20 10.6	+54.0	5.5	79
80	14 06.2	+53.7	4.8	15 06.0	+53.7	4.8	16 05.7	+53.8	4.9	17 05.5	+53.8	4.9	18 05.3	+53.8	4.9	19 05.1	+53.9	4.9	20 04.9	+53.9	5.0	21 04.6	+54.0	5.0	80
81	14 59.9	+53.6	4.4	15 59.7	+53.6	4.4	16 59.5	+53.7	4.4	17 59.3	+53.8	4.4	18 59.1	+53.8	4.5	19 59.0	+53.8	4.5	20 58.8	+53.8	4.5	21 58.6	+53.9	4.5	81
82	15 53.5	+53.6	3.9	16 53.3	+53.6	3.9	17 53.2	+53.6	3.9	18 53.1	+53.6	4.0	19 52.9	+53.7	4.0	20 52.8	+53.7	4.0	21 52.6	+53.8	4.0	22 52.5	+53.8	4.1	82
83	16 47.1	+53.5	3.4	17 46.9	+53.6	3.4	18 46.8	+53.6	3.5	19 46.7	+53.6	3.5	20 46.6	+53.6	3.5	21 46.5	+53.7	3.5	22 46.4	+53.7	3.6	23 46.3	+53.7	3.6	83
84	17 40.6	+53.4	3.0	18 40.5	+53.4	3.0	19 40.4	+53.5	3.0	20 40.3	+53.5	3.0	21 40.2	+53.6	3.0	22 40.2	+53.5	3.0	23 40.1	+53.6	3.1	24 40.0	+53.6	3.1	84
85	18 34.0	+53.4	2.5	19 33.9	+53.4	2.5	20 33.9	+53.4	2.5	21 33.8	+53.5	2.5	22 33.8	+53.4	2.5	23 33.7	+53.5	2.6	24 33.7	+53.4	2.6	25 33.6	+53.5	2.6	85
86	19 27.4	+53.3	2.0	20 27.3	+53.3	2.0	21 27.3	+53.3	2.0	22 27.3	+53.3	2.0	23 27.2	+53.4	2.0	24 27.2	+53.3	2.1	25 27.1	+53.4	2.1	26 27.1	+53.4	2.1	86
87	20 20.7	+53.2	1.5	21 20.6	+53.2	1.5	22 20.6	+53.2	1.5	23 20.6	+53.2	1.5	24 20.6	+53.2	1.5	25 20.5	+53.3	1.6	26 20.5	+53.3	1.6	27 20.5	+53.3	1.6	87
88	21 13.9	+53.1	1.0	22 13.8	+53.2	1.0	23 13.8	+53.2	1.0	24 13.8	+53.2	1.0	25 13.8	+53.2	1.0	26 13.8	+53.2	1.0	27 13.8	+53.2	1.1	28 13.8	+53.2	1.1	88
89	22 07.0	+53.0	0.5	23 07.0	+52.9	0.5	24 07.0	+53.0	0.5	25 07.0	+53.0	0.5	26 07.0	+53.0	0.5	27 07.0	+53.0	0.5	28 07.0	+53.0	0.5	29 07.0	+53.0	0.5	89
90	23 00.0	+52.9	0.0	24 00.0	+52.9	0.0	25 00.0	+52.9	0.0	26 00.0	+52.9	0.0	27 00.0	+52.9	0.0	28 00.0	+52.9	0.0	29 00.0	+52.9	0.0	30 00.0	+52.9	0.0	90
	23°			24°			25°			26°			27°			28°			29°			30°			

S. Lat. {L.H.A. greater than 180° ....Zn=180°−Z; L.H.A. less than 180°...........Zn=180°+Z

29°, 331° L.H.A. LATITUDE SAME NAME AS DECLINATION N. Lat. {L.H.A. greater than 180° .....Zn=Z / L.H.A. less than 180°............Zn=360°−Z}

Dec.	23° Hc	23° d	23° Z	24° Hc	24° d	24° Z	25° Hc	25° d	25° Z	26° Hc	26° d	26° Z	Dec.
°	° ′	′	°	° ′	′	°	° ′	′	°	° ′	′	°	°
0	53 37.1	+39.2	125.2	53 02.1	+40.2	126.3	52 26.2	+41.2	127.3	51 49.4	+42.2	128.3	0
1	54 16.3	+38.2	123.9	53 42.3	+39.4	125.0	53 07.4	+40.5	126.1	52 31.6	+41.5	127.2	1
2	54 54.5	+37.4	122.6	54 21.7	+38.6	123.7	53 47.9	+39.7	124.9	53 13.1	+40.8	126.0	2
3	55 31.9	+36.4	121.2	55 00.3	+37.6	122.4	54 27.6	+38.8	123.6	53 53.9	+40.0	124.7	3
4	56 08.3	+35.4	119.8	55 37.9	+36.8	121.0	55 06.4	+38.0	122.3	54 33.9	+39.1	123.5	4
5	56 43.7	+34.4	118.3	56 14.7	+35.7	119.6	55 44.4	+37.0	120.9	55 13.0	+38.3	122.2	5
6	57 18.1	+33.2	116.8	56 50.4	+34.7	118.2	56 21.4	+36.1	119.5	55 51.3	+37.3	120.8	6
7	57 51.3	+32.1	115.3	57 25.1	+33.5	116.7	56 57.5	+35.0	118.1	56 28.6	+36.4	119.4	7
8	58 23.4	+30.8	113.7	57 58.6	+32.4	115.1	57 32.5	+33.9	116.6	57 05.0	+35.3	117.9	8
9	58 54.2	+29.6	112.0	58 31.0	+31.2	113.5	58 06.4	+32.7	115.0	57 40.3	+34.2	116.4	9
10	59 23.8	+28.2	110.3	59 02.2	+29.9	111.9	58 39.1	+31.5	113.4	58 14.5	+33.1	114.9	10
11	59 52.0	+26.7	108.6	59 32.1	+28.5	110.2	59 10.6	+30.2	111.8	58 47.6	+31.8	113.3	11
12	60 18.7	+25.3	106.8	60 00.6	+27.1	108.4	59 40.8	+28.9	110.1	59 19.4	+30.6	111.6	12
13	60 44.0	+23.7	104.9	60 27.7	+25.6	106.6	60 09.7	+27.4	108.3	59 50.0	+29.2	109.9	13
14	61 07.7	+22.1	103.0	60 53.3	+24.0	104.8	60 37.1	+25.9	106.5	60 19.2	+27.8	108.2	14
15	61 29.8	+20.4	101.1	61 17.3	+22.4	102.9	61 03.0	+24.4	104.7	60 47.0	+26.3	106.4	15
16	61 50.2	+18.6	99.1	61 39.7	+20.8	100.9	61 27.4	+22.8	102.8	61 13.3	+24.7	104.5	16
17	62 08.8	+16.9	97.1	62 00.5	+18.9	99.0	61 50.2	+21.0	100.8	61 38.0	+23.1	102.6	17
18	62 25.7	+15.0	95.0	62 19.4	+17.2	96.9	62 11.2	+19.3	98.8	62 01.1	+21.4	100.7	18
19	62 40.7	+13.0	92.9	62 36.6	+15.3	94.9	62 30.5	+17.5	96.8	62 22.5	+19.6	98.7	19
20	62 53.7	+11.1	90.8	62 51.9	+13.3	92.7	62 48.0	+15.6	94.7	62 42.1	+17.8	96.6	20
21	63 04.8	+9.1•	88.6	63 05.2	+11.4	90.6	63 03.6	+13.6	92.6	62 59.9	+15.9	94.5	21
22	63 13.9	+7.1•	86.4	63 16.6	+9.4•	88.4	63 17.2	+11.7•	90.4	63 15.8	+13.9	92.4	22
23	63 21.0	+5.0•	84.2	63 26.0	+7.3•	86.2	63 28.9	+9.6•	88.2	63 29.7	+12.0•	90.2	23
24	63 26.0	+2.9•	82.0	63 33.3	+5.2•	84.0	63 38.5	+7.6•	86.0	63 41.7	+9.9•	88.0	24
25	63 28.9	+0.8•	79.8	63 38.5	+3.2•	81.8	63 46.1	+5.5•	83.8	63 51.6	+7.8•	85.8	25
26	63 29.7	-1.3•	77.5	63 41.7	+1.0•	79.5	63 51.6	+3.3•	81.5	63 59.4	+5.7•	83.5	26
27	63 28.4	-3.4•	75.3	63 42.7	-1.1•	77.2	63 54.9	+1.2•	79.2	64 05.1	+3.5•	81.3	27
28	63 25.0	-5.4•	73.1	63 41.6	-3.3•	75.0	63 56.1	-0.9•	77.0	64 08.6	+1.4•	79.0	28
29	63 19.6	-7.5•	70.8	63 38.3	-5.3•	72.7	63 55.2	-3.1•	74.7	64 10.0	-0.7•	76.7	29
30	63 12.1	-9.6•	68.6	63 33.0	-7.4•	70.5	63 52.1	-5.2•	72.4	64 09.3	-3.0•	74.4	30
31	63 02.5	-11.5	66.4	63 25.6	-9.4•	68.3	63 46.9	-7.3•	70.2	64 06.3	-5.0•	72.1	31
32	62 51.0	-13.5	64.3	63 16.2	-11.5•	66.1	63 39.6	-9.3•	67.9	64 01.3	-7.2•	69.8	32
33	62 37.5	-15.4	62.2	63 04.7	-13.4	63.9	63 30.3	-11.5•	65.7	63 54.1	-9.3•	67.6	33
34	62 22.1	-17.3	60.1	62 51.3	-15.4	61.8	63 18.8	-13.4	63.5	63 44.8	-11.4•	65.3	34
35	62 04.8	-19.0	58.0	62 35.9	-17.2	59.6	63 05.4	-15.3	61.3	63 33.4	-13.4	63.1	35
36	61 45.8	-20.8	56.0	62 18.7	-19.1	57.6	62 50.1	-17.2	59.2	63 20.0	-15.3	60.9	36
37	61 25.0	-22.5	54.0	61 59.6	-20.8	55.5	62 32.9	-19.1	57.1	63 04.7	-17.2	58.8	37
38	61 02.5	-24.0	52.1	61 38.8	-22.5	53.6	62 13.8	-20.8	55.1	62 47.5	-19.1	56.7	38
39	60 38.5	-25.6	50.2	61 16.3	-24.1	51.6	61 53.0	-22.6	53.1	62 28.4	-20.9	54.6	39
40	60 12.9	-27.1	48.4	60 52.2	-25.7	49.7	61 30.4	-24.1	51.1	62 07.5	-22.6	52.6	40
41	59 45.8	-28.5	46.6	60 26.5	-27.1	47.9	61 06.3	-25.8	49.2	61 44.9	-24.3	50.6	41
42	59 17.3	-29.8	44.9	59 59.4	-28.6	46.1	60 40.5	-27.2	47.4	61 20.6	-25.8	48.7	42
43	58 47.5	-31.1	43.2	59 30.8	-29.9	44.3	60 13.3	-28.7	45.6	60 54.8	-27.3	46.8	43
44	58 16.4	-32.4	41.5	59 00.9	-31.2	42.6	59 44.6	-30.0	43.8	60 27.5	-28.8	45.0	44
45	57 44.0	-33.5	40.0	58 29.7	-32.5	41.0	59 14.6	-31.4	42.1	59 58.7	-30.2	43.2	45
46	57 10.5	-34.6	38.4	57 57.2	-33.6	39.4	58 43.2	-32.5	40.4	59 28.5	-31.4	41.5	46
47	56 35.9	-35.6	36.9	57 23.6	-34.7	37.8	58 10.7	-33.8	38.8	58 57.1	-32.8	39.9	47
48	56 00.3	-36.7	35.5	56 48.9	-35.8	36.3	57 36.9	-34.8	37.3	58 24.3	-33.8	38.3	48
49	55 23.6	-37.5	34.1	56 13.1	-36.8	34.9	57 02.1	-36.0	35.8	57 50.5	-35.1	36.7	49
50	54 46.1	-38.5	32.7	55 36.3	-37.7	33.5	56 26.1	-36.9	34.3	57 15.4	-36.0	35.2	50
51	54 07.6	-39.3	31.4	54 58.6	-38.6	32.1	55 49.2	-37.8	32.9	56 39.4	-37.1	33.7	51
52	53 28.3	-40.1	30.1	54 20.0	-39.4	30.8	55 11.4	-38.8	31.5	56 02.3	-38.0	32.3	52
53	52 48.2	-40.8	28.9	53 40.6	-40.2	29.5	54 32.6	-39.5	30.2	55 24.3	-38.9	30.9	53
54	52 07.4	-41.6	27.7	53 00.4	-41.0	28.3	53 53.1	-40.4	28.9	54 45.4	-39.7	29.6	54
55	51 25.8	-42.2	26.5	52 19.4	-41.7	27.1	53 12.7	-41.2	27.7	54 05.7	-40.6	28.3	55
56	50 43.6	-42.9	25.4	51 37.7	-42.4	25.9	52 31.5	-41.8	26.5	53 25.1	-41.3	27.1	56
57	50 00.7	-43.4	24.3	50 55.3	-43.0	24.8	51 49.7	-42.5	25.3	52 43.8	-42.0	25.9	57
58	49 17.3	-44.1	23.2	50 12.3	-43.6	23.7	51 07.2	-43.2	24.2	52 01.8	-42.7	24.7	58
59	48 33.2	-44.6	22.2	49 28.7	-44.2	22.6	50 24.0	-43.8	23.1	51 19.1	-43.3	23.5	59
60	47 48.6	-45.1	21.2	48 44.5	-44.7	21.6	49 40.2	-44.3	22.0	50 35.8	-44.0	22.4	60
61	47 03.5	-45.5	20.2	47 59.8	-45.2	20.6	48 55.9	-44.9	21.0	49 51.8	-44.4	21.4	61
62	46 18.0	-46.0	19.2	47 14.6	-45.7	19.6	48 11.0	-45.3	20.0	49 07.4	-45.1	20.4	62
63	45 32.0	-46.5	18.3	46 28.9	-46.2	18.6	47 25.7	-45.9	19.0	48 22.3	-45.5	19.3	63
64	44 45.5	-46.9	17.4	45 42.7	-46.6	17.7	46 39.8	-46.3	18.0	47 36.8	-46.0	18.4	64
65	43 58.6	-47.2	16.5	44 56.1	-47.0	16.8	45 53.5	-46.8	17.1	46 50.8	-46.5	17.4	65
66	43 11.4	-47.7	15.7	44 09.1	-47.4	16.0	45 06.7	-47.1	16.2	46 04.3	-46.9	16.5	66
67	42 23.7	-47.9	14.9	43 21.7	-47.8	15.1	44 19.6	-47.6	15.4	45 17.4	-47.3	15.6	67
68	41 35.8	-48.4	14.1	42 33.9	-48.1	14.3	43 32.0	-47.9	14.5	44 30.1	-47.7	14.8	68
69	40 47.4	-48.6	13.3	41 45.8	-48.4	13.5	42 44.1	-48.2	13.7	43 42.4	-48.0	13.9	69
70	39 58.8	-48.9	12.5	40 57.4	-48.8	12.7	41 55.9	-48.6	12.9	42 54.4	-48.4	13.1	70
71	39 09.9	-49.2	11.7	40 08.6	-49.0	11.9	41 07.3	-48.9	12.1	42 06.0	-48.8	12.3	71
72	38 20.7	-49.5	11.0	39 19.6	-49.4	11.2	40 18.4	-49.2	11.3	41 17.2	-49.0	11.5	72
73	37 31.2	-49.7	10.3	38 30.2	-49.6	10.4	39 29.2	-49.4	10.6	40 28.2	-49.3	10.7	73
74	36 41.5	-50.0	9.6	37 40.6	-49.8	9.7	38 39.8	-49.8	9.9	39 38.9	-49.6	10.0	74
75	35 51.5	-50.2	8.9	36 50.8	-50.1	9.0	37 50.0	-49.9	9.1	38 49.3	-49.9	9.3	75
76	35 01.3	-50.4	8.2	36 00.7	-50.3	8.3	37 00.1	-50.3	8.4	37 59.4	-50.1	8.6	76
77	34 10.9	-50.6	7.6	35 10.4	-50.5	7.7	36 09.8	-50.4	7.8	37 09.3	-50.4	7.9	77
78	33 20.3	-50.8	6.9	34 19.9	-50.8	7.0	35 19.4	-50.7	7.1	36 18.9	-50.5	7.2	78
79	32 29.5	-51.0	6.3	33 29.1	-50.9	6.4	34 28.7	-50.8	6.4	35 28.4	-50.8	6.5	79
80	31 38.5	-51.2	5.7	32 38.2	-51.1	5.7	33 37.9	-51.1	5.8	34 37.6	-51.0	5.9	80
81	30 47.3	-51.4	5.1	31 47.1	-51.3	5.1	32 46.8	-51.2	5.2	33 46.6	-51.2	5.2	81
82	29 55.9	-51.5	4.5	30 55.8	-51.5	4.5	31 55.6	-51.5	4.6	32 55.4	-51.4	4.6	82
83	29 04.4	-51.6	3.9	30 04.3	-51.6	3.9	31 04.1	-51.5	4.0	32 04.0	-51.5	4.0	83
84	28 12.8	-51.8	3.3	29 12.7	-51.8	3.3	30 12.6	-51.8	3.4	31 12.5	-51.8	3.4	84
85	27 21.0	-52.0	2.7	28 20.9	-51.9	2.8	29 20.8	-51.9	2.8	30 20.7	-51.8	2.8	85
86	26 29.0	-52.1	2.2	27 29.0	-52.1	2.2	28 28.9	-52.0	2.2	29 28.9	-52.0	2.2	86
87	25 36.9	-52.2	1.6	26 36.9	-52.2	1.6	27 36.9	-52.2	1.6	28 36.9	-52.2	1.7	87
88	24 44.7	-52.3	1.1	25 44.7	-52.3	1.1	26 44.7	-52.3	1.1	27 44.7	-52.3	1.1	88
89	23 52.4	-52.4	0.5	24 52.4	-52.4	0.5	25 52.4	-52.4	0.5	26 52.4	-52.4	0.5	89
90	23 00.0	-52.5	0.0	24 00.0	-52.5	0.0	25 00.0	-52.5	0.0	26 00.0	-52.5	0.0	90
	23°			24°			25°			26°			

Dec.	27° Hc	27° d	27° Z	28° Hc	28° d	28° Z	29° Hc	29° d	29° Z	30° Hc	30° d	30° Z	Dec.
°	° ′	′	°	° ′	′	°	° ′	′	°	° ′	′	°	°
0	51 11.7	+43.2	129.3	50 33.3	+44.1	130.3	49 54.2	+44.9	131.2	49 14.4	+45.6	132.1	0
1	51 54.9	+42.5	128.2	51 17.4	+43.4	129.2	50 39.1	+44.3	130.1	50 00.0	+45.2	131.1	1
2	52 37.4	+41.8	127.0	52 00.8	+42.8	128.1	51 23.4	+43.7	129.1	50 45.2	+44.6	130.0	2
3	53 19.2	+41.1	125.9	52 43.6	+42.1	126.9	52 07.1	+43.1	128.0	51 29.8	+44.0	129.0	3
4	54 00.3	+40.3	124.6	53 25.7	+41.4	125.7	52 50.2	+42.4	126.8	52 13.8	+43.4	127.9	4
5	54 40.6	+39.4	123.4	54 07.1	+40.5	124.5	53 32.6	+41.6	125.6	52 57.2	+42.6	126.7	5
6	55 20.0	+38.6	122.0	54 47.6	+39.8	123.2	54 14.2	+40.9	124.4	53 39.8	+42.0	125.5	6
7	55 58.6	+37.7	120.7	55 27.4	+38.9	121.9	54 55.1	+40.1	123.1	54 21.8	+41.2	124.3	7
8	56 36.3	+36.7	119.3	56 06.3	+38.0	120.6	55 35.2	+39.3	121.8	55 03.0	+40.4	123.1	8
9	57 13.0	+35.6	117.8	56 44.3	+37.0	119.2	56 14.5	+38.3	120.5	55 43.4	+39.6	121.8	9
10	57 48.6	+34.6	116.3	57 21.3	+36.0	117.7	56 52.8	+37.3	119.1	56 23.0	+38.6	120.4	10
11	58 23.2	+33.4	114.8	57 57.3	+34.9	116.2	57 30.1	+36.4	117.7	57 01.6	+37.7	119.0	11
12	58 56.6	+32.1	113.2	58 32.2	+33.8	114.7	58 06.5	+35.2	116.2	57 39.3	+36.7	117.6	12
13	59 28.7	+30.9	111.5	59 06.0	+32.5	113.1	58 41.7	+34.1	114.6	58 16.0	+35.6	116.1	13
14	59 59.6	+29.6	109.8	59 38.5	+31.2	111.4	59 15.8	+32.9	113.0	58 51.6	+34.4	114.5	14
15	60 29.2	+28.1	108.1	60 09.7	+29.9	109.7	59 48.7	+31.6	111.4	59 26.0	+33.3	112.9	15
16	60 57.3	+26.6	106.3	60 39.6	+28.5	108.0	60 20.3	+30.2	109.7	59 59.3	+31.9	111.3	16
17	61 23.9	+25.1	104.4	61 08.1	+27.0	106.2	60 50.5	+28.8	107.9	60 31.2	+30.6	109.6	17
18	61 49.0	+23.4	102.5	61 35.1	+25.4	104.3	61 19.3	+27.4	106.1	61 01.8	+29.2	107.8	18
19	62 12.4	+21.8	100.5	62 00.5	+23.8	102.4	61 46.7	+25.7	104.2	61 31.0	+27.7	106.0	19
20	62 34.2	+19.9	98.5	62 24.3	+22.0	100.4	62 12.4	+24.2	102.3	61 58.7	+26.1	104.1	20
21	62 54.1	+18.1	96.5	62 46.3	+20.3	98.4	62 36.6	+22.4	100.3	62 24.8	+24.5	102.2	21
22	63 12.2	+16.2	94.4	63 06.6	+18.4	96.3	62 59.0	+20.6	98.3	62 49.3	+22.8	100.2	22
23	63 28.4	+14.3•	92.2	63 25.0	+16.6	94.2	63 19.6	+18.7	96.2	63 12.1	+20.9	98.2	23
24	63 42.7	+12.2•	90.0	63 41.6	+14.5•	92.1	63 38.3	+16.9	94.1	63 33.0	+19.1	96.1	24
25	63 54.9	+10.2•	87.8	63 56.1	+12.5•	89.9	63 55.2	+14.8•	91.9	63 52.1	+17.2•	93.9	25
26	64 05.1	+8.0•	85.6	64 08.6	+10.5•	87.6	64 10.0	+12.8•	89.7	64 09.3	+15.1•	91.8	26
27	64 13.1	+6.0•	83.3	64 19.1	+8.3•	85.4	64 22.8	+10.7•	87.4	64 24.4	+13.1•	89.5	27
28	64 19.1	+3.7•	81.0	64 27.4	+6.1•	83.1	64 33.5	+8.6•	85.2	64 37.5	+10.9•	87.3	28
29	64 22.8	+1.6•	78.7	64 33.5	+4.0•	80.8	64 42.1	+6.3•	82.9	64 48.4	+8.8•	85.0	29
30	64 24.4	-0.6•	76.4	64 37.5	+1.7•	78.4	64 48.4	+4.2•	80.5	64 57.2	+6.6•	82.6	30
31	64 23.8	-2.8•	74.1	64 39.2	-0.4•	76.1	64 52.6	+1.9•	78.2	65 03.8	+4.4•	80.3	31
32	64 21.0	-5.0•	71.8	64 38.8	-2.7•	73.8	64 54.5	-0.3•	75.8	65 08.2	+2.1•	77.9	32
33	64 16.0	-7.1•	69.5	64 36.1	-4.8•	71.4	64 54.2	-2.5•	73.5	65 10.3	-0.2•	75.5	33
34	64 08.9	-9.2•	67.2	64 31.3	-7.1•	69.1	64 51.7	-4.8•	71.1	65 10.1	-2.4•	73.2	34
35	63 59.7	-11.3•	64.9	64 24.2	-9.1•	66.8	64 46.9	-6.9•	68.8	65 07.7	-4.7•	70.8	35
36	63 48.4	-13.4•	62.7	64 15.1	-11.3•	64.5	64 40.0	-9.2•	66.4	65 03.0	-6.9•	68.4	36
37	63 35.0	-15.3	60.5	64 03.8	-13.4•	62.3	64 30.8	-11.2•	64.1	64 56.1	-9.1•	66.1	37
38	63 19.7	-17.3	58.3	63 50.4	-15.3	60.1	64 19.6	-13.4•	61.9	64 47.0	-11.3•	63.7	38
39	63 02.4	-19.1	56.2	63 35.1	-17.3	57.9	64 06.2	-15.4	59.6	64 35.7	-13.3•	61.4	39
40	62 43.3	-20.9	54.1	63 17.8	-19.2	55.7	63 50.8	-17.3	57.4	64 22.4	-15.4•	59.2	40
41	62 22.4	-22.7	52.1	62 58.6	-21.0	53.6	63 33.5	-19.3	55.3	64 07.0	-17.5	56.9	41
42	61 59.7	-24.3	50.1	62 37.6	-22.8	51.6	63 14.2	-21.1	53.1	63 49.5	-19.3	54.8	42
43	61 35.4	-26.0	48.2	62 14.8	-24.4	49.6	62 53.1	-22.9	51.1	63 30.2	-21.2	52.6	43
44	61 09.4	-27.4	46.3	61 50.4	-26.1	47.6	62 30.2	-24.5	49.1	63 09.0	-23.0	50.5	44
45	60 42.0	-29.0	44.5	61 24.3	-27.6	45.7	62 05.7	-26.2	47.1	62 46.0	-24.7	48.5	45
46	60 13.0	-30.3	42.7	60 56.7	-29.1	43.9	61 39.5	-27.8	45.2	62 21.3	-26.4	46.5	46
47	59 42.7	-31.6	41.0	60 27.6	-30.4	42.1	61 11.7	-29.2	43.3	61 54.9	-27.9	44.6	47
48	59 11.1	-32.8	39.3	59 57.2	-31.8	40.4	60 42.5	-30.6	41.5	61 27.0	-29.4	42.7	48
49	58 38.3	-34.1	37.7	59 25.4	-33.0	38.7	60 11.9	-32.0	39.8	60 57.6	-30.8	40.9	49
50	58 04.2	-35.2	36.1	58 52.4	-34.2	37.1	59 39.9	-33.2	38.1	60 26.8	-32.1	39.2	50
51	57 29.0	-36.2	34.6	58 18.2	-35.4	35.5	59 06.7	-34.4	36.5	59 54.7	-33.5	37.5	51
52	56 52.8	-37.2	33.1	57 42.8	-36.4	34.0	58 32.3	-35.5	34.9	59 21.2	-34.6	35.8	52
53	56 15.6	-38.2	31.7	57 06.4	-37.4	32.5	57 56.8	-36.6	33.4	58 46.6	-35.7	34.3	53
54	55 37.4	-39.1	30.3	56 29.0	-38.4	31.1	57 20.2	-37.6	31.9	58 10.9	-36.8	32.7	54
55	54 58.3	-39.9	29.0	55 50.6	-39.2	29.7	56 42.6	-38.6	30.4	57 34.1	-37.9	31.2	55
56	54 18.4	-40.7	27.7	55 11.4	-40.2	28.4	56 04.0	-39.5	29.1	56 56.2	-38.7	29.8	56
57	53 37.7	-41.5	26.4	54 31.2	-40.9	27.1	55 24.5	-40.3	27.7	56 17.5	-39.7	28.4	57
58	52 56.2	-42.2	25.2	53 50.3	-41.6	25.8	54 44.2	-41.1	26.4	55 37.8	-40.5	27.1	58
59	52 14.0	-42.9	24.1	53 08.7	-42.4	24.6	54 03.1	-41.9	25.2	54 57.3	-41.4	25.8	59
60	51 31.1	-43.5	22.9	52 26.3	-43.1	23.4	53 21.2	-42.5	24.0	54 15.9	-42.0	24.5	60
61	50 47.6	-44.1	21.8	51 43.2	-43.6	22.3	52 38.7	-43.3	22.8	53 33.9	-42.8	23.3	61
62	50 03.5	-44.6	20.8	50 59.6	-44.3	21.2	51 55.4	-43.9	21.7	52 51.1	-43.5	22.1	62
63	49 18.9	-45.2	19.7	50 15.3	-44.9	20.1	51 11.5	-44.4	20.6	52 07.6	-44.1	21.0	63
64	48 33.7	-45.7	18.7	49 30.4	-45.3	19.1	50 27.1	-45.1	19.5	51 23.5	-44.6	19.9	64
65	47 48.0	-46.2	17.8	48 45.1	-45.9	18.1	49 42.0	-45.5	18.5	50 38.9	-45.3	18.9	65
66	47 01.8	-46.7	16.8	47 59.2	-46.4	17.1	48 56.5	-46.1	17.5	49 53.6	-45.7	17.8	66
67	46 15.1	-47.0	15.9	47 12.8	-46.8	16.2	48 10.4	-46.6	16.5	49 07.9	-46.3	16.8	67
68	45 28.1	-47.5	15.0	46 26.0	-47.2	15.3	47 23.8	-46.9	15.6	48 21.6	-46.7	15.9	68
69	44 40.6	-47.8	14.2	45 38.8	-47.7	14.4	46 36.9	-47.5	14.7	47 34.9	-47.2	14.9	69
70	43 52.8	-48.2	13.3	44 51.1	-48.0	13.5	45 49.4	-47.8	13.8	46 47.7	-47.6	14.0	70
71	43 04.6	-48.6	12.5	44 03.1	-48.3	12.7	45 01.6	-48.2	12.9	46 00.1	-48.0	13.1	71
72	42 16.0	-48.9	11.7	43 14.8	-48.8	11.9	44 13.4	-48.5	12.1	45 12.1	-48.4	12.3	72
73	41 27.1	-49.1	10.9	42 26.0	-49.0	11.1	43 24.9	-48.9	11.3	44 23.7	-48.7	11.4	73
74	40 38.0	-49.5	10.1	41 37.0	-49.3	10.3	42 36.0	-49.2	10.5	43 35.0	-49.1	10.6	74
75	39 48.5	-49.8	9.4	40 47.7	-49.7	9.5	41 46.8	-49.5	9.7	42 45.9	-49.3	9.8	75
76	38 58.7	-50.0	8.7	39 58.0	-49.9	8.8	40 57.3	-49.8	8.9	41 56.6	-49.7	9.1	76
77	38 08.7	-50.2	8.0	39 08.1	-50.1	8.1	40 07.5	-50.0	8.2	41 06.9	-50.0	8.3	77
78	37 18.5	-50.5	7.3	38 18.0	-50.4	7.4	39 17.5	-50.4	7.5	40 16.9	-50.2	7.6	78
79	36 28.0	-50.8	6.6	37 27.6	-50.7	6.7	38 27.1	-50.5	6.8	39 26.7	-50.5	6.9	79
80	35 37.2	-50.9	5.9	36 36.9	-50.9	6.0	37 36.6	-50.8	6.1	38 36.2	-50.7	6.2	80
81	34 46.3	-51.1	5.3	35 46.0	-51.0	5.4	36 45.8	-51.0	5.4	37 45.5	-50.9	5.5	81
82	33 55.2	-51.3	4.7	34 55.0	-51.3	4.7	35 54.8	-51.3	4.8	36 54.6	-51.2	4.8	82
83	33 03.9	-51.6	4.0	34 03.7	-51.5	4.1	35 03.5	-51.4	4.1	36 03.4	-51.4	4.2	83
84	32 12.3	-51.6	3.4	33 12.2	-51.6	3.5	34 12.1	-51.6	3.5	35 12.0	-51.6	3.6	84
85	31 20.7	-51.9	2.8	32 20.6	-51.8	2.9	33 20.5	-51.8	2.9	34 20.4	-51.7	2.9	85
86	30 28.8	-52.0	2.2	31 28.8	-52.0	2.3	32 28.7	-51.9	2.3	33 28.7	-51.9	2.3	86
87	29 36.8	-52.1	1.7	30 36.8	-52.1	1.7	31 36.8	-52.1	1.7	32 36.8	-52.1	1.7	87
88	28 44.7	-52.3	1.1	29 44.7	-52.3	1.1	30 44.7	-52.3	1.1	31 44.7	-52.3	1.1	88
89	27 52.4	-52.4	0.5	28 52.4	-52.4	0.6	29 52.4	-52.4	0.6	30 52.4	-52.4	0.6	89
90	27 00.0	-52.5	0.0	28 00.0	-52.5	0.0	29 00.0	-52.5	0.0	30 00.0	-52.5	0.0	90
	27°			28°			29°			30°			

29°, 331° L.H.A. LATITUDE SAME NAME AS DECLINATION

242

LATITUDE **CONTRARY** NAME TO DECLINATION **L.H.A. 29°, 331°**

Dec.	23° Hc	d	Z	24° Hc	d	Z	25° Hc	d	Z	26° Hc	d	Z
°	° ′	′	°	° ′	′	°	° ′	′	°	° ′	′	°
0	53 37.1	−39.9	125.2	53 02.1	−40.9	126.3	52 26.2	−42.0	127.3	51 49.4	−42.9	128.3
1	52 57.2	−40.7	126.4	52 21.2	−41.7	127.5	51 44.2	−42.6	128.5	51 06.5	−43.5	129.5
2	52 16.5	−41.4	127.6	51 39.5	−42.4	128.6	51 01.6	−43.2	129.6	50 23.0	−44.1	130.5
3	51 35.1	−42.0	128.8	50 57.1	−42.9	129.8	50 18.4	−43.9	130.7	49 38.9	−44.7	131.6
4	50 53.1	−42.8	130.0	50 14.2	−43.6	130.9	49 34.5	−44.4	131.8	48 54.2	−45.1	132.6
5	50 10.3	−43.3	131.1	49 30.6	−44.2	131.9	48 50.1	−44.9	132.8	48 09.1	−45.7	133.6
6	49 27.0	−43.9	132.1	48 46.4	−44.7	133.0	48 05.2	−45.4	133.8	47 23.4	−46.2	134.6
7	48 43.1	−44.5	133.2	48 01.7	−45.2	134.0	47 19.8	−46.0	134.8	46 37.2	−46.6	135.5
8	47 58.6	−45.0	134.2	47 16.5	−45.7	135.0	46 33.8	−46.3	135.7	45 50.6	−47.0	136.4
9	47 13.6	−45.4	135.2	46 30.8	−46.1	135.9	45 47.5	−46.8	136.6	45 03.6	−47.4	137.3
10	46 28.2	−45.9	136.1	45 44.7	−46.6	136.8	45 00.7	−47.2	137.5	44 16.2	−47.8	138.2
11	45 42.3	−46.4	137.0	44 58.1	−47.0	137.7	44 13.5	−47.6	138.4	43 28.4	−48.2	139.0
12	44 55.9	−46.8	137.9	44 11.1	−47.4	138.6	43 25.9	−48.0	139.2	42 40.2	−48.5	139.8
13	44 09.1	−47.2	138.8	43 23.7	−47.7	139.5	42 37.9	−48.3	140.1	41 51.7	−48.8	140.6
14	43 21.9	−47.5	139.7	42 36.0	−48.1	140.3	41 49.6	−48.6	140.9	41 02.9	−49.1	141.4
15	42 34.4	−47.9	140.5	41 47.9	−48.4	141.1	41 01.0	−48.9	141.6	40 13.8	−49.4	142.2
16	41 46.5	−48.3	141.3	40 59.5	−48.8	141.9	40 12.1	−49.2	142.4	39 24.4	−49.7	142.9
17	40 58.2	−48.5	142.1	40 10.7	−49.0	142.6	39 22.9	−49.5	143.1	38 34.7	−49.9	143.6
18	40 09.7	−48.9	142.9	39 21.7	−49.3	143.4	38 33.4	−49.8	143.9	37 44.8	−50.2	144.3
19	39 20.8	−49.1	143.6	38 32.4	−49.6	144.1	37 43.6	−50.0	144.6	36 54.6	−50.4	145.0
20	38 31.7	−49.4	144.4	37 42.8	−49.9	144.8	36 53.6	−50.3	145.3	36 04.2	−50.7	145.7
21	37 42.3	−49.7	145.1	36 52.9	−50.0	145.5	36 03.3	−50.4	146.0	35 13.5	−50.8	146.4
22	36 52.6	−49.9	145.8	36 02.9	−50.3	146.2	35 12.9	−50.7	146.6	34 22.7	−51.1	147.0
23	36 02.7	−50.1	146.5	35 12.6	−50.6	146.9	34 22.2	−50.9	147.3	33 31.6	−51.2	147.6
24	35 12.6	−50.4	147.2	34 22.0	−50.7	147.6	33 31.3	−51.1	147.9	32 40.4	−51.5	148.3
25	34 22.2	−50.6	147.8	33 31.3	−50.9	148.2	32 40.2	−51.3	148.5	31 48.9	−51.6	148.9
26	33 31.6	−50.8	148.5	32 40.4	−51.2	148.8	31 48.9	−51.4	149.2	30 57.3	−51.7	149.5
27	32 40.8	−50.9	149.1	31 49.2	−51.2	149.4	30 57.5	−51.6	149.8	30 05.6	−51.9	150.0
28	31 49.9	−51.2	149.7	30 58.0	−51.5	150.1	30 05.9	−51.8	150.3	29 13.7	−52.1	150.6
29	30 58.7	−51.3	150.4	30 06.5	−51.6	150.6	29 14.1	−51.9	150.9	28 21.6	−52.2	151.2
30	30 07.4	−51.5	151.0	29 14.9	−51.8	151.2	28 22.2	−52.0	151.5	27 29.4	−52.3	151.8
31	29 15.9	−51.6	151.6	28 23.1	−51.9	151.8	27 30.2	−52.2	152.1	26 37.1	−52.5	152.3
32	28 24.3	−51.8	152.1	27 31.2	−52.1	152.4	26 38.0	−52.3	152.6	25 44.6	−52.5	152.8
33	27 32.5	−51.9	152.7	26 39.1	−52.1	152.9	25 45.7	−52.5	153.2	24 52.1	−52.7	153.4
34	26 40.6	−52.0	153.3	25 47.0	−52.3	153.5	24 53.2	−52.5	153.7	23 59.4	−52.8	153.9
35	25 48.6	−52.2	153.8	24 54.7	−52.4	154.0	24 00.7	−52.7	154.2	23 06.6	−52.9	154.4
36	24 56.4	−52.3	154.4	24 02.3	−52.6	154.6	23 08.0	−52.7	154.8	22 13.7	−53.0	154.9
37	24 04.1	−52.4	154.9	23 09.7	−52.6	155.1	22 15.3	−52.9	155.3	21 20.7	−53.0	155.4
38	23 11.7	−52.5	155.4	22 17.1	−52.7	155.6	21 22.4	−52.9	155.8	20 27.7	−53.2	155.9
39	22 19.2	−52.6	156.0	21 24.4	−52.9	156.1	20 29.5	−53.1	156.3	19 34.5	−53.2	156.4
40	21 26.6	−52.7	156.5	20 31.5	−52.9	156.6	19 36.4	−53.1	156.8	18 41.3	−53.3	156.9
41	20 33.9	−52.8	157.0	19 38.6	−53.0	157.1	18 43.3	−53.2	157.3	17 48.0	−53.4	157.4
42	19 41.1	−52.9	157.5	18 45.6	−53.0	157.6	17 50.1	−53.2	157.8	16 54.6	−53.5	157.9
43	18 48.2	−52.9	158.0	17 52.6	−53.2	158.1	16 56.9	−53.4	158.2	16 01.1	−53.5	158.4
44	17 55.3	−53.1	158.5	16 59.4	−53.2	158.6	16 03.5	−53.4	158.7	15 07.6	−53.6	158.8
45	17 02.2	−53.0	159.0	16 06.2	−53.3	159.1	15 10.1	−53.4	159.2	14 14.0	−53.6	159.3
46	16 09.2	−53.2	159.5	15 12.9	−53.3	159.6	14 16.7	−53.5	159.7	13 20.4	−53.6	159.8
47	15 16.0	−53.2	160.0	14 19.6	−53.4	160.0	13 23.2	−53.6	160.1	12 26.8	−53.8	160.2
48	14 22.8	−53.3	160.4	13 26.2	−53.4	160.5	12 29.6	−53.6	160.6	11 33.0	−53.7	160.7
49	13 29.5	−53.4	160.9	12 32.8	−53.5	161.0	11 36.0	−53.6	161.1	10 39.3	−53.8	161.1
50	12 36.1	−53.3	161.4	11 39.3	−53.6	161.4	10 42.4	−53.7	161.5	9 45.5	−53.9	161.6
51	11 42.8	−53.5	161.8	10 45.7	−53.5	161.9	9 48.7	−53.7	162.0	8 51.6	−53.8	162.0
52	10 49.3	−53.4	162.3	9 52.2	−53.6	162.4	8 55.0	−53.8	162.4	7 57.8	−53.9	162.5
53	9 55.9	−53.5	162.8	8 58.6	−53.7	162.8	8 01.2	−53.8	162.9	7 03.9	−53.9	162.9
54	9 02.4	−53.6	163.2	8 04.9	−53.7	163.3	7 07.4	−53.8	163.3	6 10.0	−54.0	163.3
55	8 08.8	−53.6	163.7	7 11.2	−53.7	163.7	6 13.6	−53.8	163.8	5 16.0	−53.9	163.8
56	7 15.2	−53.5	164.1	6 17.5	−53.7	164.2	5 19.8	−53.9	164.2	4 22.1	−54.0	164.2
57	6 21.7	−53.7	164.6	5 23.8	−53.7	164.6	4 25.9	−53.8	164.6	3 28.1	−54.0	164.7
58	5 28.0	−53.6	165.0	4 30.1	−53.8	165.1	3 32.1	−53.9	165.1	2 34.1	−54.0	165.1
59	4 34.4	−53.7	165.5	3 36.3	−53.8	165.5	2 38.2	−53.9	165.5	1 40.1	−54.0	165.5
60	3 40.7	−53.6	165.9	2 42.5	−53.8	166.0	1 44.3	−53.9	166.0	0 46.1	−54.0	166.0
61	2 47.1	−53.7	166.4	1 48.7	−53.8	166.4	0 50.4	−53.9	166.4	0 07.9	+54.0	13.6
62	1 53.4	−53.7	166.8	0 54.9	−53.7	166.8	0 03.5	+53.9	13.2	1 01.9	+54.0	13.2
63	0 59.7	−53.7	167.3	0 01.2	−53.8	167.3	0 57.4	+53.9	12.7	1 55.9	+54.0	12.7
64	0 06.0	−53.7	167.7	0 52.6	+53.8	12.3	1 51.3	+53.9	12.3	2 49.9	+54.0	12.3
65	0 47.7	+53.7	11.8	1 46.4	+53.8	11.8	2 45.2	+53.8	11.8	3 43.9	+53.9	11.8
66	1 41.4	+53.7	11.4	2 40.2	+53.8	11.4	3 39.0	+53.9	11.4	4 37.8	+54.0	11.4
67	2 35.1	+53.7	10.9	3 34.0	+53.8	10.9	4 32.9	+53.8	11.0	5 31.8	+53.9	11.0
68	3 28.8	+53.6	10.5	4 27.8	+53.7	10.5	5 26.7	+53.9	10.5	6 25.7	+53.9	10.5
69	4 22.4	+53.7	10.0	5 21.5	+53.7	10.0	6 20.6	+53.8	10.1	7 19.6	+53.9	10.1
70	5 16.1	+53.6	9.6	6 15.2	+53.7	9.6	7 14.4	+53.8	9.6	8 13.5	+53.9	9.6
71	6 09.7	+53.6	9.1	7 08.9	+53.7	9.2	8 08.2	+53.7	9.2	9 07.4	+53.8	9.2
72	7 03.3	+53.6	8.7	8 02.6	+53.7	8.7	9 01.9	+53.7	8.7	10 01.2	+53.8	8.8
73	7 56.9	+53.5	8.2	8 56.3	+53.6	8.2	9 55.6	+53.7	8.3	10 55.0	+53.8	8.3
74	8 50.4	+53.5	7.8	9 49.9	+53.5	7.8	10 49.3	+53.7	7.8	11 48.8	+53.7	7.8
75	9 43.9	+53.5	7.3	10 43.4	+53.6	7.3	11 43.0	+53.5	7.4	12 42.5	+53.6	7.4
76	10 37.4	+53.5	6.9	11 37.0	+53.5	6.9	12 36.5	+53.6	6.9	13 36.1	+53.6	6.9
77	11 30.9	+53.3	6.4	12 30.5	+53.4	6.4	13 30.1	+53.5	6.4	14 29.7	+53.6	6.5
78	12 24.2	+53.4	5.9	13 23.9	+53.4	5.9	14 23.6	+53.4	6.0	15 23.3	+53.5	6.0
79	13 17.6	+53.3	5.5	14 17.3	+53.4	5.5	15 17.0	+53.4	5.5	16 16.8	+53.4	5.5
80	14 10.9	+53.2	5.0	15 10.7	+53.2	5.0	16 10.4	+53.3	5.0	17 10.2	+53.4	5.1
81	15 04.1	+53.2	4.5	16 03.9	+53.2	4.5	17 03.7	+53.3	4.6	18 03.6	+53.2	4.6
82	15 57.3	+53.1	4.0	16 57.1	+53.2	4.0	17 57.0	+53.2	4.1	18 56.8	+53.3	4.1
83	16 50.4	+53.1	3.5	17 50.3	+53.1	3.6	18 50.2	+53.1	3.6	19 50.1	+53.1	3.6
84	17 43.5	+52.9	3.0	18 43.4	+53.0	3.1	19 43.3	+53.0	3.1	20 43.2	+53.0	3.1
85	18 36.4	+52.9	2.6	19 36.4	+52.9	2.6	20 36.3	+52.9	2.6	21 36.2	+53.0	2.6
86	19 29.3	+52.8	2.1	20 29.3	+52.8	2.1	21 29.2	+52.8	2.1	22 29.2	+52.9	2.1
87	20 22.1	+52.7	1.6	21 22.1	+52.7	1.6	22 22.1	+52.7	1.6	23 22.1	+52.7	1.6
88	21 14.8	+52.7	1.0	22 14.8	+52.7	1.0	23 14.8	+52.7	1.1	24 14.8	+52.7	1.1
89	22 07.5	+52.5	0.5	23 07.5	+52.5	0.5	24 07.5	+52.5	0.5	25 07.5	+52.5	0.5
90	23 00.0	+52.4	0.0	24 00.0	+52.4	0.0	25 00.0	+52.4	0.0	26 00.0	+52.4	0.0
	23°			24°			25°			26°		

Dec.	27° Hc	d	Z	28° Hc	d	Z	29° Hc	d	Z	30° Hc	d	Z
°	° ′	′	°	° ′	′	°	° ′	′	°	° ′	′	°
0	51 11.7	−43.7	129.3	50 33.3	−44.6	130.3	49 54.2	−45.4	131.2	49 14.4	−46.2	132.1
1	50 28.0	−44.4	130.4	49 48.7	−45.1	131.3	49 08.8	−46.0	132.2	48 28.2	−46.7	133.0
2	49 43.6	−44.9	131.5	49 03.6	−45.7	132.3	48 22.8	−46.4	133.2	47 41.5	−47.1	134.0
3	48 58.7	−45.4	132.5	48 17.9	−46.2	133.3	47 36.4	−46.8	134.1	46 54.4	−47.6	134.9
4	48 13.3	−45.9	133.5	47 31.7	−46.6	134.3	46 49.6	−47.3	135.0	46 06.8	−47.9	135.8
5	47 27.4	−46.4	134.4	46 45.1	−47.1	135.2	46 02.3	−47.8	135.9	45 18.9	−48.3	136.6
6	46 41.0	−46.9	135.3	45 58.0	−47.5	136.1	45 14.5	−48.0	136.8	44 30.6	−48.7	137.5
7	45 54.1	−47.2	136.3	45 10.5	−47.8	137.0	44 26.5	−48.5	137.6	43 41.9	−49.0	138.3
8	45 06.9	−47.6	137.1	44 22.7	−48.2	137.8	43 38.0	−48.8	138.4	42 52.9	−49.3	139.1
9	44 19.3	−48.1	138.0	43 34.5	−48.6	138.6	42 49.2	−49.1	139.2	42 03.6	−49.7	139.8
10	43 31.2	−48.3	138.8	42 45.9	−48.9	139.4	42 00.1	−49.4	140.0	41 13.9	−49.9	140.6
11	42 42.9	−48.7	139.6	41 57.0	−49.2	140.2	41 10.7	−49.7	140.8	40 24.0	−50.2	141.3
12	41 54.2	−49.0	140.4	41 07.8	−49.6	141.0	40 21.0	−50.0	141.5	39 33.8	−50.4	142.0
13	41 05.2	−49.3	141.2	40 18.2	−49.8	141.7	39 31.0	−50.3	142.2	38 43.4	−50.7	142.7
14	40 15.9	−49.6	141.9	39 28.4	−50.0	142.5	38 40.7	−50.5	142.9	37 52.7	−50.9	143.4
15	39 26.3	−49.9	142.7	38 38.4	−50.3	143.2	37 50.2	−50.7	143.6	37 01.8	−51.2	144.1
16	38 36.4	−50.1	143.4	37 48.1	−50.6	143.9	36 59.5	−51.0	144.3	36 10.6	−51.3	144.7
17	37 46.3	−50.4	144.1	36 57.5	−50.8	144.5	36 08.5	−51.1	145.0	35 19.3	−51.6	145.4
18	36 55.9	−50.6	144.8	36 06.7	−50.9	145.2	35 17.4	−51.4	145.6	34 27.7	−51.7	146.0
19	36 05.3	−50.8	145.4	35 15.8	−51.2	145.8	34 26.0	−51.6	146.2	33 36.0	−51.9	146.6
20	35 14.5	−51.0	146.1	34 24.6	−51.4	146.5	33 34.4	−51.7	146.9	32 44.1	−52.1	147.2
21	34 23.5	−51.3	146.7	33 33.2	−51.6	147.1	32 42.7	−51.9	147.5	31 52.0	−52.2	147.8
22	33 32.2	−51.4	147.4	32 41.6	−51.7	147.7	31 50.8	−52.1	148.1	30 59.8	−52.4	148.4
23	32 40.8	−51.6	148.0	31 49.9	−51.9	148.3	30 58.7	−52.2	148.6	30 07.4	−52.5	148.9
24	31 49.2	−51.7	148.6	30 58.0	−52.1	148.9	30 06.5	−52.4	149.2	29 14.9	−52.7	149.5
25	30 57.5	−51.9	149.2	30 05.9	−52.2	149.5	29 14.1	−52.5	149.8	28 22.2	−52.8	150.0
26	30 05.6	−52.1	149.8	29 13.7	−52.4	150.0	28 21.6	−52.6	150.3	27 29.4	−52.9	150.6
27	29 13.5	−52.2	150.3	28 21.3	−52.5	150.6	27 29.0	−52.8	150.9	26 36.5	−53.0	151.1
28	28 21.3	−52.3	150.9	27 28.8	−52.6	151.2	26 36.2	−52.9	151.4	25 43.5	−53.2	151.6
29	27 29.0	−52.5	151.4	26 36.2	−52.7	151.7	25 43.3	−53.0	151.9	24 50.3	−53.2	152.1
30	26 36.5	−52.6	152.0	25 43.5	−52.9	152.2	24 50.3	−53.1	152.4	23 57.1	−53.3	152.7
31	25 43.9	−52.7	152.5	24 50.6	−52.9	152.7	23 57.2	−53.2	153.0	23 03.8	−53.5	153.1
32	24 51.2	−52.8	153.1	23 57.7	−53.1	153.3	23 04.0	−53.3	153.5	22 10.3	−53.5	153.6
33	23 58.4	−52.9	153.6	23 04.6	−53.1	153.8	22 10.7	−53.3	154.0	21 16.8	−53.6	154.1
34	23 05.5	−53.1	154.1	22 11.5	−53.3	154.3	21 17.4	−53.5	154.4	20 23.2	−53.7	154.6
35	22 12.4	−53.1	154.6	21 18.2	−53.3	154.8	20 23.9	−53.6	154.9	19 29.5	−53.7	155.1
36	21 19.3	−53.2	155.1	20 24.9	−53.4	155.3	19 30.3	−53.6	155.4	18 35.8	−53.9	155.6
37	20 26.1	−53.3	155.6	19 31.5	−53.5	155.7	18 36.7	−53.7	155.9	17 41.9	−53.9	156.0
38	19 32.8	−53.3	156.1	18 38.0	−53.6	156.2	17 43.0	−53.7	156.4	16 48.0	−53.9	156.5
39	18 39.5	−53.5	156.6	17 44.4	−53.6	156.7	16 49.3	−53.9	156.8	15 54.1	−54.0	156.9
40	17 46.0	−53.5	157.0	16 50.8	−53.7	157.2	15 55.4	−53.8	157.3	15 00.1	−54.1	157.4
41	16 52.5	−53.5	157.5	15 57.1	−53.8	157.6	15 01.6	−54.0	157.7	14 06.0	−54.1	157.8
42	15 59.0	−53.7	158.0	15 03.3	−53.8	158.1	14 07.6	−54.0	158.2	13 11.9	−54.1	158.3
43	15 05.3	−53.7	158.5	14 09.5	−53.9	158.6	13 13.6	−54.0	158.6	12 17.8	−54.2	158.7
44	14 11.6	−53.7	158.9	13 15.6	−53.9	159.0	12 19.6	−54.1	159.1	11 23.6	−54.3	159.2
45	13 17.9	−53.8	159.4	12 21.7	−53.9	159.5	11 25.5	−54.1	159.5	10 29.3	−54.3	159.6
46	12 24.1	−53.8	159.8	11 27.8	−54.0	159.9	10 31.4	−54.1	160.0	9 35.0	−54.3	160.0
47	11 30.3	−53.9	160.3	10 33.8	−54.0	160.3	9 37.3	−54.2	160.4	8 40.7	−54.3	160.5
48	10 36.4	−53.9	160.7	9 39.8	−54.1	160.8	8 43.1	−54.2	160.8	7 46.4	−54.4	160.9
49	9 42.5	−54.0	161.2	8 45.7	−54.1	161.2	7 48.9	−54.3	161.3	6 52.0	−54.3	161.3
50	8 48.5	−53.9	161.6	7 51.6	−54.1	161.7	6 54.6	−54.2	161.7	5 57.7	−54.4	161.7
51	7 54.6	−54.0	162.1	6 57.5	−54.2	162.1	6 00.4	−54.3	162.1	5 03.3	−54.5	162.2
52	7 00.6	−54.1	162.5	6 03.3	−54.1	162.5	5 06.1	−54.3	162.6	4 08.8	−54.4	162.6
53	6 06.5	−54.0	162.9	5 09.2	−54.2	163.0	4 11.8	−54.3	163.0	3 14.4	−54.4	163.0
54	5 12.5	−54.1	163.4	4 15.0	−54.2	163.4	3 17.5	−54.3	163.4	2 20.0	−54.5	163.4
55	4 18.4	−54.1	163.8	3 20.8	−54.2	163.8	2 23.2	−54.4	163.8	1 25.5	−54.4	163.8
56	3 24.3	−54.1	164.2	2 26.6	−54.2	164.3	1 28.8	−54.3	164.3	0 31.1	−54.5	164.3
57	2 30.2	−54.1	164.7	1 32.4	−54.3	164.7	0 34.5	−54.4	164.7	0 23.4	+54.4	15.3
58	1 36.1	−54.1	165.1	0 38.1	−54.2	165.1	0 19.9	+54.3	14.9	1 17.8	+54.5	14.9
59	0 42.0	−54.1	165.5	0 16.1	+54.2	14.5	1 14.2	+54.3	14.5	2 12.3	+54.4	14.5
60	0 12.1	+54.1	14.0	1 10.3	+54.2	14.0	2 08.5	+54.4	14.0	3 06.7	+54.5	14.0
61	1 06.2	+54.1	13.6	2 04.5	+54.2	13.6	3 02.9	+54.3	13.6	4 01.2	+54.4	13.6
62	2 00.3	+54.1	13.2	2 58.7	+54.3	13.2	3 57.2	+54.3	13.2	4 55.6	+54.4	13.2
63	2 54.4	+54.1	12.7	3 53.0	+54.1	12.7	4 51.5	+54.3	12.8	5 50.0	+54.4	12.8
64	3 48.5	+54.1	12.3	4 47.1	+54.2	12.3	5 45.8	+54.2	12.3	6 44.4	+54.3	12.4
65	4 42.6	+54.1	11.9	5 41.3	+54.2	11.9	6 40.0	+54.3	11.9	7 38.7	+54.4	11.9
66	5 36.7	+54.0	11.4	6 35.5	+54.1	11.4	7 34.3	+54.2	11.5	8 33.1	+54.3	11.5
67	6 30.7	+54.0	11.0	7 29.6	+54.1	11.0	8 28.5	+54.2	11.0	9 27.4	+54.3	11.1
68	7 24.7	+54.0	10.6	8 23.7	+54.1	10.6	9 22.7	+54.1	10.6	10 21.7	+54.2	10.6
69	8 18.7	+54.0	10.1	9 17.8	+54.0	10.1	10 16.8	+54.2	10.2	11 15.9	+54.2	10.2
70	9 12.7	+53.9	9.7	10 11.8	+54.0	9.7	11 11.0	+54.1	9.7	12 10.1	+54.2	9.8
71	10 06.6	+53.9	9.2	11 05.8	+54.0	9.3	12 05.1	+54.0	9.3	13 04.3	+54.1	9.3
72	11 00.5	+53.9	8.8	11 59.8	+53.9	8.8	12 59.1	+54.0	8.8	13 58.4	+54.1	8.9
73	11 54.4	+53.8	8.3	12 53.7	+53.9	8.4	13 53.1	+53.9	8.4	14 52.5	+54.0	8.4
74	12 48.2	+53.8	7.9	13 47.6	+53.9	7.9	14 47.0	+53.9	7.9	15 46.5	+53.9	8.0
75	13 42.0	+53.7	7.4	14 41.5	+53.7	7.5	15 40.9	+53.9	7.5	16 40.4	+53.9	7.5
76	14 35.7	+53.6	7.0	15 35.2	+53.7	7.0	16 34.8	+53.8	7.0	17 34.3	+53.9	7.1
77	15 29.3	+53.6	6.5	16 28.9	+53.7	6.5	17 28.6	+53.7	6.6	18 28.2	+53.7	6.6
78	16 22.9	+53.6	6.0	17 22.6	+53.6	6.1	18 22.3	+53.6	6.1	19 21.9	+53.7	6.1
79	17 16.5	+53.5	5.6	18 16.2	+53.5	5.6	19 15.9	+53.6	5.6	20 15.6	+53.6	5.7
80	18 10.0	+53.4	5.1	19 09.7	+53.5	5.1	20 09.5	+53.5	5.1	21 09.2	+53.6	5.2
81	19 03.4	+53.3	4.6	20 03.2	+53.3	4.6	21 03.0	+53.4	4.7	22 02.8	+53.4	4.7
82	19 56.7	+53.2	4.1	20 56.5	+53.3	4.1	21 56.4	+53.3	4.2	22 56.2	+53.4	4.2
83	20 49.9	+53.2	3.6	21 49.8	+53.2	3.6	22 49.7	+53.2	3.7	23 49.6	+53.2	3.7
84	21 43.1	+53.1	3.1	22 43.0	+53.1	3.1	23 42.9	+53.2	3.2	24 42.8	+53.2	3.2
85	22 36.2	+53.0	2.6	23 36.1	+53.0	2.6	24 36.1	+53.0	2.7	25 36.0	+53.0	2.7
86	23 29.2	+52.8	2.1	24 29.1	+52.9	2.1	25 29.1	+52.9	2.1	26 29.0	+53.0	2.2
87	24 22.0	+52.8	1.6	25 22.0	+52.8	1.6	26 22.0	+52.8	1.6	27 22.0	+52.8	1.6
88	25 14.8	+52.7	1.1	26 14.8	+52.7	1.1	27 14.8	+52.7	1.1	28 14.8	+52.7	1.1
89	26 07.5	+52.5	0.5	27 07.5	+52.5	0.5	28 07.5	+52.5	0.5	29 07.5	+52.5	0.6
90	27 00.0	+52.4	0.0	28 00.0	+52.4	0.0	29 00.0	+52.4	0.0	30 00.0	+52.4	0.0
	27°			28°			29°			30°		

S. Lat. { L.H.A. greater than 180° ....Zn=180°−Z
L.H.A. less than 180°............Zn=180°+Z

LATITUDE **SAME** NAME AS DECLINATION **L.H.A. 151°, 209°**

243

Dec.	23° Hc	d	Z	24° Hc	d	Z	25° Hc	d	Z	26° Hc	d	Z	Dec.
°	° ′	′	°	° ′	′	°	° ′	′	°	° ′	′	°	°
0	52 51.7	+38.4	124.1	52 17.6	+39.5	125.2	51 42.6	+40.6	126.2	51 06.7	+41.6	127.2	0
1	53 30.1	+37.6	122.8	52 57.1	+38.7	123.9	52 23.2	+39.8	125.0	51 48.3	+40.9	126.1	1
2	54 07.7	+36.7	121.5	53 35.8	+37.9	122.6	53 03.0	+39.0	123.8	52 29.2	+40.1	124.9	2
3	54 44.4	+35.7	120.1	54 13.7	+37.0	121.3	53 42.0	+38.2	122.5	53 09.3	+39.3	123.6	3
4	55 20.1	+34.8	118.7	54 50.7	+36.1	120.0	54 20.2	+37.3	121.2	53 48.6	+38.5	122.4	4
5	55 54.9	+33.7	117.3	55 26.8	+35.0	118.6	54 57.5	+36.4	119.8	54 27.1	+37.6	121.0	5
6	56 28.6	+32.6	115.8	56 01.8	+34.1	117.1	55 33.9	+35.4	118.4	55 04.7	+36.7	119.7	6
7	57 01.2	+31.4	114.3	56 35.9	+32.9	115.6	56 09.3	+34.3	117.0	55 41.4	+35.7	118.3	7
8	57 32.6	+30.3	112.7	57 08.8	+31.8	114.1	56 43.6	+33.3	115.5	56 17.1	+34.7	116.9	8
9	58 02.9	+28.9	111.1	57 40.6	+30.6	112.5	57 16.9	+32.1	114.0	56 51.8	+33.6	115.4	9
10	58 31.8	+27.7	109.4	58 11.2	+29.3	110.9	57 49.0	+30.9	112.4	57 25.4	+32.5	113.9	10
11	58 59.5	+26.2	107.7	58 40.5	+27.9	109.3	58 19.9	+29.7	110.8	57 57.9	+31.3	112.3	11
12	59 25.7	+24.8	105.9	59 08.4	+26.6	107.5	58 49.6	+28.3	109.1	58 29.2	+30.0	110.7	12
13	59 50.5	+23.3	104.1	59 35.0	+25.2	105.8	59 17.9	+26.9	107.4	58 59.2	+28.6	109.0	13
14	60 13.8	+21.7	102.3	60 00.2	+23.6	104.0	59 44.8	+25.5	105.6	59 27.8	+27.3	107.3	14
15	60 35.5	+20.1	100.4	60 23.8	+22.1	102.1	60 10.3	+24.0	103.8	59 55.1	+25.9	105.5	15
16	60 55.6	+18.4	98.5	60 45.9	+20.4	100.2	60 34.3	+22.4	102.0	60 21.0	+24.3	103.7	16
17	61 14.0	+16.6	96.5	61 06.3	+18.7	98.3	60 56.7	+20.7	100.1	60 45.3	+22.7	101.8	17
18	61 30.6	+14.9	94.5	61 25.0	+17.0	96.3	61 17.4	+19.1	98.1	61 08.0	+21.1	99.9	18
19	61 45.5	+13.0	92.5	61 42.0	+15.1	94.3	61 36.5	+17.3	96.2	61 29.1	+19.4	98.0	19
20	61 58.5	+11.1	90.4	61 57.1	+13.3	92.3	61 53.8	+15.4	94.1	61 48.5	+17.6	96.0	20
21	62 09.6	+9.2	88.3	62 10.4	+11.4	90.2	62 09.2	+13.7	92.1	62 06.1	+15.8	94.0	21
22	62 18.8	+7.2	86.2	62 21.8	+9.5	88.1	62 22.9	+11.6	90.0	62 21.9	+13.9	91.9	22
23	62 26.0	+5.3•	84.0	62 31.3	+7.5•	85.9	62 34.5	+9.8	87.9	62 35.8	+12.0	89.8	23
24	62 31.3	+3.2•	81.9	62 38.8	+5.5•	83.8	62 44.3	+7.7•	85.7	62 47.8	+10.0•	87.6	24
25	62 34.5	+1.3•	79.7	62 44.3	+3.5•	81.6	62 52.0	+5.8•	83.5	62 57.8	+8.0•	85.5	25
26	62 35.8	-0.8•	77.5	62 47.8	+1.4•	79.4	62 57.8	+3.7•	81.4	63 05.8	+6.0•	83.3	26
27	62 35.0	-2.8•	75.4	62 49.2	-0.6•	77.2	63 01.5	+1.6•	79.2	63 11.8	+3.9•	81.1	27
28	62 32.2	-4.8•	73.2	62 48.6	-2.6•	75.1	63 03.1	-0.4•	76.9	63 15.7	+1.8•	78.9	28
29	62 27.4	-6.8•	71.0	62 46.0	-4.7•	72.9	63 02.7	-2.4•	74.7	63 17.5	-0.2•	76.7	29
30	62 20.6	-8.8	68.9	62 41.3	-6.6•	70.7	63 00.3	-4.6•	72.5	63 17.3	-2.3•	74.4	30
31	62 11.8	-10.7	66.8	62 34.7	-8.7•	68.5	62 55.7	-6.5•	70.3	63 15.0	-4.4•	72.2	31
32	62 01.1	-12.5	64.7	62 26.0	-10.6	66.4	62 49.2	-8.6•	68.2	63 10.6	-6.4•	70.0	32
33	61 48.6	-14.5	62.6	62 15.4	-12.5	64.3	62 40.6	-10.5	66.0	63 04.2	-8.5•	67.8	33
34	61 34.1	-16.2	60.5	62 02.9	-14.4	62.2	62 30.1	-12.5	63.9	62 55.7	-10.5	65.6	34
35	61 17.9	-18.0	58.5	61 48.5	-16.2	60.1	62 17.6	-14.3	61.8	62 45.2	-12.4	63.5	35
36	60 59.9	-19.8	56.5	61 32.3	-18.0	58.1	62 03.3	-16.2	59.7	62 32.8	-14.3	61.3	36
37	60 40.1	-21.3	54.6	61 14.3	-19.8	56.1	61 47.1	-18.0	57.6	62 18.5	-16.2	59.2	37
38	60 18.8	-23.0	52.7	60 54.5	-21.3	54.1	61 29.1	-19.8	55.6	62 02.3	-18.0	57.2	38
39	59 55.8	-24.4	50.9	60 33.2	-23.0	52.2	61 09.3	-21.4	53.7	61 44.3	-19.8	55.1	39
40	59 31.4	-26.0	49.0	60 10.2	-24.5	50.4	60 47.9	-23.0	51.7	61 24.5	-21.5	53.2	40
41	59 05.4	-27.3	47.3	59 45.7	-26.0	48.5	60 24.9	-24.6	49.8	61 03.0	-23.1	51.2	41
42	58 38.1	-28.7	45.6	59 19.7	-27.4	46.8	60 00.3	-26.1	48.0	60 39.9	-24.6	49.3	42
43	58 09.4	-29.9	43.9	58 52.3	-28.8	45.0	59 34.2	-27.5	46.2	60 15.3	-26.2	47.5	43
44	57 39.5	-31.2	42.2	58 23.5	-30.1	43.3	59 06.7	-28.8	44.5	59 49.1	-27.6	45.7	44
45	57 08.3	-32.4	40.7	57 53.4	-31.2	41.7	58 37.9	-30.2	42.8	59 21.5	-29.0	43.9	45
46	56 35.9	-33.4	39.1	57 22.2	-32.5	40.1	58 07.7	-31.4	41.1	58 52.5	-30.3	42.2	46
47	56 02.5	-34.6	37.6	56 49.7	-33.6	38.6	57 36.3	-32.6	39.5	58 22.2	-31.5	40.6	47
48	55 27.9	-35.5	36.2	56 16.1	-34.6	37.0	57 03.7	-33.7	38.0	57 50.7	-32.7	38.9	48
49	54 52.4	-36.5	34.8	55 41.5	-35.7	35.6	56 30.0	-34.8	36.5	57 18.0	-33.9	37.4	49
50	54 15.9	-37.3	33.4	55 05.8	-36.6	34.2	55 55.2	-35.8	35.0	56 44.1	-34.9	35.9	50
51	53 38.6	-38.3	32.1	54 29.2	-37.5	32.8	55 19.4	-36.7	33.6	56 09.2	-36.0	34.4	51
52	53 00.3	-39.0	30.8	53 51.7	-38.4	31.5	54 42.7	-37.7	32.2	55 33.2	-36.9	33.0	52
53	52 21.3	-39.8	29.5	53 13.3	-39.2	30.2	54 05.0	-38.5	30.9	54 56.3	-37.8	31.6	53
54	51 41.5	-40.6	28.3	52 34.1	-39.9	28.9	53 26.5	-39.3	29.6	54 18.5	-38.7	30.2	54
55	51 00.9	-41.2	27.1	51 54.2	-40.7	27.7	52 47.2	-40.2	28.3	53 39.8	-39.5	28.9	55
56	50 19.7	-41.9	26.0	51 13.5	-41.4	26.5	52 07.0	-40.8	27.1	53 00.3	-40.3	27.7	56
57	49 37.8	-42.6	24.9	50 32.1	-42.1	25.4	51 26.2	-41.6	25.9	52 20.0	-41.0	26.5	57
58	48 55.2	-43.1	23.8	49 50.0	-42.6	24.3	50 44.6	-42.2	24.8	51 39.0	-41.7	25.3	58
59	48 12.1	-43.6	22.7	49 07.4	-43.3	23.2	50 02.4	-42.8	23.6	50 57.3	-42.4	24.1	59
60	47 28.5	-44.2	21.7	48 24.1	-43.8	22.1	49 19.6	-43.4	22.6	50 14.9	-43.0	23.0	60
61	46 44.3	-44.8	20.7	47 40.3	-44.3	21.1	48 36.2	-44.0	21.5	49 31.9	-43.5	21.9	61
62	45 59.5	-45.1	19.7	46 56.0	-44.9	20.1	47 52.2	-44.5	20.5	48 48.4	-44.2	20.9	62
63	45 14.4	-45.7	18.8	46 11.1	-45.3	19.1	47 07.7	-45.0	19.5	48 04.2	-44.6	19.9	63
64	44 28.7	-46.0	17.9	45 25.8	-45.8	18.2	46 22.7	-45.4	18.5	47 19.6	-45.2	18.9	64
65	43 42.7	-46.5	17.0	44 40.0	-46.2	17.3	45 37.3	-46.0	17.6	46 34.4	-45.6	17.9	65
66	42 56.2	-46.8	16.1	43 53.8	-46.6	16.4	44 51.3	-46.3	16.7	45 48.8	-46.1	17.0	66
67	42 09.4	-47.2	15.3	43 07.2	-47.0	15.5	44 05.0	-46.8	15.8	45 02.7	-46.5	16.1	67
68	41 22.2	-47.6	14.5	42 20.2	-47.3	14.7	43 18.2	-47.1	14.9	44 16.2	-46.9	15.2	68
69	40 34.6	-47.9	13.6	41 32.9	-47.7	13.9	42 31.1	-47.5	14.1	43 29.3	-47.3	14.3	69
70	39 46.7	-48.2	12.9	40 45.2	-48.1	13.0	41 43.6	-47.8	13.2	42 42.0	-47.7	13.5	70
71	38 58.5	-48.5	12.1	39 57.1	-48.3	12.3	40 55.8	-48.2	12.4	41 54.3	-48.0	12.6	71
72	38 10.0	-48.8	11.3	39 08.8	-48.6	11.5	40 07.6	-48.5	11.7	41 06.3	-48.3	11.8	72
73	37 21.2	-49.0	10.6	38 20.2	-48.9	10.7	39 19.1	-48.8	10.9	40 18.0	-48.6	11.1	73
74	36 32.2	-49.3	9.9	37 31.3	-49.2	10.0	38 30.3	-49.0	10.1	39 29.4	-48.9	10.3	74
75	35 42.9	-49.6	9.2	36 42.1	-49.5	9.3	37 41.3	-49.3	9.4	38 40.5	-49.2	9.5	75
76	34 53.3	-49.8	8.5	35 52.6	-49.6	8.6	36 52.0	-49.6	8.7	37 51.3	-49.5	8.8	76
77	34 03.5	-50.0	7.8	35 03.0	-49.9	7.9	36 02.4	-49.8	8.0	37 01.8	-49.7	8.1	77
78	33 13.5	-50.2	7.1	34 13.1	-50.2	7.2	35 12.6	-50.1	7.3	36 12.1	-50.0	7.4	78
79	32 23.3	-50.4	6.5	33 22.9	-50.3	6.6	34 22.5	-50.2	6.6	35 22.1	-50.1	6.7	79
80	31 32.9	-50.6	5.8	32 32.6	-50.5	5.9	33 32.3	-50.5	6.0	34 32.0	-50.4	6.0	80
81	30 42.3	-50.7	5.2	31 42.1	-50.7	5.3	32 41.8	-50.6	5.3	33 41.6	-50.6	5.4	81
82	29 51.6	-51.0	4.6	30 51.4	-50.9	4.6	31 51.2	-50.9	4.7	32 51.0	-50.8	4.8	82
83	29 00.6	-51.1	4.0	30 00.5	-51.1	4.0	31 00.3	-51.0	4.1	32 00.2	-51.0	4.1	83
84	28 09.5	-51.2	3.4	29 09.4	-51.2	3.4	30 09.3	-51.2	3.5	31 09.2	-51.1	3.5	84
85	27 18.3	-51.4	2.8	28 18.2	-51.4	2.8	29 18.1	-51.3	2.9	30 18.1	-51.4	2.9	85
86	26 26.9	-51.5	2.2	27 26.8	-51.5	2.3	28 26.8	-51.5	2.3	29 26.7	-51.4	2.3	86
87	25 35.4	-51.7	1.7	26 35.3	-51.6	1.7	27 35.3	-51.6	1.7	28 35.3	-51.6	1.7	87
88	24 43.7	-51.8	1.1	25 43.7	-51.8	1.1	26 43.7	-51.8	1.1	27 43.7	-51.8	1.1	88
89	23 51.9	-51.9	0.5	24 51.9	-51.9	0.6	25 51.9	-51.9	0.6	26 51.9	-51.9	0.6	89
90	23 00.0	-52.0	0.0	24 00.0	-52.0	0.0	25 00.0	-52.0	0.0	26 00.0	-52.0	0.0	90
	23°			24°			25°			26°			

Dec.	27° Hc	d	Z	28° Hc	d	Z	29° Hc	d	Z	30° Hc	d	Z	Dec.
°	° ′	′	°	° ′	′	°	° ′	′	°	° ′	′	°	°
0	50 30.1	+42.5	128.2	49 52.6	+43.4	129.1	49 14.4	+44.2	130.0	48 35.4	+45.1	130.9	0
1	51 12.6	+41.8	127.1	50 36.0	+42.8	128.0	49 58.6	+43.7	129.0	49 20.5	+44.6	129.9	1
2	51 54.4	+41.2	125.9	51 18.8	+42.1	126.9	50 42.3	+43.1	127.9	50 05.1	+44.0	128.9	2
3	52 35.6	+40.4	124.7	52 00.9	+41.5	125.8	51 25.4	+42.5	126.8	50 49.1	+43.3	127.8	3
4	53 16.0	+39.6	123.5	52 42.4	+40.7	124.6	52 07.9	+41.7	125.7	51 32.4	+42.8	126.7	4
5	53 55.6	+38.8	122.2	53 23.1	+40.0	123.4	52 49.6	+41.1	124.5	52 15.2	+42.1	125.5	5
6	54 34.4	+38.0	120.9	54 03.1	+39.1	122.1	53 30.7	+40.2	123.3	52 57.3	+41.3	124.4	6
7	55 12.4	+37.0	119.6	54 42.2	+38.3	120.8	54 10.9	+39.5	122.0	53 38.6	+40.6	123.2	7
8	55 49.4	+36.0	118.2	55 20.5	+37.3	119.5	54 50.4	+38.6	120.7	54 19.2	+39.8	121.9	8
9	56 25.4	+35.1	116.8	55 57.8	+36.4	118.1	55 29.0	+37.7	119.4	54 59.0	+38.9	120.6	9
10	57 00.5	+33.9	115.3	56 34.2	+35.4	116.6	56 06.7	+36.7	118.0	55 37.9	+38.1	119.3	10
11	57 34.4	+32.8	113.7	57 09.6	+34.3	115.2	56 43.4	+35.7	116.6	56 16.0	+37.0	117.9	11
12	58 07.2	+31.7	112.2	57 43.9	+33.1	113.6	57 19.1	+34.7	115.1	56 53.0	+36.1	116.5	12
13	58 38.9	+30.3	110.6	58 17.0	+32.0	112.1	57 53.8	+33.5	113.6	57 29.1	+35.0	115.0	13
14	59 09.2	+29.0	108.9	58 49.0	+30.7	110.4	58 27.3	+32.3	112.0	58 04.1	+33.9	113.5	14
15	59 38.2	+27.7	107.2	59 19.7	+29.4	108.8	58 59.6	+31.1	110.4	58 38.0	+32.7	111.9	15
16	60 05.9	+26.2	105.4	59 49.1	+28.0	107.1	59 30.7	+29.8	108.7	59 10.7	+31.4	110.3	16
17	60 32.1	+24.6	103.6	60 17.1	+26.6	105.3	60 00.5	+28.3	107.0	59 42.1	+30.1	108.6	17
18	60 56.7	+23.1	101.7	60 43.7	+25.0	103.5	60 28.8	+26.9	105.2	60 12.2	+28.8	106.9	18
19	61 19.8	+21.4	99.8	61 08.7	+23.4	101.6	60 55.7	+25.4	103.4	60 41.0	+27.2	105.1	19
20	61 41.2	+19.8	97.8	61 32.1	+21.8	99.7	61 21.1	+23.8	101.5	61 08.2	+25.8	103.3	20
21	62 01.0	+17.9	95.8	61 53.9	+20.0	97.7	61 44.9	+22.1	99.6	61 34.0	+24.1	101.4	21
22	62 18.9	+16.1	93.8	62 13.9	+18.3	95.7	62 07.0	+20.4	97.6	61 58.1	+22.5	99.4	22
23	62 35.0	+14.2	91.7	62 32.2	+16.4	93.6	62 27.4	+18.6	95.6	62 20.6	+20.7	97.5	23
24	62 49.2	+12.3	89.6	62 48.6	+14.5	91.5	62 46.0	+16.7	93.5	62 41.3	+19.0	95.4	24
25	63 01.5	+10.3•	87.4	63 03.1	+12.6	89.4	63 02.7	+14.8	91.4	63 00.3	+17.0	93.3	25
26	63 11.8	+8.2•	85.3	63 15.7	+10.6•	87.2	63 17.5	+12.9•	89.2	63 17.3	+15.1	91.2	26
27	63 20.0	+6.3•	83.1	63 26.3	+8.5•	85.0	63 30.4	+10.8•	87.0	63 32.4	+13.2•	89.1	27
28	63 26.3	+4.1•	80.8	63 34.8	+6.4•	82.8	63 41.2	+8.8•	84.8	63 45.6	+11.1•	86.9	28
29	63 30.4	+2.0•	78.6	63 41.2	+4.4•	80.6	63 50.0	+6.7•	82.6	63 56.7	+9.0•	84.6	29
30	63 32.4	0.0•	76.4	63 45.6	+2.2•	78.3	63 56.7	+4.5•	80.3	64 05.7	+6.9•	82.4	30
31	63 32.4	-2.2•	74.1	63 47.8	+0.1•	76.1	64 01.2	+2.4•	78.1	64 12.6	+4.8•	80.1	31
32	63 30.2	-4.3•	71.9	63 47.9	-2.0•	73.8	64 03.6	+0.3•	75.8	64 17.4	+2.5•	77.8	32
33	63 25.9	-6.3•	69.6	63 45.9	-4.2•	71.5	64 03.9	-1.9•	73.5	64 19.9	+0.5•	75.5	33
34	63 19.6	-8.4•	67.4	63 41.7	-6.2•	69.3	64 02.0	-4.0•	71.2	64 20.4	-1.8•	73.2	34
35	63 11.2	-10.4•	65.2	63 35.5	-8.3•	67.1	63 58.0	-6.2•	68.9	64 18.6	-3.9•	70.9	35
36	63 00.8	-12.4	63.1	63 27.2	-10.4•	64.8	63 51.8	-8.2•	66.7	64 14.7	-6.1•	68.6	36
37	62 48.4	-14.3	60.9	63 16.8	-12.4	62.6	63 43.6	-10.4•	64.4	64 08.6	-8.2•	66.3	37
38	62 34.1	-16.2	58.8	63 04.4	-14.3	60.5	63 33.2	-12.3•	62.2	64 00.4	-10.4•	64.0	38
39	62 17.9	-18.1	56.7	62 50.1	-16.2	58.3	63 20.9	-14.4•	60.0	63 50.0	-12.3•	61.8	39
40	61 59.8	-19.8	54.7	62 33.9	-18.1	56.2	63 06.5	-16.3	57.9	63 37.7	-14.4•	59.6	40
41	61 40.0	-21.5	52.7	62 15.8	-19.9	54.2	62 50.2	-18.1	55.8	63 23.3	-16.3	57.4	41
42	61 18.5	-23.2	50.7	61 55.9	-21.6	52.2	62 32.1	-20.0	53.7	63 07.0	-18.3	55.3	42
43	60 55.3	-24.7	48.8	61 34.3	-23.3	50.2	62 12.1	-21.7	51.6	62 48.7	-20.0	53.2	43
44	60 30.6	-26.3	46.9	61 11.0	-24.9	48.3	61 50.4	-23.4	49.7	62 28.7	-21.8	51.1	44
45	60 04.3	-27.7	45.1	60 46.1	-26.3	46.4	61 27.0	-25.0	47.7	62 06.9	-23.5	49.1	45
46	59 36.6	-29.2	43.4	60 19.8	-27.9	44.6	61 02.0	-26.5	45.8	61 43.4	-25.2	47.2	46
47	59 07.4	-30.4	41.6	59 51.9	-29.3	42.8	60 35.5	-28.0	44.0	61 18.2	-26.7	45.2	47
48	58 37.0	-31.7	40.0	59 22.6	-30.6	41.1	60 07.5	-29.4	42.2	60 51.5	-28.2	43.4	48
49	58 05.3	-32.9	38.4	58 52.0	-31.8	39.4	59 38.1	-30.8	40.5	60 23.3	-29.6	41.6	49
50	57 32.4	-34.0	36.8	58 20.2	-33.1	37.8	59 07.3	-32.0	38.8	59 53.7	-30.9	39.8	50
51	56 58.4	-35.1	35.3	57 47.1	-34.1	36.2	58 35.3	-33.3	37.1	59 22.8	-32.2	38.2	51
52	56 23.3	-36.1	33.8	57 13.0	-35.3	34.6	58 02.0	-34.3	35.6	58 50.6	-33.5	36.5	52
53	55 47.2	-37.1	32.4	56 37.7	-36.3	33.2	57 27.7	-35.5	34.0	58 17.1	-34.5	34.9	53
54	55 10.1	-38.0	31.0	56 01.4	-37.3	31.7	56 52.2	-36.5	32.5	57 42.6	-35.7	33.4	54
55	54 32.1	-38.8	29.6	55 24.1	-38.2	30.3	56 15.7	-37.5	31.1	57 06.9	-36.7	31.9	55
56	53 53.3	-39.7	28.3	54 45.9	-39.0	29.0	55 38.2	-38.3	29.7	56 30.2	-37.7	30.4	56
57	53 13.6	-40.5	27.1	54 06.9	-39.9	27.7	54 59.9	-39.3	28.3	55 52.5	-38.6	29.0	57
58	52 33.1	-41.2	25.8	53 27.0	-40.6	26.4	54 20.6	-40.1	27.0	55 13.9	-39.5	27.7	58
59	51 51.9	-41.8	24.6	52 46.4	-41.4	25.2	53 40.5	-40.8	25.8	54 34.4	-40.3	26.4	59
60	51 10.1	-42.6	23.5	52 05.0	-42.1	24.0	52 59.7	-41.6	24.5	53 54.1	-41.0	25.1	60
61	50 27.5	-43.2	22.4	51 22.9	-42.7	22.9	52 18.1	-42.3	23.4	53 13.1	-41.8	23.9	61
62	49 44.3	-43.7	21.3	50 40.2	-43.4	21.7	51 35.8	-42.9	22.2	52 31.3	-42.5	22.7	62
63	49 00.6	-44.3	20.2	49 56.8	-43.9	20.7	50 52.9	-43.6	21.1	51 48.8	-43.2	21.5	63
64	48 16.3	-44.9	19.2	49 12.9	-44.5	19.6	50 09.3	-44.1	20.0	51 05.6	-43.7	20.4	64
65	47 31.4	-45.3	18.2	48 28.4	-45.0	18.6	49 25.2	-44.7	19.0	50 21.9	-44.4	19.3	65
66	46 46.1	-45.8	17.3	47 43.4	-45.6	17.6	48 40.5	-45.2	17.9	49 37.5	-44.9	18.3	66
67	46 00.3	-46.2	16.3	46 57.8	-45.9	16.6	47 55.3	-45.7	16.9	48 52.6	-45.4	17.3	67
68	45 14.1	-46.7	15.4	46 11.9	-46.5	15.7	47 09.6	-46.2	16.0	48 07.2	-45.9	16.3	68
69	44 27.4	-47.1	14.5	45 25.4	-46.8	14.8	46 23.4	-46.6	15.1	47 21.3	-46.4	15.3	69
70	43 40.3	-47.4	13.7	44 38.6	-47.3	13.9	45 36.8	-47.0	14.2	46 34.9	-46.8	14.4	70
71	42 52.9	-47.9	12.8	43 51.3	-47.6	13.0	44 49.8	-47.5	13.3	45 48.1	-47.2	13.5	71
72	42 05.0	-48.1	12.0	43 03.7	-48.0	12.2	44 02.3	-47.8	12.4	45 00.9	-47.6	12.6	72
73	41 16.9	-48.5	11.2	42 15.7	-48.3	11.4	43 14.5	-48.1	11.6	44 13.3	-48.0	11.8	73
74	40 28.4	-48.8	10.4	41 27.4	-48.6	10.6	42 26.4	-48.5	10.8	43 25.3	-48.4	10.9	74
75	39 39.6	-49.1	9.7	40 38.8	-49.0	9.8	41 37.9	-48.9	10.0	42 36.9	-48.6	10.1	75
76	38 50.5	-49.3	8.9	39 49.8	-49.2	9.1	40 49.0	-49.1	9.2	41 48.3	-49.0	9.3	76
77	38 01.2	-49.6	8.2	39 00.6	-49.5	8.3	39 59.9	-49.4	8.4	40 59.3	-49.3	8.6	77
78	37 11.6	-49.9	7.5	38 11.1	-49.8	7.6	39 10.5	-49.7	7.7	40 10.0	-49.6	7.8	78
79	36 21.7	-50.1	6.8	37 21.3	-50.0	6.9	38 20.8	-49.9	7.0	39 20.4	-49.8	7.1	79
80	35 31.6	-50.3	6.1	36 31.3	-50.3	6.2	37 30.9	-50.2	6.3	38 30.6	-50.2	6.4	80
81	34 41.3	-50.5	5.5	35 41.0	-50.5	5.5	36 40.7	-50.4	5.6	37 40.4	-50.3	5.7	81
82	33 50.8	-50.8	4.8	34 50.5	-50.6	4.9	35 50.3	-50.6	4.9	36 50.1	-50.6	5.0	82
83	33 00.0	-50.9	4.2	33 59.9	-50.9	4.2	34 59.7	-50.8	4.3	35 59.5	-50.8	4.3	83
84	32 09.1	-51.1	3.5	33 09.0	-51.1	3.6	34 08.9	-51.1	3.6	35 08.7	-51.0	3.7	84
85	31 18.0	-51.3	2.9	32 17.9	-51.2	3.0	33 17.8	-51.2	3.0	34 17.7	-51.2	3.0	85
86	30 26.7	-51.4	2.3	31 26.7	-51.5	2.3	32 26.6	-51.4	2.4	33 26.5	-51.3	2.4	86
87	29 35.3	-51.6	1.7	30 35.2	-51.6	1.7	31 35.2	-51.6	1.8	32 35.2	-51.6	1.8	87
88	28 43.6	-51.7	1.1	29 43.6	-51.7	1.2	30 43.6	-51.7	1.2	31 43.6	-51.7	1.2	88
89	27 51.9	-51.9	0.6	28 51.9	-51.9	0.6	29 51.9	-51.9	0.6	30 51.9	-51.9	0.6	89
90	27 00.0	-52.0	0.0	28 00.0	-52.0	0.0	29 00.0	-52.0	0.0	30 00.0	-52.0	0.0	90
	27°			28°			29°			30°			

LATITUDE CONTRARY NAME TO DECLINATION L.H.A. 30°, 330°

Dec.	23° Hc	d	Z	24° Hc	d	Z	25° Hc	d	Z	26° Hc	d	Z
°	° ′	′	°	° ′	′	°	° ′	′	°	° ′	′	°
0	52 51.7	-39.2	124.1	52 17.6	-40.3	125.2	51 42.6	-41.3	126.2	51 06.7	-42.2	127.2
1	52 12.5	-40.0	125.3	51 37.3	-41.0	126.4	51 01.3	-41.9	127.4	50 24.5	-42.8	128.3
2	51 32.5	-40.7	126.5	50 56.3	-41.6	127.5	50 19.4	-42.6	128.5	49 41.7	-43.5	129.4
3	50 51.8	-41.4	127.7	50 14.7	-42.3	128.7	49 36.8	-43.2	129.6	48 58.2	-44.0	130.5
4	50 10.4	-42.1	128.9	49 32.4	-42.9	129.8	48 53.6	-43.7	130.7	48 14.2	-44.5	131.5
5	49 28.3	-42.6	130.0	48 49.5	-43.5	130.8	48 09.9	-44.3	131.7	47 29.7	-45.1	132.5
6	48 45.7	-43.3	131.0	48 06.0	-44.1	131.9	47 25.6	-44.8	132.7	46 44.6	-45.5	133.5
7	48 02.4	-43.7	132.1	47 21.9	-44.5	132.9	46 40.8	-45.3	133.7	45 59.1	-46.0	134.4
8	47 18.7	-44.4	133.1	46 37.4	-45.1	133.9	45 55.5	-45.7	134.6	45 13.1	-46.4	135.3
9	46 34.3	-44.8	134.1	45 52.3	-45.5	134.8	45 09.8	-46.2	135.5	44 26.7	-46.8	136.2
10	45 49.5	-45.3	135.0	45 06.8	-45.9	135.8	44 23.6	-46.6	136.4	43 39.9	-47.3	137.1
11	45 04.2	-45.7	136.0	44 20.9	-46.4	136.7	43 37.0	-47.0	137.3	42 52.6	-47.5	138.0
12	44 18.5	-46.1	136.9	43 34.5	-46.8	137.5	42 50.0	-47.4	138.2	42 05.1	-47.9	138.8
13	43 32.4	-46.6	137.8	42 47.7	-47.1	138.4	42 02.6	-47.7	139.0	41 17.2	-48.3	139.6
14	42 45.8	-46.9	138.6	42 00.6	-47.5	139.2	41 14.9	-48.0	139.8	40 28.9	-48.6	140.4
15	41 58.9	-47.3	139.5	41 13.1	-47.9	140.1	40 26.9	-48.4	140.6	39 40.3	-48.8	141.1
16	41 11.6	-47.6	140.3	40 25.2	-48.1	140.9	39 38.5	-48.6	141.4	38 51.5	-49.2	141.9
17	40 24.0	-48.0	141.1	39 37.1	-48.5	141.6	38 49.9	-49.0	142.1	38 02.3	-49.4	142.6
18	39 36.0	-48.3	141.9	38 48.6	-48.7	142.4	38 00.9	-49.2	142.9	37 12.9	-49.6	143.3
19	38 47.7	-48.5	142.7	37 59.9	-49.1	143.1	37 11.7	-49.5	143.6	36 23.3	-49.9	144.0
20	37 59.2	-48.9	143.4	37 10.8	-49.3	143.9	36 22.2	-49.7	144.3	35 33.4	-50.1	144.7
21	37 10.3	-49.1	144.1	36 21.5	-49.5	144.6	35 32.5	-49.9	145.0	34 43.3	-50.4	145.4
22	36 21.2	-49.4	144.9	35 32.0	-49.8	145.3	34 42.6	-50.2	145.7	33 52.9	-50.5	146.1
23	35 31.8	-49.6	145.6	34 42.2	-50.0	146.0	33 52.4	-50.4	146.3	33 02.4	-50.8	146.7
24	34 42.2	-49.8	146.2	33 52.2	-50.2	146.6	33 02.0	-50.5	147.0	32 11.6	-50.9	147.3
25	33 52.4	-50.0	146.9	33 02.0	-50.4	147.3	32 11.5	-50.8	147.6	31 20.7	-51.1	148.0
26	33 02.4	-50.3	147.6	32 11.6	-50.6	147.9	31 20.7	-51.0	148.3	30 29.6	-51.3	148.6
27	32 12.1	-50.4	148.2	31 21.0	-50.8	148.6	30 29.7	-51.1	148.9	29 38.3	-51.4	149.2
28	31 21.7	-50.7	148.9	30 30.2	-50.9	149.2	29 38.6	-51.3	149.5	28 46.9	-51.6	149.8
29	30 31.0	-50.8	149.5	29 39.3	-51.2	149.8	28 47.3	-51.4	150.1	27 55.3	-51.8	150.3
30	29 40.2	-50.9	150.1	28 48.1	-51.2	150.4	27 55.9	-51.6	150.7	27 03.5	-51.8	150.9
31	28 49.3	-51.2	150.7	27 56.9	-51.5	151.0	27 04.3	-51.7	151.2	26 11.7	-52.0	151.5
32	27 58.1	-51.3	151.3	27 05.4	-51.5	151.6	26 12.6	-51.8	151.8	25 19.7	-52.1	152.0
33	27 06.8	-51.4	151.9	26 13.9	-51.7	152.1	25 20.8	-52.0	152.4	24 27.6	-52.3	152.6
34	26 15.4	-51.5	152.5	25 22.2	-51.9	152.7	24 28.8	-52.1	152.9	23 35.3	-52.3	153.1
35	25 23.9	-51.7	153.0	24 30.3	-51.9	153.2	23 36.7	-52.2	153.4	22 43.0	-52.5	153.6
36	24 32.2	-51.8	153.6	23 38.4	-52.1	153.8	22 44.5	-52.3	154.0	21 50.5	-52.5	154.2
37	23 40.4	-52.0	154.2	22 46.3	-52.2	154.3	21 52.2	-52.4	154.5	20 58.0	-52.6	154.7
38	22 48.4	-52.0	154.7	21 54.1	-52.2	154.9	20 59.8	-52.5	155.0	20 05.4	-52.8	155.2
39	21 56.4	-52.2	155.2	21 01.9	-52.4	155.4	20 07.3	-52.6	155.6	19 12.6	-52.8	155.7
40	21 04.2	-52.2	155.8	20 09.5	-52.5	155.9	19 14.7	-52.7	156.1	18 19.8	-52.9	156.2
41	20 12.0	-52.3	156.3	19 17.0	-52.5	156.4	18 22.0	-52.8	156.6	17 26.9	-52.9	156.7
42	19 19.7	-52.5	156.8	18 24.5	-52.6	156.9	17 29.2	-52.8	157.1	16 34.0	-53.1	157.2
43	18 27.2	-52.5	157.3	17 31.9	-52.8	157.5	16 36.4	-52.9	157.6	15 40.9	-53.1	157.7
44	17 34.7	-52.5	157.8	16 39.1	-52.7	158.0	15 43.5	-53.0	158.1	14 47.8	-53.1	158.2
45	16 42.2	-52.7	158.3	15 46.4	-52.9	158.4	14 50.5	-53.0	158.5	13 54.7	-53.2	158.6
46	15 49.5	-52.7	158.8	14 53.5	-52.9	158.9	13 57.5	-53.1	159.0	13 01.5	-53.3	159.1
47	14 56.8	-52.8	159.3	14 00.6	-52.9	159.4	13 04.4	-53.1	159.5	12 08.2	-53.3	159.6
48	14 04.0	-52.9	159.8	13 07.7	-53.1	159.9	12 11.3	-53.2	160.0	11 14.9	-53.3	160.1
49	13 11.1	-52.9	160.3	12 14.6	-53.0	160.4	11 18.1	-53.2	160.5	10 21.6	-53.4	160.5
50	12 18.2	-52.9	160.8	11 21.6	-53.1	160.9	10 24.9	-53.2	160.9	9 28.2	-53.5	161.0
51	11 25.3	-53.0	161.3	10 28.5	-53.2	161.3	9 31.6	-53.3	161.4	8 34.7	-53.4	161.4
52	10 32.3	-53.0	161.8	9 35.3	-53.2	161.8	8 38.3	-53.3	161.9	7 41.3	-53.5	161.9
53	9 39.3	-53.1	162.2	8 42.1	-53.2	162.3	7 45.0	-53.4	162.3	6 47.8	-53.5	162.4
54	8 46.2	-53.1	162.7	7 48.9	-53.3	162.7	6 51.6	-53.4	162.8	5 54.3	-53.6	162.8
55	7 53.1	-53.2	163.2	6 55.6	-53.3	163.2	5 58.2	-53.4	163.2	5 00.7	-53.5	163.3
56	6 59.9	-53.2	163.6	6 02.3	-53.3	163.7	5 04.8	-53.5	163.7	4 07.2	-53.6	163.7
57	6 06.7	-53.1	164.1	5 09.0	-53.3	164.1	4 11.3	-53.4	164.2	3 13.6	-53.6	164.2
58	5 13.6	-53.3	164.6	4 15.7	-53.3	164.6	3 17.9	-53.5	164.6	2 20.0	-53.6	164.6
59	4 20.3	-53.2	165.0	3 22.4	-53.4	165.1	2 24.4	-53.5	165.1	1 26.4	-53.6	165.1
60	3 27.1	-53.2	165.5	2 29.0	-53.4	165.5	1 30.9	-53.5	165.5	0 32.8	-53.6	165.5
61	2 33.9	-53.3	166.0	1 35.6	-53.3	166.0	0 37.4	-53.4	166.0	0 20.8	+53.6	14.0
62	1 40.6	-53.3	166.4	0 42.3	-53.4	166.4	0 16.0	+53.5	13.6	1 14.4	+53.6	13.6
63	0 47.3	-53.2	166.9	0 11.1	+53.4	13.1	1 09.5	+53.5	13.1	2 08.0	+53.6	13.1
64	0 05.9	+53.3	12.7	1 04.5	+53.3	12.7	2 03.0	+53.5	12.7	3 01.6	+53.5	12.7
65	0 59.2	+53.3	12.2	1 57.8	+53.4	12.2	2 56.5	+53.4	12.2	3 55.1	+53.6	12.2
66	1 52.5	+53.2	11.7	2 51.2	+53.4	11.7	3 49.9	+53.5	11.8	4 48.7	+53.5	11.8
67	2 45.7	+53.3	11.3	3 44.6	+53.3	11.3	4 43.4	+53.4	11.3	5 42.2	+53.5	11.3
68	3 39.0	+53.2	10.8	4 37.9	+53.3	10.8	5 36.8	+53.4	10.8	6 35.7	+53.5	10.9
69	4 32.2	+53.2	10.4	5 31.2	+53.3	10.4	6 30.2	+53.4	10.4	7 29.2	+53.5	10.4
70	5 25.4	+53.2	9.9	6 24.5	+53.3	9.9	7 23.6	+53.4	9.9	8 22.7	+53.5	10.0
71	6 18.6	+53.2	9.4	7 17.8	+53.2	9.4	8 17.0	+53.3	9.5	9 16.2	+53.4	9.5
72	7 11.8	+53.1	9.0	8 11.0	+53.2	9.0	9 10.3	+53.3	9.0	10 09.6	+53.3	9.0
73	8 04.9	+53.1	8.5	9 04.2	+53.2	8.5	10 03.6	+53.2	8.5	11 02.9	+53.3	8.6
74	8 58.0	+53.1	8.0	9 57.4	+53.2	8.0	10 56.8	+53.2	8.1	11 56.2	+53.3	8.1
75	9 51.1	+53.0	7.5	10 50.6	+53.1	7.6	11 50.0	+53.2	7.6	12 49.5	+53.2	7.6
76	10 44.1	+53.0	7.1	11 43.7	+53.0	7.1	12 43.2	+53.1	7.1	13 42.7	+53.2	7.2
77	11 37.1	+52.9	6.6	12 36.7	+53.0	6.6	13 36.3	+53.0	6.6	14 35.9	+53.1	6.7
78	12 30.0	+52.9	6.1	13 29.7	+52.9	6.1	14 29.3	+53.0	6.2	15 29.0	+53.0	6.2
79	13 22.9	+52.9	5.6	14 22.6	+52.9	5.7	15 22.3	+53.0	5.7	16 22.0	+53.0	5.7
80	14 15.8	+52.7	5.1	15 15.5	+52.8	5.2	16 15.3	+52.8	5.2	17 15.0	+52.9	5.2
81	15 08.5	+52.7	4.6	16 08.3	+52.8	4.7	17 08.1	+52.8	4.7	18 07.9	+52.9	4.7
82	16 01.2	+52.7	4.2	17 01.1	+52.7	4.2	18 00.9	+52.7	4.2	19 00.8	+52.7	4.2
83	16 53.9	+52.5	3.7	17 53.8	+52.5	3.7	18 53.6	+52.7	3.7	19 53.5	+52.7	3.7
84	17 46.4	+52.5	3.1	18 46.3	+52.6	3.2	19 46.3	+52.5	3.2	20 46.2	+52.5	3.2
85	18 38.9	+52.4	2.6	19 38.9	+52.4	2.7	20 38.8	+52.4	2.7	21 38.7	+52.5	2.7
86	19 31.3	+52.3	2.1	20 31.3	+52.3	2.1	21 31.2	+52.4	2.1	22 31.2	+52.4	2.2
87	20 23.6	+52.3	1.6	21 23.6	+52.3	1.6	22 23.6	+52.2	1.6	23 23.6	+52.2	1.6
88	21 15.9	+52.1	1.1	22 15.9	+52.1	1.1	23 15.8	+52.2	1.1	24 15.8	+52.2	1.1
89	22 08.0	+52.0	0.5	23 08.0	+52.0	0.5	24 08.0	+52.0	0.5	25 08.0	+52.0	0.6
90	23 00.0	+51.9	0.0	24 00.0	+51.9	0.0	25 00.0	+51.9	0.0	26 00.0	+51.9	0.0
	23°			24°			25°			26°		

27° Hc	d	Z	28° Hc	d	Z	29° Hc	d	Z	30° Hc	d	Z	Dec.
° ′	′	°	° ′	′	°	° ′	′	°	° ′	′	°	°
50 30.1	-43.2	128.2	49 52.6	-44.0	129.1	49 14.4	-44.9	130.0	48 35.4	-45.6	130.9	0
49 46.9	-43.7	129.3	49 08.6	-44.6	130.2	48 29.5	-45.3	131.0	47 49.8	-46.1	131.9	1
49 03.2	-44.3	130.3	48 24.0	-45.0	131.2	47 44.2	-45.8	132.0	47 03.7	-46.5	132.8	2
48 18.9	-44.8	131.3	47 39.0	-45.6	132.2	46 58.4	-46.3	133.0	46 17.2	-47.0	133.7	3
47 34.1	-45.3	132.3	46 53.4	-46.0	133.1	46 12.1	-46.7	133.9	45 30.2	-47.4	134.6	4
46 48.8	-45.8	133.3	46 07.4	-46.5	134.1	45 25.4	-47.2	134.8	44 42.8	-47.7	135.5	5
46 03.0	-46.2	134.2	45 20.9	-46.9	135.0	44 38.2	-47.5	135.7	43 55.1	-48.2	136.3	6
45 16.8	-46.6	135.1	44 34.0	-47.3	135.8	43 50.7	-47.9	136.5	43 06.9	-48.4	137.2	7
44 30.2	-47.1	136.0	43 46.7	-47.6	136.7	43 02.8	-48.2	137.3	42 18.5	-48.8	138.0	8
43 43.1	-47.4	136.9	42 59.1	-48.1	137.5	42 14.6	-48.6	138.2	41 29.7	-49.1	138.8	9
42 55.7	-47.8	137.7	42 11.0	-48.3	138.4	41 26.0	-48.9	138.9	40 40.6	-49.4	139.5	10
42 07.9	-48.2	138.6	41 22.7	-48.7	139.1	40 37.1	-49.2	139.7	39 51.2	-49.7	140.3	11
41 19.7	-48.4	139.4	40 34.0	-49.0	139.9	39 47.9	-49.4	140.5	39 01.5	-50.0	141.0	12
40 31.3	-48.8	140.1	39 45.0	-49.2	140.7	38 58.5	-49.8	141.2	38 11.5	-50.2	141.7	13
39 42.5	-49.0	140.9	38 55.8	-49.6	141.4	38 08.7	-50.0	141.9	37 21.3	-50.4	142.4	14
38 53.5	-49.4	141.6	38 06.2	-49.7	142.1	37 18.7	-50.2	142.6	36 30.9	-50.7	143.1	15
38 04.1	-49.6	142.4	37 16.5	-50.1	142.8	36 28.5	-50.5	143.3	35 40.2	-50.8	143.7	16
37 14.5	-49.8	143.1	36 26.4	-50.3	143.5	35 38.0	-50.7	144.0	34 49.4	-51.1	144.4	17
36 24.7	-50.1	143.8	35 36.1	-50.5	144.2	34 47.3	-50.8	144.6	33 58.3	-51.3	145.0	18
35 34.6	-50.3	144.5	34 45.6	-50.7	144.9	33 56.5	-51.1	145.3	33 07.0	-51.4	145.6	19
34 44.3	-50.5	145.1	33 54.9	-50.9	145.5	33 05.4	-51.3	145.9	32 15.6	-51.6	146.2	20
33 53.8	-50.8	145.8	33 04.0	-51.1	146.2	32 14.1	-51.4	146.5	31 24.0	-51.8	146.8	21
33 03.0	-50.9	146.4	32 12.9	-51.2	146.8	31 22.7	-51.7	147.1	30 32.2	-52.0	147.4	22
32 12.1	-51.1	147.0	31 21.7	-51.5	147.4	30 31.0	-51.7	147.7	29 40.2	-52.1	148.0	23
31 21.0	-51.3	147.7	30 30.2	-51.6	148.0	29 39.3	-52.0	148.3	28 48.1	-52.2	148.6	24
30 29.7	-51.4	148.3	29 38.6	-51.7	148.6	28 47.3	-52.0	148.9	27 55.9	-52.4	149.1	25
29 38.3	-51.6	148.9	28 46.9	-51.9	149.2	27 55.3	-52.2	149.4	27 03.5	-52.4	149.7	26
28 46.7	-51.7	149.5	27 55.0	-52.1	149.7	27 03.1	-52.4	150.0	26 11.1	-52.7	150.2	27
27 55.0	-51.9	150.0	27 02.9	-52.2	150.3	26 10.7	-52.4	150.5	25 18.4	-52.7	150.8	28
27 03.1	-52.0	150.6	26 10.7	-52.3	150.8	25 18.3	-52.6	151.1	24 25.7	-52.8	151.3	29
26 11.1	-52.2	151.1	25 18.4	-52.4	151.4	24 25.7	-52.7	151.6	23 32.9	-52.9	151.8	30
25 18.9	-52.3	151.7	24 26.0	-52.5	151.9	23 33.0	-52.7	152.1	22 40.0	-53.1	152.3	31
24 26.6	-52.3	152.2	23 33.5	-52.6	152.4	22 40.3	-52.9	152.6	21 46.9	-53.1	152.8	32
23 34.3	-52.5	152.8	22 40.9	-52.8	153.0	21 47.4	-53.0	153.2	20 53.8	-53.2	153.3	33
22 41.8	-52.6	153.3	21 48.1	-52.8	153.5	20 54.4	-53.1	153.7	20 00.6	-53.3	153.8	34
21 49.2	-52.7	153.8	20 55.3	-52.9	154.0	20 01.3	-53.1	154.2	19 07.3	-53.4	154.3	35
20 56.5	-52.8	154.3	20 02.4	-53.0	154.5	19 08.2	-53.2	154.6	18 13.9	-53.4	154.8	36
20 03.7	-52.8	154.8	19 09.4	-53.1	155.0	18 15.0	-53.3	155.1	17 20.5	-53.5	155.3	37
19 10.9	-53.0	155.3	18 16.3	-53.2	155.5	17 21.7	-53.4	155.6	16 27.0	-53.6	155.7	38
18 17.9	-53.0	155.8	17 23.1	-53.2	156.0	16 28.3	-53.4	156.1	15 33.4	-53.6	156.2	39
17 24.9	-53.1	156.3	16 29.9	-53.3	156.5	15 34.9	-53.5	156.6	14 39.8	-53.7	156.7	40
16 31.8	-53.2	156.8	15 36.6	-53.3	156.9	14 41.4	-53.6	157.0	13 46.1	-53.7	157.1	41
15 38.6	-53.2	157.3	14 43.3	-53.5	157.4	13 47.8	-53.6	157.5	12 52.4	-53.8	157.6	42
14 45.4	-53.3	157.8	13 49.8	-53.4	157.9	12 54.2	-53.6	158.0	11 58.6	-53.8	158.0	43
13 52.1	-53.3	158.3	12 56.4	-53.5	158.3	12 00.6	-53.7	158.4	11 04.8	-53.9	158.5	44
12 58.8	-53.4	158.7	12 02.9	-53.6	158.8	11 06.9	-53.7	158.9	10 10.9	-53.9	158.9	45
12 05.4	-53.4	159.2	11 09.3	-53.6	159.3	10 13.2	-53.8	159.3	9 17.0	-53.9	159.4	46
11 12.0	-53.5	159.7	10 15.7	-53.6	159.7	9 19.4	-53.8	159.8	8 23.1	-54.0	159.8	47
10 18.5	-53.5	160.1	9 22.1	-53.7	160.2	8 25.6	-53.8	160.2	7 29.1	-54.0	160.3	48
9 25.0	-53.6	160.6	8 28.4	-53.7	160.6	7 31.8	-53.9	160.7	6 35.1	-54.0	160.7	49
8 31.4	-53.6	161.0	7 34.7	-53.8	161.1	6 37.9	-53.9	161.1	5 41.1	-54.0	161.2	50
7 37.8	-53.6	161.5	6 40.9	-53.7	161.5	5 44.0	-53.9	161.6	4 47.1	-54.0	161.6	51
6 44.2	-53.6	161.9	5 47.2	-53.8	162.0	4 50.1	-53.9	162.0	3 53.1	-54.1	162.0	52
5 50.6	-53.7	162.4	4 53.4	-53.8	162.4	3 56.2	-53.9	162.4	2 59.0	-54.1	162.5	53
4 56.9	-53.6	162.8	3 59.6	-53.8	162.9	3 02.3	-54.0	162.9	2 04.9	-54.1	162.9	54
4 03.3	-53.7	163.3	3 05.8	-53.8	163.3	2 08.3	-53.9	163.3	1 10.8	-54.0	163.3	55
3 09.6	-53.7	163.7	2 12.0	-53.9	163.8	1 14.4	-54.0	163.8	0 16.8	-54.1	163.8	56
2 15.9	-53.7	164.2	1 18.1	-53.8	164.2	0 20.4	-53.9	164.2	0 37.3	+54.1	15.8	57
1 22.2	-53.8	164.6	0 24.3	-53.8	164.6	0 33.5	+54.0	15.4	1 31.4	+54.1	15.4	58
0 28.4	-53.7	165.1	0 29.5	+53.9	14.9	1 27.5	+54.0	14.9	2 25.5	+54.0	14.9	59
0 25.3	+53.7	14.5	1 23.4	+53.8	14.5	2 21.5	+53.9	14.5	3 19.5	+54.1	14.5	60
1 19.0	+53.7	14.0	2 17.2	+53.8	14.0	3 15.4	+53.9	14.1	4 13.6	+54.0	14.1	61
2 12.7	+53.7	13.6	3 11.0	+53.8	13.6	4 09.3	+53.9	13.6	5 07.6	+54.1	13.6	62
3 06.4	+53.7	13.1	4 04.8	+53.8	13.2	5 03.2	+53.9	13.2	6 01.7	+54.0	13.2	63
4 00.1	+53.7	12.7	4 58.6	+53.8	12.7	5 57.1	+53.9	12.7	6 55.7	+53.9	12.8	64
4 53.8	+53.6	12.2	5 52.4	+53.8	12.3	6 51.0	+53.9	12.3	7 49.6	+54.0	12.3	65
5 47.4	+53.7	11.8	6 46.2	+53.7	11.8	7 44.9	+53.8	11.8	8 43.6	+53.9	11.9	66
6 41.1	+53.6	11.3	7 39.9	+53.7	11.4	8 38.7	+53.8	11.4	9 37.5	+53.9	11.4	67
7 34.7	+53.6	10.9	8 33.6	+53.7	10.9	9 32.5	+53.8	10.9	10 31.4	+53.9	11.0	68
8 28.3	+53.5	10.4	9 27.3	+53.6	10.5	10 26.3	+53.7	10.5	11 25.3	+53.8	10.5	69
9 21.8	+53.5	10.0	10 20.9	+53.6	10.0	11 20.0	+53.7	10.0	12 19.1	+53.7	10.1	70
10 15.3	+53.5	9.5	11 14.5	+53.6	9.6	12 13.7	+53.6	9.6	13 12.8	+53.7	9.6	71
11 08.8	+53.4	9.1	12 08.1	+53.5	9.1	13 07.3	+53.6	9.1	14 06.5	+53.7	9.2	72
12 02.2	+53.4	8.6	13 01.6	+53.4	8.6	14 00.9	+53.5	8.7	15 00.2	+53.6	8.7	73
12 55.6	+53.4	8.1	13 55.0	+53.4	8.2	14 54.4	+53.5	8.2	15 53.8	+53.5	8.2	74
13 49.0	+53.3	7.7	14 48.4	+53.4	7.7	15 47.9	+53.4	7.7	16 47.3	+53.5	7.8	75
14 42.3	+53.2	7.2	15 41.8	+53.3	7.2	16 41.3	+53.4	7.3	17 40.8	+53.4	7.3	76
15 35.5	+53.1	6.7	16 35.1	+53.2	6.7	17 34.7	+53.2	6.8	18 34.2	+53.4	6.8	77
16 28.6	+53.1	6.2	17 28.3	+53.1	6.3	18 27.9	+53.2	6.3	19 27.6	+53.2	6.3	78
17 21.7	+53.1	5.7	18 21.4	+53.1	5.8	19 21.1	+53.2	5.8	20 20.8	+53.2	5.8	79
18 14.8	+52.9	5.2	19 14.5	+53.0	5.3	20 14.3	+53.0	5.3	21 14.0	+53.1	5.3	80
19 07.7	+52.9	4.7	20 07.5	+52.9	4.8	21 07.3	+53.0	4.8	22 07.1	+53.0	4.8	81
20 00.6	+52.8	4.2	21 00.4	+52.8	4.3	22 00.3	+52.8	4.3	23 00.1	+52.9	4.3	82
20 53.4	+52.7	3.7	21 53.2	+52.8	3.8	22 53.1	+52.8	3.8	23 53.0	+52.8	3.8	83
21 46.1	+52.6	3.2	22 46.0	+52.6	3.2	23 45.9	+52.6	3.3	24 45.8	+52.7	3.3	84
22 38.7	+52.5	2.7	23 38.6	+52.5	2.7	24 38.5	+52.6	2.7	25 38.5	+52.5	2.8	85
23 31.2	+52.3	2.2	24 31.1	+52.4	2.2	25 31.1	+52.4	2.2	26 31.0	+52.5	2.2	86
24 23.5	+52.3	1.6	25 23.5	+52.3	1.7	26 23.5	+52.3	1.7	27 23.5	+52.3	1.7	87
25 15.8	+52.2	1.1	26 15.8	+52.2	1.1	27 15.8	+52.2	1.1	28 15.8	+52.2	1.1	88
26 08.0	+52.0	0.6	27 08.0	+52.0	0.6	28 08.0	+52.0	0.6	29 08.0	+52.0	0.6	89
27 00.0	+51.9	0.0	28 00.0	+51.9	0.0	29 00.0	+51.9	0.0	30 00.0	+51.9	0.0	90
27°			28°			29°			30°			

S. Lat. { L.H.A. greater than 180° ....Zn=180°−Z; L.H.A. less than 180°...........Zn=180°+Z

LATITUDE SAME NAME AS DECLINATION L.H.A. 150°, 210°

31°, 329° L.H.A. LATITUDE SAME NAME AS DECLINATION N. Lat. {L.H.A. greater than 180° .....Zn=Z; L.H.A. less than 180°............Zn=360°−Z}

Dec.	23° Hc	d	Z	24° Hc	d	Z	25° Hc	d	Z	26° Hc	d	Z	27° Hc	d	Z	28° Hc	d	Z	29° Hc	d	Z	30° Hc	d	Z	Dec.
°	° ′	′	°	° ′	′	°	° ′	′	°	° ′	′	°	° ′	′	°	° ′	′	°	° ′	′	°	° ′	′	°	°
0	52 05.7	+37.7	123.0	51 32.5	+38.9	124.1	50 58.4	+39.9	125.1	50 23.5	+40.9	126.1	49 47.7	+41.9	127.1	49 11.2	+42.7	128.0	48 33.8	+43.7	128.9	47 55.8	+44.5	129.8	0
1	52 43.4	+36.9	121.8	52 11.4	+38.0	122.9	51 38.3	+39.2	123.9	51 04.4	+40.2	125.0	50 29.6	+41.2	126.0	49 53.9	+42.2	126.9	49 17.5	+43.1	127.9	48 40.3	+44.0	128.8	1
2	53 20.3	+36.1	120.5	52 49.4	+37.2	121.6	52 17.5	+38.4	122.7	51 44.6	+39.5	123.8	51 10.8	+40.5	124.8	50 36.1	+41.6	125.8	50 00.6	+42.5	126.8	49 24.3	+43.4	127.7	2
3	53 56.4	+35.1	119.1	53 26.6	+36.4	120.3	52 55.9	+37.5	121.4	52 24.1	+38.7	122.5	51 51.3	+39.8	123.6	51 17.7	+40.8	124.7	50 43.1	+41.8	125.7	50 07.7	+42.8	126.6	3
4	54 31.5	+34.1	117.7	54 03.0	+35.4	118.9	53 33.4	+36.7	120.1	53 02.8	+37.8	121.3	52 31.1	+39.0	122.4	51 58.5	+40.1	123.5	51 24.9	+41.2	124.5	50 50.5	+42.1	125.5	4
5	55 05.6	+33.0	116.3	54 38.4	+34.4	117.6	54 10.1	+35.7	118.8	53 40.6	+37.0	120.0	53 10.1	+38.2	121.1	52 38.6	+39.3	122.3	52 06.1	+40.4	123.4	51 32.6	+41.5	124.4	5
6	55 38.6	+32.0	114.8	55 12.8	+33.4	116.1	54 45.8	+34.8	117.4	54 17.6	+36.1	118.6	53 48.3	+37.3	119.8	53 17.9	+38.5	121.0	52 46.5	+39.7	122.1	52 14.1	+40.7	123.2	6
7	56 10.6	+30.9	113.3	55 46.2	+32.4	114.7	55 20.6	+33.7	116.0	54 53.7	+35.1	117.3	54 25.6	+36.4	118.5	53 56.4	+37.7	119.7	53 26.2	+38.8	120.9	52 54.8	+40.0	122.0	7
8	56 41.5	+29.7	111.8	56 18.6	+31.2	113.2	55 54.3	+32.7	114.5	55 28.8	+34.1	115.8	55 02.0	+35.5	117.1	54 34.1	+36.7	118.4	54 05.0	+38.0	119.6	53 34.8	+39.2	120.8	8
9	57 11.2	+28.4	110.2	56 49.8	+30.0	111.6	56 27.0	+31.6	113.0	56 02.9	+33.0	114.4	55 37.5	+34.4	115.7	55 10.8	+35.8	117.0	54 43.0	+37.1	118.3	54 14.0	+38.4	119.5	9
10	57 39.6	+27.1	108.5	57 19.8	+28.8	110.0	56 58.6	+30.3	111.5	56 35.9	+31.9	112.9	56 11.9	+33.4	114.3	55 46.6	+34.8	115.6	55 20.1	+36.2	116.9	54 52.4	+37.4	118.2	10
11	58 06.7	+25.8	106.9	57 48.6	+27.5	108.4	57 28.9	+29.2	109.9	57 07.8	+30.7	111.3	56 45.3	+32.3	112.7	56 21.4	+33.8	114.1	55 56.3	+35.1	115.5	55 29.8	+36.5	116.8	11
12	58 32.5	+24.4	105.1	58 16.1	+26.1	106.7	57 58.1	+27.8	108.2	57 38.5	+29.5	109.7	57 17.6	+31.0	111.2	56 55.2	+32.6	112.6	56 31.4	+34.1	114.0	56 06.3	+35.5	115.4	12
13	58 56.9	+22.9	103.4	58 42.2	+24.7	105.0	58 25.9	+26.5	106.5	58 08.0	+28.2	108.1	57 48.6	+29.9	109.6	57 27.8	+31.4	111.1	57 05.5	+33.0	112.5	56 41.8	+34.5	113.9	13
14	59 19.8	+21.3	101.6	59 06.9	+23.2	103.2	58 52.4	+25.0	104.8	58 36.2	+26.9	106.4	58 18.5	+28.5	108.0	57 59.2	+30.2	109.5	57 38.5	+31.8	111.0	57 16.3	+33.3	112.4	14
15	59 41.1	+19.8	99.7	59 30.1	+21.8	101.4	59 17.4	+23.6	103.1	59 03.1	+25.4	104.7	58 47.0	+27.2	106.3	58 29.4	+28.9	107.8	58 10.3	+30.6	109.4	57 49.6	+32.2	110.9	15
16	60 00.9	+18.2	97.8	59 51.9	+20.1	99.6	59 41.0	+22.1	101.2	59 28.5	+23.9	102.9	59 14.2	+25.8	104.5	58 58.3	+27.6	106.2	58 40.9	+29.2	107.7	58 21.8	+30.9	109.3	16
17	60 19.1	+16.5	95.9	60 12.0	+18.5	97.7	60 03.1	+20.5	99.4	59 52.4	+22.4	101.1	59 40.0	+24.3	102.8	59 25.9	+26.1	104.4	59 10.1	+28.0	106.0	58 52.7	+29.7	107.6	17
18	60 35.6	+14.7	94.0	60 30.5	+16.8	95.7	60 23.6	+18.8	97.5	60 14.8	+20.8	99.2	60 04.3	+22.8	100.9	59 52.0	+24.7	102.6	59 38.1	+26.5	104.3	59 22.4	+28.3	105.9	18
19	60 50.3	+13.0	92.0	60 47.3	+15.0	93.8	60 42.4	+17.1	95.6	60 35.6	+19.2	97.3	60 27.1	+21.1	99.1	60 16.7	+23.1	100.8	60 04.6	+25.0	102.5	59 50.7	+26.9	104.2	19
20	61 03.3	+11.1	90.0	61 02.3	+13.3	91.8	60 59.5	+15.4	93.6	60 54.8	+17.5	95.4	60 48.2	+19.5	97.2	60 39.8	+21.5	98.9	60 29.6	+23.5	100.7	60 17.6	+25.4	102.4	20
21	61 14.4	+9.3	88.0	61 15.6	+11.5	89.8	61 14.9	+13.6	91.6	61 12.3	+15.7	93.4	61 07.7	+17.8	95.2	61 01.3	+19.9	97.0	60 53.1	+21.8	98.8	60 43.0	+23.8	100.6	21
22	61 23.7	+7.4	85.9	61 27.1	+9.5	87.7	61 28.5	+11.7	89.6	61 28.0	+13.9	91.4	61 25.5	+16.1	93.2	61 21.2	+18.1	95.1	61 14.9	+20.2	96.9	61 06.8	+22.2	98.7	22
23	61 31.1	+5.5	83.8	61 36.6	+7.7	85.7	61 40.2	+9.9	87.5	61 41.9	+12.0	89.4	61 41.6	+14.2	91.2	61 39.3	+16.4	93.1	61 35.1	+18.5	94.9	61 29.0	+20.6	96.8	23
24	61 36.6	+3.6	81.7	61 44.3	+5.8	83.6	61 50.1	+7.9	85.4	61 53.9	+10.1	87.3	61 55.8	+12.3	89.2	61 55.7	+14.5	91.0	61 53.6	+16.7	92.9	61 49.6	+18.8	94.8	24
25	61 40.2	+1.7	79.6	61 50.1	+3.8	81.5	61 58.0	+6.0	83.3	62 04.0	+8.3	85.2	62 08.1	+10.4	87.1	62 10.2	+12.6	89.0	62 10.3	+14.8	90.9	62 08.4	+17.0	92.8	25
26	61 41.9	-0.3•	77.5	61 53.9	+1.9	79.3	62 04.0	+4.1	81.2	62 12.3	+6.2•	83.1	62 18.5	+8.5	85.0	62 22.8	+10.7	86.9	62 25.1	+12.9	88.8	62 25.4	+15.1	90.7	26
27	61 41.6	-2.3	75.4	61 55.8	-0.1•	77.2	62 08.1	+2.1•	79.1	62 18.5	+4.3	80.9	62 27.0	+6.5•	82.8	62 33.5	+8.7	84.7	62 38.0	+11.0	86.7	62 40.5	+13.2	88.6	27
28	61 39.3	-4.2	73.3	61 55.7	-2.1	75.1	62 10.2	+0.1•	76.9	62 22.8	+2.3•	78.8	62 33.5	+4.5•	80.7	62 42.2	+6.8•	82.6	62 49.0	+9.0•	84.5	62 53.7	+11.3•	86.5	28
29	61 35.1	-6.1	71.2	61 53.6	-4.0	73.0	62 10.3	-1.9•	74.8	62 25.1	+0.3•	76.6	62 38.0	+2.5•	78.5	62 49.0	+4.7•	80.4	62 58.0	+7.0•	82.3	63 05.0	+9.2•	84.3	29
30	61 29.0	-8.0	69.1	61 49.6	-6.0	70.9	62 08.4	-3.9	72.6	62 25.4	-1.8•	74.5	62 40.5	+0.4•	76.3	62 53.7	+2.7•	78.2	63 05.0	+4.9•	80.2	63 14.2	+7.2•	82.1	30
31	61 21.0	-9.8	67.0	61 43.6	-7.9	68.8	62 04.5	-5.8	70.5	62 23.6	-3.7	72.3	62 40.9	-1.5•	74.2	62 56.4	+0.6•	76.0	63 09.9	+2.9•	77.9	63 21.4	+5.2•	79.9	31
32	61 11.2	-11.8	65.0	61 35.7	-9.7	66.7	61 58.7	-7.8	68.4	62 19.9	-5.7•	70.2	62 39.4	-3.6•	72.0	62 57.0	-1.4•	73.8	63 12.8	+0.8•	75.7	63 26.6	+3.0•	77.7	32
33	60 59.4	-13.5	63.0	61 26.0	-11.7	64.6	61 50.9	-9.7	66.3	62 14.2	-7.7	68.0	62 35.8	-5.6•	69.8	62 55.6	-3.4•	71.6	63 13.6	-1.3•	73.5	63 29.6	+1.0•	75.4	33
34	60 45.9	-15.3	61.0	61 14.3	-13.4	62.5	61 41.2	-11.6	64.2	62 06.5	-9.6	65.9	62 30.2	-7.6	67.6	62 52.2	-5.5•	69.4	63 12.3	-3.3•	71.3	63 30.6	-1.1•	73.2	34
35	60 30.6	-17.0	59.0	61 00.9	-15.3	60.5	61 29.6	-13.4	62.1	61 56.9	-11.5	63.8	62 22.6	-9.5	65.5	62 46.7	-7.5•	67.3	63 09.0	-5.4•	69.1	63 29.5	-3.2•	71.0	35
36	60 13.6	-18.6	57.0	60 45.6	-17.0	58.5	61 16.2	-15.2	60.1	61 45.4	-13.4	61.7	62 13.1	-11.5	63.4	62 39.2	-9.5	65.1	63 03.6	-7.4•	66.9	63 26.3	-5.3•	68.7	36
37	59 55.0	-20.3	55.1	60 28.6	-18.6	56.6	61 01.0	-16.9	58.1	61 32.0	-15.2	59.7	62 01.6	-13.3	61.3	62 29.7	-11.4	63.0	62 56.2	-9.5•	64.7	63 21.0	-7.4•	66.5	37
38	59 34.7	-21.9	53.3	60 10.0	-20.3	54.7	60 44.1	-18.7	56.1	61 16.8	-16.9	57.6	61 48.3	-15.2	59.2	62 18.3	-13.4	60.8	62 46.7	-11.4	62.5	63 13.6	-9.4•	64.3	38
39	59 12.8	-23.3	51.4	59 49.7	-21.9	52.8	60 25.4	-20.3	54.2	60 59.9	-18.7	55.6	61 33.1	-17.0	57.2	62 04.9	-15.2	58.7	62 35.3	-13.3	60.4	63 04.2	-11.4•	62.1	39
40	58 49.5	-24.8	49.7	59 27.8	-23.4	50.9	60 05.1	-22.0	52.3	60 41.2	-20.4	53.7	61 16.1	-18.7	55.2	61 49.7	-17.0	56.7	62 22.0	-15.3	58.3	62 52.8	-13.4	59.9	40
41	58 24.7	-26.2	47.9	59 04.4	-24.9	49.1	59 43.1	-23.4	50.4	60 20.8	-21.9	51.8	60 57.4	-20.4	53.2	61 32.7	-18.8	54.7	62 06.7	-17.0	56.2	62 39.4	-15.3	57.8	41
42	57 58.5	-27.6	46.2	58 39.5	-26.2	47.4	59 19.7	-24.9	48.6	59 58.9	-23.6	49.9	60 37.0	-22.1	51.3	61 13.9	-20.5	52.7	61 49.7	-18.9	54.2	62 24.1	-17.1	55.7	42
43	57 30.9	-28.8	44.5	58 13.3	-27.6	45.7	58 54.8	-26.4	46.8	59 35.3	-25.0	48.1	60 14.9	-23.6	49.4	60 53.4	-22.1	50.7	61 30.8	-20.5	52.2	62 07.0	-18.9	53.7	43
44	57 02.1	-30.1	42.9	57 45.7	-29.0	44.0	58 28.4	-27.7	45.1	59 10.3	-26.4	46.3	59 51.3	-25.1	47.5	60 31.3	-23.7	48.8	61 10.3	-22.3	50.2	61 48.1	-20.7	51.6	44
45	56 32.0	-31.2	41.3	57 16.7	-30.1	42.4	58 00.7	-29.0	43.4	58 43.9	-27.8	44.6	59 26.2	-26.6	45.7	60 07.6	-25.2	47.0	60 48.0	-23.8	48.3	61 27.4	-22.3	49.7	45
46	56 00.8	-32.3	39.8	56 46.6	-31.3	40.8	57 31.7	-30.3	41.8	58 16.1	-29.2	42.9	58 59.6	-27.9	44.0	59 42.4	-26.7	45.2	60 24.2	-25.3	46.4	61 05.1	-24.0	47.7	46
47	55 28.5	-33.4	38.3	56 15.3	-32.5	39.2	57 01.4	-31.4	40.2	57 46.9	-30.4	41.2	58 31.7	-29.3	42.3	59 15.7	-28.1	43.4	59 58.9	-26.9	44.6	60 41.1	-25.5	45.8	47
48	54 55.1	-34.4	36.8	55 42.8	-33.5	37.7	56 30.0	-32.6	38.6	57 16.5	-31.5	39.6	58 02.4	-30.5	40.6	58 47.6	-29.4	41.7	59 32.0	-28.2	42.8	60 15.6	-27.0	44.0	48
49	54 20.7	-35.4	35.4	55 09.3	-34.5	36.3	55 57.4	-33.6	37.1	56 45.0	-32.7	38.0	57 31.9	-31.7	39.0	58 18.2	-30.7	40.0	59 03.8	-29.6	41.1	59 48.6	-28.4	42.2	49
50	53 45.3	-36.3	34.1	54 34.8	-35.5	34.8	55 23.8	-34.7	35.7	56 12.3	-33.8	36.5	57 00.2	-32.9	37.4	57 47.5	-31.9	38.4	58 34.2	-30.8	39.4	59 20.2	-29.7	40.5	50
51	53 09.0	-37.2	32.7	53 59.3	-36.5	33.5	54 49.1	-35.7	34.2	55 38.5	-34.9	35.1	56 27.3	-33.9	35.9	57 15.6	-33.0	36.8	58 03.4	-32.1	37.8	58 50.5	-31.1	38.8	51
52	52 31.8	-38.0	31.4	53 22.8	-37.3	32.1	54 13.4	-36.5	32.8	55 03.6	-35.8	33.6	55 53.4	-35.0	34.4	56 42.6	-34.1	35.3	57 31.3	-33.2	36.2	58 19.4	-32.2	37.1	52
53	51 53.8	-38.8	30.2	52 45.5	-38.1	30.8	53 36.9	-37.5	31.5	54 27.8	-36.7	32.2	55 18.4	-36.0	33.0	56 08.5	-35.2	33.8	56 58.1	-34.4	34.7	57 47.2	-33.5	35.6	53
54	51 15.0	-39.5	28.9	52 07.4	-39.0	29.5	52 59.4	-38.3	30.2	53 51.1	-37.6	30.9	54 42.4	-36.9	31.6	55 33.3	-36.2	32.4	56 23.7	-35.3	33.2	57 13.7	-34.5	34.0	54
55	50 35.5	-40.3	27.7	51 28.4	-39.7	28.3	52 21.1	-39.1	28.9	53 13.5	-38.5	29.6	54 05.5	-37.8	30.2	54 57.1	-37.1	31.0	55 48.4	-36.4	31.7	56 39.2	-35.6	32.5	55
56	49 55.2	-40.9	26.6	50 48.7	-40.3	27.1	51 42.0	-39.8	27.7	52 35.0	-39.3	28.3	53 27.7	-38.7	28.9	54 20.0	-38.0	29.6	55 12.0	-37.3	30.3	56 03.6	-36.6	31.1	56
57	49 14.3	-41.6	25.4	50 08.4	-41.1	26.0	51 02.2	-40.6	26.5	51 55.7	-40.0	27.1	52 49.0	-39.4	27.7	53 42.0	-38.8	28.3	54 34.7	-38.2	28.9	55 27.0	-37.5	29.6	57
58	48 32.7	-42.2	24.3	49 27.3	-41.7	24.8	50 21.6	-41.2	25.3	51 15.7	-40.7	25.9	52 09.6	-40.2	26.4	53 03.2	-39.6	27.0	53 56.5	-39.0	27.6	54 49.5	-38.4	28.3	58
59	47 50.5	-42.7	23.3	48 45.6	-42.4	23.7	49 40.4	-41.9	24.2	50 35.0	-41.4	24.7	51 29.4	-40.9	25.2	52 23.6	-40.4	25.8	53 17.5	-39.9	26.3	54 11.1	-39.2	27.0	59
60	47 07.8	-43.3	22.2	48 03.2	-42.9	22.7	48 58.5	-42.5	23.1	49 53.6	-42.0	23.6	50 48.5	-41.6	24.0	51 43.2	-41.1	24.6	52 37.6	-40.5	25.1	53 31.9	-40.1	25.7	60
61	46 24.5	-43.8	21.2	47 20.3	-43.4	21.6	48 16.0	-43.0	22.0	49 11.6	-42.7	22.5	50 06.9	-42.2	22.9	51 02.1	-41.8	23.4	51 57.1	-41.3	23.9	52 51.8	-40.8	24.4	61
62	45 40.7	-44.4	20.2	46 36.9	-44.0	20.6	47 33.0	-43.6	21.0	48 28.9	-43.2	21.4	49 24.7	-42.8	21.8	50 20.3	-42.4	22.3	51 15.8	-42.0	22.7	52 11.0	-41.5	23.2	62
63	44 56.3	-44.7	19.3	45 52.9	-44.4	19.6	46 49.4	-44.2	20.0	47 45.7	-43.8	20.4	48 41.9	-43.4	20.7	49 37.9	-43.0	21.2	50 33.8	-42.6	21.6	51 29.5	-42.2	22.1	63
64	44 11.6	-45.3	18.4	45 08.5	-45.0	18.7	46 05.2	-44.6	19.0	47 01.9	-44.3	19.3	47 58.5	-44.0	19.7	48 54.9	-43.6	20.1	49 51.2	-43.3	20.5	50 47.3	-42.9	20.9	64
65	43 26.3	-45.6	17.4	44 23.5	-45.4	17.7	45 20.6	-45.1	18.0	46 17.6	-44.8	18.4	47 14.5	-44.5	18.7	48 11.3	-44.2	19.1	49 07.9	-43.8	19.4	50 04.4	-43.4	19.8	65
66	42 40.7	-46.1	16.6	43 38.1	-45.7	16.8	44 35.5	-45.5	17.1	45 32.8	-45.2	17.4	46 30.0	-44.9	17.7	47 27.1	-44.6	18.0	48 24.1	-44.3	18.4	49 21.0	-44.0	18.8	66
67	41 54.6	-46.4	15.7	42 52.4	-46.2	15.9	43 50.0	-45.9	16.2	44 47.6	-45.7	16.5	45 45.1	-45.4	16.8	46 42.5	-45.2	17.1	47 39.8	-44.9	17.4	48 37.0	-44.6	17.7	67
68	41 08.2	-46.8	14.8	42 06.2	-46.6	15.1	43 04.1	-46.4	15.3	44 01.9	-46.1	15.6	44 59.7	-45.9	15.8	45 57.3	-45.6	16.1	46 54.9	-45.3	16.4	47 52.4	-45.0	16.7	68
69	40 21.4	-47.2	14.0	41 19.6	-47.0	14.2	42 17.7	-46.7	14.4	43 15.8	-46.5	14.7	44 13.8	-46.3	14.9	45 11.7	-46.0	15.2	46 09.6	-45.8	15.5	47 07.4	-45.6	15.7	69
70	39 34.2	-47.4	13.2	40 32.6	-47.3	13.4	41 31.0	-47.1	13.6	42 29.3	-46.9	13.8	43 27.5	-46.7	14.0	44 25.7	-46.5	14.3	45 23.8	-46.3	14.5	46 21.8	-46.0	14.8	70
71	38 46.8	-47.8	12.4	39 45.3	-47.6	12.6	40 43.9	-47.5	12.8	41 42.4	-47.3	13.0	42 40.8	-47.0	13.2	43 39.2	-46.9	13.4	44 37.5	-46.6	13.6	45 35.8	-46.4	13.9	71
72	37 59.0	-48.1	11.6	38 57.7	-47.9	11.8	39 56.4	-47.7	12.0	40 55.1	-47.6	12.2	41 53.8	-47.5	12.3	42 52.3	-47.2	12.5	43 50.9	-47.1	12.7	44 49.4	-46.9	13.0	72
73	37 10.9	-48.3	10.9	38 09.8	-48.2	11.0	39 08.7	-48.1	11.2	40 07.5	-47.9	11.4	41 06.3	-47.7	11.5	42 05.1	-47.6	11.7	43 03.8	-47.4	11.9	44 02.5	-47.2	12.1	73
74	36 22.6	-48.7	10.2	37 21.6	-48.5	10.3	38 20.6	-48.3	10.4	39 19.6	-48.2	10.6	40 18.6	-48.1	10.7	41 17.5	-47.9	10.9	42 16.4	-47.8	11.1	43 15.3	-47.6	11.2	74
75	35 33.9	-48.9	9.4	36 33.1	-48.8	9.6	37 32.3	-48.7	9.7	38 31.4	-48.5	9.8	39 30.5	-48.4	9.9	40 29.6	-48.3	10.1	41 28.6	-48.1	10.2	42 27.7	-48.0	10.4	75
76	34 45.0	-49.1	8.7	35 44.3	-49.0	8.8	36 43.6	-48.9	8.9	37 42.9	-48.8	9.1	38 42.1	-48.6	9.2	39 41.3	-48.5	9.3	40 40.5	-48.4	9.5	41 39.7	-48.3	9.6	76
77	33 55.9	-49.3	8.0	34 55.3	-49.2	8.1	35 54.7	-49.1	8.2	36 54.1	-49.1	8.3	37 53.5	-49.0	8.4	38 52.8	-48.8	8.6	39 52.1	-48.7	8.7	40 51.4	-48.6	8.8	77
78	33 06.6	-49.6	7.3	34 06.1	-49.5	7.4	35 05.6	-49.4	7.5	36 05.0	-49.3	7.6	37 04.5	-49.2	7.7	38 04.0	-49.2	7.8	39 03.4	-49.0	7.9	40 02.8	-48.9	8.0	78
79	32 17.0	-49.8	6.7	33 16.6	-49.7	6.8	34 16.2	-49.7	6.8	35 15.7	-49.5	6.9	36 15.3	-49.5	7.0	37 14.8	-49.3	7.1	38 14.4	-49.3	7.2	39 13.9	-49.2	7.3	79
80	31 27.2	-50.0	6.0	32 26.9	-49.9	6.1	33 26.5	-49.8	6.2	34 26.2	-49.8	6.2	35 25.8	-49.7	6.3	36 25.5	-49.7	6.4	37 25.1	-49.6	6.5	38 24.7	-49.5	6.6	80
81	30 37.2	-50.1	5.4	31 37.0	-50.1	5.4	32 36.7	-50.0	5.5	33 36.4	-50.0	5.6	34 36.1	-49.9	5.6	35 35.8	-49.8	5.7	36 35.5	-49.7	5.8	37 35.2	-49.7	5.8	81
82	29 47.1	-50.4	4.7	30 46.9	-50.3	4.8	31 46.7	-50.3	4.8	32 46.4	-50.2	4.9	33 46.2	-50.1	4.9	34 46.0	-50.1	5.0	35 45.8	-50.1	5.1	36 45.5	-49.9	5.1	82
83	28 56.7	-50.5	4.1	29 56.6	-50.5	4.2	30 56.4	-50.4	4.2	31 56.2	-50.3	4.2	32 56.1	-50.4	4.3	33 55.9	-50.3	4.3	34 55.7	-50.2	4.4	35 55.6	-50.2	4.4	83
84	28 06.2	-50.7	3.5	29 06.1	-50.6	3.5	30 06.0	-50.6	3.6	31 05.9	-50.6	3.6	32 05.7	-50.5	3.6	33 05.6	-50.5	3.7	34 05.5	-50.5	3.7	35 05.4	-50.4	3.8	84
85	27 15.5	-50.8	2.9	28 15.5	-50.8	2.9	29 15.4	-50.8	2.9	30 15.3	-50.7	3.0	31 15.2	-50.7	3.0	32 15.1	-50.6	3.0	33 15.0	-50.6	3.1	34 15.0	-50.7	3.1	85
86	26 24.7	-51.0	2.3	27 24.7	-51.0	2.3	28 24.6	-50.9	2.3	29 24.6	-51.0	2.4	30 24.5	-50.9	2.4	31 24.5	-50.9	2.4	32 24.4	-50.8	2.4	33 24.3	-50.8	2.5	86
87	25 33.7	-51.1	1.7	26 33.7	-51.1	1.7	27 33.7	-51.1	1.7	28 33.6	-51.0	1.8	29 33.6	-51.0	1.8	30 33.6	-51.0	1.8	31 33.6	-51.1	1.8	32 33.5	-51.0	1.8	87
88	24 42.6	-51.2	1.1	25 42.6	-51.2	1.1	26 42.6	-51.2	1.2	27 42.6	-51.2	1.2	28 42.6	-51.2	1.2	29 42.6	-51.2	1.2	30 42.5	-51.1	1.2	31 42.5	-51.2	1.2	88
89	23 51.4	-51.4	0.6	24 51.4	-51.4	0.6	25 51.4	-51.4	0.6	26 51.4	-51.4	0.6	27 51.4	-51.4	0.6	28 51.4	-51.4	0.6	29 51.4	-51.4	0.6	30 51.3	-51.3	0.6	89
90	23 00.0	-51.5	0.0	24 00.0	-51.5	0.0	25 00.0	-51.5	0.0	26 00.0	-51.5	0.0	27 00.0	-51.5	0.0	28 00.0	-51.5	0.0	29 00.0	-51.5	0.0	30 00.0	-51.5	0.0	90
	23°			24°			25°			26°			27°			28°			29°			30°			

31°, 329° L.H.A. LATITUDE SAME NAME AS DECLINATION

246

LATITUDE **CONTRARY** NAME TO DECLINATION **L.H.A. 31°, 329°**

Dec.	23° Hc	23° d	23° Z	24° Hc	24° d	24° Z	25° Hc	25° d	25° Z	26° Hc	26° d	26° Z
°	° ′	′	°	° ′	′	°	° ′	′	°	° ′	′	°
0	52 05.7	−38.6	123.0	51 32.5	−39.6	124.1	50 58.4	−40.6	125.1	50 23.5	−41.6	126.1
1	51 27.1	−39.3	124.3	50 52.9	−40.3	125.3	50 17.8	−41.3	126.3	49 41.9	−42.2	127.2
2	50 47.8	−40.0	125.5	50 12.6	−41.0	126.5	49 36.5	−41.9	127.4	48 59.7	−42.8	128.3
3	50 07.8	−40.7	126.6	49 31.6	−41.7	127.6	48 54.6	−42.6	128.5	48 16.9	−43.4	129.4
4	49 27.1	−41.4	127.8	48 49.9	−42.2	128.7	48 12.0	−43.1	129.6	47 33.5	−43.9	130.4
5	48 45.7	−42.0	128.9	48 07.7	−42.9	129.8	47 28.9	−43.6	130.6	46 49.6	−44.5	131.4
6	48 03.7	−42.6	130.0	47 24.8	−43.4	130.8	46 45.3	−44.2	131.6	46 05.1	−44.9	132.4
7	47 21.1	−43.1	131.0	46 41.4	−43.9	131.8	46 01.1	−44.7	132.6	45 20.2	−45.4	133.3
8	46 38.0	−43.7	132.0	45 57.5	−44.4	132.8	45 16.4	−45.1	133.6	44 34.8	−45.8	134.3
9	45 54.3	−44.2	133.0	45 13.1	−44.9	133.8	44 31.3	−45.6	134.5	43 49.0	−46.2	135.2
10	45 10.1	−44.6	134.0	44 28.2	−45.3	134.7	43 45.7	−46.0	135.4	43 02.8	−46.6	136.0
11	44 25.5	−45.1	134.9	43 42.9	−45.8	135.6	42 59.7	−46.3	136.3	42 16.2	−47.0	136.9
12	43 40.4	−45.5	135.9	42 57.1	−46.1	136.5	42 13.4	−46.8	137.1	41 29.2	−47.4	137.7
13	42 54.9	−46.0	136.7	42 11.0	−46.6	137.4	41 26.6	−47.1	138.0	40 41.8	−47.7	138.6
14	42 08.9	−46.3	137.6	41 24.4	−46.9	138.2	40 39.5	−47.5	138.8	39 54.1	−48.0	139.4
15	41 22.6	−46.7	138.5	40 37.5	−47.2	139.0	39 52.0	−47.8	139.6	39 06.1	−48.3	140.1
16	40 35.9	−47.0	139.3	39 50.3	−47.6	139.9	39 04.2	−48.1	140.4	38 17.8	−48.6	140.9
17	39 48.9	−47.4	140.1	39 02.7	−47.9	140.6	38 16.1	−48.4	141.1	37 29.2	−48.8	141.6
18	39 01.5	−47.7	140.9	38 14.8	−48.2	141.4	37 27.7	−48.6	141.9	36 40.4	−49.2	142.4
19	38 13.8	−47.9	141.7	37 26.6	−48.5	142.2	36 39.1	−49.0	142.6	35 51.2	−49.3	143.1
20	37 25.9	−48.3	142.4	36 38.1	−48.7	142.9	35 50.1	−49.1	143.3	35 01.9	−49.6	143.8
21	36 37.6	−48.6	143.2	35 49.4	−49.0	143.6	35 01.0	−49.5	144.0	34 12.3	−49.9	144.5
22	35 49.0	−48.8	143.9	35 00.4	−49.2	144.3	34 11.5	−49.6	144.7	33 22.4	−50.0	145.1
23	35 00.2	−49.0	144.6	34 11.2	−49.5	145.0	33 21.9	−49.9	145.4	32 32.4	−50.2	145.8
24	34 11.2	−49.3	145.3	33 21.7	−49.7	145.7	32 32.0	−50.0	146.1	31 42.2	−50.5	146.4
25	33 21.9	−49.5	146.0	32 32.0	−49.8	146.4	31 42.0	−50.3	146.7	30 51.7	−50.6	147.1
26	32 32.4	−49.7	146.7	31 42.2	−50.1	147.0	30 51.7	−50.4	147.4	30 01.1	−50.8	147.7
27	31 42.7	−49.9	147.4	30 52.1	−50.3	147.7	30 01.3	−50.6	148.0	29 10.3	−50.9	148.3
28	30 52.8	−50.1	148.0	30 01.8	−50.5	148.3	29 10.7	−50.8	148.6	28 19.4	−51.2	148.9
29	30 02.7	−50.3	148.6	29 11.3	−50.6	148.9	28 19.9	−51.0	149.2	27 28.2	−51.2	149.5
30	29 12.4	−50.5	149.3	28 20.7	−50.8	149.5	27 28.9	−51.1	149.8	26 37.0	−51.4	150.1
31	28 21.9	−50.6	149.9	27 29.9	−50.9	150.2	26 37.8	−51.2	150.4	25 45.6	−51.5	150.6
32	27 31.3	−50.8	150.5	26 39.0	−51.1	150.7	25 46.6	−51.4	151.0	24 54.1	−51.7	151.2
33	26 40.5	−50.9	151.1	25 47.9	−51.2	151.3	24 55.2	−51.5	151.6	24 02.4	−51.8	151.8
34	25 49.6	−51.1	151.7	24 56.7	−51.4	151.9	24 03.7	−51.6	152.1	23 10.6	−51.9	152.3
35	24 58.5	−51.2	152.3	24 05.3	−51.5	152.5	23 12.1	−51.8	152.7	22 18.7	−52.0	152.9
36	24 07.3	−51.4	152.8	23 13.8	−51.5	153.0	22 20.3	−51.8	153.2	21 26.7	−52.1	153.4
37	23 15.9	−51.4	153.4	22 22.3	−51.8	153.6	21 28.5	−52.0	153.8	20 34.6	−52.2	153.9
38	22 24.5	−51.6	154.0	21 30.5	−51.8	154.1	20 36.5	−52.0	154.3	19 42.4	−52.3	154.5
39	21 32.9	−51.6	154.5	20 38.7	−51.9	154.7	19 44.5	−52.2	154.8	18 50.1	−52.4	155.0
40	20 41.3	−51.8	155.1	19 46.8	−52.0	155.2	18 52.3	−52.2	155.4	17 57.7	−52.4	155.5
41	19 49.5	−51.9	155.6	18 54.8	−52.1	155.7	18 00.1	−52.3	155.9	17 05.3	−52.5	156.0
42	18 57.6	−52.0	156.1	18 02.7	−52.2	156.3	17 07.8	−52.4	156.4	16 12.8	−52.6	156.5
43	18 05.6	−52.0	156.7	17 10.5	−52.2	156.8	16 15.4	−52.5	156.9	15 20.2	−52.7	157.0
44	17 13.6	−52.1	157.2	16 18.3	−52.4	157.3	15 22.9	−52.5	157.4	14 27.5	−52.7	157.5
45	16 21.5	−52.2	157.7	15 25.9	−52.4	157.8	14 30.4	−52.6	157.9	13 34.8	−52.8	158.0
46	15 29.3	−52.3	158.2	14 33.5	−52.4	158.3	13 37.8	−52.7	158.4	12 42.0	−52.9	158.5
47	14 37.0	−52.3	158.7	13 41.1	−52.5	158.8	12 45.1	−52.7	158.9	11 49.1	−52.9	159.0
48	13 44.7	−52.4	159.2	12 48.6	−52.6	159.3	11 52.4	−52.7	159.4	10 56.2	−52.9	159.5
49	12 52.3	−52.5	159.7	11 56.0	−52.7	159.8	10 59.7	−52.9	159.9	10 03.3	−53.0	159.9
50	11 59.8	−52.5	160.2	11 03.3	−52.6	160.3	10 06.8	−52.8	160.3	9 10.3	−53.0	160.4
51	11 07.3	−52.5	160.7	10 10.7	−52.8	160.8	9 14.0	−52.9	160.8	8 17.3	−53.0	160.9
52	10 14.8	−52.6	161.2	9 17.9	−52.7	161.3	8 21.1	−52.9	161.3	7 24.3	−53.1	161.4
53	9 22.2	−52.7	161.7	8 25.2	−52.8	161.7	7 28.2	−53.0	161.8	6 31.2	−53.1	161.8
54	8 29.5	−52.7	162.2	7 32.4	−52.8	162.2	6 35.2	−52.9	162.3	5 38.1	−53.1	162.3
55	7 36.8	−52.7	162.7	6 39.6	−52.9	162.7	5 42.3	−53.0	162.7	4 45.0	−53.2	162.8
56	6 44.1	−52.7	163.1	5 46.7	−52.9	163.2	4 49.3	−53.0	163.2	3 51.8	−53.1	163.2
57	5 51.4	−52.8	163.6	4 53.8	−52.9	163.6	3 56.3	−53.1	163.7	2 58.7	−53.2	163.7
58	4 58.6	−52.7	164.1	4 00.9	−52.9	164.1	3 03.2	−53.0	164.1	2 05.5	−53.2	164.2
59	4 05.9	−52.8	164.6	3 08.0	−52.9	164.6	2 10.2	−53.1	164.6	1 12.3	−53.2	164.6
60	3 13.1	−52.8	165.1	2 15.1	−52.9	165.1	1 17.1	−53.0	165.1	0 19.1	−53.1	165.1
61	2 20.3	−52.9	165.5	1 22.2	−53.0	165.5	0 24.1	−53.1	165.5	0 34.0	+53.2	14.5
62	1 27.4	−52.8	166.0	0 29.2	−52.9	166.0	0 29.0	+53.1	14.0	1 27.2	+53.2	14.0
63	0 34.6	−52.8	166.5	0 23.7	+53.0	13.5	1 22.1	+53.0	13.5	2 20.4	+53.2	13.5
64	0 18.2	+52.8	13.0	1 16.7	+52.9	13.1	2 15.1	+53.0	13.1	3 13.6	+53.1	13.1
65	1 11.0	+52.9	12.6	2 09.6	+52.9	12.6	3 08.2	+53.0	12.6	4 06.7	+53.2	12.6
66	2 03.9	+52.8	12.1	3 02.5	+53.0	12.1	4 01.2	+53.0	12.1	4 59.9	+53.1	12.1
67	2 56.7	+52.8	11.6	3 55.5	+52.9	11.6	4 54.2	+53.0	11.7	5 53.0	+53.1	11.7
68	3 49.5	+52.8	11.1	4 48.4	+52.8	11.2	5 47.2	+53.0	11.2	6 46.1	+53.0	11.2
69	4 42.3	+52.7	10.7	5 41.2	+52.9	10.7	6 40.2	+52.9	10.7	7 39.1	+53.1	10.7
70	5 35.0	+52.8	10.2	6 34.1	+52.8	10.2	7 33.1	+53.0	10.2	8 32.2	+53.0	10.3
71	6 27.8	+52.7	9.7	7 26.9	+52.8	9.7	8 26.1	+52.8	9.8	9 25.2	+52.9	9.8
72	7 20.5	+52.7	9.2	8 19.7	+52.8	9.3	9 18.9	+52.9	9.3	10 18.1	+53.0	9.3
73	8 13.2	+52.6	8.8	9 12.5	+52.7	8.8	10 11.8	+52.8	8.8	11 11.1	+52.8	8.8
74	9 05.8	+52.6	8.3	10 05.2	+52.7	8.3	11 04.6	+52.7	8.3	12 03.9	+52.9	8.3
75	9 58.4	+52.6	7.8	10 57.9	+52.6	7.8	11 57.3	+52.7	7.8	12 56.8	+52.7	7.9
76	10 51.0	+52.5	7.3	11 50.5	+52.6	7.3	12 50.0	+52.7	7.3	13 49.5	+52.8	7.4
77	11 43.5	+52.5	6.8	12 43.1	+52.5	6.8	13 42.7	+52.6	6.8	14 42.3	+52.6	6.9
78	12 36.0	+52.4	6.3	13 35.6	+52.5	6.3	14 35.3	+52.5	6.4	15 34.9	+52.6	6.4
79	13 28.4	+52.4	5.8	14 28.1	+52.4	5.8	15 27.8	+52.5	5.9	16 27.5	+52.5	5.9
80	14 20.8	+52.3	5.3	15 20.5	+52.4	5.3	16 20.3	+52.3	5.3	17 20.0	+52.4	5.4
81	15 13.1	+52.2	4.8	16 12.9	+52.2	4.8	17 12.6	+52.4	4.8	18 12.4	+52.4	4.9
82	16 05.3	+52.1	4.3	17 05.1	+52.2	4.3	18 05.0	+52.2	4.3	19 04.8	+52.2	4.3
83	16 57.4	+52.1	3.8	17 57.3	+52.1	3.8	18 57.2	+52.1	3.8	19 57.0	+52.2	3.8
84	17 49.5	+52.0	3.2	18 49.4	+52.0	3.3	19 49.3	+52.1	3.3	20 49.2	+52.1	3.3
85	18 41.5	+51.9	2.7	19 41.4	+52.0	2.7	20 41.4	+51.9	2.8	21 41.3	+52.0	2.8
86	19 33.4	+51.8	2.2	20 33.4	+51.8	2.2	21 33.3	+51.9	2.2	22 33.3	+51.8	2.2
87	20 25.2	+51.7	1.6	21 25.2	+51.7	1.7	22 25.2	+51.7	1.7	23 25.1	+51.8	1.7
88	21 16.9	+51.6	1.1	22 16.9	+51.6	1.1	23 16.9	+51.6	1.1	24 16.9	+51.6	1.1
89	22 08.5	+51.5	0.6	23 08.5	+51.5	0.6	24 08.5	+51.5	0.6	25 08.5	+51.5	0.6
90	23 00.0	+51.4	0.0	24 00.0	+51.4	0.0	25 00.0	+51.4	0.0	26 00.0	+51.4	0.0
	23°			24°			25°			26°		

Dec.	27° Hc	27° d	27° Z	28° Hc	28° d	28° Z	29° Hc	29° d	29° Z	30° Hc	30° d	30° Z
°	° ′	′	°	° ′	′	°	° ′	′	°	° ′	′	°
0	49 47.7	−42.5	127.1	49 11.2	−43.4	128.0	48 33.8	−44.2	128.9	47 55.8	−45.0	129.8
1	49 05.2	−43.1	128.2	48 27.8	−44.0	129.1	47 49.6	−44.7	129.9	47 10.8	−45.5	130.7
2	48 22.1	−43.7	129.2	47 43.8	−44.4	130.1	47 04.9	−45.3	130.9	46 25.3	−46.0	131.7
3	47 38.4	−44.1	130.2	46 59.4	−45.0	131.1	46 19.6	−45.7	131.9	45 39.3	−46.4	132.6
4	46 54.3	−44.7	131.2	46 14.4	−45.4	132.0	45 33.9	−46.1	132.8	44 52.9	−46.8	133.5
5	46 09.6	−45.2	132.2	45 29.0	−45.9	133.0	44 47.8	−46.6	133.7	44 06.1	−47.3	134.4
6	45 24.4	−45.7	133.1	44 43.1	−46.3	133.9	44 01.2	−47.0	134.6	43 18.8	−47.5	135.3
7	44 38.7	−46.0	134.1	43 56.8	−46.8	134.8	43 14.2	−47.3	135.4	42 31.3	−48.0	136.1
8	43 52.7	−46.5	135.0	43 10.0	−47.1	135.6	42 26.9	−47.7	136.3	41 43.3	−48.2	136.9
9	43 06.2	−46.8	135.8	42 22.9	−47.4	136.5	41 39.2	−48.0	137.1	40 55.1	−48.6	137.7
10	42 19.4	−47.3	136.7	41 35.5	−47.8	137.3	40 51.2	−48.4	137.9	40 06.5	−48.9	138.5
11	41 32.1	−47.5	137.5	40 47.7	−48.2	138.1	40 02.8	−48.6	138.7	39 17.6	−49.2	139.2
12	40 44.6	−47.9	138.3	39 59.5	−48.4	138.9	39 14.2	−49.0	139.4	38 28.4	−49.4	139.9
13	39 56.7	−48.3	139.1	39 11.1	−48.7	139.7	38 25.2	−49.2	140.2	37 39.0	−49.7	140.7
14	39 08.4	−48.5	139.9	38 22.4	−49.0	140.4	37 36.0	−49.5	140.9	36 49.3	−50.0	141.4
15	38 19.9	−48.8	140.6	37 33.4	−49.3	141.1	36 46.5	−49.7	141.6	35 59.3	−50.2	142.1
16	37 31.1	−49.1	141.4	36 44.1	−49.5	141.8	35 56.8	−50.0	142.3	35 09.1	−50.3	142.7
17	36 42.0	−49.3	142.1	35 54.6	−49.8	142.5	35 06.8	−50.2	143.0	34 18.8	−50.7	143.4
18	35 52.7	−49.5	142.8	35 04.8	−50.0	143.2	34 16.6	−50.4	143.6	33 28.1	−50.8	144.0
19	35 03.2	−49.8	143.5	34 14.8	−50.2	143.9	33 26.2	−50.6	144.3	32 37.3	−50.9	144.7
20	34 13.4	−50.1	144.2	33 24.6	−50.4	144.6	32 35.6	−50.8	144.9	31 46.4	−51.2	145.3
21	33 23.3	−50.2	144.8	32 34.2	−50.6	145.2	31 44.8	−51.0	145.6	30 55.2	−51.3	145.9
22	32 33.1	−50.4	145.5	31 43.6	−50.8	145.8	30 53.8	−51.1	146.2	30 03.9	−51.5	146.5
23	31 42.7	−50.6	146.1	30 52.8	−51.0	146.5	30 02.7	−51.4	146.8	29 12.4	−51.7	147.1
24	30 52.1	−50.8	146.8	30 01.8	−51.1	147.1	29 11.3	−51.4	147.4	28 20.7	−51.8	147.7
25	30 01.3	−51.0	147.4	29 10.7	−51.3	147.7	28 19.9	−51.7	148.0	27 28.9	−51.9	148.3
26	29 10.3	−51.1	148.0	28 19.4	−51.5	148.3	27 28.2	−51.7	148.6	26 37.0	−52.1	148.8
27	28 19.2	−51.3	148.6	27 27.9	−51.6	148.9	26 36.5	−51.9	149.1	25 44.9	−52.2	149.4
28	27 27.9	−51.4	149.2	26 36.3	−51.7	149.4	25 44.6	−52.0	149.7	24 52.7	−52.3	149.9
29	26 36.5	−51.6	149.7	25 44.6	−51.9	150.0	24 52.6	−52.2	150.2	24 00.4	−52.4	150.5
30	25 44.9	−51.7	150.3	24 52.7	−51.9	150.6	24 00.4	−52.2	150.8	23 08.0	−52.5	151.0
31	24 53.2	−51.8	150.9	24 00.8	−52.1	151.1	23 08.2	−52.4	151.3	22 15.5	−52.6	151.5
32	24 01.4	−51.9	151.4	23 08.7	−52.2	151.6	22 15.8	−52.4	151.8	21 22.9	−52.7	152.0
33	23 09.5	−52.1	152.0	22 16.5	−52.3	152.2	21 23.4	−52.6	152.4	20 30.2	−52.8	152.5
34	22 17.4	−52.1	152.5	21 24.2	−52.5	152.7	20 30.8	−52.7	152.9	19 37.4	−52.9	153.0
35	21 25.3	−52.3	153.1	20 31.7	−52.4	153.2	19 38.1	−52.7	153.4	18 44.5	−53.0	153.5
36	20 33.0	−52.3	153.6	19 39.3	−52.6	153.7	18 45.4	−52.8	153.9	17 51.5	−53.0	154.0
37	19 40.7	−52.5	154.1	18 46.7	−52.7	154.2	17 52.6	−52.9	154.4	16 58.5	−53.2	154.5
38	18 48.2	−52.5	154.6	17 54.0	−52.7	154.8	16 59.7	−53.0	154.9	16 05.3	−53.1	155.0
39	17 55.7	−52.6	155.1	17 01.3	−52.9	155.3	16 06.7	−53.0	155.4	15 12.2	−53.3	155.5
40	17 03.1	−52.6	155.6	16 08.4	−52.8	155.7	15 13.7	−53.1	155.9	14 18.9	−53.3	156.0
41	16 10.5	−52.8	156.1	15 15.6	−53.0	156.2	14 20.6	−53.1	156.3	13 25.6	−53.3	156.4
42	15 17.7	−52.8	156.6	14 22.6	−53.0	156.7	13 27.5	−53.2	156.8	12 32.3	−53.4	156.9
43	14 24.9	−52.9	157.1	13 29.6	−53.1	157.2	12 34.3	−53.3	157.3	11 38.9	−53.4	157.4
44	13 32.0	−52.9	157.6	12 36.5	−53.1	157.7	11 41.0	−53.3	157.8	10 45.5	−53.5	157.8
45	12 39.1	−53.0	158.1	11 43.4	−53.1	158.2	10 47.7	−53.3	158.2	9 52.0	−53.5	158.3
46	11 46.1	−53.0	158.6	10 50.3	−53.2	158.6	9 54.4	−53.4	158.7	8 58.5	−53.6	158.8
47	10 53.1	−53.1	159.0	9 57.1	−53.3	159.1	9 01.0	−53.4	159.2	8 04.9	−53.6	159.2
48	10 00.0	−53.1	159.5	9 03.8	−53.2	159.6	8 07.6	−53.4	159.6	7 11.3	−53.6	159.7
49	9 06.9	−53.1	160.0	8 10.6	−53.4	160.0	7 14.2	−53.5	160.1	6 17.7	−53.6	160.1
50	8 13.8	−53.2	160.5	7 17.2	−53.3	160.5	6 20.7	−53.5	160.5	5 24.1	−53.7	160.6
51	7 20.6	−53.2	160.9	6 23.9	−53.4	161.0	5 27.2	−53.5	161.0	4 30.4	−53.6	161.0
52	6 27.4	−53.2	161.4	5 30.5	−53.3	161.4	4 33.7	−53.6	161.5	3 36.8	−53.7	161.5
53	5 34.2	−53.3	161.9	4 37.2	−53.4	161.9	3 40.1	−53.5	161.9	2 43.1	−53.7	161.9
54	4 40.9	−53.2	162.3	3 43.8	−53.4	162.3	2 46.6	−53.6	162.4	1 49.4	−53.7	162.4
55	3 47.7	−53.3	162.8	2 50.4	−53.5	162.8	1 53.0	−53.5	162.8	0 55.7	−53.7	162.8
56	2 54.4	−53.3	163.2	1 56.9	−53.4	163.3	0 59.5	−53.6	163.3	0 02.0	−53.7	163.3
57	2 01.1	−53.3	163.7	1 03.5	−53.4	163.7	0 05.9	−53.6	163.7	0 51.7	+53.7	16.3
58	1 07.8	−53.3	164.2	0 10.1	−53.5	164.2	0 47.7	+53.5	15.8	1 45.4	+53.7	15.8
59	0 14.5	−53.3	164.6	0 43.4	+53.4	15.4	1 41.2	+53.6	15.4	2 39.1	+53.7	15.4
60	0 38.8	+53.3	14.9	1 36.8	+53.4	14.9	2 34.8	+53.5	14.9	3 32.8	+53.6	15.0
61	1 32.1	+53.3	14.5	2 30.2	+53.5	14.5	3 28.3	+53.6	14.5	4 26.4	+53.7	14.5
62	2 25.4	+53.3	14.0	3 23.7	+53.4	14.0	4 21.9	+53.5	14.0	5 20.1	+53.6	14.1
63	3 18.7	+53.3	13.5	4 17.1	+53.4	13.6	5 15.4	+53.5	13.6	6 13.7	+53.6	13.6
64	4 12.0	+53.3	13.1	5 10.5	+53.3	13.1	6 08.9	+53.5	13.1	7 07.3	+53.6	13.2
65	5 05.3	+53.2	12.6	6 03.8	+53.4	12.6	7 02.4	+53.4	12.7	8 00.9	+53.6	12.7
66	5 58.5	+53.2	12.2	6 57.2	+53.3	12.2	7 55.8	+53.4	12.2	8 54.5	+53.5	12.2
67	6 51.7	+53.2	11.7	7 50.5	+53.3	11.7	8 49.2	+53.4	11.8	9 48.0	+53.5	11.8
68	7 44.9	+53.2	11.2	8 43.8	+53.2	11.3	9 42.6	+53.4	11.3	10 41.5	+53.4	11.3
69	8 38.1	+53.1	10.8	9 37.0	+53.2	10.8	10 36.0	+53.3	10.8	11 34.9	+53.4	10.9
70	9 31.2	+53.1	10.3	10 30.2	+53.2	10.3	11 29.3	+53.2	10.4	12 28.3	+53.3	10.4
71	10 24.3	+53.1	9.8	11 23.4	+53.2	9.8	12 22.5	+53.3	9.9	13 21.6	+53.3	9.9
72	11 17.4	+53.0	9.3	12 16.6	+53.0	9.4	13 15.8	+53.1	9.4	14 14.9	+53.3	9.5
73	12 10.4	+52.9	8.9	13 09.6	+53.1	8.9	14 08.9	+53.1	8.9	15 08.2	+53.2	9.0
74	13 03.3	+52.9	8.4	14 02.7	+52.9	8.4	15 02.0	+53.1	8.5	16 01.4	+53.1	8.5
75	13 56.2	+52.8	7.9	14 55.6	+52.9	7.9	15 55.1	+52.9	8.0	16 54.5	+53.0	8.0
76	14 49.0	+52.8	7.4	15 48.5	+52.9	7.4	16 48.0	+52.9	7.5	17 47.5	+53.0	7.5
77	15 41.8	+52.7	6.9	16 41.4	+52.8	6.9	17 40.9	+52.9	7.0	18 40.5	+52.9	7.0
78	16 34.5	+52.7	6.4	17 34.2	+52.6	6.4	18 33.8	+52.7	6.5	19 33.4	+52.8	6.5
79	17 27.2	+52.5	5.9	18 26.8	+52.7	5.9	19 26.5	+52.7	6.0	20 26.2	+52.7	6.0
80	18 19.7	+52.5	5.4	19 19.5	+52.5	5.4	20 19.2	+52.6	5.5	21 18.9	+52.6	5.5
81	19 12.2	+52.4	4.9	20 12.0	+52.4	4.9	21 11.8	+52.5	5.0	22 11.5	+52.6	5.0
82	20 04.6	+52.3	4.4	21 04.4	+52.4	4.4	22 04.3	+52.3	4.4	23 04.1	+52.4	4.5
83	20 56.9	+52.2	3.9	21 56.8	+52.2	3.9	22 56.6	+52.3	3.9	23 56.5	+52.3	3.9
84	21 49.1	+52.1	3.3	22 49.0	+52.2	3.3	23 48.9	+52.2	3.4	24 48.8	+52.2	3.4
85	22 41.2	+52.0	2.8	23 41.2	+52.0	2.8	24 41.1	+52.0	2.8	25 41.0	+52.1	2.9
86	23 33.2	+51.9	2.2	24 33.2	+51.9	2.3	25 33.1	+52.0	2.3	26 33.1	+51.9	2.3
87	24 25.1	+51.8	1.7	25 25.1	+51.8	1.7	26 25.1	+51.7	1.7	27 25.0	+51.8	1.7
88	25 16.9	+51.6	1.1	26 16.9	+51.6	1.1	27 16.8	+51.7	1.2	28 16.8	+51.7	1.2
89	26 08.5	+51.5	0.6	27 08.5	+51.5	0.6	28 08.5	+51.5	0.6	29 08.5	+51.5	0.6
90	27 00.0	+51.4	0.0	28 00.0	+51.4	0.0	29 00.0	+51.4	0.0	30 00.0	+51.3	0.0
	27°			28°			29°			30°		

S. Lat. { L.H.A. greater than 180° ....Zn=180°–Z
{ L.H.A. less than 180°...........Zn=180°+Z

LATITUDE **SAME** NAME AS DECLINATION **L.H.A. 149°, 211°**

247

32°, 328° L.H.A. LATITUDE SAME NAME AS DECLINATION

N. Lat. {L.H.A. greater than 180° .....Zn=Z; L.H.A. less than 180°............Zn=360°-Z}

Dec.	23° Hc	d	Z	24° Hc	d	Z	25° Hc	d	Z	26° Hc	d	Z	27° Hc	d	Z	28° Hc	d	Z	29° Hc	d	Z	30° Hc	d	Z	Dec.
°	° ′	′	°	° ′	′	°	° ′	′	°	° ′	′	°	° ′	′	°	° ′	′	°	° ′	′	°	° ′	′	°	°
0	51 19.1	+37.1	122.0	50 46.8	+38.3	123.1	50 13.7	+39.2	124.1	49 39.6	+40.3	125.1	49 04.8	+41.2	126.0	48 29.1	+42.2	126.9	47 52.7	+43.1	127.8	47 15.6	+43.9	128.7	0
1	51 56.2	+36.3	120.8	51 25.1	+37.4	121.8	50 52.9	+38.6	122.9	50 19.9	+39.6	123.9	49 46.0	+40.6	124.9	49 11.3	+41.6	125.8	48 35.8	+42.5	126.8	47 59.5	+43.4	127.7	1
2	52 32.5	+35.4	119.5	52 02.5	+36.6	120.6	51 31.5	+37.7	121.7	50 59.5	+38.9	122.7	50 26.6	+39.9	123.7	49 52.9	+40.9	124.7	49 18.3	+41.9	125.7	48 42.9	+42.8	126.6	2
3	53 07.9	+34.4	118.1	52 39.1	+35.7	119.3	52 09.2	+36.9	120.4	51 38.4	+38.0	121.5	51 06.5	+39.2	122.6	50 33.8	+40.2	123.6	50 00.2	+41.2	124.6	49 25.7	+42.2	125.5	3
4	53 42.3	+33.5	116.7	53 14.8	+34.8	117.9	52 46.1	+36.1	119.1	52 16.4	+37.3	120.2	51 45.7	+38.4	121.3	51 14.0	+39.5	122.4	50 41.4	+40.6	123.4	50 07.9	+41.6	124.4	4
5	54 15.8	+32.5	115.3	53 49.6	+33.8	116.6	53 22.2	+35.1	117.8	52 53.7	+36.4	118.9	52 24.1	+37.6	120.1	51 53.5	+38.8	121.2	51 22.0	+39.8	122.3	50 49.5	+40.9	123.3	5
6	54 48.3	+31.4	113.9	54 23.4	+32.8	115.2	53 57.3	+34.2	116.4	53 30.1	+35.4	117.6	53 01.7	+36.7	118.8	52 32.3	+37.9	120.0	52 01.8	+39.1	121.1	51 30.4	+40.1	122.1	6
7	55 19.7	+30.3	112.4	54 56.2	+31.8	113.7	54 31.5	+33.2	115.0	54 05.5	+34.6	116.3	53 38.4	+35.8	117.5	53 10.2	+37.1	118.7	52 40.9	+38.2	119.8	52 10.5	+39.4	120.9	7
8	55 50.0	+29.2	110.9	55 28.0	+30.7	112.2	55 04.7	+32.1	113.6	54 40.1	+33.5	114.9	54 14.2	+34.9	116.1	53 47.3	+36.1	117.3	53 19.1	+37.5	118.5	52 49.9	+38.7	119.7	8
9	56 19.2	+27.9	109.3	55 58.7	+29.5	110.7	55 36.8	+31.0	112.1	55 13.6	+32.5	113.4	54 49.1	+33.9	114.7	54 23.4	+35.3	116.0	53 56.6	+36.5	117.2	53 28.6	+37.7	118.4	9
10	56 47.1	+26.7	107.7	56 28.2	+28.2	109.1	56 07.8	+29.8	110.5	55 46.1	+31.3	111.9	55 23.0	+32.8	113.3	54 58.7	+34.2	114.6	54 33.1	+35.6	115.9	54 06.3	+36.9	117.1	10
11	57 13.8	+25.3	106.0	56 56.4	+27.0	107.5	56 37.6	+28.7	109.0	56 17.4	+30.2	110.4	55 55.8	+31.8	111.8	55 32.9	+33.2	113.1	55 08.7	+34.6	114.5	54 43.2	+36.0	115.8	11
12	57 39.1	+24.0	104.4	57 23.4	+25.7	105.9	57 06.3	+27.4	107.4	56 47.6	+29.0	108.8	56 27.6	+30.5	110.3	56 06.1	+32.1	111.7	55 43.3	+33.5	113.0	55 19.2	+34.9	114.4	12
13	58 03.1	+22.5	102.6	57 49.1	+24.4	104.2	57 33.7	+26.0	105.7	57 16.6	+27.8	107.2	56 58.1	+29.4	108.7	56 38.2	+30.9	110.1	56 16.8	+32.5	111.5	55 54.1	+34.0	112.9	13
14	58 25.6	+21.1	100.9	58 13.5	+22.8	102.5	57 59.7	+24.7	104.0	57 44.4	+26.4	105.6	57 27.5	+28.1	107.1	57 09.1	+29.8	108.6	56 49.3	+31.3	110.0	56 28.1	+32.8	111.4	14
15	58 46.7	+19.5	99.1	58 36.3	+21.5	100.7	58 24.4	+23.2	102.3	58 10.8	+25.0	103.9	57 55.6	+26.8	105.4	57 38.9	+28.5	107.0	57 20.6	+30.1	108.4	57 00.9	+31.7	109.9	15
16	59 06.2	+17.9	97.2	58 57.8	+19.8	98.9	58 47.6	+21.8	100.5	58 35.8	+23.6	102.1	58 22.4	+25.4	103.7	58 07.4	+27.1	105.3	57 50.7	+28.9	106.8	57 32.6	+30.5	108.3	16
17	59 24.1	+16.4	95.4	59 17.6	+18.3	97.1	59 09.4	+20.2	98.7	58 59.4	+22.1	100.4	58 47.8	+24.0	102.0	58 34.5	+25.8	103.6	58 19.6	+27.5	105.2	58 03.1	+29.2	106.7	17
18	59 40.5	+14.6	93.5	59 35.9	+16.7	95.2	59 29.6	+18.6	96.9	59 21.5	+20.6	98.6	59 11.8	+22.4	100.2	59 00.3	+24.3	101.9	58 47.1	+26.2	103.5	58 32.3	+27.9	105.1	18
19	59 55.1	+12.9	91.6	59 52.6	+14.9	93.3	59 48.2	+17.0	95.0	59 42.1	+19.0	96.7	59 34.2	+21.0	98.4	59 24.6	+22.8	100.1	59 13.3	+24.7	101.7	59 00.2	+26.6	103.4	19
20	60 08.0	+11.2	89.6	60 07.5	+13.3	91.3	60 05.2	+15.3	93.1	60 01.1	+17.3	94.8	59 55.2	+19.3	96.5	59 47.4	+21.3	98.2	59 38.0	+23.2	99.9	59 26.8	+25.0	101.6	20
21	60 19.2	+9.4	87.6	60 20.8	+11.5	89.4	60 20.5	+13.6	91.1	60 18.4	+15.7	92.9	60 14.5	+17.6	94.6	60 08.7	+19.7	96.4	60 01.2	+21.6	98.1	59 51.8	+23.6	99.8	21
22	60 28.6	+7.6	85.6	60 32.3	+9.7	87.4	60 34.1	+11.8	89.2	60 34.1	+13.8	90.9	60 32.1	+16.0	92.7	60 28.4	+18.0	94.5	60 22.8	+20.0	96.2	60 15.4	+22.0	98.0	22
23	60 36.2	+5.8	83.6	60 42.0	+7.9	85.4	60 45.9	+10.0	87.2	60 47.9	+12.1	88.9	60 48.1	+14.2	90.7	60 46.4	+16.3	92.5	60 42.8	+18.4	94.3	60 37.4	+20.4	96.1	23
24	60 42.0	+3.9	81.6	60 49.9	+6.0	83.3	60 55.9	+8.1	85.1	61 00.0	+10.3	86.9	61 02.3	+12.4	88.7	61 02.7	+14.5	90.5	61 01.2	+16.6	92.3	60 57.8	+18.7	94.1	24
25	60 45.9	+2.0	79.5	60 55.9	+4.1	81.3	61 04.0	+6.3	83.1	61 10.3	+8.4	84.9	61 14.7	+10.6	86.7	61 17.2	+12.7	88.5	61 17.8	+14.8	90.4	61 16.5	+16.9	92.2	25
26	60 47.9	+0.2	77.5	61 00.0	+2.3	79.2	61 10.3	+4.4	81.0	61 18.7	+6.6	82.8	61 25.3	+8.7	84.7	61 29.9	+10.9	86.5	61 32.6	+13.0	88.3	61 33.4	+15.1	90.2	26
27	60 48.1	-1.7	75.4	61 02.3	+0.4	77.2	61 14.7	+2.5	79.0	61 25.3	+4.6	80.8	61 34.0	+6.8	82.6	61 40.8	+8.9	84.4	61 45.6	+11.2	86.3	61 48.5	+13.3	88.1	27
28	60 46.4	-3.6	73.4	61 02.7	-1.5	75.1	61 17.2	+0.6	76.9	61 29.9	+2.7	78.7	61 40.8	+4.8	80.5	61 49.7	+7.1	82.3	61 56.8	+9.2	84.2	62 01.8	+11.5	86.1	28
29	60 42.8	-5.4	71.3	61 01.2	-3.4	73.1	61 17.8	-1.3	74.8	61 32.6	+0.8	76.6	61 45.6	+2.9	78.4	61 56.8	+5.0	80.2	62 06.0	+7.3	82.1	62 13.3	+9.5 •	84.0	29
30	60 37.4	-7.3	69.3	60 57.8	-5.3	71.0	61 16.5	-3.3	72.7	61 33.4	-1.2	74.5	61 48.5	+1.0	76.3	62 01.8	+3.2	78.1	62 13.3	+5.3 •	80.0	62 22.8	+7.5 •	81.8	30
31	60 30.1	-9.1	67.3	60 52.5	-7.1	68.9	61 13.2	-5.1	70.6	61 32.2	-3.0	72.4	61 49.5	-1.0	74.2	62 05.0	+1.1 •	76.0	62 18.6	+3.3	77.8	62 30.3	+5.5	79.7	31
32	60 21.0	-10.8	65.3	60 45.4	-9.0	66.9	61 08.1	-7.0	68.6	61 29.2	-5.0	70.3	61 48.5	-2.9	72.0	62 06.1	-0.8	73.8	62 21.9	+1.4 •	75.7	62 35.8	+3.6 •	77.5	32
33	60 10.2	-12.7	63.3	60 36.4	-10.8	64.9	61 01.1	-8.9	66.5	61 24.2	-6.9	68.2	61 45.6	-4.9	69.9	62 05.3	-2.8	71.7	62 23.3	-0.7 •	73.5	62 39.4	+1.5 •	75.4	33
34	59 57.5	-14.3	61.3	60 25.6	-12.6	62.9	60 52.2	-10.7	64.5	61 17.3	-8.8	66.1	61 40.7	-6.8	67.8	62 02.5	-4.7	69.6	62 22.6	-2.7	71.4	62 40.9	-0.5 •	73.2	34
35	59 43.2	-16.0	59.4	60 13.0	-14.2	60.9	60 41.5	-12.5	62.5	61 08.5	-10.6	64.1	61 33.9	-8.7	65.7	61 57.8	-6.7 •	67.4	62 19.9	-4.6	69.2	62 40.4	-2.6 •	71.0	35
36	59 27.2	-17.7	57.5	59 58.8	-16.0	59.0	60 29.0	-14.2	60.5	60 57.9	-12.5	62.0	61 25.2	-10.5	63.7	61 51.1	-8.7	65.3	62 15.3	-6.6 •	67.1	62 37.8	-4.5 •	68.8	36
37	59 09.5	-19.2	55.6	59 42.8	-17.7	57.1	60 14.8	-16.0	58.5	60 45.4	-14.2	60.0	61 14.7	-12.4	61.6	61 42.4	-10.5	63.2	62 08.7	-8.6	64.9	62 33.3	-6.6 •	66.7	37
38	58 50.3	-20.8	53.8	59 25.1	-19.2	55.2	59 58.8	-17.6	56.6	60 31.2	-16.0	58.1	61 02.3	-14.2	59.6	61 31.9	-12.4	61.2	62 00.1	-10.5	62.8	62 26.7	-8.5	64.5	38
39	58 29.5	-22.3	52.0	59 05.9	-20.8	53.3	59 41.2	-19.3	54.7	60 15.2	-17.6	56.1	60 48.1	-16.0	57.6	61 19.5	-14.2	59.1	61 49.6	-12.4	60.7	62 18.2	-10.5	62.4	39
40	58 07.2	-23.7	50.2	58 45.1	-22.3	51.5	59 21.9	-20.8	52.8	59 57.6	-19.3	54.2	60 32.1	-17.7	55.6	61 05.3	-15.9	57.1	61 37.2	-14.2	58.7	62 07.7	-12.3	60.3	40
41	57 43.5	-25.1	48.5	58 22.8	-23.8	49.7	59 01.1	-22.4	51.0	59 38.3	-20.9	52.3	60 14.4	-19.3	53.7	60 49.4	-17.8	55.1	61 23.0	-16.0	56.6	61 55.4	-14.3	58.2	41
42	57 18.4	-26.4	46.8	57 59.0	-25.1	48.0	58 38.7	-23.8	49.2	59 17.4	-22.4	50.5	59 55.1	-20.9	51.8	60 31.6	-19.3	53.2	61 07.0	-17.8	54.6	61 41.1	-16.1	56.1	42
43	56 52.0	-27.7	45.2	57 33.9	-26.5	46.3	58 14.9	-25.2	47.4	58 55.0	-23.9	48.6	59 34.2	-22.5	49.9	60 12.3	-21.0	51.3	60 49.2	-19.4	52.6	61 25.0	-17.8	54.1	43
44	56 24.3	-29.0	43.5	57 07.4	-27.8	44.6	57 49.7	-26.6	45.7	58 31.1	-25.3	46.9	59 11.7	-24.0	48.1	59 51.3	-22.6	49.4	60 29.8	-21.1	50.7	61 07.2	-19.5	52.1	44
45	55 55.3	-30.1	42.0	56 39.6	-29.0	43.0	57 23.1	-27.9	44.0	58 05.8	-26.6	45.2	58 47.7	-25.4	46.3	59 28.7	-24.1	47.5	60 08.7	-22.7	48.8	60 47.7	-21.2	50.2	45
46	55 25.2	-31.2	40.4	56 10.6	-30.2	41.4	56 55.2	-29.1	42.4	57 39.2	-28.0	43.5	58 22.3	-26.8	44.6	59 04.6	-25.5	45.8	59 46.0	-24.2	47.0	60 26.5	-22.8	48.3	46
47	54 54.0	-32.3	38.9	55 40.4	-31.3	39.9	56 26.1	-30.3	40.8	57 11.2	-29.3	41.8	57 55.5	-28.1	42.9	58 39.1	-26.9	44.0	59 21.8	-25.6	45.2	60 03.7	-24.4	46.4	47
48	54 21.7	-33.3	37.5	55 09.1	-32.5	38.4	55 55.8	-31.4	39.3	56 41.9	-30.4	40.2	57 27.4	-29.4	41.2	58 12.2	-28.3	42.3	58 56.2	-27.1	43.4	59 39.3	-25.8	44.6	48
49	53 48.4	-34.3	36.1	54 36.6	-33.4	36.9	55 24.4	-32.6	37.8	56 11.5	-31.6	38.7	56 58.0	-30.5	39.6	57 43.9	-29.5	40.6	58 29.1	-28.4	41.7	59 13.5	-27.2	42.8	49
50	53 14.1	-35.2	34.7	54 03.2	-34.4	35.5	54 51.8	-33.5	36.3	55 39.9	-32.7	37.2	56 27.5	-31.8	38.1	57 14.4	-30.7	39.0	58 00.7	-29.7	40.0	58 46.3	-28.6	41.1	50
51	52 38.9	-36.1	33.3	53 28.8	-35.4	34.1	54 18.3	-34.6	34.9	55 07.2	-33.7	35.7	55 55.7	-32.8	36.5	56 43.7	-31.9	37.4	57 31.0	-30.9	38.4	58 17.7	-29.9	39.4	51
52	52 02.8	-37.0	32.0	52 53.4	-36.2	32.7	53 43.7	-35.5	33.5	54 33.5	-34.7	34.2	55 22.9	-33.9	35.0	56 11.8	-33.1	35.9	57 00.1	-32.1	36.8	57 47.8	-31.1	37.7	52
53	51 25.8	-37.8	30.8	52 17.2	-37.1	31.4	53 08.2	-36.4	32.1	53 58.8	-35.6	32.8	54 49.0	-34.9	33.6	55 38.7	-34.0	34.4	56 28.0	-33.2	35.3	57 16.7	-32.3	36.2	53
54	50 48.0	-38.5	29.5	51 40.1	-37.9	30.1	52 31.8	-37.2	30.8	53 23.2	-36.6	31.5	54 14.1	-35.8	32.2	55 04.7	-35.1	33.0	55 54.8	-34.3	33.8	56 44.4	-33.4	34.6	54
55	50 09.5	-39.2	28.3	51 02.2	-38.7	28.9	51 54.6	-38.1	29.5	52 46.6	-37.4	30.2	53 38.3	-36.7	30.8	54 29.6	-36.0	31.6	55 20.5	-35.2	32.3	56 11.0	-34.4	33.1	55
56	49 30.3	-40.0	27.1	50 23.5	-39.4	27.7	51 16.5	-38.8	28.3	52 09.2	-38.2	28.9	53 01.6	-37.6	29.5	53 53.6	-36.9	30.2	54 45.3	-36.2	30.9	55 36.6	-35.5	31.6	56
57	48 50.3	-40.6	26.0	49 44.1	-40.1	26.5	50 37.7	-39.6	27.1	51 31.0	-39.0	27.6	52 24.0	-38.4	28.2	53 16.7	-37.8	28.9	54 09.1	-37.2	29.5	55 01.1	-36.4	30.2	57
58	48 09.7	-41.2	24.9	49 04.0	-40.7	25.4	49 58.1	-40.2	25.9	50 52.0	-39.8	26.4	51 45.6	-39.2	27.0	52 38.9	-38.6	27.6	53 31.9	-37.9	28.2	54 24.7	-37.4	28.9	58
59	47 28.5	-41.9	23.8	48 23.3	-41.4	24.3	49 17.9	-40.9	24.7	50 12.2	-40.4	25.2	51 06.4	-39.9	25.8	52 00.3	-39.4	26.3	52 54.0	-38.8	26.9	53 47.3	-38.2	27.5	59
60	46 46.6	-42.3	22.8	47 41.9	-42.0	23.2	48 37.0	-41.6	23.6	49 31.8	-41.1	24.1	50 26.5	-40.6	24.6	51 20.9	-40.1	25.1	52 15.2	-39.6	25.6	53 09.1	-39.0	26.2	60
61	46 04.3	-43.0	21.7	46 59.9	-42.5	22.1	47 55.4	-42.1	22.5	48 50.7	-41.7	23.0	49 45.9	-41.3	23.4	50 40.8	-40.8	23.9	51 35.6	-40.3	24.4	52 30.1	-39.8	25.0	61
62	45 21.3	-43.4	20.7	46 17.4	-43.1	21.1	47 13.3	-42.7	21.5	48 09.0	-42.3	21.9	49 04.6	-41.9	22.3	50 00.0	-41.4	22.8	50 55.3	-41.1	23.2	51 50.3	-40.5	23.7	62
63	44 37.9	-43.9	19.8	45 34.3	-43.6	20.1	46 30.6	-43.3	20.5	47 26.7	-42.9	20.8	48 22.7	-42.5	21.2	49 18.6	-42.1	21.7	50 14.2	-41.6	22.1	51 09.8	-41.3	22.6	63
64	43 54.0	-44.4	18.8	44 50.7	-44.1	19.1	45 47.3	-43.7	19.5	46 43.8	-43.4	19.8	47 40.2	-43.0	20.2	48 36.5	-42.7	20.6	49 32.6	-42.3	21.0	50 28.5	-41.9	21.4	64
65	43 09.6	-44.9	17.9	44 06.6	-44.5	18.2	45 03.6	-44.3	18.5	46 00.4	-43.9	18.8	46 57.2	-43.6	19.2	47 53.8	-43.3	19.5	48 50.3	-42.9	19.9	49 46.6	-42.5	20.3	65
66	42 24.7	-45.2	17.0	43 22.1	-45.0	17.2	44 19.3	-44.6	17.5	45 16.5	-44.4	17.8	46 13.6	-44.1	18.2	47 10.5	-43.8	18.5	48 07.4	-43.5	18.8	49 04.1	-43.1	19.2	66
67	41 39.5	-45.6	16.1	42 37.1	-45.4	16.3	43 34.7	-45.2	16.6	44 32.1	-44.9	16.9	45 29.5	-44.6	17.2	46 26.7	-44.2	17.5	47 23.9	-44.0	17.8	48 21.0	-43.7	18.2	67
68	40 53.9	-46.1	15.2	41 51.7	-45.8	15.5	42 49.5	-45.5	15.7	43 47.2	-45.3	16.0	44 44.9	-45.1	16.2	45 42.5	-44.8	16.5	46 39.9	-44.5	16.8	47 37.3	-44.2	17.1	68
69	40 07.8	-46.3	14.4	41 05.9	-46.1	14.6	42 04.0	-46.0	14.8	43 01.9	-45.7	15.1	43 59.8	-45.4	15.3	44 57.7	-45.3	15.6	45 55.4	-44.9	15.8	46 53.1	-44.7	16.1	69
70	39 21.5	-46.8	13.6	40 19.8	-46.6	13.8	41 18.0	-46.3	14.0	42 16.2	-46.1	14.2	43 14.4	-45.9	14.4	44 12.4	-45.6	14.6	45 10.5	-45.5	14.9	46 08.4	-45.2	15.2	70
71	38 34.7	-47.0	12.7	39 33.2	-46.8	12.9	40 31.7	-46.7	13.1	41 30.1	-46.5	13.3	42 28.5	-46.3	13.5	43 26.8	-46.1	13.7	44 25.0	-45.8	14.0	45 23.2	-45.6	14.2	71
72	37 47.7	-47.4	12.0	38 46.4	-47.2	12.1	39 45.0	-47.0	12.3	40 43.6	-46.8	12.5	41 42.2	-46.7	12.7	42 40.7	-46.5	12.9	43 39.2	-46.3	13.1	44 37.6	-46.1	13.3	72
73	37 00.3	-47.6	11.2	37 59.2	-47.5	11.3	38 58.0	-47.4	11.5	39 56.8	-47.2	11.7	40 55.5	-47.0	11.8	41 54.2	-46.8	12.0	42 52.9	-46.7	12.2	43 51.5	-46.5	12.4	73
74	36 12.7	-47.9	10.4	37 11.7	-47.8	10.6	38 10.6	-47.6	10.7	39 09.6	-47.5	10.9	40 08.5	-47.4	11.0	41 07.4	-47.2	11.2	42 06.2	-47.0	11.4	43 05.0	-46.8	11.5	74
75	35 24.8	-48.2	9.7	36 23.9	-48.1	9.8	37 23.0	-47.9	9.9	38 22.1	-47.8	10.1	39 21.1	-47.6	10.2	40 20.2	-47.5	10.4	41 19.2	-47.4	10.5	42 18.2	-47.3	10.7	75
76	34 36.6	-48.5	9.0	35 35.8	-48.3	9.1	36 35.1	-48.3	9.2	37 34.3	-48.1	9.3	38 33.5	-48.0	9.4	39 32.7	-47.9	9.6	40 31.8	-47.7	9.7	41 30.9	-47.5	9.9	76
77	33 48.1	-48.7	8.2	34 47.5	-48.6	8.3	35 46.8	-48.5	8.4	36 46.2	-48.4	8.6	37 45.5	-48.3	8.7	38 44.8	-48.2	8.8	39 44.1	-48.0	8.9	40 43.4	-48.0	9.0	77
78	32 59.4	-48.9	7.5	33 58.9	-48.8	7.6	34 58.3	-48.7	7.7	35 57.8	-48.6	7.8	36 57.2	-48.5	7.9	37 56.6	-48.4	8.0	38 56.1	-48.4	8.1	39 55.4	-48.2	8.3	78
79	32 10.5	-49.2	6.9	33 10.1	-49.1	6.9	34 09.6	-49.0	7.0	35 09.2	-48.9	7.1	36 08.7	-48.8	7.2	37 08.2	-48.7	7.3	38 07.7	-48.6	7.4	39 07.2	-48.5	7.5	79
80	31 21.3	-49.3	6.2	32 21.0	-49.3	6.3	33 20.6	-49.2	6.3	34 20.3	-49.2	6.4	35 19.9	-49.1	6.5	36 19.5	-49.0	6.6	37 19.1	-48.9	6.6	38 18.7	-48.8	6.7	80
81	30 32.0	-49.6	5.5	31 31.7	-49.5	5.6	32 31.4	-49.4	5.6	33 31.1	-49.3	5.7	34 30.8	-49.3	5.8	35 30.5	-49.2	5.8	36 30.2	-49.1	5.9	37 29.9	-49.1	6.0	81
82	29 42.4	-49.7	4.9	30 42.2	-49.7	4.9	31 42.0	-49.6	5.0	32 41.8	-49.6	5.0	33 41.5	-49.5	5.1	34 41.3	-49.5	5.1	35 41.1	-49.4	5.2	36 40.8	-49.3	5.3	82
83	28 52.7	-49.9	4.2	29 52.5	-49.8	4.3	30 52.4	-49.8	4.3	31 52.2	-49.8	4.4	32 52.0	-49.7	4.4	33 51.8	-49.6	4.5	34 51.7	-49.7	4.5	35 51.5	-49.6	4.6	83
84	28 02.8	-50.1	3.6	29 02.7	-50.1	3.6	30 02.6	-50.1	3.7	31 02.4	-49.9	3.7	32 02.3	-49.9	3.7	33 02.2	-49.9	3.8	34 02.0	-49.8	3.8	35 01.9	-49.8	3.9	84
85	27 12.7	-50.2	3.0	28 12.6	-50.2	3.0	29 12.5	-50.1	3.0	30 12.5	-50.2	3.1	31 12.4	-50.2	3.1	32 12.3	-50.1	3.1	33 12.2	-50.1	3.2	34 12.1	-50.0	3.2	85
86	26 22.5	-50.4	2.4	27 22.4	-50.4	2.4	28 22.4	-50.4	2.4	29 22.3	-50.3	2.4	30 22.2	-50.3	2.5	31 22.2	-50.3	2.5	32 22.1	-50.3	2.5	33 22.1	-50.3	2.5	86
87	25 32.1	-50.6	1.8	26 32.0	-50.5	1.8	27 32.0	-50.5	1.8	28 32.0	-50.5	1.8	29 31.9	-50.4	1.8	30 31.9	-50.5	1.8	31 31.9	-50.5	1.9	32 31.8	-50.4	1.9	87
88	24 41.5	-50.7	1.2	25 41.5	-50.7	1.2	26 41.5	-50.7	1.2	27 41.5	-50.7	1.2	28 41.5	-50.7	1.2	29 41.4	-50.6	1.2	30 41.4	-50.6	1.2	31 41.4	-50.6	1.2	88
89	23 50.8	-50.8	0.6	24 50.8	-50.8	0.6	25 50.8	-50.8	0.6	26 50.8	-50.8	0.6	27 50.8	-50.8	0.6	28 50.8	-50.8	0.6	29 50.8	-50.8	0.6	30 50.8	-50.8	0.6	89
90	23 00.0	-50.9	0.0	24 00.0	-50.9	0.0	25 00.0	-51.0	0.0	26 00.0	-51.0	0.0	27 00.0	-51.0	0.0	28 00.0	-51.0	0.0	29 00.0	-51.0	0.0	30 00.0	-51.0	0.0	90
	23°			24°			25°			26°			27°			28°			29°			30°			

32°, 328° L.H.A. LATITUDE SAME NAME AS DECLINATION

248

LATITUDE CONTRARY NAME TO DECLINATION L.H.A. 32°, 328°

Dec.	23° Hc	d	Z	24° Hc	d	Z	25° Hc	d	Z	26° Hc	d	Z	27° Hc	d	Z	28° Hc	d	Z	29° Hc	d	Z	30° Hc	d	Z	Dec.
°	° ′	′	°	° ′	′	°	° ′	′	°	° ′	′	°	° ′	′	°	° ′	′	°	° ′	′	°	° ′	′	°	°
0	51 19.1	−37.9	122.0	50 46.8	−38.9	123.1	50 13.7	−40.0	124.1	49 39.6	−40.9	125.1	49 04.8	−41.9	126.0	48 29.1	−42.8	126.9	47 52.7	−43.7	127.8	47 15.6	−44.5	128.7	0
1	50 41.2	−38.7	123.2	50 07.9	−39.7	124.3	49 33.7	−40.7	125.2	48 58.7	−41.6	126.2	48 22.9	−42.5	127.1	47 46.3	−43.3	128.0	47 09.0	−44.1	128.8	46 31.1	−45.0	129.6	1
2	50 02.5	−39.3	124.4	49 28.2	−40.4	125.4	48 53.0	−41.3	126.4	48 17.1	−42.2	127.3	47 40.4	−43.1	128.1	47 03.0	−43.9	129.0	46 24.9	−44.7	129.8	45 46.1	−45.4	130.6	2
3	49 23.2	−40.1	125.6	48 47.8	−41.0	126.5	48 11.7	−41.9	127.5	47 34.9	−42.8	128.3	46 57.3	−43.6	129.2	46 19.1	−44.4	130.0	45 40.2	−45.1	130.8	45 00.7	−45.8	131.5	3
4	48 43.1	−40.7	126.8	48 06.8	−41.6	127.6	47 29.8	−42.5	128.5	46 52.1	−43.3	129.4	46 13.7	−44.1	130.2	45 34.7	−44.9	131.0	44 55.1	−45.6	131.7	44 14.9	−46.3	132.4	4
5	48 02.4	−41.4	127.9	47 25.2	−42.2	128.7	46 47.3	−43.0	129.6	46 08.8	−43.8	130.4	45 29.6	−44.6	131.1	44 49.8	−45.3	131.9	44 09.5	−46.0	132.6	43 28.6	−46.7	133.3	5
6	47 21.0	−41.9	128.9	46 43.0	−42.8	129.8	46 04.3	−43.6	130.6	45 25.0	−44.4	131.3	44 45.0	−45.0	132.1	44 04.5	−45.7	132.8	43 23.5	−46.4	133.5	42 41.9	−47.0	134.2	6
7	46 39.1	−42.5	130.0	46 00.2	−43.3	130.8	45 20.7	−44.0	131.6	44 40.6	−44.7	132.3	44 00.0	−45.5	133.0	43 18.8	−46.2	133.7	42 37.1	−46.8	134.4	41 54.9	−47.4	135.0	7
8	45 56.6	−43.0	131.0	45 16.9	−43.7	131.8	44 36.7	−44.5	132.5	43 55.9	−45.3	133.2	43 14.5	−45.9	133.9	42 32.6	−46.5	134.6	41 50.3	−47.2	135.2	41 07.5	−47.8	135.8	8
9	45 13.6	−43.5	132.0	44 33.2	−44.3	132.7	43 52.2	−45.0	133.4	43 10.6	−45.6	134.1	42 28.6	−46.3	134.8	41 46.1	−46.9	135.4	41 03.1	−47.5	136.0	40 19.7	−48.0	136.6	9
10	44 30.1	−44.0	133.0	43 48.9	−44.7	133.7	43 07.2	−45.4	134.4	42 25.0	−46.0	135.0	41 42.3	−46.6	135.7	40 59.2	−47.3	136.3	40 15.6	−47.8	136.9	39 31.7	−48.4	137.4	10
11	43 46.1	−44.5	133.9	43 04.2	−45.2	134.6	42 21.8	−45.8	135.3	41 39.0	−46.5	135.9	40 55.7	−47.0	136.5	40 11.9	−47.5	137.1	39 27.8	−48.1	137.6	38 43.3	−48.7	138.2	11
12	43 01.6	−44.9	134.8	42 19.0	−45.5	135.5	41 36.0	−46.2	136.1	40 52.5	−46.7	136.7	40 08.7	−47.4	137.3	39 24.4	−47.9	137.9	38 39.7	−48.5	138.4	37 54.6	−48.9	138.9	12
13	42 16.7	−45.3	135.7	41 33.5	−46.0	136.4	40 49.8	−46.5	137.0	40 05.8	−47.1	137.5	39 21.3	−47.7	138.1	38 36.5	−48.2	138.6	37 51.2	−48.7	139.2	37 05.7	−49.2	139.7	13
14	41 31.4	−45.7	136.6	40 47.5	−46.3	137.2	40 03.3	−46.9	137.8	39 18.7	−47.5	138.4	38 33.6	−47.9	138.9	37 48.3	−48.5	139.4	37 02.5	−49.0	139.9	36 16.5	−49.5	140.4	14
15	40 45.7	−46.1	137.5	40 01.2	−46.6	138.1	39 16.4	−47.2	138.6	38 31.2	−47.7	139.1	37 45.7	−48.3	139.6	36 59.8	−48.8	140.1	36 13.5	−49.2	140.6	35 27.0	−49.7	141.1	15
16	39 59.6	−46.5	138.3	39 14.6	−47.0	138.9	38 29.2	−47.5	139.4	37 43.5	−48.1	139.9	36 57.4	−48.6	140.4	36 11.0	−49.0	140.9	35 24.3	−49.5	141.3	34 37.3	−49.9	141.8	16
17	39 13.1	−46.8	139.1	38 27.6	−47.4	139.7	37 41.7	−47.9	140.2	36 55.4	−48.3	140.7	36 08.8	−48.8	141.1	35 22.0	−49.3	141.6	34 34.8	−49.7	142.0	33 47.4	−50.1	142.4	17
18	38 26.3	−47.1	140.0	37 40.2	−47.6	140.5	36 53.8	−48.1	140.9	36 07.1	−48.6	141.4	35 20.0	−49.0	141.8	34 32.7	−49.5	142.3	33 45.1	−49.9	142.7	32 57.3	−50.3	143.1	18
19	37 39.2	−47.4	140.7	36 52.6	−47.9	141.2	36 05.7	−48.4	141.7	35 18.5	−48.9	142.1	34 31.0	−49.3	142.5	33 43.2	−49.7	143.0	32 55.2	−50.1	143.4	32 07.0	−50.6	143.7	19
20	36 51.8	−47.7	141.5	36 04.7	−48.2	142.0	35 17.3	−48.6	142.4	34 29.6	−49.0	142.8	33 41.7	−49.5	143.2	32 53.5	−49.9	143.6	32 05.1	−50.3	144.0	31 16.4	−50.7	144.4	20
21	36 04.1	−47.9	142.3	35 16.5	−48.4	142.7	34 28.7	−48.9	143.1	33 40.6	−49.4	143.5	32 52.2	−49.7	143.9	32 03.6	−50.1	144.3	31 14.8	−50.5	144.6	30 25.7	−50.9	145.0	21
22	35 16.2	−48.3	143.0	34 28.1	−48.7	143.4	33 39.8	−49.1	143.8	32 51.2	−49.5	144.2	32 02.5	−50.0	144.6	31 13.5	−50.4	144.9	30 24.3	−50.7	145.3	29 34.8	−51.0	145.6	22
23	34 27.9	−48.5	143.7	33 39.4	−48.9	144.1	32 50.7	−49.4	144.5	32 01.7	−49.7	144.9	31 12.5	−50.1	145.2	30 23.1	−50.4	145.6	29 33.6	−50.9	145.9	28 43.8	−51.2	146.2	23
24	33 39.4	−48.7	144.4	32 50.5	−49.2	144.8	32 01.3	−49.5	145.2	31 12.0	−50.0	145.5	30 22.4	−50.3	145.9	29 32.7	−50.7	146.2	28 42.7	−51.0	146.5	27 52.6	−51.4	146.8	24
25	32 50.7	−49.0	145.1	32 01.3	−49.3	145.5	31 11.8	−49.8	145.8	30 22.0	−50.1	146.2	29 32.1	−50.5	146.5	28 42.0	−50.8	146.8	27 51.7	−51.2	147.1	27 01.2	−51.5	147.4	25
26	32 01.7	−49.2	145.8	31 12.0	−49.6	146.2	30 22.0	−49.9	146.5	29 31.9	−50.3	146.8	28 41.6	−50.6	147.1	27 51.2	−51.0	147.4	27 00.5	−51.3	147.7	26 09.7	−51.6	148.0	26
27	31 12.5	−49.4	146.5	30 22.4	−49.7	146.8	29 32.1	−50.1	147.1	28 41.6	−50.4	147.4	27 51.0	−50.8	147.7	27 00.2	−51.2	148.0	26 09.2	−51.4	148.3	25 18.1	−51.7	148.5	27
28	30 23.1	−49.5	147.2	29 32.7	−50.0	147.5	28 42.0	−50.3	147.8	27 51.2	−50.7	148.0	27 00.2	−51.0	148.3	26 09.0	−51.2	148.6	25 17.8	−51.6	148.8	24 26.4	−51.9	149.1	28
29	29 33.6	−49.8	147.8	28 42.7	−50.1	148.1	27 51.7	−50.5	148.4	27 00.5	−50.8	148.7	26 09.2	−51.1	148.9	25 17.8	−51.4	149.2	24 26.2	−51.7	149.4	23 34.5	−52.0	149.6	29
30	28 43.8	−50.0	148.4	27 52.6	−50.3	148.7	27 01.2	−50.6	149.0	26 09.7	−50.9	149.2	25 18.1	−51.2	149.5	24 26.4	−51.6	149.7	23 34.5	−51.8	150.0	22 42.5	−52.1	150.2	30
31	27 53.8	−50.1	149.1	27 02.3	−50.4	149.3	26 10.6	−50.7	149.6	25 18.8	−51.0	149.8	24 26.9	−51.4	150.1	23 34.8	−51.6	150.3	22 42.7	−52.0	150.5	21 50.4	−52.2	150.7	31
32	27 03.7	−50.2	149.7	26 11.9	−50.6	149.9	25 19.9	−50.9	150.2	24 27.8	−51.2	150.4	23 35.5	−51.5	150.6	22 43.2	−51.8	150.8	21 50.7	−52.0	151.0	20 58.2	−52.3	151.2	32
33	26 13.5	−50.5	150.3	25 21.3	−50.8	150.5	24 29.0	−51.1	150.8	23 36.6	−51.4	151.0	22 44.0	−51.6	151.2	21 51.4	−51.9	151.4	20 58.7	−52.1	151.6	20 05.9	−52.4	151.8	33
34	25 23.0	−50.5	150.9	24 30.5	−50.8	151.1	23 37.9	−51.1	151.3	22 45.2	−51.4	151.5	21 52.4	−51.7	151.7	20 59.5	−51.9	151.9	20 06.6	−52.3	152.1	19 13.5	−52.5	152.3	34
35	24 32.5	−50.8	151.5	23 39.7	−51.0	151.7	22 46.8	−51.3	151.9	21 53.8	−51.5	152.1	21 00.7	−51.8	152.3	20 07.6	−52.1	152.5	19 14.3	−52.3	152.6	18 21.0	−52.6	152.8	35
36	23 41.7	−50.8	152.1	22 48.7	−51.1	152.3	21 55.5	−51.4	152.5	21 02.3	−51.7	152.7	20 08.9	−51.9	152.8	19 15.5	−52.2	153.0	18 22.0	−52.4	153.1	17 28.4	−52.6	153.3	36
37	22 50.9	−51.0	152.7	21 57.6	−51.3	152.9	21 04.1	−51.5	153.0	20 10.6	−51.7	153.2	19 17.0	−52.0	153.4	18 23.3	−52.2	153.5	17 29.6	−52.5	153.7	16 35.8	−52.7	153.8	37
38	21 59.9	−51.0	153.2	21 06.3	−51.3	153.4	20 12.6	−51.6	153.6	19 18.9	−51.9	153.7	18 25.0	−52.1	153.9	17 31.1	−52.3	154.0	16 37.1	−52.5	154.2	15 43.1	−52.8	154.3	38
39	21 08.9	−51.2	153.8	20 15.0	−51.5	154.0	19 21.0	−51.7	154.1	18 27.0	−51.9	154.3	17 32.9	−52.1	154.4	16 38.8	−52.4	154.5	15 44.6	−52.6	154.7	14 50.3	−52.8	154.8	39
40	20 17.7	−51.3	154.4	19 23.5	−51.5	154.5	18 29.3	−51.7	154.7	17 35.1	−52.0	154.8	16 40.8	−52.3	154.9	15 46.4	−52.5	155.1	14 52.0	−52.7	155.2	13 57.5	−52.9	155.3	40
41	19 26.4	−51.4	154.9	18 32.0	−51.6	155.1	17 37.6	−51.9	155.2	16 43.1	−52.1	155.3	15 48.5	−52.3	155.4	14 53.9	−52.5	155.6	13 59.3	−52.8	155.7	13 04.6	−53.0	155.8	41
42	18 35.0	−51.5	155.5	17 40.4	−51.8	155.6	16 45.7	−52.0	155.7	15 51.0	−52.2	155.8	14 56.2	−52.4	155.9	14 01.4	−52.6	156.1	13 06.5	−52.8	156.1	12 11.6	−53.0	156.2	42
43	17 43.5	−51.6	156.0	16 48.6	−51.8	156.1	15 53.7	−52.0	156.2	14 58.8	−52.2	156.3	14 03.8	−52.4	156.5	13 08.8	−52.6	156.5	12 13.7	−52.8	156.6	11 18.6	−53.0	156.7	43
44	16 51.9	−51.7	156.5	15 56.8	−51.8	156.6	15 01.7	−52.1	156.8	14 06.6	−52.3	156.9	13 11.4	−52.5	157.0	12 16.2	−52.7	157.0	11 20.9	−52.9	157.1	10 25.6	−53.1	157.2	44
45	16 00.2	−51.7	157.1	15 05.0	−52.0	157.2	14 09.6	−52.1	157.3	13 14.3	−52.4	157.4	12 18.9	−52.6	157.4	11 23.5	−52.8	157.5	10 28.0	−52.9	157.6	9 32.5	−53.1	157.7	45
46	15 08.5	−51.8	157.6	14 13.0	−52.0	157.7	13 17.5	−52.2	157.8	12 21.9	−52.4	157.9	11 26.3	−52.6	157.9	10 30.7	−52.8	158.0	9 35.1	−53.0	158.1	8 39.4	−53.2	158.1	46
47	14 16.7	−51.9	158.1	13 21.0	−52.1	158.2	12 25.3	−52.3	158.3	11 29.5	−52.4	158.4	10 33.7	−52.6	158.4	9 37.9	−52.8	158.5	8 42.1	−53.0	158.6	7 46.2	−53.2	158.6	47
48	13 24.8	−51.9	158.6	12 28.9	−52.1	158.7	11 33.0	−52.3	158.8	10 37.1	−52.6	158.9	9 41.1	−52.7	158.9	8 45.1	−52.9	159.0	7 49.1	−53.1	159.0	6 53.0	−53.2	159.1	48
49	12 32.9	−52.0	159.1	11 36.8	−52.2	159.2	10 40.7	−52.4	159.3	9 44.5	−52.5	159.3	8 48.4	−52.7	159.4	7 52.2	−52.9	159.5	6 56.0	−53.0	159.5	5 59.8	−53.2	159.5	49
50	11 40.9	−52.1	159.6	10 44.6	−52.2	159.7	9 48.3	−52.4	159.8	8 52.0	−52.6	159.8	7 55.7	−52.8	159.9	6 59.3	−52.9	159.9	6 03.0	−53.1	160.0	5 06.6	−53.3	160.0	50
51	10 48.8	−52.1	160.2	9 52.4	−52.3	160.2	8 55.9	−52.5	160.3	7 59.4	−52.6	160.3	7 02.9	−52.8	160.4	6 06.4	−53.0	160.4	5 09.9	−53.2	160.4	4 13.3	−53.3	160.5	51
52	9 56.7	−52.1	160.7	9 00.1	−52.3	160.7	8 03.4	−52.4	160.8	7 06.8	−52.7	160.8	6 10.1	−52.8	160.8	5 13.4	−52.9	160.9	4 16.7	−53.1	160.9	3 20.0	−53.3	160.9	52
53	9 04.6	−52.2	161.2	8 07.8	−52.4	161.2	7 11.0	−52.6	161.3	6 14.1	−52.6	161.3	5 17.3	−52.8	161.3	4 20.5	−53.0	161.3	3 23.6	−53.1	161.4	2 26.7	−53.3	161.4	53
54	8 12.4	−52.3	161.7	7 15.4	−52.4	161.7	6 18.4	−52.5	161.7	5 21.5	−52.7	161.8	4 24.5	−52.9	161.8	3 27.5	−53.0	161.8	2 30.5	−53.2	161.8	1 33.4	−53.3	161.8	54
55	7 20.1	−52.2	162.2	6 23.0	−52.4	162.2	5 25.9	−52.6	162.2	4 28.8	−52.8	162.2	3 31.6	−52.9	162.3	2 34.5	−53.1	162.3	1 37.3	−53.2	162.3	0 40.1	−53.3	162.3	55
56	6 27.9	−52.3	162.6	5 30.6	−52.4	162.7	4 33.3	−52.6	162.7	3 36.0	−52.7	162.7	2 38.7	−52.8	162.7	1 41.4	−53.0	162.8	0 44.1	−53.1	162.8	0 13.2	+53.3	17.2	56
57	5 35.6	−52.3	163.1	4 38.2	−52.5	163.2	3 40.7	−52.6	163.2	2 43.3	−52.7	163.2	1 45.9	−52.9	163.2	0 48.4	−53.0	163.2	0 09.0	+53.2	16.8	1 06.5	+53.3	16.8	57
58	4 43.3	−52.3	163.6	3 45.7	−52.5	163.7	2 48.1	−52.6	163.7	1 50.6	−52.8	163.7	0 53.0	−52.9	163.7	0 04.6	+53.0	16.3	1 02.2	+53.2	16.3	1 59.8	+53.3	16.3	58
59	3 51.0	−52.4	164.1	2 53.2	−52.4	164.1	1 55.5	−52.6	164.2	0 57.8	−52.7	164.2	0 00.1	−52.9	164.2	0 57.6	+53.1	15.8	1 55.4	+53.1	15.8	2 53.1	+53.3	15.9	59
60	2 58.6	−52.3	164.6	2 00.8	−52.5	164.6	1 02.9	−52.6	164.6	0 05.1	−52.8	164.6	0 52.8	+52.9	15.4	1 50.7	+53.0	15.4	2 48.5	+53.2	15.4	3 46.4	+53.2	15.4	60
61	2 06.3	−52.4	165.1	1 08.3	−52.5	165.1	0 10.3	−52.6	165.1	0 47.7	+52.8	14.9	1 45.7	+52.9	14.9	2 43.7	+53.0	14.9	3 41.7	+53.1	14.9	4 39.6	+53.3	14.9	61
62	1 13.9	−52.4	165.6	0 15.8	−52.5	165.6	0 42.3	+52.7	14.4	1 40.5	+52.7	14.4	2 38.6	+52.8	14.4	3 36.7	+53.0	14.4	4 34.8	+53.1	14.5	5 32.9	+53.2	14.5	62
63	0 21.5	−52.4	166.1	0 36.7	+52.5	13.9	1 35.0	+52.6	13.9	2 33.2	+52.7	13.9	3 31.4	+52.9	13.9	4 29.7	+52.9	14.0	5 27.9	+53.1	14.0	6 26.1	+53.2	14.0	63
64	0 30.9	+52.3	13.4	1 29.2	+52.5	13.4	2 27.6	+52.6	13.4	3 25.9	+52.8	13.5	4 24.3	+52.8	13.5	5 22.6	+53.0	13.5	6 21.0	+53.0	13.5	7 19.3	+53.2	13.5	64
65	1 23.2	+52.4	12.9	2 21.7	+52.5	13.0	3 20.2	+52.6	13.0	4 18.7	+52.7	13.0	5 17.1	+52.8	13.0	6 15.6	+52.9	13.0	7 14.0	+53.1	13.0	8 12.5	+53.1	13.1	65
66	2 15.6	+52.4	12.5	3 14.2	+52.5	12.5	4 12.8	+52.6	12.5	5 11.4	+52.6	12.5	6 09.9	+52.8	12.5	7 08.5	+52.9	12.5	8 07.1	+53.0	12.6	9 05.6	+53.1	12.6	66
67	3 08.0	+52.3	12.0	4 06.7	+52.4	12.0	5 05.4	+52.5	12.0	6 04.0	+52.7	12.0	7 02.7	+52.8	12.0	8 01.4	+52.9	12.1	9 00.1	+52.9	12.1	9 58.7	+53.1	12.1	67
68	4 00.3	+52.3	11.5	4 59.1	+52.4	11.5	5 57.9	+52.5	11.5	6 56.7	+52.6	11.5	7 55.5	+52.7	11.6	8 54.3	+52.8	11.6	9 53.0	+53.0	11.6	10 51.8	+53.0	11.7	68
69	4 52.6	+52.4	11.0	5 51.5	+52.4	11.0	6 50.4	+52.5	11.0	7 49.3	+52.6	11.1	8 48.2	+52.7	11.1	9 47.1	+52.8	11.1	10 46.0	+52.8	11.1	11 44.8	+53.0	11.2	69
70	5 45.0	+52.2	10.5	6 43.9	+52.4	10.5	7 42.9	+52.5	10.5	8 41.9	+52.6	10.6	9 40.9	+52.7	10.6	10 39.9	+52.7	10.6	11 38.8	+52.9	10.7	12 37.8	+52.9	10.7	70
71	6 37.2	+52.3	10.0	7 36.3	+52.4	10.0	8 35.4	+52.4	10.0	9 34.5	+52.5	10.1	10 33.6	+52.6	10.1	11 32.6	+52.7	10.1	12 31.7	+52.8	10.2	13 30.7	+52.9	10.2	71
72	7 29.5	+52.2	9.5	8 28.7	+52.3	9.5	9 27.8	+52.4	9.6	10 27.0	+52.5	9.6	11 26.2	+52.5	9.6	12 25.3	+52.6	9.7	13 24.5	+52.7	9.7	14 23.6	+52.8	9.7	72
73	8 21.7	+52.2	9.0	9 21.0	+52.2	9.0	10 20.2	+52.4	9.1	11 19.5	+52.4	9.1	12 18.7	+52.5	9.1	13 17.9	+52.6	9.2	14 17.2	+52.6	9.2	15 16.4	+52.7	9.2	73
74	9 13.9	+52.1	8.5	10 13.2	+52.2	8.5	11 12.6	+52.3	8.6	12 11.9	+52.4	8.6	13 11.2	+52.5	8.6	14 10.5	+52.5	8.7	15 09.8	+52.6	8.7	16 09.1	+52.7	8.7	74
75	10 06.0	+52.1	8.0	11 05.4	+52.2	8.0	12 04.9	+52.2	8.1	13 04.3	+52.3	8.1	14 03.7	+52.3	8.1	15 03.0	+52.5	8.2	16 02.4	+52.6	8.2	17 01.8	+52.6	8.2	75
76	10 58.1	+52.1	7.5	11 57.6	+52.1	7.5	12 57.1	+52.2	7.6	13 56.6	+52.2	7.6	14 56.0	+52.3	7.6	15 55.5	+52.4	7.7	16 55.0	+52.4	7.7	17 54.4	+52.5	7.7	76
77	11 50.2	+52.0	7.0	12 49.7	+52.1	7.0	13 49.3	+52.1	7.1	14 48.8	+52.2	7.1	15 48.3	+52.3	7.1	16 47.9	+52.3	7.2	17 47.4	+52.4	7.2	18 46.9	+52.5	7.2	77
78	12 42.2	+51.9	6.5	13 41.8	+52.0	6.5	14 41.4	+52.0	6.5	15 41.0	+52.1	6.6	16 40.6	+52.2	6.6	17 40.2	+52.2	6.6	18 39.8	+52.3	6.7	19 39.4	+52.3	6.7	78
79	13 34.1	+51.9	6.0	14 33.8	+51.9	6.0	15 33.4	+52.0	6.0	16 33.1	+52.0	6.1	17 32.8	+52.0	6.1	18 32.4	+52.2	6.1	19 32.1	+52.2	6.2	20 31.7	+52.3	6.2	79
80	14 26.0	+51.7	5.5	15 25.7	+51.8	5.5	16 25.4	+51.9	5.5	17 25.1	+52.0	5.5	18 24.8	+52.0	5.6	19 24.6	+52.0	5.6	20 24.3	+52.1	5.6	21 24.0	+52.1	5.7	80
81	15 17.7	+51.8	4.9	16 17.5	+51.8	5.0	17 17.3	+51.8	5.0	18 17.1	+51.8	5.0	19 16.8	+52.0	5.0	20 16.6	+52.0	5.1	21 16.4	+52.0	5.1	22 16.1	+52.1	5.1	81
82	16 09.5	+51.6	4.4	17 09.3	+51.7	4.4	18 09.1	+51.7	4.5	19 08.9	+51.8	4.5	20 08.8	+51.8	4.5	21 08.6	+51.8	4.5	22 08.4	+51.9	4.6	23 08.2	+51.9	4.6	82
83	17 01.1	+51.6	3.9	18 01.0	+51.6	3.9	19 00.8	+51.7	3.9	20 00.7	+51.7	3.9	21 00.6	+51.7	4.0	22 00.4	+51.8	4.0	23 00.3	+51.8	4.0	24 00.1	+51.8	4.1	83
84	17 52.7	+51.5	3.3	18 52.6	+51.5	3.4	19 52.5	+51.5	3.4	20 52.4	+51.5	3.4	21 52.3	+51.6	3.4	22 52.2	+51.6	3.4	23 52.1	+51.6	3.5	24 51.9	+51.7	3.5	84
85	18 44.2	+51.3	2.8	19 44.1	+51.4	2.8	20 44.0	+51.4	2.8	21 43.9	+51.5	2.8	22 43.9	+51.4	2.9	23 43.8	+51.5	2.9	24 43.7	+51.5	2.9	25 43.6	+51.6	2.9	85
86	19 35.5	+51.3	2.2	20 35.5	+51.3	2.3	21 35.4	+51.4	2.3	22 35.4	+51.3	2.3	23 35.3	+51.4	2.3	24 35.3	+51.4	2.3	25 35.2	+51.5	2.3	26 35.2	+51.4	2.4	86
87	20 26.8	+51.2	1.7	21 26.8	+51.2	1.7	22 26.8	+51.2	1.7	23 26.7	+51.3	1.7	24 26.7	+51.2	1.7	25 26.7	+51.2	1.8	26 26.7	+51.2	1.8	27 26.6	+51.3	1.8	87
88	21 18.0	+51.1	1.1	22 18.0	+51.1	1.1	23 18.0	+51.0	1.2	24 18.0	+51.0	1.2	25 17.9	+51.1	1.2	26 17.9	+51.1	1.2	27 17.9	+51.1	1.2	28 17.9	+51.1	1.2	88
89	22 09.1	+50.9	0.6	23 09.1	+50.9	0.6	24 09.0	+51.0	0.6	25 09.0	+51.0	0.6	26 09.0	+51.0	0.6	27 09.0	+51.0	0.6	28 09.0	+51.0	0.6	29 09.0	+51.0	0.6	89
90	23 00.0	+50.8	0.0	24 00.0	+50.8	0.0	25 00.0	+50.8	0.0	26 00.0	+50.8	0.0	27 00.0	+50.8	0.0	28 00.0	+50.8	0.0	29 00.0	+50.8	0.0	30 00.0	+50.8	0.0	90
	23°			24°			25°			26°			27°			28°			29°			30°			

S. Lat. {L.H.A. greater than 180° ....Zn=180°−Z
{L.H.A. less than 180°...........Zn=180°+Z

LATITUDE SAME NAME AS DECLINATION L.H.A. 148°, 212°

LATITUDE SAME NAME AS DECLINATION N. Lat. {L.H.A. greater than 180° .....Zn=Z / L.H.A. less than 180°...........Zn=360°-Z

Dec.	23° Hc	d	Z	24° Hc	d	Z	25° Hc	d	Z	26° Hc	d	Z	27° Hc	d	Z	28° Hc	d	Z	29° Hc	d	Z	30° Hc	d	Z	Dec.
0	50 32.0	+36.5	121.0	50 00.6	+37.6	122.1	49 28.3	+38.7	123.1	48 55.2	+39.7	124.0	48 21.2	+40.7	125.0	47 46.5	+41.6	125.9	47 10.9	+42.5	126.7	46 34.7	+43.4	127.6	0
1	51 08.5	+35.7	119.8	50 38.2	+36.8	120.8	50 07.0	+37.9	121.9	49 34.9	+39.0	122.9	49 01.9	+40.0	123.8	48 28.1	+41.0	124.8	47 53.4	+42.0	125.7	47 18.1	+42.8	126.6	1
2	51 44.2	+34.7	118.5	51 15.0	+36.0	119.6	50 44.9	+37.2	120.7	50 13.9	+38.2	121.7	49 41.9	+39.3	122.7	49 09.1	+40.3	123.7	48 35.4	+41.3	124.6	48 00.9	+42.2	125.5	2
3	52 18.9	+33.9	117.2	51 51.0	+35.1	118.3	51 22.1	+36.3	119.4	50 52.1	+37.5	120.5	50 21.2	+38.6	121.5	49 49.4	+39.6	122.5	49 16.7	+40.7	123.5	48 43.1	+41.7	124.5	3
4	52 52.8	+32.9	115.8	52 26.1	+34.3	117.0	51 58.4	+35.5	118.1	51 29.6	+36.7	119.2	50 59.8	+37.8	120.3	50 29.0	+39.0	121.4	49 57.4	+39.9	122.4	49 24.8	+41.0	123.4	4
5	53 25.7	+31.9	114.4	53 00.4	+33.2	115.6	52 33.9	+34.5	116.8	52 06.3	+35.8	118.0	51 37.6	+37.0	119.1	51 08.0	+38.1	120.2	50 37.3	+39.3	121.2	50 05.8	+40.3	122.2	5
6	53 57.6	+30.9	113.0	53 33.6	+32.3	114.2	53 08.4	+33.6	115.4	52 42.1	+34.9	116.6	52 14.6	+36.2	117.8	51 46.1	+37.4	118.9	51 16.6	+38.5	120.0	50 46.1	+39.6	121.1	6
7	54 28.5	+29.8	111.5	54 05.9	+31.2	112.8	53 42.0	+32.6	114.1	53 17.0	+33.9	115.3	52 50.8	+35.2	116.5	52 23.5	+36.5	117.6	51 55.1	+37.7	118.8	51 25.7	+38.9	119.9	7
8	54 58.3	+28.6	110.0	54 37.1	+30.1	111.3	54 14.6	+31.6	112.6	53 50.9	+33.0	113.9	53 26.0	+34.4	115.1	53 00.0	+35.6	116.3	52 32.8	+36.9	117.5	52 04.6	+38.0	118.7	8
9	55 26.9	+27.5	108.5	55 07.2	+29.0	109.8	54 46.2	+30.5	111.2	54 23.9	+32.0	112.5	54 00.4	+33.3	113.7	53 35.6	+34.7	115.0	53 09.7	+36.0	116.2	52 42.6	+37.3	117.4	9
10	55 54.4	+26.2	106.9	55 36.2	+27.9	108.3	55 16.7	+29.4	109.7	54 55.9	+30.8	111.0	54 33.7	+32.3	112.3	54 10.3	+33.7	113.6	53 45.7	+35.0	114.9	53 19.9	+36.3	116.1	10
11	56 20.6	+24.9	105.3	56 04.1	+26.5	106.7	55 46.1	+28.2	108.1	55 26.7	+29.8	109.5	55 06.0	+31.3	110.9	54 44.0	+32.7	112.2	54 20.7	+34.1	113.5	53 56.2	+35.5	114.7	11
12	56 45.5	+23.6	103.6	56 30.6	+25.3	105.1	56 14.3	+26.9	106.5	55 56.5	+28.5	108.0	55 37.3	+30.1	109.4	55 16.7	+31.6	110.7	54 54.8	+33.1	112.1	54 31.7	+34.4	113.4	12
13	57 09.1	+22.2	101.9	56 55.9	+24.0	103.4	56 41.2	+25.7	104.9	56 25.0	+27.3	106.4	56 07.4	+28.9	107.8	55 48.3	+30.5	109.2	55 27.9	+32.0	110.6	55 06.1	+33.4	111.9	13
14	57 31.3	+20.8	100.2	57 19.9	+22.5	101.8	57 06.9	+24.3	103.3	56 52.3	+26.1	104.8	56 36.3	+27.7	106.2	56 18.8	+29.3	107.7	55 59.9	+30.8	109.1	55 39.5	+32.4	110.5	14
15	57 52.1	+19.3	98.5	57 42.4	+21.2	100.0	57 31.2	+22.9	101.6	57 18.4	+24.6	103.1	57 04.0	+26.4	104.6	56 48.1	+28.1	106.1	56 30.7	+29.7	107.5	56 11.9	+31.3	109.0	15
16	58 11.4	+17.7	96.7	58 03.6	+19.6	98.3	57 54.1	+21.5	99.8	57 43.0	+23.3	101.4	57 30.4	+25.0	103.0	57 16.2	+26.7	104.5	57 00.4	+28.4	106.0	56 43.2	+30.0	107.4	16
17	58 29.1	+16.2	94.9	58 23.2	+18.1	96.5	58 15.6	+20.0	98.1	58 06.3	+21.9	99.7	57 55.4	+23.7	101.3	57 42.9	+25.5	102.8	57 28.8	+27.2	104.3	57 13.2	+28.9	105.8	17
18	58 45.3	+14.6	93.0	58 41.3	+16.5	94.6	58 35.6	+18.4	96.3	58 28.2	+20.3	97.9	58 19.1	+22.2	99.5	58 08.4	+24.0	101.1	57 56.0	+25.8	102.7	57 42.1	+27.5	104.2	18
19	58 59.9	+12.9	91.1	58 57.8	+14.9	92.8	58 54.0	+16.9	94.4	58 48.5	+18.8	96.1	58 41.3	+20.7	97.7	58 32.4	+22.6	99.4	58 21.8	+24.4	101.0	58 09.6	+26.2	102.5	19
20	59 12.8	+11.3	89.2	59 12.7	+13.3	90.9	59 10.9	+15.3	92.6	59 07.3	+17.3	94.3	59 02.0	+19.2	95.9	58 55.0	+21.0	97.6	58 46.2	+23.0	99.2	58 35.8	+24.8	100.8	20
21	59 24.1	+9.5	87.3	59 26.0	+11.5	89.0	59 26.2	+13.5	90.7	59 24.6	+15.5	92.4	59 21.2	+17.5	94.1	59 16.0	+19.6	95.7	59 09.2	+21.4	97.4	59 00.6	+23.3	99.1	21
22	59 33.6	+7.8	85.4	59 37.5	+9.9	87.1	59 39.7	+11.9	88.8	59 40.1	+13.9	90.5	59 38.7	+15.9	92.2	59 35.6	+17.9	93.9	59 30.6	+19.9	95.6	59 23.9	+21.8	97.3	22
23	59 41.4	+6.0	83.4	59 47.4	+8.0	85.1	59 51.6	+10.1	86.8	59 54.0	+12.2	88.5	59 54.6	+14.3	90.3	59 53.5	+16.2	92.0	59 50.5	+18.2	93.7	59 45.7	+20.2	95.4	23
24	59 47.4	+4.2	81.4	59 55.4	+6.3	83.1	60 01.7	+8.4	84.9	60 06.2	+10.4	86.6	60 08.9	+12.4	88.3	60 09.7	+14.5	90.1	60 08.7	+16.6	91.8	60 05.9	+18.6	93.5	24
25	59 51.6	+2.4	79.4	60 01.7	+4.5	81.1	60 10.1	+6.5	82.9	60 16.6	+8.6	84.6	60 21.3	+10.8	86.4	60 24.2	+12.8	88.1	60 25.3	+14.9	89.8	60 24.5	+16.9	91.6	25
26	59 54.0	+0.6	77.4	60 06.2	+2.7	79.1	60 16.6	+4.7	80.9	60 25.2	+6.9	82.6	60 32.1	+8.9	84.4	60 37.0	+11.0	86.1	60 40.2	+13.1	87.9	60 41.4	+15.2	89.7	26
27	59 54.6	-1.1	75.5	60 08.9	+0.8	77.1	60 21.3	+2.9	78.8	60 32.1	+4.9	80.6	60 41.0	+7.0	82.3	60 48.0	+9.2	84.1	60 53.3	+11.3	85.9	60 56.6	+13.4	87.7	27
28	59 53.5	-3.0	73.5	60 09.7	-1.0	75.1	60 24.2	+1.1	76.8	60 37.0	+3.2	78.6	60 48.0	+5.3	80.3	60 57.2	+7.4	82.1	61 04.6	+9.4	83.9	61 10.0	+11.6	85.7	28
29	59 50.5	-4.8	71.5	60 08.7	-2.8	73.1	60 25.3	-0.8	74.8	60 40.2	+1.2	76.5	60 53.3	+3.3	78.3	61 04.6	+5.4	80.0	61 14.0	+7.6	81.8	61 21.6	+9.7	83.6	29
30	59 45.7	-6.6	69.5	60 05.9	-4.6	71.1	60 24.5	-2.6	72.8	60 41.4	-0.6	74.5	60 56.6	+1.5	76.2	61 10.0	+3.6	78.0	61 21.6	+5.7	79.8	61 31.3	+7.9	81.6	30
31	59 39.1	-8.3	67.5	60 01.3	-6.4	69.1	60 21.9	-4.5	70.8	60 40.8	-2.4	72.4	60 58.1	-0.4	74.2	61 13.6	+1.7	75.9	61 27.3	+3.8	77.7	61 39.2	+5.9	79.5	31
32	59 30.8	-10.0	65.6	59 54.9	-8.2	67.1	60 17.4	-6.2	68.7	60 38.4	-4.3	70.4	60 57.7	-2.3	72.1	61 15.3	-0.3	73.8	61 31.1	+1.8	75.6	61 45.1	+4.0	77.4	32
33	59 20.8	-11.8	63.6	59 46.7	-10.0	65.2	60 11.2	-8.1	66.7	60 34.1	-6.2	68.4	60 55.4	-4.2	70.0	61 15.0	-2.1	71.7	61 32.9	0.0	73.5	61 49.1	+2.0	75.3	33
34	59 09.0	-13.5	61.7	59 36.7	-11.6	63.2	60 03.1	-9.9	64.7	60 27.9	-8.0	66.3	60 51.2	-6.0	68.0	61 12.9	-4.1	69.7	61 32.9	-2.0•	71.4	61 51.1	+0.1	73.2	34
35	58 55.5	-15.0	59.8	59 25.1	-13.4	61.3	59 53.2	-11.6	62.8	60 19.9	-9.7	64.3	60 45.2	-7.9	65.9	61 08.8	-5.9	67.6	61 30.9	-4.0	69.3	61 51.2	-1.8•	71.0	35
36	58 40.5	-16.7	57.9	59 11.7	-15.0	59.4	59 41.6	-13.3	60.8	60 10.2	-11.6	62.3	60 37.3	-9.7	63.9	61 02.9	-7.8	65.5	61 26.9	-5.8	67.2	61 49.4	-3.9	68.9	36
37	58 23.8	-18.2	56.1	58 56.7	-16.7	57.5	59 28.3	-15.0	58.9	59 58.6	-13.3	60.4	60 27.6	-11.5	61.9	60 55.1	-9.7	63.5	61 21.1	-7.7	65.1	61 45.5	-5.7	66.8	37
38	58 05.6	-19.8	54.3	58 40.0	-18.2	55.6	59 13.3	-16.6	57.0	59 45.3	-14.9	58.4	60 16.1	-13.3	59.9	60 45.4	-11.4	61.5	61 13.4	-9.6	63.1	61 39.8	-7.7	64.7	38
39	57 45.8	-21.2	52.5	58 21.8	-19.8	53.8	58 56.7	-18.3	55.1	59 30.4	-16.7	56.5	60 02.8	-14.9	58.0	60 34.0	-13.2	59.5	61 03.8	-11.5	61.0	61 32.1	-9.6	62.6	39
40	57 24.6	-22.7	50.8	58 02.0	-21.2	52.0	58 38.4	-19.7	53.3	59 13.7	-18.2	54.6	59 47.9	-16.7	56.0	60 20.8	-15.0	57.5	60 52.3	-13.2	59.0	61 22.5	-11.4	60.6	40
41	57 01.9	-24.0	49.1	57 40.8	-22.7	50.2	58 18.7	-21.3	51.5	58 55.5	-19.8	52.8	59 31.2	-18.2	54.1	60 05.8	-16.7	55.5	60 39.1	-15.0	57.0	61 11.1	-13.2	58.5	41
42	56 37.9	-25.3	47.4	57 18.1	-24.0	48.5	57 57.4	-22.7	49.7	58 35.7	-21.3	51.0	59 13.0	-19.9	52.3	59 49.1	-18.3	53.6	60 24.1	-16.7	55.0	60 57.9	-15.1	56.5	42
43	56 12.6	-26.6	45.7	56 54.1	-25.4	46.8	57 34.7	-24.1	48.0	58 14.4	-22.8	49.2	58 53.1	-21.4	50.4	59 30.8	-19.9	51.7	60 07.4	-18.4	53.1	60 42.8	-16.7	54.5	43
44	55 46.0	-27.8	44.1	56 28.7	-26.7	45.2	57 10.6	-25.5	46.3	57 51.6	-24.2	47.4	58 31.7	-22.8	48.6	59 10.9	-21.5	49.9	59 49.0	-20.0	51.2	60 26.1	-18.5	52.6	44
45	55 18.2	-29.0	42.6	56 02.0	-27.9	43.6	56 45.1	-26.7	44.6	57 27.4	-25.5	45.7	58 08.9	-24.3	46.9	58 49.4	-22.9	48.1	59 29.0	-21.5	49.3	60 07.6	-20.1	50.6	45
46	54 49.2	-30.1	41.0	55 34.1	-29.1	42.0	56 18.4	-28.0	43.0	57 01.9	-26.9	44.0	57 44.6	-25.7	45.1	58 26.5	-24.4	46.3	59 07.5	-23.1	47.5	59 47.5	-21.6	48.8	46
47	54 19.1	-31.2	39.6	55 05.0	-30.2	40.5	55 50.4	-29.2	41.4	56 35.0	-28.1	42.4	57 18.9	-26.9	43.5	58 02.1	-25.8	44.6	58 44.4	-24.5	45.7	59 25.9	-23.2	46.9	47
48	53 47.9	-32.3	38.1	54 34.8	-31.3	39.0	55 21.2	-30.4	39.9	56 06.9	-29.3	40.8	56 52.0	-28.3	41.8	57 36.3	-27.1	42.9	58 19.9	-25.9	44.0	59 02.7	-24.7	45.1	48
49	53 15.6	-33.2	36.7	54 03.5	-32.3	37.5	54 50.8	-31.4	38.4	55 37.6	-30.5	39.3	56 23.7	-29.4	40.2	57 09.2	-28.4	41.2	57 54.0	-27.3	42.3	58 38.0	-26.0	43.4	49
50	52 42.4	-34.1	35.3	53 31.2	-33.4	36.1	54 19.4	-32.5	36.9	55 07.1	-31.5	37.7	55 54.3	-30.6	38.6	56 40.8	-29.6	39.6	57 26.7	-28.5	40.6	58 12.0	-27.5	41.6	50
51	52 08.3	-35.1	33.9	52 57.8	-34.2	34.7	53 46.9	-33.4	35.5	54 35.6	-32.6	36.3	55 23.7	-31.7	37.1	56 11.2	-30.7	38.0	56 58.2	-29.8	39.0	57 44.5	-28.7	40.0	51
52	51 33.2	-35.9	32.6	52 23.6	-35.2	33.3	53 13.5	-34.3	34.1	54 03.0	-33.7	34.8	54 52.0	-32.8	35.6	55 40.5	-31.9	36.5	56 28.4	-30.9	37.4	57 15.8	-29.9	38.3	52
53	50 57.3	-36.7	31.4	51 48.4	-36.1	32.0	52 39.1	-35.4	32.7	53 29.3	-34.5	33.4	54 19.2	-33.8	34.2	55 08.6	-33.0	35.0	55 57.5	-32.1	35.8	56 45.9	-31.2	36.7	53
54	50 20.6	-37.5	30.1	51 12.3	-36.8	30.7	52 03.7	-36.2	31.4	52 54.8	-35.5	32.1	53 45.4	-34.7	32.8	54 35.6	-33.9	33.5	55 25.4	-33.1	34.3	56 14.7	-32.3	35.2	54
55	49 43.1	-38.3	28.9	50 35.5	-37.7	29.5	51 27.5	-37.0	30.1	52 19.3	-36.4	30.7	53 10.7	-35.7	31.4	54 01.7	-35.0	32.1	54 52.3	-34.2	32.9	55 42.4	-33.3	33.7	55
56	49 04.8	-38.9	27.7	49 57.8	-38.4	28.3	50 50.5	-37.8	28.8	51 42.9	-37.2	29.4	52 35.0	-36.5	30.1	53 26.7	-35.8	30.8	54 18.1	-35.1	31.5	55 09.1	-34.4	32.2	56
57	48 25.9	-39.7	26.6	49 19.4	-39.1	27.1	50 12.7	-38.6	27.6	51 05.7	-37.9	28.2	51 58.5	-37.4	28.8	52 50.9	-36.7	29.4	53 43.0	-36.1	30.1	54 34.7	-35.3	30.8	57
58	47 46.2	-40.3	25.4	48 40.3	-39.8	25.9	49 34.1	-39.2	26.4	50 27.8	-38.8	27.0	51 21.1	-38.2	27.5	52 14.2	-37.6	28.1	53 06.9	-36.9	28.7	53 59.4	-36.3	29.4	58
59	47 05.9	-40.8	24.3	48 00.5	-40.4	24.8	48 54.9	-40.0	25.3	49 49.0	-39.4	25.8	50 42.9	-38.9	26.3	51 36.6	-38.4	26.9	52 30.0	-37.8	27.4	53 23.1	-37.2	28.1	59
60	46 25.1	-41.5	23.3	47 20.1	-41.1	23.7	48 14.9	-40.6	24.1	49 09.6	-40.1	24.6	50 04.0	-39.6	25.1	50 58.2	-39.1	25.6	51 52.2	-38.5	26.2	52 45.9	-38.0	26.7	60
61	45 43.6	-42.0	22.2	46 39.0	-41.6	22.6	47 34.3	-41.2	23.0	48 29.5	-40.8	23.5	49 24.4	-40.3	23.9	50 19.1	-39.8	24.4	51 13.7	-39.4	24.9	52 07.9	-38.7	25.5	61
62	45 01.6	-42.6	21.2	45 57.4	-42.2	21.6	46 53.1	-41.7	22.0	47 48.7	-41.4	22.4	48 44.1	-40.9	22.8	49 39.3	-40.5	23.3	50 34.3	-40.0	23.7	51 29.2	-39.6	24.2	62
63	44 19.0	-43.0	20.2	45 15.2	-42.7	20.6	46 11.4	-42.4	20.9	47 07.3	-41.9	21.3	48 03.2	-41.6	21.7	48 58.8	-41.1	22.1	49 54.3	-40.7	22.6	50 49.6	-40.2	23.0	63
64	43 36.0	-43.6	19.2	44 32.5	-43.2	19.6	45 29.0	-42.9	19.9	46 25.4	-42.5	20.3	47 21.6	-42.2	20.6	48 17.7	-41.8	21.0	49 13.6	-41.4	21.4	50 09.4	-41.0	21.9	64
65	42 52.4	-44.0	18.3	43 49.3	-43.7	18.6	44 46.1	-43.3	18.9	45 42.9	-43.1	19.2	46 39.4	-42.7	19.6	47 35.9	-42.4	20.0	48 32.2	-41.9	20.3	49 28.4	-41.6	20.7	65
66	42 08.4	-44.4	17.4	43 05.6	-44.1	17.7	44 02.8	-43.9	18.0	44 59.8	-43.5	18.3	45 56.7	-43.2	18.6	46 53.6	-43.0	18.9	47 50.3	-42.6	19.3	48 46.8	-42.2	19.6	66
67	41 24.0	-44.8	16.5	42 21.5	-44.6	16.7	43 18.9	-44.3	17.0	44 16.3	-44.1	17.3	45 13.5	-43.7	17.6	46 10.6	-43.4	17.9	47 07.7	-43.1	18.2	48 04.6	-42.8	18.5	67
68	40 39.2	-45.2	15.6	41 36.9	-45.0	15.8	42 34.6	-44.7	16.1	43 32.2	-44.4	16.3	44 29.8	-44.2	16.6	45 27.2	-43.9	16.9	46 24.6	-43.7	17.2	47 21.8	-43.3	17.5	68
69	39 54.0	-45.6	14.7	40 51.9	-45.3	15.0	41 49.9	-45.2	15.2	42 47.8	-45.0	15.4	43 45.6	-44.7	15.7	44 43.3	-44.4	15.9	45 40.9	-44.1	16.2	46 38.5	-43.8	16.5	69
70	39 08.4	-46.0	13.9	40 06.6	-45.8	14.1	41 04.7	-45.5	14.3	42 02.8	-45.3	14.5	43 00.9	-45.1	14.8	43 58.9	-44.9	15.0	44 56.8	-44.6	15.3	45 54.7	-44.4	15.5	70
71	38 22.4	-46.3	13.1	39 20.8	-46.1	13.3	40 19.2	-45.9	13.4	41 17.5	-45.7	13.7	42 15.8	-45.5	13.9	43 14.0	-45.3	14.1	44 12.2	-45.1	14.3	45 10.3	-44.8	14.6	71
72	37 36.1	-46.6	12.3	38 34.7	-46.4	12.4	39 33.3	-46.3	12.6	40 31.8	-46.1	12.8	41 30.3	-45.9	13.0	42 28.7	-45.6	13.2	43 27.1	-45.4	13.4	44 25.5	-45.3	13.6	72
73	36 49.5	-46.9	11.5	37 48.3	-46.8	11.6	38 47.0	-46.6	11.8	39 45.7	-46.4	11.9	40 44.4	-46.2	12.1	41 43.1	-46.1	12.3	42 41.7	-45.9	12.5	43 40.2	-45.7	12.7	73
74	36 02.6	-47.3	10.7	37 01.5	-47.1	10.8	38 00.4	-46.9	11.0	38 59.3	-46.8	11.1	39 58.2	-46.7	11.3	40 57.0	-46.5	11.5	41 55.8	-46.3	11.6	42 54.5	-46.1	11.8	74
75	35 15.3	-47.5	9.9	36 14.4	-47.3	10.1	37 13.5	-47.2	10.2	38 12.5	-47.1	10.3	39 11.5	-46.9	10.5	40 10.5	-46.8	10.6	41 09.5	-46.7	10.8	42 08.4	-46.5	11.0	75
76	34 27.8	-47.9	9.2	35 27.1	-47.7	9.3	36 26.3	-47.6	9.4	37 25.4	-47.4	9.6	38 24.7	-47.3	9.7	39 23.7	-47.1	9.8	40 22.8	-47.0	10.0	41 21.9	-46.8	10.1	76
77	33 40.1	-48.0	8.5	34 39.4	-47.9	8.6	35 38.7	-47.8	8.7	36 38.0	-47.6	8.8	37 37.3	-47.5	8.9	38 36.6	-47.4	9.0	39 35.8	-47.3	9.1	40 35.1	-47.2	9.3	77
78	32 52.1	-48.3	7.7	33 51.5	-48.2	7.8	34 50.9	-48.0	7.9	35 50.4	-48.0	8.0	36 49.8	-47.9	8.1	37 49.2	-47.8	8.2	38 48.5	-47.6	8.4	39 47.9	-47.5	8.5	78
79	32 03.8	-48.5	7.0	33 03.3	-48.4	7.1	34 02.9	-48.3	7.2	35 02.4	-48.2	7.3	36 01.4	-48.1	7.4	37 01.4	-48.0	7.5	38 00.9	-48.0	7.6	39 00.4	-47.9	7.7	79
80	31 15.3	-48.7	6.4	32 14.9	-48.6	6.4	33 14.6	-48.6	6.5	34 14.2	-48.5	6.6	35 13.8	-48.4	6.6	36 13.4	-48.3	6.7	37 12.9	-48.2	6.8	38 12.5	-48.1	6.9	80
81	30 26.6	-48.9	5.7	31 26.3	-48.8	5.7	32 26.0	-48.8	5.8	33 25.7	-48.7	5.9	34 25.4	-48.6	5.9	35 25.1	-48.6	6.0	36 24.7	-48.5	6.1	37 24.4	-48.4	6.2	81
82	29 37.7	-49.1	5.0	30 37.5	-49.1	5.1	31 37.2	-49.0	5.1	32 37.0	-49.0	5.2	33 36.7	-48.8	5.3	34 36.5	-48.8	5.3	35 36.2	-48.7	5.4	36 36.0	-48.7	5.4	82
83	28 48.6	-49.3	4.3	29 48.4	-49.2	4.4	30 48.2	-49.2	4.4	31 48.0	-49.1	4.5	32 47.9	-49.1	4.5	33 47.7	-49.1	4.6	34 47.5	-49.0	4.6	35 47.3	-49.0	4.7	83
84	27 59.3	-49.5	3.7	28 59.2	-49.4	3.7	29 59.0	-49.4	3.8	30 58.9	-49.4	3.8	31 58.8	-49.4	3.8	32 58.6	-49.2	3.9	33 58.5	-49.2	3.9	34 58.3	-49.1	4.0	84
85	27 09.8	-49.7	3.1	28 09.7	-49.6	3.1	29 09.6	-49.5	3.1	30 09.5	-49.5	3.1	31 09.4	-49.5	3.2	32 09.4	-49.5	3.2	33 09.3	-49.5	3.3	34 09.2	-49.5	3.3	85
86	26 20.1	-49.8	2.4	27 20.1	-49.8	2.5	28 20.0	-49.8	2.5	29 20.0	-49.8	2.5	30 19.9	-49.7	2.5	31 19.9	-49.7	2.5	32 19.8	-49.7	2.6	33 19.7	-49.6	2.6	86
87	25 30.3	-49.9	1.8	26 30.3	-49.9	1.8	27 30.3	-50.0	1.8	28 30.2	-49.9	1.9	29 30.2	-49.9	1.9	30 30.2	-49.9	1.9	31 30.1	-49.8	1.9	32 30.1	-49.8	1.9	87
88	24 40.4	-50.1	1.2	25 40.4	-50.2	1.2	26 40.3	-50.1	1.2	27 40.3	-50.1	1.2	28 40.3	-50.1	1.2	29 40.3	-50.1	1.3	30 40.3	-50.1	1.3	31 40.3	-50.1	1.3	88
89	23 50.3	-50.3	0.6	24 50.2	-50.2	0.6	25 50.2	-50.2	0.6	26 50.2	-50.2	0.6	27 50.2	-50.2	0.6	28 50.2	-50.2	0.6	29 50.2	-50.2	0.6	30 50.2	-50.2	0.6	89
90	23 00.0	-50.4	0.0	24 00.0	-50.4	0.0	25 00.0	-50.4	0.0	26 00.0	-50.4	0.0	27 00.0	-50.4	0.0	28 00.0	-50.4	0.0	29 00.0	-50.4	0.0	30 00.0	-50.4	0.0	90
	23°			24°			25°			26°			27°			28°			29°			30°			

33°, 327° L.H.A.   LATITUDE SAME NAME AS DECLINATION

LATITUDE CONTRARY NAME TO DECLINATION L.H.A. 33°, 327°

Dec.	23° Hc	23° d	23° Z	24° Hc	24° d	24° Z	25° Hc	25° d	25° Z	26° Hc	26° d	26° Z	27° Hc	27° d	27° Z	28° Hc	28° d	28° Z	29° Hc	29° d	29° Z	30° Hc	30° d	30° Z	Dec.
°	° ′	′	°	° ′	′	°	° ′	′	°	° ′	′	°	° ′	′	°	° ′	′	°	° ′	′	°	° ′	′	°	°
0	50 32.0	-37.2	121.0	50 00.6	-38.3	122.1	49 28.3	-39.3	123.1	48 55.2	-40.4	124.0	48 21.2	-41.3	125.0	47 46.5	-42.3	125.9	47 10.9	-43.0	126.7	46 34.7	-43.9	127.6	0
1	49 54.8	-38.1	122.3	49 22.3	-39.1	123.2	48 49.0	-40.1	124.2	48 14.8	-40.9	125.1	47 39.9	-41.9	126.0	47 04.2	-42.7	126.9	46 27.9	-43.6	127.8	45 50.8	-44.4	128.6	1
2	49 16.7	-38.7	123.5	48 43.2	-39.7	124.4	48 08.9	-40.6	125.3	47 33.9	-41.6	126.2	46 58.0	-42.4	127.1	46 21.5	-43.3	127.9	45 44.3	-44.1	128.8	45 06.4	-44.9	129.5	2
3	48 38.0	-39.4	124.6	48 03.5	-40.4	125.5	47 28.3	-41.3	126.4	46 52.3	-42.2	127.3	46 15.6	-43.0	128.1	45 38.2	-43.8	128.9	45 00.2	-44.6	129.7	44 21.5	-45.3	130.5	3
4	47 58.6	-40.1	125.7	47 23.1	-41.0	126.6	46 47.0	-41.9	127.5	46 10.1	-42.7	128.3	45 32.6	-43.6	129.1	44 54.4	-44.3	129.9	44 15.6	-45.0	130.7	43 36.2	-45.7	131.4	4
5	47 18.5	-40.7	126.9	46 42.1	-41.5	127.7	46 05.1	-42.4	128.5	45 27.4	-43.2	129.3	44 49.0	-44.0	130.1	44 10.1	-44.8	130.9	43 30.6	-45.5	131.6	42 50.5	-46.2	132.3	5
6	46 37.8	-41.3	127.9	46 00.6	-42.2	128.8	45 22.7	-43.0	129.5	44 44.2	-43.8	130.3	44 05.0	-44.4	131.1	43 25.3	-45.1	131.8	42 45.1	-45.9	132.5	42 04.3	-46.5	133.1	6
7	45 56.5	-41.9	129.0	45 18.4	-42.7	129.8	44 39.7	-43.4	130.5	44 00.4	-44.2	131.3	43 20.6	-44.9	132.0	42 40.2	-45.6	132.7	41 59.2	-46.2	133.3	41 17.8	-46.9	134.0	7
8	45 14.6	-42.4	130.0	44 35.7	-43.1	130.8	43 56.3	-43.9	131.5	43 16.2	-44.6	132.2	42 35.7	-45.4	132.9	41 54.6	-46.0	133.6	41 13.0	-46.6	134.2	40 30.9	-47.2	134.8	8
9	44 32.2	-42.9	131.0	43 52.6	-43.7	131.7	43 12.4	-44.4	132.4	42 31.6	-45.1	133.1	41 50.3	-45.7	133.8	41 08.6	-46.4	134.4	40 26.4	-47.0	135.0	39 43.7	-47.5	135.6	9
10	43 49.3	-43.4	132.0	43 08.9	-44.1	132.7	42 28.0	-44.8	133.4	41 46.5	-45.4	134.0	41 04.6	-46.1	134.6	40 22.2	-46.7	135.3	39 39.4	-47.3	135.8	38 56.2	-47.9	136.4	10
11	43 05.9	-43.8	132.9	42 24.8	-44.5	133.6	41 43.2	-45.2	134.3	41 01.1	-45.9	134.9	40 18.5	-46.4	135.5	39 35.5	-47.0	136.1	38 52.1	-47.6	136.6	38 08.3	-48.2	137.2	11
12	42 22.1	-44.3	133.9	41 40.3	-45.0	134.5	40 58.0	-45.6	135.1	40 15.2	-46.2	135.7	39 32.1	-46.8	136.3	38 48.5	-47.4	136.9	38 04.5	-47.9	137.4	37 20.1	-48.4	137.9	12
13	41 37.8	-44.7	134.8	40 55.3	-45.3	135.4	40 12.4	-46.0	136.0	39 29.0	-46.5	136.6	38 45.3	-47.2	137.1	38 01.1	-47.7	137.7	37 16.6	-48.2	138.2	36 31.7	-48.7	138.7	13
14	40 53.1	-45.1	135.7	40 10.0	-45.8	136.2	39 26.4	-46.3	136.8	38 42.5	-46.9	137.4	37 58.1	-47.4	137.9	37 13.4	-47.9	138.4	36 28.4	-48.5	138.9	35 43.0	-49.0	139.4	14
15	40 08.0	-45.5	136.5	39 24.2	-46.0	137.1	38 40.1	-46.6	137.6	37 55.6	-47.2	138.2	37 10.7	-47.7	138.7	36 25.5	-48.3	139.2	35 39.9	-48.7	139.6	34 54.0	-49.2	140.1	15
16	39 22.5	-45.8	137.4	38 38.2	-46.5	137.9	37 53.5	-47.0	138.4	37 08.4	-47.5	138.9	36 23.0	-48.0	139.4	35 37.2	-48.5	139.9	34 51.2	-49.0	140.4	34 04.8	-49.4	140.8	16
17	38 36.7	-46.2	138.2	37 51.7	-46.7	138.7	37 06.5	-47.3	139.2	36 20.9	-47.8	139.7	35 35.0	-48.3	140.2	34 48.7	-48.7	140.6	34 02.2	-49.2	141.1	33 15.4	-49.7	141.5	17
18	37 50.5	-46.6	139.0	37 05.0	-47.0	139.5	36 19.2	-47.6	140.0	35 33.1	-48.1	140.5	34 46.7	-48.6	140.9	34 00.0	-49.0	141.3	33 13.0	-49.5	141.7	32 25.7	-49.8	142.1	18
19	37 03.9	-46.8	139.8	36 18.0	-47.4	140.3	35 31.6	-47.8	140.7	34 45.0	-48.3	141.2	33 58.1	-48.7	141.6	33 11.0	-49.2	142.0	32 23.5	-49.6	142.4	31 35.9	-50.1	142.8	19
20	36 17.1	-47.1	140.6	35 30.6	-47.6	141.0	34 43.8	-48.1	141.5	33 56.7	-48.5	141.9	33 09.4	-49.0	142.3	32 21.8	-49.5	142.7	31 33.9	-49.8	143.1	30 45.8	-50.2	143.4	20
21	35 30.0	-47.4	141.4	34 43.0	-47.9	141.8	33 55.7	-48.3	142.2	33 08.2	-48.8	142.6	32 20.4	-49.3	143.0	31 32.3	-49.6	143.4	30 44.1	-50.1	143.7	29 55.6	-50.4	144.1	21
22	34 42.6	-47.7	142.1	33 55.1	-48.2	142.5	33 07.4	-48.6	142.9	32 19.4	-49.1	143.3	31 31.1	-49.4	143.7	30 42.7	-49.8	144.0	29 54.0	-50.2	144.4	29 05.2	-50.6	144.7	22
23	33 54.9	-48.0	142.8	33 06.9	-48.3	143.2	32 18.8	-48.9	143.6	31 30.3	-49.2	144.0	30 41.7	-49.6	144.3	29 52.9	-50.1	144.7	29 03.8	-50.4	145.0	28 14.6	-50.8	145.3	23
24	33 06.9	-48.1	143.6	32 18.6	-48.7	143.9	31 29.9	-49.0	144.3	30 41.1	-49.4	144.7	29 52.1	-49.8	145.0	29 02.8	-50.2	145.3	28 13.4	-50.5	145.6	27 23.8	-50.9	145.9	24
25	32 18.8	-48.5	144.3	31 29.9	-48.8	144.6	30 40.9	-49.2	145.0	29 51.7	-49.6	145.3	29 02.3	-50.0	145.6	28 12.6	-50.3	145.9	27 22.9	-50.8	146.2	26 32.9	-51.1	146.5	25
26	31 30.3	-48.6	145.0	30 41.1	-49.0	145.3	29 51.7	-49.4	145.6	29 02.1	-49.8	146.0	28 12.3	-50.2	146.3	27 22.3	-50.5	146.5	26 32.1	-50.8	146.8	25 41.8	-51.2	147.1	26
27	30 41.7	-48.8	145.6	29 52.1	-49.3	146.0	29 02.3	-49.7	146.3	28 12.3	-50.0	146.6	27 22.1	-50.3	146.9	26 31.8	-50.7	147.2	25 41.3	-51.0	147.4	24 50.6	-51.3	147.7	27
28	29 52.9	-49.1	146.3	29 02.8	-49.4	146.6	28 12.6	-49.7	146.9	27 22.3	-50.2	147.2	26 31.8	-50.5	147.5	25 41.1	-50.8	147.8	24 50.3	-51.2	148.0	23 59.5	-51.4	148.2	28
29	29 03.8	-49.2	147.0	28 13.4	-49.6	147.3	27 22.9	-50.0	147.6	26 32.1	-50.3	147.8	25 41.3	-50.7	148.1	24 50.3	-51.0	148.3	23 59.1	-51.2	148.6	23 07.9	-51.6	148.8	29
30	28 14.6	-49.5	147.6	27 23.8	-49.8	147.9	26 32.9	-50.1	148.2	25 41.8	-50.4	148.4	24 50.6	-50.7	148.7	23 59.3	-51.1	148.9	23 07.9	-51.4	149.1	22 16.3	-51.7	149.4	30
31	27 25.1	-49.6	148.3	26 34.0	-49.9	148.5	25 42.8	-50.3	148.8	24 51.4	-50.6	149.0	23 59.9	-50.9	149.3	23 08.2	-51.2	149.5	22 16.5	-51.5	149.7	21 24.6	-51.7	149.9	31
32	26 35.5	-49.7	148.9	25 44.1	-50.1	149.2	24 52.5	-50.4	149.4	24 00.8	-50.7	149.6	23 09.0	-51.0	149.8	22 17.0	-51.3	150.1	21 25.0	-51.6	150.3	20 32.9	-51.9	150.4	32
33	25 45.8	-50.0	149.5	24 54.0	-50.2	149.8	24 02.1	-50.6	150.0	23 10.1	-50.9	150.2	22 18.0	-51.2	150.4	21 25.7	-51.4	150.6	20 33.4	-51.7	150.8	19 41.0	-52.0	151.0	33
34	24 55.8	-50.0	150.1	24 03.8	-50.4	150.4	23 11.5	-50.6	150.6	22 19.2	-50.9	150.8	21 26.8	-51.2	151.0	20 34.3	-51.5	151.2	19 41.7	-51.8	151.3	18 49.0	-52.1	151.5	34
35	24 05.8	-50.2	150.7	23 13.4	-50.5	151.0	22 20.9	-50.8	151.2	21 28.3	-51.1	151.4	20 35.6	-51.4	151.5	19 42.8	-51.7	151.7	18 49.9	-51.9	151.9	17 56.9	-52.1	152.0	35
36	23 15.6	-50.4	151.3	22 22.9	-50.7	151.5	21 30.1	-50.9	151.7	20 37.2	-51.2	151.9	19 44.2	-51.5	152.1	18 51.1	-51.7	152.3	17 58.0	-52.0	152.4	17 04.8	-52.2	152.6	36
37	22 25.2	-50.5	151.9	21 32.2	-50.7	152.1	20 39.2	-51.1	152.3	19 46.0	-51.3	152.5	18 52.7	-51.5	152.6	17 59.4	-51.8	152.8	17 06.0	-52.0	152.9	16 12.6	-52.3	153.1	37
38	21 34.7	-50.5	152.5	20 41.5	-50.9	152.7	19 48.1	-51.1	152.9	18 54.7	-51.4	153.0	18 01.2	-51.7	153.2	17 07.6	-51.9	153.3	16 14.0	-52.2	153.4	15 20.3	-52.4	153.6	38
39	20 44.2	-50.7	153.1	19 50.6	-51.0	153.3	18 57.0	-51.2	153.4	18 03.3	-51.5	153.6	17 09.5	-51.7	153.7	16 15.7	-51.9	153.8	15 21.8	-52.2	154.0	14 27.9	-52.4	154.1	39
40	19 53.5	-50.9	153.7	18 59.6	-51.0	153.8	18 05.8	-51.4	154.0	17 11.8	-51.5	154.1	16 17.8	-51.8	154.2	15 23.8	-52.1	154.4	14 29.6	-52.2	154.5	13 35.5	-52.5	154.6	40
41	19 02.6	-50.9	154.2	18 08.6	-51.2	154.4	17 14.4	-51.4	154.5	16 20.3	-51.7	154.6	15 26.0	-51.9	154.8	14 31.7	-52.1	154.9	13 37.4	-52.4	155.0	12 43.0	-52.6	155.1	41
42	18 11.7	-51.0	154.8	17 17.4	-51.2	154.9	16 23.0	-51.5	155.0	15 28.6	-51.7	155.2	14 34.1	-51.9	155.3	13 39.6	-52.2	155.4	12 45.0	-52.3	155.5	11 50.4	-52.6	155.6	42
43	17 20.7	-51.1	155.3	16 26.2	-51.4	155.5	15 31.5	-51.5	155.6	14 36.9	-51.8	155.7	13 42.2	-52.0	155.8	12 47.4	-52.2	155.9	11 52.7	-52.5	156.0	10 57.8	-52.6	156.1	43
44	16 29.6	-51.2	155.9	15 34.8	-51.4	156.0	14 40.0	-51.7	156.1	13 45.1	-51.9	156.2	12 50.2	-52.1	156.3	11 55.2	-52.3	156.4	11 00.2	-52.5	156.5	10 05.2	-52.7	156.6	44
45	15 38.4	-51.2	156.4	14 43.4	-51.5	156.5	13 48.3	-51.7	156.6	12 53.2	-51.9	156.7	11 58.1	-52.1	156.8	11 02.9	-52.3	156.9	10 07.7	-52.5	157.0	9 12.5	-52.7	157.0	45
46	14 47.2	-51.4	157.0	13 51.9	-51.5	157.1	12 56.6	-51.7	157.2	12 01.3	-51.9	157.2	11 06.0	-52.2	157.3	10 10.6	-52.4	157.4	9 15.2	-52.6	157.5	8 19.8	-52.8	157.5	46
47	13 55.8	-51.4	157.5	13 00.4	-51.7	157.6	12 04.9	-51.8	157.7	11 09.4	-52.1	157.8	10 13.8	-52.2	157.8	9 18.2	-52.4	157.9	8 22.6	-52.6	157.9	7 27.0	-52.8	158.0	47
48	13 04.4	-51.5	158.0	12 08.7	-51.6	158.1	11 13.1	-51.9	158.2	10 17.3	-52.0	158.3	9 21.6	-52.3	158.3	8 25.8	-52.4	158.4	7 30.0	-52.6	158.4	6 34.2	-52.8	158.5	48
49	12 12.9	-51.5	158.6	11 17.1	-51.8	158.6	10 21.2	-51.9	158.7	9 25.3	-52.1	158.8	8 29.3	-52.3	158.8	7 33.4	-52.5	158.9	6 37.4	-52.7	158.9	5 41.4	-52.8	159.0	49
50	11 21.4	-51.6	159.1	10 25.3	-51.7	159.1	9 29.3	-52.0	159.2	8 33.2	-52.2	159.3	7 37.0	-52.3	159.3	6 40.9	-52.5	159.4	5 44.7	-52.7	159.4	4 48.6	-52.9	159.4	50
51	10 29.8	-51.6	159.6	9 33.6	-51.9	159.7	8 37.3	-52.0	159.7	7 41.0	-52.2	159.8	6 44.7	-52.4	159.8	5 48.4	-52.6	159.8	4 52.0	-52.7	159.9	3 55.7	-52.9	159.9	51
52	9 38.2	-51.7	160.1	8 41.7	-51.8	160.2	7 45.3	-52.1	160.2	6 48.8	-52.2	160.3	5 52.3	-52.4	160.3	4 55.8	-52.5	160.3	3 59.3	-52.7	160.4	3 02.8	-52.9	160.4	52
53	8 46.5	-51.7	160.6	7 49.9	-51.9	160.7	6 53.2	-52.0	160.7	5 56.6	-52.2	160.8	4 59.9	-52.4	160.8	4 03.3	-52.6	160.8	3 06.6	-52.7	160.8	2 09.9	-52.9	160.9	53
54	7 54.8	-51.8	161.1	6 58.0	-52.0	161.2	6 01.2	-52.1	161.2	5 04.4	-52.3	161.3	4 07.5	-52.4	161.3	3 10.7	-52.6	161.3	2 13.9	-52.8	161.3	1 17.0	-52.9	161.3	54
55	7 03.0	-51.8	161.7	6 06.0	-51.9	161.7	5 09.1	-52.2	161.7	4 12.1	-52.3	161.7	3 15.1	-52.4	161.8	2 18.1	-52.6	161.8	1 21.1	-52.7	161.8	0 24.1	-52.9	161.8	55
56	6 11.2	-51.8	162.2	5 14.1	-52.0	162.2	4 16.9	-52.1	162.2	3 19.8	-52.3	162.2	2 22.7	-52.5	162.3	1 25.5	-52.6	162.3	0 28.4	-52.8	162.3	0 28.8	+52.9	17.7	56
57	5 19.4	-51.9	162.7	4 22.1	-52.0	162.7	3 24.8	-52.2	162.7	2 27.5	-52.3	162.7	1 30.2	-52.4	162.7	0 32.9	-52.6	162.7	0 24.4	+52.7	17.3	1 21.7	+52.9	17.3	57
58	4 27.5	-51.9	163.2	3 30.1	-52.0	163.2	2 32.6	-52.1	163.2	1 35.2	-52.3	163.2	0 37.8	-52.5	163.2	0 19.7	+52.6	16.8	1 17.1	+52.8	16.8	2 14.6	+52.9	16.8	58
59	3 35.6	-51.8	163.7	2 38.1	-52.1	163.7	1 40.5	-52.2	163.7	0 42.9	-52.3	163.7	0 14.7	+52.5	16.3	1 12.3	+52.6	16.3	2 09.9	+52.7	16.3	3 07.5	+52.8	16.3	59
60	2 43.8	-51.9	164.2	1 46.0	-52.0	164.2	0 48.3	-52.2	164.2	0 09.4	+52.4	15.8	1 07.2	+52.4	15.8	2 04.9	+52.6	15.8	3 02.6	+52.8	15.8	4 00.3	+52.9	15.8	60
61	1 51.9	-52.0	164.7	0 54.0	-52.1	164.7	0 03.9	+52.2	15.3	1 01.8	+52.3	15.3	1 59.6	+52.5	15.3	2 57.5	+52.6	15.3	3 55.4	+52.7	15.3	4 53.2	+52.8	15.4	61
62	0 59.9	-51.9	165.2	0 01.9	-52.0	165.2	0 56.1	+52.1	14.8	1 54.1	+52.3	14.8	2 52.1	+52.4	14.8	3 50.1	+52.5	14.8	4 48.1	+52.7	14.9	5 46.0	+52.9	14.9	62
63	0 08.0	-51.9	165.7	0 50.1	+52.0	14.3	1 48.2	+52.2	14.3	2 46.4	+52.3	14.3	3 44.5	+52.4	14.3	4 42.6	+52.6	14.4	5 40.8	+52.6	14.4	6 38.9	+52.8	14.4	63
64	0 43.9	+51.9	13.8	1 42.1	+52.1	13.8	2 40.4	+52.2	13.8	3 38.7	+52.2	13.8	4 36.9	+52.4	13.9	5 35.2	+52.5	13.9	6 33.4	+52.7	13.9	7 31.7	+52.7	13.9	64
65	1 35.8	+51.9	13.3	2 34.2	+52.0	13.3	3 32.6	+52.1	13.3	4 30.9	+52.3	13.3	5 29.3	+52.4	13.4	6 27.7	+52.5	13.4	7 26.1	+52.6	13.4	8 24.4	+52.7	13.5	65
66	2 27.7	+51.9	12.8	3 26.2	+52.0	12.8	4 24.7	+52.1	12.8	5 23.2	+52.2	12.9	6 21.7	+52.3	12.9	7 20.2	+52.4	12.9	8 18.7	+52.5	12.9	9 17.1	+52.7	13.0	66
67	3 19.6	+51.9	12.3	4 18.2	+52.0	12.3	5 16.8	+52.1	12.3	6 15.4	+52.2	12.4	7 14.0	+52.4	12.4	8 12.6	+52.5	12.4	9 11.2	+52.6	12.4	10 09.8	+52.7	12.5	67
68	4 11.5	+51.8	11.8	5 10.2	+52.0	11.8	6 08.9	+52.1	11.8	7 07.6	+52.2	11.9	8 06.4	+52.2	11.9	9 05.1	+52.3	11.9	10 03.8	+52.5	12.0	11 02.5	+52.6	12.0	68
69	5 03.3	+51.9	11.3	6 02.2	+51.9	11.3	7 01.0	+52.0	11.3	7 59.8	+52.2	11.4	8 58.6	+52.3	11.4	9 57.4	+52.4	11.4	10 56.3	+52.4	11.5	11 55.1	+52.5	11.5	69
70	5 55.2	+51.8	10.8	6 54.1	+51.9	10.8	7 53.0	+52.0	10.8	8 52.0	+52.1	10.9	9 50.9	+52.2	10.9	10 49.8	+52.3	10.9	11 48.7	+52.4	11.0	12 47.6	+52.5	11.0	70
71	6 47.0	+51.7	10.3	7 46.0	+51.9	10.3	8 45.0	+52.0	10.3	9 44.1	+52.0	10.4	10 43.1	+52.1	10.4	11 42.1	+52.2	10.4	12 41.1	+52.3	10.5	13 40.1	+52.4	10.5	71
72	7 38.7	+51.8	9.8	8 37.9	+51.8	9.8	9 37.0	+51.9	9.8	10 36.1	+52.0	9.9	11 35.2	+52.1	9.9	12 34.3	+52.2	9.9	13 33.4	+52.3	10.0	14 32.5	+52.4	10.0	72
73	8 30.5	+51.7	9.3	9 29.7	+51.8	9.3	10 28.9	+51.9	9.3	11 28.1	+52.0	9.4	12 27.3	+52.0	9.4	13 26.5	+52.1	9.4	14 25.7	+52.2	9.5	15 24.9	+52.3	9.5	73
74	9 22.2	+51.6	8.8	10 21.5	+51.7	8.8	11 20.8	+51.8	8.8	12 20.1	+51.9	8.8	13 19.3	+52.0	8.9	14 18.6	+52.1	8.9	15 17.9	+52.1	9.0	16 17.2	+52.2	9.0	74
75	10 13.8	+51.6	8.2	11 13.2	+51.7	8.3	12 12.6	+51.7	8.3	13 12.0	+51.8	8.3	14 11.3	+51.9	8.4	15 10.7	+52.0	8.4	16 10.0	+52.1	8.4	17 09.4	+52.1	8.5	75
76	11 05.4	+51.6	7.7	12 04.9	+51.6	7.7	13 04.3	+51.7	7.8	14 03.8	+51.8	7.8	15 03.2	+51.9	7.8	16 02.7	+51.9	7.9	17 02.1	+52.0	7.9	18 01.5	+52.1	8.0	76
77	11 57.0	+51.5	7.2	12 56.5	+51.6	7.2	13 56.0	+51.7	7.3	14 55.6	+51.6	7.3	15 55.1	+51.7	7.3	16 54.6	+51.8	7.4	17 54.1	+51.9	7.4	18 53.6	+51.9	7.4	77
78	12 48.5	+51.4	6.7	13 48.1	+51.5	6.7	14 47.7	+51.5	6.7	15 47.2	+51.7	6.8	16 46.8	+51.7	6.8	17 46.4	+51.7	6.8	18 46.0	+51.8	6.9	19 45.5	+51.9	6.9	78
79	13 39.9	+51.4	6.1	14 39.6	+51.4	6.2	15 39.2	+51.5	6.2	16 38.9	+51.5	6.2	17 38.5	+51.6	6.3	18 38.1	+51.7	6.3	19 37.8	+51.7	6.3	20 37.4	+51.8	6.4	79
80	14 31.3	+51.3	5.6	15 31.0	+51.3	5.6	16 30.7	+51.4	5.7	17 30.4	+51.4	5.7	18 30.1	+51.5	5.7	19 29.8	+51.6	5.8	20 29.5	+51.6	5.8	21 29.2	+51.7	5.8	80
81	15 22.6	+51.2	5.1	16 22.3	+51.3	5.1	17 22.1	+51.3	5.1	18 21.8	+51.4	5.2	19 21.6	+51.4	5.2	20 21.4	+51.4	5.2	21 21.1	+51.5	5.2	22 20.9	+51.5	5.3	81
82	16 13.8	+51.1	4.5	17 13.6	+51.2	4.6	18 13.4	+51.2	4.6	19 13.2	+51.3	4.6	20 13.0	+51.3	4.6	21 12.8	+51.4	4.7	22 12.6	+51.4	4.7	23 12.4	+51.4	4.7	82
83	17 04.9	+51.0	4.0	18 04.8	+51.0	4.0	19 04.6	+51.1	4.0	20 04.5	+51.1	4.1	21 04.3	+51.2	4.1	22 04.2	+51.2	4.1	23 04.0	+51.3	4.1	24 03.8	+51.4	4.2	83
84	17 55.9	+51.0	3.4	18 55.8	+51.0	3.5	19 55.7	+51.0	3.5	20 55.6	+51.1	3.5	21 55.5	+51.1	3.5	22 55.4	+51.1	3.5	23 55.3	+51.1	3.6	24 55.2	+51.1	3.6	84
85	18 46.9	+50.8	2.9	19 46.8	+50.9	2.9	20 46.7	+50.9	2.9	21 46.7	+50.9	2.9	22 46.6	+50.9	3.0	23 46.5	+51.0	3.0	24 46.4	+51.0	3.0	25 46.3	+51.1	3.0	85
86	19 37.7	+50.8	2.3	20 37.7	+50.7	2.3	21 37.6	+50.8	2.3	22 37.6	+50.8	2.4	23 37.5	+50.9	2.4	24 37.5	+50.8	2.4	25 37.4	+50.9	2.4	26 37.4	+50.9	2.4	86
87	20 28.5	+50.6	1.7	21 28.4	+50.7	1.8	22 28.4	+50.7	1.8	23 28.4	+50.7	1.8	24 28.4	+50.7	1.8	25 28.3	+50.7	1.8	26 28.3	+50.7	1.8	27 28.3	+50.7	1.8	87
88	21 19.1	+50.5	1.2	22 19.1	+50.5	1.2	23 19.1	+50.5	1.2	24 19.1	+50.5	1.2	25 19.1	+50.5	1.2	26 19.0	+50.6	1.2	27 19.0	+50.6	1.2	28 19.0	+50.6	1.2	88
89	22 09.6	+50.4	0.6	23 09.6	+50.4	0.6	24 09.6	+50.4	0.6	25 09.6	+50.4	0.6	26 09.6	+50.4	0.6	27 09.6	+50.4	0.6	28 09.6	+50.4	0.6	29 09.6	+50.4	0.6	89
90	23 00.0	+50.3	0.0	24 00.0	+50.2	0.0	25 00.0	+50.2	0.0	26 00.0	+50.2	0.0	27 00.0	+50.2	0.0	28 00.0	+50.2	0.0	29 00.0	+50.2	0.0	30 00.0	+50.2	0.0	90
	23°			24°			25°			26°			27°			28°			29°			30°			

S. Lat. {L.H.A. greater than 180° ....Zn=180°−Z
L.H.A. less than 180°...........Zn=180°+Z

LATITUDE SAME NAME AS DECLINATION L.H.A. 147°, 213°

34°, 326° L.H.A. LATITUDE SAME NAME AS DECLINATION

N. Lat. {L.H.A. greater than 180° .....Zn=Z; L.H.A. less than 180°............Zn=360°–Z}

Dec.	23° Hc	d	Z	24° Hc	d	Z	25° Hc	d	Z	26° Hc	d	Z	27° Hc	d	Z	28° Hc	d	Z	29° Hc	d	Z	30° Hc	d	Z	Dec.
°	° ′	′	°	° ′	′	°	° ′	′	°	° ′	′	°	° ′	′	°	° ′	′	°	° ′	′	°	° ′	′	°	°
0	49 44.5	+35.9	120.1	49 13.9	+37.0	121.1	48 42.5	+38.1	122.1	48 10.2	+39.1	123.0	47 37.1	+40.1	123.9	47 03.2	+41.1	124.8	46 28.6	+42.0	125.7	45 53.2	+42.8	126.5	0
1	50 20.4	+35.0	118.8	49 50.9	+36.3	119.9	49 20.6	+37.3	120.9	48 49.3	+38.4	121.9	48 17.2	+39.5	122.8	47 44.3	+40.4	123.8	47 10.6	+41.3	124.7	46 36.0	+42.3	125.5	1
2	50 55.4	+34.2	117.6	50 27.2	+35.3	118.6	49 57.9	+36.6	119.7	49 27.7	+37.7	120.7	48 56.7	+38.7	121.7	48 24.7	+39.8	122.7	47 51.9	+40.8	123.6	47 18.3	+41.7	124.5	2
3	51 29.6	+33.3	116.2	51 02.5	+34.6	117.4	50 34.5	+35.7	118.4	50 05.4	+36.9	119.5	49 35.4	+38.0	120.5	49 04.5	+39.1	121.5	48 32.7	+40.1	122.5	48 00.0	+41.1	123.4	3
4	52 02.9	+32.4	114.9	51 37.1	+33.6	116.0	51 10.2	+34.9	117.2	50 42.3	+36.1	118.3	50 13.4	+37.3	119.3	49 43.6	+38.3	120.4	49 12.8	+39.4	121.4	48 41.1	+40.5	122.3	4
5	52 35.3	+31.3	113.5	52 10.7	+32.8	114.7	51 45.1	+34.0	115.9	51 18.4	+35.3	117.0	50 50.7	+36.4	118.1	50 21.9	+37.6	119.2	49 52.2	+38.7	120.2	49 21.6	+39.8	121.2	5
6	53 06.6	+30.4	112.1	52 43.5	+31.7	113.3	52 19.1	+33.1	114.5	51 53.7	+34.3	115.7	51 27.1	+35.6	116.8	50 59.5	+36.8	117.9	50 30.9	+38.0	119.0	50 01.4	+39.0	120.0	6
7	53 37.0	+29.3	110.7	53 15.2	+30.7	111.9	52 52.2	+32.1	113.1	52 28.0	+33.5	114.3	52 02.7	+34.8	115.5	51 36.3	+36.0	116.7	51 08.9	+37.2	117.8	50 40.4	+38.4	118.9	7
8	54 06.3	+28.1	109.2	53 45.9	+29.6	110.5	53 24.3	+31.1	111.7	53 01.5	+32.4	113.0	52 37.5	+33.8	114.2	52 12.3	+35.1	115.4	51 46.1	+36.3	116.5	51 18.8	+37.5	117.6	8
9	54 34.4	+27.0	107.7	54 15.5	+28.6	109.0	53 55.4	+30.0	110.3	53 33.9	+31.5	111.6	53 11.3	+32.8	112.8	52 47.4	+34.2	114.0	52 22.4	+35.5	115.2	51 56.3	+36.7	116.4	9
10	55 01.4	+25.8	106.1	54 44.1	+27.3	107.5	54 25.4	+28.9	108.8	54 05.4	+30.4	110.1	53 44.1	+31.8	111.4	53 21.6	+33.2	112.7	52 57.9	+34.5	113.9	52 33.0	+35.8	115.1	10
11	55 27.2	+24.6	104.5	55 11.4	+26.2	105.9	54 54.3	+27.7	107.3	54 35.8	+29.2	108.6	54 15.9	+30.8	110.0	53 54.8	+32.2	111.3	53 32.4	+33.6	112.5	53 08.8	+35.0	113.8	11
12	55 51.8	+23.2	102.9	55 37.6	+24.9	104.3	55 22.0	+26.6	105.8	55 05.0	+28.2	107.1	54 46.7	+29.7	108.5	54 27.0	+31.2	109.8	54 06.0	+32.6	111.1	53 43.8	+34.0	112.4	12
13	56 15.0	+21.9	101.3	56 02.5	+23.6	102.7	55 48.6	+25.3	104.2	55 33.2	+26.9	105.6	55 16.4	+28.5	107.0	54 58.2	+30.0	108.3	54 38.6	+31.5	109.7	54 17.8	+32.9	111.0	13
14	56 36.9	+20.5	99.6	56 26.1	+22.3	101.1	56 13.9	+23.9	102.5	56 00.1	+25.7	104.0	55 44.9	+27.3	105.4	55 28.2	+28.9	106.8	55 10.1	+30.5	108.2	54 50.7	+31.9	109.6	14
15	56 57.4	+19.1	97.9	56 48.4	+20.9	99.4	56 37.8	+22.7	100.9	56 25.8	+24.3	102.4	56 12.2	+26.0	103.8	55 57.1	+27.7	105.3	55 40.6	+29.2	106.7	55 22.6	+30.9	108.1	15
16	57 16.5	+17.6	96.1	57 09.3	+19.4	97.7	57 00.5	+21.2	99.2	56 50.1	+23.0	100.7	56 38.2	+24.7	102.2	56 24.8	+26.4	103.7	56 09.8	+28.1	105.1	55 53.5	+29.6	106.6	16
17	57 34.1	+16.0	94.3	57 28.7	+18.0	95.9	57 21.7	+19.8	97.5	57 13.1	+21.6	99.0	57 02.9	+23.4	100.5	56 51.2	+25.1	102.0	56 37.9	+26.8	103.5	56 23.1	+28.5	105.0	17
18	57 50.1	+14.6	92.5	57 46.7	+16.4	94.1	57 41.5	+18.3	95.7	57 34.7	+20.2	97.3	57 26.3	+22.0	98.8	57 16.3	+23.8	100.4	57 04.7	+25.5	101.9	56 51.6	+27.2	103.4	18
19	58 04.7	+12.9	90.7	58 03.1	+14.8	92.3	57 59.8	+16.8	93.9	57 54.9	+18.6	95.5	57 48.3	+20.5	97.1	57 40.1	+22.3	98.7	57 30.2	+24.2	100.2	57 18.8	+25.9	101.8	19
20	58 17.6	+11.3	88.9	58 17.9	+13.3	90.5	58 16.6	+15.2	92.1	58 13.5	+17.2	93.7	58 08.8	+19.0	95.3	58 02.4	+20.9	96.9	57 54.4	+22.7	98.5	57 44.7	+24.5	100.1	20
21	58 28.9	+9.6	87.0	58 31.2	+11.6	88.6	58 31.8	+13.6	90.3	58 30.7	+15.5	91.9	58 27.8	+17.5	93.5	58 23.3	+19.4	95.1	58 17.1	+21.3	96.8	58 09.2	+23.1	98.4	21
22	58 38.5	+8.0	85.1	58 42.8	+10.0	86.7	58 45.4	+11.9	88.4	58 46.2	+13.9	90.0	58 45.3	+15.9	91.7	58 42.7	+17.8	93.3	58 38.4	+19.7	95.0	58 32.3	+21.6	96.6	22
23	58 46.5	+6.3	83.2	58 52.8	+8.2	84.8	58 57.3	+10.3	86.5	59 00.1	+12.3	88.1	59 01.2	+14.2	89.8	59 00.5	+16.2	91.5	58 58.1	+18.2	93.1	58 53.9	+20.1	94.8	23
24	58 52.8	+4.5	81.3	59 01.0	+6.6	82.9	59 07.6	+8.5	84.6	59 12.4	+10.5	86.2	59 15.4	+12.6	87.9	59 16.7	+14.6	89.6	59 16.3	+16.5	91.3	59 14.0	+18.6	93.0	24
25	58 57.3	+2.8	79.3	59 07.6	+4.8	81.0	59 16.1	+6.8	82.6	59 22.9	+8.9	84.3	59 28.0	+10.9	86.0	59 31.3	+12.9	87.7	59 32.8	+14.9	89.4	59 32.6	+16.9	91.1	25
26	59 00.1	+1.1	77.4	59 12.4	+3.0	79.0	59 22.9	+5.1	80.7	59 31.8	+7.1	82.4	59 38.9	+9.1	84.1	59 44.2	+11.2	85.8	59 47.7	+13.2	87.5	59 49.5	+15.2	89.2	26
27	59 01.2	-0.7	75.5	59 15.4	+1.3	77.1	59 28.0	+3.3	78.7	59 38.9	+5.3	80.4	59 48.0	+7.4	82.1	59 55.4	+9.4	83.8	60 00.9	+11.5	85.5	60 04.7	+13.5	87.3	27
28	59 00.5	-2.4	73.5	59 16.7	-0.4	75.1	59 31.3	+1.5	76.8	59 44.2	+3.5	78.4	59 55.4	+5.5	80.1	60 04.8	+7.6	81.8	60 12.4	+9.7	83.6	60 18.2	+11.8	85.3	28
29	58 58.1	-4.2	71.6	59 16.3	-2.3	73.2	59 32.8	-0.2	74.8	59 47.7	+1.8	76.4	60 00.9	+3.8	78.1	60 12.4	+5.8	79.8	60 22.1	+7.9	81.6	60 30.0	+10.0	83.3	29
30	58 53.9	-5.8	69.6	59 14.0	-3.9	71.2	59 32.6	-2.1	72.8	59 49.5	-0.1	74.5	60 04.7	+2.0	76.1	60 18.2	+4.0	77.8	60 30.0	+6.1	79.6	60 40.0	+8.1	81.3	30
31	58 48.1	-7.6	67.7	59 10.1	-5.8	69.3	59 30.5	-3.8	70.8	59 49.4	-1.8	72.5	60 06.7	+0.1	74.1	60 22.2	+2.2	75.8	60 36.1	+4.2	77.5	60 48.1	+6.3	79.3	31
32	58 40.5	-9.3	65.8	59 04.3	-7.4	67.3	59 26.7	-5.5	68.9	59 47.6	-3.7	70.5	60 06.8	-1.7	72.1	60 24.4	+0.3	73.8	60 40.3	+2.3	75.5	60 54.4	+4.5	77.2	32
33	58 31.2	-10.9	63.9	58 56.9	-9.1	65.4	59 21.2	-7.4	66.9	59 43.9	-5.4	68.5	60 05.1	-3.5	70.1	60 24.7	-1.5	71.8	60 42.6	+0.5	73.5	60 58.9	+2.5	75.2	33
34	58 20.3	-12.6	62.0	58 47.8	-10.9	63.5	59 13.8	-9.0	65.0	59 38.5	-7.2	66.5	60 01.6	-5.3	68.1	60 23.2	-3.4	69.7	60 43.1	-1.3	71.4	61 01.4	+0.7	73.1	34
35	58 07.7	-14.1	60.2	58 36.9	-12.5	61.6	59 04.8	-10.8	63.1	59 31.3	-9.0	64.6	59 56.3	-7.1	66.1	60 19.8	-5.2	67.7	60 41.8	-3.3	69.4	61 02.1	-1.2	71.1	35
36	57 53.6	-15.8	58.3	58 24.4	-14.1	59.7	58 54.0	-12.4	61.1	59 22.3	-10.6	62.6	59 49.2	-8.9	64.1	60 14.6	-7.0	65.7	60 38.5	-5.0	67.3	61 00.9	-3.2	69.0	36
37	57 37.8	-17.2	56.5	58 10.3	-15.6	57.9	58 41.6	-14.0	59.3	59 11.7	-12.4	60.7	59 40.3	-10.6	62.2	60 07.6	-8.8	63.7	60 33.5	-7.0	65.3	60 57.7	-4.9	66.9	37
38	57 20.6	-18.8	54.7	57 54.7	-17.3	56.0	58 27.6	-15.7	57.4	58 59.3	-14.0	58.8	59 29.7	-12.3	60.2	59 58.8	-10.5	61.7	60 26.5	-8.7	63.3	60 52.8	-6.9	64.9	38
39	57 01.8	-20.2	53.0	57 37.4	-18.7	54.2	58 11.9	-17.2	55.6	58 45.3	-15.7	56.9	59 17.4	-14.0	58.3	59 48.3	-12.3	59.8	60 17.8	-10.5	61.3	60 45.9	-8.7	62.8	39
40	56 41.6	-21.5	51.3	57 18.7	-20.2	52.5	57 54.7	-18.7	53.7	58 29.6	-17.2	55.1	59 03.4	-15.6	56.4	59 36.0	-14.0	57.8	60 07.3	-12.3	59.3	60 37.2	-10.5	60.8	40
41	56 20.1	-23.0	49.6	56 58.5	-21.6	50.7	57 36.0	-20.2	52.0	58 12.4	-18.7	53.2	58 47.8	-17.3	54.5	59 22.0	-15.6	55.9	59 55.0	-14.0	57.3	60 26.7	-12.3	58.8	41
42	55 57.1	-24.2	47.9	56 36.9	-23.0	49.0	57 15.8	-21.7	50.2	57 53.7	-20.3	51.4	58 30.5	-18.7	52.7	59 06.4	-17.3	54.0	59 41.0	-15.7	55.4	60 14.4	-14.0	56.8	42
43	55 32.9	-25.5	46.3	56 13.9	-24.3	47.4	56 54.1	-23.0	48.5	57 33.4	-21.7	49.7	58 11.8	-20.3	50.9	58 49.1	-18.9	52.2	59 25.3	-17.3	53.5	60 00.4	-15.7	54.9	43
44	55 07.4	-26.8	44.7	55 49.6	-25.6	45.7	56 31.1	-24.4	46.8	57 11.7	-23.1	47.9	57 51.5	-21.8	49.1	58 30.2	-20.3	50.3	59 08.0	-18.9	51.6	59 44.7	-17.4	53.0	44
45	54 40.6	-27.9	43.1	55 24.0	-26.8	44.1	56 06.7	-25.6	45.2	56 48.6	-24.4	46.2	57 29.7	-23.2	47.4	58 09.9	-21.9	48.6	58 49.1	-20.5	49.8	59 27.3	-19.0	51.1	45
46	54 12.7	-29.0	41.6	54 57.2	-27.9	42.6	55 41.1	-26.9	43.6	56 24.2	-25.8	44.6	57 06.5	-24.5	45.7	57 48.0	-23.2	46.8	58 28.6	-21.9	48.0	59 08.3	-20.5	49.2	46
47	53 43.7	-30.1	40.1	54 29.3	-29.2	41.0	55 14.2	-28.1	42.0	55 58.4	-26.9	43.0	56 42.0	-25.9	44.0	57 24.8	-24.7	45.1	58 06.7	-23.4	46.2	58 47.8	-22.1	47.4	47
48	53 13.6	-31.2	38.7	54 00.1	-30.2	39.5	54 46.1	-29.2	40.4	55 31.5	-28.2	41.4	56 16.1	-27.1	42.4	57 00.1	-26.0	43.4	57 43.3	-24.8	44.5	58 25.7	-23.5	45.6	48
49	52 42.4	-32.1	37.3	53 29.9	-31.2	38.1	54 16.9	-30.3	38.9	55 03.3	-29.4	39.8	55 49.0	-28.3	40.8	56 34.1	-27.2	41.8	57 18.5	-26.1	42.8	58 02.2	-24.9	43.9	49
50	52 10.3	-33.1	35.9	52 58.7	-32.3	36.7	53 46.6	-31.4	37.5	54 33.9	-30.5	38.3	55 20.7	-29.5	39.2	56 06.9	-28.5	40.1	56 52.4	-27.4	41.1	57 37.3	-26.3	42.2	50
51	51 37.2	-34.0	34.5	52 26.4	-33.2	35.3	53 15.2	-32.4	36.0	54 03.4	-31.5	36.8	54 51.2	-30.6	37.7	55 38.4	-29.6	38.6	56 25.0	-28.6	39.5	57 11.0	-27.6	40.5	51
52	51 03.2	-34.9	33.2	51 53.2	-34.1	33.9	52 42.8	-33.4	34.6	53 31.9	-32.5	35.4	54 20.6	-31.7	36.2	55 08.8	-30.8	37.0	55 56.4	-29.8	37.9	56 43.4	-28.8	38.9	52
53	50 28.3	-35.7	31.9	51 19.1	-35.0	32.6	52 09.4	-34.2	33.3	52 59.4	-33.5	34.0	53 48.9	-32.7	34.8	54 38.0	-31.8	35.6	55 26.6	-31.0	36.4	56 14.6	-30.0	37.3	53
54	49 52.6	-36.4	30.7	50 44.1	-35.8	31.3	51 35.2	-35.2	31.9	52 25.9	-34.4	32.6	53 16.2	-33.6	33.3	54 06.2	-32.9	34.1	54 55.6	-32.0	34.9	55 44.6	-31.2	35.7	54
55	49 16.2	-37.3	29.4	50 08.3	-36.7	30.0	51 00.0	-35.9	30.6	51 51.5	-35.3	31.3	52 42.6	-34.6	32.0	53 33.3	-33.9	32.7	54 23.6	-33.1	33.4	55 13.4	-32.2	34.2	55
56	48 38.9	-38.0	28.2	49 31.6	-37.4	28.8	50 24.1	-36.8	29.4	51 16.2	-36.2	30.0	52 08.0	-35.5	30.6	52 59.4	-34.7	31.3	53 50.5	-34.0	32.0	54 41.2	-33.3	32.7	56
57	48 00.9	-38.6	27.1	48 54.2	-38.1	27.6	49 47.3	-37.6	28.1	50 40.0	-36.9	28.7	51 32.5	-36.3	29.3	52 24.7	-35.7	30.0	53 16.5	-35.0	30.6	54 07.9	-34.2	31.3	57
58	47 22.3	-39.3	25.9	48 16.1	-38.8	26.4	49 09.7	-38.2	26.9	50 03.1	-37.7	27.5	50 56.2	-37.2	28.0	51 49.0	-36.5	28.6	52 41.5	-35.9	29.3	53 33.7	-35.2	29.9	58
59	46 43.0	-40.0	24.8	47 37.3	-39.5	25.3	48 31.5	-39.0	25.8	49 25.4	-38.5	26.3	50 19.0	-37.9	26.8	51 12.5	-37.4	27.4	52 05.6	-36.7	28.0	52 58.5	-36.2	28.6	59
60	46 03.0	-40.5	23.8	46 57.8	-40.0	24.2	47 52.5	-39.6	24.6	48 46.9	-39.1	25.1	49 41.1	-38.6	25.6	50 35.1	-38.1	26.1	51 28.9	-37.6	26.7	52 22.3	-36.9	27.3	60
61	45 22.5	-41.1	22.7	46 17.8	-40.7	23.1	47 12.9	-40.3	23.5	48 07.8	-39.8	24.0	49 02.5	-39.3	24.4	49 57.0	-38.8	24.9	50 51.3	-38.3	25.4	51 45.4	-37.8	26.0	61
62	44 41.4	-41.7	21.7	45 37.1	-41.3	22.0	46 32.6	-40.9	22.4	47 28.0	-40.5	22.9	48 23.2	-40.0	23.3	49 18.2	-39.5	23.7	50 13.0	-39.0	24.2	51 07.6	-38.5	24.7	62
63	43 59.7	-42.2	20.7	44 55.8	-41.8	21.0	45 51.7	-41.4	21.4	46 47.5	-41.0	21.8	47 43.2	-40.7	22.2	48 38.7	-40.2	22.6	49 34.0	-39.8	23.0	50 29.1	-39.3	23.5	63
64	43 17.5	-42.6	19.7	44 14.0	-42.3	20.0	45 10.3	-42.0	20.3	46 06.5	-41.6	20.7	47 02.5	-41.2	21.1	47 58.5	-40.9	21.5	48 54.2	-40.4	21.9	49 49.8	-40.0	22.3	64
65	42 34.9	-43.2	18.7	43 31.7	-42.9	19.0	44 28.3	-42.5	19.3	45 24.9	-42.2	19.7	46 21.3	-41.8	20.0	47 17.6	-41.4	20.4	48 13.8	-41.1	20.8	49 09.8	-40.6	21.2	65
66	41 51.7	-43.5	17.8	42 48.8	-43.3	18.1	43 45.8	-43.0	18.4	44 42.7	-42.6	18.7	45 39.5	-42.3	19.0	46 36.2	-42.0	19.3	47 32.7	-41.6	19.7	48 29.2	-41.3	20.1	66
67	41 08.2	-44.0	16.9	42 05.5	-43.7	17.1	43 02.8	-43.4	17.4	44 00.1	-43.2	17.7	44 57.2	-42.9	18.0	45 54.2	-42.6	18.3	46 51.1	-42.2	18.6	47 47.9	-41.9	19.0	67
68	40 24.2	-44.5	16.0	41 21.8	-44.2	16.2	42 19.4	-43.9	16.5	43 16.9	-43.7	16.7	44 14.3	-43.3	17.0	45 11.6	-43.0	17.3	46 08.9	-42.8	17.6	47 06.0	-42.4	17.9	68
69	39 39.7	-44.8	15.1	40 37.6	-44.5	15.3	41 35.5	-44.4	15.5	42 33.2	-44.0	15.8	43 31.0	-43.9	16.0	44 28.6	-43.6	16.3	45 26.1	-43.3	16.6	46 23.6	-43.0	16.9	69
70	38 54.9	-45.1	14.2	39 53.1	-45.0	14.4	40 51.1	-44.7	14.6	41 49.2	-44.5	14.9	42 47.1	-44.3	15.1	43 45.0	-44.0	15.4	44 42.8	-43.7	15.6	45 40.6	-43.5	15.9	70
71	38 09.8	-45.6	13.4	39 08.1	-45.3	13.6	40 06.4	-45.1	13.8	41 04.7	-45.0	14.0	42 02.8	-44.6	14.2	43 01.0	-44.5	14.4	43 59.1	-44.3	14.7	44 57.1	-44.0	14.9	71
72	37 24.2	-45.8	12.6	38 22.8	-45.7	12.7	39 21.3	-45.5	12.9	40 19.7	-45.3	13.1	41 18.2	-45.2	13.3	42 16.5	-44.9	13.5	43 14.8	-44.7	13.7	44 13.1	-44.5	14.0	72
73	36 38.4	-46.2	11.8	37 37.1	-46.0	11.9	38 35.8	-45.9	12.1	39 34.4	-45.6	12.2	40 33.0	-45.4	12.4	41 31.6	-45.3	12.6	42 30.1	-45.1	12.8	43 28.6	-44.9	13.0	73
74	35 52.2	-46.5	11.0	36 51.1	-46.4	11.1	37 49.9	-46.2	11.3	38 48.8	-46.1	11.4	39 47.6	-45.9	11.6	40 46.3	-45.7	11.7	41 45.0	-45.5	11.9	42 43.7	-45.3	12.1	74
75	35 05.7	-46.8	10.2	36 04.7	-46.6	10.3	37 03.7	-46.5	10.4	38 02.7	-46.3	10.6	39 01.7	-46.2	10.7	40 00.6	-46.0	10.9	40 59.5	-45.8	11.1	41 58.4	-45.7	11.2	75
76	34 18.9	-47.1	9.4	35 18.1	-47.0	9.5	36 17.2	-46.8	9.7	37 16.4	-46.7	9.8	38 15.5	-46.5	9.9	39 14.6	-46.4	10.1	40 13.7	-46.3	10.2	41 12.7	-46.1	10.4	76
77	33 31.8	-47.3	8.7	34 31.1	-47.2	8.8	35 30.4	-47.1	8.9	36 29.7	-47.0	9.0	37 29.0	-46.9	9.1	38 28.2	-46.7	9.2	39 27.4	-46.6	9.4	40 26.6	-46.5	9.5	77
78	32 44.5	-47.6	7.9	33 43.9	-47.4	8.0	34 43.3	-47.3	8.1	35 42.7	-47.2	8.2	36 42.1	-47.2	8.3	37 41.5	-47.1	8.4	38 40.8	-46.9	8.6	39 40.1	-46.8	8.7	78
79	31 56.9	-47.8	7.2	32 56.5	-47.8	7.3	33 56.0	-47.7	7.4	34 55.5	-47.6	7.5	35 54.9	-47.4	7.6	36 54.4	-47.3	7.7	37 53.9	-47.3	7.8	38 53.3	-47.1	7.9	79
80	31 09.1	-48.0	6.5	32 08.7	-47.9	6.6	33 08.3	-47.9	6.7	34 07.9	-47.8	6.7	35 07.5	-47.7	6.8	36 07.1	-47.7	6.9	37 06.6	-47.5	7.0	38 06.2	-47.5	7.1	80
81	30 21.1	-48.3	5.8	31 20.8	-48.2	5.9	32 20.4	-48.1	5.9	33 20.1	-48.0	6.0	34 19.8	-48.0	6.1	35 19.4	-47.9	6.2	36 19.1	-47.8	6.2	37 18.7	-47.7	6.3	81
82	29 32.8	-48.5	5.1	30 32.6	-48.4	5.2	31 32.3	-48.3	5.2	32 32.1	-48.3	5.3	33 31.8	-48.2	5.4	34 31.5	-48.1	5.4	35 31.3	-48.1	5.5	36 31.0	-48.0	5.6	82
83	28 44.3	-48.6	4.5	29 44.2	-48.7	4.5	30 44.0	-48.6	4.5	31 43.8	-48.5	4.6	32 43.6	-48.5	4.6	33 43.4	-48.4	4.7	34 43.2	-48.4	4.8	35 43.0	-48.3	4.8	83
84	27 55.7	-48.9	3.8	28 55.5	-48.8	3.8	29 55.4	-48.8	3.9	30 55.3	-48.8	3.9	31 55.1	-48.7	3.9	32 55.0	-48.7	4.0	33 54.8	-48.6	4.0	34 54.7	-48.6	4.1	84
85	27 06.8	-49.0	3.1	28 06.7	-49.0	3.2	29 06.6	-48.9	3.2	30 06.5	-48.9	3.2	31 06.4	-48.9	3.3	32 06.3	-48.8	3.3	33 06.2	-48.8	3.3	34 06.1	-48.7	3.4	85
86	26 17.8	-49.2	2.5	27 17.7	-49.2	2.5	28 17.7	-49.2	2.5	29 17.6	-49.1	2.6	30 17.5	-49.1	2.6	31 17.5	-49.1	2.6	32 17.4	-49.0	2.6	33 17.4	-49.1	2.7	86
87	25 28.6	-49.4	1.9	26 28.5	-49.3	1.9	27 28.5	-49.3	1.9	28 28.5	-49.3	1.9	29 28.4	-49.3	1.9	30 28.4	-49.3	1.9	31 28.4	-49.3	2.0	32 28.3	-49.2	2.0	87
88	24 39.2	-49.5	1.2	25 39.2	-49.5	1.2	26 39.2	-49.5	1.3	27 39.2	-49.5	1.3	28 39.1	-49.4	1.3	29 39.1	-49.4	1.3	30 39.1	-49.5	1.3	31 39.1	-49.5	1.3	88
89	23 49.7	-49.7	0.6	24 49.7	-49.7	0.6	25 49.7	-49.7	0.6	26 49.7	-49.7	0.6	27 49.7	-49.7	0.6	28 49.7	-49.7	0.6	29 49.6	-49.6	0.6	30 49.6	-49.6	0.7	89
90	23 00.0	-49.8	0.0	24 00.0	-49.8	0.0	25 00.0	-49.8	0.0	26 00.0	-49.8	0.0	27 00.0	-49.8	0.0	28 00.0	-49.8	0.0	29 00.0	-49.8	0.0	30 00.0	-49.8	0.0	90
	23°			24°			25°			26°			27°			28°			29°			30°			

34°, 326° L.H.A. LATITUDE SAME NAME AS DECLINATION

252

LATITUDE CONTRARY NAME TO DECLINATION L.H.A. 34°, 326°

Dec.	23°			24°			25°			26°		
	Hc	d	Z	Hc	d	Z	Hc	d	Z	Hc	d	Z
°	° ′	′	°	° ′	′	°	° ′	′	°	° ′	′	°
0	49 44.5	-36.7	120.1	49 13.9	-37.7	121.1	48 42.5	-38.8	122.1	48 10.2	-39.7	123.0
1	49 07.8	-37.4	121.3	48 36.2	-38.4	122.3	48 03.7	-39.4	123.2	47 30.5	-40.4	124.1
2	48 30.4	-38.1	122.5	47 57.8	-39.2	123.4	47 24.3	-40.1	124.3	46 50.1	-41.0	125.2
3	47 52.3	-38.8	123.6	47 18.6	-39.7	124.6	46 44.2	-40.7	125.4	46 09.1	-41.6	126.3
4	47 13.5	-39.5	124.8	46 38.9	-40.4	125.6	46 03.5	-41.2	126.5	45 27.5	-42.1	127.3
5	46 34.0	-40.1	125.9	45 58.5	-41.0	126.7	45 22.3	-41.9	127.5	44 45.4	-42.7	128.3
6	45 53.9	-40.7	127.0	45 17.5	-41.5	127.8	44 40.4	-42.3	128.6	44 02.7	-43.1	129.3
7	45 13.2	-41.2	128.0	44 36.0	-42.1	128.8	43 58.1	-42.9	129.5	43 19.6	-43.6	130.3
8	44 32.0	-41.8	129.0	43 53.9	-42.5	129.8	43 15.2	-43.3	130.5	42 36.0	-44.1	131.2
9	43 50.2	-42.2	130.0	43 11.4	-43.1	130.8	42 31.9	-43.8	131.5	41 51.9	-44.5	132.1
10	43 08.0	-42.8	131.0	42 28.3	-43.5	131.7	41 48.1	-44.2	132.4	41 07.4	-44.8	133.0
11	42 25.2	-43.3	132.0	41 44.8	-43.9	132.6	41 03.9	-44.6	133.3	40 22.6	-45.3	133.9
12	41 41.9	-43.6	132.9	41 00.9	-44.4	133.5	40 19.3	-45.0	134.2	39 37.3	-45.7	134.8
13	40 58.3	-44.1	133.8	40 16.5	-44.8	134.4	39 34.3	-45.4	135.0	38 51.6	-46.0	135.6
14	40 14.2	-44.5	134.7	39 31.7	-45.1	135.3	38 48.9	-45.8	135.9	38 05.6	-46.3	136.4
15	39 29.7	-44.9	135.6	38 46.6	-45.5	136.1	38 03.1	-46.1	136.7	37 19.3	-46.7	137.2
16	38 44.8	-45.3	136.4	38 01.1	-45.8	137.0	37 17.0	-46.4	137.5	36 32.6	-46.9	138.0
17	37 59.5	-45.6	137.3	37 15.3	-46.2	137.8	36 30.6	-46.7	138.3	35 45.7	-47.3	138.8
18	37 13.9	-45.9	138.1	36 29.1	-46.5	138.6	35 43.9	-47.0	139.1	34 58.4	-47.5	139.5
19	36 28.0	-46.3	138.9	35 42.6	-46.8	139.4	34 56.9	-47.3	139.8	34 10.9	-47.8	140.3
20	35 41.7	-46.5	139.7	34 55.8	-47.1	140.1	34 09.6	-47.6	140.6	33 23.1	-48.0	141.0
21	34 55.2	-46.9	140.5	34 08.7	-47.3	140.9	33 22.0	-47.8	141.3	32 35.1	-48.3	141.7
22	34 08.3	-47.1	141.2	33 21.4	-47.6	141.6	32 34.2	-48.0	142.0	31 46.8	-48.5	142.4
23	33 21.2	-47.4	142.0	32 33.8	-47.8	142.4	31 46.2	-48.3	142.7	30 58.3	-48.7	143.1
24	32 33.8	-47.6	142.7	31 46.0	-48.1	143.1	30 57.9	-48.5	143.4	30 09.6	-48.9	143.8
25	31 46.2	-47.9	143.4	30 57.9	-48.3	143.8	30 09.4	-48.7	144.1	29 20.7	-49.2	144.5
26	30 58.3	-48.1	144.1	30 09.6	-48.5	144.5	29 20.7	-49.0	144.8	28 31.5	-49.3	145.1
27	30 10.2	-48.3	144.8	29 21.1	-48.7	145.1	28 31.7	-49.1	145.5	27 42.2	-49.4	145.8
28	29 21.9	-48.5	145.5	28 32.4	-49.0	145.8	27 42.6	-49.2	146.1	26 52.8	-49.7	146.4
29	28 33.4	-48.7	146.2	27 43.4	-49.0	146.5	26 53.4	-49.5	146.7	26 03.1	-49.8	147.0
30	27 44.7	-48.9	146.8	26 54.4	-49.3	147.1	26 03.9	-49.6	147.4	25 13.3	-50.0	147.6
31	26 55.8	-49.1	147.5	26 05.1	-49.4	147.7	25 14.3	-49.8	148.0	24 23.3	-50.1	148.2
32	26 06.7	-49.3	148.1	25 15.7	-49.6	148.4	24 24.5	-49.9	148.6	23 33.2	-50.2	148.8
33	25 17.4	-49.4	148.8	24 26.1	-49.8	149.0	23 34.6	-50.1	149.2	22 43.0	-50.4	149.4
34	24 28.0	-49.5	149.4	23 36.3	-49.8	149.6	22 44.5	-50.2	149.8	21 52.6	-50.5	150.0
35	23 38.5	-49.7	150.0	22 46.5	-50.1	150.2	21 54.3	-50.3	150.4	21 02.1	-50.6	150.6
36	22 48.8	-49.9	150.6	21 56.4	-50.1	150.8	21 04.0	-50.4	151.0	20 11.5	-50.7	151.2
37	21 58.9	-49.9	151.2	21 06.3	-50.3	151.4	20 13.6	-50.6	151.6	19 20.8	-50.9	151.8
38	21 09.0	-50.1	151.8	20 16.0	-50.3	152.0	19 23.0	-50.6	152.2	18 29.9	-50.9	152.3
39	20 18.9	-50.2	152.4	19 25.7	-50.5	152.6	18 32.4	-50.8	152.7	17 39.0	-51.0	152.9
40	19 28.7	-50.4	153.0	18 35.2	-50.6	153.1	17 41.6	-50.8	153.3	16 48.0	-51.1	153.4
41	18 38.3	-50.4	153.6	17 44.6	-50.7	153.7	16 50.8	-51.0	153.8	15 56.9	-51.2	154.0
42	17 47.9	-50.5	154.1	16 53.9	-50.8	154.3	15 59.8	-51.0	154.4	15 05.7	-51.3	154.5
43	16 57.4	-50.6	154.7	16 03.1	-50.9	154.8	15 08.8	-51.1	154.9	14 14.4	-51.3	155.0
44	16 06.8	-50.7	155.2	15 12.2	-50.9	155.4	14 17.7	-51.2	155.5	13 23.1	-51.4	155.6
45	15 16.1	-50.8	155.8	14 21.3	-51.0	155.9	13 26.5	-51.2	156.0	12 31.7	-51.5	156.1
46	14 25.3	-50.9	156.4	13 30.3	-51.1	156.5	12 35.3	-51.3	156.5	11 40.2	-51.5	156.6
47	13 34.4	-50.9	156.9	12 39.2	-51.1	157.0	11 44.0	-51.4	157.1	10 48.7	-51.6	157.2
48	12 43.5	-51.0	157.4	11 48.1	-51.3	157.5	10 52.6	-51.4	157.6	9 57.1	-51.6	157.7
49	11 52.5	-51.1	158.0	10 56.8	-51.2	158.1	10 01.2	-51.5	158.1	9 05.5	-51.7	158.2
50	11 01.4	-51.1	158.5	10 05.6	-51.3	158.6	9 09.7	-51.5	158.6	8 13.8	-51.7	158.7
51	10 10.3	-51.2	159.1	9 14.3	-51.4	159.1	8 18.2	-51.6	159.2	7 22.1	-51.7	159.2
52	9 19.1	-51.2	159.6	8 22.9	-51.4	159.6	7 26.6	-51.5	159.7	6 30.4	-51.8	159.7
53	8 27.9	-51.2	160.1	7 31.5	-51.4	160.2	6 35.1	-51.7	160.2	5 38.6	-51.8	160.2
54	7 36.7	-51.3	160.6	6 40.1	-51.5	160.7	5 43.4	-51.6	160.7	4 46.8	-51.8	160.7
55	6 45.4	-51.3	161.2	5 48.6	-51.5	161.2	4 51.8	-51.7	161.2	3 55.0	-51.9	161.2
56	5 54.1	-51.4	161.7	4 57.1	-51.5	161.7	4 00.1	-51.7	161.7	3 03.1	-51.8	161.8
57	5 02.7	-51.4	162.2	4 05.6	-51.6	162.2	3 08.4	-51.7	162.2	2 11.3	-51.9	162.3
58	4 11.3	-51.4	162.7	3 14.0	-51.5	162.7	2 16.7	-51.7	162.7	1 19.4	-51.8	162.8
59	3 19.9	-51.4	163.2	2 22.5	-51.6	163.2	1 25.0	-51.7	163.3	0 27.6	-51.9	163.3
60	2 28.5	-51.4	163.7	1 30.9	-51.6	163.8	0 33.3	-51.7	163.8	0 24.3	+51.9	16.2
61	1 37.1	-51.5	164.3	0 39.3	-51.6	164.3	0 18.4	+51.8	15.7	1 16.2	+51.8	15.7
62	0 45.6	-51.4	164.8	0 12.3	+51.5	15.2	1 10.2	+51.7	15.2	2 08.0	+51.9	15.2
63	0 05.8	+51.4	14.7	1 03.8	+51.6	14.7	2 01.9	+51.7	14.7	2 59.9	+51.8	14.7
64	0 57.2	+51.5	14.2	1 55.4	+51.6	14.2	2 53.6	+51.7	14.2	3 51.7	+51.9	14.2
65	1 48.7	+51.4	13.7	2 47.0	+51.5	13.7	3 45.3	+51.6	13.7	4 43.6	+51.8	13.7
66	2 40.1	+51.4	13.2	3 38.5	+51.6	13.2	4 36.9	+51.7	13.2	5 35.4	+51.7	13.2
67	3 31.5	+51.4	12.6	4 30.1	+51.5	12.7	5 28.6	+51.6	12.7	6 27.1	+51.8	12.7
68	4 22.9	+51.4	12.1	5 21.6	+51.5	12.1	6 20.2	+51.6	12.2	7 18.9	+51.7	12.2
69	5 14.3	+51.3	11.6	6 13.1	+51.4	11.6	7 11.8	+51.6	11.7	8 10.6	+51.7	11.7
70	6 05.6	+51.4	11.1	7 04.5	+51.4	11.1	8 03.4	+51.5	11.1	9 02.3	+51.6	11.2
71	6 57.0	+51.2	10.6	7 55.9	+51.4	10.6	8 54.9	+51.5	10.6	9 53.9	+51.6	10.6
72	7 48.2	+51.3	10.0	8 47.3	+51.4	10.1	9 46.4	+51.4	10.1	10 45.5	+51.5	10.1
73	8 39.5	+51.2	9.5	9 38.7	+51.3	9.5	10 37.8	+51.4	9.6	11 37.0	+51.5	9.6
74	9 30.7	+51.1	9.0	10 30.0	+51.2	9.0	11 29.2	+51.3	9.0	12 28.5	+51.4	9.1
75	10 21.8	+51.2	8.5	11 21.2	+51.2	8.5	12 20.5	+51.3	8.5	13 19.9	+51.3	8.6
76	11 13.0	+51.0	7.9	12 12.4	+51.1	8.0	13 11.8	+51.2	8.0	14 11.2	+51.3	8.0
77	12 04.0	+51.0	7.4	13 03.5	+51.1	7.4	14 03.0	+51.1	7.5	15 02.5	+51.2	7.5
78	12 55.0	+50.9	6.9	13 54.6	+50.9	6.9	14 54.1	+51.1	6.9	15 53.7	+51.1	6.9
79	13 45.9	+50.8	6.3	14 45.5	+50.9	6.3	15 45.2	+50.9	6.4	16 44.8	+51.0	6.4
80	14 36.7	+50.8	5.8	15 36.4	+50.9	5.8	16 36.1	+50.9	5.8	17 35.8	+51.0	5.8
81	15 27.5	+50.7	5.2	16 27.3	+50.7	5.2	17 27.0	+50.8	5.3	18 26.8	+50.8	5.3
82	16 18.2	+50.6	4.7	17 18.0	+50.6	4.7	18 17.8	+50.7	4.7	19 17.6	+50.7	4.7
83	17 08.8	+50.5	4.1	18 08.6	+50.6	4.1	19 08.5	+50.6	4.1	20 08.3	+50.6	4.2
84	17 59.3	+50.4	3.5	18 59.2	+50.4	3.5	19 59.1	+50.4	3.6	20 58.9	+50.6	3.6
85	18 49.7	+50.3	3.0	19 49.6	+50.3	3.0	20 49.5	+50.4	3.0	21 49.5	+50.3	3.0
86	19 40.0	+50.2	2.4	20 39.9	+50.3	2.4	21 39.9	+50.2	2.4	22 39.8	+50.3	2.4
87	20 30.2	+50.0	1.8	21 30.2	+50.0	1.8	22 30.1	+50.1	1.8	23 30.1	+50.1	1.8
88	21 20.2	+50.0	1.2	22 20.2	+50.0	1.2	23 20.2	+50.0	1.2	24 20.2	+50.0	1.2
89	22 10.2	+49.8	0.6	23 10.2	+49.8	0.6	24 10.2	+49.8	0.6	25 10.2	+49.8	0.6
90	23 00.0	+49.7	0.0	24 00.0	+49.7	0.0	25 00.0	+49.7	0.0	26 00.0	+49.7	0.0
	23°			24°			25°			26°		

27°			28°			29°			30°			Dec.
Hc	d	Z	Hc	d	Z	Hc	d	Z	Hc	d	Z	
° ′	′	°	° ′	′	°	° ′	′	°	° ′	′	°	°
47 37.1	-40.7	123.9	47 03.2	-41.6	124.8	46 28.6	-42.5	125.7	45 53.2	-43.3	126.5	0
46 56.4	-41.3	125.0	46 21.6	-42.2	125.9	45 46.1	-43.1	126.7	45 09.9	-43.9	127.5	1
46 15.1	-41.9	126.1	45 39.4	-42.7	126.9	45 03.0	-43.5	127.7	44 26.0	-44.3	128.5	2
45 33.2	-42.4	127.1	44 56.7	-43.3	127.9	44 19.5	-44.0	128.7	43 41.7	-44.8	129.4	3
44 50.8	-43.0	128.1	44 13.4	-43.7	128.9	43 35.5	-44.5	129.6	42 56.9	-45.2	130.4	4
44 07.8	-43.4	129.1	43 29.7	-44.2	129.8	42 51.0	-44.9	130.6	42 11.7	-45.6	131.2	5
43 24.4	-43.9	130.0	42 45.5	-44.6	130.8	42 06.1	-45.3	131.4	41 26.1	-46.0	132.1	6
42 40.5	-44.3	131.0	42 00.9	-45.0	131.7	41 20.8	-45.8	132.3	40 40.1	-46.3	133.0	7
41 56.2	-44.8	131.9	41 15.9	-45.5	132.5	40 35.0	-46.0	133.2	39 53.8	-46.8	133.8	8
41 11.4	-45.1	132.8	40 30.4	-45.8	133.4	39 49.0	-46.5	134.0	39 07.0	-47.0	134.6	9
40 26.3	-45.6	133.7	39 44.6	-46.2	134.3	39 02.5	-46.8	134.8	38 20.0	-47.4	135.4	10
39 40.7	-45.9	134.5	38 58.4	-46.5	135.1	38 15.7	-47.0	135.6	37 32.6	-47.6	136.2	11
38 54.8	-46.2	135.3	38 11.9	-46.8	135.9	37 28.7	-47.5	136.4	36 45.0	-48.0	136.9	12
38 08.6	-46.6	136.1	37 25.1	-47.2	136.7	36 41.2	-47.6	137.2	35 57.0	-48.2	137.7	13
37 22.0	-46.9	136.9	36 37.9	-47.4	137.5	35 53.6	-48.0	138.0	35 08.8	-48.4	138.4	14
36 35.1	-47.2	137.7	35 50.5	-47.7	138.2	35 05.6	-48.2	138.7	34 20.4	-48.8	139.1	15
35 47.9	-47.5	138.5	35 02.8	-48.0	139.0	34 17.4	-48.5	139.4	33 31.6	-48.9	139.8	16
35 00.4	-47.8	139.2	34 14.8	-48.3	139.7	33 28.9	-48.7	140.1	32 42.7	-49.2	140.5	17
34 12.6	-48.0	140.0	33 26.5	-48.5	140.4	32 40.2	-49.0	140.8	31 53.5	-49.4	141.2	18
33 24.6	-48.3	140.7	32 38.0	-48.7	141.1	31 51.2	-49.1	141.5	31 04.1	-49.6	141.9	19
32 36.3	-48.4	141.4	31 49.3	-48.9	141.8	31 02.1	-49.4	142.2	30 14.5	-49.7	142.5	20
31 47.9	-48.8	142.1	31 00.4	-49.2	142.5	30 12.7	-49.6	142.8	29 24.8	-50.0	143.2	21
30 59.1	-48.9	142.8	30 11.2	-49.3	143.1	29 23.1	-49.7	143.5	28 34.8	-50.1	143.8	22
30 10.2	-49.1	143.5	29 21.9	-49.5	143.8	28 33.4	-50.0	144.1	27 44.7	-50.3	144.4	23
29 21.1	-49.4	144.1	28 32.4	-49.8	144.4	27 43.4	-50.0	144.8	26 54.4	-50.5	145.1	24
28 31.7	-49.5	144.8	27 42.6	-49.8	145.1	26 53.4	-50.3	145.4	26 03.9	-50.6	145.7	25
27 42.2	-49.6	145.4	26 52.8	-50.1	145.7	26 03.1	-50.4	146.0	25 13.3	-50.8	146.3	26
26 52.6	-49.9	146.0	26 02.7	-50.2	146.3	25 12.7	-50.5	146.6	24 22.5	-50.8	146.8	27
26 02.7	-50.0	146.7	25 12.5	-50.3	146.9	24 22.2	-50.7	147.2	23 31.7	-51.0	147.4	28
25 12.7	-50.2	147.3	24 22.2	-50.5	147.5	23 31.5	-50.8	147.8	22 40.7	-51.2	148.0	29
24 22.5	-50.3	147.9	23 31.7	-50.7	148.1	22 40.7	-51.0	148.3	21 49.5	-51.2	148.6	30
23 32.2	-50.4	148.5	22 41.0	-50.7	148.7	21 49.7	-51.0	148.9	20 58.3	-51.4	149.1	31
22 41.8	-50.5	149.1	21 50.3	-50.9	149.3	20 58.7	-51.2	149.5	20 06.9	-51.4	149.7	32
21 51.3	-50.7	149.6	20 59.4	-51.0	149.8	20 07.5	-51.3	150.0	19 15.5	-51.6	150.2	33
21 00.6	-50.8	150.2	20 08.4	-51.0	150.4	19 16.2	-51.3	150.6	18 23.9	-51.6	150.8	34
20 09.8	-50.9	150.8	19 17.4	-51.2	151.0	18 24.9	-51.5	151.1	17 32.3	-51.8	151.3	35
19 18.9	-51.0	151.4	18 26.2	-51.3	151.5	17 33.4	-51.5	151.7	16 40.5	-51.8	151.8	36
18 27.9	-51.1	151.9	17 34.9	-51.4	152.1	16 41.9	-51.7	152.2	15 48.7	-51.8	152.3	37
17 36.8	-51.2	152.5	16 43.5	-51.4	152.6	15 50.2	-51.7	152.7	14 56.9	-52.0	152.9	38
16 45.6	-51.3	153.0	15 52.1	-51.6	153.1	14 58.5	-51.8	153.3	14 04.9	-52.0	153.4	39
15 54.3	-51.4	153.5	15 00.5	-51.6	153.7	14 06.7	-51.8	153.8	13 12.9	-52.1	153.9	40
15 02.9	-51.4	154.1	14 08.9	-51.6	154.2	13 14.9	-51.9	154.3	12 20.8	-52.1	154.4	41
14 11.5	-51.5	154.6	13 17.3	-51.8	154.7	12 23.0	-52.0	154.8	11 28.7	-52.2	154.9	42
13 20.0	-51.6	155.1	12 25.5	-51.8	155.2	11 31.0	-52.0	155.3	10 36.5	-52.3	155.4	43
12 28.4	-51.6	155.7	11 33.7	-51.8	155.8	10 39.0	-52.1	155.8	9 44.2	-52.2	155.9	44
11 36.8	-51.7	156.2	10 41.9	-51.9	156.3	9 46.9	-52.1	156.3	8 52.0	-52.3	156.4	45
10 45.1	-51.7	156.7	9 50.0	-52.0	156.8	8 54.8	-52.1	156.8	7 59.7	-52.4	156.9	46
9 53.4	-51.8	157.2	8 58.0	-51.9	157.3	8 02.7	-52.2	157.3	7 07.3	-52.4	157.4	47
9 01.6	-51.8	157.7	8 06.1	-52.1	157.8	7 10.5	-52.2	157.8	6 14.9	-52.4	157.9	48
8 09.8	-51.9	158.2	7 14.0	-52.0	158.3	6 18.3	-52.3	158.3	5 22.5	-52.4	158.4	49
7 17.9	-51.9	158.8	6 22.0	-52.1	158.8	5 26.0	-52.2	158.8	4 30.1	-52.5	158.9	50
6 26.0	-51.9	159.3	5 29.9	-52.1	159.3	4 33.8	-52.3	159.3	3 37.6	-52.5	159.4	51
5 34.1	-52.0	159.8	4 37.8	-52.2	159.8	3 41.5	-52.3	159.8	2 45.1	-52.4	159.8	52
4 42.1	-52.0	160.3	3 45.6	-52.1	160.3	2 49.2	-52.4	160.3	1 52.7	-52.5	160.3	53
3 50.1	-51.9	160.8	2 53.5	-52.2	160.8	1 56.8	-52.3	160.8	1 00.2	-52.5	160.8	54
2 58.2	-52.0	161.3	2 01.3	-52.1	161.3	1 04.5	-52.3	161.3	0 07.7	-52.5	161.3	55
2 06.2	-52.1	161.8	1 09.2	-52.2	161.8	0 12.2	-52.4	161.8	0 44.8	+52.5	18.2	56
1 14.1	-52.0	162.3	0 17.0	-52.2	162.3	0 40.2	+52.3	17.7	1 37.3	+52.5	17.7	57
0 22.1	-52.0	162.8	0 35.2	+52.2	17.2	1 32.5	+52.3	17.2	2 29.8	+52.5	17.3	58
0 29.9	+52.0	16.7	1 27.4	+52.1	16.7	2 24.8	+52.3	16.8	3 22.3	+52.4	16.8	59
1 21.9	+52.0	16.2	2 19.5	+52.2	16.2	3 17.1	+52.3	16.3	4 14.7	+52.5	16.3	60
2 13.9	+52.0	15.7	3 11.7	+52.1	15.8	4 09.4	+52.3	15.8	5 07.2	+52.4	15.8	61
3 05.9	+52.0	15.2	4 03.8	+52.2	15.3	5 01.7	+52.3	15.3	5 59.6	+52.4	15.3	62
3 57.9	+52.0	14.7	4 56.0	+52.1	14.8	5 54.0	+52.2	14.8	6 52.0	+52.3	14.8	63
4 49.9	+52.0	14.2	5 48.1	+52.0	14.3	6 46.2	+52.2	14.3	7 44.3	+52.4	14.3	64
5 41.9	+51.9	13.7	6 40.1	+52.1	13.8	7 38.4	+52.2	13.8	8 36.7	+52.3	13.8	65
6 33.8	+51.9	13.2	7 32.2	+52.0	13.3	8 30.6	+52.1	13.3	9 29.0	+52.2	13.3	66
7 25.7	+51.8	12.7	8 24.2	+52.0	12.8	9 22.7	+52.1	12.8	10 21.2	+52.2	12.8	67
8 17.5	+51.8	12.2	9 16.2	+51.9	12.3	10 14.8	+52.0	12.3	11 13.4	+52.2	12.3	68
9 09.3	+51.8	11.7	10 08.1	+51.9	11.7	11 06.8	+52.0	11.8	12 05.6	+52.1	11.8	69
10 01.1	+51.7	11.2	11 00.0	+51.8	11.2	11 58.8	+52.0	11.3	12 57.7	+52.0	11.3	70
10 52.8	+51.7	10.7	11 51.8	+51.8	10.7	12 50.8	+51.8	10.8	13 49.7	+52.0	10.8	71
11 44.5	+51.6	10.2	12 43.6	+51.7	10.2	13 42.6	+51.8	10.2	14 41.7	+51.9	10.3	72
12 36.1	+51.6	9.6	13 35.3	+51.6	9.7	14 34.4	+51.8	9.7	15 33.6	+51.8	9.8	73
13 27.7	+51.5	9.1	14 26.9	+51.6	9.2	15 26.2	+51.6	9.2	16 25.4	+51.8	9.2	74
14 19.2	+51.4	8.6	15 18.5	+51.5	8.6	16 17.8	+51.6	8.7	17 17.2	+51.6	8.7	75
15 10.6	+51.4	8.1	16 10.0	+51.5	8.1	17 09.4	+51.5	8.1	18 08.8	+51.6	8.2	76
16 02.0	+51.2	7.5	17 01.5	+51.3	7.6	18 00.9	+51.4	7.6	19 00.4	+51.5	7.6	77
16 53.2	+51.2	7.0	17 52.8	+51.2	7.0	18 52.3	+51.4	7.1	19 51.9	+51.4	7.1	78
17 44.4	+51.1	6.4	18 44.0	+51.2	6.5	19 43.7	+51.2	6.5	20 43.3	+51.2	6.6	79
18 35.5	+51.0	5.9	19 35.2	+51.0	5.9	20 34.9	+51.1	6.0	21 34.5	+51.2	6.0	80
19 26.5	+50.9	5.3	20 26.2	+51.0	5.4	21 26.0	+51.0	5.4	22 25.7	+51.1	5.4	81
20 17.4	+50.8	4.8	21 17.2	+50.8	4.8	22 17.0	+50.8	4.8	23 16.8	+50.9	4.9	82
21 08.2	+50.6	4.2	22 08.0	+50.7	4.2	23 07.8	+50.8	4.2	24 07.7	+50.8	4.3	83
21 58.8	+50.6	3.6	22 58.7	+50.6	3.6	23 58.6	+50.6	3.7	24 58.5	+50.6	3.7	84
22 49.4	+50.4	3.0	23 49.3	+50.4	3.1	24 49.2	+50.5	3.1	25 49.1	+50.5	3.1	85
23 39.8	+50.3	2.4	24 39.7	+50.3	2.5	25 39.7	+50.3	2.5	26 39.6	+50.4	2.5	86
24 30.1	+50.1	1.8	25 30.0	+50.2	1.9	26 30.0	+50.2	1.9	27 30.0	+50.1	1.9	87
25 20.2	+50.0	1.2	26 20.2	+50.0	1.2	27 20.2	+50.0	1.3	28 20.1	+50.1	1.3	88
26 10.2	+49.8	0.6	27 10.2	+49.8	0.6	28 10.2	+49.8	0.6	29 10.2	+49.8	0.6	89
27 00.0	+49.7	0.0	28 00.0	+49.7	0.0	29 00.0	+49.6	0.0	30 00.0	+49.6	0.0	90
27°			28°			29°			30°			

S. Lat. {L.H.A. greater than 180° ....Zn=180°–Z
{L.H.A. less than 180°...........Zn=180°+Z

LATITUDE SAME NAME AS DECLINATION L.H.A. 146°, 214°

35°, 325° L.H.A. LATITUDE SAME NAME AS DECLINATION N. Lat. {L.H.A. greater than 180° .....Zn=Z
L.H.A. less than 180°............Zn=360°-Z

Dec.	23°			24°			25°			26°			27°			28°			29°			30°			Dec.
	Hc	d	Z	Hc	d	Z	Hc	d	Z	Hc	d	Z	Hc	d	Z	Hc	d	Z	Hc	d	Z	Hc	d	Z	
°	° ′	′	°	° ′	′	°	° ′	′	°	° ′	′	°	° ′	′	°	° ′	′	°	° ′	′	°	° ′	′	°	°
0	48 56.5	+35.3	119.2	48 26.8	+36.4	120.2	47 56.2	+37.5	121.1	47 24.8	+38.5	122.0	46 52.5	+39.6	123.0	46 19.5	+40.5	123.8	45 45.7	+41.4	124.7	45 11.2	+42.3	125.5	0
1	49 31.8	+34.4	117.9	49 03.2	+35.6	118.9	48 33.7	+36.8	119.9	48 03.3	+37.8	120.9	47 32.1	+38.8	121.9	47 00.0	+39.9	122.8	46 27.1	+40.9	123.7	45 53.5	+41.7	124.5	1
2	50 06.2	+33.7	116.7	49 38.8	+34.9	117.7	49 10.5	+35.9	118.7	48 41.1	+37.2	119.7	48 10.9	+38.2	120.7	47 39.9	+39.2	121.7	47 08.0	+40.2	122.6	46 35.2	+41.2	123.5	2
3	50 39.9	+32.7	115.4	50 13.7	+34.0	116.4	49 46.4	+35.2	117.5	49 18.3	+36.3	118.5	48 49.1	+37.5	119.6	48 19.1	+38.5	120.5	47 48.2	+39.5	121.5	47 16.4	+40.6	122.4	3
4	51 12.6	+31.9	114.0	50 47.7	+33.1	115.2	50 21.6	+34.4	116.2	49 54.6	+35.6	117.3	49 26.6	+36.7	118.4	48 57.6	+37.8	119.4	48 27.7	+38.9	120.4	47 57.0	+39.9	121.3	4
5	51 44.5	+30.8	112.7	51 20.8	+32.2	113.8	50 56.0	+33.5	115.0	50 30.2	+34.7	116.1	50 03.3	+35.9	117.1	49 35.4	+37.1	118.2	49 06.6	+38.2	119.2	48 36.9	+39.3	120.2	5
6	52 15.3	+29.9	111.3	51 53.0	+31.2	112.5	51 29.5	+32.5	113.6	51 04.9	+33.8	114.8	50 39.2	+35.1	115.9	50 12.5	+36.3	117.0	49 44.8	+37.5	118.0	49 16.2	+38.5	119.0	6
7	52 45.2	+28.8	109.8	52 24.2	+30.2	111.1	52 02.0	+31.6	112.3	51 38.7	+33.0	113.4	51 14.3	+34.2	114.6	50 48.8	+35.5	115.7	50 22.3	+36.6	116.8	49 54.7	+37.8	117.9	7
8	53 14.0	+27.7	108.4	52 54.4	+29.2	109.6	52 33.6	+30.6	110.9	52 11.7	+31.9	112.1	51 48.5	+33.3	113.3	51 24.3	+34.6	114.4	50 58.9	+35.8	115.6	50 32.5	+37.0	116.7	8
9	53 41.7	+26.6	106.9	53 23.6	+28.1	108.2	53 04.2	+29.6	109.5	52 43.6	+31.0	110.7	52 21.8	+32.4	111.9	51 58.9	+33.6	113.1	51 34.7	+35.0	114.3	51 09.5	+36.3	115.4	9
10	54 08.3	+25.4	105.4	53 51.7	+26.9	106.7	53 33.8	+28.5	108.0	53 14.6	+29.9	109.3	52 54.2	+31.3	110.5	52 32.5	+32.8	111.8	52 09.7	+34.1	113.0	51 45.8	+35.3	114.1	10
11	54 33.7	+24.2	103.8	54 18.6	+25.8	105.2	54 02.3	+27.3	106.5	53 44.5	+28.9	107.8	53 25.5	+30.4	109.1	53 05.3	+31.7	110.4	52 43.8	+33.1	111.6	52 21.1	+34.5	112.8	11
12	54 57.9	+22.9	102.2	54 44.4	+24.6	103.6	54 29.6	+26.2	105.0	54 13.4	+27.7	106.3	53 55.9	+29.2	107.6	53 37.0	+30.7	108.9	53 16.9	+32.2	110.2	52 55.6	+33.5	111.5	12
13	55 20.8	+21.6	100.6	55 09.0	+23.3	102.0	54 55.8	+24.9	103.4	54 41.1	+26.6	104.8	54 25.1	+28.1	106.2	54 07.7	+29.7	107.5	53 49.1	+31.1	108.8	53 29.1	+32.5	110.1	13
14	55 42.4	+20.3	99.0	55 32.3	+22.0	100.4	55 20.7	+23.7	101.8	55 07.7	+25.3	103.2	54 53.2	+27.0	104.6	54 37.4	+28.5	106.0	54 20.2	+30.0	107.3	54 01.6	+31.5	108.7	14
15	56 02.7	+18.8	97.3	55 54.3	+20.6	98.8	55 44.4	+22.3	100.2	55 33.0	+24.1	101.7	55 20.2	+25.7	103.1	55 05.9	+27.3	104.5	54 50.2	+28.9	105.8	54 33.1	+30.5	107.2	15
16	56 21.5	+17.5	95.6	56 14.9	+19.3	97.1	56 06.7	+21.1	98.6	55 57.1	+22.7	100.0	55 45.9	+24.4	101.5	55 33.2	+26.1	102.9	55 19.1	+27.7	104.3	55 03.6	+29.2	105.7	16
17	56 39.0	+16.0	93.9	56 34.2	+17.8	95.4	56 27.8	+19.6	96.9	56 19.8	+21.4	98.4	56 10.3	+23.1	99.8	55 59.3	+24.8	101.3	55 46.8	+26.5	102.7	55 32.8	+28.2	104.2	17
18	56 55.0	+14.4	92.1	56 52.0	+16.3	93.6	56 47.4	+18.1	95.2	56 41.2	+20.0	96.7	56 33.4	+21.8	98.2	56 24.1	+23.6	99.7	56 13.3	+25.2	101.1	56 01.0	+26.9	102.6	18
19	57 09.4	+13.0	90.3	57 08.3	+14.8	91.9	57 05.5	+16.7	93.4	57 01.2	+18.5	94.9	56 55.2	+20.4	96.5	56 47.7	+22.1	98.0	56 38.5	+23.9	99.5	56 27.9	+25.6	101.0	19
20	57 22.4	+11.3	88.5	57 23.1	+13.3	90.1	57 22.2	+15.2	91.6	57 19.7	+17.1	93.2	57 15.6	+18.9	94.7	57 09.8	+20.7	96.3	57 02.4	+22.5	97.8	56 53.5	+24.3	99.3	20
21	57 33.7	+9.8	86.7	57 36.4	+11.7	88.3	57 37.4	+13.6	89.8	57 36.8	+15.5	91.4	57 34.5	+17.4	93.0	57 30.5	+19.3	94.5	57 24.9	+21.1	96.1	57 17.8	+22.9	97.7	21
22	57 43.5	+8.2	84.8	57 48.1	+10.1	86.4	57 51.0	+12.0	88.0	57 52.3	+13.9	89.6	57 51.9	+15.8	91.2	57 49.8	+17.7	92.8	57 46.0	+19.7	94.4	57 40.7	+21.4	95.9	22
23	57 51.7	+6.5	83.0	57 58.2	+8.4	84.6	58 03.0	+10.4	86.2	58 06.2	+12.4	87.8	58 07.7	+14.3	89.4	58 07.5	+16.3	91.0	58 05.7	+18.1	92.6	58 02.1	+20.0	94.2	23
24	57 58.2	+4.8	81.1	58 06.6	+6.8	82.7	58 13.4	+8.8	84.3	58 18.6	+10.7	85.9	58 22.0	+12.7	87.5	58 23.8	+14.6	89.1	58 23.8	+16.6	90.8	58 21.1	+18.5	92.4	24
25	58 03.0	+3.2	79.2	58 13.4	+5.2	80.8	58 22.2	+7.1	82.4	58 29.3	+9.0	84.0	58 34.7	+11.0	85.7	58 38.4	+13.0	87.3	58 40.4	+14.9	88.9	58 40.6	+16.9	90.6	25
26	58 06.2	+1.5	77.3	58 18.6	+3.4	78.9	58 29.3	+5.4	80.5	58 38.3	+7.4	82.1	58 45.7	+9.4	83.8	58 51.4	+11.3	85.4	58 55.3	+13.3	87.1	58 57.5	+15.3	88.7	26
27	58 07.7	-0.2	75.4	58 22.0	+1.8	77.0	58 34.7	+3.7	78.6	58 45.7	+5.7	80.2	58 55.1	+7.6	81.9	59 02.7	+9.6	83.5	59 08.6	+11.7	85.2	59 12.8	+13.6	86.8	27
28	58 07.5	-1.8	73.5	58 23.8	0.0	75.1	58 38.4	+2.0	76.7	58 51.4	+3.9	78.3	59 02.7	+5.9	79.9	59 12.3	+8.0	81.6	59 20.3	+9.9	83.2	59 26.4	+12.0	84.9	28
29	58 05.7	-3.6	71.7	58 23.8	-1.7	73.2	58 40.4	+0.2	74.8	58 55.3	+2.2	76.4	59 08.6	+4.2	78.0	59 20.3	+6.1	79.6	59 30.2	+8.2	81.3	59 38.4	+10.2	83.0	29
30	58 02.1	-5.2	69.8	58 22.1	-3.3	71.3	58 40.6	-1.4	72.8	58 57.5	+0.5	74.4	59 12.8	+2.4	76.0	59 26.4	+4.5	77.7	59 38.4	+6.4	79.4	59 48.6	+8.5	81.0	30
31	57 56.9	-6.8	67.9	58 18.8	-5.1	69.4	58 39.2	-3.2	70.9	58 58.0	-1.3	72.5	59 15.2	+0.7	74.1	59 30.9	+2.6	75.7	59 44.8	+4.7	77.4	59 57.1	+6.7	79.1	31
32	57 50.1	-8.5	66.0	58 13.7	-6.7	67.5	58 36.0	-4.9	69.0	58 56.7	-3.0	70.6	59 15.9	-1.1	72.1	59 33.5	+0.9	73.8	59 49.5	+2.8	75.4	60 03.8	+4.8	77.1	32
33	57 41.6	-10.2	64.2	58 07.0	-8.3	65.6	58 31.1	-6.6	67.1	58 53.7	-4.7	68.6	59 14.8	-2.8	70.2	59 34.4	-0.9	71.8	59 52.3	+1.1	73.4	60 08.6	+3.1	75.1	33
34	57 31.4	-11.7	62.3	57 58.7	-10.1	63.7	58 24.5	-8.2	65.2	58 49.0	-6.5	66.7	59 12.0	-4.6	68.2	59 33.5	-2.7	69.8	59 53.4	-0.8	71.4	60 11.7	+1.2	73.1	34
35	57 19.7	-13.2	60.5	57 48.6	-11.6	61.9	58 16.3	-9.9	63.3	58 42.5	-8.1	64.8	59 07.4	-6.3	66.3	59 30.8	-4.5	67.8	59 52.6	-2.5	69.4	60 12.9	-0.6	71.1	35
36	57 06.5	-14.8	58.7	57 37.0	-13.2	60.0	58 06.4	-11.6	61.4	58 34.4	-9.8	62.9	59 01.1	-8.1	64.3	59 26.3	-6.2	65.9	59 50.1	-4.4	67.4	60 12.3	-2.4	69.0	36
37	56 51.7	-16.3	56.9	57 23.8	-14.7	58.2	57 54.8	-13.1	59.6	58 24.6	-11.5	61.0	58 53.0	-9.7	62.4	59 20.1	-8.0	63.9	59 45.7	-6.1	65.5	60 09.9	-4.2	67.0	37
38	56 35.4	-17.8	55.2	57 09.1	-16.3	56.4	57 41.7	-14.7	57.8	58 13.1	-13.1	59.1	58 43.3	-11.5	60.5	59 12.1	-9.7	62.0	59 39.6	-7.9	63.5	60 05.7	-6.1	65.0	38
39	56 17.6	-19.2	53.4	56 52.8	-17.7	54.7	57 27.0	-16.3	55.9	58 00.0	-14.7	57.3	58 31.8	-13.0	58.6	59 02.4	-11.3	60.1	59 31.7	-9.6	61.5	59 59.6	-7.8	63.0	39
40	55 58.4	-20.5	51.7	56 35.1	-19.2	52.9	57 10.7	-17.7	54.2	57 45.3	-16.2	55.4	58 18.8	-14.7	56.8	58 51.1	-13.1	58.2	59 22.1	-11.4	59.6	59 51.8	-9.6	61.1	40
41	55 37.9	-21.9	50.1	56 15.9	-20.6	51.2	56 53.0	-19.2	52.4	57 29.1	-17.7	53.6	58 04.1	-16.2	54.9	58 38.0	-14.6	56.3	59 10.7	-13.0	57.7	59 42.2	-11.3	59.1	41
42	55 16.0	-23.2	48.4	55 55.3	-21.9	49.5	56 33.8	-20.6	50.7	57 11.4	-19.2	51.9	57 47.9	-17.8	53.1	58 23.4	-16.3	54.4	58 57.7	-14.7	55.8	59 30.9	-13.1	57.2	42
43	54 52.8	-24.5	46.8	55 33.4	-23.2	47.9	56 13.2	-21.9	49.0	56 52.2	-20.7	50.1	57 30.1	-19.2	51.3	58 07.1	-17.8	52.6	58 43.0	-16.3	53.9	59 17.8	-14.7	55.2	43
44	54 28.3	-25.6	45.2	55 10.2	-24.5	46.3	55 51.3	-23.3	47.3	56 31.5	-22.0	48.4	57 10.9	-20.7	49.6	57 49.3	-19.3	50.8	58 26.7	-17.8	52.0	59 03.1	-16.3	53.4	44
45	54 02.7	-26.9	43.7	54 45.7	-25.7	44.7	55 28.0	-24.6	45.7	56 09.5	-23.3	46.7	56 50.2	-22.1	47.9	57 30.0	-20.7	49.0	58 08.9	-19.4	50.2	58 46.8	-18.0	51.5	45
46	53 35.8	-27.9	42.2	54 20.0	-26.9	43.1	55 03.4	-25.8	44.1	55 46.2	-24.7	45.1	56 28.1	-23.4	46.2	57 09.3	-22.2	47.3	57 49.5	-20.8	48.4	58 28.8	-19.4	49.7	46
47	53 07.9	-29.1	40.7	53 53.1	-28.1	41.6	54 37.6	-27.0	42.5	55 21.5	-25.9	43.5	56 04.7	-24.8	44.5	56 47.1	-23.6	45.6	57 28.7	-22.3	46.7	58 09.4	-21.0	47.9	47
48	52 38.8	-30.0	39.2	53 25.0	-29.1	40.1	54 10.6	-28.1	41.0	54 55.6	-27.1	41.9	55 39.9	-26.0	42.9	56 23.5	-24.8	43.9	57 06.4	-23.7	45.0	57 48.4	-22.4	46.1	48
49	52 08.8	-31.1	37.8	52 55.9	-30.2	38.6	53 42.5	-29.2	39.5	54 28.5	-28.2	40.4	55 13.9	-27.2	41.3	55 58.7	-26.2	42.3	56 42.7	-25.0	43.3	57 26.0	-23.8	44.4	49
50	51 37.7	-32.0	36.4	52 25.7	-31.1	37.2	53 13.3	-30.3	38.0	54 00.3	-29.4	38.9	54 46.7	-28.4	39.7	55 32.5	-27.3	40.7	56 17.7	-26.3	41.6	57 02.2	-25.1	42.7	50
51	51 05.7	-33.0	35.1	51 54.6	-32.2	35.8	52 43.0	-31.3	36.6	53 30.9	-30.4	37.4	54 18.3	-29.5	38.2	55 05.2	-28.6	39.1	55 51.4	-27.5	40.0	56 37.1	-26.5	41.0	51
52	50 32.7	-33.8	33.8	51 22.4	-33.1	34.5	52 11.7	-32.3	35.2	53 00.5	-31.5	35.9	53 48.8	-30.5	36.7	54 36.6	-29.6	37.6	55 23.9	-28.7	38.5	56 10.6	-27.7	39.4	52
53	49 58.9	-34.7	32.5	50 49.3	-33.9	33.1	51 39.4	-33.2	33.8	52 29.0	-32.4	34.5	53 18.3	-31.6	35.3	54 07.0	-30.8	36.1	54 55.2	-29.8	36.9	55 42.9	-28.9	37.8	53
54	49 24.2	-35.4	31.2	50 15.4	-34.8	31.8	51 06.2	-34.1	32.5	51 56.6	-33.3	33.2	52 46.7	-32.6	33.9	53 36.2	-31.7	34.6	54 25.4	-30.9	35.4	55 14.0	-30.0	36.2	54
55	48 48.8	-36.3	30.0	49 40.6	-35.6	30.6	50 32.1	-34.9	31.2	51 23.3	-34.3	31.8	52 14.1	-33.6	32.5	53 04.5	-32.8	33.2	53 54.5	-32.0	34.0	54 44.0	-31.1	34.7	55
56	48 12.5	-36.9	28.8	49 05.0	-36.4	29.3	49 57.2	-35.8	29.9	50 49.0	-35.1	30.5	51 40.5	-34.4	31.1	52 31.7	-33.7	31.8	53 22.5	-33.0	32.5	54 12.9	-32.2	33.3	56
57	47 35.6	-37.7	27.6	48 28.6	-37.1	28.1	49 21.4	-36.5	28.7	50 13.9	-35.9	29.2	51 06.1	-35.3	29.8	51 58.0	-34.6	30.5	52 49.5	-33.9	31.1	53 40.7	-33.2	31.8	57
58	46 57.9	-38.4	26.4	47 51.5	-37.8	26.9	48 44.9	-37.3	27.4	49 38.0	-36.7	28.0	50 30.8	-36.1	28.6	51 23.4	-35.5	29.1	52 15.6	-34.8	29.8	53 07.5	-34.1	30.4	58
59	46 19.5	-38.9	25.3	47 13.7	-38.5	25.8	48 07.6	-38.0	26.3	49 01.3	-37.5	26.8	49 54.7	-36.9	27.3	50 47.9	-36.3	27.9	51 40.8	-35.7	28.5	52 33.4	-35.0	29.1	59
60	45 40.6	-39.6	24.2	46 35.2	-39.2	24.7	47 29.6	-38.7	25.1	48 23.8	-38.1	25.6	49 17.8	-37.6	26.1	50 11.6	-37.1	26.6	51 05.1	-36.5	27.2	51 58.4	-36.0	27.7	60
61	45 01.0	-40.2	23.2	45 56.0	-39.7	23.6	46 50.9	-39.3	24.0	47 45.7	-38.9	24.4	48 40.2	-38.4	24.9	49 34.5	-37.8	25.4	50 28.6	-37.3	25.9	51 22.4	-36.7	26.5	61
62	44 20.8	-40.8	22.1	45 16.3	-40.4	22.5	46 11.6	-39.9	22.9	47 06.8	-39.5	23.3	48 01.8	-39.0	23.7	48 56.7	-38.6	24.2	49 51.3	-38.1	24.7	50 45.7	-37.5	25.2	62
63	43 40.0	-41.2	21.1	44 35.9	-40.9	21.5	45 31.7	-40.5	21.8	46 27.3	-40.1	22.2	47 22.8	-39.7	22.6	48 18.1	-39.2	23.0	49 13.2	-38.7	23.5	50 08.2	-38.3	24.0	63
64	42 58.8	-41.8	20.1	43 55.0	-41.4	20.4	44 51.2	-41.1	20.8	45 47.2	-40.7	21.1	46 43.1	-40.3	21.5	47 38.9	-39.9	21.9	48 34.5	-39.5	22.3	49 29.9	-39.0	22.8	64
65	42 17.0	-42.3	19.1	43 13.6	-41.9	19.4	44 10.1	-41.6	19.8	45 06.5	-41.2	20.1	46 02.8	-40.9	20.4	46 59.0	-40.5	20.8	47 55.0	-40.1	21.2	48 50.9	-39.7	21.6	65
66	41 34.7	-42.7	18.2	42 31.7	-42.5	18.5	43 28.5	-42.1	18.8	44 25.3	-41.8	19.1	45 21.9	-41.4	19.4	46 18.5	-41.1	19.7	47 14.9	-40.7	20.1	48 11.2	-40.4	20.5	66
67	40 52.0	-43.2	17.2	41 49.2	-42.9	17.5	42 46.4	-42.6	17.8	43 43.5	-42.3	18.1	44 40.5	-42.0	18.4	45 37.4	-41.7	18.7	46 34.2	-41.4	19.0	47 30.8	-40.9	19.4	67
68	40 08.8	-43.6	16.3	41 06.3	-43.3	16.6	42 03.8	-43.1	16.8	43 01.2	-42.8	17.1	43 58.5	-42.5	17.4	44 55.7	-42.2	17.7	45 52.8	-41.8	18.0	46 49.9	-41.6	18.3	68
69	39 25.2	-44.0	15.4	40 23.0	-43.7	15.7	41 20.7	-43.5	15.9	42 18.4	-43.2	16.1	43 16.0	-43.0	16.4	44 13.5	-42.7	16.7	45 11.0	-42.4	17.0	46 08.3	-42.1	17.3	69
70	38 41.2	-44.4	14.6	39 39.3	-44.2	14.8	40 37.2	-43.9	15.0	41 35.2	-43.7	15.2	42 33.0	-43.4	15.4	43 30.8	-43.1	15.7	44 28.6	-43.0	16.0	45 26.2	-42.6	16.2	70
71	37 56.8	-44.7	13.7	38 55.1	-44.5	13.9	39 53.3	-44.3	14.1	40 51.5	-44.1	14.3	41 49.6	-43.9	14.5	42 47.7	-43.7	14.7	43 45.6	-43.4	15.0	44 43.6	-43.2	15.2	71
72	37 12.1	-45.1	12.9	38 10.6	-45.0	13.0	39 09.0	-44.7	13.2	40 07.4	-44.5	13.4	41 05.7	-44.3	13.6	42 04.0	-44.1	13.8	43 02.2	-43.8	14.0	44 00.4	-43.6	14.3	72
73	36 27.0	-45.5	12.0	37 25.6	-45.2	12.2	38 24.3	-45.1	12.4	39 22.9	-44.9	12.5	40 21.4	-44.7	12.7	41 19.9	-44.5	12.9	42 18.4	-44.3	13.1	43 16.8	-44.1	13.3	73
74	35 41.5	-45.7	11.2	36 40.4	-45.6	11.4	37 39.2	-45.4	11.5	38 38.0	-45.3	11.7	39 36.7	-45.1	11.8	40 35.4	-44.9	12.0	41 34.1	-44.7	12.2	42 32.7	-44.5	12.4	74
75	34 55.8	-46.1	10.4	35 54.8	-45.9	10.6	36 53.8	-45.8	10.7	37 52.7	-45.6	10.8	38 51.6	-45.4	11.0	39 50.5	-45.3	11.1	40 49.4	-45.2	11.3	41 48.2	-45.0	11.5	75
76	34 09.7	-46.3	9.7	35 08.9	-46.2	9.8	36 08.0	-46.1	9.9	37 07.1	-45.9	10.0	38 06.2	-45.8	10.2	39 05.2	-45.6	10.3	40 04.2	-45.5	10.4	41 03.2	-45.3	10.6	76
77	33 23.4	-46.6	8.9	34 22.7	-46.5	9.0	35 21.9	-46.3	9.1	36 21.2	-46.3	9.2	37 20.4	-46.1	9.3	38 19.6	-46.0	9.5	39 18.7	-45.8	9.6	40 17.9	-45.7	9.7	77
78	32 36.8	-46.9	8.1	33 36.2	-46.8	8.2	34 35.6	-46.7	8.3	35 34.9	-46.5	8.4	36 34.3	-46.5	8.5	37 33.6	-46.3	8.7	38 32.9	-46.2	8.8	39 32.2	-46.1	8.9	78
79	31 49.9	-47.1	7.4	32 49.4	-47.0	7.5	33 48.9	-46.9	7.6	34 48.4	-46.9	7.7	35 47.8	-46.7	7.8	36 47.3	-46.7	7.9	37 46.7	-46.5	8.0	38 46.1	-46.4	8.1	79
80	31 02.8	-47.4	6.7	32 02.4	-47.3	6.7	33 02.0	-47.3	6.8	34 01.5	-47.1	6.9	35 01.1	-47.0	7.0	36 00.6	-46.9	7.1	37 00.2	-46.9	7.2	37 59.7	-46.7	7.3	80
81	30 15.4	-47.6	6.0	31 15.1	-47.5	6.0	32 14.7	-47.4	6.1	33 14.4	-47.4	6.2	34 14.1	-47.3	6.2	35 13.7	-47.2	6.3	36 13.3	-47.1	6.4	37 13.0	-47.1	6.5	81
82	29 27.8	-47.8	5.3	30 27.6	-47.8	5.3	31 27.3	-47.7	5.4	32 27.0	-47.6	5.4	33 26.8	-47.6	5.5	34 26.5	-47.5	5.6	35 26.2	-47.4	5.6	36 25.9	-47.3	5.7	82
83	28 40.0	-48.0	4.6	29 39.8	-48.0	4.6	30 39.6	-47.9	4.7	31 39.4	-47.9	4.7	32 39.2	-47.8	4.8	33 39.0	-47.8	4.8	34 38.8	-47.7	4.9	35 38.6	-47.7	4.9	83
84	27 52.0	-48.2	3.9	28 51.8	-48.1	3.9	29 51.7	-48.1	4.0	30 51.5	-48.0	4.0	31 51.4	-48.0	4.0	32 51.2	-47.9	4.1	33 51.1	-48.0	4.1	34 50.9	-47.9	4.2	84
85	27 03.8	-48.5	3.2	28 03.7	-48.4	3.2	29 03.6	-48.4	3.3	30 03.5	-48.3	3.3	31 03.4	-48.3	3.3	32 03.3	-48.3	3.4	33 03.1	-48.1	3.4	34 03.0	-48.1	3.5	85
86	26 15.3	-48.5	2.6	27 15.3	-48.6	2.6	28 15.2	-48.5	2.6	29 15.2	-48.5	2.6	30 15.1	-48.5	2.7	31 15.0	-48.4	2.7	32 15.0	-48.5	2.7	33 14.9	-48.4	2.7	86
87	25 26.8	-48.8	1.9	26 26.7	-48.7	1.9	27 26.7	-48.7	1.9	28 26.7	-48.7	2.0	29 26.6	-48.7	2.0	30 26.6	-48.7	2.0	31 26.5	-48.6	2.0	32 26.5	-48.6	2.0	87
88	24 38.0	-48.9	1.3	25 38.0	-48.9	1.3	26 38.0	-48.9	1.3	27 38.0	-48.9	1.3	28 37.9	-48.8	1.3	29 37.9	-48.8	1.3	30 37.9	-48.8	1.3	31 37.9	-48.9	1.3	88
89	23 49.1	-49.1	0.6	24 49.1	-49.1	0.6	25 49.1	-49.1	0.6	26 49.1	-49.1	0.6	27 49.1	-49.1	0.6	28 49.1	-49.1	0.7	29 49.1	-49.1	0.7	30 49.0	-49.0	0.7	89
90	23 00.0	-49.2	0.0	24 00.0	-49.2	0.0	25 00.0	-49.2	0.0	26 00.0	-49.2	0.0	27 00.0	-49.2	0.0	28 00.0	-49.2	0.0	29 00.0	-49.2	0.0	30 00.0	-49.2	0.0	90
	23°			24°			25°			26°			27°			28°			29°			30°			

35°, 325° L.H.A. LATITUDE SAME NAME AS DECLINATION

254

LATITUDE CONTRARY NAME TO DECLINATION L.H.A. 35°, 325°

Dec.	23° Hc	d	Z	24° Hc	d	Z	25° Hc	d	Z	26° Hc	d	Z	27° Hc	d	Z	28° Hc	d	Z	29° Hc	d	Z	30° Hc	d	Z	Dec.
°	° ′	′	°	° ′	′	°	° ′	′	°	° ′	′	°	° ′	′	°	° ′	′	°	° ′	′	°	° ′	′	°	°
0	48 56.5	-36.1	119.2	48 26.8	-37.2	120.2	47 56.2	-38.2	121.1	47 24.8	-39.2	122.0	46 52.5	-40.1	123.0	46 19.5	-41.1	123.8	45 45.7	-42.0	124.7	45 11.2	-42.8	125.5	0
1	48 20.4	-36.8	120.4	47 49.6	-37.8	121.3	47 18.0	-38.9	122.3	46 45.6	-39.8	123.2	46 12.4	-40.8	124.0	45 38.4	-41.6	124.9	45 03.7	-42.5	125.7	44 28.4	-43.3	126.5	1
2	47 43.6	-37.6	121.6	47 11.8	-38.6	122.5	46 39.1	-39.5	123.4	46 05.8	-40.5	124.2	45 31.6	-41.3	125.1	44 56.8	-42.2	125.9	44 21.2	-43.0	126.7	43 45.1	-43.8	127.5	2
3	47 06.0	-38.2	122.7	46 33.2	-39.1	123.6	45 59.6	-40.1	124.5	45 25.3	-41.0	125.3	44 50.3	-41.9	126.1	44 14.6	-42.7	126.9	43 38.2	-43.4	127.7	43 01.3	-44.3	128.4	3
4	46 27.8	-38.8	123.8	45 54.1	-39.8	124.7	45 19.5	-40.6	125.5	44 44.3	-41.5	126.3	44 08.4	-42.3	127.1	43 31.9	-43.2	127.9	42 54.8	-44.0	128.6	42 17.0	-44.7	129.3	4
5	45 49.0	-39.5	124.9	45 14.3	-40.4	125.8	44 38.9	-41.3	126.6	44 02.8	-42.1	127.3	43 26.1	-42.9	128.1	42 48.7	-43.6	128.8	42 10.8	-44.4	129.5	41 32.3	-45.0	130.2	5
6	45 09.5	-40.1	126.0	44 33.9	-40.9	126.8	43 57.6	-41.7	127.6	43 20.7	-42.5	128.3	42 43.2	-43.3	129.1	42 05.1	-44.1	129.8	41 26.4	-44.7	130.5	40 47.3	-45.5	131.1	6
7	44 29.4	-40.6	127.1	43 53.0	-41.5	127.8	43 15.9	-42.3	128.6	42 38.2	-43.1	129.3	41 59.9	-43.8	130.0	41 21.0	-44.5	130.7	40 41.7	-45.2	131.3	40 01.8	-45.9	132.0	7
8	43 48.8	-41.1	128.1	43 11.5	-42.0	128.8	42 33.6	-42.7	129.5	41 55.1	-43.5	130.2	41 16.1	-44.2	130.9	40 36.5	-44.9	131.6	39 56.5	-45.6	132.2	39 15.9	-46.2	132.8	8
9	43 07.7	-41.7	129.1	42 29.5	-42.4	129.8	41 50.9	-43.2	130.5	41 11.6	-43.9	131.2	40 31.9	-44.6	131.8	39 51.6	-45.2	132.4	39 10.9	-45.9	133.0	38 29.7	-46.5	133.6	9
10	42 26.0	-42.2	130.1	41 47.1	-42.9	130.8	41 07.7	-43.7	131.4	40 27.7	-44.3	132.1	39 47.3	-45.0	132.7	39 06.4	-45.7	133.3	38 25.0	-46.3	133.9	37 43.2	-46.8	134.4	10
11	41 43.8	-42.6	131.0	41 04.2	-43.4	131.7	40 24.0	-44.0	132.3	39 43.4	-44.7	132.9	39 02.3	-45.4	133.5	38 20.7	-46.0	134.1	37 38.7	-46.5	134.7	36 56.4	-47.2	135.2	11
12	41 01.2	-43.1	132.0	40 20.8	-43.8	132.6	39 40.0	-44.5	133.2	38 58.7	-45.1	133.8	38 16.9	-45.7	134.4	37 34.7	-46.3	134.9	36 52.2	-46.9	135.5	36 09.2	-47.4	136.0	12
13	40 18.1	-43.5	132.9	39 37.0	-44.1	133.5	38 55.5	-44.8	134.1	38 13.6	-45.5	134.6	37 31.2	-46.1	135.2	36 48.4	-46.6	135.7	36 05.3	-47.2	136.2	35 21.8	-47.8	136.7	13
14	39 34.6	-43.9	133.8	38 52.9	-44.6	134.4	38 10.7	-45.2	134.9	37 28.1	-45.8	135.5	36 45.1	-46.3	136.0	36 01.8	-46.9	136.5	35 18.1	-47.5	137.0	34 34.0	-47.9	137.5	14
15	38 50.7	-44.3	134.7	38 08.3	-44.9	135.2	37 25.5	-45.5	135.8	36 42.3	-46.1	136.3	35 58.8	-46.7	136.8	35 14.9	-47.2	137.3	34 30.6	-47.7	137.8	33 46.1	-48.3	138.2	15
16	38 06.4	-44.7	135.5	37 23.4	-45.3	136.1	36 40.0	-45.9	136.6	35 56.2	-46.4	137.1	35 12.1	-46.9	137.6	34 27.7	-47.5	138.0	33 42.9	-48.0	138.5	32 57.8	-48.5	138.9	16
17	37 21.7	-45.0	136.4	36 38.1	-45.6	136.9	35 54.1	-46.1	137.4	35 09.8	-46.7	137.9	34 25.2	-47.3	138.3	33 40.2	-47.8	138.8	32 54.9	-48.2	139.2	32 09.3	-48.7	139.6	17
18	36 36.7	-45.4	137.2	35 52.5	-45.9	137.7	35 08.0	-46.5	138.2	34 23.1	-47.0	138.6	33 37.9	-47.5	139.1	32 52.4	-47.9	139.5	32 06.7	-48.5	139.9	31 20.6	-48.9	140.3	18
19	35 51.3	-45.7	138.0	35 06.6	-46.3	138.5	34 21.5	-46.8	138.9	33 36.1	-47.3	139.4	32 50.4	-47.7	139.8	32 04.5	-48.3	140.2	31 18.2	-48.7	140.6	30 31.7	-49.1	141.0	19
20	35 05.6	-45.9	138.8	34 20.3	-46.5	139.3	33 34.7	-47.0	139.7	32 48.8	-47.5	140.1	32 02.7	-48.0	140.5	31 16.2	-48.4	140.9	30 29.5	-48.8	141.3	29 42.6	-49.3	141.6	20
21	34 19.7	-46.3	139.6	33 33.8	-46.8	140.0	32 47.7	-47.3	140.4	32 01.3	-47.7	140.8	31 14.7	-48.2	141.2	30 27.8	-48.7	141.6	29 40.7	-49.1	142.0	28 53.3	-49.5	142.3	21
22	33 33.4	-46.6	140.3	32 47.0	-47.0	140.8	32 00.4	-47.5	141.2	31 13.6	-48.0	141.5	30 26.5	-48.4	141.9	29 39.1	-48.8	142.3	28 51.6	-49.3	142.6	28 03.8	-49.7	142.9	22
23	32 46.8	-46.8	141.1	32 00.0	-47.3	141.5	31 12.9	-47.7	141.9	30 25.6	-48.2	142.2	29 38.1	-48.7	142.6	28 50.3	-49.1	142.9	28 02.3	-49.5	143.3	27 14.1	-49.8	143.6	23
24	32 00.0	-47.1	141.8	31 12.7	-47.5	142.2	30 25.2	-48.0	142.6	29 37.4	-48.4	142.9	28 49.4	-48.8	143.3	28 01.2	-49.2	143.6	27 12.8	-49.6	143.9	26 24.3	-50.0	144.2	24
25	31 12.9	-47.3	142.6	30 25.2	-47.8	142.9	29 37.2	-48.2	143.3	28 49.0	-48.6	143.6	28 00.6	-49.0	143.9	27 12.0	-49.4	144.2	26 23.2	-49.8	144.5	25 34.3	-50.2	144.8	25
26	30 25.6	-47.5	143.3	29 37.4	-48.0	143.6	28 49.0	-48.4	144.0	28 00.4	-48.8	144.3	27 11.6	-49.2	144.6	26 22.6	-49.6	144.9	25 33.4	-49.9	145.1	24 44.1	-50.3	145.4	26
27	29 38.1	-47.8	144.0	28 49.4	-48.2	144.3	28 00.6	-48.6	144.6	27 11.6	-49.0	144.9	26 22.4	-49.4	145.2	25 33.0	-49.7	145.5	24 43.5	-50.1	145.8	23 53.8	-50.4	146.0	27
28	28 50.3	-48.0	144.7	28 01.2	-48.4	145.0	27 12.0	-48.8	145.3	26 22.6	-49.2	145.6	25 33.0	-49.5	145.9	24 43.3	-49.9	146.1	23 53.4	-50.2	146.4	23 03.4	-50.6	146.6	28
29	28 02.3	-48.2	145.4	27 12.8	-48.5	145.7	26 23.2	-48.9	145.9	25 33.4	-49.3	146.2	24 43.5	-49.7	146.5	23 53.4	-50.0	146.7	23 03.2	-50.4	147.0	22 12.8	-50.7	147.2	29
30	27 14.1	-48.3	146.0	26 24.3	-48.8	146.3	25 34.3	-49.1	146.6	24 44.1	-49.5	146.8	23 53.8	-49.8	147.1	23 03.4	-50.2	147.3	22 12.8	-50.5	147.6	21 22.1	-50.8	147.8	30
31	26 25.8	-48.6	146.7	25 35.5	-48.9	147.0	24 45.2	-49.3	147.2	23 54.6	-49.6	147.5	23 04.0	-50.0	147.7	22 13.2	-50.3	147.9	21 22.3	-50.6	148.1	20 31.3	-50.9	148.3	31
32	25 37.2	-48.7	147.4	24 46.6	-49.1	147.6	23 55.9	-49.4	147.8	23 05.0	-49.7	148.1	22 14.0	-50.1	148.3	21 22.9	-50.4	148.5	20 31.7	-50.7	148.7	19 40.4	-51.0	148.9	32
33	24 48.5	-48.9	148.0	23 57.5	-49.2	148.2	23 06.5	-49.6	148.5	22 15.3	-49.9	148.7	21 23.9	-50.2	148.9	20 32.5	-50.5	149.1	19 41.0	-50.8	149.3	18 49.4	-51.2	149.5	33
34	23 59.6	-49.1	148.6	23 08.3	-49.4	148.9	22 16.9	-49.7	149.1	21 25.4	-50.1	149.3	20 33.7	-50.3	149.5	19 42.0	-50.6	149.7	18 50.2	-51.0	149.8	17 58.2	-51.2	150.0	34
35	23 10.5	-49.1	149.3	22 18.9	-49.5	149.5	21 27.2	-49.9	149.7	20 35.3	-50.1	149.9	19 43.4	-50.5	150.1	18 51.4	-50.8	150.2	17 59.2	-51.0	150.4	17 07.0	-51.3	150.6	35
36	22 21.4	-49.4	149.9	21 29.4	-49.6	150.1	20 37.3	-49.9	150.3	19 45.2	-50.3	150.5	18 52.9	-50.5	150.6	18 00.6	-50.8	150.8	17 08.2	-51.1	150.9	16 15.7	-51.4	151.1	36
37	21 32.0	-49.4	150.5	20 39.8	-49.8	150.7	19 47.4	-50.1	150.9	18 54.9	-50.3	151.0	18 02.4	-50.6	151.2	17 09.8	-50.9	151.4	16 17.1	-51.2	151.5	15 24.3	-51.4	151.6	37
38	20 42.6	-49.6	151.1	19 50.0	-49.9	151.3	18 57.3	-50.2	151.5	18 04.6	-50.5	151.6	17 11.8	-50.8	151.8	16 18.9	-51.0	151.9	15 25.9	-51.3	152.0	14 32.9	-51.6	152.2	38
39	19 53.0	-49.7	151.7	19 00.1	-50.0	151.9	18 07.1	-50.2	152.0	17 14.1	-50.5	152.2	16 21.0	-50.8	152.3	15 27.9	-51.1	152.5	14 34.6	-51.3	152.6	13 41.3	-51.6	152.7	39
40	19 03.3	-49.9	152.3	18 10.1	-50.1	152.5	17 16.9	-50.4	152.6	16 23.6	-50.7	152.7	15 30.2	-50.9	152.9	14 36.8	-51.2	153.0	13 43.3	-51.4	153.1	12 49.7	-51.6	153.2	40
41	18 13.4	-49.9	152.9	17 20.0	-50.2	153.0	16 26.5	-50.5	153.2	15 32.9	-50.7	153.3	14 39.3	-51.0	153.4	13 45.6	-51.2	153.5	12 51.9	-51.5	153.6	11 58.1	-51.7	153.7	41
42	17 23.5	-50.0	153.5	16 29.8	-50.3	153.6	15 36.0	-50.5	153.7	14 42.2	-50.8	153.9	13 48.3	-51.0	154.0	12 54.4	-51.3	154.1	12 00.4	-51.5	154.2	11 06.4	-51.8	154.3	42
43	16 33.5	-50.1	154.0	15 39.5	-50.4	154.2	14 45.5	-50.7	154.3	13 51.4	-50.9	154.4	12 57.3	-51.2	154.5	12 03.1	-51.4	154.6	11 08.9	-51.6	154.7	10 14.6	-51.8	154.8	43
44	15 43.4	-50.3	154.6	14 49.1	-50.4	154.7	13 54.8	-50.7	154.8	13 00.5	-50.9	154.9	12 06.1	-51.1	155.0	11 11.7	-51.4	155.1	10 17.3	-51.6	155.2	9 22.8	-51.9	155.3	44
45	14 53.1	-50.2	155.2	13 58.7	-50.6	155.3	13 04.1	-50.7	155.4	12 09.6	-51.0	155.5	11 15.0	-51.3	155.6	10 20.3	-51.5	155.7	9 25.6	-51.7	155.7	8 30.9	-51.9	155.8	45
46	14 02.9	-50.4	155.7	13 08.1	-50.6	155.8	12 13.4	-50.9	155.9	11 18.6	-51.1	156.0	10 23.7	-51.3	156.1	9 28.8	-51.5	156.2	8 33.9	-51.7	156.2	7 39.0	-51.9	156.3	46
47	13 12.5	-50.5	156.3	12 17.5	-50.7	156.4	11 22.5	-50.9	156.5	10 27.5	-51.1	156.6	9 32.4	-51.3	156.6	8 37.3	-51.5	156.7	7 42.2	-51.7	156.8	6 47.1	-52.0	156.8	47
48	12 22.0	-50.5	156.9	11 26.8	-50.7	156.9	10 31.6	-50.9	157.0	9 36.4	-51.2	157.1	8 41.1	-51.4	157.2	7 45.8	-51.6	157.2	6 50.5	-51.8	157.3	5 55.1	-52.0	157.3	48
49	11 31.5	-50.6	157.4	10 36.1	-50.8	157.5	9 40.7	-51.0	157.6	8 45.2	-51.2	157.6	7 49.7	-51.4	157.7	6 54.2	-51.6	157.7	5 58.7	-51.9	157.8	5 03.1	-52.0	157.8	49
50	10 40.9	-50.6	158.0	9 45.3	-50.8	158.0	8 49.7	-51.1	158.1	7 54.0	-51.3	158.1	6 58.3	-51.5	158.2	6 02.6	-51.7	158.2	5 06.8	-51.8	158.3	4 11.1	-52.0	158.3	50
51	9 50.3	-50.7	158.5	8 54.5	-50.9	158.6	7 58.6	-51.1	158.6	7 02.7	-51.3	158.7	6 06.8	-51.4	158.7	5 10.9	-51.7	158.7	4 15.0	-51.9	158.8	3 19.1	-52.1	158.8	51
52	8 59.6	-50.7	159.1	8 03.6	-50.9	159.1	7 07.5	-51.1	159.2	6 11.4	-51.3	159.2	5 15.4	-51.6	159.2	4 19.2	-51.7	159.3	3 23.1	-51.9	159.3	2 27.0	-52.1	159.3	52
53	8 08.9	-50.8	159.6	7 12.7	-51.0	159.6	6 16.4	-51.2	159.7	5 20.1	-51.3	159.7	4 23.8	-51.5	159.7	3 27.5	-51.7	159.8	2 31.2	-51.8	159.8	1 34.9	-52.0	159.8	53
54	7 18.1	-50.8	160.1	6 21.7	-51.0	160.2	5 25.2	-51.1	160.2	4 28.8	-51.4	160.2	3 32.3	-51.5	160.3	2 35.8	-51.7	160.3	1 39.4	-51.9	160.3	0 42.9	-52.1	160.3	54
55	6 27.3	-50.8	160.7	5 30.7	-51.0	160.7	4 34.1	-51.2	160.7	3 37.4	-51.4	160.8	2 40.8	-51.6	160.8	1 44.1	-51.7	160.8	0 47.5	-51.9	160.8	0 09.2	+52.1	19.2	55
56	5 36.5	-50.9	161.2	4 39.7	-51.1	161.2	3 42.9	-51.3	161.3	2 46.0	-51.4	161.3	1 49.2	-51.6	161.3	0 52.4	-51.8	161.3	0 04.4	+52.0	18.7	1 01.3	+52.0	18.7	56
57	4 45.6	-50.9	161.7	3 48.6	-51.1	161.8	2 51.6	-51.2	161.8	1 54.6	-51.4	161.8	0 57.6	-51.5	161.8	0 00.6	-51.7	161.8	0 56.4	+51.8	18.2	1 53.3	+52.1	18.2	57
58	3 54.7	-50.9	162.3	2 57.5	-51.0	162.3	2 00.4	-51.3	162.3	1 03.2	-51.4	162.3	0 06.1	-51.6	162.3	0 51.1	+51.7	17.7	1 48.2	+51.9	17.7	2 45.4	+52.1	17.7	58
59	3 03.8	-51.0	162.8	2 06.5	-51.1	162.8	1 09.1	-51.2	162.8	0 11.8	-51.4	162.8	0 45.5	+51.6	17.2	1 42.8	+51.7	17.2	2 40.1	+51.9	17.2	3 37.5	+52.0	17.2	59
60	2 12.8	-50.9	163.3	1 15.4	-51.1	163.3	0 17.9	-51.3	163.3	0 39.6	+51.4	16.7	1 37.1	+51.5	16.7	2 34.5	+51.8	16.7	3 32.0	+51.9	16.7	4 29.5	+52.0	16.7	60
61	1 21.9	-51.0	163.8	0 24.3	-51.1	163.9	0 33.4	+51.2	16.1	1 31.0	+51.4	16.2	2 28.6	+51.6	16.2	3 26.3	+51.7	16.2	4 23.9	+51.8	16.2	5 21.5	+52.0	16.2	61
62	0 30.9	-50.9	164.4	0 26.8	+51.1	15.6	1 24.6	+51.3	15.6	2 22.4	+51.4	15.6	3 20.2	+51.5	15.6	4 18.0	+51.6	15.7	5 15.7	+51.8	15.7	6 13.5	+51.9	15.7	62
63	0 20.0	+51.0	15.1	1 17.9	+51.1	15.1	2 15.9	+51.2	15.1	3 13.8	+51.4	15.1	4 11.7	+51.5	15.1	5 09.6	+51.7	15.2	6 07.5	+51.8	15.2	7 05.4	+52.0	15.2	63
64	1 11.0	+50.9	14.6	2 09.0	+51.1	14.6	3 07.1	+51.2	14.6	4 05.2	+51.3	14.6	5 03.2	+51.5	14.6	6 01.3	+51.6	14.6	6 59.3	+51.8	14.7	7 57.4	+51.9	14.7	64
65	2 01.9	+50.9	14.0	3 00.1	+51.1	14.0	3 58.3	+51.2	14.1	4 56.5	+51.3	14.1	5 54.7	+51.5	14.1	6 52.9	+51.6	14.1	7 51.1	+51.7	14.2	8 49.3	+51.8	14.2	65
66	2 52.8	+51.0	13.5	3 51.2	+51.0	13.5	4 49.5	+51.2	13.5	5 47.8	+51.4	13.6	6 46.2	+51.4	13.6	7 44.5	+51.5	13.6	8 42.8	+51.7	13.7	9 41.1	+51.8	13.7	66
67	3 43.8	+50.9	13.0	4 42.2	+51.1	13.0	5 40.7	+51.1	13.0	6 39.2	+51.2	13.0	7 37.6	+51.4	13.1	8 36.0	+51.6	13.1	9 34.5	+51.6	13.1	10 32.9	+51.8	13.2	67
68	4 34.7	+50.9	12.4	5 33.3	+51.0	12.5	6 31.8	+51.2	12.5	7 30.4	+51.2	12.5	8 29.0	+51.3	12.5	9 27.6	+51.4	12.6	10 26.1	+51.6	12.6	11 24.7	+51.7	12.7	68
69	5 25.6	+50.8	11.9	6 24.3	+50.9	11.9	7 23.0	+51.0	12.0	8 21.6	+51.2	12.0	9 20.3	+51.3	12.0	10 19.0	+51.4	12.1	11 17.7	+51.5	12.1	12 16.4	+51.6	12.1	69
70	6 16.4	+50.8	11.4	7 15.2	+50.9	11.4	8 14.0	+51.1	11.4	9 12.8	+51.2	11.5	10 11.6	+51.3	11.5	11 10.4	+51.4	11.5	12 09.2	+51.5	11.6	13 08.0	+51.6	11.6	70
71	7 07.2	+50.8	10.8	8 06.1	+50.9	10.9	9 05.1	+51.0	10.9	10 04.0	+51.1	10.9	11 02.9	+51.2	11.0	12 01.8	+51.3	11.0	13 00.7	+51.4	11.0	13 59.6	+51.5	11.1	71
72	7 58.0	+50.7	10.3	8 57.0	+50.9	10.3	9 56.1	+50.9	10.4	10 55.1	+51.0	10.4	11 54.1	+51.1	10.4	12 53.1	+51.2	10.5	13 52.1	+51.3	10.5	14 51.1	+51.4	10.6	72
73	8 48.7	+50.7	9.8	9 47.9	+50.8	9.8	10 47.0	+50.9	9.8	11 46.1	+51.0	9.9	12 45.2	+51.1	9.9	13 44.3	+51.2	9.9	14 43.4	+51.3	10.0	15 42.5	+51.4	10.0	73
74	9 39.4	+50.7	9.2	10 38.7	+50.7	9.3	11 37.9	+50.8	9.3	12 37.1	+50.9	9.3	13 36.3	+51.0	9.4	14 35.5	+51.1	9.4	15 34.7	+51.2	9.4	16 33.9	+51.2	9.5	74
75	10 30.1	+50.6	8.7	11 29.4	+50.7	8.7	12 28.7	+50.8	8.7	13 28.0	+50.8	8.8	14 27.3	+50.9	8.8	15 26.6	+51.0	8.9	16 25.9	+51.1	8.9	17 25.1	+51.2	9.0	75
76	11 20.7	+50.5	8.1	12 20.1	+50.6	8.2	13 19.5	+50.6	8.2	14 18.8	+50.8	8.2	15 18.2	+50.9	8.3	16 17.6	+50.9	8.3	17 17.0	+51.0	8.4	18 16.3	+51.1	8.4	76
77	12 11.2	+50.5	7.6	13 10.7	+50.5	7.6	14 10.1	+50.6	7.6	15 09.6	+50.7	7.7	16 09.1	+50.7	7.7	17 08.5	+50.8	7.8	18 08.0	+50.9	7.8	19 07.4	+51.0	7.8	77
78	13 01.7	+50.3	7.0	14 01.2	+50.5	7.1	15 00.7	+50.6	7.1	16 00.3	+50.6	7.1	16 59.8	+50.7	7.2	17 59.3	+50.8	7.2	18 58.9	+50.8	7.2	19 58.4	+50.9	7.3	78
79	13 52.0	+50.4	6.5	14 51.7	+50.3	6.5	15 51.3	+50.4	6.5	16 50.9	+50.5	6.6	17 50.5	+50.6	6.6	18 50.1	+50.6	6.6	19 49.7	+50.7	6.7	20 49.3	+50.7	6.7	79
80	14 42.4	+50.2	5.9	15 42.0	+50.3	5.9	16 41.7	+50.4	6.0	17 41.4	+50.4	6.0	18 41.1	+50.4	6.0	19 40.7	+50.5	6.1	20 40.4	+50.6	6.1	21 40.0	+50.7	6.2	80
81	15 32.6	+50.1	5.3	16 32.3	+50.2	5.4	17 32.1	+50.2	5.4	18 31.8	+50.3	5.4	19 31.5	+50.4	5.5	20 31.2	+50.5	5.5	21 31.0	+50.4	5.5	22 30.7	+50.5	5.6	81
82	16 22.7	+50.1	4.8	17 22.5	+50.1	4.8	18 22.3	+50.2	4.8	19 22.1	+50.2	4.9	20 21.9	+50.2	4.9	21 21.7	+50.3	4.9	22 21.4	+50.4	5.0	23 21.2	+50.4	5.0	82
83	17 12.8	+49.9	4.2	18 12.6	+50.0	4.2	19 12.5	+50.0	4.2	20 12.3	+50.1	4.3	21 12.1	+50.1	4.3	22 12.0	+50.1	4.3	23 11.8	+50.2	4.4	24 11.6	+50.3	4.4	83
84	18 02.7	+49.9	3.6	19 02.6	+49.9	3.6	20 02.5	+49.9	3.7	21 02.4	+49.9	3.7	22 02.2	+50.0	3.7	23 02.1	+50.0	3.7	24 02.0	+50.1	3.8	25 01.9	+50.1	3.8	84
85	18 52.6	+49.7	3.0	19 52.5	+49.8	3.0	20 52.4	+49.8	3.1	21 52.3	+49.8	3.1	22 52.2	+49.9	3.1	23 52.1	+49.9	3.1	24 52.1	+49.9	3.2	25 52.0	+49.9	3.2	85
86	19 42.3	+49.6	2.4	20 42.3	+49.6	2.5	21 42.2	+49.7	2.5	22 42.1	+49.7	2.5	23 42.1	+49.7	2.5	24 42.0	+49.8	2.5	25 42.0	+49.7	2.5	26 41.9	+49.8	2.6	86
87	20 31.9	+49.5	1.8	21 31.9	+49.5	1.8	22 31.9	+49.5	1.9	23 31.8	+49.6	1.9	24 31.8	+49.6	1.9	25 31.8	+49.5	1.9	26 31.7	+49.6	1.9	27 31.7	+49.6	1.9	87
88	21 21.4	+49.4	1.2	22 21.4	+49.4	1.2	23 21.4	+49.4	1.2	24 21.4	+49.4	1.3	25 21.4	+49.4	1.3	26 21.3	+49.5	1.3	27 21.3	+49.5	1.3	28 21.3	+49.5	1.3	88
89	22 10.8	+49.2	0.6	23 10.8	+49.2	0.6	24 10.8	+49.2	0.6	25 10.8	+49.2	0.6	26 10.8	+49.2	0.6	27 10.8	+49.2	0.6	28 10.8	+49.2	0.7	29 10.8	+49.2	0.7	89
90	23 00.0	+49.1	0.0	24 00.0	+49.1	0.0	25 00.0	+49.1	0.0	26 00.0	+49.1	0.0	27 00.0	+49.1	0.0	28 00.0	+49.1	0.0	29 00.0	+49.1	0.0	30 00.0	+49.0	0.0	90
	23°			24°			25°			26°			27°			28°			29°			30°			

S. Lat. { L.H.A. greater than 180° ....Zn=180°–Z; L.H.A. less than 180°...........Zn=180°+Z

LATITUDE SAME NAME AS DECLINATION L.H.A. 145°, 215°

255

36°, 324° L.H.A. LATITUDE SAME NAME AS DECLINATION N. Lat. {L.H.A. greater than 180° .....Zn=Z; L.H.A. less than 180°............Zn=360°–Z}

Dec.	23° Hc	d	Z	24° Hc	d	Z	25° Hc	d	Z	26° Hc	d	Z	27° Hc	d	Z	28° Hc	d	Z	29° Hc	d	Z	30° Hc	d	Z	Dec.
°	° ′	′	°	° ′	′	°	° ′	′	°	° ′	′	°	° ′	′	°	° ′	′	°	° ′	′	°	° ′	′	°	°
0	48 08.0	+34.8	118.3	47 39.2	+35.8	119.2	47 09.4	+37.0	120.2	46 38.8	+38.0	121.1	46 07.4	+39.0	122.0	45 35.2	+40.0	122.9	45 02.3	+40.9	123.7	44 28.7	+41.7	124.5	0
1	48 42.8	+33.9	117.0	48 15.0	+35.1	118.0	47 46.4	+36.2	119.0	47 16.8	+37.3	120.0	46 46.4	+38.3	120.9	46 15.2	+39.3	121.8	45 43.2	+40.3	122.7	45 10.4	+41.3	123.5	1
2	49 16.7	+33.1	115.8	48 50.1	+34.3	116.8	48 22.6	+35.4	117.8	47 54.1	+36.6	118.8	47 24.7	+37.7	119.8	46 54.5	+38.7	120.7	46 23.5	+39.7	121.6	45 51.7	+40.6	122.5	2
3	49 49.8	+32.2	114.5	49 24.4	+33.5	115.6	48 58.0	+34.7	116.6	48 30.7	+35.8	117.6	48 02.4	+36.9	118.6	47 33.2	+38.0	119.6	47 03.2	+39.0	120.5	46 32.3	+40.1	121.4	3
4	50 22.0	+31.3	113.2	49 57.9	+32.6	114.3	49 32.7	+33.8	115.4	49 06.5	+35.0	116.4	48 39.3	+36.2	117.4	48 11.2	+37.3	118.4	47 42.2	+38.4	119.4	47 12.4	+39.4	120.3	4
5	50 53.3	+30.4	111.8	50 30.5	+31.7	113.0	50 06.5	+33.0	114.1	49 41.5	+34.2	115.2	49 15.5	+35.4	116.2	48 48.5	+36.6	117.2	48 20.6	+37.7	118.2	47 51.8	+38.7	119.2	5
6	51 23.7	+29.4	110.5	51 02.2	+30.7	111.6	50 39.5	+32.1	112.8	50 15.7	+33.4	113.9	49 50.9	+34.6	115.0	49 25.1	+35.8	116.0	48 58.3	+36.9	117.1	48 30.5	+38.1	118.1	6
7	51 53.1	+28.3	109.1	51 32.9	+29.8	110.3	51 11.6	+31.1	111.4	50 49.1	+32.4	112.6	50 25.5	+33.7	113.7	50 00.9	+34.9	114.8	49 35.2	+36.2	115.9	49 08.6	+37.3	116.9	7
8	52 21.4	+27.3	107.6	52 02.7	+28.7	108.8	51 42.7	+30.1	110.1	51 21.5	+31.5	111.2	50 59.2	+32.9	112.4	50 35.8	+34.2	113.5	50 11.4	+35.3	114.6	49 45.9	+36.5	115.7	8
9	52 48.7	+26.2	106.2	52 31.4	+27.7	107.4	52 12.8	+29.2	108.6	51 53.0	+30.6	109.9	51 32.1	+31.9	111.0	51 10.0	+33.2	112.2	50 46.7	+34.5	113.3	50 22.4	+35.8	114.5	9
10	53 14.9	+25.1	104.7	52 59.1	+26.6	105.9	52 42.0	+28.0	107.2	52 23.6	+29.5	108.5	52 04.0	+30.9	109.7	51 43.2	+32.3	110.9	51 21.2	+33.7	112.0	50 58.2	+34.9	113.2	10
11	53 40.0	+23.8	103.1	53 25.7	+25.4	104.5	53 10.0	+27.0	105.7	52 53.1	+28.5	107.0	52 34.9	+29.9	108.3	52 15.5	+31.3	109.5	51 54.9	+32.6	110.7	51 33.1	+34.0	111.9	11
12	54 03.8	+22.6	101.6	53 51.1	+24.2	102.9	53 37.0	+25.8	104.2	53 21.6	+27.3	105.6	53 04.8	+28.9	106.8	52 46.8	+30.3	108.1	52 27.5	+31.8	109.3	52 07.1	+33.1	110.6	12
13	54 26.4	+21.4	100.0	54 15.3	+23.0	101.4	54 02.8	+24.6	102.7	53 48.9	+26.2	104.1	53 33.7	+27.7	105.4	53 17.1	+29.2	106.7	52 59.3	+30.7	107.9	52 40.2	+32.1	109.2	13
14	54 47.8	+20.0	98.4	54 38.3	+21.8	99.8	54 27.4	+23.4	101.2	54 15.1	+25.0	102.5	54 01.4	+26.6	103.9	53 46.3	+28.2	105.2	53 30.0	+29.6	106.5	53 12.3	+31.1	107.8	14
15	55 07.8	+18.7	96.7	55 00.1	+20.4	98.2	54 50.8	+22.1	99.6	54 40.1	+23.8	101.0	54 28.0	+25.4	102.3	54 14.5	+27.0	103.7	53 59.6	+28.6	105.0	53 43.4	+30.0	106.4	15
16	55 26.5	+17.4	95.1	55 20.5	+19.1	96.5	55 12.9	+20.8	97.9	55 03.9	+22.5	99.4	54 53.4	+24.2	100.8	54 41.5	+25.8	102.2	54 28.2	+27.3	103.5	54 13.4	+29.0	104.9	16
17	55 43.9	+15.9	93.4	55 39.6	+17.6	94.8	55 33.7	+19.5	96.3	55 26.4	+21.2	97.7	55 17.6	+22.9	99.2	55 07.3	+24.6	100.6	54 55.5	+26.3	102.0	54 42.4	+27.8	103.4	17
18	55 59.8	+14.4	91.7	55 57.2	+16.3	93.1	55 53.2	+18.0	94.6	55 47.6	+19.8	96.1	55 40.5	+21.6	97.5	55 31.9	+23.2	99.0	55 21.8	+24.9	100.4	55 10.2	+26.6	101.8	18
19	56 14.2	+13.0	89.9	56 13.5	+14.8	91.4	56 11.2	+16.7	92.9	56 07.4	+18.5	94.4	56 02.1	+20.2	95.9	55 55.1	+22.0	97.3	55 46.7	+23.7	98.8	55 36.8	+25.3	100.3	19
20	56 27.2	+11.4	88.2	56 28.3	+13.3	89.7	56 27.9	+15.1	91.2	56 25.9	+16.9	92.7	56 22.3	+18.8	94.2	56 17.1	+20.6	95.7	56 10.4	+22.3	97.2	56 02.1	+24.1	98.6	20
21	56 38.6	+9.9	86.4	56 41.6	+11.8	87.9	56 43.0	+13.7	89.4	56 42.8	+15.5	90.9	56 41.1	+17.3	92.5	56 37.7	+19.2	94.0	56 32.7	+21.0	95.5	56 26.2	+22.7	97.0	21
22	56 48.5	+8.4	84.6	56 53.4	+10.2	86.1	56 56.7	+12.1	87.6	56 58.3	+14.0	89.2	56 58.4	+15.9	90.7	56 56.9	+17.7	92.2	56 53.7	+19.5	93.8	56 48.9	+21.4	95.3	22
23	56 56.9	+6.7	82.8	57 03.6	+8.7	84.3	57 08.8	+10.5	85.8	57 12.3	+12.5	87.4	57 14.3	+14.3	88.9	57 14.6	+16.2	90.5	57 13.2	+18.1	92.0	57 10.3	+19.9	93.6	23
24	57 03.6	+5.2	80.9	57 12.3	+7.0	82.5	57 19.3	+9.0	84.0	57 24.8	+10.9	85.6	57 28.6	+12.8	87.1	57 30.8	+14.7	88.7	57 31.3	+16.6	90.3	57 30.2	+18.5	91.8	24
25	57 08.8	+3.5	79.1	57 19.3	+5.5	80.6	57 28.3	+7.4	82.2	57 35.7	+9.2	83.7	57 41.4	+11.2	85.3	57 45.5	+13.1	86.9	57 47.9	+15.0	88.5	57 48.7	+16.9	90.1	25
26	57 12.3	+2.0	77.3	57 24.8	+3.8	78.8	57 35.7	+5.7	80.3	57 44.9	+7.7	81.9	57 52.6	+9.6	83.5	57 58.6	+11.5	85.1	58 02.9	+13.5	86.7	58 05.6	+15.3	88.3	26
27	57 14.3	+0.3	75.4	57 28.6	+2.2	76.9	57 41.4	+4.1	78.5	57 52.6	+6.0	80.0	58 02.2	+7.9	81.6	58 10.1	+9.9	83.2	58 16.4	+11.8	84.8	58 20.9	+13.8	86.4	27
28	57 14.6	−1.4	73.6	57 30.8	+0.5	75.1	57 45.5	+2.4	76.6	57 58.6	+4.3	78.2	58 10.1	+6.3	79.7	58 20.0	+8.2	81.3	58 28.2	+10.1	82.9	58 34.7	+12.1	84.6	28
29	57 13.2	−2.9	71.7	57 31.3	−1.1	73.2	57 47.9	+0.8	74.7	58 02.9	+2.7	76.3	58 16.4	+4.5	77.8	58 28.2	+6.5	79.4	58 38.3	+8.5	81.0	58 46.8	+10.5	82.7	29
30	57 10.3	−4.6	69.9	57 30.2	−2.7	71.4	57 48.7	−0.9	72.9	58 05.6	+1.0	74.4	58 20.9	+2.9	75.9	58 34.7	+4.8	77.5	58 46.8	+6.8	79.1	58 57.3	+8.8	80.8	30
31	57 05.7	−6.1	68.0	57 27.5	−4.4	69.5	57 47.8	−2.6	71.0	58 06.6	−0.7	72.5	58 23.8	+1.2	74.0	58 39.5	+3.2	75.6	58 53.6	+5.1	77.2	59 06.1	+7.0	78.8	31
32	56 59.6	−7.8	66.2	57 23.1	−6.0	67.6	57 45.2	−4.2	69.1	58 05.9	−2.4	70.6	58 25.0	−0.5	72.1	58 42.7	+1.4	73.7	58 58.7	+3.4	75.3	59 13.1	+5.3	76.9	32
33	56 51.8	−9.3	64.4	57 17.1	−7.7	65.8	57 41.0	−5.9	67.2	58 03.5	−4.1	68.7	58 24.5	−2.2	70.2	58 44.1	−0.4	71.8	59 02.1	+1.6	73.4	59 18.4	+3.6	75.0	33
34	56 42.5	−10.9	62.6	57 09.4	−9.2	64.0	57 35.1	−7.5	65.4	57 59.4	−5.7	66.8	58 22.3	−3.9	68.3	58 43.7	−2.0	69.8	59 03.7	−0.2	71.4	59 22.0	+1.8	73.0	34
35	56 31.6	−12.4	60.8	57 00.2	−10.7	62.1	57 27.6	−9.1	63.5	57 53.7	−7.4	65.0	58 18.4	−5.6	66.4	58 41.7	−3.8	67.9	59 03.5	−1.9	69.5	59 23.8	0.0	71.0	35
36	56 19.2	−13.9	59.0	56 49.5	−12.4	60.3	57 18.5	−10.6	61.7	57 46.3	−9.0	63.1	58 12.8	−7.2	64.5	58 37.9	−5.4	66.0	59 01.6	−3.6	67.5	59 23.8	−1.7	69.1	36
37	56 05.3	−15.4	57.3	56 37.1	−13.8	58.6	57 07.9	−12.3	59.9	57 37.3	−10.6	61.2	58 05.6	−8.9	62.6	58 32.5	−7.2	64.1	58 58.0	−5.4	65.6	59 22.1	−3.5	67.1	37
38	55 49.9	−16.8	55.6	56 23.3	−15.3	56.8	56 55.6	−13.8	58.1	57 26.7	−12.1	59.4	57 56.7	−10.6	60.8	58 25.3	−8.8	62.2	58 52.6	−7.0	63.7	59 18.6	−5.3	65.2	38
39	55 33.1	−18.2	53.9	56 08.0	−16.8	55.1	56 41.8	−15.2	56.3	57 14.6	−13.8	57.6	57 46.1	−12.1	58.9	58 16.5	−10.5	60.3	58 45.6	−8.8	61.7	59 13.3	−7.0	63.2	39
40	55 14.9	−19.5	52.2	55 51.2	−18.1	53.3	56 26.6	−16.8	54.5	57 00.8	−15.2	55.8	57 34.0	−13.7	57.1	58 06.0	−12.1	58.4	58 36.8	−10.5	59.8	59 06.3	−8.7	61.3	40
41	54 55.4	−20.9	50.5	55 33.1	−19.6	51.6	56 09.8	−18.2	52.8	56 45.6	−16.8	54.0	57 20.3	−15.3	55.3	57 53.9	−13.7	56.6	58 26.3	−12.1	57.9	58 57.6	−10.5	59.3	41
42	54 34.5	−22.2	48.9	55 13.5	−20.9	50.0	55 51.6	−19.5	51.1	56 28.8	−18.2	52.3	57 05.0	−16.7	53.5	57 40.2	−15.3	54.8	58 14.2	−13.7	56.1	58 47.1	−12.0	57.4	42
43	54 12.3	−23.4	47.3	54 52.6	−22.2	48.3	55 32.1	−20.9	49.4	56 10.6	−19.6	50.6	56 48.3	−18.2	51.7	57 24.9	−16.7	53.0	58 00.5	−15.2	54.2	58 35.1	−13.8	55.6	43
44	53 48.9	−24.6	45.7	54 30.4	−23.4	46.7	55 11.2	−22.3	47.8	55 51.0	−20.9	48.9	56 30.1	−19.7	50.0	57 08.2	−18.3	51.2	57 45.3	−16.9	52.4	58 21.3	−15.3	53.7	44
45	53 24.3	−25.7	44.2	54 07.0	−24.7	45.2	54 48.9	−23.5	46.2	55 30.1	−22.3	47.2	56 10.4	−21.0	48.3	56 49.9	−19.7	49.4	57 28.4	−18.3	50.6	58 06.0	−16.9	51.9	45
46	52 58.6	−26.9	42.7	53 42.3	−25.8	43.6	54 25.4	−24.7	44.6	55 07.8	−23.6	45.6	55 49.4	−22.4	46.6	56 30.2	−21.1	47.7	57 10.1	−19.8	48.9	57 49.1	−18.4	50.1	46
47	52 31.7	−28.0	41.2	53 16.5	−27.0	42.1	54 00.7	−25.9	43.0	54 44.2	−24.8	44.0	55 27.0	−23.6	45.0	56 09.1	−22.5	46.0	56 50.3	−21.2	47.1	57 30.7	−19.9	48.3	47
48	52 03.7	−29.0	39.8	52 49.5	−28.0	40.6	53 34.8	−27.1	41.5	54 19.4	−26.0	42.4	55 03.4	−24.9	43.4	55 46.6	−23.7	44.4	56 29.1	−22.5	45.4	57 10.8	−21.3	46.5	48
49	51 34.7	−30.0	38.4	52 21.5	−29.1	39.2	53 07.7	−28.1	40.0	53 53.4	−27.1	40.9	54 38.5	−26.1	41.8	55 22.9	−25.1	42.7	56 06.6	−23.9	43.8	56 49.5	−22.7	44.8	49
50	51 04.7	−31.0	37.0	51 52.4	−30.1	37.7	52 39.6	−29.2	38.5	53 26.3	−28.3	39.4	54 12.4	−27.3	40.2	54 57.8	−26.2	41.2	55 42.7	−25.2	42.1	56 26.8	−24.0	43.1	50
51	50 33.7	−31.9	35.6	51 22.3	−31.1	36.3	52 10.4	−30.3	37.1	52 58.0	−29.4	37.9	53 45.1	−28.4	38.7	54 31.6	−27.4	39.6	55 17.5	−26.4	40.5	56 02.8	−25.3	41.5	51
52	50 01.8	−32.8	34.3	50 51.2	−32.0	35.0	51 40.1	−31.2	35.7	52 28.6	−30.3	36.5	53 16.7	−29.5	37.2	54 04.2	−28.6	38.1	54 51.1	−27.6	38.9	55 37.5	−26.6	39.9	52
53	49 29.0	−33.6	33.0	50 19.2	−32.9	33.6	51 08.9	−32.1	34.3	51 58.3	−31.4	35.0	52 47.2	−30.5	35.8	53 35.6	−29.6	36.6	54 23.5	−28.7	37.4	55 10.9	−27.8	38.3	53
54	48 55.4	−34.4	31.7	49 46.3	−33.8	32.3	50 36.8	−33.0	33.0	51 26.9	−32.3	33.7	52 16.7	−31.6	34.4	53 06.0	−30.7	35.1	53 54.8	−29.8	35.9	54 43.1	−28.9	36.7	54
55	48 21.0	−35.3	30.5	49 12.5	−34.6	31.1	50 03.8	−34.0	31.7	50 54.6	−33.2	32.3	51 45.1	−32.4	33.0	52 35.3	−31.7	33.7	53 25.0	−30.9	34.4	54 14.2	−30.0	35.2	55
56	47 45.7	−35.9	29.3	48 37.9	−35.3	29.8	49 29.8	−34.7	30.4	50 21.4	−34.0	31.0	51 12.7	−33.4	31.6	52 03.6	−32.7	32.3	52 54.1	−31.9	33.0	53 44.2	−31.1	33.8	56
57	47 09.8	−36.7	28.1	48 02.6	−36.1	28.6	48 55.1	−35.5	29.2	49 47.4	−34.9	29.7	50 39.3	−34.2	30.3	51 30.9	−33.5	31.0	52 22.2	−32.8	31.6	53 13.1	−32.1	32.3	57
58	46 33.1	−37.4	26.9	47 26.5	−36.9	27.4	48 19.6	−36.3	27.9	49 12.5	−35.7	28.5	50 05.1	−35.1	29.0	50 57.4	−34.5	29.6	51 49.4	−33.8	30.3	52 41.0	−33.0	30.9	58
59	45 55.7	−38.0	25.8	46 49.6	−37.5	26.3	47 43.3	−37.0	26.7	48 36.8	−36.5	27.3	49 30.0	−35.9	27.8	50 22.9	−35.2	28.3	51 15.6	−34.6	28.9	52 08.0	−34.0	29.5	59
60	45 17.7	−38.7	24.7	46 12.1	−38.2	25.1	47 06.3	−37.7	25.6	48 00.3	−37.1	26.1	48 54.1	−36.6	26.6	49 47.7	−36.1	27.1	50 41.0	−35.5	27.6	51 34.0	−34.9	28.2	60
61	44 39.0	−39.2	23.6	45 33.9	−38.8	24.0	46 28.6	−38.3	24.4	47 23.2	−37.9	24.9	48 17.5	−37.4	25.4	49 11.6	−36.8	25.9	50 05.5	−36.3	26.4	50 59.1	−35.7	26.9	61
62	43 59.8	−39.8	22.6	44 55.1	−39.4	22.9	45 50.3	−39.0	23.3	46 45.3	−38.5	23.8	47 40.1	−38.0	24.2	48 34.8	−37.6	24.7	49 29.2	−37.1	25.1	50 23.4	−36.5	25.6	62
63	43 20.0	−40.4	21.5	44 15.7	−40.0	21.9	45 11.3	−39.6	22.2	46 06.8	−39.2	22.6	47 02.1	−38.8	23.0	47 57.2	−38.3	23.5	48 52.1	−37.8	23.9	49 46.9	−37.3	24.4	63
64	42 39.6	−40.9	20.5	43 35.7	−40.5	20.8	44 31.7	−40.1	21.2	45 27.6	−39.8	21.6	46 23.3	−39.3	21.9	47 18.9	−38.9	22.3	48 14.3	−38.5	22.8	49 09.6	−38.1	23.2	64
65	41 58.7	−41.4	19.5	42 55.2	−41.1	19.8	43 51.6	−40.7	20.2	44 47.8	−40.3	20.5	45 44.0	−40.0	20.8	46 40.0	−39.6	21.2	47 35.8	−39.1	21.6	48 31.5	−38.7	22.0	65
66	41 17.3	−41.9	18.6	42 14.1	−41.5	18.8	43 10.9	−41.3	19.1	44 07.5	−40.9	19.5	45 04.0	−40.5	19.8	46 00.4	−40.2	20.1	46 56.7	−39.8	20.5	47 52.8	−39.4	20.9	66
67	40 35.4	−42.3	17.6	41 32.6	−42.1	17.9	42 29.6	−41.7	18.1	43 26.6	−41.4	18.4	44 23.5	−41.1	18.7	45 20.2	−40.7	19.1	46 16.9	−40.4	19.4	47 13.4	−40.0	19.8	67
68	39 53.1	−42.8	16.7	40 50.5	−42.4	16.9	41 47.9	−42.2	17.2	42 45.2	−41.9	17.4	43 42.4	−41.6	17.7	44 39.5	−41.3	18.0	45 36.5	−41.0	18.3	46 33.4	−40.6	18.7	68
69	39 10.3	−43.1	15.8	40 08.1	−43.0	16.0	41 05.7	−42.7	16.2	42 03.3	−42.4	16.5	43 00.8	−42.1	16.7	43 58.2	−41.8	17.0	44 55.5	−41.5	17.3	45 52.8	−41.3	17.6	69
70	38 27.2	−43.6	14.9	39 25.1	−43.3	15.1	40 23.0	−43.1	15.3	41 20.9	−42.9	15.5	42 18.7	−42.6	15.8	43 16.4	−42.4	16.0	44 14.0	−42.1	16.3	45 11.5	−41.7	16.6	70
71	37 43.6	−44.0	14.0	38 41.8	−43.7	14.2	39 39.9	−43.5	14.4	40 38.0	−43.3	14.6	41 36.1	−43.1	14.8	42 34.0	−42.8	15.1	43 31.9	−42.5	15.3	44 29.8	−42.3	15.6	71
72	36 59.6	−44.3	13.1	37 58.1	−44.2	13.3	38 56.4	−43.9	13.5	39 54.7	−43.7	13.7	40 53.0	−43.5	13.9	41 51.2	−43.2	14.1	42 49.4	−43.0	14.3	43 47.5	−42.8	14.6	72
73	36 15.3	−44.6	12.3	37 13.9	−44.4	12.5	38 12.5	−44.3	12.6	39 11.0	−44.1	12.8	40 09.5	−43.9	13.0	41 08.0	−43.7	13.2	42 06.4	−43.5	13.4	43 04.7	−43.3	13.6	73
74	35 30.7	−45.0	11.5	36 29.5	−44.9	11.6	37 28.2	−44.6	11.8	38 26.9	−44.4	11.9	39 25.6	−44.3	12.1	40 24.3	−44.1	12.3	41 22.9	−43.9	12.5	42 21.4	−43.7	12.7	74
75	34 45.7	−45.3	10.7	35 44.6	−45.1	10.8	36 43.6	−45.0	10.9	37 42.5	−44.9	11.1	38 41.3	−44.7	11.2	39 40.2	−44.6	11.4	40 39.0	−44.4	11.6	41 37.7	−44.1	11.7	75
76	34 00.4	−45.6	9.9	34 59.5	−45.5	10.0	35 58.6	−45.4	10.1	36 57.6	−45.2	10.3	37 56.6	−45.0	10.4	38 55.6	−44.8	10.5	39 54.6	−44.7	10.7	40 53.6	−44.6	10.8	76
77	33 14.8	−45.9	9.1	34 14.0	−45.8	9.2	35 13.2	−45.6	9.3	36 12.4	−45.5	9.4	37 11.6	−45.4	9.6	38 10.8	−45.3	9.7	39 09.9	−45.1	9.8	40 09.0	−44.9	10.0	77
78	32 28.9	−46.2	8.3	33 28.2	−46.0	8.4	34 27.6	−46.0	8.5	35 26.9	−45.8	8.6	36 26.2	−45.7	8.7	37 25.5	−45.6	8.9	38 24.8	−45.5	9.0	39 24.1	−45.4	9.1	78
79	31 42.7	−46.4	7.6	32 42.2	−46.3	7.7	33 41.6	−46.2	7.7	34 41.1	−46.1	7.8	35 40.5	−46.0	7.9	36 39.9	−45.9	8.0	37 39.3	−45.8	8.1	38 38.7	−45.7	8.3	79
80	30 56.3	−46.7	6.8	31 55.9	−46.6	6.9	32 55.4	−46.5	7.0	33 55.0	−46.4	7.1	34 54.5	−46.3	7.1	35 54.0	−46.2	7.2	36 53.5	−46.1	7.3	37 53.0	−46.0	7.4	80
81	30 09.6	−46.9	6.1	31 09.3	−46.9	6.2	32 08.9	−46.8	6.2	33 08.6	−46.7	6.3	34 08.2	−46.6	6.4	35 07.8	−46.5	6.5	36 07.4	−46.4	6.5	37 07.0	−46.3	6.6	81
82	29 22.7	−47.2	5.4	30 22.4	−47.1	5.4	31 22.1	−47.0	5.5	32 21.9	−47.0	5.6	33 21.6	−46.9	5.6	34 21.3	−46.8	5.7	35 21.0	−46.7	5.8	36 20.7	−46.7	5.8	82
83	28 35.5	−47.3	4.7	29 35.3	−47.3	4.7	30 35.1	−47.2	4.8	31 34.9	−47.2	4.8	32 34.7	−47.1	4.9	33 34.5	−47.1	4.9	34 34.3	−47.0	5.0	35 34.0	−46.9	5.1	83
84	27 48.2	−47.6	4.0	28 48.0	−47.5	4.0	29 47.9	−47.5	4.1	30 47.7	−47.4	4.1	31 47.6	−47.4	4.1	32 47.4	−47.3	4.2	33 47.3	−47.3	4.2	34 47.1	−47.2	4.3	84
85	27 00.6	−47.8	3.3	28 00.5	−47.7	3.3	29 00.4	−47.7	3.4	30 00.3	−47.6	3.4	31 00.2	−47.6	3.4	32 00.1	−47.6	3.5	33 00.0	−47.5	3.5	33 59.9	−47.5	3.5	85
86	26 12.8	−47.9	2.6	27 12.8	−47.9	2.6	28 12.7	−47.9	2.7	29 12.7	−47.9	2.7	30 12.6	−47.8	2.7	31 12.5	−47.8	2.7	32 12.5	−47.8	2.8	33 12.4	−47.8	2.8	86
87	25 24.9	−48.1	2.0	26 24.9	−48.2	2.0	27 24.8	−48.1	2.0	28 24.8	−48.1	2.0	29 24.8	−48.1	2.0	30 24.7	−48.0	2.0	31 24.7	−48.0	2.1	32 24.6	−47.9	2.1	87
88	24 36.8	−48.3	1.3	25 36.7	−48.2	1.3	26 36.7	−48.2	1.3	27 36.7	−48.2	1.3	28 36.7	−48.3	1.3	29 36.7	−48.3	1.4	30 36.7	−48.3	1.4	31 36.7	−48.3	1.4	88
89	23 48.5	−48.5	0.6	24 48.5	−48.5	0.6	25 48.5	−48.5	0.7	26 48.5	−48.5	0.7	27 48.4	−48.4	0.7	28 48.4	−48.4	0.7	29 48.4	−48.4	0.7	30 48.4	−48.4	0.7	89
90	23 00.0	−48.6	0.0	24 00.0	−48.6	0.0	25 00.0	−48.6	0.0	26 00.0	−48.6	0.0	27 00.0	−48.6	0.0	28 00.0	−48.6	0.0	29 00.0	−48.6	0.0	30 00.0	−48.6	0.0	90
	23°			24°			25°			26°			27°			28°			29°			30°			

36°, 324° L.H.A. LATITUDE SAME NAME AS DECLINATION

256

LATITUDE **CONTRARY** NAME TO DECLINATION L.H.A. 36°, 324°

Dec.	23° Hc	23° d	23° Z	24° Hc	24° d	24° Z	25° Hc	25° d	25° Z	26° Hc	26° d	26° Z	27° Hc	27° d	27° Z	28° Hc	28° d	28° Z	29° Hc	29° d	29° Z	30° Hc	30° d	30° Z	Dec.
°	° ′	′	°	° ′	′	°	° ′	′	°	° ′	′	°	° ′	′	°	° ′	′	°	° ′	′	°	° ′	′	°	°
0	48 08.0	−35.5	118.3	47 39.2	−36.6	119.2	47 09.4	−37.6	120.2	46 38.8	−38.6	121.1	46 07.4	−39.6	122.0	45 35.2	−40.5	122.9	45 02.3	−41.4	123.7	44 28.7	−42.4	124.5	0
1	47 32.5	−36.2	119.5	47 02.6	−37.3	120.4	46 31.8	−38.3	121.3	46 00.2	−39.3	122.2	45 27.8	−40.2	123.1	44 54.7	−41.1	123.9	44 20.9	−42.0	124.7	43 46.3	−42.8	125.5	1
2	46 56.3	−37.0	120.6	46 25.3	−38.0	121.6	45 53.5	−38.9	122.4	45 20.9	−39.8	123.3	44 47.6	−40.7	124.1	44 13.6	−41.6	124.9	43 38.9	−42.5	125.7	43 03.5	−43.2	126.5	2
3	46 19.3	−37.6	121.8	45 47.3	−38.6	122.7	45 14.6	−39.6	123.5	44 41.1	−40.5	124.4	44 06.9	−41.4	125.2	43 32.0	−42.2	125.9	42 56.4	−42.9	126.7	42 20.3	−43.8	127.4	3
4	45 41.7	−38.3	122.9	45 08.7	−39.2	123.8	44 35.0	−40.1	124.6	44 00.6	−41.0	125.4	43 25.5	−41.8	126.2	42 49.8	−42.6	126.9	42 13.5	−43.4	127.6	41 36.5	−44.1	128.4	4
5	45 03.4	−38.8	124.0	44 29.5	−39.8	124.8	43 54.9	−40.6	125.6	43 19.6	−41.5	126.4	42 43.7	−42.3	127.1	42 07.2	−43.1	127.9	41 30.1	−43.9	128.6	40 52.4	−44.6	129.3	5
6	44 24.6	−39.5	125.1	43 49.7	−40.3	125.9	43 14.3	−41.2	126.6	42 38.1	−42.0	127.4	42 01.4	−42.8	128.1	41 24.1	−43.5	128.8	40 46.2	−44.2	129.5	40 07.8	−44.9	130.1	6
7	43 45.1	−40.0	126.1	43 09.4	−40.9	126.9	42 33.1	−41.7	127.6	41 56.1	−42.4	128.3	41 18.6	−43.2	129.0	40 40.6	−44.0	129.7	40 02.0	−44.7	130.4	39 22.9	−45.4	131.0	7
8	43 05.1	−40.6	127.2	42 28.5	−41.4	127.9	41 51.4	−42.2	128.6	41 13.7	−43.0	129.3	40 35.4	−43.7	130.0	39 56.6	−44.4	130.6	39 17.3	−45.0	131.2	38 37.5	−45.7	131.8	8
9	42 24.5	−41.1	128.2	41 47.1	−41.8	128.9	41 09.2	−42.6	129.6	40 30.7	−43.3	130.2	39 51.7	−44.0	130.9	39 12.2	−44.7	131.5	38 32.3	−45.4	132.1	37 51.8	−46.0	132.7	9
10	41 43.4	−41.5	129.1	41 05.3	−42.4	129.8	40 26.6	−43.1	130.5	39 47.4	−43.8	131.1	39 07.7	−44.5	131.7	38 27.5	−45.1	132.3	37 46.9	−45.8	132.9	37 05.8	−46.4	133.5	10
11	41 01.9	−42.1	130.1	40 22.9	−42.7	130.8	39 43.5	−43.5	131.4	39 03.6	−44.2	132.0	38 23.2	−44.8	132.6	37 42.4	−45.5	133.2	37 01.1	−46.0	133.7	36 19.4	−46.6	134.3	11
12	40 19.8	−42.5	131.0	39 40.2	−43.2	131.7	39 00.0	−43.8	132.3	38 19.4	−44.5	132.9	37 38.4	−45.2	133.4	36 56.9	−45.8	134.0	36 15.1	−46.4	134.5	35 32.8	−47.0	135.0	12
13	39 37.3	−42.9	132.0	38 57.0	−43.6	132.6	38 16.2	−44.3	133.2	37 34.9	−44.9	133.7	36 53.2	−45.5	134.3	36 11.1	−46.1	134.8	35 28.7	−46.7	135.3	34 45.8	−47.2	135.8	13
14	38 54.4	−43.3	132.9	38 13.4	−44.0	133.5	37 31.9	−44.6	134.0	36 50.0	−45.2	134.6	36 07.7	−45.8	135.1	35 25.0	−46.4	135.6	34 42.0	−47.0	136.1	33 58.6	−47.5	136.5	14
15	38 11.1	−43.7	133.8	37 29.4	−44.4	134.3	36 47.3	−45.0	134.9	36 04.8	−45.6	135.4	35 21.9	−46.2	135.9	34 38.6	−46.7	136.4	33 55.0	−47.2	136.8	33 11.1	−47.7	137.3	15
16	37 27.4	−44.1	134.6	36 45.0	−44.7	135.2	36 02.3	−45.3	135.7	35 19.2	−45.9	136.2	34 35.7	−46.4	136.7	33 51.9	−46.9	137.1	33 07.8	−47.5	137.6	32 23.4	−48.0	138.0	16
17	36 43.3	−44.5	135.5	36 00.3	−45.0	136.0	35 17.0	−45.6	136.5	34 33.3	−46.2	137.0	33 49.3	−46.7	137.4	33 05.0	−47.3	137.9	32 20.3	−47.7	138.3	31 35.4	−48.3	138.7	17
18	35 58.8	−44.7	136.3	35 15.3	−45.4	136.8	34 31.4	−45.9	137.3	33 47.1	−46.4	137.7	33 02.6	−47.0	138.2	32 17.7	−47.5	138.6	31 32.6	−48.0	139.0	30 47.1	−48.4	139.4	18
19	35 14.1	−45.1	137.1	34 29.9	−45.6	137.6	33 45.5	−46.3	138.1	33 00.7	−46.8	138.5	32 15.6	−47.2	138.9	31 30.2	−47.7	139.3	30 44.6	−48.2	139.7	29 58.7	−48.6	140.1	19
20	34 29.0	−45.5	137.9	33 44.3	−46.0	138.4	32 59.2	−46.4	138.8	32 13.9	−46.9	139.2	31 28.4	−47.5	139.6	30 42.5	−47.9	140.0	29 56.4	−48.4	140.4	29 10.1	−48.9	140.8	20
21	33 43.5	−45.7	138.7	32 58.3	−46.2	139.1	32 12.8	−46.8	139.6	31 27.0	−47.3	140.0	30 40.9	−47.7	140.4	29 54.6	−48.2	140.7	29 08.0	−48.6	141.1	28 21.2	−49.0	141.4	21
22	32 57.8	−46.0	139.5	32 12.1	−46.5	139.9	31 26.0	−47.0	140.3	30 39.7	−47.4	140.7	29 53.2	−47.9	141.1	29 06.4	−48.4	141.4	28 19.4	−48.8	141.7	27 32.2	−49.2	142.1	22
23	32 11.8	−46.2	140.3	31 25.6	−46.8	140.6	30 39.0	−47.2	141.0	29 52.3	−47.7	141.4	29 05.3	−48.2	141.7	28 18.0	−48.5	142.1	27 30.6	−49.0	142.4	26 43.0	−49.4	142.7	23
24	31 25.6	−46.6	141.0	30 38.8	−47.0	141.4	29 51.8	−47.5	141.7	29 04.6	−47.9	142.1	28 17.1	−48.3	142.4	27 29.5	−48.8	142.7	26 41.6	−49.1	143.1	25 53.6	−49.6	143.4	24
25	30 39.0	−46.7	141.7	29 51.8	−47.2	142.1	29 04.3	−47.6	142.4	28 16.7	−48.1	142.8	27 28.8	−48.5	143.1	26 40.7	−48.9	143.4	25 52.5	−49.4	143.7	25 04.0	−49.7	144.0	25
26	29 52.3	−47.0	142.5	29 04.6	−47.5	142.8	28 16.7	−47.9	143.1	27 28.6	−48.3	143.5	26 40.3	−48.7	143.8	25 51.8	−49.1	144.0	25 03.1	−49.4	144.3	24 14.3	−49.8	144.6	26
27	29 05.3	−47.3	143.2	28 17.1	−47.6	143.5	27 28.8	−48.1	143.8	26 40.3	−48.5	144.1	25 51.6	−48.9	144.4	25 02.7	−49.3	144.7	24 13.7	−49.7	144.9	23 24.5	−50.0	145.2	27
28	28 18.0	−47.4	143.9	27 29.5	−47.9	144.2	26 40.7	−48.2	144.5	25 51.8	−48.7	144.8	25 02.7	−49.0	145.1	24 13.4	−49.4	145.3	23 24.0	−49.8	145.6	22 34.5	−50.2	145.8	28
29	27 30.6	−47.6	144.6	26 41.6	−48.0	144.9	25 52.5	−48.5	145.2	25 03.1	−48.8	145.4	24 13.7	−49.2	145.7	23 24.0	−49.5	145.9	22 34.2	−49.9	146.2	21 44.3	−50.2	146.4	29
30	26 43.0	−47.9	145.3	25 53.6	−48.3	145.5	25 04.0	−48.6	145.8	24 14.3	−49.0	146.1	23 24.5	−49.4	146.3	22 34.5	−49.7	146.5	21 44.3	−50.0	146.8	20 54.1	−50.4	147.0	30
31	25 55.1	−48.0	145.9	25 05.3	−48.4	146.2	24 15.4	−48.8	146.5	23 25.3	−49.1	146.7	22 35.1	−49.5	146.9	21 44.8	−49.9	147.2	20 54.3	−50.2	147.4	20 03.7	−50.5	147.6	31
32	25 07.1	−48.2	146.6	24 16.9	−48.5	146.8	23 26.6	−48.9	147.1	22 36.2	−49.3	147.3	21 45.6	−49.6	147.5	20 54.9	−49.9	147.7	20 04.1	−50.2	147.9	19 13.2	−50.5	148.1	32
33	24 18.9	−48.4	147.3	23 28.4	−48.7	147.5	22 37.7	−49.1	147.7	21 46.9	−49.4	147.9	20 56.0	−49.7	148.1	20 05.0	−50.1	148.3	19 13.9	−50.4	148.5	18 22.7	−50.7	148.7	33
34	23 30.5	−48.5	147.9	22 39.7	−48.9	148.1	21 48.6	−49.2	148.3	20 57.5	−49.5	148.5	20 06.3	−49.9	148.7	19 14.9	−50.1	148.9	18 23.5	−50.5	149.1	17 32.0	−50.8	149.3	34
35	22 42.0	−48.7	148.5	21 50.8	−49.0	148.8	20 59.4	−49.3	149.0	20 08.0	−49.7	149.1	19 16.4	−50.0	149.3	18 24.8	−50.3	149.5	17 33.0	−50.6	149.7	16 41.2	−50.9	149.8	35
36	21 53.3	−48.8	149.2	21 01.8	−49.2	149.4	20 10.1	−49.5	149.6	19 18.3	−49.8	149.7	18 26.4	−50.0	149.9	17 34.5	−50.4	150.1	16 42.4	−50.6	150.2	15 50.3	−50.9	150.4	36
37	21 04.5	−48.9	149.8	20 12.6	−49.2	150.0	19 20.6	−49.6	150.2	18 28.5	−49.8	150.3	17 36.4	−50.2	150.5	16 44.1	−50.5	150.6	15 51.8	−50.8	150.8	14 59.4	−51.1	150.9	37
38	20 15.6	−49.1	150.4	19 23.4	−49.4	150.6	18 31.0	−49.6	150.8	17 38.7	−50.0	150.9	16 46.2	−50.3	151.1	15 53.6	−50.5	151.2	15 01.0	−50.8	151.3	14 08.3	−51.1	151.5	38
39	19 26.5	−49.2	151.0	18 34.0	−49.5	151.2	17 41.4	−49.8	151.3	16 48.7	−50.1	151.5	15 55.9	−50.4	151.6	15 03.1	−50.7	151.8	14 10.2	−50.9	151.9	13 17.2	−51.1	152.0	39
40	18 37.3	−49.3	151.6	17 44.5	−49.6	151.8	16 51.6	−49.9	151.9	15 58.6	−50.2	152.1	15 05.5	−50.4	152.2	14 12.4	−50.7	152.3	13 19.3	−51.0	152.4	12 26.1	−51.3	152.5	40
41	17 48.0	−49.4	152.2	16 54.9	−49.7	152.4	16 01.7	−50.0	152.5	15 08.4	−50.2	152.6	14 15.1	−50.5	152.8	13 21.7	−50.8	152.9	12 28.3	−51.0	153.0	11 34.8	−51.3	153.1	41
42	16 58.6	−49.6	152.8	16 05.2	−49.8	153.0	15 11.7	−50.1	153.1	14 18.2	−50.4	153.2	13 24.6	−50.6	153.3	12 30.9	−50.8	153.4	11 37.3	−51.1	153.5	10 43.5	−51.3	153.6	42
43	16 09.0	−49.6	153.4	15 15.4	−49.9	153.5	14 21.6	−50.1	153.7	13 27.8	−50.4	153.8	12 34.0	−50.7	153.9	11 40.1	−50.9	154.0	10 46.2	−51.2	154.1	9 52.2	−51.4	154.1	43
44	15 19.4	−49.7	154.0	14 25.5	−50.0	154.1	13 31.5	−50.3	154.2	12 37.4	−50.5	154.3	11 43.3	−50.7	154.4	10 49.2	−51.0	154.5	9 55.0	−51.2	154.6	9 00.8	−51.4	154.7	44
45	14 29.7	−49.8	154.6	13 35.5	−50.1	154.7	12 41.2	−50.3	154.8	11 46.9	−50.5	154.9	10 52.6	−50.8	155.0	9 58.2	−51.0	155.0	9 03.8	−51.3	155.1	8 09.4	−51.5	155.2	45
46	13 39.9	−49.9	155.2	12 45.4	−50.1	155.3	11 50.9	−50.3	155.3	10 56.4	−50.6	155.4	10 01.8	−50.8	155.5	9 07.2	−51.1	155.6	8 12.5	−51.2	155.6	7 17.9	−51.5	155.7	46
47	12 50.0	−49.9	155.7	11 55.3	−50.2	155.8	11 00.6	−50.5	155.9	10 05.8	−50.7	156.0	9 11.0	−50.9	156.0	8 16.1	−51.1	156.1	7 21.3	−51.4	156.2	6 26.4	−51.6	156.2	47
48	12 00.1	−50.0	156.3	11 05.1	−50.2	156.4	10 10.1	−50.4	156.4	9 15.1	−50.7	156.5	8 20.1	−50.9	156.6	7 25.0	−51.1	156.6	6 29.9	−51.3	156.7	5 34.8	−51.6	156.7	48
49	11 10.1	−50.1	156.9	10 14.9	−50.3	156.9	9 19.7	−50.6	157.0	8 24.4	−50.7	157.1	7 29.2	−51.0	157.1	6 33.9	−51.2	157.2	5 38.6	−51.4	157.2	4 43.2	−51.5	157.2	49
50	10 20.0	−50.2	157.4	9 24.6	−50.4	157.5	8 29.1	−50.5	157.5	7 33.7	−50.8	157.6	6 38.2	−51.0	157.6	5 42.7	−51.2	157.7	4 47.2	−51.4	157.7	3 51.7	−51.7	157.7	50
51	9 29.8	−50.1	158.0	8 34.2	−50.4	158.0	7 38.6	−50.7	158.1	6 42.9	−50.8	158.1	5 47.2	−51.0	158.2	4 51.5	−51.2	158.2	3 55.8	−51.4	158.2	3 00.0	−51.6	158.3	51
52	8 39.7	−50.3	158.5	7 43.8	−50.4	158.6	6 47.9	−50.6	158.6	5 52.1	−50.9	158.7	4 56.2	−51.1	158.7	4 00.3	−51.3	158.7	3 04.3	−51.4	158.8	2 08.4	−51.6	158.8	52
53	7 49.4	−50.3	159.1	6 53.4	−50.5	159.1	5 57.3	−50.7	159.2	5 01.2	−50.9	159.2	4 05.1	−51.1	159.2	3 09.0	−51.3	159.3	2 12.9	−51.5	159.3	1 16.8	−51.7	159.3	53
54	6 59.1	−50.3	159.6	6 02.9	−50.5	159.7	5 06.6	−50.7	159.7	4 10.3	−50.9	159.7	3 14.0	−51.1	159.8	2 17.7	−51.2	159.8	1 21.4	−51.4	159.8	0 25.1	−51.6	159.8	54
55	6 08.8	−50.3	160.2	5 12.4	−50.6	160.2	4 15.9	−50.7	160.2	3 19.4	−50.9	160.3	2 22.9	−51.1	160.3	1 26.5	−51.3	160.3	0 30.0	−51.5	160.3	0 26.5	+51.7	19.7	55
56	5 18.5	−50.4	160.7	4 21.8	−50.6	160.8	3 25.2	−50.8	160.8	2 28.5	−50.9	160.8	1 31.8	−51.1	160.8	0 35.2	−51.3	160.8	0 21.5	+51.4	19.2	1 18.2	+51.6	19.2	56
57	4 28.1	−50.4	161.3	3 31.2	−50.5	161.3	2 34.4	−50.8	161.3	1 37.6	−51.0	161.3	0 40.7	−51.1	161.3	0 16.1	+51.3	18.7	1 12.9	+51.5	18.7	2 09.8	+51.6	18.7	57
58	3 37.7	−50.5	161.8	2 40.7	−50.6	161.8	1 43.6	−50.7	161.8	0 46.6	−50.9	161.8	0 10.4	+51.1	18.1	1 07.4	+51.3	18.2	2 04.4	+51.5	18.2	3 01.4	+51.6	18.2	58
59	2 47.2	−50.4	162.4	1 50.1	−50.6	162.4	0 52.9	−50.8	162.4	0 04.3	+50.9	17.6	1 01.5	+51.1	17.6	1 58.7	+51.2	17.6	2 55.9	+51.4	17.6	3 53.0	+51.6	17.7	59
60	1 56.8	−50.5	162.9	0 59.5	−50.7	162.9	0 02.1	−50.8	162.9	0 55.2	+51.0	17.1	1 52.6	+51.1	17.1	2 49.9	+51.3	17.1	3 47.3	+51.4	17.1	4 44.6	+51.6	17.2	60
61	1 06.3	−50.4	163.4	0 08.8	−50.6	163.4	0 48.7	+50.7	16.6	1 46.2	+50.9	16.6	2 43.7	+51.1	16.6	3 41.2	+51.2	16.6	4 38.7	+51.4	16.6	5 36.2	+51.5	16.6	61
62	0 15.9	−50.5	164.0	0 41.8	+50.6	16.0	1 39.4	+50.8	16.0	2 37.1	+50.9	16.0	3 34.8	+51.0	16.1	4 32.4	+51.3	16.1	5 30.1	+51.4	16.1	6 27.7	+51.5	16.1	62
63	0 34.6	+50.4	15.5	1 32.4	+50.6	15.5	2 30.2	+50.8	15.5	3 28.0	+50.9	15.5	4 25.8	+51.1	15.5	5 23.7	+51.2	15.5	6 21.5	+51.3	15.6	7 19.2	+51.5	15.6	63
64	1 25.0	+50.5	14.9	2 23.0	+50.6	14.9	3 21.0	+50.7	15.0	4 18.9	+50.9	15.0	5 16.9	+51.0	15.0	6 14.8	+51.2	15.0	7 12.8	+51.3	15.1	8 10.7	+51.5	15.1	64
65	2 15.5	+50.4	14.4	3 13.6	+50.6	14.4	4 11.7	+50.7	14.4	5 09.8	+50.9	14.4	6 07.9	+51.0	14.5	7 06.0	+51.1	14.5	8 04.1	+51.2	14.5	9 02.2	+51.4	14.6	65
66	3 05.9	+50.4	13.9	4 04.2	+50.5	13.9	5 02.4	+50.7	13.9	6 00.7	+50.8	13.9	6 58.9	+50.9	13.9	7 57.1	+51.1	14.0	8 55.3	+51.3	14.0	9 53.6	+51.3	14.0	66
67	3 56.3	+50.4	13.3	4 54.7	+50.5	13.3	5 53.1	+50.7	13.3	6 51.5	+50.8	13.4	7 49.8	+51.0	13.4	8 48.2	+51.0	13.4	9 46.6	+51.1	13.5	10 44.9	+51.3	13.5	67
68	4 46.7	+50.4	12.8	5 45.2	+50.5	12.8	6 43.8	+50.6	12.8	7 42.3	+50.7	12.8	8 40.8	+50.8	12.9	9 39.2	+51.0	12.9	10 37.7	+51.1	12.9	11 36.2	+51.2	13.0	68
69	5 37.1	+50.3	12.2	6 35.7	+50.5	12.2	7 34.4	+50.5	12.3	8 33.0	+50.7	12.3	9 31.6	+50.8	12.3	10 30.2	+51.0	12.4	11 28.8	+51.1	12.4	12 27.4	+51.2	12.5	69
70	6 27.4	+50.3	11.7	7 26.2	+50.4	11.7	8 24.9	+50.6	11.8	9 23.7	+50.6	11.8	10 22.4	+50.8	11.8	11 21.2	+50.8	11.8	12 19.9	+51.0	11.9	13 18.6	+51.1	11.9	70
71	7 17.7	+50.3	11.1	8 16.6	+50.4	11.2	9 15.5	+50.5	11.2	10 14.3	+50.6	11.2	11 13.2	+50.7	11.3	12 12.0	+50.8	11.3	13 10.9	+50.9	11.3	14 09.7	+51.0	11.4	71
72	8 08.0	+50.2	10.6	9 07.0	+50.3	10.6	10 06.0	+50.4	10.6	11 04.9	+50.6	10.7	12 03.9	+50.6	10.7	13 02.8	+50.8	10.7	14 01.8	+50.8	10.8	15 00.7	+51.0	10.8	72
73	8 58.2	+50.2	10.0	9 57.3	+50.3	10.0	10 56.4	+50.4	10.1	11 55.5	+50.4	10.1	12 54.5	+50.6	10.2	13 53.6	+50.7	10.2	14 52.6	+50.8	10.2	15 51.7	+50.8	10.3	73
74	9 48.4	+50.1	9.5	10 47.6	+50.2	9.5	11 46.8	+50.3	9.5	12 45.9	+50.4	9.6	13 45.1	+50.5	9.6	14 44.3	+50.5	9.6	15 43.4	+50.7	9.7	16 42.5	+50.8	9.7	74
75	10 38.5	+50.1	8.9	11 37.8	+50.1	8.9	12 37.1	+50.2	9.0	13 36.3	+50.4	9.0	14 35.6	+50.4	9.0	15 34.8	+50.5	9.1	16 34.1	+50.6	9.1	17 33.3	+50.7	9.2	75
76	11 28.6	+50.0	8.3	12 27.9	+50.1	8.4	13 27.3	+50.2	8.4	14 26.7	+50.2	8.4	15 26.0	+50.3	8.5	16 25.3	+50.5	8.5	17 24.7	+50.5	8.6	18 24.0	+50.6	8.6	76
77	12 18.6	+49.9	7.8	13 18.0	+50.0	7.8	14 17.5	+50.0	7.8	15 16.9	+50.2	7.9	16 16.3	+50.3	7.9	17 15.8	+50.3	8.0	18 15.2	+50.4	8.0	19 14.6	+50.5	8.1	77
78	13 08.5	+49.8	7.2	14 08.0	+49.9	7.2	15 07.5	+50.0	7.3	16 07.1	+50.0	7.3	17 06.6	+50.1	7.3	18 06.1	+50.2	7.4	19 05.6	+50.3	7.4	20 05.1	+50.3	7.5	78
79	13 58.3	+49.8	6.6	14 57.9	+49.9	6.7	15 57.5	+49.9	6.7	16 57.1	+50.0	6.7	17 56.7	+50.0	6.8	18 56.3	+50.1	6.8	19 55.9	+50.1	6.9	20 55.4	+50.3	6.9	79
80	14 48.1	+49.7	6.1	15 47.8	+49.7	6.1	16 47.4	+49.8	6.1	17 47.1	+49.9	6.2	18 46.7	+50.0	6.2	19 46.4	+50.0	6.2	20 46.0	+50.1	6.3	21 45.7	+50.1	6.3	80
81	15 37.8	+49.6	5.5	16 37.5	+49.7	5.5	17 37.2	+49.7	5.5	18 37.0	+49.7	5.6	19 36.7	+49.8	5.6	20 36.4	+49.9	5.6	21 36.1	+49.9	5.7	22 35.8	+50.0	5.7	81
82	16 27.4	+49.5	4.9	17 27.2	+49.5	4.9	18 26.9	+49.6	4.9	19 26.7	+49.7	5.0	20 26.5	+49.7	5.0	21 26.3	+49.7	5.0	22 26.0	+49.8	5.1	23 25.8	+49.8	5.1	82
83	17 16.9	+49.4	4.3	18 16.7	+49.4	4.3	19 16.5	+49.5	4.4	20 16.4	+49.5	4.4	21 16.2	+49.5	4.4	22 16.0	+49.6	4.4	23 15.8	+49.7	4.5	24 15.6	+49.7	4.5	83
84	18 06.3	+49.2	3.7	19 06.1	+49.3	3.7	20 06.0	+49.4	3.8	21 05.9	+49.4	3.8	22 05.7	+49.5	3.8	23 05.6	+49.5	3.8	24 05.5	+49.5	3.9	25 05.3	+49.6	3.9	84
85	18 55.5	+49.2	3.1	19 55.4	+49.2	3.1	20 55.4	+49.2	3.1	21 55.3	+49.2	3.2	22 55.2	+49.3	3.2	23 55.1	+49.3	3.2	24 55.0	+49.3	3.2	25 54.9	+49.4	3.3	85
86	19 44.7	+49.0	2.5	20 44.6	+49.1	2.5	21 44.6	+49.1	2.5	22 44.5	+49.1	2.5	23 44.5	+49.1	2.6	24 44.4	+49.2	2.6	25 44.3	+49.2	2.6	26 44.3	+49.2	2.6	86
87	20 33.7	+48.9	1.9	21 33.7	+48.9	1.9	22 33.7	+48.9	1.9	23 33.6	+49.0	1.9	24 33.6	+49.0	1.9	25 33.6	+48.9	2.0	26 33.5	+49.0	2.0	27 33.5	+49.0	2.0	87
88	21 22.6	+48.8	1.3	22 22.6	+48.8	1.3	23 22.6	+48.8	1.3	24 22.6	+48.8	1.3	25 22.6	+48.8	1.3	26 22.5	+48.9	1.3	27 22.5	+48.9	1.3	28 22.5	+48.9	1.3	88
89	22 11.4	+48.6	0.6	23 11.4	+48.6	0.6	24 11.4	+48.6	0.6	25 11.4	+48.6	0.6	26 11.4	+48.6	0.7	27 11.4	+48.6	0.7	28 11.4	+48.6	0.7	29 11.4	+48.6	0.7	89
90	23 00.0	+48.5	0.0	24 00.0	+48.5	0.0	25 00.0	+48.5	0.0	26 00.0	+48.5	0.0	27 00.0	+48.4	0.0	28 00.0	+48.4	0.0	29 00.0	+48.4	0.0	30 00.0	+48.4	0.0	90
	23°			24°			25°			26°			27°			28°			29°			30°			

S. Lat. {L.H.A. greater than 180° ....Zn=180°−Z; L.H.A. less than 180°...........Zn=180°+Z}

LATITUDE **SAME** NAME AS DECLINATION L.H.A. 144°, 216°

257

37°, 323° L.H.A. LATITUDE SAME NAME AS DECLINATION N. Lat. {L.H.A. greater than 180° .....Zn=Z; L.H.A. less than 180°............Zn=360°–Z}

Dec.	23°			24°			25°			26°			27°			28°			29°			30°			Dec.
°	Hc ° ′	d ′	Z °	Hc ° ′	d ′	Z °	Hc ° ′	d ′	Z °	Hc ° ′	d ′	Z °	Hc ° ′	d ′	Z °	Hc ° ′	d ′	Z °	Hc ° ′	d ′	Z °	Hc ° ′	d ′	Z °	°
0	47 19.2	+34.2	117.4	46 51.1	+35.3	118.4	46 22.2	+36.4	119.3	45 52.4	+37.5	120.2	45 21.9	+38.4	121.1	44 50.5	+39.4	121.9	44 18.4	+40.4	122.8	43 45.6	+41.3	123.6	0
1	47 53.4	+33.4	116.2	47 26.4	+34.6	117.2	46 58.6	+35.7	118.1	46 29.9	+36.7	119.1	46 00.3	+37.8	120.0	45 29.9	+38.9	120.9	44 58.8	+39.8	121.7	44 26.9	+40.7	122.6	1
2	48 26.8	+32.6	114.9	48 01.0	+33.8	116.0	47 34.3	+34.9	116.9	47 06.6	+36.1	117.9	46 38.1	+37.2	118.8	46 08.8	+38.1	119.8	45 38.6	+39.2	120.7	45 07.6	+40.1	121.5	2
3	48 59.4	+31.7	113.7	48 34.8	+32.9	114.7	48 09.2	+34.2	115.7	47 42.7	+35.3	116.7	47 15.3	+36.4	117.7	46 46.9	+37.5	118.6	46 17.8	+38.5	119.6	45 47.7	+39.6	120.5	3
4	49 31.1	+30.8	112.4	49 07.7	+32.1	113.4	48 43.4	+33.3	114.5	48 18.0	+34.5	115.5	47 51.7	+35.7	116.5	47 24.4	+36.8	117.5	46 56.3	+37.9	118.4	46 27.3	+38.9	119.4	4
5	50 01.9	+29.9	111.0	49 39.8	+31.3	112.1	49 16.7	+32.5	113.2	48 52.5	+33.8	114.3	48 27.4	+34.9	115.3	48 01.2	+36.1	116.3	47 34.2	+37.2	117.3	47 06.2	+38.3	118.3	5
6	50 31.8	+29.0	109.7	50 11.1	+30.2	110.8	49 49.2	+31.6	111.9	49 26.3	+32.8	113.0	49 02.3	+34.1	114.1	48 37.3	+35.3	115.1	48 11.4	+36.4	116.1	47 44.5	+37.5	117.1	6
7	51 00.8	+27.9	108.3	50 41.3	+29.4	109.5	50 20.8	+30.7	110.6	49 59.1	+32.0	111.7	49 36.4	+33.3	112.8	49 12.6	+34.5	113.9	48 47.8	+35.7	114.9	48 22.0	+36.9	116.0	7
8	51 28.7	+26.9	106.9	51 10.7	+28.3	108.1	50 51.5	+29.7	109.2	50 31.1	+31.1	110.4	50 09.7	+32.3	111.5	49 47.1	+33.7	112.6	49 23.5	+34.9	113.7	48 58.9	+36.1	114.8	8
9	51 55.6	+25.8	105.4	51 39.0	+27.3	106.7	51 21.2	+28.7	107.9	51 02.2	+30.1	109.0	50 42.0	+31.5	110.2	50 20.8	+32.7	111.3	49 58.4	+34.0	112.4	49 35.0	+35.2	113.5	9
10	52 21.4	+24.7	104.0	52 06.3	+26.2	105.2	51 49.9	+27.7	106.5	51 32.3	+29.1	107.7	51 13.5	+30.5	108.9	50 53.5	+31.9	110.0	50 32.4	+33.2	111.2	50 10.2	+34.5	112.3	10
11	52 46.1	+23.5	102.5	52 32.5	+25.1	103.7	52 17.6	+26.6	105.0	52 01.4	+28.1	106.2	51 44.0	+29.5	107.5	51 25.4	+30.9	108.7	51 05.6	+32.3	109.8	50 44.7	+33.6	111.0	11
12	53 09.6	+22.4	100.9	52 57.6	+23.9	102.2	52 44.2	+25.5	103.5	52 29.5	+27.0	104.8	52 13.5	+28.5	106.1	51 56.3	+29.9	107.3	51 37.9	+31.3	108.5	51 18.3	+32.7	109.7	12
13	53 32.0	+21.1	99.4	53 21.5	+22.8	100.7	53 09.7	+24.3	102.0	52 56.5	+25.9	103.3	52 42.0	+27.4	104.6	52 26.2	+28.9	105.9	52 09.2	+30.3	107.1	51 51.0	+31.7	108.3	13
14	53 53.1	+19.9	97.8	53 44.3	+21.5	99.2	53 34.0	+23.1	100.5	53 22.4	+24.7	101.8	53 09.4	+26.3	103.1	52 55.1	+27.8	104.4	52 39.5	+29.3	105.7	52 22.7	+30.7	106.9	14
15	54 13.0	+18.5	96.2	54 05.8	+20.2	97.6	53 57.1	+21.9	98.9	53 47.1	+23.5	100.3	53 35.7	+25.1	101.6	53 22.9	+26.7	102.9	53 08.8	+28.3	104.2	52 53.4	+29.7	105.5	15
16	54 31.5	+17.2	94.6	54 26.0	+18.9	96.0	54 19.0	+20.7	97.4	54 10.6	+22.3	98.7	54 00.8	+24.0	100.1	53 49.6	+25.6	101.4	53 37.1	+27.0	102.8	53 23.1	+28.6	104.1	16
17	54 48.7	+15.8	92.9	54 44.9	+17.6	94.3	54 39.7	+19.3	95.7	54 32.9	+21.0	97.1	54 24.8	+22.6	98.5	54 15.2	+24.3	99.9	54 04.1	+26.0	101.3	53 51.7	+27.6	102.6	17
18	55 04.5	+14.5	91.2	55 02.5	+16.2	92.7	54 59.0	+17.9	94.1	54 53.9	+19.7	95.5	54 47.4	+21.4	96.9	54 39.5	+23.1	98.3	54 30.1	+24.7	99.7	54 19.3	+26.3	101.1	18
19	55 19.0	+13.0	89.5	55 18.7	+14.8	91.0	55 16.9	+16.6	92.4	55 13.6	+18.4	93.9	55 08.8	+20.1	95.3	55 02.6	+21.8	96.7	54 54.8	+23.5	98.1	54 45.6	+25.1	99.5	19
20	55 32.0	+11.5	87.8	55 33.5	+13.3	89.3	55 33.5	+15.2	90.7	55 32.0	+16.9	92.2	55 28.9	+18.7	93.6	55 24.4	+20.4	95.1	55 18.3	+22.2	96.5	55 10.7	+23.9	98.0	20
21	55 43.5	+10.1	86.1	55 46.8	+11.9	87.5	55 48.7	+13.7	89.0	55 48.9	+15.5	90.5	55 47.6	+17.4	92.0	55 44.8	+19.1	93.4	55 40.5	+20.8	94.9	55 34.6	+22.6	96.3	21
22	55 53.6	+8.5	84.3	55 58.7	+10.4	85.8	56 02.4	+12.2	87.3	56 04.4	+14.1	88.8	56 05.0	+15.8	90.2	56 03.9	+17.7	91.7	56 01.3	+19.5	93.2	55 57.2	+21.2	94.7	22
23	56 02.1	+7.0	82.6	56 09.1	+8.9	84.0	56 14.6	+10.7	85.5	56 18.5	+12.5	87.0	56 20.8	+14.4	88.5	56 21.6	+16.2	90.0	56 20.8	+18.0	91.5	56 18.4	+19.9	93.0	23
24	56 09.1	+5.5	80.8	56 18.0	+7.3	82.3	56 25.3	+9.2	83.7	56 31.0	+11.1	85.2	56 35.2	+12.9	86.8	56 37.8	+14.8	88.3	56 38.8	+16.6	89.8	56 38.3	+18.4	91.3	24
25	56 14.6	+3.9	79.0	56 25.3	+5.7	80.5	56 34.5	+7.6	82.0	56 42.1	+9.5	83.5	56 48.1	+11.4	85.0	56 52.6	+13.2	86.5	56 55.4	+15.1	88.0	56 56.7	+16.9	89.6	25
26	56 18.5	+2.3	77.2	56 31.0	+4.2	78.7	56 42.1	+6.0	80.1	56 51.6	+7.9	81.7	56 59.5	+9.8	83.2	57 05.8	+11.7	84.7	57 10.5	+13.6	86.3	57 13.6	+15.5	87.8	26
27	56 20.8	+0.8	75.4	56 35.2	+2.6	76.8	56 48.1	+4.5	78.3	56 59.5	+6.3	79.8	57 09.3	+8.2	81.4	57 17.5	+10.1	82.9	57 24.1	+12.0	84.5	57 29.1	+13.9	86.0	27
28	56 21.6	−0.8	73.6	56 37.8	+1.0	75.0	56 52.6	+2.8	76.5	57 05.8	+4.7	78.0	57 17.5	+6.6	79.5	57 27.6	+8.5	81.1	57 36.1	+10.4	82.6	57 43.0	+12.3	84.2	28
29	56 20.8	−2.4	71.8	56 38.8	−0.5	73.2	56 55.4	+1.3	74.7	57 10.5	+3.1	76.2	57 24.1	+5.0	77.7	57 36.1	+6.9	79.2	57 46.5	+8.8	80.8	57 55.3	+10.7	82.4	29
30	56 18.4	−3.9	70.0	56 38.3	−2.2	71.4	56 56.7	−0.4	72.8	57 13.6	+1.5	74.3	57 29.1	+3.3	75.8	57 43.0	+5.2	77.4	57 55.3	+7.2	78.9	58 06.0	+9.1	80.5	30
31	56 14.5	−5.5	68.2	56 36.1	−3.7	69.6	56 56.3	−1.9	71.0	57 15.1	−0.1	72.5	57 32.4	+1.8	74.0	57 48.2	+3.6	75.5	58 02.5	+5.5	77.1	58 15.1	+7.4	78.6	31
32	56 09.0	−7.1	66.4	56 32.4	−5.4	67.8	56 54.4	−3.6	69.2	57 15.0	−1.8	70.6	57 34.2	0.0	72.1	57 51.8	+2.0	73.6	58 08.0	+3.8	75.2	58 22.5	+5.8	76.7	32
33	56 01.9	−8.5	64.6	56 27.0	−6.8	66.0	56 50.8	−5.1	67.4	57 13.2	−3.4	68.8	57 34.2	−1.6	70.3	57 53.8	+0.2	71.7	58 11.8	+2.1	73.3	58 28.3	+4.0	74.8	33
34	55 53.4	−10.1	62.8	56 20.2	−8.5	64.2	56 45.7	−6.8	65.5	57 09.8	−5.0	66.9	57 32.6	−3.2	68.4	57 54.0	−1.4	69.9	58 13.9	+0.5	71.4	58 32.3	+2.3	72.9	34
35	55 43.3	−11.6	61.1	56 11.7	−9.9	62.4	56 38.9	−8.3	63.7	57 04.8	−6.6	65.1	57 29.4	−4.9	66.5	57 52.6	−3.1	68.0	58 14.4	−1.3	69.5	58 34.6	+0.7	71.0	35
36	55 31.7	−13.0	59.3	56 01.8	−11.5	60.6	56 30.6	−9.8	61.9	56 58.2	−8.2	63.3	57 24.5	−6.4	64.7	57 49.5	−4.7	66.1	58 13.1	−2.9	67.6	58 35.3	−1.1	69.1	36
37	55 18.7	−14.4	57.6	55 50.3	−12.9	58.9	56 20.8	−11.4	60.1	56 50.0	−9.7	61.5	57 18.1	−8.1	62.8	57 44.8	−6.4	64.2	58 10.2	−4.6	65.7	58 34.2	−2.8	67.2	37
38	55 04.3	−15.9	55.9	55 37.4	−14.4	57.1	56 09.4	−12.9	58.4	56 40.3	−11.3	59.7	57 10.0	−9.7	61.0	57 38.4	−8.0	62.4	58 05.6	−6.3	63.8	58 31.4	−4.5	65.3	38
39	54 48.4	−17.2	54.2	55 23.0	−15.8	55.4	55 56.5	−14.3	56.6	56 29.0	−12.9	57.9	57 00.3	−11.3	59.2	57 30.4	−9.6	60.5	57 59.3	−7.9	61.9	58 26.9	−6.2	63.4	39
40	54 31.2	−18.6	52.6	55 07.2	−17.3	53.7	55 42.2	−15.8	54.9	56 16.1	−14.3	56.1	56 49.0	−12.7	57.4	57 20.8	−11.2	58.7	57 51.4	−9.6	60.1	58 20.7	−7.9	61.5	40
41	54 12.6	−19.9	51.0	54 49.9	−18.5	52.1	55 26.4	−17.2	53.2	56 01.8	−15.7	54.4	56 36.3	−14.3	55.6	57 09.6	−12.8	56.9	57 41.8	−11.2	58.2	58 12.8	−9.5	59.6	41
42	53 52.7	−21.1	49.3	54 31.4	−19.9	50.4	55 09.2	−18.6	51.5	55 46.1	−17.2	52.7	56 22.0	−15.8	53.8	56 56.8	−14.2	55.1	57 30.6	−12.7	56.4	58 03.3	−11.2	57.7	42
43	53 31.6	−22.4	47.8	54 11.5	−21.1	48.8	54 50.6	−19.9	49.9	55 28.9	−18.6	51.0	56 06.2	−17.2	52.1	56 42.6	−15.8	53.3	57 17.9	−14.3	54.6	57 52.1	−12.7	55.8	43
44	53 09.2	−23.5	46.2	53 50.4	−22.4	47.2	54 30.7	−21.1	48.2	55 10.3	−19.9	49.3	55 49.0	−18.6	50.4	56 26.8	−17.3	51.6	57 03.6	−15.8	52.8	57 39.4	−14.4	54.0	44
45	52 45.7	−24.8	44.7	53 28.0	−23.6	45.6	54 09.6	−22.5	46.6	54 50.4	−21.3	47.6	55 30.4	−20.0	48.7	56 09.5	−18.6	49.8	56 47.8	−17.3	51.0	57 25.0	−15.8	52.2	45
46	52 20.9	−25.8	43.2	53 04.4	−24.8	44.1	53 47.1	−23.7	45.0	54 29.1	−22.5	46.0	55 10.4	−21.3	47.1	55 50.9	−20.1	48.1	56 30.5	−18.7	49.3	57 09.2	−17.4	50.4	46
47	51 55.1	−26.9	41.7	52 39.6	−25.9	42.6	53 23.4	−24.8	43.5	54 06.6	−23.7	44.4	54 49.1	−22.6	45.4	55 30.8	−21.4	46.5	56 11.8	−20.2	47.5	56 51.8	−18.8	48.7	47
48	51 28.2	−28.0	40.3	52 13.7	−27.0	41.1	52 58.6	−26.0	42.0	53 42.9	−24.9	42.9	54 26.5	−23.8	43.8	55 09.4	−22.6	44.8	55 51.6	−21.5	45.9	56 33.0	−20.2	46.9	48
49	51 00.2	−28.9	38.9	51 46.7	−28.0	39.7	52 32.6	−27.1	40.5	53 18.0	−26.1	41.3	54 02.7	−25.1	42.3	54 46.8	−24.0	43.2	55 30.1	−22.8	44.2	56 12.8	−21.6	45.2	49
50	50 31.3	−29.9	37.5	51 18.7	−29.1	38.2	52 05.5	−28.1	39.0	52 51.9	−27.2	39.8	53 37.6	−26.2	40.7	54 22.8	−25.1	41.6	55 07.3	−24.0	42.6	55 51.2	−23.0	43.6	50
51	50 01.4	−30.9	36.1	50 49.6	−30.0	36.8	51 37.4	−29.2	37.6	52 24.7	−28.3	38.4	53 11.4	−27.3	39.2	53 57.7	−26.4	40.1	54 43.3	−25.3	41.0	55 28.2	−24.2	41.9	51
52	49 30.5	−31.7	34.8	50 19.6	−31.0	35.5	51 08.2	−30.1	36.2	51 56.4	−29.3	36.9	52 44.1	−28.4	37.7	53 31.3	−27.5	38.6	54 18.0	−26.5	39.4	55 04.0	−25.5	40.3	52
53	48 58.8	−32.6	33.5	49 48.6	−31.8	34.1	50 38.1	−31.1	34.8	51 27.1	−30.3	35.5	52 15.7	−29.4	36.3	53 03.8	−28.5	37.1	53 51.5	−27.7	37.9	54 38.5	−26.6	38.7	53
54	48 26.2	−33.5	32.2	49 16.8	−32.8	32.8	50 07.0	−32.0	33.5	50 56.8	−31.2	34.2	51 46.3	−30.5	34.9	52 35.3	−29.6	35.6	53 23.8	−28.7	36.4	54 11.9	−27.8	37.2	54
55	47 52.7	−34.2	31.0	48 44.0	−33.5	31.6	49 35.0	−32.9	32.2	50 25.6	−32.1	32.8	51 15.8	−31.4	33.5	52 05.7	−30.6	34.2	52 55.1	−29.8	34.9	53 44.1	−29.0	35.7	55
56	47 18.5	−34.9	29.8	48 10.5	−34.4	30.3	49 02.1	−33.7	30.9	49 53.5	−33.1	31.5	50 44.4	−32.3	32.1	51 35.1	−31.6	32.8	52 25.3	−30.8	33.5	53 15.1	−29.9	34.2	56
57	46 43.6	−35.7	28.6	47 36.1	−35.1	29.1	48 28.4	−34.5	29.6	49 20.4	−33.8	30.2	50 12.1	−33.2	30.8	51 03.5	−32.5	31.4	51 54.5	−31.8	32.1	52 45.2	−31.1	32.8	57
58	46 07.9	−36.4	27.4	47 01.0	−35.8	27.9	47 53.9	−35.2	28.4	48 46.6	−34.7	28.9	49 38.9	−34.0	29.5	50 31.0	−33.4	30.1	51 22.7	−32.7	30.7	52 14.1	−31.9	31.4	58
59	45 31.5	−37.1	26.3	46 25.2	−36.6	26.7	47 18.7	−36.0	27.2	48 11.9	−35.4	27.7	49 04.9	−34.9	28.2	49 57.6	−34.2	28.8	50 50.0	−33.6	29.4	51 42.2	−33.0	30.0	59
60	44 54.4	−37.7	25.1	45 48.6	−37.2	25.6	46 42.7	−36.8	26.0	47 36.5	−36.2	26.5	48 30.0	−35.6	27.0	49 23.4	−35.1	27.5	50 16.4	−34.4	28.1	51 09.2	−33.8	28.7	60
61	44 16.7	−38.3	24.0	45 11.4	−37.8	24.5	46 05.9	−37.3	24.9	47 00.3	−36.9	25.3	47 54.4	−36.4	25.8	48 48.3	−35.8	26.3	49 42.0	−35.3	26.8	50 35.4	−34.7	27.4	61
62	43 38.4	−38.9	23.0	44 33.6	−38.5	23.4	45 28.6	−38.1	23.8	46 23.4	−37.6	24.2	47 18.0	−37.0	24.6	48 12.5	−36.6	25.1	49 06.7	−36.0	25.6	50 00.7	−35.5	26.1	62
63	42 59.5	−39.4	21.9	43 55.1	−39.1	22.3	44 50.5	−38.6	22.7	45 45.8	−38.2	23.1	46 41.0	−37.8	23.5	47 35.9	−37.3	23.9	48 30.7	−36.8	24.4	49 25.2	−36.3	24.8	63
64	42 20.1	−40.0	20.9	43 16.0	−39.6	21.2	44 11.9	−39.2	21.6	45 07.6	−38.8	22.0	46 03.2	−38.4	22.3	46 58.6	−38.0	22.7	47 53.9	−37.6	23.2	48 48.9	−37.0	23.6	64
65	41 40.1	−40.5	19.9	42 36.4	−40.1	20.2	43 32.7	−39.8	20.5	44 28.8	−39.4	20.9	45 24.8	−39.0	21.2	46 20.6	−38.6	21.6	47 16.3	−38.2	22.0	48 11.9	−37.8	22.4	65
66	40 59.6	−41.0	18.9	41 56.3	−40.7	19.2	42 52.9	−40.4	19.5	43 49.4	−40.0	19.8	44 45.8	−39.7	20.2	45 42.0	−39.2	20.5	46 38.1	−38.8	20.9	47 34.1	−38.4	21.3	66
67	40 18.6	−41.5	18.0	41 15.6	−41.2	18.2	42 12.5	−40.8	18.5	43 09.4	−40.5	18.8	44 06.1	−40.2	19.1	45 02.8	−39.9	19.4	45 59.3	−39.5	19.8	46 55.7	−39.1	20.1	67
68	39 37.1	−41.9	17.0	40 34.4	−41.6	17.3	41 31.7	−41.3	17.5	42 28.9	−41.1	17.8	43 25.9	−40.7	18.1	44 22.9	−40.4	18.4	45 19.8	−40.0	18.7	46 16.6	−39.7	19.0	68
69	38 55.2	−42.4	16.1	39 52.8	−42.1	16.3	40 50.4	−41.9	16.6	41 47.8	−41.5	16.8	42 45.2	−41.2	17.1	43 42.5	−40.9	17.4	44 39.8	−40.7	17.7	45 36.9	−40.3	18.0	69
70	38 12.8	−42.7	15.2	39 10.7	−42.5	15.4	40 08.5	−42.2	15.6	41 06.3	−42.0	15.9	42 04.0	−41.8	16.1	43 01.6	−41.5	16.4	43 59.1	−41.2	16.6	44 56.6	−40.9	16.9	70
71	37 30.1	−43.1	14.3	38 28.2	−42.9	14.5	39 26.3	−42.7	14.7	40 24.3	−42.5	14.9	41 22.2	−42.2	15.1	42 20.1	−41.9	15.4	43 17.9	−41.6	15.6	44 15.7	−41.4	15.9	71
72	36 47.0	−43.6	13.4	37 45.3	−43.3	13.6	38 43.6	−43.1	13.8	39 41.8	−42.8	14.0	40 40.0	−42.6	14.2	41 38.2	−42.5	14.4	42 36.3	−42.2	14.6	43 34.3	−42.0	14.9	72
73	36 03.4	−43.8	12.6	37 02.0	−43.7	12.7	38 00.5	−43.5	12.9	38 59.0	−43.3	13.1	39 57.4	−43.1	13.3	40 55.7	−42.8	13.5	41 54.1	−42.7	13.7	42 52.3	−42.4	13.9	73
74	35 19.6	−44.3	11.7	36 18.3	−44.0	11.9	37 17.0	−43.9	12.0	38 15.7	−43.7	12.2	39 14.3	−43.5	12.4	40 12.9	−43.3	12.5	41 11.4	−43.1	12.7	42 09.9	−42.9	12.9	74
75	34 35.3	−44.5	10.9	35 34.3	−44.4	11.0	36 33.1	−44.2	11.2	37 32.0	−44.1	11.3	38 30.8	−43.9	11.5	39 29.6	−43.7	11.6	40 28.3	−43.5	11.8	41 27.0	−43.3	12.0	75
76	33 50.8	−44.9	10.1	34 49.9	−44.8	10.2	35 48.9	−44.6	10.3	36 47.9	−44.4	10.5	37 46.9	−44.3	10.6	38 45.9	−44.1	10.8	39 44.8	−43.9	10.9	40 43.7	−43.8	11.1	76
77	33 05.9	−45.1	9.3	34 05.1	−45.0	9.4	35 04.3	−44.9	9.5	36 03.5	−44.8	9.6	37 02.6	−44.6	9.8	38 01.8	−44.5	9.9	39 00.9	−44.4	10.0	39 59.9	−44.2	10.2	77
78	32 20.8	−45.4	8.5	33 20.1	−45.3	8.6	34 19.4	−45.2	8.7	35 18.7	−45.0	8.8	36 18.0	−44.9	8.9	37 17.3	−44.8	9.0	38 16.5	−44.7	9.2	39 15.7	−44.5	9.3	78
79	31 35.4	−45.8	7.7	32 34.8	−45.6	7.8	33 34.2	−45.5	7.9	34 33.7	−45.4	8.0	35 33.1	−45.3	8.1	36 32.5	−45.2	8.2	37 31.8	−45.0	8.3	38 31.2	−44.9	8.4	79
80	30 49.6	−45.9	7.0	31 49.2	−45.9	7.1	32 48.7	−45.8	7.1	33 48.3	−45.7	7.2	34 47.8	−45.6	7.3	35 47.3	−45.5	7.4	36 46.8	−45.4	7.5	37 46.3	−45.3	7.6	80
81	30 03.7	−46.3	6.2	31 03.3	−46.1	6.3	32 02.9	−46.0	6.4	33 02.6	−46.0	6.4	34 02.2	−45.9	6.5	35 01.8	−45.8	6.6	36 01.4	−45.7	6.7	37 01.0	−45.7	6.8	81
82	29 17.4	−46.4	5.5	30 17.2	−46.4	5.6	31 16.9	−46.3	5.6	32 16.6	−46.3	5.7	33 16.3	−46.2	5.7	34 16.0	−46.1	5.8	35 15.7	−46.1	5.9	36 15.3	−45.9	6.0	82
83	28 31.0	−46.7	4.8	29 30.8	−46.7	4.8	30 30.6	−46.6	4.9	31 30.3	−46.5	4.9	32 30.1	−46.4	5.0	33 29.9	−46.4	5.0	34 29.6	−46.3	5.1	35 29.4	−46.2	5.2	83
84	27 44.3	−46.9	4.1	28 44.1	−46.8	4.1	29 44.0	−46.8	4.2	30 43.8	−46.7	4.2	31 43.7	−46.7	4.2	32 43.5	−46.6	4.3	33 43.3	−46.6	4.3	34 43.2	−46.6	4.4	84
85	26 57.4	−47.1	3.4	27 57.3	−47.1	3.4	28 57.2	−47.0	3.4	29 57.1	−47.0	3.5	30 57.0	−47.0	3.5	31 56.9	−46.9	3.5	32 56.7	−46.8	3.6	33 56.6	−46.8	3.6	85
86	26 10.3	−47.3	2.7	27 10.2	−47.2	2.7	28 10.2	−47.3	2.7	29 10.1	−47.2	2.8	30 10.0	−47.2	2.8	31 10.0	−47.2	2.8	32 09.9	−47.1	2.8	33 09.8	−47.1	2.9	86
87	25 23.0	−47.5	2.0	26 23.0	−47.5	2.0	27 22.9	−47.4	2.0	28 22.9	−47.4	2.1	29 22.8	−47.4	2.1	30 22.8	−47.4	2.1	31 22.8	−47.4	2.1	32 22.7	−47.3	2.1	87
88	24 35.5	−47.7	1.3	25 35.5	−47.7	1.3	26 35.5	−47.7	1.3	27 35.5	−47.7	1.4	28 35.4	−47.6	1.4	29 35.4	−47.6	1.4	30 35.4	−47.6	1.4	31 35.4	−47.6	1.4	88
89	23 47.8	−47.8	0.7	24 47.8	−47.8	0.7	25 47.8	−47.8	0.7	26 47.8	−47.8	0.7	27 47.8	−47.8	0.7	28 47.8	−47.8	0.7	29 47.8	−47.8	0.7	30 47.8	−47.8	0.7	89
90	23 00.0	−48.0	0.0	24 00.0	−48.0	0.0	25 00.0	−48.0	0.0	26 00.0	−48.0	0.0	27 00.0	−48.0	0.0	28 00.0	−48.0	0.0	29 00.0	−48.0	0.0	30 00.0	−48.0	0.0	90
	23°			24°			25°			26°			27°			28°			29°			30°			

37°, 323° L.H.A. LATITUDE SAME NAME AS DECLINATION

258

LATITUDE CONTRARY NAME TO DECLINATION L.H.A. 37°, 323°

Dec.	23°			24°			25°			26°			27°			28°			29°			30°			Dec.
	Hc	d	Z	Hc	d	Z	Hc	d	Z	Hc	d	Z	Hc	d	Z	Hc	d	Z	Hc	d	Z	Hc	d	Z	
°	° ′	′	°	° ′	′	°	° ′	′	°	° ′	′	°	° ′	′	°	° ′	′	°	° ′	′	°	° ′	′	°	°
0	47 19.2	-35.0	117.4	46 51.1	-36.0	118.4	46 22.2	-37.1	119.3	45 52.4	-38.1	120.2	45 21.9	-39.1	121.1	44 50.5	-40.0	121.9	44 18.4	-40.9	122.8	43 45.6	-41.8	123.6	0
1	46 44.2	-35.7	118.6	46 15.1	-36.8	119.5	45 45.1	-37.7	120.4	45 14.3	-38.7	121.3	44 42.8	-39.7	122.1	44 10.5	-40.6	123.0	43 37.5	-41.5	123.8	43 03.8	-42.3	124.6	1
2	46 08.5	-36.3	119.8	45 38.3	-37.3	120.7	45 07.4	-38.4	121.5	44 35.6	-39.3	122.4	44 03.1	-40.2	123.2	43 29.9	-41.1	124.0	42 56.0	-41.9	124.8	42 21.5	-42.8	125.5	2
3	45 32.2	-37.1	120.9	45 01.0	-38.1	121.8	44 29.0	-39.0	122.6	43 56.3	-39.9	123.4	43 22.9	-40.8	124.2	42 48.8	-41.6	125.0	42 14.1	-42.4	125.7	41 38.7	-43.2	126.5	3
4	44 55.1	-37.7	122.0	44 22.9	-38.6	122.9	43 50.0	-39.5	123.7	43 16.4	-40.4	124.5	42 42.1	-41.3	125.2	42 07.2	-42.1	126.0	41 31.7	-42.9	126.7	40 55.5	-43.6	127.4	4
5	44 17.4	-38.3	123.1	43 44.3	-39.2	123.9	43 10.5	-40.1	124.7	42 36.0	-41.0	125.5	42 00.8	-41.7	126.2	41 25.1	-42.6	126.9	40 48.8	-43.4	127.6	40 11.9	-44.1	128.3	5
6	43 39.1	-38.9	124.2	43 05.1	-39.8	125.0	42 30.4	-40.7	125.7	41 55.0	-41.4	126.5	41 19.1	-42.3	127.2	40 42.5	-43.0	127.9	40 05.4	-43.7	128.5	39 27.8	-44.5	129.2	6
7	43 00.2	-39.4	125.2	42 25.3	-40.3	126.0	41 49.7	-41.1	126.7	41 13.6	-41.9	127.4	40 36.8	-42.7	128.1	39 59.5	-43.4	128.8	39 21.7	-44.1	129.4	38 43.3	-44.8	130.0	7
8	42 20.8	-40.0	126.3	41 45.0	-40.8	127.0	41 08.6	-41.6	127.7	40 31.7	-42.4	128.4	39 54.1	-43.1	129.0	39 16.1	-43.8	129.7	38 37.6	-44.6	130.3	37 58.5	-45.2	130.9	8
9	41 40.8	-40.5	127.3	41 04.2	-41.3	128.0	40 27.0	-42.1	128.6	39 49.3	-42.8	129.3	39 11.0	-43.5	129.9	38 32.3	-44.3	130.5	37 53.0	-44.9	131.1	37 13.3	-45.5	131.7	9
10	41 00.3	-41.0	128.2	40 22.9	-41.8	128.9	39 44.9	-42.5	129.6	39 06.5	-43.3	130.2	38 27.5	-43.9	130.8	37 48.0	-44.5	131.4	37 08.1	-45.2	132.0	36 27.8	-45.9	132.5	10
11	40 19.3	-41.4	129.2	39 41.1	-42.2	129.9	39 02.4	-42.9	130.5	38 23.2	-43.6	131.1	37 43.6	-44.3	131.7	37 03.5	-45.0	132.2	36 22.9	-45.6	132.8	35 41.9	-46.1	133.3	11
12	39 37.9	-41.9	130.2	38 58.9	-42.6	130.8	38 19.5	-43.3	131.4	37 39.6	-44.0	132.0	36 59.3	-44.7	132.5	36 18.5	-45.3	133.1	35 37.3	-45.8	133.6	34 55.8	-46.5	134.1	12
13	38 56.0	-42.4	131.1	38 16.3	-43.0	131.7	37 36.2	-43.7	132.3	36 55.6	-44.3	132.8	36 14.6	-44.9	133.4	35 33.2	-45.5	133.9	34 51.5	-46.2	134.4	34 09.3	-46.7	134.9	13
14	38 13.6	-42.7	132.0	37 33.3	-43.4	132.6	36 52.5	-44.1	133.1	36 11.3	-44.7	133.7	35 29.7	-45.4	134.2	34 47.7	-45.9	134.7	34 05.3	-46.5	135.2	33 22.6	-47.0	135.6	14
15	37 30.9	-43.1	132.9	36 49.9	-43.8	133.4	36 08.4	-44.4	134.0	35 26.6	-45.1	134.5	34 44.3	-45.6	135.0	34 01.8	-46.2	135.5	33 18.8	-46.7	135.9	32 35.6	-47.3	136.4	15
16	36 47.8	-43.5	133.7	36 06.1	-44.2	134.3	35 24.0	-44.8	134.8	34 41.5	-45.3	135.3	33 58.7	-45.9	135.8	33 15.6	-46.5	136.2	32 32.1	-47.0	136.7	31 48.3	-47.5	137.1	16
17	36 04.3	-43.9	134.6	35 21.9	-44.4	135.1	34 39.2	-45.0	135.6	33 56.2	-45.6	136.1	33 12.8	-46.2	136.5	32 29.1	-46.7	137.0	31 45.1	-47.3	137.4	31 00.8	-47.8	137.8	17
18	35 20.4	-44.2	135.4	34 37.5	-44.8	135.9	33 54.2	-45.4	136.4	33 10.6	-46.0	136.9	32 26.6	-46.4	137.3	31 42.4	-47.0	137.7	30 57.8	-47.4	138.1	30 13.0	-47.9	138.5	18
19	34 36.2	-44.6	136.3	33 52.7	-45.2	136.7	33 08.8	-45.7	137.2	32 24.6	-46.2	137.6	31 40.2	-46.8	138.0	30 55.4	-47.2	138.4	30 10.4	-47.7	138.8	29 25.1	-48.2	139.2	19
20	33 51.6	-44.8	137.1	33 07.5	-45.4	137.5	32 23.1	-45.9	138.0	31 38.4	-46.4	138.4	30 53.4	-46.9	138.8	30 08.2	-47.5	139.2	29 22.7	-48.0	139.5	28 36.9	-48.4	139.9	20
21	33 06.8	-45.2	137.9	32 22.1	-45.6	138.3	31 37.2	-46.2	138.7	30 52.0	-46.7	139.1	30 06.5	-47.2	139.5	29 20.7	-47.6	139.9	28 34.7	-48.1	140.2	27 48.5	-48.6	140.6	21
22	32 21.6	-45.4	138.7	31 36.5	-46.0	139.1	30 51.0	-46.5	139.5	30 05.3	-47.0	139.8	29 19.3	-47.4	140.2	28 33.1	-47.9	140.6	27 46.6	-48.3	140.9	26 59.9	-48.7	141.2	22
23	31 36.2	-45.7	139.4	30 50.5	-46.2	139.8	30 04.5	-46.7	140.2	29 18.3	-47.2	140.6	28 31.9	-47.7	140.9	27 45.2	-48.1	141.2	26 58.3	-48.5	141.6	26 11.2	-49.0	141.9	23
24	30 50.5	-46.0	140.2	30 04.3	-46.5	140.5	29 17.8	-46.9	140.9	28 31.1	-47.4	141.3	27 44.2	-47.8	141.6	26 57.1	-48.3	141.9	26 09.8	-48.7	142.2	25 22.2	-49.0	142.5	24
25	30 04.5	-46.2	140.9	29 17.8	-46.7	141.3	28 30.9	-47.2	141.6	27 43.7	-47.5	142.0	26 56.4	-48.0	142.3	26 08.8	-48.4	142.6	25 21.1	-48.9	142.9	24 33.2	-49.3	143.2	25
26	29 18.3	-46.4	141.7	28 31.1	-46.9	142.0	27 43.7	-47.3	142.3	26 56.2	-47.8	142.6	26 08.4	-48.2	142.9	25 20.4	-48.6	143.2	24 32.2	-49.0	143.5	23 43.9	-49.4	143.8	26
27	28 31.9	-46.7	142.4	27 44.2	-47.1	142.7	26 56.4	-47.6	143.0	26 08.4	-48.0	143.3	25 20.2	-48.4	143.6	24 31.8	-48.8	143.9	23 43.2	-49.2	144.1	22 54.5	-49.5	144.4	27
28	27 45.2	-46.9	143.1	26 57.1	-47.3	143.4	26 08.8	-47.7	143.7	25 20.4	-48.2	144.0	24 31.8	-48.6	144.3	23 43.0	-49.0	144.5	22 54.0	-49.3	144.8	22 05.0	-49.7	145.0	28
29	26 58.3	-47.1	143.8	26 09.8	-47.6	144.1	25 21.1	-47.9	144.4	24 32.2	-48.3	144.6	23 43.2	-48.7	144.9	22 54.0	-49.0	145.2	22 04.7	-49.4	145.4	21 15.3	-49.8	145.6	29
30	26 11.2	-47.3	144.5	25 22.2	-47.7	144.8	24 33.2	-48.1	145.0	23 43.9	-48.5	145.3	22 54.5	-48.9	145.5	22 05.0	-49.3	145.8	21 15.3	-49.6	146.0	20 25.5	-49.9	146.2	30
31	25 23.9	-47.5	145.2	24 34.5	-47.8	145.4	23 45.1	-48.3	145.7	22 55.4	-48.6	145.9	22 05.6	-49.0	146.2	21 15.7	-49.3	146.4	20 25.7	-49.7	146.6	19 35.6	-50.1	146.8	31
32	24 36.4	-47.7	145.9	23 46.7	-48.1	146.1	22 56.8	-48.4	146.3	22 06.8	-48.8	146.6	21 16.6	-49.1	146.8	20 26.4	-49.5	147.0	19 36.0	-49.8	147.2	18 45.5	-50.1	147.4	32
33	23 48.7	-47.8	146.5	22 58.6	-48.2	146.8	22 08.4	-48.6	147.0	21 18.0	-48.9	147.2	20 27.5	-49.3	147.4	19 36.9	-49.6	147.6	18 46.2	-49.9	147.8	17 55.4	-50.3	148.0	33
34	23 00.9	-48.0	147.2	22 10.4	-48.3	147.4	21 19.8	-48.7	147.6	20 29.1	-49.1	147.8	19 38.2	-49.3	148.0	18 47.3	-49.7	148.2	17 56.3	-50.1	148.4	17 05.1	-50.3	148.5	34
35	22 12.9	-48.1	147.8	21 22.1	-48.5	148.0	20 31.1	-48.8	148.2	19 40.0	-49.1	148.4	18 48.9	-49.5	148.6	17 57.6	-49.8	148.8	17 06.2	-50.1	148.9	16 14.8	-50.4	149.1	35
36	21 24.8	-48.3	148.5	20 33.6	-48.7	148.7	19 42.3	-49.0	148.9	18 50.9	-49.3	149.0	17 59.4	-49.7	149.2	17 07.8	-49.9	149.4	16 16.1	-50.2	149.5	15 24.4	-50.6	149.7	36
37	20 36.5	-48.5	149.1	19 44.9	-48.7	149.3	18 53.3	-49.1	149.5	18 01.6	-49.4	149.6	17 09.7	-49.7	149.8	16 17.9	-50.1	150.0	15 25.9	-50.3	150.1	14 33.8	-50.6	150.2	37
38	19 48.0	-48.5	149.7	18 56.2	-48.9	149.9	18 04.2	-49.2	150.1	17 12.2	-49.5	150.2	16 20.0	-49.8	150.4	15 27.8	-50.1	150.5	14 35.6	-50.4	150.7	13 43.2	-50.6	150.8	38
39	18 59.5	-48.7	150.4	18 07.3	-49.0	150.5	17 15.0	-49.3	150.7	16 22.7	-49.6	150.8	15 30.2	-49.9	151.0	14 37.7	-50.1	151.1	13 45.2	-50.5	151.2	12 52.6	-50.8	151.3	39
40	18 10.8	-48.8	151.0	17 18.3	-49.1	151.1	16 25.7	-49.4	151.3	15 33.1	-49.7	151.4	14 40.3	-49.9	151.5	13 47.6	-50.3	151.7	12 54.7	-50.5	151.8	12 01.8	-50.8	151.9	40
41	17 22.0	-48.9	151.6	16 29.2	-49.2	151.7	15 36.3	-49.5	151.9	14 43.4	-49.8	152.0	13 50.4	-50.1	152.1	12 57.3	-50.3	152.2	12 04.2	-50.6	152.3	11 11.0	-50.8	152.4	41
42	16 33.1	-49.0	152.2	15 40.0	-49.3	152.3	14 46.8	-49.6	152.4	13 53.6	-49.9	152.6	13 00.3	-50.1	152.7	12 07.0	-50.4	152.8	11 13.6	-50.7	152.9	10 20.2	-50.9	153.0	42
43	15 44.1	-49.2	152.8	14 50.7	-49.4	152.9	13 57.2	-49.7	153.0	13 03.7	-49.9	153.1	12 10.2	-50.2	153.2	11 16.6	-50.5	153.3	10 22.9	-50.7	153.4	9 29.3	-51.0	153.5	43
44	14 54.9	-49.2	153.4	14 01.3	-49.5	153.5	13 07.5	-49.7	153.6	12 13.8	-50.0	153.7	11 20.0	-50.3	153.8	10 26.1	-50.5	153.9	9 32.2	-50.7	154.0	8 38.3	-51.0	154.0	44
45	14 05.7	-49.3	154.0	13 11.8	-49.6	154.1	12 17.8	-49.8	154.2	11 23.8	-50.1	154.3	10 29.7	-50.3	154.4	9 35.6	-50.6	154.4	8 41.5	-50.9	154.5	7 47.3	-51.1	154.6	45
46	13 16.4	-49.3	154.6	12 22.2	-49.6	154.7	11 28.0	-49.9	154.7	10 33.7	-50.1	154.8	9 39.4	-50.4	154.9	8 45.0	-50.6	155.0	7 50.6	-50.8	155.0	6 56.2	-51.0	155.1	46
47	12 27.1	-49.5	155.1	11 32.6	-49.6	155.2	10 38.1	-49.9	155.3	9 43.6	-50.2	155.4	8 49.0	-50.4	155.5	7 54.4	-50.6	155.5	6 59.8	-50.9	155.6	6 05.2	-51.2	155.6	47
48	11 37.6	-49.5	155.7	10 42.9	-49.7	155.8	9 48.2	-50.0	155.9	8 53.4	-50.2	155.9	7 58.6	-50.5	156.0	7 03.8	-50.7	156.1	6 08.9	-50.9	156.1	5 14.0	-51.1	156.1	48
49	10 48.1	-49.6	156.3	9 53.2	-49.9	156.4	8 58.2	-50.1	156.4	8 03.2	-50.3	156.5	7 08.1	-50.5	156.6	6 13.1	-50.8	156.6	5 18.0	-51.0	156.6	4 22.9	-51.2	156.7	49
50	9 58.5	-49.6	156.9	9 03.3	-49.8	156.9	8 08.1	-50.1	157.0	7 12.9	-50.3	157.1	6 17.6	-50.5	157.1	5 22.3	-50.7	157.1	4 27.0	-50.9	157.2	3 31.7	-51.1	157.2	50
51	9 08.9	-49.7	157.4	8 13.5	-49.9	157.5	7 18.0	-50.1	157.6	6 22.6	-50.4	157.6	5 27.1	-50.6	157.6	4 31.6	-50.8	157.7	3 36.1	-51.0	157.7	2 40.6	-51.2	157.7	51
52	8 19.2	-49.7	158.0	7 23.6	-50.0	158.1	6 27.9	-50.2	158.1	5 32.2	-50.4	158.1	4 36.5	-50.6	158.2	3 40.8	-50.8	158.2	2 45.1	-51.0	158.2	1 49.4	-51.2	158.2	52
53	7 29.5	-49.8	158.6	6 33.6	-50.0	158.6	5 37.7	-50.2	158.7	4 41.8	-50.4	158.7	3 45.9	-50.6	158.7	2 50.0	-50.8	158.7	1 54.1	-51.0	158.8	0 58.2	-51.2	158.8	53
54	6 39.7	-49.8	159.1	5 43.6	-50.0	159.2	4 47.5	-50.2	159.2	3 51.4	-50.4	159.2	2 55.3	-50.6	159.3	1 59.2	-50.8	159.3	1 03.1	-51.0	159.3	0 07.0	-51.2	159.3	54
55	5 49.9	-49.9	159.7	4 53.6	-50.1	159.7	3 57.3	-50.3	159.8	3 01.0	-50.4	159.8	2 04.7	-50.6	159.8	1 08.4	-50.8	159.8	0 12.1	-51.0	159.8	0 44.2	+51.2	20.2	55
56	5 00.0	-49.9	160.3	4 03.5	-50.0	160.3	3 07.0	-50.2	160.3	2 10.6	-50.5	160.3	1 14.1	-50.7	160.3	0 17.6	-50.9	160.3	0 38.9	+51.1	19.7	1 35.4	+51.2	19.7	56
57	4 10.1	-49.9	160.8	3 13.5	-50.1	160.8	2 16.8	-50.3	160.9	1 20.1	-50.5	160.9	0 23.4	-50.6	160.9	0 33.3	+50.8	19.1	1 30.0	+51.0	19.1	2 26.6	+51.2	19.2	57
58	3 20.2	-49.9	161.4	2 23.4	-50.1	161.4	1 26.5	-50.3	161.4	0 29.6	-50.4	161.4	0 27.2	+50.7	18.6	1 24.1	+50.8	18.6	2 21.0	+51.0	18.6	3 17.8	+51.2	18.6	58
59	2 30.3	-49.9	161.9	1 33.3	-50.2	161.9	0 36.2	-50.3	161.9	0 20.8	+50.5	18.1	1 17.9	+50.6	18.1	2 14.9	+50.8	18.1	3 12.0	+50.9	18.1	4 09.0	+51.1	18.1	59
60	1 40.4	-50.0	162.5	0 43.1	-50.1	162.5	0 14.1	+50.3	17.5	1 11.3	+50.4	17.5	2 08.5	+50.6	17.5	3 05.7	+50.8	17.5	4 02.9	+51.0	17.6	5 00.1	+51.2	17.6	60
61	0 50.4	-49.9	163.0	0 07.0	+50.1	17.0	1 04.4	+50.2	17.0	2 01.7	+50.5	17.0	2 59.1	+50.6	17.0	3 56.5	+50.8	17.0	4 53.9	+50.9	17.0	5 51.3	+51.0	17.1	61
62	0 00.5	-50.0	163.6	0 57.1	+50.1	16.4	1 54.6	+50.3	16.4	2 52.2	+50.4	16.4	3 49.7	+50.6	16.4	4 47.3	+50.7	16.5	5 44.8	+50.9	16.5	6 42.3	+51.1	16.5	62
63	0 49.5	+49.9	15.9	1 47.2	+50.1	15.9	2 44.9	+50.3	15.9	3 42.6	+50.4	15.9	4 40.3	+50.6	15.9	5 38.0	+50.7	15.9	6 35.7	+50.9	16.0	7 33.4	+51.0	16.0	63
64	1 39.4	+50.0	15.3	2 37.3	+50.1	15.3	3 35.2	+50.2	15.3	4 33.0	+50.4	15.3	5 30.9	+50.5	15.4	6 28.7	+50.7	15.4	7 26.6	+50.8	15.4	8 24.4	+51.0	15.5	64
65	2 29.4	+49.9	14.7	3 27.4	+50.1	14.8	4 25.4	+50.2	14.8	5 23.4	+50.4	14.8	6 21.4	+50.5	14.8	7 19.4	+50.7	14.9	8 17.4	+50.8	14.9	9 15.4	+50.9	14.9	65
66	3 19.3	+49.9	14.2	4 17.5	+50.0	14.2	5 15.6	+50.2	14.2	6 13.8	+50.3	14.3	7 11.9	+50.5	14.3	8 10.1	+50.6	14.3	9 08.2	+50.7	14.4	10 06.3	+50.9	14.4	66
67	4 09.2	+49.9	13.6	5 07.5	+50.0	13.7	6 05.8	+50.2	13.7	7 04.1	+50.3	13.7	8 02.4	+50.4	13.7	9 00.7	+50.5	13.8	9 58.9	+50.7	13.8	10 57.2	+50.8	13.9	67
68	4 59.1	+49.8	13.1	5 57.5	+50.0	13.1	6 56.0	+50.1	13.1	7 54.4	+50.2	13.2	8 52.8	+50.4	13.2	9 51.2	+50.5	13.2	10 49.6	+50.6	13.3	11 48.0	+50.8	13.3	68
69	5 48.9	+49.9	12.5	6 47.5	+49.9	12.5	7 46.1	+50.0	12.6	8 44.6	+50.2	12.6	9 43.2	+50.3	12.6	10 41.7	+50.5	12.7	11 40.2	+50.6	12.7	12 38.8	+50.7	12.8	69
70	6 38.8	+49.7	12.0	7 37.4	+49.9	12.0	8 36.1	+50.1	12.0	9 34.8	+50.2	12.0	10 33.5	+50.2	12.1	11 32.2	+50.3	12.1	12 30.8	+50.5	12.2	13 29.5	+50.6	12.2	70
71	7 28.5	+49.8	11.4	8 27.3	+49.9	11.4	9 26.2	+49.9	11.5	10 25.0	+50.0	11.5	11 23.7	+50.2	11.5	12 22.5	+50.3	11.6	13 21.3	+50.4	11.6	14 20.1	+50.5	11.7	71
72	8 18.3	+49.7	10.8	9 17.2	+49.8	10.9	10 16.1	+49.9	10.9	11 15.0	+50.1	10.9	12 13.9	+50.2	11.0	13 12.8	+50.3	11.0	14 11.7	+50.4	11.1	15 10.6	+50.5	11.1	72
73	9 08.0	+49.6	10.3	10 07.0	+49.7	10.3	11 06.0	+49.9	10.3	12 05.1	+49.9	10.4	13 04.1	+50.0	10.4	14 03.1	+50.1	10.5	15 02.1	+50.2	10.5	16 01.1	+50.3	10.5	73
74	9 57.6	+49.6	9.7	10 56.7	+49.7	9.7	11 55.9	+49.8	9.8	12 55.0	+49.9	9.8	13 54.1	+50.0	9.8	14 53.2	+50.1	9.9	15 52.3	+50.2	9.9	16 51.4	+50.3	10.0	74
75	10 47.2	+49.5	9.1	11 46.4	+49.6	9.2	12 45.7	+49.7	9.2	13 44.9	+49.8	9.2	14 44.1	+49.9	9.3	15 43.3	+50.0	9.3	16 42.5	+50.1	9.4	17 41.7	+50.2	9.4	75
76	11 36.7	+49.4	8.5	12 36.0	+49.6	8.6	13 35.4	+49.6	8.6	14 34.7	+49.7	8.7	15 34.0	+49.8	8.7	16 33.3	+49.9	8.7	17 32.6	+50.0	8.8	18 31.9	+50.1	8.8	76
77	12 26.1	+49.4	8.0	13 25.6	+49.4	8.0	14 25.0	+49.5	8.0	15 24.4	+49.6	8.1	16 23.8	+49.7	8.1	17 23.2	+49.8	8.2	18 22.6	+49.8	8.2	19 22.0	+49.9	8.3	77
78	13 15.5	+49.3	7.4	14 15.0	+49.4	7.4	15 14.5	+49.5	7.5	16 14.0	+49.5	7.5	17 13.5	+49.6	7.5	18 13.0	+49.6	7.6	19 12.4	+49.8	7.6	20 11.9	+49.8	7.7	78
79	14 04.8	+49.2	6.8	15 04.4	+49.3	6.8	16 04.0	+49.3	6.9	17 03.5	+49.4	6.9	18 03.1	+49.5	6.9	19 02.6	+49.6	7.0	20 02.2	+49.6	7.0	21 01.7	+49.8	7.1	79
80	14 54.0	+49.1	6.2	15 53.7	+49.1	6.2	16 53.3	+49.3	6.3	17 52.9	+49.4	6.3	18 52.6	+49.4	6.3	19 52.2	+49.5	6.4	20 51.8	+49.5	6.4	21 51.5	+49.5	6.5	80
81	15 43.1	+49.1	5.6	16 42.8	+49.1	5.6	17 42.6	+49.1	5.7	18 42.3	+49.2	5.7	19 42.0	+49.2	5.7	20 41.7	+49.3	5.8	21 41.3	+49.4	5.8	22 41.0	+49.5	5.9	81
82	16 32.2	+48.9	5.0	17 31.9	+49.0	5.0	18 31.7	+49.0	5.1	19 31.5	+49.0	5.1	20 31.2	+49.1	5.1	21 31.0	+49.2	5.2	22 30.7	+49.3	5.2	23 30.5	+49.3	5.2	82
83	17 21.1	+48.8	4.4	18 20.9	+48.8	4.4	19 20.7	+48.9	4.5	20 20.5	+49.0	4.5	21 20.3	+49.0	4.5	22 20.2	+49.0	4.5	23 20.0	+49.1	4.6	24 19.8	+49.1	4.6	83
84	18 09.9	+48.7	3.8	19 09.7	+48.8	3.8	20 09.6	+48.8	3.8	21 09.5	+48.8	3.9	22 09.3	+48.9	3.9	23 09.2	+48.9	3.9	24 09.1	+48.9	4.0	25 08.9	+49.0	4.0	84
85	18 58.6	+48.5	3.2	19 58.5	+48.6	3.2	20 58.4	+48.6	3.2	21 58.3	+48.6	3.2	22 58.2	+48.7	3.3	23 58.1	+48.7	3.3	24 58.0	+48.7	3.3	25 57.9	+48.8	3.3	85
86	19 47.1	+48.5	2.6	20 47.1	+48.4	2.6	21 47.0	+48.5	2.6	22 46.9	+48.6	2.6	23 46.9	+48.5	2.6	24 46.8	+48.6	2.7	25 46.7	+48.6	2.7	26 46.7	+48.6	2.7	86
87	20 35.6	+48.3	1.9	21 35.5	+48.3	1.9	22 35.5	+48.3	2.0	23 35.5	+48.3	2.0	24 35.4	+48.4	2.0	25 35.4	+48.4	2.0	26 35.3	+48.5	2.0	27 35.3	+48.4	2.0	87
88	21 23.9	+48.1	1.3	22 23.8	+48.2	1.3	23 23.8	+48.2	1.3	24 23.8	+48.2	1.3	25 23.8	+48.2	1.3	26 23.8	+48.2	1.3	27 23.8	+48.2	1.4	28 23.7	+48.3	1.4	88
89	22 12.0	+48.0	0.6	23 12.0	+48.0	0.7	24 12.0	+48.0	0.7	25 12.0	+48.0	0.7	26 12.0	+48.0	0.7	27 12.0	+48.0	0.7	28 12.0	+48.0	0.7	29 12.0	+48.0	0.7	89
90	23 00.0	+47.8	0.0	24 00.0	+47.8	0.0	25 00.0	+47.8	0.0	26 00.0	+47.8	0.0	27 00.0	+47.8	0.0	28 00.0	+47.8	0.0	29 00.0	+47.8	0.0	30 00.0	+47.8	0.0	90
	23°			24°			25°			26°			27°			28°			29°			30°			

S. Lat. {L.H.A. greater than 180° ....Zn=180°–Z
{L.H.A. less than 180°...........Zn=180°+Z

LATITUDE SAME NAME AS DECLINATION L.H.A. 143°, 217°

38°, 322° L.H.A. LATITUDE SAME NAME AS DECLINATION

N. Lat. {L.H.A. greater than 180° .....Zn=Z
{L.H.A. less than 180°............Zn=360°–Z

Dec.	23° Hc	d	Z	24° Hc	d	Z	25° Hc	d	Z	26° Hc	d	Z	27° Hc	d	Z	28° Hc	d	Z	29° Hc	d	Z	30° Hc	d	Z	Dec.
°	° ′	′	°	° ′	′	°	° ′	′	°	° ′	′	°	° ′	′	°	° ′	′	°	° ′	′	°	° ′	′	°	°
0	46 30.0	+33.6	116.6	46 02.7	+34.8	117.5	45 34.6	+35.8	118.4	45 05.6	+36.9	119.3	44 35.9	+37.9	120.2	44 05.3	+38.9	121.0	43 34.1	+39.8	121.8	43 02.1	+40.7	122.6	0
1	47 03.6	+32.9	115.4	46 37.5	+34.0	116.3	46 10.4	+35.2	117.3	45 42.5	+36.3	118.2	45 13.8	+37.3	119.1	44 44.2	+38.4	119.9	44 13.9	+39.3	120.8	43 42.8	+40.3	121.6	1
2	47 36.5	+32.1	114.1	47 11.5	+33.3	115.1	46 45.6	+34.5	116.1	46 18.8	+35.5	117.0	45 51.1	+36.6	117.9	45 22.6	+37.6	118.8	44 53.2	+38.7	119.7	44 23.1	+39.6	120.6	2
3	48 08.6	+31.3	112.9	47 44.8	+32.5	113.9	47 20.1	+33.6	114.9	46 54.3	+34.9	115.9	46 27.7	+36.0	116.8	46 00.2	+37.1	117.7	45 31.9	+38.1	118.6	45 02.7	+39.1	119.5	3
4	48 39.9	+30.3	111.6	48 17.3	+31.6	112.6	47 53.7	+32.9	113.7	47 29.2	+34.0	114.7	47 03.7	+35.2	115.6	46 37.3	+36.3	116.6	46 10.0	+37.4	117.5	45 41.8	+38.4	118.4	4
5	49 10.2	+29.5	110.3	48 48.9	+30.8	111.3	48 26.6	+32.0	112.4	48 03.2	+33.3	113.4	47 38.9	+34.4	114.4	47 13.6	+35.6	115.4	46 47.4	+36.7	116.4	46 20.2	+37.8	117.3	5
6	49 39.7	+28.5	108.9	49 19.7	+29.8	110.0	48 58.6	+31.2	111.1	48 36.5	+32.4	112.2	48 13.3	+33.7	113.2	47 49.2	+34.8	114.2	47 24.1	+36.0	115.2	46 58.0	+37.1	116.2	6
7	50 08.2	+27.6	107.6	49 49.5	+29.0	108.7	49 29.8	+30.2	109.8	49 08.9	+31.5	110.9	48 47.0	+32.8	112.0	48 24.0	+34.1	113.0	48 00.1	+35.2	114.0	47 35.1	+36.4	115.0	7
8	50 35.8	+26.5	106.2	50 18.5	+27.9	107.3	50 00.0	+29.3	108.5	49 40.4	+30.7	109.6	49 19.8	+31.9	110.7	48 58.1	+33.2	111.8	48 35.3	+34.4	112.8	48 11.5	+35.7	113.9	8
9	51 02.3	+25.4	104.8	50 46.4	+26.9	105.9	50 29.3	+28.4	107.1	50 11.1	+29.7	108.3	49 51.7	+31.1	109.4	49 31.3	+32.3	110.5	49 09.7	+33.7	111.6	48 47.2	+34.8	112.6	9
10	51 27.7	+24.4	103.3	51 13.3	+25.9	104.5	50 57.7	+27.3	105.7	50 40.8	+28.8	106.9	50 22.8	+30.1	108.1	50 03.6	+31.5	109.2	49 43.4	+32.7	110.3	49 22.0	+34.0	111.4	10
11	51 52.1	+23.3	101.8	51 39.2	+24.8	103.1	51 25.0	+26.2	104.3	51 09.6	+27.7	105.5	50 52.9	+29.2	106.7	50 35.1	+30.5	107.9	50 16.1	+31.9	109.0	49 56.0	+33.2	110.1	11
12	52 15.4	+22.1	100.3	52 04.0	+23.6	101.6	51 51.2	+25.2	102.8	51 37.3	+26.7	104.1	51 22.1	+28.1	105.3	51 05.6	+29.6	106.5	50 48.0	+31.0	107.7	50 29.2	+32.3	108.8	12
13	52 37.5	+20.9	98.8	52 27.6	+22.5	100.1	52 16.4	+24.1	101.4	52 04.0	+25.5	102.6	51 50.2	+27.1	103.9	51 35.2	+28.5	105.1	51 19.0	+29.9	106.3	51 01.5	+31.4	107.5	13
14	52 58.4	+19.6	97.3	52 50.1	+21.3	98.6	52 40.5	+22.9	99.9	52 29.5	+24.5	101.2	52 17.3	+26.0	102.4	52 03.7	+27.5	103.7	51 48.9	+29.0	104.9	51 32.9	+30.4	106.1	14
15	53 18.0	+18.4	95.7	53 11.4	+20.1	97.0	53 03.4	+21.7	98.3	52 54.0	+23.3	99.6	52 43.3	+24.9	100.9	52 31.2	+26.4	102.2	52 17.9	+27.9	103.5	52 03.3	+29.3	104.7	15
16	53 36.4	+17.1	94.1	53 31.5	+18.7	95.4	53 25.1	+20.4	96.8	53 17.3	+22.1	98.1	53 08.2	+23.7	99.4	52 57.6	+25.3	100.7	52 45.8	+26.8	102.0	52 32.6	+28.4	103.3	16
17	53 53.5	+15.8	92.5	53 50.2	+17.5	93.8	53 45.5	+19.2	95.2	53 39.4	+20.8	96.5	53 31.9	+22.4	97.9	53 22.9	+24.1	99.2	53 12.6	+25.7	100.5	53 01.0	+27.2	101.9	17
18	54 09.3	+14.4	90.8	54 07.7	+16.2	92.2	54 04.7	+17.9	93.6	54 00.2	+19.6	95.0	53 54.3	+21.3	96.3	53 47.0	+22.9	97.7	53 38.3	+24.5	99.0	53 28.2	+26.1	100.4	18
19	54 23.7	+13.1	89.2	54 23.9	+14.8	90.6	54 22.6	+16.5	91.9	54 19.8	+18.3	93.3	54 15.6	+20.0	94.7	54 09.9	+21.7	96.1	54 02.8	+23.3	97.5	53 54.3	+24.9	98.8	19
20	54 36.8	+11.6	87.5	54 38.7	+13.4	88.9	54 39.1	+15.2	90.3	54 38.1	+16.9	91.7	54 35.6	+18.6	93.1	54 31.6	+20.3	94.5	54 26.1	+22.1	95.9	54 19.2	+23.7	97.3	20
21	54 48.4	+10.2	85.8	54 52.1	+12.0	87.2	54 54.3	+13.7	88.6	54 55.0	+15.5	90.0	54 54.2	+17.3	91.5	54 51.9	+19.1	92.9	54 48.2	+20.7	94.3	54 42.9	+22.5	95.7	21
22	54 58.6	+8.7	84.1	55 04.1	+10.5	85.5	55 08.0	+12.4	86.9	55 10.5	+14.1	88.4	55 11.5	+15.9	89.8	55 11.0	+17.6	91.2	55 08.9	+19.4	92.7	55 05.4	+21.1	94.1	22
23	55 07.3	+7.3	82.3	55 14.6	+9.1	83.8	55 20.4	+10.8	85.2	55 24.6	+12.7	86.6	55 27.4	+14.5	88.1	55 28.6	+16.3	89.5	55 28.3	+18.1	91.0	55 26.5	+19.8	92.5	23
24	55 14.6	+5.8	80.6	55 23.7	+7.5	82.0	55 31.2	+9.4	83.5	55 37.3	+11.2	84.9	55 41.9	+13.0	86.4	55 44.9	+14.8	87.8	55 46.4	+16.6	89.3	55 46.3	+18.4	90.8	24
25	55 20.4	+4.2	78.9	55 31.2	+6.1	80.3	55 40.6	+7.9	81.7	55 48.5	+9.7	83.2	55 54.9	+11.5	84.6	55 59.7	+13.4	86.1	56 03.0	+15.2	87.6	56 04.7	+17.0	89.1	25
26	55 24.6	+2.8	77.1	55 37.3	+4.6	78.5	55 48.5	+6.4	80.0	55 58.2	+8.2	81.4	56 06.4	+10.0	82.9	56 13.1	+11.8	84.4	56 18.2	+13.7	85.9	56 21.7	+15.6	87.4	26
27	55 27.4	+1.2	75.3	55 41.9	+3.0	76.8	55 54.9	+4.8	78.2	56 06.4	+6.7	79.6	56 16.4	+8.5	81.1	56 24.9	+10.4	82.6	56 31.9	+12.2	84.1	56 37.3	+14.0	85.6	27
28	55 28.6	−0.3	73.6	55 44.9	+1.5	75.0	55 59.7	+3.3	76.4	56 13.1	+5.1	77.9	56 24.9	+7.0	79.3	56 35.3	+8.8	80.8	56 44.1	+10.6	82.3	56 51.3	+12.5	83.8	28
29	55 28.3	−1.8	71.8	55 46.4	−0.1	73.2	56 03.0	+1.7	74.6	56 18.2	+3.5	76.1	56 31.9	+5.4	77.5	56 44.1	+7.2	79.0	56 54.7	+9.1	80.5	57 03.8	+11.0	82.0	29
30	55 26.5	−3.3	70.0	55 46.3	−1.6	71.4	56 04.7	+0.2	72.8	56 21.7	+2.0	74.3	56 37.3	+3.8	75.7	56 51.3	+5.7	77.2	57 03.8	+7.5	78.7	57 14.8	+9.4	80.2	30
31	55 23.2	−4.8	68.3	55 44.7	−3.1	69.6	56 04.9	−1.4	71.0	56 23.7	+0.4	72.5	56 41.1	+2.2	73.9	56 57.0	+4.0	75.4	57 11.3	+6.0	76.9	57 24.2	+7.8	78.4	31
32	55 18.4	−6.4	66.5	55 41.6	−4.6	67.9	56 03.5	−2.9	69.2	56 24.1	−1.2	70.7	56 43.3	+0.6	72.1	57 01.0	+2.4	73.6	57 17.3	+4.2	75.0	57 32.0	+6.1	76.6	32
33	55 12.0	−7.8	64.8	55 37.0	−6.2	66.1	56 00.6	−4.5	67.5	56 22.9	−2.7	68.8	56 43.9	−1.0	70.3	57 03.4	+0.9	71.7	57 21.5	+2.7	73.2	57 38.1	+4.5	74.7	33
34	55 04.2	−9.3	63.1	55 30.8	−7.7	64.3	55 56.1	−6.0	65.7	56 20.2	−4.3	67.0	56 42.9	−2.6	68.4	57 04.3	−0.8	69.9	57 24.2	+1.0	71.3	57 42.6	+2.9	72.8	34
35	54 54.9	−10.7	61.3	55 23.1	−9.2	62.6	55 50.1	−7.5	63.9	56 15.9	−5.9	65.2	56 40.3	−4.1	66.6	57 03.5	−2.4	68.0	57 25.2	−0.6	69.5	57 45.5	+1.2	71.0	35
36	54 44.2	−12.2	59.6	55 13.9	−10.6	60.9	55 42.6	−9.1	62.1	56 10.0	−7.4	63.5	56 36.2	−5.7	64.8	57 01.1	−4.0	66.2	57 24.6	−2.3	67.6	57 46.7	−0.4	69.1	36
37	54 32.0	−13.6	57.9	55 03.3	−12.1	59.1	55 33.5	−10.5	60.4	56 02.6	−8.9	61.7	56 30.5	−7.3	63.0	56 57.1	−5.7	64.4	57 22.3	−3.8	65.8	57 46.3	−2.1	67.2	37
38	54 18.4	−14.9	56.3	54 51.2	−13.5	57.4	55 23.0	−12.0	58.7	55 53.7	−10.5	59.9	56 23.2	−8.9	61.2	56 51.4	−7.2	62.5	57 18.5	−5.5	63.9	57 44.2	−3.8	65.3	38
39	54 03.5	−16.3	54.6	54 37.7	−14.8	55.7	55 11.0	−13.4	56.9	55 43.2	−11.9	58.2	56 14.3	−10.4	59.4	56 44.2	−8.7	60.7	57 13.0	−7.2	62.1	57 40.4	−5.4	63.5	39
40	53 47.2	−17.6	53.0	54 22.9	−16.3	54.1	54 57.6	−14.9	55.2	55 31.3	−13.4	56.4	56 03.9	−11.8	57.7	56 35.5	−10.3	58.9	57 05.8	−8.7	60.3	57 35.0	−7.0	61.6	40
41	53 29.6	−18.9	51.4	54 06.6	−17.6	52.4	54 42.7	−16.2	53.5	55 17.9	−14.8	54.7	55 52.1	−13.4	55.9	56 25.2	−11.9	57.1	56 57.1	−10.2	58.4	57 28.0	−8.7	59.8	41
42	53 10.7	−20.1	49.8	53 49.0	−18.8	50.8	54 26.5	−17.6	51.9	55 03.1	−16.2	53.0	55 38.7	−14.8	54.2	56 13.3	−13.3	55.4	56 46.9	−11.9	56.6	57 19.3	−10.2	57.9	42
43	52 50.6	−21.4	48.2	53 30.2	−20.2	49.2	54 08.9	−18.8	50.2	54 46.9	−17.6	51.3	55 23.9	−16.2	52.5	56 00.0	−14.8	53.6	56 35.0	−13.3	54.8	57 09.1	−11.9	56.1	43
44	52 29.2	−22.5	46.7	53 10.0	−21.4	47.6	53 50.1	−20.2	48.6	54 29.3	−18.9	49.7	55 07.7	−17.6	50.8	55 45.2	−16.3	51.9	56 21.7	−14.8	53.1	56 57.2	−13.3	54.3	44
45	52 06.7	−23.7	45.1	52 48.6	−22.5	46.1	53 29.9	−21.4	47.0	54 10.4	−20.2	48.1	54 50.1	−19.0	49.1	55 28.9	−17.6	50.2	56 06.9	−16.3	51.3	56 43.9	−14.9	52.5	45
46	51 43.0	−24.8	43.7	52 26.1	−23.8	44.5	53 08.5	−22.6	45.5	53 50.2	−21.5	46.4	54 31.1	−20.2	47.5	55 11.3	−19.0	48.5	55 50.6	−17.7	49.6	56 29.0	−16.3	50.8	46
47	51 18.2	−25.9	42.2	52 02.3	−24.8	43.0	52 45.9	−23.8	43.9	53 28.7	−22.7	44.9	54 10.9	−21.5	45.8	54 52.3	−20.3	46.9	55 32.9	−19.1	47.9	56 12.7	−17.8	49.0	47
48	50 52.3	−26.9	40.8	51 37.5	−26.0	41.6	52 22.1	−25.0	42.4	53 06.0	−23.8	43.3	53 49.4	−22.8	44.3	54 32.0	−21.7	45.2	55 13.8	−20.4	46.3	55 54.9	−19.1	47.3	48
49	50 25.4	−27.9	39.3	51 11.5	−26.9	40.1	51 57.1	−26.0	40.9	52 42.2	−25.1	41.8	53 26.6	−24.0	42.7	54 10.3	−22.8	43.6	54 53.4	−21.7	44.6	55 35.8	−20.6	45.6	49
50	49 57.5	−28.9	38.0	50 44.6	−28.0	38.7	51 31.1	−27.1	39.5	52 17.1	−26.1	40.3	53 02.6	−25.1	41.2	53 47.5	−24.1	42.1	54 31.7	−23.0	43.0	55 15.2	−21.8	44.0	50
51	49 28.6	−29.8	36.6	50 16.6	−29.0	37.3	51 04.0	−28.1	38.1	51 51.0	−27.2	38.8	52 37.5	−26.3	39.7	53 23.4	−25.3	40.5	54 08.7	−24.2	41.4	54 53.4	−23.2	42.3	51
52	48 58.8	−30.7	35.3	49 47.6	−29.9	36.0	50 35.9	−29.1	36.7	51 23.8	−28.2	37.4	52 11.2	−27.3	38.2	52 58.1	−26.4	39.0	53 44.5	−25.4	39.9	54 30.2	−24.3	40.8	52
53	48 28.1	−31.6	34.0	49 17.7	−30.9	34.6	50 06.8	−30.0	35.3	50 55.6	−29.2	36.0	51 43.9	−28.4	36.7	52 31.7	−27.4	37.5	53 19.1	−26.6	38.3	54 05.9	−25.6	39.2	53
54	47 56.5	−32.4	32.7	48 46.8	−31.6	33.3	49 36.8	−30.9	34.0	50 26.4	−30.2	34.6	51 15.5	−29.3	35.3	52 04.3	−28.6	36.1	52 52.5	−27.6	36.8	53 40.3	−26.7	37.7	54
55	47 24.1	−33.2	31.4	48 15.2	−32.6	32.0	49 05.9	−31.9	32.6	49 56.2	−31.1	33.3	50 46.2	−30.4	33.9	51 35.7	−29.5	34.6	52 24.9	−28.7	35.4	53 13.6	−27.9	36.1	55
56	46 50.9	−33.9	30.2	47 42.6	−33.3	30.8	48 34.0	−32.6	31.3	49 25.1	−32.0	32.0	50 15.8	−31.2	32.6	51 06.2	−30.5	33.2	51 56.2	−29.7	33.9	52 45.7	−28.9	34.7	56
57	46 17.0	−34.7	29.0	47 09.3	−34.1	29.5	48 01.4	−33.5	30.1	48 53.1	−32.8	30.7	49 44.6	−32.2	31.3	50 35.7	−31.5	31.9	51 26.5	−30.7	32.5	52 16.8	−29.9	33.2	57
58	45 42.3	−35.5	27.9	46 35.2	−34.9	28.3	47 27.9	−34.3	28.9	48 20.3	−33.7	29.4	49 12.4	−33.0	30.0	50 04.2	−32.3	30.6	50 55.8	−31.7	31.2	51 46.9	−30.9	31.8	58
59	45 06.8	−36.0	26.7	46 00.3	−35.5	27.2	46 53.6	−35.0	27.6	47 46.6	−34.4	28.2	48 39.4	−33.8	28.7	49 31.9	−33.2	29.2	50 24.1	−32.5	29.8	51 16.0	−31.9	30.4	59
60	44 30.8	−36.8	25.6	45 24.8	−36.3	26.0	46 18.6	−35.7	26.5	47 12.2	−35.2	26.9	48 05.6	−34.6	27.4	48 58.7	−34.0	28.0	49 51.6	−33.5	28.5	50 44.1	−32.8	29.1	60
61	43 54.0	−37.3	24.5	44 48.5	−36.9	24.9	45 42.9	−36.4	25.3	46 37.0	−35.9	25.8	47 31.0	−35.4	26.2	48 24.7	−34.9	26.7	49 18.1	−34.2	27.2	50 11.3	−33.6	27.8	61
62	43 16.7	−38.0	23.4	44 11.6	−37.5	23.8	45 06.5	−37.1	24.2	46 01.1	−36.6	24.6	46 55.6	−36.1	25.0	47 49.8	−35.5	25.5	48 43.9	−35.1	26.0	49 37.7	−34.5	26.5	62
63	42 38.7	−38.5	22.3	43 34.1	−38.1	22.7	44 29.4	−37.7	23.1	45 24.5	−37.2	23.5	46 19.5	−36.8	23.9	47 14.3	−36.3	24.3	48 08.8	−35.8	24.8	49 03.2	−35.3	25.2	63
64	42 00.2	−39.1	21.3	42 56.0	−38.7	21.6	43 51.7	−38.3	22.0	44 47.3	−37.9	22.4	45 42.7	−37.5	22.7	46 38.0	−37.0	23.1	47 33.0	−36.5	23.6	48 27.9	−36.0	24.0	64
65	41 21.1	−39.6	20.3	42 17.3	−39.2	20.6	43 13.4	−38.9	20.9	44 09.4	−38.5	21.3	45 05.2	−38.0	21.6	46 01.0	−37.7	22.0	46 56.5	−37.2	22.4	47 51.9	−36.8	22.8	65
66	40 41.5	−40.1	19.3	41 38.1	−39.8	19.6	42 34.5	−39.4	19.9	43 30.9	−39.1	20.2	44 27.2	−38.7	20.5	45 23.3	−38.3	20.9	46 19.3	−37.9	21.3	47 15.1	−37.5	21.6	66
67	40 01.4	−40.6	18.3	40 58.3	−40.3	18.6	41 55.1	−39.9	18.9	42 51.8	−39.6	19.2	43 48.5	−39.3	19.5	44 45.0	−38.9	19.8	45 41.4	−38.6	20.1	46 37.6	−38.1	20.5	67
68	39 20.8	−41.1	17.4	40 18.0	−40.7	17.6	41 15.2	−40.5	17.9	42 12.2	−40.1	18.1	43 09.2	−39.8	18.4	44 06.1	−39.5	18.7	45 02.8	−39.1	19.1	45 59.5	−38.8	19.4	68
69	38 39.7	−41.5	16.4	39 37.3	−41.3	16.6	40 34.7	−40.9	16.9	41 32.1	−40.7	17.1	42 29.4	−40.4	17.4	43 26.6	−40.1	17.7	44 23.7	−39.7	18.0	45 20.7	−39.4	18.3	69
70	37 58.2	−41.9	15.5	38 56.0	−41.6	15.7	39 53.8	−41.5	15.9	40 51.4	−41.1	16.2	41 49.0	−40.9	16.4	42 46.5	−40.6	16.7	43 44.0	−40.3	16.9	44 41.3	−40.0	17.2	70
71	37 16.3	−42.3	14.6	38 14.4	−42.1	14.8	39 12.3	−41.8	15.0	40 10.3	−41.6	15.2	41 08.1	−41.3	15.4	42 05.9	−41.0	15.7	43 03.7	−40.8	15.9	44 01.3	−40.5	16.2	71
72	36 34.0	−42.7	13.7	37 32.3	−42.5	13.9	38 30.5	−42.3	14.1	39 28.7	−42.1	14.3	40 26.8	−41.8	14.5	41 24.9	−41.6	14.7	42 22.9	−41.4	14.9	43 20.8	−41.1	15.2	72
73	35 51.3	−43.1	12.8	36 49.8	−42.9	13.0	37 48.2	−42.7	13.2	38 46.6	−42.5	13.3	39 45.0	−42.3	13.5	40 43.3	−42.1	13.7	41 41.5	−41.8	13.9	42 39.7	−41.5	14.2	73
74	35 08.2	−43.4	12.0	36 06.9	−43.3	12.1	37 05.5	−43.0	12.3	38 04.1	−42.8	12.4	39 02.7	−42.7	12.6	40 01.2	−42.4	12.8	40 59.7	−42.2	13.0	41 58.2	−42.1	13.2	74
75	34 24.8	−43.8	11.1	35 23.6	−43.6	11.3	36 22.5	−43.5	11.4	37 21.3	−43.3	11.6	38 20.0	−43.1	11.7	39 18.8	−42.9	11.9	40 17.5	−42.8	12.1	41 16.1	−42.5	12.2	75
76	33 41.0	−44.1	10.3	34 40.0	−43.9	10.4	35 39.0	−43.8	10.6	36 38.0	−43.6	10.7	37 36.9	−43.4	10.8	38 35.9	−43.3	11.0	39 34.7	−43.1	11.1	40 33.6	−43.0	11.3	76
77	32 56.9	−44.4	9.5	33 56.1	−44.3	9.6	34 55.2	−44.1	9.7	35 54.4	−44.0	9.8	36 53.5	−43.9	10.0	37 52.6	−43.7	10.1	38 51.6	−43.5	10.2	39 50.6	−43.3	10.4	77
78	32 12.5	−44.7	8.7	33 11.8	−44.6	8.8	34 11.1	−44.4	8.9	35 10.4	−44.3	9.0	36 09.6	−44.2	9.1	37 08.9	−44.1	9.2	38 08.1	−44.0	9.4	39 07.3	−43.8	9.5	78
79	31 27.8	−45.0	7.9	32 27.2	−44.8	8.0	33 26.7	−44.8	8.1	34 26.1	−44.7	8.2	35 25.4	−44.5	8.3	36 24.8	−44.4	8.4	37 24.1	−44.2	8.5	38 23.5	−44.0	8.6	79
80	30 42.8	−45.2	7.1	31 42.4	−45.2	7.2	32 41.9	−45.1	7.3	33 41.4	−45.0	7.4	34 40.9	−44.9	7.5	35 40.4	−44.8	7.6	36 39.9	−44.7	7.7	37 39.3	−44.5	7.8	80
81	29 57.6	−45.5	6.4	30 57.2	−45.4	6.4	31 56.8	−45.3	6.5	32 56.4	−45.2	6.6	33 56.0	−45.1	6.7	34 55.6	−45.0	6.7	35 55.2	−45.0	6.8	36 54.8	−44.9	6.9	81
82	29 12.1	−45.8	5.6	30 11.8	−45.7	5.7	31 11.5	−45.6	5.7	32 11.2	−45.6	5.8	33 10.9	−45.5	5.9	34 10.6	−45.4	5.9	35 10.2	−45.3	6.0	36 09.9	−45.2	6.1	82
83	28 26.3	−46.0	4.9	29 26.1	−45.9	4.9	30 25.9	−45.9	5.0	31 25.6	−45.8	5.0	32 25.4	−45.7	5.1	33 25.2	−45.7	5.2	34 24.9	−45.6	5.2	35 24.7	−45.6	5.3	83
84	27 40.3	−46.2	4.2	28 40.2	−46.2	4.2	29 40.0	−46.1	4.2	30 39.8	−46.0	4.3	31 39.7	−46.0	4.3	32 39.5	−46.0	4.4	33 39.3	−45.9	4.4	34 39.1	−45.8	4.5	84
85	26 54.1	−46.4	3.4	27 54.0	−46.4	3.5	28 53.9	−46.4	3.5	29 53.8	−46.3	3.5	30 53.7	−46.3	3.6	31 53.5	−46.2	3.6	32 53.4	−46.2	3.7	33 53.3	−46.1	3.7	85
86	26 07.7	−46.7	2.7	27 07.6	−46.6	2.8	28 07.5	−46.5	2.8	29 07.5	−46.6	2.8	30 07.4	−46.5	2.8	31 07.3	−46.5	2.9	32 07.2	−46.4	2.9	33 07.2	−46.4	2.9	86
87	25 21.0	−46.8	2.0	26 21.0	−46.8	2.1	27 21.0	−46.7	2.1	28 20.9	−46.7	2.1	29 20.9	−46.8	2.1	30 20.8	−46.7	2.1	31 20.8	−46.7	2.2	32 20.8	−46.7	2.2	87
88	24 34.2	−47.0	1.4	25 34.2	−47.0	1.4	26 34.2	−47.0	1.4	27 34.2	−47.0	1.4	28 34.1	−46.9	1.4	29 34.1	−46.9	1.4	30 34.1	−46.9	1.4	31 34.1	−46.9	1.4	88
89	23 47.2	−47.2	0.7	24 47.2	−47.2	0.7	25 47.2	−47.2	0.7	26 47.2	−47.2	0.7	27 47.2	−47.2	0.7	28 47.2	−47.2	0.7	29 47.2	−47.2	0.7	30 47.2	−47.2	0.7	89
90	23 00.0	−47.4	0.0	24 00.0	−47.4	0.0	25 00.0	−47.4	0.0	26 00.0	−47.4	0.0	27 00.0	−47.4	0.0	28 00.0	−47.4	0.0	29 00.0	−47.4	0.0	30 00.0	−47.4	0.0	90
	23°			24°			25°			26°			27°			28°			29°			30°			

38°, 322° L.H.A. LATITUDE SAME NAME AS DECLINATION

260

LATITUDE CONTRARY NAME TO DECLINATION L.H.A. 38°, 322°

Dec.	23°			24°			25°			26°		
	Hc	d	Z	Hc	d	Z	Hc	d	Z	Hc	d	Z
°	° ′	′	°	° ′	′	°	° ′	′	°	° ′	′	°
0	46 30.0	-34.5	116.6	46 02.7	-35.5	117.5	45 34.6	-36.6	118.4	45 05.6	-37.6	119.3
1	45 55.5	-35.1	117.8	45 27.2	-36.2	118.7	44 58.0	-37.2	119.5	44 28.0	-38.2	120.4
2	45 20.4	-35.8	118.9	44 51.0	-36.9	119.8	44 20.8	-37.8	120.6	43 49.8	-38.7	121.5
3	44 44.6	-36.5	120.0	44 14.1	-37.4	120.9	43 43.0	-38.5	121.7	43 11.1	-39.4	122.5
4	44 08.1	-37.2	121.2	43 36.7	-38.1	122.0	43 04.5	-39.0	122.8	42 31.7	-39.9	123.6
5	43 30.9	-37.7	122.2	42 58.6	-38.7	123.0	42 25.5	-39.5	123.8	41 51.8	-40.4	124.6
6	42 53.2	-38.3	123.3	42 19.9	-39.2	124.1	41 46.0	-40.1	124.8	41 11.4	-40.9	125.5
7	42 14.9	-38.9	124.4	41 40.7	-39.7	125.1	41 05.9	-40.6	125.8	40 30.5	-41.4	126.5
8	41 36.0	-39.4	125.4	41 01.0	-40.3	126.1	40 25.3	-41.0	126.8	39 49.1	-41.8	127.5
9	40 56.6	-39.9	126.4	40 20.7	-40.7	127.1	39 44.3	-41.5	127.7	39 07.3	-42.3	128.4
10	40 16.7	-40.4	127.4	39 40.0	-41.2	128.0	39 02.8	-42.0	128.7	38 25.0	-42.7	129.3
11	39 36.3	-40.9	128.3	38 58.8	-41.6	129.0	38 20.8	-42.4	129.6	37 42.3	-43.1	130.2
12	38 55.4	-41.3	129.3	38 17.2	-42.1	129.9	37 38.4	-42.7	130.5	36 59.2	-43.4	131.1
13	38 14.1	-41.8	130.2	37 35.1	-42.5	130.8	36 55.7	-43.2	131.4	36 15.8	-43.8	131.9
14	37 32.3	-42.2	131.1	36 52.6	-42.8	131.7	36 12.5	-43.5	132.2	35 32.0	-44.2	132.8
15	36 50.1	-42.5	132.0	36 09.8	-43.3	132.6	35 29.0	-43.9	133.1	34 47.8	-44.5	133.6
16	36 07.6	-43.0	132.9	35 26.5	-43.5	133.4	34 45.1	-44.2	133.9	34 03.3	-44.8	134.4
17	35 24.6	-43.3	133.7	34 43.0	-44.0	134.3	34 00.9	-44.5	134.7	33 18.5	-45.1	135.2
18	34 41.3	-43.6	134.6	33 59.0	-44.2	135.1	33 16.4	-44.9	135.5	32 33.4	-45.4	136.0
19	33 57.7	-44.0	135.4	33 14.8	-44.6	135.9	32 31.5	-45.1	136.3	31 48.0	-45.7	136.8
20	33 13.7	-44.3	136.2	32 30.2	-44.8	136.7	31 46.4	-45.4	137.1	31 02.3	-45.9	137.5
21	32 29.4	-44.5	137.0	31 45.4	-45.2	137.5	31 01.0	-45.7	137.9	30 16.4	-46.2	138.3
22	31 44.9	-44.9	137.8	31 00.2	-45.4	138.2	30 15.3	-45.9	138.6	29 30.2	-46.4	139.0
23	31 00.0	-45.2	138.6	30 14.8	-45.6	139.0	29 29.4	-46.2	139.4	28 43.8	-46.7	139.7
24	30 14.8	-45.4	139.4	29 29.2	-46.0	139.8	28 43.2	-46.4	140.1	27 57.1	-46.9	140.5
25	29 29.4	-45.6	140.1	28 43.2	-46.1	140.5	27 56.8	-46.6	140.8	27 10.2	-47.1	141.2
26	28 43.8	-46.0	140.9	27 57.1	-46.4	141.2	27 10.2	-46.8	141.5	26 23.1	-47.2	141.9
27	27 57.8	-46.1	141.6	27 10.7	-46.6	141.9	26 23.4	-47.1	142.2	25 35.9	-47.5	142.5
28	27 11.7	-46.3	142.3	26 24.1	-46.8	142.6	25 36.3	-47.2	142.9	24 48.4	-47.7	143.2
29	26 25.4	-46.6	143.0	25 37.3	-47.0	143.3	24 49.1	-47.4	143.6	24 00.7	-47.8	143.9
30	25 38.8	-46.8	143.7	24 50.3	-47.1	144.0	24 01.7	-47.6	144.3	23 12.9	-48.0	144.5
31	24 52.0	-46.9	144.4	24 03.2	-47.4	144.7	23 14.1	-47.7	144.9	22 24.9	-48.1	145.2
32	24 05.1	-47.1	145.1	23 15.8	-47.5	145.4	22 26.4	-47.9	145.6	21 36.8	-48.3	145.8
33	23 18.0	-47.3	145.8	22 28.3	-47.7	146.0	21 38.5	-48.1	146.3	20 48.5	-48.4	146.5
34	22 30.7	-47.5	146.5	21 40.6	-47.8	146.7	20 50.4	-48.2	146.9	20 00.1	-48.6	147.1
35	21 43.2	-47.6	147.1	20 52.8	-48.0	147.3	20 02.2	-48.3	147.5	19 11.5	-48.7	147.7
36	20 55.6	-47.8	147.8	20 04.8	-48.1	148.0	19 13.9	-48.5	148.2	18 22.8	-48.8	148.3
37	20 07.8	-47.9	148.4	19 16.7	-48.3	148.6	18 25.4	-48.6	148.8	17 34.0	-48.9	149.0
38	19 19.9	-48.0	149.1	18 28.4	-48.4	149.2	17 36.8	-48.7	149.4	16 45.1	-49.0	149.6
39	18 31.9	-48.2	149.7	17 40.0	-48.5	149.9	16 48.1	-48.8	150.0	15 56.1	-49.1	150.2
40	17 43.7	-48.3	150.3	16 51.5	-48.6	150.5	15 59.3	-48.9	150.6	15 07.0	-49.2	150.8
41	16 55.4	-48.4	150.9	16 02.9	-48.7	151.1	15 10.4	-49.0	151.2	14 17.8	-49.3	151.3
42	16 07.0	-48.5	151.6	15 14.2	-48.8	151.7	14 21.4	-49.1	151.8	13 28.5	-49.4	151.9
43	15 18.5	-48.6	152.2	14 25.4	-48.8	152.3	13 32.3	-49.2	152.4	12 39.1	-49.5	152.5
44	14 29.9	-48.7	152.8	13 36.6	-49.0	152.9	12 43.1	-49.2	153.0	11 49.6	-49.5	153.1
45	13 41.2	-48.7	153.4	12 47.6	-49.1	153.5	11 53.9	-49.4	153.6	11 00.1	-49.6	153.7
46	12 52.5	-48.9	154.0	11 58.5	-49.1	154.1	11 04.5	-49.4	154.2	10 10.5	-49.6	154.2
47	12 03.6	-48.9	154.6	11 09.4	-49.2	154.7	10 15.1	-49.4	154.7	9 20.9	-49.7	154.8
48	11 14.7	-49.0	155.2	10 20.2	-49.3	155.2	9 25.7	-49.5	155.3	8 31.2	-49.8	155.4
49	10 25.7	-49.1	155.8	9 30.9	-49.3	155.8	8 36.2	-49.6	155.9	7 41.4	-49.8	155.9
50	9 36.6	-49.1	156.3	8 41.6	-49.3	156.4	7 46.6	-49.6	156.5	6 51.6	-49.8	156.5
51	8 47.5	-49.2	156.9	7 52.3	-49.5	157.0	6 57.0	-49.6	157.0	6 01.8	-49.9	157.1
52	7 58.3	-49.2	157.5	7 02.8	-49.4	157.5	6 07.4	-49.7	157.6	5 11.9	-49.9	157.6
53	7 09.1	-49.3	158.1	6 13.4	-49.5	158.1	5 17.7	-49.7	158.2	4 22.0	-49.9	158.2
54	6 19.8	-49.3	158.6	5 23.9	-49.5	158.7	4 28.0	-49.7	158.7	3 32.1	-50.0	158.7
55	5 30.5	-49.4	159.2	4 34.4	-49.6	159.3	3 38.3	-49.8	159.3	2 42.1	-49.9	159.3
56	4 41.1	-49.3	159.8	3 44.8	-49.5	159.8	2 48.5	-49.8	159.8	1 52.2	-50.0	159.9
57	3 51.8	-49.4	160.4	2 55.3	-49.6	160.4	1 58.7	-49.7	160.4	1 02.2	-50.0	160.4
58	3 02.4	-49.4	160.9	2 05.7	-49.6	160.9	1 09.0	-49.8	161.0	0 12.2	-49.9	161.0
59	2 13.0	-49.5	161.5	1 16.1	-49.6	161.5	0 19.2	-49.8	161.5	0 37.7	+50.0	18.5
60	1 23.5	-49.4	162.1	0 26.5	-49.6	162.1	0 30.6	+49.8	17.9	1 27.7	+50.0	17.9
61	0 34.1	-49.4	162.6	0 23.1	+49.7	17.4	1 20.4	+49.8	17.4	2 17.7	+49.9	17.4
62	0 15.3	+49.4	16.8	1 12.8	+49.6	16.8	2 10.2	+49.8	16.8	3 07.6	+50.0	16.8
63	1 04.7	+49.5	16.2	2 02.4	+49.5	16.2	3 00.0	+49.7	16.3	3 57.6	+49.9	16.3
64	1 54.2	+49.4	15.7	2 51.9	+49.6	15.7	3 49.7	+49.7	15.7	4 47.5	+49.9	15.7
65	2 43.6	+49.4	15.1	3 41.5	+49.6	15.1	4 39.4	+49.7	15.1	5 37.4	+49.8	15.2
66	3 33.0	+49.4	14.5	4 31.1	+49.5	14.5	5 29.1	+49.7	14.6	6 27.2	+49.8	14.6
67	4 22.4	+49.3	14.0	5 20.6	+49.5	14.0	6 18.8	+49.6	14.0	7 17.0	+49.8	14.0
68	5 11.7	+49.3	13.4	6 10.1	+49.4	13.4	7 08.4	+49.6	13.4	8 06.8	+49.7	13.5
69	6 01.0	+49.3	12.8	6 59.5	+49.5	12.8	7 58.0	+49.6	12.9	8 56.5	+49.7	12.9
70	6 50.3	+49.3	12.2	7 49.0	+49.3	12.3	8 47.6	+49.5	12.3	9 46.2	+49.6	12.3
71	7 39.6	+49.2	11.7	8 38.3	+49.3	11.7	9 37.1	+49.4	11.7	10 35.8	+49.6	11.8
72	8 28.8	+49.1	11.1	9 27.6	+49.3	11.1	10 26.5	+49.4	11.2	11 25.4	+49.5	11.2
73	9 17.9	+49.1	10.5	10 16.9	+49.2	10.5	11 15.9	+49.3	10.6	12 14.9	+49.4	10.6
74	10 07.0	+49.0	9.9	11 06.1	+49.1	10.0	12 05.2	+49.2	10.0	13 04.3	+49.3	10.0
75	10 56.0	+49.0	9.3	11 55.2	+49.1	9.4	12 54.4	+49.2	9.4	13 53.6	+49.3	9.4
76	11 45.0	+48.9	8.8	12 44.3	+49.0	8.8	13 43.6	+49.1	8.8	14 42.9	+49.1	8.9
77	12 33.9	+48.8	8.2	13 33.3	+48.9	8.2	14 32.7	+48.9	8.2	15 32.0	+49.1	8.3
78	13 22.7	+48.7	7.6	14 22.2	+48.8	7.6	15 21.6	+48.9	7.6	16 21.1	+49.0	7.7
79	14 11.4	+48.7	7.0	15 11.0	+48.7	7.0	16 10.5	+48.8	7.0	17 10.1	+48.8	7.1
80	15 00.1	+48.5	6.4	15 59.7	+48.6	6.4	16 59.3	+48.7	6.4	17 58.9	+48.8	6.5
81	15 48.6	+48.4	5.7	16 48.3	+48.5	5.8	17 48.0	+48.5	5.8	18 47.7	+48.6	5.8
82	16 37.0	+48.4	5.1	17 36.8	+48.4	5.2	18 36.5	+48.5	5.2	19 36.3	+48.5	5.2
83	17 25.4	+48.2	4.5	18 25.2	+48.2	4.5	19 25.0	+48.3	4.6	20 24.8	+48.4	4.6
84	18 13.6	+48.1	3.9	19 13.4	+48.2	3.9	20 13.3	+48.2	3.9	21 13.2	+48.2	4.0
85	19 01.7	+47.9	3.3	20 01.6	+48.0	3.3	21 01.5	+48.0	3.3	22 01.4	+48.0	3.3
86	19 49.6	+47.8	2.6	20 49.6	+47.8	2.6	21 49.5	+47.9	2.7	22 49.4	+47.9	2.7
87	20 37.4	+47.7	2.0	21 37.4	+47.7	2.0	22 37.4	+47.7	2.0	23 37.3	+47.8	2.0
88	21 25.1	+47.5	1.3	22 25.1	+47.5	1.3	23 25.1	+47.5	1.3	24 25.1	+47.5	1.4
89	22 12.6	+47.4	0.7	23 12.6	+47.4	0.7	24 12.6	+47.4	0.7	25 12.6	+47.4	0.7
90	23 00.0	+47.2	0.0	24 00.0	+47.2	0.0	25 00.0	+47.2	0.0	26 00.0	+47.2	0.0
	23°			24°			25°			26°		

27°			28°			29°			30°			Dec.
Hc	d	Z	Hc	d	Z	Hc	d	Z	Hc	d	Z	
° ′	′	°	° ′	′	°	° ′	′	°	° ′	′	°	°
44 35.9	-38.6	120.2	44 05.3	-39.5	121.0	43 34.1	-40.5	121.8	43 02.1	-41.3	122.6	0
43 57.3	-39.1	121.2	43 25.8	-40.0	122.0	42 53.6	-40.9	122.8	42 20.8	-41.8	123.6	1
43 18.2	-39.7	122.3	42 45.8	-40.6	123.1	42 12.7	-41.5	123.8	41 39.0	-42.3	124.6	2
42 38.5	-40.3	123.3	42 05.2	-41.1	124.1	41 31.2	-41.9	124.8	40 56.7	-42.7	125.5	3
41 58.2	-40.7	124.3	41 24.1	-41.6	125.0	40 49.3	-42.4	125.7	40 14.0	-43.2	126.4	4
41 17.5	-41.3	125.3	40 42.5	-42.1	126.0	40 06.9	-42.8	126.7	39 30.8	-43.5	127.3	5
40 36.2	-41.7	126.2	40 00.4	-42.4	126.9	39 24.1	-43.2	127.6	38 47.3	-44.0	128.2	6
39 54.5	-42.2	127.2	39 18.0	-43.0	127.8	38 40.9	-43.7	128.5	38 03.3	-44.3	129.1	7
39 12.3	-42.5	128.1	38 35.0	-43.3	128.7	37 57.2	-44.0	129.4	37 19.0	-44.7	130.0	8
38 29.8	-43.0	129.0	37 51.7	-43.7	129.6	37 13.2	-44.4	130.2	36 34.3	-45.1	130.8	9
37 46.8	-43.4	129.9	37 08.0	-44.0	130.5	36 28.8	-44.7	131.1	35 49.2	-45.3	131.6	10
37 03.4	-43.8	130.8	36 24.0	-44.5	131.3	35 44.1	-45.0	131.9	35 03.9	-45.7	132.4	11
36 19.6	-44.1	131.6	35 39.5	-44.7	132.2	34 59.1	-45.4	132.7	34 18.2	-46.0	133.2	12
35 35.5	-44.5	132.5	34 54.8	-45.1	133.0	34 13.7	-45.7	133.5	33 32.2	-46.3	134.0	13
34 51.0	-44.8	133.3	34 09.7	-45.4	133.8	33 28.0	-46.0	134.3	32 45.9	-46.5	134.7	14
34 06.2	-45.1	134.1	33 24.3	-45.7	134.6	32 42.0	-46.2	135.0	31 59.4	-46.8	135.5	15
33 21.1	-45.4	134.9	32 38.6	-45.9	135.3	31 55.8	-46.5	135.8	31 12.6	-47.0	136.2	16
32 35.7	-45.6	135.7	31 52.7	-46.3	136.1	31 09.3	-46.8	136.5	30 25.6	-47.3	136.9	17
31 50.1	-46.0	136.4	31 06.4	-46.4	136.9	30 22.5	-47.0	137.3	29 38.3	-47.5	137.6	18
31 04.1	-46.2	137.2	30 20.0	-46.8	137.6	29 35.5	-47.2	138.0	28 50.8	-47.7	138.3	19
30 17.9	-46.4	137.9	29 33.2	-46.9	138.3	28 48.3	-47.4	138.7	28 03.1	-47.9	139.0	20
29 31.5	-46.7	138.7	28 46.3	-47.2	139.0	28 00.9	-47.7	139.4	27 15.2	-48.1	139.7	21
28 44.8	-47.0	139.4	27 59.1	-47.4	139.7	27 13.2	-47.8	140.1	26 27.1	-48.3	140.4	22
27 57.8	-47.1	140.1	27 11.7	-47.6	140.4	26 25.4	-48.1	140.7	25 38.8	-48.5	141.0	23
27 10.7	-47.3	140.8	26 24.1	-47.8	141.1	25 37.3	-48.2	141.4	24 50.3	-48.6	141.7	24
26 23.4	-47.5	141.5	25 36.3	-47.9	141.8	24 49.1	-48.4	142.1	24 01.7	-48.8	142.3	25
25 35.9	-47.8	142.2	24 48.4	-48.2	142.4	24 00.7	-48.5	142.7	23 12.9	-48.9	143.0	26
24 48.1	-47.9	142.8	24 00.2	-48.3	143.1	23 12.2	-48.7	143.4	22 24.0	-49.1	143.6	27
24 00.2	-48.0	143.5	23 11.9	-48.4	143.7	22 23.5	-48.9	144.0	21 34.9	-49.2	144.2	28
23 12.2	-48.2	144.1	22 23.5	-48.6	144.4	21 34.6	-48.9	144.6	20 45.7	-49.4	144.8	29
22 24.0	-48.4	144.8	21 34.9	-48.8	145.0	20 45.7	-49.2	145.2	19 56.3	-49.5	145.4	30
21 35.6	-48.5	145.4	20 46.1	-48.9	145.6	19 56.5	-49.2	145.8	19 06.8	-49.6	146.0	31
20 47.1	-48.7	146.1	19 57.2	-49.0	146.3	19 07.3	-49.4	146.5	18 17.2	-49.7	146.6	32
19 58.4	-48.8	146.7	19 08.2	-49.1	146.9	18 17.9	-49.4	147.1	17 27.5	-49.8	147.2	33
19 09.6	-48.9	147.3	18 19.1	-49.2	147.5	17 28.5	-49.6	147.6	16 37.7	-49.9	147.8	34
18 20.7	-49.0	147.9	17 29.9	-49.4	148.1	16 38.9	-49.7	148.2	15 47.8	-50.0	148.4	35
17 31.7	-49.1	148.5	16 40.5	-49.5	148.7	15 49.2	-49.8	148.8	14 57.8	-50.0	149.0	36
16 42.6	-49.3	149.1	15 51.0	-49.5	149.3	14 59.4	-49.8	149.4	14 07.8	-50.2	149.5	37
15 53.3	-49.3	149.7	15 01.5	-49.6	149.8	14 09.6	-50.0	150.0	13 17.6	-50.2	150.1	38
15 04.0	-49.4	150.3	14 11.9	-49.8	150.4	13 19.6	-50.0	150.5	12 27.4	-50.3	150.7	39
14 14.6	-49.5	150.9	13 22.1	-49.8	151.0	12 29.6	-50.0	151.1	11 37.1	-50.4	151.2	40
13 25.1	-49.6	151.5	12 32.3	-49.8	151.6	11 39.6	-50.2	151.7	10 46.7	-50.4	151.8	41
12 35.5	-49.7	152.0	11 42.5	-50.0	152.1	10 49.4	-50.2	152.2	9 56.3	-50.5	152.3	42
11 45.8	-49.7	152.6	10 52.5	-50.0	152.7	9 59.2	-50.3	152.8	9 05.8	-50.5	152.9	43
10 56.1	-49.8	153.2	10 02.5	-50.0	153.3	9 08.9	-50.3	153.3	8 15.3	-50.6	153.4	44
10 06.3	-49.8	153.8	9 12.5	-50.1	153.8	8 18.6	-50.3	153.9	7 24.7	-50.6	154.0	45
9 16.5	-49.9	154.3	8 22.4	-50.2	154.4	7 28.3	-50.4	154.4	6 34.1	-50.6	154.5	46
8 26.6	-50.0	154.9	7 32.2	-50.2	154.9	6 37.9	-50.5	155.0	5 43.5	-50.7	155.0	47
7 36.6	-50.0	155.4	6 42.0	-50.2	155.5	5 47.4	-50.5	155.5	4 52.8	-50.7	155.6	48
6 46.6	-50.0	156.0	5 51.8	-50.3	156.0	4 56.9	-50.4	156.1	4 02.1	-50.7	156.1	49
5 56.6	-50.1	156.6	5 01.5	-50.3	156.6	4 06.5	-50.6	156.6	3 11.4	-50.8	156.6	50
5 06.5	-50.1	157.1	4 11.2	-50.3	157.1	3 15.9	-50.5	157.2	2 20.6	-50.7	157.2	51
4 16.4	-50.1	157.7	3 20.9	-50.3	157.7	2 25.4	-50.5	157.7	1 29.9	-50.8	157.7	52
3 26.3	-50.1	158.2	2 30.6	-50.4	158.2	1 34.9	-50.6	158.2	0 39.1	-50.7	158.3	53
2 36.2	-50.2	158.8	1 40.2	-50.3	158.8	0 44.3	-50.6	158.8	0 11.6	+50.8	21.2	54
1 46.0	-50.1	159.3	0 49.9	-50.4	159.3	0 06.3	+50.5	20.7	1 02.4	+50.7	20.7	55
0 55.9	-50.2	159.9	0 00.5	+50.3	20.1	0 56.8	+50.6	20.1	1 53.1	+50.8	20.1	56
0 05.7	-50.2	160.4	0 50.8	+50.4	19.6	1 47.4	+50.5	19.6	2 43.9	+50.7	19.6	57
0 44.5	+50.1	19.0	1 41.2	+50.3	19.0	2 37.9	+50.5	19.1	3 34.6	+50.7	19.1	58
1 34.6	+50.2	18.5	2 31.5	+50.4	18.5	3 28.4	+50.5	18.5	4 25.3	+50.7	18.5	59
2 24.8	+50.1	17.9	3 21.9	+50.3	18.0	4 18.9	+50.5	18.0	5 16.0	+50.7	18.0	60
3 14.9	+50.2	17.4	4 12.2	+50.3	17.4	5 09.4	+50.5	17.4	6 06.7	+50.6	17.5	61
4 05.1	+50.1	16.8	5 02.5	+50.2	16.9	5 59.9	+50.4	16.9	6 57.3	+50.6	16.9	62
4 55.2	+50.0	16.3	5 52.7	+50.3	16.3	6 50.3	+50.4	16.4	7 47.9	+50.5	16.4	63
5 45.2	+50.1	15.7	6 43.0	+50.2	15.8	7 40.7	+50.4	15.8	8 38.4	+50.5	15.8	64
6 35.3	+50.0	15.2	7 33.2	+50.1	15.2	8 31.1	+50.3	15.3	9 28.9	+50.5	15.3	65
7 25.3	+49.9	14.6	8 23.3	+50.1	14.7	9 21.4	+50.2	14.7	10 19.4	+50.4	14.7	66
8 15.2	+49.9	14.1	9 13.4	+50.1	14.1	10 11.6	+50.2	14.1	11 09.8	+50.3	14.2	67
9 05.1	+49.9	13.5	10 03.5	+50.0	13.5	11 01.8	+50.1	13.6	12 00.1	+50.3	13.6	68
9 55.0	+49.8	12.9	10 53.5	+49.9	13.0	11 51.9	+50.1	13.0	12 50.4	+50.2	13.1	69
10 44.8	+49.8	12.4	11 43.4	+49.9	12.4	12 42.0	+50.0	12.5	13 40.6	+50.1	12.5	70
11 34.6	+49.6	11.8	12 33.3	+49.8	11.8	13 32.0	+49.9	11.9	14 30.7	+50.0	11.9	71
12 24.2	+49.6	11.2	13 23.1	+49.7	11.3	14 21.9	+49.9	11.3	15 20.7	+50.0	11.4	72
13 13.8	+49.6	10.7	14 12.8	+49.6	10.7	15 11.8	+49.7	10.7	16 10.7	+49.9	10.8	73
14 03.4	+49.4	10.1	15 02.4	+49.6	10.1	16 01.5	+49.7	10.2	17 00.6	+49.8	10.2	74
14 52.8	+49.4	9.5	15 52.0	+49.4	9.5	16 51.2	+49.5	9.6	17 50.3	+49.7	9.6	75
15 42.2	+49.2	8.9	16 41.4	+49.4	8.9	17 40.7	+49.4	9.0	18 40.0	+49.5	9.0	76
16 31.4	+49.2	8.3	17 30.8	+49.2	8.4	18 30.1	+49.4	8.4	19 29.5	+49.4	8.4	77
17 20.6	+49.0	7.7	18 20.0	+49.2	7.7	19 19.5	+49.2	7.8	20 18.9	+49.3	7.8	78
18 09.6	+49.0	7.1	19 09.2	+49.0	7.1	20 08.7	+49.1	7.2	21 08.2	+49.2	7.2	79
18 58.6	+48.8	6.5	19 58.2	+48.9	6.5	20 57.8	+48.9	6.6	21 57.4	+49.0	6.6	80
19 47.4	+48.7	5.9	20 47.1	+48.7	5.9	21 46.7	+48.8	6.0	22 46.4	+48.9	6.0	81
20 36.1	+48.5	5.3	21 35.8	+48.6	5.3	22 35.5	+48.7	5.3	23 35.3	+48.7	5.4	82
21 24.6	+48.4	4.6	22 24.4	+48.5	4.7	23 24.2	+48.5	4.7	24 24.0	+48.6	4.7	83
22 13.0	+48.3	4.0	23 12.9	+48.3	4.0	24 12.7	+48.4	4.0	25 12.6	+48.3	4.1	84
23 01.3	+48.1	3.3	24 01.2	+48.1	3.4	25 01.1	+48.1	3.4	26 00.9	+48.3	3.4	85
23 49.4	+47.9	2.7	24 49.3	+48.0	2.7	25 49.2	+48.0	2.7	26 49.2	+48.0	2.8	86
24 37.3	+47.7	2.0	25 37.3	+47.7	2.0	26 37.2	+47.8	2.1	27 37.2	+47.8	2.1	87
25 25.0	+47.6	1.4	26 25.0	+47.6	1.4	27 25.0	+47.6	1.4	28 25.0	+47.6	1.4	88
26 12.6	+47.4	0.7	27 12.6	+47.4	0.7	28 12.6	+47.4	0.7	29 12.6	+47.4	0.7	89
27 00.0	+47.2	0.0	28 00.0	+47.2	0.0	29 00.0	+47.2	0.0	30 00.0	+47.2	0.0	90
27°			28°			29°			30°			

S. Lat. { L.H.A. greater than 180° ....Zn=180°−Z
L.H.A. less than 180°...........Zn=180°+Z

LATITUDE SAME NAME AS DECLINATION L.H.A. 142°, 218°

39°, 321° L.H.A. LATITUDE SAME NAME AS DECLINATION N. Lat. {L.H.A. greater than 180° .....Zn=Z
L.H.A. less than 180°............Zn=360°-Z

Dec.	23° Hc	d	Z	24° Hc	d	Z	25° Hc	d	Z	26° Hc	d	Z	27° Hc	d	Z	28° Hc	d	Z	29° Hc	d	Z	30° Hc	d	Z	Dec.
°	° ′	′	°	° ′	′	°	° ′	′	°	° ′	′	°	° ′	′	°	° ′	′	°	° ′	′	°	° ′	′	°	°
0	45 40.4	+33.2	115.8	45 13.9	+34.3	116.7	44 46.5	+35.4	117.6	44 18.4	+36.4	118.4	43 49.4	+37.5	119.3	43 19.7	+38.4	120.1	42 49.2	+39.4	120.9	42 18.1	+40.3	121.7	0
1	46 13.6	+32.4	114.6	45 48.2	+33.6	115.5	45 21.9	+34.7	116.4	44 54.8	+35.8	117.3	44 26.9	+36.8	118.2	43 58.1	+37.9	119.0	43 28.6	+38.8	119.9	42 58.4	+39.7	120.7	1
2	46 46.0	+31.6	113.3	46 21.8	+32.8	114.3	45 56.6	+34.0	115.2	45 30.6	+35.0	116.2	45 03.7	+36.1	117.1	44 36.0	+37.2	118.0	44 07.4	+38.2	118.8	43 38.1	+39.2	119.7	2
3	47 17.6	+30.8	112.1	46 54.6	+32.0	113.1	46 30.6	+33.2	114.1	46 05.6	+34.4	115.0	45 39.8	+35.5	115.9	45 13.2	+36.5	116.8	44 45.6	+37.6	117.7	44 17.3	+38.6	118.6	3
4	47 48.4	+29.9	110.8	47 26.6	+31.1	111.8	47 03.8	+32.4	112.8	46 40.0	+33.6	113.8	46 15.3	+34.7	114.8	45 49.7	+35.9	115.7	45 23.2	+37.0	116.6	44 55.9	+38.0	117.5	4
5	48 18.3	+29.0	109.5	47 57.7	+30.4	110.6	47 36.2	+31.5	111.6	47 13.6	+32.8	112.6	46 50.0	+34.0	113.6	46 25.6	+35.1	114.6	46 00.2	+36.2	115.5	45 33.9	+37.3	116.4	5
6	48 47.3	+28.2	108.2	48 28.1	+29.4	109.3	48 07.7	+30.8	110.3	47 46.4	+32.0	111.4	47 24.0	+33.2	112.4	47 00.7	+34.4	113.4	46 36.4	+35.6	114.4	46 11.2	+36.7	115.3	6
7	49 15.5	+27.1	106.9	48 57.5	+28.5	108.0	48 38.5	+29.8	109.0	48 18.4	+31.1	110.1	47 57.2	+32.4	111.1	47 35.1	+33.6	112.2	47 12.0	+34.8	113.2	46 47.9	+35.9	114.2	7
8	49 42.6	+26.2	105.5	49 26.0	+27.6	106.6	49 08.3	+29.0	107.7	48 49.5	+30.3	108.8	48 29.6	+31.6	109.9	48 08.7	+32.8	110.9	47 46.8	+34.0	112.0	47 23.8	+35.2	113.0	8
9	50 08.8	+25.1	104.1	49 53.6	+26.6	105.2	49 37.3	+27.9	106.4	49 19.8	+29.3	107.5	49 01.2	+30.7	108.6	48 41.5	+32.0	109.7	48 20.8	+33.2	110.7	47 59.0	+34.5	111.8	9
10	50 33.9	+24.1	102.7	50 20.2	+25.5	103.8	50 05.2	+27.0	105.0	49 49.1	+28.4	106.1	49 31.9	+29.7	107.3	49 13.5	+31.1	108.4	48 54.0	+32.4	109.5	48 33.5	+33.6	110.5	10
11	50 58.0	+23.0	101.2	50 45.7	+24.5	102.4	50 32.2	+26.0	103.6	50 17.5	+27.4	104.8	50 01.6	+28.8	105.9	49 44.6	+30.1	107.1	49 26.4	+31.5	108.2	49 07.1	+32.8	109.3	11
12	51 21.0	+21.8	99.7	51 10.2	+23.4	101.0	50 58.2	+24.9	102.2	50 44.9	+26.4	103.4	50 30.4	+27.8	104.6	50 14.7	+29.3	105.7	49 57.9	+30.6	106.9	49 39.9	+31.9	108.0	12
13	51 42.8	+20.7	98.2	51 33.6	+22.3	99.5	51 23.1	+23.8	100.7	51 11.3	+25.3	101.9	50 58.2	+26.8	103.2	50 44.0	+28.2	104.4	50 28.5	+29.6	105.5	50 11.8	+31.1	106.7	13
14	52 03.5	+19.5	96.7	51 55.9	+21.1	98.0	51 46.9	+22.6	99.2	51 36.6	+24.2	100.5	51 25.0	+25.7	101.7	51 12.2	+27.2	102.9	50 58.1	+28.7	104.2	50 42.9	+30.0	105.3	14
15	52 23.0	+18.3	95.2	52 17.0	+19.9	96.5	52 09.5	+21.5	97.7	52 00.8	+23.1	99.0	51 50.7	+24.7	100.3	51 39.4	+26.1	101.5	51 26.8	+27.6	102.8	51 12.9	+29.1	104.0	15
16	52 41.3	+17.1	93.6	52 36.9	+18.6	94.9	52 31.0	+20.4	96.2	52 23.9	+21.9	97.5	52 15.4	+23.5	98.8	52 05.5	+25.1	100.1	51 54.4	+26.6	101.3	51 42.0	+28.0	102.6	16
17	52 58.4	+15.7	92.0	52 55.5	+17.5	93.3	52 51.4	+19.0	94.7	52 45.8	+20.7	96.0	52 38.9	+22.3	97.3	52 30.6	+23.9	98.6	52 21.0	+25.4	99.9	52 10.0	+27.0	101.1	17
18	53 14.1	+14.4	90.4	53 13.0	+16.1	91.8	53 10.4	+17.8	93.1	53 06.5	+19.5	94.4	53 01.2	+21.1	95.7	52 54.5	+22.7	97.1	52 46.4	+24.4	98.4	52 37.0	+25.9	99.7	18
19	53 28.5	+13.1	88.8	53 29.1	+14.8	90.1	53 28.2	+16.5	91.5	53 26.0	+18.2	92.8	53 22.3	+19.9	94.2	53 17.2	+21.5	95.5	53 10.8	+23.1	96.9	53 02.9	+24.7	98.2	19
20	53 41.6	+11.7	87.1	53 43.9	+13.5	88.5	53 44.7	+15.2	89.9	53 44.2	+16.9	91.2	53 42.2	+18.6	92.6	53 38.7	+20.3	94.0	53 33.9	+21.9	95.3	53 27.6	+23.6	96.6	20
21	53 53.3	+10.4	85.5	53 57.4	+12.0	86.9	53 59.9	+13.9	88.2	54 01.1	+15.5	89.6	54 00.8	+17.2	91.0	53 59.0	+19.0	92.4	53 55.8	+20.7	93.7	53 51.2	+22.3	95.1	21
22	54 03.7	+8.9	83.8	54 09.4	+10.7	85.2	54 13.8	+12.4	86.6	54 16.6	+14.2	88.0	54 18.0	+16.0	89.3	54 18.0	+17.6	90.7	54 16.5	+19.4	92.1	54 13.5	+21.1	93.5	22
23	54 12.6	+7.5	82.1	54 20.1	+9.3	83.5	54 26.2	+11.0	84.9	54 30.8	+12.8	86.3	54 34.0	+14.5	87.7	54 35.6	+16.4	89.1	54 35.9	+18.0	90.5	54 34.6	+19.8	91.9	23
24	54 20.1	+6.1	80.4	54 29.4	+7.8	81.8	54 37.2	+9.6	83.2	54 43.6	+11.4	84.6	54 48.5	+13.2	86.0	54 52.0	+14.9	87.4	54 53.9	+16.7	88.8	54 54.4	+18.4	90.3	24
25	54 26.2	+4.6	78.7	54 37.2	+6.4	80.1	54 46.8	+8.2	81.5	54 55.0	+9.9	82.9	55 01.7	+11.7	84.3	55 06.9	+13.5	85.7	55 10.6	+15.3	87.2	55 12.8	+17.0	88.6	25
26	54 30.8	+3.2	77.0	54 43.6	+4.9	78.4	54 55.0	+6.7	79.8	55 04.9	+8.5	81.2	55 13.4	+10.2	82.6	55 20.4	+12.0	84.0	55 25.9	+13.8	85.5	55 29.8	+15.7	86.9	26
27	54 34.0	+1.6	75.3	54 48.5	+3.5	76.6	55 01.7	+5.2	78.0	55 13.4	+7.0	79.4	55 23.6	+8.8	80.9	55 32.4	+10.6	82.3	55 39.7	+12.4	83.8	55 45.5	+14.2	85.2	27
28	54 35.6	+0.3	73.6	54 52.0	+1.9	74.9	55 06.9	+3.7	76.3	55 20.4	+5.5	77.7	55 32.4	+7.3	79.1	55 43.0	+9.1	80.6	55 52.1	+10.9	82.0	55 59.7	+12.7	83.5	28
29	54 35.9	-1.3	71.8	54 53.9	+0.5	73.2	55 10.6	+2.2	74.5	55 25.9	+3.9	75.9	55 39.7	+5.8	77.4	55 52.1	+7.6	78.8	56 03.0	+9.4	80.3	56 12.4	+11.2	81.7	29
30	54 34.6	-2.7	70.1	54 54.4	-1.1	71.4	55 12.8	+0.7	72.8	55 29.8	+2.5	74.2	55 45.5	+4.2	75.6	55 59.7	+6.0	77.0	56 12.4	+7.9	78.5	56 23.6	+9.7	80.0	30
31	54 31.9	-4.2	68.4	54 53.3	-2.5	69.7	55 13.5	-0.8	71.0	55 32.3	+0.9	72.4	55 49.7	+2.7	73.8	56 05.7	+4.5	75.3	56 20.3	+6.3	76.7	56 33.3	+8.2	78.2	31
32	54 27.7	-5.7	66.7	54 50.8	-4.0	68.0	55 12.7	-2.3	69.3	55 33.2	-0.6	70.7	55 52.4	+1.2	72.0	56 10.2	+3.0	73.5	56 26.6	+4.7	74.9	56 41.5	+6.5	76.4	32
33	54 22.0	-7.1	64.9	54 46.8	-5.5	66.2	55 10.4	-3.8	67.5	55 32.6	-2.1	68.9	55 53.6	-0.4	70.3	56 13.2	+1.3	71.7	56 31.3	+3.2	73.1	56 48.0	+5.0	74.6	33
34	54 14.9	-8.5	63.2	54 41.3	-6.9	64.5	55 06.6	-5.4	65.8	55 30.5	-3.6	67.1	55 53.2	-1.9	68.5	56 14.5	-0.2	69.9	56 34.5	+1.6	71.3	56 53.0	+3.4	72.7	34
35	54 06.4	-9.9	61.6	54 34.4	-8.4	62.8	55 01.2	-6.7	64.1	55 26.9	-5.2	65.4	55 51.3	-3.5	66.7	56 14.3	-1.7	68.1	56 36.1	0.0	69.5	56 56.4	+1.8	70.9	35
36	53 56.5	-11.4	59.9	54 26.0	-9.8	61.1	54 54.5	-8.3	62.3	55 21.7	-6.6	63.6	55 47.8	-5.0	64.9	56 12.6	-3.3	66.3	56 36.1	-1.6	67.7	56 58.2	+0.2	69.1	36
37	53 45.1	-12.7	58.2	54 16.2	-11.2	59.4	54 46.2	-9.7	60.6	55 15.1	-8.2	61.9	55 42.8	-6.5	63.1	56 09.3	-4.9	64.5	56 34.5	-3.2	65.8	56 58.4	-1.5	67.2	37
38	53 32.4	-14.0	56.6	54 05.0	-12.6	57.7	54 36.5	-11.1	58.9	55 06.9	-9.6	60.1	55 36.3	-8.1	61.4	56 04.4	-6.4	62.7	56 31.3	-4.7	64.0	56 56.9	-3.0	65.4	38
39	53 18.4	-15.4	54.9	53 52.4	-14.0	56.1	54 25.4	-12.6	57.2	54 57.3	-11.0	58.4	55 28.2	-9.5	59.6	55 58.0	-8.0	60.9	56 26.6	-6.4	62.2	56 53.9	-4.7	63.6	39
40	53 03.0	-16.7	53.3	53 38.4	-15.3	54.4	54 12.8	-13.9	55.5	54 46.3	-12.5	56.7	55 18.7	-11.0	57.9	55 50.0	-9.4	59.1	56 20.2	-7.8	60.4	56 49.2	-6.2	61.8	40
41	52 46.3	-17.9	51.7	53 23.1	-16.7	52.8	53 58.9	-15.3	53.9	54 33.8	-13.9	55.0	55 07.7	-12.4	56.2	55 40.6	-11.0	57.4	56 12.4	-9.4	58.6	56 43.0	-7.8	59.9	41
42	52 28.4	-19.2	50.2	53 06.4	-17.9	51.2	53 43.6	-16.6	52.2	54 19.9	-15.2	53.3	54 55.3	-13.9	54.5	55 29.6	-12.4	55.6	56 03.0	-10.9	56.9	56 35.2	-9.3	58.1	42
43	52 09.2	-20.3	48.6	52 48.5	-19.1	49.6	53 27.0	-17.9	50.6	54 04.7	-16.6	51.7	54 41.4	-15.2	52.8	55 17.2	-13.8	53.9	55 52.1	-12.4	55.1	56 25.9	-10.9	56.3	43
44	51 48.9	-21.5	47.1	52 29.4	-20.4	48.0	53 09.1	-19.1	49.0	53 48.1	-17.9	50.0	54 26.2	-16.6	51.1	55 03.4	-15.3	52.2	55 39.7	-13.9	53.4	56 15.0	-12.4	54.6	44
45	51 27.4	-22.7	45.6	52 09.0	-21.5	46.5	52 50.0	-20.4	47.4	53 30.2	-19.2	48.4	54 09.6	-18.0	49.5	54 48.1	-16.6	50.5	55 25.8	-15.3	51.7	56 02.6	-13.9	52.8	45
46	51 04.7	-23.8	44.1	51 47.5	-22.7	45.0	52 29.6	-21.6	45.9	53 11.0	-20.5	46.8	53 51.6	-19.2	47.8	54 31.5	-18.0	48.9	55 10.5	-16.6	50.0	55 48.7	-15.3	51.1	46
47	50 40.9	-24.8	42.6	51 24.8	-23.9	43.5	52 08.0	-22.8	44.4	52 50.5	-21.6	45.3	53 32.4	-20.5	46.2	54 13.5	-19.3	47.2	54 53.9	-18.1	48.3	55 33.4	-16.8	49.4	47
48	50 16.1	-25.9	41.2	51 00.9	-24.9	42.0	51 45.2	-23.9	42.9	52 28.9	-22.8	43.7	53 11.9	-21.7	44.7	53 54.2	-20.5	45.6	54 35.8	-19.4	46.6	55 16.6	-18.1	47.7	48
49	49 50.2	-26.9	39.8	50 36.0	-25.9	40.6	51 21.3	-24.9	41.4	52 06.1	-24.0	42.2	52 50.2	-22.9	43.1	53 33.7	-21.9	44.0	54 16.4	-20.6	45.0	54 58.5	-19.5	46.0	49
50	49 23.3	-27.8	38.4	50 10.1	-26.9	39.2	50 56.4	-26.1	39.9	51 42.1	-25.1	40.7	52 27.3	-24.1	41.6	53 11.8	-23.0	42.5	53 55.8	-22.0	43.4	54 39.0	-20.8	44.4	50
51	48 55.5	-28.8	37.1	49 43.2	-28.0	37.8	50 30.3	-27.0	38.5	51 17.0	-26.1	39.3	52 03.2	-25.2	40.1	52 48.8	-24.2	40.9	53 33.8	-23.1	41.8	54 18.2	-22.0	42.7	51
52	48 26.7	-29.7	35.7	49 15.2	-28.9	36.4	50 03.3	-28.1	37.1	50 50.9	-27.2	37.9	51 38.0	-26.2	38.6	52 24.6	-25.3	39.4	53 10.7	-24.3	40.3	53 56.2	-23.3	41.2	52
53	47 57.0	-30.5	34.4	48 46.3	-29.7	35.1	49 35.2	-28.9	35.7	50 23.7	-28.1	36.4	51 11.8	-27.3	37.2	51 59.3	-26.4	38.0	52 46.4	-25.5	38.8	53 32.9	-24.5	39.6	53
54	47 26.5	-31.4	33.2	48 16.6	-30.7	33.8	49 06.3	-30.0	34.4	49 55.6	-29.2	35.1	50 44.5	-28.3	35.8	51 32.9	-27.4	36.5	52 20.9	-26.6	37.3	53 08.4	-25.6	38.1	54
55	46 55.1	-32.2	31.9	47 45.9	-31.5	32.5	48 36.3	-30.7	33.1	49 26.4	-30.0	33.7	50 16.2	-29.3	34.4	51 05.5	-28.5	35.1	51 54.3	-27.6	35.8	52 42.8	-26.8	36.6	55
56	46 22.9	-32.9	30.7	47 14.4	-32.3	31.2	48 05.6	-31.7	31.8	48 56.4	-31.0	32.4	49 46.9	-30.2	33.0	50 37.0	-29.5	33.7	51 26.7	-28.6	34.4	52 16.0	-27.8	35.1	56
57	45 50.0	-33.7	29.5	46 42.1	-33.1	30.0	47 33.9	-32.5	30.5	48 25.4	-31.8	31.1	49 16.7	-31.2	31.7	50 07.5	-30.4	32.3	50 58.1	-29.7	33.0	51 48.2	-28.9	33.7	57
58	45 16.3	-34.5	28.3	46 09.0	-33.9	28.8	47 01.4	-33.2	29.3	47 53.6	-32.6	29.8	48 45.5	-31.9	30.4	49 37.1	-31.3	31.0	50 28.4	-30.6	31.6	51 19.3	-29.8	32.3	58
59	44 41.8	-35.1	27.1	45 35.1	-34.5	27.6	46 28.2	-34.0	28.1	47 21.0	-33.4	28.6	48 13.6	-32.8	29.1	49 05.8	-32.1	29.7	49 57.8	-31.5	30.3	50 49.5	-30.8	30.9	59
60	44 06.7	-35.7	26.0	45 00.6	-35.3	26.4	45 54.2	-34.7	26.9	46 47.6	-34.2	27.4	47 40.8	-33.6	27.9	48 33.7	-33.0	28.4	49 26.3	-32.4	28.9	50 18.7	-31.7	29.5	60
61	43 31.0	-36.4	24.9	44 25.3	-35.9	25.3	45 19.5	-35.5	25.7	46 13.4	-34.9	26.2	47 07.2	-34.4	26.6	48 00.7	-33.8	27.1	48 53.9	-33.2	27.7	49 47.0	-32.7	28.2	61
62	42 54.6	-37.1	23.8	43 49.4	-36.6	24.2	44 44.0	-36.1	24.6	45 38.5	-35.6	25.0	46 32.8	-35.1	25.4	47 26.9	-34.6	25.9	48 20.7	-34.0	26.4	49 14.3	-33.4	26.9	62
63	42 17.5	-37.6	22.7	43 12.8	-37.2	23.1	44 07.9	-36.7	23.5	45 02.9	-36.3	23.9	45 57.7	-35.8	24.3	46 52.3	-35.3	24.7	47 46.7	-34.8	25.2	48 40.9	-34.3	25.6	63
64	41 39.9	-38.1	21.7	42 35.6	-37.7	22.0	43 31.2	-37.4	22.4	44 26.6	-36.9	22.7	45 21.9	-36.5	23.1	46 17.0	-36.1	23.5	47 11.9	-35.6	24.0	48 06.6	-35.0	24.4	64
65	41 01.8	-38.7	20.6	41 57.9	-38.4	21.0	42 53.8	-37.9	21.3	43 49.7	-37.6	21.6	44 45.4	-37.2	22.0	45 40.9	-36.7	22.4	46 36.3	-36.2	22.8	47 31.6	-35.8	23.2	65
66	40 23.1	-39.2	19.6	41 19.5	-38.8	19.9	42 15.9	-38.5	20.2	43 12.1	-38.1	20.6	44 08.2	-37.7	20.9	45 04.2	-37.3	21.3	46 00.1	-37.0	21.6	46 55.8	-36.5	22.0	66
67	39 43.9	-39.7	18.6	40 40.7	-39.4	18.9	41 37.4	-39.1	19.2	42 34.0	-38.7	19.5	43 30.5	-38.4	19.8	44 26.9	-38.0	20.1	45 23.1	-37.5	20.5	46 19.3	-37.2	20.9	67
68	39 04.2	-40.2	17.7	40 01.3	-39.9	17.9	40 58.3	-39.5	18.2	41 55.3	-39.3	18.5	42 52.1	-38.9	18.8	43 48.9	-38.6	19.1	44 45.6	-38.3	19.4	45 42.1	-37.8	19.7	68
69	38 24.0	-40.7	16.7	39 21.4	-40.3	17.0	40 18.8	-40.1	17.2	41 16.0	-39.7	17.5	42 13.2	-39.4	17.7	43 10.3	-39.1	18.0	44 07.3	-38.8	18.3	45 04.3	-38.5	18.6	69
70	37 43.3	-41.0	15.8	38 41.1	-40.9	16.0	39 38.7	-40.6	16.2	40 36.3	-40.3	16.5	41 33.8	-40.0	16.7	42 31.2	-39.7	17.0	43 28.5	-39.3	17.3	44 25.8	-39.1	17.5	70
71	37 02.3	-41.5	14.9	38 00.2	-41.2	15.1	38 58.1	-41.0	15.3	39 56.0	-40.7	15.5	40 53.8	-40.5	15.7	41 51.5	-40.2	16.0	42 49.2	-40.0	16.2	43 46.7	-39.6	16.5	71
72	36 20.8	-41.9	14.0	37 19.0	-41.7	14.2	38 17.1	-41.4	14.3	39 15.3	-41.2	14.5	40 13.3	-41.0	14.8	41 11.3	-40.7	15.0	42 09.2	-40.4	15.2	43 07.1	-40.2	15.5	72
73	35 38.9	-42.3	13.1	36 37.3	-42.0	13.3	37 35.7	-41.8	13.4	38 34.1	-41.7	13.6	39 32.3	-41.4	13.8	40 30.6	-41.2	14.0	41 28.8	-41.0	14.2	42 26.9	-40.7	14.4	73
74	34 56.6	-42.6	12.2	35 55.3	-42.5	12.4	36 53.9	-42.3	12.5	37 52.4	-42.0	12.7	38 50.9	-41.8	12.9	39 49.4	-41.6	13.1	40 47.8	-41.4	13.2	41 46.2	-41.2	13.4	74
75	34 14.0	-43.0	11.4	35 12.8	-42.8	11.5	36 11.6	-42.6	11.6	37 10.4	-42.5	11.8	38 09.1	-42.3	12.0	39 07.8	-42.1	12.1	40 06.4	-41.9	12.3	41 05.0	-41.7	12.5	75
76	33 31.0	-43.3	10.5	34 30.0	-43.1	10.6	35 29.0	-43.0	10.8	36 27.9	-42.8	10.9	37 26.8	-42.7	11.1	38 25.7	-42.5	11.2	39 24.5	-42.3	11.4	40 23.3	-42.1	11.5	76
77	32 47.7	-43.6	9.7	33 46.9	-43.5	9.8	34 46.0	-43.4	9.9	35 45.1	-43.3	10.0	36 44.1	-43.0	10.2	37 43.2	-42.9	10.3	38 42.2	-42.8	10.5	39 41.2	-42.6	10.6	77
78	32 04.1	-44.0	8.9	33 03.4	-43.9	9.0	34 02.6	-43.7	9.1	35 01.8	-43.5	9.2	36 01.1	-43.5	9.3	37 00.3	-43.3	9.4	37 59.4	-43.1	9.6	38 58.6	-43.0	9.7	78
79	31 20.1	-44.2	8.1	32 19.5	-44.1	8.2	33 18.9	-44.0	8.3	34 18.3	-43.9	8.4	35 17.6	-43.7	8.5	36 17.0	-43.7	8.6	37 16.3	-43.5	8.7	38 15.6	-43.4	8.8	79
80	30 35.9	-44.5	7.3	31 35.4	-44.4	7.4	32 34.9	-44.3	7.5	33 34.4	-44.2	7.5	34 33.9	-44.1	7.6	35 33.3	-44.0	7.7	36 32.8	-43.9	7.8	37 32.2	-43.7	7.9	80
81	29 51.4	-44.8	6.5	30 51.0	-44.7	6.6	31 50.6	-44.6	6.7	32 50.2	-44.5	6.7	33 49.8	-44.5	6.8	34 49.3	-44.3	6.9	35 48.9	-44.2	7.0	36 48.5	-44.2	7.1	81
82	29 06.6	-45.0	5.8	30 06.3	-45.0	5.8	31 06.0	-44.9	5.9	32 05.7	-44.8	5.9	33 05.3	-44.7	6.0	34 05.0	-44.6	6.1	35 04.7	-44.6	6.1	36 04.3	-44.5	6.2	82
83	28 21.6	-45.3	5.0	29 21.3	-45.2	5.0	30 21.1	-45.2	5.1	31 20.9	-45.1	5.2	32 20.6	-45.0	5.2	33 20.4	-45.0	5.3	34 20.1	-44.9	5.3	35 19.8	-44.8	5.4	83
84	27 36.3	-45.5	4.3	28 36.1	-45.5	4.3	29 35.9	-45.4	4.3	30 35.8	-45.4	4.4	31 35.6	-45.3	4.4	32 35.4	-45.2	4.5	33 35.2	-45.2	4.5	34 35.0	-45.1	4.6	84
85	26 50.8	-45.8	3.5	27 50.6	-45.7	3.6	28 50.5	-45.6	3.6	29 50.4	-45.6	3.6	30 50.3	-45.6	3.7	31 50.2	-45.6	3.7	32 50.0	-45.4	3.7	33 49.9	-45.4	3.8	85
86	26 05.0	-45.9	2.8	27 04.9	-45.9	2.8	28 04.9	-45.9	2.9	29 04.8	-45.9	2.9	30 04.7	-45.8	2.9	31 04.6	-45.8	2.9	32 04.6	-45.8	3.0	33 04.5	-45.7	3.0	86
87	25 19.1	-46.2	2.1	26 19.0	-46.1	2.1	27 19.0	-46.1	2.1	28 18.9	-46.1	2.1	29 18.9	-46.1	2.2	30 18.8	-46.0	2.2	31 18.8	-46.0	2.2	32 18.8	-46.0	2.2	87
88	24 32.9	-46.4	1.4	25 32.9	-46.4	1.4	26 32.9	-46.4	1.4	27 32.8	-46.3	1.4	28 32.8	-46.3	1.4	29 32.8	-46.3	1.4	30 32.8	-46.3	1.5	31 32.8	-46.3	1.5	88
89	23 46.5	-46.5	0.7	24 46.5	-46.5	0.7	25 46.5	-46.5	0.7	26 46.5	-46.5	0.7	27 46.5	-46.5	0.7	28 46.5	-46.5	0.7	29 46.5	-46.5	0.7	30 46.5	-46.5	0.7	89
90	23 00.0	-46.7	0.0	24 00.0	-46.7	0.0	25 00.0	-46.7	0.0	26 00.0	-46.7	0.0	27 00.0	-46.7	0.0	28 00.0	-46.7	0.0	29 00.0	-46.7	0.0	30 00.0	-46.7	0.0	90
	23°			24°			25°			26°			27°			28°			29°			30°			

39°, 321° L.H.A. LATITUDE SAME NAME AS DECLINATION

262

LATITUDE CONTRARY NAME TO DECLINATION — L.H.A. 39°, 321°

Dec.	23° Hc	d	Z	24° Hc	d	Z	25° Hc	d	Z	26° Hc	d	Z
°	° ′	′	°	° ′	′	°	° ′	′	°	° ′	′	°
0	45 40.4	−33.9	115.8	45 13.9	−35.0	116.7	44 46.5	−36.0	117.6	44 18.4	−37.1	118.4
1	45 06.5	−34.6	116.9	44 38.9	−35.7	117.8	44 10.5	−36.7	118.7	43 41.3	−37.7	119.5
2	44 31.9	−35.3	118.1	44 03.2	−36.3	118.9	43 33.8	−37.3	119.8	43 03.6	−38.2	120.6
3	43 56.6	−36.0	119.2	43 26.9	−37.0	120.0	42 56.5	−37.9	120.9	42 25.4	−38.9	121.6
4	43 20.6	−36.6	120.3	42 49.9	−37.5	121.1	42 18.6	−38.5	121.9	41 46.5	−39.3	122.7
5	42 44.0	−37.2	121.4	42 12.4	−38.1	122.2	41 40.1	−39.0	122.9	41 07.2	−39.9	123.7
6	42 06.8	−37.7	122.5	41 34.3	−38.7	123.2	41 01.1	−39.5	124.0	40 27.3	−40.4	124.7
7	41 29.1	−38.4	123.5	40 55.6	−39.2	124.2	40 21.6	−40.1	124.9	39 46.9	−40.9	125.6
8	40 50.7	−38.8	124.5	40 16.4	−39.7	125.2	39 41.5	−40.5	125.9	39 06.0	−41.3	126.6
9	40 11.9	−39.4	125.5	39 36.7	−40.1	126.2	39 01.0	−41.0	126.9	38 24.7	−41.7	127.5
10	39 32.5	−39.8	126.5	38 56.6	−40.7	127.2	38 20.0	−41.4	127.8	37 43.0	−42.1	128.4
11	38 52.7	−40.3	127.5	38 15.9	−41.1	128.1	37 38.6	−41.8	128.7	37 00.9	−42.6	129.3
12	38 12.4	−40.8	128.4	37 34.8	−41.5	129.0	36 56.8	−42.2	129.6	36 18.3	−42.9	130.2
13	37 31.6	−41.2	129.4	36 53.3	−41.9	129.9	36 14.6	−42.6	130.5	35 35.4	−43.3	131.1
14	36 50.4	−41.6	130.3	36 11.4	−42.3	130.8	35 32.0	−43.0	131.4	34 52.1	−43.6	131.9
15	36 08.8	−42.0	131.2	35 29.1	−42.6	131.7	34 49.0	−43.3	132.2	34 08.5	−44.0	132.7
16	35 26.8	−42.3	132.0	34 46.5	−43.1	132.6	34 05.7	−43.7	133.1	33 24.5	−44.3	133.6
17	34 44.5	−42.8	132.9	34 03.4	−43.3	133.4	33 22.0	−44.0	133.9	32 40.2	−44.6	134.4
18	34 01.7	−43.0	133.8	33 20.1	−43.7	134.2	32 38.0	−44.3	134.7	31 55.6	−44.8	135.2
19	33 18.7	−43.5	134.6	32 36.4	−44.1	135.1	31 53.7	−44.6	135.5	31 10.8	−45.2	135.9
20	32 35.2	−43.7	135.4	31 52.3	−44.3	135.9	31 09.1	−44.8	136.3	30 25.6	−45.4	136.7
21	31 51.5	−44.0	136.2	31 08.0	−44.6	136.7	30 24.3	−45.2	137.1	29 40.2	−45.7	137.5
22	31 07.5	−44.3	137.0	30 23.4	−44.8	137.4	29 39.1	−45.4	137.8	28 54.5	−45.9	138.2
23	30 23.2	−44.6	137.8	29 38.6	−45.1	138.2	28 53.7	−45.6	138.6	28 08.6	−46.1	138.9
24	29 38.6	−44.9	138.6	28 53.5	−45.4	139.0	28 08.1	−45.9	139.3	27 22.5	−46.4	139.7
25	28 53.7	−45.1	139.3	28 08.1	−45.6	139.7	27 22.2	−46.1	140.0	26 36.1	−46.6	140.4
26	28 08.6	−45.3	140.1	27 22.5	−45.9	140.4	26 36.1	−46.3	140.8	25 49.5	−46.7	141.1
27	27 23.3	−45.6	140.8	26 36.6	−46.0	141.2	25 49.8	−46.5	141.5	25 02.8	−47.0	141.8
28	26 37.7	−45.8	141.6	25 50.6	−46.3	141.9	25 03.3	−46.7	142.2	24 15.8	−47.1	142.4
29	25 51.9	−46.0	142.3	25 04.3	−46.5	142.6	24 16.6	−46.9	142.9	23 28.7	−47.4	143.1
30	25 05.9	−46.3	143.0	24 17.8	−46.6	143.3	23 29.7	−47.1	143.5	22 41.3	−47.4	143.8
31	24 19.6	−46.4	143.7	23 31.2	−46.8	144.0	22 42.6	−47.2	144.2	21 53.9	−47.7	144.5
32	23 33.2	−46.6	144.4	22 44.4	−47.0	144.6	21 55.4	−47.4	144.9	21 06.2	−47.8	145.1
33	22 46.6	−46.7	145.1	21 57.4	−47.2	145.3	21 08.0	−47.6	145.5	20 18.4	−47.9	145.8
34	21 59.9	−47.0	145.8	21 10.2	−47.3	146.0	20 20.4	−47.7	146.2	19 30.5	−48.1	146.4
35	21 12.9	−47.0	146.4	20 22.9	−47.5	146.6	19 32.7	−47.8	146.8	18 42.4	−48.2	147.0
36	20 25.9	−47.3	147.1	19 35.4	−47.6	147.3	18 44.9	−48.0	147.5	17 54.2	−48.3	147.7
37	19 38.6	−47.4	147.7	18 47.8	−47.7	147.9	17 56.9	−48.1	148.1	17 05.9	−48.4	148.3
38	18 51.2	−47.5	148.4	18 00.1	−47.9	148.6	17 08.8	−48.1	148.7	16 17.5	−48.5	148.9
39	18 03.7	−47.6	149.0	17 12.2	−47.9	149.2	16 20.7	−48.4	149.4	15 29.0	−48.6	149.5
40	17 16.1	−47.8	149.7	16 24.3	−48.1	149.8	15 32.3	−48.4	150.0	14 40.4	−48.8	150.1
41	16 28.3	−47.8	150.3	15 36.2	−48.2	150.5	14 43.9	−48.5	150.6	13 51.6	−48.8	150.7
42	15 40.5	−48.0	150.9	14 48.0	−48.3	151.1	13 55.4	−48.6	151.2	13 02.8	−48.9	151.3
43	14 52.5	−48.1	151.6	13 59.7	−48.4	151.7	13 06.8	−48.6	151.8	12 13.9	−48.9	151.9
44	14 04.4	−48.2	152.2	13 11.3	−48.4	152.3	12 18.2	−48.8	152.4	11 25.0	−49.1	152.5
45	13 16.2	−48.2	152.8	12 22.9	−48.6	152.9	11 29.4	−48.8	153.0	10 35.9	−49.1	153.1
46	12 28.0	−48.4	153.4	11 34.3	−48.6	153.5	10 40.6	−48.9	153.6	9 46.8	−49.1	153.7
47	11 39.6	−48.4	154.0	10 45.7	−48.7	154.1	9 51.7	−49.0	154.2	8 57.7	−49.2	154.2
48	10 51.2	−48.5	154.6	9 57.0	−48.7	154.7	9 02.7	−49.0	154.8	8 08.5	−49.3	154.8
49	10 02.7	−48.5	155.2	9 08.3	−48.8	155.3	8 13.7	−49.0	155.3	7 19.2	−49.3	155.4
50	9 14.2	−48.6	155.8	8 19.5	−48.9	155.9	7 24.7	−49.1	155.9	6 29.9	−49.4	156.0
51	8 25.6	−48.7	156.4	7 30.6	−48.9	156.5	6 35.6	−49.2	156.5	5 40.5	−49.3	156.5
52	7 36.9	−48.7	157.0	6 41.7	−49.0	157.0	5 46.4	−49.1	157.1	4 51.2	−49.4	157.1
53	6 48.2	−48.7	157.6	5 52.7	−48.9	157.6	4 57.3	−49.3	157.7	4 01.8	−49.5	157.7
54	5 59.5	−48.8	158.2	5 03.8	−49.0	158.2	4 08.0	−49.2	158.2	3 12.3	−49.4	158.3
55	5 10.7	−48.8	158.7	4 14.8	−49.1	158.8	3 18.8	−49.2	158.8	2 22.9	−49.5	158.8
56	4 21.9	−48.9	159.3	3 25.7	−49.0	159.4	2 29.6	−49.3	159.4	1 33.4	−49.5	159.4
57	3 33.0	−48.9	159.9	2 36.7	−49.1	159.9	1 40.3	−49.3	159.9	0 43.9	−49.4	160.0
58	2 44.1	−48.8	160.5	1 47.6	−49.1	160.5	0 51.0	−49.3	160.5	0 05.5	+49.5	19.5
59	1 55.3	−48.9	161.1	0 58.5	−49.1	161.1	0 01.7	−49.3	161.1	0 55.0	+49.5	18.9
60	1 06.4	−49.0	161.7	0 09.4	−49.1	161.7	0 47.6	+49.2	18.3	1 44.5	+49.5	18.3
61	0 17.4	−48.9	162.2	0 39.7	+49.1	17.8	1 36.8	+49.3	17.8	2 34.0	+49.4	17.8
62	0 31.5	+48.9	17.2	1 28.8	+49.1	17.2	2 26.1	+49.3	17.2	3 23.4	+49.4	17.2
63	1 20.4	+48.9	16.6	2 17.9	+49.0	16.6	3 15.4	+49.2	16.6	4 12.8	+49.4	16.6
64	2 09.3	+48.8	16.0	3 06.9	+49.1	16.0	4 04.6	+49.2	16.1	5 02.2	+49.4	16.1
65	2 58.1	+48.9	15.4	3 56.0	+49.0	15.5	4 53.8	+49.2	15.5	5 51.6	+49.4	15.5
66	3 47.0	+48.8	14.9	4 45.0	+49.0	14.9	5 43.0	+49.1	14.9	6 41.0	+49.3	14.9
67	4 35.8	+48.9	14.3	5 34.0	+48.9	14.3	6 32.1	+49.1	14.3	7 30.3	+49.2	14.4
68	5 24.7	+48.7	13.7	6 22.9	+49.0	13.7	7 21.2	+49.1	13.8	8 19.5	+49.2	13.8
69	6 13.4	+48.8	13.1	7 11.9	+48.8	13.1	8 10.3	+49.0	13.2	9 08.7	+49.2	13.2
70	7 02.2	+48.7	12.5	8 00.7	+48.9	12.6	8 59.3	+49.0	12.6	9 57.9	+49.0	12.6
71	7 50.9	+48.6	11.9	8 49.6	+48.7	12.0	9 48.3	+48.9	12.0	10 46.9	+49.1	12.0
72	8 39.5	+48.6	11.3	9 38.3	+48.8	11.4	10 37.2	+48.8	11.4	11 36.0	+48.9	11.5
73	9 28.1	+48.5	10.8	10 27.1	+48.6	10.8	11 26.0	+48.7	10.8	12 24.9	+48.9	10.9
74	10 16.6	+48.5	10.2	11 15.7	+48.6	10.2	12 14.7	+48.7	10.2	13 13.8	+48.8	10.3
75	11 05.1	+48.4	9.6	12 04.3	+48.5	9.6	13 03.4	+48.6	9.6	14 02.6	+48.7	9.7
76	11 53.5	+48.3	9.0	12 52.8	+48.4	9.0	13 52.0	+48.5	9.0	14 51.3	+48.6	9.1
77	12 41.8	+48.3	8.3	13 41.2	+48.3	8.4	14 40.5	+48.4	8.4	15 39.9	+48.5	8.5
78	13 30.1	+48.1	7.7	14 29.5	+48.2	7.8	15 28.9	+48.4	7.8	16 28.4	+48.4	7.8
79	14 18.2	+48.0	7.1	15 17.7	+48.2	7.2	16 17.3	+48.2	7.2	17 16.8	+48.3	7.2
80	15 06.2	+48.0	6.5	16 05.9	+48.0	6.5	17 05.5	+48.1	6.6	18 05.1	+48.1	6.6
81	15 54.2	+47.8	5.9	16 53.9	+47.9	5.9	17 53.6	+47.9	5.9	18 53.2	+48.1	6.0
82	16 42.0	+47.8	5.2	17 41.8	+47.8	5.3	18 41.5	+47.9	5.3	19 41.3	+47.9	5.3
83	17 29.8	+47.6	4.6	18 29.6	+47.6	4.6	19 29.4	+47.7	4.7	20 29.2	+47.7	4.7
84	18 17.4	+47.4	4.0	19 17.2	+47.5	4.0	20 17.1	+47.5	4.0	21 16.9	+47.6	4.0
85	19 04.8	+47.4	3.3	20 04.7	+47.4	3.3	21 04.6	+47.4	3.4	22 04.5	+47.5	3.4
86	19 52.2	+47.2	2.7	20 52.1	+47.2	2.7	21 52.0	+47.3	2.7	22 52.0	+47.2	2.7
87	20 39.4	+47.0	2.0	21 39.3	+47.1	2.0	22 39.3	+47.1	2.0	23 39.2	+47.2	2.1
88	21 26.4	+46.9	1.4	22 26.4	+46.9	1.4	23 26.4	+46.9	1.4	24 26.4	+46.9	1.4
89	22 13.3	+46.7	0.7	23 13.3	+46.7	0.7	24 13.3	+46.7	0.7	25 13.3	+46.7	0.7
90	23 00.0	+46.5	0.0	24 00.0	+46.5	0.0	25 00.0	+46.5	0.0	26 00.0	+46.5	0.0
	23°			24°			25°			26°		

Dec.	27° Hc	d	Z	28° Hc	d	Z	29° Hc	d	Z	30° Hc	d	Z
°	° ′	′	°	° ′	′	°	° ′	′	°	° ′	′	°
0	43 49.4	−38.0	119.3	43 19.7	−39.0	120.1	42 49.2	−39.9	120.9	42 18.1	−40.8	121.7
1	43 11.4	−38.7	120.3	42 40.7	−39.6	121.1	42 09.3	−40.4	121.9	41 37.3	−41.4	122.7
2	42 32.7	−39.2	121.4	42 01.1	−40.0	122.2	41 28.9	−41.0	122.9	40 55.9	−41.7	123.6
3	41 53.5	−39.7	122.4	41 21.1	−40.6	123.2	40 47.9	−41.4	123.9	40 14.2	−42.3	124.6
4	41 13.8	−40.2	123.4	40 40.5	−41.1	124.1	40 06.5	−41.9	124.8	39 31.9	−42.6	125.5
5	40 33.6	−40.7	124.4	39 59.4	−41.6	125.1	39 24.6	−42.3	125.8	38 49.3	−43.1	126.4
6	39 52.9	−41.2	125.4	39 17.8	−41.9	126.0	38 42.3	−42.8	126.7	38 06.2	−43.5	127.3
7	39 11.7	−41.7	126.3	38 35.9	−42.4	126.9	37 59.5	−43.1	127.6	37 22.7	−43.8	128.2
8	38 30.0	−42.0	127.2	37 53.5	−42.8	127.8	37 16.4	−43.5	128.4	36 38.9	−44.3	129.0
9	37 48.0	−42.5	128.1	37 10.7	−43.2	128.7	36 32.9	−43.9	129.3	35 54.6	−44.5	129.9
10	37 05.5	−42.9	129.0	36 27.5	−43.6	129.6	35 49.0	−44.2	130.2	35 10.1	−44.9	130.7
11	36 22.6	−43.2	129.9	35 43.9	−43.9	130.4	35 04.8	−44.6	131.0	34 25.2	−45.2	131.5
12	35 39.4	−43.6	130.7	35 00.0	−44.3	131.3	34 20.2	−44.9	131.8	33 40.0	−45.5	132.3
13	34 55.8	−44.0	131.6	34 15.7	−44.5	132.1	33 35.3	−45.2	132.6	32 54.5	−45.8	133.1
14	34 11.8	−44.2	132.4	33 31.2	−44.9	132.9	32 50.1	−45.4	133.4	32 08.7	−46.0	133.8
15	33 27.6	−44.6	133.2	32 46.3	−45.2	133.7	32 04.7	−45.8	134.2	31 22.7	−46.3	134.6
16	32 43.0	−44.9	134.0	32 01.1	−45.4	134.5	31 18.9	−46.0	134.9	30 36.4	−46.6	135.3
17	31 58.1	−45.2	134.8	31 15.7	−45.8	135.2	30 32.9	−46.3	135.7	29 49.8	−46.8	136.1
18	31 12.9	−45.4	135.6	30 29.9	−46.0	136.0	29 46.6	−46.5	136.4	29 03.0	−47.0	136.8
19	30 27.5	−45.7	136.3	29 43.9	−46.2	136.7	29 00.1	−46.7	137.1	28 16.0	−47.2	137.5
20	29 41.8	−45.9	137.1	28 57.7	−46.4	137.5	28 13.4	−47.0	137.8	27 28.8	−47.5	138.2
21	28 55.9	−46.2	137.8	28 11.3	−46.7	138.2	27 26.4	−47.2	138.5	26 41.3	−47.6	138.9
22	28 09.7	−46.4	138.6	27 24.6	−46.9	138.9	26 39.2	−47.3	139.2	25 53.7	−47.8	139.6
23	27 23.3	−46.7	139.3	26 37.7	−47.1	139.6	25 51.9	−47.6	139.9	25 05.9	−48.1	140.2
24	26 36.6	−46.8	140.0	25 50.6	−47.3	140.3	25 04.3	−47.7	140.6	24 17.8	−48.1	140.9
25	25 49.8	−47.0	140.7	25 03.3	−47.5	141.0	24 16.6	−47.9	141.3	23 29.7	−48.4	141.5
26	25 02.8	−47.3	141.4	24 15.8	−47.7	141.7	23 28.7	−48.1	141.9	22 41.3	−48.5	142.2
27	24 15.5	−47.4	142.0	23 28.1	−47.8	142.3	22 40.6	−48.3	142.6	21 52.8	−48.6	142.8
28	23 28.1	−47.5	142.7	22 40.3	−48.0	143.0	21 52.3	−48.3	143.2	21 04.2	−48.8	143.5
29	22 40.6	−47.8	143.4	21 52.3	−48.1	143.6	21 04.0	−48.6	143.9	20 15.4	−48.9	144.1
30	21 52.8	−47.8	144.0	21 04.2	−48.3	144.3	20 15.4	−48.6	144.5	19 26.5	−49.0	144.7
31	21 05.0	−48.1	144.7	20 15.9	−48.4	144.9	19 26.8	−48.8	145.1	18 37.5	−49.1	145.3
32	20 16.9	−48.1	145.3	19 27.5	−48.5	145.5	18 38.0	−48.9	145.7	17 48.4	−49.3	145.9
33	19 28.8	−48.3	146.0	18 39.0	−48.7	146.1	17 49.1	−49.0	146.3	16 59.1	−49.3	146.5
34	18 40.5	−48.4	146.6	17 50.3	−48.7	146.8	17 00.1	−49.1	146.9	16 09.8	−49.5	147.1
35	17 52.1	−48.6	147.2	17 01.6	−48.9	147.4	16 11.0	−49.2	147.5	15 20.3	−49.5	147.7
36	17 03.5	−48.6	147.8	16 12.7	−49.0	148.0	15 21.8	−49.3	148.1	14 30.8	−49.7	148.3
37	16 14.9	−48.8	148.4	15 23.7	−49.1	148.6	14 32.5	−49.4	148.7	13 41.1	−49.7	148.8
38	15 26.1	−48.8	149.0	14 34.6	−49.1	149.2	13 43.1	−49.5	149.3	12 51.4	−49.8	149.4
39	14 37.3	−49.0	149.6	13 45.5	−49.3	149.8	12 53.6	−49.6	149.9	12 01.6	−49.8	150.0
40	13 48.3	−49.0	150.2	12 56.2	−49.3	150.4	12 04.0	−49.6	150.5	11 11.8	−49.9	150.6
41	12 59.3	−49.1	150.8	12 06.9	−49.4	150.9	11 14.4	−49.7	151.0	10 21.9	−50.0	151.1
42	12 10.2	−49.2	151.4	11 17.5	−49.5	151.5	10 24.7	−49.8	151.6	9 31.9	−50.0	151.7
43	11 21.0	−49.3	152.0	10 28.0	−49.5	152.1	9 34.9	−49.8	152.2	8 41.9	−50.1	152.3
44	10 31.7	−49.3	152.6	9 38.5	−49.6	152.7	8 45.1	−49.8	152.7	7 51.8	−50.1	152.8
45	9 42.4	−49.4	153.2	8 48.9	−49.7	153.2	7 55.3	−49.9	153.3	7 01.7	−50.2	153.4
46	8 53.0	−49.4	153.7	7 59.2	−49.7	153.8	7 05.4	−50.0	153.9	6 11.5	−50.2	153.9
47	8 03.6	−49.5	154.3	7 09.5	−49.7	154.4	6 15.4	−49.9	154.4	5 21.3	−50.2	154.5
48	7 14.1	−49.5	154.9	6 19.8	−49.8	154.9	5 25.5	−50.1	155.0	4 31.1	−50.3	155.0
49	6 24.6	−49.5	155.5	5 30.0	−49.7	155.5	4 35.4	−50.0	155.5	3 40.8	−50.2	155.6
50	5 35.1	−49.6	156.0	4 40.3	−49.9	156.1	3 45.4	−50.0	156.1	2 50.6	−50.3	156.1
51	4 45.5	−49.6	156.6	3 50.4	−49.8	156.6	2 55.4	−50.1	156.6	2 00.3	−50.3	156.7
52	3 55.9	−49.7	157.1	3 00.6	−49.9	157.2	2 05.3	−50.1	157.2	1 10.0	−50.3	157.2
53	3 06.2	−49.6	157.7	2 10.7	−49.9	157.7	1 15.2	−50.1	157.7	0 19.7	−50.3	157.7
54	2 16.6	−49.7	158.3	1 20.8	−49.8	158.3	0 25.1	−50.1	158.3	0 30.6	+50.3	21.7
55	1 26.9	−49.7	158.8	0 31.0	−49.9	158.8	0 25.0	+50.1	21.2	1 20.9	+50.3	21.2
56	0 37.2	−49.6	159.4	0 18.9	+49.9	20.6	1 15.1	+50.1	20.6	2 11.2	+50.3	20.6
57	0 12.4	+49.7	20.0	1 08.8	+49.9	20.0	2 05.2	+50.0	20.1	3 01.5	+50.3	20.1
58	1 02.1	+49.7	19.5	1 58.7	+49.8	19.5	2 55.2	+50.1	19.5	3 51.8	+50.2	19.5
59	1 51.8	+49.6	18.9	2 48.5	+49.9	18.9	3 45.3	+50.0	19.0	4 42.0	+50.3	19.0
60	2 41.4	+49.7	18.4	3 38.4	+49.8	18.4	4 35.3	+50.0	18.4	5 32.3	+50.1	18.4
61	3 31.1	+49.6	17.8	4 28.2	+49.8	17.8	5 25.3	+50.0	17.8	6 22.4	+50.2	17.9
62	4 20.7	+49.6	17.2	5 18.0	+49.8	17.3	6 15.3	+50.0	17.3	7 12.6	+50.1	17.3
63	5 10.3	+49.6	16.7	6 07.8	+49.7	16.7	7 05.3	+49.9	16.7	8 02.7	+50.1	16.8
64	5 59.9	+49.5	16.1	6 57.5	+49.7	16.1	7 55.2	+49.8	16.2	8 52.8	+50.0	16.2
65	6 49.4	+49.5	15.5	7 47.2	+49.7	15.6	8 45.0	+49.8	15.6	9 42.8	+50.0	15.7
66	7 38.9	+49.5	15.0	8 36.9	+49.6	15.0	9 34.8	+49.8	15.0	10 32.8	+49.9	15.1
67	8 28.4	+49.4	14.4	9 26.5	+49.5	14.4	10 24.6	+49.7	14.5	11 22.7	+49.8	14.5
68	9 17.8	+49.3	13.8	10 16.0	+49.5	13.9	11 14.3	+49.6	13.9	12 12.5	+49.8	14.0
69	10 07.1	+49.3	13.2	11 05.5	+49.4	13.3	12 03.9	+49.6	13.3	13 02.3	+49.7	13.4
70	10 56.4	+49.2	12.7	11 54.9	+49.4	12.7	12 53.5	+49.4	12.8	13 52.0	+49.6	12.8
71	11 45.6	+49.2	12.1	12 44.3	+49.3	12.1	13 42.9	+49.4	12.2	14 41.6	+49.5	12.2
72	12 34.8	+49.0	11.5	13 33.6	+49.2	11.5	14 32.3	+49.4	11.6	15 31.1	+49.4	11.6
73	13 23.8	+49.0	10.9	14 22.8	+49.1	10.9	15 21.7	+49.2	11.0	16 20.5	+49.4	11.1
74	14 12.8	+48.9	10.3	15 11.9	+49.0	10.4	16 10.9	+49.1	10.4	17 09.9	+49.2	10.5
75	15 01.7	+48.8	9.7	16 00.9	+48.9	9.8	17 00.0	+49.0	9.8	17 59.1	+49.1	9.9
76	15 50.5	+48.7	9.1	16 49.8	+48.8	9.2	17 49.0	+48.9	9.2	18 48.2	+49.0	9.3
77	16 39.2	+48.6	8.5	17 38.6	+48.7	8.5	18 37.9	+48.8	8.6	19 37.2	+48.9	8.6
78	17 27.8	+48.5	7.9	18 27.3	+48.5	7.9	19 26.7	+48.6	8.0	20 26.1	+48.7	8.0
79	18 16.3	+48.4	7.3	19 15.8	+48.5	7.3	20 15.3	+48.6	7.4	21 14.8	+48.6	7.4
80	19 04.7	+48.2	6.6	20 04.3	+48.3	6.7	21 03.9	+48.3	6.7	22 03.4	+48.5	6.8
81	19 52.9	+48.1	6.0	20 52.6	+48.1	6.0	21 52.2	+48.3	6.1	22 51.9	+48.3	6.1
82	20 41.0	+48.0	5.4	21 40.7	+48.1	5.4	22 40.5	+48.0	5.4	23 40.2	+48.1	5.5
83	21 29.0	+47.8	4.7	22 28.8	+47.8	4.8	23 28.5	+48.0	4.8	24 28.3	+48.0	4.8
84	22 16.8	+47.6	4.1	23 16.6	+47.7	4.1	24 16.5	+47.7	4.1	25 16.3	+47.8	4.2
85	23 04.4	+47.5	3.4	24 04.3	+47.5	3.4	25 04.2	+47.6	3.5	26 04.1	+47.6	3.5
86	23 51.9	+47.3	2.8	24 51.8	+47.4	2.8	25 51.8	+47.3	2.8	26 51.7	+47.4	2.8
87	24 39.2	+47.1	2.1	25 39.2	+47.1	2.1	26 39.1	+47.2	2.1	27 39.1	+47.2	2.1
88	25 26.3	+47.0	1.4	26 26.3	+47.0	1.4	27 26.3	+47.0	1.4	28 26.3	+47.0	1.4
89	26 13.3	+46.7	0.7	27 13.3	+46.7	0.7	28 13.3	+46.7	0.7	29 13.3	+46.7	0.7
90	27 00.0	+46.5	0.0	28 00.0	+46.5	0.0	29 00.0	+46.5	0.0	30 00.0	+46.5	0.0
	27°			28°			29°			30°		

S. Lat. {L.H.A. greater than 180° ....Zn=180°−Z
{L.H.A. less than 180°...........Zn=180°+Z

LATITUDE SAME NAME AS DECLINATION — L.H.A. 141°, 219°

Dec.	23° Hc	d	Z	24° Hc	d	Z	25° Hc	d	Z	26° Hc	d	Z	27° Hc	d	Z	28° Hc	d	Z	29° Hc	d	Z	30° Hc	d	Z	Dec.
°	° ′	′	°	° ′	′	°	° ′	′	°	° ′	′	°	° ′	′	°	° ′	′	°	° ′	′	°	° ′	′	°	°
0	44 50.5	+32.7	115.0	44 24.7	+33.8	115.9	43 58.2	+34.9	116.7	43 30.8	+35.9	117.6	43 02.6	+37.0	118.4	42 33.7	+37.9	119.2	42 04.0	+38.9	120.0	41 33.6	+39.9	120.8	0
1	45 23.2	+31.9	113.8	44 58.5	+33.1	114.7	44 33.1	+34.2	115.6	44 06.7	+35.3	116.5	43 39.6	+36.3	117.3	43 11.6	+37.4	118.2	42 42.9	+38.4	119.0	42 13.5	+39.3	119.8	1
2	45 55.1	+31.2	112.6	45 31.6	+32.4	113.5	45 07.3	+33.4	114.4	44 42.0	+34.6	115.3	44 15.9	+35.7	116.2	43 49.0	+36.7	117.1	43 21.3	+37.7	117.9	42 52.8	+38.7	118.8	2
3	46 26.3	+30.3	111.3	46 04.0	+31.5	112.3	45 40.7	+32.8	113.3	45 16.6	+33.9	114.2	44 51.6	+35.0	115.1	44 25.7	+36.1	116.0	43 59.0	+37.1	116.9	43 31.5	+38.2	117.7	3
4	46 56.6	+29.5	110.1	46 35.5	+30.8	111.1	46 13.5	+32.0	112.1	45 50.5	+33.2	113.0	45 26.6	+34.3	113.9	45 01.8	+35.4	114.9	44 36.1	+36.5	115.8	44 09.7	+37.5	116.6	4
5	47 26.1	+28.7	108.8	47 06.3	+29.9	109.8	46 45.5	+31.1	110.8	46 23.7	+32.3	111.8	46 00.9	+33.6	112.8	45 37.2	+34.7	113.7	45 12.6	+35.9	114.6	44 47.2	+36.9	115.5	5
6	47 54.8	+27.7	107.5	47 36.2	+29.1	108.5	47 16.6	+30.4	109.6	46 56.0	+31.6	110.6	46 34.5	+32.8	111.6	46 11.9	+34.0	112.5	45 48.5	+35.1	113.5	45 24.1	+36.2	114.4	6
7	48 22.5	+26.8	106.2	48 05.3	+28.1	107.2	47 47.0	+29.4	108.3	47 27.6	+30.8	109.3	47 07.3	+31.9	110.3	46 45.9	+33.2	111.3	46 23.6	+34.4	112.3	46 00.3	+35.5	113.3	7
8	48 49.3	+25.8	104.8	48 33.4	+27.2	105.9	48 16.4	+28.6	107.0	47 58.4	+29.8	108.1	47 39.2	+31.2	109.1	47 19.1	+32.4	110.1	46 58.0	+33.6	111.1	46 35.8	+34.9	112.1	8
9	49 15.1	+24.9	103.4	49 00.6	+26.3	104.6	48 45.0	+27.6	105.7	48 28.2	+29.0	106.7	48 10.4	+30.3	107.8	47 51.5	+31.6	108.9	47 31.6	+32.8	109.9	47 10.7	+34.0	110.9	9
10	49 40.0	+23.8	102.0	49 26.9	+25.2	103.2	49 12.6	+26.7	104.3	48 57.2	+28.1	105.4	48 40.7	+29.4	106.5	48 23.1	+30.7	107.6	48 04.4	+32.0	108.7	47 44.7	+33.3	109.7	10
11	50 03.8	+22.7	100.6	49 52.1	+24.2	101.8	49 39.3	+25.6	102.9	49 25.3	+27.1	104.1	49 10.1	+28.5	105.2	48 53.8	+29.9	106.3	48 36.4	+31.2	107.4	48 18.0	+32.4	108.5	11
12	50 26.5	+21.6	99.2	50 16.3	+23.2	100.4	50 04.9	+24.7	101.5	49 52.4	+26.0	102.7	49 38.6	+27.5	103.8	49 23.7	+28.9	105.0	49 07.6	+30.2	106.1	48 50.4	+31.6	107.2	12
13	50 48.1	+20.6	97.7	50 39.5	+22.0	98.9	50 29.6	+23.5	100.1	50 18.4	+25.1	101.3	50 06.1	+26.5	102.5	49 52.6	+27.9	103.6	49 37.8	+29.4	104.8	49 22.0	+30.7	105.9	13
14	51 08.7	+19.3	96.2	51 01.5	+21.0	97.4	50 53.1	+22.5	98.6	50 43.5	+24.0	99.9	50 32.6	+25.5	101.1	50 20.5	+26.9	102.2	50 07.2	+28.3	103.4	49 52.7	+29.7	104.6	14
15	51 28.0	+18.2	94.7	51 22.5	+19.7	95.9	51 15.6	+21.4	97.2	51 07.5	+22.9	98.4	50 58.1	+24.4	99.6	50 47.4	+25.9	100.8	50 35.5	+27.4	102.0	50 22.4	+28.8	103.2	15
16	51 46.2	+17.0	93.1	51 42.2	+18.6	94.4	51 37.0	+20.1	95.7	51 30.4	+21.7	96.9	51 22.5	+23.3	98.2	51 13.3	+24.9	99.4	51 02.9	+26.3	100.6	50 51.2	+27.8	101.8	16
17	52 03.2	+15.7	91.6	52 00.8	+17.4	92.9	51 57.1	+19.0	94.2	51 52.1	+20.6	95.4	51 45.8	+22.2	96.7	51 38.2	+23.7	97.9	51 29.2	+25.3	99.2	51 19.0	+26.8	100.4	17
18	52 18.9	+14.4	90.0	52 18.2	+16.1	91.3	52 16.1	+17.8	92.6	52 12.7	+19.4	93.9	52 08.0	+21.0	95.2	52 01.9	+22.6	96.5	51 54.5	+24.1	97.7	51 45.8	+25.6	99.0	18
19	52 33.3	+13.2	88.4	52 34.3	+14.8	89.7	52 33.9	+16.5	91.0	52 32.1	+18.1	92.3	52 29.0	+19.7	93.6	52 24.5	+21.4	94.9	52 18.6	+23.0	96.2	52 11.4	+24.6	97.5	19
20	52 46.5	+11.8	86.8	52 49.1	+13.5	88.1	52 50.4	+15.2	89.5	52 50.2	+16.9	90.8	52 48.7	+18.6	92.1	52 45.9	+20.2	93.4	52 41.6	+21.8	94.7	52 36.0	+23.4	96.0	20
21	52 58.3	+10.5	85.2	53 02.6	+12.2	86.5	53 05.6	+13.9	87.8	53 07.1	+15.6	89.2	53 07.3	+17.3	90.5	53 06.1	+18.9	91.8	53 03.4	+20.6	93.2	52 59.4	+22.3	94.5	21
22	53 08.8	+9.1	83.6	53 14.8	+10.9	84.9	53 19.5	+12.5	86.2	53 22.7	+14.3	87.6	53 24.6	+16.0	88.9	53 25.0	+17.7	90.3	53 24.0	+19.4	91.6	53 21.7	+21.0	93.0	22
23	53 17.9	+7.8	81.9	53 25.7	+9.5	83.2	53 32.0	+11.2	84.6	53 37.0	+12.9	85.9	53 40.6	+14.6	87.3	53 42.7	+16.3	88.6	53 43.4	+18.0	90.0	53 42.7	+19.7	91.4	23
24	53 25.7	+6.3	80.2	53 35.2	+8.0	81.6	53 43.2	+9.9	82.9	53 49.9	+11.6	84.3	53 55.2	+13.3	85.6	53 59.0	+15.1	87.0	54 01.4	+16.8	88.4	54 02.4	+18.4	89.8	24
25	53 32.0	+5.0	78.6	53 43.2	+6.7	79.9	53 53.1	+8.4	81.3	54 01.5	+10.1	82.6	54 08.5	+11.9	84.0	54 14.1	+13.6	85.4	54 18.2	+15.4	86.8	54 20.8	+17.2	88.1	25
26	53 37.0	+3.6	76.9	53 49.9	+5.3	78.2	54 01.5	+7.0	79.6	54 11.6	+8.8	80.9	54 20.4	+10.5	82.3	54 27.7	+12.2	83.7	54 33.6	+14.0	85.1	54 38.0	+15.7	86.5	26
27	53 40.6	+2.1	75.2	53 55.2	+3.8	76.5	54 08.5	+5.6	77.9	54 20.4	+7.3	79.2	54 30.9	+9.0	80.6	54 39.9	+10.9	82.0	54 47.6	+12.6	83.4	54 53.7	+14.4	84.8	27
28	53 42.7	+0.7	73.5	53 59.0	+2.4	74.8	54 14.1	+4.1	76.2	54 27.7	+5.9	77.5	54 39.9	+7.7	78.9	54 50.8	+9.4	80.3	55 00.2	+11.1	81.7	55 08.1	+12.9	83.1	28
29	53 43.4	−0.7	71.8	54 01.4	+1.0	73.1	54 18.2	+2.6	74.5	54 33.6	+4.4	75.8	54 47.6	+6.1	77.2	55 00.2	+7.9	78.6	55 11.3	+9.7	80.0	55 21.0	+11.5	81.4	29
30	53 42.7	−2.2	70.1	54 02.4	−0.5	71.4	54 20.8	+1.3	72.8	54 38.0	+2.9	74.1	54 53.7	+4.7	75.5	55 08.1	+6.4	76.9	55 21.0	+8.2	78.3	55 32.5	+10.0	79.7	30
31	53 40.5	−3.6	68.5	54 01.9	−1.9	69.7	54 22.1	−0.3	71.0	54 40.9	+1.4	72.4	54 58.4	+3.2	73.7	55 14.5	+4.9	75.1	55 29.2	+6.7	76.5	55 42.5	+8.5	77.9	31
32	53 36.9	−5.0	66.8	54 00.0	−3.4	68.0	54 21.8	−1.7	69.3	54 42.3	0.0	70.6	55 01.6	+1.7	72.0	55 19.4	+3.5	73.4	55 35.9	+5.2	74.8	55 51.0	+7.0	76.2	32
33	53 31.9	−6.3	65.1	53 56.6	−4.8	66.3	54 20.1	−3.2	67.6	54 42.3	−1.5	68.9	55 03.3	+0.2	70.2	55 22.9	+1.9	71.6	55 41.1	+3.7	73.0	55 58.0	+5.4	74.4	33
34	53 25.6	−7.8	63.4	53 51.8	−6.2	64.6	54 16.9	−4.6	65.9	54 40.8	−3.0	67.2	55 03.5	−1.3	68.5	55 24.8	+0.4	69.8	55 44.8	+2.1	71.2	56 03.4	+3.9	72.6	34
35	53 17.8	−9.2	61.8	53 45.6	−7.6	63.0	54 12.3	−6.0	64.2	54 37.8	−4.4	65.5	55 02.2	−2.8	66.8	55 25.2	−1.1	68.1	55 46.9	+0.6	69.4	56 07.3	+2.4	70.8	35
36	53 08.6	−10.5	60.1	53 38.0	−9.0	61.3	54 06.3	−7.5	62.5	54 33.4	−5.9	63.7	54 59.4	−4.3	65.0	55 24.1	−2.7	66.3	55 47.5	−0.9	67.7	56 09.7	+0.7	69.0	36
37	52 58.1	−11.9	58.5	53 29.0	−10.4	59.6	53 58.8	−8.9	60.8	54 27.5	−7.4	62.0	54 55.1	−5.8	63.3	55 21.4	−4.1	64.6	55 46.6	−2.5	65.9	56 10.4	−0.7	67.2	37
38	52 46.2	−13.1	56.8	53 18.6	−11.8	58.0	53 49.9	−10.3	59.1	54 20.1	−8.7	60.3	54 49.3	−7.2	61.5	55 17.3	−5.6	62.8	55 44.1	−4.0	64.1	56 09.7	−2.4	65.5	38
39	52 33.1	−14.5	55.2	53 06.8	−13.1	56.3	53 39.6	−11.7	57.5	54 11.4	−10.3	58.6	54 42.1	−8.7	59.8	55 11.7	−7.2	61.1	55 40.1	−5.5	62.3	56 07.3	−3.8	63.7	39
40	52 18.6	−15.7	53.6	52 53.7	−14.4	54.7	53 27.9	−13.0	55.8	54 01.1	−11.5	56.9	54 33.4	−10.2	58.1	55 04.5	−8.6	59.3	55 34.6	−7.1	60.6	56 03.5	−5.5	61.9	40
41	52 02.9	−17.0	52.1	52 39.3	−15.7	53.1	53 14.9	−14.4	54.2	53 49.6	−13.0	55.3	54 23.2	−11.5	56.4	54 55.9	−10.1	57.6	55 27.5	−8.5	58.8	55 58.0	−7.0	60.1	41
42	51 45.9	−18.2	50.5	52 23.6	−16.9	51.5	53 00.5	−15.6	52.6	53 36.6	−14.3	53.6	54 11.7	−12.9	54.7	54 45.8	−11.4	55.9	55 19.0	−10.0	57.1	55 51.0	−8.4	58.3	42
43	51 27.7	−19.4	49.0	52 06.7	−18.2	50.0	52 44.9	−16.9	51.0	53 22.3	−15.7	52.0	53 58.8	−14.3	53.1	54 34.4	−13.0	54.2	55 09.0	−11.5	55.4	55 42.6	−10.0	56.6	43
44	51 08.3	−20.5	47.5	51 48.5	−19.4	48.4	52 28.0	−18.2	49.4	53 06.6	−16.9	50.4	53 44.5	−15.7	51.4	54 21.4	−14.3	52.5	54 57.5	−12.9	53.6	55 32.6	−11.5	54.8	44
45	50 47.8	−21.7	46.0	51 29.1	−20.5	46.9	52 09.8	−19.4	47.8	52 49.7	−18.2	48.8	53 28.8	−16.9	49.8	54 07.1	−15.6	50.8	54 44.6	−14.3	51.9	55 21.1	−12.9	53.1	45
46	50 26.1	−22.7	44.5	51 08.6	−21.7	45.4	51 50.4	−20.6	46.3	52 31.5	−19.4	47.2	53 11.9	−18.2	48.2	53 51.5	−17.0	49.2	54 30.3	−15.7	50.3	55 08.2	−14.4	51.4	46
47	50 03.4	−23.9	43.1	50 46.9	−22.8	43.9	51 29.8	−21.7	44.8	52 12.1	−20.6	45.7	52 53.7	−19.5	46.6	53 34.5	−18.3	47.6	54 14.6	−17.0	48.6	54 53.8	−15.7	49.7	47
48	49 39.5	−24.8	41.6	50 24.1	−23.9	42.4	51 08.1	−22.9	43.3	51 51.5	−21.8	44.1	52 34.2	−20.7	45.0	53 16.2	−19.5	46.0	53 57.6	−18.4	47.0	54 38.1	−17.1	48.0	48
49	49 14.7	−25.9	40.2	50 00.2	−24.9	41.0	50 45.2	−23.9	41.8	51 29.7	−22.9	42.6	52 13.5	−21.9	43.5	52 56.7	−20.8	44.4	53 39.2	−19.6	45.4	54 21.0	−18.4	46.3	49
50	48 48.8	−26.8	38.9	49 35.3	−25.9	39.6	50 21.3	−25.0	40.4	51 06.8	−24.1	41.2	51 51.6	−23.0	42.0	52 35.9	−21.9	42.9	53 19.6	−20.9	43.8	54 02.6	−19.8	44.7	50
51	48 22.0	−27.7	37.5	49 09.4	−26.9	38.2	49 56.3	−26.0	38.9	50 42.7	−25.1	39.7	51 28.6	−24.1	40.5	52 14.0	−23.2	41.3	52 58.7	−22.1	42.2	53 42.8	−21.0	43.1	51
52	47 54.3	−28.7	36.2	48 42.5	−27.8	36.8	49 30.3	−27.0	37.5	50 17.6	−26.1	38.3	51 04.5	−25.2	39.0	51 50.8	−24.2	39.8	52 36.6	−23.2	40.7	53 21.8	−22.2	41.5	52
53	47 25.6	−29.5	34.9	48 14.7	−28.8	35.5	49 03.3	−27.9	36.2	49 51.5	−27.1	36.9	50 39.3	−26.2	37.6	51 26.6	−25.3	38.4	52 13.4	−24.4	39.2	52 59.6	−23.4	40.0	53
54	46 56.1	−30.3	33.6	47 45.9	−29.6	34.2	48 35.4	−28.9	34.8	49 24.4	−28.1	35.5	50 13.1	−27.3	36.2	51 01.3	−26.4	36.9	51 49.0	−25.5	37.7	52 36.2	−24.5	38.5	54
55	46 25.8	−31.2	32.3	47 16.3	−30.5	32.9	48 06.5	−29.8	33.5	48 56.3	−29.0	34.1	49 45.8	−28.2	34.8	50 34.9	−27.5	35.5	51 23.5	−26.6	36.2	52 11.7	−25.7	37.0	55
56	45 54.6	−32.0	31.1	46 45.8	−31.3	31.6	47 36.7	−30.6	32.2	48 27.3	−29.9	32.8	49 17.6	−29.2	33.4	50 07.4	−28.3	34.1	50 56.9	−27.6	34.8	51 46.0	−26.8	35.5	56
57	45 22.6	−32.7	29.9	46 14.5	−32.1	30.4	47 06.1	−31.4	31.0	47 57.4	−30.8	31.5	48 48.4	−30.1	32.1	49 39.1	−29.4	32.7	50 29.3	−28.5	33.4	51 19.2	−27.7	34.1	57
58	44 49.9	−33.4	28.7	45 42.4	−32.8	29.2	46 34.7	−32.3	29.7	47 26.6	−31.6	30.2	48 18.3	−30.9	30.8	49 09.7	−30.2	31.4	50 00.8	−29.6	32.0	50 51.5	−28.8	32.7	58
59	44 16.5	−34.1	27.5	45 09.6	−33.6	28.0	46 02.4	−33.0	28.5	46 55.0	−32.4	29.0	47 47.4	−31.8	29.5	48 39.5	−31.2	30.1	49 31.2	−30.4	30.7	50 22.7	−29.8	31.3	59
60	43 42.4	−34.8	26.4	44 36.0	−34.3	26.8	45 29.4	−33.7	27.3	46 22.6	−33.1	27.8	47 15.6	−32.6	28.3	48 08.3	−32.0	28.8	49 00.8	−31.4	29.3	49 52.9	−30.7	29.9	60
61	43 07.6	−35.5	25.3	44 01.7	−34.9	25.7	44 55.7	−34.5	26.1	45 49.5	−34.0	26.6	46 43.0	−33.3	27.0	47 36.3	−32.7	27.5	48 29.4	−32.2	28.0	49 22.2	−31.5	28.6	61
62	42 32.1	−36.1	24.2	43 26.8	−35.6	24.6	44 21.2	−35.1	25.0	45 15.5	−34.6	25.4	46 09.7	−34.2	25.8	47 03.6	−33.6	26.3	47 57.2	−33.0	26.8	48 50.7	−32.4	27.3	62
63	41 56.0	−36.6	23.1	42 51.2	−36.3	23.5	43 46.1	−35.8	23.8	44 40.9	−35.3	24.2	45 35.5	−34.8	24.6	46 30.0	−34.3	25.1	47 24.2	−33.8	25.5	48 18.3	−33.3	26.0	63
64	41 19.4	−37.3	22.0	42 14.9	−36.8	22.4	43 10.3	−36.4	22.7	44 05.6	−36.0	23.1	45 00.7	−35.5	23.5	45 55.7	−35.1	23.9	46 50.4	−34.5	24.3	47 45.0	−34.0	24.8	64
65	40 42.1	−37.7	21.0	41 38.1	−37.4	21.3	42 33.9	−37.0	21.6	43 29.6	−36.6	22.0	44 25.2	−36.2	22.4	45 20.6	−35.7	22.7	46 15.9	−35.3	23.1	47 11.0	−34.8	23.6	65
66	40 04.4	−38.3	20.0	41 00.7	−37.9	20.3	41 56.9	−37.6	20.6	42 53.0	−37.2	20.9	43 49.0	−36.8	21.2	44 44.9	−36.4	21.6	45 40.6	−36.0	22.0	46 36.2	−35.6	22.4	66
67	39 26.1	−38.9	19.0	40 22.8	−38.5	19.3	41 19.3	−38.1	19.5	42 15.8	−37.7	19.8	43 12.2	−37.4	20.2	44 08.5	−37.0	20.5	45 04.6	−36.6	20.8	46 00.6	−36.2	21.2	67
68	38 47.2	−39.3	18.0	39 44.3	−39.0	18.2	40 41.2	−38.7	18.5	41 38.1	−38.4	18.8	42 34.8	−38.0	19.1	43 31.5	−37.7	19.4	44 28.0	−37.3	19.7	45 24.4	−36.9	20.1	68
69	38 07.9	−39.7	17.0	39 05.3	−39.5	17.3	40 02.5	−39.1	17.5	40 59.7	−38.9	17.8	41 56.8	−38.5	18.0	42 53.8	−38.2	18.3	43 50.7	−37.9	18.6	44 47.5	−37.5	18.9	69
70	37 28.2	−40.2	16.1	38 25.8	−39.9	16.3	39 23.4	−39.7	16.5	40 20.8	−39.3	16.8	41 18.3	−39.1	17.0	42 15.6	−38.8	17.3	43 12.8	−38.4	17.6	44 10.0	−38.1	17.8	70
71	36 48.0	−40.7	15.2	37 45.9	−40.4	15.4	38 43.7	−40.1	15.6	39 41.5	−39.9	15.8	40 39.2	−39.6	16.0	41 36.8	−39.3	16.3	42 34.4	−39.1	16.5	43 31.9	−38.8	16.8	71
72	36 07.3	−41.0	14.2	37 05.5	−40.9	14.4	38 03.6	−40.6	14.6	39 01.6	−40.4	14.8	39 59.6	−40.1	15.0	40 57.5	−39.9	15.2	41 55.3	−39.5	15.5	42 53.1	−39.3	15.7	72
73	35 26.3	−41.5	13.3	36 24.6	−41.2	13.5	37 23.0	−41.0	13.7	38 21.2	−40.8	13.9	39 19.5	−40.6	14.1	40 17.6	−40.3	14.3	41 15.8	−40.1	14.5	42 13.8	−39.8	14.7	73
74	34 44.8	−41.8	12.5	35 43.4	−41.6	12.6	36 42.0	−41.5	12.8	37 40.4	−41.2	12.9	38 38.9	−41.0	13.1	39 37.3	−40.8	13.3	40 35.7	−40.6	13.5	41 34.0	−40.3	13.7	74
75	34 03.0	−42.2	11.6	35 01.8	−42.0	11.7	36 00.5	−41.8	11.9	36 59.2	−41.6	12.0	37 57.9	−41.5	12.2	38 56.5	−41.2	12.4	39 55.1	−41.0	12.5	40 53.7	−40.9	12.7	75
76	33 20.8	−42.5	10.7	34 19.8	−42.4	10.9	35 18.7	−42.2	11.0	36 17.6	−42.0	11.1	37 16.4	−41.8	11.3	38 15.3	−41.7	11.4	39 14.1	−41.5	11.6	40 12.8	−41.3	11.7	76
77	32 38.3	−42.8	9.9	33 37.4	−42.7	10.0	34 36.5	−42.6	10.1	35 35.6	−42.5	10.2	36 34.6	−42.3	10.4	37 33.6	−42.1	10.5	38 32.6	−42.0	10.7	39 31.5	−41.7	10.8	77
78	31 55.5	−43.2	9.1	32 54.7	−43.0	9.2	33 53.9	−42.9	9.3	34 53.1	−42.7	9.4	35 52.3	−42.6	9.5	36 51.5	−42.5	9.6	37 50.6	−42.3	9.7	38 49.8	−42.2	9.9	78
79	31 12.3	−43.5	8.2	32 11.7	−43.4	8.3	33 11.0	−43.2	8.4	34 10.4	−43.1	8.5	35 09.7	−43.0	8.6	36 09.0	−42.8	8.7	37 08.3	−42.7	8.9	38 07.6	−42.6	9.0	79
80	30 28.8	−43.7	7.4	31 28.3	−43.7	7.5	32 27.8	−43.6	7.6	33 27.3	−43.5	7.7	34 26.7	−43.3	7.8	35 26.2	−43.3	7.9	36 25.6	−43.1	8.0	37 25.0	−43.0	8.1	80
81	29 45.1	−44.1	6.7	30 44.6	−43.9	6.7	31 44.2	−43.8	6.8	32 43.8	−43.8	6.9	33 43.4	−43.7	6.9	34 42.9	−43.5	7.0	35 42.5	−43.5	7.1	36 42.0	−43.4	7.2	81
82	29 01.0	−44.3	5.9	30 00.7	−44.2	5.9	31 00.4	−44.2	6.0	32 00.0	−44.0	6.1	32 59.7	−44.0	6.1	33 59.4	−44.0	6.2	34 59.0	−43.8	6.3	35 58.6	−43.7	6.3	82
83	28 16.7	−44.6	5.1	29 16.5	−44.5	5.2	30 16.2	−44.4	5.2	31 16.0	−44.4	5.3	32 15.7	−44.3	5.3	33 15.4	−44.2	5.4	34 15.2	−44.2	5.4	35 14.9	−44.1	5.5	83
84	27 32.1	−44.8	4.3	28 32.0	−44.8	4.4	29 31.8	−44.7	4.4	30 31.6	−44.6	4.5	31 31.4	−44.6	4.5	32 31.2	−44.5	4.6	33 31.0	−44.4	4.6	34 30.8	−44.4	4.7	84
85	26 47.3	−45.0	3.6	27 47.2	−45.0	3.6	28 47.1	−45.0	3.7	29 47.0	−44.9	3.7	30 46.8	−44.8	3.7	31 46.7	−44.8	3.8	32 46.6	−44.8	3.8	33 46.4	−44.7	3.9	85
86	26 02.3	−45.3	2.9	27 02.2	−45.2	2.9	28 02.1	−45.2	2.9	29 02.1	−45.2	2.9	30 02.0	−45.2	3.0	31 01.9	−45.1	3.0	32 01.8	−45.0	3.0	33 01.7	−45.0	3.1	86
87	25 17.0	−45.5	2.1	26 17.0	−45.5	2.2	27 16.9	−45.4	2.2	28 16.9	−45.4	2.2	29 16.8	−45.3	2.2	30 16.8	−45.3	2.2	31 16.8	−45.4	2.3	32 16.7	−45.3	2.3	87
88	24 31.5	−45.6	1.4	25 31.5	−45.6	1.4	26 31.5	−45.6	1.4	27 31.5	−45.6	1.4	28 31.5	−45.6	1.5	29 31.5	−45.7	1.5	30 31.4	−45.6	1.5	31 31.4	−45.6	1.5	88
89	23 45.9	−45.9	0.7	24 45.9	−45.9	0.7	25 45.9	−45.9	0.7	26 45.9	−45.9	0.7	27 45.9	−45.9	0.7	28 45.8	−45.8	0.7	29 45.8	−45.8	0.7	30 45.8	−45.8	0.7	89
90	23 00.0	−46.1	0.0	24 00.0	−46.1	0.0	25 00.0	−46.1	0.0	26 00.0	−46.1	0.0	27 00.0	−46.1	0.0	28 00.0	−46.1	0.0	29 00.0	−46.1	0.0	30 00.0	−46.1	0.0	90
	23°			24°			25°			26°			27°			28°			29°			30°			

LATITUDE CONTRARY NAME TO DECLINATION L.H.A. 40°, 320°

Dec.	23° Hc	d	Z	24° Hc	d	Z	25° Hc	d	Z	26° Hc	d	Z
°	° ′	′	°	° ′	′	°	° ′	′	°	° ′	′	°
0	44 50.5	−33.4	115.0	44 24.7	−34.5	115.9	43 58.2	−35.6	116.7	43 30.8	−36.6	117.6
1	44 17.1	−34.2	116.1	43 50.2	−35.1	117.0	43 22.6	−36.2	117.8	42 54.2	−37.2	118.7
2	43 42.9	−34.7	117.3	43 15.1	−35.9	118.1	42 46.4	−36.8	118.9	42 17.0	−37.8	119.7
3	43 08.2	−35.5	118.4	42 39.2	−36.4	119.2	42 09.6	−37.4	120.0	41 39.2	−38.3	120.8
4	42 32.7	−36.0	119.5	42 02.8	−37.0	120.3	41 32.2	−37.9	121.1	41 00.9	−38.8	121.8
5	41 56.7	−36.7	120.6	41 25.8	−37.6	121.3	40 54.3	−38.5	122.1	40 22.1	−39.4	122.8
6	41 20.0	−37.2	121.6	40 48.2	−38.1	122.4	40 15.8	−39.0	123.1	39 42.7	−39.9	123.8
7	40 42.8	−37.8	122.7	40 10.1	−38.7	123.4	39 36.8	−39.6	124.1	39 02.8	−40.3	124.8
8	40 05.0	−38.3	123.7	39 31.4	−39.1	124.4	38 57.2	−39.9	125.1	38 22.5	−40.8	125.7
9	39 26.7	−38.8	124.7	38 52.3	−39.7	125.4	38 17.3	−40.5	126.0	37 41.7	−41.2	126.6
10	38 47.9	−39.3	125.7	38 12.6	−40.0	126.3	37 36.8	−40.8	127.0	37 00.5	−41.6	127.6
11	38 08.6	−39.7	126.6	37 32.6	−40.6	127.3	36 56.0	−41.3	127.9	36 18.9	−42.0	128.5
12	37 28.9	−40.2	127.6	36 52.0	−40.9	128.2	36 14.7	−41.7	128.8	35 36.9	−42.4	129.3
13	36 48.7	−40.7	128.5	36 11.1	−41.4	129.1	35 33.0	−42.1	129.7	34 54.5	−42.8	130.2
14	36 08.0	−41.0	129.4	35 29.7	−41.8	130.0	34 50.9	−42.4	130.5	34 11.7	−43.1	131.1
15	35 27.0	−41.4	130.3	34 47.9	−42.1	130.9	34 08.5	−42.8	131.4	33 28.6	−43.4	131.9
16	34 45.6	−41.8	131.2	34 05.8	−42.5	131.7	33 25.7	−43.2	132.2	32 45.2	−43.8	132.7
17	34 03.8	−42.2	132.1	33 23.3	−42.8	132.6	32 42.5	−43.4	133.1	32 01.4	−44.1	133.5
18	33 21.6	−42.5	133.0	32 40.5	−43.1	133.4	31 59.1	−43.8	133.9	31 17.3	−44.3	134.3
19	32 39.1	−42.9	133.8	31 57.4	−43.5	134.2	31 15.3	−44.0	134.7	30 33.0	−44.7	135.1
20	31 56.2	−43.2	134.6	31 13.9	−43.8	135.1	30 31.3	−44.4	135.5	29 48.3	−44.9	135.9
21	31 13.0	−43.4	135.4	30 30.1	−44.0	135.9	29 46.9	−44.6	136.3	29 03.4	−45.1	136.6
22	30 29.6	−43.8	136.2	29 46.1	−44.3	136.6	29 02.3	−44.8	137.0	28 18.3	−45.4	137.4
23	29 45.8	−44.0	137.0	29 01.8	−44.6	137.4	28 17.5	−45.2	137.8	27 32.9	−45.6	138.1
24	29 01.8	−44.3	137.8	28 17.2	−44.9	138.2	27 32.3	−45.3	138.5	26 47.3	−45.9	138.9
25	28 17.5	−44.6	138.6	27 32.3	−45.0	138.9	26 47.0	−45.6	139.3	26 01.4	−46.0	139.6
26	27 32.9	−44.8	139.3	26 47.3	−45.3	139.7	26 01.4	−45.8	140.0	25 15.4	−46.3	140.3
27	26 48.1	−45.0	140.1	26 02.0	−45.6	140.4	25 15.6	−46.0	140.7	24 29.1	−46.4	141.0
28	26 03.1	−45.3	140.8	25 16.4	−45.7	141.1	24 29.6	−46.1	141.4	23 42.7	−46.7	141.7
29	25 17.8	−45.5	141.6	24 30.7	−45.9	141.8	23 43.5	−46.4	142.1	22 56.0	−46.8	142.4
30	24 32.3	−45.6	142.3	23 44.8	−46.1	142.5	22 57.1	−46.6	142.8	22 09.2	−47.0	143.1
31	23 46.7	−45.9	143.0	22 58.7	−46.3	143.2	22 10.5	−46.7	143.5	21 22.2	−47.1	143.7
32	23 00.8	−46.1	143.7	22 12.4	−46.5	143.9	21 23.8	−46.9	144.2	20 35.1	−47.3	144.4
33	22 14.7	−46.2	144.4	21 25.9	−46.6	144.6	20 36.9	−47.0	144.8	19 47.8	−47.4	145.0
34	21 28.5	−46.4	145.1	20 39.3	−46.8	145.3	19 49.9	−47.2	145.5	19 00.4	−47.6	145.7
35	20 42.1	−46.5	145.7	19 52.5	−47.0	146.0	19 02.7	−47.3	146.1	18 12.8	−47.7	146.3
36	19 55.6	−46.7	146.4	19 05.5	−47.0	146.6	18 15.4	−47.5	146.8	17 25.1	−47.8	147.0
37	19 08.9	−46.9	147.1	18 18.5	−47.3	147.3	17 27.9	−47.5	147.4	16 37.3	−47.9	147.6
38	18 22.0	−46.9	147.7	17 31.2	−47.3	147.9	16 40.4	−47.7	148.1	15 49.4	−48.0	148.2
39	17 35.1	−47.2	148.4	16 43.9	−47.4	148.6	15 52.7	−47.8	148.7	15 01.4	−48.2	148.9
40	16 47.9	−47.2	149.0	15 56.5	−47.6	149.2	15 04.9	−47.9	149.3	14 13.2	−48.2	149.5
41	16 00.7	−47.3	149.7	15 08.9	−47.7	149.8	14 17.0	−48.0	150.0	13 25.0	−48.3	150.1
42	15 13.4	−47.5	150.3	14 21.2	−47.8	150.5	13 29.0	−48.1	150.6	12 36.7	−48.4	150.7
43	14 25.9	−47.5	151.0	13 33.4	−47.8	151.1	12 40.9	−48.2	151.2	11 48.3	−48.5	151.3
44	13 38.4	−47.7	151.6	12 45.6	−48.0	151.7	11 52.7	−48.2	151.8	10 59.8	−48.5	151.9
45	12 50.7	−47.7	152.2	11 57.6	−48.0	152.3	11 04.5	−48.3	152.4	10 11.3	−48.6	152.5
46	12 03.0	−47.8	152.8	11 09.6	−48.1	152.9	10 16.2	−48.4	153.0	9 22.7	−48.7	153.1
47	11 15.2	−47.9	153.5	10 21.5	−48.2	153.5	9 27.8	−48.5	153.6	8 34.0	−48.7	153.7
48	10 27.3	−47.9	154.1	9 33.3	−48.2	154.1	8 39.3	−48.5	154.2	7 45.3	−48.8	154.3
49	9 39.4	−48.1	154.7	8 45.1	−48.3	154.7	7 50.8	−48.5	154.8	6 56.5	−48.8	154.9
50	8 51.3	−48.1	155.3	7 56.8	−48.3	155.3	7 02.3	−48.6	155.4	6 07.7	−48.8	155.4
51	8 03.2	−48.1	155.9	7 08.5	−48.4	155.9	6 13.7	−48.7	156.0	5 18.9	−48.9	156.0
52	7 15.1	−48.2	156.5	6 20.1	−48.4	156.5	5 25.0	−48.6	156.6	4 30.0	−48.9	156.6
53	6 26.9	−48.2	157.1	5 31.7	−48.5	157.1	4 36.4	−48.7	157.2	3 41.1	−49.0	157.2
54	5 38.7	−48.3	157.7	4 43.2	−48.5	157.7	3 47.7	−48.8	157.7	2 52.1	−48.9	157.8
55	4 50.4	−48.2	158.3	3 54.7	−48.5	158.3	2 58.9	−48.7	158.3	2 03.2	−49.0	158.4
56	4 02.2	−48.4	158.9	3 06.2	−48.6	158.9	2 10.2	−48.8	158.9	1 14.2	−49.0	158.9
57	3 13.8	−48.3	159.5	2 17.6	−48.5	159.5	1 21.4	−48.7	159.5	0 25.2	−48.9	159.5
58	2 25.5	−48.4	160.1	1 29.1	−48.6	160.1	0 32.7	−48.8	160.1	0 23.7	+49.0	19.9
59	1 37.1	−48.3	160.7	0 40.5	−48.5	160.7	0 16.1	+48.7	19.3	1 12.7	+49.0	19.3
60	0 48.8	−48.4	161.3	0 08.0	+48.6	18.7	1 04.8	+48.8	18.8	2 01.7	+48.9	18.8
61	0 00.4	−48.4	161.8	0 56.6	+48.6	18.2	1 53.6	+48.8	18.2	2 50.6	+48.9	18.2
62	0 48.0	+48.3	17.6	1 45.2	+48.5	17.6	2 42.4	+48.7	17.6	3 39.5	+49.0	17.6
63	1 36.3	+48.4	17.0	2 33.7	+48.5	17.0	3 31.1	+48.7	17.0	4 28.5	+48.8	17.0
64	2 24.7	+48.3	16.4	3 22.2	+48.5	16.4	4 19.8	+48.7	16.4	5 17.3	+48.9	16.4
65	3 13.0	+48.3	15.8	4 10.7	+48.5	15.8	5 08.5	+48.6	15.8	6 06.2	+48.8	15.9
66	4 01.3	+48.3	15.2	4 59.2	+48.5	15.2	5 57.1	+48.6	15.2	6 55.0	+48.8	15.3
67	4 49.6	+48.3	14.6	5 47.7	+48.4	14.6	6 45.7	+48.6	14.7	7 43.8	+48.7	14.7
68	5 37.9	+48.2	14.0	6 36.1	+48.4	14.0	7 34.3	+48.5	14.1	8 32.5	+48.7	14.1
69	6 26.1	+48.2	13.4	7 24.5	+48.3	13.4	8 22.8	+48.5	13.5	9 21.2	+48.6	13.5
70	7 14.3	+48.1	12.8	8 12.8	+48.3	12.8	9 11.3	+48.4	12.9	10 09.8	+48.5	12.9
71	8 02.4	+48.1	12.2	9 01.1	+48.2	12.2	9 59.7	+48.3	12.3	10 58.3	+48.5	12.3
72	8 50.5	+48.0	11.6	9 49.3	+48.1	11.6	10 48.0	+48.3	11.7	11 46.8	+48.4	11.7
73	9 38.5	+48.0	11.0	10 37.4	+48.1	11.0	11 36.3	+48.2	11.1	12 35.2	+48.3	11.1
74	10 26.5	+47.9	10.4	11 25.5	+48.0	10.4	12 24.5	+48.1	10.5	13 23.5	+48.2	10.5
75	11 14.4	+47.8	9.8	12 13.5	+47.9	9.8	13 12.6	+48.0	9.8	14 11.7	+48.2	9.9
76	12 02.2	+47.7	9.1	13 01.4	+47.9	9.2	14 00.6	+48.0	9.2	14 59.9	+48.0	9.3
77	12 49.9	+47.7	8.5	13 49.3	+47.7	8.6	14 48.6	+47.8	8.6	15 47.9	+47.9	8.6
78	13 37.6	+47.5	7.9	14 37.0	+47.6	7.9	15 36.4	+47.7	8.0	16 35.8	+47.8	8.0
79	14 25.1	+47.5	7.3	15 24.6	+47.6	7.3	16 24.1	+47.7	7.3	17 23.6	+47.7	7.4
80	15 12.6	+47.3	6.6	16 12.2	+47.4	6.7	17 11.8	+47.4	6.7	18 11.3	+47.6	6.7
81	15 59.9	+47.2	6.0	16 59.6	+47.3	6.0	17 59.2	+47.4	6.1	18 58.9	+47.4	6.1
82	16 47.1	+47.1	5.4	17 46.9	+47.1	5.4	18 46.6	+47.2	5.4	19 46.3	+47.3	5.5
83	17 34.2	+47.0	4.7	18 34.0	+47.1	4.7	19 33.8	+47.1	4.8	20 33.6	+47.2	4.8
84	18 21.2	+46.9	4.1	19 21.1	+46.9	4.1	20 20.9	+47.0	4.1	21 20.8	+46.9	4.1
85	19 08.1	+46.7	3.4	20 08.0	+46.7	3.4	21 07.9	+46.7	3.4	22 07.7	+46.9	3.5
86	19 54.8	+46.5	2.7	20 54.7	+46.6	2.8	21 54.6	+46.6	2.8	22 54.6	+46.6	2.8
87	20 41.3	+46.4	2.1	21 41.3	+46.4	2.1	22 41.2	+46.5	2.1	23 41.2	+46.5	2.1
88	21 27.7	+46.2	1.4	22 27.7	+46.2	1.4	23 27.7	+46.2	1.4	24 27.7	+46.2	1.4
89	22 13.9	+46.1	0.7	23 13.9	+46.1	0.7	24 13.9	+46.1	0.7	25 13.9	+46.1	0.7
90	23 00.0	+45.9	0.0	24 00.0	+45.9	0.0	25 00.0	+45.9	0.0	26 00.0	+45.9	0.0
	23°			24°			25°			26°		

Dec.	27° Hc	d	Z	28° Hc	d	Z	29° Hc	d	Z	30° Hc	d	Z
°	° ′	′	°	° ′	′	°	° ′	′	°	° ′	′	°
0	43 02.6	−37.6	118.4	42 33.7	−38.6	119.2	42 04.0	−39.4	120.0	41 33.6	−40.3	120.8
1	42 25.0	−38.1	119.5	41 55.1	−39.0	120.3	41 24.6	−40.0	121.0	40 53.3	−40.8	121.8
2	41 46.9	−38.7	120.5	41 16.1	−39.6	121.3	40 44.6	−40.5	122.0	40 12.5	−41.3	122.7
3	41 08.2	−39.2	121.5	40 36.5	−40.1	122.3	40 04.1	−40.9	123.0	39 31.2	−41.8	123.7
4	40 29.0	−39.8	122.5	39 56.4	−40.6	123.2	39 23.2	−41.4	123.9	38 49.4	−42.2	124.6
5	39 49.2	−40.2	123.5	39 15.8	−41.0	124.2	38 41.8	−41.8	124.9	38 07.2	−42.6	125.5
6	39 09.0	−40.7	124.5	38 34.8	−41.5	125.1	38 00.0	−42.3	125.8	37 24.6	−43.0	126.4
7	38 28.3	−41.1	125.4	37 53.3	−41.9	126.1	37 17.7	−42.6	126.7	36 41.6	−43.4	127.3
8	37 47.2	−41.5	126.3	37 11.4	−42.3	127.0	36 35.1	−43.1	127.6	35 58.2	−43.7	128.1
9	37 05.7	−42.0	127.3	36 29.1	−42.7	127.8	35 52.0	−43.4	128.4	35 14.5	−44.1	129.0
10	36 23.7	−42.4	128.1	35 46.4	−43.1	128.7	35 08.6	−43.7	129.3	34 30.4	−44.4	129.8
11	35 41.3	−42.7	129.0	35 03.3	−43.4	129.6	34 24.9	−44.1	130.1	33 46.0	−44.7	130.6
12	34 58.6	−43.1	129.9	34 19.9	−43.7	130.4	33 40.8	−44.4	130.9	33 01.3	−45.0	131.4
13	34 15.5	−43.4	130.7	33 36.2	−44.1	131.2	32 56.4	−44.7	131.7	32 16.3	−45.3	132.2
14	33 32.1	−43.8	131.6	32 52.1	−44.4	132.0	32 11.7	−45.0	132.5	31 31.0	−45.6	133.0
15	32 48.3	−44.0	132.4	32 07.7	−44.7	132.8	31 26.7	−45.2	133.3	30 45.4	−45.8	133.7
16	32 04.3	−44.4	133.2	31 23.0	−44.9	133.6	30 41.5	−45.6	134.1	29 59.6	−46.1	134.5
17	31 19.9	−44.7	134.0	30 38.1	−45.2	134.4	29 55.9	−45.7	134.8	29 13.5	−46.3	135.2
18	30 35.2	−44.9	134.8	29 52.9	−45.5	135.2	29 10.2	−46.1	135.6	28 27.2	−46.6	135.9
19	29 50.3	−45.2	135.5	29 07.4	−45.8	135.9	28 24.1	−46.2	136.3	27 40.6	−46.8	136.7
20	29 05.1	−45.4	136.3	28 21.6	−45.9	136.7	27 37.9	−46.5	137.0	26 53.8	−46.9	137.4
21	28 19.7	−45.7	137.0	27 35.7	−46.2	137.4	26 51.4	−46.7	137.7	26 06.9	−47.2	138.1
22	27 34.0	−45.9	137.8	26 49.5	−46.4	138.1	26 04.7	−46.9	138.4	25 19.7	−47.4	138.7
23	26 48.1	−46.1	138.5	26 03.1	−46.7	138.8	25 17.8	−47.1	139.1	24 32.3	−47.5	139.4
24	26 02.0	−46.4	139.2	25 16.4	−46.8	139.5	24 30.7	−47.2	139.8	23 44.8	−47.7	140.1
25	25 15.6	−46.5	139.9	24 29.6	−46.9	140.2	23 43.5	−47.5	140.5	22 57.1	−47.9	140.8
26	24 29.1	−46.7	140.6	23 42.7	−47.2	140.9	22 56.0	−47.6	141.1	22 09.2	−48.0	141.4
27	23 42.4	−46.9	141.3	22 55.5	−47.4	141.5	22 08.4	−47.8	141.8	21 21.2	−48.2	142.1
28	22 55.5	−47.1	142.0	22 08.1	−47.5	142.2	21 20.6	−47.9	142.4	20 33.0	−48.3	142.7
29	22 08.4	−47.2	142.6	21 20.6	−47.6	142.9	20 32.7	−48.0	143.1	19 44.7	−48.5	143.3
30	21 21.2	−47.4	143.3	20 33.0	−47.8	143.5	19 44.7	−48.2	143.7	18 56.2	−48.5	143.9
31	20 33.8	−47.6	144.0	19 45.2	−47.9	144.2	18 56.5	−48.3	144.4	18 07.7	−48.7	144.6
32	19 46.2	−47.6	144.6	18 57.3	−48.1	144.8	18 08.2	−48.4	145.0	17 19.0	−48.8	145.2
33	18 58.6	−47.8	145.2	18 09.2	−48.2	145.4	17 19.8	−48.6	145.6	16 30.2	−48.9	145.8
34	18 10.8	−48.0	145.9	17 21.0	−48.3	146.1	16 31.2	−48.6	146.2	15 41.3	−49.0	146.4
35	17 22.8	−48.0	146.5	16 32.7	−48.4	146.7	15 42.6	−48.8	146.8	14 52.3	−49.1	147.0
36	16 34.8	−48.2	147.1	15 44.3	−48.5	147.3	14 53.8	−48.9	147.4	14 03.2	−49.2	147.6
37	15 46.6	−48.3	147.8	14 55.8	−48.6	147.9	14 04.9	−48.9	148.0	13 14.0	−49.3	148.2
38	14 58.3	−48.3	148.4	14 07.2	−48.7	148.5	13 16.0	−49.0	148.6	12 24.7	−49.3	148.8
39	14 10.0	−48.5	149.0	13 18.5	−48.8	149.1	12 27.0	−49.1	149.2	11 35.4	−49.4	149.3
40	13 21.5	−48.5	149.6	12 29.7	−48.8	149.7	11 37.9	−49.2	149.8	10 46.0	−49.5	149.9
41	12 33.0	−48.7	150.2	11 40.9	−49.0	150.3	10 48.7	−49.2	150.4	9 56.5	−49.5	150.5
42	11 44.3	−48.7	150.8	10 51.9	−49.0	150.9	9 59.5	−49.3	151.0	9 07.0	−49.6	151.1
43	10 55.6	−48.7	151.4	10 02.9	−49.0	151.5	9 10.2	−49.3	151.6	8 17.4	−49.6	151.6
44	10 06.9	−48.9	152.0	9 13.9	−49.1	152.1	8 20.9	−49.4	152.1	7 27.8	−49.7	152.2
45	9 18.0	−48.8	152.6	8 24.8	−49.2	152.6	7 31.5	−49.5	152.7	6 38.1	−49.7	152.8
46	8 29.2	−49.0	153.2	7 35.6	−49.2	153.2	6 42.0	−49.5	153.3	5 48.4	−49.7	153.3
47	7 40.2	−49.0	153.7	6 46.4	−49.3	153.8	5 52.5	−49.5	153.9	4 58.7	−49.8	153.9
48	6 51.2	−49.0	154.3	5 57.1	−49.3	154.4	5 03.0	−49.5	154.4	4 08.9	−49.8	154.5
49	6 02.2	−49.1	154.9	5 07.8	−49.3	155.0	4 13.5	−49.6	155.0	3 19.1	−49.8	155.0
50	5 13.1	−49.1	155.5	4 18.5	−49.3	155.5	3 23.9	−49.6	155.6	2 29.3	−49.8	155.6
51	4 24.0	−49.1	156.1	3 29.2	−49.4	156.1	2 34.3	−49.6	156.1	1 39.5	−49.9	156.1
52	3 34.9	−49.1	156.6	2 39.8	−49.4	156.7	1 44.7	−49.6	156.7	0 49.6	−49.8	156.7
53	2 45.8	−49.2	157.2	1 50.4	−49.4	157.2	0 55.1	−49.6	157.2	0 00.2	+49.9	22.8
54	1 56.6	−49.2	157.8	1 01.0	−49.4	157.8	0 05.5	−49.6	157.8	0 50.1	+49.8	22.2
55	1 07.4	−49.2	158.4	0 11.6	−49.4	158.4	0 44.1	+49.7	21.6	1 39.9	+49.8	21.6
56	0 18.2	−49.2	158.9	0 37.8	+49.4	21.1	1 33.8	+49.6	21.1	2 29.7	+49.9	21.1
57	0 31.0	+49.1	20.5	1 27.2	+49.3	20.5	2 23.4	+49.5	20.5	3 19.6	+49.7	20.5
58	1 20.1	+49.2	19.9	2 16.5	+49.4	19.9	3 12.9	+49.6	19.9	4 09.3	+49.8	20.0
59	2 09.3	+49.2	19.3	3 05.9	+49.4	19.4	4 02.5	+49.6	19.4	4 59.1	+49.8	19.4
60	2 58.5	+49.1	18.8	3 55.3	+49.3	18.8	4 52.1	+49.5	18.8	5 48.9	+49.7	18.8
61	3 47.6	+49.1	18.2	4 44.6	+49.3	18.2	5 41.6	+49.5	18.3	6 38.6	+49.6	18.3
62	4 36.7	+49.1	17.6	5 33.9	+49.3	17.6	6 31.1	+49.4	17.7	7 28.2	+49.7	17.7
63	5 25.8	+49.1	17.0	6 23.2	+49.2	17.1	7 20.5	+49.4	17.1	8 17.9	+49.6	17.2
64	6 14.9	+49.0	16.5	7 12.4	+49.2	16.5	8 09.9	+49.4	16.5	9 07.5	+49.5	16.6
65	7 03.9	+49.0	15.9	8 01.6	+49.1	15.9	8 59.3	+49.3	16.0	9 57.0	+49.4	16.0
66	7 52.9	+48.9	15.3	8 50.7	+49.1	15.3	9 48.6	+49.3	15.4	10 46.4	+49.5	15.4
67	8 41.8	+48.9	14.7	9 39.8	+49.1	14.8	10 37.9	+49.1	14.8	11 35.9	+49.3	14.9
68	9 30.7	+48.8	14.1	10 28.9	+48.9	14.2	11 27.0	+49.1	14.2	12 25.2	+49.2	14.3
69	10 19.5	+48.8	13.5	11 17.8	+48.9	13.6	12 16.1	+49.1	13.6	13 14.4	+49.2	13.7
70	11 08.3	+48.6	12.9	12 06.7	+48.8	13.0	13 05.2	+48.9	13.0	14 03.6	+49.1	13.1
71	11 56.9	+48.6	12.4	12 55.5	+48.8	12.4	13 54.1	+48.9	12.4	14 52.7	+49.0	12.5
72	12 45.5	+48.6	11.8	13 44.3	+48.6	11.8	14 43.0	+48.8	11.9	15 41.7	+48.9	11.9
73	13 34.1	+48.4	11.1	14 32.9	+48.6	11.2	15 31.8	+48.7	11.2	16 30.6	+48.8	11.3
74	14 22.5	+48.3	10.5	15 21.5	+48.4	10.6	16 20.5	+48.5	10.6	17 19.4	+48.7	10.7
75	15 10.8	+48.3	9.9	16 09.9	+48.4	10.0	17 09.0	+48.5	10.0	18 08.1	+48.6	10.1
76	15 59.1	+48.1	9.3	16 58.3	+48.2	9.4	17 57.5	+48.3	9.4	18 56.7	+48.4	9.5
77	16 47.2	+48.0	8.7	17 46.5	+48.1	8.7	18 45.8	+48.2	8.8	19 45.1	+48.3	8.8
78	17 35.2	+47.9	8.1	18 34.6	+48.0	8.1	19 34.0	+48.1	8.2	20 33.4	+48.2	8.2
79	18 23.1	+47.8	7.4	19 22.6	+47.9	7.5	20 22.1	+48.0	7.5	21 21.6	+48.0	7.6
80	19 10.9	+47.7	6.8	20 10.5	+47.7	6.8	21 10.1	+47.8	6.9	22 09.6	+47.9	6.9
81	19 58.6	+47.5	6.1	20 58.2	+47.6	6.2	21 57.9	+47.6	6.2	22 57.5	+47.7	6.3
82	20 46.1	+47.3	5.5	21 45.8	+47.4	5.5	22 45.5	+47.5	5.6	23 45.2	+47.6	5.6
83	21 33.4	+47.2	4.8	22 33.2	+47.2	4.9	23 33.0	+47.3	4.9	24 32.8	+47.3	4.9
84	22 20.6	+47.0	4.2	23 20.4	+47.1	4.2	24 20.3	+47.1	4.2	25 20.1	+47.2	4.3
85	23 07.6	+46.9	3.5	24 07.5	+46.9	3.5	25 07.4	+46.9	3.5	26 07.3	+47.0	3.6
86	23 54.5	+46.7	2.8	24 54.4	+46.7	2.8	25 54.3	+46.8	2.9	26 54.3	+46.7	2.9
87	24 41.2	+46.4	2.1	25 41.1	+46.5	2.1	26 41.1	+46.5	2.2	27 41.0	+46.6	2.2
88	25 27.6	+46.3	1.4	26 27.6	+46.3	1.4	27 27.6	+46.3	1.4	28 27.6	+46.3	1.5
89	26 13.9	+46.1	0.7	27 13.9	+46.1	0.7	28 13.9	+46.1	0.7	29 13.9	+46.1	0.7
90	27 00.0	+45.9	0.0	28 00.0	+45.8	0.0	29 00.0	+45.8	0.0	30 00.0	+45.8	0.0
	27°			28°			29°			30°		

S. Lat. {L.H.A. greater than 180° ....Zn=180°−Z; L.H.A. less than 180°...........Zn=180°+Z}

LATITUDE SAME NAME AS DECLINATION L.H.A. 140°, 220°

265

41°, 319° L.H.A. LATITUDE SAME NAME AS DECLINATION

N. Lat. {L.H.A. greater than 180° .....Zn=Z; L.H.A. less than 180°............Zn=360°−Z}

Dec.	23° Hc	d	Z	24° Hc	d	Z	25° Hc	d	Z	26° Hc	d	Z	27° Hc	d	Z	28° Hc	d	Z	29° Hc	d	Z	30° Hc	d	Z	Dec.
°	° ′	′	°	° ′	′	°	° ′	′	°	° ′	′	°	° ′	′	°	° ′	′	°	° ′	′	°	° ′	′	°	°
0	44 00.3	+32.2	114.2	43 35.2	+33.4	115.1	43 09.4	+34.4	115.9	42 42.8	+35.5	116.8	42 15.4	+36.5	117.6	41 47.2	+37.5	118.4	41 18.4	+38.4	119.1	40 48.8	+39.4	119.9	0
1	44 32.5	+31.5	113.0	44 08.6	+32.6	113.9	43 43.8	+33.8	114.8	43 18.3	+34.8	115.7	42 51.9	+35.9	116.5	42 24.7	+36.9	117.3	41 56.8	+37.9	118.1	41 28.2	+38.8	118.9	1
2	45 04.0	+30.7	111.8	44 41.2	+31.9	112.7	44 17.6	+33.0	113.6	43 53.1	+34.2	114.5	43 27.8	+35.2	115.4	43 01.6	+36.3	116.2	42 34.7	+37.3	117.1	42 07.0	+38.3	117.9	2
3	45 34.7	+29.9	110.6	45 13.1	+31.2	111.6	44 50.6	+32.4	112.5	44 27.3	+33.4	113.4	44 03.0	+34.6	114.3	43 37.9	+35.7	115.2	43 12.0	+36.7	116.0	42 45.3	+37.7	116.8	3
4	46 04.6	+29.1	109.4	45 44.3	+30.3	110.3	45 23.0	+31.5	111.3	45 00.7	+32.8	112.2	44 37.6	+33.9	113.1	44 13.6	+35.0	114.0	43 48.7	+36.1	114.9	43 23.0	+37.1	115.8	4
5	46 33.7	+28.3	108.1	46 14.6	+29.5	109.1	45 54.5	+30.8	110.1	45 33.5	+31.9	111.0	45 11.5	+33.1	112.0	44 48.6	+34.3	112.9	44 24.8	+35.4	113.8	44 00.1	+36.5	114.7	5
6	47 02.0	+27.4	106.8	46 44.1	+28.7	107.8	46 25.3	+29.9	108.8	46 05.4	+31.2	109.8	45 44.6	+32.4	110.8	45 22.9	+33.5	111.7	45 00.2	+34.7	112.7	44 36.6	+35.8	113.6	6
7	47 29.4	+26.4	105.5	47 12.8	+27.8	106.5	46 55.2	+29.1	107.6	46 36.6	+30.4	108.6	46 17.0	+31.6	109.6	45 56.4	+32.8	110.5	45 34.9	+34.0	111.5	45 12.4	+35.2	112.4	7
8	47 55.8	+25.5	104.2	47 40.6	+26.9	105.2	47 24.3	+28.2	106.3	47 07.0	+29.5	107.3	46 48.6	+30.8	108.3	46 29.2	+32.1	109.3	46 08.9	+33.2	110.3	45 47.6	+34.4	111.3	8
9	48 21.3	+24.6	102.8	48 07.5	+25.9	103.9	47 52.5	+27.3	105.0	47 36.5	+28.6	106.0	47 19.4	+30.0	107.1	47 01.3	+31.2	108.1	46 42.1	+32.5	109.1	46 22.0	+33.7	110.1	9
10	48 45.9	+23.5	101.4	48 33.4	+25.0	102.5	48 19.8	+26.4	103.6	48 05.1	+27.8	104.7	47 49.4	+29.0	105.8	47 32.5	+30.4	106.8	47 14.6	+31.6	107.9	46 55.7	+32.9	108.9	10
11	49 09.4	+22.5	100.0	48 58.4	+24.0	101.2	48 46.2	+25.4	102.3	48 32.9	+26.8	103.4	48 18.4	+28.2	104.5	48 02.9	+29.5	105.6	47 46.2	+30.9	106.6	47 28.6	+32.0	107.7	11
12	49 31.9	+21.5	98.6	49 22.4	+22.9	99.8	49 11.6	+24.4	100.9	48 59.7	+25.8	102.0	48 46.6	+27.2	103.1	48 32.4	+28.6	104.3	48 17.1	+29.9	105.3	48 00.6	+31.3	106.4	12
13	49 53.4	+20.3	97.2	49 45.3	+21.9	98.3	49 36.0	+23.3	99.5	49 25.5	+24.8	100.6	49 13.8	+26.3	101.8	49 01.0	+27.6	102.9	48 47.0	+29.0	104.0	48 31.9	+30.4	105.1	13
14	50 13.7	+19.3	95.7	50 07.2	+20.7	96.9	49 59.3	+22.3	98.1	49 50.3	+23.8	99.2	49 40.1	+25.2	100.4	49 28.6	+26.7	101.6	49 16.0	+28.1	102.7	49 02.3	+29.4	103.8	14
15	50 33.0	+18.0	94.2	50 27.9	+19.7	95.4	50 21.6	+21.2	96.6	50 14.1	+22.7	97.8	50 05.3	+24.2	99.0	49 55.3	+25.7	100.2	49 44.1	+27.2	101.3	49 31.7	+28.6	102.5	15
16	50 51.0	+16.9	92.7	50 47.6	+18.5	93.9	50 42.8	+20.1	95.1	50 36.8	+21.6	96.4	50 29.5	+23.2	97.6	50 21.0	+24.6	98.8	50 11.3	+26.1	100.0	50 00.3	+27.5	101.1	16
17	51 07.9	+15.7	91.2	51 06.1	+17.3	92.4	51 02.9	+18.9	93.7	50 58.4	+20.5	94.9	50 52.7	+22.0	96.1	50 45.6	+23.6	97.3	50 37.4	+25.0	98.5	50 27.8	+26.6	99.7	17
18	51 23.6	+14.5	89.6	51 23.4	+16.1	90.9	51 21.8	+17.7	92.1	51 18.9	+19.3	93.4	51 14.7	+20.9	94.6	51 09.2	+22.5	95.9	51 02.4	+24.0	97.1	50 54.4	+25.5	98.3	18
19	51 38.1	+13.2	88.1	51 39.5	+14.8	89.3	51 39.5	+16.5	90.6	51 38.2	+18.1	91.9	51 35.6	+19.7	93.1	51 31.7	+21.3	94.4	51 26.4	+22.9	95.6	51 19.9	+24.4	96.9	19
20	51 51.3	+12.0	86.5	51 54.3	+13.6	87.8	51 56.0	+15.2	89.0	51 56.3	+16.9	90.3	51 55.3	+18.5	91.6	51 53.0	+20.1	92.9	51 49.3	+21.7	94.1	51 44.3	+23.3	95.4	20
21	52 03.3	+10.6	84.9	52 07.9	+12.4	86.2	52 11.2	+14.0	87.5	52 13.2	+15.7	88.8	52 13.8	+17.3	90.1	52 13.1	+18.9	91.3	52 11.0	+20.6	92.6	52 07.6	+22.1	93.9	21
22	52 13.9	+9.4	83.3	52 20.3	+11.0	84.6	52 25.2	+12.7	85.9	52 28.9	+14.3	87.2	52 31.1	+16.1	88.5	52 32.0	+17.7	89.8	52 31.6	+19.3	91.1	52 29.7	+21.0	92.4	22
23	52 23.3	+8.0	81.7	52 31.3	+9.7	83.0	52 37.9	+11.4	84.3	52 43.2	+13.1	85.6	52 47.2	+14.7	86.9	52 49.7	+16.4	88.2	52 50.9	+18.1	89.5	52 50.7	+19.7	90.9	23
24	52 31.3	+6.6	80.1	52 41.0	+8.3	81.4	52 49.3	+10.0	82.7	52 56.3	+11.7	84.0	53 01.9	+13.4	85.3	53 06.1	+15.2	86.6	53 09.0	+16.8	87.9	53 10.4	+18.5	89.3	24
25	52 37.9	+5.3	78.4	52 49.3	+7.0	79.7	52 59.3	+8.7	81.0	53 08.0	+10.4	82.3	53 15.3	+12.1	83.7	53 21.3	+13.8	85.0	53 25.8	+15.5	86.3	53 28.9	+17.2	87.7	25
26	52 43.2	+4.0	76.8	52 56.3	+5.6	78.1	53 08.0	+7.3	79.4	53 18.4	+9.0	80.7	53 27.4	+10.8	82.0	53 35.1	+12.4	83.4	53 41.3	+14.1	84.7	53 46.1	+15.9	86.1	26
27	52 47.2	+2.5	75.1	53 01.9	+4.2	76.4	53 15.3	+6.0	77.7	53 27.4	+7.7	79.0	53 38.2	+9.3	80.4	53 47.5	+11.1	81.7	53 55.4	+12.8	83.1	54 02.0	+14.5	84.4	27
28	52 49.7	+1.2	73.5	53 06.1	+2.9	74.8	53 21.3	+4.5	76.1	53 35.1	+6.2	77.4	53 47.5	+7.9	78.7	53 58.6	+9.6	80.0	54 08.2	+11.4	81.4	54 16.5	+13.1	82.8	28
29	52 50.9	−0.2	71.8	53 09.0	+1.4	73.1	53 25.8	+3.1	74.4	53 41.3	+4.8	75.7	53 55.4	+6.6	77.0	54 08.2	+8.3	78.4	54 19.6	+10.0	79.7	54 29.6	+11.8	81.1	29
30	52 50.7	−1.6	70.2	53 10.4	+0.1	71.4	53 28.9	+1.7	72.7	53 46.1	+3.4	74.0	54 02.0	+5.1	75.3	54 16.5	+6.8	76.7	54 29.6	+8.6	78.0	54 41.4	+10.3	79.4	30
31	52 49.1	−2.9	68.5	53 10.5	−1.4	69.8	53 30.6	+0.3	71.0	53 49.5	+2.0	72.3	54 07.1	+3.6	73.6	54 23.3	+5.4	75.0	54 38.2	+7.1	76.3	54 51.7	+8.8	77.7	31
32	52 46.2	−4.4	66.9	53 09.1	−2.7	68.1	53 30.9	−1.1	69.3	53 51.5	+0.5	70.6	54 10.7	+2.3	71.9	54 28.7	+3.9	73.3	54 45.3	+5.6	74.6	55 00.5	+7.4	76.0	32
33	52 41.8	−5.7	65.2	53 06.4	−4.1	66.4	53 29.8	−2.5	67.7	53 52.0	−0.9	68.9	54 13.0	+0.7	70.2	54 32.6	+2.5	71.5	54 50.9	+4.2	72.9	55 07.9	+5.9	74.2	33
34	52 36.1	−7.0	63.6	53 02.3	−5.5	64.8	53 27.3	−4.0	66.0	53 51.1	−2.3	67.2	54 13.7	−0.7	68.5	54 35.1	+0.9	69.8	54 55.1	+2.7	71.1	55 13.8	+4.4	72.5	34
35	52 29.1	−8.4	61.9	52 56.8	−6.9	63.1	53 23.3	−5.3	64.3	53 48.8	−3.8	65.5	54 13.0	−2.1	66.8	54 36.0	−0.4	68.1	54 57.8	+1.2	69.4	55 18.2	+2.9	70.8	35
36	52 20.7	−9.7	60.3	52 49.9	−8.3	61.5	53 18.0	−6.7	62.6	53 45.0	−5.2	63.8	54 10.9	−3.6	65.1	54 35.6	−2.0	66.4	54 59.0	−0.3	67.7	55 21.1	+1.4	69.0	36
37	52 11.0	−11.1	58.7	52 41.6	−9.6	59.8	53 11.3	−8.1	61.0	53 39.8	−6.6	62.2	54 07.3	−5.0	63.4	54 33.6	−3.4	64.6	54 58.7	−1.8	65.9	55 22.5	−0.1	67.2	37
38	51 59.9	−12.3	57.1	52 32.0	−10.9	58.2	53 03.2	−9.5	59.3	53 33.2	−7.9	60.5	54 02.3	−6.5	61.7	54 30.2	−4.9	62.9	54 56.9	−3.3	64.2	55 22.4	−1.6	65.5	38
39	51 47.6	−13.6	55.5	52 21.1	−12.2	56.6	52 53.7	−10.8	57.7	53 25.3	−9.4	58.8	53 55.8	−7.9	60.0	54 25.3	−6.4	61.2	54 53.6	−4.8	62.4	55 20.8	−3.2	63.7	39
40	51 34.0	−14.8	54.0	52 08.9	−13.5	55.0	52 42.9	−12.2	56.1	53 15.9	−10.7	57.2	53 47.9	−9.3	58.3	54 18.9	−7.8	59.5	54 48.8	−6.2	60.7	55 17.6	−4.7	62.0	40
41	51 19.2	−16.0	52.4	51 55.4	−14.8	53.4	52 30.7	−13.4	54.4	53 05.2	−12.1	55.5	53 38.6	−10.6	56.6	54 11.1	−9.2	57.8	54 42.6	−7.7	59.0	55 12.9	−6.1	60.2	41
42	51 03.2	−17.3	50.9	51 40.6	−16.0	51.8	52 17.3	−14.7	52.8	52 53.1	−13.4	53.9	53 28.0	−12.0	55.0	54 01.9	−10.6	56.1	54 34.9	−9.2	57.3	55 06.8	−7.6	58.5	42
43	50 45.9	−18.4	49.3	51 24.6	−17.2	50.3	52 02.6	−16.0	51.3	52 39.7	−14.7	52.3	53 16.0	−13.4	53.3	53 51.3	−12.0	54.4	54 25.7	−10.5	55.6	54 59.2	−9.2	56.7	43
44	50 27.5	−19.6	47.8	51 07.4	−18.4	48.8	51 46.6	−17.2	49.7	52 25.0	−16.0	50.7	53 02.6	−14.7	51.7	53 39.3	−13.3	52.8	54 15.2	−12.0	53.9	54 50.0	−10.5	55.0	44
45	50 07.9	−20.6	46.4	50 49.0	−19.6	47.2	51 29.4	−18.4	48.2	52 09.0	−17.2	49.1	52 47.9	−16.0	50.1	53 26.0	−14.7	51.1	54 03.2	−13.4	52.2	54 39.5	−12.0	53.3	45
46	49 47.3	−21.8	44.9	50 29.4	−20.6	45.8	51 11.0	−19.6	46.6	51 51.8	−18.4	47.6	52 31.9	−17.2	48.5	53 11.3	−16.0	49.5	53 49.8	−14.7	50.6	54 27.5	−13.4	51.6	46
47	49 25.5	−22.8	43.5	50 08.8	−21.8	44.3	50 51.4	−20.7	45.1	51 33.4	−19.6	46.0	52 14.7	−18.5	46.9	52 55.3	−17.3	47.9	53 35.1	−16.0	48.9	54 14.1	−14.7	50.0	47
48	49 02.7	−23.8	42.0	49 47.0	−22.9	42.8	50 30.7	−21.8	43.7	51 13.8	−20.8	44.5	51 56.2	−19.6	45.4	52 38.0	−18.5	46.3	53 19.1	−17.3	47.3	53 59.4	−16.1	48.3	48
49	48 38.9	−24.9	40.7	49 24.1	−23.9	41.4	50 08.9	−23.0	42.2	50 53.0	−21.9	43.0	51 36.6	−20.9	43.9	52 19.5	−19.7	44.8	53 01.8	−18.6	45.7	53 43.3	−17.4	46.7	49
50	48 14.0	−25.8	39.3	49 00.2	−24.9	40.0	49 45.9	−23.9	40.8	50 31.1	−23.0	41.5	51 15.7	−21.9	42.4	51 59.8	−21.0	43.2	52 43.2	−19.9	44.1	53 25.9	−18.7	45.1	50
51	47 48.2	−26.7	37.9	48 35.3	−25.8	38.6	49 22.0	−25.0	39.3	50 08.1	−24.0	40.1	50 53.8	−23.1	40.9	51 38.8	−22.0	41.7	52 23.3	−21.0	42.6	53 07.2	−19.9	43.5	51
52	47 21.5	−27.6	36.6	48 09.5	−26.8	37.3	48 57.0	−25.9	38.0	49 44.1	−25.1	38.7	50 30.7	−24.2	39.4	51 16.8	−23.2	40.2	52 02.3	−22.2	41.0	52 47.3	−21.2	41.9	52
53	46 53.9	−28.5	35.3	47 42.7	−27.8	35.9	48 31.1	−27.0	36.6	49 19.0	−26.1	37.3	50 06.5	−25.2	38.0	50 53.6	−24.3	38.8	51 40.1	−23.3	39.5	52 26.1	−22.3	40.4	53
54	46 25.4	−29.4	34.0	47 14.9	−28.6	34.6	48 04.1	−27.8	35.2	48 52.9	−27.0	35.9	49 41.3	−26.2	36.6	50 29.3	−25.4	37.3	51 16.8	−24.5	38.1	52 03.8	−23.5	38.8	54
55	45 56.0	−30.1	32.8	46 46.3	−29.4	33.3	47 36.3	−28.7	33.9	48 25.9	−28.0	34.6	49 15.1	−27.2	35.2	50 03.9	−26.3	35.9	50 52.3	−25.5	36.6	51 40.3	−24.6	37.4	55
56	45 25.9	−31.0	31.5	46 16.9	−30.3	32.1	47 07.6	−29.6	32.6	47 57.9	−28.8	33.2	48 47.9	−28.1	33.8	49 37.6	−27.3	34.5	50 26.8	−26.5	35.2	51 15.7	−25.7	35.9	56
57	44 54.9	−31.7	30.3	45 46.6	−31.1	30.8	46 38.0	−30.4	31.4	47 29.1	−29.8	31.9	48 19.8	−29.0	32.5	49 10.3	−28.3	33.1	50 00.3	−27.5	33.8	50 50.0	−26.7	34.5	57
58	44 23.2	−32.4	29.1	45 15.5	−31.8	29.6	46 07.6	−31.3	30.1	46 59.3	−30.6	30.6	47 50.8	−29.9	31.2	48 42.0	−29.3	31.8	49 32.8	−28.5	32.4	50 23.3	−27.8	33.0	58
59	43 50.8	−33.2	27.9	44 43.7	−32.6	28.4	45 36.3	−32.0	28.9	46 28.7	−31.3	29.4	47 20.9	−30.8	29.9	48 12.7	−30.0	30.5	49 04.3	−29.4	31.0	49 55.5	−28.6	31.7	59
60	43 17.6	−33.8	26.8	44 11.1	−33.3	27.2	45 04.3	−32.7	27.7	45 57.4	−32.2	28.2	46 50.1	−31.5	28.7	47 42.7	−31.0	29.2	48 34.9	−30.3	29.7	49 26.9	−29.7	30.3	60
61	42 43.8	−34.5	25.7	43 37.8	−34.0	26.1	44 31.6	−33.5	26.5	45 25.2	−32.9	26.9	46 18.6	−32.4	27.4	47 11.7	−31.8	27.9	48 04.6	−31.2	28.4	48 57.2	−30.5	29.0	61
62	42 09.3	−35.1	24.5	43 03.8	−34.6	24.9	43 58.1	−34.1	25.3	44 52.3	−33.7	25.8	45 46.2	−33.1	26.2	46 39.9	−32.5	26.7	47 33.4	−32.0	27.2	48 26.7	−31.4	27.7	62
63	41 34.2	−35.7	23.5	42 29.2	−35.3	23.8	43 24.0	−34.8	24.2	44 18.6	−34.3	24.6	45 13.1	−33.8	25.0	46 07.4	−33.4	25.4	47 01.4	−32.7	25.9	47 55.3	−32.2	26.4	63
64	40 58.5	−36.3	22.4	41 53.9	−35.9	22.7	42 49.2	−35.5	23.1	43 44.3	−35.0	23.5	44 39.3	−34.6	23.8	45 34.0	−34.0	24.3	46 28.7	−33.6	24.7	47 23.1	−33.1	25.1	64
65	40 22.2	−36.9	21.3	41 18.0	−36.4	21.7	42 13.7	−36.0	22.0	43 09.3	−35.6	22.3	44 04.7	−35.2	22.7	45 00.0	−34.8	23.1	45 55.1	−34.3	23.5	46 50.0	−33.8	23.9	65
66	39 45.3	−37.3	20.3	40 41.6	−37.1	20.6	41 37.7	−36.7	20.9	42 33.7	−36.3	21.2	43 29.5	−35.8	21.6	44 25.2	−35.4	21.9	45 20.8	−35.0	22.3	46 16.2	−34.5	22.7	66
67	39 08.0	−38.0	19.3	40 04.5	−37.5	19.6	41 01.0	−37.2	19.9	41 57.4	−36.9	20.2	42 53.7	−36.5	20.5	43 49.8	−36.1	20.8	44 45.8	−35.6	21.2	45 41.7	−35.2	21.5	67
68	38 30.0	−38.4	18.3	39 27.0	−38.1	18.6	40 23.8	−37.8	18.8	41 20.5	−37.4	19.1	42 17.2	−37.1	19.4	43 13.7	−36.7	19.7	44 10.2	−36.4	20.0	45 06.5	−36.0	20.4	68
69	37 51.6	−38.8	17.3	38 48.9	−38.6	17.6	39 46.0	−38.2	17.8	40 43.1	−37.9	18.1	41 40.1	−37.6	18.3	42 37.0	−37.3	18.6	43 33.8	−36.9	18.9	44 30.5	−36.6	19.2	69
70	37 12.8	−39.4	16.4	38 10.3	−39.1	16.6	39 07.8	−38.8	16.8	40 05.2	−38.5	17.1	41 02.5	−38.2	17.3	41 59.7	−37.9	17.6	42 56.9	−37.6	17.9	43 53.9	−37.2	18.1	70
71	36 33.4	−39.8	15.4	37 31.2	−39.5	15.6	38 29.0	−39.3	15.8	39 26.7	−39.0	16.1	40 24.3	−38.7	16.3	41 21.8	−38.4	16.5	42 19.3	−38.1	16.8	43 16.7	−37.8	17.1	71
72	35 53.6	−40.2	14.5	36 51.7	−40.0	14.7	37 49.7	−39.7	14.9	38 47.7	−39.5	15.1	39 45.6	−39.2	15.3	40 43.4	−38.9	15.5	41 41.2	−38.7	15.8	42 38.9	−38.4	16.0	72
73	35 13.4	−40.6	13.6	36 11.7	−40.4	13.7	37 10.0	−40.2	13.9	38 08.2	−39.9	14.1	39 06.4	−39.7	14.3	40 04.5	−39.5	14.5	41 02.5	−39.2	14.7	42 00.5	−38.9	15.0	73
74	34 32.8	−41.0	12.7	35 31.3	−40.7	12.8	36 29.8	−40.6	13.0	37 28.3	−40.4	13.2	38 26.7	−40.2	13.3	39 25.0	−39.9	13.5	40 23.3	−39.7	13.7	41 21.6	−39.5	13.9	74
75	33 51.8	−41.3	11.8	34 50.6	−41.2	11.9	35 49.2	−41.0	12.1	36 47.9	−40.8	12.2	37 46.5	−40.6	12.4	38 45.1	−40.4	12.6	39 43.6	−40.2	12.8	40 42.1	−39.9	12.9	75
76	33 10.5	−41.7	10.9	34 09.4	−41.6	11.1	35 08.2	−41.3	11.2	36 07.1	−41.2	11.3	37 05.9	−41.0	11.5	38 04.7	−40.9	11.6	39 03.4	−40.6	11.8	40 02.2	−40.5	12.0	76
77	32 28.8	−42.1	10.1	33 27.8	−41.9	10.2	34 26.9	−41.8	10.3	35 25.9	−41.6	10.4	36 24.9	−41.5	10.6	37 23.8	−41.2	10.7	38 22.8	−41.1	10.9	39 21.7	−40.9	11.0	77
78	31 46.7	−42.4	9.2	32 45.9	−42.3	9.3	33 45.1	−42.1	9.4	34 44.3	−42.0	9.6	35 43.4	−41.8	9.7	36 42.6	−41.7	9.8	37 41.7	−41.5	9.9	38 40.8	−41.4	10.1	78
79	31 04.3	−42.7	8.4	32 03.6	−42.5	8.5	33 03.0	−42.5	8.6	34 02.3	−42.3	8.7	35 01.6	−42.2	8.8	36 00.9	−42.1	8.9	37 00.2	−42.0	9.0	37 59.4	−41.8	9.1	79
80	30 21.6	−43.0	7.6	31 21.1	−42.9	7.7	32 20.5	−42.8	7.7	33 20.0	−42.7	7.8	34 19.4	−42.6	7.9	35 18.8	−42.4	8.0	36 18.2	−42.3	8.1	37 17.6	−42.2	8.2	80
81	29 38.6	−43.3	6.8	30 38.2	−43.2	6.9	31 37.7	−43.1	6.9	32 37.3	−43.0	7.0	33 36.8	−42.9	7.1	34 36.4	−42.8	7.2	35 35.9	−42.7	7.3	36 35.4	−42.6	7.3	81
82	28 55.3	−43.6	6.0	29 55.0	−43.5	6.0	30 54.6	−43.4	6.1	31 54.3	−43.3	6.2	32 53.9	−43.2	6.2	33 53.6	−43.2	6.3	34 53.2	−43.0	6.4	35 52.8	−42.9	6.5	82
83	28 11.7	−43.8	5.2	29 11.5	−43.8	5.3	30 11.2	−43.7	5.3	31 11.0	−43.6	5.4	32 10.7	−43.5	5.4	33 10.4	−43.4	5.5	34 10.2	−43.4	5.5	35 09.9	−43.3	5.6	83
84	27 27.9	−44.1	4.4	28 27.7	−44.0	4.5	29 27.5	−43.9	4.5	30 27.4	−44.0	4.6	31 27.2	−43.9	4.6	32 27.0	−43.8	4.7	33 26.8	−43.8	4.7	34 26.6	−43.7	4.8	84
85	26 43.8	−44.3	3.7	27 43.7	−44.3	3.7	28 43.6	−44.3	3.7	29 43.4	−44.1	3.8	30 43.3	−44.1	3.8	31 43.2	−44.1	3.9	32 43.0	−44.0	3.9	33 42.9	−44.0	3.9	85
86	25 59.5	−44.6	2.9	26 59.4	−44.5	2.9	27 59.3	−44.4	3.0	28 59.3	−44.5	3.0	29 59.2	−44.4	3.0	30 59.1	−44.4	3.1	31 59.0	−44.3	3.1	32 58.9	−44.3	3.1	86
87	25 14.9	−44.7	2.2	26 14.9	−44.7	2.2	27 14.9	−44.8	2.2	28 14.8	−44.7	2.2	29 14.8	−44.7	2.3	30 14.7	−44.6	2.3	31 14.7	−44.7	2.3	32 14.6	−44.6	2.3	87
88	24 30.2	−45.0	1.4	25 30.2	−45.0	1.5	26 30.1	−44.9	1.5	27 30.1	−44.9	1.5	28 30.1	−44.9	1.5	29 30.1	−44.9	1.5	30 30.0	−44.8	1.5	31 30.0	−44.8	1.5	88
89	23 45.2	−45.2	0.7	24 45.2	−45.2	0.7	25 45.2	−45.2	0.7	26 45.2	−45.2	0.7	27 45.2	−45.2	0.7	28 45.2	−45.2	0.7	29 45.2	−45.2	0.8	30 45.2	−45.2	0.8	89
90	23 00.0	−45.4	0.0	24 00.0	−45.4	0.0	25 00.0	−45.4	0.0	26 00.0	−45.4	0.0	27 00.0	−45.4	0.0	28 00.0	−45.4	0.0	29 00.0	−45.4	0.0	30 00.0	−45.4	0.0	90
	23°			24°			25°			26°			27°			28°			29°			30°			

41°, 319° L.H.A. LATITUDE SAME NAME AS DECLINATION

LATITUDE **CONTRARY** NAME TO DECLINATION **L.H.A. 41°, 319°**

Dec.	23°			24°			25°			26°			27°			28°			29°			30°			Dec.
	Hc	d	Z	Hc	d	Z	Hc	d	Z	Hc	d	Z	Hc	d	Z	Hc	d	Z	Hc	d	Z	Hc	d	Z	
°	° ′	′	°	° ′	′	°	° ′	′	°	° ′	′	°	° ′	′	°	° ′	′	°	° ′	′	°	° ′	′	°	°
0	44 00.3	-33.0	114.2	43 35.2	-34.0	115.1	43 09.4	-35.1	115.9	42 42.8	-36.1	116.8	42 15.4	-37.1	117.6	41 47.2	-38.0	118.4	41 18.4	-39.0	119.1	40 48.8	-39.9	119.9	0
1	43 27.3	-33.6	115.4	43 01.2	-34.7	116.2	42 34.3	-35.7	117.0	42 06.7	-36.7	117.8	41 38.3	-37.7	118.6	41 09.2	-38.6	119.4	40 39.4	-39.5	120.2	40 08.9	-40.4	120.9	1
2	42 53.7	-34.3	116.5	42 26.5	-35.3	117.3	41 58.6	-36.3	118.1	41 30.0	-37.3	118.9	41 00.6	-38.2	119.7	40 30.6	-39.1	120.4	39 59.9	-40.0	121.1	39 28.5	-40.8	121.9	2
3	42 19.4	-34.9	117.6	41 51.2	-35.9	118.4	41 22.3	-36.9	119.2	40 52.7	-37.8	119.9	40 22.4	-38.7	120.7	39 51.5	-39.6	121.4	39 19.9	-40.5	122.1	38 47.7	-41.3	122.8	3
4	41 44.5	-35.6	118.7	41 15.3	-36.5	119.5	40 45.4	-37.4	120.2	40 14.9	-38.4	121.0	39 43.7	-39.3	121.7	39 11.9	-40.1	122.4	38 39.4	-40.9	123.1	38 06.4	-41.7	123.7	4
5	41 08.9	-36.1	119.8	40 38.8	-37.1	120.5	40 08.0	-38.0	121.3	39 36.5	-38.8	122.0	39 04.4	-39.7	122.7	38 31.8	-40.6	123.3	37 58.5	-41.4	124.0	37 24.7	-42.2	124.6	5
6	40 32.8	-36.7	120.8	40 01.7	-37.6	121.6	39 30.0	-38.5	122.3	38 57.7	-39.4	123.0	38 24.7	-40.2	123.6	37 51.2	-41.0	124.3	37 17.1	-41.7	124.9	36 42.5	-42.5	125.5	6
7	39 56.1	-37.2	121.9	39 24.1	-38.1	122.6	38 51.5	-39.0	123.3	38 18.3	-39.8	123.9	37 44.5	-40.6	124.6	37 10.2	-41.4	125.2	36 35.4	-42.2	125.8	36 00.0	-42.9	126.4	7
8	39 18.9	-37.8	122.9	38 46.0	-38.6	123.6	38 12.5	-39.4	124.2	37 38.5	-40.3	124.9	37 03.9	-41.0	125.5	36 28.8	-41.8	126.1	35 53.2	-42.5	126.7	35 17.1	-43.2	127.3	8
9	38 41.1	-38.3	123.9	38 07.4	-39.1	124.5	37 33.1	-40.0	125.2	36 58.2	-40.7	125.8	36 22.9	-41.5	126.4	35 47.0	-42.2	127.0	35 10.7	-42.9	127.6	34 33.9	-43.6	128.1	9
10	38 02.8	-38.7	124.9	37 28.3	-39.6	125.5	36 53.1	-40.3	126.1	36 17.5	-41.1	126.7	35 41.4	-41.8	127.3	35 04.8	-42.6	127.9	34 27.8	-43.3	128.4	33 50.3	-44.0	128.9	10
11	37 24.1	-39.2	125.8	36 48.7	-40.0	126.4	36 12.8	-40.8	127.0	35 36.4	-41.5	127.6	34 59.6	-42.3	128.2	34 22.2	-42.9	128.7	33 44.5	-43.6	129.2	33 06.3	-44.2	129.8	11
12	36 44.9	-39.7	126.8	36 08.7	-40.4	127.4	35 32.0	-41.1	127.9	34 54.9	-41.9	128.5	34 17.3	-42.5	129.0	33 39.3	-43.2	129.6	33 00.9	-43.9	130.1	32 22.1	-44.5	130.6	12
13	36 05.2	-40.1	127.7	35 28.3	-40.8	128.3	34 50.9	-41.6	128.8	34 13.0	-42.2	129.4	33 34.8	-43.0	129.9	32 56.1	-43.6	130.4	32 17.0	-44.2	130.9	31 37.6	-44.9	131.3	13
14	35 25.1	-40.4	128.6	34 47.5	-41.3	129.2	34 09.3	-41.9	129.7	33 30.8	-42.6	130.2	32 51.8	-43.2	130.7	32 12.5	-43.9	131.2	31 32.8	-44.5	131.7	30 52.7	-45.1	132.1	14
15	34 44.7	-40.9	129.5	34 06.2	-41.5	130.1	33 27.4	-42.2	130.6	32 48.2	-42.9	131.1	32 08.6	-43.6	131.5	31 28.6	-44.2	132.0	30 48.3	-44.8	132.5	30 07.6	-45.4	132.9	15
16	34 03.8	-41.3	130.4	33 24.7	-42.0	130.9	32 45.2	-42.6	131.4	32 05.3	-43.3	131.9	31 25.0	-43.8	132.4	30 44.4	-44.4	132.8	30 03.5	-45.0	133.2	29 22.2	-45.6	133.6	16
17	33 22.5	-41.6	131.3	32 42.7	-42.3	131.8	32 02.6	-43.0	132.3	31 22.0	-43.5	132.7	30 41.2	-44.2	133.2	30 00.0	-44.8	133.6	29 18.5	-45.4	134.0	28 36.6	-45.8	134.4	17
18	32 40.9	-42.0	132.2	32 00.4	-42.6	132.6	31 19.6	-43.2	133.1	30 38.5	-43.8	133.5	29 57.0	-44.4	133.9	29 15.2	-45.0	134.3	28 33.1	-45.5	134.7	27 50.8	-46.1	135.1	18
19	31 58.9	-42.3	133.0	31 17.8	-42.9	133.5	30 36.4	-43.5	133.9	29 54.7	-44.2	134.3	29 12.6	-44.7	134.7	28 30.2	-45.2	135.1	27 47.6	-45.8	135.5	27 04.7	-46.3	135.8	19
20	31 16.6	-42.6	133.8	30 34.9	-43.2	134.3	29 52.9	-43.8	134.7	29 10.5	-44.3	135.1	28 27.9	-44.9	135.5	27 45.0	-45.5	135.8	27 01.8	-46.0	136.2	26 18.4	-46.5	136.6	20
21	30 34.0	-42.9	134.7	29 51.7	-43.5	135.1	29 09.1	-44.1	135.5	28 26.2	-44.7	135.9	27 43.0	-45.2	136.2	26 59.5	-45.7	136.6	26 15.8	-46.2	136.9	25 31.9	-46.7	137.3	21
22	29 51.1	-43.2	135.5	29 08.2	-43.8	135.9	28 25.0	-44.3	136.2	27 41.5	-44.9	136.6	26 57.8	-45.4	137.0	26 13.8	-45.9	137.3	25 29.6	-46.4	137.6	24 45.2	-46.9	137.9	22
23	29 07.9	-43.5	136.3	28 24.4	-44.0	136.6	27 40.7	-44.6	137.0	26 56.6	-45.1	137.4	26 12.4	-45.6	137.7	25 27.9	-46.1	138.0	24 43.2	-46.6	138.3	23 58.3	-47.1	138.6	23
24	28 24.4	-43.7	137.0	27 40.4	-44.3	137.4	26 56.1	-44.9	137.8	26 11.5	-45.3	138.1	25 26.8	-45.9	138.4	24 41.8	-46.3	138.7	23 56.6	-46.8	139.0	23 11.2	-47.3	139.3	24
25	27 40.7	-44.1	137.8	26 56.1	-44.6	138.2	26 11.2	-45.0	138.5	25 26.2	-45.6	138.8	24 40.9	-46.0	139.1	23 55.5	-46.6	139.4	23 09.8	-47.0	139.7	22 23.9	-47.4	140.0	25
26	26 56.6	-44.2	138.6	26 11.5	-44.7	138.9	25 26.2	-45.3	139.2	24 40.6	-45.7	139.5	23 54.9	-46.2	139.8	23 08.9	-46.6	140.1	22 22.8	-47.1	140.4	21 36.5	-47.6	140.6	26
27	26 12.4	-44.5	139.3	25 26.8	-45.0	139.7	24 40.9	-45.4	140.0	23 54.9	-46.0	140.2	23 08.7	-46.4	140.5	22 22.3	-46.9	140.8	21 35.7	-47.3	141.0	20 48.9	-47.7	141.3	27
28	25 27.9	-44.7	140.1	24 41.8	-45.2	140.4	23 55.5	-45.7	140.7	23 08.9	-46.1	141.0	22 22.3	-46.6	141.2	21 35.4	-47.0	141.5	20 48.4	-47.4	141.7	20 01.2	-47.8	141.9	28
29	24 43.2	-44.9	140.8	23 56.6	-45.4	141.1	23 09.8	-45.9	141.4	22 22.8	-46.3	141.6	21 35.7	-46.8	141.9	20 48.4	-47.2	142.1	20 01.0	-47.6	142.4	19 13.4	-48.0	142.6	29
30	23 58.3	-45.2	141.6	23 11.2	-45.6	141.8	22 23.9	-46.0	142.1	21 36.5	-46.5	142.3	20 48.9	-46.8	142.6	20 01.2	-47.3	142.8	19 13.4	-47.7	143.0	18 25.4	-48.1	143.2	30
31	23 13.1	-45.3	142.3	22 25.6	-45.8	142.5	21 37.9	-46.2	142.8	20 50.0	-46.6	143.0	20 02.1	-47.1	143.2	19 13.9	-47.4	143.4	18 25.7	-47.9	143.6	17 37.3	-48.3	143.8	31
32	22 27.8	-45.5	143.0	21 39.8	-45.9	143.2	20 51.7	-46.4	143.5	20 03.4	-46.8	143.7	19 15.0	-47.2	143.9	18 26.5	-47.6	144.1	17 37.8	-48.0	144.3	16 49.0	-48.3	144.5	32
33	21 42.3	-45.7	143.7	20 53.9	-46.1	143.9	20 05.3	-46.5	144.1	19 16.6	-46.9	144.3	18 27.8	-47.3	144.5	17 38.9	-47.7	144.7	16 49.8	-48.0	144.9	16 00.7	-48.4	145.1	33
34	20 56.6	-45.8	144.4	20 07.8	-46.3	144.6	19 18.8	-46.7	144.8	18 29.7	-47.0	145.0	17 40.5	-47.4	145.2	16 51.2	-47.8	145.4	16 01.8	-48.2	145.5	15 12.3	-48.6	145.7	34
35	20 10.8	-46.0	145.1	19 21.5	-46.4	145.3	18 32.1	-46.8	145.5	17 42.7	-47.2	145.7	16 53.1	-47.6	145.8	16 03.4	-48.0	146.0	15 13.6	-48.3	146.2	14 23.7	-48.6	146.3	35
36	19 24.8	-46.2	145.8	18 35.1	-46.5	145.9	17 45.3	-46.9	146.1	16 55.5	-47.3	146.3	16 05.5	-47.7	146.5	15 15.4	-48.0	146.6	14 25.3	-48.4	146.8	13 35.1	-48.8	146.9	36
37	18 38.6	-46.3	146.4	17 48.6	-46.7	146.6	16 58.4	-47.1	146.8	16 08.2	-47.5	146.9	15 17.8	-47.7	147.1	14 27.4	-48.1	147.2	13 36.9	-48.5	147.4	12 46.3	-48.8	147.5	37
38	17 52.3	-46.4	147.1	17 01.9	-46.8	147.3	16 11.3	-47.1	147.4	15 20.7	-47.5	147.6	14 30.1	-47.9	147.7	13 39.3	-48.2	147.9	12 48.4	-48.5	148.0	11 57.5	-48.8	148.1	38
39	17 05.9	-46.6	147.8	16 15.1	-47.0	147.9	15 24.2	-47.3	148.1	14 33.2	-47.6	148.2	13 42.2	-48.0	148.3	12 51.1	-48.3	148.5	11 59.9	-48.6	148.6	11 08.7	-49.0	148.7	39
40	16 19.3	-46.7	148.4	15 28.1	-47.0	148.6	14 36.9	-47.4	148.7	13 45.6	-47.7	148.8	12 54.2	-48.1	149.0	12 02.8	-48.4	149.1	11 11.3	-48.7	149.2	10 19.7	-49.0	149.3	40
41	15 32.6	-46.8	149.1	14 41.1	-47.2	149.2	13 49.5	-47.5	149.3	12 57.9	-47.9	149.5	12 06.1	-48.1	149.6	11 14.4	-48.5	149.7	10 22.6	-48.8	149.8	9 30.7	-49.1	149.9	41
42	14 45.8	-46.9	149.7	13 53.9	-47.2	149.9	13 02.0	-47.6	150.0	12 10.0	-47.9	150.1	11 18.0	-48.2	150.2	10 25.9	-48.5	150.3	9 33.8	-48.8	150.4	8 41.6	-49.1	150.4	42
43	13 58.9	-47.0	150.4	13 06.7	-47.3	150.5	12 14.4	-47.6	150.6	11 22.1	-47.9	150.7	10 29.8	-48.3	150.8	9 37.4	-48.6	150.9	8 45.0	-48.9	151.0	7 52.5	-49.2	151.0	43
44	13 11.9	-47.2	151.0	12 19.4	-47.5	151.1	11 26.8	-47.7	151.2	10 34.2	-48.1	151.3	9 41.5	-48.3	151.4	8 48.8	-48.6	151.5	7 56.1	-48.9	151.5	7 03.3	-49.2	151.6	44
45	12 24.7	-47.1	151.6	11 31.9	-47.5	151.7	10 39.1	-47.9	151.8	9 46.1	-48.1	151.9	8 53.2	-48.4	152.0	8 00.2	-48.7	152.1	7 07.2	-49.0	152.1	6 14.1	-49.2	152.2	45
46	11 37.6	-47.3	152.3	10 44.4	-47.6	152.4	9 51.2	-47.8	152.4	8 58.0	-48.1	152.5	8 04.8	-48.5	152.6	7 11.5	-48.7	152.7	6 18.2	-49.0	152.7	5 24.9	-49.3	152.8	46
47	10 50.3	-47.4	152.9	9 56.8	-47.6	153.0	9 03.4	-48.0	153.1	8 09.9	-48.3	153.1	7 16.3	-48.5	153.2	6 22.8	-48.8	153.2	5 29.2	-49.1	153.3	4 35.6	-49.3	153.3	47
48	10 02.9	-47.4	153.5	9 09.2	-47.7	153.6	8 15.4	-48.0	153.7	7 21.6	-48.2	153.7	6 27.8	-48.5	153.8	5 34.0	-48.8	153.8	4 40.1	-49.0	153.9	3 46.3	-49.4	153.9	48
49	9 15.5	-47.5	154.1	8 21.5	-47.8	154.2	7 27.4	-48.0	154.3	6 33.4	-48.3	154.3	5 39.3	-48.6	154.4	4 45.2	-48.8	154.4	3 51.1	-49.1	154.4	2 56.9	-49.3	154.5	49
50	8 28.0	-47.5	154.8	7 33.7	-47.8	154.8	6 39.4	-48.1	154.9	5 45.1	-48.4	154.9	4 50.7	-48.6	155.0	3 56.4	-48.9	155.0	3 02.0	-49.1	155.0	2 07.6	-49.4	155.0	50
51	7 40.5	-47.6	155.4	6 45.9	-47.9	155.4	5 51.3	-48.1	155.5	4 56.7	-48.3	155.5	4 02.1	-48.6	155.6	3 07.5	-48.9	155.6	2 12.9	-49.2	155.6	1 18.2	-49.4	155.6	51
52	6 52.9	-47.7	156.0	5 58.0	-47.9	156.0	5 03.2	-48.1	156.1	4 08.4	-48.5	156.1	3 13.5	-48.7	156.1	2 18.6	-48.9	156.2	1 23.7	-49.1	156.2	0 28.8	-49.3	156.2	52
53	6 05.2	-47.7	156.6	5 10.1	-47.9	156.6	4 15.1	-48.2	156.7	3 19.9	-48.4	156.7	2 24.8	-48.6	156.7	1 29.7	-48.9	156.7	0 34.6	-49.1	156.7	0 20.5	+49.4	23.3	53
54	5 17.5	-47.7	157.2	4 22.2	-48.0	157.2	3 26.9	-48.2	157.3	2 31.5	-48.4	157.3	1 36.2	-48.7	157.3	0 40.8	-48.9	157.3	0 14.5	+49.2	22.7	1 09.9	+49.4	22.7	54
55	4 29.8	-47.7	157.8	3 34.2	-47.9	157.9	2 38.7	-48.3	157.9	1 43.1	-48.5	157.9	0 47.5	-48.7	157.9	0 08.1	+48.9	22.1	1 03.7	+49.1	22.1	1 59.3	+49.3	22.1	55
56	3 42.1	-47.8	158.4	2 46.3	-48.1	158.5	1 50.4	-48.2	158.5	0 54.6	-48.4	158.5	0 01.2	+48.7	21.5	0 57.0	+48.9	21.5	1 52.8	+49.1	21.5	2 48.6	+49.4	21.5	56
57	2 54.3	-47.8	159.0	1 58.2	-48.0	159.1	1 02.2	-48.2	159.1	0 06.2	-48.5	159.1	0 49.9	+48.6	20.9	1 45.9	+48.9	20.9	2 41.9	+49.1	21.0	3 38.0	+49.3	21.0	57
58	2 06.5	-47.8	159.6	1 10.2	-48.0	159.7	0 14.0	-48.3	159.7	0 42.3	+48.4	20.3	1 38.5	+48.7	20.4	2 34.8	+48.9	20.4	3 31.0	+49.1	20.4	4 27.3	+49.3	20.4	58
59	1 18.7	-47.8	160.2	0 22.2	-48.0	160.3	0 34.3	+48.2	19.7	1 30.7	+48.5	19.8	2 27.2	+48.7	19.8	3 23.7	+48.8	19.8	4 20.1	+49.1	19.8	5 16.6	+49.2	19.8	59
60	0 30.9	-47.9	160.8	0 25.8	+48.1	19.1	1 22.5	+48.2	19.2	2 19.2	+48.4	19.2	3 15.9	+48.6	19.2	4 12.5	+48.9	19.2	5 09.2	+49.0	19.2	6 05.8	+49.2	19.3	60
61	0 17.0	+47.8	18.5	1 13.9	+48.0	18.6	2 10.7	+48.3	18.6	3 07.6	+48.4	18.6	4 04.5	+48.6	18.6	5 01.4	+48.7	18.6	5 58.2	+49.0	18.7	6 55.0	+49.2	18.7	61
62	1 04.8	+47.8	17.9	2 01.9	+48.0	18.0	2 59.0	+48.1	18.0	3 56.0	+48.4	18.0	4 53.1	+48.6	18.0	5 50.1	+48.8	18.0	6 47.2	+48.9	18.1	7 44.2	+49.2	18.1	62
63	1 52.6	+47.8	17.3	2 49.9	+48.0	17.4	3 47.1	+48.2	17.4	4 44.4	+48.4	17.4	5 41.7	+48.5	17.4	6 38.9	+48.7	17.4	7 36.1	+48.9	17.5	8 33.4	+49.0	17.5	63
64	2 40.4	+47.8	16.7	3 37.9	+47.9	16.7	4 35.3	+48.2	16.8	5 32.8	+48.3	16.8	6 30.2	+48.5	16.8	7 27.6	+48.7	16.8	8 25.0	+48.9	16.9	9 22.4	+49.1	16.9	64
65	3 28.2	+47.8	16.1	4 25.8	+48.0	16.1	5 23.5	+48.1	16.2	6 21.1	+48.3	16.2	7 18.7	+48.4	16.2	8 16.3	+48.6	16.3	9 13.9	+48.8	16.3	10 11.5	+48.9	16.4	65
66	4 16.0	+47.7	15.5	5 13.8	+47.9	15.5	6 11.6	+48.0	15.6	7 09.4	+48.2	15.6	8 07.1	+48.4	15.6	9 04.9	+48.6	15.7	10 02.7	+48.7	15.7	11 00.4	+48.9	15.8	66
67	5 03.7	+47.7	14.9	6 01.7	+47.8	14.9	6 59.6	+48.0	15.0	7 57.6	+48.2	15.0	8 55.5	+48.4	15.0	9 53.5	+48.5	15.1	10 51.4	+48.7	15.1	11 49.3	+48.8	15.2	67
68	5 51.4	+47.6	14.3	6 49.5	+47.8	14.3	7 47.6	+48.0	14.4	8 45.8	+48.1	14.4	9 43.9	+48.3	14.4	10 42.0	+48.4	14.5	11 40.1	+48.5	14.5	12 38.1	+48.8	14.6	68
69	6 39.0	+47.7	13.7	7 37.3	+47.8	13.7	8 35.6	+47.9	13.8	9 33.9	+48.0	13.8	10 32.2	+48.2	13.8	11 30.4	+48.4	13.9	12 28.6	+48.6	13.9	13 26.9	+48.6	14.0	69
70	7 26.7	+47.5	13.1	8 25.1	+47.7	13.1	9 23.5	+47.9	13.1	10 21.9	+48.0	13.2	11 20.4	+48.1	13.2	12 18.8	+48.2	13.3	13 17.2	+48.4	13.3	14 15.5	+48.6	13.4	70
71	8 14.2	+47.5	12.5	9 12.8	+47.6	12.5	10 11.4	+47.8	12.5	11 09.9	+48.0	12.6	12 08.5	+48.0	12.6	13 07.0	+48.2	12.7	14 05.6	+48.3	12.7	15 04.1	+48.5	12.8	71
72	9 01.7	+47.5	11.8	10 00.4	+47.6	11.9	10 59.2	+47.7	11.9	11 57.9	+47.8	12.0	12 56.5	+48.0	12.0	13 55.2	+48.1	12.1	14 53.9	+48.2	12.1	15 52.6	+48.3	12.2	72
73	9 49.2	+47.3	11.2	10 48.0	+47.5	11.3	11 46.9	+47.6	11.3	12 45.7	+47.7	11.3	13 44.5	+47.9	11.4	14 43.3	+48.0	11.4	15 42.1	+48.2	11.5	16 40.9	+48.3	11.6	73
74	10 36.5	+47.3	10.6	11 35.5	+47.4	10.6	12 34.5	+47.5	10.7	13 33.4	+47.7	10.7	14 32.4	+47.8	10.8	15 31.3	+47.9	10.8	16 30.3	+48.0	10.9	17 29.2	+48.1	10.9	74
75	11 23.8	+47.3	10.0	12 22.9	+47.4	10.0	13 22.0	+47.5	10.1	14 21.1	+47.5	10.1	15 20.2	+47.6	10.1	16 19.2	+47.8	10.2	17 18.3	+47.9	10.2	18 17.3	+48.0	10.3	75
76	12 11.1	+47.1	9.3	13 10.3	+47.2	9.4	14 09.5	+47.3	9.4	15 08.6	+47.5	9.5	16 07.8	+47.6	9.5	17 07.0	+47.7	9.6	18 06.2	+47.7	9.6	19 05.3	+47.9	9.7	76
77	12 58.2	+47.0	8.7	13 57.5	+47.1	8.7	14 56.8	+47.2	8.8	15 56.1	+47.3	8.8	16 55.4	+47.4	8.9	17 54.7	+47.5	8.9	18 53.9	+47.7	9.0	19 53.2	+47.7	9.0	77
78	13 45.2	+47.0	8.1	14 44.6	+47.1	8.1	15 44.0	+47.2	8.1	16 43.4	+47.2	8.2	17 42.8	+47.3	8.2	18 42.2	+47.4	8.3	19 41.6	+47.5	8.3	20 40.9	+47.6	8.4	78
79	14 32.2	+46.8	7.4	15 31.7	+46.9	7.5	16 31.2	+47.0	7.5	17 30.6	+47.1	7.5	18 30.1	+47.2	7.6	19 29.6	+47.3	7.6	20 29.1	+47.3	7.7	21 28.5	+47.5	7.7	79
80	15 19.0	+46.7	6.8	16 18.6	+46.8	6.8	17 18.2	+46.9	6.9	18 17.7	+47.0	6.9	19 17.3	+47.0	6.9	20 16.9	+47.1	7.0	21 16.4	+47.2	7.0	22 16.0	+47.2	7.1	80
81	16 05.7	+46.7	6.1	17 05.4	+46.7	6.2	18 05.1	+46.7	6.2	19 04.7	+46.8	6.2	20 04.3	+46.9	6.3	21 04.0	+46.9	6.3	22 03.6	+47.0	6.4	23 03.2	+47.2	6.4	81
82	16 52.4	+46.4	5.5	17 52.1	+46.5	5.5	18 51.8	+46.6	5.5	19 51.5	+46.7	5.6	20 51.2	+46.8	5.6	21 50.9	+46.8	5.6	22 50.6	+46.9	5.7	23 50.4	+46.9	5.7	82
83	17 38.8	+46.4	4.8	18 38.6	+46.4	4.8	19 38.4	+46.5	4.9	20 38.2	+46.5	4.9	21 38.0	+46.5	4.9	22 37.7	+46.7	5.0	23 37.5	+46.7	5.0	24 37.3	+46.7	5.0	83
84	18 25.2	+46.2	4.1	19 25.0	+46.3	4.2	20 24.9	+46.3	4.2	21 24.7	+46.3	4.2	22 24.5	+46.4	4.3	23 24.4	+46.4	4.3	24 24.2	+46.5	4.3	25 24.0	+46.6	4.4	84
85	19 11.4	+46.0	3.5	20 11.3	+46.1	3.5	21 11.2	+46.1	3.5	22 11.0	+46.2	3.5	23 10.9	+46.2	3.6	24 10.8	+46.3	3.6	25 10.7	+46.3	3.6	26 10.6	+46.3	3.7	85
86	19 57.4	+45.9	2.8	20 57.4	+45.9	2.8	21 57.3	+45.9	2.8	22 57.2	+46.0	2.8	23 57.1	+46.1	2.9	24 57.1	+46.0	2.9	25 57.0	+46.1	2.9	26 56.9	+46.1	2.9	86
87	20 43.3	+45.8	2.1	21 43.3	+45.7	2.1	22 43.2	+45.8	2.1	23 43.2	+45.8	2.1	24 43.2	+45.8	2.2	25 43.1	+45.9	2.2	26 43.1	+45.9	2.2	27 43.0	+45.9	2.2	87
88	21 29.1	+45.5	1.4	22 29.0	+45.6	1.4	23 29.0	+45.6	1.4	24 29.0	+45.6	1.4	25 29.0	+45.6	1.5	26 29.0	+45.6	1.5	27 29.0	+45.6	1.5	28 28.9	+45.7	1.5	88
89	22 14.6	+45.4	0.7	23 14.6	+45.4	0.7	24 14.6	+45.4	0.7	25 14.6	+45.4	0.7	26 14.6	+45.4	0.7	27 14.6	+45.4	0.7	28 14.6	+45.4	0.7	29 14.6	+45.4	0.8	89
90	23 00.0	+45.2	0.0	24 00.0	+45.2	0.0	25 00.0	+45.2	0.0	26 00.0	+45.2	0.0	27 00.0	+45.2	0.0	28 00.0	+45.2	0.0	29 00.0	+45.2	0.0	30 00.0	+45.2	0.0	90
	23°			24°			25°			26°			27°			28°			29°			30°			

S. Lat. {L.H.A. greater than 180° ....Zn=180°−Z
L.H.A. less than 180°...........Zn=180°+Z

LATITUDE **SAME** NAME AS DECLINATION **L.H.A. 139°, 221°**

267

42°, 318° L.H.A. LATITUDE SAME NAME AS DECLINATION N. Lat. {L.H.A. greater than 180° .....Zn=Z; L.H.A. less than 180°............Zn=360°−Z

Dec.	23° Hc	d	Z	24° Hc	d	Z	25° Hc	d	Z	26° Hc	d	Z	27° Hc	d	Z	28° Hc	d	Z	29° Hc	d	Z	30° Hc	d	Z	Dec.
°	° ′	′	°	° ′	′	°	° ′	′	°	° ′	′	°	° ′	′	°	° ′	′	°	° ′	′	°	° ′	′	°	°
0	43 09.7	+31.8	113.5	42 45.4	+32.9	114.3	42 20.3	+34.0	115.1	41 54.5	+35.0	116.0	41 27.8	+36.1	116.8	41 00.5	+37.0	117.5	40 32.4	+38.0	118.3	40 03.6	+38.9	119.0	0
1	43 41.5	+31.1	112.3	43 18.3	+32.2	113.2	42 54.3	+33.3	114.0	42 29.5	+34.4	114.9	42 03.9	+35.4	115.7	41 37.5	+36.5	116.5	41 10.4	+37.4	117.3	40 42.5	+38.4	118.0	1
2	44 12.6	+30.3	111.1	43 50.5	+31.5	112.0	43 27.6	+32.7	112.9	43 03.9	+33.7	113.7	42 39.3	+34.8	114.6	42 14.0	+35.8	115.4	41 47.8	+36.9	116.2	41 20.9	+37.9	117.0	2
3	44 42.9	+29.5	109.9	44 22.0	+30.8	110.8	44 00.3	+31.9	111.7	43 37.6	+33.1	112.6	43 14.1	+34.2	113.5	42 49.8	+35.2	114.3	42 24.7	+36.3	115.2	41 58.8	+37.3	116.0	3
4	45 12.4	+28.7	108.7	44 52.8	+29.9	109.6	44 32.2	+31.1	110.5	44 10.7	+32.3	111.5	43 48.3	+33.4	112.3	43 25.0	+34.6	113.2	43 01.0	+35.6	114.1	42 36.1	+36.7	114.9	4
5	45 41.1	+27.9	107.4	45 22.7	+29.2	108.4	45 03.3	+30.4	109.3	44 43.0	+31.6	110.3	44 21.7	+32.8	111.2	43 59.6	+33.9	112.1	43 36.6	+35.0	113.0	43 12.8	+36.0	113.8	5
6	46 09.0	+27.1	106.1	45 51.9	+28.3	107.1	45 33.7	+29.6	108.1	45 14.6	+30.8	109.1	44 54.5	+32.0	110.0	44 33.5	+33.2	110.9	44 11.6	+34.3	111.9	43 48.8	+35.5	112.7	6
7	46 36.1	+26.1	104.8	46 20.2	+27.4	105.9	46 03.3	+28.7	106.9	45 45.4	+30.0	107.8	45 26.5	+31.3	108.8	45 06.7	+32.4	109.8	44 45.9	+33.6	110.7	44 24.3	+34.7	111.6	7
8	47 02.2	+25.2	103.5	46 47.6	+26.6	104.6	46 32.0	+27.9	105.6	46 15.4	+29.2	106.6	45 57.8	+30.4	107.6	45 39.1	+31.7	108.6	45 19.5	+32.9	109.5	44 59.0	+34.1	110.5	8
9	47 27.4	+24.3	102.2	47 14.2	+25.7	103.3	46 59.9	+27.0	104.3	46 44.6	+28.3	105.3	46 28.2	+29.6	106.3	46 10.8	+30.9	107.3	45 52.4	+32.1	108.3	45 33.1	+33.3	109.3	9
10	47 51.7	+23.3	100.8	47 39.9	+24.7	101.9	47 26.9	+26.1	103.0	47 12.9	+27.4	104.0	46 57.8	+28.8	105.1	46 41.7	+30.1	106.1	46 24.5	+31.4	107.1	46 06.4	+32.5	108.1	10
11	48 15.0	+22.3	99.5	48 04.6	+23.7	100.6	47 53.0	+25.2	101.6	47 40.3	+26.6	102.7	47 26.6	+27.9	103.8	47 11.8	+29.2	104.8	46 55.9	+30.5	105.9	46 38.9	+31.8	106.9	11
12	48 37.3	+21.2	98.1	48 28.3	+22.7	99.2	48 18.2	+24.1	100.3	48 06.9	+25.5	101.4	47 54.5	+26.9	102.5	47 41.0	+28.3	103.5	47 26.4	+29.6	104.6	47 10.7	+31.0	105.7	12
13	48 58.5	+20.2	96.6	48 51.0	+21.7	97.8	48 42.3	+23.2	98.9	48 32.4	+24.6	100.0	48 21.4	+26.0	101.1	48 09.3	+27.4	102.2	47 56.0	+28.8	103.3	47 41.7	+30.0	104.4	13
14	49 18.7	+19.2	95.2	49 12.7	+20.6	96.4	49 05.5	+22.1	97.5	48 57.0	+23.6	98.6	48 47.4	+25.1	99.8	48 36.7	+26.4	100.9	48 24.8	+27.8	102.0	48 11.7	+29.2	103.1	14
15	49 37.9	+18.0	93.7	49 33.3	+19.6	94.9	49 27.6	+21.0	96.1	49 20.6	+22.6	97.2	49 12.5	+24.0	98.4	49 03.1	+25.5	99.5	48 52.6	+26.9	100.7	48 40.9	+28.3	101.8	15
16	49 55.9	+16.8	92.3	49 52.9	+18.4	93.4	49 48.6	+20.0	94.6	49 43.2	+21.5	95.8	49 36.5	+23.0	97.0	49 28.6	+24.5	98.1	49 19.5	+25.9	99.3	49 09.2	+27.4	100.4	16
17	50 12.7	+15.7	90.8	50 11.3	+17.3	92.0	50 08.6	+18.8	93.2	50 04.7	+20.3	94.4	49 59.5	+21.9	95.5	49 53.1	+23.4	96.7	49 45.4	+24.9	97.9	49 36.6	+26.3	99.1	17
18	50 28.4	+14.5	89.3	50 28.6	+16.1	90.5	50 27.4	+17.7	91.7	50 25.0	+19.3	92.9	50 21.4	+20.8	94.1	50 16.5	+22.3	95.3	50 10.3	+23.9	96.5	50 02.9	+25.4	97.7	18
19	50 42.9	+13.3	87.7	50 44.7	+14.9	88.9	50 45.1	+16.5	90.2	50 44.3	+18.1	91.4	50 42.2	+19.7	92.6	50 38.8	+21.3	93.8	50 34.2	+22.7	95.0	50 28.3	+24.2	96.3	19
20	50 56.2	+12.1	86.2	50 59.6	+13.7	87.4	51 01.6	+15.3	88.6	51 02.4	+16.9	89.9	51 01.9	+18.5	91.1	51 00.1	+20.0	92.4	50 56.9	+21.7	93.6	50 52.5	+23.2	94.8	20
21	51 08.3	+10.8	84.6	51 13.3	+12.4	85.9	51 16.9	+14.1	87.1	51 19.3	+15.7	88.4	51 20.4	+17.3	89.6	51 20.1	+19.0	90.9	51 18.6	+20.5	92.1	51 15.7	+22.1	93.3	21
22	51 19.1	+9.5	83.1	51 25.7	+11.2	84.3	51 31.0	+12.8	85.5	51 35.0	+14.5	86.8	51 37.7	+16.1	88.1	51 39.1	+17.7	89.3	51 39.1	+19.3	90.6	51 37.8	+20.9	91.9	22
23	51 28.6	+8.3	81.5	51 36.9	+9.9	82.7	51 43.8	+11.6	84.0	51 49.5	+13.2	85.2	51 53.8	+14.8	86.5	51 56.8	+16.5	87.8	51 58.4	+18.2	89.1	51 58.7	+19.8	90.3	23
24	51 36.9	+6.9	79.9	51 46.8	+8.6	81.1	51 55.4	+10.2	82.4	52 02.7	+11.9	83.7	52 08.6	+13.6	84.9	52 13.3	+15.2	86.2	52 16.6	+16.8	87.5	52 18.5	+18.5	88.8	24
25	51 43.8	+5.7	78.3	51 55.4	+7.3	79.5	52 05.6	+9.0	80.8	52 14.6	+10.6	82.1	52 22.2	+12.3	83.3	52 28.5	+14.0	84.6	52 33.4	+15.7	85.9	52 37.0	+17.3	87.2	25
26	51 49.5	+4.3	76.7	52 02.7	+5.9	77.9	52 14.6	+7.6	79.2	52 25.2	+9.3	80.4	52 34.5	+11.0	81.7	52 42.5	+12.6	83.0	52 49.1	+14.3	84.3	52 54.3	+16.0	85.7	26
27	51 53.8	+3.0	75.1	52 08.6	+4.7	76.3	52 22.2	+6.3	77.6	52 34.5	+8.0	78.8	52 45.5	+9.6	80.1	52 55.1	+11.3	81.4	53 03.4	+13.0	82.7	53 10.3	+14.7	84.1	27
28	51 56.8	+1.6	73.4	52 13.3	+3.3	74.7	52 28.5	+4.9	75.9	52 42.5	+6.6	77.2	52 55.1	+8.3	78.5	53 06.4	+10.0	79.8	53 16.4	+11.6	81.1	53 25.0	+13.3	82.4	28
29	51 58.4	+0.3	71.8	52 16.6	+1.9	73.0	52 33.4	+3.6	74.3	52 49.1	+5.2	75.5	53 03.4	+6.9	76.8	53 16.4	+8.6	78.1	53 28.0	+10.3	79.5	53 38.3	+12.0	80.8	29
30	51 58.7	−1.0	70.2	52 18.5	+0.6	71.4	52 37.0	+2.2	72.6	52 54.3	+3.8	73.9	53 10.3	+5.5	75.2	53 25.0	+7.2	76.5	53 38.3	+8.9	77.8	53 50.3	+10.6	79.1	30
31	51 57.7	−2.3	68.6	52 19.1	−0.8	69.8	52 39.2	+0.8	71.0	52 58.1	+2.5	72.2	53 15.8	+4.1	73.5	53 32.2	+5.8	74.8	53 47.2	+7.5	76.1	54 00.9	+9.2	77.5	31
32	51 55.4	−3.7	66.9	52 18.3	−2.1	68.1	52 40.0	−0.5	69.3	53 00.6	+1.1	70.6	53 19.9	+2.8	71.8	53 38.0	+4.4	73.1	53 54.7	+6.1	74.4	54 10.1	+7.8	75.8	32
33	51 51.7	−5.1	65.3	52 16.2	−3.5	66.5	52 39.5	−1.9	67.7	53 01.7	−0.3	68.9	53 22.7	+1.3	70.2	53 42.4	+2.9	71.5	54 00.8	+4.7	72.8	54 17.9	+6.4	74.1	33
34	51 46.6	−6.3	63.7	52 12.7	−4.9	64.9	52 37.6	−3.3	66.0	53 01.4	−1.7	67.3	53 24.0	−0.1	68.5	53 45.3	+1.6	69.8	54 05.5	+3.2	71.1	54 24.3	+4.9	72.4	34
35	51 40.3	−7.6	62.1	52 07.8	−6.1	63.2	52 34.3	−4.6	64.4	52 59.7	−3.1	65.6	53 23.9	−1.5	66.8	53 46.9	+0.1	68.1	54 08.7	+1.8	69.4	54 29.2	+3.4	70.7	35
36	51 32.7	−9.0	60.5	52 01.7	−7.5	61.6	52 29.7	−6.0	62.8	52 56.6	−4.5	63.9	53 22.4	−2.9	65.1	53 47.0	−1.3	66.4	54 10.5	+0.3	67.6	54 32.6	+2.0	68.9	36
37	51 23.7	−10.2	58.9	51 54.2	−8.8	60.0	52 23.7	−7.4	61.1	52 52.1	−5.8	62.3	53 19.5	−4.3	63.5	53 45.7	−2.7	64.7	54 10.8	−1.2	65.9	54 34.6	+0.5	67.2	37
38	51 13.5	−11.5	57.3	51 45.4	−10.1	58.4	52 16.3	−8.6	59.5	52 46.3	−7.2	60.6	53 15.2	−5.7	61.8	53 43.0	−4.2	63.0	54 09.6	−2.5	64.2	54 35.1	−0.9	65.5	38
39	51 02.0	−12.7	55.8	51 35.3	−11.4	56.8	52 07.7	−10.0	57.9	52 39.1	−8.6	59.0	53 09.5	−7.1	60.1	53 38.8	−5.6	61.3	54 07.1	−4.1	62.5	54 34.2	−2.5	63.8	39
40	50 49.3	−13.9	54.2	51 23.9	−12.6	55.2	51 57.7	−11.3	56.3	52 30.5	−9.9	57.4	53 02.4	−8.5	58.5	53 33.2	−6.9	59.6	54 03.0	−5.4	60.8	54 31.7	−3.9	62.0	40
41	50 35.4	−15.2	52.7	51 11.3	−13.9	53.7	51 46.4	−12.5	54.7	52 20.6	−11.2	55.8	52 53.9	−9.8	56.8	53 26.3	−8.4	58.0	53 57.6	−6.9	59.1	54 27.8	−5.3	60.3	41
42	50 20.2	−16.3	51.2	50 57.4	−15.0	52.1	51 33.9	−13.8	53.1	52 09.4	−12.4	54.1	52 44.1	−11.1	55.2	53 17.9	−9.7	56.3	53 50.7	−8.3	57.4	54 22.5	−6.8	58.6	42
43	50 03.9	−17.5	49.7	50 42.4	−16.3	50.6	51 20.1	−15.1	51.6	51 57.0	−13.8	52.6	52 33.0	−12.5	53.6	53 08.2	−11.1	54.7	53 42.4	−9.7	55.8	54 15.7	−8.3	56.9	43
44	49 46.4	−18.6	48.2	50 26.1	−17.5	49.1	51 05.0	−16.2	50.0	51 43.2	−15.0	51.0	52 20.5	−13.7	52.0	52 57.1	−12.5	53.0	53 32.7	−11.1	54.1	54 07.4	−9.6	55.2	44
45	49 27.8	−19.7	46.7	50 08.6	−18.5	47.6	50 48.8	−17.5	48.5	51 28.2	−16.3	49.4	52 06.8	−15.0	50.4	52 44.6	−13.7	51.4	53 21.6	−12.4	52.5	53 57.8	−11.1	53.5	45
46	49 08.1	−20.7	45.3	49 50.1	−19.7	46.1	50 31.3	−18.6	47.0	51 11.9	−17.4	47.9	51 51.8	−16.3	48.8	52 30.9	−15.0	49.8	53 09.2	−13.7	50.8	53 46.7	−12.4	51.9	46
47	48 47.4	−21.8	43.8	49 30.4	−20.8	44.6	50 12.7	−19.7	45.5	50 54.5	−18.6	46.4	51 35.5	−17.4	47.3	52 15.9	−16.3	48.2	52 55.5	−15.1	49.2	53 34.3	−13.8	50.2	47
48	48 25.6	−22.9	42.4	49 09.6	−21.9	43.2	49 53.0	−20.8	44.0	50 35.9	−19.8	44.9	51 18.1	−18.7	45.7	51 59.6	−17.5	46.6	52 40.4	−16.3	47.6	53 20.5	−15.1	48.6	48
49	48 02.7	−23.8	41.0	48 47.7	−22.8	41.8	49 32.2	−21.9	42.6	50 16.1	−20.9	43.4	50 59.4	−19.8	44.2	51 42.1	−18.7	45.1	52 24.1	−17.6	46.0	53 05.4	−16.4	47.0	49
50	47 38.9	−24.8	39.7	48 24.9	−23.9	40.4	49 10.3	−22.9	41.1	49 55.2	−21.9	41.9	50 39.6	−21.0	42.7	51 23.4	−19.9	43.6	52 06.5	−18.8	44.5	52 49.0	−17.6	45.4	50
51	47 14.1	−25.7	38.3	48 01.0	−24.9	39.0	48 47.4	−24.0	39.7	49 33.3	−23.0	40.5	50 18.6	−22.0	41.3	51 03.5	−21.1	42.1	51 47.7	−20.0	42.9	52 31.4	−19.0	43.8	51
52	46 48.4	−26.6	37.0	47 36.1	−25.7	37.7	48 23.4	−24.9	38.3	49 10.3	−24.1	39.1	49 56.6	−23.1	39.8	50 42.4	−22.1	40.6	51 27.7	−21.1	41.4	52 12.4	−20.1	42.2	52
53	46 21.8	−27.5	35.7	47 10.4	−26.7	36.3	47 58.5	−25.9	37.0	48 46.2	−25.0	37.7	49 33.5	−24.2	38.4	50 20.3	−23.3	39.1	51 06.6	−22.3	39.9	51 52.3	−21.3	40.7	53
54	45 54.3	−28.3	34.4	46 43.7	−27.6	35.0	47 32.6	−26.8	35.6	48 21.2	−26.0	36.3	49 09.3	−25.1	37.0	49 57.0	−24.2	37.7	50 44.3	−23.4	38.4	51 31.0	−22.4	39.2	54
55	45 26.0	−29.2	33.2	46 16.1	−28.5	33.7	47 05.8	−27.7	34.3	47 55.2	−27.0	34.9	48 44.2	−26.2	35.6	49 32.8	−25.4	36.3	50 20.9	−24.4	37.0	51 08.6	−23.5	37.7	55
56	44 56.8	−29.9	31.9	45 47.6	−29.2	32.5	46 38.1	−28.6	33.0	47 28.2	−27.8	33.6	48 18.0	−27.1	34.2	49 07.4	−26.2	34.9	49 56.5	−25.5	35.5	50 45.1	−24.6	36.3	56
57	44 26.9	−30.7	30.7	45 18.4	−30.1	31.2	46 09.5	−29.4	31.7	47 00.4	−28.7	32.3	47 50.9	−28.0	32.9	48 41.2	−27.3	33.5	49 31.0	−26.5	34.1	50 20.5	−25.7	34.8	57
58	43 56.2	−31.5	29.5	44 48.3	−30.9	30.0	45 40.1	−30.2	30.5	46 31.7	−29.6	31.0	47 22.9	−28.8	31.6	48 13.9	−28.2	32.2	49 04.5	−27.4	32.8	49 54.8	−26.7	33.4	58
59	43 24.7	−32.1	28.3	44 17.4	−31.5	28.8	45 09.9	−31.0	29.3	46 02.1	−30.3	29.8	46 54.1	−29.8	30.3	47 45.7	−29.0	30.8	48 37.1	−28.4	31.4	49 28.1	−27.6	32.0	59
60	42 52.6	−32.9	27.2	43 45.9	−32.4	27.6	44 38.9	−31.7	28.1	45 31.8	−31.2	28.5	46 24.3	−30.5	29.0	47 16.7	−29.9	29.5	48 08.7	−29.2	30.1	49 00.5	−28.6	30.7	60
61	42 19.7	−33.5	26.0	43 13.5	−32.9	26.4	44 07.2	−32.5	26.9	45 00.6	−31.9	27.3	45 53.8	−31.4	27.8	46 46.8	−30.8	28.3	47 39.5	−30.2	28.8	48 31.9	−29.5	29.3	61
62	41 46.2	−34.1	24.9	42 40.6	−33.7	25.3	43 34.7	−33.2	25.7	44 28.7	−32.7	26.1	45 22.4	−32.1	26.6	46 16.0	−31.5	27.0	47 09.3	−30.9	27.5	48 02.4	−30.3	28.0	62
63	41 12.1	−34.8	23.8	42 06.9	−34.3	24.2	43 01.5	−33.8	24.6	43 56.0	−33.3	25.0	44 50.3	−32.8	25.4	45 44.5	−32.4	25.8	46 38.4	−31.8	26.3	47 32.1	−31.2	26.7	63
64	40 37.3	−35.3	22.7	41 32.6	−35.0	23.1	42 27.7	−34.5	23.4	43 22.7	−34.0	23.8	44 17.5	−33.6	24.2	45 12.1	−33.0	24.6	46 06.6	−32.6	25.0	47 00.9	−32.1	25.5	64
65	40 02.0	−36.0	21.7	40 57.6	−35.5	22.0	41 53.2	−35.1	22.3	42 48.7	−34.7	22.7	43 43.9	−34.2	23.0	44 39.1	−33.8	23.4	45 34.0	−33.2	23.8	46 28.8	−32.7	24.2	65
66	39 26.0	−36.4	20.6	40 22.1	−36.1	20.9	41 18.1	−35.7	21.2	42 14.0	−35.3	21.6	43 09.7	−34.9	21.9	44 05.3	−34.5	22.3	45 00.8	−34.1	22.6	45 56.1	−33.6	23.0	66
67	38 49.6	−37.0	19.6	39 46.0	−36.6	19.9	40 42.4	−36.3	20.2	41 38.7	−35.9	20.5	42 34.8	−35.5	20.8	43 30.8	−35.1	21.1	44 26.7	−34.7	21.5	45 22.5	−34.3	21.9	67
68	38 12.6	−37.5	18.6	39 09.4	−37.2	18.9	40 06.1	−36.8	19.1	41 02.8	−36.5	19.4	41 59.3	−36.1	19.7	42 55.7	−35.7	20.0	43 52.0	−35.3	20.3	44 48.2	−34.9	20.7	68
69	37 35.1	−38.0	17.6	38 32.2	−37.7	17.9	39 29.3	−37.4	18.1	40 26.3	−37.1	18.4	41 23.2	−36.8	18.6	42 20.0	−36.4	18.9	43 16.7	−36.0	19.2	44 13.3	−35.7	19.5	69
70	36 57.1	−38.5	16.6	37 54.5	−38.2	16.9	38 51.9	−37.9	17.1	39 49.2	−37.6	17.3	40 46.4	−37.2	17.6	41 43.6	−36.9	17.9	42 40.7	−36.6	18.1	43 37.6	−36.2	18.4	70
71	36 18.6	−38.9	15.7	37 16.3	−38.6	15.9	38 14.0	−38.4	16.1	39 11.6	−38.1	16.3	40 09.2	−37.6	16.6	41 06.7	−37.6	16.8	42 04.1	−37.3	17.1	43 01.4	−36.9	17.3	71
72	35 39.7	−39.3	14.7	36 37.7	−39.1	14.9	37 35.6	−38.8	15.1	38 33.5	−38.6	15.3	39 31.4	−38.4	15.5	40 29.1	−38.0	15.8	41 26.8	−37.7	16.0	42 24.5	−37.5	16.3	72
73	35 00.4	−39.8	13.8	35 58.6	−39.5	14.0	36 56.8	−39.3	14.2	37 54.9	−39.0	14.4	38 53.0	−38.8	14.6	39 51.1	−38.6	14.8	40 49.1	−38.3	15.0	41 47.0	−38.0	15.2	73
74	34 20.6	−40.2	12.9	35 19.1	−40.0	13.1	36 17.5	−39.7	13.2	37 15.9	−39.5	13.4	38 14.2	−39.3	13.6	39 12.5	−39.0	13.8	40 10.8	−38.9	14.0	41 09.0	−38.6	14.2	74
75	33 40.4	−40.5	12.0	34 39.1	−40.3	12.2	35 37.8	−40.2	12.3	36 36.4	−40.0	12.5	37 34.9	−39.7	12.6	38 33.5	−39.6	12.8	39 31.9	−39.3	13.0	40 30.4	−39.1	13.2	75
76	32 59.9	−40.9	11.1	33 58.8	−40.8	11.3	34 57.6	−40.6	11.4	35 56.4	−40.4	11.5	36 55.2	−40.2	11.7	37 53.9	−40.0	11.8	38 52.6	−39.8	12.0	39 51.3	−39.6	12.2	76
77	32 19.0	−41.3	10.3	33 18.0	−41.1	10.4	34 17.0	−40.9	10.5	35 16.0	−40.8	10.6	36 15.0	−40.6	10.8	37 13.9	−40.4	10.9	38 12.8	−40.2	11.0	39 11.7	−40.1	11.2	77
78	31 37.7	−41.5	9.4	32 36.9	−41.4	9.5	33 36.1	−41.3	9.6	34 35.2	−41.1	9.7	35 34.4	−41.0	9.8	36 33.5	−40.9	10.0	37 32.6	−40.7	10.1	38 31.6	−40.5	10.2	78
79	30 56.2	−42.0	8.6	31 55.5	−41.8	8.7	32 54.8	−41.7	8.7	33 54.1	−41.6	8.8	34 53.4	−41.4	9.0	35 52.6	−41.2	9.1	36 51.9	−41.2	9.2	37 51.1	−41.0	9.3	79
80	30 14.2	−42.2	7.7	31 13.7	−42.1	7.8	32 13.1	−42.0	7.9	33 12.5	−41.8	8.0	34 12.0	−41.8	8.1	35 11.4	−41.7	8.2	36 10.7	−41.5	8.3	37 10.1	−41.4	8.4	80
81	29 32.0	−42.5	6.9	30 31.6	−42.5	7.0	31 31.1	−42.3	7.1	32 30.7	−42.3	7.1	33 30.2	−42.1	7.2	34 29.7	−42.0	7.3	35 29.2	−41.9	7.4	36 28.7	−41.8	7.5	81
82	28 49.5	−42.8	6.1	29 49.1	−42.7	6.2	30 48.8	−42.6	6.2	31 48.4	−42.5	6.3	32 48.1	−42.5	6.4	33 47.7	−42.4	6.4	34 47.3	−42.3	6.5	35 46.9	−42.2	6.6	82
83	28 06.7	−43.1	5.3	29 06.4	−43.0	5.4	30 06.2	−43.0	5.4	31 05.9	−42.9	5.5	32 05.6	−42.8	5.5	33 05.3	−42.7	5.6	34 05.0	−42.6	5.7	35 04.7	−42.5	5.7	83
84	27 23.6	−43.3	4.5	28 23.4	−43.3	4.6	29 23.2	−43.2	4.6	30 23.0	−43.1	4.7	31 22.8	−43.1	4.7	32 22.6	−43.0	4.8	33 22.4	−43.0	4.8	34 22.2	−42.9	4.9	84
85	26 40.3	−43.6	3.7	27 40.1	−43.5	3.8	28 40.0	−43.5	3.8	29 39.9	−43.5	3.8	30 39.7	−43.4	3.9	31 39.6	−43.4	3.9	32 39.4	−43.3	4.0	33 39.3	−43.2	4.0	85
86	25 56.7	−43.9	3.0	26 56.6	−43.8	3.0	27 56.5	−43.8	3.0	28 56.4	−43.7	3.1	29 56.3	−43.7	3.1	30 56.2	−43.6	3.1	31 56.1	−43.6	3.2	32 56.1	−43.6	3.2	86
87	25 12.8	−44.0	2.2	26 12.8	−44.1	2.2	27 12.7	−44.0	2.3	28 12.7	−44.0	2.3	29 12.6	−43.9	2.3	30 12.6	−43.9	2.3	31 12.5	−43.9	2.3	32 12.5	−43.9	2.4	87
88	24 28.8	−44.3	1.5	25 28.7	−44.2	1.5	26 28.7	−44.2	1.5	27 28.7	−44.2	1.5	28 28.7	−44.2	1.5	29 28.7	−44.2	1.5	30 28.6	−44.1	1.6	31 28.6	−44.1	1.6	88
89	23 44.5	−44.5	0.7	24 44.5	−44.5	0.7	25 44.5	−44.5	0.7	26 44.5	−44.5	0.7	27 44.5	−44.5	0.8	28 44.5	−44.5	0.8	29 44.5	−44.5	0.8	30 44.5	−44.5	0.8	89
90	23 00.0	−44.7	0.0	24 00.0	−44.7	0.0	25 00.0	−44.7	0.0	26 00.0	−44.7	0.0	27 00.0	−44.7	0.0	28 00.0	−44.7	0.0	29 00.0	−44.7	0.0	30 00.0	−44.7	0.0	90
	23°			24°			25°			26°			27°			28°			29°			30°			

42°, 318° L.H.A. LATITUDE SAME NAME AS DECLINATION

268

LATITUDE **CONTRARY** NAME TO DECLINATION **L.H.A. 42°, 318°**

Dec.	23° Hc	d	Z	24° Hc	d	Z	25° Hc	d	Z	26° Hc	d	Z
°	° ′	′	°	° ′	′	°	° ′	′	°	° ′	′	°
0	43 09.7	−32.4	113.5	42 45.4	−33.5	114.3	42 20.3	−34.6	115.1	41 54.5	−35.7	116.0
1	42 37.3	−33.2	114.6	42 11.9	−34.2	115.4	41 45.7	−35.2	116.2	41 18.8	−36.2	117.0
2	42 04.1	−33.8	115.7	41 37.7	−34.9	116.5	41 10.5	−35.8	117.3	40 42.6	−36.8	118.1
3	41 30.3	−34.5	116.8	41 02.8	−35.4	117.6	40 34.7	−36.5	118.4	40 05.8	−37.4	119.1
4	40 55.8	−35.0	117.9	40 27.4	−36.0	118.7	39 58.2	−36.9	119.4	39 28.4	−37.8	120.1
5	40 20.8	−35.6	119.0	39 51.4	−36.6	119.7	39 21.3	−37.5	120.4	38 50.6	−38.4	121.1
6	39 45.2	−36.2	120.1	39 14.8	−37.1	120.8	38 43.8	−38.0	121.5	38 12.2	−38.9	122.1
7	39 09.0	−36.7	121.1	38 37.7	−37.6	121.8	38 05.8	−38.5	122.4	37 33.3	−39.3	123.1
8	38 32.3	−37.3	122.1	38 00.1	−38.1	122.8	37 27.3	−38.9	123.4	36 54.0	−39.7	124.0
9	37 55.0	−37.7	123.1	37 22.0	−38.6	123.7	36 48.4	−39.4	124.4	36 14.3	−40.2	125.0
10	37 17.3	−38.2	124.1	36 43.4	−39.0	124.7	36 09.0	−39.8	125.3	35 34.1	−40.6	125.9
11	36 39.1	−38.7	125.0	36 04.4	−39.5	125.6	35 29.2	−40.3	126.2	34 53.5	−41.0	126.8
12	36 00.4	−39.1	126.0	35 24.9	−39.9	126.6	34 48.9	−40.6	127.1	34 12.5	−41.4	127.7
13	35 21.3	−39.5	126.9	34 45.0	−40.3	127.5	34 08.3	−41.0	128.0	33 31.1	−41.7	128.6
14	34 41.8	−40.0	127.8	34 04.7	−40.7	128.4	33 27.3	−41.4	128.9	32 49.4	−42.1	129.4
15	34 01.8	−40.3	128.7	33 24.0	−41.0	129.3	32 45.9	−41.8	129.8	32 07.3	−42.4	130.3
16	33 21.5	−40.7	129.6	32 43.0	−41.4	130.1	32 04.1	−42.0	130.6	31 24.9	−42.7	131.1
17	32 40.8	−41.1	130.5	32 01.6	−41.7	131.0	31 22.1	−42.4	131.5	30 42.2	−43.1	131.9
18	31 59.7	−41.4	131.4	31 19.9	−42.1	131.8	30 39.7	−42.7	132.3	29 59.1	−43.3	132.7
19	31 18.3	−41.8	132.2	30 37.8	−42.4	132.7	29 57.0	−43.0	133.1	29 15.8	−43.6	133.5
20	30 36.5	−42.0	133.1	29 55.4	−42.7	133.5	29 14.0	−43.3	133.9	28 32.2	−43.9	134.3
21	29 54.5	−42.4	133.9	29 12.7	−42.9	134.3	28 30.7	−43.6	134.7	27 48.3	−44.1	135.1
22	29 12.1	−42.7	134.7	28 29.8	−43.3	135.1	27 47.1	−43.8	135.5	27 04.2	−44.4	135.8
23	28 29.4	−42.9	135.5	27 46.5	−43.5	135.9	27 03.3	−44.1	136.2	26 19.8	−44.6	136.6
24	27 46.5	−43.2	136.3	27 03.0	−43.8	136.7	26 19.2	−44.3	137.0	25 35.2	−44.8	137.3
25	27 03.3	−43.5	137.1	26 19.2	−44.0	137.4	25 34.9	−44.5	137.8	24 50.4	−45.0	138.1
26	26 19.8	−43.7	137.9	25 35.2	−44.2	138.2	24 50.4	−44.7	138.5	24 05.4	−45.3	138.8
27	25 36.1	−43.9	138.6	24 51.0	−44.4	138.9	24 05.7	−45.0	139.2	23 20.1	−45.4	139.5
28	24 52.2	−44.2	139.4	24 06.6	−44.7	139.7	23 20.7	−45.1	139.9	22 34.7	−45.6	140.2
29	24 08.0	−44.3	140.1	23 21.9	−44.9	140.4	22 35.6	−45.4	140.7	21 49.1	−45.8	140.9
30	23 23.7	−44.6	140.8	22 37.0	−45.0	141.1	21 50.2	−45.5	141.4	21 03.3	−46.0	141.6
31	22 39.1	−44.8	141.6	21 52.0	−45.3	141.8	21 04.7	−45.7	142.1	20 17.3	−46.1	142.3
32	21 54.3	−45.0	142.3	21 06.7	−45.4	142.5	20 19.0	−45.8	142.8	19 31.2	−46.3	143.0
33	21 09.3	−45.1	143.0	20 21.3	−45.5	143.2	19 33.2	−46.0	143.4	18 44.9	−46.4	143.7
34	20 24.2	−45.3	143.7	19 35.8	−45.8	143.9	18 47.2	−46.1	144.1	17 58.5	−46.5	144.3
35	19 38.9	−45.5	144.4	18 50.0	−45.8	144.6	18 01.1	−46.3	144.8	17 12.0	−46.7	145.0
36	18 53.4	−45.6	145.1	18 04.2	−46.1	145.3	17 14.8	−46.4	145.5	16 25.3	−46.8	145.6
37	18 07.8	−45.8	145.8	17 18.1	−46.1	146.0	16 28.4	−46.6	146.1	15 38.5	−46.9	146.3
38	17 22.0	−45.9	146.5	16 32.0	−46.3	146.6	15 41.8	−46.6	146.8	14 51.6	−47.0	146.9
39	16 36.1	−46.0	147.1	15 45.7	−46.4	147.3	14 55.2	−46.8	147.4	14 04.6	−47.2	147.6
40	15 50.1	−46.1	147.8	14 59.3	−46.5	148.0	14 08.4	−46.9	148.1	13 17.4	−47.2	148.2
41	15 04.0	−46.3	148.5	14 12.8	−46.6	148.6	13 21.5	−46.9	148.7	12 30.2	−47.3	148.9
42	14 17.7	−46.4	149.1	13 26.2	−46.8	149.3	12 34.6	−47.1	149.4	11 42.9	−47.4	149.5
43	13 31.3	−46.5	149.8	12 39.4	−46.8	149.9	11 47.5	−47.1	150.0	10 55.5	−47.5	150.1
44	12 44.8	−46.5	150.4	11 52.6	−46.9	150.5	11 00.4	−47.3	150.6	10 08.0	−47.5	150.7
45	11 58.3	−46.7	151.1	11 05.7	−46.9	151.2	10 13.1	−47.2	151.3	9 20.5	−47.6	151.3
46	11 11.6	−46.7	151.7	10 18.8	−47.1	151.8	9 25.9	−47.4	151.9	8 32.9	−47.6	152.0
47	10 24.9	−46.8	152.4	9 31.7	−47.1	152.4	8 38.5	−47.4	152.5	7 45.3	−47.8	152.6
48	9 38.1	−46.9	153.0	8 44.6	−47.2	153.1	7 51.1	−47.5	153.1	6 57.5	−47.7	153.2
49	8 51.2	−47.0	153.6	7 57.4	−47.2	153.7	7 03.6	−47.5	153.7	6 09.8	−47.8	153.8
50	8 04.2	−47.0	154.3	7 10.2	−47.3	154.3	6 16.1	−47.6	154.4	5 22.0	−47.8	154.4
51	7 17.2	−47.0	154.9	6 22.9	−47.3	154.9	5 28.5	−47.6	155.0	4 34.2	−47.9	155.0
52	6 30.2	−47.1	155.5	5 35.6	−47.4	155.5	4 40.9	−47.6	155.6	3 46.3	−47.9	155.6
53	5 43.1	−47.2	156.1	4 48.2	−47.4	156.2	3 53.3	−47.6	156.2	2 58.4	−47.9	156.2
54	4 55.9	−47.1	156.7	4 00.8	−47.4	156.8	3 05.7	−47.7	156.8	2 10.5	−47.9	156.8
55	4 08.8	−47.2	157.4	3 13.4	−47.5	157.4	2 18.0	−47.7	157.4	1 22.6	−48.0	157.4
56	3 21.6	−47.3	158.0	2 25.9	−47.4	158.0	1 30.3	−47.7	158.0	0 34.6	−47.9	158.0
57	2 34.3	−47.2	158.6	1 38.5	−47.5	158.6	0 42.6	−47.7	158.6	0 13.3	+47.9	21.4
58	1 47.1	−47.3	159.2	0 51.0	−47.5	159.2	0 05.1	+47.7	20.8	1 01.2	+48.0	20.8
59	0 59.8	−47.2	159.8	0 03.5	−47.5	159.8	0 52.8	+47.7	20.2	1 49.2	+47.9	20.2
60	0 12.6	−47.3	160.5	0 44.0	+47.5	19.5	1 40.5	+47.7	19.6	2 37.1	+47.9	19.6
61	0 34.7	+47.3	18.9	1 31.5	+47.4	18.9	2 28.2	+47.7	18.9	3 25.0	+47.8	19.0
62	1 22.0	+47.2	18.3	2 18.9	+47.5	18.3	3 15.9	+47.6	18.3	4 12.8	+47.9	18.4
63	2 09.2	+47.3	17.7	3 06.4	+47.4	17.7	4 03.5	+47.7	17.7	5 00.7	+47.8	17.8
64	2 56.5	+47.2	17.1	3 53.8	+47.4	17.1	4 51.2	+47.6	17.1	5 48.5	+47.8	17.1
65	3 43.7	+47.2	16.5	4 41.2	+47.4	16.5	5 38.8	+47.5	16.5	6 36.3	+47.7	16.5
66	4 30.9	+47.1	15.8	5 28.6	+47.3	15.9	6 26.3	+47.5	15.9	7 24.0	+47.7	15.9
67	5 18.0	+47.2	15.2	6 15.9	+47.3	15.2	7 13.8	+47.5	15.3	8 11.7	+47.6	15.3
68	6 05.2	+47.0	14.6	7 03.2	+47.3	14.6	8 01.3	+47.4	14.7	8 59.3	+47.6	14.7
69	6 52.2	+47.1	14.0	7 50.5	+47.2	14.0	8 48.7	+47.3	14.0	9 46.9	+47.5	14.1
70	7 39.3	+47.0	13.4	8 37.7	+47.1	13.4	9 36.0	+47.3	13.4	10 34.4	+47.4	13.5
71	8 26.3	+46.9	12.7	9 24.8	+47.0	12.8	10 23.3	+47.2	12.8	11 21.8	+47.3	12.8
72	9 13.2	+46.8	12.1	10 11.8	+47.0	12.1	11 10.5	+47.1	12.2	12 09.1	+47.3	12.2
73	10 00.0	+46.8	11.5	10 58.8	+46.9	11.5	11 57.6	+47.1	11.5	12 56.4	+47.2	11.6
74	10 46.8	+46.7	10.8	11 45.7	+46.9	10.9	12 44.7	+46.9	10.9	13 43.6	+47.0	10.9
75	11 33.5	+46.6	10.2	12 32.6	+46.7	10.2	13 31.6	+46.9	10.3	14 30.6	+47.0	10.3
76	12 20.1	+46.5	9.5	13 19.3	+46.6	9.6	14 18.5	+46.7	9.6	15 17.6	+46.9	9.7
77	13 06.6	+46.5	8.9	14 05.9	+46.6	8.9	15 05.2	+46.6	9.0	16 04.5	+46.7	9.0
78	13 53.1	+46.3	8.2	14 52.5	+46.4	8.3	15 51.8	+46.5	8.3	16 51.2	+46.6	8.4
79	14 39.4	+46.2	7.6	15 38.9	+46.3	7.6	16 38.3	+46.4	7.7	17 37.8	+46.5	7.7
80	15 25.6	+46.1	6.9	16 25.2	+46.1	7.0	17 24.7	+46.3	7.0	18 24.3	+46.3	7.0
81	16 11.7	+46.0	6.3	17 11.3	+46.1	6.3	18 11.0	+46.1	6.3	19 10.6	+46.2	6.4
82	16 57.7	+45.8	5.6	17 57.4	+45.9	5.6	18 57.1	+46.0	5.7	19 56.8	+46.0	5.7
83	17 43.5	+45.7	4.9	18 43.3	+45.7	4.9	19 43.1	+45.8	5.0	20 42.8	+45.9	5.0
84	18 29.2	+45.6	4.2	19 29.0	+45.6	4.3	20 28.9	+45.6	4.3	21 28.7	+45.7	4.3
85	19 14.8	+45.3	3.5	20 14.6	+45.5	3.6	21 14.5	+45.5	3.6	22 14.4	+45.5	3.6
86	20 00.1	+45.3	2.8	21 00.1	+45.2	2.9	22 00.0	+45.3	2.9	22 59.9	+45.4	2.9
87	20 45.4	+45.0	2.1	21 45.3	+45.1	2.2	22 45.3	+45.1	2.2	23 45.3	+45.1	2.2
88	21 30.4	+44.9	1.4	22 30.4	+44.9	1.4	23 30.4	+44.9	1.5	24 30.4	+44.9	1.5
89	22 15.3	+44.7	0.7	23 15.3	+44.7	0.7	24 15.3	+44.7	0.7	25 15.3	+44.7	0.7
90	23 00.0	+44.5	0.0	24 00.0	+44.5	0.0	25 00.0	+44.5	0.0	26 00.0	+44.5	0.0
	23°			24°			25°			26°		

Dec.	27° Hc	d	Z	28° Hc	d	Z	29° Hc	d	Z	30° Hc	d	Z
°	° ′	′	°	° ′	′	°	° ′	′	°	° ′	′	°
0	41 27.8	−36.6	116.8	41 00.5	−37.7	117.5	40 32.4	−38.6	118.3	40 03.6	−39.5	119.0
1	40 51.2	−37.2	117.8	40 22.8	−38.1	118.6	39 53.8	−39.0	119.3	39 24.1	−39.9	120.0
2	40 14.0	−37.8	118.8	39 44.7	−38.6	119.6	39 14.8	−39.6	120.3	38 44.2	−40.4	121.0
3	39 36.2	−38.2	119.9	39 06.1	−39.2	120.6	38 35.2	−40.0	121.3	38 03.8	−40.8	121.9
4	38 58.0	−38.8	120.9	38 26.9	−39.6	121.5	37 55.2	−40.4	122.2	37 23.0	−41.3	122.9
5	38 19.2	−39.2	121.8	37 47.3	−40.1	122.5	37 14.8	−40.9	123.1	36 41.7	−41.7	123.8
6	37 40.0	−39.7	122.8	37 07.2	−40.5	123.4	36 33.9	−41.3	124.1	36 00.0	−42.0	124.7
7	37 00.3	−40.1	123.7	36 26.7	−40.9	124.3	35 52.6	−41.7	125.0	35 18.0	−42.5	125.5
8	36 20.2	−40.6	124.7	35 45.8	−41.3	125.3	35 10.9	−42.1	125.8	34 35.5	−42.8	126.4
9	35 39.6	−41.0	125.6	35 04.5	−41.8	126.1	34 28.8	−42.4	126.7	33 52.7	−43.1	127.2
10	34 58.6	−41.3	126.5	34 22.7	−42.0	127.0	33 46.4	−42.8	127.6	33 09.6	−43.5	128.1
11	34 17.3	−41.7	127.3	33 40.7	−42.5	127.9	33 03.6	−43.1	128.4	32 26.1	−43.7	128.9
12	33 35.6	−42.1	128.2	32 58.2	−42.7	128.7	32 20.5	−43.4	129.2	31 42.4	−44.1	129.7
13	32 53.5	−42.4	129.1	32 15.5	−43.1	129.6	31 37.1	−43.8	130.0	30 58.3	−44.4	130.5
14	32 11.1	−42.8	129.9	31 32.4	−43.4	130.4	30 53.3	−44.0	130.8	30 13.9	−44.6	131.3
15	31 28.3	−43.0	130.7	30 49.0	−43.7	131.2	30 09.3	−44.3	131.6	29 29.3	−44.9	132.1
16	30 45.3	−43.4	131.5	30 05.3	−44.0	132.0	29 25.0	−44.6	132.4	28 44.4	−45.2	132.8
17	30 01.9	−43.6	132.3	29 21.3	−44.2	132.8	28 40.4	−44.8	133.2	27 59.2	−45.4	133.6
18	29 18.3	−44.0	133.1	28 37.1	−44.5	133.5	27 55.6	−45.1	133.9	27 13.8	−45.6	134.3
19	28 34.3	−44.1	133.9	27 52.6	−44.8	134.3	27 10.5	−45.3	134.7	26 28.2	−45.8	135.0
20	27 50.2	−44.5	134.7	27 07.8	−45.0	135.0	26 25.2	−45.5	135.4	25 42.4	−46.1	135.7
21	27 05.7	−44.7	135.4	26 22.8	−45.2	135.8	25 39.7	−45.7	136.1	24 56.3	−46.2	136.5
22	26 21.0	−44.9	136.2	25 37.6	−45.4	136.5	24 54.0	−46.0	136.8	24 10.1	−46.4	137.2
23	25 36.1	−45.1	136.9	24 52.2	−45.6	137.2	24 08.0	−46.1	137.6	23 23.7	−46.7	137.8
24	24 51.0	−45.3	137.7	24 06.6	−45.9	138.0	23 21.9	−46.3	138.2	22 37.0	−46.8	138.5
25	24 05.7	−45.6	138.4	23 20.7	−46.0	138.7	22 35.6	−46.5	138.9	21 50.2	−46.9	139.2
26	23 20.1	−45.7	139.1	22 34.7	−46.2	139.4	21 49.1	−46.7	139.6	21 03.3	−47.1	139.9
27	22 34.4	−45.9	139.8	21 48.5	−46.4	140.0	21 02.4	−46.8	140.3	20 16.2	−47.3	140.5
28	21 48.5	−46.1	140.5	21 02.1	−46.5	140.7	20 15.6	−47.0	141.0	19 28.9	−47.4	141.2
29	21 02.4	−46.2	141.2	20 15.6	−46.7	141.4	19 28.6	−47.1	141.6	18 41.5	−47.5	141.8
30	20 16.2	−46.4	141.8	19 28.9	−46.8	142.1	18 41.5	−47.2	142.3	17 54.0	−47.6	142.5
31	19 29.8	−46.6	142.5	18 42.1	−47.0	142.7	17 54.3	−47.4	142.9	17 06.4	−47.8	143.1
32	18 43.2	−46.7	143.2	17 55.1	−47.1	143.4	17 06.9	−47.5	143.6	16 18.6	−47.9	143.8
33	17 56.5	−46.8	143.9	17 08.0	−47.2	144.0	16 19.4	−47.6	144.2	15 30.7	−48.0	144.4
34	17 09.7	−46.9	144.5	16 20.8	−47.3	144.7	15 31.8	−47.7	144.8	14 42.7	−48.1	145.0
35	16 22.8	−47.1	145.2	15 33.5	−47.5	145.3	14 44.1	−47.8	145.5	13 54.6	−48.2	145.6
36	15 35.7	−47.2	145.8	14 46.0	−47.5	146.0	13 56.3	−47.9	146.1	13 06.4	−48.2	146.2
37	14 48.5	−47.3	146.4	13 58.5	−47.7	146.6	13 08.4	−48.0	146.7	12 18.2	−48.4	146.8
38	14 01.2	−47.3	147.1	13 10.8	−47.7	147.2	12 20.4	−48.1	147.3	11 29.8	−48.4	147.4
39	13 13.9	−47.5	147.7	12 23.1	−47.8	147.8	11 32.3	−48.2	147.9	10 41.4	−48.5	148.0
40	12 26.4	−47.6	148.3	11 35.3	−47.9	148.4	10 44.1	−48.2	148.6	9 52.9	−48.5	148.6
41	11 38.8	−47.6	149.0	10 47.4	−48.0	149.1	9 55.9	−48.3	149.2	9 04.4	−48.6	149.2
42	10 51.2	−47.7	149.6	9 59.4	−48.0	149.7	9 07.6	−48.3	149.8	8 15.8	−48.7	149.8
43	10 03.5	−47.8	150.2	9 11.4	−48.1	150.3	8 19.3	−48.4	150.4	7 27.1	−48.7	150.4
44	9 15.7	−47.9	150.8	8 23.3	−48.2	150.9	7 30.9	−48.5	151.0	6 38.4	−48.8	151.0
45	8 27.8	−47.9	151.4	7 35.1	−48.2	151.5	6 42.4	−48.5	151.5	5 49.6	−48.8	151.6
46	7 39.9	−47.9	152.0	6 46.9	−48.2	152.1	5 53.9	−48.5	152.1	5 00.8	−48.8	152.2
47	6 52.0	−48.0	152.6	5 58.7	−48.3	152.7	5 05.4	−48.6	152.7	4 12.0	−48.8	152.8
48	6 04.0	−48.1	153.2	5 10.4	−48.3	153.3	4 16.8	−48.6	153.3	3 23.2	−48.9	153.4
49	5 15.9	−48.0	153.8	4 22.1	−48.4	153.9	3 28.2	−48.6	153.9	2 34.3	−48.9	153.9
50	4 27.9	−48.1	154.4	3 33.7	−48.3	154.5	2 39.6	−48.6	154.5	1 45.4	−48.9	154.5
51	3 39.8	−48.2	155.0	2 45.4	−48.4	155.1	1 51.0	−48.7	155.1	0 56.5	−48.9	155.1
52	2 51.6	−48.1	155.6	1 57.0	−48.4	155.7	1 02.3	−48.6	155.7	0 07.6	−48.9	155.7
53	2 03.5	−48.2	156.2	1 08.6	−48.4	156.2	0 13.7	−48.7	156.3	0 41.3	+48.8	23.7
54	1 15.3	−48.1	156.8	0 20.2	−48.4	156.8	0 35.0	+48.6	23.2	1 30.1	+48.9	23.2
55	0 27.2	−48.2	157.4	0 28.2	+48.4	22.6	1 23.6	+48.7	22.6	2 19.0	+48.9	22.6
56	0 21.0	+48.2	22.0	1 16.6	+48.4	22.0	2 12.3	+48.6	22.0	3 07.9	+48.9	22.0
57	1 09.2	+48.1	21.4	2 05.0	+48.4	21.4	3 00.9	+48.6	21.4	3 56.8	+48.8	21.4
58	1 57.3	+48.2	20.8	2 53.4	+48.4	20.8	3 49.5	+48.6	20.8	4 45.6	+48.8	20.8
59	2 45.5	+48.1	20.2	3 41.8	+48.3	20.2	4 38.1	+48.5	20.2	5 34.4	+48.7	20.3
60	3 33.6	+48.1	19.6	4 30.1	+48.3	19.6	5 26.6	+48.6	19.6	6 23.1	+48.8	19.7
61	4 21.7	+48.1	19.0	5 18.4	+48.3	19.0	6 15.2	+48.4	19.0	7 11.9	+48.6	19.1
62	5 09.8	+48.0	18.4	6 06.7	+48.3	18.4	7 03.6	+48.5	18.5	8 00.5	+48.7	18.5
63	5 57.8	+48.0	17.8	6 55.0	+48.1	17.8	7 52.1	+48.4	17.9	8 49.2	+48.5	17.9
64	6 45.8	+48.0	17.2	7 43.1	+48.2	17.2	8 40.5	+48.3	17.3	9 37.7	+48.6	17.3
65	7 33.8	+47.9	16.6	8 31.3	+48.1	16.6	9 28.8	+48.2	16.7	10 26.3	+48.4	16.7
66	8 21.7	+47.9	16.0	9 19.4	+48.0	16.0	10 17.0	+48.2	16.1	11 14.7	+48.4	16.1
67	9 09.6	+47.7	15.4	10 07.4	+48.0	15.4	11 05.2	+48.2	15.5	12 03.1	+48.3	15.5
68	9 57.3	+47.8	14.7	10 55.4	+47.9	14.8	11 53.4	+48.0	14.8	12 51.4	+48.2	14.9
69	10 45.1	+47.6	14.1	11 43.3	+47.8	14.2	12 41.4	+48.0	14.2	13 39.6	+48.1	14.3
70	11 32.7	+47.6	13.5	12 31.1	+47.7	13.6	13 29.4	+47.8	13.6	14 27.7	+48.0	13.7
71	12 20.3	+47.5	12.9	13 18.8	+47.6	12.9	14 17.2	+47.8	13.0	15 15.7	+47.9	13.1
72	13 07.8	+47.4	12.3	14 06.4	+47.5	12.3	15 05.0	+47.7	12.4	16 03.6	+47.8	12.4
73	13 55.2	+47.3	11.6	14 53.9	+47.5	11.7	15 52.7	+47.6	11.7	16 51.4	+47.7	11.8
74	14 42.5	+47.2	11.0	15 41.4	+47.3	11.0	16 40.3	+47.4	11.1	17 39.1	+47.6	11.2
75	15 29.7	+47.0	10.4	16 28.7	+47.2	10.4	17 27.7	+47.3	10.5	18 26.7	+47.4	10.5
76	16 16.7	+47.0	9.7	17 15.9	+47.1	9.8	18 15.0	+47.2	9.8	19 14.1	+47.3	9.9
77	17 03.7	+46.9	9.1	18 03.0	+46.9	9.1	19 02.2	+47.0	9.2	20 01.4	+47.2	9.2
78	17 50.6	+46.7	8.4	18 49.9	+46.8	8.5	19 49.2	+46.9	8.5	20 48.6	+47.0	8.6
79	18 37.3	+46.5	7.7	19 36.7	+46.7	7.8	20 36.1	+46.8	7.8	21 35.6	+46.8	7.9
80	19 23.8	+46.4	7.1	20 23.4	+46.5	7.1	21 22.9	+46.6	7.2	22 22.4	+46.7	7.2
81	20 10.2	+46.3	6.4	21 09.9	+46.3	6.4	22 09.5	+46.4	6.5	23 09.1	+46.5	6.5
82	20 56.5	+46.1	5.7	21 56.2	+46.2	5.8	22 55.9	+46.2	5.8	23 55.6	+46.3	5.8
83	21 42.6	+45.9	5.0	22 42.4	+46.0	5.1	23 42.1	+46.1	5.1	24 41.9	+46.1	5.1
84	22 28.5	+45.8	4.3	23 28.4	+45.8	4.4	24 28.2	+45.8	4.4	25 28.0	+45.9	4.4
85	23 14.3	+45.5	3.6	24 14.2	+45.6	3.7	25 14.0	+45.7	3.7	26 13.9	+45.7	3.7
86	23 59.8	+45.4	2.9	24 59.8	+45.4	3.0	25 59.7	+45.4	3.0	26 59.6	+45.5	3.0
87	24 45.2	+45.2	2.2	25 45.2	+45.1	2.2	26 45.1	+45.2	2.2	27 45.1	+45.2	2.3
88	25 30.4	+44.9	1.5	26 30.3	+45.0	1.5	27 30.3	+45.0	1.5	28 30.3	+45.0	1.5
89	26 15.3	+44.7	0.7	27 15.3	+44.7	0.8	28 15.3	+44.7	0.8	29 15.3	+44.7	0.8
90	27 00.0	+44.5	0.0	28 00.0	+44.5	0.0	29 00.0	+44.5	0.0	30 00.0	+44.5	0.0
	27°			28°			29°			30°		

S. Lat. {L.H.A. greater than 180° ....Zn=180°−Z; L.H.A. less than 180°............Zn=180°+Z}

LATITUDE **SAME** NAME AS DECLINATION **L.H.A. 138°, 222°**

269

43°, 317° L.H.A. LATITUDE SAME NAME AS DECLINATION

N. Lat. {L.H.A. greater than 180° .....Zn=Z
{L.H.A. less than 180°............Zn=360°–Z

Dec.	23° Hc	23° d	23° Z	24° Hc	24° d	24° Z	25° Hc	25° d	25° Z	26° Hc	26° d	26° Z	27° Hc	27° d	27° Z	28° Hc	28° d	28° Z	29° Hc	29° d	29° Z	30° Hc	30° d	30° Z	Dec.
°	° ′	′	°	° ′	′	°	° ′	′	°	° ′	′	°	° ′	′	°	° ′	′	°	° ′	′	°	° ′	′	°	°
0	42 18.9	+31.4	112.7	41 55.4	+32.4	113.6	41 31.0	+33.5	114.4	41 05.8	+34.6	115.2	40 39.9	+35.6	116.0	40 13.3	+36.6	116.7	39 46.0	+37.5	117.5	39 18.0	+38.5	118.2	0
1	42 50.3	+30.6	111.6	42 27.8	+31.8	112.4	42 04.5	+32.9	113.3	41 40.4	+34.0	114.1	41 15.5	+35.1	114.9	40 49.9	+36.1	115.7	40 23.5	+37.1	116.5	39 56.5	+38.0	117.2	1
2	43 20.9	+30.0	110.4	42 59.6	+31.1	111.3	42 37.4	+32.2	112.1	42 14.4	+33.3	113.0	41 50.6	+34.4	113.8	41 26.0	+35.4	114.6	41 00.6	+36.4	115.4	40 34.5	+37.4	116.2	2
3	43 50.9	+29.1	109.2	43 30.7	+30.3	110.1	43 09.6	+31.5	111.0	42 47.7	+32.6	111.9	42 25.0	+33.7	112.7	42 01.4	+34.8	113.5	41 37.0	+35.9	114.4	41 11.9	+36.9	115.2	3
4	44 20.0	+28.4	108.0	44 01.0	+29.6	108.9	43 41.1	+30.8	109.8	43 20.3	+32.0	110.7	42 58.7	+33.1	111.6	42 36.2	+34.2	112.4	42 12.9	+35.3	113.3	41 48.8	+36.3	114.1	4
5	44 48.4	+27.5	106.7	44 30.6	+28.8	107.7	44 11.9	+30.0	108.6	43 52.3	+31.2	109.5	43 31.8	+32.3	110.4	43 10.4	+33.5	111.3	42 48.2	+34.6	112.2	42 25.1	+35.7	113.0	5
6	45 15.9	+26.7	105.5	44 59.4	+28.0	106.5	44 41.9	+29.2	107.4	44 23.5	+30.4	108.3	44 04.1	+31.7	109.3	43 43.9	+32.8	110.2	43 22.8	+33.9	111.1	43 00.8	+35.0	111.9	6
7	45 42.6	+25.8	104.2	45 27.4	+27.1	105.2	45 11.1	+28.5	106.2	44 53.9	+29.7	107.1	44 35.8	+30.9	108.1	44 16.7	+32.1	109.0	43 56.7	+33.3	109.9	43 35.8	+34.4	110.8	7
8	46 08.4	+25.0	102.9	45 54.5	+26.3	103.9	45 39.6	+27.6	104.9	45 23.6	+28.9	105.9	45 06.7	+30.1	106.9	44 48.8	+31.3	107.8	44 30.0	+32.5	108.8	44 10.2	+33.7	109.7	8
9	46 33.4	+24.0	101.6	46 20.8	+25.4	102.6	46 07.2	+26.7	103.6	45 52.5	+28.0	104.6	45 36.8	+29.3	105.6	45 20.1	+30.6	106.6	45 02.5	+31.8	107.6	44 43.9	+33.0	108.5	9
10	46 57.4	+23.1	100.3	46 46.2	+24.4	101.3	46 33.9	+25.8	102.3	46 20.5	+27.2	103.4	46 06.1	+28.5	104.4	45 50.7	+29.8	105.4	45 34.3	+31.0	106.4	45 16.9	+32.2	107.3	10
11	47 20.5	+22.1	98.9	47 10.6	+23.5	100.0	46 59.7	+24.9	101.0	46 47.7	+26.2	102.1	46 34.6	+27.6	103.1	46 20.5	+28.9	104.1	46 05.3	+30.2	105.1	45 49.1	+31.5	106.1	11
12	47 42.6	+21.1	97.5	47 34.1	+22.6	98.6	47 24.6	+23.9	99.7	47 13.9	+25.4	100.8	47 02.2	+26.7	101.8	46 49.4	+28.0	102.9	46 35.5	+29.4	103.9	46 20.6	+30.6	104.9	12
13	48 03.7	+20.0	96.1	47 56.7	+21.5	97.2	47 48.5	+23.0	98.3	47 39.3	+24.4	99.4	47 28.9	+25.8	100.5	47 17.4	+27.2	101.6	47 04.9	+28.5	102.6	46 51.2	+29.9	103.7	13
14	48 23.7	+19.0	94.7	48 18.2	+20.5	95.8	48 11.5	+22.0	96.9	48 03.7	+23.4	98.1	47 54.7	+24.9	99.2	47 44.6	+26.2	100.2	47 33.4	+27.6	101.3	47 21.1	+28.9	102.4	14
15	48 42.7	+18.0	93.3	48 38.7	+19.4	94.4	48 33.5	+20.9	95.5	48 27.1	+22.4	96.7	48 19.6	+23.8	97.8	48 10.8	+25.3	98.9	48 01.0	+26.7	100.0	47 50.0	+28.1	101.1	15
16	49 00.7	+16.8	91.8	48 58.1	+18.4	93.0	48 54.4	+19.9	94.1	48 49.5	+21.4	95.3	48 43.4	+22.9	96.4	48 36.1	+24.3	97.5	48 27.7	+25.7	98.7	48 18.1	+27.1	99.8	16
17	49 17.5	+15.7	90.4	49 16.5	+17.2	91.5	49 14.3	+18.8	92.7	49 10.9	+20.3	93.8	49 06.3	+21.8	95.0	49 00.4	+23.3	96.1	48 53.4	+24.8	97.3	48 45.2	+26.2	98.4	17
18	49 33.2	+14.5	88.9	49 33.7	+16.2	90.1	49 33.1	+17.6	91.2	49 31.2	+19.2	92.4	49 28.1	+20.7	93.6	49 23.7	+22.2	94.7	49 18.2	+23.7	95.9	49 11.4	+25.2	97.0	18
19	49 47.7	+13.4	87.4	49 49.9	+14.9	88.6	49 50.7	+16.6	89.7	49 50.4	+18.1	90.9	49 48.8	+19.6	92.1	49 45.9	+21.2	93.3	49 41.9	+22.7	94.5	49 36.6	+24.1	95.7	19
20	50 01.1	+12.2	85.9	50 04.8	+13.8	87.1	50 07.3	+15.3	88.3	50 08.5	+16.9	89.5	50 08.4	+18.5	90.6	50 07.1	+20.1	91.8	50 04.6	+21.5	93.0	50 00.7	+23.2	94.2	20
21	50 13.3	+11.0	84.3	50 18.6	+12.6	85.5	50 22.6	+14.2	86.7	50 25.4	+15.8	88.0	50 26.9	+17.4	89.2	50 27.2	+18.9	90.4	50 26.1	+20.5	91.6	50 23.9	+22.0	92.8	21
22	50 24.3	+9.7	82.8	50 31.2	+11.3	84.0	50 36.8	+13.0	85.2	50 41.2	+14.5	86.4	50 44.3	+16.1	87.7	50 46.1	+17.8	88.9	50 46.6	+19.4	90.1	50 45.9	+20.9	91.3	22
23	50 34.0	+8.5	81.3	50 42.5	+10.1	82.5	50 49.8	+11.7	83.7	50 55.7	+13.4	84.9	51 00.4	+15.0	86.1	51 03.9	+16.5	87.4	51 06.0	+18.1	88.6	51 06.8	+19.7	89.8	23
24	50 42.5	+7.3	79.7	50 52.6	+8.9	80.9	51 01.5	+10.5	82.1	51 09.1	+12.1	83.3	51 15.4	+13.7	84.6	51 20.4	+15.4	85.8	51 24.1	+17.0	87.1	51 26.5	+18.6	88.3	24
25	50 49.8	+5.9	78.1	51 01.5	+7.6	79.3	51 12.0	+9.2	80.5	51 21.2	+10.9	81.8	51 29.1	+12.5	83.0	51 35.8	+14.1	84.3	51 41.1	+15.7	85.5	51 45.1	+17.4	86.8	25
26	50 55.7	+4.7	76.5	51 09.1	+6.3	77.7	51 21.2	+7.9	79.0	51 32.1	+9.5	80.2	51 41.6	+11.2	81.4	51 49.9	+12.8	82.7	51 56.8	+14.5	84.0	52 02.5	+16.1	85.2	26
27	51 00.4	+3.5	75.0	51 15.4	+5.0	76.2	51 29.1	+6.7	77.4	51 41.6	+8.3	78.6	51 52.8	+9.9	79.9	52 02.7	+11.6	81.1	52 11.3	+13.3	82.4	52 18.6	+14.9	83.7	27
28	51 03.9	+2.1	73.4	51 20.4	+3.7	74.6	51 35.8	+5.3	75.8	51 49.9	+6.9	77.0	52 02.7	+8.6	78.3	52 14.3	+10.3	79.5	52 24.6	+11.9	80.8	52 33.5	+13.6	82.1	28
29	51 06.0	+0.8	71.8	51 24.1	+2.4	73.0	51 41.1	+4.0	74.2	51 56.8	+5.7	75.4	52 11.3	+7.3	76.6	52 24.6	+8.9	77.9	52 36.5	+10.6	79.2	52 47.1	+12.2	80.5	29
30	51 06.8	−0.5	70.2	51 26.5	+1.1	71.4	51 45.1	+2.7	72.6	52 02.5	+4.3	73.8	52 18.6	+6.0	75.0	52 33.5	+7.6	76.3	52 47.1	+9.2	77.6	52 59.3	+10.9	78.9	30
31	51 06.3	−1.8	68.6	51 27.6	−0.2	69.8	51 47.8	+1.4	71.0	52 06.8	+3.0	72.2	52 24.6	+4.5	73.4	52 41.1	+6.2	74.7	52 56.3	+7.9	75.9	53 10.2	+9.6	77.2	31
32	51 04.5	−3.0	67.0	51 27.4	−1.5	68.2	51 49.2	0.0	69.3	52 09.8	+1.6	70.5	52 29.1	+3.3	71.8	52 47.3	+4.9	73.0	53 04.2	+6.5	74.3	53 19.8	+8.2	75.6	32
33	51 01.5	−4.4	65.4	51 25.9	−2.9	66.6	51 49.2	−1.3	67.7	52 11.4	+0.2	68.9	52 32.4	+1.8	70.1	52 52.2	+3.5	71.4	53 10.7	+5.1	72.6	53 28.0	+6.8	73.9	33
34	50 57.1	−5.6	63.8	51 23.0	−4.1	65.0	51 47.9	−2.6	66.1	52 11.6	−1.0	67.3	52 34.2	+0.5	68.5	52 55.7	+2.1	69.7	53 15.8	+3.8	71.0	53 34.8	+5.4	72.2	34
35	50 51.5	−7.0	62.3	51 18.9	−5.5	63.4	51 45.3	−4.0	64.5	52 10.6	−2.5	65.6	52 34.7	−0.8	66.8	52 57.8	+0.7	68.0	53 19.6	+2.3	69.3	53 40.2	+4.0	70.6	35
36	50 44.5	−8.1	60.7	51 13.4	−6.7	61.8	51 41.3	−5.3	62.9	52 08.1	−3.7	64.0	52 33.9	−2.3	65.2	52 58.5	−0.7	66.4	53 21.9	+1.0	67.6	53 44.2	+2.5	68.9	36
37	50 36.4	−9.5	59.1	51 06.7	−8.0	60.2	51 36.0	−6.6	61.3	52 04.4	−5.2	62.4	52 31.6	−3.6	63.5	52 57.8	−2.0	64.7	53 22.9	−0.5	65.9	53 46.7	+1.1	67.2	37
38	50 26.9	−10.6	57.6	50 58.7	−9.3	58.6	51 29.4	−7.8	59.7	51 59.2	−6.4	60.8	52 28.0	−4.9	61.9	52 55.8	−3.5	63.1	53 22.4	−1.9	64.3	53 47.8	−0.3	65.5	38
39	50 16.3	−11.9	56.0	50 49.4	−10.6	57.0	51 21.6	−9.2	58.1	51 52.8	−7.7	59.2	52 23.1	−6.3	60.3	52 52.3	−4.8	61.4	53 20.5	−3.3	62.6	53 47.5	−1.7	63.8	39
40	50 04.4	−13.1	54.5	50 38.8	−11.7	55.5	51 12.4	−10.4	56.5	51 45.1	−9.1	57.6	52 16.8	−7.7	58.6	52 47.5	−6.2	59.8	53 17.2	−4.7	60.9	53 45.8	−3.1	62.1	40
41	49 51.3	−14.2	53.0	50 27.1	−13.0	53.9	51 02.0	−11.7	54.9	51 36.0	−10.3	56.0	52 09.1	−8.9	57.0	52 41.3	−7.5	58.1	53 12.5	−6.1	59.3	53 42.7	−4.6	60.4	41
42	49 37.1	−15.4	51.5	50 14.1	−14.2	52.4	50 50.3	−12.9	53.4	51 25.7	−11.6	54.4	52 00.2	−10.3	55.4	52 33.8	−8.9	56.5	53 06.4	−7.4	57.6	53 38.1	−6.0	58.7	42
43	49 21.7	−16.5	50.0	49 59.9	−15.3	50.9	50 37.4	−14.1	51.8	51 14.1	−12.9	52.8	51 49.9	−11.5	53.8	52 24.9	−10.2	54.9	52 59.0	−8.9	55.9	53 32.1	−7.4	57.1	43
44	49 05.2	−17.7	48.5	49 44.6	−16.5	49.4	50 23.3	−15.3	50.3	51 01.2	−14.1	51.3	51 38.4	−12.9	52.2	52 14.7	−11.5	53.2	52 50.1	−10.1	54.3	53 24.7	−8.8	55.4	44
45	48 47.5	−18.7	47.1	49 28.1	−17.6	47.9	50 08.0	−16.5	48.8	50 47.1	−15.3	49.7	51 25.5	−14.0	50.7	52 03.2	−12.8	51.6	52 40.0	−11.5	52.7	53 15.9	−10.1	53.7	45
46	48 28.8	−19.8	45.6	49 10.5	−18.8	46.4	49 51.5	−17.6	47.3	50 31.8	−16.5	48.2	51 11.5	−15.3	49.1	51 50.4	−14.1	50.1	52 28.5	−12.8	51.1	53 05.8	−11.5	52.1	46
47	48 09.0	−20.8	44.2	48 51.7	−19.8	45.0	49 33.9	−18.8	45.8	50 15.3	−17.6	46.7	50 56.2	−16.5	47.6	51 36.3	−15.3	48.5	52 15.7	−14.1	49.5	52 54.3	−12.8	50.5	47
48	47 48.2	−21.9	42.8	48 31.9	−20.8	43.6	49 15.1	−19.8	44.4	49 57.7	−18.7	45.2	50 39.7	−17.7	46.0	51 21.0	−16.5	46.9	52 01.6	−15.3	47.9	52 41.5	−14.2	48.8	48
49	47 26.3	−22.8	41.4	48 11.1	−21.9	42.2	48 55.3	−20.9	42.9	49 39.0	−19.9	43.7	50 22.0	−18.8	44.5	51 04.5	−17.8	45.4	51 46.3	−16.6	46.3	52 27.3	−15.4	47.2	49
50	47 03.5	−23.8	40.1	47 49.2	−22.9	40.8	48 34.4	−21.9	41.5	49 19.1	−21.0	42.3	50 03.2	−19.9	43.1	50 46.7	−18.8	43.9	51 29.7	−17.8	44.8	52 11.9	−16.6	45.7	50
51	46 39.7	−24.7	38.7	47 26.3	−23.8	39.4	48 12.5	−22.9	40.1	48 58.1	−22.0	40.8	49 43.3	−21.1	41.6	50 27.9	−20.1	42.4	51 11.9	−19.0	43.2	51 55.3	−17.9	44.1	51
52	46 15.0	−25.6	37.4	47 02.5	−24.8	38.0	47 49.6	−24.0	38.7	48 36.1	−23.0	39.4	49 22.2	−22.0	40.2	50 07.8	−21.1	40.9	50 52.9	−20.1	41.7	51 37.4	−19.1	42.6	52
53	45 49.4	−26.4	36.1	46 37.7	−25.6	36.7	47 25.6	−24.8	37.4	48 13.1	−24.0	38.0	49 00.2	−23.2	38.7	49 46.7	−22.2	39.5	50 32.8	−21.2	40.2	51 18.3	−20.2	41.0	53
54	45 23.0	−27.4	34.8	46 12.1	−26.6	35.4	47 00.8	−25.8	36.0	47 49.1	−25.0	36.7	48 37.0	−24.1	37.3	49 24.5	−23.2	38.0	50 11.6	−22.4	38.8	50 58.1	−21.4	39.5	54
55	44 55.6	−28.1	33.5	45 45.5	−27.4	34.1	46 35.0	−26.7	34.7	47 24.1	−25.9	35.3	48 12.9	−25.1	35.9	49 01.3	−24.3	36.6	49 49.2	−23.4	37.3	50 36.7	−22.5	38.1	55
56	44 27.5	−29.0	32.3	45 18.1	−28.3	32.8	46 08.3	−27.5	33.4	46 58.2	−26.8	34.0	47 47.8	−26.0	34.6	48 37.0	−25.2	35.2	49 25.8	−24.4	35.9	50 14.2	−23.5	36.6	56
57	43 58.5	−29.7	31.1	44 49.8	−29.1	31.6	45 40.8	−28.4	32.1	46 31.4	−27.7	32.7	47 21.8	−27.0	33.3	48 11.8	−26.2	33.9	49 01.4	−25.4	34.5	49 50.7	−24.6	35.2	57
58	43 28.8	−30.4	29.9	44 20.7	−29.8	30.4	45 12.4	−29.2	30.9	46 03.7	−28.5	31.4	46 54.8	−27.8	31.9	47 45.6	−27.2	32.5	48 36.0	−26.4	33.1	49 26.1	−25.7	33.8	58
59	42 58.4	−31.2	28.7	43 50.9	−30.6	29.1	44 43.2	−30.0	29.6	45 35.2	−29.4	30.1	46 27.0	−28.7	30.7	47 18.4	−28.0	31.2	48 09.6	−27.3	31.8	49 00.4	−26.5	32.4	59
60	42 27.2	−31.9	27.5	43 20.3	−31.3	28.0	44 13.2	−30.7	28.4	45 05.8	−30.1	28.9	45 58.3	−29.6	29.4	46 50.4	−28.9	29.9	47 42.3	−28.2	30.4	48 33.9	−27.6	31.0	60
61	41 55.3	−32.5	26.4	42 49.0	−32.0	26.8	43 42.5	−31.5	27.2	44 35.7	−30.9	27.7	45 28.7	−30.3	28.1	46 21.5	−29.7	28.6	47 14.1	−29.1	29.1	48 06.3	−28.4	29.7	61
62	41 22.8	−33.2	25.3	42 17.0	−32.7	25.6	43 11.0	−32.2	26.0	44 04.8	−31.7	26.5	44 58.4	−31.1	26.9	45 51.8	−30.5	27.4	46 45.0	−30.0	27.9	47 37.9	−29.3	28.4	62
63	40 49.6	−33.8	24.2	41 44.3	−33.4	24.5	42 38.8	−32.9	24.9	43 33.1	−32.3	25.3	44 27.3	−31.9	25.7	45 21.3	−31.4	26.1	46 15.0	−30.7	26.6	47 08.6	−30.2	27.1	63
64	40 15.8	−34.4	23.1	41 10.9	−33.9	23.4	42 05.9	−33.5	23.8	43 00.8	−33.1	24.1	43 55.4	−32.5	24.5	44 49.9	−32.0	24.9	45 44.3	−31.6	25.4	46 38.4	−31.0	25.8	64
65	39 41.4	−35.0	22.0	40 37.0	−34.6	22.3	41 32.4	−34.1	22.6	42 27.7	−33.7	23.0	43 22.9	−33.3	23.4	44 17.9	−32.8	23.7	45 12.7	−32.3	24.2	46 07.4	−31.8	24.6	65
66	39 06.4	−35.5	20.9	40 02.4	−35.2	21.2	40 58.3	−34.8	21.6	41 54.0	−34.3	21.9	42 49.6	−33.9	22.2	43 45.1	−33.5	22.6	44 40.4	−33.0	23.0	45 35.6	−32.6	23.4	66
67	38 30.9	−36.1	19.9	39 27.2	−35.7	20.2	40 23.5	−35.3	20.5	41 19.7	−35.0	20.8	42 15.7	−34.6	21.1	43 11.6	−34.1	21.4	44 07.4	−33.7	21.8	45 03.0	−33.3	22.2	67
68	37 54.8	−36.6	18.9	38 51.5	−36.2	19.2	39 48.2	−35.9	19.4	40 44.7	−35.6	19.7	41 41.1	−35.2	20.0	42 37.5	−34.8	20.3	43 33.7	−34.4	20.6	44 29.7	−33.9	21.0	68
69	37 18.2	−37.1	17.9	38 15.3	−36.8	18.1	39 12.3	−36.5	18.4	40 09.1	−36.1	18.6	41 05.9	−35.7	18.9	42 02.7	−35.5	19.2	42 59.3	−35.1	19.5	43 55.8	−34.7	19.8	69
70	36 41.1	−37.5	16.9	37 38.5	−37.3	17.1	38 35.8	−37.0	17.4	39 33.0	−36.6	17.6	40 30.2	−36.4	17.9	41 27.2	−36.0	18.1	42 24.2	−35.7	18.4	43 21.1	−35.3	18.7	70
71	36 03.6	−38.1	15.9	37 01.2	−37.7	16.1	37 58.8	−37.5	16.4	38 56.4	−37.2	16.6	39 53.8	−36.9	16.8	40 51.2	−36.6	17.1	41 48.5	−36.2	17.3	42 45.8	−36.0	17.6	71
72	35 25.5	−38.4	15.0	36 23.5	−38.3	15.2	37 21.3	−37.9	15.4	38 19.2	−37.7	15.6	39 16.9	−37.4	15.8	40 14.6	−37.1	16.0	41 12.3	−36.9	16.3	42 09.8	−36.5	16.5	72
73	34 47.1	−38.9	14.1	35 45.2	−38.6	14.2	36 43.4	−38.5	14.4	37 41.5	−38.2	14.6	38 39.5	−37.8	14.8	39 37.5	−37.7	15.0	40 35.4	−37.4	15.2	41 33.3	−37.2	15.5	73
74	34 08.2	−39.3	13.1	35 06.6	−39.1	13.3	36 04.9	−38.8	13.5	37 03.3	−38.7	13.6	38 01.6	−38.5	13.8	38 59.8	−38.2	14.0	39 58.0	−37.9	14.2	40 56.1	−37.6	14.4	74
75	33 28.9	−39.7	12.2	34 27.5	−39.5	12.4	35 26.1	−39.3	12.5	36 24.6	−39.1	12.7	37 23.1	−38.8	12.8	38 21.6	−38.6	13.0	39 20.1	−38.5	13.2	40 18.5	−38.3	13.4	75
76	32 49.2	−40.1	11.3	33 48.0	−39.9	11.5	34 46.8	−39.8	11.6	35 45.5	−39.5	11.7	36 44.3	−39.4	11.9	37 43.0	−39.2	12.0	38 41.6	−38.9	12.2	39 40.2	−38.7	12.4	76
77	32 09.1	−40.5	10.4	33 08.1	−40.3	10.6	34 07.0	−40.1	10.7	35 06.0	−39.9	10.8	36 04.9	−39.8	10.9	37 03.8	−39.6	11.1	38 02.7	−39.4	11.2	39 01.5	−39.2	11.4	77
78	31 28.6	−40.7	9.6	32 27.8	−40.6	9.7	33 26.9	−40.5	9.8	34 26.1	−40.4	9.9	35 25.1	−40.1	10.0	36 24.2	−40.0	10.1	37 23.3	−39.9	10.3	38 22.3	−39.7	10.4	78
79	30 47.9	−41.2	8.7	31 47.2	−41.0	8.8	32 46.4	−40.8	8.9	33 45.7	−40.7	9.0	34 45.0	−40.6	9.1	35 44.2	−40.4	9.2	36 43.4	−40.3	9.3	37 42.6	−40.1	9.5	79
80	30 06.7	−41.4	7.9	31 06.2	−41.4	8.0	32 05.6	−41.2	8.0	33 05.0	−41.1	8.1	34 04.4	−41.0	8.2	35 03.8	−40.9	8.3	36 03.1	−40.7	8.4	37 02.5	−40.6	8.5	80
81	29 25.3	−41.7	7.0	30 24.8	−41.6	7.1	31 24.4	−41.6	7.2	32 23.9	−41.4	7.3	33 23.4	−41.3	7.3	34 22.9	−41.2	7.4	35 22.4	−41.1	7.5	36 21.9	−41.0	7.6	81
82	28 43.6	−42.1	6.2	29 43.2	−41.9	6.3	30 42.8	−41.8	6.3	31 42.5	−41.8	6.4	32 42.1	−41.7	6.5	33 41.7	−41.6	6.6	34 41.3	−41.5	6.6	35 40.9	−41.4	6.7	82
83	28 01.5	−42.3	5.4	29 01.3	−42.3	5.5	30 01.0	−42.2	5.5	31 00.7	−42.1	5.6	32 00.4	−42.0	5.6	33 00.1	−41.9	5.7	33 59.8	−41.8	5.8	34 59.5	−41.7	5.8	83
84	27 19.2	−42.6	4.6	28 19.0	−42.5	4.6	29 18.8	−42.5	4.7	30 18.6	−42.4	4.7	31 18.4	−42.3	4.8	32 18.2	−42.3	4.8	33 18.0	−42.2	4.9	34 17.8	−42.2	5.0	84
85	26 36.6	−42.8	3.8	27 36.5	−42.8	3.8	28 36.3	−42.7	3.9	29 36.2	−42.7	3.9	30 36.1	−42.7	4.0	31 35.9	−42.6	4.0	32 35.8	−42.6	4.0	33 35.6	−42.5	4.1	85
86	25 53.8	−43.1	3.0	26 53.7	−43.1	3.1	27 53.6	−43.0	3.1	28 53.5	−43.0	3.1	29 53.4	−42.9	3.1	30 53.3	−42.9	3.2	31 53.2	−42.8	3.2	32 53.1	−42.8	3.2	86
87	25 10.7	−43.4	2.3	26 10.6	−43.3	2.3	27 10.6	−43.3	2.3	28 10.5	−43.2	2.3	29 10.5	−43.2	2.3	30 10.4	−43.2	2.4	31 10.4	−43.2	2.4	32 10.3	−43.1	2.4	87
88	24 27.3	−43.5	1.5	25 27.3	−43.5	1.5	26 27.3	−43.5	1.5	27 27.3	−43.5	1.5	28 27.3	−43.5	1.6	29 27.2	−43.5	1.6	30 27.2	−43.5	1.6	31 27.2	−43.5	1.6	88
89	23 43.8	−43.8	0.7	24 43.8	−43.8	0.8	25 43.8	−43.8	0.8	26 43.8	−43.8	0.8	27 43.8	−43.8	0.8	28 43.7	−43.7	0.8	29 43.7	−43.7	0.8	30 43.7	−43.7	0.8	89
90	23 00.0	−44.0	0.0	24 00.0	−44.0	0.0	25 00.0	−44.0	0.0	26 00.0	−44.0	0.0	27 00.0	−44.0	0.0	28 00.0	−44.0	0.0	29 00.0	−44.0	0.0	30 00.0	−44.0	0.0	90
	23°			24°			25°			26°			27°			28°			29°			30°			

43°, 317° L.H.A. LATITUDE SAME NAME AS DECLINATION

270

LATITUDE **CONTRARY** NAME TO DECLINATION — L.H.A. 43°, 317°

Dec.	23°			24°			25°			26°			27°			28°			29°			30°			Dec.
	Hc	d	Z	Hc	d	Z	Hc	d	Z	Hc	d	Z	Hc	d	Z	Hc	d	Z	Hc	d	Z	Hc	d	Z	
°	° ′	′	°	° ′	′	°	° ′	′	°	° ′	′	°	° ′	′	°	° ′	′	°	° ′	′	°	° ′	′	°	°
0	42 18.9	-32.0	112.7	41 55.4	-33.2	113.6	41 31.0	-34.2	114.4	41 05.8	-35.2	115.2	40 39.9	-36.2	116.0	40 13.3	-37.2	116.7	39 46.0	-38.1	117.5	39 18.0	-39.1	118.2	0
1	41 46.9	-32.7	113.9	41 22.2	-33.7	114.7	40 56.8	-34.8	115.5	40 30.6	-35.8	116.2	40 03.7	-36.7	117.0	39 36.1	-37.7	117.7	39 07.9	-38.6	118.5	38 38.9	-39.5	119.2	1
2	41 14.2	-33.4	115.0	40 48.5	-34.4	115.8	40 22.0	-35.4	116.5	39 54.8	-36.3	117.3	39 27.0	-37.3	118.0	38 58.4	-38.2	118.8	38 29.3	-39.1	119.5	37 59.4	-39.9	120.1	2
3	40 40.8	-33.9	116.1	40 14.1	-35.0	116.9	39 46.6	-35.9	117.6	39 18.5	-36.9	118.3	38 49.7	-37.8	119.0	38 20.2	-38.6	119.7	37 50.2	-39.6	120.4	37 19.5	-40.4	121.1	3
4	40 06.9	-34.6	117.2	39 39.1	-35.5	117.9	39 10.7	-36.5	118.6	38 41.6	-37.4	119.3	38 11.9	-38.3	120.0	37 41.6	-39.2	120.7	37 10.6	-40.0	121.4	36 39.1	-40.8	122.0	4
5	39 32.3	-35.1	118.2	39 03.6	-36.1	119.0	38 34.2	-37.0	119.7	38 04.2	-37.9	120.3	37 33.6	-38.8	121.0	37 02.4	-39.6	121.7	36 30.6	-40.4	122.3	35 58.3	-41.2	122.9	5
6	38 57.2	-35.7	119.3	38 27.5	-36.6	120.0	37 57.2	-37.5	120.7	37 26.3	-38.3	121.3	36 54.8	-39.2	122.0	36 22.8	-40.0	122.6	35 50.2	-40.8	123.2	35 17.1	-41.6	123.8	6
7	38 21.5	-36.2	120.3	37 50.9	-37.1	121.0	37 19.7	-38.0	121.6	36 48.0	-38.9	122.3	36 15.6	-39.6	122.9	35 42.8	-40.5	123.5	35 09.4	-41.3	124.1	34 35.5	-42.0	124.7	7
8	37 45.3	-36.7	121.3	37 13.8	-37.6	122.0	36 41.7	-38.4	122.6	36 09.1	-39.3	123.2	35 36.0	-40.1	123.8	35 02.3	-40.8	124.4	34 28.1	-41.6	125.0	33 53.5	-42.4	125.6	8
9	37 08.6	-37.3	122.3	36 36.2	-38.1	123.0	36 03.3	-38.9	123.6	35 29.8	-39.6	124.2	34 55.9	-40.5	124.8	34 21.5	-41.3	125.3	33 46.5	-41.9	125.9	33 11.1	-42.6	126.4	9
10	36 31.3	-37.6	123.3	35 58.1	-38.5	123.9	35 24.4	-39.3	124.5	34 50.2	-40.2	125.1	34 15.4	-40.8	125.6	33 40.2	-41.6	126.2	33 04.6	-42.3	126.7	32 28.5	-43.0	127.2	10
11	35 53.7	-38.2	124.3	35 19.6	-38.9	124.9	34 45.1	-39.8	125.4	34 10.0	-40.4	126.0	33 34.6	-41.3	126.5	32 58.6	-41.9	127.1	32 22.3	-42.7	127.6	31 45.5	-43.3	128.1	11
12	35 15.5	-38.6	125.2	34 40.7	-39.4	125.8	34 05.3	-40.1	126.3	33 29.6	-40.9	126.9	32 53.3	-41.6	127.4	32 16.7	-42.3	127.9	31 39.6	-42.9	128.4	31 02.2	-43.7	128.9	12
13	34 36.9	-39.0	126.2	34 01.3	-39.8	126.7	33 25.2	-40.5	127.2	32 48.7	-41.2	127.8	32 11.7	-41.9	128.3	31 34.4	-42.6	128.7	30 56.7	-43.3	129.2	30 18.5	-43.9	129.7	13
14	33 57.9	-39.4	127.1	33 21.5	-40.1	127.6	32 44.7	-40.9	128.1	32 07.5	-41.6	128.6	31 29.8	-42.2	129.1	30 51.8	-42.9	129.6	30 13.4	-43.6	130.0	29 34.6	-44.1	130.5	14
15	33 18.5	-39.8	128.0	32 41.4	-40.5	128.5	32 03.8	-41.2	129.0	31 25.9	-41.9	129.5	30 47.6	-42.6	129.9	30 08.9	-43.2	130.4	29 29.8	-43.8	130.8	28 50.5	-44.5	131.2	15
16	32 38.7	-40.2	128.9	32 00.9	-40.9	129.4	31 22.6	-41.5	129.8	30 44.0	-42.2	130.3	30 05.0	-42.9	130.7	29 25.7	-43.5	131.2	28 46.0	-44.1	131.6	28 06.0	-44.7	132.0	16
17	31 58.5	-40.5	129.7	31 20.0	-41.2	130.2	30 41.1	-41.9	130.7	30 01.8	-42.5	131.1	29 22.1	-43.1	131.5	28 42.2	-43.8	132.0	28 01.9	-44.3	132.4	27 21.3	-44.9	132.8	17
18	31 18.0	-40.9	130.6	30 38.8	-41.6	131.1	29 59.2	-42.2	131.5	29 19.3	-42.9	131.9	28 39.0	-43.4	132.3	27 58.4	-44.0	132.7	27 17.6	-44.6	133.1	26 36.4	-45.2	133.5	18
19	30 37.1	-41.2	131.5	29 57.2	-41.8	131.9	29 17.0	-42.5	132.3	28 36.4	-43.1	132.7	27 55.6	-43.7	133.1	27 14.4	-44.3	133.5	26 33.0	-44.9	133.9	25 51.2	-45.3	134.2	19
20	29 55.9	-41.5	132.3	29 15.4	-42.2	132.7	28 34.5	-42.7	133.1	27 53.3	-43.3	133.5	27 11.9	-44.0	133.9	26 30.1	-44.5	134.3	25 48.1	-45.0	134.6	25 05.9	-45.6	135.0	20
21	29 14.4	-41.8	133.1	28 33.2	-42.4	133.5	27 51.8	-43.1	133.9	27 10.0	-43.6	134.3	26 27.9	-44.1	134.7	25 45.6	-44.7	135.0	25 03.1	-45.3	135.3	24 20.3	-45.8	135.7	21
22	28 32.6	-42.1	134.0	27 50.8	-42.7	134.3	27 08.7	-43.3	134.7	26 26.4	-43.9	135.1	25 43.8	-44.4	135.4	25 00.9	-44.9	135.7	24 17.8	-45.4	136.1	23 34.5	-46.0	136.4	22
23	27 50.5	-42.4	134.8	27 08.1	-43.0	135.1	26 25.4	-43.5	135.5	25 42.5	-44.1	135.8	24 59.4	-44.7	136.2	24 16.0	-45.2	136.5	23 32.4	-45.7	136.8	22 48.5	-46.1	137.1	23
24	27 08.1	-42.7	135.6	26 25.1	-43.2	135.9	25 41.9	-43.8	136.3	24 58.4	-44.3	136.6	24 14.7	-44.8	136.9	23 30.8	-45.3	137.2	22 46.7	-45.8	137.5	22 02.4	-46.4	137.8	24
25	26 25.4	-42.9	136.4	25 41.9	-43.5	136.7	24 58.1	-44.0	137.0	24 14.1	-44.5	137.3	23 29.9	-45.0	137.6	22 45.5	-45.6	137.9	22 00.9	-46.1	138.2	21 16.0	-46.5	138.5	25
26	25 42.5	-43.1	137.1	24 58.4	-43.7	137.5	24 14.1	-44.2	137.8	23 29.6	-44.7	138.1	22 44.9	-45.3	138.3	21 59.9	-45.7	138.6	21 14.8	-46.2	138.9	20 29.5	-46.6	139.1	26
27	24 59.4	-43.4	137.9	24 14.7	-43.9	138.2	23 29.9	-44.4	138.5	22 44.9	-45.0	138.8	21 59.6	-45.4	139.1	21 14.2	-45.9	139.3	20 28.6	-46.3	139.6	19 42.9	-46.8	139.8	27
28	24 16.0	-43.6	138.7	23 30.8	-44.1	139.0	22 45.5	-44.6	139.2	21 59.9	-45.1	139.5	21 14.2	-45.6	139.8	20 28.3	-46.0	140.0	19 42.3	-46.5	140.2	18 56.1	-46.9	140.5	28
29	23 32.4	-43.9	139.4	22 46.7	-44.3	139.7	22 00.9	-44.9	140.0	21 14.8	-45.3	140.2	20 28.6	-45.7	140.5	19 42.3	-46.2	140.7	18 55.8	-46.6	140.9	18 09.2	-47.1	141.1	29
30	22 48.5	-44.0	140.2	22 02.4	-44.6	140.4	21 16.0	-45.0	140.7	20 29.5	-45.4	140.9	19 42.9	-45.9	141.1	18 56.1	-46.3	141.4	18 09.2	-46.8	141.6	17 22.1	-47.2	141.8	30
31	22 04.5	-44.2	140.9	21 17.8	-44.7	141.1	20 31.0	-45.1	141.4	19 44.1	-45.6	141.6	18 57.0	-46.1	141.8	18 09.8	-46.5	142.0	17 22.4	-46.9	142.2	16 34.9	-47.3	142.4	31
32	21 20.3	-44.5	141.6	20 33.1	-44.8	141.9	19 45.9	-45.3	142.1	18 58.5	-45.8	142.3	18 10.9	-46.1	142.5	17 23.3	-46.6	142.7	16 35.5	-47.0	142.9	15 47.6	-47.4	143.1	32
33	20 35.8	-44.6	142.3	19 48.3	-45.1	142.6	19 00.6	-45.5	142.8	18 12.7	-45.9	143.0	17 24.8	-46.4	143.2	16 36.7	-46.8	143.4	15 48.5	-47.2	143.5	15 00.2	-47.5	143.7	33
34	19 51.2	-44.7	143.0	19 03.2	-45.2	143.3	18 15.1	-45.6	143.5	17 26.8	-46.0	143.7	16 38.4	-46.4	143.8	15 49.9	-46.8	144.0	15 01.3	-47.2	144.2	14 12.7	-47.7	144.3	34
35	19 06.5	-44.9	143.8	18 18.0	-45.3	144.0	17 29.5	-45.8	144.1	16 40.8	-46.2	144.3	15 52.0	-46.6	144.5	15 03.1	-47.0	144.7	14 14.1	-47.3	144.8	13 25.0	-47.7	144.9	35
36	18 21.6	-45.1	144.5	17 32.7	-45.5	144.6	16 43.7	-45.9	144.8	15 54.6	-46.3	145.0	15 05.4	-46.7	145.1	14 16.1	-47.0	145.3	13 26.8	-47.5	145.4	12 37.3	-47.8	145.6	36
37	17 36.5	-45.2	145.1	16 47.2	-45.6	145.3	15 57.8	-46.0	145.5	15 08.3	-46.4	145.6	14 18.7	-46.8	145.8	13 29.1	-47.2	145.9	12 39.3	-47.5	146.1	11 49.5	-47.9	146.2	37
38	16 51.3	-45.4	145.8	16 01.6	-45.8	146.0	15 11.8	-46.2	146.2	14 21.9	-46.5	146.3	13 31.9	-46.8	146.4	12 41.9	-47.2	146.6	11 51.8	-47.6	146.7	11 01.6	-47.9	146.8	38
39	16 05.9	-45.5	146.5	15 15.8	-45.8	146.7	14 25.6	-46.2	146.8	13 35.4	-46.6	147.0	12 45.1	-47.0	147.1	11 54.7	-47.4	147.2	11 04.2	-47.7	147.3	10 13.7	-48.1	147.4	39
40	15 20.4	-45.6	147.2	14 30.0	-46.0	147.3	13 39.4	-46.3	147.5	12 48.8	-46.7	147.6	11 58.1	-47.1	147.7	11 07.3	-47.4	147.8	10 16.5	-47.7	147.9	9 25.6	-48.0	148.0	40
41	14 34.8	-45.7	147.9	13 44.0	-46.1	148.0	12 53.1	-46.5	148.1	12 02.1	-46.8	148.2	11 11.0	-47.1	148.4	10 19.9	-47.5	148.5	9 28.8	-47.9	148.5	8 37.6	-48.2	148.6	41
42	13 49.1	-45.8	148.5	12 57.9	-46.2	148.7	12 06.6	-46.5	148.8	11 15.3	-46.9	148.9	10 23.9	-47.2	149.0	9 32.4	-47.5	149.1	8 40.9	-47.8	149.2	7 49.4	-48.2	149.2	42
43	13 03.3	-46.0	149.2	12 11.7	-46.3	149.3	11 20.1	-46.6	149.4	10 28.4	-47.0	149.5	9 36.7	-47.3	149.6	8 44.9	-47.6	149.7	7 53.1	-48.0	149.8	7 01.2	-48.2	149.8	43
44	12 17.3	-46.0	149.9	11 25.4	-46.3	150.0	10 33.5	-46.7	150.1	9 41.4	-47.0	150.2	8 49.4	-47.4	150.2	7 57.3	-47.7	150.3	7 05.1	-47.9	150.4	6 13.0	-48.3	150.4	44
45	11 31.3	-46.1	150.5	10 39.1	-46.5	150.6	9 46.8	-46.8	150.7	8 54.4	-47.1	150.8	8 02.0	-47.4	150.9	7 09.6	-47.7	150.9	6 17.2	-48.0	151.0	5 24.7	-48.3	151.0	45
46	10 45.2	-46.2	151.2	9 52.6	-46.5	151.3	9 00.0	-46.8	151.3	8 07.3	-47.1	151.4	7 14.6	-47.4	151.5	6 21.9	-47.7	151.5	5 29.2	-48.1	151.6	4 36.4	-48.4	151.6	46
47	9 59.0	-46.2	151.8	9 06.1	-46.6	151.9	8 13.2	-46.9	152.0	7 20.2	-47.2	152.0	6 27.2	-47.5	152.1	5 34.2	-47.8	152.1	4 41.1	-48.1	152.2	3 48.0	-48.3	152.2	47
48	9 12.8	-46.4	152.5	8 19.5	-46.6	152.5	7 26.3	-47.0	152.6	6 33.0	-47.2	152.7	5 39.7	-47.5	152.7	4 46.4	-47.9	152.7	3 53.0	-48.1	152.8	2 59.7	-48.4	152.8	48
49	8 26.4	-46.4	153.1	7 32.9	-46.7	153.2	6 39.3	-46.9	153.2	5 45.8	-47.3	153.3	4 52.2	-47.6	153.3	3 58.5	-47.8	153.4	3 04.9	-48.1	153.4	2 11.3	-48.4	153.4	49
50	7 40.0	-46.4	153.7	6 46.2	-46.7	153.8	5 52.4	-47.1	153.9	4 58.5	-47.3	153.9	4 04.6	-47.6	153.9	3 10.7	-47.9	154.0	2 16.8	-48.2	154.0	1 22.9	-48.5	154.0	50
51	6 53.6	-46.5	154.4	5 59.5	-46.8	154.4	5 05.3	-47.0	154.5	4 11.2	-47.4	154.5	3 17.0	-47.6	154.5	2 22.8	-47.9	154.6	1 28.6	-48.1	154.6	0 34.4	-48.4	154.6	51
52	6 07.1	-46.6	155.0	5 12.7	-46.9	155.1	4 18.3	-47.1	155.1	3 23.8	-47.3	155.1	2 29.4	-47.6	155.1	1 34.9	-47.9	155.2	0 40.5	-48.2	155.2	0 14.0	+48.4	24.8	52
53	5 20.5	-46.6	155.7	4 25.8	-46.8	155.7	3 31.2	-47.2	155.7	2 36.5	-47.4	155.7	1 41.8	-47.7	155.8	0 47.0	-47.9	155.8	0 07.7	+48.1	24.2	1 02.4	+48.4	24.2	53
54	4 33.9	-46.6	156.3	3 39.0	-46.9	156.3	2 44.0	-47.1	156.3	1 49.1	-47.4	156.4	0 54.1	-47.6	156.4	0 00.9	+47.9	23.6	0 55.8	+48.2	23.6	1 50.8	+48.4	23.6	54
55	3 47.3	-46.6	156.9	2 52.1	-46.9	156.9	1 56.9	-47.2	157.0	1 01.7	-47.4	157.0	0 06.5	-47.7	157.0	0 48.8	+47.9	23.0	1 44.0	+48.1	23.0	2 39.2	+48.4	23.1	55
56	3 00.7	-46.7	157.5	2 05.2	-46.9	157.6	1 09.7	-47.1	157.6	0 14.3	-47.4	157.6	0 41.2	+47.6	22.4	1 36.7	+47.8	22.4	2 32.1	+48.1	22.4	3 27.6	+48.3	22.5	56
57	2 14.0	-46.7	158.2	1 18.3	-46.9	158.2	0 22.6	-47.2	158.2	0 33.1	+47.4	21.8	1 28.8	+47.7	21.8	2 24.5	+47.9	21.8	3 20.2	+48.1	21.8	4 15.9	+48.4	21.9	57
58	1 27.3	-46.7	158.8	0 31.4	-47.0	158.8	0 24.6	+47.2	21.2	1 20.5	+47.4	21.2	2 16.5	+47.6	21.2	3 12.4	+47.9	21.2	4 08.3	+48.1	21.2	5 04.3	+48.3	21.3	58
59	0 40.6	-46.7	159.4	0 15.6	+46.9	20.6	1 11.8	+47.1	20.6	2 07.9	+47.4	20.6	3 04.1	+47.6	20.6	4 00.3	+47.8	20.6	4 56.4	+48.1	20.6	5 52.6	+48.2	20.7	59
60	0 06.1	+46.7	19.9	1 02.5	+46.9	19.9	1 58.9	+47.1	20.0	2 55.3	+47.4	20.0	3 51.7	+47.6	20.0	4 48.1	+47.8	20.0	5 44.5	+48.0	20.0	6 40.8	+48.2	20.1	60
61	0 52.8	+46.7	19.3	1 49.4	+46.9	19.3	2 46.0	+47.2	19.3	3 42.7	+47.3	19.3	4 39.3	+47.5	19.4	5 35.9	+47.7	19.4	6 32.5	+47.9	19.4	7 29.0	+48.2	19.5	61
62	1 39.5	+46.7	18.7	2 36.3	+46.9	18.7	3 33.2	+47.1	18.7	4 30.0	+47.3	18.7	5 26.8	+47.5	18.8	6 23.6	+47.7	18.8	7 20.4	+47.9	18.8	8 17.2	+48.1	18.9	62
63	2 26.2	+46.7	18.1	3 23.2	+46.9	18.1	4 20.3	+47.0	18.1	5 17.3	+47.3	18.1	6 14.3	+47.5	18.1	7 11.3	+47.7	18.2	8 08.3	+47.9	18.2	9 05.3	+48.1	18.3	63
64	3 12.9	+46.6	17.4	4 10.1	+46.8	17.4	5 07.3	+47.1	17.5	6 04.6	+47.2	17.5	7 01.8	+47.4	17.5	7 59.0	+47.6	17.6	8 56.2	+47.8	17.6	9 53.4	+47.9	17.7	64
65	3 59.5	+46.6	16.8	4 56.9	+46.8	16.8	5 54.4	+47.0	16.8	6 51.8	+47.2	16.9	7 49.2	+47.4	16.9	8 46.6	+47.5	17.0	9 44.0	+47.7	17.0	10 41.3	+48.0	17.1	65
66	4 46.1	+46.6	16.2	5 43.7	+46.8	16.2	6 41.4	+46.9	16.2	7 39.0	+47.1	16.3	8 36.6	+47.3	16.3	9 34.1	+47.5	16.3	10 31.7	+47.7	16.4	11 29.3	+47.8	16.4	66
67	5 32.7	+46.5	15.5	6 30.5	+46.7	15.6	7 28.3	+46.9	15.6	8 26.1	+47.0	15.6	9 23.9	+47.2	15.7	10 21.6	+47.4	15.7	11 19.4	+47.5	15.8	12 17.1	+47.8	15.8	67
68	6 19.2	+46.5	14.9	7 17.2	+46.7	14.9	8 15.2	+46.8	15.0	9 13.1	+47.0	15.0	10 11.1	+47.2	15.0	11 09.0	+47.4	15.1	12 06.9	+47.5	15.1	13 04.9	+47.6	15.2	68
69	7 05.7	+46.5	14.3	8 03.9	+46.6	14.3	9 02.0	+46.8	14.3	10 00.1	+47.0	14.4	10 58.3	+47.0	14.4	11 56.4	+47.2	14.5	12 54.4	+47.5	14.5	13 52.5	+47.6	14.6	69
70	7 52.2	+46.3	13.6	8 50.5	+46.5	13.7	9 48.8	+46.7	13.7	10 47.1	+46.8	13.7	11 45.3	+47.0	13.8	12 43.6	+47.2	13.8	13 41.9	+47.3	13.9	14 40.1	+47.5	14.0	70
71	8 38.5	+46.4	13.0	9 37.0	+46.5	13.0	10 35.5	+46.6	13.1	11 33.9	+46.8	13.1	12 32.3	+46.9	13.1	13 30.8	+47.0	13.2	14 29.2	+47.2	13.3	15 27.6	+47.3	13.3	71
72	9 24.9	+46.2	12.3	10 23.5	+46.4	12.4	11 22.1	+46.5	12.4	12 20.7	+46.6	12.5	13 19.2	+46.9	12.5	14 17.8	+47.0	12.6	15 16.4	+47.1	12.6	16 14.9	+47.3	12.7	72
73	10 11.1	+46.2	11.7	11 09.9	+46.3	11.7	12 08.6	+46.4	11.8	13 07.3	+46.6	11.8	14 06.1	+46.7	11.9	15 04.8	+46.8	11.9	16 03.5	+47.0	12.0	17 02.2	+47.1	12.0	73
74	10 57.3	+46.1	11.0	11 56.2	+46.2	11.1	12 55.0	+46.4	11.1	13 53.9	+46.5	11.2	14 52.8	+46.6	11.2	15 51.6	+46.7	11.3	16 50.5	+46.8	11.3	17 49.3	+47.0	11.4	74
75	11 43.4	+46.0	10.4	12 42.4	+46.1	10.4	13 41.4	+46.2	10.5	14 40.4	+46.3	10.5	15 39.4	+46.5	10.6	16 38.3	+46.7	10.6	17 37.3	+46.7	10.7	18 36.3	+46.8	10.7	75
76	12 29.4	+45.9	9.7	13 28.5	+46.0	9.8	14 27.6	+46.2	9.8	15 26.7	+46.3	9.9	16 25.9	+46.3	9.9	17 25.0	+46.4	10.0	18 24.0	+46.6	10.0	19 23.1	+46.7	10.1	76
77	13 15.3	+45.8	9.1	14 14.5	+45.9	9.1	15 13.8	+46.0	9.1	16 13.0	+46.1	9.2	17 12.2	+46.2	9.2	18 11.4	+46.4	9.3	19 10.6	+46.5	9.3	20 09.8	+46.6	9.4	77
78	14 01.1	+45.7	8.4	15 00.4	+45.8	8.4	15 59.8	+45.9	8.5	16 59.1	+46.0	8.5	17 58.4	+46.1	8.6	18 57.8	+46.2	8.6	19 57.1	+46.3	8.7	20 56.4	+46.4	8.7	78
79	14 46.8	+45.5	7.7	15 46.2	+45.7	7.8	16 45.7	+45.7	7.8	17 45.1	+45.8	7.9	18 44.5	+46.0	7.9	19 44.0	+46.0	7.9	20 43.4	+46.1	8.0	21 42.8	+46.2	8.1	79
80	15 32.3	+45.5	7.1	16 31.9	+45.5	7.1	17 31.4	+45.6	7.1	18 30.9	+45.8	7.2	19 30.5	+45.8	7.2	20 30.0	+45.9	7.3	21 29.5	+46.0	7.3	22 29.0	+46.1	7.4	80
81	16 17.8	+45.3	6.4	17 17.4	+45.4	6.4	18 17.0	+45.5	6.5	19 16.7	+45.5	6.5	20 16.3	+45.6	6.5	21 15.9	+45.7	6.6	22 15.5	+45.8	6.6	23 15.1	+45.8	6.7	81
82	17 03.1	+45.2	5.7	18 02.8	+45.3	5.7	19 02.5	+45.3	5.8	20 02.2	+45.4	5.8	21 01.9	+45.4	5.8	22 01.6	+45.5	5.9	23 01.3	+45.6	5.9	24 00.9	+45.7	6.0	82
83	17 48.3	+45.0	5.0	18 48.1	+45.1	5.0	19 47.8	+45.2	5.1	20 47.6	+45.2	5.1	21 47.3	+45.3	5.1	22 47.1	+45.3	5.2	23 46.9	+45.4	5.2	24 46.6	+45.5	5.3	83
84	18 33.3	+44.9	4.3	19 33.2	+44.9	4.3	20 33.0	+45.0	4.4	21 32.8	+45.0	4.4	22 32.6	+45.1	4.4	23 32.4	+45.2	4.5	24 32.3	+45.2	4.5	25 32.1	+45.2	4.5	84
85	19 18.2	+44.7	3.6	20 18.1	+44.7	3.6	21 18.0	+44.8	3.7	22 17.8	+44.9	3.7	23 17.7	+44.9	3.7	24 17.6	+44.9	3.7	25 17.5	+44.9	3.8	26 17.3	+45.1	3.8	85
86	20 02.9	+44.6	2.9	21 02.8	+44.6	2.9	22 02.8	+44.6	2.9	23 02.7	+44.6	3.0	24 02.6	+44.7	3.0	25 02.5	+44.7	3.0	26 02.4	+44.8	3.0	27 02.4	+44.7	3.1	86
87	20 47.5	+44.3	2.2	21 47.4	+44.4	2.2	22 47.4	+44.4	2.2	23 47.3	+44.5	2.2	24 47.3	+44.5	2.3	25 47.2	+44.5	2.3	26 47.2	+44.5	2.3	27 47.1	+44.6	2.3	87
88	21 31.8	+44.2	1.5	22 31.8	+44.2	1.5	23 31.8	+44.2	1.5	24 31.8	+44.2	1.5	25 31.8	+44.2	1.5	26 31.7	+44.3	1.5	27 31.7	+44.3	1.5	28 31.7	+44.3	1.6	88
89	22 16.0	+44.0	0.7	23 16.0	+44.0	0.7	24 16.0	+44.0	0.7	25 16.0	+44.0	0.8	26 16.0	+44.0	0.8	27 16.0	+44.0	0.8	28 16.0	+44.0	0.8	29 16.0	+44.0	0.8	89
90	23 00.0	+43.8	0.0	24 00.0	+43.8	0.0	25 00.0	+43.8	0.0	26 00.0	+43.8	0.0	27 00.0	+43.8	0.0	28 00.0	+43.7	0.0	29 00.0	+43.7	0.0	30 00.0	+43.7	0.0	90
	23°			24°			25°			26°			27°			28°			29°			30°			

S. Lat. { L.H.A. greater than 180° ....Zn=180°–Z; L.H.A. less than 180°...........Zn=180°+Z

LATITUDE **SAME** NAME AS DECLINATION — L.H.A. 137°, 223°

44°, 316° L.H.A.
LATITUDE SAME NAME AS DECLINATION N. Lat. {L.H.A. greater than 180° .....Zn=Z; L.H.A. less than 180°............Zn=360°−Z}

Dec.	23° Hc	d	Z	24° Hc	d	Z	25° Hc	d	Z	26° Hc	d	Z	27° Hc	d	Z	28° Hc	d	Z	29° Hc	d	Z	30° Hc	d	Z	Dec.
°	° ′	′	°	° ′	′	°	° ′	′	°	° ′	′	°	° ′	′	°	° ′	′	°	° ′	′	°	° ′	′	°	°
0	41 27.9	+30.9	112.0	41 05.0	+32.0	112.8	40 41.3	+33.1	113.6	40 16.9	+34.1	114.4	39 51.7	+35.2	115.2	39 25.8	+36.2	115.9	38 59.2	+37.2	116.7	38 32.0	+38.1	117.4	0
1	41 58.8	+30.3	110.9	41 37.0	+31.4	111.7	41 14.4	+32.5	112.5	40 51.0	+33.6	113.3	40 26.9	+34.6	114.1	40 02.0	+35.6	114.9	39 36.4	+36.6	115.6	39 10.1	+37.6	116.4	1
2	42 29.1	+29.5	109.7	42 08.4	+30.7	110.6	41 46.9	+31.8	111.4	41 24.6	+32.9	112.2	41 01.5	+34.0	113.0	40 37.6	+35.1	113.8	40 13.0	+36.1	114.6	39 47.7	+37.0	115.4	2
3	42 58.6	+28.8	108.5	42 39.1	+30.0	109.4	42 18.7	+31.1	110.3	41 57.5	+32.3	111.1	41 35.5	+33.4	111.9	41 12.7	+34.4	112.8	40 49.1	+35.5	113.6	40 24.7	+36.5	114.3	3
4	43 27.4	+28.0	107.3	43 09.1	+29.2	108.2	42 49.8	+30.5	109.1	42 29.8	+31.5	110.0	42 08.9	+32.7	110.8	41 47.1	+33.8	111.7	41 24.6	+34.8	112.5	41 01.2	+35.9	113.3	4
5	43 55.4	+27.2	106.1	43 38.3	+28.4	107.0	43 20.3	+29.6	107.9	43 01.3	+30.9	108.8	42 41.6	+32.0	109.7	42 20.9	+33.2	110.6	41 59.4	+34.3	111.4	41 37.1	+35.4	112.2	5
6	44 22.6	+26.4	104.9	44 06.7	+27.7	105.8	43 49.9	+28.9	106.7	43 32.2	+30.1	107.6	43 13.6	+31.3	108.5	42 54.1	+32.4	109.4	42 33.7	+33.6	110.3	42 12.5	+34.6	111.1	6
7	44 49.0	+25.5	103.6	44 34.4	+26.8	104.6	44 18.8	+28.1	105.5	44 02.3	+29.4	106.4	43 44.9	+30.5	107.4	43 26.5	+31.8	108.3	43 07.3	+32.9	109.2	42 47.1	+34.1	110.0	7
8	45 14.5	+24.7	102.3	45 01.2	+26.0	103.3	44 46.9	+27.3	104.3	44 31.7	+28.5	105.2	44 15.4	+29.8	106.2	43 58.3	+31.0	107.1	43 40.2	+32.2	108.0	43 21.2	+33.3	108.9	8
9	45 39.2	+23.8	101.0	45 27.2	+25.2	102.0	45 14.2	+26.5	103.0	45 00.2	+27.8	104.0	44 45.2	+29.1	104.9	44 29.3	+30.2	105.9	44 12.4	+31.4	106.8	43 54.5	+32.7	107.8	9
10	46 03.0	+22.9	99.7	45 52.4	+24.2	100.7	45 40.7	+25.6	101.7	45 28.0	+26.9	102.7	45 14.3	+28.2	103.7	44 59.5	+29.5	104.7	44 43.8	+30.8	105.6	44 27.2	+31.9	106.6	10
11	46 25.9	+21.9	98.4	46 16.6	+23.3	99.4	46 06.3	+24.6	100.4	45 54.9	+26.0	101.4	45 42.5	+27.3	102.5	45 29.0	+28.7	103.4	45 14.6	+29.9	104.4	44 59.1	+31.2	105.4	11
12	46 47.8	+20.9	97.0	46 39.9	+22.4	98.1	46 30.9	+23.8	99.1	46 20.9	+25.1	100.1	46 09.8	+26.5	101.2	45 57.7	+27.8	102.2	45 44.5	+29.1	103.2	45 30.3	+30.4	104.2	12
13	47 08.7	+20.0	95.6	47 02.3	+21.3	96.7	46 54.7	+22.8	97.8	46 46.0	+24.3	98.8	46 36.3	+25.6	99.9	46 25.5	+26.9	100.9	46 13.6	+28.3	101.9	46 00.7	+29.5	102.9	13
14	47 28.7	+18.9	94.2	47 23.6	+20.4	95.3	47 17.5	+21.8	96.4	47 10.3	+23.2	97.5	47 01.9	+24.6	98.5	46 52.4	+26.1	99.6	46 41.9	+27.4	100.7	46 30.2	+28.8	101.7	14
15	47 47.6	+17.9	92.8	47 44.0	+19.4	93.9	47 39.3	+20.9	95.0	47 33.5	+22.3	96.1	47 26.5	+23.8	97.2	47 18.5	+25.1	98.3	47 09.3	+26.5	99.4	46 59.0	+27.8	100.4	15
16	48 05.5	+16.8	91.4	48 03.4	+18.3	92.5	48 00.2	+19.8	93.6	47 55.8	+21.3	94.7	47 50.3	+22.7	95.8	47 43.6	+24.1	96.9	47 35.8	+25.5	98.0	47 26.8	+27.0	99.1	16
17	48 22.3	+15.7	90.0	48 21.7	+17.2	91.1	48 20.0	+18.7	92.2	48 17.1	+20.2	93.3	48 13.0	+21.7	94.5	48 07.7	+23.2	95.6	48 01.3	+24.6	96.7	47 53.8	+26.0	97.8	17
18	48 38.0	+14.6	88.5	48 38.9	+16.2	89.6	48 38.7	+17.7	90.8	48 37.3	+19.2	91.9	48 34.7	+20.7	93.1	48 30.9	+22.1	94.2	48 25.9	+23.6	95.3	48 19.8	+25.0	96.4	18
19	48 52.6	+13.4	87.0	48 55.1	+15.0	88.2	48 56.4	+16.5	89.3	48 56.5	+18.0	90.5	48 55.4	+19.6	91.6	48 53.0	+21.2	92.8	48 49.5	+22.6	93.9	48 44.8	+24.1	95.1	19
20	49 06.0	+12.4	85.6	49 10.1	+13.9	86.7	49 12.9	+15.5	87.9	49 14.5	+17.0	89.0	49 15.0	+18.5	90.2	49 14.2	+20.0	91.3	49 12.1	+21.6	92.5	49 08.9	+23.0	93.7	20
21	49 18.4	+11.1	84.1	49 24.0	+12.7	85.2	49 28.4	+14.2	86.4	49 31.5	+15.9	87.6	49 33.5	+17.4	88.7	49 34.2	+18.9	89.9	49 33.7	+20.4	91.1	49 31.9	+22.0	92.2	21
22	49 29.5	+10.0	82.5	49 36.7	+11.5	83.7	49 42.6	+13.1	84.9	49 47.4	+14.6	86.1	49 50.9	+16.2	87.2	49 53.1	+17.8	88.4	49 54.1	+19.4	89.6	49 53.9	+20.9	90.8	22
23	49 39.5	+8.7	81.0	49 48.2	+10.3	82.2	49 55.7	+12.0	83.4	50 02.0	+13.5	84.6	50 07.1	+15.1	85.7	50 10.9	+16.7	86.9	50 13.5	+18.2	88.1	50 14.8	+19.8	89.3	23
24	49 48.2	+7.5	79.5	49 58.5	+9.2	80.7	50 07.7	+10.7	81.8	50 15.5	+12.3	83.0	50 22.2	+13.9	84.2	50 27.6	+15.5	85.4	50 31.7	+17.1	86.6	50 34.6	+18.6	87.9	24
25	49 55.7	+6.3	78.0	50 07.7	+7.8	79.1	50 18.4	+9.4	80.3	50 27.8	+11.1	81.5	50 36.1	+12.7	82.7	50 43.1	+14.3	83.9	50 48.8	+15.9	85.1	50 53.2	+17.5	86.4	25
26	50 02.0	+5.1	76.4	50 15.5	+6.7	77.6	50 27.8	+8.3	78.8	50 38.9	+9.9	80.0	50 48.8	+11.4	81.2	50 57.4	+13.0	82.4	51 04.7	+14.6	83.6	51 10.7	+16.3	84.8	26
27	50 07.1	+3.8	74.9	50 22.2	+5.4	76.0	50 36.1	+7.0	77.2	50 48.8	+8.6	78.4	51 00.2	+10.2	79.6	51 10.4	+11.8	80.8	51 19.3	+13.5	82.1	51 27.0	+15.0	83.3	27
28	50 10.9	+2.6	73.3	50 27.6	+4.1	74.5	50 43.1	+5.7	75.6	50 57.4	+7.3	76.8	51 10.4	+8.9	78.0	51 22.2	+10.6	79.3	51 32.8	+12.1	80.5	51 42.0	+13.8	81.7	28
29	50 13.5	+1.3	71.7	50 31.7	+2.9	72.9	50 48.8	+4.4	74.1	51 04.7	+6.0	75.3	51 19.3	+7.7	76.5	51 32.8	+9.2	77.7	51 44.9	+10.9	78.9	51 55.8	+12.6	80.2	29
30	50 14.8	+0.1	70.2	50 34.6	+1.6	71.3	50 53.2	+3.2	72.5	51 10.7	+4.8	73.7	51 27.0	+6.3	74.9	51 42.0	+8.0	76.1	51 55.8	+9.6	77.3	52 08.4	+11.2	78.6	30
31	50 14.9	-1.2	68.6	50 36.2	+0.3	69.7	50 56.4	+1.9	70.9	51 15.5	+3.4	72.1	51 33.3	+5.1	73.3	51 50.0	+6.7	74.5	52 05.4	+8.3	75.7	52 19.6	+9.9	77.0	31
32	50 13.7	-2.5	67.1	50 36.5	-0.9	68.2	50 58.3	+0.6	69.3	51 18.9	+2.2	70.5	51 38.4	+3.7	71.7	51 56.7	+5.3	72.9	52 13.7	+7.0	74.1	52 29.5	+8.6	75.4	32
33	50 11.2	-3.7	65.5	50 35.6	-2.2	66.6	50 58.9	-0.7	67.7	51 21.1	+0.8	68.9	51 42.1	+2.4	70.1	52 02.0	+4.0	71.3	52 20.7	+5.6	72.5	52 38.1	+7.2	73.7	33
34	50 07.5	-5.0	63.9	50 33.4	-3.5	65.0	50 58.2	-2.0	66.1	51 21.9	-0.5	67.3	51 44.5	+1.1	68.4	52 06.0	+2.6	69.6	52 26.3	+4.2	70.9	52 45.3	+5.9	72.1	34
35	50 02.5	-6.2	62.4	50 29.9	-4.8	63.5	50 56.2	-3.3	64.5	51 21.4	-1.8	65.7	51 45.6	-0.3	66.8	52 08.6	+1.3	68.0	52 30.5	+2.9	69.2	52 51.2	+4.5	70.4	35
36	49 56.3	-7.4	60.8	50 25.1	-6.0	61.9	50 52.9	-4.6	63.0	51 19.6	-3.0	64.1	51 45.3	-1.5	65.2	52 09.9	0.0	66.4	52 33.4	+1.5	67.6	52 55.7	+3.1	68.8	36
37	49 48.9	-8.6	59.3	50 19.1	-7.3	60.3	50 48.3	-5.8	61.4	51 16.6	-4.4	62.5	51 43.8	-2.9	63.6	52 09.9	-1.4	64.7	52 34.9	+0.2	65.9	52 58.8	+1.8	67.1	37
38	49 40.3	-9.9	57.8	50 11.8	-8.5	58.8	50 42.5	-7.1	59.8	51 12.2	-5.7	60.9	51 40.9	-4.3	62.0	52 08.5	-2.7	63.1	52 35.1	-1.2	64.3	53 00.6	+0.3	65.5	38
39	49 30.4	-11.0	56.2	50 03.3	-9.7	57.2	50 35.4	-8.4	58.2	51 06.5	-7.0	59.3	51 36.6	-5.5	60.4	52 05.8	-4.1	61.5	52 33.9	-2.6	62.6	53 00.9	-1.0	63.8	39
40	49 19.4	-12.2	54.7	49 53.6	-10.9	55.7	50 27.0	-9.6	56.7	50 59.5	-8.2	57.7	51 31.1	-6.9	58.8	52 01.7	-5.4	59.9	52 31.3	-3.9	61.0	52 59.9	-2.5	62.2	40
41	49 07.2	-13.4	53.2	49 42.7	-12.1	54.2	50 17.4	-10.8	55.1	50 51.3	-9.5	56.1	51 24.2	-8.1	57.2	51 56.3	-6.7	58.3	52 27.4	-5.3	59.4	52 57.4	-3.8	60.5	41
42	48 53.8	-14.5	51.7	49 30.6	-13.3	52.7	50 06.6	-12.0	53.6	50 41.8	-10.8	54.6	51 16.1	-9.4	55.6	51 49.6	-8.1	56.6	52 22.1	-6.7	57.7	52 53.6	-5.2	58.8	42
43	48 39.3	-15.6	50.3	49 17.3	-14.4	51.2	49 54.6	-13.3	52.1	50 31.0	-11.9	53.0	51 06.7	-10.7	54.0	51 41.5	-9.3	55.0	52 15.4	-7.9	56.1	52 48.4	-6.5	57.2	43
44	48 23.7	-16.7	48.8	49 02.9	-15.6	49.7	49 41.3	-14.3	50.6	50 19.1	-13.2	51.5	50 56.0	-11.9	52.5	51 32.2	-10.6	53.5	52 07.5	-9.3	54.5	52 41.9	-7.9	55.5	44
45	48 07.0	-17.8	47.4	48 47.3	-16.7	48.2	49 27.0	-15.6	49.1	50 05.9	-14.4	50.0	50 44.1	-13.1	50.9	51 21.6	-11.9	51.9	51 58.2	-10.6	52.9	52 34.0	-9.3	53.9	45
46	47 49.2	-18.8	45.9	48 30.6	-17.7	46.8	49 11.4	-16.6	47.6	49 51.5	-15.5	48.5	50 31.0	-14.4	49.4	51 09.7	-13.2	50.3	51 47.6	-11.9	51.3	52 24.7	-10.5	52.3	46
47	47 30.4	-19.9	44.5	48 12.9	-18.9	45.3	48 54.8	-17.8	46.1	49 36.0	-16.6	47.0	50 16.6	-15.5	47.8	50 56.5	-14.3	48.8	51 35.7	-13.1	49.7	52 14.2	-11.9	50.7	47
48	47 10.5	-20.8	43.1	47 54.0	-19.8	43.9	48 37.0	-18.8	44.7	49 19.4	-17.8	45.5	50 01.1	-16.7	46.3	50 42.2	-15.6	47.2	51 22.6	-14.4	48.1	52 02.3	-13.2	49.1	48
49	46 49.7	-21.9	41.8	47 34.2	-20.9	42.5	48 18.2	-19.9	43.2	49 01.6	-18.9	44.0	49 44.4	-17.8	44.8	50 26.6	-16.7	45.7	51 08.2	-15.6	46.6	51 49.1	-14.4	47.5	49
50	46 27.8	-22.7	40.4	47 13.3	-21.9	41.1	47 58.3	-21.0	41.8	48 42.7	-19.9	42.6	49 26.6	-18.9	43.4	50 09.9	-17.9	44.2	50 52.6	-16.8	45.0	51 34.7	-15.7	45.9	50
51	46 05.1	-23.7	39.1	46 51.4	-22.8	39.7	47 37.3	-21.9	40.4	48 22.8	-21.0	41.2	49 07.7	-20.0	41.9	49 52.0	-19.0	42.7	50 35.8	-17.9	43.5	51 19.0	-16.8	44.4	51
52	45 41.4	-24.6	37.8	46 28.6	-23.8	38.4	47 15.4	-22.9	39.1	48 01.8	-22.0	39.8	48 47.7	-21.1	40.5	49 33.0	-20.1	41.2	50 17.9	-19.1	42.0	51 02.2	-18.1	42.9	52
53	45 16.8	-25.5	36.5	46 04.8	-24.6	37.1	46 52.5	-23.8	37.7	47 39.8	-23.0	38.4	48 26.6	-22.1	39.1	49 12.9	-21.1	39.8	49 58.8	-20.2	40.5	50 44.1	-19.2	41.3	53
54	44 51.3	-26.3	35.2	45 40.2	-25.6	35.8	46 28.7	-24.8	36.4	47 16.8	-24.0	37.0	48 04.5	-23.1	37.7	48 51.8	-22.2	38.4	49 38.6	-21.3	39.1	50 24.9	-20.3	39.8	54
55	44 25.0	-27.2	33.9	45 14.6	-26.4	34.5	46 03.9	-25.7	35.0	46 52.8	-24.8	35.7	47 41.4	-24.1	36.3	48 29.6	-23.3	37.0	49 17.3	-22.4	37.7	50 04.6	-21.5	38.4	55
56	43 57.8	-27.9	32.7	44 48.2	-27.3	33.2	45 38.2	-26.5	33.7	46 28.0	-25.8	34.3	47 17.3	-25.0	34.9	48 06.3	-24.2	35.6	48 54.9	-23.3	36.2	49 43.1	-22.5	36.9	56
57	43 29.9	-28.7	31.4	44 20.9	-28.0	31.9	45 11.7	-27.4	32.5	46 02.2	-26.7	33.0	46 52.3	-25.9	33.6	47 42.1	-25.2	34.2	48 31.6	-24.4	34.8	49 20.6	-23.6	35.5	57
58	43 01.2	-29.5	30.2	43 52.9	-28.8	30.7	44 44.3	-28.1	31.2	45 35.5	-27.5	31.7	46 26.4	-26.8	32.3	47 16.9	-26.0	32.9	48 07.2	-25.4	33.5	48 57.0	-24.5	34.1	58
59	42 31.7	-30.2	29.0	43 24.1	-29.6	29.5	44 16.2	-29.0	30.0	45 08.0	-28.3	30.5	45 59.6	-27.7	31.0	46 50.9	-27.0	31.5	47 41.8	-26.2	32.1	48 32.5	-25.6	32.7	59
60	42 01.5	-30.9	27.9	42 54.5	-30.4	28.3	43 47.2	-29.8	28.8	44 39.7	-29.2	29.2	45 31.9	-28.5	29.7	46 23.9	-27.9	30.2	47 15.6	-27.2	30.8	48 06.9	-26.4	31.3	60
61	41 30.6	-31.5	26.7	42 24.1	-31.0	27.1	43 17.4	-30.4	27.6	44 10.5	-29.9	28.0	45 03.4	-29.3	28.5	45 56.0	-28.7	29.0	46 48.4	-28.1	29.5	47 40.5	-27.4	30.0	61
62	40 59.1	-32.2	25.6	41 53.1	-31.7	26.0	42 47.0	-31.2	26.4	43 40.6	-30.6	26.8	44 34.1	-30.1	27.2	45 27.3	-29.5	27.7	46 20.3	-28.9	28.2	47 13.1	-28.3	28.7	62
63	40 26.9	-32.9	24.5	41 21.4	-32.4	24.8	42 15.8	-31.9	25.2	43 10.0	-31.4	25.6	44 04.0	-30.9	26.0	44 57.8	-30.3	26.5	45 51.4	-29.8	26.9	46 44.8	-29.2	27.4	63
64	39 54.0	-33.4	23.4	40 49.0	-33.0	23.7	41 43.9	-32.6	24.1	42 38.6	-32.1	24.5	43 33.1	-31.6	24.8	44 27.5	-31.1	25.3	45 21.6	-30.5	25.7	46 15.6	-30.0	26.1	64
65	39 20.6	-34.1	22.3	40 16.0	-33.6	22.6	41 11.3	-33.1	23.0	42 06.5	-32.7	23.3	43 01.5	-32.2	23.7	43 56.4	-31.8	24.1	44 51.1	-31.3	24.5	45 45.6	-30.7	24.9	65
66	38 46.5	-34.6	21.2	39 42.4	-34.2	21.5	40 38.2	-33.8	21.9	41 33.8	-33.4	22.2	42 29.3	-33.0	22.5	43 24.6	-32.5	22.9	44 19.8	-32.0	23.3	45 14.9	-31.6	23.7	66
67	38 11.9	-35.1	20.2	39 08.2	-34.8	20.5	40 04.4	-34.4	20.8	41 00.4	-34.0	21.1	41 56.3	-33.6	21.4	42 52.1	-33.2	21.7	43 47.8	-32.8	22.1	44 43.3	-32.3	22.5	67
68	37 36.8	-35.7	19.2	38 33.4	-35.3	19.4	39 30.0	-35.0	19.7	40 26.4	-34.6	20.0	41 22.7	-34.2	20.3	42 18.9	-33.8	20.6	43 15.0	-33.4	20.9	44 11.0	-33.0	21.3	68
69	37 01.1	-36.2	18.2	37 58.1	-35.9	18.4	38 55.0	-35.6	18.7	39 51.8	-35.2	18.9	40 48.5	-34.8	19.2	41 45.1	-34.5	19.5	42 41.6	-34.1	19.8	43 38.0	-33.7	20.1	69
70	36 24.9	-36.6	17.2	37 22.2	-36.3	17.4	38 19.4	-36.0	17.6	39 16.6	-35.8	17.9	40 13.7	-35.5	18.1	41 10.6	-35.0	18.4	42 07.5	-34.7	18.7	43 04.3	-34.4	19.0	70
71	35 48.3	-37.2	16.2	36 45.9	-36.9	16.4	37 43.4	-36.6	16.6	38 40.8	-36.2	16.8	39 38.2	-35.9	17.1	40 35.6	-35.7	17.3	41 32.8	-35.4	17.6	42 29.9	-35.0	17.9	71
72	35 11.1	-37.6	15.2	36 09.0	-37.3	15.4	37 06.8	-37.1	15.6	38 04.6	-36.8	15.8	39 02.3	-36.6	16.0	39 59.9	-36.2	16.3	40 57.4	-35.9	16.5	41 54.9	-35.6	16.8	72
73	34 33.5	-38.0	14.3	35 31.7	-37.8	14.5	36 29.7	-37.5	14.6	37 27.8	-37.3	14.8	38 25.7	-37.0	15.0	39 23.7	-36.8	15.2	40 21.5	-36.5	15.5	41 19.3	-36.2	15.7	73
74	33 55.5	-38.4	13.3	34 53.9	-38.3	13.5	35 52.2	-38.0	13.7	36 50.5	-37.8	13.8	37 48.7	-37.5	14.0	38 46.9	-37.3	14.2	39 45.0	-37.0	14.4	40 43.1	-36.8	14.6	74
75	33 17.1	-38.9	12.4	34 15.6	-38.6	12.6	35 14.2	-38.4	12.7	36 12.7	-38.2	12.9	37 11.2	-38.0	13.0	38 09.6	-37.8	13.2	39 08.0	-37.6	13.4	40 06.3	-37.3	13.6	75
76	32 38.2	-39.2	11.5	33 37.0	-39.1	11.6	34 35.8	-38.9	11.8	35 34.5	-38.7	11.9	36 33.2	-38.5	12.1	37 31.8	-38.3	12.2	38 30.4	-38.0	12.4	39 29.0	-37.8	12.6	76
77	31 59.0	-39.6	10.6	32 57.9	-39.4	10.7	33 56.9	-39.3	10.9	34 55.8	-39.1	11.0	35 54.7	-38.9	11.1	36 53.5	-38.7	11.3	37 52.4	-38.6	11.4	38 51.2	-38.4	11.6	77
78	31 19.4	-40.0	9.7	32 18.5	-39.8	9.8	33 17.6	-39.6	9.9	34 16.7	-39.5	10.1	35 15.8	-39.4	10.2	36 14.8	-39.2	10.3	37 13.8	-39.0	10.5	38 12.8	-38.8	10.6	78
79	30 39.4	-40.3	8.9	31 38.7	-40.2	9.0	32 38.0	-40.1	9.1	33 37.2	-39.9	9.2	34 36.4	-39.7	9.3	35 35.6	-39.6	9.4	36 34.8	-39.4	9.5	37 34.0	-39.3	9.6	79
80	29 59.1	-40.6	8.0	30 58.5	-40.5	8.1	31 57.9	-40.4	8.2	32 57.3	-40.3	8.3	33 56.7	-40.2	8.4	34 56.0	-40.0	8.5	35 55.4	-39.9	8.6	36 54.7	-39.8	8.7	80
81	29 18.5	-41.0	7.2	30 18.0	-40.8	7.2	31 17.5	-40.7	7.3	32 17.0	-40.6	7.4	33 16.5	-40.5	7.5	34 16.0	-40.4	7.6	35 15.5	-40.3	7.6	36 14.9	-40.1	7.7	81
82	28 37.5	-41.2	6.3	29 37.2	-41.2	6.4	30 36.8	-41.1	6.4	31 36.4	-41.0	6.5	32 36.0	-40.9	6.6	33 35.6	-40.8	6.7	34 35.2	-40.7	6.7	35 34.8	-40.6	6.8	82
83	27 56.3	-41.6	5.5	28 56.0	-41.5	5.6	29 55.7	-41.4	5.6	30 55.4	-41.3	5.7	31 55.1	-41.2	5.7	32 54.8	-41.1	5.8	33 54.5	-41.0	5.9	34 54.2	-41.0	5.9	83
84	27 14.7	-41.8	4.7	28 14.5	-41.7	4.7	29 14.3	-41.7	4.8	30 14.1	-41.6	4.8	31 13.9	-41.6	4.9	32 13.7	-41.5	4.9	33 13.5	-41.5	5.0	34 13.2	-41.3	5.0	84
85	26 32.9	-42.1	3.9	27 32.8	-42.1	3.9	28 32.6	-42.0	4.0	29 32.5	-42.0	4.0	30 32.3	-41.8	4.0	31 32.2	-41.8	4.1	32 32.0	-41.7	4.1	33 31.9	-41.7	4.2	85
86	25 50.8	-42.3	3.1	26 50.7	-42.3	3.1	27 50.6	-42.2	3.1	28 50.5	-42.2	3.2	29 50.5	-42.2	3.2	30 50.4	-42.2	3.2	31 50.3	-42.1	3.3	32 50.2	-42.1	3.3	86
87	25 08.5	-42.6	2.3	26 08.4	-42.5	2.3	27 08.4	-42.6	2.3	28 08.3	-42.5	2.4	29 08.3	-42.5	2.4	30 08.2	-42.4	2.4	31 08.2	-42.5	2.4	32 08.1	-42.4	2.5	87
88	24 25.9	-42.8	1.5	25 25.9	-42.9	1.5	26 25.8	-42.8	1.6	27 25.8	-42.8	1.6	28 25.8	-42.8	1.6	29 25.8	-42.8	1.6	30 25.7	-42.7	1.6	31 25.7	-42.7	1.6	88
89	23 43.1	-43.1	0.8	24 43.0	-43.0	0.8	25 43.0	-43.0	0.8	26 43.0	-43.0	0.8	27 43.0	-43.0	0.8	28 43.0	-43.0	0.8	29 43.0	-43.0	0.8	30 43.0	-43.0	0.8	89
90	23 00.0	-43.3	0.0	24 00.0	-43.3	0.0	25 00.0	-43.3	0.0	26 00.0	-43.3	0.0	27 00.0	-43.3	0.0	28 00.0	-43.3	0.0	29 00.0	-43.3	0.0	30 00.0	-43.3	0.0	90
	23°			24°			25°			26°			27°			28°			29°			30°			

44°, 316° L.H.A. LATITUDE SAME NAME AS DECLINATION
272

LATITUDE CONTRARY NAME TO DECLINATION — L.H.A. 44°, 316°

Dec.	23°			24°			25°			26°			Dec.
	Hc	d	Z	Hc	d	Z	Hc	d	Z	Hc	d	Z	
°	° ′	′	°	° ′	′	°	° ′	′	°	° ′	′	°	°
0	41 27.9	−31.6	112.0	41 05.0	−32.7	112.8	40 41.3	−33.8	113.6	40 16.9	−34.8	114.4	0
1	40 56.3	−32.3	113.2	40 32.3	−33.3	113.9	40 07.5	−34.3	114.7	39 42.1	−35.3	115.5	1
2	40 24.0	−32.9	114.3	39 59.0	−34.0	115.0	39 33.2	−34.9	115.8	39 06.8	−35.9	116.5	2
3	39 51.1	−33.5	115.4	39 25.0	−34.5	116.1	38 58.3	−35.5	116.8	38 30.9	−36.5	117.6	3
4	39 17.6	−34.1	116.4	38 50.5	−35.0	117.2	38 22.8	−36.0	117.9	37 54.4	−36.9	118.6	4
5	38 43.5	−34.7	117.5	38 15.5	−35.6	118.2	37 46.8	−36.5	118.9	37 17.5	−37.4	119.6	5
6	38 08.8	−35.2	118.5	37 39.9	−36.2	119.2	37 10.3	−37.1	119.9	36 40.1	−37.9	120.5	6
7	37 33.6	−35.7	119.6	37 03.7	−36.6	120.2	36 33.2	−37.5	120.9	36 02.2	−38.4	121.5	7
8	36 57.9	−36.2	120.6	36 27.1	−37.1	121.2	35 55.7	−37.9	121.8	35 23.8	−38.8	122.4	8
9	36 21.7	−36.7	121.6	35 50.0	−37.6	122.2	35 17.8	−38.4	122.8	34 45.0	−39.2	123.4	9
10	35 45.0	−37.2	122.5	35 12.4	−38.0	123.1	34 39.4	−38.8	123.7	34 05.8	−39.6	124.3	10
11	35 07.8	−37.6	123.5	34 34.4	−38.4	124.1	34 00.6	−39.3	124.7	33 26.2	−40.0	125.2	11
12	34 30.2	−38.1	124.5	33 56.0	−38.9	125.0	33 21.3	−39.6	125.6	32 46.2	−40.4	126.1	12
13	33 52.1	−38.5	125.4	33 17.1	−39.2	125.9	32 41.7	−40.0	126.5	32 05.8	−40.7	127.0	13
14	33 13.6	−38.8	126.3	32 37.9	−39.7	126.8	32 01.7	−40.4	127.3	31 25.1	−41.1	127.8	14
15	32 34.8	−39.3	127.2	31 58.2	−40.0	127.7	31 21.3	−40.7	128.2	30 44.0	−41.4	128.7	15
16	31 55.5	−39.7	128.1	31 18.2	−40.3	128.6	30 40.6	−41.0	129.1	30 02.6	−41.7	129.5	16
17	31 15.8	−39.9	129.0	30 37.9	−40.7	129.5	29 59.6	−41.4	129.9	29 20.9	−42.0	130.3	17
18	30 35.9	−40.4	129.9	29 57.2	−41.0	130.3	29 18.2	−41.6	130.7	28 38.9	−42.3	131.2	18
19	29 55.5	−40.6	130.7	29 16.2	−41.3	131.2	28 36.6	−42.0	131.6	27 56.6	−42.6	132.0	19
20	29 14.9	−41.0	131.6	28 34.9	−41.6	132.0	27 54.6	−42.2	132.4	27 14.0	−42.8	132.8	20
21	28 33.9	−41.3	132.4	27 53.3	−41.9	132.8	27 12.4	−42.6	133.2	26 31.2	−43.2	133.5	21
22	27 52.6	−41.6	133.2	27 11.4	−42.2	133.6	26 29.8	−42.7	134.0	25 48.0	−43.3	134.3	22
23	27 11.0	−41.8	134.0	26 29.2	−42.5	134.4	25 47.1	−43.1	134.8	25 04.7	−43.6	135.1	23
24	26 29.2	−42.1	134.8	25 46.7	−42.7	135.2	25 04.0	−43.2	135.5	24 21.1	−43.8	135.8	24
25	25 47.1	−42.4	135.6	25 04.0	−42.9	136.0	24 20.8	−43.5	136.3	23 37.3	−44.0	136.6	25
26	25 04.7	−42.6	136.4	24 21.1	−43.1	136.7	23 37.3	−43.7	137.0	22 53.3	−44.2	137.3	26
27	24 22.1	−42.9	137.2	23 38.0	−43.4	137.5	22 53.6	−43.9	137.8	22 09.1	−44.4	138.1	27
28	23 39.2	−43.0	138.0	22 54.6	−43.6	138.3	22 09.7	−44.1	138.5	21 24.7	−44.6	138.8	28
29	22 56.2	−43.3	138.7	22 11.0	−43.8	139.0	21 25.6	−44.3	139.3	20 40.1	−44.8	139.5	29
30	22 12.9	−43.5	139.5	21 27.2	−44.0	139.7	20 41.3	−44.4	140.0	19 55.3	−44.9	140.2	30
31	21 29.4	−43.7	140.2	20 43.2	−44.2	140.5	19 56.9	−44.7	140.7	19 10.4	−45.1	140.9	31
32	20 45.7	−43.9	140.9	19 59.0	−44.3	141.2	19 12.2	−44.8	141.4	18 25.3	−45.3	141.6	32
33	20 01.8	−44.0	141.7	19 14.7	−44.5	141.9	18 27.4	−44.9	142.1	17 40.0	−45.4	142.3	33
34	19 17.8	−44.2	142.4	18 30.2	−44.7	142.6	17 42.5	−45.1	142.8	16 54.6	−45.5	143.0	34
35	18 33.6	−44.4	143.1	17 45.5	−44.8	143.3	16 57.4	−45.3	143.5	16 09.1	−45.7	143.7	35
36	17 49.2	−44.5	143.8	17 00.7	−44.9	144.0	16 12.1	−45.4	144.2	15 23.4	−45.8	144.3	36
37	17 04.7	−44.7	144.5	16 15.8	−45.1	144.7	15 26.7	−45.4	144.9	14 37.6	−45.9	145.0	37
38	16 20.0	−44.8	145.2	15 30.7	−45.2	145.4	14 41.3	−45.7	145.5	13 51.7	−46.0	145.7	38
39	15 35.2	−44.9	145.9	14 45.5	−45.4	146.1	13 55.6	−45.7	146.2	13 05.7	−46.1	146.3	39
40	14 50.3	−45.1	146.6	14 00.1	−45.4	146.7	13 09.9	−45.8	146.9	12 19.6	−46.1	147.0	40
41	14 05.2	−45.2	147.3	13 14.7	−45.6	147.4	12 24.1	−45.9	147.5	11 33.5	−46.3	147.6	41
42	13 20.0	−45.2	148.0	12 29.1	−45.6	148.1	11 38.2	−46.0	148.2	10 47.2	−46.4	148.3	42
43	12 34.8	−45.4	148.6	11 43.5	−45.7	148.7	10 52.2	−46.1	148.8	10 00.8	−46.4	148.9	43
44	11 49.4	−45.5	149.3	10 57.8	−45.9	149.4	10 06.1	−46.2	149.5	9 14.4	−46.5	149.6	44
45	11 03.9	−45.5	150.0	10 11.9	−45.9	150.1	9 19.9	−46.2	150.1	8 27.9	−46.6	150.2	45
46	10 18.4	−45.7	150.6	9 26.0	−45.9	150.7	8 33.7	−46.3	150.8	7 41.3	−46.6	150.9	46
47	9 32.7	−45.7	151.3	8 40.1	−46.1	151.4	7 47.4	−46.4	151.4	6 54.7	−46.7	151.5	47
48	8 47.0	−45.8	151.9	7 54.0	−46.1	152.0	7 01.0	−46.4	152.1	6 08.0	−46.7	152.1	48
49	8 01.2	−45.8	152.6	7 07.9	−46.1	152.7	6 14.6	−46.4	152.7	5 21.3	−46.8	152.8	49
50	7 15.4	−45.9	153.2	6 21.8	−46.2	153.3	5 28.2	−46.5	153.3	4 34.5	−46.7	153.4	50
51	6 29.5	−46.0	153.9	5 35.6	−46.3	153.9	4 41.7	−46.6	154.0	3 47.8	−46.9	154.0	51
52	5 43.5	−46.0	154.5	4 49.3	−46.2	154.6	3 55.1	−46.5	154.6	3 00.9	−46.8	154.6	52
53	4 57.5	−46.0	155.2	4 03.1	−46.3	155.2	3 08.6	−46.6	155.2	2 14.1	−46.9	155.3	53
54	4 11.5	−46.0	155.8	3 16.8	−46.4	155.9	2 22.0	−46.6	155.9	1 27.2	−46.8	155.9	54
55	3 25.5	−46.1	156.5	2 30.4	−46.3	156.5	1 35.4	−46.6	156.5	0 40.4	−46.9	156.5	55
56	2 39.4	−46.1	157.1	1 44.1	−46.4	157.1	0 48.8	−46.6	157.1	0 06.5	+46.9	22.9	56
57	1 53.3	−46.2	157.8	0 57.7	−46.3	157.8	0 02.2	−46.6	157.8	0 53.4	+46.8	22.2	57
58	1 07.1	−46.1	158.4	0 11.4	−46.4	158.4	0 44.4	+46.6	21.6	1 40.2	+46.9	21.6	58
59	0 21.0	−46.1	159.0	0 35.0	+46.4	21.0	1 31.0	+46.6	21.0	2 27.1	+46.8	21.0	59
60	0 25.1	+46.1	20.3	1 21.4	+46.3	20.3	2 17.6	+46.6	20.3	3 13.9	+46.8	20.4	60
61	1 11.2	+46.2	19.7	2 07.7	+46.4	19.7	3 04.2	+46.6	19.7	4 00.7	+46.8	19.7	61
62	1 57.4	+46.1	19.0	2 54.1	+46.3	19.1	3 50.8	+46.5	19.1	4 47.5	+46.7	19.1	62
63	2 43.5	+46.0	18.4	3 40.4	+46.3	18.4	4 37.3	+46.5	18.4	5 34.2	+46.7	18.5	63
64	3 29.5	+46.1	17.8	4 26.7	+46.2	17.8	5 23.8	+46.5	17.8	6 20.9	+46.7	17.8	64
65	4 15.6	+46.0	17.1	5 12.9	+46.3	17.1	6 10.3	+46.4	17.2	7 07.6	+46.6	17.2	65
66	5 01.6	+46.0	16.5	5 59.2	+46.1	16.5	6 56.7	+46.3	16.5	7 54.2	+46.5	16.6	66
67	5 47.6	+46.0	15.8	6 45.3	+46.2	15.9	7 43.0	+46.4	15.9	8 40.7	+46.5	15.9	67
68	6 33.6	+45.9	15.2	7 31.5	+46.0	15.2	8 29.4	+46.2	15.3	9 27.2	+46.4	15.3	68
69	7 19.5	+45.8	14.5	8 17.5	+46.0	14.6	9 15.6	+46.2	14.6	10 13.6	+46.4	14.7	69
70	8 05.3	+45.8	13.9	9 03.5	+46.0	13.9	10 01.8	+46.1	14.0	11 00.0	+46.2	14.0	70
71	8 51.1	+45.7	13.2	9 49.5	+45.8	13.3	10 47.9	+46.0	13.3	11 46.2	+46.2	13.4	71
72	9 36.8	+45.6	12.6	10 35.3	+45.8	12.6	11 33.9	+45.9	12.7	12 32.4	+46.1	12.7	72
73	10 22.4	+45.6	11.9	11 21.1	+45.7	12.0	12 19.8	+45.8	12.0	13 18.5	+46.0	12.0	73
74	11 08.0	+45.4	11.3	12 06.8	+45.6	11.3	13 05.6	+45.8	11.3	14 04.5	+45.8	11.4	74
75	11 53.4	+45.4	10.6	12 52.4	+45.5	10.6	13 51.4	+45.6	10.7	14 50.3	+45.8	10.7	75
76	12 38.8	+45.3	9.9	13 37.9	+45.4	10.0	14 37.0	+45.5	10.0	15 36.1	+45.6	10.0	76
77	13 24.1	+45.1	9.2	14 23.3	+45.2	9.3	15 22.5	+45.4	9.3	16 21.7	+45.5	9.4	77
78	14 09.2	+45.1	8.6	15 08.5	+45.2	8.6	16 07.9	+45.2	8.6	17 07.2	+45.3	8.7	78
79	14 54.3	+44.9	7.9	15 53.7	+45.0	7.9	16 53.1	+45.1	8.0	17 52.5	+45.2	8.0	79
80	15 39.2	+44.8	7.2	16 38.7	+44.9	7.2	17 38.2	+45.0	7.3	18 37.7	+45.1	7.3	80
81	16 24.0	+44.6	6.5	17 23.6	+44.7	6.5	18 23.2	+44.8	6.6	19 22.8	+44.9	6.6	81
82	17 08.6	+44.6	5.8	18 08.3	+44.6	5.8	19 08.0	+44.7	5.9	20 07.7	+44.7	5.9	82
83	17 53.2	+44.3	5.1	18 52.9	+44.4	5.1	19 52.7	+44.5	5.2	20 52.4	+44.6	5.2	83
84	18 37.5	+44.2	4.4	19 37.3	+44.3	4.4	20 37.2	+44.3	4.4	21 37.0	+44.3	4.5	84
85	19 21.7	+44.0	3.7	20 21.6	+44.1	3.7	21 21.5	+44.1	3.7	22 21.3	+44.2	3.8	85
86	20 05.7	+43.9	3.0	21 05.7	+43.9	3.0	22 05.6	+43.9	3.0	23 05.5	+44.0	3.0	86
87	20 49.6	+43.7	2.2	21 49.6	+43.6	2.2	22 49.5	+43.7	2.3	23 49.5	+43.8	2.3	87
88	21 33.3	+43.4	1.5	22 33.2	+43.5	1.5	23 33.2	+43.5	1.5	24 33.2	+43.5	1.5	88
89	22 16.7	+43.3	0.8	23 16.7	+43.3	0.8	24 16.7	+43.3	0.8	25 16.7	+43.3	0.8	89
90	23 00.0	+43.1	0.0	24 00.0	+43.0	0.0	25 00.0	+43.0	0.0	26 00.0	+43.0	0.0	90
	23°			24°			25°			26°			

Dec.	27°			28°			29°			30°			Dec.
	Hc	d	Z	Hc	d	Z	Hc	d	Z	Hc	d	Z	
°	° ′	′	°	° ′	′	°	° ′	′	°	° ′	′	°	°
0	39 51.7	−35.8	115.2	39 25.8	−36.7	115.9	38 59.2	−37.6	116.7	38 32.0	−38.6	117.4	0
1	39 15.9	−36.3	116.2	38 49.1	−37.3	116.9	38 21.6	−38.2	117.7	37 53.4	−39.1	118.3	1
2	38 39.6	−36.8	117.2	38 11.8	−37.7	117.9	37 43.4	−38.7	118.6	37 14.3	−39.5	119.3	2
3	38 02.8	−37.4	118.3	37 34.1	−38.3	118.9	37 04.7	−39.1	119.6	36 34.8	−40.0	120.2	3
4	37 25.4	−37.8	119.2	36 55.8	−38.7	119.9	36 25.6	−39.5	120.5	35 54.8	−40.3	121.2	4
5	36 47.6	−38.3	120.2	36 17.1	−39.1	120.9	35 46.1	−40.0	121.5	35 14.5	−40.8	122.1	5
6	36 09.3	−38.8	121.2	35 38.0	−39.6	121.8	35 06.1	−40.4	122.4	34 33.7	−41.2	123.0	6
7	35 30.5	−39.1	122.1	34 58.4	−40.0	122.7	34 25.7	−40.8	123.3	33 52.5	−41.5	123.9	7
8	34 51.4	−39.6	123.0	34 18.4	−40.4	123.6	33 44.9	−41.1	124.2	33 11.0	−41.9	124.7	8
9	34 11.8	−40.0	124.0	33 38.0	−40.8	124.5	33 03.8	−41.5	125.0	32 29.1	−42.2	125.6	9
10	33 31.8	−40.4	124.8	32 57.2	−41.1	125.4	32 22.3	−41.9	125.9	31 46.9	−42.6	126.4	10
11	32 51.4	−40.8	125.7	32 16.1	−41.4	126.2	31 40.4	−42.1	126.8	31 04.3	−42.8	127.2	11
12	32 10.6	−41.1	126.6	31 34.7	−41.9	127.1	30 58.3	−42.5	127.6	30 21.5	−43.2	128.1	12
13	31 29.5	−41.4	127.5	30 52.8	−42.1	127.9	30 15.8	−42.8	128.4	29 38.3	−43.4	128.9	13
14	30 48.1	−41.8	128.3	30 10.7	−42.4	128.8	29 33.0	−43.1	129.2	28 54.9	−43.8	129.6	14
15	30 06.3	−42.0	129.1	29 28.3	−42.7	129.6	28 49.9	−43.4	130.0	28 11.1	−43.9	130.4	15
16	29 24.3	−42.4	130.0	28 45.6	−43.0	130.4	28 06.5	−43.6	130.8	27 27.2	−44.3	131.2	16
17	28 41.9	−42.7	130.8	28 02.6	−43.3	131.2	27 22.9	−43.9	131.6	26 42.9	−44.4	132.0	17
18	27 59.2	−42.9	131.6	27 19.3	−43.6	132.0	26 39.0	−44.1	132.3	25 58.5	−44.7	132.7	18
19	27 16.3	−43.2	132.4	26 35.7	−43.7	132.7	25 54.9	−44.4	133.1	25 13.8	−45.0	133.4	19
20	26 33.1	−43.4	133.1	25 52.0	−44.1	133.5	25 10.5	−44.6	133.8	24 28.8	−45.1	134.2	20
21	25 49.7	−43.7	133.9	25 07.9	−44.2	134.2	24 25.9	−44.7	134.6	23 43.7	−45.3	134.9	21
22	25 06.0	−43.9	134.7	24 23.7	−44.5	135.0	23 41.2	−45.0	135.3	22 58.4	−45.5	135.6	22
23	24 22.1	−44.1	135.4	23 39.2	−44.6	135.7	22 56.2	−45.2	136.0	22 12.9	−45.7	136.3	23
24	23 38.0	−44.4	136.2	22 54.6	−44.9	136.5	22 11.0	−45.4	136.7	21 27.2	−45.9	137.0	24
25	22 53.6	−44.5	136.9	22 09.7	−45.0	137.2	21 25.6	−45.5	137.4	20 41.3	−46.0	137.7	25
26	22 09.1	−44.8	137.6	21 24.7	−45.3	137.9	20 40.1	−45.7	138.1	19 55.3	−46.2	138.4	26
27	21 24.3	−44.9	138.3	20 39.4	−45.4	138.6	19 54.4	−45.9	138.8	19 09.1	−46.3	139.1	27
28	20 39.4	−45.0	139.0	19 54.0	−45.5	139.3	19 08.5	−46.0	139.5	18 22.8	−46.5	139.7	28
29	19 54.4	−45.3	139.7	19 08.5	−45.7	140.0	18 22.5	−46.2	140.2	17 36.3	−46.6	140.4	29
30	19 09.1	−45.4	140.4	18 22.8	−45.9	140.7	17 36.3	−46.3	140.9	16 49.7	−46.7	141.1	30
31	18 23.7	−45.5	141.1	17 36.9	−46.0	141.3	16 50.0	−46.4	141.5	16 03.0	−46.9	141.7	31
32	17 38.2	−45.7	141.8	16 50.9	−46.1	142.0	16 03.6	−46.6	142.2	15 16.1	−46.9	142.4	32
33	16 52.5	−45.9	142.5	16 04.8	−46.2	142.7	15 17.0	−46.6	142.8	14 29.2	−47.1	143.0	33
34	16 06.6	−45.9	143.2	15 18.6	−46.4	143.3	14 30.4	−46.8	143.5	13 42.1	−47.2	143.6	34
35	15 20.7	−46.1	143.8	14 32.2	−46.5	144.0	13 43.6	−46.9	144.1	12 54.9	−47.2	144.3	35
36	14 34.6	−46.2	144.5	13 45.7	−46.6	144.6	12 56.7	−46.9	144.8	12 07.7	−47.4	144.9	36
37	13 48.4	−46.3	145.2	12 59.1	−46.6	145.3	12 09.8	−47.1	145.4	11 20.3	−47.4	145.5	37
38	13 02.1	−46.3	145.8	12 12.5	−46.8	145.9	11 22.7	−47.1	146.1	10 32.9	−47.5	146.2	38
39	12 15.8	−46.5	146.5	11 25.7	−46.8	146.6	10 35.6	−47.2	146.7	9 45.4	−47.5	146.8	39
40	11 29.3	−46.6	147.1	10 38.9	−46.9	147.2	9 48.4	−47.3	147.3	8 57.9	−47.6	147.4	40
41	10 42.7	−46.6	147.8	9 52.0	−47.0	147.9	9 01.1	−47.3	147.9	8 10.3	−47.7	148.0	41
42	9 56.1	−46.7	148.4	9 05.0	−47.1	148.5	8 13.8	−47.4	148.6	7 22.6	−47.7	148.6	42
43	9 09.4	−46.8	149.0	8 17.9	−47.1	149.1	7 26.4	−47.4	149.2	6 34.9	−47.8	149.2	43
44	8 22.6	−46.8	149.7	7 30.8	−47.2	149.7	6 39.0	−47.5	149.8	5 47.1	−47.8	149.8	44
45	7 35.8	−46.9	150.3	6 43.6	−47.2	150.4	5 51.5	−47.5	150.4	4 59.3	−47.8	150.5	45
46	6 48.9	−47.0	150.9	5 56.4	−47.2	151.0	5 04.0	−47.6	151.0	4 11.5	−47.9	151.1	46
47	6 01.9	−46.9	151.5	5 09.2	−47.3	151.6	4 16.4	−47.6	151.6	3 23.6	−47.9	151.7	47
48	5 15.0	−47.1	152.2	4 21.9	−47.3	152.2	3 28.8	−47.6	152.2	2 35.7	−47.9	152.3	48
49	4 27.9	−47.0	152.8	3 34.6	−47.4	152.8	2 41.2	−47.7	152.9	1 47.8	−47.9	152.9	49
50	3 40.9	−47.1	153.4	2 47.2	−47.3	153.4	1 53.5	−47.6	153.5	0 59.9	−48.0	153.5	50
51	2 53.8	−47.1	154.0	1 59.9	−47.4	154.1	1 05.9	−47.7	154.1	0 11.9	−47.9	154.1	51
52	2 06.7	−47.1	154.7	1 12.5	−47.4	154.7	0 18.2	−47.6	154.7	0 36.0	+47.9	25.3	52
53	1 19.6	−47.1	155.3	0 25.1	−47.4	155.3	0 29.4	+47.7	24.7	1 23.9	+47.9	24.7	53
54	0 32.5	−47.1	155.9	0 22.3	+47.4	24.1	1 17.1	+47.6	24.1	2 11.8	+47.9	24.1	54
55	0 14.6	+47.2	23.5	1 09.7	+47.4	23.5	2 04.7	+47.6	23.5	2 59.7	+47.9	23.5	55
56	1 01.8	+47.1	22.9	1 57.1	+47.3	22.9	2 52.3	+47.6	22.9	3 47.6	+47.9	22.9	56
57	1 48.9	+47.1	22.2	2 44.4	+47.4	22.3	3 39.9	+47.6	22.3	4 35.5	+47.8	22.3	57
58	2 36.0	+47.1	21.6	3 31.8	+47.3	21.6	4 27.5	+47.6	21.7	5 23.3	+47.8	21.7	58
59	3 23.1	+47.0	21.0	4 19.1	+47.3	21.0	5 15.1	+47.5	21.1	6 11.1	+47.7	21.1	59
60	4 10.1	+47.1	20.4	5 06.4	+47.2	20.4	6 02.6	+47.5	20.4	6 58.8	+47.7	20.5	60
61	4 57.2	+47.0	19.8	5 53.6	+47.3	19.8	6 50.1	+47.4	19.8	7 46.5	+47.7	19.9	61
62	5 44.2	+46.9	19.1	6 40.9	+47.1	19.2	7 37.5	+47.4	19.2	8 34.2	+47.6	19.3	62
63	6 31.1	+46.9	18.5	7 28.0	+47.1	18.5	8 24.9	+47.3	18.6	9 21.8	+47.5	18.6	63
64	7 18.0	+46.9	17.9	8 15.1	+47.1	17.9	9 12.2	+47.3	18.0	10 09.3	+47.4	18.0	64
65	8 04.9	+46.8	17.2	9 02.2	+47.0	17.3	9 59.5	+47.2	17.3	10 56.7	+47.4	17.4	65
66	8 51.7	+46.7	16.6	9 49.2	+46.9	16.7	10 46.7	+47.1	16.7	11 44.1	+47.3	16.8	66
67	9 38.4	+46.7	16.0	10 36.1	+46.9	16.0	11 33.8	+47.0	16.1	12 31.4	+47.2	16.1	67
68	10 25.1	+46.6	15.3	11 23.0	+46.7	15.4	12 20.8	+46.9	15.4	13 18.6	+47.1	15.5	68
69	11 11.7	+46.5	14.7	12 09.7	+46.7	14.8	13 07.7	+46.9	14.8	14 05.7	+47.0	14.9	69
70	11 58.2	+46.4	14.1	12 56.4	+46.6	14.1	13 54.6	+46.7	14.2	14 52.7	+46.9	14.2	70
71	12 44.6	+46.3	13.4	13 43.0	+46.5	13.5	14 41.3	+46.7	13.5	15 39.6	+46.8	13.6	71
72	13 30.9	+46.3	12.8	14 29.5	+46.3	12.8	15 28.0	+46.5	12.9	16 26.4	+46.7	12.9	72
73	14 17.2	+46.1	12.1	15 15.8	+46.3	12.2	16 14.5	+46.4	12.2	17 13.1	+46.5	12.3	73
74	15 03.3	+46.0	11.4	16 02.1	+46.1	11.5	17 00.9	+46.2	11.6	17 59.6	+46.4	11.6	74
75	15 49.3	+45.8	10.8	16 48.2	+46.0	10.8	17 47.1	+46.2	10.9	18 46.0	+46.3	10.9	75
76	16 35.1	+45.8	10.1	17 34.2	+45.9	10.2	18 33.3	+45.9	10.2	19 32.3	+46.1	10.3	76
77	17 20.9	+45.6	9.4	18 20.1	+45.7	9.5	19 19.2	+45.9	9.5	20 18.4	+46.0	9.6	77
78	18 06.5	+45.4	8.7	19 05.8	+45.6	8.8	20 05.1	+45.7	8.8	21 04.4	+45.7	8.9	78
79	18 51.9	+45.4	8.1	19 51.4	+45.4	8.1	20 50.8	+45.5	8.2	21 50.1	+45.6	8.2	79
80	19 37.3	+45.1	7.4	20 36.8	+45.2	7.4	21 36.3	+45.3	7.5	22 35.7	+45.5	7.5	80
81	20 22.4	+45.0	6.7	21 22.0	+45.1	6.7	22 21.6	+45.1	6.7	23 21.2	+45.2	6.8	81
82	21 07.4	+44.8	5.9	22 07.1	+44.8	6.0	23 06.7	+45.0	6.0	24 06.4	+45.0	6.1	82
83	21 52.2	+44.6	5.2	22 51.9	+44.7	5.3	23 51.7	+44.7	5.3	24 51.4	+44.8	5.4	83
84	22 36.8	+44.4	4.5	23 36.6	+44.5	4.5	24 36.4	+44.5	4.6	25 36.2	+44.6	4.6	84
85	23 21.2	+44.2	3.8	24 21.1	+44.2	3.8	25 20.9	+44.3	3.8	26 20.8	+44.4	3.9	85
86	24 05.4	+44.0	3.0	25 05.3	+44.1	3.1	26 05.2	+44.1	3.1	27 05.2	+44.1	3.1	86
87	24 49.4	+43.8	2.3	25 49.4	+43.8	2.3	26 49.3	+43.8	2.3	27 49.3	+43.8	2.4	87
88	25 33.2	+43.5	1.5	26 33.2	+43.5	1.6	27 33.1	+43.6	1.6	28 33.1	+43.6	1.6	88
89	26 16.7	+43.3	0.8	27 16.7	+43.3	0.8	28 16.7	+43.3	0.8	29 16.7	+43.3	0.8	89
90	27 00.0	+43.0	0.0	28 00.0	+43.0	0.0	29 00.0	+43.0	0.0	30 00.0	+43.0	0.0	90
	27°			28°			29°			30°			

S. Lat. {L.H.A. greater than 180°....Zn=180°−Z
{L.H.A. less than 180°...........Zn=180°+Z

LATITUDE SAME NAME AS DECLINATION — L.H.A. 136°, 224°

45°, 315° L.H.A. LATITUDE SAME NAME AS DECLINATION

N. Lat. {L.H.A. greater than 180° .....Zn=Z; L.H.A. less than 180°............Zn=360°−Z}

Dec.	23°			24°			25°			26°			27°			28°			29°			30°			Dec.
°	Hc ° ′	d ′	Z °	Hc ° ′	d ′	Z °	Hc ° ′	d ′	Z °	Hc ° ′	d ′	Z °	Hc ° ′	d ′	Z °	Hc ° ′	d ′	Z °	Hc ° ′	d ′	Z °	Hc ° ′	d ′	Z °	°
0	40 36.5	+30.6	111.3	40 14.3	+31.7	112.1	39 51.3	+32.8	112.9	39 27.6	+33.8	113.7	39 03.2	+34.8	114.4	38 38.0	+35.8	115.1	38 12.2	+36.7	115.9	37 45.7	+37.7	116.6	0
1	41 07.1	+29.9	110.2	40 46.0	+31.0	111.0	40 24.1	+32.1	111.8	40 01.4	+33.2	112.6	39 38.0	+34.2	113.4	39 13.8	+35.2	114.1	38 48.9	+36.3	114.9	38 23.4	+37.2	115.6	1
2	41 37.0	+29.1	109.0	41 17.0	+30.3	109.9	40 56.2	+31.4	110.7	40 34.6	+32.5	111.5	40 12.2	+33.6	112.3	39 49.0	+34.7	113.1	39 25.2	+35.6	113.8	39 00.6	+36.6	114.6	2
3	42 06.1	+28.5	107.9	41 47.3	+29.6	108.7	41 27.6	+30.8	109.6	41 07.1	+31.9	110.4	40 45.8	+33.0	111.2	40 23.7	+34.1	112.0	40 00.8	+35.1	112.8	39 37.2	+36.2	113.5	3
4	42 34.6	+27.6	106.7	42 16.9	+28.9	107.6	41 58.4	+30.0	108.4	41 39.0	+31.2	109.3	41 18.8	+32.3	110.1	40 57.8	+33.4	110.9	40 35.9	+34.5	111.7	40 13.4	+35.5	112.5	4
5	43 02.2	+26.9	105.5	42 45.8	+28.1	106.4	42 28.4	+29.4	107.2	42 10.2	+30.5	108.1	41 51.1	+31.7	109.0	41 31.2	+32.8	109.8	41 10.4	+33.9	110.6	40 48.9	+35.0	111.4	5
6	43 29.1	+26.1	104.2	43 13.9	+27.4	105.2	42 57.8	+28.5	106.1	42 40.7	+29.8	106.9	42 22.8	+31.0	107.8	42 04.0	+32.1	108.7	41 44.3	+33.3	109.5	41 23.9	+34.3	110.4	6
7	43 55.2	+25.3	103.0	43 41.3	+26.5	103.9	43 26.3	+27.9	104.9	43 10.5	+29.1	105.8	42 53.8	+30.2	106.7	42 36.1	+31.4	107.5	42 17.6	+32.6	108.4	41 58.2	+33.7	109.3	7
8	44 20.5	+24.5	101.7	44 07.8	+25.8	102.7	43 54.2	+27.0	103.6	43 39.6	+28.2	104.6	43 24.0	+29.5	105.5	43 07.5	+30.7	106.4	42 50.2	+31.9	107.3	42 31.9	+33.0	108.2	8
9	44 45.0	+23.5	100.5	44 33.6	+24.9	101.4	44 21.2	+26.2	102.4	44 07.8	+27.5	103.3	43 53.5	+28.8	104.3	43 38.2	+30.0	105.2	43 22.1	+31.1	106.1	43 04.9	+32.4	107.0	9
10	45 08.5	+22.7	99.2	44 58.5	+24.0	100.1	44 47.4	+25.3	101.1	44 35.3	+26.7	102.1	44 22.3	+27.9	103.1	44 08.2	+29.2	104.0	43 53.2	+30.5	104.9	43 37.3	+31.6	105.9	10
11	45 31.2	+21.7	97.8	45 22.5	+23.1	98.8	45 12.7	+24.5	99.8	45 02.0	+25.8	100.8	44 50.2	+27.1	101.8	44 37.4	+28.4	102.8	44 23.7	+29.6	103.7	44 08.9	+30.9	104.7	11
12	45 52.9	+20.8	96.5	45 45.6	+22.2	97.5	45 37.2	+23.6	98.5	45 27.8	+24.9	99.5	45 17.3	+26.3	100.5	45 05.8	+27.6	101.5	44 53.3	+28.9	102.5	44 39.8	+30.2	103.5	12
13	46 13.7	+19.9	95.2	46 07.8	+21.3	96.2	46 00.8	+22.6	97.2	45 52.7	+24.1	98.2	45 43.6	+25.4	99.3	45 33.4	+26.7	100.3	45 22.2	+28.0	101.3	45 10.0	+29.3	102.3	13
14	46 33.6	+18.8	93.8	46 29.1	+20.2	94.8	46 23.4	+21.8	95.9	46 16.8	+23.1	96.9	46 09.0	+24.5	98.0	46 00.1	+25.9	99.0	45 50.2	+27.2	100.0	45 39.3	+28.5	101.0	14
15	46 52.4	+17.8	92.4	46 49.3	+19.3	93.5	46 45.2	+20.7	94.5	46 39.9	+22.1	95.6	46 33.5	+23.5	96.6	46 26.0	+25.0	97.7	46 17.4	+26.4	98.7	46 07.8	+27.7	99.7	15
16	47 10.2	+16.8	91.0	47 08.6	+18.3	92.1	47 05.9	+19.7	93.2	47 02.0	+21.2	94.2	46 57.0	+22.7	95.3	46 51.0	+24.0	96.4	46 43.8	+25.4	97.4	46 35.5	+26.8	98.5	16
17	47 27.0	+15.8	89.6	47 26.9	+17.2	90.7	47 25.6	+18.7	91.8	47 23.2	+20.2	92.8	47 19.7	+21.6	93.9	47 15.0	+23.0	95.0	47 09.2	+24.5	96.1	47 02.3	+25.8	97.2	17
18	47 42.8	+14.6	88.2	47 44.1	+16.2	89.3	47 44.3	+17.7	90.4	47 43.4	+19.1	91.5	47 41.3	+20.6	92.6	47 38.0	+22.1	93.6	47 33.7	+23.5	94.7	47 28.1	+25.0	95.8	18
19	47 57.4	+13.6	86.7	48 00.3	+15.1	87.8	48 02.0	+16.6	88.9	48 02.5	+18.1	90.0	48 01.9	+19.6	91.2	48 00.1	+21.1	92.3	47 57.2	+22.5	93.4	47 53.1	+23.9	94.5	19
20	48 11.0	+12.4	85.3	48 15.4	+13.9	86.4	48 18.6	+15.5	87.5	48 20.6	+17.1	88.6	48 21.5	+18.5	89.7	48 21.2	+20.0	90.9	48 19.7	+21.5	92.0	48 17.0	+23.0	93.1	20
21	48 23.4	+11.3	83.8	48 29.3	+12.9	84.9	48 34.1	+14.4	86.0	48 37.7	+15.9	87.2	48 40.0	+17.5	88.3	48 41.2	+19.0	89.4	48 41.2	+20.5	90.6	48 40.0	+22.0	91.7	21
22	48 34.7	+10.2	82.3	48 42.2	+11.7	83.4	48 48.5	+13.2	84.6	48 53.6	+14.8	85.7	48 57.5	+16.3	86.8	49 00.2	+17.8	88.0	49 01.7	+19.4	89.1	49 02.0	+20.9	90.3	22
23	48 44.9	+9.0	80.8	48 53.9	+10.6	81.9	49 01.7	+12.1	83.1	49 08.4	+13.6	84.2	49 13.8	+15.2	85.4	49 18.0	+16.8	86.5	49 21.1	+18.3	87.7	49 22.9	+19.8	88.9	23
24	48 53.9	+7.8	79.3	49 04.5	+9.3	80.4	49 13.8	+11.0	81.6	49 22.0	+12.5	82.7	49 29.0	+14.1	83.9	49 34.8	+15.6	85.1	49 39.4	+17.1	86.2	49 42.7	+18.7	87.4	24
25	49 01.7	+6.7	77.8	49 13.8	+8.2	78.9	49 24.8	+9.7	80.1	49 34.5	+11.3	81.2	49 43.1	+12.9	82.4	49 50.4	+14.5	83.6	49 56.5	+16.0	84.7	50 01.4	+17.6	85.9	25
26	49 08.4	+5.4	76.3	49 22.0	+7.0	77.4	49 34.5	+8.6	78.6	49 45.8	+10.2	79.7	49 56.0	+11.7	80.9	50 04.9	+13.2	82.1	50 12.5	+14.9	83.2	50 19.0	+16.4	84.4	26
27	49 13.8	+4.2	74.8	49 29.0	+5.8	75.9	49 43.1	+7.3	77.0	49 56.0	+8.9	78.2	50 07.7	+10.4	79.3	50 18.1	+12.1	80.5	50 27.4	+13.6	81.7	50 35.4	+15.2	82.9	27
28	49 18.0	+3.1	73.2	49 34.8	+4.6	74.3	49 50.4	+6.1	75.5	50 04.9	+7.6	76.6	50 18.1	+9.3	77.8	50 30.2	+10.8	79.0	50 41.0	+12.5	80.2	50 50.6	+14.1	81.4	28
29	49 21.1	+1.8	71.7	49 39.4	+3.3	72.8	49 56.5	+4.9	73.9	50 12.5	+6.5	75.1	50 27.4	+8.0	76.3	50 41.0	+9.6	77.4	50 53.5	+11.2	78.6	51 04.7	+12.7	79.9	29
30	49 22.9	+0.6	70.2	49 42.7	+2.1	71.3	50 01.4	+3.6	72.4	50 19.0	+5.2	73.5	50 35.4	+6.8	74.7	50 50.6	+8.4	75.9	51 04.7	+9.9	77.1	51 17.4	+11.6	78.3	30
31	49 23.5	-0.7	68.6	49 44.8	+0.9	69.7	50 05.0	+2.4	70.8	50 24.2	+3.9	72.0	50 42.2	+5.4	73.1	50 59.0	+7.0	74.3	51 14.6	+8.7	75.5	51 29.0	+10.3	76.7	31
32	49 22.8	-1.8	67.1	49 45.7	-0.4	68.2	50 07.4	+1.2	69.3	50 28.1	+2.7	70.4	50 47.6	+4.3	71.6	51 06.0	+5.8	72.7	51 23.3	+7.3	73.9	51 39.3	+8.9	75.1	32
33	49 21.0	-3.1	65.6	49 45.3	-1.6	66.6	50 08.6	-0.2	67.7	50 30.8	+1.4	68.8	50 51.9	+2.9	70.0	51 11.8	+4.5	71.1	51 30.6	+6.1	72.3	51 48.2	+7.7	73.5	33
34	49 17.9	-4.3	64.0	49 43.7	-2.9	65.1	50 08.4	-1.3	66.2	50 32.2	+0.1	67.3	50 54.8	+1.6	68.4	51 16.3	+3.2	69.6	51 36.7	+4.8	70.7	51 55.9	+6.4	71.9	34
35	49 13.6	-5.5	62.5	49 40.8	-4.1	63.5	50 07.1	-2.7	64.6	50 32.3	-1.2	65.7	50 56.4	+0.4	66.8	51 19.5	+1.9	68.0	51 41.5	+3.4	69.1	52 02.3	+5.0	70.3	35
36	49 08.1	-6.7	61.0	49 36.7	-5.3	62.0	50 04.4	-3.8	63.0	50 31.1	-2.4	64.1	50 56.8	-0.9	65.2	51 21.4	+0.6	66.4	51 44.9	+2.1	67.5	52 07.3	+3.7	68.7	36
37	49 01.4	-7.9	59.4	49 31.4	-6.5	60.5	50 00.6	-5.2	61.5	50 28.7	-3.7	62.5	50 55.9	-2.3	63.6	51 22.0	-0.8	64.8	51 47.0	+0.8	65.9	52 11.0	+2.3	67.1	37
38	48 53.5	-9.0	57.9	49 24.9	-7.7	58.9	49 55.4	-6.3	59.9	50 25.0	-4.9	61.0	50 53.6	-3.5	62.1	51 21.2	-2.0	63.2	51 47.8	-0.5	64.3	52 13.3	+1.0	65.4	38
39	48 44.5	-10.3	56.4	49 17.2	-8.9	57.4	49 49.1	-7.6	58.4	50 20.1	-6.2	59.4	50 50.1	-4.8	60.5	51 19.2	-3.3	61.6	51 47.3	-1.9	62.7	52 14.3	-0.4	63.8	39
40	48 34.2	-11.3	54.9	49 08.3	-10.1	55.9	49 41.5	-8.8	56.9	50 13.9	-7.5	57.9	50 45.3	-6.0	58.9	51 15.9	-4.7	60.0	51 45.4	-3.2	61.1	52 13.9	-1.7	62.2	40
41	48 22.9	-12.5	53.5	48 58.2	-11.3	54.4	49 32.7	-9.9	55.3	50 06.4	-8.6	56.3	50 39.3	-7.3	57.3	51 11.2	-5.9	58.4	51 42.2	-4.5	59.4	52 12.2	-3.0	60.5	41
42	48 10.4	-13.6	52.0	48 46.9	-12.4	52.9	49 22.8	-11.2	53.8	49 57.8	-9.9	54.8	50 32.0	-8.6	55.8	51 05.3	-7.2	56.8	51 37.7	-5.8	57.8	52 09.2	-4.5	58.9	42
43	47 56.8	-14.8	50.5	48 34.5	-13.5	51.4	49 11.6	-12.3	52.3	49 47.9	-11.1	53.2	50 23.4	-9.8	54.2	50 58.1	-8.5	55.2	51 31.9	-7.2	56.2	52 04.7	-5.7	57.3	43
44	47 42.0	-15.7	49.1	48 21.0	-14.7	49.9	48 59.3	-13.5	50.8	49 36.8	-12.3	51.7	50 13.6	-11.0	52.7	50 49.6	-9.8	53.6	51 24.7	-8.4	54.6	51 59.0	-7.1	55.7	44
45	47 26.3	-16.9	47.7	48 06.3	-15.7	48.5	48 45.8	-14.6	49.3	49 24.5	-13.4	50.2	50 02.6	-12.3	51.1	50 39.8	-11.0	52.1	51 16.3	-9.7	53.1	51 51.9	-8.3	54.1	45
46	47 09.4	-17.9	46.2	47 50.6	-16.8	47.0	48 31.2	-15.7	47.9	49 11.1	-14.6	48.7	49 50.3	-13.4	49.6	50 28.8	-12.2	50.5	51 06.6	-11.0	51.5	51 43.6	-9.7	52.5	46
47	46 51.5	-18.9	44.8	47 33.8	-17.9	45.6	48 15.5	-16.8	46.4	48 56.5	-15.7	47.2	49 36.9	-14.6	48.1	50 16.6	-13.4	49.0	50 55.6	-12.2	49.9	51 33.9	-11.0	50.9	47
48	46 32.6	-19.8	43.5	47 15.9	-18.9	44.2	47 58.7	-17.9	45.0	48 40.8	-16.8	45.8	49 22.3	-15.7	46.6	50 03.2	-14.6	47.5	50 43.4	-13.4	48.4	51 22.9	-12.2	49.3	48
49	46 12.8	-20.9	42.1	46 57.0	-19.9	42.8	47 40.8	-18.9	43.6	48 24.0	-17.9	44.3	49 06.6	-16.8	45.1	49 48.6	-15.7	46.0	50 30.0	-14.6	46.8	51 10.7	-13.4	47.7	49
50	45 51.9	-21.8	40.7	46 37.1	-20.8	41.4	47 21.9	-20.0	42.1	48 06.1	-18.9	42.9	48 49.8	-18.0	43.7	49 32.9	-16.9	44.5	50 15.4	-15.8	45.3	50 57.3	-14.7	46.2	50
51	45 30.1	-22.7	39.4	46 16.3	-21.9	40.1	47 01.9	-20.9	40.8	47 47.2	-20.0	41.5	48 31.8	-19.0	42.2	49 16.0	-18.0	43.0	49 59.6	-16.9	43.8	50 42.6	-15.9	44.6	51
52	45 07.4	-23.6	38.1	45 54.4	-22.7	38.7	46 41.0	-21.9	39.4	47 27.2	-21.0	40.1	48 12.8	-20.0	40.8	48 58.0	-19.1	41.5	49 42.7	-18.1	42.3	50 26.7	-17.0	43.1	52
53	44 43.8	-24.5	36.8	45 31.7	-23.7	37.4	46 19.1	-22.8	38.0	47 06.2	-22.0	38.7	47 52.8	-21.1	39.4	48 38.9	-20.1	40.1	49 24.6	-19.2	40.8	50 09.7	-18.2	41.6	53
54	44 19.3	-25.3	35.5	45 08.0	-24.5	36.1	45 56.3	-23.8	36.7	46 44.2	-22.9	37.3	47 31.7	-22.1	38.0	48 18.8	-21.2	38.7	49 05.4	-20.3	39.4	49 51.5	-19.3	40.1	54
55	43 54.0	-26.1	34.3	44 43.5	-25.5	34.8	45 32.5	-24.6	35.4	46 21.3	-23.9	36.0	47 09.6	-23.0	36.6	47 57.6	-22.2	37.3	48 45.1	-21.3	38.0	49 32.2	-20.4	38.7	55
56	43 27.9	-27.0	33.0	44 18.0	-26.2	33.5	45 07.9	-25.5	34.1	45 57.4	-24.7	34.7	46 46.6	-24.0	35.3	47 35.4	-23.2	35.9	48 23.8	-22.3	36.5	49 11.8	-21.5	37.2	56
57	43 00.9	-27.7	31.8	43 51.8	-27.0	32.3	44 42.4	-26.4	32.8	45 32.7	-25.7	33.4	46 22.6	-24.9	33.9	47 12.2	-24.1	34.5	48 01.5	-23.4	35.2	48 50.3	-22.5	35.8	57
58	42 33.2	-28.4	30.6	43 24.8	-27.9	31.1	44 16.0	-27.2	31.6	45 07.0	-26.5	32.1	45 57.7	-25.8	32.6	46 48.1	-25.1	33.2	47 38.1	-24.3	33.8	48 27.8	-23.5	34.4	58
59	42 04.8	-29.2	29.4	42 56.9	-28.6	29.8	43 48.8	-27.9	30.3	44 40.5	-27.3	30.8	45 31.9	-26.7	31.3	46 23.0	-26.0	31.9	47 13.8	-25.2	32.4	48 04.3	-24.5	33.0	59
60	41 35.6	-29.9	28.2	42 28.3	-29.3	28.6	43 20.9	-28.8	29.1	44 13.2	-28.1	29.6	45 05.2	-27.4	30.1	45 57.0	-26.8	30.6	46 48.6	-26.2	31.1	47 39.8	-25.5	31.7	60
61	41 05.7	-30.6	27.1	41 59.0	-30.0	27.5	42 52.1	-29.4	27.9	43 45.1	-28.9	28.3	44 37.8	-28.3	28.8	45 30.2	-27.7	29.3	46 22.4	-27.0	29.8	47 14.3	-26.3	30.3	61
62	40 35.1	-31.3	25.9	41 29.0	-30.8	26.3	42 22.7	-30.2	26.7	43 16.2	-29.7	27.1	44 09.5	-29.1	27.6	45 02.5	-28.5	28.0	45 55.4	-27.9	28.5	46 48.0	-27.3	29.0	62
63	40 03.8	-31.8	24.8	40 58.2	-31.4	25.2	41 52.5	-30.9	25.5	42 46.5	-30.4	25.9	43 40.4	-29.9	26.3	44 34.0	-29.3	26.8	45 27.5	-28.7	27.2	46 20.7	-28.1	27.7	63
64	39 32.0	-32.5	23.7	40 26.8	-32.0	24.0	41 21.6	-31.6	24.4	42 16.1	-31.1	24.8	43 10.5	-30.6	25.2	44 04.7	-30.0	25.6	44 58.8	-29.5	26.0	45 52.6	-29.0	26.4	64
65	38 59.5	-33.1	22.6	39 54.8	-32.7	22.9	40 50.0	-32.2	23.3	41 45.0	-31.7	23.6	42 39.9	-31.2	24.0	43 34.7	-30.8	24.4	44 29.3	-30.3	24.8	45 23.6	-29.7	25.2	65
66	38 26.4	-33.7	21.5	39 22.1	-33.2	21.8	40 17.8	-32.9	22.2	41 13.3	-32.4	22.5	42 08.7	-32.0	22.8	43 03.9	-31.5	23.2	43 59.0	-31.1	23.6	44 53.9	-30.6	24.0	66
67	37 52.7	-34.2	20.5	38 48.9	-33.8	20.8	39 44.9	-33.4	21.1	40 40.9	-33.1	21.4	41 36.7	-32.6	21.7	42 32.4	-32.2	22.0	43 27.9	-31.7	22.4	44 23.3	-31.3	22.7	67
68	37 18.5	-34.7	19.5	38 15.1	-34.4	19.7	39 11.5	-34.0	20.0	40 07.8	-33.6	20.3	41 04.1	-33.3	20.6	42 00.2	-32.9	20.9	42 56.2	-32.5	21.2	43 52.0	-32.0	21.6	68
69	36 43.8	-35.3	18.4	37 40.7	-35.0	18.7	38 37.5	-34.6	18.9	39 34.2	-34.3	19.2	40 30.8	-33.9	19.5	41 27.3	-33.5	19.8	42 23.7	-33.1	20.1	43 20.0	-32.7	20.4	69
70	36 08.5	-35.7	17.4	37 05.7	-35.4	17.7	38 02.9	-35.2	17.9	38 59.9	-34.8	18.1	39 56.9	-34.5	18.4	40 53.8	-34.1	18.7	41 50.6	-33.8	18.9	42 47.3	-33.4	19.2	70
71	35 32.8	-36.3	16.4	36 30.3	-36.0	16.6	37 27.7	-35.6	16.9	38 25.1	-35.3	17.1	39 22.4	-35.0	17.3	40 19.7	-34.8	17.6	41 16.8	-34.4	17.8	42 13.9	-34.1	18.1	71
72	34 56.5	-36.7	15.5	35 54.3	-36.4	15.7	36 52.1	-36.2	15.9	37 49.8	-35.9	16.1	38 47.4	-35.6	16.3	39 44.9	-35.3	16.5	40 42.4	-35.0	16.8	41 39.8	-34.6	17.0	72
73	34 19.8	-37.1	14.5	35 17.9	-36.9	14.7	36 15.9	-36.7	14.9	37 13.9	-36.4	15.0	38 11.8	-36.1	15.3	39 09.6	-35.8	15.5	40 07.4	-35.5	15.7	41 05.2	-35.3	15.9	73
74	33 42.7	-37.6	13.6	34 41.0	-37.4	13.7	35 39.2	-37.1	13.9	36 37.5	-36.9	14.1	37 35.7	-36.7	14.2	38 33.8	-36.4	14.4	39 31.9	-36.2	14.6	40 29.9	-35.9	14.9	74
75	33 05.1	-38.0	12.6	34 03.6	-37.7	12.8	35 02.1	-37.5	12.9	36 00.6	-37.4	13.1	36 59.0	-37.1	13.2	37 57.4	-36.9	13.4	38 55.7	-36.6	13.6	39 54.0	-36.4	13.8	75
76	32 27.1	-38.4	11.7	33 25.9	-38.2	11.8	34 24.6	-38.0	12.0	35 23.2	-37.8	12.1	36 21.9	-37.6	12.3	37 20.5	-37.4	12.4	38 19.1	-37.2	12.6	39 17.6	-36.9	12.8	76
77	31 48.7	-38.7	10.8	32 47.7	-38.6	10.9	33 46.6	-38.5	11.0	34 45.4	-38.2	11.2	35 44.3	-38.1	11.3	36 43.1	-37.9	11.4	37 41.9	-37.7	11.6	38 40.7	-37.5	11.8	77
78	31 10.0	-39.2	9.9	32 09.1	-39.0	10.0	33 08.1	-38.8	10.1	34 07.2	-38.7	10.2	35 06.2	-38.5	10.4	36 05.2	-38.3	10.5	37 04.2	-38.1	10.6	38 03.2	-38.0	10.8	78
79	30 30.8	-39.4	9.0	31 30.1	-39.4	9.1	32 29.3	-39.2	9.2	33 28.5	-39.0	9.3	34 27.7	-38.9	9.4	35 26.9	-38.7	9.5	36 26.1	-38.6	9.7	37 25.2	-38.4	9.8	79
80	29 51.4	-39.9	8.1	30 50.7	-39.6	8.2	31 50.1	-39.5	8.3	32 49.5	-39.5	8.4	33 48.8	-39.3	8.5	34 48.2	-39.2	8.6	35 47.5	-39.1	8.7	36 46.8	-38.9	8.8	80
81	29 11.5	-40.1	7.3	30 11.1	-40.1	7.4	31 10.6	-40.0	7.4	32 10.0	-39.8	7.5	33 09.5	-39.7	7.6	34 09.0	-39.6	7.7	35 08.4	-39.4	7.8	36 07.9	-39.3	7.9	81
82	28 31.4	-40.5	6.4	29 31.0	-40.3	6.5	30 30.6	-40.2	6.6	31 30.2	-40.1	6.6	32 29.8	-40.0	6.7	33 29.4	-40.0	6.8	34 29.0	-39.9	6.9	35 28.6	-39.8	6.9	82
83	27 50.9	-40.7	5.6	28 50.7	-40.7	5.6	29 50.4	-40.6	5.7	30 50.1	-40.6	5.8	31 49.8	-40.5	5.8	32 49.4	-40.3	5.9	33 49.1	-40.2	6.0	34 48.8	-40.2	6.0	83
84	27 10.2	-41.1	4.8	28 10.0	-41.0	4.8	29 09.8	-41.0	4.9	30 09.5	-40.8	4.9	31 09.3	-40.8	5.0	32 09.1	-40.7	5.0	33 08.9	-40.7	5.1	34 08.6	-40.5	5.1	84
85	26 29.1	-41.3	3.9	27 29.0	-41.3	4.0	28 28.8	-41.2	4.0	29 28.7	-41.2	4.1	30 28.5	-41.1	4.1	31 28.4	-41.1	4.1	32 28.2	-41.0	4.2	33 28.1	-41.0	4.2	85
86	25 47.8	-41.6	3.1	26 47.7	-41.5	3.2	27 47.6	-41.5	3.2	28 47.5	-41.4	3.2	29 47.4	-41.4	3.3	30 47.3	-41.3	3.3	31 47.2	-41.3	3.3	32 47.1	-41.2	3.4	86
87	25 06.2	-41.8	2.3	26 06.2	-41.8	2.4	27 06.1	-41.7	2.4	28 06.1	-41.8	2.4	29 06.0	-41.7	2.4	30 06.0	-41.7	2.5	31 05.9	-41.6	2.5	32 05.9	-41.7	2.5	87
88	24 24.4	-42.1	1.6	25 24.4	-42.1	1.6	26 24.4	-42.1	1.6	27 24.3	-42.0	1.6	28 24.3	-42.0	1.6	29 24.3	-42.0	1.6	30 24.3	-42.0	1.6	31 24.2	-41.9	1.7	88
89	23 42.3	-42.3	0.8	24 42.3	-42.3	0.8	25 42.3	-42.3	0.8	26 42.3	-42.3	0.8	27 42.3	-42.3	0.8	28 42.3	-42.3	0.8	29 42.3	-42.3	0.8	30 42.3	-42.3	0.8	89
90	23 00.0	-42.5	0.0	24 00.0	-42.5	0.0	25 00.0	-42.5	0.0	26 00.0	-42.6	0.0	27 00.0	-42.6	0.0	28 00.0	-42.6	0.0	29 00.0	-42.6	0.0	30 00.0	-42.6	0.0	90
	23°			24°			25°			26°			27°			28°			29°			30°			

LATITUDE **CONTRARY** NAME TO DECLINATION **L.H.A. 45°, 315°**

Dec. °	23° Hc ° ′	d ′	Z °	24° Hc ° ′	d ′	Z °	25° Hc ° ′	d ′	Z °	26° Hc ° ′	d ′	Z °
0	40 36.5	–31.2	111.3	40 14.3	–32.3	112.1	39 51.3	–33.3	112.9	39 27.6	–34.3	113.7
1	40 05.3	–31.8	112.5	39 42.0	–32.9	113.2	39 18.0	–33.9	114.0	38 53.3	–35.0	114.7
2	39 33.5	–32.5	113.6	39 09.1	–33.4	114.3	38 44.1	–34.5	115.1	38 18.3	–35.4	115.8
3	39 01.0	–33.0	114.7	38 35.7	–34.1	115.4	38 09.6	–35.0	116.1	37 42.9	–36.0	116.8
4	38 28.0	–33.7	115.7	38 01.6	–34.6	116.4	37 34.6	–35.6	117.1	37 06.9	–36.5	117.8
5	37 54.3	–34.1	116.8	37 27.0	–35.2	117.5	36 59.0	–36.1	118.1	36 30.4	–37.0	118.8
6	37 20.2	–34.8	117.8	36 51.8	–35.6	118.5	36 22.9	–36.5	119.1	35 53.4	–37.4	119.8
7	36 45.4	–35.2	118.8	36 16.2	–36.1	119.5	35 46.4	–37.0	120.1	35 16.0	–37.9	120.7
8	36 10.2	–35.7	119.8	35 40.1	–36.7	120.5	35 09.4	–37.5	121.1	34 38.1	–38.3	121.7
9	35 34.5	–36.3	120.8	35 03.4	–37.0	121.4	34 31.9	–37.9	122.0	33 59.8	–38.7	122.6
10	34 58.2	–36.6	121.8	34 26.4	–37.6	122.4	33 54.0	–38.4	123.0	33 21.1	–39.2	123.5
11	34 21.6	–37.2	122.8	33 48.8	–37.9	123.3	33 15.6	–38.7	123.9	32 41.9	–39.5	124.4
12	33 44.4	–37.5	123.7	33 10.9	–38.4	124.3	32 36.9	–39.2	124.8	32 02.4	–39.9	125.3
13	33 06.9	–38.0	124.7	32 32.5	–38.7	125.2	31 57.7	–39.5	125.7	31 22.5	–40.2	126.2
14	32 28.9	–38.3	125.6	31 53.8	–39.1	126.1	31 18.2	–39.8	126.6	30 42.3	–40.6	127.1
15	31 50.6	–38.8	126.5	31 14.7	–39.5	127.0	30 38.4	–40.2	127.5	30 01.7	–40.9	127.9
16	31 11.8	–39.1	127.4	30 35.2	–39.8	127.9	29 58.2	–40.6	128.3	29 20.8	–41.2	128.8
17	30 32.7	–39.5	128.3	29 55.4	–40.2	128.7	29 17.6	–40.8	129.2	28 39.6	–41.5	129.6
18	29 53.2	–39.8	129.1	29 15.2	–40.5	129.6	28 36.8	–41.2	130.0	27 58.1	–41.8	130.4
19	29 13.4	–40.1	130.0	28 34.7	–40.8	130.4	27 55.6	–41.4	130.8	27 16.3	–42.1	131.2
20	28 33.3	–40.4	130.8	27 53.9	–41.1	131.2	27 14.2	–41.7	131.6	26 34.2	–42.4	132.0
21	27 52.9	–40.8	131.7	27 12.8	–41.4	132.1	26 32.5	–42.0	132.4	25 51.8	–42.6	132.8
22	27 12.1	–41.0	132.5	26 31.4	–41.6	132.9	25 50.5	–42.3	133.2	25 09.2	–42.8	133.6
23	26 31.1	–41.3	133.3	25 49.8	–41.9	133.7	25 08.2	–42.5	134.0	24 26.4	–43.1	134.4
24	25 49.8	–41.6	134.1	25 07.9	–42.2	134.5	24 25.7	–42.7	134.8	23 43.3	–43.3	135.1
25	25 08.2	–41.8	134.9	24 25.7	–42.4	135.3	23 43.0	–43.0	135.6	23 00.0	–43.5	135.9
26	24 26.4	–42.1	135.7	23 43.3	–42.6	136.0	23 00.0	–43.2	136.3	22 16.5	–43.7	136.6
27	23 44.3	–42.3	136.5	23 00.7	–42.9	136.8	22 16.8	–43.3	137.1	21 32.8	–43.9	137.4
28	23 02.0	–42.5	137.3	22 17.8	–43.0	137.6	21 33.5	–43.6	137.8	20 48.9	–44.1	138.1
29	22 19.5	–42.8	138.0	21 34.8	–43.3	138.3	20 49.9	–43.8	138.6	20 04.8	–44.3	138.8
30	21 36.7	–42.9	138.8	20 51.5	–43.4	139.1	20 06.1	–43.9	139.3	19 20.5	–44.4	139.5
31	20 53.8	–43.1	139.6	20 08.1	–43.7	139.8	19 22.2	–44.2	140.0	18 36.1	–44.6	140.2
32	20 10.7	–43.4	140.3	19 24.4	–43.8	140.5	18 38.0	–44.2	140.7	17 51.5	–44.7	140.9
33	19 27.3	–43.5	141.0	18 40.6	–43.9	141.2	17 53.8	–44.5	141.5	17 06.8	–44.9	141.6
34	18 43.8	–43.6	141.8	17 56.7	–44.2	142.0	17 09.3	–44.5	142.2	16 21.9	–45.0	142.3
35	18 00.2	–43.8	142.5	17 12.5	–44.2	142.7	16 24.8	–44.7	142.9	15 36.9	–45.2	143.0
36	17 16.4	–44.0	143.2	16 28.3	–44.5	143.4	15 40.1	–44.9	143.5	14 51.7	–45.2	143.7
37	16 32.4	–44.1	143.9	15 43.8	–44.5	144.1	14 55.2	–45.0	144.2	14 06.5	–45.4	144.4
38	15 48.3	–44.3	144.6	14 59.3	–44.7	144.8	14 10.2	–45.0	144.9	13 21.1	–45.5	145.1
39	15 04.0	–44.4	145.3	14 14.6	–44.8	145.5	13 25.2	–45.2	145.6	12 35.6	–45.6	145.7
40	14 19.6	–44.5	146.0	13 29.8	–44.9	146.1	12 40.0	–45.3	146.3	11 50.0	–45.6	146.4
41	13 35.1	–44.6	146.7	12 44.9	–45.0	146.8	11 54.7	–45.4	146.9	11 04.4	–45.8	147.1
42	12 50.5	–44.7	147.4	11 59.9	–45.1	147.5	11 09.3	–45.5	147.6	10 18.6	–45.8	147.7
43	12 05.8	–44.8	148.1	11 14.8	–45.2	148.2	10 23.8	–45.5	148.3	9 32.8	–46.0	148.4
44	11 21.0	–45.0	148.7	10 29.6	–45.2	148.8	9 38.3	–45.7	148.9	8 46.8	–45.9	149.0
45	10 36.0	–45.0	149.4	9 44.4	–45.4	149.5	8 52.6	–45.7	149.6	8 00.9	–46.1	149.7
46	9 51.0	–45.0	150.1	8 59.0	–45.4	150.2	8 06.9	–45.7	150.3	7 14.8	–46.1	150.3
47	9 06.0	–45.2	150.8	8 13.6	–45.5	150.8	7 21.2	–45.8	150.9	6 28.7	–46.1	151.0
48	8 20.8	–45.2	151.4	7 28.1	–45.6	151.5	6 35.4	–45.9	151.6	5 42.6	–46.2	151.6
49	7 35.6	–45.3	152.1	6 42.5	–45.6	152.2	5 49.5	–45.9	152.2	4 56.4	–46.2	152.2
50	6 50.3	–45.3	152.8	5 56.9	–45.6	152.8	5 03.6	–46.0	152.9	4 10.2	–46.3	152.9
51	6 05.0	–45.4	153.4	5 11.3	–45.7	153.5	4 17.6	–46.0	153.5	3 23.9	–46.3	153.5
52	5 19.6	–45.4	154.1	4 25.6	–45.7	154.1	3 31.6	–46.0	154.1	2 37.6	–46.3	154.2
53	4 34.2	–45.5	154.7	3 39.9	–45.7	154.8	2 45.6	–46.0	154.8	1 51.3	–46.3	154.8
54	3 48.7	–45.5	155.4	2 54.2	–45.8	155.4	1 59.6	–46.1	155.4	1 05.0	–46.3	155.4
55	3 03.2	–45.5	156.0	2 08.4	–45.8	156.1	1 13.5	–46.0	156.1	0 18.7	–46.3	156.1
56	2 17.7	–45.5	156.7	1 22.6	–45.8	156.7	0 27.5	–46.1	156.7	0 27.6	+46.3	23.3
57	1 32.2	–45.6	157.3	0 36.8	–45.8	157.3	0 18.6	+46.0	22.7	1 13.9	+46.4	22.7
58	0 46.6	–45.5	158.0	0 09.0	+45.8	22.0	1 04.6	+46.1	22.0	2 00.3	+46.2	22.0
59	0 01.1	–45.6	158.6	0 54.8	+45.8	21.4	1 50.7	+46.0	21.4	2 46.5	+46.3	21.4
60	0 44.5	+45.5	20.7	1 40.6	+45.8	20.7	2 36.7	+46.0	20.7	3 32.8	+46.3	20.7
61	1 30.0	+45.5	20.1	2 26.4	+45.7	20.1	3 22.7	+46.0	20.1	4 19.1	+46.2	20.1
62	2 15.5	+45.6	19.4	3 12.1	+45.8	19.4	4 08.7	+46.0	19.4	5 05.3	+46.2	19.5
63	3 01.1	+45.5	18.8	3 57.9	+45.7	18.8	4 54.7	+45.9	18.8	5 51.5	+46.1	18.8
64	3 46.6	+45.4	18.1	4 43.6	+45.6	18.1	5 40.6	+45.9	18.1	6 37.6	+46.1	18.2
65	4 32.0	+45.4	17.4	5 29.2	+45.7	17.5	6 26.5	+45.8	17.5	7 23.7	+46.0	17.5
66	5 17.4	+45.4	16.8	6 14.9	+45.6	16.8	7 12.3	+45.8	16.9	8 09.7	+46.0	16.9
67	6 02.8	+45.4	16.1	7 00.5	+45.5	16.2	7 58.1	+45.7	16.2	8 55.7	+45.9	16.2
68	6 48.2	+45.2	15.5	7 46.0	+45.4	15.5	8 43.8	+45.6	15.5	9 41.6	+45.8	15.6
69	7 33.4	+45.3	14.8	8 31.4	+45.4	14.8	9 29.4	+45.6	14.9	10 27.4	+45.8	14.9
70	8 18.7	+45.1	14.1	9 16.8	+45.4	14.2	10 15.0	+45.5	14.2	11 13.2	+45.6	14.3
71	9 03.8	+45.1	13.5	10 02.2	+45.2	13.5	11 00.5	+45.4	13.6	11 58.8	+45.6	13.6
72	9 48.9	+45.0	12.8	10 47.4	+45.2	12.9	11 45.9	+45.3	12.9	12 44.4	+45.4	12.9
73	10 33.9	+44.9	12.1	11 32.6	+45.0	12.2	12 31.2	+45.2	12.2	13 29.8	+45.4	12.3
74	11 18.8	+44.9	11.5	12 17.6	+45.0	11.5	13 16.4	+45.1	11.6	14 15.2	+45.2	11.6
75	12 03.7	+44.7	10.8	13 02.6	+44.9	10.8	14 01.5	+45.0	10.9	15 00.4	+45.2	10.9
76	12 48.4	+44.6	10.1	13 47.5	+44.7	10.1	14 46.5	+44.9	10.2	15 45.6	+45.0	10.2
77	13 33.0	+44.5	9.4	14 32.2	+44.6	9.5	15 31.4	+44.7	9.5	16 30.6	+44.8	9.5
78	14 17.5	+44.4	8.7	15 16.8	+44.5	8.8	16 16.1	+44.6	8.8	17 15.4	+44.7	8.9
79	15 01.9	+44.3	8.0	16 01.3	+44.4	8.1	17 00.7	+44.5	8.1	18 00.1	+44.6	8.2
80	15 46.2	+44.1	7.3	16 45.7	+44.2	7.4	17 45.2	+44.3	7.4	18 44.7	+44.4	7.5
81	16 30.3	+44.0	6.6	17 29.9	+44.1	6.7	18 29.5	+44.1	6.7	19 29.1	+44.2	6.7
82	17 14.3	+43.8	5.9	18 14.0	+43.9	5.9	19 13.6	+44.0	6.0	20 13.3	+44.1	6.0
83	17 58.1	+43.7	5.2	18 57.9	+43.7	5.2	19 57.6	+43.8	5.3	20 57.4	+43.8	5.3
84	18 41.8	+43.5	4.5	19 41.6	+43.6	4.5	20 41.4	+43.6	4.5	21 41.2	+43.7	4.6
85	19 25.3	+43.3	3.7	20 25.2	+43.3	3.8	21 25.0	+43.5	3.8	22 24.9	+43.5	3.8
86	20 08.6	+43.2	3.0	21 08.5	+43.2	3.0	22 08.5	+43.2	3.1	23 08.4	+43.2	3.1
87	20 51.8	+42.9	2.3	21 51.7	+43.0	2.3	22 51.7	+43.0	2.3	23 51.6	+43.1	2.3
88	21 34.7	+42.8	1.5	22 34.7	+42.8	1.5	23 34.7	+42.8	1.5	24 34.7	+42.7	1.6
89	22 17.5	+42.5	0.8	23 17.5	+42.5	0.8	24 17.5	+42.5	0.8	25 17.4	+42.6	0.8
90	23 00.0	+42.3	0.0	24 00.0	+42.3	0.0	25 00.0	+42.3	0.0	26 00.0	+42.3	0.0
	23°			24°			25°			26°		

Dec. °	27° Hc ° ′	d ′	Z °	28° Hc ° ′	d ′	Z °	29° Hc ° ′	d ′	Z °	30° Hc ° ′	d ′	Z °
0	39 03.2	–35.4	114.4	38 38.0	–36.3	115.1	38 12.2	–37.3	115.9	37 45.7	–38.2	116.6
1	38 27.8	–35.9	115.5	38 01.7	–36.8	116.2	37 34.9	–37.7	116.9	37 07.5	–38.7	117.5
2	37 51.9	–36.4	116.5	37 24.9	–37.4	117.2	36 57.2	–38.3	117.8	36 28.8	–39.1	118.5
3	37 15.5	–36.9	117.5	36 47.5	–37.8	118.1	36 18.9	–38.7	118.8	35 49.7	–39.5	119.4
4	36 38.6	–37.4	118.5	36 09.7	–38.3	119.1	35 40.2	–39.1	119.7	35 10.2	–40.0	120.4
5	36 01.2	–37.8	119.4	35 31.4	–38.7	120.1	35 01.1	–39.5	120.7	34 30.2	–40.3	121.3
6	35 23.4	–38.3	120.4	34 52.7	–39.1	121.0	34 21.6	–40.0	121.6	33 49.9	–40.7	122.2
7	34 45.1	–38.8	121.3	34 13.6	–39.5	121.9	33 41.6	–40.3	122.5	33 09.2	–41.1	123.0
8	34 06.3	–39.1	122.3	33 34.1	–40.0	122.8	33 01.3	–40.7	123.4	32 28.1	–41.5	123.9
9	33 27.2	–39.5	123.2	32 54.1	–40.3	123.7	32 20.6	–41.0	124.2	31 46.6	–41.8	124.8
10	32 47.7	–39.9	124.1	32 13.8	–40.6	124.6	31 39.6	–41.4	125.1	31 04.8	–42.1	125.6
11	32 07.8	–40.3	125.0	31 33.2	–41.0	125.5	30 58.2	–41.8	126.0	30 22.7	–42.4	126.4
12	31 27.5	–40.6	125.8	30 52.2	–41.4	126.3	30 16.4	–42.0	126.8	29 40.3	–42.7	127.2
13	30 46.9	–41.0	126.7	30 10.8	–41.6	127.2	29 34.4	–42.3	127.6	28 57.6	–43.0	128.1
14	30 05.9	–41.3	127.5	29 29.2	–42.0	128.0	28 52.1	–42.6	128.4	28 14.6	–43.3	128.8
15	29 24.6	–41.5	128.4	28 47.2	–42.2	128.8	28 09.5	–42.9	129.2	27 31.3	–43.5	129.6
16	28 43.1	–41.9	129.2	28 05.0	–42.6	129.6	27 26.6	–43.2	130.0	26 47.8	–43.8	130.4
17	28 01.2	–42.2	130.0	27 22.4	–42.8	130.4	26 43.4	–43.4	130.8	26 04.0	–44.0	131.2
18	27 19.0	–42.4	130.8	26 39.6	–43.0	131.2	26 00.0	–43.7	131.6	25 20.0	–44.2	131.9
19	26 36.6	–42.7	131.6	25 56.6	–43.3	132.0	25 16.3	–43.9	132.3	24 35.8	–44.5	132.7
20	25 53.9	–43.0	132.4	25 13.3	–43.6	132.7	24 32.4	–44.1	133.1	23 51.3	–44.6	133.4
21	25 10.9	–43.2	133.2	24 29.7	–43.7	133.5	23 48.3	–44.3	133.8	23 06.7	–44.9	134.1
22	24 27.7	–43.4	133.9	23 46.0	–44.0	134.2	23 04.0	–44.5	134.6	22 21.8	–45.1	134.9
23	23 44.3	–43.6	134.7	23 02.0	–44.2	135.0	22 19.5	–44.7	135.3	21 36.7	–45.2	135.6
24	23 00.7	–43.9	135.4	22 17.8	–44.3	135.7	21 34.8	–44.9	136.0	20 51.5	–45.4	136.3
25	22 16.8	–44.0	136.2	21 33.5	–44.6	136.4	20 49.9	–45.1	136.7	20 06.1	–45.6	137.0
26	21 32.8	–44.2	136.9	20 48.9	–44.8	137.2	20 04.8	–45.2	137.4	19 20.5	–45.7	137.7
27	20 48.6	–44.5	137.6	20 04.1	–44.9	137.9	19 19.6	–45.4	138.1	18 34.8	–45.9	138.3
28	20 04.1	–44.5	138.3	19 19.2	–45.0	138.6	18 34.2	–45.6	138.8	17 48.9	–46.0	139.0
29	19 19.6	–44.8	139.1	18 34.2	–45.3	139.3	17 48.6	–45.7	139.5	17 02.9	–46.1	139.7
30	18 34.8	–44.9	139.8	17 48.9	–45.3	140.0	17 02.9	–45.8	140.2	16 16.8	–46.3	140.4
31	17 49.9	–45.0	140.5	17 03.6	–45.5	140.7	16 17.1	–45.9	140.8	15 30.5	–46.4	141.0
32	17 04.9	–45.2	141.1	16 18.1	–45.7	141.3	15 31.2	–46.1	141.5	14 44.1	–46.4	141.7
33	16 19.7	–45.4	141.8	15 32.4	–45.7	142.0	14 45.1	–46.2	142.2	13 57.7	–46.6	142.3
34	15 34.3	–45.4	142.5	14 46.7	–45.9	142.7	13 58.9	–46.3	142.8	13 11.1	–46.7	143.0
35	14 48.9	–45.6	143.2	14 00.8	–46.0	143.3	13 12.6	–46.4	143.5	12 24.4	–46.8	143.6
36	14 03.3	–45.6	143.9	13 14.8	–46.1	144.0	12 26.2	–46.4	144.1	11 37.6	–46.9	144.3
37	13 17.7	–45.8	144.5	12 28.7	–46.1	144.7	11 39.8	–46.6	144.8	10 50.7	–46.9	144.9
38	12 31.9	–45.9	145.2	11 42.6	–46.3	145.3	10 53.2	–46.6	145.4	10 03.8	–47.1	145.5
39	11 46.0	–46.0	145.9	10 56.3	–46.3	146.0	10 06.6	–46.8	146.1	9 16.7	–47.0	146.2
40	11 00.0	–46.0	146.5	10 10.0	–46.5	146.6	9 19.8	–46.8	146.7	8 29.7	–47.2	146.8
41	10 14.0	–46.2	147.2	9 23.5	–46.5	147.3	8 33.0	–46.8	147.3	7 42.5	–47.2	147.4
42	9 27.8	–46.2	147.8	8 37.0	–46.5	147.9	7 46.2	–46.9	148.0	6 55.3	–47.2	148.0
43	8 41.6	–46.2	148.5	7 50.5	–46.6	148.5	6 59.3	–47.0	148.6	6 08.1	–47.3	148.7
44	7 55.4	–46.3	149.1	7 03.9	–46.7	149.2	6 12.3	–47.0	149.2	5 20.8	–47.4	149.3
45	7 09.1	–46.4	149.7	6 17.2	–46.7	149.8	5 25.3	–47.0	149.9	4 33.4	–47.3	149.9
46	6 22.7	–46.4	150.4	5 30.5	–46.7	150.4	4 38.3	–47.1	150.5	3 46.1	–47.4	150.5
47	5 36.3	–46.5	151.0	4 43.8	–46.8	151.1	3 51.2	–47.1	151.1	2 58.7	–47.4	151.1
48	4 49.8	–46.5	151.7	3 57.0	–46.8	151.7	3 04.1	–47.1	151.7	2 11.3	–47.4	151.7
49	4 03.3	–46.5	152.3	3 10.2	–46.9	152.3	2 17.0	–47.1	152.3	1 23.9	–47.4	152.4
50	3 16.8	–46.6	152.9	2 23.3	–46.8	152.9	1 29.9	–47.2	153.0	0 36.5	–47.5	153.0
51	2 30.2	–46.6	153.5	1 36.5	–46.9	153.6	0 42.7	–47.1	153.6	0 11.0	+47.4	26.4
52	1 43.6	–46.6	154.2	0 49.6	–46.9	154.2	0 04.4	+47.1	25.8	0 58.4	+47.4	25.8
53	0 57.0	–46.5	154.8	0 02.7	–46.8	154.8	0 51.5	+47.2	25.2	1 45.8	+47.5	25.2
54	0 10.5	–46.6	155.4	0 44.1	+46.9	24.6	1 38.7	+47.1	24.6	2 33.3	+47.4	24.6
55	0 36.1	+46.6	23.9	1 31.0	+46.8	23.9	2 25.8	+47.1	24.0	3 20.7	+47.3	24.0
56	1 22.7	+46.6	23.3	2 17.8	+46.9	23.3	3 12.9	+47.1	23.3	4 08.0	+47.4	23.4
57	2 09.3	+46.6	22.7	3 04.7	+46.8	22.7	4 00.0	+47.1	22.7	4 55.4	+47.3	22.7
58	2 55.9	+46.5	22.0	3 51.5	+46.8	22.1	4 47.1	+47.0	22.1	5 42.7	+47.2	22.1
59	3 42.4	+46.5	21.4	4 38.3	+46.7	21.4	5 34.1	+47.0	21.5	6 29.9	+47.3	21.5
60	4 28.9	+46.5	20.8	5 25.0	+46.7	20.8	6 21.1	+47.0	20.8	7 17.2	+47.1	20.9
61	5 15.4	+46.5	20.1	6 11.7	+46.7	20.2	7 08.1	+46.8	20.2	8 04.3	+47.2	20.3
62	6 01.9	+46.4	19.5	6 58.4	+46.6	19.5	7 54.9	+46.9	19.6	8 51.5	+47.0	19.6
63	6 48.3	+46.3	18.9	7 45.0	+46.6	18.9	8 41.8	+46.8	19.0	9 38.5	+47.0	19.0
64	7 34.6	+46.3	18.2	8 31.6	+46.5	18.3	9 28.6	+46.7	18.3	10 25.5	+46.9	18.4
65	8 20.9	+46.2	17.6	9 18.1	+46.4	17.6	10 15.3	+46.6	17.7	11 12.4	+46.9	17.7
66	9 07.1	+46.2	16.9	10 04.5	+46.4	17.0	11 01.9	+46.5	17.0	11 59.3	+46.7	17.1
67	9 53.3	+46.1	16.3	10 50.9	+46.2	16.3	11 48.4	+46.5	16.4	12 46.0	+46.6	16.5
68	10 39.4	+46.0	15.6	11 37.1	+46.2	15.7	12 34.9	+46.4	15.7	13 32.6	+46.6	15.8
69	11 25.4	+45.9	15.0	12 23.3	+46.1	15.0	13 21.3	+46.2	15.1	14 19.2	+46.4	15.2
70	12 11.3	+45.8	14.3	13 09.4	+46.0	14.4	14 07.5	+46.2	14.4	15 05.6	+46.4	14.5
71	12 57.1	+45.8	13.7	13 55.4	+45.9	13.7	14 53.7	+46.0	13.8	15 52.0	+46.2	13.8
72	13 42.9	+45.6	13.0	14 41.3	+45.8	13.1	15 39.7	+46.0	13.1	16 38.2	+46.1	13.2
73	14 28.5	+45.5	12.3	15 27.1	+45.6	12.4	16 25.7	+45.8	12.4	17 24.3	+45.9	12.5
74	15 14.0	+45.4	11.7	16 12.7	+45.5	11.7	17 11.5	+45.6	11.8	18 10.2	+45.8	11.8
75	15 59.4	+45.2	11.0	16 58.2	+45.4	11.0	17 57.1	+45.6	11.1	18 56.0	+45.7	11.2
76	16 44.6	+45.1	10.3	17 43.6	+45.3	10.3	18 42.7	+45.3	10.4	19 41.7	+45.5	10.5
77	17 29.7	+45.0	9.6	18 28.9	+45.1	9.7	19 28.0	+45.2	9.7	20 27.2	+45.3	9.8
78	18 14.7	+44.8	8.9	19 14.0	+44.9	9.0	20 13.2	+45.1	9.0	21 12.5	+45.1	9.1
79	18 59.5	+44.7	8.2	19 58.9	+44.8	8.3	20 58.3	+44.8	8.3	21 57.6	+45.0	8.4
80	19 44.2	+44.5	7.5	20 43.7	+44.5	7.5	21 43.1	+44.7	7.6	22 42.6	+44.8	7.6
81	20 28.7	+44.3	6.8	21 28.2	+44.4	6.8	22 27.8	+44.5	6.9	23 27.4	+44.5	6.9
82	21 13.0	+44.1	6.1	22 12.6	+44.2	6.1	23 12.3	+44.3	6.1	24 11.9	+44.4	6.2
83	21 57.1	+43.9	5.3	22 56.8	+44.0	5.4	23 56.6	+44.0	5.4	24 56.3	+44.1	5.5
84	22 41.0	+43.8	4.6	23 40.8	+43.8	4.6	24 40.6	+43.9	4.7	25 40.4	+43.9	4.7
85	23 24.8	+43.5	3.9	24 24.6	+43.6	3.9	25 24.5	+43.6	3.9	26 24.3	+43.7	3.9
86	24 08.3	+43.3	3.1	25 08.2	+43.3	3.1	26 08.1	+43.4	3.1	27 08.0	+43.4	3.2
87	24 51.6	+43.0	2.3	25 51.5	+43.1	2.4	26 51.5	+43.1	2.4	27 51.4	+43.2	2.4
88	25 34.6	+42.8	1.6	26 34.6	+42.8	1.6	27 34.6	+42.8	1.6	28 34.6	+42.8	1.6
89	26 17.4	+42.6	0.8	27 17.4	+42.6	0.8	28 17.4	+42.6	0.8	29 17.4	+42.6	0.8
90	27 00.0	+42.3	0.0	28 00.0	+42.3	0.0	29 00.0	+42.3	0.0	30 00.0	+42.3	0.0
	27°			28°			29°			30°		

S. Lat. {L.H.A. greater than 180° ....Zn=180°–Z; L.H.A. less than 180°...........Zn=180°+Z

LATITUDE **SAME** NAME AS DECLINATION **L.H.A. 135°, 225°**

275

46°, 314° L.H.A. LATITUDE SAME NAME AS DECLINATION

N. Lat. {L.H.A. greater than 180° .....Zn=Z
{L.H.A. less than 180°............Zn=360°–Z

Dec.	23°			24°			25°			26°			27°			28°			29°			30°			Dec.
	Hc	d	Z	Hc	d	Z	Hc	d	Z	Hc	d	Z	Hc	d	Z	Hc	d	Z	Hc	d	Z	Hc	d	Z	
°	° ′	′	°	° ′	′	°	° ′	′	°	° ′	′	°	° ′	′	°	° ′	′	°	° ′	′	°	° ′	′	°	°
0	39 45.0	+30.2	110.7	39 23.4	+31.3	111.4	39 01.1	+32.4	112.2	38 38.1	+33.4	112.9	38 14.3	+34.5	113.7	37 49.9	+35.4	114.4	37 24.8	+36.4	115.1	36 59.0	+37.4	115.8	0
1	40 15.2	+29.5	109.5	39 54.7	+30.6	110.3	39 33.5	+31.7	111.1	39 11.5	+32.8	111.9	38 48.8	+33.8	112.6	38 25.3	+34.9	113.4	38 01.2	+35.8	114.1	37 36.4	+36.8	114.8	1
2	40 44.7	+28.8	108.4	40 25.3	+30.0	109.2	40 05.2	+31.1	110.0	39 44.3	+32.1	110.8	39 22.6	+33.2	111.6	39 00.2	+34.3	112.3	38 37.0	+35.3	113.1	38 13.2	+36.3	113.8	2
3	41 13.5	+28.1	107.2	40 55.3	+29.2	108.1	40 36.3	+30.4	108.9	40 16.4	+31.6	109.7	39 55.8	+32.7	110.5	39 34.5	+33.6	111.3	39 12.3	+34.8	112.0	38 49.5	+35.7	112.8	3
4	41 41.6	+27.3	106.1	41 24.5	+28.6	106.9	41 06.7	+29.7	107.7	40 48.0	+30.8	108.6	40 28.5	+31.9	109.4	40 08.1	+33.1	110.2	39 47.1	+34.1	111.0	39 25.2	+35.2	111.7	4
5	42 08.9	+26.6	104.9	41 53.1	+27.8	105.7	41 36.4	+29.0	106.6	41 18.8	+30.2	107.4	41 00.4	+31.4	108.3	40 41.2	+32.5	109.1	40 21.2	+33.6	109.9	40 00.4	+34.6	110.7	5
6	42 35.5	+25.9	103.6	42 20.9	+27.1	104.5	42 05.4	+28.3	105.4	41 49.0	+29.5	106.3	41 31.8	+30.6	107.1	41 13.7	+31.8	108.0	40 54.8	+32.9	108.8	40 35.0	+34.0	109.6	6
7	43 01.4	+25.0	102.4	42 48.0	+26.3	103.3	42 33.7	+27.6	104.2	42 18.5	+28.8	105.1	42 02.4	+30.0	106.0	41 45.5	+31.1	106.8	41 27.7	+32.3	107.7	41 09.0	+33.4	108.5	7
8	43 26.4	+24.2	101.2	43 14.3	+25.5	102.1	43 01.3	+26.7	103.0	42 47.3	+28.0	103.9	42 32.4	+29.2	104.8	42 16.6	+30.4	105.7	42 00.0	+31.6	106.6	41 42.4	+32.8	107.4	8
9	43 50.6	+23.4	99.9	43 39.8	+24.7	100.8	43 28.0	+26.0	101.8	43 15.3	+27.2	102.7	43 01.6	+28.5	103.6	42 47.0	+29.7	104.5	42 31.6	+30.8	105.4	42 15.2	+32.0	106.3	9
10	44 14.0	+22.4	98.6	44 04.5	+23.8	99.6	43 54.0	+25.1	100.5	43 42.5	+26.5	101.5	43 30.1	+27.7	102.4	43 16.7	+29.0	103.3	43 02.4	+30.2	104.2	42 47.2	+31.4	105.1	10
11	44 36.4	+21.6	97.3	44 28.3	+22.9	98.3	44 19.1	+24.3	99.3	44 09.0	+25.6	100.2	43 57.8	+26.9	101.2	43 45.7	+28.2	102.1	43 32.6	+29.4	103.1	43 18.6	+30.6	104.0	11
12	44 58.0	+20.7	96.0	44 51.2	+22.1	97.0	44 43.4	+23.4	98.0	44 34.6	+24.7	99.0	44 24.7	+26.1	99.9	44 13.9	+27.3	100.9	44 02.0	+28.7	101.8	43 49.2	+29.9	102.8	12
13	45 18.7	+19.7	94.7	45 13.3	+21.1	95.7	45 06.8	+22.5	96.7	44 59.3	+23.9	97.7	44 50.8	+25.2	98.7	44 41.2	+26.6	99.6	44 30.7	+27.8	100.6	44 19.1	+29.1	101.6	13
14	45 38.4	+18.8	93.3	45 34.4	+20.2	94.4	45 29.3	+21.6	95.4	45 23.2	+23.0	96.4	45 16.0	+24.3	97.4	45 07.8	+25.7	98.4	44 58.5	+27.0	99.4	44 48.2	+28.3	100.4	14
15	45 57.2	+17.8	92.0	45 54.6	+19.2	93.0	45 50.9	+20.7	94.0	45 46.2	+22.0	95.1	45 40.3	+23.5	96.1	45 33.5	+24.8	97.1	45 25.5	+26.2	98.1	45 16.5	+27.5	99.1	15
16	46 15.0	+16.8	90.6	46 13.8	+18.3	91.6	46 11.6	+19.7	92.7	46 08.2	+21.1	93.7	46 03.8	+22.5	94.8	45 58.3	+23.9	95.8	45 51.7	+25.3	96.8	45 44.0	+26.7	97.8	16
17	46 31.8	+15.8	89.2	46 32.1	+17.2	90.3	46 31.3	+18.7	91.3	46 29.3	+20.2	92.4	46 26.3	+21.6	93.4	46 22.2	+23.0	94.5	46 17.0	+24.3	95.5	46 10.7	+25.7	96.5	17
18	46 47.6	+14.7	87.8	46 49.3	+16.2	88.9	46 50.0	+17.6	89.9	46 49.5	+19.1	91.0	46 47.9	+20.6	92.1	46 45.2	+22.0	93.1	46 41.3	+23.5	94.2	46 36.4	+24.8	95.2	18
19	47 02.3	+13.7	86.4	47 05.5	+15.2	87.5	47 07.6	+16.7	88.5	47 08.6	+18.1	89.6	47 08.5	+19.5	90.7	47 07.2	+21.0	91.8	47 04.8	+22.4	92.8	47 01.2	+23.9	93.9	19
20	47 16.0	+12.5	84.9	47 20.7	+14.1	86.0	47 24.3	+15.6	87.1	47 26.7	+17.1	88.2	47 28.0	+18.6	89.3	47 28.2	+20.0	90.4	47 27.2	+21.5	91.5	47 25.1	+23.0	92.6	20
21	47 28.5	+11.5	83.5	47 34.8	+13.0	84.6	47 39.9	+14.5	85.7	47 43.8	+16.0	86.8	47 46.6	+17.5	87.9	47 48.2	+19.0	89.0	47 48.7	+20.5	90.1	47 48.1	+21.9	91.2	21
22	47 40.0	+10.4	82.0	47 47.8	+11.9	83.1	47 54.4	+13.4	84.2	47 59.8	+14.9	85.3	48 04.1	+16.4	86.5	48 07.2	+18.0	87.6	48 09.2	+19.4	88.7	48 10.0	+20.9	89.8	22
23	47 50.4	+9.3	80.6	47 59.7	+10.7	81.7	48 07.8	+12.3	82.8	48 14.7	+13.9	83.9	48 20.5	+15.4	85.0	48 25.2	+16.8	86.1	48 28.6	+18.4	87.3	48 30.9	+19.9	88.4	23
24	47 59.7	+8.1	79.1	48 10.4	+9.7	80.2	48 20.1	+11.1	81.3	48 28.6	+12.7	82.4	48 35.9	+14.2	83.5	48 42.0	+15.8	84.7	48 47.0	+17.3	85.8	48 50.8	+18.8	87.0	24
25	48 07.8	+6.9	77.6	48 20.1	+8.5	78.7	48 31.2	+10.1	79.8	48 41.3	+11.5	80.9	48 50.1	+13.1	82.1	48 57.8	+14.6	83.2	49 04.3	+16.2	84.4	49 09.6	+17.7	85.5	25
26	48 14.7	+5.8	76.1	48 28.6	+7.3	77.2	48 41.3	+8.8	78.3	48 52.8	+10.4	79.5	49 03.2	+11.9	80.6	49 12.4	+13.5	81.7	49 20.5	+15.0	82.9	49 27.3	+16.6	84.0	26
27	48 20.5	+4.7	74.6	48 35.9	+6.1	75.7	48 50.1	+7.7	76.8	49 03.2	+9.2	78.0	49 15.1	+10.8	79.1	49 25.9	+12.3	80.2	49 35.5	+13.9	81.4	49 43.9	+15.4	82.6	27
28	48 25.2	+3.4	73.1	48 42.0	+5.0	74.2	48 57.8	+6.5	75.3	49 12.4	+8.1	76.4	49 25.9	+9.6	77.6	49 38.2	+11.2	78.7	49 49.4	+12.6	79.9	49 59.3	+14.2	81.1	28
29	48 28.6	+2.3	71.6	48 47.0	+3.8	72.7	49 04.3	+5.3	73.8	49 20.5	+6.8	74.9	49 35.5	+8.4	76.1	49 49.4	+9.9	77.2	50 02.0	+11.5	78.4	50 13.5	+13.1	79.5	29
30	48 30.9	+1.1	70.1	48 50.8	+2.6	71.2	49 09.6	+4.1	72.3	49 27.3	+5.6	73.4	49 43.9	+7.1	74.5	49 59.3	+8.7	75.7	50 13.5	+10.3	76.8	50 26.6	+11.8	78.0	30
31	48 32.0	−0.1	68.6	48 53.4	+1.4	69.7	49 13.7	+2.9	70.8	49 32.9	+4.4	71.9	49 51.0	+5.9	73.0	50 08.0	+7.5	74.1	50 23.8	+9.1	75.3	50 38.4	+10.7	76.5	31
32	48 31.9	−1.2	67.1	48 54.8	+0.2	68.2	49 16.6	+1.6	69.2	49 37.3	+3.2	70.3	49 56.9	+4.7	71.4	50 15.5	+6.2	72.6	50 32.9	+7.7	73.7	50 49.1	+9.3	74.9	32
33	48 30.7	−2.5	65.6	48 55.0	−1.1	66.6	49 18.2	+0.5	67.7	49 40.5	+1.9	68.8	50 01.6	+3.5	69.9	50 21.7	+5.0	71.0	50 40.6	+6.6	72.2	50 58.4	+8.1	73.4	33
34	48 28.2	−3.6	64.1	48 53.9	−2.2	65.1	49 18.7	−0.8	66.2	49 42.4	+0.7	67.2	50 05.1	+2.2	68.3	50 26.7	+3.7	69.5	50 47.2	+5.2	70.6	51 06.5	+6.8	71.8	34
35	48 24.6	−4.8	62.6	48 51.7	−3.4	63.6	49 17.9	−2.0	64.6	49 43.1	−0.5	65.7	50 07.3	+1.0	66.8	50 30.4	+2.5	67.9	50 52.4	+4.0	69.0	51 13.3	+5.6	70.2	35
36	48 19.8	−6.0	61.1	48 48.3	−4.6	62.1	49 15.9	−3.1	63.1	49 42.6	−1.8	64.2	50 08.3	−0.3	65.2	50 32.9	+1.2	66.3	50 56.4	+2.7	67.5	51 18.9	+4.2	68.6	36
37	48 13.8	−7.1	59.6	48 43.7	−5.8	60.6	49 12.8	−4.4	61.6	49 40.8	−3.0	62.6	50 08.0	−1.6	63.7	50 34.1	−0.1	64.8	50 59.1	+1.4	65.9	51 23.1	+2.9	67.0	37
38	48 06.7	−8.3	58.1	48 37.9	−6.9	59.1	49 08.4	−5.7	60.0	49 37.8	−4.2	61.1	50 06.4	−2.8	62.1	50 34.0	−1.4	63.2	51 00.5	+0.1	64.3	51 26.0	+1.7	65.4	38
39	47 58.4	−9.4	56.6	48 31.0	−8.1	57.6	49 02.7	−6.8	58.5	49 33.6	−5.4	59.5	50 03.6	−4.1	60.6	50 32.6	−2.6	61.6	51 00.6	−1.1	62.7	51 27.7	+0.3	63.8	39
40	47 49.0	−10.6	55.1	48 22.9	−9.3	56.1	48 55.9	−7.9	57.0	49 28.2	−6.7	58.0	49 59.5	−5.2	59.0	50 30.0	−3.9	60.0	50 59.5	−2.5	61.1	51 28.0	−1.0	62.2	40
41	47 38.4	−11.6	53.7	48 13.6	−10.4	54.6	48 48.0	−9.2	55.5	49 21.5	−7.8	56.5	49 54.3	−6.6	57.4	50 26.1	−5.2	58.5	50 57.0	−3.8	59.5	51 27.0	−2.4	60.6	41
42	47 26.8	−12.8	52.2	48 03.2	−11.6	53.1	48 38.8	−10.3	54.0	49 13.7	−9.1	54.9	49 47.7	−7.7	55.9	50 20.9	−6.4	56.9	50 53.2	−5.0	57.9	51 24.6	−3.6	59.0	42
43	47 14.0	−13.8	50.8	47 51.6	−12.6	51.6	48 28.5	−11.5	52.5	49 04.6	−10.2	53.4	49 40.0	−9.0	54.4	50 14.5	−7.6	55.3	50 48.2	−6.3	56.4	51 21.0	−4.9	57.4	43
44	47 00.2	−14.9	49.4	47 39.0	−13.8	50.2	48 17.0	−12.5	51.0	48 54.4	−11.4	51.9	49 31.0	−10.1	52.8	50 06.9	−8.9	53.8	50 41.9	−7.6	54.8	51 16.1	−6.3	55.8	44
45	46 45.3	−15.9	47.9	47 25.2	−14.8	48.7	48 04.5	−13.7	49.6	48 43.0	−12.5	50.4	49 20.9	−11.4	51.3	49 58.0	−10.1	52.3	50 34.3	−8.8	53.2	51 09.8	−7.5	54.2	45
46	46 29.4	−16.9	46.5	47 10.4	−15.9	47.3	47 50.8	−14.8	48.1	48 30.5	−13.7	49.0	49 09.5	−12.4	49.8	49 47.9	−11.3	50.7	50 25.5	−10.1	51.7	51 02.3	−8.8	52.6	46
47	46 12.5	−18.0	45.1	46 54.5	−16.9	45.9	47 36.0	−15.9	46.7	48 16.8	−14.7	47.5	48 57.1	−13.7	48.3	49 36.6	−12.5	49.2	50 15.4	−11.2	50.1	50 53.5	−10.0	51.1	47
48	45 54.5	−18.9	43.8	46 37.6	−17.9	44.5	47 20.1	−16.9	45.3	48 02.1	−15.9	46.0	48 43.4	−14.7	46.9	49 24.1	−13.6	47.7	50 04.2	−12.5	48.6	50 43.5	−11.3	49.5	48
49	45 35.6	−19.8	42.4	46 19.7	−18.9	43.1	47 03.2	−17.9	43.8	47 46.2	−16.9	44.6	48 28.7	−15.9	45.4	49 10.5	−14.8	46.2	49 51.7	−13.7	47.1	50 32.2	−12.5	47.9	49
50	45 15.8	−20.9	41.1	46 00.8	−19.9	41.7	46 45.3	−19.0	42.4	47 29.3	−18.0	43.2	48 12.8	−17.0	43.9	48 55.7	−15.9	44.7	49 38.0	−14.8	45.6	50 19.7	−13.7	46.4	50
51	44 54.9	−21.7	39.7	45 40.9	−20.9	40.4	46 26.3	−19.9	41.1	47 11.3	−19.0	41.8	47 55.8	−18.0	42.5	48 39.8	−17.0	43.3	49 23.2	−16.0	44.1	50 06.0	−14.9	44.9	51
52	44 33.2	−22.6	38.4	45 20.0	−21.7	39.0	46 06.4	−20.9	39.7	46 52.3	−19.9	40.4	47 37.8	−19.0	41.1	48 22.8	−18.1	41.8	49 07.2	−17.1	42.6	49 51.1	−16.0	43.4	52
53	44 10.6	−23.5	37.1	44 58.3	−22.7	37.7	45 45.5	−21.8	38.4	46 32.4	−21.0	39.0	47 18.8	−20.1	39.7	48 04.7	−19.1	40.4	48 50.1	−18.1	41.1	49 35.1	−17.2	41.9	53
54	43 47.1	−24.3	35.9	44 35.6	−23.6	36.4	45 23.7	−22.8	37.0	46 11.4	−21.9	37.6	46 58.7	−21.1	38.3	47 45.6	−20.2	39.0	48 32.0	−19.3	39.7	49 17.9	−18.3	40.4	54
55	43 22.8	−25.1	34.6	44 12.0	−24.4	35.1	45 00.9	−23.6	35.7	45 49.5	−22.9	36.3	46 37.6	−22.0	36.9	47 25.4	−21.2	37.6	48 12.7	−20.3	38.3	48 59.6	−19.4	39.0	55
56	42 57.7	−26.0	33.3	43 47.6	−25.2	33.9	44 37.3	−24.5	34.4	45 26.6	−23.7	35.0	46 15.6	−23.0	35.6	47 04.2	−22.1	36.2	47 52.4	−21.3	36.8	48 40.2	−20.4	37.5	56
57	42 31.7	−26.7	32.1	43 22.4	−26.1	32.6	44 12.8	−25.4	33.1	45 02.9	−24.7	33.7	45 52.6	−23.8	34.2	46 42.1	−23.1	34.8	47 31.1	−22.3	35.5	48 19.8	−21.5	36.1	57
58	42 05.0	−27.5	30.9	42 56.3	−26.8	31.4	43 47.4	−26.1	31.9	44 38.2	−25.4	32.4	45 28.8	−24.8	32.9	46 19.0	−24.1	33.5	47 08.8	−23.3	34.1	47 58.3	−22.4	34.7	58
59	41 37.5	−28.2	29.7	42 29.5	−27.6	30.2	43 21.3	−27.0	30.6	44 12.8	−26.3	31.1	45 04.0	−25.6	31.6	45 54.9	−24.9	32.2	46 45.5	−24.2	32.7	47 35.9	−23.5	33.3	59
60	41 09.3	−28.9	28.5	42 01.9	−28.3	29.0	42 54.3	−27.7	29.4	43 46.5	−27.2	29.9	44 38.4	−26.5	30.4	45 30.0	−25.8	30.9	46 21.3	−25.1	31.4	47 12.4	−24.4	32.0	60
61	40 40.4	−29.6	27.4	41 33.6	−29.1	27.8	42 26.6	−28.5	28.2	43 19.3	−27.9	28.6	44 11.9	−27.3	29.1	45 04.2	−26.7	29.6	45 56.2	−26.0	30.1	46 48.0	−25.3	30.6	61
62	40 10.8	−30.3	26.2	41 04.5	−29.7	26.6	41 58.1	−29.2	27.0	42 51.4	−28.6	27.4	43 44.6	−28.1	27.9	44 37.5	−27.5	28.3	45 30.2	−26.8	28.8	46 22.7	−26.3	29.3	62
63	39 40.5	−30.9	25.1	40 34.8	−30.4	25.5	41 28.9	−29.9	25.8	42 22.8	−29.4	26.2	43 16.5	−28.8	26.7	44 10.0	−28.2	27.1	45 03.4	−27.7	27.5	45 56.4	−27.1	28.0	63
64	39 09.6	−31.5	24.0	40 04.4	−31.1	24.3	40 59.0	−30.6	24.7	41 53.4	−30.1	25.1	42 47.7	−29.6	25.5	43 41.8	−29.1	25.9	44 35.7	−28.5	26.3	45 29.3	−27.9	26.7	64
65	38 38.1	−32.1	22.9	39 33.3	−31.7	23.2	40 28.4	−31.3	23.6	41 23.3	−30.8	23.9	42 18.1	−30.3	24.3	43 12.7	−29.8	24.7	44 07.2	−29.3	25.1	45 01.4	−28.7	25.5	65
66	38 06.0	−32.7	21.8	39 01.6	−32.3	22.1	39 57.1	−31.8	22.4	40 52.5	−31.4	22.8	41 47.8	−31.0	23.1	42 42.9	−30.5	23.5	43 37.9	−30.1	23.8	44 32.7	−29.6	24.2	66
67	37 33.3	−33.3	20.8	38 29.3	−32.9	21.0	39 25.3	−32.5	21.3	40 21.1	−32.1	21.6	41 16.8	−31.6	22.0	42 12.4	−31.2	22.3	43 07.8	−30.7	22.7	44 03.1	−30.3	23.0	67
68	37 00.0	−33.8	19.7	37 56.4	−33.4	20.0	38 52.8	−33.1	20.3	39 49.0	−32.7	20.5	40 45.2	−32.3	20.8	41 41.2	−31.9	21.2	42 37.1	−31.5	21.5	43 32.8	−31.0	21.8	68
69	36 26.2	−34.3	18.7	37 23.0	−34.0	18.9	38 19.7	−33.7	19.2	39 16.3	−33.3	19.5	40 12.9	−33.0	19.7	41 09.3	−32.6	20.0	42 05.6	−32.2	20.3	43 01.8	−31.7	20.6	69
70	35 51.9	−34.9	17.7	36 49.0	−34.5	17.9	37 46.0	−34.2	18.1	38 43.0	−33.8	18.4	39 39.9	−33.5	18.6	40 36.7	−33.1	18.9	41 33.4	−32.8	19.2	42 30.1	−32.5	19.5	70
71	35 17.0	−35.3	16.7	36 14.5	−35.1	16.9	37 11.8	−34.7	17.1	38 09.2	−34.5	17.3	39 06.4	−34.1	17.6	40 03.6	−33.8	17.8	41 00.6	−33.4	18.1	41 57.6	−33.1	18.4	71
72	34 41.7	−35.8	15.7	35 39.4	−35.5	15.9	36 37.1	−35.2	16.1	37 34.7	−34.9	16.3	38 32.3	−34.7	16.5	39 29.8	−34.4	16.7	40 27.2	−34.1	17.0	41 24.5	−33.7	17.2	72
73	34 05.9	−36.3	14.7	35 03.9	−36.0	14.9	36 01.9	−35.8	15.1	36 59.8	−35.5	15.3	37 57.6	−35.2	15.5	38 55.4	−34.9	15.7	39 53.1	−34.6	15.9	40 50.8	−34.3	16.1	73
74	33 29.6	−36.7	13.8	34 27.9	−36.5	13.9	35 26.1	−36.2	14.1	36 24.3	−36.0	14.3	37 22.4	−35.7	14.4	38 20.5	−35.5	14.6	39 18.5	−35.2	14.8	40 16.5	−35.0	15.1	74
75	32 52.9	−37.1	12.8	33 51.4	−36.9	13.0	34 49.9	−36.7	13.1	35 48.3	−36.5	13.3	36 46.7	−36.3	13.4	37 45.0	−36.0	13.6	38 43.3	−35.7	13.8	39 41.5	−35.5	14.0	75
76	32 15.8	−37.5	11.9	33 14.5	−37.3	12.0	34 13.2	−37.1	12.1	35 11.8	−36.9	12.3	36 10.4	−36.7	12.4	37 09.0	−36.5	12.6	38 07.6	−36.3	12.8	39 06.0	−36.0	13.0	76
77	31 38.3	−37.9	11.0	32 37.2	−37.7	11.1	33 36.1	−37.6	11.2	34 34.9	−37.3	11.3	35 33.7	−37.1	11.5	36 32.5	−37.0	11.6	37 31.3	−36.8	11.8	38 30.0	−36.6	11.9	77
78	31 00.4	−38.3	10.0	31 59.5	−38.2	10.2	32 58.5	−37.9	10.3	33 57.6	−37.8	10.4	34 56.6	−37.7	10.5	35 55.5	−37.4	10.6	36 54.5	−37.3	10.8	37 53.4	−37.1	10.9	78
79	30 22.1	−38.6	9.2	31 21.3	−38.5	9.2	32 20.6	−38.4	9.3	33 19.8	−38.3	9.5	34 18.9	−38.0	9.6	35 18.1	−37.9	9.7	36 17.2	−37.7	9.8	37 16.3	−37.5	9.9	79
80	29 43.5	−39.0	8.3	30 42.8	−38.8	8.4	31 42.2	−38.7	8.4	32 41.5	−38.6	8.5	33 40.9	−38.5	8.6	34 40.2	−38.3	8.7	35 39.5	−38.2	8.8	36 38.8	−38.1	9.0	80
81	29 04.5	−39.3	7.4	30 04.0	−39.2	7.5	31 03.5	−39.1	7.5	32 02.9	−38.9	7.6	33 02.4	−38.9	7.7	34 01.9	−38.8	7.8	35 01.3	−38.6	7.9	36 00.7	−38.5	8.0	81
82	28 25.2	−39.7	6.5	29 24.8	−39.6	6.6	30 24.4	−39.5	6.7	31 24.0	−39.4	6.7	32 23.5	−39.2	6.8	33 23.1	−39.1	6.9	34 22.7	−39.1	7.0	35 22.2	−38.9	7.1	82
83	27 45.5	−39.9	5.7	28 45.2	−39.9	5.7	29 44.9	−39.8	5.8	30 44.6	−39.7	5.9	31 44.3	−39.6	5.9	32 44.0	−39.6	6.0	33 43.6	−39.4	6.1	34 43.3	−39.4	6.1	83
84	27 05.6	−40.3	4.8	28 05.3	−40.1	4.9	29 05.1	−40.1	4.9	30 04.9	−40.1	5.0	31 04.7	−40.0	5.0	32 04.4	−39.9	5.1	33 04.2	−39.8	5.1	34 03.9	−39.7	5.2	84
85	26 25.3	−40.5	4.0	27 25.2	−40.5	4.1	28 25.0	−40.4	4.1	29 24.8	−40.3	4.1	30 24.7	−40.3	4.2	31 24.5	−40.2	4.2	32 24.4	−40.2	4.3	33 24.2	−40.1	4.3	85
86	25 44.8	−40.8	3.2	26 44.7	−40.8	3.2	27 44.6	−40.7	3.3	28 44.5	−40.7	3.3	29 44.4	−40.7	3.3	30 44.3	−40.6	3.3	31 44.2	−40.6	3.4	32 44.1	−40.6	3.4	86
87	25 04.0	−41.1	2.4	26 03.9	−41.0	2.4	27 03.9	−41.1	2.4	28 03.8	−41.0	2.4	29 03.7	−40.9	2.5	30 03.7	−40.9	2.5	31 03.6	−40.9	2.5	32 03.6	−40.9	2.5	87
88	24 22.9	−41.3	1.6	25 22.9	−41.3	1.6	26 22.8	−41.2	1.6	27 22.8	−41.3	1.6	28 22.8	−41.3	1.6	29 22.8	−41.3	1.7	30 22.7	−41.2	1.7	31 22.7	−41.2	1.7	88
89	23 41.6	−41.6	0.8	24 41.6	−41.6	0.8	25 41.6	−41.6	0.8	26 41.5	−41.5	0.8	27 41.5	−41.5	0.8	28 41.5	−41.5	0.8	29 41.5	−41.5	0.8	30 41.5	−41.5	0.8	89
90	23 00.0	−41.8	0.0	24 00.0	−41.8	0.0	25 00.0	−41.8	0.0	26 00.0	−41.8	0.0	27 00.0	−41.8	0.0	28 00.0	−41.8	0.0	29 00.0	−41.8	0.0	30 00.0	−41.8	0.0	90
	23°			24°			25°			26°			27°			28°			29°			30°			

46°, 314° L.H.A. LATITUDE SAME NAME AS DECLINATION

276

LATITUDE CONTRARY NAME TO DECLINATION L.H.A. 46°, 314°

Dec.	23°			24°			25°			26°		
°	Hc ° ′	d ′	Z °	Hc ° ′	d ′	Z °	Hc ° ′	d ′	Z °	Hc ° ′	d ′	Z °
0	39 45.0	-30.8	110.7	39 23.4	-31.9	111.4	39 01.1	-32.9	112.2	38 38.1	-34.0	112.9
1	39 14.2	-31.5	111.8	38 51.5	-32.4	112.5	38 28.2	-33.5	113.3	38 04.1	-34.5	114.0
2	38 42.7	-32.0	112.9	38 19.1	-33.1	113.6	37 54.7	-34.1	114.3	37 29.6	-35.0	115.0
3	38 10.7	-32.6	114.0	37 46.0	-33.6	114.7	37 20.6	-34.6	115.4	36 54.6	-35.6	116.0
4	37 38.1	-33.2	115.0	37 12.4	-34.2	115.7	36 46.0	-35.1	116.4	36 19.0	-36.0	117.1
5	37 04.9	-33.8	116.1	36 38.2	-34.7	116.7	36 10.9	-35.6	117.4	35 43.0	-36.6	118.0
6	36 31.1	-34.2	117.1	36 03.5	-35.2	117.8	35 35.3	-36.1	118.4	35 06.4	-36.9	119.0
7	35 56.9	-34.8	118.1	35 28.3	-35.7	118.8	34 59.2	-36.6	119.4	34 29.5	-37.5	120.0
8	35 22.1	-35.2	119.1	34 52.6	-36.1	119.7	34 22.6	-37.0	120.3	33 52.0	-37.8	120.9
9	34 46.9	-35.8	120.1	34 16.5	-36.6	120.7	33 45.6	-37.5	121.3	33 14.2	-38.3	121.8
10	34 11.1	-36.2	121.1	33 39.9	-37.1	121.7	33 08.1	-37.8	122.2	32 35.9	-38.7	122.8
11	33 34.9	-36.6	122.0	33 02.8	-37.4	122.6	32 30.3	-38.3	123.1	31 57.2	-39.0	123.7
12	32 58.3	-37.0	123.0	32 25.4	-37.9	123.5	31 52.0	-38.6	124.1	31 18.2	-39.4	124.6
13	32 21.3	-37.5	123.9	31 47.5	-38.2	124.4	31 13.4	-39.0	125.0	30 38.8	-39.8	125.4
14	31 43.8	-37.9	124.9	31 09.3	-38.6	125.4	30 34.4	-39.4	125.8	29 59.0	-40.1	126.3
15	31 05.9	-38.2	125.8	30 30.7	-39.0	126.2	29 55.0	-39.7	126.7	29 18.9	-40.4	127.2
16	30 27.7	-38.6	126.7	29 51.7	-39.3	127.1	29 15.3	-40.0	127.6	28 38.5	-40.7	128.0
17	29 49.1	-38.9	127.5	29 12.4	-39.7	128.0	28 35.3	-40.4	128.4	27 57.8	-41.0	128.8
18	29 10.2	-39.3	128.4	28 32.7	-40.0	128.8	27 54.9	-40.6	129.3	27 16.8	-41.3	129.7
19	28 30.9	-39.6	129.3	27 52.7	-40.2	129.7	27 14.3	-41.0	130.1	26 35.5	-41.6	130.5
20	27 51.3	-39.9	130.1	27 12.5	-40.6	130.5	26 33.3	-41.2	130.9	25 53.9	-41.9	131.3
21	27 11.4	-40.2	131.0	26 31.9	-40.9	131.4	25 52.1	-41.5	131.7	25 12.0	-42.1	132.1
22	26 31.2	-40.5	131.8	25 51.0	-41.1	132.2	25 10.6	-41.7	132.5	24 29.9	-42.3	132.9
23	25 50.7	-40.8	132.6	25 09.9	-41.4	133.0	24 28.9	-42.0	133.3	23 47.6	-42.6	133.6
24	25 09.9	-41.0	133.4	24 28.5	-41.6	133.8	23 46.9	-42.2	134.1	23 05.0	-42.8	134.4
25	24 28.9	-41.3	134.2	23 46.9	-41.9	134.6	23 04.7	-42.5	134.9	22 22.2	-43.0	135.2
26	23 47.6	-41.5	135.0	23 05.0	-42.1	135.3	22 22.2	-42.6	135.6	21 39.2	-43.2	135.9
27	23 06.1	-41.8	135.8	22 22.9	-42.3	136.1	21 39.6	-42.9	136.4	20 56.0	-43.4	136.7
28	22 24.3	-42.0	136.6	21 40.6	-42.5	136.9	20 56.7	-43.0	137.2	20 12.6	-43.5	137.4
29	21 42.3	-42.2	137.4	20 58.1	-42.7	137.6	20 13.7	-43.3	137.9	19 29.1	-43.8	138.1
30	21 00.1	-42.4	138.1	20 15.4	-43.0	138.4	19 30.4	-43.4	138.6	18 45.3	-43.9	138.9
31	20 17.7	-42.6	138.9	19 32.4	-43.1	139.1	18 47.0	-43.6	139.4	18 01.4	-44.1	139.6
32	19 35.1	-42.7	139.6	18 49.3	-43.2	139.9	18 03.4	-43.8	140.1	17 17.3	-44.2	140.3
33	18 52.4	-43.0	140.4	18 06.1	-43.5	140.6	17 19.6	-43.9	140.8	16 33.1	-44.4	141.0
34	18 09.4	-43.1	141.1	17 22.6	-43.5	141.3	16 35.7	-44.0	141.5	15 48.7	-44.5	141.7
35	17 26.3	-43.3	141.9	16 39.1	-43.8	142.0	15 51.7	-44.2	142.2	15 04.2	-44.6	142.4
36	16 43.0	-43.4	142.6	15 55.3	-43.8	142.8	15 07.5	-44.3	142.9	14 19.6	-44.8	143.1
37	15 59.6	-43.6	143.3	15 11.5	-44.1	143.5	14 23.2	-44.4	143.6	13 34.8	-44.8	143.8
38	15 16.0	-43.7	144.0	14 27.4	-44.1	144.2	13 38.8	-44.6	144.3	12 50.0	-45.0	144.5
39	14 32.3	-43.8	144.7	13 43.3	-44.2	144.9	12 54.2	-44.7	145.0	12 05.0	-45.0	145.1
40	13 48.5	-43.9	145.4	12 59.1	-44.4	145.6	12 09.5	-44.7	145.7	11 20.0	-45.2	145.8
41	13 04.6	-44.1	146.1	12 14.7	-44.4	146.3	11 24.8	-44.9	146.4	10 34.8	-45.2	146.5
42	12 20.5	-44.2	146.8	11 30.3	-44.6	146.9	10 39.9	-44.9	147.0	9 49.6	-45.3	147.1
43	11 36.3	-44.2	147.5	10 45.7	-44.6	147.6	9 55.0	-45.0	147.7	9 04.3	-45.4	147.8
44	10 52.1	-44.4	148.2	10 01.1	-44.8	148.3	9 10.0	-45.1	148.4	8 18.9	-45.5	148.5
45	10 07.7	-44.4	148.9	9 16.3	-44.8	149.0	8 24.9	-45.2	149.1	7 33.4	-45.5	149.1
46	9 23.3	-44.5	149.6	8 31.5	-44.8	149.7	7 39.7	-45.2	149.7	6 47.9	-45.6	149.8
47	8 38.8	-44.6	150.2	7 46.7	-45.0	150.3	6 54.5	-45.3	150.4	6 02.3	-45.6	150.4
48	7 54.2	-44.7	150.9	7 01.7	-45.0	151.0	6 09.2	-45.3	151.0	5 16.7	-45.6	151.1
49	7 09.5	-44.7	151.6	6 16.7	-45.0	151.7	5 23.9	-45.4	151.7	4 31.1	-45.7	151.7
50	6 24.8	-44.8	152.3	5 31.7	-45.1	152.3	4 38.5	-45.4	152.4	3 45.4	-45.7	152.4
51	5 40.0	-44.8	152.9	4 46.6	-45.1	153.0	3 53.1	-45.4	153.0	2 59.7	-45.8	153.0
52	4 55.2	-44.8	153.6	4 01.5	-45.2	153.6	3 07.7	-45.4	153.7	2 13.9	-45.7	153.7
53	4 10.4	-44.9	154.3	3 16.3	-45.2	154.3	2 22.3	-45.5	154.3	1 28.2	-45.8	154.3
54	3 25.5	-44.9	154.9	2 31.1	-45.2	155.0	1 36.8	-45.5	155.0	0 42.4	-45.8	155.0
55	2 40.6	-44.9	155.6	1 45.9	-45.2	155.6	0 51.3	-45.5	155.6	0 03.4	+45.7	24.4
56	1 55.7	-45.0	156.3	1 00.7	-45.2	156.3	0 05.8	-45.5	156.3	0 49.1	+45.8	23.7
57	1 10.7	-44.9	156.9	0 15.5	-45.2	156.9	0 39.7	+45.5	23.1	1 34.9	+45.8	23.1
58	0 25.8	-45.0	157.6	0 29.7	+45.2	22.4	1 25.2	+45.5	22.4	2 20.7	+45.7	22.4
59	0 19.2	+45.0	21.7	1 14.9	+45.3	21.8	2 10.7	+45.4	21.8	3 06.4	+45.7	21.8
60	1 04.2	+44.9	21.1	2 00.2	+45.1	21.1	2 56.1	+45.5	21.1	3 52.1	+45.7	21.1
61	1 49.1	+45.0	20.4	2 45.3	+45.2	20.4	3 41.6	+45.4	20.5	4 37.8	+45.6	20.5
62	2 34.1	+44.9	19.8	3 30.5	+45.2	19.8	4 27.0	+45.4	19.8	5 23.4	+45.6	19.8
63	3 19.0	+44.9	19.1	4 15.7	+45.1	19.1	5 12.4	+45.3	19.1	6 09.0	+45.6	19.2
64	4 03.9	+44.8	18.4	5 00.8	+45.1	18.5	5 57.7	+45.3	18.5	6 54.6	+45.5	18.5
65	4 48.7	+44.8	17.8	5 45.9	+45.0	17.8	6 43.0	+45.2	17.8	7 40.1	+45.4	17.9
66	5 33.5	+44.8	17.1	6 30.9	+45.0	17.1	7 28.2	+45.2	17.2	8 25.5	+45.4	17.2
67	6 18.3	+44.7	16.4	7 15.9	+44.9	16.5	8 13.4	+45.1	16.5	9 10.9	+45.3	16.5
68	7 03.0	+44.7	15.8	8 00.8	+44.8	15.8	8 58.5	+45.0	15.8	9 56.2	+45.2	15.9
69	7 47.7	+44.6	15.1	8 45.6	+44.8	15.1	9 43.5	+45.0	15.2	10 41.4	+45.2	15.2
70	8 32.3	+44.5	14.4	9 30.4	+44.7	14.4	10 28.5	+44.9	14.5	11 26.6	+45.0	14.5
71	9 16.8	+44.5	13.7	10 15.1	+44.6	13.8	11 13.4	+44.7	13.8	12 11.6	+45.0	13.9
72	10 01.3	+44.3	13.0	10 59.7	+44.5	13.1	11 58.1	+44.7	13.1	12 56.6	+44.8	13.2
73	10 45.6	+44.3	12.4	11 44.2	+44.5	12.4	12 42.8	+44.6	12.5	13 41.4	+44.7	12.5
74	11 29.9	+44.2	11.7	12 28.7	+44.3	11.7	13 27.4	+44.5	11.8	14 26.1	+44.7	11.8
75	12 14.1	+44.1	11.0	13 13.0	+44.2	11.0	14 11.9	+44.3	11.1	15 10.8	+44.4	11.1
76	12 58.2	+43.9	10.3	13 57.2	+44.1	10.3	14 56.2	+44.2	10.4	15 55.2	+44.4	10.4
77	13 42.1	+43.9	9.6	14 41.3	+44.0	9.6	15 40.4	+44.1	9.7	16 39.6	+44.2	9.7
78	14 26.0	+43.7	8.9	15 25.3	+43.8	8.9	16 24.5	+44.0	9.0	17 23.8	+44.0	9.0
79	15 09.7	+43.6	8.2	16 09.1	+43.7	8.2	17 08.5	+43.8	8.3	18 07.8	+43.9	8.3
80	15 53.3	+43.4	7.5	16 52.8	+43.5	7.5	17 52.3	+43.6	7.5	18 51.7	+43.8	7.6
81	16 36.7	+43.3	6.7	17 36.3	+43.4	6.8	18 35.9	+43.5	6.8	19 35.5	+43.6	6.9
82	17 20.0	+43.2	6.0	18 19.7	+43.2	6.1	19 19.4	+43.2	6.1	20 19.0	+43.4	6.1
83	18 03.2	+42.9	5.3	19 02.9	+43.0	5.3	20 02.6	+43.1	5.4	21 02.4	+43.2	5.4
84	18 46.1	+42.8	4.6	19 45.9	+42.9	4.6	20 45.7	+43.0	4.6	21 45.6	+42.9	4.6
85	19 28.9	+42.6	3.8	20 28.8	+42.7	3.8	21 28.7	+42.7	3.9	22 28.5	+42.8	3.9
86	20 11.5	+42.5	3.1	21 11.5	+42.4	3.1	22 11.4	+42.5	3.1	23 11.3	+42.5	3.1
87	20 54.0	+42.2	2.3	21 53.9	+42.3	2.3	22 53.9	+42.2	2.3	23 53.8	+42.3	2.4
88	21 36.2	+42.0	1.5	22 36.2	+42.0	1.6	23 36.1	+42.1	1.6	24 36.1	+42.1	1.6
89	22 18.2	+41.8	0.8	23 18.2	+41.8	0.8	24 18.2	+41.8	0.8	25 18.2	+41.8	0.8
90	23 00.0	+41.6	0.0	24 00.0	+41.6	0.0	25 00.0	+41.6	0.0	26 00.0	+41.5	0.0
	23°			24°			25°			26°		

Dec.	27°			28°			29°			30°		
°	Hc ° ′	d ′	Z °	Hc ° ′	d ′	Z °	Hc ° ′	d ′	Z °	Hc ° ′	d ′	Z °
0	38 14.3	-34.9	113.7	37 49.9	-35.9	114.4	37 24.8	-36.9	115.1	36 59.0	-37.8	115.8
1	37 39.4	-35.5	114.7	37 14.0	-36.4	115.4	36 47.9	-37.3	116.1	36 21.2	-38.2	116.7
2	37 03.9	-36.0	115.7	36 37.6	-37.0	116.4	36 10.6	-37.8	117.1	35 43.0	-38.7	117.7
3	36 27.9	-36.5	116.7	36 00.6	-37.3	117.4	35 32.8	-38.3	118.0	35 04.3	-39.1	118.6
4	35 51.4	-36.9	117.7	35 23.3	-37.9	118.3	34 54.5	-38.7	119.0	34 25.2	-39.6	119.6
5	35 14.5	-37.4	118.7	34 45.4	-38.3	119.3	34 15.8	-39.1	119.9	33 45.6	-39.9	120.5
6	34 37.1	-37.9	119.6	34 07.1	-38.7	120.2	33 36.7	-39.5	120.8	33 05.7	-40.3	121.4
7	33 59.2	-38.3	120.6	33 28.4	-39.0	121.1	32 57.2	-39.9	121.7	32 25.4	-40.7	122.2
8	33 20.9	-38.6	121.5	32 49.4	-39.5	122.0	32 17.3	-40.3	122.6	31 44.7	-41.0	123.1
9	32 42.3	-39.1	122.4	32 09.9	-39.9	122.9	31 37.0	-40.6	123.5	31 03.7	-41.3	124.0
10	32 03.2	-39.4	123.3	31 30.0	-40.2	123.8	30 56.4	-40.9	124.3	30 22.4	-41.7	124.8
11	31 23.8	-39.9	124.2	30 49.8	-40.5	124.7	30 15.5	-41.3	125.2	29 40.7	-42.0	125.6
12	30 43.9	-40.1	125.1	30 09.3	-40.9	125.5	29 34.2	-41.6	126.0	28 58.7	-42.2	126.5
13	30 03.8	-40.5	125.9	29 28.4	-41.2	126.4	28 52.6	-41.9	126.8	28 16.5	-42.6	127.3
14	29 23.3	-40.8	126.8	28 47.2	-41.5	127.2	28 10.7	-42.1	127.6	27 33.9	-42.8	128.1
15	28 42.5	-41.1	127.6	28 05.7	-41.8	128.0	27 28.6	-42.5	128.4	26 51.1	-43.1	128.8
16	28 01.4	-41.4	128.4	27 23.9	-42.0	128.8	26 46.1	-42.7	129.2	26 08.0	-43.3	129.6
17	27 20.0	-41.7	129.3	26 41.9	-42.4	129.6	26 03.4	-42.9	130.0	25 24.7	-43.6	130.4
18	26 38.3	-41.9	130.1	25 59.5	-42.5	130.4	25 20.5	-43.2	130.8	24 41.1	-43.8	131.2
19	25 56.4	-42.3	130.9	25 17.0	-42.9	131.2	24 37.3	-43.4	131.6	23 57.3	-44.0	131.9
20	25 14.1	-42.4	131.6	24 34.1	-43.0	132.0	23 53.9	-43.7	132.3	23 13.3	-44.2	132.6
21	24 31.7	-42.7	132.4	23 51.1	-43.3	132.8	23 10.2	-43.8	133.1	22 29.1	-44.4	133.4
22	23 49.0	-42.9	133.2	23 07.8	-43.5	133.5	22 26.4	-44.1	133.8	21 44.7	-44.6	134.1
23	23 06.1	-43.2	134.0	22 24.3	-43.7	134.3	21 42.3	-44.2	134.5	21 00.1	-44.7	134.8
24	22 22.9	-43.3	134.7	21 40.6	-43.9	135.0	20 58.1	-44.4	135.3	20 15.4	-45.0	135.5
25	21 39.6	-43.6	135.5	20 56.7	-44.1	135.7	20 13.7	-44.6	136.0	19 30.4	-45.1	136.2
26	20 56.0	-43.7	136.2	20 12.6	-44.2	136.5	19 29.1	-44.8	136.7	18 45.3	-45.3	136.9
27	20 12.3	-43.9	136.9	19 28.4	-44.5	137.2	18 44.3	-44.9	137.4	18 00.0	-45.4	137.6
28	19 28.4	-44.1	137.6	18 43.9	-44.5	137.9	17 59.4	-45.1	138.1	17 14.6	-45.5	138.3
29	18 44.3	-44.3	138.4	17 59.4	-44.8	138.6	17 14.3	-45.2	138.8	16 29.1	-45.7	139.0
30	18 00.0	-44.4	139.1	17 14.6	-44.9	139.3	16 29.1	-45.4	139.5	15 43.4	-45.8	139.7
31	17 15.6	-44.5	139.8	16 29.7	-45.0	140.0	15 43.7	-45.4	140.2	14 57.6	-45.9	140.3
32	16 31.1	-44.7	140.5	15 44.7	-45.1	140.7	14 58.3	-45.6	140.8	14 11.7	-46.0	141.0
33	15 46.4	-44.8	141.2	14 59.6	-45.3	141.4	14 12.7	-45.7	141.5	13 25.7	-46.2	141.7
34	15 01.6	-45.0	141.9	14 14.3	-45.4	142.0	13 27.0	-45.8	142.2	12 39.5	-46.2	142.3
35	14 16.6	-45.0	142.6	13 28.9	-45.4	142.7	12 41.2	-45.9	142.8	11 53.3	-46.3	143.0
36	13 31.6	-45.2	143.2	12 43.5	-45.6	143.4	11 55.3	-46.0	143.5	11 07.0	-46.4	143.6
37	12 46.4	-45.3	143.9	11 57.9	-45.7	144.0	11 09.3	-46.1	144.2	10 20.6	-46.5	144.3
38	12 01.1	-45.3	144.6	11 12.2	-45.8	144.7	10 23.2	-46.2	144.8	9 34.1	-46.5	144.9
39	11 15.8	-45.5	145.2	10 26.4	-45.8	145.4	9 37.0	-46.2	145.5	8 47.6	-46.6	145.6
40	10 30.3	-45.5	145.9	9 40.6	-45.9	146.0	8 50.8	-46.3	146.1	8 01.0	-46.7	146.2
41	9 44.8	-45.7	146.6	8 54.7	-46.0	146.7	8 04.5	-46.4	146.7	7 14.3	-46.7	146.8
42	8 59.1	-45.6	147.2	8 08.7	-46.1	147.3	7 18.1	-46.4	147.4	6 27.6	-46.8	147.5
43	8 13.5	-45.8	147.9	7 22.6	-46.1	148.0	6 31.7	-46.4	148.0	5 40.8	-46.8	148.1
44	7 27.7	-45.8	148.5	6 36.5	-46.2	148.6	5 45.3	-46.5	148.7	4 54.0	-46.8	148.7
45	6 41.9	-45.9	149.2	5 50.3	-46.2	149.2	4 58.8	-46.6	149.3	4 07.2	-46.9	149.3
46	5 56.0	-45.9	149.8	5 04.1	-46.2	149.9	4 12.2	-46.5	149.9	3 20.3	-46.9	150.0
47	5 10.1	-45.9	150.5	4 17.9	-46.3	150.5	3 25.7	-46.6	150.6	2 33.4	-46.9	150.6
48	4 24.2	-46.0	151.1	3 31.6	-46.3	151.2	2 39.1	-46.6	151.2	1 46.5	-46.9	151.2
49	3 38.2	-46.0	151.8	2 45.3	-46.3	151.8	1 52.5	-46.7	151.8	0 59.6	-47.0	151.8
50	2 52.2	-46.0	152.4	1 59.0	-46.3	152.4	1 05.8	-46.6	152.5	0 12.6	-46.9	152.5
51	2 06.2	-46.1	153.1	1 12.7	-46.3	153.1	0 19.2	-46.6	153.1	0 34.3	+46.9	26.9
52	1 20.1	-46.0	153.7	0 26.4	-46.4	153.7	0 27.4	+46.7	26.3	1 21.2	+47.0	26.3
53	0 34.1	-46.1	154.3	0 20.0	+46.3	25.7	1 14.1	+46.6	25.7	2 08.2	+46.9	25.7
54	0 12.0	+46.0	25.0	1 06.3	+46.4	25.0	2 00.7	+46.6	25.0	2 55.1	+46.8	25.0
55	0 58.0	+46.1	24.4	1 52.7	+46.3	24.4	2 47.3	+46.6	24.4	3 41.9	+46.9	24.4
56	1 44.1	+46.0	23.7	2 39.0	+46.3	23.7	3 33.9	+46.6	23.8	4 28.8	+46.8	23.8
57	2 30.1	+46.0	23.1	3 25.3	+46.3	23.1	4 20.5	+46.5	23.1	5 15.6	+46.8	23.2
58	3 16.1	+46.0	22.4	4 11.6	+46.2	22.5	5 07.0	+46.5	22.5	6 02.4	+46.8	22.5
59	4 02.1	+46.0	21.8	4 57.8	+46.2	21.8	5 53.5	+46.4	21.9	6 49.2	+46.7	21.9
60	4 48.1	+45.9	21.2	5 44.0	+46.2	21.2	6 39.9	+46.4	21.2	7 35.9	+46.6	21.3
61	5 34.0	+45.9	20.5	6 30.2	+46.1	20.5	7 26.3	+46.4	20.6	8 22.5	+46.6	20.6
62	6 19.9	+45.8	19.9	7 16.3	+46.0	19.9	8 12.7	+46.3	20.0	9 09.1	+46.5	20.0
63	7 05.7	+45.8	19.2	8 02.3	+46.0	19.3	8 59.0	+46.2	19.3	9 55.6	+46.4	19.4
64	7 51.5	+45.7	18.6	8 48.3	+46.0	18.6	9 45.2	+46.1	18.7	10 42.0	+46.4	18.7
65	8 37.2	+45.6	17.9	9 34.3	+45.8	18.0	10 31.3	+46.1	18.0	11 28.4	+46.3	18.1
66	9 22.8	+45.6	17.3	10 20.1	+45.8	17.3	11 17.4	+46.0	17.4	12 14.7	+46.1	17.4
67	10 08.4	+45.5	16.6	11 05.9	+45.7	16.6	12 03.4	+45.9	16.7	13 00.8	+46.1	16.8
68	10 53.9	+45.4	15.9	11 51.6	+45.6	16.0	12 49.3	+45.8	16.0	13 46.9	+46.0	16.1
69	11 39.3	+45.3	15.3	12 37.2	+45.5	15.3	13 35.1	+45.6	15.4	14 32.9	+45.9	15.4
70	12 24.6	+45.3	14.6	13 22.7	+45.4	14.6	14 20.7	+45.6	14.7	15 18.8	+45.7	14.8
71	13 09.9	+45.1	13.9	14 08.1	+45.3	14.0	15 06.3	+45.5	14.0	16 04.5	+45.6	14.1
72	13 55.0	+45.0	13.2	14 53.4	+45.1	13.3	15 51.8	+45.3	13.4	16 50.1	+45.5	13.4
73	14 40.0	+44.9	12.6	15 38.5	+45.1	12.6	16 37.1	+45.2	12.7	17 35.6	+45.4	12.7
74	15 24.9	+44.7	11.9	16 23.6	+44.9	11.9	17 22.3	+45.0	12.0	18 21.0	+45.2	12.1
75	16 09.6	+44.6	11.2	17 08.5	+44.7	11.2	18 07.3	+44.9	11.3	19 06.2	+45.0	11.4
76	16 54.2	+44.5	10.5	17 53.2	+44.6	10.5	18 52.2	+44.8	10.6	19 51.2	+44.9	10.7
77	17 38.7	+44.3	9.8	18 37.8	+44.5	9.8	19 37.0	+44.5	9.9	20 36.1	+44.6	10.0
78	18 23.0	+44.2	9.1	19 22.3	+44.3	9.1	20 21.5	+44.4	9.2	21 20.7	+44.6	9.2
79	19 07.2	+44.0	8.4	20 06.6	+44.1	8.4	21 05.9	+44.2	8.5	22 05.3	+44.3	8.5
80	19 51.2	+43.8	7.6	20 50.7	+43.9	7.7	21 50.1	+44.0	7.7	22 49.6	+44.1	7.8
81	20 35.0	+43.7	6.9	21 34.6	+43.7	7.0	22 34.1	+43.9	7.0	23 33.7	+43.9	7.1
82	21 18.7	+43.4	6.2	22 18.3	+43.5	6.2	23 18.0	+43.6	6.3	24 17.6	+43.7	6.3
83	22 02.1	+43.3	5.4	23 01.8	+43.4	5.5	24 01.6	+43.3	5.5	25 01.3	+43.4	5.6
84	22 45.4	+43.0	4.7	23 45.2	+43.0	4.7	24 44.9	+43.2	4.7	25 44.7	+43.3	4.8
85	23 28.4	+42.8	3.9	24 28.2	+42.9	3.9	25 28.1	+42.9	4.0	26 28.0	+42.9	4.0
86	24 11.2	+42.6	3.2	25 11.1	+42.6	3.2	26 11.0	+42.7	3.2	27 10.9	+42.7	3.2
87	24 53.8	+42.3	2.4	25 53.7	+42.4	2.4	26 53.7	+42.4	2.4	27 53.6	+42.4	2.4
88	25 36.1	+42.1	1.6	26 36.1	+42.1	1.6	27 36.1	+42.1	1.6	28 36.0	+42.2	1.6
89	26 18.2	+41.8	0.8	27 18.2	+41.8	0.8	28 18.2	+41.8	0.8	29 18.2	+41.8	0.8
90	27 00.0	+41.5	0.0	28 00.0	+41.5	0.0	29 00.0	+41.5	0.0	30 00.0	+41.5	0.0
	27°			28°			29°			30°		

S. Lat. { L.H.A. greater than 180° ....Zn=180°−Z
L.H.A. less than 180°...........Zn=180°+Z

LATITUDE SAME NAME AS DECLINATION L.H.A. 134°, 226°

Dec.	23°			24°			25°			26°			Dec.
	Hc	d	Z	Hc	d	Z	Hc	d	Z	Hc	d	Z	
°	° ′	′	°	° ′	′	°	° ′	′	°	° ′	′	°	°
0	38 53.2	+29.8	110.0	38 32.3	+30.9	110.8	38 10.7	+31.9	111.5	37 48.3	+33.0	112.2	0
1	39 23.0	+29.1	108.9	39 03.2	+30.2	109.7	38 42.6	+31.4	110.4	38 21.3	+32.4	111.2	1
2	39 52.1	+28.5	107.8	39 33.4	+29.7	108.6	39 14.0	+30.7	109.3	38 53.7	+31.8	110.1	2
3	40 20.6	+27.8	106.6	40 03.1	+28.9	107.4	39 44.7	+30.1	108.2	39 25.5	+31.2	109.0	3
4	40 48.4	+27.1	105.4	40 32.0	+28.3	106.3	40 14.8	+29.4	107.1	39 56.7	+30.6	107.9	4
5	41 15.5	+26.3	104.3	41 00.3	+27.5	105.1	40 44.2	+28.7	105.9	40 27.3	+29.9	106.8	5
6	41 41.8	+25.6	103.1	41 27.8	+26.8	103.9	41 12.9	+28.0	104.8	40 57.2	+29.2	105.6	6
7	42 07.4	+24.8	101.9	41 54.6	+26.0	102.7	41 40.9	+27.3	103.6	41 26.4	+28.5	104.5	7
8	42 32.2	+23.9	100.6	42 20.6	+25.3	101.5	42 08.2	+26.5	102.4	41 54.9	+27.7	103.3	8
9	42 56.1	+23.2	99.4	42 45.9	+24.5	100.3	42 34.7	+25.8	101.2	42 22.6	+27.0	102.1	9
10	43 19.3	+22.3	98.1	43 10.4	+23.6	99.0	43 00.5	+24.9	100.0	42 49.6	+26.2	100.9	10
11	43 41.6	+21.5	96.8	43 34.0	+22.8	97.8	43 25.4	+24.1	98.7	43 15.8	+25.4	99.6	11
12	44 03.1	+20.5	95.5	43 56.8	+21.9	96.5	43 49.5	+23.3	97.4	43 41.2	+24.6	98.4	12
13	44 23.6	+19.7	94.2	44 18.7	+21.0	95.2	44 12.8	+22.4	96.2	44 05.8	+23.8	97.1	13
14	44 43.3	+18.7	92.9	44 39.7	+20.2	93.9	44 35.2	+21.5	94.9	44 29.6	+22.8	95.8	14
15	45 02.0	+17.8	91.6	44 59.9	+19.1	92.6	44 56.7	+20.5	93.6	44 52.4	+22.0	94.5	15
16	45 19.8	+16.8	90.2	45 19.0	+18.3	91.2	45 17.2	+19.7	92.2	45 14.4	+21.0	93.2	16
17	45 36.6	+15.8	88.8	45 37.3	+17.2	89.9	45 36.9	+18.7	90.9	45 35.4	+20.1	91.9	17
18	45 52.4	+14.8	87.4	45 54.5	+16.3	88.5	45 55.6	+17.7	89.5	45 55.5	+19.2	90.5	18
19	46 07.2	+13.8	86.1	46 10.8	+15.2	87.1	46 13.3	+16.7	88.1	46 14.7	+18.1	89.2	19
20	46 21.0	+12.7	84.6	46 26.0	+14.2	85.7	46 30.0	+15.6	86.7	46 32.8	+17.2	87.8	20
21	46 33.7	+11.6	83.2	46 40.2	+13.2	84.3	46 45.6	+14.7	85.3	46 50.0	+16.1	86.4	21
22	46 45.3	+10.6	81.8	46 53.4	+12.0	82.9	47 00.3	+13.5	83.9	47 06.1	+15.0	85.0	22
23	46 55.9	+9.5	80.4	47 05.4	+11.0	81.4	47 13.8	+12.5	82.5	47 21.1	+14.0	83.6	23
24	47 05.4	+8.4	78.9	47 16.4	+9.9	80.0	47 26.3	+11.4	81.0	47 35.1	+12.9	82.1	24
25	47 13.8	+7.3	77.5	47 26.3	+8.8	78.5	47 37.7	+10.3	79.6	47 48.0	+11.8	80.7	25
26	47 21.1	+6.2	76.0	47 35.1	+7.7	77.1	47 48.0	+9.2	78.1	47 59.8	+10.7	79.2	26
27	47 27.3	+5.0	74.5	47 42.8	+6.5	75.6	47 57.2	+8.0	76.6	48 10.5	+9.5	77.7	27
28	47 32.3	+3.9	73.0	47 49.3	+5.4	74.1	48 05.2	+6.9	75.2	48 20.0	+8.4	76.3	28
29	47 36.2	+2.8	71.6	47 54.7	+4.2	72.6	48 12.1	+5.7	73.7	48 28.4	+7.2	74.8	29
30	47 39.0	+1.6	70.1	47 58.9	+3.1	71.1	48 17.8	+4.6	72.2	48 35.6	+6.1	73.3	30
31	47 40.6	+0.5	68.6	48 02.0	+1.9	69.6	48 22.4	+3.3	70.7	48 41.7	+4.8	71.8	31
32	47 41.1	−0.7	67.1	48 03.9	+0.7	68.1	48 25.7	+2.2	69.2	48 46.5	+3.7	70.2	32
33	47 40.4	−1.9	65.6	48 04.6	−0.4	66.6	48 27.9	+1.1	67.7	48 50.2	+2.5	68.7	33
34	47 38.5	−3.0	64.1	48 04.2	−1.6	65.1	48 29.0	−0.2	66.2	48 52.7	+1.3	67.2	34
35	47 35.5	−4.1	62.7	48 02.6	−2.7	63.6	48 28.8	−1.4	64.7	48 54.0	+0.1	65.7	35
36	47 31.4	−5.3	61.2	47 59.9	−3.9	62.2	48 27.4	−2.5	63.1	48 54.1	−1.1	64.2	36
37	47 26.1	−6.4	59.7	47 56.0	−5.1	60.7	48 24.9	−3.7	61.6	48 53.0	−2.4	62.6	37
38	47 19.7	−7.5	58.2	47 50.9	−6.2	59.2	48 21.2	−4.9	60.1	48 50.6	−3.5	61.1	38
39	47 12.2	−8.6	56.8	47 44.7	−7.4	57.7	48 16.3	−6.0	58.6	48 47.1	−4.7	59.6	39
40	47 03.6	−9.7	55.3	47 37.3	−8.4	56.2	48 10.3	−7.2	57.1	48 42.4	−5.9	58.1	40
41	46 53.9	−10.8	53.9	47 28.9	−9.6	54.8	48 03.1	−8.3	55.7	48 36.5	−7.0	56.6	41
42	46 43.1	−11.9	52.4	47 19.3	−10.7	53.3	47 54.8	−9.5	54.2	48 29.5	−8.2	55.1	42
43	46 31.2	−13.0	51.0	47 08.6	−11.8	51.8	47 45.3	−10.6	52.7	48 21.3	−9.4	53.6	43
44	46 18.2	−13.9	49.6	46 56.8	−12.9	50.4	47 34.7	−11.7	51.2	48 11.9	−10.5	52.1	44
45	46 04.3	−15.1	48.2	46 43.9	−13.9	49.0	47 23.0	−12.8	49.8	48 01.4	−11.6	50.6	45
46	45 49.2	−16.0	46.8	46 30.0	−14.9	47.6	47 10.2	−13.9	48.4	47 49.8	−12.8	49.2	46
47	45 33.2	−17.0	45.4	46 15.1	−16.0	46.2	46 56.3	−14.9	46.9	47 37.0	−13.8	47.7	47
48	45 16.2	−17.9	44.1	45 59.1	−17.0	44.8	46 41.4	−15.9	45.5	47 23.2	−14.9	46.3	48
49	44 58.3	−18.9	42.7	45 42.1	−17.9	43.4	46 25.5	−17.0	44.1	47 08.3	−16.0	44.9	49
50	44 39.4	−19.9	41.4	45 24.2	−19.0	42.0	46 08.5	−18.0	42.7	46 52.3	−17.0	43.4	50
51	44 19.5	−20.7	40.0	45 05.2	−19.8	40.7	45 50.5	−18.9	41.4	46 35.3	−18.0	42.0	51
52	43 58.8	−21.7	38.7	44 45.4	−20.8	39.4	45 31.6	−19.9	40.0	46 17.3	−19.0	40.7	52
53	43 37.1	−22.4	37.4	44 24.6	−21.7	38.0	45 11.7	−20.9	38.7	45 58.3	−20.0	39.3	53
54	43 14.7	−23.4	36.2	44 02.9	−22.5	36.7	44 50.8	−21.7	37.3	45 38.3	−20.9	37.9	54
55	42 51.3	−24.1	34.9	43 40.4	−23.4	35.4	44 29.1	−22.7	36.0	45 17.4	−21.8	36.6	55
56	42 27.2	−25.0	33.7	43 17.0	−24.3	34.2	44 06.4	−23.5	34.7	44 55.6	−22.8	35.3	56
57	42 02.2	−25.7	32.4	42 52.7	−25.0	32.9	43 42.9	−24.3	33.4	44 32.8	−23.6	34.0	57
58	41 36.5	−26.5	31.2	42 27.7	−25.9	31.7	43 18.6	−25.2	32.2	44 09.2	−24.4	32.7	58
59	41 10.0	−27.2	30.0	42 01.8	−26.6	30.5	42 53.4	−25.9	30.9	43 44.8	−25.3	31.4	59
60	40 42.8	−27.9	28.8	41 35.2	−27.3	29.3	42 27.5	−26.8	29.7	43 19.5	−26.1	30.2	60
61	40 14.9	−28.6	27.7	41 07.9	−28.0	28.1	42 00.7	−27.4	28.5	42 53.4	−26.9	28.9	61
62	39 46.3	−29.3	26.5	40 39.9	−28.8	26.9	41 33.3	−28.2	27.3	42 26.5	−27.7	27.7	62
63	39 17.0	−29.9	25.4	40 11.1	−29.4	25.8	41 05.1	−29.0	26.1	41 58.8	−28.4	26.5	63
64	38 47.1	−30.6	24.3	39 41.7	−30.1	24.6	40 36.1	−29.6	25.0	41 30.4	−29.1	25.3	64
65	38 16.5	−31.2	23.2	39 11.6	−30.7	23.5	40 06.5	−30.2	23.8	41 01.3	−29.7	24.2	65
66	37 45.3	−31.7	22.1	38 40.9	−31.4	22.4	39 36.3	−30.9	22.7	40 31.6	−30.5	23.0	66
67	37 13.6	−32.3	21.0	38 09.5	−31.9	21.3	39 05.4	−31.6	21.6	40 01.1	−31.1	21.9	67
68	36 41.3	−32.9	20.0	37 37.6	−32.5	20.2	38 33.8	−32.1	20.5	39 30.0	−31.7	20.8	68
69	36 08.4	−33.4	18.9	37 05.1	−33.1	19.2	38 01.7	−32.7	19.4	38 58.3	−32.4	19.7	69
70	35 35.0	−33.9	17.9	36 32.0	−33.6	18.1	37 29.0	−33.3	18.4	38 25.9	−32.9	18.6	70
71	35 01.1	−34.4	16.9	35 58.4	−34.1	17.1	36 55.7	−33.8	17.3	37 53.0	−33.5	17.6	71
72	34 26.7	−34.9	15.9	35 24.3	−34.6	16.1	36 21.9	−34.3	16.3	37 19.5	−34.0	16.5	72
73	33 51.8	−35.4	14.9	34 49.7	−35.1	15.1	35 47.6	−34.8	15.3	36 45.5	−34.6	15.5	73
74	33 16.4	−35.8	14.0	34 14.6	−35.5	14.1	35 12.8	−35.3	14.3	36 10.9	−35.1	14.5	74
75	32 40.6	−36.2	13.0	33 39.1	−36.1	13.1	34 37.5	−35.8	13.3	35 35.8	−35.5	13.5	75
76	32 04.4	−36.7	12.1	33 03.0	−36.4	12.2	34 01.7	−36.3	12.3	35 00.3	−36.1	12.5	76
77	31 27.7	−37.0	11.1	32 26.6	−36.9	11.2	33 25.4	−36.6	11.4	34 24.2	−36.4	11.5	77
78	30 50.7	−37.4	10.2	31 49.7	−37.2	10.3	32 48.8	−37.1	10.4	33 47.8	−37.0	10.5	78
79	30 13.3	−37.8	9.3	31 12.5	−37.7	9.4	32 11.7	−37.5	9.5	33 10.8	−37.3	9.6	79
80	29 35.5	−38.2	8.4	30 34.8	−38.0	8.5	31 34.2	−37.9	8.6	32 33.5	−37.8	8.7	80
81	28 57.3	−38.5	7.5	29 56.8	−38.4	7.6	30 56.3	−38.3	7.7	31 55.7	−38.1	7.7	81
82	28 18.8	−38.8	6.6	29 18.4	−38.7	6.7	30 18.0	−38.6	6.8	31 17.6	−38.5	6.8	82
83	27 40.0	−39.1	5.8	28 39.7	−39.1	5.8	29 39.4	−39.0	5.9	30 39.1	−38.9	5.9	83
84	27 00.9	−39.5	4.9	28 00.6	−39.3	5.0	29 00.4	−39.3	5.0	30 00.2	−39.3	5.1	84
85	26 21.4	−39.7	4.1	27 21.3	−39.7	4.1	28 21.1	−39.6	4.2	29 20.9	−39.5	4.2	85
86	25 41.7	−40.1	3.2	26 41.6	−40.0	3.3	27 41.5	−40.0	3.3	28 41.4	−39.9	3.3	86
87	25 01.6	−40.2	2.4	26 01.6	−40.3	2.4	27 01.5	−40.2	2.5	28 01.5	−40.2	2.5	87
88	24 21.4	−40.6	1.6	25 21.3	−40.5	1.6	26 21.3	−40.5	1.6	27 21.3	−40.5	1.6	88
89	23 40.8	−40.8	0.8	24 40.8	−40.8	0.8	25 40.8	−40.8	0.8	26 40.8	−40.8	0.8	89
90	23 00.0	−41.0	0.0	24 00.0	−41.0	0.0	25 00.0	−41.0	0.0	26 00.0	−41.1	0.0	90
	23°			24°			25°			26°			

Dec.	27°			28°			29°			30°			Dec.
	Hc	d	Z	Hc	d	Z	Hc	d	Z	Hc	d	Z	
°	° ′	′	°	° ′	′	°	° ′	′	°	° ′	′	°	°
0	37 25.3	+34.0	112.9	37 01.5	+35.0	113.6	36 37.1	+36.0	114.3	36 12.1	+36.9	115.0	0
1	37 59.3	+33.4	111.9	37 36.5	+34.5	112.6	37 13.1	+35.5	113.3	36 49.0	+36.5	114.0	1
2	38 32.7	+32.9	110.8	38 11.0	+34.0	111.6	37 48.6	+34.9	112.3	37 25.5	+35.9	113.0	2
3	39 05.6	+32.3	109.8	38 45.0	+33.3	110.5	38 23.5	+34.4	111.3	38 01.4	+35.4	112.0	3
4	39 37.9	+31.7	108.7	39 18.3	+32.8	109.5	38 57.9	+33.9	110.2	38 36.8	+34.9	111.0	4
5	40 09.6	+31.0	107.6	39 51.1	+32.1	108.4	39 31.8	+33.2	109.2	39 11.7	+34.3	109.9	5
6	40 40.6	+30.4	106.5	40 23.2	+31.5	107.3	40 05.0	+32.6	108.1	39 46.0	+33.7	108.9	6
7	41 11.0	+29.6	105.3	40 54.7	+30.8	106.1	40 37.6	+32.0	107.0	40 19.7	+33.1	107.8	7
8	41 40.6	+29.0	104.2	41 25.5	+30.2	105.0	41 09.6	+31.3	105.9	40 52.8	+32.4	106.7	8
9	42 09.6	+28.2	103.0	41 55.7	+29.4	103.9	41 40.9	+30.6	104.7	41 25.2	+31.8	105.6	9
10	42 37.8	+27.5	101.8	42 25.1	+28.7	102.7	42 11.5	+29.9	103.6	41 57.0	+31.1	104.4	10
11	43 05.3	+26.7	100.6	42 53.8	+28.0	101.5	42 41.4	+29.2	102.4	42 28.1	+30.4	103.3	11
12	43 32.0	+25.9	99.3	43 21.8	+27.2	100.3	43 10.6	+28.4	101.2	42 58.5	+29.7	102.1	12
13	43 57.9	+25.0	98.1	43 49.0	+26.3	99.0	43 39.0	+27.7	100.0	43 28.2	+28.9	100.9	13
14	44 22.9	+24.3	96.8	44 15.3	+25.6	97.8	44 06.7	+26.8	98.8	43 57.1	+28.1	99.7	14
15	44 47.2	+23.3	95.5	44 40.9	+24.6	96.5	44 33.5	+26.0	97.5	44 25.2	+27.3	98.5	15
16	45 10.5	+22.4	94.2	45 05.5	+23.8	95.2	44 59.5	+25.2	96.2	44 52.5	+26.5	97.2	16
17	45 32.9	+21.5	92.9	45 29.3	+22.9	93.9	45 24.7	+24.3	94.9	45 19.0	+25.6	96.0	17
18	45 54.4	+20.6	91.6	45 52.2	+22.0	92.6	45 49.0	+23.3	93.6	45 44.6	+24.8	94.7	18
19	46 15.0	+19.6	90.2	46 14.2	+21.0	91.3	46 12.3	+22.5	92.3	46 09.4	+23.8	93.3	19
20	46 34.6	+18.6	88.9	46 35.2	+20.1	89.9	46 34.8	+21.5	91.0	46 33.2	+22.9	92.0	20
21	46 53.2	+17.6	87.5	46 55.3	+19.0	88.5	46 56.3	+20.5	89.6	46 56.1	+21.9	90.7	21
22	47 10.8	+16.5	86.1	47 14.3	+18.0	87.1	47 16.8	+19.4	88.2	47 18.0	+21.0	89.3	22
23	47 27.3	+15.5	84.6	47 32.3	+17.0	85.7	47 36.2	+18.5	86.8	47 39.0	+19.9	87.9	23
24	47 42.8	+14.4	83.2	47 49.3	+15.9	84.3	47 54.7	+17.4	85.4	47 58.9	+18.9	86.5	24
25	47 57.2	+13.3	81.8	48 05.2	+14.8	82.9	48 12.1	+16.3	84.0	48 17.8	+17.8	85.1	25
26	48 10.5	+12.2	80.3	48 20.0	+13.7	81.4	48 28.4	+15.2	82.5	48 35.6	+16.8	83.6	26
27	48 22.7	+11.0	78.8	48 33.7	+12.6	79.9	48 43.6	+14.1	81.1	48 52.4	+15.6	82.2	27
28	48 33.7	+9.9	77.4	48 46.3	+11.4	78.5	48 57.7	+13.0	79.6	49 08.0	+14.5	80.7	28
29	48 43.6	+8.8	75.9	48 57.7	+10.3	77.0	49 10.7	+11.8	78.1	49 22.5	+13.3	79.2	29
30	48 52.4	+7.5	74.4	49 08.0	+9.1	75.5	49 22.5	+10.6	76.6	49 35.8	+12.1	77.7	30
31	48 59.9	+6.4	72.8	49 17.1	+7.8	74.0	49 33.1	+9.4	75.1	49 47.9	+11.0	76.2	31
32	49 06.3	+5.2	71.3	49 24.9	+6.7	72.4	49 42.5	+8.2	73.6	49 58.9	+9.8	74.7	32
33	49 11.5	+3.9	69.8	49 31.6	+5.5	70.9	49 50.7	+7.0	72.0	50 08.7	+8.5	73.2	33
34	49 15.4	+2.8	68.3	49 37.1	+4.2	69.4	49 57.7	+5.8	70.5	50 17.2	+7.3	71.6	34
35	49 18.2	+1.5	66.7	49 41.3	+3.1	67.8	50 03.5	+4.5	68.9	50 24.5	+6.0	70.1	35
36	49 19.7	+0.3	65.2	49 44.4	+1.7	66.3	50 08.0	+3.2	67.4	50 30.5	+4.8	68.5	36
37	49 20.0	−0.9	63.7	49 46.1	+0.6	64.7	50 11.2	+2.1	65.8	50 35.3	+3.5	66.9	37
38	49 19.1	−2.1	62.1	49 46.7	−0.7	63.2	50 13.3	+0.7	64.3	50 38.8	+2.2	65.3	38
39	49 17.0	−3.3	60.6	49 46.0	−1.9	61.6	50 14.0	−0.5	62.7	50 41.0	+1.0	63.8	39
40	49 13.7	−4.5	59.1	49 44.1	−3.2	60.1	50 13.5	−1.7	61.1	50 42.0	−0.3	62.2	40
41	49 09.2	−5.8	57.6	49 40.9	−4.4	58.5	50 11.8	−3.0	59.6	50 41.7	−1.6	60.6	41
42	49 03.4	−6.9	56.0	49 36.5	−5.6	57.0	50 08.8	−4.3	58.0	50 40.1	−2.9	59.0	42
43	48 56.5	−8.1	54.5	49 30.9	−6.8	55.5	50 04.5	−5.5	56.5	50 37.2	−4.1	57.5	43
44	48 48.4	−9.3	53.0	49 24.1	−8.1	53.9	49 59.0	−6.7	54.9	50 33.1	−5.4	55.9	44
45	48 39.1	−10.5	51.5	49 16.0	−9.2	52.4	49 52.3	−8.0	53.4	50 27.7	−6.7	54.3	45
46	48 28.6	−11.6	50.0	49 06.8	−10.4	50.9	49 44.3	−9.2	51.8	50 21.0	−7.9	52.8	46
47	48 17.0	−12.7	48.6	48 56.4	−11.5	49.4	49 35.1	−10.4	50.3	50 13.1	−9.2	51.2	47
48	48 04.3	−13.8	47.1	48 44.9	−12.7	47.9	49 24.7	−11.5	48.8	50 03.9	−10.3	49.7	48
49	47 50.5	−14.9	45.6	48 32.2	−13.9	46.4	49 13.2	−12.7	47.3	49 53.6	−11.6	48.1	49
50	47 35.6	−16.0	44.2	48 18.3	−14.9	45.0	49 00.5	−13.9	45.8	49 42.0	−12.7	46.6	50
51	47 19.6	−17.0	42.8	48 03.4	−16.0	43.5	48 46.6	−15.0	44.3	49 29.3	−13.9	45.1	51
52	47 02.6	−18.1	41.4	47 47.4	−17.1	42.1	48 31.6	−16.1	42.8	49 15.4	−15.1	43.6	52
53	46 44.5	−19.1	40.0	47 30.3	−18.2	40.7	48 15.5	−17.1	41.4	49 00.3	−16.2	42.1	53
54	46 25.4	−20.0	38.6	47 12.1	−19.1	39.3	47 58.4	−18.3	39.9	48 44.1	−17.3	40.7	54
55	46 05.4	−21.0	37.2	46 53.0	−20.2	37.9	47 40.1	−19.2	38.5	48 26.8	−18.3	39.2	55
56	45 44.4	−22.0	35.9	46 32.8	−21.1	36.5	47 20.9	−20.3	37.1	48 08.5	−19.4	37.8	56
57	45 22.4	−22.8	34.5	46 11.7	−22.1	35.1	47 00.6	−21.3	35.7	47 49.1	−20.5	36.4	57
58	44 59.6	−23.8	33.2	45 49.6	−23.0	33.8	46 39.3	−22.2	34.4	47 28.6	−21.4	35.0	58
59	44 35.8	−24.6	31.9	45 26.6	−23.9	32.5	46 17.1	−23.2	33.0	47 07.2	−22.4	33.6	59
60	44 11.2	−25.4	30.7	45 02.7	−24.8	31.2	45 53.9	−24.1	31.7	46 44.8	−23.4	32.3	60
61	43 45.8	−26.3	29.4	44 37.9	−25.6	29.9	45 29.8	−25.0	30.4	46 21.4	−24.3	30.9	61
62	43 19.5	−27.1	28.2	44 12.3	−26.5	28.6	45 04.8	−25.8	29.1	45 57.1	−25.2	29.6	62
63	42 52.4	−27.8	26.9	43 45.8	−27.3	27.4	44 39.0	−26.7	27.8	45 31.9	−26.0	28.3	63
64	42 24.6	−28.6	25.7	43 18.5	−28.0	26.1	44 12.3	−27.5	26.6	45 05.9	−26.9	27.0	64
65	41 56.0	−29.3	24.5	42 50.5	−28.8	24.9	43 44.8	−28.3	25.3	44 39.0	−27.8	25.8	65
66	41 26.7	−30.0	23.4	42 21.7	−29.5	23.7	43 16.5	−29.0	24.1	44 11.2	−28.5	24.5	66
67	40 56.7	−30.7	22.2	41 52.2	−30.3	22.6	42 47.5	−29.8	22.9	43 42.7	−29.3	23.3	67
68	40 26.0	−31.3	21.1	41 21.9	−30.9	21.4	42 17.7	−30.4	21.7	43 13.4	−30.0	22.1	68
69	39 54.7	−32.0	20.0	40 51.0	−31.5	20.3	41 47.3	−31.2	20.6	42 43.4	−30.8	20.9	69
70	39 22.7	−32.5	18.9	40 19.5	−32.3	19.2	41 16.1	−31.9	19.4	42 12.6	−31.4	19.7	70
71	38 50.2	−33.2	17.8	39 47.2	−32.8	18.1	40 44.2	−32.4	18.3	41 41.2	−32.2	18.6	71
72	38 17.0	−33.7	16.7	39 14.4	−33.4	17.0	40 11.8	−33.1	17.2	41 09.0	−32.7	17.5	72
73	37 43.3	−34.3	15.7	38 41.0	−34.0	15.9	39 38.7	−33.7	16.1	40 36.3	−33.4	16.4	73
74	37 09.0	−34.8	14.7	38 07.0	−34.5	14.8	39 05.0	−34.3	15.1	40 02.9	−34.0	15.3	74
75	36 34.2	−35.4	13.6	37 32.5	−35.1	13.8	38 30.7	−34.8	14.0	39 28.9	−34.6	14.2	75
76	35 58.8	−35.8	12.6	36 57.4	−35.6	12.8	37 55.9	−35.4	13.0	38 54.3	−35.1	13.1	76
77	35 23.0	−36.3	11.6	36 21.8	−36.1	11.8	37 20.5	−35.9	11.9	38 19.2	−35.7	12.1	77
78	34 46.7	−36.7	10.7	35 45.7	−36.6	10.8	36 44.6	−36.4	10.9	37 43.5	−36.2	11.1	78
79	34 10.0	−37.2	9.7	35 09.1	−37.0	9.8	36 08.2	−36.8	10.0	37 07.3	−36.7	10.1	79
80	33 32.8	−37.6	8.8	34 32.1	−37.5	8.9	35 31.4	−37.4	9.0	36 30.6	−37.2	9.1	80
81	32 55.2	−38.1	7.8	33 54.6	−37.9	7.9	34 54.0	−37.7	8.0	35 53.4	−37.6	8.1	81
82	32 17.1	−38.4	6.9	33 16.7	−38.3	7.0	34 16.3	−38.2	7.1	35 15.8	−38.1	7.2	82
83	31 38.7	−38.8	6.0	32 38.4	−38.7	6.1	33 38.1	−38.7	6.1	34 37.7	−38.5	6.2	83
84	30 59.9	−39.1	5.1	31 59.7	−39.1	5.2	32 59.4	−39.0	5.2	33 59.2	−38.9	5.3	84
85	30 20.8	−39.5	4.2	31 20.6	−39.4	4.3	32 20.4	−39.3	4.3	33 20.3	−39.4	4.4	85
86	29 41.3	−39.9	3.4	30 41.2	−39.8	3.4	31 41.1	−39.8	3.4	32 40.9	−39.7	3.5	86
87	29 01.4	−40.1	2.5	30 01.4	−40.2	2.5	31 01.3	−40.1	2.6	32 01.2	−40.0	2.6	87
88	28 21.3	−40.5	1.7	29 21.2	−40.4	1.7	30 21.2	−40.4	1.7	31 21.2	−40.4	1.7	88
89	27 40.8	−40.8	0.8	28 40.8	−40.8	0.8	29 40.8	−40.8	0.8	30 40.8	−40.8	0.9	89
90	27 00.0	−41.1	0.0	28 00.0	−41.1	0.0	29 00.0	−41.1	0.0	30 00.0	−41.1	0.0	90
	27°			28°			29°			30°			

LATITUDE **CONTRARY** NAME TO DECLINATION **L.H.A. 47°, 313°**

Dec.	23° Hc	d	Z	24° Hc	d	Z	25° Hc	d	Z	26° Hc	d	Z	27° Hc	d	Z	28° Hc	d	Z	29° Hc	d	Z	30° Hc	d	Z	Dec.
°	° ′	′	°	° ′	′	°	° ′	′	°	° ′	′	°	° ′	′	°	° ′	′	°	° ′	′	°	° ′	′	°	°
0	38 53.2	−30.4	110.0	38 32.3	−31.5	110.8	38 10.7	−32.6	111.5	37 48.3	−33.6	112.2	37 25.3	−34.6	112.9	37 01.5	−35.5	113.6	36 37.1	−36.5	114.3	36 12.1	−37.4	115.0	0
1	38 22.8	−31.1	111.1	38 00.8	−32.1	111.9	37 38.1	−33.1	112.6	37 14.7	−34.1	113.3	36 50.7	−35.1	114.0	36 26.0	−36.0	114.6	36 00.6	−36.9	115.3	35 34.7	−37.9	116.0	1
2	37 51.7	−31.6	112.2	37 28.7	−32.7	112.9	37 05.0	−33.7	113.6	36 40.6	−34.6	114.3	36 15.6	−35.6	115.0	35 50.0	−36.6	115.6	35 23.7	−37.4	116.3	34 56.8	−38.3	116.9	2
3	37 20.1	−32.2	113.3	36 56.0	−33.2	114.0	36 31.3	−34.1	114.7	36 06.0	−35.2	115.3	35 40.0	−36.1	116.0	35 13.4	−36.9	116.6	34 46.3	−37.9	117.2	34 18.5	−38.7	117.8	3
4	36 47.9	−32.8	114.3	36 22.8	−33.7	115.0	35 57.2	−34.7	115.7	35 30.8	−35.6	116.3	35 03.9	−36.5	117.0	34 36.5	−37.5	117.6	34 08.4	−38.3	118.2	33 39.8	−39.1	118.8	4
5	36 15.1	−33.3	115.4	35 49.1	−34.3	116.0	35 22.5	−35.2	116.7	34 55.2	−36.1	117.3	34 27.4	−37.0	117.9	33 59.0	−37.8	118.5	33 30.1	−38.7	119.1	33 00.7	−39.5	119.7	5
6	35 41.8	−33.8	116.4	35 14.8	−34.7	117.0	34 47.3	−35.7	117.7	34 19.1	−36.5	118.3	33 50.4	−37.4	118.9	33 21.2	−38.3	119.5	32 51.4	−39.1	120.0	32 21.2	−39.9	120.6	6
7	35 08.0	−34.3	117.4	34 40.1	−35.2	118.0	34 11.6	−36.1	118.6	33 42.6	−37.0	119.2	33 13.0	−37.8	119.8	32 42.9	−38.6	120.4	32 12.3	−39.4	120.9	31 41.3	−40.3	121.5	7
8	34 33.7	−34.8	118.4	34 04.9	−35.7	119.0	33 35.5	−36.6	119.6	33 05.6	−37.4	120.2	32 35.2	−38.3	120.7	32 04.3	−39.1	121.3	31 32.9	−39.8	121.8	31 01.0	−40.6	122.3	8
9	33 58.9	−35.3	119.4	33 29.2	−36.2	120.0	32 58.9	−37.0	120.6	32 28.2	−37.8	121.1	31 56.9	−38.6	121.6	31 25.2	−39.4	122.2	30 53.1	−40.2	122.7	30 20.4	−40.9	123.2	9
10	33 23.6	−35.7	120.4	32 53.0	−36.5	120.9	32 21.9	−37.3	121.5	31 50.4	−38.2	122.0	31 18.3	−39.0	122.5	30 45.8	−39.7	123.1	30 12.9	−40.5	123.5	29 39.5	−41.2	124.0	10
11	32 47.9	−36.1	121.3	32 16.5	−37.0	121.9	31 44.6	−37.8	122.4	31 12.2	−38.6	122.9	30 39.3	−39.3	123.4	30 06.1	−40.1	123.9	29 32.4	−40.9	124.4	28 58.3	−41.6	124.9	11
12	32 11.8	−36.6	122.3	31 39.5	−37.4	122.8	31 06.8	−38.2	123.3	30 33.6	−38.9	123.8	30 00.0	−39.7	124.3	29 26.0	−40.5	124.8	28 51.5	−41.1	125.2	28 16.7	−41.8	125.7	12
13	31 35.2	−36.9	123.2	31 02.1	−37.7	123.7	30 28.6	−38.5	124.2	29 54.7	−39.3	124.7	29 20.3	−40.0	125.2	28 45.5	−40.7	125.6	28 10.4	−41.4	126.1	27 34.9	−42.1	126.5	13
14	30 58.3	−37.4	124.1	30 24.4	−38.1	124.6	29 50.1	−38.9	125.1	29 15.4	−39.6	125.6	28 40.3	−40.4	126.0	28 04.8	−41.0	126.5	27 29.0	−41.7	126.9	26 52.8	−42.4	127.3	14
15	30 20.9	−37.7	125.1	29 46.3	−38.5	125.5	29 11.2	−39.2	126.0	28 35.8	−40.0	126.4	27 59.9	−40.6	126.9	27 23.8	−41.3	127.3	26 47.3	−42.0	127.7	26 10.4	−42.6	128.1	15
16	29 43.2	−38.1	126.0	29 07.8	−38.8	126.4	28 32.0	−39.6	126.8	27 55.8	−40.2	127.3	27 19.3	−40.9	127.7	26 42.5	−41.6	128.1	26 05.3	−42.3	128.5	25 27.8	−42.9	128.9	16
17	29 05.1	−38.4	126.8	28 29.0	−39.2	127.3	27 52.4	−39.8	127.7	27 15.6	−40.6	128.1	26 38.4	−41.2	128.5	26 00.9	−41.9	128.9	25 23.0	−42.5	129.3	24 44.9	−43.1	129.6	17
18	28 26.7	−38.8	127.7	27 49.8	−39.4	128.1	27 12.6	−40.2	128.5	26 35.0	−40.8	128.9	25 57.2	−41.5	129.3	25 19.0	−42.1	129.7	24 40.5	−42.7	130.1	24 01.8	−43.4	130.4	18
19	27 47.9	−39.0	128.6	27 10.4	−39.8	129.0	26 32.4	−40.4	129.4	25 54.2	−41.1	129.8	25 15.7	−41.7	130.1	24 36.9	−42.4	130.5	23 57.8	−43.0	130.8	23 18.4	−43.5	131.2	19
20	27 08.9	−39.4	129.4	26 30.6	−40.1	129.8	25 52.0	−40.7	130.2	25 13.1	−41.3	130.6	24 34.0	−42.0	130.9	23 54.5	−42.5	131.3	23 14.8	−43.1	131.6	22 34.9	−43.8	131.9	20
21	26 29.5	−39.7	130.3	25 50.5	−40.3	130.7	25 11.3	−41.0	131.0	24 31.8	−41.6	131.4	23 52.0	−42.2	131.7	23 12.0	−42.9	132.0	22 31.7	−43.4	132.3	21 51.1	−43.9	132.6	21
22	25 49.8	−40.0	131.1	25 10.2	−40.6	131.5	24 30.3	−41.2	131.8	23 50.2	−41.9	132.2	23 09.8	−42.5	132.5	22 29.1	−43.0	132.8	21 48.3	−43.6	133.1	21 07.2	−44.2	133.4	22
23	25 09.8	−40.2	131.9	24 29.6	−40.9	132.3	23 49.1	−41.5	132.6	23 08.3	−42.0	132.9	22 27.3	−42.6	133.2	21 46.1	−43.2	133.5	21 04.7	−43.8	133.8	20 23.0	−44.3	134.1	23
24	24 29.6	−40.5	132.8	23 48.7	−41.1	133.1	23 07.6	−41.7	133.4	22 26.3	−42.3	133.7	21 44.7	−42.9	134.0	21 02.9	−43.4	134.3	20 20.9	−43.9	134.6	19 38.7	−44.5	134.8	24
25	23 49.1	−40.8	133.6	23 07.6	−41.3	133.9	22 25.9	−41.9	134.2	21 44.0	−42.5	134.5	21 01.8	−43.0	134.8	20 19.5	−43.6	135.0	19 37.0	−44.2	135.3	18 54.2	−44.6	135.5	25
26	23 08.3	−41.0	134.4	22 26.3	−41.6	134.7	21 44.0	−42.2	135.0	21 01.5	−42.7	135.2	20 18.8	−43.3	135.5	19 35.9	−43.8	135.8	18 52.8	−44.3	136.0	18 09.6	−44.8	136.2	26
27	22 27.3	−41.2	135.2	21 44.7	−41.8	135.4	21 01.8	−42.3	135.7	20 18.8	−42.9	136.0	19 35.5	−43.4	136.2	18 52.1	−43.9	136.5	18 08.5	−44.4	136.7	17 24.8	−45.0	136.9	27
28	21 46.1	−41.4	135.9	21 02.9	−42.0	136.2	20 19.5	−42.5	136.5	19 35.9	−43.1	136.7	18 52.1	−43.6	137.0	18 08.2	−44.1	137.2	17 24.1	−44.6	137.4	16 39.8	−45.0	137.6	28
29	21 04.7	−41.7	136.7	20 20.9	−42.2	137.0	19 37.0	−42.8	137.2	18 52.8	−43.2	137.5	18 08.5	−43.7	137.7	17 24.1	−44.3	137.9	16 39.5	−44.7	138.1	15 54.8	−45.3	138.3	29
30	20 23.0	−41.8	137.5	19 38.7	−42.4	137.7	18 54.2	−42.9	138.0	18 09.6	−43.4	138.2	17 24.8	−43.9	138.4	16 39.8	−44.4	138.6	15 54.8	−44.9	138.8	15 09.5	−45.3	139.0	30
31	19 41.2	−42.1	138.3	18 56.3	−42.5	138.5	18 11.3	−43.0	138.7	17 26.2	−43.6	138.9	16 40.9	−44.1	139.1	15 55.4	−44.5	139.3	15 09.9	−45.0	139.5	14 24.2	−45.4	139.7	31
32	18 59.1	−42.2	139.0	18 13.8	−42.7	139.2	17 28.3	−43.3	139.4	16 42.6	−43.7	139.6	15 56.8	−44.2	139.8	15 10.9	−44.6	140.0	14 24.9	−45.1	140.2	13 38.8	−45.6	140.3	32
33	18 16.9	−42.4	139.8	17 31.1	−42.9	140.0	16 45.0	−43.3	140.2	15 58.9	−43.8	140.4	15 12.6	−44.3	140.5	14 26.3	−44.8	140.7	13 39.8	−45.2	140.9	12 53.2	−45.7	141.0	33
34	17 34.5	−42.5	140.5	16 48.2	−43.1	140.7	16 01.7	−43.6	140.9	15 15.1	−44.0	141.1	14 28.3	−44.4	141.2	13 41.5	−44.9	141.4	12 54.6	−45.4	141.5	12 07.5	−45.7	141.7	34
35	16 52.0	−42.8	141.2	16 05.1	−43.2	141.4	15 18.1	−43.6	141.6	14 31.1	−44.1	141.8	13 43.9	−44.6	141.9	12 56.6	−45.0	142.1	12 09.2	−45.4	142.2	11 21.8	−45.9	142.3	35
36	16 09.2	−42.8	142.0	15 21.9	−43.3	142.1	14 34.5	−43.8	142.3	13 47.0	−44.3	142.5	12 59.3	−44.6	142.6	12 11.6	−45.1	142.7	11 23.8	−45.5	142.9	10 35.9	−45.9	143.0	36
37	15 26.4	−43.0	142.7	14 38.6	−43.5	142.9	13 50.7	−43.9	143.0	13 02.7	−44.3	143.2	12 14.7	−44.8	143.3	11 26.5	−45.2	143.4	10 38.3	−45.6	143.5	9 50.0	−46.0	143.6	37
38	14 43.4	−43.2	143.4	13 55.1	−43.6	143.6	13 06.8	−44.0	143.7	12 18.4	−44.4	143.9	11 29.9	−44.8	144.0	10 41.3	−45.2	144.1	9 52.7	−45.7	144.2	9 04.0	−46.0	144.3	38
39	14 00.2	−43.3	144.1	13 11.5	−43.7	144.3	12 22.8	−44.1	144.4	11 34.0	−44.6	144.5	10 45.1	−45.0	144.7	9 56.1	−45.4	144.8	9 07.0	−45.7	144.9	8 18.0	−46.2	144.9	39
40	13 16.9	−43.3	144.9	12 27.8	−43.8	145.0	11 38.7	−44.3	145.1	10 49.4	−44.6	145.2	10 00.1	−45.0	145.3	9 10.7	−45.4	145.4	8 21.3	−45.8	145.5	7 31.8	−46.2	145.6	40
41	12 33.6	−43.5	145.6	11 44.0	−43.9	145.7	10 54.4	−44.3	145.8	10 04.8	−44.7	145.9	9 15.1	−45.1	146.0	8 25.3	−45.5	146.1	7 35.5	−45.9	146.2	6 45.6	−46.2	146.2	41
42	11 50.1	−43.6	146.3	11 00.1	−44.0	146.4	10 10.1	−44.4	146.5	9 20.1	−44.8	146.6	8 30.0	−45.2	146.7	7 39.8	−45.5	146.7	6 49.6	−45.9	146.8	5 59.4	−46.3	146.9	42
43	11 06.5	−43.7	147.0	10 16.1	−44.1	147.1	9 25.7	−44.4	147.2	8 35.3	−44.9	147.3	7 44.8	−45.2	147.3	6 54.3	−45.6	147.4	6 03.7	−45.9	147.5	5 13.1	−46.3	147.5	43
44	10 22.8	−43.8	147.7	9 32.0	−44.1	147.8	8 41.3	−44.6	147.8	7 50.4	−44.9	147.9	6 59.6	−45.3	148.0	6 08.7	−45.7	148.1	5 17.8	−46.0	148.1	4 26.8	−46.3	148.2	44
45	9 39.0	−43.9	148.4	8 47.9	−44.3	148.4	7 56.7	−44.6	148.5	7 05.5	−45.0	148.6	6 14.3	−45.3	148.7	5 23.0	−45.6	148.7	4 31.8	−46.1	148.8	3 40.5	−46.4	148.8	45
46	8 55.1	−44.0	149.1	8 03.6	−44.3	149.1	7 12.1	−44.7	149.2	6 20.5	−45.0	149.3	5 29.0	−45.4	149.3	4 37.4	−45.8	149.4	3 45.7	−46.0	149.4	2 54.1	−46.4	149.4	46
47	8 11.1	−44.0	149.7	7 19.3	−44.4	149.8	6 27.4	−44.7	149.9	5 35.5	−45.1	149.9	4 43.6	−45.4	150.0	3 51.6	−45.7	150.0	2 59.7	−46.1	150.0	2 07.7	−46.4	150.1	47
48	7 27.1	−44.1	150.4	6 34.9	−44.4	150.5	5 42.7	−44.8	150.5	4 50.4	−45.1	150.6	3 58.2	−45.5	150.6	3 05.9	−45.8	150.7	2 13.6	−46.1	150.7	1 21.3	−46.5	150.7	48
49	6 43.0	−44.1	151.1	5 50.5	−44.5	151.2	4 57.9	−44.8	151.2	4 05.3	−45.1	151.2	3 12.7	−45.4	151.3	2 20.1	−45.8	151.3	1 27.5	−46.1	151.3	0 34.8	−46.4	151.3	49
50	5 58.9	−44.2	151.8	5 06.0	−44.5	151.8	4 13.1	−44.8	151.9	3 20.2	−45.2	151.9	2 27.3	−45.5	151.9	1 34.3	−45.8	151.9	0 41.4	−46.2	152.0	0 11.6	+46.4	28.0	50
51	5 14.7	−44.2	152.5	4 21.5	−44.5	152.5	3 28.3	−44.9	152.5	2 35.0	−45.2	152.6	1 41.8	−45.5	152.6	0 48.5	−45.8	152.6	0 04.8	+46.1	27.4	0 58.0	+46.4	27.4	51
52	4 30.5	−44.3	153.1	3 37.0	−44.6	153.2	2 43.4	−44.9	153.2	1 49.8	−45.2	153.2	0 56.3	−45.5	153.2	0 02.7	−45.8	153.2	0 50.9	+46.1	26.8	1 44.4	+46.5	26.8	52
53	3 46.2	−44.3	153.8	2 52.4	−44.6	153.9	1 58.5	−44.9	153.9	1 04.6	−45.2	153.9	0 10.8	−45.6	153.9	0 43.1	+45.8	26.1	1 37.0	+46.1	26.1	2 30.9	+46.3	26.1	53
54	3 01.9	−44.3	154.5	2 07.8	−44.7	154.5	1 13.6	−44.9	154.5	0 19.4	−45.2	154.5	0 34.8	+45.5	25.5	1 28.9	+45.8	25.5	2 23.1	+46.1	25.5	3 17.2	+46.4	25.5	54
55	2 17.6	−44.4	155.2	1 23.1	−44.6	155.2	0 28.7	−45.0	155.2	0 25.8	+45.2	24.8	1 20.3	+45.5	24.8	2 14.7	+45.8	24.8	3 09.2	+46.0	24.8	4 03.6	+46.4	24.9	55
56	1 33.2	−44.3	155.9	0 38.5	−44.6	155.9	0 16.3	+44.9	24.1	1 11.0	+45.2	24.1	2 05.8	+45.4	24.2	3 00.5	+45.8	24.2	3 55.2	+46.1	24.2	4 50.0	+46.3	24.2	56
57	0 48.9	−44.4	156.5	0 06.1	+44.7	23.5	1 01.2	+44.9	23.5	1 56.2	+45.2	23.5	2 51.2	+45.5	23.5	3 46.3	+45.7	23.5	4 41.3	+46.0	23.6	5 36.3	+46.2	23.6	57
58	0 04.5	−44.3	157.2	0 50.8	+44.6	22.8	1 46.1	+44.9	22.8	2 41.4	+45.2	22.8	3 36.7	+45.4	22.9	4 32.0	+45.7	22.9	5 27.3	+45.9	22.9	6 22.5	+46.2	23.0	58
59	0 39.8	+44.4	22.1	1 35.4	+44.6	22.1	2 31.0	+44.9	22.2	3 26.6	+45.1	22.2	4 22.1	+45.4	22.2	5 17.7	+45.6	22.2	6 13.2	+45.9	22.3	7 08.7	+46.2	22.3	59
60	1 24.2	+44.4	21.5	2 20.0	+44.6	21.5	3 15.9	+44.8	21.5	4 11.7	+45.1	21.5	5 07.5	+45.4	21.5	6 03.3	+45.6	21.6	6 59.1	+45.9	21.6	7 54.9	+46.1	21.7	60
61	2 08.6	+44.3	20.8	3 04.6	+44.6	20.8	4 00.7	+44.9	20.8	4 56.8	+45.1	20.8	5 52.9	+45.3	20.9	6 48.9	+45.6	20.9	7 45.0	+45.8	21.0	8 41.0	+46.0	21.0	61
62	2 52.9	+44.3	20.1	3 49.2	+44.6	20.1	4 45.6	+44.7	20.2	5 41.9	+45.0	20.2	6 38.2	+45.2	20.2	7 34.5	+45.5	20.3	8 30.8	+45.7	20.3	9 27.0	+46.0	20.4	62
63	3 37.2	+44.3	19.4	4 33.8	+44.5	19.5	5 30.3	+44.8	19.5	6 26.9	+45.0	19.5	7 23.4	+45.2	19.6	8 20.0	+45.4	19.6	9 16.5	+45.6	19.7	10 13.0	+45.9	19.7	63
64	4 21.5	+44.2	18.8	5 18.3	+44.4	18.8	6 15.1	+44.7	18.8	7 11.9	+44.9	18.9	8 08.6	+45.2	18.9	9 05.4	+45.4	18.9	10 02.1	+45.6	19.0	10 58.9	+45.8	19.1	64
65	5 05.7	+44.2	18.1	6 02.7	+44.5	18.1	6 59.8	+44.6	18.1	7 56.8	+44.8	18.2	8 53.8	+45.0	18.2	9 50.8	+45.2	18.3	10 47.7	+45.5	18.3	11 44.7	+45.7	18.4	65
66	5 49.9	+44.2	17.4	6 47.2	+44.3	17.4	7 44.4	+44.6	17.5	8 41.6	+44.8	17.5	9 38.8	+45.0	17.6	10 36.0	+45.2	17.6	11 33.2	+45.4	17.7	12 30.4	+45.6	17.7	66
67	6 34.1	+44.1	16.7	7 31.5	+44.3	16.8	8 29.0	+44.5	16.8	9 26.4	+44.7	16.8	10 23.8	+44.9	16.9	11 21.2	+45.1	16.9	12 18.6	+45.3	17.0	13 16.0	+45.5	17.1	67
68	7 18.2	+44.0	16.0	8 15.8	+44.2	16.1	9 13.5	+44.4	16.1	10 11.1	+44.6	16.2	11 08.7	+44.8	16.2	12 06.3	+45.0	16.3	13 03.9	+45.2	16.3	14 01.5	+45.4	16.4	68
69	8 02.2	+43.9	15.3	9 00.0	+44.2	15.4	9 57.9	+44.3	15.4	10 55.7	+44.5	15.5	11 53.5	+44.7	15.5	12 51.3	+44.9	15.6	13 49.1	+45.1	15.7	14 46.9	+45.2	15.7	69
70	8 46.1	+43.9	14.7	9 44.2	+44.1	14.7	10 42.2	+44.3	14.7	11 40.2	+44.5	14.8	12 38.2	+44.6	14.9	13 36.2	+44.8	14.9	14 34.2	+45.0	15.0	15 32.1	+45.2	15.0	70
71	9 30.0	+43.8	14.0	10 28.3	+43.9	14.0	11 26.5	+44.1	14.1	12 24.7	+44.3	14.1	13 22.8	+44.5	14.2	14 21.0	+44.7	14.2	15 19.2	+44.8	14.3	16 17.3	+45.0	14.4	71
72	10 13.8	+43.8	13.3	11 12.2	+43.9	13.3	12 10.6	+44.1	13.4	13 09.0	+44.2	13.4	14 07.3	+44.4	13.5	15 05.7	+44.5	13.5	16 04.0	+44.7	13.6	17 02.3	+44.9	13.7	72
73	10 57.6	+43.6	12.6	11 56.1	+43.8	12.6	12 54.7	+43.9	12.7	13 53.2	+44.1	12.7	14 51.7	+44.3	12.8	15 50.2	+44.4	12.8	16 48.7	+44.6	12.9	17 47.2	+44.7	13.0	73
74	11 41.2	+43.5	11.9	12 39.9	+43.7	11.9	13 38.6	+43.8	12.0	14 37.3	+43.9	12.0	15 36.0	+44.1	12.1	16 34.6	+44.3	12.1	17 33.3	+44.4	12.2	18 31.9	+44.6	12.3	74
75	12 24.7	+43.4	11.2	13 23.6	+43.5	11.2	14 22.4	+43.7	11.3	15 21.2	+43.9	11.3	16 20.1	+43.9	11.4	17 18.9	+44.1	11.4	18 17.7	+44.3	11.5	19 16.5	+44.4	11.6	75
76	13 08.1	+43.3	10.5	14 07.1	+43.4	10.5	15 06.1	+43.6	10.6	16 05.1	+43.7	10.6	17 04.0	+43.9	10.7	18 03.0	+44.0	10.7	19 02.0	+44.0	10.8	20 00.9	+44.2	10.9	76
77	13 51.4	+43.2	9.8	14 50.5	+43.3	9.8	15 49.7	+43.4	9.8	16 48.8	+43.5	9.9	17 47.9	+43.6	9.9	18 47.0	+43.8	10.0	19 46.0	+44.0	10.1	20 45.1	+44.1	10.1	77
78	14 34.6	+43.0	9.0	15 33.8	+43.2	9.1	16 33.1	+43.2	9.1	17 32.3	+43.4	9.2	18 31.5	+43.5	9.2	19 30.8	+43.6	9.3	20 30.0	+43.7	9.3	21 29.2	+43.8	9.4	78
79	15 17.6	+42.9	8.3	16 17.0	+43.0	8.4	17 16.3	+43.2	8.4	18 15.7	+43.2	8.5	19 15.0	+43.4	8.5	20 14.4	+43.4	8.6	21 13.7	+43.6	8.6	22 13.0	+43.7	8.7	79
80	16 00.5	+42.8	7.6	17 00.0	+42.8	7.6	17 59.5	+42.9	7.7	18 58.9	+43.1	7.7	19 58.4	+43.1	7.8	20 57.8	+43.3	7.8	21 57.3	+43.3	7.9	22 56.7	+43.4	7.9	80
81	16 43.3	+42.6	6.9	17 42.8	+42.7	6.9	18 42.4	+42.8	6.9	19 42.0	+42.8	7.0	20 41.5	+43.0	7.0	21 41.1	+43.0	7.1	22 40.6	+43.1	7.1	23 40.1	+43.3	7.2	81
82	17 25.9	+42.4	6.1	18 25.5	+42.5	6.2	19 25.2	+42.6	6.2	20 24.8	+42.7	6.2	21 24.5	+42.7	6.3	22 24.1	+42.8	6.3	23 23.7	+42.9	6.4	24 23.4	+43.0	6.4	82
83	18 08.3	+42.3	5.4	19 08.0	+42.4	5.4	20 07.8	+42.4	5.4	21 07.5	+42.5	5.5	22 07.2	+42.6	5.5	23 06.9	+42.6	5.6	24 06.6	+42.7	5.6	25 06.4	+42.7	5.6	83
84	18 50.6	+42.0	4.6	19 50.4	+42.1	4.7	20 50.2	+42.2	4.7	21 50.0	+42.2	4.7	22 49.8	+42.3	4.8	23 49.5	+42.4	4.8	24 49.3	+42.5	4.8	25 49.1	+42.5	4.9	84
85	19 32.6	+41.9	3.9	20 32.5	+41.9	3.9	21 32.4	+41.9	3.9	22 32.2	+42.1	4.0	23 32.1	+42.1	4.0	24 31.9	+42.2	4.0	25 31.8	+42.2	4.1	26 31.6	+42.3	4.1	85
86	20 14.5	+41.7	3.1	21 14.4	+41.8	3.1	22 14.3	+41.8	3.2	23 14.3	+41.8	3.2	24 14.2	+41.8	3.2	25 14.1	+41.9	3.2	26 14.0	+41.9	3.3	27 13.9	+41.9	3.3	86
87	20 56.2	+41.5	2.3	21 56.2	+41.5	2.4	22 56.1	+41.6	2.4	23 56.1	+41.5	2.4	24 56.0	+41.6	2.4	25 56.0	+41.6	2.4	26 55.9	+41.7	2.5	27 55.8	+41.7	2.5	87
88	21 37.7	+41.3	1.6	22 37.7	+41.3	1.6	23 37.7	+41.3	1.6	24 37.6	+41.3	1.6	25 37.6	+41.3	1.6	26 37.6	+41.3	1.6	27 37.6	+41.3	1.7	28 37.5	+41.4	1.7	88
89	22 19.0	+41.0	0.8	23 19.0	+41.0	0.8	24 19.0	+41.0	0.8	25 18.9	+41.1	0.8	26 18.9	+41.1	0.8	27 18.9	+41.1	0.8	28 18.9	+41.1	0.8	29 18.9	+41.1	0.8	89
90	23 00.0	+40.8	0.0	24 00.0	+40.8	0.0	25 00.0	+40.8	0.0	26 00.0	+40.8	0.0	27 00.0	+40.8	0.0	28 00.0	+40.8	0.0	29 00.0	+40.8	0.0	30 00.0	+40.8	0.0	90
	23°			24°			25°			26°			27°			28°			29°			30°			

S. Lat. {L.H.A. greater than 180° ....Zn=180°−Z
{L.H.A. less than 180°...........Zn=180°+Z

LATITUDE **SAME** NAME AS DECLINATION **L.H.A. 133°, 227°**

279

48°, 312° L.H.A. LATITUDE SAME NAME AS DECLINATION N. Lat. {L.H.A. greater than 180° .....Zn=Z
L.H.A. less than 180°............Zn=360°–Z

Dec.	23°			24°			25°			26°			27°			28°			29°			30°			Dec.
	Hc	d	Z	Hc	d	Z	Hc	d	Z	Hc	d	Z	Hc	d	Z	Hc	d	Z	Hc	d	Z	Hc	d	Z	
°	° ′	′	°	° ′	′	°	° ′	′	°	° ′	′	°	° ′	′	°	° ′	′	°	° ′	′	°	° ′	′	°	°
0	38 01.2	+29.5	109.4	37 40.9	+30.6	110.1	37 19.9	+31.6	110.8	36 58.3	+32.6	111.5	36 35.9	+33.7	112.2	36 12.9	+34.6	112.9	35 49.2	+35.6	113.6	35 24.9	+36.5	114.2	0
1	38 30.7	+28.8	108.3	38 11.5	+29.9	109.0	37 51.5	+31.1	109.8	37 30.9	+32.1	110.5	37 09.6	+33.1	111.2	36 47.5	+34.1	111.9	36 24.8	+35.1	112.6	36 01.4	+36.1	113.3	1
2	38 59.5	+28.1	107.1	38 41.4	+29.3	107.9	38 22.6	+30.3	108.7	38 03.0	+31.5	109.4	37 42.7	+32.5	110.1	37 21.6	+33.6	110.9	36 59.9	+34.6	111.6	36 37.5	+35.6	112.3	2
3	39 27.6	+27.5	106.0	39 10.7	+28.6	106.8	38 52.9	+29.8	107.6	38 34.5	+30.8	108.3	38 15.2	+32.0	109.1	37 55.2	+33.1	109.8	37 34.5	+34.1	110.5	37 13.1	+35.1	111.3	3
4	39 55.1	+26.8	104.9	39 39.3	+28.0	105.7	39 22.7	+29.1	106.4	39 05.3	+30.3	107.2	38 47.2	+31.3	108.0	38 28.3	+32.4	108.8	38 08.6	+33.5	109.5	37 48.2	+34.5	110.2	4
5	40 21.9	+26.0	103.7	40 07.3	+27.2	104.5	39 51.8	+28.5	105.3	39 35.6	+29.6	106.1	39 18.5	+30.7	106.9	39 00.7	+31.8	107.7	38 42.1	+32.9	108.4	38 22.7	+34.0	109.2	5
6	40 47.9	+25.4	102.5	40 34.5	+26.6	103.3	40 20.3	+27.7	104.2	40 05.2	+28.9	105.0	39 49.2	+30.1	105.8	39 32.5	+31.2	106.6	39 15.0	+32.3	107.4	38 56.7	+33.4	108.1	6
7	41 13.3	+24.5	101.3	41 01.1	+25.8	102.1	40 48.0	+27.0	103.0	40 34.1	+28.2	103.8	40 19.3	+29.4	104.7	40 03.7	+30.6	105.5	39 47.3	+31.7	106.3	39 30.1	+32.8	107.1	7
8	41 37.8	+23.8	100.1	41 26.9	+25.0	100.9	41 15.0	+26.3	101.8	41 02.3	+27.5	102.7	40 48.7	+28.7	103.5	40 34.3	+29.9	104.3	40 19.0	+31.0	105.2	40 02.9	+32.2	106.0	8
9	42 01.6	+23.0	98.8	41 51.9	+24.3	99.7	41 41.3	+25.6	100.6	41 29.8	+26.8	101.5	41 17.4	+28.0	102.3	41 04.2	+29.2	103.2	40 50.0	+30.4	104.0	40 35.1	+31.5	104.9	9
10	42 24.6	+22.2	97.6	42 16.2	+23.5	98.5	42 06.9	+24.7	99.4	41 56.6	+26.0	100.3	41 45.4	+27.3	101.2	41 33.4	+28.5	102.0	41 20.4	+29.7	102.9	41 06.6	+30.9	103.8	10
11	42 46.8	+21.3	96.3	42 39.7	+22.6	97.3	42 31.6	+24.0	98.2	42 22.6	+25.3	99.1	42 12.7	+26.5	100.0	42 01.9	+27.7	100.9	41 50.1	+29.0	101.7	41 37.5	+30.1	102.6	11
12	43 08.1	+20.4	95.1	43 02.3	+21.8	96.0	42 55.6	+23.1	96.9	42 47.9	+24.4	97.8	42 39.2	+25.7	98.8	42 29.6	+27.0	99.7	42 19.1	+28.2	100.6	42 07.6	+29.5	101.4	12
13	43 28.5	+19.6	93.8	43 24.1	+20.9	94.7	43 18.7	+22.3	95.7	43 12.3	+23.6	96.6	43 04.9	+24.9	97.5	42 56.6	+26.2	98.4	42 47.3	+27.5	99.4	42 37.1	+28.7	100.3	13
14	43 48.1	+18.7	92.5	43 45.0	+20.1	93.4	43 41.0	+21.4	94.4	43 35.9	+22.8	95.3	43 29.8	+24.1	96.3	43 22.8	+25.4	97.2	43 14.8	+26.7	98.1	43 05.8	+28.0	99.1	14
15	44 06.8	+17.8	91.1	44 05.1	+19.1	92.1	44 02.4	+20.5	93.1	43 58.7	+21.8	94.0	43 53.9	+23.3	95.0	43 48.2	+24.6	96.0	43 41.5	+25.9	96.9	43 33.8	+27.1	97.9	15
16	44 24.6	+16.8	89.8	44 24.2	+18.3	90.8	44 22.9	+19.6	91.8	44 20.5	+21.0	92.7	44 17.2	+22.3	93.7	44 12.8	+23.7	94.7	44 07.4	+25.0	95.7	44 00.9	+26.4	96.6	16
17	44 41.4	+15.8	88.5	44 42.5	+17.2	89.4	44 42.5	+18.7	90.4	44 41.5	+20.1	91.4	44 39.5	+21.5	92.4	44 36.5	+22.8	93.4	44 32.4	+24.2	94.4	44 27.3	+25.5	95.4	17
18	44 57.2	+14.9	87.1	44 59.7	+16.3	88.1	45 01.2	+17.7	89.1	45 01.6	+19.2	90.1	45 01.0	+20.5	91.1	44 59.3	+22.0	92.1	44 56.6	+23.3	93.1	44 52.8	+24.7	94.1	18
19	45 12.1	+13.9	85.7	45 16.0	+15.4	86.7	45 18.9	+16.8	87.7	45 20.8	+18.2	88.8	45 21.5	+19.6	89.8	45 21.3	+21.0	90.8	45 19.9	+22.4	91.8	45 17.5	+23.8	92.8	19
20	45 26.0	+12.9	84.3	45 31.4	+14.3	85.4	45 35.7	+15.8	86.4	45 39.0	+17.2	87.4	45 41.1	+18.7	88.4	45 42.3	+20.0	89.4	45 42.3	+21.5	90.5	45 41.3	+22.9	91.5	20
21	45 38.9	+11.8	83.0	45 45.7	+13.3	84.0	45 51.5	+14.7	85.0	45 56.2	+16.2	86.0	45 59.8	+17.6	87.1	46 02.3	+19.1	88.1	46 03.8	+20.5	89.1	46 04.2	+21.9	90.2	21
22	45 50.7	+10.8	81.5	45 59.0	+12.3	82.6	46 06.2	+13.8	83.6	46 12.4	+15.2	84.6	46 17.4	+16.7	85.7	46 21.4	+18.1	86.7	46 24.3	+19.5	87.8	46 26.1	+21.0	88.8	22
23	46 01.5	+9.8	80.1	46 11.3	+11.2	81.2	46 20.0	+12.6	82.2	46 27.6	+14.1	83.2	46 34.1	+15.6	84.3	46 39.5	+17.1	85.3	46 43.8	+18.6	86.4	46 47.1	+20.0	87.5	23
24	46 11.3	+8.7	78.7	46 22.5	+10.1	79.7	46 32.6	+11.7	80.8	46 41.7	+13.1	81.8	46 49.7	+14.6	82.9	46 56.6	+16.1	83.9	47 02.4	+17.5	85.0	47 07.1	+18.9	86.1	24
25	46 20.0	+7.6	77.3	46 32.6	+9.1	78.3	46 44.3	+10.5	79.3	46 54.8	+12.1	80.4	47 04.3	+13.5	81.5	47 12.7	+15.0	82.5	47 19.9	+16.5	83.6	47 26.0	+18.0	84.7	25
26	46 27.6	+6.5	75.8	46 41.7	+8.0	76.9	46 54.8	+9.5	77.9	47 06.9	+10.9	79.0	47 17.8	+12.4	80.0	47 27.7	+13.9	81.1	47 36.4	+15.4	82.2	47 44.0	+16.9	83.3	26
27	46 34.1	+5.4	74.4	46 49.7	+6.9	75.4	47 04.3	+8.4	76.5	47 17.8	+9.9	77.5	47 30.2	+11.4	78.6	47 41.6	+12.8	79.6	47 51.8	+14.3	80.7	48 00.9	+15.8	81.8	27
28	46 39.5	+4.3	72.9	46 56.6	+5.8	74.0	47 12.7	+7.2	75.0	47 27.7	+8.7	76.1	47 41.6	+10.2	77.1	47 54.4	+11.7	78.2	48 06.1	+13.2	79.3	48 16.7	+14.7	80.4	28
29	46 43.8	+3.3	71.5	47 02.4	+4.7	72.5	47 19.9	+6.1	73.5	47 36.4	+7.6	74.6	47 51.8	+9.1	75.7	48 06.1	+10.6	76.7	48 19.3	+12.1	77.8	48 31.4	+13.6	78.9	29
30	46 47.1	+2.1	70.0	47 07.1	+3.5	71.0	47 26.0	+5.0	72.1	47 44.0	+6.5	73.1	48 00.9	+8.0	74.2	48 16.7	+9.5	75.3	48 31.4	+11.0	76.3	48 45.0	+12.5	77.4	30
31	46 49.2	+1.0	68.6	47 10.6	+2.4	69.6	47 31.0	+3.9	70.6	47 50.5	+5.3	71.6	48 08.9	+6.8	72.7	48 26.2	+8.3	73.8	48 42.4	+9.8	74.9	48 57.5	+11.3	76.0	31
32	46 50.2	−0.2	67.1	47 13.0	+1.3	68.1	47 34.9	+2.7	69.1	47 55.8	+4.2	70.1	48 15.7	+5.6	71.2	48 34.5	+7.1	72.3	48 52.2	+8.6	73.4	49 08.8	+10.2	74.5	32
33	46 50.0	−1.2	65.6	47 14.3	+0.2	66.6	47 37.6	+1.6	67.6	48 00.0	+3.0	68.7	48 21.3	+4.5	69.7	48 41.6	+5.9	70.8	49 00.8	+7.5	71.9	49 19.0	+8.9	73.0	33
34	46 48.8	−2.3	64.2	47 14.5	−1.0	65.2	47 39.2	+0.4	66.2	48 03.0	+1.8	67.2	48 25.8	+3.3	68.2	48 47.5	+4.8	69.3	49 08.3	+6.2	70.3	49 27.9	+7.8	71.4	34
35	46 46.5	−3.5	62.7	47 13.5	−2.1	63.7	47 39.6	−0.7	64.7	48 04.8	+0.7	65.7	48 29.1	+2.1	66.7	48 52.3	+3.6	67.7	49 14.5	+5.1	68.8	49 35.7	+6.5	69.9	35
36	46 43.0	−4.6	61.3	47 11.4	−3.2	62.2	47 38.9	−1.9	63.2	48 05.5	−0.5	64.2	48 31.2	+0.9	65.2	48 55.9	+2.3	66.2	49 19.6	+3.8	67.3	49 42.2	+5.3	68.4	36
37	46 38.4	−5.7	59.8	47 08.2	−4.4	60.7	47 37.0	−3.0	61.7	48 05.0	−1.6	62.7	48 32.1	−0.2	63.7	48 58.2	+1.2	64.7	49 23.4	+2.6	65.8	49 47.5	+4.1	66.8	37
38	46 32.7	−6.7	58.4	47 03.8	−5.5	59.3	47 34.0	−4.1	60.2	48 03.4	−2.8	61.2	48 31.9	−1.5	62.2	48 59.4	0.0	63.2	49 26.0	+1.4	64.2	49 51.6	+2.8	65.3	38
39	46 26.0	−7.9	56.9	46 58.3	−6.6	57.8	47 29.9	−5.3	58.7	48 00.6	−4.0	59.7	48 30.4	−2.6	60.7	48 59.4	−1.3	61.7	49 27.4	+0.2	62.7	49 54.4	+1.6	63.7	39
40	46 18.1	−8.9	55.5	46 51.7	−7.6	56.4	47 24.6	−6.4	57.3	47 56.6	−5.1	58.2	48 27.8	−3.8	59.2	48 58.1	−2.4	60.1	49 27.6	−1.1	61.1	49 56.0	+0.4	62.2	40
41	46 09.2	−10.0	54.1	46 44.1	−8.8	54.9	47 18.2	−7.6	55.8	47 51.5	−6.3	56.7	48 24.0	−4.9	57.6	48 55.7	−3.6	58.6	49 26.5	−2.3	59.6	49 56.4	−0.9	60.6	41
42	45 59.2	−11.0	52.6	46 35.3	−9.9	53.5	47 10.6	−8.6	54.3	47 45.2	−7.4	55.2	48 19.1	−6.2	56.1	48 52.1	−4.9	57.1	49 24.2	−3.5	58.1	49 55.5	−2.1	59.1	42
43	45 48.2	−12.1	51.2	46 25.4	−10.9	52.0	47 02.0	−9.8	52.9	47 37.8	−8.5	53.8	48 12.9	−7.3	54.7	48 47.2	−6.0	55.6	49 20.7	−4.7	56.5	49 53.4	−3.4	57.5	43
44	45 36.1	−13.1	49.8	46 14.5	−12.0	50.6	46 52.2	−10.8	51.4	47 29.3	−9.7	52.3	48 05.6	−8.4	53.2	48 41.2	−7.2	54.1	49 16.0	−5.9	55.0	49 50.0	−4.6	56.0	44
45	45 23.0	−14.1	48.4	46 02.5	−13.0	49.2	46 41.4	−11.9	50.0	47 19.6	−10.7	50.8	47 57.2	−9.6	51.7	48 34.0	−8.3	52.6	49 10.1	−7.1	53.5	49 45.4	−5.8	54.4	45
46	45 08.9	−15.1	47.1	45 49.5	−14.0	47.8	46 29.5	−13.0	48.6	47 08.9	−11.9	49.4	47 47.6	−10.7	50.2	48 25.7	−9.6	51.1	49 03.0	−8.3	52.0	49 39.6	−7.1	52.9	46
47	44 53.8	−16.1	45.7	45 35.5	−15.1	46.4	46 16.5	−14.0	47.2	46 57.0	−12.9	47.9	47 36.9	−11.8	48.8	48 16.1	−10.6	49.6	48 54.7	−9.5	50.5	49 32.5	−8.2	51.4	47
48	44 37.7	−17.0	44.3	45 20.4	−16.0	45.0	46 02.5	−15.0	45.8	46 44.1	−14.0	46.5	47 25.1	−12.9	47.3	48 05.5	−11.8	48.1	48 45.2	−10.6	49.0	49 24.3	−9.5	49.8	48
49	44 20.7	−17.9	43.0	45 04.4	−17.0	43.7	45 47.5	−16.0	44.4	46 30.1	−15.0	45.1	47 12.2	−13.9	45.9	47 53.7	−12.9	46.6	48 34.6	−11.8	47.5	49 14.8	−10.6	48.3	49
50	44 02.8	−18.9	41.6	44 47.4	−18.0	42.3	45 31.5	−17.0	43.0	46 15.1	−16.0	43.7	46 58.3	−15.1	44.4	47 40.8	−14.0	45.2	48 22.8	−12.9	46.0	49 04.2	−11.8	46.8	50
51	43 43.9	−19.8	40.3	44 29.4	−18.9	41.0	45 14.5	−18.0	41.6	45 59.1	−17.0	42.3	46 43.2	−16.0	43.0	47 26.8	−15.0	43.8	48 09.9	−14.0	44.5	48 52.4	−13.0	45.3	51
52	43 24.1	−20.6	39.0	44 10.5	−19.8	39.6	44 56.5	−18.9	40.3	45 42.1	−18.0	40.9	46 27.2	−17.1	41.6	47 11.8	−16.1	42.3	47 55.9	−15.1	43.1	48 39.4	−14.0	43.8	52
53	43 03.5	−21.6	37.7	43 50.7	−20.7	38.3	44 37.6	−19.9	38.9	45 24.1	−19.0	39.6	46 10.1	−18.1	40.2	46 55.7	−17.2	40.9	47 40.8	−16.2	41.6	48 25.4	−15.2	42.4	53
54	42 41.9	−22.3	36.5	43 30.0	−21.5	37.0	44 17.7	−20.7	37.6	45 05.1	−19.9	38.2	45 52.0	−19.0	38.9	46 38.5	−18.1	39.5	47 24.6	−17.3	40.2	48 10.2	−16.3	40.9	54
55	42 19.6	−23.2	35.2	43 08.5	−22.5	35.7	43 57.0	−21.7	36.3	44 45.2	−20.9	36.9	45 33.0	−20.0	37.5	46 20.4	−19.2	38.1	47 07.3	−18.2	38.8	47 53.9	−17.4	39.5	55
56	41 56.4	−23.9	34.0	42 46.0	−23.2	34.5	43 35.3	−22.4	35.0	44 24.3	−21.7	35.6	45 13.0	−21.0	36.2	46 01.2	−20.1	36.8	46 49.1	−19.3	37.4	47 36.5	−18.3	38.1	56
57	41 32.5	−24.8	32.7	42 22.8	−24.0	33.2	43 12.9	−23.4	33.7	44 02.6	−22.6	34.3	44 52.0	−21.8	34.8	45 41.1	−21.1	35.4	46 29.8	−20.2	36.0	47 18.2	−19.5	36.6	57
58	41 07.7	−25.5	31.5	41 58.8	−24.9	32.0	42 49.5	−24.1	32.5	43 40.0	−23.5	33.0	44 30.2	−22.8	33.5	45 20.0	−22.0	34.1	46 09.6	−21.3	34.6	46 58.7	−20.4	35.3	58
59	40 42.2	−26.2	30.3	41 33.9	−25.6	30.8	42 25.4	−25.0	31.2	43 16.5	−24.3	31.7	44 07.4	−23.6	32.2	44 58.0	−22.8	32.8	45 48.3	−22.1	33.3	46 38.3	−21.4	33.9	59
60	40 16.0	−26.9	29.1	41 08.3	−26.3	29.6	42 00.4	−25.7	30.0	42 52.2	−25.1	30.5	43 43.8	−24.4	30.9	44 35.2	−23.8	31.4	45 26.2	−23.1	32.0	46 16.9	−22.3	32.5	60
61	39 49.1	−27.6	28.0	40 42.0	−27.1	28.4	41 34.7	−26.5	28.8	42 27.1	−25.8	29.2	43 19.4	−25.3	29.7	44 11.4	−24.6	30.2	45 03.1	−23.9	30.7	45 54.6	−23.3	31.2	61
62	39 21.5	−28.3	26.8	40 14.9	−27.7	27.2	41 08.2	−27.2	27.6	42 01.3	−26.7	28.0	42 54.1	−26.0	28.4	43 46.8	−25.5	28.9	44 39.2	−24.8	29.4	45 31.3	−24.1	29.9	62
63	38 53.2	−29.0	25.7	39 47.2	−28.5	26.0	40 41.0	−27.9	26.4	41 34.6	−27.4	26.8	42 28.1	−26.9	27.2	43 21.3	−26.2	27.6	44 14.4	−25.7	28.1	45 07.2	−25.0	28.6	63
64	38 24.2	−29.6	24.6	39 18.7	−29.1	24.9	40 13.1	−28.7	25.3	41 07.2	−28.1	25.6	42 01.2	−27.5	26.0	42 55.1	−27.1	26.4	43 48.7	−26.4	26.8	44 42.2	−25.9	27.3	64
65	37 54.6	−30.2	23.5	38 49.6	−29.7	23.8	39 44.4	−29.2	24.1	40 39.1	−28.8	24.5	41 33.7	−28.3	24.8	42 28.0	−27.7	25.2	43 22.3	−27.3	25.6	44 16.3	−26.7	26.0	65
66	37 24.4	−30.8	22.4	38 19.9	−30.4	22.7	39 15.2	−30.0	23.0	40 10.3	−29.4	23.3	41 05.4	−29.0	23.6	42 00.3	−28.6	24.0	42 55.0	−28.0	24.4	43 49.6	−27.6	24.8	66
67	36 53.6	−31.3	21.3	37 49.5	−31.0	21.6	38 45.2	−30.5	21.9	39 40.9	−30.2	22.2	40 36.4	−29.7	22.5	41 31.7	−29.2	22.8	42 27.0	−28.8	23.2	43 22.0	−28.2	23.5	67
68	36 22.3	−32.0	20.2	37 18.5	−31.5	20.5	38 14.7	−31.2	20.8	39 10.7	−30.7	21.0	40 06.7	−30.4	21.3	41 02.5	−29.9	21.7	41 58.2	−29.5	22.0	42 53.8	−29.1	22.3	68
69	35 50.3	−32.4	19.2	36 47.0	−32.1	19.4	37 43.5	−31.7	19.7	38 40.0	−31.4	19.9	39 36.3	−31.0	20.2	40 32.6	−30.6	20.5	41 28.7	−30.2	20.8	42 24.7	−29.7	21.1	69
70	35 17.9	−33.0	18.1	36 14.9	−32.7	18.4	37 11.8	−32.3	18.6	38 08.6	−32.0	18.9	39 05.3	−31.6	19.1	40 02.0	−31.3	19.4	40 58.5	−30.8	19.7	41 55.0	−30.5	20.0	70
71	34 44.9	−33.5	17.1	35 42.2	−33.2	17.3	36 39.5	−32.9	17.6	37 36.6	−32.5	17.8	38 33.7	−32.2	18.0	39 30.7	−31.8	18.3	40 27.7	−31.6	18.5	41 24.5	−31.1	18.8	71
72	34 11.4	−34.0	16.1	35 09.0	−33.7	16.3	36 06.6	−33.4	16.5	37 04.1	−33.1	16.7	38 01.5	−32.8	16.9	38 58.9	−32.5	17.2	39 56.1	−32.1	17.4	40 53.4	−31.8	17.7	72
73	33 37.4	−34.4	15.1	34 35.3	−34.1	15.3	35 33.2	−33.9	15.5	36 31.0	−33.7	15.7	37 28.7	−33.3	15.9	38 26.4	−33.1	16.1	39 24.0	−32.7	16.3	40 21.6	−32.5	16.6	73
74	33 03.0	−34.9	14.1	34 01.2	−34.7	14.3	34 59.3	−34.4	14.5	35 57.3	−34.1	14.7	36 55.4	−33.9	14.8	37 53.3	−33.6	15.0	38 51.3	−33.4	15.3	39 49.1	−33.0	15.5	74
75	32 28.1	−35.3	13.2	33 26.5	−35.1	13.3	34 24.9	−34.9	13.5	35 23.2	−34.7	13.6	36 21.5	−34.4	13.8	37 19.7	−34.1	14.0	38 17.9	−33.9	14.2	39 16.1	−33.7	14.4	75
76	31 52.8	−35.8	12.2	32 51.4	−35.6	12.4	33 50.0	−35.4	12.5	34 48.5	−35.1	12.6	35 47.1	−34.9	12.8	36 45.6	−34.7	13.0	37 44.0	−34.4	13.1	38 42.4	−34.2	13.3	76
77	31 17.0	−36.2	11.3	32 15.8	−35.9	11.4	33 14.6	−35.8	11.5	34 13.4	−35.6	11.7	35 12.2	−35.4	11.8	36 10.9	−35.2	12.0	37 09.6	−35.0	12.1	38 08.2	−34.8	12.3	77
78	30 40.8	−36.5	10.3	31 39.9	−36.4	10.5	32 38.8	−36.2	10.6	33 37.8	−36.0	10.7	34 36.8	−35.9	10.8	35 35.7	−35.7	11.0	36 34.6	−35.5	11.1	37 33.4	−35.3	11.2	78
79	30 04.3	−37.0	9.4	31 03.5	−36.8	9.5	32 02.6	−36.6	9.6	33 01.8	−36.5	9.7	34 00.9	−36.3	9.9	35 00.0	−36.1	10.0	35 59.1	−36.0	10.1	36 58.1	−35.8	10.2	79
80	29 27.3	−37.3	8.5	30 26.7	−37.2	8.6	31 26.0	−37.0	8.7	32 25.3	−36.9	8.8	33 24.6	−36.8	8.9	34 23.9	−36.7	9.0	35 23.1	−36.4	9.1	36 22.3	−36.3	9.2	80
81	28 50.0	−37.6	7.6	29 49.5	−37.5	7.7	30 49.0	−37.5	7.8	31 48.4	−37.3	7.9	32 47.8	−37.1	7.9	33 47.2	−37.0	8.0	34 46.7	−37.0	8.1	35 46.0	−36.7	8.2	81
82	28 12.4	−38.0	6.7	29 12.0	−37.9	6.8	30 11.5	−37.7	6.9	31 11.1	−37.7	6.9	32 10.7	−37.6	7.0	33 10.2	−37.5	7.1	34 09.7	−37.3	7.2	35 09.3	−37.3	7.3	82
83	27 34.4	−38.3	5.9	28 34.1	−38.3	5.9	29 33.8	−38.2	6.0	30 33.4	−38.0	6.0	31 33.1	−38.0	6.1	32 32.7	−37.8	6.2	33 32.4	−37.8	6.2	34 32.0	−37.6	6.3	83
84	26 56.1	−38.7	5.0	27 55.8	−38.5	5.0	28 55.6	−38.5	5.1	29 55.4	−38.4	5.1	30 55.1	−38.3	5.2	31 54.9	−38.3	5.3	32 54.6	−38.1	5.3	33 54.4	−38.1	5.4	84
85	26 17.4	−38.9	4.1	27 17.3	−38.9	4.2	28 17.1	−38.8	4.2	29 17.0	−38.8	4.3	30 16.8	−38.7	4.3	31 16.6	−38.6	4.3	32 16.5	−38.6	4.4	33 16.3	−38.5	4.4	85
86	25 38.5	−39.2	3.3	26 38.4	−39.2	3.3	27 38.3	−39.1	3.4	28 38.2	−39.1	3.4	29 38.1	−39.0	3.4	30 38.0	−39.0	3.5	31 37.9	−39.0	3.5	32 37.8	−38.9	3.5	86
87	24 59.3	−39.5	2.5	25 59.2	−39.4	2.5	26 59.2	−39.5	2.5	27 59.1	−39.4	2.5	28 59.1	−39.4	2.5	29 59.0	−39.3	2.5	30 58.9	−39.3	2.6	31 58.9	−39.3	2.6	87
88	24 19.8	−39.8	1.6	25 19.8	−39.8	1.6	26 19.7	−39.7	1.7	27 19.7	−39.7	1.7	28 19.7	−39.7	1.7	29 19.7	−39.7	1.7	30 19.6	−39.6	1.7	31 19.6	−39.6	1.7	88
89	23 40.0	−40.0	0.8	24 40.0	−40.0	0.8	25 40.0	−40.0	0.8	26 40.0	−40.0	0.8	27 40.0	−40.0	0.8	28 40.0	−40.0	0.8	29 40.0	−40.0	0.9	30 40.0	−40.0	0.9	89
90	23 00.0	−40.3	0.0	24 00.0	−40.3	0.0	25 00.0	−40.3	0.0	26 00.0	−40.3	0.0	27 00.0	−40.3	0.0	28 00.0	−40.3	0.0	29 00.0	−40.3	0.0	30 00.0	−40.3	0.0	90
	23°			24°			25°			26°			27°			28°			29°			30°			

48°, 312° L.H.A. LATITUDE SAME NAME AS DECLINATION

280

LATITUDE CONTRARY NAME TO DECLINATION L.H.A. 48°, 312°

Dec.	23°			24°			25°			26°		
	Hc	d	Z	Hc	d	Z	Hc	d	Z	Hc	d	Z
°	° ′	′	°	° ′	′	°	° ′	′	°	° ′	′	°
0	38 01.2	-30.1	109.4	37 40.9	-31.1	110.1	37 19.9	-32.1	110.8	36 58.3	-33.2	111.5
1	37 31.1	-30.6	110.5	37 09.8	-31.7	111.2	36 47.8	-32.8	111.9	36 25.1	-33.8	112.6
2	37 00.5	-31.3	111.6	36 38.1	-32.3	112.3	36 15.0	-33.2	112.9	35 51.3	-34.2	113.6
3	36 29.2	-31.8	112.6	36 05.8	-32.8	113.3	35 41.8	-33.8	114.0	35 17.1	-34.7	114.6
4	35 57.4	-32.3	113.7	35 33.0	-33.3	114.3	35 08.0	-34.3	115.0	34 42.4	-35.3	115.6
5	35 25.1	-32.9	114.7	34 59.7	-33.8	115.4	34 33.7	-34.7	116.0	34 07.1	-35.6	116.6
6	34 52.2	-33.4	115.7	34 25.9	-34.3	116.4	33 59.0	-35.3	117.0	33 31.5	-36.2	117.6
7	34 18.8	-33.8	116.7	33 51.6	-34.8	117.3	33 23.7	-35.7	117.9	32 55.3	-36.5	118.5
8	33 45.0	-34.4	117.7	33 16.8	-35.3	118.3	32 48.0	-36.1	118.9	32 18.8	-37.0	119.5
9	33 10.6	-34.8	118.7	32 41.5	-35.6	119.3	32 11.9	-36.5	119.8	31 41.8	-37.3	120.4
10	32 35.8	-35.2	119.7	32 05.9	-36.1	120.2	31 35.4	-36.9	120.8	31 04.5	-37.8	121.3
11	32 00.6	-35.7	120.7	31 29.8	-36.5	121.2	30 58.5	-37.3	121.7	30 26.7	-38.1	122.2
12	31 24.9	-36.0	121.6	30 53.3	-36.9	122.1	30 21.2	-37.7	122.6	29 48.6	-38.5	123.1
13	30 48.9	-36.5	122.5	30 16.4	-37.3	123.0	29 43.5	-38.1	123.5	29 10.1	-38.8	124.0
14	30 12.4	-36.9	123.5	29 39.1	-37.6	123.9	29 05.4	-38.4	124.4	28 31.3	-39.1	124.8
15	29 35.5	-37.2	124.4	29 01.5	-38.0	124.8	28 27.0	-38.7	125.3	27 52.2	-39.5	125.7
16	28 58.3	-37.6	125.3	28 23.5	-38.4	125.7	27 48.3	-39.1	126.1	27 12.7	-39.8	126.6
17	28 20.7	-37.9	126.1	27 45.1	-38.6	126.6	27 09.2	-39.3	127.0	26 32.9	-40.0	127.4
18	27 42.8	-38.2	127.0	27 06.5	-39.0	127.4	26 29.9	-39.7	127.8	25 52.9	-40.3	128.2
19	27 04.6	-38.6	127.9	26 27.5	-39.2	128.3	25 50.2	-39.9	128.7	25 12.6	-40.6	129.0
20	26 26.0	-38.9	128.8	25 48.3	-39.6	129.1	25 10.3	-40.3	129.5	24 32.0	-40.9	129.9
21	25 47.1	-39.1	129.6	25 08.7	-39.8	130.0	24 30.0	-40.4	130.3	23 51.1	-41.1	130.7
22	25 08.0	-39.5	130.4	24 28.9	-40.1	130.8	23 49.6	-40.8	131.1	23 10.0	-41.4	131.5
23	24 28.5	-39.7	131.3	23 48.8	-40.3	131.6	23 08.8	-40.9	131.9	22 28.6	-41.5	132.2
24	23 48.8	-40.0	132.1	23 08.5	-40.6	132.4	22 27.9	-41.2	132.7	21 47.1	-41.8	133.0
25	23 08.8	-40.2	132.9	22 27.9	-40.8	133.2	21 46.7	-41.4	133.5	21 05.3	-42.0	133.8
26	22 28.6	-40.4	133.7	21 47.1	-41.1	134.0	21 05.3	-41.7	134.3	20 23.3	-42.2	134.6
27	21 48.2	-40.7	134.5	21 06.0	-41.2	134.8	20 23.6	-41.8	135.1	19 41.1	-42.4	135.3
28	21 07.5	-40.9	135.3	20 24.8	-41.5	135.6	19 41.8	-42.0	135.8	18 58.7	-42.6	136.1
29	20 26.6	-41.1	136.1	19 43.3	-41.7	136.3	18 59.8	-42.2	136.6	18 16.1	-42.7	136.8
30	19 45.5	-41.3	136.9	19 01.6	-41.8	137.1	18 17.6	-42.4	137.3	17 33.4	-42.9	137.5
31	19 04.2	-41.5	137.6	18 19.8	-42.0	137.9	17 35.2	-42.5	138.1	16 50.5	-43.0	138.3
32	18 22.7	-41.7	138.4	17 37.8	-42.2	138.6	16 52.7	-42.7	138.8	16 07.5	-43.2	139.0
33	17 41.0	-41.8	139.1	16 55.6	-42.4	139.3	16 10.0	-42.9	139.5	15 24.3	-43.4	139.7
34	16 59.2	-42.0	139.9	16 13.2	-42.5	140.1	15 27.1	-43.0	140.3	14 40.9	-43.4	140.4
35	16 17.2	-42.2	140.6	15 30.7	-42.6	140.8	14 44.1	-43.1	141.0	13 57.5	-43.6	141.2
36	15 35.0	-42.3	141.4	14 48.1	-42.8	141.5	14 01.0	-43.2	141.7	13 13.9	-43.7	141.9
37	14 52.7	-42.5	142.1	14 05.3	-42.9	142.3	13 17.8	-43.4	142.4	12 30.2	-43.8	142.6
38	14 10.2	-42.6	142.8	13 22.4	-43.1	143.0	12 34.4	-43.5	143.1	11 46.4	-44.0	143.3
39	13 27.6	-42.7	143.6	12 39.3	-43.1	143.7	11 50.9	-43.6	143.8	11 02.4	-44.0	144.0
40	12 44.9	-42.8	144.3	11 56.2	-43.3	144.4	11 07.3	-43.6	144.5	10 18.4	-44.1	144.6
41	12 02.1	-42.9	145.0	11 12.9	-43.3	145.1	10 23.7	-43.8	145.2	9 34.3	-44.1	145.3
42	11 19.2	-43.1	145.7	10 29.6	-43.5	145.8	9 39.9	-43.9	145.9	8 50.2	-44.3	146.0
43	10 36.1	-43.1	146.4	9 46.1	-43.5	146.5	8 56.0	-43.9	146.6	8 05.9	-44.3	146.7
44	9 53.0	-43.2	147.1	9 02.6	-43.6	147.2	8 12.1	-44.0	147.3	7 21.6	-44.4	147.4
45	9 09.8	-43.3	147.8	8 19.0	-43.7	147.9	7 28.1	-44.1	148.0	6 37.2	-44.4	148.1
46	8 26.5	-43.4	148.5	7 35.3	-43.8	148.6	6 44.0	-44.1	148.7	5 52.8	-44.5	148.7
47	7 43.1	-43.4	149.2	6 51.5	-43.8	149.3	5 59.9	-44.1	149.4	5 08.3	-44.5	149.4
48	6 59.7	-43.5	149.9	6 07.7	-43.8	150.0	5 15.8	-44.3	150.0	4 23.8	-44.6	150.1
49	6 16.2	-43.6	150.6	5 23.9	-43.9	150.7	4 31.5	-44.2	150.7	3 39.2	-44.6	150.8
50	5 32.6	-43.6	151.3	4 40.0	-44.0	151.4	3 47.3	-44.3	151.4	2 54.6	-44.6	151.4
51	4 49.0	-43.6	152.0	3 56.0	-44.0	152.0	3 03.0	-44.3	152.1	2 10.0	-44.7	152.1
52	4 05.4	-43.7	152.7	3 12.0	-44.0	152.7	2 18.7	-44.3	152.7	1 25.3	-44.6	152.8
53	3 21.7	-43.7	153.4	2 28.0	-44.0	153.4	1 34.4	-44.4	153.4	0 40.7	-44.7	153.4
54	2 38.0	-43.8	154.1	1 44.0	-44.1	154.1	0 50.0	-44.3	154.1	0 04.0	+44.6	25.9
55	1 54.2	-43.7	154.8	0 59.9	-44.0	154.8	0 05.7	-44.4	154.8	0 48.6	+44.6	25.2
56	1 10.5	-43.8	155.4	0 15.9	-44.1	155.4	0 38.7	+44.3	24.6	1 33.2	+44.7	24.6
57	0 26.7	-43.8	156.1	0 28.2	+44.0	23.9	1 23.0	+44.4	23.9	2 17.9	+44.6	23.9
58	0 17.1	+43.7	23.2	1 12.2	+44.0	23.2	2 07.4	+44.3	23.2	3 02.5	+44.6	23.2
59	1 00.8	+43.8	22.5	1 56.2	+44.1	22.5	2 51.7	+44.3	22.5	3 47.1	+44.5	22.6
60	1 44.6	+43.7	21.8	2 40.3	+44.0	21.8	3 36.0	+44.2	21.9	4 31.6	+44.6	21.9
61	2 28.3	+43.7	21.1	3 24.3	+43.9	21.2	4 20.2	+44.2	21.2	5 16.2	+44.4	21.2
62	3 12.0	+43.7	20.5	4 08.2	+44.0	20.5	5 04.4	+44.2	20.5	6 00.6	+44.5	20.5
63	3 55.7	+43.7	19.8	4 52.2	+44.0	19.8	5 48.6	+44.2	19.8	6 45.1	+44.3	19.9
64	4 39.4	+43.6	19.1	5 36.1	+43.8	19.1	6 32.8	+44.0	19.1	7 29.4	+44.3	19.2
65	5 23.0	+43.6	18.4	6 19.9	+43.8	18.4	7 16.8	+44.1	18.5	8 13.7	+44.3	18.5
66	6 06.6	+43.5	17.7	7 03.7	+43.7	17.7	8 00.9	+43.9	17.8	8 58.0	+44.2	17.8
67	6 50.1	+43.4	17.0	7 47.4	+43.7	17.0	8 44.8	+43.9	17.1	9 42.2	+44.0	17.1
68	7 33.5	+43.4	16.3	8 31.1	+43.6	16.3	9 28.7	+43.8	16.4	10 26.2	+44.0	16.4
69	8 16.9	+43.3	15.6	9 14.7	+43.5	15.7	10 12.5	+43.7	15.7	11 10.2	+43.9	15.8
70	9 00.2	+43.3	14.9	9 58.2	+43.4	15.0	10 56.2	+43.6	15.0	11 54.1	+43.8	15.1
71	9 43.5	+43.1	14.2	10 41.6	+43.4	14.3	11 39.8	+43.5	14.3	12 37.9	+43.7	14.4
72	10 26.6	+43.1	13.5	11 25.0	+43.2	13.5	12 23.3	+43.4	13.6	13 21.6	+43.6	13.7
73	11 09.7	+42.9	12.8	12 08.2	+43.1	12.8	13 06.7	+43.3	12.9	14 05.2	+43.4	12.9
74	11 52.6	+42.9	12.1	12 51.3	+43.0	12.1	13 50.0	+43.1	12.2	14 48.6	+43.3	12.2
75	12 35.5	+42.7	11.4	13 34.3	+42.9	11.4	14 33.1	+43.1	11.5	15 31.9	+43.2	11.5
76	13 18.2	+42.6	10.6	14 17.2	+42.7	10.7	15 16.2	+42.8	10.7	16 15.1	+43.0	10.8
77	14 00.8	+42.5	9.9	14 59.9	+42.7	10.0	15 59.0	+42.8	10.0	16 58.1	+42.9	10.1
78	14 43.3	+42.4	9.2	15 42.6	+42.4	9.2	16 41.8	+42.6	9.3	17 41.0	+42.7	9.3
79	15 25.7	+42.2	8.5	16 25.0	+42.3	8.5	17 24.4	+42.4	8.5	18 23.7	+42.5	8.6
80	16 07.9	+42.0	7.7	17 07.3	+42.2	7.8	18 06.8	+42.2	7.8	19 06.2	+42.4	7.8
81	16 49.9	+41.9	7.0	17 49.5	+41.9	7.0	18 49.0	+42.1	7.1	19 48.6	+42.1	7.1
82	17 31.8	+41.7	6.2	18 31.4	+41.8	6.3	19 31.1	+41.9	6.3	20 30.7	+42.0	6.3
83	18 13.5	+41.6	5.5	19 13.2	+41.7	5.5	20 13.0	+41.6	5.5	21 12.7	+41.7	5.6
84	18 55.1	+41.3	4.7	19 54.9	+41.4	4.7	20 54.6	+41.5	4.8	21 54.4	+41.6	4.8
85	19 36.4	+41.2	3.9	20 36.3	+41.2	4.0	21 36.1	+41.3	4.0	22 36.0	+41.3	4.0
86	20 17.6	+40.9	3.2	21 17.5	+40.9	3.2	22 17.4	+41.0	3.2	23 17.3	+41.0	3.2
87	20 58.5	+40.7	2.4	21 58.4	+40.8	2.4	22 58.4	+40.8	2.4	23 58.3	+40.9	2.4
88	21 39.2	+40.5	1.6	22 39.2	+40.5	1.6	23 39.2	+40.5	1.6	24 39.2	+40.5	1.6
89	22 19.7	+40.3	0.8	23 19.7	+40.3	0.8	24 19.7	+40.3	0.8	25 19.7	+40.3	0.8
90	23 00.0	+40.0	0.0	24 00.0	+40.0	0.0	25 00.0	+40.0	0.0	26 00.0	+40.0	0.0
	23°			24°			25°			26°		

Dec.	27°			28°			29°			30°			Dec.
	Hc	d	Z	Hc	d	Z	Hc	d	Z	Hc	d	Z	
°	° ′	′	°	° ′	′	°	° ′	′	°	° ′	′	°	°
0	36 35.9	-34.2	112.2	36 12.9	-35.2	112.9	35 49.2	-36.1	113.6	35 24.9	-37.1	114.2	0
1	36 01.7	-34.7	113.3	35 37.7	-35.7	113.9	35 13.1	-36.6	114.6	34 47.8	-37.5	115.2	1
2	35 27.0	-35.2	114.3	35 02.0	-36.1	114.9	34 36.5	-37.1	115.5	34 10.3	-37.9	116.1	2
3	34 51.8	-35.7	115.2	34 25.9	-36.6	115.9	33 59.4	-37.4	116.5	33 32.4	-38.3	117.1	3
4	34 16.1	-36.1	116.2	33 49.3	-37.0	116.8	33 22.0	-37.9	117.4	32 54.1	-38.7	118.0	4
5	33 40.0	-36.6	117.2	33 12.3	-37.4	117.8	32 44.1	-38.3	118.3	32 15.4	-39.2	118.9	5
6	33 03.4	-37.0	118.1	32 34.9	-37.9	118.7	32 05.8	-38.7	119.3	31 36.2	-39.4	119.8	6
7	32 26.4	-37.4	119.1	31 57.0	-38.2	119.6	31 27.1	-39.0	120.2	30 56.8	-39.9	120.7	7
8	31 49.0	-37.8	120.0	31 18.8	-38.6	120.5	30 48.1	-39.4	121.0	30 16.9	-40.1	121.5	8
9	31 11.2	-38.1	120.9	30 40.2	-39.0	121.4	30 08.7	-39.8	121.9	29 36.8	-40.5	122.4	9
10	30 33.1	-38.6	121.8	30 01.2	-39.3	122.3	29 28.9	-40.0	122.8	28 56.3	-40.9	123.3	10
11	29 54.5	-38.9	122.7	29 21.9	-39.6	123.2	28 48.9	-40.4	123.6	28 15.4	-41.1	124.1	11
12	29 15.6	-39.2	123.6	28 42.3	-40.0	124.0	28 08.5	-40.7	124.5	27 34.3	-41.4	124.9	12
13	28 36.4	-39.6	124.4	28 02.3	-40.3	124.9	27 27.8	-41.0	125.3	26 52.9	-41.7	125.7	13
14	27 56.8	-39.8	125.3	27 22.0	-40.6	125.7	26 46.8	-41.3	126.1	26 11.2	-41.9	126.5	14
15	27 17.0	-40.2	126.1	26 41.4	-40.8	126.5	26 05.5	-41.5	126.9	25 29.3	-42.2	127.3	15
16	26 36.8	-40.5	127.0	26 00.6	-41.2	127.4	25 24.0	-41.8	127.7	24 47.1	-42.4	128.1	16
17	25 56.3	-40.7	127.8	25 19.4	-41.4	128.2	24 42.2	-42.0	128.5	24 04.7	-42.7	128.9	17
18	25 15.6	-41.0	128.6	24 38.0	-41.6	129.0	24 00.2	-42.3	129.3	23 22.0	-42.9	129.7	18
19	24 34.6	-41.2	129.4	23 56.4	-41.9	129.8	23 17.9	-42.5	130.1	22 39.1	-43.1	130.4	19
20	23 53.4	-41.5	130.2	23 14.5	-42.1	130.5	22 35.4	-42.7	130.9	21 56.0	-43.3	131.2	20
21	23 11.9	-41.8	131.0	22 32.4	-42.4	131.3	21 52.7	-43.0	131.6	21 12.7	-43.5	131.9	21
22	22 30.1	-41.9	131.8	21 50.0	-42.5	132.1	21 09.7	-43.1	132.4	20 29.2	-43.7	132.6	22
23	21 48.2	-42.2	132.5	21 07.5	-42.7	132.8	20 26.6	-43.3	133.1	19 45.5	-43.9	133.4	23
24	21 06.0	-42.4	133.3	20 24.8	-43.0	133.6	19 43.3	-43.5	133.8	19 01.6	-44.0	134.1	24
25	20 23.6	-42.5	134.1	19 41.8	-43.1	134.3	18 59.8	-43.7	134.6	18 17.6	-44.2	134.8	25
26	19 41.1	-42.8	134.8	18 58.7	-43.3	135.1	18 16.1	-43.8	135.3	17 33.4	-44.3	135.5	26
27	18 58.3	-42.9	135.6	18 15.4	-43.4	135.8	17 32.3	-44.0	136.0	16 49.1	-44.5	136.2	27
28	18 15.4	-43.1	136.3	17 32.0	-43.6	136.5	16 48.3	-44.1	136.7	16 04.6	-44.6	136.9	28
29	17 32.3	-43.2	137.0	16 48.3	-43.7	137.2	16 04.2	-44.2	137.4	15 20.0	-44.8	137.6	29
30	16 49.1	-43.4	137.8	16 04.6	-43.9	138.0	15 20.0	-44.4	138.1	14 35.2	-44.9	138.3	30
31	16 05.7	-43.6	138.5	15 20.7	-44.1	138.7	14 35.6	-44.5	138.8	13 50.3	-44.9	139.0	31
32	15 22.1	-43.7	139.2	14 36.6	-44.1	139.4	13 51.1	-44.7	139.5	13 05.4	-45.1	139.7	32
33	14 38.4	-43.8	139.9	13 52.5	-44.3	140.1	13 06.4	-44.7	140.2	12 20.3	-45.2	140.4	33
34	13 54.6	-43.9	140.6	13 08.2	-44.4	140.8	12 21.7	-44.8	140.9	11 35.1	-45.3	141.0	34
35	13 10.7	-44.1	141.3	12 23.8	-44.5	141.4	11 36.9	-45.0	141.6	10 49.8	-45.4	141.7	35
36	12 26.6	-44.1	142.0	11 39.3	-44.6	142.1	10 51.9	-45.0	142.3	10 04.4	-45.4	142.4	36
37	11 42.5	-44.3	142.7	10 54.7	-44.6	142.8	10 06.9	-45.1	142.9	9 19.0	-45.5	143.0	37
38	10 58.2	-44.3	143.4	10 10.1	-44.8	143.5	9 21.8	-45.2	143.6	8 33.5	-45.6	143.7	38
39	10 13.9	-44.4	144.1	9 25.3	-44.9	144.2	8 36.6	-45.2	144.3	7 47.9	-45.7	144.3	39
40	9 29.5	-44.5	144.7	8 40.4	-44.9	144.8	7 51.4	-45.3	144.9	7 02.2	-45.7	145.0	40
41	8 45.0	-44.6	145.4	7 55.5	-44.9	145.5	7 06.1	-45.4	145.6	6 16.5	-45.7	145.7	41
42	8 00.4	-44.7	146.1	7 10.6	-45.1	146.2	6 20.7	-45.4	146.2	5 30.8	-45.8	146.3	42
43	7 15.7	-44.7	146.8	6 25.5	-45.1	146.8	5 35.3	-45.5	146.9	4 45.0	-45.8	146.9	43
44	6 31.0	-44.7	147.4	5 40.4	-45.1	147.5	4 49.8	-45.5	147.6	3 59.2	-45.9	147.6	44
45	5 46.3	-44.8	148.1	4 55.3	-45.2	148.2	4 04.3	-45.5	148.2	3 13.3	-45.9	148.2	45
46	5 01.5	-44.9	148.8	4 10.1	-45.2	148.8	3 18.8	-45.6	148.9	2 27.4	-45.9	148.9	46
47	4 16.6	-44.9	149.5	3 24.9	-45.2	149.5	2 33.2	-45.5	149.5	1 41.5	-45.9	149.5	47
48	3 31.7	-44.9	150.1	2 39.7	-45.2	150.1	1 47.7	-45.6	150.2	0 55.6	-45.9	150.2	48
49	2 46.8	-44.9	150.8	1 54.5	-45.3	150.8	1 02.1	-45.6	150.8	0 09.7	-45.9	150.8	49
50	2 01.9	-44.9	151.4	1 09.2	-45.3	151.5	0 16.5	-45.6	151.5	0 36.2	+45.9	28.5	50
51	1 17.0	-45.0	152.1	0 23.9	-45.3	152.1	0 29.1	+45.6	27.9	1 22.1	+45.9	27.9	51
52	0 32.0	-45.0	152.8	0 21.4	+45.2	27.2	1 14.7	+45.6	27.2	2 08.0	+45.9	27.2	52
53	0 13.0	+44.9	26.6	1 06.6	+45.3	26.6	2 00.3	+45.6	26.6	2 53.9	+45.9	26.6	53
54	0 57.9	+45.0	25.9	1 51.9	+45.2	25.9	2 45.9	+45.5	25.9	3 39.8	+45.9	26.0	54
55	1 42.9	+44.9	25.2	2 37.1	+45.3	25.3	3 31.4	+45.5	25.3	4 25.7	+45.8	25.3	55
56	2 27.8	+44.9	24.6	3 22.4	+45.2	24.6	4 16.9	+45.5	24.6	5 11.5	+45.7	24.7	56
57	3 12.7	+44.9	23.9	4 07.6	+45.1	23.9	5 02.4	+45.5	24.0	5 57.2	+45.7	24.0	57
58	3 57.6	+44.9	23.3	4 52.7	+45.2	23.3	5 47.9	+45.4	23.3	6 42.9	+45.7	23.4	58
59	4 42.5	+44.8	22.6	5 37.9	+45.1	22.6	6 33.3	+45.3	22.7	7 28.6	+45.6	22.7	59
60	5 27.3	+44.8	21.9	6 23.0	+45.0	22.0	7 18.6	+45.3	22.0	8 14.2	+45.6	22.1	60
61	6 12.1	+44.7	21.2	7 08.0	+45.0	21.3	8 03.9	+45.2	21.3	8 59.8	+45.5	21.4	61
62	6 56.8	+44.7	20.6	7 53.0	+44.9	20.6	8 49.1	+45.2	20.7	9 45.3	+45.4	20.7	62
63	7 41.5	+44.6	19.9	8 37.9	+44.8	20.0	9 34.3	+45.1	20.0	10 30.7	+45.3	20.1	63
64	8 26.1	+44.5	19.2	9 22.7	+44.8	19.3	10 19.4	+45.0	19.3	11 16.0	+45.2	19.4	64
65	9 10.6	+44.5	18.6	10 07.5	+44.7	18.6	11 04.4	+44.9	18.7	12 01.2	+45.1	18.7	65
66	9 55.1	+44.4	17.9	10 52.2	+44.6	17.9	11 49.3	+44.8	18.0	12 46.3	+45.1	18.1	66
67	10 39.5	+44.3	17.2	11 36.8	+44.5	17.2	12 34.1	+44.7	17.3	13 31.4	+44.9	17.4	67
68	11 23.8	+44.2	16.5	12 21.3	+44.4	16.6	13 18.8	+44.6	16.6	14 16.3	+44.8	16.7	68
69	12 08.0	+44.1	15.8	13 05.7	+44.3	15.9	14 03.4	+44.5	15.9	15 01.1	+44.7	16.0	69
70	12 52.1	+43.9	15.1	13 50.0	+44.1	15.2	14 47.9	+44.3	15.2	15 45.8	+44.5	15.3	70
71	13 36.0	+43.9	14.4	14 34.1	+44.1	14.5	15 32.2	+44.2	14.5	16 30.3	+44.4	14.6	71
72	14 19.9	+43.7	13.7	15 18.2	+43.9	13.8	16 16.4	+44.1	13.8	17 14.7	+44.3	13.9	72
73	15 03.6	+43.6	13.0	16 02.1	+43.8	13.1	17 00.5	+44.0	13.1	17 59.0	+44.1	13.2	73
74	15 47.2	+43.5	12.3	16 45.9	+43.6	12.4	17 44.5	+43.7	12.4	18 43.1	+43.9	12.5	74
75	16 30.7	+43.3	11.6	17 29.5	+43.4	11.6	18 28.2	+43.7	11.7	19 27.0	+43.8	11.8	75
76	17 14.0	+43.2	10.8	18 12.9	+43.3	10.9	19 11.9	+43.4	11.0	20 10.8	+43.5	11.0	76
77	17 57.2	+43.0	10.1	18 56.2	+43.2	10.2	19 55.3	+43.3	10.2	20 54.3	+43.4	10.3	77
78	18 40.2	+42.8	9.4	19 39.4	+42.9	9.4	20 38.6	+43.0	9.5	21 37.7	+43.2	9.6	78
79	19 23.0	+42.7	8.6	20 22.3	+42.8	8.7	21 21.6	+42.9	8.8	22 20.9	+43.0	8.8	79
80	20 05.7	+42.4	7.9	21 05.1	+42.5	7.9	22 04.5	+42.7	8.0	23 03.9	+42.8	8.1	80
81	20 48.1	+42.3	7.1	21 47.6	+42.4	7.2	22 47.2	+42.4	7.2	23 46.7	+42.5	7.3	81
82	21 30.4	+42.0	6.4	22 30.0	+42.1	6.4	23 29.6	+42.2	6.5	24 29.2	+42.3	6.5	82
83	22 12.4	+41.8	5.6	23 12.1	+41.9	5.7	24 11.8	+42.0	5.7	25 11.5	+42.1	5.7	83
84	22 54.2	+41.6	4.8	23 54.0	+41.7	4.9	24 53.8	+41.7	4.9	25 53.6	+41.8	5.0	84
85	23 35.8	+41.4	4.1	24 35.7	+41.4	4.1	25 35.5	+41.5	4.1	26 35.4	+41.5	4.2	85
86	24 17.2	+41.1	3.3	25 17.1	+41.1	3.3	26 17.0	+41.2	3.3	27 16.9	+41.2	3.3	86
87	24 58.3	+40.8	2.5	25 58.2	+40.9	2.5	26 58.2	+40.9	2.5	27 58.1	+41.0	2.5	87
88	25 39.1	+40.6	1.6	26 39.1	+40.6	1.7	27 39.1	+40.6	1.7	28 39.1	+40.6	1.7	88
89	26 19.7	+40.3	0.8	27 19.7	+40.3	0.8	28 19.7	+40.3	0.8	29 19.7	+40.3	0.9	89
90	27 00.0	+40.0	0.0	28 00.0	+40.0	0.0	29 00.0	+40.0	0.0	30 00.0	+40.0	0.0	90
	27°			28°			29°			30°			

S. Lat. { L.H.A. greater than 180° ....Zn=180°−Z; L.H.A. less than 180°..........Zn=180°+Z

LATITUDE SAME NAME AS DECLINATION L.H.A. 132°, 228°

49°, 311° L.H.A. LATITUDE SAME NAME AS DECLINATION

N. Lat. {L.H.A. greater than 180° .....Zn=Z
{L.H.A. less than 180°............Zn=360°−Z

Dec.	23° Hc	23° d	23° Z	24° Hc	24° d	24° Z	25° Hc	25° d	25° Z	26° Hc	26° d	26° Z	27° Hc	27° d	27° Z	28° Hc	28° d	28° Z	29° Hc	29° d	29° Z	30° Hc	30° d	30° Z	Dec.
°	° ′	′	°	° ′	′	°	° ′	′	°	° ′	′	°	° ′	′	°	° ′	′	°	° ′	′	°	° ′	′	°	°
0	37 09.0	+29.1	108.8	36 49.4	+30.1	109.5	36 29.0	+31.3	110.2	36 08.0	+32.3	110.9	35 46.3	+33.3	111.5	35 23.9	+34.3	112.2	35 00.9	+35.3	112.9	34 37.3	+36.3	113.5	0
1	37 38.1	+28.5	107.7	37 19.5	+29.6	108.4	37 00.3	+30.6	109.1	36 40.3	+31.7	109.8	36 19.6	+32.8	110.5	35 58.2	+33.8	111.2	35 36.2	+34.8	111.9	35 13.6	+35.7	112.5	1
2	38 06.6	+27.9	106.5	37 49.1	+29.0	107.3	37 30.9	+30.1	108.0	37 12.0	+31.2	108.8	36 52.4	+32.2	109.5	36 32.0	+33.3	110.2	36 11.0	+34.3	110.9	35 49.3	+35.3	111.5	2
3	38 34.5	+27.1	105.4	38 18.1	+28.3	106.2	38 01.0	+29.5	106.9	37 43.2	+30.5	107.7	37 24.6	+31.6	108.4	37 05.3	+32.7	109.1	36 45.3	+33.7	109.8	36 24.6	+34.7	110.5	3
4	39 01.6	+26.5	104.3	38 46.4	+27.7	105.1	38 30.5	+28.8	105.8	38 13.7	+30.0	106.6	37 56.2	+31.1	107.3	37 38.0	+32.1	108.1	37 19.0	+33.2	108.8	36 59.3	+34.2	109.5	4
5	39 28.1	+25.9	103.1	39 14.1	+27.0	103.9	38 59.3	+28.2	104.7	38 43.7	+29.3	105.5	38 27.3	+30.4	106.2	38 10.1	+31.6	107.0	37 52.2	+32.6	107.7	37 33.5	+33.7	108.5	5
6	39 54.0	+25.0	101.9	39 41.1	+26.3	102.8	39 27.5	+27.5	103.6	39 13.0	+28.7	104.4	38 57.7	+29.8	105.1	38 41.7	+30.9	105.9	38 24.8	+32.1	106.7	38 07.2	+33.1	107.4	6
7	40 19.0	+24.4	100.8	40 07.4	+25.6	101.6	39 55.0	+26.8	102.4	39 41.7	+27.9	103.2	39 27.5	+29.2	104.0	39 12.6	+30.3	104.8	38 56.9	+31.4	105.6	38 40.3	+32.6	106.4	7
8	40 43.4	+23.6	99.6	40 33.0	+24.9	100.4	40 21.8	+26.0	101.2	40 09.6	+27.3	102.1	39 56.7	+28.5	102.9	39 42.9	+29.6	103.7	39 28.3	+30.8	104.5	39 12.9	+31.9	105.3	8
9	41 07.0	+22.8	98.3	40 57.9	+24.0	99.2	40 47.8	+25.4	100.0	40 36.9	+26.6	100.9	40 25.2	+27.7	101.7	40 12.5	+29.0	102.6	39 59.1	+30.1	103.4	39 44.8	+31.2	104.2	9
10	41 29.8	+22.0	97.1	41 21.9	+23.4	98.0	41 13.2	+24.5	98.8	41 03.5	+25.8	99.7	40 52.9	+27.1	100.6	40 41.5	+28.3	101.4	40 29.2	+29.5	102.2	40 16.0	+30.7	103.1	10
11	41 51.8	+21.2	95.9	41 45.3	+22.5	96.7	41 37.7	+23.8	97.6	41 29.3	+25.1	98.5	41 20.0	+26.3	99.4	41 09.8	+27.5	100.2	40 58.7	+28.7	101.1	40 46.7	+29.9	101.9	11
12	42 13.0	+20.4	94.6	42 07.8	+21.7	95.5	42 01.5	+23.0	96.4	41 54.4	+24.3	97.3	41 46.3	+25.6	98.2	41 37.3	+26.9	99.1	41 27.4	+28.1	99.9	41 16.6	+29.3	100.8	12
13	42 33.4	+19.5	93.3	42 29.5	+20.8	94.2	42 24.5	+22.2	95.2	42 18.7	+23.5	96.1	42 11.9	+24.8	97.0	42 04.2	+26.0	97.9	41 55.5	+27.3	98.7	41 45.9	+28.5	99.6	13
14	42 52.9	+18.7	92.0	42 50.3	+20.0	93.0	42 46.7	+21.4	93.9	42 42.2	+22.6	94.8	42 36.7	+23.9	95.7	42 30.2	+25.3	96.6	42 22.8	+26.5	97.5	42 14.4	+27.9	98.4	14
15	43 11.6	+17.7	90.7	43 10.3	+19.1	91.7	43 08.1	+20.4	92.6	43 04.8	+21.9	93.5	43 00.6	+23.2	94.5	42 55.5	+24.4	95.4	42 49.3	+25.8	96.3	42 42.3	+27.0	97.2	15
16	43 29.3	+16.9	89.4	43 29.4	+18.3	90.4	43 28.5	+19.6	91.3	43 26.7	+20.9	92.3	43 23.8	+22.3	93.2	43 19.9	+23.7	94.2	43 15.1	+25.0	95.1	43 09.3	+26.2	96.0	16
17	43 46.2	+15.9	88.1	43 47.7	+17.3	89.1	43 48.1	+18.7	90.0	43 47.6	+20.1	91.0	43 46.1	+21.4	91.9	43 43.6	+22.8	92.9	43 40.1	+24.1	93.8	43 35.5	+25.5	94.8	17
18	44 02.1	+14.9	86.8	44 05.0	+16.3	87.7	44 06.8	+17.8	88.7	44 07.7	+19.2	89.7	44 07.5	+20.6	90.6	44 06.4	+21.9	91.6	44 04.2	+23.2	92.6	44 01.0	+24.6	93.5	18
19	44 17.0	+14.0	85.4	44 21.3	+15.4	86.4	44 24.6	+16.8	87.4	44 26.9	+18.2	88.3	44 28.1	+19.6	89.3	44 28.3	+21.0	90.3	44 27.4	+22.4	91.3	44 25.6	+23.7	92.3	19
20	44 31.0	+13.1	84.0	44 36.7	+14.5	85.0	44 41.4	+15.9	86.0	44 45.1	+17.3	87.0	44 47.7	+18.7	88.0	44 49.3	+20.1	89.0	44 49.8	+21.5	90.0	44 49.3	+22.9	91.0	20
21	44 44.1	+12.0	82.7	44 51.2	+13.5	83.7	44 57.3	+14.9	84.7	45 02.4	+16.3	85.6	45 06.4	+17.7	86.6	45 09.4	+19.1	87.7	45 11.3	+20.6	88.7	45 12.2	+21.9	89.7	21
22	44 56.1	+11.0	81.3	45 04.7	+12.4	82.3	45 12.2	+13.9	83.3	45 18.7	+15.3	84.3	45 24.1	+16.8	85.3	45 28.5	+18.2	86.3	45 31.9	+19.6	87.3	45 34.1	+21.1	88.3	22
23	45 07.1	+10.0	79.9	45 17.1	+11.5	80.9	45 26.1	+12.9	81.9	45 34.0	+14.4	82.9	45 40.9	+15.8	83.9	45 46.7	+17.2	84.9	45 51.5	+18.6	86.0	45 55.2	+20.0	87.0	23
24	45 17.1	+9.0	78.5	45 28.6	+10.4	79.5	45 39.0	+11.9	80.5	45 48.4	+13.3	81.5	45 56.7	+14.8	82.5	46 03.9	+16.3	83.6	46 10.1	+17.7	84.6	46 15.2	+19.1	85.6	24
25	45 26.1	+7.9	77.1	45 39.0	+9.4	78.1	45 50.9	+10.8	79.1	46 01.7	+12.3	80.1	46 11.5	+13.7	81.1	46 20.2	+15.1	82.2	46 27.8	+16.6	83.2	46 34.3	+18.1	84.3	25
26	45 34.0	+6.9	75.7	45 48.4	+8.3	76.7	46 01.7	+9.8	77.7	46 14.0	+11.2	78.7	46 25.2	+12.7	79.7	46 35.3	+14.2	80.8	46 44.4	+15.6	81.8	46 52.4	+17.1	82.9	26
27	45 40.9	+5.8	74.3	45 56.7	+7.2	75.3	46 11.5	+8.7	76.3	46 25.2	+10.1	77.3	46 37.9	+11.6	78.3	46 49.5	+13.1	79.4	47 00.0	+14.6	80.4	47 09.5	+16.0	81.5	27
28	45 46.7	+4.8	72.8	46 03.9	+6.2	73.8	46 20.2	+7.6	74.8	46 35.3	+9.1	75.8	46 49.5	+10.5	76.9	47 02.6	+12.0	77.9	47 14.6	+13.5	79.0	47 25.5	+15.0	80.0	28
29	45 51.5	+3.7	71.4	46 10.1	+5.1	72.4	46 27.8	+6.5	73.4	46 44.4	+8.0	74.4	47 00.0	+9.5	75.4	47 14.6	+10.9	76.5	47 28.1	+12.4	77.5	47 40.5	+13.9	78.6	29
30	45 55.2	+2.6	70.0	46 15.2	+4.1	71.0	46 34.3	+5.5	71.9	46 52.4	+6.9	73.0	47 09.5	+8.3	74.0	47 25.5	+9.8	75.0	47 40.5	+11.3	76.1	47 54.4	+12.7	77.2	30
31	45 57.8	+1.5	68.5	46 19.3	+2.9	69.5	46 39.8	+4.3	70.5	46 59.3	+5.8	71.5	47 17.8	+7.3	72.5	47 35.3	+8.7	73.6	47 51.8	+10.1	74.6	48 07.1	+11.7	75.7	31
32	45 59.3	+0.4	67.1	46 22.2	+1.8	68.1	46 44.1	+3.3	69.0	47 05.1	+4.7	70.0	47 25.1	+6.1	71.1	47 44.0	+7.6	72.1	48 01.9	+9.1	73.2	48 18.8	+10.5	74.2	32
33	45 59.7	−0.6	65.7	46 24.0	+0.7	66.6	46 47.4	+2.1	67.6	47 09.8	+3.5	68.6	47 31.2	+4.9	69.6	47 51.6	+6.4	70.6	48 11.0	+7.9	71.7	48 29.3	+9.4	72.7	33
34	45 59.1	−1.7	64.2	46 24.7	−0.3	65.2	46 49.5	+1.0	66.1	47 13.3	+2.4	67.1	47 36.1	+3.9	68.1	47 58.0	+5.3	69.1	48 18.9	+6.7	70.2	48 38.7	+8.2	71.3	34
35	45 57.4	−2.9	62.8	46 24.4	−1.5	63.7	46 50.5	−0.1	64.7	47 15.7	+1.3	65.6	47 40.0	+2.7	66.6	48 03.3	+4.1	67.7	48 25.6	+5.6	68.7	48 46.9	+7.0	69.8	35
36	45 54.5	−3.8	61.3	46 22.9	−2.6	62.3	46 50.4	−1.2	63.2	47 17.0	+0.1	64.2	47 42.7	+1.5	65.2	48 07.4	+3.0	66.2	48 31.2	+4.3	67.2	48 53.9	+5.9	68.2	36
37	45 50.7	−5.0	59.9	46 20.3	−3.6	60.8	46 49.2	−2.4	61.7	47 17.1	−1.0	62.7	47 44.2	+0.4	63.7	48 10.4	+1.7	64.7	48 35.5	+3.3	65.7	48 59.8	+4.6	66.7	37
38	45 45.7	−6.0	58.5	46 16.7	−4.8	59.4	46 46.8	−3.4	60.3	47 16.1	−2.1	61.2	47 44.6	−0.8	62.2	48 12.1	+0.7	63.2	48 38.8	+2.0	64.2	49 04.4	+3.5	65.2	38
39	45 39.7	−7.1	57.1	46 11.9	−5.8	57.9	46 43.4	−4.6	58.8	47 14.0	−3.2	59.7	47 43.8	−1.9	60.7	48 12.8	−0.6	61.7	48 40.8	+0.8	62.7	49 07.9	+2.2	63.7	39
40	45 32.6	−8.2	55.6	46 06.1	−6.9	56.5	46 38.8	−5.6	57.4	47 10.8	−4.4	58.3	47 41.9	−3.1	59.2	48 12.2	−1.7	60.2	48 41.6	−0.4	61.1	49 10.1	+1.0	62.2	40
41	45 24.4	−9.1	54.2	45 59.2	−8.0	55.1	46 33.2	−6.8	55.9	47 06.4	−5.5	56.8	47 38.8	−4.2	57.7	48 10.5	−2.9	58.7	48 41.2	−1.5	59.6	49 11.1	−0.2	60.6	41
42	45 15.3	−10.2	52.8	45 51.2	−9.1	53.6	46 26.4	−7.8	54.5	47 00.9	−6.6	55.3	47 34.6	−5.3	56.2	48 07.6	−4.1	57.2	48 39.7	−2.8	58.1	49 10.9	−1.4	59.1	42
43	45 05.1	−11.3	51.4	45 42.1	−10.0	52.2	46 18.6	−8.9	53.0	46 54.3	−7.7	53.9	47 29.3	−6.5	54.8	48 03.5	−5.2	55.7	48 36.9	−3.9	56.6	49 09.5	−2.6	57.6	43
44	44 53.8	−12.2	50.0	45 32.1	−11.1	50.8	46 09.7	−10.0	51.6	46 46.6	−8.8	52.4	47 22.8	−7.6	53.3	47 58.3	−6.4	54.2	48 33.0	−5.1	55.1	49 06.9	−3.8	56.0	44
45	44 41.6	−13.2	48.7	45 21.0	−12.2	49.4	45 59.7	−11.0	50.2	46 37.8	−9.9	51.0	47 15.2	−8.7	51.8	47 51.9	−7.5	52.7	48 27.9	−6.3	53.6	49 03.1	−5.0	54.5	45
46	44 28.4	−14.2	47.3	45 08.8	−13.1	48.0	45 48.7	−12.1	48.8	46 27.9	−11.0	49.6	47 06.5	−9.8	50.4	47 44.4	−8.6	51.2	48 21.6	−7.4	52.1	48 58.1	−6.2	53.0	46
47	44 14.2	−15.1	45.9	44 55.7	−14.2	46.6	45 36.6	−13.1	47.4	46 16.9	−12.0	48.1	46 56.7	−10.9	48.9	47 35.8	−9.8	49.8	48 14.2	−8.6	50.6	48 51.9	−7.4	51.5	47
48	43 59.1	−16.1	44.6	44 41.5	−15.1	45.3	45 23.5	−14.1	46.0	46 04.9	−13.0	46.7	46 45.8	−12.0	47.5	47 26.0	−10.9	48.3	48 05.6	−9.7	49.1	48 44.5	−8.5	50.0	48
49	43 43.0	−17.0	43.2	44 26.4	−16.0	43.9	45 09.4	−15.1	44.6	45 51.9	−14.1	45.3	46 33.8	−13.0	46.1	47 15.1	−11.9	46.8	47 55.9	−10.9	47.6	48 36.0	−9.8	48.5	49
50	43 26.0	−18.0	41.9	44 10.4	−17.0	42.6	44 54.3	−16.0	43.2	45 37.8	−15.1	43.9	46 20.8	−14.1	44.6	47 03.2	−13.1	45.4	47 45.0	−12.0	46.2	48 26.2	−10.8	47.0	50
51	43 08.0	−18.8	40.6	43 53.4	−18.0	41.2	44 38.3	−17.0	41.9	45 22.7	−16.0	42.5	46 06.7	−15.1	43.2	46 50.1	−14.1	44.0	47 33.0	−13.0	44.7	48 15.4	−12.0	45.5	51
52	42 49.2	−19.7	39.3	43 35.4	−18.8	39.9	44 21.3	−18.0	40.5	45 06.7	−17.1	41.2	45 51.6	−16.1	41.9	46 36.0	−15.1	42.6	47 20.0	−14.2	43.3	48 03.4	−13.1	44.0	52
53	42 29.5	−20.5	38.0	43 16.6	−19.7	38.6	44 03.3	−18.9	39.2	44 49.6	−18.0	39.8	45 35.5	−17.1	40.5	46 20.9	−16.2	41.1	47 05.8	−15.2	41.9	47 50.3	−14.2	42.6	53
54	42 09.0	−21.4	36.8	42 56.9	−20.6	37.3	43 44.4	−19.7	37.9	44 31.6	−18.9	38.5	45 18.4	−18.1	39.1	46 04.7	−17.1	39.8	46 50.6	−16.2	40.4	47 36.1	−15.3	41.1	54
55	41 47.6	−22.1	35.5	42 36.3	−21.4	36.0	43 24.7	−20.7	36.6	44 12.7	−19.8	37.2	45 00.3	−19.0	37.8	45 47.6	−18.2	38.4	46 34.4	−17.3	39.0	47 20.8	−16.4	39.7	55
56	41 25.5	−23.0	34.3	42 14.9	−22.2	34.8	43 04.0	−21.5	35.3	43 52.9	−20.8	35.8	44 41.3	−19.9	36.4	45 29.4	−19.1	37.0	46 17.1	−18.2	37.6	47 04.4	−17.3	38.3	56
57	41 02.5	−23.8	33.0	41 52.7	−23.1	33.5	42 42.5	−22.3	34.0	43 32.1	−21.6	34.5	44 21.4	−20.9	35.1	45 10.3	−20.0	35.7	45 58.9	−19.3	36.3	46 47.1	−18.4	36.9	57
58	40 38.7	−24.5	31.8	41 29.6	−23.8	32.3	42 20.2	−23.2	32.8	43 10.5	−22.4	33.3	44 00.5	−21.7	33.8	44 50.3	−21.0	34.3	45 39.6	−20.2	34.9	46 28.7	−19.4	35.5	58
59	40 14.2	−25.2	30.6	41 05.8	−24.6	31.1	41 57.0	−23.9	31.5	42 48.1	−23.3	32.0	43 38.8	−22.6	32.5	44 29.3	−21.9	33.0	45 19.4	−21.1	33.6	46 09.3	−20.4	34.1	59
60	39 49.0	−25.9	29.4	40 41.2	−25.4	29.8	41 33.1	−24.7	30.3	42 24.8	−24.1	30.7	43 16.2	−23.4	31.2	44 07.4	−22.7	31.7	44 58.3	−22.0	32.2	45 48.9	−21.3	32.8	60
61	39 23.1	−26.7	28.3	40 15.8	−26.1	28.7	41 08.4	−25.5	29.1	42 00.7	−24.9	29.5	42 52.8	−24.2	30.0	43 44.7	−23.6	30.4	44 36.3	−23.0	30.9	45 27.6	−22.2	31.4	61
62	38 56.4	−27.3	27.1	39 49.7	−26.7	27.5	40 42.9	−26.2	27.9	41 35.8	−25.6	28.3	42 28.6	−25.1	28.7	43 21.1	−24.5	29.2	44 13.3	−23.7	29.6	45 05.4	−23.2	30.1	62
63	38 29.1	−28.0	26.0	39 23.0	−27.5	26.3	40 16.7	−27.0	26.7	41 10.2	−26.4	27.1	42 03.5	−25.8	27.5	42 56.6	−25.2	27.9	43 49.6	−24.7	28.4	44 42.2	−24.0	28.8	63
64	38 01.1	−28.6	24.8	38 55.5	−28.1	25.2	39 49.7	−27.6	25.5	40 43.8	−27.1	25.9	41 37.7	−26.6	26.3	42 31.4	−26.0	26.7	43 24.9	−25.4	27.1	44 18.2	−24.8	27.5	64
65	37 32.5	−29.2	23.7	38 27.4	−28.8	24.0	39 22.1	−28.3	24.4	40 16.7	−27.8	24.7	41 11.1	−27.3	25.1	42 05.4	−26.8	25.5	42 59.5	−26.3	25.9	43 53.4	−25.7	26.3	65
66	37 03.3	−29.8	22.6	37 58.6	−29.4	22.9	38 53.8	−28.9	23.2	39 48.9	−28.5	23.6	40 43.8	−28.0	23.9	41 38.6	−27.5	24.3	42 33.2	−27.0	24.6	43 27.7	−26.5	25.0	66
67	36 33.5	−30.4	21.5	37 29.2	−30.0	21.8	38 24.9	−29.6	22.1	39 20.4	−29.1	22.4	40 15.8	−28.7	22.7	41 11.1	−28.3	23.1	42 06.2	−27.8	23.4	43 01.2	−27.3	23.8	67
68	36 03.1	−31.0	20.5	36 59.2	−30.6	20.7	37 55.3	−30.2	21.0	38 51.3	−29.8	21.3	39 47.1	−29.4	21.6	40 42.8	−28.9	21.9	41 38.4	−28.4	22.2	42 33.9	−28.0	22.6	68
69	35 32.1	−31.5	19.4	36 28.6	−31.1	19.7	37 25.1	−30.8	19.9	38 21.5	−30.4	20.2	39 17.7	−30.0	20.5	40 13.9	−29.6	20.7	41 10.0	−29.2	21.1	42 05.9	−28.8	21.4	69
70	35 00.6	−32.1	18.4	35 57.5	−31.7	18.6	36 54.3	−31.3	18.8	37 51.1	−31.0	19.1	38 47.7	−30.6	19.3	39 44.3	−30.3	19.6	40 40.8	−29.9	19.9	41 37.1	−29.5	20.2	70
71	34 28.5	−32.5	17.3	35 25.8	−32.3	17.6	36 23.0	−32.0	17.8	37 20.1	−31.6	18.0	38 17.1	−31.3	18.2	39 14.0	−30.9	18.5	40 10.9	−30.6	18.8	41 07.6	−30.1	19.0	71
72	33 56.0	−33.1	16.3	34 53.5	−32.7	16.5	35 51.0	−32.4	16.7	36 48.5	−32.2	16.9	37 45.8	−31.8	17.2	38 43.1	−31.5	17.4	39 40.3	−31.1	17.6	40 37.5	−30.9	17.9	72
73	33 22.9	−33.5	15.3	34 20.8	−33.3	15.5	35 18.6	−33.0	15.7	36 16.3	−32.7	15.9	37 14.0	−32.4	16.1	38 11.6	−32.1	16.3	39 09.2	−31.8	16.5	40 06.6	−31.4	16.8	73
74	32 49.4	−34.0	14.3	33 47.5	−33.7	14.5	34 45.6	−33.5	14.7	35 43.6	−33.2	14.8	36 41.6	−33.0	15.0	37 39.5	−32.7	15.2	38 37.4	−32.4	15.4	39 35.2	−32.1	15.7	74
75	32 15.4	−34.4	13.4	33 13.8	−34.2	13.5	34 12.1	−34.0	13.7	35 10.4	−33.7	13.8	36 08.6	−33.5	14.0	37 06.8	−33.2	14.2	38 05.0	−33.0	14.4	39 03.1	−32.7	14.6	75
76	31 41.0	−34.9	12.4	32 39.6	−34.7	12.5	33 38.1	−34.4	12.7	34 36.7	−34.3	12.8	35 35.1	−33.9	13.0	36 33.6	−33.8	13.1	37 32.0	−33.5	13.3	38 30.4	−33.3	13.5	76
77	31 06.1	−35.2	11.4	32 04.9	−35.1	11.6	33 03.7	−34.9	11.7	34 02.4	−34.7	11.8	35 01.2	−34.5	12.0	35 59.8	−34.3	12.1	36 58.5	−34.1	12.3	37 57.1	−33.9	12.4	77
78	30 30.9	−35.7	10.5	31 29.8	−35.5	10.6	32 28.8	−35.3	10.7	33 27.7	−35.1	10.8	34 26.7	−35.0	11.0	35 25.5	−34.7	11.1	36 24.4	−34.6	11.2	37 23.2	−34.3	11.4	78
79	29 55.2	−36.1	9.6	30 54.3	−35.9	9.7	31 53.5	−35.8	9.8	32 52.6	−35.6	9.9	33 51.7	−35.4	10.0	34 50.8	−35.3	10.1	35 49.8	−35.1	10.2	36 48.9	−34.9	10.4	79
80	29 19.1	−36.4	8.6	30 18.4	−36.3	8.7	31 17.7	−36.2	8.8	32 17.0	−36.0	8.9	33 16.3	−35.9	9.0	34 15.5	−35.7	9.1	35 14.7	−35.5	9.2	36 14.0	−35.5	9.4	80
81	28 42.7	−36.8	7.7	29 42.1	−36.7	7.8	30 41.5	−36.5	7.9	31 41.0	−36.5	8.0	32 40.4	−36.3	8.1	33 39.8	−36.2	8.2	34 39.2	−36.1	8.3	35 38.5	−35.9	8.4	81
82	28 05.9	−37.2	6.8	29 05.4	−37.0	6.9	30 05.0	−36.9	7.0	31 04.5	−36.8	7.0	32 04.1	−36.7	7.1	33 03.6	−36.6	7.2	34 03.1	−36.4	7.3	35 02.6	−36.3	7.4	82
83	27 28.7	−37.5	6.0	28 28.4	−37.4	6.0	29 28.1	−37.3	6.1	30 27.7	−37.2	6.1	31 27.4	−37.1	6.2	32 27.0	−37.0	6.3	33 26.7	−37.0	6.3	34 26.3	−36.8	6.4	83
84	26 51.2	−37.8	5.1	27 51.0	−37.7	5.1	28 50.8	−37.7	5.2	29 50.5	−37.6	5.2	30 50.3	−37.5	5.3	31 50.0	−37.4	5.3	32 49.7	−37.3	5.4	33 49.5	−37.3	5.4	84
85	26 13.4	−38.1	4.2	27 13.3	−38.1	4.2	28 13.1	−38.0	4.3	29 12.9	−37.9	4.3	30 12.8	−37.9	4.4	31 12.6	−37.8	4.4	32 12.4	−37.7	4.5	33 12.2	−37.7	4.5	85
86	25 35.3	−38.4	3.3	26 35.2	−38.4	3.4	27 35.1	−38.3	3.4	28 35.0	−38.3	3.4	29 34.9	−38.2	3.5	30 34.8	−38.2	3.5	31 34.7	−38.2	3.5	32 34.5	−38.0	3.6	86
87	24 56.9	−38.7	2.5	25 56.8	−38.6	2.5	26 56.8	−38.6	2.5	27 56.7	−38.6	2.6	28 56.7	−38.6	2.6	29 56.6	−38.5	2.6	30 56.5	−38.5	2.6	31 56.5	−38.5	2.7	87
88	24 18.2	−39.0	1.7	25 18.2	−39.0	1.7	26 18.2	−39.0	1.7	27 18.1	−38.9	1.7	28 18.1	−38.9	1.7	29 18.1	−38.9	1.7	30 18.0	−38.8	1.7	31 18.0	−38.8	1.8	88
89	23 39.2	−39.2	0.8	24 39.2	−39.2	0.8	25 39.2	−39.2	0.8	26 39.2	−39.2	0.8	27 39.2	−39.2	0.9	28 39.2	−39.2	0.9	29 39.2	−39.2	0.9	30 39.2	−39.2	0.9	89
90	23 00.0	−39.5	0.0	24 00.0	−39.5	0.0	25 00.0	−39.5	0.0	26 00.0	−39.5	0.0	27 00.0	−39.5	0.0	28 00.0	−39.5	0.0	29 00.0	−39.5	0.0	30 00.0	−39.5	0.0	90
	23°			24°			25°			26°			27°			28°			29°			30°			

49°, 311° L.H.A. LATITUDE SAME NAME AS DECLINATION

282

LATITUDE **CONTRARY** NAME TO DECLINATION **L.H.A. 49°, 311°**

Dec.	23° Hc	d	Z	24° Hc	d	Z	25° Hc	d	Z	26° Hc	d	Z	27° Hc	d	Z	28° Hc	d	Z	29° Hc	d	Z	30° Hc	d	Z	Dec.
°	° ′	′	°	° ′	′	°	° ′	′	°	° ′	′	°	° ′	′	°	° ′	′	°	° ′	′	°	° ′	′	°	°
0	37 09.0	−29.7	108.8	36 49.4	−30.8	109.5	36 29.0	−31.8	110.2	36 08.0	−32.9	110.9	35 46.3	−33.8	111.5	35 23.9	−34.8	112.2	35 00.9	−35.7	112.9	34 37.3	−36.6	113.5	0
1	36 39.3	−30.3	109.8	36 18.6	−31.4	110.5	35 57.2	−32.4	111.2	35 35.1	−33.3	111.9	35 12.5	−34.4	112.6	34 49.1	−35.2	113.2	34 25.2	−36.2	113.8	34 00.7	−37.2	114.5	1
2	36 09.0	−30.9	110.9	35 47.2	−31.8	111.6	35 24.8	−32.8	112.3	35 01.8	−33.9	112.9	34 38.1	−34.8	113.6	34 13.9	−35.8	114.2	33 49.0	−36.7	114.8	33 23.5	−37.5	115.4	2
3	35 38.1	−31.4	112.0	35 15.4	−32.4	112.6	34 52.0	−33.4	113.3	34 27.9	−34.3	113.9	34 03.3	−35.3	114.5	33 38.1	−36.2	115.1	33 12.3	−37.1	115.7	32 46.0	−38.0	116.3	3
4	35 06.7	−31.9	113.0	34 43.0	−33.0	113.7	34 18.6	−33.9	114.3	33 53.6	−34.8	114.9	33 28.0	−35.7	115.5	33 01.9	−36.6	116.1	32 35.2	−37.4	116.7	32 08.0	−38.3	117.2	4
5	34 34.8	−32.5	114.1	34 10.0	−33.4	114.7	33 44.7	−34.4	115.3	33 18.8	−35.3	115.9	32 52.3	−36.2	116.5	32 25.3	−37.0	117.0	31 57.8	−37.9	117.6	31 29.7	−38.7	118.1	5
6	34 02.3	−32.9	115.1	33 36.6	−33.9	115.7	33 10.3	−34.8	116.3	32 43.5	−35.7	116.9	32 16.1	−36.5	117.4	31 48.3	−37.5	118.0	31 19.9	−38.3	118.5	30 51.0	−39.1	119.0	6
7	33 29.4	−33.5	116.1	33 02.7	−34.3	116.7	32 35.5	−35.2	117.2	32 07.8	−36.1	117.8	31 39.6	−37.0	118.4	31 10.8	−37.8	118.9	30 41.6	−38.6	119.4	30 11.9	−39.4	119.9	7
8	32 55.9	−33.9	117.1	32 28.4	−34.8	117.6	32 00.3	−35.7	118.2	31 31.7	−36.6	118.7	31 02.6	−37.4	119.3	30 33.0	−38.2	119.8	30 03.0	−39.0	120.3	29 32.5	−39.8	120.8	8
9	32 22.0	−34.3	118.1	31 53.6	−35.3	118.6	31 24.6	−36.1	119.1	30 55.1	−36.9	119.7	30 25.2	−37.7	120.2	29 54.8	−38.5	120.7	29 24.0	−39.4	121.2	28 52.7	−40.1	121.6	9
10	31 47.7	−34.8	119.0	31 18.3	−35.6	119.6	30 48.5	−36.5	120.1	30 18.2	−37.3	120.6	29 47.5	−38.1	121.1	29 16.3	−38.9	121.6	28 44.6	−39.6	122.0	28 12.6	−40.4	122.5	10
11	31 12.9	−35.2	120.0	30 42.7	−36.0	120.5	30 12.0	−36.8	121.0	29 40.9	−37.7	121.5	29 09.4	−38.5	122.0	28 37.4	−39.2	122.4	28 05.0	−40.0	122.9	27 32.2	−40.7	123.3	11
12	30 37.7	−35.6	120.9	30 06.7	−36.5	121.4	29 35.2	−37.3	121.9	29 03.2	−38.0	122.4	28 30.9	−38.8	122.8	27 58.2	−39.6	123.3	27 25.0	−40.2	123.7	26 51.5	−41.0	124.2	12
13	30 02.1	−36.0	121.9	29 30.2	−36.8	122.3	28 57.9	−37.6	122.8	28 25.2	−38.3	123.3	27 52.1	−39.1	123.7	27 18.6	−39.8	124.1	26 44.8	−40.6	124.6	26 10.5	−41.2	125.0	13
14	29 26.1	−36.4	122.8	28 53.4	−37.1	123.2	28 20.3	−37.9	123.7	27 46.9	−38.7	124.1	27 13.0	−39.4	124.6	26 38.8	−40.1	125.0	26 04.2	−40.8	125.4	25 29.3	−41.5	125.8	14
15	28 49.7	−36.7	123.7	28 16.3	−37.5	124.1	27 42.4	−38.2	124.6	27 08.2	−39.0	125.0	26 33.6	−39.7	125.4	25 58.7	−40.5	125.8	25 23.4	−41.1	126.2	24 47.8	−41.8	126.6	15
16	28 13.0	−37.1	124.6	27 38.8	−37.9	125.0	27 04.2	−38.6	125.4	26 29.2	−39.3	125.9	25 53.9	−40.0	126.2	25 18.2	−40.6	126.6	24 42.3	−41.4	127.0	24 06.0	−42.0	127.4	16
17	27 35.9	−37.4	125.5	27 00.9	−38.1	125.9	26 25.6	−38.9	126.3	25 49.9	−39.6	126.7	25 13.9	−40.3	127.1	24 37.6	−41.0	127.4	24 00.9	−41.6	127.8	23 24.0	−42.2	128.1	17
18	26 58.5	−37.7	126.4	26 22.8	−38.5	126.8	25 46.7	−39.2	127.1	25 10.3	−39.8	127.5	24 33.6	−40.5	127.9	23 56.6	−41.2	128.2	23 19.3	−41.8	128.6	22 41.8	−42.5	128.9	18
19	26 20.8	−38.1	127.2	25 44.3	−38.7	127.6	25 07.5	−39.4	128.0	24 30.5	−40.2	128.3	23 53.1	−40.8	128.7	23 15.4	−41.4	129.0	22 37.5	−42.0	129.4	21 59.3	−42.6	129.7	19
20	25 42.7	−38.3	128.1	25 05.6	−39.1	128.5	24 28.1	−39.7	128.8	23 50.3	−40.3	129.2	23 12.3	−41.0	129.5	22 34.0	−41.6	129.8	21 55.5	−42.3	130.1	21 16.7	−42.9	130.4	20
21	25 04.4	−38.7	128.9	24 26.5	−39.3	129.3	23 48.4	−40.0	129.6	23 10.0	−40.7	130.0	22 31.3	−41.3	130.3	21 52.4	−41.9	130.6	21 13.2	−42.5	130.9	20 33.8	−43.1	131.2	21
22	24 25.7	−38.9	129.8	23 47.2	−39.6	130.1	23 08.4	−40.2	130.4	22 29.3	−40.8	130.8	21 50.0	−41.4	131.1	21 10.5	−42.1	131.4	20 30.7	−42.6	131.7	19 50.7	−43.2	131.9	22
23	23 46.8	−39.2	130.6	23 07.6	−39.8	130.9	22 28.2	−40.5	131.3	21 48.5	−41.1	131.6	21 08.6	−41.7	131.9	20 28.4	−42.2	132.1	19 48.1	−42.9	132.4	19 07.5	−43.4	132.7	23
24	23 07.6	−39.4	131.4	22 27.8	−40.1	131.7	21 47.7	−40.7	132.1	21 07.4	−41.3	132.3	20 26.9	−41.9	132.6	19 46.2	−42.5	132.9	19 05.2	−43.0	133.1	18 24.1	−43.6	133.4	24
25	22 28.2	−39.7	132.3	21 47.7	−40.3	132.6	21 07.0	−40.9	132.8	20 26.1	−41.5	133.1	19 45.0	−42.1	133.4	19 03.7	−42.6	133.6	18 22.2	−43.2	133.9	17 40.5	−43.7	134.1	25
26	21 48.5	−39.9	133.1	21 07.4	−40.5	133.3	20 26.1	−41.1	133.6	19 44.6	−41.7	133.9	19 02.9	−42.2	134.1	18 21.1	−42.8	134.4	17 39.0	−43.3	134.6	16 56.8	−43.9	134.8	26
27	21 08.6	−40.2	133.9	20 26.9	−40.7	134.1	19 45.0	−41.3	134.4	19 02.9	−41.8	134.7	18 20.7	−42.4	134.9	17 38.3	−43.0	135.1	16 55.7	−43.6	135.3	16 12.9	−44.0	135.5	27
28	20 28.4	−40.3	134.7	19 46.2	−41.0	134.9	19 03.7	−41.5	135.2	18 21.1	−42.1	135.4	17 38.3	−42.6	135.6	16 55.3	−43.2	135.9	16 12.1	−43.6	136.1	15 28.9	−44.2	136.3	28
29	19 48.1	−40.6	135.4	19 05.2	−41.1	135.7	18 22.2	−41.7	135.9	17 39.0	−42.2	136.2	16 55.7	−42.8	136.4	16 12.1	−43.2	136.6	15 28.5	−43.8	136.8	14 44.7	−44.3	137.0	29
30	19 07.5	−40.8	136.2	18 24.1	−41.3	136.5	17 40.5	−41.8	136.7	16 56.8	−42.4	136.9	16 12.9	−42.9	137.1	15 28.9	−43.4	137.3	14 44.7	−43.9	137.5	14 00.4	−44.4	137.7	30
31	18 26.7	−40.9	137.0	17 42.8	−41.5	137.2	16 58.7	−42.1	137.4	16 14.4	−42.5	137.6	15 30.0	−43.0	137.8	14 45.5	−43.6	138.0	14 00.8	−44.0	138.2	13 16.0	−44.5	138.3	31
32	17 45.8	−41.1	137.8	17 01.3	−41.7	138.0	16 16.6	−42.1	138.2	15 31.9	−42.7	138.4	14 47.0	−43.2	138.6	14 01.9	−43.6	138.7	13 16.8	−44.2	138.9	12 31.5	−44.6	139.0	32
33	17 04.7	−41.3	138.5	16 19.6	−41.8	138.7	15 34.5	−42.3	138.9	14 49.2	−42.8	139.1	14 03.8	−43.3	139.3	13 18.3	−43.8	139.4	12 32.6	−44.2	139.6	11 46.9	−44.7	139.7	33
34	16 23.4	−41.5	139.3	15 37.8	−41.9	139.5	14 52.2	−42.5	139.7	14 06.4	−43.0	139.8	13 20.5	−43.5	140.0	12 34.5	−43.9	140.1	11 48.4	−44.4	140.3	11 02.2	−44.8	140.4	34
35	15 41.9	−41.6	140.0	14 55.9	−42.1	140.2	14 09.7	−42.6	140.4	13 23.4	−43.0	140.5	12 37.0	−43.5	140.7	11 50.6	−44.0	140.8	11 04.0	−44.4	141.0	10 17.4	−44.9	141.1	35
36	15 00.3	−41.8	140.8	14 13.8	−42.3	141.0	13 27.1	−42.7	141.1	12 40.4	−43.2	141.3	11 53.5	−43.6	141.4	11 06.6	−44.1	141.5	10 19.6	−44.6	141.6	9 32.5	−45.0	141.7	36
37	14 18.5	−41.8	141.5	13 31.5	−42.4	141.7	12 44.4	−42.8	141.8	11 57.2	−43.3	142.0	11 09.9	−43.8	142.1	10 22.5	−44.2	142.2	9 35.0	−44.6	142.3	8 47.5	−45.0	142.4	37
38	13 36.7	−42.1	142.3	12 49.1	−42.4	142.4	12 01.6	−43.0	142.6	11 13.9	−43.4	142.7	10 26.1	−43.8	142.8	9 38.3	−44.2	142.9	8 50.4	−44.7	143.0	8 02.5	−45.1	143.1	38
39	12 54.6	−42.1	143.0	12 06.7	−42.6	143.1	11 18.6	−43.0	143.3	10 30.5	−43.5	143.4	9 42.3	−43.9	143.5	8 54.1	−44.4	143.6	8 05.7	−44.7	143.7	7 17.4	−45.2	143.8	39
40	12 12.5	−42.3	143.7	11 24.1	−42.7	143.9	10 35.6	−43.2	144.0	9 47.0	−43.5	144.1	8 58.4	−44.0	144.2	8 09.7	−44.4	144.3	7 21.0	−44.8	144.3	6 32.2	−45.2	144.4	40
41	11 30.2	−42.3	144.5	10 41.4	−42.8	144.6	9 52.4	−43.2	144.7	9 03.5	−43.7	144.8	8 14.4	−44.0	144.9	7 25.3	−44.4	144.9	6 36.2	−44.9	145.0	5 47.0	−45.3	145.1	41
42	10 47.9	−42.5	145.2	9 58.6	−42.9	145.3	9 09.2	−43.3	145.4	8 19.8	−43.7	145.5	7 30.4	−44.2	145.5	6 40.9	−44.6	145.6	5 51.3	−44.9	145.7	5 01.7	−45.2	145.7	42
43	10 05.4	−42.6	145.9	9 15.7	−43.0	146.0	8 25.9	−43.4	146.1	7 36.1	−43.8	146.2	6 46.2	−44.1	146.2	5 56.3	−44.5	146.3	5 06.4	−44.9	146.3	4 16.5	−45.4	146.4	43
44	9 22.8	−42.6	146.6	8 32.7	−43.1	146.7	7 42.5	−43.5	146.8	6 52.3	−43.8	146.9	6 02.1	−44.3	146.9	5 11.8	−44.6	147.0	4 21.5	−45.0	147.0	3 31.1	−45.3	147.0	44
45	8 40.2	−42.7	147.3	7 49.6	−43.1	147.4	6 59.1	−43.5	147.5	6 08.5	−43.9	147.5	5 17.8	−44.2	147.6	4 27.2	−44.7	147.6	3 36.5	−45.0	147.7	2 45.8	−45.4	147.7	45
46	7 57.5	−42.8	148.0	7 06.5	−43.2	148.1	6 15.6	−43.6	148.2	5 24.6	−44.0	148.2	4 33.6	−44.4	148.3	3 42.5	−44.7	148.3	2 51.5	−45.1	148.3	2 00.4	−45.4	148.4	46
47	7 14.7	−42.9	148.7	6 23.3	−43.2	148.8	5 32.0	−43.6	148.9	4 40.6	−43.9	148.9	3 49.2	−44.3	148.9	2 57.8	−44.7	149.0	2 06.4	−45.0	149.0	1 15.0	−45.4	149.0	47
48	6 31.8	−42.9	149.4	5 40.1	−43.3	149.5	4 48.4	−43.7	149.6	3 56.7	−44.1	149.6	3 04.9	−44.4	149.6	2 13.1	−44.7	149.6	1 21.4	−45.1	149.7	0 29.6	−45.4	149.7	48
49	5 48.9	−43.0	150.2	4 56.8	−43.3	150.2	4 04.7	−43.6	150.2	3 12.6	−44.0	150.3	2 20.5	−44.3	150.3	1 28.4	−44.7	150.3	0 36.3	−45.1	150.3	0 15.8	+45.4	29.7	49
50	5 05.9	−43.0	150.9	4 13.5	−43.4	150.9	3 21.1	−43.8	150.9	2 28.6	−44.0	151.0	1 36.2	−44.4	151.0	0 43.7	−44.7	151.0	0 08.8	+45.0	29.0	1 01.2	+45.4	29.0	50
51	4 22.9	−43.1	151.6	3 30.1	−43.4	151.6	2 37.3	−43.7	151.6	1 44.6	−44.1	151.6	0 51.8	−44.5	151.6	0 01.0	+44.8	28.4	0 53.8	+45.1	28.4	1 46.6	+45.4	28.4	51
52	3 39.8	−43.1	152.3	2 46.7	−43.4	152.3	1 53.6	−43.8	152.3	1 00.5	−44.1	152.3	0 07.3	−44.4	152.3	0 45.8	+44.7	27.7	1 38.9	+45.1	27.7	2 32.0	+45.4	27.7	52
53	2 56.7	−43.1	152.9	2 03.3	−43.4	153.0	1 09.8	−43.7	153.0	0 16.4	−44.1	153.0	0 37.1	+44.4	27.0	1 30.5	+44.7	27.0	2 24.0	+45.0	27.0	3 17.4	+45.3	27.1	53
54	2 13.6	−43.1	153.6	1 19.9	−43.5	153.7	0 26.1	−43.8	153.7	0 27.7	+44.1	26.3	1 21.5	+44.4	26.3	2 15.2	+44.7	26.4	3 09.0	+45.0	26.4	4 02.7	+45.3	26.4	54
55	1 30.5	−43.2	154.3	0 36.4	−43.5	154.3	0 17.7	+43.8	25.7	1 11.8	+44.0	25.7	2 05.9	+44.3	25.7	2 59.9	+44.7	25.7	3 54.0	+45.0	25.7	4 48.0	+45.3	25.7	55
56	0 47.3	−43.1	155.0	0 07.1	+43.4	25.0	1 01.5	+43.7	25.0	1 55.8	+44.1	25.0	2 50.2	+44.4	25.0	3 44.6	+44.6	25.0	4 39.0	+44.9	25.1	5 33.3	+45.2	25.1	56
57	0 04.2	−43.2	155.7	0 50.5	+43.5	24.3	1 45.2	+43.8	24.3	2 39.9	+44.0	24.3	3 34.6	+44.3	24.3	4 29.2	+44.7	24.3	5 23.9	+44.9	24.4	6 18.5	+45.2	24.4	57
58	0 39.0	+43.1	23.6	1 34.0	+43.4	23.6	2 29.0	+43.7	23.6	3 23.9	+44.0	23.6	4 18.9	+44.3	23.6	5 13.9	+44.5	23.7	6 08.8	+44.8	23.7	7 03.7	+45.1	23.8	58
59	1 22.1	+43.2	22.9	2 17.4	+43.4	22.9	3 12.7	+43.7	22.9	4 07.9	+44.0	22.9	5 03.2	+44.2	23.0	5 58.4	+44.5	23.0	6 53.6	+44.8	23.1	7 48.8	+45.1	23.1	59
60	2 05.3	+43.1	22.2	3 00.8	+43.4	22.2	3 56.4	+43.6	22.2	4 51.9	+43.9	22.3	5 47.4	+44.2	22.3	6 42.9	+44.5	22.3	7 38.4	+44.8	22.4	8 33.9	+45.0	22.4	60
61	2 48.4	+43.1	21.5	3 44.2	+43.4	21.5	4 40.0	+43.6	21.5	5 35.8	+43.9	21.6	6 31.6	+44.2	21.6	7 27.4	+44.4	21.7	8 23.2	+44.6	21.7	9 18.9	+44.9	21.8	61
62	3 31.5	+43.0	20.8	4 27.6	+43.3	20.8	5 23.6	+43.6	20.8	6 19.7	+43.8	20.9	7 15.8	+44.0	20.9	8 11.8	+44.3	21.0	9 07.8	+44.6	21.0	10 03.8	+44.8	21.1	62
63	4 14.5	+43.1	20.1	5 10.9	+43.3	20.1	6 07.2	+43.5	20.2	7 03.5	+43.8	20.2	7 59.8	+44.1	20.2	8 56.1	+44.3	20.3	9 52.4	+44.5	20.4	10 48.6	+44.8	20.4	63
64	4 57.6	+43.0	19.4	5 54.2	+43.2	19.4	6 50.7	+43.5	19.5	7 47.3	+43.7	19.5	8 43.9	+43.9	19.6	9 40.4	+44.2	19.6	10 36.9	+44.4	19.7	11 33.4	+44.6	19.7	64
65	5 40.6	+42.9	18.7	6 37.4	+43.1	18.7	7 34.2	+43.4	18.8	8 31.0	+43.6	18.8	9 27.8	+43.8	18.9	10 24.6	+44.0	18.9	11 21.3	+44.3	19.0	12 18.0	+44.6	19.1	65
66	6 23.5	+42.9	18.0	7 20.5	+43.1	18.0	8 17.6	+43.3	18.1	9 14.6	+43.6	18.1	10 11.6	+43.8	18.2	11 08.6	+44.0	18.2	12 05.6	+44.2	18.3	13 02.6	+44.4	18.4	66
67	7 06.4	+42.8	17.3	8 03.6	+43.1	17.3	9 00.9	+43.3	17.4	9 58.2	+43.4	17.4	10 55.4	+43.7	17.5	11 52.6	+43.9	17.5	12 49.8	+44.1	17.6	13 47.0	+44.3	17.7	67
68	7 49.2	+42.7	16.6	8 46.7	+42.9	16.6	9 44.2	+43.1	16.7	10 41.6	+43.4	16.7	11 39.1	+43.5	16.8	12 36.5	+43.8	16.8	13 33.9	+44.0	16.9	14 31.3	+44.2	17.0	68
69	8 31.9	+42.7	15.9	9 29.6	+42.9	15.9	10 27.3	+43.1	16.0	11 25.0	+43.2	16.0	12 22.6	+43.5	16.1	13 20.3	+43.7	16.1	14 17.9	+43.9	16.2	15 15.5	+44.1	16.3	69
70	9 14.6	+42.5	15.2	10 12.5	+42.7	15.2	11 10.4	+42.9	15.3	12 08.2	+43.2	15.3	13 06.1	+43.4	15.4	14 04.0	+43.5	15.4	15 01.8	+43.7	15.5	15 59.6	+43.9	15.6	70
71	9 57.1	+42.5	14.4	10 55.2	+42.7	14.5	11 53.3	+42.9	14.5	12 51.4	+43.0	14.6	13 49.5	+43.2	14.7	14 47.5	+43.4	14.7	15 45.5	+43.6	14.8	16 43.5	+43.8	14.9	71
72	10 39.6	+42.4	13.7	11 37.9	+42.6	13.8	12 36.2	+42.7	13.8	13 34.4	+43.0	13.9	14 32.7	+43.1	13.9	15 30.9	+43.3	14.0	16 29.1	+43.5	14.1	17 27.3	+43.6	14.2	72
73	11 22.0	+42.3	13.0	12 20.5	+42.4	13.1	13 18.9	+42.6	13.1	14 17.4	+42.7	13.2	15 15.8	+42.9	13.2	16 14.2	+43.1	13.3	17 12.6	+43.2	13.4	18 10.9	+43.5	13.4	73
74	12 04.3	+42.2	12.3	13 02.9	+42.4	12.3	14 01.5	+42.5	12.4	15 00.1	+42.7	12.4	15 58.7	+42.8	12.5	16 57.3	+43.0	12.6	17 55.8	+43.2	12.6	18 54.4	+43.3	12.7	74
75	12 46.5	+42.0	11.6	13 45.3	+42.1	11.6	14 44.0	+42.4	11.7	15 42.8	+42.5	11.7	16 41.5	+42.7	11.8	17 40.3	+42.8	11.8	18 39.0	+42.9	11.9	19 37.7	+43.1	12.0	75
76	13 28.5	+41.9	10.8	14 27.4	+42.1	10.9	15 26.4	+42.2	10.9	16 25.3	+42.3	11.0	17 24.2	+42.5	11.0	18 23.1	+42.6	11.1	19 21.9	+42.8	11.2	20 20.8	+42.9	11.2	76
77	14 10.4	+41.8	10.1	15 09.5	+41.9	10.1	16 08.6	+42.0	10.2	17 07.6	+42.2	10.2	18 06.7	+42.3	10.3	19 05.7	+42.4	10.3	20 04.7	+42.6	10.4	21 03.7	+42.7	10.5	77
78	14 52.2	+41.7	9.3	15 51.4	+41.8	9.4	16 50.6	+41.9	9.4	17 49.8	+42.0	9.5	18 49.0	+42.1	9.5	19 48.1	+42.3	9.6	20 47.3	+42.4	9.7	21 46.4	+42.6	9.7	78
79	15 33.9	+41.5	8.6	16 33.2	+41.6	8.6	17 32.5	+41.7	8.7	18 31.8	+41.8	8.7	19 31.1	+42.0	8.8	20 30.4	+42.1	8.8	21 29.7	+42.2	8.9	22 29.0	+42.3	9.0	79
80	16 15.4	+41.3	7.8	17 14.8	+41.4	7.9	18 14.2	+41.6	7.9	19 13.6	+41.7	8.0	20 13.1	+41.7	8.0	21 12.5	+41.8	8.1	22 11.9	+41.9	8.1	23 11.3	+42.0	8.2	80
81	16 56.7	+41.1	7.1	17 56.2	+41.3	7.1	18 55.8	+41.3	7.2	19 55.3	+41.4	7.2	20 54.8	+41.5	7.3	21 54.3	+41.7	7.3	22 53.8	+41.8	7.4	23 53.3	+41.9	7.4	81
82	17 37.8	+41.0	6.3	18 37.5	+41.0	6.4	19 37.1	+41.2	6.4	20 36.7	+41.3	6.4	21 36.3	+41.4	6.5	22 36.0	+41.4	6.5	23 35.6	+41.5	6.6	24 35.2	+41.6	6.6	82
83	18 18.8	+40.8	5.6	19 18.5	+40.9	5.6	20 18.3	+40.9	5.6	21 18.0	+41.0	5.7	22 17.7	+41.1	5.7	23 17.4	+41.1	5.7	24 17.1	+41.2	5.8	25 16.8	+41.3	5.8	83
84	18 59.6	+40.6	4.8	19 59.4	+40.7	4.8	20 59.2	+40.7	4.8	21 59.0	+40.8	4.9	22 58.8	+40.8	4.9	23 58.5	+41.0	5.0	24 58.3	+41.0	5.0	25 58.1	+41.1	5.0	84
85	19 40.2	+40.4	4.0	20 40.1	+40.4	4.0	21 39.9	+40.5	4.1	22 39.8	+40.5	4.1	23 39.6	+40.6	4.1	24 39.5	+40.6	4.2	25 39.3	+40.7	4.2	26 39.2	+40.7	4.2	85
86	20 20.6	+40.2	3.2	21 20.5	+40.3	3.2	22 20.4	+40.3	3.3	23 20.3	+40.4	3.3	24 20.2	+40.4	3.3	25 20.1	+40.4	3.3	26 20.0	+40.5	3.4	27 19.9	+40.5	3.4	86
87	21 00.8	+40.0	2.4	22 00.8	+40.0	2.4	23 00.7	+40.0	2.5	24 00.7	+40.0	2.5	25 00.6	+40.1	2.5	26 00.5	+40.2	2.5	27 00.5	+40.1	2.5	28 00.4	+40.2	2.6	87
88	21 40.8	+39.7	1.6	22 40.8	+39.7	1.6	23 40.7	+39.8	1.6	24 40.7	+39.8	1.7	25 40.7	+39.8	1.7	26 40.7	+39.8	1.7	27 40.6	+39.9	1.7	28 40.6	+39.9	1.7	88
89	22 20.5	+39.5	0.8	23 20.5	+39.5	0.8	24 20.5	+39.5	0.8	25 20.5	+39.5	0.8	26 20.5	+39.5	0.8	27 20.5	+39.5	0.8	28 20.5	+39.5	0.9	29 20.5	+39.5	0.9	89
90	23 00.0	+39.2	0.0	24 00.0	+39.2	0.0	25 00.0	+39.2	0.0	26 00.0	+39.2	0.0	27 00.0	+39.2	0.0	28 00.0	+39.2	0.0	29 00.0	+39.2	0.0	30 00.0	+39.2	0.0	90
	23°			24°			25°			26°			27°			28°			29°			30°			

S. Lat. { L.H.A. greater than 180° ....Zn=180°−Z
L.H.A. less than 180°...........Zn=180°+Z

LATITUDE **SAME** NAME AS DECLINATION **L.H.A. 131°, 229°**

283

Dec.	23° Hc	23° d	23° Z	24° Hc	24° d	24° Z	25° Hc	25° d	25° Z	26° Hc	26° d	26° Z	27° Hc	27° d	27° Z	28° Hc	28° d	28° Z	29° Hc	29° d	29° Z	30° Hc	30° d	30° Z	Dec.
°	° ′	′	°	° ′	′	°	° ′	′	°	° ′	′	°	° ′	′	°	° ′	′	°	° ′	′	°	° ′	′	°	°
0	36 16.6	+28.8	108.2	35 57.6	+29.8	108.8	35 37.9	+30.9	109.5	35 17.5	+31.9	110.2	34 56.4	+33.0	110.9	34 34.8	+33.9	111.5	34 12.5	+34.9	112.1	33 49.6	+35.8	112.8	0
1	36 45.4	+28.2	107.1	36 27.4	+29.3	107.8	36 08.8	+30.3	108.5	35 49.4	+31.4	109.2	35 29.4	+32.5	109.8	35 08.7	+33.5	110.5	34 47.4	+34.5	111.2	34 25.4	+35.5	111.8	1
2	37 13.6	+27.5	106.0	36 56.7	+28.7	106.7	36 39.1	+29.8	107.4	36 20.8	+30.9	108.1	36 01.9	+31.9	108.8	35 42.2	+32.9	109.5	35 21.9	+33.9	110.1	35 00.9	+34.9	110.8	2
3	37 41.1	+26.9	104.8	37 25.4	+28.0	105.6	37 08.9	+29.2	106.3	36 51.7	+30.3	107.0	36 33.8	+31.3	107.7	36 15.1	+32.4	108.4	35 55.8	+33.4	109.1	35 35.8	+34.4	109.8	3
4	38 08.0	+26.3	103.7	37 53.4	+27.5	104.5	37 38.1	+28.5	105.2	37 22.0	+29.6	105.9	37 05.1	+30.8	106.7	36 47.5	+31.9	107.4	36 29.2	+32.9	108.1	36 10.2	+34.0	108.8	4
5	38 34.3	+25.6	102.6	38 20.9	+26.7	103.3	38 06.6	+27.9	104.1	37 51.6	+29.1	104.9	37 35.9	+30.1	105.6	37 19.4	+31.2	106.3	37 02.1	+32.4	107.1	36 44.2	+33.4	107.8	5
6	38 59.9	+24.8	101.4	38 47.6	+26.1	102.2	38 34.5	+27.3	103.0	38 20.7	+28.4	103.7	38 06.0	+29.6	104.5	37 50.6	+30.7	105.3	37 34.5	+31.7	106.0	37 17.6	+32.8	106.7	6
7	39 24.7	+24.2	100.2	39 13.7	+25.4	101.0	39 01.8	+26.6	101.8	38 49.1	+27.7	102.6	38 35.6	+28.9	103.4	38 21.3	+30.0	104.2	38 06.2	+31.2	104.9	37 50.4	+32.2	105.7	7
8	39 48.9	+23.4	99.0	39 39.1	+24.6	99.9	39 28.4	+25.8	100.7	39 16.8	+27.1	101.5	39 04.5	+28.3	102.3	38 51.3	+29.5	103.1	38 37.4	+30.5	103.8	38 22.6	+31.7	104.6	8
9	40 12.3	+22.7	97.8	40 03.7	+23.9	98.7	39 54.2	+25.2	99.5	39 43.9	+26.4	100.3	39 32.8	+27.5	101.1	39 20.8	+28.7	101.9	39 07.9	+30.0	102.7	38 54.3	+31.1	103.5	9
10	40 35.0	+21.9	96.6	40 27.6	+23.2	97.5	40 19.4	+24.4	98.3	40 10.3	+25.7	99.1	40 00.3	+26.9	100.0	39 49.5	+28.1	100.8	39 37.9	+29.2	101.6	39 25.4	+30.4	102.4	10
11	40 56.9	+21.1	95.4	40 50.8	+22.4	96.2	40 43.8	+23.7	97.1	40 36.0	+24.9	98.0	40 27.2	+26.2	98.8	40 17.6	+27.4	99.6	40 07.1	+28.6	100.5	39 55.8	+29.7	101.3	11
12	41 18.0	+20.3	94.1	41 13.2	+21.6	95.0	41 07.5	+22.9	95.9	41 00.9	+24.1	96.8	40 53.4	+25.4	97.6	40 45.0	+26.6	98.5	40 35.7	+27.9	99.3	40 25.5	+29.1	100.2	12
13	41 38.3	+19.4	92.9	41 34.8	+20.8	93.8	41 30.4	+22.1	94.7	41 25.0	+23.4	95.5	41 18.8	+24.7	96.4	41 11.6	+26.0	97.3	41 03.6	+27.1	98.2	40 54.6	+28.4	99.0	13
14	41 57.7	+18.6	91.6	41 55.6	+19.9	92.5	41 52.5	+21.2	93.4	41 48.4	+22.6	94.3	41 43.5	+23.8	95.2	41 37.6	+25.1	96.1	41 30.7	+26.5	97.0	41 23.0	+27.7	97.8	14
15	42 16.3	+17.8	90.3	42 15.5	+19.1	91.2	42 13.7	+20.5	92.2	42 11.0	+21.8	93.1	42 07.3	+23.1	94.0	42 02.7	+24.4	94.9	41 57.2	+25.6	95.8	41 50.7	+26.9	96.7	15
16	42 34.1	+16.9	89.0	42 34.6	+18.2	90.0	42 34.2	+19.6	90.9	42 32.8	+20.9	91.8	42 30.4	+22.3	92.7	42 27.1	+23.6	93.6	42 22.8	+24.9	94.5	42 17.6	+26.1	95.4	16
17	42 51.0	+15.9	87.7	42 52.8	+17.4	88.7	42 53.8	+18.7	89.6	42 53.7	+20.1	90.5	42 52.7	+21.4	91.5	42 50.7	+22.7	92.4	42 47.7	+24.0	93.3	42 43.7	+25.4	94.2	17
18	43 06.9	+15.1	86.4	43 10.2	+16.4	87.4	43 12.5	+17.8	88.3	43 13.8	+19.2	89.2	43 14.1	+20.5	90.2	43 13.4	+21.9	91.1	43 11.7	+23.3	92.1	43 09.1	+24.6	93.0	18
19	43 22.0	+14.1	85.1	43 26.6	+15.6	86.0	43 30.3	+16.9	87.0	43 33.0	+18.2	87.9	43 34.6	+19.7	88.9	43 35.3	+21.0	89.8	43 35.0	+22.4	90.8	43 33.7	+23.7	91.7	19
20	43 36.1	+13.2	83.8	43 42.2	+14.5	84.7	43 47.2	+16.0	85.7	43 51.2	+17.4	86.6	43 54.3	+18.7	87.6	43 56.3	+20.2	88.5	43 57.4	+21.5	89.5	43 57.4	+22.8	90.5	20
21	43 49.3	+12.2	82.4	43 56.7	+13.7	83.4	44 03.2	+15.0	84.3	44 08.6	+16.5	85.3	44 13.0	+17.9	86.3	44 16.5	+19.2	87.2	44 18.9	+20.6	88.2	44 20.2	+22.0	89.2	21
22	44 01.5	+11.3	81.0	44 10.4	+12.6	82.0	44 18.2	+14.1	83.0	44 25.1	+15.4	83.9	44 30.9	+16.9	84.9	44 35.7	+18.3	85.9	44 39.5	+19.7	86.9	44 42.2	+21.1	87.9	22
23	44 12.8	+10.2	79.7	44 23.0	+11.7	80.6	44 32.3	+13.1	81.6	44 40.5	+14.5	82.6	44 47.8	+15.9	83.6	44 54.0	+17.3	84.6	44 59.2	+18.7	85.5	45 03.3	+20.1	86.5	23
24	44 23.0	+9.3	78.3	44 34.7	+10.7	79.3	44 45.4	+12.1	80.2	44 55.0	+13.6	81.2	45 03.7	+15.0	82.2	45 11.3	+16.4	83.2	45 17.9	+17.8	84.2	45 23.4	+19.2	85.2	24
25	44 32.3	+8.2	76.9	44 45.4	+9.6	77.9	44 57.5	+11.1	78.9	45 08.6	+12.5	79.8	45 18.7	+13.9	80.8	45 27.7	+15.4	81.8	45 35.7	+16.8	82.8	45 42.6	+18.3	83.9	25
26	44 40.5	+7.3	75.5	44 55.0	+8.7	76.5	45 08.6	+10.1	77.5	45 21.1	+11.5	78.4	45 32.6	+12.9	79.4	45 43.1	+14.4	80.5	45 52.5	+15.8	81.5	46 00.9	+17.2	82.5	26
27	44 47.8	+6.2	74.1	45 03.7	+7.6	75.1	45 18.7	+9.0	76.1	45 32.6	+10.5	77.0	45 45.5	+12.0	78.0	45 57.5	+13.3	79.1	46 08.3	+14.8	80.1	46 18.1	+16.3	81.1	27
28	44 54.0	+5.2	72.7	45 11.3	+6.6	73.7	45 27.7	+8.0	74.7	45 43.1	+9.4	75.6	45 57.5	+10.8	76.6	46 10.8	+12.3	77.7	46 23.1	+13.8	78.7	46 34.4	+15.2	79.7	28
29	44 59.2	+4.1	71.3	45 17.9	+5.5	72.3	45 35.7	+6.9	73.2	45 52.5	+8.4	74.2	46 08.3	+9.8	75.2	46 23.1	+11.3	76.2	46 36.9	+12.7	77.3	46 49.6	+14.1	78.3	29
30	45 03.3	+3.1	69.9	45 23.4	+4.5	70.9	45 42.6	+5.9	71.8	46 00.9	+7.3	72.8	46 18.1	+8.8	73.8	46 34.4	+10.1	74.8	46 49.6	+11.6	75.8	47 03.7	+13.1	76.9	30
31	45 06.4	+2.0	68.5	45 27.9	+3.4	69.4	45 48.5	+4.9	70.4	46 08.2	+6.2	71.4	46 26.9	+7.6	72.4	46 44.5	+9.1	73.4	47 01.2	+10.5	74.4	47 16.8	+12.0	75.4	31
32	45 08.4	+1.0	67.1	45 31.3	+2.4	68.0	45 53.4	+3.7	69.0	46 14.4	+5.2	69.9	46 34.5	+6.6	70.9	46 53.6	+8.0	71.9	47 11.7	+9.5	73.0	47 28.8	+10.9	74.0	32
33	45 09.4	−0.1	65.7	45 33.7	+1.3	66.6	45 57.1	+2.7	67.5	46 19.6	+4.0	68.5	46 41.1	+5.5	69.5	47 01.6	+6.9	70.5	47 21.2	+8.3	71.5	47 39.7	+9.8	72.5	33
34	45 09.3	−1.1	64.2	45 35.0	+0.2	65.2	45 59.8	+1.5	66.1	46 23.6	+3.0	67.0	46 46.6	+4.3	68.0	47 08.5	+5.8	69.0	47 29.5	+7.2	70.0	47 49.5	+8.7	71.1	34
35	45 08.2	−2.1	62.8	45 35.2	−0.8	63.7	46 01.3	+0.5	64.6	46 26.6	+1.9	65.6	46 50.9	+3.3	66.6	47 14.3	+4.7	67.6	47 36.7	+6.1	68.6	47 58.2	+7.5	69.6	35
36	45 06.1	−3.3	61.4	45 34.4	−1.9	62.3	46 01.8	−0.5	63.2	46 28.5	+0.7	64.1	46 54.2	+2.1	65.1	47 19.0	+3.5	66.1	47 42.8	+4.9	67.1	48 05.7	+6.3	68.1	36
37	45 02.8	−4.2	60.0	45 32.5	−3.0	60.9	46 01.3	−1.7	61.8	46 29.2	−0.3	62.7	46 56.3	+1.0	63.6	47 22.5	+2.4	64.6	47 47.7	+3.8	65.6	48 12.0	+5.2	66.6	37
38	44 58.6	−5.3	58.6	45 29.5	−4.1	59.4	45 59.6	−2.8	60.3	46 28.9	−1.5	61.2	46 57.3	−0.1	62.2	47 24.9	+1.2	63.1	47 51.5	+2.7	64.1	48 17.2	+4.1	65.1	38
39	44 53.3	−6.4	57.2	45 25.4	−5.1	58.0	45 56.8	−3.8	58.9	46 27.4	−2.5	59.8	46 57.2	−1.2	60.7	47 26.1	+0.1	61.7	47 54.2	+1.4	62.6	48 21.3	+2.9	63.6	39
40	44 46.9	−7.3	55.8	45 20.3	−6.1	56.6	45 53.0	−4.9	57.5	46 24.9	−3.7	58.3	46 56.0	−2.4	59.2	47 26.2	−1.0	60.2	47 55.6	+0.4	61.1	48 24.2	+1.6	62.1	40
41	44 39.6	−8.4	54.4	45 14.2	−7.2	55.2	45 48.1	−6.0	56.0	46 21.2	−4.7	56.9	46 53.6	−3.4	57.8	47 25.2	−2.2	58.7	47 56.0	−0.9	59.6	48 25.8	+0.6	60.6	41
42	44 31.2	−9.4	53.0	45 07.0	−8.2	53.8	45 42.1	−7.0	54.6	46 16.5	−5.8	55.4	46 50.2	−4.6	56.3	47 23.0	−3.3	57.2	47 55.1	−2.0	58.2	48 26.4	−0.7	59.1	42
43	44 21.8	−10.4	51.6	44 58.8	−9.3	52.4	45 35.1	−8.1	53.2	46 10.7	−6.9	54.0	46 45.6	−5.7	54.9	47 19.7	−4.4	55.7	47 53.1	−3.1	56.7	48 25.7	−1.9	57.6	43
44	44 11.4	−11.3	50.2	44 49.5	−10.2	51.0	45 27.0	−9.1	51.8	46 03.8	−8.0	52.6	46 39.9	−6.8	53.4	47 15.3	−5.6	54.3	47 50.0	−4.4	55.2	48 23.8	−3.0	56.1	44
45	44 00.1	−12.4	48.9	44 39.3	−11.3	49.6	45 17.9	−10.2	50.4	45 55.8	−9.0	51.2	46 33.1	−7.8	52.0	47 09.7	−6.6	52.8	47 45.6	−5.4	53.7	48 20.8	−4.2	54.6	45
46	43 47.7	−13.2	47.5	44 28.0	−12.2	48.2	45 07.7	−11.2	49.0	45 46.8	−10.1	49.7	46 25.3	−9.0	50.5	47 03.1	−7.8	51.4	47 40.2	−6.6	52.2	48 16.6	−5.4	53.1	46
47	43 34.5	−14.3	46.1	44 15.8	−13.3	46.8	44 56.5	−12.2	47.6	45 36.7	−11.1	48.3	46 16.3	−10.0	49.1	46 55.3	−8.9	49.9	47 33.6	−7.7	50.7	48 11.2	−6.5	51.6	47
48	43 20.2	−15.2	44.8	44 02.5	−14.2	45.5	44 44.3	−13.1	46.2	45 25.6	−12.1	46.9	46 06.3	−11.1	47.7	46 46.4	−10.0	48.5	47 25.9	−8.9	49.3	48 04.7	−7.7	50.1	48
49	43 05.0	−16.0	43.5	43 48.3	−15.1	44.1	44 31.2	−14.2	44.8	45 13.5	−13.2	45.5	45 55.2	−12.1	46.3	46 36.4	−11.0	47.0	47 17.0	−9.9	47.8	47 57.0	−8.8	48.6	49
50	42 49.0	−17.0	42.2	43 33.2	−16.0	42.8	44 17.0	−15.1	43.5	45 00.3	−14.1	44.1	45 43.1	−13.1	44.9	46 25.4	−12.1	45.6	47 07.1	−11.1	46.4	47 48.2	−9.9	47.1	50
51	42 32.0	−17.9	40.9	43 17.2	−17.0	41.5	44 01.9	−16.1	42.1	44 46.2	−15.1	42.8	45 30.0	−14.2	43.5	46 13.3	−13.2	44.2	46 56.0	−12.1	44.9	47 38.3	−11.1	45.7	51
52	42 14.1	−18.7	39.6	43 00.2	−17.9	40.2	43 45.8	−16.9	40.8	44 31.1	−16.1	41.4	45 15.8	−15.1	42.1	46 00.1	−14.1	42.8	46 43.9	−13.2	43.5	47 27.2	−12.2	44.2	52
53	41 55.4	−19.5	38.3	42 42.3	−18.7	38.9	43 28.9	−17.9	39.4	44 15.0	−17.0	40.1	45 00.7	−16.1	40.7	45 46.0	−15.2	41.4	46 30.7	−14.2	42.1	47 15.0	−13.2	42.8	53
54	41 35.9	−20.4	37.0	42 23.6	−19.6	37.6	43 11.0	−18.8	38.1	43 58.0	−18.0	38.7	44 44.6	−17.1	39.3	45 30.8	−16.2	40.0	46 16.5	−15.2	40.7	47 01.8	−14.3	41.3	54
55	41 15.5	−21.2	35.8	42 04.0	−20.5	36.3	42 52.2	−19.7	36.8	43 40.0	−18.8	37.4	44 27.5	−18.0	38.0	45 14.6	−17.2	38.6	46 01.3	−16.3	39.3	46 47.5	−15.3	39.9	55
56	40 54.3	−22.0	34.5	41 43.5	−21.2	35.0	42 32.5	−20.5	35.5	43 21.2	−19.8	36.1	44 09.5	−18.9	36.7	44 57.4	−18.1	37.3	45 45.0	−17.3	37.9	46 32.2	−16.4	38.5	56
57	40 32.3	−22.8	33.3	41 22.3	−22.1	33.8	42 12.0	−21.3	34.3	43 01.4	−20.6	34.8	43 50.6	−19.9	35.3	44 39.3	−19.0	35.9	45 27.7	−18.2	36.5	46 15.8	−17.4	37.1	57
58	40 09.5	−23.5	32.1	41 00.2	−22.8	32.5	41 50.7	−22.2	33.0	42 40.8	−21.4	33.5	43 30.7	−20.7	34.0	44 20.3	−20.0	34.6	45 09.5	−19.2	35.1	45 58.4	−18.4	35.7	58
59	39 46.0	−24.2	30.9	40 37.4	−23.6	31.3	41 28.5	−22.9	31.8	42 19.4	−22.3	32.3	43 10.0	−21.6	32.7	44 00.3	−20.8	33.3	44 50.3	−20.1	33.8	45 40.0	−19.3	34.4	59
60	39 21.8	−25.0	29.7	40 13.8	−24.4	30.1	41 05.6	−23.8	30.5	41 57.1	−23.1	31.0	42 48.4	−22.4	31.5	43 39.5	−21.8	32.0	44 30.2	−21.0	32.5	45 20.7	−20.3	33.0	60
61	38 56.8	−25.7	28.5	39 49.4	−25.1	28.9	40 41.8	−24.4	29.3	41 34.0	−23.8	29.8	42 26.0	−23.2	30.2	43 17.7	−22.5	30.7	44 09.2	−21.9	31.2	45 00.4	−21.2	31.7	61
62	38 31.1	−26.3	27.4	39 24.3	−25.7	27.7	40 17.4	−25.3	28.1	41 10.2	−24.7	28.5	42 02.8	−24.1	29.0	42 55.2	−23.5	29.4	43 47.3	−22.8	29.9	44 39.2	−22.1	30.4	62
63	38 04.8	−27.0	26.2	38 58.6	−26.5	26.6	39 52.1	−25.9	26.9	40 45.5	−25.3	27.3	41 38.7	−24.8	27.7	42 31.7	−24.2	28.2	43 24.5	−23.6	28.6	44 17.1	−23.0	29.1	63
64	37 37.8	−27.6	25.1	38 32.1	−27.1	25.4	39 26.2	−26.6	25.8	40 20.2	−26.2	26.1	41 13.9	−25.5	26.5	42 07.5	−25.0	26.9	43 00.9	−24.4	27.3	43 54.1	−23.8	27.8	64
65	37 10.2	−28.3	24.0	38 05.0	−27.8	24.3	38 59.6	−27.3	24.6	39 54.0	−26.8	25.0	40 48.4	−26.3	25.3	41 42.5	−25.8	25.7	42 36.5	−25.2	26.1	43 30.3	−24.7	26.5	65
66	36 41.9	−28.8	22.9	37 37.2	−28.4	23.2	38 32.3	−28.0	23.5	39 27.2	−27.5	23.8	40 22.1	−27.1	24.1	41 16.7	−26.5	24.5	42 11.3	−26.0	24.9	43 05.6	−25.5	25.3	66
67	36 13.1	−29.5	21.8	37 08.8	−29.1	22.1	38 04.3	−28.6	22.3	38 59.7	−28.1	22.7	39 55.0	−27.7	23.0	40 50.2	−27.2	23.3	41 45.3	−26.8	23.7	42 40.1	−26.2	24.0	67
68	35 43.6	−30.0	20.7	36 39.7	−29.6	21.0	37 35.7	−29.2	21.2	38 31.6	−28.8	21.5	39 27.3	−28.3	21.8	40 23.0	−28.0	22.1	41 18.5	−27.5	22.5	42 13.9	−27.0	22.8	68
69	35 13.6	−30.5	19.6	36 10.1	−30.2	19.9	37 06.5	−29.8	20.1	38 02.8	−29.5	20.4	38 59.0	−29.1	20.7	39 55.0	−28.6	21.0	40 51.0	−28.2	21.3	41 46.9	−27.8	21.6	69
70	34 43.1	−31.1	18.6	35 39.9	−30.7	18.8	36 36.7	−30.4	19.1	37 33.3	−30.0	19.3	38 29.9	−29.7	19.6	39 26.4	−29.3	19.8	40 22.8	−28.9	20.1	41 19.1	−28.5	20.4	70
71	34 12.0	−31.6	17.6	35 09.2	−31.3	17.8	36 06.3	−31.0	18.0	37 03.3	−30.6	18.2	38 00.2	−30.2	18.5	38 57.1	−29.9	18.7	39 53.9	−29.6	19.0	40 50.6	−29.2	19.2	71
72	33 40.4	−32.1	16.5	34 37.9	−31.9	16.7	35 35.3	−31.5	16.9	36 32.7	−31.2	17.1	37 30.0	−30.9	17.4	38 27.2	−30.6	17.6	39 24.3	−30.2	17.8	40 21.4	−29.8	18.1	72
73	33 08.3	−32.6	15.5	34 06.0	−32.3	15.7	35 03.8	−32.1	15.9	36 01.5	−31.8	16.1	36 59.1	−31.5	16.3	37 56.6	−31.1	16.5	38 54.1	−30.8	16.7	39 51.6	−30.5	17.0	73
74	32 35.7	−33.1	14.5	33 33.7	−32.8	14.7	34 31.7	−32.5	14.9	35 29.7	−32.3	15.0	36 27.6	−32.0	15.2	37 25.5	−31.7	15.4	38 23.3	−31.4	15.6	39 21.1	−31.2	15.8	74
75	32 02.6	−33.5	13.5	33 00.9	−33.3	13.7	33 59.2	−33.1	13.8	34 57.4	−32.8	14.0	35 55.6	−32.5	14.2	36 53.8	−32.3	14.4	37 51.9	−32.1	14.5	38 49.9	−31.7	14.7	75
76	31 29.1	−34.0	12.6	32 27.6	−33.7	12.7	33 26.1	−33.5	12.8	34 24.6	−33.3	13.0	35 23.1	−33.1	13.1	36 21.5	−32.9	13.3	37 19.8	−32.5	13.5	38 18.2	−32.4	13.7	76
77	30 55.1	−34.4	11.6	31 53.9	−34.2	11.7	32 52.6	−34.0	11.8	33 51.3	−33.8	12.0	34 50.0	−33.6	12.1	35 48.6	−33.3	12.3	36 47.3	−33.2	12.4	37 45.8	−32.9	12.6	77
78	30 20.7	−34.8	10.6	31 19.7	−34.6	10.7	32 18.6	−34.4	10.9	33 17.5	−34.2	11.0	34 16.4	−34.0	11.1	35 15.3	−33.9	11.2	36 14.1	−33.7	11.4	37 12.9	−33.4	11.5	78
79	29 45.9	−35.2	9.7	30 45.1	−35.1	9.8	31 44.2	−34.9	9.9	32 43.3	−34.7	10.0	33 42.4	−34.6	10.1	34 41.4	−34.3	10.2	35 40.4	−34.1	10.4	36 39.5	−34.0	10.5	79
80	29 10.7	−35.5	8.8	30 10.0	−35.4	8.9	31 09.3	−35.3	8.9	32 08.6	−35.2	9.0	33 07.8	−35.0	9.1	34 07.1	−34.9	9.2	35 06.3	−34.7	9.4	36 05.5	−34.6	9.5	80
81	28 35.2	−36.0	7.8	29 34.6	−35.8	7.9	30 34.0	−35.7	8.0	31 33.4	−35.5	8.1	32 32.8	−35.4	8.2	33 32.2	−35.3	8.3	34 31.6	−35.2	8.4	35 30.9	−35.0	8.5	81
82	27 59.2	−36.3	6.9	28 58.8	−36.2	7.0	29 58.3	−36.0	7.1	30 57.9	−36.0	7.1	31 57.4	−35.8	7.2	32 56.9	−35.7	7.3	33 56.4	−35.6	7.4	34 55.9	−35.5	7.5	82
83	27 22.9	−36.6	6.0	28 22.6	−36.5	6.1	29 22.3	−36.5	6.1	30 21.9	−36.3	6.2	31 21.6	−36.3	6.3	32 21.2	−36.2	6.3	33 20.8	−36.0	6.4	34 20.4	−35.9	6.5	83
84	26 46.3	−37.0	5.1	27 46.1	−36.9	5.2	28 45.8	−36.8	5.2	29 45.6	−36.8	5.3	30 45.3	−36.6	5.3	31 45.0	−36.5	5.4	32 44.8	−36.5	5.5	33 44.5	−36.4	5.5	84
85	26 09.3	−37.2	4.3	27 09.2	−37.2	4.3	28 09.0	−37.1	4.3	29 08.8	−37.1	4.4	30 08.7	−37.1	4.4	31 08.5	−37.0	4.5	32 08.3	−36.9	4.5	33 08.1	−36.8	4.6	85
86	25 32.1	−37.6	3.4	26 32.0	−37.6	3.4	27 31.9	−37.5	3.5	28 31.7	−37.4	3.5	29 31.6	−37.4	3.5	30 31.5	−37.3	3.6	31 31.4	−37.3	3.6	32 31.3	−37.3	3.6	86
87	24 54.5	−37.9	2.5	25 54.4	−37.8	2.6	26 54.4	−37.9	2.6	27 54.3	−37.8	2.6	28 54.2	−37.7	2.6	29 54.2	−37.7	2.7	30 54.1	−37.7	2.7	31 54.0	−37.6	2.7	87
88	24 16.6	−38.2	1.7	25 16.6	−38.2	1.7	26 16.5	−38.1	1.7	27 16.5	−38.1	1.7	28 16.5	−38.1	1.7	29 16.5	−38.1	1.8	30 16.4	−38.0	1.8	31 16.4	−38.0	1.8	88
89	23 38.4	−38.4	0.8	24 38.4	−38.4	0.8	25 38.4	−38.4	0.8	26 38.4	−38.4	0.9	27 38.4	−38.4	0.9	28 38.4	−38.4	0.9	29 38.4	−38.4	0.9	30 38.4	−38.4	0.9	89
90	23 00.0	−38.7	0.0	24 00.0	−38.7	0.0	25 00.0	−38.7	0.0	26 00.0	−38.7	0.0	27 00.0	−38.7	0.0	28 00.0	−38.7	0.0	29 00.0	−38.7	0.0	30 00.0	−38.7	0.0	90
	23°			24°			25°			26°			27°			28°			29°			30°			

LATITUDE **CONTRARY** NAME TO DECLINATION — L.H.A. 50°, 310°

Dec.	23° Hc	d	Z	24° Hc	d	Z	25° Hc	d	Z	26° Hc	d	Z
°	° ′	′	°	° ′	′	°	° ′	′	°	° ′	′	°
0	36 16.6	-29.4	108.2	35 57.6	-30.5	108.8	35 37.9	-31.5	109.5	35 17.5	-32.5	110.2
1	35 47.2	-29.9	109.2	35 27.1	-30.9	109.9	35 06.4	-32.0	110.6	34 45.0	-33.0	111.2
2	35 17.3	-30.5	110.3	34 56.2	-31.5	111.0	34 34.4	-32.5	111.6	34 12.0	-33.5	112.2
3	34 46.8	-31.0	111.3	34 24.7	-32.1	112.0	34 01.9	-33.0	112.6	33 38.5	-34.0	113.2
4	34 15.8	-31.6	112.4	33 52.6	-32.5	113.0	33 28.9	-33.5	113.6	33 04.5	-34.4	114.2
5	33 44.2	-32.0	113.4	33 20.1	-33.0	114.0	32 55.4	-34.0	114.6	32 30.1	-34.9	115.2
6	33 12.2	-32.6	114.4	32 47.1	-33.5	115.0	32 21.4	-34.4	115.6	31 55.2	-35.3	116.2
7	32 39.6	-33.0	115.4	32 13.6	-33.9	116.0	31 47.0	-34.8	116.6	31 19.9	-35.7	117.1
8	32 06.6	-33.4	116.4	31 39.7	-34.4	117.0	31 12.2	-35.3	117.5	30 44.2	-36.1	118.0
9	31 33.2	-34.0	117.4	31 05.3	-34.8	117.9	30 36.9	-35.6	118.5	30 08.1	-36.5	119.0
10	30 59.2	-34.3	118.4	30 30.5	-35.2	118.9	30 01.3	-36.0	119.4	29 31.6	-36.8	119.9
11	30 24.9	-34.7	119.3	29 55.3	-35.6	119.8	29 25.3	-36.5	120.3	28 54.8	-37.3	120.8
12	29 50.2	-35.2	120.3	29 19.7	-36.0	120.7	28 48.8	-36.7	121.2	28 17.5	-37.5	121.7
13	29 15.0	-35.5	121.2	28 43.7	-36.3	121.7	28 12.1	-37.2	122.1	27 40.0	-38.0	122.6
14	28 39.5	-35.9	122.1	28 07.4	-36.7	122.6	27 34.9	-37.4	123.0	27 02.0	-38.2	123.4
15	28 03.6	-36.2	123.0	27 30.7	-37.0	123.5	26 57.5	-37.8	123.9	26 23.8	-38.5	124.3
16	27 27.4	-36.6	123.9	26 53.7	-37.4	124.3	26 19.7	-38.1	124.8	25 45.3	-38.8	125.2
17	26 50.8	-37.0	124.8	26 16.3	-37.6	125.2	25 41.6	-38.4	125.6	25 06.5	-39.1	126.0
18	26 13.8	-37.2	125.7	25 38.7	-38.0	126.1	25 03.2	-38.7	126.5	24 27.4	-39.4	126.8
19	25 36.6	-37.5	126.6	25 00.7	-38.3	126.9	24 24.5	-39.0	127.3	23 48.0	-39.7	127.7
20	24 59.1	-37.9	127.4	24 22.4	-38.5	127.8	23 45.5	-39.2	128.1	23 08.3	-39.9	128.5
21	24 21.2	-38.1	128.3	23 43.9	-38.8	128.6	23 06.3	-39.5	129.0	22 28.4	-40.1	129.3
22	23 43.1	-38.4	129.1	23 05.1	-39.1	129.5	22 26.8	-39.7	129.8	21 48.3	-40.4	130.1
23	23 04.7	-38.7	130.0	22 26.0	-39.3	130.3	21 47.1	-40.0	130.6	21 07.9	-40.6	130.9
24	22 26.0	-38.9	130.8	21 46.7	-39.6	131.1	21 07.1	-40.2	131.4	20 27.3	-40.8	131.7
25	21 47.1	-39.2	131.6	21 07.1	-39.8	131.9	20 26.9	-40.4	132.2	19 46.5	-40.9	132.5
26	21 07.9	-39.4	132.4	20 27.3	-40.0	132.7	19 46.5	-40.6	133.0	19 05.6	-41.2	133.2
27	20 28.5	-39.6	133.2	19 47.3	-40.2	133.5	19 05.9	-40.8	133.8	18 24.4	-41.4	134.0
28	19 48.9	-39.8	134.0	19 07.1	-40.4	134.3	18 25.1	-40.9	134.5	17 43.0	-41.6	134.8
29	19 09.1	-40.0	134.8	18 26.7	-40.6	135.1	17 44.2	-41.2	135.3	17 01.4	-41.7	135.5
30	18 29.1	-40.2	135.6	17 46.1	-40.8	135.8	17 03.0	-41.3	136.1	16 19.7	-41.9	136.3
31	17 48.9	-40.4	136.4	17 05.3	-40.9	136.6	16 21.7	-41.5	136.8	15 37.8	-42.0	137.0
32	17 08.5	-40.6	137.2	16 24.4	-41.1	137.4	15 40.2	-41.7	137.6	14 55.8	-42.1	137.8
33	16 27.9	-40.8	137.9	15 43.3	-41.3	138.1	14 58.5	-41.8	138.3	14 13.7	-42.3	138.5
34	15 47.1	-40.9	138.7	15 02.0	-41.4	138.9	14 16.7	-41.9	139.1	13 31.4	-42.5	139.2
35	15 06.2	-41.0	139.5	14 20.6	-41.6	139.6	13 34.8	-42.1	139.8	12 48.9	-42.5	139.9
36	14 25.2	-41.2	140.2	13 39.0	-41.7	140.4	12 52.7	-42.1	140.5	12 06.4	-42.7	140.7
37	13 44.0	-41.4	141.0	12 57.3	-41.8	141.1	12 10.6	-42.3	141.3	11 23.7	-42.7	141.4
38	13 02.6	-41.4	141.7	12 15.5	-41.9	141.8	11 28.3	-42.4	142.0	10 41.0	-42.9	142.1
39	12 21.2	-41.6	142.5	11 33.6	-42.1	142.6	10 45.9	-42.5	142.7	9 58.1	-42.9	142.8
40	11 39.6	-41.7	143.2	10 51.5	-42.1	143.3	10 03.4	-42.6	143.4	9 15.2	-43.1	143.5
41	10 57.9	-41.8	143.9	10 09.4	-42.3	144.0	9 20.8	-42.7	144.1	8 32.1	-43.1	144.2
42	10 16.1	-41.9	144.7	9 27.1	-42.3	144.8	8 38.1	-42.7	144.8	7 49.0	-43.1	144.9
43	9 34.2	-42.0	145.4	8 44.8	-42.4	145.5	7 55.4	-42.9	145.6	7 05.9	-43.3	145.6
44	8 52.2	-42.0	146.1	8 02.4	-42.5	146.2	7 12.5	-42.9	146.3	6 22.6	-43.3	146.3
45	8 10.2	-42.2	146.8	7 19.9	-42.5	146.9	6 29.6	-42.9	147.0	5 39.3	-43.3	147.0
46	7 28.0	-42.2	147.5	6 37.4	-42.6	147.6	5 46.7	-43.0	147.7	4 56.0	-43.4	147.7
47	6 45.8	-42.3	148.3	5 54.8	-42.7	148.3	5 03.7	-43.1	148.4	4 12.6	-43.4	148.4
48	6 03.5	-42.3	149.0	5 12.1	-42.7	149.0	4 20.6	-43.0	149.1	3 29.2	-43.5	149.1
49	5 21.2	-42.4	149.7	4 29.4	-42.8	149.7	3 37.6	-43.2	149.8	2 45.7	-43.5	149.8
50	4 38.8	-42.4	150.4	3 46.6	-42.8	150.4	2 54.4	-43.1	150.5	2 02.2	-43.5	150.5
51	3 56.4	-42.5	151.1	3 03.8	-42.8	151.1	2 11.3	-43.2	151.2	1 18.7	-43.5	151.2
52	3 13.9	-42.5	151.8	2 21.0	-42.8	151.8	1 28.1	-43.1	151.9	0 35.2	-43.5	151.9
53	2 31.4	-42.5	152.5	1 38.2	-42.9	152.5	0 45.0	-43.2	152.5	0 08.3	+43.5	27.5
54	1 48.9	-42.5	153.2	0 55.3	-42.8	153.2	0 01.8	-43.2	153.2	0 51.8	+43.5	26.8
55	1 06.4	-42.6	153.9	0 12.5	-42.9	153.9	0 41.4	+43.2	26.1	1 35.3	+43.5	26.1
56	0 23.8	-42.5	154.6	0 30.4	+42.8	25.4	1 24.6	+43.1	25.4	2 18.8	+43.5	25.4
57	0 18.7	+42.5	24.7	1 13.2	+42.9	24.7	2 07.7	+43.2	24.7	3 02.3	+43.4	24.7
58	1 01.2	+42.6	24.0	1 56.1	+42.8	24.0	2 50.9	+43.1	24.0	3 45.7	+43.4	24.0
59	1 43.8	+42.5	23.2	2 38.9	+42.8	23.3	3 34.0	+43.1	23.3	4 29.1	+43.4	23.3
60	2 26.3	+42.5	22.5	3 21.7	+42.8	22.6	4 17.1	+43.0	22.6	5 12.5	+43.3	22.6
61	3 08.8	+42.4	21.8	4 04.5	+42.7	21.9	5 00.1	+43.1	21.9	5 55.8	+43.3	21.9
62	3 51.2	+42.5	21.1	4 47.2	+42.7	21.2	5 43.2	+42.9	21.2	6 39.1	+43.2	21.2
63	4 33.7	+42.4	20.4	5 29.9	+42.6	20.4	6 26.1	+42.9	20.5	7 22.3	+43.2	20.5
64	5 16.1	+42.3	19.7	6 12.5	+42.6	19.7	7 09.0	+42.8	19.8	8 05.5	+43.0	19.8
65	5 58.4	+42.3	19.0	6 55.1	+42.5	19.0	7 51.8	+42.8	19.1	8 48.5	+43.0	19.1
66	6 40.7	+42.2	18.3	7 37.6	+42.5	18.3	8 34.6	+42.7	18.4	9 31.5	+42.9	18.4
67	7 22.9	+42.2	17.6	8 20.1	+42.4	17.6	9 17.3	+42.6	17.7	10 14.4	+42.9	17.7
68	8 05.1	+42.0	16.8	9 02.5	+42.3	16.9	9 59.9	+42.5	16.9	10 57.3	+42.7	17.0
69	8 47.1	+42.0	16.1	9 44.8	+42.2	16.2	10 42.4	+42.4	16.2	11 40.0	+42.6	16.3
70	9 29.1	+41.9	15.4	10 27.0	+42.1	15.5	11 24.8	+42.3	15.5	12 22.6	+42.5	15.6
71	10 11.0	+41.8	14.7	11 09.1	+42.0	14.7	12 07.1	+42.2	14.8	13 05.1	+42.4	14.8
72	10 52.8	+41.8	13.9	11 51.1	+41.9	14.0	12 49.3	+42.0	14.1	13 47.5	+42.2	14.1
73	11 34.6	+41.5	13.2	12 33.0	+41.7	13.3	13 31.3	+42.0	13.3	14 29.7	+42.1	13.4
74	12 16.1	+41.5	12.5	13 14.7	+41.7	12.5	14 13.3	+41.8	12.6	15 11.8	+42.0	12.6
75	12 57.6	+41.4	11.7	13 56.4	+41.5	11.8	14 55.1	+41.6	11.8	15 53.8	+41.8	11.9
76	13 39.0	+41.2	11.0	14 37.9	+41.3	11.0	15 36.7	+41.6	11.1	16 35.6	+41.7	11.1
77	14 20.2	+41.1	10.2	15 19.2	+41.2	10.3	16 18.3	+41.3	10.3	17 17.3	+41.5	10.4
78	15 01.3	+40.9	9.5	16 00.4	+41.1	9.5	16 59.6	+41.2	9.6	17 58.8	+41.3	9.6
79	15 42.2	+40.8	8.7	16 41.5	+40.9	8.8	17 40.8	+41.0	8.8	18 40.1	+41.1	8.9
80	16 23.0	+40.6	8.0	17 22.4	+40.7	8.0	18 21.8	+40.8	8.1	19 21.2	+40.9	8.1
81	17 03.6	+40.4	7.2	18 03.1	+40.5	7.2	19 02.6	+40.6	7.3	20 02.1	+40.7	7.3
82	17 44.0	+40.2	6.4	18 43.6	+40.3	6.5	19 43.2	+40.4	6.5	20 42.8	+40.5	6.5
83	18 24.2	+40.1	5.6	19 23.9	+40.2	5.7	20 23.6	+40.2	5.7	21 23.3	+40.3	5.8
84	19 04.3	+39.8	4.9	20 04.1	+39.9	4.9	21 03.8	+40.0	4.9	22 03.6	+40.1	5.0
85	19 44.1	+39.7	4.1	20 44.0	+39.7	4.1	21 43.8	+39.8	4.1	22 43.7	+39.8	4.2
86	20 23.8	+39.4	3.3	21 23.7	+39.4	3.3	22 23.6	+39.5	3.3	23 23.5	+39.5	3.3
87	21 03.2	+39.2	2.5	22 03.1	+39.2	2.5	23 03.1	+39.2	2.5	24 03.0	+39.3	2.5
88	21 42.4	+38.9	1.6	22 42.3	+39.0	1.7	23 42.3	+39.0	1.7	24 42.3	+39.0	1.7
89	22 21.3	+38.7	0.8	23 21.3	+38.7	0.8	24 21.3	+38.7	0.8	25 21.3	+38.7	0.8
90	23 00.0	+38.4	0.0	24 00.0	+38.4	0.0	25 00.0	+38.4	0.0	26 00.0	+38.4	0.0
	23°			24°			25°			26°		

Dec.	27° Hc	d	Z	28° Hc	d	Z	29° Hc	d	Z	30° Hc	d	Z
°	° ′	′	°	° ′	′	°	° ′	′	°	° ′	′	°
0	34 56.4	-33.4	110.9	34 34.8	-34.5	111.5	34 12.5	-35.4	112.1	33 49.6	-36.4	112.8
1	34 23.0	-34.0	111.9	34 00.3	-34.9	112.5	33 37.1	-35.9	113.1	33 13.2	-36.7	113.7
2	33 49.0	-34.5	112.9	33 25.4	-35.4	113.5	33 01.2	-36.3	114.1	32 36.5	-37.2	114.7
3	33 14.5	-34.9	113.8	32 50.0	-35.8	114.4	32 24.9	-36.7	115.0	31 59.3	-37.6	115.6
4	32 39.6	-35.3	114.8	32 14.2	-36.2	115.4	31 48.2	-37.1	115.9	31 21.7	-38.0	116.5
5	32 04.3	-35.8	115.8	31 38.0	-36.7	116.3	31 11.1	-37.5	116.9	30 43.7	-38.3	117.4
6	31 28.5	-36.1	116.7	31 01.3	-37.0	117.3	30 33.6	-37.9	117.8	30 05.4	-38.7	118.3
7	30 52.4	-36.6	117.6	30 24.3	-37.4	118.2	29 55.7	-38.2	118.7	29 26.7	-39.0	119.2
8	30 15.8	-37.0	118.6	29 46.9	-37.8	119.1	29 17.5	-38.6	119.6	28 47.7	-39.4	120.0
9	29 38.8	-37.3	119.5	29 09.1	-38.1	120.0	28 38.9	-38.9	120.4	28 08.3	-39.7	120.9
10	29 01.5	-37.7	120.4	28 31.0	-38.5	120.8	28 00.0	-39.3	121.3	27 28.6	-40.0	121.8
11	28 23.8	-38.0	121.3	27 52.5	-38.8	121.7	27 20.7	-39.5	122.2	26 48.6	-40.3	122.6
12	27 45.8	-38.3	122.1	27 13.7	-39.1	122.6	26 41.2	-39.8	123.0	26 08.3	-40.5	123.4
13	27 07.5	-38.7	123.0	26 34.6	-39.4	123.4	26 01.4	-40.2	123.8	25 27.8	-40.9	124.2
14	26 28.8	-39.0	123.9	25 55.2	-39.7	124.3	25 21.2	-40.4	124.7	24 46.9	-41.0	125.0
15	25 49.8	-39.2	124.7	25 15.5	-40.0	125.1	24 40.8	-40.6	125.5	24 05.9	-41.4	125.8
16	25 10.6	-39.6	125.5	24 35.5	-40.2	125.9	24 00.2	-40.9	126.3	23 24.5	-41.6	126.6
17	24 31.0	-39.8	126.4	23 55.3	-40.5	126.7	23 19.3	-41.2	127.1	22 42.9	-41.8	127.4
18	23 51.2	-40.0	127.2	23 14.8	-40.7	127.5	22 38.1	-41.4	127.9	22 01.1	-42.0	128.2
19	23 11.2	-40.3	128.0	22 34.1	-41.0	128.3	21 56.7	-41.6	128.7	21 19.1	-42.2	129.0
20	22 30.9	-40.6	128.8	21 53.1	-41.2	129.1	21 15.1	-41.8	129.4	20 36.9	-42.4	129.7
21	21 50.3	-40.8	129.6	21 11.9	-41.4	129.9	20 33.3	-42.0	130.2	19 54.5	-42.6	130.5
22	21 09.5	-41.0	130.4	20 30.5	-41.6	130.7	19 51.3	-42.2	131.0	19 11.9	-42.8	131.2
23	20 28.5	-41.2	131.2	19 48.9	-41.8	131.5	19 09.1	-42.4	131.7	18 29.1	-43.0	132.0
24	19 47.3	-41.4	131.9	19 07.1	-42.0	132.2	18 26.7	-42.5	132.5	17 46.1	-43.1	132.7
25	19 05.9	-41.5	132.7	18 25.1	-42.1	133.0	17 44.2	-42.8	133.2	17 03.0	-43.3	133.4
26	18 24.4	-41.8	133.5	17 43.0	-42.3	133.7	17 01.4	-42.9	133.9	16 19.7	-43.4	134.2
27	17 42.6	-41.9	134.2	17 00.7	-42.5	134.5	16 18.5	-43.0	134.7	15 36.3	-43.6	134.9
28	17 00.7	-42.2	135.0	16 18.2	-42.7	135.2	15 35.5	-43.2	135.4	14 52.7	-43.7	135.6
29	16 18.5	-42.2	135.7	15 35.5	-42.8	135.9	14 52.3	-43.3	136.1	14 09.0	-43.8	136.3
30	15 36.3	-42.4	136.5	14 52.7	-42.9	136.7	14 09.0	-43.4	136.8	13 25.2	-43.9	137.0
31	14 53.9	-42.6	137.2	14 09.8	-43.1	137.4	13 25.6	-43.6	137.5	12 41.3	-44.1	137.7
32	14 11.3	-42.6	137.9	13 26.7	-43.1	138.1	12 42.0	-43.6	138.2	11 57.2	-44.1	138.4
33	13 28.7	-42.8	138.7	12 43.6	-43.3	138.8	11 58.4	-43.8	138.9	11 13.1	-44.3	139.1
34	12 45.9	-42.9	139.4	12 00.3	-43.4	139.5	11 14.6	-43.9	139.6	10 28.8	-44.3	139.8
35	12 03.0	-43.1	140.1	11 16.9	-43.5	140.2	10 30.7	-43.9	140.3	9 44.5	-44.4	140.5
36	11 19.9	-43.1	140.8	10 33.4	-43.6	140.9	9 46.8	-44.1	141.0	9 00.1	-44.5	141.1
37	10 36.8	-43.2	141.5	9 49.8	-43.7	141.6	9 02.7	-44.1	141.7	8 15.6	-44.5	141.8
38	9 53.6	-43.3	142.2	9 06.1	-43.7	142.3	8 18.6	-44.2	142.4	7 31.1	-44.7	142.5
39	9 10.3	-43.4	142.9	8 22.4	-43.8	143.0	7 34.4	-44.2	143.1	6 46.4	-44.6	143.2
40	8 26.9	-43.5	143.6	7 38.6	-43.9	143.7	6 50.2	-44.3	143.8	6 01.8	-44.8	143.8
41	7 43.4	-43.5	144.3	6 54.7	-44.0	144.4	6 05.9	-44.4	144.4	5 17.0	-44.7	144.5
42	6 59.9	-43.6	145.0	6 10.7	-44.0	145.1	5 21.5	-44.4	145.1	4 32.3	-44.8	145.2
43	6 16.3	-43.6	145.7	5 26.7	-44.0	145.8	4 37.1	-44.4	145.8	3 47.5	-44.8	145.8
44	5 32.7	-43.7	146.4	4 42.7	-44.1	146.4	3 52.7	-44.5	146.5	3 02.7	-44.9	146.5
45	4 49.0	-43.8	147.1	3 58.6	-44.1	147.1	3 08.2	-44.5	147.1	2 17.8	-44.9	147.2
46	4 05.2	-43.7	147.8	3 14.5	-44.2	147.8	2 23.7	-44.5	147.8	1 32.9	-44.9	147.8
47	3 21.5	-43.8	148.4	2 30.3	-44.1	148.5	1 39.2	-44.5	148.5	0 48.0	-44.9	148.5
48	2 37.7	-43.8	149.1	1 46.2	-44.2	149.1	0 54.7	-44.6	149.2	0 03.1	-44.9	149.2
49	1 53.9	-43.9	149.8	1 02.0	-44.2	149.8	0 10.1	-44.5	149.8	0 41.8	+44.8	30.2
50	1 10.0	-43.8	150.5	0 17.8	-44.2	150.5	0 34.4	+44.6	29.5	1 26.6	+44.9	29.5
51	0 26.2	-43.9	151.2	0 26.4	+44.2	28.8	1 19.0	+44.5	28.8	2 11.5	+44.9	28.8
52	0 17.7	+43.8	28.1	1 10.6	+44.2	28.1	2 03.5	+44.5	28.2	2 56.4	+44.8	28.2
53	1 01.5	+43.9	27.5	1 54.8	+44.1	27.5	2 48.0	+44.5	27.5	3 41.2	+44.8	27.5
54	1 45.4	+43.8	26.8	2 38.9	+44.2	26.8	3 32.5	+44.4	26.8	4 26.0	+44.8	26.8
55	2 29.2	+43.8	26.1	3 23.1	+44.1	26.1	4 16.9	+44.5	26.1	5 10.8	+44.7	26.2
56	3 13.0	+43.8	25.4	4 07.2	+44.1	25.4	5 01.4	+44.3	25.5	5 55.5	+44.7	25.5
57	3 56.8	+43.7	24.7	4 51.3	+44.0	24.8	5 45.7	+44.4	24.8	6 40.2	+44.6	24.8
58	4 40.5	+43.7	24.0	5 35.3	+44.0	24.1	6 30.1	+44.2	24.1	7 24.8	+44.6	24.2
59	5 24.2	+43.7	23.3	6 19.3	+43.9	23.4	7 14.3	+44.3	23.4	8 09.4	+44.5	23.5
60	6 07.9	+43.6	22.7	7 03.2	+43.9	22.7	7 58.6	+44.1	22.8	8 53.9	+44.4	22.8
61	6 51.5	+43.5	22.0	7 47.1	+43.8	22.0	8 42.7	+44.1	22.1	9 38.3	+44.3	22.1
62	7 35.0	+43.5	21.3	8 30.9	+43.7	21.3	9 26.8	+44.0	21.4	10 22.6	+44.3	21.4
63	8 18.5	+43.4	20.6	9 14.6	+43.7	20.6	10 10.8	+43.9	20.7	11 06.9	+44.2	20.8
64	9 01.9	+43.3	19.9	9 58.3	+43.6	19.9	10 54.7	+43.8	20.0	11 51.1	+44.0	20.1
65	9 45.2	+43.2	19.2	10 41.9	+43.4	19.2	11 38.5	+43.7	19.3	12 35.1	+44.0	19.4
66	10 28.4	+43.2	18.5	11 25.3	+43.4	18.5	12 22.2	+43.6	18.6	13 19.1	+43.8	18.7
67	11 11.6	+43.0	17.8	12 08.7	+43.3	17.8	13 05.8	+43.5	17.9	14 02.9	+43.7	18.0
68	11 54.6	+43.0	17.1	12 52.0	+43.1	17.1	13 49.3	+43.4	17.2	14 46.6	+43.6	17.3
69	12 37.6	+42.8	16.3	13 35.1	+43.1	16.4	14 32.7	+43.2	16.5	15 30.2	+43.5	16.6
70	13 20.4	+42.7	15.6	14 18.2	+42.9	15.7	15 15.9	+43.1	15.8	16 13.7	+43.3	15.8
71	14 03.1	+42.6	14.9	15 01.1	+42.7	15.0	15 59.0	+43.0	15.0	16 57.0	+43.1	15.1
72	14 45.7	+42.4	14.2	15 43.8	+42.6	14.2	16 42.0	+42.8	14.3	17 40.1	+43.0	14.4
73	15 28.1	+42.3	13.4	16 26.4	+42.5	13.5	17 24.8	+42.6	13.6	18 23.1	+42.8	13.7
74	16 10.4	+42.1	12.7	17 08.9	+42.3	12.8	18 07.4	+42.5	12.8	19 05.9	+42.6	12.9
75	16 52.5	+42.0	12.0	17 51.2	+42.1	12.0	18 49.9	+42.3	12.1	19 48.5	+42.5	12.2
76	17 34.5	+41.8	11.2	18 33.3	+42.0	11.3	19 32.2	+42.1	11.3	20 31.0	+42.2	11.4
77	18 16.3	+41.6	10.5	19 15.3	+41.7	10.5	20 14.3	+41.9	10.6	21 13.2	+42.1	10.7
78	18 57.9	+41.4	9.7	19 57.0	+41.6	9.8	20 56.2	+41.7	9.8	21 55.3	+41.8	9.9
79	19 39.3	+41.3	8.9	20 38.6	+41.4	9.0	21 37.9	+41.5	9.0	22 37.1	+41.6	9.1
80	20 20.6	+41.0	8.2	21 20.0	+41.1	8.2	22 19.4	+41.2	8.3	23 18.7	+41.4	8.3
81	21 01.6	+40.8	7.4	22 01.1	+40.9	7.4	23 00.6	+41.0	7.5	24 00.1	+41.1	7.5
82	21 42.4	+40.6	6.6	22 42.0	+40.7	6.6	23 41.6	+40.8	6.7	24 41.2	+40.9	6.7
83	22 23.0	+40.4	5.8	23 22.7	+40.5	5.8	24 22.4	+40.5	5.9	25 22.1	+40.6	5.9
84	23 03.4	+40.1	5.0	24 03.2	+40.1	5.0	25 02.9	+40.3	5.1	26 02.7	+40.3	5.1
85	23 43.5	+39.9	4.2	24 43.3	+39.9	4.2	25 43.2	+39.9	4.2	26 43.0	+40.0	4.3
86	24 23.4	+39.5	3.4	25 23.2	+39.7	3.4	26 23.1	+39.7	3.4	27 23.0	+39.8	3.5
87	25 02.9	+39.4	2.5	26 02.9	+39.3	2.6	27 02.8	+39.4	2.6	28 02.8	+39.4	2.6
88	25 42.3	+39.0	1.7	26 42.2	+39.1	1.7	27 42.2	+39.1	1.7	28 42.2	+39.1	1.7
89	26 21.3	+38.7	0.9	27 21.3	+38.7	0.9	28 21.3	+38.7	0.9	29 21.3	+38.7	0.9
90	27 00.0	+38.4	0.0	28 00.0	+38.4	0.0	29 00.0	+38.4	0.0	30 00.0	+38.4	0.0
	27°			28°			29°			30°		

S. Lat. { L.H.A. greater than 180° ....Zn=180°–Z
L.H.A. less than 180°...........Zn=180°+Z

LATITUDE **SAME** NAME AS DECLINATION — L.H.A. 130°, 230°

285

51°, 309° L.H.A. LATITUDE SAME NAME AS DECLINATION

N. Lat. {L.H.A. greater than 180° .....Zn=Z; L.H.A. less than 180°............Zn=360°−Z

Dec.	23° Hc	d	Z	24° Hc	d	Z	25° Hc	d	Z	26° Hc	d	Z	27° Hc	d	Z	28° Hc	d	Z	29° Hc	d	Z	30° Hc	d	Z	Dec.
°	° ′	′	°	° ′	′	°	° ′	′	°	° ′	′	°	° ′	′	°	° ′	′	°	° ′	′	°	° ′	′	°	°
0	35 24.0	+28.5	107.6	35 05.6	+29.6	108.2	34 46.5	+30.6	108.9	34 26.8	+31.6	109.5	34 06.4	+32.6	110.2	33 45.4	+33.6	110.8	33 23.7	+34.6	111.4	33 01.5	+35.6	112.0	0
1	35 52.5	+27.9	106.5	35 35.2	+28.9	107.2	35 17.1	+30.1	107.8	34 58.4	+31.1	108.5	34 39.0	+32.2	109.2	34 19.0	+33.1	109.8	33 58.3	+34.2	110.5	33 37.1	+35.1	111.1	1
2	36 20.4	+27.3	105.4	36 04.1	+28.4	106.1	35 47.2	+29.4	106.8	35 29.5	+30.5	107.5	35 11.2	+31.6	108.1	34 52.1	+32.7	108.8	34 32.5	+33.6	109.5	34 12.2	+34.6	110.1	2
3	36 47.7	+26.6	104.3	36 32.5	+27.8	105.0	36 16.6	+28.9	105.7	36 00.0	+30.0	106.4	35 42.8	+31.0	107.1	35 24.8	+32.1	107.8	35 06.1	+33.2	108.4	34 46.8	+34.2	109.1	3
4	37 14.3	+26.0	103.1	37 00.3	+27.2	103.9	36 45.5	+28.3	104.6	36 30.0	+29.4	105.3	36 13.8	+30.5	106.0	35 56.9	+31.5	106.7	35 39.3	+32.6	107.4	35 21.0	+33.6	108.1	4
5	37 40.3	+25.4	102.0	37 27.5	+26.5	102.8	37 13.8	+27.7	103.5	36 59.4	+28.8	104.2	36 44.3	+29.9	105.0	36 28.4	+31.0	105.7	36 11.9	+32.0	106.4	35 54.6	+33.1	107.1	5
6	38 05.7	+24.6	100.9	37 54.0	+25.8	101.6	37 41.5	+27.0	102.4	37 28.2	+28.2	103.1	37 14.2	+29.3	103.9	36 59.4	+30.5	104.6	36 43.9	+31.5	105.3	36 27.7	+32.6	106.1	6
7	38 30.3	+24.0	99.7	38 19.8	+25.2	100.5	38 08.5	+26.4	101.3	37 56.4	+27.5	102.0	37 43.5	+28.7	102.8	37 29.9	+29.8	103.5	37 15.4	+31.0	104.3	37 00.3	+32.0	105.0	7
8	38 54.3	+23.3	98.5	38 45.0	+24.5	99.3	38 34.9	+25.7	100.1	38 23.9	+26.9	100.9	38 12.2	+28.0	101.7	37 59.7	+29.2	102.4	37 46.4	+30.3	103.2	37 32.3	+31.4	103.9	8
9	39 17.6	+22.5	97.3	39 09.5	+23.8	98.1	39 00.6	+25.0	99.0	38 50.8	+26.2	99.7	38 40.2	+27.4	100.5	38 28.9	+28.5	101.3	38 16.7	+29.7	102.1	38 03.7	+30.9	102.9	9
10	39 40.1	+21.8	96.1	39 33.3	+23.0	97.0	39 25.6	+24.2	97.8	39 17.0	+25.5	98.6	39 07.6	+26.7	99.4	38 57.4	+27.9	100.2	38 46.4	+29.1	101.0	38 34.6	+30.2	101.8	10
11	40 01.9	+21.0	94.9	39 56.3	+22.3	95.8	39 49.8	+23.6	96.6	39 42.5	+24.8	97.4	39 34.3	+26.0	98.2	39 25.3	+27.2	99.1	39 15.5	+28.4	99.9	39 04.8	+29.5	100.7	11
12	40 22.9	+20.2	93.7	40 18.6	+21.5	94.5	40 13.4	+22.8	95.4	40 07.3	+24.0	96.2	40 00.3	+25.3	97.1	39 52.5	+26.6	97.9	39 43.9	+27.7	98.7	39 34.3	+29.0	99.5	12
13	40 43.1	+19.4	92.5	40 40.1	+20.7	93.3	40 36.2	+22.0	94.2	40 31.3	+23.3	95.0	40 25.6	+24.6	95.9	40 19.1	+25.8	96.7	40 11.6	+27.0	97.6	40 03.3	+28.2	98.4	13
14	41 02.5	+18.6	91.2	41 00.8	+19.9	92.1	40 58.2	+21.2	92.9	40 54.6	+22.5	93.8	40 50.2	+23.8	94.7	40 44.9	+25.0	95.5	40 38.6	+26.3	96.4	40 31.5	+27.5	97.2	14
15	41 21.1	+17.8	89.9	41 20.7	+19.1	90.8	41 19.4	+20.4	91.7	41 17.1	+21.8	92.6	41 14.0	+23.0	93.5	41 09.9	+24.3	94.3	41 04.9	+25.6	95.2	40 59.0	+26.8	96.1	15
16	41 38.9	+16.9	88.7	41 39.8	+18.3	89.6	41 39.8	+19.6	90.4	41 38.9	+20.9	91.3	41 37.0	+22.2	92.2	41 34.2	+23.5	93.1	41 30.5	+24.8	94.0	41 25.8	+26.1	94.9	16
17	41 55.8	+16.0	87.4	41 58.1	+17.3	88.3	41 59.4	+18.7	89.2	41 59.8	+20.0	90.1	41 59.2	+21.4	91.0	41 57.7	+22.7	91.9	41 55.3	+24.0	92.8	41 51.9	+25.3	93.7	17
18	42 11.8	+15.2	86.1	42 15.4	+16.6	87.0	42 18.1	+17.9	87.9	42 19.8	+19.3	88.8	42 20.6	+20.6	89.7	42 20.4	+21.9	90.6	42 19.3	+23.2	91.5	42 17.2	+24.5	92.5	18
19	42 27.0	+14.2	84.8	42 32.0	+15.6	85.7	42 36.0	+17.0	86.6	42 39.1	+18.3	87.5	42 41.2	+19.7	88.4	42 42.3	+21.1	89.4	42 42.5	+22.4	90.3	42 41.7	+23.7	91.2	19
20	42 41.2	+13.4	83.5	42 47.6	+14.7	84.4	42 53.0	+16.1	85.3	42 57.4	+17.5	86.2	43 00.9	+18.8	87.2	43 03.4	+20.2	88.1	43 04.9	+21.5	89.0	43 05.4	+22.9	90.0	20
21	42 54.6	+12.4	82.1	43 02.3	+13.8	83.1	43 09.1	+15.2	84.0	43 14.9	+16.5	84.9	43 19.7	+17.9	85.9	43 23.6	+19.3	86.8	43 26.4	+20.7	87.7	43 28.3	+22.0	88.7	21
22	43 07.0	+11.4	80.8	43 16.1	+12.9	81.7	43 24.3	+14.2	82.7	43 31.4	+15.7	83.6	43 37.6	+17.1	84.5	43 42.9	+18.4	85.5	43 47.1	+19.8	86.4	43 50.3	+21.1	87.4	22
23	43 18.4	+10.6	79.4	43 29.0	+11.9	80.4	43 38.5	+13.3	81.3	43 47.1	+14.7	82.3	43 54.7	+16.1	83.2	44 01.3	+17.4	84.2	44 06.9	+18.8	85.1	44 11.4	+20.3	86.1	23
24	43 29.0	+9.5	78.1	43 40.9	+10.9	79.0	43 51.8	+12.3	80.0	44 01.8	+13.7	80.9	44 10.8	+15.1	81.9	44 18.7	+16.6	82.8	44 25.7	+17.9	83.8	44 31.7	+19.3	84.8	24
25	43 38.5	+8.6	76.7	43 51.8	+10.0	77.7	44 04.1	+11.4	78.6	44 15.5	+12.8	79.6	44 25.9	+14.2	80.5	44 35.3	+15.6	81.5	44 43.6	+17.0	82.5	44 51.0	+18.4	83.5	25
26	43 47.1	+7.6	75.4	44 01.8	+9.0	76.3	44 15.5	+10.4	77.2	44 28.3	+11.8	78.2	44 40.1	+13.2	79.2	44 50.9	+14.6	80.1	45 00.6	+16.1	81.1	45 09.4	+17.4	82.1	26
27	43 54.7	+6.6	74.0	44 10.8	+7.9	74.9	44 25.9	+9.4	75.9	44 40.1	+10.8	76.8	44 53.3	+12.2	77.8	45 05.5	+13.6	78.8	45 16.7	+15.0	79.7	45 26.8	+16.5	80.7	27
28	44 01.3	+5.6	72.6	44 18.7	+7.0	73.5	44 35.3	+8.3	74.5	44 50.9	+9.7	75.4	45 05.5	+11.2	76.4	45 19.1	+12.6	77.4	45 31.7	+14.0	78.4	45 43.3	+15.4	79.4	28
29	44 06.9	+4.5	71.2	44 25.7	+6.0	72.1	44 43.6	+7.4	73.1	45 00.6	+8.8	74.0	45 16.7	+10.1	75.0	45 31.7	+11.6	76.0	45 45.7	+13.0	77.0	45 58.7	+14.4	78.0	29
30	44 11.4	+3.6	69.8	44 31.7	+4.9	70.7	44 51.0	+6.3	71.7	45 09.4	+7.7	72.6	45 26.8	+9.1	73.6	45 43.3	+10.5	74.6	45 58.7	+12.0	75.6	46 13.1	+13.4	76.6	30
31	44 15.0	+2.6	68.4	44 36.6	+3.9	69.3	44 57.3	+5.3	70.3	45 17.1	+6.7	71.2	45 35.9	+8.1	72.2	45 53.8	+9.5	73.2	46 10.7	+10.9	74.2	46 26.5	+12.4	75.2	31
32	44 17.6	+1.5	67.0	44 40.5	+2.9	67.9	45 02.6	+4.3	68.9	45 23.8	+5.6	69.8	45 44.0	+7.0	70.8	46 03.3	+8.4	71.7	46 21.6	+9.8	72.7	46 38.9	+11.3	73.8	32
33	44 19.1	+0.5	65.6	44 43.4	+1.9	66.5	45 06.9	+3.2	67.5	45 29.4	+4.6	68.4	45 51.0	+6.0	69.3	46 11.7	+7.4	70.3	46 31.4	+8.8	71.3	46 50.2	+10.2	72.3	33
34	44 19.6	-0.5	64.2	44 45.3	+0.8	65.1	45 10.1	+2.1	66.0	45 34.0	+3.5	67.0	45 57.0	+4.9	67.9	46 19.1	+6.3	68.9	46 40.2	+7.7	69.9	47 00.4	+9.1	70.9	34
35	44 19.1	-1.5	62.8	44 46.1	-0.3	63.7	45 12.2	+1.1	64.6	45 37.5	+2.4	65.5	46 01.9	+3.8	66.5	46 25.4	+5.1	67.4	46 47.9	+6.6	68.4	47 09.5	+8.0	69.4	35
36	44 17.6	-2.6	61.4	44 45.8	-1.2	62.3	45 13.3	0.0	63.2	45 39.9	+1.4	64.1	46 05.7	+2.7	65.0	46 30.5	+4.1	66.0	46 54.5	+5.5	67.0	47 17.5	+6.9	68.0	36
37	44 15.0	-3.6	60.1	44 44.6	-2.3	60.9	45 13.3	-1.0	61.8	45 41.3	+0.3	62.7	46 08.4	+1.6	63.6	46 34.6	+3.0	64.5	47 00.0	+4.3	65.5	47 24.4	+5.7	66.5	37
38	44 11.4	-4.6	58.7	44 42.3	-3.4	59.5	45 12.3	-2.0	60.4	45 41.6	-0.8	61.3	46 10.0	+0.6	62.2	46 37.6	+1.9	63.1	47 04.3	+3.3	64.0	47 30.1	+4.7	65.0	38
39	44 06.8	-5.5	57.3	44 38.9	-4.3	58.1	45 10.3	-3.2	58.9	45 40.8	-1.8	59.8	46 10.6	-0.6	60.7	46 39.5	+0.8	61.6	47 07.6	+2.1	62.6	47 34.8	+3.4	63.5	39
40	44 01.3	-6.6	55.9	44 34.6	-5.4	56.7	45 07.1	-4.1	57.5	45 39.0	-2.9	58.4	46 10.0	-1.6	59.3	46 40.3	-0.4	60.2	47 09.7	+1.0	61.1	47 38.2	+2.4	62.1	40
41	43 54.7	-7.6	54.5	44 29.2	-6.5	55.3	45 03.0	-5.2	56.1	45 36.1	-4.0	57.0	46 08.4	-2.7	57.8	46 39.9	-1.4	58.7	47 10.7	-0.2	59.6	47 40.6	+1.2	60.6	41
42	43 47.1	-8.6	53.1	44 22.7	-7.4	53.9	44 57.8	-6.3	54.7	45 32.1	-5.1	55.5	46 05.7	-3.9	56.4	46 38.5	-2.6	57.3	47 10.5	-1.2	58.2	47 41.8	0.0	59.1	42
43	43 38.5	-9.6	51.8	44 15.3	-8.4	52.5	44 51.5	-7.3	53.3	45 27.0	-6.1	54.1	46 01.8	-4.9	55.0	46 35.9	-3.6	55.8	47 09.3	-2.4	56.7	47 41.8	-1.1	57.6	43
44	43 28.9	-10.5	50.4	44 06.9	-9.4	51.1	44 44.2	-8.3	51.9	45 20.9	-7.1	52.7	45 56.9	-5.9	53.5	46 32.3	-4.8	54.4	47 06.9	-3.6	55.2	47 40.7	-2.3	56.1	44
45	43 18.4	-11.4	49.0	43 57.5	-10.4	49.8	44 35.9	-9.3	50.5	45 13.8	-8.2	51.3	45 51.0	-7.1	52.1	46 27.5	-5.8	52.9	47 03.3	-4.6	53.8	47 38.4	-3.4	54.6	45
46	43 07.0	-12.4	47.7	43 47.1	-11.4	48.4	44 26.6	-10.3	49.1	45 05.6	-9.2	49.9	45 43.9	-8.0	50.7	46 21.7	-7.0	51.5	46 58.7	-5.8	52.3	47 35.0	-4.5	53.2	46
47	42 54.6	-13.4	46.4	43 35.7	-12.3	47.0	44 16.3	-11.3	47.7	44 56.4	-10.2	48.5	45 35.9	-9.2	49.2	46 14.7	-8.0	50.0	46 52.9	-6.8	50.8	47 30.5	-5.7	51.7	47
48	42 41.2	-14.2	45.0	43 23.4	-13.3	45.7	44 05.0	-12.2	46.4	44 46.2	-11.3	47.1	45 26.7	-10.2	47.8	46 06.7	-9.1	48.6	46 46.1	-8.0	49.4	47 24.8	-6.8	50.2	48
49	42 27.0	-15.2	43.7	43 10.1	-14.2	44.4	43 52.8	-13.3	45.0	44 34.9	-12.2	45.7	45 16.5	-11.2	46.4	45 57.6	-10.1	47.2	46 38.1	-9.0	47.9	47 18.0	-7.9	48.7	49
50	42 11.8	-16.0	42.4	42 55.9	-15.1	43.0	43 39.5	-14.1	43.7	44 22.7	-13.2	44.3	45 05.3	-12.2	45.0	45 47.5	-11.2	45.8	46 29.1	-10.2	46.5	47 10.1	-9.1	47.3	50
51	41 55.8	-16.9	41.1	42 40.8	-16.0	41.7	43 25.4	-15.2	42.3	44 09.5	-14.2	43.0	44 53.1	-13.2	43.7	45 36.3	-12.2	44.4	46 18.9	-11.1	45.1	47 01.0	-10.1	45.8	51
52	41 38.9	-17.8	39.8	42 24.8	-17.0	40.4	43 10.2	-16.0	41.0	43 55.3	-15.1	41.6	44 39.9	-14.1	42.3	45 24.1	-13.2	43.0	46 07.8	-12.3	43.7	46 50.9	-11.2	44.4	52
53	41 21.1	-18.6	38.5	42 07.8	-17.7	39.1	42 54.2	-16.9	39.7	43 40.2	-16.1	40.3	44 25.8	-15.2	40.9	45 10.9	-14.2	41.6	45 55.5	-13.2	42.3	46 39.7	-12.3	43.0	53
54	41 02.5	-19.4	37.3	41 50.1	-18.7	37.8	42 37.3	-17.8	38.4	43 24.1	-16.9	39.0	44 10.6	-16.1	39.6	44 56.7	-15.3	40.2	45 42.3	-14.3	40.9	46 27.4	-13.3	41.5	54
55	40 43.1	-20.2	36.0	41 31.4	-19.4	36.5	42 19.5	-18.7	37.1	43 07.2	-17.9	37.6	43 54.5	-17.0	38.2	44 41.4	-16.1	38.8	45 28.0	-15.3	39.5	46 14.1	-14.4	40.1	55
56	40 22.9	-21.0	34.8	41 12.0	-20.3	35.3	42 00.8	-19.5	35.8	42 49.3	-18.7	36.3	43 37.5	-18.0	36.9	44 25.3	-17.1	37.5	45 12.7	-16.3	38.1	45 59.7	-15.4	38.7	56
57	40 01.9	-21.8	33.6	40 51.7	-21.1	34.0	41 41.3	-20.4	34.5	42 30.6	-19.6	35.0	43 19.5	-18.8	35.6	44 08.2	-18.1	36.1	44 56.4	-17.2	36.7	45 44.3	-16.3	37.3	57
58	39 40.1	-22.5	32.3	40 30.6	-21.8	32.8	41 20.9	-21.1	33.3	42 11.0	-20.5	33.8	43 00.7	-19.7	34.3	43 50.1	-18.9	34.8	44 39.2	-18.2	35.4	45 28.0	-17.4	36.0	58
59	39 17.6	-23.3	31.1	40 08.8	-22.6	31.6	40 59.8	-22.0	32.0	41 50.5	-21.3	32.5	42 41.0	-20.6	33.0	43 31.2	-19.9	33.5	44 21.0	-19.1	34.0	45 10.6	-18.3	34.6	59
60	38 54.3	-24.0	30.0	39 46.2	-23.4	30.4	40 37.8	-22.7	30.8	41 29.2	-22.0	31.2	42 20.4	-21.4	31.7	43 11.3	-20.7	32.2	44 01.9	-20.0	32.7	44 52.3	-19.3	33.3	60
61	38 30.3	-24.6	28.8	39 22.8	-24.1	29.2	40 15.1	-23.5	29.6	41 07.2	-22.9	30.0	41 59.0	-22.2	30.5	42 50.6	-21.6	30.9	43 41.9	-20.8	31.4	44 33.0	-20.2	31.9	61
62	38 05.7	-25.4	27.6	38 58.7	-24.8	28.0	39 51.6	-24.2	28.4	40 44.3	-23.6	28.8	41 36.8	-23.0	29.2	42 29.0	-22.4	29.7	43 21.1	-21.8	30.1	44 12.8	-21.0	30.6	62
63	37 40.3	-26.0	26.5	38 33.9	-25.4	26.8	39 27.4	-24.9	27.2	40 20.7	-24.4	27.6	41 13.8	-23.8	28.0	42 06.6	-23.2	28.4	42 59.3	-22.6	28.8	43 51.8	-22.0	29.3	63
64	37 14.3	-26.6	25.3	38 08.5	-26.2	25.7	39 02.5	-25.7	26.0	39 56.3	-25.1	26.4	40 50.0	-24.6	26.8	41 43.4	-24.0	27.2	42 36.7	-23.4	27.6	43 29.8	-22.8	28.0	64
65	36 47.7	-27.3	24.2	37 42.3	-26.8	24.5	38 36.8	-26.3	24.9	39 31.2	-25.8	25.2	40 25.4	-25.3	25.6	41 19.4	-24.7	25.9	42 13.3	-24.2	26.3	43 07.0	-23.7	26.7	65
66	36 20.4	-27.9	23.1	37 15.5	-27.4	23.4	38 10.5	-27.0	23.7	39 05.4	-26.5	24.0	40 00.1	-26.0	24.4	40 54.7	-25.5	24.7	41 49.1	-25.0	25.1	42 43.3	-24.4	25.5	66
67	35 52.5	-28.5	22.0	36 48.1	-28.1	22.3	37 43.5	-27.6	22.6	38 38.9	-27.2	22.9	39 34.1	-26.7	23.2	40 29.2	-26.3	23.5	41 24.1	-25.7	23.9	42 18.9	-25.3	24.2	67
68	35 24.0	-29.0	20.9	36 20.0	-28.6	21.2	37 15.9	-28.2	21.5	38 11.7	-27.8	21.7	39 07.4	-27.4	22.0	40 02.9	-26.9	22.4	40 58.4	-26.5	22.7	41 53.6	-26.0	23.0	68
69	34 55.0	-29.6	19.9	35 51.4	-29.3	20.1	36 47.7	-28.9	20.4	37 43.9	-28.5	20.6	38 40.0	-28.1	20.9	39 36.0	-27.7	21.2	40 31.9	-27.2	21.5	41 27.6	-26.7	21.8	69
70	34 25.4	-30.2	18.8	35 22.1	-29.8	19.0	36 18.8	-29.4	19.3	37 15.4	-29.1	19.5	38 11.9	-28.7	19.8	39 08.3	-28.3	20.0	40 04.7	-27.9	20.3	41 00.9	-27.5	20.6	70
71	33 55.2	-30.6	17.8	34 52.3	-30.3	18.0	35 49.4	-30.0	18.2	36 46.3	-29.6	18.4	37 43.2	-29.3	18.7	38 40.0	-28.9	18.9	39 36.8	-28.6	19.2	40 33.4	-28.2	19.5	71
72	33 24.6	-31.2	16.7	34 22.0	-30.9	16.9	35 19.4	-30.6	17.1	36 16.7	-30.3	17.3	37 13.9	-29.9	17.6	38 11.1	-29.6	17.8	39 08.2	-29.2	18.0	40 05.2	-28.9	18.3	72
73	32 53.4	-31.7	15.7	33 51.1	-31.4	15.9	34 48.8	-31.1	16.1	35 46.4	-30.8	16.3	36 44.0	-30.5	16.5	37 41.5	-30.2	16.7	38 39.0	-29.9	16.9	39 36.3	-29.5	17.2	73
74	32 21.7	-32.1	14.7	33 19.7	-31.8	14.9	34 17.7	-31.6	15.0	35 15.6	-31.3	15.2	36 13.5	-31.0	15.4	37 11.3	-30.7	15.6	38 09.1	-30.5	15.8	39 06.8	-30.2	16.0	74
75	31 49.6	-32.6	13.7	32 47.9	-32.4	13.8	33 46.1	-32.1	14.0	34 44.3	-31.9	14.2	35 42.5	-31.7	14.3	36 40.6	-31.4	14.5	37 38.6	-31.1	14.7	38 36.6	-30.8	14.9	75
76	31 17.0	-33.1	12.7	32 15.5	-32.8	12.8	33 14.0	-32.6	13.0	34 12.4	-32.3	13.1	35 10.8	-32.1	13.3	36 09.2	-31.9	13.5	37 07.5	-31.6	13.6	38 05.8	-31.4	13.8	76
77	30 43.9	-33.4	11.7	31 42.7	-33.3	11.9	32 41.4	-33.1	12.0	33 40.1	-32.9	12.1	34 38.7	-32.6	12.3	35 37.3	-32.4	12.4	36 35.9	-32.2	12.6	37 34.4	-31.9	12.7	77
78	30 10.5	-33.9	10.8	31 09.4	-33.7	10.9	32 08.3	-33.5	11.0	33 07.2	-33.3	11.1	34 06.1	-33.2	11.3	35 04.9	-33.0	11.4	36 03.7	-32.8	11.5	37 02.5	-32.6	11.7	78
79	29 36.6	-34.3	9.8	30 35.7	-34.2	9.9	31 34.8	-34.0	10.0	32 33.9	-33.8	10.1	33 32.9	-33.6	10.2	34 31.9	-33.4	10.4	35 30.9	-33.2	10.5	36 29.9	-33.1	10.6	79
80	29 02.3	-34.7	8.9	30 01.5	-34.5	9.0	31 00.8	-34.4	9.1	32 00.1	-34.3	9.2	32 59.3	-34.1	9.3	33 58.5	-33.9	9.4	34 57.7	-33.8	9.5	35 56.8	-33.6	9.6	80
81	28 27.6	-35.1	7.9	29 27.0	-34.9	8.0	30 26.4	-34.8	8.1	31 25.8	-34.7	8.2	32 25.2	-34.6	8.3	33 24.6	-34.4	8.4	34 23.9	-34.2	8.5	35 23.2	-34.1	8.6	81
82	27 52.5	-35.4	7.0	28 52.1	-35.3	7.1	29 51.6	-35.2	7.2	30 51.1	-35.1	7.2	31 50.6	-34.9	7.3	32 50.2	-34.9	7.4	33 49.7	-34.8	7.5	34 49.1	-34.6	7.6	82
83	27 17.1	-35.8	6.1	28 16.8	-35.7	6.2	29 16.4	-35.6	6.2	30 16.0	-35.4	6.3	31 15.7	-35.4	6.4	32 15.3	-35.3	6.4	33 14.9	-35.2	6.5	34 14.5	-35.0	6.6	83
84	26 41.3	-36.1	5.2	27 41.1	-36.1	5.3	28 40.8	-35.9	5.3	29 40.6	-35.9	5.4	30 40.3	-35.8	5.4	31 40.0	-35.7	5.5	32 39.7	-35.6	5.5	33 39.5	-35.6	5.6	84
85	26 05.2	-36.4	4.3	27 05.0	-36.3	4.4	28 04.9	-36.3	4.4	29 04.7	-36.3	4.4	30 04.5	-36.2	4.5	31 04.3	-36.1	4.5	32 04.1	-36.0	4.6	33 03.9	-35.9	4.6	85
86	25 28.8	-36.8	3.4	26 28.7	-36.7	3.5	27 28.6	-36.7	3.5	28 28.4	-36.6	3.5	29 28.3	-36.5	3.6	30 28.2	-36.5	3.6	31 28.1	-36.5	3.6	32 28.0	-36.4	3.7	86
87	24 52.0	-37.0	2.6	25 52.0	-37.1	2.6	26 51.9	-37.0	2.6	27 51.8	-36.9	2.6	28 51.8	-36.9	2.7	29 51.7	-36.9	2.7	30 51.6	-36.8	2.7	31 51.6	-36.8	2.7	87
88	24 15.0	-37.4	1.7	25 14.9	-37.3	1.7	26 14.9	-37.3	1.7	27 14.9	-37.3	1.7	28 14.9	-37.3	1.8	29 14.8	-37.2	1.8	30 14.8	-37.2	1.8	31 14.8	-37.2	1.8	88
89	23 37.6	-37.6	0.8	24 37.6	-37.6	0.9	25 37.6	-37.6	0.9	26 37.6	-37.6	0.9	27 37.6	-37.6	0.9	28 37.6	-37.6	0.9	29 37.6	-37.6	0.9	30 37.6	-37.6	0.9	89
90	23 00.0	-37.9	0.0	24 00.0	-37.9	0.0	25 00.0	-37.9	0.0	26 00.0	-37.9	0.0	27 00.0	-37.9	0.0	28 00.0	-37.9	0.0	29 00.0	-37.9	0.0	30 00.0	-37.9	0.0	90
	23°			24°			25°			26°			27°			28°			29°			30°			

51°, 309° L.H.A. LATITUDE SAME NAME AS DECLINATION

286

LATITUDE **CONTRARY** NAME TO DECLINATION **L.H.A. 51°, 309°**

Dec.	23° Hc	23° d	23° Z	24° Hc	24° d	24° Z	25° Hc	25° d	25° Z	26° Hc	26° d	26° Z	Dec.
°	° ′	′	°	° ′	′	°	° ′	′	°	° ′	′	°	°
0	35 24.0	-29.0	107.6	35 05.6	-30.1	108.2	34 46.5	-31.1	108.9	34 26.8	-32.2	109.5	0
1	34 55.0	-29.6	108.6	34 35.5	-30.6	109.3	34 15.4	-31.7	109.9	33 54.6	-32.6	110.6	1
2	34 25.4	-30.1	109.7	34 04.9	-31.2	110.3	33 43.7	-32.1	111.0	33 22.0	-33.2	111.6	2
3	33 55.3	-30.7	110.7	33 33.7	-31.6	111.4	33 11.6	-32.7	112.0	32 48.8	-33.6	112.6	3
4	33 24.6	-31.2	111.8	33 02.1	-32.2	112.4	32 38.9	-33.1	113.0	32 15.2	-34.0	113.6	4
5	32 53.4	-31.6	112.8	32 29.9	-32.6	113.4	32 05.8	-33.5	114.0	31 41.2	-34.5	114.5	5
6	32 21.8	-32.2	113.8	31 57.3	-33.1	114.4	31 32.3	-34.0	114.9	31 06.7	-34.9	115.5	6
7	31 49.6	-32.6	114.8	31 24.2	-33.5	115.3	30 58.3	-34.5	115.9	30 31.8	-35.3	116.4	7
8	31 17.0	-33.0	115.8	30 50.7	-34.0	116.3	30 23.8	-34.8	116.8	29 56.5	-35.7	117.4	8
9	30 44.0	-33.5	116.7	30 16.7	-34.3	117.3	29 49.0	-35.2	117.8	29 20.8	-36.1	118.3	9
10	30 10.5	-33.9	117.7	29 42.4	-34.8	118.2	29 13.8	-35.7	118.7	28 44.7	-36.4	119.2	10
11	29 36.6	-34.3	118.7	29 07.6	-35.2	119.2	28 38.1	-35.9	119.6	28 08.3	-36.8	120.1	11
12	29 02.3	-34.7	119.6	28 32.4	-35.5	120.1	28 02.2	-36.4	120.5	27 31.5	-37.2	121.0	12
13	28 27.6	-35.0	120.5	27 56.9	-35.9	121.0	27 25.8	-36.7	121.4	26 54.3	-37.4	121.9	13
14	27 52.6	-35.5	121.5	27 21.0	-36.2	121.9	26 49.1	-37.0	122.3	26 16.9	-37.8	122.8	14
15	27 17.1	-35.7	122.4	26 44.8	-36.5	122.8	26 12.1	-37.3	123.2	25 39.1	-38.1	123.6	15
16	26 41.4	-36.2	123.3	26 08.3	-36.9	123.7	25 34.8	-37.6	124.1	25 01.0	-38.3	124.5	16
17	26 05.2	-36.4	124.2	25 31.4	-37.2	124.6	24 57.2	-37.9	124.9	24 22.7	-38.7	125.3	17
18	25 28.8	-36.7	125.0	24 54.2	-37.5	125.4	24 19.3	-38.3	125.8	23 44.0	-38.9	126.2	18
19	24 52.1	-37.1	125.9	24 16.7	-37.8	126.3	23 41.0	-38.4	126.6	23 05.1	-39.2	127.0	19
20	24 15.0	-37.3	126.8	23 38.9	-38.0	127.1	23 02.6	-38.8	127.5	22 25.9	-39.4	127.8	20
21	23 37.7	-37.7	127.6	23 00.9	-38.3	128.0	22 23.8	-39.0	128.3	21 46.5	-39.7	128.6	21
22	23 00.0	-37.9	128.5	22 22.6	-38.6	128.8	21 44.8	-39.2	129.1	21 06.8	-39.8	129.4	22
23	22 22.1	-38.1	129.3	21 44.0	-38.8	129.6	21 05.6	-39.5	129.9	20 27.0	-40.1	130.2	23
24	21 44.0	-38.4	130.2	21 05.2	-39.1	130.5	20 26.1	-39.7	130.7	19 46.9	-40.3	131.0	24
25	21 05.6	-38.6	131.0	20 26.1	-39.2	131.3	19 46.4	-39.8	131.5	19 06.6	-40.5	131.8	25
26	20 27.0	-38.9	131.8	19 46.9	-39.5	132.1	19 06.6	-40.1	132.3	18 26.1	-40.7	132.6	26
27	19 48.1	-39.1	132.6	19 07.4	-39.7	132.9	18 26.5	-40.3	133.1	17 45.4	-40.9	133.4	27
28	19 09.0	-39.3	133.4	18 27.7	-39.9	133.7	17 46.2	-40.5	133.9	17 04.5	-41.1	134.1	28
29	18 29.7	-39.5	134.2	17 47.8	-40.1	134.4	17 05.7	-40.6	134.7	16 23.4	-41.2	134.9	29
30	17 50.2	-39.6	135.0	17 07.7	-40.2	135.2	16 25.1	-40.9	135.4	15 42.2	-41.3	135.6	30
31	17 10.6	-39.9	135.8	16 27.5	-40.4	136.0	15 44.2	-40.9	136.2	15 00.9	-41.5	136.4	31
32	16 30.7	-40.0	136.6	15 47.1	-40.6	136.8	15 03.3	-41.2	137.0	14 19.4	-41.7	137.1	32
33	15 50.7	-40.2	137.4	15 06.5	-40.8	137.5	14 22.1	-41.2	137.7	13 37.7	-41.8	137.9	33
34	15 10.5	-40.4	138.1	14 25.7	-40.8	138.3	13 40.9	-41.4	138.5	12 55.9	-41.9	138.6	34
35	14 30.1	-40.5	138.9	13 44.9	-41.1	139.1	12 59.5	-41.5	139.2	12 14.0	-42.0	139.4	35
36	13 49.6	-40.6	139.6	13 03.8	-41.1	139.8	12 18.0	-41.7	139.9	11 32.0	-42.1	140.1	36
37	13 09.0	-40.8	140.4	12 22.7	-41.3	140.5	11 36.3	-41.7	140.7	10 49.9	-42.3	140.8	37
38	12 28.2	-40.9	141.2	11 41.4	-41.3	141.3	10 54.6	-41.9	141.4	10 07.6	-42.3	141.5	38
39	11 47.3	-41.0	141.9	11 00.1	-41.5	142.0	10 12.7	-41.9	142.1	9 25.3	-42.4	142.3	39
40	11 06.3	-41.1	142.6	10 18.6	-41.6	142.8	9 30.8	-42.1	142.9	8 42.9	-42.5	143.0	40
41	10 25.2	-41.3	143.4	9 37.0	-41.7	143.5	8 48.7	-42.1	143.6	8 00.4	-42.6	143.7	41
42	9 43.9	-41.3	144.1	8 55.3	-41.8	144.2	8 06.6	-42.2	144.3	7 17.8	-42.6	144.4	42
43	9 02.6	-41.4	144.9	8 13.5	-41.8	145.0	7 24.4	-42.3	145.0	6 35.2	-42.7	145.1	43
44	8 21.2	-41.5	145.6	7 31.7	-41.9	145.7	6 42.1	-42.3	145.7	5 52.5	-42.7	145.8	44
45	7 39.7	-41.5	146.3	6 49.8	-42.0	146.4	5 59.8	-42.4	146.5	5 09.8	-42.8	146.5	45
46	6 58.2	-41.7	147.1	6 07.8	-42.0	147.1	5 17.4	-42.4	147.2	4 27.0	-42.9	147.2	46
47	6 16.5	-41.6	147.8	5 25.8	-42.1	147.8	4 35.0	-42.5	147.9	3 44.1	-42.8	147.9	47
48	5 34.9	-41.8	148.5	4 43.7	-42.1	148.5	3 52.5	-42.5	148.6	3 01.3	-42.9	148.6	48
49	4 53.1	-41.8	149.2	4 01.6	-42.2	149.3	3 10.0	-42.6	149.3	2 18.4	-42.9	149.3	49
50	4 11.3	-41.8	149.9	3 19.4	-42.2	150.0	2 27.4	-42.5	150.0	1 35.5	-43.0	150.0	50
51	3 29.5	-41.9	150.7	2 37.2	-42.2	150.7	1 44.9	-42.6	150.7	0 52.5	-42.9	150.7	51
52	2 47.6	-41.8	151.4	1 55.0	-42.3	151.4	1 02.3	-42.6	151.4	0 09.6	-42.9	151.4	52
53	2 05.8	-41.9	152.1	1 12.7	-42.2	152.1	0 19.7	-42.6	152.1	0 33.3	+43.0	27.9	53
54	1 23.9	-42.0	152.8	0 30.5	-42.3	152.8	0 22.9	+42.6	27.2	1 16.3	+42.9	27.2	54
55	0 41.9	-41.9	153.5	0 11.8	+42.2	26.5	1 05.5	+42.6	26.5	1 59.2	+42.9	26.5	55
56	0 00.0	-41.9	154.2	0 54.0	+42.3	25.8	1 48.1	+42.5	25.8	2 42.1	+42.9	25.8	56
57	0 41.9	+41.9	25.0	1 36.3	+42.2	25.1	2 30.6	+42.6	25.1	3 25.0	+42.8	25.1	57
58	1 23.8	+41.9	24.3	2 18.5	+42.2	24.3	3 13.2	+42.5	24.4	4 07.8	+42.8	24.4	58
59	2 05.7	+41.9	23.6	3 00.7	+42.2	23.6	3 55.7	+42.4	23.7	4 50.6	+42.8	23.7	59
60	2 47.6	+41.9	22.9	3 42.9	+42.1	22.9	4 38.1	+42.5	22.9	5 33.4	+42.7	23.0	60
61	3 29.5	+41.8	22.2	4 25.0	+42.1	22.2	5 20.6	+42.4	22.2	6 16.1	+42.7	22.3	61
62	4 11.3	+41.8	21.5	5 07.1	+42.1	21.5	6 03.0	+42.3	21.5	6 58.8	+42.6	21.6	62
63	4 53.1	+41.7	20.7	5 49.2	+42.0	20.8	6 45.3	+42.2	20.8	7 41.4	+42.5	20.9	63
64	5 34.8	+41.7	20.0	6 31.2	+41.9	20.1	7 27.5	+42.2	20.1	8 23.9	+42.4	20.1	64
65	6 16.5	+41.6	19.3	7 13.1	+41.9	19.3	8 09.7	+42.2	19.4	9 06.3	+42.4	19.4	65
66	6 58.1	+41.6	18.6	7 55.0	+41.8	18.6	8 51.9	+42.0	18.7	9 48.7	+42.3	18.7	66
67	7 39.7	+41.5	17.8	8 36.8	+41.7	17.9	9 33.9	+41.9	17.9	10 31.0	+42.1	18.0	67
68	8 21.2	+41.4	17.1	9 18.5	+41.6	17.2	10 15.8	+41.9	17.2	11 13.1	+42.1	17.3	68
69	9 02.6	+41.3	16.4	10 00.1	+41.6	16.4	10 57.7	+41.7	16.5	11 55.2	+42.0	16.5	69
70	9 43.9	+41.2	15.6	10 41.7	+41.4	15.7	11 39.4	+41.7	15.7	12 37.2	+41.8	15.8	70
71	10 25.1	+41.2	14.9	11 23.1	+41.3	15.0	12 21.1	+41.5	15.0	13 19.0	+41.7	15.1	71
72	11 06.3	+41.0	14.2	12 04.4	+41.2	14.2	13 02.6	+41.4	14.3	14 00.7	+41.6	14.3	72
73	11 47.3	+40.9	13.4	12 45.6	+41.1	13.5	13 44.0	+41.2	13.5	14 42.3	+41.4	13.6	73
74	12 28.2	+40.7	12.7	13 26.7	+40.9	12.7	14 25.2	+41.1	12.8	15 23.7	+41.3	12.8	74
75	13 08.9	+40.7	11.9	14 07.6	+40.8	12.0	15 06.3	+41.0	12.0	16 05.0	+41.1	12.1	75
76	13 49.6	+40.5	11.2	14 48.4	+40.7	11.2	15 47.3	+40.8	11.3	16 46.1	+41.0	11.3	76
77	14 30.1	+40.3	10.4	15 29.1	+40.5	10.5	16 28.1	+40.6	10.5	17 27.1	+40.8	10.6	77
78	15 10.4	+40.2	9.6	16 09.6	+40.3	9.7	17 08.7	+40.5	9.7	18 07.9	+40.6	9.8	78
79	15 50.6	+40.1	8.9	16 49.9	+40.2	8.9	17 49.2	+40.3	9.0	18 48.5	+40.3	9.0	79
80	16 30.7	+39.8	8.1	17 30.1	+39.9	8.1	18 29.5	+40.0	8.2	19 28.8	+40.2	8.2	80
81	17 10.5	+39.7	7.3	18 10.0	+39.8	7.4	19 09.5	+39.9	7.4	20 09.0	+40.0	7.4	81
82	17 50.2	+39.5	6.5	18 49.8	+39.6	6.6	19 49.4	+39.7	6.6	20 49.0	+39.8	6.6	82
83	18 29.7	+39.3	5.7	19 29.4	+39.4	5.8	20 29.1	+39.4	5.8	21 28.8	+39.5	5.8	83
84	19 09.0	+39.1	4.9	20 08.8	+39.1	5.0	21 08.5	+39.2	5.0	22 08.3	+39.3	5.0	84
85	19 48.1	+38.8	4.1	20 47.9	+38.9	4.2	21 47.7	+39.0	4.2	22 47.6	+39.0	4.2	85
86	20 26.9	+38.7	3.3	21 26.8	+38.7	3.3	22 26.7	+38.7	3.4	23 26.6	+38.8	3.4	86
87	21 05.6	+38.4	2.5	22 05.5	+38.4	2.5	23 05.4	+38.5	2.5	24 05.4	+38.5	2.6	87
88	21 44.0	+38.1	1.7	22 43.9	+38.2	1.7	23 43.9	+38.2	1.7	24 43.9	+38.2	1.7	88
89	22 22.1	+37.9	0.8	23 22.1	+37.9	0.8	24 22.1	+37.9	0.9	25 22.1	+37.9	0.9	89
90	23 00.0	+37.6	0.0	24 00.0	+37.6	0.0	25 00.0	+37.6	0.0	26 00.0	+37.6	0.0	90
	23°			24°			25°			26°			

Dec.	27° Hc	27° d	27° Z	28° Hc	28° d	28° Z	29° Hc	29° d	29° Z	30° Hc	30° d	30° Z	Dec.
°	° ′	′	°	° ′	′	°	° ′	′	°	° ′	′	°	°
0	34 06.4	-33.2	110.2	33 45.4	-34.2	110.8	33 23.7	-35.0	111.4	33 01.5	-36.0	112.0	0
1	33 33.2	-33.6	111.2	33 11.2	-34.5	111.8	32 48.7	-35.5	112.4	32 25.5	-36.4	113.0	1
2	32 59.6	-34.1	112.2	32 36.7	-35.1	112.8	32 13.2	-36.0	113.4	31 49.1	-36.8	113.9	2
3	32 25.5	-34.5	113.2	32 01.6	-35.4	113.7	31 37.2	-36.3	114.3	31 12.3	-37.3	114.9	3
4	31 51.0	-35.0	114.1	31 26.2	-35.9	114.7	31 00.9	-36.8	115.2	30 35.0	-37.6	115.8	4
5	31 16.0	-35.4	115.1	30 50.3	-36.2	115.6	30 24.1	-37.1	116.2	29 57.4	-37.9	116.7	5
6	30 40.6	-35.7	116.0	30 14.1	-36.7	116.5	29 47.0	-37.5	117.1	29 19.5	-38.3	117.6	6
7	30 04.9	-36.2	116.9	29 37.4	-37.0	117.5	29 09.5	-37.8	118.0	28 41.2	-38.7	118.4	7
8	29 28.7	-36.6	117.9	29 00.4	-37.4	118.4	28 31.7	-38.2	118.8	28 02.5	-39.0	119.3	8
9	28 52.1	-36.9	118.8	28 23.0	-37.7	119.3	27 53.5	-38.5	119.7	27 23.5	-39.3	120.2	9
10	28 15.2	-37.2	119.7	27 45.3	-38.1	120.1	27 15.0	-38.9	120.6	26 44.2	-39.5	121.0	10
11	27 38.0	-37.6	120.6	27 07.2	-38.3	121.0	26 36.1	-39.1	121.4	26 04.7	-39.9	121.9	11
12	27 00.4	-37.9	121.4	26 28.9	-38.7	121.9	25 57.0	-39.4	122.3	25 24.8	-40.2	122.7	12
13	26 22.5	-38.3	122.3	25 50.2	-39.0	122.7	25 17.6	-39.7	123.1	24 44.6	-40.4	123.5	13
14	25 44.2	-38.5	123.2	25 11.2	-39.2	123.6	24 37.9	-40.0	123.9	24 04.2	-40.7	124.3	14
15	25 05.7	-38.8	124.0	24 32.0	-39.6	124.4	23 57.9	-40.2	124.8	23 23.5	-40.9	125.1	15
16	24 26.9	-39.1	124.9	23 52.4	-39.7	125.2	23 17.7	-40.5	125.6	22 42.6	-41.1	125.9	16
17	23 47.8	-39.3	125.7	23 12.7	-40.1	126.0	22 37.2	-40.7	126.4	22 01.5	-41.4	126.7	17
18	23 08.5	-39.6	126.5	22 32.6	-40.3	126.8	21 56.5	-40.9	127.2	21 20.1	-41.6	127.5	18
19	22 28.9	-39.9	127.3	21 52.3	-40.5	127.6	21 15.6	-41.2	128.0	20 38.5	-41.8	128.3	19
20	21 49.0	-40.1	128.1	21 11.8	-40.7	128.4	20 34.4	-41.4	128.7	19 56.7	-41.9	129.0	20
21	21 08.9	-40.3	128.9	20 31.1	-40.9	129.2	19 53.0	-41.5	129.5	19 14.8	-42.2	129.8	21
22	20 28.6	-40.5	129.7	19 50.2	-41.2	130.0	19 11.5	-41.8	130.3	18 32.6	-42.4	130.5	22
23	19 48.1	-40.7	130.5	19 09.0	-41.3	130.8	18 29.7	-41.9	131.0	17 50.2	-42.5	131.3	23
24	19 07.4	-40.9	131.3	18 27.7	-41.5	131.5	17 47.8	-42.1	131.8	17 07.7	-42.6	132.0	24
25	18 26.5	-41.1	132.1	17 46.2	-41.7	132.3	17 05.7	-42.3	132.5	16 25.1	-42.9	132.8	25
26	17 45.4	-41.3	132.8	17 04.5	-41.9	133.1	16 23.4	-42.4	133.3	15 42.2	-42.9	133.5	26
27	17 04.1	-41.5	133.6	16 22.6	-42.0	133.8	15 41.0	-42.5	134.0	14 59.3	-43.2	134.2	27
28	16 22.6	-41.6	134.3	15 40.6	-42.1	134.5	14 58.5	-42.8	134.7	14 16.1	-43.2	134.9	28
29	15 41.0	-41.7	135.1	14 58.5	-42.4	135.3	14 15.7	-42.8	135.5	13 32.9	-43.3	135.6	29
30	14 59.3	-41.9	135.8	14 16.1	-42.4	136.0	13 32.9	-42.9	136.2	12 49.6	-43.5	136.4	30
31	14 17.4	-42.1	136.6	13 33.7	-42.6	136.7	12 50.0	-43.1	136.9	12 06.1	-43.6	137.1	31
32	13 35.3	-42.2	137.3	12 51.1	-42.6	137.5	12 06.9	-43.2	137.6	11 22.5	-43.7	137.8	32
33	12 53.1	-42.3	138.0	12 08.5	-42.8	138.2	11 23.7	-43.3	138.3	10 38.8	-43.7	138.5	33
34	12 10.8	-42.4	138.8	11 25.7	-42.9	138.9	10 40.4	-43.4	139.0	9 55.1	-43.9	139.2	34
35	11 28.4	-42.5	139.5	10 42.8	-43.0	139.6	9 57.0	-43.4	139.7	9 11.2	-43.9	139.8	35
36	10 45.9	-42.6	140.2	9 59.8	-43.1	140.3	9 13.6	-43.6	140.4	8 27.3	-44.0	140.5	36
37	10 03.3	-42.7	140.9	9 16.7	-43.2	141.0	8 30.0	-43.6	141.1	7 43.3	-44.1	141.2	37
38	9 20.6	-42.8	141.6	8 33.5	-43.2	141.7	7 46.4	-43.7	141.8	6 59.2	-44.1	141.9	38
39	8 37.8	-42.8	142.3	7 50.3	-43.3	142.4	7 02.7	-43.7	142.5	6 15.1	-44.2	142.6	39
40	7 55.0	-43.0	143.1	7 07.0	-43.4	143.1	6 19.0	-43.8	143.2	5 30.9	-44.2	143.3	40
41	7 12.0	-43.0	143.8	6 23.6	-43.4	143.8	5 35.2	-43.9	143.9	4 46.7	-44.3	143.9	41
42	6 29.0	-43.0	144.5	5 40.2	-43.5	144.5	4 51.3	-43.9	144.6	4 02.4	-44.3	144.6	42
43	5 46.0	-43.1	145.2	4 56.7	-43.5	145.2	4 07.4	-43.9	145.3	3 18.1	-44.3	145.3	43
44	5 02.9	-43.2	145.9	4 13.2	-43.6	145.9	3 23.5	-44.0	145.9	2 33.8	-44.4	146.0	44
45	4 19.7	-43.2	146.6	3 29.6	-43.6	146.6	2 39.5	-43.9	146.6	1 49.4	-44.3	146.6	45
46	3 36.5	-43.2	147.3	2 46.0	-43.6	147.3	1 55.6	-44.0	147.3	1 05.1	-44.4	147.3	46
47	2 53.3	-43.3	147.9	2 02.4	-43.6	148.0	1 11.6	-44.0	148.0	0 20.7	-44.4	148.0	47
48	2 10.0	-43.2	148.6	1 18.8	-43.6	148.7	0 27.6	-44.0	148.7	0 23.7	+44.4	31.3	48
49	1 26.8	-43.3	149.3	0 35.2	-43.7	149.3	0 16.4	+44.1	30.7	1 08.1	+44.3	30.7	49
50	0 43.5	-43.3	150.0	0 08.5	+43.6	30.0	1 00.5	+44.0	30.0	1 52.4	+44.4	30.0	50
51	0 00.2	-43.3	150.7	0 52.1	+43.7	29.3	1 44.5	+43.9	29.3	2 36.8	+44.3	29.3	51
52	0 43.1	+43.3	28.6	1 35.8	+43.6	28.6	2 28.4	+44.0	28.6	3 21.1	+44.3	28.6	52
53	1 26.4	+43.2	27.9	2 19.4	+43.6	27.9	3 12.4	+43.9	27.9	4 05.4	+44.3	28.0	53
54	2 09.6	+43.3	27.2	3 03.0	+43.6	27.2	3 56.3	+43.9	27.3	4 49.7	+44.2	27.3	54
55	2 52.9	+43.2	26.5	3 46.6	+43.5	26.5	4 40.2	+43.9	26.6	5 33.9	+44.2	26.6	55
56	3 36.1	+43.2	25.8	4 30.1	+43.5	25.8	5 24.1	+43.8	25.9	6 18.1	+44.1	25.9	56
57	4 19.3	+43.1	25.1	5 13.6	+43.5	25.2	6 07.9	+43.8	25.2	7 02.2	+44.1	25.2	57
58	5 02.4	+43.2	24.4	5 57.1	+43.4	24.5	6 51.7	+43.7	24.5	7 46.3	+44.0	24.6	58
59	5 45.6	+43.0	23.7	6 40.5	+43.3	23.8	7 35.4	+43.6	23.8	8 30.3	+43.9	23.9	59
60	6 28.6	+43.0	23.0	7 23.8	+43.3	23.1	8 19.0	+43.6	23.1	9 14.2	+43.8	23.2	60
61	7 11.6	+43.0	22.3	8 07.1	+43.2	22.4	9 02.6	+43.5	22.4	9 58.0	+43.8	22.5	61
62	7 54.6	+42.8	21.6	8 50.3	+43.2	21.7	9 46.1	+43.4	21.7	10 41.8	+43.7	21.8	62
63	8 37.4	+42.8	20.9	9 33.5	+43.0	21.0	10 29.5	+43.3	21.0	11 25.5	+43.5	21.1	63
64	9 20.2	+42.7	20.2	10 16.5	+43.0	20.3	11 12.8	+43.2	20.3	12 09.0	+43.5	20.4	64
65	10 02.9	+42.6	19.5	10 59.5	+42.8	19.5	11 56.0	+43.1	19.6	12 52.5	+43.3	19.7	65
66	10 45.5	+42.5	18.8	11 42.3	+42.8	18.8	12 39.1	+43.0	18.9	13 35.8	+43.3	19.0	66
67	11 28.0	+42.4	18.0	12 25.1	+42.6	18.1	13 22.1	+42.8	18.2	14 19.1	+43.1	18.3	67
68	12 10.4	+42.3	17.3	13 07.7	+42.5	17.4	14 04.9	+42.8	17.5	15 02.2	+42.9	17.5	68
69	12 52.7	+42.2	16.6	13 50.2	+42.4	16.7	14 47.7	+42.6	16.7	15 45.1	+42.8	16.8	69
70	13 34.9	+42.0	15.9	14 32.6	+42.3	15.9	15 30.3	+42.4	16.0	16 27.9	+42.7	16.1	70
71	14 16.9	+42.0	15.1	15 14.9	+42.1	15.2	16 12.7	+42.3	15.3	17 10.6	+42.5	15.4	71
72	14 58.9	+41.7	14.4	15 57.0	+41.9	14.5	16 55.0	+42.2	14.5	17 53.1	+42.4	14.6	72
73	15 40.6	+41.6	13.7	16 38.9	+41.8	13.7	17 37.2	+42.0	13.8	18 35.5	+42.1	13.9	73
74	16 22.2	+41.5	12.9	17 20.7	+41.6	13.0	18 19.2	+41.8	13.0	19 17.6	+42.0	13.1	74
75	17 03.7	+41.3	12.1	18 02.3	+41.5	12.2	19 01.0	+41.6	12.3	19 59.6	+41.8	12.4	75
76	17 45.0	+41.1	11.4	18 43.8	+41.2	11.5	19 42.6	+41.4	11.5	20 41.4	+41.5	11.6	76
77	18 26.1	+40.9	10.6	19 25.0	+41.1	10.7	20 24.0	+41.2	10.7	21 22.9	+41.4	10.8	77
78	19 07.0	+40.7	9.8	20 06.1	+40.9	9.9	21 05.2	+41.0	10.0	22 04.3	+41.1	10.0	78
79	19 47.7	+40.5	9.1	20 47.0	+40.6	9.1	21 46.2	+40.8	9.2	22 45.4	+40.9	9.3	79
80	20 28.2	+40.3	8.3	21 27.6	+40.4	8.3	22 27.0	+40.5	8.4	23 26.3	+40.7	8.5	80
81	21 08.5	+40.1	7.5	22 08.0	+40.2	7.5	23 07.5	+40.3	7.6	24 07.0	+40.4	7.7	81
82	21 48.6	+39.9	6.7	22 48.2	+39.9	6.7	23 47.8	+40.0	6.8	24 47.4	+40.1	6.8	82
83	22 28.5	+39.6	5.9	23 28.1	+39.7	5.9	24 27.8	+39.8	6.0	25 27.5	+39.9	6.0	83
84	23 08.1	+39.3	5.1	24 07.8	+39.5	5.1	25 07.6	+39.5	5.1	26 07.4	+39.5	5.2	84
85	23 47.4	+39.1	4.2	24 47.3	+39.1	4.3	25 47.1	+39.2	4.3	26 46.9	+39.3	4.4	85
86	24 26.5	+38.8	3.4	25 26.4	+38.9	3.4	26 26.3	+38.9	3.5	27 26.2	+38.9	3.5	86
87	25 05.3	+38.6	2.6	26 05.3	+38.5	2.6	27 05.2	+38.6	2.6	28 05.1	+38.7	2.6	87
88	25 43.9	+38.2	1.7	26 43.8	+38.3	1.7	27 43.8	+38.3	1.8	28 43.8	+38.3	1.8	88
89	26 22.1	+37.9	0.9	27 22.1	+37.9	0.9	28 22.1	+37.9	0.9	29 22.1	+37.9	0.9	89
90	27 00.0	+37.6	0.0	28 00.0	+37.6	0.0	29 00.0	+37.6	0.0	30 00.0	+37.6	0.0	90
	27°			28°			29°			30°			

S. Lat. {L.H.A. greater than 180° ....Zn=180°–Z
{L.H.A. less than 180°...........Zn=180°+Z

LATITUDE **SAME** NAME AS DECLINATION **L.H.A. 129°, 231°**

287

52°, 308° L.H.A. LATITUDE SAME NAME AS DECLINATION N. Lat. {L.H.A. greater than 180° .....Zn=Z / L.H.A. less than 180°............Zn=360°−Z

Dec.	23°			24°			25°			26°			27°			28°			29°			30°			Dec.
	Hc	d	Z	Hc	d	Z	Hc	d	Z	Hc	d	Z	Hc	d	Z	Hc	d	Z	Hc	d	Z	Hc	d	Z	
°	° ′	′	°	° ′	′	°	° ′	′	°	° ′	′	°	° ′	′	°	° ′	′	°	° ′	′	°	° ′	′	°	°
0	34 31.3	+28.2	107.0	34 13.5	+29.2	107.6	33 55.0	+30.3	108.3	33 35.8	+31.4	108.9	33 16.1	+32.3	109.5	32 55.7	+33.4	110.1	32 34.8	+34.3	110.7	32 13.2	+35.3	111.3	0
1	34 59.5	+27.6	105.9	34 42.7	+28.7	106.6	34 25.3	+29.7	107.2	34 07.2	+30.8	107.9	33 48.4	+31.9	108.5	33 29.1	+32.8	109.1	33 09.1	+33.8	109.8	32 48.5	+34.8	110.4	1
2	35 27.1	+27.0	104.8	35 11.4	+28.1	105.5	34 55.0	+29.2	106.2	34 38.0	+30.2	106.8	34 20.3	+31.3	107.5	34 01.9	+32.3	108.1	33 42.9	+33.3	108.8	33 23.3	+34.3	109.4	2
3	35 54.1	+26.4	103.7	35 39.5	+27.5	104.4	35 24.2	+28.6	105.1	35 08.2	+29.8	105.8	34 51.6	+30.8	106.5	34 34.2	+31.9	107.1	34 16.2	+32.9	107.8	33 57.6	+33.9	108.4	3
4	36 20.5	+25.8	102.6	36 07.0	+26.9	103.3	35 52.8	+28.1	104.0	35 38.0	+29.1	104.7	35 22.4	+30.2	105.4	35 06.1	+31.3	106.1	34 49.1	+32.3	106.8	34 31.5	+33.3	107.4	4
5	36 46.3	+25.1	101.5	36 33.9	+26.3	102.2	36 20.9	+27.4	102.9	36 07.1	+28.6	103.6	35 52.6	+29.6	104.3	35 37.4	+30.7	105.0	35 21.4	+31.9	105.7	35 04.8	+32.9	106.4	5
6	37 11.4	+24.5	100.3	37 00.2	+25.7	101.1	36 48.3	+26.8	101.8	36 35.7	+27.9	102.6	36 22.2	+29.1	103.3	36 08.1	+30.2	104.0	35 53.3	+31.2	104.7	35 37.7	+32.3	105.4	6
7	37 35.9	+23.8	99.2	37 25.9	+25.0	100.0	37 15.1	+26.2	100.7	37 03.6	+27.3	101.4	36 51.3	+28.5	102.2	36 38.3	+29.6	102.9	36 24.5	+30.7	103.6	36 10.0	+31.8	104.3	7
8	37 59.7	+23.1	98.0	37 50.9	+24.3	98.8	37 41.3	+25.5	99.6	37 30.9	+26.7	100.3	37 19.8	+27.8	101.1	37 07.9	+29.0	101.8	36 55.2	+30.1	102.6	36 41.8	+31.2	103.3	8
9	38 22.8	+22.4	96.9	38 15.2	+23.6	97.6	38 06.8	+24.8	98.4	37 57.6	+26.1	99.2	37 47.6	+27.2	100.0	37 36.9	+28.3	100.7	37 25.3	+29.5	101.5	37 13.0	+30.6	102.2	9
10	38 45.2	+21.6	95.7	38 38.8	+22.9	96.5	38 31.6	+24.2	97.3	38 23.7	+25.3	98.0	38 14.8	+26.6	98.8	38 05.2	+27.8	99.6	37 54.8	+28.9	100.4	37 43.6	+30.1	101.1	10
11	39 06.8	+20.9	94.5	39 01.7	+22.2	95.3	38 55.8	+23.4	96.1	38 49.0	+24.7	96.9	38 41.4	+25.9	97.7	38 33.0	+27.0	98.5	38 23.7	+28.3	99.3	38 13.7	+29.4	100.0	11
12	39 27.7	+20.2	93.3	39 23.9	+21.4	94.1	39 19.2	+22.7	94.9	39 13.7	+23.9	95.7	39 07.3	+25.1	96.5	39 00.0	+26.4	97.3	38 52.0	+27.5	98.1	38 43.1	+28.7	98.9	12
13	39 47.9	+19.4	92.0	39 45.3	+20.7	92.9	39 41.9	+21.9	93.7	39 37.6	+23.2	94.5	39 32.4	+24.5	95.4	39 26.4	+25.7	96.2	39 19.5	+26.9	97.0	39 11.8	+28.1	97.8	13
14	40 07.3	+18.6	90.8	40 06.0	+19.9	91.6	40 03.8	+21.2	92.5	40 00.8	+22.5	93.3	39 56.9	+23.7	94.2	39 52.1	+25.0	95.0	39 46.4	+26.2	95.8	39 39.9	+27.4	96.7	14
15	40 25.9	+17.8	89.6	40 25.9	+19.1	90.4	40 25.0	+20.4	91.3	40 23.3	+21.6	92.1	40 20.6	+23.0	93.0	40 17.1	+24.2	93.8	40 12.6	+25.5	94.7	40 07.3	+26.7	95.5	15
16	40 43.7	+16.9	88.3	40 45.0	+18.3	89.2	40 45.4	+19.6	90.0	40 44.9	+20.9	90.9	40 43.6	+22.2	91.7	40 41.3	+23.5	92.6	40 38.1	+24.8	93.5	40 34.0	+26.0	94.3	16
17	41 00.6	+16.1	87.0	41 03.3	+17.4	87.9	41 05.0	+18.8	88.8	41 05.8	+20.1	89.6	41 05.8	+21.4	90.5	41 04.8	+22.7	91.4	41 02.9	+23.9	92.3	41 00.0	+25.3	93.1	17
18	41 16.7	+15.3	85.8	41 20.7	+16.6	86.6	41 23.8	+17.9	87.5	41 25.9	+19.3	88.4	41 27.2	+20.5	89.3	41 27.5	+21.9	90.2	41 26.8	+23.2	91.0	41 25.3	+24.5	91.9	18
19	41 32.0	+14.4	84.5	41 37.3	+15.8	85.3	41 41.7	+17.1	86.2	41 45.2	+18.4	87.1	41 47.7	+19.8	88.0	41 49.4	+21.0	88.9	41 50.0	+22.4	89.8	41 49.8	+23.7	90.7	19
20	41 46.4	+13.5	83.2	41 53.1	+14.8	84.1	41 58.8	+16.2	84.9	42 03.6	+17.6	85.8	42 07.5	+18.9	86.7	42 10.4	+20.3	87.7	42 12.4	+21.6	88.6	42 13.5	+22.8	89.5	20
21	41 59.9	+12.6	81.9	42 07.9	+14.0	82.7	42 15.0	+15.3	83.6	42 21.2	+16.7	84.6	42 26.4	+18.0	85.5	42 30.7	+19.4	86.4	42 34.0	+20.7	87.3	42 36.3	+22.1	88.2	21
22	42 12.5	+11.7	80.5	42 21.9	+13.0	81.4	42 30.3	+14.5	82.3	42 37.9	+15.8	83.3	42 44.4	+17.2	84.2	42 50.1	+18.5	85.1	42 54.7	+19.9	86.0	42 58.4	+21.2	86.9	22
23	42 24.2	+10.7	79.2	42 34.9	+12.2	80.1	42 44.8	+13.5	81.0	42 53.7	+14.8	81.9	43 01.6	+16.3	82.9	43 08.6	+17.6	83.8	43 14.6	+19.0	84.7	43 19.6	+20.3	85.7	23
24	42 34.9	+9.9	77.9	42 47.1	+11.2	78.8	42 58.3	+12.6	79.7	43 08.5	+14.0	80.6	43 17.9	+15.3	81.5	43 26.2	+16.7	82.5	43 33.6	+18.0	83.4	43 39.9	+19.5	84.4	24
25	42 44.8	+8.9	76.5	42 58.3	+10.2	77.4	43 10.9	+11.6	78.4	43 22.5	+13.0	79.3	43 33.2	+14.4	80.2	43 42.9	+15.8	81.2	43 51.6	+17.2	82.1	43 59.4	+18.5	83.1	25
26	42 53.7	+7.9	75.2	43 08.5	+9.4	76.1	43 22.5	+10.7	77.0	43 35.5	+12.1	77.9	43 47.6	+13.4	78.9	43 58.7	+14.8	79.8	44 08.8	+16.2	80.8	44 17.9	+17.7	81.7	26
27	43 01.6	+7.0	73.8	43 17.9	+8.3	74.7	43 33.2	+9.7	75.6	43 47.6	+11.1	76.6	44 01.0	+12.5	77.5	44 13.5	+13.9	78.5	44 25.0	+15.3	79.4	44 35.6	+16.6	80.4	27
28	43 08.6	+6.0	72.5	43 26.2	+7.4	73.4	43 42.9	+8.7	74.3	43 58.7	+10.1	75.2	44 13.5	+11.5	76.2	44 27.4	+12.9	77.1	44 40.3	+14.3	78.1	44 52.2	+15.7	79.0	28
29	43 14.6	+5.0	71.1	43 33.6	+6.3	72.0	43 51.6	+7.8	72.9	44 08.8	+9.1	73.8	44 25.0	+10.6	74.8	44 40.3	+11.9	75.7	44 54.6	+13.3	76.7	45 07.9	+14.7	77.7	29
30	43 19.6	+4.1	69.7	43 39.9	+5.4	70.6	43 59.4	+6.8	71.5	44 17.9	+8.2	72.5	44 35.6	+9.5	73.4	44 52.2	+10.9	74.4	45 07.9	+12.3	75.3	45 22.6	+13.7	76.3	30
31	43 23.7	+3.0	68.4	43 45.3	+4.4	69.3	44 06.2	+5.7	70.2	44 26.1	+7.1	71.1	44 45.1	+8.5	72.0	45 03.1	+9.9	73.0	45 20.2	+11.3	73.9	45 36.3	+12.7	74.9	31
32	43 26.7	+2.1	67.0	43 49.7	+3.4	67.9	44 11.9	+4.8	68.8	44 33.2	+6.1	69.7	44 53.6	+7.4	70.6	45 13.0	+8.9	71.6	45 31.5	+10.3	72.5	45 49.0	+11.7	73.5	32
33	43 28.8	+1.1	65.6	43 53.1	+2.4	66.5	44 16.7	+3.7	67.4	44 39.3	+5.1	68.3	45 01.0	+6.5	69.2	45 21.9	+7.8	70.2	45 41.8	+9.2	71.1	46 00.7	+10.6	72.1	33
34	43 29.9	0.0	64.2	43 55.5	+1.4	65.1	44 20.4	+2.7	66.0	44 44.4	+4.0	66.9	45 07.5	+5.4	67.8	45 29.7	+6.8	68.7	45 51.0	+8.1	69.7	46 11.3	+9.6	70.7	34
35	43 29.9	-0.9	62.9	43 56.9	+0.4	63.7	44 23.1	+1.7	64.6	44 48.4	+3.0	65.5	45 12.9	+4.3	66.4	45 36.5	+5.7	67.3	45 59.1	+7.1	68.3	46 20.9	+8.4	69.2	35
36	43 29.0	-1.9	61.5	43 57.3	-0.6	62.3	44 24.8	+0.6	63.2	44 51.4	+2.0	64.1	45 17.2	+3.3	65.0	45 42.2	+4.6	65.9	46 06.2	+6.0	66.8	46 29.3	+7.4	67.8	36
37	43 27.1	-2.9	60.1	43 56.7	-1.7	60.9	44 25.4	-0.3	61.8	44 53.4	+0.9	62.7	45 20.5	+2.3	63.6	45 46.8	+3.6	64.5	46 12.2	+5.0	65.4	46 36.7	+6.3	66.4	37
38	43 24.2	-3.8	58.7	43 55.0	-2.6	59.5	44 25.1	-1.4	60.4	44 54.3	-0.1	61.2	45 22.8	+1.1	62.1	45 50.4	+2.5	63.0	46 17.2	+3.8	64.0	46 43.0	+5.2	64.9	38
39	43 20.4	-4.9	57.4	43 52.4	-3.7	58.2	44 23.7	-2.5	59.0	44 54.2	-1.2	59.8	45 23.9	+0.2	60.7	45 52.9	+1.4	61.6	46 21.0	+2.7	62.5	46 48.2	+4.1	63.5	39
40	43 15.5	-5.8	56.0	43 48.7	-4.6	56.8	44 21.2	-3.4	57.6	44 53.0	-2.2	58.4	45 24.1	-1.0	59.3	45 54.3	+0.4	60.2	46 23.7	+1.7	61.1	46 52.3	+3.0	62.0	40
41	43 09.7	-6.8	54.6	43 44.1	-5.7	55.4	44 17.8	-4.5	56.2	44 50.8	-3.2	57.0	45 23.1	-2.0	57.9	45 54.7	-0.8	58.7	46 25.4	+0.5	59.6	46 55.3	+1.9	60.5	41
42	43 02.9	-7.8	53.3	43 38.4	-6.6	54.0	44 13.3	-5.4	54.8	44 47.6	-4.3	55.6	45 21.1	-3.0	56.4	45 53.9	-1.8	57.3	46 25.9	-0.5	58.2	46 57.2	+0.7	59.1	42
43	42 55.1	-8.8	51.9	43 31.8	-7.6	52.6	44 07.9	-6.5	53.4	44 43.3	-5.3	54.2	45 18.1	-4.2	55.0	45 52.1	-2.9	55.9	46 25.4	-1.7	56.7	46 57.9	-0.4	57.6	43
44	42 46.3	-9.6	50.6	43 24.2	-8.6	51.3	44 01.4	-7.5	52.0	44 38.0	-6.3	52.8	45 13.9	-5.1	53.6	45 49.2	-4.0	54.4	46 23.7	-2.7	55.3	46 57.5	-1.5	56.2	44
45	42 36.7	-10.6	49.2	43 15.6	-9.6	49.9	43 53.9	-8.4	50.7	44 31.7	-7.4	51.4	45 08.8	-6.2	52.2	45 45.2	-5.0	53.0	46 21.0	-3.9	53.8	46 56.0	-2.6	54.7	45
46	42 26.1	-11.6	47.9	43 06.0	-10.5	48.6	43 45.5	-9.5	49.3	44 24.3	-8.3	50.0	45 02.6	-7.3	50.8	45 40.2	-6.1	51.6	46 17.1	-4.9	52.4	46 53.4	-3.7	53.2	46
47	42 14.5	-12.4	46.5	42 55.5	-11.4	47.2	43 36.0	-10.4	47.9	44 16.0	-9.4	48.6	44 55.3	-8.3	49.4	45 34.1	-7.2	50.1	46 12.2	-6.0	50.9	46 49.7	-4.9	51.8	47
48	42 02.1	-13.4	45.2	42 44.1	-12.4	45.9	43 25.6	-11.4	46.6	44 06.6	-10.3	47.3	44 47.0	-9.2	48.0	45 26.9	-8.2	48.7	46 06.2	-7.1	49.5	46 44.8	-5.9	50.3	48
49	41 48.7	-14.2	43.9	42 31.7	-13.3	44.5	43 14.2	-12.3	45.2	43 56.3	-11.4	45.9	44 37.8	-10.3	46.6	45 18.7	-9.2	47.3	45 59.1	-8.2	48.1	46 38.9	-7.1	48.9	49
50	41 34.5	-15.1	42.6	42 18.4	-14.2	43.2	43 01.9	-13.2	43.9	43 44.9	-12.2	44.5	44 27.5	-11.3	45.2	45 09.5	-10.3	45.9	45 50.9	-9.2	46.7	46 31.8	-8.1	47.4	50
51	41 19.4	-16.0	41.3	42 04.2	-15.0	41.9	42 48.7	-14.2	42.5	43 32.7	-13.3	43.2	44 16.2	-12.3	43.8	44 59.2	-11.3	44.5	45 41.7	-10.2	45.2	46 23.7	-9.2	46.0	51
52	41 03.4	-16.8	40.0	41 49.2	-16.0	40.6	42 34.5	-15.1	41.2	43 19.4	-14.1	41.8	44 03.9	-13.2	42.5	44 47.9	-12.2	43.1	45 31.5	-11.3	43.8	46 14.5	-10.3	44.5	52
53	40 46.6	-17.6	38.8	41 33.2	-16.8	39.3	42 19.4	-15.9	39.9	43 05.3	-15.1	40.5	43 50.7	-14.2	41.1	44 35.7	-13.3	41.8	45 20.2	-12.3	42.4	46 04.2	-11.3	43.1	53
54	40 29.0	-18.5	37.5	41 16.4	-17.7	38.0	42 03.5	-16.9	38.6	42 50.2	-16.0	39.2	43 36.5	-15.1	39.8	44 22.4	-14.2	40.4	45 07.9	-13.3	41.0	45 52.9	-12.4	41.7	54
55	40 10.5	-19.2	36.3	40 58.7	-18.5	36.8	41 46.6	-17.7	37.3	42 34.2	-16.9	37.9	43 21.4	-16.1	38.4	44 08.2	-15.2	39.0	44 54.6	-14.3	39.7	45 40.5	-13.4	40.3	55
56	39 51.3	-20.1	35.0	40 40.2	-19.3	35.5	41 28.9	-18.5	36.0	42 17.3	-17.8	36.6	43 05.3	-17.0	37.1	43 53.0	-16.2	37.7	44 40.3	-15.3	38.3	45 27.1	-14.3	38.9	56
57	39 31.2	-20.8	33.8	40 20.9	-20.0	34.3	41 10.4	-19.4	34.8	41 59.5	-18.6	35.3	42 48.3	-17.8	35.8	43 36.8	-17.0	36.4	44 25.0	-16.2	36.9	45 12.8	-15.4	37.5	57
58	39 10.4	-21.5	32.6	40 00.9	-20.9	33.0	40 51.0	-20.2	33.5	41 40.9	-19.5	34.0	42 30.5	-18.7	34.5	43 19.8	-18.0	35.0	44 08.8	-17.2	35.6	44 57.4	-16.4	36.2	58
59	38 48.9	-22.3	31.4	39 40.0	-21.6	31.8	40 30.8	-20.9	32.3	41 21.4	-20.2	32.7	42 11.8	-19.6	33.2	43 01.8	-18.8	33.7	43 51.6	-18.1	34.3	44 41.0	-17.3	34.8	59
60	38 26.6	-23.0	30.2	39 18.4	-22.4	30.6	40 09.9	-21.7	31.0	41 01.2	-21.1	31.5	41 52.2	-20.4	31.9	42 43.0	-19.7	32.4	43 33.5	-19.0	32.9	44 23.7	-18.2	33.5	60
61	38 03.6	-23.7	29.0	38 56.0	-23.1	29.4	39 48.2	-22.5	29.8	40 40.1	-21.9	30.2	41 31.8	-21.2	30.7	42 23.3	-20.6	31.1	43 14.5	-19.9	31.6	44 05.5	-19.2	32.1	61
62	37 39.9	-24.3	27.9	38 32.9	-23.8	28.2	39 25.7	-23.3	28.6	40 18.2	-22.6	29.0	41 10.6	-22.0	29.4	42 02.7	-21.3	29.9	42 54.6	-20.7	30.3	43 46.3	-20.1	30.8	62
63	37 15.6	-25.0	26.7	38 09.1	-24.5	27.1	39 02.4	-23.9	27.4	39 55.6	-23.4	27.8	40 48.6	-22.8	28.2	41 41.4	-22.2	28.6	42 33.9	-21.6	29.1	43 26.2	-20.9	29.5	63
64	36 50.6	-25.7	25.6	37 44.6	-25.2	25.9	38 38.5	-24.6	26.2	39 32.2	-24.1	26.6	40 25.8	-23.6	27.0	41 19.2	-23.0	27.4	42 12.3	-22.4	27.8	43 05.3	-21.8	28.2	64
65	36 24.9	-26.3	24.4	37 19.4	-25.8	24.8	38 13.9	-25.4	25.1	39 08.1	-24.8	25.4	40 02.2	-24.3	25.8	40 56.2	-23.8	26.2	41 49.9	-23.2	26.5	42 43.5	-22.6	27.0	65
66	35 58.6	-26.9	23.3	36 53.6	-26.4	23.6	37 48.5	-25.9	23.9	38 43.3	-25.5	24.3	39 37.9	-25.0	24.6	40 32.4	-24.5	24.9	41 26.7	-23.9	25.3	42 20.9	-23.4	25.7	66
67	35 31.7	-27.5	22.2	36 27.2	-27.1	22.5	37 22.6	-26.7	22.8	38 17.8	-26.2	23.1	39 12.9	-25.7	23.4	40 07.9	-25.2	23.7	41 02.8	-24.8	24.1	41 57.5	-24.3	24.5	67
68	35 04.2	-28.1	21.1	36 00.1	-27.7	21.4	36 55.9	-27.2	21.7	37 51.6	-26.8	22.0	38 47.2	-26.4	22.3	39 42.7	-26.0	22.6	40 38.0	-25.5	22.9	41 33.2	-25.0	23.2	68
69	34 36.1	-28.6	20.1	35 32.4	-28.2	20.3	36 28.7	-27.9	20.6	37 24.8	-27.5	20.8	38 20.8	-27.0	21.1	39 16.7	-26.6	21.4	40 12.5	-26.2	21.7	41 08.2	-25.7	22.0	69
70	34 07.5	-29.2	19.0	35 04.2	-28.9	19.2	36 00.8	-28.5	19.5	36 57.3	-28.1	19.7	37 53.8	-27.7	20.0	38 50.1	-27.3	20.2	39 46.3	-26.9	20.5	40 42.5	-26.5	20.8	70
71	33 38.3	-29.7	17.9	34 35.3	-29.3	18.2	35 32.3	-29.0	18.4	36 29.2	-28.7	18.6	37 26.1	-28.4	18.8	38 22.8	-28.0	19.1	39 19.4	-27.5	19.4	40 16.0	-27.2	19.6	71
72	33 08.6	-30.2	16.9	34 06.0	-29.9	17.1	35 03.3	-29.6	17.3	36 00.5	-29.2	17.5	36 57.7	-28.9	17.7	37 54.8	-28.6	18.0	38 51.9	-28.3	18.2	39 48.8	-27.9	18.5	72
73	32 38.4	-30.8	15.9	33 36.1	-30.5	16.1	34 33.7	-30.2	16.2	35 31.3	-29.9	16.4	36 28.8	-29.6	16.7	37 26.2	-29.2	16.9	38 23.6	-28.9	17.1	39 20.9	-28.5	17.3	73
74	32 07.6	-31.2	14.9	33 05.6	-30.9	15.0	34 03.5	-30.6	15.2	35 01.4	-30.4	15.4	35 59.2	-30.1	15.6	36 57.0	-29.8	15.8	37 54.7	-29.5	16.0	38 52.4	-29.2	16.2	74
75	31 36.4	-31.6	13.9	32 34.7	-31.5	14.0	33 32.9	-31.2	14.2	34 31.0	-30.9	14.3	35 29.1	-30.6	14.5	36 27.2	-30.4	14.7	37 25.2	-30.1	14.9	38 23.2	-29.9	15.1	75
76	31 04.8	-32.2	12.9	32 03.2	-31.9	13.0	33 01.7	-31.7	13.1	34 00.1	-31.4	13.3	34 58.5	-31.2	13.5	35 56.8	-30.9	13.6	36 55.1	-30.7	13.8	37 53.3	-30.4	14.0	76
77	30 32.6	-32.5	11.9	31 31.3	-32.3	12.0	32 30.0	-32.1	12.1	33 28.7	-32.0	12.3	34 27.3	-31.7	12.4	35 25.9	-31.5	12.6	36 24.4	-31.3	12.7	37 22.9	-31.0	12.9	77
78	30 00.1	-33.0	10.9	30 59.0	-32.8	11.0	31 57.9	-32.6	11.1	32 56.7	-32.4	11.3	33 55.6	-32.3	11.4	34 54.4	-32.1	11.5	35 53.1	-31.8	11.7	36 51.9	-31.6	11.8	78
79	29 27.1	-33.4	9.9	30 26.2	-33.2	10.0	31 25.3	-33.1	10.1	32 24.3	-32.9	10.3	33 23.3	-32.7	10.4	34 22.3	-32.5	10.5	35 21.3	-32.3	10.6	36 20.3	-32.2	10.8	79
80	28 53.7	-33.8	9.0	29 53.0	-33.7	9.1	30 52.2	-33.5	9.2	31 51.4	-33.3	9.3	32 50.6	-33.2	9.4	33 49.8	-33.0	9.5	34 49.0	-32.9	9.6	35 48.1	-32.7	9.7	80
81	28 19.9	-34.2	8.1	29 19.3	-34.0	8.1	30 18.7	-33.9	8.2	31 18.1	-33.8	8.3	32 17.4	-33.6	8.4	33 16.8	-33.5	8.5	34 16.1	-33.3	8.6	35 15.4	-33.2	8.7	81
82	27 45.7	-34.5	7.1	28 45.3	-34.5	7.2	29 44.8	-34.3	7.3	30 44.3	-34.2	7.3	31 43.8	-34.1	7.4	32 43.3	-34.0	7.5	33 42.8	-33.9	7.6	34 42.2	-33.7	7.7	82
83	27 11.2	-34.9	6.2	28 10.8	-34.8	6.3	29 10.5	-34.6	6.3	30 10.1	-34.6	6.4	31 09.7	-34.5	6.4	32 09.3	-34.4	6.5	33 08.9	-34.3	6.6	34 08.5	-34.1	6.7	83
84	26 36.3	-35.3	5.3	27 36.0	-35.2	5.3	28 35.7	-35.0	5.4	29 35.5	-35.0	5.4	30 35.2	-34.9	5.5	31 34.9	-34.8	5.5	32 34.6	-34.7	5.6	33 34.4	-34.7	5.7	84
85	26 01.0	-35.6	4.4	27 00.8	-35.5	4.4	28 00.7	-35.5	4.5	29 00.5	-35.4	4.5	30 00.3	-35.3	4.5	31 00.1	-35.2	4.6	31 59.9	-35.2	4.6	32 59.7	-35.1	4.7	85
86	25 25.4	-35.9	3.5	26 25.3	-35.8	3.5	27 25.2	-35.8	3.6	28 25.1	-35.8	3.6	29 25.0	-35.7	3.6	30 24.9	-35.7	3.7	31 24.7	-35.6	3.7	32 24.6	-35.5	3.7	86
87	24 49.5	-36.2	2.6	25 49.5	-36.2	2.6	26 49.4	-36.1	2.6	27 49.3	-36.1	2.7	28 49.3	-36.1	2.7	29 49.2	-36.0	2.7	30 49.1	-36.0	2.8	31 49.1	-36.0	2.8	87
88	24 13.3	-36.5	1.7	25 13.3	-36.5	1.7	26 13.3	-36.5	1.8	27 13.2	-36.4	1.8	28 13.2	-36.4	1.8	29 13.2	-36.4	1.8	30 13.1	-36.3	1.8	31 13.1	-36.4	1.8	88
89	23 36.8	-36.8	0.9	24 36.8	-36.8	0.9	25 36.8	-36.8	0.9	26 36.8	-36.8	0.9	27 36.8	-36.8	0.9	28 36.8	-36.8	0.9	29 36.8	-36.8	0.9	30 36.7	-36.7	0.9	89
90	23 00.0	-37.1	0.0	24 00.0	-37.1	0.0	25 00.0	-37.1	0.0	26 00.0	-37.1	0.0	27 00.0	-37.1	0.0	28 00.0	-37.1	0.0	29 00.0	-37.1	0.0	30 00.0	-37.1	0.0	90
	23°			24°			25°			26°			27°			28°			29°			30°			

52°, 308° L.H.A. LATITUDE SAME NAME AS DECLINATION

288

Dec.	23° Hc	d	Z	24° Hc	d	Z	25° Hc	d	Z	26° Hc	d	Z
°	° ′	′	°	° ′	′	°	° ′	′	°	° ′	′	°
0	34 31.3	−28.7	107.0	34 13.5	−29.8	107.6	33 55.0	−30.8	108.3	33 35.8	−31.8	108.9
1	34 02.6	−29.3	108.0	33 43.7	−30.3	108.7	33 24.2	−31.4	109.3	33 04.0	−32.3	109.9
2	33 33.3	−29.8	109.1	33 13.4	−30.8	109.7	32 52.8	−31.8	110.3	32 31.7	−32.8	110.9
3	33 03.5	−30.3	110.1	32 42.6	−31.3	110.7	32 21.0	−32.3	111.3	31 58.9	−33.2	111.9
4	32 33.2	−30.8	111.2	32 11.3	−31.8	111.7	31 48.7	−32.7	112.3	31 25.7	−33.7	112.9
5	32 02.4	−31.3	112.2	31 39.5	−32.3	112.7	31 16.0	−33.2	113.3	30 52.0	−34.1	113.9
6	31 31.1	−31.7	113.2	31 07.2	−32.7	113.7	30 42.8	−33.6	114.3	30 17.9	−34.5	114.8
7	30 59.4	−32.2	114.2	30 34.5	−33.1	114.7	30 09.2	−34.0	115.2	29 43.4	−34.9	115.8
8	30 27.2	−32.7	115.1	30 01.4	−33.5	115.7	29 35.2	−34.5	116.2	29 08.5	−35.3	116.7
9	29 54.5	−33.0	116.1	29 27.9	−34.0	116.6	29 00.7	−34.8	117.1	28 33.2	−35.7	117.6
10	29 21.5	−33.5	117.1	28 53.9	−34.3	117.6	28 25.9	−35.2	118.1	27 57.5	−36.1	118.5
11	28 48.0	−33.9	118.0	28 19.6	−34.7	118.5	27 50.7	−35.5	119.0	27 21.4	−36.3	119.4
12	28 14.1	−34.2	119.0	27 44.9	−35.1	119.4	27 15.2	−35.9	119.9	26 45.1	−36.7	120.3
13	27 39.9	−34.6	119.9	27 09.8	−35.5	120.3	26 39.3	−36.3	120.8	26 08.4	−37.1	121.2
14	27 05.3	−35.0	120.8	26 34.3	−35.7	121.3	26 03.0	−36.5	121.7	25 31.3	−37.3	122.1
15	26 30.3	−35.3	121.7	25 58.6	−36.1	122.1	25 26.5	−36.9	122.6	24 54.0	−37.6	122.9
16	25 55.0	−35.6	122.6	25 22.5	−36.4	123.0	24 49.6	−37.2	123.4	24 16.4	−37.9	123.8
17	25 19.4	−36.0	123.5	24 46.1	−36.8	123.9	24 12.4	−37.4	124.3	23 38.5	−38.2	124.7
18	24 43.4	−36.3	124.4	24 09.3	−37.0	124.8	23 35.0	−37.8	125.1	23 00.3	−38.5	125.5
19	24 07.1	−36.5	125.3	23 32.3	−37.3	125.6	22 57.2	−38.0	126.0	22 21.8	−38.7	126.3
20	23 30.6	−36.9	126.1	22 55.0	−37.5	126.5	22 19.2	−38.2	126.8	21 43.1	−38.9	127.1
21	22 53.7	−37.1	127.0	22 17.5	−37.8	127.3	21 41.0	−38.5	127.7	21 04.2	−39.2	128.0
22	22 16.6	−37.4	127.9	21 39.7	−38.1	128.2	21 02.5	−38.8	128.5	20 25.0	−39.4	128.8
23	21 39.2	−37.6	128.7	21 01.6	−38.3	129.0	20 23.7	−39.0	129.3	19 45.6	−39.6	129.6
24	21 01.6	−37.9	129.5	20 23.3	−38.6	129.8	19 44.7	−39.1	130.1	19 06.0	−39.8	130.4
25	20 23.7	−38.1	130.4	19 44.7	−38.7	130.6	19 05.6	−39.4	130.9	18 26.2	−40.1	131.2
26	19 45.6	−38.3	131.2	19 06.0	−39.0	131.5	18 26.2	−39.6	131.7	17 46.1	−40.2	131.9
27	19 07.3	−38.6	132.0	18 27.0	−39.2	132.3	17 46.6	−39.8	132.5	17 05.9	−40.3	132.7
28	18 28.7	−38.8	132.8	17 47.8	−39.3	133.1	17 06.8	−40.0	133.3	16 25.6	−40.6	133.5
29	17 49.9	−38.9	133.6	17 08.5	−39.6	133.8	16 26.8	−40.1	134.1	15 45.0	−40.7	134.3
30	17 11.0	−39.1	134.4	16 28.9	−39.7	134.6	15 46.7	−40.3	134.8	15 04.3	−40.8	135.0
31	16 31.9	−39.4	135.2	15 49.2	−39.9	135.4	15 06.4	−40.4	135.6	14 23.5	−41.0	135.8
32	15 52.5	−39.5	136.0	15 09.3	−40.0	136.2	14 26.0	−40.6	136.4	13 42.5	−41.2	136.5
33	15 13.0	−39.6	136.8	14 29.3	−40.2	137.0	13 45.4	−40.8	137.1	13 01.3	−41.2	137.3
34	14 33.4	−39.8	137.5	13 49.1	−40.4	137.7	13 04.6	−40.8	137.9	12 20.1	−41.4	138.0
35	13 53.6	−39.9	138.3	13 08.7	−40.4	138.5	12 23.8	−41.0	138.6	11 38.7	−41.5	138.8
36	13 13.7	−40.1	139.1	12 28.3	−40.6	139.2	11 42.8	−41.1	139.4	10 57.2	−41.6	139.5
37	12 33.6	−40.2	139.9	11 47.7	−40.8	140.0	11 01.7	−41.2	140.1	10 15.6	−41.7	140.2
38	11 53.4	−40.4	140.6	11 06.9	−40.8	140.7	10 20.5	−41.4	140.9	9 33.9	−41.8	141.0
39	11 13.0	−40.4	141.4	10 26.1	−40.9	141.5	9 39.1	−41.4	141.6	8 52.1	−41.9	141.7
40	10 32.6	−40.6	142.1	9 45.2	−41.0	142.2	8 57.7	−41.5	142.3	8 10.2	−41.9	142.4
41	9 52.0	−40.6	142.9	9 04.2	−41.1	143.0	8 16.2	−41.5	143.1	7 28.3	−42.1	143.1
42	9 11.4	−40.8	143.6	8 23.1	−41.2	143.7	7 34.7	−41.7	143.8	6 46.2	−42.1	143.9
43	8 30.6	−40.8	144.4	7 41.9	−41.3	144.4	6 53.0	−41.7	144.5	6 04.1	−42.1	144.6
44	7 49.8	−40.9	145.1	7 00.6	−41.4	145.2	6 11.3	−41.8	145.2	5 22.0	−42.2	145.3
45	7 08.9	−41.0	145.8	6 19.2	−41.4	145.9	5 29.5	−41.8	146.0	4 39.8	−42.2	146.0
46	6 27.9	−41.0	146.6	5 37.8	−41.4	146.6	4 47.7	−41.8	146.7	3 57.6	−42.3	146.7
47	5 46.9	−41.1	147.3	4 56.4	−41.5	147.4	4 05.9	−41.9	147.4	3 15.3	−42.2	147.4
48	5 05.8	−41.1	148.0	4 14.9	−41.5	148.1	3 24.0	−42.0	148.1	2 33.0	−42.3	148.1
49	4 24.7	−41.2	148.8	3 33.4	−41.6	148.8	2 42.0	−41.9	148.8	1 50.7	−42.4	148.9
50	3 43.5	−41.2	149.5	2 51.8	−41.6	149.5	2 00.1	−42.0	149.5	1 08.3	−42.3	149.6
51	3 02.3	−41.3	150.2	2 10.2	−41.6	150.2	1 18.1	−42.0	150.3	0 26.0	−42.4	150.3
52	2 21.0	−41.3	151.0	1 28.6	−41.7	151.0	0 36.1	−42.0	151.0	0 16.4	+42.3	29.0
53	1 39.7	−41.3	151.7	0 46.9	−41.6	151.7	0 05.9	+42.0	28.3	0 58.7	+42.4	28.3
54	0 58.4	−41.3	152.4	0 05.3	−41.7	152.4	0 47.9	+42.0	27.6	1 41.1	+42.3	27.6
55	0 17.1	−41.3	153.1	0 36.4	+41.6	26.9	1 29.9	+42.0	26.9	2 23.4	+42.3	26.9
56	0 24.2	+41.2	26.1	1 18.0	+41.6	26.2	2 11.9	+41.9	26.2	3 05.7	+42.3	26.2
57	1 05.4	+41.3	25.4	1 59.6	+41.6	25.4	2 53.8	+41.9	25.5	3 48.0	+42.2	25.5
58	1 46.7	+41.3	24.7	2 41.2	+41.6	24.7	3 35.7	+41.9	24.7	4 30.2	+42.2	24.8
59	2 28.0	+41.3	24.0	3 22.8	+41.6	24.0	4 17.6	+41.9	24.0	5 12.4	+42.2	24.1
60	3 09.3	+41.2	23.2	4 04.4	+41.5	23.3	4 59.5	+41.8	23.3	5 54.6	+42.1	23.3
61	3 50.5	+41.1	22.5	4 45.9	+41.5	22.5	5 41.3	+41.8	22.6	6 36.7	+42.0	22.6
62	4 31.6	+41.2	21.8	5 27.4	+41.4	21.8	6 23.1	+41.6	21.9	7 18.7	+42.0	21.9
63	5 12.8	+41.1	21.1	6 08.8	+41.3	21.1	7 04.7	+41.7	21.1	8 00.7	+41.9	21.2
64	5 53.9	+41.0	20.3	6 50.1	+41.3	20.4	7 46.4	+41.5	20.4	8 42.6	+41.8	20.5
65	6 34.9	+41.0	19.6	7 31.4	+41.2	19.6	8 27.9	+41.5	19.7	9 24.4	+41.7	19.7
66	7 15.9	+40.8	18.9	8 12.6	+41.2	18.9	9 09.4	+41.4	18.9	10 06.1	+41.7	19.0
67	7 56.7	+40.9	18.1	8 53.8	+41.0	18.2	9 50.8	+41.3	18.2	10 47.8	+41.5	18.3
68	8 37.6	+40.7	17.4	9 34.8	+41.0	17.4	10 32.1	+41.1	17.5	11 29.3	+41.4	17.5
69	9 18.3	+40.6	16.6	10 15.8	+40.8	16.7	11 13.2	+41.1	16.7	12 10.7	+41.3	16.8
70	9 58.9	+40.6	15.9	10 56.6	+40.8	15.9	11 54.3	+41.0	16.0	12 52.0	+41.1	16.0
71	10 39.5	+40.4	15.1	11 37.4	+40.6	15.2	12 35.3	+40.8	15.2	13 33.1	+41.1	15.3
72	11 19.9	+40.3	14.4	12 18.0	+40.5	14.4	13 16.1	+40.7	14.5	14 14.2	+40.9	14.5
73	12 00.2	+40.2	13.6	12 58.5	+40.4	13.7	13 56.8	+40.5	13.7	14 55.1	+40.7	13.8
74	12 40.4	+40.0	12.9	13 38.9	+40.2	12.9	14 37.3	+40.4	13.0	15 35.8	+40.6	13.0
75	13 20.4	+40.0	12.1	14 19.1	+40.1	12.2	15 17.7	+40.3	12.2	16 16.4	+40.4	12.3
76	14 00.4	+39.7	11.3	14 59.2	+39.9	11.4	15 58.0	+40.1	11.4	16 56.8	+40.2	11.5
77	14 40.1	+39.7	10.6	15 39.1	+39.8	10.6	16 38.1	+39.9	10.7	17 37.0	+40.1	10.7
78	15 19.8	+39.4	9.8	16 18.9	+39.6	9.8	17 18.0	+39.7	9.9	18 17.1	+39.9	9.9
79	15 59.2	+39.3	9.0	16 58.5	+39.4	9.0	17 57.7	+39.6	9.1	18 57.0	+39.6	9.1
80	16 38.5	+39.1	8.2	17 37.9	+39.2	8.3	18 37.3	+39.3	8.3	19 36.6	+39.5	8.4
81	17 17.6	+38.9	7.4	18 17.1	+39.0	7.5	19 16.6	+39.1	7.5	20 16.1	+39.2	7.6
82	17 56.5	+38.8	6.6	18 56.1	+38.8	6.7	19 55.7	+38.9	6.7	20 55.3	+39.0	6.7
83	18 35.3	+38.5	5.8	19 34.9	+38.6	5.9	20 34.6	+38.7	5.9	21 34.3	+38.8	5.9
84	19 13.8	+38.3	5.0	20 13.5	+38.4	5.0	21 13.3	+38.4	5.1	22 13.1	+38.5	5.1
85	19 52.1	+38.0	4.2	20 51.9	+38.1	4.2	21 51.7	+38.2	4.2	22 51.6	+38.2	4.3
86	20 30.1	+37.9	3.4	21 30.0	+37.9	3.4	22 29.9	+38.0	3.4	23 29.8	+38.0	3.4
87	21 08.0	+37.6	2.5	22 07.9	+37.7	2.6	23 07.9	+37.6	2.6	24 07.8	+37.7	2.6
88	21 45.6	+37.3	1.7	22 45.6	+37.3	1.7	23 45.5	+37.4	1.7	24 45.5	+37.4	1.7
89	22 22.9	+37.1	0.9	23 22.9	+37.1	0.9	24 22.9	+37.1	0.9	25 22.9	+37.1	0.9
90	23 00.0	+36.8	0.0	24 00.0	+36.8	0.0	25 00.0	+36.8	0.0	26 00.0	+36.8	0.0
	23°			24°			25°			26°		

Dec.	27° Hc	d	Z	28° Hc	d	Z	29° Hc	d	Z	30° Hc	d	Z
°	° ′	′	°	° ′	′	°	° ′	′	°	° ′	′	°
0	33 16.1	−32.8	109.5	32 55.7	−33.8	110.1	32 34.8	−34.8	110.7	32 13.2	−35.6	111.3
1	32 43.3	−33.3	110.5	32 21.9	−34.2	111.1	32 00.0	−35.1	111.7	31 37.6	−36.1	112.3
2	32 10.0	−33.8	111.5	31 47.7	−34.7	112.1	31 24.9	−35.6	112.7	31 01.5	−36.5	113.2
3	31 36.2	−34.1	112.5	31 13.0	−35.1	113.1	30 49.3	−36.0	113.6	30 25.0	−36.9	114.1
4	31 02.1	−34.6	113.4	30 37.9	−35.5	114.0	30 13.3	−36.4	114.5	29 48.1	−37.2	115.1
5	30 27.5	−35.0	114.4	30 02.4	−35.9	114.9	29 36.9	−36.8	115.4	29 10.9	−37.6	116.0
6	29 52.5	−35.4	115.3	29 26.5	−36.2	115.9	29 00.1	−37.1	116.4	28 33.3	−38.0	116.8
7	29 17.1	−35.8	116.3	28 50.3	−36.7	116.8	28 23.0	−37.4	117.3	27 55.3	−38.3	117.7
8	28 41.3	−36.2	117.2	28 13.6	−37.0	117.7	27 45.6	−37.8	118.1	27 17.0	−38.5	118.6
9	28 05.1	−36.5	118.1	27 36.6	−37.3	118.6	27 07.8	−38.2	119.0	26 38.5	−38.9	119.5
10	27 28.6	−36.8	119.0	26 59.3	−37.6	119.4	26 29.6	−38.4	119.9	25 59.6	−39.2	120.3
11	26 51.8	−37.2	119.9	26 21.7	−38.0	120.3	25 51.2	−38.7	120.7	25 20.4	−39.5	121.1
12	26 14.6	−37.5	120.8	25 43.7	−38.2	121.2	25 12.5	−39.0	121.6	24 40.9	−39.8	122.0
13	25 37.1	−37.8	121.6	25 05.5	−38.6	122.0	24 33.5	−39.3	122.4	24 01.1	−40.0	122.8
14	24 59.3	−38.1	122.5	24 26.9	−38.8	122.9	23 54.2	−39.6	123.2	23 21.1	−40.2	123.6
15	24 21.2	−38.4	123.3	23 48.1	−39.1	123.7	23 14.6	−39.8	124.1	22 40.9	−40.5	124.4
16	23 42.8	−38.6	124.2	23 09.0	−39.4	124.5	22 34.8	−40.0	124.9	22 00.4	−40.8	125.2
17	23 04.2	−38.9	125.0	22 29.6	−39.6	125.4	21 54.8	−40.3	125.7	21 19.6	−40.9	126.0
18	22 25.3	−39.2	125.8	21 50.0	−39.8	126.2	21 14.5	−40.5	126.5	20 38.7	−41.2	126.8
19	21 46.1	−39.3	126.7	21 10.2	−40.1	127.0	20 34.0	−40.7	127.3	19 57.5	−41.3	127.6
20	21 06.8	−39.7	127.5	20 30.1	−40.2	127.8	19 53.3	−40.9	128.1	19 16.2	−41.6	128.3
21	20 27.1	−39.8	128.3	19 49.9	−40.5	128.6	19 12.4	−41.2	128.8	18 34.6	−41.7	129.1
22	19 47.3	−40.0	129.1	19 09.4	−40.7	129.3	18 31.2	−41.3	129.6	17 52.9	−41.9	129.9
23	19 07.3	−40.3	129.9	18 28.7	−40.9	130.1	17 49.9	−41.4	130.4	17 11.0	−42.1	130.6
24	18 27.0	−40.4	130.6	17 47.8	−41.0	130.9	17 08.5	−41.7	131.1	16 28.9	−42.2	131.3
25	17 46.6	−40.7	131.4	17 06.8	−41.2	131.6	16 26.8	−41.8	131.9	15 46.7	−42.4	132.1
26	17 05.9	−40.8	132.2	16 25.6	−41.4	132.4	15 45.0	−41.9	132.6	15 04.3	−42.5	132.8
27	16 25.1	−40.9	132.9	15 44.2	−41.5	133.2	15 03.1	−42.1	133.4	14 21.8	−42.6	133.5
28	15 44.2	−41.1	133.7	15 02.7	−41.7	133.9	14 21.0	−42.3	134.1	13 39.2	−42.8	134.3
29	15 03.1	−41.3	134.5	14 21.0	−41.8	134.7	13 38.7	−42.3	134.8	12 56.4	−42.9	135.0
30	14 21.8	−41.4	135.2	13 39.2	−42.0	135.4	12 56.4	−42.5	135.6	12 13.5	−43.0	135.7
31	13 40.4	−41.5	136.0	12 57.2	−42.1	136.1	12 13.9	−42.6	136.3	11 30.5	−43.1	136.4
32	12 58.9	−41.7	136.7	12 15.1	−42.2	136.9	11 31.3	−42.7	137.0	10 47.4	−43.2	137.1
33	12 17.2	−41.8	137.4	11 32.9	−42.3	137.6	10 48.6	−42.8	137.7	10 04.2	−43.3	137.8
34	11 35.4	−41.9	138.2	10 50.6	−42.4	138.3	10 05.8	−42.9	138.4	9 20.9	−43.4	138.5
35	10 53.5	−42.0	138.9	10 08.2	−42.4	139.0	9 22.9	−43.0	139.1	8 37.5	−43.5	139.2
36	10 11.5	−42.1	139.6	9 25.8	−42.6	139.7	8 39.9	−43.0	139.8	7 54.0	−43.5	139.9
37	9 29.4	−42.2	140.4	8 43.2	−42.7	140.5	7 56.9	−43.1	140.5	7 10.5	−43.6	140.6
38	8 47.2	−42.2	141.1	8 00.5	−42.7	141.2	7 13.8	−43.2	141.2	6 26.9	−43.6	141.3
39	8 05.0	−42.4	141.8	7 17.8	−42.8	141.9	6 30.6	−43.3	141.9	5 43.3	−43.7	142.0
40	7 22.6	−42.4	142.5	6 35.0	−42.9	142.6	5 47.3	−43.3	142.6	4 59.6	−43.7	142.7
41	6 40.2	−42.4	143.2	5 52.1	−42.9	143.3	5 04.0	−43.3	143.3	4 15.9	−43.8	143.4
42	5 57.8	−42.6	143.9	5 09.2	−42.9	144.0	4 20.7	−43.4	144.0	3 32.1	−43.8	144.1
43	5 15.2	−42.5	144.6	4 26.3	−43.0	144.7	3 37.3	−43.4	144.7	2 48.3	−43.8	144.8
44	4 32.7	−42.6	145.3	3 43.3	−43.0	145.4	2 53.9	−43.4	145.4	2 04.5	−43.8	145.4
45	3 50.1	−42.7	146.1	3 00.3	−43.1	146.1	2 10.5	−43.5	146.1	1 20.7	−43.9	146.1
46	3 07.4	−42.7	146.8	2 17.2	−43.1	146.8	1 27.0	−43.4	146.8	0 36.8	−43.8	146.8
47	2 24.7	−42.7	147.5	1 34.1	−43.0	147.5	0 43.6	−43.5	147.5	0 07.0	+43.9	32.5
48	1 42.0	−42.7	148.2	0 51.1	−43.1	148.2	0 00.1	−43.5	148.2	0 50.9	+43.9	31.8
49	0 59.3	−42.7	148.9	0 08.0	−43.1	148.9	0 43.4	+43.5	31.1	1 34.8	+43.8	31.1
50	0 16.6	−42.7	149.6	0 35.1	+43.1	30.4	1 26.9	+43.4	30.4	2 18.6	+43.8	30.5
51	0 26.1	+42.7	29.7	1 18.2	+43.1	29.7	2 10.3	+43.4	29.8	3 02.4	+43.8	29.8
52	1 08.8	+42.7	29.0	2 01.3	+43.1	29.0	2 53.7	+43.5	29.1	3 46.2	+43.7	29.1
53	1 51.5	+42.7	28.3	2 44.4	+43.0	28.3	3 37.2	+43.3	28.4	4 29.9	+43.8	28.4
54	2 34.2	+42.7	27.6	3 27.4	+43.0	27.6	4 20.5	+43.4	27.7	5 13.7	+43.6	27.7
55	3 16.9	+42.6	26.9	4 10.4	+43.0	26.9	5 03.9	+43.3	27.0	5 57.3	+43.7	27.0
56	3 59.5	+42.7	26.2	4 53.4	+42.9	26.2	5 47.2	+43.2	26.3	6 41.0	+43.5	26.3
57	4 42.2	+42.5	25.5	5 36.3	+42.9	25.5	6 30.4	+43.2	25.6	7 24.5	+43.5	25.6
58	5 24.7	+42.5	24.8	6 19.2	+42.8	24.8	7 13.6	+43.1	24.9	8 08.0	+43.4	24.9
59	6 07.2	+42.5	24.1	7 02.0	+42.7	24.1	7 56.7	+43.1	24.2	8 51.4	+43.4	24.3
60	6 49.7	+42.4	23.4	7 44.7	+42.7	23.4	8 39.8	+43.0	23.5	9 34.8	+43.3	23.6
61	7 32.1	+42.3	22.7	8 27.4	+42.6	22.7	9 22.8	+42.8	22.8	10 18.1	+43.1	22.8
62	8 14.4	+42.2	22.0	9 10.0	+42.6	22.0	10 05.6	+42.8	22.1	11 01.2	+43.1	22.1
63	8 56.6	+42.2	21.2	9 52.6	+42.4	21.3	10 48.4	+42.7	21.4	11 44.3	+43.0	21.4
64	9 38.8	+42.1	20.5	10 35.0	+42.3	20.6	11 31.1	+42.6	20.6	12 27.3	+42.8	20.7
65	10 20.9	+41.9	19.8	11 17.3	+42.2	19.9	12 13.7	+42.5	19.9	13 10.1	+42.8	20.0
66	11 02.8	+41.9	19.1	11 59.5	+42.2	19.1	12 56.2	+42.4	19.2	13 52.9	+42.6	19.3
67	11 44.7	+41.8	18.3	12 41.7	+42.0	18.4	13 38.6	+42.2	18.5	14 35.5	+42.5	18.6
68	12 26.5	+41.6	17.6	13 23.7	+41.8	17.7	14 20.8	+42.1	17.7	15 18.0	+42.3	17.8
69	13 08.1	+41.5	16.9	14 05.5	+41.8	16.9	15 02.9	+42.0	17.0	16 00.3	+42.2	17.1
70	13 49.6	+41.4	16.1	14 47.3	+41.6	16.2	15 44.9	+41.8	16.3	16 42.5	+42.0	16.3
71	14 31.0	+41.2	15.4	15 28.9	+41.4	15.4	16 26.7	+41.6	15.5	17 24.5	+41.8	15.6
72	15 12.2	+41.1	14.6	16 10.3	+41.3	14.7	17 08.3	+41.5	14.8	18 06.3	+41.7	14.8
73	15 53.3	+40.9	13.9	16 51.6	+41.1	13.9	17 49.8	+41.3	14.0	18 48.0	+41.5	14.1
74	16 34.2	+40.8	13.1	17 32.7	+40.9	13.2	18 31.1	+41.1	13.2	19 29.5	+41.3	13.3
75	17 15.0	+40.6	12.3	18 13.6	+40.8	12.4	19 12.2	+40.9	12.5	20 10.8	+41.1	12.5
76	17 55.6	+40.4	11.6	18 54.4	+40.5	11.6	19 53.1	+40.7	11.7	20 51.9	+40.9	11.8
77	18 36.0	+40.2	10.8	19 34.9	+40.4	10.8	20 33.8	+40.5	10.9	21 32.8	+40.6	11.0
78	19 16.2	+40.0	10.0	20 15.3	+40.1	10.1	21 14.3	+40.3	10.1	22 13.4	+40.4	10.2
79	19 56.2	+39.8	9.2	20 55.4	+39.9	9.3	21 54.6	+40.1	9.3	22 53.8	+40.2	9.4
80	20 36.0	+39.6	8.4	21 35.3	+39.7	8.5	22 34.7	+39.8	8.5	23 34.0	+39.9	8.6
81	21 15.6	+39.3	7.6	22 15.0	+39.5	7.7	23 14.5	+39.5	7.7	24 13.9	+39.7	7.8
82	21 54.9	+39.1	6.8	22 54.5	+39.2	6.8	23 54.0	+39.3	6.9	24 53.6	+39.4	6.9
83	22 34.0	+38.8	6.0	23 33.7	+38.9	6.0	24 33.3	+39.0	6.1	25 33.0	+39.1	6.1
84	23 12.8	+38.6	5.1	24 12.6	+38.6	5.2	25 12.3	+38.8	5.2	26 12.1	+38.8	5.3
85	23 51.4	+38.3	4.3	24 51.2	+38.4	4.3	25 51.1	+38.4	4.4	26 50.9	+38.5	4.4
86	24 29.7	+38.0	3.5	25 29.6	+38.1	3.5	26 29.5	+38.1	3.5	27 29.4	+38.2	3.6
87	25 07.7	+37.8	2.6	26 07.7	+37.8	2.6	27 07.6	+37.8	2.7	28 07.6	+37.8	2.7
88	25 45.5	+37.4	1.7	26 45.4	+37.5	1.8	27 45.4	+37.5	1.8	28 45.4	+37.5	1.8
89	26 22.9	+37.1	0.9	27 22.9	+37.1	0.9	28 22.9	+37.1	0.9	29 22.9	+37.1	0.9
90	27 00.0	+36.8	0.0	28 00.0	+36.8	0.0	29 00.0	+36.8	0.0	30 00.0	+36.7	0.0
	27°			28°			29°			30°		

S. Lat. {L.H.A. greater than 180° ....Zn=180°−Z
{L.H.A. less than 180°...........Zn=180°+Z

53°, 307° L.H.A. LATITUDE **SAME** NAME AS DECLINATION N. Lat. {L.H.A. greater than 180° .....Zn=Z / L.H.A. less than 180°............Zn=360°–Z

Dec.	23° Hc	d	Z	24° Hc	d	Z	25° Hc	d	Z	26° Hc	d	Z
°	° ′	′	°	° ′	′	°	° ′	′	°	° ′	′	°
0	33 38.4	+27.9	106.4	33 21.1	+29.0	107.0	33 03.2	+30.0	107.7	32 44.7	+31.1	108.3
1	34 06.3	+27.3	105.3	33 50.1	+28.4	106.0	33 33.2	+29.5	106.6	33 15.8	+30.5	107.3
2	34 33.6	+26.8	104.3	34 18.5	+27.8	104.9	34 02.7	+28.9	105.6	33 46.3	+30.0	106.2
3	35 00.4	+26.1	103.2	34 46.3	+27.3	103.9	34 31.6	+28.4	104.5	34 16.3	+29.4	105.2
4	35 26.5	+25.6	102.1	35 13.6	+26.7	102.8	35 00.0	+27.8	103.4	34 45.7	+28.9	104.1
5	35 52.1	+24.9	101.0	35 40.3	+26.1	101.7	35 27.8	+27.2	102.4	35 14.6	+28.4	103.1
6	36 17.0	+24.3	99.8	36 06.4	+25.5	100.6	35 55.0	+26.6	101.3	35 43.0	+27.7	102.0
7	36 41.3	+23.6	98.7	36 31.9	+24.8	99.4	36 21.6	+26.0	100.2	36 10.7	+27.1	100.9
8	37 04.9	+23.0	97.5	36 56.7	+24.1	98.3	36 47.6	+25.4	99.0	36 37.8	+26.5	99.8
9	37 27.9	+22.3	96.4	37 20.8	+23.5	97.1	37 13.0	+24.7	97.9	37 04.3	+25.9	98.6
10	37 50.2	+21.5	95.2	37 44.3	+22.8	96.0	37 37.7	+24.0	96.8	37 30.2	+25.2	97.5
11	38 11.7	+20.9	94.0	38 07.1	+22.1	94.8	38 01.7	+23.3	95.6	37 55.4	+24.6	96.4
12	38 32.6	+20.1	92.8	38 29.2	+21.4	93.6	38 25.0	+22.6	94.4	38 20.0	+23.8	95.2
13	38 52.7	+19.4	91.6	38 50.6	+20.6	92.4	38 47.6	+21.9	93.2	38 43.8	+23.2	94.0
14	39 12.1	+18.6	90.4	39 11.2	+19.9	91.2	39 09.5	+21.2	92.0	39 07.0	+22.4	92.8
15	39 30.7	+17.8	89.2	39 31.1	+19.1	90.0	39 30.7	+20.3	90.8	39 29.4	+21.6	91.6
16	39 48.5	+17.0	87.9	39 50.2	+18.3	88.8	39 51.0	+19.7	89.6	39 51.0	+20.9	90.4
17	40 05.5	+16.2	86.7	40 08.5	+17.5	87.5	40 10.7	+18.8	88.4	40 11.9	+20.1	89.2
18	40 21.7	+15.3	85.4	40 26.0	+16.7	86.3	40 29.5	+18.0	87.1	40 32.0	+19.4	88.0
19	40 37.0	+14.6	84.2	40 42.7	+15.9	85.0	40 47.5	+17.2	85.9	40 51.4	+18.5	86.7
20	40 51.6	+13.6	82.9	40 58.6	+15.0	83.7	41 04.7	+16.3	84.6	41 09.9	+17.6	85.5
21	41 05.2	+12.8	81.6	41 13.6	+14.1	82.4	41 21.0	+15.5	83.3	41 27.5	+16.8	84.2
22	41 18.0	+11.9	80.3	41 27.7	+13.3	81.2	41 36.5	+14.6	82.0	41 44.3	+16.0	82.9
23	41 29.9	+11.1	79.0	41 41.0	+12.3	79.8	41 51.1	+13.7	80.7	42 00.3	+15.1	81.6
24	41 41.0	+10.1	77.7	41 53.3	+11.5	78.5	42 04.8	+12.8	79.4	42 15.4	+14.1	80.3
25	41 51.1	+9.2	76.3	42 04.8	+10.6	77.2	42 17.6	+11.9	78.1	42 29.5	+13.3	79.0
26	42 00.3	+8.3	75.0	42 15.4	+9.6	75.9	42 29.5	+11.0	76.8	42 42.8	+12.4	77.7
27	42 08.6	+7.3	73.7	42 25.0	+8.7	74.6	42 40.5	+10.1	75.4	42 55.2	+11.4	76.3
28	42 15.9	+6.4	72.3	42 33.7	+7.8	73.2	42 50.6	+9.1	74.1	43 06.6	+10.4	75.0
29	42 22.3	+5.5	71.0	42 41.5	+6.8	71.9	42 59.7	+8.1	72.7	43 17.0	+9.5	73.6
30	42 27.8	+4.5	69.6	42 48.3	+5.8	70.5	43 07.8	+7.2	71.4	43 26.5	+8.6	72.3
31	42 32.3	+3.6	68.3	42 54.1	+4.9	69.2	43 15.0	+6.2	70.0	43 35.1	+7.5	70.9
32	42 35.9	+2.6	66.9	42 59.0	+3.9	67.8	43 21.2	+5.3	68.7	43 42.6	+6.6	69.5
33	42 38.5	+1.6	65.6	43 02.9	+2.9	66.4	43 26.5	+4.2	67.3	43 49.2	+5.6	68.2
34	42 40.1	+0.7	64.2	43 05.8	+2.0	65.1	43 30.7	+3.3	65.9	43 54.8	+4.6	66.8
35	42 40.8	-0.3	62.9	43 07.8	+1.0	63.7	43 34.0	+2.2	64.5	43 59.4	+3.5	65.4
36	42 40.5	-1.3	61.5	43 08.8	0.0	62.3	43 36.2	+1.3	63.2	44 02.9	+2.6	64.0
37	42 39.2	-2.2	60.1	43 08.8	-1.0	60.9	43 37.5	+0.3	61.8	44 05.5	+1.5	62.6
38	42 37.0	-3.2	58.8	43 07.8	-2.0	59.6	43 37.8	-0.7	60.4	44 07.0	+0.6	61.2
39	42 33.8	-4.1	57.4	43 05.8	-2.9	58.2	43 37.1	-1.8	59.0	44 07.6	-0.5	59.8
40	42 29.7	-5.1	56.1	43 02.9	-4.0	56.8	43 35.3	-2.7	57.6	44 07.1	-1.5	58.5
41	42 24.6	-6.0	54.7	42 58.9	-4.9	55.5	43 32.6	-3.7	56.3	44 05.6	-2.5	57.1
42	42 18.6	-7.0	53.4	42 54.0	-5.8	54.1	43 28.9	-4.7	54.9	44 03.1	-3.6	55.7
43	42 11.6	-7.9	52.0	42 48.2	-6.8	52.8	43 24.2	-5.7	53.5	43 59.5	-4.5	54.3
44	42 03.7	-8.9	50.7	42 41.4	-7.8	51.4	43 18.5	-6.7	52.1	43 55.0	-5.5	52.9
45	41 54.8	-9.8	49.4	42 33.6	-8.7	50.1	43 11.8	-7.6	50.8	43 49.5	-6.5	51.5
46	41 45.0	-10.6	48.0	42 24.9	-9.6	48.7	43 04.2	-8.6	49.4	43 43.0	-7.6	50.1
47	41 34.4	-11.6	46.7	42 15.3	-10.6	47.4	42 55.6	-9.5	48.1	43 35.4	-8.4	48.8
48	41 22.8	-12.5	45.4	42 04.7	-11.5	46.1	42 46.1	-10.5	46.7	43 27.0	-9.5	47.4
49	41 10.3	-13.3	44.1	41 53.2	-12.4	44.7	42 35.6	-11.4	45.4	43 17.5	-10.4	46.0
50	40 57.0	-14.2	42.8	41 40.8	-13.3	43.4	42 24.2	-12.4	44.0	43 07.1	-11.4	44.7
51	40 42.8	-15.0	41.5	41 27.5	-14.1	42.1	42 11.8	-13.2	42.7	42 55.7	-12.3	43.3
52	40 27.8	-15.9	40.3	41 13.4	-15.0	40.8	41 58.6	-14.1	41.4	42 43.4	-13.2	42.0
53	40 11.9	-16.7	39.0	40 58.4	-15.9	39.5	41 44.5	-15.0	40.1	42 30.2	-14.2	40.7
54	39 55.2	-17.5	37.7	40 42.5	-16.7	38.3	41 29.5	-15.9	38.8	42 16.0	-15.0	39.4
55	39 37.7	-18.2	36.5	40 25.8	-17.5	37.0	41 13.6	-16.8	37.5	42 01.0	-15.9	38.1
56	39 19.5	-19.1	35.3	40 08.3	-18.3	35.7	40 56.8	-17.5	36.2	41 45.1	-16.8	36.8
57	39 00.4	-19.8	34.0	39 50.0	-19.1	34.5	40 39.3	-18.4	35.0	41 28.3	-17.6	35.5
58	38 40.6	-20.6	32.8	39 30.9	-19.9	33.3	40 20.9	-19.2	33.7	41 10.7	-18.5	34.2
59	38 20.0	-21.3	31.6	39 11.0	-20.6	32.0	40 01.7	-19.9	32.5	40 52.2	-19.3	33.0
60	37 58.7	-22.0	30.4	38 50.4	-21.4	30.8	39 41.8	-20.8	31.3	40 32.9	-20.1	31.7
61	37 36.7	-22.7	29.3	38 29.0	-22.1	29.6	39 21.0	-21.5	30.0	40 12.8	-20.8	30.5
62	37 14.0	-23.3	28.1	38 06.9	-22.8	28.5	38 59.5	-22.2	28.8	39 52.0	-21.6	29.2
63	36 50.7	-24.1	26.9	37 44.1	-23.5	27.3	38 37.3	-22.9	27.7	39 30.4	-22.4	28.0
64	36 26.6	-24.7	25.8	37 20.6	-24.2	26.1	38 14.4	-23.7	26.5	39 08.0	-23.1	26.8
65	36 01.9	-25.3	24.7	36 56.4	-24.8	25.0	37 50.7	-24.3	25.3	38 44.9	-23.8	25.6
66	35 36.6	-25.9	23.6	36 31.6	-25.5	23.8	37 26.4	-25.0	24.1	38 21.1	-24.5	24.5
67	35 10.7	-26.5	22.4	36 06.1	-26.1	22.7	37 01.4	-25.7	23.0	37 56.6	-25.2	23.3
68	34 44.2	-27.1	21.3	35 40.0	-26.7	21.6	36 35.7	-26.2	21.9	37 31.4	-25.9	22.2
69	34 17.1	-27.7	20.3	35 13.3	-27.3	20.5	36 09.5	-26.9	20.8	37 05.5	-26.5	21.0
70	33 49.4	-28.2	19.2	34 46.0	-27.8	19.4	35 42.6	-27.5	19.7	36 39.0	-27.1	19.9
71	33 21.2	-28.8	18.1	34 18.2	-28.4	18.3	35 15.1	-28.1	18.6	36 11.9	-27.7	18.8
72	32 52.4	-29.2	17.1	33 49.8	-29.0	17.3	34 47.0	-28.6	17.5	35 44.2	-28.3	17.7
73	32 23.2	-29.8	16.1	33 20.8	-29.5	16.2	34 18.4	-29.2	16.4	35 15.9	-28.9	16.6
74	31 53.4	-30.3	15.0	32 51.3	-30.0	15.2	33 49.2	-29.7	15.4	34 47.0	-29.4	15.5
75	31 23.1	-30.7	14.0	32 21.3	-30.5	14.2	33 19.5	-30.2	14.3	34 17.6	-30.0	14.5
76	30 52.4	-31.2	13.0	31 50.8	-30.9	13.1	32 49.3	-30.8	13.3	33 47.6	-30.5	13.4
77	30 21.2	-31.6	12.0	31 19.9	-31.5	12.1	32 18.5	-31.2	12.3	33 17.1	-31.0	12.4
78	29 49.6	-32.1	11.0	30 48.4	-31.8	11.1	31 47.3	-31.7	11.3	32 46.1	-31.5	11.4
79	29 17.5	-32.5	10.1	30 16.6	-32.4	10.2	31 15.6	-32.1	10.3	32 14.6	-31.9	10.4
80	28 45.0	-32.9	9.1	29 44.2	-32.7	9.2	30 43.5	-32.6	9.3	31 42.7	-32.5	9.4
81	28 12.1	-33.3	8.1	29 11.5	-33.1	8.2	30 10.9	-33.0	8.3	31 10.2	-32.8	8.4
82	27 38.8	-33.6	7.2	28 38.4	-33.6	7.3	29 37.9	-33.5	7.3	30 37.4	-33.3	7.4
83	27 05.2	-34.1	6.3	28 04.8	-33.9	6.3	29 04.4	-33.8	6.4	30 04.1	-33.8	6.5
84	26 31.1	-34.3	5.4	27 30.9	-34.3	5.4	28 30.6	-34.2	5.5	29 30.3	-34.1	5.5
85	25 56.8	-34.8	4.4	26 56.6	-34.7	4.5	27 56.4	-34.6	4.5	28 56.2	-34.5	4.6
86	25 22.0	-35.0	3.5	26 21.9	-35.0	3.6	27 21.8	-34.9	3.6	28 21.7	-34.9	3.6
87	24 47.0	-35.4	2.6	25 46.9	-35.3	2.7	26 46.9	-35.3	2.7	27 46.8	-35.2	2.7
88	24 11.6	-35.6	1.8	25 11.6	-35.6	1.8	26 11.6	-35.6	1.8	27 11.6	-35.7	1.8
89	23 36.0	-36.0	0.9	24 36.0	-36.0	0.9	25 36.0	-36.0	0.9	26 35.9	-35.9	0.9
90	23 00.0	-36.2	0.0	24 00.0	-36.3	0.0	25 00.0	-36.3	0.0	26 00.0	-36.3	0.0
	23°			24°			25°			26°		

27° Hc	d	Z	28° Hc	d	Z	29° Hc	d	Z	30° Hc	d	Z	Dec.
° ′	′	°	° ′	′	°	° ′	′	°	° ′	′	°	°
32 25.6	+32.0	108.9	32 05.9	+33.0	109.5	31 45.6	+34.0	110.1	31 24.7	+35.0	110.6	0
32 57.6	+31.6	107.9	32 38.9	+32.6	108.5	32 19.6	+33.5	109.1	31 59.7	+34.5	109.7	1
33 29.2	+31.0	106.9	33 11.5	+32.0	107.5	32 53.1	+33.1	108.1	32 34.2	+34.0	108.7	2
34 00.2	+30.5	105.8	33 43.5	+31.6	106.5	33 26.2	+32.6	107.1	33 08.2	+33.6	107.7	3
34 30.7	+30.0	104.8	34 15.1	+31.0	105.5	33 58.8	+32.1	106.1	33 41.8	+33.1	106.7	4
35 00.7	+29.5	103.7	34 46.1	+30.5	104.4	34 30.9	+31.5	105.1	34 14.9	+32.6	105.7	5
35 30.2	+28.8	102.7	35 16.6	+30.0	103.4	35 02.4	+31.0	104.0	34 47.5	+32.1	104.7	6
35 59.0	+28.3	101.6	35 46.6	+29.4	102.3	35 33.4	+30.5	103.0	35 19.6	+31.6	103.7	7
36 27.3	+27.6	100.5	36 16.0	+28.8	101.2	36 03.9	+29.9	101.9	35 51.2	+31.0	102.6	8
36 54.9	+27.1	99.4	36 44.8	+28.2	100.1	36 33.8	+29.4	100.9	36 22.2	+30.4	101.6	9
37 22.0	+26.4	98.3	37 13.0	+27.5	99.0	37 03.2	+28.7	99.8	36 52.6	+29.8	100.5	10
37 48.4	+25.7	97.1	37 40.5	+27.0	97.9	37 31.9	+28.1	98.7	37 22.4	+29.3	99.4	11
38 14.1	+25.1	96.0	38 07.5	+26.2	96.8	38 00.0	+27.4	97.6	37 51.7	+28.6	98.3	12
38 39.2	+24.4	94.8	38 33.7	+25.6	95.6	38 27.4	+26.8	96.4	38 20.3	+28.0	97.2	13
39 03.6	+23.6	93.7	38 59.3	+24.9	94.5	38 54.2	+26.1	95.3	38 48.3	+27.3	96.1	14
39 27.2	+22.9	92.5	39 24.2	+24.2	93.3	39 20.3	+25.4	94.1	39 15.6	+26.6	94.9	15
39 50.1	+22.2	91.3	39 48.4	+23.4	92.1	39 45.7	+24.7	92.9	39 42.2	+25.9	93.8	16
40 12.3	+21.4	90.1	40 11.8	+22.7	90.9	40 10.4	+24.0	91.7	40 08.1	+25.2	92.6	17
40 33.7	+20.6	88.8	40 34.5	+21.9	89.7	40 34.4	+23.2	90.5	40 33.3	+24.5	91.4	18
40 54.3	+19.8	87.6	40 56.4	+21.1	88.5	40 57.6	+22.4	89.3	40 57.8	+23.7	90.2	19
41 14.1	+19.0	86.3	41 17.5	+20.3	87.2	41 20.0	+21.6	88.1	41 21.5	+22.9	89.0	20
41 33.1	+18.2	85.1	41 37.8	+19.5	86.0	41 41.6	+20.8	86.8	41 44.4	+22.1	87.7	21
41 51.3	+17.3	83.8	41 57.3	+18.6	84.7	42 02.4	+19.9	85.6	42 06.5	+21.3	86.5	22
42 08.6	+16.4	82.5	42 15.9	+17.8	83.4	42 22.3	+19.2	84.3	42 27.8	+20.5	85.2	23
42 25.0	+15.5	81.2	42 33.7	+16.9	82.1	42 41.5	+18.2	83.0	42 48.3	+19.5	83.9	24
42 40.5	+14.7	79.9	42 50.6	+16.0	80.8	42 59.7	+17.3	81.7	43 07.8	+18.7	82.7	25
42 55.2	+13.7	78.6	43 06.6	+15.1	79.5	43 17.0	+16.5	80.4	43 26.5	+17.8	81.4	26
43 08.9	+12.8	77.2	43 21.7	+14.1	78.2	43 33.5	+15.5	79.1	43 44.3	+16.9	80.0	27
43 21.7	+11.8	75.9	43 35.8	+13.2	76.8	43 49.0	+14.6	77.8	44 01.2	+16.0	78.7	28
43 33.5	+10.8	74.6	43 49.0	+12.2	75.5	44 03.6	+13.6	76.4	44 17.2	+15.0	77.4	29
43 44.3	+9.9	73.2	44 01.2	+11.3	74.1	44 17.2	+12.6	75.1	44 32.2	+14.0	76.0	30
43 54.2	+9.0	71.8	44 12.5	+10.3	72.7	44 29.8	+11.7	73.7	44 46.2	+13.0	74.6	31
44 03.2	+7.9	70.5	44 22.8	+9.3	71.4	44 41.5	+10.6	72.3	44 59.2	+12.1	73.3	32
44 11.1	+6.9	69.1	44 32.1	+8.2	70.0	44 52.1	+9.7	70.9	45 11.3	+11.0	71.9	33
44 18.0	+5.9	67.7	44 40.3	+7.3	68.6	45 01.8	+8.6	69.5	45 22.3	+10.0	70.5	34
44 23.9	+4.9	66.3	44 47.6	+6.2	67.2	45 10.4	+7.6	68.1	45 32.3	+9.0	69.1	35
44 28.8	+3.9	64.9	44 53.8	+5.2	65.8	45 18.0	+6.5	66.7	45 41.3	+7.9	67.7	36
44 32.7	+2.8	63.5	44 59.0	+4.2	64.4	45 24.5	+5.5	65.3	45 49.2	+6.8	66.2	37
44 35.5	+1.8	62.1	45 03.2	+3.1	63.0	45 30.0	+4.5	63.9	45 56.0	+5.8	64.8	38
44 37.3	+0.8	60.7	45 06.3	+2.1	61.6	45 34.5	+3.3	62.5	46 01.8	+4.7	63.4	39
44 38.1	-0.3	59.3	45 08.4	+1.0	60.1	45 37.8	+2.3	61.0	46 06.5	+3.6	61.9	40
44 37.8	-1.2	57.9	45 09.4	-0.1	58.7	45 40.1	+1.3	59.6	46 10.1	+2.5	60.5	41
44 36.6	-2.4	56.5	45 09.3	-1.1	57.3	45 41.4	+0.1	58.2	46 12.6	+1.4	59.1	42
44 34.2	-3.3	55.1	45 08.2	-2.1	55.9	45 41.5	-0.9	56.7	46 14.0	+0.4	57.6	43
44 30.9	-4.4	53.7	45 06.1	-3.2	54.5	45 40.6	-2.0	55.3	46 14.4	-0.8	56.2	44
44 26.5	-5.4	52.3	45 02.9	-4.2	53.1	45 38.6	-3.0	53.9	46 13.6	-1.8	54.7	45
44 21.1	-6.4	50.9	44 58.7	-5.3	51.7	45 35.6	-4.2	52.4	46 11.8	-3.0	53.3	46
44 14.7	-7.4	49.5	44 53.4	-6.3	50.2	45 31.4	-5.1	51.0	46 08.8	-4.0	51.8	47
44 07.3	-8.4	48.1	44 47.1	-7.4	48.8	45 26.3	-6.3	49.6	46 04.8	-5.1	50.4	48
43 58.9	-9.4	46.7	44 39.7	-8.3	47.4	45 20.0	-7.3	48.2	45 59.7	-6.2	49.0	49
43 49.5	-10.4	45.4	44 31.4	-9.4	46.1	45 12.7	-8.3	46.8	45 53.5	-7.2	47.5	50
43 39.1	-11.3	44.0	44 22.0	-10.3	44.7	45 04.4	-9.3	45.4	45 46.3	-8.3	46.1	51
43 27.8	-12.3	42.6	44 11.7	-11.4	43.3	44 55.1	-10.4	44.0	45 38.0	-9.3	44.7	52
43 15.5	-13.3	41.3	44 00.3	-12.3	41.9	44 44.7	-11.3	42.6	45 28.7	-10.4	43.3	53
43 02.2	-14.2	40.0	43 48.0	-13.3	40.6	44 33.4	-12.4	41.2	45 18.3	-11.4	41.9	54
42 48.0	-15.0	38.6	43 34.7	-14.2	39.2	44 21.0	-13.3	39.8	45 06.9	-12.5	40.5	55
42 33.0	-16.0	37.3	43 20.5	-15.1	37.9	44 07.7	-14.3	38.5	44 54.4	-13.4	39.1	56
42 17.0	-16.9	36.0	43 05.4	-16.1	36.6	43 53.4	-15.3	37.1	44 41.0	-14.4	37.7	57
42 00.1	-17.7	34.7	42 49.3	-17.0	35.2	43 38.1	-16.1	35.8	44 26.6	-15.3	36.4	58
41 42.4	-18.6	33.4	42 32.3	-17.8	33.9	43 22.0	-17.1	34.5	44 11.3	-16.3	35.0	59
41 23.8	-19.4	32.2	42 14.5	-18.7	32.6	43 04.9	-18.0	33.1	43 55.0	-17.3	33.7	60
41 04.4	-20.2	30.9	41 55.8	-19.5	31.4	42 46.9	-18.8	31.8	43 37.7	-18.1	32.3	61
40 44.2	-21.0	29.7	41 36.3	-20.4	30.1	42 28.1	-19.8	30.5	43 19.6	-19.0	31.0	62
40 23.2	-21.8	28.4	41 15.9	-21.2	28.8	42 08.3	-20.5	29.3	43 00.6	-20.0	29.7	63
40 01.4	-22.5	27.2	40 54.7	-22.0	27.6	41 47.8	-21.4	28.0	42 40.6	-20.7	28.4	64
39 38.9	-23.3	26.0	40 32.7	-22.7	26.4	41 26.4	-22.2	26.8	42 19.9	-21.6	27.2	65
39 15.6	-24.0	24.8	40 10.0	-23.5	25.2	41 04.2	-22.9	25.5	41 58.3	-22.4	25.9	66
38 51.6	-24.7	23.6	39 46.5	-24.2	24.0	40 41.3	-23.8	24.3	41 35.9	-23.2	24.7	67
38 26.9	-25.4	22.5	39 22.3	-25.0	22.8	40 17.5	-24.4	23.1	41 12.7	-24.0	23.4	68
38 01.5	-26.1	21.3	38 57.3	-25.6	21.6	39 53.1	-25.2	21.9	40 48.7	-24.8	22.2	69
37 35.4	-26.7	20.2	38 31.7	-26.3	20.4	39 27.9	-25.9	20.7	40 23.9	-25.5	21.0	70
37 08.7	-27.4	19.0	38 05.4	-27.0	19.3	39 02.0	-26.6	19.6	39 58.4	-26.1	19.8	71
36 41.3	-27.9	17.9	37 38.4	-27.6	18.2	38 35.4	-27.3	18.4	39 32.3	-26.9	18.7	72
36 13.4	-28.6	16.8	37 10.8	-28.3	17.0	38 08.1	-27.9	17.3	39 05.4	-27.6	17.5	73
35 44.8	-29.1	15.7	36 42.5	-28.8	15.9	37 40.2	-28.5	16.1	38 37.8	-28.2	16.4	74
35 15.7	-29.7	14.7	36 13.7	-29.4	14.8	37 11.7	-29.2	15.0	38 09.6	-28.9	15.2	75
34 46.0	-30.3	13.6	35 44.3	-30.0	13.8	36 42.5	-29.7	13.9	37 40.7	-29.4	14.1	76
34 15.7	-30.8	12.6	35 14.3	-30.6	12.7	36 12.8	-30.3	12.9	37 11.3	-30.1	13.0	77
33 44.9	-31.2	11.5	34 43.7	-31.1	11.7	35 42.5	-30.9	11.8	36 41.2	-30.7	12.0	78
33 13.7	-31.8	10.5	34 12.6	-31.6	10.6	35 11.6	-31.4	10.7	36 10.5	-31.2	10.9	79
32 41.9	-32.3	9.5	33 41.0	-32.1	9.6	34 40.2	-31.9	9.7	35 39.3	-31.7	9.8	80
32 09.6	-32.7	8.5	33 08.9	-32.6	8.6	34 08.3	-32.5	8.7	35 07.6	-32.3	8.8	81
31 36.9	-33.2	7.5	32 36.3	-33.0	7.6	33 35.8	-32.9	7.7	34 35.3	-32.8	7.8	82
31 03.7	-33.6	6.5	32 03.3	-33.5	6.6	33 02.9	-33.4	6.7	34 02.5	-33.3	6.7	83
30 30.1	-34.1	5.6	31 29.8	-34.0	5.6	32 29.5	-33.9	5.7	33 29.2	-33.8	5.7	84
29 56.0	-34.4	4.6	30 55.8	-34.3	4.7	31 55.6	-34.3	4.7	32 55.4	-34.2	4.8	85
29 21.6	-34.9	3.7	30 21.5	-34.8	3.7	31 21.3	-34.7	3.7	32 21.2	-34.7	3.8	86
28 46.7	-35.2	2.7	29 46.7	-35.2	2.8	30 46.6	-35.1	2.8	31 46.5	-35.1	2.8	87
28 11.5	-35.6	1.8	29 11.5	-35.6	1.8	30 11.5	-35.6	1.8	31 11.4	-35.5	1.9	88
27 35.9	-35.9	0.9	28 35.9	-35.9	0.9	29 35.9	-35.9	0.9	30 35.9	-35.9	0.9	89
27 00.0	-36.3	0.0	28 00.0	-36.3	0.0	29 00.0	-36.3	0.0	30 00.0	-36.3	0.0	90
27°			28°			29°			30°			

53°, 307° L.H.A. LATITUDE **SAME** NAME AS DECLINATION

290

Dec.	23° Hc	d	Z	24° Hc	d	Z	25° Hc	d	Z	26° Hc	d	Z
°	° ′	′	°	° ′	′	°	° ′	′	°	° ′	′	°
0	33 38.4	−28.4	106.4	33 21.1	−29.4	107.0	33 03.2	−30.5	107.7	32 44.7	−31.5	108.3
1	33 10.0	−29.0	107.5	32 51.7	−30.0	108.1	32 32.7	−31.0	108.7	32 13.2	−32.0	109.3
2	32 41.0	−29.5	108.5	32 21.7	−30.5	109.1	32 01.7	−31.4	109.7	31 41.2	−32.4	110.3
3	32 11.5	−29.9	109.5	31 51.2	−31.0	110.1	31 30.3	−32.0	110.7	31 08.8	−32.9	111.3
4	31 41.6	−30.5	110.6	31 20.2	−31.4	111.1	30 58.3	−32.4	111.7	30 35.9	−33.3	112.2
5	31 11.1	−30.9	111.6	30 48.8	−31.9	112.1	30 25.9	−32.8	112.7	30 02.6	−33.8	113.2
6	30 40.2	−31.4	112.6	30 16.9	−32.3	113.1	29 53.1	−33.2	113.6	29 28.8	−34.1	114.2
7	30 08.8	−31.8	113.6	29 44.6	−32.7	114.1	29 19.9	−33.7	114.6	28 54.7	−34.6	115.1
8	29 37.0	−32.2	114.5	29 11.9	−33.2	115.0	28 46.2	−34.0	115.5	28 20.1	−34.9	116.0
9	29 04.8	−32.7	115.5	28 38.7	−33.5	116.0	28 12.2	−34.4	116.5	27 45.2	−35.2	117.0
10	28 32.1	−33.0	116.5	28 05.2	−33.9	116.9	27 37.8	−34.8	117.4	27 10.0	−35.7	117.9
11	27 59.1	−33.4	117.4	27 31.3	−34.3	117.9	27 03.0	−35.1	118.3	26 34.3	−35.9	118.8
12	27 25.7	−33.8	118.3	26 57.0	−34.7	118.8	26 27.9	−35.5	119.2	25 58.4	−36.3	119.7
13	26 51.9	−34.2	119.3	26 22.3	−35.0	119.7	25 52.4	−35.8	120.1	25 22.1	−36.6	120.5
14	26 17.7	−34.5	120.2	25 47.3	−35.3	120.6	25 16.6	−36.1	121.0	24 45.5	−36.9	121.4
15	25 43.2	−34.9	121.1	25 12.0	−35.6	121.5	24 40.5	−36.5	121.9	24 08.6	−37.2	122.3
16	25 08.3	−35.1	122.0	24 36.4	−36.0	122.4	24 04.0	−36.7	122.8	23 31.4	−37.5	123.1
17	24 33.2	−35.5	122.9	24 00.4	−36.2	123.3	23 27.3	−37.0	123.6	22 53.9	−37.7	124.0
18	23 57.7	−35.8	123.8	23 24.2	−36.6	124.1	22 50.3	−37.3	124.5	22 16.2	−38.0	124.8
19	23 21.9	−36.1	124.7	22 47.6	−36.8	125.0	22 13.0	−37.5	125.3	21 38.2	−38.2	125.7
20	22 45.8	−36.4	125.5	22 10.8	−37.1	125.9	21 35.5	−37.8	126.2	21 00.0	−38.5	126.5
21	22 09.4	−36.6	126.4	21 33.7	−37.3	126.7	20 57.7	−38.0	127.0	20 21.5	−38.7	127.3
22	21 32.8	−36.9	127.2	20 56.4	−37.6	127.5	20 19.7	−38.3	127.8	19 42.8	−39.0	128.1
23	20 55.9	−37.1	128.1	20 18.8	−37.8	128.4	19 41.4	−38.4	128.7	19 03.8	−39.1	128.9
24	20 18.8	−37.4	128.9	19 41.0	−38.0	129.2	19 03.0	−38.7	129.5	18 24.7	−39.3	129.7
25	19 41.4	−37.6	129.8	19 03.0	−38.3	130.0	18 24.3	−38.9	130.3	17 45.4	−39.6	130.5
26	19 03.8	−37.8	130.6	18 24.7	−38.5	130.8	17 45.4	−39.1	131.1	17 05.8	−39.7	131.3
27	18 26.0	−38.0	131.4	17 46.2	−38.6	131.6	17 06.3	−39.3	131.9	16 26.1	−39.8	132.1
28	17 48.0	−38.2	132.2	17 07.6	−38.9	132.4	16 27.0	−39.5	132.7	15 46.3	−40.1	132.9
29	17 09.8	−38.5	133.0	16 28.7	−39.0	133.2	15 47.5	−39.6	133.5	15 06.2	−40.2	133.7
30	16 31.3	−38.6	133.8	15 49.7	−39.2	134.0	15 07.9	−39.7	134.2	14 26.0	−40.3	134.4
31	15 52.7	−38.7	134.6	15 10.5	−39.3	134.8	14 28.2	−40.0	135.0	13 45.7	−40.5	135.2
32	15 14.0	−39.0	135.4	14 31.2	−39.6	135.6	13 48.2	−40.0	135.8	13 05.2	−40.7	135.9
33	14 35.0	−39.1	136.2	13 51.6	−39.6	136.4	13 08.2	−40.3	136.5	12 24.5	−40.7	136.7
34	13 55.9	−39.2	137.0	13 12.0	−39.8	137.2	12 27.9	−40.3	137.3	11 43.8	−40.9	137.5
35	13 16.7	−39.4	137.8	12 32.2	−39.9	137.9	11 47.6	−40.4	138.1	11 02.9	−40.9	138.2
36	12 37.3	−39.5	138.5	11 52.3	−40.1	138.7	11 07.2	−40.6	138.8	10 22.0	−41.1	138.9
37	11 57.8	−39.7	139.3	11 12.2	−40.2	139.4	10 26.6	−40.7	139.6	9 40.9	−41.2	139.7
38	11 18.1	−39.7	140.1	10 32.1	−40.3	140.2	9 45.9	−40.7	140.3	8 59.7	−41.2	140.4
39	10 38.4	−39.9	140.8	9 51.8	−40.4	141.0	9 05.2	−40.9	141.1	8 18.5	−41.4	141.2
40	9 58.5	−40.0	141.6	9 11.4	−40.4	141.7	8 24.3	−40.9	141.8	7 37.1	−41.4	141.9
41	9 18.5	−40.1	142.4	8 31.0	−40.6	142.4	7 43.4	−41.1	142.5	6 55.7	−41.5	142.6
42	8 38.4	−40.1	143.1	7 50.4	−40.6	143.2	7 02.3	−41.0	143.3	6 14.2	−41.5	143.3
43	7 58.3	−40.3	143.9	7 09.8	−40.7	143.9	6 21.3	−41.2	144.0	5 32.7	−41.6	144.1
44	7 18.0	−40.3	144.6	6 29.1	−40.8	144.7	5 40.1	−41.2	144.7	4 51.1	−41.6	144.8
45	6 37.7	−40.4	145.4	5 48.3	−40.8	145.4	4 58.9	−41.2	145.5	4 09.5	−41.7	145.5
46	5 57.3	−40.4	146.1	5 07.5	−40.9	146.2	4 17.7	−41.3	146.2	3 27.8	−41.7	146.2
47	5 16.9	−40.5	146.8	4 26.6	−40.9	146.9	3 36.4	−41.4	146.9	2 46.1	−41.7	147.0
48	4 36.4	−40.6	147.6	3 45.7	−40.9	147.6	2 55.0	−41.3	147.7	2 04.4	−41.8	147.7
49	3 55.8	−40.5	148.3	3 04.8	−41.0	148.4	2 13.7	−41.4	148.4	1 22.6	−41.8	148.4
50	3 15.3	−40.6	149.1	2 23.8	−41.0	149.1	1 32.3	−41.4	149.1	0 40.8	−41.7	149.1
51	2 34.7	−40.7	149.8	1 42.8	−41.0	149.8	0 50.9	−41.4	149.8	0 00.9	+41.8	30.2
52	1 54.0	−40.6	150.5	1 01.8	−41.1	150.5	0 09.5	−41.4	150.5	0 42.7	+41.8	29.5
53	1 13.4	−40.7	151.3	0 20.7	−41.0	151.3	0 31.9	+41.4	28.7	1 24.5	+41.7	28.7
54	0 32.7	−40.7	152.0	0 20.3	+41.0	28.0	1 13.3	+41.3	28.0	2 06.2	+41.8	28.0
55	0 08.0	+40.7	27.3	1 01.3	+41.0	27.3	1 54.6	+41.4	27.3	2 48.0	+41.7	27.3
56	0 48.7	+40.6	26.5	1 42.3	+41.0	26.5	2 36.0	+41.3	26.6	3 29.7	+41.6	26.6
57	1 29.3	+40.7	25.8	2 23.3	+41.0	25.8	3 17.3	+41.4	25.8	4 11.3	+41.7	25.9
58	2 10.0	+40.6	25.1	3 04.3	+41.0	25.1	3 58.7	+41.2	25.1	4 53.0	+41.6	25.1
59	2 50.6	+40.6	24.3	3 45.3	+40.9	24.3	4 39.9	+41.3	24.4	5 34.6	+41.5	24.4
60	3 31.2	+40.6	23.6	4 26.2	+40.9	23.6	5 21.2	+41.1	23.6	6 16.1	+41.5	23.7
61	4 11.8	+40.5	22.8	5 07.1	+40.8	22.9	6 02.3	+41.1	22.9	6 57.6	+41.4	23.0
62	4 52.3	+40.5	22.1	5 47.9	+40.7	22.1	6 43.4	+41.1	22.2	7 39.0	+41.3	22.2
63	5 32.8	+40.4	21.4	6 28.6	+40.7	21.4	7 24.5	+41.0	21.4	8 20.3	+41.3	21.5
64	6 13.2	+40.3	20.6	7 09.3	+40.7	20.7	8 05.5	+40.9	20.7	9 01.6	+41.1	20.8
65	6 53.5	+40.3	19.9	7 50.0	+40.5	19.9	8 46.4	+40.8	20.0	9 42.7	+41.1	20.0
66	7 33.8	+40.2	19.1	8 30.5	+40.5	19.2	9 27.2	+40.7	19.2	10 23.8	+41.0	19.3
67	8 14.0	+40.2	18.4	9 11.0	+40.3	18.4	10 07.9	+40.6	18.5	11 04.8	+40.8	18.5
68	8 54.2	+40.0	17.6	9 51.3	+40.3	17.7	10 48.5	+40.5	17.7	11 45.6	+40.8	17.8
69	9 34.2	+39.9	16.9	10 31.6	+40.2	16.9	11 29.0	+40.4	17.0	12 26.4	+40.6	17.0
70	10 14.1	+39.9	16.1	11 11.8	+40.0	16.2	12 09.4	+40.3	16.2	13 07.0	+40.5	16.3
71	10 54.0	+39.7	15.4	11 51.8	+39.9	15.4	12 49.7	+40.1	15.5	13 47.5	+40.3	15.5
72	11 33.7	+39.6	14.6	12 31.7	+39.8	14.6	13 29.8	+40.0	14.7	14 27.8	+40.2	14.8
73	12 13.3	+39.5	13.8	13 11.5	+39.7	13.9	14 09.8	+39.8	13.9	15 08.0	+40.1	14.0
74	12 52.8	+39.3	13.1	13 51.2	+39.5	13.1	14 49.6	+39.7	13.2	15 48.1	+39.8	13.2
75	13 32.1	+39.2	12.3	14 30.7	+39.4	12.3	15 29.3	+39.6	12.4	16 27.9	+39.7	12.4
76	14 11.3	+39.0	11.5	15 10.1	+39.2	11.5	16 08.9	+39.3	11.6	17 07.6	+39.5	11.7
77	14 50.3	+38.9	10.7	15 49.3	+39.0	10.8	16 48.2	+39.2	10.8	17 47.1	+39.4	10.9
78	15 29.2	+38.7	9.9	16 28.3	+38.8	10.0	17 27.4	+39.0	10.0	18 26.5	+39.1	10.1
79	16 07.9	+38.5	9.1	17 07.1	+38.7	9.2	18 06.4	+38.8	9.2	19 05.6	+38.9	9.3
80	16 46.4	+38.4	8.3	17 45.8	+38.5	8.4	18 45.2	+38.5	8.4	19 44.5	+38.7	8.5
81	17 24.8	+38.1	7.5	18 24.3	+38.2	7.6	19 23.7	+38.4	7.6	20 23.2	+38.5	7.7
82	18 02.9	+38.0	6.7	19 02.5	+38.1	6.8	20 02.1	+38.1	6.8	21 01.7	+38.2	6.8
83	18 40.9	+37.7	5.9	19 40.6	+37.8	5.9	20 40.2	+37.9	6.0	21 39.9	+38.0	6.0
84	19 18.6	+37.5	5.1	20 18.4	+37.6	5.1	21 18.1	+37.7	5.1	22 17.9	+37.7	5.2
85	19 56.1	+37.3	4.2	20 56.0	+37.3	4.3	21 55.8	+37.4	4.3	22 55.6	+37.5	4.3
86	20 33.4	+37.0	3.4	21 33.3	+37.1	3.4	22 33.2	+37.1	3.5	23 33.1	+37.2	3.5
87	21 10.4	+36.8	2.6	22 10.4	+36.8	2.6	23 10.3	+36.9	2.6	24 10.3	+36.8	2.6
88	21 47.2	+36.6	1.7	22 47.2	+36.5	1.7	23 47.2	+36.5	1.7	24 47.1	+36.6	1.8
89	22 23.8	+36.2	0.9	23 23.7	+36.3	0.9	24 23.7	+36.3	0.9	25 23.7	+36.3	0.9
90	23 00.0	+36.0	0.0	24 00.0	+36.0	0.0	25 00.0	+36.0	0.0	26 00.0	+35.9	0.0
	23°			24°			25°			26°		

27° Hc	d	Z	28° Hc	d	Z	29° Hc	d	Z	30° Hc	d	Z	Dec.
° ′	′	°	° ′	′	°	° ′	′	°	° ′	′	°	°
32 25.6	−32.5	108.9	32 05.9	−33.5	109.5	31 45.6	−34.4	110.1	31 24.7	−35.3	110.6	0
31 53.1	−33.0	109.9	31 32.4	−33.9	110.5	31 11.2	−34.9	111.0	30 49.4	−35.8	111.6	1
31 20.1	−33.4	110.9	30 58.5	−34.3	111.4	30 36.3	−35.2	112.0	30 13.6	−36.2	112.5	2
30 46.7	−33.8	111.8	30 24.2	−34.8	112.4	30 01.1	−35.7	112.9	29 37.4	−36.5	113.4	3
30 12.9	−34.2	112.8	29 49.4	−35.1	113.3	29 25.4	−36.0	113.8	29 00.9	−36.9	114.4	4
29 38.7	−34.7	113.7	29 14.3	−35.6	114.3	28 49.4	−36.4	114.8	28 24.0	−37.2	115.3	5
29 04.0	−35.0	114.7	28 38.7	−35.9	115.2	28 13.0	−36.8	115.7	27 46.8	−37.6	116.1	6
28 29.0	−35.4	115.6	28 02.8	−36.2	116.1	27 36.2	−37.1	116.6	27 09.2	−37.9	117.0	7
27 53.6	−35.8	116.5	27 26.6	−36.6	117.0	26 59.1	−37.4	117.4	26 31.3	−38.3	117.9	8
27 17.8	−36.1	117.4	26 50.0	−37.0	117.9	26 21.7	−37.7	118.3	25 53.0	−38.5	118.7	9
26 41.7	−36.4	118.3	26 13.0	−37.2	118.8	25 44.0	−38.1	119.2	25 14.5	−38.8	119.6	10
26 05.3	−36.8	119.2	25 35.8	−37.6	119.6	25 05.9	−38.3	120.0	24 35.7	−39.1	120.4	11
25 28.5	−37.1	120.1	24 58.2	−37.8	120.5	24 27.6	−38.6	120.9	23 56.6	−39.3	121.3	12
24 51.4	−37.4	121.0	24 20.4	−38.2	121.3	23 49.0	−38.9	121.7	23 17.3	−39.6	122.1	13
24 14.0	−37.6	121.8	23 42.2	−38.4	122.2	23 10.1	−39.1	122.6	22 37.7	−39.9	122.9	14
23 36.4	−38.0	122.7	23 03.8	−38.6	123.0	22 31.0	−39.4	123.4	21 57.8	−40.1	123.7	15
22 58.4	−38.2	123.5	22 25.2	−39.0	123.9	21 51.6	−39.6	124.2	21 17.7	−40.3	124.5	16
22 20.2	−38.4	124.3	21 46.2	−39.1	124.7	21 12.0	−39.9	125.0	20 37.4	−40.5	125.3	17
21 41.8	−38.7	125.2	21 07.1	−39.4	125.5	20 32.1	−40.1	125.8	19 56.9	−40.7	126.1	18
21 03.1	−39.0	126.0	20 27.7	−39.6	126.3	19 52.0	−40.2	126.6	19 16.2	−41.0	126.9	19
20 24.1	−39.1	126.8	19 48.1	−39.9	127.1	19 11.8	−40.5	127.4	18 35.2	−41.1	127.6	20
19 45.0	−39.4	127.6	19 08.2	−40.0	127.9	18 31.3	−40.7	128.2	17 54.1	−41.3	128.4	21
19 05.6	−39.6	128.4	18 28.2	−40.2	128.7	17 50.6	−40.8	128.9	17 12.8	−41.5	129.2	22
18 26.0	−39.8	129.2	17 48.0	−40.4	129.5	17 09.8	−41.1	129.7	16 31.3	−41.6	129.9	23
17 46.2	−39.9	130.0	17 07.6	−40.6	130.2	16 28.7	−41.2	130.5	15 49.7	−41.8	130.7	24
17 06.3	−40.2	130.8	16 27.0	−40.7	131.0	15 47.5	−41.3	131.2	15 07.9	−41.9	131.4	25
16 26.1	−40.3	131.5	15 46.3	−41.0	131.8	15 06.2	−41.5	132.0	14 26.0	−42.1	132.2	26
15 45.8	−40.5	132.3	15 05.3	−41.0	132.5	14 24.7	−41.6	132.7	13 43.9	−42.2	132.9	27
15 05.3	−40.6	133.1	14 24.3	−41.2	133.3	13 43.1	−41.8	133.5	13 01.7	−42.3	133.6	28
14 24.7	−40.8	133.8	13 43.1	−41.4	134.0	13 01.3	−41.9	134.2	12 19.4	−42.4	134.4	29
13 43.9	−40.9	134.6	13 01.7	−41.4	134.8	12 19.4	−42.0	134.9	11 37.0	−42.5	135.1	30
13 03.0	−41.0	135.4	12 20.3	−41.6	135.5	11 37.4	−42.1	135.7	10 54.5	−42.7	135.8	31
12 22.0	−41.2	136.1	11 38.7	−41.7	136.2	10 55.3	−42.2	136.4	10 11.8	−42.7	136.5	32
11 40.8	−41.3	136.8	10 57.0	−41.8	137.0	10 13.1	−42.3	137.1	9 29.1	−42.8	137.2	33
10 59.5	−41.3	137.6	10 15.2	−41.9	137.7	9 30.8	−42.4	137.8	8 46.3	−42.9	137.9	34
10 18.2	−41.5	138.3	9 33.3	−42.0	138.4	8 48.4	−42.5	138.5	8 03.4	−43.0	138.6	35
9 36.7	−41.6	139.1	8 51.3	−42.1	139.2	8 05.9	−42.6	139.3	7 20.4	−43.0	139.3	36
8 55.1	−41.7	139.8	8 09.2	−42.1	139.9	7 23.3	−42.6	140.0	6 37.4	−43.1	140.1	37
8 13.4	−41.7	140.5	7 27.1	−42.2	140.6	6 40.7	−42.7	140.7	5 54.3	−43.2	140.8	38
7 31.7	−41.8	141.2	6 44.9	−42.3	141.3	5 58.0	−42.7	141.4	5 11.1	−43.2	141.4	39
6 49.9	−41.9	142.0	6 02.6	−42.3	142.0	5 15.3	−42.8	142.1	4 27.9	−43.2	142.1	40
6 08.0	−41.9	142.7	5 20.3	−42.4	142.7	4 32.5	−42.8	142.8	3 44.7	−43.3	142.8	41
5 26.1	−42.0	143.4	4 37.9	−42.4	143.5	3 49.7	−42.9	143.5	3 01.4	−43.3	143.5	42
4 44.1	−42.0	144.1	3 55.5	−42.5	144.2	3 06.8	−42.9	144.2	2 18.1	−43.3	144.2	43
4 02.1	−42.1	144.8	3 13.0	−42.5	144.9	2 23.9	−42.9	144.9	1 34.8	−43.3	144.9	44
3 20.0	−42.1	145.6	2 30.5	−42.5	145.6	1 41.0	−42.9	145.6	0 51.5	−43.3	145.6	45
2 37.9	−42.1	146.3	1 48.0	−42.5	146.3	0 58.1	−42.9	146.3	0 08.2	−43.4	146.3	46
1 55.8	−42.2	147.0	1 05.5	−42.6	147.0	0 15.2	−43.0	147.0	0 35.2	+43.3	33.0	47
1 13.6	−42.1	147.7	0 22.9	−42.5	147.7	0 27.8	+42.9	32.3	1 18.5	+43.3	32.3	48
0 31.5	−42.2	148.4	0 19.6	+42.5	31.6	1 10.7	+42.9	31.6	2 01.8	+43.3	31.6	49
0 10.7	+42.1	30.9	1 02.1	+42.6	30.9	1 53.6	+42.9	30.9	2 45.1	+43.3	30.9	50
0 52.8	+42.2	30.2	1 44.7	+42.5	30.2	2 36.5	+42.9	30.2	3 28.4	+43.2	30.2	51
1 35.0	+42.1	29.5	2 27.2	+42.5	29.5	3 19.4	+42.9	29.5	4 11.6	+43.2	29.5	52
2 17.1	+42.1	28.8	3 09.7	+42.5	28.8	4 02.3	+42.8	28.8	4 54.8	+43.2	28.8	53
2 59.2	+42.1	28.0	3 52.2	+42.4	28.1	4 45.1	+42.8	28.1	5 38.0	+43.1	28.1	54
3 41.3	+42.0	27.3	4 34.6	+42.4	27.4	5 27.9	+42.7	27.4	6 21.1	+43.1	27.4	55
4 23.3	+42.0	26.6	5 17.0	+42.3	26.6	6 10.6	+42.6	26.7	7 04.2	+43.0	26.7	56
5 05.3	+42.0	25.9	5 59.3	+42.3	25.9	6 53.2	+42.7	26.0	7 47.2	+42.9	26.0	57
5 47.3	+41.9	25.2	6 41.6	+42.2	25.2	7 35.9	+42.5	25.3	8 30.1	+42.8	25.3	58
6 29.2	+41.8	24.5	7 23.8	+42.2	24.5	8 18.4	+42.4	24.6	9 12.9	+42.8	24.6	59
7 11.0	+41.8	23.7	8 06.0	+42.0	23.8	9 00.8	+42.4	23.8	9 55.7	+42.7	23.9	60
7 52.8	+41.7	23.0	8 48.0	+42.0	23.1	9 43.2	+42.3	23.1	10 38.4	+42.6	23.2	61
8 34.5	+41.6	22.3	9 30.0	+41.9	22.3	10 25.5	+42.2	22.4	11 21.0	+42.4	22.5	62
9 16.1	+41.6	21.6	10 11.9	+41.8	21.6	11 07.7	+42.1	21.7	12 03.4	+42.4	21.8	63
9 57.7	+41.4	20.8	10 53.7	+41.7	20.9	11 49.8	+42.0	21.0	12 45.8	+42.2	21.0	64
10 39.1	+41.3	20.1	11 35.4	+41.6	20.2	12 31.8	+41.8	20.2	13 28.0	+42.2	20.3	65
11 20.4	+41.3	19.3	12 17.0	+41.5	19.4	13 13.6	+41.7	19.5	14 10.2	+41.9	19.6	66
12 01.7	+41.1	18.6	12 58.5	+41.4	18.7	13 55.3	+41.6	18.8	14 52.1	+41.9	18.8	67
12 42.8	+40.9	17.9	13 39.9	+41.2	17.9	14 36.9	+41.5	18.0	15 34.0	+41.7	18.1	68
13 23.7	+40.9	17.1	14 21.1	+41.0	17.2	15 18.4	+41.3	17.3	16 15.7	+41.5	17.3	69
14 04.6	+40.7	16.4	15 02.1	+41.0	16.4	15 59.7	+41.1	16.5	16 57.2	+41.4	16.6	70
14 45.3	+40.5	15.6	15 43.1	+40.7	15.7	16 40.8	+41.0	15.7	17 38.6	+41.1	15.8	71
15 25.8	+40.4	14.8	16 23.8	+40.6	14.9	17 21.8	+40.8	15.0	18 19.7	+41.0	15.1	72
16 06.2	+40.3	14.1	17 04.4	+40.4	14.1	18 02.6	+40.6	14.2	19 00.7	+40.9	14.3	73
16 46.5	+40.0	13.3	17 44.8	+40.3	13.4	18 43.2	+40.4	13.4	19 41.6	+40.6	13.5	74
17 26.5	+39.9	12.5	18 25.1	+40.0	12.6	19 23.6	+40.2	12.7	20 22.2	+40.4	12.7	75
18 06.4	+39.7	11.7	19 05.1	+39.9	11.8	20 03.8	+40.1	11.9	21 02.6	+40.1	11.9	76
18 46.1	+39.4	10.9	19 45.0	+39.6	11.0	20 43.9	+39.7	11.1	21 42.7	+40.0	11.1	77
19 25.5	+39.3	10.1	20 24.6	+39.4	10.2	21 23.6	+39.6	10.3	22 22.7	+39.7	10.3	78
20 04.8	+39.1	9.3	21 04.0	+39.2	9.4	22 03.2	+39.3	9.5	23 02.4	+39.4	9.5	79
20 43.9	+38.8	8.5	21 43.2	+38.9	8.6	22 42.5	+39.1	8.6	23 41.8	+39.2	8.7	80
21 22.7	+38.6	7.7	22 22.1	+38.7	7.8	23 21.6	+38.8	7.8	24 21.0	+38.9	7.9	81
22 01.3	+38.3	6.9	23 00.8	+38.4	6.9	24 00.4	+38.5	7.0	24 59.9	+38.7	7.0	82
22 39.6	+38.1	6.1	23 39.2	+38.2	6.1	24 38.9	+38.2	6.1	25 38.6	+38.3	6.2	83
23 17.7	+37.8	5.2	24 17.4	+37.9	5.3	25 17.1	+38.0	5.3	26 16.9	+38.0	5.3	84
23 55.5	+37.5	4.4	24 55.3	+37.6	4.4	25 55.1	+37.6	4.4	26 54.9	+37.7	4.5	85
24 33.0	+37.2	3.5	25 32.9	+37.2	3.5	26 32.7	+37.4	3.6	27 32.6	+37.4	3.6	86
25 10.2	+36.9	2.6	26 10.1	+37.0	2.7	27 10.1	+37.0	2.7	28 10.0	+37.0	2.7	87
25 47.1	+36.6	1.8	26 47.1	+36.6	1.8	27 47.1	+36.6	1.8	28 47.0	+36.7	1.8	88
26 23.7	+36.3	0.9	27 23.7	+36.3	0.9	28 23.7	+36.3	0.9	29 23.7	+36.3	0.9	89
27 00.0	+35.9	0.0	28 00.0	+35.9	0.0	29 00.0	+35.9	0.0	30 00.0	+35.9	0.0	90
27°			28°			29°			30°			

S. Lat. {L.H.A. greater than 180° ....Zn=180°−Z; L.H.A. less than 180°...........Zn=180°+Z}

54°, 306° L.H.A. LATITUDE SAME NAME AS DECLINATION

N. Lat. {L.H.A. greater than 180° .....Zn=Z
{L.H.A. less than 180°............Zn=360°−Z

Dec.	23°			24°			25°			26°			27°			28°			29°			30°			Dec.
°	Hc ° ′	d ′	Z °	Hc ° ′	d ′	Z °	Hc ° ′	d ′	Z °	Hc ° ′	d ′	Z °	Hc ° ′	d ′	Z °	Hc ° ′	d ′	Z °	Hc ° ′	d ′	Z °	Hc ° ′	d ′	Z °	°
0	32 45.3	+27.7	105.8	32 28.7	+28.6	106.5	32 11.3	+29.8	107.1	31 53.4	+30.8	107.7	31 34.9	+31.8	108.3	31 15.8	+32.8	108.8	30 56.2	+33.7	109.4	30 36.0	+34.6	110.0	0
1	33 13.0	+27.0	104.8	32 57.3	+28.2	105.4	32 41.1	+29.2	106.0	32 24.2	+30.2	106.7	32 06.7	+31.2	107.3	31 48.6	+32.2	107.9	31 29.9	+33.2	108.4	31 10.6	+34.2	109.0	1
2	33 40.0	+26.5	103.7	33 25.5	+27.6	104.4	33 10.3	+28.6	105.0	32 54.4	+29.7	105.6	32 37.9	+30.8	106.2	32 20.8	+31.8	106.9	32 03.1	+32.8	107.5	31 44.8	+33.8	108.1	2
3	34 06.5	+26.0	102.6	33 53.1	+27.0	103.3	33 38.9	+28.2	103.9	33 24.1	+29.3	104.6	33 08.7	+30.3	105.2	32 52.6	+31.3	105.8	32 35.9	+32.4	106.5	32 18.6	+33.4	107.1	3
4	34 32.5	+25.3	101.5	34 20.1	+26.5	102.2	34 07.1	+27.6	102.9	33 53.4	+28.6	103.5	33 39.0	+29.7	104.2	33 23.9	+30.8	104.8	33 08.3	+31.8	105.5	32 52.0	+32.8	106.1	4
5	34 57.8	+24.8	100.4	34 46.6	+25.9	101.1	34 34.7	+27.0	101.8	34 22.0	+28.1	102.5	34 08.7	+29.2	103.1	33 54.7	+30.3	103.8	33 40.1	+31.3	104.4	33 24.8	+32.4	105.1	5
6	35 22.6	+24.1	99.3	35 12.5	+25.2	100.0	35 01.7	+26.4	100.7	34 50.1	+27.6	101.4	34 37.9	+28.7	102.1	34 25.0	+29.8	102.8	34 11.4	+30.9	103.4	33 57.2	+31.8	104.1	6
7	35 46.7	+23.5	98.2	35 37.7	+24.7	98.9	35 28.1	+25.8	99.6	35 17.7	+26.9	100.3	35 06.6	+28.1	101.0	34 54.8	+29.2	101.7	34 42.3	+30.2	102.4	34 29.0	+31.4	103.1	7
8	36 10.2	+22.8	97.1	36 02.4	+24.0	97.8	35 53.9	+25.2	98.5	35 44.6	+26.4	99.2	35 34.7	+27.5	99.9	35 24.0	+28.6	100.6	35 12.5	+29.7	101.3	35 00.4	+30.8	102.0	8
9	36 33.0	+22.2	95.9	36 26.4	+23.4	96.7	36 19.1	+24.5	97.4	36 11.0	+25.7	98.1	36 02.2	+26.8	98.8	35 52.6	+28.0	99.5	35 42.2	+29.2	100.3	35 31.2	+30.3	101.0	9
10	36 55.2	+21.4	94.8	36 49.8	+22.7	95.5	36 43.6	+23.9	96.3	36 36.7	+25.1	97.0	36 29.0	+26.3	97.7	36 20.6	+27.4	98.5	36 11.4	+28.6	99.2	36 01.5	+29.6	99.9	10
11	37 16.6	+20.8	93.6	37 12.5	+22.0	94.3	37 07.5	+23.3	95.1	37 01.8	+24.5	95.9	36 55.3	+25.6	96.6	36 48.0	+26.8	97.3	36 40.0	+27.9	98.1	36 31.1	+29.1	98.8	11
12	37 37.4	+20.1	92.4	37 34.5	+21.3	93.2	37 30.8	+22.5	93.9	37 26.3	+23.7	94.7	37 20.9	+25.0	95.5	37 14.8	+26.2	96.2	37 07.9	+27.3	97.0	37 00.2	+28.5	97.7	12
13	37 57.5	+19.3	91.2	37 55.8	+20.6	92.0	37 53.3	+21.9	92.8	37 50.0	+23.1	93.5	37 45.9	+24.3	94.3	37 41.0	+25.5	95.1	37 35.2	+26.7	95.9	37 28.7	+27.9	96.6	13
14	38 16.8	+18.6	90.0	38 16.4	+19.9	90.8	38 15.2	+21.1	91.6	38 13.1	+22.4	92.4	38 10.2	+23.6	93.2	38 06.5	+24.8	93.9	38 01.9	+26.1	94.7	37 56.6	+27.2	95.5	14
15	38 35.4	+17.9	88.8	38 36.3	+19.1	89.6	38 36.3	+20.4	90.4	38 35.5	+21.6	91.2	38 33.8	+22.9	92.0	38 31.3	+24.1	92.8	38 28.0	+25.3	93.6	38 23.8	+26.5	94.4	15
16	38 53.3	+17.0	87.6	38 55.4	+18.4	88.4	38 56.7	+19.6	89.2	38 57.1	+20.9	90.0	38 56.7	+22.1	90.8	38 55.4	+23.4	91.6	38 53.3	+24.7	92.4	38 50.3	+25.9	93.2	16
17	39 10.3	+16.3	86.3	39 13.8	+17.5	87.2	39 16.3	+18.9	88.0	39 18.0	+20.1	88.8	39 18.8	+21.5	89.6	39 18.8	+22.7	90.4	39 18.0	+23.9	91.2	39 16.2	+25.2	92.1	17
18	39 26.6	+15.5	85.1	39 31.3	+16.8	85.9	39 35.2	+18.1	86.7	39 38.1	+19.4	87.6	39 40.3	+20.6	88.4	39 41.5	+21.9	89.2	39 41.9	+23.2	90.1	39 41.4	+24.4	90.9	18
19	39 42.1	+14.7	83.8	39 48.1	+16.0	84.7	39 53.3	+17.2	85.5	39 57.5	+18.6	86.3	40 00.9	+19.9	87.2	40 03.4	+21.2	88.0	40 05.1	+22.4	88.9	40 05.8	+23.7	89.7	19
20	39 56.8	+13.8	82.6	40 04.1	+15.1	83.4	40 10.5	+16.5	84.3	40 16.1	+17.8	85.1	40 20.8	+19.1	85.9	40 24.6	+20.4	86.8	40 27.5	+21.7	87.6	40 29.5	+23.0	88.5	20
21	40 10.6	+13.0	81.3	40 19.2	+14.4	82.1	40 27.0	+15.6	83.0	40 33.9	+16.9	83.8	40 39.9	+18.3	84.7	40 45.0	+19.6	85.5	40 49.2	+20.9	86.4	40 52.5	+22.2	87.3	21
22	40 23.6	+12.1	80.0	40 33.6	+13.4	80.9	40 42.6	+14.8	81.7	40 50.8	+16.2	82.6	40 58.2	+17.4	83.4	41 04.6	+18.7	84.3	41 10.1	+20.0	85.2	41 14.7	+21.3	86.0	22
23	40 35.7	+11.3	78.7	40 47.0	+12.6	79.6	40 57.4	+14.0	80.4	41 07.0	+15.2	81.3	41 15.6	+16.6	82.2	41 23.3	+17.9	83.0	41 30.1	+19.3	83.9	41 36.0	+20.6	84.8	23
24	40 47.0	+10.4	77.4	40 59.6	+11.8	78.3	41 11.4	+13.0	79.1	41 22.2	+14.4	80.0	41 32.2	+15.7	80.9	41 41.2	+17.1	81.8	41 49.4	+18.4	82.6	41 56.6	+19.7	83.5	24
25	40 57.4	+9.6	76.1	41 11.4	+10.8	77.0	41 24.4	+12.2	77.8	41 36.6	+13.6	78.7	41 47.9	+14.9	79.6	41 58.3	+16.2	80.5	42 07.8	+17.5	81.4	42 16.3	+18.9	82.3	25
26	41 07.0	+8.6	74.8	41 22.2	+10.0	75.7	41 36.6	+11.3	76.5	41 50.2	+12.6	77.4	42 02.8	+14.0	78.3	42 14.5	+15.3	79.2	42 25.3	+16.7	80.1	42 35.2	+18.0	81.0	26
27	41 15.6	+7.7	73.5	41 32.2	+9.0	74.4	41 47.9	+10.4	75.2	42 02.8	+11.7	76.1	42 16.8	+13.0	77.0	42 29.8	+14.4	77.9	42 42.0	+15.7	78.8	42 53.2	+17.1	79.7	27
28	41 23.3	+6.8	72.2	41 41.2	+8.2	73.0	41 58.3	+9.5	73.9	42 14.5	+10.8	74.8	42 29.8	+12.2	75.7	42 44.2	+13.5	76.5	42 57.7	+14.9	77.5	43 10.3	+16.2	78.4	28
29	41 30.1	+5.9	70.9	41 49.4	+7.2	71.7	42 07.8	+8.5	72.6	42 25.3	+9.9	73.4	42 42.0	+11.2	74.3	42 57.7	+12.6	75.2	43 12.6	+13.9	76.1	43 26.5	+15.3	77.0	29
30	41 36.0	+5.0	69.5	41 56.6	+6.3	70.4	42 16.3	+7.6	71.2	42 35.2	+8.9	72.1	42 53.2	+10.3	73.0	43 10.3	+11.6	73.9	43 26.5	+13.0	74.8	43 41.8	+14.3	75.7	30
31	41 41.0	+4.1	68.2	42 02.9	+5.4	69.0	42 23.9	+6.7	69.9	42 44.1	+8.0	70.8	43 03.5	+9.3	71.6	43 21.9	+10.7	72.5	43 39.5	+12.0	73.4	43 56.1	+13.4	74.4	31
32	41 45.1	+3.1	66.9	42 08.3	+4.4	67.7	42 30.6	+5.7	68.5	42 52.1	+7.1	69.4	43 12.8	+8.4	70.3	43 32.6	+9.7	71.2	43 51.5	+11.1	72.1	44 09.5	+12.4	73.0	32
33	41 48.2	+2.2	65.5	42 12.7	+3.4	66.4	42 36.3	+4.8	67.2	42 59.2	+6.0	68.1	43 21.2	+7.4	68.9	43 42.3	+8.7	69.8	44 02.6	+10.1	70.7	44 21.9	+11.5	71.6	33
34	41 50.4	+1.3	64.2	42 16.1	+2.6	65.0	42 41.1	+3.8	65.8	43 05.2	+5.1	66.7	43 28.6	+6.4	67.6	43 51.0	+7.8	68.4	44 12.7	+9.0	69.3	44 33.4	+10.4	70.3	34
35	41 51.7	+0.3	62.9	42 18.7	+1.5	63.7	42 44.9	+2.8	64.5	43 10.3	+4.2	65.3	43 35.0	+5.4	66.2	43 58.8	+6.7	67.1	44 21.7	+8.1	68.0	44 43.8	+9.4	68.9	35
36	41 52.0	−0.7	61.5	42 20.2	+0.6	62.3	42 47.7	+1.9	63.1	43 14.5	+3.1	64.0	43 40.4	+4.4	64.8	44 05.5	+5.8	65.7	44 29.8	+7.1	66.6	44 53.2	+8.4	67.5	36
37	41 51.3	−1.5	60.2	42 20.8	−0.3	61.0	42 49.6	+0.9	61.8	43 17.6	+2.2	62.6	43 44.8	+3.5	63.4	44 11.3	+4.7	64.3	44 36.9	+6.0	65.2	45 01.6	+7.4	66.1	37
38	41 49.8	−2.5	58.8	42 20.5	−1.3	59.6	42 50.5	−0.1	60.4	43 19.8	+1.1	61.2	43 48.3	+2.4	62.0	44 16.0	+3.7	62.9	44 42.9	+5.0	63.8	45 09.0	+6.3	64.7	38
39	41 47.3	−3.4	57.5	42 19.2	−2.2	58.2	42 50.4	−1.0	59.0	43 20.9	+0.2	59.8	43 50.7	+1.4	60.7	44 19.7	+2.7	61.5	44 47.9	+4.0	62.4	45 15.3	+5.3	63.3	39
40	41 43.9	−4.4	56.1	42 17.0	−3.2	56.9	42 49.4	−2.0	57.7	43 21.1	−0.8	58.5	43 52.1	+0.5	59.3	44 22.4	+1.7	60.1	44 51.9	+3.0	61.0	45 20.6	+4.3	61.9	40
41	41 39.5	−5.3	54.8	42 13.8	−4.2	55.5	42 47.4	−3.0	56.3	43 20.3	−1.8	57.1	43 52.6	−0.6	57.9	44 24.1	+0.6	58.7	44 54.9	+1.9	59.6	45 24.9	+3.2	60.4	41
42	41 34.2	−6.2	53.5	42 09.6	−5.1	54.2	42 44.4	−4.0	54.9	43 18.5	−2.8	55.7	43 52.0	−1.6	56.5	44 24.7	−0.3	57.3	44 56.8	+0.8	58.2	45 28.1	+2.1	59.0	42
43	41 28.0	−7.1	52.1	42 04.5	−6.0	52.9	42 40.4	−4.9	53.6	43 15.7	−3.7	54.3	43 50.4	−2.6	55.1	44 24.4	−1.4	55.9	44 57.6	−0.2	56.7	45 30.2	+1.0	57.6	43
44	41 20.9	−8.1	50.8	41 58.5	−7.0	51.5	42 35.5	−5.8	52.2	43 12.0	−4.8	53.0	43 47.8	−3.6	53.7	44 23.0	−2.5	54.5	44 57.4	−1.2	55.3	45 31.2	0.0	56.2	44
45	41 12.8	−8.9	49.5	41 51.5	−7.8	50.2	42 29.7	−6.8	50.9	43 07.2	−5.7	51.6	43 44.2	−4.6	52.3	44 20.5	−3.4	53.1	44 56.2	−2.3	53.9	45 31.2	−1.1	54.7	45
46	41 03.9	−9.8	48.2	41 43.7	−8.8	48.9	42 22.9	−7.8	49.5	43 01.5	−6.6	50.2	43 39.6	−5.6	51.0	44 17.1	−4.5	51.7	44 53.9	−3.3	52.5	45 30.1	−2.1	53.3	46
47	40 54.1	−10.7	46.9	41 34.9	−9.7	47.5	42 15.1	−8.7	48.2	42 54.9	−7.7	48.9	43 34.0	−6.5	49.6	44 12.6	−5.4	50.3	44 50.6	−4.3	51.1	45 28.0	−3.2	51.9	47
48	40 43.4	−11.6	45.6	41 25.2	−10.6	46.2	42 06.4	−9.6	46.9	42 47.2	−8.6	47.5	43 27.5	−7.6	48.2	44 07.2	−6.5	48.9	44 46.3	−5.4	49.7	45 24.8	−4.3	50.5	48
49	40 31.8	−12.4	44.3	41 14.6	−11.5	44.9	41 56.8	−10.5	45.5	42 38.6	−9.5	46.2	43 19.9	−8.5	46.9	44 00.7	−7.5	47.6	44 40.9	−6.4	48.3	45 20.5	−5.3	49.0	49
50	40 19.4	−13.3	43.0	41 03.1	−12.4	43.6	41 46.3	−11.4	44.2	42 29.1	−10.5	44.8	43 11.4	−9.5	45.5	43 53.2	−8.5	46.2	44 34.5	−7.5	46.9	45 15.2	−6.4	47.6	50
51	40 06.1	−14.1	41.7	40 50.7	−13.2	42.3	41 34.9	−12.3	42.9	42 18.6	−11.4	43.5	43 01.9	−10.4	44.1	43 44.7	−9.4	44.8	44 27.0	−8.4	45.5	45 08.8	−7.4	46.2	51
52	39 52.0	−14.9	40.5	40 37.5	−14.1	41.0	41 22.6	−13.2	41.6	42 07.2	−12.3	42.2	42 51.5	−11.4	42.8	43 35.3	−10.4	43.4	44 18.6	−9.4	44.1	45 01.4	−8.4	44.8	52
53	39 37.1	−15.7	39.2	40 23.4	−14.9	39.7	41 09.4	−14.1	40.3	41 54.9	−13.2	40.9	42 40.1	−12.3	41.5	43 24.9	−11.4	42.1	44 09.2	−10.5	42.7	44 53.0	−9.5	43.4	53
54	39 21.4	−16.6	38.0	40 08.5	−15.7	38.5	40 55.3	−14.9	39.0	41 41.7	−14.0	39.6	42 27.8	−13.2	40.1	43 13.5	−12.3	40.7	43 58.7	−11.4	41.4	44 43.5	−10.4	42.0	54
55	39 04.8	−17.3	36.7	39 52.8	−16.6	37.2	40 40.4	−15.8	37.7	41 27.7	−15.0	38.3	42 14.6	−14.1	38.8	43 01.2	−13.3	39.4	43 47.3	−12.3	40.0	44 33.1	−11.5	40.6	55
56	38 47.5	−18.1	35.5	39 36.2	−17.4	36.0	40 24.6	−16.6	36.5	41 12.7	−15.8	37.0	42 00.5	−15.0	37.5	42 47.9	−14.2	38.1	43 35.0	−13.4	38.6	44 21.6	−12.4	39.3	56
57	38 29.4	−18.9	34.3	39 18.8	−18.1	34.7	40 08.0	−17.4	35.2	40 56.9	−16.6	35.7	41 45.5	−15.9	36.2	42 33.7	−15.0	36.7	43 21.6	−14.2	37.3	44 09.2	−13.4	37.9	57
58	38 10.5	−19.5	33.0	39 00.7	−18.9	33.5	39 50.6	−18.2	33.9	40 40.3	−17.5	34.4	41 29.6	−16.7	34.9	42 18.7	−16.0	35.4	43 07.4	−15.2	36.0	43 55.8	−14.4	36.5	58
59	37 51.0	−20.3	31.8	38 41.8	−19.6	32.3	39 32.4	−19.0	32.7	40 22.8	−18.3	33.2	41 12.9	−17.6	33.6	42 02.7	−16.9	34.1	42 52.2	−16.1	34.6	43 41.4	−15.3	35.2	59
60	37 30.7	−21.1	30.7	38 22.2	−20.4	31.1	39 13.4	−19.7	31.5	40 04.5	−19.1	31.9	40 55.3	−18.4	32.4	41 45.8	−17.6	32.8	42 36.1	−17.0	33.3	43 26.1	−16.2	33.9	60
61	37 09.6	−21.7	29.5	38 01.8	−21.1	29.9	38 53.7	−20.5	30.3	39 45.4	−19.8	30.7	40 36.9	−19.2	31.1	41 28.2	−18.6	31.6	42 19.1	−17.8	32.0	43 09.9	−17.2	32.5	61
62	36 47.9	−22.4	28.3	37 40.7	−21.9	28.7	38 33.2	−21.2	29.1	39 25.6	−20.7	29.5	40 17.7	−20.0	29.9	41 09.6	−19.4	30.3	42 01.3	−18.7	30.7	42 52.7	−18.0	31.2	62
63	36 25.5	−23.0	27.2	37 18.8	−22.5	27.5	38 12.0	−22.0	27.9	39 04.9	−21.3	28.2	39 57.7	−20.8	28.6	40 50.2	−20.1	29.0	41 42.6	−19.5	29.5	42 34.7	−18.9	29.9	63
64	36 02.5	−23.7	26.0	36 56.3	−23.1	26.3	37 50.0	−22.6	26.7	38 43.6	−22.1	27.0	39 36.9	−21.5	27.4	40 30.1	−21.0	27.8	41 23.1	−20.4	28.2	42 15.8	−19.7	28.6	64
65	35 38.8	−24.3	24.9	36 33.2	−23.9	25.2	37 27.4	−23.4	25.5	38 21.5	−22.9	25.9	39 15.4	−22.3	26.2	40 09.1	−21.7	26.6	41 02.7	−21.2	27.0	41 56.1	−20.6	27.4	65
66	35 14.5	−25.0	23.8	36 09.3	−24.5	24.1	37 04.0	−24.0	24.4	37 58.6	−23.5	24.7	38 53.1	−23.0	25.0	39 47.4	−22.5	25.4	40 41.5	−21.9	25.7	41 35.5	−21.4	26.1	66
67	34 49.5	−25.5	22.6	35 44.8	−25.1	22.9	36 40.0	−24.6	23.2	37 35.1	−24.2	23.5	38 30.1	−23.7	23.8	39 24.9	−23.2	24.2	40 19.6	−22.7	24.5	41 14.1	−22.2	24.9	67
68	34 24.0	−26.1	21.5	35 19.7	−25.7	21.8	36 15.4	−25.3	22.1	37 10.9	−24.8	22.4	38 06.4	−24.4	22.7	39 01.7	−24.0	23.0	39 56.9	−23.5	23.3	40 51.9	−23.0	23.6	68
69	33 57.9	−26.7	20.5	34 54.0	−26.3	20.7	35 50.1	−25.9	21.0	36 46.1	−25.5	21.2	37 42.0	−25.1	21.5	38 37.7	−24.6	21.8	39 33.4	−24.2	22.1	40 28.9	−23.7	22.4	69
70	33 31.2	−27.3	19.4	34 27.7	−26.9	19.6	35 24.2	−26.5	19.8	36 20.6	−26.1	20.1	37 16.9	−25.7	20.4	38 13.1	−25.3	20.6	39 09.2	−24.9	20.9	40 05.2	−24.5	21.2	70
71	33 03.9	−27.8	18.3	34 00.8	−27.4	18.5	34 57.7	−27.1	18.7	35 54.5	−26.8	19.0	36 51.2	−26.4	19.2	37 47.8	−26.0	19.5	38 44.3	−25.6	19.7	39 40.7	−25.1	20.0	71
72	32 36.1	−28.3	17.3	33 33.4	−28.0	17.5	34 30.6	−27.7	17.7	35 27.7	−27.3	17.9	36 24.8	−27.0	18.1	37 21.8	−26.6	18.3	38 18.7	−26.2	18.6	39 15.6	−25.9	18.8	72
73	32 07.8	−28.8	16.2	33 05.4	−28.5	16.4	34 02.9	−28.2	16.6	35 00.4	−27.9	16.8	35 57.8	−27.6	17.0	36 55.2	−27.3	17.2	37 52.5	−27.0	17.4	38 49.7	−26.6	17.7	73
74	31 39.0	−29.3	15.2	32 36.9	−29.0	15.4	33 34.7	−28.7	15.5	34 32.5	−28.5	15.7	35 30.2	−28.1	15.9	36 27.9	−27.8	16.1	37 25.5	−27.5	16.3	38 23.1	−27.2	16.5	74
75	31 09.7	−29.8	14.2	32 07.9	−29.6	14.3	33 06.0	−29.3	14.5	34 04.0	−29.0	14.6	35 02.1	−28.8	14.8	36 00.1	−28.5	15.0	36 58.0	−28.2	15.2	37 55.9	−27.9	15.4	75
76	30 39.9	−30.3	13.2	31 38.3	−30.0	13.3	32 36.7	−29.8	13.4	33 35.0	−29.5	13.6	34 33.3	−29.3	13.7	35 31.6	−29.0	13.9	36 29.8	−28.8	14.1	37 28.0	−28.5	14.3	76
77	30 09.6	−30.7	12.2	31 08.3	−30.5	12.3	32 06.9	−30.3	12.4	33 05.5	−30.1	12.5	34 04.0	−29.8	12.7	35 02.6	−29.6	12.8	36 01.0	−29.3	13.0	36 59.5	−29.1	13.2	77
78	29 38.9	−31.1	11.2	30 37.8	−31.0	11.3	31 36.6	−30.7	11.4	32 35.4	−30.5	11.5	33 34.2	−30.3	11.6	34 33.0	−30.2	11.8	35 31.7	−29.9	11.9	36 30.4	−29.7	12.1	78
79	29 07.8	−31.6	10.2	30 06.8	−31.4	10.3	31 05.9	−31.3	10.4	32 04.9	−31.1	10.5	33 03.9	−30.9	10.6	34 02.8	−30.6	10.7	35 01.8	−30.5	10.9	36 00.7	−30.3	11.0	79
80	28 36.2	−32.0	9.2	29 35.4	−31.8	9.3	30 34.6	−31.6	9.4	31 33.8	−31.5	9.5	32 33.0	−31.3	9.6	33 32.2	−31.2	9.7	34 31.3	−31.0	9.8	35 30.4	−30.8	9.9	80
81	28 04.2	−32.3	8.2	29 03.6	−32.2	8.3	30 03.0	−32.1	8.4	31 02.3	−31.9	8.5	32 01.7	−31.9	8.6	33 01.0	−31.7	8.7	34 00.3	−31.5	8.8	34 59.6	−31.4	8.9	81
82	27 31.9	−32.8	7.3	28 31.4	−32.7	7.4	29 30.9	−32.6	7.4	30 30.4	−32.4	7.5	31 29.8	−32.2	7.6	32 29.3	−32.1	7.7	33 28.8	−32.0	7.8	34 28.2	−31.9	7.8	82
83	26 59.1	−33.1	6.4	27 58.7	−33.0	6.4	28 58.3	−32.9	6.5	29 58.0	−32.9	6.5	30 57.6	−32.7	6.6	31 57.2	−32.6	6.7	32 56.8	−32.5	6.7	33 56.3	−32.3	6.8	83
84	26 26.0	−33.5	5.4	27 25.7	−33.4	5.5	28 25.4	−33.3	5.5	29 25.1	−33.2	5.6	30 24.9	−33.2	5.6	31 24.6	−33.1	5.7	32 24.3	−33.0	5.7	33 24.0	−32.9	5.8	84
85	25 52.5	−33.9	4.5	26 52.3	−33.8	4.5	27 52.1	−33.7	4.6	28 51.9	−33.6	4.6	29 51.7	−33.6	4.7	30 51.5	−33.5	4.7	31 51.3	−33.4	4.8	32 51.1	−33.4	4.8	85
86	25 18.6	−34.2	3.6	26 18.5	−34.1	3.6	27 18.4	−34.1	3.6	28 18.3	−34.1	3.7	29 18.1	−33.9	3.7	30 18.0	−33.9	3.7	31 17.9	−33.9	3.8	32 17.7	−33.7	3.8	86
87	24 44.4	−34.5	2.7	25 44.4	−34.5	2.7	26 44.3	−34.4	2.7	27 44.2	−34.4	2.7	28 44.2	−34.4	2.8	29 44.1	−34.3	2.8	30 44.0	−34.2	2.8	31 44.0	−34.3	2.9	87
88	24 09.9	−34.8	1.8	25 09.9	−34.8	1.8	26 09.9	−34.8	1.8	27 09.8	−34.7	1.8	28 09.8	−34.7	1.8	29 09.8	−34.7	1.9	30 09.8	−34.7	1.9	31 09.7	−34.6	1.9	88
89	23 35.1	−35.1	0.9	24 35.1	−35.1	0.9	25 35.1	−35.1	0.9	26 35.1	−35.1	0.9	27 35.1	−35.1	0.9	28 35.1	−35.1	0.9	29 35.1	−35.1	0.9	30 35.1	−35.1	0.9	89
90	23 00.0	−35.4	0.0	24 00.0	−35.4	0.0	25 00.0	−35.4	0.0	26 00.0	−35.4	0.0	27 00.0	−35.4	0.0	28 00.0	−35.4	0.0	29 00.0	−35.5	0.0	30 00.0	−35.5	0.0	90
	23°			24°			25°			26°			27°			28°			29°			30°			

54°, 306° L.H.A. LATITUDE SAME NAME AS DECLINATION

292

LATITUDE CONTRARY NAME TO DECLINATION L.H.A. 54°, 306°

Dec.	23° Hc	d	Z	24° Hc	d	Z	25° Hc	d	Z	26° Hc	d	Z
°	° ′	′	°	° ′	′	°	° ′	′	°	° ′	′	°
0	32 45.3	-28.1	105.8	32 28.7	-29.2	106.5	32 11.3	-30.2	107.1	31 53.4	-31.2	107.7
1	32 17.2	-28.6	106.9	31 59.5	-29.7	107.5	31 41.1	-30.7	108.1	31 22.2	-31.7	108.7
2	31 48.6	-29.2	107.9	31 29.8	-30.2	108.5	31 10.4	-31.1	109.1	30 50.5	-32.1	109.7
3	31 19.4	-29.6	109.0	30 59.6	-30.6	109.5	30 39.3	-31.6	110.1	30 18.4	-32.5	110.6
4	30 49.8	-30.1	110.0	30 29.0	-31.1	110.5	30 07.7	-32.0	111.1	29 45.9	-33.0	111.6
5	30 19.7	-30.6	111.0	29 57.9	-31.5	111.5	29 35.7	-32.5	112.1	29 12.9	-33.4	112.6
6	29 49.1	-31.0	112.0	29 26.4	-31.9	112.5	29 03.2	-32.9	113.0	28 39.5	-33.8	113.5
7	29 18.1	-31.4	113.0	28 54.5	-32.4	113.5	28 30.3	-33.3	114.0	28 05.7	-34.2	114.5
8	28 46.7	-31.9	113.9	28 22.1	-32.8	114.4	27 57.0	-33.6	114.9	27 31.5	-34.5	115.4
9	28 14.8	-32.2	114.9	27 49.3	-33.1	115.4	27 23.4	-34.0	115.8	26 57.0	-34.9	116.3
10	27 42.6	-32.7	115.9	27 16.2	-33.5	116.3	26 49.4	-34.4	116.8	26 22.1	-35.2	117.2
11	27 09.9	-33.0	116.8	26 42.7	-33.9	117.2	26 15.0	-34.7	117.7	25 46.9	-35.5	118.1
12	26 36.9	-33.4	117.7	26 08.8	-34.2	118.2	25 40.3	-35.1	118.6	25 11.4	-35.9	119.0
13	26 03.5	-33.7	118.7	25 34.6	-34.6	119.1	25 05.2	-35.4	119.5	24 35.5	-36.2	119.9
14	25 29.8	-34.1	119.6	25 00.0	-34.9	120.0	24 29.8	-35.7	120.4	23 59.3	-36.5	120.8
15	24 55.7	-34.4	120.5	24 25.1	-35.2	120.9	23 54.1	-35.9	121.3	23 22.8	-36.7	121.6
16	24 21.3	-34.7	121.4	23 49.9	-35.5	121.8	23 18.2	-36.3	122.1	22 46.1	-37.0	122.5
17	23 46.6	-35.0	122.3	23 14.4	-35.8	122.6	22 41.9	-36.6	123.0	22 09.1	-37.3	123.4
18	23 11.6	-35.3	123.2	22 38.6	-36.1	123.5	22 05.3	-36.8	123.9	21 31.8	-37.6	124.2
19	22 36.3	-35.6	124.0	22 02.5	-36.3	124.4	21 28.5	-37.1	124.7	20 54.2	-37.8	125.0
20	22 00.7	-35.9	124.9	21 26.2	-36.6	125.2	20 51.4	-37.3	125.6	20 16.4	-38.0	125.9
21	21 24.8	-36.1	125.8	20 49.6	-36.9	126.1	20 14.1	-37.5	126.4	19 38.4	-38.2	126.7
22	20 48.7	-36.4	126.6	20 12.7	-37.0	126.9	19 36.6	-37.8	127.2	19 00.2	-38.5	127.5
23	20 12.3	-36.6	127.5	19 35.7	-37.4	127.8	18 58.8	-38.0	128.0	18 21.7	-38.7	128.3
24	19 35.7	-36.9	128.3	18 58.3	-37.5	128.6	18 20.8	-38.2	128.9	17 43.0	-38.8	129.1
25	18 58.8	-37.1	129.2	18 20.8	-37.8	129.4	17 42.6	-38.4	129.7	17 04.2	-39.1	129.9
26	18 21.7	-37.3	130.0	17 43.0	-37.9	130.2	17 04.2	-38.6	130.5	16 25.1	-39.2	130.7
27	17 44.4	-37.5	130.8	17 05.1	-38.2	131.1	16 25.6	-38.8	131.3	15 45.9	-39.4	131.5
28	17 06.9	-37.7	131.6	16 26.9	-38.3	131.9	15 46.8	-38.9	132.1	15 06.5	-39.5	132.3
29	16 29.2	-37.9	132.4	15 48.6	-38.5	132.7	15 07.9	-39.1	132.9	14 27.0	-39.7	133.1
30	15 51.3	-38.1	133.3	15 10.1	-38.7	133.5	14 28.8	-39.3	133.6	13 47.3	-39.9	133.8
31	15 13.2	-38.2	134.1	14 31.4	-38.8	134.2	13 49.5	-39.4	134.4	13 07.4	-39.9	134.6
32	14 35.0	-38.4	134.9	13 52.6	-39.0	135.0	13 10.1	-39.5	135.2	12 27.5	-40.1	135.4
33	13 56.6	-38.5	135.6	13 13.6	-39.1	135.8	12 30.6	-39.7	136.0	11 47.4	-40.3	136.1
34	13 18.1	-38.7	136.4	12 34.5	-39.2	136.6	11 50.9	-39.8	136.7	11 07.1	-40.3	136.9
35	12 39.4	-38.9	137.2	11 55.3	-39.4	137.4	11 11.1	-39.9	137.5	10 26.8	-40.5	137.6
36	12 00.5	-38.9	138.0	11 15.9	-39.5	138.1	10 31.2	-40.1	138.3	9 46.3	-40.5	138.4
37	11 21.6	-39.1	138.8	10 36.4	-39.6	138.9	9 51.1	-40.1	139.0	9 05.8	-40.6	139.1
38	10 42.5	-39.2	139.5	9 56.8	-39.7	139.7	9 11.0	-40.2	139.8	8 25.2	-40.8	139.9
39	10 03.3	-39.3	140.3	9 17.1	-39.8	140.4	8 30.8	-40.3	140.5	7 44.4	-40.8	140.6
40	9 24.0	-39.4	141.1	8 37.3	-39.9	141.2	7 50.5	-40.4	141.3	7 03.6	-40.8	141.4
41	8 44.6	-39.5	141.8	7 57.4	-40.0	141.9	7 10.1	-40.5	142.0	6 22.8	-41.0	142.1
42	8 05.1	-39.6	142.6	7 17.4	-40.1	142.7	6 29.6	-40.5	142.8	5 41.8	-40.9	142.8
43	7 25.5	-39.7	143.4	6 37.3	-40.1	143.4	5 49.1	-40.6	143.5	5 00.9	-41.1	143.6
44	6 45.8	-39.7	144.1	5 57.2	-40.2	144.2	5 08.5	-40.6	144.2	4 19.8	-41.1	144.3
45	6 06.1	-39.8	144.9	5 17.0	-40.2	144.9	4 27.9	-40.7	145.0	3 38.7	-41.1	145.0
46	5 26.3	-39.8	145.6	4 36.8	-40.3	145.7	3 47.2	-40.7	145.7	2 57.6	-41.1	145.8
47	4 46.5	-39.9	146.4	3 56.5	-40.3	146.4	3 06.5	-40.7	146.5	2 16.5	-41.2	146.5
48	4 06.6	-39.9	147.1	3 16.2	-40.4	147.2	2 25.8	-40.8	147.2	1 35.3	-41.1	147.2
49	3 26.7	-40.0	147.9	2 35.8	-40.3	147.9	1 45.0	-40.8	147.9	0 54.2	-41.2	147.9
50	2 46.7	-40.0	148.6	1 55.5	-40.4	148.6	1 04.2	-40.8	148.7	0 13.0	-41.2	148.7
51	2 06.7	-40.0	149.4	1 15.1	-40.5	149.4	0 23.4	-40.8	149.4	0 28.2	+41.2	30.6
52	1 26.7	-40.1	150.1	0 34.6	-40.4	150.1	0 17.4	+40.8	29.9	1 09.4	+41.2	29.9
53	0 46.6	-40.0	150.9	0 05.8	+40.4	29.1	0 58.2	+40.8	29.1	1 50.6	+41.1	29.2
54	0 06.6	-40.0	151.6	0 46.2	+40.4	28.4	1 39.0	+40.7	28.4	2 31.7	+41.2	28.4
55	0 33.4	+40.1	27.6	1 26.6	+40.4	27.7	2 19.7	+40.8	27.7	3 12.9	+41.1	27.7
56	1 13.5	+40.0	26.9	2 07.0	+40.4	26.9	3 00.5	+40.7	26.9	3 54.0	+41.0	27.0
57	1 53.5	+40.0	26.2	2 47.4	+40.3	26.2	3 41.2	+40.7	26.2	4 35.0	+41.0	26.2
58	2 33.5	+40.0	25.4	3 27.7	+40.3	25.4	4 21.9	+40.6	25.5	5 16.0	+41.0	25.5
59	3 13.5	+39.9	24.7	4 08.0	+40.3	24.7	5 02.5	+40.6	24.7	5 57.0	+40.9	24.8
60	3 53.4	+39.9	23.9	4 48.3	+40.2	23.9	5 43.1	+40.5	24.0	6 37.9	+40.9	24.0
61	4 33.3	+39.9	23.2	5 28.5	+40.2	23.2	6 23.6	+40.5	23.2	7 18.8	+40.7	23.3
62	5 13.2	+39.8	22.4	6 08.7	+40.1	22.5	7 04.1	+40.4	22.5	7 59.5	+40.7	22.6
63	5 53.0	+39.8	21.7	6 48.8	+40.0	21.7	7 44.5	+40.3	21.8	8 40.2	+40.6	21.8
64	6 32.8	+39.6	20.9	7 28.8	+40.0	21.0	8 24.8	+40.3	21.0	9 20.8	+40.5	21.1
65	7 12.4	+39.6	20.2	8 08.8	+39.8	20.2	9 05.1	+40.1	20.3	10 01.3	+40.4	20.3
66	7 52.0	+39.6	19.4	8 48.6	+39.8	19.5	9 45.2	+40.0	19.5	10 41.7	+40.3	19.6
67	8 31.6	+39.4	18.6	9 28.4	+39.7	18.7	10 25.2	+40.0	18.7	11 22.0	+40.2	18.8
68	9 11.0	+39.3	17.9	10 08.1	+39.6	17.9	11 05.2	+39.8	18.0	12 02.2	+40.1	18.1
69	9 50.3	+39.3	17.1	10 47.7	+39.4	17.2	11 45.0	+39.7	17.2	12 42.3	+39.9	17.3
70	10 29.6	+39.1	16.3	11 27.1	+39.4	16.4	12 24.7	+39.6	16.5	13 22.2	+39.8	16.5
71	11 08.7	+39.0	15.6	12 06.5	+39.2	15.6	13 04.3	+39.4	15.7	14 02.0	+39.7	15.8
72	11 47.7	+38.9	14.8	12 45.7	+39.1	14.9	13 43.7	+39.3	14.9	14 41.7	+39.5	15.0
73	12 26.6	+38.7	14.0	13 24.8	+38.9	14.1	14 23.0	+39.1	14.1	15 21.2	+39.3	14.2
74	13 05.3	+38.6	13.2	14 03.7	+38.8	13.3	15 02.1	+39.0	13.4	16 00.5	+39.1	13.4
75	13 43.9	+38.5	12.4	14 42.5	+38.6	12.5	15 41.1	+38.8	12.6	16 39.6	+39.0	12.6
76	14 22.4	+38.3	11.7	15 21.1	+38.5	11.7	16 19.9	+38.6	11.8	17 18.6	+38.8	11.8
77	15 00.7	+38.1	10.9	15 59.6	+38.3	10.9	16 58.5	+38.4	11.0	17 57.4	+38.6	11.0
78	15 38.8	+37.9	10.1	16 37.9	+38.0	10.1	17 36.9	+38.3	10.2	18 36.0	+38.4	10.2
79	16 16.7	+37.8	9.3	17 15.9	+37.9	9.3	18 15.2	+38.0	9.4	19 14.4	+38.1	9.4
80	16 54.5	+37.6	8.4	17 53.8	+37.7	8.5	18 53.2	+37.8	8.5	19 52.5	+38.0	8.6
81	17 32.1	+37.3	7.6	18 31.5	+37.5	7.7	19 31.0	+37.6	7.7	20 30.5	+37.6	7.8
82	18 09.4	+37.2	6.8	19 09.0	+37.3	6.8	20 08.6	+37.3	6.9	21 08.1	+37.5	6.9
83	18 46.6	+36.9	6.0	19 46.3	+37.0	6.0	20 45.9	+37.1	6.1	21 45.6	+37.2	6.1
84	19 23.5	+36.7	5.1	20 23.3	+36.8	5.2	21 23.0	+36.9	5.2	22 22.8	+36.9	5.2
85	20 00.2	+36.5	4.3	21 00.1	+36.5	4.3	21 59.9	+36.6	4.4	22 59.7	+36.7	4.4
86	20 36.7	+36.2	3.5	21 36.6	+36.3	3.5	22 36.5	+36.3	3.5	23 36.4	+36.3	3.5
87	21 12.9	+36.0	2.6	22 12.9	+36.0	2.6	23 12.8	+36.0	2.6	24 12.7	+36.1	2.7
88	21 48.9	+35.7	1.7	22 48.9	+35.7	1.8	23 48.8	+35.8	1.8	24 48.8	+35.8	1.8
89	22 24.6	+35.4	0.9	23 24.6	+35.4	0.9	24 24.6	+35.4	0.9	25 24.6	+35.4	0.9
90	23 00.0	+35.1	0.0	24 00.0	+35.1	0.0	25 00.0	+35.1	0.0	26 00.0	+35.1	0.0
	23°			24°			25°			26°		

27° Hc	d	Z	28° Hc	d	Z	29° Hc	d	Z	30° Hc	d	Z	Dec.
° ′	′	°	° ′	′	°	° ′	′	°	° ′	′	°	°
31 34.9	-32.2	108.3	31 15.8	-33.1	108.8	30 56.2	-34.1	109.4	30 36.0	-35.1	110.0	0
31 02.7	-32.6	109.2	30 42.7	-33.6	109.8	30 22.1	-34.6	110.4	30 00.9	-35.4	110.9	1
30 30.1	-33.1	110.2	30 09.1	-34.0	110.8	29 47.5	-34.9	111.3	29 25.5	-35.9	111.8	2
29 57.0	-33.5	111.2	29 35.1	-34.5	111.7	29 12.6	-35.3	112.2	28 49.6	-36.2	112.8	3
29 23.5	-33.9	112.1	29 00.6	-34.8	112.7	28 37.3	-35.7	113.2	28 13.4	-36.5	113.7	4
28 49.6	-34.3	113.1	28 25.8	-35.2	113.6	28 01.6	-36.1	114.1	27 36.9	-36.9	114.6	5
28 15.3	-34.7	114.0	27 50.6	-35.5	114.5	27 25.5	-36.4	115.0	27 00.0	-37.3	115.4	6
27 40.6	-35.0	114.9	27 15.1	-35.9	115.4	26 49.1	-36.7	115.9	26 22.7	-37.5	116.3	7
27 05.6	-35.4	115.9	26 39.2	-36.2	116.3	26 12.4	-37.0	116.8	25 45.2	-37.9	117.2	8
26 30.2	-35.7	116.8	26 03.0	-36.6	117.2	25 35.4	-37.4	117.6	25 07.3	-38.1	118.0	9
25 54.5	-36.1	117.7	25 26.4	-36.8	118.1	24 58.0	-37.7	118.5	24 29.2	-38.4	118.9	10
25 18.4	-36.3	118.5	24 49.6	-37.2	119.0	24 20.3	-37.9	119.4	23 50.8	-38.7	119.7	11
24 42.1	-36.7	119.4	24 12.4	-37.4	119.8	23 42.4	-38.2	120.2	23 12.1	-39.0	120.6	12
24 05.4	-37.0	120.3	23 35.0	-37.8	120.7	23 04.2	-38.5	121.0	22 33.1	-39.2	121.4	13
23 28.4	-37.2	121.2	22 57.2	-38.0	121.5	22 25.7	-38.7	121.9	21 53.9	-39.5	122.2	14
22 51.2	-37.5	122.0	22 19.2	-38.2	122.4	21 47.0	-39.0	122.7	21 14.4	-39.7	123.0	15
22 13.7	-37.8	122.8	21 41.0	-38.5	123.2	21 08.0	-39.2	123.5	20 34.7	-39.9	123.8	16
21 35.9	-38.0	123.7	21 02.5	-38.7	124.0	20 28.8	-39.4	124.3	19 54.8	-40.1	124.6	17
20 57.9	-38.3	124.5	20 23.8	-39.0	124.8	19 49.4	-39.7	125.1	19 14.7	-40.3	125.4	18
20 19.6	-38.5	125.3	19 44.8	-39.2	125.6	19 09.7	-39.8	125.9	18 34.4	-40.5	126.2	19
19 41.1	-38.7	126.2	19 05.6	-39.4	126.4	18 29.9	-40.1	126.7	17 53.9	-40.7	127.0	20
19 02.4	-38.9	127.0	18 26.2	-39.5	127.2	17 49.8	-40.2	127.5	17 13.2	-40.9	127.7	21
18 23.5	-39.1	127.8	17 46.7	-39.8	128.0	17 09.6	-40.4	128.3	16 32.3	-41.0	128.5	22
17 44.4	-39.3	128.6	17 06.9	-40.0	128.8	16 29.2	-40.6	129.0	15 51.3	-41.2	129.3	23
17 05.1	-39.5	129.4	16 26.9	-40.1	129.6	15 48.6	-40.7	129.8	15 10.1	-41.3	130.0	24
16 25.6	-39.7	130.1	15 46.8	-40.3	130.4	15 07.9	-40.9	130.6	14 28.8	-41.5	130.8	25
15 45.9	-39.8	130.9	15 06.5	-40.4	131.1	14 27.0	-41.0	131.3	13 47.3	-41.6	131.5	26
15 06.1	-40.0	131.7	14 26.1	-40.6	131.9	13 46.0	-41.2	132.1	13 05.7	-41.8	132.3	27
14 26.1	-40.1	132.5	13 45.5	-40.7	132.7	13 04.8	-41.3	132.8	12 23.9	-41.8	133.0	28
13 46.0	-40.3	133.2	13 04.8	-40.9	133.4	12 23.5	-41.4	133.6	11 42.1	-42.0	133.7	29
13 05.7	-40.4	134.0	12 23.9	-40.9	134.2	11 42.1	-41.6	134.3	11 00.1	-42.1	134.5	30
12 25.3	-40.6	134.8	11 43.0	-41.1	134.9	11 00.5	-41.6	135.1	10 18.0	-42.1	135.2	31
11 44.7	-40.6	135.5	11 01.9	-41.2	135.7	10 18.9	-41.7	135.8	9 35.9	-42.3	135.9	32
11 04.1	-40.8	136.3	10 20.7	-41.3	136.4	9 37.2	-41.9	136.5	8 53.6	-42.3	136.6	33
10 23.3	-40.9	137.0	9 39.4	-41.4	137.1	8 55.3	-41.9	137.2	8 11.3	-42.5	137.3	34
9 42.4	-41.0	137.8	8 58.0	-41.5	137.9	8 13.4	-42.0	138.0	7 28.8	-42.5	138.1	35
9 01.4	-41.0	138.5	8 16.5	-41.6	138.6	7 31.4	-42.0	138.7	6 46.3	-42.5	138.8	36
8 20.4	-41.2	139.2	7 34.9	-41.6	139.3	6 49.4	-42.1	139.4	6 03.8	-42.6	139.5	37
7 39.2	-41.2	140.0	6 53.3	-41.7	140.0	6 07.3	-42.2	140.1	5 21.2	-42.7	140.2	38
6 58.0	-41.2	140.7	6 11.6	-41.8	140.8	5 25.1	-42.2	140.8	4 38.5	-42.7	140.9	39
6 16.8	-41.4	141.4	5 29.8	-41.8	141.5	4 42.9	-42.3	141.5	3 55.8	-42.7	141.6	40
5 35.4	-41.4	142.2	4 48.0	-41.8	142.2	4 00.6	-42.3	142.3	3 13.1	-42.7	142.3	41
4 54.0	-41.4	142.9	4 06.2	-41.9	142.9	3 18.3	-42.4	143.0	2 30.4	-42.8	143.0	42
4 12.6	-41.5	143.6	3 24.3	-42.0	143.6	2 35.9	-42.3	143.7	1 47.6	-42.8	143.7	43
3 31.1	-41.5	144.3	2 42.3	-41.9	144.4	1 53.6	-42.4	144.4	1 04.8	-42.8	144.4	44
2 49.6	-41.6	145.1	2 00.4	-42.0	145.1	1 11.2	-42.4	145.1	0 22.0	-42.8	145.1	45
2 08.0	-41.5	145.8	1 18.4	-42.0	145.8	0 28.8	-42.4	145.8	0 20.8	+42.9	34.2	46
1 26.5	-41.6	146.5	0 36.4	-42.0	146.5	0 13.6	+42.4	33.5	1 03.7	+42.8	33.5	47
0 44.9	-41.6	147.2	0 05.6	+41.9	32.8	0 56.0	+42.4	32.8	1 46.5	+42.7	32.8	48
0 03.3	-41.6	147.9	0 47.5	+42.0	32.1	1 38.4	+42.4	32.1	2 29.2	+42.8	32.1	49
0 38.3	+41.6	31.3	1 29.5	+42.0	31.3	2 20.8	+42.3	31.4	3 12.0	+42.7	31.4	50
1 19.9	+41.5	30.6	2 11.5	+41.9	30.6	3 03.1	+42.3	30.7	3 54.7	+42.7	30.7	51
2 01.4	+41.6	29.9	2 53.4	+42.0	29.9	3 45.4	+42.3	29.9	4 37.4	+42.7	30.0	52
2 43.0	+41.5	29.2	3 35.4	+41.8	29.2	4 27.7	+42.3	29.2	5 20.1	+42.6	29.3	53
3 24.5	+41.5	28.4	4 17.2	+41.9	28.5	5 10.0	+42.2	28.5	6 02.7	+42.5	28.6	54
4 06.0	+41.4	27.7	4 59.1	+41.8	27.8	5 52.2	+42.1	27.8	6 45.2	+42.5	27.9	55
4 47.4	+41.4	27.0	5 40.9	+41.7	27.0	6 34.3	+42.1	27.1	7 27.7	+42.4	27.1	56
5 28.8	+41.4	26.3	6 22.6	+41.7	26.3	7 16.4	+42.0	26.4	8 10.1	+42.4	26.4	57
6 10.2	+41.3	25.5	7 04.3	+41.6	25.6	7 58.4	+42.0	25.7	8 52.5	+42.3	25.7	58
6 51.5	+41.2	24.8	7 45.9	+41.6	24.9	8 40.4	+41.8	24.9	9 34.8	+42.1	25.0	59
7 32.7	+41.2	24.1	8 27.5	+41.4	24.1	9 22.2	+41.8	24.2	10 16.9	+42.1	24.3	60
8 13.9	+41.0	23.3	9 08.9	+41.4	23.4	10 04.0	+41.7	23.5	10 59.0	+42.0	23.5	61
8 54.9	+41.0	22.6	9 50.3	+41.3	22.7	10 45.7	+41.5	22.7	11 41.0	+41.8	22.8	62
9 35.9	+40.9	21.9	10 31.6	+41.2	21.9	11 27.2	+41.5	22.0	12 22.8	+41.8	22.1	63
10 16.8	+40.8	21.1	11 12.8	+41.0	21.2	12 08.7	+41.3	21.3	13 04.6	+41.6	21.4	64
10 57.6	+40.7	20.4	11 53.8	+41.0	20.5	12 50.0	+41.2	20.5	13 46.2	+41.5	20.6	65
11 38.3	+40.5	19.6	12 34.8	+40.8	19.7	13 31.2	+41.1	19.8	14 27.7	+41.3	19.9	66
12 18.8	+40.5	18.9	13 15.6	+40.7	19.0	14 12.3	+41.0	19.0	15 09.0	+41.2	19.1	67
12 59.3	+40.3	18.1	13 56.3	+40.5	18.2	14 53.3	+40.8	18.3	15 50.2	+41.1	18.4	68
13 39.6	+40.1	17.4	14 36.8	+40.4	17.4	15 34.1	+40.6	17.5	16 31.3	+40.8	17.6	69
14 19.7	+40.1	16.6	15 17.2	+40.3	16.7	16 14.7	+40.5	16.8	17 12.1	+40.7	16.8	70
14 59.8	+39.8	15.8	15 57.5	+40.0	15.9	16 55.2	+40.3	16.0	17 52.8	+40.5	16.1	71
15 39.6	+39.7	15.0	16 37.5	+39.9	15.1	17 35.5	+40.1	15.2	18 33.3	+40.4	15.3	72
16 19.3	+39.5	14.3	17 17.4	+39.8	14.3	18 15.6	+39.9	14.4	19 13.7	+40.1	14.5	73
16 58.8	+39.4	13.5	17 57.2	+39.5	13.6	18 55.5	+39.7	13.6	19 53.8	+39.9	13.7	74
17 38.2	+39.1	12.7	18 36.7	+39.3	12.8	19 35.2	+39.5	12.8	20 33.7	+39.7	12.9	75
18 17.3	+39.0	11.9	19 16.0	+39.1	12.0	20 14.7	+39.3	12.0	21 13.4	+39.4	12.1	76
18 56.3	+38.7	11.1	19 55.1	+38.9	11.2	20 54.0	+39.1	11.2	21 52.8	+39.3	11.3	77
19 35.0	+38.5	10.3	20 34.0	+38.7	10.3	21 33.1	+38.8	10.4	22 32.1	+38.9	10.5	78
20 13.5	+38.3	9.5	21 12.7	+38.5	9.5	22 11.9	+38.6	9.6	23 11.0	+38.7	9.7	79
20 51.8	+38.1	8.6	21 51.2	+38.1	8.7	22 50.5	+38.3	8.8	23 49.7	+38.5	8.8	80
21 29.9	+37.8	7.8	22 29.3	+38.0	7.9	23 28.8	+38.0	7.9	24 28.2	+38.1	8.0	81
22 07.7	+37.6	7.0	23 07.3	+37.6	7.0	24 06.8	+37.8	7.1	25 06.3	+37.9	7.1	82
22 45.3	+37.2	6.1	23 44.9	+37.4	6.2	24 44.6	+37.4	6.2	25 44.2	+37.6	6.3	83
23 22.5	+37.1	5.3	24 22.3	+37.1	5.3	25 22.0	+37.2	5.4	26 21.8	+37.2	5.4	84
23 59.6	+36.7	4.4	24 59.4	+36.8	4.5	25 59.2	+36.8	4.5	26 59.0	+36.9	4.5	85
24 36.3	+36.4	3.6	25 36.2	+36.4	3.6	26 36.0	+36.5	3.6	27 35.9	+36.6	3.7	86
25 12.7	+36.1	2.7	26 12.6	+36.2	2.7	27 12.5	+36.2	2.7	28 12.5	+36.2	2.8	87
25 48.8	+35.8	1.8	26 48.8	+35.8	1.8	27 48.7	+35.8	1.8	28 48.7	+35.8	1.8	88
26 24.6	+35.4	0.9	27 24.6	+35.4	0.9	28 24.5	+35.5	0.9	29 24.5	+35.5	0.9	89
27 00.0	+35.1	0.0	28 00.0	+35.1	0.0	29 00.0	+35.1	0.0	30 00.0	+35.1	0.0	90
27°			28°			29°			30°			

S. Lat. {L.H.A. greater than 180° ....Zn=180°–Z
{L.H.A. less than 180°............Zn=180°+Z

LATITUDE SAME NAME AS DECLINATION L.H.A. 126°, 234°

55°, 305° L.H.A. LATITUDE SAME NAME AS DECLINATION N. Lat. {L.H.A. greater than 180° .....Zn=Z; L.H.A. less than 180°.............Zn=360°−Z}

Dec.	23° Hc	d	Z	24° Hc	d	Z	25° Hc	d	Z	26° Hc	d	Z	27° Hc	d	Z	28° Hc	d	Z	29° Hc	d	Z	30° Hc	d	Z	Dec.
°	° ′	′	°	° ′	′	°	° ′	′	°	° ′	′	°	° ′	′	°	° ′	′	°	° ′	′	°	° ′	′	°	°
0	31 52.1	+27.4	105.3	31 36.0	+28.4	105.9	31 19.3	+29.4	106.5	31 02.0	+30.4	107.1	30 44.1	+31.4	107.6	30 25.6	+32.5	108.2	30 06.6	+33.4	108.8	29 47.0	+34.4	109.3	0
1	32 19.5	+26.8	104.3	32 04.4	+27.9	104.9	31 48.7	+29.0	105.5	31 32.4	+30.0	106.1	31 15.5	+31.0	106.6	30 58.1	+32.0	107.2	30 40.0	+33.0	107.8	30 21.4	+34.0	108.3	1
2	32 46.3	+26.3	103.2	32 32.3	+27.4	103.8	32 17.7	+28.4	104.4	32 02.4	+29.5	105.0	31 46.5	+30.6	105.6	31 30.1	+31.5	106.2	31 13.0	+32.5	106.8	30 55.4	+33.5	107.4	2
3	33 12.6	+25.7	102.1	32 59.7	+26.8	102.8	32 46.1	+27.9	103.4	32 31.9	+29.0	104.0	32 17.1	+30.0	104.6	32 01.6	+31.1	105.2	31 45.5	+32.1	105.8	31 28.9	+33.0	106.4	3
4	33 38.3	+25.2	101.0	33 26.5	+26.3	101.7	33 14.0	+27.4	102.3	33 00.9	+28.4	103.0	32 47.1	+29.5	103.6	32 32.7	+30.5	104.2	32 17.6	+31.6	104.8	32 01.9	+32.7	105.4	4
5	34 03.5	+24.5	99.9	33 52.8	+25.6	100.6	33 41.4	+26.8	101.3	33 29.3	+27.9	101.9	33 16.6	+29.0	102.6	33 03.2	+30.1	103.2	32 49.2	+31.1	103.8	32 34.6	+32.1	104.4	5
6	34 28.0	+24.0	98.8	34 18.4	+25.2	99.5	34 08.2	+26.2	100.2	33 57.2	+27.4	100.8	33 45.6	+28.5	101.5	33 33.3	+29.5	102.2	33 20.3	+30.6	102.8	33 06.7	+31.7	103.4	6
7	34 52.0	+23.3	97.7	34 43.6	+24.5	98.4	34 34.4	+25.7	99.1	34 24.6	+26.8	99.8	34 14.1	+27.9	100.4	34 02.8	+29.0	101.1	33 50.9	+30.1	101.8	33 38.4	+31.1	102.4	7
8	35 15.3	+22.7	96.6	35 08.1	+23.8	97.3	35 00.1	+25.0	98.0	34 51.4	+26.2	98.7	34 42.0	+27.3	99.4	34 31.8	+28.5	100.1	34 21.0	+29.6	100.7	34 09.5	+30.6	101.4	8
9	35 38.0	+22.1	95.5	35 31.9	+23.3	96.2	35 25.1	+24.5	96.9	35 17.6	+25.6	97.6	35 09.3	+26.7	98.3	35 00.3	+27.9	99.0	34 50.6	+29.0	99.7	34 40.1	+30.1	100.4	9
10	36 00.1	+21.4	94.3	35 55.2	+22.6	95.0	35 49.6	+23.8	95.8	35 43.2	+24.9	96.5	35 36.0	+26.2	97.2	35 28.2	+27.2	97.9	35 19.6	+28.4	98.6	35 10.2	+29.6	99.3	10
11	36 21.5	+20.7	93.2	36 17.8	+22.0	93.9	36 13.4	+23.1	94.6	36 08.1	+24.4	95.4	36 02.2	+25.5	96.1	35 55.4	+26.7	96.8	35 48.0	+27.8	97.5	35 39.8	+28.9	98.2	11
12	36 42.2	+20.1	92.0	36 39.8	+21.2	92.7	36 36.5	+22.5	93.5	36 32.5	+23.7	94.2	36 27.7	+24.9	95.0	36 22.1	+26.1	95.7	36 15.8	+27.2	96.4	36 08.7	+28.4	97.1	12
13	37 02.3	+19.3	90.8	37 01.0	+20.6	91.6	36 59.0	+21.8	92.3	36 56.2	+23.0	93.1	36 52.6	+24.2	93.8	36 48.2	+25.4	94.6	36 43.0	+26.6	95.3	36 37.1	+27.7	96.1	13
14	37 21.6	+18.6	89.6	37 21.6	+19.9	90.4	37 20.8	+21.1	91.1	37 19.2	+22.3	91.9	37 16.8	+23.6	92.7	37 13.6	+24.8	93.4	37 09.6	+26.0	94.2	37 04.8	+27.2	94.9	14
15	37 40.2	+17.9	88.4	37 41.5	+19.1	89.2	37 41.9	+20.4	90.0	37 41.5	+21.7	90.7	37 40.4	+22.8	91.5	37 38.4	+24.1	92.3	37 35.6	+25.3	93.1	37 32.0	+26.5	93.8	15
16	37 58.1	+17.1	87.2	38 00.6	+18.4	88.0	38 02.3	+19.7	88.8	38 03.2	+20.9	89.6	38 03.2	+22.2	90.3	38 02.5	+23.3	91.1	38 00.9	+24.6	91.9	37 58.5	+25.8	92.7	16
17	38 15.2	+16.4	86.0	38 19.0	+17.7	86.8	38 22.0	+18.9	87.6	38 24.1	+20.2	88.4	38 25.4	+21.4	89.2	38 25.8	+22.7	90.0	38 25.5	+23.9	90.7	38 24.3	+25.1	91.5	17
18	38 31.6	+15.6	84.8	38 36.7	+16.8	85.6	38 40.9	+18.2	86.4	38 44.3	+19.4	87.2	38 46.8	+20.7	88.0	38 48.5	+22.0	88.8	38 49.4	+23.2	89.6	38 49.4	+24.5	90.4	18
19	38 47.2	+14.8	83.5	38 53.5	+16.2	84.3	38 59.1	+17.3	85.1	39 03.7	+18.7	85.9	39 07.5	+20.0	86.8	39 10.5	+21.2	87.6	39 12.6	+22.5	88.4	39 13.9	+23.7	89.2	19
20	39 02.0	+14.0	82.3	39 09.7	+15.3	83.1	39 16.4	+16.6	83.9	39 22.4	+17.9	84.7	39 27.5	+19.2	85.5	39 31.7	+20.5	86.4	39 35.1	+21.7	87.2	39 37.6	+23.0	88.0	20
21	39 16.0	+13.2	81.0	39 25.0	+14.5	81.8	39 33.0	+15.9	82.7	39 40.3	+17.1	83.5	39 46.7	+18.4	84.3	39 52.2	+19.7	85.1	39 56.8	+21.0	86.0	40 00.6	+22.2	86.8	21
22	39 29.2	+12.4	79.8	39 39.5	+13.6	80.6	39 48.9	+14.9	81.4	39 57.4	+16.3	82.2	40 05.1	+17.6	83.1	40 11.9	+18.9	83.9	40 17.8	+20.2	84.7	40 22.8	+21.5	85.6	22
23	39 41.6	+11.5	78.5	39 53.1	+12.9	79.3	40 03.8	+14.2	80.1	40 13.7	+15.4	81.0	40 22.7	+16.7	81.8	40 30.8	+18.0	82.7	40 38.0	+19.4	83.5	40 44.3	+20.7	84.4	23
24	39 53.1	+10.7	77.2	40 06.0	+12.0	78.0	40 18.0	+13.3	78.9	40 29.1	+14.7	79.7	40 39.4	+16.0	80.6	40 48.8	+17.3	81.4	40 57.4	+18.5	82.3	41 05.0	+19.9	83.1	24
25	40 03.8	+9.9	75.9	40 18.0	+11.1	76.8	40 31.3	+12.5	77.6	40 43.8	+13.8	78.4	40 55.4	+15.1	79.3	41 06.1	+16.4	80.1	41 15.9	+17.8	81.0	41 24.9	+19.0	81.9	25
26	40 13.7	+9.0	74.7	40 29.1	+10.3	75.5	40 43.8	+11.6	76.3	40 57.6	+12.9	77.1	41 10.5	+14.2	78.0	41 22.5	+15.6	78.9	41 33.7	+16.8	79.7	41 43.9	+18.2	80.6	26
27	40 22.7	+8.1	73.4	40 39.4	+9.4	74.2	40 55.4	+10.7	75.0	41 10.5	+12.0	75.8	41 24.7	+13.4	76.7	41 38.1	+14.6	77.6	41 50.5	+16.0	78.4	42 02.1	+17.3	79.3	27
28	40 30.8	+7.2	72.1	40 48.8	+8.6	72.9	41 06.1	+9.8	73.7	41 22.5	+11.2	74.5	41 38.1	+12.4	75.4	41 52.7	+13.8	76.3	42 06.5	+15.2	77.1	42 19.4	+16.5	78.0	28
29	40 38.0	+6.3	70.7	40 57.4	+7.6	71.6	41 15.9	+9.0	72.4	41 33.7	+10.2	73.2	41 50.5	+11.6	74.1	42 06.5	+12.9	75.0	42 21.7	+14.2	75.8	42 35.9	+15.6	76.7	29
30	40 44.3	+5.5	69.4	41 05.0	+6.7	70.2	41 24.9	+8.0	71.1	41 43.9	+9.4	71.9	42 02.1	+10.7	72.8	42 19.4	+12.0	73.6	42 35.9	+13.3	74.5	42 51.5	+14.6	75.4	30
31	40 49.8	+4.5	68.1	41 11.7	+5.9	68.9	41 32.9	+7.1	69.8	41 53.3	+8.4	70.6	42 12.8	+9.7	71.4	42 31.4	+11.1	72.3	42 49.2	+12.4	73.2	43 06.1	+13.8	74.1	31
32	40 54.3	+3.6	66.8	41 17.6	+4.9	67.6	41 40.0	+6.2	68.4	42 01.7	+7.5	69.3	42 22.5	+8.8	70.1	42 42.5	+10.1	71.0	43 01.6	+11.5	71.9	43 19.9	+12.8	72.7	32
33	40 57.9	+2.8	65.5	41 22.5	+4.0	66.3	41 46.2	+5.3	67.1	42 09.2	+6.5	67.9	42 31.3	+7.9	68.8	42 52.6	+9.2	69.6	43 13.1	+10.5	70.5	43 32.7	+11.8	71.4	33
34	41 00.7	+1.8	64.2	41 26.5	+3.0	64.9	41 51.5	+4.3	65.8	42 15.7	+5.7	66.6	42 39.2	+6.9	67.4	43 01.8	+8.2	68.3	43 23.6	+9.5	69.2	43 44.5	+10.9	70.0	34
35	41 02.5	+0.9	62.8	41 29.5	+2.2	63.6	41 55.8	+3.4	64.4	42 21.4	+4.6	65.2	42 46.1	+6.0	66.1	43 10.0	+7.3	66.9	43 33.1	+8.6	67.8	43 55.4	+9.9	68.7	35
36	41 03.4	0.0	61.5	41 31.7	+1.2	62.3	41 59.2	+2.5	63.1	42 26.0	+3.7	63.9	42 52.1	+4.9	64.7	43 17.3	+6.3	65.6	43 41.7	+7.6	66.4	44 05.3	+8.9	67.3	36
37	41 03.4	−0.9	60.2	41 32.9	+0.3	60.9	42 01.7	+1.5	61.7	42 29.7	+2.8	62.5	42 57.0	+4.1	63.4	43 23.6	+5.3	64.2	43 49.3	+6.6	65.1	44 14.2	+7.9	65.9	37
38	41 02.5	−1.8	58.9	41 33.2	−0.6	59.6	42 03.2	+0.6	60.4	42 32.5	+1.8	61.2	43 01.1	+3.0	62.0	43 28.9	+4.3	62.8	43 55.9	+5.6	63.7	44 22.1	+6.9	64.6	38
39	41 00.7	−2.7	57.5	41 32.6	−1.6	58.3	42 03.8	−0.4	59.0	42 34.3	+0.9	59.8	43 04.1	+2.1	60.6	43 33.2	+3.3	61.4	44 01.5	+4.6	62.3	44 29.0	+5.8	63.2	39
40	40 58.0	−3.7	56.2	41 31.0	−2.5	56.9	42 03.4	−1.3	57.7	42 35.2	−0.2	58.5	43 06.2	+1.1	59.3	43 36.5	+2.3	60.1	44 06.1	+3.5	60.9	44 34.8	+4.9	61.8	40
41	40 54.3	−4.5	54.9	41 28.5	−3.4	55.6	42 02.1	−2.2	56.3	42 35.0	−1.0	57.1	43 07.3	+0.1	57.9	43 38.8	+1.4	58.7	44 09.6	+2.6	59.5	44 39.7	+3.8	60.4	41
42	40 49.8	−5.4	53.6	41 25.1	−4.3	54.3	41 59.9	−3.2	55.0	42 34.0	−2.1	55.7	43 07.4	−0.9	56.5	43 40.2	+0.3	57.3	44 12.2	+1.6	58.1	44 43.5	+2.8	59.0	42
43	40 44.4	−6.4	52.2	41 20.8	−5.2	52.9	41 56.7	−4.2	53.7	42 31.9	−3.0	54.4	43 06.5	−1.8	55.1	43 40.5	−0.7	55.9	44 13.8	+0.5	56.7	44 46.3	+1.8	57.6	43
44	40 38.0	−7.2	50.9	41 15.6	−6.2	51.6	41 52.5	−5.0	52.3	42 28.9	−3.9	53.0	43 04.7	−2.8	53.8	43 39.8	−1.7	54.5	44 14.3	−0.5	55.3	44 48.1	+0.7	56.1	44
45	40 30.8	−8.1	49.6	41 09.4	−7.1	50.3	41 47.5	−6.0	51.0	42 25.0	−5.0	51.7	43 01.9	−3.8	52.4	43 38.1	−2.6	53.2	44 13.8	−1.5	53.9	44 48.8	−0.3	54.7	45
46	40 22.7	−9.0	48.3	41 02.3	−7.9	49.0	41 41.5	−6.9	49.6	42 20.0	−5.8	50.3	42 58.1	−4.8	51.0	43 35.5	−3.7	51.8	44 12.3	−2.5	52.5	44 48.5	−1.4	53.3	46
47	40 13.7	−9.8	47.0	40 54.4	−8.9	47.7	41 34.6	−7.9	48.3	42 14.2	−6.8	49.0	42 53.3	−5.7	49.7	43 31.8	−4.6	50.4	44 09.8	−3.6	51.1	44 47.1	−2.4	51.9	47
48	40 03.9	−10.7	45.7	40 45.5	−9.7	46.4	41 26.7	−8.7	47.0	42 07.4	−7.7	47.6	42 47.6	−6.7	48.3	43 27.2	−5.7	49.0	44 06.2	−4.5	49.8	44 44.7	−3.4	50.5	48
49	39 53.2	−11.5	44.5	40 35.8	−10.6	45.1	41 18.0	−9.7	45.7	41 59.7	−8.7	46.3	42 40.9	−7.7	47.0	43 21.5	−6.6	47.7	44 01.7	−5.6	48.4	44 41.3	−4.5	49.1	49
50	39 41.7	−12.4	43.2	40 25.2	−11.4	43.8	41 08.3	−10.5	44.4	41 51.0	−9.6	45.0	42 33.2	−8.6	45.6	43 14.9	−7.6	46.3	43 56.1	−6.5	47.0	44 36.8	−5.5	47.7	50
51	39 29.3	−13.2	41.9	40 13.8	−12.3	42.5	40 57.8	−11.4	43.1	41 41.4	−10.4	43.7	42 24.6	−9.5	44.3	43 07.3	−8.5	44.9	43 49.6	−7.6	45.6	44 31.3	−6.5	46.3	51
52	39 16.1	−14.0	40.6	40 01.5	−13.2	41.2	40 46.4	−12.3	41.8	41 31.0	−11.4	42.3	42 15.1	−10.4	42.9	42 58.8	−9.5	43.6	43 42.0	−8.5	44.2	44 24.8	−7.6	44.9	52
53	39 02.1	−14.8	39.4	39 48.3	−14.0	39.9	40 34.1	−13.1	40.5	41 19.6	−12.3	41.0	42 04.7	−11.4	41.6	42 49.3	−10.4	42.2	43 33.5	−9.5	42.9	44 17.2	−8.5	43.5	53
54	38 47.3	−15.6	38.1	39 34.3	−14.8	38.7	40 21.0	−14.0	39.2	41 07.3	−13.1	39.7	41 53.3	−12.3	40.3	42 38.9	−11.4	40.9	43 24.0	−10.5	41.5	44 08.7	−9.5	42.1	54
55	38 31.7	−16.4	36.9	39 19.5	−15.6	37.4	40 07.0	−14.8	37.9	40 54.2	−14.0	38.4	41 41.0	−13.1	39.0	42 27.5	−12.3	39.6	43 13.5	−11.4	40.2	43 59.2	−10.5	40.8	55
56	38 15.3	−17.1	35.7	39 03.9	−16.3	36.2	39 52.2	−15.6	36.6	40 40.2	−14.8	37.2	41 27.9	−14.1	37.7	42 15.2	−13.2	38.2	43 02.1	−12.3	38.8	43 48.7	−11.5	39.4	56
57	37 58.2	−17.9	34.5	38 47.6	−17.2	34.9	39 36.6	−16.4	35.4	40 25.4	−15.7	35.9	41 13.8	−14.9	36.4	42 02.0	−14.1	36.9	42 49.8	−13.3	37.5	43 37.2	−12.4	38.0	57
58	37 40.3	−18.6	33.3	38 30.4	−17.9	33.7	39 20.2	−17.2	34.1	40 09.7	−16.5	34.6	40 58.9	−15.7	35.1	41 47.9	−15.0	35.6	42 36.5	−14.2	36.1	43 24.8	−13.4	36.7	58
59	37 21.7	−19.3	32.1	38 12.5	−18.7	32.5	39 03.0	−18.0	32.9	39 53.2	−17.3	33.4	40 43.2	−16.6	33.8	41 32.9	−15.9	34.3	42 22.3	−15.1	34.8	43 11.4	−14.3	35.4	59
60	37 02.4	−20.0	30.9	37 53.8	−19.4	31.3	38 45.0	−18.8	31.7	39 35.9	−18.1	32.1	40 26.6	−17.4	32.6	41 17.0	−16.7	33.0	42 07.2	−16.0	33.5	42 57.1	−15.2	34.0	60
61	36 42.4	−20.8	29.7	37 34.4	−20.1	30.1	38 26.2	−19.5	30.5	39 17.8	−18.8	30.9	40 09.2	−18.2	31.3	41 00.3	−17.5	31.8	41 51.2	−16.8	32.2	42 41.9	−16.2	32.7	61
62	36 21.6	−21.4	28.5	37 14.3	−20.9	28.9	38 06.7	−20.2	29.3	38 59.0	−19.7	29.7	39 51.0	−19.0	30.1	40 42.8	−18.3	30.5	41 34.4	−17.7	30.9	42 25.7	−17.0	31.4	62
63	36 00.2	−22.0	27.4	36 53.4	−21.5	27.7	37 46.5	−21.0	28.1	38 39.3	−20.3	28.4	39 32.0	−19.8	28.8	40 24.5	−19.2	29.2	41 16.7	−18.5	29.7	42 08.7	−17.9	30.1	63
64	35 38.2	−22.7	26.2	36 31.9	−22.2	26.5	37 25.5	−21.6	26.9	38 19.0	−21.1	27.2	39 12.2	−20.5	27.6	40 05.3	−20.0	28.0	40 58.2	−19.4	28.4	41 50.8	−18.7	28.8	64
65	35 15.5	−23.4	25.1	36 09.7	−22.8	25.4	37 03.9	−22.4	25.7	37 57.9	−21.9	26.0	38 51.7	−21.3	26.4	39 45.3	−20.7	26.8	40 38.8	−20.1	27.1	41 32.1	−19.5	27.5	65
66	34 52.1	−23.9	24.0	35 46.9	−23.5	24.2	36 41.5	−23.0	24.6	37 36.0	−22.5	24.9	38 30.4	−22.0	25.2	39 24.6	−21.5	25.5	40 18.7	−21.0	25.9	41 12.6	−20.4	26.3	66
67	34 28.2	−24.6	22.8	35 23.4	−24.1	23.1	36 18.5	−23.6	23.4	37 13.5	−23.2	23.7	38 08.4	−22.7	24.0	39 03.1	−22.2	24.3	39 57.7	−21.7	24.7	40 52.2	−21.2	25.0	67
68	34 03.6	−25.1	21.7	34 59.3	−24.7	22.0	35 54.9	−24.3	22.3	36 50.3	−23.8	22.5	37 45.7	−23.4	22.8	38 40.9	−22.9	23.1	39 36.0	−22.4	23.5	40 31.0	−21.9	23.8	68
69	33 38.5	−25.7	20.6	34 34.6	−25.3	20.9	35 30.6	−24.9	21.1	36 26.5	−24.5	21.4	37 22.3	−24.1	21.7	38 18.0	−23.6	22.0	39 13.6	−23.2	22.3	40 09.1	−22.8	22.6	69
70	33 12.8	−26.3	19.6	34 09.3	−26.0	19.8	35 05.7	−25.6	20.0	36 02.0	−25.1	20.3	36 58.2	−24.7	20.5	37 54.4	−24.3	20.8	38 50.4	−23.9	21.1	39 46.3	−23.4	21.4	70
71	32 46.5	−26.8	18.5	33 43.3	−26.4	18.7	34 40.1	−26.1	18.9	35 36.9	−25.8	19.2	36 33.5	−25.4	19.4	37 30.1	−25.0	19.6	38 26.5	−24.6	19.9	39 22.9	−24.2	20.2	71
72	32 19.7	−27.4	17.4	33 16.9	−27.0	17.6	34 14.0	−26.7	17.8	35 11.1	−26.3	18.0	36 08.1	−26.0	18.3	37 05.1	−25.7	18.5	38 01.9	−25.2	18.7	38 58.7	−24.9	19.0	72
73	31 52.3	−27.8	16.4	32 49.9	−27.6	16.6	33 47.3	−27.2	16.7	34 44.8	−27.0	16.9	35 42.1	−26.6	17.2	36 39.4	−26.2	17.4	37 36.7	−26.0	17.6	38 33.8	−25.6	17.8	73
74	31 24.5	−28.4	15.3	32 22.3	−28.1	15.5	33 20.1	−27.8	15.7	34 17.8	−27.5	15.9	35 15.5	−27.2	16.1	36 13.2	−26.9	16.3	37 10.7	−26.5	16.5	38 08.2	−26.2	16.7	74
75	30 56.1	−28.8	14.3	31 54.2	−28.6	14.5	32 52.3	−28.3	14.6	33 50.3	−28.0	14.8	34 48.3	−27.7	15.0	35 46.3	−27.5	15.1	36 44.2	−27.2	15.3	37 42.0	−26.9	15.5	75
76	30 27.3	−29.3	13.3	31 25.6	−29.0	13.4	32 24.0	−28.8	13.6	33 22.3	−28.6	13.7	34 20.6	−28.4	13.9	35 18.8	−28.1	14.1	36 17.0	−27.8	14.2	37 15.1	−27.5	14.4	76
77	29 58.0	−29.8	12.3	30 56.6	−29.6	12.4	31 55.2	−29.4	12.5	32 53.7	−29.1	12.7	33 52.2	−28.8	12.8	34 50.7	−28.6	13.0	35 49.2	−28.4	13.1	36 47.6	−28.2	13.3	77
78	29 28.2	−30.2	11.3	30 27.0	−30.0	11.4	31 25.8	−29.8	11.5	32 24.6	−29.6	11.6	33 23.4	−29.4	11.8	34 22.1	−29.2	11.9	35 20.8	−29.0	12.1	36 19.4	−28.7	12.2	78
79	28 58.0	−30.7	10.3	29 57.0	−30.5	10.4	30 56.0	−30.3	10.5	31 55.0	−30.1	10.6	32 54.0	−30.0	10.7	33 52.9	−29.7	10.9	34 51.8	−29.5	11.0	35 50.7	−29.3	11.1	79
80	28 27.3	−31.0	9.3	29 26.5	−30.9	9.4	30 25.7	−30.7	9.5	31 24.9	−30.6	9.6	32 24.0	−30.4	9.7	33 23.2	−30.3	9.8	34 22.3	−30.1	9.9	35 21.4	−29.9	10.0	80
81	27 56.3	−31.5	8.3	28 55.6	−31.3	8.4	29 55.0	−31.2	8.5	30 54.3	−31.0	8.6	31 53.6	−30.9	8.7	32 52.9	−30.7	8.8	33 52.2	−30.6	8.9	34 51.5	−30.4	9.0	81
82	27 24.8	−31.8	7.4	28 24.3	−31.7	7.4	29 23.8	−31.6	7.5	30 23.3	−31.5	7.6	31 22.7	−31.3	7.7	32 22.2	−31.2	7.8	33 21.6	−31.0	7.8	34 21.1	−31.0	7.9	82
83	26 53.0	−32.3	6.4	27 52.6	−32.2	6.5	28 52.2	−32.0	6.5	29 51.8	−31.9	6.6	30 51.4	−31.8	6.7	31 51.0	−31.7	6.7	32 50.6	−31.6	6.8	33 50.1	−31.4	6.9	83
84	26 20.7	−32.6	5.5	27 20.4	−32.5	5.5	28 20.2	−32.5	5.6	29 19.9	−32.4	5.6	30 19.6	−32.3	5.7	31 19.3	−32.2	5.8	32 19.0	−32.1	5.8	33 18.7	−32.0	5.9	84
85	25 48.1	−32.9	4.5	26 47.9	−32.9	4.6	27 47.7	−32.8	4.6	28 47.5	−32.7	4.7	29 47.3	−32.6	4.7	30 47.1	−32.6	4.8	31 46.9	−32.5	4.8	32 46.7	−32.4	4.9	85
86	25 15.2	−33.3	3.6	26 15.0	−33.2	3.7	27 14.9	−33.2	3.7	28 14.8	−33.2	3.7	29 14.7	−33.1	3.8	30 14.5	−33.0	3.8	31 14.4	−33.0	3.8	32 14.3	−32.9	3.9	86
87	24 41.9	−33.7	2.7	25 41.8	−33.6	2.7	26 41.7	−33.5	2.8	27 41.6	−33.5	2.8	28 41.6	−33.5	2.8	29 41.5	−33.4	2.8	30 41.4	−33.4	2.9	31 41.4	−33.4	2.9	87
88	24 08.2	−33.9	1.8	25 08.2	−33.9	1.8	26 08.2	−34.0	1.8	27 08.1	−33.9	1.8	28 08.1	−33.9	1.9	29 08.1	−33.9	1.9	30 08.0	−33.8	1.9	31 08.0	−33.8	1.9	88
89	23 34.3	−34.3	0.9	24 34.3	−34.3	0.9	25 34.2	−34.2	0.9	26 34.2	−34.2	0.9	27 34.2	−34.2	0.9	28 34.2	−34.2	0.9	29 34.2	−34.2	0.9	30 34.2	−34.2	1.0	89
90	23 00.0	−34.6	0.0	24 00.0	−34.6	0.0	25 00.0	−34.6	0.0	26 00.0	−34.6	0.0	27 00.0	−34.6	0.0	28 00.0	−34.6	0.0	29 00.0	−34.6	0.0	30 00.0	−34.6	0.0	90
	23°			24°			25°			26°			27°			28°			29°			30°			

55°, 305° L.H.A. LATITUDE SAME NAME AS DECLINATION

294

LATITUDE **CONTRARY** NAME TO DECLINATION L.H.A. 55°, 305°

Dec.	23° Hc	d	Z	24° Hc	d	Z	25° Hc	d	Z	26° Hc	d	Z	27° Hc	d	Z	28° Hc	d	Z	29° Hc	d	Z	30° Hc	d	Z	Dec.
°	° ′	′	°	° ′	′	°	° ′	′	°	° ′	′	°	° ′	′	°	° ′	′	°	° ′	′	°	° ′	′	°	°
0	31 52.1	−27.8	105.3	31 36.0	−28.9	105.9	31 19.3	−29.9	106.5	31 02.0	−31.0	107.1	30 44.1	−31.9	107.6	30 25.6	−32.9	108.2	30 06.6	−33.8	108.8	29 47.0	−34.7	109.3	0
1	31 24.3	−28.4	106.3	31 07.1	−29.4	106.9	30 49.4	−30.4	107.5	30 31.0	−31.3	108.1	30 12.2	−32.4	108.6	29 52.7	−33.3	109.2	29 32.8	−34.3	109.7	29 12.3	−35.2	110.2	1
2	30 55.9	−28.8	107.4	30 37.7	−29.8	107.9	30 19.0	−30.9	108.5	29 59.7	−31.9	109.0	29 39.8	−32.8	109.6	29 19.4	−33.7	110.1	28 58.5	−34.6	110.6	28 37.1	−35.5	111.2	2
3	30 27.1	−29.3	108.4	30 07.9	−30.3	108.9	29 48.1	−31.3	109.5	29 27.8	−32.2	110.0	29 07.0	−33.1	110.6	28 45.7	−34.1	111.1	28 23.9	−35.0	111.6	28 01.6	−35.9	112.1	3
4	29 57.8	−29.8	109.4	29 37.6	−30.8	109.9	29 16.8	−31.7	110.5	28 55.6	−32.6	111.0	28 33.9	−33.6	111.5	28 11.6	−34.4	112.0	27 48.9	−35.4	112.5	27 25.7	−36.2	113.0	4
5	29 28.0	−30.2	110.4	29 06.8	−31.2	110.9	28 45.1	−32.1	111.4	28 23.0	−33.1	111.9	28 00.3	−34.0	112.4	27 37.2	−34.9	112.9	27 13.5	−35.7	113.4	26 49.5	−36.6	113.9	5
6	28 57.8	−30.7	111.4	28 35.6	−31.5	111.9	28 13.0	−32.5	112.4	27 49.9	−33.4	112.9	27 26.3	−34.3	113.4	27 02.3	−35.2	113.8	26 37.8	−36.0	114.3	26 12.9	−36.9	114.8	6
7	28 27.1	−31.0	112.4	28 04.1	−32.0	112.9	27 40.5	−32.9	113.4	27 16.5	−33.8	113.8	26 52.0	−34.6	114.3	26 27.1	−35.5	114.8	26 01.8	−36.4	115.2	25 36.0	−37.2	115.6	7
8	27 56.1	−31.5	113.3	27 32.1	−32.4	113.8	27 07.6	−33.3	114.3	26 42.7	−34.2	114.8	26 17.4	−35.1	115.2	25 51.6	−35.9	115.7	25 25.4	−36.7	116.1	24 58.8	−37.5	116.5	8
9	27 24.6	−31.9	114.3	26 59.7	−32.8	114.8	26 34.3	−33.6	115.2	26 08.5	−34.5	115.7	25 42.3	−35.3	116.1	25 15.7	−36.1	116.5	24 48.7	−37.0	117.0	24 21.3	−37.7	117.4	9
10	26 52.7	−32.2	115.3	26 26.9	−33.1	115.7	26 00.7	−34.0	116.2	25 34.0	−34.8	116.6	25 07.0	−35.7	117.0	24 39.6	−36.5	117.4	24 11.7	−37.2	117.8	23 43.6	−38.1	118.2	10
11	26 20.5	−32.6	116.2	25 53.8	−33.5	116.6	25 26.7	−34.3	117.1	24 59.2	−35.1	117.5	24 31.3	−35.9	117.9	24 03.1	−36.8	118.3	23 34.5	−37.6	118.7	23 05.5	−38.3	119.1	11
12	25 47.9	−33.0	117.1	25 20.3	−33.8	117.6	24 52.4	−34.7	118.0	24 24.1	−35.5	118.4	23 55.4	−36.3	118.8	23 26.3	−37.1	119.2	22 56.9	−37.8	119.5	22 27.2	−38.6	119.9	12
13	25 14.9	−33.3	118.1	24 46.5	−34.1	118.5	24 17.7	−34.9	118.9	23 48.6	−35.8	119.3	23 19.1	−36.6	119.6	22 49.2	−37.3	120.0	22 19.1	−38.1	120.4	21 48.6	−38.8	120.7	13
14	24 41.6	−33.6	119.0	24 12.4	−34.5	119.4	23 42.8	−35.3	119.8	23 12.8	−36.0	120.1	22 42.5	−36.8	120.5	22 11.9	−37.6	120.9	21 41.0	−38.3	121.2	21 09.8	−39.1	121.5	14
15	24 08.0	−34.0	119.9	23 37.9	−34.7	120.3	23 07.5	−35.5	120.6	22 36.8	−36.4	121.0	22 05.7	−37.1	121.4	21 34.3	−37.8	121.7	21 02.7	−38.6	122.0	20 30.7	−39.3	122.3	15
16	23 34.0	−34.2	120.8	23 03.2	−35.1	121.2	22 32.0	−35.9	121.5	22 00.4	−36.6	121.9	21 28.6	−37.3	122.2	20 56.5	−38.1	122.5	20 24.1	−38.8	122.8	19 51.4	−39.5	123.2	16
17	22 59.8	−34.6	121.7	22 28.1	−35.3	122.0	21 56.1	−36.1	122.4	21 23.8	−36.8	122.7	20 51.3	−37.6	123.0	20 18.4	−38.3	123.4	19 45.3	−39.0	123.7	19 11.9	−39.7	124.0	17
18	22 25.2	−34.8	122.6	21 52.8	−35.7	122.9	21 20.0	−36.3	123.2	20 47.0	−37.1	123.6	20 13.7	−37.8	123.9	19 40.1	−38.5	124.2	19 06.3	−39.2	124.5	18 32.2	−39.9	124.7	18
19	21 50.4	−35.2	123.4	21 17.1	−35.8	123.8	20 43.7	−36.7	124.1	20 09.9	−37.4	124.4	19 35.9	−38.1	124.7	19 01.6	−38.8	125.0	18 27.1	−39.5	125.3	17 52.3	−40.1	125.5	19
20	21 15.2	−35.4	124.3	20 41.3	−36.2	124.6	20 07.0	−36.8	124.9	19 32.5	−37.5	125.2	18 57.8	−38.3	125.5	18 22.8	−38.9	125.8	17 47.6	−39.6	126.1	17 12.2	−40.3	126.3	20
21	20 39.8	−35.6	125.2	20 05.1	−36.3	125.5	19 30.2	−37.1	125.8	18 55.0	−37.8	126.1	18 19.5	−38.4	126.3	17 43.9	−39.1	126.6	17 08.0	−39.8	126.8	16 31.9	−40.4	127.1	21
22	20 04.2	−35.9	126.0	19 28.8	−36.6	126.3	18 53.1	−37.3	126.6	18 17.2	−38.0	126.9	17 41.1	−38.7	127.1	17 04.8	−39.4	127.4	16 28.2	−39.9	127.6	15 51.5	−40.6	127.9	22
23	19 28.3	−36.1	126.9	18 52.2	−36.9	127.2	18 15.8	−37.5	127.4	17 39.2	−38.2	127.7	17 02.4	−38.8	127.9	16 25.4	−39.5	128.2	15 48.3	−40.2	128.4	15 10.9	−40.8	128.6	23
24	18 52.2	−36.4	127.7	18 15.3	−37.0	128.0	17 38.3	−37.7	128.3	17 01.0	−38.4	128.5	16 23.6	−39.1	128.7	15 45.9	−39.6	129.0	15 08.1	−40.3	129.2	14 30.1	−40.9	129.4	24
25	18 15.8	−36.6	128.6	17 38.3	−37.3	128.8	17 00.6	−38.0	129.1	16 22.6	−38.5	129.3	15 44.5	−39.2	129.5	15 06.3	−39.8	129.7	14 27.8	−40.4	129.9	13 49.2	−41.0	130.1	25
26	17 39.2	−36.8	129.4	17 01.0	−37.4	129.6	16 22.6	−38.1	129.9	15 44.1	−38.8	130.1	15 05.3	−39.3	130.3	14 26.5	−40.0	130.5	13 47.4	−40.6	130.7	13 08.2	−41.2	130.9	26
27	17 02.4	−37.0	130.2	16 23.6	−37.7	130.5	15 44.5	−38.2	130.7	15 05.3	−38.8	130.9	14 26.0	−39.5	131.1	13 46.5	−40.1	131.3	13 06.8	−40.7	131.5	12 27.0	−41.3	131.6	27
28	16 25.4	−37.1	131.1	15 45.9	−37.8	131.3	15 06.3	−38.5	131.5	14 26.5	−39.1	131.7	13 46.5	−39.7	131.9	13 06.4	−40.3	132.0	12 26.1	−40.8	132.2	11 45.7	−41.4	132.4	28
29	15 48.3	−37.4	131.9	15 08.1	−38.0	132.1	14 27.8	−38.6	132.3	13 47.4	−39.2	132.5	13 06.8	−39.8	132.6	12 26.1	−40.4	132.8	11 45.3	−41.0	133.0	11 04.3	−41.5	133.1	29
30	15 10.9	−37.5	132.7	14 30.1	−38.1	132.9	13 49.2	−38.7	133.1	13 08.2	−39.3	133.2	12 27.0	−39.9	133.4	11 45.7	−40.5	133.6	11 04.3	−41.0	133.7	10 22.8	−41.6	133.8	30
31	14 33.4	−37.7	133.5	13 52.0	−38.3	133.7	13 10.5	−38.9	133.9	12 28.9	−39.5	134.0	11 47.1	−40.0	134.2	11 05.2	−40.6	134.3	10 23.3	−41.2	134.5	9 41.2	−41.7	134.6	31
32	13 55.7	−37.9	134.3	13 13.7	−38.5	134.5	12 31.6	−39.0	134.6	11 49.4	−39.6	134.8	11 07.1	−40.2	134.9	10 24.6	−40.7	135.1	9 42.1	−41.2	135.2	8 59.5	−41.8	135.3	32
33	13 17.8	−38.0	135.1	12 35.2	−38.5	135.3	11 52.6	−39.2	135.4	11 09.8	−39.7	135.6	10 26.9	−40.3	135.7	9 43.9	−40.8	135.8	9 00.9	−41.4	135.9	8 17.7	−41.9	136.0	33
34	12 39.8	−38.1	135.9	11 56.7	−38.8	136.0	11 13.4	−39.3	136.2	10 30.1	−39.8	136.3	9 46.6	−40.3	136.4	9 03.1	−40.9	136.6	8 19.5	−41.4	136.7	7 35.8	−41.9	136.8	34
35	12 01.7	−38.3	136.7	11 17.9	−38.8	136.8	10 34.1	−39.3	137.0	9 50.3	−40.0	137.1	9 06.3	−40.5	137.2	8 22.2	−41.0	137.3	7 38.1	−41.5	137.4	6 53.9	−42.0	137.5	35
36	11 23.4	−38.4	137.5	10 39.1	−38.9	137.6	9 54.8	−39.5	137.7	9 10.3	−40.0	137.8	8 25.8	−40.5	137.9	7 41.2	−41.0	138.0	6 56.6	−41.6	138.1	6 11.9	−42.1	138.2	36
37	10 45.0	−38.5	138.2	10 00.2	−39.1	138.4	9 15.3	−39.6	138.5	8 30.3	−40.1	138.6	7 45.3	−40.6	138.7	7 00.2	−41.1	138.8	6 15.0	−41.6	138.8	5 29.8	−42.1	138.9	37
38	10 06.5	−38.7	139.0	9 21.1	−39.1	139.1	8 35.7	−39.7	139.2	7 50.2	−40.2	139.3	7 04.7	−40.7	139.4	6 19.1	−41.2	139.5	5 33.4	−41.7	139.6	4 47.7	−42.1	139.6	38
39	9 27.8	−38.7	139.8	8 42.0	−39.3	139.9	7 56.0	−39.7	140.0	7 10.0	−40.2	140.1	6 24.0	−40.8	140.2	5 37.9	−41.3	140.2	4 51.7	−41.7	140.3	4 05.6	−42.2	140.3	39
40	8 49.1	−38.8	140.6	8 02.7	−39.3	140.7	7 16.3	−39.9	140.8	6 29.8	−40.4	140.8	5 43.2	−40.8	140.9	4 56.6	−41.2	141.0	4 10.0	−41.7	141.0	3 23.4	−42.3	141.1	40
41	8 10.3	−39.0	141.3	7 23.4	−39.4	141.4	6 36.4	−39.9	141.5	5 49.4	−40.3	141.6	5 02.4	−40.8	141.6	4 15.4	−41.4	141.7	3 28.3	−41.8	141.7	2 41.1	−42.2	141.8	41
42	7 31.3	−38.9	142.1	6 44.0	−39.5	142.2	5 56.5	−39.9	142.3	5 09.1	−40.5	142.3	4 21.6	−40.9	142.4	3 34.0	−41.3	142.4	2 46.5	−41.8	142.4	1 58.9	−42.3	142.5	42
43	6 52.4	−39.1	142.9	6 04.5	−39.6	143.0	5 16.6	−40.0	143.0	4 28.6	−40.4	143.1	3 40.7	−41.0	143.1	2 52.7	−41.4	143.1	2 04.7	−41.9	143.2	1 16.6	−42.3	143.2	43
44	6 13.3	−39.1	143.6	5 24.9	−39.6	143.7	4 36.6	−40.1	143.8	3 48.2	−40.6	143.8	2 59.7	−40.9	143.8	2 11.3	−41.4	143.9	1 22.8	−41.8	143.9	0 34.3	−42.2	143.9	44
45	5 34.2	−39.2	144.4	4 45.3	−39.6	144.5	3 56.5	−40.1	144.5	3 07.6	−40.5	144.5	2 18.8	−41.0	144.6	1 29.9	−41.5	144.6	0 41.0	−41.9	144.6	0 07.9	+42.3	35.4	45
46	4 55.0	−39.3	145.2	4 05.7	−39.7	145.2	3 16.4	−40.1	145.3	2 27.1	−40.6	145.3	1 37.8	−41.0	145.3	0 48.4	−41.4	145.3	0 00.9	+41.8	34.7	0 50.2	+42.3	34.7	46
47	4 15.7	−39.3	145.9	3 26.0	−39.7	146.0	2 36.3	−40.2	146.0	1 46.5	−40.6	146.0	0 56.8	−41.0	146.0	0 07.0	−41.4	146.0	0 42.7	+41.9	34.0	1 32.5	+42.3	34.0	47
48	3 36.4	−39.3	146.7	2 46.3	−39.8	146.7	1 56.1	−40.2	146.7	1 05.9	−40.6	146.8	0 15.8	−41.1	146.8	0 34.4	+41.4	33.2	1 24.6	+41.8	33.2	2 14.8	+42.2	33.3	48
49	2 57.1	−39.3	147.4	2 06.5	−39.7	147.5	1 15.9	−40.1	147.5	0 25.3	−40.6	147.5	0 25.3	+41.0	32.5	1 15.8	+41.5	32.5	2 06.4	+41.9	32.5	2 57.0	+42.2	32.6	49
50	2 17.8	−39.4	148.2	1 26.8	−39.8	148.2	0 35.8	−40.2	148.2	0 15.3	+40.6	31.8	1 06.3	+41.0	31.8	1 57.3	+41.4	31.8	2 48.3	+41.7	31.8	3 39.2	+42.2	31.8	50
51	1 38.4	−39.4	149.0	0 47.0	−39.8	149.0	0 04.4	+40.2	31.0	0 55.9	+40.5	31.0	1 47.3	+40.9	31.0	2 38.7	+41.3	31.1	3 30.0	+41.8	31.1	4 21.4	+42.2	31.1	51
52	0 59.0	−39.4	149.7	0 07.2	−39.8	149.7	0 44.6	+40.2	30.3	1 36.4	+40.6	30.3	2 28.2	+41.0	30.3	3 20.0	+41.4	30.3	4 11.8	+41.7	30.4	5 03.6	+42.1	30.4	52
53	0 19.6	−39.4	150.5	0 32.6	+39.8	29.5	1 24.8	+40.2	29.5	2 17.0	+40.6	29.6	3 09.2	+40.9	29.6	4 01.4	+41.3	29.6	4 53.5	+41.7	29.7	5 45.7	+42.0	29.7	53
54	0 19.8	+39.4	28.8	1 12.4	+39.8	28.8	2 05.0	+40.2	28.8	2 57.6	+40.5	28.8	3 50.1	+40.9	28.9	4 42.7	+41.2	28.9	5 35.2	+41.6	28.9	6 27.7	+42.0	29.0	54
55	0 59.2	+39.4	28.0	1 52.2	+39.8	28.0	2 45.2	+40.1	28.1	3 38.1	+40.5	28.1	4 31.0	+40.9	28.1	5 23.9	+41.2	28.2	6 16.8	+41.6	28.2	7 09.7	+41.9	28.3	55
56	1 38.6	+39.4	27.3	2 32.0	+39.7	27.3	3 25.3	+40.1	27.3	4 18.6	+40.4	27.3	5 11.9	+40.8	27.4	6 05.1	+41.2	27.4	6 58.4	+41.5	27.5	7 51.6	+41.8	27.5	56
57	2 18.0	+39.4	26.5	3 11.7	+39.7	26.5	4 05.4	+40.0	26.6	4 59.0	+40.4	26.6	5 52.7	+40.7	26.6	6 46.3	+41.1	26.7	7 39.9	+41.4	26.8	8 33.4	+41.8	26.8	57
58	2 57.4	+39.3	25.8	3 51.4	+39.7	25.8	4 45.4	+40.0	25.8	5 39.4	+40.4	25.9	6 33.4	+40.7	25.9	7 27.4	+41.0	26.0	8 21.3	+41.3	26.0	9 15.2	+41.7	26.1	58
59	3 36.7	+39.3	25.0	4 31.1	+39.6	25.0	5 25.4	+40.0	25.1	6 19.8	+40.2	25.1	7 14.1	+40.6	25.2	8 08.4	+40.9	25.2	9 02.6	+41.3	25.3	9 56.9	+41.5	25.4	59
60	4 16.0	+39.2	24.2	5 10.7	+39.5	24.3	6 05.4	+39.8	24.3	7 00.0	+40.2	24.4	7 54.7	+40.5	24.4	8 49.3	+40.8	24.5	9 43.9	+41.1	24.6	10 38.4	+41.5	24.6	60
61	4 55.2	+39.2	23.5	5 50.2	+39.5	23.5	6 45.2	+39.9	23.6	7 40.2	+40.2	23.6	8 35.2	+40.4	23.7	9 30.1	+40.8	23.7	10 25.0	+41.1	23.8	11 19.9	+41.4	23.9	61
62	5 34.4	+39.1	22.7	6 29.7	+39.5	22.8	7 25.1	+39.7	22.8	8 20.4	+40.0	22.9	9 15.6	+40.4	22.9	10 10.9	+40.6	23.0	11 06.1	+40.9	23.1	12 01.3	+41.2	23.2	62
63	6 13.5	+39.1	22.0	7 09.2	+39.3	22.0	8 04.8	+39.7	22.1	9 00.4	+39.9	22.1	9 56.0	+40.2	22.2	10 51.5	+40.5	22.3	11 47.0	+40.9	22.3	12 42.5	+41.1	22.4	63
64	6 52.6	+39.0	21.2	7 48.5	+39.3	21.3	8 44.5	+39.5	21.3	9 40.3	+39.9	21.4	10 36.2	+40.1	21.4	11 32.0	+40.5	21.5	12 27.9	+40.7	21.6	13 23.6	+41.0	21.7	64
65	7 31.6	+38.9	20.4	8 27.8	+39.2	20.5	9 24.0	+39.5	20.5	10 20.2	+39.7	20.6	11 16.3	+40.1	20.7	12 12.5	+40.3	20.7	13 08.6	+40.5	20.8	14 04.6	+40.9	20.9	65
66	8 10.5	+38.8	19.7	9 07.0	+39.1	19.7	10 03.5	+39.3	19.8	10 59.9	+39.7	19.8	11 56.4	+39.8	19.9	12 52.8	+40.1	20.0	13 49.1	+40.5	20.1	14 45.5	+40.7	20.2	66
67	8 49.3	+38.8	18.9	9 46.1	+39.0	19.0	10 42.8	+39.3	19.0	11 39.6	+39.5	19.1	12 36.2	+39.8	19.1	13 32.9	+40.0	19.2	14 29.6	+40.2	19.3	15 26.2	+40.5	19.4	67
68	9 28.1	+38.6	18.1	10 25.1	+38.9	18.2	11 22.1	+39.1	18.2	12 19.1	+39.3	18.3	13 16.0	+39.6	18.4	14 12.9	+39.9	18.5	15 09.8	+40.2	18.5	16 06.7	+40.4	18.6	68
69	10 06.7	+38.5	17.3	11 04.0	+38.7	17.4	12 01.2	+39.0	17.5	12 58.4	+39.3	17.5	13 55.6	+39.5	17.6	14 52.8	+39.7	17.7	15 50.0	+39.9	17.8	16 47.1	+40.2	17.9	69
70	10 45.2	+38.4	16.6	11 42.7	+38.7	16.6	12 40.2	+38.9	16.7	13 37.7	+39.1	16.8	14 35.1	+39.3	16.8	15 32.5	+39.6	16.9	16 29.9	+39.8	17.0	17 27.3	+40.0	17.1	70
71	11 23.6	+38.3	15.8	12 21.4	+38.4	15.8	13 19.1	+38.7	15.9	14 16.8	+38.9	16.0	15 14.4	+39.2	16.0	16 12.1	+39.4	16.1	17 09.7	+39.6	16.2	18 07.3	+39.8	16.3	71
72	12 01.9	+38.1	15.0	12 59.8	+38.4	15.1	13 57.8	+38.5	15.1	14 55.7	+38.8	15.2	15 53.6	+39.0	15.3	16 51.5	+39.2	15.3	17 49.3	+39.4	15.4	18 47.1	+39.7	15.5	72
73	12 40.0	+38.0	14.2	13 38.2	+38.2	14.3	14 36.3	+38.4	14.3	15 34.5	+38.6	14.4	16 32.6	+38.8	14.5	17 30.7	+39.0	14.5	18 28.7	+39.2	14.6	19 26.8	+39.4	14.7	73
74	13 18.0	+37.9	13.4	14 16.4	+38.1	13.5	15 14.7	+38.3	13.5	16 13.1	+38.4	13.6	17 11.4	+38.6	13.7	18 09.7	+38.8	13.7	19 07.9	+39.1	13.8	20 06.2	+39.2	13.9	74
75	13 55.9	+37.7	12.6	14 54.5	+37.8	12.7	15 53.0	+38.0	12.7	16 51.5	+38.2	12.8	17 50.0	+38.4	12.9	18 48.5	+38.6	12.9	19 47.0	+38.7	13.0	20 45.4	+39.0	13.1	75
76	14 33.6	+37.5	11.8	15 32.3	+37.7	11.9	16 31.0	+37.9	11.9	17 29.7	+38.1	12.0	18 28.4	+38.2	12.1	19 27.1	+38.4	12.1	20 25.7	+38.6	12.2	21 24.4	+38.7	12.3	76
77	15 11.1	+37.4	11.0	16 10.0	+37.5	11.1	17 08.9	+37.7	11.1	18 07.8	+37.8	11.2	19 06.6	+38.0	11.2	20 05.5	+38.1	11.3	21 04.3	+38.3	11.4	22 03.1	+38.5	11.5	77
78	15 48.5	+37.2	10.2	16 47.5	+37.4	10.2	17 46.6	+37.5	10.3	18 45.6	+37.6	10.4	19 44.6	+37.8	10.4	20 43.6	+38.0	10.5	21 42.6	+38.1	10.6	22 41.6	+38.2	10.6	78
79	16 25.7	+37.0	9.4	17 24.9	+37.1	9.4	18 24.1	+37.2	9.5	19 23.2	+37.4	9.5	20 22.4	+37.5	9.6	21 21.6	+37.6	9.7	22 20.7	+37.8	9.7	23 19.8	+38.0	9.8	79
80	17 02.7	+36.7	8.6	18 02.0	+36.9	8.6	19 01.3	+37.0	8.7	20 00.6	+37.2	8.7	20 59.9	+37.3	8.8	21 59.2	+37.4	8.8	22 58.5	+37.6	8.9	23 57.8	+37.7	9.0	80
81	17 39.4	+36.6	7.7	18 38.9	+36.7	7.8	19 38.3	+36.9	7.8	20 37.8	+36.9	7.9	21 37.2	+37.0	7.9	22 36.6	+37.2	8.0	23 36.1	+37.2	8.0	24 35.5	+37.3	8.1	81
82	18 16.0	+36.4	6.9	19 15.6	+36.5	6.9	20 15.2	+36.5	7.0	21 14.7	+36.7	7.0	22 14.2	+36.8	7.1	23 13.8	+36.9	7.1	24 13.3	+37.0	7.2	25 12.8	+37.1	7.2	82
83	18 52.4	+36.1	6.1	19 52.1	+36.2	6.1	20 51.7	+36.3	6.1	21 51.4	+36.4	6.2	22 51.0	+36.5	6.2	23 50.7	+36.5	6.3	24 50.3	+36.7	6.3	25 49.9	+36.8	6.4	83
84	19 28.5	+35.9	5.2	20 28.3	+35.9	5.2	21 28.0	+36.1	5.3	22 27.8	+36.1	5.3	23 27.5	+36.2	5.4	24 27.2	+36.3	5.4	25 27.0	+36.3	5.4	26 26.7	+36.4	5.5	84
85	20 04.4	+35.7	4.4	21 04.2	+35.8	4.4	22 04.1	+35.7	4.4	23 03.9	+35.8	4.5	24 03.7	+35.9	4.5	25 03.5	+36.0	4.5	26 03.3	+36.1	4.6	27 03.1	+36.1	4.6	85
86	20 40.1	+35.4	3.5	21 40.0	+35.4	3.5	22 39.8	+35.5	3.6	23 39.7	+35.6	3.6	24 39.6	+35.6	3.6	25 39.5	+35.6	3.6	26 39.4	+35.7	3.7	27 39.2	+35.8	3.7	86
87	21 15.5	+35.1	2.6	22 15.4	+35.2	2.7	23 15.3	+35.2	2.7	24 15.3	+35.2	2.7	25 15.2	+35.3	2.7	26 15.1	+35.3	2.7	27 15.1	+35.3	2.8	28 15.0	+35.4	2.8	87
88	21 50.6	+34.8	1.8	22 50.6	+34.8	1.8	23 50.5	+34.9	1.8	24 50.5	+34.9	1.8	25 50.5	+34.9	1.8	26 50.4	+35.0	1.8	27 50.4	+35.0	1.9	28 50.4	+35.0	1.9	88
89	22 25.4	+34.6	0.9	23 25.4	+34.6	0.9	24 25.4	+34.6	0.9	25 25.4	+34.6	0.9	26 25.4	+34.6	0.9	27 25.4	+34.6	0.9	28 25.4	+34.6	0.9	29 25.4	+34.6	0.9	89
90	23 00.0	+34.3	0.0	24 00.0	+34.3	0.0	25 00.0	+34.2	0.0	26 00.0	+34.2	0.0	27 00.0	+34.2	0.0	28 00.0	+34.2	0.0	29 00.0	+34.2	0.0	30 00.0	+34.2	0.0	90
	23°			24°			25°			26°			27°			28°			29°			30°			

S. Lat. {L.H.A. greater than 180° ....Zn=180°−Z; L.H.A. less than 180°...........Zn=180°+Z}

LATITUDE **SAME** NAME AS DECLINATION L.H.A. 125°, 235°

295

Dec.	23° Hc	d	Z	24° Hc	d	Z	25° Hc	d	Z	26° Hc	d	Z
°	° ′	′	°	° ′	′	°	° ′	′	°	° ′	′	°
0	30 58.8	+27.1	104.8	30 43.2	+28.2	105.3	30 27.1	+29.1	105.9	30 10.3	+30.2	106.5
1	31 25.9	+26.6	103.7	31 11.4	+27.6	104.3	30 56.2	+28.7	104.9	30 40.5	+29.8	105.5
2	31 52.5	+26.0	102.7	31 39.0	+27.1	103.3	31 24.9	+28.2	103.9	31 10.3	+29.2	104.5
3	32 18.5	+25.5	101.6	32 06.1	+26.7	102.2	31 53.1	+27.7	102.8	31 39.5	+28.8	103.4
4	32 44.0	+25.0	100.5	32 32.8	+26.0	101.2	32 20.8	+27.2	101.8	32 08.3	+28.2	102.4
5	33 09.0	+24.4	99.4	32 58.8	+25.5	100.1	32 48.0	+26.6	100.7	32 36.5	+27.7	101.4
6	33 33.4	+23.8	98.4	33 24.3	+25.0	99.0	33 14.6	+26.1	99.7	33 04.2	+27.2	100.3
7	33 57.2	+23.2	97.3	33 49.3	+24.4	97.9	33 40.7	+25.5	98.6	33 31.4	+26.6	99.2
8	34 20.4	+22.6	96.1	34 13.7	+23.7	96.8	34 06.2	+24.9	97.5	33 58.0	+26.1	98.2
9	34 43.0	+22.0	95.0	34 37.4	+23.2	95.7	34 31.1	+24.3	96.4	34 24.1	+25.5	97.1
10	35 05.0	+21.3	93.9	35 00.6	+22.5	94.6	34 55.4	+23.7	95.3	34 49.6	+24.8	96.0
11	35 26.3	+20.7	92.7	35 23.1	+21.9	93.4	35 19.1	+23.1	94.2	35 14.4	+24.3	94.9
12	35 47.0	+20.0	91.6	35 45.0	+21.2	92.3	35 42.2	+22.5	93.0	35 38.7	+23.6	93.7
13	36 07.0	+19.4	90.4	36 06.2	+20.6	91.1	36 04.7	+21.7	91.9	36 02.3	+23.0	92.6
14	36 26.4	+18.6	89.2	36 26.8	+19.9	90.0	36 26.4	+21.1	90.7	36 25.3	+22.3	91.5
15	36 45.0	+17.9	88.1	36 46.7	+19.1	88.8	36 47.5	+20.4	89.5	36 47.6	+21.6	90.3
16	37 02.9	+17.3	86.9	37 05.8	+18.5	87.6	37 07.9	+19.7	88.4	37 09.2	+21.0	89.1
17	37 20.2	+16.4	85.7	37 24.3	+17.7	86.4	37 27.6	+19.0	87.2	37 30.2	+20.2	88.0
18	37 36.6	+15.7	84.4	37 42.0	+17.0	85.2	37 46.6	+18.3	86.0	37 50.4	+19.5	86.8
19	37 52.3	+15.0	83.2	37 59.0	+16.3	84.0	38 04.9	+17.5	84.8	38 09.9	+18.8	85.6
20	38 07.3	+14.2	82.0	38 15.3	+15.4	82.8	38 22.4	+16.7	83.6	38 28.7	+18.0	84.4
21	38 21.5	+13.4	80.8	38 30.7	+14.7	81.5	38 39.1	+16.0	82.3	38 46.7	+17.3	83.1
22	38 34.9	+12.6	79.5	38 45.4	+13.9	80.3	38 55.1	+15.2	81.1	39 04.0	+16.4	81.9
23	38 47.5	+11.8	78.3	38 59.3	+13.1	79.1	39 10.3	+14.4	79.9	39 20.4	+15.7	80.7
24	38 59.3	+11.0	77.0	39 12.4	+12.3	77.8	39 24.7	+13.5	78.6	39 36.1	+14.9	79.4
25	39 10.3	+10.1	75.7	39 24.7	+11.4	76.5	39 38.2	+12.8	77.3	39 51.0	+14.0	78.1
26	39 20.4	+9.4	74.5	39 36.1	+10.6	75.3	39 51.0	+11.9	76.1	40 05.0	+13.2	76.9
27	39 29.8	+8.4	73.2	39 46.7	+9.8	74.0	40 02.9	+11.0	74.8	40 18.2	+12.4	75.6
28	39 38.2	+7.7	71.9	39 56.5	+8.9	72.7	40 13.9	+10.2	73.5	40 30.6	+11.5	74.3
29	39 45.9	+6.7	70.6	40 05.4	+8.0	71.4	40 24.1	+9.4	72.2	40 42.1	+10.6	73.0
30	39 52.6	+5.9	69.3	40 13.4	+7.2	70.1	40 33.5	+8.4	70.9	40 52.7	+9.7	71.7
31	39 58.5	+5.1	68.0	40 20.6	+6.3	68.8	40 41.9	+7.6	69.6	41 02.4	+8.9	70.4
32	40 03.6	+4.1	66.7	40 26.9	+5.4	67.5	40 49.5	+6.6	68.3	41 11.3	+7.9	69.1
33	40 07.7	+3.3	65.4	40 32.3	+4.5	66.2	40 56.1	+5.8	67.0	41 19.2	+7.1	67.8
34	40 11.0	+2.4	64.1	40 36.8	+3.7	64.9	41 01.9	+4.9	65.7	41 26.3	+6.1	66.5
35	40 13.4	+1.5	62.8	40 40.5	+2.7	63.6	41 06.8	+4.0	64.3	41 32.4	+5.2	65.1
36	40 14.9	+0.6	61.5	40 43.2	+1.8	62.2	41 10.8	+3.0	63.0	41 37.6	+4.3	63.8
37	40 15.5	−0.3	60.2	40 45.0	+0.9	60.9	41 13.8	+2.2	61.7	41 41.9	+3.4	62.5
38	40 15.2	−1.1	58.9	40 45.9	+0.1	59.6	41 16.0	+1.2	60.4	41 45.3	+2.4	61.1
39	40 14.1	−2.0	57.6	40 46.0	−0.9	58.3	41 17.2	+0.3	59.0	41 47.7	+1.5	59.8
40	40 12.1	−3.0	56.3	40 45.1	−1.8	57.0	41 17.5	−0.7	57.7	41 49.2	+0.6	58.4
41	40 09.1	−3.8	54.9	40 43.3	−2.7	55.6	41 16.8	−1.5	56.4	41 49.8	−0.4	57.1
42	40 05.3	−4.6	53.6	40 40.6	−3.6	54.3	41 15.3	−2.4	55.0	41 49.4	−1.3	55.8
43	40 00.7	−5.6	52.3	40 37.0	−4.4	53.0	41 12.9	−3.4	53.7	41 48.1	−2.3	54.4
44	39 55.1	−6.4	51.0	40 32.6	−5.4	51.7	41 09.5	−4.3	52.4	41 45.8	−3.2	53.1
45	39 48.7	−7.3	49.7	40 27.2	−6.2	50.4	41 05.2	−5.2	51.1	41 42.6	−4.1	51.7
46	39 41.4	−8.1	48.5	40 21.0	−7.2	49.1	41 00.0	−6.1	49.7	41 38.5	−5.0	50.4
47	39 33.3	−9.0	47.2	40 13.8	−8.0	47.8	40 53.9	−7.0	48.4	41 33.5	−6.0	49.1
48	39 24.3	−9.8	45.9	40 05.8	−8.8	46.5	40 46.9	−7.9	47.1	41 27.5	−6.9	47.7
49	39 14.5	−10.7	44.6	39 57.0	−9.7	45.2	40 39.0	−8.7	45.8	41 20.6	−7.7	46.4
50	39 03.8	−11.4	43.3	39 47.3	−10.6	43.9	40 30.3	−9.7	44.5	41 12.9	−8.7	45.1
51	38 52.4	−12.3	42.1	39 36.7	−11.4	42.6	40 20.6	−10.5	43.2	41 04.2	−9.6	43.8
52	38 40.1	−13.1	40.8	39 25.3	−12.2	41.4	40 10.1	−11.3	41.9	40 54.6	−10.5	42.5
53	38 27.0	−13.9	39.6	39 13.1	−13.1	40.1	39 58.8	−12.2	40.6	40 44.1	−11.3	41.2
54	38 13.1	−14.6	38.3	39 00.0	−13.8	38.8	39 46.6	−13.0	39.3	40 32.8	−12.2	39.9
55	37 58.5	−15.4	37.1	38 46.2	−14.7	37.6	39 33.6	−13.9	38.1	40 20.6	−13.0	38.6
56	37 43.1	−16.2	35.9	38 31.5	−15.4	36.3	39 19.7	−14.7	36.8	40 07.6	−13.9	37.3
57	37 26.9	−16.9	34.7	38 16.1	−16.2	35.1	39 05.0	−15.4	35.6	39 53.7	−14.7	36.1
58	37 10.0	−17.7	33.5	37 59.9	−16.9	33.9	38 49.6	−16.3	34.3	39 39.0	−15.5	34.8
59	36 52.3	−18.3	32.3	37 43.0	−17.7	32.7	38 33.3	−17.0	33.1	39 23.5	−16.3	33.5
60	36 34.0	−19.1	31.1	37 25.3	−18.5	31.5	38 16.3	−17.7	31.9	39 07.2	−17.1	32.3
61	36 14.9	−19.7	29.9	37 06.8	−19.1	30.3	37 58.6	−18.5	30.7	38 50.1	−17.9	31.1
62	35 55.2	−20.4	28.7	36 47.7	−19.8	29.1	37 40.1	−19.3	29.5	38 32.2	−18.6	29.8
63	35 34.8	−21.1	27.6	36 27.9	−20.6	27.9	37 20.8	−19.9	28.3	38 13.6	−19.4	28.6
64	35 13.7	−21.7	26.4	36 07.3	−21.1	26.7	37 00.9	−20.7	27.1	37 54.2	−20.1	27.4
65	34 52.0	−22.4	25.3	35 46.2	−21.9	25.6	36 40.2	−21.3	25.9	37 34.1	−20.8	26.2
66	34 29.6	−23.0	24.2	35 24.3	−22.5	24.4	36 18.9	−22.0	24.7	37 13.3	−21.5	25.1
67	34 06.6	−23.5	23.0	35 01.8	−23.1	23.3	35 56.9	−22.7	23.6	36 51.8	−22.2	23.9
68	33 43.1	−24.2	21.9	34 38.7	−23.7	22.2	35 34.2	−23.3	22.4	36 29.6	−22.9	22.7
69	33 18.9	−24.7	20.8	34 15.0	−24.4	21.1	35 10.9	−23.9	21.3	36 06.7	−23.5	21.6
70	32 54.2	−25.3	19.7	33 50.6	−24.9	20.0	34 47.0	−24.6	20.2	35 43.2	−24.1	20.4
71	32 28.9	−25.9	18.7	33 25.7	−25.5	18.9	34 22.4	−25.1	19.1	35 19.1	−24.8	19.3
72	32 03.0	−26.3	17.6	33 00.2	−26.0	17.8	33 57.3	−25.7	18.0	34 54.3	−25.3	18.2
73	31 36.7	−26.9	16.5	32 34.2	−26.6	16.7	33 31.6	−26.3	16.9	34 29.0	−26.0	17.1
74	31 09.8	−27.4	15.5	32 07.6	−27.1	15.7	33 05.3	−26.8	15.8	34 03.0	−26.5	16.0
75	30 42.4	−27.9	14.5	31 40.5	−27.6	14.6	32 38.5	−27.3	14.8	33 36.5	−27.1	14.9
76	30 14.5	−28.3	13.4	31 12.9	−28.2	13.6	32 11.2	−27.9	13.7	33 09.4	−27.6	13.9
77	29 46.2	−28.9	12.4	30 44.7	−28.6	12.5	31 43.3	−28.4	12.7	32 41.8	−28.1	12.8
78	29 17.3	−29.2	11.4	30 16.1	−29.0	11.5	31 14.9	−28.8	11.6	32 13.7	−28.7	11.8
79	28 48.1	−29.7	10.4	29 47.1	−29.6	10.5	30 46.1	−29.4	10.6	31 45.0	−29.1	10.7
80	28 18.4	−30.2	9.4	29 17.5	−29.9	9.5	30 16.7	−29.8	9.6	31 15.9	−29.7	9.7
81	27 48.2	−30.5	8.4	28 47.6	−30.4	8.5	29 46.9	−30.3	8.6	30 46.2	−30.1	8.7
82	27 17.7	−31.0	7.5	28 17.2	−30.9	7.5	29 16.6	−30.6	7.6	30 16.1	−30.6	7.7
83	26 46.7	−31.3	6.5	27 46.3	−31.2	6.6	28 46.0	−31.2	6.6	29 45.5	−31.0	6.7
84	26 15.4	−31.7	5.5	27 15.1	−31.6	5.6	28 14.8	−31.5	5.6	29 14.5	−31.4	5.7
85	25 43.7	−32.1	4.6	26 43.5	−32.0	4.6	27 43.3	−31.9	4.7	28 43.1	−31.8	4.7
86	25 11.6	−32.4	3.7	26 11.5	−32.3	3.7	27 11.4	−32.3	3.7	28 11.3	−32.3	3.8
87	24 39.2	−32.7	2.7	25 39.2	−32.8	2.8	26 39.1	−32.7	2.8	27 39.0	−32.6	2.8
88	24 06.5	−33.1	1.8	25 06.4	−33.0	1.8	26 06.4	−33.0	1.8	27 06.4	−33.0	1.9
89	23 33.4	−33.4	0.9	24 33.4	−33.4	0.9	25 33.4	−33.4	0.9	26 33.4	−33.4	0.9
90	23 00.0	−33.7	0.0	24 00.0	−33.7	0.0	25 00.0	−33.7	0.0	26 00.0	−33.7	0.0
	23°			24°			25°			26°		

27° Hc	d	Z	28° Hc	d	Z	29° Hc	d	Z	30° Hc	d	Z	Dec.
° ′	′	°	° ′	′	°	° ′	′	°	° ′	′	°	°
29 53.0	+31.2	107.0	29 35.2	+32.2	107.6	29 16.8	+33.2	108.1	28 57.9	+34.1	108.6	0
30 24.2	+30.8	106.0	30 07.4	+31.7	106.6	29 50.0	+32.7	107.1	29 32.0	+33.7	107.7	1
30 55.0	+30.3	105.0	30 39.1	+31.3	105.6	30 22.7	+32.3	106.2	30 05.7	+33.2	106.7	2
31 25.3	+29.8	104.0	31 10.4	+30.8	104.6	30 55.0	+31.8	105.2	30 38.9	+32.9	105.8	3
31 55.1	+29.3	103.0	31 41.2	+30.4	103.6	31 26.8	+31.4	104.2	31 11.8	+32.4	104.8	4
32 24.4	+28.8	102.0	32 11.6	+29.9	102.6	31 58.2	+30.9	103.2	31 44.2	+31.9	103.8	5
32 53.2	+28.2	100.9	32 41.5	+29.3	101.6	32 29.1	+30.4	102.2	32 16.1	+31.5	102.8	6
33 21.4	+27.8	99.9	33 10.8	+28.8	100.5	32 59.5	+29.9	101.2	32 47.6	+30.9	101.8	7
33 49.2	+27.2	98.8	33 39.6	+28.3	99.5	33 29.4	+29.3	100.1	33 18.5	+30.5	100.8	8
34 16.4	+26.6	97.7	34 07.9	+27.7	98.4	33 58.8	+28.8	99.1	33 49.0	+29.9	99.7	9
34 43.0	+26.0	96.7	34 35.6	+27.2	97.3	34 27.6	+28.3	98.0	34 18.9	+29.4	98.7	10
35 09.0	+25.4	95.6	35 02.8	+26.6	96.3	34 55.9	+27.7	97.0	34 48.3	+28.8	97.6	11
35 34.4	+24.8	94.4	35 29.4	+26.0	95.2	35 23.6	+27.1	95.9	35 17.1	+28.3	96.6	12
35 59.2	+24.2	93.3	35 55.4	+25.3	94.0	35 50.7	+26.6	94.8	35 45.4	+27.6	95.5	13
36 23.4	+23.5	92.2	36 20.7	+24.7	92.9	36 17.3	+25.9	93.7	36 13.0	+27.1	94.4	14
36 46.9	+22.9	91.0	36 45.4	+24.1	91.8	36 43.2	+25.2	92.5	36 40.1	+26.4	93.3	15
37 09.8	+22.1	89.9	37 09.5	+23.4	90.6	37 08.4	+24.6	91.4	37 06.5	+25.8	92.2	16
37 31.9	+21.5	88.7	37 32.9	+22.7	89.5	37 33.0	+23.9	90.3	37 32.3	+25.2	91.0	17
37 53.4	+20.8	87.5	37 55.6	+22.0	88.3	37 56.9	+23.3	89.1	37 57.5	+24.4	89.9	18
38 14.2	+20.0	86.3	38 17.6	+21.3	87.1	38 20.2	+22.5	87.9	38 21.9	+23.8	88.7	19
38 34.2	+19.3	85.1	38 38.9	+20.5	85.9	38 42.7	+21.8	86.7	38 45.7	+23.0	87.5	20
38 53.5	+18.5	83.9	38 59.4	+19.8	84.7	39 04.5	+21.1	85.5	39 08.7	+22.4	86.4	21
39 12.0	+17.8	82.7	39 19.2	+19.0	83.5	39 25.6	+20.3	84.3	39 31.1	+21.5	85.2	22
39 29.8	+16.9	81.5	39 38.2	+18.3	82.3	39 45.9	+19.5	83.1	39 52.6	+20.8	83.9	23
39 46.7	+16.2	80.2	39 56.5	+17.4	81.0	40 05.4	+18.7	81.9	40 13.4	+20.1	82.7	24
40 02.9	+15.3	79.0	40 13.9	+16.7	79.8	40 24.1	+18.0	80.6	40 33.5	+19.2	81.5	25
40 18.2	+14.5	77.7	40 30.6	+15.8	78.5	40 42.1	+17.1	79.4	40 52.7	+18.4	80.2	26
40 32.7	+13.7	76.4	40 46.4	+14.9	77.3	40 59.2	+16.2	78.1	41 11.1	+17.5	79.0	27
40 46.4	+12.8	75.1	41 01.3	+14.1	76.0	41 15.4	+15.4	76.8	41 28.6	+16.8	77.7	28
40 59.2	+11.9	73.9	41 15.4	+13.2	74.7	41 30.8	+14.6	75.5	41 45.4	+15.8	76.4	29
41 11.1	+11.0	72.6	41 28.6	+12.4	73.4	41 45.4	+13.6	74.2	42 01.2	+15.0	75.1	30
41 22.1	+10.2	71.2	41 41.0	+11.4	72.1	41 59.0	+12.8	72.9	42 16.2	+14.1	73.8	31
41 32.3	+9.2	69.9	41 52.4	+10.6	70.8	42 11.8	+11.8	71.6	42 30.3	+13.1	72.5	32
41 41.5	+8.3	68.6	42 03.0	+9.6	69.4	42 23.6	+11.0	70.3	42 43.4	+12.3	71.2	33
41 49.8	+7.5	67.3	42 12.6	+8.7	68.1	42 34.6	+10.0	69.0	42 55.7	+11.3	69.8	34
41 57.3	+6.4	65.9	42 21.3	+7.8	66.8	42 44.6	+9.0	67.6	43 07.0	+10.3	68.5	35
42 03.7	+5.6	64.6	42 29.1	+6.8	65.4	42 53.6	+8.1	66.3	43 17.3	+9.4	67.1	36
42 09.3	+4.6	63.3	42 35.9	+5.9	64.1	43 01.7	+7.2	64.9	43 26.7	+8.5	65.8	37
42 13.9	+3.6	61.9	42 41.8	+4.9	62.7	43 08.9	+6.1	63.6	43 35.2	+7.4	64.4	38
42 17.5	+2.8	60.6	42 46.7	+3.9	61.4	43 15.0	+5.2	62.2	43 42.6	+6.5	63.0	39
42 20.3	+1.7	59.2	42 50.6	+3.0	60.0	43 20.2	+4.2	60.8	43 49.1	+5.4	61.7	40
42 22.0	+0.8	57.9	42 53.6	+2.0	58.7	43 24.4	+3.3	59.5	43 54.5	+4.5	60.3	41
42 22.8	−0.1	56.5	42 55.6	+1.0	57.3	43 27.7	+2.2	58.1	43 59.0	+3.5	58.9	42
42 22.7	−1.2	55.2	42 56.6	+0.1	55.9	43 29.9	+1.2	56.7	44 02.5	+2.4	57.5	43
42 21.5	−2.0	53.8	42 56.7	−1.0	54.6	43 31.1	+0.3	55.3	44 04.9	+1.5	56.1	44
42 19.5	−3.0	52.5	42 55.7	−1.9	53.2	43 31.4	−0.8	53.9	44 06.4	+0.4	54.7	45
42 16.5	−4.0	51.1	42 53.8	−2.8	51.8	43 30.6	−1.7	52.6	44 06.8	−0.6	53.3	46
42 12.5	−4.9	49.8	42 51.0	−3.8	50.5	43 28.9	−2.7	51.2	44 06.2	−1.6	51.9	47
42 07.6	−5.9	48.4	42 47.2	−4.8	49.1	43 26.2	−3.8	49.8	44 04.6	−2.6	50.5	48
42 01.7	−6.7	47.1	42 42.4	−5.8	47.7	43 22.4	−4.7	48.4	44 02.0	−3.7	49.2	49
41 55.0	−7.7	45.7	42 36.6	−6.7	46.4	43 17.7	−5.7	47.1	43 58.3	−4.6	47.8	50
41 47.3	−8.7	44.4	42 29.9	−7.7	45.0	43 12.0	−6.6	45.7	43 53.7	−5.6	46.4	51
41 38.6	−9.5	43.1	42 22.2	−8.6	43.7	43 05.4	−7.6	44.3	43 48.1	−6.7	45.0	52
41 29.1	−10.4	41.8	42 13.6	−9.5	42.4	42 57.8	−8.6	43.0	43 41.4	−7.6	43.6	53
41 18.7	−11.4	40.4	42 04.1	−10.4	41.0	42 49.2	−9.5	41.6	43 33.8	−8.6	42.3	54
41 07.3	−12.2	39.1	41 53.7	−11.4	39.7	42 39.7	−10.5	40.3	43 25.2	−9.5	40.9	55
40 55.1	−13.0	37.8	41 42.3	−12.2	38.4	42 29.2	−11.4	39.0	43 15.7	−10.6	39.5	56
40 42.1	−14.0	36.6	41 30.1	−13.1	37.1	42 17.8	−12.3	37.6	43 05.1	−11.4	38.2	57
40 28.1	−14.7	35.3	41 17.0	−14.0	35.8	42 05.5	−13.2	36.3	42 53.7	−12.4	36.8	58
40 13.4	−15.6	34.0	41 03.0	−14.9	34.5	41 52.3	−14.1	35.0	42 41.3	−13.4	35.5	59
39 57.8	−16.4	32.7	40 48.1	−15.7	33.2	41 38.2	−15.0	33.7	42 27.9	−14.2	34.2	60
39 41.4	−17.3	31.5	40 32.4	−16.5	31.9	41 23.2	−15.8	32.4	42 13.7	−15.1	32.9	61
39 24.1	−18.0	30.2	40 15.9	−17.4	30.7	41 07.4	−16.7	31.1	41 58.6	−16.0	31.6	62
39 06.1	−18.7	29.0	39 58.5	−18.1	29.4	40 50.7	−17.6	29.8	41 42.6	−16.9	30.3	63
38 47.4	−19.6	27.8	39 40.4	−19.0	28.2	40 33.1	−18.3	28.6	41 25.7	−17.7	29.0	64
38 27.8	−20.2	26.6	39 21.4	−19.7	26.9	40 14.8	−19.1	27.3	41 08.0	−18.5	27.7	65
38 07.6	−21.0	25.4	39 01.7	−20.5	25.7	39 55.7	−19.9	26.1	40 49.5	−19.4	26.5	66
37 46.6	−21.7	24.2	38 41.2	−21.2	24.5	39 35.8	−20.7	24.9	40 30.1	−20.1	25.2	67
37 24.9	−22.4	23.0	38 20.0	−21.9	23.3	39 15.1	−21.5	23.6	40 10.0	−21.0	24.0	68
37 02.5	−23.1	21.9	37 58.1	−22.6	22.1	38 53.6	−22.1	22.4	39 49.0	−21.7	22.8	69
36 39.4	−23.7	20.7	37 35.5	−23.3	21.0	38 31.5	−22.9	21.2	39 27.3	−22.4	21.5	70
36 15.7	−24.4	19.6	37 12.2	−24.0	19.8	38 08.6	−23.6	20.1	39 04.9	−23.2	20.3	71
35 51.3	−25.0	18.4	36 48.2	−24.7	18.7	37 45.0	−24.3	18.9	38 41.7	−23.9	19.2	72
35 26.3	−25.6	17.3	36 23.5	−25.2	17.5	37 20.7	−24.9	17.8	38 17.8	−24.5	18.0	73
35 00.7	−26.2	16.2	35 58.3	−25.9	16.4	36 55.8	−25.6	16.6	37 53.3	−25.3	16.8	74
34 34.5	−26.8	15.1	35 32.4	−26.5	15.3	36 30.2	−26.2	15.5	37 28.0	−25.9	15.7	75
34 07.7	−27.4	14.0	35 05.9	−27.1	14.2	36 04.0	−26.8	14.4	37 02.1	−26.5	14.6	76
33 40.3	−27.9	12.9	34 38.8	−27.7	13.1	35 37.2	−27.4	13.3	36 35.6	−27.2	13.4	77
33 12.4	−28.4	11.9	34 11.1	−28.2	12.0	35 09.8	−28.0	12.2	36 08.4	−27.8	12.3	78
32 44.0	−29.0	10.8	33 42.9	−28.8	11.0	34 41.8	−28.6	11.1	35 40.6	−28.3	11.2	79
32 15.0	−29.5	9.8	33 14.1	−29.3	9.9	34 13.2	−29.1	10.0	35 12.3	−29.0	10.1	80
31 45.5	−29.9	8.8	32 44.8	−29.8	8.9	33 44.1	−29.7	9.0	34 43.3	−29.4	9.1	81
31 15.6	−30.5	7.8	32 15.0	−30.3	7.8	33 14.4	−30.1	7.9	34 13.9	−30.1	8.0	82
30 45.1	−30.9	6.8	31 44.7	−30.8	6.8	32 44.3	−30.7	6.9	33 43.8	−30.5	7.0	83
30 14.2	−31.3	5.8	31 13.9	−31.2	5.8	32 13.6	−31.1	5.9	33 13.3	−31.0	5.9	84
29 42.9	−31.8	4.8	30 42.7	−31.7	4.8	31 42.5	−31.6	4.9	32 42.3	−31.6	4.9	85
29 11.1	−32.2	3.8	30 11.0	−32.1	3.8	31 10.9	−32.1	3.9	32 10.7	−32.0	3.9	86
28 38.9	−32.5	2.8	29 38.9	−32.6	2.9	30 38.8	−32.5	2.9	31 38.7	−32.4	2.9	87
28 06.4	−33.0	1.9	29 06.3	−32.9	1.9	30 06.3	−33.0	1.9	31 06.3	−33.0	1.9	88
27 33.4	−33.4	0.9	28 33.4	−33.4	0.9	29 33.3	−33.3	1.0	30 33.3	−33.3	1.0	89
27 00.0	−33.7	0.0	28 00.0	−33.7	0.0	29 00.0	−33.7	0.0	30 00.0	−33.8	0.0	90
27°			28°			29°			30°			

LATITUDE CONTRARY NAME TO DECLINATION — L.H.A. 56°, 304°

Dec.	23° Hc	d	Z	24° Hc	d	Z	25° Hc	d	Z	26° Hc	d	Z	27° Hc	d	Z	28° Hc	d	Z	29° Hc	d	Z	30° Hc	d	Z	Dec.
°	° ′	′	°	° ′	′	°	° ′	′	°	° ′	′	°	° ′	′	°	° ′	′	°	° ′	′	°	° ′	′	°	°
0	30 58.8	-27.6	104.8	30 43.2	-28.6	105.3	30 27.1	-29.7	105.9	30 10.3	-30.6	106.5	29 53.0	-31.6	107.0	29 35.2	-32.6	107.6	29 16.8	-33.5	108.1	28 57.9	-34.5	108.6	0
1	30 31.2	-28.1	105.8	30 14.6	-29.1	106.4	29 57.4	-30.1	106.9	29 39.7	-31.1	107.5	29 21.4	-32.1	108.0	29 02.6	-33.0	108.5	28 43.3	-34.0	109.1	28 23.4	-34.8	109.6	1
2	30 03.1	-28.5	106.8	29 45.5	-29.6	107.4	29 27.3	-30.5	107.9	29 08.6	-31.5	108.4	28 49.3	-32.4	109.0	28 29.6	-33.4	109.5	28 09.3	-34.3	110.0	27 48.6	-35.3	110.5	2
3	29 34.6	-29.0	107.8	29 15.9	-29.9	108.4	28 56.8	-31.0	108.9	28 37.1	-31.9	109.4	28 16.9	-32.9	109.9	27 56.2	-33.8	110.4	27 35.0	-34.7	110.9	27 13.3	-35.5	111.4	3
4	29 05.6	-29.5	108.8	28 46.0	-30.5	109.4	28 25.8	-31.4	109.9	28 05.2	-32.4	110.4	27 44.0	-33.2	110.9	27 22.4	-34.2	111.4	27 00.3	-35.0	111.8	26 37.8	-36.0	112.3	4
5	28 36.1	-29.8	109.8	28 15.5	-30.8	110.3	27 54.4	-31.8	110.8	27 32.8	-32.7	111.3	27 10.8	-33.6	111.8	26 48.2	-34.5	112.3	26 25.3	-35.4	112.7	26 01.8	-36.2	113.2	5
6	28 06.3	-30.3	110.8	27 44.7	-31.3	111.3	27 22.6	-32.1	111.8	27 00.1	-33.1	112.3	26 37.2	-34.0	112.7	26 13.7	-34.8	113.2	25 49.9	-35.7	113.6	25 25.6	-36.5	114.1	6
7	27 36.0	-30.7	111.8	27 13.4	-31.6	112.3	26 50.5	-32.6	112.7	26 27.0	-33.4	113.2	26 03.2	-34.3	113.7	25 38.9	-35.2	114.1	25 14.2	-36.1	114.5	24 49.1	-36.9	115.0	7
8	27 05.3	-31.1	112.8	26 41.8	-32.0	113.2	26 17.9	-32.9	113.7	25 53.6	-33.8	114.1	25 28.9	-34.7	114.6	25 03.7	-35.5	115.0	24 38.1	-36.3	115.4	24 12.2	-37.1	115.8	8
9	26 34.2	-31.5	113.7	26 09.8	-32.4	114.2	25 45.0	-33.2	114.6	25 19.8	-34.1	115.1	24 54.2	-35.0	115.5	24 28.2	-35.8	115.9	24 01.8	-36.6	116.3	23 35.1	-37.5	116.7	9
10	26 02.7	-31.9	114.7	25 37.4	-32.7	115.1	25 11.8	-33.6	115.5	24 45.7	-34.5	116.0	24 19.2	-35.3	116.4	23 52.4	-36.1	116.8	23 25.2	-36.9	117.2	22 57.6	-37.7	117.5	10
11	25 30.8	-32.2	115.6	25 04.7	-33.1	116.0	24 38.2	-34.0	116.5	24 11.2	-34.7	116.9	23 43.9	-35.5	117.3	23 16.3	-36.4	117.6	22 48.3	-37.2	118.0	22 19.9	-37.9	118.4	11
12	24 58.6	-32.5	116.5	24 31.6	-33.4	117.0	24 04.2	-34.2	117.4	23 36.5	-35.1	117.8	23 08.4	-35.9	118.1	22 39.9	-36.7	118.5	22 11.1	-37.5	118.9	21 42.0	-38.2	119.2	12
13	24 26.1	-32.9	117.5	23 58.2	-33.7	117.9	23 30.0	-34.6	118.3	23 01.4	-35.4	118.6	22 32.5	-36.2	119.0	22 03.2	-36.9	119.4	21 33.6	-37.7	119.7	21 03.8	-38.5	120.0	13
14	23 53.2	-33.2	118.4	23 24.5	-34.1	118.8	22 55.4	-34.8	119.1	22 26.0	-35.6	119.5	21 56.3	-36.4	119.9	21 26.3	-37.2	120.2	20 55.9	-37.9	120.5	20 25.3	-38.7	120.9	14
15	23 20.0	-33.6	119.3	22 50.4	-34.3	119.7	22 20.6	-35.2	120.0	21 50.4	-35.9	120.4	21 19.9	-36.7	120.7	20 49.1	-37.4	121.0	20 18.0	-38.2	121.4	19 46.6	-38.9	121.7	15
16	22 46.4	-33.8	120.2	22 16.1	-34.6	120.6	21 45.4	-35.4	120.9	21 14.5	-36.2	121.2	20 43.2	-36.9	121.6	20 11.7	-37.7	121.9	19 39.8	-38.4	122.2	19 07.7	-39.1	122.5	16
17	22 12.6	-34.1	121.1	21 41.5	-34.9	121.4	21 10.0	-35.6	121.8	20 38.3	-36.4	122.1	20 06.3	-37.2	122.4	19 34.0	-37.9	122.7	19 01.4	-38.6	123.0	18 28.6	-39.3	123.3	17
18	21 38.5	-34.4	122.0	21 06.6	-35.2	122.3	20 34.4	-35.9	122.6	20 01.9	-36.7	122.9	19 29.1	-37.4	123.2	18 56.1	-38.1	123.5	18 22.8	-38.8	123.8	17 49.3	-39.5	124.1	18
19	21 04.1	-34.6	122.9	20 31.4	-35.4	123.2	19 58.5	-36.2	123.5	19 25.2	-36.9	123.8	18 51.7	-37.6	124.1	18 18.0	-38.3	124.3	17 44.0	-39.0	124.6	17 09.8	-39.6	124.9	19
20	20 29.5	-35.0	123.7	19 56.0	-35.7	124.0	19 22.3	-36.4	124.3	18 48.3	-37.1	124.6	18 14.1	-37.8	124.9	17 39.7	-38.5	125.2	17 05.0	-39.2	125.4	16 30.2	-39.9	125.7	20
21	19 54.5	-35.1	124.6	19 20.3	-35.9	124.9	18 45.9	-36.6	125.2	18 11.2	-37.3	125.4	17 36.3	-38.0	125.7	17 01.2	-38.7	126.0	16 25.8	-39.3	126.2	15 50.3	-40.0	126.4	21
22	19 19.4	-35.5	125.5	18 44.4	-36.1	125.7	18 09.3	-36.9	126.0	17 33.9	-37.5	126.3	16 58.3	-38.2	126.5	16 22.5	-38.9	126.8	15 46.5	-39.5	127.0	15 10.3	-40.2	127.2	22
23	18 43.9	-35.6	126.3	18 08.3	-36.3	126.6	17 32.4	-37.0	126.8	16 56.4	-37.8	127.1	16 20.1	-38.4	127.3	15 43.6	-39.0	127.6	15 07.0	-39.7	127.8	14 30.1	-40.3	128.0	23
24	18 08.3	-35.9	127.2	17 32.0	-36.6	127.4	16 55.4	-37.2	127.7	16 18.6	-37.9	127.9	15 41.7	-38.6	128.1	15 04.6	-39.2	128.3	14 27.3	-39.9	128.5	13 49.8	-40.5	128.7	24
25	17 32.4	-36.0	128.0	16 55.4	-36.8	128.2	16 18.2	-37.5	128.5	15 40.7	-38.0	128.7	15 03.1	-38.7	128.9	14 25.4	-39.4	129.1	13 47.4	-40.0	129.3	13 09.3	-40.6	129.5	25
26	16 56.4	-36.3	128.8	16 18.6	-36.9	129.1	15 40.7	-37.6	129.3	15 02.7	-38.3	129.5	14 24.4	-38.9	129.7	13 46.0	-39.5	129.9	13 07.4	-40.1	130.1	12 28.7	-40.7	130.3	26
27	16 20.1	-36.5	129.7	15 41.7	-37.1	129.9	15 03.1	-37.7	130.1	14 24.4	-38.4	130.3	13 45.5	-39.0	130.5	13 06.5	-39.7	130.7	12 27.3	-40.2	130.8	11 48.0	-40.8	131.0	27
28	15 43.6	-36.6	130.5	15 04.6	-37.3	130.7	14 25.4	-38.0	130.9	13 46.0	-38.6	131.1	13 06.5	-39.2	131.3	12 26.8	-39.7	131.4	11 47.1	-40.4	131.6	11 07.2	-41.0	131.8	28
29	15 07.0	-36.9	131.3	14 27.3	-37.5	131.5	13 47.4	-38.1	131.7	13 07.4	-38.7	131.9	12 27.3	-39.3	132.0	11 47.1	-39.9	132.2	11 06.7	-40.5	132.4	10 26.2	-41.0	132.5	29
30	14 30.1	-37.0	132.1	13 49.8	-37.6	132.3	13 09.3	-38.2	132.5	12 28.7	-38.8	132.7	11 48.0	-39.4	132.8	11 07.2	-40.0	133.0	10 26.2	-40.6	133.1	9 45.2	-41.2	133.2	30
31	13 53.1	-37.2	132.9	13 12.2	-37.8	133.1	12 31.1	-38.4	133.3	11 49.9	-39.0	133.4	11 08.6	-39.6	133.6	10 27.2	-40.2	133.7	9 45.6	-40.7	133.9	9 04.0	-41.2	134.0	31
32	13 15.9	-37.3	133.8	12 34.4	-37.9	133.9	11 52.7	-38.5	134.1	11 10.9	-39.1	134.2	10 29.0	-39.6	134.4	9 47.0	-40.2	134.5	9 04.9	-40.7	134.6	8 22.8	-41.3	134.7	32
33	12 38.6	-37.4	134.6	11 56.5	-38.1	134.7	11 14.2	-38.6	134.9	10 31.8	-39.2	135.0	9 49.4	-39.8	135.1	9 06.8	-40.3	135.2	8 24.2	-40.9	135.3	7 41.5	-41.4	135.4	33
34	12 01.2	-37.6	135.4	11 18.4	-38.1	135.5	10 35.6	-38.8	135.6	9 52.6	-39.3	135.8	9 09.6	-39.8	135.9	8 26.5	-40.4	136.0	7 43.3	-40.9	136.1	7 00.1	-41.5	136.2	34
35	11 23.6	-37.7	136.2	10 40.3	-38.3	136.3	9 56.8	-38.8	136.4	9 13.3	-39.4	136.5	8 29.8	-40.0	136.6	7 46.1	-40.5	136.7	7 02.4	-41.0	136.8	6 18.6	-41.5	136.9	35
36	10 45.9	-37.9	136.9	10 02.0	-38.4	137.1	9 18.0	-39.0	137.2	8 33.9	-39.4	137.3	7 49.8	-40.0	137.4	7 05.6	-40.5	137.5	6 21.4	-41.1	137.6	5 37.1	-41.6	137.6	36
37	10 08.0	-37.9	137.7	9 23.6	-38.5	137.8	8 39.0	-39.0	138.0	7 54.5	-39.6	138.1	7 09.8	-40.1	138.1	6 25.1	-40.6	138.2	5 40.3	-41.1	138.3	4 55.5	-41.6	138.4	37
38	9 30.1	-38.1	138.5	8 45.1	-38.6	138.6	8 00.0	-39.1	138.7	7 14.9	-39.7	138.8	6 29.7	-40.2	138.9	5 44.5	-40.7	139.0	4 59.2	-41.2	139.0	4 13.9	-41.7	139.1	38
39	8 52.0	-38.2	139.3	8 06.5	-38.7	139.4	7 20.9	-39.2	139.5	6 35.2	-39.7	139.6	5 49.5	-40.2	139.6	5 03.8	-40.7	139.7	4 18.0	-41.2	139.8	3 32.2	-41.7	139.8	39
40	8 13.8	-38.2	140.1	7 27.8	-38.8	140.2	6 41.7	-39.3	140.2	5 55.5	-39.7	140.3	5 09.3	-40.2	140.4	4 23.1	-40.8	140.4	3 36.8	-41.2	140.5	2 50.5	-41.7	140.5	40
41	7 35.6	-38.3	140.9	6 49.0	-38.8	140.9	6 02.4	-39.3	141.0	5 15.8	-39.9	141.1	4 29.1	-40.4	141.1	3 42.3	-40.8	141.2	2 55.6	-41.3	141.2	2 08.8	-41.7	141.2	41
42	6 57.3	-38.5	141.6	6 10.2	-38.9	141.7	5 23.1	-39.4	141.8	4 35.9	-39.9	141.8	3 48.7	-40.3	141.9	3 01.5	-40.8	141.9	2 14.3	-41.3	141.9	1 27.1	-41.8	142.0	42
43	6 18.8	-38.4	142.4	5 31.3	-39.0	142.5	4 43.7	-39.5	142.5	3 56.0	-39.9	142.6	3 08.4	-40.4	142.6	2 20.7	-40.8	142.6	1 33.0	-41.3	142.7	0 45.3	-41.8	142.7	43
44	5 40.4	-38.6	143.2	4 52.3	-39.0	143.2	4 04.2	-39.4	143.3	3 16.1	-39.9	143.3	2 28.0	-40.4	143.4	1 39.9	-40.9	143.4	0 51.7	-41.3	143.4	0 03.5	-41.7	143.4	44
45	5 01.8	-38.6	144.0	4 13.3	-39.0	144.0	3 24.8	-39.6	144.0	2 36.2	-40.0	144.1	1 47.6	-40.5	144.1	0 59.0	-40.9	144.1	0 10.4	-41.3	144.1	0 38.2	+41.8	35.9	45
46	4 23.2	-38.6	144.7	3 34.3	-39.1	144.8	2 45.2	-39.5	144.8	1 56.2	-40.0	144.8	1 07.2	-40.5	144.8	0 18.1	-40.9	144.8	0 30.9	+41.3	35.2	1 20.0	+41.7	35.2	46
47	3 44.6	-38.7	145.5	2 55.2	-39.2	145.5	2 05.7	-39.6	145.5	1 16.2	-40.0	145.6	0 26.7	-40.4	145.6	0 22.8	+40.8	34.4	1 12.2	+41.4	34.4	2 01.7	+41.8	34.5	47
48	3 05.9	-38.7	146.3	2 16.0	-39.1	146.3	1 26.1	-39.6	146.3	0 36.2	-40.0	146.3	0 13.7	+40.5	33.7	1 03.6	+40.9	33.7	1 53.6	+41.2	33.7	2 43.5	+41.7	33.7	48
49	2 27.2	-38.7	147.0	1 36.9	-39.2	147.0	0 46.5	-39.6	147.0	0 03.8	+40.0	32.9	0 54.2	+40.4	33.0	1 44.5	+40.8	33.0	2 34.8	+41.3	33.0	3 25.2	+41.6	33.0	49
50	1 48.5	-38.8	147.8	0 57.7	-39.2	147.8	0 06.9	-39.5	147.8	0 43.8	+40.0	32.2	1 34.6	+40.4	32.2	2 25.3	+40.9	32.2	3 16.1	+41.2	32.3	4 06.8	+41.7	32.3	50
51	1 09.7	-38.7	148.5	0 18.5	-39.1	148.6	0 32.6	+39.6	31.4	1 23.8	+40.0	31.5	2 15.0	+40.4	31.5	3 06.2	+40.8	31.5	3 57.3	+41.2	31.5	4 48.5	+41.5	31.6	51
52	0 31.0	-38.8	149.3	0 20.6	+39.2	30.7	1 12.2	+39.6	30.7	2 03.8	+40.0	30.7	2 55.4	+40.4	30.7	3 47.0	+40.7	30.8	4 38.5	+41.2	30.8	5 30.0	+41.6	30.8	52
53	0 07.8	+38.8	29.9	0 59.8	+39.2	29.9	1 51.8	+39.6	29.9	2 43.8	+39.9	30.0	3 35.8	+40.3	30.0	4 27.7	+40.7	30.0	5 19.7	+41.0	30.1	6 11.6	+41.4	30.1	53
54	0 46.6	+38.8	29.2	1 39.0	+39.1	29.2	2 31.4	+39.5	29.2	3 23.7	+39.9	29.2	4 16.1	+40.3	29.3	5 08.4	+40.7	29.3	6 00.7	+41.1	29.3	6 53.0	+41.4	29.4	54
55	1 25.4	+38.7	28.4	2 18.1	+39.2	28.4	3 10.9	+39.5	28.4	4 03.6	+39.9	28.5	4 56.4	+40.2	28.5	5 49.1	+40.6	28.6	6 41.8	+40.9	28.6	7 34.4	+41.4	28.7	55
56	2 04.1	+38.7	27.6	2 57.3	+39.0	27.7	3 50.4	+39.4	27.7	4 43.5	+39.8	27.7	5 36.6	+40.2	27.8	6 29.7	+40.5	27.8	7 22.7	+40.9	27.9	8 15.8	+41.2	27.9	56
57	2 42.8	+38.7	26.9	3 36.3	+39.1	26.9	4 29.8	+39.5	26.9	5 23.3	+39.8	27.0	6 16.8	+40.1	27.0	7 10.2	+40.5	27.1	8 03.6	+40.9	27.1	8 57.0	+41.2	27.2	57
58	3 21.5	+38.7	26.1	4 15.4	+39.0	26.1	5 09.3	+39.3	26.2	6 03.1	+39.7	26.2	6 56.9	+40.1	26.3	7 50.7	+40.4	26.3	8 44.5	+40.7	26.4	9 38.2	+41.1	26.5	58
59	4 00.2	+38.6	25.3	4 54.4	+39.0	25.4	5 48.6	+39.3	25.4	6 42.8	+39.6	25.5	7 37.0	+39.9	25.5	8 31.1	+40.3	25.6	9 25.2	+40.6	25.6	10 19.3	+40.9	25.7	59
60	4 38.8	+38.6	24.6	5 33.4	+38.9	24.6	6 27.9	+39.2	24.7	7 22.4	+39.6	24.7	8 16.9	+39.9	24.8	9 11.4	+40.2	24.8	10 05.8	+40.6	24.9	11 00.2	+40.9	25.0	60
61	5 17.4	+38.5	23.8	6 12.3	+38.8	23.8	7 07.1	+39.2	23.9	8 02.0	+39.4	23.9	8 56.8	+39.8	24.0	9 51.6	+40.1	24.1	10 46.4	+40.4	24.2	11 41.1	+40.7	24.2	61
62	5 55.9	+38.4	23.0	6 51.1	+38.8	23.1	7 46.3	+39.1	23.1	8 41.4	+39.4	23.2	9 36.6	+39.7	23.3	10 31.7	+40.0	23.3	11 26.8	+40.3	23.4	12 21.8	+40.7	23.5	62
63	6 34.3	+38.4	22.3	7 29.9	+38.6	22.3	8 25.4	+38.9	22.4	9 20.8	+39.3	22.4	10 16.3	+39.6	22.5	11 11.7	+39.9	22.6	12 07.1	+40.2	22.6	13 02.5	+40.4	22.7	63
64	7 12.7	+38.3	21.5	8 08.5	+38.6	21.5	9 04.3	+38.9	21.6	10 00.1	+39.2	21.7	10 55.9	+39.4	21.7	11 51.6	+39.8	21.8	12 47.3	+40.0	21.9	13 42.9	+40.4	22.0	64
65	7 51.0	+38.2	20.7	8 47.1	+38.5	20.8	9 43.2	+38.8	20.8	10 39.3	+39.1	20.9	11 35.3	+39.4	21.0	12 31.4	+39.6	21.0	13 27.3	+40.0	21.1	14 23.3	+40.2	21.2	65
66	8 29.2	+38.1	19.9	9 25.6	+38.4	20.0	10 22.0	+38.7	20.0	11 18.4	+38.9	20.1	12 14.7	+39.2	20.2	13 11.0	+39.5	20.3	14 07.3	+39.7	20.3	15 03.5	+40.0	20.4	66
67	9 07.3	+38.1	19.2	10 04.0	+38.3	19.2	11 00.7	+38.5	19.3	11 57.3	+38.8	19.3	12 53.9	+39.1	19.4	13 50.5	+39.3	19.5	14 47.0	+39.6	19.6	15 43.5	+39.9	19.7	67
68	9 45.4	+37.9	18.4	10 42.3	+38.2	18.4	11 39.2	+38.4	18.5	12 36.1	+38.7	18.6	13 33.0	+38.9	18.6	14 29.8	+39.2	18.7	15 26.6	+39.5	18.8	16 23.4	+39.7	18.9	68
69	10 23.3	+37.8	17.6	11 20.5	+38.0	17.6	12 17.6	+38.3	17.7	13 14.8	+38.5	17.8	14 11.9	+38.8	17.8	15 09.0	+39.0	17.9	16 06.1	+39.3	18.0	17 03.1	+39.6	18.1	69
70	11 01.1	+37.6	16.8	11 58.5	+37.9	16.8	12 55.9	+38.2	16.9	13 53.3	+38.4	17.0	14 50.7	+38.6	17.1	15 48.0	+38.9	17.1	16 45.4	+39.1	17.2	17 42.7	+39.3	17.3	70
71	11 38.7	+37.6	16.0	12 36.4	+37.8	16.1	13 34.1	+38.0	16.1	14 31.7	+38.2	16.2	15 29.3	+38.5	16.3	16 26.9	+38.7	16.3	17 24.5	+38.9	16.4	18 22.0	+39.1	16.5	71
72	12 16.3	+37.4	15.2	13 14.2	+37.6	15.3	14 12.1	+37.8	15.3	15 09.9	+38.1	15.4	16 07.8	+38.2	15.5	17 05.6	+38.5	15.5	18 03.4	+38.7	15.6	19 01.1	+39.0	15.7	72
73	12 53.7	+37.2	14.4	13 51.8	+37.5	14.5	14 49.9	+37.7	14.5	15 48.0	+37.8	14.6	16 46.0	+38.1	14.7	17 44.1	+38.2	14.7	18 42.1	+38.5	14.8	19 40.1	+38.7	14.9	73
74	13 30.9	+37.1	13.6	14 29.3	+37.3	13.7	15 27.6	+37.4	13.7	16 25.8	+37.7	13.8	17 24.1	+37.9	13.9	18 22.3	+38.1	13.9	19 20.6	+38.3	14.0	20 18.8	+38.5	14.1	74
75	14 08.0	+37.0	12.8	15 06.6	+37.1	12.8	16 05.0	+37.4	12.9	17 03.5	+37.5	13.0	18 02.0	+37.7	13.0	19 00.4	+37.9	13.1	19 58.9	+38.0	13.2	20 57.3	+38.2	13.3	75
76	14 45.0	+36.8	12.0	15 43.7	+36.9	12.0	16 42.4	+37.1	12.1	17 41.0	+37.3	12.2	18 39.7	+37.4	12.2	19 38.3	+37.6	12.3	20 36.9	+37.8	12.4	21 35.5	+38.0	12.5	76
77	15 21.8	+36.5	11.2	16 20.6	+36.8	11.2	17 19.5	+36.9	11.3	18 18.3	+37.1	11.3	19 17.1	+37.3	11.4	20 15.9	+37.4	11.5	21 14.7	+37.6	11.5	22 13.5	+37.8	11.6	77
78	15 58.3	+36.4	10.3	16 57.4	+36.5	10.4	17 56.4	+36.7	10.4	18 55.4	+36.8	10.5	19 54.4	+37.0	10.6	20 53.3	+37.2	10.6	21 52.3	+37.3	10.7	22 51.3	+37.4	10.8	78
79	16 34.7	+36.2	9.5	17 33.9	+36.3	9.6	18 33.1	+36.4	9.6	19 32.2	+36.6	9.7	20 31.4	+36.7	9.7	21 30.5	+36.9	9.8	22 29.6	+37.1	9.9	23 28.7	+37.2	9.9	79
80	17 10.9	+36.0	8.7	18 10.2	+36.2	8.7	19 09.5	+36.3	8.8	20 08.8	+36.4	8.8	21 08.1	+36.5	8.9	22 07.4	+36.6	8.9	23 06.7	+36.7	9.0	24 05.9	+36.9	9.1	80
81	17 46.9	+35.8	7.8	18 46.4	+35.9	7.9	19 45.8	+36.0	7.9	20 45.2	+36.1	8.0	21 44.6	+36.3	8.0	22 44.0	+36.4	8.1	23 43.4	+36.5	8.1	24 42.8	+36.6	8.2	81
82	18 22.7	+35.6	7.0	19 22.3	+35.6	7.0	20 21.8	+35.8	7.1	21 21.3	+35.9	7.1	22 20.9	+35.9	7.2	23 20.4	+36.1	7.2	24 19.9	+36.2	7.3	25 19.4	+36.3	7.3	82
83	18 58.3	+35.3	6.1	19 57.9	+35.4	6.2	20 57.6	+35.5	6.2	21 57.2	+35.6	6.3	22 56.8	+35.7	6.3	23 56.5	+35.8	6.3	24 56.1	+35.9	6.4	25 55.7	+36.0	6.5	83
84	19 33.6	+35.0	5.3	20 33.3	+35.2	5.3	21 33.1	+35.2	5.3	22 32.8	+35.3	5.4	23 32.5	+35.4	5.4	24 32.3	+35.4	5.5	25 32.0	+35.5	5.5	26 31.7	+35.6	5.6	84
85	20 08.6	+34.9	4.4	21 08.5	+34.8	4.4	22 08.3	+34.9	4.5	23 08.1	+35.0	4.5	24 07.9	+35.1	4.5	25 07.7	+35.2	4.6	26 07.5	+35.2	4.6	27 07.3	+35.3	4.7	85
86	20 43.5	+34.5	3.5	21 43.3	+34.7	3.6	22 43.2	+34.7	3.6	23 43.1	+34.7	3.6	24 43.0	+34.8	3.7	25 42.9	+34.8	3.7	26 42.7	+34.9	3.7	27 42.6	+34.9	3.7	86
87	21 18.0	+34.3	2.7	22 18.0	+34.3	2.7	23 17.9	+34.3	2.7	24 17.8	+34.4	2.7	25 17.8	+34.4	2.8	26 17.7	+34.4	2.8	27 17.6	+34.5	2.8	28 17.5	+34.6	2.8	87
88	21 52.3	+34.0	1.8	22 52.3	+34.0	1.8	23 52.2	+34.1	1.8	24 52.2	+34.1	1.8	25 52.2	+34.1	1.8	26 52.1	+34.2	1.9	27 52.1	+34.2	1.9	28 52.1	+34.1	1.9	88
89	22 26.3	+33.7	0.9	23 26.3	+33.7	0.9	24 26.3	+33.7	0.9	25 26.3	+33.7	0.9	26 26.3	+33.7	0.9	27 26.3	+33.7	0.9	28 26.3	+33.7	0.9	29 26.2	+33.8	1.0	89
90	23 00.0	+33.4	0.0	24 00.0	+33.4	0.0	25 00.0	+33.4	0.0	26 00.0	+33.4	0.0	27 00.0	+33.4	0.0	28 00.0	+33.4	0.0	29 00.0	+33.3	0.0	30 00.0	+33.3	0.0	90
	23°			24°			25°			26°			27°			28°			29°			30°			

S. Lat. {L.H.A. greater than 180° ....Zn=180°−Z; L.H.A. less than 180°...........Zn=180°+Z}

LATITUDE SAME NAME AS DECLINATION — L.H.A. 124°, 236°

Dec.	23°			24°			25°			26°			27°			28°			29°			30°			Dec.
°	Hc ° ′	d ′	Z °	Hc ° ′	d ′	Z °	Hc ° ′	d ′	Z °	Hc ° ′	d ′	Z °	Hc ° ′	d ′	Z °	Hc ° ′	d ′	Z °	Hc ° ′	d ′	Z °	Hc ° ′	d ′	Z °	°
0	30 05.3	+26.9	104.2	29 50.3	+27.9	104.8	29 34.7	+28.9	105.3	29 18.5	+30.0	105.9	29 01.8	+31.0	106.4	28 44.6	+31.9	107.0	28 26.8	+32.9	107.5	28 08.6	+33.8	108.0	0
1	30 32.2	+26.3	103.2	30 18.2	+27.4	103.8	30 03.6	+28.5	104.3	29 48.5	+29.5	104.9	29 32.8	+30.5	105.4	29 16.5	+31.5	106.0	28 59.7	+32.5	106.5	28 42.4	+33.4	107.0	1
2	30 58.5	+25.9	102.2	30 45.6	+26.9	102.7	30 32.1	+28.0	103.3	30 18.0	+29.0	103.9	30 03.3	+30.0	104.5	29 48.0	+31.1	105.0	29 32.2	+32.1	105.6	29 15.8	+33.1	106.1	2
3	31 24.4	+25.3	101.1	31 12.5	+26.4	101.7	31 00.1	+27.4	102.3	30 47.0	+28.5	102.9	30 33.3	+29.6	103.4	30 19.1	+30.6	104.0	30 04.3	+31.6	104.6	29 48.9	+32.6	105.1	3
4	31 49.7	+24.8	100.0	31 38.9	+25.9	100.6	31 27.5	+27.0	101.2	31 15.5	+28.1	101.8	31 02.9	+29.1	102.4	30 49.7	+30.1	103.0	30 35.9	+31.1	103.6	30 21.5	+32.2	104.2	4
5	32 14.5	+24.2	99.0	32 04.8	+25.4	99.6	31 54.5	+26.5	100.2	31 43.6	+27.5	100.8	31 32.0	+28.6	101.4	31 19.8	+29.7	102.0	31 07.0	+30.7	102.6	30 53.7	+31.7	103.2	5
6	32 38.7	+23.7	97.9	32 30.2	+24.8	98.5	32 21.0	+25.9	99.1	32 11.1	+27.0	99.8	32 00.6	+28.1	100.4	31 49.5	+29.2	101.0	31 37.7	+30.3	101.6	31 25.4	+31.2	102.2	6
7	33 02.4	+23.1	96.8	32 55.0	+24.2	97.4	32 46.9	+25.3	98.1	32 38.1	+26.5	98.7	32 28.7	+27.6	99.3	32 18.7	+28.6	100.0	32 08.0	+29.7	100.6	31 56.6	+30.8	101.2	7
8	33 25.5	+22.5	95.7	33 19.2	+23.7	96.3	33 12.2	+24.8	97.0	33 04.6	+25.9	97.6	32 56.3	+27.0	98.3	32 47.3	+28.2	98.9	32 37.7	+29.2	99.6	32 27.4	+30.3	100.2	8
9	33 48.0	+21.9	94.6	33 42.9	+23.0	95.2	33 37.0	+24.3	95.9	33 30.5	+25.4	96.6	33 23.3	+26.5	97.2	33 15.5	+27.6	97.9	33 06.9	+28.7	98.5	32 57.7	+29.8	99.2	9
10	34 09.9	+21.3	93.4	34 05.9	+22.5	94.1	34 01.3	+23.6	94.8	33 55.9	+24.8	95.5	33 49.8	+26.0	96.1	33 43.1	+27.0	96.8	33 35.6	+28.2	97.5	33 27.5	+29.3	98.1	10
11	34 31.2	+20.6	92.3	34 28.4	+21.8	93.0	34 24.9	+23.0	93.7	34 20.7	+24.2	94.4	34 15.8	+25.3	95.0	34 10.1	+26.5	95.7	34 03.8	+27.6	96.4	33 56.8	+28.7	97.1	11
12	34 51.8	+20.0	91.2	34 50.2	+21.2	91.9	34 47.9	+22.4	92.6	34 44.9	+23.5	93.3	34 41.1	+24.7	93.9	34 36.6	+25.9	94.6	34 31.4	+27.0	95.3	34 25.5	+28.1	96.0	12
13	35 11.8	+19.4	90.0	35 11.4	+20.6	90.7	35 10.3	+21.8	91.4	35 08.4	+23.0	92.1	35 05.8	+24.2	92.8	35 02.5	+25.3	93.5	34 58.4	+26.5	94.2	34 53.6	+27.6	94.9	13
14	35 31.2	+18.6	88.9	35 32.0	+19.9	89.6	35 32.1	+21.1	90.3	35 31.4	+22.3	91.0	35 30.0	+23.5	91.7	35 27.8	+24.7	92.4	35 24.9	+25.8	93.1	35 21.2	+27.0	93.8	14
15	35 49.8	+18.0	87.7	35 51.9	+19.2	88.4	35 53.2	+20.4	89.1	35 53.7	+21.6	89.9	35 53.5	+22.8	90.6	35 52.5	+24.0	91.3	35 50.7	+25.2	92.0	35 48.2	+26.4	92.7	15
16	36 07.8	+17.3	86.5	36 11.1	+18.5	87.2	36 13.6	+19.7	88.0	36 15.3	+21.0	88.7	36 16.3	+22.2	89.4	36 16.5	+23.4	90.2	36 15.9	+24.6	90.9	36 14.6	+25.8	91.6	16
17	36 25.1	+16.6	85.3	36 29.6	+17.8	86.1	36 33.3	+19.1	86.8	36 36.3	+20.3	87.5	36 38.5	+21.5	88.3	36 39.9	+22.7	89.0	36 40.5	+24.0	89.8	36 40.4	+25.1	90.5	17
18	36 41.7	+15.8	84.1	36 47.4	+17.1	84.9	36 52.4	+18.3	85.6	36 56.6	+19.6	86.4	37 00.0	+20.8	87.1	37 02.6	+22.1	87.9	37 04.5	+23.2	88.6	37 05.5	+24.5	89.4	18
19	36 57.5	+15.1	82.9	37 04.5	+16.4	83.7	37 10.7	+17.7	84.4	37 16.2	+18.9	85.2	37 20.8	+20.1	85.9	37 24.7	+21.3	86.7	37 27.7	+22.6	87.5	37 30.0	+23.8	88.2	19
20	37 12.6	+14.4	81.7	37 20.9	+15.6	82.5	37 28.4	+16.9	83.2	37 35.1	+18.1	84.0	37 40.9	+19.4	84.8	37 46.0	+20.7	85.5	37 50.3	+21.9	86.3	37 53.8	+23.1	87.1	20
21	37 27.0	+13.6	80.5	37 36.5	+14.9	81.2	37 45.3	+16.1	82.0	37 53.2	+17.4	82.8	38 00.3	+18.7	83.6	38 06.7	+19.9	84.3	38 12.2	+21.2	85.1	38 16.9	+22.4	85.9	21
22	37 40.6	+12.9	79.3	37 51.4	+14.1	80.0	38 01.4	+15.4	80.8	38 10.6	+16.7	81.6	38 19.0	+17.9	82.3	38 26.6	+19.2	83.1	38 33.4	+20.4	83.9	38 39.3	+21.7	84.7	22
23	37 53.5	+12.0	78.0	38 05.5	+13.3	78.8	38 16.8	+14.6	79.6	38 27.3	+15.8	80.3	38 36.9	+17.2	81.1	38 45.8	+18.4	81.9	38 53.8	+19.7	82.7	39 01.0	+20.9	83.5	23
24	38 05.5	+11.3	76.8	38 18.8	+12.6	77.5	38 31.4	+13.8	78.3	38 43.1	+15.1	79.1	38 54.1	+16.3	79.9	39 04.2	+17.6	80.7	39 13.5	+18.9	81.5	39 21.9	+20.2	82.3	24
25	38 16.8	+10.5	75.5	38 31.4	+11.7	76.3	38 45.2	+13.0	77.1	38 58.2	+14.3	77.9	39 10.4	+15.6	78.7	39 21.8	+16.9	79.5	39 32.4	+18.1	80.3	39 42.1	+19.4	81.1	25
26	38 27.3	+9.6	74.3	38 43.1	+11.0	75.0	38 58.2	+12.2	75.8	39 12.5	+13.5	76.6	39 26.0	+14.8	77.4	39 38.7	+16.0	78.2	39 50.5	+17.3	79.0	40 01.5	+18.6	79.9	26
27	38 36.9	+8.9	73.0	38 54.1	+10.1	73.8	39 10.4	+11.4	74.6	39 26.0	+12.7	75.4	39 40.8	+13.9	76.2	39 54.7	+15.3	77.0	40 07.8	+16.6	77.8	40 20.1	+17.8	78.6	27
28	38 45.8	+8.0	71.7	39 04.2	+9.3	72.5	39 21.8	+10.6	73.3	39 38.7	+11.8	74.1	39 54.7	+13.1	74.9	40 10.0	+14.4	75.7	40 24.4	+15.6	76.5	40 37.9	+17.0	77.4	28
29	38 53.8	+7.2	70.5	39 13.5	+8.4	71.2	39 32.4	+9.7	72.0	39 50.5	+11.0	72.8	40 07.8	+12.3	73.6	40 24.4	+13.5	74.4	40 40.0	+14.9	75.3	40 54.9	+16.1	76.1	29
30	39 01.0	+6.3	69.2	39 21.9	+7.6	70.0	39 42.1	+8.9	70.7	40 01.5	+10.1	71.5	40 20.1	+11.4	72.3	40 37.9	+12.7	73.1	40 54.9	+14.0	74.0	41 11.0	+15.3	74.8	30
31	39 07.3	+5.5	67.9	39 29.5	+6.8	68.7	39 51.0	+8.0	69.5	40 11.6	+9.3	70.2	40 31.5	+10.6	71.0	40 50.6	+11.9	71.9	41 08.9	+13.1	72.7	41 26.3	+14.5	73.5	31
32	39 12.8	+4.7	66.6	39 36.3	+5.9	67.4	39 59.0	+7.1	68.2	40 20.9	+8.4	68.9	40 42.1	+9.7	69.7	41 02.5	+10.9	70.6	41 22.0	+12.3	71.4	41 40.8	+13.5	72.2	32
33	39 17.5	+3.8	65.3	39 42.2	+5.0	66.1	40 06.1	+6.3	66.9	40 29.3	+7.6	67.6	40 51.8	+8.8	68.4	41 13.4	+10.1	69.3	41 34.3	+11.3	70.1	41 54.3	+12.6	70.9	33
34	39 21.3	+3.0	64.1	39 47.2	+4.2	64.8	40 12.4	+5.4	65.6	40 36.9	+6.6	66.3	41 00.6	+7.9	67.1	41 23.5	+9.2	67.9	41 45.6	+10.5	68.8	42 06.9	+11.8	69.6	34
35	39 24.3	+2.1	62.8	39 51.4	+3.3	63.5	40 17.8	+4.5	64.3	40 43.5	+5.8	65.0	41 08.5	+7.0	65.8	41 32.7	+8.2	66.6	41 56.1	+9.5	67.4	42 18.7	+10.8	68.3	35
36	39 26.4	+1.2	61.5	39 54.7	+2.4	62.2	40 22.3	+3.7	62.9	40 49.3	+4.8	63.7	41 15.5	+6.1	64.5	41 40.9	+7.4	65.3	42 05.6	+8.6	66.1	42 29.5	+9.9	66.9	36
37	39 27.6	+0.4	60.2	39 57.1	+1.6	60.9	40 26.0	+2.7	61.6	40 54.1	+4.0	62.4	41 21.6	+5.1	63.2	41 48.3	+6.4	64.0	42 14.2	+7.7	64.8	42 39.4	+8.9	65.6	37
38	39 28.0	-0.5	58.9	39 58.7	+0.6	59.6	40 28.7	+1.9	60.3	40 58.1	+3.0	61.1	41 26.7	+4.3	61.8	41 54.7	+5.5	62.6	42 21.9	+6.7	63.4	42 48.3	+8.0	64.3	38
39	39 27.5	-1.4	57.6	39 59.3	-0.2	58.3	40 30.6	+0.9	59.0	41 01.1	+2.2	59.8	41 31.0	+3.3	60.5	42 00.2	+4.5	61.3	42 28.6	+5.8	62.1	42 56.3	+7.1	62.9	39
40	39 26.1	-2.2	56.3	39 59.1	-1.1	57.0	40 31.5	+0.1	57.7	41 03.3	+1.2	58.4	41 34.3	+2.4	59.2	42 04.7	+3.6	59.9	42 34.4	+4.8	60.7	43 03.4	+6.0	61.6	40
41	39 23.9	-3.1	55.0	39 58.0	-1.9	55.7	40 31.6	-0.9	56.4	41 04.5	+0.3	57.1	41 36.7	+1.5	57.8	42 08.3	+2.7	58.6	42 39.2	+3.9	59.4	43 09.4	+5.1	60.2	41
42	39 20.8	-3.9	53.7	39 56.1	-2.9	54.4	40 30.7	-1.7	55.1	41 04.8	-0.6	55.8	41 38.2	+0.6	56.5	42 11.0	+1.7	57.3	42 43.1	+2.9	58.0	43 14.5	+4.2	58.8	42
43	39 16.9	-4.8	52.4	39 53.2	-3.7	53.1	40 29.0	-2.6	53.7	41 04.2	-1.5	54.4	41 38.8	-0.4	55.2	42 12.7	+0.8	55.9	42 46.0	+2.0	56.7	43 18.7	+3.1	57.5	43
44	39 12.1	-5.6	51.1	39 49.5	-4.5	51.8	40 26.4	-3.5	52.4	41 02.7	-2.4	53.1	41 38.4	-1.3	53.8	42 13.5	-0.2	54.6	42 48.0	+0.9	55.3	43 21.8	+2.1	56.1	44
45	39 06.5	-6.5	49.8	39 45.0	-5.5	50.5	40 22.9	-4.4	51.1	41 00.3	-3.4	51.8	41 37.1	-2.3	52.5	42 13.3	-1.1	53.2	42 48.9	+0.1	53.9	43 23.9	+1.2	54.7	45
46	39 00.0	-7.3	48.6	39 39.5	-6.3	49.2	40 18.5	-5.3	49.8	40 56.9	-4.2	50.5	41 34.8	-3.1	51.2	42 12.2	-2.1	51.9	42 49.0	-1.0	52.6	43 25.1	+0.2	53.3	46
47	38 52.7	-8.1	47.3	39 33.2	-7.1	47.9	40 13.2	-6.2	48.5	40 52.7	-5.1	49.2	41 31.7	-4.1	49.8	42 10.1	-3.0	50.5	42 48.0	-1.9	51.2	43 25.3	-0.9	52.0	47
48	38 44.6	-9.0	46.0	39 26.1	-8.1	46.6	40 07.0	-7.0	47.2	40 47.6	-6.1	47.8	41 27.6	-5.0	48.5	42 07.1	-4.0	49.2	42 46.1	-2.9	49.9	43 24.4	-1.8	50.6	48
49	38 35.6	-9.7	44.7	39 18.0	-8.8	45.3	40 00.0	-7.9	45.9	40 41.5	-6.9	46.5	41 22.6	-5.9	47.2	42 03.1	-4.9	47.8	42 43.2	-3.9	48.5	43 22.6	-2.8	49.2	49
50	38 25.9	-10.6	43.5	39 09.2	-9.7	44.0	39 52.1	-8.7	44.6	40 34.6	-7.8	45.2	41 16.7	-6.9	45.8	41 58.2	-5.8	46.5	42 39.3	-4.8	47.1	43 19.8	-3.8	47.8	50
51	38 15.3	-11.4	42.2	38 59.5	-10.5	42.8	39 43.4	-9.6	43.3	40 26.8	-8.7	43.9	41 09.8	-7.7	44.5	41 52.4	-6.8	45.1	42 34.5	-5.8	45.8	43 16.0	-4.7	46.5	51
52	38 03.9	-12.2	41.0	38 49.0	-11.3	41.5	39 33.8	-10.5	42.0	40 18.1	-9.5	42.6	41 02.1	-8.7	43.2	41 45.6	-7.7	43.8	42 28.7	-6.7	44.4	43 11.3	-5.8	45.1	52
53	37 51.7	-12.9	39.7	38 37.7	-12.1	40.2	39 23.3	-11.2	40.8	40 08.6	-10.4	41.3	40 53.4	-9.5	41.9	41 37.9	-8.6	42.5	42 22.0	-7.7	43.1	43 05.5	-6.7	43.7	53
54	37 38.8	-13.7	38.5	38 25.6	-12.9	39.0	39 12.1	-12.1	39.5	39 58.2	-11.3	40.0	40 43.9	-10.4	40.6	41 29.3	-9.5	41.2	42 14.3	-8.6	41.7	42 58.8	-7.6	42.4	54
55	37 25.1	-14.5	37.3	38 12.7	-13.7	37.8	39 00.0	-12.9	38.2	39 46.9	-12.1	38.8	40 33.5	-11.2	39.3	41 19.8	-10.4	39.8	42 05.7	-9.5	40.4	42 51.2	-8.7	41.0	55
56	37 10.6	-15.2	36.1	37 59.0	-14.5	36.5	38 47.1	-13.7	37.0	39 34.8	-12.9	37.5	40 22.3	-12.1	38.0	41 09.4	-11.3	38.5	41 56.2	-10.5	39.1	42 42.5	-9.5	39.7	56
57	36 55.4	-16.0	34.8	37 44.5	-15.2	35.3	38 33.4	-14.5	35.7	39 21.9	-13.7	36.2	40 10.2	-13.0	36.7	40 58.1	-12.2	37.2	41 45.7	-11.3	37.8	42 33.0	-10.5	38.3	57
58	36 39.4	-16.6	33.6	37 29.3	-16.0	34.1	38 18.9	-15.3	34.5	39 08.2	-14.6	35.0	39 57.2	-13.8	35.4	40 45.9	-13.0	35.9	41 34.4	-12.3	36.4	42 22.5	-11.5	37.0	58
59	36 22.8	-17.4	32.4	37 13.3	-16.7	32.9	38 03.6	-16.1	33.3	38 53.6	-15.3	33.7	39 43.4	-14.6	34.2	40 32.9	-13.9	34.6	41 22.1	-13.1	35.1	42 11.0	-12.3	35.7	59
60	36 05.4	-18.1	31.3	36 56.6	-17.5	31.6	37 47.5	-16.7	32.0	38 38.3	-16.1	32.5	39 28.8	-15.4	32.9	40 19.0	-14.7	33.4	41 09.0	-14.0	33.8	41 58.7	-13.2	34.3	60
61	35 47.3	-18.7	30.1	36 39.1	-18.1	30.5	37 30.8	-17.6	30.8	38 22.2	-16.9	31.2	39 13.4	-16.3	31.7	40 04.3	-15.5	32.1	40 55.0	-14.8	32.6	41 45.5	-14.2	33.0	61
62	35 28.6	-19.5	28.9	36 21.0	-18.9	29.3	37 13.2	-18.2	29.6	38 05.3	-17.6	30.0	38 57.1	-17.0	30.4	39 48.8	-16.4	30.8	40 40.2	-15.7	31.3	41 31.3	-15.0	31.7	62
63	35 09.1	-20.1	27.8	36 02.1	-19.5	28.1	36 55.0	-19.0	28.4	37 47.7	-18.4	28.8	38 40.1	-17.7	29.2	39 32.4	-17.1	29.6	40 24.5	-16.5	30.0	41 16.3	-15.8	30.4	63
64	34 49.0	-20.7	26.6	35 42.6	-20.2	26.9	36 36.0	-19.6	27.3	37 29.3	-19.1	27.6	38 22.4	-18.6	28.0	39 15.3	-18.0	28.3	40 08.0	-17.3	28.7	41 00.5	-16.7	29.2	64
65	34 28.3	-21.4	25.5	35 22.4	-20.9	25.8	36 16.4	-20.4	26.1	37 10.2	-19.8	26.4	38 03.8	-19.2	26.8	38 57.3	-18.7	27.1	39 50.7	-18.2	27.5	40 43.8	-17.5	27.9	65
66	34 06.9	-21.9	24.3	35 01.5	-21.5	24.6	35 56.0	-21.0	24.9	36 50.4	-20.5	25.2	37 44.6	-20.0	25.6	38 38.6	-19.4	25.9	39 32.5	-18.9	26.3	40 26.3	-18.4	26.6	66
67	33 45.0	-22.6	23.2	34 40.0	-22.1	23.5	35 35.0	-21.6	23.8	36 29.9	-21.2	24.1	37 24.6	-20.7	24.4	38 19.2	-20.2	24.7	39 13.6	-19.6	25.0	40 07.9	-19.1	25.4	67
68	33 22.4	-23.2	22.1	34 17.9	-22.7	22.4	35 13.4	-22.3	22.6	36 08.7	-21.9	22.9	37 03.9	-21.4	23.2	37 59.0	-20.9	23.5	38 54.0	-20.5	23.8	39 48.8	-19.9	24.1	68
69	32 59.2	-23.7	21.0	33 55.2	-23.4	21.2	34 51.1	-23.0	21.5	35 46.8	-22.5	21.7	36 42.5	-22.1	22.0	37 38.1	-21.6	22.3	38 33.5	-21.1	22.6	39 28.9	-20.7	22.9	69
70	32 35.5	-24.4	19.9	33 31.8	-23.9	20.1	34 28.1	-23.5	20.4	35 24.3	-23.1	20.6	36 20.4	-22.7	20.9	37 16.5	-22.3	21.1	38 12.4	-21.9	21.4	39 08.2	-21.4	21.7	70
71	32 11.1	-24.8	18.8	33 07.9	-24.5	19.0	34 04.6	-24.2	19.2	35 01.2	-23.8	19.5	35 57.7	-23.4	19.7	36 54.2	-23.0	20.0	37 50.5	-22.6	20.2	38 46.8	-22.2	20.5	71
72	31 46.3	-25.4	17.7	32 43.4	-25.1	17.9	33 40.4	-24.7	18.1	34 37.4	-24.3	18.4	35 34.3	-24.0	18.6	36 31.2	-23.7	18.8	37 27.9	-23.2	19.1	38 24.6	-22.9	19.3	72
73	31 20.9	-25.9	16.7	32 18.3	-25.6	16.9	33 15.7	-25.3	17.1	34 13.1	-25.0	17.2	35 10.3	-24.6	17.5	36 07.5	-24.3	17.7	37 04.7	-24.0	17.9	38 01.7	-23.5	18.1	73
74	30 55.0	-26.5	15.6	31 52.7	-26.1	15.8	32 50.4	-25.8	16.0	33 48.1	-25.5	16.2	34 45.7	-25.2	16.3	35 43.2	-24.9	16.5	36 40.7	-24.6	16.8	37 38.2	-24.3	17.0	74
75	30 28.5	-26.9	14.6	31 26.6	-26.7	14.7	32 24.6	-26.4	14.9	33 22.6	-26.1	15.1	34 20.5	-25.8	15.2	35 18.3	-25.5	15.4	36 16.1	-25.2	15.6	37 13.9	-24.9	15.8	75
76	30 01.6	-27.4	13.6	30 59.9	-27.1	13.7	31 58.2	-26.9	13.8	32 56.5	-26.7	14.0	33 54.7	-26.4	14.2	34 52.8	-26.1	14.3	35 50.9	-25.8	14.5	36 49.0	-25.6	14.7	76
77	29 34.2	-27.8	12.5	30 32.8	-27.7	12.7	31 31.3	-27.4	12.8	32 29.8	-27.2	12.9	33 28.3	-27.0	13.1	34 26.7	-26.7	13.2	35 25.1	-26.5	13.4	36 23.4	-26.1	13.6	77
78	29 06.4	-28.4	11.5	30 05.1	-28.1	11.6	31 03.9	-27.9	11.7	32 02.6	-27.7	11.9	33 01.3	-27.4	12.0	34 00.0	-27.3	12.1	34 58.6	-27.0	12.3	35 57.3	-26.8	12.4	78
79	28 38.0	-28.7	10.5	29 37.0	-28.6	10.6	30 36.0	-28.4	10.7	31 34.9	-28.2	10.8	32 33.9	-28.1	10.9	33 32.7	-27.8	11.1	34 31.6	-27.6	11.2	35 30.5	-27.4	11.3	79
80	28 09.3	-29.2	9.5	29 08.4	-29.0	9.6	30 07.6	-28.9	9.7	31 06.7	-28.7	9.8	32 05.8	-28.5	9.9	33 04.9	-28.3	10.0	34 04.0	-28.1	10.1	35 03.1	-28.0	10.2	80
81	27 40.1	-29.6	8.5	28 39.4	-29.5	8.6	29 38.7	-29.3	8.7	30 38.0	-29.1	8.8	31 37.3	-29.0	8.9	32 36.6	-28.9	9.0	33 35.9	-28.7	9.1	34 35.1	-28.5	9.2	81
82	27 10.5	-30.0	7.5	28 09.9	-29.8	7.6	29 09.4	-29.7	7.7	30 08.9	-29.7	7.8	31 08.3	-29.5	7.8	32 07.7	-29.3	7.9	33 07.2	-29.2	8.0	34 06.6	-29.1	8.1	82
83	26 40.5	-30.5	6.6	27 40.1	-30.3	6.6	28 39.7	-30.2	6.7	29 39.2	-30.0	6.8	30 38.8	-29.9	6.8	31 38.4	-29.9	6.9	32 38.0	-29.8	7.0	33 37.5	-29.6	7.1	83
84	26 10.0	-30.7	5.6	27 09.8	-30.7	5.7	28 09.5	-30.6	5.7	29 09.2	-30.6	5.8	30 08.9	-30.5	5.8	31 08.5	-30.3	5.9	32 08.2	-30.2	5.9	33 07.9	-30.1	6.0	84
85	25 39.3	-31.2	4.7	26 39.1	-31.1	4.7	27 38.9	-31.1	4.7	28 38.6	-30.9	4.8	29 38.4	-30.8	4.8	30 38.2	-30.8	4.9	31 38.0	-30.7	4.9	32 37.8	-30.6	5.0	85
86	25 08.1	-31.5	3.7	26 08.0	-31.5	3.7	27 07.8	-31.4	3.8	28 07.7	-31.3	3.8	29 07.6	-31.3	3.8	30 07.4	-31.2	3.9	31 07.3	-31.2	3.9	32 07.2	-31.1	4.0	86
87	24 36.6	-31.9	2.8	25 36.5	-31.8	2.8	26 36.4	-31.7	2.8	27 36.4	-31.8	2.8	28 36.3	-31.7	2.9	29 36.2	-31.6	2.9	30 36.1	-31.6	2.9	31 36.1	-31.6	3.0	87
88	24 04.7	-32.2	1.8	25 04.7	-32.2	1.9	26 04.7	-32.2	1.9	27 04.6	-32.1	1.9	28 04.6	-32.1	1.9	29 04.6	-32.1	1.9	30 04.5	-32.0	1.9	31 04.5	-32.0	2.0	88
89	23 32.5	-32.5	0.9	24 32.5	-32.5	0.9	25 32.5	-32.5	0.9	26 32.5	-32.5	0.9	27 32.5	-32.5	0.9	28 32.5	-32.5	1.0	29 32.5	-32.5	1.0	30 32.5	-32.5	1.0	89
90	23 00.0	-32.8	0.0	24 00.0	-32.8	0.0	25 00.0	-32.8	0.0	26 00.0	-32.9	0.0	27 00.0	-32.9	0.0	28 00.0	-32.9	0.0	29 00.0	-32.9	0.0	30 00.0	-32.9	0.0	90
	23°			24°			25°			26°			27°			28°			29°			30°			

LATITUDE **CONTRARY** NAME TO DECLINATION L.H.A. 57°, 303°

Dec.	23°			24°			25°			26°			27°			28°			29°			30°			Dec.
	Hc	d	Z	Hc	d	Z	Hc	d	Z	Hc	d	Z	Hc	d	Z	Hc	d	Z	Hc	d	Z	Hc	d	Z	
°	° ′	′	°	° ′	′	°	° ′	′	°	° ′	′	°	° ′	′	°	° ′	′	°	° ′	′	°	° ′	′	°	°
0	30 05.3	-27.3	104.2	29 50.3	-28.4	104.8	29 34.7	-29.4	105.3	29 18.5	-30.3	105.9	29 01.8	-31.3	106.4	28 44.6	-32.3	107.0	28 26.8	-33.2	107.5	28 08.6	-34.2	108.0	0
1	29 38.0	-27.8	105.3	29 21.9	-28.8	105.8	29 05.3	-29.8	106.3	28 48.2	-30.9	106.9	28 30.5	-31.8	107.4	28 12.3	-32.8	107.9	27 53.6	-33.7	108.4	27 34.4	-34.6	108.9	1
2	29 10.2	-28.3	106.3	28 53.1	-29.3	106.8	28 35.5	-30.3	107.3	28 17.3	-31.2	107.9	27 58.7	-32.2	108.4	27 39.5	-33.1	108.9	27 19.9	-34.0	109.4	26 59.8	-34.9	109.8	2
3	28 41.9	-28.7	107.3	28 23.8	-29.7	107.8	28 05.2	-30.6	108.3	27 46.1	-31.6	108.8	27 26.5	-32.5	109.3	27 06.4	-33.4	109.8	26 45.9	-34.4	110.3	26 24.9	-35.3	110.7	3
4	28 13.2	-29.1	108.3	27 54.1	-30.1	108.8	27 34.6	-31.1	109.3	27 14.5	-32.0	109.8	26 54.0	-33.0	110.3	26 33.0	-33.9	110.7	26 11.5	-34.7	111.2	25 49.6	-35.6	111.6	4
5	27 44.1	-29.6	109.3	27 24.0	-30.5	109.8	27 03.5	-31.5	110.3	26 42.5	-32.4	110.7	26 21.0	-33.3	111.2	25 59.1	-34.2	111.7	25 36.8	-35.1	112.1	25 14.0	-35.9	112.5	5
6	27 14.5	-29.9	110.3	26 53.5	-30.9	110.7	26 32.0	-31.8	111.2	26 10.1	-32.7	111.7	25 47.7	-33.6	112.1	25 24.9	-34.5	112.6	25 01.7	-35.4	113.0	24 38.1	-36.3	113.4	6
7	26 44.6	-30.4	111.2	26 22.6	-31.3	111.7	26 00.2	-32.2	112.2	25 37.4	-33.1	112.6	25 14.1	-34.0	113.0	24 50.4	-34.8	113.5	24 26.3	-35.7	113.9	24 01.8	-36.5	114.3	7
8	26 14.2	-30.7	112.2	25 51.3	-31.6	112.6	25 28.0	-32.5	113.1	25 04.3	-33.5	113.5	24 40.1	-34.3	113.9	24 15.6	-35.2	114.4	23 50.6	-36.0	114.8	23 25.3	-36.8	115.2	8
9	25 43.5	-31.1	113.2	25 19.7	-32.0	113.6	24 55.5	-32.9	114.0	24 30.8	-33.7	114.4	24 05.8	-34.6	114.8	23 40.4	-35.4	115.2	23 14.6	-36.2	115.6	22 48.5	-37.1	116.0	9
10	25 12.4	-31.5	114.1	24 47.7	-32.4	114.5	24 22.6	-33.3	114.9	23 57.1	-34.1	115.3	23 31.2	-34.9	115.7	23 05.0	-35.8	116.1	22 38.4	-36.6	116.5	22 11.4	-37.3	116.9	10
11	24 40.9	-31.8	115.0	24 15.3	-32.7	115.4	23 49.3	-33.5	115.9	23 23.0	-34.4	116.2	22 56.3	-35.2	116.6	22 29.2	-36.0	117.0	22 01.8	-36.8	117.4	21 34.1	-37.6	117.7	11
12	24 09.1	-32.2	116.0	23 42.6	-33.0	116.4	23 15.8	-33.9	116.8	22 48.6	-34.7	117.1	22 21.1	-35.5	117.5	21 53.2	-36.3	117.9	21 25.0	-37.1	118.2	20 56.5	-37.9	118.6	12
13	23 36.9	-32.4	116.9	23 09.6	-33.3	117.3	22 41.9	-34.1	117.7	22 13.9	-34.9	118.0	21 45.6	-35.8	118.4	21 16.9	-36.5	118.7	20 47.9	-37.3	119.1	20 18.6	-38.0	119.4	13
14	23 04.5	-32.8	117.8	22 36.3	-33.6	118.2	22 07.8	-34.4	118.5	21 39.0	-35.3	118.9	21 09.8	-36.0	119.2	20 40.4	-36.8	119.6	20 10.6	-37.6	119.9	19 40.6	-38.3	120.2	14
15	22 31.7	-33.1	118.7	22 02.7	-33.9	119.1	21 33.4	-34.8	119.4	21 03.7	-35.5	119.8	20 33.8	-36.3	120.1	20 03.6	-37.1	120.4	19 33.0	-37.7	120.7	19 02.3	-38.5	121.0	15
16	21 58.6	-33.4	119.6	21 28.8	-34.2	120.0	20 58.6	-34.9	120.3	20 28.2	-35.7	120.6	19 57.5	-36.5	120.9	19 26.5	-37.2	121.2	18 55.3	-38.0	121.5	18 23.8	-38.8	121.8	16
17	21 25.2	-33.7	120.5	20 54.6	-34.5	120.8	20 23.7	-35.3	121.2	19 52.5	-36.0	121.5	19 21.0	-36.7	121.8	18 49.3	-37.5	122.1	18 17.3	-38.2	122.4	17 45.0	-38.9	122.6	17
18	20 51.5	-33.9	121.4	20 20.1	-34.7	121.7	19 48.4	-35.5	122.0	19 16.5	-36.3	122.3	18 44.3	-37.0	122.6	18 11.8	-37.7	122.9	17 39.1	-38.4	123.2	17 06.1	-39.1	123.4	18
19	20 17.6	-34.2	122.3	19 45.4	-35.0	122.6	19 12.9	-35.7	122.9	18 40.2	-36.4	123.2	18 07.3	-37.2	123.5	17 34.1	-37.9	123.7	17 00.7	-38.6	124.0	16 27.0	-39.2	124.2	19
20	19 43.4	-34.5	123.2	19 10.4	-35.2	123.4	18 37.2	-35.9	123.7	18 03.8	-36.7	124.0	17 30.1	-37.4	124.3	16 56.2	-38.1	124.5	16 22.1	-38.8	124.8	15 47.8	-39.5	125.0	20
21	19 08.9	-34.7	124.0	18 35.2	-35.4	124.3	18 01.3	-36.2	124.6	17 27.1	-36.9	124.8	16 52.7	-37.5	125.1	16 18.1	-38.2	125.3	15 43.3	-38.9	125.6	15 08.3	-39.6	125.8	21
22	18 34.2	-34.9	124.9	17 59.8	-35.7	125.2	17 25.1	-36.3	125.4	16 50.2	-37.0	125.7	16 15.2	-37.8	125.9	15 39.9	-38.5	126.1	15 04.4	-39.1	126.4	14 28.7	-39.7	126.6	22
23	17 59.3	-35.2	125.7	17 24.1	-35.8	126.0	16 48.8	-36.6	126.2	16 13.2	-37.3	126.5	15 37.4	-37.9	126.7	15 01.4	-38.6	126.9	14 25.3	-39.3	127.1	13 49.0	-39.9	127.3	23
24	17 24.1	-35.3	126.6	16 48.3	-36.1	126.8	16 12.2	-36.8	127.1	15 35.9	-37.4	127.3	14 59.5	-38.1	127.5	14 22.8	-38.7	127.7	13 46.0	-39.4	127.9	13 09.1	-40.0	128.1	24
25	16 48.8	-35.6	127.4	16 12.2	-36.3	127.7	15 35.4	-36.9	127.9	14 58.5	-37.6	128.1	14 21.4	-38.3	128.3	13 44.1	-38.9	128.5	13 06.6	-39.5	128.7	12 29.1	-40.2	128.9	25
26	16 13.2	-35.8	128.3	15 35.9	-36.4	128.5	14 58.5	-37.1	128.7	14 20.9	-37.8	128.9	13 43.1	-38.4	129.1	13 05.2	-39.1	129.3	12 27.1	-39.7	129.5	11 48.9	-40.3	129.6	26
27	15 37.4	-36.0	129.1	14 59.5	-36.7	129.3	14 21.4	-37.3	129.5	13 43.1	-37.9	129.7	13 04.7	-38.6	129.9	12 26.1	-39.2	130.1	11 47.4	-39.8	130.2	11 08.6	-40.4	130.4	27
28	15 01.4	-36.1	129.9	14 22.8	-36.8	130.1	13 44.1	-37.5	130.3	13 05.2	-38.1	130.5	12 26.1	-38.7	130.7	11 46.9	-39.3	130.8	11 07.6	-39.9	131.0	10 28.2	-40.5	131.1	28
29	14 25.3	-36.3	130.8	13 46.0	-36.9	131.0	13 06.6	-37.5	131.1	12 27.1	-38.2	131.3	11 47.4	-38.8	131.5	11 07.6	-39.4	131.6	10 27.7	-40.0	131.8	9 47.7	-40.6	131.9	29
30	13 49.0	-36.5	131.6	13 09.1	-37.1	131.8	12 29.1	-37.8	131.9	11 48.9	-38.3	132.1	11 08.6	-38.9	132.2	10 28.2	-39.5	132.4	9 47.7	-40.1	132.5	9 07.1	-40.7	132.6	30
31	13 12.5	-36.6	132.4	12 32.0	-37.3	132.6	11 51.3	-37.8	132.7	11 10.6	-38.5	132.9	10 29.7	-39.1	133.0	9 48.7	-39.7	133.2	9 07.6	-40.2	133.3	8 26.4	-40.7	133.4	31
32	12 35.9	-36.8	133.2	11 54.7	-37.4	133.4	11 13.5	-38.0	133.5	10 32.1	-38.6	133.7	9 50.6	-39.1	133.8	9 09.0	-39.7	133.9	8 27.4	-40.3	134.0	7 45.7	-40.9	134.1	32
33	11 59.1	-36.9	134.0	11 17.3	-37.5	134.2	10 35.5	-38.1	134.3	9 53.5	-38.7	134.4	9 11.5	-39.3	134.6	8 29.3	-39.8	134.7	7 47.1	-40.4	134.8	7 04.8	-40.9	134.9	33
34	11 22.2	-37.1	134.8	10 39.8	-37.6	135.0	9 57.4	-38.2	135.1	9 14.8	-38.7	135.2	8 32.2	-39.3	135.3	7 49.5	-39.9	135.4	7 06.7	-40.4	135.5	6 23.9	-41.0	135.6	34
35	10 45.1	-37.1	135.6	10 02.2	-37.8	135.8	9 19.2	-38.3	135.9	8 36.1	-38.9	136.0	7 52.9	-39.5	136.1	7 09.6	-40.0	136.2	6 26.3	-40.5	136.3	5 42.9	-41.0	136.3	35
36	10 08.0	-37.3	136.4	9 24.4	-37.8	136.5	8 40.9	-38.5	136.7	7 57.2	-39.0	136.8	7 13.4	-39.5	136.8	6 29.6	-40.0	136.9	5 45.8	-40.6	137.0	5 01.9	-41.1	137.1	36
37	9 30.7	-37.4	137.2	8 46.6	-37.9	137.3	8 02.4	-38.5	137.4	7 18.2	-39.0	137.5	6 33.9	-39.5	137.6	5 49.6	-40.1	137.7	5 05.2	-40.6	137.7	4 20.8	-41.1	137.8	37
38	8 53.3	-37.5	138.0	8 08.7	-38.1	138.1	7 23.9	-38.5	138.2	6 39.2	-39.1	138.3	5 54.4	-39.7	138.4	5 09.5	-40.1	138.4	4 24.6	-40.7	138.5	3 39.7	-41.2	138.5	38
39	8 15.8	-37.6	138.8	7 30.6	-38.1	138.9	6 45.4	-38.7	139.0	6 00.1	-39.2	139.1	5 14.7	-39.6	139.1	4 29.4	-40.2	139.2	3 43.9	-40.7	139.2	2 58.5	-41.2	139.3	39
40	7 38.2	-37.7	139.6	6 52.5	-38.2	139.7	6 06.7	-38.7	139.7	5 20.9	-39.2	139.8	4 35.1	-39.8	139.9	3 49.2	-40.3	139.9	3 03.2	-40.7	140.0	2 17.3	-41.2	140.0	40
41	7 00.5	-37.7	140.4	6 14.3	-38.3	140.5	5 28.0	-38.8	140.5	4 41.7	-39.3	140.6	3 55.3	-39.8	140.6	3 08.9	-40.2	140.7	2 22.5	-40.7	140.7	1 36.1	-41.2	140.7	41
42	6 22.8	-37.8	141.2	5 36.0	-38.3	141.2	4 49.2	-38.8	141.3	4 02.4	-39.3	141.3	3 15.5	-39.8	141.4	2 28.7	-40.3	141.4	1 41.8	-40.8	141.4	0 54.9	-41.3	141.4	42
43	5 45.0	-37.9	141.9	4 57.7	-38.4	142.0	4 10.4	-38.9	142.0	3 23.1	-39.4	142.1	2 35.7	-39.8	142.1	1 48.4	-40.3	142.1	1 01.0	-40.8	142.2	0 13.6	-41.2	142.2	43
44	5 07.1	-37.9	142.7	4 19.3	-38.4	142.8	3 31.5	-38.9	142.8	2 43.7	-39.3	142.8	1 55.9	-39.8	142.9	1 08.1	-40.3	142.9	0 20.2	-40.8	142.9	0 27.6	+41.3	37.1	44
45	4 29.2	-38.0	143.5	3 40.9	-38.5	143.5	2 52.6	-38.9	143.6	2 04.4	-39.4	143.6	1 16.1	-39.9	143.6	0 27.8	-40.4	143.6	0 20.6	+40.7	36.4	1 08.9	+41.2	36.4	45
46	3 51.2	-38.1	144.3	3 02.4	-38.4	144.3	2 13.7	-38.9	144.3	1 25.0	-39.5	144.4	0 36.2	-39.9	144.4	0 12.6	+40.3	35.6	1 01.3	+40.8	35.6	1 50.1	+41.2	35.7	46
47	3 13.1	-38.0	145.0	2 24.0	-38.6	145.1	1 34.8	-39.0	145.1	0 45.5	-39.4	145.1	0 03.7	+39.8	34.9	0 52.9	+40.3	34.9	1 42.1	+40.8	34.9	2 31.3	+41.2	34.9	47
48	2 35.1	-38.1	145.8	1 45.4	-38.5	145.8	0 55.8	-39.0	145.9	0 06.1	-39.4	145.9	0 43.5	+39.9	34.1	1 33.2	+40.3	34.2	2 22.9	+40.7	34.2	3 12.5	+41.1	34.2	48
49	1 57.0	-38.1	146.6	1 06.9	-38.6	146.6	0 16.8	-39.0	146.6	0 33.3	+39.4	33.4	1 23.4	+39.9	33.4	2 13.5	+40.3	33.4	3 03.6	+40.7	33.4	3 53.6	+41.2	33.5	49
50	1 18.9	-38.2	147.4	0 28.3	-38.5	147.4	0 22.2	+39.0	32.6	1 12.7	+39.4	32.6	2 03.3	+39.8	32.6	2 53.8	+40.2	32.7	3 44.3	+40.6	32.7	4 34.8	+41.0	32.7	50
51	0 40.7	-38.1	148.1	0 10.2	+38.6	31.9	1 01.2	+39.0	31.9	1 52.1	+39.4	31.9	2 43.1	+39.8	31.9	3 34.0	+40.2	31.9	4 24.9	+40.6	32.0	5 15.8	+41.0	32.0	51
52	0 02.6	-38.1	148.9	0 48.8	+38.5	31.1	1 40.2	+38.9	31.1	2 31.5	+39.4	31.1	3 22.9	+39.8	31.1	4 14.2	+40.2	31.2	5 05.5	+40.6	31.2	5 56.8	+41.0	31.3	52
53	0 35.5	+38.2	30.3	1 27.3	+38.6	30.3	2 19.1	+38.9	30.3	3 10.9	+39.3	30.4	4 02.7	+39.7	30.4	4 54.4	+40.1	30.4	5 46.1	+40.5	30.5	6 37.8	+40.9	30.5	53
54	1 13.7	+38.1	29.5	2 05.9	+38.5	29.6	2 58.0	+38.9	29.6	3 50.2	+39.3	29.6	4 42.4	+39.7	29.6	5 34.5	+40.1	29.7	6 26.6	+40.5	29.7	7 18.7	+40.8	29.8	54
55	1 51.8	+38.1	28.8	2 44.4	+38.4	28.8	3 36.9	+38.9	28.8	4 29.5	+39.2	28.9	5 22.1	+39.6	28.9	6 14.6	+40.0	28.9	7 07.1	+40.3	29.0	7 59.5	+40.8	29.1	55
56	2 29.9	+38.0	28.0	3 22.8	+38.5	28.0	4 15.8	+38.8	28.1	5 08.7	+39.2	28.1	6 01.7	+39.5	28.1	6 54.6	+39.9	28.2	7 47.4	+40.3	28.3	8 40.3	+40.6	28.3	56
57	3 07.9	+38.1	27.2	4 01.3	+38.4	27.3	4 54.6	+38.8	27.3	5 47.9	+39.2	27.3	6 41.2	+39.5	27.4	7 34.5	+39.8	27.4	8 27.7	+40.2	27.5	9 20.9	+40.6	27.6	57
58	3 46.0	+38.0	26.4	4 39.7	+38.3	26.5	5 33.4	+38.7	26.5	6 27.1	+39.0	26.6	7 20.7	+39.4	26.6	8 14.3	+39.8	26.7	9 07.9	+40.1	26.8	10 01.5	+40.5	26.8	58
59	4 24.0	+37.9	25.7	5 18.0	+38.3	25.7	6 12.1	+38.6	25.8	7 06.1	+39.0	25.8	8 00.1	+39.4	25.9	8 54.1	+39.7	25.9	9 48.0	+40.1	26.0	10 42.0	+40.3	26.1	59
60	5 01.9	+37.9	24.9	5 56.3	+38.3	24.9	6 50.7	+38.6	25.0	7 45.1	+38.9	25.0	8 39.5	+39.2	25.1	9 33.8	+39.5	25.2	10 28.1	+39.9	25.2	11 22.3	+40.3	25.3	60
61	5 39.8	+37.8	24.1	6 34.6	+38.1	24.2	7 29.3	+38.5	24.2	8 24.0	+38.8	24.3	9 18.7	+39.1	24.3	10 13.3	+39.5	24.4	11 08.0	+39.8	24.5	12 02.6	+40.1	24.6	61
62	6 17.6	+37.8	23.3	7 12.7	+38.1	23.4	8 07.8	+38.4	23.4	9 02.8	+38.7	23.5	9 57.8	+39.1	23.6	10 52.8	+39.4	23.6	11 47.8	+39.6	23.7	12 42.7	+40.0	23.8	62
63	6 55.4	+37.7	22.6	7 50.8	+38.0	22.6	8 46.2	+38.3	22.7	9 41.5	+38.6	22.7	10 36.9	+38.9	22.8	11 32.2	+39.2	22.9	12 27.4	+39.6	23.0	13 22.7	+39.8	23.0	63
64	7 33.1	+37.6	21.8	8 28.8	+37.9	21.8	9 24.5	+38.2	21.9	10 20.1	+38.5	21.9	11 15.8	+38.8	22.0	12 11.4	+39.1	22.1	13 07.0	+39.4	22.2	14 02.5	+39.7	22.3	64
65	8 10.7	+37.5	21.0	9 06.7	+37.8	21.0	10 02.7	+38.1	21.1	10 58.6	+38.4	21.2	11 54.6	+38.6	21.2	12 50.5	+38.9	21.3	13 46.4	+39.2	21.4	14 42.2	+39.6	21.5	65
66	8 48.2	+37.4	20.2	9 44.5	+37.7	20.2	10 40.8	+37.9	20.3	11 37.0	+38.3	20.4	12 33.2	+38.6	20.5	13 29.4	+38.9	20.5	14 25.6	+39.1	20.6	15 21.8	+39.3	20.7	66
67	9 25.6	+37.3	19.4	10 22.2	+37.5	19.5	11 18.7	+37.9	19.5	12 15.3	+38.1	19.6	13 11.8	+38.4	19.7	14 08.3	+38.6	19.8	15 04.7	+39.0	19.8	16 01.1	+39.3	19.9	67
68	10 02.9	+37.2	18.6	10 59.7	+37.5	18.7	11 56.6	+37.7	18.7	12 53.4	+37.9	18.8	13 50.2	+38.2	18.9	14 46.9	+38.5	19.0	15 43.7	+38.7	19.0	16 40.4	+39.0	19.1	68
69	10 40.1	+37.0	17.8	11 37.2	+37.3	17.9	12 34.3	+37.5	17.9	13 31.3	+37.9	18.0	14 28.4	+38.1	18.1	15 25.4	+38.3	18.2	16 22.4	+38.6	18.3	17 19.4	+38.8	18.4	69
70	11 17.1	+37.0	17.0	12 14.5	+37.2	17.1	13 11.8	+37.5	17.1	14 09.2	+37.6	17.2	15 06.5	+37.9	17.3	16 03.7	+38.2	17.4	17 01.0	+38.4	17.5	17 58.2	+38.7	17.6	70
71	11 54.1	+36.8	16.2	12 51.7	+37.0	16.3	13 49.3	+37.2	16.3	14 46.8	+37.5	16.4	15 44.4	+37.7	16.5	16 41.9	+38.0	16.6	17 39.4	+38.2	16.7	18 36.9	+38.4	16.7	71
72	12 30.9	+36.6	15.4	13 28.7	+36.9	15.5	14 26.5	+37.1	15.5	15 24.3	+37.3	15.6	16 22.1	+37.5	15.7	17 19.9	+37.7	15.8	18 17.6	+38.0	15.8	19 15.3	+38.2	15.9	72
73	13 07.5	+36.5	14.6	14 05.6	+36.7	14.6	15 03.6	+36.9	14.7	16 01.6	+37.2	14.8	16 59.6	+37.4	14.9	17 57.6	+37.6	14.9	18 55.6	+37.8	15.0	19 53.5	+38.0	15.1	73
74	13 44.0	+36.3	13.8	14 42.3	+36.5	13.8	15 40.5	+36.8	13.9	16 38.8	+36.9	14.0	17 37.0	+37.1	14.0	18 35.2	+37.3	14.1	19 33.4	+37.5	14.2	20 31.5	+37.8	14.3	74
75	14 20.3	+36.2	12.9	15 18.8	+36.4	13.0	16 17.3	+36.5	13.1	17 15.7	+36.7	13.1	18 14.1	+37.0	13.2	19 12.5	+37.1	13.3	20 10.9	+37.3	13.4	21 09.3	+37.5	13.5	75
76	14 56.5	+36.0	12.1	15 55.2	+36.1	12.2	16 53.8	+36.4	12.2	17 52.4	+36.6	12.3	18 51.1	+36.7	12.4	19 49.6	+36.9	12.5	20 48.2	+37.1	12.5	21 46.8	+37.2	12.6	76
77	15 32.5	+35.8	11.3	16 31.3	+36.0	11.3	17 30.2	+36.1	11.4	18 29.0	+36.3	11.5	19 27.8	+36.4	11.5	20 26.5	+36.7	11.6	21 25.3	+36.8	11.7	22 24.0	+37.0	11.8	77
78	16 08.3	+35.6	10.5	17 07.3	+35.8	10.5	18 06.3	+35.9	10.6	19 05.3	+36.0	10.6	20 04.2	+36.3	10.7	21 03.2	+36.4	10.8	22 02.1	+36.6	10.8	23 01.0	+36.7	10.9	78
79	16 43.9	+35.4	9.6	17 43.1	+35.5	9.7	18 42.2	+35.7	9.7	19 41.3	+35.9	9.8	20 40.5	+35.9	9.8	21 39.6	+36.1	9.9	22 38.7	+36.2	10.0	23 37.7	+36.5	10.1	79
80	17 19.3	+35.2	8.8	18 18.6	+35.3	8.8	19 17.9	+35.4	8.9	20 17.2	+35.5	8.9	21 16.4	+35.7	9.0	22 15.7	+35.8	9.1	23 14.9	+36.0	9.1	24 14.2	+36.1	9.2	80
81	17 54.5	+35.0	7.9	18 53.9	+35.1	8.0	19 53.3	+35.2	8.0	20 52.7	+35.4	8.1	21 52.1	+35.5	8.1	22 51.5	+35.6	8.2	23 50.9	+35.7	8.2	24 50.3	+35.8	8.3	81
82	18 29.5	+34.7	7.1	19 29.0	+34.8	7.1	20 28.5	+35.0	7.2	21 28.1	+35.0	7.2	22 27.6	+35.1	7.3	23 27.1	+35.3	7.3	24 26.6	+35.4	7.4	25 26.1	+35.5	7.4	82
83	19 04.2	+34.5	6.2	20 03.8	+34.6	6.2	21 03.5	+34.7	6.3	22 03.1	+34.8	6.3	23 02.7	+34.9	6.4	24 02.4	+34.9	6.4	25 02.0	+35.1	6.5	26 01.6	+35.2	6.5	83
84	19 38.7	+34.2	5.3	20 38.4	+34.3	5.4	21 38.2	+34.4	5.4	22 37.9	+34.5	5.5	23 37.6	+34.6	5.5	24 37.3	+34.7	5.5	25 37.1	+34.7	5.6	26 36.8	+34.8	5.6	84
85	20 12.9	+34.0	4.5	21 12.7	+34.1	4.5	22 12.6	+34.1	4.5	23 12.4	+34.1	4.6	24 12.2	+34.2	4.6	25 12.0	+34.3	4.6	26 11.8	+34.4	4.7	27 11.6	+34.4	4.7	85
86	20 46.9	+33.7	3.6	21 46.8	+33.7	3.6	22 46.7	+33.8	3.6	23 46.5	+33.9	3.7	24 46.4	+33.9	3.7	25 46.3	+34.0	3.7	26 46.2	+34.0	3.8	27 46.0	+34.1	3.8	86
87	21 20.6	+33.4	2.7	22 20.5	+33.5	2.7	23 20.5	+33.5	2.7	24 20.4	+33.5	2.8	25 20.3	+33.6	2.8	26 20.3	+33.6	2.8	27 20.2	+33.6	2.8	28 20.1	+33.7	2.9	87
88	21 54.0	+33.2	1.8	22 54.0	+33.2	1.8	23 54.0	+33.2	1.8	24 53.9	+33.2	1.8	25 53.9	+33.2	1.9	26 53.9	+33.2	1.9	27 53.8	+33.3	1.9	28 53.8	+33.3	1.9	88
89	22 27.2	+32.8	0.9	23 27.2	+32.8	0.9	24 27.2	+32.8	0.9	25 27.1	+32.9	0.9	26 27.1	+32.9	0.9	27 27.1	+32.9	0.9	28 27.1	+32.9	1.0	29 27.1	+32.9	1.0	89
90	23 00.0	+32.5	0.0	24 00.0	+32.5	0.0	25 00.0	+32.5	0.0	26 00.0	+32.5	0.0	27 00.0	+32.5	0.0	28 00.0	+32.5	0.0	29 00.0	+32.5	0.0	30 00.0	+32.5	0.0	90
	23°			24°			25°			26°			27°			28°			29°			30°			

S. Lat. {L.H.A. greater than 180° ....Zn=180°−Z
{L.H.A. less than 180°...........Zn=180°+Z

LATITUDE **SAME** NAME AS DECLINATION L.H.A. 123°, 237°

299

58°, 302° L.H.A. LATITUDE SAME NAME AS DECLINATION N. Lat. {L.H.A. greater than 180° .....Zn=Z / L.H.A. less than 180°............Zn=360°–Z}

Dec.	23°			24°			25°			26°			27°			28°			29°			30°			Dec.
	Hc	d	Z	Hc	d	Z	Hc	d	Z	Hc	d	Z	Hc	d	Z	Hc	d	Z	Hc	d	Z	Hc	d	Z	
°	° ′	′	°	° ′	′	°	° ′	′	°	° ′	′	°	° ′	′	°	° ′	′	°	° ′	′	°	° ′	′	°	°
0	29 11.7	+26.7	103.7	28 57.2	+27.7	104.3	28 42.2	+28.7	104.8	28 26.6	+29.7	105.3	28 10.5	+30.7	105.8	27 53.8	+31.7	106.3	27 36.7	+32.6	106.9	27 19.1	+33.5	107.4	0
1	29 38.4	+26.1	102.7	29 24.9	+27.2	103.2	29 10.9	+28.2	103.8	28 56.3	+29.3	104.3	28 41.2	+30.2	104.9	28 25.5	+31.3	105.4	28 09.3	+32.3	105.9	27 52.6	+33.2	106.4	1
2	30 04.5	+25.6	101.7	29 52.1	+26.7	102.2	29 39.1	+27.8	102.8	29 25.6	+28.8	103.3	29 11.4	+29.9	103.9	28 56.8	+30.8	104.4	28 41.6	+31.8	104.9	28 25.8	+32.8	105.5	2
3	30 30.1	+25.2	100.6	30 18.8	+26.2	101.2	30 06.9	+27.3	101.8	29 54.4	+28.3	102.3	29 41.3	+29.3	102.9	29 27.6	+30.4	103.4	29 13.4	+31.4	104.0	28 58.6	+32.4	104.5	3
4	30 55.3	+24.6	99.6	30 45.0	+25.7	100.1	30 34.2	+26.8	100.7	30 22.7	+27.9	101.3	30 10.6	+29.0	101.9	29 58.0	+30.0	102.4	29 44.8	+31.0	103.0	29 31.0	+32.0	103.6	4
5	31 19.9	+24.1	98.5	31 10.7	+25.2	99.1	31 01.0	+26.2	99.7	30 50.6	+27.3	100.3	30 39.6	+28.4	100.9	30 28.0	+29.4	101.4	30 15.8	+30.5	102.0	30 03.0	+31.5	102.6	5
6	31 44.0	+23.5	97.4	31 35.9	+24.7	98.0	31 27.2	+25.8	98.6	31 17.9	+26.9	99.2	31 08.0	+27.9	99.8	30 57.4	+29.0	100.4	30 46.3	+30.0	101.0	30 34.5	+31.1	101.6	6
7	32 07.5	+23.0	96.3	32 00.6	+24.1	96.9	31 53.0	+25.2	97.6	31 44.8	+26.3	98.2	31 35.9	+27.5	98.8	31 26.4	+28.6	99.4	31 16.3	+29.6	100.0	31 05.6	+30.6	100.6	7
8	32 30.5	+22.4	95.2	32 24.7	+23.6	95.9	32 18.2	+24.7	96.5	32 11.1	+25.8	97.1	32 03.4	+26.9	97.7	31 55.0	+28.0	98.4	31 45.9	+29.1	99.0	31 36.2	+30.2	99.6	8
9	32 52.9	+21.8	94.1	32 48.3	+22.9	94.8	32 42.9	+24.2	95.4	32 36.9	+25.3	96.1	32 30.3	+26.4	96.7	32 23.0	+27.4	97.3	32 15.0	+28.6	97.9	32 06.4	+29.6	98.6	9
10	33 14.7	+21.3	93.0	33 11.2	+22.4	93.7	33 07.1	+23.5	94.3	33 02.2	+24.7	95.0	32 56.7	+25.8	95.6	32 50.4	+27.0	96.3	32 43.6	+28.0	96.9	32 36.0	+29.2	97.5	10
11	33 36.0	+20.6	91.9	33 33.6	+21.8	92.6	33 30.6	+23.0	93.2	33 26.9	+24.1	93.9	33 22.5	+25.2	94.5	33 17.4	+26.4	95.2	33 11.6	+27.5	95.9	33 05.2	+28.6	96.5	11
12	33 56.6	+20.0	90.8	33 55.4	+21.2	91.4	33 53.6	+22.3	92.1	33 51.0	+23.5	92.8	33 47.7	+24.7	93.5	33 43.8	+25.8	94.1	33 39.1	+27.0	94.8	33 33.8	+28.0	95.4	12
13	34 16.6	+19.3	89.6	34 16.6	+20.6	90.3	34 15.9	+21.8	91.0	34 14.5	+23.0	91.7	34 12.4	+24.1	92.4	34 09.6	+25.2	93.0	34 06.1	+26.4	93.7	34 01.8	+27.6	94.4	13
14	34 35.9	+18.7	88.5	34 37.2	+19.9	89.2	34 37.7	+21.1	89.9	34 37.5	+22.3	90.6	34 36.5	+23.5	91.2	34 34.8	+24.7	91.9	34 32.5	+25.8	92.6	34 29.4	+26.9	93.3	14
15	34 54.6	+18.1	87.3	34 57.1	+19.2	88.0	34 58.8	+20.5	88.7	34 59.8	+21.6	89.4	35 00.0	+22.8	90.1	34 59.5	+24.0	90.8	34 58.3	+25.2	91.5	34 56.3	+26.4	92.2	15
16	35 12.7	+17.4	86.2	35 16.3	+18.6	86.9	35 19.3	+19.8	87.6	35 21.4	+21.0	88.3	35 22.8	+22.3	89.0	35 23.5	+23.4	89.7	35 23.5	+24.6	90.4	35 22.7	+25.7	91.1	16
17	35 30.1	+16.6	85.0	35 34.9	+17.9	85.7	35 39.1	+19.1	86.4	35 42.4	+20.4	87.1	35 45.1	+21.5	87.9	35 46.9	+22.8	88.6	35 48.1	+23.9	89.3	35 48.4	+25.2	90.0	17
18	35 46.7	+16.0	83.8	35 52.8	+17.3	84.5	35 58.2	+18.4	85.2	36 02.8	+19.7	86.0	36 06.6	+20.9	86.7	36 09.7	+22.1	87.4	36 12.0	+23.3	88.2	36 13.6	+24.5	88.9	18
19	36 02.7	+15.3	82.6	36 10.1	+16.5	83.3	36 16.6	+17.8	84.1	36 22.5	+18.9	84.8	36 27.5	+20.2	85.5	36 31.8	+21.4	86.3	36 35.3	+22.7	87.0	36 38.1	+23.8	87.8	19
20	36 18.0	+14.6	81.4	36 26.6	+15.8	82.1	36 34.4	+17.0	82.9	36 41.4	+18.3	83.6	36 47.7	+19.5	84.4	36 53.2	+20.8	85.1	36 58.0	+21.9	85.9	37 01.9	+23.2	86.6	20
21	36 32.6	+13.8	80.2	36 42.4	+15.0	80.9	36 51.4	+16.4	81.7	36 59.7	+17.6	82.4	37 07.2	+18.8	83.2	37 14.0	+20.0	83.9	37 19.9	+21.3	84.7	37 25.1	+22.5	85.5	21
22	36 46.4	+13.0	79.0	36 57.4	+14.4	79.7	37 07.8	+15.5	80.5	37 17.3	+16.8	81.2	37 26.0	+18.1	82.0	37 34.0	+19.3	82.7	37 41.2	+20.6	83.5	37 47.6	+21.8	84.3	22
23	36 59.4	+12.4	77.8	37 11.8	+13.5	78.5	37 23.3	+14.9	79.3	37 34.1	+16.1	80.0	37 44.1	+17.4	80.8	37 53.3	+18.6	81.5	38 01.8	+19.8	82.3	38 09.4	+21.0	83.1	23
24	37 11.8	+11.5	76.6	37 25.3	+12.9	77.3	37 38.2	+14.0	78.0	37 50.2	+15.3	78.8	38 01.5	+16.5	79.6	38 11.9	+17.9	80.3	38 21.6	+19.1	81.1	38 30.4	+20.4	81.9	24
25	37 23.3	+10.8	75.3	37 38.2	+12.0	76.1	37 52.2	+13.3	76.8	38 05.5	+14.6	77.6	38 18.0	+15.9	78.3	38 29.8	+17.0	79.1	38 40.7	+18.3	79.9	38 50.8	+19.6	80.7	25
26	37 34.1	+10.0	74.1	37 50.2	+11.3	74.8	38 05.5	+12.5	75.6	38 20.1	+13.8	76.3	38 33.9	+15.0	77.1	38 46.8	+16.3	77.9	38 59.0	+17.6	78.7	39 10.4	+18.8	79.5	26
27	37 44.1	+9.2	72.8	38 01.5	+10.4	73.6	38 18.0	+11.8	74.3	38 33.9	+12.9	75.1	38 48.9	+14.2	75.9	39 03.1	+15.5	76.7	39 16.6	+16.8	77.5	39 29.2	+18.0	78.3	27
28	37 53.3	+8.5	71.6	38 11.9	+9.7	72.3	38 29.8	+10.9	73.1	38 46.8	+12.2	73.8	39 03.1	+13.5	74.6	39 18.6	+14.8	75.4	39 33.4	+15.9	76.2	39 47.2	+17.3	77.0	28
29	38 01.8	+7.6	70.3	38 21.6	+8.8	71.1	38 40.7	+10.1	71.8	38 59.0	+11.4	72.6	39 16.6	+12.6	73.4	39 33.4	+13.8	74.2	39 49.3	+15.2	75.0	40 04.5	+16.4	75.8	29
30	38 09.4	+6.8	69.1	38 30.4	+8.1	69.8	38 50.8	+9.3	70.6	39 10.4	+10.5	71.3	39 29.2	+11.8	72.1	39 47.2	+13.1	72.9	40 04.5	+14.3	73.7	40 20.9	+15.6	74.5	30
31	38 16.2	+6.0	67.8	38 38.5	+7.2	68.5	39 00.1	+8.4	69.3	39 20.9	+9.7	70.1	39 41.0	+11.0	70.8	40 00.3	+12.2	71.6	40 18.8	+13.5	72.4	40 36.5	+14.8	73.2	31
32	38 22.2	+5.1	66.5	38 45.7	+6.4	67.3	39 08.5	+7.6	68.0	39 30.6	+8.9	68.8	39 52.0	+10.1	69.6	40 12.5	+11.4	70.3	40 32.3	+12.7	71.1	40 51.3	+13.9	72.0	32
33	38 27.3	+4.4	65.3	38 52.1	+5.5	66.0	39 16.1	+6.8	66.7	39 39.5	+8.0	67.5	40 02.1	+9.2	68.3	40 23.9	+10.5	69.1	40 45.0	+11.7	69.9	41 05.2	+13.1	70.7	33
34	38 31.7	+3.5	64.0	38 57.6	+4.7	64.7	39 22.9	+5.9	65.5	39 47.5	+7.1	66.2	40 11.3	+8.4	67.0	40 34.4	+9.7	67.8	40 56.7	+10.9	68.6	41 18.3	+12.1	69.4	34
35	38 35.2	+2.6	62.7	39 02.3	+3.9	63.4	39 28.8	+5.1	64.2	39 54.6	+6.3	64.9	40 19.7	+7.5	65.7	40 44.1	+8.7	66.5	41 07.6	+10.1	67.3	41 30.4	+11.3	68.1	35
36	38 37.8	+1.9	61.4	39 06.2	+3.0	62.1	39 33.9	+4.2	62.9	40 00.9	+5.4	63.6	40 27.2	+6.7	64.4	40 52.8	+7.9	65.2	41 17.7	+9.1	65.9	41 41.7	+10.4	66.8	36
37	38 39.7	+1.0	60.2	39 09.2	+2.2	60.9	39 38.1	+3.4	61.6	40 06.3	+4.6	62.3	40 33.9	+5.7	63.1	41 00.7	+7.0	63.8	41 26.8	+8.2	64.6	41 52.1	+9.5	65.4	37
38	38 40.7	+0.2	58.9	39 11.4	+1.3	59.6	39 41.5	+2.4	60.3	40 10.9	+3.6	61.0	40 39.6	+4.9	61.8	41 07.7	+6.0	62.5	41 35.0	+7.3	63.3	42 01.6	+8.5	64.1	38
39	38 40.9	−0.7	57.6	39 12.7	+0.5	58.3	39 43.9	+1.6	59.0	40 14.5	+2.8	59.7	40 44.5	+3.9	60.4	41 13.7	+5.2	61.2	41 42.3	+6.4	62.0	42 10.1	+7.6	62.8	39
40	38 40.2	−1.5	56.3	39 13.2	−0.4	57.0	39 45.5	+0.8	57.7	40 17.3	+1.9	58.4	40 48.4	+3.1	59.1	41 18.9	+4.2	59.9	41 48.7	+5.4	60.6	42 17.7	+6.7	61.4	40
41	38 38.7	−2.4	55.0	39 12.8	−1.3	55.7	39 46.3	−0.1	56.4	40 19.2	+1.0	57.1	40 51.5	+2.1	57.8	41 23.1	+3.4	58.5	41 54.1	+4.5	59.3	42 24.4	+5.7	60.1	41
42	38 36.3	−3.2	53.8	39 11.5	−2.1	54.4	39 46.2	−1.1	55.1	40 20.2	+0.1	55.8	40 53.6	+1.3	56.5	41 26.5	+2.4	57.2	41 58.6	+3.6	58.0	42 30.1	+4.8	58.7	42
43	38 33.1	−4.0	52.5	39 09.4	−2.9	53.1	39 45.1	−1.8	53.8	40 20.3	−0.8	54.5	40 54.9	+0.3	55.2	41 28.9	+1.4	55.9	42 02.2	+2.6	56.6	42 34.9	+3.8	57.4	43
44	38 29.1	−4.8	51.2	39 06.5	−3.8	51.8	39 43.3	−2.8	52.5	40 19.5	−1.6	53.1	40 55.2	−0.5	53.8	41 30.3	+0.6	54.5	42 04.8	+1.7	55.3	42 38.7	+2.8	56.0	44
45	38 24.3	−5.7	49.9	39 02.7	−4.7	50.5	39 40.5	−3.6	51.2	40 17.9	−2.6	51.8	40 54.7	−1.5	52.5	41 30.9	−0.4	53.2	42 06.5	+0.8	53.9	42 41.5	+1.9	54.7	45
46	38 18.6	−6.5	48.7	38 58.0	−5.5	49.3	39 36.9	−4.5	49.9	40 15.3	−3.4	50.5	40 53.2	−2.4	51.2	41 30.5	−1.3	51.9	42 07.3	−0.2	52.6	42 43.4	+1.0	53.3	46
47	38 12.1	−7.3	47.4	38 52.5	−6.3	48.0	39 32.4	−5.3	48.6	40 11.9	−4.3	49.2	40 50.8	−3.3	49.9	41 29.2	−2.2	50.5	42 07.1	−1.2	51.2	42 44.4	−0.1	52.0	47
48	38 04.8	−8.1	46.1	38 46.2	−7.2	46.7	39 27.1	−6.2	47.3	40 07.6	−5.2	47.9	40 47.5	−4.1	48.5	41 27.0	−3.2	49.2	42 05.9	−2.1	49.9	42 44.3	−1.0	50.6	48
49	37 56.7	−8.9	44.9	38 39.0	−7.9	45.4	39 20.9	−7.0	46.0	40 02.4	−6.1	46.6	40 43.4	−5.1	47.2	41 23.8	−4.0	47.9	42 03.8	−3.0	48.5	42 43.3	−2.0	49.2	49
50	37 47.8	−9.7	43.6	38 31.1	−8.8	44.2	39 13.9	−7.9	44.7	39 56.3	−6.9	45.3	40 38.3	−6.0	45.9	41 19.8	−5.0	46.5	42 00.8	−4.0	47.2	42 41.3	−2.9	47.9	50
51	37 38.1	−10.5	42.4	38 22.3	−9.6	42.9	39 06.0	−8.7	43.4	39 49.4	−7.8	44.0	40 32.3	−6.8	44.6	41 14.8	−5.9	45.2	41 56.8	−4.9	45.9	42 38.4	−3.9	46.5	51
52	37 27.6	−11.2	41.1	38 12.7	−10.5	41.6	38 57.3	−9.5	42.2	39 41.6	−8.7	42.7	40 25.5	−7.8	43.3	41 08.9	−6.8	43.9	41 51.9	−5.8	44.5	42 34.5	−4.9	45.2	52
53	37 16.4	−12.0	39.9	38 02.2	−11.2	40.4	38 47.8	−10.4	40.9	39 32.9	−9.5	41.4	40 17.7	−8.6	42.0	41 02.1	−7.7	42.6	41 46.1	−6.8	43.2	42 29.6	−5.8	43.8	53
54	37 04.4	−12.8	38.7	37 51.0	−11.9	39.1	38 37.4	−11.2	39.6	39 23.4	−10.3	40.2	40 09.1	−9.5	40.7	40 54.4	−8.6	41.3	41 39.3	−7.7	41.8	42 23.8	−6.8	42.5	54
55	36 51.6	−13.6	37.4	37 39.1	−12.8	37.9	38 26.2	−11.9	38.4	39 13.1	−11.1	38.9	39 59.6	−10.3	39.4	40 45.8	−9.5	40.0	41 31.6	−8.6	40.5	42 17.0	−7.7	41.1	55
56	36 38.0	−14.2	36.2	37 26.3	−13.5	36.7	38 14.3	−12.8	37.1	39 02.0	−12.0	37.6	39 49.3	−11.1	38.1	40 36.3	−10.3	38.7	41 23.0	−9.5	39.2	42 09.3	−8.6	39.8	56
57	36 23.8	−15.0	35.0	37 12.8	−14.3	35.4	38 01.5	−13.5	35.9	38 50.0	−12.8	36.4	39 38.2	−12.1	36.9	40 26.0	−11.2	37.4	41 13.5	−10.4	37.9	42 00.7	−9.5	38.4	57
58	36 08.8	−15.7	33.8	36 58.5	−15.0	34.2	37 48.0	−14.3	34.7	38 37.2	−13.6	35.1	39 26.1	−12.8	35.6	40 14.8	−12.1	36.1	41 03.1	−11.2	36.6	41 51.2	−10.5	37.1	58
59	35 53.1	−16.4	32.6	36 43.5	−15.7	33.0	37 33.7	−15.1	33.4	38 23.6	−14.3	33.9	39 13.3	−13.6	34.3	40 02.7	−12.9	34.8	40 51.9	−12.2	35.3	41 40.7	−11.4	35.8	59
60	35 36.7	−17.1	31.4	36 27.8	−16.5	31.8	37 18.6	−15.8	32.2	38 09.3	−15.2	32.6	38 59.7	−14.5	33.1	39 49.8	−13.7	33.5	40 39.7	−13.0	34.0	41 29.3	−12.2	34.5	60
61	35 19.6	−17.8	30.3	36 11.3	−17.2	30.6	37 02.8	−16.5	31.0	37 54.1	−15.9	31.4	38 45.2	−15.2	31.8	39 36.1	−14.5	32.2	40 26.7	−13.8	32.7	41 17.1	−13.2	33.2	61
62	35 01.8	−18.5	29.1	35 54.1	−17.8	29.4	36 46.3	−17.3	29.8	37 38.2	−16.6	30.2	38 30.0	−16.0	30.6	39 21.6	−15.4	31.0	40 12.9	−14.7	31.4	41 03.9	−13.9	31.9	62
63	34 43.3	−19.1	27.9	35 36.3	−18.6	28.3	36 29.0	−17.9	28.6	37 21.6	−17.4	29.0	38 14.0	−16.8	29.3	39 06.2	−16.2	29.7	39 58.2	−15.5	30.2	40 50.0	−14.9	30.6	63
64	34 24.2	−19.7	26.8	35 17.7	−19.2	27.1	36 11.1	−18.7	27.4	37 04.2	−18.1	27.8	37 57.2	−17.5	28.1	38 50.0	−16.9	28.5	39 42.7	−16.3	28.9	40 35.1	−15.7	29.3	64
65	34 04.5	−20.4	25.6	34 58.5	−19.9	25.9	35 52.4	−19.4	26.3	36 46.1	−18.8	26.6	37 39.7	−18.3	26.9	38 33.1	−17.7	27.3	39 26.4	−17.2	27.7	40 19.4	−16.5	28.0	65
66	33 44.1	−21.0	24.5	34 38.6	−20.5	24.8	35 33.0	−20.0	25.1	36 27.3	−19.5	25.4	37 21.4	−18.9	25.7	38 15.4	−18.4	26.1	39 09.2	−17.8	26.4	40 02.9	−17.3	26.8	66
67	33 23.1	−21.6	23.4	34 18.1	−21.1	23.6	35 13.0	−20.6	23.9	36 07.8	−20.2	24.2	37 02.5	−19.7	24.5	37 57.0	−19.2	24.8	38 51.4	−18.7	25.2	39 45.6	−18.1	25.5	67
68	33 01.5	−22.2	22.3	33 57.0	−21.8	22.5	34 52.4	−21.3	22.8	35 47.6	−20.8	23.1	36 42.8	−20.4	23.3	37 37.8	−19.9	23.6	38 32.7	−19.4	24.0	39 27.5	−18.9	24.3	68
69	32 39.3	−22.7	21.2	33 35.2	−22.3	21.4	34 31.1	−22.0	21.6	35 26.8	−21.5	21.9	36 22.4	−21.1	22.2	37 17.9	−20.6	22.5	38 13.3	−20.1	22.8	39 08.6	−19.7	23.1	69
70	32 16.6	−23.3	20.1	33 12.9	−22.9	20.3	34 09.1	−22.5	20.5	35 05.3	−22.2	20.8	36 01.3	−21.7	21.0	36 57.3	−21.3	21.3	37 53.2	−20.9	21.6	38 48.9	−20.4	21.9	70
71	31 53.3	−23.9	19.0	32 50.0	−23.6	19.2	33 46.6	−23.2	19.4	34 43.1	−22.7	19.6	35 39.6	−22.4	19.9	36 36.0	−22.0	20.1	37 32.3	−21.6	20.4	38 28.5	−21.2	20.7	71
72	31 29.4	−24.4	17.9	32 26.4	−24.0	18.1	33 23.4	−23.7	18.3	34 20.4	−23.4	18.5	35 17.2	−23.0	18.7	36 14.0	−22.6	19.0	37 10.7	−22.2	19.2	38 07.3	−21.8	19.5	72
73	31 05.0	−25.0	16.8	32 02.4	−24.7	17.0	32 59.7	−24.3	17.2	33 57.0	−24.0	17.4	34 54.2	−23.6	17.6	35 51.4	−23.3	17.8	36 48.5	−23.0	18.0	37 45.5	−22.6	18.3	73
74	30 40.0	−25.4	15.8	31 37.7	−25.1	15.9	32 35.4	−24.8	16.1	33 33.0	−24.5	16.3	34 30.6	−24.2	16.5	35 28.1	−23.9	16.7	36 25.5	−23.5	16.9	37 22.9	−23.2	17.1	74
75	30 14.6	−26.0	14.7	31 12.6	−25.7	14.9	32 10.6	−25.4	15.0	33 08.5	−25.1	15.2	34 06.4	−24.9	15.4	35 04.2	−24.5	15.6	36 02.0	−24.3	15.7	36 59.7	−23.9	16.0	75
76	29 48.6	−26.4	13.7	30 46.9	−26.2	13.8	31 45.2	−26.0	14.0	32 43.4	−25.7	14.1	33 41.5	−25.4	14.3	34 39.7	−25.2	14.4	35 37.7	−24.8	14.6	36 35.8	−24.6	14.8	76
77	29 22.2	−26.9	12.6	30 20.7	−26.7	12.8	31 19.2	−26.4	12.9	32 17.7	−26.2	13.0	33 16.1	−25.9	13.2	34 14.5	−25.7	13.3	35 12.9	−25.5	13.5	36 11.2	−25.2	13.7	77
78	28 55.3	−27.4	11.6	29 54.0	−27.1	11.7	30 52.8	−27.0	11.9	31 51.5	−26.7	12.0	32 50.2	−26.5	12.1	33 48.8	−26.3	12.3	34 47.4	−26.0	12.4	35 46.0	−25.8	12.6	78
79	28 27.9	−27.8	10.6	29 26.9	−27.6	10.7	30 25.8	−27.4	10.8	31 24.8	−27.3	10.9	32 23.7	−27.1	11.0	33 22.5	−26.8	11.2	34 21.4	−26.6	11.3	35 20.2	−26.4	11.4	79
80	28 00.1	−28.2	9.6	28 59.3	−28.1	9.7	29 58.4	−27.9	9.8	30 57.5	−27.7	9.9	31 56.6	−27.5	10.0	32 55.7	−27.4	10.1	33 54.8	−27.2	10.2	34 53.8	−27.0	10.3	80
81	27 31.9	−28.7	8.6	28 31.2	−28.5	8.7	29 30.5	−28.4	8.8	30 29.8	−28.2	8.9	31 29.1	−28.1	8.9	32 28.3	−27.9	9.0	33 27.6	−27.8	9.1	34 26.8	−27.6	9.3	81
82	27 03.2	−29.1	7.6	28 02.7	−29.0	7.7	29 02.1	−28.8	7.8	30 01.6	−28.7	7.8	31 01.0	−28.6	7.9	32 00.4	−28.4	8.0	32 59.8	−28.3	8.1	33 59.2	−28.1	8.2	82
83	26 34.1	−29.5	6.6	27 33.7	−29.4	6.7	28 33.3	−29.3	6.8	29 32.9	−29.2	6.8	30 32.4	−29.0	6.9	31 32.0	−28.9	7.0	32 31.5	−28.7	7.0	33 31.1	−28.7	7.1	83
84	26 04.6	−29.8	5.7	27 04.3	−29.8	5.7	28 04.0	−29.7	5.8	29 03.7	−29.6	5.8	30 03.4	−29.5	5.9	31 03.1	−29.4	5.9	32 02.8	−29.3	6.0	33 02.4	−29.2	6.1	84
85	25 34.8	−30.3	4.7	26 34.5	−30.1	4.7	27 34.3	−30.1	4.8	28 34.1	−30.0	4.8	29 33.9	−29.9	4.9	30 33.7	−29.9	4.9	31 33.5	−29.8	5.0	32 33.2	−29.6	5.0	85
86	25 04.5	−30.6	3.7	26 04.4	−30.6	3.8	27 04.2	−30.4	3.8	28 04.1	−30.4	3.8	29 04.0	−30.4	3.9	30 03.8	−30.3	3.9	31 03.7	−30.3	4.0	32 03.6	−30.2	4.0	86
87	24 33.9	−31.0	2.8	25 33.8	−30.9	2.8	26 33.8	−30.9	2.8	27 33.7	−30.9	2.9	28 33.6	−30.8	2.9	29 33.5	−30.7	2.9	30 33.4	−30.7	3.0	31 33.4	−30.7	3.0	87
88	24 02.9	−31.3	1.9	25 02.9	−31.3	1.9	26 02.9	−31.3	1.9	27 02.8	−31.2	1.9	28 02.8	−31.2	1.9	29 02.8	−31.2	1.9	30 02.7	−31.1	2.0	31 02.7	−31.1	2.0	88
89	23 31.6	−31.6	0.9	24 31.6	−31.6	0.9	25 31.6	−31.6	0.9	26 31.6	−31.6	0.9	27 31.6	−31.6	1.0	28 31.6	−31.6	1.0	29 31.6	−31.6	1.0	30 31.6	−31.6	1.0	89
90	23 00.0	−32.0	0.0	24 00.0	−32.0	0.0	25 00.0	−32.0	0.0	26 00.0	−32.0	0.0	27 00.0	−32.0	0.0	28 00.0	−32.0	0.0	29 00.0	−32.0	0.0	30 00.0	−32.0	0.0	90
	23°			24°			25°			26°			27°			28°			29°			30°			

58°, 302° L.H.A. LATITUDE SAME NAME AS DECLINATION

300

LATITUDE CONTRARY NAME TO DECLINATION   L.H.A. 58°, 302°

Dec.	23° Hc	d	Z	24° Hc	d	Z	25° Hc	d	Z	26° Hc	d	Z	Dec.
°	° ′	′	°	° ′	′	°	° ′	′	°	° ′	′	°	°
0	29 11.7	−27.0	103.7	28 57.2	−28.1	104.3	28 42.2	−29.1	104.8	28 26.6	−30.1	105.3	0
1	28 44.7	−27.6	104.7	28 29.1	−28.5	105.3	28 13.1	−29.6	105.8	27 56.5	−30.6	106.3	1
2	28 17.1	−28.0	105.8	28 00.6	−29.0	106.3	27 43.5	−30.0	106.8	27 25.9	−30.9	107.3	2
3	27 49.1	−28.4	106.8	27 31.6	−29.4	107.3	27 13.5	−30.3	107.7	26 55.0	−31.3	108.2	3
4	27 20.7	−28.8	107.7	27 02.2	−29.8	108.2	26 43.2	−30.8	108.7	26 23.7	−31.7	109.2	4
5	26 51.9	−29.3	108.7	26 32.4	−30.2	109.2	26 12.4	−31.1	109.7	25 52.0	−32.1	110.1	5
6	26 22.6	−29.6	109.7	26 02.2	−30.6	110.2	25 41.3	−31.6	110.6	25 19.9	−32.4	111.1	6
7	25 53.0	−30.0	110.7	25 31.6	−31.0	111.1	25 09.7	−31.8	111.6	24 47.5	−32.8	112.0	7
8	25 23.0	−30.4	111.6	25 00.6	−31.3	112.1	24 37.9	−32.2	112.5	24 14.7	−33.1	112.9	8
9	24 52.6	−30.8	112.6	24 29.3	−31.6	113.0	24 05.7	−32.6	113.4	23 41.6	−33.4	113.8	9
10	24 21.8	−31.1	113.5	23 57.7	−32.0	113.9	23 33.1	−32.8	114.3	23 08.2	−33.7	114.7	10
11	23 50.7	−31.4	114.5	23 25.7	−32.3	114.9	23 00.3	−33.2	115.3	22 34.5	−34.0	115.6	11
12	23 19.3	−31.7	115.4	22 53.4	−32.6	115.8	22 27.1	−33.5	116.2	22 00.5	−34.3	116.5	12
13	22 47.6	−32.1	116.3	22 20.8	−33.0	116.7	21 53.6	−33.7	117.1	21 26.2	−34.6	117.4	13
14	22 15.5	−32.4	117.2	21 47.8	−33.2	117.6	21 19.9	−34.0	117.9	20 51.6	−34.8	118.3	14
15	21 43.1	−32.7	118.1	21 14.6	−33.5	118.5	20 45.9	−34.3	118.8	20 16.8	−35.1	119.2	15
16	21 10.4	−32.9	119.0	20 41.1	−33.7	119.4	20 11.6	−34.6	119.7	19 41.7	−35.4	120.0	16
17	20 37.5	−33.3	119.9	20 07.4	−34.1	120.3	19 37.0	−34.8	120.6	19 06.3	−35.5	120.9	17
18	20 04.2	−33.5	120.8	19 33.3	−34.2	121.1	19 02.2	−35.1	121.4	18 30.8	−35.8	121.7	18
19	19 30.7	−33.7	121.7	18 59.1	−34.6	122.0	18 27.1	−35.2	122.3	17 55.0	−36.1	122.6	19
20	18 57.0	−34.0	122.6	18 24.5	−34.7	122.9	17 51.9	−35.5	123.1	17 18.9	−36.2	123.4	20
21	18 23.0	−34.2	123.5	17 49.8	−35.0	123.7	17 16.4	−35.8	124.0	16 42.7	−36.4	124.2	21
22	17 48.8	−34.5	124.3	17 14.8	−35.2	124.6	16 40.6	−35.9	124.8	16 06.3	−36.6	125.1	22
23	17 14.3	−34.7	125.2	16 39.6	−35.4	125.4	16 04.7	−36.1	125.7	15 29.7	−36.9	125.9	23
24	16 39.6	−34.9	126.0	16 04.2	−35.6	126.3	15 28.6	−36.3	126.5	14 52.8	−36.9	126.7	24
25	16 04.7	−35.0	126.9	15 28.6	−35.8	127.1	14 52.3	−36.4	127.3	14 15.9	−37.2	127.5	25
26	15 29.7	−35.3	127.7	14 52.8	−35.9	127.9	14 15.9	−36.7	128.1	13 38.7	−37.3	128.3	26
27	14 54.4	−35.5	128.6	14 16.9	−36.1	128.8	13 39.2	−36.7	129.0	13 01.4	−37.4	129.1	27
28	14 18.9	−35.6	129.4	13 40.8	−36.3	129.6	13 02.5	−37.0	129.8	12 24.0	−37.6	129.9	28
29	13 43.3	−35.8	130.2	13 04.5	−36.5	130.4	12 25.5	−37.1	130.6	11 46.4	−37.7	130.7	29
30	13 07.5	−36.0	131.1	12 28.0	−36.6	131.2	11 48.4	−37.2	131.4	11 08.7	−37.8	131.5	30
31	12 31.5	−36.1	131.9	11 51.4	−36.7	132.0	11 11.2	−37.3	132.2	10 30.9	−38.0	132.3	31
32	11 55.4	−36.2	132.7	11 14.7	−36.9	132.8	10 33.9	−37.5	133.0	9 52.9	−38.1	133.1	32
33	11 19.2	−36.4	133.5	10 37.8	−36.9	133.6	9 56.4	−37.6	133.8	9 14.8	−38.1	133.9	33
34	10 42.8	−36.5	134.3	10 00.9	−37.1	134.4	9 18.8	−37.7	134.6	8 36.7	−38.3	134.7	34
35	10 06.3	−36.6	135.1	9 23.8	−37.2	135.2	8 41.1	−37.8	135.4	7 58.4	−38.3	135.5	35
36	9 29.7	−36.7	135.9	8 46.6	−37.3	136.0	8 03.3	−37.8	136.1	7 20.1	−38.5	136.2	36
37	8 53.0	−36.8	136.7	8 09.3	−37.4	136.8	7 25.5	−38.0	136.9	6 41.6	−38.5	137.0	37
38	8 16.2	−37.0	137.5	7 31.9	−37.5	137.6	6 47.5	−38.0	137.7	6 03.1	−38.5	137.8	38
39	7 39.2	−37.0	138.3	6 54.4	−37.6	138.4	6 09.5	−38.1	138.5	5 24.6	−38.7	138.5	39
40	7 02.2	−37.1	139.1	6 16.8	−37.6	139.2	5 31.4	−38.1	139.3	4 45.9	−38.6	139.3	40
41	6 25.1	−37.1	139.9	5 39.2	−37.7	140.0	4 53.3	−38.2	140.0	4 07.3	−38.8	140.1	41
42	5 48.0	−37.2	140.7	5 01.5	−37.7	140.8	4 15.1	−38.3	140.8	3 28.5	−38.7	140.8	42
43	5 10.8	−37.3	141.5	4 23.8	−37.8	141.5	3 36.8	−38.3	141.6	2 49.8	−38.8	141.6	43
44	4 33.5	−37.4	142.3	3 46.0	−37.8	142.3	2 58.5	−38.3	142.3	2 11.0	−38.8	142.4	44
45	3 56.1	−37.4	143.1	3 08.2	−37.9	143.1	2 20.2	−38.4	143.1	1 32.2	−38.8	143.1	45
46	3 18.7	−37.4	143.8	2 30.3	−37.9	143.9	1 41.8	−38.3	143.9	0 53.4	−38.9	143.9	46
47	2 41.3	−37.4	144.6	1 52.4	−37.9	144.6	1 03.5	−38.4	144.7	0 14.5	−38.8	144.7	47
48	2 03.9	−37.5	145.4	1 14.5	−37.9	145.4	0 25.1	−38.4	145.4	0 24.3	+38.9	34.6	48
49	1 26.4	−37.5	146.2	0 36.6	−38.0	146.2	0 13.3	+38.4	33.8	1 03.2	+38.8	33.8	49
50	0 48.9	−37.5	147.0	0 01.4	+37.9	33.0	0 51.7	+38.4	33.0	1 42.0	+38.8	33.0	50
51	0 11.4	−37.5	147.7	0 39.3	+37.9	32.3	1 30.1	+38.3	32.3	2 20.8	+38.8	32.3	51
52	0 26.1	+37.5	31.5	1 17.2	+38.0	31.5	2 08.4	+38.3	31.5	2 59.6	+38.7	31.5	52
53	1 03.6	+37.5	30.7	1 55.2	+37.9	30.7	2 46.7	+38.3	30.7	3 38.3	+38.7	30.8	53
54	1 41.1	+37.4	29.9	2 33.1	+37.8	29.9	3 25.0	+38.3	30.0	4 17.0	+38.7	30.0	54
55	2 18.5	+37.5	29.1	3 10.9	+37.9	29.2	4 03.3	+38.2	29.2	4 55.7	+38.6	29.2	55
56	2 56.0	+37.4	28.3	3 48.8	+37.7	28.4	4 41.5	+38.2	28.4	5 34.3	+38.5	28.5	56
57	3 33.4	+37.3	27.6	4 26.5	+37.8	27.6	5 19.7	+38.1	27.6	6 12.8	+38.5	27.7	57
58	4 10.7	+37.3	26.8	5 04.3	+37.7	26.8	5 57.8	+38.1	26.9	6 51.3	+38.4	26.9	58
59	4 48.0	+37.3	26.0	5 42.0	+37.6	26.0	6 35.9	+37.9	26.1	7 29.7	+38.4	26.1	59
60	5 25.3	+37.2	25.2	6 19.6	+37.5	25.3	7 13.8	+37.9	25.3	8 08.1	+38.2	25.4	60
61	6 02.5	+37.1	24.4	6 57.1	+37.5	24.5	7 51.7	+37.8	24.5	8 46.3	+38.1	24.6	61
62	6 39.6	+37.1	23.6	7 34.6	+37.4	23.7	8 29.5	+37.8	23.7	9 24.4	+38.1	23.8	62
63	7 16.7	+37.0	22.8	8 12.0	+37.3	22.9	9 07.3	+37.6	23.0	10 02.5	+37.9	23.0	63
64	7 53.7	+36.9	22.0	8 49.3	+37.2	22.1	9 44.9	+37.5	22.2	10 40.4	+37.8	22.2	64
65	8 30.6	+36.8	21.2	9 26.5	+37.1	21.3	10 22.4	+37.4	21.4	11 18.2	+37.7	21.4	65
66	9 07.4	+36.6	20.4	10 03.6	+36.9	20.5	10 59.8	+37.2	20.6	11 55.9	+37.6	20.6	66
67	9 44.0	+36.6	19.6	10 40.5	+36.9	19.7	11 37.0	+37.1	19.8	12 33.5	+37.4	19.8	67
68	10 20.6	+36.5	18.8	11 17.4	+36.7	18.9	12 14.1	+37.0	19.0	13 10.9	+37.2	19.0	68
69	10 57.1	+36.3	18.0	11 54.1	+36.6	18.1	12 51.1	+36.9	18.2	13 48.1	+37.1	18.2	69
70	11 33.4	+36.2	17.2	12 30.7	+36.4	17.3	13 28.0	+36.6	17.4	14 25.2	+37.0	17.4	70
71	12 09.6	+36.0	16.4	13 07.1	+36.3	16.5	14 04.6	+36.6	16.5	15 02.2	+36.7	16.6	71
72	12 45.6	+35.9	15.6	13 43.4	+36.1	15.7	14 41.2	+36.3	15.7	15 38.9	+36.6	15.8	72
73	13 21.5	+35.7	14.8	14 19.5	+36.0	14.8	15 17.5	+36.2	14.9	16 15.5	+36.4	15.0	73
74	13 57.2	+35.6	13.9	14 55.5	+35.7	14.0	15 53.7	+35.9	14.1	16 51.9	+36.1	14.1	74
75	14 32.8	+35.4	13.1	15 31.2	+35.6	13.2	16 29.6	+35.8	13.2	17 28.0	+36.0	13.3	75
76	15 08.2	+35.2	12.3	16 06.8	+35.4	12.3	17 05.4	+35.6	12.4	18 04.0	+35.8	12.5	76
77	15 43.4	+35.0	11.4	16 42.2	+35.2	11.5	17 41.0	+35.3	11.6	18 39.8	+35.5	11.6	77
78	16 18.4	+34.8	10.6	17 17.4	+34.9	10.6	18 16.3	+35.1	10.7	19 15.3	+35.3	10.8	78
79	16 53.2	+34.6	9.7	17 52.3	+34.8	9.8	18 51.4	+34.9	9.8	19 50.6	+35.0	9.9	79
80	17 27.8	+34.4	8.9	18 27.1	+34.5	8.9	19 26.3	+34.7	9.0	20 25.6	+34.8	9.0	80
81	18 02.2	+34.1	8.0	19 01.6	+34.2	8.1	20 01.0	+34.4	8.1	21 00.4	+34.5	8.2	81
82	18 36.3	+33.9	7.2	19 35.8	+34.0	7.2	20 35.4	+34.1	7.2	21 34.9	+34.2	7.3	82
83	19 10.2	+33.7	6.3	20 09.8	+33.8	6.3	21 09.5	+33.8	6.4	22 09.1	+33.9	6.4	83
84	19 43.9	+33.3	5.4	20 43.6	+33.5	5.4	21 43.3	+33.6	5.5	22 43.0	+33.7	5.5	84
85	20 17.2	+33.2	4.5	21 17.1	+33.2	4.5	22 16.9	+33.2	4.6	23 16.7	+33.3	4.6	85
86	20 50.4	+32.8	3.6	21 50.3	+32.9	3.7	22 50.1	+33.0	3.7	23 50.0	+33.0	3.7	86
87	21 23.2	+32.6	2.7	22 23.2	+32.6	2.8	23 23.1	+32.6	2.8	24 23.0	+32.7	2.8	87
88	21 55.8	+32.2	1.8	22 55.8	+32.2	1.8	23 55.7	+32.3	1.9	24 55.7	+32.3	1.9	88
89	22 28.0	+32.0	0.9	23 28.0	+32.0	0.9	24 28.0	+32.0	0.9	25 28.0	+32.0	0.9	89
90	23 00.0	+31.6	0.0	24 00.0	+31.6	0.0	25 00.0	+31.6	0.0	26 00.0	+31.6	0.0	90
	23°			24°			25°			26°			

Dec.	27° Hc	d	Z	28° Hc	d	Z	29° Hc	d	Z	30° Hc	d	Z	Dec.
°	° ′	′	°	° ′	′	°	° ′	′	°	° ′	′	°	°
0	28 10.5	−31.1	105.8	27 53.8	−32.0	106.3	27 36.7	−33.0	106.9	27 19.1	−34.0	107.4	0
1	27 39.4	−31.5	106.8	27 21.8	−32.5	107.3	27 03.7	−33.4	107.8	26 45.1	−34.3	108.3	1
2	27 07.9	−31.9	107.8	26 49.3	−32.8	108.2	26 30.3	−33.7	108.7	26 10.8	−34.6	109.2	2
3	26 36.0	−32.3	108.7	26 16.5	−33.2	109.2	25 56.6	−34.1	109.6	25 36.2	−35.0	110.1	3
4	26 03.7	−32.6	109.7	25 43.3	−33.5	110.1	25 22.5	−34.5	110.6	25 01.2	−35.3	111.0	4
5	25 31.1	−33.0	110.6	25 09.8	−33.9	111.0	24 48.0	−34.7	111.5	24 25.9	−35.6	111.9	5
6	24 58.1	−33.3	111.5	24 35.9	−34.2	111.9	24 13.3	−35.1	112.4	23 50.3	−36.0	112.8	6
7	24 24.8	−33.7	112.4	24 01.7	−34.5	112.8	23 38.2	−35.3	113.2	23 14.3	−36.2	113.6	7
8	23 51.1	−33.9	113.3	23 27.2	−34.8	113.7	23 02.9	−35.7	114.1	22 38.1	−36.4	114.5	8
9	23 17.2	−34.3	114.2	22 52.4	−35.1	114.6	22 27.2	−35.9	115.0	22 01.7	−36.8	115.4	9
10	22 42.9	−34.5	115.1	22 17.3	−35.4	115.5	21 51.3	−36.2	115.9	21 24.9	−37.0	116.2	10
11	22 08.4	−34.9	116.0	21 41.9	−35.7	116.4	21 15.1	−36.5	116.7	20 47.9	−37.2	117.1	11
12	21 33.5	−35.1	116.9	21 06.2	−35.9	117.2	20 38.6	−36.7	117.6	20 10.7	−37.5	117.9	12
13	20 58.4	−35.4	117.8	20 30.3	−36.2	118.1	20 01.9	−36.9	118.4	19 33.2	−37.7	118.7	13
14	20 23.0	−35.6	118.6	19 54.1	−36.4	118.9	19 25.0	−37.2	119.3	18 55.5	−37.9	119.6	14
15	19 47.4	−35.9	119.5	19 17.7	−36.6	119.8	18 47.8	−37.4	120.1	18 17.6	−38.1	120.4	15
16	19 11.5	−36.1	120.3	18 41.1	−36.9	120.6	18 10.4	−37.6	120.9	17 39.5	−38.4	121.2	16
17	18 35.4	−36.3	121.2	18 04.2	−37.0	121.5	17 32.8	−37.8	121.7	17 01.1	−38.5	122.0	17
18	17 59.1	−36.6	122.0	17 27.2	−37.3	122.3	16 55.0	−38.0	122.5	16 22.6	−38.7	122.8	18
19	17 22.5	−36.7	122.8	16 49.9	−37.5	123.1	16 17.0	−38.2	123.3	15 43.9	−38.9	123.6	19
20	16 45.8	−37.0	123.7	16 12.4	−37.6	123.9	15 38.8	−38.3	124.1	15 05.0	−39.0	124.4	20
21	16 08.8	−37.1	124.5	15 34.8	−37.9	124.7	15 00.5	−38.5	124.9	14 26.0	−39.2	125.2	21
22	15 31.7	−37.3	125.3	14 56.9	−38.0	125.5	14 22.0	−38.7	125.7	13 46.8	−39.3	125.9	22
23	14 54.4	−37.5	126.1	14 18.9	−38.1	126.3	13 43.3	−38.8	126.5	13 07.5	−39.5	126.7	23
24	14 16.9	−37.7	126.9	13 40.8	−38.3	127.1	13 04.5	−39.0	127.3	12 28.0	−39.6	127.5	24
25	13 39.2	−37.8	127.7	13 02.5	−38.5	127.9	12 25.5	−39.1	128.1	11 48.4	−39.7	128.3	25
26	13 01.4	−37.9	128.5	12 24.0	−38.6	128.7	11 46.4	−39.2	128.9	11 08.7	−39.8	129.0	26
27	12 23.5	−38.1	129.3	11 45.4	−38.7	129.5	11 07.2	−39.3	129.6	10 28.9	−40.0	129.8	27
28	11 45.4	−38.2	130.1	11 06.7	−38.8	130.3	10 27.9	−39.5	130.4	9 48.9	−40.0	130.5	28
29	11 07.2	−38.3	130.9	10 27.9	−39.0	131.0	9 48.4	−39.5	131.2	9 08.9	−40.2	131.3	29
30	10 28.9	−38.5	131.7	9 48.9	−39.0	131.8	9 08.9	−39.7	131.9	8 28.7	−40.2	132.1	30
31	9 50.4	−38.6	132.5	9 09.9	−39.2	132.6	8 29.2	−39.7	132.7	7 48.5	−40.3	132.8	31
32	9 11.8	−38.6	133.2	8 30.7	−39.2	133.3	7 49.5	−39.8	133.5	7 08.2	−40.4	133.5	32
33	8 33.2	−38.8	134.0	7 51.5	−39.4	134.1	7 09.7	−39.9	134.2	6 27.8	−40.4	134.3	33
34	7 54.4	−38.8	134.8	7 12.1	−39.4	134.9	6 29.8	−40.0	135.0	5 47.4	−40.6	135.0	34
35	7 15.6	−38.9	135.5	6 32.7	−39.4	135.6	5 49.8	−40.0	135.7	5 06.8	−40.5	135.8	35
36	6 36.7	−39.0	136.3	5 53.3	−39.6	136.4	5 09.8	−40.1	136.5	4 26.3	−40.6	136.5	36
37	5 57.7	−39.0	137.1	5 13.7	−39.5	137.1	4 29.7	−40.1	137.2	3 45.7	−40.6	137.3	37
38	5 18.7	−39.1	137.8	4 34.2	−39.7	137.9	3 49.6	−40.1	138.0	3 05.1	−40.7	138.0	38
39	4 39.6	−39.2	138.6	3 54.5	−39.6	138.7	3 09.5	−40.2	138.7	2 24.4	−40.7	138.7	39
40	4 00.4	−39.2	139.4	3 14.9	−39.7	139.4	2 29.3	−40.2	139.4	1 43.7	−40.7	139.5	40
41	3 21.2	−39.2	140.1	2 35.2	−39.8	140.2	1 49.1	−40.2	140.2	1 03.0	−40.7	140.2	41
42	2 42.0	−39.3	140.9	1 55.4	−39.7	140.9	1 08.9	−40.3	140.9	0 22.3	−40.7	140.9	42
43	2 02.7	−39.2	141.6	1 15.7	−39.8	141.7	0 28.6	−40.2	141.7	0 18.4	+40.8	38.3	43
44	1 23.5	−39.3	142.4	0 35.9	−39.7	142.4	0 11.6	+40.3	37.6	0 59.2	+40.7	37.6	44
45	0 44.2	−39.3	143.2	0 03.8	+39.8	36.8	0 51.9	+40.2	36.9	1 39.9	+40.7	36.9	45
46	0 04.9	−39.3	143.9	0 43.6	+39.8	36.1	1 32.1	+40.2	36.1	2 20.6	+40.6	36.1	46
47	0 34.4	+39.3	35.3	1 23.4	+39.7	35.3	2 12.3	+40.2	35.4	3 01.2	+40.7	35.4	47
48	1 13.7	+39.3	34.6	2 03.1	+39.7	34.6	2 52.5	+40.2	34.6	3 41.9	+40.6	34.7	48
49	1 53.0	+39.3	33.8	2 42.8	+39.7	33.8	3 32.7	+40.1	33.9	4 22.5	+40.5	33.9	49
50	2 32.3	+39.2	33.1	3 22.5	+39.7	33.1	4 12.8	+40.1	33.1	5 03.0	+40.5	33.2	50
51	3 11.5	+39.2	32.3	4 02.2	+39.7	32.3	4 52.9	+40.0	32.4	5 43.5	+40.5	32.4	51
52	3 50.7	+39.2	31.6	4 41.8	+39.6	31.6	5 32.9	+40.0	31.6	6 24.0	+40.4	31.7	52
53	4 29.9	+39.1	30.8	5 21.4	+39.5	30.8	6 12.9	+39.9	30.9	7 04.4	+40.3	30.9	53
54	5 09.0	+39.0	30.0	6 00.9	+39.5	30.1	6 52.8	+39.9	30.1	7 44.7	+40.2	30.2	54
55	5 48.0	+39.0	29.3	6 40.4	+39.3	29.3	7 32.7	+39.7	29.4	8 24.9	+40.2	29.5	55
56	6 27.0	+39.0	28.5	7 19.7	+39.4	28.6	8 12.4	+39.7	28.6	9 05.1	+40.0	28.7	56
57	7 06.0	+38.8	27.7	7 59.1	+39.2	27.8	8 52.1	+39.6	27.9	9 45.1	+40.0	27.9	57
58	7 44.8	+38.8	27.0	8 38.3	+39.1	27.0	9 31.7	+39.5	27.1	10 25.1	+39.8	27.2	58
59	8 23.6	+38.7	26.2	9 17.4	+39.0	26.3	10 11.2	+39.4	26.3	11 04.9	+39.8	26.4	59
60	9 02.3	+38.6	25.4	9 56.4	+39.0	25.5	10 50.6	+39.3	25.6	11 44.7	+39.6	25.7	60
61	9 40.9	+38.4	24.7	10 35.4	+38.8	24.7	11 29.9	+39.1	24.8	12 24.3	+39.5	24.9	61
62	10 19.3	+38.4	23.9	11 14.2	+38.7	23.9	12 09.0	+39.0	24.0	13 03.8	+39.3	24.1	62
63	10 57.7	+38.2	23.1	11 52.9	+38.5	23.2	12 48.0	+38.9	23.3	13 43.1	+39.2	23.3	63
64	11 35.9	+38.2	22.3	12 31.4	+38.5	22.4	13 26.9	+38.7	22.5	14 22.3	+39.1	22.6	64
65	12 14.1	+37.9	21.5	13 09.9	+38.2	21.6	14 05.6	+38.6	21.7	15 01.4	+38.9	21.8	65
66	12 52.0	+37.9	20.7	13 48.1	+38.2	20.8	14 44.2	+38.4	20.9	15 40.3	+38.7	21.0	66
67	13 29.9	+37.7	19.9	14 26.3	+37.9	20.0	15 22.6	+38.3	20.1	16 19.0	+38.5	20.2	67
68	14 07.6	+37.5	19.1	15 04.2	+37.8	19.2	16 00.9	+38.1	19.3	16 57.5	+38.3	19.4	68
69	14 45.1	+37.4	18.3	15 42.0	+37.7	18.4	16 39.0	+37.8	18.5	17 35.8	+38.2	18.6	69
70	15 22.5	+37.1	17.5	16 19.7	+37.4	17.6	17 16.8	+37.7	17.7	18 14.0	+37.9	17.8	70
71	15 59.6	+37.0	16.7	16 57.1	+37.2	16.8	17 54.5	+37.5	16.9	18 51.9	+37.8	17.0	71
72	16 36.6	+36.8	15.9	17 34.3	+37.1	16.0	18 32.0	+37.3	16.0	19 29.7	+37.5	16.1	72
73	17 13.4	+36.6	15.0	18 11.4	+36.8	15.1	19 09.3	+37.0	15.2	20 07.2	+37.2	15.3	73
74	17 50.0	+36.4	14.2	18 48.2	+36.6	14.3	19 46.3	+36.8	14.4	20 44.4	+37.0	14.5	74
75	18 26.4	+36.2	13.4	19 24.8	+36.3	13.5	20 23.1	+36.6	13.5	21 21.4	+36.8	13.6	75
76	19 02.6	+35.9	12.5	20 01.1	+36.2	12.6	20 59.7	+36.3	12.7	21 58.2	+36.5	12.8	76
77	19 38.5	+35.7	11.7	20 37.3	+35.8	11.8	21 36.0	+36.0	11.8	22 34.7	+36.2	11.9	77
78	20 14.2	+35.5	10.8	21 13.1	+35.6	10.9	22 12.0	+35.8	11.0	23 10.9	+36.0	11.1	78
79	20 49.7	+35.1	10.0	21 48.7	+35.4	10.0	22 47.8	+35.5	10.1	23 46.9	+35.6	10.2	79
80	21 24.8	+34.9	9.1	22 24.1	+35.0	9.2	23 23.3	+35.2	9.2	24 22.5	+35.4	9.3	80
81	21 59.7	+34.7	8.2	22 59.1	+34.8	8.3	23 58.5	+34.9	8.3	24 57.9	+35.0	8.4	81
82	22 34.4	+34.3	7.3	23 33.9	+34.4	7.4	24 33.4	+34.5	7.5	25 32.9	+34.7	7.5	82
83	23 08.7	+34.1	6.5	24 08.3	+34.2	6.5	25 07.9	+34.3	6.6	26 07.6	+34.3	6.6	83
84	23 42.8	+33.7	5.6	24 42.5	+33.8	5.6	25 42.2	+33.9	5.6	26 41.9	+34.0	5.7	84
85	24 16.5	+33.4	4.7	25 16.3	+33.5	4.7	26 16.1	+33.5	4.7	27 15.9	+33.6	4.8	85
86	24 49.9	+33.0	3.7	25 49.8	+33.1	3.8	26 49.6	+33.2	3.8	27 49.5	+33.2	3.8	86
87	25 22.9	+32.8	2.8	26 22.9	+32.7	2.8	27 22.8	+32.8	2.9	28 22.7	+32.9	2.9	87
88	25 55.7	+32.3	1.9	26 55.6	+32.4	1.9	27 55.6	+32.4	1.9	28 55.6	+32.4	1.9	88
89	26 28.0	+32.0	0.9	27 28.0	+32.0	1.0	28 28.0	+32.0	1.0	29 28.0	+32.0	1.0	89
90	27 00.0	+31.6	0.0	28 00.0	+31.6	0.0	29 00.0	+31.6	0.0	30 00.0	+31.6	0.0	90
	27°			28°			29°			30°			

S. Lat. {L.H.A. greater than 180° ....Zn=180°−Z
{L.H.A. less than 180°...........Zn=180°+Z

LATITUDE SAME NAME AS DECLINATION   L.H.A. 122°, 238°

Dec.	23° Hc	d	Z	24° Hc	d	Z	25° Hc	d	Z	26° Hc	d	Z	27° Hc	d	Z	28° Hc	d	Z	29° Hc	d	Z	30° Hc	d	Z	Dec.
°	° ′	′	°	° ′	′	°	° ′	′	°	° ′	′	°	° ′	′	°	° ′	′	°	° ′	′	°	° ′	′	°	°
0	28 18.0	+26.4	103.2	28 04.0	+27.5	103.7	27 49.5	+28.5	104.2	27 34.5	+29.5	104.8	27 19.0	+30.4	105.3	27 02.9	+31.5	105.8	26 46.4	+32.4	106.2	26 29.4	+33.3	106.7	0
1	28 44.4	+26.0	102.2	28 31.5	+27.0	102.7	28 18.0	+28.0	103.3	28 04.0	+29.0	103.8	27 49.4	+30.1	104.3	27 34.4	+31.0	104.8	27 18.8	+32.0	105.3	27 02.7	+33.0	105.8	1
2	29 10.4	+25.4	101.2	28 58.5	+26.5	101.7	28 46.0	+27.6	102.2	28 33.0	+28.6	102.8	28 19.5	+29.6	103.3	28 05.4	+30.6	103.8	27 50.8	+31.6	104.3	27 35.7	+32.6	104.9	2
3	29 35.8	+25.0	100.1	29 25.0	+26.0	100.7	29 13.6	+27.1	101.2	29 01.6	+28.2	101.8	28 49.1	+29.2	102.3	28 36.0	+30.2	102.8	28 22.4	+31.2	103.4	28 08.3	+32.1	103.9	3
4	30 00.8	+24.4	99.1	29 51.0	+25.6	99.6	29 40.7	+26.6	100.2	29 29.8	+27.7	100.8	29 18.3	+28.7	101.3	29 06.2	+29.8	101.9	28 53.6	+30.8	102.4	28 40.4	+31.8	102.9	4
5	30 25.2	+24.0	98.0	30 16.6	+25.0	98.6	30 07.3	+26.1	99.2	29 57.5	+27.2	99.7	29 47.0	+28.3	100.3	29 36.0	+29.3	100.9	29 24.4	+30.3	101.4	29 12.2	+31.4	102.0	5
6	30 49.2	+23.4	97.0	30 41.6	+24.6	97.5	30 33.4	+25.7	98.1	30 24.7	+26.7	98.7	30 15.3	+27.8	99.3	30 05.3	+28.8	99.9	29 54.7	+29.9	100.4	29 43.6	+30.9	101.0	6
7	31 12.6	+22.9	95.9	31 06.2	+24.0	96.5	30 59.1	+25.1	97.1	30 51.4	+26.2	97.7	30 43.1	+27.3	98.3	30 34.1	+28.4	98.8	30 24.6	+29.4	99.4	30 14.5	+30.5	100.0	7
8	31 35.5	+22.3	94.8	31 30.2	+23.4	95.4	31 24.2	+24.6	96.0	31 17.6	+25.7	96.6	31 10.4	+26.8	97.2	31 02.5	+27.9	97.8	30 54.0	+29.0	98.4	30 45.0	+30.0	99.0	8
9	31 57.8	+21.8	93.7	31 53.6	+22.9	94.3	31 48.8	+24.0	94.9	31 43.3	+25.2	95.6	31 37.2	+26.2	96.2	31 30.4	+27.4	96.8	31 23.0	+28.4	97.4	31 15.0	+29.5	98.0	9
10	32 19.6	+21.2	92.6	32 16.5	+22.4	93.2	32 12.8	+23.5	93.9	32 08.5	+24.6	94.5	32 03.4	+25.8	95.1	31 57.8	+26.8	95.7	31 51.4	+28.0	96.4	31 44.5	+29.0	97.0	10
11	32 40.8	+20.6	91.5	32 38.9	+21.7	92.1	32 36.3	+22.9	92.8	32 33.1	+24.0	93.4	32 29.2	+25.2	94.0	32 24.6	+26.3	94.7	32 19.4	+27.4	95.3	32 13.5	+28.5	95.9	11
12	33 01.4	+20.0	90.4	33 00.6	+21.2	91.0	32 59.2	+22.4	91.7	32 57.1	+23.5	92.3	32 54.4	+24.6	93.0	32 50.9	+25.8	93.6	32 46.8	+26.9	94.3	32 42.0	+28.0	94.9	12
13	33 21.4	+19.3	89.2	33 21.8	+20.6	89.9	33 21.6	+21.7	90.6	33 20.6	+22.9	91.2	33 19.0	+24.1	91.9	33 16.7	+25.2	92.5	33 13.7	+26.3	93.2	33 10.0	+27.5	93.8	13
14	33 40.7	+18.8	88.1	33 42.4	+19.9	88.8	33 43.3	+21.1	89.4	33 43.5	+22.3	90.1	33 43.1	+23.4	90.8	33 41.9	+24.6	91.4	33 40.0	+25.8	92.1	33 37.5	+26.9	92.8	14
15	33 59.5	+18.1	87.0	34 02.3	+19.3	87.6	34 04.4	+20.5	88.3	34 05.8	+21.7	89.0	34 06.5	+22.9	89.7	34 06.5	+24.1	90.3	34 05.8	+25.2	91.0	34 04.4	+26.3	91.7	15
16	34 17.6	+17.5	85.8	34 21.6	+18.7	86.5	34 24.9	+19.9	87.2	34 27.5	+21.1	87.9	34 29.4	+22.2	88.6	34 30.6	+23.4	89.2	34 31.0	+24.6	89.9	34 30.7	+25.8	90.6	16
17	34 35.1	+16.8	84.7	34 40.3	+18.0	85.3	34 44.8	+19.2	86.0	34 48.6	+20.4	86.7	34 51.6	+21.7	87.4	34 54.0	+22.8	88.1	34 55.6	+24.0	88.8	34 56.5	+25.1	89.5	17
18	34 51.9	+16.1	83.5	34 58.3	+17.3	84.2	35 04.0	+18.6	84.9	35 09.0	+19.8	85.6	35 13.3	+20.9	86.3	35 16.8	+22.2	87.0	35 19.6	+23.3	87.7	35 21.6	+24.5	88.4	18
19	35 08.0	+15.4	82.3	35 15.6	+16.7	83.0	35 22.6	+17.9	83.7	35 28.8	+19.1	84.4	35 34.2	+20.3	85.1	35 39.0	+21.5	85.8	35 42.9	+22.7	86.6	35 46.1	+23.9	87.3	19
20	35 23.4	+14.7	81.1	35 32.3	+16.0	81.8	35 40.5	+17.2	82.5	35 47.9	+18.4	83.3	35 54.5	+19.7	84.0	36 00.5	+20.8	84.7	36 05.6	+22.1	85.4	36 10.0	+23.3	86.1	20
21	35 38.1	+14.1	79.9	35 48.3	+15.2	80.6	35 57.7	+16.4	81.4	36 06.3	+17.7	82.1	36 14.2	+18.9	82.8	36 21.3	+20.2	83.5	36 27.7	+21.4	84.3	36 33.3	+22.6	85.0	21
22	35 52.2	+13.3	78.7	36 03.5	+14.6	79.5	36 14.1	+15.8	80.2	36 24.0	+17.0	80.9	36 33.1	+18.3	81.6	36 41.5	+19.5	82.4	36 49.1	+20.7	83.1	36 55.9	+21.9	83.8	22
23	36 05.5	+12.6	77.5	36 18.1	+13.8	78.2	36 29.9	+15.1	79.0	36 41.0	+16.3	79.7	36 51.4	+17.5	80.4	37 01.0	+18.7	81.2	37 09.8	+20.0	81.9	37 17.8	+21.2	82.7	23
24	36 18.1	+11.8	76.3	36 31.9	+13.1	77.0	36 45.0	+14.3	77.8	36 57.3	+15.6	78.5	37 08.9	+16.8	79.2	37 19.7	+18.1	80.0	37 29.8	+19.2	80.7	37 39.0	+20.5	81.5	24
25	36 29.9	+11.1	75.1	36 45.0	+12.3	75.8	36 59.3	+13.6	76.6	37 12.9	+14.8	77.3	37 25.7	+16.1	78.0	37 37.8	+17.3	78.8	37 49.0	+18.6	79.5	37 59.5	+19.8	80.3	25
26	36 41.0	+10.4	73.9	36 57.3	+11.6	74.6	37 12.9	+12.8	75.3	37 27.7	+14.1	76.1	37 41.8	+15.3	76.8	37 55.1	+16.5	77.6	38 07.6	+17.8	78.3	38 19.3	+19.1	79.1	26
27	36 51.4	+9.6	72.7	37 08.9	+10.8	73.4	37 25.7	+12.1	74.1	37 41.8	+13.3	74.8	37 57.1	+14.5	75.6	38 11.6	+15.8	76.4	38 25.4	+17.0	77.1	38 38.4	+18.2	77.9	27
28	37 01.0	+8.8	71.4	37 19.7	+10.1	72.1	37 37.8	+11.2	72.9	37 55.1	+12.5	73.6	38 11.6	+13.8	74.4	38 27.4	+15.0	75.1	38 42.4	+16.3	75.9	38 56.6	+17.6	76.7	28
29	37 09.8	+8.0	70.2	37 29.8	+9.2	70.9	37 49.0	+10.5	71.6	38 07.6	+11.7	72.4	38 25.4	+13.0	73.1	38 42.4	+14.2	73.9	38 58.7	+15.5	74.7	39 14.2	+16.7	75.4	29
30	37 17.8	+7.3	68.9	37 39.0	+8.5	69.6	37 59.5	+9.7	70.4	38 19.3	+11.0	71.1	38 38.4	+12.1	71.9	38 56.6	+13.5	72.6	39 14.2	+14.6	73.4	39 30.9	+15.9	74.2	30
31	37 25.1	+6.4	67.7	37 47.5	+7.7	68.4	38 09.2	+8.9	69.1	38 30.3	+10.1	69.9	38 50.5	+11.4	70.6	39 10.1	+12.6	71.4	39 28.8	+13.9	72.2	39 46.8	+15.1	73.0	31
32	37 31.5	+5.7	66.4	37 55.2	+6.8	67.1	38 18.1	+8.1	67.9	38 40.4	+9.3	68.6	39 01.9	+10.5	69.4	39 22.7	+11.8	70.1	39 42.7	+13.0	70.9	40 01.9	+14.3	71.7	32
33	37 37.2	+4.8	65.2	38 02.0	+6.1	65.9	38 26.2	+7.3	66.6	38 49.7	+8.5	67.3	39 12.4	+9.8	68.1	39 34.5	+10.9	68.9	39 55.7	+12.2	69.6	40 16.2	+13.5	70.4	33
34	37 42.0	+4.1	63.9	38 08.1	+5.2	64.6	38 33.5	+6.4	65.3	38 58.2	+7.6	66.1	39 22.2	+8.8	66.8	39 45.4	+10.1	67.6	40 07.9	+11.4	68.3	40 29.7	+12.6	69.1	34
35	37 46.1	+3.2	62.7	38 13.3	+4.5	63.3	38 39.9	+5.6	64.1	39 05.8	+6.8	64.8	39 31.0	+8.1	65.5	39 55.5	+9.3	66.3	40 19.3	+10.5	67.1	40 42.3	+11.7	67.9	35
36	37 49.3	+2.5	61.4	38 17.8	+3.6	62.1	38 45.5	+4.8	62.8	39 12.6	+6.0	63.5	39 39.1	+7.1	64.2	40 04.8	+8.4	65.0	40 29.8	+9.6	65.8	40 54.0	+10.9	66.6	36
37	37 51.8	+1.6	60.1	38 21.4	+2.7	60.8	38 50.3	+4.0	61.5	39 18.6	+5.1	62.2	39 46.2	+6.3	63.0	40 13.2	+7.5	63.7	40 39.4	+8.7	64.5	41 04.9	+9.9	65.3	37
38	37 53.4	+0.8	58.9	38 24.1	+2.0	59.5	38 54.3	+3.0	60.2	39 23.7	+4.3	60.9	39 52.5	+5.5	61.7	40 20.7	+6.6	62.4	40 48.1	+7.9	63.2	41 14.8	+9.1	63.9	38
39	37 54.2	0.0	57.6	38 26.1	+1.1	58.3	38 57.3	+2.3	58.9	39 28.0	+3.4	59.6	39 58.0	+4.6	60.4	40 27.3	+5.8	61.1	40 56.0	+6.9	61.9	41 23.9	+8.2	62.6	39
40	37 54.2	-0.8	56.3	38 27.2	+0.3	57.0	38 59.6	+1.4	57.7	39 31.4	+2.5	58.3	40 02.6	+3.7	59.1	40 33.1	+4.9	59.8	41 02.9	+6.1	60.5	41 32.1	+7.3	61.3	40
41	37 53.4	-1.6	55.1	38 27.5	-0.6	55.7	39 01.0	+0.6	56.4	39 33.9	+1.7	57.1	40 06.3	+2.8	57.8	40 38.0	+3.9	58.5	41 09.0	+5.1	59.2	41 39.4	+6.3	60.0	41
42	37 51.8	-2.5	53.8	38 26.9	-1.3	54.4	39 01.6	-0.3	55.1	39 35.6	+0.8	55.8	40 09.1	+1.9	56.4	40 41.9	+3.1	57.2	41 14.1	+4.3	57.9	41 45.7	+5.4	58.6	42
43	37 49.3	-3.2	52.5	38 25.6	-2.2	53.2	39 01.3	-1.2	53.8	39 36.4	0.0	54.5	40 11.0	+1.1	55.1	40 45.0	+2.2	55.8	41 18.4	+3.3	56.6	41 51.1	+4.5	57.3	43
44	37 46.1	-4.1	51.3	38 23.4	-3.1	51.9	39 00.1	-2.0	52.5	39 36.4	-0.9	53.2	40 12.1	+0.1	53.8	40 47.2	+1.3	54.5	41 21.7	+2.4	55.2	41 55.6	+3.6	56.0	44
45	37 42.0	-4.9	50.0	38 20.3	-3.8	50.6	38 58.1	-2.8	51.2	39 35.5	-1.8	51.9	40 12.2	-0.7	52.5	40 48.5	+0.3	53.2	41 24.1	+1.5	53.9	41 59.2	+2.6	54.6	45
46	37 37.1	-5.7	48.7	38 16.5	-4.7	49.3	38 55.3	-3.7	49.9	39 33.7	-2.7	50.6	40 11.5	-1.6	51.2	40 48.8	-0.5	51.9	41 25.6	+0.6	52.6	42 01.8	+1.6	53.3	46
47	37 31.4	-6.4	47.5	38 11.8	-5.5	48.1	38 51.6	-4.5	48.7	39 31.0	-3.5	49.3	40 09.9	-2.4	49.9	40 48.3	-1.4	50.6	41 26.2	-0.4	51.2	42 03.4	+0.8	51.9	47
48	37 25.0	-7.3	46.2	38 06.3	-6.3	46.8	38 47.1	-5.3	47.4	39 27.5	-4.3	48.0	40 07.5	-3.4	48.6	40 46.9	-2.4	49.2	41 25.8	-1.3	49.9	42 04.2	-0.3	50.6	48
49	37 17.7	-8.0	45.0	38 00.0	-7.2	45.5	38 41.8	-6.2	46.1	39 23.2	-5.3	46.7	40 04.1	-4.3	47.3	40 44.5	-3.2	47.9	41 24.5	-2.2	48.6	42 03.9	-1.1	49.2	49
50	37 09.7	-8.8	43.7	37 52.8	-7.9	44.3	38 35.6	-7.0	44.8	39 17.9	-6.0	45.4	39 59.8	-5.1	46.0	40 41.3	-4.1	46.6	41 22.3	-3.1	47.2	42 02.8	-2.1	47.9	50
51	37 00.9	-9.6	42.5	37 44.9	-8.7	43.0	38 28.6	-7.8	43.6	39 11.9	-6.9	44.1	39 54.7	-5.9	44.7	40 37.2	-5.1	45.3	41 19.2	-4.1	45.9	42 00.7	-3.1	46.6	51
52	36 51.3	-10.4	41.3	37 36.2	-9.5	41.8	38 20.8	-8.7	42.3	39 05.0	-7.8	42.8	39 48.8	-6.9	43.4	40 32.1	-5.9	44.0	41 15.1	-5.0	44.6	41 57.6	-4.0	45.2	52
53	36 40.9	-11.1	40.0	37 26.7	-10.3	40.5	38 12.1	-9.4	41.0	38 57.2	-8.6	41.6	39 41.9	-7.7	42.1	40 26.2	-6.8	42.7	41 10.1	-5.8	43.3	41 53.6	-4.9	43.9	53
54	36 29.8	-11.9	38.8	37 16.4	-11.1	39.3	38 02.7	-10.3	39.8	38 48.6	-9.4	40.3	39 34.2	-8.5	40.8	40 19.4	-7.6	41.4	41 04.3	-6.8	41.9	41 48.7	-5.9	42.5	54
55	36 17.9	-12.6	37.6	37 05.3	-11.8	38.0	37 52.4	-11.0	38.5	38 39.2	-10.2	39.0	39 25.7	-9.4	39.5	40 11.8	-8.6	40.1	40 57.5	-7.7	40.6	41 42.8	-6.7	41.2	55
56	36 05.3	-13.3	36.4	36 53.5	-12.6	36.8	37 41.4	-11.8	37.3	38 29.0	-11.0	37.8	39 16.3	-10.3	38.3	40 03.2	-9.4	38.8	40 49.8	-8.5	39.3	41 36.1	-7.7	39.9	56
57	35 52.0	-14.0	35.2	36 40.9	-13.3	35.6	37 29.6	-12.6	36.0	38 18.0	-11.9	36.5	39 06.0	-11.0	37.0	39 53.8	-10.2	37.5	40 41.3	-9.5	38.0	41 28.4	-8.6	38.5	57
58	35 38.0	-14.8	34.0	36 27.6	-14.0	34.4	37 17.0	-13.3	34.8	38 06.1	-12.6	35.3	38 55.0	-11.9	35.7	39 43.6	-11.1	36.2	40 31.8	-10.3	36.7	41 19.8	-9.5	37.2	58
59	35 23.2	-15.4	32.8	36 13.6	-14.8	33.2	37 03.7	-14.1	33.6	37 53.5	-13.4	34.0	38 43.1	-12.6	34.5	39 32.5	-12.0	34.9	40 21.5	-11.2	35.4	41 10.3	-10.4	35.9	59
60	35 07.8	-16.1	31.6	35 58.8	-15.5	32.0	36 49.6	-14.9	32.4	37 40.1	-14.1	32.8	38 30.5	-13.5	33.2	39 20.5	-12.7	33.7	40 10.3	-12.0	34.1	40 59.9	-11.3	34.6	60
61	34 51.7	-16.8	30.4	35 43.3	-16.2	30.8	36 34.7	-15.5	31.2	37 26.0	-14.9	31.6	38 17.0	-14.3	32.0	39 07.8	-13.6	32.4	39 58.3	-12.8	32.8	40 48.6	-12.1	33.3	61
62	34 34.9	-17.5	29.3	35 27.1	-16.9	29.6	36 19.2	-16.3	30.0	37 11.1	-15.7	30.3	38 02.7	-15.0	30.7	38 54.2	-14.3	31.1	39 45.5	-13.7	31.6	40 36.5	-13.0	32.0	62
63	34 17.4	-18.1	28.1	35 10.2	-17.5	28.4	36 02.9	-17.0	28.8	36 55.4	-16.4	29.1	37 47.7	-15.7	29.5	38 39.9	-15.2	29.9	39 31.8	-14.5	30.3	40 23.5	-13.9	30.7	63
64	33 59.3	-18.8	26.9	34 52.7	-18.2	27.3	35 45.9	-17.6	27.6	36 39.0	-17.1	27.9	37 32.0	-16.6	28.3	38 24.7	-15.9	28.7	39 17.3	-15.4	29.0	40 09.6	-14.7	29.5	64
65	33 40.5	-19.4	25.8	34 34.5	-18.9	26.1	35 28.3	-18.4	26.4	36 21.9	-17.8	26.7	37 15.4	-17.2	27.1	38 08.8	-16.7	27.4	39 01.9	-16.1	27.8	39 54.9	-15.5	28.2	65
66	33 21.1	-20.0	24.7	34 15.6	-19.5	25.0	35 09.9	-19.0	25.2	36 04.1	-18.5	25.6	36 58.2	-18.0	25.9	37 52.1	-17.4	26.2	38 45.8	-16.8	26.6	39 39.4	-16.3	26.9	66
67	33 01.1	-20.6	23.5	33 56.1	-20.2	23.8	34 50.9	-19.7	24.1	35 45.6	-19.2	24.4	36 40.2	-18.7	24.7	37 34.7	-18.2	25.0	38 29.0	-17.7	25.3	39 23.1	-17.1	25.7	67
68	32 40.5	-21.2	22.4	33 35.9	-20.7	22.7	34 31.2	-20.3	22.9	35 26.4	-19.8	23.2	36 21.5	-19.3	23.5	37 16.5	-18.9	23.8	38 11.3	-18.4	24.1	39 06.0	-17.9	24.4	68
69	32 19.3	-21.7	21.3	33 15.2	-21.4	21.6	34 10.9	-20.9	21.8	35 06.6	-20.5	22.1	36 02.2	-20.1	22.3	36 57.6	-19.6	22.6	37 52.9	-19.1	22.9	38 48.1	-18.6	23.2	69
70	31 57.6	-22.4	20.2	32 53.8	-21.9	20.4	33 50.0	-21.5	20.7	34 46.1	-21.1	20.9	35 42.1	-20.7	21.2	36 38.0	-20.3	21.4	37 33.8	-19.8	21.7	38 29.5	-19.4	22.0	70
71	31 35.2	-22.9	19.1	32 31.9	-22.5	19.3	33 28.5	-22.2	19.5	34 25.0	-21.8	19.8	35 21.4	-21.4	20.0	36 17.7	-21.0	20.3	37 14.0	-20.6	20.5	38 10.1	-20.1	20.8	71
72	31 12.3	-23.4	18.0	32 09.4	-23.1	18.2	33 06.3	-22.7	18.4	34 03.2	-22.4	18.6	35 00.0	-22.0	18.9	35 56.7	-21.6	19.1	36 53.4	-21.2	19.3	37 50.0	-20.9	19.6	72
73	30 48.9	-23.9	17.0	31 46.3	-23.7	17.1	32 43.6	-23.3	17.3	33 40.8	-23.0	17.5	34 38.0	-22.6	17.7	35 35.1	-22.3	17.9	36 32.2	-22.0	18.2	37 29.1	-21.5	18.4	73
74	30 25.0	-24.5	15.9	31 22.6	-24.1	16.1	32 20.3	-23.9	16.2	33 17.8	-23.5	16.4	34 15.4	-23.3	16.6	35 12.8	-22.9	16.8	36 10.2	-22.5	17.0	37 07.6	-22.3	17.2	74
75	30 00.5	-25.0	14.8	30 58.5	-24.7	15.0	31 56.4	-24.4	15.2	32 54.3	-24.1	15.3	33 52.1	-23.8	15.5	34 49.9	-23.5	15.7	35 47.7	-23.3	15.9	36 45.3	-22.9	16.1	75
76	29 35.5	-25.4	13.8	30 33.8	-25.2	13.9	31 32.0	-25.0	14.1	32 30.2	-24.7	14.2	33 28.3	-24.4	14.4	34 26.4	-24.1	14.6	35 24.4	-23.8	14.7	36 22.4	-23.5	14.9	76
77	29 10.1	-26.0	12.8	30 08.6	-25.8	12.9	31 07.0	-25.4	13.0	32 05.5	-25.3	13.2	33 03.9	-25.0	13.3	34 02.3	-24.8	13.5	35 00.6	-24.5	13.6	35 58.9	-24.2	13.8	77
78	28 44.1	-26.4	11.7	29 42.8	-26.1	11.8	30 41.6	-26.0	12.0	31 40.2	-25.7	12.1	32 38.9	-25.5	12.2	33 37.5	-25.3	12.4	34 36.1	-25.1	12.5	35 34.7	-24.8	12.7	78
79	28 17.7	-26.8	10.7	29 16.7	-26.7	10.8	30 15.6	-26.5	10.9	31 14.5	-26.3	11.0	32 13.4	-26.1	11.1	33 12.2	-25.8	11.3	34 11.0	-25.6	11.4	35 09.9	-25.5	11.5	79
80	27 50.9	-27.3	9.7	28 50.0	-27.1	9.8	29 49.1	-26.9	9.9	30 48.2	-26.8	10.0	31 47.3	-26.6	10.1	32 46.4	-26.5	10.2	33 45.4	-26.2	10.3	34 44.4	-26.0	10.4	80
81	27 23.6	-27.8	8.7	28 22.9	-27.6	8.8	29 22.2	-27.5	8.9	30 21.4	-27.2	8.9	31 20.7	-27.1	9.0	32 19.9	-26.9	9.1	33 19.2	-26.8	9.2	34 18.4	-26.6	9.3	81
82	26 55.8	-28.1	7.7	27 55.3	-28.0	7.8	28 54.7	-27.8	7.8	29 54.2	-27.8	7.9	30 53.6	-27.6	8.0	31 53.0	-27.5	8.1	32 52.4	-27.3	8.2	33 51.8	-27.2	8.3	82
83	26 27.7	-28.6	6.7	27 27.3	-28.5	6.8	28 26.9	-28.4	6.8	29 26.4	-28.2	6.9	30 26.0	-28.1	7.0	31 25.5	-27.9	7.0	32 25.1	-27.9	7.1	33 24.6	-27.7	7.2	83
84	25 59.1	-28.9	5.7	26 58.8	-28.8	5.8	27 58.5	-28.7	5.8	28 58.2	-28.6	5.9	29 57.9	-28.6	5.9	30 57.6	-28.5	6.0	31 57.2	-28.3	6.1	32 56.9	-28.2	6.1	84
85	25 30.2	-29.3	4.7	26 30.0	-29.3	4.8	27 29.8	-29.2	4.8	28 29.6	-29.1	4.9	29 29.3	-29.0	4.9	30 29.1	-28.9	5.0	31 28.9	-28.8	5.0	32 28.7	-28.8	5.1	85
86	25 00.9	-29.7	3.8	26 00.7	-29.6	3.8	27 00.6	-29.6	3.8	28 00.5	-29.5	3.9	29 00.3	-29.4	3.9	30 00.2	-29.4	4.0	31 00.1	-29.4	4.0	31 59.9	-29.3	4.0	86
87	24 31.2	-30.1	2.8	25 31.1	-30.0	2.8	26 31.0	-29.9	2.9	27 31.0	-30.0	2.9	28 30.9	-29.9	2.9	29 30.8	-29.8	3.0	30 30.7	-29.8	3.0	31 30.6	-29.7	3.0	87
88	24 01.1	-30.4	1.9	25 01.1	-30.4	1.9	26 01.1	-30.4	1.9	27 01.0	-30.3	1.9	28 01.0	-30.3	1.9	29 01.0	-30.3	2.0	30 00.9	-30.2	2.0	31 00.9	-30.2	2.0	88
89	23 30.7	-30.7	0.9	24 30.7	-30.7	0.9	25 30.7	-30.7	0.9	26 30.7	-30.7	1.0	27 30.7	-30.7	1.0	28 30.7	-30.7	1.0	29 30.7	-30.7	1.0	30 30.7	-30.7	1.0	89
90	23 00.0	-31.1	0.0	24 00.0	-31.1	0.0	25 00.0	-31.1	0.0	26 00.0	-31.1	0.0	27 00.0	-31.1	0.0	28 00.0	-31.1	0.0	29 00.0	-31.1	0.0	30 00.0	-31.1	0.0	90
	23°			24°			25°			26°			27°			28°			29°			30°			

LATITUDE **CONTRARY** NAME TO DECLINATION **L.H.A. 59°, 301°**

Dec.	23° Hc	d	Z	24° Hc	d	Z	25° Hc	d	Z	26° Hc	d	Z	27° Hc	d	Z	28° Hc	d	Z	29° Hc	d	Z	30° Hc	d	Z	Dec.
°	° ′	′	°	° ′	′	°	° ′	′	°	° ′	′	°	° ′	′	°	° ′	′	°	° ′	′	°	° ′	′	°	°
0	28 18.0	−26.8	103.2	28 04.0	−27.8	103.7	27 49.5	−28.8	104.2	27 34.5	−29.9	104.8	27 19.0	−30.9	105.3	27 02.9	−31.8	105.8	26 46.4	−32.8	106.2	26 29.4	−33.7	106.7	0
1	27 51.2	−27.3	104.2	27 36.2	−28.3	104.7	27 20.7	−29.3	105.2	27 04.6	−30.2	105.7	26 48.1	−31.2	106.2	26 31.1	−32.2	106.7	26 13.6	−33.1	107.2	25 55.7	−34.1	107.6	1
2	27 23.9	−27.7	105.2	27 07.9	−28.7	105.7	26 51.4	−29.7	106.2	26 34.4	−30.7	106.7	26 16.9	−31.6	107.2	25 58.9	−32.5	107.6	25 40.5	−33.5	108.1	25 21.6	−34.3	108.6	2
3	26 56.2	−28.2	106.2	26 39.2	−29.2	106.7	26 21.7	−30.1	107.2	26 03.7	−31.1	107.7	25 45.3	−32.0	108.1	25 26.4	−32.9	108.6	25 07.0	−33.8	109.0	24 47.3	−34.7	109.5	3
4	26 28.0	−28.5	107.2	26 10.0	−29.5	107.7	25 51.6	−30.5	108.2	25 32.6	−31.4	108.6	25 13.3	−32.4	109.1	24 53.5	−33.3	109.5	24 33.2	−34.1	109.9	24 12.6	−35.1	110.4	4
5	25 59.5	−29.0	108.2	25 40.5	−29.9	108.7	25 21.1	−30.8	109.1	25 01.2	−31.7	109.6	24 40.9	−32.6	110.0	24 20.2	−33.5	110.4	23 59.1	−34.5	110.8	23 37.5	−35.3	111.2	5
6	25 30.5	−29.3	109.2	25 10.6	−30.2	109.6	24 50.3	−31.2	110.1	24 29.5	−32.1	110.5	24 08.3	−33.0	110.9	23 46.7	−33.9	111.3	23 24.6	−34.7	111.7	23 02.2	−35.6	112.1	6
7	25 01.2	−29.7	110.1	24 40.4	−30.7	110.6	24 19.1	−31.6	111.0	23 57.4	−32.5	111.4	23 35.3	−33.4	111.8	23 12.8	−34.2	112.2	22 49.9	−35.1	112.6	22 26.6	−35.9	113.0	7
8	24 31.5	−30.0	111.1	24 09.7	−30.9	111.5	23 47.5	−31.8	111.9	23 24.9	−32.7	112.3	23 01.9	−33.6	112.7	22 38.6	−34.5	113.1	22 14.8	−35.3	113.5	21 50.7	−36.1	113.9	8
9	24 01.5	−30.4	112.0	23 38.8	−31.3	112.5	23 15.7	−32.2	112.9	22 52.2	−33.1	113.2	22 28.3	−33.9	113.6	22 04.1	−34.8	114.0	21 39.5	−35.6	114.4	21 14.6	−36.4	114.7	9
10	23 31.1	−30.7	113.0	23 07.5	−31.6	113.4	22 43.5	−32.5	113.8	22 19.1	−33.3	114.1	21 54.4	−34.2	114.5	21 29.3	−35.0	114.9	21 03.9	−35.8	115.2	20 38.2	−36.7	115.6	10
11	23 00.4	−31.1	113.9	22 35.9	−32.0	114.3	22 11.0	−32.8	114.7	21 45.8	−33.7	115.0	21 20.2	−34.5	115.4	20 54.3	−35.3	115.7	20 28.1	−36.1	116.1	20 01.5	−36.9	116.4	11
12	22 29.3	−31.4	114.8	22 03.9	−32.2	115.2	21 38.2	−33.1	115.6	21 12.1	−33.9	115.9	20 45.7	−34.7	116.3	20 19.0	−35.6	116.6	19 52.0	−36.4	116.9	19 24.6	−37.1	117.3	12
13	21 57.9	−31.7	115.8	21 31.7	−32.6	116.1	21 05.1	−33.4	116.5	20 38.2	−34.2	116.8	20 11.0	−35.0	117.1	19 43.4	−35.8	117.5	19 15.6	−36.6	117.8	18 47.5	−37.3	118.1	13
14	21 26.2	−31.9	116.7	20 59.1	−32.8	117.0	20 31.7	−33.6	117.4	20 04.0	−34.5	117.7	19 36.0	−35.3	118.0	19 07.6	−36.0	118.3	18 39.0	−36.8	118.6	18 10.2	−37.6	118.9	14
15	20 54.3	−32.3	117.6	20 26.3	−33.1	117.9	19 58.1	−33.9	118.2	19 29.5	−34.7	118.6	19 00.7	−35.5	118.9	18 31.6	−36.2	119.2	18 02.2	−37.0	119.5	17 32.6	−37.8	119.7	15
16	20 22.0	−32.5	118.5	19 53.2	−33.3	118.8	19 24.2	−34.2	119.1	18 54.8	−34.9	119.4	18 25.2	−35.7	119.7	17 55.4	−36.5	120.0	17 25.2	−37.2	120.3	16 54.8	−37.9	120.5	16
17	19 49.5	−32.8	119.4	19 19.9	−33.6	119.7	18 50.0	−34.4	120.0	18 19.9	−35.2	120.3	17 49.5	−35.9	120.6	17 18.9	−36.7	120.8	16 48.0	−37.4	121.1	16 16.9	−38.1	121.4	17
18	19 16.7	−33.1	120.3	18 46.3	−33.9	120.6	18 15.6	−34.6	120.9	17 44.7	−35.3	121.1	17 13.6	−36.1	121.4	16 42.2	−36.9	121.7	16 10.6	−37.6	121.9	15 38.8	−38.3	122.2	18
19	18 43.6	−33.3	121.2	18 12.4	−34.0	121.4	17 41.0	−34.8	121.7	17 09.4	−35.6	122.0	16 37.5	−36.4	122.2	16 05.3	−37.0	122.5	15 33.0	−37.8	122.7	15 00.5	−38.5	123.0	19
20	18 10.3	−33.5	122.0	17 38.4	−34.3	122.3	17 06.2	−35.1	122.6	16 33.8	−35.8	122.8	16 01.1	−36.5	123.1	15 28.3	−37.2	123.3	14 55.2	−37.9	123.5	14 22.0	−38.6	123.7	20
21	17 36.8	−33.8	122.9	17 04.1	−34.6	123.2	16 31.1	−35.2	123.4	15 58.0	−36.0	123.7	15 24.6	−36.7	123.9	14 51.1	−37.5	124.1	14 17.3	−38.1	124.3	13 43.4	−38.8	124.5	21
22	17 03.0	−34.0	123.8	16 29.5	−34.7	124.0	15 55.9	−35.5	124.3	15 22.0	−36.2	124.5	14 47.9	−36.9	124.7	14 13.6	−37.5	124.9	13 39.2	−38.2	125.1	13 04.6	−38.9	125.3	22
23	16 29.0	−34.2	124.6	15 54.8	−34.9	124.9	15 20.4	−35.6	125.1	14 45.8	−36.3	125.3	14 11.0	−37.0	125.5	13 36.1	−37.7	125.7	13 01.0	−38.4	125.9	12 25.7	−39.1	126.1	23
24	15 54.8	−34.4	125.5	15 19.9	−35.1	125.7	14 44.8	−35.9	125.9	14 09.5	−36.6	126.1	13 34.0	−37.2	126.3	12 58.4	−37.9	126.5	12 22.6	−38.6	126.7	11 46.6	−39.1	126.9	24
25	15 20.4	−34.6	126.3	14 44.8	−35.3	126.6	14 08.9	−36.0	126.8	13 32.9	−36.6	127.0	12 56.8	−37.4	127.1	12 20.5	−38.0	127.3	11 44.0	−38.6	127.5	11 07.5	−39.3	127.7	25
26	14 45.8	−34.8	127.2	14 09.5	−35.5	127.4	13 32.9	−36.1	127.6	12 56.3	−36.9	127.8	12 19.4	−37.4	127.9	11 42.5	−38.1	128.1	11 05.4	−38.8	128.3	10 28.2	−39.4	128.4	26
27	14 11.0	−34.9	128.0	13 34.0	−35.6	128.2	12 56.8	−36.3	128.4	12 19.4	−36.9	128.6	11 42.0	−37.6	128.7	11 04.4	−38.3	128.9	10 26.6	−38.9	129.0	9 48.8	−39.6	129.2	27
28	13 36.1	−35.1	128.9	12 58.4	−35.8	129.0	12 20.5	−36.5	129.2	11 42.5	−37.1	129.4	11 04.4	−37.8	129.5	10 26.1	−38.4	129.7	9 47.7	−39.0	129.8	9 09.2	−39.6	130.0	28
29	13 01.0	−35.3	129.7	12 22.6	−36.0	129.9	11 44.0	−36.5	130.0	11 05.4	−37.2	130.2	10 26.6	−37.8	130.3	9 47.7	−38.5	130.5	9 08.7	−39.1	130.6	8 29.6	−39.6	130.7	29
30	12 25.7	−35.4	130.5	11 46.6	−36.0	130.7	11 07.5	−36.8	130.8	10 28.2	−37.4	131.0	9 48.8	−38.0	131.1	9 09.2	−38.5	131.2	8 29.6	−39.1	131.4	7 50.0	−39.8	131.5	30
31	11 50.3	−35.6	131.3	11 10.6	−36.3	131.5	10 30.7	−36.8	131.6	9 50.8	−37.4	131.8	9 10.8	−38.1	131.9	8 30.7	−38.7	132.0	7 50.5	−39.3	132.1	7 10.2	−39.9	132.2	31
32	11 14.7	−35.7	132.2	10 34.3	−36.3	132.3	9 53.9	−36.9	132.4	9 13.4	−37.6	132.6	8 32.7	−38.1	132.7	7 52.0	−38.7	132.8	7 11.2	−39.3	132.9	6 30.3	−39.9	133.0	32
33	10 39.0	−35.9	133.0	9 58.0	−36.4	133.1	9 17.0	−37.1	133.2	8 35.8	−37.7	133.4	7 54.6	−38.3	133.5	7 13.3	−38.9	133.6	6 31.9	−39.4	133.6	5 50.4	−39.9	133.7	33
34	10 03.1	−35.9	133.8	9 21.6	−36.6	133.9	8 39.9	−37.2	134.0	7 58.1	−37.7	134.1	7 16.3	−38.3	134.2	6 34.4	−38.9	134.3	5 52.5	−39.5	134.4	5 10.5	−40.1	134.5	34
35	9 27.2	−36.1	134.6	8 45.0	−36.7	134.7	8 02.7	−37.2	134.8	7 20.4	−37.8	134.9	6 38.0	−38.4	135.0	5 55.5	−38.9	135.1	5 13.0	−39.5	135.2	4 30.4	−40.0	135.2	35
36	8 51.1	−36.1	135.4	8 08.3	−36.7	135.5	7 25.5	−37.3	135.6	6 42.6	−37.9	135.7	5 59.6	−38.5	135.8	5 16.6	−39.1	135.9	4 33.5	−39.6	135.9	3 50.4	−40.2	136.0	36
37	8 15.0	−36.3	136.2	7 31.6	−36.8	136.3	6 48.2	−37.4	136.4	6 04.7	−38.0	136.5	5 21.1	−38.5	136.6	4 37.5	−39.0	136.6	3 53.9	−39.6	136.7	3 10.2	−40.1	136.7	37
38	7 38.7	−36.4	137.0	6 54.8	−37.0	137.1	6 10.8	−37.5	137.2	5 26.7	−38.0	137.3	4 42.6	−38.6	137.3	3 58.5	−39.1	137.4	3 14.3	−39.6	137.4	2 30.1	−40.2	137.5	38
39	7 02.3	−36.4	137.8	6 17.8	−37.0	137.9	5 33.3	−37.6	138.0	4 48.7	−38.1	138.0	4 04.0	−38.6	138.1	3 19.4	−39.2	138.1	2 34.7	−39.7	138.2	1 49.9	−40.1	138.2	39
40	6 25.9	−36.5	138.6	5 40.8	−37.0	138.7	4 55.7	−37.5	138.8	4 10.6	−38.1	138.8	3 25.4	−38.6	138.9	2 40.2	−39.2	138.9	1 55.0	−39.7	138.9	1 09.8	−40.2	138.9	40
41	5 49.4	−36.6	139.4	5 03.8	−37.1	139.5	4 18.2	−37.7	139.6	3 32.5	−38.2	139.6	2 46.8	−38.7	139.6	2 01.0	−39.1	139.7	1 15.3	−39.7	139.7	0 29.6	−40.2	139.7	41
42	5 12.8	−36.6	140.2	4 26.7	−37.2	140.3	3 40.5	−37.7	140.3	2 54.3	−38.2	140.4	2 08.1	−38.7	140.4	1 21.9	−39.3	140.4	0 35.6	−39.7	140.4	0 10.6	+40.2	39.6	42
43	4 36.2	−36.7	141.0	3 49.5	−37.2	141.1	3 02.8	−37.7	141.1	2 16.1	−38.2	141.1	1 29.4	−38.7	141.2	0 42.6	−39.2	141.2	0 04.1	+39.7	38.8	0 50.8	+40.2	38.8	43
44	3 59.5	−36.7	141.8	3 12.3	−37.2	141.9	2 25.1	−37.7	141.9	1 37.9	−38.2	141.9	0 50.7	−38.8	141.9	0 03.4	−39.2	141.9	0 43.8	+39.7	38.1	1 31.0	+40.2	38.1	44
45	3 22.8	−36.8	142.6	2 35.1	−37.3	142.6	1 47.4	−37.8	142.7	0 59.7	−38.3	142.7	0 11.9	−38.7	142.7	0 35.8	+39.2	37.3	1 23.5	+39.7	37.3	2 11.2	+40.2	37.3	45
46	2 46.0	−36.8	143.4	1 57.8	−37.3	143.4	1 09.6	−37.8	143.4	0 21.4	−38.2	143.5	0 26.8	+38.7	36.5	1 15.0	+39.2	36.6	2 03.2	+39.6	36.6	2 51.4	+40.1	36.6	46
47	2 09.2	−36.8	144.2	1 20.5	−37.3	144.2	0 31.8	−37.7	144.2	0 16.8	+38.3	35.8	1 05.5	+38.7	35.8	1 54.2	+39.2	35.8	2 42.8	+39.7	35.8	3 31.5	+40.1	35.9	47
48	1 32.4	−36.9	145.0	0 43.2	−37.3	145.0	0 05.9	+37.8	35.0	0 55.1	+38.2	35.0	1 44.2	+38.7	35.0	2 33.4	+39.1	35.0	3 22.5	+39.6	35.1	4 11.6	+40.0	35.1	48
49	0 55.5	−36.9	145.8	0 05.9	−37.3	145.8	0 43.7	+37.8	34.2	1 33.3	+38.2	34.2	2 22.9	+38.7	34.3	3 12.5	+39.1	34.3	4 02.1	+39.5	34.3	4 51.6	+40.0	34.4	49
50	0 18.6	−36.8	146.6	0 31.4	+37.3	33.4	1 21.5	+37.7	33.4	2 11.5	+38.2	33.5	3 01.6	+38.6	33.5	3 51.6	+39.1	33.5	4 41.6	+39.5	33.6	5 31.6	+40.0	33.6	50
51	0 18.2	+36.9	32.6	1 08.7	+37.3	32.7	1 59.2	+37.8	32.7	2 49.7	+38.2	32.7	3 40.2	+38.6	32.7	4 30.7	+39.0	32.8	5 21.1	+39.5	32.8	6 11.6	+39.8	32.9	51
52	0 55.1	+36.8	31.9	1 46.0	+37.3	31.9	2 37.0	+37.7	31.9	3 27.9	+38.1	31.9	4 18.8	+38.6	32.0	5 09.7	+39.0	32.0	6 00.6	+39.4	32.0	6 51.4	+39.8	32.1	52
53	1 31.9	+36.8	31.1	2 23.3	+37.3	31.1	3 14.7	+37.7	31.1	4 06.0	+38.1	31.1	4 57.4	+38.5	31.2	5 48.7	+38.9	31.2	6 40.0	+39.3	31.3	7 31.2	+39.8	31.4	53
54	2 08.7	+36.9	30.3	3 00.6	+37.2	30.3	3 52.4	+37.6	30.3	4 44.1	+38.1	30.4	5 35.9	+38.4	30.4	6 27.6	+38.9	30.5	7 19.3	+39.3	30.5	8 11.0	+39.6	30.6	54
55	2 45.6	+36.7	29.5	3 37.8	+37.1	29.5	4 30.0	+37.6	29.5	5 22.2	+37.9	29.6	6 14.3	+38.4	29.6	7 06.5	+38.7	29.7	7 58.6	+39.1	29.8	8 50.6	+39.6	29.8	55
56	3 22.3	+36.8	28.7	4 14.9	+37.2	28.7	5 07.6	+37.5	28.8	6 00.1	+37.9	28.8	6 52.7	+38.3	28.9	7 45.2	+38.7	28.9	8 37.7	+39.1	29.0	9 30.2	+39.4	29.1	56
57	3 59.1	+36.7	27.9	4 52.1	+37.0	27.9	5 45.1	+37.4	28.0	6 38.0	+37.9	28.0	7 31.0	+38.2	28.1	8 23.9	+38.6	28.2	9 16.8	+39.0	28.2	10 09.6	+39.4	28.3	57
58	4 35.8	+36.6	27.1	5 29.1	+37.1	27.1	6 22.5	+37.4	27.2	7 15.9	+37.7	27.3	8 09.2	+38.1	27.3	9 02.5	+38.5	27.4	9 55.8	+38.8	27.5	10 49.0	+39.2	27.5	58
59	5 12.4	+36.6	26.3	6 06.2	+36.9	26.4	6 59.9	+37.3	26.4	7 53.6	+37.7	26.5	8 47.3	+38.1	26.5	9 41.0	+38.4	26.6	10 34.6	+38.8	26.7	11 28.2	+39.1	26.8	59
60	5 49.0	+36.5	25.5	6 43.1	+36.9	25.6	7 37.2	+37.2	25.6	8 31.3	+37.6	25.7	9 25.4	+37.9	25.8	10 19.4	+38.3	25.8	11 13.4	+38.6	25.9	12 07.3	+39.0	26.0	60
61	6 25.5	+36.4	24.7	7 20.0	+36.7	24.8	8 14.4	+37.2	24.8	9 08.9	+37.4	24.9	10 03.3	+37.8	25.0	10 57.7	+38.1	25.0	11 52.0	+38.5	25.1	12 46.3	+38.8	25.2	61
62	7 01.9	+36.4	23.9	7 56.7	+36.7	24.0	8 51.6	+37.0	24.0	9 46.3	+37.4	24.1	10 41.1	+37.7	24.2	11 35.8	+38.0	24.3	12 30.5	+38.4	24.3	13 25.1	+38.7	24.4	62
63	7 38.3	+36.2	23.1	8 33.4	+36.6	23.2	9 28.6	+36.9	23.2	10 23.7	+37.2	23.3	11 18.8	+37.6	23.4	12 13.8	+37.9	23.5	13 08.9	+38.2	23.6	14 03.8	+38.6	23.7	63
64	8 14.5	+36.2	22.3	9 10.0	+36.5	22.4	10 05.5	+36.8	22.4	11 00.9	+37.2	22.5	11 56.4	+37.4	22.6	12 51.7	+37.8	22.7	13 47.1	+38.0	22.8	14 42.4	+38.4	22.9	64
65	8 50.7	+36.1	21.5	9 46.5	+36.4	21.6	10 42.3	+36.7	21.6	11 38.1	+36.9	21.7	12 33.8	+37.3	21.8	13 29.5	+37.6	21.9	14 25.1	+38.0	22.0	15 20.8	+38.2	22.1	65
66	9 26.8	+35.9	20.7	10 22.9	+36.2	20.8	11 19.0	+36.5	20.8	12 15.0	+36.9	20.9	13 11.1	+37.1	21.0	14 07.1	+37.4	21.1	15 03.1	+37.7	21.2	15 59.0	+38.0	21.3	66
67	10 02.7	+35.9	19.9	10 59.1	+36.1	19.9	11 55.5	+36.4	20.0	12 51.9	+36.7	20.1	13 48.2	+37.0	20.2	14 44.5	+37.3	20.3	15 40.8	+37.5	20.4	16 37.0	+37.9	20.5	67
68	10 38.6	+35.7	19.1	11 35.2	+36.0	19.1	12 31.9	+36.3	19.2	13 28.6	+36.5	19.3	14 25.2	+36.8	19.4	15 21.8	+37.1	19.5	16 18.3	+37.4	19.5	17 14.9	+37.6	19.6	68
69	11 14.3	+35.5	18.3	12 11.2	+35.9	18.3	13 08.2	+36.1	18.4	14 05.1	+36.4	18.5	15 02.0	+36.6	18.5	15 58.9	+36.9	18.6	16 55.7	+37.2	18.7	17 52.5	+37.5	18.8	69
70	11 49.8	+35.5	17.4	12 47.1	+35.6	17.5	13 44.3	+35.9	17.6	14 41.5	+36.2	17.6	15 38.6	+36.5	17.7	16 35.8	+36.7	17.8	17 32.9	+36.9	17.9	18 30.0	+37.2	18.0	70
71	12 25.3	+35.2	16.6	13 22.7	+35.6	16.7	14 20.2	+35.8	16.7	15 17.7	+36.0	16.8	16 15.1	+36.2	16.9	17 12.5	+36.5	17.0	18 09.8	+36.8	17.1	19 07.2	+37.0	17.2	71
72	13 00.5	+35.2	15.8	13 58.3	+35.3	15.8	14 56.0	+35.6	15.9	15 53.7	+35.8	16.0	16 51.3	+36.1	16.1	17 49.0	+36.3	16.2	18 46.6	+36.5	16.2	19 44.2	+36.8	16.3	72
73	13 35.7	+34.9	14.9	14 33.6	+35.2	15.0	15 31.6	+35.4	15.1	16 29.5	+35.6	15.2	17 27.4	+35.8	15.2	18 25.3	+36.0	15.3	19 23.1	+36.3	15.4	20 21.0	+36.5	15.5	73
74	14 10.6	+34.8	14.1	15 08.8	+35.0	14.2	16 07.0	+35.2	14.2	17 05.1	+35.4	14.3	18 03.2	+35.7	14.4	19 01.3	+35.9	14.5	19 59.4	+36.1	14.6	20 57.5	+36.3	14.7	74
75	14 45.4	+34.6	13.3	15 43.8	+34.8	13.3	16 42.2	+35.0	13.4	17 40.5	+35.2	13.5	18 38.9	+35.4	13.5	19 37.2	+35.6	13.6	20 35.5	+35.8	13.7	21 33.8	+36.0	13.8	75
76	15 20.0	+34.4	12.4	16 18.6	+34.6	12.5	17 17.2	+34.7	12.5	18 15.7	+35.0	12.6	19 14.3	+35.1	12.7	20 12.8	+35.3	12.8	21 11.3	+35.5	12.9	22 09.8	+35.7	12.9	76
77	15 54.4	+34.2	11.6	16 53.2	+34.3	11.6	17 51.9	+34.6	11.7	18 50.7	+34.7	11.8	19 49.4	+34.9	11.8	20 48.1	+35.1	11.9	21 46.8	+35.3	12.0	22 45.5	+35.5	12.1	77
78	16 28.6	+34.0	10.7	17 27.5	+34.2	10.8	18 26.5	+34.3	10.8	19 25.4	+34.5	10.9	20 24.3	+34.7	11.0	21 23.2	+34.8	11.0	22 22.1	+35.0	11.1	23 21.0	+35.1	11.2	78
79	17 02.6	+33.8	9.8	18 01.7	+33.9	9.9	19 00.8	+34.1	10.0	19 59.9	+34.2	10.0	20 59.0	+34.3	10.1	21 58.0	+34.6	10.2	22 57.1	+34.7	10.2	23 56.1	+34.9	10.3	79
80	17 36.4	+33.5	9.0	18 35.6	+33.7	9.0	19 34.9	+33.8	9.1	20 34.1	+34.0	9.1	21 33.3	+34.1	9.2	22 32.6	+34.2	9.3	23 31.8	+34.4	9.3	24 31.0	+34.5	9.4	80
81	18 09.9	+33.3	8.1	19 09.3	+33.4	8.2	20 08.7	+33.5	8.2	21 08.1	+33.7	8.3	22 07.4	+33.9	8.3	23 06.8	+33.9	8.4	24 06.2	+34.0	8.4	25 05.5	+34.2	8.5	81
82	18 43.2	+33.1	7.2	19 42.7	+33.2	7.3	20 42.2	+33.3	7.3	21 41.8	+33.3	7.4	22 41.3	+33.5	7.4	23 40.7	+33.7	7.5	24 40.2	+33.8	7.5	25 39.7	+33.9	7.6	82
83	19 16.3	+32.8	6.4	20 15.9	+32.9	6.4	21 15.5	+33.0	6.4	22 15.1	+33.1	6.5	23 14.8	+33.2	6.5	24 14.4	+33.3	6.6	25 14.0	+33.4	6.6	26 13.6	+33.5	6.7	83
84	19 49.1	+32.5	5.5	20 48.8	+32.6	5.5	21 48.5	+32.7	5.5	22 48.2	+32.8	5.6	23 48.0	+32.8	5.6	24 47.7	+32.9	5.7	25 47.4	+33.0	5.7	26 47.1	+33.1	5.8	84
85	20 21.6	+32.3	4.6	21 21.4	+32.4	4.6	22 21.2	+32.4	4.6	23 21.0	+32.5	4.7	24 20.8	+32.6	4.7	25 20.6	+32.7	4.7	26 20.4	+32.7	4.8	27 20.2	+32.8	4.8	85
86	20 53.9	+32.0	3.7	21 53.8	+32.0	3.7	22 53.6	+32.1	3.7	23 53.5	+32.2	3.7	24 53.4	+32.2	3.8	25 53.3	+32.2	3.8	26 53.1	+32.3	3.8	27 53.0	+32.4	3.9	86
87	21 25.9	+31.7	2.8	22 25.8	+31.7	2.8	23 25.7	+31.7	2.8	24 25.7	+31.8	2.8	25 25.6	+31.8	2.8	26 25.5	+31.9	2.9	27 25.4	+32.0	2.9	28 25.4	+31.9	2.9	87
88	21 57.6	+31.3	1.8	22 57.5	+31.4	1.9	23 57.5	+31.4	1.9	24 57.5	+31.4	1.9	25 57.4	+31.5	1.9	26 57.4	+31.5	1.9	27 57.4	+31.5	1.9	28 57.3	+31.6	2.0	88
89	22 28.9	+31.1	0.9	23 28.9	+31.1	0.9	24 28.9	+31.1	0.9	25 28.9	+31.1	0.9	26 28.9	+31.1	1.0	27 28.9	+31.1	1.0	28 28.9	+31.1	1.0	29 28.9	+31.1	1.0	89
90	23 00.0	+30.7	0.0	24 00.0	+30.7	0.0	25 00.0	+30.7	0.0	26 00.0	+30.7	0.0	27 00.0	+30.7	0.0	28 00.0	+30.7	0.0	29 00.0	+30.7	0.0	30 00.0	+30.7	0.0	90
	23°			24°			25°			26°			27°			28°			29°			30°			

S. Lat. {L.H.A. greater than 180° ....Zn=180°−Z; L.H.A. less than 180°............Zn=180°+Z

LATITUDE **SAME** NAME AS DECLINATION **L.H.A. 121°, 239°**

303

Dec.	23° Hc	d	Z	24° Hc	d	Z	25° Hc	d	Z	26° Hc	d	Z	27° Hc	d	Z	28° Hc	d	Z	29° Hc	d	Z	30° Hc	d	Z	Dec.
°	° ′	′	°	° ′	′	°	° ′	′	°	° ′	′	°	° ′	′	°	° ′	′	°	° ′	′	°	° ′	′	°	°
0	27 24.2	+26.2	102.7	27 10.7	+27.3	103.2	26 56.8	+28.2	103.7	26 42.3	+29.2	104.2	26 27.3	+30.3	104.7	26 11.9	+31.2	105.2	25 55.9	+32.2	105.6	25 39.5	+33.1	106.1	0
1	27 50.4	+25.7	101.7	27 38.0	+26.7	102.2	27 25.0	+27.8	102.7	27 11.5	+28.9	103.2	26 57.6	+29.8	103.7	26 43.1	+30.8	104.2	26 28.1	+31.8	104.7	26 12.6	+32.8	105.2	1
2	28 16.1	+25.3	100.7	28 04.7	+26.4	101.2	27 52.8	+27.4	101.7	27 40.4	+28.4	102.2	27 27.4	+29.4	102.7	27 13.9	+30.4	103.2	26 59.9	+31.4	103.7	26 45.4	+32.4	104.2	2
3	28 41.4	+24.8	99.6	28 31.1	+25.8	100.2	28 20.2	+26.9	100.7	28 08.8	+27.9	101.2	27 56.8	+29.0	101.8	27 44.3	+30.0	102.3	27 31.3	+31.0	102.8	27 17.8	+31.9	103.3	3
4	29 06.2	+24.3	98.6	28 56.9	+25.4	99.1	28 47.1	+26.5	99.7	28 36.7	+27.6	100.2	28 25.8	+28.6	100.8	28 14.3	+29.6	101.3	28 02.3	+30.6	101.8	27 49.7	+31.6	102.3	4
5	29 30.5	+23.8	97.6	29 22.3	+25.0	98.1	29 13.6	+26.0	98.7	29 04.3	+27.0	99.2	28 54.4	+28.1	99.8	28 43.9	+29.2	100.3	28 32.9	+30.2	100.8	28 21.3	+31.2	101.4	5
6	29 54.3	+23.4	96.5	29 47.3	+24.4	97.1	29 39.6	+25.5	97.6	29 31.3	+26.6	98.2	29 22.5	+27.6	98.8	29 13.1	+28.7	99.3	29 03.1	+29.7	99.9	28 52.5	+30.8	100.4	6
7	30 17.7	+22.7	95.4	30 11.7	+23.9	96.0	30 05.1	+25.0	96.6	29 57.9	+26.1	97.2	29 50.1	+27.2	97.7	29 41.8	+28.2	98.3	29 32.8	+29.3	98.9	29 23.3	+30.3	99.4	7
8	30 40.4	+22.3	94.4	30 35.6	+23.4	94.9	30 30.1	+24.5	95.5	30 24.0	+25.6	96.1	30 17.3	+26.7	96.7	30 10.0	+27.8	97.3	30 02.1	+28.8	97.9	29 53.6	+29.9	98.4	8
9	31 02.7	+21.7	93.3	30 59.0	+22.8	93.9	30 54.6	+24.0	94.5	30 49.6	+25.1	95.1	30 44.0	+26.2	95.7	30 37.8	+27.2	96.3	30 30.9	+28.4	96.8	30 23.5	+29.4	97.4	9
10	31 24.4	+21.2	92.2	31 21.8	+22.3	92.8	31 18.6	+23.4	93.4	31 14.7	+24.5	94.0	31 10.2	+25.6	94.6	31 05.0	+26.8	95.2	30 59.3	+27.8	95.8	30 52.9	+28.9	96.4	10
11	31 45.6	+20.5	91.1	31 44.1	+21.7	91.7	31 42.0	+22.9	92.3	31 39.2	+24.0	92.9	31 35.8	+25.2	93.6	31 31.8	+26.2	94.2	31 27.1	+27.4	94.8	31 21.8	+28.4	95.4	11
12	32 06.1	+20.0	90.0	32 05.8	+21.2	90.6	32 04.9	+22.3	91.2	32 03.2	+23.5	91.9	32 01.0	+24.6	92.5	31 58.0	+25.8	93.1	31 54.5	+26.8	93.7	31 50.2	+28.0	94.4	12
13	32 26.1	+19.4	88.9	32 27.0	+20.6	89.5	32 27.2	+21.7	90.1	32 26.7	+22.9	90.8	32 25.6	+24.0	91.4	32 23.8	+25.1	92.0	32 21.3	+26.3	92.7	32 18.2	+27.4	93.3	13
14	32 45.5	+18.8	87.7	32 47.6	+20.0	88.4	32 48.9	+21.2	89.0	32 49.6	+22.3	89.7	32 49.6	+23.5	90.3	32 48.9	+24.6	91.0	32 47.6	+25.7	91.6	32 45.6	+26.8	92.3	14
15	33 04.3	+18.2	86.6	33 07.6	+19.3	87.3	33 10.1	+20.5	87.9	33 11.9	+21.7	88.6	33 13.1	+22.9	89.2	33 13.5	+24.1	89.9	33 13.3	+25.2	90.5	33 12.4	+26.3	91.2	15
16	33 22.5	+17.6	85.5	33 26.9	+18.8	86.1	33 30.6	+20.0	86.8	33 33.6	+21.2	87.5	33 36.0	+22.3	88.1	33 37.6	+23.4	88.8	33 38.5	+24.6	89.4	33 38.7	+25.8	90.1	16
17	33 40.1	+16.9	84.3	33 45.7	+18.1	85.0	33 50.6	+19.3	85.7	33 54.8	+20.5	86.3	33 58.3	+21.6	87.0	34 01.0	+22.9	87.7	34 03.1	+24.0	88.3	34 04.5	+25.2	89.0	17
18	33 57.0	+16.3	83.2	34 03.8	+17.5	83.8	34 09.9	+18.6	84.5	34 15.3	+19.8	85.2	34 19.9	+21.1	85.9	34 23.9	+22.2	86.6	34 27.1	+23.5	87.2	34 29.7	+24.6	87.9	18
19	34 13.3	+15.6	82.0	34 21.3	+16.8	82.7	34 28.5	+18.1	83.4	34 35.1	+19.2	84.0	34 41.0	+20.4	84.7	34 46.1	+21.6	85.4	34 50.6	+22.7	86.1	34 54.3	+23.9	86.8	19
20	34 28.9	+14.9	80.8	34 38.1	+16.1	81.5	34 46.6	+17.3	82.2	34 54.3	+18.6	82.9	35 01.4	+19.8	83.6	35 07.7	+21.0	84.3	35 13.3	+22.2	85.0	35 18.2	+23.4	85.7	20
21	34 43.8	+14.2	79.7	34 54.2	+15.5	80.3	35 03.9	+16.7	81.0	35 12.9	+17.9	81.7	35 21.2	+19.1	82.4	35 28.7	+20.3	83.1	35 35.5	+21.5	83.8	35 41.6	+22.7	84.6	21
22	34 58.0	+13.6	78.5	35 09.7	+14.7	79.2	35 20.6	+16.0	79.9	35 30.8	+17.2	80.6	35 40.3	+18.4	81.3	35 49.0	+19.6	82.0	35 57.0	+20.8	82.7	36 04.3	+22.0	83.4	22
23	35 11.6	+12.8	77.3	35 24.4	+14.1	78.0	35 36.6	+15.3	78.7	35 48.0	+16.5	79.4	35 58.7	+17.7	80.1	36 08.6	+19.0	80.8	36 17.8	+20.2	81.5	36 26.3	+21.4	82.3	23
24	35 24.4	+12.2	76.1	35 38.5	+13.4	76.8	35 51.9	+14.6	77.5	36 04.5	+15.8	78.2	36 16.4	+17.0	78.9	36 27.6	+18.2	79.6	36 38.0	+19.5	80.4	36 47.7	+20.6	81.1	24
25	35 36.6	+11.4	74.9	35 51.9	+12.6	75.6	36 06.5	+13.8	76.3	36 20.3	+15.1	77.0	36 33.4	+16.4	77.7	36 45.8	+17.6	78.4	36 57.5	+18.7	79.2	37 08.3	+20.0	79.9	25
26	35 48.0	+10.7	73.7	36 04.5	+11.9	74.4	36 20.3	+13.1	75.1	36 35.4	+14.4	75.8	36 49.8	+15.5	76.5	37 03.4	+16.8	77.3	37 16.2	+18.1	78.0	37 28.3	+19.3	78.7	26
27	35 58.7	+9.9	72.5	36 16.4	+11.2	73.2	36 33.4	+12.4	73.9	36 49.8	+13.6	74.6	37 05.3	+14.9	75.3	37 20.2	+16.0	76.0	37 34.3	+17.3	76.8	37 47.6	+18.5	77.5	27
28	36 08.6	+9.2	71.2	36 27.6	+10.4	71.9	36 45.8	+11.7	72.6	37 03.4	+12.8	73.4	37 20.2	+14.1	74.1	37 36.2	+15.4	74.8	37 51.6	+16.5	75.6	38 06.1	+17.8	76.3	28
29	36 17.8	+8.5	70.0	36 38.0	+9.7	70.7	36 57.5	+10.8	71.4	37 16.2	+12.1	72.1	37 34.3	+13.3	72.9	37 51.6	+14.5	73.6	38 08.1	+15.8	74.4	38 23.9	+17.0	75.1	29
30	36 26.3	+7.7	68.8	36 47.7	+8.9	69.5	37 08.3	+10.2	70.2	37 28.3	+11.4	70.9	37 47.6	+12.5	71.6	38 06.1	+13.8	72.4	38 23.9	+15.0	73.1	38 40.9	+16.3	73.9	30
31	36 34.0	+6.9	67.6	36 56.6	+8.1	68.2	37 18.5	+9.3	69.0	37 39.7	+10.5	69.7	38 00.1	+11.8	70.4	38 19.9	+13.0	71.1	38 38.9	+14.2	71.9	38 57.2	+15.4	72.7	31
32	36 40.9	+6.2	66.3	37 04.7	+7.3	67.0	37 27.8	+8.5	67.7	37 50.2	+9.8	68.4	38 11.9	+11.0	69.2	38 32.9	+12.2	69.9	38 53.1	+13.5	70.7	39 12.6	+14.7	71.4	32
33	36 47.1	+5.4	65.1	37 12.0	+6.6	65.8	37 36.3	+7.8	66.5	38 00.0	+8.9	67.2	38 22.9	+10.1	67.9	38 45.1	+11.4	68.6	39 06.6	+12.6	69.4	39 27.3	+13.9	70.2	33
34	36 52.5	+4.6	63.8	37 18.6	+5.8	64.5	37 44.1	+6.9	65.2	38 08.9	+8.2	65.9	38 33.0	+9.4	66.6	38 56.5	+10.5	67.4	39 19.2	+11.8	68.1	39 41.2	+13.0	68.9	34
35	36 57.1	+3.8	62.6	37 24.4	+4.9	63.3	37 51.0	+6.2	64.0	38 17.1	+7.3	64.7	38 42.4	+8.5	65.4	39 07.0	+9.8	66.1	39 31.0	+10.9	66.9	39 54.2	+12.2	67.6	35
36	37 00.9	+3.0	61.3	37 29.3	+4.2	62.0	37 57.2	+5.3	62.7	38 24.4	+6.5	63.4	38 50.9	+7.7	64.1	39 16.8	+8.9	64.8	39 41.9	+10.2	65.6	40 06.4	+11.3	66.4	36
37	37 03.9	+2.2	60.1	37 33.5	+3.4	60.7	38 02.5	+4.6	61.4	38 30.9	+5.7	62.1	38 58.6	+6.9	62.8	39 25.7	+8.1	63.6	39 52.1	+9.2	64.3	40 17.7	+10.5	65.1	37
38	37 06.1	+1.5	58.8	37 36.9	+2.6	59.5	38 07.1	+3.7	60.2	38 36.6	+4.9	60.8	39 05.5	+6.0	61.6	39 33.8	+7.2	62.3	40 01.3	+8.4	63.0	40 28.2	+9.6	63.8	38
39	37 07.6	+0.7	57.6	37 39.5	+1.7	58.2	38 10.8	+2.9	58.9	38 41.5	+4.0	59.6	39 11.5	+5.2	60.3	39 41.0	+6.3	61.0	40 09.7	+7.6	61.7	40 37.8	+8.7	62.5	39
40	37 08.3	−0.2	56.3	37 41.2	+1.0	57.0	38 13.7	+2.0	57.6	38 45.5	+3.2	58.3	39 16.7	+4.4	59.0	39 47.3	+5.5	59.7	40 17.3	+6.6	60.4	40 46.5	+7.9	61.2	40
41	37 08.1	−0.9	55.1	37 42.2	+0.2	55.7	38 15.7	+1.3	56.3	38 48.7	+2.3	57.0	39 21.1	+3.4	57.7	39 52.8	+4.6	58.4	40 23.9	+5.8	59.1	40 54.4	+7.0	59.9	41
42	37 07.2	−1.7	53.8	37 42.4	−0.7	54.4	38 17.0	+0.4	55.1	38 51.0	+1.6	55.7	39 24.5	+2.7	56.4	39 57.4	+3.8	57.1	40 29.7	+4.9	57.8	41 01.4	+6.0	58.5	42
43	37 05.5	−2.5	52.6	37 41.7	−1.5	53.2	38 17.4	−0.4	53.8	38 52.6	+0.6	54.4	39 27.2	+1.7	55.1	40 01.2	+2.9	55.8	40 34.6	+4.0	56.5	41 07.4	+5.2	57.2	43
44	37 03.0	−3.3	51.3	37 40.2	−2.3	51.9	38 17.0	−1.3	52.5	38 53.2	−0.2	53.2	39 28.9	+0.9	53.8	40 04.1	+2.0	54.5	40 38.6	+3.1	55.2	41 12.6	+4.2	55.9	44
45	36 59.7	−4.1	50.1	37 37.9	−3.0	50.6	38 15.7	−2.0	51.3	38 53.0	−1.0	51.9	39 29.8	+0.1	52.5	40 06.1	+1.1	53.2	40 41.7	+2.2	53.9	41 16.8	+3.3	54.6	45
46	36 55.6	−4.9	48.8	37 34.9	−3.9	49.4	38 13.7	−2.9	50.0	38 52.0	−1.8	50.6	39 29.9	−0.9	51.2	40 07.2	+0.2	51.9	40 43.9	+1.3	52.6	41 20.1	+2.4	53.2	46
47	36 50.7	−5.6	47.6	37 31.0	−4.7	48.1	38 10.8	−3.7	48.7	38 50.2	−2.8	49.3	39 29.0	−1.7	49.9	40 07.4	−0.7	50.6	40 45.2	+0.4	51.2	41 22.5	+1.5	51.9	47
48	36 45.1	−6.5	46.3	37 26.3	−5.5	46.9	38 07.1	−4.5	47.4	38 47.4	−3.5	48.0	39 27.3	−2.5	48.6	40 06.7	−1.5	49.3	40 45.6	−0.5	49.9	41 24.0	+0.6	50.6	48
49	36 38.6	−7.1	45.1	37 20.8	−6.3	45.6	38 02.6	−5.4	46.2	38 43.9	−4.4	46.7	39 24.8	−3.4	47.3	40 05.2	−2.4	48.0	40 45.1	−1.4	48.6	41 24.6	−0.4	49.2	49
50	36 31.5	−8.0	43.8	37 14.5	−7.0	44.4	37 57.2	−6.1	44.9	38 39.5	−5.2	45.5	39 21.4	−4.3	46.0	40 02.8	−3.3	46.7	40 43.7	−2.3	47.3	41 24.2	−1.3	47.9	50
51	36 23.5	−8.7	42.6	37 07.5	−7.9	43.1	37 51.1	−7.0	43.6	38 34.3	−6.0	44.2	39 17.1	−5.1	44.8	39 59.5	−4.2	45.3	40 41.4	−3.2	46.0	41 22.9	−2.2	46.6	51
52	36 14.8	−9.5	41.4	36 59.6	−8.6	41.9	37 44.1	−7.7	42.4	38 28.3	−6.9	42.9	39 12.0	−6.0	43.5	39 55.3	−5.0	44.0	40 38.2	−4.0	44.6	41 20.7	−3.1	45.3	52
53	36 05.3	−10.2	40.2	36 51.0	−9.4	40.6	37 36.4	−8.6	41.1	38 21.4	−7.7	41.7	39 06.0	−6.8	42.2	39 50.3	−5.9	42.7	40 34.2	−5.0	43.3	41 17.6	−4.1	43.9	53
54	35 55.1	−10.9	38.9	36 41.6	−10.1	39.4	37 27.8	−9.3	39.9	38 13.7	−8.5	40.4	38 59.2	−7.6	40.9	39 44.4	−6.8	41.5	40 29.2	−5.9	42.0	41 13.5	−4.9	42.6	54
55	35 44.2	−11.7	37.7	36 31.5	−10.9	38.2	37 18.5	−10.1	38.6	38 05.2	−9.3	39.1	38 51.6	−8.5	39.6	39 37.6	−7.6	40.2	40 23.3	−6.8	40.7	41 08.6	−5.9	41.3	55
56	35 32.5	−12.4	36.5	36 20.6	−11.6	37.0	37 08.4	−10.9	37.4	37 55.9	−10.1	37.9	38 43.1	−9.3	38.4	39 30.0	−8.5	38.9	40 16.5	−7.6	39.4	41 02.7	−6.7	39.9	56
57	35 20.1	−13.0	35.3	36 09.0	−12.4	35.7	36 57.5	−11.6	36.2	37 45.8	−10.8	36.6	38 33.8	−10.1	37.1	39 21.5	−9.3	37.6	40 08.9	−8.5	38.1	40 56.0	−7.7	38.6	57
58	35 07.1	−13.8	34.1	35 56.6	−13.1	34.5	36 45.9	−12.4	35.0	37 35.0	−11.7	35.4	38 23.7	−10.9	35.8	39 12.2	−10.1	36.3	40 00.4	−9.3	36.8	40 48.3	−8.6	37.3	58
59	34 53.3	−14.5	32.9	35 43.5	−13.8	33.3	36 33.5	−13.1	33.7	37 23.3	−12.4	34.2	38 12.8	−11.7	34.6	39 02.1	−11.0	35.0	39 51.1	−10.2	35.5	40 39.7	−9.4	36.0	59
60	34 38.8	−15.2	31.8	35 29.7	−14.5	32.1	36 20.4	−13.9	32.5	37 10.9	−13.2	32.9	38 01.1	−12.5	33.3	38 51.1	−11.8	33.8	39 40.9	−11.1	34.2	40 30.3	−10.3	34.7	60
61	34 23.6	−15.8	30.6	35 15.2	−15.2	30.9	36 06.5	−14.5	31.3	36 57.7	−13.9	31.7	37 48.6	−13.2	32.1	38 39.3	−12.5	32.5	39 29.8	−11.9	33.0	40 20.0	−11.1	33.4	61
62	34 07.8	−16.5	29.4	35 00.0	−15.9	29.8	35 52.0	−15.3	30.1	36 43.8	−14.7	30.5	37 35.4	−14.1	30.9	38 26.8	−13.4	31.3	39 17.9	−12.7	31.7	40 08.9	−12.0	32.1	62
63	33 51.3	−17.1	28.3	34 44.1	−16.6	28.6	35 36.7	−16.0	28.9	36 29.1	−15.4	29.3	37 21.3	−14.7	29.6	38 13.4	−14.2	30.0	39 05.2	−13.5	30.4	39 56.9	−12.9	30.9	63
64	33 34.2	−17.8	27.1	34 27.5	−17.2	27.4	35 20.7	−16.7	27.7	36 13.7	−16.1	28.1	37 06.6	−15.6	28.4	37 59.2	−14.9	28.8	38 51.7	−14.3	29.2	39 44.0	−13.7	29.6	64
65	33 16.4	−18.4	26.0	34 10.3	−17.9	26.3	35 04.0	−17.3	26.6	35 57.6	−16.8	26.9	36 51.0	−16.2	27.2	37 44.3	−15.7	27.6	38 37.4	−15.1	27.9	39 30.3	−14.5	28.3	65
66	32 58.0	−19.0	24.8	33 52.4	−18.5	25.1	34 46.7	−18.0	25.4	35 40.8	−17.5	25.7	36 34.8	−17.0	26.0	37 28.6	−16.4	26.4	38 22.3	−15.8	26.7	39 15.8	−15.3	27.1	66
67	32 39.0	−19.6	23.7	33 33.9	−19.2	24.0	34 28.7	−18.7	24.2	35 23.3	−18.2	24.5	36 17.8	−17.6	24.8	37 12.2	−17.1	25.1	38 06.5	−16.7	25.5	39 00.5	−16.0	25.8	67
68	32 19.4	−20.2	22.6	33 14.7	−19.7	22.8	34 10.0	−19.3	23.1	35 05.1	−18.8	23.4	36 00.2	−18.4	23.6	36 55.1	−17.9	23.9	37 49.8	−17.4	24.3	38 44.5	−16.9	24.6	68
69	31 59.2	−20.8	21.5	32 55.0	−20.4	21.7	33 50.7	−19.9	21.9	34 46.3	−19.5	22.2	35 41.8	−19.1	22.5	36 37.2	−18.6	22.7	37 32.4	−18.1	23.0	38 27.6	−17.6	23.3	69
70	31 38.4	−21.3	20.4	32 34.6	−20.9	20.6	33 30.8	−20.6	20.8	34 26.8	−20.1	21.0	35 22.7	−19.7	21.3	36 18.6	−19.3	21.6	37 14.3	−18.8	21.8	38 10.0	−18.4	22.1	70
71	31 17.1	−21.9	19.3	32 13.7	−21.6	19.5	33 10.2	−21.1	19.7	34 06.7	−20.8	19.9	35 03.0	−20.3	20.1	35 59.3	−19.9	20.4	36 55.5	−19.5	20.7	37 51.6	−19.1	20.9	71
72	30 55.2	−22.5	18.2	31 52.1	−22.0	18.4	32 49.1	−21.8	18.6	33 45.9	−21.4	18.8	34 42.7	−21.0	19.0	35 39.4	−20.7	19.2	36 36.0	−20.3	19.5	37 32.5	−19.8	19.7	72
73	30 32.7	−22.9	17.1	31 30.1	−22.7	17.3	32 27.3	−22.3	17.5	33 24.5	−22.0	17.7	34 21.7	−21.7	17.9	35 18.7	−21.2	18.1	36 15.7	−20.9	18.3	37 12.7	−20.6	18.5	73
74	30 09.8	−23.5	16.0	31 07.4	−23.2	16.2	32 05.0	−22.9	16.4	33 02.5	−22.5	16.5	34 00.0	−22.2	16.7	34 57.5	−21.9	16.9	35 54.8	−21.5	17.1	36 52.1	−21.2	17.4	74
75	29 46.3	−24.0	15.0	30 44.2	−23.7	15.1	31 42.1	−23.4	15.3	32 40.0	−23.2	15.4	33 37.8	−22.8	15.6	34 35.6	−22.6	15.8	35 33.3	−22.3	16.0	36 30.9	−21.9	16.2	75
76	29 22.3	−24.5	13.9	30 20.5	−24.2	14.0	31 18.7	−24.0	14.2	32 16.8	−23.7	14.3	33 15.0	−23.5	14.5	34 13.0	−23.1	14.7	35 11.0	−22.8	14.9	36 09.0	−22.6	15.0	76
77	28 57.8	−25.0	12.9	29 56.3	−24.7	13.0	30 54.7	−24.5	13.1	31 53.1	−24.2	13.3	32 51.5	−24.0	13.4	33 49.9	−23.8	13.6	34 48.2	−23.5	13.7	35 46.4	−23.2	13.9	77
78	28 32.8	−25.4	11.8	29 31.6	−25.3	11.9	30 30.2	−25.0	12.1	31 28.9	−24.8	12.2	32 27.5	−24.5	12.3	33 26.1	−24.3	12.5	34 24.7	−24.1	12.6	35 23.2	−23.8	12.8	78
79	28 07.4	−25.9	10.8	29 06.3	−25.7	10.9	30 05.2	−25.5	11.0	31 04.1	−25.3	11.1	32 03.0	−25.1	11.2	33 01.8	−24.9	11.4	34 00.6	−24.6	11.5	34 59.4	−24.4	11.6	79
80	27 41.5	−26.3	9.8	28 40.6	−26.1	9.9	29 39.7	−25.9	10.0	30 38.8	−25.8	10.1	31 37.9	−25.6	10.2	32 36.9	−25.4	10.3	33 36.0	−25.3	10.4	34 35.0	−25.1	10.5	80
81	27 15.2	−26.8	8.8	28 14.5	−26.6	8.8	29 13.8	−26.5	8.9	30 13.0	−26.3	9.0	31 12.3	−26.2	9.1	32 11.5	−26.0	9.2	33 10.7	−25.8	9.3	34 09.9	−25.6	9.4	81
82	26 48.4	−27.2	7.8	27 47.9	−27.1	7.8	28 47.3	−26.9	7.9	29 46.7	−26.8	8.0	30 46.1	−26.6	8.1	31 45.5	−26.5	8.1	32 44.9	−26.3	8.2	33 44.3	−26.2	8.3	82
83	26 21.2	−27.6	6.8	27 20.8	−27.5	6.8	28 20.4	−27.4	6.9	29 19.9	−27.2	7.0	30 19.5	−27.2	7.0	31 19.0	−27.0	7.1	32 18.6	−26.9	7.2	33 18.1	−26.8	7.3	83
84	25 53.6	−28.0	5.8	26 53.3	−27.9	5.8	27 53.0	−27.8	5.9	28 52.7	−27.7	5.9	29 52.3	−27.6	6.0	30 52.0	−27.5	6.1	31 51.7	−27.4	6.1	32 51.3	−27.3	6.2	84
85	25 25.6	−28.4	4.8	26 25.4	−28.3	4.8	27 25.2	−28.3	4.9	28 25.0	−28.2	4.9	29 24.7	−28.0	5.0	30 24.5	−28.0	5.0	31 24.3	−27.9	5.1	32 24.0	−27.8	5.1	85
86	24 57.2	−28.7	3.8	25 57.1	−28.7	3.9	26 56.9	−28.6	3.9	27 56.8	−28.6	3.9	28 56.7	−28.6	4.0	29 56.5	−28.4	4.0	30 56.4	−28.4	4.0	31 56.2	−28.3	4.1	86
87	24 28.5	−29.2	2.9	25 28.4	−29.1	2.9	26 28.3	−29.0	2.9	27 28.2	−29.0	2.9	28 28.1	−28.9	3.0	29 28.1	−29.0	3.0	30 28.0	−28.9	3.0	31 27.9	−28.8	3.0	87
88	23 59.3	−29.5	1.9	24 59.3	−29.5	1.9	25 59.3	−29.5	1.9	26 59.2	−29.4	1.9	27 59.2	−29.4	2.0	28 59.1	−29.3	2.0	29 59.1	−29.3	2.0	30 59.1	−29.3	2.0	88
89	23 29.8	−29.8	0.9	24 29.8	−29.8	1.0	25 29.8	−29.8	1.0	26 29.8	−29.8	1.0	27 29.8	−29.8	1.0	28 29.8	−29.8	1.0	29 29.8	−29.8	1.0	30 29.8	−29.8	1.0	89
90	23 00.0	−30.2	0.0	24 00.0	−30.2	0.0	25 00.0	−30.2	0.0	26 00.0	−30.2	0.0	27 00.0	−30.2	0.0	28 00.0	−30.2	0.0	29 00.0	−30.2	0.0	30 00.0	−30.2	0.0	90
	23°			24°			25°			26°			27°			28°			29°			30°			

LATITUDE CONTRARY NAME TO DECLINATION — L.H.A. 60°, 300°

Dec.	23° Hc	d	Z	24° Hc	d	Z	25° Hc	d	Z	26° Hc	d	Z	27° Hc	d	Z	28° Hc	d	Z	29° Hc	d	Z	30° Hc	d	Z	Dec.
°	° ′	′	°	° ′	′	°	° ′	′	°	° ′	′	°	° ′	′	°	° ′	′	°	° ′	′	°	° ′	′	°	°
0	27 24.2	-26.6	102.7	27 10.7	-27.6	103.2	26 56.8	-28.7	103.7	26 42.3	-29.6	104.2	26 27.3	-30.6	104.7	26 11.9	-31.6	105.2	25 55.9	-32.5	105.6	25 39.5	-33.4	106.1	0
1	26 57.6	-27.1	103.7	26 43.1	-28.1	104.2	26 28.1	-29.0	104.7	26 12.7	-30.1	105.2	25 56.7	-31.0	105.6	25 40.3	-31.9	106.1	25 23.4	-32.9	106.6	25 06.1	-33.8	107.0	1
2	26 30.5	-27.4	104.7	26 15.0	-28.4	105.2	25 59.1	-29.5	105.7	25 42.6	-30.4	106.1	25 25.7	-31.3	106.6	25 08.4	-32.3	107.0	24 50.5	-33.2	107.5	24 32.3	-34.1	107.9	2
3	26 03.1	-27.9	105.7	25 46.6	-28.9	106.2	25 29.6	-29.8	106.6	25 12.2	-30.7	107.1	24 54.4	-31.7	107.5	24 36.1	-32.7	108.0	24 17.3	-33.5	108.4	23 58.2	-34.5	108.8	3
4	25 35.2	-28.3	106.7	25 17.7	-29.2	107.1	24 59.8	-30.2	107.6	24 41.5	-31.2	108.0	24 22.7	-32.1	108.5	24 03.4	-32.9	108.9	23 43.8	-33.9	109.3	23 23.7	-34.7	109.7	4
5	25 06.9	-28.6	107.7	24 48.5	-29.6	108.1	24 29.6	-30.5	108.5	24 10.3	-31.4	109.0	23 50.6	-32.4	109.4	23 30.5	-33.3	109.8	23 09.9	-34.1	110.2	22 49.0	-35.0	110.6	5
6	24 38.3	-29.0	108.6	24 18.9	-29.9	109.1	23 59.1	-30.9	109.5	23 38.9	-31.8	109.9	23 18.2	-32.7	110.3	22 57.2	-33.6	110.7	22 35.8	-34.5	111.1	22 14.0	-35.3	111.5	6
7	24 09.3	-29.4	109.6	23 49.0	-30.3	110.0	23 28.2	-31.2	110.4	23 07.1	-32.1	110.8	22 45.5	-33.0	111.2	22 23.6	-33.9	111.6	22 01.3	-34.7	112.0	21 38.7	-35.6	112.4	7
8	23 39.9	-29.7	110.6	23 18.7	-30.7	111.0	22 57.0	-31.5	111.4	22 35.0	-32.5	111.7	22 12.5	-33.3	112.1	21 49.7	-34.1	112.5	21 26.6	-35.0	112.9	21 03.1	-35.8	113.2	8
9	23 10.2	-30.0	111.5	22 48.0	-30.9	111.9	22 25.5	-31.9	112.3	22 02.5	-32.7	112.7	21 39.2	-33.6	113.0	21 15.6	-34.4	113.4	20 51.6	-35.3	113.7	20 27.3	-36.1	114.1	9
10	22 40.2	-30.4	112.4	22 17.1	-31.3	112.8	21 53.6	-32.1	113.2	21 29.8	-33.0	113.6	21 05.6	-33.8	113.9	20 41.2	-34.7	114.3	20 16.3	-35.5	114.6	19 51.2	-36.3	114.9	10
11	22 09.8	-30.7	113.4	21 45.8	-31.6	113.7	21 21.5	-32.5	114.1	20 56.8	-33.3	114.5	20 31.8	-34.1	114.8	20 06.5	-35.0	115.1	19 40.8	-35.8	115.5	19 14.9	-36.6	115.8	11
12	21 39.1	-31.0	114.3	21 14.2	-31.9	114.7	20 49.0	-32.7	115.0	20 23.5	-33.6	115.3	19 57.7	-34.4	115.7	19 31.5	-35.2	116.0	19 05.0	-35.9	116.3	18 38.3	-36.8	116.6	12
13	21 08.1	-31.3	115.2	20 42.3	-32.1	115.6	20 16.3	-33.0	115.9	19 49.9	-33.8	116.2	19 23.3	-34.7	116.5	18 56.3	-35.4	116.9	18 29.1	-36.3	117.2	18 01.5	-37.0	117.5	13
14	20 36.8	-31.6	116.1	20 10.2	-32.4	116.5	19 43.3	-33.2	116.8	19 16.1	-34.1	117.1	18 48.6	-34.8	117.4	18 20.9	-35.7	117.7	17 52.8	-36.4	118.0	17 24.5	-37.2	118.3	14
15	20 05.2	-31.9	117.0	19 37.8	-32.7	117.4	19 10.1	-33.6	117.7	18 42.0	-34.3	118.0	18 13.8	-35.1	118.3	17 45.2	-35.9	118.6	17 16.4	-36.6	118.8	16 47.3	-37.3	119.1	15
16	19 33.3	-32.1	117.9	19 05.1	-33.0	118.2	18 36.5	-33.7	118.5	18 07.7	-34.5	118.8	17 38.7	-35.4	119.1	17 09.3	-36.0	119.4	16 39.8	-36.9	119.7	16 10.0	-37.6	119.9	16
17	19 01.2	-32.4	118.8	18 32.1	-33.1	119.1	18 02.8	-34.0	119.4	17 33.2	-34.8	119.7	17 03.3	-35.5	120.0	16 33.3	-36.3	120.2	16 02.9	-37.0	120.5	15 32.4	-37.8	120.7	17
18	18 28.8	-32.6	119.7	17 59.0	-33.5	120.0	17 28.8	-34.2	120.3	16 58.4	-34.9	120.6	16 27.8	-35.7	120.8	15 57.0	-36.5	121.1	15 25.9	-37.2	121.3	14 54.6	-37.9	121.5	18
19	17 56.2	-32.9	120.6	17 25.5	-33.6	120.9	16 54.6	-34.4	121.1	16 23.5	-35.2	121.4	15 52.1	-35.9	121.6	15 20.5	-36.6	121.9	14 48.7	-37.4	122.1	14 16.7	-38.1	122.3	19
20	17 23.3	-33.1	121.5	16 51.9	-33.9	121.7	16 20.2	-34.6	122.0	15 48.3	-35.4	122.2	15 16.2	-36.1	122.5	14 43.9	-36.9	122.7	14 11.3	-37.5	122.9	13 38.6	-38.2	123.1	20
21	16 50.2	-33.3	122.4	16 18.0	-34.1	122.6	15 45.6	-34.8	122.9	15 12.9	-35.5	123.1	14 40.1	-36.3	123.3	14 07.0	-36.9	123.5	13 33.8	-37.7	123.7	13 00.4	-38.4	123.9	21
22	16 16.9	-33.5	123.2	15 43.9	-34.2	123.5	15 10.8	-35.0	123.7	14 37.4	-35.8	123.9	14 03.8	-36.4	124.1	13 30.1	-37.2	124.3	12 56.1	-37.8	124.5	12 22.0	-38.5	124.7	22
23	15 43.4	-33.7	124.1	15 09.7	-34.5	124.3	14 35.8	-35.2	124.5	14 01.6	-35.9	124.7	13 27.4	-36.6	124.9	12 52.9	-37.3	125.1	12 18.3	-38.0	125.3	11 43.5	-38.6	125.5	23
24	15 09.7	-33.9	124.9	14 35.2	-34.6	125.2	14 00.6	-35.4	125.4	13 25.7	-36.0	125.6	12 50.8	-36.8	125.8	12 15.6	-37.4	125.9	11 40.3	-38.1	126.1	11 04.9	-38.8	126.3	24
25	14 35.8	-34.2	125.8	14 00.6	-34.9	126.0	13 25.2	-35.5	126.2	12 49.7	-36.2	126.4	12 14.0	-36.9	126.6	11 38.2	-37.6	126.7	11 02.2	-38.2	126.9	10 26.1	-38.8	127.1	25
26	14 01.6	-34.2	126.6	13 25.7	-34.9	126.8	12 49.7	-35.7	127.0	12 13.5	-36.4	127.2	11 37.1	-37.0	127.4	11 00.6	-37.6	127.5	10 24.0	-38.3	127.7	9 47.3	-39.0	127.8	26
27	13 27.4	-34.5	127.5	12 50.8	-35.2	127.7	12 14.0	-35.8	127.9	11 37.1	-36.5	128.0	11 00.1	-37.1	128.2	10 23.0	-37.8	128.3	9 45.7	-38.4	128.5	9 08.3	-39.1	128.6	27
28	12 52.9	-34.6	128.3	12 15.6	-35.3	128.5	11 38.2	-36.0	128.7	11 00.6	-36.6	128.8	10 23.0	-37.3	129.0	9 45.2	-37.9	129.1	9 07.3	-38.6	129.2	8 29.2	-39.1	129.4	28
29	12 18.3	-34.8	129.2	11 40.3	-35.4	129.3	11 02.2	-36.1	129.5	10 24.0	-36.7	129.6	9 45.7	-37.4	129.8	9 07.3	-38.1	129.9	8 28.7	-38.6	130.0	7 50.1	-39.3	130.1	29
30	11 43.5	-34.9	130.0	11 04.9	-35.6	130.2	10 26.1	-36.2	130.3	9 47.3	-36.9	130.4	9 08.3	-37.5	130.6	8 29.2	-38.1	130.7	7 50.1	-38.7	130.8	7 10.8	-39.3	130.9	30
31	11 08.6	-35.0	130.8	10 29.3	-35.7	131.0	9 49.9	-36.3	131.1	9 10.4	-36.9	131.2	8 30.8	-37.5	131.4	7 51.1	-38.1	131.5	7 11.4	-38.8	131.6	6 31.5	-39.4	131.7	31
32	10 33.6	-35.2	131.7	9 53.6	-35.8	131.8	9 13.6	-36.4	131.9	8 33.5	-37.1	132.0	7 53.3	-37.7	132.1	7 13.0	-38.3	132.2	6 32.6	-38.9	132.3	5 52.1	-39.4	132.4	32
33	9 58.4	-35.3	132.5	9 17.8	-35.9	132.6	8 37.2	-36.6	132.7	7 56.4	-37.1	132.8	7 15.6	-37.8	132.9	6 34.7	-38.3	133.0	5 53.7	-38.9	133.1	5 12.7	-39.5	133.2	33
34	9 23.1	-35.4	133.3	8 41.9	-36.0	133.4	8 00.6	-36.6	133.5	7 19.3	-37.3	133.6	6 37.8	-37.8	133.7	5 56.4	-38.4	133.8	5 14.8	-39.0	133.9	4 33.2	-39.5	133.9	34
35	8 47.7	-35.5	134.1	8 05.9	-36.1	134.2	7 24.0	-36.7	134.3	6 42.0	-37.3	134.4	6 00.0	-37.9	134.5	5 18.0	-38.5	134.6	4 35.8	-39.0	134.6	3 53.7	-39.6	134.7	35
36	8 12.2	-35.6	134.9	7 29.8	-36.2	135.0	6 47.3	-36.8	135.1	6 04.7	-37.3	135.2	5 22.1	-37.9	135.3	4 39.5	-38.5	135.3	3 56.8	-39.1	135.4	3 14.1	-39.7	135.4	36
37	7 36.6	-35.7	135.8	6 53.6	-36.3	135.8	6 10.5	-36.9	135.9	5 27.4	-37.5	136.0	4 44.2	-38.0	136.1	4 01.0	-38.6	136.1	3 17.7	-39.1	136.1	2 34.4	-39.6	136.2	37
38	7 00.9	-35.8	136.6	6 17.3	-36.4	136.6	5 33.6	-36.9	136.7	4 49.9	-37.4	136.8	4 06.2	-38.0	136.8	3 22.4	-38.6	136.9	2 38.6	-39.1	136.9	1 54.8	-39.7	136.9	38
39	6 25.1	-35.9	137.4	5 40.9	-36.4	137.4	4 56.7	-37.0	137.5	4 12.5	-37.6	137.6	3 28.2	-38.1	137.6	2 43.8	-38.6	137.6	1 59.5	-39.2	137.7	1 15.1	-39.6	137.7	39
40	5 49.2	-35.9	138.2	5 04.5	-36.5	138.2	4 19.7	-37.0	138.3	3 34.9	-37.5	138.3	2 50.1	-38.1	138.4	2 05.2	-38.6	138.4	1 20.3	-39.1	138.4	0 35.5	-39.7	138.4	40
41	5 13.3	-36.0	139.0	4 28.0	-36.5	139.0	3 42.7	-37.1	139.1	2 57.4	-37.7	139.1	2 12.0	-38.2	139.2	1 26.6	-38.7	139.2	0 41.2	-39.2	139.2	0 04.2	+39.7	40.8	41
42	4 37.3	-36.0	139.8	3 51.5	-36.6	139.8	3 05.6	-37.1	139.9	2 19.7	-37.6	139.9	1 33.8	-38.1	139.9	0 47.9	-38.6	139.9	0 02.0	-39.2	139.9	0 43.9	+39.7	40.1	42
43	4 01.3	-36.1	140.6	3 14.9	-36.6	140.6	2 28.5	-37.1	140.7	1 42.1	-37.6	140.7	0 55.7	-38.2	140.7	0 09.3	-38.7	140.7	0 37.2	+39.1	39.3	1 23.6	+39.7	39.3	43
44	3 25.2	-36.1	141.4	2 38.3	-36.6	141.4	1 51.4	-37.2	141.4	1 04.5	-37.7	141.5	0 17.5	-38.1	141.5	0 29.4	+38.7	38.5	1 16.3	+39.2	38.5	2 03.3	+39.6	38.6	44
45	2 49.1	-36.2	142.2	2 01.7	-36.7	142.2	1 14.2	-37.1	142.2	0 26.8	-37.7	142.2	0 20.6	+38.2	37.8	1 08.1	+38.6	37.8	1 55.5	+39.1	37.8	2 42.9	+39.6	37.8	45
46	2 12.9	-36.2	143.0	1 25.0	-36.7	143.0	0 37.1	-37.2	143.0	0 10.9	+37.6	37.0	0 58.8	+38.1	37.0	1 46.7	+38.6	37.0	2 34.6	+39.1	37.0	3 22.5	+39.6	37.1	46
47	1 36.7	-36.2	143.8	0 48.3	-36.7	143.8	0 00.1	+37.2	36.2	0 48.5	+37.7	36.2	1 36.9	+38.2	36.2	2 25.3	+38.6	36.2	3 13.7	+39.1	36.3	4 02.1	+39.5	36.3	47
48	1 00.5	-36.2	144.6	0 11.6	-36.7	144.6	0 37.3	+37.2	35.4	1 26.2	+37.6	35.4	2 15.1	+38.1	35.4	3 03.9	+38.6	35.5	3 52.8	+39.0	35.5	4 41.6	+39.5	35.6	48
49	0 24.3	-36.2	145.4	0 25.1	+36.7	34.6	1 14.5	+37.1	34.6	2 03.8	+37.6	34.6	2 53.2	+38.1	34.7	3 42.5	+38.5	34.7	4 31.8	+39.0	34.7	5 21.1	+39.4	34.8	49
50	0 11.9	+36.3	33.8	1 01.8	+36.7	33.8	1 51.6	+37.2	33.8	2 41.4	+37.6	33.9	3 31.3	+38.0	33.9	4 21.0	+38.5	33.9	5 10.8	+38.9	34.0	6 00.5	+39.4	34.0	50
51	0 48.2	+36.2	33.0	1 38.5	+36.6	33.0	2 28.8	+37.1	33.1	3 19.0	+37.6	33.1	4 09.3	+38.0	33.1	4 59.5	+38.5	33.2	5 49.7	+38.9	33.2	6 39.9	+39.3	33.3	51
52	1 24.4	+36.2	32.2	2 15.1	+36.7	32.2	3 05.9	+37.0	32.3	3 56.6	+37.5	32.3	4 47.3	+37.9	32.3	5 38.0	+38.3	32.4	6 28.6	+38.8	32.5	7 19.2	+39.2	32.5	52
53	2 00.6	+36.1	31.4	2 51.8	+36.6	31.5	3 42.9	+37.1	31.5	4 34.1	+37.4	31.5	5 25.2	+37.9	31.6	6 16.3	+38.3	31.6	7 07.4	+38.7	31.7	7 58.4	+39.2	31.8	53
54	2 36.7	+36.2	30.6	3 28.4	+36.5	30.7	4 20.0	+36.9	30.7	5 11.5	+37.4	30.7	6 03.1	+37.8	30.8	6 54.6	+38.3	30.8	7 46.1	+38.7	30.9	8 37.6	+39.0	31.0	54
55	3 12.9	+36.1	29.8	4 04.9	+36.5	29.9	4 56.9	+37.0	29.9	5 48.9	+37.4	30.0	6 40.9	+37.8	30.0	7 32.9	+38.1	30.1	8 24.8	+38.5	30.1	9 16.6	+39.0	30.2	55
56	3 49.0	+36.0	29.0	4 41.4	+36.5	29.1	5 33.9	+36.8	29.1	6 26.3	+37.2	29.2	7 18.7	+37.6	29.2	8 11.0	+38.1	29.3	9 03.3	+38.5	29.4	9 55.6	+38.8	29.4	56
57	4 25.0	+36.1	28.2	5 17.9	+36.4	28.3	6 10.7	+36.8	28.3	7 03.5	+37.2	28.4	7 56.3	+37.6	28.4	8 49.1	+37.9	28.5	9 41.8	+38.3	28.6	10 34.4	+38.7	28.7	57
58	5 01.1	+35.9	27.4	5 54.3	+36.3	27.5	6 47.5	+36.7	27.5	7 40.7	+37.1	27.6	8 33.9	+37.5	27.7	9 27.0	+37.9	27.7	10 20.1	+38.2	27.8	11 13.1	+38.7	27.9	58
59	5 37.0	+35.9	26.6	6 30.6	+36.3	26.7	7 24.2	+36.7	26.7	8 17.8	+37.0	26.8	9 11.4	+37.3	26.9	10 04.9	+37.7	26.9	10 58.3	+38.1	27.0	11 51.8	+38.4	27.1	59
60	6 12.9	+35.8	25.8	7 06.9	+36.2	25.9	8 00.9	+36.5	25.9	8 54.8	+36.9	26.0	9 48.7	+37.3	26.1	10 42.6	+37.6	26.1	11 36.4	+38.0	26.2	12 30.2	+38.4	26.3	60
61	6 48.7	+35.7	25.0	7 43.1	+36.0	25.1	8 37.4	+36.4	25.1	9 31.7	+36.8	25.2	10 26.0	+37.1	25.3	11 20.2	+37.5	25.4	12 14.4	+37.9	25.4	13 08.6	+38.2	25.5	61
62	7 24.4	+35.7	24.2	8 19.1	+36.0	24.3	9 13.8	+36.4	24.3	10 08.5	+36.7	24.4	11 03.1	+37.0	24.5	11 57.7	+37.4	24.6	12 52.3	+37.7	24.6	13 46.8	+38.0	24.7	62
63	8 00.1	+35.5	23.4	8 55.1	+35.9	23.5	9 50.2	+36.2	23.5	10 45.2	+36.5	23.6	11 40.1	+36.9	23.7	12 35.1	+37.2	23.8	13 30.0	+37.5	23.8	14 24.8	+37.9	24.0	63
64	8 35.6	+35.5	22.6	9 31.0	+35.8	22.6	10 26.4	+36.1	22.7	11 21.7	+36.4	22.8	12 17.0	+36.7	22.9	13 12.3	+37.0	23.0	14 07.5	+37.4	23.0	15 02.7	+37.7	23.1	64
65	9 11.1	+35.3	21.8	10 06.8	+35.6	21.8	11 02.5	+35.9	21.9	11 58.1	+36.3	22.0	12 53.7	+36.6	22.1	13 49.3	+36.9	22.1	14 44.9	+37.2	22.2	15 40.4	+37.5	22.3	65
66	9 46.4	+35.2	20.9	10 42.4	+35.5	21.0	11 38.4	+35.8	21.1	12 34.4	+36.1	21.2	13 30.3	+36.5	21.2	14 26.2	+36.8	21.3	15 22.1	+37.0	21.4	16 17.9	+37.4	21.5	66
67	10 21.6	+35.1	20.1	11 17.9	+35.4	20.2	12 14.2	+35.7	20.3	13 10.5	+36.0	20.3	14 06.8	+36.2	20.4	15 03.0	+36.5	20.5	15 59.1	+36.9	20.6	16 55.3	+37.1	20.7	67
68	10 56.7	+35.0	19.3	11 53.3	+35.3	19.4	12 49.9	+35.5	19.4	13 46.5	+35.8	19.5	14 43.0	+36.1	19.6	15 39.5	+36.4	19.7	16 36.0	+36.7	19.8	17 32.4	+37.0	19.9	68
69	11 31.7	+34.8	18.5	12 28.6	+35.0	18.5	13 25.4	+35.4	18.6	14 22.3	+35.6	18.7	15 19.1	+35.9	18.8	16 15.9	+36.2	18.9	17 12.7	+36.4	19.0	18 09.4	+36.7	19.1	69
70	12 06.5	+34.6	17.6	13 03.6	+35.0	17.7	14 00.8	+35.2	17.8	14 57.9	+35.5	17.9	15 55.0	+35.7	17.9	16 52.1	+35.9	18.0	17 49.1	+36.3	18.1	18 46.1	+36.5	18.2	70
71	12 41.1	+34.5	16.8	13 38.6	+34.7	16.9	14 36.0	+35.0	16.9	15 33.4	+35.2	17.0	16 30.7	+35.5	17.1	17 28.0	+35.8	17.2	18 25.4	+36.0	17.3	19 22.6	+36.3	17.4	71
72	13 15.6	+34.4	16.0	14 13.3	+34.6	16.0	15 11.0	+34.8	16.1	16 08.6	+35.1	16.2	17 06.2	+35.3	16.3	18 03.8	+35.6	16.3	19 01.4	+35.8	16.4	19 58.9	+36.0	16.5	72
73	13 50.0	+34.1	15.1	14 47.9	+34.4	15.2	15 45.8	+34.6	15.3	16 43.7	+34.8	15.3	17 41.5	+35.1	15.4	18 39.4	+35.3	15.5	19 37.2	+35.5	15.6	20 34.9	+35.8	15.7	73
74	14 24.1	+34.0	14.3	15 22.3	+34.2	14.3	16 20.4	+34.4	14.4	17 18.5	+34.7	14.5	18 16.6	+34.9	14.6	19 14.7	+35.0	14.6	20 12.7	+35.3	14.7	21 10.7	+35.5	14.8	74
75	14 58.1	+33.8	13.4	15 56.5	+34.0	13.5	16 54.8	+34.2	13.5	17 53.2	+34.4	13.6	18 51.5	+34.6	13.7	19 49.7	+34.9	13.8	20 48.0	+35.0	13.9	21 46.2	+35.3	14.0	75
76	15 31.9	+33.6	12.6	16 30.5	+33.8	12.6	17 29.0	+34.0	12.7	18 27.6	+34.1	12.8	19 26.1	+34.3	12.8	20 24.6	+34.5	12.9	21 23.0	+34.8	13.0	22 21.5	+34.9	13.1	76
77	16 05.5	+33.4	11.7	17 04.3	+33.5	11.8	18 03.0	+33.8	11.8	19 01.7	+34.0	11.9	20 00.4	+34.1	12.0	20 59.1	+34.3	12.0	21 57.8	+34.5	12.1	22 56.4	+34.7	12.2	77
78	16 38.9	+33.2	10.8	17 37.8	+33.4	10.9	18 36.8	+33.5	11.0	19 35.7	+33.6	11.0	20 34.5	+33.9	11.1	21 33.4	+34.0	11.2	22 32.3	+34.2	11.2	23 31.1	+34.4	11.3	78
79	17 12.1	+32.9	10.0	18 11.2	+33.1	10.0	19 10.3	+33.2	10.1	20 09.3	+33.4	10.1	21 08.4	+33.5	10.2	22 07.4	+33.8	10.3	23 06.5	+33.8	10.3	24 05.5	+34.0	10.4	79
80	17 45.0	+32.7	9.1	18 44.3	+32.8	9.1	19 43.5	+33.0	9.2	20 42.7	+33.2	9.3	21 41.9	+33.3	9.3	22 41.2	+33.4	9.4	23 40.3	+33.6	9.5	24 39.5	+33.7	9.5	80
81	18 17.7	+32.5	8.2	19 17.1	+32.6	8.3	20 16.5	+32.7	8.3	21 15.9	+32.8	8.4	22 15.2	+33.0	8.4	23 14.6	+33.1	8.5	24 13.9	+33.3	8.5	25 13.2	+33.4	8.6	81
82	18 50.2	+32.2	7.3	19 49.7	+32.3	7.4	20 49.2	+32.5	7.4	21 48.7	+32.6	7.5	22 48.2	+32.7	7.5	23 47.7	+32.8	7.6	24 47.2	+32.9	7.6	25 46.6	+33.1	7.7	82
83	19 22.4	+32.0	6.4	20 22.0	+32.1	6.5	21 21.7	+32.1	6.5	22 21.3	+32.2	6.6	23 20.9	+32.3	6.6	24 20.5	+32.4	6.7	25 20.1	+32.5	6.7	26 19.7	+32.6	6.8	83
84	19 54.4	+31.6	5.5	20 54.1	+31.8	5.6	21 53.8	+31.9	5.6	22 53.5	+32.0	5.6	23 53.2	+32.0	5.7	24 52.9	+32.1	5.7	25 52.6	+32.2	5.8	26 52.3	+32.3	5.8	84
85	20 26.0	+31.4	4.6	21 25.9	+31.4	4.7	22 25.7	+31.5	4.7	23 25.5	+31.6	4.7	24 25.2	+31.7	4.8	25 25.0	+31.8	4.8	26 24.8	+31.9	4.8	27 24.6	+31.9	4.9	85
86	20 57.4	+31.1	3.7	21 57.3	+31.2	3.7	22 57.2	+31.2	3.8	23 57.1	+31.2	3.8	24 56.9	+31.3	3.8	25 56.8	+31.4	3.9	26 56.7	+31.4	3.9	27 56.5	+31.5	3.9	86
87	21 28.5	+30.8	2.8	22 28.5	+30.8	2.8	23 28.4	+30.9	2.8	24 28.3	+30.9	2.9	25 28.3	+30.9	2.9	26 28.2	+31.0	2.9	27 28.1	+31.0	2.9	28 28.0	+31.1	3.0	87
88	21 59.3	+30.5	1.9	22 59.3	+30.5	1.9	23 59.3	+30.5	1.9	24 59.2	+30.6	1.9	25 59.2	+30.6	1.9	26 59.2	+30.6	1.9	27 59.1	+30.7	2.0	28 59.1	+30.7	2.0	88
89	22 29.8	+30.2	0.9	23 29.8	+30.2	0.9	24 29.8	+30.2	1.0	25 29.8	+30.2	1.0	26 29.8	+30.2	1.0	27 29.8	+30.2	1.0	28 29.8	+30.2	1.0	29 29.8	+30.2	1.0	89
90	23 00.0	+29.8	0.0	24 00.0	+29.8	0.0	25 00.0	+29.8	0.0	26 00.0	+29.8	0.0	27 00.0	+29.8	0.0	28 00.0	+29.8	0.0	29 00.0	+29.8	0.0	30 00.0	+29.8	0.0	90
	23°			24°			25°			26°			27°			28°			29°			30°			

S. Lat. {L.H.A. greater than 180° ....Zn=180°−Z; L.H.A. less than 180°...........Zn=180°+Z}

LATITUDE SAME NAME AS DECLINATION — L.H.A. 120°, 240°

N. Lat. {L.H.A. greater than 180° .....Zn=Z
L.H.A. less than 180°............Zn=360°−Z}

Dec.	23° Hc	23° d	23° Z	24° Hc	24° d	24° Z	25° Hc	25° d	25° Z	26° Hc	26° d	26° Z
°	° ′	′	°	° ′	′	°	° ′	′	°	° ′	′	°
0	26 30.3	+26.0	102.2	26 17.3	+27.0	102.7	26 03.9	+28.0	103.2	25 50.0	+29.0	103.7
1	26 56.3	+25.5	101.2	26 44.3	+26.6	101.7	26 31.9	+27.6	102.2	26 19.0	+28.6	102.7
2	27 21.8	+25.1	100.2	27 10.9	+26.2	100.7	26 59.5	+27.2	101.2	26 47.6	+28.2	101.7
3	27 46.9	+24.7	99.2	27 37.1	+25.7	99.7	27 26.7	+26.8	100.2	27 15.8	+27.8	100.7
4	28 11.6	+24.1	98.1	28 02.8	+25.2	98.7	27 53.5	+26.3	99.2	27 43.6	+27.4	99.7
5	28 35.7	+23.7	97.1	28 28.0	+24.8	97.6	28 19.8	+25.9	98.2	28 11.0	+26.9	98.7
6	28 59.4	+23.2	96.0	28 52.8	+24.3	96.6	28 45.7	+25.3	97.1	28 37.9	+26.5	97.7
7	29 22.6	+22.8	95.0	29 17.1	+23.8	95.6	29 11.0	+24.9	96.1	29 04.4	+26.0	96.7
8	29 45.4	+22.1	93.9	29 40.9	+23.4	94.5	29 35.9	+24.5	95.1	29 30.4	+25.5	95.6
9	30 07.5	+21.7	92.9	30 04.3	+22.7	93.4	30 00.4	+23.9	94.0	29 55.9	+25.0	94.6
10	30 29.2	+21.1	91.8	30 27.0	+22.3	92.4	30 24.3	+23.3	93.0	30 20.9	+24.5	93.5
11	30 50.3	+20.6	90.7	30 49.3	+21.7	91.3	30 47.6	+22.9	91.9	30 45.4	+23.9	92.5
12	31 10.9	+20.0	89.6	31 11.0	+21.2	90.2	31 10.5	+22.3	90.8	31 09.3	+23.5	91.4
13	31 30.9	+19.5	88.5	31 32.2	+20.6	89.1	31 32.8	+21.8	89.7	31 32.8	+22.9	90.3
14	31 50.4	+18.8	87.4	31 52.8	+20.0	88.0	31 54.6	+21.1	88.6	31 55.7	+22.3	89.2
15	32 09.2	+18.3	86.3	32 12.8	+19.4	86.9	32 15.7	+20.6	87.5	32 18.0	+21.8	88.1
16	32 27.5	+17.6	85.1	32 32.2	+18.9	85.8	32 36.3	+20.1	86.4	32 39.8	+21.2	87.0
17	32 45.1	+17.1	84.0	32 51.1	+18.2	84.6	32 56.4	+19.4	85.3	33 01.0	+20.5	85.9
18	33 02.2	+16.4	82.9	33 09.3	+17.6	83.5	33 15.8	+18.7	84.2	33 21.5	+20.0	84.8
19	33 18.6	+15.8	81.7	33 26.9	+17.0	82.4	33 34.5	+18.2	83.0	33 41.5	+19.3	83.7
20	33 34.4	+15.1	80.5	33 43.9	+16.3	81.2	33 52.7	+17.5	81.9	34 00.8	+18.8	82.5
21	33 49.5	+14.4	79.4	34 00.2	+15.7	80.0	34 10.2	+16.9	80.7	34 19.6	+18.0	81.4
22	34 03.9	+13.8	78.2	34 15.9	+15.0	78.9	34 27.1	+16.2	79.6	34 37.6	+17.4	80.2
23	34 17.7	+13.2	77.0	34 30.9	+14.3	77.7	34 43.3	+15.5	78.4	34 55.0	+16.8	79.1
24	34 30.9	+12.4	75.9	34 45.2	+13.6	76.5	34 58.8	+14.9	77.2	35 11.8	+16.0	77.9
25	34 43.3	+11.7	74.7	34 58.8	+13.0	75.3	35 13.7	+14.1	76.0	35 27.8	+15.4	76.7
26	34 55.0	+11.1	73.5	35 11.8	+12.2	74.1	35 27.8	+13.4	74.8	35 43.2	+14.6	75.5
27	35 06.1	+10.3	72.3	35 24.0	+11.5	72.9	35 41.2	+12.8	73.6	35 57.8	+13.9	74.3
28	35 16.4	+9.6	71.1	35 35.5	+10.8	71.7	35 54.0	+12.0	72.4	36 11.7	+13.2	73.1
29	35 26.0	+8.8	69.9	35 46.3	+10.1	70.5	36 06.0	+11.2	71.2	36 24.9	+12.5	71.9
30	35 34.8	+8.2	68.6	35 56.4	+9.3	69.3	36 17.2	+10.5	70.0	36 37.4	+11.7	70.7
31	35 43.0	+7.4	67.4	36 05.7	+8.6	68.1	36 27.7	+9.8	68.8	36 49.1	+11.0	69.5
32	35 50.4	+6.6	66.2	36 14.3	+7.8	66.9	36 37.5	+9.0	67.5	37 00.1	+10.2	68.2
33	35 57.0	+5.9	65.0	36 22.1	+7.0	65.6	36 46.5	+8.2	66.3	37 10.3	+9.4	67.0
34	36 02.9	+5.1	63.7	36 29.1	+6.3	64.4	36 54.7	+7.5	65.1	37 19.7	+8.6	65.8
35	36 08.0	+4.4	62.5	36 35.4	+5.6	63.2	37 02.2	+6.7	63.8	37 28.3	+7.9	64.5
36	36 12.4	+3.6	61.3	36 41.0	+4.7	61.9	37 08.9	+5.9	62.6	37 36.2	+7.1	63.3
37	36 16.0	+2.9	60.0	36 45.7	+4.0	60.7	37 14.8	+5.1	61.3	37 43.3	+6.2	62.0
38	36 18.9	+2.1	58.8	36 49.7	+3.2	59.4	37 19.9	+4.3	60.1	37 49.5	+5.5	60.8
39	36 21.0	+1.3	57.6	36 52.9	+2.4	58.2	37 24.2	+3.6	58.8	37 55.0	+4.6	59.5
40	36 22.3	+0.5	56.3	36 55.3	+1.6	56.9	37 27.8	+2.7	57.6	37 59.6	+3.9	58.2
41	36 22.8	-0.2	55.1	36 56.9	+0.9	55.7	37 30.5	+1.9	56.3	38 03.5	+3.0	57.0
42	36 22.6	-1.0	53.8	36 57.8	0.0	54.4	37 32.4	+1.1	55.1	38 06.5	+2.2	55.7
43	36 21.6	-1.8	52.6	36 57.8	-0.7	53.2	37 33.5	+0.3	53.8	38 08.7	+1.4	54.4
44	36 19.8	-2.5	51.3	36 57.1	-1.6	51.9	37 33.8	-0.5	52.5	38 10.1	+0.5	53.2
45	36 17.3	-3.3	50.1	36 55.5	-2.3	50.7	37 33.3	-1.3	51.3	38 10.6	-0.3	51.9
46	36 14.0	-4.1	48.9	36 53.2	-3.1	49.4	37 32.0	-2.1	50.0	38 10.3	-1.0	50.6
47	36 09.9	-4.8	47.6	36 50.1	-3.8	48.2	37 29.9	-2.9	48.8	38 09.3	-2.0	49.3
48	36 05.1	-5.6	46.4	36 46.3	-4.7	46.9	37 27.0	-3.7	47.5	38 07.3	-2.7	48.1
49	35 59.5	-6.3	45.2	36 41.6	-5.4	45.7	37 23.3	-4.5	46.2	38 04.6	-3.5	46.8
50	35 53.2	-7.1	43.9	36 36.2	-6.2	44.5	37 18.8	-5.3	45.0	38 01.1	-4.4	45.5
51	35 46.1	-7.9	42.7	36 30.0	-7.0	43.2	37 13.5	-6.1	43.7	37 56.7	-5.2	44.3
52	35 38.2	-8.5	41.5	36 23.0	-7.7	42.0	37 07.4	-6.8	42.5	37 51.5	-6.0	43.0
53	35 29.7	-9.3	40.3	36 15.3	-8.5	40.7	37 00.6	-7.7	41.2	37 45.5	-6.8	41.7
54	35 20.4	-10.1	39.1	36 06.8	-9.2	39.5	36 52.9	-8.4	40.0	37 38.7	-7.6	40.5
55	35 10.3	-10.7	37.9	35 57.6	-10.0	38.3	36 44.5	-9.2	38.8	37 31.1	-8.3	39.2
56	34 59.6	-11.4	36.7	35 47.6	-10.7	37.1	36 35.3	-9.9	37.5	37 22.8	-9.2	38.0
57	34 48.2	-12.2	35.5	35 36.9	-11.4	35.9	36 25.4	-10.7	36.3	37 13.6	-9.9	36.7
58	34 36.0	-12.8	34.3	35 25.5	-12.2	34.7	36 14.7	-11.4	35.1	37 03.7	-10.7	35.5
59	34 23.2	-13.6	33.1	35 13.3	-12.8	33.5	36 03.3	-12.2	33.9	36 53.0	-11.5	34.3
60	34 09.6	-14.1	31.9	35 00.5	-13.6	32.3	35 51.1	-12.9	32.7	36 41.5	-12.2	33.0
61	33 55.5	-14.9	30.7	34 46.9	-14.2	31.1	35 38.2	-13.6	31.4	36 29.3	-12.9	31.8
62	33 40.6	-15.5	29.6	34 32.7	-14.9	29.9	35 24.6	-14.3	30.3	36 16.4	-13.7	30.6
63	33 25.1	-16.2	28.4	34 17.8	-15.6	28.7	35 10.3	-15.0	29.1	36 02.7	-14.4	29.4
64	33 08.9	-16.7	27.3	34 02.2	-16.2	27.6	34 55.3	-15.7	27.9	35 48.3	-15.1	28.2
65	32 52.2	-17.4	26.1	33 46.0	-16.9	26.4	34 39.6	-16.3	26.7	35 33.2	-15.8	27.0
66	32 34.8	-18.1	25.0	33 29.1	-17.5	25.2	34 23.3	-17.0	25.5	35 17.4	-16.5	25.8
67	32 16.7	-18.6	23.8	33 11.6	-18.2	24.1	34 06.3	-17.7	24.4	35 00.9	-17.2	24.7
68	31 58.1	-19.2	22.7	32 53.4	-18.7	23.0	33 48.6	-18.3	23.2	34 43.7	-17.8	23.5
69	31 38.9	-19.8	21.6	32 34.7	-19.4	21.8	33 30.3	-18.9	22.1	34 25.9	-18.5	22.3
70	31 19.1	-20.3	20.5	32 15.3	-20.0	20.7	33 11.4	-19.6	20.9	34 07.4	-19.2	21.2
71	30 58.8	-20.9	19.4	31 55.3	-20.5	19.6	32 51.8	-20.1	19.8	33 48.2	-19.7	20.0
72	30 37.9	-21.5	18.3	31 34.8	-21.1	18.5	32 31.7	-20.8	18.7	33 28.5	-20.4	18.9
73	30 16.4	-21.9	17.2	31 13.7	-21.6	17.4	32 10.9	-21.3	17.6	33 08.1	-21.0	17.8
74	29 54.5	-22.5	16.1	30 52.1	-22.2	16.3	31 49.6	-21.9	16.5	32 47.1	-21.5	16.7
75	29 32.0	-23.0	15.1	30 29.9	-22.7	15.2	31 27.7	-22.4	15.4	32 25.6	-22.2	15.6
76	29 09.0	-23.5	14.0	30 07.2	-23.3	14.2	31 05.3	-23.0	14.3	32 03.4	-22.7	14.5
77	28 45.5	-24.0	13.0	29 43.9	-23.7	13.1	30 42.3	-23.5	13.2	31 40.7	-23.2	13.4
78	28 21.5	-24.5	11.9	29 20.2	-24.3	12.0	30 18.8	-24.0	12.2	31 17.5	-23.8	12.3
79	27 57.0	-24.9	10.9	28 55.9	-24.7	11.0	29 54.8	-24.5	11.1	30 53.7	-24.3	11.2
80	27 32.1	-25.4	9.9	28 31.2	-25.2	10.0	29 30.3	-25.0	10.0	30 29.4	-24.9	10.2
81	27 06.7	-25.8	8.8	28 06.0	-25.6	8.9	29 05.3	-25.5	9.0	30 04.5	-25.3	9.1
82	26 40.9	-26.2	7.8	27 40.4	-26.1	7.9	28 39.8	-26.0	8.0	29 39.2	-25.8	8.1
83	26 14.7	-26.7	6.8	27 14.3	-26.6	6.9	28 13.8	-26.4	6.9	29 13.4	-26.3	7.0
84	25 48.0	-27.0	5.8	26 47.7	-26.9	5.9	27 47.4	-26.9	5.9	28 47.1	-26.8	6.0
85	25 21.0	-27.5	4.8	26 20.8	-27.4	4.9	27 20.5	-27.3	4.9	28 20.3	-27.2	5.0
86	24 53.5	-27.8	3.9	25 53.4	-27.8	3.9	26 53.2	-27.7	3.9	27 53.1	-27.6	4.0
87	24 25.7	-28.2	2.9	25 25.6	-28.2	2.9	26 25.5	-28.1	2.9	27 25.5	-28.1	3.0
88	23 57.5	-28.6	1.9	24 57.4	-28.5	1.9	25 57.4	-28.5	1.9	26 57.4	-28.5	2.0
89	23 28.9	-28.9	1.0	24 28.9	-28.9	1.0	25 28.9	-28.9	1.0	26 28.9	-28.9	1.0
90	23 00.0	-29.3	0.0	24 00.0	-29.3	0.0	25 00.0	-29.3	0.0	26 00.0	-29.3	0.0
	23°			24°			25°			26°		

27° Hc	27° d	27° Z	28° Hc	28° d	28° Z	29° Hc	29° d	29° Z	30° Hc	30° d	30° Z	Dec.
° ′	′	°	° ′	′	°	° ′	′	°	° ′	′	°	°
25 35.6	+30.0	104.1	25 20.7	+31.0	104.6	25 05.3	+32.0	105.0	24 49.5	+32.9	105.5	0
26 05.6	+29.6	103.2	25 51.7	+30.6	103.6	25 37.3	+31.6	104.1	25 22.4	+32.6	104.6	1
26 35.2	+29.2	102.2	26 22.3	+30.2	102.7	26 08.9	+31.2	103.2	25 55.0	+32.1	103.6	2
27 04.4	+28.8	101.2	26 52.5	+29.8	101.7	26 40.1	+30.8	102.2	26 27.1	+31.8	102.7	3
27 33.2	+28.4	100.2	27 22.3	+29.4	100.7	27 10.9	+30.4	101.2	26 58.9	+31.4	101.7	4
28 01.6	+28.0	99.2	27 51.7	+29.0	99.8	27 41.3	+30.0	100.3	27 30.3	+31.1	100.8	5
28 29.6	+27.5	98.2	28 20.7	+28.6	98.8	28 11.3	+29.6	99.3	28 01.4	+30.6	99.8	6
28 57.1	+27.1	97.2	28 49.3	+28.1	97.8	28 40.9	+29.2	98.3	28 32.0	+30.2	98.8	7
29 24.2	+26.6	96.2	29 17.4	+27.7	96.7	29 10.1	+28.7	97.3	29 02.2	+29.7	97.9	8
29 50.8	+26.1	95.2	29 45.1	+27.1	95.7	29 38.8	+28.2	96.3	29 31.9	+29.3	96.9	9
30 16.9	+25.6	94.1	30 12.2	+26.7	94.7	30 07.0	+27.8	95.3	30 01.2	+28.8	95.9	10
30 42.5	+25.0	93.1	30 38.9	+26.2	93.7	30 34.8	+27.3	94.3	30 30.0	+28.4	94.8	11
31 07.5	+24.6	92.0	31 05.1	+25.7	92.6	31 02.1	+26.8	93.2	30 58.4	+27.9	93.8	12
31 32.1	+24.0	90.9	31 30.8	+25.2	91.6	31 28.9	+26.2	92.2	31 26.3	+27.3	92.8	13
31 56.1	+23.5	89.9	31 56.0	+24.6	90.5	31 55.1	+25.8	91.1	31 53.6	+26.9	91.7	14
32 19.6	+22.9	88.8	32 20.6	+24.0	89.4	32 20.9	+25.1	90.0	32 20.5	+26.3	90.7	15
32 42.5	+22.4	87.7	32 44.6	+23.5	88.3	32 46.0	+24.7	89.0	32 46.8	+25.8	89.6	16
33 04.9	+21.7	86.6	33 08.1	+22.9	87.2	33 10.7	+24.0	87.9	33 12.6	+25.2	88.5	17
33 26.6	+21.2	85.5	33 31.0	+22.3	86.1	33 34.7	+23.5	86.8	33 37.8	+24.6	87.4	18
33 47.8	+20.5	84.3	33 53.3	+21.7	85.0	33 58.2	+22.9	85.7	34 02.4	+24.0	86.4	19
34 08.3	+19.9	83.2	34 15.0	+21.1	83.9	34 21.1	+22.2	84.6	34 26.4	+23.4	85.2	20
34 28.2	+19.2	82.1	34 36.1	+20.5	82.7	34 43.3	+21.7	83.4	34 49.8	+22.9	84.1	21
34 47.4	+18.7	80.9	34 56.6	+19.8	81.6	35 05.0	+21.0	82.3	35 12.7	+22.1	83.0	22
35 06.1	+17.9	79.8	35 16.4	+19.1	80.4	35 26.0	+20.3	81.1	35 34.8	+21.6	81.9	23
35 24.0	+17.2	78.6	35 35.5	+18.5	79.3	35 46.3	+19.7	80.0	35 56.4	+20.8	80.7	24
35 41.2	+16.6	77.4	35 54.0	+17.7	78.1	36 06.0	+18.9	78.8	36 17.2	+20.2	79.5	25
35 57.8	+15.9	76.2	36 11.7	+17.1	76.9	36 24.9	+18.3	77.6	36 37.4	+19.5	78.4	26
36 13.7	+15.1	75.0	36 28.8	+16.3	75.7	36 43.2	+17.6	76.5	36 56.9	+18.8	77.2	27
36 28.8	+14.4	73.8	36 45.1	+15.7	74.5	37 00.8	+16.8	75.3	37 15.7	+18.0	76.0	28
36 43.2	+13.7	72.6	37 00.8	+14.9	73.3	37 17.6	+16.1	74.1	37 33.7	+17.3	74.8	29
36 56.9	+12.9	71.4	37 15.7	+14.1	72.1	37 33.7	+15.4	72.8	37 51.0	+16.6	73.6	30
37 09.8	+12.2	70.2	37 29.8	+13.4	70.9	37 49.1	+14.6	71.6	38 07.6	+15.8	72.4	31
37 22.0	+11.4	68.9	37 43.2	+12.6	69.7	38 03.7	+13.8	70.4	38 23.4	+15.1	71.1	32
37 33.4	+10.6	67.7	37 55.8	+11.8	68.4	38 17.5	+13.0	69.2	38 38.5	+14.2	69.9	33
37 44.0	+9.8	66.5	38 07.6	+11.0	67.2	38 30.5	+12.3	67.9	38 52.7	+13.5	68.7	34
37 53.8	+9.1	65.2	38 18.6	+10.3	65.9	38 42.8	+11.4	66.7	39 06.2	+12.6	67.4	35
38 02.9	+8.2	64.0	38 28.9	+9.4	64.7	38 54.2	+10.6	65.4	39 18.8	+11.8	66.1	36
38 11.1	+7.4	62.7	38 38.3	+8.6	63.4	39 04.8	+9.8	64.1	39 30.6	+11.0	64.9	37
38 18.5	+6.6	61.4	38 46.9	+7.8	62.1	39 14.6	+8.9	62.9	39 41.6	+10.2	63.6	38
38 25.1	+5.8	60.2	38 54.7	+6.9	60.9	39 23.5	+8.2	61.6	39 51.8	+9.3	62.3	39
38 30.9	+5.0	58.9	39 01.6	+6.1	59.6	39 31.7	+7.2	60.3	40 01.1	+8.4	61.0	40
38 35.9	+4.1	57.6	39 07.7	+5.3	58.3	39 38.9	+6.4	59.0	40 09.5	+7.6	59.7	41
38 40.0	+3.3	56.4	39 13.0	+4.4	57.0	39 45.3	+5.6	57.7	40 17.1	+6.6	58.4	42
38 43.3	+2.5	55.1	39 17.4	+3.5	55.7	39 50.9	+4.6	56.4	40 23.7	+5.9	57.1	43
38 45.8	+1.6	53.8	39 20.9	+2.7	54.4	39 55.5	+3.8	55.1	40 29.6	+4.9	55.8	44
38 47.4	+0.8	52.5	39 23.6	+1.9	53.2	39 59.3	+3.0	53.8	40 34.5	+4.0	54.5	45
38 48.2	-0.1	51.2	39 25.5	+1.0	51.9	40 02.3	+2.0	52.5	40 38.5	+3.1	53.2	46
38 48.1	-0.9	49.9	39 26.5	+0.1	50.6	40 04.3	+1.2	51.2	40 41.6	+2.3	51.9	47
38 47.2	-1.7	48.7	39 26.6	-0.7	49.3	40 05.5	+0.3	49.9	40 43.9	+1.3	50.6	48
38 45.5	-2.6	47.4	39 25.9	-1.6	48.0	40 05.8	-0.6	48.6	40 45.2	+0.4	49.2	49
38 42.9	-3.5	46.1	39 24.3	-2.5	46.7	40 05.2	-1.5	47.3	40 45.6	-0.4	47.9	50
38 39.4	-4.2	44.8	39 21.8	-3.3	45.4	40 03.7	-2.3	46.0	40 45.2	-1.4	46.6	51
38 35.2	-5.1	43.5	39 18.5	-4.2	44.1	40 01.4	-3.3	44.7	40 43.8	-2.3	45.3	52
38 30.1	-5.9	42.3	39 14.3	-5.0	42.8	39 58.1	-4.1	43.4	40 41.5	-3.1	44.0	53
38 24.2	-6.7	41.0	39 09.3	-5.9	41.5	39 54.0	-5.0	42.1	40 38.4	-4.1	42.6	54
38 17.5	-7.6	39.7	39 03.4	-6.7	40.2	39 49.0	-5.8	40.8	40 34.3	-5.0	41.3	55
38 09.9	-8.4	38.5	38 56.7	-7.5	39.0	39 43.2	-6.7	39.5	40 29.3	-5.8	40.0	56
38 01.5	-9.1	37.2	38 49.2	-8.4	37.7	39 36.5	-7.6	38.2	40 23.5	-6.7	38.7	57
37 52.4	-10.0	36.0	38 40.8	-9.2	36.4	39 28.9	-8.4	36.9	40 16.8	-7.6	37.4	58
37 42.4	-10.7	34.7	38 31.6	-10.0	35.2	39 20.5	-9.2	35.6	40 09.2	-8.5	36.1	59
37 31.7	-11.5	33.5	38 21.6	-10.8	33.9	39 11.3	-10.1	34.3	40 00.7	-9.3	34.8	60
37 20.2	-12.3	32.2	38 10.8	-11.6	32.6	39 01.2	-10.9	33.1	39 51.4	-10.2	33.5	61
37 07.9	-13.0	31.0	37 59.2	-12.4	31.4	38 50.3	-11.7	31.8	39 41.2	-11.0	32.2	62
36 54.9	-13.8	29.8	37 46.8	-13.1	30.2	38 38.6	-12.5	30.6	39 30.2	-11.9	31.0	63
36 41.1	-14.6	28.6	37 33.7	-14.0	28.9	38 26.1	-13.3	29.3	39 18.3	-12.7	29.7	64
36 26.5	-15.2	27.4	37 19.7	-14.6	27.7	38 12.8	-14.1	28.1	39 05.6	-13.5	28.4	65
36 11.3	-16.0	26.2	37 05.1	-15.5	26.5	37 58.7	-14.9	26.8	38 52.1	-14.2	27.2	66
35 55.3	-16.6	25.0	36 49.6	-16.1	25.3	37 43.8	-15.6	25.6	38 37.9	-15.1	25.9	67
35 38.7	-17.4	23.8	36 33.5	-16.9	24.1	37 28.2	-16.3	24.4	38 22.8	-15.8	24.7	68
35 21.3	-18.0	22.6	36 16.6	-17.5	22.9	37 11.9	-17.1	23.2	38 07.0	-16.7	23.5	69
35 03.3	-18.7	21.4	35 59.1	-18.3	21.7	36 54.8	-17.9	22.0	37 50.3	-17.3	22.3	70
34 44.6	-19.4	20.3	35 40.8	-18.9	20.5	36 36.9	-18.5	20.8	37 33.0	-18.1	21.0	71
34 25.2	-20.0	19.1	35 21.9	-19.7	19.4	36 18.4	-19.2	19.6	37 14.9	-18.8	19.8	72
34 05.2	-20.6	18.0	35 02.2	-20.2	18.2	35 59.2	-19.9	18.4	36 56.1	-19.5	18.7	73
33 44.6	-21.3	16.9	34 42.0	-20.9	17.1	35 39.3	-20.6	17.3	36 36.6	-20.2	17.5	74
33 23.3	-21.8	15.7	34 21.1	-21.6	15.9	35 18.7	-21.2	16.1	36 16.4	-20.9	16.3	75
33 01.5	-22.4	14.6	33 59.5	-22.1	14.8	34 57.5	-21.8	15.0	35 55.5	-21.6	15.1	76
32 39.1	-23.0	13.5	33 37.4	-22.7	13.7	34 35.7	-22.5	13.8	35 33.9	-22.2	14.0	77
32 16.1	-23.6	12.4	33 14.7	-23.4	12.6	34 13.2	-23.1	12.7	35 11.7	-22.8	12.9	78
31 52.5	-24.1	11.3	32 51.3	-23.9	11.5	33 50.1	-23.7	11.6	34 48.9	-23.5	11.7	79
31 28.4	-24.6	10.3	32 27.4	-24.4	10.4	33 26.4	-24.2	10.5	34 25.4	-24.0	10.6	80
31 03.8	-25.2	9.2	32 03.0	-25.0	9.3	33 02.2	-24.8	9.4	34 01.4	-24.7	9.5	81
30 38.6	-25.7	8.1	31 38.0	-25.5	8.2	32 37.4	-25.4	8.3	33 36.7	-25.2	8.4	82
30 12.9	-26.2	7.1	31 12.5	-26.1	7.2	32 12.0	-25.9	7.2	33 11.5	-25.8	7.3	83
29 46.7	-26.6	6.0	30 46.4	-26.5	6.1	31 46.1	-26.5	6.2	32 45.7	-26.3	6.2	84
29 20.1	-27.1	5.0	30 19.9	-27.1	5.1	31 19.6	-26.9	5.1	32 19.4	-26.9	5.2	85
28 53.0	-27.6	4.0	29 52.8	-27.5	4.0	30 52.7	-27.5	4.1	31 52.5	-27.4	4.1	86
28 25.4	-28.1	3.0	29 25.3	-28.0	3.0	30 25.2	-27.9	3.0	31 25.1	-27.9	3.1	87
27 57.3	-28.4	2.0	28 57.3	-28.4	2.0	29 57.3	-28.4	2.0	30 57.2	-28.3	2.0	88
27 28.9	-28.9	1.0	28 28.9	-28.9	1.0	29 28.9	-28.9	1.0	30 28.9	-28.9	1.0	89
27 00.0	-29.3	0.0	28 00.0	-29.3	0.0	29 00.0	-29.3	0.0	30 00.0	-29.3	0.0	90
27°			28°			29°			30°			

LATITUDE CONTRARY NAME TO DECLINATION L.H.A. 61°, 299°

Dec.	23° Hc	d	Z	24° Hc	d	Z	25° Hc	d	Z	26° Hc	d	Z	27° Hc	d	Z	28° Hc	d	Z	29° Hc	d	Z	30° Hc	d	Z	Dec.
°	° ′	′	°	° ′	′	°	° ′	′	°	° ′	′	°	° ′	′	°	° ′	′	°	° ′	′	°	° ′	′	°	°
0	26 30.3	-26.4	102.2	26 17.3	-27.4	102.7	26 03.9	-28.4	103.2	25 50.0	-29.5	103.7	25 35.6	-30.4	104.1	25 20.7	-31.4	104.6	25 05.3	-32.3	105.0	24 49.5	-33.2	105.5	0
1	26 03.9	-26.8	103.2	25 49.9	-27.8	103.7	25 35.5	-28.9	104.2	25 20.5	-29.7	104.6	25 05.2	-30.8	105.1	24 49.3	-31.7	105.5	24 33.0	-32.6	106.0	24 16.3	-33.5	106.4	1
2	25 37.1	-27.3	104.2	25 22.1	-28.2	104.7	25 06.6	-29.1	105.1	24 50.8	-30.2	105.6	24 34.4	-31.1	106.0	24 17.6	-32.0	106.5	24 00.4	-32.9	106.9	23 42.8	-33.9	107.3	2
3	25 09.8	-27.6	105.2	24 53.9	-28.6	105.7	24 37.5	-29.6	106.1	24 20.6	-30.5	106.5	24 03.3	-31.4	107.0	23 45.6	-32.4	107.4	23 27.5	-33.3	107.8	23 08.9	-34.2	108.2	3
4	24 42.2	-28.0	106.2	24 25.3	-29.0	106.6	24 07.9	-29.9	107.1	23 50.1	-30.9	107.5	23 31.9	-31.8	107.9	23 13.2	-32.7	108.3	22 54.2	-33.6	108.7	22 34.7	-34.4	109.1	4
5	24 14.2	-28.3	107.2	23 56.3	-29.3	107.6	23 38.0	-30.3	108.0	23 19.2	-31.1	108.4	23 00.1	-32.1	108.8	22 40.5	-32.9	109.2	22 20.6	-33.9	109.6	22 00.3	-34.8	110.0	5
6	23 45.9	-28.7	108.1	23 27.0	-29.6	108.5	23 07.7	-30.5	108.9	22 48.1	-31.5	109.3	22 28.0	-32.4	109.7	22 07.6	-33.3	110.1	21 46.7	-34.1	110.5	21 25.5	-35.0	110.9	6
7	23 17.2	-29.1	109.1	22 57.4	-30.0	109.5	22 37.2	-30.9	109.9	22 16.6	-31.8	110.3	21 55.6	-32.7	110.6	21 34.3	-33.6	111.0	21 12.6	-34.5	111.4	20 50.5	-35.3	111.7	7
8	22 48.1	-29.4	110.0	22 27.4	-30.3	110.4	22 06.3	-31.3	110.8	21 44.8	-32.1	111.2	21 22.9	-33.0	111.5	21 00.7	-33.8	111.9	20 38.1	-34.7	112.3	20 15.2	-35.5	112.6	8
9	22 18.7	-29.7	111.0	21 57.1	-30.7	111.4	21 35.0	-31.5	111.7	21 12.7	-32.4	112.1	20 49.9	-33.2	112.4	20 26.9	-34.2	112.8	20 03.4	-34.9	113.1	19 39.7	-35.7	113.5	9
10	21 49.0	-30.0	111.9	21 26.4	-30.9	112.3	21 03.5	-31.8	112.6	20 40.3	-32.7	113.0	20 16.7	-33.6	113.3	19 52.7	-34.3	113.7	19 28.5	-35.2	114.0	19 04.0	-36.1	114.3	10
11	21 19.0	-30.4	112.8	20 55.5	-31.2	113.2	20 31.7	-32.1	113.5	20 07.6	-33.0	113.9	19 43.1	-33.7	114.2	19 18.4	-34.6	114.5	18 53.3	-35.4	114.8	18 27.9	-36.2	115.2	11
12	20 48.6	-30.6	113.8	20 24.3	-31.5	114.1	19 59.6	-32.3	114.4	19 34.6	-33.2	114.8	19 09.4	-34.1	115.1	18 43.8	-34.9	115.4	18 17.9	-35.7	115.7	17 51.7	-36.4	116.0	12
13	20 18.0	-30.9	114.7	19 52.8	-31.8	115.0	19 27.3	-32.7	115.3	19 01.4	-33.4	115.7	18 35.3	-34.3	116.0	18 08.9	-35.1	116.3	17 42.2	-35.8	116.5	17 15.3	-36.7	116.8	13
14	19 47.1	-31.2	115.6	19 21.0	-32.0	115.9	18 54.6	-32.8	116.2	18 28.0	-33.7	116.5	18 01.0	-34.5	116.8	17 33.8	-35.3	117.1	17 06.4	-36.1	117.4	16 38.6	-36.8	117.7	14
15	19 15.9	-31.5	116.5	18 49.0	-32.3	116.8	18 21.8	-33.1	117.1	17 54.3	-33.9	117.4	17 26.5	-34.7	117.7	16 58.5	-35.5	118.0	16 30.3	-36.3	118.2	16 01.8	-37.0	118.5	15
16	18 44.4	-31.7	117.4	18 16.7	-32.6	117.7	17 48.7	-33.4	118.0	17 20.4	-34.2	118.3	16 51.8	-34.9	118.5	16 23.0	-35.7	118.8	15 54.0	-36.4	119.1	15 24.8	-37.2	119.3	16
17	18 12.7	-32.0	118.3	17 44.1	-32.7	118.6	17 15.3	-33.6	118.9	16 46.2	-34.3	119.1	16 16.9	-35.1	119.4	15 47.3	-35.8	119.6	15 17.6	-36.7	119.9	14 47.6	-37.4	120.1	17
18	17 40.7	-32.2	119.2	17 11.4	-33.0	119.5	16 41.7	-33.8	119.7	16 11.9	-34.6	120.0	15 41.8	-35.4	120.2	15 11.5	-36.1	120.5	14 40.9	-36.8	120.7	14 10.2	-37.5	120.9	18
19	17 08.5	-32.4	120.1	16 38.4	-33.3	120.3	16 07.9	-34.0	120.6	15 37.3	-34.8	120.8	15 06.4	-35.5	121.1	14 35.4	-36.3	121.3	14 04.1	-37.0	121.5	13 32.7	-37.7	121.7	19
20	16 36.1	-32.6	120.9	16 05.1	-33.4	121.2	15 33.9	-34.1	121.4	15 02.5	-34.9	121.7	14 30.9	-35.6	121.9	13 59.1	-36.4	122.1	13 27.1	-37.1	122.3	12 55.0	-37.9	122.5	20
21	16 03.5	-32.9	121.8	15 31.7	-33.6	122.1	14 59.8	-34.4	122.3	14 27.6	-35.1	122.5	13 55.3	-35.9	122.7	13 22.7	-36.5	122.9	12 50.0	-37.3	123.1	12 17.1	-37.9	123.3	21
22	15 30.6	-33.1	122.7	14 58.1	-33.8	122.9	14 25.4	-34.6	123.1	13 52.5	-35.3	123.4	13 19.4	-36.0	123.6	12 46.2	-36.8	123.7	12 12.7	-37.4	123.9	11 39.2	-38.1	124.1	22
23	14 57.5	-33.2	123.6	14 24.3	-34.0	123.8	13 50.8	-34.7	124.0	13 17.2	-35.5	124.2	12 43.4	-36.2	124.4	12 09.4	-36.8	124.6	11 35.3	-37.5	124.7	11 01.1	-38.2	124.9	23
24	14 24.3	-33.5	124.4	13 50.3	-34.2	124.6	13 16.1	-34.9	124.8	12 41.7	-35.6	125.0	12 07.2	-36.3	125.2	11 32.6	-37.0	125.4	10 57.8	-37.7	125.5	10 22.9	-38.4	125.7	24
25	13 50.8	-33.6	125.3	13 16.1	-34.4	125.5	12 41.2	-35.1	125.7	12 06.1	-35.7	125.8	11 30.9	-36.4	126.0	10 55.6	-37.1	126.2	10 20.1	-37.8	126.3	9 44.5	-38.4	126.5	25
26	13 17.2	-33.8	126.1	12 41.7	-34.5	126.3	12 06.1	-35.2	126.5	11 30.4	-35.9	126.7	10 54.5	-36.6	126.8	10 18.5	-37.3	127.0	9 42.3	-37.9	127.1	9 06.1	-38.6	127.2	26
27	12 43.4	-34.0	127.0	12 07.2	-34.6	127.1	11 30.9	-35.3	127.3	10 54.5	-36.0	127.5	10 17.9	-36.7	127.6	9 41.2	-37.3	127.8	9 04.4	-38.0	127.9	8 27.5	-38.6	128.0	27
28	12 09.4	-34.1	127.8	11 32.6	-34.8	128.0	10 55.6	-35.5	128.1	10 18.5	-36.2	128.3	9 41.2	-36.8	128.4	9 03.9	-37.5	128.6	8 26.4	-38.0	128.7	7 48.9	-38.7	128.8	28
29	11 35.3	-34.2	128.7	10 57.8	-34.9	128.8	10 20.1	-35.6	129.0	9 42.3	-36.2	129.1	9 04.4	-36.9	129.2	8 26.4	-37.5	129.3	7 48.4	-38.2	129.5	7 10.2	-38.8	129.6	29
30	11 01.1	-34.4	129.5	10 22.9	-35.1	129.6	9 44.5	-35.7	129.8	9 06.1	-36.4	129.9	8 27.5	-37.0	130.0	7 48.9	-37.6	130.1	7 10.2	-38.3	130.2	6 31.4	-38.9	130.3	30
31	10 26.7	-34.5	130.3	9 47.8	-35.2	130.5	9 08.8	-35.8	130.6	8 29.7	-36.4	130.7	7 50.5	-37.0	130.8	7 11.3	-37.7	130.9	6 31.9	-38.3	131.0	5 52.5	-38.9	131.1	31
32	9 52.2	-34.7	131.2	9 12.6	-35.3	131.3	8 33.0	-35.9	131.4	7 53.3	-36.6	131.5	7 13.5	-37.2	131.6	6 33.6	-37.8	131.7	5 53.6	-38.4	131.8	5 13.6	-39.0	131.9	32
33	9 17.5	-34.7	132.0	8 37.3	-35.4	132.1	7 57.1	-36.1	132.2	7 16.7	-36.6	132.3	6 36.3	-37.3	132.4	5 55.8	-37.9	132.5	5 15.2	-38.4	132.6	4 34.6	-39.0	132.6	33
34	8 42.8	-34.9	132.8	8 01.9	-35.4	132.9	7 21.0	-36.1	133.0	6 40.1	-36.7	133.1	5 59.0	-37.3	133.2	5 17.9	-37.9	133.3	4 36.8	-38.5	133.3	3 55.6	-39.1	133.4	34
35	8 07.9	-35.0	133.6	7 26.5	-35.6	133.7	6 44.9	-36.1	133.8	6 03.4	-36.8	133.9	5 21.7	-37.3	134.0	4 40.0	-37.9	134.0	3 58.3	-38.5	134.1	3 16.5	-39.1	134.1	35
36	7 32.9	-35.0	134.5	6 50.9	-35.7	134.5	6 08.8	-36.3	134.6	5 26.6	-36.9	134.7	4 44.4	-37.5	134.8	4 02.1	-38.0	134.8	3 19.8	-38.6	134.9	2 37.4	-39.1	134.9	36
37	6 57.9	-35.2	135.3	6 15.2	-35.7	135.4	5 32.5	-36.3	135.4	4 49.7	-36.9	135.5	4 06.9	-37.4	135.5	3 24.1	-38.1	135.6	2 41.2	-38.6	135.6	1 58.3	-39.2	135.7	37
38	6 22.7	-35.2	136.1	5 39.5	-35.8	136.2	4 56.2	-36.4	136.2	4 12.8	-36.9	136.3	3 29.5	-37.6	136.3	2 46.0	-38.0	136.4	2 02.6	-38.6	136.4	1 19.1	-39.1	136.4	38
39	5 47.5	-35.2	136.9	5 03.7	-35.9	137.0	4 19.8	-36.4	137.0	3 35.9	-37.0	137.1	2 51.9	-37.5	137.1	2 08.0	-38.1	137.1	1 24.0	-38.6	137.2	0 40.0	-39.2	137.2	39
40	5 12.3	-35.4	137.7	4 27.8	-35.9	137.8	3 43.4	-36.5	137.8	2 58.9	-37.0	137.9	2 14.4	-37.6	137.9	1 29.9	-38.1	137.9	0 45.4	-38.7	137.9	0 00.8	-39.2	137.9	40
41	4 36.9	-35.4	138.5	3 51.9	-35.9	138.6	3 06.9	-36.5	138.6	2 21.9	-37.1	138.7	1 36.8	-37.5	138.7	0 51.8	-38.1	138.7	0 06.7	-38.6	138.7	0 38.4	+39.1	41.3	41
42	4 01.5	-35.4	139.3	3 16.0	-36.0	139.4	2 30.4	-36.5	139.4	1 44.8	-37.0	139.4	0 59.3	-37.6	139.5	0 13.7	-38.2	139.5	0 31.9	+38.7	40.5	1 17.5	+39.2	40.6	42
43	3 26.1	-35.5	140.1	2 40.0	-36.0	140.2	1 53.9	-36.6	140.2	1 07.8	-37.1	140.2	0 21.7	-37.6	140.2	0 24.5	+38.1	39.8	1 10.6	+38.6	39.8	1 56.7	+39.1	39.8	43
44	2 50.6	-35.6	141.0	2 04.0	-36.1	141.0	1 17.3	-36.5	141.0	0 30.7	-37.1	141.0	0 15.9	+37.6	39.0	1 02.6	+38.1	39.0	1 49.2	+38.6	39.0	2 35.8	+39.1	39.0	44
45	2 15.0	-35.5	141.8	1 27.9	-36.1	141.8	0 40.8	-36.6	141.8	0 06.4	+37.1	38.2	0 53.5	+37.6	38.2	1 40.7	+38.1	38.2	2 27.8	+38.6	38.2	3 14.9	+39.1	38.3	45
46	1 39.5	-35.6	142.6	0 51.8	-36.0	142.6	0 04.2	-36.6	142.6	0 43.5	+37.0	37.4	1 31.1	+37.6	37.4	2 18.8	+38.0	37.4	3 06.4	+38.5	37.5	3 54.0	+39.0	37.5	46
47	1 03.9	-35.6	143.4	0 15.8	-36.1	143.4	0 32.4	+36.6	36.6	1 20.5	+37.1	36.6	2 08.7	+37.5	36.6	2 56.8	+38.0	36.7	3 44.9	+38.5	36.7	4 33.0	+39.0	36.8	47
48	0 28.3	-35.6	144.2	0 20.3	+36.1	35.8	1 09.0	+36.5	35.8	1 57.6	+37.0	35.8	2 46.2	+37.6	35.9	3 34.8	+38.0	35.9	4 23.4	+38.5	35.9	5 12.0	+38.9	36.0	48
49	0 07.3	+35.5	35.0	0 56.4	+36.1	35.0	1 45.5	+36.6	35.0	2 34.6	+37.1	35.1	3 23.8	+37.4	35.1	4 12.8	+38.0	35.1	5 01.9	+38.4	35.2	5 50.9	+38.9	35.2	49
50	0 42.8	+35.6	34.2	1 32.5	+36.0	34.2	2 22.1	+36.5	34.2	3 11.7	+36.9	34.3	4 01.2	+37.5	34.3	4 50.8	+37.9	34.3	5 40.3	+38.3	34.4	6 29.8	+38.8	34.5	50
51	1 18.4	+35.6	33.4	2 08.5	+36.0	33.4	2 58.6	+36.4	33.4	3 48.6	+37.0	33.5	4 38.7	+37.3	33.5	5 28.7	+37.8	33.6	6 18.6	+38.3	33.6	7 08.6	+38.7	33.7	51
52	1 54.0	+35.5	32.6	2 44.5	+36.0	32.6	3 35.0	+36.5	32.7	4 25.6	+36.8	32.7	5 16.0	+37.4	32.7	6 06.5	+37.8	32.8	6 56.9	+38.2	32.9	7 47.3	+38.6	32.9	52
53	2 29.5	+35.5	31.8	3 20.5	+36.0	31.8	4 11.5	+36.4	31.9	5 02.4	+36.9	31.9	5 53.4	+37.2	31.9	6 44.3	+37.6	32.0	7 35.1	+38.1	32.1	8 25.9	+38.6	32.1	53
54	3 05.0	+35.5	31.0	3 56.5	+35.9	31.0	4 47.9	+36.3	31.1	5 39.3	+36.7	31.1	6 30.6	+37.2	31.2	7 21.9	+37.6	31.2	8 13.2	+38.1	31.3	9 04.5	+38.4	31.4	54
55	3 40.5	+35.4	30.2	4 32.4	+35.8	30.2	5 24.2	+36.3	30.3	6 16.0	+36.7	30.3	7 07.8	+37.1	30.4	7 59.5	+37.6	30.4	8 51.3	+37.9	30.5	9 42.9	+38.4	30.6	55
56	4 15.9	+35.4	29.4	5 08.2	+35.8	29.4	6 00.5	+36.2	29.5	6 52.7	+36.6	29.5	7 44.9	+37.0	29.6	8 37.1	+37.4	29.6	9 29.2	+37.8	29.7	10 21.3	+38.2	29.8	56
57	4 51.3	+35.3	28.6	5 44.0	+35.7	28.6	6 36.7	+36.1	28.7	7 29.3	+36.5	28.7	8 21.9	+36.9	28.8	9 14.5	+37.3	28.9	10 07.0	+37.7	28.9	10 59.5	+38.1	29.0	57
58	5 26.6	+35.3	27.7	6 19.7	+35.7	27.8	7 12.8	+36.0	27.9	8 05.8	+36.4	27.9	8 58.8	+36.8	28.0	9 51.8	+37.2	28.1	10 44.7	+37.6	28.1	11 37.6	+38.0	28.2	58
59	6 01.9	+35.2	26.9	6 55.4	+35.5	27.0	7 48.8	+36.0	27.0	8 42.2	+36.4	27.1	9 35.6	+36.7	27.2	10 29.0	+37.1	27.3	11 22.3	+37.5	27.4	12 15.6	+37.8	27.5	59
60	6 37.1	+35.1	26.1	7 30.9	+35.5	26.2	8 24.8	+35.8	26.2	9 18.6	+36.2	26.3	10 12.3	+36.6	26.4	11 06.1	+36.9	26.5	11 59.8	+37.3	26.6	12 53.4	+37.7	26.7	60
61	7 12.2	+35.0	25.3	8 06.4	+35.4	25.4	9 00.6	+35.8	25.4	9 54.8	+36.1	25.5	10 48.9	+36.5	25.6	11 43.0	+36.8	25.7	12 37.1	+37.2	25.8	13 31.1	+37.6	25.9	61
62	7 47.2	+34.9	24.5	8 41.8	+35.3	24.5	9 36.4	+35.6	24.6	10 30.9	+36.0	24.7	11 25.4	+36.3	24.8	12 19.8	+36.7	24.9	13 14.3	+37.0	24.9	14 08.7	+37.3	25.1	62
63	8 22.1	+34.8	23.7	9 17.1	+35.1	23.7	10 12.0	+35.5	23.8	11 06.9	+35.8	23.9	12 01.7	+36.2	24.0	12 56.5	+36.6	24.0	13 51.3	+36.9	24.1	14 46.0	+37.2	24.2	63
64	8 56.9	+34.8	22.8	9 52.2	+35.1	22.9	10 47.5	+35.3	23.0	11 42.7	+35.7	23.1	12 37.9	+36.0	23.1	13 33.1	+36.3	23.2	14 28.2	+36.7	23.3	15 23.2	+37.1	23.4	64
65	9 31.7	+34.5	22.0	10 27.3	+34.9	22.1	11 22.8	+35.3	22.2	12 18.4	+35.6	22.2	13 13.9	+35.9	22.3	14 09.4	+36.2	22.4	15 04.9	+36.5	22.5	16 00.3	+36.8	22.6	65
66	10 06.2	+34.5	21.2	11 02.2	+34.8	21.3	11 58.1	+35.1	21.3	12 54.0	+35.4	21.4	13 49.8	+35.7	21.5	14 45.6	+36.0	21.6	15 41.4	+36.3	21.7	16 37.1	+36.7	21.8	66
67	10 40.7	+34.3	20.4	11 37.0	+34.6	20.4	12 33.2	+34.9	20.5	13 29.4	+35.2	20.6	14 25.5	+35.6	20.7	15 21.6	+35.9	20.8	16 17.7	+36.2	20.9	17 13.8	+36.4	21.0	67
68	11 15.0	+34.2	19.5	12 11.6	+34.5	19.6	13 08.1	+34.8	19.7	14 04.6	+35.1	19.7	15 01.1	+35.3	19.8	15 57.5	+35.6	19.9	16 53.9	+35.9	20.0	17 50.2	+36.3	20.1	68
69	11 49.2	+34.1	18.7	12 46.1	+34.3	18.7	13 42.9	+34.6	18.8	14 39.7	+34.8	18.9	15 36.4	+35.2	19.0	16 33.1	+35.5	19.1	17 29.8	+35.7	19.2	18 26.5	+36.0	19.3	69
70	12 23.3	+33.9	17.8	13 20.4	+34.2	17.9	14 17.5	+34.4	18.0	15 14.5	+34.7	18.1	16 11.6	+34.9	18.1	17 08.6	+35.2	18.2	18 05.5	+35.5	18.3	19 02.5	+35.7	18.4	70
71	12 57.2	+33.7	17.0	13 54.6	+33.9	17.1	14 51.9	+34.2	17.1	15 49.2	+34.5	17.2	16 46.5	+34.8	17.3	17 43.8	+35.0	17.4	18 41.0	+35.3	17.5	19 38.2	+35.6	17.6	71
72	13 30.9	+33.6	16.1	14 28.5	+33.8	16.2	15 26.1	+34.1	16.3	16 23.7	+34.3	16.4	17 21.3	+34.5	16.4	18 18.8	+34.8	16.5	19 16.3	+35.0	16.6	20 13.8	+35.3	16.7	72
73	14 04.5	+33.3	15.3	15 02.3	+33.6	15.4	16 00.2	+33.8	15.4	16 58.0	+34.1	15.5	17 55.8	+34.3	15.6	18 53.6	+34.5	15.7	19 51.3	+34.8	15.8	20 49.1	+35.0	15.9	73
74	14 37.8	+33.2	14.4	15 35.9	+33.4	14.5	16 34.0	+33.6	14.6	17 32.1	+33.8	14.6	18 30.1	+34.1	14.7	19 28.1	+34.3	14.8	20 26.1	+34.6	14.9	21 24.1	+34.7	15.0	74
75	15 11.0	+33.0	13.6	16 09.3	+33.2	13.6	17 07.6	+33.4	13.7	18 05.9	+33.6	13.8	19 04.2	+33.8	13.9	20 02.4	+34.1	13.9	21 00.7	+34.2	14.0	21 58.8	+34.5	14.1	75
76	15 44.0	+32.8	12.7	16 42.5	+33.0	12.8	17 41.0	+33.2	12.8	18 39.5	+33.4	12.9	19 38.0	+33.6	13.0	20 36.5	+33.7	13.1	21 34.9	+34.0	13.2	22 33.3	+34.2	13.2	76
77	16 16.8	+32.6	11.8	17 15.5	+32.8	11.9	18 14.2	+32.9	12.0	19 12.9	+33.1	12.0	20 11.6	+33.3	12.1	21 10.2	+33.5	12.2	22 08.9	+33.7	12.3	23 07.5	+33.9	12.4	77
78	16 49.4	+32.3	11.0	17 48.3	+32.5	11.0	18 47.1	+32.7	11.1	19 46.0	+32.9	11.1	20 44.9	+33.0	11.2	21 43.7	+33.2	11.3	22 42.6	+33.3	11.4	23 41.4	+33.5	11.5	78
79	17 21.7	+32.1	10.1	18 20.8	+32.2	10.1	19 19.8	+32.4	10.2	20 18.9	+32.6	10.3	21 17.9	+32.7	10.3	22 16.9	+32.9	10.4	23 15.9	+33.1	10.5	24 14.9	+33.3	10.5	79
80	17 53.8	+31.9	9.2	18 53.0	+32.0	9.2	19 52.2	+32.2	9.3	20 51.5	+32.2	9.4	21 50.6	+32.5	9.4	22 49.8	+32.6	9.5	23 49.0	+32.8	9.6	24 48.2	+32.9	9.6	80
81	18 25.7	+31.6	8.3	19 25.0	+31.8	8.3	20 24.4	+31.9	8.4	21 23.7	+32.1	8.5	22 23.1	+32.1	8.5	23 22.4	+32.3	8.6	24 21.8	+32.4	8.6	25 21.1	+32.5	8.7	81
82	18 57.3	+31.3	7.4	19 56.8	+31.4	7.4	20 56.3	+31.6	7.5	21 55.8	+31.7	7.5	22 55.2	+31.9	7.6	23 54.7	+31.9	7.7	24 54.2	+32.0	7.7	25 53.6	+32.2	7.8	82
83	19 28.6	+31.1	6.5	20 28.2	+31.2	6.5	21 27.9	+31.3	6.6	22 27.5	+31.3	6.6	23 27.1	+31.4	6.7	24 26.6	+31.6	6.7	25 26.2	+31.7	6.8	26 25.8	+31.8	6.8	83
84	19 59.7	+30.8	5.6	20 59.4	+30.9	5.6	21 59.1	+31.0	5.7	22 58.8	+31.1	5.7	23 58.5	+31.2	5.7	24 58.2	+31.3	5.8	25 57.9	+31.4	5.8	26 57.6	+31.5	5.9	84
85	20 30.5	+30.5	4.7	21 30.3	+30.6	4.7	22 30.1	+30.7	4.7	23 29.9	+30.7	4.8	24 29.7	+30.8	4.8	25 29.5	+30.9	4.8	26 29.3	+30.9	4.9	27 29.1	+31.0	4.9	85
86	21 01.0	+30.3	3.7	22 00.9	+30.3	3.8	23 00.8	+30.3	3.8	24 00.6	+30.4	3.8	25 00.5	+30.5	3.9	26 00.4	+30.5	3.9	27 00.2	+30.6	3.9	28 00.1	+30.6	4.0	86
87	21 31.3	+29.9	2.8	22 31.2	+29.9	2.8	23 31.1	+30.0	2.9	24 31.0	+30.1	2.9	25 31.0	+30.0	2.9	26 30.9	+30.1	2.9	27 30.8	+30.2	3.0	28 30.7	+30.2	3.0	87
88	22 01.2	+29.5	1.9	23 01.1	+29.6	1.9	24 01.1	+29.6	1.9	25 01.1	+29.6	1.9	26 01.0	+29.7	1.9	27 01.0	+29.7	2.0	28 01.0	+29.7	2.0	29 00.9	+29.8	2.0	88
89	22 30.7	+29.3	0.9	23 30.7	+29.3	1.0	24 30.7	+29.3	1.0	25 30.7	+29.3	1.0	26 30.7	+29.3	1.0	27 30.7	+29.3	1.0	28 30.7	+29.3	1.0	29 30.7	+29.3	1.0	89
90	23 00.0	+28.9	0.0	24 00.0	+28.9	0.0	25 00.0	+28.9	0.0	26 00.0	+28.9	0.0	27 00.0	+28.9	0.0	28 00.0	+28.9	0.0	29 00.0	+28.9	0.0	30 00.0	+28.9	0.0	90
	23°			24°			25°			26°			27°			28°			29°			30°			

S. Lat. {L.H.A. greater than 180° ....Zn=180°–Z
{L.H.A. less than 180°...........Zn=180°+Z

LATITUDE SAME NAME AS DECLINATION L.H.A. 119°, 241°

62°, 298° L.H.A. LATITUDE SAME NAME AS DECLINATION

N. Lat. {L.H.A. greater than 180° .....Zn=Z
{L.H.A. less than 180°............Zn=360°–Z

Dec.	23°			24°			25°			26°			27°			28°			29°			30°			Dec.
	Hc	d	Z	Hc	d	Z	Hc	d	Z	Hc	d	Z	Hc	d	Z	Hc	d	Z	Hc	d	Z	Hc	d	Z	
°	° ′	′	°	° ′	′	°	° ′	′	°	° ′	′	°	° ′	′	°	° ′	′	°	° ′	′	°	° ′	′	°	°
0	25 36.2	+25.8	101.7	25 23.8	+26.8	102.2	25 10.9	+27.8	102.7	24 57.5	+28.8	103.1	24 43.6	+29.9	103.6	24 29.3	+30.8	104.0	24 14.6	+31.7	104.5	23 59.4	+32.7	104.9	0
1	26 02.0	+25.4	100.7	25 50.6	+26.4	101.2	25 38.7	+27.4	101.7	25 26.3	+28.5	102.2	25 13.5	+29.4	102.6	25 00.1	+30.4	103.1	24 46.3	+31.4	103.5	24 32.1	+32.3	104.0	1
2	26 27.4	+25.0	99.7	26 17.0	+26.0	100.2	26 06.1	+27.1	100.7	25 54.8	+28.0	101.2	25 42.9	+29.0	101.6	25 30.5	+30.1	102.1	25 17.7	+31.0	102.6	25 04.4	+32.0	103.0	2
3	26 52.4	+24.5	98.7	26 43.0	+25.6	99.2	26 33.2	+26.6	99.7	26 22.8	+27.6	100.2	26 11.9	+28.7	100.7	26 00.6	+29.6	101.2	25 48.7	+30.7	101.6	25 36.4	+31.6	102.1	3
4	27 16.9	+24.0	97.7	27 08.6	+25.1	98.2	26 59.8	+26.1	98.7	26 50.4	+27.3	99.2	26 40.6	+28.2	99.7	26 30.2	+29.3	100.2	26 19.4	+30.2	100.7	26 08.0	+31.3	101.2	4
5	27 40.9	+23.6	96.6	27 33.7	+24.7	97.2	27 25.9	+25.8	97.7	27 17.7	+26.7	98.2	27 08.8	+27.9	98.7	26 59.5	+28.8	99.2	26 49.6	+29.9	99.7	26 39.3	+30.8	100.2	5
6	28 04.5	+23.1	95.6	27 58.4	+24.2	96.1	27 51.7	+25.2	96.7	27 44.4	+26.4	97.2	27 36.7	+27.4	97.7	27 28.3	+28.5	98.2	27 19.5	+29.5	98.7	27 10.1	+30.5	99.2	6
7	28 27.6	+22.6	94.6	28 22.6	+23.7	95.1	28 16.9	+24.9	95.6	28 10.8	+25.9	96.2	28 04.1	+26.9	96.7	27 56.8	+28.0	97.2	27 49.0	+29.0	97.8	27 40.6	+30.0	98.3	7
8	28 50.2	+22.2	93.5	28 46.3	+23.2	94.1	28 41.8	+24.3	94.6	28 36.7	+25.4	95.1	28 31.0	+26.5	95.7	28 24.8	+27.5	96.2	28 18.0	+28.6	96.8	28 10.6	+29.7	97.3	8
9	29 12.4	+21.6	92.4	29 09.5	+22.8	93.0	29 06.1	+23.8	93.6	29 02.1	+24.9	94.1	28 57.5	+26.0	94.7	28 52.3	+27.1	95.2	28 46.6	+28.1	95.8	28 40.3	+29.2	96.3	9
10	29 34.0	+21.1	91.4	29 32.3	+22.2	91.9	29 29.9	+23.4	92.5	29 27.0	+24.5	93.1	29 23.5	+25.6	93.6	29 19.4	+26.7	94.2	29 14.7	+27.7	94.8	29 09.5	+28.7	95.3	10
11	29 55.1	+20.6	90.3	29 54.5	+21.7	90.9	29 53.3	+22.8	91.4	29 51.5	+23.9	92.0	29 49.1	+25.0	92.6	29 46.1	+26.1	93.2	29 42.4	+27.3	93.7	29 38.2	+28.3	94.3	11
12	30 15.7	+20.0	89.2	30 16.2	+21.2	89.8	30 16.1	+22.3	90.4	30 15.4	+23.5	91.0	30 14.1	+24.6	91.5	30 12.2	+25.6	92.1	30 09.7	+26.7	92.7	30 06.5	+27.9	93.3	12
13	30 35.7	+19.5	88.1	30 37.4	+20.6	88.7	30 38.4	+21.8	89.3	30 38.9	+22.9	89.9	30 38.7	+24.0	90.5	30 37.8	+25.2	91.1	30 36.4	+26.2	91.7	30 34.4	+27.3	92.3	13
14	30 55.2	+18.9	87.0	30 58.0	+20.1	87.6	31 00.2	+21.2	88.2	31 01.8	+22.3	88.8	31 02.7	+23.5	89.4	31 03.0	+24.6	90.0	31 02.6	+25.8	90.6	31 01.7	+26.8	91.2	14
15	31 14.1	+18.4	85.9	31 18.1	+19.5	86.5	31 21.4	+20.7	87.1	31 24.1	+21.8	87.7	31 26.2	+22.9	88.3	31 27.6	+24.1	89.0	31 28.4	+25.2	89.6	31 28.5	+26.3	90.2	15
16	31 32.5	+17.7	84.8	31 37.6	+18.9	85.4	31 42.1	+20.1	86.0	31 45.9	+21.3	86.6	31 49.1	+22.4	87.3	31 51.7	+23.5	87.9	31 53.6	+24.6	88.5	31 54.8	+25.8	89.1	16
17	31 50.2	+17.2	83.7	31 56.5	+18.4	84.3	32 02.2	+19.5	84.9	32 07.2	+20.6	85.5	32 11.5	+21.8	86.2	32 15.2	+23.0	86.8	32 18.2	+24.2	87.4	32 20.6	+25.3	88.1	17
18	32 07.4	+16.6	82.5	32 14.9	+17.7	83.2	32 21.7	+18.9	83.8	32 27.8	+20.1	84.4	32 33.3	+21.3	85.1	32 38.2	+22.4	85.7	32 42.4	+23.5	86.3	32 45.9	+24.6	87.0	18
19	32 24.0	+15.9	81.4	32 32.6	+17.1	82.0	32 40.6	+18.3	82.7	32 47.9	+19.5	83.3	32 54.6	+20.6	83.9	33 00.6	+21.8	84.6	33 05.9	+23.0	85.2	33 10.5	+24.2	85.9	19
20	32 39.9	+15.3	80.3	32 49.7	+16.5	80.9	32 58.9	+17.7	81.5	33 07.4	+18.9	82.2	33 15.2	+20.1	82.8	33 22.4	+21.2	83.5	33 28.9	+22.3	84.1	33 34.7	+23.5	84.8	20
21	32 55.2	+14.7	79.1	33 06.2	+15.9	79.7	33 16.6	+17.0	80.4	33 26.3	+18.2	81.0	33 35.3	+19.4	81.7	33 43.6	+20.6	82.4	33 51.2	+21.8	83.0	33 58.2	+22.9	83.7	21
22	33 09.9	+14.0	78.0	33 22.1	+15.2	78.6	33 33.6	+16.5	79.2	33 44.5	+17.6	79.9	33 54.7	+18.8	80.6	34 04.2	+20.0	81.2	34 13.0	+21.1	81.9	34 21.1	+22.3	82.6	22
23	33 23.9	+13.4	76.8	33 37.3	+14.6	77.4	33 50.1	+15.7	78.1	34 02.1	+17.0	78.7	34 13.5	+18.1	79.4	34 24.2	+19.3	80.1	34 34.1	+20.5	80.8	34 43.4	+21.7	81.4	23
24	33 37.3	+12.8	75.6	33 51.9	+13.9	76.3	34 05.8	+15.1	76.9	34 19.1	+16.2	77.6	34 31.6	+17.5	78.3	34 43.5	+18.7	78.9	34 54.6	+19.9	79.6	35 05.1	+21.0	80.3	24
25	33 50.1	+12.0	74.4	34 05.8	+13.3	75.1	34 20.9	+14.4	75.8	34 35.3	+15.7	76.4	34 49.1	+16.8	77.1	35 02.2	+18.0	77.8	35 14.5	+19.2	78.5	35 26.1	+20.4	79.2	25
26	34 02.1	+11.4	73.3	34 19.1	+12.5	73.9	34 35.3	+13.8	74.6	34 51.0	+14.9	75.2	35 05.9	+16.1	75.9	35 20.2	+17.3	76.6	35 33.7	+18.5	77.3	35 46.5	+19.8	78.0	26
27	34 13.5	+10.7	72.1	34 31.6	+11.9	72.7	34 49.1	+13.1	73.4	35 05.9	+14.3	74.1	35 22.0	+15.5	74.7	35 37.5	+16.6	75.4	35 52.2	+17.9	76.1	36 06.3	+19.0	76.8	27
28	34 24.2	+9.9	70.9	34 43.5	+11.1	71.5	35 02.2	+12.3	72.2	35 20.2	+13.5	72.9	35 37.5	+14.7	73.6	35 54.1	+16.0	74.2	36 10.1	+17.1	74.9	36 25.3	+18.3	75.7	28
29	34 34.1	+9.3	69.7	34 54.6	+10.5	70.3	35 14.5	+11.6	71.0	35 33.7	+12.8	71.7	35 52.2	+14.1	72.4	36 10.1	+15.2	73.1	36 27.2	+16.4	73.8	36 43.6	+17.6	74.5	29
30	34 43.4	+8.6	68.5	35 05.1	+9.8	69.1	35 26.1	+11.0	69.8	35 46.5	+12.1	70.5	36 06.3	+13.3	71.2	36 25.3	+14.5	71.9	36 43.6	+15.7	72.6	37 01.2	+16.9	73.3	30
31	34 52.0	+7.9	67.3	35 14.9	+9.0	67.9	35 37.1	+10.2	68.6	35 58.6	+11.4	69.3	36 19.6	+12.5	70.0	36 39.8	+13.7	70.6	36 59.3	+15.0	71.4	37 18.1	+16.2	72.1	31
32	34 59.9	+7.1	66.1	35 23.9	+8.3	66.7	35 47.3	+9.4	67.4	36 10.0	+10.7	68.1	36 32.1	+11.8	68.7	36 53.5	+13.1	69.4	37 14.3	+14.2	70.1	37 34.3	+15.4	70.9	32
33	35 07.0	+6.4	64.9	35 32.2	+7.5	65.5	35 56.7	+8.8	66.2	36 20.7	+9.9	66.8	36 43.9	+11.1	67.5	37 06.6	+12.2	68.2	37 28.5	+13.4	68.9	37 49.7	+14.7	69.6	33
34	35 13.4	+5.7	63.6	35 39.7	+6.8	64.3	36 05.5	+7.9	64.9	36 30.6	+9.1	65.6	36 55.0	+10.3	66.3	37 18.8	+11.5	67.0	37 41.9	+12.7	67.7	38 04.4	+13.8	68.4	34
35	35 19.1	+4.9	62.4	35 46.5	+6.1	63.1	36 13.4	+7.2	63.7	36 39.7	+8.4	64.4	37 05.3	+9.6	65.1	37 30.3	+10.7	65.7	37 54.6	+11.9	66.5	38 18.2	+13.1	67.2	35
36	35 24.0	+4.2	61.2	35 52.6	+5.3	61.8	36 20.6	+6.5	62.5	36 48.1	+7.6	63.1	37 14.9	+8.7	63.8	37 41.0	+9.9	64.5	38 06.5	+11.1	65.2	38 31.3	+12.3	65.9	36
37	35 28.2	+3.5	60.0	35 57.9	+4.6	60.6	36 27.1	+5.7	61.2	36 55.7	+6.8	61.9	37 23.6	+8.0	62.6	37 50.9	+9.2	63.3	38 17.6	+10.3	64.0	38 43.6	+11.5	64.7	37
38	35 31.7	+2.7	58.8	36 02.5	+3.8	59.4	36 32.8	+4.9	60.0	37 02.5	+6.0	60.7	37 31.6	+7.2	61.3	38 00.1	+8.3	62.0	38 27.9	+9.5	62.7	38 55.1	+10.7	63.4	38
39	35 34.4	+1.9	57.5	36 06.3	+3.1	58.1	36 37.7	+4.2	58.8	37 08.5	+5.3	59.4	37 38.8	+6.4	60.1	38 08.4	+7.5	60.7	38 37.4	+8.7	61.4	39 05.8	+9.8	62.1	39
40	35 36.3	+1.3	56.3	36 09.4	+2.3	56.9	36 41.9	+3.3	57.5	37 13.8	+4.5	58.2	37 45.2	+5.6	58.8	38 15.9	+6.8	59.5	38 46.1	+7.9	60.2	39 15.6	+9.0	60.9	40
41	35 37.6	+0.4	55.1	36 11.7	+1.5	55.7	36 45.2	+2.6	56.3	37 18.3	+3.7	56.9	37 50.8	+4.7	57.6	38 22.7	+5.9	58.2	38 54.0	+7.0	58.9	39 24.6	+8.2	59.6	41
42	35 38.0	-0.3	53.8	36 13.2	+0.7	54.4	36 47.8	+1.8	55.0	37 22.0	+2.8	55.6	37 55.5	+4.0	56.3	38 28.6	+5.0	56.9	39 01.0	+6.2	57.6	39 32.8	+7.3	58.3	42
43	35 37.7	-1.0	52.6	36 13.9	0.0	53.2	36 49.6	+1.1	53.8	37 24.8	+2.1	54.4	37 59.5	+3.2	55.0	38 33.6	+4.3	55.7	39 07.2	+5.3	56.3	39 40.1	+6.5	57.0	43
44	35 36.7	-1.8	51.4	36 13.9	-0.8	51.9	36 50.7	+0.2	52.5	37 26.9	+1.3	53.1	38 02.7	+2.3	53.8	38 37.9	+3.4	54.4	39 12.5	+4.5	55.1	39 46.6	+5.6	55.7	44
45	35 34.9	-2.5	50.1	36 13.1	-1.5	50.7	36 50.9	-0.5	51.3	37 28.2	+0.5	51.9	38 05.0	+1.5	52.5	38 41.3	+2.5	53.1	39 17.0	+3.6	53.8	39 52.2	+4.7	54.4	45
46	35 32.4	-3.3	48.9	36 11.6	-2.3	49.5	36 50.4	-1.4	50.0	37 28.7	-0.4	50.6	38 06.5	+0.7	51.2	38 43.8	+1.8	51.8	39 20.6	+2.8	52.5	39 56.9	+3.9	53.1	46
47	35 29.1	-4.0	47.7	36 09.3	-3.1	48.2	36 49.0	-2.1	48.8	37 28.3	-1.1	49.4	38 07.2	-0.1	49.9	38 45.6	+0.9	50.6	39 23.4	+2.0	51.2	40 00.8	+3.0	51.8	47
48	35 25.1	-4.8	46.5	36 06.2	-3.8	47.0	36 46.9	-2.9	47.5	37 27.2	-1.9	48.1	38 07.1	-1.0	48.7	38 46.5	0.0	49.3	39 25.4	+1.0	49.9	40 03.8	+2.1	50.5	48
49	35 20.3	-5.5	45.2	36 02.4	-4.6	45.8	36 44.0	-3.6	46.3	37 25.3	-2.7	46.8	38 06.1	-1.8	47.4	38 46.5	-0.8	48.0	39 26.4	+0.2	48.6	40 05.9	+1.2	49.2	49
50	35 14.8	-6.2	44.0	35 57.8	-5.4	44.5	36 40.4	-4.5	45.0	37 22.6	-3.6	45.6	38 04.3	-2.5	46.1	38 45.7	-1.6	46.7	39 26.6	-0.6	47.3	40 07.1	+0.3	47.9	50
51	35 08.6	-7.0	42.8	35 52.4	-6.1	43.3	36 35.9	-5.2	43.8	37 19.0	-4.3	44.3	38 01.8	-3.5	44.9	38 44.1	-2.5	45.4	39 26.0	-1.6	46.0	40 07.4	-0.5	46.6	51
52	35 01.6	-7.7	41.6	35 46.3	-6.8	42.1	36 30.7	-6.0	42.6	37 14.7	-5.1	43.1	37 58.3	-4.2	43.6	38 41.6	-3.3	44.1	39 24.4	-2.3	44.7	40 06.9	-1.5	45.3	52
53	34 53.9	-8.4	40.4	35 39.5	-7.6	40.8	36 24.7	-6.8	41.3	37 09.6	-5.9	41.8	37 54.1	-5.0	42.3	38 38.3	-4.2	42.9	39 22.1	-3.3	43.4	40 05.4	-2.3	44.0	53
54	34 45.5	-9.1	39.2	35 31.9	-8.3	39.6	36 17.9	-7.5	40.1	37 03.7	-6.7	40.6	37 49.1	-5.8	41.1	38 34.1	-4.9	41.6	39 18.8	-4.1	42.1	40 03.1	-3.1	42.7	54
55	34 36.4	-9.8	38.0	35 23.6	-9.1	38.4	36 10.4	-8.2	38.9	36 57.0	-7.5	39.3	37 43.3	-6.7	39.8	38 29.2	-5.8	40.3	39 14.7	-4.9	40.8	40 00.0	-4.1	41.4	55
56	34 26.6	-10.5	36.8	35 14.5	-9.8	37.2	36 02.2	-9.0	37.6	36 49.5	-8.2	38.1	37 36.6	-7.4	38.6	38 23.4	-6.6	39.0	39 09.8	-5.8	39.6	39 55.9	-4.9	40.1	56
57	34 16.1	-11.2	35.6	35 04.7	-10.4	36.0	35 53.2	-9.8	36.4	36 41.3	-9.0	36.8	37 29.2	-8.2	37.3	38 16.8	-7.5	37.8	39 04.0	-6.6	38.3	39 51.0	-5.8	38.8	57
58	34 04.9	-11.9	34.4	34 54.3	-11.2	34.8	35 43.4	-10.5	35.2	36 32.3	-9.7	35.6	37 21.0	-9.1	36.1	38 09.3	-8.2	36.5	38 57.4	-7.5	37.0	39 45.2	-6.7	37.5	58
59	33 53.0	-12.6	33.2	34 43.1	-11.9	33.6	35 32.9	-11.2	34.0	36 22.6	-10.5	34.4	37 11.9	-9.7	34.8	38 01.1	-9.1	35.3	38 49.9	-8.3	35.7	39 38.5	-7.5	36.2	59
60	33 40.4	-13.2	32.0	34 31.2	-12.6	32.4	35 21.7	-11.9	32.8	36 12.1	-11.3	33.2	37 02.2	-10.6	33.6	37 52.0	-9.8	34.0	38 41.6	-9.1	34.4	39 31.0	-8.4	34.9	60
61	33 27.2	-13.9	30.9	34 18.6	-13.3	31.2	35 09.8	-12.6	31.6	36 00.8	-12.0	32.0	36 51.6	-11.3	32.3	37 42.2	-10.6	32.8	38 32.5	-9.9	33.2	39 22.6	-9.2	33.6	61
62	33 13.3	-14.5	29.7	34 05.3	-13.9	30.0	34 57.2	-13.3	30.4	35 48.8	-12.7	30.7	36 40.3	-12.0	31.1	37 31.6	-11.4	31.5	38 22.6	-10.7	31.9	39 13.4	-10.0	32.3	62
63	32 58.8	-15.2	28.5	33 51.4	-14.6	28.9	34 43.9	-14.1	29.2	35 36.1	-13.4	29.5	36 28.3	-12.8	29.9	37 20.2	-12.2	30.3	38 11.9	-11.5	30.7	39 03.4	-10.9	31.1	63
64	32 43.6	-15.8	27.4	33 36.8	-15.3	27.7	34 29.8	-14.7	28.0	35 22.7	-14.1	28.3	36 15.5	-13.6	28.7	37 08.0	-12.9	29.0	38 00.4	-12.4	29.4	38 52.5	-11.7	29.8	64
65	32 27.8	-16.4	26.2	33 21.5	-15.9	26.5	34 15.1	-15.3	26.8	35 08.6	-14.8	27.2	36 01.9	-14.2	27.5	36 55.1	-13.7	27.8	37 48.0	-13.0	28.2	38 40.8	-12.4	28.6	65
66	32 11.4	-17.1	25.1	33 05.6	-16.5	25.4	33 59.8	-16.0	25.7	34 53.8	-15.5	26.0	35 47.7	-15.0	26.3	36 41.4	-14.4	26.6	37 35.0	-13.9	26.9	38 28.4	-13.3	27.3	66
67	31 54.3	-17.6	24.0	32 49.1	-17.1	24.2	33 43.8	-16.7	24.5	34 38.3	-16.2	24.8	35 32.7	-15.7	25.1	36 27.0	-15.2	25.4	37 21.1	-14.6	25.7	38 15.1	-14.1	26.1	67
68	31 36.7	-18.2	22.9	32 32.0	-17.8	23.1	33 27.1	-17.3	23.4	34 22.1	-16.8	23.6	35 17.0	-16.3	23.9	36 11.8	-15.8	24.2	37 06.5	-15.3	24.5	38 01.0	-14.8	24.8	68
69	31 18.5	-18.8	21.7	32 14.2	-18.4	22.0	33 09.8	-17.9	22.2	34 05.3	-17.5	22.5	35 00.7	-17.0	22.7	35 56.0	-16.6	23.0	36 51.2	-16.1	23.3	37 46.2	-15.6	23.6	69
70	30 59.7	-19.3	20.6	31 55.8	-18.9	20.8	32 51.9	-18.6	21.1	33 47.8	-18.1	21.3	34 43.7	-17.7	21.6	35 39.4	-17.2	21.8	36 35.1	-16.8	22.1	37 30.6	-16.3	22.4	70
71	30 40.4	-19.9	19.5	31 36.9	-19.5	19.7	32 33.3	-19.1	19.9	33 29.7	-18.7	20.2	34 26.0	-18.4	20.4	35 22.2	-18.0	20.6	36 18.3	-17.5	20.9	37 14.3	-17.1	21.2	71
72	30 20.5	-20.5	18.4	31 17.4	-20.1	18.6	32 14.2	-19.7	18.8	33 11.0	-19.4	19.0	34 07.6	-18.9	19.2	35 04.2	-18.6	19.5	36 00.8	-18.2	19.7	36 57.2	-17.8	20.0	72
73	30 00.0	-21.0	17.3	30 57.3	-20.7	17.5	31 54.5	-20.4	17.7	32 51.6	-20.0	17.9	33 48.7	-19.7	18.1	34 45.6	-19.2	18.3	35 42.6	-18.9	18.5	36 39.4	-18.5	18.8	73
74	29 39.0	-21.5	16.3	30 36.6	-21.2	16.4	31 34.1	-20.8	16.6	32 31.6	-20.5	16.8	33 29.0	-20.2	17.0	34 26.4	-19.9	17.2	35 23.7	-19.6	17.4	36 20.9	-19.2	17.6	74
75	29 17.5	-22.0	15.2	30 15.4	-21.7	15.3	31 13.3	-21.5	15.5	32 11.1	-21.2	15.7	33 08.8	-20.8	15.8	34 06.5	-20.5	16.0	35 04.1	-20.2	16.2	36 01.7	-19.8	16.4	75
76	28 55.5	-22.5	14.1	29 53.7	-22.3	14.3	30 51.8	-22.0	14.4	31 49.9	-21.7	14.6	32 48.0	-21.5	14.7	33 46.0	-21.2	14.9	34 43.9	-20.8	15.1	35 41.9	-20.6	15.2	76
77	28 33.0	-23.0	13.1	29 31.4	-22.7	13.2	30 29.8	-22.5	13.3	31 28.2	-22.3	13.5	32 26.5	-22.0	13.6	33 24.8	-21.7	13.8	34 23.1	-21.5	13.9	35 21.3	-21.2	14.1	77
78	28 10.0	-23.5	12.0	29 08.7	-23.3	12.1	30 07.3	-23.0	12.3	31 06.0	-22.9	12.4	32 04.5	-22.5	12.5	33 03.1	-22.3	12.7	34 01.6	-22.1	12.8	35 00.1	-21.8	13.0	78
79	27 46.5	-23.9	11.0	28 45.4	-23.7	11.1	29 44.3	-23.5	11.2	30 43.1	-23.3	11.3	31 42.0	-23.1	11.4	32 40.8	-22.9	11.5	33 39.5	-22.6	11.7	34 38.3	-22.5	11.8	79
80	27 22.6	-24.4	9.9	28 21.7	-24.2	10.0	29 20.8	-24.1	10.1	30 19.8	-23.8	10.2	31 18.9	-23.7	10.3	32 17.9	-23.5	10.5	33 16.9	-23.3	10.6	34 15.8	-23.0	10.7	80
81	26 58.2	-24.8	8.9	27 57.5	-24.7	9.0	28 56.7	-24.5	9.1	29 56.0	-24.4	9.2	30 55.2	-24.2	9.3	31 54.4	-24.0	9.4	32 53.6	-23.9	9.5	33 52.8	-23.7	9.6	81
82	26 33.4	-25.3	7.9	27 32.8	-25.1	8.0	28 32.2	-25.0	8.0	29 31.6	-24.8	8.1	30 31.0	-24.7	8.2	31 30.4	-24.6	8.3	32 29.7	-24.4	8.4	33 29.1	-24.2	8.5	82
83	26 08.1	-25.7	6.9	27 07.7	-25.6	6.9	28 07.2	-25.4	7.0	29 06.8	-25.4	7.1	30 06.3	-25.2	7.1	31 05.8	-25.1	7.2	32 05.3	-24.9	7.3	33 04.9	-24.9	7.4	83
84	25 42.4	-26.1	5.9	26 42.1	-26.0	5.9	27 41.8	-26.0	6.0	28 41.4	-25.8	6.0	29 41.1	-25.7	6.1	30 40.7	-25.5	6.2	31 40.4	-25.5	6.2	32 40.0	-25.3	6.3	84
85	25 16.3	-26.5	4.9	26 16.1	-26.4	4.9	27 15.8	-26.3	5.0	28 15.6	-26.2	5.0	29 15.4	-26.2	5.1	30 15.2	-26.1	5.1	31 14.9	-26.0	5.2	32 14.7	-25.9	5.2	85
86	24 49.8	-26.9	3.9	25 49.7	-26.9	3.9	26 49.5	-26.8	4.0	27 49.4	-26.7	4.0	28 49.2	-26.6	4.0	29 49.1	-26.6	4.1	30 48.9	-26.5	4.1	31 48.8	-26.5	4.2	86
87	24 22.9	-27.3	2.9	25 22.8	-27.2	2.9	26 22.7	-27.1	3.0	27 22.7	-27.2	3.0	28 22.6	-27.1	3.0	29 22.5	-27.0	3.0	30 22.4	-27.0	3.1	31 22.3	-26.9	3.1	87
88	23 55.6	-27.6	1.9	24 55.6	-27.6	1.9	25 55.6	-27.6	2.0	26 55.5	-27.5	2.0	27 55.5	-27.5	2.0	28 55.5	-27.6	2.0	29 55.4	-27.5	2.0	30 55.4	-27.5	2.1	88
89	23 28.0	-28.0	1.0	24 28.0	-28.0	1.0	25 28.0	-28.0	1.0	26 28.0	-28.0	1.0	27 28.0	-28.0	1.0	28 27.9	-27.9	1.0	29 27.9	-27.9	1.0	30 27.9	-27.9	1.0	89
90	23 00.0	-28.3	0.0	24 00.0	-28.3	0.0	25 00.0	-28.4	0.0	26 00.0	-28.4	0.0	27 00.0	-28.4	0.0	28 00.0	-28.4	0.0	29 00.0	-28.4	0.0	30 00.0	-28.4	0.0	90
	23°			24°			25°			26°			27°			28°			29°			30°			

62°, 298° L.H.A. LATITUDE SAME NAME AS DECLINATION

308

LATITUDE **CONTRARY** NAME TO DECLINATION **L.H.A. 62°, 298°**

Dec.	23° Hc	d	Z	24° Hc	d	Z	25° Hc	d	Z	26° Hc	d	Z	27° Hc	d	Z	28° Hc	d	Z	29° Hc	d	Z	30° Hc	d	Z	Dec.
°	° ′	′	°	° ′	′	°	° ′	′	°	° ′	′	°	° ′	′	°	° ′	′	°	° ′	′	°	° ′	′	°	°
0	25 36.2	-26.2	101.7	25 23.8	-27.2	102.2	25 10.9	-28.2	102.7	24 57.5	-29.2	103.1	24 43.6	-30.1	103.6	24 29.3	-31.1	104.0	24 14.6	-32.1	104.5	23 59.4	-33.0	104.9	0
1	25 10.0	-26.5	102.7	24 56.6	-27.6	103.2	24 42.7	-28.6	103.6	24 28.3	-29.6	104.1	24 13.5	-30.5	104.5	23 58.2	-31.4	105.0	23 42.5	-32.4	105.4	23 26.4	-33.3	105.8	1
2	24 43.5	-27.0	103.7	24 29.0	-28.0	104.2	24 14.1	-29.0	104.6	23 58.7	-29.9	105.0	23 43.0	-30.9	105.5	23 26.8	-31.8	105.9	23 10.1	-32.7	106.3	22 53.1	-33.6	106.7	2
3	24 16.5	-27.4	104.7	24 01.0	-28.3	105.1	23 45.1	-29.3	105.6	23 28.8	-30.2	106.0	23 12.1	-31.2	106.4	22 55.0	-32.2	106.8	22 37.4	-33.0	107.2	22 19.5	-34.0	107.6	3
4	23 49.1	-27.7	105.7	23 32.7	-28.7	106.1	23 15.8	-29.6	106.5	22 58.6	-30.6	106.9	22 40.9	-31.5	107.3	22 22.8	-32.4	107.7	22 04.4	-33.3	108.1	21 45.5	-34.1	108.5	4
5	23 21.4	-28.1	106.6	23 04.0	-29.0	107.1	22 46.2	-30.0	107.5	22 28.0	-30.9	107.9	22 09.4	-31.8	108.2	21 50.4	-32.7	108.6	21 31.1	-33.6	109.0	21 11.4	-34.5	109.4	5
6	22 53.3	-28.4	107.6	22 35.0	-29.4	108.0	22 16.2	-30.3	108.4	21 57.1	-31.2	108.8	21 37.6	-32.1	109.2	21 17.7	-33.0	109.5	20 57.5	-33.9	109.9	20 36.9	-34.7	110.3	6
7	22 24.9	-28.8	108.6	22 05.6	-29.7	108.9	21 45.9	-30.6	109.3	21 25.9	-31.5	109.7	21 05.5	-32.4	110.1	20 44.7	-33.3	110.4	20 23.6	-34.1	110.8	20 02.2	-35.0	111.1	7
8	21 56.1	-29.0	109.5	21 35.9	-30.0	109.9	21 15.3	-30.9	110.3	20 54.4	-31.8	110.6	20 33.1	-32.7	111.0	20 11.4	-33.5	111.3	19 49.5	-34.4	111.7	19 27.2	-35.3	112.0	8
9	21 27.1	-29.4	110.4	21 05.9	-30.3	110.8	20 44.4	-31.2	111.2	20 22.6	-32.1	111.5	20 00.4	-32.9	111.9	19 37.9	-33.8	112.2	19 15.1	-34.7	112.5	18 51.9	-35.4	112.8	9
10	20 57.7	-29.7	111.4	20 35.6	-30.6	111.7	20 13.2	-31.4	112.1	19 50.5	-32.3	112.4	19 27.5	-33.2	112.7	19 04.1	-34.0	113.1	18 40.4	-34.8	113.4	18 16.5	-35.7	113.7	10
11	20 28.0	-30.0	112.3	20 05.0	-30.8	112.7	19 41.8	-31.8	113.0	19 18.2	-32.6	113.3	18 54.3	-33.5	113.6	18 30.1	-34.3	113.9	18 05.6	-35.1	114.2	17 40.8	-35.9	114.5	11
12	19 58.0	-30.3	113.2	19 34.2	-31.2	113.6	19 10.0	-32.0	113.9	18 45.6	-32.9	114.2	18 20.8	-33.7	114.5	17 55.8	-34.5	114.8	17 30.5	-35.3	115.1	17 04.9	-36.1	115.4	12
13	19 27.7	-30.5	114.2	19 03.0	-31.4	114.5	18 38.0	-32.3	114.8	18 12.7	-33.1	115.1	17 47.1	-33.9	115.4	17 21.3	-34.7	115.7	16 55.2	-35.6	115.9	16 28.8	-36.3	116.2	13
14	18 57.2	-30.9	115.1	18 31.6	-31.7	115.4	18 05.7	-32.5	115.7	17 39.6	-33.3	116.0	17 13.2	-34.1	116.2	16 46.6	-35.0	116.5	16 19.6	-35.7	116.8	15 52.5	-36.5	117.0	14
15	18 26.3	-31.0	116.0	17 59.9	-31.9	116.3	17 33.2	-32.7	116.6	17 06.3	-33.6	116.8	16 39.1	-34.4	117.1	16 11.6	-35.1	117.4	15 43.9	-35.9	117.6	15 16.0	-36.7	117.9	15
16	17 55.3	-31.3	116.9	17 28.0	-32.1	117.2	17 00.5	-32.9	117.4	16 32.7	-33.7	117.7	16 04.7	-34.5	118.0	15 36.5	-35.3	118.2	15 08.0	-36.1	118.4	14 39.3	-36.8	118.7	16
17	17 24.0	-31.6	117.8	16 55.9	-32.4	118.0	16 27.6	-33.2	118.3	15 59.0	-34.0	118.6	15 30.2	-34.8	118.8	15 01.2	-35.5	119.0	14 31.9	-36.2	119.3	14 02.5	-37.0	119.5	17
18	16 52.4	-31.8	118.7	16 23.5	-32.6	118.9	15 54.4	-33.4	119.2	15 25.0	-34.1	119.4	14 55.4	-34.9	119.7	14 25.7	-35.7	119.9	13 55.7	-36.5	120.1	13 25.5	-37.2	120.3	18
19	16 20.6	-32.0	119.5	15 50.9	-32.8	119.8	15 21.0	-33.6	120.0	14 50.9	-34.4	120.3	14 20.5	-35.1	120.5	13 50.0	-35.9	120.7	13 19.2	-36.5	120.9	12 48.3	-37.3	121.1	19
20	15 48.6	-32.2	120.4	15 18.1	-33.0	120.7	14 47.4	-33.8	120.9	14 16.5	-34.5	121.1	13 45.4	-35.3	121.3	13 14.1	-36.0	121.5	12 42.7	-36.8	121.7	12 11.0	-37.4	121.9	20
21	15 16.4	-32.4	121.3	14 45.1	-33.2	121.5	14 13.6	-33.9	121.7	13 42.0	-34.7	122.0	13 10.1	-35.4	122.2	12 38.1	-36.1	122.4	12 05.9	-36.8	122.5	11 33.6	-37.6	122.7	21
22	14 44.0	-32.6	122.2	14 11.9	-33.3	122.4	13 39.7	-34.1	122.6	13 07.3	-34.9	122.8	12 34.7	-35.6	123.0	12 02.0	-36.3	123.2	11 29.1	-37.1	123.3	10 56.0	-37.7	123.5	22
23	14 11.4	-32.8	123.0	13 38.6	-33.6	123.2	13 05.6	-34.3	123.4	12 32.4	-35.0	123.6	11 59.1	-35.7	123.8	11 25.7	-36.5	124.0	10 52.0	-37.1	124.1	10 18.3	-37.8	124.3	23
24	13 38.6	-33.0	123.9	13 05.0	-33.7	124.1	12 31.3	-34.5	124.3	11 57.4	-35.1	124.5	11 23.4	-35.9	124.6	10 49.2	-36.5	124.8	10 14.9	-37.2	124.9	9 40.5	-37.9	125.1	24
25	13 05.6	-33.2	124.8	12 31.3	-33.9	124.9	11 56.8	-34.5	125.1	11 22.3	-35.3	125.3	10 47.5	-36.0	125.4	10 12.7	-36.7	125.6	9 37.7	-37.4	125.7	9 02.6	-38.1	125.9	25
26	12 32.4	-33.3	125.6	11 57.4	-34.0	125.8	11 22.3	-34.8	126.0	10 47.0	-35.5	126.1	10 11.5	-36.1	126.3	9 36.0	-36.8	126.4	9 00.3	-37.4	126.5	8 24.5	-38.1	126.7	26
27	11 59.1	-33.4	126.5	11 23.4	-34.2	126.6	10 47.5	-34.8	126.8	10 11.5	-35.5	126.9	9 35.4	-36.2	127.1	8 59.2	-36.9	127.2	8 22.9	-37.6	127.3	7 46.4	-38.2	127.4	27
28	11 25.7	-33.7	127.3	10 49.2	-34.3	127.5	10 12.7	-35.0	127.6	9 36.0	-35.7	127.8	8 59.2	-36.3	127.9	8 22.3	-37.0	128.0	7 45.3	-37.6	128.1	7 08.2	-38.2	128.2	28
29	10 52.0	-33.7	128.2	10 14.9	-34.4	128.3	9 37.7	-35.1	128.4	9 00.3	-35.8	128.6	8 22.9	-36.5	128.7	7 45.3	-37.1	128.8	7 07.7	-37.7	128.9	6 30.0	-38.4	129.0	29
30	10 18.3	-33.9	129.0	9 40.5	-34.6	129.1	9 02.6	-35.2	129.3	8 24.5	-35.8	129.4	7 46.4	-36.5	129.5	7 08.2	-37.1	129.6	6 30.0	-37.8	129.7	5 51.6	-38.4	129.8	30
31	9 44.4	-34.0	129.8	9 05.9	-34.6	130.0	8 27.4	-35.4	130.1	7 48.7	-36.0	130.2	7 09.9	-36.6	130.3	6 31.1	-37.2	130.4	5 52.2	-37.9	130.5	5 13.2	-38.5	130.5	31
32	9 10.4	-34.1	130.7	8 31.3	-34.8	130.8	7 52.0	-35.4	130.9	7 12.7	-36.0	131.0	6 33.3	-36.7	131.1	5 53.9	-37.3	131.2	5 14.3	-37.9	131.2	4 34.7	-38.5	131.3	32
33	8 36.3	-34.2	131.5	7 56.5	-34.9	131.6	7 16.6	-35.5	131.7	6 36.7	-36.2	131.8	5 56.6	-36.7	131.9	5 16.6	-37.4	132.0	4 36.4	-37.9	132.0	3 56.2	-38.5	132.1	33
34	8 02.1	-34.3	132.3	7 21.6	-34.9	132.4	6 41.1	-35.6	132.5	6 00.5	-36.2	132.6	5 19.9	-36.8	132.7	4 39.2	-37.4	132.7	3 58.5	-38.0	132.8	3 17.7	-38.6	132.8	34
35	7 27.8	-34.4	133.2	6 46.7	-35.0	133.3	6 05.5	-35.6	133.3	5 24.3	-36.2	133.4	4 43.1	-36.9	133.5	4 01.8	-37.5	133.5	3 20.5	-38.1	133.6	2 39.1	-38.6	133.6	35
36	6 53.4	-34.5	134.0	6 11.7	-35.2	134.1	5 29.9	-35.7	134.1	4 48.1	-36.3	134.2	4 06.2	-36.9	134.3	3 24.3	-37.5	134.3	2 42.4	-38.1	134.3	2 00.5	-38.7	134.4	36
37	6 18.9	-34.6	134.8	5 36.5	-35.1	134.9	4 54.2	-35.8	134.9	4 11.8	-36.4	135.0	3 29.3	-36.9	135.1	2 46.8	-37.5	135.1	2 04.3	-38.1	135.1	1 21.8	-38.6	135.1	37
38	5 44.3	-34.7	135.6	5 01.4	-35.3	135.7	4 18.4	-35.8	135.8	3 35.4	-36.4	135.8	2 52.4	-37.0	135.8	2 09.3	-37.5	135.9	1 26.2	-38.1	135.9	0 43.2	-38.7	135.9	38
39	5 09.6	-34.7	136.5	4 26.1	-35.3	136.5	3 42.6	-35.9	136.6	2 59.0	-36.4	136.6	2 15.4	-37.0	136.6	1 31.8	-37.6	136.7	0 48.1	-38.1	136.7	0 04.5	-38.7	136.7	39
40	4 34.9	-34.7	137.3	3 50.8	-35.3	137.3	3 06.7	-35.9	137.4	2 22.6	-36.5	137.4	1 38.4	-37.0	137.4	0 54.2	-37.6	137.4	0 10.0	-38.1	137.4	0 34.2	+38.6	42.6	40
41	4 00.2	-34.8	138.1	3 15.5	-35.4	138.1	2 30.8	-35.9	138.2	1 46.1	-36.5	138.2	1 01.4	-37.1	138.2	0 16.6	-37.5	138.2	0 28.1	+38.1	41.8	1 12.8	+38.7	41.8	41
42	3 25.4	-34.9	138.9	2 40.1	-35.4	138.9	1 54.9	-36.0	139.0	1 09.6	-36.5	139.0	0 24.3	-37.0	139.0	0 20.9	+37.6	41.0	1 06.2	+38.1	41.0	1 51.5	+38.6	41.0	42
43	2 50.5	-34.9	139.7	2 04.7	-35.4	139.7	1 18.9	-35.9	139.8	0 33.1	-36.5	139.8	0 12.7	+37.0	40.2	0 58.5	+37.6	40.2	1 44.3	+38.1	40.2	2 30.1	+38.6	40.3	43
44	2 15.6	-34.9	140.5	1 29.3	-35.3	140.6	0 43.0	-36.0	140.6	0 03.4	+36.5	39.4	0 49.7	+37.1	39.4	1 36.1	+37.5	39.4	2 22.4	+38.1	39.5	3 08.7	+38.6	39.5	44
45	1 40.7	-34.9	141.3	0 53.8	-35.4	141.4	0 07.0	-36.0	141.4	0 39.9	+36.5	38.6	1 26.8	+37.0	38.6	2 13.6	+37.5	38.7	3 00.5	+38.0	38.7	3 47.3	+38.5	38.7	45
46	1 05.8	-35.0	142.2	0 18.4	-35.5	142.2	0 29.0	+36.0	37.8	1 16.4	+36.5	37.8	2 03.8	+37.0	37.9	2 51.1	+37.5	37.9	3 38.5	+38.0	37.9	4 25.8	+38.5	38.0	46
47	0 30.8	-34.9	143.0	0 17.1	+35.4	37.0	1 05.0	+36.0	37.0	1 52.9	+36.4	37.0	2 40.8	+36.9	37.1	3 28.6	+37.5	37.1	4 16.5	+37.9	37.1	5 04.3	+38.4	37.2	47
48	0 04.1	+35.0	36.2	0 52.5	+35.5	36.2	1 41.0	+35.9	36.2	2 29.3	+36.5	36.3	3 17.7	+36.9	36.3	4 06.1	+37.4	36.3	4 54.4	+37.9	36.4	5 42.7	+38.4	36.4	48
49	0 39.1	+34.9	35.4	1 28.0	+35.4	35.4	2 16.9	+35.9	35.4	3 05.8	+36.4	35.5	3 54.6	+36.9	35.5	4 43.5	+37.3	35.5	5 32.3	+37.8	35.6	6 21.1	+38.2	35.7	49
50	1 14.0	+35.0	34.6	2 03.4	+35.4	34.6	2 52.8	+35.9	34.6	3 42.2	+36.3	34.7	4 31.5	+36.8	34.7	5 20.8	+37.3	34.8	6 10.1	+37.8	34.8	6 59.3	+38.3	34.9	50
51	1 49.0	+34.9	33.8	2 38.8	+35.4	33.8	3 28.7	+35.8	33.8	4 18.5	+36.3	33.9	5 08.3	+36.8	33.9	5 58.1	+37.2	34.0	6 47.9	+37.6	34.0	7 37.6	+38.1	34.1	51
52	2 23.9	+34.9	33.0	3 14.2	+35.4	33.0	4 04.5	+35.8	33.0	4 54.8	+36.3	33.1	5 45.1	+36.7	33.1	6 35.3	+37.2	33.2	7 25.5	+37.6	33.2	8 15.7	+38.0	33.3	52
53	2 58.8	+34.8	32.1	3 49.6	+35.2	32.2	4 40.3	+35.8	32.2	5 31.1	+36.2	32.3	6 21.8	+36.6	32.3	7 12.5	+37.1	32.4	8 03.1	+37.5	32.5	8 53.7	+38.0	32.5	53
54	3 33.6	+34.8	31.3	4 24.8	+35.3	31.4	5 16.1	+35.6	31.4	6 07.3	+36.1	31.5	6 58.4	+36.6	31.5	7 49.6	+36.9	31.6	8 40.6	+37.4	31.7	9 31.7	+37.8	31.8	54
55	4 08.4	+34.8	30.5	5 00.1	+35.2	30.6	5 51.7	+35.7	30.6	6 43.4	+36.0	30.7	7 35.0	+36.4	30.7	8 26.5	+36.9	30.8	9 18.0	+37.3	30.9	10 09.5	+37.7	31.0	55
56	4 43.2	+34.7	29.7	5 35.3	+35.1	29.7	6 27.4	+35.5	29.8	7 19.4	+36.0	29.9	8 11.4	+36.4	29.9	9 03.4	+36.8	30.0	9 55.3	+37.2	30.1	10 47.2	+37.6	30.2	56
57	5 17.9	+34.6	28.9	6 10.4	+35.0	28.9	7 02.9	+35.4	29.0	7 55.4	+35.8	29.0	8 47.8	+36.2	29.1	9 40.2	+36.6	29.2	10 32.5	+37.1	29.3	11 24.8	+37.5	29.4	57
58	5 52.5	+34.5	28.1	6 45.4	+35.0	28.1	7 38.3	+35.4	28.2	8 31.2	+35.8	28.2	9 24.0	+36.2	28.3	10 16.8	+36.6	28.4	11 09.6	+37.0	28.5	12 02.3	+37.4	28.6	58
59	6 27.0	+34.5	27.2	7 20.4	+34.8	27.3	8 13.7	+35.2	27.4	9 07.0	+35.6	27.4	10 00.2	+36.0	27.5	10 53.4	+36.4	27.6	11 46.6	+36.8	27.7	12 39.7	+37.2	27.8	59
60	7 01.5	+34.4	26.4	7 55.2	+34.8	26.5	8 48.9	+35.2	26.5	9 42.6	+35.5	26.6	10 36.2	+35.9	26.7	11 29.8	+36.3	26.8	12 23.4	+36.6	26.9	13 16.9	+37.0	27.0	60
61	7 35.9	+34.3	25.6	8 30.0	+34.7	25.6	9 24.1	+35.0	25.7	10 18.1	+35.4	25.8	11 12.1	+35.8	25.9	12 06.1	+36.1	26.0	13 00.0	+36.5	26.1	13 53.9	+36.9	26.2	61
62	8 10.2	+34.2	24.8	9 04.7	+34.5	24.8	9 59.1	+34.9	24.9	10 53.5	+35.3	25.0	11 47.9	+35.6	25.1	12 42.2	+36.0	25.1	13 36.5	+36.4	25.2	14 30.8	+36.7	25.4	62
63	8 44.4	+34.1	23.9	9 39.2	+34.5	24.0	10 34.0	+34.8	24.1	11 28.8	+35.1	24.1	12 23.5	+35.5	24.2	13 18.2	+35.9	24.3	14 12.9	+36.2	24.4	15 07.5	+36.5	24.5	63
64	9 18.5	+34.0	23.1	10 13.7	+34.3	23.2	11 08.8	+34.7	23.2	12 03.9	+35.0	23.3	12 59.0	+35.3	23.4	13 54.1	+35.6	23.5	14 49.1	+36.0	23.6	15 44.0	+36.4	23.7	64
65	9 52.5	+33.8	22.3	10 48.0	+34.1	22.3	11 43.5	+34.5	22.4	12 38.9	+34.8	22.5	13 34.3	+35.2	22.6	14 29.7	+35.5	22.7	15 25.1	+35.8	22.8	16 20.4	+36.1	22.9	65
66	10 26.3	+33.7	21.4	11 22.1	+34.1	21.5	12 18.0	+34.3	21.6	13 13.7	+34.7	21.6	14 09.5	+35.0	21.7	15 05.2	+35.3	21.8	16 00.9	+35.6	21.9	16 56.5	+36.0	22.1	66
67	11 00.0	+33.6	20.6	11 56.2	+33.9	20.6	12 52.3	+34.2	20.7	13 48.4	+34.5	20.8	14 44.5	+34.8	20.9	15 40.5	+35.1	21.0	16 36.5	+35.4	21.1	17 32.5	+35.7	21.2	67
68	11 33.6	+33.4	19.7	12 30.1	+33.7	19.8	13 26.5	+34.0	19.9	14 22.9	+34.3	20.0	15 19.3	+34.6	20.1	16 15.6	+34.9	20.2	17 11.9	+35.2	20.3	18 08.2	+35.5	20.4	68
69	12 07.0	+33.3	18.9	13 03.8	+33.5	19.0	14 00.5	+33.9	19.0	14 57.2	+34.1	19.1	15 53.9	+34.4	19.2	16 50.5	+34.7	19.3	17 47.1	+35.0	19.4	18 43.7	+35.3	19.5	69
70	12 40.3	+33.1	18.0	13 37.3	+33.4	18.1	14 34.4	+33.6	18.2	15 31.3	+34.0	18.3	16 28.3	+34.2	18.4	17 25.2	+34.5	18.5	18 22.1	+34.8	18.6	19 19.0	+35.0	18.7	70
71	13 13.4	+32.9	17.2	14 10.7	+33.2	17.2	15 08.0	+33.5	17.3	16 05.3	+33.7	17.4	17 02.5	+34.0	17.5	17 59.7	+34.3	17.6	18 56.9	+34.5	17.7	19 54.0	+34.8	17.8	71
72	13 46.3	+32.8	16.3	14 43.9	+33.0	16.4	15 41.5	+33.2	16.5	16 39.0	+33.5	16.5	17 36.5	+33.8	16.6	18 34.0	+34.0	16.7	19 31.4	+34.3	16.8	20 28.8	+34.6	16.9	72
73	14 19.1	+32.6	15.5	15 16.9	+32.8	15.5	16 14.7	+33.1	15.6	17 12.5	+33.3	15.7	18 10.3	+33.5	15.8	19 08.0	+33.8	15.9	20 05.7	+34.0	16.0	21 03.4	+34.2	16.1	73
74	14 51.7	+32.3	14.6	15 49.7	+32.6	14.7	16 47.8	+32.8	14.7	17 45.8	+33.0	14.8	18 43.8	+33.3	14.9	19 41.8	+33.5	15.0	20 39.7	+33.7	15.1	21 37.6	+34.0	15.2	74
75	15 24.0	+32.2	13.7	16 22.3	+32.4	13.8	17 20.6	+32.6	13.9	18 18.8	+32.8	13.9	19 17.1	+33.0	14.0	20 15.3	+33.2	14.1	21 13.4	+33.5	14.2	22 11.6	+33.7	14.3	75
76	15 56.2	+32.0	12.8	16 54.7	+32.2	12.9	17 53.2	+32.3	13.0	18 51.6	+32.6	13.0	19 50.1	+32.7	13.1	20 48.5	+33.0	13.2	21 46.9	+33.2	13.3	22 45.3	+33.4	13.4	76
77	16 28.2	+31.7	12.0	17 26.9	+31.9	12.0	18 25.5	+32.1	12.1	19 24.2	+32.3	12.2	20 22.8	+32.5	12.2	21 21.5	+32.7	12.3	22 20.1	+32.9	12.4	23 18.7	+33.0	12.5	77
78	16 59.9	+31.5	11.1	17 58.8	+31.7	11.1	18 57.6	+31.9	11.2	19 56.5	+32.0	11.3	20 55.3	+32.2	11.3	21 54.2	+32.3	11.4	22 53.0	+32.5	11.5	23 51.7	+32.8	11.6	78
79	17 31.4	+31.3	10.2	18 30.5	+31.4	10.2	19 29.5	+31.6	10.3	20 28.5	+31.8	10.4	21 27.5	+31.9	10.4	22 26.5	+32.1	10.5	23 25.5	+32.3	10.6	24 24.5	+32.4	10.7	79
80	18 02.7	+31.0	9.3	19 01.9	+31.1	9.3	20 01.1	+31.3	9.4	21 00.3	+31.4	9.5	21 59.4	+31.6	9.5	22 58.6	+31.8	9.6	23 57.8	+31.9	9.7	24 56.9	+32.1	9.7	80
81	18 33.7	+30.7	8.4	19 33.0	+30.9	8.4	20 32.4	+31.0	8.5	21 31.7	+31.2	8.5	22 31.0	+31.3	8.6	23 30.4	+31.4	8.7	24 29.7	+31.5	8.7	25 29.0	+31.7	8.8	81
82	19 04.4	+30.5	7.5	20 03.9	+30.6	7.5	21 03.4	+30.7	7.6	22 02.9	+30.8	7.6	23 02.3	+31.0	7.7	24 01.8	+31.1	7.7	25 01.2	+31.3	7.8	26 00.7	+31.3	7.9	82
83	19 34.9	+30.2	6.6	20 34.5	+30.3	6.6	21 34.1	+30.4	6.6	22 33.7	+30.5	6.7	23 33.3	+30.6	6.7	24 32.9	+30.7	6.8	25 32.5	+30.8	6.8	26 32.0	+31.0	6.9	83
84	20 05.1	+29.9	5.6	21 04.8	+30.0	5.7	22 04.5	+30.1	5.7	23 04.2	+30.2	5.8	24 03.9	+30.3	5.8	25 03.6	+30.4	5.8	26 03.3	+30.5	5.9	27 03.0	+30.5	5.9	84
85	20 35.0	+29.7	4.7	21 34.8	+29.7	4.7	22 34.6	+29.8	4.8	23 34.4	+29.9	4.8	24 34.2	+29.9	4.9	25 34.0	+30.0	4.9	26 33.8	+30.0	4.9	27 33.5	+30.2	5.0	85
86	21 04.7	+29.3	3.8	22 04.5	+29.4	3.8	23 04.4	+29.4	3.8	24 04.3	+29.5	3.9	25 04.1	+29.6	3.9	26 04.0	+29.6	3.9	27 03.8	+29.7	4.0	28 03.7	+29.7	4.0	86
87	21 34.0	+29.0	2.8	22 33.9	+29.1	2.9	23 33.8	+29.1	2.9	24 33.8	+29.1	2.9	25 33.7	+29.1	2.9	26 33.6	+29.2	3.0	27 33.5	+29.3	3.0	28 33.4	+29.3	3.0	87
88	22 03.0	+28.7	1.9	23 03.0	+28.7	1.9	24 02.9	+28.7	1.9	25 02.9	+28.7	1.9	26 02.8	+28.8	2.0	27 02.8	+28.8	2.0	28 02.8	+28.8	2.0	29 02.7	+28.9	2.0	88
89	22 31.7	+28.3	1.0	23 31.7	+28.3	1.0	24 31.6	+28.4	1.0	25 31.6	+28.4	1.0	26 31.6	+28.4	1.0	27 31.6	+28.4	1.0	28 31.6	+28.4	1.0	29 31.6	+28.4	1.0	89
90	23 00.0	+28.0	0.0	24 00.0	+28.0	0.0	25 00.0	+28.0	0.0	26 00.0	+28.0	0.0	27 00.0	+28.0	0.0	28 00.0	+27.9	0.0	29 00.0	+27.9	0.0	30 00.0	+27.9	0.0	90
	23°			24°			25°			26°			27°			28°			29°			30°			

S. Lat. {L.H.A. greater than 180° ....Zn=180°−Z
L.H.A. less than 180°............Zn=180°+Z

LATITUDE **SAME** NAME AS DECLINATION **L.H.A. 118°, 242°**

309

LATITUDE SAME NAME AS DECLINATION   N. Lat. { L.H.A. greater than 180° .....Zn=Z / L.H.A. less than 180°...........Zn=360°-Z

Dec.	23° Hc	d	Z	24° Hc	d	Z	25° Hc	d	Z	26° Hc	d	Z	27° Hc	d	Z	28° Hc	d	Z	29° Hc	d	Z	30° Hc	d	Z	Dec.
0	24 42.1	+25.6	101.3	24 30.2	+26.6	101.7	24 17.8	+27.6	102.2	24 04.9	+28.6	102.6	23 51.6	+29.6	103.0	23 37.9	+30.6	103.5	23 23.7	+31.5	103.9	23 09.1	+32.5	104.3	0
1	25 07.7	+25.2	100.3	24 56.8	+26.2	100.7	24 45.4	+27.3	101.2	24 33.5	+28.3	101.6	24 21.2	+29.3	102.1	24 08.5	+30.2	102.5	23 55.2	+31.2	102.9	23 41.6	+32.1	103.4	1
2	25 32.9	+24.8	99.3	25 23.0	+25.9	99.7	25 12.7	+26.8	100.2	25 01.8	+27.9	100.7	24 50.5	+28.9	101.1	24 38.7	+29.8	101.6	24 26.4	+30.9	102.0	24 13.7	+31.8	102.5	2
3	25 57.7	+24.4	98.2	25 48.9	+25.4	98.7	25 39.5	+26.5	99.2	25 29.7	+27.5	99.7	25 19.4	+28.5	100.1	25 08.5	+29.5	100.6	24 57.3	+30.5	101.1	24 45.5	+31.5	101.5	3
4	26 22.1	+23.9	97.2	26 14.3	+25.0	97.7	26 06.0	+26.0	98.2	25 57.2	+27.0	98.7	25 47.9	+28.1	99.2	25 38.0	+29.2	99.6	25 27.8	+30.1	100.1	25 17.0	+31.1	100.6	4
5	26 46.0	+23.5	96.2	26 39.3	+24.5	96.7	26 32.0	+25.6	97.2	26 24.2	+26.7	97.7	26 16.0	+27.6	98.2	26 07.2	+28.7	98.7	25 57.9	+29.7	99.2	25 48.1	+30.7	99.6	5
6	27 09.5	+23.0	95.2	27 03.8	+24.1	95.7	26 57.6	+25.2	96.2	26 50.9	+26.2	96.7	26 43.6	+27.3	97.2	26 35.9	+28.3	97.7	26 27.6	+29.3	98.2	26 18.8	+30.3	98.7	6
7	27 32.5	+22.6	94.1	27 27.9	+23.7	94.7	27 22.8	+24.7	95.2	27 17.1	+25.8	95.7	27 10.9	+26.9	96.2	27 04.2	+27.9	96.7	26 56.9	+28.9	97.2	26 49.1	+30.0	97.7	7
8	27 55.1	+22.1	93.1	27 51.6	+23.2	93.6	27 47.5	+24.3	94.1	27 42.9	+25.4	94.7	27 37.8	+26.4	95.2	27 32.1	+27.5	95.7	27 25.8	+28.6	96.2	27 19.1	+29.5	96.7	8
9	28 17.2	+21.6	92.0	28 14.8	+22.7	92.6	28 11.8	+23.8	93.1	28 08.3	+24.9	93.6	28 04.2	+26.0	94.2	27 59.6	+27.0	94.7	27 54.4	+28.0	95.2	27 48.6	+29.1	95.8	9
10	28 38.8	+21.1	91.0	28 37.5	+22.2	91.5	28 35.6	+23.3	92.1	28 33.2	+24.4	92.6	28 30.2	+25.4	93.1	28 26.6	+26.5	93.7	28 22.4	+27.7	94.2	28 17.7	+28.7	94.8	10
11	28 59.9	+20.6	89.9	28 59.7	+21.7	90.5	28 58.9	+22.8	91.0	28 57.6	+23.9	91.6	28 55.6	+25.1	92.1	28 53.1	+26.1	92.7	28 50.1	+27.1	93.2	28 46.4	+28.2	93.8	11
12	29 20.5	+20.0	88.8	29 21.4	+21.2	89.4	29 21.7	+22.4	90.0	29 21.5	+23.4	90.5	29 20.7	+24.5	91.1	29 19.2	+25.7	91.6	29 17.2	+26.7	92.2	29 14.6	+27.8	92.8	12
13	29 40.5	+19.6	87.7	29 42.6	+20.7	88.3	29 44.1	+21.8	88.9	29 44.9	+22.9	89.5	29 45.2	+24.0	90.0	29 44.9	+25.1	90.6	29 43.9	+26.3	91.2	29 42.4	+27.3	91.7	13
14	30 00.1	+18.9	86.7	30 03.3	+20.1	87.2	30 05.9	+21.2	87.8	30 07.8	+22.4	88.4	30 09.2	+23.5	89.0	30 10.0	+24.6	89.5	30 10.2	+25.7	90.1	30 09.7	+26.9	90.7	14
15	30 19.0	+18.5	85.6	30 23.4	+19.6	86.1	30 27.1	+20.8	86.7	30 30.2	+21.9	87.3	30 32.7	+23.0	87.9	30 34.6	+24.1	88.5	30 35.9	+25.2	89.1	30 36.6	+26.3	89.7	15
16	30 37.5	+17.9	84.5	30 43.0	+19.0	85.0	30 47.9	+20.1	85.6	30 52.1	+21.3	86.2	30 55.7	+22.5	86.8	30 58.7	+23.6	87.4	31 01.1	+24.7	88.0	31 02.9	+25.8	88.6	16
17	30 55.4	+17.3	83.3	31 02.0	+18.5	83.9	31 08.0	+19.6	84.5	31 13.4	+20.8	85.1	31 18.2	+21.9	85.7	31 22.3	+23.1	86.4	31 25.8	+24.2	87.0	31 28.7	+25.3	87.6	17
18	31 12.7	+16.7	82.2	31 20.5	+17.8	82.8	31 27.6	+19.1	83.4	31 34.2	+20.2	84.0	31 40.1	+21.3	84.7	31 45.4	+22.5	85.3	31 50.0	+23.6	85.9	31 54.0	+24.7	86.5	18
19	31 29.4	+16.1	81.1	31 38.3	+17.3	81.7	31 46.7	+18.4	82.3	31 54.4	+19.6	82.9	32 01.4	+20.8	83.6	32 07.9	+21.9	84.2	32 13.6	+23.1	84.8	32 18.7	+24.2	85.4	19
20	31 45.5	+15.5	80.0	31 55.6	+16.7	80.6	32 05.1	+17.9	81.2	32 14.0	+19.0	81.8	32 22.2	+20.2	82.4	32 29.8	+21.3	83.1	32 36.7	+22.5	83.7	32 42.9	+23.7	84.3	20
21	32 01.0	+14.9	78.8	32 12.3	+16.1	79.4	32 23.0	+17.2	80.1	32 33.0	+18.4	80.7	32 42.4	+19.6	81.3	32 51.1	+20.8	82.0	32 59.2	+21.9	82.6	33 06.6	+23.0	83.2	21
22	32 15.9	+14.3	77.7	32 28.4	+15.5	78.3	32 40.2	+16.7	78.9	32 51.4	+17.8	79.6	33 02.0	+19.0	80.2	33 11.9	+20.1	80.8	33 21.1	+21.3	81.5	33 29.6	+22.5	82.1	22
23	32 30.2	+13.7	76.5	32 43.9	+14.8	77.2	32 56.9	+16.0	77.8	33 09.2	+17.2	78.4	33 21.0	+18.3	79.1	33 32.0	+19.5	79.7	33 42.4	+20.7	80.4	33 52.1	+21.8	81.0	23
24	32 43.9	+13.0	75.4	32 58.7	+14.2	76.0	33 12.9	+15.3	76.6	33 26.4	+16.6	77.3	33 39.3	+17.7	77.9	33 51.5	+18.9	78.6	34 03.1	+20.0	79.2	34 13.9	+21.2	79.9	24
25	32 56.9	+12.3	74.2	33 12.9	+13.5	74.8	33 28.2	+14.8	75.5	33 43.0	+15.9	76.1	33 57.0	+17.1	76.8	34 10.4	+18.3	77.4	34 23.1	+19.4	78.1	34 35.1	+20.6	78.8	25
26	33 09.2	+11.8	73.0	33 26.4	+12.9	73.7	33 43.0	+14.0	74.3	33 58.9	+15.2	75.0	34 14.1	+16.4	75.6	34 28.7	+17.5	76.3	34 42.5	+18.8	77.0	34 55.7	+20.0	77.6	26
27	33 21.0	+11.0	71.9	33 39.3	+12.2	72.5	33 57.0	+13.4	73.1	34 14.1	+14.6	73.8	34 30.5	+15.7	74.5	34 46.2	+17.0	75.1	35 01.3	+18.1	75.8	35 15.7	+19.3	76.5	27
28	33 32.0	+10.4	70.7	33 51.5	+11.6	71.3	34 10.4	+12.7	72.0	34 28.7	+13.9	72.6	34 46.2	+15.1	73.3	35 03.2	+16.2	73.9	35 19.4	+17.5	74.6	35 35.0	+18.6	75.3	28
29	33 42.4	+9.7	69.5	34 03.1	+10.8	70.1	34 23.1	+12.0	70.8	34 42.5	+13.2	71.4	35 01.3	+14.4	72.1	35 19.4	+15.6	72.8	35 36.9	+16.7	73.5	35 53.6	+17.9	74.1	29
30	33 52.1	+9.0	68.3	34 13.9	+10.2	69.0	34 35.1	+11.4	69.6	34 55.7	+12.6	70.3	35 15.7	+13.7	70.9	35 35.0	+14.8	71.6	35 53.6	+16.0	72.3	36 11.5	+17.2	73.0	30
31	34 01.1	+8.3	67.1	34 24.1	+9.5	67.8	34 46.5	+10.6	68.4	35 08.2	+11.8	69.1	35 29.4	+12.9	69.7	35 49.8	+14.2	70.4	36 09.6	+15.4	71.1	36 28.7	+16.6	71.8	31
32	34 09.4	+7.6	65.9	34 33.6	+8.7	66.6	34 57.1	+9.9	67.2	35 20.0	+11.1	67.9	35 42.3	+12.3	68.6	36 04.0	+13.4	69.2	36 25.0	+14.6	69.9	36 45.3	+15.7	70.6	32
33	34 17.0	+6.9	64.7	34 42.3	+8.1	65.4	35 07.0	+9.2	66.0	35 31.1	+10.4	66.6	35 54.6	+11.5	67.3	36 17.4	+12.7	68.0	36 39.6	+13.8	68.7	37 01.0	+15.1	69.4	33
34	34 23.9	+6.2	63.5	34 50.4	+7.3	64.2	35 16.2	+8.5	64.8	35 41.5	+9.6	65.4	36 06.1	+10.8	66.1	36 30.1	+11.9	66.8	36 53.4	+13.1	67.5	37 16.1	+14.3	68.2	34
35	34 30.1	+5.5	62.3	34 57.7	+6.6	62.9	35 24.7	+7.7	63.6	35 51.1	+8.9	64.2	36 16.9	+10.0	64.9	36 42.0	+11.2	65.6	37 06.5	+12.4	66.2	37 30.4	+13.5	66.9	35
36	34 35.6	+4.8	61.1	35 04.3	+5.9	61.7	35 32.4	+7.1	62.4	36 00.0	+8.1	63.0	36 26.9	+9.3	63.7	36 53.2	+10.5	64.3	37 18.9	+11.6	65.0	37 43.9	+12.8	65.7	36
37	34 40.4	+4.1	59.9	35 10.2	+5.2	60.5	35 39.5	+6.2	61.1	36 08.1	+7.4	61.8	36 36.2	+8.5	62.4	37 03.7	+9.6	63.1	37 30.5	+10.8	63.8	37 56.7	+12.0	64.5	37
38	34 44.5	+3.3	58.7	35 15.4	+4.4	59.3	35 45.7	+5.5	59.9	36 15.5	+6.6	60.5	36 44.7	+7.8	61.2	37 13.3	+8.9	61.9	37 41.3	+10.1	62.5	38 08.7	+11.2	63.2	38
39	34 47.8	+2.6	57.5	35 19.8	+3.7	58.1	35 51.2	+4.8	58.7	36 22.1	+5.9	59.3	36 52.5	+7.0	60.0	37 22.2	+8.1	60.6	37 51.4	+9.2	61.3	38 19.9	+10.4	62.0	39
40	34 50.4	+1.9	56.3	35 23.5	+2.9	56.9	35 56.0	+4.0	57.5	36 28.0	+5.1	58.1	36 59.5	+6.2	58.7	37 30.3	+7.4	59.4	38 00.6	+8.5	60.0	38 30.3	+9.6	60.7	40
41	34 52.3	+1.1	55.0	35 26.4	+2.2	55.6	36 00.0	+3.3	56.2	36 33.1	+4.3	56.8	37 05.7	+5.4	57.5	37 37.7	+6.5	58.1	38 09.1	+7.6	58.8	38 39.9	+8.7	59.5	41
42	34 53.4	+0.5	53.8	35 28.6	+1.5	54.4	36 03.3	+2.5	55.0	36 37.4	+3.6	55.6	37 11.1	+4.6	56.2	37 44.2	+5.7	56.9	38 16.7	+6.8	57.5	38 48.6	+8.0	58.2	42
43	34 53.9	-0.4	52.6	35 30.1	+0.7	53.2	36 05.8	+1.7	53.8	36 41.0	+2.8	54.3	37 15.7	+3.9	55.0	37 49.9	+4.9	55.6	38 23.5	+6.0	56.2	38 56.6	+7.1	56.9	43
44	34 53.5	-1.0	51.4	35 30.8	-0.1	51.9	36 07.5	+1.0	52.5	36 43.8	+2.0	53.1	37 19.6	+3.0	53.7	37 54.8	+4.1	54.3	38 29.5	+5.2	55.0	39 03.7	+6.2	55.6	44
45	34 52.5	-1.8	50.2	35 30.7	-0.8	50.7	36 08.5	+0.2	51.3	36 45.8	+1.2	51.9	37 22.6	+2.2	52.5	37 58.9	+3.3	53.1	38 34.7	+4.3	53.7	39 09.9	+5.5	54.4	45
46	34 50.7	-2.5	49.0	35 29.9	-1.5	49.5	36 08.7	-0.6	50.0	36 47.0	+0.4	50.6	37 24.8	+1.5	51.2	38 02.2	+2.5	51.8	38 39.0	+3.6	52.4	39 15.4	+4.5	53.1	46
47	34 48.2	-3.2	47.7	35 28.4	-2.3	48.3	36 08.1	-1.3	48.8	36 47.4	-0.3	49.4	37 26.3	+0.6	49.9	38 04.7	+1.6	50.5	38 42.6	+2.6	51.1	39 19.9	+3.8	51.8	47
48	34 45.0	-3.9	46.5	35 26.1	-3.0	47.0	36 06.8	-2.1	47.6	36 47.1	-1.2	48.1	37 26.9	-0.1	48.7	38 06.3	+0.8	49.3	38 45.2	+1.9	49.9	39 23.7	+2.8	50.5	48
49	34 41.1	-4.7	45.3	35 23.1	-3.8	45.8	36 04.7	-2.8	46.3	36 45.9	-1.9	46.9	37 26.8	-1.0	47.4	38 07.1	0.0	48.0	38 47.1	+1.0	48.6	39 26.5	+2.0	49.2	49
50	34 36.4	-5.4	44.1	35 19.3	-4.5	44.6	36 01.9	-3.7	45.1	36 44.0	-2.7	45.6	37 25.8	-1.8	46.2	38 07.1	-0.8	46.7	38 48.1	+0.1	47.3	39 28.5	+1.2	47.9	50
51	34 31.0	-6.1	42.9	35 14.8	-5.2	43.4	35 58.2	-4.3	43.9	36 41.3	-3.4	44.4	37 24.0	-2.5	44.9	38 06.3	-1.6	45.4	38 48.2	-0.7	46.0	39 29.7	+0.2	46.6	51
52	34 24.9	-6.8	41.7	35 09.6	-6.0	42.1	35 53.9	-5.1	42.6	36 37.9	-4.3	43.1	37 21.5	-3.4	43.6	38 04.7	-2.5	44.2	38 47.5	-1.5	44.7	39 29.9	-0.6	45.3	52
53	34 18.1	-7.5	40.5	35 03.6	-6.7	40.9	35 48.8	-5.9	41.4	36 33.6	-5.0	41.9	37 18.1	-4.2	42.4	38 02.2	-3.2	42.9	38 46.0	-2.4	43.5	39 29.3	-1.4	44.0	53
54	34 10.6	-8.2	39.3	34 56.9	-7.4	39.7	35 42.9	-6.6	40.2	36 28.6	-5.8	40.6	37 13.9	-4.9	41.1	37 59.0	-4.1	41.6	38 43.6	-3.2	42.2	39 27.9	-2.3	42.7	54
55	34 02.4	-8.9	38.1	34 49.5	-8.2	38.5	35 36.3	-7.4	38.9	36 22.8	-6.6	39.4	37 09.0	-5.7	39.9	37 54.9	-4.9	40.4	38 40.4	-4.0	40.9	39 25.6	-3.2	41.4	55
56	33 53.5	-9.6	36.9	34 41.3	-8.8	37.3	35 28.9	-8.1	37.7	36 16.2	-7.3	38.2	37 03.3	-6.6	38.6	37 50.0	-5.7	39.1	38 36.4	-4.9	39.6	39 22.4	-4.0	40.1	56
57	33 43.9	-10.3	35.7	34 32.5	-9.6	36.1	35 20.8	-8.8	36.5	36 08.9	-8.0	36.9	36 56.7	-7.2	37.4	37 44.3	-6.5	37.9	38 31.5	-5.7	38.3	39 18.4	-4.9	38.8	57
58	33 33.6	-10.9	34.5	34 22.9	-10.2	34.9	35 12.0	-9.5	35.3	36 00.9	-8.8	35.7	36 49.5	-8.1	36.1	37 37.8	-7.3	36.6	38 25.8	-6.5	37.1	39 13.5	-5.7	37.6	58
59	33 22.7	-11.6	33.3	34 12.7	-11.0	33.7	35 02.5	-10.3	34.1	35 52.1	-9.6	34.5	36 41.4	-8.8	34.9	37 30.5	-8.1	35.3	38 19.3	-7.4	35.8	39 07.8	-6.6	36.3	59
60	33 11.1	-12.3	32.2	34 01.7	-11.6	32.5	34 52.2	-10.9	32.9	35 42.5	-10.3	33.3	36 32.6	-9.6	33.7	37 22.4	-8.9	34.1	38 11.9	-8.1	34.5	39 01.2	-7.4	35.0	60
61	32 58.8	-12.9	31.0	33 50.1	-12.3	31.3	34 41.3	-11.7	31.7	35 32.2	-11.0	32.1	36 23.0	-10.4	32.4	37 13.5	-9.7	32.9	38 03.8	-9.0	33.3	38 53.8	-8.2	33.7	61
62	32 45.9	-13.6	29.8	33 37.8	-12.9	30.2	34 29.6	-12.3	30.5	35 21.2	-11.7	30.9	36 12.6	-11.0	31.2	37 03.8	-10.4	31.6	37 54.8	-9.7	32.0	38 45.6	-9.1	32.4	62
63	32 32.3	-14.2	28.7	33 24.9	-13.6	29.0	34 17.3	-13.1	29.3	35 09.5	-12.4	29.7	36 01.6	-11.9	30.0	36 53.4	-11.2	30.4	37 45.1	-10.6	30.8	38 36.5	-9.9	31.2	63
64	32 18.1	-14.8	27.5	33 11.3	-14.3	27.8	34 04.2	-13.7	28.1	34 57.1	-13.1	28.5	35 49.7	-12.5	28.8	36 42.2	-11.9	29.2	37 34.5	-11.3	29.5	38 26.6	-10.6	29.9	64
65	32 03.3	-15.4	26.4	32 57.0	-14.9	26.7	33 50.5	-14.3	27.0	34 44.0	-13.9	27.3	35 37.2	-13.2	27.6	36 30.3	-12.7	27.9	37 23.2	-12.1	28.3	38 16.0	-11.5	28.6	65
66	31 47.9	-16.1	25.2	32 42.1	-15.5	25.5	33 36.2	-15.0	25.8	34 30.1	-14.5	26.1	35 24.0	-14.0	26.4	36 17.6	-13.4	26.7	37 11.1	-12.8	27.1	38 04.5	-12.3	27.4	66
67	31 31.8	-16.6	24.1	32 26.6	-16.2	24.4	33 21.2	-15.7	24.6	34 15.6	-15.1	24.9	35 10.0	-14.7	25.2	36 04.2	-14.1	25.5	36 58.3	-13.6	25.8	37 52.2	-13.0	26.2	67
68	31 15.2	-17.2	23.0	32 10.4	-16.8	23.2	33 05.5	-16.3	23.5	34 00.5	-15.9	23.7	34 55.3	-15.3	24.0	35 50.1	-14.9	24.3	36 44.7	-14.3	24.6	37 39.2	-13.8	24.9	68
69	30 58.0	-17.8	21.9	31 53.6	-17.3	22.1	32 49.2	-16.9	22.3	33 44.6	-16.4	22.6	34 40.0	-16.0	22.8	35 35.2	-15.5	23.1	36 30.4	-15.1	23.4	37 25.4	-14.6	23.7	69
70	30 40.2	-18.3	20.8	31 36.3	-18.0	21.0	32 32.3	-17.6	21.2	33 28.2	-17.1	21.4	34 24.0	-16.7	21.7	35 19.7	-16.3	21.9	36 15.3	-15.8	22.2	37 10.8	-15.3	22.5	70
71	30 21.9	-18.9	19.6	31 18.3	-18.5	19.8	32 14.7	-18.1	20.1	33 11.1	-17.8	20.3	34 07.3	-17.3	20.5	35 03.4	-16.9	20.8	35 59.5	-16.5	21.0	36 55.5	-16.1	21.3	71
72	30 03.0	-19.5	18.5	30 59.8	-19.1	18.7	31 56.6	-18.7	18.9	32 53.3	-18.3	19.1	33 50.0	-18.0	19.4	34 46.5	-17.5	19.6	35 43.0	-17.2	19.8	36 39.4	-16.7	20.1	72
73	29 43.5	-20.0	17.5	30 40.7	-19.6	17.6	31 37.9	-19.3	17.8	32 35.0	-18.9	18.0	33 32.0	-18.6	18.2	34 29.0	-18.3	18.4	35 25.8	-17.9	18.6	36 22.7	-17.5	18.9	73
74	29 23.5	-20.5	16.4	30 21.1	-20.2	16.5	31 18.6	-19.9	16.7	32 16.1	-19.5	16.9	33 13.4	-19.2	17.1	34 10.7	-18.9	17.3	35 08.0	-18.6	17.5	36 05.2	-18.2	17.7	74
75	29 03.0	-21.0	15.3	30 00.9	-20.8	15.4	30 58.7	-20.4	15.6	31 56.5	-20.2	15.8	32 54.2	-19.9	15.9	33 51.8	-19.5	16.1	34 49.4	-19.1	16.3	35 47.0	-18.9	16.5	75
76	28 42.0	-21.6	14.2	29 40.1	-21.2	14.4	30 38.3	-21.0	14.5	31 36.3	-20.7	14.7	32 34.3	-20.4	14.8	33 32.3	-20.1	15.0	34 30.3	-19.9	15.2	35 28.1	-19.5	15.3	76
77	28 20.5	-22.0	13.2	29 18.9	-21.8	13.3	30 17.3	-21.5	13.4	31 15.6	-21.2	13.6	32 13.9	-21.0	13.7	33 12.2	-20.7	13.9	34 10.4	-20.4	14.0	35 08.6	-20.2	14.2	77
78	27 58.5	-22.5	12.1	28 57.1	-22.2	12.2	29 55.8	-22.1	12.3	30 54.4	-21.9	12.5	31 52.9	-21.6	12.6	32 51.5	-21.4	12.7	33 50.0	-21.1	12.9	34 48.4	-20.8	13.0	78
79	27 36.0	-23.0	11.1	28 34.9	-22.8	11.2	29 33.7	-22.5	11.3	30 32.5	-22.3	11.4	31 31.3	-22.1	11.5	32 30.1	-21.9	11.6	33 28.9	-21.7	11.8	34 27.6	-21.4	11.9	79
80	27 13.0	-23.4	10.0	28 12.1	-23.2	10.1	29 11.2	-23.1	10.2	30 10.2	-22.9	10.3	31 09.2	-22.7	10.4	32 08.2	-22.5	10.5	33 07.2	-22.3	10.6	34 06.2	-22.1	10.8	80
81	26 49.6	-23.9	9.0	27 48.9	-23.7	9.1	28 48.1	-23.5	9.2	29 47.3	-23.3	9.2	30 46.5	-23.2	9.3	31 45.7	-23.0	9.4	32 44.9	-22.8	9.5	33 44.1	-22.7	9.6	81
82	26 25.7	-24.3	8.0	27 25.2	-24.2	8.0	28 24.6	-24.1	8.1	29 24.0	-23.9	8.2	30 23.3	-23.7	8.3	31 22.7	-23.6	8.4	32 22.1	-23.4	8.4	33 21.4	-23.2	8.5	82
83	26 01.4	-24.7	6.9	27 01.0	-24.6	7.0	28 00.5	-24.4	7.1	29 00.1	-24.4	7.1	29 59.6	-24.2	7.2	30 59.1	-24.1	7.3	31 58.7	-24.0	7.4	32 58.2	-23.9	7.4	83
84	25 36.7	-25.1	5.9	26 36.4	-25.0	6.0	27 36.1	-25.0	6.0	28 35.7	-24.8	6.1	29 35.4	-24.7	6.1	30 35.0	-24.6	6.2	31 34.7	-24.5	6.3	32 34.3	-24.4	6.3	84
85	25 11.6	-25.5	4.9	26 11.3	-25.4	5.0	27 11.1	-25.4	5.0	28 10.9	-25.3	5.1	29 10.7	-25.3	5.1	30 10.4	-25.1	5.2	31 10.2	-25.1	5.2	32 09.9	-24.9	5.3	85
86	24 46.0	-25.9	3.9	25 45.9	-25.9	4.0	26 45.7	-25.8	4.0	27 45.6	-25.8	4.0	28 45.4	-25.7	4.1	29 45.3	-25.6	4.1	30 45.1	-25.5	4.1	31 45.0	-25.5	4.2	86
87	24 20.1	-26.3	2.9	25 20.0	-26.3	3.0	26 19.9	-26.2	3.0	27 19.8	-26.1	3.0	28 19.7	-26.2	3.0	29 19.7	-26.1	3.1	30 19.6	-26.1	3.1	31 19.5	-26.0	3.1	87
88	23 53.8	-26.7	1.9	24 53.7	-26.6	2.0	25 53.7	-26.7	2.0	26 53.7	-26.7	2.0	27 53.6	-26.6	2.0	28 53.6	-26.6	2.0	29 53.5	-26.5	2.1	30 53.5	-26.5	2.1	88
89	23 27.1	-27.1	1.0	24 27.1	-27.1	1.0	25 27.0	-27.0	1.0	26 27.0	-27.0	1.0	27 27.0	-27.0	1.0	28 27.0	-27.0	1.0	29 27.0	-27.0	1.0	30 27.0	-27.0	1.0	89
90	23 00.0	-27.4	0.0	24 00.0	-27.4	0.0	25 00.0	-27.4	0.0	26 00.0	-27.4	0.0	27 00.0	-27.4	0.0	28 00.0	-27.5	0.0	29 00.0	-27.5	0.0	30 00.0	-27.5	0.0	90
	23°			24°			25°			26°			27°			28°			29°			30°			

63°, 297° L.H.A.   LATITUDE SAME NAME AS DECLINATION

LATITUDE **CONTRARY** NAME TO DECLINATION　　　**L.H.A. 63°, 297°**

Dec.	23° Hc	d	Z	24° Hc	d	Z	25° Hc	d	Z	26° Hc	d	Z	27° Hc	d	Z	28° Hc	d	Z	29° Hc	d	Z	30° Hc	d	Z	Dec.
°	° ′	′	°	° ′	′	°	° ′	′	°	° ′	′	°	° ′	′	°	° ′	′	°	° ′	′	°	° ′	′	°	°
0	24 42.1	−26.0	101.3	24 30.2	−27.0	101.7	24 17.8	−28.0	102.2	24 04.9	−29.0	102.6	23 51.6	−29.9	103.0	23 37.9	−30.9	103.5	23 23.7	−31.9	103.9	23 09.1	−32.8	104.3	0
1	24 16.1	−26.4	102.2	24 03.2	−27.4	102.7	23 49.8	−28.4	103.1	23 35.9	−29.3	103.5	23 21.7	−30.3	104.0	23 07.0	−31.3	104.4	22 51.8	−32.1	104.8	22 36.3	−33.1	105.2	1
2	23 49.7	−26.7	103.2	23 35.8	−27.7	103.7	23 21.4	−28.7	104.1	23 06.6	−29.7	104.5	22 51.4	−30.7	104.9	22 35.7	−31.5	105.3	22 19.7	−32.5	105.7	22 03.2	−33.4	106.1	2
3	23 23.0	−27.1	104.2	23 08.1	−28.1	104.6	22 52.7	−29.1	105.0	22 36.9	−30.0	105.4	22 20.7	−30.9	105.8	22 04.2	−31.9	106.2	21 47.2	−32.8	106.6	21 29.8	−33.6	107.0	3
4	22 55.9	−27.5	105.2	22 40.0	−28.5	105.6	22 23.6	−29.3	106.0	22 06.9	−30.3	106.4	21 49.8	−31.2	106.8	21 32.3	−32.2	107.1	21 14.4	−33.0	107.5	20 56.2	−34.0	107.9	4
5	22 28.4	−27.8	106.1	22 11.5	−28.7	106.5	21 54.3	−29.8	106.9	21 36.6	−30.6	107.3	21 18.6	−31.6	107.7	21 00.1	−32.4	108.1	20 41.4	−33.4	108.4	20 22.2	−34.2	108.8	5
6	22 00.6	−28.1	107.1	21 42.8	−29.1	107.5	21 24.5	−30.0	107.9	21 06.0	−31.0	108.2	20 47.0	−31.8	108.6	20 27.7	−32.7	109.0	20 08.0	−33.6	109.3	19 48.0	−34.4	109.6	6
7	21 32.5	−28.5	108.1	21 13.7	−29.4	108.4	20 54.5	−30.3	108.8	20 35.0	−31.2	109.1	20 15.2	−32.1	109.5	19 55.0	−33.0	109.8	19 34.4	−33.8	110.2	19 13.6	−34.7	110.5	7
8	21 04.0	−28.8	109.0	20 44.3	−29.7	109.4	20 24.2	−30.6	109.7	20 03.8	−31.5	110.1	19 43.1	−32.4	110.4	19 22.0	−33.2	110.7	19 00.6	−34.1	111.1	18 38.9	−35.0	111.4	8
9	20 35.2	−29.0	109.9	20 14.6	−30.0	110.3	19 53.6	−30.9	110.6	19 32.3	−31.7	111.0	19 10.7	−32.6	111.3	18 48.8	−33.5	111.6	18 26.5	−34.3	111.9	18 03.9	−35.1	112.2	9
10	20 06.2	−29.4	110.9	19 44.6	−30.3	111.2	19 22.7	−31.1	111.5	19 00.6	−32.1	111.9	18 38.1	−32.9	112.2	18 15.3	−33.8	112.5	17 52.2	−34.6	112.8	17 28.8	−35.4	113.1	10
11	19 36.8	−29.7	111.8	19 14.3	−30.5	112.1	18 51.6	−31.4	112.4	18 28.5	−32.2	112.8	18 05.2	−33.1	113.1	17 41.5	−33.9	113.4	17 17.6	−34.8	113.6	16 53.4	−35.6	113.9	11
12	19 07.1	−29.9	112.7	18 43.8	−30.8	113.0	18 20.2	−31.7	113.3	17 56.3	−32.5	113.6	17 32.1	−33.4	113.9	17 07.6	−34.2	114.2	16 42.8	−34.9	114.5	16 17.8	−35.7	114.8	12
13	18 37.2	−30.2	113.6	18 13.0	−31.0	113.9	17 48.5	−31.9	114.2	17 23.8	−32.8	114.5	16 58.7	−33.5	114.8	16 33.4	−34.4	115.1	16 07.9	−35.2	115.3	15 42.1	−36.0	115.6	13
14	18 07.0	−30.4	114.5	17 42.0	−31.3	114.8	17 16.6	−32.1	115.1	16 51.0	−32.9	115.4	16 25.2	−33.8	115.7	15 59.0	−34.5	115.9	15 32.7	−35.4	116.2	15 06.1	−36.2	116.4	14
15	17 36.6	−30.7	115.5	17 10.7	−31.6	115.7	16 44.5	−32.4	116.0	16 18.1	−33.2	116.3	15 51.4	−34.0	116.5	15 24.5	−34.8	116.8	14 57.3	−35.6	117.0	14 29.9	−36.3	117.3	15
16	17 05.9	−30.9	116.4	16 39.1	−31.7	116.6	16 12.1	−32.5	116.9	15 44.9	−33.4	117.1	15 17.4	−34.2	117.4	14 49.7	−35.0	117.6	14 21.7	−35.7	117.9	13 53.6	−36.5	118.1	16
17	16 35.0	−31.2	117.2	16 07.4	−32.0	117.5	15 39.6	−32.8	117.8	15 11.5	−33.6	118.0	14 43.2	−34.3	118.2	14 14.7	−35.1	118.5	13 46.0	−35.9	118.7	13 17.1	−36.6	118.9	17
18	16 03.8	−31.4	118.1	15 35.4	−32.2	118.4	15 06.8	−33.0	118.6	14 37.9	−33.7	118.9	14 08.9	−34.6	119.1	13 39.6	−35.3	119.3	13 10.1	−36.0	119.5	12 40.5	−36.8	119.7	18
19	15 32.4	−31.5	119.0	15 03.2	−32.4	119.3	14 33.8	−33.2	119.5	14 04.2	−34.0	119.7	13 34.3	−34.7	119.9	13 04.3	−35.5	120.1	12 34.1	−36.2	120.3	12 03.7	−36.9	120.5	19
20	15 00.9	−31.8	119.9	14 30.8	−32.5	120.1	14 00.6	−33.3	120.4	13 30.2	−34.1	120.6	12 59.6	−34.9	120.8	12 28.8	−35.6	121.0	11 57.9	−36.4	121.1	11 26.8	−37.1	121.3	20
21	14 29.1	−32.0	120.8	13 58.3	−32.8	121.0	13 27.3	−33.6	121.2	12 56.1	−34.3	121.4	12 24.7	−35.0	121.6	11 53.2	−35.7	121.8	11 21.5	−36.4	122.0	10 49.7	−37.2	122.1	21
22	13 57.1	−32.2	121.7	13 25.5	−32.9	121.9	12 53.7	−33.6	122.1	12 21.8	−34.4	122.2	11 49.7	−35.1	122.4	11 17.5	−35.9	122.6	10 45.1	−36.6	122.8	10 12.5	−37.3	122.9	22
23	13 24.9	−32.3	122.5	12 52.6	−33.1	122.7	12 20.1	−33.9	122.9	11 47.4	−34.6	123.1	11 14.6	−35.3	123.3	10 41.6	−36.0	123.4	10 08.5	−36.7	123.6	9 35.2	−37.4	123.7	23
24	12 52.6	−32.5	123.4	12 19.5	−33.3	123.6	11 46.2	−34.0	123.8	11 12.8	−34.7	123.9	10 39.3	−35.5	124.1	10 05.6	−36.2	124.2	9 31.8	−36.9	124.4	8 57.8	−37.5	124.5	24
25	12 20.1	−32.7	124.2	11 46.2	−33.4	124.4	11 12.2	−34.1	124.6	10 38.1	−34.9	124.8	10 03.8	−35.5	124.9	9 29.4	−36.2	125.0	8 54.9	−36.9	125.2	8 20.3	−37.6	125.3	25
26	11 47.4	−32.8	125.1	11 12.8	−33.5	125.3	10 38.1	−34.3	125.4	10 03.2	−34.9	125.6	9 28.3	−35.7	125.7	8 53.2	−36.4	125.8	8 18.0	−37.0	126.0	7 42.7	−37.7	126.1	26
27	11 14.6	−33.0	126.0	10 39.3	−33.7	126.1	10 03.8	−34.4	126.3	9 28.3	−35.1	126.4	8 52.6	−35.8	126.5	8 16.8	−36.4	126.7	7 41.0	−37.1	126.8	7 05.0	−37.7	126.9	27
28	10 41.6	−33.1	126.8	10 05.6	−33.8	127.0	9 29.4	−34.5	127.1	8 53.2	−35.2	127.2	8 16.8	−35.8	127.3	7 40.4	−36.5	127.5	7 03.9	−37.2	127.6	6 27.3	−37.9	127.7	28
29	10 08.5	−33.3	127.7	9 31.8	−34.0	127.8	8 54.9	−34.6	127.9	8 18.0	−35.3	128.0	7 41.0	−36.0	128.2	7 03.9	−36.6	128.3	6 26.7	−37.3	128.3	5 49.4	−37.9	128.4	29
30	9 35.2	−33.3	128.5	8 57.8	−34.0	128.6	8 20.3	−34.7	128.8	7 42.7	−35.4	128.9	7 05.0	−36.0	129.0	6 27.3	−36.7	129.1	5 49.4	−37.3	129.1	5 11.5	−37.9	129.2	30
31	9 01.9	−33.5	129.3	8 23.8	−34.2	129.5	7 45.6	−34.8	129.6	7 07.3	−35.4	129.7	6 29.0	−36.1	129.8	5 50.6	−36.8	129.8	5 12.1	−37.4	129.9	4 33.6	−38.0	130.0	31
32	8 28.4	−33.6	130.2	7 49.6	−34.2	130.3	7 10.8	−34.9	130.4	6 31.9	−35.6	130.5	5 52.9	−36.2	130.6	5 13.8	−36.8	130.6	4 34.7	−37.4	130.7	3 55.6	−38.1	130.8	32
33	7 54.8	−33.7	131.0	7 15.4	−34.4	131.1	6 35.9	−35.0	131.2	5 56.3	−35.6	131.3	5 16.7	−36.3	131.4	4 37.0	−36.9	131.4	3 57.3	−37.5	131.5	3 17.5	−38.1	131.5	33
34	7 21.1	−33.8	131.9	6 41.0	−34.4	131.9	6 00.9	−35.1	132.0	5 20.7	−35.7	132.1	4 40.4	−36.3	132.2	4 00.1	−36.9	132.2	3 19.8	−37.5	132.3	2 39.4	−38.1	132.3	34
35	6 47.3	−33.8	132.7	6 06.6	−34.5	132.8	5 25.8	−35.1	132.8	4 45.0	−35.7	132.9	4 04.1	−36.3	133.0	3 23.2	−36.9	133.0	2 42.3	−37.6	133.1	2 01.3	−38.1	133.1	35
36	6 13.5	−34.0	133.5	5 32.1	−34.5	133.6	4 50.7	−35.2	133.7	4 09.3	−35.8	133.7	3 27.8	−36.4	133.8	2 46.3	−37.0	133.8	2 04.7	−37.6	133.8	1 23.2	−38.2	133.9	36
37	5 39.5	−34.0	134.4	4 57.6	−34.7	134.4	4 15.5	−35.2	134.5	3 33.5	−35.8	134.5	2 51.4	−36.4	134.6	2 09.3	−37.0	134.6	1 27.1	−37.5	134.6	0 45.0	−38.2	134.6	37
38	5 05.5	−34.1	135.2	4 22.9	−34.6	135.2	3 40.3	−35.3	135.3	2 57.7	−35.9	135.3	2 15.0	−36.5	135.4	1 32.3	−37.1	135.4	0 49.6	−37.6	135.4	0 06.8	−38.1	135.4	38
39	4 31.4	−34.1	136.0	3 48.3	−34.8	136.1	3 05.0	−35.3	136.1	2 21.8	−35.9	136.1	1 38.5	−36.4	136.2	0 55.2	−37.0	136.2	0 12.0	−37.6	136.2	0 31.3	+38.2	43.8	39
40	3 57.3	−34.2	136.8	3 13.5	−34.7	136.9	2 29.7	−35.3	136.9	1 45.9	−35.9	136.9	1 02.1	−36.5	136.9	0 18.2	−37.0	137.0	0 25.6	+37.6	43.0	1 09.5	+38.1	43.1	40
41	3 23.1	−34.2	137.7	2 38.8	−34.8	137.7	1 54.4	−35.4	137.7	1 10.0	−35.9	137.7	0 25.6	−36.5	137.7	0 18.8	+37.1	42.3	1 03.2	+37.6	42.3	1 47.6	+38.2	42.3	41
42	2 48.9	−34.3	138.5	2 04.0	−34.9	138.5	1 19.0	−35.4	138.5	0 34.1	−36.0	138.5	0 10.9	+36.5	41.5	0 55.9	+37.0	41.5	1 40.8	+37.6	41.5	2 25.8	+38.1	41.5	42
43	2 14.6	−34.2	139.3	1 29.1	−34.8	139.3	0 43.6	−35.3	139.3	0 01.9	+35.9	40.7	0 47.4	+36.5	40.7	1 32.9	+37.0	40.7	2 18.4	+37.5	40.7	3 03.9	+38.0	40.7	43
44	1 40.4	−34.4	140.1	0 54.3	−34.8	140.1	0 08.3	−35.4	140.1	0 37.8	+35.9	39.9	1 23.9	+36.4	39.9	2 09.9	+37.0	39.9	2 55.9	+37.5	39.9	3 41.9	+38.0	40.0	44
45	1 06.0	−34.3	140.9	0 19.5	−34.9	140.9	0 27.1	+35.4	39.1	1 13.7	+35.9	39.1	2 00.3	+36.4	39.1	2 46.9	+36.9	39.1	3 33.4	+37.5	39.1	4 19.9	+38.0	39.2	45
46	0 31.7	−34.3	141.8	0 15.4	+34.8	38.2	1 02.5	+35.4	38.2	1 49.6	+35.9	38.3	2 36.7	+36.4	38.3	3 23.8	+36.9	38.3	4 10.9	+37.4	38.4	4 57.9	+37.9	38.4	46
47	0 02.6	+34.3	37.4	0 50.2	+34.9	37.4	1 37.9	+35.3	37.4	2 25.5	+35.9	37.5	3 13.1	+36.4	37.5	4 00.7	+36.9	37.5	4 48.3	+37.4	37.6	5 35.8	+37.9	37.6	47
48	0 36.9	+34.3	36.6	1 25.1	+34.8	36.6	2 13.2	+35.4	36.6	3 01.4	+35.8	36.7	3 49.5	+36.3	36.7	4 37.6	+36.8	36.7	5 25.7	+37.3	36.8	6 13.7	+37.8	36.9	48
49	1 11.2	+34.3	35.8	1 59.9	+34.8	35.8	2 48.6	+35.3	35.8	3 37.2	+35.8	35.9	4 25.8	+36.3	35.9	5 14.4	+36.8	35.9	6 03.0	+37.2	36.0	6 51.5	+37.7	36.1	49
50	1 45.5	+34.3	35.0	2 34.7	+34.8	35.0	3 23.9	+35.2	35.0	4 13.0	+35.7	35.0	5 02.1	+36.2	35.1	5 51.2	+36.7	35.2	6 40.2	+37.2	35.2	7 29.2	+37.6	35.3	50
51	2 19.8	+34.3	34.1	3 09.5	+34.7	34.2	3 59.1	+35.2	34.2	4 48.7	+35.7	34.2	5 38.3	+36.2	34.3	6 27.9	+36.6	34.4	7 17.4	+37.1	34.4	8 06.8	+37.6	34.5	51
52	2 54.1	+34.2	33.3	3 44.2	+34.7	33.3	4 34.3	+35.2	33.4	5 24.4	+35.6	33.4	6 14.5	+36.0	33.5	7 04.5	+36.5	33.6	7 54.5	+36.9	33.6	8 44.4	+37.4	33.7	52
53	3 28.3	+34.2	32.5	4 18.9	+34.6	32.5	5 09.5	+35.1	32.6	6 00.0	+35.6	32.6	6 50.5	+36.0	32.7	7 41.0	+36.4	32.8	8 31.4	+36.9	32.8	9 21.8	+37.4	32.9	53
54	4 02.5	+34.1	31.7	4 53.5	+34.6	31.7	5 44.6	+35.0	31.8	6 35.6	+35.4	31.8	7 26.5	+35.9	31.9	8 17.4	+36.4	32.0	9 08.3	+36.8	32.0	9 59.2	+37.2	32.1	54
55	4 36.6	+34.1	30.8	5 28.1	+34.5	30.9	6 19.6	+34.9	30.9	7 11.0	+35.4	31.0	8 02.4	+35.8	31.1	8 53.8	+36.2	31.2	9 45.1	+36.7	31.2	10 36.4	+37.1	31.3	55
56	5 10.7	+34.0	30.0	6 02.6	+34.4	30.1	6 54.5	+34.9	30.1	7 46.4	+35.3	30.2	8 38.2	+35.7	30.3	9 30.0	+36.2	30.3	10 21.8	+36.5	30.4	11 13.5	+37.0	30.5	56
57	5 44.7	+33.9	29.2	6 37.0	+34.4	29.2	7 29.4	+34.7	29.3	8 21.7	+35.2	29.4	9 13.9	+35.6	29.4	10 06.2	+36.0	29.5	10 58.3	+36.5	29.6	11 50.5	+36.8	29.7	57
58	6 18.6	+33.8	28.4	7 11.4	+34.2	28.4	8 04.1	+34.7	28.5	8 56.9	+35.0	28.6	9 49.5	+35.5	28.6	10 42.2	+35.9	28.7	11 34.8	+36.3	28.8	12 27.3	+36.7	28.9	58
59	6 52.4	+33.8	27.5	7 45.6	+34.2	27.6	8 38.8	+34.6	27.7	9 31.9	+35.0	27.7	10 25.0	+35.4	27.8	11 18.1	+35.7	27.9	12 11.1	+36.1	28.0	13 04.0	+36.6	28.1	59
60	7 26.2	+33.7	26.7	8 19.8	+34.1	26.8	9 13.4	+34.4	26.8	10 06.9	+34.8	26.9	11 00.4	+35.2	27.0	11 53.8	+35.6	27.1	12 47.2	+36.0	27.2	13 40.6	+36.3	27.3	60
61	7 59.9	+33.6	25.9	8 53.9	+33.9	25.9	9 47.8	+34.3	26.0	10 41.7	+34.7	26.1	11 35.6	+35.1	26.2	12 29.4	+35.5	26.3	13 23.2	+35.8	26.4	14 16.9	+36.2	26.5	61
62	8 33.5	+33.4	25.0	9 27.8	+33.8	25.1	10 22.1	+34.2	25.2	11 16.4	+34.6	25.2	12 10.7	+34.9	25.3	13 04.9	+35.3	25.4	13 59.0	+35.7	25.5	14 53.1	+36.1	25.6	62
63	9 06.9	+33.4	24.2	10 01.6	+33.7	24.3	10 56.3	+34.1	24.3	11 51.0	+34.4	24.4	12 45.6	+34.8	24.5	13 40.2	+35.1	24.6	14 34.7	+35.5	24.7	15 29.2	+35.8	24.8	63
64	9 40.3	+33.2	23.3	10 35.3	+33.6	23.4	11 30.4	+33.9	23.5	12 25.4	+34.3	23.6	13 20.4	+34.6	23.7	14 15.3	+35.0	23.8	15 10.2	+35.3	23.9	16 05.0	+35.7	24.0	64
65	10 13.5	+33.1	22.5	11 08.9	+33.4	22.6	12 04.3	+33.8	22.6	12 59.7	+34.0	22.7	13 55.0	+34.4	22.8	14 50.3	+34.7	22.9	15 45.5	+35.1	23.0	16 40.7	+35.4	23.1	65
66	10 46.6	+32.9	21.6	11 42.3	+33.3	21.7	12 38.1	+33.6	21.8	13 33.7	+34.0	21.9	14 29.4	+34.3	22.0	15 25.0	+34.6	22.1	16 20.6	+34.9	22.2	17 16.1	+35.3	22.3	66
67	11 19.5	+32.8	20.8	12 15.6	+33.1	20.9	13 11.7	+33.4	21.0	14 07.7	+33.7	21.0	15 03.7	+34.0	21.1	15 59.6	+34.4	21.2	16 55.5	+34.7	21.3	17 51.4	+35.0	21.5	67
68	11 52.3	+32.7	19.9	12 48.7	+33.0	20.0	13 45.1	+33.2	20.1	14 41.4	+33.6	20.2	15 37.7	+33.9	20.3	16 34.0	+34.1	20.4	17 30.2	+34.5	20.5	18 26.4	+34.8	20.6	68
69	12 25.0	+32.5	19.1	13 21.7	+32.8	19.2	14 18.3	+33.1	19.2	15 15.0	+33.3	19.3	16 11.6	+33.6	19.4	17 08.1	+34.0	19.5	18 04.7	+34.2	19.6	19 01.2	+34.5	19.7	69
70	12 57.5	+32.3	18.2	13 54.5	+32.6	18.3	14 51.4	+32.9	18.4	15 48.3	+33.2	18.5	16 45.2	+33.5	18.6	17 42.1	+33.7	18.7	18 38.9	+34.0	18.8	19 35.7	+34.3	18.9	70
71	13 29.8	+32.1	17.4	14 27.1	+32.4	17.4	15 24.3	+32.7	17.5	16 21.5	+32.9	17.6	17 18.7	+33.2	17.7	18 15.8	+33.5	17.8	19 12.9	+33.8	17.9	20 10.0	+34.1	18.0	71
72	14 01.9	+32.0	16.5	14 59.5	+32.2	16.6	15 57.0	+32.4	16.6	16 54.4	+32.8	16.7	17 51.9	+33.0	16.8	18 49.3	+33.2	16.9	19 46.7	+33.5	17.0	20 44.1	+33.7	17.1	72
73	14 33.9	+31.7	15.6	15 31.7	+32.0	15.7	16 29.4	+32.3	15.8	17 27.2	+32.4	15.8	18 24.9	+32.7	15.9	19 22.5	+33.0	16.0	20 20.2	+33.2	16.1	21 17.8	+33.5	16.2	73
74	15 05.6	+31.6	14.7	16 03.7	+31.7	14.8	17 01.7	+32.0	14.9	17 59.6	+32.3	15.0	18 57.6	+32.5	15.1	19 55.5	+32.7	15.1	20 53.4	+33.0	15.2	21 51.3	+33.2	15.3	74
75	15 37.2	+31.3	13.9	16 35.4	+31.6	13.9	17 33.7	+31.8	14.0	18 31.9	+32.0	14.1	19 30.1	+32.2	14.2	20 28.2	+32.5	14.3	21 26.4	+32.6	14.3	22 24.5	+32.9	14.4	75
76	16 08.5	+31.2	13.0	17 07.0	+31.3	13.0	18 05.5	+31.5	13.1	19 03.9	+31.7	13.2	20 02.3	+31.9	13.3	21 00.7	+32.1	13.4	21 59.0	+32.4	13.4	22 57.4	+32.6	13.5	76
77	16 39.7	+30.9	12.1	17 38.3	+31.1	12.1	18 37.0	+31.3	12.2	19 35.6	+31.5	12.3	20 34.2	+31.7	12.4	21 32.8	+31.9	12.4	22 31.4	+32.1	12.5	23 30.0	+32.2	12.6	77
78	17 10.6	+30.6	11.2	18 09.4	+30.8	11.2	19 08.3	+31.0	11.3	20 07.1	+31.2	11.4	21 05.9	+31.4	11.5	22 04.7	+31.5	11.5	23 03.5	+31.7	11.6	24 02.2	+32.0	11.7	78
79	17 41.2	+30.4	10.3	18 40.2	+30.6	10.3	19 39.3	+30.7	10.4	20 38.3	+30.9	10.5	21 37.3	+31.0	10.5	22 36.2	+31.3	10.6	23 35.2	+31.4	10.7	24 34.2	+31.5	10.8	79
80	18 11.6	+30.2	9.4	19 10.8	+30.3	9.4	20 10.0	+30.4	9.5	21 09.2	+30.6	9.5	22 08.3	+30.8	9.6	23 07.5	+30.9	9.7	24 06.6	+31.1	9.8	25 05.7	+31.3	9.8	80
81	18 41.8	+29.8	8.5	19 41.1	+30.0	8.5	20 40.4	+30.2	8.6	21 39.8	+30.3	8.6	22 39.1	+30.4	8.7	23 38.4	+30.6	8.8	24 37.7	+30.7	8.8	25 37.0	+30.8	8.9	81
82	19 11.6	+29.6	7.5	20 11.1	+29.7	7.6	21 10.6	+29.8	7.6	22 10.1	+29.9	7.7	23 09.5	+30.1	7.8	24 09.0	+30.2	7.8	25 08.4	+30.3	7.9	26 07.8	+30.5	7.9	82
83	19 41.2	+29.4	6.6	20 40.8	+29.5	6.7	21 40.4	+29.6	6.7	22 40.0	+29.7	6.8	23 39.6	+29.8	6.8	24 39.2	+29.8	6.9	25 38.7	+30.0	6.9	26 38.3	+30.1	7.0	83
84	20 10.6	+29.0	5.7	21 10.3	+29.1	5.7	22 10.0	+29.2	5.8	23 09.7	+29.3	5.8	24 09.4	+29.3	5.9	25 09.0	+29.5	5.9	26 08.7	+29.6	6.0	27 08.4	+29.7	6.0	84
85	20 39.6	+28.7	4.8	21 39.4	+28.8	4.8	22 39.2	+28.9	4.8	23 39.0	+28.9	4.9	24 38.7	+29.1	4.9	25 38.5	+29.1	4.9	26 38.3	+29.2	5.0	27 38.1	+29.2	5.0	85
86	21 08.3	+28.4	3.8	22 08.2	+28.5	3.8	23 08.1	+28.5	3.9	24 07.9	+28.6	3.9	25 07.8	+28.6	3.9	26 07.6	+28.7	4.0	27 07.5	+28.8	4.0	28 07.3	+28.9	4.0	86
87	21 36.7	+28.1	2.9	22 36.7	+28.1	2.9	23 36.6	+28.2	2.9	24 36.5	+28.2	2.9	25 36.4	+28.3	3.0	26 36.3	+28.4	3.0	27 36.3	+28.3	3.0	28 36.2	+28.4	3.0	87
88	22 04.8	+27.8	1.9	23 04.8	+27.8	1.9	24 04.8	+27.8	2.0	25 04.7	+27.9	2.0	26 04.7	+27.9	2.0	27 04.7	+27.8	2.0	28 04.6	+27.9	2.0	29 04.6	+27.9	2.0	88
89	22 32.6	+27.4	1.0	23 32.6	+27.4	1.0	24 32.6	+27.4	1.0	25 32.6	+27.4	1.0	26 32.6	+27.4	1.0	27 32.5	+27.5	1.0	28 32.5	+27.5	1.0	29 32.5	+27.5	1.0	89
90	23 00.0	+27.1	0.0	24 00.0	+27.1	0.0	25 00.0	+27.0	0.0	26 00.0	+27.0	0.0	27 00.0	+27.0	0.0	28 00.0	+27.0	0.0	29 00.0	+27.0	0.0	30 00.0	+27.0	0.0	90
	23°			24°			25°			26°			27°			28°			29°			30°			

S. Lat. {L.H.A. greater than 180° ....Zn=180°−Z; L.H.A. less than 180°..........Zn=180°+Z

LATITUDE **SAME** NAME AS DECLINATION　　　**L.H.A. 117°, 243°**

311

Dec.	23° Hc	d	Z	24° Hc	d	Z	25° Hc	d	Z	26° Hc	d	Z	27° Hc	d	Z	28° Hc	d	Z	29° Hc	d	Z	30° Hc	d	Z	Dec.
°	° ′	′	°	° ′	′	°	° ′	′	°	° ′	′	°	° ′	′	°	° ′	′	°	° ′	′	°	° ′	′	°	°
0	23 47.9	+25.4	100.8	23 36.5	+26.4	101.2	23 24.6	+27.4	101.6	23 12.2	+28.5	102.1	22 59.5	+29.4	102.5	22 46.3	+30.4	102.9	22 32.7	+31.3	103.3	22 18.7	+32.3	103.7	0
1	24 13.3	+25.1	99.8	24 02.9	+26.1	100.2	23 52.0	+27.1	100.7	23 40.7	+28.1	101.1	23 28.9	+29.1	101.5	23 16.7	+30.0	102.0	23 04.0	+31.0	102.4	22 51.0	+31.9	102.8	1
2	24 38.4	+24.6	98.8	24 29.0	+25.7	99.3	24 19.1	+26.7	99.7	24 08.8	+27.7	100.1	23 58.0	+28.7	100.6	23 46.7	+29.7	101.0	23 35.0	+30.7	101.4	23 22.9	+31.7	101.9	2
3	25 03.0	+24.3	97.8	24 54.7	+25.2	98.3	24 45.8	+26.3	98.7	24 36.5	+27.3	99.2	24 26.7	+28.3	99.6	24 16.4	+29.4	100.1	24 05.7	+30.3	100.5	23 54.6	+31.2	100.9	3
4	25 27.3	+23.8	96.8	25 19.9	+24.9	97.3	25 12.1	+25.9	97.7	25 03.8	+27.0	98.2	24 55.0	+28.0	98.6	24 45.8	+29.0	99.1	24 36.0	+30.0	99.6	24 25.8	+31.0	100.0	4
5	25 51.1	+23.4	95.8	25 44.8	+24.5	96.2	25 38.0	+25.5	96.7	25 30.8	+26.5	97.2	25 23.0	+27.6	97.7	25 14.8	+28.5	98.1	25 06.0	+29.6	98.6	24 56.8	+30.6	99.1	5
6	26 14.5	+22.9	94.7	26 09.3	+24.0	95.2	26 03.5	+25.1	95.7	25 57.3	+26.2	96.2	25 50.6	+27.2	96.7	25 43.3	+28.2	97.2	25 35.6	+29.2	97.6	25 27.4	+30.2	98.1	6
7	26 37.4	+22.5	93.7	26 33.3	+23.6	94.2	26 28.6	+24.7	94.7	26 23.5	+25.7	95.2	26 17.8	+26.7	95.7	26 11.5	+27.8	96.2	26 04.8	+28.9	96.7	25 57.6	+29.8	97.2	7
8	26 59.9	+22.1	92.7	26 56.9	+23.1	93.2	26 53.3	+24.2	93.7	26 49.2	+25.2	94.2	26 44.5	+26.4	94.7	26 39.3	+27.4	95.2	26 33.7	+28.4	95.7	26 27.4	+29.5	96.2	8
9	27 22.0	+21.6	91.6	27 20.0	+22.7	92.1	27 17.5	+23.8	92.7	27 14.4	+24.9	93.2	27 10.9	+25.9	93.7	27 06.7	+27.0	94.2	27 02.1	+28.0	94.7	26 56.9	+29.0	95.2	9
10	27 43.6	+21.0	90.6	27 42.7	+22.2	91.1	27 41.3	+23.2	91.6	27 39.3	+24.4	92.1	27 36.8	+25.4	92.7	27 33.7	+26.5	93.2	27 30.1	+27.6	93.7	27 25.9	+28.6	94.2	10
11	28 04.6	+20.6	89.5	28 04.9	+21.7	90.0	28 04.5	+22.9	90.6	28 03.7	+23.9	91.1	28 02.2	+25.0	91.6	28 00.2	+26.1	92.2	27 57.7	+27.1	92.7	27 54.5	+28.2	93.2	11
12	28 25.2	+20.1	88.4	28 26.6	+21.2	89.0	28 27.4	+22.3	89.5	28 27.6	+23.4	90.1	28 27.2	+24.5	90.6	28 26.3	+25.6	91.2	28 24.8	+26.7	91.7	28 22.7	+27.8	92.2	12
13	28 45.3	+19.6	87.4	28 47.8	+20.7	87.9	28 49.7	+21.8	88.5	28 51.0	+22.9	89.0	28 51.7	+24.1	89.6	28 51.9	+25.1	90.1	28 51.5	+26.2	90.7	28 50.5	+27.3	91.2	13
14	29 04.9	+19.1	86.3	29 08.5	+20.2	86.8	29 11.5	+21.3	87.4	29 13.9	+22.5	88.0	29 15.8	+23.5	88.5	29 17.0	+24.7	89.1	29 17.7	+25.7	89.6	29 17.8	+26.8	90.2	14
15	29 24.0	+18.5	85.2	29 28.7	+19.7	85.8	29 32.8	+20.8	86.3	29 36.4	+21.9	86.9	29 39.3	+23.1	87.5	29 41.7	+24.1	88.0	29 43.4	+25.3	88.6	29 44.6	+26.3	89.2	15
16	29 42.5	+18.0	84.1	29 48.4	+19.1	84.7	29 53.6	+20.3	85.3	29 58.3	+21.4	85.8	30 02.4	+22.5	86.4	30 05.8	+23.7	87.0	30 08.7	+24.7	87.6	30 10.9	+25.9	88.1	16
17	30 00.5	+17.5	83.0	30 07.5	+18.6	83.6	30 13.9	+19.7	84.2	30 19.7	+20.9	84.7	30 24.9	+22.0	85.3	30 29.5	+23.1	85.9	30 33.4	+24.3	86.5	30 36.8	+25.3	87.1	17
18	30 18.0	+16.8	81.9	30 26.1	+18.0	82.5	30 33.6	+19.2	83.1	30 40.6	+20.3	83.7	30 46.9	+21.4	84.3	30 52.6	+22.6	84.8	30 57.7	+23.7	85.4	31 02.1	+24.8	86.0	18
19	30 34.8	+16.3	80.8	30 44.1	+17.5	81.4	30 52.8	+18.6	82.0	31 00.9	+19.7	82.6	31 08.3	+20.9	83.2	31 15.2	+22.0	83.8	31 21.4	+23.1	84.4	31 26.9	+24.3	85.0	19
20	30 51.1	+15.8	79.7	31 01.6	+16.9	80.3	31 11.4	+18.1	80.9	31 20.6	+19.2	81.5	31 29.2	+20.4	82.1	31 37.2	+21.5	82.7	31 44.5	+22.7	83.3	31 51.2	+23.8	83.9	20
21	31 06.9	+15.1	78.5	31 18.5	+16.3	79.1	31 29.5	+17.4	79.7	31 39.8	+18.6	80.3	31 49.6	+19.7	81.0	31 58.7	+20.9	81.6	32 07.2	+22.0	82.2	32 15.0	+23.2	82.8	21
22	31 22.0	+14.5	77.4	31 34.8	+15.6	78.0	31 46.9	+16.9	78.6	31 58.4	+18.0	79.2	32 09.3	+19.2	79.8	32 19.6	+20.3	80.5	32 29.2	+21.5	81.1	32 38.2	+22.6	81.7	22
23	31 36.5	+13.9	76.3	31 50.4	+15.1	76.9	32 03.8	+16.2	77.5	32 16.4	+17.4	78.1	32 28.5	+18.6	78.7	32 39.9	+19.7	79.4	32 50.7	+20.8	80.0	33 00.8	+22.0	80.6	23
24	31 50.4	+13.4	75.1	32 05.5	+14.5	75.7	32 20.0	+15.6	76.4	32 33.8	+16.8	77.0	32 47.1	+17.9	77.6	32 59.6	+19.1	78.2	33 11.5	+20.3	78.9	33 22.8	+21.4	79.5	24
25	32 03.8	+12.6	74.0	32 20.0	+13.8	74.6	32 35.6	+15.0	75.2	32 50.6	+16.2	75.8	33 05.0	+17.3	76.5	33 18.7	+18.5	77.1	33 31.8	+19.7	77.7	33 44.2	+20.8	78.4	25
26	32 16.4	+12.1	72.8	32 33.8	+13.3	73.4	32 50.6	+14.4	74.1	33 06.8	+15.5	74.7	33 22.3	+16.7	75.3	33 37.2	+17.9	76.0	33 51.5	+19.0	76.6	34 05.0	+20.2	77.3	26
27	32 28.5	+11.4	71.7	32 47.1	+12.5	72.3	33 05.0	+13.7	72.9	33 22.3	+14.9	73.5	33 39.0	+16.1	74.2	33 55.1	+17.2	74.8	34 10.5	+18.4	75.5	34 25.2	+19.6	76.1	27
28	32 39.9	+10.8	70.5	32 59.6	+11.9	71.1	33 18.7	+13.1	71.7	33 37.2	+14.3	72.4	33 55.1	+15.4	73.0	34 12.3	+16.6	73.7	34 28.9	+17.7	74.3	34 44.8	+18.9	75.0	28
29	32 50.7	+10.1	69.3	33 11.5	+11.3	69.9	33 31.8	+12.4	70.6	33 51.5	+13.5	71.2	34 10.5	+14.7	71.8	34 28.9	+15.9	72.5	34 46.6	+17.1	73.1	35 03.7	+18.2	73.8	29
30	33 00.8	+9.4	68.2	33 22.8	+10.6	68.8	33 44.2	+11.8	69.4	34 05.0	+12.9	70.0	34 25.2	+14.1	70.7	34 44.8	+15.2	71.3	35 03.7	+16.3	72.0	35 21.9	+17.5	72.6	30
31	33 10.2	+8.8	67.0	33 33.4	+9.9	67.6	33 56.0	+11.0	68.2	34 17.9	+12.2	68.8	34 39.3	+13.3	69.5	35 00.0	+14.5	70.1	35 20.0	+15.7	70.8	35 39.4	+16.9	71.5	31
32	33 19.0	+8.1	65.8	33 43.3	+9.2	66.4	34 07.0	+10.4	67.0	34 30.1	+11.5	67.7	34 52.6	+12.7	68.3	35 14.5	+13.8	68.9	35 35.7	+15.0	69.6	35 56.3	+16.2	70.3	32
33	33 27.1	+7.4	64.6	33 52.5	+8.6	65.2	34 17.4	+9.7	65.8	34 41.6	+10.9	66.5	35 05.3	+12.0	67.1	35 28.3	+13.2	67.8	35 50.7	+14.3	68.4	36 12.5	+15.4	69.1	33
34	33 34.5	+6.7	63.4	34 01.1	+7.8	64.0	34 27.1	+8.9	64.6	34 52.5	+10.1	65.3	35 17.3	+11.2	65.9	35 41.5	+12.4	66.6	36 05.0	+13.6	67.2	36 27.9	+14.7	67.9	34
35	33 41.2	+6.1	62.2	34 08.9	+7.2	62.8	34 36.0	+8.3	63.4	35 02.6	+9.4	64.1	35 28.5	+10.6	64.7	35 53.9	+11.6	65.4	36 18.6	+12.8	66.0	36 42.6	+14.0	66.7	35
36	33 47.3	+5.3	61.0	34 16.1	+6.4	61.6	34 44.3	+7.6	62.2	35 12.0	+8.6	62.9	35 39.1	+9.8	63.5	36 05.5	+11.0	64.1	36 31.4	+12.1	64.8	36 56.6	+13.3	65.5	36
37	33 52.6	+4.7	59.8	34 22.5	+5.8	60.4	34 51.9	+6.8	61.0	35 20.6	+8.0	61.6	35 48.9	+9.0	62.3	36 16.5	+10.2	62.9	36 43.5	+11.3	63.6	37 09.9	+12.4	64.3	37
38	33 57.3	+3.9	58.6	34 28.3	+5.0	59.2	34 58.7	+6.1	59.8	35 28.6	+7.2	60.4	35 57.9	+8.3	61.1	36 26.7	+9.4	61.7	36 54.8	+10.6	62.4	37 22.3	+11.8	63.0	38
39	34 01.2	+3.3	57.4	34 33.3	+4.3	58.0	35 04.8	+5.4	58.6	35 35.8	+6.5	59.2	36 06.2	+7.6	59.8	36 36.1	+8.7	60.5	37 05.4	+9.8	61.1	37 34.1	+10.9	61.8	39
40	34 04.5	+2.5	56.2	34 37.6	+3.6	56.8	35 10.2	+4.6	57.4	35 42.3	+5.7	58.0	36 13.8	+6.8	58.6	36 44.8	+7.9	59.2	37 15.2	+9.0	59.9	37 45.0	+10.1	60.5	40
41	34 07.0	+1.9	55.0	34 41.2	+2.8	55.6	35 14.8	+4.0	56.2	35 48.0	+5.0	56.8	36 20.6	+6.1	57.4	36 52.7	+7.1	58.0	37 24.2	+8.3	58.6	37 55.1	+9.4	59.3	41
42	34 08.9	+1.1	53.8	34 44.0	+2.2	54.4	35 18.8	+3.1	54.9	35 53.0	+4.2	55.5	36 26.7	+5.3	56.1	36 59.8	+6.4	56.8	37 32.5	+7.4	57.4	38 04.5	+8.6	58.0	42
43	34 10.0	+0.4	52.6	34 46.2	+1.4	53.2	35 21.9	+2.5	53.7	35 57.2	+3.5	54.3	36 32.0	+4.5	54.9	37 06.2	+5.6	55.5	37 39.9	+6.7	56.1	38 13.1	+7.7	56.8	43
44	34 10.4	−0.3	51.4	34 47.6	+0.7	51.9	35 24.4	+1.7	52.5	36 00.7	+2.7	53.1	36 36.5	+3.7	53.7	37 11.8	+4.8	54.3	37 46.6	+5.8	54.9	38 20.8	+6.9	55.5	44
45	34 10.1	−1.0	50.2	34 48.3	−0.1	50.7	35 26.1	+0.9	51.3	36 03.4	+1.9	51.8	36 40.2	+3.0	52.4	37 16.6	+4.0	53.0	37 52.4	+5.1	53.6	38 27.7	+6.1	54.3	45
46	34 09.1	−1.7	49.0	34 48.2	−0.7	49.5	35 27.0	+0.2	50.0	36 05.3	+1.2	50.6	36 43.2	+2.2	51.2	37 20.6	+3.2	51.8	37 57.5	+4.2	52.4	38 33.8	+5.3	53.0	46
47	34 07.4	−2.5	47.8	34 47.5	−1.5	48.3	35 27.2	−0.5	48.8	36 06.5	+0.4	49.4	36 45.4	+1.4	49.9	37 23.8	+2.4	50.5	38 01.7	+3.4	51.1	38 39.1	+4.5	51.7	47
48	34 04.9	−3.1	46.6	34 46.0	−2.2	47.1	35 26.7	−1.3	47.6	36 06.9	−0.3	48.1	36 46.8	+0.6	48.7	37 26.2	+1.6	49.2	38 05.1	+2.6	49.8	38 43.6	+3.6	50.4	48
49	34 01.8	−3.9	45.4	34 43.8	−3.0	45.8	35 25.4	−2.1	46.4	36 06.6	−1.1	46.9	36 47.4	−0.2	47.4	37 27.8	+0.8	48.0	38 07.7	+1.8	48.6	38 47.2	+2.8	49.2	49
50	33 57.9	−4.5	44.2	34 40.8	−3.7	44.6	35 23.3	−2.7	45.1	36 05.5	−1.9	45.6	36 47.2	−0.9	46.2	37 28.6	0.0	46.7	38 09.5	+1.0	47.3	38 50.0	+1.9	47.9	50
51	33 53.4	−5.2	43.0	34 37.1	−4.3	43.4	35 20.6	−3.6	43.9	36 03.6	−2.6	44.4	36 46.3	−1.7	44.9	37 28.6	−0.8	45.5	38 10.5	+0.1	46.0	38 51.9	+1.1	46.6	51
52	33 48.2	−6.0	41.8	34 32.8	−5.1	42.2	35 17.0	−4.2	42.7	36 01.0	−3.4	43.2	36 44.6	−2.6	43.7	37 27.8	−1.6	44.2	38 10.6	−0.7	44.7	38 53.0	+0.2	45.3	52
53	33 42.2	−6.6	40.6	34 27.7	−5.9	41.0	35 12.8	−5.0	41.5	35 57.6	−4.2	41.9	36 42.0	−3.2	42.4	37 26.2	−2.5	42.9	38 09.9	−1.5	43.5	38 53.2	−0.6	44.0	53
54	33 35.6	−7.3	39.4	34 21.8	−6.5	39.8	35 07.8	−5.7	40.2	35 53.4	−4.9	40.7	36 38.8	−4.1	41.2	37 23.7	−3.2	41.7	38 08.4	−2.4	42.2	38 52.6	−1.4	42.7	54
55	33 28.3	−8.0	38.2	34 15.3	−7.2	38.6	35 02.1	−6.5	39.0	35 48.5	−5.6	39.5	36 34.7	−4.8	39.9	37 20.5	−4.0	40.4	38 06.0	−3.1	40.9	38 51.2	−2.3	41.5	55
56	33 20.3	−8.7	37.0	34 08.1	−7.9	37.4	34 55.6	−7.1	37.8	35 42.9	−6.4	38.2	36 29.9	−5.6	38.7	37 16.5	−4.8	39.2	38 02.9	−4.0	39.7	38 48.9	−3.1	40.2	56
57	33 11.6	−9.3	35.8	34 00.2	−8.7	36.2	34 48.5	−7.9	36.6	35 36.5	−7.1	37.0	36 24.3	−6.4	37.5	37 11.7	−5.5	37.9	37 58.9	−4.8	38.4	38 45.8	−4.0	38.9	57
58	33 02.3	−10.0	34.6	33 51.5	−9.3	35.0	34 40.6	−8.6	35.4	35 29.4	−7.9	35.8	36 17.9	−7.1	36.2	37 06.2	−6.4	36.7	37 54.1	−5.6	37.1	38 41.8	−4.8	37.6	58
59	32 52.3	−10.7	33.4	33 42.2	−10.0	33.8	34 32.0	−9.3	34.2	35 21.5	−8.6	34.6	36 10.8	−7.9	35.0	36 59.8	−7.2	35.4	37 48.5	−6.4	35.9	38 37.0	−5.6	36.3	59
60	32 41.6	−11.3	32.3	33 32.2	−10.6	32.6	34 22.7	−10.0	33.0	35 12.9	−9.3	33.4	36 02.9	−8.6	33.8	36 52.6	−7.9	34.2	37 42.1	−7.1	34.6	38 31.4	−6.5	35.1	60
61	32 30.3	−12.0	31.1	33 21.6	−11.3	31.4	34 12.7	−10.7	31.8	35 03.6	−10.1	32.2	35 54.3	−9.4	32.5	36 44.7	−8.7	32.9	37 35.0	−8.0	33.4	38 24.9	−7.2	33.8	61
62	32 18.3	−12.5	29.9	33 10.3	−12.0	30.3	34 02.0	−11.4	30.6	34 53.5	−10.7	31.0	35 44.9	−10.1	31.3	36 36.0	−9.4	31.7	37 27.0	−8.8	32.1	38 17.7	−8.1	32.5	62
63	32 05.8	−13.3	28.8	32 58.3	−12.7	29.1	33 50.6	−12.0	29.4	34 42.8	−11.5	29.8	35 34.8	−10.9	30.1	36 26.6	−10.2	30.5	37 18.2	−9.6	30.9	38 09.6	−8.9	31.3	63
64	31 52.5	−13.8	27.6	32 45.6	−13.3	27.9	33 38.6	−12.8	28.2	34 31.3	−12.1	28.6	35 23.9	−11.5	28.9	36 16.4	−11.0	29.3	37 08.6	−10.3	29.6	38 00.7	−9.7	30.0	64
65	31 38.7	−14.4	26.5	32 32.3	−13.9	26.8	33 25.8	−13.3	27.1	34 19.2	−12.8	27.4	35 12.4	−12.3	27.7	36 05.4	−11.6	28.0	36 58.3	−11.1	28.4	37 51.0	−10.5	28.8	65
66	31 24.3	−15.1	25.4	32 18.4	−14.5	25.6	33 12.5	−14.1	25.9	34 06.4	−13.5	26.2	35 00.1	−12.9	26.5	35 53.8	−12.5	26.8	36 47.2	−11.8	27.2	37 40.5	−11.2	27.5	66
67	31 09.2	−15.6	24.2	32 03.9	−15.2	24.5	32 58.4	−14.6	24.7	33 52.9	−14.2	25.0	34 47.2	−13.7	25.3	35 41.3	−13.1	25.6	36 35.4	−12.6	25.9	37 29.3	−12.1	26.3	67
68	30 53.6	−16.2	23.1	31 48.7	−15.7	23.3	32 43.8	−15.3	23.6	33 38.7	−14.8	23.9	34 33.5	−14.3	24.1	35 28.2	−13.8	24.4	36 22.8	−13.3	24.7	37 17.2	−12.8	25.0	68
69	30 37.4	−16.8	22.0	31 33.0	−16.4	22.2	32 28.5	−15.9	22.4	33 23.9	−15.5	22.7	34 19.2	−15.0	23.0	35 14.4	−14.5	23.2	36 09.5	−14.1	23.5	37 04.4	−13.5	23.8	69
70	30 20.6	−17.4	20.9	31 16.6	−16.9	21.1	32 12.6	−16.6	21.3	33 08.4	−16.1	21.5	34 04.2	−15.7	21.8	34 59.9	−15.3	22.0	35 55.4	−14.8	22.3	36 50.9	−14.3	22.6	70
71	30 03.2	−17.9	19.8	30 59.7	−17.5	20.0	31 56.0	−17.1	20.2	32 52.3	−16.7	20.4	33 48.5	−16.3	20.6	34 44.6	−15.9	20.9	35 40.6	−15.4	21.1	36 36.6	−15.1	21.4	71
72	29 45.3	−18.4	18.7	30 42.2	−18.1	18.8	31 38.9	−17.7	19.0	32 35.6	−17.4	19.2	33 32.2	−17.0	19.5	34 28.7	−16.5	19.7	35 25.2	−16.2	19.9	36 21.5	−15.7	20.2	72
73	29 26.9	−19.0	17.6	30 24.1	−18.7	17.7	31 21.2	−18.3	17.9	32 18.2	−17.9	18.1	33 15.2	−17.6	18.3	34 12.2	−17.3	18.5	35 09.0	−16.8	18.7	36 05.8	−16.5	19.0	73
74	29 07.9	−19.5	16.5	30 05.4	−19.2	16.6	31 02.9	−18.9	16.8	32 00.3	−18.5	17.0	32 57.6	−18.2	17.2	33 54.9	−17.8	17.4	34 52.2	−17.5	17.6	35 49.3	−17.1	17.8	74
75	28 48.4	−20.0	15.4	29 46.2	−19.7	15.5	30 44.0	−19.4	15.7	31 41.8	−19.2	15.9	32 39.4	−18.8	16.0	33 37.1	−18.5	16.2	34 34.7	−18.2	16.4	35 32.2	−17.8	16.6	75
76	28 28.4	−20.5	14.3	29 26.5	−20.3	14.5	30 24.6	−20.0	14.6	31 22.6	−19.7	14.8	32 20.6	−19.4	14.9	33 18.6	−19.1	15.1	34 16.5	−18.8	15.3	35 14.4	−18.6	15.4	76
77	28 07.9	−21.1	13.3	29 06.2	−20.7	13.4	30 04.6	−20.5	13.5	31 02.9	−20.2	13.7	32 01.2	−20.0	13.8	32 59.5	−19.8	13.9	33 57.7	−19.5	14.1	34 55.8	−19.1	14.3	77
78	27 46.8	−21.5	12.2	28 45.5	−21.3	12.3	29 44.1	−21.1	12.4	30 42.7	−20.8	12.6	31 41.2	−20.5	12.7	32 39.7	−20.3	12.8	33 38.2	−20.0	13.0	34 36.7	−19.8	13.1	78
79	27 25.3	−21.9	11.1	28 24.2	−21.8	11.2	29 23.0	−21.5	11.4	30 21.9	−21.4	11.5	31 20.7	−21.2	11.6	32 19.4	−20.9	11.7	33 18.2	−20.7	11.8	34 16.9	−20.5	12.0	79
80	27 03.4	−22.5	10.1	28 02.4	−22.2	10.2	29 01.5	−22.1	10.3	30 00.5	−21.9	10.4	30 59.5	−21.7	10.5	31 58.5	−21.5	10.6	32 57.5	−21.3	10.7	33 56.4	−21.1	10.8	80
81	26 40.9	−22.8	9.1	27 40.2	−22.7	9.1	28 39.4	−22.5	9.2	29 38.6	−22.3	9.3	30 37.8	−22.2	9.4	31 37.0	−22.0	9.5	32 36.2	−21.9	9.6	33 35.3	−21.6	9.7	81
82	26 18.1	−23.4	8.0	27 17.5	−23.2	8.1	28 16.9	−23.1	8.2	29 16.3	−22.9	8.2	30 15.6	−22.7	8.3	31 15.0	−22.6	8.4	32 14.3	−22.4	8.5	33 13.7	−22.3	8.6	82
83	25 54.7	−23.7	7.0	26 54.3	−23.6	7.1	27 53.8	−23.5	7.1	28 53.4	−23.4	7.2	29 52.9	−23.3	7.3	30 52.4	−23.1	7.3	31 51.9	−23.0	7.4	32 51.4	−22.8	7.5	83
84	25 31.0	−24.2	6.0	26 30.7	−24.1	6.0	27 30.3	−23.9	6.1	28 30.0	−23.9	6.1	29 29.6	−23.7	6.2	30 29.3	−23.7	6.3	31 28.9	−23.5	6.3	32 28.6	−23.5	6.4	84
85	25 06.8	−24.6	5.0	26 06.6	−24.5	5.0	27 06.4	−24.5	5.0	28 06.1	−24.3	5.1	29 05.9	−24.3	5.1	30 05.6	−24.1	5.2	31 05.4	−24.1	5.2	32 05.1	−23.9	5.3	85
86	24 42.2	−25.0	4.0	25 42.1	−24.9	4.0	26 41.9	−24.8	4.0	27 41.8	−24.8	4.1	28 41.6	−24.7	4.1	29 41.5	−24.7	4.1	30 41.3	−24.6	4.2	31 41.2	−24.5	4.2	86
87	24 17.2	−25.3	3.0	25 17.2	−25.4	3.0	26 17.1	−25.3	3.0	27 17.0	−25.2	3.0	28 16.9	−25.2	3.1	29 16.8	−25.1	3.1	30 16.7	−25.1	3.1	31 16.7	−25.1	3.2	87
88	23 51.9	−25.8	2.0	24 51.8	−25.7	2.0	25 51.8	−25.7	2.0	26 51.8	−25.7	2.0	27 51.7	−25.6	2.0	28 51.7	−25.6	2.1	29 51.6	−25.5	2.1	30 51.6	−25.5	2.1	88
89	23 26.1	−26.1	1.0	24 26.1	−26.1	1.0	25 26.1	−26.1	1.0	26 26.1	−26.1	1.0	27 26.1	−26.1	1.0	28 26.1	−26.1	1.0	29 26.1	−26.1	1.0	30 26.1	−26.1	1.0	89
90	23 00.0	−26.5	0.0	24 00.0	−26.5	0.0	25 00.0	−26.5	0.0	26 00.0	−26.5	0.0	27 00.0	−26.5	0.0	28 00.0	−26.5	0.0	29 00.0	−26.5	0.0	30 00.0	−26.5	0.0	90
	23°			24°			25°			26°			27°			28°			29°			30°			

LATITUDE **CONTRARY** NAME TO DECLINATION   L.H.A. 64°, 296°

Dec.	23° Hc	23° d	23° Z	24° Hc	24° d	24° Z	25° Hc	25° d	25° Z	26° Hc	26° d	26° Z
°	° ′	′	°	° ′	′	°	° ′	′	°	° ′	′	°
0	23 47.9	−25.8	100.8	23 36.5	−26.9	101.2	23 24.6	−27.8	101.6	23 12.2	−28.8	102.1
1	23 22.1	−26.2	101.8	23 09.6	−27.1	102.2	22 56.8	−28.2	102.6	22 43.4	−29.1	103.0
2	22 55.9	−26.5	102.8	22 42.5	−27.5	103.2	22 28.6	−28.5	103.6	22 14.3	−29.4	104.0
3	22 29.4	−26.9	103.7	22 15.0	−27.9	104.1	22 00.1	−28.8	104.5	21 44.9	−29.8	104.9
4	22 02.5	−27.2	104.7	21 47.1	−28.2	105.1	21 31.3	−29.1	105.5	21 15.1	−30.1	105.8
5	21 35.3	−27.6	105.7	21 18.9	−28.5	106.0	21 02.2	−29.5	106.4	20 45.0	−30.3	106.8
6	21 07.7	−27.8	106.6	20 50.4	−28.8	107.0	20 32.7	−29.7	107.3	20 14.7	−30.7	107.7
7	20 39.9	−28.2	107.6	20 21.6	−29.1	107.9	20 03.0	−30.1	108.3	19 44.0	−30.9	108.6
8	20 11.7	−28.5	108.5	19 52.5	−29.4	108.8	19 32.9	−30.3	109.2	19 13.1	−31.2	109.5
9	19 43.2	−28.7	109.4	19 23.1	−29.7	109.8	19 02.6	−30.5	110.1	18 41.9	−31.5	110.4
10	19 14.5	−29.1	110.4	18 53.4	−29.9	110.7	18 32.1	−30.9	111.0	18 10.4	−31.7	111.3
11	18 45.4	−29.3	111.3	18 23.5	−30.2	111.6	18 01.2	−31.0	111.9	17 38.7	−31.9	112.2
12	18 16.1	−29.6	112.2	17 53.3	−30.5	112.5	17 30.2	−31.4	112.8	17 06.8	−32.2	113.1
13	17 46.5	−29.8	113.1	17 22.8	−30.7	113.4	16 58.8	−31.5	113.7	16 34.6	−32.4	114.0
14	17 16.7	−30.1	114.0	16 52.1	−30.9	114.3	16 27.3	−31.8	114.6	16 02.2	−32.6	114.9
15	16 46.6	−30.3	114.9	16 21.2	−31.2	115.2	15 55.5	−32.0	115.5	15 29.6	−32.8	115.7
16	16 16.3	−30.5	115.8	15 50.0	−31.4	116.1	15 23.5	−32.2	116.3	14 56.8	−33.0	116.6
17	15 45.8	−30.8	116.7	15 18.6	−31.5	117.0	14 51.3	−32.4	117.2	14 23.8	−33.2	117.5
18	15 15.0	−31.0	117.6	14 47.1	−31.8	117.9	14 18.9	−32.6	118.1	13 50.6	−33.4	118.3
19	14 44.0	−31.1	118.5	14 15.3	−32.0	118.7	13 46.3	−32.7	119.0	13 17.2	−33.6	119.2
20	14 12.9	−31.4	119.4	13 43.3	−32.1	119.6	13 13.6	−33.0	119.8	12 43.6	−33.7	120.0
21	13 41.5	−31.6	120.3	13 11.2	−32.4	120.5	12 40.6	−33.1	120.7	12 09.9	−33.8	120.9
22	13 09.9	−31.7	121.1	12 38.8	−32.5	121.3	12 07.5	−33.2	121.5	11 36.1	−34.0	121.7
23	12 38.2	−31.9	122.0	12 06.3	−32.6	122.2	11 34.3	−33.4	122.4	11 02.1	−34.2	122.5
24	12 06.3	−32.0	122.9	11 33.7	−32.8	123.1	11 00.9	−33.6	123.2	10 27.9	−34.3	123.4
25	11 34.3	−32.2	123.7	11 00.9	−33.0	123.9	10 27.3	−33.7	124.1	9 53.6	−34.4	124.2
26	11 02.1	−32.4	124.6	10 27.9	−33.1	124.8	9 53.6	−33.8	124.9	9 19.2	−34.5	125.1
27	10 29.7	−32.5	125.5	9 54.8	−33.2	125.6	9 19.8	−33.9	125.8	8 44.7	−34.6	125.9
28	9 57.2	−32.6	126.3	9 21.6	−33.3	126.5	8 45.9	−34.0	126.6	8 10.1	−34.7	126.7
29	9 24.6	−32.7	127.2	8 48.3	−33.4	127.3	8 11.9	−34.1	127.4	7 35.4	−34.8	127.5
30	8 51.9	−32.9	128.0	8 14.9	−33.6	128.1	7 37.8	−34.3	128.2	7 00.6	−34.9	128.3
31	8 19.0	−33.0	128.9	7 41.3	−33.6	129.0	7 03.5	−34.3	129.1	6 25.7	−35.0	129.2
32	7 46.0	−33.0	129.7	7 07.7	−33.8	129.8	6 29.2	−34.4	129.9	5 50.7	−35.1	130.0
33	7 13.0	−33.2	130.6	6 33.9	−33.8	130.6	5 54.8	−34.5	130.7	5 15.6	−35.1	130.8
34	6 39.8	−33.2	131.4	6 00.1	−33.9	131.5	5 20.3	−34.5	131.5	4 40.5	−35.1	131.6
35	6 06.6	−33.3	132.2	5 26.2	−33.9	132.3	4 45.8	−34.6	132.4	4 05.4	−35.3	132.4
36	5 33.3	−33.4	133.1	4 52.3	−34.1	133.1	4 11.2	−34.6	133.2	3 30.1	−35.2	133.2
37	4 59.9	−33.5	133.9	4 18.2	−34.0	134.0	3 36.6	−34.7	134.0	2 54.9	−35.3	134.0
38	4 26.4	−33.5	134.7	3 44.2	−34.1	134.8	3 01.9	−34.7	134.8	2 19.6	−35.3	134.9
39	3 52.9	−33.5	135.6	3 10.1	−34.2	135.6	2 27.2	−34.8	135.6	1 44.3	−35.4	135.7
40	3 19.4	−33.6	136.4	2 35.9	−34.2	136.4	1 52.4	−34.8	136.5	1 08.9	−35.3	136.5
41	2 45.8	−33.7	137.2	2 01.7	−34.2	137.3	1 17.6	−34.8	137.3	0 33.6	−35.4	137.3
42	2 12.1	−33.6	138.1	1 27.5	−34.2	138.1	0 42.8	−34.8	138.1	0 01.8	+35.4	41.9
43	1 38.5	−33.7	138.9	0 53.3	−34.3	138.9	0 08.0	−34.8	138.9	0 37.2	+35.3	41.1
44	1 04.8	−33.7	139.7	0 19.0	−34.2	139.7	0 26.8	+34.8	40.3	1 12.5	+35.4	40.3
45	0 31.1	−33.7	140.5	0 15.2	+34.3	39.5	1 01.6	+34.7	39.5	1 47.9	+35.3	39.5
46	0 02.6	+33.7	38.6	0 49.5	+34.2	38.6	1 36.3	+34.8	38.7	2 23.2	+35.3	38.7
47	0 36.3	+33.7	37.8	1 23.7	+34.2	37.8	2 11.1	+34.7	37.8	2 58.5	+35.2	37.9
48	1 10.0	+33.7	37.0	1 57.9	+34.2	37.0	2 45.8	+34.7	37.0	3 33.7	+35.2	37.1
49	1 43.7	+33.6	36.2	2 32.1	+34.2	36.2	3 20.5	+34.7	36.2	4 08.9	+35.2	36.2
50	2 17.3	+33.7	35.3	3 06.3	+34.1	35.4	3 55.2	+34.6	35.4	4 44.1	+35.1	35.4
51	2 51.0	+33.6	34.5	3 40.4	+34.1	34.5	4 29.8	+34.6	34.6	5 19.2	+35.1	34.6
52	3 24.6	+33.5	33.7	4 14.5	+34.0	33.7	5 04.4	+34.5	33.7	5 54.3	+34.9	33.8
53	3 58.1	+33.5	32.8	4 48.5	+34.0	32.9	5 38.9	+34.4	32.9	6 29.2	+34.9	33.0
54	4 31.6	+33.4	32.0	5 22.5	+33.9	32.0	6 13.3	+34.4	32.1	7 04.1	+34.8	32.2
55	5 05.0	+33.4	31.2	5 56.4	+33.8	31.2	6 47.7	+34.2	31.3	7 38.9	+34.7	31.3
56	5 38.4	+33.3	30.3	6 30.2	+33.7	30.4	7 21.9	+34.2	30.4	8 13.6	+34.7	30.5
57	6 11.7	+33.3	29.5	7 03.9	+33.7	29.6	7 56.1	+34.1	29.6	8 48.3	+34.5	29.7
58	6 45.0	+33.1	28.7	7 37.6	+33.5	28.7	8 30.2	+34.0	28.8	9 22.8	+34.3	28.9
59	7 18.1	+33.0	27.8	8 11.1	+33.5	27.9	9 04.2	+33.8	28.0	9 57.1	+34.3	28.0
60	7 51.1	+33.0	27.0	8 44.6	+33.3	27.0	9 38.0	+33.8	27.1	10 31.4	+34.1	27.2
61	8 24.1	+32.8	26.1	9 17.9	+33.3	26.2	10 11.8	+33.6	26.3	11 05.5	+34.0	26.4
62	8 56.9	+32.8	25.3	9 51.2	+33.1	25.4	10 45.4	+33.4	25.4	11 39.5	+33.9	25.5
63	9 29.7	+32.6	24.4	10 24.3	+32.9	24.5	11 18.8	+33.4	24.6	12 13.4	+33.7	24.7
64	10 02.3	+32.4	23.6	10 57.2	+32.8	23.7	11 52.2	+33.1	23.7	12 47.1	+33.5	23.8
65	10 34.7	+32.4	22.7	11 30.0	+32.7	22.8	12 25.3	+33.1	22.9	13 20.6	+33.4	23.0
66	11 07.1	+32.1	21.9	12 02.7	+32.5	22.0	12 58.4	+32.8	22.0	13 54.0	+33.1	22.1
67	11 39.2	+32.1	21.0	12 35.2	+32.4	21.1	13 31.2	+32.7	21.2	14 27.1	+33.0	21.3
68	12 11.3	+31.8	20.1	13 07.6	+32.2	20.2	14 03.9	+32.5	20.3	15 00.1	+32.8	20.4
69	12 43.1	+31.7	19.3	13 39.8	+32.0	19.4	14 36.4	+32.2	19.4	15 32.9	+32.6	19.5
70	13 14.8	+31.6	18.4	14 11.8	+31.8	18.5	15 08.6	+32.1	18.6	16 05.5	+32.4	18.7
71	13 46.4	+31.3	17.5	14 43.6	+31.6	17.6	15 40.7	+31.9	17.7	16 37.9	+32.1	17.8
72	14 17.7	+31.1	16.7	15 15.2	+31.4	16.7	16 12.6	+31.7	16.8	17 10.0	+32.0	16.9
73	14 48.8	+31.0	15.8	15 46.6	+31.1	15.8	16 44.3	+31.4	15.9	17 42.0	+31.6	16.0
74	15 19.8	+30.7	14.9	16 17.7	+31.0	15.0	17 15.7	+31.2	15.0	18 13.6	+31.5	15.1
75	15 50.5	+30.5	14.0	16 48.7	+30.7	14.1	17 46.9	+30.9	14.1	18 45.1	+31.1	14.2
76	16 21.0	+30.3	13.1	17 19.4	+30.5	13.2	18 17.8	+30.7	13.2	19 16.2	+30.9	13.3
77	16 51.3	+30.0	12.2	17 49.9	+30.2	12.3	18 48.5	+30.5	12.3	19 47.1	+30.7	12.4
78	17 21.3	+29.8	11.3	18 20.1	+30.0	11.4	19 19.0	+30.1	11.4	20 17.8	+30.3	11.5
79	17 51.1	+29.5	10.4	18 50.1	+29.7	10.4	19 49.1	+29.9	10.5	20 48.1	+30.1	10.6
80	18 20.6	+29.3	9.5	19 19.8	+29.5	9.5	20 19.0	+29.6	9.6	21 18.2	+29.7	9.6
81	18 49.9	+29.0	8.5	19 49.3	+29.1	8.6	20 48.6	+29.3	8.7	21 47.9	+29.4	8.7
82	19 18.9	+28.7	7.6	20 18.4	+28.8	7.7	21 17.9	+28.9	7.7	22 17.3	+29.1	7.8
83	19 47.6	+28.5	6.7	20 47.2	+28.6	6.7	21 46.8	+28.7	6.8	22 46.4	+28.8	6.8
84	20 16.1	+28.1	5.7	21 15.8	+28.2	5.8	22 15.5	+28.3	5.8	23 15.2	+28.4	5.9
85	20 44.2	+27.8	4.8	21 44.0	+27.9	4.8	22 43.8	+27.9	4.9	23 43.6	+28.0	4.9
86	21 12.0	+27.5	3.9	22 11.9	+27.5	3.9	23 11.7	+27.7	3.9	24 11.6	+27.7	3.9
87	21 39.5	+27.2	2.9	22 39.4	+27.3	2.9	23 39.4	+27.2	2.9	24 39.3	+27.3	3.0
88	22 06.7	+26.8	1.9	23 06.7	+26.8	2.0	24 06.6	+26.9	2.0	25 06.6	+26.9	2.0
89	22 33.5	+26.5	1.0	23 33.5	+26.5	1.0	24 33.5	+26.5	1.0	25 33.5	+26.5	1.0
90	23 00.0	+26.1	0.0	24 00.0	+26.1	0.0	25 00.0	+26.1	0.0	26 00.0	+26.1	0.0
	23°			24°			25°			26°		

27° Hc	27° d	27° Z	28° Hc	28° d	28° Z	29° Hc	29° d	29° Z	30° Hc	30° d	30° Z	Dec.
° ′	′	°	° ′	′	°	° ′	′	°	° ′	′	°	°
22 59.5	−29.8	102.5	22 46.3	−30.7	102.9	22 32.7	−31.7	103.3	22 18.7	−32.6	103.7	0
22 29.7	−30.1	103.4	22 15.6	−31.0	103.8	22 01.0	−31.9	104.2	21 46.1	−32.9	104.6	1
21 59.6	−30.4	104.4	21 44.6	−31.4	104.8	21 29.1	−32.3	105.1	21 13.2	−33.1	105.5	2
21 29.2	−30.7	105.3	21 13.2	−31.6	105.7	20 56.8	−32.5	106.0	20 40.1	−33.4	106.4	3
20 58.5	−31.0	106.2	20 41.6	−31.9	106.6	20 24.3	−32.8	106.9	20 06.7	−33.7	107.3	4
20 27.5	−31.2	107.1	20 09.7	−32.2	107.5	19 51.5	−33.1	107.8	19 33.0	−34.0	108.2	5
19 56.3	−31.6	108.0	19 37.5	−32.4	108.4	19 18.4	−33.3	108.7	18 59.0	−34.2	109.0	6
19 24.7	−31.8	108.9	19 05.1	−32.7	109.3	18 45.1	−33.6	109.6	18 24.8	−34.4	109.9	7
18 52.9	−32.1	109.8	18 32.4	−33.0	110.2	18 11.5	−33.8	110.5	17 50.4	−34.7	110.8	8
18 20.8	−32.3	110.7	17 59.4	−33.2	111.0	17 37.7	−34.0	111.3	17 15.7	−34.8	111.6	9
17 48.5	−32.6	111.6	17 26.2	−33.4	111.9	17 03.7	−34.3	112.2	16 40.9	−35.1	112.5	10
17 15.9	−32.8	112.5	16 52.8	−33.6	112.8	16 29.4	−34.4	113.1	16 05.8	−35.3	113.3	11
16 43.1	−33.0	113.4	16 19.2	−33.9	113.6	15 55.0	−34.7	113.9	15 30.5	−35.4	114.2	12
16 10.1	−33.2	114.2	15 45.3	−34.0	114.5	15 20.3	−34.8	114.8	14 55.1	−35.7	115.0	13
15 36.9	−33.5	115.1	15 11.3	−34.3	115.4	14 45.5	−35.1	115.6	14 19.4	−35.8	115.8	14
15 03.4	−33.6	116.0	14 37.0	−34.4	116.2	14 10.4	−35.2	116.4	13 43.6	−36.0	116.7	15
14 29.8	−33.8	116.8	14 02.6	−34.6	117.1	13 35.2	−35.3	117.3	13 07.6	−36.1	117.5	16
13 56.0	−34.0	117.7	13 28.0	−34.7	117.9	12 59.9	−35.6	118.1	12 31.5	−36.3	118.3	17
13 22.0	−34.1	118.5	12 53.3	−35.0	118.7	12 24.3	−35.7	118.9	11 55.2	−36.4	119.1	18
12 47.9	−34.4	119.4	12 18.3	−35.0	119.6	11 48.6	−35.8	119.7	11 18.8	−36.6	119.9	19
12 13.5	−34.4	120.2	11 43.3	−35.3	120.4	11 12.8	−35.9	120.6	10 42.2	−36.6	120.7	20
11 39.1	−34.6	121.0	11 08.0	−35.3	121.2	10 36.9	−36.1	121.4	10 05.6	−36.8	121.5	21
11 04.5	−34.8	121.9	10 32.7	−35.5	122.0	10 00.8	−36.2	122.2	9 28.8	−36.9	122.3	22
10 29.7	−34.9	122.7	9 57.2	−35.6	122.9	9 24.6	−36.3	123.0	8 51.9	−37.0	123.1	23
9 54.8	−35.0	123.5	9 21.6	−35.7	123.7	8 48.3	−36.4	123.8	8 14.9	−37.1	123.9	24
9 19.8	−35.1	124.4	8 45.9	−35.8	124.5	8 11.9	−36.5	124.6	7 37.8	−37.2	124.7	25
8 44.7	−35.2	125.2	8 10.1	−35.9	125.3	7 35.4	−36.6	125.4	7 00.6	−37.3	125.5	26
8 09.5	−35.3	126.0	7 34.2	−36.0	126.1	6 58.8	−36.7	126.2	6 23.3	−37.3	126.3	27
7 34.2	−35.4	126.8	6 58.2	−36.1	126.9	6 22.1	−36.7	127.0	5 46.0	−37.4	127.1	28
6 58.8	−35.5	127.6	6 22.1	−36.1	127.7	5 45.4	−36.8	127.8	5 08.6	−37.5	127.9	29
6 23.3	−35.6	128.4	5 46.0	−36.3	128.5	5 08.6	−36.9	128.6	4 31.1	−37.5	128.7	30
5 47.7	−35.6	129.3	5 09.7	−36.2	129.3	4 31.7	−36.9	129.4	3 53.6	−37.6	129.4	31
5 12.1	−35.7	130.1	4 33.5	−36.4	130.1	3 54.8	−37.0	130.2	3 16.0	−37.6	130.2	32
4 36.4	−35.7	130.9	3 57.1	−36.4	130.9	3 17.8	−37.0	131.0	2 38.4	−37.6	131.0	33
4 00.7	−35.8	131.7	3 20.7	−36.4	131.7	2 40.8	−37.0	131.8	2 00.8	−37.6	131.8	34
3 24.9	−35.9	132.5	2 44.3	−36.4	132.5	2 03.8	−37.1	132.5	1 23.2	−37.7	132.6	35
2 49.0	−35.9	133.3	2 07.9	−36.5	133.3	1 26.7	−37.1	133.3	0 45.5	−37.6	133.3	36
2 13.1	−35.8	134.1	1 31.4	−36.5	134.1	0 49.6	−37.0	134.1	0 07.9	−37.7	134.1	37
1 37.3	−36.0	134.9	0 54.9	−36.5	134.9	0 12.6	−37.1	134.9	0 29.8	+37.7	45.1	38
1 01.3	−35.9	135.7	0 18.4	−36.5	135.7	0 24.5	+37.1	44.3	1 07.5	+37.6	44.3	39
0 25.4	−35.9	136.5	0 18.1	+36.5	43.5	1 01.6	+37.1	43.5	1 45.1	+37.6	43.5	40
0 10.5	+36.0	42.7	0 54.6	+36.5	42.7	1 38.7	+37.0	42.7	2 22.7	+37.6	42.8	41
0 46.5	+35.9	41.9	1 31.1	+36.5	41.9	2 15.7	+37.1	41.9	3 00.3	+37.6	42.0	42
1 22.4	+35.9	41.1	2 07.6	+36.4	41.1	2 52.8	+37.0	41.2	3 37.9	+37.5	41.2	43
1 58.3	+35.9	40.3	2 44.0	+36.4	40.3	3 29.8	+36.9	40.4	4 15.4	+37.5	40.4	44
2 34.2	+35.8	39.5	3 20.4	+36.4	39.5	4 06.7	+36.9	39.6	4 52.9	+37.5	39.6	45
3 10.0	+35.8	38.7	3 56.8	+36.4	38.7	4 43.6	+36.9	38.8	5 30.4	+37.3	38.8	46
3 45.8	+35.8	37.9	4 33.2	+36.2	37.9	5 20.5	+36.8	38.0	6 07.7	+37.3	38.1	47
4 21.6	+35.7	37.1	5 09.4	+36.3	37.1	5 57.3	+36.7	37.2	6 45.0	+37.2	37.3	48
4 57.3	+35.7	36.3	5 45.7	+36.1	36.3	6 34.0	+36.6	36.4	7 22.2	+37.2	36.5	49
5 33.0	+35.6	35.5	6 21.8	+36.1	35.5	7 10.6	+36.6	35.6	7 59.4	+37.0	35.7	50
6 08.6	+35.5	34.7	6 57.9	+36.0	34.7	7 47.2	+36.5	34.8	8 36.4	+37.0	34.9	51
6 44.1	+35.4	33.9	7 33.9	+35.9	33.9	8 23.7	+36.3	34.0	9 13.4	+36.8	34.1	52
7 19.5	+35.4	33.0	8 09.8	+35.8	33.1	9 00.0	+36.3	33.2	9 50.2	+36.7	33.3	53
7 54.9	+35.3	32.2	8 45.6	+35.7	32.3	9 36.3	+36.2	32.4	10 26.9	+36.7	32.5	54
8 30.2	+35.1	31.4	9 21.3	+35.6	31.5	10 12.5	+36.0	31.6	11 03.6	+36.4	31.7	55
9 05.3	+35.1	30.6	9 56.9	+35.5	30.7	10 48.5	+35.9	30.8	11 40.0	+36.4	30.9	56
9 40.4	+34.9	29.8	10 32.4	+35.4	29.9	11 24.4	+35.8	30.0	12 16.4	+36.2	30.1	57
10 15.3	+34.8	28.9	11 07.8	+35.2	29.0	12 00.2	+35.6	29.1	12 52.6	+36.0	29.2	58
10 50.1	+34.7	28.1	11 43.0	+35.1	28.2	12 35.8	+35.5	28.3	13 28.6	+35.9	28.4	59
11 24.8	+34.5	27.3	12 18.1	+34.9	27.4	13 11.3	+35.3	27.5	14 04.5	+35.7	27.6	60
11 59.3	+34.4	26.5	12 53.0	+34.7	26.6	13 46.6	+35.2	26.7	14 40.2	+35.6	26.8	61
12 33.7	+34.2	25.6	13 27.7	+34.6	25.7	14 21.8	+34.9	25.8	15 15.8	+35.3	25.9	62
13 07.9	+34.0	24.8	14 02.3	+34.5	24.9	14 56.7	+34.8	25.0	15 51.1	+35.2	25.1	63
13 41.9	+33.9	23.9	14 36.8	+34.2	24.0	15 31.5	+34.6	24.1	16 26.3	+34.9	24.3	64
14 15.8	+33.7	23.1	15 11.0	+34.0	23.2	16 06.1	+34.4	23.3	17 01.2	+34.8	23.4	65
14 49.5	+33.5	22.2	15 45.0	+33.9	22.3	16 40.5	+34.2	22.4	17 36.0	+34.5	22.6	66
15 23.0	+33.3	21.4	16 18.9	+33.6	21.5	17 14.7	+34.0	21.6	18 10.5	+34.3	21.7	67
15 56.3	+33.1	20.5	16 52.5	+33.4	20.6	17 48.7	+33.7	20.7	18 44.8	+34.0	20.8	68
16 29.4	+32.9	19.6	17 25.9	+33.2	19.7	18 22.4	+33.5	19.8	19 18.8	+33.8	20.0	69
17 02.3	+32.7	18.8	17 59.1	+33.0	18.9	18 55.9	+33.2	19.0	19 52.6	+33.6	19.1	70
17 35.0	+32.4	17.9	18 32.1	+32.7	18.0	19 29.1	+33.0	18.1	20 26.2	+33.2	18.2	71
18 07.4	+32.2	17.0	19 04.8	+32.4	17.1	20 02.1	+32.7	17.2	20 59.4	+33.0	17.3	72
18 39.6	+31.9	16.1	19 37.2	+32.2	16.2	20 34.8	+32.5	16.3	21 32.4	+32.7	16.4	73
19 11.5	+31.7	15.2	20 09.4	+31.9	15.3	21 07.3	+32.1	15.4	22 05.1	+32.4	15.5	74
19 43.2	+31.4	14.3	20 41.3	+31.7	14.4	21 39.4	+31.9	14.5	22 37.5	+32.1	14.6	75
20 14.6	+31.1	13.4	21 13.0	+31.3	13.5	22 11.3	+31.6	13.6	23 09.6	+31.8	13.7	76
20 45.7	+30.9	12.5	21 44.3	+31.0	12.6	22 42.9	+31.2	12.7	23 41.4	+31.4	12.8	77
21 16.6	+30.5	11.6	22 15.3	+30.7	11.6	23 14.1	+30.9	11.7	24 12.8	+31.1	11.8	78
21 47.1	+30.2	10.6	22 46.0	+30.4	10.7	23 45.0	+30.6	10.8	24 43.9	+30.8	10.9	79
22 17.3	+29.9	9.7	23 16.4	+30.1	9.8	24 15.6	+30.2	9.9	25 14.7	+30.3	9.9	80
22 47.2	+29.6	8.8	23 46.5	+29.7	8.8	24 45.8	+29.8	8.9	25 45.0	+30.0	9.0	81
23 16.8	+29.2	7.8	24 16.2	+29.3	7.9	25 15.6	+29.5	8.0	26 15.0	+29.6	8.0	82
23 46.0	+28.8	6.9	24 45.5	+29.0	6.9	25 45.1	+29.1	7.0	26 44.6	+29.3	7.0	83
24 14.8	+28.5	5.9	25 14.5	+28.6	6.0	26 14.2	+28.7	6.0	27 13.9	+28.8	6.1	84
24 43.3	+28.2	4.9	25 43.1	+28.2	5.0	26 42.9	+28.3	5.0	27 42.7	+28.3	5.1	85
25 11.5	+27.7	4.0	26 11.3	+27.8	4.0	27 11.2	+27.8	4.0	28 11.0	+28.0	4.1	86
25 39.2	+27.3	3.0	26 39.1	+27.4	3.0	27 39.0	+27.5	3.0	28 39.0	+27.4	3.1	87
26 06.5	+27.0	2.0	27 06.5	+27.0	2.0	28 06.5	+27.0	2.0	29 06.4	+27.1	2.1	88
26 33.5	+26.5	1.0	27 33.5	+26.5	1.0	28 33.5	+26.5	1.0	29 33.5	+26.5	1.0	89
27 00.0	+26.1	0.0	28 00.0	+26.1	0.0	29 00.0	+26.1	0.0	30 00.0	+26.1	0.0	90
27°			28°			29°			30°			

S. Lat. {L.H.A. greater than 180° ....Zn=180°−Z; L.H.A. less than 180°...........Zn=180°+Z}

LATITUDE **SAME** NAME AS DECLINATION   L.H.A. 116°, 244°

313

Dec.	23° Hc	d	Z	24° Hc	d	Z	25° Hc	d	Z	26° Hc	d	Z	27° Hc	d	Z	28° Hc	d	Z	29° Hc	d	Z	30° Hc	d	Z	Dec.
°	° ′	′	°	° ′	′	°	° ′	′	°	° ′	′	°	° ′	′	°	° ′	′	°	° ′	′	°	° ′	′	°	°
0	22 53.6	+25.3	100.3	22 42.7	+26.2	100.7	22 31.3	+27.2	101.1	22 19.5	+28.2	101.6	22 07.2	+29.3	102.0	21 54.6	+30.2	102.3	21 41.6	+31.1	102.7	21 28.1	+32.1	103.1	0
1	23 18.9	+24.9	99.3	23 08.9	+25.9	99.8	22 58.5	+27.0	100.2	22 47.7	+27.9	100.6	22 36.5	+28.9	101.0	22 24.8	+29.9	101.4	22 12.7	+30.9	101.8	22 00.2	+31.8	102.2	1
2	23 43.8	+24.5	98.3	23 34.8	+25.6	98.8	23 25.5	+26.5	99.2	23 15.6	+27.6	99.6	23 05.4	+28.5	100.1	22 54.7	+29.5	100.5	22 43.6	+30.5	100.9	22 32.0	+31.5	101.3	2
3	24 08.3	+24.1	97.3	24 00.4	+25.1	97.8	23 52.0	+26.2	98.2	23 43.2	+27.2	98.7	23 33.9	+28.2	99.1	23 24.2	+29.2	99.5	23 14.1	+30.2	100.0	23 03.5	+31.1	100.4	3
4	24 32.4	+23.7	96.3	24 25.5	+24.8	96.8	24 18.2	+25.8	97.2	24 10.4	+26.8	97.7	24 02.1	+27.9	98.1	23 53.4	+28.9	98.6	23 44.3	+29.8	99.0	23 34.6	+30.8	99.4	4
5	24 56.1	+23.3	95.3	24 50.3	+24.4	95.8	24 44.0	+25.4	96.3	24 37.2	+26.5	96.7	24 30.0	+27.5	97.2	24 22.3	+28.5	97.6	24 14.1	+29.5	98.1	24 05.4	+30.5	98.5	5
6	25 19.4	+22.9	94.3	25 14.7	+23.9	94.8	25 09.4	+25.0	95.3	25 03.7	+26.0	95.7	24 57.5	+27.0	96.2	24 50.8	+28.1	96.6	24 43.6	+29.1	97.1	24 35.9	+30.1	97.6	6
7	25 42.3	+22.5	93.3	25 38.6	+23.5	93.8	25 34.4	+24.6	94.2	25 29.7	+25.7	94.7	25 24.5	+26.7	95.2	25 18.9	+27.7	95.7	25 12.7	+28.7	96.1	25 06.0	+29.8	96.6	7
8	26 04.8	+22.0	92.3	26 02.1	+23.1	92.7	25 59.0	+24.2	93.2	25 55.4	+25.2	93.7	25 51.2	+26.3	94.2	25 46.6	+27.3	94.7	25 41.4	+28.4	95.2	25 35.8	+29.3	95.6	8
9	26 26.8	+21.5	91.2	26 25.2	+22.7	91.7	26 23.2	+23.7	92.2	26 20.6	+24.8	92.7	26 17.5	+25.8	93.2	26 13.9	+26.9	93.7	26 09.8	+27.9	94.2	26 05.1	+29.0	94.7	9
10	26 48.3	+21.1	90.2	26 47.9	+22.2	90.7	26 46.9	+23.3	91.2	26 45.4	+24.3	91.7	26 43.3	+25.5	92.2	26 40.8	+26.5	92.7	26 37.7	+27.5	93.2	26 34.1	+28.6	93.7	10
11	27 09.4	+20.6	89.1	27 10.1	+21.7	89.6	27 10.2	+22.8	90.2	27 09.7	+23.9	90.7	27 08.8	+25.0	91.2	27 07.3	+26.0	91.7	27 05.2	+27.1	92.2	27 02.7	+28.1	92.7	11
12	27 30.0	+20.2	88.1	27 31.8	+21.2	88.6	27 33.0	+22.3	89.1	27 33.6	+23.5	89.6	27 33.8	+24.5	90.2	27 33.3	+25.6	90.7	27 32.3	+26.7	91.2	27 30.8	+27.7	91.7	12
13	27 50.2	+19.6	87.0	27 53.0	+20.8	87.5	27 55.3	+21.9	88.1	27 57.1	+23.0	88.6	27 58.3	+24.0	89.1	27 58.9	+25.2	89.7	27 59.0	+26.2	90.2	27 58.5	+27.3	90.7	13
14	28 09.8	+19.2	85.9	28 13.8	+20.3	86.5	28 17.2	+21.4	87.0	28 20.1	+22.4	87.5	28 22.3	+23.6	88.1	28 24.1	+24.6	88.6	28 25.2	+25.8	89.2	28 25.8	+26.8	89.7	14
15	28 29.0	+18.6	84.9	28 34.1	+19.7	85.4	28 38.6	+20.9	85.9	28 42.5	+22.0	86.5	28 45.9	+23.1	87.0	28 48.7	+24.2	87.6	28 51.0	+25.3	88.1	28 52.6	+26.4	88.7	15
16	28 47.6	+18.1	83.8	28 53.8	+19.3	84.3	28 59.5	+20.3	84.9	29 04.5	+21.5	85.4	29 09.0	+22.6	86.0	29 12.9	+23.7	86.5	29 16.3	+24.8	87.1	29 19.0	+25.9	87.7	16
17	29 05.7	+17.6	82.7	29 13.1	+18.7	83.2	29 19.8	+19.9	83.8	29 26.0	+21.0	84.4	29 31.6	+22.1	84.9	29 36.6	+23.2	85.5	29 41.1	+24.3	86.1	29 44.9	+25.4	86.6	17
18	29 23.3	+17.0	81.6	29 31.8	+18.2	82.2	29 39.7	+19.3	82.7	29 47.0	+20.4	83.3	29 53.7	+21.6	83.9	29 59.8	+22.7	84.4	30 05.4	+23.8	85.0	30 10.3	+24.9	85.6	18
19	29 40.3	+16.5	80.5	29 50.0	+17.6	81.1	29 59.0	+18.8	81.6	30 07.4	+19.9	82.2	30 15.3	+21.0	82.8	30 22.5	+22.2	83.4	30 29.2	+23.2	83.9	30 35.2	+24.4	84.5	19
20	29 56.8	+16.0	79.4	30 07.6	+17.1	80.0	30 17.8	+18.2	80.5	30 27.3	+19.4	81.1	30 36.3	+20.5	81.7	30 44.7	+21.6	82.3	30 52.4	+22.8	82.9	30 59.6	+23.8	83.5	20
21	30 12.8	+15.3	78.3	30 24.7	+16.5	78.8	30 36.0	+17.6	79.4	30 46.7	+18.8	80.0	30 56.8	+19.9	80.6	31 06.3	+21.1	81.2	31 15.2	+22.2	81.8	31 23.4	+23.4	82.4	21
22	30 28.1	+14.8	77.1	30 41.2	+15.9	77.7	30 53.6	+17.1	78.3	31 05.5	+18.2	78.9	31 16.7	+19.4	79.5	31 27.4	+20.5	80.1	31 37.4	+21.6	80.7	31 46.8	+22.7	81.3	22
23	30 42.9	+14.2	76.0	30 57.1	+15.3	76.6	31 10.7	+16.5	77.2	31 23.7	+17.6	77.8	31 36.1	+18.8	78.4	31 47.9	+19.9	79.0	31 59.0	+21.1	79.6	32 09.5	+22.2	80.2	23
24	30 57.1	+13.6	74.9	31 12.4	+14.8	75.5	31 27.2	+15.9	76.1	31 41.3	+17.1	76.7	31 54.9	+18.2	77.3	32 07.8	+19.3	77.9	32 20.1	+20.5	78.5	32 31.7	+21.7	79.1	24
25	31 10.7	+13.0	73.8	31 27.2	+14.1	74.3	31 43.1	+15.3	74.9	31 58.4	+16.4	75.5	32 13.1	+17.6	76.1	32 27.1	+18.8	76.8	32 40.6	+19.8	77.4	32 53.4	+21.0	78.0	25
26	31 23.7	+12.4	72.6	31 41.3	+13.6	73.2	31 58.4	+14.7	73.8	32 14.8	+15.9	74.4	32 30.7	+16.9	75.0	32 45.9	+18.1	75.6	33 00.4	+19.3	76.3	33 14.4	+20.4	76.9	26
27	31 36.1	+11.8	71.5	31 54.9	+12.9	72.1	32 13.1	+14.0	72.6	32 30.7	+15.2	73.3	32 47.6	+16.4	73.9	33 04.0	+17.5	74.5	33 19.7	+18.7	75.1	33 34.8	+19.8	75.8	27
28	31 47.9	+11.1	70.3	32 07.8	+12.3	70.9	32 27.1	+13.5	71.5	32 45.9	+14.5	72.1	33 04.0	+15.7	72.7	33 21.5	+16.9	73.3	33 38.4	+18.0	74.0	33 54.6	+19.2	74.6	28
29	31 59.0	+10.5	69.2	32 20.1	+11.6	69.7	32 40.6	+12.8	70.3	33 00.4	+14.0	71.0	33 19.7	+15.1	71.6	33 38.4	+16.2	72.2	33 56.4	+17.4	72.8	34 13.8	+18.5	73.5	29
30	32 09.5	+9.9	68.0	32 31.7	+11.0	68.6	32 53.4	+12.1	69.2	33 14.4	+13.3	69.8	33 34.8	+14.4	70.4	33 54.6	+15.6	71.0	34 13.8	+16.7	71.7	34 32.3	+17.9	72.3	30
31	32 19.4	+9.2	66.8	32 42.7	+10.4	67.4	33 05.5	+11.5	68.0	33 27.7	+12.6	68.6	33 49.2	+13.8	69.2	34 10.2	+14.9	69.9	34 30.5	+16.1	70.5	34 50.2	+17.2	71.2	31
32	32 28.6	+8.6	65.7	32 53.1	+9.7	66.2	33 17.0	+10.8	66.8	33 40.3	+11.9	67.4	34 03.0	+13.1	68.1	34 25.1	+14.2	68.7	34 46.6	+15.4	69.3	35 07.4	+16.6	70.0	32
33	32 37.2	+7.9	64.5	33 02.8	+9.0	65.1	33 27.8	+10.2	65.7	33 52.2	+11.3	66.3	34 16.1	+12.4	66.9	34 39.3	+13.6	67.5	35 02.0	+14.7	68.2	35 24.0	+15.8	68.8	33
34	32 45.1	+7.3	63.3	33 11.8	+8.4	63.9	33 38.0	+9.4	64.5	34 03.5	+10.6	65.1	34 28.5	+11.7	65.7	34 52.9	+12.8	66.3	35 16.7	+14.0	67.0	35 39.8	+15.2	67.6	34
35	32 52.4	+6.6	62.1	33 20.2	+7.7	62.7	33 47.4	+8.8	63.3	34 14.1	+9.9	63.9	34 40.2	+11.0	64.5	35 05.7	+12.2	65.1	35 30.7	+13.2	65.8	35 55.0	+14.4	66.4	35
36	32 59.0	+5.9	60.9	33 27.9	+7.0	61.5	33 56.2	+8.1	62.1	34 24.0	+9.2	62.7	34 51.2	+10.4	63.3	35 17.9	+11.4	63.9	35 43.9	+12.6	64.6	36 09.4	+13.7	65.2	36
37	33 04.9	+5.2	59.8	33 34.9	+6.3	60.3	34 04.3	+7.4	60.9	34 33.2	+8.5	61.5	35 01.6	+9.6	62.1	35 29.3	+10.8	62.7	35 56.5	+11.9	63.4	36 23.1	+13.0	64.0	37
38	33 10.1	+4.6	58.6	33 41.2	+5.6	59.1	34 11.7	+6.7	59.7	34 41.7	+7.8	60.3	35 11.2	+8.8	60.9	35 40.1	+9.9	61.5	36 08.4	+11.1	62.2	36 36.1	+12.2	62.8	38
39	33 14.7	+3.9	57.4	33 46.8	+4.9	57.9	34 18.4	+6.0	58.5	34 49.5	+7.1	59.1	35 20.0	+8.2	59.7	35 50.0	+9.3	60.3	36 19.5	+10.3	61.0	36 48.3	+11.5	61.6	39
40	33 18.6	+3.2	56.2	33 51.7	+4.3	56.7	34 24.4	+5.3	57.3	34 56.6	+6.3	57.9	35 28.2	+7.4	58.5	35 59.3	+8.5	59.1	36 29.8	+9.6	59.7	36 59.8	+10.7	60.4	40
41	33 21.8	+2.5	55.0	33 56.0	+3.5	55.5	34 29.7	+4.6	56.1	35 02.9	+5.6	56.7	35 35.6	+6.7	57.3	36 07.8	+7.8	57.9	36 39.4	+8.9	58.5	37 10.5	+9.9	59.1	41
42	33 24.3	+1.8	53.8	33 59.5	+2.8	54.3	34 34.3	+3.8	54.9	35 08.5	+4.9	55.5	35 42.3	+5.9	56.0	36 15.6	+7.0	56.6	36 48.3	+8.1	57.3	37 20.4	+9.2	57.9	42
43	33 26.1	+1.1	52.6	34 02.3	+2.2	53.1	34 38.1	+3.1	53.7	35 13.4	+4.2	54.2	35 48.2	+5.2	54.8	36 22.6	+6.2	55.4	36 56.4	+7.3	56.0	37 29.6	+8.4	56.7	43
44	33 27.2	+0.5	51.4	34 04.5	+1.4	51.9	34 41.2	+2.4	52.5	35 17.6	+3.4	53.0	35 53.4	+4.5	53.6	36 28.8	+5.5	54.2	37 03.7	+6.5	54.8	37 38.0	+7.6	55.4	44
45	33 27.7	-0.3	50.2	34 05.9	+0.7	50.7	34 43.6	+1.7	51.2	35 21.0	+2.7	51.8	35 57.9	+3.7	52.4	36 34.3	+4.7	52.9	37 10.2	+5.7	53.5	37 45.6	+6.8	54.2	45
46	33 27.4	-1.0	49.0	34 06.6	0.0	49.5	34 45.3	+1.0	50.0	35 23.7	+1.9	50.6	36 01.6	+2.9	51.1	36 39.0	+3.9	51.7	37 15.9	+5.0	52.3	37 52.4	+6.0	52.9	46
47	33 26.4	-1.6	47.8	34 06.6	-0.8	48.3	34 46.3	+0.2	48.8	35 25.6	+1.2	49.3	36 04.5	+2.1	49.9	36 42.9	+3.2	50.4	37 20.9	+4.1	51.0	37 58.4	+5.1	51.6	47
48	33 24.8	-2.3	46.6	34 05.8	-1.4	47.1	34 46.5	-0.5	47.6	35 26.8	+0.4	48.1	36 06.6	+1.4	48.6	36 46.1	+2.3	49.2	37 25.0	+3.4	49.8	38 03.5	+4.4	50.4	48
49	33 22.5	-3.0	45.4	34 04.4	-2.1	45.9	34 46.0	-1.2	46.4	35 27.2	-0.3	46.9	36 08.0	+0.7	47.4	36 48.4	+1.6	48.0	37 28.4	+2.5	48.5	38 07.9	+3.5	49.1	49
50	33 19.5	-3.8	44.2	34 02.3	-2.8	44.7	34 44.8	-2.0	45.2	35 26.9	-1.0	45.7	36 08.7	-0.2	46.2	36 50.0	+0.8	46.7	37 30.9	+1.8	47.3	38 11.4	+2.8	47.8	50
51	33 15.7	-4.3	43.0	33 59.5	-3.6	43.5	34 42.8	-2.6	43.9	35 25.9	-1.8	44.4	36 08.5	-0.9	44.9	36 50.8	0.0	45.5	37 32.7	+0.9	46.0	38 14.2	+1.9	46.6	51
52	33 11.4	-5.1	41.8	33 55.9	-4.2	42.3	34 40.2	-3.4	42.7	35 24.1	-2.6	43.2	36 07.6	-1.6	43.7	36 50.8	-0.7	44.2	37 33.6	+0.2	44.7	38 16.1	+1.0	45.3	52
53	33 06.3	-5.8	40.6	33 51.7	-5.0	41.1	34 36.8	-4.2	41.5	35 21.5	-3.2	42.0	36 06.0	-2.5	42.5	36 50.1	-1.6	43.0	37 33.8	-0.7	43.5	38 17.1	+0.3	44.0	53
54	33 00.5	-6.4	39.4	33 46.7	-5.6	39.9	34 32.6	-4.8	40.3	35 18.3	-4.1	40.8	36 03.5	-3.1	41.2	36 48.5	-2.3	41.7	37 33.1	-1.4	42.2	38 17.4	-0.6	42.7	54
55	32 54.1	-7.1	38.3	33 41.1	-6.3	38.7	34 27.8	-5.5	39.1	35 14.2	-4.7	39.5	36 00.4	-4.0	40.0	36 46.2	-3.1	40.5	37 31.7	-2.3	41.0	38 16.8	-1.4	41.5	55
56	32 47.0	-7.7	37.1	33 34.8	-7.0	37.5	34 22.3	-6.3	37.9	35 09.5	-5.5	38.3	35 56.4	-4.7	38.8	36 43.1	-3.9	39.2	37 29.4	-3.1	39.7	38 15.4	-2.2	40.2	56
57	32 39.3	-8.4	35.9	33 27.8	-7.7	36.3	34 16.0	-7.0	36.7	35 04.0	-6.2	37.1	35 51.7	-5.4	37.5	36 39.2	-4.7	38.0	37 26.3	-3.9	38.4	38 13.2	-3.1	38.9	57
58	32 30.9	-9.1	34.7	33 20.1	-8.4	35.1	34 09.0	-7.6	35.5	34 57.8	-7.0	35.9	35 46.3	-6.2	36.3	36 34.5	-5.4	36.7	37 22.4	-4.6	37.2	38 10.1	-3.9	37.7	58
59	32 21.8	-9.7	33.5	33 11.7	-9.1	33.9	34 01.4	-8.4	34.3	34 50.8	-7.6	34.7	35 40.1	-7.0	35.1	36 29.1	-6.3	35.5	37 17.8	-5.5	35.9	38 06.2	-4.7	36.4	59
60	32 12.1	-10.4	32.4	33 02.6	-9.7	32.7	33 53.0	-9.0	33.1	34 43.2	-8.4	33.5	35 33.1	-7.6	33.8	36 22.8	-6.9	34.3	37 12.3	-6.2	34.7	38 01.5	-5.5	35.1	60
61	32 01.7	-11.0	31.2	32 52.9	-10.3	31.5	33 44.0	-9.7	31.9	34 34.8	-9.1	32.3	35 25.5	-8.5	32.6	36 15.9	-7.7	33.0	37 06.1	-7.1	33.4	37 56.0	-6.3	33.9	61
62	31 50.7	-11.6	30.1	32 42.6	-11.0	30.4	33 34.3	-10.5	30.7	34 25.7	-9.7	31.1	35 17.0	-9.1	31.4	36 08.2	-8.5	31.8	36 59.0	-7.8	32.2	37 49.7	-7.1	32.6	62
63	31 39.1	-12.2	28.9	32 31.6	-11.7	29.2	33 23.8	-11.0	29.5	34 16.0	-10.5	29.9	35 07.9	-9.8	30.2	35 59.7	-9.2	30.6	36 51.2	-8.5	30.9	37 42.6	-7.9	31.3	63
64	31 26.9	-12.9	27.8	32 19.9	-12.3	28.0	33 12.8	-11.8	28.4	34 05.5	-11.2	28.7	34 58.1	-10.6	29.0	35 50.5	-10.0	29.3	36 42.7	-9.4	29.7	37 34.7	-8.7	30.1	64
65	31 14.0	-13.4	26.6	32 07.6	-12.9	26.9	33 01.0	-12.3	27.2	33 54.3	-11.8	27.5	34 47.5	-11.3	27.8	35 40.5	-10.7	28.1	36 33.3	-10.1	28.5	37 26.0	-9.5	28.8	65
66	31 00.6	-14.1	25.5	31 54.7	-13.6	25.7	32 48.7	-13.1	26.0	33 42.5	-12.5	26.3	34 36.2	-11.9	26.6	35 29.8	-11.4	26.9	36 23.2	-10.8	27.3	37 16.5	-10.3	27.6	66
67	30 46.5	-14.6	24.3	31 41.1	-14.1	24.6	32 35.6	-13.6	24.9	33 30.0	-13.1	25.1	34 24.3	-12.7	25.4	35 18.4	-12.1	25.7	36 12.4	-11.6	26.0	37 06.2	-11.0	26.4	67
68	30 31.9	-15.2	23.2	31 27.0	-14.8	23.5	32 22.0	-14.3	23.7	33 16.9	-13.9	24.0	34 11.6	-13.3	24.2	35 06.3	-12.9	24.5	36 00.8	-12.3	24.8	36 55.2	-11.8	25.1	68
69	30 16.7	-15.8	22.1	31 12.2	-15.3	22.3	32 07.7	-14.9	22.6	33 03.0	-14.4	22.8	33 58.3	-14.0	23.1	34 53.4	-13.5	23.3	35 48.5	-13.0	23.6	36 43.4	-12.5	23.9	69
70	30 00.9	-16.4	21.0	30 56.9	-16.0	21.2	31 52.8	-15.6	21.4	32 48.6	-15.1	21.6	33 44.3	-14.7	21.9	34 39.9	-14.2	22.1	35 35.5	-13.8	22.4	36 30.9	-13.3	22.7	70
71	29 44.5	-16.9	19.9	30 40.9	-16.5	20.1	31 37.2	-16.1	20.3	32 33.5	-15.7	20.5	33 29.6	-15.3	20.7	34 25.7	-14.9	21.0	35 21.7	-14.4	21.2	36 17.6	-14.0	21.5	71
72	29 27.6	-17.4	18.8	30 24.4	-17.1	18.9	31 21.1	-16.7	19.1	32 17.8	-16.4	19.3	33 14.3	-15.9	19.6	34 10.8	-15.5	19.8	35 07.3	-15.2	20.0	36 03.6	-14.7	20.3	72
73	29 10.2	-18.0	17.7	30 07.3	-17.6	17.8	31 04.4	-17.3	18.0	32 01.4	-16.9	18.2	32 58.4	-16.6	18.4	33 55.3	-16.2	18.6	34 52.1	-15.8	18.8	35 48.9	-15.5	19.1	73
74	28 52.2	-18.5	16.6	29 49.7	-18.2	16.7	30 47.1	-17.8	16.9	31 44.5	-17.5	17.1	32 41.8	-17.2	17.3	33 39.1	-16.9	17.5	34 36.3	-16.5	17.7	35 33.4	-16.1	17.9	74
75	28 33.7	-19.0	15.5	29 31.5	-18.7	15.6	30 29.3	-18.5	15.8	31 27.0	-18.2	16.0	32 24.6	-17.8	16.1	33 22.2	-17.4	16.3	34 19.8	-17.2	16.5	35 17.3	-16.8	16.7	75
76	28 14.7	-19.5	14.4	29 12.8	-19.3	14.5	30 10.8	-18.9	14.7	31 08.8	-18.6	14.8	32 06.8	-18.4	15.0	33 04.8	-18.1	15.2	34 02.6	-17.8	15.3	35 00.5	-17.5	15.5	76
77	27 55.2	-20.1	13.3	28 53.5	-19.7	13.5	29 51.9	-19.6	13.6	30 50.2	-19.3	13.7	31 48.4	-19.0	13.9	32 46.7	-18.8	14.0	33 44.8	-18.4	14.2	34 43.0	-18.2	14.4	77
78	27 35.1	-20.5	12.3	28 33.8	-20.3	12.4	29 32.3	-20.0	12.5	30 30.9	-19.8	12.6	31 29.4	-19.5	12.8	32 27.9	-19.3	12.9	33 26.4	-19.0	13.1	34 24.8	-18.8	13.2	78
79	27 14.6	-20.9	11.2	28 13.5	-20.8	11.3	29 12.3	-20.6	11.4	30 11.1	-20.3	11.5	31 09.9	-20.1	11.7	32 08.6	-19.9	11.8	33 07.4	-19.7	11.9	34 06.0	-19.4	12.1	79
80	26 53.7	-21.5	10.2	27 52.7	-21.2	10.3	28 51.7	-21.0	10.4	29 50.8	-20.9	10.5	30 49.8	-20.7	10.6	31 48.7	-20.4	10.7	32 47.7	-20.3	10.8	33 46.6	-20.1	10.9	80
81	26 32.2	-21.9	9.1	27 31.5	-21.8	9.2	28 30.7	-21.6	9.3	29 29.9	-21.4	9.4	30 29.1	-21.2	9.5	31 28.3	-21.1	9.6	32 27.4	-20.9	9.7	33 26.5	-20.6	9.8	81
82	26 10.3	-22.3	8.1	27 09.7	-22.2	8.2	28 09.1	-22.0	8.2	29 08.5	-21.9	8.3	30 07.9	-21.8	8.4	31 07.2	-21.6	8.5	32 06.5	-21.4	8.6	33 05.9	-21.3	8.7	82
83	25 48.0	-22.8	7.0	26 47.5	-22.6	7.1	27 47.1	-22.6	7.2	28 46.6	-22.4	7.2	29 46.1	-22.3	7.3	30 45.6	-22.1	7.4	31 45.1	-22.0	7.5	32 44.6	-21.9	7.5	83
84	25 25.2	-23.2	6.0	26 24.9	-23.1	6.1	27 24.5	-22.9	6.1	28 24.2	-22.9	6.2	29 23.8	-22.7	6.2	30 23.5	-22.7	6.3	31 23.1	-22.5	6.4	32 22.7	-22.4	6.4	84
85	25 02.0	-23.6	5.0	26 01.8	-23.5	5.0	27 01.6	-23.5	5.1	28 01.3	-23.3	5.1	29 01.1	-23.3	5.2	30 00.8	-23.2	5.2	31 00.6	-23.1	5.3	32 00.3	-23.0	5.3	85
86	24 38.4	-24.0	4.0	25 38.3	-24.0	4.0	26 38.1	-23.9	4.1	27 38.0	-23.9	4.1	28 37.8	-23.8	4.1	29 37.6	-23.6	4.2	30 37.5	-23.6	4.2	31 37.3	-23.5	4.3	86
87	24 14.4	-24.4	3.0	25 14.3	-24.4	3.0	26 14.2	-24.3	3.0	27 14.1	-24.2	3.1	28 14.0	-24.2	3.1	29 14.0	-24.2	3.1	30 13.9	-24.2	3.1	31 13.8	-24.1	3.2	87
88	23 50.0	-24.8	2.0	24 49.9	-24.7	2.0	25 49.9	-24.7	2.0	26 49.9	-24.8	2.0	27 49.8	-24.7	2.0	28 49.8	-24.7	2.1	29 49.7	-24.6	2.1	30 49.7	-24.6	2.1	88
89	23 25.2	-25.2	1.0	24 25.2	-25.2	1.0	25 25.2	-25.2	1.0	26 25.1	-25.1	1.0	27 25.1	-25.1	1.0	28 25.1	-25.1	1.0	29 25.1	-25.1	1.0	30 25.1	-25.1	1.1	89
90	23 00.0	-25.5	0.0	24 00.0	-25.5	0.0	25 00.0	-25.6	0.0	26 00.0	-25.6	0.0	27 00.0	-25.6	0.0	28 00.0	-25.6	0.0	29 00.0	-25.6	0.0	30 00.0	-25.6	0.0	90
	23°			24°			25°			26°			27°			28°			29°			30°			

LATITUDE **CONTRARY** NAME TO DECLINATION **L.H.A. 65°, 295°**

Dec.	23°			24°			25°			26°			27°			28°			29°			30°			Dec.
°	Hc ° ′	d ′	Z °	Hc ° ′	d ′	Z °	Hc ° ′	d ′	Z °	Hc ° ′	d ′	Z °	Hc ° ′	d ′	Z °	Hc ° ′	d ′	Z °	Hc ° ′	d ′	Z °	Hc ° ′	d ′	Z °	°
0	22 53.6	-25.6	100.3	22 42.7	-26.7	100.7	22 31.3	-27.7	101.1	22 19.5	-28.6	101.6	22 07.2	-29.5	102.0	21 54.6	-30.5	102.3	21 41.6	-31.5	102.7	21 28.1	-32.3	103.1	0
1	22 28.0	-26.0	101.3	22 16.0	-27.0	101.7	22 03.6	-27.9	102.1	21 50.9	-29.0	102.5	21 37.7	-29.9	102.9	21 24.1	-30.8	103.3	21 10.1	-31.7	103.7	20 55.8	-32.7	104.0	1
2	22 02.0	-26.3	102.3	21 49.0	-27.3	102.7	21 35.7	-28.3	103.1	21 21.9	-29.2	103.4	21 07.8	-30.2	103.8	20 53.3	-31.1	104.2	20 38.4	-32.1	104.6	20 23.1	-32.9	104.9	2
3	21 35.7	-26.7	103.2	21 21.7	-27.6	103.6	21 07.4	-28.6	104.0	20 52.7	-29.5	104.4	20 37.6	-30.5	104.7	20 22.2	-31.4	105.1	20 06.3	-32.3	105.5	19 50.2	-33.2	105.8	3
4	21 09.0	-27.0	104.2	20 54.1	-27.9	104.6	20 38.8	-28.9	104.9	20 23.2	-29.9	105.3	20 07.1	-30.7	105.7	19 50.8	-31.7	106.0	19 34.0	-32.5	106.4	19 17.0	-33.5	106.7	4
5	20 42.0	-27.3	105.2	20 26.2	-28.3	105.5	20 09.9	-29.2	105.9	19 53.3	-30.1	106.2	19 36.4	-31.1	106.6	19 19.1	-31.9	106.9	19 01.5	-32.9	107.2	18 43.5	-33.7	107.6	5
6	20 14.7	-27.6	106.1	19 57.9	-28.5	106.5	19 40.7	-29.4	106.8	19 23.2	-30.4	107.2	19 05.3	-31.3	107.5	18 47.2	-32.2	107.8	18 28.6	-33.0	108.1	18 09.8	-33.9	108.4	6
7	19 47.1	-27.9	107.1	19 29.4	-28.9	107.4	19 11.3	-29.8	107.7	18 52.8	-30.6	108.1	18 34.0	-31.5	108.4	18 15.0	-32.5	108.7	17 55.6	-33.3	109.0	17 35.9	-34.2	109.3	7
8	19 19.2	-28.1	108.0	19 00.5	-29.1	108.3	18 41.5	-30.0	108.7	18 22.2	-31.0	109.0	18 02.5	-31.8	109.3	17 42.5	-32.6	109.6	17 22.3	-33.6	109.9	17 01.7	-34.4	110.2	8
9	18 51.1	-28.5	108.9	18 31.4	-29.3	109.3	18 11.5	-30.3	109.6	17 51.2	-31.1	109.9	17 30.7	-32.0	110.2	17 09.9	-32.9	110.5	16 48.7	-33.7	110.8	16 27.3	-34.5	111.0	9
10	18 22.6	-28.7	109.9	18 02.1	-29.7	110.2	17 41.2	-30.5	110.5	17 20.1	-31.4	110.8	16 58.7	-32.3	111.1	16 37.0	-33.1	111.3	16 15.0	-34.0	111.6	15 52.8	-34.8	111.9	10
11	17 53.9	-29.0	110.8	17 32.4	-29.9	111.1	17 10.7	-30.8	111.4	16 48.7	-31.6	111.7	16 26.4	-32.5	111.9	16 03.9	-33.4	112.2	15 41.0	-34.1	112.5	15 18.0	-35.0	112.7	11
12	17 24.9	-29.3	111.7	17 02.5	-30.1	112.0	16 39.9	-31.0	112.3	16 17.1	-31.9	112.5	15 53.9	-32.7	112.8	15 30.5	-33.5	113.1	15 06.9	-34.3	113.3	14 43.0	-35.1	113.6	12
13	16 55.6	-29.5	112.6	16 32.4	-30.3	112.9	16 08.9	-31.2	113.2	15 45.2	-32.0	113.4	15 21.2	-32.9	113.7	14 57.0	-33.7	113.9	14 32.6	-34.6	114.2	14 07.9	-35.4	114.4	13
14	16 26.1	-29.7	113.5	16 02.1	-30.6	113.8	15 37.7	-31.4	114.1	15 13.2	-32.3	114.3	14 48.3	-33.1	114.6	14 23.3	-33.9	114.8	13 58.0	-34.7	115.0	13 32.5	-35.4	115.2	14
15	15 56.4	-29.9	114.4	15 31.5	-30.8	114.7	15 06.3	-31.6	114.9	14 40.9	-32.5	115.2	14 15.2	-33.2	115.4	13 49.4	-34.1	115.6	13 23.3	-34.8	115.9	12 57.1	-35.7	116.1	15
16	15 26.5	-30.2	115.3	15 00.7	-31.0	115.6	14 34.7	-31.9	115.8	14 08.4	-32.6	116.0	13 42.0	-33.5	116.3	13 15.3	-34.2	116.5	12 48.5	-35.1	116.7	12 21.4	-35.8	116.9	16
17	14 56.3	-30.3	116.2	14 29.7	-31.2	116.5	14 02.8	-32.0	116.7	13 35.8	-32.8	116.9	13 08.5	-33.6	117.1	12 41.1	-34.4	117.3	12 13.4	-35.1	117.5	11 45.6	-35.9	117.7	17
18	14 26.0	-30.6	117.1	13 58.5	-31.4	117.3	13 30.8	-32.2	117.6	13 03.0	-33.0	117.8	12 34.9	-33.8	118.0	12 06.7	-34.6	118.2	11 38.3	-35.3	118.4	11 09.7	-36.1	118.5	18
19	13 55.4	-30.8	118.0	13 27.1	-31.6	118.2	12 58.6	-32.3	118.4	12 30.0	-33.2	118.6	12 01.1	-33.9	118.8	11 32.1	-34.7	119.0	11 03.0	-35.5	119.2	10 33.6	-36.2	119.3	19
20	13 24.6	-30.9	118.9	12 55.5	-31.7	119.1	12 26.3	-32.6	119.3	11 56.8	-33.3	119.5	11 27.2	-34.1	119.7	10 57.4	-34.8	119.8	10 27.5	-35.6	120.0	9 57.4	-36.3	120.2	20
21	12 53.7	-31.1	119.8	12 23.8	-31.9	120.0	11 53.7	-32.6	120.2	11 23.5	-33.4	120.3	10 53.1	-34.2	120.5	10 22.6	-34.9	120.7	9 51.9	-35.6	120.8	9 21.1	-36.4	121.0	21
22	12 22.6	-31.3	120.6	11 51.9	-32.1	120.8	11 21.1	-32.9	121.0	10 50.1	-33.6	121.2	10 18.9	-34.3	121.3	9 47.7	-35.1	121.5	9 16.3	-35.8	121.6	8 44.7	-36.5	121.8	22
23	11 51.3	-31.5	121.5	11 19.8	-32.2	121.7	10 48.2	-33.0	121.9	10 16.5	-33.7	122.0	9 44.6	-34.5	122.2	9 12.6	-35.2	122.3	8 40.5	-35.9	122.4	8 08.2	-36.6	122.6	23
24	11 19.8	-31.6	122.4	10 47.6	-32.4	122.6	10 15.2	-33.1	122.7	9 42.8	-33.9	122.9	9 10.1	-34.5	123.0	8 37.4	-35.3	123.1	8 04.6	-36.0	123.3	7 31.6	-36.7	123.4	24
25	10 48.2	-31.7	123.3	10 15.2	-32.4	123.4	9 42.1	-33.2	123.6	9 08.9	-33.9	123.7	8 35.6	-34.7	123.8	8 02.1	-35.4	123.9	7 28.6	-36.1	124.1	6 54.9	-36.8	124.2	25
26	10 16.5	-31.9	124.1	9 42.8	-32.7	124.3	9 08.9	-33.3	124.4	8 35.0	-34.1	124.5	8 00.9	-34.8	124.7	7 26.7	-35.4	124.8	6 52.5	-36.2	124.9	6 18.1	-36.8	125.0	26
27	9 44.6	-32.0	125.0	9 10.1	-32.7	125.1	8 35.6	-33.5	125.2	8 00.9	-34.2	125.4	7 26.1	-34.8	125.5	6 51.3	-35.6	125.6	6 16.3	-36.2	125.7	5 41.3	-36.9	125.8	27
28	9 12.6	-32.1	125.8	8 37.4	-32.8	126.0	8 02.1	-33.5	126.1	7 26.7	-34.2	126.2	6 51.3	-35.0	126.3	6 15.7	-35.6	126.4	5 40.1	-36.3	126.5	5 04.4	-37.0	126.5	28
29	8 40.5	-32.3	126.7	8 04.6	-33.0	126.8	7 28.6	-33.7	126.9	6 52.5	-34.4	127.0	6 16.3	-35.0	127.1	5 40.1	-35.7	127.2	5 03.8	-36.4	127.3	4 27.4	-37.0	127.3	29
30	8 08.2	-32.3	127.5	7 31.6	-33.0	127.7	6 54.9	-33.7	127.8	6 18.1	-34.4	127.8	5 41.3	-35.1	127.9	5 04.4	-35.8	128.0	4 27.4	-36.4	128.1	3 50.4	-37.1	128.1	30
31	7 35.9	-32.5	128.4	6 58.6	-33.2	128.5	6 21.2	-33.9	128.6	5 43.7	-34.5	128.7	5 06.2	-35.2	128.7	4 28.6	-35.8	128.8	3 51.0	-36.5	128.9	3 13.3	-37.1	128.9	31
32	7 03.4	-32.5	129.2	6 25.4	-33.2	129.3	5 47.3	-33.8	129.4	5 09.2	-34.5	129.5	4 31.0	-35.2	129.6	3 52.8	-35.9	129.6	3 14.5	-36.5	129.7	2 36.2	-37.1	129.7	32
33	6 30.9	-32.7	130.1	5 52.2	-33.3	130.2	5 13.5	-34.0	130.2	4 34.7	-34.6	130.3	3 55.8	-35.2	130.4	3 16.9	-35.9	130.4	2 38.0	-36.5	130.5	1 59.1	-37.2	130.5	33
34	5 58.2	-32.7	130.9	5 18.9	-33.4	131.0	4 39.5	-34.0	131.1	4 00.1	-34.7	131.1	3 20.6	-35.3	131.2	2 41.0	-35.9	131.2	2 01.5	-36.6	131.3	1 21.9	-37.1	131.3	34
35	5 25.5	-32.7	131.8	4 45.5	-33.4	131.8	4 05.5	-34.1	131.9	3 25.4	-34.7	131.9	2 45.3	-35.4	132.0	2 05.1	-35.9	132.0	1 24.9	-36.5	132.0	0 44.8	-37.2	132.1	35
36	4 52.8	-32.9	132.6	4 12.1	-33.5	132.7	3 31.4	-34.1	132.7	2 50.7	-34.7	132.8	2 09.9	-35.3	132.8	1 29.2	-36.0	132.8	0 48.4	-36.6	132.8	0 07.6	-37.2	132.8	36
37	4 19.9	-32.9	133.5	3 38.6	-33.5	133.5	2 57.3	-34.1	133.5	2 16.0	-34.8	133.6	1 34.6	-35.4	133.6	0 53.2	-36.0	133.6	0 11.8	-36.6	133.6	0 29.6	+37.2	46.4	37
38	3 47.0	-32.9	134.3	3 05.1	-33.5	134.3	2 23.2	-34.2	134.4	1 41.2	-34.8	134.4	0 59.2	-35.4	134.4	0 17.2	-36.0	134.4	0 24.8	+36.5	45.6	1 06.8	+37.1	45.6	38
39	3 14.1	-33.0	135.1	2 31.6	-33.6	135.2	1 49.0	-34.2	135.2	1 06.4	-34.8	135.2	0 23.8	-35.4	135.2	0 18.8	+35.9	44.8	1 01.3	+36.6	44.8	1 43.9	+37.2	44.8	39
40	2 41.1	-33.0	136.0	1 58.0	-33.6	136.0	1 14.8	-34.2	136.0	0 31.6	-34.8	136.0	0 11.6	+35.3	44.0	0 54.7	+36.0	44.0	1 37.9	+36.6	44.0	2 21.1	+37.1	44.0	40
41	2 08.1	-33.0	136.8	1 24.4	-33.7	136.8	0 40.6	-34.2	136.8	0 03.2	+34.8	43.2	0 46.9	+35.4	43.2	1 30.7	+36.0	43.2	2 14.5	+36.5	43.2	2 58.2	+37.1	43.2	41
42	1 35.1	-33.1	137.6	0 50.7	-33.6	137.7	0 06.4	-34.2	137.7	0 38.0	+34.8	42.3	1 22.3	+35.4	42.4	2 06.7	+35.9	42.4	2 51.0	+36.5	42.4	3 35.3	+37.0	42.4	42
43	1 02.0	-33.1	138.5	0 17.1	-33.7	138.5	0 27.8	+34.3	41.5	1 12.8	+34.7	41.5	1 57.7	+35.3	41.5	2 42.6	+35.9	41.6	3 27.5	+36.4	41.6	4 12.3	+37.0	41.7	43
44	0 28.9	-33.1	139.3	0 16.6	+33.6	40.7	1 02.1	+34.2	40.7	1 47.5	+34.8	40.7	2 33.0	+35.3	40.7	3 18.5	+35.8	40.8	4 03.9	+36.4	40.8	4 49.3	+36.9	40.9	44
45	0 04.2	+33.0	39.9	0 50.2	+33.6	39.9	1 36.3	+34.1	39.9	2 22.3	+34.7	39.9	3 08.3	+35.3	39.9	3 54.3	+35.8	40.0	4 40.3	+36.3	40.0	5 26.2	+36.9	40.1	45
46	0 37.2	+33.1	39.0	1 23.8	+33.7	39.0	2 10.4	+34.2	39.1	2 57.0	+34.7	39.1	3 43.6	+35.2	39.1	4 30.1	+35.8	39.2	5 16.6	+36.3	39.2	6 03.1	+36.8	39.3	46
47	1 10.3	+33.1	38.2	1 57.5	+33.6	38.2	2 44.6	+34.1	38.2	3 31.7	+34.7	38.3	4 18.8	+35.2	38.3	5 05.9	+35.7	38.4	5 52.9	+36.2	38.4	6 39.9	+36.7	38.5	47
48	1 43.4	+33.0	37.4	2 31.1	+33.5	37.4	3 18.7	+34.1	37.4	4 06.4	+34.6	37.4	4 54.0	+35.1	37.5	5 41.6	+35.6	37.5	6 29.1	+36.2	37.6	7 16.6	+36.7	37.7	48
49	2 16.4	+33.0	36.5	3 04.6	+33.5	36.5	3 52.8	+34.0	36.6	4 41.0	+34.5	36.6	5 29.1	+35.1	36.7	6 17.2	+35.6	36.7	7 05.3	+36.0	36.8	7 53.3	+36.5	36.9	49
50	2 49.4	+33.0	35.7	3 38.1	+33.5	35.7	4 26.8	+34.0	35.8	5 15.5	+34.5	35.8	6 04.2	+34.9	35.9	6 52.8	+35.4	35.9	7 41.3	+36.0	36.0	8 29.8	+36.5	36.1	50
51	3 22.4	+32.9	34.8	4 11.6	+33.4	34.9	5 00.8	+33.9	34.9	5 50.0	+34.4	35.0	6 39.1	+34.9	35.0	7 28.2	+35.4	35.1	8 17.3	+35.9	35.2	9 06.3	+36.3	35.3	51
52	3 55.3	+32.9	34.0	4 45.0	+33.4	34.0	5 34.7	+33.9	34.1	6 24.4	+34.3	34.2	7 14.0	+34.8	34.2	8 03.6	+35.3	34.3	8 53.2	+35.7	34.4	9 42.6	+36.3	34.5	52
53	4 28.2	+32.8	33.2	5 18.4	+33.3	33.2	6 08.6	+33.7	33.3	6 58.7	+34.3	33.3	7 48.8	+34.7	33.4	8 38.9	+35.2	33.5	9 28.9	+35.7	33.6	10 18.9	+36.1	33.7	53
54	5 01.0	+32.8	32.3	5 51.7	+33.2	32.4	6 42.3	+33.7	32.4	7 33.0	+34.1	32.5	8 23.5	+34.7	32.6	9 14.1	+35.0	32.7	10 04.6	+35.5	32.8	10 55.0	+36.0	32.9	54
55	5 33.8	+32.6	31.5	6 24.9	+33.1	31.5	7 16.0	+33.6	31.6	8 07.1	+34.1	31.7	8 58.2	+34.5	31.8	9 49.1	+35.0	31.8	10 40.1	+35.4	31.9	11 31.0	+35.8	32.0	55
56	6 06.4	+32.6	30.6	6 58.0	+33.1	30.7	7 49.6	+33.5	30.8	8 41.2	+33.9	30.8	9 32.7	+34.3	30.9	10 24.1	+34.8	31.0	11 15.5	+35.3	31.1	12 06.8	+35.7	31.2	56
57	6 39.0	+32.6	29.8	7 31.1	+33.0	29.9	8 23.1	+33.4	29.9	9 15.1	+33.8	30.0	10 07.0	+34.3	30.1	10 58.9	+34.7	30.2	11 50.8	+35.1	30.3	12 42.5	+35.6	30.4	57
58	7 11.6	+32.4	29.0	8 04.1	+32.8	29.0	8 56.5	+33.3	29.1	9 48.9	+33.7	29.2	10 41.3	+34.1	29.3	11 33.6	+34.5	29.4	12 25.9	+34.9	29.5	13 18.1	+35.4	29.6	58
59	7 44.0	+32.3	28.1	8 36.9	+32.7	28.2	9 29.8	+33.1	28.2	10 22.6	+33.6	28.3	11 15.4	+34.0	28.4	12 08.1	+34.4	28.5	13 00.8	+34.8	28.6	13 53.5	+35.2	28.7	59
60	8 16.3	+32.2	27.3	9 09.6	+32.7	27.3	10 02.9	+33.1	27.4	10 56.2	+33.4	27.5	11 49.4	+33.8	27.6	12 42.5	+34.3	27.7	13 35.6	+34.7	27.8	14 28.7	+35.0	27.9	60
61	8 48.5	+32.1	26.4	9 42.3	+32.5	26.5	10 36.0	+32.8	26.6	11 29.6	+33.3	26.6	12 23.2	+33.7	26.7	13 16.8	+34.0	26.8	14 10.3	+34.4	26.9	15 03.7	+34.9	27.1	61
62	9 20.6	+32.0	25.5	10 14.8	+32.3	25.6	11 08.8	+32.8	25.7	12 02.9	+33.1	25.8	12 56.9	+33.5	25.9	13 50.8	+33.9	26.0	14 44.7	+34.3	26.1	15 38.6	+34.7	26.2	62
63	9 52.6	+31.9	24.7	10 47.1	+32.2	24.8	11 41.6	+32.6	24.8	12 36.0	+33.0	24.9	13 30.4	+33.3	25.0	14 24.7	+33.7	25.1	15 19.0	+34.1	25.3	16 13.3	+34.4	25.4	63
64	10 24.5	+31.7	23.8	11 19.3	+32.1	23.9	12 14.2	+32.4	24.0	13 09.0	+32.8	24.1	14 03.7	+33.2	24.2	14 58.4	+33.6	24.3	15 53.1	+33.9	24.4	16 47.7	+34.3	24.5	64
65	10 56.2	+31.5	23.0	11 51.4	+31.9	23.0	12 46.6	+32.3	23.1	13 41.8	+32.6	23.2	14 36.9	+32.9	23.3	15 32.0	+33.3	23.4	16 27.0	+33.7	23.5	17 22.0	+34.0	23.7	65
66	11 27.7	+31.4	22.1	12 23.3	+31.8	22.2	13 18.9	+32.0	22.3	14 14.4	+32.4	22.4	15 09.8	+32.8	22.5	16 05.3	+33.1	22.6	17 00.7	+33.4	22.7	17 56.0	+33.8	22.8	66
67	11 59.1	+31.3	21.2	12 55.1	+31.5	21.3	13 50.9	+31.9	21.4	14 46.8	+32.2	21.5	15 42.6	+32.6	21.6	16 38.4	+32.9	21.7	17 34.1	+33.2	21.8	18 29.8	+33.5	21.9	67
68	12 30.4	+31.1	20.4	13 26.6	+31.4	20.4	14 22.8	+31.7	20.5	15 19.0	+32.0	20.6	16 15.2	+32.3	20.7	17 11.3	+32.6	20.8	18 07.3	+33.0	20.9	19 03.3	+33.3	21.1	68
69	13 01.5	+30.9	19.5	13 58.0	+31.2	19.6	14 54.5	+31.5	19.6	15 51.0	+31.8	19.7	16 47.5	+32.1	19.8	17 43.9	+32.4	19.9	18 40.3	+32.7	20.0	19 36.6	+33.1	20.2	69
70	13 32.4	+30.7	18.6	14 29.2	+31.0	18.7	15 26.0	+31.3	18.8	16 22.8	+31.6	18.8	17 19.6	+31.9	18.9	18 16.3	+32.2	19.1	19 13.0	+32.5	19.2	20 09.7	+32.8	19.3	70
71	14 03.1	+30.5	17.7	15 00.2	+30.8	17.8	15 57.3	+31.1	17.9	16 54.4	+31.4	18.0	17 51.5	+31.6	18.1	18 48.5	+31.9	18.2	19 45.5	+32.2	18.3	20 42.5	+32.5	18.4	71
72	14 33.6	+30.3	16.8	15 31.0	+30.6	16.9	16 28.4	+30.9	17.0	17 25.8	+31.1	17.1	18 23.1	+31.4	17.2	19 20.4	+31.7	17.3	20 17.7	+32.0	17.4	21 15.0	+32.2	17.5	72
73	15 03.9	+30.1	15.9	16 01.6	+30.4	16.0	16 59.3	+30.6	16.1	17 56.9	+30.9	16.2	18 54.5	+31.1	16.3	19 52.1	+31.4	16.4	20 49.7	+31.6	16.5	21 47.2	+31.9	16.6	73
74	15 34.0	+29.9	15.0	16 32.0	+30.1	15.1	17 29.9	+30.3	15.2	18 27.8	+30.6	15.3	19 25.6	+30.9	15.4	20 23.5	+31.1	15.5	21 21.3	+31.3	15.6	22 19.1	+31.6	15.7	74
75	16 03.9	+29.7	14.1	17 02.1	+29.9	14.2	18 00.2	+30.2	14.3	18 58.4	+30.3	14.4	19 56.5	+30.6	14.4	20 54.6	+30.8	14.5	21 52.6	+31.1	14.6	22 50.7	+31.3	14.7	75
76	16 33.6	+29.4	13.2	17 32.0	+29.6	13.3	18 30.4	+29.8	13.4	19 28.7	+30.1	13.4	20 27.1	+30.2	13.5	21 25.4	+30.5	13.6	22 23.7	+30.7	13.7	23 22.0	+30.9	13.8	76
77	17 03.0	+29.2	12.3	18 01.6	+29.4	12.4	19 00.2	+29.6	12.5	19 58.8	+29.8	12.5	20 57.3	+30.0	12.6	21 55.9	+30.2	12.7	22 54.4	+30.4	12.8	23 52.9	+30.6	12.9	77
78	17 32.2	+28.9	11.4	18 31.0	+29.1	11.5	19 29.8	+29.3	11.5	20 28.6	+29.5	11.6	21 27.3	+29.7	11.7	22 26.1	+29.8	11.8	23 24.8	+30.1	11.8	24 23.5	+30.3	11.9	78
79	18 01.1	+28.7	10.5	19 00.1	+28.8	10.5	19 59.1	+29.0	10.6	20 58.1	+29.1	10.7	21 57.0	+29.4	10.7	22 55.9	+29.6	10.8	23 54.9	+29.7	10.9	24 53.8	+29.9	11.0	79
80	18 29.8	+28.4	9.6	19 28.9	+28.6	9.6	20 28.1	+28.7	9.7	21 27.2	+28.9	9.7	22 26.4	+29.0	9.8	23 25.5	+29.2	9.9	24 24.6	+29.3	10.0	25 23.7	+29.5	10.0	80
81	18 58.2	+28.1	8.6	19 57.5	+28.2	8.7	20 56.8	+28.4	8.7	21 56.1	+28.5	8.8	22 55.4	+28.7	8.9	23 54.7	+28.8	8.9	24 53.9	+29.0	9.0	25 53.2	+29.1	9.1	81
82	19 26.3	+27.8	7.7	20 25.7	+28.0	7.7	21 25.2	+28.1	7.8	22 24.6	+28.2	7.8	23 24.1	+28.3	7.9	24 23.5	+28.5	8.0	25 22.9	+28.6	8.0	26 22.3	+28.7	8.1	82
83	19 54.1	+27.5	6.7	20 53.7	+27.6	6.8	21 53.3	+27.7	6.8	22 52.8	+27.9	6.9	23 52.4	+28.0	6.9	24 52.0	+28.0	7.0	25 51.5	+28.2	7.1	26 51.0	+28.4	7.1	83
84	20 21.6	+27.3	5.8	21 21.3	+27.3	5.8	22 21.0	+27.4	5.9	23 20.7	+27.5	5.9	24 20.4	+27.6	6.0	25 20.0	+27.7	6.0	26 19.7	+27.8	6.1	27 19.4	+27.9	6.1	84
85	20 48.9	+26.9	4.8	21 48.6	+27.0	4.9	22 48.4	+27.1	4.9	23 48.2	+27.1	5.0	24 48.0	+27.2	5.0	25 47.7	+27.3	5.0	26 47.5	+27.4	5.1	27 47.3	+27.4	5.1	85
86	21 15.8	+26.5	3.9	22 15.6	+26.7	3.9	23 15.5	+26.7	3.9	24 15.3	+26.8	4.0	25 15.2	+26.8	4.0	26 15.0	+26.9	4.0	27 14.9	+26.9	4.1	28 14.7	+27.1	4.1	86
87	21 42.3	+26.3	2.9	22 42.3	+26.2	2.9	23 42.2	+26.3	3.0	24 42.1	+26.4	3.0	25 42.0	+26.4	3.0	26 41.9	+26.5	3.0	27 41.8	+26.5	3.1	28 41.8	+26.5	3.1	87
88	22 08.6	+25.9	2.0	23 08.5	+26.0	2.0	24 08.5	+25.9	2.0	25 08.5	+25.9	2.0	26 08.4	+26.0	2.0	27 08.4	+26.0	2.0	28 08.3	+26.1	2.0	29 08.3	+26.1	2.1	88
89	22 34.5	+25.5	1.0	23 34.5	+25.5	1.0	24 34.4	+25.6	1.0	25 34.4	+25.6	1.0	26 34.4	+25.6	1.0	27 34.4	+25.6	1.0	28 34.4	+25.6	1.0	29 34.4	+25.6	1.0	89
90	23 00.0	+25.2	0.0	24 00.0	+25.2	0.0	25 00.0	+25.2	0.0	26 00.0	+25.1	0.0	27 00.0	+25.1	0.0	28 00.0	+25.1	0.0	29 00.0	+25.1	0.0	30 00.0	+25.1	0.0	90
	23°			24°			25°			26°			27°			28°			29°			30°			

S. Lat. {L.H.A. greater than 180° ....Zn=180°−Z
{L.H.A. less than 180°...........Zn=180°+Z

LATITUDE **SAME** NAME AS DECLINATION **L.H.A. 115°, 245°**

66°, 294° L.H.A. LATITUDE SAME NAME AS DECLINATION

N. Lat. {L.H.A. greater than 180° .....Zn=Z; L.H.A. less than 180°............Zn=360°−Z}

Dec.	23° Hc	d	Z	24° Hc	d	Z	25° Hc	d	Z	26° Hc	d	Z	27° Hc	d	Z	28° Hc	d	Z	29° Hc	d	Z	30° Hc	d	Z	Dec.
°	° ′	′	°	° ′	′	°	° ′	′	°	° ′	′	°	° ′	′	°	° ′	′	°	° ′	′	°	° ′	′	°	°
0	21 59.2	+25.2	99.9	21 48.8	+26.1	100.3	21 37.9	+27.1	100.7	21 26.6	+28.1	101.0	21 14.9	+29.0	101.4	21 02.8	+30.0	101.8	20 50.3	+31.0	102.2	20 37.5	+31.9	102.6	0
1	22 24.4	+24.7	98.9	22 14.9	+25.7	99.3	22 05.0	+26.7	99.7	21 54.7	+27.7	100.1	21 43.9	+28.8	100.5	21 32.8	+29.7	100.9	21 21.3	+30.7	101.3	21 09.4	+31.6	101.6	1
2	22 49.1	+24.4	97.9	22 40.6	+25.4	98.3	22 31.7	+26.5	98.7	22 22.4	+27.5	99.1	22 12.7	+28.4	99.5	22 02.5	+29.4	99.9	21 52.0	+30.3	100.3	21 41.0	+31.3	100.7	2
3	23 13.5	+24.0	96.9	23 06.0	+25.1	97.3	22 58.2	+26.0	97.8	22 49.9	+27.0	98.2	22 41.1	+28.1	98.6	22 31.9	+29.1	99.0	22 22.3	+30.1	99.4	22 12.3	+31.0	99.8	3
4	23 37.5	+23.6	95.9	23 31.1	+24.7	96.3	23 24.2	+25.7	96.8	23 16.9	+26.8	97.2	23 09.2	+27.7	97.6	23 01.0	+28.7	98.1	22 52.4	+29.7	98.5	22 43.3	+30.7	98.9	4
5	24 01.1	+23.2	94.9	23 55.8	+24.2	95.3	23 49.9	+25.3	95.8	23 43.7	+26.3	96.2	23 36.9	+27.4	96.7	23 29.7	+28.4	97.1	23 22.1	+29.4	97.5	23 14.0	+30.4	98.0	5
6	24 24.3	+22.9	93.9	24 20.0	+23.9	94.3	24 15.2	+25.0	94.8	24 10.0	+26.0	95.2	24 04.3	+27.0	95.7	23 58.1	+28.0	96.1	23 51.5	+29.0	96.6	23 44.4	+30.0	97.0	6
7	24 47.2	+22.4	92.9	24 43.9	+23.5	93.3	24 40.2	+24.5	93.8	24 36.0	+25.5	94.3	24 31.3	+26.6	94.7	24 26.1	+27.7	95.2	24 20.5	+28.6	95.6	24 14.4	+29.6	96.1	7
8	25 09.6	+21.9	91.9	25 07.4	+23.0	92.3	25 04.7	+24.1	92.8	25 01.5	+25.2	93.3	24 57.9	+26.2	93.7	24 53.8	+27.2	94.2	24 49.1	+28.3	94.6	24 44.0	+29.3	95.1	8
9	25 31.5	+21.6	90.8	25 30.4	+22.7	91.3	25 28.8	+23.7	91.8	25 26.7	+24.8	92.3	25 24.1	+25.8	92.7	25 21.0	+26.9	93.2	25 17.4	+27.9	93.7	25 13.3	+28.9	94.1	9
10	25 53.1	+21.1	89.8	25 53.1	+22.2	90.3	25 52.5	+23.3	90.8	25 51.5	+24.3	91.2	25 49.9	+25.4	91.7	25 47.9	+26.4	92.2	25 45.3	+27.5	92.7	25 42.2	+28.5	93.2	10
11	26 14.2	+20.6	88.7	26 15.3	+21.7	89.2	26 15.8	+22.8	89.7	26 15.8	+23.9	90.2	26 15.3	+25.0	90.7	26 14.3	+26.0	91.2	26 12.8	+27.1	91.7	26 10.7	+28.2	92.2	11
12	26 34.8	+20.2	87.7	26 37.0	+21.3	88.2	26 38.6	+22.4	88.7	26 39.7	+23.5	89.2	26 40.3	+24.5	89.7	26 40.3	+25.6	90.2	26 39.9	+26.6	90.7	26 38.9	+27.7	91.2	12
13	26 55.0	+19.7	86.6	26 58.3	+20.8	87.2	27 01.0	+21.9	87.7	27 03.2	+23.0	88.2	27 04.8	+24.1	88.7	27 05.9	+25.2	89.2	27 06.5	+26.3	89.7	27 06.6	+27.3	90.2	13
14	27 14.7	+19.3	85.6	27 19.1	+20.3	86.1	27 22.9	+21.5	86.6	27 26.2	+22.5	87.1	27 28.9	+23.7	87.6	27 31.1	+24.7	88.2	27 32.8	+25.7	88.7	27 33.9	+26.8	89.2	14
15	27 34.0	+18.7	84.5	27 39.4	+19.9	85.0	27 44.4	+20.9	85.6	27 48.7	+22.1	86.1	27 52.6	+23.1	86.6	27 55.8	+24.3	87.1	27 58.5	+25.4	87.7	28 00.7	+26.4	88.2	15
16	27 52.7	+18.3	83.4	27 59.3	+19.4	84.0	28 05.3	+20.5	84.5	28 10.8	+21.6	85.0	28 15.7	+22.7	85.6	28 20.1	+23.7	86.1	28 23.9	+24.8	86.6	28 27.1	+25.9	87.2	16
17	28 11.0	+17.7	82.4	28 18.7	+18.8	82.9	28 25.8	+20.0	83.4	28 32.4	+21.1	84.0	28 38.4	+22.2	84.5	28 43.8	+23.3	85.1	28 48.7	+24.4	85.6	28 53.0	+25.5	86.2	17
18	28 28.7	+17.2	81.3	28 37.5	+18.3	81.8	28 45.8	+19.4	82.4	28 53.5	+20.5	82.9	29 00.6	+21.7	83.5	29 07.1	+22.8	84.0	29 13.1	+23.9	84.6	29 18.5	+25.0	85.1	18
19	28 45.9	+16.7	80.2	28 55.8	+17.8	80.7	29 05.2	+18.9	81.3	29 14.0	+20.1	81.8	29 22.3	+21.1	82.4	29 29.9	+22.3	82.9	29 37.0	+23.4	83.5	29 43.5	+24.5	84.1	19
20	29 02.6	+16.1	79.1	29 13.6	+17.3	79.6	29 24.1	+18.4	80.2	29 34.1	+19.5	80.7	29 43.4	+20.7	81.3	29 52.2	+21.8	81.9	30 00.4	+22.9	82.4	30 08.0	+24.0	83.0	20
21	29 18.7	+15.6	78.0	29 30.9	+16.7	78.5	29 42.5	+17.9	79.1	29 53.6	+19.0	79.7	30 04.1	+20.1	80.2	30 14.0	+21.2	80.8	30 23.3	+22.3	81.4	30 32.0	+23.4	82.0	21
22	29 34.3	+15.0	76.9	29 47.6	+16.2	77.4	30 00.4	+17.3	78.0	30 12.6	+18.4	78.6	30 24.2	+19.6	79.1	30 35.2	+20.7	79.7	30 45.6	+21.8	80.3	30 55.4	+23.0	80.9	22
23	29 49.3	+14.5	75.8	30 03.8	+15.6	76.3	30 17.7	+16.8	76.9	30 31.0	+17.9	77.5	30 43.8	+19.0	78.0	30 55.9	+20.1	78.6	31 07.4	+21.3	79.2	31 18.4	+22.3	79.8	23
24	30 03.8	+13.9	74.6	30 19.4	+15.1	75.2	30 34.5	+16.1	75.8	30 48.9	+17.3	76.3	31 02.8	+18.4	76.9	31 16.0	+19.6	77.5	31 28.7	+20.7	78.1	31 40.7	+21.9	78.7	24
25	30 17.7	+13.3	73.5	30 34.5	+14.4	74.1	30 50.6	+15.6	74.7	31 06.2	+16.7	75.2	31 21.2	+17.9	75.8	31 35.6	+19.0	76.4	31 49.4	+20.1	77.0	32 02.6	+21.2	77.6	25
26	30 31.0	+12.8	72.4	30 48.9	+13.9	73.0	31 06.2	+15.0	73.5	31 22.9	+16.2	74.1	31 39.1	+17.2	74.7	31 54.6	+18.4	75.3	32 09.5	+19.5	75.9	32 23.8	+20.7	76.5	26
27	30 43.8	+12.1	71.3	31 02.8	+13.2	71.8	31 21.2	+14.4	72.4	31 39.1	+15.5	73.0	31 56.3	+16.7	73.6	32 13.0	+17.8	74.2	32 29.0	+19.0	74.8	32 44.5	+20.1	75.4	27
28	30 55.9	+11.5	70.1	31 16.0	+12.7	70.7	31 35.6	+13.8	71.3	31 54.6	+14.9	71.8	32 13.0	+16.0	72.4	32 30.8	+17.2	73.0	32 48.0	+18.3	73.7	33 04.6	+19.4	74.3	28
29	31 07.4	+11.0	69.0	31 28.7	+12.0	69.5	31 49.4	+13.2	70.1	32 09.5	+14.3	70.7	32 29.0	+15.5	71.3	32 48.0	+16.6	71.9	33 06.3	+17.7	72.5	33 24.0	+18.9	73.2	29
30	31 18.4	+10.3	67.8	31 40.7	+11.5	68.4	32 02.6	+12.5	69.0	32 23.8	+13.7	69.6	32 44.5	+14.8	70.2	33 04.6	+15.9	70.8	33 24.0	+17.1	71.4	33 42.9	+18.2	72.0	30
31	31 28.7	+9.6	66.7	31 52.2	+10.8	67.2	32 15.1	+11.9	67.8	32 37.5	+13.0	68.4	32 59.3	+14.1	69.0	33 20.5	+15.3	69.6	33 41.1	+16.4	70.2	34 01.1	+17.5	70.9	31
32	31 38.3	+9.1	65.5	32 03.0	+10.1	66.1	32 27.0	+11.3	66.6	32 50.5	+12.4	67.2	33 13.4	+13.6	67.8	33 35.8	+14.6	68.5	33 57.5	+15.8	69.1	34 18.6	+17.0	69.7	32
33	31 47.4	+8.4	64.3	32 13.1	+9.5	64.9	32 38.3	+10.6	65.5	33 02.9	+11.7	66.1	33 27.0	+12.8	66.7	33 50.4	+14.0	67.3	34 13.3	+15.1	67.9	34 35.6	+16.2	68.5	33
34	31 55.8	+7.8	63.2	32 22.6	+8.9	63.7	32 48.9	+10.0	64.3	33 14.6	+11.1	64.9	33 39.8	+12.2	65.5	34 04.4	+13.3	66.1	34 28.4	+14.4	66.7	34 51.8	+15.6	67.4	34
35	32 03.6	+7.1	62.0	32 31.5	+8.2	62.6	32 58.9	+9.3	63.1	33 25.7	+10.4	63.7	33 52.0	+11.5	64.3	34 17.7	+12.6	64.9	34 42.8	+13.8	65.6	35 07.4	+14.8	66.2	35
36	32 10.7	+6.5	60.8	32 39.7	+7.6	61.4	33 08.2	+8.6	62.0	33 36.1	+9.8	62.5	34 03.5	+10.8	63.1	34 30.3	+12.0	63.7	34 56.6	+13.0	64.4	35 22.2	+14.2	65.0	36
37	32 17.2	+5.8	59.7	32 47.3	+6.9	60.2	33 16.8	+8.0	60.8	33 45.9	+9.0	61.4	34 14.3	+10.2	61.9	34 42.3	+11.2	62.6	35 09.6	+12.4	63.2	35 36.4	+13.5	63.8	37
38	32 23.0	+5.2	58.5	32 54.2	+6.2	59.0	33 24.8	+7.3	59.6	33 54.9	+8.4	60.2	34 24.5	+9.4	60.8	34 53.5	+10.6	61.4	35 22.0	+11.6	62.0	35 49.9	+12.7	62.6	38
39	32 28.2	+4.5	57.3	33 00.4	+5.5	57.8	33 32.1	+6.6	58.4	34 03.3	+7.6	59.0	34 33.9	+8.8	59.6	35 04.1	+9.8	60.2	35 33.6	+10.9	60.8	36 02.6	+12.1	61.4	39
40	32 32.7	+3.9	56.1	33 05.9	+4.9	56.7	33 38.7	+5.9	57.2	34 10.9	+7.0	57.8	34 42.7	+8.0	58.4	35 13.9	+9.1	59.0	35 44.5	+10.2	59.6	36 14.7	+11.2	60.2	40
41	32 36.6	+3.1	54.9	33 10.8	+4.2	55.5	33 44.6	+5.2	56.0	34 17.9	+6.2	56.6	34 50.7	+7.3	57.1	35 23.0	+8.3	57.7	35 54.7	+9.5	58.4	36 25.9	+10.6	59.0	41
42	32 39.7	+2.5	53.7	33 15.0	+3.5	54.3	33 49.8	+4.5	54.8	34 24.1	+5.6	55.4	34 58.0	+6.6	55.9	35 31.3	+7.7	56.5	36 04.2	+8.7	57.1	36 36.5	+9.7	57.7	42
43	32 42.2	+1.9	52.6	33 18.5	+2.8	53.1	33 54.3	+3.8	53.6	34 29.7	+4.8	54.2	35 04.6	+5.8	54.7	35 39.0	+6.9	55.3	36 12.9	+7.9	55.9	36 46.2	+9.1	56.5	43
44	32 44.1	+1.1	51.4	33 21.3	+2.2	51.9	33 58.1	+3.2	52.4	34 34.5	+4.1	53.0	35 10.4	+5.2	53.5	35 45.9	+6.1	54.1	36 20.8	+7.2	54.7	36 55.3	+8.2	55.3	44
45	32 45.2	+0.5	50.2	33 23.5	+1.4	50.7	34 01.3	+2.4	51.2	34 38.6	+3.4	51.7	35 15.6	+4.4	52.3	35 52.0	+5.4	52.9	36 28.0	+6.4	53.4	37 03.5	+7.5	54.0	45
46	32 45.7	-0.2	49.0	33 24.9	+0.7	49.5	34 03.7	+1.7	50.0	34 42.0	+2.7	50.5	35 20.0	+3.6	51.1	35 57.4	+4.7	51.6	36 34.4	+5.7	52.2	37 11.0	+6.6	52.8	46
47	32 45.5	-0.8	47.8	33 25.6	+0.1	48.3	34 05.4	+1.0	48.8	34 44.7	+1.9	49.3	35 23.6	+2.9	49.8	36 02.1	+3.9	50.4	36 40.1	+4.9	51.0	37 17.6	+5.9	51.6	47
48	32 44.7	-1.6	46.6	33 25.7	-0.6	47.1	34 06.4	+0.3	47.6	34 46.6	+1.3	48.1	35 26.5	+2.2	48.6	36 06.0	+3.1	49.2	36 45.0	+4.1	49.7	37 23.5	+5.1	50.3	48
49	32 43.1	-2.2	45.4	33 25.1	-1.3	45.9	34 06.7	-0.5	46.4	34 47.9	+0.5	46.9	35 28.7	+1.4	47.4	36 09.1	+2.4	47.9	36 49.1	+3.3	48.5	37 28.6	+4.3	49.0	49
50	32 40.9	-2.8	44.2	33 23.8	-2.1	44.7	34 06.2	-1.1	45.2	34 48.4	-0.3	45.7	35 30.1	+0.7	46.2	36 11.5	+1.6	46.7	36 52.4	+2.6	47.2	37 32.9	+3.5	47.8	50
51	32 38.1	-3.6	43.1	33 21.7	-2.7	43.5	34 05.1	-1.8	44.0	34 48.1	-1.0	44.4	35 30.8	-0.1	44.9	36 13.1	+0.8	45.4	36 55.0	+1.7	46.0	37 36.4	+2.7	46.5	51
52	32 34.5	-4.2	41.9	33 19.0	-3.3	42.3	34 03.3	-2.6	42.8	34 47.1	-1.6	43.2	35 30.7	-0.8	43.7	36 13.9	+0.1	44.2	36 56.7	+1.0	44.7	37 39.1	+1.9	45.3	52
53	32 30.3	-4.9	40.7	33 15.7	-4.1	41.1	34 00.7	-3.2	41.5	34 45.5	-2.5	42.0	35 29.9	-1.6	42.5	36 14.0	-0.7	43.0	36 57.7	+0.2	43.5	37 41.0	+1.1	44.0	53
54	32 25.4	-5.5	39.5	33 11.6	-4.8	39.9	33 57.5	-4.0	40.3	34 43.0	-3.1	40.8	35 28.3	-2.3	41.2	36 13.3	-1.5	41.7	36 57.9	-0.6	42.2	37 42.1	+0.3	42.7	54
55	32 19.9	-6.2	38.3	33 06.8	-5.4	38.7	33 53.5	-4.7	39.1	34 39.9	-3.9	39.6	35 26.0	-3.1	40.0	36 11.8	-2.2	40.5	36 57.3	-1.4	41.0	37 42.4	-0.6	41.5	55
56	32 13.7	-6.8	37.1	33 01.4	-6.1	37.5	33 48.8	-5.3	37.9	34 36.0	-4.5	38.4	35 22.9	-3.8	38.8	36 09.6	-3.0	39.3	36 55.9	-2.2	39.7	37 41.8	-1.3	40.2	56
57	32 06.9	-7.5	36.0	32 55.3	-6.8	36.4	33 43.5	-6.0	36.7	34 31.5	-5.3	37.2	35 19.1	-4.5	37.6	36 06.6	-3.8	38.0	36 53.7	-3.0	38.5	37 40.5	-2.2	38.9	57
58	31 59.4	-8.2	34.8	32 48.5	-7.4	35.2	33 37.5	-6.8	35.5	34 26.2	-6.1	35.9	35 14.6	-5.3	36.4	36 02.8	-4.5	36.8	36 50.7	-3.7	37.2	37 38.3	-2.9	37.7	58
59	31 51.2	-8.7	33.6	32 41.1	-8.1	34.0	33 30.7	-7.4	34.4	34 20.1	-6.7	34.7	35 09.3	-6.0	35.1	35 58.3	-5.3	35.5	36 47.0	-4.6	36.0	37 35.4	-3.8	36.4	59
60	31 42.5	-9.4	32.5	32 33.0	-8.8	32.8	33 23.3	-8.1	33.2	34 13.4	-7.4	33.5	35 03.3	-6.7	33.9	35 53.0	-6.0	34.3	36 42.4	-5.3	34.7	37 31.6	-4.5	35.2	60
61	31 33.1	-10.1	31.3	32 24.2	-9.4	31.6	33 15.2	-8.8	32.0	34 06.0	-8.1	32.3	34 56.6	-7.4	32.7	35 47.0	-6.8	33.1	36 37.1	-6.0	33.5	37 27.1	-5.4	33.9	61
62	31 23.0	-10.6	30.2	32 14.8	-10.0	30.5	33 06.4	-9.4	30.8	33 57.9	-8.8	31.1	34 49.2	-8.2	31.5	35 40.2	-7.5	31.9	36 31.1	-6.9	32.3	37 21.7	-6.2	32.7	62
63	31 12.4	-11.3	29.0	32 04.8	-10.7	29.3	32 57.0	-10.1	29.6	33 49.1	-9.5	29.9	34 41.0	-8.9	30.3	35 32.7	-8.2	30.6	36 24.2	-7.6	31.0	37 15.5	-6.9	31.4	63
64	31 01.1	-11.9	27.9	31 54.1	-11.3	28.1	32 46.9	-10.7	28.4	33 39.6	-10.2	28.8	34 32.1	-9.6	29.1	35 24.5	-9.0	29.4	36 16.6	-8.3	29.8	37 08.6	-7.7	30.2	64
65	30 49.2	-12.4	26.7	31 42.8	-12.0	27.0	32 36.2	-11.4	27.3	33 29.4	-10.8	27.6	34 22.5	-10.2	27.9	35 15.5	-9.7	28.2	36 08.3	-9.1	28.6	37 00.9	-8.5	28.9	65
66	30 36.8	-13.1	25.6	31 30.8	-12.5	25.8	32 24.8	-12.1	26.1	33 18.6	-11.5	26.4	34 12.3	-11.0	26.7	35 05.8	-10.4	27.0	35 59.2	-9.9	27.3	36 52.4	-9.3	27.7	66
67	30 23.7	-13.6	24.4	31 18.3	-13.2	24.7	32 12.7	-12.6	25.0	33 07.1	-12.2	25.2	34 01.3	-11.7	25.5	34 55.4	-11.1	25.8	35 49.3	-10.6	26.1	36 43.1	-10.0	26.4	67
68	30 10.1	-14.3	23.3	31 05.1	-13.7	23.6	32 00.1	-13.3	23.8	32 54.9	-12.8	24.1	33 49.6	-12.3	24.3	34 44.3	-11.9	24.6	35 38.7	-11.3	24.9	36 33.1	-10.8	25.2	68
69	29 55.8	-14.7	22.2	30 51.4	-14.4	22.4	31 46.8	-13.9	22.7	32 42.1	-13.5	22.9	33 37.3	-13.0	23.2	34 32.4	-12.5	23.4	35 27.4	-12.0	23.7	36 22.3	-11.5	24.0	69
70	29 41.1	-15.4	21.1	30 37.0	-14.9	21.3	31 32.9	-14.5	21.5	32 28.6	-14.0	21.7	33 24.3	-13.6	22.0	34 19.9	-13.2	22.2	35 15.4	-12.7	22.5	36 10.8	-12.3	22.8	70
71	29 25.7	-15.9	20.0	30 22.1	-15.5	20.2	31 18.4	-15.2	20.4	32 14.6	-14.7	20.6	33 10.7	-14.3	20.8	34 06.7	-13.8	21.1	35 02.7	-13.5	21.3	35 58.5	-13.0	21.6	71
72	29 09.8	-16.4	18.9	30 06.6	-16.1	19.0	31 03.2	-15.7	19.2	31 59.9	-15.4	19.4	32 56.4	-14.9	19.7	33 52.9	-14.6	19.9	34 49.2	-14.1	20.1	35 45.5	-13.7	20.4	72
73	28 53.4	-17.0	17.8	29 50.5	-16.6	17.9	30 47.5	-16.2	18.1	31 44.5	-15.9	18.3	32 41.5	-15.6	18.5	33 38.3	-15.2	18.7	34 35.1	-14.8	18.9	35 31.8	-14.4	19.2	73
74	28 36.4	-17.5	16.7	29 33.9	-17.2	16.8	30 31.3	-16.9	17.0	31 28.6	-16.5	17.2	32 25.9	-16.2	17.4	33 23.1	-15.8	17.6	34 20.3	-15.4	17.8	35 17.4	-15.1	18.0	74
75	28 18.9	-18.0	15.6	29 16.7	-17.7	15.7	30 14.4	-17.4	15.9	31 12.1	-17.1	16.0	32 09.7	-16.8	16.2	33 07.3	-16.4	16.4	34 04.9	-16.2	16.6	35 02.3	-15.8	16.8	75
76	28 00.9	-18.5	14.5	28 59.0	-18.3	14.6	29 57.0	-18.0	14.8	30 55.0	-17.7	14.9	31 52.9	-17.3	15.1	32 50.9	-17.1	15.3	33 48.7	-16.8	15.4	34 46.5	-16.4	15.6	76
77	27 42.4	-19.0	13.4	28 40.7	-18.7	13.5	29 39.0	-18.5	13.7	30 37.3	-18.2	13.8	31 35.6	-18.0	14.0	32 33.8	-17.7	14.1	33 31.9	-17.4	14.3	34 30.1	-17.2	14.4	77
78	27 23.4	-19.5	12.4	28 22.0	-19.3	12.5	29 20.5	-19.0	12.6	30 19.1	-18.8	12.7	31 17.6	-18.6	12.8	32 16.1	-18.3	13.0	33 14.5	-18.0	13.1	34 12.9	-17.7	13.3	78
79	27 03.9	-20.0	11.3	28 02.7	-19.8	11.4	29 01.5	-19.6	11.5	30 00.3	-19.4	11.6	30 59.0	-19.1	11.7	31 57.8	-18.9	11.9	32 56.5	-18.7	12.0	33 55.2	-18.5	12.1	79
80	26 43.9	-20.5	10.2	27 42.9	-20.2	10.3	28 41.9	-20.0	10.4	29 40.9	-19.8	10.5	30 39.9	-19.6	10.6	31 38.9	-19.5	10.7	32 37.8	-19.2	10.9	33 36.7	-19.0	11.0	80
81	26 23.4	-20.9	9.2	27 22.7	-20.8	9.3	28 21.9	-20.6	9.3	29 21.1	-20.4	9.4	30 20.3	-20.3	9.5	31 19.4	-20.0	9.6	32 18.6	-19.9	9.7	33 17.7	-19.7	9.8	81
82	26 02.5	-21.3	8.1	27 01.9	-21.2	8.2	28 01.3	-21.0	8.3	29 00.7	-20.9	8.4	30 00.0	-20.7	8.4	30 59.4	-20.6	8.5	31 58.7	-20.4	8.6	32 58.0	-20.2	8.7	82
83	25 41.2	-21.8	7.1	26 40.7	-21.6	7.2	27 40.3	-21.6	7.2	28 39.8	-21.4	7.3	29 39.3	-21.3	7.4	30 38.8	-21.2	7.4	31 38.3	-21.0	7.5	32 37.8	-20.9	7.6	83
84	25 19.4	-22.2	6.1	26 19.1	-22.1	6.1	27 18.7	-22.0	6.2	28 18.4	-21.9	6.2	29 18.0	-21.8	6.3	30 17.6	-21.6	6.3	31 17.3	-21.6	6.4	32 16.9	-21.4	6.5	84
85	24 57.2	-22.7	5.0	25 57.0	-22.6	5.1	26 56.7	-22.5	5.1	27 56.5	-22.4	5.2	28 56.2	-22.3	5.2	29 56.0	-22.2	5.3	30 55.7	-22.1	5.3	31 55.5	-22.1	5.4	85
86	24 34.5	-23.0	4.0	25 34.4	-23.0	4.1	26 34.2	-22.9	4.1	27 34.1	-22.9	4.1	28 33.9	-22.7	4.2	29 33.8	-22.7	4.2	30 33.6	-22.6	4.2	31 33.4	-22.5	4.3	86
87	24 11.5	-23.4	3.0	25 11.4	-23.4	3.0	26 11.3	-23.3	3.1	27 11.2	-23.3	3.1	28 11.2	-23.3	3.1	29 11.1	-23.2	3.1	30 11.0	-23.2	3.2	31 10.9	-23.1	3.2	87
88	23 48.1	-23.9	2.0	24 48.0	-23.8	2.0	25 48.0	-23.8	2.0	26 47.9	-23.7	2.0	27 47.9	-23.7	2.1	28 47.9	-23.7	2.1	29 47.8	-23.6	2.1	30 47.8	-23.7	2.1	88
89	23 24.2	-24.2	1.0	24 24.2	-24.2	1.0	25 24.2	-24.2	1.0	26 24.2	-24.2	1.0	27 24.2	-24.2	1.0	28 24.2	-24.2	1.0	29 24.2	-24.2	1.0	30 24.1	-24.1	1.1	89
90	23 00.0	-24.6	0.0	24 00.0	-24.6	0.0	25 00.0	-24.6	0.0	26 00.0	-24.6	0.0	27 00.0	-24.6	0.0	28 00.0	-24.6	0.0	29 00.0	-24.6	0.0	30 00.0	-24.7	0.0	90
	23°			24°			25°			26°			27°			28°			29°			30°			

66°, 294° L.H.A. LATITUDE SAME NAME AS DECLINATION

316

LATITUDE **CONTRARY** NAME TO DECLINATION **L.H.A. 66°, 294°**

Dec.	23° Hc	d	Z	24° Hc	d	Z	25° Hc	d	Z	26° Hc	d	Z	27° Hc	d	Z	28° Hc	d	Z	29° Hc	d	Z	30° Hc	d	Z	Dec.
°	° ′	′	°	° ′	′	°	° ′	′	°	° ′	′	°	° ′	′	°	° ′	′	°	° ′	′	°	° ′	′	°	°
0	21 59.2	-25.4	99.9	21 48.8	-26.5	100.3	21 37.9	-27.5	100.7	21 26.6	-28.4	101.0	21 14.9	-29.4	101.4	21 02.8	-30.3	101.8	20 50.3	-31.2	102.2	20 37.5	-32.2	102.6	0
1	21 33.8	-25.8	100.8	21 22.3	-26.8	101.2	21 10.4	-27.7	101.6	20 58.2	-28.8	102.0	20 45.5	-29.7	102.4	20 32.5	-30.7	102.7	20 19.1	-31.6	103.1	20 05.3	-32.5	103.5	1
2	21 08.0	-26.1	101.8	20 55.5	-27.1	102.2	20 42.7	-28.1	102.6	20 29.4	-29.0	102.9	20 15.8	-30.0	103.3	20 01.8	-30.9	103.6	19 47.5	-31.8	104.0	19 32.8	-32.7	104.3	2
3	20 41.9	-26.5	102.8	20 28.4	-27.4	103.1	20 14.6	-28.4	103.5	20 00.4	-29.3	103.9	19 45.8	-30.2	104.2	19 30.9	-31.1	104.6	19 15.7	-32.1	104.9	19 00.1	-33.0	105.2	3
4	20 15.4	-26.7	103.7	20 01.0	-27.7	104.1	19 46.2	-28.6	104.4	19 31.1	-29.6	104.8	19 15.6	-30.5	105.1	18 59.8	-31.5	105.5	18 43.6	-32.3	105.8	18 27.1	-33.2	106.1	4
5	19 48.7	-27.1	104.7	19 33.3	-28.0	105.0	19 17.6	-29.0	105.4	19 01.5	-29.9	105.7	18 45.1	-30.8	106.0	18 28.3	-31.7	106.4	18 11.3	-32.6	106.7	17 53.9	-33.5	107.0	5
6	19 21.6	-27.3	105.6	19 05.3	-28.3	106.0	18 48.6	-29.2	106.3	18 31.6	-30.1	106.6	18 14.3	-31.1	106.9	17 56.6	-31.9	107.3	17 38.7	-32.8	107.6	17 20.4	-33.6	107.9	6
7	18 54.3	-27.7	106.6	18 37.0	-28.6	106.9	18 19.4	-29.5	107.2	18 01.5	-30.4	107.5	17 43.2	-31.2	107.8	17 24.7	-32.2	108.1	17 05.9	-33.1	108.4	16 46.8	-33.9	108.7	7
8	18 26.6	-27.9	107.5	18 08.4	-28.8	107.8	17 49.9	-29.7	108.1	17 31.1	-30.7	108.4	17 12.0	-31.6	108.7	16 52.5	-32.4	109.0	16 32.8	-33.2	109.3	16 12.9	-34.1	109.6	8
9	17 58.7	-28.1	108.4	17 39.6	-29.1	108.8	17 20.2	-30.0	109.0	17 00.4	-30.8	109.3	16 40.4	-31.7	109.6	16 20.1	-32.6	109.9	15 59.6	-33.5	110.2	15 38.8	-34.4	110.4	9
10	17 30.6	-28.5	109.4	17 10.5	-29.3	109.7	16 50.2	-30.2	110.0	16 29.6	-31.1	110.2	16 08.7	-32.0	110.5	15 47.5	-32.8	110.8	15 26.1	-33.6	111.0	15 04.4	-34.4	111.3	10
11	17 02.1	-28.6	110.3	16 41.2	-29.6	110.6	16 20.0	-30.5	110.9	15 58.5	-31.3	111.1	15 36.7	-32.2	111.4	15 14.7	-33.0	111.6	14 52.5	-33.9	111.9	14 30.0	-34.7	112.1	11
12	16 33.5	-28.9	111.2	16 11.6	-29.8	111.5	15 49.5	-30.6	111.8	15 27.2	-31.6	112.0	15 04.5	-32.3	112.3	14 41.7	-33.2	112.5	14 18.6	-34.0	112.8	13 55.3	-34.9	113.0	12
13	16 04.6	-29.2	112.1	15 41.8	-30.0	112.4	15 18.9	-30.9	112.6	14 55.6	-31.7	112.9	14 32.2	-32.6	113.1	14 08.5	-33.4	113.4	13 44.6	-34.2	113.6	13 20.4	-35.0	113.8	13
14	15 35.4	-29.4	113.0	15 11.8	-30.2	113.3	14 48.0	-31.1	113.5	14 23.9	-31.9	113.8	13 59.6	-32.7	114.0	13 35.1	-33.6	114.2	13 10.4	-34.4	114.4	12 45.4	-35.1	114.7	14
15	15 06.0	-29.5	113.9	14 41.6	-30.5	114.2	14 16.9	-31.3	114.4	13 52.0	-32.1	114.6	13 26.9	-33.0	114.9	13 01.5	-33.7	115.1	12 36.0	-34.5	115.3	12 10.3	-35.3	115.5	15
16	14 36.5	-29.8	114.8	14 11.1	-30.6	115.1	13 45.6	-31.5	115.3	13 19.9	-32.3	115.5	12 53.9	-33.1	115.7	12 27.8	-33.9	115.9	12 01.5	-34.7	116.1	11 35.0	-35.5	116.3	16
17	14 06.7	-30.0	115.7	13 40.5	-30.8	116.0	13 14.1	-31.6	116.2	12 47.6	-32.5	116.4	12 20.8	-33.2	116.6	11 53.9	-34.0	116.8	11 26.8	-34.8	117.0	10 59.5	-35.6	117.1	17
18	13 36.7	-30.2	116.6	13 09.7	-31.0	116.8	12 42.5	-31.8	117.0	12 15.1	-32.6	117.2	11 47.6	-33.4	117.4	11 19.9	-34.2	117.6	10 52.0	-35.0	117.8	10 23.9	-35.7	118.0	18
19	13 06.5	-30.3	117.5	12 38.7	-31.2	117.7	12 10.7	-32.0	117.9	11 42.5	-32.7	118.1	11 14.2	-33.6	118.3	10 45.7	-34.3	118.4	10 17.0	-35.1	118.6	9 48.2	-35.8	118.8	19
20	12 36.2	-30.6	118.4	12 07.5	-31.3	118.6	11 38.7	-32.1	118.8	11 09.8	-33.0	119.0	10 40.6	-33.7	119.1	10 11.4	-34.5	119.3	9 41.9	-35.2	119.4	9 12.4	-36.0	119.6	20
21	12 05.6	-30.7	119.3	11 36.2	-31.5	119.5	11 06.6	-32.3	119.6	10 36.8	-33.0	119.8	10 06.9	-33.8	120.0	9 36.9	-34.5	120.1	9 06.7	-35.3	120.3	8 36.4	-36.0	120.4	21
22	11 34.9	-30.8	120.2	11 04.7	-31.6	120.3	10 34.3	-32.4	120.5	10 03.8	-33.2	120.7	9 33.1	-33.9	120.8	9 02.4	-34.7	120.9	8 31.4	-35.4	121.1	8 00.4	-36.1	121.2	22
23	11 04.1	-31.0	121.0	10 33.1	-31.8	121.2	10 01.9	-32.5	121.4	9 30.6	-33.3	121.5	8 59.2	-34.0	121.6	8 27.7	-34.8	121.8	7 56.0	-35.5	121.9	7 24.3	-36.2	122.0	23
24	10 33.1	-31.2	121.9	10 01.3	-31.9	122.1	9 29.4	-32.7	122.2	8 57.3	-33.4	122.3	8 25.2	-34.2	122.5	7 52.9	-34.9	122.6	7 20.5	-35.6	122.7	6 48.1	-36.3	122.8	24
25	10 01.9	-31.3	122.8	9 29.4	-32.1	122.9	8 56.7	-32.8	123.1	8 23.9	-33.5	123.2	7 51.0	-34.2	123.3	7 18.0	-34.9	123.4	6 44.9	-35.6	123.5	6 11.8	-36.4	123.6	25
26	9 30.6	-31.4	123.6	8 57.3	-32.1	123.8	8 23.9	-32.9	123.9	7 50.4	-33.6	124.0	7 16.8	-34.4	124.1	6 43.1	-35.1	124.2	6 09.3	-35.8	124.3	5 35.4	-36.4	124.4	26
27	8 59.2	-31.5	124.5	8 25.2	-32.3	124.6	7 51.0	-33.0	124.7	7 16.8	-33.7	124.9	6 42.4	-34.4	125.0	6 08.0	-35.1	125.0	5 33.5	-35.8	125.1	4 59.0	-36.5	125.2	27
28	8 27.7	-31.7	125.4	7 52.9	-32.4	125.5	7 18.0	-33.1	125.6	6 43.1	-33.8	125.7	6 08.0	-34.5	125.8	5 32.9	-35.2	125.9	4 57.7	-35.8	125.9	4 22.5	-36.6	126.0	28
29	7 56.0	-31.7	126.2	7 20.5	-32.4	126.3	6 44.9	-33.1	126.4	6 09.3	-33.9	126.5	5 33.5	-34.5	126.6	4 57.7	-35.2	126.7	4 21.9	-36.0	126.7	3 45.9	-36.5	126.8	29
30	7 24.3	-31.9	127.1	6 48.1	-32.6	127.2	6 11.8	-33.3	127.3	5 35.4	-33.9	127.4	4 59.0	-34.7	127.4	4 22.5	-35.3	127.5	3 45.9	-35.9	127.5	3 09.4	-36.7	127.6	30
31	6 52.4	-31.9	127.9	6 15.5	-32.6	128.0	5 38.5	-33.3	128.1	5 01.5	-34.0	128.2	4 24.3	-34.6	128.2	3 47.2	-35.4	128.3	3 10.0	-36.0	128.3	2 32.7	-36.6	128.4	31
32	6 20.5	-32.0	128.8	5 42.9	-32.7	128.9	5 05.2	-33.4	129.0	4 27.5	-34.1	129.0	3 49.7	-34.8	129.1	3 11.8	-35.3	129.1	2 34.0	-36.1	129.1	1 56.1	-36.7	129.2	32
33	5 48.5	-32.1	129.6	5 10.2	-32.8	129.7	4 31.8	-33.4	129.8	3 53.4	-34.1	129.8	3 14.9	-34.7	129.9	2 36.5	-35.5	129.9	1 57.9	-36.0	129.9	1 19.4	-36.7	130.0	33
34	5 16.4	-32.2	130.5	4 37.4	-32.8	130.6	3 58.4	-33.5	130.6	3 19.3	-34.2	130.7	2 40.2	-34.8	130.7	2 01.0	-35.4	130.7	1 21.9	-36.1	130.7	0 42.7	-36.7	130.8	34
35	4 44.2	-32.2	131.3	4 04.6	-32.9	131.4	3 24.9	-33.6	131.4	2 45.1	-34.1	131.5	2 05.4	-34.8	131.5	1 25.6	-35.6	131.5	0 45.8	-36.1	131.5	0 06.0	-36.7	131.6	35
36	4 12.0	-32.3	132.2	3 31.7	-33.0	132.2	2 51.3	-33.5	132.3	2 11.0	-34.2	132.3	1 30.6	-34.9	132.3	0 50.2	-35.5	132.3	0 09.7	-36.0	132.3	0 30.7	+36.7	47.7	36
37	3 39.7	-32.3	133.0	2 58.7	-32.9	133.1	2 17.8	-33.6	133.1	1 36.8	-34.3	133.1	0 55.7	-34.8	133.1	0 14.7	-35.5	133.1	0 26.3	+36.1	46.9	1 07.4	+36.6	46.9	37
38	3 07.4	-32.4	133.9	2 25.8	-33.0	133.9	1 44.2	-33.7	133.9	1 02.5	-34.2	133.9	0 20.9	-34.9	134.0	0 20.8	+35.4	46.0	1 02.4	+36.1	46.1	1 44.0	+36.7	46.1	38
39	2 35.0	-32.4	134.7	1 52.8	-33.1	134.7	1 10.5	-33.6	134.8	0 28.3	-34.3	134.8	0 14.0	+34.8	45.2	0 56.2	+35.5	45.2	1 38.5	+36.0	45.3	2 20.7	+36.6	45.3	39
40	2 02.6	-32.4	135.6	1 19.7	-33.0	135.6	0 36.9	-33.7	135.6	0 06.0	+34.2	44.4	0 48.8	+34.9	44.4	1 31.7	+35.4	44.4	2 14.5	+36.0	44.5	2 57.3	+36.6	44.5	40
41	1 30.2	-32.5	136.4	0 46.7	-33.0	136.4	0 03.2	-33.6	136.4	0 40.2	+34.2	43.6	1 23.7	+34.8	43.6	2 07.1	+35.4	43.6	2 50.5	+36.0	43.7	3 33.9	+36.6	43.7	41
42	0 57.7	-32.5	137.2	0 13.7	-33.1	137.2	0 30.4	+33.6	42.8	1 14.4	+34.3	42.8	1 58.5	+34.8	42.8	2 42.5	+35.4	42.8	3 26.5	+36.0	42.9	4 10.5	+36.5	42.9	42
43	0 25.2	-32.4	138.1	0 19.4	+33.0	41.9	1 04.0	+33.7	41.9	1 48.7	+34.2	41.9	2 33.3	+34.8	42.0	3 17.9	+35.3	42.0	4 02.5	+35.8	42.1	4 47.0	+36.4	42.1	43
44	0 07.2	+32.5	41.1	0 52.4	+33.1	41.1	1 37.7	+33.6	41.1	2 22.9	+34.1	41.1	3 08.1	+34.7	41.2	3 53.2	+35.3	41.2	4 38.3	+35.9	41.2	5 23.4	+36.4	41.3	44
45	0 39.7	+32.5	40.2	1 25.5	+33.0	40.3	2 11.3	+33.6	40.3	2 57.0	+34.2	40.3	3 42.8	+34.7	40.3	4 28.5	+35.2	40.4	5 14.2	+35.8	40.4	5 59.8	+36.3	40.5	45
46	1 12.2	+32.4	39.4	1 58.5	+33.0	39.4	2 44.9	+33.5	39.4	3 31.2	+34.1	39.5	4 17.5	+34.6	39.5	5 03.7	+35.2	39.6	5 50.0	+35.7	39.6	6 36.1	+36.3	39.7	46
47	1 44.6	+32.4	38.6	2 31.5	+33.0	38.6	3 18.4	+33.5	38.6	4 05.3	+34.0	38.7	4 52.1	+34.6	38.7	5 38.9	+35.1	38.8	6 25.7	+35.6	38.8	7 12.4	+36.2	38.9	47
48	2 17.0	+32.4	37.7	3 04.5	+32.9	37.7	3 51.9	+33.5	37.8	4 39.3	+34.0	37.8	5 26.7	+34.5	37.9	6 14.0	+35.0	37.9	7 01.3	+35.6	38.0	7 48.6	+36.0	38.1	48
49	2 49.4	+32.4	36.9	3 37.4	+32.9	36.9	4 25.4	+33.4	37.0	5 13.3	+33.9	37.0	6 01.2	+34.4	37.1	6 49.0	+35.0	37.1	7 36.9	+35.4	37.2	8 24.6	+36.0	37.3	49
50	3 21.8	+32.3	36.0	4 10.3	+32.8	36.1	4 58.8	+33.3	36.1	5 47.2	+33.9	36.2	6 35.6	+34.4	36.2	7 24.0	+34.9	36.3	8 12.3	+35.4	36.4	9 00.6	+35.9	36.5	50
51	3 54.1	+32.2	35.2	4 43.1	+32.8	35.2	5 32.1	+33.3	35.3	6 21.1	+33.7	35.3	7 10.0	+34.2	35.4	7 58.9	+34.7	35.5	8 47.7	+35.2	35.6	9 36.5	+35.7	35.7	51
52	4 26.3	+32.2	34.3	5 15.9	+32.7	34.4	6 05.4	+33.1	34.4	6 54.8	+33.7	34.5	7 44.2	+34.2	34.6	8 33.6	+34.7	34.7	9 22.9	+35.2	34.8	10 12.2	+35.6	34.9	52
53	4 58.5	+32.2	33.5	5 48.6	+32.6	33.5	6 38.5	+33.1	33.6	7 28.5	+33.6	33.7	8 18.4	+34.1	33.8	9 08.3	+34.5	33.8	9 58.1	+35.0	33.9	10 47.8	+35.5	34.0	53
54	5 30.7	+32.0	32.6	6 21.2	+32.5	32.7	7 11.6	+33.1	32.8	8 02.1	+33.5	32.8	8 52.5	+33.9	32.9	9 42.8	+34.4	33.0	10 33.1	+34.9	33.1	11 23.3	+35.4	33.2	54
55	6 02.7	+32.0	31.8	6 53.7	+32.5	31.9	7 44.7	+32.9	31.9	8 35.6	+33.3	32.0	9 26.4	+33.9	32.1	10 17.2	+34.3	32.2	11 08.0	+34.7	32.3	11 58.7	+35.2	32.4	55
56	6 34.7	+31.9	30.9	7 26.2	+32.3	31.0	8 17.6	+32.8	31.1	9 08.9	+33.3	31.2	10 00.3	+33.7	31.2	10 51.5	+34.2	31.3	11 42.7	+34.7	31.4	12 33.9	+35.1	31.6	56
57	7 06.6	+31.8	30.1	7 58.5	+32.3	30.2	8 50.4	+32.7	30.2	9 42.2	+33.1	30.3	10 34.0	+33.5	30.4	11 25.7	+34.0	30.5	12 17.4	+34.4	30.6	13 09.0	+34.9	30.7	57
58	7 38.4	+31.7	29.2	8 30.8	+32.1	29.3	9 23.1	+32.5	29.4	10 15.3	+33.0	29.5	11 07.5	+33.5	29.6	11 59.7	+33.9	29.7	12 51.8	+34.3	29.8	13 43.9	+34.7	29.9	58
59	8 10.1	+31.6	28.4	9 02.9	+32.0	28.5	9 55.6	+32.5	28.5	10 48.3	+32.9	28.6	11 41.0	+33.3	28.7	12 33.6	+33.7	28.8	13 26.1	+34.1	28.9	14 18.6	+34.5	29.1	59
60	8 41.7	+31.5	27.5	9 34.9	+31.9	27.6	10 28.1	+32.3	27.7	11 21.2	+32.7	27.8	12 14.3	+33.1	27.9	13 07.3	+33.5	28.0	14 00.2	+34.0	28.1	14 53.1	+34.4	28.2	60
61	9 13.2	+31.4	26.7	10 06.8	+31.8	26.7	11 00.4	+32.1	26.8	11 53.9	+32.6	26.9	12 47.4	+32.9	27.0	13 40.8	+33.4	27.1	14 34.2	+33.7	27.2	15 27.5	+34.2	27.4	61
62	9 44.6	+31.2	25.8	10 38.6	+31.6	25.9	11 32.5	+32.0	26.0	12 26.5	+32.4	26.1	13 20.3	+32.8	26.2	14 14.2	+33.1	26.3	15 07.9	+33.6	26.4	16 01.7	+33.9	26.5	62
63	10 15.8	+31.1	24.9	11 10.2	+31.4	25.0	12 04.5	+31.9	25.1	12 58.9	+32.2	25.2	13 53.1	+32.6	25.3	14 47.3	+33.0	25.4	15 41.5	+33.4	25.5	16 35.6	+33.8	25.6	63
64	10 46.9	+30.9	24.1	11 41.6	+31.4	24.1	12 36.4	+31.7	24.2	13 31.1	+32.0	24.3	14 25.7	+32.4	24.4	15 20.3	+32.8	24.5	16 14.9	+33.1	24.7	17 09.4	+33.5	24.8	64
65	11 17.8	+30.8	23.2	12 13.0	+31.1	23.3	13 08.1	+31.5	23.4	14 03.1	+31.9	23.5	14 58.1	+32.3	23.6	15 53.1	+32.6	23.7	16 48.0	+33.0	23.8	17 42.9	+33.3	23.9	65
66	11 48.6	+30.6	22.3	12 44.1	+31.0	22.4	13 39.6	+31.3	22.5	14 35.0	+31.6	22.6	15 30.4	+32.0	22.7	16 25.7	+32.3	22.8	17 21.0	+32.7	22.9	18 16.2	+33.1	23.0	66
67	12 19.2	+30.5	21.4	13 15.1	+30.8	21.5	14 10.9	+31.1	21.6	15 06.6	+31.5	21.7	16 02.4	+31.8	21.8	16 58.0	+32.2	21.9	17 53.7	+32.5	22.0	18 49.3	+32.8	22.2	67
68	12 49.7	+30.3	20.5	13 45.9	+30.5	20.6	14 42.0	+30.9	20.7	15 38.1	+31.2	20.8	16 34.2	+31.5	20.9	17 30.2	+31.9	21.0	18 26.2	+32.2	21.1	19 22.1	+32.5	21.3	68
69	13 20.0	+30.1	19.7	14 16.4	+30.4	19.7	15 12.9	+30.7	19.8	16 09.3	+31.1	19.9	17 05.7	+31.4	20.0	18 02.1	+31.6	20.1	18 58.4	+31.9	20.3	19 54.6	+32.3	20.4	69
70	13 50.1	+29.9	18.8	14 46.8	+30.2	18.9	15 43.6	+30.5	18.9	16 40.4	+30.7	19.0	17 37.1	+31.0	19.1	18 33.7	+31.4	19.2	19 30.3	+31.7	19.4	20 26.9	+32.0	19.5	70
71	14 20.0	+29.7	17.9	15 17.0	+30.0	18.0	16 14.1	+30.3	18.0	17 11.1	+30.6	18.1	18 08.1	+30.9	18.2	19 05.1	+31.1	18.3	20 02.0	+31.5	18.5	20 58.9	+31.8	18.6	71
72	14 49.7	+29.4	17.0	15 47.0	+29.8	17.1	16 44.4	+30.0	17.1	17 41.7	+30.3	17.2	18 39.0	+30.6	17.3	19 36.2	+30.9	17.4	20 33.5	+31.1	17.5	21 30.7	+31.4	17.7	72
73	15 19.1	+29.3	16.1	16 16.8	+29.5	16.2	17 14.4	+29.8	16.2	18 12.0	+30.0	16.3	19 09.6	+30.3	16.4	20 07.1	+30.6	16.5	21 04.6	+30.8	16.6	22 02.1	+31.1	16.7	73
74	15 48.4	+29.1	15.2	16 46.3	+29.3	15.2	17 44.2	+29.5	15.3	18 42.0	+29.8	15.4	19 39.9	+30.0	15.5	20 37.7	+30.2	15.6	21 35.4	+30.6	15.7	22 33.2	+30.8	15.8	74
75	16 17.5	+28.8	14.3	17 15.6	+29.0	14.3	18 13.7	+29.3	14.4	19 11.8	+29.5	14.5	20 09.9	+29.7	14.6	21 07.9	+30.0	14.7	22 06.0	+30.2	14.8	23 04.0	+30.4	14.9	75
76	16 46.3	+28.5	13.3	17 44.6	+28.8	13.4	18 43.0	+29.0	13.5	19 41.3	+29.2	13.6	20 39.6	+29.5	13.7	21 37.9	+29.7	13.8	22 36.2	+29.9	13.9	23 34.4	+30.2	14.0	76
77	17 14.8	+28.3	12.4	18 13.4	+28.5	12.5	19 12.0	+28.7	12.6	20 10.5	+29.0	12.6	21 09.1	+29.1	12.7	22 07.6	+29.3	12.8	23 06.1	+29.5	12.9	24 04.6	+29.7	13.0	77
78	17 43.1	+28.1	11.5	18 41.9	+28.3	11.6	19 40.7	+28.4	11.6	20 39.5	+28.6	11.7	21 38.2	+28.8	11.8	22 36.9	+29.0	11.9	23 35.6	+29.2	12.0	24 34.3	+29.4	12.1	78
79	18 11.2	+27.8	10.6	19 10.2	+27.9	10.6	20 09.1	+28.2	10.7	21 08.1	+28.3	10.8	22 07.0	+28.5	10.8	23 05.9	+28.7	10.9	24 04.8	+28.9	11.0	25 03.7	+29.1	11.1	79
80	18 39.0	+27.5	9.6	19 38.1	+27.7	9.7	20 37.3	+27.8	9.8	21 36.4	+28.0	9.8	22 35.5	+28.2	9.9	23 34.6	+28.3	10.0	24 33.7	+28.5	10.0	25 32.8	+28.6	10.1	80
81	19 06.5	+27.2	8.7	20 05.8	+27.3	8.8	21 05.1	+27.5	8.8	22 04.4	+27.6	8.9	23 03.7	+27.7	8.9	24 02.9	+28.0	9.0	25 02.2	+28.1	9.1	26 01.4	+28.3	9.2	81
82	19 33.7	+26.9	7.8	20 33.1	+27.1	7.8	21 32.6	+27.2	7.9	22 32.0	+27.3	7.9	23 31.4	+27.5	8.0	24 30.9	+27.5	8.0	25 30.3	+27.7	8.1	26 29.7	+27.8	8.2	82
83	20 00.6	+26.6	6.8	21 00.2	+26.7	6.8	21 59.8	+26.8	6.9	22 59.3	+27.0	6.9	23 58.9	+27.1	7.0	24 58.4	+27.2	7.1	25 58.0	+27.3	7.1	26 57.5	+27.4	7.2	83
84	20 27.2	+26.3	5.8	21 26.9	+26.4	5.9	22 26.6	+26.5	5.9	23 26.3	+26.6	6.0	24 26.0	+26.6	6.0	25 25.6	+26.8	6.1	26 25.3	+26.9	6.1	27 24.9	+27.0	6.2	84
85	20 53.5	+26.0	4.9	21 53.3	+26.1	4.9	22 53.1	+26.1	5.0	23 52.9	+26.2	5.0	24 52.6	+26.3	5.0	25 52.4	+26.4	5.1	26 52.2	+26.4	5.1	27 51.9	+26.6	5.2	85
86	21 19.5	+25.7	3.9	22 19.4	+25.7	4.0	23 19.2	+25.8	4.0	24 19.1	+25.8	4.0	25 18.9	+25.9	4.0	26 18.8	+25.9	4.1	27 18.6	+26.1	4.1	28 18.5	+26.1	4.2	86
87	21 45.2	+25.3	3.0	22 45.1	+25.3	3.0	23 45.0	+25.4	3.0	24 44.9	+25.5	3.0	25 44.8	+25.5	3.0	26 44.7	+25.6	3.1	27 44.7	+25.5	3.1	28 44.6	+25.6	3.1	87
88	22 10.5	+24.9	2.0	23 10.4	+25.0	2.0	24 10.4	+25.0	2.0	25 10.4	+25.0	2.0	26 10.3	+25.1	2.0	27 10.3	+25.1	2.1	28 10.2	+25.2	2.1	29 10.2	+25.1	2.1	88
89	22 35.4	+24.6	1.0	23 35.4	+24.6	1.0	24 35.4	+24.6	1.0	25 35.4	+24.6	1.0	26 35.4	+24.6	1.0	27 35.4	+24.6	1.0	28 35.4	+24.6	1.0	29 35.3	+24.7	1.1	89
90	23 00.0	+24.2	0.0	24 00.0	+24.2	0.0	25 00.0	+24.2	0.0	26 00.0	+24.2	0.0	27 00.0	+24.2	0.0	28 00.0	+24.2	0.0	29 00.0	+24.2	0.0	30 00.0	+24.1	0.0	90
	23°			24°			25°			26°			27°			28°			29°			30°			

S. Lat. {L.H.A. greater than 180° ....Zn=180°−Z; L.H.A. less than 180°...........Zn=180°+Z

LATITUDE **SAME** NAME AS DECLINATION **L.H.A. 114°, 246°**

317

N. Lat. {L.H.A. greater than 180° .....Zn=Z; L.H.A. less than 180°............Zn=360°–Z}

Dec.	23° Hc	d	Z	24° Hc	d	Z	25° Hc	d	Z	26° Hc	d	Z	27° Hc	d	Z	28° Hc	d	Z	29° Hc	d	Z	30° Hc	d	Z	Dec.
°	° ′	′	°	° ′	′	°	° ′	′	°	° ′	′	°	° ′	′	°	° ′	′	°	° ′	′	°	° ′	′	°	°
0	21 04.8	+25.0	99.4	20 54.8	+25.9	99.8	20 44.4	+26.9	100.2	20 33.6	+27.9	100.5	20 22.4	+28.9	100.9	20 10.9	+29.9	101.3	19 59.0	+30.8	101.6	19 46.7	+31.7	102.0	0
1	21 29.8	+24.6	98.4	21 20.7	+25.7	98.8	21 11.3	+26.7	99.2	21 01.5	+27.7	99.6	20 51.3	+28.6	100.0	20 40.8	+29.5	100.3	20 29.8	+30.5	100.7	20 18.4	+31.5	101.1	1
2	21 54.4	+24.2	97.5	21 46.4	+25.3	97.9	21 38.0	+26.3	98.3	21 29.2	+27.2	98.6	21 19.9	+28.3	99.0	21 10.3	+29.3	99.4	21 00.3	+30.2	99.8	20 49.9	+31.2	100.2	2
3	22 18.6	+23.9	96.5	22 11.7	+24.9	96.9	22 04.3	+25.9	97.3	21 56.4	+27.0	97.7	21 48.2	+28.0	98.1	21 39.6	+28.9	98.5	21 30.5	+29.9	98.9	21 21.1	+30.9	99.3	3
4	22 42.5	+23.6	95.5	22 36.6	+24.6	95.9	22 30.2	+25.6	96.3	22 23.4	+26.6	96.7	22 16.2	+27.6	97.1	22 08.5	+28.6	97.5	22 00.4	+29.6	97.9	21 52.0	+30.5	98.3	4
5	23 06.1	+23.1	94.5	23 01.2	+24.2	94.9	22 55.8	+25.2	95.3	22 50.0	+26.3	95.7	22 43.8	+27.3	96.2	22 37.1	+28.3	96.6	22 30.0	+29.3	97.0	22 22.5	+30.3	97.4	5
6	23 29.2	+22.8	93.5	23 25.4	+23.8	93.9	23 21.0	+24.9	94.3	23 16.3	+25.9	94.8	23 11.1	+26.9	95.2	23 05.4	+27.9	95.6	22 59.3	+28.9	96.0	22 52.8	+29.9	96.5	6
7	23 52.0	+22.4	92.5	23 49.2	+23.4	92.9	23 45.9	+24.5	93.3	23 42.2	+25.5	93.8	23 38.0	+26.5	94.2	23 33.3	+27.6	94.7	23 28.2	+28.6	95.1	23 22.7	+29.6	95.5	7
8	24 14.4	+21.9	91.5	24 12.6	+23.0	91.9	24 10.4	+24.1	92.3	24 07.7	+25.1	92.8	24 04.5	+26.2	93.2	24 00.9	+27.2	93.7	23 56.8	+28.2	94.1	23 52.3	+29.2	94.6	8
9	24 36.3	+21.6	90.4	24 35.6	+22.6	90.9	24 34.5	+23.6	91.3	24 32.8	+24.8	91.8	24 30.7	+25.8	92.3	24 28.1	+26.8	92.7	24 25.0	+27.9	93.2	24 21.5	+28.8	93.6	9
10	24 57.9	+21.1	89.4	24 58.2	+22.2	89.9	24 58.1	+23.3	90.3	24 57.6	+24.3	90.8	24 56.5	+25.4	91.3	24 54.9	+26.4	91.7	24 52.9	+27.4	92.2	24 50.3	+28.5	92.7	10
11	25 19.0	+20.7	88.4	25 20.4	+21.8	88.8	25 21.4	+22.9	89.3	25 21.9	+23.9	89.8	25 21.9	+24.9	90.3	25 21.3	+26.1	90.7	25 20.3	+27.1	91.2	25 18.8	+28.1	91.7	11
12	25 39.7	+20.2	87.3	25 42.2	+21.3	87.8	25 44.3	+22.4	88.3	25 45.8	+23.5	88.8	25 46.8	+24.6	89.3	25 47.4	+25.6	89.7	25 47.4	+26.6	90.2	25 46.9	+27.7	90.7	12
13	25 59.9	+19.8	86.3	26 03.5	+20.9	86.8	26 06.7	+21.9	87.3	26 09.3	+23.0	87.7	26 11.4	+24.1	88.2	26 13.0	+25.2	88.7	26 14.0	+26.3	89.2	26 14.6	+27.3	89.7	13
14	26 19.7	+19.3	85.2	26 24.4	+20.4	85.7	26 28.6	+21.6	86.2	26 32.3	+22.6	86.7	26 35.5	+23.7	87.2	26 38.2	+24.7	87.7	26 40.3	+25.8	88.2	26 41.9	+26.9	88.7	14
15	26 39.0	+18.9	84.2	26 44.8	+20.0	84.7	26 50.2	+21.0	85.2	26 54.9	+22.2	85.7	26 59.2	+23.2	86.2	27 02.9	+24.3	86.7	27 06.1	+25.4	87.2	27 08.8	+26.4	87.7	15
16	26 57.9	+18.3	83.1	27 04.8	+19.5	83.6	27 11.2	+20.6	84.1	27 17.1	+21.7	84.6	27 22.4	+22.8	85.2	27 27.2	+23.9	85.7	27 31.5	+24.9	86.2	27 35.2	+26.0	86.7	16
17	27 16.2	+17.9	82.0	27 24.3	+19.0	82.5	27 31.8	+20.1	83.1	27 38.8	+21.2	83.6	27 45.2	+22.3	84.1	27 51.1	+23.4	84.6	27 56.4	+24.5	85.2	28 01.2	+25.6	85.7	17
18	27 34.1	+17.4	81.0	27 43.3	+18.5	81.5	27 51.9	+19.6	82.0	28 00.0	+20.7	82.5	28 07.5	+21.8	83.1	28 14.5	+22.9	83.6	28 20.9	+24.0	84.1	28 26.8	+25.0	84.7	18
19	27 51.5	+16.9	79.9	28 01.8	+17.9	80.4	28 11.5	+19.1	80.9	28 20.7	+20.2	81.5	28 29.3	+21.3	82.0	28 37.4	+22.4	82.5	28 44.9	+23.5	83.1	28 51.8	+24.6	83.6	19
20	28 08.4	+16.3	78.8	28 19.7	+17.5	79.3	28 30.6	+18.6	79.9	28 40.9	+19.7	80.4	28 50.6	+20.8	80.9	28 59.8	+21.9	81.5	29 08.4	+23.0	82.0	29 16.4	+24.1	82.6	20
21	28 24.7	+15.8	77.7	28 37.2	+17.0	78.2	28 49.2	+18.0	78.8	29 00.6	+19.2	79.3	29 11.4	+20.3	79.9	29 21.7	+21.4	80.4	29 31.4	+22.5	81.0	29 40.5	+23.7	81.5	21
22	28 40.5	+15.3	76.6	28 54.2	+16.4	77.1	29 07.2	+17.6	77.7	29 19.8	+18.6	78.2	29 31.7	+19.8	78.8	29 43.1	+20.9	79.3	29 53.9	+22.0	79.9	30 04.2	+23.0	80.5	22
23	28 55.8	+14.8	75.5	29 10.6	+15.9	76.0	29 24.8	+17.0	76.6	29 38.4	+18.1	77.1	29 51.5	+19.2	77.7	30 04.0	+20.3	78.3	30 15.9	+21.5	78.8	30 27.2	+22.6	79.4	23
24	29 10.6	+14.2	74.4	29 26.5	+15.3	74.9	29 41.8	+16.4	75.5	29 56.5	+17.6	76.0	30 10.7	+18.7	76.6	30 24.3	+19.8	77.2	30 37.4	+20.9	77.7	30 49.8	+22.0	78.3	24
25	29 24.8	+13.6	73.3	29 41.8	+14.7	73.8	29 58.2	+15.9	74.4	30 14.1	+17.0	74.9	30 29.4	+18.1	75.5	30 44.1	+19.3	76.1	30 58.3	+20.4	76.7	31 11.8	+21.5	77.2	25
26	29 38.4	+13.1	72.2	29 56.5	+14.2	72.7	30 14.1	+15.3	73.3	30 31.1	+16.4	73.8	30 47.5	+17.6	74.4	31 03.4	+18.7	75.0	31 18.7	+19.7	75.6	31 33.3	+20.9	76.1	26
27	29 51.5	+12.5	71.0	30 10.7	+13.6	71.6	30 29.4	+14.7	72.1	30 47.5	+15.9	72.7	31 05.1	+17.0	73.3	31 22.1	+18.1	73.9	31 38.4	+19.3	74.4	31 54.2	+20.4	75.0	27
28	30 04.0	+11.9	69.9	30 24.3	+13.1	70.5	30 44.1	+14.2	71.0	31 03.4	+15.3	71.6	31 22.1	+16.3	72.2	31 40.2	+17.5	72.7	31 57.7	+18.6	73.3	32 14.6	+19.7	73.9	28
29	30 15.9	+11.3	68.8	30 37.4	+12.4	69.3	30 58.3	+13.5	69.9	31 18.7	+14.6	70.4	31 38.4	+15.8	71.0	31 57.7	+16.9	71.6	32 16.3	+18.0	72.2	32 34.3	+19.2	72.8	29
30	30 27.2	+10.8	67.6	30 49.8	+11.9	68.2	31 11.8	+13.0	68.7	31 33.3	+14.1	69.3	31 54.2	+15.2	69.9	32 14.6	+16.3	70.5	32 34.3	+17.4	71.1	32 53.5	+18.5	71.7	30
31	30 38.0	+10.1	66.5	31 01.7	+11.2	67.0	31 24.8	+12.3	67.6	31 47.4	+13.4	68.2	32 09.4	+14.6	68.7	32 30.9	+15.7	69.3	32 51.7	+16.8	69.9	33 12.0	+17.9	70.6	31
32	30 48.1	+9.5	65.3	31 12.9	+10.6	65.9	31 37.1	+11.8	66.5	32 00.8	+12.9	67.0	32 24.0	+13.9	67.6	32 46.6	+15.0	68.2	33 08.5	+16.2	68.8	33 29.9	+17.3	69.4	32
33	30 57.6	+9.0	64.2	31 23.5	+10.0	64.7	31 48.9	+11.0	65.3	32 13.7	+12.1	65.9	32 37.9	+13.3	66.4	33 01.6	+14.4	67.0	33 24.7	+15.5	67.6	33 47.2	+16.7	68.3	33
34	31 06.6	+8.3	63.0	31 33.5	+9.4	63.6	31 59.9	+10.5	64.1	32 25.8	+11.6	64.7	32 51.2	+12.7	65.3	33 16.0	+13.8	65.9	33 40.2	+14.9	66.5	34 03.9	+16.0	67.1	34
35	31 14.9	+7.6	61.9	31 42.9	+8.7	62.4	32 10.4	+9.8	63.0	32 37.4	+10.9	63.5	33 03.9	+12.0	64.1	33 29.8	+13.1	64.7	33 55.1	+14.2	65.3	34 19.9	+15.3	65.9	35
36	31 22.5	+7.1	60.7	31 51.6	+8.1	61.3	32 20.2	+9.2	61.8	32 48.3	+10.3	62.4	33 15.9	+11.3	63.0	33 42.9	+12.4	63.5	34 09.3	+13.6	64.1	34 35.2	+14.6	64.8	36
37	31 29.6	+6.4	59.6	31 59.7	+7.5	60.1	32 29.4	+8.5	60.6	32 58.6	+9.6	61.2	33 27.2	+10.7	61.8	33 55.3	+11.8	62.4	34 22.9	+12.8	63.0	34 49.8	+14.0	63.6	37
38	31 36.0	+5.8	58.4	32 07.2	+6.8	58.9	32 37.9	+7.9	59.5	33 08.2	+8.9	60.0	33 37.9	+10.0	60.6	34 07.1	+11.0	61.2	34 35.7	+12.2	61.8	35 03.8	+13.3	62.4	38
39	31 41.8	+5.1	57.2	32 14.0	+6.2	57.7	32 45.8	+7.2	58.3	33 17.1	+8.2	58.8	33 47.9	+9.3	59.4	34 18.1	+10.4	60.0	34 47.9	+11.4	60.6	35 17.1	+12.5	61.2	39
40	31 46.9	+4.5	56.0	32 20.2	+5.5	56.6	32 53.0	+6.5	57.1	33 25.3	+7.6	57.7	33 57.2	+8.6	58.2	34 28.5	+9.7	58.8	34 59.3	+10.8	59.4	35 29.6	+11.8	60.0	40
41	31 51.4	+3.8	54.9	32 25.7	+4.8	55.4	32 59.5	+5.9	55.9	33 32.9	+6.9	56.5	34 05.8	+7.9	57.0	34 38.2	+9.0	57.6	35 10.1	+10.0	58.2	35 41.4	+11.2	58.8	41
42	31 55.2	+3.2	53.7	32 30.5	+4.2	54.2	33 05.4	+5.2	54.7	33 39.8	+6.2	55.3	34 13.7	+7.3	55.8	34 47.2	+8.3	56.4	35 20.1	+9.4	57.0	35 52.6	+10.3	57.6	42
43	31 58.4	+2.5	52.5	32 34.7	+3.5	53.0	33 10.6	+4.5	53.5	33 46.0	+5.5	54.1	34 21.0	+6.5	54.6	34 55.5	+7.5	55.2	35 29.5	+8.5	55.8	36 02.9	+9.7	56.4	43
44	32 00.9	+1.9	51.3	32 38.2	+2.9	51.8	33 15.1	+3.8	52.4	33 51.5	+4.8	52.9	34 27.5	+5.8	53.4	35 03.0	+6.8	54.0	35 38.0	+7.9	54.6	36 12.6	+8.9	55.2	44
45	32 02.8	+1.2	50.2	32 41.1	+2.1	50.7	33 18.9	+3.1	51.2	33 56.3	+4.1	51.7	34 33.3	+5.1	52.2	35 09.8	+6.1	52.8	35 45.9	+7.1	53.3	36 21.5	+8.1	53.9	45
46	32 04.0	+0.6	49.0	32 43.2	+1.5	49.5	33 22.0	+2.5	50.0	34 00.4	+3.4	50.5	34 38.4	+4.4	51.0	35 15.9	+5.4	51.6	35 53.0	+6.4	52.1	36 29.6	+7.4	52.7	46
47	32 04.6	−0.1	47.8	32 44.7	+0.9	48.3	33 24.5	+1.7	48.8	34 03.8	+2.7	49.3	34 42.8	+3.6	49.8	35 21.3	+4.6	50.3	35 59.4	+5.6	50.9	36 37.0	+6.6	51.5	47
48	32 04.5	−0.7	46.6	32 45.6	+0.1	47.1	33 26.2	+1.1	47.6	34 06.5	+2.0	48.1	34 46.4	+2.9	48.6	35 25.9	+3.9	49.1	36 05.0	+4.8	49.7	36 43.6	+5.8	50.2	48
49	32 03.8	−1.4	45.4	32 45.7	−0.5	45.9	33 27.3	+0.4	46.4	34 08.5	+1.3	46.9	34 49.3	+2.2	47.4	35 29.8	+3.1	47.9	36 09.8	+4.1	48.4	36 49.4	+5.1	49.0	49
50	32 02.4	−2.1	44.3	32 45.2	−1.2	44.7	33 27.7	−0.4	45.2	34 09.8	+0.6	45.6	34 51.5	+1.5	46.1	35 32.9	+2.4	46.7	36 13.9	+3.3	47.2	36 54.5	+4.2	47.7	50
51	32 00.3	−2.7	43.1	32 44.0	−1.9	43.5	33 27.3	−1.0	44.0	34 10.4	−0.2	44.4	34 53.0	+0.8	44.9	35 35.3	+1.7	45.4	36 17.2	+2.6	45.9	36 58.7	+3.5	46.5	51
52	31 57.6	−3.3	41.9	32 42.1	−2.5	42.3	33 26.3	−1.7	42.8	34 10.2	−0.8	43.2	34 53.8	0.0	43.7	35 37.0	+0.8	44.2	36 19.8	+1.8	44.7	37 02.2	+2.7	45.2	52
53	31 54.3	−4.0	40.7	32 39.6	−3.2	41.1	33 24.6	−2.4	41.6	34 09.4	−1.6	42.0	34 53.8	−0.7	42.5	35 37.8	+0.2	43.0	36 21.6	+1.0	43.5	37 04.9	+1.9	44.0	53
54	31 50.3	−4.7	39.6	32 36.4	−3.9	40.0	33 22.2	−3.0	40.4	34 07.8	−2.3	40.8	34 53.1	−1.5	41.3	35 38.0	−0.6	41.7	36 22.6	+0.2	42.2	37 06.8	+1.2	42.7	54
55	31 45.6	−5.3	38.4	32 32.5	−4.5	38.8	33 19.2	−3.8	39.2	34 05.5	−3.0	39.6	34 51.6	−2.2	40.0	35 37.4	−1.4	40.5	36 22.8	−0.5	41.0	37 08.0	+0.3	41.5	55
56	31 40.3	−5.9	37.2	32 28.0	−5.2	37.6	33 15.4	−4.5	38.0	34 02.5	−3.6	38.4	34 49.4	−2.9	38.8	35 36.0	−2.1	39.3	36 22.3	−1.3	39.7	37 08.3	−0.5	40.2	56
57	31 34.4	−6.6	36.0	32 22.8	−5.9	36.4	33 10.9	−5.1	36.8	33 58.9	−4.4	37.2	34 46.5	−3.6	37.6	35 33.9	−2.8	38.0	36 21.0	−2.0	38.5	37 07.8	−1.2	39.0	57
58	31 27.8	−7.2	34.9	32 16.9	−6.5	35.2	33 05.8	−5.8	35.6	33 54.5	−5.1	36.0	34 42.9	−4.4	36.4	35 31.1	−3.6	36.8	36 19.0	−2.9	37.3	37 06.6	−2.1	37.7	58
59	31 20.6	−7.8	33.7	32 10.4	−7.2	34.1	33 00.0	−6.5	34.4	33 49.4	−5.8	34.8	34 38.5	−5.0	35.2	35 27.5	−4.4	35.6	36 16.1	−3.6	36.0	37 04.5	−2.8	36.5	59
60	31 12.8	−8.5	32.6	32 03.2	−7.8	32.9	32 53.5	−7.1	33.2	33 43.6	−6.5	33.6	34 33.5	−5.8	34.0	35 23.1	−5.1	34.4	36 12.5	−4.3	34.8	37 01.7	−3.7	35.2	60
61	31 04.3	−9.1	31.4	31 55.4	−8.4	31.7	32 46.4	−7.8	32.1	33 37.1	−7.1	32.4	34 27.7	−6.5	32.8	35 18.0	−5.8	33.1	36 08.2	−5.2	33.5	36 58.0	−4.4	34.0	61
62	30 55.2	−9.6	30.2	31 47.0	−9.1	30.6	32 38.6	−8.5	30.9	33 30.0	−7.9	31.2	34 21.2	−7.2	31.6	35 12.2	−6.5	31.9	36 03.0	−5.8	32.3	36 53.6	−5.2	32.7	62
63	30 45.6	−10.3	29.1	31 37.9	−9.7	29.4	32 30.1	−9.1	29.7	33 22.1	−8.5	30.0	34 14.0	−7.9	30.4	35 05.7	−7.3	30.7	35 57.2	−6.7	31.1	36 48.4	−5.9	31.5	63
64	30 35.3	−10.9	28.0	31 28.2	−10.3	28.2	32 21.0	−9.8	28.5	33 13.6	−9.2	28.8	34 06.1	−8.6	29.2	34 58.4	−8.0	29.5	35 50.5	−7.4	29.9	36 42.5	−6.8	30.2	64
65	30 24.4	−11.5	26.8	31 17.9	−11.0	27.1	32 11.2	−10.4	27.4	33 04.4	−9.8	27.7	33 57.5	−9.3	28.0	34 50.4	−8.7	28.3	35 43.1	−8.1	28.6	36 35.7	−7.5	29.0	65
66	30 12.9	−12.1	25.7	31 06.9	−11.6	25.9	32 00.8	−11.0	26.2	32 54.6	−10.5	26.5	33 48.2	−10.0	26.8	34 41.7	−9.4	27.1	35 35.0	−8.8	27.4	36 28.2	−8.3	27.7	66
67	30 00.8	−12.6	24.5	30 55.3	−12.1	24.8	31 49.8	−11.7	25.0	32 44.1	−11.2	25.3	33 38.2	−10.6	25.6	34 32.3	−10.1	25.9	35 26.2	−9.6	26.2	36 19.9	−9.0	26.5	67
68	29 48.2	−13.3	23.4	30 43.2	−12.8	23.6	31 38.1	−12.3	23.9	32 32.9	−11.8	24.1	33 27.6	−11.3	24.4	34 22.2	−10.9	24.7	35 16.6	−10.3	25.0	36 10.9	−9.8	25.3	68
69	29 34.9	−13.7	22.3	30 30.4	−13.3	22.5	31 25.8	−12.9	22.7	32 21.1	−12.5	23.0	33 16.3	−12.0	23.2	34 11.3	−11.5	23.5	35 06.3	−11.0	23.8	36 01.1	−10.5	24.1	69
70	29 21.2	−14.4	21.2	30 17.1	−14.0	21.4	31 12.9	−13.5	21.6	32 08.6	−13.0	21.8	33 04.3	−12.6	22.1	33 59.8	−12.1	22.3	34 55.3	−11.7	22.6	35 50.6	−11.2	22.9	70
71	29 06.8	−14.9	20.1	30 03.1	−14.5	20.3	30 59.4	−14.1	20.5	31 55.6	−13.7	20.7	32 51.7	−13.3	20.9	33 47.7	−12.9	21.1	34 43.6	−12.4	21.4	35 39.4	−12.0	21.6	71
72	28 51.9	−15.4	19.0	29 48.6	−15.0	19.1	30 45.3	−14.7	19.3	31 41.9	−14.3	19.5	32 38.4	−13.9	19.7	33 34.8	−13.5	20.0	34 31.2	−13.1	20.2	35 27.4	−12.6	20.4	72
73	28 36.5	−16.0	17.9	29 33.6	−15.7	18.0	30 30.6	−15.3	18.2	31 27.6	−14.9	18.4	32 24.5	−14.6	18.6	33 21.3	−14.2	18.8	34 18.1	−13.8	19.0	35 14.8	−13.4	19.2	73
74	28 20.5	−16.5	16.8	29 17.9	−16.1	16.9	30 15.3	−15.8	17.1	31 12.7	−15.5	17.3	32 09.9	−15.1	17.4	33 07.1	−14.8	17.6	34 04.3	−14.5	17.8	35 01.4	−14.1	18.0	74
75	28 04.0	−17.0	15.7	29 01.8	−16.7	15.8	29 59.5	−16.4	16.0	30 57.2	−16.1	16.1	31 54.8	−15.8	16.3	32 52.3	−15.4	16.5	33 49.8	−15.1	16.7	34 47.3	−14.8	16.9	75
76	27 47.0	−17.5	14.6	28 45.1	−17.3	14.7	29 43.1	−17.0	14.9	30 41.1	−16.7	15.0	31 39.0	−16.4	15.2	32 36.9	−16.1	15.3	33 34.7	−15.7	15.5	34 32.5	−15.4	15.7	76
77	27 29.5	−18.0	13.5	28 27.8	−17.7	13.6	29 26.1	−17.4	13.8	30 24.4	−17.2	13.9	31 22.6	−16.9	14.0	32 20.8	−16.7	14.2	33 19.0	−16.4	14.3	34 17.1	−16.1	14.5	77
78	27 11.5	−18.5	12.4	28 10.1	−18.3	12.5	29 08.7	−18.1	12.7	30 07.2	−17.8	12.8	31 05.7	−17.6	12.9	32 04.1	−17.2	13.1	33 02.6	−17.0	13.2	34 01.0	−16.8	13.3	78
79	26 53.0	−19.0	11.4	27 51.8	−18.7	11.5	28 50.6	−18.5	11.6	29 49.4	−18.3	11.7	30 48.1	−18.1	11.8	31 46.9	−17.9	11.9	32 45.6	−17.7	12.1	33 44.2	−17.4	12.2	79
80	26 34.0	−19.4	10.3	27 33.1	−19.3	10.4	28 32.1	−19.1	10.5	29 31.1	−18.9	10.6	30 30.0	−18.6	10.7	31 29.0	−18.5	10.8	32 27.9	−18.2	10.9	33 26.8	−18.0	11.0	80
81	26 14.6	−19.9	9.2	27 13.8	−19.7	9.3	28 13.0	−19.5	9.4	29 12.2	−19.4	9.5	30 11.4	−19.2	9.6	31 10.5	−19.0	9.7	32 09.7	−18.9	9.8	33 08.8	−18.7	9.9	81
82	25 54.7	−20.4	8.2	26 54.1	−20.2	8.3	27 53.5	−20.1	8.3	28 52.8	−19.9	8.4	29 52.2	−19.8	8.5	30 51.5	−19.6	8.6	31 50.8	−19.4	8.7	32 50.1	−19.2	8.8	82
83	25 34.3	−20.8	7.1	26 33.9	−20.7	7.2	27 33.4	−20.5	7.3	28 32.9	−20.4	7.3	29 32.4	−20.3	7.4	30 31.9	−20.1	7.5	31 31.4	−20.0	7.6	32 30.9	−19.9	7.6	83
84	25 13.5	−21.2	6.1	26 13.2	−21.1	6.2	27 12.9	−21.1	6.2	28 12.5	−20.9	6.3	29 12.1	−20.8	6.3	30 11.8	−20.7	6.4	31 11.4	−20.6	6.5	32 11.0	−20.4	6.5	84
85	24 52.3	−21.6	5.1	25 52.1	−21.6	5.1	26 51.8	−21.4	5.2	27 51.6	−21.4	5.2	28 51.3	−21.3	5.3	29 51.1	−21.2	5.3	30 50.8	−21.1	5.4	31 50.6	−21.1	5.4	85
86	24 30.7	−22.1	4.0	25 30.5	−22.0	4.1	26 30.4	−22.0	4.1	27 30.2	−21.9	4.2	28 30.0	−21.8	4.2	29 29.9	−21.7	4.2	30 29.7	−21.6	4.3	31 29.5	−21.5	4.3	86
87	24 08.6	−22.5	3.0	25 08.5	−22.4	3.1	26 08.4	−22.4	3.1	27 08.3	−22.3	3.1	28 08.2	−22.2	3.1	29 08.2	−22.3	3.2	30 08.1	−22.2	3.2	31 08.0	−22.2	3.2	87
88	23 46.1	−22.8	2.0	24 46.1	−22.9	2.0	25 46.0	−22.8	2.0	26 46.0	−22.8	2.1	27 46.0	−22.8	2.1	28 45.9	−22.7	2.1	29 45.9	−22.7	2.1	30 45.8	−22.6	2.1	88
89	23 23.3	−23.3	1.0	24 23.2	−23.2	1.0	25 23.2	−23.2	1.0	26 23.2	−23.2	1.0	27 23.2	−23.2	1.0	28 23.2	−23.2	1.0	29 23.2	−23.2	1.1	30 23.2	−23.2	1.1	89
90	23 00.0	−23.6	0.0	24 00.0	−23.6	0.0	25 00.0	−23.6	0.0	26 00.0	−23.7	0.0	27 00.0	−23.7	0.0	28 00.0	−23.7	0.0	29 00.0	−23.7	0.0	30 00.0	−23.7	0.0	90
	23°			24°			25°			26°			27°			28°			29°			30°			

LATITUDE CONTRARY NAME TO DECLINATION L.H.A. 67°, 293°

Dec.	23° Hc	d	Z	24° Hc	d	Z	25° Hc	d	Z	26° Hc	d	Z	27° Hc	d	Z	28° Hc	d	Z	29° Hc	d	Z	30° Hc	d	Z	Dec.
°	° ′	′	°	° ′	′	°	° ′	′	°	° ′	′	°	° ′	′	°	° ′	′	°	° ′	′	°	° ′	′	°	°
0	21 04.8	-25.3	99.4	20 54.8	-26.3	99.8	20 44.4	-27.3	100.2	20 33.6	-28.2	100.5	20 22.4	-29.2	100.9	20 10.9	-30.2	101.3	19 59.0	-31.1	101.6	19 46.7	-32.0	102.0	0
1	20 39.5	-25.6	100.4	20 28.5	-26.6	100.8	20 17.1	-27.6	101.1	20 05.4	-28.6	101.5	19 53.2	-29.5	101.8	19 40.7	-30.4	102.2	19 27.9	-31.4	102.5	19 14.7	-32.3	102.9	1
2	20 13.9	-25.9	101.4	20 01.9	-26.9	101.7	19 49.5	-27.8	102.1	19 36.8	-28.8	102.4	19 23.7	-29.7	102.8	19 10.3	-30.7	103.1	18 56.5	-31.6	103.4	18 42.4	-32.5	103.8	2
3	19 48.0	-26.3	102.3	19 35.0	-27.2	102.7	19 21.7	-28.2	103.0	19 08.0	-29.1	103.3	18 54.0	-30.1	103.7	18 39.6	-31.0	104.0	18 24.9	-31.9	104.3	18 09.9	-32.8	104.7	3
4	19 21.7	-26.5	103.3	19 07.8	-27.5	103.6	18 53.5	-28.4	103.9	18 38.9	-29.4	104.3	18 23.9	-30.3	104.6	18 08.6	-31.2	104.9	17 53.0	-32.1	105.2	17 37.1	-33.0	105.5	4
5	18 55.2	-26.8	104.2	18 40.3	-27.8	104.5	18 25.1	-28.7	104.9	18 09.5	-29.6	105.2	17 53.6	-30.5	105.5	17 37.4	-31.4	105.8	17 20.9	-32.3	106.1	17 04.1	-33.2	106.4	5
6	18 28.4	-27.1	105.2	18 12.5	-28.0	105.5	17 56.4	-29.0	105.8	17 39.9	-29.9	106.1	17 23.1	-30.8	106.4	17 06.0	-31.7	106.7	16 48.6	-32.6	107.0	16 30.9	-33.4	107.3	6
7	18 01.3	-27.4	106.1	17 44.5	-28.3	106.4	17 27.4	-29.2	106.7	17 10.0	-30.2	107.0	16 52.3	-31.1	107.3	16 34.3	-31.9	107.6	16 16.0	-32.8	107.9	15 57.5	-33.7	108.1	7
8	17 33.9	-27.6	107.0	17 16.2	-28.6	107.3	16 58.2	-29.5	107.6	16 39.8	-30.3	107.9	16 21.2	-31.2	108.2	16 02.4	-32.2	108.5	15 43.2	-33.0	108.7	15 23.8	-33.8	109.0	8
9	17 06.3	-27.9	108.0	16 47.6	-28.8	108.3	16 28.7	-29.7	108.5	16 09.5	-30.6	108.8	15 50.0	-31.5	109.1	15 30.2	-32.3	109.4	15 10.2	-33.2	109.6	14 50.0	-34.1	109.9	9
10	16 38.4	-28.1	108.9	16 18.8	-29.0	109.2	15 59.0	-29.9	109.4	15 38.9	-30.8	109.7	15 18.5	-31.7	110.0	14 57.9	-32.5	110.2	14 37.0	-33.3	110.5	14 15.9	-34.2	110.7	10
11	16 10.3	-28.4	109.8	15 49.8	-29.3	110.1	15 29.1	-30.2	110.3	15 08.1	-31.0	110.6	14 46.8	-31.8	110.8	14 25.4	-32.7	111.1	14 03.7	-33.6	111.3	13 41.7	-34.4	111.6	11
12	15 41.9	-28.6	110.7	15 20.5	-29.4	111.0	14 58.9	-30.3	111.2	14 37.1	-31.2	111.5	14 15.0	-32.1	111.7	13 52.7	-33.0	112.0	13 30.1	-33.7	112.2	13 07.3	-34.5	112.4	12
13	15 13.3	-28.8	111.6	14 51.1	-29.7	111.9	14 28.6	-30.6	112.1	14 05.9	-31.5	112.4	13 42.9	-32.2	112.6	13 19.7	-33.0	112.8	12 56.4	-33.9	113.0	12 32.8	-34.7	113.2	13
14	14 44.5	-29.0	112.5	14 21.4	-29.9	112.8	13 58.0	-30.7	113.0	13 34.4	-31.5	113.2	13 10.7	-32.5	113.5	12 46.7	-33.3	113.7	12 22.5	-34.1	113.9	11 58.1	-34.9	114.1	14
15	14 15.5	-29.3	113.5	13 51.5	-30.1	113.7	13 27.3	-31.0	113.9	13 02.9	-31.8	114.1	12 38.2	-32.5	114.3	12 13.4	-33.4	114.5	11 48.4	-34.2	114.7	11 23.2	-34.9	114.9	15
16	13 46.2	-29.4	114.4	13 21.4	-30.3	114.6	12 56.3	-31.1	114.8	12 31.1	-31.9	115.0	12 05.7	-32.8	115.2	11 40.0	-33.5	115.4	11 14.2	-34.3	115.6	10 48.3	-35.2	115.7	16
17	13 16.8	-29.6	115.2	12 51.1	-30.4	115.5	12 25.2	-31.2	115.7	11 59.2	-32.1	115.9	11 32.9	-32.9	116.0	11 06.5	-33.7	116.2	10 39.9	-34.5	116.4	10 13.1	-35.2	116.6	17
18	12 47.2	-29.8	116.1	12 20.7	-30.6	116.3	11 54.0	-31.5	116.5	11 27.1	-32.3	116.7	11 00.0	-33.0	116.9	10 32.8	-33.8	117.1	10 05.4	-34.6	117.2	9 37.9	-35.4	117.4	18
19	12 17.4	-29.9	117.0	11 50.1	-30.8	117.2	11 22.5	-31.6	117.4	10 54.8	-32.3	117.6	10 27.0	-33.2	117.7	9 59.0	-34.0	117.9	9 30.8	-34.7	118.1	9 02.5	-35.4	118.2	19
20	11 47.5	-30.2	117.9	11 19.3	-31.0	118.1	10 50.9	-31.7	118.3	10 22.5	-32.6	118.4	9 53.8	-33.3	118.6	9 25.0	-34.0	118.7	8 56.1	-34.8	118.9	8 27.1	-35.6	119.0	20
21	11 17.3	-30.3	118.8	10 48.3	-31.0	119.0	10 19.2	-31.9	119.1	9 49.9	-32.6	119.3	9 20.5	-33.4	119.4	8 51.0	-34.2	119.6	8 21.3	-34.9	119.7	7 51.5	-35.7	119.8	21
22	10 47.0	-30.4	119.7	10 17.3	-31.3	119.8	9 47.3	-32.0	120.0	9 17.3	-32.8	120.1	8 47.1	-33.5	120.3	8 16.8	-34.3	120.4	7 46.4	-35.1	120.5	7 15.8	-35.7	120.6	22
23	10 16.6	-30.6	120.6	9 46.0	-31.3	120.7	9 15.3	-32.1	120.9	8 44.5	-32.9	121.0	8 13.6	-33.7	121.1	7 42.5	-34.4	121.2	7 11.3	-35.1	121.3	6 40.1	-35.8	121.4	23
24	9 46.0	-30.7	121.4	9 14.7	-31.5	121.6	8 43.2	-32.2	121.7	8 11.6	-33.0	121.8	7 39.9	-33.7	122.0	7 08.1	-34.4	122.1	6 36.2	-35.1	122.2	6 04.3	-35.9	122.3	24
25	9 15.3	-30.8	122.3	8 43.2	-31.6	122.4	8 11.0	-32.4	122.6	7 38.6	-33.0	122.7	7 06.2	-33.8	122.8	6 33.7	-34.6	122.9	6 01.1	-35.3	123.0	5 28.4	-36.0	123.1	25
26	8 44.5	-30.9	123.2	8 11.6	-31.7	123.3	7 38.6	-32.4	123.4	7 05.6	-33.2	123.5	6 32.4	-33.9	123.6	5 59.1	-34.6	123.7	5 25.8	-35.3	123.8	4 52.4	-36.0	123.9	26
27	8 13.6	-31.1	124.0	7 39.9	-31.8	124.1	7 06.2	-32.5	124.3	6 32.4	-33.3	124.4	5 58.5	-34.0	124.4	5 24.5	-34.7	124.5	4 50.5	-35.4	124.6	4 16.4	-36.1	124.7	27
28	7 42.5	-31.2	124.9	7 08.1	-31.9	125.0	6 33.7	-32.6	125.1	5 59.1	-33.3	125.2	5 24.5	-34.0	125.3	4 49.8	-34.7	125.3	4 15.1	-35.4	125.4	3 40.3	-36.1	125.5	28
29	7 11.3	-31.2	125.8	6 36.2	-31.9	125.9	6 01.1	-32.7	125.9	5 25.8	-33.4	126.0	4 50.5	-34.1	126.1	4 15.1	-34.8	126.2	3 39.7	-35.5	126.2	3 04.2	-36.2	126.3	29
30	6 40.1	-31.4	126.6	6 04.3	-32.1	126.7	5 28.4	-32.8	126.8	4 52.4	-33.5	126.9	4 16.4	-34.2	126.9	3 40.3	-34.8	127.0	3 04.2	-35.5	127.0	2 28.0	-36.1	127.1	30
31	6 08.7	-31.4	127.5	5 32.2	-32.1	127.6	4 55.6	-32.8	127.6	4 18.9	-33.5	127.7	3 42.2	-34.2	127.8	3 05.5	-34.9	127.8	2 28.7	-35.6	127.8	1 51.9	-36.2	127.9	31
32	5 37.3	-31.5	128.3	5 00.1	-32.2	128.4	4 22.8	-32.9	128.5	3 45.4	-33.6	128.5	3 08.0	-34.2	128.6	2 30.6	-34.9	128.6	1 53.1	-35.5	128.6	1 15.7	-36.3	128.7	32
33	5 05.8	-31.6	129.2	4 27.9	-32.3	129.3	3 49.9	-33.0	129.3	3 11.8	-33.6	129.4	2 33.8	-34.3	129.4	1 55.7	-34.9	129.4	1 17.6	-35.6	129.4	0 39.4	-36.2	129.5	33
34	4 34.2	-31.6	130.0	3 55.6	-32.3	130.1	3 16.9	-32.9	130.1	2 38.2	-33.6	130.2	1 59.5	-34.3	130.2	1 20.8	-35.0	130.3	0 42.0	-35.6	130.3	0 03.2	-36.2	130.3	34
35	4 02.6	-31.7	130.9	3 23.3	-32.4	130.9	2 44.0	-33.1	131.0	2 04.6	-33.7	131.0	1 25.2	-34.3	131.0	0 45.8	-34.9	131.1	0 06.4	-35.6	131.1	0 33.0	+36.2	48.9	35
36	3 30.9	-31.7	131.7	2 50.9	-32.3	131.8	2 10.9	-33.0	131.8	1 30.9	-33.7	131.8	0 50.9	-34.3	131.9	0 10.9	-35.0	131.9	0 29.2	+35.6	48.1	1 09.2	+36.2	48.1	36
37	2 59.2	-31.8	132.6	2 18.6	-32.5	132.6	1 37.9	-33.1	132.7	0 57.2	-33.6	132.7	0 16.6	-34.4	132.7	0 24.1	+34.9	47.3	1 04.8	+35.5	47.3	1 45.4	+36.2	47.3	37
38	2 27.4	-31.8	133.4	1 46.1	-32.4	133.5	1 04.8	-33.0	133.5	0 23.6	-33.8	133.5	0 17.8	+34.3	46.5	0 59.0	+35.0	46.5	1 40.3	+35.6	46.5	2 21.6	+36.2	46.6	38
39	1 55.6	-31.8	134.3	1 13.7	-32.5	134.3	0 31.8	-33.1	134.3	0 10.2	+33.6	45.7	0 52.1	+34.3	45.7	1 34.0	+34.9	45.7	2 15.9	+35.5	45.7	2 57.8	+36.1	45.8	39
40	1 23.8	-31.9	135.1	0 41.2	-32.4	135.2	0 01.3	+33.1	44.8	0 43.8	+33.7	44.8	1 26.4	+34.3	44.9	2 08.9	+34.9	44.9	2 51.4	+35.5	44.9	3 33.9	+36.1	45.0	40
41	0 51.9	-31.8	136.0	0 08.8	-32.5	136.0	0 34.4	+33.1	44.0	1 17.5	+33.7	44.0	2 00.7	+34.2	44.0	2 43.8	+34.9	44.1	3 26.9	+35.4	44.1	4 10.0	+36.0	44.2	41
42	0 20.1	-31.9	136.8	0 23.7	+32.5	43.2	1 07.5	+33.0	43.2	1 51.2	+33.7	43.2	2 34.9	+34.3	43.2	3 18.7	+34.8	43.3	4 02.3	+35.4	43.3	4 46.0	+36.0	43.3	42
43	0 11.8	+31.9	42.3	0 56.2	+32.4	42.3	1 40.5	+33.1	42.3	2 24.9	+33.6	42.4	3 09.2	+34.2	42.4	3 53.5	+34.8	42.4	4 37.7	+35.4	42.5	5 22.0	+35.9	42.5	43
44	0 43.7	+31.8	41.5	1 28.6	+32.4	41.5	2 13.6	+33.0	41.5	2 58.5	+33.6	41.5	3 43.4	+34.1	41.6	4 28.3	+34.7	41.6	5 13.1	+35.3	41.7	5 57.9	+35.8	41.7	44
45	1 15.5	+31.8	40.6	2 01.0	+32.5	40.6	2 46.6	+32.9	40.7	3 32.1	+33.5	40.7	4 17.5	+34.1	40.7	5 03.0	+34.6	40.8	5 48.4	+35.2	40.9	6 33.7	+35.8	40.9	45
46	1 47.3	+31.9	39.8	2 33.5	+32.3	39.8	3 19.5	+33.0	39.8	4 05.6	+33.5	39.9	4 51.6	+34.1	39.9	5 37.6	+34.6	40.0	6 23.6	+35.1	40.0	7 09.5	+35.7	40.1	46
47	2 19.2	+31.7	38.9	3 05.8	+32.4	39.0	3 52.5	+32.9	39.0	4 39.1	+33.5	39.0	5 25.7	+33.9	39.1	6 12.2	+34.5	39.2	6 58.7	+35.1	39.2	7 45.2	+35.6	39.3	47
48	2 50.9	+31.8	38.1	3 38.2	+32.2	38.1	4 25.4	+32.8	38.2	5 12.5	+33.4	38.2	5 59.6	+33.9	38.3	6 46.7	+34.5	38.3	7 33.8	+34.9	38.4	8 20.8	+35.4	38.5	48
49	3 22.7	+31.7	37.2	4 10.4	+32.3	37.3	4 58.2	+32.7	37.3	5 45.9	+33.3	37.4	6 33.5	+33.9	37.4	7 21.2	+34.3	37.5	8 08.7	+34.9	37.6	8 56.2	+35.4	37.7	49
50	3 54.4	+31.6	36.4	4 42.7	+32.1	36.4	5 30.9	+32.7	36.5	6 19.2	+33.2	36.5	7 07.4	+33.7	36.6	7 55.5	+34.2	36.7	8 43.6	+34.7	36.8	9 31.6	+35.3	36.9	50
51	4 26.0	+31.6	35.5	5 14.8	+32.1	35.6	6 03.6	+32.6	35.6	6 52.4	+33.1	35.7	7 41.1	+33.6	35.8	8 29.7	+34.2	35.9	9 18.3	+34.7	35.9	10 06.9	+35.1	36.0	51
52	4 57.6	+31.5	34.7	5 46.9	+32.1	34.7	6 36.2	+32.6	34.8	7 25.5	+33.0	34.9	8 14.7	+33.5	34.9	9 03.9	+34.0	35.0	9 53.0	+34.5	35.1	10 42.0	+35.0	35.2	52
53	5 29.1	+31.5	33.8	6 19.0	+31.9	33.9	7 08.8	+32.4	33.9	7 58.5	+33.0	34.0	8 48.2	+33.5	34.1	9 37.9	+33.9	34.2	10 27.5	+34.4	34.3	11 17.0	+34.9	34.4	53
54	6 00.6	+31.4	33.0	6 50.9	+31.9	33.0	7 41.2	+32.3	33.1	8 31.5	+32.8	33.2	9 21.7	+33.3	33.3	10 11.8	+33.8	33.3	11 01.9	+34.2	33.5	11 51.9	+34.7	33.6	54
55	6 32.0	+31.2	32.1	7 22.8	+31.7	32.2	8 13.5	+32.3	32.2	9 04.3	+32.7	32.3	9 54.9	+33.2	32.4	10 45.6	+33.6	32.5	11 36.1	+34.1	32.6	12 26.6	+34.6	32.7	55
56	7 03.2	+31.2	31.2	7 54.5	+31.7	31.3	8 45.8	+32.1	31.4	9 37.0	+32.5	31.5	10 28.1	+33.0	31.6	11 19.2	+33.5	31.7	12 10.2	+34.0	31.8	13 01.2	+34.4	31.9	56
57	7 34.4	+31.1	30.4	8 26.2	+31.5	30.5	9 17.9	+32.0	30.5	10 09.5	+32.5	30.6	11 01.1	+32.9	30.7	11 52.7	+33.3	30.8	12 44.2	+33.8	30.9	13 35.6	+34.3	31.1	57
58	8 05.5	+31.0	29.5	8 57.7	+31.4	29.6	9 49.9	+31.8	29.7	10 42.0	+32.3	29.8	11 34.0	+32.8	29.9	12 26.0	+33.2	30.0	13 18.0	+33.6	30.1	14 09.9	+34.0	30.2	58
59	8 36.5	+30.9	28.7	9 29.1	+31.3	28.7	10 21.7	+31.7	28.8	11 14.3	+32.1	28.9	12 06.8	+32.6	29.0	12 59.2	+33.0	29.1	13 51.6	+33.5	29.2	14 43.9	+33.9	29.4	59
60	9 07.4	+30.7	27.8	10 00.4	+31.2	27.9	10 53.4	+31.6	27.9	11 46.4	+32.0	28.0	12 39.4	+32.4	28.1	13 32.2	+32.9	28.3	14 25.1	+33.2	28.4	15 17.8	+33.7	28.5	60
61	9 38.1	+30.6	26.9	10 31.6	+31.0	27.0	11 25.0	+31.4	27.1	12 18.4	+31.8	27.2	13 11.8	+32.2	27.3	14 05.1	+32.6	27.4	14 58.3	+33.1	27.5	15 51.5	+33.5	27.6	61
62	10 08.7	+30.5	26.0	11 02.6	+30.9	26.1	11 56.4	+31.3	26.2	12 50.2	+31.7	26.3	13 44.0	+32.1	26.4	14 37.7	+32.5	26.5	15 31.4	+32.8	26.6	16 25.0	+33.2	26.8	62
63	10 39.2	+30.3	25.2	11 33.5	+30.7	25.2	12 27.7	+31.1	25.3	13 21.9	+31.5	25.4	14 16.1	+31.8	25.5	15 10.2	+32.2	25.7	16 04.2	+32.7	25.8	16 58.2	+33.1	25.9	63
64	11 09.5	+30.2	24.3	12 04.2	+30.5	24.4	12 58.8	+30.9	24.5	13 53.4	+31.3	24.6	14 47.9	+31.7	24.7	15 42.4	+32.1	24.8	16 36.9	+32.4	24.9	17 31.3	+32.8	25.0	64
65	11 39.7	+30.0	23.4	12 34.7	+30.4	23.5	13 29.7	+30.7	23.6	14 24.7	+31.1	23.7	15 19.6	+31.5	23.8	16 14.5	+31.8	23.9	17 09.3	+32.2	24.0	18 04.1	+32.6	24.2	65
66	12 09.7	+29.8	22.5	13 05.1	+30.2	22.6	14 00.4	+30.6	22.7	14 55.8	+30.9	22.8	15 51.1	+31.2	22.9	16 46.3	+31.6	23.0	17 41.5	+32.0	23.1	18 36.7	+32.3	23.3	66
67	12 39.5	+29.7	21.6	13 35.3	+30.0	21.7	14 31.0	+30.3	21.8	15 26.7	+30.6	21.9	16 22.3	+31.0	22.0	17 17.9	+31.4	22.1	18 13.5	+31.7	22.3	19 09.0	+32.0	22.4	67
68	13 09.2	+29.4	20.7	14 05.3	+29.7	20.8	15 01.3	+30.1	20.9	15 57.3	+30.5	21.0	16 53.3	+30.8	21.1	17 49.3	+31.1	21.2	18 45.2	+31.4	21.4	19 41.0	+31.8	21.5	68
69	13 38.6	+29.3	19.8	14 35.0	+29.6	19.9	15 31.4	+29.9	20.0	16 27.8	+30.2	20.1	17 24.1	+30.6	20.2	18 20.4	+30.9	20.3	19 16.6	+31.2	20.5	20 12.8	+31.5	20.6	69
70	14 07.9	+29.1	18.9	15 04.6	+29.4	19.0	16 01.3	+29.7	19.1	16 58.0	+30.0	19.2	17 54.7	+30.3	19.3	18 51.3	+30.6	19.4	19 47.8	+30.9	19.5	20 44.3	+31.3	19.7	70
71	14 37.0	+28.9	18.0	15 34.0	+29.2	18.1	16 31.0	+29.5	18.2	17 28.0	+29.7	18.3	18 25.0	+30.0	18.4	19 21.9	+30.3	18.5	20 18.7	+30.7	18.6	21 15.6	+30.9	18.8	71
72	15 05.9	+28.6	17.1	16 03.2	+28.9	17.2	17 00.5	+29.2	17.3	17 57.7	+29.5	17.4	18 55.0	+29.7	17.5	19 52.2	+30.0	17.6	20 49.4	+30.3	17.7	21 46.5	+30.6	17.8	72
73	15 34.5	+28.4	16.2	16 32.1	+28.7	16.3	17 29.7	+28.9	16.4	18 27.2	+29.2	16.5	19 24.7	+29.5	16.6	20 22.2	+29.8	16.7	21 19.7	+30.0	16.8	22 17.1	+30.3	16.9	73
74	16 02.9	+28.2	15.3	17 00.8	+28.4	15.4	17 58.6	+28.7	15.5	18 56.4	+29.0	15.6	19 54.2	+29.2	15.7	20 52.0	+29.4	15.8	21 49.7	+29.7	15.9	22 47.4	+30.0	16.0	74
75	16 31.1	+28.0	14.4	17 29.2	+28.2	14.5	18 27.3	+28.4	14.5	19 25.4	+28.6	14.6	20 23.4	+28.9	14.7	21 21.4	+29.2	14.8	22 19.4	+29.4	14.9	23 17.4	+29.6	15.0	75
76	16 59.1	+27.7	13.5	17 57.4	+27.9	13.5	18 55.7	+28.2	13.6	19 54.0	+28.4	13.7	20 52.3	+28.6	13.8	21 50.6	+28.8	13.9	22 48.8	+29.1	14.0	23 47.0	+29.3	14.1	76
77	17 26.8	+27.4	12.5	18 25.3	+27.7	12.6	19 23.9	+27.8	12.7	20 22.4	+28.1	12.8	21 20.9	+28.3	12.8	22 19.4	+28.5	12.9	23 17.9	+28.7	13.0	24 16.3	+28.9	13.1	77
78	17 54.2	+27.2	11.6	18 53.0	+27.3	11.7	19 51.7	+27.6	11.7	20 50.5	+27.7	11.8	21 49.2	+27.9	11.9	22 47.9	+28.1	12.0	23 46.6	+28.3	12.1	24 45.2	+28.6	12.2	78
79	18 21.4	+26.9	10.7	19 20.3	+27.1	10.7	20 19.3	+27.2	10.8	21 18.2	+27.4	10.9	22 17.1	+27.6	10.9	23 16.0	+27.8	11.0	24 14.9	+28.0	11.1	25 13.8	+28.1	11.2	79
80	18 48.3	+26.6	9.7	19 47.4	+26.8	9.8	20 46.5	+27.0	9.8	21 45.6	+27.1	9.9	22 44.7	+27.3	10.0	23 43.8	+27.4	10.1	24 42.9	+27.6	10.1	25 41.9	+27.8	10.2	80
81	19 14.9	+26.3	8.8	20 14.2	+26.4	8.8	21 13.5	+26.6	8.9	22 12.7	+26.8	8.9	23 12.0	+26.9	9.0	24 11.2	+27.1	9.1	25 10.5	+27.2	9.2	26 09.7	+27.4	9.2	81
82	19 41.2	+26.0	7.8	20 40.6	+26.2	7.9	21 40.1	+26.2	7.9	22 39.5	+26.4	8.0	23 38.9	+26.5	8.0	24 38.3	+26.7	8.1	25 37.7	+26.8	8.2	26 37.1	+26.9	8.2	82
83	20 07.2	+25.7	6.9	21 06.8	+25.8	6.9	22 06.3	+25.9	7.0	23 05.9	+26.0	7.0	24 05.4	+26.2	7.1	25 05.0	+26.2	7.1	26 04.5	+26.4	7.2	27 04.0	+26.5	7.2	83
84	20 32.9	+25.4	5.9	21 32.6	+25.4	5.9	22 32.2	+25.6	6.0	23 31.9	+25.7	6.0	24 31.6	+25.8	6.1	25 31.2	+25.9	6.1	26 30.9	+26.0	6.2	27 30.5	+26.1	6.2	84
85	20 58.3	+25.0	4.9	21 58.0	+25.2	5.0	22 57.8	+25.2	5.0	23 57.6	+25.3	5.0	24 57.4	+25.3	5.1	25 57.1	+25.5	5.1	26 56.9	+25.5	5.2	27 56.6	+25.7	5.2	85
86	21 23.3	+24.7	4.0	22 23.2	+24.7	4.0	23 23.0	+24.9	4.0	24 22.9	+24.9	4.0	25 22.7	+25.0	4.1	26 22.6	+25.0	4.1	27 22.4	+25.1	4.1	28 22.3	+25.1	4.2	86
87	21 48.0	+24.4	3.0	22 47.9	+24.4	3.0	23 47.9	+24.4	3.0	24 47.8	+24.5	3.0	25 47.7	+24.5	3.1	26 47.6	+24.6	3.1	27 47.5	+24.6	3.1	28 47.4	+24.7	3.2	87
88	22 12.4	+24.0	2.0	23 12.3	+24.1	2.0	24 12.3	+24.1	2.0	25 12.3	+24.0	2.0	26 12.2	+24.1	2.1	27 12.2	+24.1	2.1	28 12.1	+24.2	2.1	29 12.1	+24.2	2.1	88
89	22 36.4	+23.6	1.0	23 36.4	+23.6	1.0	24 36.4	+23.6	1.0	25 36.3	+23.7	1.0	26 36.3	+23.7	1.0	27 36.3	+23.7	1.0	28 36.3	+23.7	1.0	29 36.3	+23.7	1.1	89
90	23 00.0	+23.3	0.0	24 00.0	+23.2	0.0	25 00.0	+23.2	0.0	26 00.0	+23.2	0.0	27 00.0	+23.2	0.0	28 00.0	+23.2	0.0	29 00.0	+23.2	0.0	30 00.0	+23.2	0.0	90
	23°			24°			25°			26°			27°			28°			29°			30°			

S. Lat. {L.H.A. greater than 180° ....Zn=180°–Z
{L.H.A. less than 180°...........Zn=180°+Z

LATITUDE SAME NAME AS DECLINATION L.H.A. 113°, 247°

68°, 292° L.H.A. LATITUDE SAME NAME AS DECLINATION

N. Lat. {L.H.A. greater than 180° .....Zn=Z; L.H.A. less than 180°............Zn=360°−Z}

Dec.	23° Hc	d	Z	24° Hc	d	Z	25° Hc	d	Z	26° Hc	d	Z	27° Hc	d	Z	28° Hc	d	Z	29° Hc	d	Z	30° Hc	d	Z	Dec.
°	° ′	′	°	° ′	′	°	° ′	′	°	° ′	′	°	° ′	′	°	° ′	′	°	° ′	′	°	° ′	′	°	°
0	20 10.3	+24.8	99.0	20 00.7	+25.8	99.3	19 50.8	+26.8	99.7	19 40.5	+27.8	100.0	19 29.9	+28.7	100.4	19 18.9	+29.7	100.7	19 07.5	+30.7	101.1	18 55.8	+31.6	101.4	0
1	20 35.1	+24.5	98.0	20 26.5	+25.5	98.4	20 17.6	+26.5	98.7	20 08.3	+27.5	99.1	19 58.6	+28.5	99.5	19 48.6	+29.4	99.8	19 38.2	+30.4	100.2	19 27.4	+31.3	100.5	1
2	20 59.6	+24.1	97.0	20 52.0	+25.2	97.4	20 44.1	+26.2	97.8	20 35.8	+27.2	98.2	20 27.1	+28.2	98.5	20 18.0	+29.1	98.9	20 08.6	+30.0	99.3	19 58.7	+31.1	99.6	2
3	21 23.7	+23.8	96.0	21 17.2	+24.8	96.4	21 10.3	+25.8	96.8	21 03.0	+26.8	97.2	20 55.3	+27.8	97.6	20 47.1	+28.9	98.0	20 38.6	+29.8	98.3	20 29.8	+30.7	98.7	3
4	21 47.5	+23.5	95.1	21 42.0	+24.5	95.5	21 36.1	+25.5	95.8	21 29.8	+26.5	96.2	21 23.1	+27.5	96.6	21 16.0	+28.5	97.0	21 08.4	+29.5	97.4	21 00.5	+30.5	97.8	4
5	22 11.0	+23.1	94.1	22 06.5	+24.2	94.5	22 01.6	+25.2	94.9	21 56.3	+26.2	95.3	21 50.6	+27.2	95.7	21 44.5	+28.2	96.1	21 37.9	+29.2	96.5	21 31.0	+30.1	96.9	5
6	22 34.1	+22.7	93.1	22 30.7	+23.7	93.5	22 26.8	+24.8	93.9	22 22.5	+25.8	94.3	22 17.8	+26.8	94.7	22 12.7	+27.8	95.1	22 07.1	+28.8	95.5	22 01.1	+29.8	95.9	6
7	22 56.8	+22.3	92.1	22 54.4	+23.4	92.5	22 51.6	+24.4	92.9	22 48.3	+25.5	93.3	22 44.6	+26.5	93.7	22 40.5	+27.5	94.2	22 35.9	+28.5	94.6	22 30.9	+29.5	95.0	7
8	23 19.1	+22.0	91.1	23 17.8	+23.0	91.5	23 16.0	+24.1	91.9	23 13.8	+25.1	92.3	23 11.1	+26.2	92.8	23 08.0	+27.2	93.2	23 04.4	+28.2	93.6	23 00.4	+29.2	94.0	8
9	23 41.1	+21.5	90.0	23 40.8	+22.6	90.5	23 40.1	+23.7	90.9	23 38.9	+24.7	91.4	23 37.3	+25.7	91.8	23 35.2	+26.8	92.2	23 32.6	+27.8	92.7	23 29.6	+28.8	93.1	9
10	24 02.6	+21.2	89.0	24 03.4	+22.3	89.5	24 03.8	+23.2	89.9	24 03.6	+24.4	90.4	24 03.0	+25.4	90.8	24 02.0	+26.4	91.2	24 00.4	+27.5	91.7	23 58.4	+28.5	92.1	10
11	24 23.8	+20.7	88.0	24 25.7	+21.8	88.4	24 27.0	+22.9	88.9	24 28.0	+23.9	89.4	24 28.4	+25.0	89.8	24 28.4	+26.0	90.3	24 27.9	+27.0	90.7	24 26.9	+28.0	91.2	11
12	24 44.5	+20.3	87.0	24 47.5	+21.3	87.4	24 49.9	+22.5	87.9	24 51.9	+23.5	88.3	24 53.4	+24.6	88.8	24 54.4	+25.6	89.3	24 54.9	+26.7	89.7	24 54.9	+27.7	90.2	12
13	25 04.8	+19.9	85.9	25 08.8	+21.0	86.4	25 12.4	+22.0	86.9	25 15.4	+23.1	87.3	25 18.0	+24.1	87.8	25 20.0	+25.2	88.3	25 21.6	+26.3	88.7	25 22.6	+27.4	89.2	13
14	25 24.7	+19.4	84.9	25 29.8	+20.5	85.4	25 34.4	+21.6	85.8	25 38.5	+22.7	86.3	25 42.1	+23.8	86.8	25 45.2	+24.8	87.3	25 47.9	+25.8	87.7	25 50.0	+26.9	88.2	14
15	25 44.1	+19.0	83.8	25 50.3	+20.0	84.3	25 56.0	+21.1	84.8	26 01.2	+22.2	85.3	26 05.9	+23.3	85.8	26 10.0	+24.4	86.3	26 13.7	+25.4	86.7	26 16.9	+26.5	87.2	15
16	26 03.1	+18.5	82.8	26 10.3	+19.7	83.3	26 17.1	+20.7	83.7	26 23.4	+21.8	84.2	26 29.2	+22.8	84.7	26 34.4	+24.0	85.2	26 39.1	+25.1	85.7	26 43.4	+26.0	86.2	16
17	26 21.6	+18.0	81.7	26 30.0	+19.1	82.2	26 37.8	+20.3	82.7	26 45.2	+21.3	83.2	26 52.0	+22.4	83.7	26 58.4	+23.4	84.2	27 04.2	+24.5	84.7	27 09.4	+25.6	85.2	17
18	26 39.6	+17.5	80.6	26 49.1	+18.6	81.1	26 58.1	+19.7	81.6	27 06.5	+20.9	82.2	27 14.4	+22.0	82.7	27 21.8	+23.1	83.2	27 28.7	+24.1	83.7	27 35.0	+25.2	84.2	18
19	26 57.1	+17.1	79.6	27 07.7	+18.2	80.1	27 17.8	+19.3	80.6	27 27.4	+20.3	81.1	27 36.4	+21.5	81.6	27 44.9	+22.5	82.1	27 52.8	+23.7	82.7	28 00.2	+24.7	83.2	19
20	27 14.2	+16.6	78.5	27 25.9	+17.7	79.0	27 37.1	+18.8	79.5	27 47.7	+19.9	80.0	27 57.9	+20.9	80.6	28 07.4	+22.1	81.1	28 16.5	+23.1	81.6	28 24.9	+24.3	82.1	20
21	27 30.8	+16.0	77.4	27 43.6	+17.2	77.9	27 55.9	+18.3	78.4	28 07.6	+19.4	79.0	28 18.8	+20.5	79.5	28 29.5	+21.6	80.0	28 39.6	+22.7	80.6	28 49.2	+23.7	81.1	21
22	27 46.8	+15.6	76.3	28 00.8	+16.6	76.8	28 14.2	+17.7	77.4	28 27.0	+18.9	77.9	28 39.3	+20.0	78.4	28 51.1	+21.1	79.0	29 02.3	+22.2	79.5	29 12.9	+23.3	80.1	22
23	28 02.4	+15.0	75.2	28 17.4	+16.2	75.8	28 31.9	+17.3	76.3	28 45.9	+18.3	76.8	28 59.3	+19.5	77.3	29 12.2	+20.5	77.9	29 24.5	+21.6	78.4	29 36.2	+22.8	79.0	23
24	28 17.4	+14.5	74.1	28 33.6	+15.6	74.7	28 49.2	+16.7	75.2	29 04.2	+17.9	75.7	29 18.8	+18.9	76.3	29 32.7	+20.1	76.8	29 46.1	+21.2	77.4	29 59.0	+22.2	77.9	24
25	28 31.9	+14.0	73.0	28 49.2	+15.0	73.6	29 05.9	+16.2	74.1	29 22.1	+17.2	74.6	29 37.7	+18.4	75.2	29 52.8	+19.5	75.7	30 07.3	+20.6	76.3	30 21.2	+21.7	76.9	25
26	28 45.9	+13.4	71.9	29 04.2	+14.6	72.5	29 22.1	+15.6	73.0	29 39.3	+16.8	73.5	29 56.1	+17.8	74.1	30 12.3	+18.9	74.6	30 27.9	+20.0	75.2	30 42.9	+21.2	75.8	26
27	28 59.3	+12.9	70.8	29 18.8	+13.9	71.3	29 37.7	+15.1	71.9	29 56.1	+16.2	72.4	30 13.9	+17.3	73.0	30 31.2	+18.4	73.5	30 47.9	+19.5	74.1	31 04.1	+20.6	74.7	27
28	29 12.2	+12.3	69.7	29 32.7	+13.4	70.2	29 52.8	+14.5	70.8	30 12.3	+15.6	71.3	30 31.2	+16.7	71.9	30 49.6	+17.8	72.4	31 07.4	+19.0	73.0	31 24.7	+20.0	73.6	28
29	29 24.5	+11.7	68.6	29 46.1	+12.9	69.1	30 07.3	+13.9	69.6	30 27.9	+15.0	70.2	30 47.9	+16.2	70.7	31 07.4	+17.3	71.3	31 26.4	+18.3	71.9	31 44.7	+19.5	72.5	29
30	29 36.2	+11.2	67.4	29 59.0	+12.2	68.0	30 21.2	+13.4	68.5	30 42.9	+14.5	69.1	31 04.1	+15.5	69.6	31 24.7	+16.6	70.2	31 44.7	+17.8	70.8	32 04.2	+18.9	71.4	30
31	29 47.4	+10.6	66.3	30 11.2	+11.7	66.8	30 34.6	+12.7	67.4	30 57.4	+13.8	67.9	31 19.6	+15.0	68.5	31 41.3	+16.1	69.1	32 02.5	+17.2	69.6	32 23.1	+18.3	70.2	31
32	29 58.0	+10.0	65.2	30 22.9	+11.1	65.7	30 47.3	+12.2	66.2	31 11.2	+13.3	66.8	31 34.6	+14.3	67.4	31 57.4	+15.5	67.9	32 19.7	+16.5	68.5	32 41.4	+17.6	69.1	32
33	30 08.0	+9.4	64.0	30 34.0	+10.5	64.6	30 59.5	+11.6	65.1	31 24.5	+12.6	65.7	31 48.9	+13.8	66.2	32 12.9	+14.8	66.8	32 36.2	+16.0	67.4	32 59.0	+17.1	68.0	33
34	30 17.4	+8.8	62.9	30 44.5	+9.8	63.4	31 11.1	+10.9	64.0	31 37.1	+12.1	64.5	32 02.7	+13.1	65.1	32 27.7	+14.2	65.6	32 52.2	+15.3	66.2	33 16.1	+16.4	66.8	34
35	30 26.2	+8.2	61.8	30 54.3	+9.3	62.3	31 22.0	+10.3	62.8	31 49.2	+11.4	63.4	32 15.8	+12.5	63.9	32 41.9	+13.6	64.5	33 07.5	+14.6	65.1	33 32.5	+15.7	65.7	35
36	30 34.4	+7.6	60.6	31 03.6	+8.7	61.1	31 32.3	+9.7	61.7	32 00.6	+10.7	62.2	32 28.3	+11.8	62.8	32 55.5	+12.9	63.3	33 22.1	+14.1	63.9	33 48.2	+15.1	64.5	36
37	30 42.0	+7.0	59.4	31 12.3	+8.0	60.0	31 42.0	+9.1	60.5	32 11.3	+10.2	61.0	32 40.1	+11.2	61.6	33 08.4	+12.3	62.2	33 36.2	+13.3	62.8	34 03.3	+14.5	63.4	37
38	30 49.0	+6.3	58.3	31 20.3	+7.4	58.8	31 51.1	+8.5	59.3	32 21.5	+9.5	59.9	32 51.3	+10.6	60.4	33 20.7	+11.6	61.0	33 49.5	+12.7	61.6	34 17.8	+13.8	62.2	38
39	30 55.3	+5.8	57.1	31 27.7	+6.7	57.6	31 59.6	+7.8	58.2	32 31.0	+8.8	58.7	33 01.9	+9.9	59.3	33 32.3	+10.9	59.8	34 02.2	+12.0	60.4	34 31.6	+13.0	61.0	39
40	31 01.1	+5.1	56.0	31 34.4	+6.2	56.5	32 07.4	+7.1	57.0	32 39.8	+8.2	57.5	33 11.8	+9.2	58.1	33 43.2	+10.3	58.6	34 14.2	+11.3	59.2	34 44.6	+12.4	59.8	40
41	31 06.2	+4.5	54.8	31 40.6	+5.5	55.3	32 14.5	+6.5	55.8	32 48.0	+7.5	56.4	33 21.0	+8.5	56.9	33 53.5	+9.6	57.5	34 25.5	+10.7	58.0	34 57.0	+11.7	58.6	41
42	31 10.7	+3.9	53.6	31 46.1	+4.8	54.1	32 21.0	+5.8	54.6	32 55.5	+6.8	55.2	33 29.5	+7.9	55.7	34 03.1	+8.9	56.3	34 36.2	+9.9	56.8	35 08.7	+11.0	57.4	42
43	31 14.6	+3.2	52.5	31 50.9	+4.2	53.0	32 26.8	+5.2	53.5	33 02.3	+6.2	54.0	33 37.4	+7.2	54.5	34 12.0	+8.2	55.1	34 46.1	+9.2	55.6	35 19.7	+10.3	56.2	43
44	31 17.8	+2.6	51.3	31 55.1	+3.6	51.8	32 32.0	+4.5	52.3	33 08.5	+5.5	52.8	33 44.6	+6.5	53.3	34 20.2	+7.5	53.9	34 55.3	+8.5	54.4	35 30.0	+9.5	55.0	44
45	31 20.4	+2.0	50.1	31 58.7	+2.9	50.6	32 36.5	+3.9	51.1	33 14.0	+4.8	51.6	33 51.1	+5.8	52.1	34 27.7	+6.8	52.7	35 03.8	+7.8	53.2	35 39.5	+8.8	53.8	45
46	31 22.4	+1.3	49.0	32 01.6	+2.2	49.4	32 40.4	+3.2	49.9	33 18.8	+4.2	50.4	33 56.9	+5.0	50.9	34 34.5	+6.0	51.5	35 11.6	+7.1	52.0	35 48.3	+8.1	52.6	46
47	31 23.7	+0.7	47.8	32 03.8	+1.6	48.3	32 43.6	+2.5	48.7	33 23.0	+3.4	49.2	34 01.9	+4.4	49.7	34 40.5	+5.4	50.3	35 18.7	+6.3	50.8	35 56.4	+7.3	51.4	47
48	31 24.4	0.0	46.6	32 05.4	+0.9	47.1	32 46.1	+1.8	47.5	33 26.4	+2.8	48.0	34 06.3	+3.7	48.5	34 45.9	+4.6	49.0	35 25.0	+5.6	49.6	36 03.7	+6.5	50.1	48
49	31 24.4	−0.6	45.5	32 06.3	+0.3	45.9	32 47.9	+1.2	46.4	33 29.2	+2.0	46.8	34 10.0	+3.0	47.3	34 50.5	+3.9	47.8	35 30.6	+4.8	48.4	36 10.2	+5.8	48.9	49
50	31 23.8	−1.2	44.3	32 06.6	−0.4	44.7	32 49.1	+0.5	45.2	33 31.2	+1.4	45.6	34 13.0	+2.3	46.1	34 54.4	+3.2	46.6	35 35.4	+4.1	47.1	36 16.0	+5.1	47.7	50
51	31 22.6	−1.9	43.1	32 06.2	−1.0	43.5	32 49.6	−0.2	44.0	33 32.6	+0.7	44.4	34 15.3	+1.5	44.9	34 57.6	+2.4	45.4	35 39.5	+3.4	45.9	36 21.1	+4.3	46.4	51
52	31 20.7	−2.5	41.9	32 05.2	−1.7	42.4	32 49.4	−0.9	42.8	33 33.3	0.0	43.2	34 16.8	+0.9	43.7	35 00.0	+1.7	44.2	35 42.9	+2.6	44.7	36 25.4	+3.5	45.2	52
53	31 18.2	−3.1	40.8	32 03.5	−2.3	41.2	32 48.5	−1.5	41.6	33 33.3	−0.8	42.0	34 17.7	+0.1	42.5	35 01.7	+1.0	43.0	35 45.5	+1.8	43.4	36 28.9	+2.7	43.9	53
54	31 15.1	−3.8	39.6	32 01.2	−3.0	40.0	32 47.0	−2.2	40.4	33 32.5	−1.4	40.8	34 17.8	−0.6	41.3	35 02.7	+0.3	41.7	35 47.3	+1.1	42.2	36 31.6	+2.0	42.7	54
55	31 11.3	−4.4	38.4	31 58.2	−3.7	38.8	32 44.8	−2.9	39.2	33 31.1	−2.1	39.6	34 17.2	−1.3	40.1	35 03.0	−0.5	40.5	35 48.4	+0.4	41.0	36 33.6	+1.1	41.5	55
56	31 06.9	−5.0	37.3	31 54.5	−4.3	37.6	32 41.9	−3.5	38.0	33 29.0	−2.8	38.4	34 15.9	−2.0	38.9	35 02.5	−1.2	39.3	35 48.8	−0.5	39.7	36 34.7	+0.5	40.2	56
57	31 01.9	−5.7	36.1	31 50.2	−4.9	36.5	32 38.4	−4.2	36.8	33 26.2	−3.4	37.2	34 13.9	−2.7	37.6	35 01.3	−2.0	38.1	35 48.3	−1.1	38.5	36 35.2	−0.4	39.0	57
58	30 56.2	−6.3	34.9	31 45.3	−5.6	35.3	32 34.1	−4.9	35.7	33 22.8	−4.2	36.0	34 11.2	−3.5	36.4	34 59.3	−2.7	36.8	35 47.2	−1.9	37.3	36 34.8	−1.2	37.7	58
59	30 49.9	−6.9	33.8	31 39.7	−6.2	34.1	32 29.2	−5.5	34.5	33 18.6	−4.9	34.8	34 07.7	−4.1	35.2	34 56.6	−3.4	35.6	35 45.3	−2.7	36.0	36 33.6	−1.9	36.5	59
60	30 43.0	−7.5	32.6	31 33.5	−6.9	33.0	32 23.7	−6.2	33.3	33 13.7	−5.5	33.7	34 03.6	−4.9	34.0	34 53.2	−4.2	34.4	35 42.6	−3.5	34.8	36 31.7	−2.7	35.2	60
61	30 35.5	−8.1	31.5	31 26.6	−7.5	31.8	32 17.5	−6.9	32.1	33 08.2	−6.2	32.5	33 58.7	−5.5	32.8	34 49.0	−4.8	33.2	35 39.1	−4.1	33.6	36 29.0	−3.5	34.0	61
62	30 27.4	−8.7	30.3	31 19.1	−8.1	30.6	32 10.6	−7.5	30.9	33 02.0	−6.9	31.3	33 53.2	−6.3	31.6	34 44.2	−5.6	32.0	35 35.0	−5.0	32.4	36 25.5	−4.2	32.8	62
63	30 18.7	−9.4	29.2	31 11.0	−8.8	29.5	32 03.1	−8.1	29.8	32 55.1	−7.5	30.1	33 46.9	−6.9	30.4	34 38.6	−6.3	30.8	35 30.0	−5.6	31.1	36 21.3	−5.0	31.5	63
64	30 09.3	−9.9	28.0	31 02.2	−9.3	28.3	31 55.0	−8.8	28.6	32 47.6	−8.2	28.9	33 40.0	−7.6	29.2	34 32.3	−7.0	29.6	35 24.4	−6.4	29.9	36 16.3	−5.8	30.3	64
65	29 59.4	−10.5	26.9	30 52.9	−10.0	27.2	31 46.2	−9.5	27.4	32 39.4	−8.9	27.7	33 32.4	−8.3	28.0	34 25.3	−7.8	28.4	35 18.0	−7.2	28.7	36 10.5	−6.5	29.0	65
66	29 48.9	−11.1	25.8	30 42.9	−10.6	26.0	31 36.7	−10.0	26.3	32 30.5	−9.5	26.6	33 24.1	−9.0	26.9	34 17.5	−8.4	27.2	35 10.8	−7.8	27.5	36 04.0	−7.3	27.8	66
67	29 37.8	−11.6	24.6	30 32.3	−11.2	24.9	31 26.7	−10.7	25.1	32 21.0	−10.2	25.4	33 15.1	−9.7	25.7	34 09.1	−9.1	26.0	35 03.0	−8.6	26.3	35 56.7	−8.0	26.6	67
68	29 26.2	−12.3	23.5	30 21.1	−11.7	23.7	31 16.0	−11.3	24.0	32 10.8	−10.8	24.2	33 05.4	−10.3	24.5	34 00.0	−9.8	24.8	34 54.4	−9.3	25.1	35 48.7	−8.8	25.4	68
69	29 13.9	−12.7	22.4	30 09.4	−12.4	22.6	31 04.7	−11.9	22.8	32 00.0	−11.5	23.1	32 55.1	−10.9	23.3	33 50.2	−10.5	23.6	34 45.1	−10.0	23.9	35 39.9	−9.5	24.1	69
70	29 01.2	−13.4	21.3	29 57.0	−12.9	21.5	30 52.8	−12.5	21.7	31 48.5	−12.0	21.9	32 44.2	−11.7	22.1	33 39.7	−11.2	22.4	34 35.1	−10.7	22.7	35 30.4	−10.2	22.9	70
71	28 47.8	−13.9	20.1	29 44.1	−13.5	20.3	30 40.3	−13.1	20.5	31 36.5	−12.7	20.8	32 32.5	−12.2	21.0	33 28.5	−11.8	21.2	34 24.4	−11.4	21.5	35 20.2	−10.9	21.7	71
72	28 33.9	−14.4	19.0	29 30.6	−14.0	19.2	30 27.2	−13.6	19.4	31 23.8	−13.3	19.6	32 20.3	−12.9	19.8	33 16.7	−12.5	20.0	34 13.0	−12.1	20.3	35 09.3	−11.7	20.5	72
73	28 19.5	−14.9	17.9	29 16.6	−14.6	18.1	30 13.6	−14.3	18.3	31 10.5	−13.9	18.5	32 07.4	−13.5	18.7	33 04.2	−13.1	18.9	34 00.9	−12.7	19.1	34 57.6	−12.4	19.3	73
74	28 04.6	−15.5	16.8	29 02.0	−15.2	17.0	29 59.3	−14.8	17.2	30 56.6	−14.5	17.3	31 53.9	−14.2	17.5	32 51.1	−13.8	17.7	33 48.2	−13.4	17.9	34 45.2	−13.0	18.1	74
75	27 49.1	−16.0	15.7	28 46.8	−15.7	15.9	29 44.5	−15.4	16.0	30 42.1	−15.0	16.2	31 39.7	−14.7	16.4	32 37.3	−14.5	16.6	33 34.8	−14.1	16.7	34 32.2	−13.8	16.9	75
76	27 33.1	−16.5	14.7	28 31.1	−16.2	14.8	29 29.1	−15.9	14.9	30 27.1	−15.7	15.1	31 25.0	−15.4	15.2	32 22.8	−15.0	15.4	33 20.7	−14.8	15.6	34 18.4	−14.4	15.8	76
77	27 16.6	−17.0	13.6	28 14.9	−16.7	13.7	29 13.2	−16.5	13.8	30 11.4	−16.2	14.0	31 09.6	−15.9	14.1	32 07.8	−15.7	14.3	33 05.9	−15.3	14.4	34 04.0	−15.1	14.6	77
78	26 59.6	−17.5	12.5	27 58.2	−17.3	12.6	28 56.7	−17.0	12.7	29 55.2	−16.8	12.9	30 53.7	−16.5	13.0	31 52.1	−16.2	13.1	32 50.6	−16.0	13.3	33 48.9	−15.7	13.4	78
79	26 42.1	−18.0	11.4	27 40.9	−17.7	11.5	28 39.7	−17.5	11.6	29 38.4	−17.3	11.7	30 37.2	−17.1	11.9	31 35.9	−16.9	12.0	32 34.6	−16.7	12.1	33 33.2	−16.4	12.3	79
80	26 24.1	−18.4	10.4	27 23.2	−18.3	10.4	28 22.2	−18.1	10.5	29 21.1	−17.8	10.6	30 20.1	−17.7	10.8	31 19.0	−17.4	10.9	32 17.9	−17.2	11.0	33 16.8	−17.0	11.1	80
81	26 05.7	−18.9	9.3	27 04.9	−18.7	9.4	28 04.1	−18.6	9.5	29 03.3	−18.4	9.6	30 02.4	−18.2	9.6	31 01.6	−18.0	9.7	32 00.7	−17.8	9.8	32 59.8	−17.6	10.0	81
82	25 46.8	−19.3	8.2	26 46.2	−19.2	8.3	27 45.5	−19.0	8.4	28 44.9	−18.9	8.5	29 44.2	−18.7	8.5	30 43.6	−18.6	8.6	31 42.9	−18.4	8.7	32 42.2	−18.3	8.8	82
83	25 27.5	−19.8	7.2	26 27.0	−19.7	7.3	27 26.5	−19.5	7.3	28 26.0	−19.4	7.4	29 25.5	−19.3	7.5	30 25.0	−19.1	7.5	31 24.5	−19.0	7.6	32 23.9	−18.8	7.7	83
84	25 07.7	−20.3	6.1	26 07.3	−20.1	6.2	27 07.0	−20.1	6.3	28 06.6	−19.9	6.3	29 06.2	−19.8	6.4	30 05.9	−19.7	6.4	31 05.5	−19.6	6.5	32 05.1	−19.5	6.6	84
85	24 47.4	−20.6	5.1	25 47.2	−20.6	5.1	26 46.9	−20.5	5.2	27 46.7	−20.4	5.2	28 46.4	−20.3	5.3	29 46.2	−20.2	5.3	30 45.9	−20.1	5.4	31 45.6	−20.0	5.5	85
86	24 26.8	−21.1	4.1	25 26.6	−21.0	4.1	26 26.4	−20.9	4.1	27 26.3	−20.9	4.2	28 26.1	−20.8	4.2	29 26.0	−20.8	4.3	30 25.8	−20.7	4.3	31 25.6	−20.6	4.3	86
87	24 05.7	−21.5	3.0	25 05.6	−21.5	3.1	26 05.5	−21.4	3.1	27 05.4	−21.3	3.1	28 05.3	−21.3	3.2	29 05.2	−21.2	3.2	30 05.1	−21.2	3.2	31 05.0	−21.1	3.2	87
88	23 44.2	−21.9	2.0	24 44.1	−21.8	2.0	25 44.1	−21.8	2.1	26 44.1	−21.8	2.1	27 44.0	−21.8	2.1	28 44.0	−21.8	2.1	29 43.9	−21.7	2.1	30 43.9	−21.7	2.2	88
89	23 22.3	−22.3	1.0	24 22.3	−22.3	1.0	25 22.3	−22.3	1.0	26 22.3	−22.3	1.0	27 22.2	−22.2	1.0	28 22.2	−22.2	1.1	29 22.2	−22.2	1.1	30 22.2	−22.2	1.1	89
90	23 00.0	−22.7	0.0	24 00.0	−22.7	0.0	25 00.0	−22.7	0.0	26 00.0	−22.7	0.0	27 00.0	−22.7	0.0	28 00.0	−22.7	0.0	29 00.0	−22.7	0.0	30 00.0	−22.7	0.0	90
	23°			24°			25°			26°			27°			28°			29°			30°			

68°, 292° L.H.A. LATITUDE SAME NAME AS DECLINATION

320

LATITUDE **CONTRARY** NAME TO DECLINATION L.H.A. 68°, 292°

Dec.	23° Hc	d	Z	24° Hc	d	Z	25° Hc	d	Z	26° Hc	d	Z	Dec.
°	° ′	′	°	° ′	′	°	° ′	′	°	° ′	′	°	°
0	20 10.3	−25.2	99.0	20 00.7	−26.1	99.3	19 50.8	−27.1	99.7	19 40.5	−28.0	100.0	0
1	19 45.1	−25.4	99.9	19 34.6	−26.4	100.3	19 23.7	−27.4	100.6	19 12.5	−28.4	101.0	1
2	19 19.7	−25.7	100.9	19 08.2	−26.7	101.2	18 56.3	−27.7	101.6	18 44.1	−28.6	101.9	2
3	18 54.0	−26.1	101.9	18 41.5	−27.0	102.2	18 28.6	−27.9	102.5	18 15.5	−28.9	102.8	3
4	18 27.9	−26.3	102.8	18 14.5	−27.3	103.1	18 00.7	−28.3	103.4	17 46.6	−29.2	103.8	4
5	18 01.6	−26.6	103.8	17 47.2	−27.6	104.1	17 32.4	−28.4	104.4	17 17.4	−29.4	104.7	5
6	17 35.0	−26.8	104.7	17 19.6	−27.8	105.0	17 04.0	−28.8	105.3	16 48.0	−29.7	105.6	6
7	17 08.2	−27.2	105.6	16 51.8	−28.0	105.9	16 35.2	−28.9	106.2	16 18.3	−29.8	106.5	7
8	16 41.0	−27.3	106.6	16 23.8	−28.3	106.8	16 06.3	−29.2	107.1	15 48.5	−30.1	107.4	8
9	16 13.7	−27.6	107.5	15 55.5	−28.5	107.8	15 37.1	−29.5	108.0	15 18.4	−30.4	108.3	9
10	15 46.1	−27.9	108.4	15 27.0	−28.8	108.7	15 07.6	−29.6	108.9	14 48.0	−30.5	109.2	10
11	15 18.2	−28.0	109.3	14 58.2	−28.9	109.6	14 38.0	−29.8	109.8	14 17.5	−30.7	110.1	11
12	14 50.2	−28.3	110.2	14 29.3	−29.2	110.5	14 08.2	−30.1	110.7	13 46.8	−30.9	111.0	12
13	14 21.9	−28.5	111.2	14 00.1	−29.4	111.4	13 38.1	−30.2	111.6	13 15.9	−31.1	111.8	13
14	13 53.4	−28.7	112.1	13 30.7	−29.5	112.3	13 07.9	−30.4	112.5	12 44.8	−31.3	112.7	14
15	13 24.7	−28.9	113.0	13 01.2	−29.8	113.2	12 37.5	−30.6	113.4	12 13.5	−31.4	113.6	15
16	12 55.8	−29.0	113.9	12 31.4	−29.9	114.1	12 06.9	−30.8	114.3	11 42.1	−31.6	114.5	16
17	12 26.8	−29.3	114.8	12 01.5	−30.0	115.0	11 36.1	−30.9	115.2	11 10.5	−31.7	115.3	17
18	11 57.5	−29.4	115.7	11 31.5	−30.3	115.8	11 05.2	−31.1	116.0	10 38.8	−31.9	116.2	18
19	11 28.1	−29.6	116.6	11 01.2	−30.4	116.7	10 34.1	−31.2	116.9	10 06.9	−32.0	117.1	19
20	10 58.5	−29.7	117.4	10 30.8	−30.5	117.6	10 02.9	−31.3	117.8	9 34.9	−32.1	117.9	20
21	10 28.8	−29.8	118.3	10 00.3	−30.7	118.5	9 31.6	−31.5	118.6	9 02.8	−32.3	118.8	21
22	9 59.0	−30.1	119.2	9 29.6	−30.8	119.4	9 00.1	−31.6	119.5	8 30.5	−32.3	119.6	22
23	9 28.9	−30.1	120.1	8 58.8	−30.9	120.2	8 28.5	−31.7	120.4	7 58.2	−32.5	120.5	23
24	8 58.8	−30.3	121.0	8 27.9	−31.1	121.1	7 56.8	−31.8	121.2	7 25.7	−32.6	121.3	24
25	8 28.5	−30.3	121.8	7 56.8	−31.1	122.0	7 25.0	−31.9	122.1	6 53.1	−32.6	122.2	25
26	7 58.2	−30.5	122.7	7 25.7	−31.3	122.8	6 53.1	−32.0	122.9	6 20.5	−32.8	123.0	26
27	7 27.7	−30.6	123.6	6 54.4	−31.3	123.7	6 21.1	−32.0	123.8	5 47.7	−32.8	123.9	27
28	6 57.1	−30.7	124.4	6 23.1	−31.4	124.5	5 49.1	−32.2	124.6	5 14.9	−32.9	124.7	28
29	6 26.4	−30.8	125.3	5 51.7	−31.5	125.4	5 16.9	−32.2	125.5	4 42.0	−32.9	125.5	29
30	5 55.6	−30.8	126.2	5 20.2	−31.6	126.2	4 44.7	−32.3	126.3	4 09.1	−33.0	126.4	30
31	5 24.8	−30.9	127.0	4 48.6	−31.6	127.1	4 12.4	−32.3	127.2	3 36.1	−33.0	127.2	31
32	4 53.9	−31.0	127.9	4 17.0	−31.7	128.0	3 40.1	−32.4	128.0	3 03.1	−33.1	128.1	32
33	4 22.9	−31.1	128.8	3 45.3	−31.8	128.8	3 07.7	−32.5	128.9	2 30.0	−33.1	128.9	33
34	3 51.8	−31.1	129.6	3 13.5	−31.7	129.7	2 35.2	−32.4	129.7	1 56.9	−33.1	129.7	34
35	3 20.7	−31.1	130.5	2 41.8	−31.9	130.5	2 02.8	−32.5	130.5	1 23.8	−33.2	130.6	35
36	2 49.6	−31.2	131.3	2 09.9	−31.8	131.4	1 30.3	−32.5	131.4	0 50.6	−33.1	131.4	36
37	2 18.4	−31.2	132.2	1 38.1	−31.9	132.2	0 57.8	−32.5	132.2	0 17.5	−33.2	132.2	37
38	1 47.2	−31.3	133.0	1 06.2	−31.9	133.0	0 25.3	−32.6	133.1	0 15.7	+33.2	46.9	38
39	1 15.9	−31.2	133.9	0 34.3	−31.9	133.9	0 07.3	+32.5	46.1	0 48.9	+33.1	46.1	39
40	0 44.7	−31.3	134.7	0 02.4	−31.8	134.7	0 39.8	+32.5	45.3	1 22.0	+33.2	45.3	40
41	0 13.4	−31.3	135.6	0 29.4	+31.9	44.4	1 12.3	+32.5	44.4	1 55.2	+33.1	44.4	41
42	0 17.9	+31.2	43.6	1 01.3	+31.9	43.6	1 44.8	+32.5	43.6	2 28.3	+33.0	43.6	42
43	0 49.1	+31.3	42.7	1 33.2	+31.9	42.7	2 17.3	+32.4	42.7	3 01.3	+33.1	42.8	43
44	1 20.4	+31.2	41.8	2 05.1	+31.8	41.9	2 49.7	+32.4	41.9	3 34.4	+33.0	41.9	44
45	1 51.6	+31.2	41.0	2 36.9	+31.8	41.0	3 22.1	+32.4	41.1	4 07.4	+32.9	41.1	45
46	2 22.8	+31.2	40.1	3 08.7	+31.7	40.2	3 54.5	+32.3	40.2	4 40.3	+32.9	40.3	46
47	2 54.0	+31.1	39.3	3 40.4	+31.7	39.3	4 26.8	+32.3	39.4	5 13.2	+32.8	39.4	47
48	3 25.1	+31.1	38.4	4 12.1	+31.7	38.5	4 59.1	+32.2	38.5	5 46.0	+32.8	38.6	48
49	3 56.2	+31.1	37.6	4 43.8	+31.6	37.6	5 31.3	+32.1	37.7	6 18.8	+32.6	37.7	49
50	4 27.3	+30.9	36.7	5 15.4	+31.5	36.8	6 03.4	+32.0	36.8	6 51.4	+32.6	36.9	50
51	4 58.2	+31.0	35.9	5 46.9	+31.4	35.9	6 35.4	+32.0	36.0	7 24.0	+32.5	36.0	51
52	5 29.2	+30.8	35.0	6 18.3	+31.4	35.1	7 07.4	+31.9	35.1	7 56.5	+32.3	35.2	52
53	6 00.0	+30.8	34.1	6 49.7	+31.2	34.2	7 39.3	+31.7	34.3	8 28.8	+32.3	34.3	53
54	6 30.8	+30.6	33.3	7 20.9	+31.2	33.3	8 11.0	+31.7	33.4	9 01.1	+32.1	33.5	54
55	7 01.4	+30.6	32.4	7 52.1	+31.0	32.5	8 42.7	+31.5	32.5	9 33.2	+32.0	32.6	55
56	7 32.0	+30.5	31.5	8 23.1	+31.0	31.6	9 14.2	+31.4	31.7	10 05.2	+31.9	31.8	56
57	8 02.5	+30.3	30.7	8 54.1	+30.8	30.7	9 45.6	+31.3	30.8	10 37.1	+31.8	30.9	57
58	8 32.8	+30.3	29.8	9 24.9	+30.7	29.9	10 16.9	+31.1	30.0	11 08.9	+31.6	30.1	58
59	9 03.1	+30.1	28.9	9 55.6	+30.5	29.0	10 48.0	+31.0	29.1	11 40.5	+31.4	29.2	59
60	9 33.2	+30.0	28.0	10 26.1	+30.5	28.1	11 19.0	+30.9	28.2	12 11.9	+31.3	28.3	60
61	10 03.2	+29.9	27.2	10 56.6	+30.2	27.2	11 49.9	+30.7	27.3	12 43.2	+31.1	27.4	61
62	10 33.1	+29.7	26.3	11 26.8	+30.1	26.4	12 20.6	+30.5	26.5	13 14.3	+30.9	26.6	62
63	11 02.8	+29.5	25.4	11 56.9	+30.0	25.5	12 51.1	+30.3	25.6	13 45.2	+30.7	25.7	63
64	11 32.3	+29.4	24.5	12 26.9	+29.7	24.6	13 21.4	+30.2	24.7	14 15.9	+30.5	24.8	64
65	12 01.7	+29.2	23.6	12 56.6	+29.6	23.7	13 51.6	+29.9	23.8	14 46.4	+30.4	23.9	65
66	12 30.9	+29.0	22.7	13 26.2	+29.4	22.8	14 21.5	+29.8	22.9	15 16.8	+30.1	23.0	66
67	12 59.9	+28.9	21.8	13 55.6	+29.2	21.9	14 51.3	+29.5	22.0	15 46.9	+29.9	22.1	67
68	13 28.8	+28.7	20.9	14 24.8	+29.0	21.0	15 20.8	+29.3	21.1	16 16.8	+29.6	21.2	68
69	13 57.5	+28.4	20.0	14 53.8	+28.8	20.1	15 50.1	+29.1	20.2	16 46.4	+29.5	20.3	69
70	14 25.9	+28.3	19.1	15 22.6	+28.5	19.2	16 19.2	+28.9	19.3	17 15.9	+29.1	19.4	70
71	14 54.2	+28.0	18.2	15 51.1	+28.4	18.3	16 48.1	+28.6	18.4	17 45.0	+28.9	18.5	71
72	15 22.2	+27.8	17.3	16 19.5	+28.1	17.4	17 16.7	+28.4	17.5	18 13.9	+28.7	17.6	72
73	15 50.0	+27.6	16.4	16 47.6	+27.8	16.4	17 45.1	+28.1	16.5	18 42.6	+28.4	16.6	73
74	16 17.6	+27.3	15.4	17 15.4	+27.6	15.5	18 13.2	+27.8	15.6	19 11.0	+28.1	15.7	74
75	16 44.9	+27.1	14.5	17 43.0	+27.3	14.6	18 41.0	+27.6	14.7	19 39.1	+27.8	14.8	75
76	17 12.0	+26.8	13.6	18 10.3	+27.0	13.7	19 08.6	+27.3	13.7	20 06.9	+27.5	13.8	76
77	17 38.8	+26.6	12.6	18 37.3	+26.8	12.7	19 35.9	+26.9	12.8	20 34.4	+27.2	12.9	77
78	18 05.4	+26.2	11.7	19 04.1	+26.5	11.8	20 02.8	+26.7	11.8	21 01.6	+26.8	11.9	78
79	18 31.6	+26.0	10.8	19 30.6	+26.1	10.8	20 29.5	+26.4	10.9	21 28.4	+26.6	11.0	79
80	18 57.6	+25.7	9.8	19 56.7	+25.9	9.9	20 55.9	+26.0	9.9	21 55.0	+26.1	10.0	80
81	19 23.3	+25.4	8.8	20 22.6	+25.6	8.9	21 21.9	+25.7	9.0	22 21.1	+25.9	9.0	81
82	19 48.7	+25.1	7.9	20 48.2	+25.2	7.9	21 47.6	+25.3	8.0	22 47.0	+25.5	8.0	82
83	20 13.8	+24.8	6.9	21 13.4	+24.9	7.0	22 12.9	+25.0	7.0	23 12.5	+25.1	7.1	83
84	20 38.6	+24.4	5.9	21 38.3	+24.5	6.0	22 37.9	+24.7	6.0	23 37.6	+24.7	6.1	84
85	21 03.0	+24.1	5.0	22 02.8	+24.2	5.0	23 02.6	+24.2	5.0	24 02.3	+24.4	5.1	85
86	21 27.1	+23.8	4.0	22 27.0	+23.8	4.0	23 26.8	+23.9	4.0	24 26.7	+23.9	4.1	86
87	21 50.9	+23.4	3.0	22 50.8	+23.5	3.0	23 50.7	+23.5	3.0	24 50.6	+23.6	3.1	87
88	22 14.3	+23.0	2.0	23 14.3	+23.0	2.0	24 14.2	+23.1	2.0	25 14.2	+23.1	2.1	88
89	22 37.3	+22.7	1.0	23 37.3	+22.7	1.0	24 37.3	+22.7	1.0	25 37.3	+22.7	1.0	89
90	23 00.0	+22.3	0.0	24 00.0	+22.3	0.0	25 00.0	+22.3	0.0	26 00.0	+22.3	0.0	90
	23°			24°			25°			26°			

Dec.	27° Hc	d	Z	28° Hc	d	Z	29° Hc	d	Z	30° Hc	d	Z	Dec.
°	° ′	′	°	° ′	′	°	° ′	′	°	° ′	′	°	°
0	19 29.9	−29.0	100.4	19 18.9	−30.0	100.7	19 07.5	−30.9	101.1	18 55.8	−31.8	101.4	0
1	19 00.9	−29.4	101.3	18 48.9	−30.2	101.7	18 36.6	−31.2	102.0	18 24.0	−32.1	102.3	1
2	18 31.5	−29.5	102.2	18 18.7	−30.6	102.6	18 05.4	−31.4	102.9	17 51.9	−32.3	103.2	2
3	18 02.0	−29.9	103.2	17 48.1	−30.7	103.5	17 34.0	−31.7	103.8	17 19.6	−32.6	104.1	3
4	17 32.1	−30.1	104.1	17 17.4	−31.0	104.4	17 02.3	−31.9	104.7	16 47.0	−32.8	105.0	4
5	17 02.0	−30.3	105.0	16 46.4	−31.2	105.3	16 30.4	−32.1	105.6	16 14.2	−33.0	105.8	5
6	16 31.7	−30.5	105.9	16 15.2	−31.5	106.2	15 58.3	−32.3	106.4	15 41.2	−33.2	106.7	6
7	16 01.2	−30.8	106.8	15 43.7	−31.7	107.0	15 26.0	−32.6	107.3	15 08.0	−33.4	107.6	7
8	15 30.4	−31.0	107.7	15 12.0	−31.8	107.9	14 53.4	−32.7	108.2	14 34.6	−33.6	108.4	8
9	14 59.4	−31.2	108.6	14 40.2	−32.1	108.8	14 20.7	−32.9	109.0	14 01.0	−33.8	109.3	9
10	14 28.2	−31.4	109.4	14 08.1	−32.2	109.7	13 47.8	−33.1	109.9	13 27.2	−33.9	110.1	10
11	13 56.8	−31.6	110.3	13 35.9	−32.5	110.5	13 14.7	−33.3	110.8	12 53.3	−34.1	111.0	11
12	13 25.2	−31.7	111.2	13 03.4	−32.6	111.4	12 41.4	−33.4	111.6	12 19.2	−34.2	111.8	12
13	12 53.5	−32.0	112.1	12 30.8	−32.7	112.3	12 08.0	−33.6	112.5	11 45.0	−34.4	112.7	13
14	12 21.5	−32.1	112.9	11 58.1	−33.0	113.1	11 34.4	−33.7	113.3	11 10.6	−34.6	113.5	14
15	11 49.4	−32.2	113.8	11 25.1	−33.0	114.0	11 00.7	−33.9	114.2	10 36.0	−34.7	114.3	15
16	11 17.2	−32.4	114.7	10 52.1	−33.3	114.8	10 26.8	−34.0	115.0	10 01.3	−34.8	115.2	16
17	10 44.8	−32.6	115.5	10 18.8	−33.3	115.7	9 52.8	−34.2	115.8	9 26.5	−34.9	116.0	17
18	10 12.2	−32.6	116.4	9 45.5	−33.5	116.5	9 18.6	−34.2	116.7	8 51.6	−35.0	116.8	18
19	9 39.6	−32.8	117.2	9 12.0	−33.5	117.4	8 44.4	−34.4	117.5	8 16.6	−35.1	117.6	19
20	9 06.8	−33.0	118.1	8 38.5	−33.7	118.2	8 10.0	−34.4	118.3	7 41.5	−35.2	118.5	20
21	8 33.8	−33.0	118.9	8 04.8	−33.8	119.0	7 35.6	−34.6	119.2	7 06.3	−35.3	119.3	21
22	8 00.8	−33.1	119.8	7 31.0	−33.9	119.9	7 01.0	−34.6	120.0	6 31.0	−35.4	120.1	22
23	7 27.7	−33.3	120.6	6 57.1	−34.0	120.7	6 26.4	−34.7	120.8	5 55.6	−35.4	120.9	23
24	6 54.4	−33.3	121.4	6 23.1	−34.0	121.5	5 51.7	−34.8	121.6	5 20.2	−35.5	121.7	24
25	6 21.1	−33.4	122.3	5 49.1	−34.2	122.4	5 16.9	−34.9	122.4	4 44.7	−35.6	122.5	25
26	5 47.7	−33.4	123.1	5 14.9	−34.2	123.2	4 42.0	−34.9	123.3	4 09.1	−35.6	123.3	26
27	5 14.3	−33.6	123.9	4 40.7	−34.2	124.0	4 07.1	−34.9	124.1	3 33.5	−35.7	124.1	27
28	4 40.7	−33.6	124.8	4 06.5	−34.3	124.8	3 32.2	−35.0	124.9	2 57.8	−35.6	124.9	28
29	4 07.1	−33.6	125.6	3 32.2	−34.4	125.7	2 57.2	−35.0	125.7	2 22.2	−35.8	125.7	29
30	3 33.5	−33.7	126.4	2 57.8	−34.3	126.5	2 22.2	−35.1	126.5	1 46.4	−35.7	126.5	30
31	2 59.8	−33.7	127.3	2 23.5	−34.4	127.3	1 47.1	−35.1	127.3	1 10.7	−35.8	127.4	31
32	2 26.1	−33.8	128.1	1 49.1	−34.5	128.1	1 12.0	−35.1	128.1	0 34.9	−35.7	128.2	32
33	1 52.3	−33.8	128.9	1 14.6	−34.4	128.9	0 36.9	−35.1	129.0	0 00.8	+35.8	51.0	33
34	1 18.5	−33.8	129.7	0 40.2	−34.5	129.8	0 01.8	−35.1	129.8	0 36.6	+35.7	50.2	34
35	0 44.7	−33.8	130.6	0 05.7	−34.4	130.6	0 33.3	+35.1	49.4	1 12.3	+35.8	49.4	35
36	0 10.9	−33.8	131.4	0 28.7	+34.5	48.6	1 08.4	+35.1	48.6	1 48.1	+35.7	48.6	36
37	0 22.9	+33.8	47.8	1 03.2	+34.4	47.8	1 43.5	+35.1	47.8	2 23.8	+35.7	47.8	37
38	0 56.7	+33.8	46.9	1 37.6	+34.4	47.0	2 18.6	+35.0	47.0	2 59.5	+35.6	47.0	38
39	1 30.5	+33.7	46.1	2 12.0	+34.4	46.1	2 53.6	+35.0	46.2	3 35.1	+35.6	46.2	39
40	2 04.2	+33.8	45.3	2 46.4	+34.4	45.3	3 28.6	+35.0	45.4	4 10.7	+35.6	45.4	40
41	2 38.0	+33.7	44.5	3 20.8	+34.3	44.5	4 03.6	+34.9	44.5	4 46.3	+35.5	44.6	41
42	3 11.7	+33.7	43.6	3 55.1	+34.3	43.7	4 38.5	+34.8	43.7	5 21.8	+35.5	43.8	42
43	3 45.4	+33.6	42.8	4 29.4	+34.2	42.9	5 13.3	+34.8	42.9	5 57.3	+35.3	43.0	43
44	4 19.0	+33.6	42.0	5 03.6	+34.1	42.0	5 48.1	+34.8	42.1	6 32.6	+35.3	42.2	44
45	4 52.6	+33.5	41.1	5 37.7	+34.1	41.2	6 22.9	+34.6	41.3	7 07.9	+35.2	41.4	45
46	5 26.1	+33.4	40.3	6 11.8	+34.0	40.4	6 57.5	+34.6	40.5	7 43.1	+35.1	40.5	46
47	5 59.5	+33.4	39.5	6 45.8	+33.9	39.6	7 32.1	+34.4	39.6	8 18.2	+35.0	39.7	47
48	6 32.9	+33.3	38.6	7 19.7	+33.9	38.7	8 06.5	+34.4	38.8	8 53.2	+35.0	38.9	48
49	7 06.2	+33.2	37.8	7 53.6	+33.7	37.9	8 40.9	+34.2	38.0	9 28.2	+34.7	38.1	49
50	7 39.4	+33.1	37.0	8 27.3	+33.6	37.1	9 15.1	+34.2	37.1	10 02.9	+34.7	37.2	50
51	8 12.5	+33.0	36.1	9 00.9	+33.5	36.2	9 49.3	+34.0	36.3	10 37.6	+34.5	36.4	51
52	8 45.5	+32.8	35.3	9 34.4	+33.4	35.4	10 23.3	+33.9	35.5	11 12.1	+34.4	35.6	52
53	9 18.3	+32.8	34.4	10 07.8	+33.3	34.5	10 57.2	+33.7	34.6	11 46.5	+34.3	34.7	53
54	9 51.1	+32.6	33.6	10 41.1	+33.1	33.7	11 30.9	+33.7	33.8	12 20.8	+34.1	33.9	54
55	10 23.7	+32.5	32.7	11 14.2	+32.9	32.8	12 04.6	+33.4	32.9	12 54.9	+33.9	33.1	55
56	10 56.2	+32.4	31.9	11 47.1	+32.9	32.0	12 38.0	+33.3	32.1	13 28.8	+33.8	32.2	56
57	11 28.6	+32.2	31.0	12 20.0	+32.6	31.1	13 11.3	+33.1	31.2	14 02.6	+33.5	31.4	57
58	12 00.8	+32.0	30.2	12 52.6	+32.5	30.3	13 44.4	+33.0	30.4	14 36.1	+33.4	30.5	58
59	12 32.8	+31.9	29.3	13 25.1	+32.3	29.4	14 17.4	+32.7	29.5	15 09.5	+33.2	29.7	59
60	13 04.7	+31.7	28.4	13 57.4	+32.2	28.5	14 50.1	+32.6	28.7	15 42.7	+33.0	28.8	60
61	13 36.4	+31.5	27.5	14 29.6	+31.9	27.7	15 22.7	+32.3	27.8	16 15.7	+32.8	27.9	61
62	14 07.9	+31.3	26.7	15 01.5	+31.7	26.8	15 55.0	+32.2	26.9	16 48.5	+32.5	27.0	62
63	14 39.2	+31.1	25.8	15 33.2	+31.5	25.9	16 27.2	+31.9	26.0	17 21.0	+32.4	26.2	63
64	15 10.3	+31.0	24.9	16 04.7	+31.3	25.0	16 59.1	+31.7	25.1	17 53.4	+32.0	25.3	64
65	15 41.3	+30.7	24.0	16 36.0	+31.1	24.1	17 30.8	+31.4	24.3	18 25.4	+31.9	24.4	65
66	16 12.0	+30.4	23.1	17 07.1	+30.9	23.2	18 02.2	+31.2	23.4	18 57.3	+31.6	23.5	66
67	16 42.4	+30.3	22.2	17 38.0	+30.6	22.3	18 33.4	+31.0	22.5	19 28.9	+31.3	22.6	67
68	17 12.7	+30.0	21.3	18 08.6	+30.3	21.4	19 04.4	+30.7	21.6	20 00.2	+31.0	21.7	68
69	17 42.7	+29.7	20.4	18 38.9	+30.1	20.5	19 35.1	+30.4	20.7	20 31.2	+30.7	20.8	69
70	18 12.4	+29.5	19.5	19 09.0	+29.8	19.6	20 05.5	+30.1	19.7	21 01.9	+30.5	19.9	70
71	18 41.9	+29.2	18.6	19 38.8	+29.5	18.7	20 35.6	+29.8	18.8	21 32.4	+30.1	18.9	71
72	19 11.1	+29.0	17.7	20 08.3	+29.2	17.8	21 05.4	+29.5	17.9	22 02.5	+29.8	18.0	72
73	19 40.1	+28.6	16.7	20 37.5	+28.9	16.8	21 34.9	+29.2	16.9	22 32.3	+29.5	17.1	73
74	20 08.7	+28.4	15.8	21 06.4	+28.7	15.9	22 04.1	+28.9	16.0	23 01.8	+29.1	16.1	74
75	20 37.1	+28.0	14.9	21 35.1	+28.2	15.0	22 33.0	+28.5	15.1	23 30.9	+28.8	15.2	75
76	21 05.1	+27.7	13.9	22 03.3	+28.0	14.0	23 01.5	+28.2	14.1	23 59.7	+28.5	14.2	76
77	21 32.8	+27.4	13.0	22 31.3	+27.6	13.0	23 29.7	+27.9	13.1	24 28.2	+28.0	13.2	77
78	22 00.2	+27.1	12.0	22 58.9	+27.3	12.1	23 57.6	+27.5	12.2	24 56.2	+27.7	12.3	78
79	22 27.3	+26.7	11.0	23 26.2	+26.9	11.1	24 25.1	+27.1	11.2	25 23.9	+27.3	11.3	79
80	22 54.0	+26.4	10.1	23 53.1	+26.5	10.1	24 52.2	+26.7	10.2	25 51.2	+26.9	10.3	80
81	23 20.4	+26.0	9.1	24 19.6	+26.2	9.2	25 18.9	+26.3	9.2	26 18.1	+26.5	9.3	81
82	23 46.4	+25.6	8.1	24 45.8	+25.8	8.2	25 45.2	+25.9	8.2	26 44.6	+26.0	8.3	82
83	24 12.0	+25.3	7.1	25 11.6	+25.3	7.2	26 11.1	+25.5	7.2	27 10.6	+25.6	7.3	83
84	24 37.3	+24.8	6.1	25 36.9	+25.0	6.2	26 36.6	+25.0	6.2	27 36.2	+25.2	6.3	84
85	25 02.1	+24.4	5.1	26 01.9	+24.5	5.2	27 01.6	+24.6	5.2	28 01.4	+24.7	5.3	85
86	25 26.5	+24.1	4.1	26 26.4	+24.1	4.1	27 26.2	+24.2	4.2	28 26.1	+24.2	4.2	86
87	25 50.6	+23.5	3.1	26 50.5	+23.6	3.1	27 50.4	+23.7	3.1	28 50.3	+23.7	3.2	87
88	26 14.1	+23.2	2.1	27 14.1	+23.2	2.1	28 14.1	+23.2	2.1	29 14.0	+23.3	2.1	88
89	26 37.3	+22.7	1.0	27 37.3	+22.7	1.0	28 37.3	+22.7	1.1	29 37.3	+22.7	1.1	89
90	27 00.0	+22.2	0.0	28 00.0	+22.2	0.0	29 00.0	+22.2	0.0	30 00.0	+22.2	0.0	90
	27°			28°			29°			30°			

S. Lat. {L.H.A. greater than 180° ....Zn=180°−Z; L.H.A. less than 180°...........Zn=180°+Z}

LATITUDE **SAME** NAME AS DECLINATION L.H.A. 112°, 248°

321

Dec.	23°			24°			25°			26°			27°			28°			29°			30°			Dec.
	Hc	d	Z	Hc	d	Z	Hc	d	Z	Hc	d	Z	Hc	d	Z	Hc	d	Z	Hc	d	Z	Hc	d	Z	
°	° ′	′	°	° ′	′	°	° ′	′	°	° ′	′	°	° ′	′	°	° ′	′	°	° ′	′	°	° ′	′	°	°
0	19 15.7	+24.7	98.5	19 06.6	+25.7	98.9	18 57.2	+26.6	99.2	18 47.4	+27.6	99.6	18 37.3	+28.6	99.9	18 26.8	+29.6	100.2	18 16.0	+30.5	100.5	18 04.8	+31.5	100.9	0
1	19 40.4	+24.3	97.6	19 32.3	+25.4	97.9	19 23.8	+26.4	98.3	19 15.0	+27.4	98.6	19 05.9	+28.3	99.0	18 56.4	+29.2	99.3	18 46.5	+30.2	99.6	18 36.3	+31.2	100.0	1
2	20 04.7	+24.1	96.6	19 57.7	+25.0	97.0	19 50.2	+26.1	97.3	19 42.4	+27.0	97.7	19 34.2	+28.0	98.0	19 25.6	+29.0	98.4	19 16.7	+30.0	98.7	19 07.5	+30.9	99.1	2
3	20 28.8	+23.7	95.6	20 22.7	+24.8	96.0	20 16.3	+25.7	96.4	20 09.4	+26.8	96.7	20 02.2	+27.8	97.1	19 54.6	+28.8	97.4	19 46.7	+29.7	97.8	19 38.4	+30.6	98.2	3
4	20 52.5	+23.4	94.6	20 47.5	+24.4	95.0	20 42.0	+25.4	95.4	20 36.2	+26.4	95.8	20 30.0	+27.4	96.1	20 23.4	+28.4	96.5	20 16.4	+29.4	96.9	20 09.0	+30.3	97.2	4
5	21 15.9	+23.0	93.6	21 11.9	+24.0	94.0	21 07.4	+25.1	94.4	21 02.6	+26.1	94.8	20 57.4	+27.1	95.2	20 51.8	+28.1	95.6	20 45.8	+29.0	95.9	20 39.3	+30.1	96.3	5
6	21 38.9	+22.7	92.7	21 35.9	+23.8	93.1	21 32.5	+24.8	93.4	21 28.7	+25.8	93.8	21 24.5	+26.8	94.2	21 19.9	+27.8	94.6	21 14.8	+28.8	95.0	21 09.4	+29.8	95.4	6
7	22 01.6	+22.3	91.7	21 59.7	+23.3	92.1	21 57.3	+24.4	92.5	21 54.5	+25.4	92.9	21 51.3	+26.4	93.3	21 47.7	+27.4	93.7	21 43.6	+28.5	94.1	21 39.2	+29.4	94.5	7
8	22 23.9	+22.0	90.7	22 23.0	+23.0	91.1	22 21.7	+24.0	91.5	22 19.9	+25.1	91.9	22 17.7	+26.1	92.3	22 15.1	+27.1	92.7	22 12.1	+28.1	93.1	22 08.6	+29.1	93.5	8
9	22 45.9	+21.5	89.6	22 46.0	+22.6	90.1	22 45.7	+23.7	90.5	22 45.0	+24.7	90.9	22 43.8	+25.8	91.3	22 42.2	+26.8	91.7	22 40.2	+27.8	92.2	22 37.7	+28.8	92.6	9
10	23 07.4	+21.2	88.6	23 08.6	+22.3	89.1	23 09.4	+23.3	89.5	23 09.7	+24.3	89.9	23 09.6	+25.3	90.3	23 09.0	+26.4	90.8	23 08.0	+27.4	91.2	23 06.5	+28.4	91.6	10
11	23 28.6	+20.8	87.6	23 30.9	+21.8	88.0	23 32.7	+22.9	88.5	23 34.0	+24.0	88.9	23 34.9	+25.0	89.4	23 35.4	+26.0	89.8	23 35.4	+27.0	90.2	23 34.9	+28.1	90.7	11
12	23 49.4	+20.3	86.6	23 52.7	+21.4	87.0	23 55.6	+22.5	87.5	23 58.0	+23.6	87.9	23 59.9	+24.6	88.4	24 01.4	+25.7	88.8	24 02.4	+26.7	89.3	24 03.0	+27.7	89.7	12
13	24 09.7	+20.0	85.6	24 14.1	+21.1	86.0	24 18.1	+22.1	86.5	24 21.6	+23.1	86.9	24 24.5	+24.3	87.4	24 27.1	+25.2	87.8	24 29.1	+26.3	88.3	24 30.7	+27.3	88.7	13
14	24 29.7	+19.5	84.5	24 35.2	+20.6	85.0	24 40.2	+21.7	85.4	24 44.7	+22.8	85.9	24 48.8	+23.8	86.4	24 52.3	+24.9	86.8	24 55.4	+25.9	87.3	24 58.0	+27.0	87.7	14
15	24 49.2	+19.1	83.5	24 55.8	+20.1	83.9	25 01.9	+21.2	84.4	25 07.5	+22.3	84.9	25 12.6	+23.4	85.3	25 17.2	+24.4	85.8	25 21.3	+25.5	86.3	25 25.0	+26.5	86.8	15
16	25 08.3	+18.6	82.4	25 15.9	+19.8	82.9	25 23.1	+20.8	83.4	25 29.8	+21.9	83.8	25 36.0	+22.9	84.3	25 41.6	+24.1	84.8	25 46.8	+25.1	85.3	25 51.5	+26.2	85.8	16
17	25 26.9	+18.2	81.4	25 35.7	+19.3	81.9	25 43.9	+20.4	82.3	25 51.7	+21.4	82.8	25 58.9	+22.6	83.3	26 05.7	+23.6	83.8	26 11.9	+24.7	84.3	26 17.7	+25.7	84.8	17
18	25 45.1	+17.8	80.3	25 55.0	+18.8	80.8	26 04.3	+19.9	81.3	26 13.1	+21.0	81.8	26 21.5	+22.0	82.3	26 29.3	+23.1	82.8	26 36.6	+24.2	83.3	26 43.4	+25.3	83.8	18
19	26 02.9	+17.2	79.3	26 13.8	+18.3	79.8	26 24.2	+19.5	80.2	26 34.1	+20.6	80.7	26 43.5	+21.7	81.2	26 52.4	+22.7	81.7	27 00.8	+23.8	82.2	27 08.7	+24.8	82.7	19
20	26 20.1	+16.8	78.2	26 32.1	+17.9	78.7	26 43.7	+18.9	79.2	26 54.7	+20.0	79.7	27 05.2	+21.1	80.2	27 15.1	+22.3	80.7	27 24.6	+23.3	81.2	27 33.5	+24.4	81.7	20
21	26 36.9	+16.3	77.1	26 50.0	+17.4	77.6	27 02.6	+18.5	78.1	27 14.7	+19.6	78.6	27 26.3	+20.7	79.1	27 37.4	+21.7	79.6	27 47.9	+22.8	80.2	27 57.9	+23.9	80.7	21
22	26 53.2	+15.8	76.1	27 07.4	+16.9	76.5	27 21.1	+18.0	77.0	27 34.3	+19.1	77.6	27 47.0	+20.2	78.1	27 59.1	+21.3	78.6	28 10.7	+22.4	79.1	28 21.8	+23.4	79.6	22
23	27 09.0	+15.3	75.0	27 24.3	+16.4	75.5	27 39.1	+17.5	76.0	27 53.4	+18.6	76.5	28 07.2	+19.7	77.0	28 20.4	+20.8	77.5	28 33.1	+21.9	78.1	28 45.2	+23.0	78.6	23
24	27 24.3	+14.8	73.9	27 40.7	+15.9	74.4	27 56.6	+17.0	74.9	28 12.0	+18.1	75.4	28 26.9	+19.1	75.9	28 41.2	+20.3	76.5	28 55.0	+21.3	77.0	29 08.2	+22.4	77.5	24
25	27 39.1	+14.3	72.8	27 56.6	+15.4	73.3	28 13.6	+16.5	73.8	28 30.1	+17.6	74.3	28 46.0	+18.7	74.8	29 01.5	+19.7	75.4	29 16.3	+20.9	75.9	29 30.6	+22.0	76.5	25
26	27 53.4	+13.8	71.7	28 12.0	+14.9	72.2	28 30.1	+15.9	72.7	28 47.7	+17.0	73.2	29 04.7	+18.2	73.8	29 21.2	+19.3	74.3	29 37.2	+20.3	74.8	29 52.6	+21.4	75.4	26
27	28 07.2	+13.2	70.6	28 26.9	+14.3	71.1	28 46.0	+15.5	71.6	29 04.7	+16.5	72.1	29 22.9	+17.6	72.7	29 40.5	+18.7	73.2	29 57.5	+19.8	73.8	30 14.0	+20.9	74.3	27
28	28 20.4	+12.7	69.5	28 41.2	+13.8	70.0	29 01.5	+14.8	70.5	29 21.2	+16.0	71.0	29 40.5	+17.0	71.6	29 59.2	+18.1	72.1	30 17.3	+19.2	72.7	30 34.9	+20.3	73.2	28
29	28 33.1	+12.1	68.4	28 55.0	+13.2	68.9	29 16.3	+14.3	69.4	29 37.2	+15.4	69.9	29 57.5	+16.5	70.5	30 17.3	+17.6	71.0	30 36.5	+18.7	71.6	30 55.2	+19.8	72.1	29
30	28 45.2	+11.6	67.3	29 08.2	+12.7	67.8	29 30.6	+13.8	68.3	29 52.6	+14.8	68.8	30 14.0	+15.9	69.4	30 34.9	+17.0	69.9	30 55.2	+18.1	70.5	31 15.0	+19.2	71.0	30
31	28 56.8	+11.1	66.1	29 20.9	+12.1	66.6	29 44.4	+13.2	67.2	30 07.4	+14.3	67.7	30 29.9	+15.4	68.2	30 51.9	+16.5	68.8	31 13.3	+17.6	69.4	31 34.2	+18.7	69.9	31
32	29 07.9	+10.4	65.0	29 33.0	+11.5	65.5	29 57.6	+12.6	66.0	30 21.7	+13.7	66.6	30 45.3	+14.8	67.1	31 08.4	+15.8	67.7	31 30.9	+16.9	68.2	31 52.9	+18.0	68.8	32
33	29 18.3	+9.9	63.9	29 44.5	+11.0	64.4	30 10.2	+12.0	64.9	30 35.4	+13.1	65.4	31 00.1	+14.2	66.0	31 24.2	+15.3	66.5	31 47.8	+16.4	67.1	32 10.9	+17.4	67.7	33
34	29 28.2	+9.4	62.7	29 55.5	+10.4	63.3	30 22.2	+11.5	63.8	30 48.5	+12.5	64.3	31 14.3	+13.5	64.9	31 39.5	+14.6	65.4	32 04.2	+15.7	66.0	32 28.3	+16.9	66.6	34
35	29 37.6	+8.7	61.6	30 05.9	+9.7	62.1	30 33.7	+10.8	62.6	31 01.0	+11.9	63.2	31 27.8	+13.0	63.7	31 54.1	+14.1	64.3	32 19.9	+15.2	64.8	32 45.2	+16.2	65.4	35
36	29 46.3	+8.2	60.5	30 15.6	+9.2	61.0	30 44.5	+10.2	61.5	31 12.9	+11.3	62.0	31 40.8	+12.4	62.6	32 08.2	+13.4	63.1	32 35.1	+14.4	63.7	33 01.4	+15.6	64.3	36
37	29 54.5	+7.5	59.3	30 24.8	+8.6	59.8	30 54.7	+9.7	60.3	31 24.2	+10.7	60.9	31 53.2	+11.7	61.4	32 21.6	+12.8	62.0	32 49.5	+13.9	62.5	33 17.0	+14.9	63.1	37
38	30 02.0	+7.0	58.2	30 33.4	+8.0	58.7	31 04.4	+9.0	59.2	31 34.9	+10.0	59.7	32 04.9	+11.1	60.3	32 34.4	+12.1	60.8	33 03.4	+13.2	61.4	33 31.9	+14.3	62.0	38
39	30 09.0	+6.3	57.0	30 41.4	+7.4	57.5	31 13.4	+8.4	58.0	31 44.9	+9.4	58.6	32 16.0	+10.4	59.1	32 46.5	+11.5	59.6	33 16.6	+12.6	60.2	33 46.2	+13.6	60.8	39
40	30 15.3	+5.8	55.9	30 48.8	+6.7	56.4	31 21.8	+7.7	56.9	31 54.3	+8.8	57.4	32 26.4	+9.8	57.9	32 58.0	+10.9	58.5	33 29.2	+11.9	59.0	33 59.8	+12.9	59.6	40
41	30 21.1	+5.2	54.7	30 55.5	+6.2	55.2	31 29.5	+7.2	55.7	32 03.1	+8.2	56.2	32 36.2	+9.2	56.8	33 08.9	+10.2	57.3	33 41.1	+11.2	57.9	34 12.7	+12.3	58.4	41
42	30 26.3	+4.5	53.6	31 01.7	+5.5	54.1	31 36.7	+6.5	54.6	32 11.3	+7.4	55.1	32 45.4	+8.5	55.6	33 19.1	+9.5	56.1	33 52.3	+10.5	56.7	34 25.0	+11.6	57.2	42
43	30 30.8	+3.9	52.4	31 07.2	+4.9	52.9	31 43.2	+5.8	53.4	32 18.7	+6.9	53.9	32 53.9	+7.8	54.4	33 28.6	+8.8	54.9	34 02.8	+9.9	55.5	34 36.6	+10.8	56.1	43
44	30 34.7	+3.3	51.3	31 12.1	+4.2	51.7	31 49.0	+5.2	52.2	32 25.6	+6.2	52.7	33 01.7	+7.2	53.2	33 37.4	+8.2	53.8	34 12.7	+9.1	54.3	34 47.4	+10.2	54.9	44
45	30 38.0	+2.7	50.1	31 16.3	+3.6	50.6	31 54.2	+4.6	51.0	32 31.8	+5.5	51.5	33 08.9	+6.5	52.0	33 45.6	+7.4	52.6	34 21.8	+8.5	53.1	34 57.6	+9.5	53.7	45
46	30 40.7	+2.1	48.9	31 19.9	+3.0	49.4	31 58.8	+3.9	49.9	32 37.3	+4.8	50.4	33 15.4	+5.8	50.9	33 53.0	+6.8	51.4	34 30.3	+7.7	51.9	35 07.1	+8.7	52.5	46
47	30 42.8	+1.4	47.8	31 22.9	+2.4	48.2	32 02.7	+3.3	48.7	32 42.1	+4.2	49.2	33 21.2	+5.1	49.7	33 59.8	+6.1	50.2	34 38.0	+7.1	50.7	35 15.8	+8.0	51.2	47
48	30 44.2	+0.9	46.6	31 25.3	+1.7	47.1	32 06.0	+2.6	47.5	32 46.3	+3.5	48.0	33 26.3	+4.4	48.5	34 05.9	+5.4	49.0	34 45.1	+6.3	49.5	35 23.8	+7.3	50.0	48
49	30 45.1	+0.2	45.5	31 27.0	+1.1	45.9	32 08.6	+1.9	46.3	32 49.8	+2.9	46.8	33 30.7	+3.8	47.3	34 11.3	+4.6	47.8	34 51.4	+5.6	48.3	35 31.1	+6.6	48.8	49
50	30 45.3	−0.5	44.3	31 28.1	+0.4	44.7	32 10.5	+1.3	45.2	32 52.7	+2.1	45.6	33 34.5	+3.0	46.1	34 15.9	+4.0	46.6	34 57.0	+4.9	47.1	35 37.7	+5.8	47.6	50
51	30 44.8	−1.0	43.1	31 28.5	−0.2	43.5	32 11.8	+0.7	44.0	32 54.8	+1.5	44.4	33 37.5	+2.4	44.9	34 19.9	+3.2	45.4	35 01.9	+4.1	45.8	35 43.5	+5.0	46.4	51
52	30 43.8	−1.7	42.0	31 28.3	−0.9	42.4	32 12.5	−0.1	42.8	32 56.3	+0.8	43.2	33 39.9	+1.7	43.7	34 23.1	+2.6	44.1	35 06.0	+3.4	44.6	35 48.5	+4.3	45.1	52
53	30 42.1	−2.2	40.8	31 27.4	−1.5	41.2	32 12.4	−0.7	41.6	32 57.1	+0.2	42.0	33 41.6	+0.9	42.5	34 25.7	+1.8	42.9	35 09.4	+2.7	43.4	35 52.8	+3.6	43.9	53
54	30 39.9	−2.9	39.6	31 25.9	−2.1	40.0	32 11.7	−1.3	40.4	32 57.3	−0.6	40.8	33 42.5	+0.3	41.3	34 27.5	+1.1	41.7	35 12.1	+1.9	42.2	35 56.4	+2.8	42.7	54
55	30 37.0	−3.6	38.5	31 23.8	−2.8	38.9	32 10.4	−2.0	39.2	32 56.7	−1.2	39.6	33 42.8	−0.4	40.1	34 28.6	+0.3	40.5	35 14.0	+1.2	41.0	35 59.2	+2.0	41.4	55
56	30 33.4	−4.1	37.3	31 21.0	−3.4	37.7	32 08.4	−2.7	38.1	32 55.5	−1.9	38.5	33 42.4	−1.2	38.9	34 28.9	−0.3	39.3	35 15.2	+0.5	39.7	36 01.2	+1.3	40.2	56
57	30 29.3	−4.8	36.2	31 17.6	−4.0	36.5	32 05.7	−3.3	36.9	32 53.6	−2.6	37.3	33 41.2	−1.8	37.7	34 28.6	−1.1	38.1	35 15.7	−0.3	38.5	36 02.5	+0.5	39.0	57
58	30 24.5	−5.3	35.0	31 13.6	−4.7	35.3	32 02.4	−4.0	35.7	32 51.0	−3.2	36.1	33 39.4	−2.5	36.5	34 27.5	−1.8	36.9	35 15.4	−1.0	37.3	36 03.0	−0.3	37.7	58
59	30 19.2	−6.0	33.8	31 08.9	−5.3	34.2	31 58.4	−4.6	34.5	32 47.8	−4.0	34.9	33 36.9	−3.3	35.3	34 25.7	−2.5	35.7	35 14.4	−1.8	36.1	36 02.7	−1.0	36.5	59
60	30 13.2	−6.6	32.7	31 03.6	−5.9	33.0	31 53.8	−5.2	33.4	32 43.8	−4.6	33.7	33 33.6	−3.9	34.1	34 23.2	−3.2	34.4	35 12.6	−2.5	34.8	36 01.7	−1.8	35.3	60
61	30 06.6	−7.1	31.5	30 57.7	−6.6	31.9	31 48.6	−6.0	32.2	32 39.2	−5.2	32.5	33 29.7	−4.6	32.9	34 20.0	−3.9	33.2	35 10.1	−3.2	33.6	35 59.9	−2.5	34.0	61
62	29 59.5	−7.8	30.4	30 51.1	−7.1	30.7	31 42.6	−6.5	31.0	32 34.0	−5.9	31.3	33 25.1	−5.3	31.7	34 16.1	−4.6	32.0	35 06.9	−4.0	32.4	35 57.4	−3.3	32.8	62
63	29 51.7	−8.4	29.3	30 44.0	−7.8	29.5	31 36.1	−7.2	29.8	32 28.1	−6.6	30.2	33 19.8	−5.9	30.5	34 11.5	−5.4	30.8	35 02.9	−4.7	31.2	35 54.1	−4.0	31.5	63
64	29 43.3	−8.9	28.1	30 36.2	−8.4	28.4	31 28.9	−7.8	28.7	32 21.5	−7.3	29.0	33 13.9	−6.7	29.3	34 06.1	−6.0	29.6	34 58.2	−5.4	30.0	35 50.1	−4.8	30.3	64
65	29 34.4	−9.5	27.0	30 27.8	−9.0	27.2	31 21.1	−8.5	27.5	32 14.2	−7.9	27.8	33 07.2	−7.3	28.1	34 00.1	−6.8	28.4	34 52.8	−6.2	28.7	35 45.3	−5.6	29.1	65
66	29 24.9	−10.1	25.8	30 18.8	−9.6	26.1	31 12.6	−9.0	26.4	32 06.3	−8.5	26.6	32 59.9	−8.0	26.9	33 53.3	−7.4	27.2	34 46.6	−6.9	27.5	35 39.7	−6.3	27.9	66
67	29 14.8	−10.7	24.7	30 09.2	−10.2	25.0	31 03.6	−9.7	25.2	31 57.8	−9.2	25.5	32 51.9	−8.6	25.7	33 45.9	−8.1	26.0	34 39.7	−7.5	26.3	35 33.4	−7.0	26.6	67
68	29 04.1	−11.2	23.6	29 59.0	−10.7	23.8	30 53.9	−10.3	24.1	31 48.6	−9.8	24.3	32 43.3	−9.4	24.6	33 37.8	−8.8	24.8	34 32.2	−8.3	25.1	35 26.4	−7.8	25.4	68
69	28 52.9	−11.8	22.5	29 48.3	−11.4	22.7	30 43.6	−10.9	22.9	31 38.8	−10.4	23.1	32 33.9	−9.9	23.4	33 29.0	−9.5	23.6	34 23.9	−9.0	23.9	35 18.6	−8.4	24.2	69
70	28 41.1	−12.3	21.3	29 36.9	−11.9	21.5	30 32.7	−11.5	21.8	31 28.4	−11.1	22.0	32 24.0	−10.6	22.2	33 19.5	−10.2	22.5	34 14.9	−9.7	22.7	35 10.2	−9.3	23.0	70
71	28 28.8	−12.9	20.2	29 25.0	−12.5	20.4	30 21.2	−12.1	20.6	31 17.3	−11.6	20.8	32 13.4	−11.3	21.1	33 09.3	−10.8	21.3	34 05.2	−10.4	21.5	35 00.9	−9.9	21.8	71
72	28 15.9	−13.4	19.1	29 12.5	−13.0	19.3	30 09.1	−12.6	19.5	31 05.7	−12.3	19.7	32 02.1	−11.9	19.9	32 58.5	−11.5	20.1	33 54.8	−11.1	20.3	34 51.0	−10.6	20.6	72
73	28 02.5	−14.0	18.0	28 59.5	−13.6	18.2	29 56.5	−13.3	18.4	30 53.4	−12.9	18.5	31 50.2	−12.5	18.7	32 47.0	−12.1	18.9	33 43.7	−11.7	19.2	34 40.4	−11.4	19.4	73
74	27 48.5	−14.4	16.9	28 45.9	−14.1	17.1	29 43.2	−13.8	17.2	30 40.5	−13.4	17.4	31 37.7	−13.1	17.6	32 34.9	−12.8	17.8	33 32.0	−12.4	18.0	34 29.0	−12.0	18.2	74
75	27 34.1	−15.0	15.8	28 31.8	−14.7	16.0	29 29.4	−14.3	16.1	30 27.1	−14.1	16.3	31 24.6	−13.7	16.4	32 22.1	−13.4	16.6	33 19.6	−13.1	16.8	34 17.0	−12.7	17.0	75
76	27 19.1	−15.5	14.7	28 17.1	−15.2	14.9	29 15.1	−14.9	15.0	30 13.0	−14.6	15.2	31 10.9	−14.3	15.3	32 08.7	−14.0	15.5	33 06.5	−13.7	15.6	34 04.3	−13.4	15.8	76
77	27 03.6	−16.0	13.6	28 01.9	−15.7	13.8	29 00.2	−15.5	13.9	29 58.4	−15.2	14.0	30 56.6	−14.9	14.2	31 54.7	−14.6	14.3	32 52.8	−14.3	14.5	33 50.9	−14.0	14.6	77
78	26 47.6	−16.5	12.6	27 46.2	−16.3	12.7	28 44.7	−16.0	12.8	29 43.2	−15.8	12.9	30 41.7	−15.5	13.0	31 40.1	−15.2	13.2	32 38.5	−15.0	13.3	33 36.9	−14.7	13.5	78
79	26 31.1	−16.9	11.5	27 29.9	−16.7	11.6	28 28.7	−16.5	11.7	29 27.4	−16.3	11.8	30 26.2	−16.1	11.9	31 24.9	−15.9	12.0	32 23.5	−15.6	12.2	33 22.2	−15.4	12.3	79
80	26 14.2	−17.4	10.4	27 13.2	−17.2	10.5	28 12.2	−17.1	10.6	29 11.1	−16.8	10.7	30 10.1	−16.6	10.8	31 09.0	−16.4	10.9	32 07.9	−16.2	11.0	33 06.8	−16.0	11.2	80
81	25 56.8	−17.9	9.3	26 56.0	−17.8	9.4	27 55.1	−17.5	9.5	28 54.3	−17.4	9.6	29 53.5	−17.2	9.7	30 52.6	−17.0	9.8	31 51.7	−16.8	9.9	32 50.8	−16.6	10.0	81
82	25 38.9	−18.4	8.3	26 38.2	−18.2	8.4	27 37.6	−18.0	8.4	28 36.9	−17.8	8.5	29 36.3	−17.8	8.6	30 35.6	−17.6	8.7	31 34.9	−17.4	8.8	32 34.2	−17.2	8.9	82
83	25 20.5	−18.8	7.2	26 20.0	−18.6	7.3	27 19.6	−18.6	7.4	28 19.1	−18.5	7.4	29 18.5	−18.2	7.5	30 18.0	−18.1	7.6	31 17.5	−18.0	7.7	32 17.0	−17.9	7.7	83
84	25 01.7	−19.2	6.2	26 01.4	−19.2	6.2	27 01.0	−19.0	6.3	28 00.6	−18.9	6.3	29 00.3	−18.8	6.4	29 59.9	−18.7	6.5	30 59.5	−18.5	6.5	31 59.1	−18.4	6.6	84
85	24 42.5	−19.7	5.1	25 42.2	−19.5	5.2	26 42.0	−19.5	5.2	27 41.7	−19.4	5.3	28 41.5	−19.3	5.3	29 41.2	−19.2	5.4	30 41.0	−19.2	5.4	31 40.7	−19.0	5.5	85
86	24 22.8	−20.1	4.1	25 22.7	−20.1	4.1	26 22.5	−20.0	4.2	27 22.3	−19.8	4.2	28 22.2	−19.8	4.2	29 22.0	−19.7	4.3	30 21.8	−19.6	4.3	31 21.7	−19.6	4.4	86
87	24 02.7	−20.5	3.1	25 02.6	−20.4	3.1	26 02.5	−20.4	3.1	27 02.5	−20.4	3.1	28 02.4	−20.3	3.2	29 02.3	−20.3	3.2	30 02.2	−20.2	3.2	31 02.1	−20.2	3.3	87
88	23 42.2	−20.9	2.0	24 42.2	−20.9	2.1	25 42.1	−20.8	2.1	26 42.1	−20.8	2.1	27 42.1	−20.8	2.1	28 42.0	−20.7	2.1	29 42.0	−20.8	2.1	30 41.9	−20.7	2.2	88
89	23 21.3	−21.3	1.0	24 21.3	−21.3	1.0	25 21.3	−21.3	1.0	26 21.3	−21.3	1.0	27 21.3	−21.3	1.1	28 21.3	−21.3	1.1	29 21.2	−21.2	1.1	30 21.2	−21.2	1.1	89
90	23 00.0	−21.7	0.0	24 00.0	−21.7	0.0	25 00.0	−21.7	0.0	26 00.0	−21.7	0.0	27 00.0	−21.7	0.0	28 00.0	−21.7	0.0	29 00.0	−21.8	0.0	30 00.0	−21.8	0.0	90
	23°			24°			25°			26°			27°			28°			29°			30°			

LATITUDE CONTRARY NAME TO DECLINATION — L.H.A. 69°, 291°

Dec.	23° Hc	23° d	23° Z	24° Hc	24° d	24° Z	25° Hc	25° d	25° Z	26° Hc	26° d	26° Z	27° Hc	27° d	27° Z	28° Hc	28° d	28° Z	29° Hc	29° d	29° Z	30° Hc	30° d	30° Z	Dec.
°	° ′	′	°	° ′	′	°	° ′	′	°	° ′	′	°	° ′	′	°	° ′	′	°	° ′	′	°	° ′	′	°	°
0	19 15.7	−25.0	98.5	19 06.6	−26.0	98.9	18 57.2	−27.0	99.2	18 47.4	−27.9	99.6	18 37.3	−28.9	99.9	18 26.8	−29.8	100.2	18 16.0	−30.8	100.5	18 04.8	−31.6	100.9	0
1	18 50.7	−25.3	99.5	18 40.6	−26.2	99.8	18 30.2	−27.2	100.2	18 19.5	−28.2	100.5	18 08.4	−29.2	100.8	17 57.0	−30.1	101.1	17 45.2	−31.0	101.4	17 33.2	−32.0	101.8	1
2	18 25.4	−25.5	100.4	18 14.4	−26.6	100.8	18 03.0	−27.5	101.1	17 51.3	−28.5	101.4	17 39.2	−29.3	101.7	17 26.9	−30.3	102.0	17 14.2	−31.2	102.3	17 01.2	−32.1	102.6	2
3	17 59.9	−25.9	101.4	17 47.8	−26.8	101.7	17 35.5	−27.8	102.0	17 22.8	−28.7	102.3	17 09.9	−29.7	102.6	16 56.6	−30.6	102.9	16 43.0	−31.5	103.2	16 29.1	−32.4	103.5	3
4	17 34.0	−26.1	102.3	17 21.0	−27.0	102.7	17 07.7	−28.0	103.0	16 54.1	−28.9	103.3	16 40.2	−29.9	103.6	16 26.0	−30.8	103.8	16 11.5	−31.7	104.1	15 56.7	−32.6	104.4	4
5	17 07.9	−26.4	103.3	16 54.0	−27.4	103.6	16 39.7	−28.3	103.9	16 25.2	−29.2	104.2	16 10.3	−30.1	104.5	15 55.2	−31.0	104.7	15 39.8	−31.9	105.0	15 24.1	−32.7	105.3	5
6	16 41.5	−26.6	104.2	16 26.6	−27.5	104.5	16 11.4	−28.4	104.8	15 56.0	−29.4	105.1	15 40.2	−30.3	105.4	15 24.2	−31.2	105.6	15 07.9	−32.1	105.9	14 51.4	−33.0	106.1	6
7	16 14.9	−26.9	105.2	15 59.1	−27.8	105.4	15 43.0	−28.8	105.7	15 26.6	−29.7	106.0	15 09.9	−30.5	106.2	14 53.0	−31.4	106.5	14 35.8	−32.3	106.8	14 18.4	−33.2	107.0	7
8	15 48.0	−27.1	106.1	15 31.3	−28.1	106.4	15 14.2	−28.9	106.6	14 56.9	−29.8	106.9	14 39.4	−30.8	107.1	14 21.6	−31.7	107.4	14 03.5	−32.5	107.6	13 45.2	−33.3	107.9	8
9	15 20.9	−27.3	107.0	15 03.2	−28.2	107.3	14 45.3	−29.2	107.5	14 27.1	−30.1	107.8	14 08.6	−30.9	108.0	13 49.9	−31.8	108.3	13 31.0	−32.6	108.5	13 11.9	−33.5	108.7	9
10	14 53.6	−27.6	107.9	14 35.0	−28.5	108.2	14 16.1	−29.3	108.4	13 57.0	−30.2	108.7	13 37.7	−31.1	108.9	13 18.1	−31.9	109.1	12 58.4	−32.9	109.4	12 38.4	−33.7	109.6	10
11	14 26.0	−27.7	108.9	14 06.5	−28.6	109.1	13 46.8	−29.6	109.3	13 26.8	−30.4	109.6	13 06.6	−31.3	109.8	12 46.2	−32.2	110.0	12 25.5	−33.0	110.2	12 04.7	−33.8	110.4	11
12	13 58.3	−28.0	109.8	13 37.9	−28.9	110.0	13 17.2	−29.7	110.2	12 56.4	−30.7	110.5	12 35.3	−31.5	110.7	12 14.0	−32.3	110.9	11 52.5	−33.1	111.1	11 30.9	−34.0	111.3	12
13	13 30.3	−28.2	110.7	13 09.0	−29.1	110.9	12 47.5	−29.9	111.1	12 25.7	−30.7	111.3	12 03.8	−31.6	111.5	11 41.7	−32.5	111.7	11 19.4	−33.3	111.9	10 56.9	−34.1	112.1	13
14	13 02.1	−28.3	111.6	12 39.9	−29.2	111.8	12 17.6	−30.1	112.0	11 55.0	−31.0	112.2	11 32.2	−31.8	112.4	11 09.2	−32.6	112.6	10 46.1	−33.4	112.8	10 22.8	−34.2	112.9	14
15	12 33.8	−28.6	112.5	12 10.7	−29.4	112.7	11 47.5	−30.3	112.9	11 24.0	−31.1	113.1	11 00.4	−31.9	113.3	10 36.6	−32.7	113.4	10 12.7	−33.6	113.6	9 48.6	−34.4	113.8	15
16	12 05.2	−28.7	113.4	11 41.3	−29.6	113.6	11 17.2	−30.4	113.8	10 52.9	−31.2	114.0	10 28.5	−32.1	114.1	10 03.9	−32.9	114.3	9 39.1	−33.7	114.5	9 14.2	−34.5	114.6	16
17	11 36.5	−28.9	114.3	11 11.7	−29.7	114.5	10 46.8	−30.6	114.7	10 21.7	−31.4	114.8	9 56.4	−32.2	115.0	9 31.0	−33.0	115.1	9 05.4	−33.8	115.3	8 39.7	−34.5	115.4	17
18	11 07.6	−29.0	115.2	10 42.0	−29.8	115.4	10 16.2	−30.7	115.5	9 50.3	−31.5	115.7	9 24.2	−32.3	115.8	8 58.0	−33.1	116.0	8 31.6	−33.9	116.1	8 05.2	−34.7	116.3	18
19	10 38.6	−29.2	116.1	10 12.2	−30.1	116.2	9 45.5	−30.8	116.4	9 18.8	−31.6	116.6	8 51.9	−32.4	116.7	8 24.9	−33.2	116.8	7 57.7	−34.0	117.0	7 30.5	−34.8	117.1	19
20	10 09.4	−29.3	117.0	9 42.1	−30.1	117.1	9 14.7	−30.9	117.3	8 47.2	−31.8	117.4	8 19.5	−32.6	117.5	7 51.7	−33.4	117.7	7 23.7	−34.1	117.8	6 55.7	−34.9	117.9	20
21	9 40.1	−29.5	117.9	9 12.0	−30.3	118.0	8 43.8	−31.1	118.1	8 15.4	−31.9	118.3	7 46.9	−32.6	118.4	7 18.3	−33.4	118.5	6 49.6	−34.1	118.6	6 20.8	−34.9	118.7	21
22	9 10.6	−29.6	118.7	8 41.7	−30.4	118.9	8 12.7	−31.2	119.0	7 43.5	−31.9	119.1	7 14.3	−32.8	119.2	6 44.9	−33.5	119.4	6 15.5	−34.3	119.4	5 45.9	−35.0	119.5	22
23	8 41.0	−29.7	119.6	8 11.3	−30.5	119.7	7 41.5	−31.3	119.9	7 11.6	−32.1	120.0	6 41.5	−32.8	120.1	6 11.4	−33.6	120.2	5 41.2	−34.3	120.3	5 10.9	−35.0	120.4	23
24	8 11.3	−29.8	120.5	7 40.8	−30.6	120.6	7 10.2	−31.4	120.7	6 39.5	−32.1	120.8	6 08.7	−32.9	120.9	5 37.8	−33.6	121.0	5 06.9	−34.4	121.1	4 35.9	−35.2	121.2	24
25	7 41.5	−29.9	121.4	7 10.2	−30.7	121.5	6 38.8	−31.4	121.6	6 07.4	−32.3	121.7	5 35.8	−33.0	121.8	5 04.2	−33.7	121.8	4 32.5	−34.5	121.9	4 00.7	−35.1	122.0	25
26	7 11.6	−30.1	122.2	6 39.5	−30.8	122.4	6 07.4	−31.6	122.4	5 35.1	−32.3	122.5	5 02.8	−33.0	122.6	4 30.5	−33.8	122.7	3 58.0	−34.5	122.7	3 25.6	−35.2	122.8	26
27	6 41.5	−30.1	123.1	6 08.7	−30.9	123.2	5 35.8	−31.6	123.3	5 02.8	−32.3	123.4	4 29.8	−33.1	123.4	3 56.7	−33.8	123.5	3 23.5	−34.5	123.6	2 50.4	−35.3	123.6	27
28	6 11.4	−30.2	124.0	5 37.8	−30.9	124.1	5 04.2	−31.7	124.2	4 30.5	−32.5	124.2	3 56.7	−33.2	124.3	3 22.9	−33.9	124.3	2 49.0	−34.6	124.4	2 15.1	−35.3	124.4	28
29	5 41.2	−30.3	124.9	5 06.9	−31.0	124.9	4 32.5	−31.8	125.0	3 58.0	−32.4	125.1	3 23.5	−33.1	125.1	2 49.0	−33.9	125.2	2 14.4	−34.6	125.2	1 39.8	−35.2	125.2	29
30	5 10.9	−30.3	125.7	4 35.9	−31.1	125.8	4 00.7	−31.8	125.9	3 25.6	−32.6	125.9	2 50.4	−33.3	126.0	2 15.1	−33.9	126.0	1 39.8	−34.6	126.0	1 04.6	−35.4	126.0	30
31	4 40.6	−30.5	126.6	4 04.8	−31.2	126.7	3 28.9	−31.8	126.7	2 53.0	−32.5	126.8	2 17.1	−33.2	126.8	1 41.2	−34.0	126.8	1 05.2	−34.6	126.8	0 29.2	−35.3	126.8	31
32	4 10.1	−30.4	127.5	3 33.6	−31.2	127.5	2 57.1	−31.9	127.6	2 20.5	−32.6	127.6	1 43.9	−33.3	127.6	1 07.2	−33.9	127.6	0 30.6	−34.6	127.7	0 06.1	+35.3	52.3	32
33	3 39.7	−30.6	128.3	3 02.4	−31.2	128.4	2 25.2	−31.9	128.4	1 47.9	−32.6	128.4	1 10.6	−33.3	128.5	0 33.3	−34.0	128.5	0 04.0	+34.7	51.5	0 41.4	+35.3	51.5	33
34	3 09.1	−30.5	129.2	2 31.2	−31.3	129.2	1 53.3	−32.0	129.2	1 15.3	−32.6	129.3	0 37.3	−33.3	129.3	0 00.7	+34.0	50.7	0 38.7	+34.6	50.7	1 16.7	+35.3	50.7	34
35	2 38.6	−30.6	130.0	1 59.9	−31.2	130.1	1 21.3	−32.0	130.1	0 42.7	−32.7	130.1	0 04.0	−33.3	130.1	0 34.7	+33.9	49.9	1 13.3	+34.6	49.9	1 52.0	+35.2	49.9	35
36	2 08.0	−30.7	130.9	1 28.7	−31.4	130.9	0 49.3	−31.9	130.9	0 10.0	−32.6	130.9	0 29.3	+33.3	49.1	1 08.6	+34.0	49.1	1 47.9	+34.6	49.1	2 27.2	+35.2	49.1	36
37	1 37.3	−30.6	131.8	0 57.3	−31.3	131.8	0 17.4	−32.0	131.8	0 22.6	+32.6	48.2	1 02.6	+33.3	48.2	1 42.6	+33.9	48.2	2 22.5	+34.6	48.3	3 02.4	+35.2	48.3	37
38	1 06.7	−30.7	132.6	0 26.0	−31.3	132.6	0 14.6	+32.0	47.4	0 55.2	+32.7	47.4	1 35.9	+33.2	47.4	2 16.5	+33.9	47.4	2 57.1	+34.5	47.4	3 37.6	+35.2	47.5	38
39	0 36.0	−30.7	133.5	0 05.3	+31.3	46.5	0 46.6	+32.0	46.5	1 27.9	+32.6	46.5	2 09.1	+33.3	46.6	2 50.4	+33.8	46.6	3 31.6	+34.5	46.6	4 12.8	+35.1	46.7	39
40	0 05.3	−30.7	134.3	0 36.6	+31.3	45.7	1 18.6	+31.9	45.7	2 00.5	+32.6	45.7	2 42.4	+33.2	45.7	3 24.2	+33.9	45.8	4 06.1	+34.4	45.8	4 47.9	+35.0	45.9	40
41	0 25.4	+30.6	44.8	1 07.9	+31.3	44.8	1 50.5	+31.9	44.8	2 33.1	+32.5	44.9	3 15.6	+33.1	44.9	3 58.1	+33.7	44.9	4 40.5	+34.4	45.0	5 22.9	+35.0	45.0	41
42	0 56.0	+30.7	43.9	1 39.2	+31.3	44.0	2 22.4	+31.9	44.0	3 05.6	+32.5	44.0	3 48.7	+33.1	44.1	4 31.8	+33.7	44.1	5 14.9	+34.3	44.2	5 57.9	+34.9	44.2	42
43	1 26.7	+30.7	43.1	2 10.5	+31.3	43.1	2 54.3	+31.9	43.1	3 38.1	+32.5	43.2	4 21.8	+33.1	43.2	5 05.5	+33.7	43.3	5 49.2	+34.3	43.3	6 32.8	+34.9	43.4	43
44	1 57.4	+30.6	42.2	2 41.8	+31.2	42.2	3 26.2	+31.8	42.3	4 10.6	+32.4	42.3	4 54.9	+33.0	42.4	5 39.2	+33.6	42.4	6 23.5	+34.1	42.5	7 07.7	+34.7	42.6	44
45	2 28.0	+30.6	41.4	3 13.0	+31.2	41.4	3 58.0	+31.8	41.4	4 43.0	+32.3	41.5	5 27.9	+32.9	41.5	6 12.8	+33.5	41.6	6 57.6	+34.1	41.7	7 42.4	+34.6	41.8	45
46	2 58.6	+30.5	40.5	3 44.2	+31.1	40.5	4 29.8	+31.7	40.6	5 15.3	+32.3	40.6	6 00.8	+32.9	40.7	6 46.3	+33.4	40.8	7 31.7	+34.0	40.9	8 17.0	+34.6	40.9	46
47	3 29.1	+30.5	39.6	4 15.3	+31.1	39.7	5 01.5	+31.6	39.7	5 47.6	+32.2	39.8	6 33.7	+32.7	39.9	7 19.7	+33.3	39.9	8 05.7	+33.8	40.0	8 51.6	+34.4	40.1	47
48	3 59.6	+30.4	38.8	4 46.4	+31.0	38.8	5 33.1	+31.5	38.9	6 19.8	+32.1	38.9	7 06.4	+32.7	39.0	7 53.0	+33.2	39.1	8 39.5	+33.8	39.2	9 26.0	+34.3	39.3	48
49	4 30.0	+30.4	37.9	5 17.4	+30.9	38.0	6 04.6	+31.5	38.0	6 51.9	+32.0	38.1	7 39.1	+32.6	38.2	8 26.2	+33.1	38.3	9 13.3	+33.7	38.4	10 00.3	+34.2	38.5	49
50	5 00.4	+30.3	37.0	5 48.3	+30.8	37.1	6 36.1	+31.4	37.2	7 23.9	+31.9	37.2	8 11.7	+32.4	37.3	8 59.3	+33.0	37.4	9 47.0	+33.5	37.5	10 34.5	+34.1	37.6	50
51	5 30.7	+30.3	36.2	6 19.1	+30.8	36.2	7 07.5	+31.3	36.3	7 55.8	+31.9	36.4	8 44.1	+32.4	36.5	9 32.3	+32.9	36.6	10 20.5	+33.4	36.7	11 08.6	+33.9	36.8	51
52	6 01.0	+30.1	35.3	6 49.9	+30.7	35.4	7 38.8	+31.2	35.4	8 27.7	+31.7	35.5	9 16.5	+32.2	35.6	10 05.2	+32.8	35.7	10 53.9	+33.3	35.8	11 42.5	+33.8	35.9	52
53	6 31.1	+30.1	34.4	7 20.6	+30.6	34.5	8 10.0	+31.1	34.6	8 59.4	+31.6	34.7	9 48.7	+32.1	34.8	10 38.0	+32.6	34.9	11 27.2	+33.1	35.0	12 16.3	+33.6	35.1	53
54	7 01.2	+29.9	33.6	7 51.2	+30.4	33.6	8 41.1	+31.0	33.7	9 31.0	+31.4	33.8	10 20.8	+32.0	33.9	11 10.6	+32.4	34.0	12 00.3	+32.9	34.1	12 49.9	+33.4	34.2	54
55	7 31.1	+29.9	32.7	8 21.6	+30.4	32.8	9 12.1	+30.8	32.9	10 02.4	+31.4	32.9	10 52.8	+31.8	33.0	11 43.0	+32.3	33.2	12 33.2	+32.8	33.3	13 23.3	+33.3	33.4	55
56	8 01.0	+29.8	31.8	8 52.0	+30.2	31.9	9 42.9	+30.7	32.0	10 33.8	+31.1	32.1	11 24.6	+31.6	32.2	12 15.3	+32.2	32.3	13 06.0	+32.6	32.4	13 56.6	+33.1	32.5	56
57	8 30.8	+29.6	30.9	9 22.2	+30.1	31.0	10 13.6	+30.6	31.1	11 04.9	+31.1	31.2	11 56.2	+31.5	31.3	12 47.5	+31.9	31.4	13 38.6	+32.5	31.5	14 29.7	+32.9	31.7	57
58	9 00.4	+29.5	30.1	9 52.3	+30.0	30.1	10 44.2	+30.4	30.2	11 36.0	+30.9	30.3	12 27.7	+31.4	30.4	13 19.4	+31.8	30.6	14 11.1	+32.2	30.7	15 02.6	+32.8	30.8	58
59	9 29.9	+29.4	29.2	10 22.3	+29.8	29.3	11 14.6	+30.3	29.4	12 06.9	+30.7	29.5	12 59.1	+31.1	29.6	13 51.2	+31.6	29.7	14 43.3	+32.1	29.8	15 35.4	+32.5	29.9	59
60	9 59.3	+29.2	28.3	10 52.1	+29.7	28.4	11 44.9	+30.1	28.5	12 37.6	+30.5	28.6	13 30.2	+31.0	28.7	14 22.8	+31.5	28.8	15 15.4	+31.8	28.9	16 07.9	+32.3	29.1	60
61	10 28.5	+29.1	27.4	11 21.8	+29.5	27.5	12 15.0	+29.9	27.6	13 08.1	+30.4	27.7	14 01.2	+30.8	27.8	14 54.3	+31.2	27.9	15 47.2	+31.7	28.1	16 40.2	+32.0	28.2	61
62	10 57.6	+28.9	26.5	11 51.3	+29.3	26.6	12 44.9	+29.8	26.7	13 38.5	+30.1	26.8	14 32.0	+30.6	26.9	15 25.5	+31.0	27.0	16 18.9	+31.4	27.2	17 12.2	+31.9	27.3	62
63	11 26.5	+28.8	25.6	12 20.6	+29.2	25.7	13 14.7	+29.5	25.8	14 08.6	+30.0	25.9	15 02.6	+30.4	26.0	15 56.5	+30.8	26.2	16 50.3	+31.2	26.3	17 44.1	+31.6	26.4	63
64	11 55.3	+28.6	24.7	12 49.8	+29.0	24.8	13 44.2	+29.4	24.9	14 38.6	+29.8	25.0	15 33.0	+30.1	25.1	16 27.3	+30.5	25.3	17 21.5	+30.9	25.4	18 15.7	+31.3	25.5	64
65	12 23.9	+28.4	23.8	13 18.8	+28.8	23.9	14 13.6	+29.2	24.0	15 08.4	+29.5	24.1	16 03.1	+30.0	24.2	16 57.8	+30.3	24.4	17 52.4	+30.7	24.5	18 47.0	+31.1	24.6	65
66	12 52.3	+28.3	22.9	13 47.6	+28.6	23.0	14 42.8	+28.9	23.1	15 37.9	+29.4	23.2	16 33.1	+29.7	23.3	17 28.1	+30.1	23.5	18 23.1	+30.5	23.6	19 18.1	+30.8	23.7	66
67	13 20.6	+28.0	22.0	14 16.2	+28.4	22.1	15 11.7	+28.8	22.2	16 07.3	+29.1	22.3	17 02.8	+29.4	22.4	17 58.2	+29.8	22.5	18 53.6	+30.1	22.7	19 48.9	+30.5	22.8	67
68	13 48.6	+27.8	21.1	14 44.6	+28.1	21.2	15 40.5	+28.5	21.3	16 36.4	+28.8	21.4	17 32.2	+29.2	21.5	18 28.0	+29.6	21.6	19 23.7	+29.9	21.8	20 19.4	+30.3	21.9	68
69	14 16.4	+27.7	20.2	15 12.7	+28.0	20.3	16 09.0	+28.3	20.4	17 05.2	+28.6	20.5	18 01.4	+29.0	20.6	18 57.6	+29.2	20.7	19 53.6	+29.7	20.8	20 49.7	+30.0	21.0	69
70	14 44.1	+27.4	19.3	15 40.7	+27.7	19.4	16 37.3	+28.0	19.5	17 33.8	+28.4	19.6	18 30.4	+28.6	19.7	19 26.8	+29.0	19.8	20 23.3	+29.3	19.9	21 19.7	+29.6	20.0	70
71	15 11.5	+27.2	18.4	16 08.4	+27.5	18.4	17 05.3	+27.8	18.5	18 02.2	+28.1	18.6	18 59.0	+28.4	18.7	19 55.8	+28.7	18.9	20 52.6	+29.0	19.0	21 49.3	+29.3	19.1	71
72	15 38.7	+26.9	17.4	16 35.9	+27.2	17.5	17 33.1	+27.5	17.6	18 30.3	+27.8	17.7	19 27.4	+28.1	17.8	20 24.5	+28.4	17.9	21 21.6	+28.7	18.0	22 18.6	+29.0	18.2	72
73	16 05.6	+26.7	16.5	17 03.1	+27.0	16.6	18 00.6	+27.3	16.7	18 58.1	+27.5	16.8	19 55.5	+27.8	16.9	20 52.9	+28.1	17.0	21 50.3	+28.4	17.1	22 47.6	+28.7	17.2	73
74	16 32.3	+26.5	15.6	17 30.1	+26.7	15.7	18 27.9	+27.0	15.7	19 25.6	+27.3	15.8	20 23.3	+27.5	15.9	21 21.0	+27.8	16.0	22 18.7	+28.0	16.2	23 16.3	+28.3	16.3	74
75	16 58.8	+26.2	14.6	17 56.8	+26.5	14.7	18 54.9	+26.7	14.8	19 52.9	+26.9	14.9	20 50.8	+27.2	15.0	21 48.8	+27.4	15.1	22 46.7	+27.7	15.2	23 44.6	+27.9	15.3	75
76	17 25.0	+25.9	13.7	18 23.3	+26.2	13.8	19 21.6	+26.4	13.9	20 19.8	+26.6	13.9	21 18.0	+26.9	14.0	22 16.2	+27.1	14.1	23 14.4	+27.3	14.2	24 12.5	+27.6	14.3	76
77	17 50.9	+25.7	12.7	18 49.5	+25.8	12.8	19 48.0	+26.0	12.9	20 46.4	+26.3	13.0	21 44.9	+26.5	13.1	22 43.3	+26.8	13.2	23 41.7	+27.0	13.3	24 40.1	+27.2	13.4	77
78	18 16.6	+25.4	11.8	19 15.3	+25.6	11.9	20 14.0	+25.8	11.9	21 12.7	+26.0	12.0	22 11.4	+26.2	12.1	23 10.1	+26.4	12.2	24 08.7	+26.6	12.3	25 07.3	+26.8	12.4	78
79	18 42.0	+25.1	10.8	19 40.9	+25.3	10.9	20 39.8	+25.5	11.0	21 38.7	+25.6	11.0	22 37.6	+25.8	11.1	23 36.5	+26.0	11.2	24 35.3	+26.2	11.3	25 34.1	+26.4	11.4	79
80	19 07.1	+24.8	9.9	20 06.2	+24.9	9.9	21 05.3	+25.1	10.0	22 04.3	+25.3	10.1	23 03.4	+25.5	10.1	24 02.5	+25.6	10.2	25 01.5	+25.8	10.3	26 00.5	+26.0	10.4	80
81	19 31.9	+24.4	8.9	20 31.1	+24.7	9.0	21 30.4	+24.8	9.0	22 29.6	+25.0	9.1	23 28.9	+25.1	9.2	24 28.1	+25.3	9.2	25 27.3	+25.4	9.3	26 26.5	+25.6	9.4	81
82	19 56.3	+24.2	7.9	20 55.8	+24.2	8.0	21 55.2	+24.4	8.1	22 54.6	+24.5	8.1	23 54.0	+24.7	8.2	24 53.4	+24.8	8.2	25 52.7	+25.0	8.3	26 52.1	+25.1	8.4	82
83	20 20.5	+23.8	7.0	21 20.0	+24.0	7.0	22 19.6	+24.1	7.1	23 19.1	+24.2	7.1	24 18.7	+24.3	7.2	25 18.2	+24.4	7.2	26 17.7	+24.6	7.3	27 17.2	+24.7	7.4	83
84	20 44.3	+23.5	6.0	21 44.0	+23.6	6.0	22 43.7	+23.7	6.1	23 43.3	+23.8	6.1	24 43.0	+23.9	6.2	25 42.6	+24.0	6.2	26 42.3	+24.1	6.3	27 41.9	+24.2	6.3	84
85	21 07.8	+23.2	5.0	22 07.6	+23.2	5.0	23 07.4	+23.3	5.1	24 07.1	+23.4	5.1	25 06.9	+23.5	5.2	26 06.6	+23.6	5.2	27 06.4	+23.7	5.2	28 06.1	+23.8	5.3	85
86	21 31.0	+22.8	4.0	22 30.8	+22.9	4.0	23 30.7	+22.9	4.1	24 30.5	+23.0	4.1	25 30.4	+23.0	4.1	26 30.2	+23.2	4.2	27 30.1	+23.2	4.2	28 29.9	+23.3	4.2	86
87	21 53.8	+22.4	3.0	22 53.7	+22.5	3.0	23 53.5	+22.6	3.1	24 53.4	+22.6	3.1	25 53.4	+22.7	3.1	26 53.4	+22.6	3.1	27 53.3	+22.7	3.2	28 53.2	+22.8	3.2	87
88	22 16.2	+22.1	2.0	23 16.2	+22.1	2.0	24 16.2	+22.1	2.0	25 16.1	+22.2	2.1	26 16.1	+22.2	2.1	27 16.0	+22.3	2.1	28 16.0	+22.2	2.1	29 16.0	+22.2	2.1	88
89	22 38.3	+21.7	1.0	23 38.3	+21.7	1.0	24 38.3	+21.7	1.0	25 38.3	+21.7	1.0	26 38.3	+21.7	1.0	27 38.3	+21.7	1.1	28 38.2	+21.8	1.1	29 38.2	+21.8	1.1	89
90	23 00.0	+21.3	0.0	24 00.0	+21.3	0.0	25 00.0	+21.3	0.0	26 00.0	+21.3	0.0	27 00.0	+21.3	0.0	28 00.0	+21.3	0.0	29 00.0	+21.2	0.0	30 00.0	+21.2	0.0	90
	23°			24°			25°			26°			27°			28°			29°			30°			

S. Lat. {L.H.A. greater than 180° ....Zn=180°−Z; L.H.A. less than 180°...........Zn=180°+Z

LATITUDE SAME NAME AS DECLINATION — L.H.A. 111°, 249°

70°, 290° L.H.A. LATITUDE SAME NAME AS DECLINATION N. Lat. {L.H.A. greater than 180° .....Zn=Z
L.H.A. less than 180°............Zn=360°−Z

Dec.	23° Hc	d	Z	24° Hc	d	Z	25° Hc	d	Z	26° Hc	d	Z	27° Hc	d	Z	28° Hc	d	Z	29° Hc	d	Z	30° Hc	d	Z	Dec.
°	° ′	′	°	° ′	′	°	° ′	′	°	° ′	′	°	° ′	′	°	° ′	′	°	° ′	′	°	° ′	′	°	°
0	18 21.0	+24.6	98.1	18 12.4	+25.6	98.4	18 03.5	+26.5	98.7	17 54.2	+27.5	99.1	17 44.6	+28.4	99.4	17 34.6	+29.4	99.7	17 24.3	+30.4	100.0	17 13.8	+31.3	100.3	0
1	18 45.6	+24.2	97.1	18 38.0	+25.2	97.5	18 30.0	+26.2	97.8	18 21.7	+27.2	98.1	18 13.0	+28.2	98.5	18 04.0	+29.2	98.8	17 54.7	+30.1	99.1	17 45.1	+31.0	99.4	1
2	19 09.8	+24.0	96.2	19 03.2	+25.0	96.5	18 56.2	+26.0	96.9	18 48.9	+27.0	97.2	18 41.2	+28.0	97.5	18 33.2	+28.9	97.9	18 24.8	+29.9	98.2	18 16.1	+30.8	98.5	2
3	19 33.8	+23.6	95.2	19 28.2	+24.6	95.5	19 22.2	+25.7	95.9	19 15.9	+26.6	96.2	19 09.2	+27.6	96.6	19 02.1	+28.6	96.9	18 54.7	+29.5	97.3	18 46.9	+30.5	97.6	3
4	19 57.4	+23.4	94.2	19 52.8	+24.4	94.6	19 47.9	+25.3	94.9	19 42.5	+26.4	95.3	19 36.8	+27.3	95.7	19 30.7	+28.3	96.0	19 24.2	+29.3	96.4	19 17.4	+30.3	96.7	4
5	20 20.8	+22.9	93.2	20 17.2	+24.0	93.6	20 13.2	+25.0	94.0	20 08.9	+26.0	94.3	20 04.1	+27.1	94.7	19 59.0	+28.1	95.1	19 53.5	+29.0	95.4	19 47.7	+29.9	95.8	5
6	20 43.7	+22.7	92.2	20 41.2	+23.7	92.6	20 38.2	+24.8	93.0	20 34.9	+25.7	93.4	20 31.2	+26.7	93.8	20 27.1	+27.7	94.1	20 22.5	+28.8	94.5	20 17.6	+29.7	94.9	6
7	21 06.4	+22.3	91.3	21 04.9	+23.3	91.6	21 03.0	+24.3	92.0	21 00.6	+25.4	92.4	20 57.9	+26.4	92.8	20 54.8	+27.4	93.2	20 51.3	+28.4	93.6	20 47.3	+29.4	93.9	7
8	21 28.7	+21.9	90.3	21 28.2	+23.0	90.7	21 27.3	+24.0	91.0	21 26.0	+25.1	91.4	21 24.3	+26.1	91.8	21 22.2	+27.1	92.2	21 19.7	+28.0	92.6	21 16.7	+29.1	93.0	8
9	21 50.6	+21.6	89.3	21 51.2	+22.6	89.7	21 51.3	+23.7	90.1	21 51.1	+24.7	90.5	21 50.4	+25.7	90.9	21 49.3	+26.7	91.3	21 47.7	+27.8	91.7	21 45.8	+28.7	92.1	9
10	22 12.2	+21.2	88.3	22 13.8	+22.3	88.7	22 15.0	+23.3	89.1	22 15.8	+24.3	89.5	22 16.1	+25.4	89.9	22 16.0	+26.4	90.3	22 15.5	+27.4	90.7	22 14.5	+28.4	91.1	10
11	22 33.4	+20.8	87.2	22 36.1	+21.9	87.7	22 38.3	+23.0	88.1	22 40.1	+24.0	88.5	22 41.5	+25.0	88.9	22 42.4	+26.1	89.3	22 42.9	+27.1	89.7	22 42.9	+28.1	90.2	11
12	22 54.2	+20.5	86.2	22 58.0	+21.5	86.6	23 01.3	+22.5	87.1	23 04.1	+23.6	87.5	23 06.5	+24.7	87.9	23 08.5	+25.6	88.3	23 10.0	+26.7	88.8	23 11.0	+27.8	89.2	12
13	23 14.7	+20.0	85.2	23 19.5	+21.1	85.6	23 23.8	+22.2	86.1	23 27.7	+23.2	86.5	23 31.2	+24.2	86.9	23 34.1	+25.4	87.4	23 36.7	+26.3	87.8	23 38.8	+27.3	88.2	13
14	23 34.7	+19.6	84.2	23 40.6	+20.7	84.6	23 46.0	+21.7	85.0	23 50.9	+22.9	85.5	23 55.4	+23.9	85.9	23 59.5	+24.9	86.4	24 03.0	+26.0	86.8	24 06.1	+27.0	87.3	14
15	23 54.3	+19.3	83.1	24 01.3	+20.3	83.6	24 07.7	+21.4	84.0	24 13.8	+22.4	84.5	24 19.3	+23.5	84.9	24 24.4	+24.5	85.4	24 29.0	+25.6	85.8	24 33.1	+26.6	86.3	15
16	24 13.6	+18.7	82.1	24 21.6	+19.8	82.6	24 29.1	+20.9	83.0	24 36.2	+22.0	83.5	24 42.8	+23.1	83.9	24 48.9	+24.1	84.4	24 54.6	+25.1	84.8	24 59.7	+26.2	85.3	16
17	24 32.3	+18.4	81.1	24 41.4	+19.5	81.5	24 50.0	+20.6	82.0	24 58.2	+21.6	82.4	25 05.9	+22.6	82.9	25 13.0	+23.7	83.4	25 19.7	+24.8	83.8	25 25.9	+25.8	84.3	17
18	24 50.7	+17.9	80.0	25 00.9	+19.0	80.5	25 10.6	+20.0	80.9	25 19.8	+21.1	81.4	25 28.5	+22.2	81.9	25 36.7	+23.3	82.3	25 44.5	+24.3	82.8	25 51.7	+25.4	83.3	18
19	25 08.6	+17.5	79.0	25 19.9	+18.5	79.4	25 30.6	+19.7	79.9	25 40.9	+20.7	80.4	25 50.7	+21.8	80.8	26 00.0	+22.9	81.3	26 08.8	+23.9	81.8	26 17.1	+25.0	82.3	19
20	25 26.1	+17.0	77.9	25 38.4	+18.1	78.4	25 50.3	+19.1	78.8	26 01.6	+20.3	79.3	26 12.5	+21.3	79.8	26 22.9	+22.4	80.3	26 32.7	+23.5	80.8	26 42.1	+24.5	81.3	20
21	25 43.1	+16.5	76.8	25 56.5	+17.6	77.3	26 09.4	+18.8	77.8	26 21.9	+19.8	78.3	26 33.8	+20.9	78.8	26 45.3	+21.9	79.3	26 56.2	+23.0	79.8	27 06.6	+24.1	80.3	21
22	25 59.6	+16.1	75.8	26 14.1	+17.2	76.2	26 28.2	+18.2	76.7	26 41.7	+19.3	77.2	26 54.7	+20.4	77.7	27 07.2	+21.5	78.2	27 19.2	+22.6	78.7	27 30.7	+23.6	79.2	22
23	26 15.7	+15.6	74.7	26 31.3	+16.7	75.2	26 46.4	+17.8	75.7	27 01.0	+18.9	76.2	27 15.1	+19.9	76.7	27 28.7	+21.0	77.2	27 41.8	+22.1	77.7	27 54.3	+23.2	78.2	23
24	26 31.3	+15.1	73.6	26 48.0	+16.2	74.1	27 04.2	+17.2	74.6	27 19.9	+18.3	75.1	27 35.0	+19.5	75.6	27 49.7	+20.5	76.1	28 03.9	+21.6	76.6	28 17.5	+22.7	77.1	24
25	26 46.4	+14.6	72.5	27 04.2	+15.7	73.0	27 21.4	+16.8	73.5	27 38.2	+17.9	74.0	27 54.5	+18.9	74.5	28 10.2	+20.1	75.0	28 25.5	+21.1	75.6	28 40.2	+22.1	76.1	25
26	27 01.0	+14.1	71.5	27 19.9	+15.1	71.9	27 38.2	+16.3	72.4	27 56.1	+17.3	72.9	28 13.4	+18.5	73.4	28 30.3	+19.5	74.0	28 46.6	+20.6	74.5	29 02.3	+21.7	75.0	26
27	27 15.1	+13.6	70.4	27 35.0	+14.7	70.8	27 54.5	+15.7	71.3	28 13.4	+16.9	71.9	28 31.9	+17.9	72.4	28 49.8	+19.0	72.9	29 07.2	+20.0	73.4	29 24.0	+21.2	74.0	27
28	27 28.7	+13.1	69.3	27 49.7	+14.2	69.8	28 10.2	+15.3	70.3	28 30.3	+16.3	70.8	28 49.8	+17.4	71.3	29 08.8	+18.4	71.8	29 27.2	+19.6	72.3	29 45.2	+20.6	72.9	28
29	27 41.8	+12.5	68.2	28 03.9	+13.6	68.7	28 25.5	+14.7	69.2	28 46.6	+15.7	69.7	29 07.2	+16.8	70.2	29 27.2	+18.0	70.7	29 46.8	+19.0	71.2	30 05.8	+20.1	71.8	29
30	27 54.3	+12.1	67.1	28 17.5	+13.1	67.5	28 40.2	+14.1	68.0	29 02.3	+15.3	68.6	29 24.0	+16.3	69.1	29 45.2	+17.4	69.6	30 05.8	+18.5	70.2	30 25.9	+19.6	70.7	30
31	28 06.4	+11.4	65.9	28 30.6	+12.5	66.4	28 54.3	+13.6	66.9	29 17.6	+14.7	67.5	29 40.3	+15.8	68.0	30 02.6	+16.8	68.5	30 24.3	+17.9	69.1	30 45.5	+19.0	69.6	31
32	28 17.8	+11.0	64.8	28 43.1	+12.0	65.3	29 07.9	+13.1	65.8	29 32.3	+14.1	66.3	29 56.1	+15.2	66.9	30 19.4	+16.3	67.4	30 42.2	+17.3	67.9	31 04.5	+18.4	68.5	32
33	28 28.8	+10.4	63.7	28 55.1	+11.5	64.2	29 21.0	+12.5	64.7	29 46.4	+13.5	65.2	30 11.3	+14.6	65.7	30 35.7	+15.7	66.3	30 59.5	+16.8	66.8	31 22.9	+17.8	67.4	33
34	28 39.2	+9.8	62.6	29 06.6	+10.8	63.1	29 33.5	+11.9	63.6	29 59.9	+13.0	64.1	30 25.9	+14.0	64.6	30 51.4	+15.1	65.2	31 16.3	+16.2	65.7	31 40.7	+17.3	66.3	34
35	28 49.0	+9.3	61.5	29 17.4	+10.3	62.0	29 45.4	+11.4	62.5	30 12.9	+12.4	63.0	30 39.9	+13.5	63.5	31 06.5	+14.5	64.0	31 32.5	+15.6	64.6	31 58.0	+16.6	65.1	35
36	28 58.3	+8.7	60.3	29 27.7	+9.8	60.8	29 56.8	+10.7	61.3	30 25.3	+11.8	61.8	30 53.4	+12.9	62.4	31 21.0	+13.9	62.9	31 48.1	+14.9	63.4	32 14.6	+16.1	64.0	36
37	29 07.0	+8.1	59.2	29 37.5	+9.1	59.7	30 07.5	+10.2	60.2	30 37.1	+11.2	60.7	31 06.3	+12.2	61.2	31 34.9	+13.3	61.8	32 03.0	+14.4	62.3	32 30.7	+15.4	62.9	37
38	29 15.1	+7.6	58.1	29 46.6	+8.6	58.6	30 17.7	+9.6	59.0	30 48.3	+10.6	59.6	31 18.5	+11.6	60.1	31 48.2	+12.7	60.6	32 17.4	+13.7	61.2	32 46.1	+14.8	61.7	38
39	29 22.7	+6.9	56.9	29 55.2	+8.0	57.4	30 27.3	+9.0	57.9	30 58.9	+10.0	58.4	31 30.1	+11.1	58.9	32 00.9	+12.0	59.5	32 31.1	+13.1	60.0	33 00.9	+14.1	60.6	39
40	29 29.6	+6.4	55.8	30 03.2	+7.3	56.3	30 36.3	+8.3	56.8	31 08.9	+9.4	57.3	31 41.2	+10.4	57.8	32 12.9	+11.4	58.3	32 44.2	+12.5	58.8	33 15.0	+13.5	59.4	40
41	29 36.0	+5.8	54.7	30 10.5	+6.8	55.1	30 44.6	+7.8	55.6	31 18.3	+8.8	56.1	31 51.6	+9.7	56.6	32 24.3	+10.8	57.1	32 56.7	+11.8	57.7	33 28.5	+12.8	58.2	41
42	29 41.8	+5.2	53.5	30 17.3	+6.2	54.0	30 52.4	+7.2	54.5	31 27.1	+8.1	54.9	32 01.3	+9.2	55.5	32 35.1	+10.2	56.0	33 08.5	+11.1	56.5	33 41.3	+12.2	57.1	42
43	29 47.0	+4.7	52.4	30 23.5	+5.6	52.8	30 59.6	+6.5	53.3	31 35.2	+7.5	53.8	32 10.5	+8.4	54.3	32 45.3	+9.4	54.8	33 19.6	+10.5	55.3	33 53.5	+11.5	55.9	43
44	29 51.7	+4.0	51.2	30 29.1	+4.9	51.7	31 06.1	+5.9	52.1	31 42.7	+6.9	52.6	32 18.9	+7.9	53.1	32 54.7	+8.8	53.6	33 30.1	+9.8	54.2	34 05.0	+10.8	54.7	44
45	29 55.7	+3.4	50.1	30 34.0	+4.3	50.5	31 12.0	+5.3	51.0	31 49.6	+6.2	51.4	32 26.8	+7.1	51.9	33 03.5	+8.2	52.4	33 39.9	+9.1	53.0	34 15.8	+10.1	53.5	45
46	29 59.1	+2.8	48.9	30 38.3	+3.8	49.3	31 17.3	+4.6	49.8	31 55.8	+5.6	50.3	32 33.9	+6.6	50.8	33 11.7	+7.5	51.3	33 49.0	+8.5	51.8	34 25.9	+9.4	52.3	46
47	30 01.9	+2.2	47.8	30 42.1	+3.1	48.2	31 21.9	+4.0	48.6	32 01.4	+4.9	49.1	32 40.5	+5.8	49.6	33 19.2	+6.7	50.1	33 57.5	+7.7	50.6	34 35.3	+8.7	51.1	47
48	30 04.1	+1.6	46.6	30 45.2	+2.4	47.0	31 25.9	+3.4	47.5	32 06.3	+4.2	47.9	32 46.3	+5.2	48.4	33 25.9	+6.2	48.9	34 05.2	+7.0	49.4	34 44.0	+8.0	49.9	48
49	30 05.7	+1.0	45.4	30 47.6	+1.9	45.9	31 29.3	+2.7	46.3	32 10.5	+3.7	46.7	32 51.5	+4.5	47.2	33 32.1	+5.4	47.7	34 12.2	+6.4	48.2	34 52.0	+7.3	48.7	49
50	30 06.7	+0.4	44.3	30 49.5	+1.2	44.7	31 32.0	+2.1	45.1	32 14.2	+2.9	45.6	32 56.0	+3.8	46.0	33 37.5	+4.7	46.5	34 18.6	+5.6	47.0	34 59.3	+6.6	47.5	50
51	30 07.1	−0.2	43.1	30 50.7	+0.6	43.5	31 34.1	+1.4	44.0	32 17.1	+2.3	44.4	32 59.8	+3.2	44.8	33 42.2	+4.0	45.3	34 24.2	+5.0	45.8	35 05.9	+5.8	46.3	51
52	30 06.9	−0.9	42.0	30 51.3	0.0	42.4	31 35.5	+0.8	42.8	32 19.4	+1.6	43.2	33 03.0	+2.5	43.6	33 46.2	+3.4	44.1	34 29.2	+4.2	44.6	35 11.7	+5.1	45.1	52
53	30 06.0	−1.4	40.8	30 51.3	−0.6	41.2	31 36.3	+0.2	41.6	32 21.0	+1.0	42.0	33 05.5	+1.8	42.5	33 49.6	+2.6	42.9	34 33.4	+3.5	43.4	35 16.8	+4.4	43.8	53
54	30 04.6	−2.0	39.7	30 50.7	−1.3	40.0	31 36.5	−0.5	40.4	32 22.0	+0.3	40.8	33 07.3	+1.1	41.3	33 52.2	+1.9	41.7	34 36.9	+2.7	42.2	35 21.2	+3.6	42.6	54
55	30 02.6	−2.7	38.5	30 49.4	−1.9	38.9	31 36.0	−1.1	39.3	32 22.3	−0.3	39.7	33 08.4	+0.4	40.1	33 54.1	+1.3	40.5	34 39.6	+2.1	40.9	35 24.8	+2.9	41.4	55
56	29 59.9	−3.2	37.4	30 47.5	−2.5	37.7	31 34.9	−1.8	38.1	32 22.0	−1.1	38.5	33 08.8	−0.3	38.9	33 55.4	+0.5	39.3	34 41.7	+1.3	39.7	35 27.7	+2.1	40.2	56
57	29 56.7	−3.9	36.2	30 45.0	−3.1	36.5	31 33.1	−2.4	36.9	32 20.9	−1.6	37.3	33 08.5	−0.9	37.7	33 55.9	−0.2	38.1	34 43.0	+0.6	38.5	35 29.8	+1.4	38.9	57
58	29 52.8	−4.4	35.1	30 41.9	−3.8	35.4	31 30.7	−3.1	35.7	32 19.3	−2.4	36.1	33 07.6	−1.6	36.5	33 55.7	−0.9	36.9	34 43.6	−0.1	37.3	35 31.2	+0.6	37.7	58
59	29 48.4	−5.1	33.9	30 38.1	−4.4	34.2	31 27.6	−3.7	34.6	32 16.9	−3.0	34.9	33 06.0	−2.3	35.3	33 54.8	−1.5	35.7	34 43.5	−0.9	36.1	35 31.8	−0.1	36.5	59
60	29 43.3	−5.6	32.8	30 33.7	−5.0	33.1	31 23.9	−4.3	33.4	32 13.9	−3.7	33.7	33 03.7	−3.0	34.1	33 53.3	−2.3	34.5	34 42.6	−1.6	34.9	35 31.7	−0.8	35.3	60
61	29 37.7	−6.2	31.6	30 28.7	−5.6	31.9	31 19.6	−5.0	32.2	32 10.2	−4.3	32.6	33 00.7	−3.7	32.9	33 51.0	−3.0	33.3	34 41.0	−2.3	33.6	35 30.9	−1.6	34.0	61
62	29 31.5	−6.8	30.5	30 23.1	−6.2	30.8	31 14.6	−5.6	31.1	32 05.9	−5.0	31.4	32 57.0	−4.3	31.7	33 48.0	−3.7	32.1	34 38.7	−3.0	32.4	35 29.3	−2.4	32.8	62
63	29 24.7	−7.4	29.3	30 16.9	−6.8	29.6	31 09.0	−6.2	29.9	32 00.9	−5.6	30.2	32 52.7	−5.0	30.5	33 44.3	−4.4	30.9	34 35.7	−3.7	31.2	35 26.9	−3.1	31.6	63
64	29 17.3	−8.0	28.2	30 10.1	−7.4	28.5	31 02.8	−6.9	28.7	31 55.3	−6.3	29.0	32 47.7	−5.7	29.3	33 39.9	−5.1	29.7	34 32.0	−4.5	30.0	35 23.8	−3.8	30.4	64
65	29 09.3	−8.5	27.0	30 02.7	−8.0	27.3	30 55.9	−7.4	27.6	31 49.0	−6.9	27.9	32 42.0	−6.3	28.2	33 34.8	−5.7	28.5	34 27.5	−5.2	28.8	35 20.0	−4.6	29.1	65
66	29 00.8	−9.1	25.9	29 54.7	−8.6	26.2	30 48.5	−8.1	26.4	31 42.1	−7.5	26.7	32 35.7	−7.0	27.0	33 29.1	−6.5	27.3	34 22.3	−5.9	27.6	35 15.4	−5.3	27.9	66
67	28 51.7	−9.7	24.8	29 46.1	−9.2	25.0	30 40.4	−8.7	25.3	31 34.6	−8.2	25.5	32 28.7	−7.7	25.8	33 22.6	−7.1	26.1	34 16.4	−6.5	26.4	35 10.1	−6.0	26.7	67
68	28 42.0	−10.3	23.7	29 36.9	−9.8	23.9	30 31.7	−9.3	24.1	31 26.4	−8.8	24.4	32 21.0	−8.3	24.6	33 15.5	−7.8	24.9	34 09.9	−7.3	25.2	35 04.1	−6.8	25.5	68
69	28 31.7	−10.7	22.5	29 27.1	−10.3	22.8	30 22.4	−9.9	23.0	31 17.6	−9.4	23.2	32 12.7	−9.0	23.5	33 07.7	−8.5	23.7	34 02.6	−8.0	24.0	34 57.3	−7.5	24.3	69
70	28 21.0	−11.4	21.4	29 16.8	−10.9	21.6	30 12.5	−10.5	21.8	31 08.2	−10.1	22.1	32 03.7	−9.6	22.3	32 59.2	−9.1	22.5	33 54.6	−8.7	22.8	34 49.8	−8.2	23.1	70
71	28 09.6	−11.8	20.3	29 05.9	−11.5	20.5	30 02.0	−11.0	20.7	30 58.1	−10.6	20.9	31 54.1	−10.2	21.1	32 50.1	−9.8	21.4	33 45.9	−9.4	21.6	34 41.6	−8.9	21.8	71
72	27 57.8	−12.4	19.2	28 54.4	−12.0	19.4	29 51.0	−11.7	19.6	30 47.5	−11.3	19.8	31 43.9	−10.9	20.0	32 40.3	−10.5	20.2	33 36.5	−10.0	20.4	34 32.7	−9.6	20.6	72
73	27 45.4	−13.0	18.1	28 42.4	−12.6	18.3	29 39.3	−12.2	18.4	30 36.2	−11.8	18.6	31 33.0	−11.4	18.8	32 29.8	−11.1	19.0	33 26.5	−10.7	19.2	34 23.1	−10.3	19.4	73
74	27 32.4	−13.4	17.0	28 29.8	−13.1	17.1	29 27.1	−12.8	17.3	30 24.4	−12.5	17.5	31 21.6	−12.1	17.7	32 18.7	−11.7	17.8	33 15.8	−11.4	18.0	34 12.8	−11.0	18.3	74
75	27 19.0	−14.0	15.9	28 16.7	−13.7	16.0	29 14.3	−13.3	16.2	30 11.9	−13.0	16.3	31 09.5	−12.7	16.5	32 07.0	−12.4	16.7	33 04.4	−12.0	16.9	34 01.8	−11.7	17.1	75
76	27 05.0	−14.5	14.8	28 03.0	−14.2	14.9	29 01.0	−13.9	15.1	29 58.9	−13.6	15.2	30 56.8	−13.3	15.4	31 54.6	−13.0	15.5	32 52.4	−12.7	15.7	33 50.1	−12.4	15.9	76
77	26 50.5	−14.9	13.7	27 48.8	−14.7	13.8	28 47.1	−14.5	14.0	29 45.3	−14.2	14.1	30 43.5	−13.9	14.2	31 41.6	−13.6	14.4	32 39.7	−13.3	14.5	33 37.7	−13.0	14.7	77
78	26 35.6	−15.5	12.6	27 34.1	−15.2	12.7	28 32.6	−14.9	12.9	29 31.1	−14.7	13.0	30 29.6	−14.5	13.1	31 28.0	−14.2	13.2	32 26.4	−14.0	13.4	33 24.7	−13.7	13.5	78
79	26 20.1	−15.9	11.5	27 18.9	−15.7	11.6	28 17.7	−15.5	11.7	29 16.4	−15.3	11.9	30 15.1	−15.1	12.0	31 13.8	−14.8	12.1	32 12.4	−14.5	12.2	33 11.0	−14.3	12.4	79
80	26 04.2	−16.4	10.5	27 03.2	−16.2	10.6	28 02.2	−16.1	10.7	29 01.1	−15.8	10.8	30 00.0	−15.6	10.9	30 59.0	−15.4	11.0	31 57.9	−15.2	11.1	32 56.7	−14.9	11.2	80
81	25 47.8	−16.9	9.4	26 47.0	−16.7	9.5	27 46.1	−16.5	9.6	28 45.3	−16.4	9.7	29 44.4	−16.1	9.7	30 43.6	−16.0	9.8	31 42.7	−15.8	10.0	32 41.8	−15.6	10.1	81
82	25 30.9	−17.4	8.3	26 30.3	−17.2	8.4	27 29.6	−17.0	8.5	28 28.9	−16.8	8.6	29 28.3	−16.8	8.6	30 27.6	−16.6	8.7	31 26.9	−16.4	8.8	32 26.2	−16.3	8.9	82
83	25 13.5	−17.7	7.3	26 13.1	−17.7	7.3	27 12.6	−17.6	7.4	28 12.1	−17.4	7.5	29 11.5	−17.2	7.5	30 11.0	−17.1	7.6	31 10.5	−17.0	7.7	32 09.9	−16.8	7.8	83
84	24 55.8	−18.3	6.2	25 55.4	−18.1	6.3	26 55.0	−18.0	6.3	27 54.7	−17.9	6.4	28 54.3	−17.8	6.4	29 53.9	−17.7	6.5	30 53.5	−17.5	6.6	31 53.1	−17.4	6.6	84
85	24 37.5	−18.6	5.2	25 37.3	−18.6	5.2	26 37.0	−18.5	5.3	27 36.8	−18.4	5.3	28 36.5	−18.3	5.4	29 36.2	−18.2	5.4	30 36.0	−18.1	5.5	31 35.7	−18.0	5.5	85
86	24 18.9	−19.1	4.1	25 18.7	−19.0	4.2	26 18.5	−18.9	4.2	27 18.4	−18.9	4.2	28 18.2	−18.8	4.3	29 18.0	−18.7	4.3	30 17.9	−18.7	4.4	31 17.7	−18.6	4.4	86
87	23 59.8	−19.6	3.1	24 59.7	−19.5	3.1	25 59.6	−19.4	3.1	26 59.5	−19.4	3.2	27 59.4	−19.3	3.2	28 59.3	−19.3	3.2	29 59.2	−19.2	3.3	30 59.1	−19.1	3.3	87
88	23 40.2	−19.9	2.1	24 40.2	−19.9	2.1	25 40.2	−19.9	2.1	26 40.1	−19.8	2.1	27 40.1	−19.8	2.1	28 40.0	−19.7	2.1	29 40.0	−19.7	2.2	30 40.0	−19.7	2.2	88
89	23 20.3	−20.3	1.0	24 20.3	−20.3	1.0	25 20.3	−20.3	1.0	26 20.3	−20.3	1.0	27 20.3	−20.3	1.1	28 20.3	−20.3	1.1	29 20.3	−20.3	1.1	30 20.3	−20.3	1.1	89
90	23 00.0	−20.7	0.0	24 00.0	−20.7	0.0	25 00.0	−20.7	0.0	26 00.0	−20.7	0.0	27 00.0	−20.8	0.0	28 00.0	−20.8	0.0	29 00.0	−20.8	0.0	30 00.0	−20.8	0.0	90
	23°			24°			25°			26°			27°			28°			29°			30°			

70°, 290° L.H.A. LATITUDE SAME NAME AS DECLINATION

324

LATITUDE **CONTRARY** NAME TO DECLINATION **L.H.A. 70°, 290°**

Dec.	23° Hc	d	Z	24° Hc	d	Z	25° Hc	d	Z	26° Hc	d	Z	27° Hc	d	Z	28° Hc	d	Z	29° Hc	d	Z	30° Hc	d	Z	Dec.
°	° ′	′	°	° ′	′	°	° ′	′	°	° ′	′	°	° ′	′	°	° ′	′	°	° ′	′	°	° ′	′	°	°
0	18 21.0	−24.8	98.1	18 12.4	−25.8	98.4	18 03.5	−26.8	98.7	17 54.2	−27.8	99.1	17 44.6	−28.8	99.4	17 34.6	−29.7	99.7	17 24.3	−30.6	100.0	17 13.8	−31.6	100.3	0
1	17 56.2	−25.1	99.1	17 46.6	−26.1	99.4	17 36.7	−27.1	99.7	17 26.4	−28.0	100.0	17 15.8	−28.9	100.3	17 04.9	−29.9	100.6	16 53.7	−30.8	100.9	16 42.2	−31.7	101.2	1
2	17 31.1	−25.4	100.0	17 20.5	−26.4	100.3	17 09.6	−27.3	100.6	16 58.4	−28.3	100.9	16 46.9	−29.3	101.2	16 35.0	−30.1	101.5	16 22.9	−31.1	101.8	16 10.5	−32.0	102.1	2
3	17 05.7	−25.7	101.0	16 54.1	−26.6	101.3	16 42.3	−27.6	101.6	16 30.1	−28.5	101.8	16 17.6	−29.4	102.1	16 04.9	−30.4	102.4	15 51.8	−31.2	102.7	15 38.5	−32.2	103.0	3
4	16 40.0	−25.9	101.9	16 27.5	−26.9	102.2	16 14.7	−27.8	102.5	16 01.6	−28.8	102.8	15 48.2	−29.7	103.0	15 34.5	−30.6	103.3	15 20.6	−31.5	103.6	15 06.3	−32.3	103.8	4
5	16 14.1	−26.2	102.8	16 00.6	−27.1	103.1	15 46.9	−28.1	103.4	15 32.8	−29.0	103.7	15 18.5	−29.9	103.9	15 03.9	−30.8	104.2	14 49.1	−31.7	104.5	14 34.0	−32.6	104.7	5
6	15 47.9	−26.4	103.8	15 33.5	−27.3	104.0	15 18.8	−28.3	104.3	15 03.8	−29.1	104.6	14 48.6	−30.1	104.8	14 33.1	−31.0	105.1	14 17.4	−31.9	105.3	14 01.4	−32.8	105.6	6
7	15 21.5	−26.6	104.7	15 06.2	−27.6	105.0	14 50.5	−28.4	105.2	14 34.7	−29.4	105.5	14 18.5	−30.3	105.7	14 02.1	−31.2	106.0	13 45.5	−32.1	106.2	13 28.6	−32.9	106.4	7
8	14 54.9	−26.8	105.6	14 38.6	−27.8	105.9	14 22.1	−28.7	106.1	14 05.3	−29.6	106.4	13 48.2	−30.5	106.6	13 30.9	−31.3	106.9	13 13.4	−32.2	107.1	12 55.7	−33.1	107.3	8
9	14 28.1	−27.1	106.6	14 10.8	−28.0	106.8	13 53.4	−28.9	107.0	13 35.7	−29.8	107.3	13 17.7	−30.7	107.5	12 59.6	−31.6	107.7	12 41.2	−32.4	107.9	12 22.6	−33.3	108.2	9
10	14 01.0	−27.3	107.5	13 42.8	−28.1	107.7	13 24.5	−29.1	107.9	13 05.9	−30.0	108.2	12 47.0	−30.8	108.4	12 28.0	−31.7	108.6	12 08.8	−32.6	108.8	11 49.3	−33.4	109.0	10
11	13 33.7	−27.5	108.4	13 14.7	−28.4	108.6	12 55.4	−29.3	108.8	12 35.9	−30.2	109.1	12 16.2	−31.0	109.3	11 56.3	−31.9	109.5	11 36.2	−32.7	109.7	11 15.9	−33.5	109.9	11
12	13 06.2	−27.7	109.3	12 46.3	−28.6	109.5	12 26.1	−29.4	109.7	12 05.7	−30.3	109.9	11 45.2	−31.2	110.1	11 24.4	−32.0	110.3	11 03.5	−32.9	110.5	10 42.4	−33.7	110.7	12
13	12 38.5	−27.8	110.2	12 17.7	−28.7	110.4	11 56.7	−29.6	110.6	11 35.4	−30.4	110.8	11 14.0	−31.3	111.0	10 52.4	−32.2	111.2	10 30.6	−33.0	111.4	10 08.7	−33.9	111.5	13
14	12 10.7	−28.0	111.1	11 49.0	−28.9	111.3	11 27.1	−29.8	111.5	11 05.0	−30.7	111.7	10 42.7	−31.5	111.9	10 20.2	−32.3	112.1	9 57.6	−33.1	112.2	9 34.8	−33.9	112.4	14
15	11 42.7	−28.2	112.0	11 20.1	−29.1	112.2	10 57.3	−29.9	112.4	10 34.3	−30.7	112.6	10 11.2	−31.6	112.7	9 47.9	−32.4	112.9	9 24.5	−33.3	113.1	9 00.9	−34.0	113.2	15
16	11 14.5	−28.4	112.9	10 51.0	−29.2	113.1	10 27.4	−30.1	113.3	10 03.6	−31.0	113.5	9 39.6	−31.7	113.6	9 15.5	−32.6	113.8	8 51.2	−33.3	113.9	8 26.9	−34.2	114.0	16
17	10 46.1	−28.5	113.8	10 21.8	−29.4	114.0	9 57.3	−30.2	114.2	9 32.6	−31.0	114.3	9 07.9	−31.9	114.5	8 42.9	−32.6	114.6	8 17.9	−33.5	114.8	7 52.7	−34.3	114.9	17
18	10 17.6	−28.7	114.7	9 52.4	−29.5	114.9	9 27.1	−30.4	115.0	9 01.6	−31.2	115.2	8 36.0	−32.0	115.3	8 10.3	−32.8	115.5	7 44.4	−33.5	115.6	7 18.4	−34.3	115.7	18
19	9 48.9	−28.8	115.6	9 22.9	−29.6	115.8	8 56.7	−30.4	115.9	8 30.4	−31.2	116.1	8 04.0	−32.0	116.2	7 37.5	−32.9	116.3	7 10.9	−33.7	116.4	6 44.1	−34.4	116.5	19
20	9 20.1	−28.9	116.5	8 53.3	−29.8	116.7	8 26.3	−30.6	116.8	7 59.2	−31.4	116.9	7 32.0	−32.2	117.0	7 04.6	−32.9	117.2	6 37.2	−33.7	117.3	6 09.7	−34.5	117.4	20
21	8 51.2	−29.1	117.4	8 23.5	−29.9	117.5	7 55.7	−30.7	117.7	7 27.8	−31.5	117.8	6 59.8	−32.3	117.9	6 31.7	−33.1	118.0	6 03.5	−33.9	118.1	5 35.2	−34.6	118.2	21
22	8 22.1	−29.2	118.3	7 53.6	−30.0	118.4	7 25.0	−30.8	118.5	6 56.3	−31.6	118.6	6 27.5	−32.3	118.7	5 58.6	−33.1	118.8	5 29.6	−33.8	118.9	5 00.6	−34.6	119.0	22
23	7 52.9	−29.3	119.2	7 23.6	−30.1	119.3	6 54.2	−30.8	119.4	6 24.7	−31.6	119.5	5 55.2	−32.5	119.6	5 25.5	−33.2	119.7	4 55.8	−34.0	119.7	4 26.0	−34.7	119.8	23
24	7 23.6	−29.4	120.0	6 53.5	−30.1	120.2	6 23.4	−31.0	120.3	5 53.1	−31.8	120.3	5 22.7	−32.5	120.4	4 52.3	−33.2	120.5	4 21.8	−34.0	120.6	3 51.3	−34.8	120.6	24
25	6 54.2	−29.5	120.9	6 23.4	−30.3	121.0	5 52.4	−31.1	121.1	5 21.3	−31.8	121.2	4 50.2	−32.5	121.3	4 19.1	−33.4	121.3	3 47.8	−34.0	121.4	3 16.5	−34.7	121.5	25
26	6 24.7	−29.5	121.8	5 53.1	−30.4	121.9	5 21.3	−31.1	122.0	4 49.5	−31.8	122.0	4 17.7	−32.6	122.1	3 45.7	−33.3	122.2	3 13.8	−34.1	122.2	2 41.8	−34.9	122.3	26
27	5 55.2	−29.7	122.7	5 22.7	−30.4	122.8	4 50.2	−31.1	122.8	4 17.7	−32.0	122.9	3 45.1	−32.7	123.0	3 12.4	−33.4	123.0	2 39.7	−34.1	123.1	2 06.9	−34.8	123.1	27
28	5 25.5	−29.7	123.5	4 52.3	−30.5	123.6	4 19.1	−31.3	123.7	3 45.7	−31.9	123.7	3 12.4	−32.7	123.8	2 39.0	−33.4	123.8	2 05.6	−34.2	123.9	1 32.1	−34.8	123.9	28
29	4 55.8	−29.8	124.4	4 21.8	−30.5	124.5	3 47.8	−31.3	124.5	3 13.8	−32.0	124.6	2 39.7	−32.8	124.6	2 05.6	−33.5	124.7	1 31.4	−34.1	124.7	0 57.3	−34.9	124.7	29
30	4 26.0	−29.9	125.3	3 51.3	−30.6	125.3	3 16.5	−31.3	125.4	2 41.8	−32.1	125.4	2 06.9	−32.7	125.5	1 32.1	−33.5	125.5	0 57.3	−34.2	125.5	0 22.4	−34.9	125.5	30
31	3 56.1	−29.9	126.2	3 20.7	−30.7	126.2	2 45.2	−31.4	126.3	2 09.7	−32.1	126.3	1 34.2	−32.8	126.3	0 58.6	−33.4	126.3	0 23.1	−34.2	126.3	0 12.5	+34.8	53.7	31
32	3 26.2	−30.0	127.0	2 50.0	−30.7	127.1	2 13.8	−31.4	127.1	1 37.6	−32.1	127.1	1 01.4	−32.8	127.2	0 25.2	−33.5	127.2	0 11.1	+34.2	52.8	0 47.3	+34.9	52.8	32
33	2 56.2	−30.0	127.9	2 19.3	−30.7	127.9	1 42.4	−31.4	128.0	1 05.5	−32.1	128.0	0 28.6	−32.8	128.0	0 08.3	+33.5	52.0	0 45.3	+34.1	52.0	1 22.2	+34.8	52.0	33
34	2 26.2	−30.0	128.8	1 48.6	−30.7	128.8	1 11.0	−31.4	128.8	0 33.4	−32.1	128.8	0 04.2	+32.8	51.2	0 41.8	+33.5	51.2	1 19.4	+34.2	51.2	1 57.0	+34.8	51.2	34
35	1 56.2	−30.1	129.6	1 17.9	−30.8	129.7	0 39.6	−31.5	129.7	0 01.3	−32.1	129.7	0 37.0	+32.8	50.3	1 15.3	+33.5	50.3	1 53.6	+34.1	50.4	2 31.8	+34.8	50.4	35
36	1 26.1	−30.1	130.5	0 47.1	−30.8	130.5	0 08.1	−31.4	130.5	0 30.8	+32.2	49.5	1 09.8	+32.8	49.5	1 48.8	+33.4	49.5	2 27.7	+34.1	49.5	3 06.6	+34.8	49.6	36
37	0 56.0	−30.1	131.4	0 16.3	−30.7	131.4	0 23.3	+31.5	48.6	1 03.0	+32.1	48.6	1 42.6	+32.8	48.7	2 22.2	+33.4	48.7	3 01.8	+34.1	48.7	3 41.4	+34.7	48.8	37
38	0 25.9	−30.1	132.2	0 14.4	+30.8	47.8	0 54.8	+31.4	47.8	1 35.1	+32.0	47.8	2 15.4	+32.7	47.8	2 55.6	+33.4	47.9	3 35.9	+34.0	47.9	4 16.1	+34.6	47.9	38
39	0 04.2	+30.1	46.9	0 45.2	+30.8	46.9	1 26.2	+31.4	46.9	2 07.1	+32.1	47.0	2 48.1	+32.7	47.0	3 29.0	+33.3	47.0	4 09.9	+34.0	47.1	4 50.7	+34.6	47.1	39
40	0 34.3	+30.1	46.0	1 16.0	+30.7	46.1	1 57.6	+31.4	46.1	2 39.2	+32.0	46.1	3 20.8	+32.6	46.1	4 02.3	+33.3	46.2	4 43.9	+33.9	46.2	5 25.3	+34.6	46.3	40
41	1 04.4	+30.1	45.2	1 46.7	+30.7	45.2	2 29.0	+31.3	45.2	3 11.2	+32.0	45.3	3 53.4	+32.6	45.3	4 35.6	+33.2	45.4	5 17.8	+33.8	45.4	5 59.9	+34.4	45.5	41
42	1 34.5	+30.1	44.3	2 17.4	+30.7	44.3	3 00.3	+31.3	44.4	3 43.2	+31.9	44.4	4 26.0	+32.6	44.5	5 08.8	+33.2	44.5	5 51.6	+33.8	44.6	6 34.3	+34.4	44.7	42
43	2 04.6	+30.0	43.4	2 48.1	+30.7	43.5	3 31.6	+31.3	43.5	4 15.1	+31.9	43.6	4 58.6	+32.5	43.6	5 42.0	+33.1	43.7	6 25.4	+33.7	43.8	7 08.7	+34.3	43.8	43
44	2 34.6	+30.0	42.6	3 18.8	+30.6	42.6	4 02.9	+31.2	42.7	4 47.0	+31.8	42.7	5 31.1	+32.4	42.8	6 15.1	+33.0	42.8	6 59.1	+33.5	42.9	7 43.0	+34.1	43.0	44
45	3 04.6	+29.9	41.7	3 49.4	+30.5	41.8	4 34.1	+31.2	41.8	5 18.8	+31.8	41.9	6 03.5	+32.3	41.9	6 48.1	+32.9	42.0	7 32.6	+33.5	42.1	8 17.1	+34.1	42.2	45
46	3 34.5	+30.0	40.8	4 19.9	+30.5	40.9	5 05.3	+31.0	40.9	5 50.6	+31.6	41.0	6 35.8	+32.3	41.1	7 21.0	+32.8	41.2	8 06.1	+33.4	41.3	8 51.2	+34.0	41.3	46
47	4 04.5	+29.8	40.0	4 50.4	+30.4	40.0	5 36.3	+31.0	40.1	6 22.2	+31.6	40.2	7 08.1	+32.1	40.2	7 53.8	+32.8	40.3	8 39.5	+33.3	40.4	9 25.2	+33.9	40.5	47
48	4 34.3	+29.8	39.1	5 20.8	+30.4	39.2	6 07.3	+31.0	39.2	6 53.8	+31.5	39.3	7 40.2	+32.1	39.4	8 26.6	+32.6	39.5	9 12.8	+33.2	39.6	9 59.1	+33.7	39.7	48
49	5 04.1	+29.7	38.2	5 51.2	+30.3	38.3	6 38.3	+30.8	38.4	7 25.3	+31.4	38.4	8 12.3	+31.9	38.5	8 59.2	+32.5	38.6	9 46.0	+33.1	38.7	10 32.8	+33.6	38.8	49
50	5 33.8	+29.6	37.4	6 21.5	+30.2	37.4	7 09.1	+30.7	37.5	7 56.7	+31.3	37.6	8 44.2	+31.8	37.7	9 31.7	+32.3	37.8	10 19.1	+32.9	37.9	11 06.4	+33.4	38.0	50
51	6 03.4	+29.6	36.5	6 51.7	+30.1	36.6	7 39.8	+30.7	36.6	8 28.0	+31.1	36.7	9 16.0	+31.7	36.8	10 04.0	+32.3	36.9	10 52.0	+32.7	37.0	11 39.8	+33.3	37.1	51
52	6 33.0	+29.5	35.6	7 21.8	+30.0	35.7	8 10.5	+30.5	35.8	8 59.1	+31.1	35.9	9 47.7	+31.6	36.0	10 36.3	+32.1	36.1	11 24.7	+32.7	36.2	12 13.1	+33.2	36.3	52
53	7 02.5	+29.3	34.7	7 51.8	+29.8	34.8	8 41.0	+30.4	34.9	9 30.2	+30.9	35.0	10 19.3	+31.4	35.1	11 08.4	+31.9	35.2	11 57.4	+32.4	35.3	12 46.3	+33.0	35.4	53
54	7 31.8	+29.3	33.9	8 21.6	+29.8	33.9	9 11.4	+30.3	34.0	10 01.1	+30.8	34.1	10 50.7	+31.3	34.2	11 40.3	+31.8	34.3	12 29.8	+32.3	34.5	13 19.3	+32.8	34.6	54
55	8 01.1	+29.1	33.0	8 51.4	+29.7	33.1	9 41.7	+30.1	33.1	10 31.9	+30.6	33.2	11 22.0	+31.2	33.4	12 12.1	+31.6	33.5	13 02.1	+32.2	33.6	13 52.1	+32.6	33.7	55
56	8 30.2	+29.1	32.1	9 21.1	+29.5	32.2	10 11.8	+30.0	32.3	11 02.5	+30.5	32.4	11 53.2	+30.9	32.5	12 43.7	+31.5	32.6	13 34.3	+31.9	32.7	14 24.7	+32.4	32.9	56
57	8 59.3	+28.9	31.2	9 50.6	+29.3	31.3	10 41.8	+29.9	31.4	11 33.0	+30.3	31.5	12 24.1	+30.8	31.6	13 15.2	+31.3	31.7	14 06.2	+31.8	31.9	14 57.1	+32.3	32.0	57
58	9 28.2	+28.7	30.3	10 19.9	+29.3	30.4	11 11.7	+29.7	30.5	12 03.3	+30.2	30.6	12 54.9	+30.7	30.7	13 46.5	+31.1	30.8	14 38.0	+31.5	31.0	15 29.4	+32.0	31.1	58
59	9 56.9	+28.7	29.4	10 49.2	+29.1	29.5	11 41.4	+29.5	29.6	12 33.5	+30.0	29.7	13 25.6	+30.4	29.8	14 17.6	+30.9	30.0	15 09.5	+31.4	30.1	16 01.4	+31.8	30.2	59
60	10 25.6	+28.4	28.5	11 18.3	+28.9	28.6	12 10.9	+29.4	28.7	13 03.5	+29.8	28.8	13 56.0	+30.3	29.0	14 48.5	+30.7	29.1	15 40.9	+31.1	29.2	16 33.2	+31.6	29.4	60
61	10 54.0	+28.4	27.6	11 47.2	+28.7	27.7	12 40.3	+29.1	27.8	13 33.3	+29.6	27.9	14 26.3	+30.0	28.1	15 19.2	+30.5	28.2	16 12.0	+30.9	28.3	17 04.8	+31.4	28.5	61
62	11 22.4	+28.1	26.7	12 15.9	+28.6	26.8	13 09.4	+29.0	26.9	14 02.9	+29.4	27.0	14 56.3	+29.8	27.2	15 49.7	+30.2	27.3	16 42.9	+30.7	27.4	17 36.2	+31.1	27.6	62
63	11 50.5	+28.0	25.8	12 44.5	+28.4	25.9	13 38.4	+28.8	26.0	14 32.3	+29.2	26.2	15 26.1	+29.7	26.3	16 19.9	+30.1	26.4	17 13.6	+30.5	26.5	18 07.3	+30.9	26.7	63
64	12 18.5	+27.8	24.9	13 12.9	+28.2	25.0	14 07.2	+28.6	25.1	15 01.5	+29.0	25.2	15 55.8	+29.4	25.4	16 50.0	+29.8	25.5	17 44.1	+30.2	25.6	18 38.2	+30.6	25.8	64
65	12 46.3	+27.6	24.0	13 41.1	+28.0	24.1	14 35.8	+28.4	24.2	15 30.5	+28.8	24.3	16 25.2	+29.1	24.5	17 19.8	+29.5	24.6	18 14.3	+29.9	24.7	19 08.8	+30.3	24.9	65
66	13 13.9	+27.5	23.1	14 09.1	+27.8	23.2	15 04.2	+28.2	23.3	15 59.3	+28.5	23.4	16 54.3	+28.9	23.5	17 49.3	+29.3	23.7	18 44.2	+29.7	23.8	19 39.1	+30.0	23.9	66
67	13 41.4	+27.2	22.2	14 36.9	+27.6	22.3	15 32.4	+27.9	22.4	16 27.8	+28.3	22.5	17 23.2	+28.7	22.6	18 18.6	+29.0	22.8	19 13.9	+29.4	22.9	20 09.1	+29.8	23.0	67
68	14 08.6	+27.0	21.3	15 04.5	+27.3	21.4	16 00.3	+27.7	21.5	16 56.1	+28.1	21.6	17 51.9	+28.4	21.7	18 47.6	+28.8	21.8	19 43.3	+29.1	22.0	20 38.9	+29.5	22.1	68
69	14 35.6	+26.8	20.4	15 31.8	+27.1	20.5	16 28.0	+27.5	20.6	17 24.2	+27.8	20.7	18 20.3	+28.1	20.8	19 16.4	+28.4	20.9	20 12.4	+28.8	21.0	21 08.4	+29.1	21.2	69
70	15 02.4	+26.6	19.4	15 58.9	+26.9	19.5	16 55.5	+27.2	19.6	17 52.0	+27.5	19.7	18 48.4	+27.9	19.8	19 44.8	+28.2	20.0	20 41.2	+28.5	20.1	21 37.5	+28.9	20.2	70
71	15 29.0	+26.3	18.5	16 25.8	+26.7	18.6	17 22.7	+26.9	18.7	18 19.5	+27.3	18.8	19 16.3	+27.5	18.9	20 13.0	+27.9	19.0	21 09.7	+28.2	19.2	22 06.4	+28.5	19.3	71
72	15 55.3	+26.1	17.6	16 52.5	+26.4	17.7	17 49.6	+26.7	17.8	18 46.8	+26.9	17.9	19 43.8	+27.3	18.0	20 40.9	+27.6	18.1	21 37.9	+27.9	18.2	22 34.9	+28.2	18.3	72
73	16 21.4	+25.8	16.6	17 18.9	+26.1	16.7	18 16.3	+26.4	16.8	19 13.7	+26.7	16.9	20 11.1	+27.0	17.0	21 08.5	+27.2	17.1	22 05.8	+27.5	17.2	23 03.1	+27.8	17.4	73
74	16 47.2	+25.6	15.7	17 45.0	+25.8	15.8	18 42.7	+26.1	15.9	19 40.4	+26.4	16.0	20 38.1	+26.6	16.1	21 35.7	+26.9	16.2	22 33.3	+27.2	16.3	23 30.9	+27.5	16.4	74
75	17 12.8	+25.3	14.8	18 10.8	+25.6	14.8	19 08.8	+25.8	14.9	20 06.8	+26.0	15.0	21 04.7	+26.3	15.1	22 02.6	+26.6	15.2	23 00.5	+26.8	15.3	23 58.4	+27.1	15.4	75
76	17 38.1	+25.1	13.8	18 36.4	+25.3	13.9	19 34.6	+25.5	14.0	20 32.8	+25.8	14.1	21 31.0	+26.0	14.1	22 29.2	+26.2	14.2	23 27.3	+26.5	14.3	24 25.5	+26.7	14.5	76
77	18 03.2	+24.7	12.8	19 01.7	+24.9	12.9	20 00.1	+25.2	13.0	20 58.6	+25.4	13.1	21 57.0	+25.7	13.2	22 55.4	+25.9	13.3	23 53.8	+26.1	13.4	24 52.2	+26.3	13.5	77
78	18 27.9	+24.5	11.9	19 26.6	+24.7	12.0	20 25.3	+24.9	12.0	21 24.0	+25.1	12.1	22 22.7	+25.2	12.2	23 21.3	+25.5	12.3	24 19.9	+25.7	12.4	25 18.5	+25.9	12.5	78
79	18 52.4	+24.2	10.9	19 51.3	+24.4	11.0	20 50.2	+24.6	11.1	21 49.1	+24.7	11.1	22 47.9	+25.0	11.2	23 46.8	+25.1	11.3	24 45.6	+25.3	11.4	25 44.4	+25.5	11.5	79
80	19 16.6	+23.8	10.0	20 15.7	+24.0	10.0	21 14.8	+24.2	10.1	22 13.8	+24.4	10.2	23 12.9	+24.5	10.2	24 11.9	+24.7	10.3	25 10.9	+24.9	10.4	26 09.9	+25.1	10.5	80
81	19 40.4	+23.6	9.0	20 39.7	+23.7	9.0	21 39.0	+23.8	9.1	22 38.2	+24.0	9.2	23 37.4	+24.2	9.2	24 36.6	+24.4	9.3	25 35.8	+24.5	9.4	26 35.0	+24.7	9.5	81
82	20 04.0	+23.2	8.0	21 03.4	+23.4	8.1	22 02.8	+23.5	8.1	23 02.2	+23.6	8.2	24 01.6	+23.8	8.2	25 01.0	+23.9	8.3	26 00.3	+24.1	8.4	26 59.7	+24.2	8.4	82
83	20 27.2	+22.9	7.0	21 26.8	+23.0	7.1	22 26.3	+23.1	7.1	23 25.8	+23.3	7.2	24 25.4	+23.3	7.2	25 24.9	+23.5	7.3	26 24.4	+23.6	7.3	27 23.9	+23.8	7.4	83
84	20 50.1	+22.6	6.0	21 49.8	+22.6	6.1	22 49.4	+22.8	6.1	23 49.1	+22.9	6.2	24 48.7	+23.0	6.2	25 48.4	+23.1	6.3	26 48.0	+23.2	6.3	27 47.7	+23.3	6.4	84
85	21 12.7	+22.2	5.0	22 12.4	+22.3	5.1	23 12.2	+22.4	5.1	24 12.0	+22.4	5.2	25 11.7	+22.6	5.2	26 11.5	+22.6	5.2	27 11.2	+22.7	5.3	28 11.0	+22.8	5.3	85
86	21 34.9	+21.8	4.0	22 34.7	+21.9	4.1	23 34.6	+21.9	4.1	24 34.4	+22.0	4.1	25 34.3	+22.1	4.2	26 34.1	+22.2	4.2	27 33.9	+22.3	4.2	28 33.8	+22.3	4.3	86
87	21 56.7	+21.5	3.0	22 56.6	+21.5	3.1	23 56.5	+21.6	3.1	24 56.4	+21.7	3.1	25 56.4	+21.6	3.1	26 56.3	+21.7	3.2	27 56.2	+21.7	3.2	28 56.1	+21.8	3.2	87
88	22 18.2	+21.1	2.0	23 18.1	+21.2	2.0	24 18.1	+21.2	2.1	25 18.1	+21.2	2.1	26 18.0	+21.2	2.1	27 18.0	+21.2	2.1	28 17.9	+21.3	2.1	29 17.9	+21.3	2.2	88
89	22 39.3	+20.7	1.0	23 39.3	+20.7	1.0	24 39.3	+20.7	1.0	25 39.3	+20.7	1.0	26 39.2	+20.8	1.1	27 39.2	+20.8	1.1	28 39.2	+20.8	1.1	29 39.2	+20.8	1.1	89
90	23 00.0	+20.3	0.0	24 00.0	+20.3	0.0	25 00.0	+20.3	0.0	26 00.0	+20.3	0.0	27 00.0	+20.3	0.0	28 00.0	+20.3	0.0	29 00.0	+20.3	0.0	30 00.0	+20.3	0.0	90
	23°			24°			25°			26°			27°			28°			29°			30°			

S. Lat. {L.H.A. greater than 180° ....Zn=180°−Z; L.H.A. less than 180°...........Zn=180°+Z}

LATITUDE **SAME** NAME AS DECLINATION **L.H.A. 110°, 250°**

325

71°, 289° L.H.A. LATITUDE SAME NAME AS DECLINATION

N. Lat. {L.H.A. greater than 180° .....Zn=Z; L.H.A. less than 180°............Zn=360°–Z}

Dec.	23° Hc	d	Z	24° Hc	d	Z	25° Hc	d	Z	26° Hc	d	Z	27° Hc	d	Z	28° Hc	d	Z	29° Hc	d	Z	30° Hc	d	Z	Dec.
°	° ′	′	°	° ′	′	°	° ′	′	°	° ′	′	°	° ′	′	°	° ′	′	°	° ′	′	°	° ′	′	°	°
0	17 26.3	+24.5	97.7	17 18.2	+25.4	98.0	17 09.7	+26.4	98.3	17 00.9	+27.4	98.6	16 51.8	+28.3	98.9	16 42.4	+29.2	99.2	16 32.6	+30.3	99.5	16 22.6	+31.2	99.8	0
1	17 50.8	+24.1	96.7	17 43.6	+25.1	97.0	17 36.1	+26.1	97.3	17 28.3	+27.1	97.7	17 20.1	+28.1	98.0	17 11.6	+29.1	98.3	17 02.9	+29.9	98.6	16 53.8	+30.9	98.9	1
2	18 14.9	+23.9	95.7	18 08.7	+24.9	96.1	18 02.2	+25.9	96.4	17 55.4	+26.8	96.7	17 48.2	+27.8	97.0	17 40.7	+28.8	97.4	17 32.8	+29.8	97.7	17 24.7	+30.7	98.0	2
3	18 38.8	+23.5	94.8	18 33.6	+24.6	95.1	18 28.1	+25.6	95.4	18 22.2	+26.6	95.8	18 16.0	+27.6	96.1	18 09.5	+28.5	96.4	18 02.6	+29.5	96.8	17 55.4	+30.4	97.1	3
4	19 02.3	+23.3	93.8	18 58.2	+24.3	94.1	18 53.7	+25.3	94.5	18 48.8	+26.3	94.8	18 43.6	+27.2	95.2	18 38.0	+28.2	95.5	18 32.1	+29.2	95.8	18 25.8	+30.2	96.2	4
5	19 25.6	+22.9	92.8	19 22.5	+23.9	93.2	19 19.0	+24.9	93.5	19 15.1	+26.0	93.9	19 10.8	+27.0	94.2	19 06.2	+28.0	94.6	19 01.3	+28.9	94.9	18 56.0	+29.9	95.3	5
6	19 48.5	+22.7	91.8	19 46.4	+23.7	92.2	19 43.9	+24.7	92.6	19 41.1	+25.6	92.9	19 37.8	+26.7	93.3	19 34.2	+27.7	93.6	19 30.2	+28.7	94.0	19 25.9	+29.6	94.3	6
7	20 11.2	+22.3	90.9	20 10.1	+23.3	91.2	20 08.6	+24.3	91.6	20 06.7	+25.4	92.0	20 04.5	+26.4	92.3	20 01.9	+27.3	92.7	19 58.9	+28.3	93.1	19 55.5	+29.3	93.4	7
8	20 33.5	+21.9	89.9	20 33.4	+23.0	90.2	20 32.9	+24.1	90.6	20 32.1	+25.0	91.0	20 30.9	+26.0	91.4	20 29.2	+27.1	91.7	20 27.2	+28.1	92.1	20 24.8	+29.0	92.5	8
9	20 55.4	+21.6	88.9	20 56.4	+22.6	89.3	20 57.0	+23.6	89.6	20 57.1	+24.8	90.0	20 56.9	+25.7	90.4	20 56.3	+26.7	90.8	20 55.3	+27.7	91.2	20 53.8	+28.8	91.6	9
10	21 17.0	+21.3	87.9	21 19.0	+22.3	88.3	21 20.6	+23.4	88.7	21 21.9	+24.3	89.0	21 22.6	+25.4	89.4	21 23.0	+26.4	89.8	21 23.0	+27.4	90.2	21 22.6	+28.4	90.6	10
11	21 38.3	+20.8	86.9	21 41.3	+22.0	87.3	21 44.0	+23.0	87.7	21 46.2	+24.0	88.1	21 48.0	+25.1	88.5	21 49.4	+26.1	88.9	21 50.4	+27.1	89.3	21 51.0	+28.1	89.7	11
12	21 59.1	+20.6	85.9	22 03.3	+21.5	86.3	22 07.0	+22.6	86.7	22 10.2	+23.7	87.1	22 13.1	+24.7	87.5	22 15.5	+25.7	87.9	22 17.5	+26.7	88.3	22 19.1	+27.7	88.7	12
13	22 19.7	+20.1	84.8	22 24.8	+21.2	85.3	22 29.6	+22.2	85.7	22 33.9	+23.3	86.1	22 37.8	+24.3	86.5	22 41.2	+25.4	86.9	22 44.2	+26.4	87.3	22 46.8	+27.4	87.7	13
14	22 39.8	+19.7	83.8	22 46.0	+20.8	84.2	22 51.8	+21.9	84.7	22 57.2	+22.9	85.1	23 02.1	+24.0	85.5	23 06.6	+25.0	85.9	23 10.6	+26.1	86.4	23 14.2	+27.1	86.8	14
15	22 59.5	+19.4	82.8	23 06.8	+20.4	83.2	23 13.7	+21.5	83.6	23 20.1	+22.5	84.1	23 26.1	+23.5	84.5	23 31.6	+24.6	84.9	23 36.7	+25.6	85.4	23 41.3	+26.6	85.8	15
16	23 18.9	+18.9	81.8	23 27.2	+20.0	82.2	23 35.2	+21.0	82.6	23 42.6	+22.2	83.1	23 49.6	+23.2	83.5	23 56.2	+24.2	83.9	24 02.3	+25.3	84.4	24 07.9	+26.3	84.8	16
17	23 37.8	+18.5	80.7	23 47.2	+19.6	81.2	23 56.2	+20.7	81.6	24 04.8	+21.7	82.0	24 12.8	+22.8	82.5	24 20.4	+23.9	82.9	24 27.6	+24.8	83.4	24 34.2	+26.0	83.8	17
18	23 56.3	+18.1	79.7	24 06.8	+19.2	80.1	24 16.9	+20.2	80.6	24 26.5	+21.3	81.0	24 35.6	+22.4	81.5	24 44.3	+23.4	81.9	24 52.4	+24.5	82.4	25 00.2	+25.5	82.9	18
19	24 14.4	+17.7	78.7	24 26.0	+18.8	79.1	24 37.1	+19.9	79.5	24 47.8	+20.9	80.0	24 58.0	+21.9	80.5	25 07.7	+23.0	80.9	25 16.9	+24.1	81.4	25 25.7	+25.1	81.8	19
20	24 32.1	+17.2	77.6	24 44.8	+18.3	78.1	24 57.0	+19.3	78.5	25 08.7	+20.4	79.0	25 19.9	+21.5	79.4	25 30.7	+22.6	79.9	25 41.0	+23.6	80.4	25 50.8	+24.7	80.8	20
21	24 49.3	+16.8	76.5	25 03.1	+17.8	77.0	25 16.3	+19.0	77.5	25 29.1	+20.0	77.9	25 41.4	+21.1	78.4	25 53.3	+22.1	78.9	26 04.6	+23.2	79.3	26 15.5	+24.2	79.8	21
22	25 06.1	+16.4	75.5	25 20.9	+17.5	75.9	25 35.3	+18.5	76.4	25 49.1	+19.6	76.9	26 02.5	+20.6	77.4	26 15.4	+21.7	77.8	26 27.8	+22.8	78.3	26 39.7	+23.8	78.8	22
23	25 22.5	+15.9	74.4	25 38.4	+16.9	74.9	25 53.8	+18.0	75.4	26 08.7	+19.1	75.8	26 23.1	+20.2	76.3	26 37.1	+21.2	76.8	26 50.6	+22.3	77.3	27 03.5	+23.4	77.8	23
24	25 38.4	+15.4	73.4	25 55.3	+16.5	73.8	26 11.8	+17.5	74.3	26 27.8	+18.6	74.8	26 43.3	+19.7	75.3	26 58.3	+20.8	75.7	27 12.9	+21.8	76.2	27 26.9	+22.9	76.7	24
25	25 53.8	+14.9	72.3	26 11.8	+16.0	72.8	26 29.3	+17.1	73.2	26 46.4	+18.2	73.7	27 03.0	+19.2	74.2	27 19.1	+20.3	74.7	27 34.7	+21.3	75.2	27 49.8	+22.4	75.7	25
26	26 08.7	+14.4	71.2	26 27.8	+15.5	71.7	26 46.4	+16.6	72.2	27 04.6	+17.6	72.6	27 22.2	+18.8	73.1	27 39.4	+19.8	73.6	27 56.0	+20.9	74.1	28 12.2	+21.9	74.6	26
27	26 23.1	+14.0	70.1	26 43.3	+15.0	70.6	27 03.0	+16.1	71.1	27 22.2	+17.2	71.6	27 41.0	+18.2	72.1	27 59.2	+19.3	72.6	28 16.9	+20.4	73.1	28 34.1	+21.5	73.6	27
28	26 37.1	+13.5	69.0	26 58.3	+14.6	69.5	27 19.1	+15.6	70.0	27 39.4	+16.6	70.5	27 59.2	+17.7	71.0	28 18.5	+18.8	71.5	28 37.3	+19.9	72.0	28 55.6	+20.9	72.5	28
29	26 50.6	+12.9	67.9	27 12.9	+14.0	68.4	27 34.7	+15.1	68.9	27 56.0	+16.2	69.4	28 16.9	+17.2	69.9	28 37.3	+18.3	70.4	28 57.2	+19.3	70.9	29 16.5	+20.4	71.5	29
30	27 03.5	+12.5	66.9	27 26.9	+13.5	67.3	27 49.8	+14.5	67.8	28 12.2	+15.6	68.3	28 34.1	+16.7	68.8	28 55.6	+17.7	69.3	29 16.5	+18.8	69.8	29 36.9	+19.9	70.4	30
31	27 16.0	+11.9	65.8	27 40.4	+13.0	66.2	28 04.3	+14.1	66.7	28 27.8	+15.1	67.2	28 50.8	+16.2	67.7	29 13.3	+17.2	68.2	29 35.3	+18.3	68.8	29 56.8	+19.4	69.3	31
32	27 27.9	+11.4	64.6	27 53.4	+12.4	65.1	28 18.4	+13.5	65.6	28 42.9	+14.6	66.1	29 07.0	+15.6	66.6	29 30.5	+16.7	67.1	29 53.6	+17.7	67.7	30 16.2	+18.8	68.2	32
33	27 39.3	+10.9	63.5	28 05.8	+11.9	64.0	28 31.9	+12.9	64.5	28 57.5	+14.0	65.0	29 22.6	+15.0	65.5	29 47.2	+16.1	66.0	30 11.3	+17.2	66.5	30 35.0	+18.2	67.1	33
34	27 50.2	+10.3	62.4	28 17.7	+11.4	62.9	28 44.8	+12.4	63.4	29 11.5	+13.4	63.9	29 37.6	+14.5	64.4	30 03.3	+15.6	64.9	30 28.5	+16.6	65.4	30 53.2	+17.7	66.0	34
35	28 00.5	+9.8	61.3	28 29.1	+10.8	61.8	28 57.2	+11.9	62.3	29 24.9	+12.9	62.8	29 52.1	+14.0	63.3	30 18.9	+15.0	63.8	30 45.1	+16.1	64.3	31 10.9	+17.1	64.9	35
36	28 10.3	+9.3	60.2	28 39.9	+10.3	60.7	29 09.1	+11.3	61.1	29 37.8	+12.3	61.6	30 06.1	+13.3	62.2	30 33.9	+14.4	62.7	31 01.2	+15.4	63.2	31 28.0	+16.5	63.7	36
37	28 19.6	+8.7	59.1	28 50.2	+9.7	59.5	29 20.4	+10.7	60.0	29 50.1	+11.8	60.5	30 19.4	+12.8	61.0	30 48.3	+13.8	61.5	31 16.6	+14.9	62.1	31 44.5	+15.9	62.6	37
38	28 28.3	+8.1	58.0	28 59.9	+9.1	58.4	29 31.1	+10.2	58.9	30 01.9	+11.1	59.4	30 32.2	+12.2	59.9	31 02.1	+13.3	60.4	31 31.5	+14.2	60.9	32 00.4	+15.3	61.5	38
39	28 36.4	+7.6	56.8	29 09.0	+8.6	57.3	29 41.3	+9.5	57.8	30 13.0	+10.6	58.2	30 44.4	+11.6	58.8	31 15.3	+12.6	59.3	31 45.7	+13.7	59.8	32 15.7	+14.6	60.3	39
40	28 44.0	+7.0	55.7	29 17.6	+8.0	56.2	29 50.8	+9.0	56.6	30 23.6	+10.0	57.1	30 56.0	+11.0	57.6	31 27.9	+12.0	58.1	31 59.4	+13.0	58.6	32 30.3	+14.1	59.2	40
41	28 51.0	+6.5	54.6	29 25.6	+7.4	55.0	29 59.8	+8.4	55.5	30 33.6	+9.4	56.0	31 07.0	+10.3	56.5	31 39.9	+11.4	57.0	32 12.4	+12.3	57.5	32 44.4	+13.4	58.0	41
42	28 57.5	+5.8	53.4	29 33.0	+6.8	53.9	30 08.2	+7.8	54.3	30 43.0	+8.7	54.8	31 17.3	+9.8	55.3	31 51.3	+10.7	55.8	32 24.7	+11.8	56.3	32 57.8	+12.7	56.9	42
43	29 03.3	+5.3	52.3	29 39.8	+6.3	52.7	30 16.0	+7.2	53.2	30 51.7	+8.2	53.7	31 27.1	+9.1	54.2	32 02.0	+10.1	54.7	32 36.5	+11.1	55.2	33 10.5	+12.1	55.7	43
44	29 08.6	+4.7	51.1	29 46.1	+5.6	51.6	30 23.2	+6.6	52.0	30 59.9	+7.5	52.5	31 36.2	+8.5	53.0	32 12.1	+9.5	53.5	32 47.6	+10.4	54.0	33 22.6	+11.5	54.5	44
45	29 13.3	+4.2	50.0	29 51.7	+5.1	50.4	30 29.8	+5.9	50.9	31 07.4	+6.9	51.4	31 44.7	+7.9	51.8	32 21.6	+8.8	52.3	32 58.0	+9.8	52.8	33 34.1	+10.7	53.4	45
46	29 17.5	+3.5	48.9	29 56.8	+4.4	49.3	30 35.7	+5.4	49.7	31 14.3	+6.3	50.2	31 52.6	+7.2	50.7	32 30.4	+8.2	51.2	33 07.8	+9.1	51.7	33 44.8	+10.1	52.2	46
47	29 21.0	+3.0	47.7	30 01.2	+3.9	48.1	30 41.1	+4.7	48.6	31 20.6	+5.7	49.0	31 59.8	+6.5	49.5	32 38.6	+7.5	50.0	33 16.9	+8.5	50.5	33 54.9	+9.4	51.0	47
48	29 24.0	+2.4	46.6	30 05.1	+3.2	47.0	30 45.8	+4.2	47.4	31 26.3	+5.0	47.9	32 06.3	+6.0	48.3	32 46.1	+6.8	48.8	33 25.4	+7.8	49.3	34 04.3	+8.7	49.8	48
49	29 26.4	+1.7	45.4	30 08.3	+2.7	45.8	30 50.0	+3.5	46.3	31 31.3	+4.4	46.7	32 12.3	+5.2	47.1	32 52.9	+6.2	47.6	33 33.2	+7.0	48.1	34 13.0	+8.0	48.6	49
50	29 28.1	+1.2	44.3	30 11.0	+2.0	44.7	30 53.5	+2.8	45.1	31 35.7	+3.7	45.5	32 17.5	+4.6	46.0	32 59.1	+5.5	46.4	33 40.2	+6.4	46.9	34 21.0	+7.3	47.4	50
51	29 29.3	+0.6	43.1	30 13.0	+1.4	43.5	30 56.3	+2.3	43.9	31 39.4	+3.1	44.4	32 22.1	+4.0	44.8	33 04.6	+4.8	45.2	33 46.6	+5.7	45.7	34 28.3	+6.6	46.2	51
52	29 29.9	0.0	42.0	30 14.4	+0.8	42.4	30 58.6	+1.6	42.8	31 42.5	+2.4	43.2	32 26.1	+3.3	43.6	33 09.4	+4.1	44.1	33 52.3	+5.0	44.5	34 34.9	+5.9	45.0	52
53	29 29.9	-0.5	40.8	30 15.2	+0.2	41.2	31 00.2	+1.0	41.6	31 44.9	+1.8	42.0	32 29.4	+2.6	42.4	33 13.5	+3.5	42.9	33 57.3	+4.3	43.3	34 40.8	+5.2	43.8	53
54	29 29.4	-1.2	39.7	30 15.4	-0.4	40.0	31 01.2	+0.4	40.4	31 46.7	+1.2	40.8	32 32.0	+2.0	41.2	33 17.0	+2.8	41.7	34 01.6	+3.6	42.1	34 46.0	+4.4	42.6	54
55	29 28.2	-1.8	38.5	30 15.0	-1.0	38.9	31 01.6	-0.3	39.3	31 47.9	+0.5	39.7	32 34.0	+1.3	40.1	33 19.8	+2.0	40.5	34 05.2	+2.9	40.9	34 50.4	+3.8	41.4	55
56	29 26.4	-2.4	37.4	30 14.0	-1.7	37.7	31 01.3	-0.9	38.1	31 48.4	-0.1	38.5	32 35.3	+0.6	38.9	33 21.8	+1.4	39.3	34 08.1	+2.2	39.7	34 54.2	+2.9	40.1	56
57	29 24.0	-2.9	36.2	30 12.3	-2.2	36.6	31 00.4	-1.5	36.9	31 48.3	-0.8	37.3	32 35.9	-0.1	37.7	33 23.2	+0.7	38.1	34 10.3	+1.5	38.5	34 57.1	+2.3	38.9	57
58	29 21.1	-3.5	35.1	30 10.1	-2.9	35.4	30 58.9	-2.2	35.8	31 47.5	-1.5	36.1	32 35.8	-0.7	36.5	33 23.9	0.0	36.9	34 11.8	+0.8	37.3	34 59.4	+1.5	37.7	58
59	29 17.6	-4.2	33.9	30 07.2	-3.4	34.3	30 56.7	-2.7	34.6	31 46.0	-2.1	34.9	32 35.1	-1.4	35.3	33 23.9	-0.6	35.7	34 12.6	0.0	36.1	35 00.9	+0.8	36.5	59
60	29 13.4	-4.7	32.8	30 03.8	-4.1	33.1	30 54.0	-3.4	33.4	31 43.9	-2.7	33.8	32 33.7	-2.1	34.1	33 23.3	-1.4	34.5	34 12.6	-0.6	34.9	35 01.7	+0.1	35.3	60
61	29 08.7	-5.2	31.7	29 59.7	-4.6	32.0	30 50.6	-4.1	32.3	31 41.2	-3.4	32.6	32 31.6	-2.7	32.9	33 21.9	-2.0	33.3	34 12.0	-1.4	33.7	35 01.8	-0.7	34.0	61
62	29 03.5	-5.9	30.5	29 55.1	-5.3	30.8	30 46.5	-4.6	31.1	31 37.8	-4.0	31.4	32 28.9	-3.4	31.8	33 19.9	-2.8	32.1	34 10.6	-2.1	32.4	35 01.1	-1.4	32.8	62
63	28 57.6	-6.4	29.4	29 49.8	-5.8	29.7	30 41.9	-5.3	29.9	31 33.8	-4.7	30.3	32 25.5	-4.0	30.6	33 17.1	-3.4	30.9	34 08.5	-2.8	31.2	34 59.7	-2.1	31.6	63
64	28 51.2	-7.0	28.2	29 44.0	-6.5	28.5	30 36.6	-5.9	28.8	31 29.1	-5.3	29.1	32 21.5	-4.7	29.4	33 13.7	-4.1	29.7	34 05.7	-3.5	30.0	34 57.6	-2.9	30.4	64
65	28 44.2	-7.6	27.1	29 37.5	-7.0	27.4	30 30.7	-6.5	27.6	31 23.8	-5.9	27.9	32 16.8	-5.4	28.2	33 09.6	-4.8	28.5	34 02.2	-4.2	28.8	34 54.7	-3.6	29.2	65
66	28 36.6	-8.1	26.0	29 30.5	-7.6	26.2	30 24.2	-7.1	26.5	31 17.9	-6.6	26.7	32 11.4	-6.0	27.0	33 04.8	-5.5	27.3	33 58.0	-4.9	27.6	34 51.1	-4.3	27.9	66
67	28 28.5	-8.7	24.9	29 22.9	-8.2	25.1	30 17.1	-7.7	25.3	31 11.3	-7.2	25.6	32 05.4	-6.7	25.9	32 59.3	-6.1	26.1	33 53.1	-5.6	26.4	34 46.8	-5.1	26.7	67
68	28 19.8	-9.3	23.7	29 14.7	-8.8	23.9	30 09.4	-8.2	24.2	31 04.1	-7.8	24.4	31 58.7	-7.3	24.7	32 53.2	-6.8	24.9	33 47.5	-6.3	25.2	34 41.7	-5.7	25.5	68
69	28 10.5	-9.7	22.6	29 05.9	-9.4	22.8	30 01.2	-8.9	23.0	30 56.3	-8.4	23.3	31 51.4	-8.0	23.5	32 46.4	-7.5	23.8	33 41.2	-7.0	24.0	34 36.0	-6.5	24.3	69
70	28 00.8	-10.4	21.5	28 56.5	-9.9	21.7	29 52.3	-9.5	21.9	30 47.9	-9.0	22.1	31 43.4	-8.6	22.3	32 38.9	-8.2	22.6	33 34.2	-7.6	22.8	34 29.5	-7.2	23.1	70
71	27 50.4	-10.8	20.4	28 46.6	-10.4	20.6	29 42.8	-10.1	20.8	30 38.9	-9.7	21.0	31 34.8	-9.2	21.2	32 30.7	-8.7	21.4	33 26.6	-8.4	21.6	34 22.3	-7.9	21.9	71
72	27 39.6	-11.4	19.3	28 36.2	-11.0	19.4	29 32.7	-10.6	19.6	30 29.2	-10.2	19.8	31 25.6	-9.8	20.0	32 22.0	-9.5	20.2	33 18.2	-9.0	20.5	34 14.4	-8.6	20.7	72
73	27 28.2	-11.9	18.2	28 25.2	-11.6	18.3	29 22.1	-11.2	18.5	30 19.0	-10.9	18.7	31 15.8	-10.5	18.9	32 12.5	-10.1	19.1	33 09.2	-9.7	19.3	34 05.8	-9.3	19.5	73
74	27 16.3	-12.5	17.1	28 13.6	-12.1	17.2	29 10.9	-11.8	17.4	30 08.1	-11.4	17.5	31 05.3	-11.1	17.7	32 02.4	-10.7	17.9	32 59.5	-10.4	18.1	33 56.5	-10.0	18.3	74
75	27 03.8	-12.9	16.0	28 01.5	-12.6	16.1	28 59.1	-12.3	16.2	29 56.7	-12.0	16.4	30 54.2	-11.6	16.6	31 51.7	-11.3	16.7	32 49.1	-11.0	16.9	33 46.5	-10.6	17.1	75
76	26 50.9	-13.5	14.9	27 48.9	-13.2	15.0	28 46.8	-12.9	15.1	29 44.7	-12.6	15.3	30 42.6	-12.3	15.4	31 40.4	-12.0	15.6	32 38.1	-11.6	15.8	33 35.9	-11.4	15.9	76
77	26 37.4	-13.9	13.8	27 35.7	-13.7	13.9	28 33.9	-13.4	14.0	29 32.1	-13.1	14.2	30 30.3	-12.9	14.3	31 28.4	-12.6	14.4	32 26.5	-12.3	14.6	33 24.5	-12.0	14.8	77
78	26 23.5	-14.5	12.7	27 22.0	-14.2	12.8	28 20.5	-13.9	12.9	29 19.0	-13.7	13.0	30 17.4	-13.4	13.2	31 15.8	-13.2	13.3	32 14.2	-12.9	13.4	33 12.5	-12.6	13.6	78
79	26 09.0	-14.9	11.6	27 07.8	-14.7	11.7	28 06.6	-14.5	11.8	29 05.3	-14.3	11.9	30 04.0	-14.1	12.0	31 02.6	-13.7	12.2	32 01.3	-13.6	12.3	32 59.9	-13.3	12.4	79
80	25 54.1	-15.4	10.5	26 53.1	-15.2	10.6	27 52.1	-15.0	10.7	28 51.0	-14.8	10.8	29 49.9	-14.5	10.9	30 48.9	-14.4	11.0	31 47.7	-14.1	11.1	32 46.6	-13.9	11.3	80
81	25 38.7	-15.8	9.4	26 37.9	-15.7	9.5	27 37.1	-15.5	9.6	28 36.2	-15.3	9.7	29 35.4	-15.2	9.8	30 34.5	-15.0	9.9	31 33.6	-14.8	10.0	32 32.7	-14.6	10.1	81
82	25 22.9	-16.4	8.4	26 22.2	-16.2	8.4	27 21.6	-16.1	8.5	28 20.9	-15.9	8.6	29 20.2	-15.7	8.7	30 19.5	-15.5	8.8	31 18.8	-15.4	8.9	32 18.1	-15.2	9.0	82
83	25 06.5	-16.7	7.3	26 06.0	-16.6	7.4	27 05.5	-16.5	7.4	28 05.0	-16.3	7.5	29 04.5	-16.2	7.6	30 04.0	-16.1	7.7	31 03.4	-15.9	7.7	32 02.9	-15.8	7.8	83
84	24 49.8	-17.3	6.3	25 49.4	-17.1	6.3	26 49.0	-17.0	6.4	27 48.7	-16.9	6.4	28 48.3	-16.8	6.5	29 47.9	-16.7	6.5	30 47.5	-16.5	6.6	31 47.1	-16.4	6.7	84
85	24 32.5	-17.6	5.2	25 32.3	-17.6	5.2	26 32.0	-17.4	5.3	27 31.8	-17.4	5.3	28 31.5	-17.3	5.4	29 31.2	-17.1	5.4	30 31.0	-17.1	5.5	31 30.7	-17.0	5.5	85
86	24 14.9	-18.1	4.1	25 14.7	-18.0	4.2	26 14.6	-18.0	4.2	27 14.4	-17.9	4.3	28 14.2	-17.8	4.3	29 14.1	-17.8	4.3	30 13.9	-17.7	4.4	31 13.7	-17.6	4.4	86
87	23 56.8	-18.5	3.1	24 56.7	-18.5	3.1	25 56.6	-18.4	3.2	26 56.5	-18.4	3.2	27 56.4	-18.3	3.2	28 56.3	-18.2	3.2	29 56.2	-18.2	3.3	30 56.1	-18.1	3.3	87
88	23 38.3	-19.0	2.1	24 38.2	-18.9	2.1	25 38.2	-18.9	2.1	26 38.1	-18.8	2.1	27 38.1	-18.8	2.1	28 38.1	-18.8	2.2	29 38.0	-18.7	2.2	30 38.0	-18.7	2.2	88
89	23 19.3	-19.3	1.0	24 19.3	-19.3	1.0	25 19.3	-19.3	1.0	26 19.3	-19.3	1.1	27 19.3	-19.3	1.1	28 19.3	-19.3	1.1	29 19.3	-19.3	1.1	30 19.3	-19.3	1.1	89
90	23 00.0	-19.7	0.0	24 00.0	-19.7	0.0	25 00.0	-19.8	0.0	26 00.0	-19.8	0.0	27 00.0	-19.8	0.0	28 00.0	-19.8	0.0	29 00.0	-19.8	0.0	30 00.0	-19.8	0.0	90
	23°			24°			25°			26°			27°			28°			29°			30°			

71°, 289° L.H.A. LATITUDE SAME NAME AS DECLINATION

326

LATITUDE **CONTRARY** NAME TO DECLINATION L.H.A. 71°, 289°

Dec.	23° Hc	23° d	23° Z	24° Hc	24° d	24° Z	25° Hc	25° d	25° Z	26° Hc	26° d	26° Z
°	° ′	′	°	° ′	′	°	° ′	′	°	° ′	′	°
0	17 26.3	-24.7	97.7	17 18.2	-25.7	98.0	17 09.7	-26.7	98.3	17 00.9	-27.6	98.6
1	17 01.6	-25.0	98.6	16 52.5	-26.0	98.9	16 43.0	-26.9	99.2	16 33.3	-27.9	99.5
2	16 36.6	-25.2	99.6	16 26.5	-26.2	99.9	16 16.1	-27.2	100.1	16 05.4	-28.1	100.4
3	16 11.4	-25.5	100.5	16 00.3	-26.4	100.8	15 48.9	-27.4	101.1	15 37.3	-28.4	101.4
4	15 45.9	-25.7	101.5	15 33.9	-26.7	101.7	15 21.5	-27.6	102.0	15 08.9	-28.5	102.3
5	15 20.2	-26.0	102.4	15 07.2	-26.9	102.7	14 53.9	-27.8	102.9	14 40.4	-28.8	103.2
6	14 54.2	-26.1	103.3	14 40.3	-27.1	103.6	14 26.1	-28.1	103.8	14 11.6	-29.0	104.1
7	14 28.1	-26.4	104.3	14 13.2	-27.4	104.5	13 58.0	-28.2	104.7	13 42.6	-29.2	105.0
8	14 01.7	-26.6	105.2	13 45.8	-27.5	105.4	13 29.8	-28.5	105.7	13 13.4	-29.3	105.9
9	13 35.1	-26.9	106.1	13 18.3	-27.7	106.3	13 01.3	-28.6	106.6	12 44.1	-29.5	106.8
10	13 08.2	-27.0	107.0	12 50.6	-28.0	107.2	12 32.7	-28.9	107.5	12 14.6	-29.8	107.7
11	12 41.2	-27.2	107.9	12 22.6	-28.1	108.2	12 03.8	-29.0	108.4	11 44.8	-29.8	108.6
12	12 14.0	-27.4	108.9	11 54.5	-28.2	109.1	11 34.8	-29.1	109.3	11 15.0	-30.1	109.4
13	11 46.6	-27.5	109.8	11 26.3	-28.5	110.0	11 05.7	-29.3	110.1	10 44.9	-30.1	110.3
14	11 19.1	-27.7	110.7	10 57.8	-28.6	110.9	10 36.4	-29.5	111.0	10 14.8	-30.4	111.2
15	10 51.4	-27.9	111.6	10 29.2	-28.7	111.7	10 06.9	-29.6	111.9	9 44.4	-30.4	112.1
16	10 23.5	-28.0	112.5	10 00.5	-28.9	112.6	9 37.3	-29.7	112.8	9 14.0	-30.6	113.0
17	9 55.5	-28.2	113.4	9 31.6	-29.0	113.5	9 07.6	-29.9	113.7	8 43.4	-30.7	113.8
18	9 27.3	-28.3	114.3	9 02.6	-29.2	114.4	8 37.7	-30.0	114.6	8 12.7	-30.8	114.7
19	8 59.0	-28.4	115.2	8 33.4	-29.2	115.3	8 07.7	-30.1	115.4	7 41.9	-30.9	115.6
20	8 30.6	-28.6	116.1	8 04.2	-29.4	116.2	7 37.6	-30.2	116.3	7 11.0	-31.0	116.4
21	8 02.0	-28.6	116.9	7 34.8	-29.5	117.1	7 07.4	-30.3	117.2	6 40.0	-31.1	117.3
22	7 33.4	-28.8	117.8	7 05.3	-29.6	117.9	6 37.1	-30.4	118.0	6 08.9	-31.2	118.1
23	7 04.6	-28.9	118.7	6 35.7	-29.7	118.8	6 06.7	-30.4	118.9	5 37.7	-31.3	119.0
24	6 35.7	-29.0	119.6	6 06.0	-29.7	119.7	5 36.3	-30.6	119.8	5 06.4	-31.3	119.9
25	6 06.7	-29.0	120.5	5 36.3	-29.9	120.6	5 05.7	-30.6	120.6	4 35.1	-31.4	120.7
26	5 37.7	-29.1	121.4	5 06.4	-29.9	121.4	4 35.1	-30.7	121.5	4 03.7	-31.4	121.6
27	5 08.6	-29.2	122.2	4 36.5	-30.0	122.3	4 04.4	-30.7	122.4	3 32.3	-31.5	122.4
28	4 39.4	-29.3	123.1	4 06.5	-30.0	123.2	3 33.7	-30.8	123.2	3 00.8	-31.5	123.3
29	4 10.1	-29.3	124.0	3 36.5	-30.1	124.0	3 02.9	-30.8	124.1	2 29.3	-31.6	124.1
30	3 40.8	-29.4	124.9	3 06.4	-30.1	124.9	2 32.1	-30.9	125.0	1 57.7	-31.6	125.0
31	3 11.4	-29.4	125.7	2 36.3	-30.1	125.8	2 01.2	-30.9	125.8	1 26.1	-31.6	125.8
32	2 42.0	-29.5	126.6	2 06.2	-30.2	126.6	1 30.3	-30.9	126.7	0 54.5	-31.6	126.7
33	2 12.5	-29.5	127.5	1 36.0	-30.2	127.5	0 59.4	-30.9	127.5	0 22.9	-31.6	127.5
34	1 43.0	-29.5	128.4	1 05.8	-30.3	128.4	0 28.5	-30.9	128.4	0 08.7	+31.7	51.6
35	1 13.5	-29.5	129.2	0 35.5	-30.2	129.2	0 02.4	+30.9	50.8	0 40.4	+31.6	50.8
36	0 44.0	-29.6	130.1	0 05.3	-30.2	130.1	0 33.3	+31.0	49.9	1 12.0	+31.6	49.9
37	0 14.4	-29.5	131.0	0 24.9	+30.2	49.0	1 04.3	+30.9	49.0	1 43.6	+31.5	49.1
38	0 15.1	+29.6	48.2	0 55.1	+30.3	48.2	1 35.2	+30.8	48.2	2 15.1	+31.6	48.2
39	0 44.7	+29.5	47.3	1 25.4	+30.2	47.3	2 06.0	+30.9	47.3	2 46.7	+31.5	47.4
40	1 14.2	+29.5	46.4	1 55.6	+30.1	46.4	2 36.9	+30.8	46.5	3 18.2	+31.5	46.5
41	1 43.7	+29.5	45.6	2 25.7	+30.2	45.6	3 07.7	+30.8	45.6	3 49.7	+31.4	45.7
42	2 13.2	+29.5	44.7	2 55.9	+30.1	44.7	3 38.5	+30.7	44.8	4 21.1	+31.3	44.8
43	2 42.7	+29.4	43.8	3 26.0	+30.0	43.8	4 09.2	+30.7	43.9	4 52.4	+31.3	43.9
44	3 12.1	+29.4	42.9	3 56.0	+30.0	43.0	4 39.9	+30.6	43.0	5 23.7	+31.2	43.1
45	3 41.5	+29.3	42.1	4 26.0	+29.9	42.1	5 10.5	+30.5	42.2	5 54.9	+31.2	42.2
46	4 10.8	+29.3	41.2	4 55.9	+29.9	41.2	5 41.0	+30.5	41.3	6 26.1	+31.0	41.4
47	4 40.1	+29.2	40.3	5 25.8	+29.8	40.4	6 11.5	+30.4	40.4	6 57.1	+31.0	40.5
48	5 09.3	+29.1	39.4	5 55.6	+29.7	39.5	6 41.9	+30.2	39.6	7 28.1	+30.8	39.6
49	5 38.4	+29.0	38.6	6 25.3	+29.6	38.6	7 12.1	+30.2	38.7	7 58.9	+30.8	38.8
50	6 07.4	+29.0	37.7	6 54.9	+29.5	37.8	7 42.3	+30.1	37.8	8 29.7	+30.6	37.9
51	6 36.4	+28.9	36.8	7 24.4	+29.5	36.9	8 12.4	+30.0	37.0	9 00.3	+30.5	37.0
52	7 05.3	+28.8	35.9	7 53.9	+29.3	36.0	8 42.4	+29.8	36.1	9 30.8	+30.4	36.2
53	7 34.1	+28.6	35.0	8 23.2	+29.2	35.1	9 12.2	+29.7	35.2	10 01.2	+30.3	35.3
54	8 02.7	+28.6	34.1	8 52.4	+29.0	34.2	9 41.9	+29.6	34.3	10 31.5	+30.1	34.4
55	8 31.3	+28.4	33.3	9 21.4	+29.0	33.3	10 11.5	+29.5	33.4	11 01.6	+29.9	33.5
56	8 59.7	+28.3	32.4	9 50.4	+28.7	32.5	10 41.0	+29.2	32.6	11 31.5	+29.8	32.7
57	9 28.0	+28.2	31.5	10 19.1	+28.7	31.6	11 10.2	+29.2	31.7	12 01.3	+29.6	31.8
58	9 56.2	+28.0	30.6	10 47.8	+28.5	30.7	11 39.4	+28.9	30.8	12 30.9	+29.4	30.9
59	10 24.2	+27.9	29.7	11 16.3	+28.3	29.8	12 08.3	+28.8	29.9	13 00.3	+29.3	30.0
60	10 52.1	+27.7	28.8	11 44.6	+28.2	28.9	12 37.1	+28.6	29.0	13 29.6	+29.1	29.1
61	11 19.8	+27.5	27.9	12 12.8	+28.0	28.0	13 05.7	+28.5	28.1	13 58.7	+28.8	28.2
62	11 47.3	+27.4	27.0	12 40.8	+27.8	27.1	13 34.2	+28.2	27.2	14 27.5	+28.7	27.3
63	12 14.7	+27.2	26.1	13 08.6	+27.6	26.2	14 02.4	+28.0	26.3	14 56.2	+28.4	26.4
64	12 41.9	+27.0	25.1	13 36.2	+27.4	25.2	14 30.4	+27.8	25.3	15 24.6	+28.2	25.5
65	13 08.9	+26.8	24.2	14 03.6	+27.2	24.3	14 58.2	+27.6	24.4	15 52.8	+28.0	24.5
66	13 35.7	+26.6	23.3	14 30.8	+27.0	23.4	15 25.8	+27.4	23.5	16 20.8	+27.8	23.6
67	14 02.3	+26.4	22.4	14 57.8	+26.7	22.5	15 53.2	+27.1	22.6	16 48.6	+27.5	22.7
68	14 28.7	+26.2	21.5	15 24.5	+26.6	21.6	16 20.3	+26.9	21.7	17 16.1	+27.2	21.8
69	14 54.9	+25.9	20.5	15 51.1	+26.2	20.6	16 47.2	+26.6	20.7	17 43.3	+27.0	20.8
70	15 20.8	+25.8	19.6	16 17.3	+26.1	19.7	17 13.8	+26.4	19.8	18 10.3	+26.6	19.9
71	15 46.6	+25.4	18.7	16 43.4	+25.8	18.7	17 40.2	+26.1	18.8	18 36.9	+26.5	19.0
72	16 12.0	+25.3	17.7	17 09.2	+25.5	17.8	18 06.3	+25.8	17.9	19 03.4	+26.1	18.0
73	16 37.3	+24.9	16.8	17 34.7	+25.2	16.9	18 32.1	+25.5	17.0	19 29.5	+25.8	17.1
74	17 02.2	+24.7	15.8	17 59.9	+25.0	15.9	18 57.6	+25.3	16.0	19 55.3	+25.5	16.1
75	17 26.9	+24.5	14.9	18 24.9	+24.7	14.9	19 22.9	+24.9	15.0	20 20.8	+25.2	15.1
76	17 51.4	+24.1	13.9	18 49.6	+24.4	14.0	19 47.8	+24.6	14.1	20 46.0	+24.8	14.2
77	18 15.5	+23.9	12.9	19 14.0	+24.0	13.0	20 12.4	+24.3	13.1	21 10.8	+24.6	13.2
78	18 39.4	+23.5	12.0	19 38.0	+23.8	12.0	20 36.7	+24.0	12.1	21 35.4	+24.1	12.2
79	19 02.9	+23.3	11.0	20 01.8	+23.4	11.1	21 00.7	+23.6	11.1	21 59.5	+23.9	11.2
80	19 26.2	+22.9	10.0	20 25.2	+23.1	10.1	21 24.3	+23.3	10.2	22 23.4	+23.4	10.2
81	19 49.1	+22.6	9.0	20 48.3	+22.8	9.1	21 47.6	+22.9	9.2	22 46.8	+23.1	9.2
82	20 11.7	+22.3	8.1	21 11.1	+22.4	8.1	22 10.5	+22.6	8.2	23 09.9	+22.7	8.2
83	20 34.0	+21.9	7.1	21 33.5	+22.1	7.1	22 33.1	+22.2	7.2	23 32.6	+22.3	7.2
84	20 55.9	+21.6	6.1	21 55.6	+21.7	6.1	22 55.3	+21.8	6.2	23 54.9	+21.9	6.2
85	21 17.5	+21.3	5.1	22 17.3	+21.3	5.1	23 17.1	+21.4	5.1	24 16.8	+21.5	5.2
86	21 38.8	+20.8	4.1	22 38.6	+21.0	4.1	23 38.5	+21.0	4.1	24 38.3	+21.1	4.2
87	21 59.6	+20.5	3.1	22 59.6	+20.5	3.1	23 59.5	+20.6	3.1	24 59.4	+20.6	3.1
88	22 20.1	+20.2	2.0	23 20.1	+20.2	2.1	24 20.1	+20.1	2.1	25 20.0	+20.2	2.1
89	22 40.3	+19.7	1.0	23 40.3	+19.7	1.0	24 40.2	+19.8	1.0	25 40.2	+19.8	1.0
90	23 00.0	+19.3	0.0	24 00.0	+19.3	0.0	25 00.0	+19.3	0.0	26 00.0	+19.3	0.0
	23°			24°			25°			26°		

Dec.	27° Hc	27° d	27° Z	28° Hc	28° d	28° Z	29° Hc	29° d	29° Z	30° Hc	30° d	30° Z	Dec.
°	° ′	′	°	° ′	′	°	° ′	′	°	° ′	′	°	°
0	16 51.8	-28.6	98.9	16 42.4	-29.6	99.2	16 32.6	-30.4	99.5	16 22.6	-31.4	99.8	0
1	16 23.2	-28.8	99.8	16 12.8	-29.7	100.1	16 02.2	-30.7	100.4	15 51.2	-31.6	100.7	1
2	15 54.4	-29.1	100.7	15 43.1	-30.0	101.0	15 31.5	-30.9	101.3	15 19.6	-31.8	101.5	2
3	15 25.3	-29.3	101.6	15 13.1	-30.2	101.9	15 00.6	-31.1	102.2	14 47.8	-32.0	102.4	3
4	14 56.0	-29.4	102.5	14 42.9	-30.4	102.8	14 29.5	-31.3	103.0	14 15.8	-32.2	103.3	4
5	14 26.6	-29.7	103.4	14 12.5	-30.6	103.7	13 58.2	-31.5	103.9	13 43.6	-32.3	104.2	5
6	13 56.9	-29.9	104.3	13 41.9	-30.8	104.6	13 26.7	-31.7	104.8	13 11.3	-32.6	105.0	6
7	13 27.0	-30.1	105.2	13 11.1	-30.9	105.4	12 55.0	-31.8	105.7	12 38.7	-32.7	105.9	7
8	12 56.9	-30.2	106.1	12 40.2	-31.2	106.3	12 23.2	-32.0	106.5	12 06.0	-32.9	106.7	8
9	12 26.7	-30.5	107.0	12 09.0	-31.3	107.2	11 51.2	-32.2	107.4	11 33.1	-33.0	107.6	9
10	11 56.2	-30.5	107.9	11 37.7	-31.4	108.1	11 19.0	-32.3	108.3	11 00.1	-33.1	108.5	10
11	11 25.7	-30.8	108.8	11 06.3	-31.6	108.9	10 46.7	-32.5	109.1	10 27.0	-33.3	109.3	11
12	10 54.9	-30.9	109.6	10 34.7	-31.8	109.8	10 14.2	-32.5	110.0	9 53.7	-33.5	110.1	12
13	10 24.0	-31.0	110.5	10 02.9	-31.9	110.7	9 41.7	-32.8	110.8	9 20.2	-33.5	111.0	13
14	9 53.0	-31.2	111.4	9 31.0	-32.0	111.5	9 08.9	-32.8	111.7	8 46.7	-33.6	111.8	14
15	9 21.8	-31.3	112.2	8 59.0	-32.1	112.4	8 36.1	-32.9	112.5	8 13.1	-33.8	112.7	15
16	8 50.5	-31.4	113.1	8 26.9	-32.2	113.2	8 03.2	-33.1	113.4	7 39.3	-33.8	113.5	16
17	8 19.1	-31.5	114.0	7 54.7	-32.4	114.1	7 30.1	-33.1	114.2	7 05.5	-34.0	114.3	17
18	7 47.6	-31.6	114.8	7 22.3	-32.4	114.9	6 57.0	-33.3	115.1	6 31.5	-34.0	115.2	18
19	7 16.0	-31.8	115.7	6 49.9	-32.5	115.8	6 23.7	-33.3	115.9	5 57.5	-34.1	116.0	19
20	6 44.2	-31.8	116.5	6 17.4	-32.6	116.6	5 50.4	-33.4	116.7	5 23.4	-34.2	116.8	20
21	6 12.4	-31.9	117.4	5 44.8	-32.7	117.5	5 17.0	-33.4	117.6	4 49.2	-34.2	117.6	21
22	5 40.5	-31.9	118.2	5 12.1	-32.7	118.3	4 43.6	-33.5	118.4	4 15.0	-34.2	118.5	22
23	5 08.6	-32.1	119.1	4 39.4	-32.9	119.2	4 10.1	-33.6	119.2	3 40.8	-34.4	119.3	23
24	4 36.5	-32.1	119.9	4 06.5	-32.8	120.0	3 36.5	-33.6	120.1	3 06.4	-34.3	120.1	24
25	4 04.4	-32.1	120.8	3 33.7	-32.9	120.8	3 02.9	-33.6	120.9	2 32.1	-34.4	120.9	25
26	3 32.3	-32.2	121.6	3 00.8	-33.0	121.7	2 29.3	-33.7	121.7	1 57.7	-34.4	121.8	26
27	3 00.1	-32.3	122.5	2 27.8	-32.9	122.5	1 55.6	-33.7	122.5	1 23.3	-34.4	122.6	27
28	2 27.8	-32.2	123.3	1 54.9	-33.0	123.4	1 21.9	-33.7	123.4	0 48.9	-34.5	123.4	28
29	1 55.6	-32.3	124.2	1 21.9	-33.0	124.2	0 48.2	-33.8	124.2	0 14.4	-34.4	124.2	29
30	1 23.3	-32.3	125.0	0 48.9	-33.1	125.0	0 14.4	-33.7	125.0	0 20.0	+34.5	55.0	30
31	0 51.0	-32.3	125.8	0 15.8	-33.0	125.9	0 19.3	+33.7	54.1	0 54.5	+34.4	54.2	31
32	0 18.7	-32.4	126.7	0 17.2	+33.0	53.3	0 53.0	+33.8	53.3	1 28.9	+34.4	53.3	32
33	0 13.7	+32.3	52.5	0 50.2	+33.0	52.5	1 26.8	+33.7	52.5	2 03.3	+34.4	52.5	33
34	0 46.0	+32.3	51.6	1 23.2	+33.0	51.6	2 00.5	+33.6	51.7	2 37.7	+34.3	51.7	34
35	1 18.3	+32.3	50.8	1 56.2	+33.0	50.8	2 34.1	+33.7	50.8	3 12.0	+34.3	50.9	35
36	1 50.6	+32.3	49.9	2 29.2	+32.9	50.0	3 07.8	+33.6	50.0	3 46.3	+34.3	50.0	36
37	2 22.9	+32.2	49.1	3 02.1	+32.9	49.1	3 41.4	+33.5	49.2	4 20.6	+34.2	49.2	37
38	2 55.1	+32.2	48.2	3 35.0	+32.9	48.3	4 14.9	+33.6	48.3	4 54.8	+34.2	48.4	38
39	3 27.3	+32.2	47.4	4 07.9	+32.8	47.5	4 48.5	+33.4	47.5	5 29.0	+34.0	47.6	39
40	3 59.5	+32.1	46.6	4 40.7	+32.7	46.6	5 21.9	+33.4	46.7	6 03.0	+34.0	46.7	40
41	4 31.6	+32.0	45.7	5 13.4	+32.7	45.8	5 55.3	+33.3	45.8	6 37.0	+34.0	45.9	41
42	5 03.6	+32.0	44.9	5 46.1	+32.6	44.9	6 28.6	+33.2	45.0	7 11.0	+33.8	45.1	42
43	5 35.6	+31.9	44.0	6 18.7	+32.5	44.1	7 01.8	+33.1	44.2	7 44.8	+33.7	44.3	43
44	6 07.5	+31.8	43.2	6 51.2	+32.5	43.2	7 34.9	+33.1	43.3	8 18.5	+33.7	43.4	44
45	6 39.3	+31.8	42.3	7 23.7	+32.3	42.4	8 08.0	+32.9	42.5	8 52.2	+33.5	42.6	45
46	7 11.1	+31.6	41.5	7 56.0	+32.2	41.5	8 40.9	+32.8	41.6	9 25.7	+33.4	41.7	46
47	7 42.7	+31.6	40.6	8 28.2	+32.2	40.7	9 13.7	+32.7	40.8	9 59.1	+33.3	40.9	47
48	8 14.3	+31.4	39.7	9 00.4	+32.0	39.8	9 46.4	+32.6	39.9	10 32.4	+33.1	40.1	48
49	8 45.7	+31.3	38.9	9 32.4	+31.8	39.0	10 19.0	+32.4	39.1	11 05.5	+33.0	39.2	49
50	9 17.0	+31.2	38.0	10 04.2	+31.8	38.1	10 51.4	+32.3	38.2	11 38.5	+32.8	38.4	50
51	9 48.2	+31.0	37.1	10 36.0	+31.6	37.3	11 23.7	+32.1	37.4	12 11.3	+32.7	37.5	51
52	10 19.2	+31.0	36.3	11 07.6	+31.4	36.4	11 55.8	+32.0	36.5	12 44.0	+32.5	36.6	52
53	10 50.2	+30.7	35.4	11 39.0	+31.3	35.5	12 27.8	+31.8	35.6	13 16.5	+32.4	35.8	53
54	11 20.9	+30.6	34.5	12 10.3	+31.1	34.6	12 59.6	+31.7	34.8	13 48.9	+32.1	34.9	54
55	11 51.5	+30.5	33.7	12 41.4	+31.0	33.8	13 31.3	+31.4	33.9	14 21.0	+32.0	34.0	55
56	12 22.0	+30.3	32.8	13 12.4	+30.8	32.9	14 02.7	+31.3	33.0	14 53.0	+31.8	33.2	56
57	12 52.3	+30.1	31.9	13 43.2	+30.6	32.0	14 34.0	+31.1	32.1	15 24.8	+31.5	32.3	57
58	13 22.4	+29.9	31.0	14 13.8	+30.4	31.1	15 05.1	+30.9	31.3	15 56.3	+31.4	31.4	58
59	13 52.3	+29.7	30.1	14 44.2	+30.1	30.2	15 36.0	+30.6	30.4	16 27.7	+31.1	30.5	59
60	14 22.0	+29.5	29.2	15 14.3	+30.0	29.3	16 06.6	+30.4	29.5	16 58.8	+30.9	29.6	60
61	14 51.5	+29.3	28.3	15 44.3	+29.8	28.4	16 37.0	+30.2	28.6	17 29.7	+30.6	28.7	61
62	15 20.8	+29.1	27.4	16 14.1	+29.5	27.5	17 07.2	+30.0	27.7	18 00.3	+30.4	27.8	62
63	15 49.9	+28.9	26.5	16 43.6	+29.3	26.6	17 37.2	+29.7	26.8	18 30.7	+30.1	26.9	63
64	16 18.8	+28.6	25.6	17 12.9	+29.0	25.7	18 06.9	+29.4	25.9	19 00.8	+29.9	26.0	64
65	16 47.4	+28.4	24.7	17 41.9	+28.8	24.8	18 36.3	+29.2	24.9	19 30.7	+29.6	25.1	65
66	17 15.8	+28.1	23.7	18 10.7	+28.5	23.9	19 05.5	+28.9	24.0	20 00.3	+29.3	24.2	66
67	17 43.9	+27.8	22.8	18 39.2	+28.2	22.9	19 34.4	+28.6	23.1	20 29.6	+28.9	23.2	67
68	18 11.7	+27.6	21.9	19 07.4	+27.9	22.0	20 03.0	+28.3	22.2	20 58.5	+28.7	22.3	68
69	18 39.3	+27.4	21.0	19 35.3	+27.7	21.1	20 31.3	+28.0	21.2	21 27.2	+28.4	21.4	69
70	19 06.7	+27.0	20.0	20 03.0	+27.4	20.1	20 59.3	+27.7	20.3	21 55.6	+28.0	20.4	70
71	19 33.7	+26.7	19.1	20 30.4	+27.0	19.2	21 27.0	+27.4	19.3	22 23.6	+27.7	19.4	71
72	20 00.4	+26.4	18.1	20 57.4	+26.7	18.2	21 54.4	+27.0	18.4	22 51.3	+27.3	18.5	72
73	20 26.8	+26.1	17.2	21 24.1	+26.4	17.3	22 21.4	+26.7	17.4	23 18.6	+27.0	17.5	73
74	20 52.9	+25.8	16.2	21 50.5	+26.1	16.3	22 48.1	+26.3	16.4	23 45.6	+26.6	16.5	74
75	21 18.7	+25.4	15.2	22 16.6	+25.7	15.3	23 14.4	+26.0	15.4	24 12.2	+26.3	15.6	75
76	21 44.1	+25.2	14.3	22 42.3	+25.3	14.4	23 40.4	+25.6	14.5	24 38.5	+25.8	14.6	76
77	22 09.3	+24.7	13.3	23 07.6	+25.0	13.4	24 06.0	+25.2	13.5	25 04.3	+25.5	13.6	77
78	22 34.0	+24.4	12.3	23 32.6	+24.6	12.4	24 31.2	+24.8	12.5	25 29.8	+25.0	12.6	78
79	22 58.4	+24.0	11.3	23 57.2	+24.2	11.4	24 56.0	+24.4	11.5	25 54.8	+24.6	11.6	79
80	23 22.4	+23.6	10.3	24 21.4	+23.8	10.4	25 20.4	+24.0	10.5	26 19.4	+24.2	10.6	80
81	23 46.0	+23.3	9.3	24 45.2	+23.4	9.4	25 44.4	+23.6	9.5	26 43.6	+23.7	9.5	81
82	24 09.3	+22.8	8.3	25 08.6	+23.0	8.4	26 08.0	+23.1	8.4	27 07.3	+23.3	8.5	82
83	24 32.1	+22.5	7.3	25 31.6	+22.6	7.3	26 31.1	+22.7	7.4	27 30.6	+22.9	7.5	83
84	24 54.6	+22.0	6.3	25 54.2	+22.1	6.3	26 53.8	+22.3	6.4	27 53.5	+22.3	6.4	84
85	25 16.6	+21.5	5.2	26 16.3	+21.7	5.3	27 16.1	+21.7	5.3	28 15.8	+21.9	5.4	85
86	25 38.1	+21.2	4.2	26 38.0	+21.2	4.2	27 37.8	+21.3	4.3	28 37.7	+21.3	4.3	86
87	25 59.3	+20.7	3.2	26 59.2	+20.7	3.2	27 59.1	+20.8	3.2	28 59.0	+20.9	3.2	87
88	26 20.0	+20.2	2.1	27 19.9	+20.3	2.1	28 19.9	+20.3	2.1	29 19.9	+20.3	2.2	88
89	26 40.2	+19.8	1.1	27 40.2	+19.8	1.1	28 40.2	+19.8	1.1	29 40.2	+19.8	1.1	89
90	27 00.0	+19.3	0.0	28 00.0	+19.3	0.0	29 00.0	+19.3	0.0	30 00.0	+19.3	0.0	90
	27°			28°			29°			30°			

S. Lat. { L.H.A. greater than 180° ....Zn=180°−Z
L.H.A. less than 180°...........Zn=180°+Z

LATITUDE **SAME** NAME AS DECLINATION L.H.A. 109°, 251°

327

72°, 288° L.H.A. **LATITUDE SAME NAME AS DECLINATION** N. Lat. {L.H.A. greater than 180° .....Zn=Z
{L.H.A. less than 180°............Zn=360°–Z

Dec.	23° Hc	23° d	23° Z	24° Hc	24° d	24° Z	25° Hc	25° d	25° Z	26° Hc	26° d	26° Z
°	° ′	′	°	° ′	′	°	° ′	′	°	° ′	′	°
0	16 31.6	+24.3	97.2	16 23.9	+25.3	97.5	16 15.8	+26.3	97.8	16 07.5	+27.3	98.1
1	16 55.9	+24.0	96.3	16 49.2	+25.0	96.6	16 42.1	+26.1	96.9	16 34.8	+27.0	97.2
2	17 19.9	+23.8	95.3	17 14.2	+24.8	95.6	17 08.2	+25.7	95.9	17 01.8	+26.8	96.2
3	17 43.7	+23.5	94.4	17 39.0	+24.5	94.7	17 33.9	+25.5	95.0	17 28.6	+26.4	95.3
4	18 07.2	+23.2	93.4	18 03.5	+24.2	93.7	17 59.4	+25.3	94.0	17 55.0	+26.3	94.4
5	18 30.4	+22.9	92.4	18 27.7	+23.9	92.8	18 24.7	+24.9	93.1	18 21.3	+25.9	93.4
6	18 53.3	+22.6	91.4	18 51.6	+23.7	91.8	18 49.6	+24.6	92.1	18 47.2	+25.6	92.5
7	19 15.9	+22.3	90.5	19 15.3	+23.3	90.8	19 14.2	+24.4	91.2	19 12.8	+25.4	91.5
8	19 38.2	+22.0	89.5	19 38.6	+23.0	89.8	19 38.6	+24.0	90.2	19 38.2	+25.0	90.6
9	20 00.2	+21.6	88.5	20 01.6	+22.7	88.9	20 02.6	+23.7	89.2	20 03.2	+24.7	89.6
10	20 21.8	+21.3	87.5	20 24.3	+22.3	87.9	20 26.3	+23.4	88.2	20 27.9	+24.4	88.6
11	20 43.1	+21.0	86.5	20 46.6	+22.0	86.9	20 49.7	+23.0	87.3	20 52.3	+24.1	87.6
12	21 04.1	+20.6	85.5	21 08.6	+21.6	85.9	21 12.7	+22.7	86.3	21 16.4	+23.7	86.7
13	21 24.7	+20.2	84.5	21 30.2	+21.3	84.9	21 35.4	+22.3	85.3	21 40.1	+23.4	85.7
14	21 44.9	+19.9	83.5	21 51.5	+20.9	83.9	21 57.7	+22.0	84.3	22 03.5	+23.0	84.7
15	22 04.8	+19.4	82.5	22 12.4	+20.6	82.9	22 19.7	+21.5	83.3	22 26.5	+22.6	83.7
16	22 24.2	+19.1	81.4	22 33.0	+20.1	81.8	22 41.2	+21.3	82.3	22 49.1	+22.3	82.7
17	22 43.3	+18.7	80.4	22 53.1	+19.8	80.8	23 02.5	+20.8	81.2	23 11.4	+21.8	81.7
18	23 02.0	+18.3	79.4	23 12.9	+19.3	79.8	23 23.3	+20.4	80.2	23 33.2	+21.5	80.7
19	23 20.3	+17.9	78.3	23 32.2	+19.0	78.8	23 43.7	+20.0	79.2	23 54.7	+21.1	79.6
20	23 38.2	+17.5	77.3	23 51.2	+18.5	77.7	24 03.7	+19.6	78.2	24 15.8	+20.6	78.6
21	23 55.7	+17.0	76.3	24 09.7	+18.1	76.7	24 23.3	+19.2	77.1	24 36.4	+20.3	77.6
22	24 12.7	+16.6	75.2	24 27.8	+17.7	75.6	24 42.5	+18.7	76.1	24 56.7	+19.7	76.5
23	24 29.3	+16.2	74.2	24 45.5	+17.2	74.6	25 01.2	+18.3	75.0	25 16.4	+19.4	75.5
24	24 45.5	+15.7	73.1	25 02.7	+16.8	73.5	25 19.5	+17.8	74.0	25 35.8	+18.9	74.4
25	25 01.2	+15.2	72.0	25 19.5	+16.3	72.5	25 37.3	+17.4	72.9	25 54.7	+18.4	73.4
26	25 16.4	+14.8	71.0	25 35.8	+15.8	71.4	25 54.7	+16.9	71.9	26 13.1	+18.0	72.3
27	25 31.2	+14.4	69.9	25 51.6	+15.4	70.3	26 11.6	+16.4	70.8	26 31.1	+17.5	71.3
28	25 45.6	+13.8	68.8	26 07.0	+14.9	69.3	26 28.0	+16.0	69.7	26 48.6	+17.0	70.2
29	25 59.4	+13.4	67.7	26 21.9	+14.4	68.2	26 44.0	+15.5	68.6	27 05.6	+16.5	69.1
30	26 12.8	+12.8	66.6	26 36.3	+14.0	67.1	26 59.5	+14.9	67.6	27 22.1	+16.0	68.0
31	26 25.6	+12.4	65.6	26 50.3	+13.4	66.0	27 14.4	+14.5	66.5	27 38.1	+15.6	67.0
32	26 38.0	+11.9	64.5	27 03.7	+12.9	64.9	27 28.9	+13.9	65.4	27 53.7	+14.9	65.9
33	26 49.9	+11.4	63.4	27 16.6	+12.4	63.8	27 42.8	+13.5	64.3	28 08.6	+14.5	64.8
34	27 01.3	+10.8	62.3	27 29.0	+11.8	62.7	27 56.3	+12.8	63.2	28 23.1	+13.9	63.7
35	27 12.1	+10.3	61.2	27 40.8	+11.4	61.6	28 09.1	+12.4	62.1	28 37.0	+13.4	62.6
36	27 22.4	+9.8	60.0	27 52.2	+10.8	60.5	28 21.5	+11.8	61.0	28 50.4	+12.8	61.4
37	27 32.2	+9.3	58.9	28 03.0	+10.2	59.4	28 33.3	+11.3	59.9	29 03.2	+12.3	60.3
38	27 41.5	+8.7	57.8	28 13.2	+9.8	58.3	28 44.6	+10.7	58.7	29 15.5	+11.7	59.2
39	27 50.2	+8.2	56.7	28 23.0	+9.1	57.2	28 55.3	+10.2	57.6	29 27.2	+11.2	58.1
40	27 58.4	+7.6	55.6	28 32.1	+8.6	56.0	29 05.5	+9.5	56.5	29 38.4	+10.5	57.0
41	28 06.0	+7.1	54.5	28 40.7	+8.1	54.9	29 15.0	+9.0	55.4	29 48.9	+10.0	55.8
42	28 13.1	+6.6	53.3	28 48.8	+7.5	53.8	29 24.0	+8.5	54.2	29 58.9	+9.4	54.7
43	28 19.7	+5.9	52.2	28 56.3	+6.9	52.6	29 32.5	+7.8	53.1	30 08.3	+8.8	53.5
44	28 25.6	+5.4	51.1	29 03.2	+6.3	51.5	29 40.3	+7.3	51.9	30 17.1	+8.2	52.4
45	28 31.0	+4.9	49.9	29 09.5	+5.7	50.4	29 47.6	+6.7	50.8	30 25.3	+7.6	51.2
46	28 35.9	+4.3	48.8	29 15.2	+5.2	49.2	29 54.3	+6.0	49.7	30 32.9	+7.0	50.1
47	28 40.2	+3.7	47.7	29 20.4	+4.6	48.1	30 00.3	+5.5	48.5	30 39.9	+6.4	48.9
48	28 43.9	+3.1	46.5	29 25.0	+4.0	46.9	30 05.8	+4.9	47.4	30 46.3	+5.8	47.8
49	28 47.0	+2.6	45.4	29 29.0	+3.4	45.8	30 10.7	+4.3	46.2	30 52.1	+5.1	46.6
50	28 49.6	+2.0	44.3	29 32.4	+2.8	44.6	30 15.0	+3.6	45.0	30 57.2	+4.5	45.5
51	28 51.6	+1.4	43.1	29 35.2	+2.3	43.5	30 18.6	+3.1	43.9	31 01.7	+3.9	44.3
52	28 53.0	+0.8	42.0	29 37.5	+1.6	42.3	30 21.7	+2.4	42.7	31 05.6	+3.3	43.1
53	28 53.8	+0.3	40.8	29 39.1	+1.0	41.2	30 24.1	+1.9	41.6	31 08.9	+2.6	42.0
54	28 54.1	−0.3	39.7	29 40.1	+0.5	40.0	30 26.0	+1.2	40.4	31 11.5	+2.0	40.8
55	28 53.8	−0.9	38.5	29 40.6	−0.2	38.9	30 27.2	+0.6	39.3	31 13.5	+1.4	39.6
56	28 52.9	−1.5	37.4	29 40.4	−0.7	37.7	30 27.8	−0.1	38.1	31 14.9	+0.7	38.5
57	28 51.4	−2.1	36.3	29 39.7	−1.4	36.6	30 27.7	−0.6	36.9	31 15.6	+0.1	37.3
58	28 49.3	−2.6	35.1	29 38.3	−1.9	35.4	30 27.1	−1.2	35.8	31 15.7	−0.6	36.1
59	28 46.7	−3.2	34.0	29 36.4	−2.6	34.3	30 25.9	−1.9	34.6	31 15.1	−1.2	35.0
60	28 43.5	−3.8	32.8	29 33.8	−3.1	33.1	30 24.0	−2.5	33.5	31 13.9	−1.8	33.8
61	28 39.7	−4.3	31.7	29 30.7	−3.7	32.0	30 21.5	−3.1	32.3	31 12.1	−2.4	32.6
62	28 35.4	−4.9	30.6	29 27.0	−4.3	30.8	30 18.4	−3.7	31.1	31 09.7	−3.1	31.5
63	28 30.5	−5.5	29.4	29 22.7	−4.9	29.7	30 14.7	−4.3	30.0	31 06.6	−3.7	30.3
64	28 25.0	−6.0	28.3	29 17.8	−5.5	28.6	30 10.4	−4.9	28.8	31 02.9	−4.3	29.1
65	28 19.0	−6.6	27.2	29 12.3	−6.1	27.4	30 05.5	−5.5	27.7	30 58.6	−5.0	28.0
66	28 12.4	−7.2	26.0	29 06.2	−6.6	26.3	30 00.0	−6.1	26.5	30 53.6	−5.6	26.8
67	28 05.2	−7.7	24.9	28 59.6	−7.2	25.1	29 53.9	−6.8	25.4	30 48.0	−6.2	25.6
68	27 57.5	−8.2	23.8	28 52.4	−7.8	24.0	29 47.1	−7.3	24.2	30 41.8	−6.8	24.5
69	27 49.3	−8.8	22.7	28 44.6	−8.3	22.9	29 39.8	−7.8	23.1	30 35.0	−7.4	23.3
70	27 40.5	−9.3	21.5	28 36.3	−8.9	21.7	29 32.0	−8.5	22.0	30 27.6	−8.1	22.2
71	27 31.2	−9.9	20.4	28 27.4	−9.5	20.6	29 23.5	−9.1	20.8	30 19.5	−8.6	21.0
72	27 21.3	−10.4	19.3	28 17.9	−10.0	19.5	29 14.4	−9.6	19.7	30 10.9	−9.2	19.9
73	27 10.9	−10.9	18.2	28 07.9	−10.5	18.4	29 04.8	−10.2	18.6	30 01.7	−9.8	18.7
74	27 00.0	−11.4	17.1	27 57.4	−11.1	17.3	28 54.6	−10.7	17.4	29 51.9	−10.5	17.6
75	26 48.6	−11.9	16.0	27 46.3	−11.6	16.2	28 43.9	−11.3	16.3	29 41.4	−10.9	16.5
76	26 36.7	−12.4	14.9	27 34.7	−12.2	15.0	28 32.6	−11.9	15.2	29 30.5	−11.6	15.3
77	26 24.3	−13.0	13.8	27 22.5	−12.6	13.9	28 20.7	−12.4	14.1	29 18.9	−12.1	14.2
78	26 11.3	−13.4	12.7	27 09.9	−13.2	12.8	28 08.3	−12.9	13.0	29 06.8	−12.7	13.1
79	25 57.9	−13.9	11.6	26 56.7	−13.7	11.7	27 55.4	−13.4	11.9	28 54.1	−13.2	12.0
80	25 44.0	−14.4	10.6	26 43.0	−14.2	10.7	27 42.0	−14.0	10.8	28 40.9	−13.8	10.9
81	25 29.6	−14.8	9.5	26 28.8	−14.6	9.6	27 28.0	−14.5	9.7	28 27.1	−14.3	9.7
82	25 14.8	−15.3	8.4	26 14.2	−15.2	8.5	27 13.5	−15.0	8.6	28 12.8	−14.8	8.6
83	24 59.5	−15.8	7.3	25 59.0	−15.6	7.4	26 58.5	−15.5	7.5	27 58.0	−15.4	7.5
84	24 43.7	−16.2	6.3	25 43.4	−16.1	6.3	26 43.0	−16.0	6.4	27 42.6	−15.8	6.4
85	24 27.5	−16.6	5.2	25 27.3	−16.6	5.3	26 27.0	−16.5	5.3	27 26.8	−16.4	5.4
86	24 10.9	−17.1	4.2	25 10.7	−17.0	4.2	26 10.5	−16.9	4.2	27 10.4	−16.9	4.3
87	23 53.8	−17.5	3.1	24 53.7	−17.5	3.1	25 53.6	−17.4	3.2	26 53.5	−17.4	3.2
88	23 36.3	−18.0	2.1	24 36.2	−17.9	2.1	25 36.2	−17.9	2.1	26 36.1	−17.8	2.1
89	23 18.3	−18.3	1.0	24 18.3	−18.3	1.0	25 18.3	−18.3	1.1	26 18.3	−18.3	1.1
90	23 00.0	−18.7	0.0	24 00.0	−18.8	0.0	25 00.0	−18.8	0.0	26 00.0	−18.8	0.0
	23°			24°			25°			26°		

27° Hc	27° d	27° Z	28° Hc	28° d	28° Z	29° Hc	29° d	29° Z	30° Hc	30° d	30° Z	Dec.
° ′	′	°	° ′	′	°	° ′	′	°	° ′	′	°	°
15 58.9	+28.2	98.4	15 50.0	+29.2	98.7	15 40.8	+30.1	99.0	15 31.3	+31.1	99.2	0
16 27.1	+28.0	97.5	16 19.2	+28.9	97.8	16 10.9	+29.9	98.1	16 02.4	+30.8	98.3	1
16 55.1	+27.7	96.5	16 48.1	+28.7	96.8	16 40.8	+29.6	97.1	16 33.2	+30.6	97.4	2
17 22.8	+27.5	95.6	17 16.8	+28.4	95.9	17 10.4	+29.4	96.2	17 03.8	+30.3	96.5	3
17 50.3	+27.2	94.7	17 45.2	+28.2	95.0	17 39.8	+29.2	95.3	17 34.1	+30.1	95.6	4
18 17.5	+26.9	93.8	18 13.4	+27.9	94.1	18 09.0	+28.8	94.4	18 04.2	+29.8	94.7	5
18 44.4	+26.7	92.8	18 41.3	+27.6	93.1	18 37.8	+28.6	93.5	18 34.0	+29.6	93.8	6
19 11.1	+26.3	91.9	19 08.9	+27.4	92.2	19 06.4	+28.4	92.6	19 03.6	+29.3	92.9	7
19 37.4	+26.1	90.9	19 36.3	+27.0	91.3	19 34.8	+28.0	91.6	19 32.9	+29.0	92.0	8
20 03.5	+25.7	89.9	20 03.3	+26.8	90.3	20 02.8	+27.7	90.7	20 01.9	+28.7	91.0	9
20 29.2	+25.4	89.0	20 30.1	+26.4	89.4	20 30.5	+27.5	89.7	20 30.6	+28.4	90.1	10
20 54.6	+25.1	88.0	20 56.5	+26.1	88.4	20 58.0	+27.1	88.8	20 59.0	+28.1	89.2	11
21 19.7	+24.7	87.0	21 22.6	+25.7	87.4	21 25.1	+26.7	87.8	21 27.1	+27.8	88.2	12
21 44.4	+24.4	86.1	21 48.3	+25.5	86.5	21 51.8	+26.5	86.9	21 54.9	+27.5	87.3	13
22 08.8	+24.1	85.1	22 13.8	+25.0	85.5	22 18.3	+26.1	85.9	22 22.4	+27.1	86.3	14
22 32.9	+23.6	84.1	22 38.8	+24.7	84.5	22 44.4	+25.7	84.9	22 49.5	+26.7	85.3	15
22 56.5	+23.3	83.1	23 03.5	+24.4	83.5	23 10.1	+25.4	83.9	23 16.2	+26.4	84.4	16
23 19.8	+23.0	82.1	23 27.9	+23.9	82.5	23 35.5	+25.0	83.0	23 42.6	+26.0	83.4	17
23 42.8	+22.5	81.1	23 51.8	+23.6	81.5	24 00.5	+24.6	82.0	24 08.6	+25.7	82.4	18
24 05.3	+22.1	80.1	24 15.4	+23.2	80.5	24 25.1	+24.2	81.0	24 34.3	+25.2	81.4	19
24 27.4	+21.7	79.0	24 38.6	+22.7	79.5	24 49.3	+23.8	80.0	24 59.5	+24.8	80.4	20
24 49.1	+21.3	78.0	25 01.3	+22.4	78.5	25 13.1	+23.4	78.9	25 24.3	+24.5	79.4	21
25 10.4	+20.8	77.0	25 23.7	+21.9	77.5	25 36.5	+22.9	77.9	25 48.8	+24.0	78.4	22
25 31.2	+20.4	76.0	25 45.6	+21.4	76.4	25 59.4	+22.5	76.9	26 12.8	+23.5	77.4	23
25 51.6	+20.0	74.9	26 07.0	+21.0	75.4	26 21.9	+22.1	75.9	26 36.3	+23.2	76.3	24
26 11.6	+19.5	73.9	26 28.0	+20.6	74.3	26 44.0	+21.6	74.8	26 59.5	+22.6	75.3	25
26 31.1	+19.0	72.8	26 48.6	+20.1	73.3	27 05.6	+21.2	73.8	27 22.1	+22.2	74.3	26
26 50.1	+18.6	71.7	27 08.7	+19.6	72.2	27 26.8	+20.6	72.7	27 44.3	+21.8	73.2	27
27 08.7	+18.1	70.7	27 28.3	+19.1	71.2	27 47.4	+20.2	71.7	28 06.1	+21.2	72.2	28
27 26.8	+17.5	69.6	27 47.4	+18.7	70.1	28 07.6	+19.7	70.6	28 27.3	+20.7	71.1	29
27 44.3	+17.1	68.5	28 06.1	+18.1	69.0	28 27.3	+19.2	69.5	28 48.0	+20.3	70.0	30
28 01.4	+16.6	67.4	28 24.2	+17.6	67.9	28 46.5	+18.6	68.4	29 08.3	+19.7	69.0	31
28 18.0	+16.0	66.4	28 41.8	+17.1	66.8	29 05.1	+18.2	67.4	29 28.0	+19.2	67.9	32
28 34.0	+15.5	65.3	28 58.9	+16.5	65.8	29 23.3	+17.5	66.3	29 47.2	+18.6	66.8	33
28 49.5	+14.9	64.2	29 15.4	+16.0	64.7	29 40.8	+17.1	65.2	30 05.8	+18.1	65.7	34
29 04.4	+14.5	63.0	29 31.4	+15.5	63.5	29 57.9	+16.5	64.1	30 23.9	+17.5	64.6	35
29 18.9	+13.8	61.9	29 46.9	+14.8	62.4	30 14.4	+15.9	62.9	30 41.4	+17.0	63.5	36
29 32.7	+13.3	60.8	30 01.7	+14.4	61.3	30 30.3	+15.4	61.8	30 58.4	+16.4	62.4	37
29 46.0	+12.7	59.7	30 16.1	+13.7	60.2	30 45.7	+14.7	60.7	31 14.8	+15.8	61.2	38
29 58.7	+12.2	58.6	30 29.8	+13.2	59.1	31 00.4	+14.2	59.6	31 30.6	+15.2	60.1	39
30 10.9	+11.5	57.4	30 43.0	+12.5	57.9	31 14.6	+13.6	58.4	31 45.8	+14.5	59.0	40
30 22.4	+11.0	56.3	30 55.5	+12.0	56.8	31 28.2	+12.9	57.3	32 00.3	+14.0	57.8	41
30 33.4	+10.4	55.2	31 07.5	+11.3	55.7	31 41.1	+12.4	56.2	32 14.3	+13.3	56.7	42
30 43.8	+9.7	54.0	31 18.8	+10.8	54.5	31 53.5	+11.7	55.0	32 27.6	+12.8	55.5	43
30 53.5	+9.2	52.9	31 29.6	+10.1	53.4	32 05.2	+11.1	53.8	32 40.4	+12.0	54.4	44
31 02.7	+8.5	51.7	31 39.7	+9.5	52.2	32 16.3	+10.4	52.7	32 52.4	+11.4	53.2	45
31 11.2	+8.0	50.6	31 49.2	+8.8	51.0	32 26.7	+9.8	51.5	33 03.8	+10.8	52.0	46
31 19.2	+7.2	49.4	31 58.0	+8.2	49.9	32 36.5	+9.1	50.4	33 14.6	+10.1	50.9	47
31 26.4	+6.7	48.2	32 06.2	+7.6	48.7	32 45.6	+8.5	49.2	33 24.7	+9.4	49.7	48
31 33.1	+6.0	47.1	32 13.8	+6.9	47.5	32 54.1	+7.8	48.0	33 34.1	+8.7	48.5	49
31 39.1	+5.4	45.9	32 20.7	+6.3	46.4	33 01.9	+7.2	46.8	33 42.8	+8.1	47.3	50
31 44.5	+4.7	44.7	32 27.0	+5.6	45.2	33 09.1	+6.5	45.6	33 50.9	+7.3	46.1	51
31 49.2	+4.1	43.6	32 32.6	+4.9	44.0	33 15.6	+5.8	44.4	33 58.2	+6.7	44.9	52
31 53.3	+3.5	42.4	32 37.5	+4.3	42.8	33 21.4	+5.1	43.3	34 04.9	+6.0	43.7	53
31 56.8	+2.8	41.2	32 41.8	+3.6	41.6	33 26.5	+4.4	42.1	34 10.9	+5.2	42.5	54
31 59.6	+2.1	40.0	32 45.4	+2.9	40.4	33 30.9	+3.7	40.9	34 16.1	+4.6	41.3	55
32 01.7	+1.5	38.9	32 48.3	+2.3	39.3	33 34.6	+3.1	39.7	34 20.7	+3.8	40.1	56
32 03.2	+0.8	37.7	32 50.6	+1.5	38.1	33 37.7	+2.3	38.5	34 24.5	+3.1	38.9	57
32 04.0	+0.2	36.5	32 52.1	+0.9	36.9	33 40.0	+1.7	37.3	34 27.6	+2.4	37.7	58
32 04.2	−0.5	35.3	32 53.0	+0.3	35.7	33 41.7	+0.9	36.1	34 30.0	+1.7	36.5	59
32 03.7	−1.1	34.1	32 53.3	−0.5	34.5	33 42.6	+0.3	34.9	34 31.7	+1.0	35.3	60
32 02.6	−1.8	33.0	32 52.8	−1.1	33.3	33 42.9	−0.5	33.7	34 32.7	+0.2	34.0	61
32 00.8	−2.5	31.8	32 51.7	−1.8	32.1	33 42.4	−1.1	32.5	34 32.9	−0.4	32.8	62
31 58.3	−3.1	30.6	32 49.9	−2.5	30.9	33 41.3	−1.9	31.3	34 32.5	−1.2	31.6	63
31 55.2	−3.7	29.4	32 47.4	−3.1	29.7	33 39.4	−2.5	30.1	34 31.3	−1.9	30.4	64
31 51.5	−4.4	28.2	32 44.3	−3.9	28.5	33 36.9	−3.2	28.9	34 29.4	−2.7	29.2	65
31 47.1	−5.1	27.1	32 40.4	−4.4	27.4	33 33.7	−4.0	27.7	34 26.7	−3.3	28.0	66
31 42.0	−5.6	25.9	32 36.0	−5.2	26.2	33 29.7	−4.6	26.5	34 23.4	−4.1	26.8	67
31 36.4	−6.4	24.7	32 30.8	−5.8	25.0	33 25.1	−5.3	25.3	34 19.3	−4.8	25.6	68
31 30.0	−6.9	23.6	32 25.0	−6.5	23.8	33 19.8	−6.0	24.1	34 14.5	−5.4	24.3	69
31 23.1	−7.6	22.4	32 18.5	−7.1	22.6	33 13.8	−6.6	22.9	34 09.1	−6.2	23.1	70
31 15.5	−8.2	21.2	32 11.4	−7.8	21.5	33 07.2	−7.4	21.7	34 02.9	−6.9	21.9	71
31 07.3	−8.8	20.1	32 03.6	−8.4	20.3	32 59.8	−8.0	20.5	33 56.0	−7.6	20.7	72
30 58.5	−9.5	18.9	31 55.2	−9.1	19.1	32 51.8	−8.6	19.3	33 48.4	−8.3	19.6	73
30 49.0	−10.0	17.8	31 46.1	−9.7	18.0	32 43.2	−9.4	18.2	33 40.1	−8.9	18.4	74
30 39.0	−10.7	16.6	31 36.4	−10.3	16.8	32 33.8	−9.9	17.0	33 31.2	−9.6	17.2	75
30 28.3	−11.2	15.5	31 26.1	−10.9	15.6	32 23.9	−10.7	15.8	33 21.6	−10.3	16.0	76
30 17.1	−11.9	14.3	31 15.2	−11.6	14.5	32 13.2	−11.2	14.6	33 11.3	−11.0	14.8	77
30 05.2	−12.4	13.2	31 03.6	−12.1	13.3	32 02.0	−11.9	13.5	33 00.3	−11.6	13.6	78
29 52.8	−13.0	12.1	30 51.5	−12.8	12.2	31 50.1	−12.5	12.3	32 48.7	−12.3	12.5	79
29 39.8	−13.6	11.0	30 38.7	−13.3	11.1	31 37.6	−13.2	11.2	32 36.4	−12.9	11.3	80
29 26.2	−14.1	9.8	30 25.4	−14.0	9.9	31 24.4	−13.7	10.0	32 23.5	−13.5	10.1	81
29 12.1	−14.6	8.7	30 11.4	−14.5	8.8	31 10.7	−14.3	8.9	32 10.0	−14.2	9.0	82
28 57.5	−15.3	7.6	29 56.9	−15.1	7.7	30 56.4	−15.0	7.8	31 55.8	−14.8	7.8	83
28 42.2	−15.7	6.5	29 41.8	−15.6	6.6	30 41.4	−15.5	6.6	31 41.0	−15.3	6.7	84
28 26.5	−16.3	5.4	29 26.2	−16.2	5.5	30 25.9	−16.0	5.5	31 25.7	−16.0	5.6	85
28 10.2	−16.8	4.3	29 10.0	−16.7	4.4	30 09.9	−16.7	4.4	31 09.7	−16.6	4.4	86
27 53.4	−17.3	3.2	28 53.3	−17.2	3.3	29 53.2	−17.2	3.3	30 53.1	−17.1	3.3	87
27 36.1	−17.8	2.1	28 36.1	−17.8	2.2	29 36.0	−17.7	2.2	30 36.0	−17.7	2.2	88
27 18.3	−18.3	1.1	28 18.3	−18.3	1.1	29 18.3	−18.3	1.1	30 18.3	−18.3	1.1	89
27 00.0	−18.8	0.0	28 00.0	−18.8	0.0	29 00.0	−18.8	0.0	30 00.0	−18.8	0.0	90
27°			28°			29°			30°			

72°, 288° L.H.A. **LATITUDE SAME NAME AS DECLINATION**

328

LATITUDE **CONTRARY** NAME TO DECLINATION **L.H.A. 72°, 288°**

Dec.	23° Hc	d	Z	24° Hc	d	Z	25° Hc	d	Z	26° Hc	d	Z
°	° ′	′	°	° ′	′	°	° ′	′	°	° ′	′	°
0	16 31.6	-24.6	97.2	16 23.9	-25.6	97.5	16 15.8	-26.5	97.8	16 07.5	-27.5	98.1
1	16 07.0	-24.9	98.2	15 58.3	-25.8	98.5	15 49.3	-26.8	98.8	15 40.0	-27.7	99.0
2	15 42.1	-25.0	99.1	15 32.5	-26.1	99.4	15 22.5	-27.0	99.7	15 12.3	-27.9	100.0
3	15 17.1	-25.3	100.1	15 06.4	-26.2	100.3	14 55.5	-27.2	100.6	14 44.4	-28.2	100.9
4	14 51.8	-25.6	101.0	14 40.2	-26.5	101.3	14 28.3	-27.4	101.5	14 16.2	-28.4	101.8
5	14 26.2	-25.7	101.9	14 13.7	-26.7	102.2	14 00.9	-27.7	102.4	13 47.8	-28.6	102.7
6	14 00.5	-26.0	102.9	13 47.0	-27.0	103.1	13 33.2	-27.8	103.4	13 19.2	-28.7	103.6
7	13 34.5	-26.2	103.8	13 20.0	-27.1	104.0	13 05.4	-28.1	104.3	12 50.5	-29.0	104.5
8	13 08.3	-26.4	104.7	12 52.9	-27.3	105.0	12 37.3	-28.2	105.2	12 21.5	-29.1	105.4
9	12 41.9	-26.5	105.7	12 25.6	-27.5	105.9	12 09.1	-28.4	106.1	11 52.4	-29.3	106.3
10	12 15.4	-26.8	106.6	11 58.1	-27.6	106.8	11 40.7	-28.5	107.0	11 23.1	-29.5	107.2
11	11 48.6	-26.9	107.5	11 30.5	-27.8	107.7	11 12.2	-28.8	107.9	10 53.6	-29.6	108.1
12	11 21.7	-27.1	108.4	11 02.7	-28.0	108.6	10 43.4	-28.8	108.8	10 24.0	-29.7	108.9
13	10 54.6	-27.3	109.3	10 34.7	-28.2	109.5	10 14.6	-29.1	109.7	9 54.3	-29.9	109.8
14	10 27.3	-27.4	110.2	10 06.5	-28.3	110.4	9 45.5	-29.1	110.6	9 24.4	-30.0	110.7
15	9 59.9	-27.5	111.1	9 38.2	-28.4	111.3	9 16.4	-29.3	111.4	8 54.4	-30.2	111.6
16	9 32.4	-27.7	112.0	9 09.8	-28.5	112.2	8 47.1	-29.4	112.3	8 24.2	-30.2	112.5
17	9 04.7	-27.8	112.9	8 41.3	-28.7	113.1	8 17.7	-29.5	113.2	7 54.0	-30.4	113.3
18	8 36.9	-28.0	113.8	8 12.6	-28.8	114.0	7 48.2	-29.7	114.1	7 23.6	-30.5	114.2
19	8 08.9	-28.0	114.7	7 43.8	-28.9	114.8	7 18.5	-29.7	115.0	6 53.1	-30.5	115.1
20	7 40.9	-28.2	115.6	7 14.9	-29.0	115.7	6 48.8	-29.8	115.8	6 22.6	-30.7	115.9
21	7 12.7	-28.3	116.5	6 45.9	-29.1	116.6	6 19.0	-30.0	116.7	5 51.9	-30.7	116.8
22	6 44.4	-28.4	117.4	6 16.8	-29.2	117.5	5 49.0	-30.0	117.6	5 21.2	-30.8	117.7
23	6 16.0	-28.4	118.3	5 47.6	-29.3	118.4	5 19.0	-30.0	118.4	4 50.4	-30.8	118.5
24	5 47.6	-28.6	119.2	5 18.3	-29.3	119.2	4 49.0	-30.2	119.3	4 19.6	-31.0	119.4
25	5 19.0	-28.6	120.0	4 49.0	-29.4	120.1	4 18.8	-30.2	120.2	3 48.6	-30.9	120.2
26	4 50.4	-28.7	120.9	4 19.6	-29.5	121.0	3 48.6	-30.2	121.1	3 17.7	-31.1	121.1
27	4 21.7	-28.7	121.8	3 50.1	-29.5	121.9	3 18.4	-30.3	121.9	2 46.6	-31.0	122.0
28	3 53.0	-28.8	122.7	3 20.6	-29.6	122.7	2 48.1	-30.3	122.8	2 15.6	-31.1	122.8
29	3 24.2	-28.9	123.6	2 51.0	-29.6	123.6	2 17.8	-30.4	123.6	1 44.5	-31.1	123.7
30	2 55.3	-28.9	124.4	2 21.4	-29.7	124.5	1 47.4	-30.4	124.5	1 13.4	-31.1	124.5
31	2 26.4	-28.9	125.3	1 51.7	-29.6	125.3	1 17.0	-30.4	125.4	0 42.3	-31.2	125.4
32	1 57.5	-29.0	126.2	1 22.1	-29.7	126.2	0 46.6	-30.4	126.2	0 11.1	-31.1	126.2
33	1 28.5	-28.9	127.1	0 52.4	-29.7	127.1	0 16.2	-30.4	127.1	0 20.0	+31.1	52.9
34	0 59.6	-29.0	127.9	0 22.7	-29.7	128.0	0 14.2	+30.5	52.0	0 51.1	+31.2	52.1
35	0 30.6	-29.0	128.8	0 07.0	+29.7	51.2	0 44.7	+30.4	51.2	1 22.3	+31.1	51.2
36	0 01.6	-29.0	129.7	0 36.7	+29.7	50.3	1 15.1	+30.3	50.3	1 53.4	+31.0	50.3
37	0 27.4	+29.0	49.4	1 06.4	+29.7	49.4	1 45.4	+30.4	49.5	2 24.4	+31.1	49.5
38	0 56.4	+29.0	48.6	1 36.1	+29.7	48.6	2 15.8	+30.3	48.6	2 55.5	+31.0	48.6
39	1 25.4	+28.9	47.7	2 05.8	+29.6	47.7	2 46.1	+30.3	47.7	3 26.5	+30.9	47.8
40	1 54.3	+29.0	46.8	2 35.4	+29.6	46.8	3 16.4	+30.3	46.9	3 57.4	+31.0	46.9
41	2 23.3	+28.9	45.9	3 05.0	+29.5	46.0	3 46.7	+30.2	46.0	4 28.4	+30.8	46.1
42	2 52.2	+28.8	45.0	3 34.5	+29.6	45.1	4 16.9	+30.1	45.1	4 59.2	+30.8	45.2
43	3 21.0	+28.8	44.2	4 04.1	+29.4	44.2	4 47.0	+30.1	44.3	5 30.0	+30.7	44.3
44	3 49.8	+28.8	43.3	4 33.5	+29.4	43.3	5 17.1	+30.0	43.4	6 00.7	+30.6	43.5
45	4 18.6	+28.7	42.4	5 02.9	+29.3	42.5	5 47.1	+29.9	42.5	6 31.3	+30.5	42.6
46	4 47.3	+28.6	41.5	5 32.2	+29.2	41.6	6 17.0	+29.9	41.7	7 01.8	+30.5	41.7
47	5 15.9	+28.6	40.6	6 01.4	+29.2	40.7	6 46.9	+29.7	40.8	7 32.3	+30.3	40.9
48	5 44.5	+28.4	39.8	6 30.6	+29.0	39.8	7 16.6	+29.7	39.9	8 02.6	+30.2	40.0
49	6 12.9	+28.4	38.9	6 59.6	+29.0	38.9	7 46.3	+29.5	39.0	8 32.8	+30.2	39.1
50	6 41.3	+28.3	38.0	7 28.6	+28.8	38.1	8 15.8	+29.4	38.2	9 03.0	+29.9	38.2
51	7 09.6	+28.2	37.1	7 57.4	+28.8	37.2	8 45.2	+29.3	37.3	9 32.9	+29.9	37.4
52	7 37.8	+28.1	36.2	8 26.2	+28.6	36.3	9 14.5	+29.2	36.4	10 02.8	+29.7	36.5
53	8 05.9	+27.9	35.3	8 54.8	+28.5	35.4	9 43.7	+29.0	35.5	10 32.5	+29.6	35.6
54	8 33.8	+27.9	34.4	9 23.3	+28.4	34.5	10 12.7	+28.9	34.6	11 02.1	+29.4	34.7
55	9 01.7	+27.7	33.5	9 51.7	+28.2	33.6	10 41.6	+28.7	33.7	11 31.5	+29.2	33.8
56	9 29.4	+27.5	32.6	10 19.9	+28.0	32.7	11 10.3	+28.6	32.8	12 00.7	+29.1	32.9
57	9 56.9	+27.5	31.7	10 47.9	+28.0	31.8	11 38.9	+28.4	31.9	12 29.8	+28.9	32.0
58	10 24.4	+27.2	30.8	11 15.9	+27.7	30.9	12 07.3	+28.2	31.0	12 58.7	+28.7	31.1
59	10 51.6	+27.1	29.9	11 43.6	+27.6	30.0	12 35.5	+28.1	30.1	13 27.4	+28.5	30.2
60	11 18.7	+27.0	29.0	12 11.2	+27.4	29.1	13 03.6	+27.8	29.2	13 55.9	+28.3	29.3
61	11 45.7	+26.8	28.1	12 38.6	+27.2	28.2	13 31.4	+27.7	28.3	14 24.2	+28.1	28.4
62	12 12.5	+26.5	27.2	13 05.8	+27.0	27.3	13 59.1	+27.5	27.4	14 52.3	+27.9	27.5
63	12 39.0	+26.4	26.3	13 32.8	+26.8	26.4	14 26.6	+27.2	26.5	15 20.2	+27.7	26.6
64	13 05.4	+26.2	25.3	13 59.6	+26.6	25.4	14 53.8	+27.0	25.6	15 47.9	+27.4	25.7
65	13 31.6	+26.0	24.4	14 26.2	+26.4	24.5	15 20.8	+26.8	24.6	16 15.3	+27.2	24.8
66	13 57.6	+25.8	23.5	14 52.6	+26.2	23.6	15 47.6	+26.6	23.7	16 42.5	+27.0	23.8
67	14 23.4	+25.6	22.6	15 18.8	+25.9	22.7	16 14.2	+26.3	22.8	17 09.5	+26.6	22.9
68	14 49.0	+25.3	21.6	15 44.7	+25.7	21.7	16 40.5	+26.0	21.8	17 36.1	+26.4	21.9
69	15 14.3	+25.1	20.7	16 10.4	+25.5	20.8	17 06.5	+25.8	20.9	18 02.5	+26.2	21.0
70	15 39.4	+24.9	19.7	16 35.9	+25.2	19.8	17 32.3	+25.5	19.9	18 28.7	+25.8	20.1
71	16 04.3	+24.6	18.8	17 01.1	+24.9	18.9	17 57.8	+25.3	19.0	18 54.5	+25.6	19.1
72	16 28.9	+24.3	17.8	17 26.0	+24.6	17.9	18 23.1	+24.9	18.0	19 20.1	+25.2	18.1
73	16 53.2	+24.1	16.9	17 50.6	+24.4	17.0	18 48.0	+24.7	17.1	19 45.3	+25.0	17.2
74	17 17.3	+23.8	15.9	18 15.0	+24.1	16.0	19 12.7	+24.3	16.1	20 10.3	+24.6	16.2
75	17 41.1	+23.6	15.0	18 39.1	+23.8	15.1	19 37.0	+24.1	15.1	20 34.9	+24.3	15.2
76	18 04.7	+23.2	14.0	19 02.9	+23.5	14.1	20 01.1	+23.7	14.2	20 59.2	+24.0	14.3
77	18 27.9	+23.0	13.0	19 26.4	+23.1	13.1	20 24.8	+23.4	13.2	21 23.2	+23.6	13.3
78	18 50.9	+22.6	12.1	19 49.5	+22.9	12.1	20 48.2	+23.0	12.2	21 46.8	+23.3	12.3
79	19 13.5	+22.3	11.1	20 12.4	+22.5	11.1	21 11.2	+22.7	11.2	22 10.1	+22.9	11.3
80	19 35.8	+22.0	10.1	20 34.9	+22.2	10.2	21 33.9	+22.4	10.2	22 33.0	+22.5	10.3
81	19 57.8	+21.7	9.1	20 57.1	+21.8	9.2	21 56.3	+22.0	9.2	22 55.5	+22.1	9.3
82	20 19.5	+21.3	8.1	21 18.9	+21.5	8.2	22 18.3	+21.6	8.2	23 17.6	+21.8	8.3
83	20 40.8	+21.0	7.1	21 40.4	+21.1	7.2	22 39.9	+21.2	7.2	23 39.4	+21.4	7.3
84	21 01.8	+20.6	6.1	22 01.5	+20.7	6.2	23 01.1	+20.9	6.2	24 00.8	+20.9	6.2
85	21 22.4	+20.3	5.1	22 22.2	+20.3	5.1	23 22.0	+20.4	5.2	24 21.7	+20.5	5.2
86	21 42.7	+19.9	4.1	22 42.5	+20.0	4.1	23 42.4	+20.0	4.2	24 42.2	+20.1	4.2
87	22 02.6	+19.5	3.1	23 02.5	+19.6	3.1	24 02.4	+19.6	3.1	25 02.3	+19.7	3.1
88	22 22.1	+19.2	2.1	23 22.1	+19.1	2.1	24 22.0	+19.2	2.1	25 22.0	+19.2	2.1
89	22 41.3	+18.7	1.0	23 41.2	+18.8	1.0	24 41.2	+18.8	1.0	25 41.2	+18.8	1.1
90	23 00.0	+18.3	0.0	24 00.0	+18.3	0.0	25 00.0	+18.3	0.0	26 00.0	+18.3	0.0
	23°			24°			25°			26°		

27° Hc	d	Z	28° Hc	d	Z	29° Hc	d	Z	30° Hc	d	Z	Dec.
° ′	′	°	° ′	′	°	° ′	′	°	° ′	′	°	°
15 58.9	-28.4	98.4	15 50.0	-29.4	98.7	15 40.8	-30.3	99.0	15 31.3	-31.2	99.2	0
15 30.5	-28.7	99.3	15 20.6	-29.6	99.6	15 10.5	-30.5	99.8	15 00.1	-31.4	100.1	1
15 01.8	-28.9	100.2	14 51.0	-29.8	100.5	14 40.0	-30.8	100.7	14 28.7	-31.7	101.0	2
14 32.9	-29.1	101.1	14 21.2	-30.0	101.4	14 09.2	-30.9	101.6	13 57.0	-31.8	101.9	3
14 03.8	-29.3	102.0	13 51.2	-30.2	102.3	13 38.3	-31.1	102.5	13 25.2	-32.0	102.7	4
13 34.5	-29.5	102.9	13 21.0	-30.4	103.2	13 07.2	-31.3	103.4	12 53.2	-32.2	103.6	5
13 05.0	-29.7	103.8	12 50.6	-30.6	104.0	12 35.9	-31.5	104.3	12 21.0	-32.3	104.5	6
12 35.3	-29.8	104.7	12 20.0	-30.7	104.9	12 04.4	-31.6	105.1	11 48.7	-32.5	105.3	7
12 05.5	-30.0	105.6	11 49.3	-31.0	105.8	11 32.8	-31.8	106.0	11 16.2	-32.7	106.2	8
11 35.5	-30.2	106.5	11 18.3	-31.0	106.7	11 01.0	-31.9	106.9	10 43.5	-32.8	107.0	9
11 05.3	-30.3	107.4	10 47.3	-31.2	107.5	10 29.1	-32.1	107.7	10 10.7	-32.9	107.9	10
10 35.0	-30.5	108.2	10 16.1	-31.4	108.4	9 57.0	-32.2	108.6	9 37.8	-33.0	108.8	11
10 04.5	-30.6	109.1	9 44.7	-31.4	109.3	9 24.8	-32.3	109.4	9 04.8	-33.2	109.6	12
9 33.9	-30.8	110.0	9 13.3	-31.6	110.1	8 52.5	-32.4	110.3	8 31.6	-33.2	110.4	13
9 03.1	-30.9	110.9	8 41.7	-31.7	111.0	8 20.1	-32.6	111.1	7 58.4	-33.4	111.3	14
8 32.2	-30.9	111.7	8 10.0	-31.9	111.9	7 47.5	-32.6	112.0	7 25.0	-33.4	112.1	15
8 01.3	-31.1	112.6	7 38.1	-31.9	112.7	7 14.9	-32.7	112.8	6 51.6	-33.6	113.0	16
7 30.2	-31.2	113.5	7 06.2	-32.0	113.6	6 42.2	-32.9	113.7	6 18.0	-33.6	113.8	17
6 59.0	-31.3	114.3	6 34.2	-32.1	114.4	6 09.3	-32.9	114.5	5 44.4	-33.7	114.6	18
6 27.7	-31.4	115.2	6 02.1	-32.2	115.3	5 36.4	-32.9	115.4	5 10.7	-33.8	115.5	19
5 56.3	-31.5	116.0	5 29.9	-32.2	116.1	5 03.5	-33.1	116.2	4 36.9	-33.8	116.3	20
5 24.8	-31.5	116.9	4 57.7	-32.3	117.0	4 30.4	-33.1	117.0	4 03.1	-33.9	117.1	21
4 53.3	-31.6	117.7	4 25.4	-32.4	117.8	3 57.3	-33.1	117.9	3 29.2	-33.9	117.9	22
4 21.7	-31.6	118.6	3 53.0	-32.4	118.7	3 24.2	-33.2	118.7	2 55.3	-33.9	118.8	23
3 50.1	-31.7	119.5	3 20.6	-32.5	119.5	2 51.0	-33.2	119.6	2 21.4	-34.0	119.6	24
3 18.4	-31.8	120.3	2 48.1	-32.5	120.3	2 17.8	-33.3	120.4	1 47.4	-34.0	120.4	25
2 46.6	-31.7	121.2	2 15.6	-32.5	121.2	1 44.5	-33.3	121.2	1 13.4	-34.0	121.2	26
2 14.9	-31.8	122.0	1 43.1	-32.6	122.0	1 11.2	-33.3	122.1	0 39.4	-34.1	122.1	27
1 43.1	-31.9	122.8	1 10.5	-32.6	122.9	0 37.9	-33.3	122.9	0 05.3	-34.0	122.9	28
1 11.2	-31.8	123.7	0 37.9	-32.6	123.7	0 04.6	-33.3	123.7	0 28.7	+34.0	56.3	29
0 39.4	-31.9	124.5	0 05.3	-32.5	124.5	0 28.7	+33.3	55.5	1 02.7	+34.0	55.5	30
0 07.5	-31.8	125.4	0 27.2	+32.6	54.6	1 02.0	+33.3	54.6	1 36.7	+34.0	54.6	31
0 24.3	+31.9	53.8	0 59.8	+32.6	53.8	1 35.3	+33.2	53.8	2 10.7	+34.0	53.8	32
0 56.2	+31.8	52.9	1 32.4	+32.5	52.9	2 08.5	+33.3	53.0	2 44.7	+33.9	53.0	33
1 28.0	+31.9	52.1	2 04.9	+32.5	52.1	2 41.8	+33.2	52.1	3 18.6	+33.9	52.2	34
1 59.9	+31.7	51.2	2 37.4	+32.5	51.2	3 15.0	+33.1	51.3	3 52.5	+33.8	51.3	35
2 31.6	+31.8	50.4	3 09.9	+32.4	50.4	3 48.1	+33.1	50.5	4 26.3	+33.8	50.5	36
3 03.4	+31.7	49.5	3 42.3	+32.4	49.6	4 21.2	+33.1	49.6	5 00.1	+33.7	49.7	37
3 35.1	+31.7	48.7	4 14.7	+32.4	48.7	4 54.3	+33.0	48.8	5 33.8	+33.6	48.9	38
4 06.8	+31.6	47.8	4 47.1	+32.2	47.9	5 27.3	+32.9	47.9	6 07.4	+33.6	48.0	39
4 38.4	+31.6	47.0	5 19.3	+32.2	47.0	6 00.2	+32.9	47.1	6 41.0	+33.5	47.2	40
5 10.0	+31.5	46.1	5 51.5	+32.2	46.2	6 33.1	+32.7	46.3	7 14.5	+33.4	46.3	41
5 41.5	+31.4	45.3	6 23.7	+32.0	45.3	7 05.8	+32.7	45.4	7 47.9	+33.3	45.5	42
6 12.9	+31.3	44.4	6 55.7	+32.0	44.5	7 38.5	+32.6	44.6	8 21.2	+33.2	44.7	43
6 44.2	+31.2	43.5	7 27.7	+31.8	43.6	8 11.1	+32.4	43.7	8 54.4	+33.1	43.8	44
7 15.4	+31.2	42.7	7 59.5	+31.8	42.8	8 43.5	+32.4	42.9	9 27.5	+32.9	43.0	45
7 46.6	+31.0	41.8	8 31.3	+31.6	41.9	9 15.9	+32.2	42.0	10 00.4	+32.8	42.1	46
8 17.6	+31.0	41.0	9 02.9	+31.5	41.1	9 48.1	+32.1	41.2	10 33.2	+32.7	41.3	47
8 48.6	+30.8	40.1	9 34.4	+31.4	40.2	10 20.2	+32.0	40.3	11 05.9	+32.6	40.4	48
9 19.4	+30.6	39.2	10 05.8	+31.3	39.3	10 52.2	+31.8	39.4	11 38.5	+32.4	39.6	49
9 50.0	+30.6	38.3	10 37.1	+31.1	38.5	11 24.0	+31.7	38.6	12 10.9	+32.2	38.7	50
10 20.6	+30.4	37.5	11 08.2	+30.9	37.6	11 55.7	+31.5	37.7	12 43.1	+32.1	37.8	51
10 51.0	+30.2	36.6	11 39.1	+30.8	36.7	12 27.2	+31.3	36.8	13 15.2	+31.8	37.0	52
11 21.2	+30.1	35.7	12 09.9	+30.7	35.8	12 58.5	+31.2	36.0	13 47.0	+31.7	36.1	53
11 51.3	+30.0	34.8	12 40.6	+30.4	35.0	13 29.7	+31.0	35.1	14 18.7	+31.5	35.2	54
12 21.3	+29.7	33.9	13 11.0	+30.3	34.1	14 00.7	+30.8	34.2	14 50.2	+31.4	34.4	55
12 51.0	+29.6	33.1	13 41.3	+30.1	33.2	14 31.5	+30.5	33.3	15 21.6	+31.0	33.5	56
13 20.6	+29.4	32.2	14 11.4	+29.9	32.3	15 02.0	+30.4	32.4	15 52.6	+30.9	32.6	57
13 50.0	+29.2	31.3	14 41.3	+29.6	31.4	15 32.4	+30.2	31.5	16 23.5	+30.7	31.7	58
14 19.2	+29.0	30.4	15 10.9	+29.5	30.5	16 02.6	+29.9	30.6	16 54.2	+30.4	30.8	59
14 48.2	+28.8	29.5	15 40.4	+29.2	29.6	16 32.5	+29.7	29.7	17 24.6	+30.2	29.9	60
15 17.0	+28.5	28.6	16 09.6	+29.0	28.7	17 02.2	+29.5	28.8	17 54.8	+29.9	29.0	61
15 45.5	+28.4	27.6	16 38.6	+28.8	27.8	17 31.7	+29.2	27.9	18 24.7	+29.6	28.1	62
16 13.9	+28.0	26.7	17 07.4	+28.5	26.9	18 00.9	+29.0	27.0	18 54.3	+29.4	27.2	63
16 41.9	+27.9	25.8	17 35.9	+28.3	25.9	18 29.9	+28.6	26.1	19 23.7	+29.1	26.2	64
17 09.8	+27.6	24.9	18 04.2	+28.0	25.0	18 58.5	+28.4	25.2	19 52.8	+28.8	25.3	65
17 37.4	+27.3	23.9	18 32.2	+27.7	24.1	19 26.9	+28.1	24.2	20 21.6	+28.5	24.4	66
18 04.7	+27.1	23.0	18 59.9	+27.4	23.1	19 55.0	+27.9	23.3	20 50.1	+28.2	23.4	67
18 31.8	+26.7	22.1	19 27.3	+27.2	22.2	20 22.9	+27.5	22.3	21 18.3	+27.9	22.5	68
18 58.5	+26.5	21.1	19 54.5	+26.8	21.3	20 50.4	+27.2	21.4	21 46.2	+27.6	21.5	69
19 25.0	+26.2	20.2	20 21.3	+26.5	20.3	21 17.6	+26.8	20.4	22 13.8	+27.2	20.6	70
19 51.2	+25.9	19.2	20 47.8	+26.2	19.3	21 44.4	+26.6	19.5	22 41.0	+26.8	19.6	71
20 17.1	+25.6	18.3	21 14.0	+25.9	18.4	22 11.0	+26.2	18.5	23 07.8	+26.5	18.6	72
20 42.7	+25.2	17.3	21 39.9	+25.6	17.4	22 37.2	+25.8	17.5	23 34.3	+26.2	17.7	73
21 07.9	+24.9	16.3	22 05.5	+25.1	16.4	23 03.0	+25.5	16.6	24 00.5	+25.7	16.7	74
21 32.8	+24.6	15.3	22 30.6	+24.9	15.5	23 28.5	+25.1	15.6	24 26.2	+25.4	15.7	75
21 57.4	+24.2	14.4	22 55.5	+24.4	14.5	23 53.6	+24.7	14.6	24 51.6	+25.0	14.7	76
22 21.6	+23.8	13.4	23 19.9	+24.1	13.5	24 18.3	+24.3	13.6	25 16.6	+24.5	13.7	77
22 45.4	+23.5	12.4	23 44.0	+23.7	12.5	24 42.6	+23.9	12.6	25 41.1	+24.2	12.7	78
23 08.9	+23.1	11.4	24 07.7	+23.3	11.5	25 06.5	+23.5	11.6	26 05.3	+23.7	11.7	79
23 32.0	+22.7	10.4	24 31.0	+22.9	10.5	25 30.0	+23.1	10.5	26 29.0	+23.2	10.6	80
23 54.7	+22.3	9.4	24 53.9	+22.5	9.4	25 53.1	+22.6	9.5	26 52.2	+22.9	9.6	81
24 17.0	+21.9	8.3	25 16.4	+22.0	8.4	26 15.7	+22.2	8.5	27 15.1	+22.3	8.6	82
24 38.9	+21.5	7.3	25 38.4	+21.6	7.4	26 37.9	+21.8	7.5	27 37.4	+21.9	7.5	83
25 00.4	+21.1	6.3	26 00.0	+21.2	6.4	26 59.7	+21.2	6.4	27 59.3	+21.4	6.5	84
25 21.5	+20.6	5.3	26 21.2	+20.7	5.3	27 20.9	+20.8	5.4	28 20.7	+20.9	5.4	85
25 42.1	+20.1	4.2	26 41.9	+20.3	4.3	27 41.7	+20.4	4.3	28 41.6	+20.4	4.3	86
26 02.2	+19.8	3.2	27 02.2	+19.7	3.2	28 02.1	+19.8	3.2	29 02.0	+19.8	3.3	87
26 22.0	+19.2	2.1	27 21.9	+19.3	2.1	28 21.9	+19.3	2.2	29 21.8	+19.4	2.2	88
26 41.2	+18.8	1.1	27 41.2	+18.8	1.1	28 41.2	+18.8	1.1	29 41.2	+18.8	1.1	89
27 00.0	+18.3	0.0	28 00.0	+18.3	0.0	29 00.0	+18.3	0.0	30 00.0	+18.3	0.0	90
27°			28°			29°			30°			

S. Lat. { L.H.A. greater than 180° ....Zn=180°−Z
L.H.A. less than 180°...........Zn=180°+Z

LATITUDE **SAME** NAME AS DECLINATION **L.H.A. 108°, 252°**

329

Dec.	23° Hc	d	Z	24° Hc	d	Z	25° Hc	d	Z	26° Hc	d	Z	27° Hc	d	Z	28° Hc	d	Z	29° Hc	d	Z	30° Hc	d	Z	Dec.
°	° ′	′	°	° ′	′	°	° ′	′	°	° ′	′	°	° ′	′	°	° ′	′	°	° ′	′	°	° ′	′	°	°
0	15 36.7	+24.3	96.8	15 29.5	+25.2	97.1	15 21.9	+26.2	97.4	15 14.1	+27.2	97.6	15 06.0	+28.1	97.9	14 57.6	+29.1	98.2	14 49.0	+29.9	98.4	14 40.0	+30.9	98.7	0
1	16 01.0	+23.9	95.9	15 54.7	+24.9	96.1	15 48.1	+26.0	96.4	15 41.3	+26.9	96.7	15 34.1	+27.9	97.0	15 26.7	+28.8	97.3	15 18.9	+29.8	97.5	15 10.9	+30.7	97.8	1
2	16 24.9	+23.7	94.9	16 19.6	+24.8	95.2	16 14.1	+25.7	95.5	16 08.2	+26.6	95.8	16 02.0	+27.6	96.1	15 55.5	+28.6	96.4	15 48.7	+29.6	96.6	15 41.6	+30.5	96.9	2
3	16 48.6	+23.5	93.9	16 44.4	+24.4	94.2	16 39.8	+25.4	94.5	16 34.8	+26.5	94.8	16 29.6	+27.4	95.1	16 24.1	+28.3	95.4	16 18.3	+29.3	95.7	16 12.1	+30.3	96.0	3
4	17 12.1	+23.1	93.0	17 08.8	+24.2	93.3	17 05.2	+25.2	93.6	17 01.3	+26.1	93.9	16 57.0	+27.1	94.2	16 52.4	+28.2	94.5	16 47.6	+29.0	94.8	16 42.4	+30.0	95.1	4
5	17 35.2	+22.9	92.0	17 33.0	+23.9	92.3	17 30.4	+24.9	92.7	17 27.4	+25.9	93.0	17 24.1	+26.9	93.3	17 20.6	+27.8	93.6	17 16.6	+28.9	93.9	17 12.4	+29.8	94.2	5
6	17 58.1	+22.6	91.0	17 56.9	+23.6	91.4	17 55.3	+24.6	91.7	17 53.3	+25.6	92.0	17 51.0	+26.6	92.3	17 48.4	+27.6	92.7	17 45.5	+28.5	93.0	17 42.2	+29.5	93.3	6
7	18 20.7	+22.3	90.1	18 20.5	+23.3	90.4	18 19.9	+24.3	90.7	18 18.9	+25.4	91.1	18 17.6	+26.4	91.4	18 16.0	+27.3	91.7	18 14.0	+28.3	92.1	18 11.7	+29.3	92.4	7
8	18 43.0	+22.0	89.1	18 43.8	+23.0	89.4	18 44.2	+24.0	89.8	18 44.3	+25.0	90.1	18 44.0	+26.0	90.5	18 43.3	+27.0	90.8	18 42.3	+28.0	91.1	18 41.0	+28.9	91.5	8
9	19 05.0	+21.7	88.1	19 06.8	+22.7	88.5	19 08.2	+23.7	88.8	19 09.3	+24.7	89.2	19 10.0	+25.7	89.5	19 10.3	+26.8	89.8	19 10.3	+27.8	90.2	19 09.9	+28.8	90.5	9
10	19 26.7	+21.3	87.1	19 29.5	+22.4	87.5	19 31.9	+23.5	87.8	19 34.0	+24.5	88.2	19 35.7	+25.5	88.5	19 37.1	+26.4	88.9	19 38.1	+27.4	89.3	19 38.7	+28.4	89.6	10
11	19 48.0	+21.0	86.1	19 51.9	+22.0	86.5	19 55.4	+23.0	86.9	19 58.5	+24.1	87.2	20 01.2	+25.1	87.6	20 03.5	+26.2	87.9	20 05.5	+27.1	88.3	20 07.1	+28.1	88.7	11
12	20 09.0	+20.7	85.1	20 13.9	+21.7	85.5	20 18.4	+22.8	85.9	20 22.6	+23.8	86.2	20 26.3	+24.8	86.6	20 29.7	+25.8	87.0	20 32.6	+26.8	87.4	20 35.2	+27.8	87.7	12
13	20 29.7	+20.3	84.1	20 35.6	+21.4	84.5	20 41.2	+22.4	84.9	20 46.4	+23.4	85.3	20 51.1	+24.5	85.6	20 55.5	+25.5	86.0	20 59.4	+26.5	86.4	21 03.0	+27.5	86.8	13
14	20 50.0	+20.0	83.1	20 57.0	+21.1	83.5	21 03.6	+22.1	83.9	21 09.8	+23.1	84.3	21 15.6	+24.1	84.7	21 21.0	+25.1	85.0	21 25.9	+26.2	85.4	21 30.5	+27.2	85.8	14
15	21 10.0	+19.6	82.1	21 18.1	+20.6	82.5	21 25.7	+21.7	82.9	21 32.9	+22.8	83.3	21 39.7	+23.8	83.7	21 46.1	+24.8	84.1	21 52.1	+25.8	84.5	21 57.7	+26.8	84.9	15
16	21 29.6	+19.3	81.1	21 38.7	+20.3	81.5	21 47.4	+21.3	81.9	21 55.7	+22.3	82.3	22 03.5	+23.4	82.7	22 10.9	+24.5	83.1	22 17.9	+25.5	83.5	22 24.5	+26.5	83.9	16
17	21 48.9	+18.9	80.1	21 59.0	+19.9	80.5	22 08.7	+21.0	80.9	22 18.0	+22.1	81.3	22 26.9	+23.1	81.7	22 35.4	+24.1	82.1	22 43.4	+25.1	82.5	22 51.0	+26.1	82.9	17
18	22 07.8	+18.5	79.1	22 18.9	+19.6	79.5	22 29.7	+20.6	79.9	22 40.1	+21.6	80.3	22 50.0	+22.7	80.7	22 59.5	+23.7	81.1	23 08.5	+24.8	81.5	23 17.1	+25.8	82.0	18
19	22 26.3	+18.1	78.0	22 38.5	+19.1	78.4	22 50.3	+20.2	78.8	23 01.7	+21.2	79.3	23 12.7	+22.2	79.7	23 23.2	+23.3	80.1	23 33.3	+24.3	80.5	23 42.9	+25.4	81.0	19
20	22 44.4	+17.6	77.0	22 57.6	+18.8	77.4	23 10.5	+19.8	77.8	23 22.9	+20.9	78.2	23 34.9	+21.9	78.7	23 46.5	+22.9	79.1	23 57.6	+24.0	79.5	24 08.3	+25.0	80.0	20
21	23 02.0	+17.3	76.0	23 16.4	+18.3	76.4	23 30.3	+19.4	76.8	23 43.8	+20.4	77.2	23 56.8	+21.5	77.7	24 09.4	+22.6	78.1	24 21.6	+23.6	78.6	24 33.3	+24.6	79.0	21
22	23 19.3	+16.9	74.9	23 34.7	+18.0	75.3	23 49.7	+19.0	75.8	24 04.2	+20.1	76.2	24 18.3	+21.1	76.6	24 32.0	+22.1	77.1	24 45.2	+23.1	77.5	24 57.9	+24.2	78.0	22
23	23 36.2	+16.5	73.9	23 52.7	+17.5	74.3	24 08.7	+18.5	74.7	24 24.3	+19.6	75.2	24 39.4	+20.7	75.6	24 54.1	+21.7	76.1	25 08.3	+22.8	76.5	25 22.1	+23.8	77.0	23
24	23 52.7	+16.0	72.8	24 10.2	+17.0	73.2	24 27.2	+18.2	73.7	24 43.9	+19.2	74.1	25 00.1	+20.2	74.6	25 15.8	+21.3	75.0	25 31.1	+22.3	75.5	25 45.9	+23.3	75.9	24
25	24 08.7	+15.6	71.8	24 27.2	+16.7	72.2	24 45.4	+17.7	72.6	25 03.1	+18.7	73.1	25 20.3	+19.8	73.5	25 37.1	+20.8	74.0	25 53.4	+21.9	74.5	26 09.2	+23.0	74.9	25
26	24 24.3	+15.1	70.7	24 43.9	+16.2	71.1	25 03.1	+17.2	71.6	25 21.8	+18.3	72.0	25 40.1	+19.3	72.5	25 57.9	+20.4	72.9	26 15.3	+21.4	73.4	26 32.2	+22.4	73.9	26
27	24 39.4	+14.7	69.6	25 00.1	+15.7	70.1	25 20.3	+16.8	70.5	25 40.1	+17.8	71.0	25 59.4	+18.9	71.4	26 18.3	+19.9	71.9	26 36.7	+21.0	72.4	26 54.6	+22.0	72.9	27
28	24 54.1	+14.2	68.6	25 15.8	+15.3	69.0	25 37.1	+16.3	69.5	25 57.9	+17.4	69.9	26 18.3	+18.4	70.4	26 38.2	+19.5	70.8	26 57.7	+20.5	71.3	27 16.6	+21.6	71.8	28
29	25 08.3	+13.8	67.5	25 31.1	+14.8	67.9	25 53.4	+15.8	68.4	26 15.3	+16.9	68.8	26 36.7	+17.9	69.3	26 57.7	+18.9	69.8	27 18.2	+20.0	70.3	27 38.2	+21.0	70.8	29
30	25 22.1	+13.3	66.4	25 45.9	+14.3	66.9	26 09.2	+15.4	67.3	26 32.2	+16.4	67.8	26 54.6	+17.5	68.2	27 16.6	+18.5	68.7	27 38.2	+19.5	69.2	27 59.2	+20.6	69.7	30
31	25 35.4	+12.8	65.3	26 00.2	+13.9	65.8	26 24.6	+14.9	66.2	26 48.6	+15.9	66.7	27 12.1	+16.9	67.2	27 35.1	+18.0	67.6	27 57.7	+19.0	68.1	28 19.8	+20.1	68.6	31
32	25 48.2	+12.4	64.3	26 14.1	+13.3	64.7	26 39.5	+14.4	65.2	27 04.5	+15.4	65.6	27 29.0	+16.5	66.1	27 53.1	+17.5	66.6	28 16.7	+18.6	67.1	28 39.9	+19.6	67.6	32
33	26 00.6	+11.8	63.2	26 27.4	+12.9	63.6	26 53.9	+13.9	64.1	27 19.9	+14.9	64.5	27 45.5	+15.9	65.0	28 10.6	+17.0	65.5	28 35.3	+18.0	66.0	28 59.5	+19.0	66.5	33
34	26 12.4	+11.4	62.1	26 40.3	+12.4	62.5	27 07.8	+13.3	63.0	27 34.8	+14.4	63.4	28 01.4	+15.4	63.9	28 27.6	+16.4	64.4	28 53.3	+17.5	64.9	29 18.5	+18.5	65.4	34
35	26 23.8	+10.8	61.0	26 52.7	+11.8	61.4	27 21.1	+12.9	61.9	27 49.2	+13.9	62.3	28 16.8	+14.9	62.8	28 44.0	+15.9	63.3	29 10.8	+16.9	63.8	29 37.0	+18.0	64.3	35
36	26 34.6	+10.3	59.9	27 04.5	+11.3	60.3	27 34.0	+12.3	60.8	28 03.1	+13.3	61.2	28 31.7	+14.4	61.7	28 59.9	+15.4	62.2	29 27.7	+16.4	62.7	29 55.0	+17.4	63.2	36
37	26 44.9	+9.9	58.8	27 15.8	+10.9	59.2	27 46.3	+11.8	59.7	28 16.4	+12.8	60.1	28 46.1	+13.8	60.6	29 15.3	+14.8	61.1	29 44.1	+15.8	61.6	30 12.4	+16.9	62.1	37
38	26 54.8	+9.3	57.7	27 26.7	+10.2	58.1	27 58.1	+11.3	58.6	28 29.2	+12.3	59.0	28 59.9	+13.3	59.5	29 30.1	+14.3	60.0	29 59.9	+15.3	60.5	30 29.3	+16.3	61.0	38
39	27 04.1	+8.8	56.6	27 36.9	+9.8	57.0	28 09.4	+10.8	57.5	28 41.5	+11.7	57.9	29 13.2	+12.7	58.4	29 44.4	+13.7	58.9	30 15.2	+14.7	59.4	30 45.6	+15.7	59.9	39
40	27 12.9	+8.2	55.5	27 46.7	+9.2	55.9	28 20.2	+10.1	56.3	28 53.2	+11.2	56.8	29 25.9	+12.1	57.3	29 58.1	+13.1	57.7	30 29.9	+14.1	58.2	31 01.3	+15.1	58.7	40
41	27 21.1	+7.8	54.3	27 55.9	+8.7	54.8	28 30.3	+9.7	55.2	29 04.4	+10.6	55.7	29 38.0	+11.6	56.1	30 11.2	+12.6	56.6	30 44.0	+13.6	57.1	31 16.4	+14.5	57.6	41
42	27 28.9	+7.1	53.2	28 04.6	+8.1	53.7	28 40.0	+9.0	54.1	29 15.0	+10.0	54.5	29 49.6	+11.0	55.0	30 23.8	+11.9	55.5	30 57.6	+12.9	56.0	31 30.9	+14.0	56.5	42
43	27 36.0	+6.7	52.1	28 12.7	+7.6	52.5	28 49.0	+8.5	53.0	29 25.0	+9.4	53.4	30 00.6	+10.4	53.9	30 35.7	+11.4	54.3	31 10.5	+12.3	54.8	31 44.9	+13.3	55.3	43
44	27 42.7	+6.1	51.0	28 20.3	+7.0	51.4	28 57.5	+8.0	51.8	29 34.4	+8.9	52.3	30 11.0	+9.8	52.7	30 47.1	+10.8	53.2	31 22.8	+11.8	53.7	31 58.2	+12.7	54.2	44
45	27 48.8	+5.6	49.9	28 27.3	+6.5	50.3	29 05.5	+7.4	50.7	29 43.3	+8.3	51.1	30 20.8	+9.2	51.6	30 57.9	+10.1	52.1	31 34.6	+11.1	52.5	32 10.9	+12.0	53.0	45
46	27 54.4	+5.0	48.7	28 33.8	+5.9	49.1	29 12.9	+6.7	49.6	29 51.6	+7.7	50.0	30 30.0	+8.6	50.4	31 08.0	+9.5	50.9	31 45.7	+10.4	51.4	32 22.9	+11.4	51.9	46
47	27 59.4	+4.4	47.6	28 39.7	+5.3	48.0	29 19.6	+6.2	48.4	29 59.3	+7.1	48.9	30 38.6	+8.0	49.3	31 17.5	+8.9	49.7	31 56.1	+9.9	50.2	32 34.3	+10.8	50.7	47
48	28 03.8	+3.9	46.5	28 45.0	+4.7	46.9	29 25.8	+5.7	47.3	30 06.4	+6.5	47.7	30 46.6	+7.4	48.1	31 26.5	+8.2	48.6	32 06.0	+9.2	49.1	32 45.1	+10.1	49.5	48
49	28 07.7	+3.4	45.4	28 49.7	+4.2	45.7	29 31.5	+5.0	46.1	30 12.9	+5.9	46.6	30 54.0	+6.8	47.0	31 34.7	+7.7	47.4	32 15.2	+8.5	47.9	32 55.2	+9.5	48.4	49
50	28 11.1	+2.7	44.2	28 53.9	+3.6	44.6	29 36.5	+4.4	45.0	30 18.8	+5.3	45.4	31 00.8	+6.1	45.8	31 42.4	+7.0	46.3	32 23.7	+7.9	46.7	33 04.7	+8.8	47.2	50
51	28 13.8	+2.3	43.1	28 57.5	+3.1	43.5	29 40.9	+3.9	43.8	30 24.1	+4.7	44.2	31 06.9	+5.5	44.7	31 49.4	+6.4	45.1	32 31.6	+7.2	45.5	33 13.5	+8.1	46.0	51
52	28 16.1	+1.6	41.9	29 00.6	+2.4	42.3	29 44.8	+3.2	42.7	30 28.8	+4.0	43.1	31 12.4	+4.9	43.5	31 55.8	+5.7	43.9	32 38.8	+6.6	44.4	33 21.6	+7.4	44.8	52
53	28 17.7	+1.1	40.8	29 03.0	+1.9	41.2	29 48.0	+2.7	41.5	30 32.8	+3.5	41.9	31 17.3	+4.3	42.3	32 01.5	+5.1	42.8	32 45.4	+5.9	43.2	33 29.0	+6.8	43.6	53
54	28 18.8	+0.6	39.7	29 04.9	+1.3	40.0	29 50.7	+2.1	40.4	30 36.3	+2.8	40.8	31 21.6	+3.6	41.2	32 06.6	+4.4	41.6	32 51.3	+5.3	42.0	33 35.8	+6.0	42.4	54
55	28 19.4	-0.1	38.5	29 06.2	+0.7	38.9	29 52.8	+1.4	39.2	30 39.1	+2.2	39.6	31 25.2	+3.0	40.0	32 11.0	+3.8	40.4	32 56.6	+4.5	40.8	33 41.8	+5.4	41.2	55
56	28 19.3	-0.6	37.4	29 06.9	+0.1	37.7	29 54.2	+0.9	38.1	30 41.3	+1.6	38.5	31 28.2	+2.3	38.8	32 14.8	+3.1	39.2	33 01.1	+3.9	39.6	33 47.2	+4.7	40.0	56
57	28 18.7	-1.1	36.3	29 07.0	-0.5	36.6	29 55.1	+0.2	36.9	30 42.9	+1.0	37.3	31 30.5	+1.7	37.7	32 17.9	+2.5	38.0	33 05.0	+3.2	38.4	33 51.9	+4.0	38.8	57
58	28 17.6	-1.8	35.1	29 06.5	-1.0	35.5	29 55.3	-0.3	35.8	30 43.9	+0.3	36.1	31 32.2	+1.1	36.5	32 20.4	+1.7	36.9	33 08.2	+2.6	37.2	33 55.9	+3.3	37.6	58
59	28 15.8	-2.3	34.0	29 05.5	-1.6	34.3	29 55.0	-1.0	34.6	30 44.2	-0.2	35.0	31 33.3	+0.4	35.3	32 22.1	+1.2	35.7	33 10.8	+1.8	36.0	33 59.2	+2.5	36.4	59
60	28 13.5	-2.8	32.9	29 03.9	-2.2	33.2	29 54.0	-1.6	33.5	30 44.0	-0.9	33.8	31 33.7	-0.2	34.1	32 23.3	+0.4	34.5	33 12.6	+1.2	34.9	34 01.7	+1.9	35.2	60
61	28 10.7	-3.4	31.7	29 01.7	-2.8	32.0	29 52.4	-2.1	32.3	30 43.1	-1.6	32.6	31 33.5	-0.9	33.0	32 23.7	-0.2	33.3	33 13.8	+0.5	33.7	34 03.6	+1.2	34.0	61
62	28 07.3	-4.0	30.6	28 58.9	-3.4	30.9	29 50.3	-2.8	31.2	30 41.5	-2.1	31.5	31 32.6	-1.5	31.8	32 23.5	-0.8	32.1	33 14.3	-0.3	32.5	34 04.8	+0.4	32.8	62
63	28 03.3	-4.5	29.5	28 55.5	-3.9	29.7	29 47.5	-3.3	30.0	30 39.4	-2.8	30.3	31 31.1	-2.1	30.6	32 22.7	-1.6	30.9	33 14.0	-0.9	31.3	34 05.2	-0.2	31.6	63
64	27 58.8	-5.1	28.3	28 51.6	-4.6	28.6	29 44.2	-4.0	28.9	30 36.6	-3.3	29.1	31 29.0	-2.8	29.4	32 21.1	-2.2	29.8	33 13.1	-1.5	30.1	34 05.0	-1.0	30.4	64
65	27 53.7	-5.6	27.2	28 47.0	-5.1	27.5	29 40.2	-4.5	27.7	30 33.3	-4.0	28.0	31 26.2	-3.5	28.3	32 18.9	-2.8	28.6	33 11.6	-2.3	28.9	34 04.0	-1.7	29.2	65
66	27 48.1	-6.2	26.1	28 41.9	-5.6	26.3	29 35.7	-5.2	26.6	30 29.3	-4.6	26.8	31 22.7	-4.0	27.1	32 16.1	-3.5	27.4	33 09.3	-3.0	27.7	34 02.3	-2.3	28.0	66
67	27 41.9	-6.7	25.0	28 36.3	-6.2	25.2	29 30.5	-5.7	25.4	30 24.7	-5.3	25.7	31 18.7	-4.7	25.9	32 12.6	-4.2	26.2	33 06.3	-3.6	26.5	34 00.0	-3.1	26.8	67
68	27 35.2	-7.2	23.8	28 30.1	-6.8	24.1	29 24.8	-6.3	24.3	30 19.4	-5.8	24.5	31 14.0	-5.3	24.8	32 08.4	-4.8	25.0	33 02.7	-4.3	25.3	33 56.9	-3.8	25.6	68
69	27 28.0	-7.8	22.7	28 23.3	-7.4	22.9	29 18.5	-6.9	23.1	30 13.6	-6.4	23.4	31 08.7	-6.0	23.6	32 03.6	-5.5	23.9	32 58.4	-5.0	24.1	33 53.1	-4.5	24.4	69
70	27 20.2	-8.3	21.6	28 15.9	-7.9	21.8	29 11.6	-7.5	22.0	30 07.2	-7.0	22.2	31 02.7	-6.6	22.4	31 58.1	-6.1	22.7	32 53.4	-5.6	22.9	33 48.6	-5.2	23.2	70
71	27 11.9	-8.9	20.5	28 08.0	-8.4	20.7	29 04.1	-8.0	20.9	30 00.2	-7.7	21.1	30 56.1	-7.2	21.3	31 52.0	-6.8	21.5	32 47.8	-6.4	21.7	33 43.4	-5.8	22.0	71
72	27 03.0	-9.4	19.4	27 59.6	-9.0	19.6	28 56.1	-8.6	19.7	29 52.5	-8.2	19.9	30 48.9	-7.8	20.1	31 45.2	-7.4	20.3	32 41.4	-7.0	20.6	33 37.6	-6.6	20.8	72
73	26 53.6	-9.8	18.3	27 50.6	-9.5	18.4	28 47.5	-9.2	18.6	29 44.3	-8.8	18.8	30 41.1	-8.4	19.0	31 37.8	-8.0	19.2	32 34.4	-7.6	19.4	33 31.0	-7.2	19.6	73
74	26 43.8	-10.4	17.2	27 41.1	-10.1	17.3	28 38.3	-9.7	17.5	29 35.5	-9.4	17.6	30 32.7	-9.1	17.8	31 29.8	-8.7	18.0	32 26.8	-8.3	18.2	33 23.8	-8.0	18.4	74
75	26 33.4	-10.9	16.1	27 31.0	-10.6	16.2	28 28.6	-10.3	16.4	29 26.1	-9.9	16.5	30 23.6	-9.6	16.7	31 21.1	-9.3	16.8	32 18.5	-9.0	17.0	33 15.8	-8.6	17.2	75
76	26 22.5	-11.5	15.0	27 20.4	-11.1	15.1	28 18.3	-10.8	15.2	29 16.2	-10.5	15.4	30 14.0	-10.2	15.5	31 11.8	-9.9	15.7	32 09.5	-9.5	15.9	33 07.2	-9.2	16.0	76
77	26 11.0	-11.9	13.9	27 09.3	-11.7	14.0	28 07.5	-11.4	14.1	29 05.7	-11.1	14.3	30 03.8	-10.8	14.4	31 01.9	-10.5	14.5	32 00.0	-10.3	14.7	32 58.0	-10.0	14.9	77
78	25 59.1	-12.3	12.8	26 57.6	-12.1	12.9	27 56.1	-11.9	13.0	28 54.6	-11.7	13.1	29 53.0	-11.4	13.3	30 51.4	-11.2	13.4	31 49.7	-10.8	13.5	32 48.0	-10.5	13.7	78
79	25 46.8	-12.9	11.7	26 45.5	-12.7	11.8	27 44.2	-12.4	11.9	28 42.9	-12.2	12.0	29 41.6	-12.0	12.1	30 40.2	-11.7	12.2	31 38.9	-11.5	12.4	32 37.5	-11.3	12.5	79
80	25 33.9	-13.4	10.6	26 32.8	-13.1	10.7	27 31.8	-13.0	10.8	28 30.7	-12.7	10.9	29 29.6	-12.5	11.0	30 28.5	-12.3	11.1	31 27.4	-12.1	11.2	32 26.2	-11.9	11.3	80
81	25 20.5	-13.8	9.5	26 19.7	-13.7	9.6	27 18.8	-13.4	9.7	28 18.0	-13.3	9.8	29 17.1	-13.1	9.9	30 16.2	-12.9	10.0	31 15.3	-12.7	10.1	32 14.3	-12.5	10.2	81
82	25 06.7	-14.3	8.5	26 06.0	-14.1	8.5	27 05.4	-14.0	8.6	28 04.7	-13.8	8.7	29 04.0	-13.6	8.8	30 03.3	-13.5	8.8	31 02.6	-13.3	8.9	32 01.8	-13.1	9.0	82
83	24 52.4	-14.7	7.4	25 51.9	-14.6	7.4	26 51.4	-14.5	7.5	27 50.9	-14.3	7.6	28 50.4	-14.2	7.6	29 49.8	-14.0	7.7	30 49.3	-13.9	7.8	31 48.7	-13.7	7.9	83
84	24 37.7	-15.2	6.3	25 37.3	-15.1	6.4	26 36.9	-14.9	6.4	27 36.6	-14.9	6.5	28 36.2	-14.8	6.5	29 35.8	-14.6	6.6	30 35.4	-14.5	6.7	31 35.0	-14.4	6.7	84
85	24 22.5	-15.7	5.3	25 22.2	-15.5	5.3	26 22.0	-15.5	5.3	27 21.7	-15.4	5.4	28 21.4	-15.2	5.4	29 21.2	-15.2	5.5	30 20.9	-15.1	5.5	31 20.6	-15.0	5.6	85
86	24 06.8	-16.0	4.2	25 06.7	-16.0	4.2	26 06.5	-15.9	4.3	27 06.3	-15.8	4.3	28 06.2	-15.8	4.3	29 06.0	-15.7	4.4	30 05.8	-15.6	4.4	31 05.6	-15.5	4.5	86
87	23 50.8	-16.5	3.1	24 50.7	-16.5	3.2	25 50.6	-16.4	3.2	26 50.5	-16.4	3.2	27 50.4	-16.3	3.2	28 50.3	-16.2	3.3	29 50.2	-16.2	3.3	30 50.1	-16.1	3.3	87
88	23 34.3	-17.0	2.1	24 34.2	-16.9	2.1	25 34.2	-16.9	2.1	26 34.1	-16.8	2.1	27 34.1	-16.8	2.2	28 34.1	-16.8	2.2	29 34.0	-16.7	2.2	30 34.0	-16.7	2.2	88
89	23 17.3	-17.3	1.0	24 17.3	-17.3	1.0	25 17.3	-17.3	1.1	26 17.3	-17.3	1.1	27 17.3	-17.3	1.1	28 17.3	-17.3	1.1	29 17.3	-17.3	1.1	30 17.3	-17.3	1.1	89
90	23 00.0	-17.7	0.0	24 00.0	-17.8	0.0	25 00.0	-17.8	0.0	26 00.0	-17.8	0.0	27 00.0	-17.8	0.0	28 00.0	-17.8	0.0	29 00.0	-17.8	0.0	30 00.0	-17.8	0.0	90
	23°			24°			25°			26°			27°			28°			29°			30°			

LATITUDE **CONTRARY** NAME TO DECLINATION **L.H.A. 73°, 287°**

Dec.	23° Hc	d	Z	24° Hc	d	Z	25° Hc	d	Z	26° Hc	d	Z	27° Hc	d	Z	28° Hc	d	Z	29° Hc	d	Z	30° Hc	d	Z	Dec.
°	° ′	′	°	° ′	′	°	° ′	′	°	° ′	′	°	° ′	′	°	° ′	′	°	° ′	′	°	° ′	′	°	°
0	15 36.7	-24.4	96.8	15 29.5	-25.5	97.1	15 21.9	-26.4	97.4	15 14.1	-27.4	97.6	15 06.0	-28.3	97.9	14 57.6	-29.2	98.2	14 49.0	-30.2	98.4	14 40.0	-31.1	98.7	0
1	15 12.3	-24.7	97.8	15 04.0	-25.6	98.0	14 55.5	-26.6	98.3	14 46.7	-27.6	98.6	14 37.7	-28.6	98.8	14 28.4	-29.5	99.1	14 18.8	-30.4	99.3	14 08.9	-31.3	99.6	1
2	14 47.6	-24.9	98.7	14 38.4	-25.9	99.0	14 28.9	-26.9	99.2	14 19.1	-27.8	99.5	14 09.1	-28.7	99.7	13 58.9	-29.7	100.0	13 48.4	-30.6	100.2	13 37.6	-31.5	100.5	2
3	14 22.7	-25.2	99.6	14 12.5	-26.1	99.9	14 02.0	-27.0	100.1	13 51.3	-28.0	100.4	13 40.4	-28.9	100.6	13 29.2	-29.8	100.9	13 17.8	-30.8	101.1	13 06.1	-31.6	101.3	3
4	13 57.5	-25.4	100.6	13 46.4	-26.4	100.8	13 35.0	-27.3	101.1	13 23.3	-28.2	101.3	13 11.5	-29.1	101.5	12 59.4	-30.1	101.8	12 47.0	-30.9	102.0	12 34.5	-31.9	102.2	4
5	13 32.1	-25.5	101.5	13 20.0	-26.5	101.7	13 07.7	-27.4	102.0	12 55.1	-28.3	102.2	12 42.4	-29.4	102.4	12 29.3	-30.2	102.6	12 16.1	-31.1	102.9	12 02.6	-32.0	103.1	5
6	13 06.6	-25.8	102.4	12 53.5	-26.7	102.7	12 40.3	-27.7	102.9	12 26.8	-28.6	103.1	12 13.0	-29.4	103.3	11 59.1	-30.4	103.5	11 45.0	-31.3	103.7	11 30.6	-32.1	103.9	6
7	12 40.8	-26.0	103.4	12 26.8	-26.9	103.6	12 12.6	-27.8	103.8	11 58.2	-28.7	104.0	11 43.6	-29.7	104.2	11 28.7	-30.5	104.4	11 13.7	-31.4	104.6	10 58.5	-32.3	104.8	7
8	12 14.8	-26.1	104.3	11 59.9	-27.1	104.5	11 44.8	-28.0	104.7	11 29.5	-28.9	104.9	11 13.9	-29.8	105.1	10 58.2	-30.7	105.3	10 42.3	-31.6	105.5	10 26.2	-32.4	105.6	8
9	11 48.7	-26.3	105.2	11 32.8	-27.2	105.4	11 16.8	-28.2	105.6	11 00.6	-29.1	105.8	10 44.1	-29.9	106.0	10 27.5	-30.8	106.2	10 10.7	-31.7	106.3	9 53.8	-32.6	106.5	9
10	11 22.4	-26.5	106.1	11 05.6	-27.4	106.3	10 48.6	-28.3	106.5	10 31.5	-29.2	106.7	10 14.2	-30.1	106.9	9 56.7	-31.0	107.0	9 39.0	-31.8	107.2	9 21.2	-32.6	107.4	10
11	10 55.9	-26.7	107.0	10 38.2	-27.6	107.2	10 20.3	-28.4	107.4	10 02.3	-29.3	107.6	9 44.1	-30.2	107.7	9 25.7	-31.0	107.9	9 07.2	-31.9	108.1	8 48.6	-32.8	108.2	11
12	10 29.2	-26.8	108.0	10 10.6	-27.7	108.1	9 51.9	-28.6	108.3	9 33.0	-29.5	108.5	9 13.9	-30.4	108.6	8 54.7	-31.3	108.8	8 35.3	-32.1	108.9	8 15.8	-32.9	109.1	12
13	10 02.4	-27.0	108.9	9 42.9	-27.8	109.0	9 23.3	-28.8	109.2	9 03.5	-29.6	109.3	8 43.5	-30.4	109.5	8 23.4	-31.3	109.6	8 03.2	-32.1	109.8	7 42.9	-33.0	109.9	13
14	9 35.4	-27.1	109.8	9 15.1	-28.0	109.9	8 54.5	-28.8	110.1	8 33.9	-29.7	110.2	8 13.1	-30.6	110.4	7 52.1	-31.4	110.5	7 31.1	-32.3	110.6	7 09.9	-33.1	110.7	14
15	9 08.3	-27.2	110.7	8 47.1	-28.1	110.8	8 25.7	-29.0	111.0	8 04.2	-29.9	111.1	7 42.5	-30.7	111.2	7 20.7	-31.5	111.4	6 58.8	-32.4	111.5	6 36.8	-33.2	111.6	15
16	8 41.1	-27.4	111.6	8 19.0	-28.3	111.7	7 56.7	-29.1	111.8	7 34.3	-29.9	112.0	7 11.8	-30.8	112.1	6 49.2	-31.6	112.2	6 26.4	-32.4	112.3	6 03.6	-33.2	112.4	16
17	8 13.7	-27.4	112.5	7 50.7	-28.3	112.6	7 27.6	-29.2	112.7	7 04.4	-30.1	112.8	6 41.0	-30.9	113.0	6 17.6	-31.7	113.1	5 54.0	-32.5	113.2	5 30.4	-33.4	113.3	17
18	7 46.3	-27.6	113.4	7 22.4	-28.4	113.5	6 58.4	-29.3	113.6	6 34.3	-30.1	113.7	6 10.1	-30.9	113.8	5 45.9	-31.8	113.9	5 21.5	-32.6	114.0	4 57.0	-33.3	114.1	18
19	7 18.7	-27.7	114.3	6 54.0	-28.6	114.4	6 29.1	-29.4	114.5	6 04.2	-30.2	114.6	5 39.2	-31.0	114.7	5 14.1	-31.8	114.8	4 48.9	-32.6	114.9	4 23.7	-33.5	114.9	19
20	6 51.0	-27.8	115.2	6 25.4	-28.6	115.3	5 59.7	-29.4	115.4	5 34.0	-30.3	115.5	5 08.2	-31.1	115.5	4 42.3	-32.0	115.6	4 16.3	-32.7	115.7	3 50.2	-33.5	115.8	20
21	6 23.2	-27.9	116.1	5 56.8	-28.8	116.2	5 30.3	-29.6	116.2	5 03.7	-30.4	116.3	4 37.1	-31.2	116.4	4 10.3	-31.9	116.5	3 43.6	-32.8	116.5	3 16.7	-33.5	116.6	21
22	5 55.3	-28.0	116.9	5 28.0	-28.8	117.0	5 00.7	-29.6	117.1	4 33.3	-30.4	117.2	4 05.9	-31.2	117.3	3 38.4	-32.0	117.3	3 10.8	-32.8	117.4	2 43.2	-33.5	117.4	22
23	5 27.3	-28.1	117.8	4 59.2	-28.8	117.9	4 31.1	-29.7	118.0	4 02.9	-30.4	118.1	3 34.7	-31.3	118.1	3 06.4	-32.1	118.2	2 38.0	-32.8	118.2	2 09.7	-33.6	118.2	23
24	4 59.2	-28.1	118.7	4 30.4	-29.0	118.8	4 01.4	-29.7	118.9	3 32.5	-30.6	118.9	3 03.4	-31.3	119.0	2 34.3	-32.0	119.0	2 05.2	-32.8	119.0	1 36.1	-33.6	119.1	24
25	4 31.1	-28.2	119.6	4 01.4	-28.9	119.7	3 31.7	-29.8	119.7	3 01.9	-30.5	119.8	2 32.1	-31.3	119.8	2 02.3	-32.2	119.9	1 32.4	-32.9	119.9	1 02.5	-33.7	119.9	25
26	4 02.9	-28.2	120.5	3 32.5	-29.1	120.6	3 01.9	-29.8	120.6	2 31.4	-30.6	120.6	2 00.8	-31.4	120.7	1 30.1	-32.1	120.7	0 59.5	-32.9	120.7	0 28.8	-33.6	120.7	26
27	3 34.7	-28.3	121.4	3 03.4	-29.1	121.4	2 32.1	-29.8	121.5	2 00.8	-30.7	121.5	1 29.4	-31.4	121.5	0 58.0	-32.1	121.5	0 26.6	-32.9	121.6	0 04.8	+33.6	58.4	27
28	3 06.4	-28.4	122.3	2 34.3	-29.1	122.3	2 02.3	-29.9	122.3	1 30.1	-30.6	122.4	0 58.0	-31.4	122.4	0 25.9	-32.2	122.4	0 06.3	+32.8	57.6	0 38.4	+33.6	57.6	28
29	2 38.0	-28.3	123.1	2 05.2	-29.1	123.2	1 32.4	-29.9	123.2	0 59.5	-30.7	123.2	0 26.6	-31.4	123.2	0 06.3	+32.1	56.8	0 39.1	+32.9	56.8	1 12.0	+33.6	56.8	29
30	2 09.7	-28.5	124.0	1 36.1	-29.2	124.1	1 02.5	-30.0	124.1	0 28.8	-30.6	124.1	0 04.8	+31.4	55.9	0 38.4	+32.1	55.9	1 12.0	+32.9	55.9	1 45.6	+33.6	56.0	30
31	1 41.2	-28.4	124.9	1 06.9	-29.2	124.9	0 32.5	-29.9	124.9	0 01.8	+30.7	55.1	0 36.2	+31.4	55.1	1 10.5	+32.2	55.1	1 44.9	+32.8	55.1	2 19.2	+33.6	55.1	31
32	1 12.8	-28.4	125.8	0 37.7	-29.2	125.8	0 02.6	-29.9	125.8	0 32.5	+30.6	54.2	1 07.6	+31.4	54.2	1 42.7	+32.1	54.2	2 17.7	+32.8	54.3	2 52.8	+33.5	54.3	32
33	0 44.4	-28.5	126.7	0 08.5	-29.2	126.7	0 27.3	+29.9	53.3	1 03.1	+30.7	53.3	1 39.0	+31.3	53.4	2 14.8	+32.0	53.4	2 50.5	+32.8	53.4	3 26.3	+33.4	53.5	33
34	0 15.9	-28.5	127.6	0 20.7	+29.2	52.5	0 57.2	+29.9	52.5	1 33.8	+30.6	52.5	2 10.3	+31.4	52.5	2 46.8	+32.1	52.5	3 23.3	+32.7	52.6	3 59.7	+33.5	52.6	34
35	0 12.6	+28.4	51.6	0 49.9	+29.1	51.6	1 27.1	+29.9	51.6	2 04.4	+30.6	51.6	2 41.7	+31.2	51.6	3 18.9	+32.0	51.7	3 56.0	+32.7	51.7	4 33.2	+33.3	51.8	35
36	0 41.0	+28.5	50.7	1 19.0	+29.2	50.7	1 57.0	+29.9	50.7	2 35.0	+30.6	50.8	3 12.9	+31.3	50.8	3 50.9	+31.9	50.8	4 28.7	+32.6	50.9	5 06.5	+33.3	51.0	36
37	1 09.5	+28.4	49.8	1 48.2	+29.1	49.8	2 26.9	+29.8	49.9	3 05.6	+30.5	49.9	3 44.2	+31.2	49.9	4 22.8	+31.9	50.0	5 01.3	+32.6	50.1	5 39.8	+33.3	50.1	37
38	1 37.9	+28.4	48.9	2 17.3	+29.1	49.0	2 56.7	+29.8	49.0	3 36.1	+30.4	49.0	4 15.4	+31.1	49.1	4 54.7	+31.8	49.1	5 33.9	+32.5	49.2	6 13.1	+33.1	49.3	38
39	2 06.3	+28.4	48.0	2 46.4	+29.1	48.1	3 26.5	+29.8	48.1	4 06.5	+30.5	48.2	4 46.5	+31.1	48.2	5 26.5	+31.7	48.3	6 06.4	+32.4	48.4	6 46.2	+33.1	48.5	39
40	2 34.7	+28.4	47.2	3 15.5	+29.0	47.2	3 56.3	+29.6	47.2	4 37.0	+30.3	47.3	5 17.6	+31.0	47.4	5 58.2	+31.7	47.4	6 38.8	+32.3	47.5	7 19.3	+32.9	47.6	40
41	3 03.1	+28.3	46.3	3 44.5	+29.0	46.3	4 25.9	+29.7	46.4	5 07.3	+30.3	46.4	5 48.6	+31.0	46.5	6 29.9	+31.6	46.6	7 11.1	+32.2	46.7	7 52.2	+32.9	46.8	41
42	3 31.4	+28.2	45.4	4 13.5	+28.9	45.4	4 55.6	+29.5	45.5	5 37.6	+30.2	45.6	6 19.6	+30.8	45.6	7 01.5	+31.5	45.7	7 43.3	+32.1	45.8	8 25.1	+32.8	45.9	42
43	3 59.6	+28.2	44.5	4 42.4	+28.8	44.6	5 25.1	+29.5	44.6	6 07.8	+30.1	44.7	6 50.4	+30.8	44.8	7 33.0	+31.3	44.9	8 15.4	+32.1	45.0	8 57.9	+32.6	45.1	43
44	4 27.8	+28.2	43.6	5 11.2	+28.8	43.7	5 54.6	+29.4	43.8	6 37.9	+30.0	43.8	7 21.2	+30.6	43.9	8 04.3	+31.3	44.0	8 47.5	+31.9	44.1	9 30.5	+32.5	44.2	44
45	4 56.0	+28.0	42.7	5 40.0	+28.7	42.8	6 24.0	+29.3	42.9	7 07.9	+30.0	43.0	7 51.8	+30.6	43.0	8 35.6	+31.2	43.1	9 19.4	+31.7	43.3	10 03.0	+32.4	43.4	45
46	5 24.0	+28.0	41.9	6 08.7	+28.6	41.9	6 53.3	+29.2	42.0	7 37.9	+29.8	42.1	8 22.4	+30.4	42.2	9 06.8	+31.0	42.3	9 51.1	+31.7	42.4	10 35.4	+32.3	42.5	46
47	5 52.0	+27.9	41.0	6 37.3	+28.5	41.0	7 22.5	+29.1	41.1	8 07.7	+29.7	41.2	8 52.8	+30.3	41.3	9 37.8	+30.9	41.4	10 22.8	+31.5	41.5	11 07.7	+32.1	41.7	47
48	6 19.9	+27.8	40.1	7 05.8	+28.4	40.2	7 51.6	+29.0	40.2	8 37.4	+29.6	40.3	9 23.1	+30.2	40.4	10 08.7	+30.8	40.5	10 54.3	+31.3	40.7	11 39.8	+31.9	40.8	48
49	6 47.7	+27.7	39.2	7 34.2	+28.3	39.3	8 20.6	+28.9	39.4	9 07.0	+29.5	39.5	9 53.3	+30.0	39.6	10 39.5	+30.6	39.7	11 25.6	+31.3	39.8	12 11.7	+31.8	39.9	49
50	7 15.4	+27.6	38.3	8 02.5	+28.2	38.4	8 49.5	+28.8	38.5	9 36.5	+29.3	38.6	10 23.3	+29.9	38.7	11 10.1	+30.5	38.8	11 56.9	+31.0	38.9	12 43.5	+31.6	39.1	50
51	7 43.0	+27.5	37.4	8 30.7	+28.0	37.5	9 18.3	+28.6	37.6	10 05.8	+29.2	37.7	10 53.2	+29.8	37.8	11 40.6	+30.3	37.9	12 27.9	+30.9	38.1	13 15.1	+31.4	38.2	51
52	8 10.5	+27.4	36.5	8 58.7	+28.0	36.6	9 46.9	+28.5	36.7	10 35.0	+29.0	36.8	11 23.0	+29.6	36.9	12 10.9	+30.2	37.0	12 58.8	+30.7	37.2	13 46.5	+31.3	37.3	52
53	8 37.9	+27.3	35.6	9 26.7	+27.8	35.7	10 15.4	+28.3	35.8	11 04.0	+28.9	35.9	11 52.6	+29.4	36.0	12 41.1	+29.9	36.2	13 29.5	+30.5	36.3	14 17.8	+31.0	36.4	53
54	9 05.2	+27.1	34.7	9 54.5	+27.6	34.8	10 43.7	+28.2	34.9	11 32.9	+28.7	35.0	12 22.0	+29.2	35.1	13 11.0	+29.8	35.3	14 00.0	+30.3	35.4	14 48.8	+30.9	35.6	54
55	9 32.3	+27.0	33.8	10 22.1	+27.5	33.9	11 11.9	+28.0	34.0	12 01.6	+28.5	34.1	12 51.2	+29.1	34.2	13 40.8	+29.6	34.4	14 30.3	+30.1	34.5	15 19.7	+30.6	34.7	55
56	9 59.3	+26.8	32.9	10 49.6	+27.4	33.0	11 39.9	+27.9	33.1	12 30.1	+28.4	33.2	13 20.3	+28.9	33.3	14 10.4	+29.4	33.5	15 00.4	+29.9	33.6	15 50.3	+30.4	33.8	56
57	10 26.1	+26.7	32.0	11 17.0	+27.1	32.1	12 07.8	+27.6	32.2	12 58.5	+28.2	32.3	13 49.2	+28.7	32.4	14 39.8	+29.2	32.6	15 30.3	+29.7	32.7	16 20.7	+30.2	32.9	57
58	10 52.8	+26.5	31.1	11 44.1	+27.0	31.2	12 35.4	+27.5	31.3	13 26.7	+28.0	31.4	14 17.9	+28.4	31.5	15 09.0	+28.9	31.7	16 00.0	+29.4	31.8	16 50.9	+30.0	32.0	58
59	11 19.3	+26.3	30.2	12 11.1	+26.9	30.3	13 02.9	+27.3	30.4	13 54.7	+27.7	30.5	14 46.3	+28.3	30.6	15 37.9	+28.8	30.8	16 29.4	+29.3	30.9	17 20.9	+29.7	31.1	59
60	11 45.6	+26.2	29.2	12 38.0	+26.6	29.3	13 30.2	+27.1	29.5	14 22.4	+27.6	29.6	15 14.6	+28.0	29.7	16 06.7	+28.5	29.8	16 58.7	+28.9	30.0	17 50.6	+29.4	30.2	60
61	12 11.8	+26.0	28.3	13 04.6	+26.4	28.4	13 57.3	+26.9	28.5	14 50.0	+27.3	28.7	15 42.6	+27.8	28.8	16 35.2	+28.2	28.9	17 27.6	+28.8	29.1	18 20.0	+29.2	29.2	61
62	12 37.8	+25.8	27.4	13 31.0	+26.3	27.5	14 24.2	+26.7	27.6	15 17.3	+27.2	27.7	16 10.4	+27.6	27.9	17 03.4	+28.0	28.0	17 56.4	+28.4	28.2	18 49.2	+28.9	28.3	62
63	13 03.6	+25.6	26.5	13 57.3	+26.0	26.6	14 50.9	+26.4	26.7	15 44.5	+26.8	26.8	16 38.0	+27.3	26.9	17 31.4	+27.8	27.1	18 24.8	+28.2	27.2	19 18.1	+28.7	27.4	63
64	13 29.2	+25.4	25.5	14 23.3	+25.8	25.6	15 17.3	+26.3	25.8	16 11.3	+26.7	25.9	17 05.3	+27.1	26.0	17 59.2	+27.5	26.2	18 53.0	+27.9	26.3	19 46.8	+28.3	26.5	64
65	13 54.6	+25.1	24.6	14 49.1	+25.6	24.7	15 43.6	+25.9	24.8	16 38.0	+26.4	24.9	17 32.4	+26.8	25.1	18 26.7	+27.2	25.2	19 20.9	+27.6	25.4	20 15.1	+28.0	25.5	65
66	14 19.7	+25.0	23.7	15 14.7	+25.3	23.8	16 09.5	+25.8	23.9	17 04.4	+26.1	24.0	17 59.2	+26.5	24.1	18 53.9	+26.9	24.3	19 48.5	+27.4	24.4	20 43.1	+27.8	24.6	66
67	14 44.7	+24.7	22.7	15 40.0	+25.1	22.8	16 35.3	+25.5	22.9	17 30.5	+25.9	23.1	18 25.7	+26.2	23.2	19 20.8	+26.6	23.3	20 15.9	+27.0	23.5	21 10.9	+27.4	23.6	67
68	15 09.4	+24.5	21.8	16 05.1	+24.9	21.9	17 00.8	+25.2	22.0	17 56.4	+25.5	22.1	18 51.9	+26.0	22.2	19 47.4	+26.4	22.4	20 42.9	+26.7	22.5	21 38.3	+27.1	22.7	68
69	15 33.9	+24.2	20.8	16 30.0	+24.6	20.9	17 26.0	+24.9	21.1	18 21.9	+25.3	21.2	19 17.9	+25.6	21.3	20 13.8	+26.0	21.4	21 09.6	+26.4	21.6	22 05.4	+26.7	21.7	69
70	15 58.1	+24.0	19.9	16 54.6	+24.3	20.0	17 50.9	+24.7	20.1	18 47.2	+25.0	20.2	19 43.5	+25.4	20.3	20 39.8	+25.7	20.5	21 36.0	+26.0	20.6	22 32.1	+26.4	20.7	70
71	16 22.1	+23.8	18.9	17 18.9	+24.0	19.0	18 15.6	+24.4	19.1	19 12.2	+24.7	19.2	20 08.9	+25.0	19.4	21 05.5	+25.3	19.5	22 02.0	+25.7	19.6	22 58.5	+26.0	19.8	71
72	16 45.9	+23.5	18.0	17 42.9	+23.8	18.1	18 40.0	+24.0	18.2	19 36.9	+24.4	18.3	20 33.9	+24.7	18.4	21 30.8	+25.0	18.5	22 27.7	+25.3	18.6	23 24.5	+25.7	18.8	72
73	17 09.4	+23.1	17.0	18 06.7	+23.5	17.1	19 04.0	+23.8	17.2	20 01.3	+24.1	17.3	20 58.6	+24.4	17.4	21 55.8	+24.7	17.5	22 53.0	+25.0	17.7	23 50.2	+25.3	17.8	73
74	17 32.5	+23.0	16.0	18 30.2	+23.2	16.1	19 27.8	+23.5	16.2	20 25.4	+23.8	16.3	21 23.0	+24.0	16.4	22 20.5	+24.3	16.6	23 18.0	+24.6	16.7	24 15.5	+24.8	16.8	74
75	17 55.5	+22.6	15.1	18 53.4	+22.9	15.2	19 51.3	+23.1	15.3	20 49.2	+23.4	15.4	21 47.0	+23.7	15.5	22 44.8	+24.0	15.6	23 42.6	+24.2	15.7	24 40.3	+24.5	15.8	75
76	18 18.1	+22.3	14.1	19 16.3	+22.5	14.2	20 14.4	+22.8	14.3	21 12.6	+23.0	14.4	22 10.7	+23.3	14.5	23 08.8	+23.5	14.6	24 06.8	+23.8	14.7	25 04.8	+24.1	14.8	76
77	18 40.4	+22.0	13.1	19 38.8	+22.3	13.2	20 37.2	+22.5	13.3	21 35.6	+22.7	13.4	22 34.0	+22.9	13.5	23 32.3	+23.2	13.6	24 30.6	+23.5	13.7	25 28.9	+23.7	13.8	77
78	19 02.4	+21.7	12.1	20 01.1	+21.9	12.2	20 59.7	+22.1	12.3	21 58.3	+22.4	12.4	22 56.9	+22.6	12.5	23 55.5	+22.8	12.6	24 54.1	+23.0	12.7	25 52.6	+23.2	12.8	78
79	19 24.1	+21.4	11.2	20 23.0	+21.6	11.2	21 21.8	+21.8	11.3	22 20.7	+21.9	11.4	23 19.5	+22.2	11.5	24 18.3	+22.4	11.5	25 17.1	+22.5	11.6	26 15.8	+22.8	11.7	79
80	19 45.5	+21.1	10.2	20 44.6	+21.2	10.2	21 43.6	+21.4	10.3	22 42.6	+21.6	10.4	23 41.7	+21.7	10.4	24 40.7	+21.9	10.5	25 39.6	+22.2	10.6	26 38.6	+22.3	10.7	80
81	20 06.6	+20.7	9.2	21 05.8	+20.9	9.2	22 05.0	+21.1	9.3	23 04.2	+21.2	9.4	24 03.4	+21.4	9.4	25 02.6	+21.6	9.5	26 01.8	+21.7	9.6	27 00.9	+21.9	9.7	81
82	20 27.3	+20.4	8.2	21 26.7	+20.5	8.2	22 26.1	+20.6	8.3	23 25.4	+20.8	8.3	24 24.8	+21.0	8.4	25 24.2	+21.1	8.5	26 23.5	+21.2	8.5	27 22.8	+21.4	8.6	82
83	20 47.7	+20.0	7.2	21 47.2	+20.2	7.2	22 46.7	+20.3	7.3	23 46.2	+20.4	7.3	24 45.8	+20.5	7.4	25 45.3	+20.6	7.4	26 44.7	+20.8	7.5	27 44.2	+21.0	7.6	83
84	21 07.7	+19.7	6.2	22 07.4	+19.7	6.2	23 07.0	+19.9	6.2	24 06.6	+20.0	6.3	25 06.3	+20.1	6.3	26 05.9	+20.2	6.4	27 05.5	+20.4	6.4	28 05.2	+20.4	6.5	84
85	21 27.4	+19.3	5.1	22 27.1	+19.4	5.2	23 26.9	+19.4	5.2	24 26.6	+19.6	5.3	25 26.4	+19.6	5.3	26 26.1	+19.8	5.3	27 25.9	+19.8	5.4	28 25.6	+19.9	5.4	85
86	21 46.7	+18.9	4.1	22 46.5	+19.0	4.1	23 46.3	+19.1	4.2	24 46.2	+19.1	4.2	25 46.0	+19.2	4.2	26 45.9	+19.2	4.3	27 45.7	+19.3	4.3	28 45.5	+19.4	4.4	86
87	22 05.6	+18.5	3.1	23 05.5	+18.6	3.1	24 05.4	+18.6	3.1	25 05.3	+18.7	3.2	26 05.2	+18.8	3.2	27 05.1	+18.8	3.2	28 05.0	+18.9	3.3	29 04.9	+18.9	3.3	87
88	22 24.1	+18.2	2.1	23 24.1	+18.1	2.1	24 24.0	+18.2	2.1	25 24.0	+18.2	2.1	26 24.0	+18.2	2.1	27 23.9	+18.3	2.2	28 23.9	+18.3	2.2	29 23.8	+18.4	2.2	88
89	22 42.3	+17.7	1.0	23 42.2	+17.8	1.0	24 42.2	+17.8	1.1	25 42.2	+17.8	1.1	26 42.2	+17.8	1.1	27 42.2	+17.8	1.1	28 42.2	+17.8	1.1	29 42.2	+17.8	1.1	89
90	23 00.0	+17.3	0.0	24 00.0	+17.3	0.0	25 00.0	+17.3	0.0	26 00.0	+17.3	0.0	27 00.0	+17.3	0.0	28 00.0	+17.3	0.0	29 00.0	+17.3	0.0	30 00.0	+17.3	0.0	90
	23°			24°			25°			26°			27°			28°			29°			30°			

S. Lat. {L.H.A. greater than 180° ....Zn=180°–Z; L.H.A. less than 180°...........Zn=180°+Z}

LATITUDE **SAME** NAME AS DECLINATION **L.H.A. 107°, 253°**

331

N. Lat. {L.H.A. greater than 180° .....Zn=Z; L.H.A. less than 180°............Zn=360°−Z}

Dec.	23°			24°			25°			26°			27°			28°			29°			30°			Dec.
	Hc	d	Z	Hc	d	Z	Hc	d	Z	Hc	d	Z	Hc	d	Z	Hc	d	Z	Hc	d	Z	Hc	d	Z	
°	° ′	′	°	° ′	′	°	° ′	′	°	° ′	′	°	° ′	′	°	° ′	′	°	° ′	′	°	° ′	′	°	°
0	14 41.9	+24.1	96.4	14 35.1	+25.1	96.7	14 28.0	+26.1	96.9	14 20.6	+27.1	97.2	14 13.0	+28.0	97.4	14 05.1	+29.0	97.7	13 57.0	+29.9	97.9	13 48.6	+30.8	98.2	0
1	15 06.0	+23.9	95.4	15 00.2	+24.8	95.7	14 54.1	+25.8	96.0	14 47.7	+26.8	96.2	14 41.0	+27.8	96.5	14 34.1	+28.7	96.8	14 26.9	+29.7	97.0	14 19.4	+30.6	97.3	1
2	15 29.9	+23.6	94.5	15 25.0	+24.7	94.8	15 19.9	+25.6	95.0	15 14.5	+26.6	95.3	15 08.8	+27.6	95.6	15 02.8	+28.5	95.9	14 56.6	+29.4	96.1	14 50.0	+30.4	96.4	2
3	15 53.5	+23.4	93.5	15 49.7	+24.4	93.8	15 45.5	+25.4	94.1	15 41.1	+26.3	94.4	15 36.4	+27.3	94.7	15 31.3	+28.3	94.9	15 26.0	+29.3	95.2	15 20.4	+30.2	95.5	3
4	16 16.9	+23.1	92.6	16 14.1	+24.1	92.9	16 10.9	+25.1	93.2	16 07.4	+26.1	93.5	16 03.7	+27.1	93.7	15 59.6	+28.1	94.0	15 55.3	+29.0	94.3	15 50.6	+29.9	94.6	4
5	16 40.0	+22.9	91.6	16 38.2	+23.9	91.9	16 36.0	+24.9	92.2	16 33.5	+25.9	92.5	16 30.8	+26.8	92.8	16 27.7	+27.8	93.1	16 24.3	+28.7	93.4	16 20.5	+29.8	93.7	5
6	17 02.9	+22.6	90.7	17 02.1	+23.6	91.0	17 00.9	+24.6	91.3	16 59.4	+25.6	91.6	16 57.6	+26.6	91.9	16 55.5	+27.5	92.2	16 53.0	+28.6	92.5	16 50.3	+29.5	92.8	6
7	17 25.5	+22.3	89.7	17 25.7	+23.3	90.0	17 25.5	+24.3	90.3	17 25.0	+25.3	90.6	17 24.2	+26.3	90.9	17 23.0	+27.3	91.3	17 21.6	+28.2	91.6	17 19.8	+29.2	91.9	7
8	17 47.8	+22.0	88.7	17 49.0	+23.0	89.0	17 49.8	+24.1	89.4	17 50.3	+25.1	89.7	17 50.5	+26.0	90.0	17 50.3	+27.1	90.3	17 49.8	+28.0	90.6	17 49.0	+29.0	91.0	8
9	18 09.8	+21.7	87.7	18 12.0	+22.7	88.1	18 13.9	+23.7	88.4	18 15.4	+24.7	88.7	18 16.5	+25.8	89.0	18 17.4	+26.7	89.4	18 17.8	+27.8	89.7	18 18.0	+28.7	90.0	9
10	18 31.5	+21.4	86.7	18 34.7	+22.5	87.1	18 37.6	+23.5	87.4	18 40.1	+24.5	87.8	18 42.3	+25.5	88.1	18 44.1	+26.5	88.4	18 45.6	+27.4	88.8	18 46.7	+28.4	89.1	10
11	18 52.9	+21.1	85.8	18 57.2	+22.1	86.1	19 01.1	+23.1	86.4	19 04.6	+24.2	86.8	19 07.8	+25.2	87.1	19 10.6	+26.2	87.5	19 13.0	+27.2	87.8	19 15.1	+28.2	88.2	11
12	19 14.0	+20.8	84.8	19 19.3	+21.8	85.1	19 24.2	+22.9	85.5	19 28.8	+23.8	85.8	19 33.0	+24.8	86.2	19 36.8	+25.8	86.5	19 40.2	+26.9	86.9	19 43.3	+27.9	87.2	12
13	19 34.8	+20.4	83.8	19 41.1	+21.5	84.1	19 47.1	+22.5	84.5	19 52.6	+23.6	84.8	19 57.8	+24.6	85.2	20 02.6	+25.6	85.6	20 07.1	+26.6	85.9	20 11.2	+27.5	86.3	13
14	19 55.2	+20.1	82.8	20 02.6	+21.1	83.1	20 09.6	+22.1	83.5	20 16.2	+23.2	83.9	20 22.4	+24.2	84.2	20 28.2	+25.3	84.6	20 33.7	+26.2	85.0	20 38.7	+27.3	85.4	14
15	20 15.3	+19.8	81.8	20 23.7	+20.8	82.1	20 31.7	+21.9	82.5	20 39.4	+22.8	82.9	20 46.6	+23.9	83.3	20 53.5	+24.9	83.6	20 59.9	+25.9	84.0	21 06.0	+26.9	84.4	15
16	20 35.1	+19.4	80.8	20 44.5	+20.5	81.1	20 53.6	+21.5	81.5	21 02.2	+22.6	81.9	21 10.5	+23.6	82.3	21 18.4	+24.5	82.7	21 25.8	+25.6	83.1	21 32.9	+26.6	83.4	16
17	20 54.5	+19.1	79.8	21 05.0	+20.1	80.1	21 15.1	+21.1	80.5	21 24.8	+22.1	80.9	21 34.1	+23.2	81.3	21 42.9	+24.3	81.7	21 51.4	+25.3	82.1	21 59.5	+26.2	82.5	17
18	21 13.6	+18.7	78.7	21 25.1	+19.7	79.1	21 36.2	+20.8	79.5	21 46.9	+21.8	79.9	21 57.3	+22.8	80.3	22 07.2	+23.8	80.7	22 16.7	+24.8	81.1	22 25.7	+25.9	81.5	18
19	21 32.3	+18.3	77.7	21 44.8	+19.4	78.1	21 57.0	+20.4	78.5	22 08.7	+21.5	78.9	22 20.1	+22.5	79.3	22 31.0	+23.5	79.7	22 41.5	+24.6	80.1	22 51.6	+25.6	80.5	19
20	21 50.6	+17.9	76.7	22 04.2	+19.0	77.1	22 17.4	+20.0	77.5	22 30.2	+21.0	77.9	22 42.6	+22.1	78.3	22 54.5	+23.2	78.7	23 06.1	+24.1	79.1	23 17.2	+25.1	79.5	20
21	22 08.5	+17.5	75.7	22 23.2	+18.5	76.1	22 37.4	+19.6	76.5	22 51.2	+20.7	76.9	23 04.7	+21.7	77.3	23 17.7	+22.7	77.7	23 30.2	+23.8	78.1	23 42.3	+24.8	78.6	21
22	22 26.0	+17.2	74.6	22 41.7	+18.2	75.0	22 57.0	+19.3	75.4	23 11.9	+20.3	75.9	23 26.4	+21.3	76.3	23 40.4	+22.3	76.7	23 54.0	+23.4	77.1	24 07.1	+24.4	77.6	22
23	22 43.2	+16.7	73.6	22 59.9	+17.8	74.0	23 16.3	+18.8	74.4	23 32.2	+19.9	74.8	23 47.7	+20.9	75.3	24 02.7	+22.0	75.7	24 17.4	+22.9	76.1	24 31.5	+24.0	76.6	23
24	22 59.9	+16.4	72.6	23 17.7	+17.4	73.0	23 35.1	+18.4	73.4	23 52.1	+19.4	73.8	24 08.6	+20.5	74.2	24 24.7	+21.5	74.7	24 40.3	+22.6	75.1	24 55.5	+23.6	75.5	24
25	23 16.3	+15.9	71.5	23 35.1	+17.0	71.9	23 53.5	+18.0	72.3	24 11.5	+19.0	72.8	24 29.1	+20.0	73.2	24 46.2	+21.1	73.6	25 02.9	+22.1	74.1	25 19.1	+23.2	74.5	25
26	23 32.2	+15.5	70.5	23 52.1	+16.5	70.9	24 11.5	+17.6	71.3	24 30.5	+18.6	71.7	24 49.1	+19.7	72.2	25 07.3	+20.7	72.6	25 25.0	+21.7	73.1	25 42.3	+22.7	73.5	26
27	23 47.7	+15.0	69.4	24 08.6	+16.1	69.8	24 29.1	+17.1	70.2	24 49.1	+18.2	70.7	25 08.8	+19.2	71.1	25 28.0	+20.2	71.6	25 46.7	+21.3	72.0	26 05.0	+22.3	72.5	27
28	24 02.7	+14.7	68.3	24 24.7	+15.6	68.8	24 46.2	+16.7	69.2	25 07.3	+17.7	69.6	25 28.0	+18.7	70.1	25 48.2	+19.8	70.5	26 08.0	+20.8	71.0	26 27.3	+21.9	71.4	28
29	24 17.4	+14.1	67.3	24 40.3	+15.2	67.7	25 02.9	+16.2	68.1	25 25.0	+17.3	68.6	25 46.7	+18.3	69.0	26 08.0	+19.3	69.5	26 28.8	+20.4	69.9	26 49.2	+21.4	70.4	29
30	24 31.5	+13.8	66.2	24 55.5	+14.8	66.6	25 19.1	+15.8	67.1	25 42.3	+16.8	67.5	26 05.0	+17.9	68.0	26 27.3	+18.9	68.4	26 49.2	+19.9	68.9	27 10.6	+20.9	69.4	30
31	24 45.3	+13.2	65.1	25 10.3	+14.3	65.6	25 34.9	+15.3	66.0	25 59.1	+16.3	66.4	26 22.9	+17.3	66.9	26 46.2	+18.4	67.3	27 09.1	+19.4	67.8	27 31.5	+20.4	68.3	31
32	24 58.5	+12.8	64.1	25 24.6	+13.8	64.5	25 50.2	+14.8	64.9	26 15.4	+15.9	65.4	26 40.2	+16.9	65.8	27 04.6	+17.9	66.3	27 28.5	+18.9	66.8	27 51.9	+20.0	67.2	32
33	25 11.3	+12.3	63.0	25 38.4	+13.3	63.4	26 05.0	+14.4	63.8	26 31.3	+15.3	64.3	26 57.1	+16.4	64.7	27 22.5	+17.4	65.2	27 47.4	+18.4	65.7	28 11.9	+19.4	66.2	33
34	25 23.6	+11.9	61.9	25 51.7	+12.9	62.3	26 19.4	+13.8	62.8	26 46.6	+14.9	63.2	27 13.5	+15.8	63.7	27 39.9	+16.9	64.1	28 05.8	+17.9	64.6	28 31.3	+19.0	65.1	34
35	25 35.5	+11.4	60.8	26 04.6	+12.3	61.2	26 33.2	+13.4	61.7	27 01.5	+14.4	62.1	27 29.3	+15.4	62.6	27 56.8	+16.3	63.0	28 23.7	+17.4	63.5	28 50.3	+18.4	64.0	35
36	25 46.9	+10.8	59.7	26 16.9	+11.9	60.2	26 46.6	+12.8	60.6	27 15.9	+13.8	61.0	27 44.7	+14.9	61.5	28 13.1	+15.9	62.0	28 41.1	+16.9	62.4	29 08.7	+17.8	62.9	36
37	25 57.7	+10.4	58.6	26 28.8	+11.4	59.1	26 59.4	+12.4	59.5	27 29.7	+13.3	59.9	27 59.6	+14.3	60.4	28 29.0	+15.3	60.9	28 58.0	+16.3	61.3	29 26.5	+17.4	61.8	37
38	26 08.1	+9.9	57.5	26 40.2	+10.8	58.0	27 11.8	+11.8	58.4	27 43.0	+12.9	58.8	28 13.9	+13.8	59.3	28 44.3	+14.8	59.8	29 14.3	+15.8	60.2	29 43.9	+16.8	60.7	38
39	26 18.0	+9.4	56.4	26 51.0	+10.4	56.9	27 23.6	+11.3	57.3	27 55.9	+12.2	57.7	28 27.7	+13.3	58.2	28 59.1	+14.3	58.7	29 30.1	+15.3	59.1	30 00.7	+16.2	59.6	39
40	26 27.4	+8.9	55.3	27 01.4	+9.8	55.8	27 34.9	+10.8	56.2	28 08.1	+11.8	56.6	28 41.0	+12.7	57.1	29 13.4	+13.7	57.5	29 45.4	+14.6	58.0	30 16.9	+15.7	58.5	40
41	26 36.3	+8.3	54.2	27 11.2	+9.3	54.6	27 45.7	+10.3	55.1	28 19.9	+11.2	55.5	28 53.7	+12.1	56.0	29 27.1	+13.1	56.4	30 00.0	+14.1	56.9	30 32.6	+15.1	57.4	41
42	26 44.6	+7.9	53.1	27 20.5	+8.7	53.5	27 56.0	+9.7	54.0	28 31.1	+10.6	54.4	29 05.8	+11.6	54.8	29 40.2	+12.5	55.3	30 14.1	+13.6	55.8	30 47.7	+14.5	56.3	42
43	26 52.5	+7.3	52.0	27 29.2	+8.3	52.4	28 05.7	+9.1	52.8	28 41.7	+10.1	53.3	29 17.4	+11.1	53.7	29 52.7	+12.0	54.2	30 27.7	+12.9	54.6	31 02.2	+13.9	55.1	43
44	26 59.8	+6.8	50.9	27 37.5	+7.7	51.3	28 14.8	+8.6	51.7	28 51.8	+9.6	52.1	29 28.5	+10.4	52.6	30 04.7	+11.4	53.0	30 40.6	+12.4	53.5	31 16.1	+13.3	54.0	44
45	27 06.6	+6.3	49.8	27 45.2	+7.1	50.2	28 23.4	+8.1	50.6	29 01.4	+8.9	51.0	29 38.9	+9.9	51.5	30 16.1	+10.8	51.9	30 53.0	+11.7	52.4	31 29.4	+12.7	52.9	45
46	27 12.9	+5.7	48.7	27 52.3	+6.6	49.1	28 31.5	+7.5	49.5	29 10.3	+8.4	49.9	29 48.8	+9.3	50.3	30 26.9	+10.3	50.8	31 04.7	+11.1	51.2	31 42.1	+12.1	51.7	46
47	27 18.6	+5.2	47.5	27 58.9	+6.1	47.9	28 39.0	+6.9	48.3	29 18.7	+7.8	48.7	29 58.1	+8.7	49.2	30 37.2	+9.6	49.6	31 15.8	+10.6	50.1	31 54.2	+11.4	50.6	47
48	27 23.8	+4.6	46.4	28 05.0	+5.5	46.8	28 45.9	+6.4	47.2	29 26.5	+7.3	47.6	30 06.8	+8.1	48.0	30 46.8	+9.0	48.5	31 26.4	+9.9	48.9	32 05.6	+10.8	49.4	48
49	27 28.4	+4.2	45.3	28 10.5	+5.0	45.7	28 52.3	+5.8	46.1	29 33.8	+6.6	46.5	30 14.9	+7.5	46.9	30 55.8	+8.4	47.3	31 36.3	+9.2	47.8	32 16.4	+10.2	48.2	49
50	27 32.6	+3.5	44.2	28 15.5	+4.3	44.5	28 58.1	+5.2	44.9	29 40.4	+6.1	45.3	30 22.4	+6.9	45.7	31 04.2	+7.7	46.2	31 45.5	+8.7	46.6	32 26.6	+9.5	47.1	50
51	27 36.1	+3.1	43.0	28 19.8	+3.9	43.4	29 03.3	+4.6	43.8	29 46.5	+5.4	44.2	30 29.3	+6.3	44.6	31 11.9	+7.2	45.0	31 54.2	+8.0	45.4	32 36.1	+8.9	45.9	51
52	27 39.2	+2.4	41.9	28 23.7	+3.2	42.3	29 07.9	+4.1	42.7	29 51.9	+4.9	43.0	30 35.6	+5.7	43.4	31 19.1	+6.5	43.8	32 02.2	+7.3	44.3	32 45.0	+8.2	44.7	52
53	27 41.6	+2.0	40.8	28 26.9	+2.7	41.1	29 12.0	+3.5	41.5	29 56.8	+4.3	41.9	30 41.3	+5.1	42.3	31 25.6	+5.9	42.7	32 09.5	+6.7	43.1	32 53.2	+7.5	43.5	53
54	27 43.6	+1.3	39.7	28 29.6	+2.2	40.0	29 15.5	+2.9	40.4	30 01.1	+3.6	40.7	30 46.4	+4.4	41.1	31 31.5	+5.2	41.5	32 16.2	+6.1	41.9	33 00.7	+6.9	42.4	54
55	27 44.9	+0.9	38.5	28 31.8	+1.5	38.9	29 18.4	+2.3	39.2	30 04.7	+3.1	39.6	30 50.8	+3.9	40.0	31 36.7	+4.6	40.3	32 22.3	+5.4	40.8	33 07.6	+6.2	41.2	55
56	27 45.8	+0.2	37.4	28 33.3	+1.0	37.7	29 20.7	+1.7	38.1	30 07.8	+2.4	38.4	30 54.7	+3.2	38.8	31 41.3	+4.0	39.2	32 27.7	+4.7	39.6	33 13.8	+5.5	40.0	56
57	27 46.0	−0.2	36.3	28 34.3	+0.4	36.6	29 22.4	+1.1	36.9	30 10.2	+1.9	37.3	30 57.9	+2.6	37.6	31 45.3	+3.3	38.0	32 32.4	+4.1	38.4	33 19.3	+4.9	38.8	57
58	27 45.8	−0.9	35.1	28 34.7	−0.1	35.5	29 23.5	+0.6	35.8	30 12.1	+1.2	36.1	31 00.5	+1.9	36.5	31 48.6	+2.7	36.8	32 36.5	+3.4	37.2	33 24.2	+4.1	37.6	58
59	27 44.9	−1.3	34.0	28 34.6	−0.7	34.3	29 24.1	−0.1	34.6	30 13.3	+0.7	35.0	31 02.4	+1.3	35.3	31 51.3	+2.0	35.7	32 39.9	+2.7	36.0	33 28.3	+3.5	36.4	59
60	27 43.6	−2.0	32.9	28 33.9	−1.3	33.2	29 24.0	−0.6	33.5	30 14.0	0.0	33.8	31 03.7	+0.7	34.1	31 53.3	+1.3	34.5	32 42.6	+2.1	34.8	33 31.8	+2.7	35.2	60
61	27 41.6	−2.4	31.8	28 32.6	−1.9	32.0	29 23.4	−1.3	32.3	30 14.0	−0.6	32.6	31 04.4	+0.1	33.0	31 54.6	+0.8	33.3	32 44.7	+1.4	33.6	33 34.5	+2.1	34.0	61
62	27 39.2	−3.1	30.6	28 30.7	−2.4	30.9	29 22.1	−1.8	31.2	30 13.4	−1.2	31.5	31 04.5	−0.6	31.8	31 55.4	0.0	32.1	32 46.1	+0.7	32.5	33 36.6	+1.4	32.8	62
63	27 36.1	−3.5	29.5	28 28.3	−3.0	29.8	29 20.3	−2.4	30.0	30 12.2	−1.8	30.3	31 03.9	−1.2	30.6	31 55.4	−0.6	30.9	32 46.8	0.0	31.3	33 38.0	+0.7	31.6	63
64	27 32.6	−4.1	28.4	28 25.3	−3.6	28.6	29 17.9	−3.0	28.9	30 10.4	−2.5	29.2	31 02.7	−1.9	29.5	31 54.8	−1.2	29.8	32 46.8	−0.6	30.1	33 38.7	0.0	30.4	64
65	27 28.5	−4.7	27.3	28 21.7	−4.1	27.5	29 14.9	−3.6	27.7	30 07.9	−3.0	28.0	31 00.8	−2.4	28.3	31 53.6	−1.9	28.6	32 46.2	−1.3	28.9	33 38.7	−0.7	29.2	65
66	27 23.8	−5.2	26.1	28 17.6	−4.7	26.4	29 11.3	−4.1	26.6	30 04.9	−3.6	26.9	30 58.4	−3.1	27.1	31 51.7	−2.5	27.4	32 44.9	−2.0	27.7	33 38.0	−1.5	28.0	66
67	27 18.6	−5.7	25.0	28 12.9	−5.2	25.2	29 07.2	−4.8	25.5	30 01.3	−4.3	25.7	30 55.3	−3.7	26.0	31 49.2	−3.2	26.2	32 42.9	−2.6	26.5	33 36.5	−2.1	26.8	67
68	27 12.9	−6.3	23.9	28 07.7	−5.8	24.1	29 02.4	−5.3	24.3	29 57.0	−4.8	24.6	30 51.6	−4.4	24.8	31 46.0	−3.9	25.1	32 40.3	−3.4	25.3	33 34.4	−2.8	25.6	68
69	27 06.6	−6.8	22.8	28 01.9	−6.3	23.0	28 57.1	−5.9	23.2	29 52.2	−5.4	23.4	30 47.2	−4.9	23.6	31 42.1	−4.4	23.9	32 36.9	−3.9	24.1	33 31.6	−3.4	24.4	69
70	26 59.8	−7.3	21.7	27 55.6	−6.9	21.8	28 51.2	−6.5	22.0	29 46.8	−6.0	22.3	30 42.3	−5.6	22.5	31 37.7	−5.2	22.7	32 33.0	−4.7	23.0	33 28.2	−4.2	23.2	70
71	26 52.5	−7.8	20.5	27 48.7	−7.5	20.7	28 44.7	−7.0	20.9	29 40.8	−6.7	21.1	30 36.7	−6.2	21.3	31 32.5	−5.7	21.5	32 28.3	−5.3	21.8	33 24.0	−4.9	22.0	71
72	26 44.7	−8.4	19.4	27 41.2	−8.0	19.6	28 37.7	−7.6	19.8	29 34.1	−7.2	20.0	30 30.5	−6.8	20.2	31 26.8	−6.4	20.4	32 23.0	−6.0	20.6	33 19.1	−5.5	20.8	72
73	26 36.3	−8.9	18.3	27 33.2	−8.5	18.5	28 30.1	−8.1	18.7	29 26.9	−7.7	18.8	30 23.7	−7.4	19.0	31 20.4	−7.0	19.2	32 17.0	−6.6	19.4	33 13.6	−6.3	19.6	73
74	26 27.4	−9.3	17.2	27 24.7	−9.0	17.4	28 22.0	−8.7	17.5	29 19.2	−8.4	17.7	30 16.3	−8.0	17.9	31 13.4	−7.7	18.0	32 10.4	−7.3	18.2	33 07.3	−6.9	18.4	74
75	26 18.1	−9.9	16.1	27 15.7	−9.6	16.3	28 13.3	−9.3	16.4	29 10.8	−8.9	16.6	30 08.3	−8.6	16.7	31 05.7	−8.2	16.9	32 03.1	−7.9	17.1	33 00.4	−7.5	17.3	75
76	26 08.2	−10.4	15.0	27 06.1	−10.1	15.1	28 04.0	−9.8	15.3	29 01.9	−9.5	15.4	29 59.7	−9.2	15.6	30 57.5	−8.9	15.7	31 55.2	−8.6	15.9	32 52.9	−8.3	16.1	76
77	25 57.8	−10.9	13.9	26 56.0	−10.6	14.0	27 54.2	−10.3	14.2	28 52.4	−10.1	14.3	29 50.5	−9.8	14.4	30 48.6	−9.5	14.6	31 46.6	−9.2	14.7	32 44.6	−8.9	14.9	77
78	25 46.9	−11.4	12.8	26 45.4	−11.1	12.9	27 43.9	−10.9	13.0	28 42.3	−10.6	13.2	29 40.7	−10.4	13.3	30 39.1	−10.1	13.4	31 37.4	−9.8	13.6	32 35.7	−9.5	13.7	78
79	25 35.5	−11.8	11.7	26 34.3	−11.7	11.8	27 33.0	−11.4	11.9	28 31.7	−11.2	12.0	29 30.3	−10.9	12.2	30 29.0	−10.7	12.3	31 27.6	−10.5	12.4	32 26.2	−10.2	12.6	79
80	25 23.7	−12.3	10.6	26 22.6	−12.1	10.7	27 21.6	−11.9	10.8	28 20.5	−11.7	10.9	29 19.4	−11.5	11.0	30 18.3	−11.3	11.1	31 17.1	−11.0	11.3	32 16.0	−10.9	11.4	80
81	25 11.4	−12.8	9.6	26 10.5	−12.6	9.6	27 09.7	−12.5	9.7	28 08.8	−12.3	9.8	29 07.9	−12.1	9.9	30 07.0	−11.9	10.0	31 06.1	−11.7	10.1	32 05.1	−11.4	10.2	81
82	24 58.6	−13.3	8.5	25 57.9	−13.1	8.6	26 57.2	−12.9	8.6	27 56.5	−12.7	8.7	28 55.8	−12.6	8.8	29 55.1	−12.4	8.9	30 54.4	−12.3	9.0	31 53.7	−12.1	9.1	82
83	24 45.3	−13.7	7.4	25 44.8	−13.6	7.5	26 44.3	−13.5	7.5	27 43.8	−13.3	7.6	28 43.2	−13.1	7.7	29 42.7	−13.0	7.8	30 42.1	−12.8	7.8	31 41.6	−12.8	7.9	83
84	24 31.6	−14.2	6.3	25 31.2	−14.0	6.4	26 30.8	−13.9	6.4	27 30.5	−13.9	6.5	28 30.1	−13.7	6.6	29 29.7	−13.6	6.6	30 29.3	−13.5	6.7	31 28.8	−13.3	6.8	84
85	24 17.4	−14.6	5.3	25 17.2	−14.6	5.3	26 16.9	−14.4	5.4	27 16.6	−14.3	5.4	28 16.4	−14.3	5.5	29 16.1	−14.2	5.5	30 15.8	−14.0	5.6	31 15.5	−13.9	5.6	85
86	24 02.8	−15.1	4.2	25 02.6	−15.0	4.2	26 02.5	−14.9	4.3	27 02.3	−14.8	4.3	28 02.1	−14.7	4.4	29 01.9	−14.6	4.4	30 01.8	−14.6	4.4	31 01.6	−14.5	4.5	86
87	23 47.7	−15.5	3.2	24 47.6	−15.4	3.2	25 47.6	−15.4	3.2	26 47.5	−15.4	3.2	27 47.4	−15.3	3.3	28 47.3	−15.3	3.3	29 47.2	−15.2	3.3	30 47.1	−15.2	3.4	87
88	23 32.2	−15.9	2.1	24 32.2	−15.9	2.1	25 32.2	−15.9	2.1	26 32.1	−15.8	2.1	27 32.1	−15.8	2.2	28 32.0	−15.7	2.2	29 32.0	−15.7	2.2	30 31.9	−15.6	2.2	88
89	23 16.3	−16.3	1.0	24 16.3	−16.3	1.1	25 16.3	−16.3	1.1	26 16.3	−16.3	1.1	27 16.3	−16.3	1.1	28 16.3	−16.3	1.1	29 16.3	−16.3	1.1	30 16.3	−16.3	1.1	89
90	23 00.0	−16.7	0.0	24 00.0	−16.8	0.0	25 00.0	−16.8	0.0	26 00.0	−16.8	0.0	27 00.0	−16.8	0.0	28 00.0	−16.8	0.0	29 00.0	−16.8	0.0	30 00.0	−16.8	0.0	90
	23°			24°			25°			26°			27°			28°			29°			30°			

74°, 286° L.H.A. LATITUDE **SAME** NAME AS DECLINATION

LATITUDE **CONTRARY** NAME TO DECLINATION L.H.A. 74°, 286°

Dec.	23° Hc	d	Z	24° Hc	d	Z	25° Hc	d	Z	26° Hc	d	Z	27° Hc	d	Z	28° Hc	d	Z	29° Hc	d	Z	30° Hc	d	Z	Dec.
°	° ′	′	°	° ′	′	°	° ′	′	°	° ′	′	°	° ′	′	°	° ′	′	°	° ′	′	°	° ′	′	°	°
0	14 41.9	−24.4	96.4	14 35.1	−25.4	96.7	14 28.0	−26.3	96.9	14 20.6	−27.2	97.2	14 13.0	−28.2	97.4	14 05.1	−29.1	97.7	13 57.0	−30.1	97.9	13 48.6	−31.0	98.2	0
1	14 17.5	−24.5	97.3	14 09.7	−25.5	97.6	14 01.7	−26.5	97.8	13 53.4	−27.5	98.1	13 44.8	−28.4	98.3	13 36.0	−29.3	98.6	13 26.9	−30.2	98.8	13 17.6	−31.1	99.0	1
2	13 53.0	−24.8	98.3	13 44.2	−25.8	98.5	13 35.2	−26.7	98.8	13 25.9	−27.6	99.0	13 16.4	−28.6	99.2	13 06.7	−29.6	99.5	12 56.7	−30.4	99.7	12 46.5	−31.4	99.9	2
3	13 28.2	−25.0	99.2	13 18.4	−25.9	99.4	13 08.5	−26.9	99.7	12 58.3	−27.9	99.9	12 47.8	−28.8	100.1	12 37.1	−29.6	100.4	12 26.3	−30.7	100.6	12 15.1	−31.5	100.8	3
4	13 03.2	−25.2	100.1	12 52.5	−26.2	100.4	12 41.6	−27.1	100.6	12 30.4	−28.0	100.8	12 19.0	−28.9	101.0	12 07.5	−29.9	101.2	11 55.6	−30.7	101.5	11 43.6	−31.6	101.7	4
5	12 38.0	−25.4	101.1	12 26.3	−26.3	101.3	12 14.5	−27.3	101.5	12 02.4	−28.2	101.7	11 50.1	−29.1	101.9	11 37.6	−30.0	102.1	11 24.9	−31.0	102.3	11 12.0	−31.9	102.5	5
6	12 12.6	−25.6	102.0	12 00.0	−26.5	102.2	11 47.2	−27.4	102.4	11 34.2	−28.4	102.6	11 21.0	−29.3	102.8	11 07.6	−30.2	103.0	10 53.9	−31.0	103.2	10 40.1	−31.9	103.4	6
7	11 47.0	−25.7	102.9	11 33.5	−26.7	103.1	11 19.8	−27.7	103.3	11 05.8	−28.5	103.5	10 51.7	−29.4	103.7	10 37.4	−30.4	103.9	10 22.9	−31.2	104.1	10 08.2	−32.1	104.3	7
8	11 21.3	−26.0	103.9	11 06.8	−26.9	104.0	10 52.1	−27.7	104.2	10 37.3	−28.7	104.4	10 22.3	−29.6	104.6	10 07.0	−30.4	104.8	9 51.7	−31.4	104.9	9 36.1	−32.2	105.1	8
9	10 55.3	−26.0	104.8	10 39.9	−27.0	105.0	10 24.4	−28.0	105.1	10 08.6	−28.8	105.3	9 52.7	−29.7	105.5	9 36.6	−30.6	105.6	9 20.3	−31.5	105.8	9 03.9	−32.3	106.0	9
10	10 29.3	−26.3	105.7	10 12.9	−27.1	105.9	9 56.4	−28.0	106.0	9 39.8	−29.0	106.2	9 23.0	−29.9	106.4	9 06.0	−30.7	106.5	8 48.8	−31.5	106.7	8 31.6	−32.5	106.8	10
11	10 03.0	−26.4	106.6	9 45.8	−27.3	106.8	9 28.4	−28.2	106.9	9 10.8	−29.1	107.1	8 53.1	−30.0	107.2	8 35.3	−30.9	107.4	8 17.3	−31.7	107.5	7 59.1	−32.5	107.7	11
12	9 36.6	−26.5	107.5	9 18.5	−27.5	107.7	9 00.2	−28.4	107.8	8 41.7	−29.2	108.0	8 23.1	−30.0	108.1	8 04.4	−30.9	108.3	7 45.6	−31.8	108.4	7 26.6	−32.7	108.5	12
13	9 10.1	−26.7	108.4	8 51.0	−27.5	108.6	8 31.8	−28.4	108.7	8 12.5	−29.3	108.9	7 53.1	−30.2	109.0	7 33.5	−31.1	109.1	7 13.8	−31.9	109.2	6 53.9	−32.7	109.4	13
14	8 43.4	−26.8	109.3	8 23.5	−27.7	109.5	8 03.4	−28.6	109.6	7 43.2	−29.4	109.7	7 22.9	−30.3	109.9	7 02.4	−31.1	110.0	6 41.9	−32.0	110.1	6 21.2	−32.8	110.2	14
15	8 16.6	−26.9	110.2	7 55.8	−27.8	110.4	7 34.8	−28.6	110.5	7 13.8	−29.6	110.6	6 52.6	−30.4	110.7	6 31.3	−31.3	110.8	6 09.9	−32.1	110.9	5 48.4	−32.9	111.0	15
16	7 49.7	−27.1	111.1	7 28.0	−27.9	111.3	7 06.2	−28.8	111.4	6 44.2	−29.6	111.5	6 22.2	−30.5	111.6	6 00.0	−31.3	111.7	5 37.8	−32.1	111.8	5 15.5	−33.0	111.9	16
17	7 22.6	−27.1	112.0	7 00.1	−28.1	112.2	6 37.4	−28.9	112.3	6 14.6	−29.7	112.4	5 51.7	−30.5	112.5	5 28.7	−31.4	112.6	5 05.7	−32.2	112.6	4 42.5	−33.0	112.7	17
18	6 55.5	−27.3	112.9	6 32.0	−28.1	113.0	6 08.5	−28.9	113.1	5 44.9	−29.8	113.2	5 21.2	−30.7	113.3	4 57.3	−31.4	113.4	4 33.5	−32.3	113.5	4 09.5	−33.1	113.6	18
19	6 28.2	−27.3	113.8	6 03.9	−28.2	113.9	5 39.6	−29.1	114.0	5 15.1	−29.9	114.1	4 50.5	−30.7	114.2	4 25.9	−31.5	114.3	4 01.2	−32.3	114.3	3 36.4	−33.1	114.4	19
20	6 00.9	−27.4	114.7	5 35.7	−28.2	114.8	5 10.5	−29.1	114.9	4 45.2	−29.9	115.0	4 19.8	−30.7	115.1	3 54.4	−31.6	115.1	3 28.9	−32.4	115.2	3 03.3	−33.1	115.2	20
21	5 33.5	−27.6	115.6	5 07.5	−28.4	115.7	4 41.4	−29.2	115.8	4 15.3	−30.0	115.9	3 49.1	−30.8	115.9	3 22.8	−31.6	116.0	2 56.5	−32.4	116.0	2 30.2	−33.2	116.1	21
22	5 05.9	−27.5	116.5	4 39.1	−28.4	116.6	4 12.2	−29.2	116.7	3 45.3	−30.1	116.7	3 18.3	−30.9	116.8	2 51.2	−31.6	116.8	2 24.1	−32.4	116.9	1 57.0	−33.2	116.9	22
23	4 38.4	−27.7	117.4	4 10.7	−28.5	117.5	3 43.0	−29.3	117.5	3 15.2	−30.1	117.6	2 47.4	−30.9	117.6	2 19.6	−31.7	117.7	1 51.7	−32.5	117.7	1 23.8	−33.3	117.7	23
24	4 10.7	−27.7	118.3	3 42.2	−28.5	118.4	3 13.7	−29.3	118.4	2 45.1	−30.1	118.5	2 16.5	−30.9	118.5	1 47.9	−31.7	118.5	1 19.2	−32.4	118.6	0 50.5	−33.2	118.6	24
25	3 43.0	−27.8	119.2	3 13.7	−28.6	119.2	2 44.4	−29.4	119.3	2 15.0	−30.1	119.3	1 45.6	−30.9	119.4	1 16.2	−31.7	119.4	0 46.8	−32.5	119.4	0 17.3	−33.2	119.4	25
26	3 15.2	−27.8	120.1	2 45.1	−28.6	120.1	2 15.0	−29.4	120.2	1 44.9	−30.2	120.2	1 14.7	−31.0	120.2	0 44.5	−31.7	120.2	0 14.3	−32.5	120.2	0 15.9	+33.3	59.8	26
27	2 47.4	−27.8	121.0	2 16.5	−28.6	121.0	1 45.6	−29.4	121.0	1 14.7	−30.2	121.1	0 43.7	−30.9	121.1	0 12.8	−31.8	121.1	0 18.2	+32.5	58.9	0 49.2	+33.2	58.9	27
28	2 19.6	−27.9	121.8	1 47.9	−28.7	121.9	1 16.2	−29.4	121.9	0 44.5	−30.2	121.9	0 12.8	−31.0	121.9	0 19.0	+31.7	58.1	0 50.7	+32.5	58.1	1 22.4	+33.2	58.1	28
29	1 51.7	−27.9	122.7	1 19.2	−28.7	122.8	0 46.8	−29.5	122.8	0 14.3	−30.2	122.8	0 18.2	+31.0	57.2	0 50.7	+31.7	57.2	1 23.2	+32.4	57.2	1 55.6	+33.2	57.3	29
30	1 23.8	−28.0	123.6	0 50.5	−28.6	123.6	0 17.3	−29.4	123.6	0 15.9	+30.2	56.4	0 49.2	+30.9	56.4	1 22.4	+31.7	56.4	1 55.6	+32.4	56.4	2 28.8	+33.2	56.4	30
31	0 55.8	−27.9	124.5	0 21.9	−28.8	124.5	0 12.1	+29.5	55.5	0 46.1	+30.2	55.5	1 20.1	+31.0	55.5	1 54.1	+31.7	55.5	2 28.0	+32.4	55.6	3 02.0	+33.1	55.6	31
32	0 27.9	−28.0	125.4	0 06.9	+28.7	54.6	0 41.6	+29.4	54.6	1 16.3	+30.2	54.6	1 51.1	+30.9	54.6	2 25.8	+31.6	54.7	3 00.4	+32.4	54.7	3 35.1	+33.1	54.8	32
33	0 00.1	+27.9	53.7	0 35.6	+28.6	53.7	1 11.0	+29.5	53.7	1 46.5	+30.2	53.8	2 22.0	+30.9	53.8	2 57.4	+31.6	53.8	3 32.8	+32.3	53.9	4 08.2	+33.0	53.9	33
34	0 28.0	+27.9	52.8	1 04.2	+28.7	52.9	1 40.5	+29.4	52.9	2 16.7	+30.1	52.9	2 52.9	+30.8	52.9	3 29.0	+31.6	53.0	4 05.1	+32.3	53.0	4 41.2	+32.9	53.1	34
35	0 55.9	+28.0	52.0	1 32.9	+28.7	52.0	2 09.9	+29.3	52.0	2 46.8	+30.1	52.0	3 23.7	+30.8	52.1	4 00.6	+31.5	52.1	4 37.4	+32.2	52.2	5 14.1	+32.9	52.3	35
36	1 23.9	+27.9	51.1	2 01.6	+28.6	51.1	2 39.2	+29.4	51.1	3 16.9	+30.0	51.2	3 54.5	+30.7	51.2	4 32.1	+31.4	51.3	5 09.6	+32.1	51.3	5 47.0	+32.8	51.4	36
37	1 51.8	+27.9	50.2	2 30.2	+28.6	50.2	3 08.6	+29.3	50.3	3 46.9	+30.0	50.3	4 25.2	+30.7	50.4	5 03.5	+31.4	50.4	5 41.7	+32.1	50.5	6 19.8	+32.8	50.6	37
38	2 19.7	+27.8	49.3	2 58.8	+28.5	49.3	3 37.9	+29.2	49.4	4 16.9	+30.0	49.4	4 55.9	+30.6	49.5	5 34.9	+31.3	49.6	6 13.8	+31.9	49.6	6 52.6	+32.6	49.7	38
39	2 47.5	+27.8	48.4	3 27.3	+28.5	48.5	4 07.1	+29.2	48.5	4 46.9	+29.8	48.6	5 26.5	+30.6	48.6	6 06.2	+31.2	48.7	6 45.7	+31.9	48.8	7 25.2	+32.6	48.9	39
40	3 15.3	+27.8	47.5	3 55.8	+28.5	47.6	4 36.3	+29.1	47.6	5 16.7	+29.8	47.7	5 57.1	+30.4	47.8	6 37.4	+31.1	47.8	7 17.6	+31.8	47.9	7 57.8	+32.4	48.0	40
41	3 43.1	+27.7	46.6	4 24.3	+28.4	46.7	5 05.4	+29.1	46.7	5 46.5	+29.7	46.8	6 27.5	+30.4	46.9	7 08.5	+31.0	47.0	7 49.4	+31.7	47.1	8 30.2	+32.4	47.2	41
42	4 10.8	+27.7	45.7	4 52.7	+28.3	45.8	5 34.5	+28.9	45.9	6 16.2	+29.6	45.9	6 57.9	+30.3	46.0	7 39.5	+31.0	46.1	8 21.1	+31.6	46.2	9 02.6	+32.2	46.3	42
43	4 38.5	+27.6	44.9	5 21.0	+28.2	44.9	6 03.4	+28.9	45.0	6 45.8	+29.6	45.1	7 28.2	+30.2	45.2	8 10.5	+30.8	45.3	8 52.7	+31.4	45.4	9 34.8	+32.1	45.5	43
44	5 06.1	+27.5	44.0	5 49.2	+28.2	44.0	6 32.3	+28.8	44.1	7 15.4	+29.4	44.2	7 58.4	+30.0	44.3	8 41.3	+30.7	44.4	9 24.1	+31.3	44.5	10 06.9	+31.9	44.6	44
45	5 33.6	+27.4	43.1	6 17.4	+28.0	43.1	7 01.1	+28.7	43.2	7 44.8	+29.3	43.3	8 28.4	+30.0	43.4	9 12.0	+30.6	43.5	9 55.4	+31.2	43.6	10 38.8	+31.8	43.8	45
46	6 01.0	+27.3	42.2	6 45.4	+28.0	42.3	7 29.8	+28.6	42.3	8 14.1	+29.2	42.4	8 58.4	+29.8	42.5	9 42.6	+30.4	42.6	10 26.6	+31.1	42.8	11 10.6	+31.7	42.9	46
47	6 28.3	+27.3	41.3	7 13.4	+27.9	41.4	7 58.4	+28.5	41.5	8 43.3	+29.1	41.5	9 28.2	+29.7	41.7	10 13.0	+30.3	41.8	10 57.7	+30.9	41.9	11 42.3	+31.5	42.0	47
48	6 55.6	+27.1	40.4	7 41.3	+27.7	40.5	8 26.9	+28.3	40.6	9 12.4	+29.0	40.7	9 57.9	+29.6	40.8	10 43.3	+30.1	40.9	11 28.6	+30.8	41.0	12 13.8	+31.4	41.2	48
49	7 22.7	+27.1	39.5	8 09.0	+27.6	39.6	8 55.2	+28.2	39.7	9 41.4	+28.8	39.8	10 27.5	+29.4	39.9	11 13.4	+30.0	40.0	11 59.4	+30.5	40.1	12 45.2	+31.2	40.3	49
50	7 49.8	+26.9	38.6	8 36.6	+27.5	38.7	9 23.4	+28.1	38.8	10 10.2	+28.7	38.9	10 56.9	+29.2	39.0	11 43.4	+29.9	39.1	12 29.9	+30.5	39.3	13 16.4	+30.9	39.4	50
51	8 16.7	+26.8	37.7	9 04.1	+27.4	37.8	9 51.5	+28.0	37.9	10 38.9	+28.5	38.0	11 26.1	+29.1	38.1	12 13.3	+29.6	38.2	13 00.4	+30.2	38.4	13 47.3	+30.9	38.5	51
52	8 43.5	+26.7	36.8	9 31.5	+27.3	36.9	10 19.5	+27.8	37.0	11 07.4	+28.3	37.1	11 55.2	+28.9	37.2	12 42.9	+29.5	37.4	13 30.6	+30.0	37.5	14 18.2	+30.6	37.6	52
53	9 10.2	+26.5	35.9	9 58.8	+27.0	36.0	10 47.3	+27.6	36.1	11 35.7	+28.2	36.2	12 24.1	+28.8	36.3	13 12.4	+29.3	36.5	14 00.6	+29.9	36.6	14 48.8	+30.4	36.8	53
54	9 36.7	+26.4	35.0	10 25.8	+27.0	35.1	11 14.9	+27.5	35.2	12 03.9	+28.1	35.3	12 52.9	+28.5	35.4	13 41.7	+29.1	35.6	14 30.5	+29.6	35.7	15 19.2	+30.2	35.9	54
55	10 03.1	+26.2	34.1	10 52.8	+26.8	34.2	11 42.4	+27.3	34.3	12 32.0	+27.8	34.4	13 21.4	+28.4	34.5	14 10.8	+28.9	34.7	15 00.1	+29.5	34.8	15 49.4	+29.9	35.0	55
56	10 29.3	+26.1	33.1	11 19.6	+26.6	33.2	12 09.7	+27.1	33.4	12 59.8	+27.6	33.5	13 49.8	+28.2	33.6	14 39.7	+28.7	33.8	15 29.6	+29.2	33.9	16 19.3	+29.8	34.1	56
57	10 55.4	+26.0	32.2	11 46.2	+26.4	32.3	12 36.8	+27.0	32.4	13 27.4	+27.5	32.6	14 18.0	+27.9	32.7	15 08.4	+28.5	32.8	15 58.8	+29.0	33.0	16 49.1	+29.4	33.2	57
58	11 21.4	+25.7	31.3	12 12.6	+26.2	31.4	13 03.8	+26.7	31.5	13 54.9	+27.2	31.7	14 45.9	+27.8	31.8	15 36.9	+28.2	31.9	16 27.8	+28.7	32.1	17 18.5	+29.3	32.2	58
59	11 47.1	+25.6	30.4	12 38.8	+26.1	30.5	13 30.5	+26.6	30.6	14 22.1	+27.1	30.7	15 13.7	+27.5	30.9	16 05.1	+28.0	31.0	16 56.5	+28.5	31.2	17 47.8	+29.0	31.3	59
60	12 12.7	+25.4	29.5	13 04.9	+25.9	29.6	13 57.1	+26.3	29.7	14 49.2	+26.8	29.8	15 41.2	+27.3	29.9	16 33.1	+27.8	30.1	17 25.0	+28.2	30.2	18 16.8	+28.7	30.4	60
61	12 38.1	+25.2	28.5	13 30.8	+25.6	28.6	14 23.4	+26.1	28.8	15 16.0	+26.5	28.9	16 08.5	+27.0	29.0	17 00.9	+27.5	29.2	17 53.2	+28.0	29.3	18 45.5	+28.5	29.5	61
62	13 03.3	+25.0	27.6	13 56.4	+25.5	27.7	14 49.5	+25.9	27.8	15 42.5	+26.4	28.0	16 35.5	+26.8	28.1	17 28.4	+27.2	28.2	18 21.2	+27.7	28.4	19 14.0	+28.1	28.6	62
63	13 28.3	+24.8	26.7	14 21.9	+25.2	26.8	15 15.4	+25.7	26.9	16 08.9	+26.1	27.0	17 02.3	+26.5	27.2	17 55.6	+27.0	27.3	18 48.9	+27.5	27.5	19 42.1	+27.9	27.6	63
64	13 53.1	+24.5	25.7	14 47.1	+25.0	25.8	15 41.1	+25.4	26.0	16 35.0	+25.8	26.1	17 28.8	+26.3	26.2	18 22.6	+26.7	26.4	19 16.4	+27.1	26.5	20 10.0	+27.6	26.7	64
65	14 17.6	+24.4	24.8	15 12.1	+24.7	24.9	16 06.5	+25.1	25.0	17 00.8	+25.6	25.1	17 55.1	+26.0	25.3	18 49.3	+26.4	25.4	19 43.5	+26.8	25.6	20 37.6	+27.2	25.7	65
66	14 42.0	+24.1	23.8	15 36.8	+24.5	24.0	16 31.6	+25.0	24.1	17 26.4	+25.3	24.2	18 21.1	+25.7	24.3	19 15.7	+26.2	24.5	20 10.3	+26.5	24.6	21 04.8	+27.0	24.8	66
67	15 06.1	+23.9	22.9	16 01.3	+24.3	23.0	16 56.6	+24.6	23.1	17 51.7	+25.0	23.2	18 46.8	+25.4	23.4	19 41.9	+25.8	23.5	20 36.8	+26.3	23.7	21 31.8	+26.6	23.8	67
68	15 30.0	+23.6	21.9	16 25.6	+24.0	22.1	17 21.2	+24.4	22.2	18 16.7	+24.8	22.3	19 12.2	+25.2	22.4	20 07.7	+25.5	22.6	21 03.1	+25.8	22.7	21 58.4	+26.2	22.8	68
69	15 53.6	+23.4	21.0	16 49.6	+23.8	21.1	17 45.6	+24.1	21.2	18 41.5	+24.4	21.3	19 37.4	+24.8	21.5	20 33.2	+25.2	21.6	21 28.9	+25.6	21.7	22 24.6	+26.0	21.9	69
70	16 17.0	+23.1	20.0	17 13.4	+23.4	20.1	18 09.7	+23.8	20.2	19 05.9	+24.2	20.4	20 02.2	+24.5	20.5	20 58.4	+24.8	20.6	21 54.5	+25.2	20.8	22 50.6	+25.5	20.9	70
71	16 40.1	+22.9	19.1	17 36.8	+23.2	19.2	18 33.5	+23.5	19.3	19 30.1	+23.8	19.4	20 26.7	+24.1	19.5	21 23.2	+24.5	19.6	22 19.7	+24.8	19.8	23 16.1	+25.2	19.9	71
72	17 03.0	+22.6	18.1	18 00.0	+22.9	18.2	18 57.0	+23.2	18.3	19 53.9	+23.5	18.4	20 50.8	+23.9	18.5	21 47.7	+24.2	18.7	22 44.5	+24.5	18.8	23 41.3	+24.8	18.9	72
73	17 25.6	+22.3	17.1	18 22.9	+22.6	17.2	19 20.2	+22.9	17.3	20 17.4	+23.2	17.4	21 14.7	+23.5	17.5	22 11.9	+23.8	17.7	23 09.0	+24.1	17.8	24 06.1	+24.4	17.9	73
74	17 47.9	+22.0	16.2	18 45.5	+22.3	16.2	19 43.1	+22.5	16.3	20 40.6	+22.9	16.5	21 38.2	+23.1	16.6	22 35.7	+23.4	16.7	23 33.1	+23.7	16.8	24 30.5	+24.0	16.9	74
75	18 09.9	+21.7	15.2	19 07.8	+21.9	15.3	20 05.6	+22.3	15.4	21 03.5	+22.5	15.5	22 01.3	+22.8	15.6	22 59.1	+23.0	15.7	23 56.8	+23.4	15.8	24 54.5	+23.7	15.9	75
76	18 31.6	+21.4	14.2	19 29.7	+21.7	14.3	20 27.9	+21.9	14.4	21 26.0	+22.1	14.5	22 24.1	+22.4	14.6	23 22.1	+22.7	14.7	24 20.2	+22.9	14.8	25 18.2	+23.1	14.9	76
77	18 53.0	+21.1	13.2	19 51.4	+21.3	13.3	20 49.8	+21.5	13.4	21 48.1	+21.8	13.5	22 46.5	+22.0	13.6	23 44.8	+22.3	13.7	24 43.1	+22.5	13.8	25 41.3	+22.8	13.9	77
78	19 14.1	+20.8	12.2	20 12.7	+21.0	12.3	21 11.3	+21.2	12.4	22 09.9	+21.4	12.5	23 08.5	+21.6	12.6	24 07.1	+21.8	12.6	25 05.6	+22.1	12.7	26 04.1	+22.3	12.9	78
79	19 34.9	+20.4	11.2	20 33.7	+20.6	11.3	21 32.5	+20.9	11.4	22 31.3	+21.1	11.5	23 30.1	+21.3	11.5	24 28.9	+21.5	11.6	25 27.7	+21.6	11.7	26 26.4	+21.9	11.8	79
80	19 55.3	+20.1	10.2	20 54.3	+20.3	10.3	21 53.4	+20.4	10.4	22 52.4	+20.6	10.4	23 51.4	+20.8	10.5	24 50.4	+21.0	10.6	25 49.3	+21.3	10.7	26 48.3	+21.4	10.8	80
81	20 15.4	+19.8	9.2	21 14.6	+20.0	9.3	22 13.8	+20.1	9.3	23 13.0	+20.3	9.4	24 12.2	+20.4	9.5	25 11.4	+20.6	9.6	26 10.6	+20.7	9.6	27 09.7	+20.9	9.7	81
82	20 35.2	+19.4	8.2	21 34.6	+19.5	8.3	22 33.9	+19.7	8.3	23 33.3	+19.8	8.4	24 32.6	+20.0	8.5	25 32.0	+20.1	8.5	26 31.3	+20.3	8.6	27 30.6	+20.5	8.7	82
83	20 54.6	+19.0	7.2	21 54.1	+19.2	7.3	22 53.6	+19.3	7.3	23 53.1	+19.5	7.4	24 52.6	+19.6	7.4	25 52.1	+19.7	7.5	26 51.6	+19.8	7.5	27 51.1	+20.0	7.6	83
84	21 13.6	+18.7	6.2	22 13.3	+18.8	6.2	23 12.9	+18.9	6.3	24 12.6	+19.0	6.3	25 12.2	+19.1	6.4	26 11.8	+19.3	6.4	27 11.4	+19.4	6.5	28 11.1	+19.4	6.5	84
85	21 32.3	+18.3	5.2	22 32.1	+18.4	5.2	23 31.8	+18.5	5.2	24 31.6	+18.6	5.3	25 31.3	+18.7	5.3	26 31.1	+18.7	5.4	27 30.8	+18.9	5.4	28 30.5	+19.0	5.5	85
86	21 50.6	+18.0	4.1	22 50.5	+18.0	4.2	23 50.3	+18.1	4.2	24 50.2	+18.1	4.2	25 50.0	+18.2	4.3	26 49.8	+18.3	4.3	27 49.7	+18.3	4.3	28 49.5	+18.4	4.4	86
87	22 08.6	+17.5	3.1	23 08.5	+17.6	3.1	24 08.4	+17.6	3.2	25 08.3	+17.7	3.2	26 08.2	+17.7	3.2	27 08.1	+17.8	3.2	28 08.0	+17.9	3.3	29 07.9	+17.9	3.3	87
88	22 26.1	+17.2	2.1	23 26.1	+17.1	2.1	24 26.0	+17.2	2.1	25 26.0	+17.2	2.1	26 25.9	+17.3	2.1	27 25.9	+17.3	2.2	28 25.9	+17.3	2.2	29 25.8	+17.4	2.2	88
89	22 43.3	+16.7	1.0	23 43.2	+16.8	1.0	24 43.2	+16.8	1.1	25 43.2	+16.8	1.1	26 43.2	+16.8	1.1	27 43.2	+16.8	1.1	28 43.2	+16.8	1.1	29 43.2	+16.8	1.1	89
90	23 00.0	+16.3	0.0	24 00.0	+16.3	0.0	25 00.0	+16.3	0.0	26 00.0	+16.3	0.0	27 00.0	+16.3	0.0	28 00.0	+16.3	0.0	29 00.0	+16.3	0.0	30 00.0	+16.3	0.0	90
	23°			24°			25°			26°			27°			28°			29°			30°			

S. Lat. {L.H.A. greater than 180° ....Zn=180°–Z
{L.H.A. less than 180°...........Zn=180°+Z

LATITUDE **SAME** NAME AS DECLINATION L.H.A. 106°, 254°

Dec.	23° Hc	d	Z	24° Hc	d	Z	25° Hc	d	Z	26° Hc	d	Z	27° Hc	d	Z	28° Hc	d	Z	29° Hc	d	Z	30° Hc	d	Z	Dec.
°	° ′	′	°	° ′	′	°	° ′	′	°	° ′	′	°	° ′	′	°	° ′	′	°	° ′	′	°	° ′	′	°	°
0	13 47.0	+24.0	96.0	13 40.6	+25.0	96.2	13 34.0	+26.0	96.5	13 27.1	+26.9	96.7	13 20.0	+27.9	96.9	13 12.6	+28.8	97.2	13 05.0	+29.8	97.4	12 57.2	+30.6	97.6	0
1	14 11.0	+23.8	95.0	14 05.6	+24.8	95.3	14 00.0	+25.7	95.5	13 54.0	+26.8	95.8	13 47.9	+27.7	96.0	13 41.4	+28.7	96.3	13 34.8	+29.6	96.5	13 27.8	+30.6	96.7	1
2	14 34.8	+23.6	94.1	14 30.4	+24.6	94.3	14 25.7	+25.6	94.6	14 20.8	+26.5	94.9	14 15.6	+27.5	95.1	14 10.1	+28.4	95.4	14 04.4	+29.3	95.6	13 58.4	+30.3	95.9	2
3	14 58.4	+23.3	93.1	14 55.0	+24.3	93.4	14 51.3	+25.3	93.7	14 47.3	+26.3	93.9	14 43.1	+27.2	94.2	14 38.5	+28.3	94.5	14 33.7	+29.2	94.7	14 28.7	+30.1	95.0	3
4	15 21.7	+23.1	92.2	15 19.3	+24.1	92.5	15 16.6	+25.1	92.7	15 13.6	+26.1	93.0	15 10.3	+27.1	93.3	15 06.8	+28.0	93.5	15 02.9	+29.0	93.8	14 58.8	+29.9	94.1	4
5	15 44.8	+22.9	91.2	15 43.4	+23.8	91.5	15 41.7	+24.8	91.8	15 39.7	+25.8	92.1	15 37.4	+26.8	92.3	15 34.8	+27.7	92.6	15 31.9	+28.7	92.9	15 28.7	+29.7	93.2	5
6	16 07.7	+22.6	90.3	16 07.2	+23.6	90.5	16 06.5	+24.6	90.8	16 05.5	+25.6	91.1	16 04.2	+26.5	91.4	16 02.5	+27.6	91.7	16 00.6	+28.5	92.0	15 58.4	+29.4	92.3	6
7	16 30.3	+22.3	89.3	16 30.8	+23.4	89.6	16 31.1	+24.3	89.9	16 31.1	+25.3	90.2	16 30.7	+26.3	90.5	16 30.1	+27.3	90.8	16 29.1	+28.3	91.1	16 27.8	+29.2	91.4	7
8	16 52.6	+22.0	88.3	16 54.2	+23.0	88.6	16 55.4	+24.1	88.9	16 56.4	+25.1	89.2	16 57.0	+26.1	89.5	16 57.4	+27.0	89.8	16 57.4	+28.0	90.2	16 57.0	+29.0	90.5	8
9	17 14.6	+21.8	87.4	17 17.2	+22.8	87.7	17 19.5	+23.8	88.0	17 21.5	+24.8	88.3	17 23.1	+25.8	88.6	17 24.4	+26.8	88.9	17 25.4	+27.7	89.2	17 26.0	+28.7	89.5	9
10	17 36.4	+21.4	86.4	17 40.0	+22.5	86.7	17 43.3	+23.5	87.0	17 46.3	+24.5	87.3	17 48.9	+25.5	87.7	17 51.2	+26.5	88.0	17 53.1	+27.5	88.3	17 54.7	+28.5	88.6	10
11	17 57.8	+21.2	85.4	18 02.5	+22.2	85.7	18 06.8	+23.2	86.0	18 10.8	+24.2	86.4	18 14.4	+25.2	86.7	18 17.7	+26.2	87.0	18 20.6	+27.2	87.4	18 23.2	+28.2	87.7	11
12	18 19.0	+20.9	84.4	18 24.7	+21.9	84.7	18 30.0	+22.9	85.1	18 35.0	+23.9	85.4	18 39.6	+25.0	85.7	18 43.9	+25.9	86.1	18 47.8	+27.0	86.4	18 51.4	+27.9	86.8	12
13	18 39.9	+20.6	83.4	18 46.6	+21.6	83.8	18 52.9	+22.7	84.1	18 58.9	+23.7	84.4	19 04.6	+24.6	84.8	19 09.8	+25.7	85.1	19 14.8	+26.6	85.5	19 19.3	+27.6	85.8	13
14	19 00.5	+20.2	82.4	19 08.2	+21.3	82.8	19 15.6	+22.3	83.1	19 22.6	+23.3	83.5	19 29.2	+24.3	83.8	19 35.5	+25.3	84.2	19 41.4	+26.3	84.5	19 46.9	+27.4	84.9	14
15	19 20.7	+19.9	81.4	19 29.5	+20.9	81.8	19 37.9	+21.9	82.1	19 45.9	+23.0	82.5	19 53.5	+24.0	82.8	20 00.8	+25.0	83.2	20 07.7	+26.1	83.6	20 14.3	+27.0	83.9	15
16	19 40.6	+19.6	80.4	19 50.4	+20.6	80.8	19 59.8	+21.7	81.1	20 08.9	+22.6	81.5	20 17.5	+23.7	81.9	20 25.8	+24.7	82.2	20 33.8	+25.7	82.6	20 41.3	+26.7	83.0	16
17	20 00.2	+19.2	79.4	20 11.0	+20.3	79.8	20 21.5	+21.3	80.2	20 31.5	+22.4	80.5	20 41.2	+23.4	80.9	20 50.5	+24.4	81.3	20 59.5	+25.3	81.6	21 08.0	+26.4	82.0	17
18	20 19.4	+18.9	78.4	20 31.3	+19.9	78.8	20 42.8	+20.9	79.2	20 53.9	+22.0	79.5	21 04.6	+23.0	79.9	21 14.9	+24.0	80.3	21 24.8	+25.1	80.7	21 34.4	+26.0	81.1	18
19	20 38.3	+18.6	77.4	20 51.2	+19.6	77.8	21 03.7	+20.6	78.1	21 15.9	+21.6	78.5	21 27.6	+22.7	78.9	21 38.9	+23.7	79.3	21 49.9	+24.7	79.7	22 00.4	+25.7	80.1	19
20	20 56.9	+18.1	76.4	21 10.8	+19.2	76.8	21 24.3	+20.3	77.1	21 37.5	+21.3	77.5	21 50.3	+22.2	77.9	22 02.6	+23.3	78.3	22 14.6	+24.3	78.7	22 26.1	+25.3	79.1	20
21	21 15.0	+17.8	75.4	21 30.0	+18.8	75.7	21 44.6	+19.8	76.1	21 58.8	+20.9	76.5	22 12.5	+22.0	76.9	22 25.9	+23.0	77.3	22 38.9	+24.0	77.7	22 51.4	+25.0	78.1	21
22	21 32.8	+17.5	74.3	21 48.8	+18.5	74.7	22 04.4	+19.5	75.1	22 19.7	+20.5	75.5	22 34.5	+21.5	75.9	22 48.9	+22.5	76.3	23 02.9	+23.6	76.7	23 16.4	+24.6	77.1	22
23	21 50.3	+17.0	73.3	22 07.3	+18.1	73.7	22 23.9	+19.1	74.1	22 40.2	+20.1	74.5	22 56.0	+21.2	74.9	23 11.4	+22.2	75.3	23 26.5	+23.2	75.7	23 41.0	+24.3	76.1	23
24	22 07.3	+16.6	72.3	22 25.4	+17.6	72.7	22 43.0	+18.7	73.1	23 00.3	+19.8	73.5	23 17.2	+20.7	73.9	23 33.6	+21.8	74.3	23 49.7	+22.8	74.7	24 05.3	+23.8	75.1	24
25	22 23.9	+16.3	71.2	22 43.0	+17.3	71.6	23 01.7	+18.4	72.0	23 20.1	+19.3	72.4	23 37.9	+20.4	72.9	23 55.4	+21.4	73.3	24 12.5	+22.4	73.7	24 29.1	+23.4	74.1	25
26	22 40.2	+15.8	70.2	23 00.3	+16.9	70.6	23 20.1	+17.8	71.0	23 39.4	+18.9	71.4	23 58.3	+20.0	71.8	24 16.8	+21.0	72.3	24 34.9	+22.0	72.7	24 52.5	+23.0	73.1	26
27	22 56.0	+15.4	69.1	23 17.2	+16.4	69.5	23 37.9	+17.5	70.0	23 58.3	+18.5	70.4	24 18.3	+19.5	70.8	24 37.8	+20.5	71.2	24 56.9	+21.5	71.7	25 15.5	+22.6	72.1	27
28	23 11.4	+15.1	68.1	23 33.6	+16.1	68.5	23 55.4	+17.1	68.9	24 16.8	+18.1	69.3	24 37.8	+19.1	69.8	24 58.3	+20.1	70.2	25 18.4	+21.2	70.6	25 38.1	+22.2	71.1	28
29	23 26.5	+14.5	67.0	23 49.7	+15.6	67.4	24 12.5	+16.6	67.9	24 34.9	+17.6	68.3	24 56.9	+18.6	68.7	25 18.4	+19.7	69.1	25 39.6	+20.7	69.6	26 00.3	+21.7	70.0	29
30	23 41.0	+14.2	66.0	24 05.3	+15.1	66.4	24 29.1	+16.2	66.8	24 52.5	+17.2	67.2	25 15.5	+18.2	67.7	25 38.1	+19.3	68.1	26 00.3	+20.2	68.6	26 22.0	+21.3	69.0	30
31	23 55.2	+13.7	64.9	24 20.4	+14.7	65.3	24 45.3	+15.7	65.7	25 09.7	+16.7	66.2	25 33.7	+17.8	66.6	25 57.4	+18.7	67.0	26 20.5	+19.8	67.5	26 43.3	+20.8	68.0	31
32	24 08.9	+13.3	63.9	24 35.1	+14.3	64.3	25 01.0	+15.3	64.7	25 26.4	+16.3	65.1	25 51.5	+17.3	65.5	26 16.1	+18.3	66.0	26 40.3	+19.3	66.4	27 04.1	+20.3	66.9	32
33	24 22.2	+12.8	62.8	24 49.4	+13.8	63.2	25 16.3	+14.8	63.6	25 42.7	+15.8	64.0	26 08.8	+16.8	64.5	26 34.4	+17.8	64.9	26 59.6	+18.9	65.4	27 24.4	+19.8	65.9	33
34	24 35.0	+12.3	61.7	25 03.2	+13.4	62.1	25 31.1	+14.3	62.5	25 58.5	+15.4	63.0	26 25.6	+16.3	63.4	26 52.2	+17.4	63.9	27 18.5	+18.3	64.3	27 44.2	+19.4	64.8	34
35	24 47.3	+11.9	60.6	25 16.6	+12.8	61.0	25 45.4	+13.9	61.5	26 13.9	+14.8	61.9	26 41.9	+15.9	62.3	27 09.6	+16.8	62.8	27 36.8	+17.9	63.2	28 03.6	+18.9	63.7	35
36	24 59.2	+11.4	59.6	25 29.4	+12.4	60.0	25 59.3	+13.3	60.4	26 28.7	+14.4	60.8	26 57.8	+15.3	61.3	27 26.4	+16.4	61.7	27 54.7	+17.3	62.2	28 22.5	+18.3	62.6	36
37	25 10.6	+11.0	58.5	25 41.8	+11.9	58.9	26 12.6	+12.9	59.3	26 43.1	+13.8	59.7	27 13.1	+14.9	60.2	27 42.8	+15.8	60.6	28 12.0	+16.8	61.1	28 40.8	+17.8	61.6	37
38	25 21.6	+10.4	57.4	25 53.7	+11.5	57.8	26 25.5	+12.4	58.2	26 56.9	+13.4	58.6	27 28.0	+14.3	59.1	27 58.6	+15.3	59.5	28 28.8	+16.3	60.0	28 58.6	+17.3	60.5	38
39	25 32.0	+10.0	56.3	26 05.2	+10.9	56.7	26 37.9	+11.9	57.1	27 10.3	+12.9	57.5	27 42.3	+13.8	58.0	28 13.9	+14.8	58.4	28 45.1	+15.8	58.9	29 15.9	+16.8	59.4	39
40	25 42.0	+9.5	55.2	26 16.1	+10.4	55.6	26 49.8	+11.4	56.0	27 23.2	+12.3	56.4	27 56.1	+13.3	56.9	28 28.7	+14.3	57.3	29 00.9	+15.2	57.8	29 32.7	+16.2	58.3	40
41	25 51.5	+9.0	54.1	26 26.5	+9.9	54.5	27 01.2	+10.8	54.9	27 35.5	+11.8	55.3	28 09.4	+12.8	55.8	28 43.0	+13.7	56.2	29 16.1	+14.7	56.7	29 48.9	+15.6	57.2	41
42	26 00.5	+8.5	53.0	26 36.4	+9.4	53.4	27 12.0	+10.4	53.8	27 47.3	+11.3	54.2	28 22.2	+12.2	54.7	28 56.7	+13.1	55.1	29 30.8	+14.1	55.6	30 04.5	+15.1	56.0	42
43	26 09.0	+8.0	51.9	26 45.8	+8.9	52.3	27 22.4	+9.8	52.7	27 58.6	+10.7	53.1	28 34.4	+11.6	53.6	29 09.8	+12.6	54.0	29 44.9	+13.6	54.5	30 19.6	+14.5	54.9	43
44	26 17.0	+7.5	50.8	26 54.7	+8.4	51.2	27 32.2	+9.3	51.6	28 09.3	+10.2	52.0	28 46.0	+11.2	52.4	29 22.4	+12.1	52.9	29 58.5	+12.9	53.3	30 34.1	+13.9	53.8	44
45	26 24.5	+6.9	49.7	27 03.1	+7.9	50.1	27 41.5	+8.7	50.5	28 19.5	+9.6	50.9	28 57.2	+10.5	51.3	29 34.5	+11.4	51.8	30 11.4	+12.4	52.2	30 48.0	+13.3	52.7	45
46	26 31.4	+6.5	48.6	27 11.0	+7.3	49.0	27 50.2	+8.2	49.4	28 29.1	+9.1	49.8	29 07.7	+10.0	50.2	29 45.9	+10.9	50.6	30 23.8	+11.8	51.1	31 01.3	+12.8	51.5	46
47	26 37.9	+5.9	47.5	27 18.3	+6.8	47.8	27 58.4	+7.6	48.2	28 38.2	+8.5	48.6	29 17.7	+9.4	49.1	29 56.8	+10.3	49.5	30 35.6	+11.2	49.9	31 14.1	+12.1	50.4	47
48	26 43.8	+5.4	46.4	27 25.1	+6.2	46.7	28 06.0	+7.2	47.1	28 46.7	+8.0	47.5	29 27.1	+8.8	47.9	30 07.1	+9.8	48.3	30 46.8	+10.6	48.8	31 26.2	+11.5	49.2	48
49	26 49.2	+4.9	45.2	27 31.3	+5.7	45.6	28 13.2	+6.5	46.0	28 54.7	+7.4	46.4	29 35.9	+8.3	46.8	30 16.9	+9.1	47.2	30 57.4	+10.0	47.6	31 37.7	+10.9	48.1	49
50	26 54.1	+4.3	44.1	27 37.0	+5.2	44.5	28 19.7	+6.0	44.9	29 02.1	+6.8	45.2	29 44.2	+7.6	45.6	30 26.0	+8.5	46.1	31 07.4	+9.4	46.5	31 48.6	+10.2	46.9	50
51	26 58.4	+3.9	43.0	27 42.2	+4.6	43.4	28 25.7	+5.4	43.7	29 08.9	+6.3	44.1	29 51.8	+7.1	44.5	30 34.5	+7.9	44.9	31 16.8	+8.8	45.3	31 58.8	+9.6	45.8	51
52	27 02.3	+3.3	41.9	27 46.8	+4.1	42.2	28 31.1	+4.9	42.6	29 15.2	+5.6	43.0	29 58.9	+6.5	43.4	30 42.4	+7.3	43.8	31 25.6	+8.1	44.2	32 08.4	+9.0	44.6	52
53	27 05.6	+2.7	40.8	27 50.9	+3.5	41.1	28 36.0	+4.3	41.5	29 20.8	+5.1	41.8	30 05.4	+5.9	42.2	30 49.7	+6.7	42.6	31 33.7	+7.5	43.0	32 17.4	+8.4	43.4	53
54	27 08.3	+2.2	39.6	27 54.4	+3.0	40.0	28 40.3	+3.7	40.3	29 25.9	+4.5	40.7	30 11.3	+5.2	41.1	30 56.4	+6.0	41.4	31 41.2	+6.9	41.9	32 25.8	+7.6	42.3	54
55	27 10.5	+1.7	38.5	27 57.4	+2.4	38.8	28 44.0	+3.1	39.2	29 30.4	+3.9	39.5	30 16.5	+4.7	39.9	31 02.4	+5.5	40.3	31 48.1	+6.2	40.7	32 33.4	+7.0	41.1	55
56	27 12.2	+1.2	37.4	27 59.8	+1.8	37.7	28 47.1	+2.6	38.0	29 34.3	+3.3	38.4	30 21.2	+4.1	38.8	31 07.9	+4.8	39.1	31 54.3	+5.6	39.5	32 40.4	+6.4	39.9	56
57	27 13.4	+0.6	36.3	28 01.6	+1.3	36.6	28 49.7	+2.0	36.9	29 37.6	+2.7	37.2	30 25.3	+3.4	37.6	31 12.7	+4.2	38.0	31 59.9	+4.9	38.3	32 46.8	+5.7	38.7	57
58	27 14.0	0.0	35.1	28 02.9	+0.8	35.4	28 51.7	+1.5	35.8	29 40.3	+2.1	36.1	30 28.7	+2.8	36.4	31 16.9	+3.5	36.8	32 04.8	+4.3	37.2	32 52.5	+5.0	37.6	58
59	27 14.0	-0.4	34.0	28 03.7	+0.2	34.3	28 53.2	+0.8	34.6	29 42.4	+1.6	34.9	30 31.5	+2.2	35.3	31 20.4	+2.9	35.6	32 09.1	+3.6	36.0	32 57.5	+4.3	36.4	59
60	27 13.6	-1.0	32.9	28 03.9	-0.4	33.2	28 54.0	+0.3	33.5	29 44.0	+0.9	33.8	30 33.7	+1.6	34.1	31 23.3	+2.3	34.5	32 12.7	+2.9	34.8	33 01.8	+3.7	35.2	60
61	27 12.6	-1.6	31.8	28 03.5	-0.9	32.0	28 54.3	-0.3	32.3	29 44.9	+0.3	32.6	30 35.3	+1.0	33.0	31 25.6	+1.6	33.3	32 15.6	+2.3	33.6	33 05.5	+3.0	34.0	61
62	27 11.0	-2.1	30.6	28 02.6	-1.5	30.9	28 54.0	-0.9	31.2	29 45.2	-0.3	31.5	30 36.3	+0.3	31.8	31 27.2	+1.0	32.1	32 17.9	+1.7	32.4	33 08.5	+2.3	32.8	62
63	27 08.9	-2.6	29.5	28 01.1	-2.1	29.8	28 53.1	-1.5	30.1	29 44.9	-0.8	30.3	30 36.6	-0.2	30.6	31 28.2	+0.3	30.9	32 19.6	+0.9	31.3	33 10.8	+1.6	31.6	63
64	27 06.3	-3.1	28.4	27 59.0	-2.6	28.7	28 51.6	-2.0	28.9	29 44.1	-1.5	29.2	30 36.4	-0.9	29.5	31 28.5	-0.3	29.8	32 20.5	+0.4	30.1	33 12.4	+0.9	30.4	64
65	27 03.2	-3.7	27.3	27 56.4	-3.1	27.5	28 49.6	-2.6	27.8	29 42.6	-2.1	28.0	30 35.5	-1.5	28.3	31 28.2	-0.9	28.6	32 20.9	-0.4	28.9	33 13.3	+0.2	29.2	65
66	26 59.5	-4.2	26.2	27 53.3	-3.7	26.4	28 47.0	-3.2	26.6	29 40.5	-2.6	26.9	30 34.0	-2.1	27.1	31 27.3	-1.6	27.4	32 20.5	-1.0	27.7	33 13.5	-0.4	28.0	66
67	26 55.3	-4.8	25.0	27 49.6	-4.3	25.3	28 43.8	-3.8	25.5	29 37.9	-3.3	25.7	30 31.9	-2.8	26.0	31 25.7	-2.2	26.3	32 19.5	-1.7	26.5	33 13.1	-1.1	26.8	67
68	26 50.5	-5.3	23.9	27 45.3	-4.8	24.1	28 40.0	-4.3	24.4	29 34.6	-3.8	24.6	30 29.1	-3.3	24.8	31 23.5	-2.8	25.1	32 17.8	-2.3	25.3	33 12.0	-1.8	25.6	68
69	26 45.2	-5.8	22.8	27 40.5	-5.4	23.0	28 35.7	-4.9	23.2	29 30.8	-4.5	23.4	30 25.8	-4.0	23.7	31 20.7	-3.5	23.9	32 15.5	-3.0	24.2	33 10.2	-2.5	24.4	69
70	26 39.4	-6.3	21.7	27 35.1	-5.8	21.9	28 30.8	-5.5	22.1	29 26.3	-5.0	22.3	30 21.8	-4.6	22.5	31 17.2	-4.1	22.7	32 12.5	-3.7	23.0	33 07.7	-3.2	23.2	70
71	26 33.1	-6.8	20.6	27 29.3	-6.5	20.8	28 25.3	-6.0	21.0	29 21.3	-5.6	21.1	30 17.2	-5.1	21.4	31 13.1	-4.8	21.6	32 08.8	-4.3	21.8	33 04.5	-3.9	22.0	71
72	26 26.3	-7.4	19.5	27 22.8	-7.0	19.6	28 19.3	-6.6	19.8	29 15.7	-6.2	20.0	30 12.1	-5.8	20.2	31 08.3	-5.4	20.4	32 04.5	-4.9	20.6	33 00.6	-4.5	20.9	72
73	26 18.9	-7.8	18.4	27 15.8	-7.5	18.5	28 12.7	-7.1	18.7	29 09.5	-6.7	18.9	30 06.3	-6.4	19.1	31 02.9	-6.0	19.2	31 59.6	-5.7	19.4	32 56.1	-5.2	19.7	73
74	26 11.1	-8.4	17.3	27 08.3	-8.0	17.4	28 05.6	-7.7	17.6	29 02.8	-7.4	17.7	29 59.9	-7.0	17.9	30 56.9	-6.6	18.1	31 53.9	-6.2	18.3	32 50.9	-5.9	18.5	74
75	26 02.7	-8.9	16.2	27 00.3	-8.5	16.3	27 57.9	-8.2	16.4	28 55.4	-7.9	16.6	29 52.9	-7.6	16.8	30 50.3	-7.2	16.9	31 47.7	-6.9	17.1	32 45.0	-6.5	17.3	75
76	25 53.8	-9.3	15.1	26 51.8	-9.1	15.2	27 49.7	-8.8	15.3	28 47.5	-8.5	15.5	29 45.3	-8.2	15.6	30 43.1	-7.9	15.8	31 40.8	-7.5	15.9	32 38.5	-7.2	16.1	76
77	25 44.5	-9.9	14.0	26 42.7	-9.6	14.1	27 40.9	-9.3	14.2	28 39.0	-9.0	14.3	29 37.1	-8.7	14.5	30 35.2	-8.4	14.6	31 33.3	-8.2	14.8	32 31.3	-7.9	14.9	77
78	25 34.6	-10.3	12.9	26 33.1	-10.1	13.0	27 31.6	-9.9	13.1	28 30.0	-9.6	13.2	29 28.4	-9.3	13.3	30 26.8	-9.1	13.5	31 25.1	-8.8	13.6	32 23.4	-8.5	13.8	78
79	25 24.3	-10.8	11.8	26 23.0	-10.6	11.9	27 21.7	-10.3	12.0	28 20.4	-10.1	12.1	29 19.1	-9.9	12.2	30 17.7	-9.7	12.3	31 16.3	-9.4	12.5	32 14.9	-9.2	12.6	79
80	25 13.5	-11.3	10.7	26 12.4	-11.1	10.8	27 11.4	-10.9	10.9	28 10.3	-10.7	11.0	29 09.2	-10.5	11.1	30 08.0	-10.2	11.2	31 06.9	-10.0	11.3	32 05.7	-9.8	11.4	80
81	25 02.2	-11.8	9.6	26 01.3	-11.6	9.7	27 00.5	-11.4	9.8	27 59.6	-11.2	9.9	28 58.7	-11.0	9.9	29 57.8	-10.9	10.0	30 56.9	-10.7	10.1	31 55.9	-10.4	10.3	81
82	24 50.4	-12.2	8.5	25 49.7	-12.0	8.6	26 49.1	-12.0	8.7	27 48.4	-11.8	8.7	28 47.7	-11.6	8.8	29 46.9	-11.4	8.9	30 46.2	-11.2	9.0	31 45.5	-11.1	9.1	82
83	24 38.2	-12.7	7.4	25 37.7	-12.6	7.5	26 37.1	-12.4	7.6	27 36.6	-12.3	7.6	28 36.1	-12.2	7.7	29 35.5	-12.0	7.8	30 35.0	-11.9	7.9	31 34.4	-11.7	7.9	83
84	24 25.5	-13.2	6.4	25 25.1	-13.0	6.4	26 24.7	-12.9	6.5	27 24.3	-12.8	6.5	28 23.9	-12.6	6.6	29 23.5	-12.5	6.7	30 23.1	-12.4	6.7	31 22.7	-12.3	6.8	84
85	24 12.3	-13.6	5.3	25 12.1	-13.5	5.3	26 11.8	-13.4	5.4	27 11.5	-13.3	5.4	28 11.3	-13.2	5.5	29 11.0	-13.1	5.5	30 10.7	-13.0	5.6	31 10.4	-12.9	5.6	85
86	23 58.7	-14.0	4.2	24 58.6	-14.0	4.3	25 58.4	-13.9	4.3	26 58.2	-13.8	4.3	27 58.1	-13.8	4.4	28 57.9	-13.7	4.4	29 57.7	-13.6	4.5	30 57.5	-13.5	4.5	86
87	23 44.7	-14.5	3.2	24 44.6	-14.4	3.2	25 44.5	-14.4	3.2	26 44.4	-14.3	3.2	27 44.3	-14.2	3.3	28 44.2	-14.2	3.3	29 44.1	-14.1	3.3	30 44.0	-14.1	3.4	87
88	23 30.2	-14.9	2.1	24 30.2	-14.9	2.1	25 30.1	-14.8	2.1	26 30.1	-14.8	2.2	27 30.1	-14.8	2.2	28 30.0	-14.7	2.2	29 30.0	-14.7	2.2	30 29.9	-14.7	2.2	88
89	23 15.3	-15.3	1.1	24 15.3	-15.3	1.1	25 15.3	-15.3	1.1	26 15.3	-15.3	1.1	27 15.3	-15.3	1.1	28 15.3	-15.3	1.1	29 15.3	-15.3	1.1	30 15.2	-15.2	1.1	89
90	23 00.0	-15.7	0.0	24 00.0	-15.7	0.0	25 00.0	-15.8	0.0	26 00.0	-15.8	0.0	27 00.0	-15.8	0.0	28 00.0	-15.8	0.0	29 00.0	-15.8	0.0	30 00.0	-15.8	0.0	90
	23°			24°			25°			26°			27°			28°			29°			30°			

LATITUDE CONTRARY NAME TO DECLINATION L.H.A. 75°, 285°

	23°			24°			25°			26°			27°			28°			29°			30°			
Dec.	Hc	d	Z	Hc	d	Z	Hc	d	Z	Hc	d	Z	Hc	d	Z	Hc	d	Z	Hc	d	Z	Hc	d	Z	Dec.
°	° ′	′	°	° ′	′	°	° ′	′	°	° ′	′	°	° ′	′	°	° ′	′	°	° ′	′	°	° ′	′	°	°
0	13 47.0	-24.3	96.0	13 40.6	-25.2	96.2	13 34.0	-26.2	96.5	13 27.1	-27.1	96.7	13 20.0	-28.1	96.9	13 12.6	-29.0	97.2	13 05.0	-30.0	97.4	12 57.2	-30.9	97.6	0
1	13 22.7	-24.4	96.9	13 15.4	-25.4	97.2	13 07.8	-26.4	97.4	13 00.0	-27.4	97.6	12 51.9	-28.3	97.8	12 43.6	-29.2	98.1	12 35.0	-30.1	98.3	12 26.3	-31.1	98.5	1
2	12 58.3	-24.7	97.9	12 50.0	-25.7	98.1	12 41.4	-26.6	98.3	12 32.6	-27.5	98.5	12 23.6	-28.4	98.7	12 14.4	-29.4	99.0	12 04.9	-30.3	99.2	11 55.2	-31.2	99.4	2
3	12 33.6	-24.8	98.8	12 24.3	-25.8	99.0	12 14.8	-26.7	99.2	12 05.1	-27.7	99.4	11 55.2	-28.7	99.6	11 45.0	-29.6	99.9	11 34.6	-30.4	100.1	11 24.0	-31.3	100.3	3
4	12 08.8	-25.1	99.7	11 58.5	-26.0	99.9	11 48.1	-27.0	100.1	11 37.4	-27.9	100.3	11 26.5	-28.8	100.5	11 15.4	-29.7	100.7	11 04.2	-30.6	100.9	10 52.7	-31.5	101.1	4
5	11 43.7	-25.2	100.7	11 32.5	-26.1	100.9	11 21.1	-27.1	101.1	11 09.5	-28.0	101.2	10 57.7	-28.9	101.4	10 45.7	-29.8	101.6	10 33.6	-30.8	101.8	10 21.2	-31.7	102.0	5
6	11 18.5	-25.4	101.6	11 06.4	-26.3	101.8	10 54.0	-27.2	102.0	10 41.5	-28.2	102.1	10 28.8	-29.1	102.3	10 15.9	-30.0	102.5	10 02.8	-30.9	102.7	9 49.5	-31.7	102.9	6
7	10 53.1	-25.5	102.5	10 40.1	-26.5	102.7	10 26.8	-27.4	102.9	10 13.3	-28.3	103.0	9 59.7	-29.2	103.2	9 45.9	-30.1	103.4	9 31.9	-31.0	103.6	9 17.8	-31.9	103.7	7
8	10 27.6	-25.7	103.4	10 13.6	-26.7	103.6	9 59.4	-27.6	103.8	9 45.0	-28.5	103.9	9 30.5	-29.4	104.1	9 15.8	-30.3	104.3	9 00.9	-31.1	104.4	8 45.9	-32.0	104.6	8
9	10 01.9	-25.9	104.3	9 46.9	-26.7	104.5	9 31.8	-27.7	104.7	9 16.5	-28.6	104.8	9 01.1	-29.5	105.0	8 45.5	-30.4	105.1	8 29.8	-31.3	105.3	8 13.9	-32.1	105.4	9
10	9 36.0	-26.0	105.3	9 20.2	-27.0	105.4	9 04.1	-27.8	105.6	8 47.9	-28.7	105.7	8 31.6	-29.6	105.9	8 15.1	-30.5	106.0	7 58.5	-31.4	106.1	7 41.8	-32.3	106.3	10
11	9 10.0	-26.1	106.2	8 53.2	-27.0	106.3	8 36.3	-28.0	106.5	8 19.2	-28.8	106.6	8 02.0	-29.7	106.7	7 44.6	-30.6	106.9	7 27.1	-31.4	107.0	7 09.5	-32.3	107.1	11
12	8 43.9	-26.3	107.1	8 26.2	-27.2	107.2	8 08.3	-28.0	107.4	7 50.4	-29.0	107.5	7 32.3	-29.9	107.6	7 14.0	-30.7	107.7	6 55.7	-31.6	107.9	6 37.2	-32.4	108.0	12
13	8 17.6	-26.4	108.0	7 59.0	-27.3	108.1	7 40.3	-28.2	108.3	7 21.4	-29.0	108.4	7 02.4	-29.9	108.5	6 43.3	-30.7	108.6	6 24.1	-31.6	108.7	6 04.8	-32.5	108.8	13
14	7 51.2	-26.5	108.9	7 31.7	-27.4	109.0	7 12.1	-28.3	109.1	6 52.4	-29.2	109.3	6 32.5	-30.0	109.4	6 12.6	-30.9	109.5	5 52.5	-31.7	109.6	5 32.3	-32.5	109.7	14
15	7 24.7	-26.6	109.8	7 04.3	-27.5	109.9	6 43.8	-28.4	110.0	6 23.2	-29.2	110.1	6 02.5	-30.1	110.2	5 41.7	-31.0	110.3	5 20.8	-31.8	110.4	4 59.8	-32.6	110.5	15
16	6 58.1	-26.7	110.7	6 36.8	-27.6	110.8	6 15.4	-28.4	110.9	5 54.0	-29.4	111.0	5 32.4	-30.2	111.1	5 10.7	-31.0	111.2	4 49.0	-31.8	111.3	4 27.2	-32.7	111.4	16
17	6 31.4	-26.9	111.6	6 09.2	-27.7	111.7	5 47.0	-28.6	111.8	5 24.6	-29.4	111.9	5 02.2	-30.2	112.0	4 39.7	-31.1	112.1	4 17.2	-32.0	112.1	3 54.5	-32.7	112.2	17
18	6 04.5	-26.9	112.5	5 41.5	-27.7	112.6	5 18.4	-28.6	112.7	4 55.2	-29.4	112.8	4 32.0	-30.3	112.8	4 08.6	-31.1	112.9	3 45.2	-31.9	113.0	3 21.8	-32.8	113.0	18
19	5 37.6	-27.0	113.4	5 13.8	-27.9	113.5	4 49.8	-28.7	113.6	4 25.8	-29.6	113.6	4 01.7	-30.4	113.7	3 37.5	-31.2	113.8	3 13.3	-32.0	113.8	2 49.0	-32.8	113.9	19
20	5 10.6	-27.0	114.3	4 45.9	-27.9	114.4	4 21.1	-28.7	114.5	3 56.2	-29.5	114.5	3 31.3	-30.4	114.6	3 06.3	-31.2	114.6	2 41.3	-32.0	114.7	2 16.2	-32.8	114.7	20
21	4 43.6	-27.2	115.2	4 18.0	-28.0	115.3	3 52.4	-28.9	115.3	3 26.7	-29.7	115.4	3 00.9	-30.5	115.4	2 35.1	-31.3	115.5	2 09.3	-32.1	115.5	1 43.4	-32.9	115.6	21
22	4 16.4	-27.2	116.1	3 50.0	-28.0	116.2	3 23.5	-28.8	116.2	2 57.0	-29.7	116.3	2 30.4	-30.4	116.3	2 03.8	-31.2	116.3	1 37.2	-32.1	116.4	1 10.5	-32.8	116.4	22
23	3 49.2	-27.2	117.0	3 22.0	-28.1	117.0	2 54.7	-28.9	117.1	2 27.3	-29.7	117.1	2 00.0	-30.5	117.2	1 32.6	-31.4	117.2	1 05.1	-32.1	117.2	0 37.7	-32.9	117.2	23
24	3 22.0	-27.3	117.9	2 53.9	-28.1	117.9	2 25.8	-28.9	118.0	1 57.6	-29.7	118.0	1 29.5	-30.6	118.0	1 01.2	-31.3	118.0	0 33.0	-32.1	118.1	0 04.8	-32.9	118.1	24
25	2 54.7	-27.4	118.8	2 25.8	-28.2	118.8	1 56.9	-29.0	118.8	1 27.9	-29.8	118.9	0 58.9	-30.5	118.9	0 29.9	-31.3	118.9	0 00.9	-32.1	118.9	0 28.1	+32.8	61.1	25
26	2 27.3	-27.3	119.7	1 57.6	-28.1	119.7	1 27.9	-29.0	119.7	0 58.1	-29.7	119.7	0 28.4	-30.6	119.8	0 01.4	+31.3	60.2	0 31.2	+32.1	60.3	1 00.9	+32.9	60.3	26
27	2 00.0	-27.4	120.6	1 29.5	-28.3	120.6	0 58.9	-29.0	120.6	0 28.4	-29.8	120.6	0 02.2	+30.5	59.4	0 32.7	+31.3	59.4	1 03.3	+32.1	59.4	1 33.8	+32.8	59.4	27
28	1 32.6	-27.5	121.4	1 01.2	-28.2	121.5	0 29.9	-29.0	121.5	0 01.4	+29.8	58.5	0 32.7	+30.6	58.5	1 04.0	+31.4	58.5	1 35.4	+32.0	58.6	2 06.6	+32.8	58.6	28
29	1 05.1	-27.4	122.3	0 33.0	-28.2	122.3	0 00.9	-29.0	122.3	0 31.2	+29.7	57.7	1 03.3	+30.5	57.7	1 35.4	+31.2	57.7	2 07.4	+32.0	57.7	2 39.4	+32.8	57.7	29
30	0 37.7	-27.5	123.2	0 04.8	-28.2	123.2	0 28.1	+29.0	56.8	1 00.9	+29.8	56.8	1 33.8	+30.5	56.8	2 06.6	+31.3	56.8	2 39.4	+32.0	56.9	3 12.2	+32.8	56.9	30
31	0 10.2	-27.4	124.1	0 23.4	+28.2	55.9	0 57.1	+28.9	55.9	1 30.7	+29.7	55.9	2 04.3	+30.5	55.9	2 37.9	+31.2	56.0	3 11.4	+32.0	56.0	3 45.0	+32.6	56.1	31
32	0 17.2	+27.5	55.0	0 51.6	+28.3	55.0	1 26.0	+29.0	55.0	2 00.4	+29.7	55.1	2 34.8	+30.4	55.1	3 09.1	+31.2	55.1	3 43.4	+31.9	55.2	4 17.6	+32.7	55.2	32
33	0 44.7	+27.4	54.1	1 19.9	+28.1	54.1	1 55.0	+28.9	54.1	2 30.1	+29.7	54.2	3 05.2	+30.4	54.2	3 40.3	+31.1	54.3	4 15.3	+31.9	54.3	4 50.3	+32.5	54.4	33
34	1 12.1	+27.5	53.2	1 48.0	+28.2	53.2	2 23.9	+28.9	53.3	2 59.8	+29.6	53.3	3 35.6	+30.4	53.4	4 11.4	+31.1	53.4	4 47.2	+31.7	53.5	5 22.8	+32.5	53.5	34
35	1 39.6	+27.4	52.3	2 16.2	+28.1	52.4	2 52.8	+28.9	52.4	3 29.4	+29.6	52.4	4 06.0	+30.3	52.5	4 42.5	+31.0	52.6	5 18.9	+31.8	52.6	5 55.3	+32.5	52.7	35
36	2 07.0	+27.3	51.4	2 44.3	+28.1	51.5	3 21.7	+28.8	51.5	3 59.0	+29.5	51.6	4 36.3	+30.2	51.6	5 13.5	+30.9	51.7	5 50.7	+31.6	51.8	6 27.8	+32.3	51.9	36
37	2 34.3	+27.4	50.6	3 12.4	+28.1	50.6	3 50.5	+28.8	50.6	4 28.5	+29.5	50.7	5 06.5	+30.2	50.8	5 44.4	+30.9	50.8	6 22.3	+31.6	50.9	7 00.1	+32.2	51.0	37
38	3 01.7	+27.3	49.7	3 40.5	+28.0	49.7	4 19.3	+28.7	49.8	4 58.0	+29.4	49.8	5 36.7	+30.1	49.9	6 15.3	+30.8	50.0	6 53.9	+31.4	50.1	7 32.3	+32.2	50.2	38
39	3 29.0	+27.2	48.8	4 08.5	+27.9	48.8	4 48.0	+28.6	48.9	5 27.4	+29.3	48.9	6 06.8	+30.0	49.0	6 46.1	+30.7	49.1	7 25.3	+31.4	49.2	8 04.5	+32.0	49.3	39
40	3 56.2	+27.2	47.9	4 36.4	+27.9	47.9	5 16.6	+28.5	48.0	5 56.7	+29.3	48.1	6 36.8	+29.9	48.2	7 16.8	+30.6	48.2	7 56.7	+31.3	48.3	8 36.5	+32.0	48.4	40
41	4 23.4	+27.1	47.0	5 04.3	+27.8	47.0	5 45.1	+28.5	47.1	6 26.0	+29.1	47.2	7 06.7	+29.8	47.3	7 47.4	+30.4	47.4	8 28.0	+31.1	47.5	9 08.5	+31.8	47.6	41
42	4 50.5	+27.0	46.1	5 32.1	+27.7	46.2	6 13.6	+28.4	46.2	6 55.1	+29.0	46.3	7 36.5	+29.7	46.4	8 17.8	+30.4	46.5	8 59.1	+31.0	46.6	9 40.3	+31.7	46.7	42
43	5 17.5	+27.0	45.2	5 59.8	+27.6	45.3	6 42.0	+28.3	45.3	7 24.1	+29.0	45.4	8 06.2	+29.6	45.5	8 48.2	+30.3	45.6	9 30.1	+30.9	45.7	10 12.0	+31.5	45.9	43
44	5 44.5	+26.9	44.3	6 27.4	+27.6	44.4	7 10.3	+28.2	44.5	7 53.1	+28.8	44.5	8 35.8	+29.5	44.6	9 18.5	+30.1	44.8	10 01.0	+30.8	44.9	10 43.5	+31.4	45.0	44
45	6 11.4	+26.8	43.4	6 55.0	+27.4	43.5	7 38.5	+28.1	43.6	8 21.9	+28.7	43.7	9 05.3	+29.3	43.8	9 48.6	+30.0	43.9	10 31.8	+30.6	44.0	11 14.9	+31.2	44.1	45
46	6 38.2	+26.7	42.5	7 22.4	+27.3	42.6	8 06.6	+27.9	42.7	8 50.6	+28.6	42.8	9 34.6	+29.3	42.9	10 18.6	+29.8	43.0	11 02.4	+30.5	43.1	11 46.1	+31.1	43.3	46
47	7 04.9	+26.6	41.6	7 49.7	+27.2	41.7	8 34.5	+27.8	41.8	9 19.2	+28.5	41.9	10 03.9	+29.0	42.0	10 48.4	+29.7	42.1	11 32.9	+30.3	42.3	12 17.2	+30.9	42.4	47
48	7 31.5	+26.5	40.7	8 16.9	+27.1	40.8	9 02.3	+27.8	40.9	9 47.7	+28.3	41.0	10 32.9	+29.0	41.1	11 18.1	+29.5	41.2	12 03.2	+30.1	41.4	12 48.1	+30.8	41.5	48
49	7 58.0	+26.3	39.8	8 44.0	+27.0	39.9	9 30.1	+27.5	40.0	10 16.0	+28.2	40.1	11 01.9	+28.7	40.2	11 47.6	+29.4	40.3	12 33.3	+30.0	40.5	13 18.9	+30.6	40.6	49
50	8 24.3	+26.3	38.9	9 11.0	+26.8	39.0	9 57.6	+27.4	39.1	10 44.2	+28.0	39.2	11 30.6	+28.6	39.3	12 17.0	+29.2	39.5	13 03.3	+29.8	39.6	13 49.5	+30.3	39.7	50
51	8 50.6	+26.1	38.0	9 37.8	+26.7	38.1	10 25.0	+27.3	38.2	11 12.2	+27.8	38.3	11 59.2	+28.4	38.4	12 46.2	+29.0	38.6	13 33.1	+29.5	38.7	14 19.8	+30.2	38.9	51
52	9 16.7	+25.9	37.1	10 04.5	+26.6	37.2	10 52.3	+27.1	37.3	11 40.0	+27.7	37.4	12 27.6	+28.3	37.5	13 15.2	+28.8	37.7	14 02.6	+29.4	37.8	14 50.0	+30.0	38.0	52
53	9 42.6	+25.9	36.1	10 31.1	+26.3	36.2	11 19.4	+27.0	36.4	12 07.7	+27.5	36.5	12 55.9	+28.1	36.6	13 44.0	+28.6	36.8	14 32.0	+29.2	36.9	15 20.0	+29.7	37.1	53
54	10 08.5	+25.6	35.2	10 57.4	+26.3	35.3	11 46.4	+26.7	35.4	12 35.2	+27.3	35.6	13 24.0	+27.8	35.7	14 12.6	+28.5	35.9	15 01.2	+29.0	36.0	15 49.7	+29.5	36.2	54
55	10 34.1	+25.5	34.3	11 23.7	+26.0	34.4	12 13.1	+26.6	34.5	13 02.5	+27.1	34.7	13 51.8	+27.7	34.8	14 41.1	+28.2	34.9	15 30.2	+28.7	35.1	16 19.2	+29.3	35.3	55
56	10 59.6	+25.4	33.4	11 49.7	+25.9	33.5	12 39.7	+26.4	33.6	13 29.6	+27.0	33.7	14 19.5	+27.4	33.9	15 09.3	+27.9	34.0	15 58.9	+28.6	34.2	16 48.5	+29.1	34.3	56
57	11 25.0	+25.2	32.5	12 15.6	+25.7	32.6	13 06.1	+26.2	32.7	13 56.6	+26.7	32.8	14 46.9	+27.3	33.0	15 37.2	+27.8	33.1	16 27.5	+28.2	33.3	17 17.6	+28.8	33.4	57
58	11 50.2	+24.9	31.5	12 41.3	+25.5	31.6	13 32.3	+26.0	31.8	14 23.3	+26.5	31.9	15 14.2	+27.0	32.0	16 05.0	+27.5	32.2	16 55.7	+28.1	32.3	17 46.4	+28.5	32.5	58
59	12 15.1	+24.8	30.6	13 06.8	+25.2	30.7	13 58.3	+25.8	30.8	14 49.8	+26.3	31.0	15 41.2	+26.8	31.1	16 32.5	+27.3	31.3	17 23.8	+27.7	31.4	18 14.9	+28.3	31.6	59
60	12 39.9	+24.6	29.7	13 32.0	+25.1	29.8	14 24.1	+25.5	29.9	15 16.1	+26.0	30.0	16 08.0	+26.5	30.2	16 59.8	+27.0	30.3	17 51.5	+27.5	30.5	18 43.2	+28.0	30.7	60
61	13 04.5	+24.4	28.7	13 57.1	+24.9	28.9	14 49.6	+25.4	29.0	15 42.1	+25.8	29.1	16 34.5	+26.3	29.2	17 26.8	+26.8	29.4	18 19.0	+27.3	29.6	19 11.2	+27.7	29.7	61
62	13 28.9	+24.2	27.8	14 22.0	+24.6	27.9	15 15.0	+25.1	28.0	16 07.9	+25.6	28.2	17 00.8	+26.0	28.3	17 53.6	+26.4	28.5	18 46.3	+26.9	28.6	19 38.9	+27.4	28.8	62
63	13 53.1	+24.0	26.9	14 46.6	+24.5	27.0	15 40.1	+24.8	27.1	16 33.5	+25.3	27.2	17 26.8	+25.7	27.4	18 20.0	+26.2	27.5	19 13.2	+26.7	27.7	20 06.3	+27.1	27.8	63
64	14 17.1	+23.8	25.9	15 11.1	+24.1	26.0	16 04.9	+24.6	26.1	16 58.8	+25.0	26.3	17 52.5	+25.5	26.4	18 46.2	+25.9	26.6	19 39.9	+26.3	26.7	20 33.4	+26.8	26.9	64
65	14 40.9	+23.5	25.0	15 35.2	+24.0	25.1	16 29.5	+24.4	25.2	17 23.8	+24.8	25.3	18 18.0	+25.2	25.5	19 12.1	+25.7	25.6	20 06.2	+26.1	25.8	21 00.2	+26.5	25.9	65
66	15 04.4	+23.3	24.0	15 59.2	+23.6	24.1	16 53.9	+24.1	24.2	17 48.6	+24.5	24.4	18 43.2	+24.9	24.5	19 37.8	+25.3	24.7	20 32.3	+25.7	24.8	21 26.7	+26.1	25.0	66
67	15 27.7	+23.0	23.1	16 22.8	+23.5	23.2	17 18.0	+23.8	23.3	18 13.1	+24.2	23.4	19 08.1	+24.6	23.5	20 03.1	+25.0	23.7	20 58.0	+25.4	23.8	21 52.8	+25.8	24.0	67
68	15 50.7	+22.8	22.1	16 46.3	+23.1	22.2	17 41.8	+23.5	22.3	18 37.3	+23.9	22.4	19 32.7	+24.3	22.6	20 28.1	+24.6	22.7	21 23.4	+25.0	22.9	22 18.6	+25.5	23.0	68
69	16 13.5	+22.5	21.1	17 09.4	+22.9	21.2	18 05.3	+23.2	21.4	19 01.2	+23.6	21.5	19 57.0	+23.9	21.6	20 52.7	+24.4	21.7	21 48.4	+24.7	21.9	22 44.1	+25.1	22.0	69
70	16 36.0	+22.2	20.2	17 32.3	+22.6	20.3	18 28.5	+23.0	20.4	19 24.8	+23.3	20.5	20 20.9	+23.7	20.6	21 17.1	+24.0	20.8	22 13.1	+24.4	20.9	23 09.2	+24.7	21.1	70
71	16 58.2	+22.0	19.2	17 54.9	+22.3	19.3	18 51.5	+22.6	19.4	19 48.1	+22.9	19.5	20 44.6	+23.3	19.6	21 41.1	+23.6	19.8	22 37.5	+24.0	19.9	23 33.9	+24.3	20.1	71
72	17 20.2	+21.7	18.2	18 17.2	+22.0	18.3	19 14.1	+22.3	18.4	20 11.0	+22.7	18.5	21 07.9	+22.9	18.7	22 04.7	+23.3	18.8	23 01.5	+23.6	18.9	23 58.2	+24.0	19.1	72
73	17 41.9	+21.4	17.2	18 39.2	+21.7	17.3	19 36.4	+22.0	17.4	20 33.7	+22.3	17.6	21 30.8	+22.6	17.7	22 28.0	+22.9	17.8	23 25.1	+23.2	17.9	24 22.2	+23.5	18.1	73
74	18 03.3	+21.1	16.3	19 00.9	+21.4	16.4	19 58.4	+21.7	16.5	20 56.0	+21.9	16.6	21 53.4	+22.3	16.7	22 50.9	+22.5	16.8	23 48.3	+22.9	16.9	24 45.7	+23.2	17.0	74
75	18 24.4	+20.8	15.3	19 22.3	+21.0	15.4	20 20.1	+21.3	15.5	21 17.9	+21.6	15.6	22 15.7	+21.9	15.7	23 13.4	+22.2	15.8	24 11.2	+22.4	15.9	25 08.9	+22.7	16.0	75
76	18 45.2	+20.5	14.3	19 43.3	+20.7	14.4	20 41.4	+21.0	14.5	21 39.5	+21.2	14.6	22 37.6	+21.5	14.7	23 35.6	+21.8	14.8	24 33.6	+22.0	14.9	25 31.6	+22.3	15.0	76
77	19 05.7	+20.1	13.3	20 04.0	+20.4	13.4	21 02.4	+20.6	13.5	22 00.7	+20.9	13.6	22 59.1	+21.1	13.7	23 57.4	+21.3	13.8	24 55.6	+21.6	13.9	25 53.9	+21.8	14.0	77
78	19 25.8	+19.8	12.3	20 24.4	+20.1	12.4	21 23.0	+20.3	12.5	22 21.6	+20.5	12.5	23 20.2	+20.7	12.6	24 18.7	+20.9	12.7	25 17.2	+21.2	12.8	26 15.7	+21.4	12.9	78
79	19 45.6	+19.5	11.3	20 44.5	+19.7	11.4	21 43.3	+19.9	11.4	22 42.1	+20.1	11.5	23 40.9	+20.3	11.6	24 39.6	+20.5	11.7	25 38.4	+20.7	11.8	26 37.1	+20.9	11.9	79
80	20 05.1	+19.2	10.3	21 04.2	+19.3	10.4	22 03.2	+19.5	10.4	23 02.2	+19.7	10.5	24 01.2	+19.9	10.6	25 00.1	+20.1	10.7	25 59.1	+20.3	10.8	26 58.0	+20.5	10.8	80
81	20 24.3	+18.8	9.3	21 23.5	+19.0	9.3	22 22.7	+19.1	9.4	23 21.9	+19.3	9.5	24 21.1	+19.4	9.5	25 20.2	+19.7	9.6	26 19.4	+19.8	9.7	27 18.5	+20.0	9.8	81
82	20 43.1	+18.4	8.3	21 42.5	+18.5	8.3	22 41.8	+18.8	8.4	23 41.2	+18.9	8.4	24 40.5	+19.1	8.5	25 39.9	+19.1	8.6	26 39.2	+19.3	8.7	27 38.5	+19.5	8.7	82
83	21 01.5	+18.1	7.2	22 01.0	+18.3	7.3	23 00.6	+18.3	7.3	24 00.1	+18.4	7.4	24 59.6	+18.6	7.5	25 59.0	+18.8	7.5	26 58.5	+18.9	7.6	27 58.0	+19.0	7.7	83
84	21 19.6	+17.7	6.2	22 19.3	+17.8	6.3	23 18.9	+17.9	6.3	24 18.5	+18.1	6.4	25 18.2	+18.1	6.4	26 17.8	+18.2	6.5	27 17.4	+18.4	6.5	28 17.0	+18.5	6.6	84
85	21 37.3	+17.3	5.2	22 37.1	+17.4	5.2	23 36.8	+17.5	5.3	24 36.6	+17.6	5.3	25 36.3	+17.7	5.4	26 36.0	+17.8	5.4	27 35.8	+17.8	5.5	28 35.5	+18.0	5.5	85
86	21 54.6	+17.0	4.2	22 54.5	+17.0	4.2	23 54.3	+17.1	4.2	24 54.2	+17.1	4.3	25 54.0	+17.2	4.3	26 53.8	+17.3	4.3	27 53.6	+17.4	4.4	28 53.5	+17.4	4.4	86
87	22 11.6	+16.5	3.1	23 11.5	+16.6	3.2	24 11.4	+16.6	3.2	25 11.3	+16.7	3.2	26 11.2	+16.8	3.2	27 11.1	+16.8	3.3	28 11.0	+16.9	3.3	29 10.9	+16.9	3.3	87
88	22 28.1	+16.2	2.1	23 28.1	+16.2	2.1	24 28.0	+16.2	2.1	25 28.0	+16.2	2.1	26 28.0	+16.2	2.2	27 27.9	+16.3	2.2	28 27.9	+16.3	2.2	29 27.8	+16.4	2.2	88
89	22 44.3	+15.7	1.0	23 44.3	+15.7	1.1	24 44.2	+15.8	1.1	25 44.2	+15.8	1.1	26 44.2	+15.8	1.1	27 44.2	+15.8	1.1	28 44.2	+15.8	1.1	29 44.2	+15.8	1.1	89
90	23 00.0	+15.3	0.0	24 00.0	+15.3	0.0	25 00.0	+15.3	0.0	26 00.0	+15.3	0.0	27 00.0	+15.3	0.0	28 00.0	+15.3	0.0	29 00.0	+15.3	0.0	30 00.0	+15.2	0.0	90
	23°			24°			25°			26°			27°			28°			29°			30°			

S. Lat. {L.H.A. greater than 180° ....Zn=180°−Z
{L.H.A. less than 180°...........Zn=180°+Z

LATITUDE SAME NAME AS DECLINATION L.H.A. 105°, 255°

335

Dec.	23°			24°			25°			26°			27°			28°			29°			30°			Dec.
	Hc	d	Z	Hc	d	Z	Hc	d	Z	Hc	d	Z	Hc	d	Z	Hc	d	Z	Hc	d	Z	Hc	d	Z	
°	° ′	′	°	° ′	′	°	° ′	′	°	° ′	′	°	° ′	′	°	° ′	′	°	° ′	′	°	° ′	′	°	°
0	12 52.0	+24.0	95.6	12 46.1	+24.9	95.8	12 39.9	+25.9	96.0	12 33.5	+26.9	96.2	12 26.9	+27.8	96.5	12 20.0	+28.8	96.7	12 12.9	+29.7	96.9	12 05.6	+30.6	97.1	0
1	13 16.0	+23.7	94.6	13 11.0	+24.7	94.9	13 05.8	+25.7	95.1	13 00.4	+26.6	95.3	12 54.7	+27.6	95.5	12 48.8	+28.5	95.8	12 42.6	+29.5	96.0	12 36.2	+30.4	96.2	1
2	13 39.7	+23.5	93.7	13 35.7	+24.5	93.9	13 31.5	+25.5	94.2	13 27.0	+26.5	94.4	13 22.3	+27.4	94.6	13 17.3	+28.4	94.9	13 12.1	+29.3	95.1	13 06.6	+30.3	95.3	2
3	14 03.2	+23.3	92.7	14 00.2	+24.3	93.0	13 57.0	+25.3	93.2	13 53.5	+26.2	93.5	13 49.7	+27.2	93.7	13 45.7	+28.2	94.0	13 41.4	+29.1	94.2	13 36.9	+30.0	94.5	3
4	14 26.5	+23.1	91.8	14 24.5	+24.1	92.0	14 22.3	+25.0	92.3	14 19.7	+26.1	92.5	14 16.9	+27.0	92.8	14 13.9	+27.9	93.1	14 10.5	+28.9	93.3	14 06.9	+29.9	93.6	4
5	14 49.6	+22.8	90.8	14 48.6	+23.8	91.1	14 47.3	+24.8	91.4	14 45.8	+25.8	91.6	14 43.9	+26.8	91.9	14 41.8	+27.8	92.1	14 39.4	+28.7	92.4	14 36.8	+29.6	92.7	5
6	15 12.4	+22.6	89.9	15 12.4	+23.6	90.1	15 12.1	+24.6	90.4	15 11.6	+25.5	90.7	15 10.7	+26.6	91.0	15 09.6	+27.5	91.2	15 08.1	+28.5	91.5	15 06.4	+29.5	91.8	6
7	15 35.0	+22.4	88.9	15 36.0	+23.4	89.2	15 36.7	+24.4	89.5	15 37.1	+25.4	89.7	15 37.3	+26.3	90.0	15 37.1	+27.3	90.3	15 36.6	+28.3	90.6	15 35.9	+29.2	90.9	7
8	15 57.4	+22.1	87.9	15 59.4	+23.1	88.2	16 01.1	+24.1	88.5	16 02.5	+25.1	88.8	16 03.6	+26.1	89.1	16 04.4	+27.0	89.4	16 04.9	+28.0	89.7	16 05.1	+29.0	90.0	8
9	16 19.5	+21.8	87.0	16 22.5	+22.8	87.3	16 25.2	+23.8	87.6	16 27.6	+24.8	87.9	16 29.7	+25.8	88.2	16 31.4	+26.8	88.4	16 32.9	+27.8	88.7	16 34.1	+28.7	89.0	9
10	16 41.3	+21.5	86.0	16 45.3	+22.6	86.3	16 49.0	+23.6	86.6	16 52.4	+24.6	86.9	16 55.5	+25.5	87.2	16 58.2	+26.6	87.5	17 00.7	+27.5	87.8	17 02.8	+28.5	88.1	10
11	17 02.8	+21.3	85.0	17 07.9	+22.2	85.3	17 12.6	+23.3	85.6	17 17.0	+24.3	86.0	17 21.0	+25.3	86.3	17 24.8	+26.3	86.6	17 28.2	+27.3	86.9	17 31.3	+28.2	87.2	11
12	17 24.1	+20.9	84.0	17 30.1	+22.0	84.4	17 35.9	+23.0	84.7	17 41.3	+24.0	85.0	17 46.3	+25.0	85.3	17 51.1	+26.0	85.6	17 55.5	+27.0	86.0	17 59.5	+28.0	86.3	12
13	17 45.0	+20.7	83.1	17 52.1	+21.7	83.4	17 58.9	+22.7	83.7	18 05.3	+23.7	84.0	18 11.3	+24.8	84.4	18 17.1	+25.7	84.7	18 22.5	+26.7	85.0	18 27.5	+27.7	85.3	13
14	18 05.7	+20.4	82.1	18 13.8	+21.4	82.4	18 21.6	+22.4	82.7	18 29.0	+23.4	83.1	18 36.1	+24.4	83.4	18 42.8	+25.4	83.7	18 49.2	+26.4	84.1	18 55.2	+27.4	84.4	14
15	18 26.1	+20.1	81.1	18 35.2	+21.1	81.4	18 44.0	+22.1	81.8	18 52.4	+23.2	82.1	19 00.5	+24.2	82.4	19 08.2	+25.2	82.8	19 15.6	+26.1	83.1	19 22.6	+27.1	83.5	15
16	18 46.2	+19.7	80.1	18 56.3	+20.8	80.4	19 06.1	+21.8	80.8	19 15.6	+22.8	81.1	19 24.7	+23.8	81.5	19 33.4	+24.8	81.8	19 41.7	+25.9	82.2	19 49.7	+26.9	82.5	16
17	19 05.9	+19.5	79.1	19 17.1	+20.5	79.4	19 27.9	+21.5	79.8	19 38.4	+22.5	80.1	19 48.5	+23.5	80.5	19 58.2	+24.5	80.8	20 07.6	+25.5	81.2	20 16.6	+26.5	81.6	17
18	19 25.4	+19.1	78.1	19 37.6	+20.1	78.4	19 49.4	+21.1	78.8	20 00.9	+22.1	79.1	20 12.0	+23.2	79.5	20 22.7	+24.2	79.9	20 33.1	+25.2	80.2	20 43.1	+26.2	80.6	18
19	19 44.5	+18.7	77.1	19 57.7	+19.8	77.4	20 10.5	+20.9	77.8	20 23.0	+21.9	78.2	20 35.2	+22.8	78.5	20 46.9	+23.9	78.9	20 58.3	+24.8	79.3	21 09.3	+25.8	79.6	19
20	20 03.2	+18.4	76.1	20 17.5	+19.4	76.4	20 31.4	+20.4	76.8	20 44.9	+21.5	77.2	20 58.0	+22.5	77.5	21 10.8	+23.5	77.9	21 23.1	+24.6	78.3	21 35.1	+25.5	78.7	20
21	20 21.6	+18.1	75.1	20 36.9	+19.1	75.4	20 51.8	+20.1	75.8	21 06.4	+21.1	76.2	21 20.5	+22.2	76.5	21 34.3	+23.1	76.9	21 47.7	+24.1	77.3	22 00.6	+25.2	77.7	21
22	20 39.7	+17.7	74.0	20 56.0	+18.7	74.4	21 11.9	+19.8	74.8	21 27.5	+20.8	75.2	21 42.7	+21.8	75.5	21 57.4	+22.8	75.9	22 11.8	+23.8	76.3	22 25.8	+24.8	76.7	22
23	20 57.4	+17.3	73.0	21 14.7	+18.4	73.4	21 31.7	+19.4	73.8	21 48.3	+20.4	74.2	22 04.5	+21.4	74.5	22 20.2	+22.5	74.9	22 35.6	+23.5	75.3	22 50.6	+24.5	75.7	23
24	21 14.7	+17.0	72.0	21 33.1	+18.0	72.4	21 51.1	+19.0	72.8	22 08.7	+20.0	73.1	22 25.9	+21.0	73.5	22 42.7	+22.0	73.9	22 59.1	+23.1	74.3	23 15.1	+24.1	74.7	24
25	21 31.7	+16.6	71.0	21 51.1	+17.6	71.3	22 10.1	+18.6	71.7	22 28.7	+19.6	72.1	22 46.9	+20.7	72.5	23 04.7	+21.7	72.9	23 22.2	+22.6	73.3	23 39.2	+23.6	73.7	25
26	21 48.3	+16.2	69.9	22 08.7	+17.2	70.3	22 28.7	+18.2	70.7	22 48.3	+19.3	71.1	23 07.6	+20.2	71.5	23 26.4	+21.3	71.9	23 44.8	+22.3	72.3	24 02.8	+23.3	72.7	26
27	22 04.5	+15.7	68.9	22 25.9	+16.8	69.3	22 46.9	+17.8	69.7	23 07.6	+18.8	70.1	23 27.8	+19.9	70.5	23 47.7	+20.8	70.9	24 07.1	+21.9	71.3	24 26.1	+22.9	71.7	27
28	22 20.2	+15.4	67.9	22 42.7	+16.4	68.2	23 04.7	+17.5	68.6	23 26.4	+18.4	69.0	23 47.7	+19.4	69.4	24 08.5	+20.5	69.9	24 29.0	+21.5	70.3	24 49.0	+22.5	70.7	28
29	22 35.6	+15.0	66.8	22 59.1	+16.0	67.2	23 22.2	+17.0	67.6	23 44.8	+18.0	68.0	24 07.1	+19.0	68.4	24 29.0	+20.0	68.8	24 50.5	+21.0	69.3	25 11.5	+22.0	69.7	29
30	22 50.6	+14.6	65.8	23 15.1	+15.6	66.1	23 39.2	+16.5	66.5	24 02.8	+17.6	66.9	24 26.1	+18.6	67.4	24 49.0	+19.6	67.8	25 11.5	+20.6	68.2	25 33.5	+21.7	68.7	30
31	23 05.2	+14.2	64.7	23 30.7	+15.1	65.1	23 55.7	+16.2	65.5	24 20.4	+17.2	65.9	24 44.7	+18.2	66.3	25 08.6	+19.2	66.7	25 32.1	+20.2	67.2	25 55.2	+21.1	67.6	31
32	23 19.4	+13.7	63.6	23 45.8	+14.7	64.0	24 11.9	+15.7	64.4	24 37.6	+16.7	64.8	25 02.9	+17.7	65.3	25 27.8	+18.7	65.7	25 52.3	+19.7	66.1	26 16.3	+20.7	66.6	32
33	23 33.1	+13.3	62.6	24 00.5	+14.3	63.0	24 27.6	+15.3	63.4	24 54.3	+16.3	63.8	25 20.6	+17.2	64.2	25 46.5	+18.2	64.6	26 12.0	+19.2	65.1	26 37.0	+20.3	65.5	33
34	23 46.4	+12.8	61.5	24 14.8	+13.8	61.9	24 42.9	+14.8	62.3	25 10.6	+15.8	62.7	25 37.8	+16.8	63.2	26 04.7	+17.8	63.6	26 31.2	+18.8	64.0	26 57.3	+19.8	64.5	34
35	23 59.2	+12.4	60.5	24 28.6	+13.4	60.8	24 57.7	+14.3	61.2	25 26.4	+15.3	61.7	25 54.6	+16.4	62.1	26 22.5	+17.3	62.5	26 50.0	+18.3	63.0	27 17.1	+19.3	63.4	35
36	24 11.6	+12.0	59.4	24 42.0	+12.9	59.8	25 12.0	+13.9	60.2	25 41.7	+14.9	60.6	26 11.0	+15.8	61.0	26 39.8	+16.9	61.5	27 08.3	+17.8	61.9	27 36.4	+18.8	62.4	36
37	24 23.6	+11.5	58.3	24 54.9	+12.5	58.7	25 25.9	+13.5	59.1	25 56.6	+14.3	59.5	26 26.8	+15.4	59.9	26 56.7	+16.3	60.4	27 26.1	+17.3	60.8	27 55.2	+18.3	61.3	37
38	24 35.1	+11.0	57.2	25 07.4	+12.0	57.6	25 39.4	+12.9	58.0	26 10.9	+14.0	58.4	26 42.2	+14.8	58.9	27 13.0	+15.8	59.3	27 43.4	+16.9	59.7	28 13.5	+17.8	60.2	38
39	24 46.1	+10.6	56.1	25 19.4	+11.5	56.5	25 52.3	+12.5	56.9	26 24.9	+13.4	57.3	26 57.0	+14.4	57.8	27 28.8	+15.4	58.2	28 00.3	+16.2	58.7	28 31.3	+17.2	59.1	39
40	24 56.7	+10.1	55.1	25 30.9	+11.0	55.4	26 04.8	+11.9	55.8	26 38.3	+12.9	56.3	27 11.4	+13.9	56.7	27 44.2	+14.8	57.1	28 16.5	+15.8	57.6	28 48.5	+16.8	58.0	40
41	25 06.8	+9.6	54.0	25 41.9	+10.6	54.4	26 16.7	+11.5	54.8	26 51.2	+12.4	55.2	27 25.3	+13.3	55.6	27 59.0	+14.3	56.0	28 32.3	+15.3	56.5	29 05.3	+16.2	56.9	41
42	25 16.4	+9.2	52.9	25 52.5	+10.0	53.3	26 28.2	+11.0	53.7	27 03.6	+11.9	54.1	27 38.6	+12.8	54.5	28 13.3	+13.7	54.9	28 47.6	+14.7	55.4	29 21.5	+15.6	55.8	42
43	25 25.6	+8.6	51.8	26 02.5	+9.6	52.2	26 39.2	+10.4	52.6	27 15.5	+11.3	53.0	27 51.4	+12.3	53.4	28 27.0	+13.2	53.8	29 02.3	+14.1	54.3	29 37.1	+15.1	54.7	43
44	25 34.2	+8.2	50.7	26 12.1	+9.0	51.1	26 49.6	+9.9	51.5	27 26.8	+10.9	51.9	28 03.7	+11.8	52.3	28 40.2	+12.7	52.7	29 16.4	+13.6	53.1	29 52.2	+14.6	53.6	44
45	25 42.4	+7.6	49.6	26 21.1	+8.5	50.0	26 59.5	+9.5	50.4	27 37.7	+10.3	50.8	28 15.5	+11.2	51.2	28 52.9	+12.1	51.6	29 30.0	+13.1	52.0	30 06.8	+13.9	52.5	45
46	25 50.0	+7.2	48.5	26 29.6	+8.1	48.9	27 09.0	+8.9	49.2	27 48.0	+9.8	49.6	28 26.7	+10.6	50.0	29 05.0	+11.6	50.5	29 43.1	+12.4	50.9	30 20.7	+13.4	51.4	46
47	25 57.2	+6.7	47.4	26 37.7	+7.5	47.8	27 17.9	+8.3	48.1	27 57.8	+9.2	48.5	28 37.3	+10.2	48.9	29 16.6	+11.0	49.3	29 55.5	+11.9	49.8	30 34.1	+12.8	50.2	47
48	26 03.9	+6.1	46.3	26 45.2	+7.0	46.6	27 26.2	+7.9	47.0	28 07.0	+8.7	47.4	28 47.5	+9.5	47.8	29 27.6	+10.4	48.2	30 07.4	+11.3	48.6	30 46.9	+12.2	49.1	48
49	26 10.0	+5.7	45.2	26 52.2	+6.4	45.5	27 34.1	+7.3	45.9	28 15.7	+8.1	46.3	28 57.0	+9.0	46.7	29 38.0	+9.9	47.1	30 18.7	+10.7	47.5	30 59.1	+11.6	47.9	49
50	26 15.7	+5.1	44.1	26 58.6	+6.0	44.4	27 41.4	+6.7	44.8	28 23.8	+7.6	45.2	29 06.0	+8.4	45.5	29 47.9	+9.2	45.9	30 29.4	+10.1	46.4	31 10.7	+10.9	46.8	50
51	26 20.8	+4.6	43.0	27 04.6	+5.4	43.3	27 48.1	+6.2	43.7	28 31.4	+7.0	44.0	29 14.4	+7.8	44.4	29 57.1	+8.7	44.8	30 39.5	+9.5	45.2	31 21.6	+10.4	45.7	51
52	26 25.4	+4.1	41.8	27 10.0	+4.9	42.2	27 54.3	+5.7	42.5	28 38.4	+6.5	42.9	29 22.2	+7.3	43.3	30 05.8	+8.1	43.7	30 49.0	+8.9	44.1	31 32.0	+9.7	44.5	52
53	26 29.5	+3.6	40.7	27 14.9	+4.3	41.1	28 00.0	+5.1	41.4	28 44.9	+5.9	41.8	29 29.5	+6.7	42.1	30 13.9	+7.4	42.5	30 57.9	+8.3	42.9	31 41.7	+9.1	43.3	53
54	26 33.1	+3.0	39.6	27 19.2	+3.8	39.9	28 05.1	+4.6	40.3	28 50.8	+5.3	40.6	29 36.2	+6.1	41.0	30 21.3	+6.9	41.4	31 06.2	+7.7	41.8	31 50.8	+8.5	42.2	54
55	26 36.1	+2.6	38.5	27 23.0	+3.3	38.8	28 09.7	+3.9	39.1	28 56.1	+4.7	39.5	29 42.3	+5.5	39.8	30 28.2	+6.3	40.2	31 13.9	+7.0	40.6	31 59.3	+7.8	41.0	55
56	26 38.7	+2.0	37.4	27 26.3	+2.7	37.7	28 13.6	+3.5	38.0	29 00.8	+4.2	38.3	29 47.8	+4.9	38.7	30 34.5	+5.6	39.1	31 20.9	+6.4	39.4	32 07.1	+7.2	39.8	56
57	26 40.7	+1.5	36.3	27 29.0	+2.2	36.6	28 17.1	+2.9	36.9	29 05.0	+3.6	37.2	29 52.7	+4.3	37.6	30 40.1	+5.0	37.9	31 27.3	+5.8	38.3	32 14.3	+6.5	38.7	57
58	26 42.2	+0.9	35.1	27 31.2	+1.6	35.4	28 20.0	+2.3	35.7	29 08.6	+3.0	36.1	29 57.0	+3.7	36.4	30 45.1	+4.4	36.7	31 33.1	+5.1	37.1	32 20.8	+5.9	37.5	58
59	26 43.1	+0.5	34.0	27 32.8	+1.1	34.3	28 22.3	+1.7	34.6	29 11.6	+2.4	34.9	30 00.7	+3.0	35.2	30 49.5	+3.8	35.6	31 38.2	+4.5	35.9	32 26.7	+5.2	36.3	59
60	26 43.6	−0.1	32.9	27 33.9	+0.5	33.2	28 24.0	+1.2	33.5	29 14.0	+1.8	33.8	30 03.7	+2.5	34.1	30 53.3	+3.2	34.4	31 42.7	+3.9	34.8	32 31.9	+4.6	35.1	60
61	26 43.5	−0.6	31.8	27 34.4	0.0	32.1	28 25.2	+0.6	32.3	29 15.8	+1.2	32.6	30 06.2	+1.9	32.9	30 56.5	+2.5	33.3	31 46.6	+3.2	33.6	32 36.5	+3.8	33.9	61
62	26 42.9	−1.2	30.7	27 34.4	−0.6	30.9	28 25.8	0.0	31.2	29 17.0	+0.7	31.5	30 08.1	+1.3	31.8	30 59.0	+2.0	32.1	31 49.8	+2.5	32.4	32 40.3	+3.2	32.8	62
63	26 41.7	−1.7	29.5	27 33.8	−1.1	29.8	28 25.8	−0.5	30.1	29 17.7	+0.1	30.3	30 09.4	+0.7	30.6	31 01.0	+1.2	30.9	31 52.3	+1.9	31.2	32 43.5	+2.6	31.6	63
64	26 40.0	−2.2	28.4	27 32.7	−1.6	28.7	28 25.3	−1.1	28.9	29 17.8	−0.5	29.2	30 10.1	0.0	29.5	31 02.2	+0.7	29.8	31 54.2	+1.3	30.1	32 46.1	+1.9	30.4	64
65	26 37.8	−2.7	27.3	27 31.1	−2.2	27.5	28 24.2	−1.6	27.8	29 17.3	−1.2	28.0	30 10.1	−0.5	28.3	31 02.9	0.0	28.6	31 55.5	+0.6	28.9	32 48.0	+1.1	29.2	65
66	26 35.1	−3.2	26.2	27 28.9	−2.7	26.4	28 22.6	−2.2	26.7	29 16.1	−1.6	26.9	30 09.6	−1.2	27.2	31 02.9	−0.6	27.4	31 56.1	−0.1	27.7	32 49.1	+0.6	28.0	66
67	26 31.9	−3.8	25.1	27 26.2	−3.3	25.3	28 20.4	−2.8	25.5	29 14.5	−2.3	25.8	30 08.4	−1.7	26.0	31 02.3	−1.2	26.3	31 56.0	−0.7	26.5	32 49.7	−0.2	26.8	67
68	26 28.1	−4.3	24.0	27 22.9	−3.8	24.2	28 17.6	−3.4	24.4	29 12.2	−2.9	24.6	30 06.7	−2.4	24.8	31 01.1	−1.9	25.1	31 55.3	−1.3	25.4	32 49.5	−0.8	25.6	68
69	26 23.8	−4.8	22.8	27 19.1	−4.4	23.0	28 14.2	−3.9	23.2	29 09.3	−3.4	23.5	30 04.3	−3.0	23.7	30 59.2	−2.5	23.9	31 54.0	−2.0	24.2	32 48.7	−1.5	24.4	69
70	26 19.0	−5.3	21.7	27 14.7	−4.9	21.9	28 10.3	−4.4	22.1	29 05.9	−4.1	22.3	30 01.3	−3.5	22.5	30 56.7	−3.1	22.8	31 52.0	−2.7	23.0	32 47.2	−2.2	23.3	70
71	26 13.7	−5.8	20.6	27 09.8	−5.4	20.8	28 05.9	−5.1	21.0	29 01.8	−4.6	21.2	29 57.8	−4.2	21.4	30 53.6	−3.8	21.6	31 49.3	−3.3	21.8	32 45.0	−2.9	22.1	71
72	26 07.9	−6.4	19.5	27 04.4	−6.0	19.7	28 00.8	−5.5	19.9	28 57.2	−5.1	20.0	29 53.6	−4.8	20.2	30 49.8	−4.3	20.4	31 46.0	−3.9	20.7	32 42.1	−3.5	20.9	72
73	26 01.5	−6.8	18.4	26 58.4	−6.5	18.6	27 55.3	−6.2	18.7	28 52.1	−5.8	18.9	29 48.8	−5.4	19.1	30 45.5	−5.0	19.3	31 42.1	−4.6	19.5	32 38.6	−4.2	19.7	73
74	25 54.7	−7.4	17.3	26 51.9	−7.0	17.4	27 49.1	−6.6	17.6	28 46.3	−6.3	17.8	29 43.4	−5.9	17.9	30 40.5	−5.6	18.1	31 37.5	−5.3	18.3	32 34.4	−4.9	18.5	74
75	25 47.3	−7.8	16.2	26 44.9	−7.5	16.3	27 42.5	−7.2	16.5	28 40.0	−6.9	16.6	29 37.5	−6.6	16.8	30 34.9	−6.2	17.0	31 32.2	−5.8	17.1	32 29.5	−5.5	17.3	75
76	25 39.5	−8.4	15.1	26 37.4	−8.1	15.2	27 35.3	−7.8	15.4	28 33.1	−7.4	15.5	29 30.9	−7.1	15.6	30 28.7	−6.9	15.8	31 26.4	−6.5	16.0	32 24.0	−6.2	16.1	76
77	25 31.1	−8.8	14.0	26 29.3	−8.5	14.1	27 27.5	−8.3	14.2	28 25.7	−8.0	14.4	29 23.8	−7.8	14.5	30 21.8	−7.4	14.7	31 19.9	−7.2	14.8	32 17.8	−6.8	15.0	77
78	25 22.3	−9.3	12.9	26 20.8	−9.1	13.0	27 19.2	−8.8	13.1	28 17.7	−8.6	13.2	29 16.0	−8.3	13.4	30 14.4	−8.0	13.5	31 12.7	−7.7	13.6	32 11.0	−7.5	13.8	78
79	25 13.0	−9.8	11.8	26 11.7	−9.5	11.9	27 10.4	−9.3	12.0	28 09.1	−9.1	12.1	29 07.7	−8.8	12.2	30 06.4	−8.7	12.4	31 05.0	−8.4	12.5	32 03.5	−8.1	12.6	79
80	25 03.2	−10.3	10.7	26 02.2	−10.1	10.8	27 01.1	−9.9	10.9	28 00.0	−9.7	11.0	28 58.9	−9.5	11.1	29 57.7	−9.2	11.2	30 56.6	−9.0	11.3	31 55.4	−8.8	11.5	80
81	24 52.9	−10.7	9.6	25 52.1	−10.6	9.7	26 51.2	−10.4	9.8	27 50.3	−10.1	9.9	28 49.4	−10.0	10.0	29 48.5	−9.8	10.1	30 47.6	−9.6	10.2	31 46.6	−9.4	10.3	81
82	24 42.2	−11.2	8.5	25 41.5	−11.0	8.6	26 40.8	−10.8	8.7	27 40.2	−10.8	8.8	28 39.4	−10.5	8.9	29 38.7	−10.4	8.9	30 38.0	−10.2	9.0	31 37.2	−10.0	9.1	82
83	24 31.0	−11.7	7.5	25 30.5	−11.5	7.5	26 30.0	−11.4	7.6	27 29.4	−11.2	7.7	28 28.9	−11.1	7.7	29 28.3	−10.9	7.8	30 27.8	−10.8	7.9	31 27.2	−10.6	8.0	83
84	24 19.3	−12.1	6.4	25 19.0	−12.0	6.4	26 18.6	−11.9	6.5	27 18.2	−11.8	6.6	28 17.8	−11.7	6.6	29 17.4	−11.5	6.7	30 17.0	−11.4	6.7	31 16.6	−11.3	6.8	84
85	24 07.2	−12.6	5.3	25 07.0	−12.5	5.4	26 06.7	−12.4	5.4	27 06.4	−12.3	5.5	28 06.1	−12.1	5.5	29 05.9	−12.1	5.6	30 05.6	−12.0	5.6	31 05.3	−11.9	5.7	85
86	23 54.6	−13.0	4.2	24 54.5	−13.0	4.3	25 54.3	−12.9	4.3	26 54.1	−12.7	4.4	27 54.0	−12.7	4.4	28 53.8	−12.6	4.4	29 53.6	−12.5	4.5	30 53.4	−12.5	4.5	86
87	23 41.6	−13.4	3.2	24 41.5	−13.4	3.2	25 41.4	−13.3	3.2	26 41.4	−13.3	3.3	27 41.3	−13.3	3.3	28 41.2	−13.2	3.3	29 41.1	−13.2	3.4	30 40.9	−13.0	3.4	87
88	23 28.2	−13.9	2.1	24 28.1	−13.8	2.1	25 28.1	−13.8	2.1	26 28.1	−13.8	2.2	27 28.0	−13.7	2.2	28 28.0	−13.7	2.2	29 27.9	−13.7	2.2	30 27.9	−13.7	2.3	88
89	23 14.3	−14.3	1.1	24 14.3	−14.3	1.1	25 14.3	−14.3	1.1	26 14.3	−14.3	1.1	27 14.3	−14.3	1.1	28 14.3	−14.3	1.1	29 14.2	−14.2	1.1	30 14.2	−14.2	1.1	89
90	23 00.0	−14.7	0.0	24 00.0	−14.7	0.0	25 00.0	−14.7	0.0	26 00.0	−14.8	0.0	27 00.0	−14.8	0.0	28 00.0	−14.8	0.0	29 00.0	−14.8	0.0	30 00.0	−14.8	0.0	90
	23°			24°			25°			26°			27°			28°			29°			30°			

76°, 284° L.H.A. LATITUDE SAME NAME AS DECLINATION

336

LATITUDE **CONTRARY** NAME TO DECLINATION **L.H.A. 76°, 284°**

	23°			24°			25°			26°			27°			28°			29°			30°			
Dec.	Hc	d	Z	Hc	d	Z	Hc	d	Z	Hc	d	Z	Hc	d	Z	Hc	d	Z	Hc	d	Z	Hc	d	Z	Dec.
°	° ′	′	°	° ′	′	°	° ′	′	°	° ′	′	°	° ′	′	°	° ′	′	°	° ′	′	°	° ′	′	°	°
0	12 52.0	-24.1	95.6	12 46.1	-25.1	95.8	12 39.9	-26.1	96.0	12 33.5	-27.0	96.2	12 26.9	-28.0	96.5	12 20.0	-28.9	96.7	12 12.9	-29.8	96.9	12 05.6	-30.7	97.1	0
1	12 27.9	-24.4	96.5	12 21.0	-25.3	96.7	12 13.8	-26.2	96.9	12 06.5	-27.2	97.2	11 58.9	-28.2	97.4	11 51.1	-29.1	97.6	11 43.1	-30.0	97.8	11 34.9	-31.0	98.0	1
2	12 03.5	-24.5	97.4	11 55.7	-25.5	97.6	11 47.6	-26.5	97.9	11 39.3	-27.4	98.1	11 30.7	-28.3	98.3	11 22.0	-29.2	98.5	11 13.1	-30.2	98.7	11 03.9	-31.0	98.9	2
3	11 39.0	-24.7	98.4	11 30.2	-25.7	98.6	11 21.1	-26.6	98.8	11 11.9	-27.6	99.0	11 02.4	-28.5	99.2	10 52.8	-29.4	99.4	10 42.9	-30.3	99.5	10 32.9	-31.2	99.7	3
4	11 14.3	-24.9	99.3	11 04.5	-25.8	99.5	10 54.5	-26.8	99.7	10 44.3	-27.7	99.9	10 33.9	-28.6	100.1	10 23.4	-29.6	100.2	10 12.6	-30.5	100.4	10 01.7	-31.4	100.6	4
5	10 49.4	-25.0	100.2	10 38.7	-26.0	100.4	10 27.7	-26.9	100.6	10 16.6	-27.8	100.8	10 05.3	-28.8	101.0	9 53.8	-29.7	101.1	9 42.1	-30.5	101.3	9 30.3	-31.5	101.5	5
6	10 24.4	-25.2	101.2	10 12.7	-26.2	101.3	10 00.8	-27.1	101.5	9 48.8	-28.0	101.7	9 36.5	-28.9	101.8	9 24.1	-29.8	102.0	9 11.6	-30.8	102.2	8 58.8	-31.6	102.3	6
7	9 59.2	-25.4	102.1	9 46.5	-26.3	102.2	9 33.7	-27.2	102.4	9 20.8	-28.2	102.6	9 07.6	-29.0	102.7	8 54.3	-29.9	102.9	8 40.8	-30.8	103.0	8 27.2	-31.7	103.2	7
8	9 33.8	-25.5	103.0	9 20.2	-26.4	103.2	9 06.5	-27.3	103.3	8 52.6	-28.2	103.5	8 38.6	-29.2	103.6	8 24.4	-30.1	103.8	8 10.0	-30.9	103.9	7 55.5	-31.8	104.0	8
9	9 08.3	-25.6	103.9	8 53.8	-26.5	104.1	8 39.2	-27.5	104.2	8 24.4	-28.4	104.4	8 09.4	-29.3	104.5	7 54.3	-30.2	104.6	7 39.1	-31.1	104.8	7 23.7	-31.9	104.9	9
10	8 42.7	-25.8	104.8	8 27.3	-26.7	105.0	8 11.7	-27.6	105.1	7 56.0	-28.5	105.3	7 40.1	-29.4	105.4	7 24.1	-30.2	105.5	7 08.0	-31.1	105.6	6 51.8	-32.0	105.8	10
11	8 16.9	-25.9	105.7	8 00.6	-26.8	105.9	7 44.1	-27.7	106.0	7 27.5	-28.6	106.1	7 10.7	-29.5	106.3	6 53.9	-30.4	106.4	6 36.9	-31.2	106.5	6 19.8	-32.1	106.6	11
12	7 51.0	-26.0	106.7	7 33.8	-27.0	106.8	7 16.4	-27.8	106.9	6 58.9	-28.7	107.0	6 41.2	-29.5	107.1	6 23.5	-30.4	107.2	6 05.7	-31.3	107.4	5 47.7	-32.1	107.5	12
13	7 25.0	-26.1	107.6	7 06.8	-27.0	107.7	6 48.6	-27.9	107.8	6 30.2	-28.8	107.9	6 11.7	-29.7	108.0	5 53.1	-30.6	108.1	5 34.4	-31.4	108.2	5 15.6	-32.3	108.3	13
14	6 58.9	-26.2	108.5	6 39.8	-27.1	108.6	6 20.7	-28.0	108.7	6 01.4	-28.9	108.8	5 42.0	-29.7	108.9	5 22.5	-30.6	109.0	5 03.0	-31.5	109.1	4 43.3	-32.3	109.1	14
15	6 32.7	-26.4	109.4	6 12.7	-27.2	109.5	5 52.7	-28.1	109.6	5 32.5	-29.0	109.7	5 12.3	-29.9	109.8	4 51.9	-30.6	109.8	4 31.5	-31.5	109.9	4 11.0	-32.3	110.0	15
16	6 06.3	-26.4	110.3	5 45.5	-27.3	110.4	5 24.6	-28.2	110.5	5 03.5	-29.0	110.6	4 42.4	-29.8	110.6	4 21.3	-30.8	110.7	4 00.0	-31.5	110.8	3 38.7	-32.4	110.8	16
17	5 39.9	-26.5	111.2	5 18.2	-27.4	111.3	4 56.4	-28.2	111.4	4 34.5	-29.1	111.4	4 12.6	-30.0	111.5	3 50.5	-30.7	111.6	3 28.5	-31.7	111.6	3 06.3	-32.4	111.7	17
18	5 13.4	-26.5	112.1	4 50.8	-27.4	112.2	4 28.2	-28.3	112.2	4 05.4	-29.1	112.3	3 42.6	-30.0	112.4	3 19.8	-30.9	112.4	2 56.8	-31.6	112.5	2 33.9	-32.5	112.5	18
19	4 46.9	-26.7	113.0	4 23.4	-27.5	113.1	3 59.9	-28.4	113.1	3 36.3	-29.2	113.2	3 12.6	-30.0	113.2	2 48.9	-30.8	113.3	2 25.2	-31.7	113.3	2 01.4	-32.5	113.4	19
20	4 20.2	-26.7	113.9	3 55.9	-27.6	113.9	3 31.5	-28.4	114.0	3 07.1	-29.3	114.1	2 42.6	-30.1	114.1	2 18.1	-30.9	114.1	1 53.5	-31.7	114.2	1 28.9	-32.5	114.2	20
21	3 53.5	-26.8	114.8	3 28.3	-27.6	114.8	3 03.1	-28.4	114.9	2 37.8	-29.2	114.9	2 12.5	-30.1	115.0	1 47.2	-30.9	115.0	1 21.8	-31.7	115.0	0 56.4	-32.5	115.0	21
22	3 26.7	-26.8	115.7	3 00.7	-27.6	115.7	2 34.7	-28.5	115.8	2 08.6	-29.3	115.8	1 42.4	-30.1	115.8	1 16.3	-31.0	115.9	0 50.1	-31.7	115.9	0 23.9	-32.5	115.9	22
23	2 59.9	-26.8	116.6	2 33.1	-27.7	116.6	2 06.2	-28.5	116.6	1 39.3	-29.4	116.7	1 12.3	-30.1	116.7	0 45.3	-30.9	116.7	0 18.4	-31.8	116.7	0 08.6	+32.6	63.3	23
24	2 33.1	-26.9	117.5	2 05.4	-27.7	117.5	1 37.7	-28.6	117.5	1 09.9	-29.3	117.6	0 42.2	-30.2	117.6	0 14.4	-31.0	117.6	0 13.4	+31.7	62.4	0 41.2	+32.5	62.4	24
25	2 06.2	-26.9	118.4	1 37.7	-27.8	118.4	1 09.1	-28.5	118.4	0 40.6	-29.4	118.4	0 12.0	-30.1	118.4	0 16.6	+30.9	61.6	0 45.1	+31.7	61.6	1 13.7	+32.5	61.6	25
26	1 39.3	-27.0	119.3	1 09.9	-27.7	119.3	0 40.6	-28.6	119.3	0 11.2	-29.3	119.3	0 18.1	+30.2	60.7	0 47.5	+30.9	60.7	1 16.8	+31.8	60.7	1 46.2	+32.4	60.8	26
27	1 12.3	-27.0	120.1	0 42.2	-27.8	120.2	0 12.0	-28.6	120.2	0 18.1	+29.4	59.8	0 48.3	+30.1	59.8	1 18.4	+30.9	59.9	1 48.6	+31.6	59.9	2 18.6	+32.5	59.9	27
28	0 45.3	-26.9	121.0	0 14.4	-27.8	121.0	0 16.6	+28.5	59.0	0 47.5	+29.3	59.0	1 18.4	+30.2	59.0	1 49.3	+30.9	59.0	2 20.2	+31.7	59.0	2 51.1	+32.4	59.1	28
29	0 18.4	-27.0	121.9	0 13.4	+27.8	58.1	0 45.1	+28.6	58.1	1 16.8	+29.4	58.1	1 48.6	+30.0	58.1	2 20.2	+30.9	58.1	2 51.9	+31.6	58.2	3 23.5	+32.4	58.2	29
30	0 08.6	+27.0	57.2	0 41.2	+27.7	57.2	1 13.7	+28.5	57.2	1 46.2	+29.3	57.2	2 18.6	+30.1	57.2	2 51.1	+30.8	57.3	3 23.5	+31.6	57.3	3 55.9	+32.3	57.4	30
31	0 35.6	+27.0	56.3	1 08.9	+27.8	56.3	1 42.2	+28.5	56.3	2 15.5	+29.2	56.3	2 48.7	+30.0	56.4	3 21.9	+30.8	56.4	3 55.1	+31.5	56.5	4 28.2	+32.2	56.5	31
32	1 02.6	+26.9	55.4	1 36.7	+27.7	55.4	2 10.7	+28.5	55.4	2 44.7	+29.3	55.5	3 18.7	+30.0	55.5	3 52.7	+30.7	55.6	4 26.6	+31.5	55.6	5 00.4	+32.2	55.7	32
33	1 29.5	+27.0	54.5	2 04.4	+27.7	54.5	2 39.2	+28.4	54.6	3 14.0	+29.2	54.6	3 48.7	+29.9	54.6	4 23.4	+30.7	54.7	4 58.1	+31.3	54.8	5 32.6	+32.2	54.8	33
34	1 56.5	+26.9	53.6	2 32.1	+27.6	53.6	3 07.6	+28.4	53.7	3 43.2	+29.1	53.7	4 18.6	+29.9	53.8	4 54.1	+30.6	53.8	5 29.4	+31.4	53.9	6 04.8	+32.0	54.0	34
35	2 23.4	+26.9	52.7	2 59.7	+27.6	52.7	3 36.0	+28.4	52.8	4 12.3	+29.1	52.8	4 48.5	+29.8	52.9	5 24.7	+30.5	53.0	6 00.8	+31.2	53.1	6 36.8	+31.9	53.1	35
36	2 50.3	+26.8	51.8	3 27.3	+27.6	51.9	4 04.4	+28.3	51.9	4 41.4	+29.0	52.0	5 18.3	+29.7	52.0	5 55.2	+30.4	52.1	6 32.0	+31.2	52.2	7 08.7	+31.9	52.3	36
37	3 17.1	+26.8	50.9	3 54.9	+27.5	51.0	4 32.7	+28.2	51.0	5 10.4	+28.9	51.1	5 48.0	+29.7	51.2	6 25.6	+30.4	51.2	7 03.2	+31.0	51.3	7 40.6	+31.8	51.4	37
38	3 43.9	+26.7	50.0	4 22.4	+27.4	50.1	5 00.9	+28.1	50.1	5 39.3	+28.9	50.2	6 17.7	+29.6	50.3	6 56.0	+30.3	50.4	7 34.2	+31.0	50.5	8 12.4	+31.6	50.6	38
39	4 10.6	+26.7	49.1	4 49.8	+27.4	49.2	5 29.0	+28.1	49.2	6 08.2	+28.8	49.3	6 47.3	+29.4	49.4	7 26.3	+30.1	49.5	8 05.2	+30.8	49.6	8 44.0	+31.5	49.7	39
40	4 37.3	+26.6	48.2	5 17.2	+27.3	48.3	5 57.1	+28.0	48.4	6 37.0	+28.6	48.4	7 16.7	+29.4	48.5	7 56.4	+30.1	48.6	8 36.0	+30.8	48.7	9 15.5	+31.5	48.9	40
41	5 03.9	+26.5	47.3	5 44.5	+27.2	47.4	6 25.1	+27.9	47.5	7 05.6	+28.6	47.6	7 46.1	+29.2	47.7	8 26.5	+29.9	47.8	9 06.8	+30.6	47.9	9 47.0	+31.2	48.0	41
42	5 30.4	+26.4	46.4	6 11.7	+27.1	46.5	6 53.0	+27.8	46.6	7 34.2	+28.5	46.7	8 15.3	+29.2	46.8	8 56.4	+29.8	46.9	9 37.4	+30.4	47.0	10 18.2	+31.2	47.1	42
43	5 56.8	+26.4	45.5	6 38.8	+27.1	45.6	7 20.8	+27.7	45.7	8 02.7	+28.3	45.8	8 44.5	+29.0	45.9	9 26.2	+29.7	46.0	10 07.8	+30.4	46.1	10 49.4	+31.0	46.3	43
44	6 23.2	+26.3	44.6	7 05.9	+26.9	44.7	7 48.5	+27.6	44.8	8 31.0	+28.3	44.9	9 13.5	+28.9	45.0	9 55.9	+29.5	45.1	10 38.2	+30.2	45.2	11 20.4	+30.8	45.4	44
45	6 49.5	+26.1	43.7	7 32.8	+26.8	43.8	8 16.1	+27.4	43.9	8 59.3	+28.1	44.0	9 42.4	+28.7	44.1	10 25.4	+29.4	44.2	11 08.4	+30.0	44.4	11 51.2	+30.7	44.5	45
46	7 15.6	+26.1	42.8	7 59.6	+26.7	42.9	8 43.5	+27.4	43.0	9 27.4	+27.9	43.1	10 11.1	+28.6	43.2	10 54.8	+29.3	43.3	11 38.4	+29.9	43.5	12 21.9	+30.5	43.6	46
47	7 41.7	+25.9	41.9	8 26.3	+26.6	42.0	9 10.9	+27.1	42.1	9 55.3	+27.9	42.2	10 39.7	+28.5	42.3	11 24.1	+29.0	42.5	12 08.3	+29.7	42.6	12 52.4	+30.3	42.8	47
48	8 07.6	+25.8	41.0	8 52.9	+26.4	41.1	9 38.0	+27.1	41.2	10 23.2	+27.6	41.3	11 08.2	+28.3	41.4	11 53.1	+28.9	41.6	12 38.0	+29.5	41.7	13 22.7	+30.2	41.9	48
49	8 33.4	+25.7	40.1	9 19.3	+26.3	40.2	10 05.1	+26.9	40.3	10 50.8	+27.5	40.4	11 36.5	+28.1	40.5	12 22.0	+28.8	40.7	13 07.5	+29.3	40.8	13 52.9	+29.9	41.0	49
50	8 59.1	+25.5	39.2	9 45.6	+26.1	39.3	10 32.0	+26.8	39.4	11 18.3	+27.4	39.5	12 04.6	+28.0	39.6	12 50.8	+28.5	39.8	13 36.8	+29.2	39.9	14 22.8	+29.7	40.1	50
51	9 24.6	+25.5	38.2	10 11.7	+26.0	38.3	10 58.8	+26.5	38.5	11 45.7	+27.2	38.6	12 32.6	+27.7	38.7	13 19.3	+28.4	38.9	14 06.0	+28.9	39.0	14 52.5	+29.6	39.2	51
52	9 50.1	+25.2	37.3	10 37.7	+25.9	37.4	11 25.3	+26.5	37.5	12 12.9	+27.0	37.7	13 00.3	+27.6	37.8	13 47.7	+28.1	38.0	14 34.9	+28.8	38.1	15 22.1	+29.3	38.3	52
53	10 15.3	+25.1	36.4	11 03.6	+25.6	36.5	11 51.8	+26.2	36.6	12 39.9	+26.8	36.8	13 27.9	+27.4	36.9	14 15.8	+28.0	37.1	15 03.7	+28.5	37.2	15 51.4	+29.1	37.4	53
54	10 40.4	+25.0	35.5	11 29.2	+25.5	35.6	12 18.0	+26.1	35.7	13 06.7	+26.6	35.8	13 55.3	+27.2	36.0	14 43.8	+27.7	36.1	15 32.2	+28.3	36.3	16 20.5	+28.8	36.5	54
55	11 05.4	+24.7	34.6	11 54.7	+25.4	34.7	12 44.1	+25.8	34.8	13 33.3	+26.4	34.9	14 22.4	+27.0	35.1	15 11.5	+27.5	35.2	16 00.5	+28.0	35.4	16 49.3	+28.7	35.6	55
56	11 30.1	+24.6	33.6	12 20.1	+25.1	33.7	13 09.9	+25.7	33.9	13 59.7	+26.2	34.0	14 49.4	+26.7	34.1	15 39.0	+27.3	34.3	16 28.5	+27.8	34.5	17 18.0	+28.3	34.6	56
57	11 54.7	+24.4	32.7	12 45.2	+24.9	32.8	13 35.6	+25.4	32.9	14 25.9	+26.0	33.1	15 16.1	+26.5	33.2	16 06.3	+27.0	33.4	16 56.3	+27.6	33.5	17 46.3	+28.1	33.7	57
58	12 19.1	+24.2	31.8	13 10.1	+24.7	31.9	14 01.0	+25.3	32.0	14 51.9	+25.7	32.1	15 42.6	+26.3	32.3	16 33.3	+26.8	32.4	17 23.9	+27.3	32.6	18 14.4	+27.8	32.8	58
59	12 43.3	+24.1	30.8	13 34.8	+24.6	30.9	14 26.3	+25.0	31.1	15 17.6	+25.5	31.2	16 08.9	+26.0	31.4	17 00.1	+26.5	31.5	17 51.2	+27.1	31.7	18 42.2	+27.6	31.8	59
60	13 07.4	+23.8	29.9	13 59.4	+24.3	30.0	14 51.3	+24.8	30.1	15 43.1	+25.3	30.3	16 34.9	+25.8	30.4	17 26.6	+26.3	30.6	18 18.3	+26.7	30.7	19 09.8	+27.2	30.9	60
61	13 31.2	+23.6	28.9	14 23.7	+24.0	29.1	15 16.1	+24.5	29.2	16 08.4	+25.1	29.3	17 00.7	+25.5	29.5	17 52.9	+26.0	29.6	18 45.0	+26.5	29.8	19 37.0	+27.0	30.0	61
62	13 54.8	+23.4	28.0	14 47.7	+23.9	28.1	15 40.6	+24.3	28.2	16 33.5	+24.7	28.4	17 26.2	+25.2	28.5	18 18.9	+25.7	28.7	19 11.5	+26.2	28.8	20 04.0	+26.7	29.0	62
63	14 18.2	+23.1	27.0	15 11.6	+23.6	27.2	16 04.9	+24.1	27.3	16 58.2	+24.5	27.4	17 51.4	+25.0	27.6	18 44.6	+25.4	27.7	19 37.7	+25.8	27.9	20 30.7	+26.3	28.1	63
64	14 41.3	+22.9	26.1	15 35.2	+23.3	26.2	16 29.0	+23.8	26.3	17 22.7	+24.3	26.5	18 16.4	+24.7	26.6	19 10.0	+25.1	26.8	20 03.5	+25.6	26.9	20 57.0	+26.0	27.1	64
65	15 04.2	+22.7	25.1	15 58.5	+23.1	25.2	16 52.8	+23.5	25.4	17 47.0	+23.9	25.5	18 41.1	+24.4	25.7	19 35.1	+24.8	25.8	20 29.1	+25.3	26.0	21 23.0	+25.7	26.1	65
66	15 26.9	+22.4	24.2	16 21.6	+22.9	24.3	17 16.3	+23.2	24.4	18 10.9	+23.7	24.5	19 05.5	+24.0	24.7	19 59.9	+24.5	24.8	20 54.4	+24.9	25.0	21 48.7	+25.3	25.2	66
67	15 49.3	+22.2	23.2	16 44.5	+22.5	23.3	17 39.5	+23.0	23.4	18 34.6	+23.3	23.6	19 29.5	+23.8	23.7	20 24.4	+24.2	23.9	21 19.3	+24.5	24.0	22 14.0	+25.0	24.2	67
68	16 11.5	+21.9	22.2	17 07.0	+22.3	22.4	18 02.5	+22.7	22.5	18 57.9	+23.1	22.6	19 53.3	+23.4	22.7	20 48.6	+23.8	22.9	21 43.8	+24.3	23.0	22 39.0	+24.7	23.2	68
69	16 33.4	+21.7	21.3	17 29.3	+22.0	21.4	18 25.2	+22.3	21.5	19 21.0	+22.7	21.6	20 16.7	+23.1	21.8	21 12.4	+23.5	21.9	22 08.1	+23.8	22.0	23 03.7	+24.2	22.2	69
70	16 55.1	+21.3	20.3	17 51.3	+21.7	20.4	18 47.5	+22.1	20.5	19 43.7	+22.4	20.6	20 39.8	+22.8	20.8	21 35.9	+23.2	20.9	22 31.9	+23.5	21.1	23 27.9	+23.9	21.2	70
71	17 16.4	+21.1	19.3	18 13.0	+21.5	19.4	19 09.6	+21.8	19.5	20 06.1	+22.1	19.7	21 02.6	+22.4	19.8	21 59.1	+22.7	19.9	22 55.4	+23.2	20.1	23 51.8	+23.5	20.2	71
72	17 37.5	+20.8	18.3	18 34.5	+21.1	18.4	19 31.4	+21.4	18.5	20 28.2	+21.8	18.7	21 25.0	+22.1	18.8	22 21.8	+22.4	18.9	23 18.6	+22.7	19.1	24 15.3	+23.0	19.2	72
73	17 58.3	+20.5	17.4	18 55.6	+20.8	17.5	19 52.8	+21.1	17.6	20 50.0	+21.4	17.7	21 47.1	+21.7	17.8	22 44.2	+22.1	17.9	23 41.3	+22.4	18.0	24 38.3	+22.7	18.2	73
74	18 18.8	+20.2	16.4	19 16.4	+20.4	16.5	20 13.9	+20.7	16.6	21 11.4	+21.0	16.7	22 08.8	+21.4	16.8	23 06.3	+21.6	16.9	24 03.7	+21.9	17.0	25 01.0	+22.2	17.2	74
75	18 39.0	+19.8	15.4	19 36.8	+20.2	15.5	20 34.6	+20.4	15.6	21 32.4	+20.7	15.7	22 30.2	+20.9	15.8	23 27.9	+21.2	15.9	24 25.6	+21.5	16.0	25 23.2	+21.9	16.1	75
76	18 58.8	+19.6	14.4	19 57.0	+19.8	14.5	20 55.0	+20.1	14.6	21 53.1	+20.3	14.7	22 51.1	+20.6	14.8	23 49.1	+20.9	14.9	24 47.1	+21.1	15.0	25 45.1	+21.3	15.1	76
77	19 18.4	+19.2	13.4	20 16.8	+19.4	13.5	21 15.1	+19.7	13.5	22 13.4	+20.0	13.6	23 11.7	+20.2	13.7	24 10.0	+20.4	13.8	25 08.2	+20.7	14.0	26 06.4	+21.0	14.1	77
78	19 37.6	+18.9	12.4	20 36.2	+19.1	12.4	21 34.8	+19.3	12.5	22 33.4	+19.5	12.6	23 31.9	+19.8	12.7	24 30.4	+20.0	12.8	25 28.9	+20.2	12.9	26 27.4	+20.4	13.0	78
79	19 56.5	+18.5	11.4	20 55.3	+18.7	11.4	21 54.1	+19.0	11.5	22 52.9	+19.1	11.6	23 51.7	+19.3	11.7	24 50.4	+19.6	11.8	25 49.1	+19.8	11.9	26 47.8	+20.0	12.0	79
80	20 15.0	+18.2	10.3	21 14.0	+18.4	10.4	22 13.1	+18.5	10.5	23 12.0	+18.8	10.6	24 11.0	+19.0	10.6	25 10.0	+19.1	10.7	26 08.9	+19.3	10.8	27 07.8	+19.6	10.9	80
81	20 33.2	+17.8	9.3	21 32.4	+18.0	9.4	22 31.6	+18.2	9.5	23 30.8	+18.3	9.5	24 30.0	+18.5	9.6	25 29.1	+18.7	9.7	26 28.2	+18.9	9.8	27 27.4	+19.0	9.8	81
82	20 51.0	+17.5	8.3	21 50.4	+17.6	8.4	22 49.8	+17.7	8.4	23 49.1	+17.9	8.5	24 48.5	+18.0	8.6	25 47.8	+18.2	8.6	26 47.1	+18.4	8.7	27 46.4	+18.5	8.8	82
83	21 08.5	+17.1	7.3	22 08.0	+17.3	7.3	23 07.5	+17.4	7.4	24 07.0	+17.5	7.4	25 06.5	+17.6	7.5	26 06.0	+17.8	7.6	27 05.5	+17.9	7.6	28 04.9	+18.1	7.7	83
84	21 25.6	+16.7	6.3	22 25.3	+16.8	6.3	23 24.9	+16.9	6.3	24 24.5	+17.1	6.4	25 24.1	+17.2	6.4	26 23.8	+17.2	6.5	27 23.4	+17.4	6.5	28 23.0	+17.5	6.6	84
85	21 42.3	+16.4	5.2	22 42.1	+16.4	5.3	23 41.8	+16.5	5.3	24 41.6	+16.6	5.3	25 41.3	+16.7	5.4	26 41.0	+16.8	5.4	27 40.8	+16.9	5.5	28 40.5	+17.0	5.5	85
86	21 58.7	+15.9	4.2	22 58.5	+16.0	4.2	23 58.3	+16.1	4.2	24 58.2	+16.1	4.3	25 58.0	+16.2	4.3	26 57.8	+16.3	4.4	27 57.7	+16.3	4.4	28 57.5	+16.4	4.4	86
87	22 14.6	+15.5	3.1	23 14.5	+15.6	3.2	24 14.4	+15.7	3.2	25 14.3	+15.7	3.2	26 14.2	+15.8	3.2	27 14.1	+15.8	3.3	28 14.0	+15.9	3.3	29 13.9	+15.9	3.3	87
88	22 30.1	+15.2	2.1	23 30.1	+15.2	2.1	24 30.1	+15.2	2.1	25 30.0	+15.2	2.2	26 30.0	+15.2	2.2	27 29.9	+15.3	2.2	28 29.9	+15.3	2.2	29 29.8	+15.4	2.2	88
89	22 45.3	+14.7	1.1	23 45.3	+14.7	1.1	24 45.3	+14.7	1.1	25 45.2	+14.8	1.1	26 45.2	+14.8	1.1	27 45.2	+14.8	1.1	28 45.2	+14.8	1.1	29 45.2	+14.8	1.1	89
90	23 00.0	+14.3	0.0	24 00.0	+14.3	0.0	25 00.0	+14.3	0.0	26 00.0	+14.3	0.0	27 00.0	+14.3	0.0	28 00.0	+14.3	0.0	29 00.0	+14.2	0.0	30 00.0	+14.2	0.0	90
	23°			24°			25°			26°			27°			28°			29°			30°			

S. Lat. {L.H.A. greater than 180° ....Zn=180°−Z
{L.H.A. less than 180°...........Zn=180°+Z

LATITUDE **SAME** NAME AS DECLINATION **L.H.A. 104°, 256°**

337

 N. Lat. {L.H.A. greater than 180° .....Zn=Z; L.H.A. less than 180°............Zn=360°−Z}

Dec.	23° Hc	d	Z	24° Hc	d	Z	25° Hc	d	Z	26° Hc	d	Z	27° Hc	d	Z	28° Hc	d	Z	29° Hc	d	Z	30° Hc	d	Z	Dec.
°	° ′	′	°	° ′	′	°	° ′	′	°	° ′	′	°	° ′	′	°	° ′	′	°	° ′	′	°	° ′	′	°	°
0	11 57.0	+23.9	95.2	11 51.5	+24.9	95.4	11 45.8	+25.8	95.6	11 39.9	+26.8	95.8	11 33.7	+27.8	96.0	11 27.4	+28.6	96.2	11 20.8	+29.6	96.4	11 14.0	+30.5	96.6	0
1	12 20.9	+23.7	94.2	12 16.4	+24.6	94.4	12 11.6	+25.7	94.6	12 06.7	+26.5	94.9	12 01.5	+27.5	95.1	11 56.0	+28.5	95.3	11 50.4	+29.4	95.5	11 44.5	+30.4	95.7	1
2	12 44.6	+23.5	93.3	12 41.0	+24.5	93.5	12 37.3	+25.4	93.7	12 33.2	+26.4	93.9	12 29.0	+27.4	94.2	12 24.5	+28.3	94.4	12 19.8	+29.3	94.6	12 14.9	+30.2	94.8	2
3	13 08.1	+23.2	92.3	13 05.5	+24.3	92.6	13 02.7	+25.2	92.8	12 59.6	+26.3	93.0	12 56.4	+27.1	93.3	12 52.8	+28.2	93.5	12 49.1	+29.0	93.7	12 45.1	+30.0	93.9	3
4	13 31.3	+23.1	91.4	13 29.8	+24.0	91.6	13 27.9	+25.1	91.9	13 25.9	+26.0	92.1	13 23.5	+27.0	92.3	13 21.0	+27.9	92.6	13 18.1	+28.9	92.8	13 15.1	+29.8	93.0	4
5	13 54.4	+22.8	90.4	13 53.8	+23.8	90.7	13 53.0	+24.8	90.9	13 51.9	+25.7	91.2	13 50.5	+26.8	91.4	13 48.9	+27.7	91.7	13 47.0	+28.7	91.9	13 44.9	+29.6	92.2	5
6	14 17.2	+22.6	89.5	14 17.6	+23.6	89.7	14 17.8	+24.6	90.0	14 17.6	+25.6	90.2	14 17.3	+26.5	90.5	14 16.6	+27.5	90.8	14 15.7	+28.5	91.0	14 14.5	+29.4	91.3	6
7	14 39.8	+22.4	88.5	14 41.2	+23.4	88.8	14 42.4	+24.3	89.0	14 43.2	+25.4	89.3	14 43.8	+26.3	89.6	14 44.1	+27.3	89.8	14 44.2	+28.2	90.1	14 43.9	+29.2	90.4	7
8	15 02.2	+22.1	87.6	15 04.6	+23.1	87.8	15 06.7	+24.2	88.1	15 08.6	+25.1	88.4	15 10.1	+26.1	88.6	15 11.4	+27.1	88.9	15 12.4	+28.0	89.2	15 13.1	+29.0	89.5	8
9	15 24.3	+21.9	86.6	15 27.7	+22.9	86.9	15 30.9	+23.8	87.2	15 33.7	+24.9	87.4	15 36.2	+25.9	87.7	15 38.5	+26.8	88.0	15 40.4	+27.9	88.3	15 42.1	+28.8	88.5	9
10	15 46.2	+21.6	85.6	15 50.6	+22.6	85.9	15 54.7	+23.7	86.2	15 58.6	+24.6	86.5	16 02.1	+25.6	86.8	16 05.3	+26.6	87.1	16 08.3	+27.5	87.3	16 10.9	+28.5	87.6	10
11	16 07.8	+21.4	84.7	16 13.2	+22.4	85.0	16 18.4	+23.3	85.2	16 23.2	+24.4	85.5	16 27.7	+25.4	85.8	16 31.9	+26.4	86.1	16 35.8	+27.3	86.4	16 39.4	+28.3	86.7	11
12	16 29.2	+21.0	83.7	16 35.6	+22.1	84.0	16 41.7	+23.1	84.3	16 47.6	+24.1	84.6	16 53.1	+25.1	84.9	16 58.3	+26.0	85.2	17 03.1	+27.1	85.5	17 07.7	+28.0	85.8	12
13	16 50.2	+20.9	82.7	16 57.7	+21.8	83.0	17 04.8	+22.9	83.3	17 11.7	+23.8	83.6	17 18.2	+24.8	83.9	17 24.3	+25.9	84.2	17 30.2	+26.8	84.6	17 35.7	+27.8	84.9	13
14	17 11.1	+20.5	81.7	17 19.5	+21.6	82.0	17 27.7	+22.5	82.3	17 35.5	+23.6	82.7	17 43.0	+24.5	83.0	17 50.2	+25.5	83.3	17 57.0	+26.5	83.6	18 03.5	+27.5	83.9	14
15	17 31.6	+20.2	80.7	17 41.1	+21.2	81.1	17 50.2	+22.3	81.4	17 59.1	+23.2	81.7	18 07.5	+24.3	82.0	18 15.7	+25.3	82.3	18 23.5	+26.3	82.7	18 31.0	+27.2	83.0	15
16	17 51.8	+19.9	79.8	18 02.3	+20.9	80.1	18 12.5	+21.9	80.4	18 22.3	+23.0	80.7	18 31.8	+24.0	81.1	18 41.0	+24.9	81.4	18 49.8	+25.9	81.7	18 58.2	+27.0	82.1	16
17	18 11.7	+19.6	78.8	18 23.2	+20.7	79.1	18 34.4	+21.7	79.4	18 45.3	+22.6	79.8	18 55.8	+23.7	80.1	19 05.9	+24.7	80.4	19 15.7	+25.7	80.8	19 25.2	+26.6	81.1	17
18	18 31.3	+19.4	77.8	18 43.9	+20.3	78.1	18 56.1	+21.3	78.4	19 07.9	+22.4	78.8	19 19.5	+23.3	79.1	19 30.6	+24.4	79.5	19 41.4	+25.4	79.8	19 51.8	+26.4	80.2	18
19	18 50.7	+18.9	76.8	19 04.2	+20.0	77.1	19 17.4	+21.1	77.4	19 30.3	+22.0	77.8	19 42.8	+23.1	78.1	19 55.0	+24.0	78.5	20 06.8	+25.0	78.8	20 18.2	+26.0	79.2	19
20	19 09.6	+18.7	75.8	19 24.2	+19.7	76.1	19 38.5	+20.6	76.5	19 52.3	+21.7	76.8	20 05.9	+22.7	77.2	20 19.0	+23.7	77.5	20 31.8	+24.7	77.9	20 44.2	+25.7	78.2	20
21	19 28.3	+18.3	74.8	19 43.9	+19.3	75.1	19 59.1	+20.4	75.5	20 14.0	+21.4	75.8	20 28.6	+22.3	76.2	20 42.7	+23.4	76.5	20 56.5	+24.4	76.9	21 09.9	+25.4	77.3	21
22	19 46.6	+18.0	73.7	20 03.2	+19.0	74.1	20 19.5	+20.0	74.5	20 35.4	+21.0	74.8	20 50.9	+22.1	75.2	21 06.1	+23.0	75.5	21 20.9	+24.0	75.9	21 35.3	+25.0	76.3	22
23	20 04.6	+17.6	72.7	20 22.2	+18.7	73.1	20 39.5	+19.7	73.4	20 56.4	+20.7	73.8	21 13.0	+21.6	74.2	21 29.1	+22.7	74.6	21 44.9	+23.7	74.9	22 00.3	+24.7	75.3	23
24	20 22.2	+17.3	71.7	20 40.9	+18.3	72.1	20 59.2	+19.3	72.4	21 17.1	+20.3	72.8	21 34.6	+21.4	73.2	21 51.8	+22.3	73.6	22 08.6	+23.3	73.9	22 25.0	+24.3	74.3	24
25	20 39.5	+16.9	70.7	20 59.2	+17.9	71.1	21 18.5	+18.9	71.4	21 37.4	+19.9	71.8	21 56.0	+20.9	72.2	22 14.1	+22.0	72.6	22 31.9	+23.0	73.0	22 49.3	+24.0	73.4	25
26	20 56.4	+16.6	69.7	21 17.1	+17.5	70.0	21 37.4	+18.6	70.4	21 57.3	+19.6	70.8	22 16.9	+20.6	71.2	22 36.1	+21.6	71.6	22 54.9	+22.6	72.0	23 13.3	+23.5	72.4	26
27	21 13.0	+16.1	68.6	21 34.6	+17.2	69.0	21 56.0	+18.1	69.4	22 16.9	+19.2	69.8	22 37.5	+20.2	70.1	22 57.7	+21.2	70.5	23 17.5	+22.1	70.9	23 36.8	+23.2	71.4	27
28	21 29.1	+15.8	67.6	21 51.8	+16.8	68.0	22 14.1	+17.8	68.3	22 36.1	+18.8	68.7	22 57.7	+19.8	69.1	23 18.9	+20.7	69.5	23 39.6	+21.8	69.9	24 00.0	+22.8	70.3	28
29	21 44.9	+15.4	66.6	22 08.6	+16.4	66.9	22 31.9	+17.4	67.3	22 54.9	+18.4	67.7	23 17.5	+19.3	68.1	23 39.6	+20.4	68.5	24 01.4	+21.4	68.9	24 22.8	+22.4	69.3	29
30	22 00.3	+15.0	65.5	22 25.0	+16.0	65.9	22 49.3	+17.0	66.3	23 13.3	+18.0	66.7	23 36.8	+19.0	67.1	24 00.0	+20.0	67.5	24 22.8	+21.0	67.9	24 45.2	+22.0	68.3	30
31	22 15.3	+14.6	64.5	22 41.0	+15.6	64.9	23 06.3	+16.6	65.2	23 31.3	+17.5	65.6	23 55.8	+18.6	66.0	24 20.0	+19.6	66.4	24 43.8	+20.5	66.9	25 07.2	+21.5	67.3	31
32	22 29.9	+14.2	63.4	22 56.6	+15.1	63.8	23 22.9	+16.1	64.2	23 48.8	+17.2	64.6	24 14.4	+18.1	65.0	24 39.6	+19.1	65.4	25 04.3	+20.1	65.8	25 28.7	+21.1	66.3	32
33	22 44.1	+13.8	62.4	23 11.7	+14.8	62.8	23 39.0	+15.8	63.1	24 06.0	+16.7	63.5	24 32.5	+17.7	63.9	24 58.7	+18.7	64.4	25 24.4	+19.7	64.8	25 49.8	+20.7	65.2	33
34	22 57.9	+13.3	61.3	23 26.5	+14.3	61.7	23 54.8	+15.3	62.1	24 22.7	+16.2	62.5	24 50.2	+17.3	62.9	25 17.4	+18.2	63.3	25 44.1	+19.2	63.7	26 10.5	+20.2	64.2	34
35	23 11.2	+13.0	60.3	23 40.8	+13.9	60.6	24 10.1	+14.8	61.0	24 38.9	+15.9	61.4	25 07.5	+16.8	61.8	25 35.6	+17.8	62.3	26 03.3	+18.8	62.7	26 30.7	+19.7	63.1	35
36	23 24.2	+12.4	59.2	23 54.7	+13.5	59.6	24 24.9	+14.4	60.0	24 54.8	+15.3	60.4	25 24.3	+16.3	60.8	25 53.4	+17.3	61.2	26 22.1	+18.3	61.6	26 50.4	+19.3	62.1	36
37	23 36.6	+12.1	58.1	24 08.2	+13.0	58.5	24 39.3	+14.0	58.9	25 10.1	+15.0	59.3	25 40.6	+15.9	59.7	26 10.7	+16.8	60.1	26 40.4	+17.8	60.6	27 09.7	+18.7	61.0	37
38	23 48.7	+11.6	57.1	24 21.2	+12.5	57.4	24 53.3	+13.5	57.8	25 25.1	+14.4	58.2	25 56.5	+15.4	58.6	26 27.5	+16.4	59.1	26 58.2	+17.3	59.5	27 28.4	+18.3	59.9	38
39	24 00.3	+11.2	56.0	24 33.7	+12.1	56.4	25 06.8	+13.0	56.7	25 39.5	+14.0	57.1	26 11.9	+14.9	57.6	26 43.9	+15.8	58.0	27 15.5	+16.8	58.4	27 46.7	+17.8	58.9	39
40	24 11.5	+10.7	54.9	24 45.8	+11.6	55.3	25 19.8	+12.6	55.7	25 53.5	+13.5	56.1	26 26.8	+14.4	56.5	26 59.7	+15.4	56.9	27 32.3	+16.3	57.3	28 04.5	+17.3	57.8	40
41	24 22.2	+10.2	53.8	24 57.4	+11.2	54.2	25 32.4	+12.0	54.6	26 07.0	+13.0	55.0	26 41.2	+13.9	55.4	27 15.1	+14.9	55.8	27 48.6	+15.8	56.2	28 21.8	+16.7	56.7	41
42	24 32.4	+9.8	52.7	25 08.6	+10.7	53.1	25 44.4	+11.6	53.5	26 20.0	+12.5	53.9	26 55.1	+13.5	54.3	27 30.0	+14.3	54.7	28 04.4	+15.3	55.2	28 38.5	+16.3	55.6	42
43	24 42.2	+9.3	51.7	25 19.3	+10.2	52.0	25 56.0	+11.1	52.4	26 32.5	+12.0	52.8	27 08.6	+12.9	53.2	27 44.3	+13.9	53.6	28 19.7	+14.8	54.1	28 54.8	+15.7	54.5	43
44	24 51.5	+8.8	50.6	25 29.5	+9.7	50.9	26 07.1	+10.6	51.3	26 44.5	+11.5	51.7	27 21.5	+12.4	52.1	27 58.2	+13.3	52.5	28 34.5	+14.2	53.0	29 10.5	+15.1	53.4	44
45	25 00.3	+8.4	49.5	25 39.2	+9.2	49.8	26 17.7	+10.1	50.2	26 56.0	+10.9	50.6	27 33.9	+11.8	51.0	28 11.5	+12.7	51.4	28 48.7	+13.7	51.8	29 25.6	+14.6	52.3	45
46	25 08.7	+7.9	48.4	25 48.4	+8.7	48.7	26 27.8	+9.6	49.1	27 06.9	+10.5	49.5	27 45.7	+11.4	49.9	28 24.2	+12.3	50.3	29 02.4	+13.1	50.7	29 40.2	+14.0	51.2	46
47	25 16.6	+7.4	47.3	25 57.1	+8.3	47.7	26 37.4	+9.1	48.0	27 17.4	+9.9	48.4	27 57.1	+10.8	48.8	28 36.5	+11.6	49.2	29 15.5	+12.6	49.6	29 54.2	+13.5	50.0	47
48	25 24.0	+6.9	46.2	26 05.4	+7.7	46.5	26 46.5	+8.6	46.9	27 27.3	+9.4	47.3	28 07.9	+10.3	47.7	28 48.1	+11.2	48.1	29 28.1	+12.0	48.5	30 07.7	+12.8	48.9	48
49	25 30.9	+6.4	45.1	26 13.1	+7.2	45.4	26 55.1	+8.0	45.8	27 36.7	+8.9	46.2	28 18.2	+9.7	46.6	28 59.3	+10.5	47.0	29 40.1	+11.4	47.4	30 20.5	+12.3	47.8	49
50	25 37.3	+5.9	44.0	26 20.3	+6.7	44.3	27 03.1	+7.5	44.7	27 45.6	+8.4	45.1	28 27.9	+9.1	45.4	29 09.8	+10.0	45.8	29 51.5	+10.8	46.2	30 32.8	+11.7	46.7	50
51	25 43.2	+5.4	42.9	26 27.0	+6.2	43.2	27 10.6	+7.0	43.6	27 54.0	+7.7	43.9	28 37.0	+8.6	44.3	29 19.8	+9.4	44.7	30 02.3	+10.3	45.1	30 44.5	+11.1	45.5	51
52	25 48.6	+4.9	41.8	26 33.2	+5.7	42.1	27 17.6	+6.5	42.5	28 01.7	+7.3	42.8	28 45.6	+8.1	43.2	29 29.2	+8.9	43.6	30 12.6	+9.6	44.0	30 55.6	+10.5	44.4	52
53	25 53.5	+4.4	40.7	26 38.9	+5.1	41.0	27 24.1	+5.9	41.3	28 09.0	+6.7	41.7	28 53.7	+7.4	42.0	29 38.1	+8.2	42.4	30 22.2	+9.1	42.8	31 06.1	+9.9	43.2	53
54	25 57.9	+3.9	39.6	26 44.0	+4.7	39.9	27 30.0	+5.3	40.2	28 15.7	+6.1	40.6	29 01.1	+6.9	40.9	29 46.3	+7.7	41.3	30 31.3	+8.5	41.7	31 16.0	+9.2	42.1	54
55	26 01.8	+3.4	38.5	26 48.7	+4.1	38.8	27 35.3	+4.9	39.1	28 21.8	+5.6	39.4	29 08.0	+6.3	39.8	29 54.0	+7.1	40.1	30 39.8	+7.8	40.5	31 25.2	+8.7	40.9	55
56	26 05.2	+2.8	37.3	26 52.8	+3.5	37.7	27 40.2	+4.3	38.0	28 27.4	+5.0	38.3	29 14.3	+5.8	38.6	30 01.1	+6.5	39.0	30 47.6	+7.2	39.4	31 33.9	+8.0	39.8	56
57	26 08.0	+2.4	36.2	26 56.3	+3.1	36.5	27 44.5	+3.7	36.8	28 32.4	+4.4	37.2	29 20.1	+5.1	37.5	30 07.6	+5.9	37.8	30 54.8	+6.7	38.2	31 41.9	+7.3	38.6	57
58	26 10.4	+1.8	35.1	26 59.4	+2.5	35.4	27 48.2	+3.2	35.7	28 36.8	+3.9	36.0	29 25.2	+4.6	36.4	30 13.5	+5.2	36.7	31 01.5	+6.0	37.1	31 49.2	+6.8	37.4	58
59	26 12.2	+1.4	34.0	27 01.9	+2.0	34.3	27 51.4	+2.6	34.6	28 40.7	+3.3	34.9	29 29.8	+4.0	35.2	30 18.7	+4.7	35.5	31 07.5	+5.3	35.9	31 56.0	+6.0	36.3	59
60	26 13.6	+0.8	32.9	27 03.9	+1.4	33.2	27 54.0	+2.1	33.5	28 44.0	+2.7	33.8	29 33.8	+3.4	34.1	30 23.4	+4.1	34.4	31 12.8	+4.8	34.7	32 02.0	+5.5	35.1	60
61	26 14.4	+0.3	31.8	27 05.3	+0.9	32.0	27 56.1	+1.5	32.3	28 46.7	+2.2	32.6	29 37.2	+2.8	32.9	30 27.5	+3.4	33.2	31 17.6	+4.1	33.6	32 07.5	+4.7	33.9	61
62	26 14.7	−0.2	30.7	27 06.2	+0.4	30.9	27 57.6	+1.0	31.2	28 48.9	+1.6	31.5	29 40.0	+2.2	31.8	30 30.9	+2.8	32.1	31 21.7	+3.4	32.4	32 12.2	+4.2	32.7	62
63	26 14.5	−0.8	29.5	27 06.6	−0.2	29.8	27 58.6	+0.4	30.1	28 50.5	+1.0	30.3	29 42.2	+1.6	30.6	30 33.7	+2.2	30.9	31 25.1	+2.9	31.2	32 16.4	+3.4	31.5	63
64	26 13.7	−1.2	28.4	27 06.4	−0.7	28.7	27 59.0	−0.1	28.9	28 51.5	+0.4	29.2	29 43.8	+1.0	29.5	30 35.9	+1.6	29.8	31 28.0	+2.1	30.1	32 19.8	+2.8	30.4	64
65	26 12.5	−1.8	27.3	27 05.7	−1.2	27.6	27 58.9	−0.7	27.8	28 51.9	−0.2	28.0	29 44.8	+0.4	28.3	30 37.5	+1.0	28.6	31 30.1	+1.6	28.9	32 22.6	+2.1	29.2	65
66	26 10.7	−2.3	26.2	27 04.5	−1.8	26.4	27 58.2	−1.3	26.7	28 51.7	−0.7	26.9	29 45.2	−0.2	27.2	30 38.5	+0.4	27.4	31 31.7	+0.9	27.7	32 24.7	+1.5	28.0	66
67	26 08.4	−2.7	25.1	27 02.7	−2.3	25.3	27 56.9	−1.8	25.5	28 51.0	−1.3	25.8	29 45.0	−0.8	26.0	30 38.9	−0.3	26.3	31 32.6	+0.3	26.5	32 26.2	+0.8	26.8	67
68	26 05.7	−3.3	24.0	27 00.4	−2.8	24.2	27 55.1	−2.3	24.4	28 49.7	−1.9	24.6	29 44.2	−1.4	24.9	30 38.6	−0.9	25.1	31 32.9	−0.4	25.4	32 27.0	+0.2	25.6	68
69	26 02.4	−3.9	22.9	26 57.6	−3.4	23.1	27 52.8	−3.0	23.3	28 47.8	−2.4	23.5	29 42.8	−2.0	23.7	30 37.7	−1.5	23.9	31 32.5	−1.0	24.2	32 27.2	−0.6	24.4	69
70	25 58.5	−4.3	21.8	26 54.2	−3.9	21.9	27 49.8	−3.4	22.1	28 45.4	−3.0	22.3	29 40.8	−2.5	22.6	30 36.2	−2.1	22.8	31 31.5	−1.7	23.0	32 26.6	−1.1	23.3	70
71	25 54.2	−4.8	20.6	26 50.3	−4.4	20.8	27 46.4	−4.0	21.0	28 42.4	−3.6	21.2	29 38.3	−3.2	21.4	30 34.1	−2.8	21.6	31 29.8	−2.3	21.8	32 25.5	−1.9	22.1	71
72	25 49.4	−5.3	19.5	26 45.9	−4.9	19.7	27 42.4	−4.6	19.9	28 38.8	−4.2	20.1	29 35.1	−3.8	20.3	30 31.3	−3.3	20.5	31 27.5	−2.9	20.7	32 23.6	−2.5	20.9	72
73	25 44.1	−5.9	18.4	26 41.0	−5.5	18.6	27 37.8	−5.1	18.8	28 34.6	−4.8	18.9	29 31.3	−4.4	19.1	30 28.0	−4.0	19.3	31 24.6	−3.6	19.5	32 21.1	−3.2	19.7	73
74	25 38.2	−6.3	17.3	26 35.5	−6.0	17.5	27 32.7	−5.7	17.6	28 29.8	−5.3	17.8	29 26.9	−4.9	18.0	30 24.0	−4.6	18.1	31 21.0	−4.2	18.3	32 17.9	−3.8	18.5	74
75	25 31.9	−6.8	16.2	26 29.5	−6.5	16.4	27 27.0	−6.1	16.5	28 24.5	−5.8	16.7	29 22.0	−5.5	16.8	30 19.4	−5.2	17.0	31 16.8	−4.9	17.2	32 14.1	−4.5	17.3	75
76	25 25.1	−7.3	15.1	26 23.0	−7.0	15.3	27 20.9	−6.8	15.4	28 18.7	−6.4	15.5	29 16.5	−6.1	15.7	30 14.2	−5.8	15.8	31 11.9	−5.5	16.0	32 09.6	−5.2	16.2	76
77	25 17.8	−7.8	14.0	26 16.0	−7.6	14.1	27 14.1	−7.2	14.3	28 12.3	−7.0	14.4	29 10.4	−6.7	14.5	30 08.4	−6.4	14.7	31 06.4	−6.1	14.8	32 04.4	−5.8	15.0	77
78	25 10.0	−8.3	12.9	26 08.4	−8.0	13.0	27 06.9	−7.8	13.2	28 05.3	−7.5	13.3	29 03.7	−7.3	13.4	30 02.0	−7.0	13.5	31 00.3	−6.7	13.7	31 58.6	−6.4	13.8	78
79	25 01.7	−8.8	11.8	26 00.4	−8.5	11.9	26 59.1	−8.3	12.0	27 57.8	−8.1	12.2	28 56.4	−7.8	12.3	29 55.0	−7.6	12.4	30 53.6	−7.3	12.5	31 52.2	−7.1	12.6	79
80	24 52.9	−9.2	10.7	25 51.9	−9.1	10.8	26 50.8	−8.8	10.9	27 49.7	−8.6	11.0	28 48.6	−8.4	11.1	29 47.4	−8.2	11.2	30 46.3	−8.0	11.4	31 45.1	−7.8	11.5	80
81	24 43.7	−9.7	9.7	25 42.8	−9.5	9.7	26 42.0	−9.4	9.8	27 41.1	−9.2	9.9	28 40.2	−9.0	10.0	29 39.2	−8.7	10.1	30 38.3	−8.6	10.2	31 37.3	−8.3	10.3	81
82	24 34.0	−10.2	8.6	25 33.3	−10.0	8.6	26 32.6	−9.8	8.7	27 31.9	−9.7	8.8	28 31.2	−9.5	8.9	29 30.5	−9.4	9.0	30 29.7	−9.1	9.1	31 29.0	−9.0	9.1	82
83	24 23.8	−10.6	7.5	25 23.3	−10.5	7.6	26 22.8	−10.4	7.6	27 22.2	−10.2	7.7	28 21.7	−10.1	7.8	29 21.1	−9.9	7.8	30 20.6	−9.8	7.9	31 20.0	−9.6	8.0	83
84	24 13.2	−11.1	6.4	25 12.8	−11.0	6.5	26 12.4	−10.8	6.5	27 12.0	−10.7	6.6	28 11.6	−10.6	6.6	29 11.2	−10.5	6.7	30 10.8	−10.4	6.8	31 10.4	−10.2	6.8	84
85	24 02.1	−11.6	5.3	25 01.8	−11.4	5.4	26 01.6	−11.4	5.4	27 01.3	−11.3	5.5	28 01.0	−11.1	5.5	29 00.7	−11.0	5.6	30 00.4	−10.9	5.6	31 00.2	−10.9	5.7	85
86	23 50.5	−11.9	4.3	24 50.4	−11.9	4.3	25 50.2	−11.8	4.3	26 50.0	−11.7	4.4	27 49.9	−11.7	4.4	28 49.7	−11.6	4.4	29 49.5	−11.5	4.5	30 49.3	−11.4	4.5	86
87	23 38.6	−12.5	3.2	24 38.5	−12.4	3.2	25 38.4	−12.3	3.2	26 38.3	−12.3	3.3	27 38.2	−12.2	3.3	28 38.1	−12.2	3.3	29 38.0	−12.1	3.4	30 37.9	−12.1	3.4	87
88	23 26.1	−12.8	2.1	24 26.1	−12.8	2.1	25 26.1	−12.8	2.2	26 26.0	−12.7	2.2	27 26.0	−12.8	2.2	28 25.9	−12.7	2.2	29 25.9	−12.7	2.2	30 25.8	−12.6	2.3	88
89	23 13.3	−13.3	1.1	24 13.3	−13.3	1.1	25 13.3	−13.3	1.1	26 13.3	−13.3	1.1	27 13.2	−13.2	1.1	28 13.2	−13.2	1.1	29 13.2	−13.2	1.1	30 13.2	−13.2	1.1	89
90	23 00.0	−13.7	0.0	24 00.0	−13.7	0.0	25 00.0	−13.7	0.0	26 00.0	−13.7	0.0	27 00.0	−13.7	0.0	28 00.0	−13.8	0.0	29 00.0	−13.8	0.0	30 00.0	−13.8	0.0	90
	23°			24°			25°			26°			27°			28°			29°			30°			

LATITUDE CONTRARY NAME TO DECLINATION L.H.A. 77°, 283°

Dec.	23° Hc	d	Z	24° Hc	d	Z	25° Hc	d	Z	26° Hc	d	Z	27° Hc	d	Z	28° Hc	d	Z	29° Hc	d	Z	30° Hc	d	Z	Dec.
°	° ′	′	°	° ′	′	°	° ′	′	°	° ′	′	°	° ′	′	°	° ′	′	°	° ′	′	°	° ′	′	°	°
0	11 57.0	−24.0	95.2	11 51.5	−25.0	95.4	11 45.8	−26.0	95.6	11 39.9	−27.0	95.8	11 33.7	−27.9	96.0	11 27.4	−28.8	96.2	11 20.8	−29.7	96.4	11 14.0	−30.6	96.6	0
1	11 33.0	−24.3	96.1	11 26.5	−25.2	96.3	11 19.8	−26.1	96.5	11 12.9	−27.1	96.7	11 05.8	−28.0	96.9	10 58.6	−29.0	97.1	10 51.1	−29.9	97.3	10 43.4	−30.8	97.5	1
2	11 08.7	−24.4	97.0	11 01.3	−25.4	97.2	10 53.7	−26.4	97.4	10 45.8	−27.2	97.6	10 37.8	−28.2	97.8	10 29.6	−29.1	98.0	10 21.2	−30.1	98.2	10 12.6	−31.0	98.3	2
3	10 44.3	−24.5	98.0	10 35.9	−25.5	98.1	10 27.3	−26.4	98.3	10 18.6	−27.4	98.5	10 09.6	−28.3	98.7	10 00.5	−29.3	98.9	9 51.1	−30.2	99.0	9 41.6	−31.1	99.2	3
4	10 19.8	−24.8	98.9	10 10.4	−25.7	99.1	10 00.9	−26.7	99.2	9 51.2	−27.6	99.4	9 41.3	−28.5	99.6	9 31.2	−29.4	99.7	9 20.9	−30.3	99.9	9 10.5	−31.2	100.1	4
5	9 55.0	−24.8	99.8	9 44.7	−25.8	100.0	9 34.2	−26.7	100.1	9 23.6	−27.7	100.3	9 12.8	−28.6	100.5	9 01.8	−29.5	100.6	8 50.6	−30.4	100.8	8 39.3	−31.3	100.9	5
6	9 30.2	−25.1	100.7	9 18.9	−26.0	100.9	9 07.5	−26.9	101.1	8 55.9	−27.8	101.2	8 44.2	−28.8	101.4	8 32.3	−29.7	101.5	8 20.2	−30.5	101.7	8 08.0	−31.4	101.8	6
7	9 05.1	−25.1	101.7	8 52.9	−26.1	101.8	8 40.6	−27.1	102.0	8 28.1	−28.0	102.1	8 15.4	−28.8	102.2	8 02.6	−29.7	102.4	7 49.7	−30.7	102.5	7 36.6	−31.5	102.7	7
8	8 40.0	−25.3	102.6	8 26.8	−26.2	102.7	8 13.5	−27.1	102.9	8 00.1	−28.0	103.0	7 46.6	−29.0	103.1	7 32.9	−29.9	103.3	7 19.0	−30.7	103.4	7 05.1	−31.7	103.5	8
9	8 14.7	−25.5	103.5	8 00.6	−26.3	103.6	7 46.4	−27.3	103.8	7 32.1	−28.2	103.9	7 17.6	−29.1	104.0	7 03.0	−30.0	104.1	6 48.3	−30.9	104.3	6 33.4	−31.7	104.4	9
10	7 49.2	−25.5	104.4	7 34.3	−26.5	104.5	7 19.1	−27.3	104.7	7 03.9	−28.3	104.8	6 48.5	−29.1	104.9	6 33.0	−30.0	105.0	6 17.4	−30.9	105.1	6 01.7	−31.8	105.2	10
11	7 23.7	−25.7	105.3	7 07.8	−26.6	105.4	6 51.8	−27.5	105.6	6 35.6	−28.4	105.7	6 19.4	−29.3	105.8	6 03.0	−30.1	105.9	5 46.5	−31.0	106.0	5 29.9	−31.8	106.1	11
12	6 58.0	−25.7	106.2	6 41.2	−26.6	106.3	6 24.3	−27.6	106.5	6 07.2	−28.4	106.6	5 50.1	−29.3	106.7	5 32.9	−30.3	106.8	5 15.5	−31.1	106.8	4 58.1	−31.9	106.9	12
13	6 32.3	−25.9	107.1	6 14.6	−26.8	107.2	5 56.7	−27.6	107.3	5 38.8	−28.5	107.4	5 20.8	−29.4	107.5	5 02.6	−30.2	107.6	4 44.4	−31.1	107.7	4 26.2	−32.0	107.8	13
14	6 06.4	−25.9	108.0	5 47.8	−26.8	108.1	5 29.1	−27.8	108.2	5 10.3	−28.7	108.3	4 51.4	−29.5	108.4	4 32.4	−30.4	108.5	4 13.3	−31.2	108.6	3 54.2	−32.1	108.6	14
15	5 40.5	−26.0	108.9	5 21.0	−27.0	109.0	5 01.3	−27.8	109.1	4 41.6	−28.6	109.2	4 21.9	−29.6	109.3	4 02.0	−30.4	109.4	3 42.1	−31.2	109.4	3 22.1	−32.0	109.5	15
16	5 14.5	−26.1	109.9	4 54.0	−26.9	109.9	4 33.5	−27.8	110.0	4 13.0	−28.8	110.1	3 52.3	−29.6	110.2	3 31.6	−30.4	110.2	3 10.9	−31.3	110.3	2 50.1	−32.2	110.3	16
17	4 48.4	−26.2	110.8	4 27.1	−27.1	110.8	4 05.7	−27.9	110.9	3 44.2	−28.7	111.0	3 22.7	−29.6	111.0	3 01.2	−30.5	111.1	2 39.6	−31.3	111.1	2 17.9	−32.1	111.2	17
18	4 22.2	−26.3	111.7	4 00.0	−27.1	111.7	3 37.8	−28.0	111.8	3 15.5	−28.9	111.8	2 53.1	−29.7	111.9	2 30.7	−30.5	111.9	2 08.3	−31.4	112.0	1 45.8	−32.2	112.0	18
19	3 55.9	−26.3	112.6	3 32.9	−27.2	112.6	3 09.8	−28.0	112.7	2 46.6	−28.8	112.7	2 23.4	−29.7	112.8	2 00.2	−30.6	112.8	1 36.9	−31.3	112.8	1 13.6	−32.2	112.9	19
20	3 29.6	−26.3	113.5	3 05.7	−27.2	113.5	2 41.8	−28.1	113.6	2 17.8	−29.0	113.6	1 53.7	−29.7	113.6	1 29.6	−30.5	113.7	1 05.6	−31.4	113.7	0 41.4	−32.2	113.7	20
21	3 03.3	−26.4	114.4	2 38.5	−27.2	114.4	2 13.7	−28.1	114.4	1 48.8	−28.9	114.5	1 24.0	−29.8	114.5	0 59.1	−30.6	114.5	0 34.2	−31.4	114.5	0 09.2	−32.1	114.5	21
22	2 36.9	−26.5	115.3	2 11.3	−27.3	115.3	1 45.6	−28.1	115.3	1 19.9	−28.9	115.4	0 54.2	−29.8	115.4	0 28.5	−30.6	115.4	0 02.8	−31.4	115.4	0 22.9	+32.2	64.6	22
23	2 10.4	−26.4	116.2	1 44.0	−27.3	116.2	1 17.5	−28.2	116.2	0 51.0	−29.0	116.2	0 24.4	−29.7	116.2	0 02.1	+30.6	63.8	0 28.6	+31.4	63.8	0 55.1	+32.2	63.8	23
24	1 44.0	−26.5	117.1	1 16.7	−27.4	117.1	0 49.3	−28.1	117.1	0 22.0	−29.0	117.1	0 05.3	+29.8	62.9	0 32.7	+30.5	62.9	1 00.0	+31.4	62.9	1 27.3	+32.2	62.9	24
25	1 17.5	−26.5	118.0	0 49.3	−27.3	118.0	0 21.2	−28.2	118.0	0 07.0	+28.9	62.0	0 35.1	+29.8	62.0	1 03.2	+30.6	62.0	1 31.4	+31.3	62.1	1 59.5	+32.1	62.1	25
26	0 51.0	−26.6	118.9	0 22.0	−27.3	118.9	0 07.0	+28.1	61.1	0 35.9	+29.0	61.1	1 04.9	+29.7	61.2	1 33.8	+30.5	61.2	2 02.7	+31.4	61.2	2 31.6	+32.1	61.2	26
27	0 24.4	−26.5	119.8	0 05.3	+27.4	60.2	0 35.1	+28.1	60.3	1 04.9	+28.9	60.3	1 34.6	+29.7	60.3	2 04.3	+30.6	60.3	2 34.1	+31.2	60.3	3 03.7	+32.1	60.4	27
28	0 02.1	+26.5	59.4	0 32.7	+27.3	59.4	1 03.2	+28.2	59.4	1 33.8	+28.9	59.4	2 04.3	+29.8	59.4	2 34.9	+30.4	59.5	3 05.3	+31.3	59.5	3 35.8	+32.0	59.5	28
29	0 28.6	+26.5	58.5	1 00.0	+27.3	58.5	1 31.4	+28.1	58.5	2 02.7	+28.9	58.5	2 34.1	+29.6	58.5	3 05.3	+30.5	58.6	3 36.6	+31.2	58.6	4 07.8	+32.0	58.7	29
30	0 55.1	+26.6	57.6	1 27.3	+27.3	57.6	1 59.5	+28.1	57.6	2 31.6	+28.9	57.6	3 03.7	+29.6	57.7	3 35.8	+30.4	57.7	4 07.8	+31.1	57.8	4 39.8	+31.9	57.8	30
31	1 21.7	+26.4	56.7	1 54.6	+27.3	56.7	2 27.6	+28.0	56.7	3 00.5	+28.8	56.8	3 33.3	+29.6	56.8	4 06.2	+30.3	56.9	4 38.9	+31.1	56.9	5 11.7	+31.8	57.0	31
32	1 48.1	+26.5	55.8	2 21.9	+27.2	55.8	2 55.6	+28.0	55.8	3 29.3	+28.7	55.9	4 02.9	+29.5	55.9	4 36.5	+30.3	56.0	5 10.0	+31.0	56.1	5 43.5	+31.7	56.1	32
33	2 14.6	+26.4	54.9	2 49.1	+27.2	54.9	3 23.6	+28.0	54.9	3 58.0	+28.7	55.0	4 32.4	+29.5	55.1	5 06.8	+30.2	55.1	5 41.0	+31.0	55.2	6 15.2	+31.7	55.3	33
34	2 41.0	+26.4	54.0	3 16.3	+27.2	54.0	3 51.6	+27.9	54.1	4 26.7	+28.7	54.1	5 01.9	+29.4	54.2	5 37.0	+30.1	54.3	6 12.0	+30.8	54.3	6 46.9	+31.6	54.4	34
35	3 07.4	+26.4	53.1	3 43.5	+27.1	53.1	4 19.5	+27.8	53.2	4 55.4	+28.6	53.2	5 31.3	+29.3	53.3	6 07.1	+30.0	53.4	6 42.8	+30.8	53.5	7 18.5	+31.5	53.6	35
36	3 33.8	+26.3	52.2	4 10.6	+27.0	52.2	4 47.3	+27.8	52.3	5 24.0	+28.5	52.4	6 00.6	+29.2	52.4	6 37.1	+30.0	52.5	7 13.6	+30.7	52.6	7 50.0	+31.4	52.7	36
37	4 00.1	+26.2	51.3	4 37.6	+26.9	51.3	5 15.1	+27.6	51.4	5 52.5	+28.4	51.5	6 29.8	+29.1	51.6	7 07.1	+29.8	51.6	7 44.3	+30.5	51.7	8 21.4	+31.2	51.9	37
38	4 26.3	+26.2	50.4	5 04.5	+26.9	50.4	5 42.7	+27.6	50.5	6 20.9	+28.3	50.6	6 58.9	+29.1	50.7	7 36.9	+29.8	50.8	8 14.8	+30.5	50.9	8 52.6	+31.2	51.0	38
39	4 52.5	+26.1	49.5	5 31.4	+26.8	49.5	6 10.3	+27.6	49.6	6 49.2	+28.2	49.7	7 28.0	+28.9	49.8	8 06.7	+29.6	49.9	8 45.3	+30.3	50.0	9 23.8	+31.0	50.1	39
40	5 18.6	+26.0	48.6	5 58.2	+26.8	48.6	6 37.9	+27.4	48.7	7 17.4	+28.1	48.8	7 56.9	+28.8	48.9	8 36.3	+29.5	49.0	9 15.6	+30.2	49.1	9 54.8	+30.9	49.3	40
41	5 44.6	+25.9	47.7	6 25.0	+26.6	47.7	7 05.3	+27.3	47.8	7 45.5	+28.0	47.9	8 25.7	+28.7	48.0	9 05.8	+29.4	48.1	9 45.8	+30.1	48.3	10 25.7	+30.7	48.4	41
42	6 10.5	+25.8	46.7	6 51.6	+26.5	46.8	7 32.6	+27.2	46.9	8 13.5	+27.9	47.0	8 54.4	+28.6	47.1	9 35.2	+29.2	47.3	10 15.9	+29.9	47.4	10 56.4	+30.6	47.5	42
43	6 36.3	+25.8	45.8	7 18.1	+26.4	45.9	7 59.8	+27.1	46.0	8 41.4	+27.8	46.1	9 23.0	+28.4	46.2	10 04.4	+29.1	46.4	10 45.8	+29.8	46.5	11 27.0	+30.5	46.6	43
44	7 02.1	+25.6	44.9	7 44.5	+26.3	45.0	8 26.9	+27.0	45.1	9 09.2	+27.6	45.2	9 51.4	+28.3	45.3	10 33.5	+29.0	45.5	11 15.6	+29.6	45.6	11 57.5	+30.2	45.8	44
45	7 27.7	+25.5	44.0	8 10.8	+26.2	44.1	8 53.9	+26.8	44.2	9 36.8	+27.5	44.3	10 19.7	+28.2	44.5	11 02.5	+28.8	44.6	11 45.2	+29.4	44.7	12 27.7	+30.1	44.9	45
46	7 53.2	+25.4	43.1	8 37.0	+26.1	43.2	9 20.7	+26.7	43.3	10 04.3	+27.4	43.4	10 47.9	+27.9	43.6	11 31.3	+28.6	43.7	12 14.6	+29.3	43.8	12 57.8	+30.0	44.0	46
47	8 18.6	+25.3	42.2	9 03.1	+25.9	42.3	9 47.4	+26.6	42.4	10 31.7	+27.2	42.5	11 15.8	+27.9	42.7	11 59.9	+28.5	42.8	12 43.9	+29.1	42.9	13 27.8	+29.7	43.1	47
48	8 43.9	+25.2	41.3	9 29.0	+25.8	41.4	10 14.0	+26.4	41.5	10 58.9	+27.0	41.6	11 43.7	+27.6	41.8	12 28.4	+28.3	41.9	13 13.0	+28.9	42.0	13 57.5	+29.5	42.2	48
49	9 09.1	+25.0	40.4	9 54.8	+25.6	40.5	10 40.4	+26.2	40.6	11 25.9	+26.9	40.7	12 11.3	+27.5	40.8	12 56.7	+28.1	41.0	13 41.9	+28.7	41.1	14 27.0	+29.4	41.3	49
50	9 34.1	+24.8	39.4	10 20.4	+25.4	39.5	11 06.6	+26.1	39.7	11 52.8	+26.6	39.8	12 38.8	+27.3	39.9	13 24.8	+27.9	40.1	14 10.6	+28.5	40.2	14 56.4	+29.1	40.4	50
51	9 58.9	+24.7	38.5	10 45.8	+25.4	38.6	11 32.7	+25.9	38.7	12 19.4	+26.5	38.9	13 06.1	+27.1	39.0	13 52.7	+27.7	39.2	14 39.1	+28.3	39.3	15 25.5	+28.9	39.5	51
52	10 23.6	+24.6	37.6	11 11.2	+25.1	37.7	11 58.6	+25.7	37.8	12 45.9	+26.3	38.0	13 33.2	+26.9	38.1	14 20.4	+27.5	38.3	15 07.4	+28.1	38.4	15 54.4	+28.6	38.6	52
53	10 48.2	+24.4	36.7	11 36.3	+24.9	36.8	12 24.3	+25.5	36.9	13 12.2	+26.2	37.0	14 00.1	+26.7	37.2	14 47.9	+27.2	37.3	15 35.5	+27.9	37.5	16 23.0	+28.5	37.7	53
54	11 12.6	+24.2	35.7	12 01.2	+24.8	35.8	12 49.8	+25.4	36.0	13 38.4	+25.9	36.1	14 26.8	+26.5	36.3	15 15.1	+27.1	36.4	16 03.4	+27.6	36.6	16 51.5	+28.2	36.8	54
55	11 36.8	+24.0	34.8	12 26.0	+24.6	34.9	13 15.2	+25.1	35.0	14 04.3	+25.6	35.2	14 53.3	+26.2	35.3	15 42.2	+26.8	35.5	16 31.0	+27.3	35.7	17 19.7	+27.9	35.8	55
56	12 00.8	+23.8	33.9	12 50.6	+24.4	34.0	13 40.3	+24.9	34.1	14 29.9	+25.5	34.2	15 19.5	+26.0	34.4	16 09.0	+26.5	34.6	16 58.3	+27.1	34.7	17 47.6	+27.6	34.9	56
57	12 24.6	+23.7	32.9	13 15.0	+24.1	33.0	14 05.2	+24.7	33.2	14 55.4	+25.3	33.3	15 45.5	+25.8	33.5	16 35.5	+26.3	33.6	17 25.4	+26.9	33.8	18 15.2	+27.4	34.0	57
58	12 48.3	+23.4	32.0	13 39.1	+24.0	32.1	14 29.9	+24.5	32.2	15 20.7	+25.0	32.4	16 11.3	+25.5	32.5	17 01.8	+26.1	32.7	17 52.3	+26.6	32.9	18 42.6	+27.1	33.0	58
59	13 11.7	+23.3	31.0	14 03.1	+23.7	31.2	14 54.4	+24.3	31.3	15 45.7	+24.7	31.4	16 36.8	+25.3	31.6	17 27.9	+25.8	31.7	18 18.9	+26.3	31.9	19 09.7	+26.9	32.1	59
60	13 35.0	+23.0	30.1	14 26.8	+23.6	30.2	15 18.7	+24.0	30.3	16 10.4	+24.5	30.5	17 02.1	+25.0	30.6	17 53.7	+25.5	30.8	18 45.2	+26.0	31.0	19 36.6	+26.5	31.1	60
61	13 58.0	+22.8	29.1	14 50.4	+23.2	29.3	15 42.7	+23.7	29.4	16 34.9	+24.3	29.5	17 27.1	+24.7	29.7	18 19.2	+25.2	29.8	19 11.2	+25.7	30.0	20 03.1	+26.2	30.2	61
62	14 20.8	+22.5	28.2	15 13.6	+23.1	28.3	16 06.4	+23.5	28.4	16 59.2	+23.9	28.6	17 51.8	+24.5	28.7	18 44.4	+24.9	28.9	19 36.9	+25.4	29.1	20 29.3	+25.9	29.2	62
63	14 43.3	+22.4	27.2	15 36.7	+22.8	27.3	16 29.9	+23.3	27.5	17 23.1	+23.7	27.6	18 16.3	+24.1	27.8	19 09.3	+24.6	27.9	20 02.3	+25.1	28.1	20 55.2	+25.6	28.3	63
64	15 05.7	+22.1	26.3	15 59.5	+22.5	26.4	16 53.2	+22.9	26.5	17 46.8	+23.5	26.7	18 40.4	+23.9	26.8	19 33.9	+24.4	27.0	20 27.4	+24.8	27.1	21 20.8	+25.2	27.3	64
65	15 27.8	+21.8	25.3	16 22.0	+22.2	25.4	17 16.1	+22.7	25.5	18 10.3	+23.1	25.7	19 04.3	+23.6	25.8	19 58.3	+24.0	26.0	20 52.2	+24.4	26.1	21 46.0	+24.9	26.3	65
66	15 49.6	+21.6	24.3	16 44.2	+22.0	24.4	17 38.8	+22.4	24.6	18 33.4	+22.8	24.7	19 27.9	+23.2	24.9	20 22.3	+23.6	25.0	21 16.6	+24.1	25.2	22 10.9	+24.5	25.3	66
67	16 11.2	+21.3	23.4	17 06.2	+21.7	23.5	18 01.2	+22.2	23.6	18 56.2	+22.5	23.7	19 51.1	+22.9	23.9	20 45.9	+23.4	24.0	21 40.7	+23.7	24.2	22 35.4	+24.2	24.4	67
68	16 32.5	+21.0	22.4	17 27.9	+21.5	22.5	18 23.4	+21.8	22.6	19 18.7	+22.2	22.8	20 14.0	+22.6	22.9	21 09.3	+23.0	23.0	22 04.4	+23.4	23.2	22 59.6	+23.8	23.4	68
69	16 53.5	+20.8	21.4	17 49.4	+21.1	21.5	18 45.2	+21.5	21.6	19 40.9	+21.9	21.8	20 36.6	+22.3	21.9	21 32.3	+22.6	22.0	22 27.8	+23.1	22.2	23 23.4	+23.4	22.4	69
70	17 14.3	+20.5	20.4	18 10.5	+20.8	20.5	19 06.7	+21.2	20.7	20 02.8	+21.5	20.8	20 58.9	+21.9	20.9	21 54.9	+22.3	21.1	22 50.9	+22.6	21.2	23 46.8	+23.0	21.4	70
71	17 34.8	+20.2	19.4	18 31.3	+20.5	19.5	19 27.9	+20.8	19.7	20 24.3	+21.2	19.8	21 20.8	+21.5	19.9	22 17.2	+21.9	20.0	23 13.5	+22.3	20.2	24 09.8	+22.6	20.3	71
72	17 55.0	+19.8	18.4	18 51.8	+20.3	18.6	19 48.7	+20.5	18.7	20 45.5	+20.9	18.8	21 42.3	+21.2	18.9	22 39.1	+21.5	19.0	23 35.8	+21.8	19.2	24 32.4	+22.2	19.3	72
73	18 14.8	+19.6	17.5	19 12.1	+19.8	17.6	20 09.2	+20.2	17.7	21 06.4	+20.5	17.8	22 03.5	+20.8	17.9	23 00.6	+21.1	18.0	23 57.6	+21.5	18.2	24 54.6	+21.8	18.3	73
74	18 34.4	+19.3	16.5	19 31.9	+19.6	16.6	20 29.4	+19.9	16.7	21 26.9	+20.1	16.8	22 24.3	+20.5	16.9	23 21.7	+20.8	17.0	24 19.1	+21.0	17.1	25 16.4	+21.3	17.3	74
75	18 53.7	+18.9	15.5	19 51.5	+19.2	15.6	20 49.3	+19.4	15.7	21 47.0	+19.8	15.8	22 44.8	+20.0	15.9	23 42.5	+20.3	16.0	24 40.1	+20.6	16.1	25 37.7	+21.0	16.2	75
76	19 12.6	+18.6	14.5	20 10.7	+18.8	14.5	21 08.7	+19.2	14.6	22 06.8	+19.4	14.7	23 04.8	+19.6	14.8	24 02.8	+19.9	15.0	25 00.7	+20.2	15.1	25 58.7	+20.4	15.2	76
77	19 31.2	+18.3	13.4	20 29.5	+18.6	13.5	21 27.9	+18.7	13.6	22 26.2	+19.0	13.7	23 24.4	+19.3	13.8	24 22.7	+19.5	13.9	25 20.9	+19.8	14.0	26 19.1	+20.0	14.2	77
78	19 49.5	+17.9	12.4	20 48.1	+18.1	12.5	21 46.6	+18.4	12.6	22 45.2	+18.6	12.7	23 43.7	+18.8	12.8	24 42.2	+19.0	12.9	25 40.7	+19.3	13.0	26 39.1	+19.6	13.1	78
79	20 07.4	+17.6	11.4	21 06.2	+17.8	11.5	22 05.0	+18.0	11.6	23 03.8	+18.2	11.7	24 02.5	+18.4	11.7	25 01.2	+18.7	11.8	26 00.0	+18.8	11.9	26 58.7	+19.0	12.0	79
80	20 25.0	+17.2	10.4	21 24.0	+17.4	10.5	22 23.0	+17.6	10.5	23 22.0	+17.7	10.6	24 20.9	+18.0	10.7	25 19.9	+18.1	10.8	26 18.8	+18.4	10.9	27 17.7	+18.6	11.0	80
81	20 42.2	+16.9	9.4	21 41.4	+17.0	9.4	22 40.6	+17.2	9.5	23 39.7	+17.4	9.6	24 38.9	+17.5	9.7	25 38.0	+17.8	9.7	26 37.2	+17.9	9.8	27 36.3	+18.1	9.9	81
82	20 59.1	+16.4	8.4	21 58.4	+16.6	8.4	22 57.8	+16.7	8.5	23 57.1	+16.9	8.5	24 56.4	+17.1	8.6	25 55.8	+17.2	8.7	26 55.1	+17.4	8.7	27 54.4	+17.5	8.8	82
83	21 15.5	+16.1	7.3	22 15.0	+16.3	7.4	23 14.5	+16.4	7.4	24 14.0	+16.5	7.5	25 13.5	+16.7	7.5	26 13.0	+16.8	7.6	27 12.5	+16.9	7.7	28 11.9	+17.1	7.7	83
84	21 31.6	+15.8	6.3	22 31.3	+15.8	6.3	23 30.9	+16.0	6.4	24 30.5	+16.1	6.4	25 30.2	+16.1	6.5	26 29.8	+16.3	6.5	27 29.4	+16.4	6.6	28 29.0	+16.5	6.7	84
85	21 47.4	+15.3	5.2	22 47.1	+15.4	5.3	23 46.9	+15.5	5.3	24 46.6	+15.6	5.4	25 46.3	+15.7	5.4	26 46.1	+15.8	5.5	27 45.8	+15.9	5.5	28 45.5	+16.0	5.6	85
86	22 02.7	+14.9	4.2	23 02.5	+15.0	4.2	24 02.4	+15.1	4.3	25 02.2	+15.2	4.3	26 02.0	+15.3	4.3	27 01.9	+15.3	4.4	28 01.7	+15.4	4.4	29 01.5	+15.5	4.5	86
87	22 17.6	+14.6	3.2	23 17.5	+14.6	3.2	24 17.5	+14.6	3.2	25 17.4	+14.6	3.2	26 17.3	+14.7	3.3	27 17.2	+14.8	3.3	28 17.1	+14.8	3.3	29 17.0	+14.9	3.4	87
88	22 32.2	+14.1	2.1	23 32.1	+14.2	2.1	24 32.1	+14.2	2.1	25 32.0	+14.3	2.2	26 32.0	+14.3	2.2	27 32.0	+14.2	2.2	28 31.9	+14.3	2.2	29 31.9	+14.3	2.2	88
89	22 46.3	+13.7	1.1	23 46.3	+13.7	1.1	24 46.3	+13.7	1.1	25 46.3	+13.7	1.1	26 46.3	+13.7	1.1	27 46.2	+13.8	1.1	28 46.2	+13.8	1.1	29 46.2	+13.8	1.1	89
90	23 00.0	+13.3	0.0	24 00.0	+13.3	0.0	25 00.0	+13.3	0.0	26 00.0	+13.3	0.0	27 00.0	+13.2	0.0	28 00.0	+13.2	0.0	29 00.0	+13.2	0.0	30 00.0	+13.2	0.0	90
	23°			24°			25°			26°			27°			28°			29°			30°			

S. Lat. { L.H.A. greater than 180° ....Zn=180°−Z
L.H.A. less than 180°...........Zn=180°+Z

LATITUDE SAME NAME AS DECLINATION L.H.A. 103°, 257°

Dec.	23°			24°			25°			26°			27°			28°			29°			30°			Dec.
	Hc	d	Z	Hc	d	Z	Hc	d	Z	Hc	d	Z	Hc	d	Z	Hc	d	Z	Hc	d	Z	Hc	d	Z	
°	° ′	′	°	° ′	′	°	° ′	′	°	° ′	′	°	° ′	′	°	° ′	′	°	° ′	′	°	° ′	′	°	°
0	11 02.0	+23.8	94.7	10 56.9	+24.8	94.9	10 51.7	+25.7	95.1	10 46.2	+26.7	95.3	10 40.5	+27.7	95.5	10 34.7	+28.6	95.7	10 28.6	+29.5	95.9	10 22.4	+30.4	96.1	0
1	11 25.8	+23.6	93.8	11 21.7	+24.6	94.0	11 17.4	+25.6	94.2	11 12.9	+26.5	94.4	11 08.2	+27.5	94.6	11 03.3	+28.4	94.8	10 58.1	+29.4	95.0	10 52.8	+30.3	95.2	1
2	11 49.4	+23.5	92.9	11 46.3	+24.4	93.1	11 43.0	+25.4	93.3	11 39.4	+26.4	93.5	11 35.7	+27.3	93.7	11 31.7	+28.2	93.9	11 27.5	+29.2	94.1	11 23.1	+30.1	94.3	2
3	12 12.9	+23.2	91.9	12 10.7	+24.3	92.1	12 08.4	+25.2	92.4	12 05.8	+26.2	92.6	12 03.0	+27.1	92.8	11 59.9	+28.1	93.0	11 56.7	+29.0	93.2	11 53.2	+30.0	93.4	3
4	12 36.1	+23.0	91.0	12 35.0	+24.0	91.2	12 33.6	+25.0	91.4	12 32.0	+25.9	91.7	12 30.1	+26.9	91.9	12 28.0	+27.9	92.1	12 25.7	+28.8	92.3	12 23.2	+29.7	92.5	4
5	12 59.1	+22.9	90.0	12 59.0	+23.8	90.3	12 58.6	+24.8	90.5	12 57.9	+25.8	90.7	12 57.0	+26.8	91.0	12 55.9	+27.7	91.2	12 54.5	+28.7	91.4	12 52.9	+29.6	91.7	5
6	13 22.0	+22.6	89.1	13 22.8	+23.6	89.3	13 23.4	+24.6	89.6	13 23.7	+25.6	89.8	13 23.8	+26.6	90.0	13 23.6	+27.5	90.3	13 23.2	+28.5	90.5	13 22.5	+29.5	90.8	6
7	13 44.6	+22.4	88.1	13 46.4	+23.4	88.4	13 48.0	+24.4	88.6	13 49.3	+25.4	88.9	13 50.4	+26.3	89.1	13 51.1	+27.4	89.4	13 51.7	+28.2	89.6	13 52.0	+29.2	89.9	7
8	14 07.0	+22.2	87.2	14 09.8	+23.2	87.4	14 12.4	+24.1	87.7	14 14.7	+25.1	87.9	14 16.7	+26.1	88.2	14 18.5	+27.0	88.4	14 19.9	+28.1	88.7	14 21.2	+29.0	89.0	8
9	14 29.2	+21.9	86.2	14 33.0	+22.9	86.5	14 36.5	+24.0	86.7	14 39.8	+24.9	87.0	14 42.8	+25.9	87.3	14 45.5	+26.9	87.5	14 48.0	+27.8	87.8	14 50.2	+28.8	88.1	9
10	14 51.1	+21.7	85.3	14 55.9	+22.8	85.5	15 00.5	+23.7	85.8	15 04.7	+24.7	86.1	15 08.7	+25.7	86.3	15 12.4	+26.7	86.6	15 15.8	+27.7	86.9	15 19.0	+28.5	87.1	10
11	15 12.8	+21.5	84.3	15 18.7	+22.4	84.6	15 24.2	+23.4	84.8	15 29.4	+24.5	85.1	15 34.4	+25.4	85.4	15 39.1	+26.4	85.7	15 43.5	+27.3	86.0	15 47.5	+28.4	86.2	11
12	15 34.3	+21.2	83.3	15 41.1	+22.2	83.6	15 47.6	+23.3	83.9	15 53.9	+24.2	84.2	15 59.8	+25.2	84.5	16 05.5	+26.2	84.7	16 10.8	+27.2	85.0	16 15.9	+28.1	85.3	12
13	15 55.5	+20.9	82.4	16 03.3	+22.0	82.6	16 10.9	+22.9	82.9	16 18.1	+23.9	83.2	16 25.0	+25.0	83.5	16 31.7	+25.9	83.8	16 38.0	+26.9	84.1	16 44.0	+27.9	84.4	13
14	16 16.4	+20.7	81.4	16 25.3	+21.6	81.7	16 33.8	+22.7	82.0	16 42.0	+23.7	82.3	16 50.0	+24.6	82.6	16 57.6	+25.6	82.9	17 04.9	+26.6	83.2	17 11.9	+27.6	83.5	14
15	16 37.1	+20.4	80.4	16 46.9	+21.4	80.7	16 56.5	+22.4	81.0	17 05.7	+23.4	81.3	17 14.6	+24.4	81.6	17 23.2	+25.4	81.9	17 31.5	+26.4	82.2	17 39.5	+27.3	82.5	15
16	16 57.5	+20.1	79.4	17 08.3	+21.2	79.7	17 18.9	+22.1	80.0	17 29.1	+23.1	80.3	17 39.0	+24.2	80.6	17 48.6	+25.1	81.0	17 57.9	+26.1	81.3	18 06.8	+27.1	81.6	16
17	17 17.6	+19.8	78.4	17 29.5	+20.8	78.7	17 41.0	+21.9	79.1	17 52.2	+22.9	79.4	18 03.2	+23.8	79.7	18 13.7	+24.9	80.0	18 24.0	+25.8	80.3	18 33.9	+26.8	80.7	17
18	17 37.4	+19.5	77.4	17 50.3	+20.5	77.8	18 02.9	+21.5	78.1	18 15.1	+22.5	78.4	18 27.0	+23.5	78.7	18 38.6	+24.5	79.0	18 49.8	+25.5	79.4	19 00.7	+26.5	79.7	18
19	17 56.9	+19.2	76.5	18 10.8	+20.3	76.8	18 24.4	+21.2	77.1	18 37.6	+22.3	77.4	18 50.5	+23.3	77.7	19 03.1	+24.2	78.1	19 15.3	+25.2	78.4	19 27.2	+26.2	78.8	19
20	18 16.1	+19.0	75.5	18 31.1	+19.9	75.8	18 45.6	+21.0	76.1	18 59.9	+21.9	76.4	19 13.8	+22.9	76.8	19 27.3	+23.9	77.1	19 40.5	+24.9	77.5	19 53.4	+25.9	77.8	20
21	18 35.1	+18.5	74.5	18 51.0	+19.6	74.8	19 06.6	+20.6	75.1	19 21.8	+21.6	75.5	19 36.7	+22.6	75.8	19 51.2	+23.6	76.1	20 05.4	+24.6	76.5	20 19.3	+25.5	76.9	21
22	18 53.6	+18.3	73.4	19 10.6	+19.2	73.8	19 27.2	+20.2	74.1	19 43.4	+21.3	74.5	19 59.3	+22.3	74.8	20 14.8	+23.3	75.2	20 30.0	+24.3	75.5	20 44.8	+25.3	75.9	22
23	19 11.9	+17.9	72.4	19 29.8	+19.0	72.8	19 47.4	+20.0	73.1	20 04.7	+20.9	73.5	20 21.6	+21.9	73.8	20 38.1	+23.0	74.2	20 54.3	+23.9	74.5	21 10.1	+24.9	74.9	23
24	19 29.8	+17.6	71.4	19 48.8	+18.6	71.8	20 07.4	+19.6	72.1	20 25.6	+20.6	72.5	20 43.5	+21.6	72.8	21 01.1	+22.6	73.2	21 18.2	+23.6	73.6	21 35.0	+24.6	73.9	24
25	19 47.4	+17.3	70.4	20 07.4	+18.2	70.8	20 27.0	+19.2	71.1	20 46.2	+20.3	71.5	21 05.1	+21.3	71.8	21 23.7	+22.2	72.2	21 41.8	+23.2	72.6	21 59.6	+24.2	73.0	25
26	20 04.7	+16.9	69.4	20 25.6	+17.9	69.7	20 46.2	+18.9	70.1	21 06.5	+19.9	70.5	21 26.4	+20.9	70.8	21 45.9	+21.9	71.2	22 05.0	+22.9	71.6	22 23.8	+23.9	72.0	26
27	20 21.6	+16.5	68.4	20 43.5	+17.6	68.7	21 05.1	+18.6	69.1	21 26.4	+19.5	69.4	21 47.3	+20.5	69.8	22 07.8	+21.5	70.2	22 27.9	+22.5	70.6	22 47.7	+23.5	71.0	27
28	20 38.1	+16.2	67.3	21 01.1	+17.1	67.7	21 23.7	+18.1	68.1	21 45.9	+19.1	68.4	22 07.8	+20.1	68.8	22 29.3	+21.1	69.2	22 50.4	+22.1	69.6	23 11.2	+23.1	70.0	28
29	20 54.3	+15.8	66.3	21 18.2	+16.8	66.7	21 41.8	+17.8	67.0	22 05.0	+18.8	67.4	22 27.9	+19.8	67.8	22 50.4	+20.8	68.2	23 12.5	+21.8	68.6	23 34.3	+22.7	69.0	29
30	21 10.1	+15.4	65.3	21 35.0	+16.4	65.6	21 59.6	+17.4	66.0	22 23.8	+18.4	66.4	22 47.7	+19.3	66.8	23 11.2	+20.3	67.2	23 34.3	+21.3	67.5	23 57.0	+22.3	68.0	30
31	21 25.5	+15.1	64.2	21 51.4	+16.0	64.6	22 17.0	+17.0	65.0	22 42.2	+18.0	65.3	23 07.0	+19.0	65.7	23 31.5	+19.9	66.1	23 55.6	+20.9	66.5	24 19.3	+21.9	66.9	31
32	21 40.6	+14.6	63.2	22 07.4	+15.7	63.6	22 34.0	+16.6	63.9	23 00.2	+17.5	64.3	23 26.0	+18.5	64.7	23 51.4	+19.6	65.1	24 16.5	+20.5	65.5	24 41.2	+21.5	65.9	32
33	21 55.2	+14.3	62.2	22 23.1	+15.2	62.5	22 50.6	+16.2	62.9	23 17.7	+17.2	63.3	23 44.5	+18.2	63.7	24 11.0	+19.1	64.1	24 37.0	+20.1	64.5	25 02.7	+21.1	64.9	33
34	22 09.5	+13.8	61.1	22 38.3	+14.8	61.5	23 06.8	+15.7	61.8	23 34.9	+16.7	62.2	24 02.7	+17.7	62.6	24 30.1	+18.7	63.0	24 57.1	+19.7	63.4	25 23.8	+20.6	63.9	34
35	22 23.3	+13.5	60.1	22 53.1	+14.4	60.4	23 22.5	+15.4	60.8	23 51.6	+16.4	61.2	24 20.4	+17.3	61.6	24 48.8	+18.2	62.0	25 16.8	+19.2	62.4	25 44.4	+20.2	62.8	35
36	22 36.8	+13.0	59.0	23 07.5	+14.0	59.4	23 37.9	+14.9	59.7	24 08.0	+15.8	60.1	24 37.7	+16.8	60.5	25 07.0	+17.8	60.9	25 36.0	+18.7	61.3	26 04.6	+19.7	61.8	36
37	22 49.8	+12.6	57.9	23 21.5	+13.5	58.3	23 52.8	+14.5	58.7	24 23.8	+15.5	59.1	24 54.5	+16.4	59.5	25 24.8	+17.3	59.9	25 54.7	+18.3	60.3	26 24.3	+19.2	60.7	37
38	23 02.4	+12.2	56.9	23 35.0	+13.1	57.2	24 07.3	+14.0	57.6	24 39.3	+14.9	58.0	25 10.9	+15.9	58.4	25 42.1	+16.9	58.8	26 13.0	+17.9	59.2	26 43.5	+18.8	59.7	38
39	23 14.6	+11.7	55.8	23 48.1	+12.7	56.2	24 21.3	+13.6	56.6	24 54.2	+14.6	56.9	25 26.8	+15.5	57.3	25 59.0	+16.4	57.7	26 30.9	+17.3	58.2	27 02.3	+18.3	58.6	39
40	23 26.3	+11.3	54.8	24 00.8	+12.2	55.1	24 34.9	+13.2	55.5	25 08.8	+14.0	55.9	25 42.3	+15.0	56.3	26 15.4	+15.9	56.7	26 48.2	+16.9	57.1	27 20.6	+17.8	57.5	40
41	23 37.6	+10.9	53.7	24 13.0	+11.8	54.0	24 48.1	+12.7	54.4	25 22.8	+13.6	54.8	25 57.3	+14.5	55.2	26 31.3	+15.5	55.6	27 05.1	+16.3	56.0	27 38.4	+17.3	56.4	41
42	23 48.5	+10.4	52.6	24 24.8	+11.3	53.0	25 00.8	+12.2	53.3	25 36.4	+13.1	53.7	26 11.8	+14.0	54.1	26 46.8	+14.9	54.5	27 21.4	+15.9	54.9	27 55.7	+16.8	55.4	42
43	23 58.9	+10.0	51.5	24 36.1	+10.8	51.9	25 13.0	+11.7	52.3	25 49.5	+12.7	52.6	26 25.8	+13.5	53.0	27 01.7	+14.5	53.4	27 37.3	+15.4	53.8	28 12.5	+16.3	54.3	43
44	24 08.9	+9.5	50.5	24 46.9	+10.4	50.8	25 24.7	+11.3	51.2	26 02.2	+12.1	51.5	26 39.3	+13.1	51.9	27 16.2	+13.9	52.3	27 52.7	+14.8	52.7	28 28.8	+15.7	53.2	44
45	24 18.4	+9.0	49.4	24 57.3	+9.9	49.7	25 36.0	+10.7	50.1	26 14.3	+11.7	50.5	26 52.4	+12.5	50.8	27 30.1	+13.4	51.2	28 07.5	+14.3	51.7	28 44.5	+15.3	52.1	45
46	24 27.4	+8.6	48.3	25 07.2	+9.5	48.6	25 46.7	+10.3	49.0	26 26.0	+11.1	49.4	27 04.9	+12.0	49.7	27 43.5	+12.9	50.1	28 21.8	+13.8	50.5	28 59.8	+14.6	51.0	46
47	24 36.0	+8.1	47.2	25 16.7	+8.9	47.5	25 57.0	+9.8	47.9	26 37.1	+10.7	48.3	27 16.9	+11.5	48.6	27 56.4	+12.4	49.0	28 35.6	+13.2	49.4	29 14.4	+14.1	49.9	47
48	24 44.1	+7.7	46.1	25 25.6	+8.5	46.4	26 06.8	+9.3	46.8	26 47.8	+10.1	47.2	27 28.4	+11.0	47.5	28 08.8	+11.8	47.9	28 48.8	+12.7	48.3	29 28.5	+13.6	48.7	48
49	24 51.8	+7.1	45.0	25 34.1	+7.9	45.3	26 16.1	+8.8	45.7	26 57.9	+9.6	46.1	27 39.4	+10.4	46.4	28 20.6	+11.3	46.8	29 01.5	+12.1	47.2	29 42.1	+13.0	47.6	49
50	24 58.9	+6.7	43.9	25 42.0	+7.5	44.2	26 24.9	+8.3	44.6	27 07.5	+9.1	44.9	27 49.8	+9.9	45.3	28 31.9	+10.7	45.7	29 13.6	+11.6	46.1	29 55.1	+12.4	46.5	50
51	25 05.6	+6.2	42.8	25 49.5	+7.0	43.1	26 33.2	+7.7	43.5	27 16.6	+8.5	43.8	27 59.7	+9.4	44.2	28 42.6	+10.2	44.6	29 25.2	+11.0	45.0	30 07.5	+11.8	45.4	51
52	25 11.8	+5.7	41.7	25 56.5	+6.4	42.0	26 40.9	+7.3	42.4	27 25.1	+8.0	42.7	28 09.1	+8.8	43.1	28 52.8	+9.6	43.5	29 36.2	+10.4	43.8	30 19.3	+11.3	44.2	52
53	25 17.5	+5.2	40.6	26 02.9	+6.0	40.9	26 48.2	+6.7	41.3	27 33.1	+7.5	41.6	28 17.9	+8.2	42.0	29 02.4	+9.0	42.3	29 46.6	+9.8	42.7	30 30.6	+10.6	43.1	53
54	25 22.7	+4.7	39.5	26 08.9	+5.5	39.8	26 54.9	+6.2	40.1	27 40.6	+7.0	40.5	28 26.1	+7.7	40.8	29 11.4	+8.5	41.2	29 56.4	+9.3	41.6	30 41.2	+10.0	42.0	54
55	25 27.4	+4.3	38.4	26 14.4	+4.9	38.7	27 01.1	+5.6	39.0	27 47.6	+6.4	39.4	28 33.8	+7.2	39.7	29 19.9	+7.9	40.1	30 05.7	+8.7	40.4	30 51.2	+9.5	40.8	55
56	25 31.7	+3.7	37.3	26 19.3	+4.4	37.6	27 06.7	+5.2	37.9	27 54.0	+5.8	38.2	28 41.0	+6.6	38.6	29 27.8	+7.3	38.9	30 14.4	+8.0	39.3	31 00.7	+8.8	39.7	56
57	25 35.4	+3.2	36.2	26 23.7	+3.9	36.5	27 11.9	+4.6	36.8	27 59.8	+5.3	37.1	28 47.6	+6.0	37.4	29 35.1	+6.7	37.8	30 22.4	+7.5	38.1	31 09.5	+8.2	38.5	57
58	25 38.6	+2.8	35.1	26 27.6	+3.4	35.4	27 16.5	+4.0	35.7	28 05.1	+4.8	36.0	28 53.6	+5.4	36.3	29 41.8	+6.2	36.6	30 29.9	+6.8	37.0	31 17.7	+7.5	37.3	58
59	25 41.4	+2.2	34.0	26 31.0	+2.9	34.3	27 20.5	+3.6	34.6	28 09.9	+4.1	34.9	28 59.0	+4.9	35.2	29 48.0	+5.5	35.5	30 36.7	+6.2	35.8	31 25.2	+7.0	36.2	59
60	25 43.6	+1.7	32.9	26 33.9	+2.3	33.1	27 24.1	+2.9	33.4	28 14.0	+3.7	33.7	29 03.9	+4.2	34.0	29 53.5	+4.9	34.3	30 42.9	+5.7	34.7	31 32.2	+6.3	35.0	60
61	25 45.3	+1.2	31.8	26 36.2	+1.9	32.0	27 27.0	+2.5	32.3	28 17.7	+3.0	32.6	29 08.1	+3.7	32.9	29 58.4	+4.4	33.2	30 48.6	+5.0	33.5	31 38.5	+5.7	33.8	61
62	25 46.5	+0.7	30.7	26 38.1	+1.3	30.9	27 29.5	+1.9	31.2	28 20.7	+2.5	31.5	29 11.8	+3.2	31.7	30 02.8	+3.7	32.0	30 53.6	+4.3	32.4	31 44.2	+5.0	32.7	62
63	25 47.2	+0.2	29.6	26 39.4	+0.7	29.8	27 31.4	+1.3	30.0	28 23.2	+2.0	30.3	29 15.0	+2.5	30.6	30 06.5	+3.2	30.9	30 57.9	+3.8	31.2	31 49.2	+4.4	31.5	63
64	25 47.4	-0.3	28.4	26 40.1	+0.3	28.7	27 32.7	+0.8	28.9	28 25.2	+1.3	29.2	29 17.5	+1.9	29.4	30 09.7	+2.5	29.7	31 01.7	+3.1	30.0	31 53.6	+3.7	30.3	64
65	25 47.1	-0.8	27.3	26 40.4	-0.3	27.6	27 33.5	+0.3	27.8	28 26.5	+0.8	28.0	29 19.4	+1.4	28.3	30 12.2	+1.9	28.6	31 04.8	+2.5	28.9	31 57.3	+3.1	29.2	65
66	25 46.3	-1.3	26.2	26 40.1	-0.8	26.4	27 33.8	-0.3	26.7	28 27.3	+0.3	26.9	29 20.8	+0.8	27.2	30 14.1	+1.3	27.4	31 07.3	+1.9	27.7	32 00.4	+2.4	28.0	66
67	25 45.0	-1.8	25.1	26 39.3	-1.3	25.3	27 33.5	-0.8	25.5	28 27.6	-0.4	25.8	29 21.6	+0.1	26.0	30 15.4	+0.7	26.3	31 09.2	+1.2	26.5	32 02.8	+1.8	26.8	67
68	25 43.2	-2.3	24.0	26 38.0	-1.9	24.2	27 32.7	-1.4	24.4	28 27.2	-0.9	24.6	29 21.7	-0.4	24.9	30 16.1	+0.1	25.1	31 10.4	+0.6	25.4	32 04.6	+1.1	25.6	68
69	25 40.9	-2.8	22.9	26 36.1	-2.4	23.1	27 31.3	-2.0	23.3	28 26.3	-1.4	23.5	29 21.3	-1.0	23.7	30 16.2	-0.5	23.9	31 11.0	0.0	24.2	32 05.7	+0.4	24.4	69
70	25 38.1	-3.4	21.8	26 33.7	-2.9	22.0	27 29.3	-2.4	22.2	28 24.9	-2.1	22.4	29 20.3	-1.6	22.6	30 15.7	-1.2	22.8	31 11.0	-0.7	23.0	32 06.1	-0.2	23.3	70
71	25 34.7	-3.8	20.7	26 30.8	-3.4	20.8	27 26.9	-3.0	21.0	28 22.8	-2.6	21.2	29 18.7	-2.1	21.4	30 14.5	-1.7	21.6	31 10.3	-1.3	21.9	32 05.9	-0.8	22.1	71
72	25 30.9	-4.3	19.6	26 27.4	-3.9	19.7	27 23.9	-3.6	19.9	28 20.2	-3.1	20.1	29 16.6	-2.8	20.3	30 12.8	-2.4	20.5	31 09.0	-2.0	20.7	32 05.1	-1.5	20.9	72
73	25 26.6	-4.8	18.5	26 23.5	-4.5	18.6	27 20.3	-4.1	18.8	28 17.1	-3.7	19.0	29 13.8	-3.4	19.1	30 10.4	-2.9	19.3	31 07.0	-2.5	19.5	32 03.6	-2.2	19.7	73
74	25 21.8	-5.3	17.4	26 19.0	-5.0	17.5	27 16.2	-4.6	17.7	28 13.4	-4.3	17.8	29 10.4	-3.9	18.0	30 07.5	-3.6	18.2	31 04.5	-3.2	18.3	32 01.4	-2.8	18.5	74
75	25 16.5	-5.8	16.3	26 14.0	-5.5	16.4	27 11.6	-5.2	16.5	28 09.1	-4.9	16.7	29 06.5	-4.5	16.8	30 03.9	-4.1	17.0	31 01.3	-3.9	17.2	31 58.6	-3.5	17.4	75
76	25 10.7	-6.3	15.2	26 08.5	-5.9	15.3	27 06.4	-5.7	15.4	28 04.2	-5.4	15.6	29 02.0	-5.1	15.7	29 59.8	-4.8	15.9	30 57.4	-4.4	16.0	31 55.1	-4.1	16.2	76
77	25 04.4	-6.8	14.1	26 02.6	-6.5	14.2	27 00.7	-6.2	14.3	27 58.8	-5.9	14.4	28 56.9	-5.6	14.6	29 55.0	-5.4	14.7	30 53.0	-5.1	14.9	31 51.0	-4.8	15.0	77
78	24 57.6	-7.3	13.0	25 56.1	-7.1	13.1	26 54.5	-6.8	13.2	27 52.9	-6.5	13.3	28 51.3	-6.3	13.4	29 49.6	-6.0	13.6	30 47.9	-5.7	13.7	31 46.2	-5.4	13.8	78
79	24 50.3	-7.7	11.9	25 49.0	-7.5	12.0	26 47.7	-7.2	12.1	27 46.4	-7.0	12.2	28 45.0	-6.8	12.3	29 43.6	-6.5	12.4	30 42.2	-6.3	12.5	31 40.8	-6.1	12.7	79
80	24 42.6	-8.2	10.8	25 41.5	-8.0	10.9	26 40.5	-7.8	11.0	27 39.4	-7.6	11.1	28 38.2	-7.3	11.2	29 37.1	-7.2	11.3	30 35.9	-6.9	11.4	31 34.7	-6.7	11.5	80
81	24 34.4	-8.7	9.7	25 33.5	-8.4	9.8	26 32.7	-8.3	9.8	27 31.8	-8.1	9.9	28 30.9	-8.0	10.0	29 29.9	-7.7	10.1	30 29.0	-7.5	10.2	31 28.0	-7.3	10.3	81
82	24 25.7	-9.1	8.6	25 25.1	-9.0	8.7	26 24.4	-8.8	8.7	27 23.7	-8.7	8.8	28 22.9	-8.4	8.9	29 22.2	-8.3	9.0	30 21.5	-8.2	9.1	31 20.7	-7.9	9.2	82
83	24 16.6	-9.6	7.5	25 16.1	-9.5	7.6	26 15.6	-9.4	7.6	27 15.0	-9.2	7.7	28 14.5	-9.1	7.8	29 13.9	-8.9	7.9	30 13.3	-8.7	7.9	31 12.8	-8.6	8.0	83
84	24 07.0	-10.1	6.4	25 06.6	-9.9	6.5	26 06.2	-9.8	6.5	27 05.8	-9.7	6.6	28 05.4	-9.5	6.7	29 05.0	-9.4	6.7	30 04.6	-9.3	6.8	31 04.2	-9.2	6.9	84
85	23 56.9	-10.5	5.4	24 56.7	-10.4	5.4	25 56.4	-10.3	5.4	26 56.1	-10.2	5.5	27 55.9	-10.2	5.5	28 55.6	-10.0	5.6	29 55.3	-9.9	5.6	30 55.0	-9.8	5.7	85
86	23 46.4	-10.9	4.3	24 46.3	-10.9	4.3	25 46.1	-10.8	4.3	26 45.9	-10.7	4.4	27 45.7	-10.6	4.4	28 45.6	-10.6	4.5	29 45.4	-10.5	4.5	30 45.2	-10.4	4.6	86
87	23 35.5	-11.4	3.2	24 35.4	-11.4	3.2	25 35.3	-11.3	3.3	26 35.2	-11.2	3.3	27 35.1	-11.2	3.3	28 35.0	-11.1	3.3	29 34.9	-11.1	3.4	30 34.8	-11.0	3.4	87
88	23 24.1	-11.8	2.1	24 24.0	-11.7	2.1	25 24.0	-11.8	2.2	26 24.0	-11.8	2.2	27 23.9	-11.7	2.2	28 23.9	-11.7	2.2	29 23.8	-11.6	2.2	30 23.8	-11.6	2.3	88
89	23 12.3	-12.3	1.1	24 12.3	-12.3	1.1	25 12.2	-12.2	1.1	26 12.2	-12.2	1.1	27 12.2	-12.2	1.1	28 12.2	-12.2	1.1	29 12.2	-12.2	1.1	30 12.2	-12.2	1.1	89
90	23 00.0	-12.7	0.0	24 00.0	-12.7	0.0	25 00.0	-12.7	0.0	26 00.0	-12.7	0.0	27 00.0	-12.7	0.0	28 00.0	-12.7	0.0	29 00.0	-12.8	0.0	30 00.0	-12.8	0.0	90
	23°			24°			25°			26°			27°			28°			29°			30°			

78°, 282° L.H.A. **LATITUDE SAME NAME AS DECLINATION**

LATITUDE CONTRARY NAME TO DECLINATION — L.H.A. 78°, 282°

Dec.	23°			24°			25°			26°			27°			28°			29°			30°			Dec.
	Hc	d	Z	Hc	d	Z	Hc	d	Z	Hc	d	Z	Hc	d	Z	Hc	d	Z	Hc	d	Z	Hc	d	Z	
°	° ′	′	°	° ′	′	°	° ′	′	°	° ′	′	°	° ′	′	°	° ′	′	°	° ′	′	°	° ′	′	°	°
0	11 02.0	−24.0	94.7	10 56.9	−24.9	94.9	10 51.7	−25.9	95.1	10 46.2	−26.8	95.3	10 40.5	−27.8	95.5	10 34.7	−28.7	95.7	10 28.6	−29.6	95.9	10 22.4	−30.6	96.1	0
1	10 38.0	−24.1	95.7	10 32.0	−25.1	95.9	10 25.8	−26.1	96.1	10 19.4	−27.0	96.2	10 12.7	−27.9	96.4	10 06.0	−28.9	96.6	9 59.0	−29.8	96.8	9 51.8	−30.7	96.9	1
2	10 13.9	−24.3	96.6	10 06.9	−25.2	96.8	9 59.7	−26.2	97.0	9 52.4	−27.2	97.1	9 44.8	−28.1	97.3	9 37.1	−29.0	97.5	9 29.2	−29.9	97.6	9 21.1	−30.8	97.8	2
3	9 49.6	−24.4	97.5	9 41.7	−25.4	97.7	9 33.5	−26.3	97.9	9 25.2	−27.3	98.0	9 16.7	−28.2	98.2	9 08.1	−29.2	98.4	8 59.3	−30.1	98.5	8 50.3	−31.0	98.7	3
4	9 25.2	−24.6	98.5	9 16.3	−25.6	98.6	9 07.2	−26.5	98.8	8 57.9	−27.4	98.9	8 48.5	−28.3	99.1	8 38.9	−29.2	99.3	8 29.2	−30.2	99.4	8 19.3	−31.0	99.5	4
5	9 00.6	−24.7	99.4	8 50.7	−25.7	99.5	8 40.7	−26.6	99.7	8 30.5	−27.5	99.8	8 20.2	−28.5	100.0	8 09.7	−29.4	100.1	7 59.0	−30.2	100.3	7 48.3	−31.2	100.4	5
6	8 35.9	−24.9	100.3	8 25.0	−25.8	100.5	8 14.1	−26.8	100.6	8 03.0	−27.7	100.7	7 51.7	−28.6	100.9	7 40.3	−29.5	101.0	7 28.8	−30.4	101.1	7 17.1	−31.3	101.3	6
7	8 11.0	−25.0	101.2	7 59.2	−25.9	101.4	7 47.3	−26.8	101.5	7 35.3	−27.8	101.6	7 23.1	−28.7	101.8	7 10.8	−29.6	101.9	6 58.4	−30.5	102.0	6 45.8	−31.3	102.1	7
8	7 46.0	−25.1	102.2	7 33.3	−26.0	102.3	7 20.5	−27.0	102.4	7 07.5	−27.8	102.5	6 54.4	−28.7	102.7	6 41.2	−29.6	102.8	6 27.9	−30.5	102.9	6 14.5	−31.5	103.0	8
9	7 20.9	−25.2	103.1	7 07.3	−26.2	103.2	6 53.5	−27.0	103.3	6 39.7	−28.0	103.4	6 25.7	−28.9	103.5	6 11.6	−29.8	103.6	5 57.4	−30.7	103.7	5 43.0	−31.5	103.8	9
10	6 55.7	−25.3	104.0	6 41.1	−26.2	104.1	6 26.5	−27.2	104.2	6 11.7	−28.1	104.3	5 56.8	−29.0	104.4	5 41.8	−29.8	104.5	5 26.7	−30.7	104.6	5 11.5	−31.6	104.7	10
11	6 30.4	−25.4	104.9	6 14.9	−26.3	105.0	5 59.3	−27.2	105.1	5 43.6	−28.1	105.2	5 27.8	−29.0	105.3	5 12.0	−29.9	105.4	4 56.0	−30.8	105.5	4 39.9	−31.6	105.6	11
12	6 05.0	−25.5	105.8	5 48.6	−26.4	105.9	5 32.1	−27.3	106.0	5 15.5	−28.2	106.1	4 58.8	−29.1	106.2	4 42.1	−30.0	106.3	4 25.2	−30.8	106.3	4 08.3	−31.7	106.4	12
13	5 39.5	−25.6	106.7	5 22.2	−26.5	106.8	5 04.8	−27.4	106.9	4 47.3	−28.3	107.0	4 29.7	−29.1	107.1	4 12.1	−30.1	107.1	3 54.4	−30.9	107.2	3 36.6	−31.7	107.3	13
14	5 13.9	−25.7	107.6	4 55.7	−26.6	107.7	4 37.4	−27.5	107.8	4 19.0	−28.3	107.9	4 00.6	−29.3	107.9	3 42.0	−30.0	108.0	3 23.5	−31.0	108.1	3 04.9	−31.8	108.1	14
15	4 48.2	−25.7	108.5	4 29.1	−26.7	108.6	4 09.9	−27.5	108.7	3 50.7	−28.4	108.7	3 31.3	−29.2	108.8	3 12.0	−30.2	108.9	2 52.5	−30.9	108.9	2 33.1	−31.8	109.0	15
16	4 22.5	−25.9	109.4	4 02.4	−26.6	109.5	3 42.4	−27.6	109.6	3 22.3	−28.5	109.6	3 02.1	−29.3	109.7	2 41.8	−30.1	109.7	2 21.6	−31.0	109.8	2 01.3	−31.9	109.8	16
17	3 56.6	−25.8	110.3	3 35.8	−26.8	110.4	3 14.8	−27.6	110.5	2 53.8	−28.5	110.5	2 32.8	−29.4	110.6	2 11.7	−30.2	110.6	1 50.6	−31.1	110.6	1 29.4	−31.9	110.7	17
18	3 30.8	−25.9	111.2	3 09.0	−26.8	111.3	2 47.2	−27.7	111.3	2 25.3	−28.5	111.4	2 03.4	−29.4	111.4	1 41.5	−30.2	111.5	1 19.5	−31.0	111.5	0 57.5	−31.8	111.5	18
19	3 04.9	−26.0	112.2	2 42.2	−26.8	112.2	2 19.5	−27.7	112.2	1 56.8	−28.5	112.3	1 34.0	−29.4	112.3	1 11.3	−30.3	112.3	0 48.5	−31.1	112.3	0 25.7	−31.9	112.3	19
20	2 38.9	−26.0	113.1	2 15.4	−26.9	113.1	1 51.8	−27.7	113.1	1 28.3	−28.6	113.2	1 04.6	−29.4	113.2	0 41.0	−30.2	113.2	0 17.4	−31.1	113.2	0 06.2	+31.9	66.8	20
21	2 12.9	−26.0	114.0	1 48.5	−26.9	114.0	1 24.1	−27.7	114.0	0 59.7	−28.6	114.0	0 35.2	−29.4	114.0	0 10.8	−30.3	114.1	0 13.7	+31.0	65.9	0 38.1	+31.9	66.0	21
22	1 46.9	−26.1	114.9	1 21.6	−26.9	114.9	0 56.4	−27.8	114.9	0 31.1	−28.6	114.9	0 05.8	−29.4	114.9	0 19.5	+30.2	65.1	0 44.7	+31.1	65.1	1 10.0	+31.8	65.1	22
23	1 20.8	−26.1	115.8	0 54.7	−26.9	115.8	0 28.6	−27.8	115.8	0 02.5	−28.6	115.8	0 23.6	+29.4	64.2	0 49.7	+30.2	64.2	1 15.8	+31.0	64.2	1 41.8	+31.9	64.3	23
24	0 54.7	−26.1	116.7	0 27.8	−27.0	116.7	0 00.8	−27.7	116.7	0 26.1	+28.6	63.3	0 53.0	+29.4	63.3	1 19.9	+30.2	63.4	1 46.8	+31.0	63.4	2 13.7	+31.8	63.4	24
25	0 28.6	−26.1	117.6	0 00.8	−26.9	117.6	0 26.9	+27.8	62.4	0 54.7	+28.5	62.5	1 22.4	+29.4	62.5	1 50.1	+30.2	62.5	2 17.8	+31.0	62.5	2 45.5	+31.8	62.6	25
26	0 02.5	−26.1	118.5	0 26.1	+26.9	61.5	0 54.7	+27.7	61.6	1 23.2	+28.6	61.6	1 51.8	+29.4	61.6	2 20.3	+30.2	61.6	2 48.8	+31.0	61.7	3 17.3	+31.7	61.7	26
27	0 23.6	+26.1	60.6	0 53.0	+26.9	60.6	1 22.4	+27.7	60.7	1 51.8	+28.5	60.7	2 21.2	+29.3	60.7	2 50.5	+30.1	60.8	3 19.8	+30.9	60.8	3 49.0	+31.7	60.9	27
28	0 49.7	+26.1	59.7	1 19.9	+26.9	59.8	1 50.1	+27.7	59.8	2 20.3	+28.5	59.8	2 50.5	+29.3	59.9	3 20.6	+30.1	59.9	3 50.7	+30.8	60.0	4 20.7	+31.6	60.0	28
29	1 15.8	+26.0	58.8	1 46.8	+26.9	58.9	2 17.8	+27.7	58.9	2 48.8	+28.5	58.9	3 19.8	+29.2	59.0	3 50.7	+30.0	59.0	4 21.5	+30.8	59.1	4 52.3	+31.6	59.2	29
30	1 41.8	+26.1	57.9	2 13.7	+26.8	58.0	2 45.5	+27.6	58.0	3 17.3	+28.4	58.0	3 49.0	+29.2	58.1	4 20.7	+29.9	58.2	4 52.3	+30.7	58.2	5 23.9	+31.4	58.3	30
31	2 07.9	+26.0	57.0	2 40.5	+26.8	57.1	3 13.1	+27.6	57.1	3 45.7	+28.3	57.2	4 18.2	+29.1	57.2	4 50.6	+29.9	57.3	5 23.0	+30.7	57.4	5 55.3	+31.4	57.5	31
32	2 33.9	+26.0	56.1	3 07.3	+26.8	56.2	3 40.7	+27.5	56.2	4 14.0	+28.3	56.3	4 47.3	+29.1	56.3	5 20.5	+29.8	56.4	5 53.7	+30.5	56.5	6 26.7	+31.4	56.6	32
33	2 59.9	+25.9	55.2	3 34.1	+26.7	55.3	4 08.2	+27.5	55.3	4 42.3	+28.2	55.4	5 16.4	+28.9	55.5	5 50.3	+29.8	55.6	6 24.2	+30.5	55.6	6 58.1	+31.2	55.7	33
34	3 25.8	+25.9	54.3	4 00.8	+26.6	54.4	4 35.7	+27.4	54.4	5 10.5	+28.2	54.5	5 45.3	+28.9	54.6	6 20.1	+29.6	54.7	6 54.7	+30.4	54.8	7 29.3	+31.1	54.9	34
35	3 51.7	+25.8	53.4	4 27.4	+26.6	53.5	5 03.1	+27.3	53.6	5 38.7	+28.1	53.6	6 14.2	+28.9	53.7	6 49.7	+29.6	53.8	7 25.1	+30.3	53.9	8 00.4	+31.0	54.0	35
36	4 17.5	+25.8	52.5	4 54.0	+26.5	52.6	5 30.4	+27.3	52.7	6 06.8	+28.0	52.7	6 43.1	+28.7	52.8	7 19.3	+29.4	52.9	7 55.4	+30.2	53.0	8 31.4	+30.9	53.1	36
37	4 43.3	+25.6	51.6	5 20.5	+26.4	51.7	5 57.7	+27.1	51.8	6 34.8	+27.8	51.8	7 11.8	+28.6	51.9	7 48.7	+29.4	52.0	8 25.6	+30.0	52.2	9 02.3	+30.8	52.3	37
38	5 08.9	+25.6	50.7	5 46.9	+26.3	50.8	6 24.8	+27.1	50.9	7 02.6	+27.8	51.0	7 40.4	+28.5	51.1	8 18.1	+29.2	51.2	8 55.6	+30.0	51.3	9 33.1	+30.7	51.4	38
39	5 34.5	+25.6	49.8	6 13.2	+26.3	49.9	6 51.9	+26.9	50.0	7 30.4	+27.7	50.1	8 08.9	+28.4	50.2	8 47.3	+29.1	50.3	9 25.6	+29.8	50.4	10 03.8	+30.5	50.5	39
40	6 00.1	+25.4	48.9	6 39.5	+26.1	49.0	7 18.8	+26.9	49.1	7 58.1	+27.6	49.2	8 37.3	+28.3	49.3	9 16.4	+29.0	49.4	9 55.4	+29.7	49.5	10 34.3	+30.4	49.7	40
41	6 25.5	+25.3	48.0	7 05.6	+26.1	48.1	7 45.7	+26.7	48.2	8 25.7	+27.4	48.3	9 05.6	+28.1	48.4	9 45.4	+28.8	48.5	10 25.1	+29.5	48.6	11 04.7	+30.2	48.8	41
42	6 50.8	+25.3	47.1	7 31.7	+25.9	47.2	8 12.4	+26.7	47.3	8 53.1	+27.3	47.4	9 33.7	+28.0	47.5	10 14.2	+28.7	47.6	10 54.6	+29.4	47.8	11 34.9	+30.0	47.9	42
43	7 16.1	+25.1	46.2	7 57.6	+25.8	46.2	8 39.1	+26.4	46.4	9 20.4	+27.2	46.5	10 01.7	+27.9	46.6	10 42.9	+28.5	46.7	11 24.0	+29.2	46.9	12 04.9	+29.9	47.0	43
44	7 41.2	+25.0	45.2	8 23.4	+25.7	45.3	9 05.5	+26.4	45.4	9 47.6	+27.0	45.6	10 29.6	+27.7	45.7	11 11.4	+28.4	45.8	11 53.2	+29.0	46.0	12 34.8	+29.7	46.1	44
45	8 06.2	+24.9	44.3	8 49.1	+25.5	44.4	9 31.9	+26.2	44.5	10 14.6	+26.9	44.7	10 57.3	+27.5	44.8	11 39.8	+28.2	44.9	12 22.2	+28.9	45.1	13 04.5	+29.6	45.2	45
46	8 31.1	+24.7	43.4	9 14.6	+25.5	43.5	9 58.1	+26.1	43.6	10 41.5	+26.7	43.7	11 24.8	+27.4	43.9	12 08.0	+28.0	44.0	12 51.1	+28.7	44.2	13 34.1	+29.3	44.3	46
47	8 55.8	+24.7	42.5	9 40.1	+25.2	42.6	10 24.2	+25.9	42.7	11 08.2	+26.6	42.8	11 52.2	+27.2	43.0	12 36.0	+27.9	43.1	13 19.8	+28.5	43.3	14 03.4	+29.1	43.4	47
48	9 20.5	+24.4	41.6	10 05.3	+25.1	41.7	10 50.1	+25.7	41.8	11 34.8	+26.4	41.9	12 19.4	+27.0	42.1	13 03.9	+27.6	42.2	13 48.3	+28.3	42.4	14 32.5	+29.0	42.5	48
49	9 44.9	+24.4	40.6	10 30.4	+25.0	40.7	11 15.8	+25.6	40.9	12 01.2	+26.2	41.0	12 46.4	+26.8	41.1	13 31.5	+27.5	41.3	14 16.6	+28.0	41.5	15 01.5	+28.7	41.6	49
50	10 09.3	+24.1	39.7	10 55.4	+24.8	39.8	11 41.4	+25.4	39.9	12 27.4	+26.0	40.1	13 13.2	+26.7	40.2	13 59.0	+27.2	40.4	14 44.6	+27.9	40.6	15 30.2	+28.4	40.7	50
51	10 33.4	+24.0	38.8	11 20.2	+24.6	38.9	12 06.8	+25.2	39.0	12 53.4	+25.8	39.2	13 39.9	+26.4	39.3	14 26.2	+27.1	39.5	15 12.5	+27.6	39.6	15 58.6	+28.3	39.8	51
52	10 57.4	+23.9	37.8	11 44.8	+24.4	38.0	12 32.0	+25.1	38.1	13 19.2	+25.6	38.2	14 06.3	+26.2	38.4	14 53.3	+26.8	38.5	15 40.1	+27.5	38.7	16 26.9	+28.0	38.9	52
53	11 21.3	+23.6	36.9	12 09.2	+24.2	37.0	12 57.1	+24.8	37.2	13 44.8	+25.4	37.3	14 32.5	+26.0	37.5	15 20.1	+26.6	37.6	16 07.6	+27.1	37.8	16 54.9	+27.8	38.0	53
54	11 44.9	+23.5	36.0	12 33.4	+24.1	36.1	13 21.9	+24.6	36.2	14 10.2	+25.2	36.4	14 58.5	+25.8	36.5	15 46.7	+26.3	36.7	16 34.7	+27.0	36.9	17 22.7	+27.5	37.0	54
55	12 08.4	+23.3	35.0	12 57.5	+23.8	35.1	13 46.5	+24.4	35.3	14 35.4	+25.0	35.4	15 24.3	+25.5	35.6	16 13.0	+26.1	35.8	17 01.7	+26.6	35.9	17 50.2	+27.2	36.1	55
56	12 31.7	+23.0	34.1	13 21.3	+23.6	34.2	14 10.9	+24.2	34.3	15 00.4	+24.7	34.5	15 49.8	+25.3	34.6	16 39.1	+25.9	34.8	17 28.3	+26.4	35.0	18 17.4	+27.0	35.2	56
57	12 54.7	+22.9	33.1	13 44.9	+23.5	33.3	14 35.1	+23.9	33.4	15 25.1	+24.5	33.5	16 15.1	+25.0	33.7	17 05.0	+25.5	33.9	17 54.7	+26.1	34.0	18 44.4	+26.7	34.2	57
58	13 17.6	+22.7	32.2	14 08.4	+23.2	32.3	14 59.0	+23.7	32.5	15 49.6	+24.3	32.6	16 40.1	+24.8	32.8	17 30.5	+25.3	32.9	18 20.8	+25.9	33.1	19 11.1	+26.3	33.3	58
59	13 40.3	+22.4	31.2	14 31.6	+22.9	31.4	15 22.7	+23.5	31.5	16 13.9	+24.0	31.6	17 04.9	+24.5	31.8	17 55.8	+25.1	32.0	18 46.7	+25.6	32.1	19 37.4	+26.1	32.3	59
60	14 02.7	+22.2	30.3	14 54.5	+22.7	30.4	15 46.2	+23.2	30.5	16 37.9	+23.7	30.7	17 29.4	+24.2	30.8	18 20.9	+24.7	31.0	19 12.3	+25.2	31.2	20 03.5	+25.8	31.4	60
61	14 24.9	+22.0	29.3	15 17.2	+22.5	29.4	16 09.4	+23.0	29.6	17 01.6	+23.4	29.7	17 53.6	+24.0	29.9	18 45.6	+24.5	30.1	19 37.5	+25.0	30.2	20 29.3	+25.5	30.4	61
62	14 46.9	+21.8	28.4	15 39.7	+22.2	28.5	16 32.4	+22.7	28.6	17 25.0	+23.2	28.8	18 17.6	+23.7	28.9	19 10.1	+24.1	29.1	20 02.5	+24.6	29.3	20 54.8	+25.1	29.4	62
63	15 08.7	+21.5	27.4	16 01.9	+22.0	27.5	16 55.1	+22.4	27.7	17 48.2	+22.9	27.8	18 41.3	+23.3	28.0	19 34.2	+23.8	28.1	20 27.1	+24.3	28.3	21 19.9	+24.8	28.5	63
64	15 30.2	+21.2	26.4	16 23.9	+21.7	26.5	17 17.5	+22.2	26.7	18 11.1	+22.6	26.8	19 04.6	+23.1	27.0	19 58.0	+23.5	27.1	20 51.4	+24.0	27.3	21 44.7	+24.4	27.5	64
65	15 51.4	+21.0	25.5	16 45.6	+21.4	25.6	17 39.7	+21.8	25.7	18 33.7	+22.3	25.9	19 27.7	+22.7	26.0	20 21.5	+23.2	26.2	21 15.4	+23.6	26.3	22 09.1	+24.1	26.5	65
66	16 12.4	+20.7	24.5	17 07.0	+21.1	24.6	18 01.5	+21.6	24.7	18 56.0	+22.0	24.9	19 50.4	+22.4	25.0	20 44.7	+22.9	25.2	21 39.0	+23.3	25.3	22 33.2	+23.7	25.5	66
67	16 33.1	+20.5	23.5	17 28.1	+20.9	23.6	18 23.1	+21.2	23.8	19 18.0	+21.6	23.9	20 12.8	+22.1	24.0	21 07.6	+22.5	24.2	22 02.3	+22.9	24.4	22 56.9	+23.3	24.5	67
68	16 53.6	+20.1	22.5	17 49.0	+20.5	22.6	18 44.3	+21.0	22.8	19 39.6	+21.4	22.9	20 34.9	+21.7	23.0	21 30.1	+22.1	23.2	22 25.2	+22.5	23.4	23 20.2	+23.0	23.5	68
69	17 13.7	+19.9	21.5	18 09.5	+20.3	21.6	19 05.3	+20.6	21.8	20 01.0	+21.0	21.9	20 56.6	+21.4	22.0	21 52.2	+21.8	22.2	22 47.7	+22.2	22.3	23 43.2	+22.5	22.5	69
70	17 33.6	+19.6	20.5	18 29.8	+19.9	20.7	19 25.9	+20.3	20.8	20 22.0	+20.6	20.9	21 18.0	+21.0	21.0	22 14.0	+21.4	21.2	23 09.9	+21.8	21.3	24 05.7	+22.2	21.5	70
71	17 53.2	+19.3	19.5	18 49.7	+19.6	19.7	19 46.2	+20.0	19.8	20 42.6	+20.4	19.9	21 39.0	+20.7	20.0	22 35.4	+21.0	20.2	23 31.7	+21.3	20.3	24 27.9	+21.7	20.5	71
72	18 12.5	+18.9	18.6	19 09.3	+19.3	18.7	20 06.2	+19.6	18.8	21 03.0	+19.9	18.9	21 59.7	+20.3	19.0	22 56.4	+20.6	19.2	23 53.0	+21.0	19.3	24 49.6	+21.4	19.5	72
73	18 31.4	+18.7	17.6	19 28.6	+19.0	17.7	20 25.8	+19.3	17.8	21 22.9	+19.6	17.9	22 20.0	+19.9	18.0	23 17.0	+20.3	18.1	24 14.0	+20.6	18.3	25 11.0	+20.9	18.4	73
74	18 50.1	+18.3	16.6	19 47.6	+18.6	16.7	20 45.1	+18.9	16.8	21 42.5	+19.2	16.9	22 39.9	+19.5	17.0	23 37.3	+19.8	17.1	24 34.6	+20.1	17.2	25 31.9	+20.4	17.4	74
75	19 08.4	+18.0	15.5	20 06.2	+18.3	15.6	21 04.0	+18.5	15.7	22 01.7	+18.8	15.8	22 59.4	+19.1	16.0	23 57.1	+19.4	16.1	24 54.7	+19.7	16.2	25 52.3	+20.0	16.3	75
76	19 26.4	+17.7	14.5	20 24.5	+17.9	14.6	21 22.5	+18.2	14.7	22 20.5	+18.5	14.8	23 18.5	+18.8	14.9	24 16.5	+19.0	15.0	25 14.4	+19.3	15.2	26 12.3	+19.6	15.3	76
77	19 44.1	+17.3	13.5	20 42.4	+17.6	13.6	21 40.7	+17.8	13.7	22 39.0	+18.0	13.8	23 37.3	+18.3	13.9	24 35.5	+18.5	14.0	25 33.7	+18.8	14.1	26 31.9	+19.0	14.2	77
78	20 01.4	+17.0	12.5	21 00.0	+17.2	12.6	21 58.5	+17.4	12.7	22 57.0	+17.7	12.8	23 55.6	+17.8	12.9	24 54.0	+18.1	13.0	25 52.5	+18.3	13.1	26 50.9	+18.6	13.2	78
79	20 18.4	+16.6	11.5	21 17.2	+16.8	11.6	22 15.9	+17.1	11.6	23 14.7	+17.2	11.7	24 13.4	+17.5	11.8	25 12.1	+17.7	11.9	26 10.8	+17.9	12.0	27 09.5	+18.1	12.1	79
80	20 35.0	+16.2	10.5	21 34.0	+16.4	10.5	22 33.0	+16.6	10.6	23 31.9	+16.8	10.7	24 30.9	+17.0	10.8	25 29.8	+17.2	10.8	26 28.7	+17.4	10.9	27 27.6	+17.6	11.0	80
81	20 51.2	+15.9	9.4	21 50.4	+16.0	9.5	22 49.6	+16.2	9.6	23 48.7	+16.4	9.6	24 47.9	+16.5	9.7	25 47.0	+16.8	9.8	26 46.1	+17.0	9.9	27 45.2	+17.1	10.0	81
82	21 07.1	+15.5	8.4	22 06.4	+15.7	8.4	23 05.8	+15.8	8.5	24 05.1	+16.0	8.6	25 04.4	+16.2	8.6	26 03.8	+16.2	8.7	27 03.1	+16.4	8.8	28 02.3	+16.6	8.9	82
83	21 22.6	+15.1	7.4	22 22.1	+15.2	7.4	23 21.6	+15.4	7.5	24 21.1	+15.5	7.5	25 20.6	+15.6	7.6	26 20.0	+15.8	7.6	27 19.5	+15.9	7.7	28 18.9	+16.1	7.8	83
84	21 37.7	+14.7	6.3	22 37.3	+14.9	6.4	23 37.0	+14.9	6.4	24 36.6	+15.1	6.5	25 36.2	+15.2	6.5	26 35.8	+15.3	6.6	27 35.4	+15.4	6.6	28 35.0	+15.6	6.7	84
85	21 52.4	+14.4	5.3	22 52.2	+14.4	5.3	23 51.9	+14.5	5.3	24 51.7	+14.6	5.4	25 51.4	+14.7	5.4	26 51.1	+14.8	5.5	27 50.8	+14.9	5.5	28 50.6	+15.0	5.6	85
86	22 06.8	+13.9	4.2	23 06.6	+14.0	4.3	24 06.4	+14.1	4.3	25 06.3	+14.1	4.3	26 06.1	+14.2	4.4	27 05.9	+14.3	4.4	28 05.7	+14.4	4.4	29 05.6	+14.4	4.5	86
87	22 20.7	+13.5	3.2	23 20.6	+13.6	3.2	24 20.5	+13.6	3.2	25 20.4	+13.7	3.2	26 20.3	+13.7	3.3	27 20.2	+13.8	3.3	28 20.1	+13.8	3.3	29 20.0	+13.9	3.4	87
88	22 34.2	+13.1	2.1	23 34.2	+13.1	2.1	24 34.1	+13.2	2.2	25 34.1	+13.2	2.2	26 34.0	+13.3	2.2	27 34.0	+13.3	2.2	28 33.9	+13.3	2.2	29 33.9	+13.3	2.2	88
89	22 47.3	+12.7	1.1	23 47.3	+12.7	1.1	24 47.3	+12.7	1.1	25 47.3	+12.7	1.1	26 47.3	+12.7	1.1	27 47.3	+12.7	1.1	28 47.2	+12.8	1.1	29 47.2	+12.8	1.1	89
90	23 00.0	+12.3	0.0	24 00.0	+12.3	0.0	25 00.0	+12.2	0.0	26 00.0	+12.2	0.0	27 00.0	+12.2	0.0	28 00.0	+12.2	0.0	29 00.0	+12.2	0.0	30 00.0	+12.2	0.0	90
	23°			24°			25°			26°			27°			28°			29°			30°			

S. Lat. {L.H.A. greater than 180° ....Zn=180°−Z; L.H.A. less than 180°...........Zn=180°+Z}

LATITUDE SAME NAME AS DECLINATION — L.H.A. 102°, 258°

79°, 281° L.H.A. LATITUDE SAME NAME AS DECLINATION

N. Lat. {L.H.A. greater than 180° .....Zn=Z
{L.H.A. less than 180°............Zn=360°−Z

Dec.	23° Hc	d	Z	24° Hc	d	Z	25° Hc	d	Z	26° Hc	d	Z	27° Hc	d	Z	28° Hc	d	Z	29° Hc	d	Z	30° Hc	d	Z	Dec.
°	° ′	′	°	° ′	′	°	° ′	′	°	° ′	′	°	° ′	′	°	° ′	′	°	° ′	′	°	° ′	′	°	°
0	10 07.0	+23.7	94.3	10 02.3	+24.7	94.5	9 57.5	+25.7	94.7	9 52.5	+26.6	94.9	9 47.3	+27.6	95.0	9 41.9	+28.6	95.2	9 36.4	+29.4	95.4	9 30.7	+30.3	95.6	0
1	10 30.7	+23.6	93.4	10 27.0	+24.6	93.6	10 23.2	+25.5	93.8	10 19.1	+26.5	94.0	10 14.9	+27.4	94.1	10 10.5	+28.3	94.3	10 05.8	+29.3	94.5	10 01.0	+30.3	94.7	1
2	10 54.3	+23.4	92.5	10 51.6	+24.3	92.7	10 48.7	+25.3	92.9	10 45.6	+26.3	93.0	10 42.3	+27.3	93.2	10 38.8	+28.2	93.4	10 35.1	+29.2	93.6	10 31.3	+30.0	93.8	2
3	11 17.7	+23.2	91.5	11 15.9	+24.3	91.7	11 14.0	+25.2	91.9	11 11.9	+26.1	92.1	11 09.6	+27.1	92.3	11 07.0	+28.1	92.5	11 04.3	+29.0	92.7	11 01.3	+29.9	92.9	3
4	11 40.9	+23.0	90.6	11 40.2	+24.0	90.8	11 39.2	+25.0	91.0	11 38.0	+26.0	91.2	11 36.7	+26.9	91.4	11 35.1	+27.8	91.6	11 33.3	+28.8	91.8	11 31.2	+29.8	92.0	4
5	12 03.9	+22.9	89.7	12 04.2	+23.8	89.9	12 04.2	+24.8	90.1	12 04.0	+25.8	90.3	12 03.6	+26.7	90.5	12 02.9	+27.8	90.7	12 02.1	+28.6	90.9	12 01.0	+29.6	91.1	5
6	12 26.8	+22.6	88.7	12 28.0	+23.6	88.9	12 29.0	+24.6	89.1	12 29.8	+25.6	89.4	12 30.3	+26.6	89.6	12 30.7	+27.5	89.8	12 30.7	+28.5	90.0	12 30.6	+29.4	90.3	6
7	12 49.4	+22.5	87.8	12 51.6	+23.5	88.0	12 53.6	+24.5	88.2	12 55.4	+25.4	88.4	12 56.9	+26.4	88.7	12 58.2	+27.3	88.9	12 59.2	+28.3	89.1	13 00.0	+29.2	89.4	7
8	13 11.9	+22.2	86.8	13 15.1	+23.2	87.0	13 18.1	+24.2	87.3	13 20.8	+25.2	87.5	13 23.3	+26.1	87.7	13 25.5	+27.1	88.0	13 27.5	+28.1	88.2	13 29.2	+29.1	88.5	8
9	13 34.1	+22.0	85.8	13 38.3	+23.0	86.1	13 42.3	+24.0	86.3	13 46.0	+25.0	86.6	13 49.4	+26.0	86.8	13 52.6	+27.0	87.1	13 55.6	+27.9	87.3	13 58.3	+28.8	87.6	9
10	13 56.1	+21.8	84.9	14 01.3	+22.8	85.1	14 06.3	+23.7	85.4	14 11.0	+24.7	85.6	14 15.4	+25.7	85.9	14 19.6	+26.7	86.1	14 23.5	+27.6	86.4	14 27.1	+28.6	86.7	10
11	14 17.9	+21.5	83.9	14 24.1	+22.6	84.2	14 30.0	+23.6	84.4	14 35.7	+24.6	84.7	14 41.1	+25.5	85.0	14 46.3	+26.5	85.2	14 51.1	+27.5	85.5	14 55.7	+28.4	85.8	11
12	14 39.4	+21.4	83.0	14 46.7	+22.3	83.2	14 53.6	+23.3	83.5	15 00.3	+24.3	83.8	15 06.6	+25.3	84.0	15 12.8	+26.2	84.3	15 18.6	+27.2	84.6	15 24.1	+28.2	84.8	12
13	15 00.8	+21.0	82.0	15 09.0	+22.1	82.3	15 16.9	+23.1	82.5	15 24.6	+24.0	82.8	15 31.9	+25.1	83.1	15 39.0	+26.0	83.4	15 45.8	+27.0	83.6	15 52.3	+28.0	83.9	13
14	15 21.8	+20.9	81.0	15 31.1	+21.8	81.3	15 40.0	+22.8	81.6	15 48.6	+23.8	81.9	15 57.0	+24.8	82.1	16 05.0	+25.8	82.4	16 12.8	+26.7	82.7	16 20.3	+27.7	83.0	14
15	15 42.7	+20.5	80.1	15 52.9	+21.5	80.3	16 02.8	+22.6	80.6	16 12.4	+23.6	80.9	16 21.8	+24.5	81.2	16 30.8	+25.5	81.5	16 39.5	+26.5	81.8	16 48.0	+27.4	82.1	15
16	16 03.2	+20.3	79.1	16 14.4	+21.3	79.4	16 25.4	+22.3	79.7	16 36.0	+23.3	79.9	16 46.3	+24.3	80.2	16 56.3	+25.3	80.5	17 06.0	+26.3	80.8	17 15.4	+27.2	81.1	16
17	16 23.5	+20.0	78.1	16 35.7	+21.1	78.4	16 47.7	+22.0	78.7	16 59.3	+23.0	79.0	17 10.6	+24.0	79.3	17 21.6	+25.0	79.6	17 32.3	+25.9	79.9	17 42.6	+27.0	80.2	17
18	16 43.5	+19.8	77.1	16 56.8	+20.7	77.4	17 09.7	+21.7	77.7	17 22.3	+22.7	78.0	17 34.6	+23.7	78.3	17 46.6	+24.7	78.6	17 58.2	+25.7	79.0	18 09.6	+26.6	79.3	18
19	17 03.3	+19.4	76.1	17 17.5	+20.5	76.4	17 31.4	+21.5	76.7	17 45.0	+22.5	77.0	17 58.3	+23.5	77.4	18 11.3	+24.4	77.7	18 23.9	+25.4	78.0	18 36.2	+26.4	78.3	19
20	17 22.7	+19.2	75.1	17 38.0	+20.1	75.4	17 52.9	+21.1	75.8	18 07.5	+22.1	76.1	18 21.8	+23.1	76.4	18 35.7	+24.2	76.7	18 49.3	+25.2	77.0	19 02.6	+26.1	77.4	20
21	17 41.9	+18.8	74.1	17 58.1	+19.9	74.5	18 14.0	+20.9	74.8	18 29.6	+21.9	75.1	18 44.9	+22.9	75.4	18 59.9	+23.8	75.7	19 14.5	+24.8	76.1	19 28.7	+25.8	76.4	21
22	18 00.7	+18.6	73.1	18 18.0	+19.5	73.5	18 34.9	+20.5	73.8	18 51.5	+21.5	74.1	19 07.8	+22.5	74.4	19 23.7	+23.5	74.8	19 39.3	+24.5	75.1	19 54.5	+25.5	75.5	22
23	18 19.3	+18.2	72.1	18 37.5	+19.3	72.5	18 55.4	+20.3	72.8	19 13.0	+21.3	73.1	19 30.3	+22.2	73.5	19 47.2	+23.2	73.8	20 03.8	+24.1	74.1	20 20.0	+25.1	74.5	23
24	18 37.5	+17.9	71.1	18 56.8	+18.9	71.5	19 15.7	+19.9	71.8	19 34.3	+20.8	72.1	19 52.5	+21.9	72.5	20 10.4	+22.9	72.8	20 27.9	+23.9	73.2	20 45.1	+24.9	73.5	24
25	18 55.4	+17.6	70.1	19 15.7	+18.6	70.5	19 35.6	+19.5	70.8	19 55.1	+20.6	71.1	20 14.4	+21.5	71.5	20 33.3	+22.5	71.8	20 51.8	+23.5	72.2	21 10.0	+24.5	72.6	25
26	19 13.0	+17.3	69.1	19 34.3	+18.2	69.5	19 55.1	+19.3	69.8	20 15.7	+20.2	70.1	20 35.9	+21.2	70.5	20 55.8	+22.2	70.8	21 15.3	+23.2	71.2	21 34.5	+24.1	71.6	26
27	19 30.3	+16.9	68.1	19 52.5	+17.9	68.4	20 14.4	+18.9	68.8	20 35.9	+19.9	69.1	20 57.1	+20.9	69.5	21 18.0	+21.8	69.8	21 38.5	+22.8	70.2	21 58.6	+23.8	70.6	27
28	19 47.2	+16.6	67.1	20 10.4	+17.5	67.4	20 33.3	+18.5	67.8	20 55.8	+19.5	68.1	21 18.0	+20.5	68.5	21 39.8	+21.5	68.8	22 01.3	+22.4	69.2	22 22.4	+23.4	69.6	28
29	20 03.8	+16.2	66.1	20 27.9	+17.2	66.4	20 51.8	+18.2	66.8	21 15.3	+19.2	67.1	21 38.5	+20.1	67.5	22 01.3	+21.1	67.8	22 23.7	+22.1	68.2	22 45.8	+23.1	68.6	29
30	20 20.0	+15.8	65.0	20 45.1	+16.9	65.4	21 10.0	+17.8	65.7	21 34.5	+18.7	66.1	21 58.6	+19.8	66.5	22 22.4	+20.7	66.8	22 45.8	+21.7	67.2	23 08.9	+22.6	67.6	30
31	20 35.8	+15.5	64.0	21 02.0	+16.4	64.4	21 27.8	+17.4	64.7	21 53.2	+18.4	65.1	22 18.4	+19.3	65.4	22 43.1	+20.4	65.8	23 07.5	+21.3	66.2	23 31.5	+22.3	66.6	31
32	20 51.3	+15.1	63.0	21 18.4	+16.1	63.3	21 45.2	+17.0	63.7	22 11.6	+18.0	64.0	22 37.7	+19.0	64.4	23 03.5	+19.9	64.8	23 28.8	+20.9	65.2	23 53.8	+21.9	65.6	32
33	21 06.4	+14.8	61.9	21 34.5	+15.7	62.3	22 02.2	+16.7	62.6	22 29.6	+17.6	63.0	22 56.7	+18.6	63.4	23 23.4	+19.5	63.8	23 49.7	+20.5	64.2	24 15.7	+21.5	64.6	33
34	21 21.2	+14.3	60.9	21 50.2	+15.3	61.2	22 18.9	+16.2	61.6	22 47.2	+17.2	62.0	23 15.3	+18.1	62.3	23 42.9	+19.2	62.7	24 10.2	+20.1	63.1	24 37.2	+21.0	63.5	34
35	21 35.5	+14.0	59.9	22 05.5	+14.9	60.2	22 35.1	+15.9	60.6	23 04.4	+16.8	60.9	23 33.4	+17.8	61.3	24 02.1	+18.7	61.7	24 30.3	+19.7	62.1	24 58.2	+20.6	62.5	35
36	21 49.5	+13.5	58.8	22 20.4	+14.5	59.2	22 51.0	+15.4	59.5	23 21.2	+16.4	59.9	23 51.2	+17.3	60.3	24 20.8	+18.2	60.7	24 50.0	+19.2	61.1	25 18.8	+20.2	61.5	36
37	22 03.0	+13.2	57.8	22 34.9	+14.1	58.1	23 06.4	+15.0	58.5	23 37.6	+16.0	58.8	24 08.5	+16.9	59.2	24 39.0	+17.9	59.6	25 09.2	+18.8	60.0	25 39.0	+19.8	60.4	37
38	22 16.2	+12.7	56.7	22 49.0	+13.6	57.1	23 21.4	+14.6	57.4	23 53.6	+15.5	57.8	24 25.4	+16.5	58.2	24 56.9	+17.4	58.6	25 28.0	+18.3	59.0	25 58.8	+19.2	59.4	38
39	22 28.9	+12.4	55.7	23 02.6	+13.3	56.0	23 36.0	+14.2	56.4	24 09.1	+15.1	56.7	24 41.9	+16.0	57.1	25 14.3	+16.9	57.5	25 46.3	+17.9	57.9	26 18.0	+18.8	58.3	39
40	22 41.3	+11.9	54.6	23 15.9	+12.8	54.9	23 50.2	+13.7	55.3	24 24.2	+14.6	55.7	24 57.9	+15.5	56.0	25 31.2	+16.5	56.4	26 04.2	+17.4	56.8	26 36.8	+18.4	57.3	40
41	22 53.2	+11.5	53.5	23 28.7	+12.4	53.9	24 03.9	+13.3	54.2	24 38.8	+14.2	54.6	25 13.4	+15.1	55.0	25 47.7	+16.0	55.4	26 21.6	+16.9	55.8	26 55.2	+17.8	56.2	41
42	23 04.7	+11.0	52.5	23 41.1	+11.9	52.8	24 17.2	+12.8	53.2	24 53.0	+13.7	53.5	25 28.5	+14.6	53.9	26 03.7	+15.5	54.3	26 38.5	+16.5	54.7	27 13.0	+17.4	55.1	42
43	23 15.7	+10.6	51.4	23 53.0	+11.5	51.7	24 30.0	+12.4	52.1	25 06.7	+13.3	52.5	25 43.1	+14.2	52.8	26 19.2	+15.1	53.2	26 55.0	+15.9	53.6	27 30.4	+16.9	54.0	43
44	23 26.3	+10.2	50.3	24 04.5	+11.0	50.7	24 42.4	+11.9	51.0	25 20.0	+12.8	51.4	25 57.3	+13.7	51.8	26 34.3	+14.5	52.1	27 10.9	+15.5	52.5	27 47.3	+16.3	53.0	44
45	23 36.5	+9.7	49.2	24 15.5	+10.6	49.6	24 54.3	+11.5	49.9	25 32.8	+12.3	50.3	26 11.0	+13.1	50.7	26 48.8	+14.1	51.1	27 26.4	+14.9	51.5	28 03.6	+15.8	51.9	45
46	23 46.2	+9.3	48.2	24 26.1	+10.2	48.5	25 05.8	+10.9	48.8	25 45.1	+11.8	49.2	26 24.1	+12.7	49.6	27 02.9	+13.6	50.0	27 41.3	+14.5	50.4	28 19.4	+15.4	50.8	46
47	23 55.5	+8.9	47.1	24 36.3	+9.6	47.4	25 16.7	+10.5	47.8	25 56.9	+11.4	48.1	26 36.8	+12.2	48.5	27 16.5	+13.0	48.9	27 55.8	+13.9	49.3	28 34.8	+14.7	49.7	47
48	24 04.4	+8.3	46.0	24 45.9	+9.2	46.3	25 27.2	+10.0	46.7	26 08.3	+10.8	47.0	26 49.0	+11.7	47.4	27 29.5	+12.5	47.8	28 09.7	+13.3	48.2	28 49.5	+14.3	48.6	48
49	24 12.7	+8.0	44.9	24 55.1	+8.7	45.2	25 37.2	+9.5	45.6	26 19.1	+10.3	45.9	27 00.7	+11.1	46.3	27 42.0	+12.0	46.7	28 23.0	+12.9	47.1	29 03.8	+13.6	47.5	49
50	24 20.7	+7.4	43.8	25 03.8	+8.2	44.2	25 46.7	+9.1	44.5	26 29.4	+9.9	44.8	27 11.8	+10.7	45.2	27 54.0	+11.5	45.6	28 35.9	+12.3	45.9	29 17.4	+13.2	46.3	50
51	24 28.1	+7.0	42.7	25 12.0	+7.8	43.1	25 55.8	+8.5	43.4	26 39.3	+9.3	43.7	27 22.5	+10.1	44.1	28 05.5	+10.9	44.4	28 48.2	+11.7	44.8	29 30.6	+12.5	45.2	51
52	24 35.1	+6.5	41.7	25 19.8	+7.3	42.0	26 04.3	+8.0	42.3	26 48.6	+8.8	42.6	27 32.6	+9.6	43.0	28 16.4	+10.3	43.3	28 59.9	+11.2	43.7	29 43.1	+12.0	44.1	52
53	24 41.6	+6.0	40.6	25 27.1	+6.7	40.9	26 12.3	+7.5	41.2	26 57.4	+8.2	41.5	27 42.2	+9.0	41.9	28 26.7	+9.9	42.2	29 11.1	+10.6	42.6	29 55.1	+11.4	43.0	53
54	24 47.6	+5.5	39.5	25 33.8	+6.3	39.8	26 19.8	+7.1	40.1	27 05.6	+7.8	40.4	27 51.2	+8.5	40.7	28 36.6	+9.2	41.1	29 21.7	+10.0	41.5	30 06.5	+10.8	41.8	54
55	24 53.1	+5.1	38.4	25 40.1	+5.8	38.7	26 26.9	+6.4	39.0	27 13.4	+7.2	39.3	27 59.7	+8.0	39.6	28 45.8	+8.7	40.0	29 31.7	+9.5	40.3	30 17.3	+10.2	40.7	55
56	24 58.2	+4.6	37.3	25 45.9	+5.2	37.6	26 33.3	+6.0	37.9	27 20.6	+6.7	38.2	28 07.7	+7.4	38.5	28 54.5	+8.2	38.8	29 41.2	+8.8	39.2	30 27.5	+9.7	39.6	56
57	25 02.8	+4.1	36.2	25 51.1	+4.8	36.4	26 39.3	+5.5	36.7	27 27.3	+6.2	37.0	28 15.1	+6.8	37.4	29 02.7	+7.5	37.7	29 50.0	+8.3	38.0	30 37.2	+9.0	38.4	57
58	25 06.9	+3.6	35.1	25 55.9	+4.3	35.3	26 44.8	+4.9	35.6	27 33.5	+5.6	35.9	28 21.9	+6.3	36.2	29 10.2	+7.0	36.6	29 58.3	+7.7	36.9	30 46.2	+8.4	37.3	58
59	25 10.5	+3.1	34.0	26 00.2	+3.7	34.2	26 49.7	+4.4	34.5	27 39.1	+5.0	34.8	28 28.2	+5.8	35.1	29 17.2	+6.4	35.4	30 06.0	+7.1	35.8	30 54.6	+7.8	36.1	59
60	25 13.6	+2.6	32.9	26 03.9	+3.3	33.1	26 54.1	+3.9	33.4	27 44.1	+4.5	33.7	28 34.0	+5.1	34.0	29 23.6	+5.9	34.3	30 13.1	+6.5	34.6	31 02.4	+7.2	34.9	60
61	25 16.2	+2.2	31.8	26 07.2	+2.7	32.0	26 58.0	+3.3	32.3	27 48.6	+4.0	32.6	28 39.1	+4.6	32.8	29 29.5	+5.2	33.1	30 19.6	+5.9	33.5	31 09.6	+6.5	33.8	61
62	25 18.4	+1.6	30.6	26 09.9	+2.2	30.9	27 01.3	+2.8	31.2	27 52.6	+3.4	31.4	28 43.7	+4.1	31.7	29 34.7	+4.6	32.0	30 25.5	+5.3	32.3	31 16.1	+5.9	32.6	62
63	25 20.0	+1.1	29.5	26 12.1	+1.7	29.8	27 04.1	+2.3	30.0	27 56.0	+2.9	30.3	28 47.8	+3.4	30.6	29 39.3	+4.1	30.9	30 30.8	+4.6	31.2	31 22.0	+5.3	31.5	63
64	25 21.1	+0.7	28.4	26 13.8	+1.2	28.7	27 06.4	+1.8	28.9	27 58.9	+2.3	29.2	28 51.2	+2.9	29.4	29 43.4	+3.5	29.7	30 35.4	+4.1	30.0	31 27.3	+4.7	30.3	64
65	25 21.8	+0.1	27.3	26 15.0	+0.7	27.6	27 08.2	+1.2	27.8	28 01.2	+1.7	28.0	28 54.1	+2.3	28.3	29 46.9	+2.8	28.6	30 39.5	+3.4	28.8	31 32.0	+4.0	29.1	65
66	25 21.9	−0.3	26.2	26 15.7	+0.2	26.4	27 09.4	+0.6	26.7	28 02.9	+1.2	26.9	28 56.4	+1.7	27.1	29 49.7	+2.3	27.4	30 42.9	+2.8	27.7	31 36.0	+3.4	28.0	66
67	25 21.6	−0.9	25.1	26 15.9	−0.4	25.3	27 10.0	+0.2	25.5	28 04.1	+0.7	25.8	28 58.1	+1.2	26.0	29 52.0	+1.6	26.3	30 45.7	+2.2	26.5	31 39.4	+2.7	26.8	67
68	25 20.7	−1.3	24.0	26 15.5	−0.9	24.2	27 10.2	−0.4	24.4	28 04.8	0.0	24.6	28 59.3	+0.5	24.9	29 53.6	+1.1	25.1	30 47.9	+1.6	25.3	31 42.1	+2.1	25.6	68
69	25 19.4	−1.8	22.9	26 14.6	−1.4	23.1	27 09.8	−1.0	23.3	28 04.8	−0.4	23.5	28 59.8	0.0	23.7	29 54.7	+0.5	23.9	30 49.5	+0.9	24.2	31 44.2	+1.4	24.4	69
70	25 17.6	−2.4	21.8	26 13.2	−1.9	22.0	27 08.8	−1.4	22.2	28 04.4	−1.1	22.4	28 59.8	−0.6	22.6	29 55.2	−0.2	22.8	30 50.4	+0.3	23.0	31 45.6	+0.8	23.3	70
71	25 15.2	−2.8	20.7	26 11.3	−2.4	20.9	27 07.4	−2.1	21.0	28 03.3	−1.6	21.2	28 59.2	−1.2	21.4	29 55.0	−0.7	21.6	30 50.7	−0.3	21.9	31 46.4	+0.1	22.1	71
72	25 12.4	−3.3	19.6	26 08.9	−2.9	19.8	27 05.3	−2.5	19.9	28 01.7	−2.1	20.1	28 58.0	−1.7	20.3	29 54.3	−1.4	20.5	30 50.4	−0.9	20.7	31 46.5	−0.5	20.9	72
73	25 09.1	−3.8	18.5	26 06.0	−3.5	18.6	27 02.8	−3.1	18.8	27 59.6	−2.8	19.0	28 56.3	−2.4	19.1	29 52.9	−1.9	19.3	30 49.5	−1.6	19.5	31 46.0	−1.1	19.7	73
74	25 05.3	−4.3	17.4	26 02.5	−3.9	17.5	26 59.7	−3.6	17.7	27 56.8	−3.2	17.8	28 53.9	−2.9	18.0	29 51.0	−2.6	18.2	30 47.9	−2.1	18.4	31 44.9	−1.8	18.6	74
75	25 01.0	−4.8	16.3	25 58.6	−4.5	16.4	26 56.1	−4.2	16.6	27 53.6	−3.8	16.7	28 51.0	−3.5	16.9	29 48.4	−3.1	17.0	30 45.8	−2.8	17.2	31 43.1	−2.5	17.4	75
76	24 56.2	−5.3	15.2	25 54.1	−5.0	15.3	26 51.9	−4.6	15.4	27 49.8	−4.4	15.6	28 47.5	−4.0	15.7	29 45.3	−3.8	15.9	30 43.0	−3.5	16.0	31 40.6	−3.1	16.2	76
77	24 50.9	−5.7	14.1	25 49.1	−5.5	14.2	26 47.3	−5.2	14.3	27 45.4	−4.9	14.4	28 43.5	−4.7	14.6	29 41.5	−4.3	14.7	30 39.5	−4.0	14.9	31 37.5	−3.7	15.0	77
78	24 45.2	−6.2	13.0	25 43.6	−5.9	13.1	26 42.1	−5.7	13.2	27 40.5	−5.5	13.3	28 38.8	−5.2	13.4	29 37.2	−5.0	13.6	30 35.5	−4.7	13.7	31 33.8	−4.4	13.9	78
79	24 39.0	−6.7	11.9	25 37.7	−6.5	12.0	26 36.4	−6.3	12.1	27 35.0	−6.0	12.2	28 33.6	−5.7	12.3	29 32.2	−5.5	12.4	30 30.8	−5.2	12.6	31 29.4	−5.0	12.7	79
80	24 32.3	−7.2	10.8	25 31.2	−7.0	10.9	26 30.1	−6.7	11.0	27 29.0	−6.5	11.1	28 27.9	−6.4	11.2	29 26.7	−6.1	11.3	30 25.6	−5.9	11.4	31 24.4	−5.7	11.5	80
81	24 25.1	−7.6	9.7	25 24.2	−7.4	9.8	26 23.4	−7.3	9.9	27 22.5	−7.1	10.0	28 21.5	−6.8	10.0	29 20.6	−6.7	10.1	30 19.7	−6.5	10.2	31 18.7	−6.3	10.4	81
82	24 17.5	−8.1	8.6	25 16.8	−8.0	8.7	26 16.1	−7.8	8.8	27 15.4	−7.6	8.8	28 14.7	−7.5	8.9	29 13.9	−7.2	9.0	30 13.2	−7.1	9.1	31 12.4	−6.9	9.2	82
83	24 09.4	−8.6	7.5	25 08.8	−8.4	7.6	26 08.3	−8.3	7.7	27 07.8	−8.2	7.7	28 07.2	−8.0	7.8	29 06.7	−7.9	7.9	30 06.1	−7.7	7.9	31 05.5	−7.5	8.0	83
84	24 00.8	−9.0	6.4	25 00.4	−8.9	6.5	26 00.0	−8.7	6.6	26 59.6	−8.6	6.6	27 59.2	−8.5	6.7	28 58.8	−8.4	6.7	29 58.4	−8.3	6.8	30 58.0	−8.2	6.9	84
85	23 51.8	−9.5	5.4	24 51.5	−9.4	5.4	25 51.3	−9.3	5.5	26 51.0	−9.2	5.5	27 50.7	−9.1	5.6	28 50.4	−9.0	5.6	29 50.1	−8.8	5.7	30 49.8	−8.7	5.7	85
86	23 42.3	−9.9	4.3	24 42.1	−9.8	4.3	25 42.0	−9.8	4.4	26 41.8	−9.7	4.4	27 41.6	−9.6	4.4	28 41.4	−9.5	4.5	29 41.3	−9.5	4.5	30 41.1	−9.4	4.6	86
87	23 32.4	−10.4	3.2	24 32.3	−10.3	3.2	25 32.2	−10.3	3.3	26 32.1	−10.2	3.3	27 32.0	−10.1	3.3	28 31.9	−10.1	3.4	29 31.8	−10.0	3.4	30 31.7	−10.0	3.4	87
88	23 22.0	−10.8	2.1	24 22.0	−10.8	2.2	25 21.9	−10.7	2.2	26 21.9	−10.7	2.2	27 21.9	−10.7	2.2	28 21.8	−10.6	2.2	29 21.8	−10.6	2.3	30 21.7	−10.5	2.3	88
89	23 11.2	−11.2	1.1	24 11.2	−11.2	1.1	25 11.2	−11.2	1.1	26 11.2	−11.2	1.1	27 11.2	−11.2	1.1	28 11.2	−11.2	1.1	29 11.2	−11.2	1.1	30 11.2	−11.2	1.1	89
90	23 00.0	−11.7	0.0	24 00.0	−11.7	0.0	25 00.0	−11.7	0.0	26 00.0	−11.7	0.0	27 00.0	−11.7	0.0	28 00.0	−11.7	0.0	29 00.0	−11.7	0.0	30 00.0	−11.7	0.0	90
	23°			24°			25°			26°			27°			28°			29°			30°			

79°, 281° L.H.A. LATITUDE SAME NAME AS DECLINATION

342

LATITUDE **CONTRARY** NAME TO DECLINATION L.H.A. 79°, 281°

Dec.	23° Hc	d	Z	24° Hc	d	Z	25° Hc	d	Z	26° Hc	d	Z	27° Hc	d	Z	28° Hc	d	Z	29° Hc	d	Z	30° Hc	d	Z	Dec.
°	° ′	′	°	° ′	′	°	° ′	′	°	° ′	′	°	° ′	′	°	° ′	′	°	° ′	′	°	° ′	′	°	°
0	10 07.0	-23.9	94.3	10 02.3	-24.8	94.5	9 57.5	-25.8	94.7	9 52.5	-26.8	94.9	9 47.3	-27.7	95.0	9 41.9	-28.6	95.2	9 36.4	-29.6	95.4	9 30.7	-30.5	95.6	0
1	9 43.1	-24.1	95.3	9 37.5	-25.0	95.4	9 31.7	-26.0	95.6	9 25.7	-26.9	95.8	9 19.6	-27.8	95.9	9 13.3	-28.8	96.1	9 06.8	-29.7	96.3	9 00.2	-30.6	96.4	1
2	9 19.0	-24.2	96.2	9 12.5	-25.2	96.4	9 05.7	-26.1	96.5	8 58.8	-27.0	96.7	8 51.8	-28.0	96.8	8 44.5	-28.9	97.0	8 37.1	-29.8	97.1	8 29.6	-30.7	97.3	2
3	8 54.8	-24.3	97.1	8 47.3	-25.3	97.3	8 39.6	-26.2	97.4	8 31.8	-27.2	97.6	8 23.8	-28.1	97.7	8 15.6	-29.0	97.9	8 07.3	-29.9	98.0	7 58.9	-30.8	98.2	3
4	8 30.5	-24.4	98.1	8 22.0	-25.4	98.2	8 13.4	-26.4	98.3	8 04.6	-27.3	98.5	7 55.7	-28.2	98.6	7 46.6	-29.1	98.8	7 37.4	-30.0	98.9	7 28.1	-31.0	99.0	4
5	8 06.1	-24.6	99.0	7 56.6	-25.5	99.1	7 47.0	-26.4	99.3	7 37.3	-27.4	99.4	7 27.5	-28.3	99.5	7 17.5	-29.2	99.6	7 07.4	-30.2	99.8	6 57.1	-31.0	99.9	5
6	7 41.5	-24.7	99.9	7 31.1	-25.6	100.0	7 20.6	-26.6	100.2	7 09.9	-27.5	100.3	6 59.2	-28.5	100.4	6 48.3	-29.4	100.5	6 37.2	-30.2	100.6	6 26.1	-31.1	100.8	6
7	7 16.8	-24.8	100.8	7 05.5	-25.8	100.9	6 54.0	-26.7	101.1	6 42.4	-27.6	101.2	6 30.7	-28.5	101.3	6 18.9	-29.4	101.4	6 07.0	-30.3	101.5	5 55.0	-31.2	101.6	7
8	6 52.0	-24.9	101.7	6 39.7	-25.8	101.9	6 27.3	-26.7	102.0	6 14.8	-27.7	102.1	6 02.2	-28.6	102.2	5 49.5	-29.5	102.3	5 36.7	-30.4	102.4	5 23.8	-31.3	102.5	8
9	6 27.1	-25.0	102.7	6 13.9	-26.0	102.8	6 00.6	-26.9	102.9	5 47.1	-27.7	103.0	5 33.6	-28.6	103.1	5 20.0	-29.5	103.2	5 06.3	-30.4	103.2	4 52.5	-31.3	103.3	9
10	6 02.1	-25.1	103.6	5 47.9	-26.0	103.7	5 33.7	-26.9	103.8	5 19.4	-27.9	103.9	5 05.0	-28.8	103.9	4 50.5	-29.7	104.0	4 35.9	-30.5	104.1	4 21.2	-31.4	104.2	10
11	5 37.0	-25.2	104.5	5 21.9	-26.1	104.6	5 06.8	-27.1	104.7	4 51.5	-27.9	104.7	4 36.2	-28.8	104.8	4 20.8	-29.7	104.9	4 05.4	-30.6	105.0	3 49.8	-31.4	105.0	11
12	5 11.8	-25.3	105.4	4 55.8	-26.2	105.5	4 39.7	-27.0	105.6	4 23.6	-28.0	105.6	4 07.4	-28.9	105.7	3 51.1	-29.7	105.8	3 34.8	-30.6	105.8	3 18.4	-31.5	105.9	12
13	4 46.5	-25.3	106.3	4 29.6	-26.2	106.4	4 12.7	-27.2	106.5	3 55.6	-28.0	106.5	3 38.5	-28.9	106.6	3 21.4	-29.8	106.6	3 04.2	-30.7	106.7	2 46.9	-31.5	106.7	13
14	4 21.2	-25.4	107.2	4 03.4	-26.3	107.3	3 45.5	-27.2	107.3	3 27.6	-28.1	107.4	3 09.6	-28.9	107.5	2 51.6	-29.8	107.5	2 33.5	-30.7	107.6	2 15.4	-31.5	107.6	14
15	3 55.8	-25.5	108.1	3 37.1	-26.4	108.2	3 18.3	-27.2	108.2	2 59.5	-28.1	108.3	2 40.7	-29.0	108.3	2 21.8	-29.9	108.4	2 02.8	-30.7	108.4	1 43.9	-31.6	108.4	15
16	3 30.3	-25.5	109.0	3 10.7	-26.4	109.1	2 51.1	-27.3	109.1	2 31.4	-28.2	109.2	2 11.7	-29.1	109.2	1 51.9	-29.9	109.2	1 32.1	-30.7	109.3	1 12.3	-31.6	109.3	16
17	3 04.8	-25.6	109.9	2 44.3	-26.4	110.0	2 23.8	-27.3	110.0	2 03.2	-28.2	110.1	1 42.6	-29.0	110.1	1 22.0	-29.9	110.1	1 01.4	-30.8	110.1	0 40.7	-31.6	110.1	17
18	2 39.2	-25.6	110.8	2 17.9	-26.5	110.9	1 56.5	-27.4	110.9	1 35.0	-28.2	110.9	1 13.6	-29.1	111.0	0 52.1	-29.9	111.0	0 30.6	-30.8	111.0	0 09.1	-31.6	111.0	18
19	2 13.6	-25.6	111.7	1 51.4	-26.5	111.8	1 29.1	-27.4	111.8	1 06.8	-28.2	111.8	0 44.5	-29.1	111.8	0 22.2	-30.0	111.8	0 00.2	+30.7	68.1	0 22.5	+31.6	68.2	19
20	1 48.0	-25.7	112.6	1 24.9	-26.5	112.7	1 01.7	-27.3	112.7	0 38.6	-28.3	112.7	0 15.4	-29.1	112.7	0 07.8	+29.9	67.3	0 30.9	+30.8	67.3	0 54.1	+31.6	67.3	20
21	1 22.3	-25.6	113.6	0 58.4	-26.6	113.6	0 34.4	-27.4	113.6	0 10.3	-28.2	113.6	0 13.7	+29.1	66.4	0 37.7	+29.9	66.4	1 01.7	+30.7	66.4	1 25.7	+31.5	66.5	21
22	0 56.7	-25.7	114.5	0 31.8	-26.5	114.5	0 07.0	-27.4	114.5	0 17.9	+28.2	65.5	0 42.8	+29.0	65.5	1 07.6	+29.9	65.6	1 32.4	+30.7	65.6	1 57.2	+31.6	65.6	22
23	0 31.0	-25.7	115.4	0 05.3	-26.6	115.4	0 20.4	+27.4	64.6	0 46.1	+28.3	64.6	1 11.8	+29.1	64.7	1 37.5	+29.9	64.7	2 03.1	+30.7	64.7	2 28.8	+31.5	64.7	23
24	0 05.3	-25.7	116.3	0 21.3	+26.5	63.7	0 47.8	+27.4	63.7	1 14.4	+28.2	63.8	1 40.9	+29.0	63.8	2 07.4	+29.8	63.8	2 33.8	+30.7	63.9	3 00.3	+31.4	63.9	24
25	0 20.4	+25.7	62.8	0 47.8	+26.6	62.8	1 15.2	+27.4	62.9	1 42.6	+28.2	62.9	2 09.9	+29.0	62.9	2 37.2	+29.8	62.9	3 04.5	+30.6	63.0	3 31.7	+31.4	63.0	25
26	0 46.1	+25.7	61.9	1 14.4	+26.5	61.9	1 42.6	+27.3	62.0	2 10.8	+28.1	62.0	2 38.9	+29.0	62.0	3 07.0	+29.8	62.1	3 35.1	+30.6	62.1	4 03.1	+31.4	62.2	26
27	1 11.8	+25.7	61.0	1 40.9	+26.5	61.0	2 09.9	+27.3	61.1	2 38.9	+28.1	61.1	3 07.9	+28.9	61.2	3 36.8	+29.7	61.2	4 05.7	+30.5	61.3	4 34.5	+31.3	61.3	27
28	1 37.5	+25.6	60.1	2 07.4	+26.4	60.1	2 37.2	+27.3	60.2	3 07.0	+28.1	60.2	3 36.8	+28.9	60.3	4 06.5	+29.7	60.3	4 36.2	+30.4	60.4	5 05.8	+31.2	60.5	28
29	2 03.1	+25.7	59.2	2 33.8	+26.5	59.3	3 04.5	+27.2	59.3	3 35.1	+28.0	59.3	4 05.7	+28.8	59.4	4 36.2	+29.6	59.5	5 06.6	+30.4	59.5	5 37.0	+31.2	59.6	29
30	2 28.8	+25.5	58.3	3 00.3	+26.3	58.4	3 31.7	+27.2	58.4	4 03.1	+28.0	58.5	4 34.5	+28.7	58.5	5 05.8	+29.5	58.6	5 37.0	+30.3	58.7	6 08.2	+31.0	58.8	30
31	2 54.3	+25.6	57.4	3 26.6	+26.4	57.5	3 58.9	+27.1	57.5	4 31.1	+27.9	57.6	5 03.2	+28.7	57.6	5 35.3	+29.5	57.7	6 07.3	+30.2	57.8	6 39.2	+31.0	57.9	31
32	3 19.9	+25.4	56.5	3 53.0	+26.2	56.6	4 26.0	+27.1	56.6	4 59.0	+27.8	56.7	5 31.9	+28.6	56.8	6 04.8	+29.3	56.8	6 37.5	+30.2	56.9	7 10.2	+30.9	57.0	32
33	3 45.3	+25.5	55.6	4 19.2	+26.2	55.7	4 53.1	+26.9	55.7	5 26.8	+27.8	55.8	6 00.5	+28.5	55.9	6 34.1	+29.3	56.0	7 07.7	+30.0	56.1	7 41.1	+30.8	56.2	33
34	4 10.8	+25.3	54.7	4 45.4	+26.2	54.7	5 20.0	+26.9	54.8	5 54.6	+27.6	54.9	6 29.0	+28.4	55.0	7 03.4	+29.2	55.1	7 37.7	+29.9	55.2	8 11.9	+30.7	55.3	34
35	4 36.1	+25.3	53.8	5 11.6	+26.0	53.8	5 46.9	+26.8	53.9	6 22.2	+27.6	54.0	6 57.4	+28.4	54.1	7 32.6	+29.1	54.2	8 07.6	+29.8	54.3	8 42.6	+30.5	54.4	35
36	5 01.4	+25.2	52.9	5 37.6	+26.0	52.9	6 13.7	+26.8	53.0	6 49.8	+27.5	53.1	7 25.8	+28.2	53.2	8 01.7	+28.9	53.3	8 37.4	+29.7	53.4	9 13.1	+30.5	53.6	36
37	5 26.6	+25.2	52.0	6 03.6	+25.9	52.0	6 40.5	+26.6	52.1	7 17.3	+27.3	52.2	7 54.0	+28.1	52.3	8 30.6	+28.8	52.4	9 07.1	+29.6	52.6	9 43.6	+30.3	52.7	37
38	5 51.8	+25.0	51.0	6 29.5	+25.8	51.1	7 07.1	+26.5	51.2	7 44.6	+27.3	51.3	8 22.1	+28.0	51.4	8 59.4	+28.8	51.6	9 36.7	+29.4	51.7	10 13.9	+30.1	51.8	38
39	6 16.8	+25.0	50.1	6 55.3	+25.6	50.2	7 33.6	+26.4	50.3	8 11.9	+27.1	50.4	8 50.1	+27.8	50.5	9 28.2	+28.5	50.7	10 06.1	+29.3	50.8	10 44.0	+30.0	50.9	39
40	6 41.8	+24.8	49.2	7 20.9	+25.6	49.3	8 00.0	+26.3	49.4	8 39.0	+27.0	49.5	9 17.9	+27.7	49.6	9 56.7	+28.5	49.8	10 35.4	+29.2	49.9	11 14.0	+29.9	50.1	40
41	7 06.6	+24.8	48.3	7 46.5	+25.5	48.4	8 26.3	+26.2	48.5	9 06.0	+26.9	48.6	9 45.6	+27.6	48.7	10 25.2	+28.2	48.9	11 04.6	+29.0	49.0	11 43.9	+29.6	49.2	41
42	7 31.4	+24.6	47.4	8 12.0	+25.3	47.5	8 52.5	+26.0	47.6	9 32.9	+26.7	47.7	10 13.2	+27.5	47.8	10 53.4	+28.2	48.0	11 33.6	+28.8	48.1	12 13.5	+29.6	48.3	42
43	7 56.0	+24.5	46.5	8 37.3	+25.2	46.6	9 18.5	+25.9	46.7	9 59.6	+26.6	46.8	10 40.7	+27.2	46.9	11 21.6	+27.9	47.1	12 02.4	+28.6	47.2	12 43.1	+29.3	47.4	43
44	8 20.5	+24.4	45.5	9 02.5	+25.1	45.6	9 44.4	+25.8	45.8	10 26.2	+26.4	45.9	11 07.9	+27.1	46.0	11 49.5	+27.8	46.2	12 31.0	+28.5	46.3	13 12.4	+29.1	46.5	44
45	8 44.9	+24.2	44.6	9 27.6	+24.9	44.7	10 10.2	+25.5	44.8	10 52.6	+26.3	45.0	11 35.0	+27.0	45.1	12 17.3	+27.6	45.3	12 59.5	+28.3	45.4	13 41.5	+29.0	45.6	45
46	9 09.1	+24.1	43.7	9 52.5	+24.7	43.8	10 35.7	+25.5	43.9	11 18.9	+26.1	44.1	12 02.0	+26.7	44.2	12 44.9	+27.5	44.4	13 27.8	+28.1	44.5	14 10.5	+28.7	44.7	46
47	9 33.2	+24.0	42.8	10 17.2	+24.7	42.9	11 01.2	+25.2	43.0	11 45.0	+25.9	43.1	12 28.7	+26.6	43.3	13 12.4	+27.2	43.4	13 55.9	+27.8	43.6	14 39.2	+28.6	43.8	47
48	9 57.2	+23.8	41.8	10 41.9	+24.4	41.9	11 26.4	+25.1	42.1	12 10.9	+25.8	42.2	12 55.3	+26.4	42.4	13 39.6	+27.0	42.5	14 23.7	+27.7	42.7	15 07.8	+28.3	42.9	48
49	10 21.0	+23.6	40.9	11 06.3	+24.3	41.0	11 51.5	+24.9	41.2	12 36.7	+25.5	41.3	13 21.7	+26.2	41.4	14 06.6	+26.8	41.6	14 51.4	+27.5	41.8	15 36.1	+28.1	42.0	49
50	10 44.6	+23.5	40.0	11 30.6	+24.1	40.1	12 16.4	+24.8	40.2	13 02.2	+25.3	40.4	13 47.9	+25.9	40.5	14 33.4	+26.6	40.7	15 18.9	+27.2	40.9	16 04.2	+27.8	41.0	50
51	11 08.1	+23.3	39.0	11 54.7	+23.9	39.1	12 41.2	+24.5	39.3	13 27.5	+25.2	39.4	14 13.8	+25.8	39.6	15 00.0	+26.4	39.8	15 46.1	+27.0	39.9	16 32.0	+27.6	40.1	51
52	11 31.4	+23.1	38.1	12 18.6	+23.7	38.2	13 05.7	+24.3	38.4	13 52.7	+24.9	38.5	14 39.6	+25.5	38.7	15 26.4	+26.1	38.8	16 13.1	+26.7	39.0	16 59.6	+27.4	39.2	52
53	11 54.5	+22.9	37.1	12 42.3	+23.5	37.3	13 30.0	+24.1	37.4	14 17.6	+24.7	37.6	15 05.1	+25.3	37.7	15 52.5	+25.9	37.9	16 39.8	+26.5	38.1	17 27.0	+27.1	38.3	53
54	12 17.4	+22.8	36.2	13 05.8	+23.3	36.3	13 54.1	+23.9	36.5	14 42.3	+24.5	36.6	15 30.4	+25.1	36.8	16 18.4	+25.7	37.0	17 06.3	+26.2	37.1	17 54.1	+26.8	37.3	54
55	12 40.2	+22.5	35.2	13 29.1	+23.1	35.4	14 18.0	+23.7	35.5	15 06.8	+24.2	35.7	15 55.5	+24.8	35.8	16 44.1	+25.4	36.0	17 32.5	+26.0	36.2	18 20.9	+26.6	36.4	55
56	13 02.7	+22.3	34.3	13 52.2	+22.9	34.4	14 41.7	+23.4	34.6	15 31.0	+24.0	34.7	16 20.3	+24.5	34.9	17 09.5	+25.1	35.1	17 58.5	+25.7	35.2	18 47.5	+26.2	35.4	56
57	13 25.0	+22.1	33.3	14 15.1	+22.6	33.5	15 05.1	+23.2	33.6	15 55.0	+23.8	33.8	16 44.8	+24.3	33.9	17 34.6	+24.8	34.1	18 24.2	+25.4	34.3	19 13.7	+26.0	34.5	57
58	13 47.1	+21.9	32.4	14 37.7	+22.5	32.5	15 28.3	+22.9	32.7	16 18.8	+23.4	32.8	17 09.1	+24.1	33.0	17 59.4	+24.6	33.2	18 49.6	+25.1	33.3	19 39.7	+25.6	33.5	58
59	14 09.0	+21.6	31.4	15 00.2	+22.1	31.6	15 51.2	+22.7	31.7	16 42.2	+23.3	31.9	17 33.2	+23.7	32.0	18 24.0	+24.3	32.2	19 14.7	+24.8	32.4	20 05.3	+25.4	32.6	59
60	14 30.6	+21.5	30.5	15 22.3	+22.0	30.6	16 13.9	+22.5	30.7	17 05.5	+22.9	30.9	17 56.9	+23.5	31.1	18 48.3	+23.9	31.2	19 39.5	+24.5	31.4	20 30.7	+25.0	31.6	60
61	14 52.1	+21.1	29.5	15 44.3	+21.6	29.6	16 36.4	+22.1	29.8	17 28.4	+22.7	29.9	18 20.4	+23.1	30.1	19 12.2	+23.7	30.3	20 04.0	+24.2	30.4	20 55.7	+24.7	30.6	61
62	15 13.2	+21.0	28.5	16 05.9	+21.4	28.7	16 58.5	+21.9	28.8	17 51.1	+22.3	29.0	18 43.5	+22.9	29.1	19 35.9	+23.4	29.3	20 28.2	+23.8	29.5	21 20.4	+24.3	29.7	62
63	15 34.2	+20.6	27.6	16 27.3	+21.2	27.7	17 20.4	+21.6	27.8	18 13.4	+22.1	28.0	19 06.4	+22.5	28.1	19 59.3	+23.0	28.3	20 52.0	+23.5	28.5	21 44.7	+24.0	28.7	63
64	15 54.8	+20.4	26.6	16 48.5	+20.8	26.7	17 42.0	+21.3	26.9	18 35.5	+21.8	27.0	19 28.9	+22.3	27.2	20 22.3	+22.7	27.3	21 15.5	+23.2	27.5	22 08.7	+23.7	27.7	64
65	16 15.2	+20.2	25.6	17 09.3	+20.6	25.7	18 03.3	+21.0	25.9	18 57.3	+21.4	26.0	19 51.2	+21.9	26.2	20 45.0	+22.3	26.3	21 38.7	+22.8	26.5	22 32.4	+23.2	26.7	65
66	16 35.4	+19.8	24.6	17 29.9	+20.3	24.7	18 24.3	+20.7	24.9	19 18.7	+21.2	25.0	20 13.1	+21.5	25.2	21 07.3	+22.0	25.3	22 01.5	+22.5	25.5	22 55.6	+22.9	25.7	66
67	16 55.2	+19.6	23.6	17 50.2	+19.9	23.8	18 45.0	+20.4	23.9	19 39.9	+20.8	24.0	20 34.6	+21.3	24.2	21 29.3	+21.7	24.3	22 24.0	+22.0	24.5	23 18.5	+22.5	24.7	67
68	17 14.8	+19.3	22.6	18 10.1	+19.7	22.8	19 05.4	+20.1	22.9	20 00.7	+20.5	23.0	20 55.9	+20.8	23.2	21 51.0	+21.3	23.3	22 46.0	+21.7	23.5	23 41.0	+22.1	23.7	68
69	17 34.1	+19.0	21.7	18 29.8	+19.4	21.8	19 25.5	+19.8	21.9	20 21.2	+20.1	22.0	21 16.7	+20.6	22.2	22 12.3	+20.9	22.3	23 07.7	+21.3	22.5	24 03.1	+21.7	22.7	69
70	17 53.1	+18.6	20.7	18 49.2	+19.0	20.8	19 45.3	+19.4	20.9	20 41.3	+19.8	21.0	21 37.3	+20.1	21.2	22 33.2	+20.5	21.3	23 29.0	+20.9	21.5	24 24.8	+21.3	21.6	70
71	18 11.7	+18.4	19.7	19 08.2	+18.7	19.8	20 04.7	+19.0	19.9	21 01.1	+19.4	20.0	21 57.4	+19.8	20.2	22 53.7	+20.1	20.3	23 49.9	+20.5	20.4	24 46.1	+20.9	20.6	71
72	18 30.1	+18.0	18.7	19 26.9	+18.4	18.8	20 23.7	+18.7	18.9	21 20.5	+19.0	19.0	22 17.2	+19.4	19.1	23 13.8	+19.8	19.3	24 10.4	+20.1	19.4	25 07.0	+20.4	19.6	72
73	18 48.1	+17.8	17.6	19 45.3	+18.0	17.8	20 42.4	+18.4	17.9	21 39.5	+18.7	18.0	22 36.6	+19.0	18.1	23 33.6	+19.3	18.2	24 30.5	+19.7	18.4	25 27.4	+20.0	18.5	73
74	19 05.9	+17.4	16.6	20 03.3	+17.7	16.7	21 00.8	+18.0	16.8	21 58.2	+18.3	17.0	22 55.6	+18.6	17.1	23 52.9	+18.9	17.2	24 50.2	+19.2	17.3	25 47.4	+19.6	17.5	74
75	19 23.3	+17.0	15.6	20 21.0	+17.4	15.7	21 18.8	+17.6	15.8	22 16.5	+17.9	15.9	23 14.2	+18.1	16.1	24 11.8	+18.5	16.2	25 09.4	+18.8	16.3	26 07.0	+19.1	16.4	75
76	19 40.3	+16.7	14.6	20 38.4	+16.9	14.7	21 36.4	+17.2	14.8	22 34.4	+17.5	14.9	23 32.3	+17.8	15.0	24 30.3	+18.0	15.1	25 28.2	+18.3	15.3	26 26.1	+18.6	15.4	76
77	19 57.0	+16.4	13.6	20 55.3	+16.6	13.7	21 53.6	+16.9	13.8	22 51.9	+17.1	13.9	23 50.1	+17.4	14.0	24 48.3	+17.6	14.1	25 46.5	+17.9	14.2	26 44.7	+18.1	14.3	77
78	20 13.4	+16.0	12.6	21 11.9	+16.3	12.6	22 10.5	+16.4	12.7	23 09.0	+16.7	12.8	24 07.5	+16.9	12.9	25 05.9	+17.2	13.0	26 04.4	+17.4	13.1	27 02.8	+17.7	13.2	78
79	20 29.4	+15.6	11.5	21 28.2	+15.8	11.6	22 26.9	+16.1	11.7	23 25.7	+16.2	11.8	24 24.4	+16.5	11.9	25 23.1	+16.7	12.0	26 21.8	+16.9	12.1	27 20.5	+17.1	12.2	79
80	20 45.0	+15.3	10.5	21 44.0	+15.5	10.6	22 43.0	+15.6	10.6	23 41.9	+15.9	10.7	24 40.9	+16.0	10.8	25 39.8	+16.2	10.9	26 38.7	+16.5	11.0	27 37.6	+16.7	11.1	80
81	21 00.3	+14.9	9.5	21 59.5	+15.0	9.5	22 58.6	+15.3	9.6	23 57.8	+15.4	9.7	24 56.9	+15.6	9.8	25 56.0	+15.8	9.8	26 55.2	+15.9	9.9	27 54.3	+16.1	10.0	81
82	21 15.2	+14.5	8.4	22 14.5	+14.7	8.5	23 13.9	+14.8	8.5	24 13.2	+14.9	8.6	25 12.5	+15.1	8.7	26 11.8	+15.3	8.8	27 11.1	+15.4	8.8	28 10.4	+15.6	8.9	82
83	21 29.7	+14.1	7.4	22 29.2	+14.2	7.4	23 28.7	+14.3	7.5	24 28.1	+14.6	7.6	25 27.6	+14.7	7.6	26 27.1	+14.8	7.7	27 26.5	+15.0	7.7	28 26.0	+15.1	7.8	83
84	21 43.8	+13.7	6.3	22 43.4	+13.9	6.4	23 43.0	+14.0	6.4	24 42.7	+14.0	6.5	25 42.3	+14.2	6.5	26 41.9	+14.3	6.6	27 41.5	+14.4	6.6	28 41.1	+14.5	6.7	84
85	21 57.5	+13.3	5.3	22 57.3	+13.4	5.3	23 57.0	+13.5	5.4	24 56.7	+13.6	5.4	25 56.5	+13.7	5.5	26 56.2	+13.8	5.5	27 55.9	+13.9	5.6	28 55.6	+14.0	5.6	85
86	22 10.8	+13.0	4.2	23 10.7	+13.0	4.3	24 10.5	+13.1	4.3	25 10.3	+13.2	4.3	26 10.2	+13.2	4.4	27 10.0	+13.3	4.4	28 09.8	+13.4	4.5	29 09.6	+13.5	4.5	86
87	22 23.8	+12.5	3.2	23 23.7	+12.5	3.2	24 23.6	+12.6	3.2	25 23.5	+12.6	3.3	26 23.4	+12.7	3.3	27 23.3	+12.7	3.3	28 23.2	+12.8	3.3	29 23.1	+12.8	3.4	87
88	22 36.3	+12.0	2.1	23 36.2	+12.1	2.1	24 36.2	+12.1	2.2	25 36.1	+12.2	2.2	26 36.1	+12.2	2.2	27 36.0	+12.3	2.2	28 36.0	+12.3	2.2	29 35.9	+12.4	2.3	88
89	22 48.3	+11.7	1.1	23 48.3	+11.7	1.1	24 48.3	+11.7	1.1	25 48.3	+11.7	1.1	26 48.3	+11.7	1.1	27 48.3	+11.7	1.1	28 48.3	+11.7	1.1	29 48.3	+11.7	1.1	89
90	23 00.0	+11.2	0.0	24 00.0	+11.2	0.0	25 00.0	+11.2	0.0	26 00.0	+11.2	0.0	27 00.0	+11.2	0.0	28 00.0	+11.2	0.0	29 00.0	+11.2	0.0	30 00.0	+11.2	0.0	90
	23°			24°			25°			26°			27°			28°			29°			30°			

S. Lat. { L.H.A. greater than 180° ....Zn=180°–Z
L.H.A. less than 180°...........Zn=180°+Z

LATITUDE **SAME** NAME AS DECLINATION L.H.A. 101°, 259°

343

Dec.	23° Hc	d	Z	24° Hc	d	Z	25° Hc	d	Z	26° Hc	d	Z	Dec.
°	° ′	′	°	° ′	′	°	° ′	′	°	° ′	′	°	°
0	9 11.9	+23.6	93.9	9 07.7	+24.6	94.1	9 03.3	+25.6	94.3	8 58.7	+26.6	94.4	0
1	9 35.5	+23.6	93.0	9 32.3	+24.5	93.2	9 28.9	+25.5	93.3	9 25.3	+26.4	93.5	1
2	9 59.1	+23.3	92.1	9 56.8	+24.4	92.3	9 54.4	+25.3	92.4	9 51.7	+26.3	92.6	2
3	10 22.4	+23.3	91.1	10 21.2	+24.1	91.3	10 19.7	+25.1	91.5	10 18.0	+26.1	91.7	3
4	10 45.7	+23.0	90.2	10 45.3	+24.1	90.4	10 44.8	+25.0	90.6	10 44.1	+26.0	90.8	4
5	11 08.7	+22.9	89.3	11 09.4	+23.8	89.5	11 09.8	+24.8	89.7	11 10.1	+25.8	89.9	5
6	11 31.6	+22.6	88.3	11 33.2	+23.7	88.5	11 34.6	+24.7	88.7	11 35.9	+25.6	88.9	6
7	11 54.2	+22.5	87.4	11 56.9	+23.5	87.6	11 59.3	+24.4	87.8	12 01.5	+25.4	88.0	7
8	12 16.7	+22.3	86.4	12 20.4	+23.2	86.6	12 23.7	+24.3	86.9	12 26.9	+25.3	87.1	8
9	12 39.0	+22.1	85.5	12 43.6	+23.1	85.7	12 48.0	+24.1	85.9	12 52.2	+25.0	86.2	9
10	13 01.1	+21.9	84.5	13 06.7	+22.9	84.8	13 12.1	+23.8	85.0	13 17.2	+24.8	85.2	10
11	13 23.0	+21.7	83.6	13 29.6	+22.7	83.8	13 35.9	+23.7	84.0	13 42.0	+24.7	84.3	11
12	13 44.7	+21.4	82.6	13 52.3	+22.4	82.8	13 59.6	+23.4	83.1	14 06.7	+24.4	83.3	12
13	14 06.1	+21.2	81.6	14 14.7	+22.2	81.9	14 23.0	+23.2	82.1	14 31.1	+24.2	82.4	13
14	14 27.3	+21.0	80.7	14 36.9	+22.0	80.9	14 46.2	+23.0	81.2	14 55.3	+23.9	81.5	14
15	14 48.3	+20.7	79.7	14 58.9	+21.7	80.0	15 09.2	+22.7	80.2	15 19.2	+23.7	80.5	15
16	15 09.0	+20.5	78.7	15 20.6	+21.5	79.0	15 31.9	+22.5	79.3	15 42.9	+23.5	79.6	16
17	15 29.5	+20.2	77.8	15 42.1	+21.2	78.0	15 54.4	+22.2	78.3	16 06.4	+23.2	78.6	17
18	15 49.7	+20.0	76.8	16 03.3	+21.0	77.1	16 16.6	+21.9	77.3	16 29.6	+22.9	77.6	18
19	16 09.7	+19.7	75.8	16 24.3	+20.6	76.1	16 38.5	+21.7	76.4	16 52.5	+22.7	76.7	19
20	16 29.4	+19.4	74.8	16 44.9	+20.5	75.1	17 00.2	+21.4	75.4	17 15.2	+22.4	75.7	20
21	16 48.8	+19.1	73.8	17 05.4	+20.1	74.1	17 21.6	+21.1	74.4	17 37.6	+22.1	74.7	21
22	17 07.9	+18.9	72.8	17 25.5	+19.8	73.1	17 42.7	+20.8	73.4	17 59.7	+21.8	73.8	22
23	17 26.8	+18.5	71.8	17 45.3	+19.5	72.1	18 03.5	+20.6	72.5	18 21.5	+21.5	72.8	23
24	17 45.3	+18.2	70.8	18 04.8	+19.3	71.2	18 24.1	+20.2	71.5	18 43.0	+21.2	71.8	24
25	18 03.5	+18.0	69.8	18 24.1	+18.9	70.2	18 44.3	+19.9	70.5	19 04.2	+20.8	70.8	25
26	18 21.5	+17.6	68.8	18 43.0	+18.6	69.2	19 04.2	+19.5	69.5	19 25.0	+20.6	69.8	26
27	18 39.1	+17.3	67.8	19 01.6	+18.2	68.2	19 23.7	+19.3	68.5	19 45.6	+20.2	68.8	27
28	18 56.4	+16.9	66.8	19 19.8	+18.0	67.1	19 43.0	+18.9	67.5	20 05.8	+19.9	67.8	28
29	19 13.3	+16.7	65.8	19 37.8	+17.6	66.1	20 01.9	+18.5	66.5	20 25.7	+19.5	66.8	29
30	19 30.0	+16.2	64.8	19 55.4	+17.2	65.1	20 20.4	+18.3	65.4	20 45.2	+19.2	65.8	30
31	19 46.2	+16.0	63.8	20 12.6	+16.9	64.1	20 38.7	+17.8	64.4	21 04.4	+18.8	64.8	31
32	20 02.2	+15.5	62.7	20 29.5	+16.5	63.1	20 56.5	+17.5	63.4	21 23.2	+18.4	63.8	32
33	20 17.7	+15.2	61.7	20 46.0	+16.2	62.0	21 14.0	+17.1	62.4	21 41.6	+18.1	62.7	33
34	20 32.9	+14.9	60.7	21 02.2	+15.8	61.0	21 31.1	+16.7	61.4	21 59.7	+17.7	61.7	34
35	20 47.8	+14.5	59.6	21 18.0	+15.4	60.0	21 47.8	+16.4	60.3	22 17.4	+17.3	60.7	35
36	21 02.3	+14.1	58.6	21 33.4	+15.0	58.9	22 04.2	+15.9	59.3	22 34.7	+16.8	59.6	36
37	21 16.4	+13.7	57.6	21 48.4	+14.6	57.9	22 20.1	+15.6	58.2	22 51.5	+16.5	58.6	37
38	21 30.1	+13.3	56.5	22 03.0	+14.2	56.9	22 35.7	+15.1	57.2	23 08.0	+16.1	57.6	38
39	21 43.4	+12.9	55.5	22 17.2	+13.9	55.8	22 50.8	+14.7	56.1	23 24.1	+15.6	56.5	39
40	21 56.3	+12.5	54.4	22 31.1	+13.4	54.8	23 05.5	+14.3	55.1	23 39.7	+15.2	55.5	40
41	22 08.8	+12.1	53.4	22 44.5	+13.0	53.7	23 19.8	+13.9	54.0	23 54.9	+14.8	54.4	41
42	22 20.9	+11.7	52.3	22 57.5	+12.5	52.6	23 33.7	+13.5	53.0	24 09.7	+14.3	53.3	42
43	22 32.6	+11.3	51.2	23 10.0	+12.2	51.6	23 47.2	+13.0	51.9	24 24.0	+13.9	52.3	43
44	22 43.9	+10.8	50.2	23 22.2	+11.7	50.5	24 00.2	+12.5	50.8	24 37.9	+13.4	51.2	44
45	22 54.7	+10.4	49.1	23 33.9	+11.2	49.4	24 12.7	+12.2	49.8	24 51.3	+13.0	50.1	45
46	23 05.1	+10.0	48.0	23 45.1	+10.8	48.4	24 24.9	+11.6	48.7	25 04.3	+12.5	49.0	46
47	23 15.1	+9.6	47.0	23 55.9	+10.4	47.3	24 36.5	+11.2	47.6	25 16.8	+12.0	48.0	47
48	23 24.7	+9.1	45.9	24 06.3	+9.9	46.2	24 47.7	+10.7	46.5	25 28.8	+11.6	46.9	48
49	23 33.8	+8.6	44.8	24 16.2	+9.5	45.1	24 58.4	+10.3	45.5	25 40.4	+11.0	45.8	49
50	23 42.4	+8.2	43.7	24 25.7	+9.0	44.0	25 08.7	+9.8	44.4	25 51.4	+10.6	44.7	50
51	23 50.6	+7.8	42.7	24 34.7	+8.5	43.0	25 18.5	+9.2	43.3	26 02.0	+10.1	43.6	51
52	23 58.4	+7.3	41.6	24 43.2	+8.0	41.9	25 27.7	+8.9	42.2	26 12.1	+9.6	42.5	52
53	24 05.7	+6.8	40.5	24 51.2	+7.6	40.8	25 36.6	+8.3	41.1	26 21.7	+9.0	41.4	53
54	24 12.5	+6.4	39.4	24 58.8	+7.1	39.7	25 44.9	+7.8	40.0	26 30.7	+8.6	40.3	54
55	24 18.9	+5.9	38.3	25 05.9	+6.6	38.6	25 52.7	+7.3	38.9	26 39.3	+8.0	39.2	55
56	24 24.8	+5.4	37.2	25 12.5	+6.1	37.5	26 00.0	+6.8	37.8	26 47.3	+7.5	38.1	56
57	24 30.2	+5.0	36.1	25 18.6	+5.6	36.4	26 06.8	+6.3	36.7	26 54.8	+7.0	37.0	57
58	24 35.2	+4.5	35.0	25 24.2	+5.2	35.3	26 13.1	+5.8	35.6	27 01.8	+6.5	35.9	58
59	24 39.7	+4.0	33.9	25 29.4	+4.6	34.2	26 18.9	+5.3	34.5	27 08.3	+5.9	34.7	59
60	24 43.7	+3.5	32.8	25 34.0	+4.1	33.1	26 24.2	+4.8	33.3	27 14.2	+5.4	33.6	60
61	24 47.2	+3.0	31.7	25 38.1	+3.7	32.0	26 29.0	+4.2	32.2	27 19.6	+4.9	32.5	61
62	24 50.2	+2.6	30.6	25 41.8	+3.1	30.9	26 33.2	+3.7	31.1	27 24.5	+4.3	31.4	62
63	24 52.8	+2.0	29.5	25 44.9	+2.7	29.8	26 36.9	+3.2	30.0	27 28.8	+3.8	30.3	63
64	24 54.8	+1.6	28.4	25 47.6	+2.1	28.7	26 40.1	+2.7	28.9	27 32.6	+3.3	29.1	64
65	24 56.4	+1.1	27.3	25 49.7	+1.6	27.5	26 42.8	+2.2	27.8	27 35.9	+2.6	28.0	65
66	24 57.5	+0.6	26.2	25 51.3	+1.1	26.4	26 45.0	+1.6	26.7	27 38.5	+2.2	26.9	66
67	24 58.1	+0.2	25.1	25 52.4	+0.6	25.3	26 46.6	+1.1	25.5	27 40.7	+1.6	25.8	67
68	24 58.3	−0.4	24.0	25 53.0	+0.1	24.2	26 47.7	+0.6	24.4	27 42.3	+1.0	24.6	68
69	24 57.9	−0.9	22.9	25 53.1	−0.4	23.1	26 48.3	0.0	23.3	27 43.3	+0.5	23.5	69
70	24 57.0	−1.3	21.8	25 52.7	−0.9	22.0	26 48.3	−0.5	22.2	27 43.8	0.0	22.4	70
71	24 55.7	−1.8	20.7	25 51.8	−1.4	20.9	26 47.8	−1.0	21.1	27 43.8	−0.6	21.2	71
72	24 53.9	−2.3	19.6	25 50.4	−2.0	19.8	26 46.8	−1.5	19.9	27 43.2	−1.2	20.1	72
73	24 51.6	−2.8	18.5	25 48.4	−2.4	18.7	26 45.3	−2.1	18.8	27 42.0	−1.7	19.0	73
74	24 48.8	−3.3	17.4	25 46.0	−2.9	17.5	26 43.2	−2.6	17.7	27 40.3	−2.2	17.8	74
75	24 45.5	−3.8	16.3	25 43.1	−3.5	16.4	26 40.6	−3.1	16.6	27 38.1	−2.8	16.7	75
76	24 41.7	−4.2	15.2	25 39.6	−3.9	15.3	26 37.5	−3.7	15.5	27 35.3	−3.4	15.6	76
77	24 37.5	−4.7	14.1	25 35.7	−4.5	14.2	26 33.8	−4.2	14.3	27 31.9	−3.9	14.5	77
78	24 32.8	−5.2	13.0	25 31.2	−4.9	13.1	26 29.6	−4.6	13.2	27 28.0	−4.4	13.3	78
79	24 27.6	−5.7	11.9	25 26.3	−5.5	12.0	26 25.0	−5.3	12.1	27 23.6	−5.0	12.2	79
80	24 21.9	−6.1	10.8	25 20.8	−5.9	10.9	26 19.7	−5.7	11.0	27 18.6	−5.5	11.1	80
81	24 15.8	−6.6	9.7	25 14.9	−6.4	9.8	26 14.0	−6.2	9.9	27 13.1	−6.0	10.0	81
82	24 09.2	−7.1	8.6	25 08.5	−6.9	8.7	26 07.8	−6.7	8.8	27 07.1	−6.6	8.9	82
83	24 02.1	−7.5	7.6	25 01.6	−7.4	7.6	26 01.1	−7.3	7.7	27 00.5	−7.1	7.7	83
84	23 54.6	−8.0	6.5	24 54.2	−7.9	6.5	25 53.8	−7.7	6.6	26 53.4	−7.6	6.6	84
85	23 46.6	−8.4	5.4	24 46.3	−8.3	5.4	25 46.1	−8.3	5.5	26 45.8	−8.1	5.5	85
86	23 38.2	−8.9	4.3	24 38.0	−8.8	4.3	25 37.8	−8.7	4.4	26 37.7	−8.7	4.4	86
87	23 29.3	−9.3	3.2	24 29.2	−9.3	3.2	25 29.1	−9.2	3.3	26 29.0	−9.2	3.3	87
88	23 20.0	−9.8	2.1	24 19.9	−9.7	2.2	25 19.9	−9.7	2.2	26 19.8	−9.6	2.2	88
89	23 10.2	−10.2	1.1	24 10.2	−10.2	1.1	25 10.2	−10.2	1.1	26 10.2	−10.2	1.1	89
90	23 00.0	−10.6	0.0	24 00.0	−10.6	0.0	25 00.0	−10.7	0.0	26 00.0	−10.7	0.0	90
	23°			24°			25°			26°			

Dec.	27° Hc	d	Z	28° Hc	d	Z	29° Hc	d	Z	30° Hc	d	Z	Dec.
°	° ′	′	°	° ′	′	°	° ′	′	°	° ′	′	°	°
0	8 54.0	+27.5	94.6	8 49.2	+28.4	94.7	8 44.1	+29.4	94.9	8 39.0	+30.2	95.0	0
1	9 21.5	+27.4	93.7	9 17.6	+28.3	93.8	9 13.5	+29.2	94.0	9 09.2	+30.2	94.2	1
2	9 48.9	+27.2	92.8	9 45.9	+28.2	92.9	9 42.7	+29.1	93.1	9 39.4	+30.0	93.3	2
3	10 16.1	+27.1	91.9	10 14.1	+28.0	92.0	10 11.8	+29.0	92.2	10 09.4	+29.9	92.4	3
4	10 43.2	+26.9	91.0	10 42.1	+27.9	91.2	10 40.8	+28.8	91.3	10 39.3	+29.7	91.5	4
5	11 10.1	+26.8	90.1	11 10.0	+27.7	90.2	11 09.6	+28.7	90.4	11 09.0	+29.6	90.6	5
6	11 36.9	+26.6	89.1	11 37.7	+27.5	89.3	11 38.3	+28.4	89.5	11 38.6	+29.4	89.8	6
7	12 03.5	+26.4	88.2	12 05.2	+27.4	88.4	12 06.7	+28.3	88.7	12 08.0	+29.3	88.9	7
8	12 29.9	+26.2	87.3	12 32.6	+27.1	87.5	12 35.0	+28.2	87.7	12 37.3	+29.0	88.0	8
9	12 56.1	+26.0	86.4	12 59.7	+27.0	86.6	13 03.2	+27.9	86.8	13 06.3	+28.9	87.1	9
10	13 22.1	+25.8	85.5	13 26.7	+26.8	85.7	13 31.1	+27.7	85.9	13 35.2	+28.7	86.2	10
11	13 47.9	+25.6	84.5	13 53.5	+26.6	84.8	13 58.8	+27.6	85.0	14 03.9	+28.5	85.3	11
12	14 13.5	+25.4	83.6	14 20.1	+26.3	83.8	14 26.4	+27.3	84.1	14 32.4	+28.3	84.4	12
13	14 38.9	+25.1	82.7	14 46.4	+26.1	82.9	14 53.7	+27.1	83.2	15 00.7	+28.0	83.4	13
14	15 04.0	+25.0	81.7	15 12.5	+25.9	82.0	15 20.8	+26.8	82.3	15 28.7	+27.8	82.5	14
15	15 29.0	+24.7	80.8	15 38.4	+25.7	81.1	15 47.6	+26.7	81.3	15 56.5	+27.6	81.6	15
16	15 53.7	+24.4	79.8	16 04.1	+25.4	80.1	16 14.3	+26.4	80.4	16 24.1	+27.4	80.7	16
17	16 18.1	+24.2	78.9	16 29.5	+25.2	79.2	16 40.7	+26.1	79.5	16 51.5	+27.1	79.8	17
18	16 42.3	+23.9	77.9	16 54.7	+24.9	78.2	17 06.8	+25.8	78.5	17 18.6	+26.8	78.8	18
19	17 06.2	+23.7	77.0	17 19.6	+24.6	77.3	17 32.6	+25.6	77.6	17 45.4	+26.6	77.9	19
20	17 29.9	+23.3	76.0	17 44.2	+24.4	76.3	17 58.2	+25.4	76.6	18 12.0	+26.2	76.9	20
21	17 53.2	+23.1	75.0	18 08.6	+24.0	75.4	18 23.6	+25.0	75.7	18 38.2	+26.0	76.0	21
22	18 16.3	+22.8	74.1	18 32.6	+23.8	74.4	18 48.6	+24.7	74.7	19 04.2	+25.8	75.0	22
23	18 39.1	+22.5	73.1	18 56.4	+23.4	73.4	19 13.3	+24.5	73.7	19 30.0	+25.4	74.1	23
24	19 01.6	+22.1	72.1	19 19.8	+23.2	72.4	19 37.8	+24.1	72.8	19 55.4	+25.0	73.1	24
25	19 23.7	+21.9	71.1	19 43.0	+22.8	71.5	20 01.9	+23.8	71.8	20 20.4	+24.8	72.2	25
26	19 45.6	+21.5	70.1	20 05.8	+22.5	70.5	20 25.7	+23.5	70.8	20 45.2	+24.5	71.2	26
27	20 07.1	+21.2	69.1	20 28.3	+22.2	69.5	20 49.2	+23.1	69.8	21 09.7	+24.1	70.2	27
28	20 28.3	+20.9	68.1	20 50.5	+21.8	68.5	21 12.3	+22.8	68.9	21 33.8	+23.7	69.2	28
29	20 49.2	+20.5	67.1	21 12.3	+21.5	67.5	21 35.1	+22.4	67.9	21 57.5	+23.4	68.2	29
30	21 09.7	+20.1	66.1	21 33.8	+21.1	66.5	21 57.5	+22.1	66.9	22 20.9	+23.0	67.2	30
31	21 29.8	+19.8	65.1	21 54.9	+20.7	65.5	22 19.6	+21.7	65.9	22 43.9	+22.7	66.2	31
32	21 49.6	+19.4	64.1	22 15.6	+20.3	64.5	22 41.3	+21.3	64.9	23 06.6	+22.2	65.2	32
33	22 09.0	+19.0	63.1	22 35.9	+20.0	63.5	23 02.6	+20.9	63.8	23 28.8	+21.9	64.2	33
34	22 28.0	+18.6	62.1	22 55.9	+19.6	62.4	23 23.5	+20.5	62.8	23 50.7	+21.5	63.2	34
35	22 46.6	+18.2	61.0	23 15.5	+19.1	61.4	23 44.0	+20.1	61.8	24 12.2	+21.1	62.2	35
36	23 04.8	+17.8	60.0	23 34.6	+18.8	60.4	24 04.1	+19.7	60.8	24 33.3	+20.6	61.2	36
37	23 22.6	+17.4	59.0	23 53.4	+18.3	59.3	24 23.8	+19.3	59.7	24 53.9	+20.2	60.1	37
38	23 40.0	+17.0	57.9	24 11.7	+18.0	58.3	24 43.1	+18.8	58.7	25 14.1	+19.8	59.1	38
39	23 57.0	+16.6	56.9	24 29.7	+17.4	57.2	25 01.9	+18.4	57.6	25 33.9	+19.3	58.0	39
40	24 13.6	+16.1	55.8	24 47.1	+17.1	56.2	25 20.3	+18.0	56.6	25 53.2	+18.9	57.0	40
41	24 29.7	+15.7	54.8	25 04.2	+16.5	55.1	25 38.3	+17.5	55.5	26 12.1	+18.4	55.9	41
42	24 45.4	+15.2	53.7	25 20.7	+16.2	54.1	25 55.8	+17.0	54.5	26 30.5	+17.9	54.9	42
43	25 00.6	+14.8	52.6	25 36.9	+15.6	53.0	26 12.8	+16.5	53.4	26 48.4	+17.5	53.8	43
44	25 15.4	+14.3	51.6	25 52.5	+15.2	51.9	26 29.3	+16.1	52.3	27 05.9	+16.9	52.7	44
45	25 29.7	+13.8	50.5	26 07.7	+14.7	50.9	26 45.4	+15.6	51.2	27 22.8	+16.5	51.6	45
46	25 43.5	+13.4	49.4	26 22.4	+14.2	49.8	27 01.0	+15.1	50.2	27 39.3	+15.9	50.6	46
47	25 56.9	+12.8	48.3	26 36.6	+13.7	48.7	27 16.1	+14.5	49.1	27 55.2	+15.4	49.5	47
48	26 09.7	+12.4	47.2	26 50.3	+13.2	47.6	27 30.6	+14.1	48.0	28 10.6	+14.9	48.4	48
49	26 22.1	+11.9	46.1	27 03.5	+12.7	46.5	27 44.7	+13.5	46.9	28 25.5	+14.4	47.3	49
50	26 34.0	+11.3	45.1	27 16.2	+12.2	45.4	27 58.2	+13.0	45.8	28 39.9	+13.8	46.2	50
51	26 45.3	+10.9	44.0	27 28.4	+11.7	44.3	28 11.2	+12.5	44.7	28 53.7	+13.3	45.1	51
52	26 56.2	+10.3	42.9	27 40.1	+11.1	43.2	28 23.7	+11.9	43.6	29 07.0	+12.7	43.9	52
53	27 06.5	+9.9	41.7	27 51.2	+10.6	42.1	28 35.6	+11.4	42.5	29 19.7	+12.2	42.8	53
54	27 16.4	+9.3	40.6	28 01.8	+10.0	41.0	28 47.0	+10.8	41.3	29 31.9	+11.6	41.7	54
55	27 25.7	+8.7	39.5	28 11.8	+9.6	39.9	28 57.8	+10.2	40.2	29 43.5	+11.0	40.6	55
56	27 34.4	+8.3	38.4	28 21.4	+8.9	38.7	29 08.0	+9.7	39.1	29 54.5	+10.4	39.4	56
57	27 42.7	+7.7	37.3	28 30.3	+8.4	37.6	29 17.7	+9.1	38.0	30 04.9	+9.9	38.3	57
58	27 50.4	+7.1	36.2	28 38.7	+7.8	36.5	29 26.8	+8.6	36.8	30 14.8	+9.2	37.2	58
59	27 57.5	+6.6	35.0	28 46.5	+7.3	35.4	29 35.4	+7.9	35.7	30 24.0	+8.7	36.0	59
60	28 04.1	+6.1	33.9	28 53.8	+6.7	34.2	29 43.3	+7.4	34.5	30 32.7	+8.0	34.9	60
61	28 10.2	+5.5	32.8	29 00.5	+6.1	33.1	29 50.7	+6.8	33.4	30 40.7	+7.4	33.7	61
62	28 15.7	+4.9	31.7	29 06.6	+5.6	32.0	29 57.5	+6.1	32.3	30 48.1	+6.8	32.6	62
63	28 20.6	+4.4	30.5	29 12.2	+5.0	30.8	30 03.6	+5.6	31.1	30 54.9	+6.2	31.4	63
64	28 25.0	+3.8	29.4	29 17.2	+4.3	29.7	30 09.2	+5.0	30.0	31 01.1	+5.6	30.2	64
65	28 28.8	+3.2	28.3	29 21.5	+3.8	28.5	30 14.2	+4.4	28.8	31 06.7	+4.9	29.1	65
66	28 32.0	+2.7	27.1	29 25.3	+3.3	27.4	30 18.6	+3.7	27.6	31 11.6	+4.4	27.9	66
67	28 34.7	+2.1	26.0	29 28.6	+2.6	26.2	30 22.3	+3.2	26.5	31 16.0	+3.6	26.8	67
68	28 36.8	+1.5	24.8	29 31.2	+2.0	25.1	30 25.5	+2.5	25.3	31 19.6	+3.1	25.6	68
69	28 38.3	+1.0	23.7	29 33.2	+1.4	23.9	30 28.0	+1.9	24.2	31 22.7	+2.4	24.4	69
70	28 39.3	+0.4	22.6	29 34.6	+0.9	22.8	30 29.9	+1.3	23.0	31 25.1	+1.8	23.2	70
71	28 39.7	−0.2	21.4	29 35.5	+0.2	21.6	30 31.2	+0.7	21.9	31 26.9	+1.1	22.1	71
72	28 39.5	−0.8	20.3	29 35.7	−0.3	20.5	30 31.9	+0.1	20.7	31 28.0	+0.5	20.9	72
73	28 38.7	−1.3	19.2	29 35.4	−1.0	19.3	30 32.0	−0.6	19.5	31 28.5	−0.2	19.7	73
74	28 37.4	−1.9	18.0	29 34.4	−1.5	18.2	30 31.4	−1.2	18.4	31 28.3	−0.8	18.6	74
75	28 35.5	−2.5	16.9	29 32.9	−2.1	17.0	30 30.2	−1.7	17.2	31 27.5	−1.4	17.4	75
76	28 33.0	−3.0	15.7	29 30.8	−2.8	15.9	30 28.5	−2.4	16.0	31 26.1	−2.1	16.2	76
77	28 30.0	−3.6	14.6	29 28.0	−3.3	14.7	30 26.1	−3.1	14.9	31 24.0	−2.7	15.0	77
78	28 26.4	−4.2	13.5	29 24.7	−3.9	13.6	30 23.0	−3.6	13.7	31 21.3	−3.3	13.9	78
79	28 22.2	−4.7	12.3	29 20.8	−4.5	12.4	30 19.4	−4.2	12.6	31 18.0	−4.0	12.7	79
80	28 17.5	−5.3	11.2	29 16.3	−5.0	11.3	30 15.2	−4.9	11.4	31 14.0	−4.6	11.5	80
81	28 12.2	−5.8	10.1	29 11.3	−5.7	10.2	30 10.3	−5.4	10.3	31 09.4	−5.3	10.4	81
82	28 06.4	−6.4	8.9	29 05.6	−6.2	9.0	30 04.9	−6.1	9.1	31 04.1	−5.9	9.2	82
83	28 00.0	−7.0	7.8	28 59.4	−6.8	7.9	29 58.8	−6.6	8.0	30 58.2	−6.4	8.0	83
84	27 53.0	−7.5	6.7	28 52.6	−7.4	6.8	29 51.8	−7.3	6.8	30 51.8	−7.2	6.9	84
85	27 45.5	−8.0	5.6	28 45.2	−7.9	5.6	29 44.9	−7.8	5.7	30 44.6	−7.7	5.7	85
86	27 37.5	−8.6	4.4	28 37.3	−8.5	4.5	29 37.1	−8.4	4.5	30 36.9	−8.3	4.6	86
87	27 28.9	−9.1	3.3	28 28.8	−9.0	3.4	29 28.7	−9.0	3.4	30 28.6	−8.9	3.4	87
88	27 19.8	−9.6	2.2	28 19.8	−9.7	2.2	29 19.7	−9.6	2.3	30 19.7	−9.6	2.3	88
89	27 10.2	−10.2	1.1	28 10.1	−10.1	1.1	29 10.1	−10.1	1.1	30 10.1	−10.1	1.1	89
90	27 00.0	−10.7	0.0	28 00.0	−10.7	0.0	29 00.0	−10.7	0.0	30 00.0	−10.7	0.0	90
	27°			28°			29°			30°			

LATITUDE **CONTRARY** NAME TO DECLINATION **L.H.A. 80°, 280°**

Dec.	23° Hc	d	Z	24° Hc	d	Z	25° Hc	d	Z	26° Hc	d	Z	27° Hc	d	Z	28° Hc	d	Z	29° Hc	d	Z	30° Hc	d	Z	Dec.
°	° ′	′	°	° ′	′	°	° ′	′	°	° ′	′	°	° ′	′	°	° ′	′	°	° ′	′	°	° ′	′	°	°
0	9 11.9	−23.8	93.9	9 07.7	−24.8	94.1	9 03.3	−25.8	94.3	8 58.7	−26.6	94.4	8 54.0	−27.6	94.6	8 49.2	−28.6	94.7	8 44.1	−29.4	94.9	8 39.0	−30.5	95.0	0
1	8 48.1	−24.0	94.9	8 42.9	−24.9	95.0	8 37.5	−25.8	95.2	8 32.1	−26.9	95.3	8 26.4	−27.8	95.5	8 20.6	−28.7	95.6	8 14.7	−29.7	95.8	8 08.5	−30.5	95.9	1
2	8 24.1	−24.1	95.8	8 18.0	−25.1	95.9	8 11.7	−26.0	96.1	8 05.2	−26.9	96.2	7 58.6	−27.8	96.4	7 51.9	−28.8	96.5	7 45.0	−29.7	96.6	7 38.0	−30.6	96.8	2
3	8 00.0	−24.2	96.7	7 52.9	−25.2	96.9	7 45.7	−26.1	97.0	7 38.3	−27.1	97.1	7 30.8	−28.0	97.3	7 23.1	−28.9	97.4	7 15.3	−29.8	97.5	7 07.4	−30.7	97.6	3
4	7 35.8	−24.3	97.6	7 27.7	−25.2	97.8	7 19.6	−26.3	97.9	7 11.2	−27.1	98.0	7 02.8	−28.1	98.2	6 54.2	−29.0	98.3	6 45.5	−29.9	98.4	6 36.7	−30.8	98.5	4
5	7 11.5	−24.5	98.6	7 02.5	−25.4	98.7	6 53.3	−26.3	98.8	6 44.1	−27.3	98.9	6 34.7	−28.2	99.0	6 25.2	−29.1	99.2	6 15.6	−30.0	99.3	6 05.9	−30.9	99.4	5
6	6 47.0	−24.5	99.5	6 37.1	−25.5	99.6	6 27.0	−26.4	99.7	6 16.8	−27.3	99.8	6 06.5	−28.2	99.9	5 56.1	−29.1	100.0	5 45.6	−30.1	100.1	5 35.0	−31.0	100.2	6
7	6 22.5	−24.6	100.4	6 11.6	−25.6	100.5	6 00.6	−26.5	100.6	5 49.5	−27.4	100.7	5 38.3	−28.4	100.8	5 27.0	−29.3	100.9	5 15.5	−30.1	101.0	5 04.0	−31.0	101.1	7
8	5 57.9	−24.8	101.3	5 46.0	−25.6	101.4	5 34.1	−26.6	101.5	5 22.1	−27.6	101.6	5 09.9	−28.4	101.7	4 57.7	−29.3	101.8	4 45.4	−30.2	101.9	4 33.0	−31.1	102.0	8
9	5 33.1	−24.8	102.2	5 20.4	−25.8	102.3	5 07.5	−26.7	102.4	4 54.5	−27.5	102.5	4 41.5	−28.5	102.6	4 28.4	−29.4	102.7	4 15.2	−30.3	102.7	4 01.9	−31.1	102.8	9
10	5 08.3	−24.9	103.2	4 54.6	−25.8	103.2	4 40.8	−26.7	103.3	4 27.0	−27.7	103.4	4 13.0	−28.5	103.5	3 59.0	−29.4	103.5	3 44.9	−30.3	103.6	3 30.8	−31.2	103.7	10
11	4 43.4	−24.9	104.1	4 28.8	−25.9	104.1	4 14.1	−26.8	104.2	3 59.3	−27.7	104.3	3 44.5	−28.6	104.4	3 29.6	−29.5	104.4	3 14.6	−30.4	104.5	2 59.6	−31.2	104.5	11
12	4 18.5	−25.1	105.0	4 02.9	−25.9	105.1	3 47.3	−26.8	105.1	3 31.6	−27.7	105.2	3 15.9	−28.7	105.2	3 00.1	−29.5	105.3	2 44.2	−30.4	105.3	2 28.4	−31.3	105.4	12
13	3 53.4	−25.0	105.9	3 37.0	−26.0	106.0	3 20.5	−26.9	106.0	3 03.9	−27.8	106.1	2 47.2	−28.6	106.1	2 30.6	−29.6	106.2	2 13.8	−30.4	106.2	1 57.1	−31.3	106.2	13
14	3 28.4	−25.2	106.8	3 11.0	−26.1	106.9	2 53.6	−27.0	106.9	2 36.1	−27.9	107.0	2 18.6	−28.8	107.0	2 01.0	−29.6	107.0	1 43.4	−30.4	107.1	1 25.8	−31.3	107.1	14
15	3 03.2	−25.2	107.7	2 44.9	−26.1	107.8	2 26.6	−27.0	107.8	2 08.2	−27.8	107.8	1 49.8	−28.7	107.9	1 31.4	−29.6	107.9	1 13.0	−30.5	107.9	0 54.5	−31.3	107.9	15
16	2 38.0	−25.2	108.6	2 18.8	−26.1	108.7	1 59.6	−27.0	108.7	1 40.4	−27.9	108.7	1 21.1	−28.8	108.8	1 01.8	−29.6	108.8	0 42.5	−30.5	108.8	0 23.2	−31.4	108.8	16
17	2 12.8	−25.3	109.5	1 52.7	−26.1	109.6	1 32.6	−27.0	109.6	1 12.5	−27.9	109.6	0 52.3	−28.7	109.6	0 32.2	−29.6	109.6	0 12.0	−30.5	109.6	0 08.2	+31.3	70.4	17
18	1 47.5	−25.2	110.4	1 26.6	−26.2	110.5	1 05.6	−27.1	110.5	0 44.6	−27.9	110.5	0 23.6	−28.8	110.5	0 02.6	−29.7	110.5	0 18.5	+30.4	69.5	0 39.5	+31.3	69.5	18
19	1 22.3	−25.3	111.3	1 00.4	−26.2	111.4	0 38.5	−27.0	111.4	0 16.7	−27.9	111.4	0 05.2	+28.8	68.6	0 27.1	+29.6	68.6	0 48.9	+30.5	68.6	1 10.8	+31.3	68.6	19
20	0 57.0	−25.4	112.2	0 34.2	−26.2	112.3	0 11.5	−27.1	112.3	0 11.2	+28.0	67.7	0 34.0	+28.7	67.7	0 56.7	+29.6	67.8	1 19.4	+30.5	67.8	1 42.1	+31.3	67.8	20
21	0 31.6	−25.3	113.2	0 08.0	−26.2	113.2	0 15.6	+27.0	66.8	0 39.2	+27.9	66.8	1 02.7	+28.8	66.9	1 26.3	+29.6	66.9	1 49.9	+30.4	66.9	2 13.4	+31.2	66.9	21
22	0 06.3	−25.3	114.1	0 18.2	+26.1	65.9	0 42.6	+27.1	65.9	1 07.1	+27.9	66.0	1 31.5	+28.7	66.0	1 55.9	+29.6	66.0	2 20.3	+30.4	66.0	2 44.6	+31.2	66.1	22
23	0 19.0	+25.3	65.0	0 44.3	+26.2	65.0	1 09.7	+27.0	65.1	1 35.0	+27.8	65.1	2 00.2	+28.7	65.1	2 25.5	+29.5	65.1	2 50.7	+30.3	65.2	3 15.8	+31.2	65.2	23
24	0 44.3	+25.4	64.1	1 10.5	+26.2	64.1	1 36.7	+27.0	64.2	2 02.8	+27.9	64.2	2 28.9	+28.7	64.2	2 55.0	+29.5	64.3	3 21.0	+30.3	64.3	3 47.0	+31.1	64.4	24
25	1 09.7	+25.3	63.2	1 36.7	+26.1	63.2	2 03.7	+27.0	63.3	2 30.7	+27.8	63.3	2 57.6	+28.6	63.3	3 24.5	+29.4	63.4	3 51.3	+30.3	63.5	4 18.1	+31.1	63.5	25
26	1 35.0	+25.2	62.3	2 02.8	+26.1	62.3	2 30.7	+26.9	62.4	2 58.5	+27.7	62.4	3 26.2	+28.6	62.5	3 53.9	+29.4	62.5	4 21.6	+30.2	62.6	4 49.2	+31.0	62.7	26
27	2 00.2	+25.3	61.4	2 28.9	+26.1	61.4	2 57.6	+26.9	61.5	3 26.2	+27.7	61.5	3 54.8	+28.5	61.6	4 23.3	+29.4	61.6	4 51.8	+30.1	61.7	5 20.2	+30.9	61.8	27
28	2 25.5	+25.2	60.5	2 55.0	+26.0	60.5	3 24.5	+26.8	60.6	3 53.9	+27.7	60.6	4 23.3	+28.5	60.7	4 52.7	+29.2	60.8	5 21.9	+30.1	60.9	5 51.1	+30.8	60.9	28
29	2 50.7	+25.1	59.6	3 21.0	+26.0	59.6	3 51.3	+26.8	59.7	4 21.6	+27.6	59.7	4 51.8	+28.4	59.8	5 21.9	+29.2	59.9	5 52.0	+29.9	60.0	6 21.9	+30.8	60.1	29
30	3 15.8	+25.2	58.7	3 47.0	+25.9	58.7	4 18.1	+26.7	58.8	4 49.2	+27.5	58.9	5 20.2	+28.3	58.9	5 51.1	+29.1	59.0	6 21.9	+29.9	59.1	6 52.7	+30.7	59.2	30
31	3 41.0	+25.0	57.8	4 12.9	+25.9	57.8	4 44.8	+26.7	57.9	5 16.7	+27.5	58.0	5 48.5	+28.2	58.0	6 20.2	+29.0	58.1	6 51.8	+29.8	58.2	7 23.4	+30.5	58.3	31
32	4 06.0	+25.0	56.9	4 38.8	+25.8	56.9	5 11.5	+26.6	57.0	5 44.2	+27.3	57.1	6 16.7	+28.2	57.2	6 49.2	+28.9	57.3	7 21.6	+29.7	57.4	7 53.9	+30.5	57.5	32
33	4 31.0	+24.9	55.9	5 04.6	+25.7	56.0	5 38.1	+26.5	56.1	6 11.5	+27.3	56.2	6 44.9	+28.0	56.3	7 18.1	+28.9	56.4	7 51.3	+29.6	56.5	8 24.4	+30.3	56.6	33
34	4 55.9	+24.9	55.0	5 30.3	+25.6	55.1	6 04.6	+26.4	55.2	6 38.8	+27.2	55.3	7 12.9	+28.0	55.4	7 47.0	+28.7	55.5	8 20.9	+29.5	55.6	8 54.7	+30.3	55.7	34
35	5 20.8	+24.8	54.1	5 55.9	+25.6	54.2	6 31.0	+26.3	54.3	7 06.0	+27.0	54.4	7 40.9	+27.8	54.5	8 15.7	+28.6	54.6	8 50.4	+29.3	54.7	9 25.0	+30.0	54.9	35
36	5 45.6	+24.6	53.2	6 21.5	+25.4	53.3	6 57.3	+26.2	53.4	7 33.0	+27.0	53.5	8 08.7	+27.7	53.6	8 44.3	+28.4	53.7	9 19.7	+29.2	53.8	9 55.0	+30.0	54.0	36
37	6 10.2	+24.6	52.3	6 46.9	+25.4	52.4	7 23.5	+26.1	52.5	8 00.0	+26.8	52.6	8 36.4	+27.6	52.7	9 12.7	+28.3	52.8	9 48.9	+29.1	53.0	10 25.0	+29.8	53.1	37
38	6 34.8	+24.5	51.4	7 12.3	+25.2	51.5	7 49.6	+26.0	51.6	8 26.8	+26.8	51.7	9 04.0	+27.5	51.8	9 41.0	+28.3	51.9	10 18.0	+28.9	52.1	10 54.8	+29.7	52.2	38
39	6 59.3	+24.4	50.4	7 37.5	+25.1	50.5	8 15.6	+25.8	50.7	8 53.6	+26.5	50.8	9 31.5	+27.3	50.9	10 09.2	+28.1	51.0	10 46.9	+28.8	51.2	11 24.5	+29.5	51.3	39
40	7 23.7	+24.3	49.5	8 02.6	+25.0	49.6	8 41.4	+25.7	49.7	9 20.1	+26.5	49.9	9 58.8	+27.1	50.0	10 37.3	+27.9	50.1	11 15.7	+28.6	50.3	11 54.0	+29.3	50.4	40
41	7 48.0	+24.1	48.6	8 27.6	+24.9	48.7	9 07.1	+25.6	48.8	9 46.6	+26.3	49.0	10 25.9	+27.1	49.1	11 05.2	+27.7	49.2	11 44.3	+28.4	49.4	12 23.3	+29.1	49.5	41
42	8 12.1	+24.0	47.7	8 52.5	+24.7	47.8	9 32.7	+25.5	47.9	10 12.9	+26.1	48.0	10 53.0	+26.8	48.2	11 32.9	+27.6	48.3	12 12.7	+28.3	48.5	12 52.4	+29.0	48.7	42
43	8 36.1	+23.9	46.8	9 17.2	+24.6	46.9	9 58.2	+25.3	47.0	10 39.0	+26.0	47.1	11 19.8	+26.7	47.3	12 00.5	+27.4	47.4	12 41.0	+28.1	47.6	13 21.4	+28.8	47.8	43
44	9 00.0	+23.8	45.8	9 41.8	+24.4	45.9	10 23.5	+25.1	46.1	11 05.0	+25.9	46.2	11 46.5	+26.5	46.4	12 27.9	+27.2	46.5	13 09.1	+27.9	46.7	13 50.2	+28.6	46.9	44
45	9 23.8	+23.6	44.9	10 06.2	+24.3	45.0	10 48.6	+25.0	45.1	11 30.9	+25.6	45.3	12 13.0	+26.4	45.4	12 55.1	+27.0	45.6	13 37.0	+27.7	45.8	14 18.8	+28.3	45.9	45
46	9 47.4	+23.4	44.0	10 30.5	+24.1	44.1	11 13.6	+24.8	44.2	11 56.5	+25.5	44.4	12 39.4	+26.1	44.5	13 22.1	+26.8	44.7	14 04.7	+27.5	44.9	14 47.1	+28.2	45.0	46
47	10 10.8	+23.3	43.0	10 54.6	+24.0	43.2	11 38.4	+24.6	43.3	12 22.0	+25.3	43.4	13 05.5	+25.9	43.6	13 48.9	+26.6	43.8	14 32.2	+27.2	43.9	15 15.3	+27.9	44.1	47
48	10 34.1	+23.1	42.1	11 18.6	+23.8	42.2	12 03.0	+24.4	42.4	12 47.3	+25.0	42.5	13 31.4	+25.8	42.7	14 15.5	+26.4	42.8	14 59.4	+27.1	43.0	15 43.2	+27.7	43.2	48
49	10 57.2	+23.0	41.2	11 42.4	+23.6	41.3	12 27.4	+24.2	41.4	13 12.3	+24.9	41.6	13 57.2	+25.5	41.7	14 41.9	+26.2	41.9	15 26.5	+26.8	42.1	16 10.9	+27.5	42.3	49
50	11 20.2	+22.8	40.2	12 06.0	+23.4	40.3	12 51.6	+24.1	40.5	13 37.2	+24.7	40.6	14 22.7	+25.3	40.8	15 08.1	+25.9	41.0	15 53.3	+26.6	41.2	16 38.4	+27.2	41.4	50
51	11 43.0	+22.5	39.3	12 29.4	+23.2	39.4	13 15.7	+23.8	39.5	14 01.9	+24.5	39.7	14 48.0	+25.1	39.9	15 34.0	+25.7	40.0	16 19.9	+26.3	40.2	17 05.6	+27.0	40.4	51
52	12 05.5	+22.4	38.3	12 52.6	+23.0	38.5	13 39.5	+23.6	38.6	14 26.4	+24.2	38.8	15 13.1	+24.8	38.9	15 59.7	+25.5	39.1	16 46.2	+26.1	39.3	17 32.6	+26.7	39.5	52
53	12 27.9	+22.2	37.4	13 15.6	+22.8	37.5	14 03.1	+23.4	37.7	14 50.6	+24.0	37.8	15 37.9	+24.6	38.0	16 25.2	+25.2	38.2	17 12.3	+25.8	38.3	17 59.3	+26.4	38.5	53
54	12 50.1	+22.0	36.4	13 38.4	+22.5	36.6	14 26.5	+23.2	36.7	15 14.6	+23.7	36.9	16 02.5	+24.4	37.0	16 50.4	+24.9	37.2	17 38.1	+25.5	37.4	18 25.7	+26.1	37.6	54
55	13 12.1	+21.8	35.5	14 00.9	+22.4	35.6	14 49.7	+22.9	35.8	15 38.3	+23.5	35.9	16 26.9	+24.1	36.1	17 15.3	+24.7	36.3	18 03.6	+25.3	36.5	18 51.8	+25.9	36.6	55
56	13 33.9	+21.5	34.5	14 23.3	+22.1	34.6	15 12.6	+22.7	34.8	16 01.8	+23.3	35.0	16 51.0	+23.8	35.1	17 40.0	+24.4	35.3	18 28.9	+25.0	35.5	19 17.7	+25.5	35.7	56
57	13 55.4	+21.4	33.5	14 45.4	+21.9	33.7	15 35.3	+22.4	33.8	16 25.1	+23.0	34.0	17 14.8	+23.5	34.2	18 04.4	+24.1	34.3	18 53.9	+24.6	34.5	19 43.2	+25.3	34.7	57
58	14 16.8	+21.1	32.6	15 07.3	+21.6	32.7	15 57.7	+22.2	32.9	16 48.1	+22.7	33.0	17 38.3	+23.3	33.2	18 28.5	+23.8	33.4	19 18.5	+24.4	33.6	20 08.5	+24.9	33.8	58
59	14 37.9	+20.8	31.6	15 28.9	+21.4	31.8	16 19.9	+21.9	31.9	17 10.8	+22.4	32.1	18 01.6	+23.0	32.2	18 52.3	+23.5	32.4	19 42.9	+24.1	32.6	20 33.4	+24.6	32.8	59
60	14 58.7	+20.6	30.6	15 50.3	+21.1	30.8	16 41.8	+21.7	30.9	17 33.2	+22.2	31.1	18 24.6	+22.6	31.3	19 15.8	+23.2	31.4	20 07.0	+23.7	31.6	20 58.0	+24.2	31.8	60
61	15 19.3	+20.4	29.7	16 11.4	+20.9	29.8	17 03.5	+21.3	30.0	17 55.4	+21.9	30.1	18 47.2	+22.4	30.3	19 39.0	+22.9	30.5	20 30.7	+23.4	30.6	21 22.2	+24.0	30.8	61
62	15 39.7	+20.1	28.7	16 32.3	+20.6	28.8	17 24.8	+21.1	29.0	18 17.3	+21.5	29.1	19 09.6	+22.1	29.3	20 01.9	+22.6	29.5	20 54.1	+23.0	29.7	21 46.2	+23.5	29.9	62
63	15 59.8	+19.8	27.7	16 52.9	+20.3	27.9	17 45.9	+20.8	28.0	18 38.8	+21.3	28.2	19 31.7	+21.7	28.3	20 24.5	+22.2	28.5	21 17.1	+22.8	28.7	22 09.7	+23.2	28.9	63
64	16 19.6	+19.6	26.7	17 13.2	+20.0	26.9	18 06.7	+20.4	27.0	19 00.1	+20.9	27.2	19 53.4	+21.4	27.3	20 46.7	+21.9	27.5	21 39.9	+22.3	27.7	22 32.9	+22.9	27.9	64
65	16 39.2	+19.2	25.7	17 33.2	+19.7	25.9	18 27.1	+20.2	26.0	19 21.0	+20.6	26.2	20 14.8	+21.1	26.3	21 08.6	+21.5	26.5	22 02.2	+22.0	26.7	22 55.8	+22.4	26.9	65
66	16 58.4	+19.0	24.8	17 52.9	+19.4	24.9	18 47.3	+19.8	25.0	19 41.6	+20.3	25.2	20 35.9	+20.7	25.3	21 30.1	+21.1	25.5	22 24.2	+21.6	25.7	23 18.2	+22.1	25.9	66
67	17 17.4	+18.7	23.8	18 12.3	+19.1	23.9	19 07.1	+19.6	24.0	20 01.9	+19.9	24.2	20 56.6	+20.4	24.3	21 51.2	+20.8	24.5	22 45.8	+21.2	24.7	23 40.3	+21.7	24.8	67
68	17 36.1	+18.4	22.8	18 31.4	+18.8	22.9	19 26.7	+19.1	23.0	20 21.8	+19.6	23.2	21 17.0	+20.0	23.3	22 12.0	+20.5	23.5	23 07.0	+20.9	23.6	24 02.0	+21.2	23.8	68
69	17 54.5	+18.1	21.8	18 50.2	+18.5	21.9	19 45.8	+18.9	22.0	20 41.4	+19.3	22.2	21 37.0	+19.6	22.3	22 32.5	+20.0	22.5	23 27.9	+20.4	22.6	24 23.2	+20.9	22.8	69
70	18 12.6	+17.8	20.8	19 08.7	+18.1	20.9	20 04.7	+18.5	21.0	21 00.7	+18.9	21.2	21 56.6	+19.3	21.3	22 52.5	+19.6	21.4	23 48.3	+20.0	21.6	24 44.1	+20.4	21.8	70
71	18 30.4	+17.4	19.8	19 26.8	+17.8	19.9	20 23.2	+18.2	20.0	21 19.6	+18.5	20.1	22 15.9	+18.8	20.3	23 12.1	+19.3	20.4	24 08.3	+19.6	20.6	25 04.5	+20.0	20.7	71
72	18 47.8	+17.1	18.8	19 44.6	+17.5	18.9	20 41.4	+17.8	19.0	21 38.1	+18.1	19.1	22 34.7	+18.5	19.2	23 31.4	+18.8	19.4	24 27.9	+19.2	19.5	25 24.5	+19.5	19.7	72
73	19 04.9	+16.8	17.7	20 02.1	+17.1	17.8	20 59.2	+17.4	18.0	21 56.2	+17.8	18.1	22 53.2	+18.1	18.2	23 50.2	+18.4	18.3	24 47.1	+18.8	18.5	25 44.0	+19.1	18.6	73
74	19 21.7	+16.5	16.7	20 19.2	+16.7	16.8	21 16.6	+17.0	16.9	22 14.0	+17.3	17.1	23 11.3	+17.7	17.2	24 08.6	+18.0	17.3	25 05.9	+18.3	17.4	26 03.1	+18.6	17.6	74
75	19 38.2	+16.1	15.7	20 35.9	+16.4	15.8	21 33.6	+16.7	15.9	22 31.3	+17.0	16.0	23 29.0	+17.2	16.1	24 26.6	+17.5	16.3	25 24.2	+17.8	16.4	26 21.7	+18.2	16.5	75
76	19 54.3	+15.7	14.7	20 52.3	+16.0	14.8	21 50.3	+16.3	14.9	22 48.3	+16.5	15.0	23 46.2	+16.9	15.1	24 44.1	+17.2	15.2	25 42.0	+17.4	15.3	26 39.9	+17.7	15.5	76
77	20 10.0	+15.4	13.7	21 08.3	+15.7	13.7	22 06.6	+15.9	13.8	23 04.8	+16.2	13.9	24 03.1	+16.4	14.0	25 01.3	+16.6	14.2	25 59.4	+16.9	14.3	26 57.6	+17.1	14.4	77
78	20 25.4	+15.0	12.6	21 24.0	+15.2	12.7	22 22.5	+15.5	12.8	23 21.0	+15.7	12.9	24 19.5	+15.9	13.0	25 17.9	+16.2	13.1	26 16.3	+16.5	13.2	27 14.7	+16.7	13.3	78
79	20 40.4	+14.7	11.6	21 39.2	+14.9	11.7	22 38.0	+15.0	11.7	23 36.7	+15.3	11.8	24 35.4	+15.5	11.9	25 34.1	+15.7	12.0	26 32.8	+15.9	12.1	27 31.4	+16.2	12.2	79
80	20 55.1	+14.3	10.5	21 54.1	+14.5	10.6	22 53.0	+14.7	10.7	23 52.0	+14.9	10.8	24 50.9	+15.1	10.9	25 49.8	+15.3	11.0	26 48.7	+15.5	11.0	27 47.6	+15.7	11.1	80
81	21 09.4	+13.9	9.5	22 08.6	+14.0	9.6	23 07.7	+14.3	9.6	24 06.9	+14.4	9.7	25 06.0	+14.6	9.8	26 05.1	+14.8	9.9	27 04.2	+15.0	10.0	28 03.3	+15.2	10.1	81
82	21 23.3	+13.5	8.5	22 22.6	+13.7	8.5	23 22.0	+13.8	8.6	24 21.3	+14.0	8.7	25 20.6	+14.1	8.7	26 19.9	+14.3	8.8	27 19.2	+14.4	8.9	28 18.5	+14.6	9.0	82
83	21 36.8	+13.1	7.4	22 36.3	+13.2	7.5	23 35.8	+13.4	7.5	24 35.3	+13.5	7.6	25 34.7	+13.7	7.6	26 34.2	+13.8	7.7	27 33.6	+14.0	7.8	28 33.1	+14.1	7.9	83
84	21 49.9	+12.7	6.4	22 49.5	+12.9	6.4	23 49.2	+12.9	6.5	24 48.8	+13.0	6.5	25 48.4	+13.2	6.6	26 48.0	+13.3	6.6	27 47.6	+13.4	6.7	28 47.2	+13.5	6.7	84
85	22 02.6	+12.3	5.3	23 02.4	+12.4	5.4	24 02.1	+12.5	5.4	25 01.8	+12.6	5.4	26 01.6	+12.6	5.5	27 01.3	+12.8	5.5	28 01.0	+12.9	5.6	29 00.7	+13.0	5.6	85
86	22 14.9	+11.9	4.3	23 14.8	+11.9	4.3	24 14.6	+12.0	4.3	25 14.4	+12.1	4.4	26 14.2	+12.2	4.4	27 14.1	+12.2	4.4	28 13.9	+12.3	4.5	29 13.7	+12.4	4.5	86
87	22 26.8	+11.5	3.2	23 26.7	+11.6	3.2	24 26.6	+11.6	3.2	25 26.5	+11.7	3.3	26 26.4	+11.7	3.3	27 26.3	+11.8	3.3	28 26.2	+11.8	3.4	29 26.1	+11.9	3.4	87
88	22 38.3	+11.1	2.1	23 38.3	+11.1	2.2	24 38.2	+11.1	2.2	25 38.2	+11.1	2.2	26 38.1	+11.2	2.2	27 38.1	+11.2	2.2	28 38.0	+11.3	2.2	29 38.0	+11.3	2.3	88
89	22 49.4	+10.6	1.1	23 49.4	+10.6	1.1	24 49.3	+10.7	1.1	25 49.3	+10.7	1.1	26 49.3	+10.7	1.1	27 49.3	+10.7	1.1	28 49.3	+10.7	1.1	29 49.3	+10.7	1.1	89
90	23 00.0	+10.2	0.0	24 00.0	+10.2	0.0	25 00.0	+10.2	0.0	26 00.0	+10.2	0.0	27 00.0	+10.2	0.0	28 00.0	+10.1	0.0	29 00.0	+10.1	0.0	30 00.0	+10.1	0.0	90
	23°			24°			25°			26°			27°			28°			29°			30°			

S. Lat. {L.H.A. greater than 180° ....Zn=180°−Z; L.H.A. less than 180°...........Zn=180°+Z}

LATITUDE **SAME** NAME AS DECLINATION **L.H.A. 100°, 260°**

345

Dec.	23° Hc	d	Z	24° Hc	d	Z	25° Hc	d	Z	26° Hc	d	Z	Dec.
°	° ′	′	°	° ′	′	°	° ′	′	°	° ′	′	°	°
0	8 16.8	+23.6	93.5	8 13.0	+24.6	93.7	8 09.0	+25.6	93.8	8 05.0	+26.5	94.0	0
1	8 40.4	+23.5	92.6	8 37.6	+24.4	92.8	8 34.6	+25.4	92.9	8 31.5	+26.3	93.1	1
2	9 03.9	+23.3	91.7	9 02.0	+24.4	91.8	9 00.0	+25.3	92.0	8 57.8	+26.3	92.2	2
3	9 27.2	+23.2	90.7	9 26.4	+24.1	90.9	9 25.3	+25.2	91.1	9 24.1	+26.1	91.2	3
4	9 50.4	+23.1	89.8	9 50.5	+24.1	90.0	9 50.5	+24.9	90.2	9 50.2	+26.0	90.3	4
5	10 13.5	+22.9	88.9	10 14.6	+23.8	89.1	10 15.4	+24.9	89.2	10 16.2	+25.8	89.4	5
6	10 36.4	+22.7	87.9	10 38.4	+23.7	88.1	10 40.3	+24.7	88.3	10 42.0	+25.6	88.5	6
7	10 59.1	+22.5	87.0	11 02.1	+23.5	87.2	11 05.0	+24.5	87.4	11 07.6	+25.5	87.6	7
8	11 21.6	+22.4	86.0	11 25.6	+23.4	86.2	11 29.5	+24.3	86.5	11 33.1	+25.3	86.7	8
9	11 44.0	+22.1	85.1	11 49.0	+23.2	85.3	11 53.8	+24.1	85.5	11 58.4	+25.1	85.7	9
10	12 06.1	+22.0	84.2	12 12.2	+22.9	84.4	12 17.9	+24.0	84.6	12 23.5	+24.9	84.8	10
11	12 28.1	+21.8	83.2	12 35.1	+22.8	83.4	12 41.9	+23.7	83.6	12 48.4	+24.7	83.9	11
12	12 49.9	+21.6	82.2	12 57.9	+22.5	82.5	13 05.6	+23.6	82.7	13 13.1	+24.6	82.9	12
13	13 11.5	+21.3	81.3	13 20.4	+22.4	81.5	13 29.2	+23.3	81.8	13 37.7	+24.3	82.0	13
14	13 32.8	+21.2	80.3	13 42.8	+22.1	80.6	13 52.5	+23.1	80.8	14 02.0	+24.1	81.1	14
15	13 54.0	+20.9	79.4	14 04.9	+21.9	79.6	14 15.6	+22.9	79.9	14 26.1	+23.8	80.1	15
16	14 14.9	+20.7	78.4	14 26.8	+21.7	78.6	14 38.5	+22.7	78.9	14 49.9	+23.7	79.2	16
17	14 35.6	+20.4	77.4	14 48.5	+21.4	77.7	15 01.2	+22.4	77.9	15 13.6	+23.3	78.2	17
18	14 56.0	+20.2	76.5	15 09.9	+21.2	76.7	15 23.6	+22.1	77.0	15 36.9	+23.2	77.3	18
19	15 16.2	+19.9	75.5	15 31.1	+20.9	75.7	15 45.7	+21.9	76.0	16 00.1	+22.9	76.3	19
20	15 36.1	+19.7	74.5	15 52.0	+20.7	74.8	16 07.6	+21.7	75.0	16 23.0	+22.6	75.3	20
21	15 55.8	+19.4	73.5	16 12.7	+20.4	73.8	16 29.3	+21.4	74.1	16 45.6	+22.3	74.4	21
22	16 15.2	+19.1	72.5	16 33.1	+20.1	72.8	16 50.7	+21.0	73.1	17 07.9	+22.1	73.4	22
23	16 34.3	+18.9	71.5	16 53.2	+19.8	71.8	17 11.7	+20.9	72.1	17 30.0	+21.8	72.4	23
24	16 53.2	+18.5	70.6	17 13.0	+19.6	70.8	17 32.6	+20.5	71.1	17 51.8	+21.5	71.4	24
25	17 11.7	+18.3	69.6	17 32.6	+19.2	69.9	17 53.1	+20.2	70.2	18 13.3	+21.2	70.5	25
26	17 30.0	+18.0	68.6	17 51.8	+18.9	68.9	18 13.3	+19.9	69.2	18 34.5	+20.9	69.5	26
27	17 48.0	+17.7	67.6	18 10.7	+18.7	67.9	18 33.2	+19.6	68.2	18 55.4	+20.5	68.5	27
28	18 05.7	+17.3	66.6	18 29.4	+18.3	66.9	18 52.8	+19.3	67.2	19 15.9	+20.3	67.5	28
29	18 23.0	+17.0	65.5	18 47.7	+18.0	65.9	19 12.1	+18.9	66.2	19 36.2	+19.9	66.5	29
30	18 40.0	+16.7	64.5	19 05.7	+17.6	64.8	19 31.0	+18.7	65.2	19 56.1	+19.6	65.5	30
31	18 56.7	+16.4	63.5	19 23.3	+17.4	63.8	19 49.7	+18.2	64.2	20 15.7	+19.2	64.5	31
32	19 13.1	+16.1	62.5	19 40.7	+17.0	62.8	20 07.9	+18.0	63.1	20 34.9	+18.9	63.5	32
33	19 29.2	+15.6	61.5	19 57.7	+16.6	61.8	20 25.9	+17.5	62.1	20 53.8	+18.5	62.5	33
34	19 44.8	+15.4	60.5	20 14.3	+16.3	60.8	20 43.4	+17.2	61.1	21 12.3	+18.1	61.4	34
35	20 00.2	+15.0	59.4	20 30.6	+15.9	59.7	21 00.6	+16.9	60.1	21 30.4	+17.8	60.4	35
36	20 15.2	+14.6	58.4	20 46.5	+15.5	58.7	21 17.5	+16.4	59.0	21 48.2	+17.4	59.4	36
37	20 29.8	+14.2	57.4	21 02.0	+15.2	57.7	21 33.9	+16.1	58.0	22 05.6	+17.0	58.4	37
38	20 44.0	+13.9	56.3	21 17.2	+14.8	56.6	21 50.0	+15.7	57.0	22 22.6	+16.6	57.3	38
39	20 57.9	+13.5	55.3	21 32.0	+14.3	55.6	22 05.7	+15.3	55.9	22 39.2	+16.2	56.3	39
40	21 11.4	+13.1	54.2	21 46.3	+14.0	54.6	22 21.0	+14.9	54.9	22 55.4	+15.7	55.2	40
41	21 24.5	+12.7	53.2	22 00.3	+13.6	53.5	22 35.9	+14.5	53.8	23 11.1	+15.4	54.2	41
42	21 37.2	+12.4	52.1	22 13.9	+13.2	52.5	22 50.4	+14.0	52.8	23 26.5	+14.9	53.1	42
43	21 49.6	+11.9	51.1	22 27.1	+12.8	51.4	23 04.4	+13.7	51.7	23 41.4	+14.5	52.1	43
44	22 01.5	+11.5	50.0	22 39.9	+12.4	50.3	23 18.1	+13.2	50.7	23 55.9	+14.1	51.0	44
45	22 13.0	+11.1	49.0	22 52.3	+11.9	49.3	23 31.3	+12.7	49.6	24 10.0	+13.6	50.0	45
46	22 24.1	+10.7	47.9	23 04.2	+11.5	48.2	23 44.0	+12.4	48.5	24 23.6	+13.2	48.9	46
47	22 34.8	+10.2	46.8	23 15.7	+11.1	47.2	23 56.4	+11.9	47.5	24 36.8	+12.7	47.8	47
48	22 45.0	+9.9	45.8	23 26.8	+10.6	46.1	24 08.3	+11.4	46.4	24 49.5	+12.3	46.7	48
49	22 54.9	+9.4	44.7	23 37.4	+10.2	45.0	24 19.7	+11.0	45.3	25 01.8	+11.8	45.7	49
50	23 04.3	+9.0	43.6	23 47.6	+9.7	43.9	24 30.7	+10.5	44.2	25 13.6	+11.3	44.6	50
51	23 13.3	+8.5	42.6	23 57.3	+9.3	42.9	24 41.2	+10.1	43.2	25 24.9	+10.8	43.5	51
52	23 21.8	+8.1	41.5	24 06.6	+8.9	41.8	24 51.3	+9.5	42.1	25 35.7	+10.3	42.4	52
53	23 29.9	+7.6	40.4	24 15.5	+8.3	40.7	25 00.8	+9.2	41.0	25 46.0	+9.9	41.3	53
54	23 37.5	+7.2	39.3	24 23.8	+7.9	39.6	25 10.0	+8.6	39.9	25 55.9	+9.3	40.2	54
55	23 44.7	+6.7	38.2	24 31.7	+7.5	38.5	25 18.6	+8.1	38.8	26 05.2	+8.9	39.1	55
56	23 51.4	+6.3	37.2	24 39.2	+6.9	37.4	25 26.7	+7.7	37.7	26 14.1	+8.3	38.0	56
57	23 57.7	+5.8	36.1	24 46.1	+6.5	36.3	25 34.4	+7.1	36.6	26 22.4	+7.9	36.9	57
58	24 03.5	+5.3	35.0	24 52.6	+6.0	35.2	25 41.5	+6.7	35.5	26 30.3	+7.3	35.8	58
59	24 08.8	+4.9	33.9	24 58.6	+5.5	34.1	25 48.2	+6.1	34.4	26 37.6	+6.8	34.7	59
60	24 13.7	+4.4	32.8	25 04.1	+5.0	33.0	25 54.3	+5.7	33.3	26 44.4	+6.3	33.6	60
61	24 18.1	+4.0	31.7	25 09.1	+4.6	31.9	26 00.0	+5.1	32.2	26 50.7	+5.7	32.5	61
62	24 22.1	+3.5	30.6	25 13.7	+4.0	30.8	26 05.1	+4.7	31.1	26 56.4	+5.3	31.3	62
63	24 25.6	+3.0	29.5	25 17.7	+3.6	29.7	26 09.8	+4.1	30.0	27 01.7	+4.7	30.2	63
64	24 28.6	+2.5	28.4	25 21.3	+3.0	28.6	26 13.9	+3.6	28.9	27 06.4	+4.1	29.1	64
65	24 31.1	+2.0	27.3	25 24.3	+2.6	27.5	26 17.5	+3.1	27.7	27 10.5	+3.7	28.0	65
66	24 33.1	+1.6	26.2	25 26.9	+2.1	26.4	26 20.6	+2.6	26.6	27 14.2	+3.1	26.9	66
67	24 34.7	+1.1	25.1	25 29.0	+1.5	25.3	26 23.2	+2.0	25.5	27 17.3	+2.5	25.7	67
68	24 35.8	+0.6	24.0	25 30.5	+1.1	24.2	26 25.2	+1.6	24.4	27 19.8	+2.0	24.6	68
69	24 36.4	+0.1	22.9	25 31.6	+0.6	23.1	26 26.8	+1.0	23.3	27 21.8	+1.5	23.5	69
70	24 36.5	−0.3	21.8	25 32.2	+0.1	22.0	26 27.8	+0.5	22.2	27 23.3	+0.9	22.4	70
71	24 36.2	−0.9	20.7	25 32.3	−0.5	20.9	26 28.3	0.0	21.1	27 24.2	+0.4	21.2	71
72	24 35.3	−1.3	19.6	25 31.8	−0.9	19.8	26 28.3	−0.6	19.9	27 24.6	−0.1	20.1	72
73	24 34.0	−1.8	18.5	25 30.9	−1.4	18.7	26 27.7	−1.0	18.8	27 24.5	−0.7	19.0	73
74	24 32.2	−2.2	17.4	25 29.5	−2.0	17.6	26 26.7	−1.6	17.7	27 23.8	−1.3	17.9	74
75	24 30.0	−2.8	16.3	25 27.5	−2.4	16.4	26 25.1	−2.1	16.6	27 22.5	−1.7	16.7	75
76	24 27.2	−3.2	15.2	25 25.1	−2.9	15.3	26 23.0	−2.7	15.5	27 20.8	−2.4	15.6	76
77	24 24.0	−3.7	14.1	25 22.2	−3.4	14.2	26 20.3	−3.1	14.4	27 18.4	−2.8	14.5	77
78	24 20.3	−4.1	13.0	25 18.8	−3.9	13.1	26 17.2	−3.7	13.2	27 15.6	−3.4	13.4	78
79	24 16.2	−4.7	11.9	25 14.9	−4.4	12.0	26 13.5	−4.1	12.1	27 12.2	−4.0	12.2	79
80	24 11.5	−5.1	10.8	25 10.5	−4.9	10.9	26 09.4	−4.7	11.0	27 08.2	−4.4	11.1	80
81	24 06.4	−5.5	9.7	25 05.6	−5.4	9.8	26 04.7	−5.2	9.9	27 03.8	−5.0	10.0	81
82	24 00.9	−6.0	8.7	25 00.2	−5.9	8.7	25 59.5	−5.7	8.8	26 58.8	−5.6	8.9	82
83	23 54.9	−6.5	7.6	24 54.3	−6.3	7.6	25 53.8	−6.2	7.7	26 53.2	−6.0	7.8	83
84	23 48.4	−7.0	6.5	24 48.0	−6.8	6.5	25 47.6	−6.7	6.6	26 47.2	−6.6	6.6	84
85	23 41.4	−7.4	5.4	24 41.2	−7.3	5.4	25 40.9	−7.2	5.5	26 40.6	−7.1	5.5	85
86	23 34.0	−7.8	4.3	24 33.9	−7.8	4.3	25 33.7	−7.7	4.4	26 33.5	−7.6	4.4	86
87	23 26.2	−8.3	3.2	24 26.1	−8.2	3.3	25 26.0	−8.2	3.3	26 25.9	−8.1	3.3	87
88	23 17.9	−8.7	2.2	24 17.9	−8.7	2.2	25 17.8	−8.7	2.2	26 17.8	−8.7	2.2	88
89	23 09.2	−9.2	1.1	24 09.2	−9.2	1.1	25 09.1	−9.1	1.1	26 09.1	−9.1	1.1	89
90	23 00.0	−9.6	0.0	24 00.0	−9.6	0.0	25 00.0	−9.6	0.0	26 00.0	−9.6	0.0	90
	23°			24°			25°			26°			

Dec.	27° Hc	d	Z	28° Hc	d	Z	29° Hc	d	Z	30° Hc	d	Z	Dec.
°	° ′	′	°	° ′	′	°	° ′	′	°	° ′	′	°	°
0	8 00.7	+27.5	94.1	7 56.4	+28.3	94.3	7 51.8	+29.3	94.4	7 47.2	+30.2	94.5	0
1	8 28.2	+27.3	93.2	8 24.7	+28.3	93.4	8 21.1	+29.2	93.5	8 17.4	+30.1	93.7	1
2	8 55.5	+27.2	92.3	8 53.0	+28.1	92.5	8 50.3	+29.1	92.6	8 47.5	+30.0	92.8	2
3	9 22.7	+27.1	91.4	9 21.1	+28.0	91.6	9 19.4	+28.9	91.7	9 17.5	+29.9	91.9	3
4	9 49.8	+26.9	90.5	9 49.1	+27.9	90.7	9 48.3	+28.8	90.9	9 47.4	+29.7	91.0	4
5	10 16.7	+26.7	89.6	10 17.0	+27.7	89.8	10 17.1	+28.7	90.0	10 17.1	+29.6	90.1	5
6	10 43.4	+26.6	88.7	10 44.7	+27.6	88.9	10 45.8	+28.5	89.1	10 46.7	+29.4	89.3	6
7	11 10.0	+26.5	87.8	11 12.3	+27.3	88.0	11 14.3	+28.3	88.2	11 16.1	+29.3	88.4	7
8	11 36.5	+26.2	86.9	11 39.6	+27.3	87.1	11 42.6	+28.2	87.3	11 45.4	+29.1	87.5	8
9	12 02.7	+26.1	85.9	12 06.9	+27.0	86.2	12 10.8	+28.0	86.4	12 14.5	+28.9	86.6	9
10	12 28.8	+25.9	85.0	12 33.9	+26.9	85.2	12 38.8	+27.8	85.5	12 43.4	+28.7	85.7	10
11	12 54.7	+25.7	84.1	13 00.8	+26.6	84.3	13 06.6	+27.6	84.6	13 12.1	+28.6	84.8	11
12	13 20.4	+25.5	83.2	13 27.4	+26.5	83.4	13 34.2	+27.4	83.6	13 40.7	+28.4	83.9	12
13	13 45.9	+25.3	82.2	13 53.9	+26.2	82.5	14 01.6	+27.2	82.7	14 09.1	+28.1	83.0	13
14	14 11.2	+25.0	81.3	14 20.1	+26.0	81.6	14 28.8	+27.0	81.8	14 37.2	+28.0	82.1	14
15	14 36.2	+24.9	80.4	14 46.1	+25.9	80.6	14 55.8	+26.8	80.9	15 05.2	+27.7	81.1	15
16	15 01.1	+24.6	79.4	15 12.0	+25.5	79.7	15 22.6	+26.5	80.0	15 32.9	+27.5	80.2	16
17	15 25.7	+24.3	78.5	15 37.5	+25.4	78.7	15 49.1	+26.3	79.0	16 00.4	+27.2	79.3	17
18	15 50.0	+24.2	77.5	16 02.9	+25.0	77.8	16 15.4	+26.0	78.1	16 27.6	+27.0	78.4	18
19	16 14.2	+23.8	76.6	16 27.9	+24.9	76.9	16 41.4	+25.8	77.1	16 54.6	+26.8	77.4	19
20	16 38.0	+23.6	75.6	16 52.8	+24.5	75.9	17 07.2	+25.6	76.2	17 21.4	+26.5	76.5	20
21	17 01.6	+23.3	74.7	17 17.3	+24.3	75.0	17 32.8	+25.2	75.3	17 47.9	+26.2	75.6	21
22	17 24.9	+23.1	73.7	17 41.6	+24.1	74.0	17 58.0	+25.0	74.3	18 14.1	+25.9	74.6	22
23	17 48.0	+22.7	72.7	18 05.7	+23.7	73.0	18 23.0	+24.7	73.3	18 40.0	+25.7	73.7	23
24	18 10.7	+22.5	71.8	18 29.4	+23.4	72.1	18 47.7	+24.4	72.4	19 05.7	+25.3	72.7	24
25	18 33.2	+22.2	70.8	18 52.8	+23.1	71.1	19 12.1	+24.1	71.4	19 31.0	+25.1	71.8	25
26	18 55.4	+21.8	69.8	19 15.9	+22.8	70.1	19 36.2	+23.8	70.4	19 56.1	+24.7	70.8	26
27	19 17.2	+21.5	68.8	19 38.7	+22.5	69.1	20 00.0	+23.4	69.5	20 20.8	+24.4	69.8	27
28	19 38.7	+21.3	67.8	20 01.2	+22.2	68.2	20 23.4	+23.1	68.5	20 45.2	+24.1	68.8	28
29	20 00.0	+20.8	66.8	20 23.4	+21.8	67.2	20 46.5	+22.8	67.5	21 09.3	+23.7	67.9	29
30	20 20.8	+20.5	65.8	20 45.2	+21.5	66.2	21 09.3	+22.4	66.5	21 33.0	+23.4	66.9	30
31	20 41.3	+20.2	64.8	21 06.7	+21.1	65.2	21 31.7	+22.1	65.5	21 56.4	+23.1	65.9	31
32	21 01.5	+19.8	63.8	21 27.8	+20.8	64.2	21 53.8	+21.7	64.5	22 19.5	+22.6	64.9	32
33	21 21.3	+19.5	62.8	21 48.6	+20.4	63.2	22 15.5	+21.4	63.5	22 42.1	+22.3	63.9	33
34	21 40.8	+19.1	61.8	22 09.0	+20.0	62.1	22 36.9	+20.9	62.5	23 04.4	+21.9	62.9	34
35	21 59.9	+18.7	60.8	22 29.0	+19.7	61.1	22 57.8	+20.6	61.5	23 26.3	+21.5	61.9	35
36	22 18.6	+18.3	59.7	22 48.7	+19.2	60.1	23 18.4	+20.2	60.5	23 47.8	+21.1	60.8	36
37	22 36.9	+17.9	58.7	23 07.9	+18.8	59.1	23 38.6	+19.7	59.4	24 08.9	+20.7	59.8	37
38	22 54.8	+17.5	57.7	23 26.7	+18.5	58.0	23 58.3	+19.4	58.4	24 29.6	+20.3	58.8	38
39	23 12.3	+17.1	56.6	23 45.2	+18.0	57.0	24 17.7	+18.9	57.4	24 49.9	+19.8	57.8	39
40	23 29.4	+16.7	55.6	24 03.2	+17.6	56.0	24 36.6	+18.5	56.3	25 09.7	+19.4	56.7	40
41	23 46.1	+16.3	54.5	24 20.8	+17.1	54.9	24 55.1	+18.0	55.3	25 29.1	+18.9	55.7	41
42	24 02.4	+15.8	53.5	24 37.9	+16.7	53.8	25 13.1	+17.6	54.2	25 48.0	+18.5	54.6	42
43	24 18.2	+15.4	52.4	24 54.6	+16.3	52.8	25 30.7	+17.2	53.2	26 06.5	+18.1	53.6	43
44	24 33.6	+14.9	51.4	25 10.9	+15.8	51.7	25 47.9	+16.6	52.1	26 24.6	+17.5	52.5	44
45	24 48.5	+14.5	50.3	25 26.7	+15.3	50.7	26 04.5	+16.2	51.0	26 42.1	+17.1	51.4	45
46	25 03.0	+14.0	49.2	25 42.0	+14.9	49.6	26 20.7	+15.8	50.0	26 59.2	+16.6	50.3	46
47	25 17.0	+13.5	48.2	25 56.9	+14.3	48.5	26 36.5	+15.2	48.9	27 15.8	+16.0	49.3	47
48	25 30.5	+13.1	47.1	26 11.2	+13.9	47.4	26 51.7	+14.7	47.8	27 31.8	+15.6	48.2	48
49	25 43.6	+12.6	46.0	26 25.1	+13.4	46.3	27 06.4	+14.2	46.7	27 47.4	+15.1	47.1	49
50	25 56.2	+12.1	44.9	26 38.5	+12.9	45.3	27 20.6	+13.8	45.6	28 02.5	+14.5	46.0	50
51	26 08.3	+11.6	43.8	26 51.4	+12.4	44.2	27 34.4	+13.1	44.5	28 17.0	+14.0	44.9	51
52	26 19.9	+11.1	42.7	27 03.8	+11.9	43.1	27 47.5	+12.7	43.4	28 31.0	+13.5	43.8	52
53	26 31.0	+10.6	41.6	27 15.7	+11.4	42.0	28 00.2	+12.1	42.3	28 44.5	+12.9	42.7	53
54	26 41.6	+10.1	40.5	27 27.1	+10.8	40.9	28 12.3	+11.6	41.2	28 57.4	+12.3	41.6	54
55	26 51.7	+9.6	39.4	27 37.9	+10.3	39.8	28 23.9	+11.1	40.1	29 09.7	+11.8	40.4	55
56	27 01.3	+9.0	38.3	27 48.2	+9.8	38.6	28 35.0	+10.5	39.0	29 21.5	+11.3	39.3	56
57	27 10.3	+8.5	37.2	27 58.0	+9.2	37.5	28 45.5	+9.9	37.9	29 32.8	+10.6	38.2	57
58	27 18.8	+8.0	36.1	28 07.2	+8.7	36.4	28 55.4	+9.4	36.7	29 43.4	+10.1	37.1	58
59	27 26.8	+7.5	35.0	28 15.9	+8.1	35.3	29 04.8	+8.8	35.6	29 53.5	+9.5	35.9	59
60	27 34.3	+6.9	33.9	28 24.0	+7.6	34.2	29 13.6	+8.2	34.5	30 03.0	+8.9	34.8	60
61	27 41.2	+6.4	32.7	28 31.6	+7.0	33.0	29 21.8	+7.7	33.3	30 11.9	+8.3	33.6	61
62	27 47.6	+5.8	31.6	28 38.6	+6.5	31.9	29 29.5	+7.1	32.2	30 20.2	+7.7	32.5	62
63	27 53.4	+5.3	30.5	28 45.1	+5.9	30.8	29 36.6	+6.4	31.0	30 27.9	+7.1	31.3	63
64	27 58.7	+4.8	29.4	28 51.0	+5.3	29.6	29 43.0	+5.9	29.9	30 35.0	+6.5	30.2	64
65	28 03.5	+4.1	28.2	28 56.3	+4.7	28.5	29 48.9	+5.3	28.8	30 41.5	+5.8	29.0	65
66	28 07.6	+3.7	27.1	29 01.0	+4.2	27.3	29 54.2	+4.7	27.6	30 47.3	+5.3	27.9	66
67	28 11.3	+3.0	26.0	29 05.2	+3.5	26.2	29 58.9	+4.1	26.5	30 52.6	+4.6	26.7	67
68	28 14.3	+2.5	24.8	29 08.7	+3.0	25.1	30 03.0	+3.5	25.3	30 57.2	+4.0	25.6	68
69	28 16.8	+2.0	23.7	29 11.7	+2.4	23.9	30 06.5	+2.9	24.2	31 01.2	+3.4	24.4	69
70	28 18.8	+1.3	22.6	29 14.1	+1.9	22.8	30 09.4	+2.3	23.0	31 04.6	+2.7	23.2	70
71	28 20.1	+0.8	21.4	29 16.0	+1.2	21.6	30 11.7	+1.7	21.8	31 07.3	+2.2	22.1	71
72	28 20.9	+0.3	20.3	29 17.2	+0.6	20.5	30 13.4	+1.0	20.7	31 09.5	+1.4	20.9	72
73	28 21.2	−0.3	19.2	29 17.8	+0.1	19.3	30 14.4	+0.5	19.5	31 10.9	+0.9	19.7	73
74	28 20.9	−0.9	18.0	29 17.9	−0.5	18.2	30 14.9	−0.2	18.4	31 11.8	+0.2	18.6	74
75	28 20.0	−1.5	16.9	29 17.4	−1.1	17.0	30 14.7	−0.8	17.2	31 12.0	−0.4	17.4	75
76	28 18.5	−2.0	15.7	29 16.3	−1.7	15.9	30 13.9	−1.3	16.1	31 11.6	−1.1	16.2	76
77	28 16.5	−2.6	14.6	29 14.6	−2.3	14.8	30 12.6	−2.0	14.9	31 10.5	−1.7	15.1	77
78	28 13.9	−3.1	13.5	29 12.3	−2.9	13.6	30 10.6	−2.6	13.7	31 08.8	−2.3	13.9	78
79	28 10.8	−3.7	12.3	29 09.4	−3.4	12.5	30 08.0	−3.2	12.6	31 06.5	−2.9	12.7	79
80	28 07.1	−4.2	11.2	29 06.0	−4.1	11.3	30 04.8	−3.8	11.4	31 03.6	−3.6	11.5	80
81	28 02.9	−4.8	10.1	29 01.9	−4.6	10.2	30 01.0	−4.4	10.3	31 00.0	−4.2	10.4	81
82	27 58.1	−5.4	9.0	28 57.3	−5.2	9.0	29 56.6	−5.0	9.1	30 55.8	−4.8	9.2	82
83	27 52.7	−5.9	7.8	28 52.1	−5.7	7.9	29 51.6	−5.7	8.0	30 51.0	−5.5	8.1	83
84	27 46.8	−6.5	6.7	28 46.4	−6.4	6.8	29 45.9	−6.2	6.8	30 45.5	−6.1	6.9	84
85	27 40.3	−7.0	5.6	28 40.0	−6.9	5.6	29 39.7	−6.7	5.7	30 39.4	−6.6	5.7	85
86	27 33.3	−7.5	4.5	28 33.1	−7.4	4.5	29 33.0	−7.4	4.5	30 32.8	−7.3	4.6	86
87	27 25.8	−8.1	3.3	28 25.7	−8.0	3.4	29 25.6	−8.0	3.4	30 25.6	−7.9	3.4	87
88	27 17.7	−8.6	2.2	28 17.7	−8.6	2.2	29 17.6	−8.5	2.3	30 17.6	−8.5	2.3	88
89	27 09.1	−9.1	1.1	28 09.1	−9.1	1.1	29 09.1	−9.1	1.1	30 09.1	−9.1	1.1	89
90	27 00.0	−9.6	0.0	28 00.0	−9.7	0.0	29 00.0	−9.7	0.0	30 00.0	−9.7	0.0	90
	27°			28°			29°			30°			

LATITUDE **CONTRARY** NAME TO DECLINATION L.H.A. 81°, 279°

Dec.	23°			24°			25°			26°		
	Hc	d	Z	Hc	d	Z	Hc	d	Z	Hc	d	Z
°	° ′	′	°	° ′	′	°	° ′	′	°	° ′	′	°
0	8 16.8	-23.8	93.5	8 13.0	-24.7	93.7	8 09.0	-25.6	93.8	8 05.0	-26.7	94.0
1	7 53.0	-23.9	94.5	7 48.3	-24.9	94.6	7 43.4	-25.8	94.7	7 38.3	-26.7	94.9
2	7 29.1	-24.0	95.4	7 23.4	-24.9	95.5	7 17.6	-25.9	95.7	7 11.6	-26.8	95.8
3	7 05.1	-24.1	96.3	6 58.5	-25.1	96.4	6 51.7	-26.0	96.6	6 44.8	-27.0	96.7
4	6 41.0	-24.2	97.2	6 33.4	-25.1	97.4	6 25.7	-26.1	97.5	6 17.8	-27.0	97.6
5	6 16.8	-24.3	98.2	6 08.3	-25.3	98.3	5 59.6	-26.2	98.4	5 50.8	-27.1	98.5
6	5 52.5	-24.4	99.1	5 43.0	-25.3	99.2	5 33.4	-26.3	99.3	5 23.7	-27.2	99.4
7	5 28.1	-24.4	100.0	5 17.7	-25.4	100.1	5 07.1	-26.3	100.2	4 56.5	-27.3	100.3
8	5 03.7	-24.6	100.9	4 52.3	-25.5	101.0	4 40.8	-26.4	101.1	4 29.2	-27.3	101.2
9	4 39.1	-24.6	101.8	4 26.8	-25.6	101.9	4 14.4	-26.5	102.0	4 01.9	-27.4	102.1
10	4 14.5	-24.7	102.7	4 01.2	-25.6	102.8	3 47.9	-26.6	102.9	3 34.5	-27.5	102.9
11	3 49.8	-24.7	103.7	3 35.6	-25.7	103.7	3 21.3	-26.5	103.8	3 07.0	-27.5	103.8
12	3 25.1	-24.8	104.6	3 09.9	-25.7	104.6	2 54.8	-26.7	104.7	2 39.5	-27.5	104.7
13	3 00.3	-24.9	105.5	2 44.2	-25.7	105.5	2 28.1	-26.6	105.6	2 12.0	-27.6	105.6
14	2 35.4	-24.9	106.4	2 18.5	-25.8	106.4	2 01.5	-26.7	106.5	1 44.4	-27.6	106.5
15	2 10.5	-24.9	107.3	1 52.7	-25.8	107.3	1 34.8	-26.7	107.4	1 16.8	-27.6	107.4
16	1 45.6	-24.9	108.2	1 26.9	-25.9	108.2	1 08.1	-26.8	108.3	0 49.2	-27.6	108.3
17	1 20.7	-25.0	109.1	1 01.0	-25.8	109.1	0 41.3	-26.7	109.2	0 21.6	-27.6	109.2
18	0 55.7	-25.0	110.0	0 35.2	-25.9	110.0	0 14.6	-26.8	110.1	0 06.0	+27.6	69.9
19	0 30.7	-24.9	110.9	0 09.3	-25.9	111.0	0 12.2	+26.7	69.0	0 33.6	+27.6	69.1
20	0 05.8	-25.0	111.9	0 16.6	+25.8	68.1	0 38.9	+26.7	68.2	1 01.2	+27.6	68.2
21	0 19.2	+25.0	67.2	0 42.4	+25.9	67.2	1 05.6	+26.8	67.3	1 28.8	+27.6	67.3
22	0 44.2	+25.0	66.3	1 08.3	+25.8	66.3	1 32.4	+26.6	66.4	1 56.4	+27.5	66.4
23	1 09.2	+24.9	65.4	1 34.1	+25.8	65.4	1 59.0	+26.7	65.5	2 23.9	+27.6	65.5
24	1 34.1	+24.9	64.5	1 59.9	+25.8	64.5	2 25.7	+26.6	64.6	2 51.5	+27.4	64.6
25	1 59.0	+24.9	63.6	2 25.7	+25.8	63.6	2 52.3	+26.6	63.7	3 18.9	+27.5	63.7
26	2 23.9	+24.9	62.7	2 51.5	+25.7	62.7	3 18.9	+26.6	62.8	3 46.4	+27.3	62.8
27	2 48.8	+24.8	61.8	3 17.2	+25.6	61.8	3 45.5	+26.5	61.9	4 13.7	+27.3	61.9
28	3 13.6	+24.8	60.9	3 42.8	+25.6	60.9	4 12.0	+26.4	61.0	4 41.0	+27.3	61.0
29	3 38.4	+24.7	60.0	4 08.4	+25.6	60.0	4 38.4	+26.3	60.1	5 08.3	+27.1	60.2
30	4 03.1	+24.7	59.0	4 34.0	+25.4	59.1	5 04.7	+26.3	59.2	5 35.4	+27.1	59.3
31	4 27.8	+24.5	58.1	4 59.4	+25.4	58.2	5 31.0	+26.2	58.3	6 02.5	+27.0	58.4
32	4 52.3	+24.6	57.2	5 24.8	+25.3	57.3	5 57.2	+26.1	57.4	6 29.5	+26.9	57.5
33	5 16.9	+24.4	56.3	5 50.1	+25.2	56.4	6 23.3	+26.0	56.5	6 56.4	+26.8	56.6
34	5 41.3	+24.3	55.4	6 15.3	+25.2	55.5	6 49.3	+25.9	55.6	7 23.2	+26.7	55.7
35	6 05.6	+24.3	54.5	6 40.5	+25.0	54.5	7 15.2	+25.8	54.6	7 49.9	+26.6	54.8
36	6 29.9	+24.1	53.5	7 05.5	+24.9	53.6	7 41.0	+25.7	53.7	8 16.5	+26.4	53.8
37	6 54.0	+24.1	52.6	7 30.4	+24.8	52.7	8 06.7	+25.6	52.8	8 42.9	+26.4	52.9
38	7 18.1	+23.9	51.7	7 55.2	+24.7	51.8	8 32.3	+25.4	51.9	9 09.3	+26.1	52.0
39	7 42.0	+23.8	50.8	8 19.9	+24.6	50.9	8 57.7	+25.3	51.0	9 35.4	+26.1	51.1
40	8 05.8	+23.7	49.8	8 44.5	+24.4	50.0	9 23.0	+25.2	50.1	10 01.5	+25.9	50.2
41	8 29.5	+23.6	48.9	9 08.9	+24.3	49.0	9 48.2	+25.0	49.2	10 27.4	+25.7	49.3
42	8 53.1	+23.4	48.0	9 33.2	+24.1	48.1	10 13.2	+24.8	48.2	10 53.1	+25.6	48.4
43	9 16.5	+23.2	47.0	9 57,3	+24.0	47.2	10 38.0	+24.7	47.3	11 18.7	+25.4	47.4
44	9 39.7	+23.2	46.1	10 21.3	+23.8	46.2	11 02.7	+24.6	46.4	11 44.1	+25.2	46.5
45	10 02.9	+22.9	45.2	10 45.1	+23.7	45.3	11 27.3	+24.3	45.4	12 09.3	+25.0	45.6
46	10 25.8	+22.8	44.2	11 08.8	+23.4	44.4	11 51.6	+24.2	44.5	12 34.3	+24.9	44.7
47	10 48.6	+22.6	43.3	11 32.2	+23.3	43.4	12 15.8	+23.9	43.6	12 59.2	+24.6	43.7
48	11 11.2	+22.5	42.4	11 55.5	+23.1	42.5	12 39.7	+23.8	42.6	13 23.8	+24.4	42.8
49	11 33.7	+22.2	41.4	12 18.6	+22.9	41.5	13 03.5	+23.6	41.7	13 48.2	+24.3	41.9
50	11 55.9	+22.1	40.5	12 41.5	+22.8	40.6	13 27.1	+23.3	40.8	14 12.5	+23.9	40.9
51	12 18.0	+21.9	39.5	13 04.3	+22.5	39.7	13 50.4	+23.1	39.8	14 36.4	+23.8	40.0
52	12 39.9	+21.7	38.6	13 26.8	+22.2	38.7	14 13.5	+22.9	38.9	15 00.2	+23.5	39.0
53	13 01.6	+21.4	37.6	13 49.0	+22.1	37.7	14 36.4	+22.7	37.9	15 23.7	+23.3	38.1
54	13 23.0	+21.2	36.6	14 11.1	+21.8	36.8	14 59.1	+22.4	36.9	15 47.0	+23.1	37.1
55	13 44.2	+21.1	35.7	14 32.9	+21.6	35.8	15 21.5	+22.2	36.0	16 10.1	+22.7	36.1
56	14 05.3	+20.7	34.7	14 54.5	+21.4	34.9	15 43.7	+22.0	35.0	16 32.8	+22.5	35.2
57	14 26.0	+20.6	33.7	15 15.9	+21.1	33.9	16 05.7	+21.6	34.0	16 55.3	+22.3	34.2
58	14 46.6	+20.3	32.8	15 37.0	+20.9	32.9	16 27.3	+21.4	33.1	17 17.6	+21.9	33.2
59	15 06.9	+20.1	31.8	15 57.9	+20.5	31.9	16 48.7	+21.1	32.1	17 39.5	+21.7	32.3
60	15 27.0	+19.7	30.8	16 18.4	+20.4	31.0	17 09.8	+20.9	31.1	18 01.2	+21.3	31.3
61	15 46.7	+19.6	29.8	16 38.8	+20.0	30.0	17 30.7	+20.5	30.1	18 22.5	+21.1	30.3
62	16 06.3	+19.2	28.9	16 58.8	+19.7	29.0	17 51.2	+20.3	29.2	18 43.6	+20.7	29.3
63	16 25.5	+19.0	27.9	17 18.5	+19.5	28.0	18 11.5	+19.9	28.2	19 04.3	+20.5	28.3
64	16 44.5	+18.7	26.9	17 38.0	+19.2	27.0	18 31.4	+19.6	27.2	19 24.8	+20.1	27.3
65	17 03.2	+18.4	25.9	17 57.2	+18.8	26.0	18 51.0	+19.4	26.2	19 44.9	+19.7	26.3
66	17 21.6	+18.1	24.9	18 16.0	+18.6	25.0	19 10.4	+18.9	25.2	20 04.6	+19.4	25.3
67	17 39.7	+17.8	23.9	18 34.6	+18.2	24.0	19 29.3	+18.7	24.2	20 24.0	+19.1	24.3
68	17 57.5	+17.5	22.9	18 52.8	+17.9	23.0	19 48.0	+18.3	23.2	20 43.1	+18.7	23.3
69	18 15.0	+17.2	21.9	19 10.7	+17.6	22.0	20 06.3	+18.0	22.1	21 01.8	+18.4	22.3
70	18 32.2	+16.9	20.9	19 28.3	+17.2	21.0	20 24.3	+17.6	21.1	21 20.2	+18.0	21.3
71	18 49.1	+16.5	19.9	19 45.5	+16.9	20.0	20 41.9	+17.2	20.1	21 38.2	+17.6	20.2
72	19 05.6	+16.2	18.8	20 02.4	+16.5	19.0	20 59.1	+16.9	19.1	21 55.8	+17.2	19.2
73	19 21.8	+15.8	17.8	20 18.9	+16.2	17.9	21 16.0	+16.5	18.1	22 13.0	+16.8	18.2
74	19 37.6	+15.6	16.8	20 35.1	+15.8	16.9	21 32.5	+16.1	17.0	22 29.8	+16.4	17.1
75	19 53.2	+15.1	15.8	20 50.9	+15.4	15.9	21 48.6	+15.7	16.0	22 46.2	+16.1	16.1
76	20 08.3	+14.8	14.7	21 06.3	+15.1	14.8	22 04.3	+15.3	14.9	23 02.3	+15.6	15.0
77	20 23.1	+14.4	13.7	21 21.4	+14.6	13.8	22 19.6	+14.9	13.9	23 17.9	+15.1	14.0
78	20 37.5	+14.1	12.7	21 36.0	+14.3	12.8	22 34.5	+14.6	12.8	23 33.0	+14.8	12.9
79	20 51.6	+13.6	11.6	21 50.3	+13.9	11.7	22 49.1	+14.1	11.8	23 47.8	+14.3	11.9
80	21 05.2	+13.3	10.6	22 04.2	+13.5	10.7	23 03.2	+13.6	10.7	24 02.1	+13.9	10.8
81	21 18.5	+12.9	9.5	22 17.7	+13.1	9.6	23 16.8	+13.3	9.7	24 16.0	+13.4	9.8
82	21 31.4	+12.5	8.5	22 30.8	+12.6	8.6	23 30.1	+12.8	8.6	24 29.4	+13.0	8.7
83	21 43.9	+12.1	7.4	22 43.4	+12.3	7.5	23 42.9	+12.4	7.6	24 42.4	+12.5	7.6
84	21 56.0	+11.7	6.4	22 55.7	+11.8	6.4	23 55.3	+11.9	6.5	24 54.9	+12.0	6.5
85	22 07.7	+11.3	5.3	23 07.5	+11.4	5.4	24 07.2	+11.5	5.4	25 06.9	+11.6	5.5
86	22 19.0	+10.9	4.3	23 18.9	+10.9	4.3	24 18.7	+11.0	4.3	25 18.5	+11.1	4.4
87	22 29.9	+10.5	3.2	23 29.8	+10.5	3.2	24 29.7	+10.6	3.3	25 29.6	+10.6	3.3
88	22 40.4	+10.0	2.1	23 40.3	+10.1	2.2	24 40.3	+10.1	2.2	25 40.2	+10.2	2.2
89	22 50.4	+9.6	1.1	23 50.4	+9.6	1.1	24 50.4	+9.6	1.1	25 50.4	+9.6	1.1
90	23 00.0	+9.2	0.0	24 00.0	+9.2	0.0	25 00.0	+9.1	0.0	26 00.0	+9.1	0.0
	23°			24°			25°			26°		

27°			28°			29°			30°			Dec.
Hc	d	Z	Hc	d	Z	Hc	d	Z	Hc	d	Z	
° ′	′	°	° ′	′	°	° ′	′	°	° ′	′	°	°
8 00.7	-27.5	94.1	7 56.4	-28.5	94.3	7 51.8	-29.4	94.4	7 47.2	-30.4	94.5	0
7 33.2	-27.7	95.0	7 27.9	-28.6	95.1	7 22.4	-29.5	95.3	7 16.8	-30.4	95.4	1
7 05.5	-27.8	95.9	6 59.3	-28.7	96.0	6 52.9	-29.6	96.1	6 46.4	-30.5	96.3	2
6 37.7	-27.9	96.8	6 30.6	-28.8	96.9	6 23.3	-29.7	97.0	6 15.9	-30.6	97.1	3
6 09.8	-27.9	97.7	6 01.8	-28.9	97.8	5 53.6	-29.8	97.9	5 45.3	-30.7	98.0	4
5 41.9	-28.1	98.6	5 32.9	-29.0	98.7	5 23.8	-29.9	98.8	5 14.6	-30.8	98.9	5
5 13.8	-28.1	99.5	5 03.9	-29.0	99.6	4 53.9	-29.9	99.6	4 43.8	-30.8	99.7	6
4 45.7	-28.2	100.4	4 34.9	-29.1	100.4	4 24.0	-30.0	100.5	4 13.0	-30.9	100.6	7
4 17.5	-28.2	101.2	4 05.8	-29.1	101.3	3 54.0	-30.0	101.4	3 42.1	-30.9	101.4	8
3 49.3	-28.3	102.1	3 36.7	-29.2	102.2	3 24.0	-30.1	102.2	3 11.2	-31.0	102.3	9
3 21.0	-28.4	103.0	3 07.5	-29.3	103.1	2 53.9	-30.2	103.1	2 40.2	-31.0	103.2	10
2 52.6	-28.3	103.9	2 38.2	-29.3	103.9	2 23.7	-30.1	104.0	2 09.2	-31.0	104.0	11
2 24.3	-28.5	104.8	2 08.9	-29.3	104.8	1 53.6	-30.2	104.8	1 38.2	-31.1	104.9	12
1 55.8	-28.4	105.7	1 39.6	-29.3	105.7	1 23.4	-30.2	105.7	1 07.1	-31.0	105.7	13
1 27.4	-28.5	106.5	1 10.3	-29.4	106.6	0 53.2	-30.2	106.6	0 36.1	-31.1	106.6	14
0 58.9	-28.5	107.4	0 40.9	-29.3	107.4	0 23.0	-30.3	107.4	0 05.0	-31.1	107.4	15
0 30.4	-28.5	108.3	0 11.6	-29.4	108.3	0 07.3	+30.2	71.7	0 26.1	+31.1	71.7	16
0 01.9	-28.5	109.2	0 17.8	+29.3	70.8	0 37.5	+30.2	70.8	0 57.2	+31.0	70.8	17
0 26.6	+28.5	69.9	0 47.1	+29.4	70.0	1 07.7	+30.2	70.0	1 28.2	+31.1	70.0	18
0 55.1	+28.4	69.1	1 16.5	+29.3	69.1	1 37.9	+30.2	69.1	1 59.3	+31.0	69.1	19
1 23.5	+28.5	68.2	1 45.8	+29.3	68.2	2 08.1	+30.1	68.2	2 30.3	+31.0	68.3	20
1 52.0	+28.4	67.3	2 15.1	+29.3	67.3	2 38.2	+30.1	67.4	3 01.3	+30.9	67.4	21
2 20.4	+28.4	66.4	2 44.4	+29.2	66.5	3 08.3	+30.1	66.5	3 32.2	+30.9	66.6	22
2 48.8	+28.4	65.5	3 13.6	+29.2	65.6	3 38.4	+30.0	65.6	4 03.1	+30.9	65.7	23
3 17.2	+28.3	64.7	3 42.8	+29.2	64.7	4 08.4	+30.0	64.8	4 34.0	+30.7	64.8	24
3 45.5	+28.2	63.8	4 12.0	+29.0	63.8	4 38.4	+29.9	63.9	5 04.7	+30.7	64.0	25
4 13.7	+28.2	62.9	4 41.0	+29.0	63.0	5 08.3	+29.8	63.0	5 35.4	+30.7	63.1	26
4 41.9	+28.1	62.0	5 10.0	+29.0	62.1	5 38.1	+29.7	62.2	6 06.1	+30.5	62.3	27
5 10.0	+28.1	61.1	5 39.0	+28.8	61.2	6 07.8	+29.7	61.3	6 36.6	+30.5	61.4	28
5 38.1	+28.0	60.2	6 07.8	+28.8	60.3	6 37.5	+29.6	60.4	7 07.1	+30.3	60.5	29
6 06.1	+27.9	59.3	6 36.6	+28.7	59.4	7 07.1	+29.5	59.5	7 37.4	+30.3	59.7	30
6 34.0	+27.7	58.5	7 05.3	+28.6	58.6	7 36.6	+29.3	58.7	8 07.7	+30.2	58.8	31
7 01.7	+27.7	57.6	7 33.9	+28.5	57.7	8 05.9	+29.3	57.8	8 37.9	+30.0	57.9	32
7 29.4	+27.6	56.7	8 02.4	+28.3	56.8	8 35.2	+29.1	56.9	9 07.9	+29.9	57.0	33
7 57.0	+27.5	55.8	8 30.7	+28.3	55.9	9 04.3	+29.0	56.0	9 37.8	+29.8	56.2	34
8 24.5	+27.3	54.9	8 59.0	+28.1	55.0	9 33.3	+28.9	55.1	10 07.6	+29.6	55.3	35
8 51.8	+27.2	54.0	9 27.1	+27.9	54.1	10 02.2	+28.7	54.2	10 37.2	+29.5	54.4	36
9 19.0	+27.1	53.1	9 55.0	+27.9	53.2	10 30.9	+28.6	53.3	11 06.7	+29.3	53.5	37
9 46.1	+26.9	52.2	10 22.9	+27.6	52.3	10 59.5	+28.4	52.5	11 36.0	+29.1	52.6	38
10 13.0	+26.8	51.3	10 50.5	+27.6	51.4	11 27.9	+28.3	51.6	12 05.1	+29.0	51.7	39
10 39.8	+26.6	50.3	11 18.1	+27.3	50.5	11 56.2	+28.0	50.7	12 34.1	+28.8	50.8	40
11 06.4	+26.5	49.4	11 45.4	+27.2	49.6	12 24.2	+27.9	49.8	13 02.9	+28.7	49.9	41
11 32.9	+26.3	48.5	12 12.6	+27.0	48.7	12 52.1	+27.8	48.8	13 31.6	+28.4	49.0	42
11 59.2	+26.1	47.6	12 39.6	+26.8	47.8	13 19.9	+27.5	47.9	14 00.0	+28.2	48.1	43
12 25.3	+25.9	46.7	13 06.4	+26.6	46.8	13 47.4	+27.3	47.0	14 28.2	+28.0	47.2	44
12 51.2	+25.7	45.8	13 33.0	+26.4	45.9	14 14.7	+27.1	46.1	14 56.2	+27.8	46.3	45
13 16.9	+25.6	44.8	13 59.4	+26.2	45.0	14 41.8	+26.9	45.2	15 24.0	+27.6	45.4	46
13 42.5	+25.3	43.9	14 25.6	+26.0	44.1	15 08.7	+26.6	44.3	15 51.6	+27.3	44.4	47
14 07.8	+25.1	43.0	14 51.6	+25.8	43.1	15 35.3	+26.5	43.3	16 18.9	+27.1	43.5	48
14 32.9	+24.8	42.0	15 17.4	+25.5	42.2	16 01.8	+26.1	42.4	16 46.0	+26.8	42.6	49
14 57.7	+24.7	41.1	15 42.9	+25.3	41.3	16 27.9	+26.0	41.5	17 12.8	+26.6	41.7	50
15 22.4	+24.4	40.1	16 08.2	+25.0	40.3	16 53.9	+25.6	40.5	17 39.4	+26.3	40.7	51
15 46.8	+24.1	39.2	16 33.2	+24.8	39.4	17 19.5	+25.4	39.6	18 05.7	+26.0	39.8	52
16 10.9	+23.9	38.2	16 58.0	+24.5	38.4	17 44.9	+25.2	38.6	18 31.7	+25.8	38.8	53
16 34.8	+23.6	37.3	17 22.5	+24.2	37.5	18 10.1	+24.8	37.7	18 57.5	+25.4	37.9	54
16 58.4	+23.4	36.3	17 46.7	+24.0	36.5	18 34.9	+24.5	36.7	19 22.9	+25.2	36.9	55
17 21.8	+23.1	35.4	18 10.7	+23.7	35.5	18 59.4	+24.3	35.7	19 48.1	+24.8	35.9	56
17 44.9	+22.8	34.4	18 34.4	+23.3	34.6	19 23.7	+23.9	34.8	20 12.9	+24.5	35.0	57
18 07.7	+22.5	33.4	18 57.7	+23.1	33.6	19 47.6	+23.7	33.8	20 37.4	+24.2	34.0	58
18 30.2	+22.2	32.4	19 20.8	+22.7	32.6	20 11.3	+23.3	32.8	21 01.6	+23.9	33.0	59
18 52.4	+21.9	31.5	19 43.5	+22.4	31.6	20 34.6	+22.9	31.8	21 25.5	+23.5	32.0	60
19 14.3	+21.6	30.5	20 05.9	+22.1	30.7	20 57.5	+22.6	30.8	21 49.0	+23.1	31.0	61
19 35.9	+21.2	29.5	20 28.0	+21.8	29.7	21 20.1	+22.3	29.9	22 12.1	+22.8	30.1	62
19 57.1	+20.9	28.5	20 49.8	+21.4	28.7	21 42.4	+21.9	28.9	22 34.9	+22.4	29.1	63
20 18.0	+20.6	27.5	21 11.2	+21.1	27.7	22 04.3	+21.5	27.9	22 57.3	+22.0	28.0	64
20 38.6	+20.2	26.5	21 32.3	+20.6	26.7	22 25.8	+21.2	26.8	23 19.3	+21.7	27.0	65
20 58.8	+19.9	25.5	21 52.9	+20.4	25.7	22 47.0	+20.8	25.8	23 41.0	+21.2	26.0	66
21 18.7	+19.5	24.5	22 13.3	+19.9	24.6	23 07.8	+20.3	24.8	24 02.2	+20.8	25.0	67
21 38.2	+19.1	23.5	22 33.2	+19.6	23.6	23 28.1	+20.0	23.8	24 23.0	+20.4	24.0	68
21 57.3	+18.8	22.4	22 52.8	+19.1	22.6	23 48.1	+19.6	22.8	24 43.4	+20.0	22.9	69
22 16.1	+18.3	21.4	23 11.9	+18.8	21.6	24 07.7	+19.1	21.7	25 03.4	+19.5	21.9	70
22 34.4	+18.0	20.4	23 30.7	+18.3	20.5	24 26.8	+18.7	20.7	25 22.9	+19.1	20.8	71
22 52.4	+17.6	19.3	23 49.0	+17.9	19.5	24 45.5	+18.3	19.6	25 42.0	+18.7	19.8	72
23 10.0	+17.1	18.3	24 06.9	+17.5	18.4	25 03.8	+17.8	18.6	26 00.7	+18.1	18.7	73
23 27.1	+16.8	17.3	24 24.4	+17.1	17.4	25 21.6	+17.4	17.5	26 18.8	+17.7	17.7	74
23 43.9	+16.3	16.2	24 41.5	+16.6	16.3	25 39.0	+16.9	16.5	26 36.5	+17.3	16.6	75
24 00.2	+15.9	15.2	24 58.1	+16.1	15.3	25 55.9	+16.5	15.4	26 53.8	+16.7	15.5	76
24 16.1	+15.4	14.1	25 14.2	+15.7	14.2	26 12.4	+16.0	14.3	27 10.5	+16.2	14.5	77
24 31.5	+15.0	13.0	25 29.9	+15.3	13.2	26 28.4	+15.4	13.3	27 26.7	+15.8	13.4	78
24 46.5	+14.5	12.0	25 45.2	+14.7	12.1	26 43.8	+15.0	12.2	27 42.5	+15.2	12.3	79
25 01.0	+14.1	10.9	25 59.9	+14.3	11.0	26 58.8	+14.5	11.1	27 57.7	+14.7	11.2	80
25 15.1	+13.6	9.8	26 14.2	+13.8	9.9	27 13.3	+14.0	10.0	28 12.4	+14.2	10.1	81
25 28.7	+13.2	8.8	26 28.0	+13.3	8.8	27 27.3	+13.5	8.9	28 26.6	+13.6	9.0	82
25 41.9	+12.6	7.7	26 41.3	+12.8	7.7	27 40.8	+12.9	7.8	28 40.2	+13.1	7.9	83
25 54.5	+12.2	6.6	26 54.1	+12.3	6.6	27 53.7	+12.4	6.7	28 53.3	+12.5	6.8	84
26 06.7	+11.6	5.5	27 06.4	+11.8	5.5	28 06.1	+11.9	5.6	29 05.8	+12.0	5.7	85
26 18.3	+11.2	4.4	27 18.2	+11.2	4.4	28 18.0	+11.3	4.5	29 17.8	+11.4	4.5	86
26 29.5	+10.7	3.3	27 29.4	+10.7	3.3	28 29.3	+10.8	3.4	29 29.2	+10.9	3.4	87
26 40.2	+10.2	2.2	27 40.1	+10.2	2.2	28 40.1	+10.2	2.3	29 40.1	+10.2	2.3	88
26 50.4	+9.6	1.1	27 50.3	+9.7	1.1	28 50.3	+9.7	1.1	29 50.3	+9.7	1.1	89
27 00.0	+9.1	0.0	28 00.0	+9.1	0.0	29 00.0	+9.1	0.0	30 00.0	+9.1	0.0	90
27°			28°			29°			30°			

S. Lat. {L.H.A. greater than 180° ....Zn=180°−Z
{L.H.A. less than 180°............Zn=180°+Z

LATITUDE **SAME** NAME AS DECLINATION L.H.A. 99°, 261°

347

82°, 278° L.H.A. LATITUDE **SAME** NAME AS DECLINATION N. Lat. {L.H.A. greater than 180° .....Zn=Z / L.H.A. less than 180°............Zn=360°–Z

Dec.	23° Hc	23° d	23° Z	24° Hc	24° d	24° Z	25° Hc	25° d	25° Z	26° Hc	26° d	26° Z	27° Hc	27° d	27° Z	28° Hc	28° d	28° Z	29° Hc	29° d	29° Z	30° Hc	30° d	30° Z	Dec.
°	° ′	′	°	° ′	′	°	° ′	′	°	° ′	′	°	° ′	′	°	° ′	′	°	° ′	′	°	° ′	′	°	°
0	7 21.6	+23.6	93.1	7 18.3	+24.5	93.3	7 14.8	+25.5	93.4	7 11.2	+26.4	93.5	7 07.4	+27.4	93.7	7 03.5	+28.3	93.8	6 59.5	+29.3	93.9	6 55.4	+30.1	94.0	0
1	7 45.2	+23.5	92.2	7 42.8	+24.4	92.4	7 40.3	+25.4	92.5	7 37.6	+26.3	92.6	7 34.8	+27.3	92.8	7 31.8	+28.3	92.9	7 28.8	+29.1	93.0	7 25.5	+30.1	93.1	1
2	8 08.7	+23.3	91.3	8 07.2	+24.3	91.4	8 05.7	+25.2	91.6	8 03.9	+26.3	91.7	8 02.1	+27.2	91.9	8 00.1	+28.1	92.0	7 57.9	+29.0	92.1	7 55.6	+30.0	92.3	2
3	8 32.0	+23.2	90.4	8 31.5	+24.2	90.5	8 30.9	+25.2	90.7	8 30.2	+26.1	90.8	8 29.3	+27.0	91.0	8 28.2	+28.0	91.1	8 26.9	+29.0	91.3	8 25.6	+29.8	91.4	3
4	8 55.2	+23.1	89.4	8 55.7	+24.1	89.6	8 56.1	+25.0	89.7	8 56.3	+25.9	89.9	8 56.3	+26.9	90.1	8 56.2	+27.8	90.2	8 55.9	+28.8	90.4	8 55.4	+29.7	90.5	4
5	9 18.3	+22.9	88.5	9 19.8	+23.8	88.7	9 21.1	+24.8	88.8	9 22.2	+25.9	89.0	9 23.2	+26.8	89.1	9 24.0	+27.7	89.3	9 24.7	+28.6	89.5	9 25.1	+29.6	89.6	5
6	9 41.2	+22.7	87.6	9 43.6	+23.8	87.7	9 45.9	+24.7	87.9	9 48.1	+25.6	88.1	9 50.0	+26.6	88.2	9 51.7	+27.6	88.4	9 53.3	+28.5	88.6	9 54.7	+29.5	88.8	6
7	10 03.9	+22.6	86.6	10 07.4	+23.6	86.8	10 10.6	+24.6	87.0	10 13.7	+25.5	87.1	10 16.6	+26.5	87.3	10 19.3	+27.5	87.5	10 21.8	+28.4	87.7	10 24.2	+29.3	87.9	7
8	10 26.5	+22.5	85.7	10 31.0	+23.4	85.9	10 35.2	+24.4	86.0	10 39.2	+25.4	86.2	10 43.1	+26.3	86.4	10 46.8	+27.2	86.6	10 50.2	+28.2	86.8	10 53.5	+29.1	87.0	8
9	10 49.0	+22.2	84.7	10 54.4	+23.2	84.9	10 59.6	+24.2	85.1	11 04.6	+25.2	85.3	11 09.4	+26.2	85.5	11 14.0	+27.1	85.7	11 18.4	+28.1	85.9	11 22.6	+29.0	86.1	9
10	11 11.2	+22.1	83.8	11 17.6	+23.1	84.0	11 23.8	+24.1	84.2	11 29.8	+25.0	84.4	11 35.6	+25.9	84.6	11 41.1	+27.0	84.8	11 46.5	+27.9	85.0	11 51.6	+28.8	85.2	10
11	11 33.3	+21.9	82.8	11 40.7	+22.9	83.0	11 47.9	+23.8	83.2	11 54.8	+24.8	83.5	12 01.5	+25.8	83.7	12 08.1	+26.7	83.9	12 14.4	+27.7	84.1	12 20.4	+28.7	84.3	11
12	11 55.2	+21.7	81.9	12 03.6	+22.7	82.1	12 11.7	+23.7	82.3	12 19.6	+24.7	82.5	12 27.3	+25.6	82.7	12 34.8	+26.6	83.0	12 42.1	+27.5	83.2	12 49.1	+28.4	83.4	12
13	12 16.9	+21.5	80.9	12 26.3	+22.5	81.1	12 35.4	+23.5	81.4	12 44.3	+24.4	81.6	12 52.9	+25.5	81.8	13 01.4	+26.3	82.0	13 09.6	+27.3	82.3	13 17.5	+28.3	82.5	13
14	12 38.4	+21.3	80.0	12 48.8	+22.2	80.2	12 58.9	+23.2	80.4	13 08.7	+24.3	80.6	13 18.4	+25.2	80.9	13 27.7	+26.2	81.1	13 36.9	+27.1	81.4	13 45.8	+28.1	81.6	14
15	12 59.7	+21.1	79.0	13 11.0	+22.1	79.2	13 22.1	+23.1	79.5	13 33.0	+24.0	79.7	13 43.6	+25.0	79.9	13 53.9	+26.0	80.2	14 04.0	+26.9	80.4	14 13.9	+27.8	80.7	15
16	13 20.8	+20.9	78.1	13 33.1	+21.9	78.3	13 45.2	+22.8	78.5	13 57.0	+23.8	78.8	14 08.6	+24.7	79.0	14 19.9	+25.7	79.3	14 30.9	+26.7	79.5	14 41.7	+27.7	79.8	16
17	13 41.7	+20.6	77.1	13 55.0	+21.6	77.3	14 08.0	+22.6	77.6	14 20.8	+23.6	77.8	14 33.3	+24.6	78.1	14 45.6	+25.5	78.3	14 57.6	+26.5	78.6	15 09.4	+27.4	78.8	17
18	14 02.3	+20.5	76.1	14 16.6	+21.4	76.4	14 30.6	+22.4	76.6	14 44.4	+23.3	76.9	14 57.9	+24.3	77.1	15 11.1	+25.3	77.4	15 24.1	+26.2	77.7	15 36.8	+27.2	77.9	18
19	14 22.8	+20.1	75.1	14 38.0	+21.2	75.4	14 53.0	+22.1	75.7	15 07.7	+23.1	75.9	15 22.2	+24.1	76.2	15 36.4	+25.0	76.4	15 50.3	+26.0	76.7	16 04.0	+26.9	77.0	19
20	14 42.9	+20.0	74.2	14 59.2	+20.9	74.4	15 15.1	+21.9	74.7	15 30.8	+22.9	75.0	15 46.3	+23.8	75.2	16 01.4	+24.8	75.5	16 16.3	+25.8	75.8	16 30.9	+26.7	76.1	20
21	15 02.9	+19.7	73.2	15 20.1	+20.6	73.5	15 37.0	+21.7	73.7	15 53.7	+22.6	74.0	16 10.1	+23.6	74.3	16 26.2	+24.6	74.6	16 42.1	+25.5	74.8	16 57.6	+26.4	75.1	21
22	15 22.6	+19.4	72.2	15 40.7	+20.4	72.5	15 58.7	+21.3	72.8	16 16.3	+22.4	73.0	16 33.7	+23.3	73.3	16 50.8	+24.2	73.6	17 07.6	+25.2	73.9	17 24.0	+26.2	74.2	22
23	15 42.0	+19.1	71.2	16 01.1	+20.2	71.5	16 20.0	+21.1	71.8	16 38.7	+22.0	72.1	16 57.0	+23.0	72.4	17 15.0	+24.0	72.6	17 32.8	+24.9	72.9	17 50.2	+25.9	73.3	23
24	16 01.1	+18.9	70.3	16 21.3	+19.8	70.5	16 41.1	+20.9	70.8	17 00.7	+21.8	71.1	17 20.0	+22.8	71.4	17 39.0	+23.7	71.7	17 57.7	+24.7	72.0	18 16.1	+25.6	72.3	24
25	16 20.0	+18.7	69.3	16 41.1	+19.6	69.5	17 02.0	+20.5	69.8	17 22.5	+21.5	70.1	17 42.8	+22.5	70.4	18 02.7	+23.5	70.7	18 22.4	+24.4	71.0	18 41.7	+25.4	71.3	25
26	16 38.7	+18.3	68.3	17 00.7	+19.3	68.6	17 22.5	+20.3	68.8	17 44.0	+21.3	69.1	18 05.3	+22.1	69.4	18 26.2	+23.1	69.8	18 46.8	+24.1	70.1	19 07.1	+25.0	70.4	26
27	16 57.0	+18.0	67.3	17 20.0	+19.0	67.6	17 42.8	+19.9	67.9	18 05.3	+20.9	68.2	18 27.4	+21.9	68.5	18 49.3	+22.8	68.8	19 10.9	+23.7	69.1	19 32.1	+24.7	69.4	27
28	17 15.0	+17.8	66.3	17 39.0	+18.7	66.6	18 02.7	+19.7	66.9	18 26.2	+20.6	67.2	18 49.3	+21.6	67.5	19 12.1	+22.5	67.8	19 34.6	+23.5	68.1	19 56.8	+24.4	68.5	28
29	17 32.8	+17.4	65.3	17 57.7	+18.4	65.6	18 22.4	+19.3	65.9	18 46.8	+20.3	66.2	19 10.9	+21.2	66.5	19 34.6	+22.2	66.8	19 58.1	+23.1	67.1	20 21.2	+24.1	67.5	29
30	17 50.2	+17.2	64.3	18 16.1	+18.1	64.6	18 41.7	+19.1	64.9	19 07.1	+20.0	65.2	19 32.1	+20.9	65.5	19 56.8	+21.9	65.8	20 21.2	+22.9	66.2	20 45.3	+23.8	66.5	30
31	18 07.4	+16.8	63.3	18 34.2	+17.8	63.6	19 00.8	+18.7	63.9	19 27.1	+19.6	64.2	19 53.0	+20.6	64.5	20 18.7	+21.5	64.8	20 44.1	+22.4	65.2	21 09.1	+23.4	65.5	31
32	18 24.2	+16.5	62.3	18 52.0	+17.4	62.6	19 19.5	+18.4	62.9	19 46.7	+19.3	63.2	20 13.6	+20.3	63.5	20 40.2	+21.2	63.8	21 06.5	+22.1	64.2	21 32.5	+23.0	64.5	32
33	18 40.7	+16.2	61.2	19 09.4	+17.1	61.5	19 37.9	+18.0	61.9	20 06.0	+19.0	62.2	20 33.9	+19.9	62.5	21 01.4	+20.8	62.8	21 28.6	+21.8	63.2	21 55.5	+22.7	63.5	33
34	18 56.9	+15.8	60.2	19 26.5	+16.8	60.5	19 55.9	+17.7	60.8	20 25.0	+18.6	61.2	20 53.8	+19.5	61.5	21 22.2	+20.5	61.8	21 50.4	+21.4	62.2	22 18.2	+22.4	62.5	34
35	19 12.7	+15.5	59.2	19 43.3	+16.4	59.5	20 13.6	+17.3	59.8	20 43.6	+18.2	60.1	21 13.3	+19.2	60.5	21 42.7	+20.1	60.8	22 11.8	+21.0	61.2	22 40.6	+21.9	61.5	35
36	19 28.2	+15.1	58.2	19 59.7	+16.0	58.5	20 30.9	+17.0	58.8	21 01.8	+17.9	59.1	21 32.5	+18.8	59.5	22 02.8	+19.7	59.8	22 32.8	+20.7	60.2	23 02.5	+21.6	60.5	36
37	19 43.3	+14.8	57.2	20 15.7	+15.7	57.5	20 47.9	+16.6	57.8	21 19.7	+17.5	58.1	21 51.3	+18.4	58.4	22 22.5	+19.4	58.8	22 53.5	+20.2	59.1	23 24.1	+21.1	59.5	37
38	19 58.1	+14.5	56.1	20 31.4	+15.4	56.4	21 04.1	+16.2	56.7	21 37.2	+17.2	57.1	22 09.7	+18.0	57.4	22 41.9	+18.9	57.8	23 13.7	+19.8	58.1	23 45.2	+20.8	58.5	38
39	20 12.6	+14.1	55.1	20 46.8	+14.9	55.4	21 20.7	+15.9	55.7	21 54.4	+16.7	56.0	22 27.7	+17.7	56.4	23 00.8	+18.5	56.7	23 33.6	+19.4	57.1	24 06.0	+20.3	57.5	39
40	20 26.7	+13.7	54.1	21 01.7	+14.6	54.4	21 36.6	+15.4	54.7	22 11.1	+16.4	55.0	22 45.4	+17.2	55.3	23 19.3	+18.2	55.7	23 53.0	+19.0	56.1	24 26.3	+20.0	56.4	40
41	20 40.4	+13.3	53.0	21 16.3	+14.2	53.3	21 52.0	+15.1	53.6	22 27.5	+15.9	54.0	23 02.6	+16.8	54.3	23 37.5	+17.7	54.7	24 12.0	+18.6	55.0	24 46.3	+19.5	55.4	41
42	20 53.7	+12.9	52.0	21 30.5	+13.8	52.3	22 07.1	+14.7	52.6	22 43.4	+15.6	52.9	23 19.4	+16.5	53.3	23 55.2	+17.3	53.6	24 30.6	+18.2	54.0	25 05.8	+19.0	54.4	42
43	21 06.6	+12.6	50.9	21 44.3	+13.5	51.2	22 21.8	+14.2	51.5	22 59.0	+15.1	51.9	23 35.9	+15.9	52.2	24 12.5	+16.8	52.6	24 48.8	+17.7	52.9	25 24.8	+18.6	53.3	43
44	21 19.2	+12.2	49.9	21 57.8	+13.0	50.2	22 36.0	+13.9	50.5	23 14.1	+14.7	50.8	23 51.8	+15.6	51.2	24 29.3	+16.4	51.5	25 06.5	+17.3	51.9	25 43.4	+18.2	52.3	44
45	21 31.4	+11.8	48.8	22 10.8	+12.6	49.1	22 49.9	+13.4	49.4	23 28.8	+14.3	49.8	24 07.4	+15.1	50.1	24 45.7	+16.0	50.5	25 23.8	+16.8	50.8	26 01.6	+17.6	51.2	45
46	21 43.2	+11.3	47.8	22 23.4	+12.2	48.1	23 03.3	+13.1	48.4	23 43.1	+13.8	48.7	24 22.5	+14.7	49.0	25 01.7	+15.5	49.4	25 40.6	+16.4	49.8	26 19.2	+17.3	50.1	46
47	21 54.5	+11.0	46.7	22 35.6	+11.7	47.0	23 16.4	+12.5	47.3	23 56.9	+13.4	47.6	24 37.2	+14.2	48.0	25 17.2	+15.1	48.3	25 57.0	+15.9	48.7	26 36.5	+16.7	49.1	47
48	22 05.5	+10.6	45.7	22 47.3	+11.4	45.9	23 28.9	+12.2	46.3	24 10.3	+13.0	46.6	24 51.4	+13.8	46.9	25 32.3	+14.6	47.3	26 12.9	+15.4	47.6	26 53.2	+16.2	48.0	48
49	22 16.1	+10.1	44.6	22 58.7	+10.9	44.9	23 41.1	+11.7	45.2	24 23.3	+12.5	45.5	25 05.2	+13.3	45.8	25 46.9	+14.1	46.2	26 28.3	+14.9	46.5	27 09.4	+15.7	46.9	49
50	22 26.2	+9.7	43.5	23 09.6	+10.5	43.8	23 52.8	+11.3	44.1	24 35.8	+12.0	44.4	25 18.5	+12.8	44.8	26 01.0	+13.6	45.1	26 43.2	+14.4	45.4	27 25.1	+15.3	45.8	50
51	22 35.9	+9.3	42.5	23 20.1	+10.0	42.7	24 04.1	+10.8	43.0	24 47.8	+11.6	43.4	25 31.3	+12.4	43.7	26 14.6	+13.1	44.0	26 57.6	+13.9	44.4	27 40.4	+14.7	44.7	51
52	22 45.2	+8.9	41.4	23 30.1	+9.7	41.7	24 14.9	+10.3	42.0	24 59.4	+11.1	42.3	25 43.7	+11.8	42.6	26 27.7	+12.6	42.9	27 11.5	+13.4	43.3	27 55.1	+14.2	43.6	52
53	22 54.1	+8.4	40.3	23 39.8	+9.1	40.6	24 25.2	+9.9	40.9	25 10.5	+10.6	41.2	25 55.5	+11.4	41.5	26 40.3	+12.2	41.8	27 24.9	+12.9	42.2	28 09.3	+13.6	42.5	53
54	23 02.5	+8.0	39.2	23 48.9	+8.7	39.5	24 35.1	+9.4	39.8	25 21.1	+10.2	40.1	26 06.9	+10.9	40.4	26 52.5	+11.6	40.7	27 37.8	+12.4	41.1	28 22.9	+13.2	41.4	54
55	23 10.5	+7.6	38.2	23 57.6	+8.3	38.4	24 44.5	+9.0	38.7	25 31.3	+9.6	39.0	26 17.8	+10.4	39.3	27 04.1	+11.1	39.6	27 50.2	+11.8	40.0	28 36.1	+12.5	40.3	55
56	23 18.1	+7.1	37.1	24 05.9	+7.8	37.3	24 53.5	+8.5	37.6	25 40.9	+9.2	37.9	26 28.2	+9.8	38.2	27 15.2	+10.6	38.5	28 02.0	+11.3	38.9	28 48.6	+12.1	39.2	56
57	23 25.2	+6.7	36.0	24 13.7	+7.3	36.3	25 02.0	+8.0	36.5	25 50.1	+8.7	36.8	26 38.0	+9.4	37.1	27 25.8	+10.0	37.4	28 13.3	+10.8	37.7	29 00.7	+11.4	38.1	57
58	23 31.9	+6.2	34.9	24 21.0	+6.8	35.2	25 10.0	+7.5	35.4	25 58.8	+8.1	35.7	26 47.4	+8.8	36.0	27 35.8	+9.6	36.3	28 24.1	+10.2	36.6	29 12.1	+10.9	37.0	58
59	23 38.1	+5.7	33.8	24 27.8	+6.4	34.1	25 17.5	+7.0	34.3	26 06.9	+7.7	34.6	26 56.2	+8.3	34.9	27 45.4	+8.9	35.2	28 34.3	+9.6	35.5	29 23.0	+10.4	35.8	59
60	23 43.8	+5.3	32.7	24 34.2	+6.0	33.0	25 24.5	+6.5	33.2	26 14.6	+7.2	33.5	27 04.5	+7.8	33.8	27 54.3	+8.5	34.1	28 43.9	+9.1	34.4	29 33.4	+9.7	34.7	60
61	23 49.1	+4.9	31.7	24 40.2	+5.4	31.9	25 31.0	+6.1	32.1	26 21.8	+6.6	32.4	27 12.3	+7.3	32.7	28 02.8	+7.9	33.0	28 53.0	+8.6	33.3	29 43.1	+9.2	33.6	61
62	23 54.0	+4.4	30.6	24 45.6	+5.0	30.8	25 37.1	+5.5	31.0	26 28.4	+6.1	31.3	27 19.6	+6.7	31.6	28 10.7	+7.3	31.8	29 01.6	+7.9	32.1	29 52.3	+8.6	32.4	62
63	23 58.4	+3.9	29.5	24 50.6	+4.4	29.7	25 42.6	+5.1	29.9	26 34.5	+5.7	30.2	27 26.3	+6.2	30.4	28 18.0	+6.8	30.7	29 09.5	+7.4	31.0	30 00.9	+8.0	31.3	63
64	24 02.3	+3.5	28.4	24 55.0	+4.0	28.6	25 47.7	+4.5	28.8	26 40.2	+5.1	29.1	27 32.5	+5.7	29.3	28 24.8	+6.2	29.6	29 16.9	+6.8	29.8	30 08.9	+7.4	30.1	64
65	24 05.8	+2.9	27.3	24 59.0	+3.5	27.5	25 52.2	+4.0	27.7	26 45.3	+4.5	27.9	27 38.2	+5.1	28.2	28 31.0	+5.7	28.4	29 23.7	+6.2	28.7	30 16.3	+6.8	29.0	65
66	24 08.7	+2.6	26.2	25 02.5	+3.1	26.4	25 56.2	+3.6	26.6	26 49.8	+4.1	26.8	27 43.3	+4.6	27.1	28 36.7	+5.1	27.3	29 29.9	+5.7	27.6	30 23.1	+6.1	27.8	66
67	24 11.3	+2.0	25.1	25 05.6	+2.5	25.3	25 59.8	+3.0	25.5	26 53.9	+3.5	25.7	27 47.9	+4.0	25.9	28 41.8	+4.5	26.2	29 35.6	+5.0	26.4	30 29.2	+5.6	26.7	67
68	24 13.3	+1.6	24.0	25 08.1	+2.0	24.2	26 02.8	+2.5	24.4	26 57.4	+3.0	24.6	27 51.9	+3.4	24.8	28 46.3	+3.9	25.0	29 40.6	+4.5	25.3	30 34.8	+5.0	25.5	68
69	24 14.9	+1.1	22.9	25 10.1	+1.6	23.1	26 05.3	+2.0	23.3	27 00.4	+2.4	23.5	27 55.3	+3.0	23.7	28 50.2	+3.4	23.9	29 45.1	+3.8	24.1	30 39.8	+4.3	24.4	69
70	24 16.0	+0.6	21.8	25 11.7	+1.0	22.0	26 07.3	+1.5	22.2	27 02.8	+1.9	22.4	27 58.3	+2.3	22.5	28 53.6	+2.8	22.8	29 48.9	+3.3	23.0	30 44.1	+3.7	23.2	70
71	24 16.6	+0.2	20.7	25 12.7	+0.6	20.9	26 08.8	+0.9	21.0	27 04.7	+1.4	21.2	28 00.6	+1.8	21.4	28 56.4	+2.3	21.6	29 52.2	+2.6	21.8	30 47.8	+3.1	22.0	71
72	24 16.8	-0.3	19.6	25 13.3	+0.1	19.8	26 09.7	+0.5	19.9	27 06.1	+0.8	20.1	28 02.4	+1.2	20.3	28 58.7	+1.6	20.5	29 54.8	+2.1	20.7	30 50.9	+2.5	20.9	72
73	24 16.5	-0.8	18.5	25 13.4	-0.5	18.7	26 10.2	-0.1	18.8	27 06.9	+0.3	19.0	28 03.6	+0.7	19.2	29 00.3	+1.1	19.3	29 56.9	+1.4	19.5	30 53.4	+1.8	19.7	73
74	24 15.7	-1.2	17.4	25 12.9	-0.9	17.6	26 10.1	-0.6	17.7	27 07.2	-0.2	17.9	28 04.3	+0.2	18.0	29 01.4	+0.4	18.2	29 58.3	+0.9	18.4	30 55.2	+1.3	18.6	74
75	24 14.5	-1.8	16.3	25 12.0	-1.4	16.5	26 09.5	-1.0	16.6	27 07.0	-0.7	16.7	28 04.5	-0.5	16.9	29 01.8	-0.1	17.0	29 59.2	+0.2	17.2	30 56.5	+0.6	17.4	75
76	24 12.7	-2.2	15.2	25 10.6	-1.9	15.4	26 08.5	-1.7	15.5	27 06.3	-1.3	15.6	28 04.0	-1.0	15.8	29 01.7	-0.6	15.9	29 59.4	-0.3	16.1	30 57.1	-0.1	16.2	76
77	24 10.5	-2.6	14.1	25 08.7	-2.4	14.2	26 06.8	-2.1	14.4	27 05.0	-1.9	14.5	28 03.0	-1.5	14.6	29 01.1	-1.3	14.8	29 59.1	-1.0	14.9	30 57.0	-0.6	15.1	77
78	24 07.9	-3.2	13.0	25 06.3	-2.9	13.1	26 04.7	-2.6	13.3	27 03.1	-2.3	13.4	28 01.5	-2.1	13.5	28 59.8	-1.8	13.6	29 58.1	-1.6	13.7	30 56.4	-1.3	13.9	78
79	24 04.7	-3.6	11.9	25 03.4	-3.3	12.0	26 02.1	-3.1	12.1	27 00.8	-3.0	12.2	27 59.4	-2.7	12.4	28 58.0	-2.4	12.5	29 56.5	-2.1	12.6	30 55.1	-1.9	12.7	79
80	24 01.1	-4.0	10.9	25 00.1	-3.9	10.9	25 59.0	-3.7	11.0	26 57.8	-3.4	11.1	27 56.7	-3.2	11.2	28 55.6	-3.0	11.3	29 54.4	-2.8	11.4	30 53.2	-2.6	11.6	80
81	23 57.1	-4.5	9.8	24 56.2	-4.3	9.8	25 55.3	-4.1	9.9	26 54.4	-3.9	10.0	27 53.5	-3.8	10.1	28 52.6	-3.6	10.2	29 51.6	-3.4	10.3	30 50.6	-3.1	10.4	81
82	23 52.6	-5.0	8.7	24 51.9	-4.9	8.7	25 51.2	-4.7	8.8	26 50.5	-4.5	8.9	27 49.7	-4.3	9.0	28 49.0	-4.2	9.1	29 48.2	-3.9	9.1	30 47.5	-3.8	9.2	82
83	23 47.6	-5.5	7.6	24 47.0	-5.3	7.6	25 46.5	-5.2	7.7	26 46.0	-5.1	7.8	27 45.4	-4.9	7.8	28 44.8	-4.7	7.9	29 44.3	-4.6	8.0	30 43.7	-4.4	8.1	83
84	23 42.1	-5.9	6.5	24 41.7	-5.7	6.5	25 41.3	-5.6	6.6	26 40.9	-5.5	6.7	27 40.5	-5.4	6.7	28 40.1	-5.3	6.8	29 39.7	-5.2	6.8	30 39.3	-5.1	6.9	84
85	23 36.2	-6.3	5.4	24 36.0	-6.3	5.4	25 35.7	-6.2	5.5	26 35.4	-6.0	5.5	27 35.1	-5.9	5.6	28 34.8	-5.8	5.6	29 34.5	-5.7	5.7	30 34.2	-5.6	5.8	85
86	23 29.9	-6.8	4.3	24 29.7	-6.7	4.4	25 29.5	-6.6	4.4	26 29.4	-6.6	4.4	27 29.2	-6.5	4.5	28 29.0	-6.4	4.5	29 28.8	-6.3	4.6	30 28.6	-6.2	4.6	86
87	23 23.1	-7.3	3.2	24 23.0	-7.2	3.3	25 22.9	-7.2	3.3	26 22.8	-7.1	3.3	27 22.7	-7.1	3.3	28 22.6	-7.0	3.4	29 22.5	-6.9	3.4	30 22.4	-6.9	3.4	87
88	23 15.8	-7.7	2.2	24 15.8	-7.7	2.2	25 15.7	-7.6	2.2	26 15.7	-7.6	2.2	27 15.6	-7.5	2.2	28 15.6	-7.5	2.2	29 15.6	-7.5	2.3	30 15.5	-7.4	2.3	88
89	23 08.1	-8.1	1.1	24 08.1	-8.1	1.1	25 08.1	-8.1	1.1	26 08.1	-8.1	1.1	27 08.1	-8.1	1.1	28 08.1	-8.1	1.1	29 08.1	-8.1	1.1	30 08.1	-8.1	1.1	89
90	23 00.0	-8.6	0.0	24 00.0	-8.6	0.0	25 00.0	-8.6	0.0	26 00.0	-8.6	0.0	27 00.0	-8.6	0.0	28 00.0	-8.6	0.0	29 00.0	-8.6	0.0	30 00.0	-8.6	0.0	90
	23°			24°			25°			26°			27°			28°			29°			30°			

82°, 278° L.H.A. LATITUDE **SAME** NAME AS DECLINATION

348

LATITUDE **CONTRARY** NAME TO DECLINATION   L.H.A. 82°, 278°

Dec.	23° Hc	d	Z	24° Hc	d	Z	25° Hc	d	Z	26° Hc	d	Z	27° Hc	d	Z	28° Hc	d	Z	29° Hc	d	Z	30° Hc	d	Z	Dec.
°	° ′	′	°	° ′	′	°	° ′	′	°	° ′	′	°	° ′	′	°	° ′	′	°	° ′	′	°	° ′	′	°	°
0	7 21.6	−23.7	93.1	7 18.3	−24.7	93.3	7 14.8	−25.6	93.4	7 11.2	−26.6	93.5	7 07.4	−27.5	93.7	7 03.5	−28.4	93.8	6 59.5	−29.4	93.9	6 55.4	−30.3	94.0	0
1	6 57.9	−23.8	94.1	6 53.6	−24.8	94.2	6 49.2	−25.8	94.3	6 44.6	−26.7	94.4	6 39.9	−27.6	94.5	6 35.1	−28.5	94.7	6 30.1	−29.4	94.8	6 25.1	−30.4	94.9	1
2	6 34.1	−23.9	95.0	6 28.8	−24.8	95.1	6 23.4	−25.8	95.2	6 17.9	−26.7	95.3	6 12.3	−27.7	95.4	6 06.6	−28.7	95.5	6 00.7	−29.5	95.7	5 54.7	−30.4	95.8	2
3	6 10.2	−24.0	95.9	6 04.0	−25.0	96.0	5 57.6	−25.9	96.1	5 51.2	−26.9	96.2	5 44.6	−27.8	96.3	5 37.9	−28.7	96.4	5 31.2	−29.6	96.5	5 24.3	−30.5	96.6	3
4	5 46.2	−24.1	96.8	5 39.0	−25.0	96.9	5 31.7	−26.0	97.0	5 24.3	−26.9	97.1	5 16.8	−27.8	97.2	5 09.2	−28.7	97.3	5 01.6	−29.7	97.4	4 53.8	−30.6	97.5	4
5	5 22.1	−24.1	97.8	5 14.0	−25.1	97.9	5 05.7	−26.0	97.9	4 57.4	−27.0	98.0	4 49.0	−27.9	98.1	4 40.5	−28.9	98.2	4 31.9	−29.8	98.3	4 23.2	−30.6	98.4	5
6	4 58.0	−24.3	98.7	4 48.9	−25.2	98.8	4 39.7	−26.1	98.8	4 30.4	−27.0	98.9	4 21.1	−28.0	99.0	4 11.6	−28.8	99.1	4 02.1	−29.7	99.1	3 52.6	−30.7	99.2	6
7	4 33.7	−24.3	99.6	4 23.7	−25.3	99.7	4 13.6	−26.2	99.7	4 03.4	−27.2	99.8	3 53.1	−28.0	99.9	3 42.8	−29.0	100.0	3 32.4	−29.9	100.0	3 21.9	−30.7	100.1	7
8	4 09.4	−24.4	100.5	3 58.4	−25.3	100.6	3 47.4	−26.3	100.6	3 36.2	−27.1	100.7	3 25.1	−28.1	100.8	3 13.8	−29.0	100.8	3 02.5	−29.9	100.9	2 51.2	−30.8	100.9	8
9	3 45.0	−24.4	101.4	3 33.1	−25.4	101.5	3 21.1	−26.3	101.5	3 09.1	−27.2	101.6	2 57.0	−28.1	101.7	2 44.8	−29.0	101.7	2 32.6	−29.9	101.8	2 20.4	−30.8	101.8	9
10	3 20.6	−24.5	102.3	3 07.7	−25.4	102.4	2 54.8	−26.3	102.4	2 41.9	−27.3	102.5	2 28.9	−28.2	102.5	2 15.8	−29.1	102.6	2 02.7	−29.9	102.6	1 49.6	−30.8	102.7	10
11	2 56.1	−24.5	103.3	2 42.3	−25.5	103.3	2 28.5	−26.4	103.3	2 14.6	−27.3	103.4	2 00.7	−28.2	103.4	1 46.7	−29.0	103.5	1 32.8	−30.0	103.5	1 18.8	−30.9	103.5	11
12	2 31.6	−24.6	104.2	2 16.8	−25.4	104.2	2 02.1	−26.4	104.2	1 47.3	−27.3	104.3	1 32.5	−28.2	104.3	1 17.7	−29.1	104.3	1 02.8	−30.0	104.4	0 47.9	−30.8	104.4	12
13	2 07.0	−24.6	105.1	1 51.4	−25.6	105.1	1 35.7	−26.4	105.1	1 20.0	−27.3	105.2	1 04.3	−28.2	105.2	0 48.6	−29.2	105.2	0 32.8	−30.0	105.2	0 17.1	−30.9	105.2	13
14	1 42.4	−24.6	106.0	1 25.8	−25.5	106.0	1 09.3	−26.5	106.0	0 52.7	−27.4	106.1	0 36.1	−28.3	106.1	0 19.4	−29.1	106.1	0 02.8	−30.0	106.1	0 13.8	+30.9	73.9	14
15	1 17.8	−24.7	106.9	1 00.3	−25.6	106.9	0 42.8	−26.4	106.9	0 25.3	−27.3	107.0	0 07.8	−28.2	107.0	0 09.7	+29.1	73.0	0 27.2	+29.9	73.0	0 44.7	+30.8	73.1	15
16	0 53.1	−24.7	107.8	0 34.7	−25.5	107.8	0 16.4	−26.5	107.8	0 02.0	+27.4	72.2	0 20.4	+28.2	72.2	0 38.8	+29.1	72.2	0 57.1	+30.0	72.2	1 15.5	+30.8	72.2	16
17	0 28.4	−24.6	108.7	0 09.2	−25.6	108.7	0 10.1	+26.5	71.3	0 29.4	+27.3	71.3	0 48.6	+28.3	71.3	1 07.9	+29.1	71.3	1 27.1	+30.0	71.3	1 46.3	+30.8	71.3	17
18	0 03.8	−24.7	109.6	0 16.4	+25.6	70.4	0 36.6	+26.4	70.4	0 56.7	+27.3	70.4	1 16.9	+28.2	70.4	1 37.0	+29.0	70.4	1 57.1	+29.9	70.4	2 17.1	+30.8	70.5	18
19	0 20.9	+24.7	69.4	0 42.0	+25.5	69.5	1 03.0	+26.5	69.5	1 24.0	+27.4	69.5	1 45.1	+28.1	69.5	2 06.0	+29.1	69.5	2 27.0	+29.9	69.6	2 47.9	+30.7	69.6	19
20	0 45.6	+24.6	68.5	1 07.5	+25.6	68.5	1 29.5	+26.4	68.6	1 51.4	+27.2	68.6	2 13.2	+28.2	68.6	2 35.1	+29.0	68.7	2 56.9	+29.8	68.7	3 18.6	+30.7	68.8	20
21	1 10.2	+24.7	67.6	1 33.1	+25.5	67.6	1 55.9	+26.3	67.7	2 18.6	+27.3	67.7	2 41.4	+28.1	67.7	3 04.1	+28.9	67.8	3 26.7	+29.8	67.8	3 49.3	+30.7	67.9	21
22	1 34.9	+24.6	66.7	1 58.6	+25.5	66.7	2 22.2	+26.4	66.8	2 45.9	+27.2	66.8	3 09.5	+28.1	66.9	3 33.0	+29.0	66.9	3 56.5	+29.8	67.0	4 20.0	+30.6	67.0	22
23	1 59.5	+24.6	65.8	2 24.1	+25.4	65.8	2 48.6	+26.3	65.9	3 13.1	+27.2	65.9	3 37.6	+28.0	66.0	4 02.0	+28.8	66.0	4 26.3	+29.7	66.1	4 50.6	+30.5	66.2	23
24	2 24.1	+24.5	64.9	2 49.5	+25.4	64.9	3 14.9	+26.3	65.0	3 40.3	+27.1	65.0	4 05.6	+27.9	65.1	4 30.8	+28.8	65.2	4 56.0	+29.6	65.2	5 21.1	+30.4	65.3	24
25	2 48.6	+24.5	64.0	3 14.9	+25.4	64.0	3 41.2	+26.2	64.1	4 07.4	+27.0	64.1	4 33.5	+27.9	64.2	4 59.6	+28.7	64.3	5 25.6	+29.5	64.4	5 51.5	+30.4	64.4	25
26	3 13.1	+24.5	63.1	3 40.3	+25.3	63.1	4 07.4	+26.1	63.2	4 34.4	+27.0	63.2	5 01.4	+27.8	63.3	5 28.3	+28.7	63.4	5 55.1	+29.5	63.5	6 21.9	+30.3	63.6	26
27	3 37.6	+24.4	62.1	4 05.6	+25.2	62.2	4 33.5	+26.1	62.3	5 01.4	+26.9	62.3	5 29.2	+27.8	62.4	5 57.0	+28.5	62.5	6 24.6	+29.4	62.6	6 52.2	+30.1	62.7	27
28	4 02.0	+24.3	61.2	4 30.8	+25.2	61.3	4 59.6	+26.0	61.4	5 28.3	+26.8	61.4	5 57.0	+27.6	61.5	6 25.5	+28.5	61.6	6 54.0	+29.2	61.7	7 22.3	+30.1	61.8	28
29	4 26.3	+24.3	60.3	4 56.0	+25.1	60.4	5 25.6	+25.9	60.5	5 55.1	+26.8	60.5	6 24.6	+27.6	60.6	6 54.0	+28.3	60.7	7 23.2	+29.2	60.9	7 52.4	+30.0	61.0	29
30	4 50.6	+24.2	59.4	5 21.1	+25.0	59.5	5 51.5	+25.9	59.6	6 21.9	+26.6	59.6	6 52.2	+27.4	59.7	7 22.3	+28.3	59.9	7 52.4	+29.1	60.0	8 22.4	+29.8	60.1	30
31	5 14.8	+24.1	58.5	5 46.1	+24.9	58.6	6 17.4	+25.7	58.6	6 48.5	+26.6	58.7	7 19.6	+27.4	58.8	7 50.6	+28.1	59.0	8 21.5	+28.9	59.1	8 52.2	+29.8	59.2	31
32	5 38.9	+24.0	57.6	6 11.0	+24.9	57.6	6 43.1	+25.6	57.7	7 15.1	+26.4	57.8	7 47.0	+27.2	58.0	8 18.7	+28.1	58.1	8 50.4	+28.8	58.2	9 22.0	+29.6	58.3	32
33	6 02.9	+23.9	56.6	6 35.9	+24.7	56.7	7 08.7	+25.6	56.8	7 41.5	+26.3	56.9	8 14.2	+27.1	57.1	8 46.8	+27.9	57.2	9 19.2	+28.7	57.3	9 51.6	+29.4	57.5	33
34	6 26.8	+23.9	55.7	7 00.6	+24.6	55.8	7 34.3	+25.4	55.9	8 07.8	+26.2	56.0	8 41.3	+27.0	56.2	9 14.7	+27.7	56.3	9 47.9	+28.6	56.4	10 21.0	+29.4	56.6	34
35	6 50.7	+23.7	54.8	7 25.2	+24.5	54.9	7 59.7	+25.3	55.0	8 34.0	+26.1	55.1	9 08.3	+26.9	55.2	9 42.4	+27.7	55.4	10 16.5	+28.4	55.5	10 50.4	+29.1	55.7	35
36	7 14.4	+23.6	53.9	7 49.7	+24.4	54.0	8 25.0	+25.1	54.1	9 00.1	+26.0	54.2	9 35.2	+26.7	54.3	10 10.1	+27.5	54.5	10 44.9	+28.2	54.6	11 19.5	+29.0	54.8	36
37	7 38.0	+23.5	52.9	8 14.1	+24.3	53.0	8 50.1	+25.1	53.2	9 26.1	+25.8	53.3	10 01.9	+26.5	53.4	10 37.6	+27.3	53.6	11 13.1	+28.1	53.7	11 48.5	+28.9	53.9	37
38	8 01.5	+23.4	52.0	8 38.4	+24.1	52.1	9 15.2	+24.9	52.2	9 51.9	+25.6	52.4	10 28.4	+26.4	52.5	11 04.9	+27.1	52.7	11 41.2	+27.9	52.8	12 17.4	+28.6	53.0	38
39	8 24.9	+23.2	51.1	9 02.5	+24.0	51.2	9 40.1	+24.7	51.3	10 17.5	+25.5	51.5	10 54.8	+26.3	51.6	11 32.0	+27.0	51.8	12 09.1	+27.7	51.9	12 46.0	+28.5	52.1	39
40	8 48.1	+23.1	50.1	9 26.5	+23.9	50.3	10 04.8	+24.6	50.4	10 43.0	+25.3	50.5	11 21.1	+26.1	50.7	11 59.0	+26.8	50.8	12 36.8	+27.6	51.0	13 14.5	+28.3	51.2	40
41	9 11.2	+23.0	49.2	9 50.4	+23.7	49.3	10 29.4	+24.4	49.5	11 08.3	+25.2	49.6	11 47.2	+25.9	49.8	12 25.8	+26.7	49.9	13 04.4	+27.4	50.1	13 42.8	+28.1	50.3	41
42	9 34.2	+22.8	48.3	10 14.1	+23.5	48.4	10 53.8	+24.3	48.5	11 33.5	+25.0	48.7	12 13.1	+25.7	48.8	12 52.5	+26.4	49.0	13 31.8	+27.1	49.2	14 10.9	+27.9	49.4	42
43	9 57.0	+22.6	47.3	10 37.6	+23.4	47.5	11 18.1	+24.1	47.6	11 58.5	+24.8	47.8	12 38.8	+25.5	47.9	13 18.9	+26.2	48.1	13 58.9	+27.0	48.3	14 38.8	+27.6	48.5	43
44	10 19.6	+22.5	46.4	11 01.0	+23.2	46.5	11 42.2	+23.9	46.7	12 23.3	+24.6	46.8	13 04.3	+25.3	47.0	13 45.1	+26.1	47.2	14 25.9	+26.7	47.4	15 06.4	+27.5	47.5	44
45	10 42.1	+22.3	45.4	11 24.2	+23.0	45.6	12 06.1	+23.7	45.7	12 47.9	+24.4	45.9	13 29.6	+25.1	46.1	14 11.2	+25.8	46.2	14 52.6	+26.5	46.4	15 33.9	+27.2	46.6	45
46	11 04.4	+22.2	44.5	11 47.2	+22.8	44.6	12 29.8	+23.5	44.8	13 12.3	+24.2	45.0	13 54.7	+24.9	45.1	14 37.0	+25.6	45.3	15 19.1	+26.3	45.5	16 01.1	+27.0	45.7	46
47	11 26.6	+21.9	43.6	12 10.0	+22.6	43.7	12 53.3	+23.3	43.9	13 36.5	+24.0	44.0	14 19.6	+24.7	44.2	15 02.6	+25.3	44.4	15 45.4	+26.0	44.6	16 28.1	+26.7	44.8	47
48	11 48.5	+21.8	42.6	12 32.6	+22.5	42.8	13 16.6	+23.2	42.9	14 00.5	+23.8	43.1	14 44.3	+24.5	43.2	15 27.9	+25.2	43.4	16 11.4	+25.8	43.6	16 54.8	+26.5	43.8	48
49	12 10.3	+21.6	41.7	12 55.1	+22.2	41.8	13 39.8	+22.8	42.0	14 24.3	+23.6	42.1	15 08.8	+24.2	42.3	15 53.1	+24.8	42.5	16 37.2	+25.6	42.7	17 21.3	+26.2	42.9	49
50	12 31.9	+21.3	40.7	13 17.3	+22.0	40.8	14 02.6	+22.7	41.0	14 47.9	+23.3	41.2	15 33.0	+23.9	41.4	16 17.9	+24.7	41.5	17 02.8	+25.2	41.7	17 47.5	+25.9	42.0	50
51	12 53.2	+21.2	39.7	13 39.3	+21.8	39.9	14 25.3	+22.4	40.1	15 11.2	+23.0	40.2	15 56.9	+23.7	40.4	16 42.6	+24.3	40.6	17 28.0	+25.1	40.8	18 13.4	+25.7	41.0	51
52	13 14.4	+20.9	38.8	14 01.1	+21.6	38.9	14 47.7	+22.2	39.1	15 34.2	+22.9	39.3	16 20.6	+23.5	39.4	17 06.9	+24.1	39.6	17 53.1	+24.7	39.8	18 39.1	+25.3	40.1	52
53	13 35.3	+20.8	37.8	14 22.7	+21.3	38.0	15 09.9	+22.0	38.1	15 57.1	+22.5	38.3	16 44.1	+23.2	38.5	17 31.0	+23.8	38.7	18 17.8	+24.4	38.9	19 04.4	+25.1	39.1	53
54	13 56.1	+20.4	36.8	14 44.0	+21.1	37.0	15 31.9	+21.7	37.2	16 19.6	+22.3	37.3	17 07.3	+22.9	37.5	17 54.8	+23.5	37.7	18 42.2	+24.2	37.9	19 29.5	+24.7	38.1	54
55	14 16.5	+20.3	35.9	15 05.1	+20.9	36.0	15 53.6	+21.4	36.2	16 41.9	+22.1	36.4	17 30.2	+22.6	36.6	18 18.3	+23.3	36.7	19 06.4	+23.8	36.9	19 54.2	+24.5	37.2	55
56	14 36.8	+20.0	34.9	15 26.0	+20.5	35.1	16 15.0	+21.2	35.2	17 04.0	+21.7	35.4	17 52.8	+22.4	35.6	18 41.6	+22.9	35.8	19 30.2	+23.5	36.0	20 18.7	+24.1	36.2	56
57	14 56.8	+19.8	33.9	15 46.5	+20.4	34.1	16 36.2	+20.9	34.2	17 25.7	+21.5	34.4	18 15.2	+22.0	34.6	19 04.5	+22.6	34.8	19 53.7	+23.2	35.0	20 42.8	+23.8	35.2	57
58	15 16.6	+19.5	33.0	16 06.9	+20.0	33.1	16 57.1	+20.6	33.3	17 47.2	+21.2	33.4	18 37.2	+21.7	33.6	19 27.1	+22.3	33.8	20 16.9	+22.9	34.0	21 06.6	+23.4	34.2	58
59	15 36.1	+19.2	32.0	16 26.9	+19.8	32.1	17 17.7	+20.3	32.3	18 08.4	+20.8	32.5	18 58.9	+21.5	32.6	19 49.4	+22.0	32.8	20 39.8	+22.5	33.0	21 30.0	+23.1	33.2	59
60	15 55.3	+19.0	31.0	16 46.7	+19.5	31.1	17 38.0	+20.1	31.3	18 29.2	+20.6	31.5	19 20.4	+21.1	31.7	20 11.4	+21.6	31.8	21 02.3	+22.2	32.0	21 53.1	+22.7	32.2	60
61	16 14.3	+18.7	30.0	17 06.2	+19.2	30.2	17 58.1	+19.7	30.3	18 49.8	+20.3	30.5	19 41.5	+20.7	30.7	20 33.0	+21.3	30.8	21 24.5	+21.8	31.0	22 15.8	+22.4	31.2	61
62	16 33.0	+18.4	29.0	17 25.4	+19.0	29.2	18 17.8	+19.4	29.3	19 10.1	+19.9	29.5	20 02.2	+20.5	29.7	20 54.3	+21.0	29.8	21 46.3	+21.5	30.0	22 38.2	+22.0	30.2	62
63	16 51.4	+18.2	28.0	17 44.4	+18.6	28.2	18 37.2	+19.1	28.3	19 30.0	+19.6	28.5	20 22.7	+20.1	28.7	21 15.3	+20.6	28.8	22 07.8	+21.1	29.0	23 00.2	+21.6	29.2	63
64	17 09.6	+17.8	27.0	18 03.0	+18.3	27.2	18 56.3	+18.8	27.3	19 49.6	+19.2	27.5	20 42.8	+19.7	27.7	21 35.9	+20.2	27.8	22 28.9	+20.7	28.0	23 21.8	+21.2	28.2	64
65	17 27.4	+17.5	26.0	18 21.3	+18.0	26.2	19 15.1	+18.4	26.3	20 08.8	+18.9	26.5	21 02.5	+19.4	26.6	21 56.1	+19.8	26.8	22 49.6	+20.3	27.0	23 43.0	+20.8	27.2	65
66	17 44.9	+17.3	25.0	18 39.3	+17.6	25.2	19 33.5	+18.2	25.3	20 27.7	+18.6	25.5	21 21.9	+19.0	25.6	22 15.9	+19.5	25.8	23 09.9	+19.9	26.0	24 03.8	+20.4	26.2	66
67	18 02.2	+16.9	24.0	18 56.9	+17.4	24.1	19 51.7	+17.7	24.3	20 46.3	+18.2	24.4	21 40.9	+18.6	24.6	22 35.4	+19.1	24.8	23 29.8	+19.6	25.0	24 24.2	+20.0	25.1	67
68	18 19.1	+16.6	23.0	19 14.3	+17.0	23.1	20 09.4	+17.4	23.3	21 04.5	+17.8	23.4	21 59.5	+18.3	23.6	22 54.5	+18.7	23.7	23 49.4	+19.1	23.9	24 44.2	+19.5	24.1	68
69	18 35.7	+16.2	22.0	19 31.3	+16.6	22.1	20 26.8	+17.1	22.3	21 22.3	+17.5	22.4	22 17.8	+17.8	22.6	23 13.2	+18.2	22.7	24 08.5	+18.7	22.9	25 03.7	+19.1	23.1	69
70	18 51.9	+16.0	21.0	19 47.9	+16.4	21.1	20 43.9	+16.7	21.2	21 39.8	+17.1	21.4	22 35.6	+17.5	21.5	23 31.4	+17.9	21.7	24 27.2	+18.2	21.8	25 22.8	+18.7	22.0	70
71	19 07.9	+15.6	20.0	20 04.3	+15.9	20.1	21 00.6	+16.3	20.2	21 56.9	+16.7	20.3	22 53.1	+17.1	20.5	23 49.3	+17.5	20.6	24 45.4	+17.8	20.8	25 41.5	+18.2	21.0	71
72	19 23.5	+15.2	18.9	20 20.2	+15.6	19.0	21 16.9	+16.0	19.2	22 13.6	+16.3	19.3	23 10.2	+16.6	19.4	24 06.7	+17.0	19.6	25 03.2	+17.4	19.7	25 59.7	+17.7	19.9	72
73	19 38.7	+14.9	17.9	20 35.8	+15.2	18.0	21 32.9	+15.5	18.1	22 29.9	+15.8	18.3	23 26.8	+16.2	18.4	24 23.7	+16.6	18.5	25 20.6	+16.9	18.7	26 17.4	+17.3	18.8	73
74	19 53.6	+14.6	16.9	20 51.0	+14.9	17.0	21 48.4	+15.2	17.1	22 45.7	+15.5	17.2	23 43.0	+15.8	17.3	24 40.3	+16.1	17.5	25 37.5	+16.4	17.6	26 34.7	+16.7	17.8	74
75	20 08.2	+14.2	15.8	21 05.9	+14.5	15.9	22 03.6	+14.7	16.1	23 01.2	+15.1	16.2	23 58.8	+15.4	16.3	24 56.4	+15.7	16.4	25 53.9	+16.0	16.6	26 51.4	+16.3	16.7	75
76	20 22.4	+13.8	14.8	21 20.4	+14.1	14.9	22 18.3	+14.4	15.0	23 16.3	+14.6	15.1	24 14.2	+14.9	15.2	25 12.1	+15.2	15.4	26 09.9	+15.5	15.5	27 07.7	+15.8	15.6	76
77	20 36.2	+13.5	13.8	21 34.5	+13.7	13.9	22 32.7	+14.0	14.0	23 30.9	+14.2	14.1	24 29.1	+14.5	14.2	25 27.3	+14.7	14.3	26 25.4	+15.0	14.4	27 23.5	+15.3	14.5	77
78	20 49.7	+13.0	12.7	21 48.2	+13.3	12.8	22 46.7	+13.5	12.9	23 45.1	+13.8	13.0	24 43.6	+14.0	13.1	25 42.0	+14.3	13.2	26 40.4	+14.5	13.3	27 38.8	+14.8	13.4	78
79	21 02.7	+12.7	11.7	22 01.5	+12.9	11.8	23 00.2	+13.1	11.8	23 58.9	+13.4	11.9	24 57.6	+13.6	12.0	25 56.3	+13.8	12.1	26 54.9	+14.0	12.2	27 53.6	+14.2	12.3	79
80	21 15.4	+12.3	10.6	22 14.4	+12.5	10.7	23 13.3	+12.7	10.8	24 12.3	+12.8	10.9	25 11.2	+13.1	11.0	26 10.1	+13.3	11.0	27 08.9	+13.5	11.1	28 07.8	+13.7	11.2	80
81	21 27.7	+11.9	9.6	22 26.9	+12.0	9.6	23 26.0	+12.3	9.7	24 25.1	+12.5	9.8	25 24.3	+12.6	9.9	26 23.4	+12.8	10.0	27 22.4	+13.0	10.0	28 21.5	+13.2	10.1	81
82	21 39.6	+11.5	8.5	22 38.9	+11.7	8.6	23 38.3	+11.8	8.7	24 37.6	+11.9	8.7	25 36.9	+12.1	8.8	26 36.2	+12.3	8.9	27 35.4	+12.5	8.9	28 34.7	+12.6	9.0	82
83	21 51.1	+11.1	7.5	22 50.6	+11.2	7.5	23 50.1	+11.3	7.6	24 49.5	+11.5	7.6	25 49.0	+11.7	7.7	26 48.5	+11.7	7.8	27 47.9	+11.9	7.8	28 47.3	+12.1	7.9	83
84	22 02.2	+10.7	6.4	23 01.8	+10.8	6.5	24 01.4	+11.0	6.5	25 01.0	+11.1	6.6	26 00.7	+11.1	6.6	27 00.2	+11.3	6.7	27 59.8	+11.4	6.8	28 59.4	+11.5	6.8	84
85	22 12.9	+10.3	5.3	23 12.6	+10.4	5.4	24 12.4	+10.4	5.4	25 12.1	+10.5	5.5	26 11.8	+10.7	5.5	27 11.5	+10.8	5.6	28 11.2	+10.9	5.6	29 10.9	+11.0	5.7	85
86	22 23.2	+9.8	4.3	23 23.0	+9.9	4.3	24 22.8	+10.0	4.3	25 22.6	+10.1	4.4	26 22.5	+10.1	4.4	27 22.3	+10.2	4.5	28 22.1	+10.3	4.5	29 21.9	+10.4	4.5	86
87	22 33.0	+9.4	3.2	23 32.9	+9.5	3.2	24 32.8	+9.5	3.3	25 32.7	+9.6	3.3	26 32.6	+9.7	3.3	27 32.5	+9.7	3.4	28 32.4	+9.8	3.4	29 32.3	+9.8	3.4	87
88	22 42.4	+9.0	2.1	23 42.4	+9.0	2.2	24 42.3	+9.1	2.2	25 42.3	+9.1	2.2	26 42.3	+9.1	2.2	27 42.2	+9.2	2.2	28 42.2	+9.2	2.3	29 42.1	+9.3	2.3	88
89	22 51.4	+8.6	1.1	23 51.4	+8.6	1.1	24 51.4	+8.6	1.1	25 51.4	+8.6	1.1	26 51.4	+8.6	1.1	27 51.4	+8.6	1.1	28 51.4	+8.6	1.1	29 51.4	+8.6	1.1	89
90	23 00.0	+8.1	0.0	24 00.0	+8.1	0.0	25 00.0	+8.1	0.0	26 00.0	+8.1	0.0	27 00.0	+8.1	0.0	28 00.0	+8.1	0.0	29 00.0	+8.1	0.0	30 00.0	+8.1	0.0	90
	23°			24°			25°			26°			27°			28°			29°			30°			

S. Lat. {L.H.A. greater than 180° ....Zn=180°–Z; L.H.A. less than 180°...........Zn=180°+Z}

LATITUDE **SAME** NAME AS DECLINATION   L.H.A. 98°, 262°

349

Dec.	23° Hc	d	Z	24° Hc	d	Z	25° Hc	d	Z	26° Hc	d	Z	27° Hc	d	Z	28° Hc	d	Z	29° Hc	d	Z	30° Hc	d	Z	Dec.
°	° ′	′	°	° ′	′	°	° ′	′	°	° ′	′	°	° ′	′	°	° ′	′	°	° ′	′	°	° ′	′	°	°
0	6 26.5	+23.5	92.7	6 23.5	+24.5	92.9	6 20.5	+25.4	93.0	6 17.3	+26.4	93.1	6 14.0	+27.4	93.2	6 10.6	+28.3	93.3	6 07.1	+29.2	93.4	6 03.5	+30.1	93.5	0
1	6 50.0	+23.4	91.8	6 48.0	+24.4	91.9	6 45.9	+25.4	92.1	6 43.7	+26.3	92.2	6 41.4	+27.2	92.3	6 38.9	+28.2	92.4	6 36.3	+29.2	92.5	6 33.6	+30.1	92.6	1
2	7 13.4	+23.4	90.9	7 12.4	+24.3	91.0	7 11.3	+25.3	91.1	7 10.0	+26.2	91.3	7 08.6	+27.2	91.4	7 07.1	+28.1	91.5	7 05.5	+29.0	91.6	7 03.7	+29.9	91.8	2
3	7 36.8	+23.2	90.0	7 36.7	+24.2	90.1	7 36.6	+25.1	90.2	7 36.2	+26.1	90.4	7 35.8	+27.0	90.5	7 35.2	+28.0	90.6	7 34.5	+28.9	90.8	7 33.6	+29.8	90.9	3
4	8 00.0	+23.0	89.0	8 00.9	+24.1	89.2	8 01.7	+25.0	89.3	8 02.3	+26.0	89.5	8 02.8	+27.0	89.6	8 03.2	+27.9	89.7	8 03.4	+28.8	89.9	8 03.4	+29.8	90.0	4
5	8 23.0	+23.0	88.1	8 25.0	+23.9	88.2	8 26.7	+24.9	88.4	8 28.3	+25.9	88.5	8 29.8	+26.8	88.7	8 31.1	+27.7	88.8	8 32.2	+28.7	89.0	8 33.2	+29.6	89.1	5
6	8 46.0	+22.8	87.2	8 48.9	+23.8	87.3	8 51.6	+24.8	87.5	8 54.2	+25.7	87.6	8 56.6	+26.6	87.8	8 58.8	+27.6	87.9	9 00.9	+28.5	88.1	9 02.8	+29.4	88.3	6
7	9 08.8	+22.7	86.2	9 12.7	+23.6	86.4	9 16.4	+24.6	86.6	9 19.9	+25.6	86.7	9 23.2	+26.6	86.9	9 26.4	+27.5	87.0	9 29.4	+28.4	87.2	9 32.2	+29.4	87.4	7
8	9 31.5	+22.5	85.3	9 36.3	+23.5	85.5	9 41.0	+24.4	85.6	9 45.5	+25.4	85.8	9 49.8	+26.3	86.0	9 53.9	+27.3	86.1	9 57.8	+28.3	86.3	10 01.6	+29.2	86.5	8
9	9 54.0	+22.3	84.4	9 59.8	+23.3	84.5	10 05.4	+24.3	84.7	10 10.9	+25.2	84.9	10 16.1	+26.3	85.1	10 21.2	+27.2	85.2	10 26.1	+28.1	85.4	10 30.8	+29.0	85.6	9
10	10 16.3	+22.2	83.4	10 23.1	+23.2	83.6	10 29.7	+24.2	83.8	10 36.1	+25.2	84.0	10 42.4	+26.0	84.1	10 48.4	+27.0	84.3	10 54.2	+28.0	84.5	10 59.8	+28.9	84.7	10
11	10 38.5	+22.1	82.5	10 46.3	+23.0	82.7	10 53.9	+24.0	82.8	11 01.3	+24.9	83.0	11 08.4	+25.9	83.2	11 15.4	+26.9	83.4	11 22.2	+27.8	83.6	11 28.7	+28.8	83.8	11
12	11 00.6	+21.8	81.5	11 09.3	+22.8	81.7	11 17.9	+23.8	81.9	11 26.2	+24.8	82.1	11 34.3	+25.8	82.3	11 42.3	+26.6	82.5	11 50.0	+27.6	82.7	11 57.5	+28.5	82.9	12
13	11 22.4	+21.7	80.6	11 32.1	+22.7	80.8	11 41.7	+23.6	81.0	11 51.0	+24.5	81.2	12 00.1	+25.5	81.4	12 08.9	+26.5	81.6	12 17.6	+27.4	81.8	12 26.0	+28.4	82.0	13
14	11 44.1	+21.4	79.6	11 54.8	+22.4	79.8	12 05.3	+23.4	80.0	12 15.5	+24.4	80.2	12 25.6	+25.4	80.5	12 35.4	+26.3	80.7	12 45.0	+27.3	80.9	12 54.4	+28.2	81.1	14
15	12 05.5	+21.3	78.7	12 17.2	+22.3	78.9	12 28.7	+23.2	79.1	12 39.9	+24.2	79.3	12 51.0	+25.1	79.5	13 01.7	+26.2	79.8	13 12.3	+27.1	80.0	13 22.6	+28.0	80.2	15
16	12 26.8	+21.1	77.7	12 39.5	+22.0	77.9	12 51.9	+23.1	78.1	13 04.1	+24.0	78.4	13 16.1	+25.0	78.6	13 27.9	+25.9	78.8	13 39.4	+26.8	79.1	13 50.6	+27.8	79.3	16
17	12 47.9	+20.9	76.7	13 01.5	+21.9	77.0	13 15.0	+22.8	77.2	13 28.1	+23.8	77.4	13 41.1	+24.7	77.7	13 53.8	+25.7	77.9	14 06.2	+26.7	78.1	14 18.4	+27.6	78.4	17
18	13 08.8	+20.6	75.8	13 23.4	+21.6	76.0	13 37.8	+22.6	76.2	13 51.9	+23.6	76.5	14 05.8	+24.5	76.7	14 19.5	+25.4	77.0	14 32.9	+26.4	77.2	14 46.0	+27.4	77.5	18
19	13 29.4	+20.4	74.8	13 45.0	+21.4	75.1	14 00.4	+22.3	75.3	14 15.5	+23.3	75.5	14 30.3	+24.3	75.8	14 44.9	+25.3	76.0	14 59.3	+26.2	76.3	15 13.4	+27.1	76.6	19
20	13 49.8	+20.2	73.9	14 06.4	+21.2	74.1	14 22.7	+22.2	74.3	14 38.8	+23.1	74.6	14 54.6	+24.1	74.8	15 10.2	+25.0	75.1	15 25.5	+26.0	75.4	15 40.5	+26.9	75.6	20
21	14 10.0	+20.0	72.9	14 27.6	+20.9	73.1	14 44.9	+21.9	73.4	15 01.9	+22.9	73.6	15 18.7	+23.8	73.9	15 35.2	+24.8	74.2	15 51.5	+25.7	74.4	16 07.4	+26.7	74.7	21
22	14 30.0	+19.7	71.9	14 48.5	+20.7	72.2	15 06.8	+21.6	72.4	15 24.8	+22.6	72.7	15 42.5	+23.6	72.9	16 00.0	+24.5	73.2	16 17.2	+25.5	73.5	16 34.1	+26.4	73.8	22
23	14 49.7	+19.5	70.9	15 09.2	+20.5	71.2	15 28.4	+21.4	71.4	15 47.4	+22.4	71.7	16 06.1	+23.3	72.0	16 24.5	+24.3	72.3	16 42.7	+25.2	72.5	17 00.5	+26.2	72.8	23
24	15 09.2	+19.2	70.0	15 29.7	+20.1	70.2	15 49.8	+21.2	70.5	16 09.8	+22.1	70.7	16 29.4	+23.1	71.0	16 48.8	+24.0	71.3	17 07.9	+24.9	71.6	17 26.7	+25.9	71.9	24
25	15 28.4	+19.0	69.0	15 49.8	+20.0	69.2	16 11.0	+20.9	69.5	16 31.9	+21.8	69.8	16 52.5	+22.8	70.1	17 12.8	+23.7	70.3	17 32.8	+24.7	70.6	17 52.6	+25.6	70.9	25
26	15 47.4	+18.7	68.0	16 09.8	+19.6	68.2	16 31.9	+20.6	68.5	16 53.7	+21.6	68.8	17 15.3	+22.5	69.1	17 36.5	+23.5	69.4	17 57.5	+24.4	69.7	18 18.2	+25.3	70.0	26
27	16 06.1	+18.4	67.0	16 29.4	+19.4	67.3	16 52.5	+20.3	67.5	17 15.3	+21.2	67.8	17 37.8	+22.2	68.1	18 00.0	+23.1	68.4	18 21.9	+24.1	68.7	18 43.5	+25.1	69.0	27
28	16 24.5	+18.2	66.0	16 48.8	+19.1	66.3	17 12.8	+20.0	66.6	17 36.5	+21.0	66.8	18 00.0	+21.9	67.1	18 23.1	+22.9	67.4	18 46.0	+23.8	67.8	19 08.6	+24.7	68.1	28
29	16 42.7	+17.8	65.0	17 07.9	+18.8	65.3	17 32.8	+19.8	65.6	17 57.5	+20.7	65.9	18 21.9	+21.6	66.2	18 46.0	+22.6	66.5	19 09.8	+23.5	66.8	19 33.3	+24.4	67.1	29
30	17 00.5	+17.6	64.0	17 26.7	+18.5	64.3	17 52.6	+19.4	64.6	18 18.2	+20.4	64.9	18 43.5	+21.3	65.2	19 08.6	+22.2	65.5	19 33.3	+23.2	65.8	19 57.7	+24.2	66.1	30
31	17 18.1	+17.3	63.0	17 45.2	+18.2	63.3	18 12.0	+19.1	63.6	18 38.6	+20.0	63.9	19 04.8	+21.0	64.2	19 30.8	+21.9	64.5	19 56.5	+22.8	64.8	20 21.9	+23.7	65.2	31
32	17 35.4	+16.9	62.0	18 03.4	+17.9	62.3	18 31.1	+18.9	62.6	18 58.6	+19.8	62.9	19 25.8	+20.7	63.2	19 52.7	+21.6	63.5	20 19.3	+22.6	63.8	20 45.6	+23.5	64.2	32
33	17 52.3	+16.7	61.0	18 21.3	+17.5	61.3	18 50.0	+18.5	61.6	19 18.4	+19.4	61.9	19 46.5	+20.3	62.2	20 14.3	+21.3	62.5	20 41.9	+22.2	62.9	21 09.1	+23.1	63.2	33
34	18 09.0	+16.3	60.0	18 38.8	+17.3	60.3	19 08.5	+18.1	60.6	19 37.8	+19.1	60.9	20 06.8	+20.0	61.2	20 35.6	+20.9	61.5	21 04.1	+21.8	61.9	21 32.2	+22.7	62.2	34
35	18 25.3	+16.0	59.0	18 56.1	+16.9	59.3	19 26.6	+17.8	59.6	19 56.9	+18.7	59.9	20 26.8	+19.7	60.2	20 56.5	+20.6	60.5	21 25.9	+21.5	60.9	21 54.9	+22.4	61.2	35
36	18 41.3	+15.7	58.0	19 13.0	+16.6	58.3	19 44.4	+17.5	58.6	20 15.6	+18.4	58.9	20 46.5	+19.3	59.2	21 17.1	+20.2	59.5	21 47.4	+21.1	59.9	22 17.3	+22.1	60.2	36
37	18 57.0	+15.3	56.9	19 29.6	+16.2	57.2	20 01.9	+17.2	57.5	20 34.0	+18.0	57.8	21 05.8	+18.9	58.2	21 37.3	+19.8	58.5	22 08.5	+20.7	58.8	22 39.4	+21.6	59.2	37
38	19 12.3	+15.0	55.9	19 45.8	+15.9	56.2	20 19.1	+16.7	56.5	20 52.0	+17.7	56.8	21 24.7	+18.6	57.2	21 57.1	+19.5	57.5	22 29.2	+20.4	57.8	23 01.0	+21.3	58.2	38
39	19 27.3	+14.7	54.9	20 01.7	+15.6	55.2	20 35.8	+16.5	55.5	21 09.7	+17.3	55.8	21 43.3	+18.2	56.1	22 16.6	+19.0	56.5	22 49.6	+19.9	56.8	23 22.3	+20.8	57.2	39
40	19 42.0	+14.3	53.9	20 17.3	+15.1	54.2	20 52.3	+16.0	54.5	21 27.0	+16.9	54.8	22 01.5	+17.8	55.1	22 35.6	+18.7	55.4	23 09.5	+19.6	55.8	23 43.1	+20.5	56.1	40
41	19 56.3	+13.9	52.8	20 32.4	+14.8	53.1	21 08.3	+15.7	53.4	21 43.9	+16.6	53.7	22 19.3	+17.4	54.1	22 54.3	+18.3	54.4	23 29.1	+19.2	54.8	24 03.6	+20.1	55.1	41
42	20 10.2	+13.6	51.8	20 47.2	+14.5	52.1	21 24.0	+15.3	52.4	22 00.5	+16.1	52.7	22 36.7	+17.0	53.0	23 12.6	+17.9	53.4	23 48.3	+18.7	53.7	24 23.6	+19.6	54.1	42
43	20 23.8	+13.2	50.8	21 01.7	+14.0	51.0	21 39.3	+14.8	51.4	22 16.6	+15.7	51.7	22 53.7	+16.6	52.0	23 30.5	+17.4	52.3	24 07.0	+18.3	52.7	24 43.2	+19.2	53.0	43
44	20 37.0	+12.9	49.7	21 15.7	+13.7	50.0	21 54.1	+14.5	50.3	22 32.3	+15.4	50.6	23 10.3	+16.2	51.0	23 47.9	+17.1	51.3	24 25.3	+17.9	51.6	25 02.4	+18.7	52.0	44
45	20 49.9	+12.4	48.7	21 29.4	+13.2	49.0	22 08.6	+14.1	49.3	22 47.7	+14.9	49.6	23 26.5	+15.7	49.9	24 05.0	+16.6	50.2	24 43.2	+17.4	50.6	25 21.1	+18.3	51.0	45
46	21 02.3	+12.1	47.6	21 42.6	+12.9	47.9	22 22.7	+13.7	48.2	23 02.6	+14.5	48.5	23 42.2	+15.3	48.9	24 21.6	+16.1	49.2	25 00.6	+17.0	49.5	25 39.4	+17.9	49.9	46
47	21 14.4	+11.7	46.6	21 55.5	+12.5	46.9	22 36.4	+13.3	47.2	23 17.1	+14.1	47.5	23 57.5	+14.9	47.8	24 37.7	+15.7	48.1	25 17.6	+16.6	48.5	25 57.3	+17.3	48.8	47
48	21 26.1	+11.2	45.5	22 08.0	+12.1	45.8	22 49.7	+12.9	46.1	23 31.2	+13.6	46.4	24 12.4	+14.5	46.7	24 53.4	+15.3	47.1	25 34.2	+16.0	47.4	26 14.6	+16.9	47.8	48
49	21 37.3	+10.9	44.5	22 20.1	+11.6	44.7	23 02.6	+12.4	45.0	23 44.8	+13.3	45.3	24 26.9	+14.0	45.7	25 08.7	+14.8	46.0	25 50.2	+15.7	46.3	26 31.5	+16.4	46.7	49
50	21 48.2	+10.5	43.4	22 31.7	+11.2	43.7	23 15.0	+12.0	44.0	23 58.1	+12.7	44.3	24 40.9	+13.5	44.6	25 23.5	+14.3	44.9	26 05.9	+15.1	45.3	26 47.9	+16.0	45.6	50
51	21 58.7	+10.1	42.3	22 42.9	+10.8	42.6	23 27.0	+11.5	42.9	24 10.8	+12.3	43.2	24 54.4	+13.1	43.5	25 37.8	+13.9	43.9	26 21.0	+14.6	44.2	27 03.9	+15.4	44.5	51
52	22 08.8	+9.6	41.3	22 53.7	+10.4	41.6	23 38.5	+11.2	41.8	24 23.1	+11.9	42.1	25 07.5	+12.6	42.4	25 51.7	+13.4	42.8	26 35.6	+14.2	43.1	27 19.3	+14.9	43.5	52
53	22 18.4	+9.2	40.2	23 04.1	+10.0	40.5	23 49.7	+10.6	40.8	24 35.0	+11.4	41.1	25 20.1	+12.2	41.4	26 05.1	+12.9	41.7	26 49.8	+13.6	42.0	27 34.2	+14.4	42.4	53
54	22 27.6	+8.8	39.1	23 14.1	+9.5	39.4	24 00.3	+10.3	39.7	24 46.4	+11.0	40.0	25 32.3	+11.6	40.3	26 18.0	+12.3	40.6	27 03.4	+13.1	40.9	27 48.6	+13.9	41.3	54
55	22 36.4	+8.4	38.1	23 23.6	+9.1	38.3	24 10.6	+9.7	38.6	24 57.4	+10.4	38.9	25 43.9	+11.2	39.2	26 30.3	+11.9	39.5	27 16.5	+12.7	39.8	28 02.5	+13.3	40.2	55
56	22 44.8	+8.0	37.0	23 32.7	+8.6	37.3	24 20.3	+9.3	37.5	25 07.8	+10.0	37.8	25 55.1	+10.7	38.1	26 42.2	+11.4	38.4	27 29.2	+12.0	38.7	28 15.8	+12.9	39.1	56
57	22 52.8	+7.5	35.9	23 41.3	+8.1	36.2	24 29.6	+8.9	36.4	25 17.8	+9.5	36.7	26 05.8	+10.2	37.0	26 53.6	+10.9	37.3	27 41.2	+11.6	37.6	28 28.7	+12.2	38.0	57
58	23 00.3	+7.1	34.8	23 49.4	+7.8	35.1	24 38.5	+8.3	35.4	25 27.3	+9.0	35.6	26 16.0	+9.7	35.9	27 04.5	+10.4	36.2	27 52.8	+11.1	36.5	28 40.9	+11.8	36.8	58
59	23 07.4	+6.6	33.8	23 57.2	+7.2	34.0	24 46.8	+7.9	34.3	25 36.3	+8.6	34.5	26 25.7	+9.2	34.8	27 14.9	+9.8	35.1	28 03.9	+10.4	35.4	28 52.7	+11.1	35.7	59
60	23 14.0	+6.2	32.7	24 04.4	+6.8	32.9	24 54.7	+7.4	33.2	25 44.9	+8.0	33.4	26 34.9	+8.6	33.7	27 24.7	+9.3	34.0	28 14.3	+10.0	34.3	29 03.8	+10.6	34.6	60
61	23 20.2	+5.7	31.6	24 11.2	+6.3	31.8	25 02.1	+7.0	32.1	25 52.9	+7.5	32.3	26 43.5	+8.2	32.6	27 34.0	+8.8	32.9	28 24.3	+9.4	33.2	29 14.4	+10.1	33.5	61
62	23 25.9	+5.3	30.5	24 17.5	+5.9	30.7	25 09.1	+6.4	31.0	26 00.4	+7.1	31.2	26 51.7	+7.6	31.5	27 42.8	+8.2	31.8	28 33.7	+8.8	32.0	29 24.5	+9.4	32.3	62
63	23 31.2	+4.9	29.4	24 23.4	+5.4	29.7	25 15.5	+6.0	29.9	26 07.5	+6.5	30.1	26 59.3	+7.1	30.4	27 51.0	+7.7	30.6	28 42.5	+8.3	30.9	29 33.9	+8.9	31.2	63
64	23 36.1	+4.3	28.3	24 28.8	+4.9	28.6	25 21.5	+5.4	28.8	26 14.0	+6.0	29.0	27 06.4	+6.6	29.3	27 58.7	+7.1	29.5	28 50.8	+7.7	29.8	29 42.8	+8.3	30.1	64
65	23 40.4	+4.0	27.3	24 33.7	+4.5	27.5	25 26.9	+5.0	27.7	26 20.0	+5.5	27.9	27 13.0	+6.0	28.1	28 05.8	+6.6	28.4	28 58.5	+7.2	28.7	29 51.1	+7.7	28.9	65
66	23 44.4	+3.4	26.2	24 38.2	+3.9	26.4	25 31.9	+4.5	26.6	26 25.5	+5.0	26.8	27 19.0	+5.5	27.0	28 12.4	+6.0	27.3	29 05.7	+6.5	27.5	29 58.8	+7.1	27.8	66
67	23 47.8	+3.0	25.1	24 42.1	+3.5	25.3	25 36.4	+3.9	25.5	26 30.5	+4.4	25.7	27 24.5	+5.0	25.9	28 18.4	+5.5	26.1	29 12.2	+6.0	26.4	30 05.9	+6.5	26.6	67
68	23 50.8	+2.6	24.0	24 45.6	+3.0	24.2	25 40.3	+3.5	24.4	26 34.9	+4.0	24.6	27 29.5	+4.4	24.8	28 23.9	+4.9	25.0	29 18.2	+5.4	25.2	30 12.4	+5.9	25.5	68
69	23 53.4	+2.1	22.9	24 48.6	+2.6	23.1	25 43.8	+3.0	23.3	26 38.9	+3.4	23.5	27 33.9	+3.9	23.7	28 28.8	+4.3	23.9	29 23.6	+4.8	24.1	30 18.3	+5.3	24.3	69
70	23 55.5	+1.6	21.8	24 51.2	+2.0	22.0	25 46.8	+2.4	22.1	26 42.3	+2.9	22.3	27 37.8	+3.3	22.5	28 33.1	+3.8	22.7	29 28.4	+4.3	23.0	30 23.6	+4.7	23.2	70
71	23 57.1	+1.2	20.7	24 53.2	+1.5	20.9	25 49.2	+2.0	21.0	26 45.2	+2.4	21.2	27 41.1	+2.8	21.4	28 36.9	+3.2	21.6	29 32.7	+3.6	21.8	30 28.3	+4.1	22.0	71
72	23 58.3	+0.6	19.6	24 54.7	+1.1	19.8	25 51.2	+1.4	19.9	26 47.6	+1.8	20.1	27 43.9	+2.2	20.3	28 40.1	+2.7	20.5	29 36.3	+3.1	20.7	30 32.4	+3.5	20.9	72
73	23 58.9	+0.3	18.5	24 55.8	+0.6	18.7	25 52.6	+1.0	18.8	26 49.4	+1.3	19.0	27 46.1	+1.7	19.1	28 42.8	+2.0	19.3	29 39.4	+2.4	19.5	30 35.9	+2.8	19.7	73
74	23 59.2	−0.3	17.4	24 56.4	+0.1	17.6	25 53.6	+0.4	17.7	26 50.7	+0.8	17.9	27 47.8	+1.1	18.0	28 44.8	+1.5	18.2	29 41.8	+1.9	18.4	30 38.7	+2.2	18.5	74
75	23 58.9	−0.7	16.3	24 56.5	−0.4	16.5	25 54.0	−0.1	16.6	26 51.5	+0.2	16.7	27 48.9	+0.6	16.9	28 46.3	+0.9	17.0	29 43.7	+1.2	17.2	30 40.9	+1.7	17.4	75
76	23 58.2	−1.2	15.2	24 56.1	−0.9	15.4	25 53.9	−0.5	15.5	26 51.7	−0.2	15.6	27 49.5	0.0	15.8	28 47.2	+0.4	15.9	29 44.9	+0.7	16.1	30 42.6	+0.9	16.2	76
77	23 57.0	−1.6	14.1	24 55.2	−1.4	14.3	25 53.4	−1.1	14.4	26 51.5	−0.9	14.5	27 49.5	−0.5	14.6	28 47.6	−0.3	14.8	29 45.6	0.0	14.9	30 43.5	+0.4	15.1	77
78	23 55.4	−2.1	13.0	24 53.8	−1.8	13.2	25 52.3	−1.6	13.3	26 50.6	−1.3	13.4	27 49.0	−1.1	13.5	28 47.3	−0.8	13.6	29 45.6	−0.5	13.8	30 43.9	−0.3	13.9	78
79	23 53.3	−2.6	12.0	24 52.0	−2.3	12.0	25 50.7	−2.1	12.1	26 49.3	−1.9	12.3	27 47.9	−1.6	12.4	28 46.5	−1.4	12.5	29 45.1	−1.1	12.6	30 43.6	−0.8	12.7	79
80	23 50.7	−3.0	10.9	24 49.7	−2.9	10.9	25 48.6	−2.7	11.0	26 47.4	−2.4	11.1	27 46.3	−2.2	11.2	28 45.1	−1.9	11.3	29 44.0	−1.8	11.4	30 42.8	−1.6	11.6	80
81	23 47.7	−3.5	9.8	24 46.8	−3.3	9.8	25 45.9	−3.1	9.9	26 45.0	−2.9	10.0	27 44.1	−2.7	10.1	28 43.2	−2.6	10.2	29 42.2	−2.3	10.3	30 41.2	−2.1	10.4	81
82	23 44.2	−3.9	8.7	24 43.5	−3.7	8.7	25 42.8	−3.6	8.8	26 42.1	−3.4	8.9	27 41.4	−3.3	9.0	28 40.6	−3.1	9.1	29 39.9	−2.9	9.1	30 39.1	−2.7	9.2	82
83	23 40.3	−4.4	7.6	24 39.8	−4.3	7.6	25 39.2	−4.1	7.7	26 38.7	−4.0	7.8	27 38.1	−3.8	7.8	28 37.5	−3.6	7.9	29 37.0	−3.6	8.0	30 36.4	−3.4	8.1	83
84	23 35.9	−4.9	6.5	24 35.5	−4.7	6.6	25 35.1	−4.6	6.6	26 34.7	−4.5	6.7	27 34.3	−4.4	6.7	28 33.9	−4.3	6.8	29 33.4	−4.1	6.9	30 33.0	−4.0	6.9	84
85	23 31.0	−5.3	5.4	24 30.8	−5.3	5.5	25 30.5	−5.1	5.5	26 30.2	−5.0	5.5	27 29.9	−4.9	5.6	28 29.6	−4.8	5.6	29 29.3	−4.7	5.7	30 29.0	−4.6	5.8	85
86	23 25.7	−5.7	4.3	24 25.5	−5.6	4.4	25 25.4	−5.6	4.4	26 25.2	−5.5	4.4	27 25.0	−5.4	4.5	28 24.8	−5.3	4.5	29 24.6	−5.3	4.6	30 24.4	−5.2	4.6	86
87	23 20.0	−6.3	3.2	24 19.9	−6.2	3.3	25 19.8	−6.1	3.3	26 19.7	−6.1	3.3	27 19.6	−6.0	3.4	28 19.5	−6.0	3.4	29 19.3	−5.8	3.4	30 19.2	−5.8	3.4	87
88	23 13.7	−6.6	2.2	24 13.7	−6.6	2.2	25 13.7	−6.6	2.2	26 13.6	−6.5	2.2	27 13.6	−6.6	2.2	28 13.5	−6.5	2.3	29 13.5	−6.5	2.3	30 13.4	−6.4	2.3	88
89	23 07.1	−7.1	1.1	24 07.1	−7.1	1.1	25 07.1	−7.1	1.1	26 07.1	−7.1	1.1	27 07.0	−7.0	1.1	28 07.0	−7.0	1.1	29 07.0	−7.0	1.1	30 07.0	−7.0	1.1	89
90	23 00.0	−7.5	0.0	24 00.0	−7.5	0.0	25 00.0	−7.6	0.0	26 00.0	−7.6	0.0	27 00.0	−7.6	0.0	28 00.0	−7.6	0.0	29 00.0	−7.6	0.0	30 00.0	−7.6	0.0	90
	23°			24°			25°			26°			27°			28°			29°			30°			

LATITUDE CONTRARY NAME TO DECLINATION — L.H.A. 83°, 277°

Dec. °	23° Hc ° ′	23° d ′	23° Z °	24° Hc ° ′	24° d ′	24° Z °	25° Hc ° ′	25° d ′	25° Z °	26° Hc ° ′	26° d ′	26° Z °
0	6 26.5	−23.7	92.7	6 23.5	−24.6	92.9	6 20.5	−25.6	93.0	6 17.3	−26.5	93.1
1	6 02.8	−23.7	93.7	5 58.9	−24.7	93.8	5 54.9	−25.6	93.9	5 50.8	−26.6	94.0
2	5 39.1	−23.8	94.6	5 34.2	−24.8	94.7	5 29.3	−25.8	94.8	5 24.2	−26.7	94.9
3	5 15.3	−23.9	95.5	5 09.4	−24.8	95.6	5 03.5	−25.8	95.7	4 57.5	−26.7	95.8
4	4 51.4	−24.0	96.4	4 44.6	−24.9	96.5	4 37.7	−25.8	96.6	4 30.8	−26.8	96.7
5	4 27.4	−24.1	97.4	4 19.7	−25.0	97.4	4 11.9	−26.0	97.5	4 04.0	−26.9	97.6
6	4 03.3	−24.1	98.3	3 54.7	−25.1	98.3	3 45.9	−26.0	98.4	3 37.1	−26.9	98.5
7	3 39.2	−24.1	99.2	3 29.6	−25.1	99.3	3 19.9	−26.0	99.3	3 10.2	−27.0	99.4
8	3 15.1	−24.3	100.1	3 04.5	−25.2	100.2	2 53.9	−26.1	100.2	2 43.2	−27.0	100.3
9	2 50.8	−24.2	101.0	2 39.3	−25.2	101.1	2 27.8	−26.1	101.1	2 16.2	−27.0	101.2
10	2 26.6	−24.3	101.9	2 14.1	−25.2	102.0	2 01.7	−26.2	102.0	1 49.2	−27.1	102.1
11	2 02.3	−24.3	102.9	1 48.9	−25.2	102.9	1 35.5	−26.2	102.9	1 22.1	−27.1	102.9
12	1 38.0	−24.4	103.8	1 23.7	−25.3	103.8	1 09.3	−26.1	103.8	0 55.0	−27.1	103.8
13	1 13.6	−24.4	104.7	0 58.4	−25.3	104.7	0 43.2	−26.3	104.7	0 27.9	−27.1	104.7
14	0 49.2	−24.3	105.6	0 33.1	−25.3	105.6	0 16.9	−26.2	105.6	0 00.8	−27.1	105.6
15	0 24.9	−24.4	106.5	0 07.8	−25.3	106.5	0 09.3	+26.2	73.5	0 26.3	+27.1	73.5
16	0 00.5	−24.4	107.4	0 17.5	+25.3	72.6	0 35.5	+26.2	72.6	0 53.4	+27.1	72.6
17	0 23.9	+24.4	71.7	0 42.8	+25.3	71.7	1 01.7	+26.1	71.7	1 20.5	+27.1	71.7
18	0 48.3	+24.4	70.7	1 08.1	+25.3	70.8	1 27.8	+26.2	70.8	1 47.6	+27.0	70.8
19	1 12.7	+24.3	69.8	1 33.4	+25.2	69.9	1 54.0	+26.1	69.9	2 14.6	+27.0	69.9
20	1 37.0	+24.4	68.9	1 58.6	+25.2	68.9	2 20.1	+26.1	69.0	2 41.6	+27.0	69.0
21	2 01.4	+24.3	68.0	2 23.8	+25.2	68.0	2 46.2	+26.1	68.1	3 08.6	+26.9	68.1
22	2 25.7	+24.2	67.1	2 49.0	+25.1	67.1	3 12.3	+26.0	67.2	3 35.5	+26.9	67.2
23	2 49.9	+24.2	66.2	3 14.1	+25.1	66.2	3 38.3	+26.0	66.3	4 02.4	+26.8	66.3
24	3 14.1	+24.2	65.3	3 39.2	+25.1	65.3	4 04.3	+25.9	65.4	4 29.2	+26.8	65.4
25	3 38.3	+24.1	64.3	4 04.3	+24.9	64.4	4 30.2	+25.8	64.5	4 56.0	+26.7	64.5
26	4 02.4	+24.1	63.4	4 29.2	+24.9	63.5	4 56.0	+25.7	63.6	5 22.7	+26.6	63.6
27	4 26.5	+23.9	62.5	4 54.1	+24.9	62.6	5 21.7	+25.7	62.7	5 49.3	+26.5	62.7
28	4 50.4	+24.0	61.6	5 19.0	+24.7	61.7	5 47.4	+25.6	61.7	6 15.8	+26.4	61.8
29	5 14.4	+23.8	60.7	5 43.7	+24.7	60.7	6 13.0	+25.5	60.8	6 42.2	+26.3	60.9
30	5 38.2	+23.7	59.7	6 08.4	+24.5	59.8	6 38.5	+25.4	59.9	7 08.5	+26.2	60.0
31	6 01.9	+23.7	58.8	6 32.9	+24.5	58.9	7 03.9	+25.3	59.0	7 34.7	+26.1	59.1
32	6 25.6	+23.5	57.9	6 57.4	+24.4	58.0	7 29.2	+25.1	58.1	8 00.8	+26.0	58.2
33	6 49.1	+23.4	57.0	7 21.8	+24.2	57.1	7 54.3	+25.1	57.2	8 26.8	+25.9	57.3
34	7 12.5	+23.4	56.0	7 46.0	+24.1	56.1	8 19.4	+24.9	56.3	8 52.7	+25.7	56.4
35	7 35.9	+23.2	55.1	8 10.1	+24.1	55.2	8 44.3	+24.8	55.3	9 18.4	+25.6	55.5
36	7 59.1	+23.1	54.2	8 34.2	+23.8	54.3	9 09.1	+24.7	54.4	9 44.0	+25.4	54.6
37	8 22.2	+22.9	53.2	8 58.0	+23.8	53.4	9 33.8	+24.5	53.5	10 09.4	+25.3	53.6
38	8 45.1	+22.8	52.3	9 21.8	+23.5	52.4	9 58.3	+24.3	52.6	10 34.7	+25.1	52.7
39	9 07.9	+22.7	51.4	9 45.3	+23.5	51.5	10 22.6	+24.2	51.6	10 59.8	+24.9	51.8
40	9 30.6	+22.5	50.4	10 08.8	+23.2	50.6	10 46.8	+24.0	50.7	11 24.7	+24.8	50.9
41	9 53.1	+22.4	49.5	10 32.0	+23.1	49.6	11 10.8	+23.9	49.8	11 49.5	+24.6	49.9
42	10 15.5	+22.2	48.6	10 55.1	+23.0	48.7	11 34.7	+23.7	48.8	12 14.1	+24.4	49.0
43	10 37.7	+22.0	47.6	11 18.1	+22.7	47.8	11 58.4	+23.4	47.9	12 38.5	+24.2	48.1
44	10 59.7	+21.9	46.7	11 40.8	+22.6	46.8	12 21.8	+23.3	47.0	13 02.7	+24.0	47.1
45	11 21.6	+21.6	45.7	12 03.4	+22.4	45.9	12 45.1	+23.1	46.0	13 26.7	+23.8	46.2
46	11 43.2	+21.5	44.8	12 25.8	+22.2	44.9	13 08.2	+22.9	45.1	13 50.5	+23.6	45.2
47	12 04.7	+21.3	43.8	12 48.0	+21.9	44.0	13 31.1	+22.7	44.1	14 14.1	+23.4	44.3
48	12 26.0	+21.1	42.9	13 09.9	+21.8	43.0	13 53.8	+22.4	43.2	14 37.5	+23.1	43.3
49	12 47.1	+20.9	41.9	13 31.7	+21.5	42.0	14 16.2	+22.2	42.2	15 00.6	+22.9	42.4
50	13 08.0	+20.6	40.9	13 53.2	+21.4	41.1	14 38.4	+22.0	41.3	15 23.5	+22.6	41.4
51	13 28.6	+20.5	40.0	14 14.6	+21.0	40.1	15 00.4	+21.7	40.3	15 46.1	+22.4	40.5
52	13 49.1	+20.2	39.0	14 35.6	+20.9	39.2	15 22.1	+21.5	39.3	16 08.5	+22.1	39.5
53	14 09.3	+20.0	38.0	14 56.5	+20.6	38.2	15 43.6	+21.2	38.4	16 30.6	+21.8	38.5
54	14 29.3	+19.7	37.1	15 17.1	+20.3	37.2	16 04.8	+21.0	37.4	16 52.4	+21.6	37.6
55	14 49.0	+19.5	36.1	15 37.4	+20.1	36.2	16 25.8	+20.7	36.4	17 14.0	+21.3	36.6
56	15 08.5	+19.2	35.1	15 57.5	+19.8	35.3	16 46.5	+20.4	35.4	17 35.3	+21.0	35.6
57	15 27.7	+19.0	34.1	16 17.3	+19.6	34.3	17 06.9	+20.1	34.4	17 56.3	+20.7	34.6
58	15 46.7	+18.7	33.1	16 36.9	+19.2	33.3	17 27.0	+19.8	33.5	18 17.0	+20.4	33.6
59	16 05.4	+18.4	32.1	16 56.1	+19.0	32.3	17 46.8	+19.5	32.5	18 37.4	+20.1	32.6
60	16 23.8	+18.2	31.2	17 15.1	+18.7	31.3	18 06.3	+19.3	31.5	18 57.5	+19.7	31.7
61	16 42.0	+17.8	30.2	17 33.8	+18.4	30.3	18 25.6	+18.9	30.5	19 17.2	+19.5	30.7
62	16 59.8	+17.6	29.2	17 52.2	+18.1	29.3	18 44.5	+18.6	29.5	19 36.7	+19.1	29.6
63	17 17.4	+17.3	28.2	18 10.3	+17.8	28.3	19 03.1	+18.2	28.5	19 55.8	+18.7	28.6
64	17 34.7	+17.0	27.2	18 28.1	+17.4	27.3	19 21.3	+18.0	27.5	20 14.5	+18.4	27.6
65	17 51.7	+16.6	26.1	18 45.5	+17.1	26.3	19 39.3	+17.5	26.5	20 32.9	+18.1	26.6
66	18 08.3	+16.4	25.1	19 02.6	+16.8	25.3	19 56.8	+17.3	25.4	20 51.0	+17.7	25.6
67	18 24.7	+16.0	24.1	19 19.4	+16.5	24.3	20 14.1	+16.9	24.4	21 08.7	+17.3	24.6
68	18 40.7	+15.7	23.1	19 35.9	+16.1	23.2	20 31.0	+16.5	23.4	21 26.0	+16.9	23.5
69	18 56.4	+15.4	22.1	19 52.0	+15.7	22.2	20 47.5	+16.1	22.4	21 42.9	+16.6	22.5
70	19 11.8	+15.0	21.1	20 07.7	+15.4	21.2	21 03.6	+15.8	21.3	21 59.5	+16.2	21.5
71	19 26.8	+14.6	20.0	20 23.1	+15.0	20.2	21 19.4	+15.4	20.3	22 15.7	+15.7	20.4
72	19 41.4	+14.4	19.0	20 38.1	+14.7	19.1	21 34.8	+15.0	19.3	22 31.4	+15.4	19.4
73	19 55.8	+13.9	18.0	20 52.8	+14.3	18.1	21 49.8	+14.6	18.2	22 46.8	+14.9	18.3
74	20 09.7	+13.6	16.9	21 07.1	+13.9	17.1	22 04.4	+14.2	17.2	23 01.7	+14.6	17.3
75	20 23.3	+13.2	15.9	21 21.0	+13.5	16.0	22 18.6	+13.9	16.1	23 16.3	+14.1	16.2
76	20 36.5	+12.9	14.9	21 34.5	+13.1	15.0	22 32.5	+13.4	15.1	23 30.4	+13.7	15.2
77	20 49.4	+12.4	13.8	21 47.6	+12.8	13.9	22 45.9	+12.9	14.0	23 44.1	+13.2	14.1
78	21 01.8	+12.1	12.8	22 00.4	+12.3	12.9	22 58.8	+12.6	13.0	23 57.3	+12.8	13.1
79	21 13.9	+11.7	11.7	22 12.7	+11.9	11.8	23 11.4	+12.1	11.9	24 10.1	+12.3	12.0
80	21 25.6	+11.3	10.7	22 24.6	+11.5	10.7	23 23.5	+11.7	10.8	24 22.4	+11.9	10.9
81	21 36.9	+10.9	9.6	22 36.1	+11.0	9.7	23 35.2	+11.3	9.8	24 34.3	+11.5	9.8
82	21 47.8	+10.5	8.6	22 47.1	+10.7	8.6	23 46.5	+10.8	8.7	24 45.8	+10.9	8.8
83	21 58.3	+10.1	7.5	22 57.8	+10.2	7.5	23 57.3	+10.3	7.6	24 56.7	+10.5	7.7
84	22 08.4	+9.6	6.4	23 08.0	+9.8	6.5	24 07.6	+9.9	6.5	25 07.2	+10.0	6.6
85	22 18.0	+9.3	5.4	23 17.8	+9.3	5.4	24 17.5	+9.4	5.4	25 17.2	+9.6	5.5
86	22 27.3	+8.8	4.3	23 27.1	+8.9	4.3	24 26.9	+9.0	4.4	25 26.8	+9.0	4.4
87	22 36.1	+8.4	3.2	23 36.0	+8.5	3.2	24 35.9	+8.5	3.3	25 35.8	+8.6	3.3
88	22 44.5	+8.0	2.2	23 44.5	+8.0	2.2	24 44.4	+8.0	2.2	25 44.4	+8.0	2.2
89	22 52.5	+7.5	1.1	23 52.5	+7.5	1.1	24 52.4	+7.6	1.1	25 52.4	+7.6	1.1
90	23 00.0	+7.1	0.0	24 00.0	+7.1	0.0	25 00.0	+7.1	0.0	26 00.0	+7.1	0.0
	23°			24°			25°			26°		

27° Hc ° ′	27° d ′	27° Z °	28° Hc ° ′	28° d ′	28° Z °	29° Hc ° ′	29° d ′	29° Z °	30° Hc ° ′	30° d ′	30° Z °	Dec. °
6 14.0	−27.4	93.2	6 10.6	−28.3	93.3	6 07.1	−29.3	93.4	6 03.5	−30.2	93.5	0
5 46.6	−27.5	94.1	5 42.3	−28.5	94.2	5 37.8	−29.3	94.3	5 33.3	−30.3	94.4	1
5 19.1	−27.7	95.0	5 13.8	−28.5	95.1	5 08.5	−29.5	95.2	5 03.0	−30.3	95.2	2
4 51.4	−27.6	95.9	4 45.3	−28.6	96.0	4 39.0	−29.5	96.0	4 32.7	−30.5	96.1	3
4 23.8	−27.8	96.8	4 16.7	−28.7	96.8	4 09.5	−29.6	96.9	4 02.2	−30.4	97.0	4
3 56.0	−27.8	97.6	3 48.0	−28.7	97.7	3 39.9	−29.6	97.8	3 31.8	−30.5	97.8	5
3 28.2	−27.8	98.5	3 19.3	−28.8	98.6	3 10.3	−29.7	98.7	3 01.3	−30.6	98.7	6
3 00.4	−27.9	99.4	2 50.5	−28.8	99.5	2 40.6	−29.7	99.5	2 30.7	−30.6	99.6	7
2 32.5	−27.9	100.3	2 21.7	−28.8	100.4	2 10.9	−29.7	100.4	2 00.1	−30.6	100.4	8
2 04.6	−28.0	101.2	1 52.9	−28.9	101.2	1 41.2	−29.7	101.3	1 29.5	−30.7	101.3	9
1 36.6	−28.0	102.1	1 24.0	−28.8	102.1	1 11.5	−29.8	102.1	0 58.8	−30.6	102.1	10
1 08.6	−28.0	103.0	0 55.2	−28.9	103.0	0 41.7	−29.8	103.0	0 28.2	−30.7	103.0	11
0 40.6	−28.0	103.9	0 26.3	−28.9	103.9	0 11.9	−29.8	103.9	0 02.5	+30.6	76.1	12
0 12.6	−28.0	104.7	0 02.6	+28.9	75.3	0 17.9	+29.8	75.3	0 33.1	+30.7	75.3	13
0 15.4	+28.0	74.4	0 31.5	+28.9	74.4	0 47.7	+29.7	74.4	1 03.8	+30.6	74.4	14
0 43.4	+28.0	73.5	1 00.4	+28.9	73.5	1 17.4	+29.8	73.5	1 34.4	+30.6	73.6	15
1 11.4	+27.9	72.6	1 29.3	+28.8	72.6	1 47.2	+29.7	72.7	2 05.0	+30.6	72.7	16
1 39.3	+28.0	71.7	1 58.1	+28.9	71.8	2 16.9	+29.7	71.8	2 35.6	+30.6	71.8	17
2 07.3	+27.9	70.8	2 27.0	+28.8	70.9	2 46.6	+29.7	70.9	3 06.2	+30.5	71.0	18
2 35.2	+27.9	70.0	2 55.8	+28.7	70.0	3 16.3	+29.6	70.1	3 36.7	+30.5	70.1	19
3 03.1	+27.8	69.1	3 24.5	+28.7	69.1	3 45.9	+29.5	69.2	4 07.2	+30.4	69.2	20
3 30.9	+27.8	68.2	3 53.2	+28.7	68.2	4 15.4	+29.5	68.3	4 37.6	+30.3	68.4	21
3 58.7	+27.8	67.3	4 21.9	+28.5	67.4	4 44.9	+29.5	67.4	5 07.9	+30.3	67.5	22
4 26.5	+27.6	66.4	4 50.4	+28.6	66.5	5 14.4	+29.3	66.6	5 38.2	+30.2	66.6	23
4 54.1	+27.6	65.5	5 19.0	+28.4	65.6	5 43.7	+29.3	65.7	6 08.4	+30.1	65.8	24
5 21.7	+27.6	64.6	5 47.4	+28.4	64.7	6 13.0	+29.2	64.8	6 38.5	+30.0	64.9	25
5 49.3	+27.4	63.7	6 15.8	+28.2	63.8	6 42.2	+29.1	63.9	7 08.5	+29.9	64.0	26
6 16.7	+27.3	62.8	6 44.0	+28.2	62.9	7 11.3	+29.0	63.0	7 38.4	+29.8	63.2	27
6 44.0	+27.3	61.9	7 12.2	+28.1	62.0	7 40.3	+28.9	62.2	8 08.2	+29.7	62.3	28
7 11.3	+27.1	61.0	7 40.3	+27.9	61.2	8 09.2	+28.7	61.3	8 37.9	+29.6	61.4	29
7 38.4	+27.1	60.1	8 08.2	+27.9	60.3	8 37.9	+28.7	60.4	9 07.5	+29.5	60.5	30
8 05.5	+26.9	59.2	8 36.1	+27.7	59.4	9 06.6	+28.5	59.5	9 37.0	+29.3	59.6	31
8 32.4	+26.8	58.3	9 03.8	+27.6	58.5	9 35.1	+28.4	58.6	10 06.3	+29.2	58.8	32
8 59.2	+26.6	57.4	9 31.4	+27.4	57.6	10 03.5	+28.2	57.7	10 35.5	+29.0	57.9	33
9 25.8	+26.5	56.5	9 58.8	+27.3	56.7	10 31.7	+28.1	56.8	11 04.5	+28.9	57.0	34
9 52.3	+26.4	55.6	10 26.1	+27.2	55.8	10 59.8	+28.0	55.9	11 33.4	+28.7	56.1	35
10 18.7	+26.2	54.7	10 53.3	+27.0	54.9	11 27.8	+27.7	55.0	12 02.1	+28.5	55.2	36
10 44.9	+26.1	53.8	11 20.3	+26.8	53.9	11 55.5	+27.6	54.1	12 30.6	+28.4	54.3	37
11 11.0	+25.8	52.9	11 47.1	+26.7	53.0	12 23.1	+27.4	53.2	12 59.0	+28.1	53.4	38
11 36.8	+25.8	52.0	12 13.8	+26.4	52.1	12 50.5	+27.2	52.3	13 27.1	+28.0	52.5	39
12 02.6	+25.5	51.0	12 40.2	+26.3	51.2	13 17.7	+27.1	51.4	13 55.1	+27.8	51.6	40
12 28.1	+25.3	50.1	13 06.5	+26.1	50.3	13 44.8	+26.8	50.5	14 22.9	+27.5	50.7	41
12 53.4	+25.2	49.2	13 32.6	+25.8	49.3	14 11.6	+26.6	49.5	14 50.4	+27.4	49.7	42
13 18.6	+24.9	48.2	13 58.4	+25.7	48.4	14 38.2	+26.4	48.6	15 17.8	+27.1	48.8	43
13 43.5	+24.7	47.3	14 24.1	+25.4	47.5	15 04.6	+26.1	47.7	15 44.9	+26.9	47.9	44
14 08.2	+24.5	46.4	14 49.5	+25.3	46.6	15 30.7	+25.9	46.7	16 11.8	+26.6	47.0	45
14 32.7	+24.3	45.4	15 14.8	+24.9	45.6	15 56.6	+25.7	45.8	16 38.4	+26.4	46.0	46
14 57.0	+24.0	44.5	15 39.7	+24.8	44.7	16 22.3	+25.4	44.9	17 04.8	+26.1	45.1	47
15 21.0	+23.8	43.5	16 04.5	+24.4	43.7	16 47.7	+25.2	43.9	17 30.9	+25.8	44.1	48
15 44.8	+23.6	42.6	16 28.9	+24.3	42.8	17 12.9	+24.9	43.0	17 56.7	+25.6	43.2	49
16 08.4	+23.3	41.6	16 53.2	+23.9	41.8	17 37.8	+24.6	42.0	18 22.3	+25.3	42.2	50
16 31.7	+23.0	40.7	17 17.1	+23.7	40.9	18 02.4	+24.4	41.1	18 47.6	+25.0	41.3	51
16 54.7	+22.8	39.7	17 40.8	+23.4	39.9	18 26.8	+24.0	40.1	19 12.6	+24.7	40.3	52
17 17.5	+22.4	38.7	18 04.2	+23.1	38.9	18 50.8	+23.8	39.1	19 37.3	+24.4	39.4	53
17 39.9	+22.2	37.8	18 27.3	+22.8	38.0	19 14.6	+23.4	38.2	20 01.7	+24.0	38.4	54
18 02.1	+21.9	36.8	18 50.1	+22.5	37.0	19 38.0	+23.1	37.2	20 25.7	+23.7	37.4	55
18 24.0	+21.6	35.8	19 12.6	+22.2	36.0	20 01.1	+22.8	36.2	20 49.4	+23.4	36.4	56
18 45.6	+21.3	34.8	19 34.8	+21.9	35.0	20 23.9	+22.4	35.2	21 12.8	+23.1	35.4	57
19 06.9	+21.0	33.8	19 56.7	+21.5	34.0	20 46.3	+22.2	34.2	21 35.9	+22.7	34.5	58
19 27.9	+20.6	32.8	20 18.2	+21.2	33.0	21 08.5	+21.7	33.2	21 58.6	+22.3	33.5	59
19 48.5	+20.3	31.8	20 39.4	+20.9	32.0	21 30.2	+21.4	32.2	22 20.9	+22.0	32.5	60
20 08.8	+20.0	30.8	21 00.3	+20.5	31.0	21 51.6	+21.1	31.2	22 42.9	+21.6	31.4	61
20 28.8	+19.6	29.8	21 20.8	+20.1	30.0	22 12.7	+20.6	30.2	23 04.5	+21.1	30.4	62
20 48.4	+19.2	28.8	21 40.9	+19.8	29.0	22 33.3	+20.3	29.2	23 25.6	+20.8	29.4	63
21 07.6	+18.9	27.8	22 00.7	+19.4	28.0	22 53.6	+19.9	28.2	23 46.4	+20.4	28.4	64
21 26.5	+18.6	26.8	22 20.1	+19.0	27.0	23 13.5	+19.5	27.2	24 06.8	+20.0	27.4	65
21 45.1	+18.1	25.8	22 39.1	+18.6	25.9	23 33.0	+19.0	26.1	24 26.8	+19.5	26.3	66
22 03.2	+17.8	24.7	22 57.7	+18.2	24.9	23 52.0	+18.7	25.1	24 46.3	+19.2	25.3	67
22 21.0	+17.3	23.7	23 15.9	+17.8	23.9	24 10.7	+18.2	24.1	25 05.5	+18.6	24.2	68
22 38.3	+17.0	22.7	23 33.7	+17.3	22.8	24 28.9	+17.8	23.0	25 24.1	+18.2	23.2	69
22 55.3	+16.6	21.6	23 51.0	+17.0	21.8	24 46.7	+17.4	22.0	25 42.3	+17.8	22.1	70
23 11.9	+16.1	20.6	24 08.0	+16.5	20.7	25 04.1	+16.9	20.9	26 00.1	+17.3	21.1	71
23 28.0	+15.7	19.5	24 24.5	+16.1	19.7	25 21.0	+16.4	19.8	26 17.4	+16.8	20.0	72
23 43.7	+15.3	18.5	24 40.6	+15.6	18.6	25 37.4	+16.0	18.8	26 34.2	+16.4	18.9	73
23 59.0	+14.9	17.4	24 56.2	+15.2	17.6	25 53.4	+15.5	17.7	26 50.6	+15.8	17.9	74
24 13.9	+14.4	16.4	25 11.4	+14.7	16.5	26 08.9	+15.1	16.6	27 06.4	+15.3	16.8	75
24 28.3	+13.9	15.3	25 26.1	+14.3	15.4	26 24.0	+14.5	15.5	27 21.7	+14.9	15.7	76
24 42.2	+13.5	14.2	25 40.4	+13.7	14.3	26 38.5	+14.0	14.5	27 36.6	+14.3	14.6	77
24 55.7	+13.1	13.2	25 54.1	+13.3	13.3	26 52.5	+13.6	13.4	27 50.9	+13.8	13.5	78
25 08.8	+12.5	12.1	26 07.4	+12.8	12.2	27 06.1	+13.0	12.3	28 04.7	+13.3	12.4	79
25 21.3	+12.1	11.0	26 20.2	+12.3	11.1	27 19.1	+12.5	11.2	28 18.0	+12.7	11.3	80
25 33.4	+11.7	9.9	26 32.5	+11.8	10.0	27 31.6	+12.0	10.1	28 30.7	+12.2	10.2	81
25 45.1	+11.1	8.8	26 44.3	+11.3	8.9	27 43.6	+11.5	9.0	28 42.9	+11.6	9.1	82
25 56.2	+10.6	7.7	26 55.6	+10.8	7.8	27 55.1	+10.9	7.9	28 54.5	+11.1	7.9	83
26 06.8	+10.2	6.6	27 06.4	+10.3	6.7	28 06.0	+10.4	6.8	29 05.6	+10.5	6.8	84
26 17.0	+9.6	5.5	27 16.7	+9.7	5.6	28 16.4	+9.8	5.6	29 16.1	+9.9	5.7	85
26 26.6	+9.1	4.4	27 26.4	+9.2	4.5	28 26.2	+9.3	4.5	29 26.0	+9.4	4.6	86
26 35.7	+8.6	3.3	27 35.6	+8.7	3.4	28 35.5	+8.7	3.4	29 35.4	+8.8	3.4	87
26 44.3	+8.1	2.2	27 44.3	+8.1	2.2	28 44.2	+8.2	2.3	29 44.2	+8.2	2.3	88
26 52.4	+7.6	1.1	27 52.4	+7.6	1.1	28 52.4	+7.6	1.1	29 52.4	+7.6	1.1	89
27 00.0	+7.0	0.0	28 00.0	+7.0	0.0	29 00.0	+7.0	0.0	30 00.0	+7.0	0.0	90
27°			28°			29°			30°			

S. Lat. {L.H.A. greater than 180° ....Zn=180°−Z; L.H.A. less than 180°...........Zn=180°+Z

LATITUDE SAME NAME AS DECLINATION — L.H.A. 97°, 263°

84°, 276° L.H.A. LATITUDE SAME NAME AS DECLINATION

N. Lat. {L.H.A. greater than 180° .....Zn=Z
{L.H.A. less than 180°............Zn=360°-Z

Dec.	23°			24°			25°			26°			27°			28°			29°			30°			Dec.
	Hc	d	Z	Hc	d	Z	Hc	d	Z	Hc	d	Z	Hc	d	Z	Hc	d	Z	Hc	d	Z	Hc	d	Z	
°	° ′	′	°	° ′	′	°	° ′	′	°	° ′	′	°	° ′	′	°	° ′	′	°	° ′	′	°	° ′	′	°	°
0	5 31.3	+23.5	92.4	5 28.8	+24.4	92.4	5 26.2	+25.4	92.5	5 23.5	+26.3	92.6	5 20.6	+27.4	92.7	5 17.7	+28.3	92.8	5 14.7	+29.2	92.9	5 11.6	+30.1	93.0	0
1	5 54.8	+23.4	91.4	5 53.2	+24.4	91.5	5 51.6	+25.3	91.6	5 49.8	+26.3	91.7	5 48.0	+27.2	91.8	5 46.0	+28.2	91.9	5 43.9	+29.1	92.0	5 41.7	+30.0	92.1	1
2	6 18.2	+23.3	90.5	6 17.6	+24.3	90.6	6 16.9	+25.3	90.7	6 16.1	+26.2	90.8	6 15.2	+27.1	90.9	6 14.2	+28.0	91.1	6 13.0	+29.0	91.2	6 11.7	+29.9	91.3	2
3	6 41.5	+23.2	89.6	6 41.9	+24.2	89.7	6 42.2	+25.1	89.8	6 42.3	+26.1	89.9	6 42.3	+27.1	90.0	6 42.2	+28.0	90.2	6 42.0	+28.9	90.3	6 41.6	+29.9	90.4	3
4	7 04.7	+23.2	88.6	7 06.1	+24.1	88.8	7 07.3	+25.1	88.9	7 08.4	+26.0	89.0	7 09.4	+26.9	89.1	7 10.2	+27.9	89.3	7 10.9	+28.8	89.4	7 11.5	+29.7	89.5	4
5	7 27.9	+22.9	87.7	7 30.2	+23.9	87.8	7 32.4	+24.9	88.0	7 34.4	+25.9	88.1	7 36.3	+26.8	88.2	7 38.1	+27.8	88.4	7 39.7	+28.7	88.5	7 41.2	+29.6	88.6	5
6	7 50.8	+22.9	86.8	7 54.1	+23.9	86.9	7 57.3	+24.8	87.1	8 00.3	+25.8	87.2	8 03.1	+26.8	87.3	8 05.9	+27.6	87.5	8 08.4	+28.6	87.6	8 10.8	+29.5	87.8	6
7	8 13.7	+22.7	85.8	8 18.0	+23.7	86.0	8 22.1	+24.7	86.1	8 26.1	+25.6	86.3	8 29.9	+26.5	86.4	8 33.5	+27.5	86.6	8 37.0	+28.5	86.7	8 40.3	+29.4	86.9	7
8	8 36.4	+22.6	84.9	8 41.7	+23.6	85.1	8 46.8	+24.5	85.2	8 51.7	+25.5	85.4	8 56.4	+26.5	85.5	9 01.0	+27.4	85.7	9 05.5	+28.3	85.8	9 09.7	+29.3	86.0	8
9	8 59.0	+22.5	84.0	9 05.3	+23.4	84.1	9 11.3	+24.4	84.3	9 17.2	+25.3	84.5	9 22.9	+26.3	84.6	9 28.4	+27.3	84.8	9 33.8	+28.2	85.0	9 39.0	+29.1	85.1	9
10	9 21.5	+22.3	83.0	9 28.7	+23.3	83.2	9 35.7	+24.2	83.4	9 42.5	+25.3	83.5	9 49.2	+26.2	83.7	9 55.7	+27.1	83.9	10 02.0	+28.0	84.1	10 08.1	+29.0	84.2	10
11	9 43.8	+22.2	82.1	9 52.0	+23.1	82.3	9 59.9	+24.1	82.4	10 07.8	+25.0	82.6	10 15.4	+26.0	82.8	10 22.8	+27.0	83.0	10 30.0	+27.9	83.2	10 37.1	+28.8	83.3	11
12	10 06.0	+21.9	81.2	10 15.1	+23.0	81.3	10 24.0	+24.0	81.5	10 32.8	+24.9	81.7	10 41.4	+25.8	81.9	10 49.8	+26.8	82.1	10 57.9	+27.8	82.3	11 05.9	+28.7	82.4	12
13	10 27.9	+21.9	80.2	10 38.1	+22.8	80.4	10 48.0	+23.7	80.6	10 57.7	+24.7	80.8	11 07.2	+25.7	81.0	11 16.6	+26.6	81.2	11 25.7	+27.6	81.4	11 34.6	+28.5	81.6	13
14	10 49.8	+21.6	79.3	11 00.9	+22.6	79.4	11 11.7	+23.6	79.6	11 22.4	+24.6	79.8	11 32.9	+25.5	80.0	11 43.2	+26.4	80.2	11 53.3	+27.4	80.4	12 03.1	+28.3	80.7	14
15	11 11.4	+21.5	78.3	11 23.5	+22.4	78.5	11 35.3	+23.4	78.7	11 47.0	+24.4	78.9	11 58.4	+25.4	79.1	12 09.6	+26.3	79.3	12 20.7	+27.2	79.5	12 31.4	+28.2	79.8	15
16	11 32.9	+21.3	77.4	11 45.9	+22.3	77.6	11 58.7	+23.3	77.8	12 11.4	+24.1	78.0	12 23.8	+25.1	78.2	12 35.9	+26.1	78.4	12 47.9	+27.0	78.6	12 59.6	+28.0	78.8	16
17	11 54.2	+21.1	76.4	12 08.2	+22.0	76.6	12 22.0	+23.0	76.8	12 35.5	+24.0	77.0	12 48.9	+24.9	77.3	13 02.0	+25.9	77.5	13 14.9	+26.8	77.7	13 27.6	+27.7	77.9	17
18	12 15.3	+20.9	75.4	12 30.2	+21.9	75.7	12 45.0	+22.8	75.9	12 59.5	+23.8	76.1	13 13.8	+24.8	76.3	13 27.9	+25.7	76.6	13 41.7	+26.7	76.8	13 55.3	+27.6	77.0	18
19	12 36.2	+20.6	74.5	12 52.1	+21.6	74.7	13 07.8	+22.6	74.9	13 23.3	+23.6	75.2	13 38.6	+24.5	75.4	13 53.6	+25.5	75.6	14 08.4	+26.4	75.9	14 22.9	+27.3	76.1	19
20	12 56.8	+20.5	73.5	13 13.7	+21.5	73.7	13 30.4	+22.4	74.0	13 46.9	+23.3	74.2	14 03.1	+24.3	74.4	14 19.1	+25.2	74.7	14 34.8	+26.2	74.9	14 50.2	+27.2	75.2	20
21	13 17.3	+20.3	72.6	13 35.2	+21.2	72.8	13 52.8	+22.2	73.0	14 10.2	+23.2	73.3	14 27.4	+24.1	73.5	14 44.3	+25.0	73.8	15 01.0	+25.9	74.0	15 17.4	+26.9	74.3	21
22	13 37.6	+20.0	71.6	13 56.4	+21.0	71.8	14 15.0	+21.9	72.1	14 33.4	+22.9	72.3	14 51.5	+23.8	72.6	15 09.3	+24.8	72.8	15 26.9	+25.8	73.1	15 44.3	+26.6	73.3	22
23	13 57.6	+19.8	70.6	14 17.4	+20.7	70.9	14 36.9	+21.7	71.1	14 56.3	+22.6	71.3	15 15.3	+23.6	71.6	15 34.1	+24.6	71.9	15 52.7	+25.4	72.1	16 10.9	+26.5	72.4	23
24	14 17.4	+19.5	69.6	14 38.1	+20.5	69.9	14 58.6	+21.5	70.1	15 18.9	+22.4	70.4	15 38.9	+23.4	70.7	15 58.7	+24.3	70.9	16 18.1	+25.3	71.2	16 37.4	+26.1	71.5	24
25	14 36.9	+19.4	68.7	14 58.6	+20.3	68.9	15 20.1	+21.2	69.2	15 41.3	+22.2	69.4	16 02.3	+23.1	69.7	16 23.0	+24.0	70.0	16 43.4	+25.0	70.2	17 03.5	+25.9	70.5	25
26	14 56.3	+19.0	67.7	15 18.9	+20.0	67.9	15 41.3	+21.0	68.2	16 03.5	+21.9	68.5	16 25.4	+22.8	68.7	16 47.0	+23.8	69.0	17 08.4	+24.7	69.3	17 29.4	+25.7	69.6	26
27	15 15.3	+18.8	66.7	15 38.9	+19.8	67.0	16 02.3	+20.7	67.2	16 25.4	+21.6	67.5	16 48.2	+22.6	67.8	17 10.8	+23.5	68.0	17 33.1	+24.4	68.3	17 55.1	+25.3	68.6	27
28	15 34.1	+18.6	65.7	15 58.7	+19.4	66.0	16 23.0	+20.4	66.2	16 47.0	+21.4	66.5	17 10.8	+22.3	66.8	17 34.3	+23.2	67.1	17 57.5	+24.2	67.4	18 20.4	+25.1	67.7	28
29	15 52.7	+18.2	64.7	16 18.1	+19.3	65.0	16 43.4	+20.1	65.3	17 08.4	+21.0	65.5	17 33.1	+22.0	65.8	17 57.5	+22.9	66.1	18 21.7	+23.8	66.4	18 45.5	+24.8	66.7	29
30	16 10.9	+18.0	63.7	16 37.4	+18.9	64.0	17 03.5	+19.9	64.3	17 29.4	+20.8	64.6	17 55.1	+21.7	64.8	18 20.4	+22.7	65.1	18 45.5	+23.6	65.4	19 10.3	+24.5	65.8	30
31	16 28.9	+17.7	62.7	16 56.3	+18.6	63.0	17 23.4	+19.5	63.3	17 50.2	+20.5	63.6	18 16.8	+21.4	63.9	18 43.1	+22.3	64.2	19 09.1	+23.2	64.5	19 34.8	+24.1	64.8	31
32	16 46.6	+17.5	61.8	17 14.9	+18.4	62.0	17 42.9	+19.3	62.3	18 10.7	+20.2	62.6	18 38.2	+21.1	62.9	19 05.4	+22.0	63.2	19 32.3	+22.9	63.5	19 58.9	+23.9	63.8	32
33	17 04.1	+17.1	60.8	17 33.3	+18.0	61.0	18 02.2	+19.0	61.3	18 30.9	+19.8	61.6	18 59.3	+20.8	61.9	19 27.4	+21.7	62.2	19 55.2	+22.7	62.5	20 22.8	+23.5	62.8	33
34	17 21.2	+16.8	59.7	17 51.3	+17.7	60.0	18 21.2	+18.6	60.3	18 50.7	+19.6	60.6	19 20.1	+20.4	60.9	19 49.1	+21.4	61.2	20 17.9	+22.2	61.5	20 46.3	+23.2	61.9	34
35	17 38.0	+16.5	58.7	18 09.0	+17.5	59.0	18 39.8	+18.3	59.3	19 10.3	+19.2	59.6	19 40.5	+20.1	59.9	20 10.5	+21.0	60.2	20 40.1	+22.0	60.5	21 09.5	+22.8	60.9	35
36	17 54.5	+16.3	57.7	18 26.5	+17.1	58.0	18 58.1	+18.0	58.3	19 29.5	+18.9	58.6	20 00.6	+19.8	58.9	20 31.5	+20.7	59.2	21 02.1	+21.5	59.5	21 32.3	+22.5	59.9	36
37	18 10.8	+15.8	56.7	18 43.6	+16.7	57.0	19 16.1	+17.7	57.3	19 48.4	+18.6	57.6	20 20.4	+19.5	57.9	20 52.2	+20.3	58.2	21 23.6	+21.3	58.5	21 54.8	+22.1	58.9	37
38	18 26.6	+15.6	55.7	19 00.3	+16.5	56.0	19 33.8	+17.3	56.3	20 07.0	+18.2	56.6	20 39.9	+19.1	56.9	21 12.5	+20.0	57.2	21 44.9	+20.8	57.5	22 16.9	+21.8	57.9	38
39	18 42.2	+15.2	54.7	19 16.8	+16.1	55.0	19 51.1	+17.0	55.3	20 25.2	+17.8	55.6	20 59.0	+18.7	55.9	21 32.5	+19.6	56.2	22 05.7	+20.5	56.5	22 38.7	+21.3	56.9	39
40	18 57.4	+14.9	53.7	19 32.9	+15.7	53.9	20 08.1	+16.6	54.2	20 43.0	+17.5	54.5	21 17.7	+18.3	54.9	21 52.1	+19.2	55.2	22 26.2	+20.1	55.5	23 00.0	+21.0	55.9	40
41	19 12.3	+14.6	52.6	19 48.6	+15.4	52.9	20 24.7	+16.2	53.2	21 00.5	+17.1	53.5	21 36.0	+18.0	53.8	22 11.3	+18.9	54.2	22 46.3	+19.7	54.5	23 21.0	+20.6	54.8	41
42	19 26.9	+14.2	51.6	20 04.0	+15.1	51.9	20 40.9	+15.9	52.2	21 17.6	+16.8	52.5	21 54.0	+17.6	52.8	22 30.2	+18.4	53.1	23 06.0	+19.3	53.5	23 41.6	+20.2	53.8	42
43	19 41.1	+13.8	50.6	20 19.1	+14.7	50.9	20 56.8	+15.6	51.2	21 34.4	+16.3	51.5	22 11.6	+17.2	51.8	22 48.6	+18.1	52.1	23 25.3	+18.9	52.4	24 01.8	+19.7	52.8	43
44	19 54.9	+13.5	49.5	20 33.8	+14.3	49.8	21 12.4	+15.1	50.1	21 50.7	+16.0	50.4	22 28.8	+16.8	50.7	23 06.7	+17.6	51.1	23 44.2	+18.5	51.4	24 21.5	+19.4	51.7	44
45	20 08.4	+13.2	48.5	20 48.1	+13.9	48.8	21 27.5	+14.8	49.1	22 06.7	+15.6	49.4	22 45.6	+16.4	49.7	23 24.3	+17.2	50.0	24 02.7	+18.1	50.4	24 40.9	+18.9	50.7	45
46	20 21.6	+12.7	47.5	21 02.0	+13.6	47.7	21 42.3	+14.3	48.0	22 22.3	+15.1	48.3	23 02.0	+16.0	48.7	23 41.5	+16.8	49.0	24 20.8	+17.6	49.3	24 59.8	+18.4	49.7	46
47	20 34.3	+12.4	46.4	21 15.6	+13.1	46.7	21 56.6	+14.0	47.0	22 37.4	+14.8	47.3	23 18.0	+15.6	47.6	23 58.3	+16.4	47.9	24 38.4	+17.2	48.3	25 18.2	+18.0	48.6	47
48	20 46.7	+12.0	45.4	21 28.7	+12.8	45.7	22 10.6	+13.5	45.9	22 52.2	+14.3	46.2	23 33.6	+15.1	46.6	24 14.7	+15.9	46.9	24 55.6	+16.7	47.2	25 36.2	+17.6	47.6	48
49	20 58.7	+11.6	44.3	21 41.5	+12.4	44.6	22 24.1	+13.2	44.9	23 06.5	+14.0	45.2	23 48.7	+14.7	45.5	24 30.6	+15.5	45.8	25 12.3	+16.3	46.1	25 53.8	+17.1	46.5	49
50	21 10.3	+11.2	43.3	21 53.9	+12.0	43.5	22 37.3	+12.7	43.8	23 20.5	+13.5	44.1	24 03.4	+14.3	44.4	24 46.1	+15.1	44.8	25 28.6	+15.9	45.1	26 10.9	+16.6	45.4	50
51	21 21.5	+10.9	42.2	22 05.9	+11.5	42.5	22 50.0	+12.3	42.8	23 34.0	+13.0	43.1	24 17.7	+13.8	43.4	25 01.2	+14.6	43.7	25 44.5	+15.3	44.0	26 27.5	+16.1	44.4	51
52	21 32.4	+10.4	41.2	22 17.4	+11.2	41.4	23 02.3	+11.9	41.7	23 47.0	+12.6	42.0	24 31.5	+13.4	42.3	25 15.8	+14.1	42.6	25 59.8	+14.9	42.9	26 43.6	+15.7	43.3	52
53	21 42.8	+10.0	40.1	22 28.6	+10.7	40.4	23 14.2	+11.5	40.6	23 59.6	+12.2	40.9	24 44.9	+12.9	41.2	25 29.9	+13.6	41.5	26 14.7	+14.4	41.9	26 59.3	+15.1	42.2	53
54	21 52.8	+9.6	39.0	22 39.3	+10.3	39.3	23 25.7	+11.0	39.6	24 11.8	+11.7	39.9	24 57.8	+12.4	40.2	25 43.5	+13.2	40.5	26 29.1	+13.9	40.8	27 14.4	+14.6	41.1	54
55	22 02.4	+9.2	38.0	22 49.6	+9.9	38.2	23 36.7	+10.5	38.5	24 23.5	+11.3	38.8	25 10.2	+12.0	39.1	25 56.7	+12.7	39.4	26 43.0	+13.4	39.7	27 29.0	+14.2	40.0	55
56	22 11.6	+8.8	36.9	22 59.5	+9.5	37.2	23 47.2	+10.2	37.4	24 34.8	+10.8	37.7	25 22.2	+11.5	38.0	26 09.4	+12.2	38.3	26 56.4	+12.9	38.6	27 43.2	+13.6	38.9	56
57	22 20.4	+8.3	35.8	23 09.0	+9.0	36.1	23 57.4	+9.6	36.3	24 45.6	+10.3	36.6	25 33.7	+11.0	36.9	26 21.6	+11.6	37.2	27 09.3	+12.3	37.5	27 56.8	+13.0	37.8	57
58	22 28.7	+8.0	34.8	23 18.0	+8.5	35.0	24 07.0	+9.2	35.3	24 55.9	+9.9	35.5	25 44.7	+10.5	35.8	26 33.2	+11.2	36.1	27 21.6	+11.9	36.4	28 09.8	+12.6	36.7	58
59	22 36.7	+7.5	33.7	23 26.5	+8.2	33.9	24 16.2	+8.8	34.2	25 05.8	+9.4	34.4	25 55.2	+10.0	34.7	26 44.4	+10.7	35.0	27 33.5	+11.3	35.3	28 22.4	+12.0	35.6	59
60	22 44.2	+7.1	32.6	23 34.7	+7.6	32.9	24 25.0	+8.3	33.1	25 15.2	+8.9	33.4	26 05.2	+9.5	33.6	26 55.1	+10.2	33.9	27 44.8	+10.8	34.2	28 34.4	+11.4	34.5	60
61	22 51.3	+6.6	31.5	23 42.3	+7.2	31.8	24 33.3	+7.8	32.0	25 24.1	+8.4	32.3	26 14.7	+9.1	32.5	27 05.3	+9.6	32.8	27 55.6	+10.3	33.1	28 45.8	+10.9	33.4	61
62	22 57.9	+6.2	30.5	23 49.5	+6.8	30.7	24 41.1	+7.3	30.9	25 32.5	+7.9	31.2	26 23.8	+8.5	31.4	27 14.9	+9.1	31.7	28 05.9	+9.7	32.0	28 56.7	+10.3	32.2	62
63	23 04.1	+5.7	29.4	23 56.3	+6.3	29.6	24 48.4	+6.9	29.8	25 40.4	+7.4	30.1	26 32.3	+8.0	30.3	27 24.0	+8.6	30.6	28 15.6	+9.2	30.8	29 07.0	+9.8	31.1	63
64	23 09.8	+5.4	28.3	24 02.6	+5.9	28.5	24 55.3	+6.4	28.7	25 47.8	+7.0	29.0	26 40.3	+7.5	29.2	27 32.6	+8.0	29.5	28 24.8	+8.6	29.7	29 16.8	+9.2	30.0	64
65	23 15.2	+4.8	27.2	24 08.5	+5.3	27.4	25 01.7	+5.9	27.6	25 54.8	+6.4	27.9	26 47.8	+6.9	28.1	27 40.6	+7.5	28.3	28 33.4	+8.0	28.6	29 26.0	+8.6	28.9	65
66	23 20.0	+4.4	26.1	24 13.8	+5.0	26.3	25 07.6	+5.4	26.5	26 01.2	+5.9	26.8	26 54.7	+6.5	27.0	27 48.1	+7.0	27.2	28 41.4	+7.5	27.5	29 34.6	+8.1	27.7	66
67	23 24.4	+4.0	25.1	24 18.8	+4.4	25.2	25 13.0	+4.9	25.4	26 07.1	+5.4	25.6	27 01.2	+5.9	25.9	27 55.1	+6.4	26.1	28 48.9	+7.0	26.3	29 42.7	+7.4	26.6	67
68	23 28.4	+3.5	24.0	24 23.2	+4.0	24.1	25 17.9	+4.4	24.3	26 12.5	+4.9	24.5	27 07.1	+5.3	24.7	28 01.5	+5.9	25.0	28 55.9	+6.3	25.2	29 50.1	+6.8	25.4	68
69	23 31.9	+3.1	22.9	24 27.2	+3.5	23.0	25 22.3	+4.0	23.2	26 17.4	+4.4	23.4	27 12.4	+4.9	23.6	28 07.4	+5.3	23.8	29 02.2	+5.8	24.1	29 56.9	+6.3	24.3	69
70	23 35.0	+2.6	21.8	24 30.7	+3.0	22.0	25 26.3	+3.4	22.1	26 21.8	+3.9	22.3	27 17.3	+4.3	22.5	28 12.7	+4.7	22.7	29 08.0	+5.2	22.9	30 03.2	+5.7	23.1	70
71	23 37.6	+2.1	20.7	24 33.7	+2.5	20.9	25 29.7	+3.0	21.0	26 25.7	+3.3	21.2	27 21.6	+3.8	21.4	28 17.4	+4.2	21.6	29 13.2	+4.6	21.8	30 08.9	+5.0	22.0	71
72	23 39.7	+1.7	19.6	24 36.2	+2.1	19.8	25 32.7	+2.4	19.9	26 29.0	+2.9	20.1	27 25.4	+3.2	20.3	28 21.6	+3.6	20.4	29 17.8	+4.0	20.6	30 13.9	+4.5	20.8	72
73	23 41.4	+1.2	18.5	24 38.3	+1.6	18.7	25 35.1	+1.9	18.8	26 31.9	+2.3	19.0	27 28.6	+2.7	19.1	28 25.2	+3.1	19.3	29 21.8	+3.5	19.5	30 18.4	+3.8	19.7	73
74	23 42.6	+0.8	17.4	24 39.9	+1.1	17.6	25 37.0	+1.5	17.7	26 34.2	+1.8	17.8	27 31.3	+2.1	18.0	28 28.3	+2.5	18.2	29 25.3	+2.8	18.3	30 22.2	+3.2	18.5	74
75	23 43.4	+0.3	16.3	24 41.0	+0.6	16.5	25 38.5	+0.9	16.6	26 36.0	+1.2	16.7	27 33.4	+1.6	16.9	28 30.8	+1.9	17.0	29 28.1	+2.3	17.2	30 25.4	+2.6	17.4	75
76	23 43.7	-0.1	15.2	24 41.6	+0.1	15.4	25 39.4	+0.5	15.5	26 37.2	+0.8	15.6	27 35.0	+1.0	15.8	28 32.7	+1.4	15.9	29 30.4	+1.7	16.0	30 28.0	+2.0	16.2	76
77	23 43.6	-0.7	14.1	24 41.7	-0.3	14.3	25 39.9	-0.1	14.4	26 38.0	+0.2	14.5	27 36.0	+0.5	14.6	28 34.1	+0.8	14.8	29 32.1	+1.1	14.9	30 30.0	+1.4	15.0	77
78	23 42.9	-1.0	13.1	24 41.4	-0.8	13.2	25 39.8	-0.6	13.3	26 38.2	-0.3	13.4	27 36.5	0.0	13.5	28 34.9	+0.2	13.6	29 33.2	+0.4	13.8	30 31.4	+0.8	13.9	78
79	23 41.9	-1.6	12.0	24 40.6	-1.4	12.1	25 39.2	-1.1	12.2	26 37.9	-0.9	12.3	27 36.5	-0.6	12.4	28 35.1	-0.4	12.5	29 33.6	-0.1	12.6	30 32.2	+0.1	12.7	79
80	23 40.3	-2.0	10.9	24 39.2	-1.7	11.0	25 38.1	-1.5	11.0	26 37.0	-1.3	11.1	27 35.9	-1.2	11.2	28 34.7	-0.9	11.3	29 33.5	-0.7	11.5	30 32.3	-0.4	11.6	80
81	23 38.3	-2.4	9.8	24 37.5	-2.3	9.9	25 36.6	-2.1	9.9	26 35.7	-1.9	10.0	27 34.7	-1.7	10.1	28 33.8	-1.5	10.2	29 32.8	-1.3	10.3	30 31.9	-1.1	10.4	81
82	23 35.9	-2.9	8.7	24 35.2	-2.7	8.8	25 34.5	-2.6	8.8	26 33.8	-2.4	8.9	27 33.0	-2.2	9.0	28 32.3	-2.1	9.1	29 31.5	-1.8	9.2	30 30.8	-1.7	9.2	82
83	23 33.0	-3.4	7.6	24 32.5	-3.3	7.7	25 31.9	-3.1	7.7	26 31.4	-3.0	7.8	27 30.8	-2.8	7.9	28 30.2	-2.6	7.9	29 29.7	-2.5	8.0	30 29.1	-2.4	8.1	83
84	23 29.6	-3.8	6.5	24 29.2	-3.7	6.6	25 28.8	-3.5	6.6	26 28.4	-3.4	6.7	27 28.0	-3.3	6.7	28 27.6	-3.2	6.8	29 27.2	-3.1	6.9	30 26.7	-2.9	6.9	84
85	23 25.8	-4.3	5.4	24 25.5	-4.1	5.5	25 25.3	-4.1	5.5	26 25.0	-4.0	5.6	27 24.7	-3.9	5.6	28 24.4	-3.8	5.7	29 24.1	-3.6	5.7	30 23.8	-3.5	5.8	85
86	23 21.5	-4.7	4.3	24 21.4	-4.7	4.4	25 21.2	-4.6	4.4	26 21.0	-4.5	4.4	27 20.8	-4.4	4.5	28 20.6	-4.3	4.5	29 20.5	-4.3	4.6	30 20.3	-4.2	4.6	86
87	23 16.8	-5.1	3.2	24 16.7	-5.1	3.3	25 16.6	-5.0	3.3	26 16.5	-5.0	3.3	27 16.4	-4.9	3.4	28 16.3	-4.9	3.4	29 16.2	-4.8	3.4	30 16.1	-4.8	3.5	87
88	23 11.7	-5.6	2.2	24 11.6	-5.6	2.2	25 11.6	-5.6	2.2	26 11.5	-5.5	2.2	27 11.5	-5.5	2.2	28 11.4	-5.4	2.3	29 11.4	-5.4	2.3	30 11.3	-5.3	2.3	88
89	23 06.1	-6.1	1.1	24 06.0	-6.0	1.1	25 06.0	-6.0	1.1	26 06.0	-6.0	1.1	27 06.0	-6.0	1.1	28 06.0	-6.0	1.1	29 06.0	-6.0	1.1	30 06.0	-6.0	1.1	89
90	23 00.0	-6.5	0.0	24 00.0	-6.5	0.0	25 00.0	-6.5	0.0	26 00.0	-6.5	0.0	27 00.0	-6.5	0.0	28 00.0	-6.5	0.0	29 00.0	-6.6	0.0	30 00.0	-6.6	0.0	90
	23°			24°			25°			26°			27°			28°			29°			30°			

84°, 276° L.H.A. LATITUDE SAME NAME AS DECLINATION

352

LATITUDE CONTRARY NAME TO DECLINATION L.H.A. 84°, 276°

Dec.	23° Hc	d	Z	24° Hc	d	Z	25° Hc	d	Z	26° Hc	d	Z
°	° ′	′	°	° ′	′	°	° ′	′	°	° ′	′	°
0	5 31.3	−23.6	92.4	5 28.8	−24.6	92.4	5 26.2	−25.5	92.5	5 23.5	−26.5	92.6
1	5 07.7	−23.7	93.3	5 04.2	−24.6	93.4	5 00.7	−25.6	93.5	4 57.0	−26.5	93.5
2	4 44.0	−23.7	94.2	4 39.6	−24.7	94.3	4 35.1	−25.7	94.4	4 30.5	−26.6	94.4
3	4 20.3	−23.8	95.1	4 14.9	−24.8	95.2	4 09.4	−25.7	95.3	4 03.9	−26.7	95.3
4	3 56.5	−23.9	96.0	3 50.1	−24.8	96.1	3 43.7	−25.8	96.2	3 37.2	−26.7	96.2
5	3 32.6	−23.9	97.0	3 25.3	−24.9	97.0	3 17.9	−25.8	97.1	3 10.5	−26.8	97.1
6	3 08.7	−24.0	97.9	3 00.4	−24.9	97.9	2 52.1	−25.9	98.0	2 43.7	−26.8	98.0
7	2 44.7	−24.0	98.8	2 35.5	−25.0	98.8	2 26.2	−25.9	98.9	2 16.9	−26.8	98.9
8	2 20.7	−24.1	99.7	2 10.5	−25.0	99.8	2 00.3	−25.9	99.8	1 50.1	−26.8	99.8
9	1 56.6	−24.1	100.6	1 45.5	−25.0	100.7	1 34.4	−26.0	100.7	1 23.3	−26.9	100.7
10	1 32.5	−24.1	101.5	1 20.5	−25.1	101.6	1 08.4	−25.9	101.6	0 56.4	−26.9	101.6
11	1 08.4	−24.1	102.5	0 55.4	−25.0	102.5	0 42.5	−26.0	102.5	0 29.5	−26.9	102.5
12	0 44.3	−24.2	103.4	0 30.4	−25.1	103.4	0 16.5	−26.0	103.4	0 02.6	−26.9	103.4
13	0 20.1	−24.1	104.3	0 05.3	−25.0	104.3	0 09.5	+26.0	75.7	0 24.3	+26.9	75.7
14	0 04.0	+24.1	74.8	0 19.7	+25.1	74.8	0 35.5	+26.0	74.8	0 51.2	+26.9	74.8
15	0 28.1	+24.2	73.9	0 44.8	+25.1	73.9	1 01.5	+25.9	73.9	1 18.1	+26.8	73.9
16	0 52.3	+24.1	73.0	1 09.9	+25.0	73.0	1 27.4	+25.9	73.0	1 44.9	+26.9	73.0
17	1 16.4	+24.1	72.0	1 34.9	+25.0	72.1	1 53.3	+26.0	72.1	2 11.8	+26.8	72.1
18	1 40.5	+24.1	71.1	1 59.9	+25.0	71.2	2 19.3	+25.8	71.2	2 38.6	+26.7	71.2
19	2 04.6	+24.0	70.2	2 24.9	+24.9	70.2	2 45.1	+25.9	70.3	3 05.3	+26.8	70.3
20	2 28.6	+24.0	69.3	2 49.8	+24.9	69.3	3 11.0	+25.8	69.4	3 32.1	+26.6	69.4
21	2 52.6	+24.0	68.4	3 14.7	+24.9	68.4	3 36.8	+25.7	68.5	3 58.7	+26.6	68.5
22	3 16.6	+23.9	67.5	3 39.6	+24.8	67.5	4 02.5	+25.7	67.6	4 25.3	+26.6	67.6
23	3 40.5	+23.9	66.5	4 04.4	+24.7	66.6	4 28.2	+25.6	66.7	4 51.9	+26.5	66.7
24	4 04.4	+23.8	65.6	4 29.1	+24.7	65.7	4 53.8	+25.5	65.8	5 18.4	+26.4	65.8
25	4 28.2	+23.7	64.7	4 53.8	+24.6	64.8	5 19.3	+25.5	64.9	5 44.8	+26.3	64.9
26	4 51.9	+23.6	63.8	5 18.4	+24.5	63.9	5 44.8	+25.3	63.9	6 11.1	+26.2	64.0
27	5 15.5	+23.6	62.9	5 42.9	+24.4	62.9	6 10.1	+25.3	63.0	6 37.3	+26.1	63.1
28	5 39.1	+23.5	61.9	6 07.3	+24.3	62.0	6 35.4	+25.2	62.1	7 03.4	+26.0	62.2
29	6 02.6	+23.4	61.0	6 31.6	+24.2	61.1	7 00.6	+25.0	61.2	7 29.4	+25.9	61.3
30	6 26.0	+23.3	60.1	6 55.8	+24.2	60.2	7 25.6	+25.0	60.3	7 55.3	+25.8	60.4
31	6 49.3	+23.1	59.2	7 20.0	+24.0	59.3	7 50.6	+24.8	59.4	8 21.1	+25.7	59.5
32	7 12.4	+23.1	58.2	7 44.0	+23.9	58.3	8 15.4	+24.7	58.5	8 46.8	+25.5	58.6
33	7 35.5	+22.9	57.3	8 07.9	+23.7	57.4	8 40.1	+24.6	57.5	9 12.3	+25.4	57.7
34	7 58.4	+22.9	56.4	8 31.6	+23.7	56.5	9 04.7	+24.4	56.6	9 37.7	+25.2	56.7
35	8 21.3	+22.7	55.4	8 55.3	+23.5	55.6	9 29.1	+24.3	55.7	10 02.9	+25.1	55.8
36	8 44.0	+22.5	54.5	9 18.8	+23.3	54.6	9 53.4	+24.2	54.8	10 28.0	+24.9	54.9
37	9 06.5	+22.4	53.6	9 42.1	+23.2	53.7	10 17.6	+23.9	53.8	10 52.9	+24.8	54.0
38	9 28.9	+22.3	52.6	10 05.3	+23.0	52.7	10 41.5	+23.9	52.9	11 17.7	+24.6	53.1
39	9 51.2	+22.1	51.7	10 28.3	+22.9	51.8	11 05.4	+23.6	52.0	11 42.3	+24.4	52.1
40	10 13.3	+21.9	50.7	10 51.2	+22.7	50.9	11 29.0	+23.5	51.0	12 06.7	+24.2	51.2
41	10 35.2	+21.8	49.8	11 13.9	+22.5	49.9	11 52.5	+23.2	50.1	12 30.9	+24.0	50.3
42	10 57.0	+21.6	48.8	11 36.4	+22.3	49.0	12 15.7	+23.1	49.1	12 54.9	+23.8	49.3
43	11 18.6	+21.4	47.9	11 58.7	+22.2	48.0	12 38.8	+22.9	48.2	13 18.7	+23.6	48.4
44	11 40.0	+21.2	46.9	12 20.9	+21.9	47.1	13 01.7	+22.7	47.2	13 42.3	+23.4	47.4
45	12 01.2	+21.0	46.0	12 42.8	+21.8	46.1	13 24.4	+22.4	46.3	14 05.7	+23.2	46.5
46	12 22.2	+20.8	45.0	13 04.6	+21.5	45.2	13 46.8	+22.2	45.3	14 28.9	+23.0	45.5
47	12 43.0	+20.7	44.1	13 26.1	+21.3	44.2	14 09.0	+22.1	44.4	14 51.9	+22.7	44.6
48	13 03.7	+20.4	43.1	13 47.4	+21.1	43.3	14 31.1	+21.7	43.4	15 14.6	+22.4	43.6
49	13 24.1	+20.1	42.1	14 08.5	+20.9	42.3	14 52.8	+21.6	42.5	15 37.0	+22.2	42.6
50	13 44.2	+20.0	41.2	14 29.4	+20.6	41.3	15 14.4	+21.2	41.5	15 59.2	+22.0	41.7
51	14 04.2	+19.7	40.2	14 50.0	+20.3	40.3	15 35.6	+21.1	40.5	16 21.2	+21.7	40.7
52	14 23.9	+19.5	39.2	15 10.3	+20.2	39.4	15 56.7	+20.7	39.6	16 42.9	+21.4	39.7
53	14 43.4	+19.2	38.2	15 30.5	+19.8	38.4	16 17.4	+20.5	38.6	17 04.3	+21.1	38.8
54	15 02.6	+19.0	37.3	15 50.3	+19.6	37.4	16 37.9	+20.2	37.6	17 25.4	+20.8	37.8
55	15 21.6	+18.7	36.3	16 09.9	+19.3	36.4	16 58.1	+20.0	36.6	17 46.2	+20.6	36.8
56	15 40.3	+18.5	35.3	16 29.2	+19.1	35.4	17 18.1	+19.6	35.6	18 06.8	+20.2	35.8
57	15 58.8	+18.1	34.3	16 48.3	+18.7	34.5	17 37.7	+19.3	34.6	18 27.0	+19.9	34.8
58	16 16.9	+17.9	33.3	17 07.0	+18.5	33.5	17 57.0	+19.1	33.6	18 46.9	+19.7	33.8
59	16 34.8	+17.7	32.3	17 25.5	+18.2	32.5	18 16.1	+18.7	32.6	19 06.6	+19.2	32.8
60	16 52.5	+17.3	31.3	17 43.7	+17.8	31.5	18 34.8	+18.4	31.6	19 25.8	+19.0	31.8
61	17 09.8	+17.0	30.3	18 01.5	+17.6	30.5	18 53.2	+18.1	30.6	19 44.8	+18.6	30.8
62	17 26.8	+16.7	29.3	18 19.1	+17.2	29.5	19 11.3	+17.8	29.6	20 03.4	+18.3	29.8
63	17 43.5	+16.5	28.3	18 36.3	+17.0	28.5	19 29.1	+17.4	28.6	20 21.7	+17.9	28.8
64	18 00.0	+16.1	27.3	18 53.3	+16.5	27.4	19 46.5	+17.0	27.6	20 39.6	+17.6	27.8
65	18 16.1	+15.7	26.3	19 09.8	+16.3	26.4	20 03.5	+16.7	26.6	20 57.2	+17.1	26.7
66	18 31.8	+15.5	25.3	19 26.1	+15.9	25.4	20 20.2	+16.4	25.6	21 14.3	+16.9	25.7
67	18 47.3	+15.1	24.2	19 42.0	+15.5	24.4	20 36.6	+16.0	24.5	21 31.2	+16.4	24.7
68	19 02.4	+14.8	23.2	19 57.5	+15.2	23.4	20 52.6	+15.6	23.5	21 47.6	+16.0	23.7
69	19 17.2	+14.4	22.2	20 12.7	+14.9	22.3	21 08.2	+15.3	22.5	22 03.6	+15.7	22.6
70	19 31.6	+14.1	21.2	20 27.6	+14.4	21.3	21 23.5	+14.8	21.4	22 19.3	+15.2	21.6
71	19 45.7	+13.8	20.1	20 42.0	+14.1	20.3	21 38.3	+14.5	20.4	22 34.5	+14.9	20.5
72	19 59.5	+13.3	19.1	20 56.1	+13.8	19.2	21 52.8	+14.1	19.3	22 49.4	+14.4	19.5
73	20 12.8	+13.0	18.1	21 09.9	+13.3	18.2	22 06.9	+13.6	18.3	23 03.8	+14.0	18.4
74	20 25.8	+12.7	17.0	21 23.2	+12.9	17.1	22 20.5	+13.3	17.2	23 17.8	+13.6	17.4
75	20 38.5	+12.2	16.0	21 36.1	+12.6	16.1	22 33.8	+12.8	16.2	23 31.4	+13.1	16.3
76	20 50.7	+11.9	14.9	21 48.7	+12.1	15.0	22 46.6	+12.4	15.1	23 44.5	+12.7	15.2
77	21 02.6	+11.5	13.9	22 00.8	+11.8	14.0	22 59.0	+12.0	14.1	23 57.2	+12.3	14.2
78	21 14.1	+11.1	12.8	22 12.6	+11.3	12.9	23 11.0	+11.6	13.0	24 09.5	+11.8	13.1
79	21 25.2	+10.7	11.8	22 23.9	+10.9	11.8	23 22.6	+11.1	11.9	24 21.3	+11.4	12.0
80	21 35.9	+10.3	10.7	22 34.8	+10.5	10.8	23 33.7	+10.7	10.9	24 32.7	+10.9	10.9
81	21 46.2	+9.8	9.6	22 45.3	+10.1	9.7	23 44.4	+10.3	9.8	24 43.6	+10.4	9.9
82	21 56.0	+9.5	8.6	22 55.4	+9.6	8.6	23 54.7	+9.8	8.7	24 54.0	+9.9	8.8
83	22 05.5	+9.1	7.5	23 05.0	+9.2	7.6	24 04.5	+9.3	7.6	25 03.9	+9.5	7.7
84	22 14.6	+8.6	6.4	23 14.2	+8.7	6.5	24 13.8	+8.9	6.5	25 13.4	+9.0	6.6
85	22 23.2	+8.2	5.4	23 22.9	+8.4	5.4	24 22.7	+8.4	5.5	25 22.4	+8.5	5.5
86	22 31.4	+7.8	4.3	23 31.3	+7.8	4.3	24 31.1	+7.9	4.4	25 30.9	+8.0	4.4
87	22 39.2	+7.4	3.2	23 39.1	+7.4	3.3	24 39.0	+7.5	3.3	25 38.9	+7.6	3.3
88	22 46.6	+6.9	2.2	23 46.5	+7.0	2.2	24 46.5	+7.0	2.2	25 46.5	+7.0	2.2
89	22 53.5	+6.5	1.1	23 53.5	+6.5	1.1	24 53.5	+6.5	1.1	25 53.5	+6.5	1.1
90	23 00.0	+6.1	0.0	24 00.0	+6.0	0.0	25 00.0	+6.0	0.0	26 00.0	+6.0	0.0
	23°			24°			25°			26°		

Dec.	27° Hc	d	Z	28° Hc	d	Z	29° Hc	d	Z	30° Hc	d	Z
°	° ′	′	°	° ′	′	°	° ′	′	°	° ′	′	°
0	5 20.6	−27.4	92.7	5 17.7	−28.3	92.8	5 14.7	−29.2	92.9	5 11.6	−30.1	93.0
1	4 53.2	−27.4	93.6	4 49.4	−28.4	93.7	4 45.5	−29.3	93.8	4 41.5	−30.3	93.9
2	4 25.8	−27.6	94.5	4 21.0	−28.4	94.6	4 16.2	−29.4	94.7	4 11.2	−30.2	94.7
3	3 58.2	−27.5	95.4	3 52.6	−28.6	95.5	3 46.8	−29.4	95.5	3 41.0	−30.4	95.6
4	3 30.7	−27.7	96.3	3 24.0	−28.5	96.4	3 17.4	−29.5	96.4	3 10.6	−30.3	96.5
5	3 03.0	−27.7	97.2	2 55.5	−28.6	97.2	2 47.9	−29.5	97.3	2 40.3	−30.4	97.3
6	2 35.3	−27.7	98.1	2 26.9	−28.6	98.1	2 18.4	−29.6	98.2	2 09.9	−30.5	98.2
7	2 07.6	−27.7	99.0	1 58.3	−28.7	99.0	1 48.8	−29.5	99.0	1 39.4	−30.4	99.1
8	1 39.9	−27.8	99.9	1 29.6	−28.7	99.9	1 19.3	−29.6	99.9	1 09.0	−30.5	99.9
9	1 12.1	−27.8	100.7	1 00.9	−28.7	100.8	0 49.7	−29.6	100.8	0 38.5	−30.5	100.8
10	0 44.3	−27.8	101.6	0 32.2	−28.7	101.6	0 20.1	−29.6	101.6	0 08.0	−30.5	101.6
11	0 16.5	−27.8	102.5	0 03.5	−28.7	102.5	0 09.5	+29.6	77.5	0 22.5	+30.5	77.5
12	0 11.3	+27.8	76.6	0 25.2	+28.7	76.6	0 39.1	+29.6	76.6	0 53.0	+30.4	76.6
13	0 39.1	+27.8	75.7	0 53.9	+28.7	75.7	1 08.7	+29.6	75.7	1 23.4	+30.5	75.8
14	1 06.9	+27.8	74.8	1 22.6	+28.7	74.9	1 38.3	+29.5	74.9	1 53.9	+30.4	74.9
15	1 34.7	+27.7	73.9	1 51.3	+28.6	74.0	2 07.8	+29.5	74.0	2 24.3	+30.4	74.0
16	2 02.4	+27.8	73.1	2 19.9	+28.6	73.1	2 37.3	+29.5	73.1	2 54.7	+30.4	73.2
17	2 30.2	+27.7	72.2	2 48.5	+28.6	72.2	3 06.8	+29.5	72.3	3 25.1	+30.3	72.3
18	2 57.9	+27.6	71.3	3 17.1	+28.5	71.3	3 36.3	+29.4	71.4	3 55.4	+30.2	71.5
19	3 25.5	+27.6	70.4	3 45.6	+28.5	70.5	4 05.7	+29.3	70.5	4 25.6	+30.2	70.6
20	3 53.1	+27.5	69.5	4 14.1	+28.4	69.6	4 35.0	+29.3	69.6	4 55.8	+30.1	69.7
21	4 20.6	+27.5	68.6	4 42.5	+28.3	68.7	5 04.3	+29.2	68.8	5 25.9	+30.1	68.9
22	4 48.1	+27.4	67.7	5 10.8	+28.3	67.8	5 33.5	+29.1	67.9	5 56.0	+30.0	68.0
23	5 15.5	+27.4	66.8	5 39.1	+28.2	66.9	6 02.6	+29.0	67.0	6 26.0	+29.8	67.1
24	5 42.9	+27.2	65.9	6 07.3	+28.1	66.0	6 31.6	+29.0	66.1	6 55.8	+29.8	66.2
25	6 10.1	+27.2	65.0	6 35.4	+28.0	65.1	7 00.6	+28.8	65.2	7 25.6	+29.7	65.4
26	6 37.3	+27.0	64.1	7 03.4	+27.9	64.2	7 29.4	+28.8	64.4	7 55.3	+29.6	64.5
27	7 04.3	+27.0	63.2	7 31.3	+27.8	63.4	7 58.2	+28.6	63.5	8 24.9	+29.4	63.6
28	7 31.3	+26.9	62.3	7 59.1	+27.7	62.5	8 26.8	+28.5	62.6	8 54.3	+29.4	62.7
29	7 58.2	+26.7	61.4	8 26.8	+27.5	61.6	8 55.3	+28.4	61.7	9 23.7	+29.2	61.8
30	8 24.9	+26.6	60.5	8 54.3	+27.5	60.7	9 23.7	+28.2	60.8	9 52.9	+29.0	61.0
31	8 51.5	+26.5	59.6	9 21.8	+27.3	59.8	9 51.9	+28.1	59.9	10 21.9	+28.9	60.1
32	9 18.0	+26.3	58.7	9 49.1	+27.1	58.9	10 20.0	+28.0	59.0	10 50.8	+28.8	59.2
33	9 44.3	+26.2	57.8	10 16.2	+27.0	58.0	10 48.0	+27.8	58.1	11 19.6	+28.6	58.3
34	10 10.5	+26.0	56.9	10 43.2	+26.8	57.0	11 15.8	+27.6	57.2	11 48.2	+28.4	57.4
35	10 36.5	+25.9	56.0	11 10.0	+26.7	56.1	11 43.4	+27.5	56.3	12 16.6	+28.3	56.5
36	11 02.4	+25.7	55.1	11 36.7	+26.5	55.2	12 10.9	+27.2	55.4	12 44.9	+28.0	55.6
37	11 28.1	+25.6	54.1	12 03.2	+26.3	54.3	12 38.1	+27.1	54.5	13 12.9	+27.9	54.7
38	11 53.7	+25.3	53.2	12 29.5	+26.2	53.4	13 05.2	+26.9	53.6	13 40.8	+27.7	53.8
39	12 19.0	+25.2	52.3	12 55.7	+25.9	52.5	13 32.1	+26.7	52.7	14 08.5	+27.4	52.8
40	12 44.2	+25.0	51.4	13 21.6	+25.7	51.5	13 58.8	+26.5	51.7	14 35.9	+27.3	51.9
41	13 09.2	+24.8	50.4	13 47.3	+25.6	50.6	14 25.3	+26.3	50.8	15 03.2	+27.0	51.0
42	13 34.0	+24.5	49.5	14 12.9	+25.3	49.7	14 51.6	+26.1	49.9	15 30.2	+26.8	50.1
43	13 58.5	+24.4	48.6	14 38.2	+25.1	48.7	15 17.7	+25.8	48.9	15 57.0	+26.5	49.2
44	14 22.9	+24.1	47.6	15 03.3	+24.8	47.8	15 43.5	+25.5	48.0	16 23.5	+26.3	48.2
45	14 47.0	+23.9	46.7	15 28.1	+24.6	46.9	16 09.0	+25.4	47.1	16 49.8	+26.1	47.3
46	15 10.9	+23.6	45.7	15 52.7	+24.4	45.9	16 34.4	+25.0	46.1	17 15.9	+25.8	46.3
47	15 34.5	+23.4	44.8	16 17.1	+24.1	45.0	16 59.4	+24.8	45.2	17 41.7	+25.5	45.4
48	15 57.9	+23.2	43.8	16 41.2	+23.8	44.0	17 24.2	+24.6	44.2	18 07.2	+25.2	44.4
49	16 21.1	+22.9	42.8	17 05.0	+23.6	43.0	17 48.8	+24.2	43.3	18 32.4	+24.9	43.5
50	16 44.0	+22.6	41.9	17 28.6	+23.3	42.1	18 13.0	+24.0	42.3	18 57.3	+24.7	42.5
51	17 06.6	+22.3	40.9	17 51.9	+23.0	41.1	18 37.0	+23.7	41.3	19 22.0	+24.3	41.6
52	17 28.9	+22.1	39.9	18 14.9	+22.7	40.1	19 00.7	+23.3	40.4	19 46.3	+24.0	40.6
53	17 51.0	+21.8	39.0	18 37.6	+22.4	39.2	19 24.0	+23.1	39.4	20 10.3	+23.7	39.6
54	18 12.8	+21.4	38.0	19 00.0	+22.1	38.2	19 47.1	+22.7	38.4	20 34.0	+23.4	38.6
55	18 34.2	+21.2	37.0	19 22.1	+21.7	37.2	20 09.8	+22.4	37.4	20 57.4	+23.0	37.7
56	18 55.4	+20.8	36.0	19 43.8	+21.5	36.2	20 32.2	+22.0	36.4	21 20.4	+22.7	36.7
57	19 16.2	+20.5	35.0	20 05.3	+21.1	35.2	20 54.2	+21.7	35.4	21 43.1	+22.3	35.7
58	19 36.7	+20.2	34.0	20 26.4	+20.8	34.2	21 15.9	+21.4	34.4	22 05.4	+21.9	34.7
59	19 56.9	+19.9	33.0	20 47.2	+20.4	33.2	21 37.3	+21.0	33.4	22 27.3	+21.6	33.7
60	20 16.8	+19.5	32.0	21 07.6	+20.0	32.2	21 58.3	+20.6	32.4	22 48.9	+21.2	32.6
61	20 36.3	+19.1	31.0	21 27.6	+19.7	31.2	22 18.9	+20.3	31.4	23 10.1	+20.7	31.6
62	20 55.4	+18.8	30.0	21 47.3	+19.4	30.2	22 39.2	+19.8	30.4	23 30.8	+20.4	30.6
63	21 14.2	+18.4	29.0	22 06.7	+18.9	29.2	22 59.0	+19.5	29.4	23 51.2	+20.0	29.6
64	21 32.6	+18.1	28.0	22 25.6	+18.5	28.1	23 18.5	+19.0	28.3	24 11.2	+19.6	28.5
65	21 50.7	+17.7	26.9	22 44.1	+18.2	27.1	23 37.5	+18.6	27.3	24 30.8	+19.1	27.5
66	22 08.4	+17.2	25.9	23 02.3	+17.7	26.1	23 56.1	+18.3	26.3	24 49.9	+18.7	26.5
67	22 25.6	+16.9	24.9	23 20.0	+17.4	25.0	24 14.4	+17.7	25.2	25 08.6	+18.2	25.4
68	22 42.5	+16.5	23.8	23 37.4	+16.9	24.0	24 32.1	+17.4	24.2	25 26.8	+17.8	24.4
69	22 59.0	+16.1	22.8	23 54.3	+16.5	22.9	24 49.5	+16.9	23.1	25 44.6	+17.4	23.3
70	23 15.1	+15.6	21.7	24 10.8	+16.0	21.9	25 06.4	+16.4	22.1	26 02.0	+16.8	22.2
71	23 30.7	+15.2	20.7	24 26.8	+15.6	20.8	25 22.8	+16.0	21.0	26 18.8	+16.4	21.2
72	23 45.9	+14.8	19.6	24 42.4	+15.2	19.8	25 38.8	+15.6	19.9	26 35.2	+15.9	20.1
73	24 00.7	+14.3	18.6	24 57.6	+14.7	18.7	25 54.4	+15.0	18.9	26 51.1	+15.4	19.0
74	24 15.0	+14.0	17.5	25 12.3	+14.2	17.6	26 09.4	+14.6	17.8	27 06.5	+14.9	17.9
75	24 29.0	+13.4	16.4	25 26.5	+13.7	16.6	26 24.0	+14.0	16.7	27 21.4	+14.4	16.8
76	24 42.4	+13.0	15.4	25 40.2	+13.3	15.5	26 38.0	+13.6	15.6	27 35.8	+13.9	15.8
77	24 55.4	+12.5	14.3	25 53.5	+12.8	14.4	26 51.6	+13.1	14.5	27 49.7	+13.3	14.7
78	25 07.9	+12.1	13.2	26 06.3	+12.3	13.3	27 04.7	+12.6	13.4	28 03.0	+12.9	13.6
79	25 20.0	+11.6	12.1	26 18.6	+11.8	12.2	27 17.3	+12.0	12.3	28 15.9	+12.2	12.4
80	25 31.6	+11.1	11.0	26 30.4	+11.3	11.1	27 29.3	+11.5	11.2	28 28.1	+11.8	11.3
81	25 42.7	+10.6	9.9	26 41.7	+10.8	10.0	27 40.8	+11.0	10.1	28 39.9	+11.2	10.2
82	25 53.3	+10.1	8.9	26 52.5	+10.3	8.9	27 51.8	+10.5	9.0	28 51.1	+10.6	9.1
83	26 03.4	+9.6	7.8	27 02.8	+9.8	7.8	28 02.3	+9.9	7.9	29 01.7	+10.1	8.0
84	26 13.0	+9.1	6.7	27 12.6	+9.2	6.7	28 12.2	+9.3	6.8	29 11.8	+9.5	6.8
85	26 22.1	+8.6	5.6	27 21.8	+8.7	5.6	28 21.5	+8.9	5.7	29 21.3	+8.9	5.7
86	26 30.7	+8.1	4.4	27 30.5	+8.2	4.5	28 30.4	+8.2	4.5	29 30.2	+8.3	4.6
87	26 38.8	+7.6	3.3	27 38.7	+7.7	3.4	28 38.6	+7.7	3.4	29 38.5	+7.8	3.4
88	26 46.4	+7.1	2.2	27 46.4	+7.1	2.2	28 46.3	+7.1	2.3	29 46.3	+7.1	2.3
89	26 53.5	+6.5	1.1	27 53.5	+6.5	1.1	28 53.4	+6.6	1.1	29 53.4	+6.6	1.1
90	27 00.0	+6.0	0.0	28 00.0	+6.0	0.0	29 00.0	+6.0	0.0	30 00.0	+6.0	0.0
	27°			28°			29°			30°		

S. Lat. {L.H.A. greater than 180° ....Zn=180°−Z
{L.H.A. less than 180°...........Zn=180°+Z

LATITUDE SAME NAME AS DECLINATION L.H.A. 96°, 264°

85°, 275° L.H.A. LATITUDE SAME NAME AS DECLINATION

N. Lat. {L.H.A. greater than 180° .....Zn=Z
L.H.A. less than 180°............Zn=360°−Z}

Dec.	23° Hc	23° d	23° Z	24° Hc	24° d	24° Z	25° Hc	25° d	25° Z	26° Hc	26° d	26° Z	27° Hc	27° d	27° Z	28° Hc	28° d	28° Z	29° Hc	29° d	29° Z	30° Hc	30° d	30° Z	Dec.
°	° ′	′	°	° ′	′	°	° ′	′	°	° ′	′	°	° ′	′	°	° ′	′	°	° ′	′	°	° ′	′	°	°
0	4 36.1	+23.5	92.0	4 34.0	+24.5	92.0	4 31.8	+25.4	92.1	4 29.6	+26.3	92.2	4 27.2	+27.3	92.3	4 24.8	+28.2	92.4	4 22.3	+29.1	92.4	4 19.7	+30.1	92.5	0
1	4 59.6	+23.4	91.0	4 58.5	+24.3	91.1	4 57.2	+25.4	91.2	4 55.9	+26.3	91.3	4 54.5	+27.2	91.4	4 53.0	+28.2	91.5	4 51.4	+29.1	91.6	4 49.8	+30.0	91.6	1
2	5 23.0	+23.3	90.1	5 22.8	+24.3	90.2	5 22.6	+25.2	90.3	5 22.2	+26.2	90.4	5 21.7	+27.2	90.5	5 21.2	+28.1	90.6	5 20.5	+29.0	90.7	5 19.8	+29.9	90.8	2
3	5 46.3	+23.2	89.2	5 47.1	+24.2	89.3	5 47.8	+25.2	89.4	5 48.4	+26.1	89.5	5 48.9	+27.0	89.6	5 49.3	+27.9	89.7	5 49.5	+28.9	89.8	5 49.7	+29.8	89.9	3
4	6 09.5	+23.2	88.3	6 11.3	+24.1	88.4	6 13.0	+25.0	88.5	6 14.5	+26.0	88.6	6 15.9	+27.0	88.7	6 17.2	+27.9	88.8	6 18.4	+28.9	88.9	6 19.5	+29.8	89.0	4
5	6 32.7	+23.0	87.3	6 35.4	+24.0	87.4	6 38.0	+25.0	87.6	6 40.5	+25.9	87.7	6 42.9	+26.9	87.8	6 45.1	+27.8	87.9	6 47.3	+28.7	88.0	6 49.3	+29.6	88.1	5
6	6 55.7	+22.9	86.4	6 59.4	+23.9	86.5	7 03.0	+24.8	86.6	7 06.4	+25.9	86.8	7 09.8	+26.7	86.9	7 12.9	+27.7	87.0	7 16.0	+28.6	87.1	7 18.9	+29.6	87.3	6
7	7 18.6	+22.8	85.5	7 23.3	+23.8	85.6	7 27.8	+24.8	85.7	7 32.3	+25.6	85.9	7 36.5	+26.7	86.0	7 40.6	+27.6	86.1	7 44.6	+28.5	86.3	7 48.5	+29.4	86.4	7
8	7 41.4	+22.7	84.5	7 47.1	+23.6	84.7	7 52.6	+24.6	84.8	7 57.9	+25.6	84.9	8 03.2	+26.5	85.1	8 08.2	+27.5	85.2	8 13.1	+28.4	85.4	8 17.9	+29.3	85.5	8
9	8 04.1	+22.6	83.6	8 10.7	+23.6	83.7	8 17.2	+24.5	83.9	8 23.5	+25.5	84.0	8 29.7	+26.4	84.2	8 35.7	+27.3	84.3	8 41.5	+28.3	84.5	8 47.2	+29.2	84.6	9
10	8 26.7	+22.4	82.7	8 34.3	+23.4	82.8	8 41.7	+24.4	83.0	8 49.0	+25.3	83.1	8 56.1	+26.3	83.3	9 03.0	+27.3	83.4	9 09.8	+28.2	83.6	9 16.4	+29.1	83.7	10
11	8 49.1	+22.3	81.7	8 57.7	+23.2	81.9	9 06.1	+24.2	82.0	9 14.3	+25.2	82.2	9 22.4	+26.1	82.4	9 30.3	+27.0	82.5	9 38.0	+28.0	82.7	9 45.5	+28.9	82.9	11
12	9 11.4	+22.2	80.8	9 20.9	+23.1	80.9	9 30.3	+24.1	81.1	9 39.5	+25.0	81.3	9 48.5	+26.0	81.4	9 57.3	+26.9	81.6	10 06.0	+27.8	81.8	10 14.4	+28.8	82.0	12
13	9 33.6	+21.9	79.8	9 44.0	+23.0	80.0	9 54.4	+23.9	80.2	10 04.5	+24.9	80.4	10 14.5	+25.8	80.5	10 24.2	+26.8	80.7	10 33.8	+27.7	80.9	10 43.2	+28.7	81.1	13
14	9 55.5	+21.9	78.9	10 07.0	+22.8	79.1	10 18.3	+23.7	79.2	10 29.4	+24.7	79.4	10 40.3	+25.7	79.6	10 51.0	+26.6	79.8	11 01.5	+27.6	80.0	11 11.9	+28.4	80.2	14
15	10 17.4	+21.6	78.0	10 29.8	+22.6	78.1	10 42.0	+23.6	78.3	10 54.1	+24.6	78.5	11 06.0	+25.5	78.7	11 17.6	+26.5	78.9	11 29.1	+27.4	79.1	11 40.3	+28.4	79.3	15
16	10 39.0	+21.5	77.0	10 52.4	+22.5	77.2	11 05.6	+23.5	77.4	11 18.7	+24.3	77.6	11 31.5	+25.3	77.8	11 44.1	+26.2	78.0	11 56.5	+27.2	78.2	12 08.7	+28.1	78.4	16
17	11 00.5	+21.3	76.1	11 14.9	+22.3	76.2	11 29.1	+23.2	76.4	11 43.0	+24.2	76.6	11 56.8	+25.1	76.8	12 10.3	+26.1	77.1	12 23.7	+27.0	77.3	12 36.8	+27.9	77.5	17
18	11 21.8	+21.2	75.1	11 37.2	+22.1	75.3	11 52.3	+23.1	75.5	12 07.2	+24.0	75.7	12 21.9	+25.0	75.9	12 36.4	+25.9	76.1	12 50.7	+26.8	76.3	13 04.7	+27.8	76.6	18
19	11 43.0	+20.9	74.1	11 59.3	+21.9	74.3	12 15.4	+22.8	74.6	12 31.2	+23.8	74.8	12 46.9	+24.7	75.0	13 02.3	+25.7	75.2	13 17.5	+26.6	75.4	13 32.5	+27.6	75.7	19
20	12 03.9	+20.8	73.2	12 21.2	+21.7	73.4	12 38.2	+22.7	73.6	12 55.0	+23.6	73.8	13 11.6	+24.6	74.0	13 28.0	+25.5	74.3	13 44.1	+26.5	74.5	14 00.1	+27.3	74.7	20
21	12 24.7	+20.5	72.2	12 42.9	+21.5	72.4	13 00.9	+22.4	72.7	13 18.6	+23.4	72.9	13 36.2	+24.3	73.1	13 53.5	+25.3	73.3	14 10.6	+26.2	73.6	14 27.4	+27.1	73.8	21
22	12 45.2	+20.3	71.3	13 04.4	+21.3	71.5	13 23.3	+22.2	71.7	13 42.0	+23.2	71.9	14 00.5	+24.1	72.2	14 18.8	+25.0	72.4	14 36.8	+26.0	72.7	14 54.5	+27.0	72.9	22
23	13 05.5	+20.2	70.3	13 25.7	+21.0	70.5	13 45.5	+22.1	70.8	14 05.2	+23.0	71.0	14 24.6	+23.9	71.2	14 43.8	+24.9	71.5	15 02.8	+25.7	71.7	15 21.5	+26.6	72.0	23
24	13 25.7	+19.8	69.3	13 46.7	+20.9	69.6	14 07.6	+21.7	69.8	14 28.2	+22.7	70.0	14 48.5	+23.7	70.3	15 08.7	+24.6	70.5	15 28.5	+25.6	70.8	15 48.1	+26.5	71.1	24
25	13 45.5	+19.7	68.4	14 07.6	+20.6	68.6	14 29.3	+21.6	68.8	14 50.9	+22.5	69.1	15 12.2	+23.4	69.3	15 33.3	+24.3	69.6	15 54.1	+25.2	69.8	16 14.6	+26.2	70.1	25
26	14 05.2	+19.4	67.4	14 28.2	+20.3	67.6	14 50.9	+21.3	67.9	15 13.4	+22.2	68.1	15 35.6	+23.2	68.4	15 57.6	+24.1	68.6	16 19.3	+25.1	68.9	16 40.8	+25.9	69.2	26
27	14 24.6	+19.2	66.4	14 48.5	+20.2	66.7	15 12.2	+21.1	66.9	15 35.6	+22.0	67.2	15 58.8	+22.9	67.4	16 21.7	+23.9	67.7	16 44.4	+24.7	68.0	17 06.7	+25.7	68.2	27
28	14 43.8	+19.0	65.4	15 08.7	+19.8	65.7	15 33.3	+20.8	65.9	15 57.6	+21.7	66.2	16 21.7	+22.7	66.5	16 45.6	+23.5	66.7	17 09.1	+24.5	67.0	17 32.4	+25.4	67.3	28
29	15 02.8	+18.7	64.5	15 28.5	+19.6	64.7	15 54.1	+20.5	65.0	16 19.3	+21.5	65.2	16 44.4	+22.3	65.5	17 09.1	+23.3	65.8	17 33.6	+24.2	66.0	17 57.8	+25.2	66.3	29
30	15 21.5	+18.4	63.5	15 48.1	+19.4	63.7	16 14.6	+20.3	64.0	16 40.8	+21.2	64.2	17 06.7	+22.2	64.5	17 32.4	+23.1	64.8	17 57.8	+24.0	65.1	18 23.0	+24.8	65.4	30
31	15 39.9	+18.2	62.5	16 07.5	+19.1	62.7	16 34.9	+20.0	63.0	17 02.0	+20.9	63.3	17 28.9	+21.8	63.5	17 55.5	+22.7	63.8	18 21.8	+23.6	64.1	18 47.8	+24.6	64.4	31
32	15 58.1	+17.8	61.5	16 26.6	+18.8	61.7	16 54.9	+19.7	62.0	17 22.9	+20.6	62.3	17 50.7	+21.5	62.6	18 18.2	+22.4	62.9	18 45.4	+23.4	63.2	19 12.4	+24.2	63.5	32
33	16 15.9	+17.7	60.5	16 45.4	+18.5	60.8	17 14.6	+19.4	61.0	17 43.5	+20.3	61.3	18 12.2	+21.2	61.6	18 40.6	+22.1	61.9	19 08.8	+23.0	62.2	19 36.6	+24.0	62.5	33
34	16 33.6	+17.3	59.5	17 03.9	+18.2	59.8	17 34.0	+19.1	60.0	18 03.8	+20.1	60.3	18 33.4	+20.9	60.6	19 02.7	+21.9	60.9	19 31.8	+22.7	61.2	20 00.6	+23.6	61.5	34
35	16 50.9	+17.0	58.5	17 22.1	+17.9	58.8	17 53.1	+18.8	59.0	18 23.9	+19.7	59.3	18 54.3	+20.6	59.6	19 24.6	+21.5	59.9	19 54.5	+22.4	60.2	20 24.2	+23.2	60.5	35
36	17 07.9	+16.7	57.5	17 40.0	+17.7	57.8	18 11.9	+18.5	58.0	18 43.6	+19.4	58.3	19 14.9	+20.3	58.6	19 46.1	+21.1	58.9	20 16.9	+22.0	59.2	20 47.4	+23.0	59.6	36
37	17 24.6	+16.5	56.5	17 57.7	+17.3	56.8	18 30.4	+18.2	57.0	19 03.0	+19.0	57.3	19 35.2	+20.0	57.6	20 07.2	+20.9	57.9	20 38.9	+21.8	58.2	21 10.4	+22.6	58.6	37
38	17 41.1	+16.1	55.5	18 15.0	+17.0	55.7	18 48.6	+17.9	56.0	19 22.0	+18.8	56.3	19 55.2	+19.6	56.6	20 28.1	+20.4	56.9	21 00.7	+21.3	57.2	21 33.0	+22.2	57.6	38
39	17 57.2	+15.8	54.5	18 32.0	+16.6	54.7	19 06.5	+17.5	55.0	19 40.8	+18.3	55.3	20 14.8	+19.2	55.6	20 48.5	+20.2	55.9	21 22.0	+21.0	56.2	21 55.2	+21.9	56.6	39
40	18 13.0	+15.5	53.5	18 48.6	+16.4	53.7	19 24.0	+17.2	54.0	19 59.1	+18.1	54.3	20 34.0	+18.9	54.6	21 08.7	+19.7	54.9	21 43.0	+20.7	55.2	22 17.1	+21.5	55.6	40
41	18 28.5	+15.2	52.4	19 05.0	+16.0	52.7	19 41.2	+16.9	53.0	20 17.2	+17.7	53.3	20 52.9	+18.6	53.6	21 28.4	+19.4	53.9	22 03.7	+20.2	54.2	22 38.6	+21.1	54.6	41
42	18 43.7	+14.8	51.4	19 21.0	+15.6	51.7	19 58.1	+16.5	52.0	20 34.9	+17.3	52.3	21 11.5	+18.2	52.6	21 47.8	+19.1	52.9	22 23.9	+19.9	53.2	22 59.7	+20.8	53.5	42
43	18 58.5	+14.5	50.4	19 36.6	+15.3	50.7	20 14.6	+16.1	50.9	20 52.2	+17.0	51.2	21 29.7	+17.8	51.5	22 06.9	+18.6	51.9	22 43.8	+19.5	52.2	23 20.5	+20.3	52.5	43
44	19 13.0	+14.1	49.4	19 51.9	+15.0	49.6	20 30.7	+15.8	49.9	21 09.2	+16.6	50.2	21 47.5	+17.4	50.5	22 25.5	+18.3	50.8	23 03.3	+19.1	51.2	23 40.8	+19.9	51.5	44
45	19 27.1	+13.8	48.3	20 06.9	+14.6	48.6	20 46.5	+15.4	48.9	21 25.8	+16.2	49.2	22 04.9	+17.0	49.5	22 43.8	+17.8	49.8	23 22.4	+18.7	50.1	24 00.7	+19.5	50.5	45
46	19 40.9	+13.5	47.3	20 21.5	+14.2	47.6	21 01.9	+15.0	47.9	21 42.0	+15.9	48.1	22 21.9	+16.7	48.4	23 01.6	+17.5	48.8	23 41.1	+18.2	49.1	24 20.2	+19.1	49.4	46
47	19 54.4	+13.0	46.3	20 35.7	+13.9	46.5	21 16.9	+14.7	46.8	21 57.9	+15.4	47.1	22 38.6	+16.2	47.4	23 19.1	+17.0	47.7	23 59.3	+17.9	48.0	24 39.3	+18.7	48.4	47
48	20 07.4	+12.8	45.2	20 49.6	+13.5	45.5	21 31.6	+14.2	45.8	22 13.3	+15.0	46.1	22 54.8	+15.8	46.4	23 36.1	+16.6	46.7	24 17.2	+17.4	47.0	24 58.0	+18.2	47.3	48
49	20 20.2	+12.3	44.2	21 03.1	+13.1	44.5	21 45.8	+13.9	44.7	22 28.3	+14.7	45.0	23 10.6	+15.4	45.3	23 52.7	+16.2	45.6	24 34.6	+16.9	45.9	25 16.2	+17.7	46.3	49
50	20 32.5	+12.0	43.1	21 16.2	+12.7	43.4	21 59.7	+13.4	43.7	22 43.0	+14.2	44.0	23 26.0	+15.0	44.3	24 08.9	+15.8	44.6	24 51.5	+16.6	44.9	25 33.9	+17.3	45.2	50
51	20 44.5	+11.5	42.1	21 28.9	+12.3	42.4	22 13.1	+13.1	42.6	22 57.2	+13.8	42.9	23 41.0	+14.6	43.2	24 24.7	+15.3	43.5	25 08.1	+16.0	43.8	25 51.2	+16.9	44.2	51
52	20 56.0	+11.2	41.0	21 41.2	+11.9	41.3	22 26.2	+12.6	41.6	23 11.0	+13.4	41.9	23 55.6	+14.1	42.1	24 40.0	+14.8	42.4	25 24.1	+15.6	42.8	26 08.1	+16.3	43.1	52
53	21 07.2	+10.8	40.0	21 53.1	+11.5	40.2	22 38.8	+12.3	40.5	23 24.4	+12.9	40.8	24 09.7	+13.6	41.1	24 54.8	+14.4	41.4	25 39.7	+15.2	41.7	26 24.4	+15.9	42.0	53
54	21 18.0	+10.5	38.9	22 04.6	+11.1	39.2	22 51.1	+11.8	39.5	23 37.3	+12.5	39.7	24 23.3	+13.3	40.0	25 09.2	+13.9	40.3	25 54.9	+14.6	40.6	26 40.3	+15.4	40.9	54
55	21 28.5	+10.0	37.9	22 15.7	+10.7	38.1	23 02.9	+11.3	38.4	23 49.8	+12.1	38.7	24 36.6	+12.7	38.9	25 23.1	+13.5	39.2	26 09.5	+14.2	39.5	26 55.7	+14.9	39.9	55
56	21 38.5	+9.6	36.8	22 26.4	+10.3	37.1	23 14.2	+11.0	37.3	24 01.9	+11.6	37.6	24 49.3	+12.3	37.9	25 36.6	+13.0	38.2	26 23.7	+13.7	38.5	27 10.6	+14.3	38.8	56
57	21 48.1	+9.2	35.8	22 36.7	+9.8	36.0	23 25.2	+10.5	36.2	24 13.5	+11.1	36.5	25 01.6	+11.8	36.8	25 49.6	+12.5	37.1	26 37.4	+13.1	37.4	27 24.9	+13.9	37.7	57
58	21 57.3	+8.8	34.7	22 46.5	+9.5	34.9	23 35.7	+10.0	35.2	24 24.6	+10.7	35.4	25 13.4	+11.4	35.7	26 02.1	+12.0	36.0	26 50.5	+12.7	36.3	27 38.8	+13.4	36.6	58
59	22 06.1	+8.3	33.6	22 56.0	+8.9	33.9	23 45.7	+9.6	34.1	24 35.3	+10.3	34.3	25 24.8	+10.9	34.6	26 14.1	+11.5	34.9	27 03.2	+12.2	35.2	27 52.2	+12.8	35.5	59
60	22 14.4	+8.0	32.6	23 04.9	+8.6	32.8	23 55.3	+9.2	33.0	24 45.6	+9.7	33.3	25 35.7	+10.3	33.5	26 25.6	+11.0	33.8	27 15.4	+11.6	34.1	28 05.0	+12.3	34.4	60
61	22 22.4	+7.5	31.5	23 13.5	+8.1	31.7	24 04.5	+8.7	31.9	24 55.3	+9.3	32.2	25 46.0	+9.9	32.4	26 36.6	+10.5	32.7	27 27.0	+11.1	33.0	28 17.3	+11.7	33.3	61
62	22 29.9	+7.1	30.4	23 21.6	+7.7	30.6	24 13.2	+8.2	30.9	25 04.6	+8.8	31.1	25 55.9	+9.4	31.3	26 47.1	+10.0	31.6	27 38.1	+10.6	31.9	28 29.0	+11.2	32.1	62
63	22 37.0	+6.7	29.3	23 29.3	+7.2	29.5	24 21.4	+7.8	29.8	25 13.4	+8.4	30.0	26 05.3	+8.9	30.2	26 57.1	+9.5	30.5	27 48.7	+10.1	30.8	28 40.2	+10.7	31.0	63
64	22 43.7	+6.2	28.3	23 36.5	+6.7	28.5	24 29.2	+7.3	28.7	25 21.8	+7.8	28.9	26 14.2	+8.4	29.1	27 06.6	+8.9	29.4	27 58.8	+9.5	29.6	28 50.9	+10.1	29.9	64
65	22 49.9	+5.8	27.2	23 43.2	+6.3	27.4	24 36.5	+6.8	27.6	25 29.6	+7.3	27.8	26 22.6	+7.9	28.0	27 15.5	+8.4	28.3	28 08.3	+9.0	28.5	29 01.0	+9.5	28.8	65
66	22 55.7	+5.4	26.1	23 49.5	+5.9	26.3	24 43.3	+6.3	26.5	25 36.9	+6.9	26.7	26 30.5	+7.4	26.9	27 23.9	+7.9	27.2	28 17.3	+8.4	27.4	29 10.5	+8.9	27.6	66
67	23 01.1	+4.9	25.0	23 55.4	+5.4	25.2	24 49.6	+5.9	25.4	25 43.8	+6.4	25.6	26 37.9	+6.8	25.8	27 31.8	+7.4	26.0	28 25.7	+7.8	26.3	29 19.4	+8.4	26.5	67
68	23 06.0	+4.5	23.9	24 00.8	+4.9	24.1	24 55.5	+5.4	24.3	25 50.2	+5.8	24.5	26 44.7	+6.3	24.7	27 39.2	+6.8	24.9	28 33.5	+7.3	25.1	29 27.8	+7.8	25.4	68
69	23 10.5	+4.0	22.9	24 05.7	+4.5	23.0	25 00.9	+4.9	23.2	25 56.0	+5.4	23.4	26 51.0	+5.8	23.6	27 46.0	+6.2	23.8	28 40.8	+6.8	24.0	29 35.6	+7.2	24.2	69
70	23 14.5	+3.6	21.8	24 10.2	+4.0	21.9	25 05.8	+4.4	22.1	26 01.4	+4.8	22.3	26 56.8	+5.3	22.5	27 52.2	+5.8	22.7	28 47.6	+6.1	22.9	29 42.8	+6.6	23.1	70
71	23 18.1	+3.1	20.7	24 14.2	+3.5	20.8	25 10.2	+3.9	21.0	26 06.2	+4.3	21.2	27 02.1	+4.8	21.4	27 58.0	+5.1	21.5	28 53.7	+5.6	21.7	29 49.4	+6.0	22.0	71
72	23 21.2	+2.7	19.6	24 17.7	+3.0	19.7	25 14.1	+3.5	19.9	26 10.5	+3.9	20.1	27 06.9	+4.2	20.2	28 03.1	+4.6	20.4	28 59.3	+5.0	20.6	29 55.4	+5.5	20.8	72
73	23 23.9	+2.2	18.5	24 20.7	+2.6	18.6	25 17.6	+2.9	18.8	26 14.4	+3.3	18.9	27 11.1	+3.6	19.1	28 07.7	+4.1	19.3	29 04.3	+4.5	19.5	30 00.9	+4.8	19.7	73
74	23 26.1	+1.8	17.4	24 23.3	+2.1	17.5	25 20.5	+2.5	17.7	26 17.7	+2.7	17.8	27 14.7	+3.2	18.0	28 11.8	+3.5	18.2	29 08.8	+3.8	18.3	30 05.7	+4.2	18.5	74
75	23 27.9	+1.3	16.3	24 25.4	+1.7	16.4	25 23.0	+1.9	16.6	26 20.4	+2.3	16.7	27 17.9	+2.6	16.9	28 15.3	+2.9	17.0	29 12.6	+3.3	17.2	30 09.9	+3.6	17.4	75
76	23 29.2	+0.9	15.2	24 27.1	+1.1	15.4	25 24.9	+1.5	15.5	26 22.7	+1.8	15.6	27 20.5	+2.0	15.7	28 18.2	+2.4	15.9	29 15.9	+2.7	16.0	30 13.5	+3.1	16.2	76
77	23 30.1	+0.4	14.1	24 28.2	+0.7	14.3	25 26.4	+0.9	14.4	26 24.5	+1.2	14.5	27 22.5	+1.6	14.6	28 20.6	+1.8	14.8	29 18.6	+2.1	14.9	30 16.6	+2.4	15.0	77
78	23 30.5	−0.1	13.1	24 28.9	+0.2	13.2	25 27.3	+0.5	13.3	26 25.7	+0.7	13.4	27 24.1	+0.9	13.5	28 22.4	+1.2	13.6	29 20.7	+1.5	13.7	30 19.0	+1.7	13.9	78
79	23 30.4	−0.5	12.0	24 29.1	−0.3	12.1	25 27.8	−0.1	12.2	26 26.4	+0.2	12.3	27 25.0	+0.5	12.4	28 23.6	+0.7	12.5	29 22.2	+0.9	12.6	30 20.7	+1.2	12.7	79
80	23 29.9	−0.9	10.9	24 28.8	−0.7	11.0	25 27.7	−0.5	11.0	26 26.6	−0.3	11.1	27 25.5	−0.1	11.2	28 24.3	+0.1	11.3	29 23.1	+0.4	11.5	30 21.9	+0.6	11.6	80
81	23 29.0	−1.5	9.8	24 28.1	−1.2	9.9	25 27.2	−1.1	9.9	26 26.3	−0.9	10.0	27 25.4	−0.7	10.1	28 24.4	−0.4	10.2	29 23.5	−0.3	10.3	30 22.5	−0.1	10.4	81
82	23 27.5	−1.8	8.7	24 26.9	−1.8	8.8	25 26.1	−1.5	8.8	26 25.4	−1.3	8.9	27 24.7	−1.2	9.0	28 24.0	−1.1	9.1	29 23.2	−0.8	9.2	30 22.4	−0.6	9.2	82
83	23 25.7	−2.3	7.6	24 25.1	−2.1	7.7	25 24.6	−2.0	7.7	26 24.1	−1.9	7.8	27 23.5	−1.7	7.9	28 22.9	−1.6	7.9	29 22.4	−1.5	8.0	30 21.8	−1.3	8.1	83
84	23 23.4	−2.8	6.5	24 23.0	−2.7	6.6	25 22.6	−2.6	6.6	26 22.2	−2.4	6.7	27 21.8	−2.3	6.7	28 21.3	−2.1	6.8	29 20.9	−2.0	6.9	30 20.5	−1.9	6.9	84
85	23 20.6	−3.2	5.4	24 20.3	−3.1	5.5	25 20.0	−3.0	5.5	26 19.8	−3.0	5.6	27 19.5	−2.8	5.6	28 19.2	−2.7	5.7	29 18.9	−2.6	5.7	30 18.6	−2.5	5.8	85
86	23 17.4	−3.7	4.3	24 17.2	−3.6	4.4	25 17.0	−3.5	4.4	26 16.8	−3.4	4.4	27 16.7	−3.4	4.5	28 16.5	−3.3	4.5	29 16.3	−3.2	4.6	30 16.1	−3.1	4.6	86
87	23 13.7	−4.1	3.3	24 13.6	−4.1	3.3	25 13.5	−4.0	3.3	26 13.4	−4.0	3.3	27 13.3	−3.9	3.4	28 13.2	−3.9	3.4	29 13.1	−3.8	3.4	30 13.0	−3.7	3.5	87
88	23 09.6	−4.6	2.2	24 09.5	−4.5	2.2	25 09.5	−4.5	2.2	26 09.4	−4.4	2.2	27 09.4	−4.4	2.2	28 09.3	−4.3	2.3	29 09.3	−4.4	2.3	30 09.3	−4.4	2.3	88
89	23 05.0	−5.0	1.1	24 05.0	−5.0	1.1	25 05.0	−5.0	1.1	26 05.0	−5.0	1.1	27 05.0	−5.0	1.1	28 05.0	−5.0	1.1	29 04.9	−4.9	1.1	30 04.9	−4.9	1.2	89
90	23 00.0	−5.4	0.0	24 00.0	−5.5	0.0	25 00.0	−5.5	0.0	26 00.0	−5.5	0.0	27 00.0	−5.5	0.0	28 00.0	−5.5	0.0	29 00.0	−5.5	0.0	30 00.0	−5.5	0.0	90
	23°			24°			25°			26°			27°			28°			29°			30°			

85°, 275° L.H.A. LATITUDE SAME NAME AS DECLINATION

354

LATITUDE **CONTRARY** NAME TO DECLINATION **L.H.A. 85°, 275°**

Dec.	23° Hc	d	Z	24° Hc	d	Z	25° Hc	d	Z	26° Hc	d	Z
°	° ′	′	°	° ′	′	°	° ′	′	°	° ′	′	°
0	4 36.1	-23.6	92.0	4 34.0	-24.5	92.0	4 31.8	-25.4	92.1	4 29.6	-26.4	92.2
1	4 12.5	-23.6	92.9	4 09.5	-24.6	93.0	4 06.4	-25.6	93.0	4 03.2	-26.5	93.1
2	3 48.9	-23.7	93.8	3 44.9	-24.6	93.9	3 40.8	-25.6	93.9	3 36.7	-26.5	94.0
3	3 25.2	-23.7	94.7	3 20.3	-24.7	94.8	3 15.2	-25.6	94.8	3 10.2	-26.6	94.9
4	3 01.5	-23.8	95.6	2 55.6	-24.7	95.7	2 49.6	-25.7	95.7	2 43.6	-26.6	95.8
5	2 37.7	-23.8	96.6	2 30.9	-24.8	96.6	2 23.9	-25.7	96.6	2 17.0	-26.7	96.7
6	2 13.9	-23.8	97.5	2 06.1	-24.8	97.5	1 58.2	-25.7	97.6	1 50.3	-26.7	97.6
7	1 50.1	-23.9	98.4	1 41.3	-24.8	98.4	1 32.5	-25.8	98.5	1 23.6	-26.7	98.5
8	1 26.2	-23.9	99.3	1 16.5	-24.9	99.3	1 06.7	-25.8	99.4	0 56.9	-26.7	99.4
9	1 02.3	-23.9	100.2	0 51.6	-24.8	100.2	0 40.9	-25.8	100.3	0 30.2	-26.7	100.3
10	0 38.4	-24.0	101.2	0 26.8	-24.9	101.2	0 15.1	-25.8	101.2	0 03.5	-26.7	101.2
11	0 14.4	-23.9	102.1	0 01.9	-24.9	102.1	0 10.7	+25.8	77.9	0 23.2	+26.7	77.9
12	0 09.5	+23.9	77.0	0 23.0	+24.8	77.0	0 36.5	+25.7	77.0	0 49.9	+26.7	77.0
13	0 33.4	+24.0	76.1	0 47.8	+24.9	76.1	1 02.2	+25.8	76.1	1 16.6	+26.7	76.1
14	0 57.4	+23.9	75.2	1 12.7	+24.8	75.2	1 28.0	+25.8	75.2	1 43.3	+26.7	75.2
15	1 21.3	+23.8	74.3	1 37.5	+24.8	74.3	1 53.8	+25.7	74.3	2 10.0	+26.6	74.4
16	1 45.1	+23.9	73.3	2 02.3	+24.8	73.4	2 19.5	+25.7	73.4	2 36.6	+26.6	73.5
17	2 09.0	+23.8	72.4	2 27.1	+24.7	72.5	2 45.2	+25.6	72.5	3 03.2	+26.5	72.6
18	2 32.8	+23.8	71.5	2 51.8	+24.7	71.6	3 10.8	+25.6	71.6	3 29.7	+26.5	71.7
19	2 56.6	+23.8	70.6	3 16.5	+24.7	70.6	3 36.4	+25.5	70.7	3 56.2	+26.4	70.8
20	3 20.4	+23.6	69.7	3 41.2	+24.6	69.7	4 01.9	+25.5	69.8	4 22.6	+26.4	69.9
21	3 44.0	+23.7	68.7	4 05.8	+24.5	68.8	4 27.4	+25.4	68.9	4 49.0	+26.3	69.0
22	4 07.7	+23.5	67.8	4 30.3	+24.4	67.9	4 52.8	+25.4	68.0	5 15.3	+26.2	68.1
23	4 31.2	+23.5	66.9	4 54.7	+24.4	67.0	5 18.2	+25.2	67.1	5 41.5	+26.1	67.2
24	4 54.7	+23.5	66.0	5 19.1	+24.3	66.1	5 43.4	+25.2	66.2	6 07.6	+26.1	66.2
25	5 18.2	+23.3	65.1	5 43.4	+24.2	65.1	6 08.6	+25.1	65.2	6 33.7	+25.9	65.3
26	5 41.5	+23.3	64.1	6 07.6	+24.2	64.2	6 33.7	+25.0	64.3	6 59.6	+25.9	64.4
27	6 04.8	+23.1	63.2	6 31.8	+24.0	63.3	6 58.7	+24.8	63.4	7 25.5	+25.7	63.5
28	6 27.9	+23.1	62.3	6 55.8	+23.9	62.4	7 23.5	+24.8	62.5	7 51.2	+25.6	62.6
29	6 51.0	+22.9	61.3	7 19.7	+23.8	61.5	7 48.3	+24.6	61.6	8 16.8	+25.5	61.7
30	7 13.9	+22.9	60.4	7 43.5	+23.7	60.5	8 12.9	+24.6	60.7	8 42.3	+25.3	60.8
31	7 36.8	+22.7	59.5	8 07.2	+23.5	59.6	8 37.5	+24.4	59.7	9 07.6	+25.3	59.9
32	7 59.5	+22.6	58.6	8 30.7	+23.4	58.7	9 01.9	+24.2	58.8	9 32.9	+25.0	58.9
33	8 22.1	+22.4	57.6	8 54.1	+23.3	57.7	9 26.1	+24.1	57.9	9 57.9	+25.0	58.0
34	8 44.5	+22.3	56.7	9 17.4	+23.1	56.8	9 50.2	+23.9	57.0	10 22.9	+24.7	57.1
35	9 06.8	+22.2	55.7	9 40.5	+23.0	55.9	10 14.1	+23.8	56.0	10 47.6	+24.6	56.2
36	9 29.0	+22.0	54.8	10 03.5	+22.9	54.9	10 37.9	+23.7	55.1	11 12.2	+24.4	55.2
37	9 51.0	+21.9	53.9	10 26.4	+22.6	54.0	11 01.6	+23.4	54.2	11 36.6	+24.3	54.3
38	10 12.9	+21.7	52.9	10 49.0	+22.5	53.1	11 25.0	+23.3	53.2	12 00.9	+24.0	53.4
39	10 34.6	+21.5	52.0	11 11.5	+22.3	52.1	11 48.3	+23.1	52.3	12 24.9	+23.9	52.4
40	10 56.1	+21.4	51.0	11 33.8	+22.1	51.2	12 11.4	+22.9	51.3	12 48.8	+23.6	51.5
41	11 17.5	+21.1	50.1	11 55.9	+22.0	50.2	12 34.3	+22.6	50.4	13 12.4	+23.5	50.6
42	11 38.6	+21.0	49.1	12 17.9	+21.7	49.3	12 56.9	+22.5	49.4	13 35.9	+23.2	49.6
43	11 59.6	+20.8	48.1	12 39.6	+21.5	48.3	13 19.4	+22.3	48.5	13 59.1	+23.1	48.7
44	12 20.4	+20.6	47.2	13 01.1	+21.3	47.4	13 41.7	+22.1	47.5	14 22.2	+22.7	47.7
45	12 41.0	+20.4	46.2	13 22.4	+21.1	46.4	14 03.8	+21.8	46.6	14 44.9	+22.6	46.8
46	13 01.4	+20.1	45.3	13 43.5	+20.9	45.4	14 25.6	+21.6	45.6	15 07.5	+22.3	45.8
47	13 21.5	+20.0	44.3	14 04.4	+20.7	44.5	14 47.2	+21.3	44.6	15 29.8	+22.0	44.8
48	13 41.5	+19.7	43.3	14 25.1	+20.4	43.5	15 08.5	+21.1	43.7	15 51.8	+21.8	43.9
49	14 01.2	+19.5	42.3	14 45.5	+20.1	42.5	15 29.6	+20.9	42.7	16 13.6	+21.6	42.9
50	14 20.7	+19.2	41.4	15 05.6	+19.9	41.5	15 50.5	+20.6	41.7	16 35.2	+21.2	41.9
51	14 39.9	+19.0	40.4	15 25.5	+19.7	40.6	16 11.1	+20.3	40.8	16 56.4	+21.0	40.9
52	14 58.9	+18.7	39.4	15 45.2	+19.4	39.6	16 31.4	+20.0	39.8	17 17.4	+20.7	40.0
53	15 17.6	+18.5	38.4	16 04.6	+19.1	38.6	16 51.4	+19.8	38.8	17 38.1	+20.4	39.0
54	15 36.1	+18.2	37.4	16 23.7	+18.8	37.6	17 11.2	+19.4	37.8	17 58.5	+20.1	38.0
55	15 54.3	+18.0	36.5	16 42.5	+18.6	36.6	17 30.6	+19.2	36.8	18 18.6	+19.8	37.0
56	16 12.3	+17.6	35.5	17 01.1	+18.3	35.6	17 49.8	+18.9	35.8	18 38.4	+19.5	36.0
57	16 29.9	+17.4	34.5	17 19.4	+17.9	34.6	18 08.7	+18.5	34.8	18 57.9	+19.1	35.0
58	16 47.3	+17.1	33.5	17 37.3	+17.7	33.6	18 27.2	+18.3	33.8	19 17.0	+18.9	34.0
59	17 04.4	+16.8	32.5	17 55.0	+17.4	32.6	18 45.5	+17.9	32.8	19 35.9	+18.4	33.0
60	17 21.2	+16.5	31.5	18 12.4	+17.0	31.6	19 03.4	+17.6	31.8	19 54.3	+18.2	32.0
61	17 37.7	+16.2	30.4	18 29.4	+16.7	30.6	19 21.0	+17.2	30.8	20 12.5	+17.8	31.0
62	17 53.9	+15.9	29.4	18 46.1	+16.4	29.6	19 38.2	+17.0	29.8	20 30.3	+17.4	30.0
63	18 09.8	+15.5	28.4	19 02.5	+16.1	28.6	19 55.2	+16.5	28.8	20 47.7	+17.1	28.9
64	18 25.3	+15.3	27.4	19 18.6	+15.7	27.6	20 11.7	+16.2	27.7	21 04.8	+16.7	27.9
65	18 40.6	+14.9	26.4	19 34.3	+15.3	26.5	20 27.9	+15.9	26.7	21 21.5	+16.3	26.9
66	18 55.5	+14.5	25.4	19 49.6	+15.1	25.5	20 43.8	+15.4	25.7	21 37.8	+15.9	25.8
67	19 10.0	+14.2	24.3	20 04.7	+14.6	24.5	20 59.2	+15.1	24.6	21 53.7	+15.6	24.8
68	19 24.2	+13.9	23.3	20 19.3	+14.3	23.5	21 14.3	+14.7	23.6	22 09.3	+15.1	23.8
69	19 38.1	+13.5	22.3	20 33.6	+13.9	22.4	21 29.0	+14.4	22.6	22 24.4	+14.8	22.7
70	19 51.6	+13.2	21.2	20 47.5	+13.6	21.4	21 43.4	+13.9	21.5	22 39.2	+14.3	21.7
71	20 04.8	+12.8	20.2	21 01.1	+13.1	20.3	21 57.3	+13.5	20.5	22 53.5	+13.9	20.6
72	20 17.6	+12.4	19.2	21 14.2	+12.8	19.3	22 10.8	+13.2	19.4	23 07.4	+13.5	19.6
73	20 30.0	+12.0	18.1	21 27.0	+12.4	18.2	22 24.0	+12.7	18.4	23 20.9	+13.0	18.5
74	20 42.0	+11.7	17.1	21 39.4	+11.9	17.2	22 36.7	+12.3	17.3	23 33.9	+12.7	17.4
75	20 53.7	+11.3	16.0	21 51.3	+11.6	16.1	22 49.0	+11.8	16.2	23 46.6	+12.1	16.4
76	21 05.0	+10.9	15.0	22 02.9	+11.2	15.1	23 00.8	+11.5	15.2	23 58.7	+11.8	15.3
77	21 15.9	+10.4	13.9	22 14.1	+10.7	14.0	23 12.3	+11.0	14.1	24 10.5	+11.2	14.2
78	21 26.3	+10.1	12.9	22 24.8	+10.4	12.9	23 23.3	+10.6	13.0	24 21.7	+10.9	13.1
79	21 36.4	+9.7	11.8	22 35.2	+9.9	11.9	23 33.9	+10.1	12.0	24 32.6	+10.3	12.1
80	21 46.1	+9.3	10.7	22 45.1	+9.5	10.8	23 44.0	+9.7	10.9	24 42.9	+9.9	11.0
81	21 55.4	+8.9	9.7	22 54.6	+9.0	9.7	23 53.7	+9.2	9.8	24 52.8	+9.4	9.9
82	22 04.3	+8.4	8.6	23 03.6	+8.6	8.7	24 02.9	+8.8	8.7	25 02.2	+9.0	8.8
83	22 12.7	+8.1	7.5	23 12.2	+8.2	7.6	24 11.7	+8.3	7.6	25 11.2	+8.4	7.7
84	22 20.8	+7.6	6.5	23 20.4	+7.7	6.5	24 20.0	+7.9	6.6	25 19.6	+8.0	6.6
85	22 28.4	+7.2	5.4	23 28.1	+7.3	5.4	24 27.9	+7.3	5.5	25 27.6	+7.5	5.5
86	22 35.6	+6.7	4.3	23 35.4	+6.8	4.3	24 35.2	+6.9	4.4	25 35.1	+6.9	4.4
87	22 42.3	+6.4	3.3	23 42.2	+6.4	3.3	24 42.1	+6.5	3.3	25 42.0	+6.5	3.3
88	22 48.7	+5.9	2.2	23 48.6	+5.9	2.2	24 48.6	+5.9	2.2	25 48.5	+6.0	2.2
89	22 54.6	+5.4	1.1	23 54.5	+5.5	1.1	24 54.5	+5.5	1.1	25 54.5	+5.5	1.1
90	23 00.0	+5.0	0.0	24 00.0	+5.0	0.0	25 00.0	+5.0	0.0	26 00.0	+5.0	0.0
	23°			24°			25°			26°		

Dec.	27° Hc	d	Z	28° Hc	d	Z	29° Hc	d	Z	30° Hc	d	Z
°	° ′	′	°	° ′	′	°	° ′	′	°	° ′	′	°
0	4 27.2	-27.3	92.3	4 24.8	-28.3	92.4	4 22.3	-29.2	92.4	4 19.7	-30.1	92.5
1	3 59.9	-27.4	93.2	3 56.5	-28.3	93.2	3 53.1	-29.3	93.3	3 49.6	-30.2	93.4
2	3 32.5	-27.5	94.1	3 28.2	-28.4	94.1	3 23.8	-29.3	94.2	3 19.4	-30.2	94.2
3	3 05.0	-27.5	94.9	2 59.8	-28.4	95.0	2 54.5	-29.3	95.1	2 49.2	-30.2	95.1
4	2 37.5	-27.5	95.8	2 31.4	-28.5	95.9	2 25.2	-29.4	95.9	2 19.0	-30.3	96.0
5	2 10.0	-27.6	96.7	2 02.9	-28.5	96.8	1 55.8	-29.4	96.8	1 48.7	-30.3	96.8
6	1 42.4	-27.6	97.6	1 34.4	-28.5	97.6	1 26.4	-29.4	97.7	1 18.4	-30.3	97.7
7	1 14.8	-27.6	98.5	1 05.9	-28.5	98.5	0 57.0	-29.5	98.5	0 48.1	-30.4	98.6
8	0 47.2	-27.7	99.4	0 37.4	-28.6	99.4	0 27.5	-29.4	99.4	0 17.7	-30.3	99.4
9	0 19.5	-27.6	100.3	0 08.8	-28.5	100.3	0 01.9	+29.4	79.7	0 12.6	+30.3	79.7
10	0 08.1	+27.6	78.8	0 19.7	+28.6	78.8	0 31.3	+29.5	78.8	0 42.9	+30.4	78.9
11	0 35.7	+27.7	77.9	0 48.3	+28.5	78.0	1 00.8	+29.4	78.0	1 13.3	+30.3	78.0
12	1 03.4	+27.6	77.1	1 16.8	+28.5	77.1	1 30.2	+29.4	77.1	1 43.6	+30.3	77.1
13	1 31.0	+27.6	76.2	1 45.3	+28.5	76.2	1 59.6	+29.4	76.2	2 13.9	+30.2	76.3
14	1 58.6	+27.5	75.3	2 13.8	+28.4	75.3	2 29.0	+29.3	75.4	2 44.1	+30.2	75.4
15	2 26.1	+27.5	74.4	2 42.2	+28.5	74.4	2 58.3	+29.3	74.5	3 14.3	+30.2	74.5
16	2 53.6	+27.5	73.5	3 10.7	+28.3	73.6	3 27.6	+29.3	73.6	3 44.5	+30.1	73.7
17	3 21.1	+27.5	72.6	3 39.0	+28.3	72.7	3 56.9	+29.2	72.7	4 14.6	+30.1	72.8
18	3 48.6	+27.3	71.7	4 07.3	+28.3	71.8	4 26.1	+29.1	71.9	4 44.7	+30.0	71.9
19	4 15.9	+27.3	70.8	4 35.6	+28.2	70.9	4 55.2	+29.1	71.0	5 14.7	+29.9	71.1
20	4 43.2	+27.3	69.9	5 03.8	+28.1	70.0	5 24.3	+28.9	70.1	5 44.6	+29.9	70.2
21	5 10.5	+27.2	69.0	5 31.9	+28.1	69.1	5 53.2	+29.0	69.2	6 14.5	+29.7	69.3
22	5 37.7	+27.1	68.1	6 00.0	+27.9	68.2	6 22.2	+28.8	68.3	6 44.2	+29.7	68.4
23	6 04.8	+27.0	67.2	6 27.9	+27.9	67.3	6 51.0	+28.7	67.5	7 13.9	+29.6	67.6
24	6 31.8	+26.9	66.3	6 55.8	+27.7	66.5	7 19.7	+28.6	66.6	7 43.5	+29.4	66.7
25	6 58.7	+26.8	65.4	7 23.5	+27.7	65.6	7 48.3	+28.5	65.7	8 12.9	+29.4	65.8
26	7 25.5	+26.7	64.5	7 51.2	+27.5	64.7	8 16.8	+28.4	64.8	8 42.3	+29.2	64.9
27	7 52.2	+26.5	63.6	8 18.7	+27.5	63.8	8 45.2	+28.3	63.9	9 11.5	+29.1	64.0
28	8 18.7	+26.5	62.7	8 46.2	+27.3	62.9	9 13.5	+28.1	63.0	9 40.6	+29.0	63.2
29	8 45.2	+26.3	61.8	9 13.5	+27.1	62.0	9 41.6	+28.0	62.1	10 09.6	+28.8	62.3
30	9 11.5	+26.2	60.9	9 40.6	+27.0	61.1	10 09.6	+27.8	61.2	10 38.4	+28.6	61.4
31	9 37.7	+26.0	60.0	10 07.6	+26.9	60.2	10 37.4	+27.7	60.3	11 07.0	+28.6	60.5
32	10 03.7	+25.9	59.1	10 34.5	+26.7	59.3	11 05.1	+27.5	59.4	11 35.6	+28.3	59.6
33	10 29.6	+25.8	58.2	11 01.2	+26.6	58.3	11 32.6	+27.4	58.5	12 03.9	+28.1	58.7
34	10 55.4	+25.5	57.3	11 27.8	+26.3	57.4	12 00.0	+27.2	57.6	12 32.0	+28.0	57.8
35	11 20.9	+25.4	56.3	11 54.1	+26.2	56.5	12 27.2	+27.0	56.7	13 00.0	+27.8	56.9
36	11 46.3	+25.3	55.4	12 20.3	+26.0	55.6	12 54.2	+26.8	55.8	13 27.8	+27.6	56.0
37	12 11.6	+25.0	54.5	12 46.3	+25.9	54.7	13 21.0	+26.6	54.9	13 55.4	+27.4	55.1
38	12 36.6	+24.8	53.6	13 12.2	+25.6	53.7	13 47.6	+26.4	53.9	14 22.8	+27.2	54.1
39	13 01.4	+24.7	52.6	13 37.8	+25.4	52.8	14 14.0	+26.1	53.0	14 50.0	+26.9	53.2
40	13 26.1	+24.4	51.7	14 03.2	+25.2	51.9	14 40.1	+26.0	52.1	15 16.9	+26.8	52.3
41	13 50.5	+24.2	50.7	14 28.4	+24.9	50.9	15 06.1	+25.7	51.1	15 43.7	+26.4	51.4
42	14 14.7	+24.0	49.8	14 53.3	+24.8	50.0	15 31.8	+25.5	50.2	16 10.1	+26.3	50.4
43	14 38.7	+23.7	48.9	15 18.1	+24.5	49.1	15 57.3	+25.3	49.3	16 36.4	+26.0	49.5
44	15 02.4	+23.6	47.9	15 42.6	+24.2	48.1	16 22.6	+25.0	48.3	17 02.4	+25.7	48.5
45	15 26.0	+23.2	47.0	16 06.8	+24.1	47.2	16 47.6	+24.7	47.4	17 28.1	+25.5	47.6
46	15 49.2	+23.1	46.0	16 30.9	+23.7	46.2	17 12.3	+24.5	46.4	17 53.6	+25.2	46.7
47	16 12.3	+22.7	45.0	16 54.6	+23.5	45.2	17 36.8	+24.1	45.5	18 18.8	+24.8	45.7
48	16 35.0	+22.5	44.1	17 18.1	+23.2	44.3	18 00.9	+23.9	44.5	18 43.6	+24.6	44.7
49	16 57.5	+22.2	43.1	17 41.3	+22.9	43.3	18 24.8	+23.6	43.5	19 08.2	+24.3	43.8
50	17 19.7	+22.0	42.1	18 04.2	+22.6	42.3	18 48.4	+23.3	42.6	19 32.5	+24.0	42.8
51	17 41.7	+21.6	41.2	18 26.8	+22.3	41.4	19 11.7	+23.0	41.6	19 56.5	+23.7	41.8
52	18 03.3	+21.4	40.2	18 49.1	+22.0	40.4	19 34.7	+22.7	40.6	20 20.2	+23.3	40.9
53	18 24.7	+21.0	39.2	19 11.1	+21.7	39.4	19 57.4	+22.4	39.6	20 43.5	+23.0	39.9
54	18 45.7	+20.8	38.2	19 32.8	+21.4	38.4	20 19.8	+22.0	38.6	21 06.5	+22.7	38.9
55	19 06.5	+20.4	37.2	19 54.2	+21.0	37.4	20 41.8	+21.6	37.6	21 29.2	+22.3	37.9
56	19 26.9	+20.1	36.2	20 15.2	+20.7	36.4	21 03.4	+21.3	36.7	21 51.5	+21.9	36.9
57	19 47.0	+19.7	35.2	20 35.9	+20.4	35.4	21 24.7	+21.0	35.6	22 13.4	+21.6	35.9
58	20 06.7	+19.4	34.2	20 56.3	+20.0	34.4	21 45.7	+20.6	34.6	22 35.0	+21.2	34.9
59	20 26.1	+19.1	33.2	21 16.3	+19.6	33.4	22 06.3	+20.2	33.6	22 56.2	+20.8	33.9
60	20 45.2	+18.7	32.2	21 35.9	+19.3	32.4	22 26.5	+19.8	32.6	23 17.0	+20.4	32.8
61	21 03.9	+18.3	31.2	21 55.2	+18.8	31.4	22 46.3	+19.5	31.6	23 37.4	+20.0	31.8
62	21 22.2	+18.0	30.1	22 14.0	+18.5	30.3	23 05.8	+19.0	30.6	23 57.4	+19.6	30.8
63	21 40.2	+17.6	29.1	22 32.5	+18.1	29.3	23 24.8	+18.6	29.5	24 17.0	+19.1	29.7
64	21 57.8	+17.2	28.1	22 50.6	+17.7	28.3	23 43.4	+18.2	28.5	24 36.1	+18.7	28.7
65	22 15.0	+16.8	27.1	23 08.3	+17.3	27.2	24 01.6	+17.8	27.4	24 54.8	+18.3	27.7
66	22 31.8	+16.4	26.0	23 25.6	+16.9	26.2	24 19.4	+17.4	26.4	25 13.1	+17.8	26.6
67	22 48.2	+16.0	25.0	23 42.5	+16.5	25.2	24 36.8	+16.9	25.3	25 30.9	+17.4	25.6
68	23 04.2	+15.5	23.9	23 59.0	+16.0	24.1	24 53.7	+16.4	24.3	25 48.3	+16.9	24.5
69	23 19.7	+15.2	22.9	24 15.0	+15.6	23.1	25 10.1	+16.1	23.2	26 05.2	+16.5	23.4
70	23 34.9	+14.7	21.8	24 30.6	+15.1	22.0	25 26.2	+15.5	22.2	26 21.7	+15.9	22.3
71	23 49.6	+14.3	20.8	24 45.7	+14.7	20.9	25 41.7	+15.1	21.1	26 37.6	+15.5	21.3
72	24 03.9	+13.9	19.7	25 00.4	+14.2	19.9	25 56.8	+14.6	20.0	26 53.1	+15.0	20.2
73	24 17.8	+13.4	18.6	25 14.6	+13.7	18.8	26 11.4	+14.1	18.9	27 08.1	+14.5	19.1
74	24 31.2	+12.9	17.6	25 28.3	+13.3	17.7	26 25.5	+13.6	17.9	27 22.6	+13.9	18.0
75	24 44.1	+12.5	16.5	25 41.6	+12.8	16.6	26 39.1	+13.1	16.8	27 36.5	+13.4	16.9
76	24 56.6	+12.0	15.4	25 54.4	+12.3	15.5	26 52.2	+12.6	15.7	27 49.9	+13.0	15.8
77	25 08.6	+11.6	14.3	26 06.7	+11.8	14.5	27 04.8	+12.1	14.6	28 02.9	+12.3	14.7
78	25 20.2	+11.0	13.2	26 18.5	+11.4	13.4	27 16.9	+11.6	13.5	28 15.2	+11.9	13.6
79	25 31.2	+10.6	12.2	26 29.9	+10.8	12.3	27 28.5	+11.0	12.4	28 27.1	+11.3	12.5
80	25 41.8	+10.1	11.1	26 40.7	+10.3	11.2	27 39.5	+10.6	11.3	28 38.4	+10.7	11.4
81	25 51.9	+9.6	10.0	26 51.0	+9.8	10.1	27 50.1	+9.9	10.2	28 49.1	+10.2	10.2
82	26 01.5	+9.1	8.9	27 00.8	+9.3	9.0	28 00.0	+9.5	9.0	28 59.3	+9.6	9.1
83	26 10.6	+8.6	7.8	27 10.1	+8.7	7.8	28 09.5	+8.9	7.9	29 08.9	+9.1	8.0
84	26 19.2	+8.1	6.7	27 18.8	+8.2	6.7	28 18.4	+8.3	6.8	29 18.0	+8.4	6.9
85	26 27.3	+7.6	5.6	27 27.0	+7.7	5.6	28 26.7	+7.8	5.7	29 26.4	+7.9	5.7
86	26 34.9	+7.0	4.5	27 34.7	+7.1	4.5	28 34.5	+7.2	4.5	29 34.3	+7.3	4.6
87	26 41.9	+6.6	3.3	27 41.8	+6.6	3.4	28 41.7	+6.7	3.4	29 41.6	+6.7	3.4
88	26 48.5	+6.0	2.2	27 48.4	+6.1	2.3	28 48.4	+6.1	2.3	29 48.3	+6.2	2.3
89	26 54.5	+5.5	1.1	27 54.5	+5.5	1.1	28 54.5	+5.5	1.1	29 54.5	+5.5	1.1
90	27 00.0	+5.0	0.0	28 00.0	+5.0	0.0	29 00.0	+4.9	0.0	30 00.0	+4.9	0.0
	27°			28°			29°			30°		

S. Lat. {L.H.A. greater than 180° ....Zn=180°–Z; L.H.A. less than 180°...........Zn=180°+Z}

LATITUDE **SAME** NAME AS DECLINATION **L.H.A. 95°, 265°**

355

86°, 274° L.H.A. LATITUDE SAME NAME AS DECLINATION

N. Lat. {L.H.A. greater than 180° .....Zn=Z
{L.H.A. less than 180°............Zn=360°−Z

Dec.	23°			24°			25°			26°			27°			28°			29°			30°			Dec.
	Hc	d	Z	Hc	d	Z	Hc	d	Z	Hc	d	Z	Hc	d	Z	Hc	d	Z	Hc	d	Z	Hc	d	Z	
°	° ′	′	°	° ′	′	°	° ′	′	°	° ′	′	°	° ′	′	°	° ′	′	°	° ′	′	°	° ′	′	°	°
0	3 40.9	+23.5	91.6	3 39.2	+24.4	91.6	3 37.5	+25.4	91.7	3 35.7	+26.3	91.8	3 33.8	+27.3	91.8	3 31.9	+28.2	91.9	3 29.9	+29.1	91.9	3 27.8	+30.0	92.0	0
1	4 04.4	+23.4	90.6	4 03.6	+24.4	90.7	4 02.9	+25.3	90.8	4 02.0	+26.3	90.9	4 01.1	+27.2	90.9	4 00.1	+28.1	91.0	3 59.0	+29.0	91.1	3 57.8	+30.0	91.1	1
2	4 27.8	+23.3	89.7	4 28.0	+24.3	89.8	4 28.2	+25.2	89.9	4 28.3	+26.2	90.0	4 28.3	+27.1	90.0	4 28.2	+28.1	90.1	4 28.0	+29.0	90.2	4 27.8	+29.9	90.3	2
3	4 51.1	+23.2	88.8	4 52.3	+24.2	88.9	4 53.4	+25.2	89.0	4 54.5	+26.1	89.1	4 55.4	+27.1	89.1	4 56.3	+28.0	89.2	4 57.0	+29.0	89.3	4 57.7	+29.9	89.4	3
4	5 14.3	+23.2	87.9	5 16.5	+24.2	88.0	5 18.6	+25.1	88.1	5 20.6	+26.0	88.1	5 22.5	+27.0	88.2	5 24.3	+27.9	88.3	5 26.0	+28.8	88.4	5 27.6	+29.7	88.5	4
5	5 37.5	+23.1	86.9	5 40.7	+24.0	87.0	5 43.7	+25.0	87.1	5 46.6	+26.0	87.2	5 49.5	+26.9	87.3	5 52.2	+27.9	87.4	5 54.8	+28.8	87.5	5 57.3	+29.7	87.7	5
6	6 00.6	+23.0	86.0	6 04.7	+24.0	86.1	6 08.7	+24.9	86.2	6 12.6	+25.9	86.3	6 16.4	+26.8	86.4	6 20.1	+27.7	86.6	6 23.6	+28.7	86.7	6 27.0	+29.6	86.8	6
7	6 23.6	+22.9	85.1	6 28.7	+23.8	85.2	6 33.6	+24.9	85.3	6 38.5	+25.7	85.4	6 43.2	+26.7	85.5	6 47.8	+27.7	85.7	6 52.3	+28.6	85.8	6 56.6	+29.5	85.9	7
8	6 46.5	+22.8	84.2	6 52.5	+23.8	84.3	6 58.5	+24.7	84.4	7 04.2	+25.7	84.5	7 09.9	+26.6	84.6	7 15.5	+27.5	84.8	7 20.9	+28.4	84.9	7 26.1	+29.4	85.0	8
9	7 09.3	+22.6	83.2	7 16.3	+23.6	83.3	7 23.2	+24.6	83.5	7 29.9	+25.6	83.6	7 36.5	+26.5	83.7	7 43.0	+27.4	83.9	7 49.3	+28.4	84.0	7 55.5	+29.3	84.1	9
10	7 31.9	+22.6	82.3	7 39.9	+23.5	82.4	7 47.8	+24.4	82.6	7 55.5	+25.4	82.7	8 03.0	+26.4	82.8	8 10.4	+27.4	83.0	8 17.7	+28.2	83.1	8 24.8	+29.2	83.3	10
11	7 54.5	+22.4	81.4	8 03.4	+23.4	81.5	8 12.2	+24.4	81.6	8 20.9	+25.3	81.8	8 29.4	+26.3	81.9	8 37.8	+27.1	82.1	8 45.9	+28.2	82.2	8 54.0	+29.0	82.4	11
12	8 16.9	+22.3	80.4	8 26.8	+23.3	80.6	8 36.6	+24.2	80.7	8 46.2	+25.2	80.9	8 55.7	+26.1	81.0	9 04.9	+27.1	81.2	9 14.1	+28.0	81.3	9 23.0	+28.9	81.5	12
13	8 39.2	+22.2	79.5	8 50.1	+23.1	79.6	9 00.8	+24.1	79.8	9 11.4	+25.0	79.9	9 21.8	+25.9	80.1	9 32.0	+26.9	80.3	9 42.1	+27.8	80.4	9 51.9	+28.8	80.6	13
14	9 01.4	+22.0	78.5	9 13.2	+23.0	78.7	9 24.9	+23.9	78.9	9 36.4	+24.9	79.0	9 47.7	+25.9	79.2	9 58.9	+26.8	79.4	10 09.9	+27.7	79.5	10 20.7	+28.6	79.7	14
15	9 23.4	+21.9	77.6	9 36.2	+22.8	77.8	9 48.8	+23.8	77.9	10 01.3	+24.7	78.1	10 13.6	+25.7	78.3	10 25.7	+26.6	78.5	10 37.6	+27.5	78.6	10 49.3	+28.5	78.8	15
16	9 45.3	+21.7	76.7	9 59.0	+22.7	76.8	10 12.6	+23.6	77.0	10 26.0	+24.6	77.2	10 39.3	+25.5	77.4	10 52.3	+26.5	77.5	11 05.1	+27.4	77.7	11 17.8	+28.3	77.9	16
17	10 07.0	+21.5	75.7	10 21.7	+22.5	75.9	10 36.2	+23.5	76.1	10 50.6	+24.4	76.2	11 04.8	+25.3	76.4	11 18.8	+26.2	76.6	11 32.5	+27.2	76.8	11 46.1	+28.1	77.0	17
18	10 28.5	+21.4	74.8	10 44.2	+22.3	74.9	10 59.7	+23.3	75.1	11 15.0	+24.2	75.3	11 30.1	+25.2	75.5	11 45.0	+26.1	75.7	11 59.7	+27.1	75.9	12 14.2	+28.0	76.1	18
19	10 49.9	+21.2	73.8	11 06.5	+22.2	74.0	11 23.0	+23.1	74.2	11 39.2	+24.1	74.4	11 55.3	+25.0	74.6	12 11.1	+26.0	74.8	12 26.8	+26.8	75.0	12 42.2	+27.8	75.2	19
20	11 11.1	+21.0	72.9	11 28.7	+22.0	73.0	11 46.1	+22.9	73.2	12 03.3	+23.9	73.4	12 20.3	+24.8	73.7	12 37.1	+25.7	73.9	12 53.6	+26.7	74.1	13 10.0	+27.6	74.3	20
21	11 32.1	+20.9	71.9	11 50.7	+21.7	72.1	12 09.0	+22.7	72.3	12 27.2	+23.6	72.5	12 45.1	+24.6	72.7	13 02.8	+25.5	72.9	13 20.3	+26.5	73.2	13 37.6	+27.3	73.4	21
22	11 53.0	+20.6	70.9	12 12.4	+21.6	71.1	12 31.7	+22.6	71.3	12 50.8	+23.5	71.6	13 09.7	+24.4	71.8	13 28.3	+25.4	72.0	13 46.8	+26.2	72.2	14 04.9	+27.2	72.5	22
23	12 13.6	+20.4	70.0	12 34.0	+21.4	70.2	12 54.3	+22.3	70.4	13 14.3	+23.2	70.6	13 34.1	+24.2	70.8	13 53.7	+25.1	71.1	14 13.0	+26.0	71.3	14 32.1	+27.0	71.6	23
24	12 34.0	+20.3	69.0	12 55.4	+21.2	69.2	13 16.6	+22.1	69.4	13 37.5	+23.1	69.7	13 58.3	+23.9	69.9	14 18.8	+24.9	70.1	14 39.0	+25.9	70.4	14 59.1	+26.7	70.6	24
25	12 54.3	+20.0	68.1	13 16.6	+20.9	68.3	13 38.7	+21.9	68.5	14 00.6	+22.8	68.7	14 22.2	+23.8	69.0	14 43.7	+24.6	69.2	15 04.9	+25.5	69.4	15 25.8	+26.5	69.7	25
26	13 14.3	+19.8	67.1	13 37.5	+20.8	67.3	14 00.6	+21.6	67.5	14 23.4	+22.6	67.8	14 46.0	+23.5	68.0	15 08.3	+24.5	68.3	15 30.4	+25.4	68.5	15 52.3	+26.3	68.8	26
27	13 34.1	+19.6	66.1	13 58.3	+20.5	66.3	14 22.2	+21.5	66.6	14 46.0	+22.3	66.8	15 09.5	+23.3	67.1	15 32.8	+24.2	67.3	15 55.8	+25.1	67.6	16 18.6	+26.0	67.8	27
28	13 53.7	+19.3	65.1	14 18.8	+20.2	65.4	14 43.7	+21.2	65.6	15 08.3	+22.1	65.8	15 32.8	+23.0	66.1	15 57.0	+23.9	66.4	16 20.9	+24.8	66.6	16 44.6	+25.7	66.9	28
29	14 13.0	+19.1	64.2	14 39.0	+20.1	64.4	15 04.9	+20.9	64.6	15 30.4	+21.9	64.9	15 55.8	+22.8	65.1	16 20.9	+23.7	65.4	16 45.7	+24.6	65.7	17 10.3	+25.5	66.0	29
30	14 32.1	+18.9	63.2	14 59.1	+19.7	63.4	15 25.8	+20.7	63.7	15 52.3	+21.6	63.9	16 18.6	+22.5	64.2	16 44.6	+23.4	64.4	17 10.3	+24.3	64.7	17 35.8	+25.2	65.0	30
31	14 51.0	+18.6	62.2	15 18.8	+19.6	62.4	15 46.5	+20.4	62.7	16 13.9	+21.3	62.9	16 41.1	+22.2	63.2	17 08.0	+23.1	63.5	17 34.6	+24.1	63.8	18 01.0	+25.0	64.0	31
32	15 09.6	+18.3	61.2	15 38.4	+19.2	61.5	16 06.9	+20.2	61.7	16 35.2	+21.1	62.0	17 03.3	+21.9	62.2	17 31.1	+22.9	62.5	17 58.7	+23.7	62.8	18 26.0	+24.6	63.1	32
33	15 27.9	+18.1	60.2	15 57.6	+19.0	60.5	16 27.1	+19.8	60.7	16 56.3	+20.8	61.0	17 25.2	+21.7	61.3	17 54.0	+22.5	61.5	18 22.4	+23.5	61.8	18 50.6	+24.4	62.1	33
34	15 46.0	+17.8	59.2	16 16.6	+18.7	59.5	16 46.9	+19.6	59.7	17 17.1	+20.4	60.0	17 46.9	+21.4	60.3	18 16.5	+22.3	60.6	18 45.9	+23.1	60.9	19 15.0	+24.0	61.2	34
35	16 03.8	+17.6	58.3	16 35.3	+18.4	58.5	17 06.5	+19.4	58.8	17 37.5	+20.2	59.0	18 08.3	+21.1	59.3	18 38.8	+22.0	59.6	19 09.0	+22.9	59.9	19 39.0	+23.7	60.2	35
36	16 21.4	+17.3	57.3	16 53.7	+18.2	57.5	17 25.9	+19.0	57.8	17 57.7	+19.9	58.0	18 29.4	+20.7	58.3	19 00.8	+21.6	58.6	19 31.9	+22.5	58.9	20 02.7	+23.4	59.2	36
37	16 38.7	+16.9	56.3	17 11.9	+17.8	56.5	17 44.9	+18.7	56.8	18 17.6	+19.6	57.0	18 50.1	+20.5	57.3	19 22.4	+21.3	57.6	19 54.4	+22.2	57.9	20 26.1	+23.1	58.2	37
38	16 55.6	+16.7	55.3	17 29.7	+17.6	55.5	18 03.6	+18.4	55.8	18 37.2	+19.3	56.0	19 10.6	+20.1	56.3	19 43.7	+21.0	56.6	20 16.6	+21.9	56.9	20 49.2	+22.7	57.2	38
39	17 12.3	+16.4	54.2	17 47.3	+17.2	54.5	18 22.0	+18.1	54.8	18 56.5	+18.9	55.0	19 30.7	+19.8	55.3	20 04.7	+20.7	55.6	20 38.5	+21.5	55.9	21 11.9	+22.4	56.3	39
40	17 28.7	+16.1	53.2	18 04.5	+16.9	53.5	18 40.1	+17.7	53.8	19 15.4	+18.6	54.0	19 50.5	+19.5	54.3	20 25.4	+20.3	54.6	21 00.0	+21.2	54.9	21 34.3	+22.1	55.3	40
41	17 44.8	+15.7	52.2	18 21.4	+16.6	52.5	18 57.8	+17.5	52.8	19 34.0	+18.3	53.0	20 10.0	+19.1	53.3	20 45.7	+20.0	53.6	21 21.2	+20.8	53.9	21 56.4	+21.6	54.3	41
42	18 00.5	+15.5	51.2	18 38.0	+16.3	51.5	19 15.3	+17.1	51.7	19 52.3	+18.0	52.0	20 29.1	+18.8	52.3	21 05.7	+19.6	52.6	21 42.0	+20.4	52.9	22 18.0	+21.3	53.3	42
43	18 16.0	+15.1	50.2	18 54.3	+15.9	50.5	19 32.4	+16.7	50.7	20 10.3	+17.5	51.0	20 47.9	+18.4	51.3	21 25.3	+19.2	51.6	22 02.4	+20.1	51.9	22 39.3	+20.9	52.2	43
44	18 31.1	+14.8	49.2	19 10.2	+15.6	49.4	19 49.1	+16.5	49.7	20 27.8	+17.3	50.0	21 06.3	+18.0	50.3	21 44.5	+18.9	50.6	22 22.5	+19.7	50.9	23 00.2	+20.5	51.2	44
45	18 45.9	+14.5	48.2	19 25.8	+15.3	48.4	20 05.6	+16.0	48.7	20 45.1	+16.8	49.0	21 24.3	+17.7	49.3	22 03.4	+18.5	49.6	22 42.2	+19.3	49.9	23 20.7	+20.1	50.2	45
46	19 00.4	+14.1	47.1	19 41.1	+14.9	47.4	20 21.6	+15.7	47.7	21 01.9	+16.5	47.9	21 42.0	+17.3	48.2	22 21.9	+18.0	48.5	23 01.5	+18.9	48.8	23 40.8	+19.7	49.2	46
47	19 14.5	+13.8	46.1	19 56.0	+14.6	46.4	20 37.3	+15.3	46.6	21 18.4	+16.1	46.9	21 59.3	+16.9	47.2	22 39.9	+17.7	47.5	23 20.4	+18.4	47.8	24 00.5	+19.3	48.1	47
48	19 28.3	+13.4	45.1	20 10.6	+14.1	45.3	20 52.6	+15.0	45.6	21 34.5	+15.8	45.9	22 16.2	+16.5	46.2	22 57.6	+17.3	46.5	23 38.8	+18.1	46.8	24 19.8	+18.9	47.1	48
49	19 41.7	+13.1	44.0	20 24.7	+13.9	44.3	21 07.6	+14.6	44.6	21 50.3	+15.3	44.8	22 32.7	+16.1	45.1	23 14.9	+16.9	45.4	23 56.9	+17.7	45.7	24 38.7	+18.4	46.1	49
50	19 54.8	+12.7	43.0	20 38.6	+13.4	43.3	21 22.2	+14.2	43.5	22 05.6	+14.9	43.8	22 48.8	+15.7	44.1	23 31.8	+16.4	44.4	24 14.6	+17.2	44.7	24 57.1	+18.0	45.0	50
51	20 07.5	+12.3	42.0	20 52.0	+13.1	42.2	21 36.4	+13.8	42.5	22 20.5	+14.6	42.7	23 04.5	+15.3	43.0	23 48.2	+16.1	43.3	24 31.8	+16.7	43.6	25 15.1	+17.5	44.0	51
52	20 19.8	+12.0	40.9	21 05.1	+12.7	41.2	21 50.2	+13.4	41.4	22 35.1	+14.1	41.7	23 19.8	+14.8	42.0	24 04.3	+15.5	42.3	24 48.5	+16.4	42.6	25 32.6	+17.1	42.9	52
53	20 31.8	+11.6	39.9	21 17.8	+12.2	40.1	22 03.6	+12.9	40.4	22 49.2	+13.7	40.6	23 34.6	+14.4	40.9	24 19.8	+15.2	41.2	25 04.9	+15.8	41.5	25 49.7	+16.6	41.8	53
54	20 43.4	+11.2	38.8	21 30.0	+11.9	39.1	22 16.5	+12.6	39.3	23 02.9	+13.3	39.6	23 49.0	+14.0	39.9	24 35.0	+14.7	40.2	25 20.7	+15.5	40.5	26 06.3	+16.1	40.8	54
55	20 54.6	+10.8	37.8	21 41.9	+11.5	38.0	22 29.1	+12.2	38.3	23 16.2	+12.8	38.5	24 03.0	+13.6	38.8	24 49.7	+14.2	39.1	25 36.2	+14.9	39.4	26 22.4	+15.7	39.7	55
56	21 05.4	+10.4	36.7	21 53.4	+11.1	37.0	22 41.3	+11.8	37.2	23 29.0	+12.4	37.5	24 16.6	+13.0	37.7	25 03.9	+13.8	38.0	25 51.1	+14.5	38.3	26 38.1	+15.1	38.6	56
57	21 15.8	+10.1	35.7	22 04.5	+10.7	35.9	22 53.1	+11.3	36.1	23 41.4	+12.0	36.4	24 29.6	+12.7	36.7	25 17.7	+13.3	36.9	26 05.6	+13.9	37.2	26 53.2	+14.7	37.5	57
58	21 25.9	+9.6	34.6	22 15.2	+10.3	34.8	23 04.4	+10.9	35.1	23 53.4	+11.5	35.3	24 42.3	+12.2	35.6	25 31.0	+12.8	35.9	26 19.5	+13.5	36.1	27 07.9	+14.2	36.4	58
59	21 35.5	+9.2	33.5	22 25.5	+9.8	33.8	23 15.3	+10.4	34.0	24 04.9	+11.1	34.2	24 54.5	+11.7	34.5	25 43.8	+12.4	34.8	26 33.0	+13.0	35.1	27 22.1	+13.6	35.3	59
60	21 44.7	+8.9	32.5	22 35.3	+9.4	32.7	23 25.7	+10.0	32.9	24 16.0	+10.6	33.2	25 06.2	+11.2	33.4	25 56.2	+11.8	33.7	26 46.0	+12.5	34.0	27 35.7	+13.1	34.2	60
61	21 53.6	+8.4	31.4	22 44.7	+9.0	31.6	23 35.7	+9.6	31.9	24 26.6	+10.2	32.1	25 17.4	+10.8	32.3	26 08.0	+11.4	32.6	26 58.5	+12.0	32.9	27 48.8	+12.6	33.1	61
62	22 02.0	+8.0	30.3	22 53.7	+8.6	30.6	23 45.3	+9.1	30.8	24 36.8	+9.7	31.0	25 28.2	+10.2	31.2	26 19.4	+10.9	31.5	27 10.5	+11.4	31.8	28 01.4	+12.1	32.0	62
63	22 10.0	+7.6	29.3	23 02.3	+8.1	29.5	23 54.4	+8.7	29.7	24 46.5	+9.2	29.9	25 38.4	+9.8	30.2	26 30.3	+10.3	30.4	27 21.9	+11.0	30.7	28 13.5	+11.5	30.9	63
64	22 17.6	+7.1	28.2	23 10.4	+7.7	28.4	24 03.1	+8.2	28.6	24 55.7	+8.8	28.8	25 48.2	+9.3	29.1	26 40.6	+9.9	29.3	27 32.9	+10.4	29.6	28 25.0	+11.0	29.8	64
65	22 24.7	+6.7	27.1	23 18.1	+7.2	27.3	24 11.3	+7.8	27.5	25 04.5	+8.2	27.7	25 57.5	+8.8	28.0	26 50.5	+9.3	28.2	27 43.3	+9.8	28.4	28 36.0	+10.4	28.7	65
66	22 31.4	+6.3	26.1	23 25.3	+6.8	26.2	24 19.1	+7.2	26.4	25 12.7	+7.8	26.6	26 06.3	+8.3	26.9	26 59.8	+8.8	27.1	27 53.1	+9.4	27.3	28 46.4	+9.9	27.6	66
67	22 37.7	+5.9	25.0	23 32.1	+6.3	25.2	24 26.3	+6.9	25.3	25 20.5	+7.3	25.5	26 14.6	+7.8	25.8	27 08.6	+8.3	26.0	28 02.5	+8.8	26.2	28 56.3	+9.3	26.4	67
68	22 43.6	+5.4	23.9	23 38.4	+5.9	24.1	24 33.2	+6.3	24.3	25 27.8	+6.8	24.5	26 22.4	+7.3	24.7	27 16.9	+7.7	24.9	28 11.3	+8.2	25.1	29 05.6	+8.7	25.3	68
69	22 49.0	+5.0	22.8	23 44.3	+5.4	23.0	24 39.5	+5.9	23.2	25 34.6	+6.3	23.3	26 29.7	+6.7	23.5	27 24.6	+7.2	23.7	28 19.5	+7.7	24.0	29 14.3	+8.1	24.2	69
70	22 54.0	+4.6	21.7	23 49.7	+5.0	21.9	24 45.4	+5.3	22.1	25 40.9	+5.8	22.2	26 36.4	+6.3	22.4	27 31.8	+6.7	22.6	28 27.2	+7.1	22.8	29 22.4	+7.6	23.0	70
71	22 58.6	+4.1	20.7	23 54.7	+4.5	20.8	24 50.7	+4.9	21.0	25 46.7	+5.3	21.1	26 42.7	+5.7	21.3	27 38.5	+6.2	21.5	28 34.3	+6.6	21.7	29 30.0	+7.0	21.9	71
72	23 02.7	+3.7	19.6	23 59.2	+4.0	19.7	24 55.6	+4.5	19.9	25 52.0	+4.8	20.0	26 48.4	+5.2	20.2	27 44.7	+5.5	20.4	28 40.9	+6.0	20.6	29 37.0	+6.4	20.8	72
73	23 06.4	+3.2	18.5	24 03.2	+3.6	18.6	25 00.1	+3.9	18.8	25 56.8	+4.3	18.9	26 53.6	+4.6	19.1	27 50.2	+5.1	19.3	28 46.9	+5.4	19.4	29 43.4	+5.8	19.6	73
74	23 09.6	+2.8	17.4	24 06.8	+3.1	17.5	25 04.0	+3.4	17.7	26 01.1	+3.8	17.8	26 58.2	+4.2	18.0	27 55.3	+4.5	18.1	28 52.3	+4.8	18.3	29 49.2	+5.2	18.5	74
75	23 12.4	+2.3	16.3	24 09.9	+2.7	16.4	25 07.4	+3.0	16.6	26 04.9	+3.3	16.7	27 02.4	+3.6	16.9	27 59.8	+3.9	17.0	28 57.1	+4.3	17.2	29 54.4	+4.7	17.3	75
76	23 14.7	+1.9	15.2	24 12.6	+2.1	15.3	25 10.4	+2.5	15.5	26 08.2	+2.8	15.6	27 06.0	+3.1	15.7	28 03.7	+3.4	15.9	29 01.4	+3.7	16.0	29 59.1	+4.0	16.2	76
77	23 16.6	+1.4	14.1	24 14.7	+1.7	14.2	25 12.9	+1.9	14.4	26 11.0	+2.2	14.5	27 09.1	+2.5	14.6	28 07.1	+2.8	14.7	29 05.1	+3.1	14.9	30 03.1	+3.4	15.0	77
78	23 18.0	+1.0	13.1	24 16.4	+1.3	13.2	25 14.8	+1.5	13.3	26 13.2	+1.8	13.4	27 11.6	+2.0	13.5	28 09.9	+2.3	13.6	29 08.2	+2.6	13.7	30 06.5	+2.8	13.9	78
79	23 19.0	+0.5	12.0	24 17.7	+0.7	12.1	25 16.3	+1.0	12.2	26 15.0	+1.2	12.3	27 13.6	+1.4	12.4	28 12.2	+1.7	12.5	29 10.8	+1.9	12.6	30 09.3	+2.2	12.7	79
80	23 19.5	+0.1	10.9	24 18.4	+0.3	11.0	25 17.3	+0.5	11.0	26 16.2	+0.7	11.1	27 15.0	+1.0	11.2	28 13.9	+1.1	11.3	29 12.7	+1.4	11.4	30 11.5	+1.6	11.6	80
81	23 19.6	−0.4	9.8	24 18.7	−0.2	9.9	25 17.8	0.0	9.9	26 16.9	+0.2	10.0	27 16.0	+0.3	10.1	28 15.0	+0.6	10.2	29 14.1	+0.7	10.3	30 13.1	+1.0	10.4	81
82	23 19.2	−0.8	8.7	24 18.5	−0.7	8.8	25 17.8	−0.5	8.8	26 17.1	−0.4	8.9	27 16.3	−0.1	9.0	28 15.6	0.0	9.1	29 14.8	+0.2	9.2	30 14.1	+0.3	9.2	82
83	23 18.4	−1.3	7.6	24 17.8	−1.1	7.7	25 17.3	−1.0	7.7	26 16.7	−0.8	7.8	27 16.2	−0.7	7.9	28 15.6	−0.5	7.9	29 15.0	−0.4	8.0	30 14.4	−0.2	8.1	83
84	23 17.1	−1.7	6.5	24 16.7	−1.6	6.6	25 16.3	−1.5	6.6	26 15.9	−1.4	6.7	27 15.5	−1.2	6.7	28 15.1	−1.1	6.8	29 14.6	−0.9	6.9	30 14.2	−0.8	6.9	84
85	23 15.4	−2.2	5.4	24 15.1	−2.1	5.5	25 14.8	−2.0	5.5	26 14.5	−1.8	5.6	27 14.3	−1.8	5.6	28 14.0	−1.7	5.7	29 13.7	−1.6	5.7	30 13.4	−1.5	5.8	85
86	23 13.2	−2.6	4.3	24 13.0	−2.5	4.4	25 12.8	−2.4	4.4	26 12.7	−2.4	4.4	27 12.5	−2.3	4.5	28 12.3	−2.2	4.5	29 12.1	−2.2	4.6	30 11.9	−2.1	4.6	86
87	23 10.6	−3.1	3.3	24 10.5	−3.1	3.3	25 10.4	−3.0	3.3	26 10.3	−2.9	3.3	27 10.2	−2.9	3.4	28 10.1	−2.8	3.4	29 09.9	−2.7	3.4	30 09.8	−2.6	3.5	87
88	23 07.5	−3.5	2.2	24 07.4	−3.4	2.2	25 07.4	−3.5	2.2	26 07.4	−3.5	2.2	27 07.3	−3.4	2.2	28 07.3	−3.4	2.3	29 07.2	−3.3	2.3	30 07.2	−3.3	2.3	88
89	23 04.0	−4.0	1.1	24 04.0	−4.0	1.1	25 03.9	−3.9	1.1	26 03.9	−3.9	1.1	27 03.9	−3.9	1.1	28 03.9	−3.9	1.1	29 03.9	−3.9	1.1	30 03.9	−3.9	1.2	89
90	23 00.0	−4.4	0.0	24 00.0	−4.4	0.0	25 00.0	−4.4	0.0	26 00.0	−4.4	0.0	27 00.0	−4.5	0.0	28 00.0	−4.5	0.0	29 00.0	−4.5	0.0	30 00.0	−4.5	0.0	90
	23°			24°			25°			26°			27°			28°			29°			30°			

86°, 274° L.H.A. LATITUDE SAME NAME AS DECLINATION

356

LATITUDE **CONTRARY** NAME TO DECLINATION   L.H.A. 86°, 274°

Dec.	23° Hc	d	Z	24° Hc	d	Z	25° Hc	d	Z	26° Hc	d	Z	27° Hc	d	Z	28° Hc	d	Z	29° Hc	d	Z	30° Hc	d	Z	Dec.
°	° ′	′	°	° ′	′	°	° ′	′	°	° ′	′	°	° ′	′	°	° ′	′	°	° ′	′	°	° ′	′	°	°
0	3 40.9	−23.5	91.6	3 39.2	−24.5	91.6	3 37.5	−25.5	91.7	3 35.7	−26.4	91.8	3 33.8	−27.3	91.8	3 31.9	−28.3	91.9	3 29.9	−29.2	91.9	3 27.8	−30.1	92.0	0
1	3 17.4	−23.6	92.5	3 14.7	−24.5	92.5	3 12.0	−25.4	92.6	3 09.3	−26.4	92.7	3 06.5	−27.4	92.7	3 03.6	−28.3	92.8	3 00.7	−29.2	92.8	2 57.7	−30.1	92.9	1
2	2 53.8	−23.6	93.4	2 50.2	−24.6	93.5	2 46.6	−25.6	93.5	2 42.9	−26.5	93.6	2 39.1	−27.4	93.6	2 35.3	−28.3	93.6	2 31.5	−29.2	93.7	2 27.6	−30.1	93.7	2
3	2 30.2	−23.7	94.3	2 25.6	−24.6	94.4	2 21.0	−25.5	94.4	2 16.4	−26.5	94.5	2 11.7	−27.4	94.5	2 07.0	−28.3	94.5	2 02.3	−29.3	94.6	1 57.5	−30.2	94.6	3
4	2 06.5	−23.7	95.2	2 01.0	−24.6	95.3	1 55.5	−25.6	95.3	1 49.9	−26.5	95.4	1 44.3	−27.5	95.4	1 38.7	−28.4	95.4	1 33.0	−29.3	95.4	1 27.3	−30.2	95.5	4
5	1 42.8	−23.7	96.2	1 36.4	−24.7	96.2	1 29.9	−25.6	96.2	1 23.4	−26.6	96.2	1 16.8	−27.4	96.3	1 10.3	−28.4	96.3	1 03.7	−29.3	96.3	0 57.1	−30.2	96.3	5
6	1 19.1	−23.7	97.1	1 11.7	−24.7	97.1	1 04.3	−25.6	97.1	0 56.8	−26.5	97.1	0 49.4	−27.5	97.2	0 41.9	−28.4	97.2	0 34.4	−29.3	97.2	0 26.9	−30.2	97.2	6
7	0 55.4	−23.7	98.0	0 47.0	−24.7	98.0	0 38.7	−25.7	98.0	0 30.3	−26.6	98.0	0 21.9	−27.5	98.0	0 13.5	−28.4	98.1	0 05.1	−29.4	98.1	0 03.3	+30.3	81.9	7
8	0 31.7	−23.8	98.9	0 22.3	−24.7	98.9	0 13.0	−25.6	98.9	0 03.7	−26.6	98.9	0 05.6	+27.5	81.1	0 14.9	+28.4	81.1	0 24.3	+29.3	81.1	0 33.6	+30.2	81.1	8
9	0 07.9	−23.8	99.8	0 02.4	+24.7	80.2	0 12.6	+25.7	80.2	0 22.9	+26.5	80.2	0 33.1	+27.5	80.2	0 43.3	+28.4	80.2	0 53.6	+29.3	80.2	1 03.8	+30.2	80.2	9
10	0 15.9	+23.7	79.2	0 27.1	+24.7	79.2	0 38.3	+25.6	79.3	0 49.4	+26.6	79.3	1 00.6	+27.5	79.3	1 11.7	+28.4	79.3	1 22.9	+29.2	79.3	1 34.0	+30.1	79.4	10
11	0 39.6	+23.8	78.3	0 51.8	+24.6	78.3	1 03.9	+25.6	78.4	1 16.0	+26.5	78.4	1 28.1	+27.4	78.4	1 40.1	+28.4	78.4	1 52.1	+29.3	78.5	2 04.1	+30.2	78.5	11
12	1 03.4	+23.7	77.4	1 16.4	+24.7	77.4	1 29.5	+25.6	77.4	1 42.5	+26.5	77.5	1 55.5	+27.4	77.5	2 08.5	+28.3	77.5	2 21.4	+29.2	77.6	2 34.3	+30.1	77.6	12
13	1 27.1	+23.7	76.5	1 41.1	+24.6	76.5	1 55.1	+25.5	76.5	2 09.0	+26.5	76.6	2 22.9	+27.4	76.6	2 36.8	+28.3	76.7	2 50.6	+29.2	76.7	3 04.4	+30.1	76.8	13
14	1 50.8	+23.7	75.6	2 05.7	+24.6	75.6	2 20.6	+25.6	75.6	2 35.5	+26.4	75.7	2 50.3	+27.4	75.7	3 05.1	+28.2	75.8	3 19.8	+29.1	75.8	3 34.5	+30.0	75.9	14
15	2 14.5	+23.6	74.6	2 30.3	+24.6	74.7	2 46.2	+25.4	74.7	3 01.9	+26.4	74.8	3 17.7	+27.3	74.8	3 33.3	+28.2	74.9	3 48.9	+29.1	75.0	4 04.5	+29.9	75.0	15
16	2 38.1	+23.6	73.7	2 54.9	+24.5	73.8	3 11.6	+25.5	73.8	3 28.3	+26.4	73.9	3 45.0	+27.2	73.9	4 01.5	+28.2	74.0	4 18.0	+29.0	74.1	4 34.4	+29.9	74.2	16
17	3 01.7	+23.6	72.8	3 19.4	+24.5	72.9	3 37.1	+25.4	72.9	3 54.7	+26.3	73.0	4 12.2	+27.2	73.0	4 29.7	+28.0	73.1	4 47.0	+29.0	73.2	5 04.3	+29.9	73.3	17
18	3 25.3	+23.5	71.9	3 43.9	+24.4	71.9	4 02.5	+25.3	72.0	4 21.0	+26.2	72.1	4 39.4	+27.1	72.2	4 57.7	+28.0	72.2	5 16.0	+28.9	72.3	5 34.2	+29.7	72.4	18
19	3 48.8	+23.4	71.0	4 08.3	+24.4	71.0	4 27.8	+25.2	71.1	4 47.2	+26.1	71.2	5 06.5	+27.0	71.3	5 25.7	+28.0	71.3	5 44.9	+28.8	71.4	6 03.9	+29.7	71.5	19
20	4 12.2	+23.4	70.0	4 32.7	+24.2	70.1	4 53.0	+25.2	70.2	5 13.3	+26.1	70.3	5 33.5	+27.0	70.4	5 53.7	+27.8	70.5	6 13.7	+28.7	70.6	6 33.6	+29.6	70.7	20
21	4 35.6	+23.3	69.1	4 56.9	+24.2	69.2	5 18.2	+25.1	69.3	5 39.4	+26.0	69.4	6 00.5	+26.9	69.5	6 21.5	+27.7	69.6	6 42.4	+28.6	69.7	7 03.2	+29.5	69.8	21
22	4 58.9	+23.2	68.2	5 21.1	+24.2	68.3	5 43.3	+25.0	68.4	6 05.4	+25.9	68.5	6 27.4	+26.7	68.6	6 49.2	+27.7	68.7	7 11.0	+28.5	68.8	7 32.7	+29.3	68.9	22
23	5 22.1	+23.2	67.3	5 45.3	+24.0	67.4	6 08.3	+24.9	67.5	6 31.3	+25.8	67.6	6 54.1	+26.7	67.7	7 16.9	+27.5	67.8	7 39.5	+28.4	67.9	8 02.0	+29.3	68.0	23
24	5 45.3	+23.0	66.3	6 09.3	+23.9	66.4	6 33.2	+24.9	66.5	6 57.1	+25.7	66.6	7 20.8	+26.6	66.8	7 44.4	+27.5	66.9	8 07.9	+28.3	67.0	8 31.3	+29.1	67.1	24
25	6 08.3	+23.0	65.4	6 33.2	+23.9	65.5	6 58.1	+24.7	65.6	7 22.8	+25.6	65.7	7 47.4	+26.4	65.9	8 11.9	+27.3	66.0	8 36.2	+28.2	66.1	9 00.4	+29.0	66.3	25
26	6 31.3	+22.8	64.5	6 57.1	+23.7	64.6	7 22.8	+24.6	64.7	7 48.4	+25.4	64.8	8 13.8	+26.3	64.9	8 39.2	+27.1	65.1	9 04.4	+28.0	65.2	9 29.4	+28.9	65.4	26
27	6 54.1	+22.8	63.6	7 20.8	+23.6	63.7	7 47.4	+24.5	63.8	8 13.8	+25.4	63.9	8 40.1	+26.2	64.0	9 06.3	+27.1	64.2	9 32.4	+27.9	64.3	9 58.3	+28.8	64.5	27
28	7 16.9	+22.6	62.6	7 44.4	+23.5	62.7	8 11.9	+24.3	62.9	8 39.2	+25.2	63.0	9 06.3	+26.1	63.1	9 33.4	+26.9	63.3	10 00.3	+27.8	63.4	10 27.1	+28.6	63.6	28
29	7 39.5	+22.5	61.7	8 07.9	+23.4	61.8	8 36.2	+24.2	61.9	9 04.4	+25.0	62.1	9 32.4	+25.9	62.2	10 00.3	+26.8	62.4	10 28.1	+27.6	62.5	10 55.7	+28.4	62.7	29
30	8 02.0	+22.4	60.7	8 31.3	+23.2	60.9	9 00.4	+24.1	61.0	9 29.4	+25.0	61.2	9 58.3	+25.8	61.3	10 27.1	+26.6	61.5	10 55.7	+27.4	61.6	11 24.1	+28.3	61.8	30
31	8 24.4	+22.3	59.8	8 54.5	+23.1	59.9	9 24.5	+24.0	60.1	9 54.4	+24.8	60.2	10 24.1	+25.6	60.4	10 53.7	+26.4	60.5	11 23.1	+27.3	60.7	11 52.4	+28.1	60.9	31
32	8 46.7	+22.1	58.9	9 17.6	+23.0	59.0	9 48.5	+23.7	59.2	10 19.2	+24.6	59.3	10 49.7	+25.5	59.5	11 20.1	+26.3	59.6	11 50.4	+27.1	59.8	12 20.5	+27.9	60.0	32
33	9 08.8	+21.9	57.9	9 40.6	+22.8	58.1	10 12.2	+23.7	58.2	10 43.8	+24.4	58.4	11 15.2	+25.2	58.5	11 46.4	+26.1	58.7	12 17.5	+26.9	58.9	12 48.4	+27.7	59.1	33
34	9 30.7	+21.9	57.0	10 03.4	+22.6	57.1	10 35.9	+23.4	57.3	11 08.2	+24.3	57.4	11 40.4	+25.1	57.6	12 12.5	+25.9	57.8	12 44.4	+26.7	58.0	13 16.1	+27.5	58.2	34
35	9 52.6	+21.6	56.0	10 26.0	+22.5	56.2	10 59.3	+23.3	56.3	11 32.5	+24.1	56.5	12 05.5	+24.9	56.7	12 38.4	+25.7	56.9	13 11.1	+26.5	57.1	13 43.6	+27.4	57.3	35
36	10 14.2	+21.5	55.1	10 48.5	+22.3	55.2	11 22.6	+23.1	55.4	11 56.6	+23.9	55.6	12 30.4	+24.8	55.8	13 04.1	+25.5	55.9	13 37.6	+26.4	56.1	14 11.0	+27.1	56.3	36
37	10 35.7	+21.3	54.1	11 10.8	+22.1	54.3	11 45.7	+22.9	54.5	12 20.5	+23.7	54.6	12 55.2	+24.5	54.8	13 29.6	+25.4	55.0	14 04.0	+26.1	55.2	14 38.1	+26.9	55.4	37
38	10 57.0	+21.2	53.2	11 32.9	+21.9	53.4	12 08.6	+22.8	53.5	12 44.2	+23.6	53.7	13 19.7	+24.3	53.9	13 55.0	+25.1	54.1	14 30.1	+25.9	54.3	15 05.0	+26.7	54.5	38
39	11 18.2	+20.9	52.2	11 54.8	+21.8	52.4	12 31.4	+22.5	52.6	13 07.8	+23.3	52.8	13 44.0	+24.1	52.9	14 20.1	+24.9	53.1	14 56.0	+25.6	53.4	15 31.7	+26.4	53.6	39
40	11 39.1	+20.8	51.3	12 16.6	+21.5	51.4	12 53.9	+22.3	51.6	13 31.1	+23.1	51.8	14 08.1	+23.9	52.0	14 45.0	+24.6	52.2	15 21.6	+25.5	52.4	15 58.1	+26.2	52.6	40
41	11 59.9	+20.6	50.3	12 38.1	+21.4	50.5	13 16.2	+22.1	50.7	13 54.2	+22.9	50.9	14 32.0	+23.6	51.1	15 09.6	+24.4	51.3	15 47.1	+25.2	51.5	16 24.3	+26.0	51.7	41
42	12 20.5	+20.3	49.4	12 59.5	+21.1	49.5	13 38.3	+21.9	49.7	14 17.1	+22.6	49.9	14 55.6	+23.4	50.1	15 34.0	+24.2	50.3	16 12.3	+24.9	50.5	16 50.3	+25.7	50.8	42
43	12 40.8	+20.2	48.4	13 20.6	+20.9	48.6	14 00.2	+21.7	48.8	14 39.7	+22.4	48.9	15 19.0	+23.2	49.2	15 58.2	+23.9	49.4	16 37.2	+24.7	49.6	17 16.0	+25.4	49.8	43
44	13 01.0	+19.9	47.4	13 41.5	+20.7	47.6	14 21.9	+21.4	47.8	15 02.1	+22.2	48.0	15 42.2	+22.9	48.2	16 22.1	+23.7	48.4	17 01.9	+24.4	48.6	17 41.4	+25.2	48.9	44
45	13 20.9	+19.8	46.5	14 02.2	+20.5	46.6	14 43.3	+21.2	46.8	15 24.3	+21.9	47.0	16 05.1	+22.7	47.2	16 45.8	+23.4	47.5	17 26.3	+24.1	47.7	18 06.6	+24.9	47.9	45
46	13 40.7	+19.5	45.5	14 22.7	+20.2	45.7	15 04.5	+21.0	45.9	15 46.2	+21.7	46.1	16 27.8	+22.4	46.3	17 09.2	+23.1	46.5	17 50.4	+23.9	46.7	18 31.5	+24.5	47.0	46
47	14 00.2	+19.2	44.5	14 42.9	+20.0	44.7	15 25.5	+20.7	44.9	16 07.9	+21.4	45.1	16 50.2	+22.1	45.3	17 32.3	+22.8	45.5	18 14.3	+23.5	45.8	18 56.0	+24.3	46.0	47
48	14 19.4	+19.1	43.5	15 02.9	+19.7	43.7	15 46.2	+20.4	43.9	16 29.3	+21.1	44.1	17 12.3	+21.8	44.3	17 55.1	+22.6	44.5	18 37.8	+23.3	44.8	19 20.3	+24.0	45.0	48
49	14 38.5	+18.7	42.6	15 22.6	+19.5	42.7	16 06.6	+20.1	42.9	16 50.4	+20.9	43.1	17 34.1	+21.6	43.4	18 17.7	+22.2	43.6	19 01.1	+22.9	43.8	19 44.3	+23.6	44.1	49
50	14 57.2	+18.6	41.6	15 42.1	+19.2	41.8	16 26.7	+19.9	42.0	17 11.3	+20.6	42.2	17 55.7	+21.2	42.4	18 39.9	+22.0	42.6	19 24.0	+22.7	42.8	20 07.9	+23.4	43.1	50
51	15 15.8	+18.2	40.6	16 01.3	+18.9	40.8	16 46.6	+19.6	41.0	17 31.9	+20.2	41.2	18 16.9	+21.0	41.4	19 01.9	+21.6	41.6	19 46.7	+22.3	41.8	20 31.3	+23.0	42.1	51
52	15 34.0	+18.0	39.6	16 20.2	+18.7	39.8	17 06.2	+19.3	40.0	17 52.1	+20.0	40.2	18 37.9	+20.6	40.4	19 23.5	+21.3	40.6	20 09.0	+22.0	40.9	20 54.3	+22.6	41.1	52
53	15 52.0	+17.8	38.6	16 38.9	+18.3	38.8	17 25.5	+19.1	39.0	18 12.1	+19.7	39.2	18 58.5	+20.4	39.4	19 44.8	+21.0	39.6	20 31.0	+21.6	39.9	21 16.9	+22.3	40.1	53
54	16 09.8	+17.4	37.6	16 57.2	+18.1	37.8	17 44.6	+18.7	38.0	18 31.8	+19.3	38.2	19 18.9	+20.0	38.4	20 05.8	+20.7	38.6	20 52.6	+21.3	38.9	21 39.2	+22.0	39.1	54
55	16 27.2	+17.2	36.6	17 15.3	+17.8	36.8	18 03.3	+18.4	37.0	18 51.1	+19.1	37.2	19 38.9	+19.6	37.4	20 26.5	+20.3	37.6	21 13.9	+20.9	37.9	22 01.2	+21.6	38.1	55
56	16 44.4	+16.9	35.6	17 33.1	+17.5	35.8	18 21.7	+18.1	36.0	19 10.2	+18.7	36.2	19 58.5	+19.4	36.4	20 46.8	+19.9	36.6	21 34.8	+20.6	36.9	22 22.8	+21.2	37.1	56
57	17 01.3	+16.5	34.6	17 50.6	+17.2	34.8	18 39.8	+17.8	35.0	19 28.9	+18.4	35.2	20 17.9	+18.9	35.4	21 06.7	+19.6	35.6	21 55.4	+20.2	35.9	22 44.0	+20.8	36.1	57
58	17 17.8	+16.3	33.6	18 07.8	+16.8	33.8	18 57.6	+17.4	34.0	19 47.3	+18.0	34.2	20 36.8	+18.7	34.4	21 26.3	+19.2	34.6	22 15.6	+19.8	34.8	23 04.8	+20.4	35.1	58
59	17 34.1	+16.0	32.6	18 24.6	+16.6	32.8	19 15.0	+17.1	33.0	20 05.3	+17.7	33.2	20 55.5	+18.2	33.4	21 45.5	+18.8	33.6	22 35.4	+19.5	33.8	23 25.2	+20.0	34.0	59
60	17 50.1	+15.7	31.6	18 41.2	+16.2	31.8	19 32.1	+16.8	32.0	20 23.0	+17.3	32.1	21 13.7	+17.9	32.4	22 04.3	+18.5	32.6	22 54.9	+19.0	32.8	23 45.2	+19.6	33.0	60
61	18 05.8	+15.3	30.6	18 57.4	+15.8	30.8	19 48.9	+16.4	30.9	20 40.3	+17.0	31.1	21 31.6	+17.5	31.3	22 22.8	+18.1	31.5	23 13.9	+18.6	31.8	24 04.8	+19.2	32.0	61
62	18 21.1	+15.0	29.6	19 13.2	+15.6	29.7	20 05.3	+16.1	29.9	20 57.3	+16.6	30.1	21 49.1	+17.1	30.3	22 40.9	+17.6	30.5	23 32.5	+18.2	30.7	24 24.0	+18.8	30.9	62
63	18 36.1	+14.7	28.5	19 28.8	+15.2	28.7	20 21.4	+15.7	28.9	21 13.9	+16.2	29.1	22 06.2	+16.8	29.3	22 58.5	+17.3	29.5	23 50.7	+17.8	29.7	24 42.8	+18.3	29.9	63
64	18 50.8	+14.4	27.5	19 44.0	+14.8	27.7	20 37.1	+15.3	27.9	21 30.1	+15.8	28.0	22 23.0	+16.3	28.2	23 15.8	+16.9	28.4	24 08.5	+17.4	28.6	25 01.1	+17.9	28.9	64
65	19 05.2	+14.0	26.5	19 58.8	+14.5	26.7	20 52.4	+15.0	26.8	21 45.9	+15.5	27.0	22 39.3	+16.0	27.2	23 32.7	+16.4	27.4	24 25.9	+16.9	27.6	25 19.0	+17.4	27.8	65
66	19 19.2	+13.6	25.5	20 13.3	+14.1	25.6	21 07.4	+14.5	25.8	22 01.4	+15.0	26.0	22 55.3	+15.5	26.1	23 49.1	+16.0	26.3	24 42.8	+16.5	26.5	25 36.4	+17.0	26.7	66
67	19 32.8	+13.3	24.4	20 27.4	+13.8	24.6	21 21.9	+14.2	24.7	22 16.4	+14.6	24.9	23 10.8	+15.1	25.1	24 05.1	+15.5	25.3	24 59.3	+16.0	25.5	25 53.4	+16.5	25.7	67
68	19 46.1	+13.0	23.4	20 41.2	+13.3	23.5	21 36.1	+13.8	23.7	22 31.0	+14.3	23.9	23 25.9	+14.7	24.0	24 20.6	+15.2	24.2	25 15.3	+15.6	24.4	26 09.9	+16.0	24.6	68
69	19 59.1	+12.6	22.4	20 54.5	+13.0	22.5	21 49.9	+13.4	22.7	22 45.3	+13.8	22.8	23 40.6	+14.2	23.0	24 35.8	+14.6	23.2	25 30.9	+15.1	23.3	26 25.9	+15.6	23.5	69
70	20 11.7	+12.2	21.3	21 07.5	+12.6	21.5	22 03.3	+13.0	21.6	22 59.1	+13.4	21.8	23 54.8	+13.8	21.9	24 50.4	+14.2	22.1	25 46.0	+14.6	22.3	26 41.5	+15.0	22.5	70
71	20 23.9	+11.8	20.3	21 20.1	+12.3	20.4	22 16.3	+12.6	20.5	23 12.5	+13.0	20.7	24 08.6	+13.4	20.8	25 04.6	+13.8	21.0	26 00.6	+14.2	21.2	26 56.5	+14.6	21.4	71
72	20 35.7	+11.5	19.2	21 32.4	+11.8	19.4	22 28.9	+12.2	19.5	23 25.5	+12.5	19.6	24 22.0	+12.9	19.8	25 18.4	+13.3	19.9	26 14.8	+13.6	20.1	27 11.1	+14.0	20.3	72
73	20 47.2	+11.1	18.2	21 44.2	+11.4	18.3	22 41.1	+11.8	18.4	23 38.0	+12.1	18.6	24 34.9	+12.4	18.7	25 31.7	+12.8	18.9	26 28.4	+13.2	19.0	27 25.1	+13.6	19.2	73
74	20 58.3	+10.7	17.1	21 55.6	+11.0	17.2	22 52.9	+11.3	17.4	23 50.1	+11.7	17.5	24 47.3	+12.0	17.6	25 44.5	+12.3	17.8	26 41.6	+12.6	17.9	27 38.7	+13.0	18.1	74
75	21 09.0	+10.3	16.1	22 06.6	+10.6	16.2	23 04.2	+10.9	16.3	24 01.8	+11.2	16.4	24 59.3	+11.5	16.6	25 56.8	+11.8	16.7	26 54.2	+12.2	16.8	27 51.7	+12.4	17.0	75
76	21 19.3	+9.9	15.0	22 17.2	+10.2	15.1	23 15.1	+10.5	15.2	24 13.0	+10.7	15.3	25 10.8	+11.1	15.5	26 08.6	+11.4	15.6	27 06.4	+11.6	15.7	28 04.1	+12.0	15.9	76
77	21 29.2	+9.5	14.0	22 27.4	+9.7	14.1	23 25.6	+10.0	14.2	24 23.7	+10.3	14.3	25 21.9	+10.5	14.4	26 20.0	+10.8	14.5	27 18.0	+11.2	14.6	28 16.1	+11.4	14.8	77
78	21 38.7	+9.0	12.9	22 37.1	+9.4	13.0	23 35.6	+9.6	13.1	24 34.0	+9.8	13.2	25 32.4	+10.1	13.3	26 30.8	+10.3	13.4	27 29.2	+10.5	13.5	28 27.5	+10.8	13.6	78
79	21 47.7	+8.7	11.8	22 46.5	+8.9	11.9	23 45.2	+9.1	12.0	24 43.8	+9.4	12.1	25 42.5	+9.6	12.2	26 41.1	+9.9	12.3	27 39.7	+10.1	12.4	28 38.3	+10.3	12.5	79
80	21 56.4	+8.3	10.8	22 55.4	+8.4	10.8	23 54.3	+8.7	10.9	24 53.2	+8.9	11.0	25 52.1	+9.1	11.1	26 51.0	+9.3	11.2	27 49.8	+9.5	11.3	28 48.6	+9.8	11.4	80
81	22 04.7	+7.9	9.7	23 03.8	+8.1	9.8	24 03.0	+8.2	9.8	25 02.1	+8.4	9.9	26 01.2	+8.6	10.0	27 00.3	+8.7	10.1	27 59.3	+9.0	10.2	28 58.4	+9.1	10.3	81
82	22 12.6	+7.4	8.6	23 11.9	+7.6	8.7	24 11.2	+7.7	8.8	25 10.5	+7.9	8.8	26 09.8	+8.0	8.9	27 09.0	+8.3	9.0	28 08.3	+8.4	9.1	29 07.5	+8.6	9.1	82
83	22 20.0	+7.0	7.6	23 19.5	+7.1	7.6	24 18.9	+7.3	7.7	25 18.4	+7.4	7.7	26 17.8	+7.6	7.8	27 17.3	+7.7	7.9	28 16.7	+7.9	7.9	29 16.1	+8.1	8.0	83
84	22 27.0	+6.6	6.5	23 26.6	+6.7	6.5	24 26.2	+6.8	6.6	25 25.8	+7.0	6.6	26 25.4	+7.1	6.7	27 25.0	+7.2	6.7	28 24.6	+7.3	6.8	29 24.2	+7.4	6.9	84
85	22 33.6	+6.1	5.4	23 33.3	+6.3	5.4	24 33.0	+6.4	5.5	25 32.8	+6.4	5.5	26 32.5	+6.5	5.6	27 32.2	+6.7	5.6	28 31.9	+6.8	5.7	29 31.6	+6.9	5.7	85
86	22 39.7	+5.8	4.3	23 39.6	+5.8	4.4	24 39.4	+5.9	4.4	25 39.2	+6.0	4.4	26 39.0	+6.1	4.5	27 38.9	+6.1	4.5	28 38.7	+6.2	4.5	29 38.5	+6.2	4.6	86
87	22 45.5	+5.2	3.2	23 45.4	+5.3	3.3	24 45.3	+5.4	3.3	25 45.2	+5.4	3.3	26 45.1	+5.5	3.4	27 45.0	+5.5	3.4	28 44.9	+5.6	3.4	29 44.7	+5.7	3.4	87
88	22 50.7	+4.9	2.2	23 50.7	+4.9	2.2	24 50.7	+4.9	2.2	25 50.6	+5.0	2.2	26 50.6	+4.9	2.2	27 50.5	+5.0	2.3	28 50.5	+5.0	2.3	29 50.4	+5.1	2.3	88
89	22 55.6	+4.4	1.1	23 55.6	+4.4	1.1	24 55.6	+4.4	1.1	25 55.6	+4.4	1.1	26 55.5	+4.5	1.1	27 55.5	+4.5	1.1	28 55.5	+4.5	1.1	29 55.5	+4.5	1.2	89
90	23 00.0	+4.0	0.0	24 00.0	+4.0	0.0	25 00.0	+3.9	0.0	26 00.0	+3.9	0.0	27 00.0	+3.9	0.0	28 00.0	+3.9	0.0	29 00.0	+3.9	0.0	30 00.0	+3.9	0.0	90
	23°			24°			25°			26°			27°			28°			29°			30°			

S. Lat. {L.H.A. greater than 180° ....Zn=180°−Z
{L.H.A. less than 180°...........Zn=180°+Z

LATITUDE **SAME** NAME AS DECLINATION   L.H.A. 94°, 266°

87°, 273° L.H.A. LATITUDE SAME NAME AS DECLINATION N. Lat. {L.H.A. greater than 180° .....Zn=Z; L.H.A. less than 180°............Zn=360°−Z}

Dec.	23° Hc	d	Z	24° Hc	d	Z	25° Hc	d	Z	26° Hc	d	Z	27° Hc	d	Z	28° Hc	d	Z	29° Hc	d	Z	30° Hc	d	Z	Dec.
°	° ′	′	°	° ′	′	°	° ′	′	°	° ′	′	°	° ′	′	°	° ′	′	°	° ′	′	°	° ′	′	°	°
0	2 45.7	+23.4	91.2	2 44.4	+24.4	91.2	2 43.1	+25.4	91.3	2 41.8	+26.3	91.3	2 40.4	+27.2	91.4	2 38.9	+28.2	91.4	2 37.4	+29.1	91.5	2 35.9	+30.0	91.5	0
1	3 09.1	+23.4	90.3	3 08.8	+24.4	90.3	3 08.5	+25.3	90.4	3 08.1	+26.2	90.4	3 07.6	+27.2	90.5	3 07.1	+28.1	90.5	3 06.5	+29.1	90.6	3 05.9	+29.9	90.6	1
2	3 32.5	+23.4	89.3	3 33.2	+24.3	89.4	3 33.8	+25.3	89.5	3 34.3	+26.3	89.5	3 34.8	+27.2	89.6	3 35.2	+28.1	89.6	3 35.6	+29.0	89.7	3 35.8	+30.0	89.8	2
3	3 55.9	+23.3	88.4	3 57.5	+24.3	88.5	3 59.1	+25.2	88.5	4 00.6	+26.1	88.6	4 02.0	+27.1	88.7	4 03.3	+28.0	88.8	4 04.6	+28.9	88.8	4 05.8	+29.8	88.9	3
4	4 19.2	+23.2	87.5	4 21.8	+24.1	87.6	4 24.3	+25.1	87.6	4 26.7	+26.1	87.7	4 29.1	+27.0	87.8	4 31.3	+28.0	87.9	4 33.5	+28.9	87.9	4 35.6	+29.8	88.0	4
5	4 42.4	+23.1	86.6	4 45.9	+24.1	86.6	4 49.4	+25.1	86.7	4 52.8	+26.0	86.8	4 56.1	+26.9	86.9	4 59.3	+27.9	87.0	5 02.4	+28.8	87.1	5 05.4	+29.8	87.2	5
6	5 05.5	+23.1	85.6	5 10.0	+24.1	85.7	5 14.5	+25.0	85.8	5 18.8	+25.9	85.9	5 23.0	+26.9	86.0	5 27.2	+27.8	86.1	5 31.2	+28.8	86.2	5 35.2	+29.6	86.3	6
7	5 28.6	+23.0	84.7	5 34.1	+23.9	84.8	5 39.5	+24.9	84.9	5 44.7	+25.9	85.0	5 49.9	+26.8	85.1	5 55.0	+27.7	85.2	6 00.0	+28.6	85.3	6 04.8	+29.6	85.4	7
8	5 51.6	+22.8	83.8	5 58.0	+23.9	83.9	6 04.4	+24.8	84.0	6 10.6	+25.7	84.1	6 16.7	+26.7	84.2	6 22.7	+27.6	84.3	6 28.6	+28.6	84.4	6 34.4	+29.5	84.5	8
9	6 14.4	+22.8	82.8	6 21.9	+23.7	83.0	6 29.2	+24.7	83.1	6 36.3	+25.7	83.2	6 43.4	+26.6	83.3	6 50.3	+27.6	83.4	6 57.2	+28.4	83.5	7 03.9	+29.3	83.7	9
10	6 37.2	+22.7	81.9	6 45.6	+23.7	82.0	6 53.9	+24.6	82.1	7 02.0	+25.6	82.3	7 10.0	+26.5	82.4	7 17.9	+27.4	82.5	7 25.6	+28.4	82.6	7 33.2	+29.3	82.8	10
11	6 59.9	+22.6	81.0	7 09.3	+23.5	81.1	7 18.5	+24.5	81.2	7 27.6	+25.4	81.4	7 36.5	+26.4	81.5	7 45.3	+27.3	81.6	7 54.0	+28.2	81.8	8 02.5	+29.2	81.9	11
12	7 22.5	+22.4	80.0	7 32.8	+23.4	80.2	7 43.0	+24.3	80.3	7 53.0	+25.3	80.4	8 02.9	+26.2	80.6	8 12.6	+27.2	80.7	8 22.2	+28.1	80.9	8 31.7	+29.0	81.0	12
13	7 44.9	+22.4	79.1	7 56.2	+23.3	79.2	8 07.3	+24.3	79.4	8 18.3	+25.2	79.5	8 29.1	+26.2	79.7	8 39.8	+27.1	79.8	8 50.3	+28.0	80.0	9 00.7	+28.9	80.1	13
14	8 07.3	+22.2	78.2	8 19.5	+23.2	78.3	8 31.6	+24.1	78.5	8 43.5	+25.1	78.6	8 55.3	+26.0	78.8	9 06.9	+26.9	78.9	9 18.3	+27.9	79.1	9 29.6	+28.8	79.2	14
15	8 29.5	+22.1	77.2	8 42.7	+23.0	77.4	8 55.7	+24.0	77.5	9 08.6	+24.9	77.7	9 21.3	+25.8	77.9	9 33.8	+26.8	78.0	9 46.2	+27.7	78.2	9 58.4	+28.6	78.4	15
16	8 51.6	+21.9	76.3	9 05.7	+22.9	76.5	9 19.7	+23.8	76.6	9 33.5	+24.8	76.8	9 47.1	+25.8	76.9	10 00.6	+26.7	77.1	10 13.9	+27.6	77.3	10 27.0	+28.5	77.5	16
17	9 13.5	+21.8	75.4	9 28.6	+22.7	75.5	9 43.5	+23.7	75.7	9 58.3	+24.6	75.8	10 12.9	+25.5	76.0	10 27.3	+26.4	76.2	10 41.5	+27.4	76.4	10 55.5	+28.3	76.6	17
18	9 35.3	+21.6	74.4	9 51.3	+22.6	74.6	10 07.2	+23.5	74.7	10 22.9	+24.5	74.9	10 38.4	+25.4	75.1	10 53.7	+26.4	75.3	11 08.9	+27.2	75.5	11 23.8	+28.2	75.7	18
19	9 56.9	+21.5	73.5	10 13.9	+22.4	73.6	10 30.7	+23.4	73.8	10 47.4	+24.2	74.0	11 03.8	+25.2	74.2	11 20.1	+26.1	74.4	11 36.1	+27.1	74.6	11 52.0	+28.0	74.8	19
20	10 18.4	+21.3	72.5	10 36.3	+22.3	72.7	10 54.1	+23.2	72.9	11 11.6	+24.2	73.1	11 29.0	+25.1	73.3	11 46.2	+26.0	73.4	12 03.2	+26.9	73.7	12 20.0	+27.8	73.9	20
21	10 39.7	+21.1	71.6	10 58.6	+22.0	71.7	11 17.3	+23.0	71.9	11 35.8	+23.9	72.1	11 54.1	+24.9	72.3	12 12.2	+25.8	72.5	12 30.1	+26.7	72.7	12 47.8	+27.6	72.9	21
22	11 00.8	+21.0	70.6	11 20.6	+21.9	70.8	11 40.3	+22.8	71.0	11 59.7	+23.8	71.2	12 19.0	+24.6	71.4	12 38.0	+25.6	71.6	12 56.8	+26.6	71.8	13 15.4	+27.5	72.0	22
23	11 21.8	+20.7	69.7	11 42.5	+21.7	69.8	12 03.1	+22.6	70.0	12 23.5	+23.5	70.2	12 43.6	+24.5	70.5	13 03.6	+25.4	70.7	13 23.4	+26.3	70.9	13 42.9	+27.2	71.1	23
24	11 42.5	+20.6	68.7	12 04.2	+21.5	68.9	12 25.7	+22.5	69.1	12 47.0	+23.4	69.3	13 08.1	+24.3	69.5	13 29.0	+25.2	69.7	13 49.7	+26.1	70.0	14 10.1	+27.0	70.2	24
25	12 03.1	+20.4	67.7	12 25.7	+21.3	67.9	12 48.2	+22.2	68.1	13 10.4	+23.1	68.4	13 32.4	+24.1	68.6	13 54.2	+25.0	68.8	14 15.8	+25.9	69.0	14 37.1	+26.8	69.3	25
26	12 23.5	+20.1	66.8	12 47.0	+21.1	67.0	13 10.4	+22.0	67.2	13 33.5	+23.0	67.4	13 56.5	+23.8	67.6	14 19.2	+24.8	67.9	14 41.7	+25.7	68.1	15 03.9	+26.6	68.4	26
27	12 43.6	+20.0	65.8	13 08.1	+20.9	66.0	13 32.4	+21.8	66.2	13 56.5	+22.7	66.5	14 20.3	+23.7	66.7	14 44.0	+24.5	66.9	15 07.4	+25.4	67.2	15 30.5	+26.3	67.4	27
28	13 03.6	+19.8	64.8	13 29.0	+20.7	65.1	13 54.2	+21.6	65.3	14 19.2	+22.5	65.5	14 44.0	+23.4	65.7	15 08.5	+24.3	66.0	15 32.8	+25.2	66.2	15 56.8	+26.1	66.5	28
29	13 23.4	+19.5	63.9	13 49.7	+20.4	64.1	14 15.8	+21.3	64.3	14 41.7	+22.2	64.5	15 07.4	+23.1	64.8	15 32.8	+24.0	65.0	15 58.0	+24.9	65.3	16 22.9	+25.9	65.6	29
30	13 42.9	+19.3	62.9	14 10.1	+20.2	63.1	14 37.1	+21.1	63.4	15 03.9	+22.0	63.6	15 30.5	+22.9	63.8	15 56.8	+23.8	64.1	16 22.9	+24.7	64.3	16 48.8	+25.6	64.6	30
31	14 02.2	+19.0	61.9	14 30.3	+20.0	62.2	14 58.2	+20.9	62.4	15 25.9	+21.8	62.6	15 53.4	+22.7	62.9	16 20.6	+23.6	63.1	16 47.6	+24.5	63.4	17 14.4	+25.3	63.7	31
32	14 21.2	+18.9	60.9	14 50.3	+19.7	61.2	15 19.1	+20.6	61.4	15 47.7	+21.5	61.7	16 16.1	+22.3	61.9	16 44.2	+23.3	62.2	17 12.1	+24.1	62.4	17 39.7	+25.1	62.7	32
33	14 40.1	+18.5	60.0	15 10.0	+19.4	60.2	15 39.7	+20.3	60.4	16 09.2	+21.2	60.7	16 38.4	+22.2	60.9	17 07.5	+23.0	61.2	17 36.2	+23.9	61.5	18 04.8	+24.7	61.8	33
34	14 58.6	+18.3	59.0	15 29.4	+19.2	59.2	16 00.0	+20.1	59.5	16 30.4	+21.0	59.7	17 00.6	+21.8	60.0	17 30.5	+22.7	60.2	18 00.1	+23.6	60.5	18 29.5	+24.5	60.8	34
35	15 16.9	+18.1	58.0	15 48.6	+19.0	58.2	16 20.1	+19.8	58.5	16 51.4	+20.7	58.7	17 22.4	+21.6	59.0	17 53.2	+22.4	59.3	18 23.7	+23.3	59.6	18 54.0	+24.2	59.8	35
36	15 35.0	+17.8	57.0	16 07.6	+18.6	57.2	16 39.9	+19.6	57.5	17 12.1	+20.4	57.8	17 44.0	+21.2	58.0	18 15.6	+22.1	58.3	18 47.0	+23.0	58.6	19 18.2	+23.8	58.9	36
37	15 52.8	+17.5	56.0	16 26.2	+18.4	56.3	16 59.5	+19.2	56.5	17 32.5	+20.1	56.8	18 05.2	+21.0	57.0	18 37.7	+21.9	57.3	19 10.0	+22.7	57.6	19 42.0	+23.6	57.9	37
38	16 10.3	+17.3	55.0	16 44.6	+18.1	55.3	17 18.7	+18.9	55.5	17 52.6	+19.8	55.8	18 26.2	+20.6	56.0	18 59.6	+21.5	56.3	19 32.7	+22.4	56.6	20 05.6	+23.2	56.9	38
39	16 27.6	+16.9	54.0	17 02.7	+17.8	54.3	17 37.6	+18.7	54.5	18 12.4	+19.4	54.8	18 46.8	+20.4	55.1	19 21.1	+21.2	55.3	19 55.1	+22.0	55.6	20 28.8	+22.9	55.9	39
40	16 44.5	+16.7	53.0	17 20.5	+17.5	53.3	17 56.3	+18.3	53.5	18 31.8	+19.2	53.8	19 07.2	+20.0	54.1	19 42.3	+20.8	54.3	20 17.1	+21.7	54.6	20 51.7	+22.6	55.0	40
41	17 01.2	+16.4	52.0	17 38.0	+17.2	52.3	18 14.6	+18.1	52.5	18 51.0	+18.9	52.8	19 27.2	+19.7	53.1	20 03.1	+20.6	53.4	20 38.8	+21.4	53.6	21 14.3	+22.2	54.0	41
42	17 17.6	+16.0	51.0	17 55.2	+16.9	51.3	18 32.7	+17.7	51.5	19 09.9	+18.5	51.8	19 46.9	+19.3	52.1	20 23.7	+20.1	52.3	21 00.2	+21.0	52.6	21 36.5	+21.8	53.0	42
43	17 33.6	+15.8	50.0	18 12.1	+16.6	50.2	18 50.4	+17.3	50.5	19 28.4	+18.2	50.8	20 06.2	+19.0	51.1	20 43.8	+19.9	51.3	21 21.2	+20.6	51.6	21 58.3	+21.5	52.0	43
44	17 49.4	+15.4	49.0	18 28.7	+16.2	49.2	19 07.7	+17.1	49.5	19 46.6	+17.9	49.8	20 25.2	+18.7	50.0	21 03.7	+19.4	50.3	21 41.8	+20.3	50.6	22 19.8	+21.1	50.9	44
45	18 04.8	+15.2	48.0	18 44.9	+15.9	48.2	19 24.8	+16.7	48.5	20 04.5	+17.5	48.7	20 43.9	+18.3	49.0	21 23.1	+19.1	49.3	22 02.1	+19.9	49.6	22 40.9	+20.7	49.9	45
46	18 20.0	+14.8	47.0	19 00.8	+15.6	47.2	19 41.5	+16.3	47.5	20 22.0	+17.1	47.7	21 02.2	+17.9	48.0	21 42.2	+18.8	48.3	22 22.0	+19.5	48.6	23 01.6	+20.3	48.9	46
47	18 34.8	+14.4	45.9	19 16.4	+15.2	46.2	19 57.8	+16.1	46.4	20 39.1	+16.8	46.7	21 20.1	+17.6	47.0	22 01.0	+18.3	47.3	22 41.5	+19.2	47.6	23 21.9	+19.9	47.9	47
48	18 49.2	+14.2	44.9	19 31.6	+14.9	45.2	20 13.9	+15.6	45.4	20 55.9	+16.4	45.7	21 37.7	+17.2	46.0	22 19.3	+18.0	46.2	23 00.7	+18.7	46.6	23 41.8	+19.5	46.9	48
49	19 03.4	+13.8	43.9	19 46.5	+14.6	44.1	20 29.5	+15.3	44.4	21 12.3	+16.0	44.6	21 54.9	+16.8	44.9	22 37.3	+17.5	45.2	23 19.4	+18.3	45.5	24 01.3	+19.1	45.8	49
50	19 17.2	+13.4	42.8	20 01.1	+14.1	43.1	20 44.8	+14.9	43.3	21 28.3	+15.7	43.6	22 11.7	+16.4	43.9	22 54.8	+17.2	44.2	23 37.7	+17.9	44.5	24 20.4	+18.7	44.8	50
51	19 30.6	+13.1	41.8	20 15.2	+13.8	42.1	20 59.7	+14.5	42.3	21 44.0	+15.2	42.6	22 28.1	+16.0	42.8	23 12.0	+16.7	43.1	23 55.6	+17.5	43.4	24 39.1	+18.2	43.7	51
52	19 43.7	+12.7	40.8	20 29.0	+13.5	41.0	21 14.2	+14.2	41.3	21 59.2	+14.9	41.5	22 44.1	+15.5	41.8	23 28.7	+16.3	42.1	24 13.1	+17.1	42.4	24 57.3	+17.8	42.7	52
53	19 56.4	+12.4	39.7	20 42.5	+13.1	40.0	21 28.4	+13.7	40.2	22 14.1	+14.5	40.5	22 59.6	+15.2	40.8	23 45.0	+15.9	41.0	24 30.2	+16.6	41.3	25 15.1	+17.3	41.6	53
54	20 08.8	+12.0	38.7	20 55.6	+12.6	38.9	21 42.1	+13.4	39.2	22 28.6	+14.0	39.4	23 14.8	+14.8	39.7	24 00.9	+15.4	40.0	24 46.8	+16.1	40.3	25 32.4	+16.9	40.6	54
55	20 20.8	+11.6	37.7	21 08.2	+12.3	37.9	21 55.5	+13.0	38.1	22 42.6	+13.7	38.4	23 29.6	+14.3	38.6	24 16.3	+15.0	38.9	25 02.9	+15.7	39.2	25 49.3	+16.4	39.5	55
56	20 32.4	+11.3	36.6	21 20.5	+11.9	36.8	22 08.5	+12.5	37.1	22 56.3	+13.2	37.3	23 43.9	+13.9	37.6	24 31.3	+14.6	37.9	25 18.6	+15.3	38.2	26 05.7	+15.9	38.4	56
57	20 43.7	+10.9	35.6	21 32.4	+11.5	35.8	22 21.0	+12.2	36.0	23 09.5	+12.8	36.3	23 57.8	+13.4	36.5	24 45.9	+14.1	36.8	25 33.9	+14.7	37.1	26 21.6	+15.5	37.4	57
58	20 54.6	+10.4	34.5	21 43.9	+11.1	34.7	22 33.2	+11.7	35.0	23 22.3	+12.3	35.2	24 11.2	+13.0	35.5	25 00.0	+13.7	35.7	25 48.6	+14.3	36.0	26 37.1	+14.9	36.3	58
59	21 05.0	+10.1	33.5	21 55.0	+10.7	33.7	22 44.9	+11.3	33.9	23 34.6	+12.0	34.1	24 24.2	+12.6	34.4	25 13.7	+13.1	34.6	26 02.9	+13.8	34.9	26 52.0	+14.5	35.2	59
60	21 15.1	+9.7	32.4	22 05.7	+10.3	32.6	22 56.2	+10.9	32.8	23 46.6	+11.4	33.1	24 36.8	+12.1	33.3	25 26.8	+12.7	33.6	26 16.7	+13.4	33.8	27 06.5	+14.0	34.1	60
61	21 24.8	+9.3	31.3	22 16.0	+9.9	31.5	23 07.1	+10.4	31.8	23 58.0	+11.1	32.0	24 48.9	+11.6	32.2	25 39.5	+12.3	32.5	26 30.1	+12.8	32.8	27 20.5	+13.4	33.0	61
62	21 34.1	+8.9	30.3	22 25.9	+9.4	30.5	23 17.5	+10.0	30.7	24 09.1	+10.5	30.9	25 00.5	+11.1	31.2	25 51.8	+11.7	31.4	26 42.9	+12.3	31.7	27 33.9	+12.9	31.9	62
63	21 43.0	+8.5	29.2	22 35.3	+9.0	29.4	23 27.5	+9.6	29.6	24 19.6	+10.1	29.8	25 11.6	+10.7	30.1	26 03.5	+11.2	30.3	26 55.2	+11.8	30.6	27 46.8	+12.4	30.8	63
64	21 51.5	+8.0	28.1	22 44.3	+8.6	28.3	23 37.1	+9.1	28.5	24 29.7	+9.7	28.8	25 22.3	+10.2	29.0	26 14.7	+10.8	29.2	27 07.0	+11.3	29.5	27 59.2	+11.9	29.7	64
65	21 59.5	+7.7	27.1	22 52.9	+8.2	27.3	23 46.2	+8.7	27.5	24 39.4	+9.2	27.7	25 32.5	+9.7	27.9	26 25.5	+10.2	28.1	27 18.3	+10.8	28.4	28 11.1	+11.3	28.6	65
66	22 07.2	+7.2	26.0	23 01.1	+7.7	26.2	23 54.9	+8.2	26.4	24 48.6	+8.7	26.6	25 42.2	+9.2	26.8	26 35.7	+9.7	27.0	27 29.1	+10.2	27.2	28 22.4	+10.7	27.5	66
67	22 14.4	+6.8	24.9	23 08.8	+7.3	25.1	24 03.1	+7.7	25.3	24 57.3	+8.2	25.5	25 51.4	+8.7	25.7	26 45.4	+9.2	25.9	27 39.3	+9.7	26.1	28 33.1	+10.3	26.4	67
68	22 21.2	+6.4	23.9	23 16.1	+6.8	24.0	24 10.8	+7.3	24.2	25 05.5	+7.8	24.4	26 00.1	+8.2	24.6	26 54.6	+8.7	24.8	27 49.0	+9.2	25.0	28 43.4	+9.6	25.3	68
69	22 27.6	+6.0	22.8	23 22.9	+6.4	22.9	24 18.1	+6.8	23.1	25 13.3	+7.2	23.3	26 08.3	+7.7	23.5	27 03.3	+8.2	23.7	27 58.2	+8.6	23.9	28 53.0	+9.1	24.1	69
70	22 33.6	+5.5	21.7	23 29.3	+5.9	21.9	24 24.9	+6.4	22.0	25 20.5	+6.8	22.2	26 16.0	+7.2	22.4	27 11.5	+7.6	22.6	28 06.8	+8.1	22.8	29 02.1	+8.5	23.0	70
71	22 39.1	+5.1	20.6	23 35.2	+5.5	20.8	24 31.3	+5.9	20.9	25 27.3	+6.3	21.1	26 23.2	+6.7	21.3	27 19.1	+7.1	21.5	28 14.9	+7.5	21.7	29 10.6	+8.0	21.9	71
72	22 44.2	+4.6	19.5	23 40.7	+5.0	19.7	24 37.2	+5.4	19.8	25 33.6	+5.8	20.0	26 29.9	+6.2	20.2	27 26.2	+6.6	20.3	28 22.4	+7.0	20.5	29 18.6	+7.4	20.7	72
73	22 48.8	+4.3	18.5	23 45.7	+4.6	18.6	24 42.6	+4.9	18.7	25 39.4	+5.3	18.9	26 36.1	+5.7	19.1	27 32.8	+6.0	19.2	28 29.4	+6.4	19.4	29 26.0	+6.8	19.6	73
74	22 53.1	+3.7	17.4	23 50.3	+4.1	17.5	24 47.5	+4.4	17.7	25 44.7	+4.7	17.8	26 41.8	+5.1	17.9	27 38.8	+5.5	18.1	28 35.8	+5.9	18.3	29 32.8	+6.2	18.4	74
75	22 56.8	+3.4	16.3	23 54.4	+3.7	16.4	24 51.9	+4.0	16.6	25 49.4	+4.3	16.7	26 46.9	+4.6	16.8	27 44.3	+4.9	17.0	28 41.7	+5.2	17.1	29 39.0	+5.6	17.3	75
76	23 00.2	+2.9	15.2	23 58.1	+3.1	15.3	24 55.9	+3.5	15.5	25 53.7	+3.8	15.6	26 51.5	+4.1	15.7	27 49.2	+4.4	15.9	28 46.9	+4.7	16.0	29 44.6	+5.0	16.2	76
77	23 03.1	+2.4	14.1	24 01.2	+2.8	14.2	24 59.4	+3.0	14.4	25 57.5	+3.3	14.5	26 55.6	+3.5	14.6	27 53.6	+3.9	14.7	28 51.6	+4.2	14.9	29 49.6	+4.4	15.0	77
78	23 05.5	+2.0	13.0	24 04.0	+2.2	13.1	25 02.4	+2.5	13.2	26 00.8	+2.7	13.4	26 59.1	+3.0	13.5	27 57.5	+3.2	13.6	28 55.8	+3.5	13.7	29 54.0	+3.9	13.9	78
79	23 07.5	+1.6	12.0	24 06.2	+1.8	12.0	25 04.9	+2.0	12.1	26 03.5	+2.3	12.2	27 02.1	+2.5	12.4	28 00.7	+2.8	12.5	28 59.3	+3.0	12.6	29 57.9	+3.2	12.7	79
80	23 09.1	+1.1	10.9	24 08.0	+1.3	11.0	25 06.9	+1.5	11.0	26 05.8	+1.7	11.1	27 04.6	+2.0	11.2	28 03.5	+2.1	11.3	29 02.3	+2.4	11.4	30 01.1	+2.6	11.6	80
81	23 10.2	+0.6	9.8	24 09.3	+0.9	9.9	25 08.4	+1.0	9.9	26 07.5	+1.2	10.0	27 06.6	+1.4	10.1	28 05.6	+1.7	10.2	29 04.7	+1.8	10.3	30 03.7	+2.0	10.4	81
82	23 10.8	+0.3	8.7	24 10.2	+0.3	8.8	25 09.4	+0.6	8.8	26 08.7	+0.7	8.9	27 08.0	+0.9	9.0	28 07.3	+1.0	9.1	29 06.5	+1.2	9.2	30 05.7	+1.4	9.2	82
83	23 11.1	−0.3	7.6	24 10.5	−0.1	7.7	25 10.0	0.0	7.7	26 09.4	+0.2	7.8	27 08.9	+0.3	7.9	28 08.3	+0.5	7.9	29 07.7	+0.7	8.0	30 07.1	+0.8	8.1	83
84	23 10.8	−0.7	6.5	24 10.4	−0.5	6.6	25 10.0	−0.4	6.6	26 09.6	−0.3	6.7	27 09.2	−0.2	6.7	28 08.8	−0.1	6.8	29 08.4	0.0	6.9	30 07.9	+0.2	6.9	84
85	23 10.1	−1.1	5.4	24 09.9	−1.1	5.5	25 09.6	−0.9	5.5	26 09.3	−0.8	5.6	27 09.0	−0.7	5.6	28 08.7	−0.6	5.7	29 08.4	−0.5	5.7	30 08.1	−0.4	5.8	85
86	23 09.0	−1.6	4.3	24 08.8	−1.5	4.4	25 08.7	−1.5	4.4	26 08.5	−1.4	4.5	27 08.3	−1.3	4.5	28 08.1	−1.2	4.5	29 07.9	−1.1	4.6	30 07.7	−1.0	4.6	86
87	23 07.4	−2.0	3.3	24 07.3	−2.0	3.3	25 07.2	−1.9	3.3	26 07.1	−1.8	3.3	27 07.0	−1.8	3.4	28 06.9	−1.7	3.4	29 06.8	−1.7	3.4	30 06.7	−1.6	3.5	87
88	23 05.4	−2.5	2.2	24 05.3	−2.4	2.2	25 05.3	−2.4	2.2	26 05.3	−2.4	2.2	27 05.2	−2.3	2.2	28 05.2	−2.3	2.3	29 05.1	−2.2	2.3	30 05.1	−2.3	2.3	88
89	23 02.9	−2.9	1.1	24 02.9	−2.9	1.1	25 02.9	−2.9	1.1	26 02.9	−2.9	1.1	27 02.9	−2.9	1.1	28 02.9	−2.9	1.1	29 02.9	−2.9	1.1	30 02.8	−2.8	1.2	89
90	23 00.0	−3.4	0.0	24 00.0	−3.4	0.0	25 00.0	−3.4	0.0	26 00.0	−3.4	0.0	27 00.0	−3.4	0.0	28 00.0	−3.4	0.0	29 00.0	−3.4	0.0	30 00.0	−3.4	0.0	90
	23°			24°			25°			26°			27°			28°			29°			30°			

87°, 273° L.H.A. LATITUDE SAME NAME AS DECLINATION

358

LATITUDE **CONTRARY** NAME TO DECLINATION **L.H.A. 87°, 273°**

Dec.	23°			24°			25°			26°			27°			28°			29°			30°			Dec.
	Hc	d	Z	Hc	d	Z	Hc	d	Z	Hc	d	Z	Hc	d	Z	Hc	d	Z	Hc	d	Z	Hc	d	Z	
°	° ′	′	°	° ′	′	°	° ′	′	°	° ′	′	°	° ′	′	°	° ′	′	°	° ′	′	°	° ′	′	°	°
0	2 45.7	-23.5	91.2	2 44.4	-24.4	91.2	2 43.1	-25.4	91.3	2 41.8	-26.4	91.3	2 40.4	-27.3	91.4	2 38.9	-28.2	91.4	2 37.4	-29.1	91.5	2 35.9	-30.1	91.5	0
1	2 22.2	-23.5	92.1	2 20.0	-24.5	92.1	2 17.7	-25.4	92.2	2 15.4	-26.4	92.2	2 13.1	-27.3	92.3	2 10.7	-28.2	92.3	2 08.3	-29.2	92.3	2 05.8	-30.1	92.4	1
2	1 58.7	-23.6	93.0	1 55.5	-24.5	93.0	1 52.3	-25.5	93.1	1 49.0	-26.4	93.1	1 45.8	-27.4	93.1	1 42.5	-28.3	93.2	1 39.1	-29.2	93.2	1 35.7	-30.1	93.2	2
3	1 35.1	-23.6	93.9	1 31.0	-24.6	94.0	1 26.8	-25.5	94.0	1 22.6	-26.4	94.0	1 18.4	-27.3	94.0	1 14.2	-28.3	94.1	1 09.9	-29.2	94.1	1 05.6	-30.1	94.1	3
4	1 11.5	-23.6	94.9	1 06.4	-24.5	94.9	1 01.3	-25.5	94.9	0 56.2	-26.5	94.9	0 51.1	-27.4	94.9	0 45.9	-28.3	94.9	0 40.7	-29.2	95.0	0 35.5	-30.1	95.0	4
5	0 47.9	-23.6	95.8	0 41.9	-24.6	95.8	0 35.8	-25.5	95.8	0 29.7	-26.4	95.8	0 23.7	-27.4	95.8	0 17.6	-28.3	95.8	0 11.5	-29.2	95.8	0 05.4	-30.1	95.8	5
6	0 24.3	-23.6	96.7	0 17.3	-24.6	96.7	0 10.3	-25.5	96.7	0 03.3	-26.5	96.7	0 03.7	+27.4	83.3	0 10.7	+28.3	83.3	0 17.7	+29.2	83.3	0 24.7	+30.1	83.3	6
7	0 00.7	-23.6	97.6	0 07.3	+24.5	82.4	0 15.2	+25.5	82.4	0 23.2	+26.4	82.4	0 31.1	+27.4	82.4	0 39.0	+28.3	82.4	0 46.9	+29.2	82.4	0 54.8	+30.1	82.4	7
8	0 22.9	+23.7	81.5	0 31.8	+24.6	81.5	0 40.7	+25.5	81.5	0 49.6	+26.4	81.5	0 58.5	+27.3	81.5	1 07.3	+28.3	81.5	1 16.1	+29.2	81.6	1 24.9	+30.1	81.6	8
9	0 46.6	+23.6	80.5	0 56.4	+24.5	80.6	1 06.2	+25.5	80.6	1 16.0	+26.5	80.6	1 25.8	+27.4	80.6	1 35.6	+28.2	80.7	1 45.3	+29.2	80.7	1 55.0	+30.1	80.7	9
10	1 10.2	+23.5	79.6	1 20.9	+24.6	79.7	1 31.7	+25.5	79.7	1 42.5	+26.3	79.7	1 53.2	+27.3	79.7	2 03.8	+28.3	79.8	2 14.5	+29.1	79.8	2 25.1	+30.0	79.8	10
11	1 33.7	+23.6	78.7	1 45.5	+24.5	78.7	1 57.2	+25.4	78.8	2 08.8	+26.4	78.8	2 20.5	+27.3	78.8	2 32.1	+28.1	78.9	2 43.6	+29.1	78.9	2 55.1	+30.0	79.0	11
12	1 57.3	+23.5	77.8	2 10.0	+24.4	77.8	2 22.6	+25.4	77.9	2 35.2	+26.3	77.9	2 47.8	+27.2	78.0	3 00.2	+28.2	78.0	3 12.7	+29.0	78.1	3 25.1	+29.9	78.1	12
13	2 20.8	+23.5	76.9	2 34.4	+24.5	76.9	2 48.0	+25.4	77.0	3 01.5	+26.3	77.0	3 15.0	+27.2	77.1	3 28.4	+28.1	77.1	3 41.7	+29.0	77.2	3 55.0	+29.9	77.2	13
14	2 44.3	+23.5	75.9	2 58.9	+24.4	76.0	3 13.4	+25.3	76.0	3 27.8	+26.2	76.1	3 42.2	+27.1	76.2	3 56.5	+28.0	76.2	4 10.7	+29.0	76.3	4 24.9	+29.8	76.4	14
15	3 07.8	+23.4	75.0	3 23.3	+24.3	75.1	3 38.7	+25.2	75.1	3 54.0	+26.2	75.2	4 09.3	+27.1	75.3	4 24.5	+28.0	75.3	4 39.7	+28.8	75.4	4 54.7	+29.8	75.5	15
16	3 31.2	+23.3	74.1	3 47.6	+24.3	74.2	4 03.9	+25.2	74.2	4 20.2	+26.1	74.3	4 36.4	+27.0	74.4	4 52.5	+27.9	74.5	5 08.5	+28.8	74.5	5 24.5	+29.7	74.6	16
17	3 54.5	+23.3	73.2	4 11.9	+24.2	73.2	4 29.1	+25.1	73.3	4 46.3	+26.0	73.4	5 03.4	+26.9	73.5	5 20.4	+27.8	73.6	5 37.3	+28.8	73.7	5 54.2	+29.6	73.8	17
18	4 17.8	+23.2	72.3	4 36.1	+24.1	72.3	4 54.2	+25.1	72.4	5 12.3	+26.0	72.5	5 30.3	+26.9	72.6	5 48.2	+27.8	72.7	6 06.1	+28.6	72.8	6 23.8	+29.5	72.9	18
19	4 41.0	+23.2	71.3	5 00.2	+24.1	71.4	5 19.3	+25.0	71.5	5 38.3	+25.9	71.6	5 57.2	+26.7	71.7	6 16.0	+27.6	71.8	6 34.7	+28.5	71.9	6 53.3	+29.4	72.0	19
20	5 04.2	+23.1	70.4	5 24.3	+23.9	70.5	5 44.3	+24.8	70.6	6 04.2	+25.7	70.7	6 23.9	+26.7	70.8	6 43.6	+27.6	70.9	7 03.2	+28.5	71.0	7 22.7	+29.3	71.1	20
21	5 27.3	+22.9	69.5	5 48.2	+23.9	69.6	6 09.1	+24.8	69.7	6 29.9	+25.7	69.8	6 50.6	+26.6	69.9	7 11.2	+27.5	70.0	7 31.7	+28.3	70.1	7 52.0	+29.2	70.2	21
22	5 50.2	+22.9	68.6	6 12.1	+23.8	68.6	6 33.9	+24.7	68.8	6 55.6	+25.6	68.9	7 17.2	+26.5	69.0	7 38.7	+27.3	69.1	8 00.0	+28.2	69.2	8 21.2	+29.1	69.4	22
23	6 13.1	+22.8	67.6	6 35.9	+23.7	67.7	6 58.6	+24.6	67.8	7 21.2	+25.5	68.0	7 43.7	+26.3	68.1	8 06.0	+27.2	68.2	8 28.2	+28.1	68.3	8 50.3	+28.9	68.5	23
24	6 35.9	+22.7	66.7	6 59.6	+23.6	66.8	7 23.2	+24.5	66.9	7 46.7	+25.3	67.0	8 10.0	+26.2	67.2	8 33.2	+27.1	67.3	8 56.3	+28.0	67.4	9 19.2	+28.9	67.6	24
25	6 58.6	+22.6	65.8	7 23.2	+23.5	65.9	7 47.7	+24.3	66.0	8 12.0	+25.2	66.1	8 36.2	+26.1	66.3	9 00.3	+27.0	66.4	9 24.3	+27.8	66.5	9 48.1	+28.7	66.7	25
26	7 21.2	+22.5	64.8	7 46.7	+23.3	64.9	8 12.0	+24.2	65.1	8 37.2	+25.1	65.2	9 02.3	+26.0	65.3	9 27.3	+26.8	65.5	9 52.1	+27.7	65.6	10 16.8	+28.5	65.8	26
27	7 43.7	+22.3	63.9	8 10.0	+23.2	64.0	8 36.2	+24.1	64.1	9 02.3	+25.0	64.3	9 28.3	+25.8	64.4	9 54.1	+26.7	64.6	10 19.8	+27.5	64.7	10 45.3	+28.4	64.9	27
28	8 06.0	+22.2	63.0	8 33.2	+23.1	63.1	9 00.3	+24.0	63.2	9 27.3	+24.8	63.4	9 54.1	+25.7	63.5	10 20.8	+26.5	63.7	10 47.3	+27.4	63.8	11 13.7	+28.2	64.0	28
29	8 28.2	+22.1	62.0	8 56.3	+22.9	62.1	9 24.3	+23.8	62.3	9 52.1	+24.7	62.4	10 19.8	+25.5	62.6	10 47.3	+26.4	62.8	11 14.7	+27.2	62.9	11 41.9	+28.1	63.1	29
30	8 50.3	+21.9	61.1	9 19.2	+22.8	61.2	9 48.1	+23.6	61.4	10 16.8	+24.5	61.5	10 45.3	+25.4	61.7	11 13.7	+26.2	61.8	11 41.9	+27.1	62.0	12 10.0	+27.9	62.2	30
31	9 12.2	+21.8	60.1	9 42.0	+22.7	60.3	10 11.7	+23.5	60.4	10 41.3	+24.3	60.6	11 10.7	+25.1	60.8	11 39.9	+26.0	60.9	12 09.0	+26.8	61.1	12 37.9	+27.6	61.3	31
32	9 34.0	+21.7	59.2	10 04.7	+22.5	59.3	10 35.2	+23.3	59.5	11 05.6	+24.2	59.7	11 35.8	+25.0	59.8	12 05.9	+25.9	60.0	12 35.8	+26.7	60.2	13 05.5	+27.5	60.4	32
33	9 55.7	+21.4	58.2	10 27.2	+22.3	58.4	10 58.5	+23.2	58.6	11 29.8	+24.0	58.7	12 00.8	+24.9	58.9	12 31.8	+25.6	59.1	13 02.5	+26.5	59.3	13 33.0	+27.4	59.5	33
34	10 17.1	+21.3	57.3	10 49.5	+22.1	57.4	11 21.7	+23.0	57.6	11 53.8	+23.8	57.8	12 25.7	+24.6	58.0	12 57.4	+25.5	58.2	13 29.0	+26.2	58.4	14 00.4	+27.0	58.6	34
35	10 38.4	+21.2	56.3	11 11.6	+22.0	56.5	11 44.7	+22.8	56.7	12 17.6	+23.6	56.8	12 50.3	+24.4	57.0	13 22.9	+25.2	57.2	13 55.2	+26.1	57.4	14 27.4	+26.9	57.6	35
36	10 59.6	+20.9	55.4	11 33.6	+21.8	55.6	12 07.5	+22.6	55.7	12 41.2	+23.4	55.9	13 14.7	+24.3	56.1	13 48.1	+25.0	56.3	14 21.3	+25.9	56.5	14 54.3	+26.7	56.7	36
37	11 20.5	+20.8	54.4	11 55.4	+21.6	54.6	12 30.1	+22.4	54.8	13 04.6	+23.2	55.0	13 39.0	+24.0	55.2	14 13.1	+24.9	55.4	14 47.2	+25.6	55.6	15 21.0	+26.4	55.8	37
38	11 41.3	+20.6	53.5	12 17.0	+21.4	53.6	12 52.5	+22.1	53.8	13 27.8	+23.0	54.0	14 03.0	+23.8	54.2	14 38.0	+24.6	54.4	15 12.8	+25.4	54.6	15 47.4	+26.2	54.9	38
39	12 01.9	+20.4	52.5	12 38.4	+21.1	52.7	13 14.6	+22.0	52.9	13 50.8	+22.8	53.1	14 26.8	+23.5	53.3	15 02.6	+24.3	53.5	15 38.2	+25.1	53.7	16 13.6	+25.9	53.9	39
40	12 22.3	+20.2	51.6	12 59.5	+21.0	51.7	13 36.6	+21.8	51.9	14 13.6	+22.5	52.1	14 50.3	+23.3	52.3	15 26.9	+24.1	52.5	16 03.3	+24.9	52.8	16 39.5	+25.7	53.0	40
41	12 42.5	+20.0	50.6	13 20.5	+20.8	50.8	13 58.4	+21.5	51.0	14 36.1	+22.3	51.2	15 13.6	+23.1	51.4	15 51.0	+23.9	51.6	16 28.2	+24.7	51.8	17 05.2	+25.4	52.0	41
42	13 02.5	+19.7	49.6	13 41.3	+20.5	49.8	14 19.9	+21.3	50.0	14 58.4	+22.1	50.2	15 36.7	+22.9	50.4	16 14.9	+23.6	50.6	16 52.9	+24.3	50.9	17 30.6	+25.2	51.1	42
43	13 22.2	+19.6	48.7	14 01.8	+20.3	48.8	14 41.2	+21.1	49.0	15 20.5	+21.8	49.2	15 59.6	+22.5	49.4	16 38.5	+23.3	49.7	17 17.2	+24.1	49.9	17 55.8	+24.9	50.1	43
44	13 41.8	+19.3	47.7	14 22.1	+20.0	47.9	15 02.3	+20.8	48.1	15 42.3	+21.5	48.3	16 22.1	+22.4	48.5	17 01.8	+23.1	48.7	17 41.3	+23.9	48.9	18 20.7	+24.5	49.2	44
45	14 01.1	+19.0	46.7	14 42.1	+19.9	46.9	15 23.1	+20.5	47.1	16 03.8	+21.3	47.3	16 44.5	+22.0	47.5	17 24.9	+22.8	47.7	18 05.2	+23.5	48.0	18 45.2	+24.3	48.2	45
46	14 20.1	+18.9	45.7	15 02.0	+19.5	45.9	15 43.6	+20.3	46.1	16 25.1	+21.1	46.3	17 06.5	+21.8	46.5	17 47.7	+22.5	46.8	18 28.7	+23.2	47.0	19 09.5	+24.0	47.3	46
47	14 39.0	+18.6	44.7	15 21.5	+19.3	44.9	16 03.9	+20.1	45.1	16 46.2	+20.7	45.3	17 28.3	+21.4	45.6	18 10.2	+22.2	45.8	18 51.9	+23.0	46.0	19 33.5	+23.7	46.3	47
48	14 57.6	+18.3	43.8	15 40.8	+19.1	44.0	16 24.0	+19.7	44.2	17 06.9	+20.5	44.4	17 49.7	+21.2	44.6	18 32.4	+21.9	44.8	19 14.9	+22.6	45.1	19 57.2	+23.3	45.3	48
49	15 15.9	+18.1	42.8	15 59.9	+18.7	43.0	16 43.7	+19.5	43.2	17 27.4	+20.2	43.4	18 10.9	+20.9	43.6	18 54.3	+21.6	43.8	19 37.5	+22.3	44.1	20 20.5	+23.0	44.3	49
50	15 34.0	+17.8	41.8	16 18.6	+18.5	42.0	17 03.2	+19.2	42.2	17 47.6	+19.8	42.4	18 31.8	+20.6	42.6	19 15.9	+21.3	42.8	19 59.8	+22.0	43.1	20 43.5	+22.7	43.3	50
51	15 51.8	+17.5	40.8	16 37.1	+18.2	41.0	17 22.4	+18.9	41.2	18 07.4	+19.6	41.4	18 52.4	+20.2	41.6	19 37.2	+20.9	41.9	20 21.8	+21.6	42.1	21 06.2	+22.3	42.3	51
52	16 09.3	+17.3	39.8	16 55.3	+18.0	40.0	17 41.3	+18.5	40.2	18 27.0	+19.3	40.4	19 12.6	+20.0	40.6	19 58.1	+20.6	40.9	20 43.4	+21.3	41.1	21 28.5	+22.0	41.4	52
53	16 26.6	+16.9	38.8	17 13.3	+17.6	39.0	17 59.8	+18.3	39.2	18 46.3	+18.9	39.4	19 32.6	+19.6	39.6	20 18.7	+20.3	39.9	21 04.7	+20.9	40.1	21 50.5	+21.6	40.4	53
54	16 43.5	+16.7	37.8	17 30.9	+17.3	38.0	18 18.1	+18.0	38.2	19 05.2	+18.6	38.4	19 52.2	+19.2	38.6	20 39.0	+19.9	38.8	21 25.6	+20.6	39.1	22 12.1	+21.2	39.3	54
55	17 00.2	+16.4	36.8	17 48.2	+17.0	37.0	18 36.1	+17.6	37.2	19 23.8	+18.3	37.4	20 11.4	+18.9	37.6	20 58.9	+19.5	37.8	21 46.2	+20.2	38.1	22 33.3	+20.9	38.3	55
56	17 16.6	+16.1	35.8	18 05.2	+16.7	36.0	18 53.7	+17.3	36.2	19 42.1	+17.9	36.4	20 30.3	+18.6	36.6	21 18.4	+19.2	36.8	22 06.4	+19.8	37.1	22 54.2	+20.4	37.3	56
57	17 32.7	+15.8	34.8	18 21.9	+16.4	35.0	19 11.0	+17.0	35.2	20 00.0	+17.6	35.4	20 48.9	+18.2	35.6	21 37.6	+18.8	35.8	22 26.2	+19.4	36.0	23 14.6	+20.1	36.3	57
58	17 48.5	+15.5	33.8	18 38.3	+16.1	34.0	19 28.0	+16.7	34.1	20 17.6	+17.3	34.3	21 07.1	+17.8	34.6	21 56.4	+18.5	34.8	22 45.6	+19.1	35.0	23 34.7	+19.7	35.3	58
59	18 04.0	+15.1	32.8	18 54.4	+15.7	32.9	19 44.7	+16.3	33.1	20 34.9	+16.8	33.3	21 24.9	+17.5	33.5	22 14.9	+18.0	33.8	23 04.7	+18.6	34.0	23 54.4	+19.2	34.2	59
60	18 19.1	+14.8	31.7	19 10.1	+15.4	31.9	20 01.0	+15.9	32.1	20 51.7	+16.5	32.3	21 42.4	+17.1	32.5	22 32.9	+17.7	32.7	23 23.3	+18.3	33.0	24 13.6	+18.8	33.2	60
61	18 33.9	+14.5	30.7	19 25.5	+15.0	30.9	20 16.9	+15.6	31.1	21 08.2	+16.2	31.3	21 59.5	+16.6	31.5	22 50.6	+17.2	31.7	23 41.6	+17.8	31.9	24 32.4	+18.4	32.2	61
62	18 48.4	+14.2	29.7	19 40.5	+14.7	29.9	20 32.5	+15.2	30.0	21 24.4	+15.7	30.2	22 16.1	+16.3	30.4	23 07.8	+16.9	30.7	23 59.4	+17.4	30.9	24 50.8	+18.0	31.1	62
63	19 02.6	+13.8	28.7	19 55.2	+14.3	28.8	20 47.7	+14.8	29.0	21 40.1	+15.4	29.2	22 32.4	+15.9	29.4	23 24.7	+16.4	29.6	24 16.8	+16.9	29.8	25 08.8	+17.5	30.1	63
64	19 16.4	+13.4	27.6	20 09.5	+14.0	27.8	21 02.5	+14.5	28.0	21 55.5	+14.9	28.2	22 48.3	+15.5	28.4	23 41.1	+16.0	28.6	24 33.7	+16.5	28.8	25 26.3	+17.0	29.0	64
65	19 29.8	+13.2	26.6	20 23.5	+13.5	26.8	21 17.0	+14.1	26.9	22 10.4	+14.6	27.1	23 03.8	+15.1	27.3	23 57.1	+15.5	27.5	24 50.2	+16.1	27.7	25 43.3	+16.6	27.9	65
66	19 43.0	+12.7	25.6	20 37.0	+13.3	25.7	21 31.1	+13.6	25.9	22 25.0	+14.2	26.1	23 18.9	+14.6	26.3	24 12.6	+15.1	26.4	25 06.3	+15.6	26.7	25 59.9	+16.1	26.9	66
67	19 55.7	+12.4	24.5	20 50.3	+12.8	24.7	21 44.7	+13.3	24.8	22 39.2	+13.7	25.0	23 33.5	+14.2	25.2	24 27.7	+14.7	25.4	25 21.9	+15.1	25.6	26 16.0	+15.6	25.8	67
68	20 08.1	+12.0	23.5	21 03.1	+12.5	23.6	21 58.0	+12.9	23.8	22 52.9	+13.3	24.0	23 47.7	+13.8	24.1	24 42.4	+14.2	24.3	25 37.0	+14.7	24.5	26 31.6	+15.1	24.7	68
69	20 20.1	+11.7	22.4	21 15.6	+12.0	22.6	22 10.9	+12.5	22.7	23 06.2	+12.9	22.9	24 01.5	+13.3	23.1	24 56.6	+13.8	23.2	25 51.7	+14.2	23.4	26 46.7	+14.7	23.6	69
70	20 31.8	+11.2	21.4	21 27.6	+11.7	21.5	22 23.4	+12.1	21.7	23 19.1	+12.5	21.8	24 14.8	+12.9	22.0	25 10.4	+13.3	22.2	26 05.9	+13.7	22.4	27 01.4	+14.1	22.5	70
71	20 43.0	+10.9	20.3	21 39.3	+11.2	20.5	22 35.5	+11.6	20.6	23 31.6	+12.0	20.8	24 27.7	+12.4	20.9	25 23.7	+12.8	21.1	26 19.6	+13.2	21.3	27 15.5	+13.6	21.5	71
72	20 53.9	+10.5	19.3	21 50.5	+10.9	19.4	22 47.1	+11.2	19.6	23 43.6	+11.6	19.7	24 40.1	+11.9	19.9	25 36.5	+12.3	20.0	26 32.8	+12.8	20.2	27 29.1	+13.1	20.4	72
73	21 04.4	+10.1	18.2	22 01.4	+10.5	18.4	22 58.3	+10.8	18.5	23 55.2	+11.2	18.6	24 52.0	+11.5	18.8	25 48.8	+11.9	18.9	26 45.6	+12.2	19.1	27 42.2	+12.6	19.3	73
74	21 14.5	+9.8	17.2	22 11.9	+10.0	17.3	23 09.1	+10.4	17.4	24 06.4	+10.6	17.6	25 03.5	+11.1	17.7	26 00.7	+11.3	17.8	26 57.8	+11.7	18.0	27 54.8	+12.1	18.1	74
75	21 24.3	+9.3	16.1	22 21.9	+9.6	16.2	23 19.5	+9.9	16.3	24 17.0	+10.3	16.5	25 14.6	+10.5	16.6	26 12.0	+10.9	16.7	27 09.5	+11.2	16.9	28 06.9	+11.5	17.0	75
76	21 33.6	+8.9	15.1	22 31.5	+9.2	15.2	23 29.4	+9.5	15.3	24 27.3	+9.7	15.4	25 25.1	+10.1	15.5	26 22.9	+10.4	15.6	27 20.7	+10.6	15.8	28 18.4	+10.9	15.9	76
77	21 42.5	+8.5	14.0	22 40.7	+8.8	14.1	23 38.9	+9.0	14.2	24 37.0	+9.3	14.3	25 35.2	+9.5	14.4	26 33.3	+9.8	14.5	27 31.3	+10.1	14.7	28 29.3	+10.5	14.8	77
78	21 51.0	+8.1	12.9	22 49.5	+8.3	13.0	23 47.9	+8.6	13.1	24 46.3	+8.9	13.2	25 44.7	+9.1	13.3	26 43.1	+9.3	13.4	27 41.4	+9.6	13.6	28 39.8	+9.8	13.7	78
79	21 59.1	+7.7	11.9	22 57.8	+7.9	11.9	23 56.5	+8.1	12.0	24 55.2	+8.3	12.1	25 53.8	+8.6	12.2	26 52.4	+8.9	12.3	27 51.0	+9.1	12.4	28 49.6	+9.3	12.6	79
80	22 06.8	+7.2	10.8	23 05.7	+7.5	10.9	24 04.6	+7.7	10.9	25 03.5	+7.9	11.0	26 02.4	+8.1	11.1	27 01.3	+8.2	11.2	28 00.1	+8.5	11.3	28 58.9	+8.7	11.4	80
81	22 14.0	+6.9	9.7	23 13.2	+7.0	9.8	24 12.3	+7.2	9.9	25 11.4	+7.4	9.9	26 10.5	+7.5	10.0	27 09.5	+7.8	10.1	28 08.6	+8.0	10.2	29 07.6	+8.2	10.3	81
82	22 20.9	+6.4	8.6	23 20.2	+6.5	8.7	24 19.5	+6.7	8.8	25 18.8	+6.9	8.8	26 18.0	+7.1	8.9	27 17.3	+7.2	9.0	28 16.6	+7.4	9.1	29 15.8	+7.6	9.2	82
83	22 27.3	+5.9	7.6	23 26.7	+6.2	7.6	24 26.2	+6.3	7.7	25 25.7	+6.4	7.7	26 25.1	+6.6	7.8	27 24.5	+6.7	7.9	28 24.0	+6.8	8.0	29 23.4	+7.0	8.0	83
84	22 33.2	+5.6	6.5	23 32.9	+5.6	6.5	24 32.5	+5.8	6.6	25 32.1	+5.9	6.6	26 31.7	+6.0	6.7	27 31.2	+6.2	6.8	28 30.8	+6.3	6.8	29 30.4	+6.4	6.9	84
85	22 38.8	+5.1	5.4	23 38.5	+5.2	5.5	24 38.3	+5.3	5.5	25 38.0	+5.4	5.5	26 37.7	+5.5	5.6	27 37.4	+5.6	5.6	28 37.1	+5.7	5.7	29 36.8	+5.8	5.7	85
86	22 43.9	+4.7	4.3	23 43.7	+4.8	4.4	24 43.6	+4.8	4.4	25 43.4	+4.9	4.4	26 43.2	+5.0	4.5	27 43.0	+5.1	4.5	28 42.8	+5.2	4.6	29 42.6	+5.3	4.6	86
87	22 48.6	+4.2	3.3	23 48.5	+4.3	3.3	24 48.4	+4.3	3.3	25 48.3	+4.4	3.3	26 48.2	+4.5	3.4	27 48.1	+4.5	3.4	28 48.0	+4.6	3.4	29 47.9	+4.6	3.5	87
88	22 52.8	+3.8	2.2	23 52.8	+3.8	2.2	24 52.7	+3.9	2.2	25 52.7	+3.9	2.2	26 52.7	+3.9	2.2	27 52.6	+4.0	2.2	28 52.6	+4.0	2.3	29 52.5	+4.1	2.3	88
89	22 56.6	+3.4	1.1	23 56.6	+3.4	1.1	24 56.6	+3.4	1.1	25 56.6	+3.4	1.1	26 56.6	+3.4	1.1	27 56.6	+3.4	1.1	28 56.6	+3.4	1.1	29 56.6	+3.4	1.2	89
90	23 00.0	+2.9	0.0	24 00.0	+2.9	0.0	25 00.0	+2.9	0.0	26 00.0	+2.9	0.0	27 00.0	+2.9	0.0	28 00.0	+2.9	0.0	29 00.0	+2.9	0.0	30 00.0	+2.8	0.0	90
	23°			24°			25°			26°			27°			28°			29°			30°			

S. Lat. {L.H.A. greater than 180° ....Zn=180°−Z
{L.H.A. less than 180°...........Zn=180°+Z

LATITUDE **SAME** NAME AS DECLINATION **L.H.A. 93°, 267°**

88°, 272° L.H.A. LATITUDE SAME NAME AS DECLINATION N. Lat. {L.H.A. greater than 180° .....Zn=Z / L.H.A. less than 180°............Zn=360°–Z}

Dec.	23° Hc	23° d	23° Z	24° Hc	24° d	24° Z	25° Hc	25° d	25° Z	26° Hc	26° d	26° Z
°	° ′	′	°	° ′	′	°	° ′	′	°	° ′	′	°
0	1 50.5	+23.4	90.8	1 49.6	+24.4	90.8	1 48.8	+25.3	90.8	1 47.9	+26.3	90.9
1	2 13.9	+23.4	89.9	2 14.0	+24.4	89.9	2 14.1	+25.3	89.9	2 14.2	+26.2	90.0
2	2 37.3	+23.4	88.9	2 38.4	+24.3	89.0	2 39.4	+25.3	89.0	2 40.4	+26.2	89.1
3	3 00.7	+23.3	88.0	3 02.7	+24.3	88.1	3 04.7	+25.2	88.1	3 06.6	+26.2	88.2
4	3 24.0	+23.3	87.1	3 27.0	+24.2	87.2	3 29.9	+25.2	87.2	3 32.8	+26.2	87.3
5	3 47.3	+23.2	86.2	3 51.2	+24.2	86.2	3 55.1	+25.2	86.3	3 59.0	+26.0	86.4
6	4 10.5	+23.1	85.2	4 15.4	+24.1	85.3	4 20.3	+25.0	85.4	4 25.0	+26.0	85.5
7	4 33.6	+23.1	84.3	4 39.5	+24.0	84.4	4 45.3	+25.0	84.5	4 51.0	+26.0	84.6
8	4 56.7	+23.0	83.4	5 03.5	+24.0	83.5	5 10.3	+24.9	83.6	5 17.0	+25.8	83.7
9	5 19.7	+22.9	82.5	5 27.5	+23.9	82.6	5 35.2	+24.8	82.7	5 42.8	+25.8	82.8
10	5 42.6	+22.8	81.5	5 51.4	+23.7	81.6	6 00.0	+24.8	81.7	6 08.6	+25.7	81.8
11	6 05.4	+22.7	80.6	6 15.1	+23.7	80.7	6 24.8	+24.6	80.8	6 34.3	+25.5	80.9
12	6 28.1	+22.6	79.7	6 38.8	+23.6	79.8	6 49.4	+24.5	79.9	6 59.8	+25.5	80.0
13	6 50.7	+22.6	78.7	7 02.4	+23.5	78.9	7 13.9	+24.4	79.0	7 25.3	+25.4	79.1
14	7 13.3	+22.4	77.8	7 25.9	+23.3	77.9	7 38.3	+24.3	78.1	7 50.7	+25.2	78.2
15	7 35.7	+22.2	76.9	7 49.2	+23.3	77.0	8 02.6	+24.2	77.1	8 15.9	+25.1	77.3
16	7 57.9	+22.2	75.9	8 12.5	+23.1	76.1	8 26.8	+24.1	76.2	8 41.0	+25.0	76.4
17	8 20.1	+22.0	75.0	8 35.6	+22.9	75.1	8 50.9	+23.9	75.3	9 06.0	+24.9	75.4
18	8 42.1	+21.9	74.1	8 58.5	+22.9	74.2	9 14.8	+23.7	74.4	9 30.9	+24.7	74.5
19	9 04.0	+21.7	73.1	9 21.4	+22.6	73.3	9 38.5	+23.7	73.4	9 55.6	+24.5	73.6
20	9 25.7	+21.6	72.2	9 44.0	+22.6	72.3	10 02.2	+23.4	72.5	10 20.1	+24.4	72.7
21	9 47.3	+21.5	71.2	10 06.6	+22.3	71.4	10 25.6	+23.3	71.6	10 44.5	+24.2	71.7
22	10 08.8	+21.2	70.3	10 28.9	+22.2	70.4	10 48.9	+23.1	70.6	11 08.7	+24.1	70.8
23	10 30.0	+21.1	69.3	10 51.1	+22.0	69.5	11 12.0	+23.0	69.7	11 32.8	+23.8	69.9
24	10 51.1	+20.9	68.4	11 13.1	+21.9	68.6	11 35.0	+22.8	68.7	11 56.6	+23.7	68.9
25	11 12.0	+20.8	67.4	11 35.0	+21.6	67.6	11 57.8	+22.5	67.8	12 20.3	+23.5	68.0
26	11 32.8	+20.5	66.5	11 56.6	+21.5	66.7	12 20.3	+22.4	66.9	12 43.8	+23.3	67.1
27	11 53.3	+20.4	65.5	12 18.1	+21.3	65.7	12 42.7	+22.2	65.9	13 07.1	+23.1	66.1
28	12 13.7	+20.1	64.5	12 39.4	+21.0	64.7	13 04.9	+21.9	64.9	13 30.2	+22.9	65.2
29	12 33.8	+20.0	63.6	13 00.4	+20.9	63.8	13 26.8	+21.8	64.0	13 53.1	+22.6	64.2
30	12 53.8	+19.7	62.6	13 21.3	+20.6	62.8	13 48.6	+21.5	63.0	14 15.7	+22.4	63.3
31	13 13.5	+19.5	61.6	13 41.9	+20.4	61.9	14 10.1	+21.3	62.1	14 38.1	+22.2	62.3
32	13 33.0	+19.3	60.7	14 02.3	+20.2	60.9	14 31.4	+21.1	61.1	15 00.3	+21.9	61.3
33	13 52.3	+19.1	59.7	14 22.5	+19.9	59.9	14 52.5	+20.8	60.1	15 22.2	+21.7	60.4
34	14 11.4	+18.8	58.7	14 42.4	+19.7	58.9	15 13.3	+20.5	59.2	15 43.9	+21.5	59.4
35	14 30.2	+18.5	57.7	15 02.1	+19.4	58.0	15 33.8	+20.3	58.2	16 05.4	+21.1	58.4
36	14 48.7	+18.4	56.8	15 21.5	+19.2	57.0	15 54.1	+20.1	57.2	16 26.5	+20.9	57.5
37	15 07.1	+18.0	55.8	15 40.7	+18.9	56.0	16 14.2	+19.7	56.2	16 47.4	+20.6	56.5
38	15 25.1	+17.8	54.8	15 59.6	+18.7	55.0	16 33.9	+19.5	55.2	17 08.0	+20.4	55.5
39	15 42.9	+17.6	53.8	16 18.3	+18.3	54.0	16 53.4	+19.2	54.3	17 28.4	+20.0	54.5
40	16 00.5	+17.2	52.8	16 36.6	+18.1	53.0	17 12.6	+18.9	53.3	17 48.4	+19.7	53.5
41	16 17.7	+17.0	51.8	16 54.7	+17.8	52.0	17 31.5	+18.7	52.3	18 08.1	+19.5	52.5
42	16 34.7	+16.7	50.8	17 12.5	+17.5	51.0	17 50.2	+18.3	51.3	18 27.6	+19.1	51.5
43	16 51.4	+16.4	49.8	17 30.0	+17.2	50.0	18 08.5	+18.0	50.3	18 46.7	+18.8	50.5
44	17 07.8	+16.1	48.8	17 47.2	+16.9	49.0	18 26.5	+17.6	49.3	19 05.5	+18.5	49.5
45	17 23.9	+15.8	47.8	18 04.1	+16.6	48.0	18 44.1	+17.4	48.3	19 24.0	+18.1	48.5
46	17 39.7	+15.4	46.8	18 20.7	+16.2	47.0	19 01.5	+17.0	47.3	19 42.1	+17.8	47.5
47	17 55.1	+15.2	45.8	18 36.9	+15.9	46.0	19 18.5	+16.7	46.2	19 59.9	+17.5	46.5
48	18 10.3	+14.8	44.7	18 52.8	+15.6	45.0	19 35.2	+16.3	45.2	20 17.4	+17.1	45.5
49	18 25.1	+14.6	43.7	19 08.4	+15.3	43.9	19 51.5	+16.0	44.2	20 34.5	+16.7	44.5
50	18 39.7	+14.1	42.7	19 23.7	+14.9	42.9	20 07.5	+15.7	43.2	20 51.2	+16.4	43.4
51	18 53.8	+13.9	41.7	19 38.6	+14.5	41.9	20 23.2	+15.2	42.1	21 07.6	+15.9	42.4
52	19 07.7	+13.5	40.6	19 53.1	+14.2	40.9	20 38.4	+14.9	41.1	21 23.5	+15.6	41.4
53	19 21.2	+13.1	39.6	20 07.3	+13.9	39.8	20 53.3	+14.5	40.1	21 39.1	+15.3	40.3
54	19 34.3	+12.8	38.6	20 21.2	+13.4	38.8	21 07.8	+14.2	39.0	21 54.4	+14.8	39.3
55	19 47.1	+12.4	37.5	20 34.6	+13.1	37.8	21 22.0	+13.7	38.0	22 09.2	+14.4	38.2
56	19 59.5	+12.1	36.5	20 47.7	+12.7	36.7	21 35.7	+13.4	36.9	22 23.6	+14.0	37.2
57	20 11.6	+11.7	35.4	21 00.4	+12.3	35.7	21 49.1	+13.0	35.9	22 37.6	+13.6	36.1
58	20 23.3	+11.3	34.4	21 12.7	+12.0	34.6	22 02.1	+12.5	34.8	22 51.2	+13.2	35.1
59	20 34.6	+11.0	33.4	21 24.7	+11.5	33.6	22 14.6	+12.2	33.8	23 04.4	+12.8	34.0
60	20 45.6	+10.5	32.3	21 36.2	+11.2	32.5	22 26.8	+11.7	32.7	23 17.2	+12.3	33.0
61	20 56.1	+10.2	31.2	21 47.4	+10.7	31.5	22 38.5	+11.3	31.7	23 29.5	+11.9	31.9
62	21 06.3	+9.8	30.2	21 58.1	+10.3	30.4	22 49.8	+10.9	30.6	23 41.4	+11.4	30.8
63	21 16.1	+9.4	29.1	22 08.4	+9.9	29.3	23 00.7	+10.4	29.5	23 52.8	+11.0	29.7
64	21 25.5	+8.9	28.1	22 18.3	+9.5	28.3	23 11.1	+10.1	28.5	24 03.8	+10.6	28.7
65	21 34.4	+8.6	27.0	22 27.8	+9.1	27.2	23 21.2	+9.5	27.4	24 14.4	+10.1	27.6
66	21 43.0	+8.2	25.9	22 36.9	+8.7	26.1	23 30.7	+9.2	26.3	24 24.5	+9.6	26.5
67	21 51.2	+7.7	24.9	22 45.6	+8.2	25.1	23 39.9	+8.7	25.2	24 34.1	+9.2	25.4
68	21 58.9	+7.3	23.8	22 53.8	+7.8	24.0	23 48.6	+8.2	24.2	24 43.3	+8.7	24.3
69	22 06.2	+7.0	22.7	23 01.6	+7.3	22.9	23 56.8	+7.8	23.1	24 52.0	+8.2	23.3
70	22 13.2	+6.5	21.7	23 08.9	+6.9	21.8	24 04.6	+7.3	22.0	25 00.2	+7.7	22.2
71	22 19.7	+6.0	20.6	23 15.8	+6.5	20.7	24 11.9	+6.8	20.9	25 07.9	+7.3	21.1
72	22 25.7	+5.7	19.5	23 22.3	+6.0	19.7	24 18.7	+6.4	19.8	25 15.2	+6.7	20.0
73	22 31.4	+5.2	18.4	23 28.3	+5.5	18.6	24 25.1	+5.9	18.7	25 21.9	+6.3	18.9
74	22 36.6	+4.8	17.4	23 33.8	+5.1	17.5	24 31.0	+5.5	17.6	25 28.2	+5.8	17.8
75	22 41.4	+4.3	16.3	23 38.9	+4.7	16.4	24 36.5	+4.9	16.5	25 34.0	+5.2	16.7
76	22 45.7	+3.9	15.2	23 43.6	+4.2	15.3	24 41.4	+4.5	15.4	25 39.2	+4.8	15.6
77	22 49.6	+3.5	14.1	23 47.8	+3.7	14.2	24 45.9	+4.0	14.3	25 44.0	+4.3	14.5
78	22 53.1	+3.0	13.0	23 51.5	+3.3	13.1	24 49.9	+3.5	13.2	25 48.3	+3.8	13.3
79	22 56.1	+2.6	12.0	23 54.8	+2.8	12.0	24 53.4	+3.1	12.1	25 52.1	+3.3	12.2
80	22 58.7	+2.1	10.9	23 57.6	+2.3	10.9	24 56.5	+2.5	11.0	25 55.4	+2.7	11.1
81	23 00.8	+1.7	9.8	23 59.9	+1.9	9.9	24 59.0	+2.1	9.9	25 58.1	+2.3	10.0
82	23 02.5	+1.2	8.7	24 01.8	+1.4	8.8	25 01.1	+1.6	8.8	26 00.4	+1.7	8.9
83	23 03.7	+0.8	7.6	24 03.2	+1.0	7.7	25 02.7	+1.1	7.7	26 02.1	+1.3	7.8
84	23 04.5	+0.4	6.5	24 04.2	+0.4	6.6	25 03.8	+0.6	6.6	26 03.4	+0.7	6.7
85	23 04.9	−0.1	5.4	24 04.6	0.0	5.5	25 04.4	+0.1	5.5	26 04.1	+0.2	5.6
86	23 04.8	−0.5	4.3	24 04.6	−0.4	4.4	25 04.5	−0.4	4.4	26 04.3	−0.3	4.5
87	23 04.3	−1.0	3.3	24 04.2	−0.9	3.3	25 04.1	−0.9	3.3	26 04.0	−0.8	3.3
88	23 03.3	−1.4	2.2	24 03.3	−1.4	2.2	25 03.2	−1.4	2.2	26 03.2	−1.4	2.2
89	23 01.9	−1.9	1.1	24 01.9	−1.9	1.1	25 01.8	−1.8	1.1	26 01.8	−1.8	1.1
90	23 00.0	−2.3	0.0	24 00.0	−2.3	0.0	25 00.0	−2.3	0.0	26 00.0	−2.3	0.0
	23°			24°			25°			26°		

Dec.	27° Hc	27° d	27° Z	28° Hc	28° d	28° Z	29° Hc	29° d	29° Z	30° Hc	30° d	30° Z
°	° ′	′	°	° ′	′	°	° ′	′	°	° ′	′	°
0	1 46.9	+27.3	90.9	1 45.9	+28.2	90.9	1 44.9	+29.1	91.0	1 43.9	+30.0	91.0
1	2 14.2	+27.2	90.0	2 14.1	+28.2	90.1	2 14.0	+29.1	90.1	2 13.9	+30.0	90.1
2	2 41.4	+27.1	89.1	2 42.3	+28.1	89.2	2 43.1	+29.0	89.2	2 43.9	+29.9	89.3
3	3 08.5	+27.1	88.2	3 10.4	+28.0	88.3	3 12.1	+29.0	88.3	3 13.8	+29.9	88.4
4	3 35.6	+27.1	87.3	3 38.4	+28.0	87.4	3 41.1	+28.9	87.5	3 43.7	+29.8	87.5
5	4 02.7	+27.0	86.4	4 06.4	+27.9	86.5	4 10.0	+28.9	86.6	4 13.5	+29.8	86.7
6	4 29.7	+27.0	85.5	4 34.3	+27.9	85.6	4 38.9	+28.8	85.7	4 43.3	+29.7	85.8
7	4 56.7	+26.8	84.7	5 02.2	+27.8	84.7	5 07.7	+28.7	84.8	5 13.0	+29.7	84.9
8	5 23.5	+26.8	83.8	5 30.0	+27.7	83.8	5 36.4	+28.6	83.9	5 42.7	+29.5	84.0
9	5 50.3	+26.7	82.9	5 57.7	+27.7	83.0	6 05.0	+28.6	83.1	6 12.2	+29.5	83.2
10	6 17.0	+26.7	82.0	6 25.4	+27.5	82.1	6 33.6	+28.5	82.2	6 41.7	+29.4	82.3
11	6 43.7	+26.5	81.1	6 52.9	+27.5	81.2	7 02.1	+28.3	81.3	7 11.1	+29.3	81.4
12	7 10.2	+26.4	80.1	7 20.4	+27.3	80.3	7 30.4	+28.3	80.4	7 40.4	+29.2	80.5
13	7 36.6	+26.3	79.2	7 47.7	+27.2	79.4	7 58.7	+28.2	79.5	8 09.6	+29.0	79.7
14	8 02.9	+26.2	78.3	8 14.9	+27.1	78.5	8 26.9	+28.0	78.6	8 38.6	+29.0	78.8
15	8 29.1	+26.0	77.4	8 42.0	+27.0	77.6	8 54.9	+27.9	77.7	9 07.6	+28.8	77.9
16	8 55.1	+25.9	76.5	9 09.0	+26.9	76.7	9 22.8	+27.7	76.8	9 36.4	+28.6	77.0
17	9 21.0	+25.8	75.6	9 35.9	+26.7	75.8	9 50.5	+27.6	75.9	10 05.0	+28.6	76.1
18	9 46.8	+25.6	74.7	10 02.6	+26.5	74.9	10 18.1	+27.5	75.0	10 33.6	+28.3	75.2
19	10 12.4	+25.5	73.8	10 29.1	+26.4	73.9	10 45.6	+27.3	74.1	11 01.9	+28.3	74.3
20	10 37.9	+25.3	72.8	10 55.5	+26.2	73.0	11 12.9	+27.2	73.2	11 30.2	+28.0	73.4
21	11 03.2	+25.2	71.9	11 21.7	+26.1	72.1	11 40.1	+26.9	72.3	11 58.2	+27.9	72.5
22	11 28.4	+24.9	71.0	11 47.8	+25.9	71.2	12 07.0	+26.8	71.4	12 26.1	+27.7	71.6
23	11 53.3	+24.8	70.1	12 13.7	+25.7	70.3	12 33.8	+26.6	70.5	12 53.8	+27.5	70.7
24	12 18.1	+24.6	69.1	12 39.4	+25.5	69.3	13 00.4	+26.4	69.6	13 21.3	+27.3	69.8
25	12 42.7	+24.4	68.2	13 04.9	+25.3	68.4	13 26.8	+26.3	68.6	13 48.6	+27.1	68.9
26	13 07.1	+24.2	67.3	13 30.2	+25.1	67.5	13 53.1	+26.0	67.7	14 15.7	+26.9	67.9
27	13 31.3	+24.0	66.3	13 55.3	+24.9	66.6	14 19.1	+25.7	66.8	14 42.6	+26.7	67.0
28	13 55.3	+23.8	65.4	14 20.2	+24.6	65.6	14 44.8	+25.6	65.8	15 09.3	+26.4	66.1
29	14 19.1	+23.5	64.4	14 44.8	+24.5	64.7	15 10.4	+25.3	64.9	15 35.7	+26.2	65.2
30	14 42.6	+23.3	63.5	15 09.3	+24.2	63.7	15 35.7	+25.1	64.0	16 01.9	+26.0	64.2
31	15 05.9	+23.1	62.5	15 33.5	+23.9	62.8	16 00.8	+24.8	63.0	16 27.9	+25.7	63.3
32	15 29.0	+22.8	61.6	15 57.4	+23.7	61.8	16 25.6	+24.6	62.1	16 53.6	+25.5	62.3
33	15 51.8	+22.6	60.6	16 21.1	+23.5	60.9	16 50.2	+24.3	61.1	17 19.1	+25.1	61.4
34	16 14.4	+22.3	59.7	16 44.6	+23.1	59.9	17 14.5	+24.1	60.2	17 44.2	+24.9	60.4
35	16 36.7	+22.0	58.7	17 07.7	+22.9	58.9	17 38.6	+23.7	59.2	18 09.1	+24.7	59.5
36	16 58.7	+21.7	57.7	17 30.6	+22.6	58.0	18 02.3	+23.5	58.2	18 33.8	+24.3	58.5
37	17 20.4	+21.5	56.7	17 53.2	+22.4	57.0	18 25.8	+23.2	57.3	18 58.1	+24.0	57.6
38	17 41.9	+21.2	55.8	18 15.6	+22.0	56.0	18 49.0	+22.8	56.3	19 22.1	+23.7	56.6
39	18 03.1	+20.9	54.8	18 37.6	+21.7	55.0	19 11.8	+22.6	55.3	19 45.8	+23.4	55.6
40	18 24.0	+20.5	53.8	18 59.3	+21.4	54.1	19 34.4	+22.2	54.3	20 09.2	+23.1	54.6
41	18 44.5	+20.3	52.8	19 20.7	+21.1	53.1	19 56.6	+21.9	53.4	20 32.3	+22.8	53.7
42	19 04.8	+19.9	51.8	19 41.8	+20.7	52.1	20 18.5	+21.6	52.4	20 55.1	+22.4	52.7
43	19 24.7	+19.6	50.8	20 02.5	+20.5	51.1	20 40.1	+21.2	51.4	21 17.5	+22.0	51.7
44	19 44.3	+19.3	49.8	20 23.0	+20.0	50.1	21 01.3	+20.9	50.4	21 39.5	+21.7	50.7
45	20 03.6	+18.9	48.8	20 43.0	+19.8	49.1	21 22.2	+20.5	49.4	22 01.2	+21.3	49.7
46	20 22.5	+18.6	47.8	21 02.8	+19.3	48.1	21 42.7	+20.2	48.4	22 22.5	+20.9	48.7
47	20 41.1	+18.2	46.8	21 22.1	+19.0	47.0	22 02.9	+19.8	47.3	22 43.4	+20.6	47.6
48	20 59.3	+17.9	45.7	21 41.1	+18.6	46.0	22 22.7	+19.3	46.3	23 04.0	+20.1	46.6
49	21 17.2	+17.5	44.7	21 59.7	+18.3	45.0	22 42.0	+19.0	45.3	23 24.1	+19.8	45.6
50	21 34.7	+17.1	43.7	22 18.0	+17.8	44.0	23 01.0	+18.6	44.3	23 43.9	+19.3	44.6
51	21 51.8	+16.7	42.7	22 35.8	+17.4	42.9	23 19.6	+18.2	43.2	24 03.2	+18.9	43.5
52	22 08.5	+16.3	41.6	22 53.2	+17.1	41.9	23 37.8	+17.8	42.2	24 22.1	+18.5	42.5
53	22 24.8	+15.9	40.6	23 10.3	+16.6	40.9	23 55.6	+17.3	41.1	24 40.6	+18.1	41.4
54	22 40.7	+15.5	39.5	23 26.9	+16.2	39.8	24 12.9	+16.9	40.1	24 58.7	+17.6	40.4
55	22 56.2	+15.1	38.5	23 43.1	+15.8	38.8	24 29.8	+16.5	39.0	25 16.3	+17.2	39.3
56	23 11.3	+14.7	37.4	23 58.9	+15.3	37.7	24 46.3	+16.0	38.0	25 33.5	+16.7	38.3
57	23 26.0	+14.3	36.4	24 14.2	+14.9	36.6	25 02.3	+15.5	36.9	25 50.2	+16.2	37.2
58	23 40.3	+13.8	35.3	24 29.1	+14.5	35.6	25 17.8	+15.1	35.9	26 06.4	+15.7	36.1
59	23 54.1	+13.3	34.3	24 43.6	+14.0	34.5	25 32.9	+14.7	34.8	26 22.1	+15.3	35.1
60	24 07.4	+13.0	33.2	24 57.6	+13.5	33.4	25 47.6	+14.1	33.7	26 37.4	+14.8	34.0
61	24 20.4	+12.5	32.1	25 11.1	+13.1	32.4	26 01.7	+13.7	32.6	26 52.2	+14.3	32.9
62	24 32.9	+12.0	31.1	25 24.2	+12.6	31.3	26 15.4	+13.2	31.5	27 06.5	+13.7	31.8
63	24 44.9	+11.5	30.0	25 36.8	+12.1	30.2	26 28.6	+12.7	30.5	27 20.2	+13.3	30.7
64	24 56.4	+11.1	28.9	25 48.9	+11.6	29.1	26 41.3	+12.1	29.4	27 33.5	+12.7	29.6
65	25 07.5	+10.6	27.8	26 00.5	+11.2	28.0	26 53.4	+11.7	28.3	27 46.2	+12.2	28.5
66	25 18.1	+10.1	26.7	26 11.7	+10.6	26.9	27 05.1	+11.1	27.2	27 58.4	+11.7	27.4
67	25 28.2	+9.7	25.6	26 22.3	+10.1	25.8	27 16.2	+10.7	26.1	28 10.1	+11.1	26.3
68	25 37.9	+9.1	24.5	26 32.4	+9.7	24.7	27 26.9	+10.1	25.0	28 21.2	+10.6	25.2
69	25 47.0	+8.7	23.4	26 42.1	+9.1	23.6	27 37.0	+9.5	23.8	28 31.8	+10.0	24.1
70	25 55.7	+8.2	22.3	26 51.2	+8.6	22.5	27 46.5	+9.1	22.7	28 41.8	+9.5	22.9
71	26 03.9	+7.6	21.2	26 59.8	+8.0	21.4	27 55.6	+8.5	21.6	28 51.3	+8.9	21.8
72	26 11.5	+7.2	20.1	27 07.8	+7.6	20.3	28 04.1	+7.9	20.5	29 00.2	+8.4	20.7
73	26 18.7	+6.6	19.0	27 15.4	+7.0	19.2	28 12.0	+7.4	19.4	29 08.6	+7.7	19.5
74	26 25.3	+6.1	17.9	27 22.4	+6.4	18.1	28 19.4	+6.8	18.2	29 16.3	+7.2	18.4
75	26 31.4	+5.6	16.8	27 28.8	+6.0	17.0	28 26.2	+6.3	17.1	29 23.5	+6.6	17.3
76	26 37.0	+5.1	15.7	27 34.8	+5.4	15.8	28 32.5	+5.7	16.0	29 30.1	+6.1	16.1
77	26 42.1	+4.6	14.6	27 40.2	+4.8	14.7	28 38.2	+5.1	14.8	29 36.2	+5.4	15.0
78	26 46.7	+4.0	13.5	27 45.0	+4.3	13.6	28 43.3	+4.6	13.7	29 41.6	+4.8	13.8
79	26 50.7	+3.5	12.3	27 49.3	+3.8	12.5	28 47.9	+4.0	12.6	29 46.4	+4.3	12.7
80	26 54.2	+3.0	11.2	27 53.1	+3.2	11.3	28 51.9	+3.4	11.4	29 50.7	+3.6	11.5
81	26 57.2	+2.5	10.1	27 56.3	+2.6	10.2	28 55.3	+2.9	10.3	29 54.3	+3.1	10.4
82	26 59.7	+1.9	9.0	27 58.9	+2.1	9.1	28 58.2	+2.2	9.1	29 57.4	+2.4	9.2
83	27 01.6	+1.3	7.9	28 01.0	+1.5	7.9	29 00.4	+1.7	8.0	29 59.8	+1.9	8.1
84	27 02.9	+0.9	6.7	28 02.5	+1.0	6.8	29 02.1	+1.1	6.9	30 01.7	+1.2	6.9
85	27 03.8	+0.3	5.6	28 03.5	+0.4	5.7	29 03.2	+0.5	5.7	30 02.9	+0.6	5.8
86	27 04.1	−0.2	4.5	28 03.9	−0.1	4.5	29 03.7	0.0	4.6	30 03.5	+0.1	4.6
87	27 03.9	−0.8	3.4	28 03.8	−0.7	3.4	29 03.7	−0.7	3.4	30 03.6	−0.6	3.5
88	27 03.1	−1.3	2.2	28 03.1	−1.3	2.3	29 03.0	−1.2	2.3	30 03.0	−1.2	2.3
89	27 01.8	−1.8	1.1	28 01.8	−1.8	1.1	29 01.8	−1.8	1.1	30 01.8	−1.8	1.2
90	27 00.0	−2.4	0.0	28 00.0	−2.4	0.0	29 00.0	−2.4	0.0	30 00.0	−2.4	0.0
	27°			28°			29°			30°		

88°, 272° L.H.A. LATITUDE SAME NAME AS DECLINATION

360

LATITUDE CONTRARY NAME TO DECLINATION L.H.A. 88°, 272°

Dec.	23° Hc	d	Z	24° Hc	d	Z	25° Hc	d	Z	26° Hc	d	Z	27° Hc	d	Z	28° Hc	d	Z	29° Hc	d	Z	30° Hc	d	Z	Dec.
°	° ′	′	°	° ′	′	°	° ′	′	°	° ′	′	°	° ′	′	°	° ′	′	°	° ′	′	°	° ′	′	°	°
0	1 50.5	-23.5	90.8	1 49.6	-24.4	90.8	1 48.8	-25.4	90.8	1 47.9	-26.4	90.9	1 46.9	-27.2	90.9	1 45.9	-28.1	90.9	1 44.9	-29.1	91.0	1 43.9	-30.0	91.0	0
1	1 27.0	-23.5	91.7	1 25.2	-24.5	91.7	1 23.4	-25.4	91.8	1 21.5	-26.3	91.8	1 19.7	-27.3	91.8	1 17.8	-28.3	91.8	1 15.8	-29.1	91.8	1 13.9	-30.0	91.9	1
2	1 03.5	-23.5	92.6	1 00.7	-24.4	92.6	0 58.0	-25.5	92.7	0 55.2	-26.4	92.7	0 52.4	-27.3	92.7	0 49.5	-28.2	92.7	0 46.7	-29.1	92.7	0 43.9	-30.1	92.7	2
3	0 40.0	-23.5	93.5	0 36.3	-24.5	93.6	0 32.5	-25.4	93.6	0 28.8	-26.4	93.6	0 25.1	-27.3	93.6	0 21.3	-28.2	93.6	0 17.6	-29.2	93.6	0 13.8	-30.1	93.6	3
4	0 16.5	-23.6	94.5	0 11.8	-24.5	94.5	0 07.1	-25.4	94.5	0 02.4	-26.3	94.5	0 02.2	+27.3	85.5	0 06.9	+28.2	85.5	0 11.6	+29.1	85.5	0 16.3	+30.0	85.5	4
5	0 07.1	+23.5	84.6	0 12.7	+24.5	84.6	0 18.3	+25.4	84.6	0 23.9	+26.4	84.6	0 29.5	+27.3	84.6	0 35.1	+28.3	84.6	0 40.7	+29.2	84.7	0 46.3	+30.0	84.7	5
6	0 30.6	+23.5	83.7	0 37.2	+24.4	83.7	0 43.7	+25.4	83.7	0 50.3	+26.3	83.7	0 56.8	+27.3	83.7	1 03.4	+28.2	83.8	1 09.9	+29.1	83.8	1 16.3	+30.1	83.8	6
7	0 54.1	+23.5	82.8	1 01.6	+24.5	82.8	1 09.1	+25.4	82.8	1 16.6	+26.4	82.8	1 24.1	+27.3	82.9	1 31.6	+28.1	82.9	1 39.0	+29.1	82.9	1 46.4	+30.0	82.9	7
8	1 17.6	+23.5	81.9	1 26.1	+24.4	81.9	1 34.5	+25.4	81.9	1 43.0	+26.3	81.9	1 51.4	+27.2	82.0	1 59.7	+28.2	82.0	2 08.1	+29.0	82.0	2 16.4	+29.9	82.1	8
9	1 41.1	+23.4	80.9	1 50.5	+24.4	81.0	1 59.9	+25.3	81.0	2 09.3	+26.2	81.0	2 18.6	+27.2	81.1	2 27.9	+28.1	81.1	2 37.1	+29.1	81.2	2 46.3	+30.0	81.2	9
10	2 04.5	+23.4	80.0	2 14.9	+24.4	80.1	2 25.2	+25.4	80.1	2 35.5	+26.3	80.1	2 45.8	+27.2	80.2	2 56.0	+28.1	80.2	3 06.2	+28.9	80.3	3 16.3	+29.8	80.3	10
11	2 27.9	+23.4	79.1	2 39.3	+24.3	79.1	2 50.6	+25.2	79.2	3 01.8	+26.2	79.2	3 13.0	+27.1	79.3	3 24.1	+28.0	79.3	3 35.1	+29.0	79.4	3 46.1	+29.9	79.5	11
12	2 51.3	+23.4	78.2	3 03.6	+24.3	78.2	3 15.8	+25.2	78.3	3 28.0	+26.1	78.3	3 40.1	+27.0	78.4	3 52.1	+28.0	78.5	4 04.1	+28.9	78.5	4 16.0	+29.8	78.6	12
13	3 14.7	+23.2	77.2	3 27.9	+24.2	77.3	3 41.0	+25.2	77.4	3 54.1	+26.1	77.4	4 07.1	+27.0	77.5	4 20.1	+27.9	77.6	4 33.0	+28.8	77.6	4 45.8	+29.7	77.7	13
14	3 37.9	+23.3	76.3	3 52.1	+24.2	76.4	4 06.2	+25.1	76.5	4 20.2	+26.0	76.5	4 34.1	+27.0	76.6	4 48.0	+27.8	76.7	5 01.8	+28.7	76.8	5 15.5	+29.6	76.9	14
15	4 01.2	+23.1	75.4	4 16.3	+24.1	75.5	4 31.3	+25.0	75.5	4 46.2	+26.0	75.6	5 01.1	+26.8	75.7	5 15.8	+27.8	75.8	5 30.5	+28.7	75.9	5 45.1	+29.5	76.0	15
16	4 24.3	+23.1	74.5	4 40.4	+24.0	74.6	4 56.3	+25.0	74.6	5 12.2	+25.8	74.7	5 27.9	+26.8	74.8	5 43.6	+27.7	74.9	5 59.2	+28.6	75.0	6 14.6	+29.5	75.1	16
17	4 47.4	+23.1	73.6	5 04.4	+23.9	73.6	5 21.3	+24.8	73.7	5 38.0	+25.8	73.8	5 54.7	+26.7	73.9	6 11.3	+27.6	74.0	6 27.8	+28.4	74.1	6 44.1	+29.4	74.2	17
18	5 10.5	+22.9	72.6	5 28.3	+23.9	72.7	5 46.1	+24.8	72.8	6 03.8	+25.7	72.9	6 21.4	+26.6	73.0	6 38.9	+27.5	73.1	6 56.2	+28.4	73.2	7 13.5	+29.3	73.4	18
19	5 33.4	+22.9	71.7	5 52.2	+23.8	71.8	6 10.9	+24.7	71.9	6 29.5	+25.6	72.0	6 48.0	+26.5	72.1	7 06.4	+27.4	72.2	7 24.6	+28.3	72.3	7 42.8	+29.1	72.5	19
20	5 56.3	+22.7	70.8	6 16.0	+23.7	70.9	6 35.6	+24.6	71.0	6 55.1	+25.5	71.1	7 14.5	+26.4	71.2	7 33.8	+27.3	71.3	7 52.9	+28.2	71.5	8 11.9	+29.1	71.6	20
21	6 19.0	+22.7	69.8	6 39.7	+23.5	69.9	7 00.2	+24.5	70.1	7 20.6	+25.4	70.2	7 40.9	+26.3	70.3	8 01.1	+27.1	70.4	8 21.1	+28.0	70.6	8 41.0	+28.9	70.7	21
22	6 41.7	+22.6	68.9	7 03.2	+23.5	69.0	7 24.7	+24.3	69.1	7 46.0	+25.2	69.3	8 07.2	+26.1	69.4	8 28.2	+27.1	69.5	8 49.1	+28.0	69.7	9 09.9	+28.8	69.8	22
23	7 04.3	+22.4	68.0	7 26.7	+23.4	68.1	7 49.0	+24.3	68.2	8 11.2	+25.2	68.3	8 33.3	+26.0	68.5	8 55.3	+26.9	68.6	9 17.1	+27.7	68.8	9 38.7	+28.7	68.9	23
24	7 26.7	+22.3	67.0	7 50.1	+23.2	67.2	8 13.3	+24.1	67.3	8 36.4	+25.0	67.4	8 59.3	+25.9	67.6	9 22.2	+26.7	67.7	9 44.8	+27.7	67.9	10 07.4	+28.5	68.0	24
25	7 49.0	+22.2	66.1	8 13.3	+23.1	66.2	8 37.4	+24.0	66.4	9 01.4	+24.9	66.5	9 25.2	+25.8	66.7	9 48.9	+26.7	66.8	10 12.5	+27.5	67.0	10 35.9	+28.3	67.1	25
26	8 11.2	+22.1	65.2	8 36.4	+22.9	65.3	9 01.4	+23.8	65.4	9 26.3	+24.7	65.6	9 51.0	+25.6	65.7	10 15.6	+26.4	65.9	10 40.0	+27.3	66.1	11 04.2	+28.2	66.2	26
27	8 33.3	+22.0	64.2	8 59.3	+22.9	64.4	9 25.2	+23.7	64.5	9 51.0	+24.6	64.7	10 16.6	+25.4	64.8	10 42.0	+26.4	65.0	11 07.3	+27.2	65.2	11 32.4	+28.1	65.3	27
28	8 55.3	+21.8	63.3	9 22.2	+22.6	63.4	9 48.9	+23.6	63.6	10 15.6	+24.4	63.7	10 42.0	+25.3	63.9	11 08.4	+26.1	64.1	11 34.5	+27.0	64.3	12 00.5	+27.8	64.4	28
29	9 17.1	+21.6	62.3	9 44.8	+22.6	62.5	10 12.5	+23.4	62.6	10 40.0	+24.2	62.8	11 07.3	+25.1	63.0	11 34.5	+26.0	63.2	12 01.5	+26.8	63.3	12 28.3	+27.7	63.5	29
30	9 38.7	+21.5	61.4	10 07.4	+22.3	61.5	10 35.9	+23.2	61.7	11 04.2	+24.1	61.9	11 32.4	+25.0	62.1	12 00.5	+25.8	62.2	12 28.3	+26.7	62.4	12 56.0	+27.5	62.6	30
31	10 00.2	+21.3	60.4	10 29.7	+22.2	60.6	10 59.1	+23.1	60.8	11 28.3	+23.9	60.9	11 57.4	+24.7	61.1	12 26.3	+25.6	61.3	12 55.0	+26.5	61.5	13 23.5	+27.3	61.7	31
32	10 21.5	+21.2	59.5	10 51.9	+22.0	59.7	11 22.2	+22.8	59.8	11 52.2	+23.7	60.0	12 22.1	+24.6	60.2	12 51.9	+25.4	60.4	13 21.4	+26.3	60.6	13 50.8	+27.1	60.8	32
33	10 42.7	+21.0	58.5	11 13.9	+21.9	58.7	11 45.0	+22.7	58.9	12 15.9	+23.6	59.1	12 46.7	+24.4	59.3	13 17.3	+25.2	59.5	13 47.7	+26.0	59.7	14 17.9	+26.9	59.9	33
34	11 03.7	+20.8	57.6	11 35.8	+21.6	57.8	12 07.7	+22.5	57.9	12 39.5	+23.3	58.1	13 11.1	+24.1	58.3	13 42.5	+25.0	58.5	14 13.7	+25.9	58.7	14 44.8	+26.6	59.0	34
35	11 24.5	+20.6	56.6	11 57.4	+21.5	56.8	12 30.2	+22.3	57.0	13 02.8	+23.1	57.2	13 35.2	+24.0	57.4	14 07.5	+24.8	57.6	14 39.6	+25.6	57.8	15 11.4	+26.5	58.0	35
36	11 45.1	+20.5	55.7	12 18.9	+21.2	55.8	12 52.5	+22.1	56.0	13 25.9	+22.9	56.2	13 59.2	+23.7	56.4	14 32.3	+24.5	56.6	15 05.2	+25.3	56.9	15 37.9	+26.2	57.1	36
37	12 05.6	+20.2	54.7	12 40.1	+21.1	54.9	13 14.6	+21.8	55.1	13 48.8	+22.7	55.3	14 22.9	+23.5	55.5	14 56.8	+24.3	55.7	15 30.5	+25.2	55.9	16 04.1	+25.9	56.2	37
38	12 25.8	+20.0	53.7	13 01.2	+20.8	53.9	13 36.4	+21.7	54.1	14 11.5	+22.5	54.3	14 46.4	+23.3	54.5	15 21.1	+24.1	54.8	15 55.7	+24.9	55.0	16 30.0	+25.7	55.2	38
39	12 45.8	+19.8	52.8	13 22.0	+20.7	53.0	13 58.1	+21.4	53.2	14 34.0	+22.2	53.4	15 09.7	+23.0	53.6	15 45.2	+23.8	53.8	16 20.6	+24.6	54.0	16 55.7	+25.4	54.3	39
40	13 05.6	+19.6	51.8	13 42.7	+20.3	52.0	14 19.5	+21.2	52.2	14 56.2	+22.0	52.4	15 32.7	+22.8	52.6	16 09.0	+23.6	52.8	16 45.2	+24.3	53.1	17 21.1	+25.2	53.3	40
41	13 25.2	+19.4	50.8	14 03.0	+20.2	51.0	14 40.7	+20.9	51.2	15 18.2	+21.7	51.4	15 55.5	+22.5	51.7	16 32.6	+23.3	51.9	17 09.5	+24.1	52.1	17 46.3	+24.9	52.4	41
42	13 44.6	+19.2	49.9	14 23.2	+19.9	50.1	15 01.6	+20.7	50.3	15 39.9	+21.5	50.5	16 18.0	+22.3	50.7	16 55.9	+23.1	50.9	17 33.6	+23.9	51.2	18 11.2	+24.6	51.4	42
43	14 03.8	+18.9	48.9	14 43.1	+19.7	49.1	15 22.3	+20.5	49.3	16 01.4	+21.2	49.5	16 40.3	+22.0	49.7	17 19.0	+22.7	50.0	17 57.5	+23.5	50.2	18 35.8	+24.3	50.5	43
44	14 22.7	+18.6	47.9	15 02.8	+19.4	48.1	15 42.8	+20.2	48.3	16 22.6	+21.0	48.5	17 02.3	+21.7	48.8	17 41.7	+22.5	49.0	18 21.0	+23.2	49.2	19 00.1	+24.0	49.5	44
45	14 41.3	+18.5	46.9	15 22.2	+19.2	47.1	16 03.0	+19.9	47.3	16 43.6	+20.6	47.6	17 24.0	+21.4	47.8	18 04.2	+22.2	48.0	18 44.2	+23.0	48.3	19 24.1	+23.7	48.5	45
46	14 59.8	+18.1	45.9	15 41.4	+18.9	46.1	16 22.9	+19.6	46.4	17 04.2	+20.4	46.6	17 45.4	+21.1	46.8	18 26.4	+21.8	47.0	19 07.2	+22.6	47.3	19 47.8	+23.3	47.5	46
47	15 17.9	+17.9	45.0	16 00.3	+18.6	45.2	16 42.5	+19.4	45.4	17 24.6	+20.1	45.6	18 06.5	+20.9	45.8	18 48.2	+21.6	46.1	19 29.8	+22.3	46.3	20 11.1	+23.1	46.6	47
48	15 35.8	+17.7	44.0	16 18.9	+18.4	44.2	17 01.9	+19.1	44.4	17 44.7	+19.8	44.6	18 27.4	+20.5	44.8	19 09.8	+21.3	45.1	19 52.1	+22.0	45.3	20 34.2	+22.7	45.6	48
49	15 53.5	+17.3	43.0	16 37.3	+18.1	43.2	17 21.0	+18.8	43.4	18 04.5	+19.5	43.6	18 47.9	+20.2	43.8	19 31.1	+20.9	44.1	20 14.1	+21.6	44.3	20 56.9	+22.4	44.6	49
50	16 10.8	+17.1	42.0	16 55.4	+17.8	42.2	17 39.8	+18.4	42.4	18 24.0	+19.2	42.6	19 08.1	+19.9	42.8	19 52.0	+20.6	43.1	20 35.7	+21.3	43.3	21 19.3	+22.0	43.6	50
51	16 27.9	+16.8	41.0	17 13.2	+17.4	41.2	17 58.2	+18.2	41.4	18 43.2	+18.8	41.6	19 28.0	+19.5	41.8	20 12.6	+20.2	42.1	20 57.0	+21.0	42.3	21 41.3	+21.6	42.6	51
52	16 44.7	+16.5	40.0	17 30.6	+17.2	40.2	18 16.4	+17.9	40.4	19 02.0	+18.6	40.6	19 47.5	+19.2	40.8	20 32.8	+19.9	41.1	21 18.0	+20.6	41.3	22 02.9	+21.3	41.6	52
53	17 01.2	+16.3	39.0	17 47.8	+16.9	39.2	18 34.3	+17.5	39.4	19 20.6	+18.2	39.6	20 06.7	+18.9	39.8	20 52.7	+19.6	40.1	21 38.6	+20.2	40.3	22 24.2	+20.9	40.6	53
54	17 17.5	+15.9	38.0	18 04.7	+16.6	38.2	18 51.8	+17.2	38.4	19 38.8	+17.8	38.6	20 25.6	+18.5	38.8	21 12.3	+19.2	39.1	21 58.8	+19.8	39.3	22 45.1	+20.5	39.6	54
55	17 33.4	+15.6	37.0	18 21.3	+16.2	37.2	19 09.0	+16.9	37.4	19 56.6	+17.6	37.6	20 44.1	+18.2	37.8	21 31.5	+18.8	38.0	22 18.6	+19.5	38.3	23 05.6	+20.2	38.5	55
56	17 49.0	+15.3	35.9	18 37.5	+15.9	36.1	19 25.9	+16.5	36.3	20 14.2	+17.1	36.6	21 02.3	+17.8	36.8	21 50.3	+18.4	37.0	22 38.1	+19.1	37.3	23 25.8	+19.7	37.5	56
57	18 04.3	+14.9	34.9	18 53.4	+15.6	35.1	19 42.4	+16.2	35.3	20 31.3	+16.8	35.5	21 20.1	+17.4	35.8	22 08.7	+18.0	36.0	22 57.2	+18.6	36.2	23 45.5	+19.3	36.5	57
58	18 19.2	+14.7	33.9	19 09.0	+15.2	34.1	19 58.6	+15.8	34.3	20 48.1	+16.4	34.5	21 37.5	+17.0	34.7	22 26.7	+17.7	35.0	23 15.8	+18.3	35.2	24 04.8	+18.9	35.5	58
59	18 33.9	+14.3	32.9	19 24.2	+14.9	33.1	20 14.4	+15.5	33.3	21 04.5	+16.1	33.5	21 54.5	+16.7	33.7	22 44.4	+17.2	33.9	23 34.1	+17.8	34.2	24 23.7	+18.4	34.4	59
60	18 48.2	+14.0	31.9	19 39.1	+14.5	32.0	20 29.9	+15.1	32.2	21 20.6	+15.7	32.4	22 11.2	+16.2	32.7	23 01.6	+16.9	32.9	23 51.9	+17.5	33.1	24 42.1	+18.0	33.4	60
61	19 02.2	+13.6	30.8	19 53.6	+14.2	31.0	20 45.0	+14.8	31.2	21 36.3	+15.3	31.4	22 27.4	+15.9	31.6	23 18.5	+16.4	31.8	24 09.4	+17.0	32.1	25 00.1	+17.6	32.3	61
62	19 15.8	+13.3	29.8	20 07.8	+13.8	30.0	20 59.8	+14.3	30.2	21 51.6	+14.9	30.4	22 43.3	+15.4	30.6	23 34.9	+16.0	30.8	24 26.4	+16.5	31.0	25 17.7	+17.1	31.3	62
63	19 29.1	+12.9	28.8	20 21.6	+13.5	28.9	21 14.1	+14.0	29.1	22 06.5	+14.5	29.3	22 58.7	+15.1	29.5	23 50.9	+15.6	29.7	24 42.9	+16.1	30.0	25 34.8	+16.7	30.2	63
64	19 42.0	+12.6	27.7	20 35.1	+13.1	27.9	21 28.1	+13.6	28.1	22 21.0	+14.1	28.3	23 13.8	+14.6	28.5	24 06.5	+15.1	28.7	24 59.0	+15.7	28.9	25 51.5	+16.2	29.1	64
65	19 54.6	+12.2	26.7	20 48.2	+12.7	26.9	21 41.7	+13.1	27.0	22 35.1	+13.6	27.2	23 28.4	+14.1	27.4	24 21.6	+14.7	27.6	25 14.7	+15.2	27.8	26 07.7	+15.7	28.1	65
66	20 06.8	+11.9	25.7	21 00.9	+12.3	25.8	21 54.8	+12.8	26.0	22 48.7	+13.3	26.2	23 42.5	+13.8	26.4	24 36.3	+14.2	26.6	25 29.9	+14.7	26.8	26 23.4	+15.2	27.0	66
67	20 18.7	+11.4	24.6	21 13.2	+11.9	24.8	22 07.6	+12.4	24.9	23 02.0	+12.8	25.1	23 56.3	+13.3	25.3	24 50.5	+13.8	25.5	25 44.6	+14.3	25.7	26 38.6	+14.8	25.9	67
68	20 30.1	+11.1	23.6	21 25.1	+11.5	23.7	22 20.0	+12.0	23.9	23 14.8	+12.4	24.0	24 09.6	+12.8	24.2	25 04.3	+13.3	24.4	25 58.9	+13.7	24.6	26 53.4	+14.2	24.8	68
69	20 41.2	+10.7	22.5	21 36.6	+11.2	22.7	22 32.0	+11.5	22.8	23 27.2	+12.0	23.0	24 22.4	+12.4	23.2	25 17.6	+12.8	23.3	26 12.6	+13.3	23.5	27 07.6	+13.7	23.7	69
70	20 51.9	+10.4	21.5	21 47.8	+10.7	21.6	22 43.5	+11.1	21.8	23 39.2	+11.5	21.9	24 34.8	+12.0	22.1	25 30.4	+12.4	22.3	26 25.9	+12.8	22.4	27 21.3	+13.2	22.6	70
71	21 02.3	+9.9	20.4	21 58.5	+10.3	20.5	22 54.6	+10.7	20.7	23 50.7	+11.1	20.8	24 46.8	+11.5	21.0	25 42.8	+11.8	21.2	26 38.7	+12.3	21.3	27 34.5	+12.7	21.5	71
72	21 12.2	+9.5	19.3	22 08.8	+9.9	19.5	23 05.3	+10.3	19.6	24 01.8	+10.7	19.8	24 58.3	+11.0	19.9	25 54.6	+11.4	20.1	26 51.0	+11.7	20.3	27 47.2	+12.2	20.4	72
73	21 21.7	+9.2	18.3	22 18.7	+9.5	18.4	23 15.6	+9.8	18.5	24 12.5	+10.1	18.7	25 09.3	+10.5	18.8	26 06.0	+10.9	19.0	27 02.7	+11.3	19.2	27 59.4	+11.6	19.3	73
74	21 30.9	+8.7	17.2	22 28.2	+9.0	17.3	23 25.4	+9.4	17.5	24 22.6	+9.8	17.6	25 19.8	+10.1	17.7	26 16.9	+10.4	17.9	27 14.0	+10.7	18.0	28 11.0	+11.1	18.2	74
75	21 39.6	+8.3	16.2	22 37.2	+8.7	16.3	23 34.8	+8.9	16.4	24 32.4	+9.2	16.5	25 29.9	+9.5	16.7	26 27.3	+9.9	16.8	27 24.7	+10.2	16.9	28 22.1	+10.5	17.1	75
76	21 47.9	+8.0	15.1	22 45.9	+8.2	15.2	23 43.7	+8.5	15.3	24 41.6	+8.8	15.4	25 39.4	+9.1	15.6	26 37.2	+9.4	15.7	27 34.9	+9.7	15.8	28 32.6	+10.0	16.0	76
77	21 55.9	+7.5	14.0	22 54.1	+7.7	14.1	23 52.2	+8.1	14.2	24 50.4	+8.3	14.3	25 48.5	+8.6	14.5	26 46.6	+8.8	14.6	27 44.6	+9.2	14.7	28 42.6	+9.5	14.9	77
78	22 03.4	+7.0	13.0	23 01.8	+7.4	13.0	24 00.3	+7.5	13.1	24 58.7	+7.8	13.3	25 57.1	+8.0	13.4	26 55.4	+8.4	13.5	27 53.8	+8.6	13.6	28 52.1	+8.8	13.7	78
79	22 10.4	+6.7	11.9	23 09.2	+6.8	12.0	24 07.8	+7.1	12.1	25 06.5	+7.3	12.2	26 05.1	+7.6	12.3	27 03.8	+7.8	12.4	28 02.4	+8.0	12.5	29 00.9	+8.3	12.6	79
80	22 17.1	+6.2	10.8	23 16.0	+6.5	10.9	24 14.9	+6.7	11.0	25 13.8	+6.9	11.1	26 12.7	+7.1	11.2	27 11.6	+7.3	11.3	28 10.4	+7.5	11.4	29 09.2	+7.8	11.5	80
81	22 23.3	+5.9	9.7	23 22.5	+6.0	9.8	24 21.6	+6.2	9.9	25 20.7	+6.4	10.0	26 19.8	+6.5	10.0	27 18.9	+6.7	10.1	28 17.9	+7.0	10.2	29 17.0	+7.1	10.3	81
82	22 29.2	+5.3	8.7	23 28.5	+5.5	8.7	24 27.8	+5.7	8.8	25 27.1	+5.8	8.9	26 26.3	+6.1	8.9	27 25.6	+6.2	9.0	28 24.9	+6.3	9.1	29 24.1	+6.6	9.2	82
83	22 34.5	+5.0	7.6	23 34.0	+5.1	7.6	24 33.5	+5.2	7.7	25 32.9	+5.4	7.8	26 32.4	+5.5	7.8	27 31.8	+5.7	7.9	28 31.2	+5.9	8.0	29 30.7	+5.9	8.0	83
84	22 39.5	+4.5	6.5	23 39.1	+4.6	6.5	24 38.7	+4.8	6.6	25 38.3	+4.9	6.7	26 37.9	+5.0	6.7	27 37.5	+5.1	6.8	28 37.1	+5.2	6.8	29 36.6	+5.4	6.9	84
85	22 44.0	+4.1	5.4	23 43.7	+4.2	5.5	24 43.5	+4.2	5.5	25 43.2	+4.4	5.5	26 42.9	+4.5	5.6	27 42.6	+4.6	5.6	28 42.3	+4.7	5.7	29 42.0	+4.8	5.8	85
86	22 48.1	+3.6	4.3	23 47.9	+3.7	4.4	24 47.7	+3.8	4.4	25 47.6	+3.8	4.4	26 47.4	+3.9	4.5	27 47.2	+4.0	4.5	28 47.0	+4.1	4.6	29 46.8	+4.2	4.6	86
87	22 51.7	+3.2	3.3	23 51.6	+3.3	3.3	24 51.5	+3.3	3.3	25 51.4	+3.4	3.3	26 51.3	+3.4	3.4	27 51.2	+3.5	3.4	28 51.1	+3.6	3.4	29 51.0	+3.6	3.5	87
88	22 54.9	+2.8	2.2	23 54.9	+2.8	2.2	24 54.8	+2.9	2.2	25 54.8	+2.9	2.2	26 54.7	+2.9	2.2	27 54.7	+2.9	2.3	28 54.7	+2.9	2.3	29 54.6	+3.0	2.3	88
89	22 57.7	+2.3	1.1	23 57.7	+2.3	1.1	24 57.7	+2.3	1.1	25 57.7	+2.3	1.1	26 57.6	+2.4	1.1	27 57.6	+2.4	1.1	28 57.6	+2.4	1.1	29 57.6	+2.4	1.2	89
90	23 00.0	+1.9	0.0	24 00.0	+1.9	0.0	25 00.0	+1.8	0.0	26 00.0	+1.8	0.0	27 00.0	+1.8	0.0	28 00.0	+1.8	0.0	29 00.0	+1.8	0.0	30 00.0	+1.8	0.0	90
	23°			24°			25°			26°			27°			28°			29°			30°			

S. Lat. {L.H.A. greater than 180° ....Zn=180°−Z; L.H.A. less than 180°...........Zn=180°+Z

LATITUDE SAME NAME AS DECLINATION L.H.A. 92°, 268°

89°, 271° L.H.A. **LATITUDE SAME NAME AS DECLINATION** N. Lat. {L.H.A. greater than 180° .....Zn=Z
L.H.A. less than 180°............Zn=360°−Z

	23°			24°			25°			26°			27°			28°			29°			30°			
Dec.	Hc	d	Z	Hc	d	Z	Hc	d	Z	Hc	d	Z	Hc	d	Z	Hc	d	Z	Hc	d	Z	Hc	d	Z	Dec.
°	° ′	′	°	° ′	′	°	° ′	′	°	° ′	′	°	° ′	′	°	° ′	′	°	° ′	′	°	° ′	′	°	°
0	0 55.2	+23.5	90.4	0 54.8	+24.4	90.4	0 54.4	+25.3	90.4	0 53.9	+26.3	90.4	0 53.5	+27.2	90.5	0 53.0	+28.1	90.5	0 52.5	+29.1	90.5	0 52.0	+30.0	90.5	0
1	1 18.7	+23.4	89.5	1 19.2	+24.4	89.5	1 19.7	+25.4	89.5	1 20.2	+26.3	89.5	1 20.7	+27.2	89.6	1 21.1	+28.2	89.6	1 21.6	+29.0	89.6	1 22.0	+29.9	89.6	1
2	1 42.1	+23.4	88.5	1 43.6	+24.3	88.6	1 45.1	+25.3	88.6	1 46.5	+26.3	88.6	1 47.9	+27.2	88.7	1 49.3	+28.1	88.7	1 50.6	+29.1	88.7	1 51.9	+30.0	88.8	2
3	2 05.5	+23.3	87.6	2 07.9	+24.4	87.7	2 10.4	+25.2	87.7	2 12.8	+26.2	87.7	2 15.1	+27.2	87.8	2 17.4	+28.1	87.8	2 19.7	+29.0	87.9	2 21.9	+29.9	87.9	3
4	2 28.8	+23.4	86.7	2 32.3	+24.2	86.7	2 35.6	+25.3	86.8	2 39.0	+26.2	86.8	2 42.3	+27.1	86.9	2 45.5	+28.0	86.9	2 48.7	+28.9	87.0	2 51.8	+29.9	87.0	4
5	2 52.2	+23.2	85.8	2 56.5	+24.3	85.8	3 00.9	+25.2	85.9	3 05.2	+26.1	85.9	3 09.4	+27.0	86.0	3 13.5	+28.0	86.0	3 17.6	+29.0	86.1	3 21.7	+29.8	86.2	5
6	3 15.4	+23.3	84.9	3 20.8	+24.2	84.9	3 26.1	+25.1	85.0	3 31.3	+26.1	85.0	3 36.4	+27.1	85.1	3 41.5	+28.0	85.2	3 46.6	+28.8	85.2	3 51.5	+29.8	85.3	6
7	3 38.7	+23.1	83.9	3 45.0	+24.1	84.0	3 51.2	+25.1	84.1	3 57.4	+26.0	84.1	4 03.5	+26.9	84.2	4 09.5	+27.9	84.3	4 15.4	+28.8	84.3	4 21.3	+29.7	84.4	7
8	4 01.8	+23.1	83.0	4 09.1	+24.1	83.1	4 16.3	+25.0	83.2	4 23.4	+26.0	83.2	4 30.4	+26.9	83.3	4 37.4	+27.8	83.4	4 44.2	+28.8	83.5	4 51.0	+29.7	83.6	8
9	4 24.9	+23.1	82.1	4 33.2	+24.0	82.2	4 41.3	+24.9	82.2	4 49.4	+25.8	82.3	4 57.3	+26.8	82.4	5 05.2	+27.7	82.5	5 13.0	+28.7	82.6	5 20.7	+29.6	82.7	9
10	4 48.0	+22.9	81.2	4 57.2	+23.9	81.2	5 06.2	+24.9	81.3	5 15.2	+25.8	81.4	5 24.1	+26.8	81.5	5 32.9	+27.7	81.6	5 41.7	+28.5	81.7	5 50.3	+29.5	81.8	10
11	5 10.9	+22.9	80.2	5 21.1	+23.8	80.3	5 31.1	+24.8	80.4	5 41.0	+25.8	80.5	5 50.9	+26.6	80.6	6 00.6	+27.6	80.7	6 10.2	+28.5	80.8	6 19.8	+29.4	80.9	11
12	5 33.8	+22.8	79.3	5 44.9	+23.8	79.4	5 55.9	+24.7	79.5	6 06.8	+25.6	79.6	6 17.5	+26.6	79.7	6 28.2	+27.5	79.8	6 38.7	+28.4	79.9	6 49.2	+29.3	80.1	12
13	5 56.6	+22.7	78.4	6 08.7	+23.6	78.5	6 20.6	+24.6	78.6	6 32.4	+25.5	78.7	6 44.1	+26.5	78.8	6 55.7	+27.4	78.9	7 07.1	+28.3	79.0	7 18.5	+29.2	79.2	13
14	6 19.3	+22.6	77.4	6 32.3	+23.6	77.6	6 45.2	+24.5	77.7	6 57.9	+25.5	77.8	7 10.6	+26.3	77.9	7 23.1	+27.2	78.0	7 35.4	+28.2	78.2	7 47.7	+29.1	78.3	14
15	6 41.9	+22.5	76.5	6 55.9	+23.4	76.6	7 09.7	+24.3	76.7	7 23.4	+25.3	76.9	7 36.9	+26.3	77.0	7 50.3	+27.2	77.1	8 03.6	+28.1	77.3	8 16.8	+29.0	77.4	15
16	7 04.4	+22.4	75.6	7 19.3	+23.3	75.7	7 34.0	+24.3	75.8	7 48.7	+25.2	76.0	8 03.2	+26.1	76.1	8 17.5	+27.1	76.2	8 31.7	+28.0	76.4	8 45.8	+28.8	76.5	16
17	7 26.8	+22.3	74.6	7 42.6	+23.2	74.8	7 58.3	+24.2	74.9	8 13.9	+25.0	75.0	8 29.3	+26.0	75.2	8 44.6	+26.9	75.3	8 59.7	+27.8	75.5	9 14.6	+28.8	75.6	17
18	7 49.1	+22.1	73.7	8 05.8	+23.1	73.8	8 22.5	+24.0	74.0	8 38.9	+25.0	74.1	8 55.3	+25.8	74.3	9 11.5	+26.8	74.4	9 27.5	+27.7	74.6	9 43.4	+28.6	74.7	18
19	8 11.2	+22.0	72.8	8 28.9	+23.0	72.9	8 46.5	+23.8	73.1	9 03.9	+24.8	73.2	9 21.1	+25.8	73.4	9 38.3	+26.6	73.5	9 55.2	+27.5	73.7	10 12.0	+28.4	73.9	19
20	8 33.2	+21.9	71.8	8 51.9	+22.8	72.0	9 10.3	+23.8	72.1	9 28.7	+24.6	72.3	9 46.9	+25.5	72.4	10 04.9	+26.5	72.6	10 22.7	+27.4	72.8	10 40.4	+28.3	73.0	20
21	8 55.1	+21.7	70.9	9 14.7	+22.6	71.0	9 34.1	+23.6	71.2	9 53.3	+24.6	71.4	10 12.4	+25.5	71.5	10 31.4	+26.3	71.7	10 50.1	+27.3	71.9	11 08.7	+28.1	72.1	21
22	9 16.8	+21.6	69.9	9 37.3	+22.5	70.1	9 57.7	+23.4	70.3	10 17.9	+24.3	70.4	10 37.9	+25.2	70.6	10 57.7	+26.2	70.8	11 17.4	+27.0	71.0	11 36.8	+28.0	71.2	22
23	9 38.4	+21.4	69.0	9 59.8	+22.4	69.2	10 21.1	+23.3	69.3	10 42.2	+24.2	69.5	11 03.1	+25.1	69.7	11 23.9	+26.0	69.9	11 44.4	+26.9	70.1	12 04.8	+27.8	70.3	23
24	9 59.8	+21.3	68.0	10 22.2	+22.2	68.2	10 44.4	+23.1	68.4	11 06.4	+24.0	68.6	11 28.2	+24.9	68.8	11 49.9	+25.8	68.9	12 11.3	+26.7	69.1	12 32.6	+27.6	69.3	24
25	10 21.1	+21.1	67.1	10 44.4	+22.0	67.3	11 07.5	+22.9	67.4	11 30.4	+23.8	67.6	11 53.1	+24.8	67.8	12 15.7	+25.6	68.0	12 38.0	+26.6	68.2	13 00.2	+27.4	68.4	25
26	10 42.2	+20.9	66.1	11 06.4	+21.8	66.3	11 30.4	+22.7	66.5	11 54.2	+23.7	66.7	12 17.9	+24.5	66.9	12 41.3	+25.5	67.1	13 04.6	+26.3	67.3	13 27.6	+27.2	67.5	26
27	11 03.1	+20.8	65.2	11 28.2	+21.7	65.4	11 53.1	+22.6	65.6	12 17.9	+23.4	65.8	12 42.4	+24.4	66.0	13 06.8	+25.2	66.2	13 30.9	+26.1	66.4	13 54.8	+27.0	66.6	27
28	11 23.9	+20.5	64.2	11 49.9	+21.4	64.4	12 15.7	+22.3	64.6	12 41.3	+23.3	64.8	13 06.8	+24.1	65.0	13 32.0	+25.0	65.2	13 57.0	+25.9	65.5	14 21.8	+26.8	65.7	28
29	11 44.4	+20.4	63.3	12 11.3	+21.3	63.5	12 38.0	+22.2	63.7	13 04.6	+23.0	63.9	13 30.9	+23.9	64.1	13 57.0	+24.8	64.3	14 22.9	+25.7	64.5	14 48.6	+26.6	64.8	29
30	12 04.8	+20.2	62.3	12 32.6	+21.1	62.5	13 00.2	+21.9	62.7	13 27.6	+22.8	62.9	13 54.8	+23.7	63.1	14 21.8	+24.6	63.4	14 48.6	+25.5	63.6	15 15.2	+26.4	63.8	30
31	12 25.0	+19.9	61.3	12 53.7	+20.8	61.5	13 22.1	+21.8	61.8	13 50.4	+22.7	62.0	14 18.5	+23.5	62.2	14 46.4	+24.4	62.4	15 14.1	+25.2	62.7	15 41.6	+26.1	62.9	31
32	12 44.9	+19.8	60.4	13 14.5	+20.6	60.6	13 43.9	+21.5	60.8	14 13.1	+22.3	61.0	14 42.0	+23.3	61.2	15 10.8	+24.1	61.5	15 39.3	+25.0	61.7	16 07.7	+25.8	62.0	32
33	13 04.7	+19.5	59.4	13 35.1	+20.4	59.6	14 05.4	+21.3	59.8	14 35.4	+22.2	60.1	15 05.3	+23.0	60.3	15 34.9	+23.9	60.5	16 04.3	+24.8	60.8	16 33.5	+25.6	61.0	33
34	13 24.2	+19.3	58.4	13 55.5	+20.2	58.7	14 26.7	+21.0	58.9	14 57.6	+21.9	59.1	15 28.3	+22.8	59.3	15 58.8	+23.6	59.6	16 29.1	+24.5	59.8	16 59.1	+25.4	60.1	34
35	13 43.5	+19.1	57.5	14 15.7	+20.0	57.7	14 47.7	+20.8	57.9	15 19.5	+21.6	58.1	15 51.1	+22.5	58.4	16 22.4	+23.4	58.6	16 53.6	+24.2	58.9	17 24.5	+25.0	59.1	35
36	14 02.6	+18.9	56.5	14 35.7	+19.7	56.7	15 08.5	+20.5	56.9	15 41.1	+21.4	57.2	16 13.6	+22.2	57.4	16 45.8	+23.1	57.6	17 17.8	+23.9	57.9	17 49.5	+24.8	58.2	36
37	14 21.5	+18.6	55.5	14 55.4	+19.4	55.7	15 29.0	+20.3	56.0	16 02.5	+21.2	56.2	16 35.8	+22.0	56.4	17 08.9	+22.8	56.7	17 41.7	+23.7	56.9	18 14.3	+24.5	57.2	37
38	14 40.1	+18.3	54.5	15 14.8	+19.2	54.7	15 49.3	+20.1	55.0	16 23.7	+20.8	55.2	16 57.8	+21.7	55.5	17 31.7	+22.5	55.7	18 05.4	+23.4	56.0	18 38.8	+24.2	56.3	38
39	14 58.4	+18.1	53.5	15 34.0	+18.9	53.8	16 09.4	+19.7	54.0	16 44.5	+20.6	54.2	17 19.5	+21.4	54.5	17 54.2	+22.3	54.7	18 28.8	+23.0	55.0	19 03.0	+24.0	55.3	39
40	15 16.5	+17.9	52.6	15 52.9	+18.7	52.8	16 29.1	+19.5	53.0	17 05.1	+20.3	53.3	17 40.9	+21.1	53.5	18 16.5	+21.9	53.8	18 51.8	+22.8	54.0	19 27.0	+23.6	54.3	40
41	15 34.4	+17.6	51.6	16 11.6	+18.4	51.8	16 48.6	+19.2	52.0	17 25.4	+20.0	52.3	18 02.0	+20.9	52.5	18 38.4	+21.7	52.8	19 14.6	+22.5	53.1	19 50.6	+23.2	53.3	41
42	15 52.0	+17.3	50.6	16 30.0	+18.1	50.8	17 07.8	+18.9	51.0	17 45.4	+19.7	51.3	18 22.9	+20.5	51.5	19 00.1	+21.3	51.8	19 37.1	+22.1	52.1	20 13.8	+23.0	52.4	42
43	16 09.3	+17.0	49.6	16 48.1	+17.8	49.8	17 26.7	+18.6	50.0	18 05.1	+19.5	50.3	18 43.4	+20.2	50.5	19 21.4	+21.0	50.8	19 59.2	+21.8	51.1	20 36.8	+22.6	51.4	43
44	16 26.3	+16.7	48.6	17 05.9	+17.5	48.8	17 45.3	+18.3	49.0	18 24.6	+19.0	49.3	19 03.6	+19.9	49.5	19 42.4	+20.7	49.8	20 21.0	+21.5	50.1	20 59.4	+22.3	50.4	44
45	16 43.0	+16.5	47.6	17 23.4	+17.2	47.8	18 03.6	+18.0	48.0	18 43.6	+18.8	48.3	19 23.5	+19.5	48.5	20 03.1	+20.3	48.8	20 42.5	+21.1	49.1	21 21.7	+21.9	49.4	45
46	16 59.5	+16.1	46.6	17 40.6	+17.0	46.8	18 21.6	+17.7	47.0	19 02.4	+18.5	47.3	19 43.0	+19.2	47.5	20 23.4	+20.0	47.8	21 03.6	+20.8	48.1	21 43.6	+21.5	48.4	46
47	17 15.6	+15.9	45.6	17 57.6	+16.6	45.8	18 39.3	+17.4	46.0	19 20.9	+18.1	46.3	20 02.2	+18.9	46.5	20 43.4	+19.7	46.8	21 24.4	+20.4	47.1	22 05.1	+21.2	47.4	47
48	17 31.5	+15.5	44.6	18 14.2	+16.2	44.8	18 56.7	+17.0	45.0	19 39.0	+17.8	45.3	20 21.1	+18.5	45.5	21 03.1	+19.2	45.8	21 44.8	+20.0	46.1	22 26.3	+20.8	46.4	48
49	17 47.0	+15.3	43.5	18 30.4	+16.0	43.8	19 13.7	+16.7	44.0	19 56.8	+17.4	44.3	20 39.6	+18.2	44.5	21 22.3	+18.9	44.8	22 04.8	+19.7	45.1	22 47.1	+20.4	45.4	49
50	18 02.3	+14.9	42.5	18 46.4	+15.6	42.8	19 30.4	+16.3	43.0	20 14.2	+17.1	43.2	20 57.8	+17.8	43.5	21 41.2	+18.6	43.8	22 24.5	+19.2	44.0	23 07.5	+20.0	44.3	50
51	18 17.2	+14.6	41.5	19 02.0	+15.3	41.7	19 46.7	+16.0	42.0	20 31.3	+16.7	42.2	21 15.6	+17.4	42.5	21 59.8	+18.1	42.7	22 43.7	+18.9	43.0	23 27.5	+19.6	43.3	51
52	18 31.8	+14.2	40.5	19 17.3	+15.0	40.7	20 02.7	+15.7	40.9	20 48.0	+16.3	41.2	21 33.0	+17.1	41.4	22 17.9	+17.8	41.7	23 02.6	+18.5	42.0	23 47.1	+19.2	42.3	52
53	18 46.0	+13.9	39.5	19 32.3	+14.6	39.7	20 18.4	+15.3	39.9	21 04.3	+16.0	40.2	21 50.1	+16.6	40.4	22 35.7	+17.3	40.7	23 21.1	+18.1	41.0	24 06.3	+18.8	41.2	53
54	18 59.9	+13.6	38.4	19 46.9	+14.2	38.6	20 33.7	+14.9	38.9	21 20.3	+15.6	39.1	22 06.7	+16.3	39.4	22 53.0	+17.0	39.6	23 39.2	+17.6	39.9	24 25.1	+18.3	40.2	54
55	19 13.5	+13.2	37.4	20 01.1	+13.9	37.6	20 48.6	+14.5	37.8	21 35.9	+15.2	38.1	22 23.0	+15.9	38.3	23 10.0	+16.5	38.6	23 56.8	+17.2	38.9	24 43.4	+17.9	39.2	55
56	19 26.7	+12.9	36.4	20 15.0	+13.5	36.6	21 03.1	+14.2	36.8	21 51.1	+14.8	37.0	22 38.9	+15.5	37.3	23 26.5	+16.2	37.5	24 14.0	+16.8	37.8	25 01.3	+17.5	38.1	56
57	19 39.6	+12.5	35.3	20 28.5	+13.2	35.5	21 17.3	+13.7	35.8	22 05.9	+14.4	36.0	22 54.4	+15.0	36.2	23 42.7	+15.7	36.5	24 30.8	+16.4	36.8	25 18.8	+17.0	37.0	57
58	19 52.1	+12.2	34.3	20 41.7	+12.7	34.5	21 31.0	+13.4	34.7	22 20.3	+14.0	34.9	23 09.4	+14.6	35.2	23 58.4	+15.2	35.4	24 47.2	+15.9	35.7	25 35.8	+16.5	36.0	58
59	20 04.3	+11.8	33.2	20 54.4	+12.4	33.5	21 44.4	+13.0	33.7	22 34.3	+13.6	33.9	23 24.0	+14.2	34.1	24 13.6	+14.8	34.4	25 03.1	+15.4	34.6	25 52.3	+16.1	34.9	59
60	20 16.1	+11.4	32.2	21 06.8	+12.0	32.4	21 57.4	+12.6	32.6	22 47.9	+13.2	32.8	23 38.2	+13.8	33.1	24 28.4	+14.4	33.3	25 18.5	+15.0	33.6	26 08.4	+15.6	33.8	60
61	20 27.5	+11.1	31.2	21 18.8	+11.6	31.4	22 10.0	+12.2	31.6	23 01.1	+12.7	31.8	23 52.0	+13.3	32.0	24 42.8	+13.9	32.2	25 33.5	+14.5	32.5	26 24.0	+15.1	32.8	61
62	20 38.6	+10.6	30.1	21 30.4	+11.2	30.3	22 22.2	+11.7	30.5	23 13.8	+12.3	30.7	24 05.3	+12.9	30.9	24 56.7	+13.5	31.2	25 48.0	+14.0	31.4	26 39.1	+14.6	31.7	62
63	20 49.2	+10.3	29.1	21 41.6	+10.8	29.2	22 33.9	+11.4	29.4	23 26.1	+11.9	29.7	24 18.2	+12.4	29.9	25 10.2	+13.0	30.1	26 02.0	+13.6	30.3	26 53.7	+14.1	30.6	63
64	20 59.5	+9.9	28.0	21 52.4	+10.4	28.2	22 45.3	+10.9	28.4	23 38.0	+11.4	28.6	24 30.6	+12.0	28.8	25 23.2	+12.5	29.0	26 15.6	+13.0	29.3	27 07.8	+13.7	29.5	64
65	21 09.4	+9.5	26.9	22 02.8	+10.0	27.1	22 56.2	+10.5	27.3	23 49.4	+11.0	27.5	24 42.6	+11.5	27.7	25 35.7	+12.0	27.9	26 28.6	+12.6	28.2	27 21.5	+13.0	28.4	65
66	21 18.9	+9.1	25.9	22 12.8	+9.6	26.1	23 06.7	+10.0	26.2	24 00.4	+10.6	26.4	24 54.1	+11.1	26.6	25 47.7	+11.5	26.9	26 41.2	+12.0	27.1	27 34.5	+12.6	27.3	66
67	21 28.0	+8.6	24.8	22 22.4	+9.1	25.0	23 16.7	+9.6	25.2	24 11.0	+10.1	25.4	25 05.2	+10.5	25.6	25 59.2	+11.1	25.8	26 53.2	+11.6	26.0	27 47.1	+12.1	26.2	67
68	21 36.6	+8.3	23.8	22 31.5	+8.7	23.9	23 26.3	+9.2	24.1	24 21.1	+9.6	24.3	25 15.7	+10.1	24.5	26 10.3	+10.5	24.7	27 04.8	+11.0	24.9	27 59.2	+11.5	25.1	68
69	21 44.9	+7.9	22.7	22 40.2	+8.3	22.8	23 35.5	+8.7	23.0	24 30.7	+9.2	23.2	25 25.8	+9.6	23.4	26 20.8	+10.1	23.6	27 15.8	+10.5	23.8	28 10.7	+10.9	24.0	69
70	21 52.8	+7.4	21.6	22 48.5	+7.9	21.8	23 44.2	+8.3	21.9	24 39.9	+8.6	22.1	25 35.4	+9.1	22.3	26 30.9	+9.5	22.5	27 26.3	+10.0	22.7	28 21.6	+10.4	22.9	70
71	22 00.2	+7.1	20.6	22 56.4	+7.4	20.7	23 52.5	+7.8	20.9	24 48.5	+8.3	21.0	25 44.5	+8.6	21.2	26 40.4	+9.1	21.4	27 36.3	+9.4	21.6	28 32.0	+9.9	21.7	71
72	22 07.3	+6.6	19.5	23 03.8	+7.0	19.6	24 00.3	+7.4	19.8	24 56.8	+7.7	19.9	25 53.1	+8.2	20.1	26 49.5	+8.5	20.3	27 45.7	+8.9	20.4	28 41.9	+9.3	20.6	72
73	22 13.9	+6.2	18.4	23 10.8	+6.6	18.5	24 07.7	+6.9	18.7	25 04.5	+7.2	18.8	26 01.3	+7.6	19.0	26 58.0	+8.0	19.1	27 54.6	+8.4	19.3	28 51.2	+8.7	19.5	73
74	22 20.1	+5.8	17.3	23 17.4	+6.1	17.5	24 14.6	+6.4	17.6	25 11.7	+6.8	17.7	26 08.9	+7.1	17.9	27 06.0	+7.4	18.0	28 03.0	+7.8	18.2	28 59.9	+8.2	18.4	74
75	22 25.9	+5.3	16.3	23 23.5	+5.6	16.4	24 21.0	+6.0	16.5	25 18.5	+6.3	16.6	26 16.0	+6.6	16.8	27 13.4	+6.9	16.9	28 10.8	+7.3	17.1	29 08.1	+7.6	17.2	75
76	22 31.2	+4.9	15.2	23 29.1	+5.2	15.3	24 27.0	+5.5	15.4	25 24.8	+5.8	15.5	26 22.6	+6.1	15.7	27 20.3	+6.4	15.8	28 18.1	+6.7	15.9	29 15.7	+7.0	16.1	76
77	22 36.1	+4.5	14.1	23 34.3	+4.8	14.2	24 32.5	+5.0	14.3	25 30.6	+5.3	14.4	26 28.7	+5.5	14.6	27 26.7	+5.9	14.7	28 24.8	+6.1	14.8	29 22.7	+6.5	15.0	77
78	22 40.6	+4.1	13.0	23 39.1	+4.2	13.1	24 37.5	+4.5	13.2	25 35.9	+4.8	13.3	26 34.2	+5.1	13.4	27 32.6	+5.3	13.6	28 30.9	+5.6	13.7	29 29.2	+5.8	13.8	78
79	22 44.7	+3.6	11.9	23 43.3	+3.9	12.0	24 42.0	+4.1	12.1	25 40.7	+4.3	12.2	26 39.3	+4.5	12.3	27 37.9	+4.8	12.4	28 36.5	+5.0	12.6	29 35.0	+5.3	12.7	79
80	22 48.3	+3.1	10.9	23 47.2	+3.3	10.9	24 46.1	+3.6	11.0	25 45.0	+3.8	11.1	26 43.8	+4.0	11.2	27 42.7	+4.2	11.3	28 41.5	+4.4	11.4	29 40.3	+4.7	11.5	80
81	22 51.4	+2.8	9.8	23 50.5	+3.0	9.8	24 49.7	+3.1	9.9	25 48.8	+3.2	10.0	26 47.8	+3.5	10.1	27 46.9	+3.7	10.2	28 45.9	+3.9	10.3	29 45.0	+4.0	10.4	81
82	22 54.2	+2.2	8.7	23 53.5	+2.4	8.8	24 52.8	+2.6	8.8	25 52.0	+2.8	8.9	26 51.3	+3.0	9.0	27 50.6	+3.1	9.1	28 49.8	+3.3	9.1	29 49.0	+3.5	9.2	82
83	22 56.4	+1.9	7.6	23 55.9	+2.0	7.7	24 55.4	+2.1	7.7	25 54.8	+2.3	7.8	26 54.3	+2.4	7.9	27 53.7	+2.6	7.9	28 53.1	+2.7	8.0	29 52.5	+2.9	8.1	83
84	22 58.3	+1.4	6.5	23 57.9	+1.5	6.6	24 57.5	+1.6	6.6	25 57.1	+1.7	6.7	26 56.7	+1.9	6.7	27 56.3	+2.0	6.8	28 55.8	+2.2	6.9	29 55.4	+2.3	6.9	84
85	22 59.7	+0.9	5.4	23 59.4	+1.1	5.5	24 59.1	+1.2	5.5	25 58.8	+1.3	5.6	26 58.6	+1.3	5.6	27 58.3	+1.4	5.7	28 58.0	+1.5	5.7	29 57.7	+1.7	5.8	85
86	23 00.6	+0.5	4.3	24 00.5	+0.5	4.4	25 00.3	+0.6	4.4	26 00.1	+0.7	4.5	26 59.9	+0.8	4.5	27 59.7	+0.9	4.5	28 59.5	+1.0	4.6	29 59.4	+1.0	4.6	86
87	23 01.1	+0.1	3.3	24 01.0	+0.2	3.3	25 00.9	+0.2	3.3	26 00.8	+0.3	3.3	27 00.7	+0.3	3.4	28 00.6	+0.4	3.4	29 00.5	+0.4	3.4	30 00.4	+0.5	3.5	87
88	23 01.2	−0.4	2.2	24 01.2	−0.4	2.2	25 01.1	−0.3	2.2	26 01.1	−0.3	2.2	27 01.0	−0.2	2.2	28 01.0	−0.2	2.3	29 00.9	−0.1	2.3	30 00.9	−0.2	2.3	88
89	23 00.8	−0.8	1.1	24 00.8	−0.8	1.1	25 00.8	−0.8	1.1	26 00.8	−0.8	1.1	27 00.8	−0.8	1.1	28 00.8	−0.8	1.1	29 00.8	−0.8	1.1	30 00.7	−0.7	1.2	89
90	23 00.0	−1.3	0.0	24 00.0	−1.3	0.0	25 00.0	−1.3	0.0	26 00.0	−1.3	0.0	27 00.0	−1.3	0.0	28 00.0	−1.3	0.0	29 00.0	−1.3	0.0	30 00.0	−1.3	0.0	90
	23°			24°			25°			26°			27°			28°			29°			30°			

89°, 271° L.H.A. **LATITUDE SAME NAME AS DECLINATION**

362

LATITUDE **CONTRARY** NAME TO DECLINATION — L.H.A. 89°, 271°

Dec.	23° Hc	d	Z	24° Hc	d	Z	25° Hc	d	Z	26° Hc	d	Z	27° Hc	d	Z	28° Hc	d	Z	29° Hc	d	Z	30° Hc	d	Z	Dec.
°	° ′	′	°	° ′	′	°	° ′	′	°	° ′	′	°	° ′	′	°	° ′	′	°	° ′	′	°	° ′	′	°	°
0	0 55.2	−23.4	90.4	0 54.8	−24.4	90.4	0 54.4	−25.4	90.4	0 53.9	−26.3	90.4	0 53.5	−27.3	90.5	0 53.0	−28.2	90.5	0 52.5	−29.1	90.5	0 52.0	−30.0	90.5	0
1	0 31.8	−23.5	91.3	0 30.4	−24.4	91.3	0 29.0	−25.4	91.3	0 27.6	−26.3	91.3	0 26.2	−27.2	91.3	0 24.8	−28.2	91.4	0 23.4	−29.1	91.4	0 22.0	−30.1	91.4	1
2	0 08.3	−23.4	92.2	0 06.0	−24.4	92.2	0 03.6	−25.3	92.2	0 01.3	−26.3	92.2	0 01.0	+27.3	87.8	0 03.4	+28.2	87.8	0 05.7	+29.1	87.8	0 08.1	+30.0	87.8	2
3	0 15.1	+23.5	86.8	0 18.4	+24.5	86.9	0 21.7	+25.4	86.9	0 25.0	+26.3	86.9	0 28.3	+27.2	86.9	0 31.6	+28.1	86.9	0 34.8	+29.1	86.9	0 38.1	+30.0	86.9	3
4	0 38.6	+23.5	85.9	0 42.9	+24.4	85.9	0 47.1	+25.4	86.0	0 51.3	+26.3	86.0	0 55.5	+27.3	86.0	0 59.7	+28.2	86.0	1 03.9	+29.1	86.0	1 08.1	+30.0	86.0	4
5	1 02.1	+23.4	85.0	1 07.3	+24.4	85.0	1 12.5	+25.3	85.0	1 17.6	+26.3	85.1	1 22.8	+27.2	85.1	1 27.9	+28.1	85.1	1 33.0	+29.1	85.1	1 38.1	+29.9	85.2	5
6	1 25.5	+23.4	84.1	1 31.7	+24.3	84.1	1 37.8	+25.3	84.1	1 43.9	+26.3	84.2	1 50.0	+27.2	84.2	1 56.0	+28.2	84.2	2 02.1	+29.0	84.3	2 08.0	+30.0	84.3	6
7	1 48.9	+23.4	83.2	1 56.0	+24.4	83.2	2 03.1	+25.3	83.2	2 10.2	+26.2	83.3	2 17.2	+27.1	83.3	2 24.2	+28.0	83.3	2 31.1	+29.0	83.4	2 38.0	+29.9	83.4	7
8	2 12.3	+23.3	82.2	2 20.4	+24.3	82.3	2 28.4	+25.2	82.3	2 36.4	+26.2	82.4	2 44.3	+27.1	82.4	2 52.2	+28.1	82.5	3 00.1	+28.9	82.5	3 07.9	+29.8	82.6	8
9	2 35.6	+23.3	81.3	2 44.7	+24.2	81.4	2 53.6	+25.2	81.4	3 02.6	+26.1	81.5	3 11.4	+27.1	81.5	3 20.3	+28.0	81.6	3 29.0	+28.9	81.6	3 37.7	+29.8	81.7	9
10	2 58.9	+23.3	80.4	3 08.9	+24.2	80.5	3 18.8	+25.2	80.5	3 28.7	+26.1	80.6	3 38.5	+27.0	80.6	3 48.3	+27.9	80.7	3 57.9	+28.9	80.8	4 07.5	+29.8	80.8	10
11	3 22.2	+23.2	79.5	3 33.1	+24.2	79.5	3 44.0	+25.1	79.6	3 54.8	+26.0	79.7	4 05.5	+27.0	79.7	4 16.2	+27.9	79.8	4 26.8	+28.8	79.9	4 37.3	+29.7	80.0	11
12	3 45.4	+23.2	78.6	3 57.3	+24.1	78.6	4 09.1	+25.0	78.7	4 20.8	+26.0	78.8	4 32.5	+26.9	78.8	4 44.1	+27.8	78.9	4 55.6	+28.7	79.0	5 07.0	+29.6	79.1	12
13	4 08.6	+23.1	77.6	4 21.4	+24.0	77.7	4 34.1	+25.0	77.8	4 46.8	+25.9	77.9	4 59.4	+26.8	77.9	5 11.9	+27.7	78.0	5 24.3	+28.6	78.1	5 36.6	+29.5	78.2	13
14	4 31.7	+23.0	76.7	4 45.4	+24.0	76.8	4 59.1	+24.9	76.9	5 12.7	+25.8	77.0	5 26.2	+26.7	77.0	5 39.6	+27.6	77.1	5 52.9	+28.6	77.2	6 06.1	+29.5	77.3	14
15	4 54.7	+22.9	75.8	5 09.4	+23.8	75.9	5 24.0	+24.8	75.9	5 38.5	+25.7	76.0	5 52.9	+26.7	76.1	6 07.2	+27.6	76.2	6 21.5	+28.4	76.3	6 35.6	+29.3	76.5	15
16	5 17.6	+22.9	74.8	5 33.2	+23.8	74.9	5 48.8	+24.7	75.0	6 04.2	+25.7	75.1	6 19.6	+26.5	75.2	6 34.8	+27.5	75.3	6 49.9	+28.4	75.5	7 04.9	+29.3	75.6	16
17	5 40.5	+22.7	73.9	5 57.0	+23.7	74.0	6 13.5	+24.6	74.1	6 29.9	+25.5	74.2	6 46.1	+26.5	74.3	7 02.3	+27.3	74.5	7 18.3	+28.2	74.6	7 34.2	+29.1	74.7	17
18	6 03.2	+22.7	73.0	6 20.7	+23.6	73.1	6 38.1	+24.6	73.2	6 55.4	+25.5	73.3	7 12.6	+26.3	73.4	7 29.6	+27.3	73.6	7 46.5	+28.2	73.7	8 03.3	+29.1	73.8	18
19	6 25.9	+22.6	72.1	6 44.3	+23.5	72.2	7 02.7	+24.4	72.3	7 20.9	+25.3	72.4	7 38.9	+26.3	72.5	7 56.9	+27.1	72.7	8 14.7	+28.0	72.8	8 32.4	+28.9	72.9	19
20	6 48.5	+22.4	71.1	7 07.8	+23.4	71.2	7 27.1	+24.3	71.4	7 46.2	+25.2	71.5	8 05.2	+26.1	71.6	8 24.0	+27.0	71.8	8 42.7	+27.9	71.9	9 01.3	+28.8	72.0	20
21	7 10.9	+22.4	70.2	7 31.2	+23.3	70.3	7 51.4	+24.1	70.4	8 11.4	+25.1	70.6	8 31.3	+26.0	70.7	8 51.0	+26.9	70.9	9 10.6	+27.8	71.0	9 30.1	+28.6	71.2	21
22	7 33.3	+22.2	69.3	7 54.5	+23.1	69.4	8 15.5	+24.1	69.5	8 36.5	+24.9	69.7	8 57.3	+25.8	69.8	9 17.9	+26.8	69.9	9 38.4	+27.6	70.1	9 58.7	+28.6	70.3	22
23	7 55.5	+22.1	68.3	8 17.6	+23.0	68.4	8 39.6	+23.9	68.6	9 01.4	+24.9	68.7	9 23.1	+25.7	68.9	9 44.7	+26.6	69.0	10 06.0	+27.5	69.2	10 27.3	+28.3	69.4	23
24	8 17.6	+22.0	67.4	8 40.6	+22.9	67.5	9 03.5	+23.8	67.7	9 26.3	+24.6	67.8	9 48.8	+25.6	68.0	10 11.3	+26.4	68.1	10 33.5	+27.4	68.3	10 55.6	+28.2	68.5	24
25	8 39.6	+21.8	66.4	9 03.5	+22.8	66.6	9 27.3	+23.6	66.7	9 50.9	+24.5	66.9	10 14.4	+25.4	67.0	10 37.7	+26.3	67.2	11 00.9	+27.1	67.4	11 23.8	+28.1	67.6	25
26	9 01.4	+21.7	65.5	9 26.3	+22.5	65.6	9 50.9	+23.5	65.8	10 15.4	+24.4	66.0	10 39.8	+25.3	66.1	11 04.0	+26.1	66.3	11 28.0	+27.0	66.5	11 51.9	+27.9	66.7	26
27	9 23.1	+21.6	64.5	9 48.8	+22.5	64.7	10 14.4	+23.3	64.9	10 39.8	+24.2	65.0	11 05.1	+25.0	65.2	11 30.1	+26.0	65.4	11 55.0	+26.9	65.6	12 19.8	+27.6	65.8	27
28	9 44.7	+21.3	63.6	10 11.3	+22.2	63.8	10 37.7	+23.2	63.9	11 04.0	+24.0	64.1	11 30.1	+24.9	64.3	11 56.1	+25.8	64.5	12 21.9	+26.6	64.7	12 47.4	+27.5	64.9	28
29	10 06.0	+21.3	62.7	10 33.5	+22.1	62.8	11 00.9	+22.9	63.0	11 28.0	+23.9	63.2	11 55.0	+24.8	63.3	12 21.9	+25.5	63.5	12 48.5	+26.4	63.7	13 14.9	+27.4	63.9	29
30	10 27.3	+21.0	61.7	10 55.6	+22.0	61.9	11 23.8	+22.8	62.0	11 51.9	+23.6	62.2	12 19.8	+24.5	62.4	12 47.4	+25.4	62.6	13 14.9	+26.3	62.8	13 42.3	+27.1	63.0	30
31	10 48.3	+20.9	60.8	11 17.6	+21.7	60.9	11 46.6	+22.6	61.1	12 15.5	+23.5	61.3	12 44.3	+24.3	61.5	13 12.8	+25.2	61.7	13 41.2	+26.0	61.9	14 09.4	+26.9	62.1	31
32	11 09.2	+20.7	59.8	11 39.3	+21.5	60.0	12 09.2	+22.5	60.2	12 39.0	+23.3	60.3	13 08.6	+24.1	60.5	13 38.0	+25.0	60.8	14 07.2	+25.9	61.0	14 36.3	+26.6	61.2	32
33	11 29.9	+20.5	58.8	12 00.8	+21.4	59.0	12 31.7	+22.2	59.2	13 02.3	+23.0	59.4	13 32.7	+24.0	59.6	14 03.0	+24.8	59.8	14 33.1	+25.6	60.0	15 02.9	+26.5	60.3	33
34	11 50.4	+20.3	57.9	12 22.2	+21.2	58.1	12 53.9	+22.0	58.3	13 25.3	+22.9	58.5	13 56.7	+23.6	58.7	14 27.8	+24.5	58.9	14 58.7	+25.4	59.1	15 29.4	+26.2	59.3	34
35	12 10.7	+20.1	56.9	12 43.4	+20.9	57.1	13 15.9	+21.8	57.3	13 48.2	+22.6	57.5	14 20.3	+23.5	57.7	14 52.3	+24.3	57.9	15 24.1	+25.1	58.2	15 55.6	+26.0	58.4	35
36	12 30.8	+19.9	56.0	13 04.3	+20.8	56.1	13 37.7	+21.5	56.3	14 10.8	+22.4	56.5	14 43.8	+23.2	56.8	15 16.6	+24.1	57.0	15 49.2	+24.9	57.2	16 21.6	+25.7	57.5	36
37	12 50.7	+19.7	55.0	13 25.1	+20.5	55.2	13 59.2	+21.4	55.4	14 33.2	+22.2	55.6	15 07.0	+23.0	55.8	15 40.7	+23.8	56.0	16 14.1	+24.6	56.3	16 47.3	+25.5	56.5	37
38	13 10.4	+19.5	54.0	13 45.6	+20.3	54.2	14 20.6	+21.1	54.4	14 55.4	+21.9	54.6	15 30.0	+22.8	54.8	16 04.5	+23.6	55.1	16 38.7	+24.4	55.3	17 12.8	+25.2	55.6	38
39	13 29.9	+19.2	53.0	14 05.9	+20.0	53.2	14 41.7	+20.9	53.4	15 17.3	+21.7	53.7	15 52.8	+22.5	53.9	16 28.1	+23.3	54.1	17 03.1	+24.1	54.4	17 38.0	+24.9	54.6	39
40	13 49.1	+19.0	52.1	14 25.9	+19.8	52.3	15 02.6	+20.6	52.5	15 39.0	+21.4	52.7	16 15.3	+22.2	52.9	16 51.4	+23.0	53.2	17 27.2	+23.9	53.4	18 02.9	+24.6	53.7	40
41	14 08.1	+18.8	51.1	14 45.7	+19.6	51.3	15 23.2	+20.3	51.5	16 00.4	+21.2	51.7	16 37.5	+22.0	52.0	17 14.4	+22.7	52.2	17 51.1	+23.5	52.4	18 27.5	+24.4	52.7	41
42	14 26.9	+18.6	50.1	15 05.3	+19.3	50.3	15 43.5	+20.1	50.5	16 21.6	+20.9	50.7	16 59.5	+21.6	51.0	17 37.1	+22.5	51.2	18 14.6	+23.3	51.5	18 51.9	+24.0	51.7	42
43	14 45.5	+18.2	49.1	15 24.6	+19.1	49.3	16 03.6	+19.9	49.5	16 42.5	+20.6	49.8	17 21.1	+21.4	50.0	17 59.6	+22.2	50.3	18 37.9	+22.9	50.5	19 15.9	+23.8	50.8	43
44	15 03.7	+18.1	48.1	15 43.7	+18.8	48.3	16 23.5	+19.5	48.6	17 03.1	+20.3	48.8	17 42.5	+21.1	49.0	18 21.8	+21.9	49.3	19 00.8	+22.7	49.5	19 39.7	+23.4	49.8	44
45	15 21.8	+17.7	47.2	16 02.5	+18.5	47.4	16 43.0	+19.3	47.6	17 23.4	+20.1	47.8	18 03.6	+20.8	48.0	18 43.7	+21.5	48.3	19 23.5	+22.3	48.5	20 03.1	+23.1	48.8	45
46	15 39.5	+17.5	46.2	16 21.0	+18.3	46.4	17 02.3	+19.0	46.6	17 43.5	+19.7	46.8	18 24.4	+20.5	47.1	19 05.2	+21.3	47.3	19 45.8	+22.0	47.6	20 26.2	+22.8	47.8	46
47	15 57.0	+17.3	45.2	16 39.3	+17.9	45.4	17 21.3	+18.7	45.6	18 03.2	+19.5	45.8	18 44.9	+20.2	46.1	19 26.5	+20.9	46.3	20 07.8	+21.7	46.6	20 49.0	+22.4	46.8	47
48	16 14.3	+16.9	44.2	16 57.2	+17.7	44.4	17 40.0	+18.4	44.6	18 22.7	+19.1	44.8	19 05.1	+19.9	45.1	19 47.4	+20.6	45.3	20 29.5	+21.3	45.6	21 11.4	+22.1	45.9	48
49	16 31.2	+16.7	43.2	17 14.9	+17.4	43.4	17 58.4	+18.1	43.6	18 41.8	+18.8	43.8	19 25.0	+19.5	44.1	20 08.0	+20.3	44.3	20 50.8	+21.0	44.6	21 33.5	+21.7	44.9	49
50	16 47.9	+16.3	42.2	17 32.3	+17.0	42.4	18 16.5	+17.8	42.6	19 00.6	+18.5	42.8	19 44.5	+19.2	43.1	20 28.3	+19.9	43.3	21 11.8	+20.6	43.6	21 55.2	+21.3	43.8	50
51	17 04.2	+16.1	41.2	17 49.3	+16.8	41.4	18 34.3	+17.4	41.6	19 19.1	+18.1	41.8	20 03.7	+18.8	42.1	20 48.2	+19.5	42.3	21 32.4	+20.3	42.6	22 16.5	+21.0	42.8	51
52	17 20.3	+15.7	40.2	18 06.1	+16.4	40.4	18 51.7	+17.1	40.6	19 37.2	+17.8	40.8	20 22.5	+18.5	41.0	21 07.7	+19.2	41.3	21 52.7	+19.9	41.6	22 37.5	+20.6	41.8	52
53	17 36.0	+15.5	39.1	18 22.5	+16.1	39.3	19 08.8	+16.8	39.6	19 55.0	+17.5	39.8	20 41.0	+18.2	40.0	21 26.9	+18.8	40.3	22 12.6	+19.5	40.5	22 58.1	+20.2	40.8	53
54	17 51.5	+15.1	38.1	18 38.6	+15.8	38.3	19 25.6	+16.5	38.5	20 12.5	+17.1	38.8	20 59.2	+17.8	39.0	21 45.7	+18.5	39.3	22 32.1	+19.1	39.5	23 18.3	+19.8	39.8	54
55	18 06.6	+14.9	37.1	18 54.4	+15.5	37.3	19 42.1	+16.1	37.5	20 29.6	+16.7	37.8	21 17.0	+17.4	38.0	22 04.2	+18.0	38.2	22 51.2	+18.7	38.5	23 38.1	+19.4	38.8	55
56	18 21.5	+14.4	36.1	19 09.9	+15.1	36.3	19 58.2	+15.7	36.5	20 46.3	+16.4	36.7	21 34.4	+17.0	37.0	22 22.2	+17.7	37.2	23 09.9	+18.3	37.5	23 57.5	+19.0	37.7	56
57	18 35.9	+14.2	35.1	19 25.0	+14.8	35.3	20 13.9	+15.4	35.5	21 02.7	+16.0	35.7	21 51.4	+16.6	35.9	22 39.9	+17.3	36.2	23 28.2	+18.0	36.4	24 16.5	+18.5	36.7	57
58	18 50.1	+13.8	34.0	19 39.8	+14.4	34.2	20 29.3	+15.0	34.4	21 18.7	+15.7	34.7	22 08.0	+16.2	34.9	22 57.2	+16.8	35.1	23 46.2	+17.4	35.4	24 35.0	+18.1	35.6	58
59	19 03.9	+13.5	33.0	19 54.2	+14.0	33.2	20 44.3	+14.7	33.4	21 34.4	+15.2	33.6	22 24.2	+15.9	33.8	23 14.0	+16.5	34.1	24 03.6	+17.1	34.3	24 53.1	+17.7	34.6	59
60	19 17.4	+13.1	32.0	20 08.2	+13.7	32.2	20 59.0	+14.2	32.4	21 49.6	+14.8	32.6	22 40.1	+15.4	32.8	23 30.5	+16.0	33.0	24 20.7	+16.6	33.3	25 10.8	+17.2	33.5	60
61	19 30.5	+12.8	30.9	20 21.9	+13.4	31.1	21 13.2	+13.9	31.3	22 04.4	+14.5	31.5	22 55.5	+15.0	31.8	23 46.5	+15.6	32.0	24 37.3	+16.2	32.2	25 28.0	+16.7	32.5	61
62	19 43.3	+12.4	29.9	20 35.3	+12.9	30.1	21 27.1	+13.5	30.3	22 18.9	+14.0	30.5	23 10.5	+14.6	30.7	24 02.1	+15.1	30.9	24 53.5	+15.7	31.2	25 44.7	+16.3	31.4	62
63	19 55.7	+12.1	28.9	20 48.2	+12.6	29.1	21 40.6	+13.1	29.2	22 32.9	+13.7	29.4	23 25.1	+14.2	29.6	24 17.2	+14.7	29.9	25 09.2	+15.2	30.1	26 01.0	+15.9	30.3	63
64	20 07.8	+11.7	27.8	21 00.8	+12.2	28.0	21 53.7	+12.7	28.2	22 46.6	+13.2	28.4	23 39.3	+13.7	28.6	24 31.9	+14.3	28.8	25 24.4	+14.8	29.0	26 16.9	+15.3	29.3	64
65	20 19.5	+11.3	26.8	21 13.0	+11.8	27.0	22 06.4	+12.3	27.1	22 59.8	+12.8	27.3	23 53.0	+13.3	27.5	24 46.2	+13.8	27.7	25 39.2	+14.4	28.0	26 32.2	+14.8	28.2	65
66	20 30.8	+10.9	25.7	21 24.8	+11.4	25.9	22 18.7	+11.9	26.1	23 12.6	+12.3	26.3	24 06.3	+12.9	26.5	25 00.0	+13.3	26.7	25 53.6	+13.8	26.9	26 47.0	+14.4	27.1	66
67	20 41.7	+10.5	24.7	21 36.2	+11.0	24.8	22 30.6	+11.5	25.0	23 24.9	+11.9	25.2	24 19.2	+12.4	25.4	25 13.3	+12.9	25.6	26 07.4	+13.4	25.8	27 01.4	+13.8	26.0	67
68	20 52.2	+10.2	23.6	21 47.2	+10.6	23.8	22 42.1	+11.0	24.0	23 36.8	+11.5	24.1	24 31.6	+11.9	24.3	25 26.2	+12.4	24.5	26 20.8	+12.8	24.7	27 15.2	+13.3	24.9	68
69	21 02.4	+9.8	22.6	21 57.8	+10.2	22.7	22 53.1	+10.6	22.9	23 48.3	+11.1	23.1	24 43.5	+11.5	23.2	25 38.6	+11.9	23.4	26 33.6	+12.4	23.6	27 28.5	+12.9	23.8	69
70	21 12.2	+9.4	21.5	22 08.0	+9.7	21.7	23 03.7	+10.2	21.8	23 59.4	+10.6	22.0	24 55.0	+11.0	22.2	25 50.5	+11.4	22.3	26 46.0	+11.8	22.5	27 41.4	+12.2	22.7	70
71	21 21.6	+8.9	20.5	22 17.7	+9.4	20.6	23 13.9	+9.7	20.7	24 10.0	+10.1	20.9	25 06.0	+10.5	21.1	26 01.9	+11.0	21.2	26 57.8	+11.4	21.4	27 53.6	+11.8	21.6	71
72	21 30.5	+8.6	19.4	22 27.1	+8.9	19.5	23 23.6	+9.3	19.7	24 20.1	+9.7	19.8	25 16.5	+10.1	20.0	26 12.9	+10.4	20.1	27 09.2	+10.8	20.3	28 05.4	+11.2	20.5	72
73	21 39.1	+8.2	18.3	22 36.0	+8.5	18.5	23 32.9	+8.9	18.6	24 29.8	+9.2	18.7	25 26.6	+9.5	18.9	26 23.3	+9.9	19.0	27 20.0	+10.3	19.2	28 16.6	+10.7	19.4	73
74	21 47.3	+7.7	17.3	22 44.5	+8.1	17.4	23 41.8	+8.4	17.5	24 39.0	+8.7	17.7	25 36.1	+9.1	17.8	26 33.2	+9.4	17.9	27 30.3	+9.7	18.1	28 27.3	+10.1	18.3	74
75	21 55.0	+7.3	16.2	22 52.6	+7.6	16.3	23 50.2	+7.9	16.4	24 47.7	+8.3	16.6	25 45.2	+8.6	16.7	26 42.6	+8.9	16.8	27 40.0	+9.3	17.0	28 37.4	+9.6	17.1	75
76	22 02.3	+7.0	15.1	23 00.2	+7.3	15.2	23 58.1	+7.5	15.3	24 56.0	+7.8	15.5	25 53.8	+8.1	15.6	26 51.5	+8.4	15.7	27 49.3	+8.7	15.9	28 47.0	+9.0	16.0	76
77	22 09.3	+6.5	14.1	23 07.5	+6.7	14.2	24 05.6	+7.0	14.3	25 03.8	+7.3	14.4	26 01.9	+7.5	14.5	26 59.9	+7.9	14.6	27 58.0	+8.1	14.8	28 56.0	+8.4	14.9	77
78	22 15.8	+6.0	13.0	23 14.2	+6.3	13.1	24 12.6	+6.6	13.2	25 11.1	+6.8	13.3	26 09.4	+7.1	13.4	27 07.8	+7.3	13.5	28 06.1	+7.6	13.6	29 04.4	+7.9	13.8	78
79	22 21.8	+5.7	11.9	23 20.5	+5.9	12.0	24 19.2	+6.1	12.1	25 17.9	+6.3	12.2	26 16.5	+6.6	12.3	27 15.1	+6.8	12.4	28 13.7	+7.1	12.5	29 12.3	+7.3	12.6	79
80	22 27.5	+5.2	10.8	23 26.4	+5.4	10.9	24 25.3	+5.6	11.0	25 24.2	+5.8	11.1	26 23.1	+6.0	11.2	27 21.9	+6.3	11.3	28 20.8	+6.4	11.4	29 19.6	+6.7	11.5	80
81	22 32.7	+4.8	9.8	23 31.8	+5.0	9.8	24 30.9	+5.2	9.9	25 30.0	+5.4	10.0	26 29.1	+5.6	10.1	27 28.2	+5.7	10.2	28 27.2	+6.0	10.2	29 26.3	+6.1	10.3	81
82	22 37.5	+4.3	8.7	23 36.8	+4.5	8.7	24 36.1	+4.7	8.8	25 35.4	+4.8	8.9	26 34.7	+5.0	9.0	27 33.9	+5.2	9.0	28 33.2	+5.3	9.1	29 32.4	+5.5	9.2	82
83	22 41.8	+3.9	7.6	23 41.3	+4.1	7.6	24 40.8	+4.2	7.7	25 40.2	+4.4	7.8	26 39.7	+4.5	7.8	27 39.1	+4.6	7.9	28 38.5	+4.8	8.0	29 37.9	+5.0	8.1	83
84	22 45.7	+3.5	6.5	23 45.4	+3.6	6.6	24 45.0	+3.7	6.6	25 44.6	+3.8	6.7	26 44.2	+3.9	6.7	27 43.7	+4.1	6.8	28 43.3	+4.2	6.8	29 42.9	+4.3	6.9	84
85	22 49.2	+3.1	5.4	23 49.0	+3.1	5.5	24 48.7	+3.2	5.5	25 48.4	+3.3	5.6	26 48.1	+3.5	5.6	27 47.8	+3.6	5.7	28 47.5	+3.7	5.7	29 47.2	+3.8	5.8	85
86	22 52.3	+2.6	4.3	23 52.1	+2.7	4.4	24 51.9	+2.8	4.4	25 51.7	+2.9	4.4	26 51.6	+2.9	4.5	27 51.4	+3.0	4.5	28 51.2	+3.1	4.6	29 51.0	+3.1	4.6	86
87	22 54.9	+2.1	3.3	23 54.8	+2.2	3.3	24 54.7	+2.2	3.3	25 54.6	+2.3	3.3	26 54.5	+2.3	3.4	27 54.4	+2.4	3.4	28 54.3	+2.4	3.4	29 54.1	+2.6	3.5	87
88	22 57.0	+1.7	2.2	23 57.0	+1.7	2.2	24 56.9	+1.8	2.2	25 56.9	+1.8	2.2	26 56.8	+1.9	2.2	27 56.8	+1.9	2.3	28 56.7	+2.0	2.3	29 56.7	+2.0	2.3	88
89	22 58.7	+1.3	1.1	23 58.7	+1.3	1.1	24 58.7	+1.3	1.1	25 58.7	+1.3	1.1	26 58.7	+1.3	1.1	27 58.7	+1.3	1.1	28 58.7	+1.3	1.1	29 58.7	+1.3	1.2	89
90	23 00.0	+0.8	0.0	24 00.0	+0.8	0.0	25 00.0	+0.8	0.0	26 00.0	+0.8	0.0	27 00.0	+0.8	0.0	28 00.0	+0.8	0.0	29 00.0	+0.8	0.0	30 00.0	+0.7	0.0	90
	23°			24°			25°			26°			27°			28°			29°			30°			

S. Lat. {L.H.A. greater than 180° ....Zn=180°−Z; L.H.A. less than 180°...........Zn=180°+Z

LATITUDE **SAME** NAME AS DECLINATION — L.H.A. 91°, 269°

363

Dec.	23°			24°			25°			26°		
	Hc	d	Z	Hc	d	Z	Hc	d	Z	Hc	d	Z
°	° ′	′	°	° ′	′	°	° ′	′	°	° ′	′	°
0	0 00.0	+23.4	90.0	0 00.0	+24.4	90.0	0 00.0	+25.4	90.0	0 00.0	+26.3	90.0
1	0 23.4	+23.5	89.1	0 24.4	+24.4	89.1	0 25.4	+25.3	89.1	0 26.3	+26.3	89.1
2	0 46.9	+23.4	88.2	0 48.8	+24.4	88.2	0 50.7	+25.3	88.2	0 52.6	+26.3	88.2
3	1 10.3	+23.4	87.2	1 13.2	+24.4	87.3	1 16.0	+25.4	87.3	1 18.9	+26.2	87.3
4	1 33.7	+23.4	86.3	1 37.6	+24.3	86.3	1 41.4	+25.3	86.4	1 45.1	+26.3	86.4
5	1 57.1	+23.3	85.4	2 01.9	+24.3	85.4	2 06.7	+25.2	85.5	2 11.4	+26.2	85.5
6	2 20.4	+23.4	84.5	2 26.2	+24.3	84.5	2 31.9	+25.2	84.6	2 37.6	+26.1	84.6
7	2 43.8	+23.2	83.6	2 50.5	+24.2	83.6	2 57.1	+25.2	83.7	3 03.7	+26.2	83.7
8	3 07.0	+23.3	82.6	3 14.7	+24.2	82.7	3 22.3	+25.1	82.7	3 29.9	+26.0	82.8
9	3 30.3	+23.1	81.7	3 38.9	+24.1	81.8	3 47.4	+25.1	81.8	3 55.9	+26.0	81.9
10	3 53.4	+23.1	80.8	4 03.0	+24.1	80.8	4 12.5	+25.0	80.9	4 21.9	+26.0	81.0
11	4 16.5	+23.1	79.9	4 27.1	+24.0	79.9	4 37.5	+25.0	80.0	4 47.9	+25.9	80.1
12	4 39.6	+23.0	78.9	4 51.1	+23.9	79.0	5 02.5	+24.8	79.1	5 13.8	+25.8	79.2
13	5 02.6	+22.8	78.0	5 15.0	+23.8	78.1	5 27.3	+24.8	78.2	5 39.6	+25.7	78.3
14	5 25.4	+22.8	77.1	5 38.8	+23.8	77.2	5 52.1	+24.7	77.3	6 05.3	+25.6	77.4
15	5 48.2	+22.8	76.1	6 02.6	+23.6	76.2	6 16.8	+24.6	76.4	6 30.9	+25.5	76.5
16	6 11.0	+22.6	75.2	6 26.2	+23.6	75.3	6 41.4	+24.5	75.4	6 56.4	+25.4	75.5
17	6 33.6	+22.5	74.3	6 49.8	+23.4	74.4	7 05.9	+24.3	74.5	7 21.8	+25.3	74.6
18	6 56.1	+22.4	73.3	7 13.2	+23.4	73.5	7 30.2	+24.3	73.6	7 47.1	+25.2	73.7
19	7 18.5	+22.3	72.4	7 36.6	+23.2	72.5	7 54.5	+24.2	72.7	8 12.3	+25.1	72.8
20	7 40.8	+22.2	71.5	7 59.8	+23.1	71.6	8 18.7	+24.0	71.7	8 37.4	+24.9	71.9
21	8 03.0	+22.0	70.5	8 22.9	+22.9	70.7	8 42.7	+23.8	70.8	9 02.3	+24.8	71.0
22	8 25.0	+21.9	69.6	8 45.8	+22.9	69.7	9 06.5	+23.8	69.9	9 27.1	+24.7	70.0
23	8 46.9	+21.8	68.7	9 08.7	+22.6	68.8	9 30.3	+23.6	69.0	9 51.8	+24.5	69.1
24	9 08.7	+21.6	67.7	9 31.3	+22.6	67.9	9 53.9	+23.4	68.0	10 16.3	+24.3	68.2
25	9 30.3	+21.5	66.8	9 53.9	+22.4	66.9	10 17.3	+23.3	67.1	10 40.6	+24.2	67.3
26	9 51.8	+21.3	65.8	10 16.3	+22.2	66.0	10 40.6	+23.1	66.2	11 04.8	+24.0	66.3
27	10 13.1	+21.1	64.9	10 38.5	+22.0	65.0	11 03.7	+22.9	65.2	11 28.8	+23.8	65.4
28	10 34.2	+21.0	63.9	11 00.5	+21.9	64.1	11 26.6	+22.8	64.3	11 52.6	+23.6	64.5
29	10 55.2	+20.8	63.0	11 22.4	+21.6	63.1	11 49.4	+22.5	63.3	12 16.2	+23.5	63.5
30	11 16.0	+20.6	62.0	11 44.0	+21.5	62.2	12 11.9	+22.4	62.4	12 39.7	+23.2	62.6
31	11 36.6	+20.4	61.1	12 05.5	+21.3	61.2	12 34.3	+22.2	61.4	13 02.9	+23.1	61.6
32	11 57.0	+20.2	60.1	12 26.8	+21.1	60.3	12 56.5	+21.9	60.5	13 26.0	+22.8	60.7
33	12 17.2	+20.0	59.1	12 47.9	+20.9	59.3	13 18.4	+21.8	59.5	13 48.8	+22.6	59.7
34	12 37.2	+19.8	58.2	13 08.8	+20.7	58.4	13 40.2	+21.5	58.6	14 11.4	+22.4	58.8
35	12 57.0	+19.6	57.2	13 29.5	+20.4	57.4	14 01.7	+21.3	57.6	14 33.8	+22.1	57.8
36	13 16.6	+19.4	56.2	13 49.9	+20.2	56.4	14 23.0	+21.1	56.6	14 55.9	+21.9	56.9
37	13 36.0	+19.2	55.3	14 10.1	+20.0	55.5	14 44.1	+20.8	55.7	15 17.8	+21.7	55.9
38	13 55.2	+18.9	54.3	14 30.1	+19.8	54.5	15 04.9	+20.5	54.7	15 39.5	+21.4	54.9
39	14 14.1	+18.7	53.3	14 49.9	+19.5	53.5	15 25.4	+20.4	53.7	16 00.9	+21.1	54.0
40	14 32.8	+18.4	52.3	15 09.4	+19.2	52.5	15 45.8	+20.0	52.7	16 22.0	+20.8	53.0
41	14 51.2	+18.2	51.3	15 28.6	+19.0	51.5	16 05.8	+19.8	51.8	16 42.8	+20.6	52.0
42	15 09.4	+17.9	50.3	15 47.6	+18.7	50.6	16 25.6	+19.5	50.8	17 03.4	+20.3	51.0
43	15 27.3	+17.6	49.4	16 06.3	+18.4	49.6	16 45.1	+19.2	49.8	17 23.7	+20.1	50.0
44	15 44.9	+17.4	48.4	16 24.7	+18.2	48.6	17 04.3	+19.0	48.8	17 43.8	+19.7	49.0
45	16 02.3	+17.1	47.4	16 42.9	+17.9	47.6	17 23.3	+18.6	47.8	18 03.5	+19.4	48.1
46	16 19.4	+16.9	46.4	17 00.8	+17.5	46.6	17 41.9	+18.3	46.8	18 22.9	+19.1	47.1
47	16 36.3	+16.5	45.4	17 18.3	+17.3	45.6	18 00.2	+18.1	45.8	18 42.0	+18.7	46.1
48	16 52.8	+16.3	44.4	17 35.6	+17.0	44.6	18 18.3	+17.7	44.8	19 00.7	+18.5	45.1
49	17 09.1	+15.9	43.4	17 52.6	+16.7	43.6	18 36.0	+17.4	43.8	19 19.2	+18.1	44.0
50	17 25.0	+15.6	42.4	18 09.3	+16.3	42.6	18 53.4	+17.0	42.8	19 37.3	+17.8	43.0
51	17 40.6	+15.4	41.3	18 25.6	+16.0	41.6	19 10.4	+16.8	41.8	19 55.1	+17.4	42.0
52	17 56.0	+15.0	40.3	18 41.6	+15.7	40.5	19 27.2	+16.3	40.8	20 12.5	+17.1	41.0
53	18 11.0	+14.7	39.3	18 57.3	+15.4	39.5	19 43.5	+16.1	39.7	20 29.6	+16.7	40.0
54	18 25.7	+14.3	38.3	19 12.7	+15.0	38.5	19 59.6	+15.7	38.7	20 46.3	+16.4	39.0
55	18 40.0	+14.0	37.3	19 27.7	+14.7	37.5	20 15.3	+15.3	37.7	21 02.7	+15.9	37.9
56	18 54.0	+13.7	36.2	19 42.4	+14.3	36.4	20 30.6	+14.9	36.7	21 18.6	+15.6	36.9
57	19 07.7	+13.4	35.2	19 56.7	+14.0	35.4	20 45.5	+14.6	35.6	21 34.2	+15.3	35.8
58	19 21.1	+13.0	34.2	20 10.7	+13.6	34.4	21 00.1	+14.2	34.6	21 49.5	+14.8	34.8
59	19 34.1	+12.6	33.1	20 24.3	+13.2	33.3	21 14.3	+13.8	33.5	22 04.3	+14.4	33.8
60	19 46.7	+12.3	32.1	20 37.5	+12.8	32.3	21 28.1	+13.5	32.5	22 18.7	+14.0	32.7
61	19 59.0	+11.9	31.1	20 50.3	+12.5	31.2	21 41.6	+13.0	31.5	22 32.7	+13.6	31.7
62	20 10.9	+11.5	30.0	21 02.8	+12.1	30.2	21 54.6	+12.6	30.4	22 46.3	+13.2	30.6
63	20 22.4	+11.2	29.0	21 14.9	+11.7	29.2	22 07.2	+12.3	29.3	22 59.5	+12.7	29.5
64	20 33.6	+10.8	27.9	21 26.6	+11.3	28.1	22 19.5	+11.8	28.3	23 12.2	+12.4	28.5
65	20 44.4	+10.4	26.9	21 37.9	+10.9	27.0	22 31.3	+11.4	27.2	23 24.6	+11.9	27.4
66	20 54.8	+10.0	25.8	21 48.8	+10.4	26.0	22 42.7	+10.9	26.2	23 36.5	+11.4	26.4
67	21 04.8	+9.6	24.8	21 59.2	+10.1	24.9	22 53.6	+10.6	25.1	23 47.9	+11.0	25.3
68	21 14.4	+9.2	23.7	22 09.3	+9.7	23.9	23 04.2	+10.1	24.0	23 58.9	+10.6	24.2
69	21 23.6	+8.9	22.6	22 19.0	+9.2	22.8	23 14.3	+9.6	23.0	24 09.5	+10.1	23.1
70	21 32.5	+8.4	21.6	22 28.2	+8.8	21.7	23 23.9	+9.3	21.9	24 19.6	+9.6	22.0
71	21 40.9	+8.0	20.5	22 37.0	+8.4	20.7	23 33.2	+8.7	20.8	24 29.2	+9.2	21.0
72	21 48.9	+7.6	19.4	22 45.4	+8.0	19.6	23 41.9	+8.4	19.7	24 38.4	+8.7	19.9
73	21 56.5	+7.2	18.4	22 53.4	+7.5	18.5	23 50.3	+7.9	18.6	24 47.1	+8.2	18.8
74	22 03.7	+6.7	17.3	23 00.9	+7.1	17.4	23 58.2	+7.4	17.6	24 55.3	+7.8	17.7
75	22 10.4	+6.4	16.2	23 08.0	+6.7	16.3	24 05.6	+6.9	16.5	25 03.1	+7.3	16.6
76	22 16.8	+5.9	15.2	23 14.7	+6.2	15.3	24 12.5	+6.5	15.4	25 10.4	+6.8	15.5
77	22 22.7	+5.5	14.1	23 20.9	+5.7	14.2	24 19.0	+6.1	14.3	25 17.2	+6.3	14.4
78	22 28.2	+5.0	13.0	23 26.6	+5.3	13.1	24 25.1	+5.5	13.2	25 23.5	+5.8	13.3
79	22 33.2	+4.7	11.9	23 31.9	+4.9	12.0	24 30.6	+5.1	12.1	25 29.3	+5.3	12.2
80	22 37.9	+4.2	10.8	23 36.8	+4.4	10.9	24 35.7	+4.6	11.0	25 34.6	+4.8	11.1
81	22 42.1	+3.7	9.8	23 41.2	+3.9	9.8	24 40.3	+4.1	9.9	25 39.4	+4.3	10.0
82	22 45.8	+3.3	8.7	23 45.1	+3.5	8.7	24 44.4	+3.7	8.8	25 43.7	+3.8	8.9
83	22 49.1	+2.9	7.6	23 48.6	+3.0	7.7	24 48.1	+3.1	7.7	25 47.5	+3.3	7.8
84	22 52.0	+2.4	6.5	23 51.6	+2.6	6.6	24 51.2	+2.7	6.6	25 50.8	+2.8	6.7
85	22 54.4	+2.0	5.4	23 54.2	+2.1	5.5	24 53.9	+2.2	5.5	25 53.6	+2.3	5.6
86	22 56.4	+1.6	4.3	23 56.3	+1.6	4.4	24 56.1	+1.7	4.4	25 55.9	+1.8	4.4
87	22 58.0	+1.1	3.3	23 57.9	+1.2	3.3	24 57.8	+1.2	3.3	25 57.7	+1.3	3.3
88	22 59.1	+0.7	2.2	23 59.1	+0.7	2.2	24 59.0	+0.8	2.2	25 59.0	+0.7	2.2
89	22 59.8	+0.2	1.1	23 59.8	+0.2	1.1	24 59.8	+0.2	1.1	25 59.7	+0.3	1.1
90	23 00.0	−0.2	0.0	24 00.0	−0.2	0.0	25 00.0	−0.2	0.0	26 00.0	−0.3	0.0
	23°			24°			25°			26°		

27°			28°			29°			30°			Dec.
Hc	d	Z	Hc	d	Z	Hc	d	Z	Hc	d	Z	
° ′	′	°	° ′	′	°	° ′	′	°	° ′	′	°	°
0 00.0	+27.2	90.0	0 00.0	+28.2	90.0	0 00.0	+29.1	90.0	0 00.0	+30.0	90.0	0
0 27.2	+27.3	89.1	0 28.2	+28.1	89.1	0 29.1	+29.1	89.1	0 30.0	+30.0	89.1	1
0 54.5	+27.2	88.2	0 56.3	+28.2	88.2	0 58.2	+29.0	88.3	1 00.0	+30.0	88.3	2
1 21.7	+27.2	87.3	1 24.5	+28.1	87.4	1 27.2	+29.1	87.4	1 30.0	+29.9	87.4	3
1 48.9	+27.2	86.4	1 52.6	+28.1	86.5	1 56.3	+29.0	86.5	1 59.9	+30.0	86.5	4
2 16.1	+27.1	85.5	2 20.7	+28.1	85.6	2 25.3	+29.0	85.6	2 29.9	+29.9	85.7	5
2 43.2	+27.1	84.6	2 48.8	+28.0	84.7	2 54.3	+28.9	84.7	2 59.8	+29.8	84.8	6
3 10.3	+27.1	83.8	3 16.8	+28.0	83.8	3 23.2	+28.9	83.9	3 29.6	+29.8	83.9	7
3 37.4	+27.0	82.9	3 44.8	+27.9	82.9	3 52.1	+28.9	83.0	3 59.4	+29.8	83.1	8
4 04.4	+26.9	82.0	4 12.7	+27.9	82.0	4 21.0	+28.8	82.1	4 29.2	+29.7	82.2	9
4 31.3	+26.9	81.1	4 40.6	+27.8	81.2	4 49.8	+28.7	81.2	4 58.9	+29.6	81.3	10
4 58.2	+26.8	80.2	5 08.4	+27.7	80.3	5 18.5	+28.6	80.4	5 28.5	+29.5	80.4	11
5 25.0	+26.7	79.3	5 36.1	+27.6	79.4	5 47.1	+28.6	79.5	5 58.0	+29.5	79.6	12
5 51.7	+26.6	78.4	6 03.7	+27.6	78.5	6 15.7	+28.4	78.6	6 27.5	+29.4	78.7	13
6 18.3	+26.6	77.5	6 31.3	+27.4	77.6	6 44.1	+28.4	77.7	6 56.9	+29.2	77.8	14
6 44.9	+26.4	76.6	6 58.7	+27.4	76.7	7 12.5	+28.3	76.8	7 26.1	+29.2	76.9	15
7 11.3	+26.4	75.7	7 26.1	+27.3	75.8	7 40.8	+28.1	75.9	7 55.3	+29.1	76.1	16
7 37.7	+26.2	74.8	7 53.4	+27.1	74.9	8 08.9	+28.1	75.0	8 24.4	+28.9	75.2	17
8 03.9	+26.1	73.9	8 20.5	+27.0	74.0	8 37.0	+27.9	74.1	8 53.3	+28.8	74.3	18
8 30.0	+26.0	72.9	8 47.5	+26.9	73.1	9 04.9	+27.8	73.2	9 22.1	+28.7	73.4	19
8 56.0	+25.8	72.0	9 14.4	+26.7	72.2	9 32.7	+27.6	72.3	9 50.8	+28.5	72.5	20
9 21.8	+25.7	71.1	9 41.1	+26.6	71.3	10 00.3	+27.5	71.4	10 19.3	+28.4	71.6	21
9 47.5	+25.6	70.2	10 07.7	+26.5	70.4	10 27.8	+27.4	70.5	10 47.7	+28.3	70.7	22
10 13.1	+25.4	69.3	10 34.2	+26.3	69.5	10 55.2	+27.2	69.6	11 16.0	+28.0	69.8	23
10 38.5	+25.2	68.4	11 00.5	+26.1	68.5	11 22.4	+27.0	68.7	11 44.0	+27.9	68.9	24
11 03.7	+25.1	67.4	11 26.6	+26.0	67.6	11 49.4	+26.8	67.8	12 11.9	+27.8	68.0	25
11 28.8	+24.9	66.5	11 52.6	+25.8	66.7	12 16.2	+26.7	66.9	12 39.7	+27.5	67.1	26
11 53.7	+24.7	65.6	12 18.4	+25.6	65.8	12 42.9	+26.5	66.0	13 07.2	+27.4	66.2	27
12 18.4	+24.5	64.7	12 44.0	+25.4	64.9	13 09.4	+26.2	65.1	13 34.6	+27.1	65.3	28
12 42.9	+24.3	63.7	13 09.4	+25.2	63.9	13 35.6	+26.1	64.1	14 01.7	+27.0	64.4	29
13 07.2	+24.1	62.8	13 34.6	+25.0	63.0	14 01.7	+25.9	63.2	14 28.7	+26.7	63.4	30
13 31.3	+23.9	61.8	13 59.6	+24.7	62.1	14 27.6	+25.6	62.3	14 55.4	+26.5	62.5	31
13 55.2	+23.7	60.9	14 24.3	+24.6	61.1	14 53.2	+25.4	61.3	15 21.9	+26.2	61.6	32
14 18.9	+23.5	59.9	14 48.9	+24.3	60.2	15 18.6	+25.2	60.4	15 48.1	+26.1	60.6	33
14 42.4	+23.2	59.0	15 13.2	+24.1	59.2	15 43.8	+24.9	59.5	16 14.2	+25.7	59.7	34
15 05.6	+23.0	58.0	15 37.3	+23.8	58.3	16 08.7	+24.7	58.5	16 39.9	+25.6	58.8	35
15 28.6	+22.8	57.1	16 01.1	+23.6	57.3	16 33.4	+24.4	57.6	17 05.5	+25.2	57.8	36
15 51.4	+22.4	56.1	16 24.7	+23.3	56.4	16 57.8	+24.2	56.6	17 30.7	+25.0	56.9	37
16 13.8	+22.3	55.2	16 48.0	+23.1	55.4	17 22.0	+23.9	55.7	17 55.7	+24.7	55.9	38
16 36.1	+21.9	54.2	17 11.1	+22.7	54.4	17 45.9	+23.5	54.7	18 20.4	+24.4	55.0	39
16 58.0	+21.7	53.2	17 33.8	+22.5	53.5	18 09.4	+23.4	53.7	18 44.8	+24.2	54.0	40
17 19.7	+21.4	52.2	17 56.3	+22.2	52.5	18 32.8	+23.0	52.8	19 09.0	+23.8	53.0	41
17 41.1	+21.1	51.3	18 18.5	+21.9	51.5	18 55.8	+22.7	51.8	19 32.8	+23.5	52.1	42
18 02.2	+20.8	50.3	18 40.4	+21.6	50.5	19 18.5	+22.3	50.8	19 56.3	+23.1	51.1	43
18 23.0	+20.5	49.3	19 02.0	+21.3	49.5	19 40.8	+22.1	49.8	20 19.4	+22.9	50.1	44
18 43.5	+20.2	48.3	19 23.3	+20.9	48.6	20 02.9	+21.7	48.8	20 42.3	+22.5	49.1	45
19 03.7	+19.8	47.3	19 44.2	+20.7	47.6	20 24.6	+21.4	47.8	21 04.8	+22.2	48.1	46
19 23.5	+19.5	46.3	20 04.9	+20.2	46.6	20 46.0	+21.1	46.8	21 27.0	+21.8	47.1	47
19 43.0	+19.2	45.3	20 25.1	+20.0	45.6	21 07.1	+20.6	45.8	21 48.8	+21.4	46.1	48
20 02.2	+18.9	44.3	20 45.1	+19.6	44.6	21 27.7	+20.4	44.8	22 10.2	+21.1	45.1	49
20 21.1	+18.5	43.3	21 04.7	+19.2	43.5	21 48.1	+19.9	43.8	22 31.3	+20.6	44.1	50
20 39.6	+18.1	42.3	21 23.9	+18.8	42.5	22 08.0	+19.6	42.8	22 51.9	+20.3	43.1	51
20 57.7	+17.8	41.2	21 42.7	+18.5	41.5	22 27.6	+19.2	41.8	23 12.2	+19.9	42.1	52
21 15.5	+17.4	40.2	22 01.2	+18.1	40.5	22 46.8	+18.8	40.7	23 32.1	+19.5	41.0	53
21 32.9	+17.0	39.2	22 19.3	+17.7	39.4	23 05.6	+18.3	39.7	23 51.6	+19.1	40.0	54
21 49.9	+16.7	38.2	22 37.0	+17.3	38.4	23 23.9	+18.0	38.7	24 10.7	+18.6	39.0	55
22 06.6	+16.2	37.1	22 54.3	+16.9	37.4	23 41.9	+17.6	37.6	24 29.3	+18.3	37.9	56
22 22.8	+15.8	36.1	23 11.2	+16.5	36.3	23 59.5	+17.1	36.6	24 47.6	+17.7	36.9	57
22 38.6	+15.5	35.0	23 27.7	+16.1	35.3	24 16.6	+16.7	35.5	25 05.3	+17.4	35.8	58
22 54.1	+15.0	34.0	23 43.8	+15.6	34.2	24 33.3	+16.2	34.5	25 22.7	+16.8	34.8	59
23 09.1	+14.6	32.9	23 59.4	+15.2	33.2	24 49.5	+15.8	33.4	25 39.5	+16.4	33.7	60
23 23.7	+14.2	31.9	24 14.6	+14.7	32.1	25 05.3	+15.4	32.4	25 55.9	+16.0	32.6	61
23 37.9	+13.7	30.8	24 29.3	+14.3	31.1	25 20.7	+14.9	31.3	26 11.9	+15.4	31.5	62
23 51.6	+13.3	29.8	24 43.6	+13.9	30.0	25 35.6	+14.4	30.2	26 27.3	+15.0	30.5	63
24 04.9	+12.9	28.7	24 57.5	+13.4	28.9	25 50.0	+13.9	29.1	26 42.3	+14.5	29.4	64
24 17.8	+12.4	27.6	25 10.9	+12.9	27.8	26 03.9	+13.4	28.1	26 56.8	+13.9	28.3	65
24 30.2	+11.9	26.6	25 23.8	+12.4	26.8	26 17.3	+13.0	27.0	27 10.7	+13.5	27.2	66
24 42.1	+11.5	25.5	25 36.2	+12.0	25.7	26 30.3	+12.4	25.9	27 24.2	+12.9	26.1	67
24 53.6	+11.0	24.4	25 48.2	+11.5	24.6	26 42.7	+12.0	24.8	27 37.1	+12.5	25.0	68
25 04.6	+10.6	23.3	25 59.7	+11.0	23.5	26 54.7	+11.4	23.7	27 49.6	+11.9	23.9	69
25 15.2	+10.0	22.2	26 10.7	+10.5	22.4	27 06.1	+10.9	22.6	28 01.5	+11.3	22.8	70
25 25.2	+9.6	21.1	26 21.2	+9.9	21.3	27 17.0	+10.4	21.5	28 12.8	+10.8	21.7	71
25 34.8	+9.1	20.0	26 31.1	+9.5	20.2	27 27.4	+9.9	20.4	28 23.6	+10.3	20.6	72
25 43.9	+8.6	18.9	26 40.6	+9.0	19.1	27 37.3	+9.3	19.3	28 33.9	+9.7	19.4	73
25 52.5	+8.1	17.8	26 49.6	+8.4	18.0	27 46.6	+8.8	18.2	28 43.6	+9.1	18.3	74
26 00.6	+7.6	16.7	26 58.0	+7.9	16.9	27 55.4	+8.2	17.0	28 52.7	+8.6	17.2	75
26 08.2	+7.1	15.6	27 05.9	+7.4	15.8	28 03.6	+7.7	15.9	29 01.3	+8.0	16.1	76
26 15.3	+6.5	14.5	27 13.3	+6.9	14.7	28 11.3	+7.2	14.8	29 09.3	+7.5	14.9	77
26 21.8	+6.1	13.4	27 20.2	+6.3	13.5	28 18.5	+6.6	13.7	29 16.8	+6.8	13.8	78
26 27.9	+5.5	12.3	27 26.5	+5.8	12.4	28 25.1	+6.0	12.5	29 23.6	+6.3	12.7	79
26 33.4	+5.1	11.2	27 32.3	+5.2	11.3	28 31.1	+5.5	11.4	29 29.9	+5.7	11.5	80
26 38.5	+4.5	10.1	27 37.5	+4.7	10.2	28 36.6	+4.9	10.3	29 35.6	+5.1	10.4	81
26 43.0	+4.0	9.0	27 42.2	+4.2	9.0	28 41.5	+4.3	9.1	29 40.7	+4.5	9.2	82
26 47.0	+3.4	7.8	27 46.4	+3.6	7.9	28 45.8	+3.8	8.0	29 45.2	+3.9	8.1	83
26 50.4	+2.9	6.7	27 50.0	+3.0	6.8	28 49.6	+3.2	6.9	29 49.1	+3.4	6.9	84
26 53.3	+2.4	5.6	27 53.0	+2.5	5.7	28 52.8	+2.6	5.7	29 52.5	+2.7	5.8	85
26 55.7	+1.9	4.5	27 55.5	+2.0	4.5	28 55.4	+2.0	4.6	29 55.2	+2.1	4.6	86
26 57.6	+1.3	3.4	27 57.5	+1.4	3.4	28 57.4	+1.4	3.4	29 57.3	+1.5	3.5	87
26 58.9	+0.8	2.2	27 58.9	+0.8	2.3	28 58.8	+0.9	2.3	29 58.8	+0.9	2.3	88
26 59.7	+0.3	1.1	27 59.7	+0.3	1.1	28 59.7	+0.3	1.1	29 59.7	+0.3	1.2	89
27 00.0	−0.3	0.0	28 00.0	−0.3	0.0	29 00.0	−0.3	0.0	30 00.0	−0.3	0.0	90
27°			28°			29°			30°			

Dec.	23° Hc	23° d	23° Z	24° Hc	24° d	24° Z	25° Hc	25° d	25° Z	26° Hc	26° d	26° Z
°	° ′	′	°	° ′	′	°	° ′	′	°	° ′	′	°
0	0 00.0	+23.4	90.0	0 00.0	+24.4	90.0	0 00.0	+25.4	90.0	0 00.0	+26.3	90.0
1	0 23.4	+23.5	89.1	0 24.4	+24.4	89.1	0 25.4	+25.3	89.1	0 26.3	+26.3	89.1
2	0 46.9	+23.4	88.2	0 48.8	+24.4	88.2	0 50.7	+25.3	88.2	0 52.6	+26.3	88.2
3	1 10.3	+23.4	87.2	1 13.2	+24.4	87.3	1 16.0	+25.4	87.3	1 18.9	+26.2	87.3
4	1 33.7	+23.4	86.3	1 37.6	+24.3	86.3	1 41.4	+25.3	86.4	1 45.1	+26.3	86.4
5	1 57.1	+23.3	85.4	2 01.9	+24.3	85.4	2 06.7	+25.2	85.5	2 11.4	+26.2	85.5
6	2 20.4	+23.4	84.5	2 26.2	+24.3	84.5	2 31.9	+25.2	84.6	2 37.6	+26.1	84.6
7	2 43.8	+23.2	83.6	2 50.5	+24.2	83.6	2 57.1	+25.2	83.7	3 03.7	+26.2	83.7
8	3 07.0	+23.3	82.6	3 14.7	+24.2	82.7	3 22.3	+25.1	82.7	3 29.9	+26.0	82.8
9	3 30.3	+23.1	81.7	3 38.9	+24.1	81.8	3 47.4	+25.1	81.8	3 55.9	+26.0	81.9
10	3 53.4	+23.1	80.8	4 03.0	+24.1	80.8	4 12.5	+25.0	80.9	4 21.9	+26.0	81.0
11	4 16.5	+23.1	79.9	4 27.1	+24.0	79.9	4 37.5	+25.0	80.0	4 47.9	+25.9	80.1
12	4 39.6	+23.0	78.9	4 51.1	+23.9	79.0	5 02.5	+24.8	79.1	5 13.8	+25.8	79.2
13	5 02.6	+22.8	78.0	5 15.0	+23.8	78.1	5 27.3	+24.8	78.2	5 39.6	+25.7	78.3
14	5 25.4	+22.9	77.1	5 38.8	+23.8	77.2	5 52.1	+24.7	77.3	6 05.3	+25.6	77.4
15	5 48.3	+22.7	76.1	6 02.6	+23.6	76.2	6 16.8	+24.6	76.4	6 30.9	+25.5	76.5
16	6 11.0	+22.6	75.2	6 26.2	+23.6	75.3	6 41.4	+24.5	75.4	6 56.4	+25.4	75.5
17	6 33.6	+22.5	74.3	6 49.8	+23.4	74.4	7 05.9	+24.3	74.5	7 21.8	+25.3	74.6
18	6 56.1	+22.4	73.3	7 13.2	+23.4	73.5	7 30.2	+24.3	73.6	7 47.1	+25.2	73.7
19	7 18.5	+22.3	72.4	7 36.6	+23.2	72.5	7 54.5	+24.2	72.7	8 12.3	+25.1	72.8
20	7 40.8	+22.2	71.5	7 59.8	+23.1	71.6	8 18.7	+24.0	71.7	8 37.4	+24.9	71.9
21	8 03.0	+22.0	70.5	8 22.9	+22.9	70.7	8 42.7	+23.8	70.8	9 02.3	+24.8	71.0
22	8 25.0	+21.9	69.6	8 45.8	+22.9	69.7	9 06.5	+23.8	69.9	9 27.1	+24.7	70.0
23	8 46.9	+21.8	68.7	9 08.7	+22.6	68.8	9 30.3	+23.6	69.0	9 51.8	+24.5	69.1
24	9 08.7	+21.6	67.7	9 31.3	+22.6	67.9	9 53.9	+23.4	68.0	10 16.3	+24.3	68.2
25	9 30.3	+21.5	66.8	9 53.9	+22.4	66.9	10 17.3	+23.3	67.1	10 40.6	+24.2	67.3
26	9 51.8	+21.3	65.8	10 16.3	+22.2	66.0	10 40.6	+23.1	66.2	11 04.8	+24.0	66.3
27	10 13.1	+21.1	64.9	10 38.5	+22.0	65.0	11 03.7	+22.9	65.2	11 28.8	+23.8	65.4
28	10 34.2	+21.0	63.9	11 00.5	+21.9	64.1	11 26.6	+22.8	64.3	11 52.6	+23.6	64.5
29	10 55.2	+20.8	63.0	11 22.4	+21.6	63.1	11 49.4	+22.5	63.3	12 16.2	+23.5	63.5
30	11 16.0	+20.6	62.0	11 44.0	+21.5	62.2	12 11.9	+22.4	62.4	12 39.7	+23.2	62.6
31	11 36.6	+20.4	61.1	12 05.5	+21.3	61.2	12 34.3	+22.2	61.4	13 02.9	+23.1	61.6
32	11 57.0	+20.2	60.1	12 26.8	+21.1	60.3	12 56.5	+21.9	60.5	13 26.0	+22.8	60.7
33	12 17.2	+20.0	59.1	12 47.9	+20.9	59.3	13 18.4	+21.8	59.5	13 48.8	+22.6	59.7
34	12 37.2	+19.8	58.2	13 08.8	+20.7	58.4	13 40.2	+21.5	58.6	14 11.4	+22.4	58.8
35	12 57.0	+19.6	57.2	13 29.5	+20.4	57.4	14 01.7	+21.3	57.6	14 33.8	+22.1	57.8
36	13 16.6	+19.4	56.2	13 49.9	+20.2	56.4	14 23.0	+21.1	56.6	14 55.9	+21.9	56.9
37	13 36.0	+19.2	55.3	14 10.1	+20.0	55.5	14 44.1	+20.8	55.7	15 17.8	+21.7	55.9
38	13 55.2	+18.9	54.3	14 30.1	+19.8	54.5	15 04.9	+20.5	54.7	15 39.5	+21.4	54.9
39	14 14.1	+18.7	53.3	14 49.9	+19.5	53.5	15 25.4	+20.4	53.7	16 00.9	+21.1	54.0
40	14 32.8	+18.4	52.3	15 09.4	+19.2	52.5	15 45.8	+20.0	52.7	16 22.0	+20.9	53.0
41	14 51.2	+18.2	51.3	15 28.6	+19.0	51.5	16 05.8	+19.8	51.8	16 42.9	+20.5	52.0
42	15 09.4	+17.9	50.3	15 47.6	+18.7	50.6	16 25.6	+19.5	50.8	17 03.4	+20.3	51.0
43	15 27.3	+17.6	49.4	16 06.3	+18.4	49.6	16 45.1	+19.2	49.8	17 23.7	+20.1	50.0
44	15 44.9	+17.4	48.4	16 24.7	+18.2	48.6	17 04.3	+19.0	48.8	17 43.8	+19.7	49.0
45	16 02.3	+17.1	47.4	16 42.9	+17.9	47.6	17 23.3	+18.6	47.8	18 03.5	+19.4	48.1
46	16 19.4	+16.9	46.4	17 00.8	+17.5	46.6	17 41.9	+18.3	46.8	18 22.9	+19.1	47.1
47	16 36.3	+16.5	45.4	17 18.3	+17.3	45.6	18 00.2	+18.1	45.8	18 42.0	+18.7	46.1
48	16 52.8	+16.3	44.4	17 35.6	+17.0	44.6	18 18.3	+17.7	44.8	19 00.7	+18.5	45.1
49	17 09.1	+15.9	43.4	17 52.6	+16.7	43.6	18 36.0	+17.4	43.8	19 19.2	+18.1	44.0
50	17 25.0	+15.6	42.4	18 09.3	+16.3	42.6	18 53.4	+17.0	42.8	19 37.3	+17.8	43.0
51	17 40.6	+15.4	41.3	18 25.6	+16.0	41.6	19 10.4	+16.8	41.8	19 55.1	+17.4	42.0
52	17 56.0	+15.0	40.3	18 41.6	+15.7	40.5	19 27.2	+16.3	40.8	20 12.5	+17.1	41.0
53	18 11.0	+14.7	39.3	18 57.3	+15.4	39.5	19 43.5	+16.1	39.7	20 29.6	+16.7	40.0
54	18 25.7	+14.3	38.3	19 12.7	+15.0	38.5	19 59.6	+15.7	38.7	20 46.3	+16.4	39.0
55	18 40.0	+14.0	37.3	19 27.7	+14.7	37.5	20 15.3	+15.3	37.7	21 02.7	+15.9	37.9
56	18 54.0	+13.7	36.2	19 42.4	+14.3	36.4	20 30.6	+14.9	36.7	21 18.6	+15.6	36.9
57	19 07.7	+13.4	35.2	19 56.7	+14.0	35.4	20 45.5	+14.6	35.6	21 34.2	+15.3	35.8
58	19 21.1	+13.0	34.2	20 10.7	+13.6	34.4	21 00.1	+14.2	34.6	21 49.5	+14.8	34.8
59	19 34.1	+12.6	33.1	20 24.3	+13.2	33.3	21 14.3	+13.8	33.5	22 04.3	+14.4	33.8
60	19 46.7	+12.3	32.1	20 37.5	+12.8	32.3	21 28.1	+13.5	32.5	22 18.7	+14.0	32.7
61	19 59.0	+11.9	31.1	20 50.3	+12.5	31.2	21 41.6	+13.0	31.5	22 32.7	+13.6	31.7
62	20 10.9	+11.5	30.0	21 02.8	+12.1	30.2	21 54.6	+12.6	30.4	22 46.3	+13.2	30.6
63	20 22.4	+11.2	29.0	21 14.9	+11.7	29.2	22 07.2	+12.3	29.3	22 59.5	+12.7	29.5
64	20 33.6	+10.8	27.9	21 26.6	+11.3	28.1	22 19.5	+11.8	28.3	23 12.2	+12.4	28.5
65	20 44.4	+10.4	26.9	21 37.9	+10.9	27.0	22 31.3	+11.4	27.2	23 24.6	+11.9	27.4
66	20 54.8	+10.0	25.8	21 48.8	+10.4	26.0	22 42.7	+10.9	26.2	23 36.5	+11.4	26.4
67	21 04.8	+9.6	24.8	21 59.2	+10.1	24.9	22 53.6	+10.6	25.1	23 47.9	+11.0	25.3
68	21 14.4	+9.2	23.7	22 09.3	+9.7	23.9	23 04.2	+10.1	24.0	23 58.9	+10.6	24.2
69	21 23.6	+8.9	22.6	22 19.0	+9.2	22.8	23 14.3	+9.6	23.0	24 09.5	+10.1	23.1
70	21 32.5	+8.4	21.6	22 28.2	+8.8	21.7	23 23.9	+9.3	21.9	24 19.6	+9.6	22.0
71	21 40.9	+8.0	20.5	22 37.0	+8.4	20.7	23 33.2	+8.7	20.8	24 29.2	+9.2	21.0
72	21 48.9	+7.6	19.4	22 45.4	+8.0	19.6	23 41.9	+8.4	19.7	24 38.4	+8.7	19.9
73	21 56.5	+7.2	18.4	22 53.4	+7.5	18.5	23 50.3	+7.9	18.6	24 47.1	+8.2	18.8
74	22 03.7	+6.7	17.3	23 00.9	+7.1	17.4	23 58.2	+7.4	17.6	24 55.3	+7.8	17.7
75	22 10.4	+6.4	16.2	23 08.0	+6.7	16.3	24 05.6	+6.9	16.5	25 03.1	+7.3	16.6
76	22 16.8	+5.9	15.2	23 14.7	+6.2	15.3	24 12.5	+6.5	15.4	25 10.4	+6.8	15.5
77	22 22.7	+5.5	14.1	23 20.9	+5.7	14.2	24 19.0	+6.1	14.3	25 17.2	+6.3	14.4
78	22 28.2	+5.0	13.0	23 26.6	+5.3	13.1	24 25.1	+5.5	13.2	25 23.5	+5.8	13.3
79	22 33.2	+4.7	11.9	23 31.9	+4.9	12.0	24 30.6	+5.1	12.1	25 29.3	+5.3	12.2
80	22 37.9	+4.2	10.8	23 36.8	+4.4	10.9	24 35.7	+4.6	11.0	25 34.6	+4.8	11.1
81	22 42.1	+3.7	9.8	23 41.2	+3.9	9.8	24 40.3	+4.1	9.9	25 39.4	+4.3	10.0
82	22 45.8	+3.3	8.7	23 45.1	+3.5	8.7	24 44.4	+3.7	8.8	25 43.7	+3.8	8.9
83	22 49.1	+2.9	7.6	23 48.6	+3.0	7.7	24 48.1	+3.1	7.7	25 47.5	+3.3	7.8
84	22 52.0	+2.4	6.5	23 51.6	+2.6	6.6	24 51.2	+2.7	6.6	25 50.8	+2.8	6.7
85	22 54.4	+2.0	5.4	23 54.2	+2.1	5.5	24 53.9	+2.2	5.5	25 53.6	+2.3	5.6
86	22 56.4	+1.6	4.3	23 56.3	+1.6	4.4	24 56.1	+1.7	4.4	25 55.9	+1.8	4.4
87	22 58.0	+1.1	3.3	23 57.9	+1.2	3.3	24 57.8	+1.2	3.3	25 57.7	+1.3	3.3
88	22 59.1	+0.7	2.2	23 59.1	+0.7	2.2	24 59.0	+0.8	2.2	25 59.0	+0.7	2.2
89	22 59.8	+0.2	1.1	23 59.8	+0.2	1.1	24 59.8	+0.2	1.1	25 59.7	+0.3	1.1
90	23 00.0	−0.2	0.0	24 00.0	−0.2	0.0	25 00.0	−0.2	0.0	26 00.0	−0.3	0.0
	23°			24°			25°			26°		

27° Hc	27° d	27° Z	28° Hc	28° d	28° Z	29° Hc	29° d	29° Z	30° Hc	30° d	30° Z	Dec.
° ′	′	°	° ′	′	°	° ′	′	°	° ′	′	°	°
0 00.0	+27.2	90.0	0 00.0	+28.2	90.0	0 00.0	+29.1	90.0	0 00.0	+30.0	90.0	0
0 27.2	+27.3	89.1	0 28.2	+28.1	89.1	0 29.1	+29.1	89.1	0 30.0	+30.0	89.1	1
0 54.5	+27.2	88.2	0 56.3	+28.2	88.2	0 58.2	+29.0	88.3	1 00.0	+30.0	88.3	2
1 21.7	+27.2	87.3	1 24.5	+28.1	87.4	1 27.2	+29.1	87.4	1 30.0	+29.9	87.4	3
1 48.9	+27.2	86.4	1 52.6	+28.1	86.5	1 56.3	+29.0	86.5	1 59.9	+30.0	86.5	4
2 16.1	+27.1	85.5	2 20.7	+28.1	85.6	2 25.3	+29.0	85.6	2 29.9	+29.9	85.7	5
2 43.2	+27.1	84.6	2 48.8	+28.0	84.7	2 54.3	+28.9	84.7	2 59.8	+29.8	84.8	6
3 10.3	+27.1	83.8	3 16.8	+28.0	83.8	3 23.2	+28.9	83.9	3 29.6	+29.8	83.9	7
3 37.4	+27.0	82.9	3 44.8	+27.9	82.9	3 52.1	+28.9	83.0	3 59.4	+29.8	83.1	8
4 04.4	+26.9	82.0	4 12.7	+27.9	82.0	4 21.0	+28.8	82.1	4 29.2	+29.7	82.2	9
4 31.3	+26.9	81.1	4 40.6	+27.8	81.2	4 49.8	+28.7	81.2	4 58.9	+29.6	81.3	10
4 58.2	+26.8	80.2	5 08.4	+27.7	80.3	5 18.5	+28.6	80.4	5 28.5	+29.5	80.4	11
5 25.0	+26.7	79.3	5 36.1	+27.6	79.4	5 47.1	+28.6	79.5	5 58.0	+29.5	79.6	12
5 51.7	+26.6	78.4	6 03.7	+27.6	78.5	6 15.7	+28.4	78.6	6 27.5	+29.4	78.7	13
6 18.3	+26.6	77.5	6 31.3	+27.4	77.6	6 44.1	+28.4	77.7	6 56.9	+29.2	77.8	14
6 44.9	+26.4	76.6	6 58.7	+27.4	76.7	7 12.5	+28.3	76.8	7 26.1	+29.2	76.9	15
7 11.3	+26.4	75.7	7 26.1	+27.3	75.8	7 40.8	+28.1	75.9	7 55.3	+29.1	76.1	16
7 37.7	+26.2	74.8	7 53.4	+27.1	74.9	8 08.9	+28.1	75.0	8 24.4	+28.9	75.2	17
8 03.9	+26.1	73.9	8 20.5	+27.0	74.0	8 37.0	+27.9	74.1	8 53.3	+28.8	74.3	18
8 30.0	+26.0	72.9	8 47.5	+26.9	73.1	9 04.9	+27.8	73.2	9 22.1	+28.7	73.4	19
8 56.0	+25.8	72.0	9 14.4	+26.7	72.2	9 32.7	+27.6	72.3	9 50.8	+28.5	72.5	20
9 21.8	+25.7	71.1	9 41.1	+26.6	71.3	10 00.3	+27.5	71.4	10 19.3	+28.4	71.6	21
9 47.5	+25.6	70.2	10 07.7	+26.5	70.4	10 27.8	+27.4	70.5	10 47.7	+28.3	70.7	22
10 13.1	+25.4	69.3	10 34.2	+26.3	69.5	10 55.2	+27.2	69.6	11 16.0	+28.0	69.8	23
10 38.5	+25.2	68.4	11 00.5	+26.1	68.5	11 22.4	+27.0	68.7	11 44.0	+27.9	68.9	24
11 03.7	+25.1	67.4	11 26.6	+26.0	67.6	11 49.4	+26.8	67.8	12 11.9	+27.8	68.0	25
11 28.8	+24.9	66.5	11 52.6	+25.8	66.7	12 16.2	+26.7	66.9	12 39.7	+27.5	67.1	26
11 53.7	+24.7	65.6	12 18.4	+25.6	65.8	12 42.9	+26.5	66.0	13 07.2	+27.4	66.2	27
12 18.4	+24.5	64.7	12 44.0	+25.4	64.9	13 09.4	+26.2	65.1	13 34.6	+27.1	65.3	28
12 42.9	+24.3	63.7	13 09.4	+25.2	63.9	13 35.6	+26.1	64.1	14 01.7	+27.0	64.4	29
13 07.2	+24.1	62.8	13 34.6	+25.0	63.0	14 01.7	+25.9	63.2	14 28.7	+26.7	63.4	30
13 31.3	+23.9	61.8	13 59.6	+24.7	62.1	14 27.6	+25.6	62.3	14 55.4	+26.5	62.5	31
13 55.2	+23.7	60.9	14 24.3	+24.6	61.1	14 53.2	+25.4	61.3	15 21.9	+26.2	61.6	32
14 18.9	+23.5	59.9	14 48.9	+24.3	60.2	15 18.6	+25.2	60.4	15 48.1	+26.1	60.6	33
14 42.4	+23.2	59.0	15 13.2	+24.1	59.2	15 43.8	+24.9	59.5	16 14.2	+25.7	59.7	34
15 05.6	+23.0	58.0	15 37.3	+23.8	58.3	16 08.7	+24.7	58.5	16 39.9	+25.6	58.8	35
15 28.6	+22.8	57.1	16 01.1	+23.6	57.3	16 33.4	+24.4	57.6	17 05.5	+25.2	57.8	36
15 51.4	+22.4	56.1	16 24.7	+23.3	56.4	16 57.8	+24.2	56.6	17 30.7	+25.0	56.9	37
16 13.8	+22.3	55.2	16 48.0	+23.1	55.4	17 22.0	+23.9	55.7	17 55.7	+24.7	55.9	38
16 36.1	+21.9	54.2	17 11.1	+22.7	54.4	17 45.9	+23.5	54.7	18 20.4	+24.4	55.0	39
16 58.0	+21.7	53.2	17 33.8	+22.5	53.5	18 09.4	+23.4	53.7	18 44.8	+24.2	54.0	40
17 19.7	+21.4	52.2	17 56.3	+22.2	52.5	18 32.8	+23.0	52.8	19 09.0	+23.8	53.0	41
17 41.1	+21.1	51.3	18 18.5	+21.9	51.5	18 55.8	+22.7	51.8	19 32.8	+23.5	52.1	42
18 02.2	+20.8	50.3	18 40.4	+21.6	50.5	19 18.5	+22.3	50.8	19 56.3	+23.1	51.1	43
18 23.0	+20.5	49.3	19 02.0	+21.3	49.5	19 40.8	+22.1	49.8	20 19.4	+22.9	50.1	44
18 43.5	+20.2	48.3	19 23.3	+20.9	48.6	20 02.9	+21.7	48.8	20 42.3	+22.5	49.1	45
19 03.7	+19.8	47.3	19 44.2	+20.7	47.6	20 24.6	+21.4	47.8	21 04.8	+22.2	48.1	46
19 23.5	+19.5	46.3	20 04.9	+20.2	46.6	20 46.0	+21.1	46.8	21 27.0	+21.8	47.1	47
19 43.0	+19.2	45.3	20 25.1	+20.0	45.6	21 07.1	+20.6	45.8	21 48.8	+21.4	46.1	48
20 02.2	+18.9	44.3	20 45.1	+19.6	44.6	21 27.7	+20.4	44.8	22 10.2	+21.1	45.1	49
20 21.1	+18.5	43.3	21 04.7	+19.2	43.5	21 48.1	+19.9	43.8	22 31.3	+20.6	44.1	50
20 39.6	+18.1	42.3	21 23.9	+18.8	42.5	22 08.0	+19.6	42.8	22 51.9	+20.3	43.1	51
20 57.7	+17.8	41.2	21 42.7	+18.5	41.5	22 27.6	+19.2	41.8	23 12.2	+19.9	42.1	52
21 15.5	+17.4	40.2	22 01.2	+18.1	40.5	22 46.8	+18.8	40.7	23 32.1	+19.5	41.0	53
21 32.9	+17.0	39.2	22 19.3	+17.7	39.4	23 05.6	+18.3	39.7	23 51.6	+19.1	40.0	54
21 49.9	+16.7	38.2	22 37.0	+17.3	38.4	23 23.9	+18.0	38.7	24 10.7	+18.6	39.0	55
22 06.6	+16.2	37.1	22 54.3	+16.9	37.4	23 41.9	+17.6	37.6	24 29.3	+18.3	37.9	56
22 22.8	+15.8	36.1	23 11.2	+16.5	36.3	23 59.5	+17.1	36.6	24 47.6	+17.7	36.9	57
22 38.6	+15.5	35.0	23 27.7	+16.1	35.3	24 16.6	+16.7	35.5	25 05.3	+17.4	35.8	58
22 54.1	+15.0	34.0	23 43.8	+15.6	34.2	24 33.3	+16.2	34.5	25 22.7	+16.8	34.8	59
23 09.1	+14.6	32.9	23 59.4	+15.2	33.2	24 49.5	+15.8	33.4	25 39.5	+16.4	33.7	60
23 23.7	+14.2	31.9	24 14.6	+14.7	32.1	25 05.3	+15.4	32.4	25 55.9	+16.0	32.6	61
23 37.9	+13.7	30.8	24 29.3	+14.3	31.1	25 20.7	+14.9	31.3	26 11.9	+15.4	31.5	62
23 51.6	+13.3	29.8	24 43.6	+13.9	30.0	25 35.6	+14.4	30.2	26 27.3	+15.0	30.5	63
24 04.9	+12.9	28.7	24 57.5	+13.4	28.9	25 50.0	+13.9	29.1	26 42.3	+14.5	29.4	64
24 17.8	+12.4	27.6	25 10.9	+12.9	27.8	26 03.9	+13.4	28.1	26 56.8	+13.9	28.3	65
24 30.2	+11.9	26.6	25 23.8	+12.4	26.8	26 17.3	+13.0	27.0	27 10.7	+13.5	27.2	66
24 42.1	+11.5	25.5	25 36.2	+12.0	25.7	26 30.3	+12.4	25.9	27 24.2	+12.9	26.1	67
24 53.6	+11.0	24.4	25 48.2	+11.5	24.6	26 42.7	+12.0	24.8	27 37.1	+12.5	25.0	68
25 04.6	+10.6	23.3	25 59.7	+11.0	23.5	26 54.7	+11.4	23.7	27 49.6	+11.9	23.9	69
25 15.2	+10.0	22.2	26 10.7	+10.5	22.4	27 06.1	+10.9	22.6	28 01.5	+11.3	22.8	70
25 25.2	+9.6	21.1	26 21.2	+9.9	21.3	27 17.0	+10.4	21.5	28 12.8	+10.8	21.7	71
25 34.8	+9.1	20.0	26 31.1	+9.5	20.2	27 27.4	+9.9	20.4	28 23.6	+10.3	20.6	72
25 43.9	+8.6	18.9	26 40.6	+9.0	19.1	27 37.3	+9.3	19.3	28 33.9	+9.7	19.4	73
25 52.5	+8.1	17.8	26 49.6	+8.4	18.0	27 46.6	+8.8	18.2	28 43.6	+9.1	18.3	74
26 00.6	+7.6	16.7	26 58.0	+7.9	16.9	27 55.4	+8.2	17.0	28 52.7	+8.6	17.2	75
26 08.2	+7.1	15.6	27 05.9	+7.4	15.8	28 03.6	+7.7	15.9	29 01.3	+8.0	16.1	76
26 15.3	+6.5	14.5	27 13.3	+6.9	14.7	28 11.3	+7.2	14.8	29 09.3	+7.5	14.9	77
26 21.8	+6.1	13.4	27 20.2	+6.3	13.5	28 18.5	+6.6	13.7	29 16.8	+6.8	13.8	78
26 27.9	+5.5	12.3	27 26.5	+5.8	12.4	28 25.1	+6.0	12.5	29 23.6	+6.3	12.7	79
26 33.4	+5.1	11.2	27 32.3	+5.2	11.3	28 31.1	+5.5	11.4	29 29.9	+5.7	11.5	80
26 38.5	+4.5	10.1	27 37.5	+4.7	10.2	28 36.6	+4.9	10.3	29 35.6	+5.1	10.4	81
26 43.0	+4.0	9.0	27 42.2	+4.2	9.0	28 41.5	+4.3	9.1	29 40.7	+4.5	9.2	82
26 47.0	+3.4	7.8	27 46.4	+3.6	7.9	28 45.8	+3.8	8.0	29 45.2	+3.9	8.1	83
26 50.4	+2.9	6.7	27 50.0	+3.0	6.8	28 49.6	+3.2	6.9	29 49.1	+3.4	6.9	84
26 53.3	+2.4	5.6	27 53.0	+2.5	5.7	28 52.8	+2.6	5.7	29 52.5	+2.7	5.8	85
26 55.7	+1.9	4.5	27 55.5	+2.0	4.5	28 55.4	+2.0	4.6	29 55.2	+2.1	4.6	86
26 57.6	+1.3	3.4	27 57.5	+1.4	3.4	28 57.4	+1.4	3.4	29 57.3	+1.5	3.5	87
26 58.9	+0.8	2.2	27 58.9	+0.8	2.3	28 58.8	+0.9	2.3	29 58.8	+0.9	2.3	88
26 59.7	+0.3	1.1	27 59.7	+0.3	1.1	28 59.7	+0.3	1.1	29 59.7	+0.3	1.2	89
27 00.0	−0.3	0.0	28 00.0	−0.3	0.0	29 00.0	−0.3	0.0	30 00.0	−0.3	0.0	90
27°			28°			29°			30°			

S. Lat. {L.H.A. greater than 180° ....Zn=180°−Z
{L.H.A. less than 180°...........Zn=180°+Z

LATITUDE SAME NAME AS DECLINATION L.H.A. 90°, 270°

*No entries for contrary name appear on this page.

Made in the USA
San Bernardino, CA
13 January 2016